BALLENTINE'S LAW DICTIONARY

WITH PRONUNCIATIONS

JAMES A. BALLENTINE

THIRD EDITION

Edited by William S. Anderson

THE LAWYERS CO-OPERATIVE PUBLISHING COMPANY
ROCHESTER, N. Y.
BANCROFT–WHITNEY CO., SAN FRANCISCO, CALIF.
1969

Copyright © 1930, 1948
by
THE LAWYERS CO-OPERATIVE PUBLISHING COMPANY

Copyright © 1969
by
THE LAWYERS CO-OPERATIVE PUBLISHING COMPANY

Key To Pronunciation reproduced from THE NEW CENTURY DICTIONARY OF THE ENGLISH LANGUAGE, Edited by H. G. Emery and K. G. Brewster. Copyright © 1963, by Meredith Publishing Company. Reproduced by permission of Appleton-Century-Crofts, Division of Meredith Corporation.

Library of Congress Catalog Card Number 68–30931

FOREWORD TO THE THIRD EDITION

"A word is not a crystal, transparent and unchanged, it is the skin of a living thought and may vary greatly in color and content according to the circumstances in which it is used," wrote Justice Oliver Wendall Holmes in Towne v Eisner, 245 US 418, 425 (1918).

True it is, words are chameleons reflecting the color of their environment and as that environment, social, economic, and legal, changes, so too do words, and their meanings, change. Thus are new words created.

Language is alive! To remain relevant, a dictionary requires periodic revision and updating. This third edition of Ballentine's Law Dictionary is the publisher's response to its recognition that law and language change too quickly for a practicing attorney to rely on a dictionary a generation old.

Every effort has been expended to assure the authority and reliability of this work. The definitions of the more than 30,000 terms contained herein are largely based on the actual construction of those terms by courts of last resort, with each case cited to the page on which the definition appears. The use of these primary sources should give the lawyer-researcher that added measure of confidence which, itself, is perhaps the indefinable element of success.

The scope of this third edition is larger than its predecessors. Within these pages the reader will find precise explanations of many federal statutes and all uniform acts, together with the particular terms used in each, and a listing of the states adopting such enactments as patterns or in their entirety. Further, current definitions of tax terms, all in accord with the latest revenue rulings and tax court cases, are included.

The pronunciation feature, which first brought this dictionary to the legal profession's immediate attention in 1930, has been retained and improved by the adoption of the simplest, clearest available keys and guides.

Finally, the attention of the Bar should be directed to the fact that the accomplishment of this particular edition is directly attributable to the prodigious efforts of its editor the late William S. Anderson who, after almost 33 years of service as a lawyer-editor, retired as Managing Editor of the Lawyers Cooperative Publishing Company in February 1962. During his long and distinguished career, Mr. Anderson authored a number of scholarly legal treatises which were relied upon by lawyers in all the states of this Union. As Managing Editor of the 58-volume encyclopedia Ohio Jurisprudence (2d edition), of Carmody-Wait Cyclopedia of New York Practice (1st edition), and of New York Jurisprudence, his contribution to the development of legal knowledge was profound and lasting. William S. Anderson passed away just as this dictionary, his final and perhaps greatest achievement, was going to press. To him can justly be applied Lord Coke's comment: "When a great learned man, who is long in making, dieth, much learning dieth with him."

FOREWORD TO THE FIRST EDITION
BY ROSCOE POUND
LATE DEAN OF HARVARD UNIVERSITY LAW SCHOOL

My first advice to the beginner in the study of law has always been to buy a good law dictionary and turn to it constantly. It was the custom formerly to give an elementary course in which everyday terms and ordinary legal conceptions were explained. But law school experience has shown the futility of such courses.

The sure way of acquiring an enduring grasp upon legal terminology is to look up every word as it is encountered in the student's reading, get its meaning concretely in view of the context, and keep up this process until there is an assured conviction that it is no longer necessary.

The popular use of legal terms is so loose, so many words have technical legal meanings different from those which they bear in ordinary speech, and intelligent understanding of the cases and of law books depends so much upon a clear grasp of the terms used, that the beginner cannot be too assiduous in pulling down his law dictionary whenever he has the slightest reason to suspect that a word he meets in his reading may have a technical legal meaning. By resorting constantly to his law dictionary he will acquire a sure and accurate use of legal terms, and incidentally a mass of legal information, in such a way that they will become permanent possessions; not something to be crammed for examination in abstract definitions, disgorged at the examination, and then reacquired painfully and more concretely in the course of study and practice.

Accurate use of legal terms is important much beyond the exigencies of the student's reading and study. He will be judged not only by his teachers, but by his elders and his contemporaries in the profession. Few things can harm him more than a reputation for slovenliness and inaccuracy. If he uses legal terms carelessly or ignorantly, he will create a bad impression not easy to live down. He should from the very beginning exert himself to be sure that he knows the exact meaning of the terms he uses, and strive to avoid slovenly usages and popular misuses when he is writing or speaking to judges or lawyers, or in professional connections.

Another matter of importance is the pronunciation of legal terms. Now that the English pronunciation of Latin is no longer taught in our schools, the traditional pronunciation of law terms is being replaced by a slovenly jargon. It is well worth the student's time and effort to acquire the pronunciation traditional in the profession. Indeed, the educated lawyer will be as careful in his pronunciations of law Latin as in his pronunciation of English.

I am glad to take advantage of the request to write a foreword for Mr. Ballentine's dictionary in order to say to law students generally what I have been saying to my own students with all earnestness for the past thirty years.

PREFACE TO THE FIRST EDITION

Where shall the lawyer turn for the meaning of a word, a term, an expression, or a maxim which has been employed in a statute, a decision, a pleading, a treaty, a will, a contract, or any other document? As stated by Justice Harrison in Estate of Nelson, 132 Cal. 182, 194, 64 Pac. Rep. 294: "Philology at best is an unsafe criterion for ascertaining the meaning of words which are in common use, and the definition thus obtained is always subordinate to the meaning derived from the context, or from the circumstances under which the word is used."

It is submitted that one of the hopeful sources of such information should be found in the law dictionaries, but, to quote from the opinion of Bigelow, C. J., in Dole v. New England Mutual Marine Insurance Co., 88 Mass. (6 Allen) 373, 386: "It is not always safe to adopt the mere etymological meaning of words, or the definitions which lexicographers give to them. It is often necessary to inquire and ascertain whether a particular word or phrase has acquired a special or peculiar meaning, as applied to the subject-matter of the contract, or whether it is used with any restricted signification by authors or jurists or those conversant with the business to which the contract relates."

From all these considerations, it would seem that an ideal lawyers' dictionary, the star to which the editor has, perhaps with some presumption, hitched his wagon, may one day be published. Adopting the language of Lumpkin, J., in Hargroves v. Cooke, 15 Ga. 321, 333, "I would not thoughtlessly aggravate the bibliomania or extravagant desire of multiplying books abroad in the land; still, if there be any member of the bar who feels burdened to discharge the duty which Sir Edward Coke says every man owes to his profession, to bring forth something of this sort, according to his power, place and capacity, I would suggest" the publication of a law dictionary containing every word, term and expression which has been defined or construed by the judges of the courts of last resort and the more eminent text-writers, citing the cases and works and stating the pages on which the definitions appear.

In the preface of a pocket-size law dictionary published by the editor in 1916, it was stated that the main effort in the work had been directed at the omission of whatever belonged exclusively to the encyclopedias and the inclusion of as many words, terms and phrases as possible which are peculiar to the law, or which have meanings which are peculiar to the law. The same effort has been made in the present work, which contains all of the matter in the small book and very much more besides. The number of words, terms and phrases has been more than doubled; the definitions are much more full and complete; a great many authorities have been cited; the cross-references have been multiplied, and the pronunciation feature has been added, all with a view to making a book more useful to the law student and to the profession.

As to the pronunciation, it is the editor's belief that this is the first law dictionary in the English language which contains this feature. His experience and that of other lawyers and law teachers has proved the need and importance of a law dictionary giving the correct pronunciation of legal terms. As Dean Pound says in his Foreword in this dictionary,

"Another matter of importance is the pronunciation of legal terms. Now that the English pronunciation of Latin is no longer taught in our schools, the traditional pronunciation of law terms is being replaced by a slovenly jargon. It is well worth the student's time and effort to acquire the pronunciation traditional in the profession. Indeed, the educated lawyer will be as careful in his pronunciations of law Latin as in his pronunciation of English."

If this book shall meet the generous reception which was accorded its small predecessor, its editor will be well rewarded.

San Francisco.

JAMES A. BALLENTINE.

CONTENTS

	Page
Key to Pronunciation	Inside Front Cover
Foreword to the Third Edition	iii
Foreword to the First Edition	v
Preface to the First Edition	vii
Editor's Acknowledgment	ix
Dictionary with Pronunciations	1
Abbreviations of Legal Reports, Treatises, and Phrases	1389

A LAW DICTIONARY
WITH
PRONUNCIATIONS

A

A (ạ;ā, for emphasis). The first letter of the English alphabet, deriving from the Greek "alpha." The indefinite article. One or any one, depending upon the entire context in which it appears. State v Martin, 60 Ark 343, 30 SW 421 (holding that a constitutional provision of a constitution for "a judge" for each circuit is not a limitation upon the power of the legislature to provide for an additional judge;) First Trust Joint Stock Land Bank v Armstrong, 222 Iowa 425, 269 NW 502; Snowden v Guion, 101 NY 458, 5 NE 322 (holding that a policy insuring against loss by "a sea" covers damage to ship or cargo caused by a succession of heavy waves.)

An abbreviation, although not recommended, of **acre.** An algebraic symbol of a known quantity. Symbolizing, when encircled, computation at a designated rate, for example, "interest @ 6%." An abbreviation of the Welsh **ap.**

Latin: Used interchangeably with "ab" and "abs," as the context requires, for prepositions:— from; after; in; on; of; out of; because of; with.

French: Often appearing in the form "à" in expressions having legal significance as a preposition: —to; from; at; on; in; for; with.

See **an.**

AAA. Abbreviation of Agricultural Adjustment Administration. Also abbreviation of American Automobile Association.

a aver et tener (ā ā′vĕr et te′nĕr). To have and to hold.

Ab (ab). The eleventh month of the year according to the Jewish lunisolar calendar.

a.b. An abbreviation of able-bodied, where used in ship's papers after the name of a sailor.

A. B. An abbreviation of Bachelor of Arts.

ABA. Abbreviation of American Bar Association. See **bar association.**

abacinate. Same as **abbacinate.**

abaction (ab-ak′shon). An abactor's theft.

ab actis (ab ak′tis). A clerk or recorder.

abactor (ab-ak′tor). A cattle thief who takes in numbers.

ab aeterno (ab ē-ter′nō). From eternity.

ab agendo (ab ā-jen′dō). Incapacitated.

abalienare (ab-ā-li-ē-nā′re). (Civil law.) To transfer an interest or right in, or a title to, real or personal property.

abandon. To withdraw entirely from a person or a thing, putting aside all care for him or it.

To abandon a person is to withdraw from one entitled to support. A child is abandoned by his parent; a wife by her husband. Pidge v Pidge, 44 Mass (3 Met) 257,265. A patient may be the subject of abandonment by a physician. 41 Am J1st Phys & S § 102.

abandoned property. Property to which an owner has voluntarily relinquished all right, title, claim and possession with the intention of terminating his ownership, but without vesting it in any other person and with the intention of not reclaiming future possession or resuming ownership, possession, or enjoyment. 1 Am J2d Aband § 1.

abandonee (a-ban-do-ne′). A person to whom property or rights are abandoned or relinquished.

abandonment for torts or wrongs. (Civil law.) The relinquishment of an animal or a slave in settlement of liability.

abandonment of attachment lien. Affirmative act or conduct of the creditor inconsistent with the continuance of the lien. 6 Am J2d Attach § 412.

abandonment of child. An actual desertion accompanied by an intention, express or implied, to sever the relation entirely and throw off the obligations growing out of the relation. 39 Am J1st P & C §§ 2, 104.

abandonment of copyright. Publication without obtaining a copyright. 18 Am J2d Copyr § 84.

abandonment of homestead. An actual relinquishment of possession of the premises and removal therefrom, coupled with an intention to abandon the use of the property as a homestead, or an intention to remain away after such removal. See 26 Am J1st Home § 193.

abandonment of invention. Voluntary declaration of a purpose to abandon or conduct inconsistent with the right to obtain patent protection. Electric Storage Battery Co. v Shimadzu, 307 US 5, 83 L Ed 1071, 59 S Ct 675.

If an inventor, after perfecting his invention and applying for a patent, and thereby irretrievably committing himself to the proposition that his invention is ripe for introduction to the public, accept the decision rejecting his application, and cast aside his invention as no longer of any value to him, he thereby makes it forever public property and forever abandons it. See Consolidated Fruit Jar Co. v Bellaire Stamping Co. (CC Ohio) 27 F 337, 381.

abandonment of patent. A defense sometimes asserted in infringement cases. 40 Am J1st P § 184. See **abandonment of invention.**

abandonment of property. Intentional and absolute relinquishment of property without reference to any particular person or for any particular purpose. 1 Am J2d Aband § 1; 3 Am J2d Adv P § 77.

Abandoned property is that to which the owner has voluntarily relinquished all right, title, claim, and possession with the intention of terminating his ownership, but without vesting it in any other person, and with no intention of reclaiming possession or resuming ownership and enjoyment in the future. 1 Am J2d Aband § 1.

Abandonment is the relinquishment of a right or property with the intention of not reclaiming it or reassuming its ownership or enjoyment. Ellis v Brown (CA6 Ky) 177 F2d 677, 13 ALR2d 945.

In marine insurance, the act of the insured in notifying the insurer that owing to damage done to the subject of the insurance, he elects to take the amount of the insurance in the place of the subject thereof, the remnant of which he cedes to the insurer. 29A Am J Rev ed Ins § 1572.

(Mining Law). "The term 'forfeiture' is often employed by miners as synonymous with abandonment." See Wiseman v McNulty, 25 Cal 230.

See **derelict; dereliction; presumed dereliction; renunciation; res derelicta.**

abandonment of spouse. The unjustified separation of one spouse from the other with the deliberate intention of the offender to terminate the matrimonial relation. Bennett v Bennett, 197 Md 408, 79 A2d 513, 29 ALR2d 467.

As the word is used in the state of Kentucky in a statute relative to divorce, it has been construed to include the refusal by the offending spouse to recognize and contribute to the marital relation for a period of one year, although the spouses sleep beneath the same roof. See McQuinn v McQuinn, 110 Ky 321, 328, 61 SW 360.

See **desertion.**

abandonment of trademark or tradename. Something more than temporary disuse; something showing not only a practical abandonment but an actual intent to abandon. 52 Am J1st Tradem § 30.

abandonment of use. A voluntary, affirmative, completed act whereby the right to resume a noncomforming use under the zoning law is lost to the owner. 58 Am J1st Zon § 153.

abandonment to insurer. The act of the insured in notifying the insurer that owing to damage done to the subject of the insurance he elects to take the amount of the insurance in the place of the subject thereof, the remnant of which he cedes to the insurer. 29A Am J Rev ed Ins § 1572.

See **fifty percent rule,** i.

abandum (a-ban'dum). A chattel confiscated or forfeited.

abannition (ab-a-nish'on). The punishment of banishment.

ab ante (ab an'tē). In advance. Beforehand.

ab antecedente (ab an-te-sē-den'te). In advance; beforehand.

ab antiquo (ab an-tī'quō). From antiquity; anciently. See 3 Bl Comm 96.

abarnare (ab-ar-nā're). To expose a concealed crime.

ab assuetis non fit injuria (ab as-su-ē'tis non fit in-jū'ri-a). The violation of a legal right is not affected by acquiescence.

abatable. Capable of abatement.

abatable nuisance. A nuisance that is not permanent, because it can be eliminated. Bischof v Merchants Nat. Bank, 75 Neb 838, 106 NW 996.

abatamentum (ab″a-ta-men′tum). The wrongful entry and taking possession of real property by a stranger, before the heir or devisee has entered.

See **abatement.**

abatare (ab-a-tā′re). To put an end to; to cut down; to reduce; to diminish.

abate. To quash, beat down, or destroy, as in the case of a nuisance or an objectionable writ.

abatement of action. The entire overthrow or destruction of an action, resulting from the fact that the defendant pleads a matter which defeats the action either for the time being or permanently. 1 Am J2d Abat & R § 1.

A suit at law, when it abates as at common law, is absolutely dead; any further enforcement of the cause of action necessitates the bringing of a new suit. But in courts of equity and also in some law courts proceeding under modern practice statutes or rules, an abatement signifies only a present suspension of all proceedings in the suit because of the want of proper parties capable of proceeding therein; the suit can be revived or put in motion by a bill of revivor and proceed to its regular determination. 1 Am J2d Abat & R § 1.

"Abatement" and "stay of proceedings" are in some respects similar, but are not identical; to abate a suit is to put an end to it, at least for the time. Simmons v Superior Court, 96 Cal App 2d 119, 214 P2d 844, 19 ALR2d 288.

See **plea in abatement.**

abatement of bequest. The process of determining the distribution of the assets left by a testator at his death among the various beneficiaries named in the will, where it appears that such assets are insufficient to pay both the debts of the testator and the expenses of administrating his estate and also all of the legacies and devices called for by the will. 57 Am J1st Wills § 1457.

abatement of cause of action. The extinguishment of a cause of action upon the death of a party, where the cause is not one which survives. 1 Am J2d Abat & R § 1.

abatement of debt. Proportionate reduction of satisfaction where the fund for payment is insufficient to meet full payment. See Brown v Brown, 79 Va 648, 650.

abatement of freehold. The extinguishment of the freehold of heir or devisee by the entry of a stranger between the death of the ancestor or testator who died seized and the entry of the heir or devisee. 3 Bl Comm 167.

abatement of nuisance. The extinction or termination of a nuisance whether effected physically by or under the direction of the party injured by the nuisance, or by suit instituted by him.

See **summary abatement.**

abatement of tax assessment. The relief granted against an assessment for illegality or irregularity in the imposition of the tax or, under some statutes, because of the impoverishment of the taxpayer. 51 Am J1st Tax §§ 743 et seq.

abator (a-bā′tor). An occupier without color of title.

A stranger was so called if where a person died seized of an inheritance, and before the heir or devisee entered, the stranger, who had no right, made an entry and got possession of the freehold. See Brown v Burdick, 25 Ohio St 260, 268.

ab auctoritate (ab âk-tō-ri-tā'te). From authority or precedent.

abavus (ab'a-vus). A great-great-grandfather. See 2 Bl Comm 207.
　The feminine form "abavia" stands for great-great-grandmother.

abbacinate (a-bas'i-nāt). To put out the eyes.

abbacy (ab'a̧-si). An abbey and its appurtenances; the jurisdiction of an abbot; the rights and privileges of an abbot.

abbatial (a-bā'shial). Pertaining to an abbey or an abbot.

abbess (ab'es). The female head of a nuns' convent, corresponding to the abbot of a monastery.

abbey (ab'e). A monastery of monks or a convent of nuns.

abbey-land. An estate in real property annexed to an abbey.

abbot. The head monk of a monastery; an Episcopal rector who is head clergyman of a parish.

abbreviate. Verb: to shorten. Noun: an abstract of a longer instrument or writing.

abbreviate of adjudication. Abstract of judgment.

abbreviations. Shortened forms of words obtained by omitting one or more letters or syllables, or by using various signs, symbols, and characters.
　The abbreviations more commonly used in modern times consist of initial letters or syllables, the omissions of intermediate syllables, etc., usually being designated contractions. 1 Am J2d Abbr § 1.

abbreviationum, ille numerus et sensus accipiendus est, ut concessio non sit inanis (ab-bre-vi-ā-she-ō'-num, il'le nu'me-rus et sēn'sus ak-si-pi-en'dus est, ut kon-se'she-ō non sit in-ā'nis). In abbreviations, that number and sense should be taken which will not avoid the grant.

abbrochment (a-broch'ment). The ancient offense of forestalling.

ABC. A game of chance, prohibited as gambling where played for a stake. Anno: 135 ALR 120.

ABC Powers. Argentina, Brazil, and Chile.

ABC transaction. A tax-law term for three-party arrangement in financing the purchase of a mineral lease.

abdicate. Entirely to renounce, throw off, disown, relinquish. People v Board of Police (NY) 26 Barb 487, 501.

abdication (ab-di-kā'shon). The renunciation or abandonment by a person of an office, trust, or sovereignty to which he is entitled.
　The word is also frequently applied to a government, as where a government is said to abdicate its taxing power.

abdicatio tutelae (ab-di-kā'she-ō tū-tē'lē). (Civil Law). The resignation of a guardian.

abditorium (ab-di-tō'ri-um). A hiding place for the safe-keeping of valuables and relics.

abduct. To take a child from its parent or a wife from her spouse surreptitiously or by force. Doss v State, 220 Ala 30, 123 So 231, 68 ALR 712; 1 Am J2d Abduct § 2.
　The word is derived from the Latin word "abducere" and means "to lead away." Anno: 68 ALR 719.

abduction. Unlawful interference with a family relationship by taking or leading a person away, for example, the taking of a child from its parent, irrespective of the consent of the person taken. 1 Am J2d Abduct § 2. Illegally leading away or carrying off a person, more especially the taking or carrying away of a wife, child, a ward, or a voter, by fraud, persuasion, or open violence.
　The offense is against the family relationship rather than the person taken and may be committed irrespective of his consent to the taking. 1 Am J2d Abduct § 2.
　See **kidnapping; ravishment.**

abductor (ab-duk'tor). One who abducts.
　See **abduction.**

abearance (a-bār'ans). "Recognizance with sureties for good behavior. It includes security for the peace, and somewhat more." See 4 Bl Comm 256.

ab epistolis (ab e-pis'to-lus). A subordinate in charge of correspondence.

abet (a-bet'). To give aid, to assist, especially in the commission of a criminal offense. To exertion of a force, physical or moral, joined with that of another in the perpetration of a criminal offense. Anno: 5 ALR 786.
　Although there are some offenses which are so defined by statute or by common law that they may be committed only by certain persons or classes of persons, nevertheless a person not within the class of those by whom the crime may be directly perpetrated may, by aiding and abetting a person who is within the scope of the definition, render himself criminally liable. Anno: 131 ALR 1322.
　See **accessory; accomplice; aiding and abetting.**

abetment (a-bet'ment). The act of abetting.

abettare (a-bet-tā're). To aid or abet.

abettor (a-bet'or). One who aids, abets or instigates; one who advises, counsels, procures, or encourages another to commit a crime. 21 Am J2d Crim L § 119.

ab extra (ab eks'trä). From without; from outside.
　Extraneous evidence introduced to explain a writing is sometimes called "ab extra." Lunt v Holland, 14 Mass 149, 151.

abeyance. In expectation, remembrance, and contemplation in law.
　An estate in fee is in abeyance where there is no person in esse in whom it may vest and abide, although the law considers it as always potentially existing and ready to vest when a proper person in whom it may vest appears. 28 Am J2d Est § 10.

abeyant (a̧-bā'ant). The state or condition of an estate or fee which is in abeyance.

abide. To dwell, to obey; to comply with; to perform; to execute; to conform to; as to abide the judgment or order of the court. Jackson v State, 30 Kan 88, 1 P 317.
　See **costs to abide event.**

abiding conviction. An expression sometimes used in instructing juries respecting reasonable doubt and there having the signification of settled and fixed, a conviction which may follow a careful examination and comparison of the whole evidence. Hopt v Utah, 120 US 430, 30 L Ed 708, 7 S Ct 614.

abiding faith. A belief or confidence in the guilt of one accused of crime, which remains or continues in the minds of the jury. See Patzwald v United States, 7 Okla 232, 54 P 458.

abiding place. A place of abode. See **domicil; residence.**

abigeus (ab-i′jē-us). A cattle-stealer, singular of "abigei."

ability to act or perform. See **capacity.**

ability to pay debts. See **able to pay; insolvency.**

ability to support. As an element of nonsupport constituting a ground for divorce:—the capacity to work gainfully and opportunity to do so; in some jurisdictions, the possession of property or funds from which support may be provided. 24 Am J2d Divorce & S § 143.

ab impossibili (ab im-pos-sib′lī). From an impossibility.

ab inconvenienti (ab in-kon-ve-ni-en′tī). From inconvenience.

ab initio (ab i-nish′i-ō). From the beginning. See **trespass ab initio; unlawful ab initio.**

ab initio mundi (ab in-i′she-ō mun′dī). From the beginning of the world.

ab intestato (ab in-tes-tā′tō). From one who left no will, that is, succession to the property of one who dies intestate.

ab intra (ab in′trä). From within.

ab invito (ab in-vī′tō). Against one's will.

ab irato (ab ī-rā′tō). In anger.

abishering (a-bish′er-ing). The right or privilege of being freed and exempt from forfeitures and amercements.

abjudicate (ab-jö′di-kāt). To deprive by a judgment; to adjudge to be wrong or unlawful.

abjuration of the realm (ab-jö-rā′shọn). Originally a renunciation of one's country, upon oath of perpetual banishment, and the doctrine of abjuring the realm, by which a husband became civilly dead, was an incident of the right of sanctuary, which was abolished by statute under James the First. The meaning of the word has changed until it implies simply a total abandonment of the state; a departure from the state without intention of returning. Mead v Hughes' Adm. 15 Ala 141. See **expatriation.**

able. Legally qualified; legally authorized. Fit for a task. See **capacity; infancy; insanity.**

able and willing. See **ready.**

able-bodied. The absence of those palpable and visible defects, which evidently incapacitate the person from performing ordinary duties but not necessarily absence from all physical defects. Darling v Bowen, 10 Vt 148, 152.

able buyer. A purchaser who has the money at the time to make any cash payment that is required and who is in condition financially to meet any deferred payments. Reynor v Mackrill, 181 Iowa 210, 164 NW 335, 1 ALR 523. Not one who might have property upon which he could raise the necessary money. Reynor v Mackrill, 181 Iowa 210, 164 NW 335, 1 ALR 523, 528.

A purchaser is not "able" where he is depending upon third parties who are in no way bound to furnish the funds to make the purchase. Anno: 1 ALR 528.

ablegate (ab′li-gāt). An envoy of the Pope.

able to pay. In a majority of the jurisdictions it is held that a promise to pay when the promisor "is able" is a conditional, and not an absolute promise to pay, and that the promisee is not entitled to recover on such a promise unless the promisor is able to pay the debt.

The minority view is that this is an absolute and not a conditional promise. 17 Am J2d Contr § 341.

ablocate (ab′lō-kāt). To lease; to let for hire.

abnegate (ab′nē-gāt). To give up; to surrender; to renounce.

abnormally dangerous. Fraught with peril not necessarily or inherently connected with the place or thing.

Employees act within their rights in quitting work on the ground that the premises have become "abnormally dangerous," where an accumulation of dust, grit, and dangerous abrasives is consequent upon the failure of a blower. NLRB v Knight Morley Corp. (CA6) 251 F2d 753, cert den 357 US 927, 2 L Ed 2d 1370, 78 S Ct 1372, reh den 358 US 858, 3 L Ed 2d 93, 79 S Ct 15.

abode. A dwelling-place; a residence. Central Mfrs. Mut. Ins. Co. v Friedman, 213 Ark 9, 209 SW2d 102, 1 ALR2d 557. Sometimes, but not necessarily, synonymous with domicil. 25 Am J2d Dom § 4.

The term "abode" or "usual place of abode" is often synonymous with domicil, but it is not necessarily so, since in some instances one's domicil may be different from his abode. But the "permanent abode" prescribed by statute as necessary to qualify one to vote means nothing more than a domicil or home. 25 Am J2d Dom § 8.

ab olim (ab ō′lim). Formerly; in times past. 3 Bl Comm 96.

ab olim ordinatum (ab ō′lim or-di-nā′tum). Formerly ordained. See 3 Bl Comm 96.

abolish (ạ-bol′ish). To repeal; to recall; to revoke; to cancel and eliminate entirely.

abolitio legis (ab-o-li′she-ó lē′jis). The repeal of a law.

abolition. In the broad sense, an entire elimination or extinguishment, for example, the abolition of slavery by the Thirteenth Amendment; in a narrower sense, leave to stop a prosecution. See **letters of abolition.**

aborticide (a-bôr′ti-sīd). The killing of the fetus in the uterus.

abortifacient (a-bôr-ti-fā′shient). Anything used to cause an abortion.

abortion (a-bôr′shon). The explusion of the fetus at a period of utero-gestation so early that it has not acquired the power of sustaining an independent life. 1 Am J2d Abort § 1.

The crime of "abortion" is the wilful bringing about of an abortion without justification or excuse. 1 Am J2d Abort § 1.

Although there may be a technical distinction recognized in medicine between abortion and miscarriage, the words are usually synonymous in law. Anderson v Commonwealth, 190 Va 665, 58 SE2d 72, 16 ALR2d 942; 1 Am J2d Abort § 1.

See **Miscarriage.**

abortionist (a-bôr′shon-ist). One who commits the crime of producing an abortion.

abortive (ạ-bôr′tiv). Anything used to produce an abortion or miscarriage.

abortive child. Such a child as by an untimely birth is either born dead, or incapable of living. Cottin v Cottin (La) 5 Mart 93, 94.

abortive trial. A trial in which no verdict is reached involving no misconduct of a party.

abortus (a-bôr′tus). An aborted fetus.

about. In reference to time:—a word of flexible significance, denoting an approximation to exactness. 52 Am J1st Time § 30. Signifying present and not future action, as in a representation that one is "about to abandon" a business. 37 Am J2d Fraud § 65. In reference to area, quantity, dimension:—a word whose precise meaning depends upon the surrounding circumstances, frequently used as a synonym for "nearly" or "approximately" and for the purpose of giving a margin for excess or deficiency. 17 Am J2d Contr § 282. A qualifying word in the description of a boundary which is usually to be disregarded if not controlled or explained by monuments or other markers, but may be given meaning in effect when so controlled and explained. 12 Am J2d Bound § 57.

As used in a description of the subject matter in a contract for the sale of real estate, the term "about" is one of precaution or safety, being intended to cover slight and unimportant inaccuracies. 56 Am J1st V & P § 131.

As used in a conveyance in connection with area, the word is generally one of precaution and safety, intended to cover some unimportant inaccuracy, and has been held not to estop either party from setting up a deficiency, or surplus, sufficiently large to raise the presumption that there was not a meeting of the minds. But it has also been held that the obvious common sense meaning of such words is that the parties shall run the risk of gain or loss, and if the area proves greater or less than the area sold, they shall abide by their bargain. See 23 Am J2d Deeds § 247.

In contracts of sale of personalty in estimating the quantity to be delivered, the word is given practically the same meaning as the phrase "more or less," its use being only for the purpose of providing against accidental variations arising from slight and unimportant excesses or deficiencies in number, weight, or measure. See 46 Am J1st Sales § 156.

As used in Workmen's Compensation statutes to describe the locus of the industrial enterprise, it has been treated as enlarging the application of the act, and has been spoken of as an "elastic word." Thus, a workman may be employed "about" or "in," or "on" a factory, although he is on the street adjoining the factory, if the work he is performing is part of the factory business; and also where he is employed in a building adjoining the factory proper, although at some distance from it. 58 Am J1st Workm Comp § 86.

about to. In ordinary grammatical construction, "about" before an infinitive means "on the point of" or "in the act of." It signifies present and not future action. For example, the words "about to abandon" are synonymous with "intended now to abandon." See Sallies v Johnson, 85 Conn 77, 81 A 974.

about to remove. An act in removing property, which will soon be performed, rather than one which will be performed within a definite period of time. 6 Am J2d Attach § 242.

above. Higher in the sense of position, as where something is described as above high-water mark; or in the sense of superiority, for example, a higher court. In a higher place; preceding, as where there is a reference in a will to "above bequests." 28 Am J Rev ed Inher T § 493.
See **bail above**.

above named. A sufficient reference in a certificate of acknowledgment to the party acknowledging. 1 Am J2d Ack § 66.

ab ovo (ab ō′vō). From the egg; that is, from the beginning.

Abp. Abbreviation of **Archbishop**.

abridge. To reduce; to cut down; to omit a part of a prayer or demand for relief.

To abridge within the meaning of the law of copyright is to preserve the substance, the essence, of the work in more terse language suited to the purpose. 18 Am J2d Copyr § 115.

abridgment. A shortened version. 18 Am J2d Copyr § 42.

abridgment of damages. Reduction of damages by order of court.

abroach (a̱-brōch′). See **broach**.

abroachment (a̱-brōch′ment). The purchase of goods wholesale and the sale of them at retail, without offering them in open market.

abroad. Beyond the seas or out of the country.
See **traveling abroad**.

abrogate. To repeal; to make void; to annul.

abrogatio legis (ab-ro-gā′she-ō lē′jis). The repeal of a law.

abrogation. The repeal of a law; an avoidance; an annulment.
See **implied abrogation**.

abrogative (ab′rō-gā-tiv). Annulling or repealing: as an abrogative statute.

abscond. To withdraw clandestinely, to hide or conceal one's self, for the purpose of avoiding legal proceedings. McMorran v Moore, 113 Mich 101, 104.

absconder (ab-skon′dėr). One who absconds.

absconding debtor. A person who has gone out of the state, or one who has intentionally concealed himself from his creditors, or withdrawn himself from the reach of their suits, with intent to frustrate their just demand. Fitch v Waite, 5 Conn 117, 121.

absence. The state of being away, not being present.
See **effective absence**.

Absence as Evidence of Death Act. One of the Uniform Laws. 1 Am J2d Absent § 2.

absence for seven years. See **presumption of death**.

absence from the state. Out of the state, having left the state. Montgomery v. Cleveland, 134 Miss 132, 98 So 111, 32 ALR 1151.

In statutes of limitation which provide that the running of the statute is suspended during the defendant's absence from the state, mere temporary absence in another state is insufficient to stop the running of the statute. 34 Am J1st Lim Ac § 218.

The provision found in limitation statutes that the statute is not to run when the defendant is absent from the state has been interpreted by most courts not to apply if process could be served notwithstanding such absence. Some courts, however, giving a literal construction to the statute, have held that the provision still applies. 34 Am J1st Lim Ac § 221.

The expressions "absent from" and "out of the state" have been employed by a majority of the states having limitation statutes with a suspensory provision, and the courts in each of those jurisdictions, with few exceptions have construed such a statute as applying to a defendant who was a nonresident when the cause of action accrued. Anno: 17 ALR2d 506.

Within the meaning of the statute of limitations a corporation's absence from the state begins when it ceases to do business therein, cancels its license, files its resolution of withdrawal and removes its officers and representatives from the state. The Secretary of State and the Commissioner of Securities, its designated attorneys for the service of process, are its agents in no such sense as to represent the continued corporate presence of the corporation in the state. City Co. of New York, Inc. v Stern (CA8 Minn) 110 F2d 601.

absence of jurisdiction. See **lack of jurisdiction.**

absent. The state of being away from a place; withdrawal from a place; not existing.
See **absence; absence from the state.**

absentee. A person who, for whatsoever reason, is missing from his residence or who has departed to parts unknown, concerning whose whereabouts no information is forthcoming. 1 Am J2d Absent § 1.

Absentees may be those of whom little or nothing may be known. They may be dead. See Re Estate of Kite, 194 Iowa 129, 187 NW 585, 24 ALR 850.

See **absence; absence from the state; absence out of the state.**

absenteeism (ab-sęn-tē'izm). Wilful misconduct of an employee for the purposes of unemployment compensation, where persistent or chronic, without notice or excuse, and continued in the face of warnings by the employer. Kelleher v Unemployment Compensation Board of Review 175 Pa Super 261, 104 A2d 171, 41 ALR2d 1155; Anno: 41 ALR2d 1158.

Absentees' Property Act. One of the Uniform Laws. 1 Am J2d Absent § 2.

absente reo (ab-sen'tē rē'ō). In the absence of the defendant.

absentia. See **absence; durante absentia.**

absent out of the state. Beyond the boundaries of the state so that one cannot be reached by process. 34 Am J1st Lim Ac § 215.

absinthe (ab'sinth). A highly aromatic but potent liquor of an opaline green color and bitter taste, prepared by steeping in alcohol or strong spirit bitter herbs, the chief of them being wormwood. Erhardt v Steinhardt, 153 US 177, 182, 38 L Ed 678, 679, 14 S Ct 715.

absoluta sententia expositore non indiget (ab-so-lū'ta sen-ten'she-a ex-po-zi-tō're non īn'di-jet). Clear sense requires no explanation.

absolute (ab'so-lūt). Free; unconditional; unrestricted; not dependent upon or appurtenant to something else. Anno: 36 ALR2d 151 (absolute gift to spouse.)

The most ordinary signification of the adjective absolute is "unrestricted" or "unconditional." Thus, an absolute estate in land is an estate in fee simple. Also, in the law of insurance, an absolute interest in property is one which is so completely vested in the individual that there could be no danger of his being deprived of it without his own consent. See Columbia Water Power Co. v Columbia Electric Street Railway Light & Power Co., 172 US 475, 491, 43 L Ed 520, 527, 19 S Ct 247.
See **conditional; rule absolute.**

absolute acceptance. The unqualified assent to liability by the drawee on a bill of exchange.
Words written on a bill of exchange which demonstrate the intention to accept it are sufficient for that purpose. 11 Am J2d B & N § 507.

absolute assignment. An outright transfer of title, as distinguished from a transfer by way of security.

absolute control. The term imports that the person having such control is able to direct operations as he thinks best, without let or hindrance or direction by any other person, and that he is free to do what he thinks best in directing such operations. People v Boggess 75 Cal App 499, 243 P 478.

absolute conveyance. A conveyance free from conditions.

absolute covenant. An unconditional covenant.

absolute deed. See **absolute conveyance.**

absolute deed as mortgage. An instrument in the form of a deed which is given effect as a mortgage. 36 Am J1st Mtg §§ 125 et seq.

absolute delivery of deed. The simplest mode of delivering a deed is by manual transfer of it to the grantee, with the intention of relinquishing all control over the instrument and of passing title to the property. This delivery is defined as "absolute delivery," and undoubtedly it constitutes a consummation of the deed. 23 Am J2d Deeds § 91.

absolute divorce. A judicial dissolution or termination of the bonds of matrimony, because of marital misconduct or other statutory cause arising after the marriage ceremony, with the result that the status of the parties is changed from coverture to that of single persons. 24 Am J2d Div & S § 1.

absolute embargo. See **embargo.**

absolute estate. An estate in real property of which the owner has complete, unqualified and unconditional possession, control, dominion, and right of disposition, and which descends to his heirs upon his death, if his will does not otherwise direct.
See **absolute owner; fee; fee simple.**

The words "absolute estate" which appear in a will making bequests in trust as well as bequests of a full and complete interest has reference to the bequests other than those in trust. Hills v Hart, 136 Conn 536, 72 A2d 807.

absolute gift. So long as the condition or qualification imposed in the making of a gift is not inconsistent with the vesting of title in the donee, the gift is not invalidated for want of absolute character in the transfer. 24 Am J1st Gifts § 44.

absolute guaranty. An unconditional undertaking on the part of the guarantor that the debtor will pay the debt or perform the obligation. 24 Am J1st Guar § 16; Anno: 53 ALR2d 525.

A contract of guaranty is absolute where one absolutely guarantees the payment of money to another, where the amount of the payment is certain and definite, and where the time of payment is likewise determined certainly. Schulderberg-Kurdle Co. v Trice, 198 Va 85, 92 SE2d 374, 57 ALR2d 1204.

absolute interest. The nature of ownership of a thing objectively and lawfully appropriated by a person to his own use in exclusion of all others. Griffith v Charlotte, C & A R Co., 23 SC 25.

In the law of insurance, an absolute interest in property is one which is so completely vested in the individual that there could be no danger of his being deprived of it without his own consent. Columbia Water Power Co. v Columbia Electric Street Railway, Light & Power Co., 172 US 475, 491, 43 L Ed 520, 527, 19 S Ct 247.

See **absolute estate; limited interest.**

absolute liability. Liability for an injury resulting to another where no account is taken of the standard of care exercised, often called insurer's liability. 38 Am J1st Negl § 4. Criminal liability of which intent not an element. 21 Am J2d Crim L § 91. Liability of a principal as distinguished from that of a guarantor or surety.

The word as used in a Motor Vehicle Financial Responsibility Act providing that the liability of the insurer under the policy shall become absolute upon occurrence of the accident means that there shall be no defenses to liability of the insurer based upon any statement made by or on behalf of the insured or upon exclusions, conditions, terms, or language contained in the policy. Farm Bureau Auto. Ins. Co. v Martin, 97 NH 196, 84 A2d 823, 29 ALR2d 811.

absolutely (ab'so-lūt-li). Independently or unconditionally; wholly; positively. Collins v Hartford Acci. & Indem. Co. 178 Va 501, 17 SE2d 413, 137 ALR 1046; Anno: 36 ALR2d 151 (gift to spouse "absolutely").

absolutely privileged communications. See **absolute privilege.**

absolute nuisance A distinct civil wrong arising or resulting from the invasion of a legally protected interest, and consisting of an unreasonable interference with the use and enjoyment of the property of another; the doing of anything or the permitting of anything under one's control or direction to be done without just cause or excuse, the necessary consequence of which interferes with or annoys another in the enjoyment of his legal rights; the unlawful doing of anything or the permitting of anything under one's control or direction to be done which results in injury to another; or the collecting and keeping on one's premises of anything inherently dangerous or likely to do mischief if it escapes, which, escaping, injures another in the enjoyment of his legal rights. Anno: 73 ALR2d 1395.

absolute owner. A person in whom are combined at one time the right of possession, and the right of property. Harris v Southeast Portland Lumber Co., 123 Or 549, 262 P 243.

A vendee in possession under an executory contract for the purchase of the property is an absolute owner for purposes of fire insurance. Libby Lumber Co. v Pacific States Fire Ins. Co. 79 Mont 166, 255 P 340.

Each of two persons owning in severalty respective shares of personal property insured is the absolute owner of the property, within the meaning of a question and answer as to such ownership in an application for insurance thereon. Beebe v Ohio Farmers Ins. Co., 93 Mich 514, 53 NW 818.

absolute pardon. A pardon to which no conditions are attached by the authority granting it. 39 Am J1st Pard §§ 4, 5.

absolute predestination. A doctrine of some religious denominations that God foreknew and predestined all things whatsoever that may come to pass. See Bennett v Morgan, 112 Ky 512, 519, 66 SW 289.

absolute privilege. The privilege which exists in the law of defamation when by reason of the occasion on which a defamatory communication is made or the matter in reference to which the communication is made, no remedy can be had in a civil action. Anno: 13 ALR2d 893; 33 Am J1st L & S § 125.

absolute rights. Rights incident to the ownership of property, rights growing out of contractual relations, or the right to enter or refuse to enter into contractual relations.

These rights the individual may exercise without reference to his motive as to any injury resulting therefrom directly, since the courts, apparently on the ground of expediency, have consistently held that such an injury is not a legal injury in the sense that it is actionable. On the other hand, under the guise of exercising an absolute right, it is not lawful, according to some authorities, indirectly to interfere with the business, employment, or occupation of a third person, where the exercise of the right is with the object of injuring the latter rather than primarily benefiting the person exercising such right. 30 Am J Rev ed Interf § 51.

See **absolute estate; absolute owner.**

absolute rule. Same as **rule absolute.**

absolute warrandice (Scotch). An absolute warranty, whereby the grantor warrants against every imperfection in the thing or right conveyed.

absolute warranty. A warranty of personalty, made in a sale thereof, to which no conditions are attached. 46 Am J1st Sales § 301.

The covenant of warranty in a deed of real estate is an assurance by the grantor that the grantee and his heirs and assigns shall enjoy it without interruption by virtue of a paramount title and that they shall not, by force of a paramount title, be evicted from the land or deprived of possession thereof. 20 Am J2d Cov § 50.

absolution (Civil Law). A judgment declaring a defendant to be innocent of the crime charged.

absolutism. The principle of absolute power in the sovereign.

absolutist. An advocate of the principle of absolute power in the sovereign.

absolve. To acquit; to set free; to release.

absolvitor (ab-sol'vi-tor). A judgment of absolution.

absorbed tax. Where the price designated in the contract is a composite price, made up of various unspecified elements of cost in which is included the tax, not as a separate item, but as an integral part thereof, the tax is generally regarded as "absorbed or buried" in the price. 46 Am J1st Sales § 184; Anno: 115 ALR 667, supplemented in 132 ALR 706.

absque (abz'kwē). Without.

absque aliquo inde redendo (abz'kwē a'li-quō īn'de re-den'dō). Without reservation of rent.

absque consideratione curiae (abz'kwē kon-si-de-rā-she-ō'ne kū'ri-ē). Without the consideration of the court.

absque damno. See **injuria absque damno.**

absque hoc (abz'kwē hok). Without this.
See **special traverse.**

absque impetitione vasti (abz'kwē im-pē-ti-she-ō'ne vās'tī). Without impeachment of waste, a clause in a deed or lease signifying that the grantee or lessee shall not be liable for waste. See 2 Bl Comm 283.

absque injuria (abz'kwē in-jū'ri-a). Without violation of a legal right.
See **damnum absque injuria.**

absque tali causa (abz'kwē tā'lī kâ'zä). Without such cause.

abstract. Verb: to take without right. 10 Am J2d Banks § 224. To glean and state the pith of a discussion. Noun: an abridgment.

abstracter. One who prepares abstracts of title.
See **certificate of abstracter.**

abstract idea. A concept which has not been put in tangible form so as to be a subject of copyright, but which may be a subject of protection by contract. 18 Am J2d Copyr § 3.

abstract instruction. An instruction to the jury, which is generally regarded as insufficient and erroneous, that does not apply the law to the facts but is merely an abstract proposition of law. 53 Am J1st Tr § 573.

abstraction. A taking; a removal, especially a wrongful taking or removal.

Under the National Bank Act, the act of one who, being an officer of a national banking association, wrongfully takes or withdraws from it any of its moneys, funds, or credits, with intent to injure or defraud it or some other person or company, and, without its knowledge or consent, or that of its board of directors, converts them to the use of himself or of some person or company other than the bank. It is not necessarily the same as embezzlement, larceny or misapplication of funds. US v Northway, 120 US 327, 39 L Ed 664, 7 S Ct 580.

abstract of a fine. An abstract of the writ of covenant and the concord, naming the parties, the parcels of land, and the agreement, in a proceeding to alienate land by levying a fine. See 2 Bl Comm 351.

abstract of article. An abridgment, a less quantity containing the virtue and force of a greater quantity. That which comprises or concentrates in itself the essential qualities of a larger thing, or of several things; a compendium, epitome, or synopsis. Hess v Draffen & Co. 99 Mo App 580, 585, 74 SW 440.

abstract of judgment. A brief transcript of the essentials of a judgment.

abstract of record on appeal. A complete history in short, abbreviated form of the case as found in the record, complete enough to show that the questions presented for review have been properly preserved in the case, and to give a full understanding of the questions presented. 4 Am J2d A & E §§ 407, 408.

abstract of title. A short account of the state of the title to real estate, or a synopsis of the instruments which show title—an epitome of the record evidence of title. 1 Am J2d Abstr T § 1.

It should contain a full summary of all grants, conveyances, wills and all records and judicial proceedings whereby the title is in any way affected, and all incumbrances and liens of record, showing whether they have been released or not. 1 Am J2d Abstr T § 1.

A proper abstract requires a certification by an abstracter. 55 Am J1st V & P § 295.

abstract on appeal. See **abstract of record.**

abstract question. A moot, theoretical, academic, hypothetical, or speculative question. 20 Am J2d Cts § 81; 22 Am J2d Dec J § 10.

absurdity. Not only that which is physically impossible, but also that which is morally so. That is to be regarded as morally impossible which is contrary to reason, or in other words, which cannot be attributed to a man in his right senses. State v Hays, 81 Mo 574, 585.

Ab uno disce omnes (ab u'nō di'se om'nēz). From one part all may be learned. Nicholas' Estate, 8 Pa Dist 725, 726.

ab urbe condita (ab ėr'bē kon'di-tä). From the founding of the city. The Roman era began with the founding of Rome in 753 B. C.

abuse (a̤-būz'). From the Latin, "ab" and "utor;" to injure; to diminish in value; to wear away by using improperly. To wrong in speech, reproach coarsely, disparage, revile, malign. Campf v State, 80 Ohio St 321, 88 NE 887.

abuse (a̤-būs'). Ill treatment by physical means or by coarse insulting speech; improper treatment or use of something such as process.

Under a statute punishing the abuse in an attempt to have carnal knowledge of a female child, the word "abuse" applies only to injuries to the genital organs in an unsuccessful attempt at rape, and does not include mere forcible or wrongful illusage. 44 Am J1st Rape § 18.

abuse of discretion. Decision by whim or caprice, arbitrarily, or from a bad motive which amounts practically to a denial of justice as a clearly erroneous conclusion, one that is clearly against logic and effect of the facts presented. 5 Am J2d A & E § 774.

Abuse of judicial discretion, within the rule that an appellate court will not disturb the discretionary action of the court below unless the discretion was abused, is an exercise of discretionary power to an end or purpose not justified by, and clearly against, reason and evidence. Re Crane's Estate, 201 Okla 354, 206 P2d 726, 9 ALR2d 524.

There is no hard and fast rule by which an abuse of discretion may be determined, but in general an exercise of discretion, not to amount to an abuse, must be legally sound; there must be an honest attempt by the court to do what is right and equitable under the circumstances and the law, without the dictates of whim or caprice. 5 Am J2d A & E § 774.

abuse of distress. Making use of a distrained animal or chattel and thereby committing a conversion of it.

abuse of privilege. See **excess of privilege.**

abuse of process. The malicious perversion of a regularly issued civil or criminal process, for a purpose, and to obtain a result not lawfully warranted or properly attainable thereby, and for which perversion an action will lie to recover the pecuniary loss sustained. 1 Am J2d Abuse P § 1.

Malicious use of process is the employment of process for its ostensible purpose, but without reasonable or probable cause, whereas the malicious abuse of process is the employment of a process in a manner not contemplated by law, or to effect a purpose which such a process is not intended by law to effect. 1 Am J2d Abuse P § 2.

abusive language. Cruelty amounting to a ground for divorce, where it is so intense as to cause mental suffering sufficient to impair health. 24 Am J2d Div & S § 48.

abut (a̤-but'). To end at; to border on; to reach or touch with an end, as where a lot touches the highway. Hensler v Anacortes, 140 Wash 184, 248 P 406.

See **abutting owners.**

abutments (a-but'ments). The masses of stone or solid work at the ends of a bridge by which the extreme arches or timbers are sustained.

They are as much a part of the bridge itself as are the pier, the arch, or the timbers. Freeholders of Sussex v Strader, 18 NJL 108.

abuttal (a-but'al). The part of a tract of land which abuts; a boundary line.

abutting. See **abutting owners; fronting and abutting.**

abutting owners (a-but'ing ō'nėrs). Those owners whose lands touch a highway or other public place. 1 Am J2d Adj L § 1; 25 Am J1st High § 153.

It is arbitrary to limit the meaning of "abutting owners" to lands bordering a highway and not to speak of lands as "adjoining" a highway, but the usefulness of a distinction in legal articles between lands that abut on a highway and adjoining lands generally, arbitrary and fanciful although it may be, is not to be denied. 1 Am J2d Adj L § 1.

academic question. A theoretical, abstract, hypothetical, or speculative question, involving no actual controversy over rights. 20 Am J2d Cts § 81; 22 Am J2d Dec J § 10.

academy. The word originally meant a garden, grove, or villa, near Athens, where Plato and his followers held their philosophical conferences; but now it is most commonly used to mean a school or seminary of learning (holding a rank between a university or college, and a common school), in which the arts and sciences in general are taught. See Academy of Fine Arts v Philadelphia County, 22 Pa 496, 498; Anno: 95 ALR 63.

acc. An abbreviation for in accord with or consonant with.

accedas ad vice comitem (ak-sē'dās ad vi'se ko'mitem). A writ directed to the coroner to compel a sheriff to make return of a writ.

accede (ak-sēd'). To attain an office or dignity; to give consent; to assent to a treaty.
See **accession.**

acceleration clause. A clause in a note or mortgage stipulating that the whole debt secured thereby shall become due and payable upon the failure of the maker to pay the interest annually or to comply with any other condition of the contract. 11 Am J2d B & N § 181; 36 Am J1st Mtg § 385.

acceleration of estate. The shortening of the time at which a future estate is to vest, as where the precedent estate fails to come into existence, or, having come into existence, terminates prematurely. 28 Am J2d Est § 304.

The most familiar case of acceleration is that where a widow given a life estate renounces the will and elects to take her dower or statutory interest instead, whereby the remainderman takes immediately as if the widow had died. 28 Am J2d Est § 307.

acceleration of maturity. The shortening of the time for the payment of a note or the payment of money called for by a contract. 11 Am J2d B & N §§ 179 et seq; 17 Am J2d Contr § 337. Making an instrument to become due and payable prior to the maturity date stated therein by the payee's exercise of an option provided him. The operation of an automatic provision for acceleration upon default. 11 Am J2d B & N §§ 179 et seq.

acceleration of remainder. See **acceleration of estate.**

accept. To receive with the intent to retain; to give assent. Kidd v New Hampshire Traction Co. 74 NH 160, 171, 66 A 127.

acceptance. The actual or implied receipt and retention of that which is tendered or offered.

A receipt alone does not amount to an acceptance, but anything done by the receiptor as owner is evidence of an acceptance. Patterson & Holden v Sargent, 83 Vt 516, 77 A 338.

The acceptance of the goods constituting the subject of a sale has an important bearing upon the passing of title from the seller to the buyer where the contract is executory; it is also a material consideration in respect of the satisfaction of the statute of frauds where the contract is parol. 46 Am J1st Sales § 411. In a sale of personal property the term covers more than a mere receipt of the goods by the purchaser and implies some act done by him after he has exercised, or has had the means of exercising, his right of rejection. Patterson & Holden v Sargent, 83 Vt 516, 77 A 338.

acceptance by mail. The acceptance of an offer made by mail is complete upon depositing the letter of acceptance in the postoffice, postage prepaid, and directed to the offeror's proper address, provided it is done in proper season and before receiving any intimation of a revocation of the offer; it is immaterial whether the letter actually reaches the offeror. 17 Am J2d Contr § 48.

acceptance for honor. The acceptance of a bill of exchange by a person other than the drawee, voluntarily and without consideration.

It is allowed for the convenience of commerce, that such a person may, after presentation, refusal, and protest, accept for the honor of the drawer, or any of the indorsers, or all of the parties, as he may see fit, but this is done supra protest and in accord with settled forms. Heenan v Nash, 8 Minn 407. Provisions for acceptance for honor have been eliminated from the Commercial Code as unnecessary in this day of rapid communications whereby notice of dishonor is given so rapidly that an acceptance for honor is no longer necessary to protect the credit of the drawer. 11 Am J2d B & N § 506.

acceptance in blank. The act of the drawee of a bill of exchange in merely signing his name across the face of the bill.

acceptance of bill of exchange. The drawee's signed engagement to honor the bill as presented; the signification by the drawee of his assent to the order of the drawer and his agreement to pay the bill when it falls due. 11 Am J2d B & N § 500.

The contract of the acceptor, by his acceptance, is, that he will pay the bill, upon due presentment thereof, at its maturity, or its becoming due. 11 Am J2d B & N § 500.

acceptance of bribe. See **bribery.**

acceptance of charter. An act essential to the existence of a corporation when the mode of its creation is by special grant to a designated person or persons.

This act may be express, as where it appears on the records of the corporation, or it may be presumed or inferred, as where corporate powers have been assumed or exercised after the granting of the charter. 18 Am J2d Corp § 27.

acceptance of check. The certification of a check. The purpose and effect of procuring a check to be

ACCEPTANCE

accepted or certified by the bank on which it is drawn is to impart strength and credit to the paper by obtaining an acknowledgment from the bank that the drawer has funds therein sufficient to cover the check, and securing the engagement of the bank that the check will be paid upon presentation. 10 Am J2d Banks § 578.

Any act on the part of the bank upon which a check is drawn which demonstrates an intention to become bound for payment will constitute an acceptance. It is not essential that the acceptance be written upon the check itself. A drawee bank makes itself liable by a contract of acceptance extrinsic to the check itself whenever the plain import of the language used is that of a contract of acceptance. 10 Am J2d Banks § 581.

acceptance of dedication. An essential element of a completed dedication, which may be either express or implied, by formal action or by public use. 23 Am J2d Ded § 50.

acceptance of deed. A manifestation by act, conduct, or declaration of an intention to take the legal title to the property which the instrument purports to convey, after an antecedent delivery or tender of the deed to the knowledge of the grantee accepting. 23 Am J2d Deeds § 128.

acceptance of draft. Same as **acceptance of bill of exchange.**

acceptance of gift. A donee's exercise of dominion over, or the assertion of rights to, the subject of the gift. 24 Am J1st Gifts § 40.

acceptance of goods. See **acceptance.**

acceptance of issue. Formally to accept the tender of an issue made by the pleadings.
The technical term is **similiter.**

acceptance of nomination. A filed approval by the candidate of a nomination as a candidate for public office, sometimes required as a condition of having the name of the candidate printed on the ballot. 25 Am J2d Elect § 133. A formal speech of acceptance by a candidate for President, following his nomination at a national convention of a political party.

acceptance of offer. A fundamental element of a binding contract; the assent of the offeree to the offer as made by the offeror, whereby the engagement is made and the parties become bound as contracting parties. 17 Am J2d Contr § 18.

The assent requisite to the creation of a contract is an objective thing manifested by intelligible conduct, act, or sign; it is not determined by secret intentions but by expressed or manifested intentions. 17 Am J2d Contr § 19.

acceptance of office. The assumption of the powers and prerogatives of an office to which one has been legally elected or appointed. Ekwall v Stadelman, 146 Or 439, 30 P2d 1037.

acceptance of performance. The waiver of perfect and complete performance of the terms of a contract by accepting performance different from that stipulated in the contract.
Such acceptance may be express or it may be implied from conduct. 17 Am J2d Contr § 393.

acceptance of plea. The reception by the court in a criminal prosecution of a plea of guilty.
There are statutory limitations upon the acceptance of a plea in a capital case and in any case where it is open to the accused to plead guilty, the court is under a duty to determine whether the plea is voluntary and to admonish the accused of the consequences of the plea. 21 Am J2d Crim L §§ 484 et seq.

acceptance of service. Dispensing with the formalities attending service of process by acknowledging the service, which acknowledgment is generally effective to confer the same jurisdiction as would have been conferred by a formal service of the process. 42 Am J1st Proc § 33.

acceptance supra protest. See **acceptance for honor.**

accepter (ak-sep′ter). Same **as acceptor.**

accepting wagers. Taking bets. Acting as the "banker" in a gambling game.

acceptor (ak-sep′tor). One who accepts a bill of exchange and trust binds himself to pay it.

acceptor for honor. See **acceptance for honor.**

acceptor supra protest. (ak-sep′tor sū′prạ prō′test). See **acceptance for honor.**

access. Opportunity to come and go from premises. An easement of way, whether arising from express or implied grant, express or implied reservation. The right of a parson to a designated benefice which is temporarily in abeyance. The opportunity of a husband for sexual intercourse with his wife.
See **presumption of access.**

accessary (ak-ses′a-ri). Same as **accessory.**

accessio. See **accession.** The right of an owner of personal property to the personal property of another which is incorporated into or united with his property.
Sometimes the term is given a broader significance to include rights which an owner of real or personal property has to any increase thereto from any cause, natural or artificial. In any event, rights by accession include accession of other materials as well as additions by skill or labor. 1 Am J2d Access § 1. They also include the right of the mortgagee under a chattel mortgage to additions to the mortgaged chattel. 15 Am J2d Chat Mtg § 68.

accession (ak-sesh′ọn). A nation's assent to a treaty. See **specification.**

accessio possessionis (ak-se′she-ō po-ze-she-ō′nis). See **tacking.**

accessorial (ak-se-sō′ri-al). Pertaining to an accessory.

Accessorium non ducit, sed sequitur suum principale (ak-ses-sō′ri-um non dū′sit, sed se′qui-ter su′um prin-si-pā′le). That which is but accessory does not lead, but follows the principal thing.
"The land is the principal thing, the accretion is but an accessory." Plaintiff's brief in Banks v Ogden, US 2 Wall 57, 17 L Ed 818.

Accessorium non trahit principale (ak-ses-sō′ri-um non tra′hit prin-si-pā′le). The accessory right does not control the principal.

Accessorius sequitur naturam sui principalis (ak-ses-sō′ri-us se′qui-ter nă-tū′ram su′ī prin-si-pā′lis). The accessory follows the condition of his principal. Hence, an accessory cannot be guilty of a higher crime than his principal. See 4 Bl Comm 36.

accessory (ak-ses′ọ-ri or ak′se-sọ-ri). A subordinate working part of a larger machine or instrumentality, for example, the windshield wipers on an automobile. A person who in some manner is connected with a crime, either before or after its perpetration, but who is not present at the time the crime is committed. 21 Am J2d Crim L § 115.
See **accomplice.**

accessory after the fact. A person who, knowing a felony to have been committed, receives, relieves, comforts, or assists the felon, or in any manner aids him to escape arrest. 21 Am J2d Crim L § 126.

accessory at the fact. Persons who were present at the commission of a crime only for the purpose of aiding, countenancing, or encouraging its perpetration, were, by the most ancient writers on the common law of England, described as accessories at the fact. Hence, they could not be brought to trial until the principal offenders had been convicted or outlawed. See note to State v Hildreth, 51 Am Dec 373. There seems to be no room for this classification under modern views.
See **accessory**.

accessory before the fact. One whose will contributes to a felony committed by another as principal, yet who is too far away to aid in the felonious act. There are statutes which abolish the distinction between an accessory before the fact and a principal, providing that the latter is subject to prosecution and conviction as a principal. 21 Am J2d Crim L § 124.

accessory building. An outbuilding so detached from the dwelling on the premises as not to be considered properly a component part thereof. 58 Am J1st Zon § 50 supp.

accessory contract. A contract subordinate to the main or principal one, usually made for the purpose of securing the performance of the principal contract.
See **subcontract**.

accessory obligation. An obligation subordinate to the main or principal one.

accessory use. A use of premises which is dependent on or pertains to the principal or main use. 58 Am J1st Zon § 46.

access to courts. The right to resort to the courts on equal terms with others for the enforcement of one's rights and the obtaining of justice on the presentation of one's defenses. 16 Am J2d Const L § 382.

accident. An occurrence by chance or not as expected. Haser v Maryland Casualty Co. 78 ND 893, 53 NW2d 508, 33 ALR2d 1018; Anno: 8 ALR2d 409. In lesser scope, an occurrence which could not have been foreseen by the exercise of reasonable prudence, one which happens unexpectedly from the uncontrollable operations of nature alone, and without human agency. 38 Am J1st Neg § 6.

The word "accident" in a bill of lading, which refers to events involving damage to the property carried for which the carrier is to be liable, includes the result of any human fault for which the carrier may be liable; it is not synonymous with "mere accident" or "purely accidental." Ullman v Chicago & N. W. R. Co. 112 Wis 150, 88 NW 41.

The word "accident" in a policy of insurance insuring against injury by accident means an event that takes place without one's foresight or expectation—an event that proceeds from an unknown cause, or is an unusual effect of a known cause, and therefore not expected. 29A Am J Rev ed Ins § 1164.

An "accident" within the meaning of an automobile insurance policy indemnifying against loss by collision or upset includes any event which takes place without the foresight or expectation of the person acted upon or affected thereby. Riley v National Auto Ins. Co. 162 Neb 658, 77 NW2d 241, 57 ALR2d 1219.

As the word is used in an automobile liability insurance policy, it means an undesigned, unexpected happening which produces injury or damage. It does not include injuries caused intentionally. Anno: 117 ALR 1175; 18 ALR2d 456.

An "accident" within the meaning of a policy insuring against liability incident to ownership or use of premises does not include an event which has its inception in a wilful act of the insured. 29A Am J Rev ed Ins § 1359.

As used in the phrase "injury arising by accident" in compensation statutes the term is interpreted in the popular and ordinary sense, and is generally construed as meaning an occurrence which is neither expected, designed, nor intentionally caused, by the workman. 58 Am J1st Workm Comp § 196.

In the phrase "by accidents arising out of and in the course of the employment," found in Employers' Liability Acts, "accident" signifies any untoward and unexpected event, the term being used in its popular sense. 35 Am J1st M & S § 422.

The term within the meaning of the equitable principle under which relief is granted for "accident" means an occurrence without intention on the part of the complainant and one which he was unable to see and avert. 19 Am J2d Equity § 44.

See **inevitable accident; unavoidable accident**.

accidental. By accident; by chance or fortuitously, without intention or design; unexpected, unusual, and unforeseen. 29A Am J Rev ed Ins § 1164.

The word is used in its ordinary popular sense in accident policies and means happening by chance, unexpectedly taking place, not according to the usual course of things, or not as expected; so, if in the preceding act something unexpected or unusual occurred, which produced the catastrophe which caused the injury, then the injury was accidental. Anno: 105 ALR 1428; 148 ALR 611; 27 ALR2d 1013; 33 ALR2d 1027; 56 ALR2d 800; 57 ALR2d 1229; 85 ALR2d 1057.

The mere apprehension that an injury might occur does not deprive the actual occurrence of accidental character within the meaning of a workmen's compensation act. 58 Am J1st Workm Comp § 196.

accidental cause. An unavoidable cause, one which cannot be avoided by the exercise of due diligence and foresight, and which reasonably prudent men would not ordinarily anticipate and avoid. Chicago, Burlington & Quincy R. Co. v United States, (CA8 Neb) 194 F 342, 334.

accidental death. One that occurs unforeseen, undesigned, and unexpected. 29 Am J Rev ed Ins § 1166. One which occurs by accident, that is, was not designed or anticipated, albeit it may occur in consequence of a voluntary act. Anno: 26 ALR 119; 56 ALR 1091; 166 ALR 469; 12 ALR2d 1270; 52 ALR2d 1083.

accidental injury. An injury which occurs by accident, being undesigned and not anticipated, although it may result from a voluntary act. Anno: 29 ALR 691; 39 ALR 871; 44 ALR 372; 56 ALR 1091; 90 ALR 620; 109 ALR 892; 166 ALR 469. An injury incurred in a manner and by a force that is unforeseen, undesigned, and unexpected, 29A Am J Rev ed Ins § 1166.

The mere apprehension that an injury such as did

ACCIDENTALLY [12] ACCOMMODATION

occur was likely to occur in some indefinite time in the future does not deprive the actual occurrence of its accidental character. 58 Am J1st Workm Comp § 196.

accidentally thrown from. A hurling or catapulting of a person from a vehicle. 29A Am J Rev ed Ins § 1243.

accidental means. Characterizing the nature of the cause of a happening by chance and without intention or design, which is unforeseen, unexpected and unusual at the time it occurs. 29A Am J Rev ed Ins § 1165; Anno: 17 ALR 1199.

Where the death is the result of some act, but was not designed, and not anticipated by the deceased, though it be in consequence of some act voluntarily done by him, it is accidental death; but where death is caused by some act of the deceased, not designed by him, or not intentionally done by him, it is death by accidental means. See Ogilvie v Aetna Life Ins. Co., 189 Cal 406, 411, 209 P 26, 26 ALR 116, 119.

An injury received by making an intentional assault on another person by striking him in the face with the fist has been held not to have been by accidental means, within the meaning of an accident policy insuring against injuries received through accidental means. See Fidelity & Casualty Co. v Carroll, (CA4 SC) 143 F 271.

For a death to occur by accidental means within the meaning of a life insurance policy, the immediate and proximate cause of the death must be accidental; a death is not by accidental means of it results as the natural and probable consequence of the voluntary act of the insured. Prudential Ins. Co. v Gutowski (Sup) 49 Del 233, 113 A2d 579, 52 ALR2d 1073.

Although the courts in the past have drawn a distinction between "accident" and "accidental means," in recent years the terms have come to be regarded as legally synonymous. 29A Am J Rev ed § 1166.

To attempt such a fine distinction is to plunge this branch of the law of insurance into a "Serbogian Bog." Dissenting opinion of Mr. Justice Cardoza in Landress v Phoenix Mut. Life Ins. Co. 291 US 491, 78 L Ed 934, 54 S Ct 461, 90 ALR 1382, which appears to have been of great weight on the side of eliminating the distinction.

accidental result. An unusual or unexpected result of an intentional act. 29A Am J Rev ed Ins § 1166.

accident insurance. A policy or contract of insurance whereunder the insurer agrees to pay to the insured or a beneficiary named in the policy a stated sum for disability of the insured incurred by accident, for the death of the insured caused by accident, for the loss suffered by the insured through accident of a leg, arm, or other member of the body, or, in the terms of some policies, a stated sum upon the sustaining of any of such losses by accidental means.

See **accident**; **accidental**; **accidental means**; **general accident policy**.

accident report. The report of a motor vehicle accident made to a police officer or other public official by the operator of a vehicle involved therein, the giving of which is a most common statutory requirement. 8 Am J2d Auto § 959. A common requirement in industry and the transportation business, an employee being required by the terms of employment to report all accidents to the employer, the superintendent or foreman. A require-

ment under boating regulations. 12 Am J2d Boats § 19.

accion (ak-thē-on'). A word from the Spanish law which appears to stand for what is known in American and English law as a right of action. See Welder v Lambert, 91 Tex 510, 44 SW 281.

Accipere quid ut justitiam facias, non est tam accipere quam extorquere (ak-si'pe-re quid ut jūs-ti'-she-am fa'she-as non est tam ak-si'pe-re quam ex-tor-kwe're). The acceptance of something for doing justice is not so much an acceptance as an extortion.

acclamation (ak-la-mā'shon). Approval. The spontaneous approval in a deliberative assembly of a resolution, measure or candidate by voice, without counting heads.

accola (a'ko-la). A tenant farmer under the feudal law.

accollade (ak-ō-lād'). An award; words of praise, the word having been first used to denote the ceremony by which knighthood was conferred.

accomenda (a-kom-men'da). A contract by which the master of a vessel agrees to sell the goods of the shipper for their joint account.

accommodated indorser. See **accommodated party**.

accommodated party. The person for whose benefit another known as the accomodation party signs a bill or note as maker, drawer, acceptor or indorser, thereby lending the credit of his name to the former. 11 Am J2d B & N § 121.

An indorser is accommodated when the maker, drawer or acceptor of a negotiable instrument makes, draws, or accepts it for his benefit, without consideration. Lucas v Swan, (CA4 W Va) 67 F2d 106, 90 ALR 210.

accommodation (a-kom-ō-dā'shon). An obligation assumed without consideration. A **favor**.

accommodation acceptance. The acceptance of a bill of exchange for the purpose of lending credit to another party. 11 Am J2d B & N § 121.

accommodation bill. A bill of exchange on which the maker, indorser, or acceptor has assumed liability, in order to lend the credit of his name to another party. 11 Am J2d B & N § 121.

accommodation indorser. A person who has indorsed a bill or note for the purpose of lending the credit of his name to another party. 11 Am J2d B & N § 121.

accommodation land. Land which a speculator or builder has built upon or improved in order to secure increased rents.

accommodation maker. The drawer of a bill, or the maker of a note, to which he has put his name for the purpose of accommodating, by a loan of his credit, some other person who is to provide for the bill or note when it falls due. 11 Am J2d B & N § 121.

accommodation note. A promissory note on which the maker or indorser has assumed liability in order to lend his name to another person. 11 Am J2d B & N § 121.

accommodation paper. A bill or note which one has signed as a maker, drawer, acceptor, or indorser for the purpose of lending the credit of his name to another. 11 Am J2d B & N § 121.

accommodation party. A person who has signed a bill or note as maker, drawer, acceptor, or indorser

ACCOMMODATION [13] ACCOUNT

for the purpose of lending his name to the credit of some other person. 11 Am J2d B & N § 121.

Under the Commercial Code, absence of consideration is not a requisite of status as an accomodation party, the essential characteristic being that he signed as a surety, not that he signed gratuitously. 11 Am J2d B & N § 121.

accommodation road. A road for access to private property; a spur track of a railroad.

accommodation train. One which is scheduled to stop at local or way stations. Gray v Chicago, Milwaukee & St. Paul Railway Co. 189 Ill 400, 59 NE 950.

accommodation works. Structures such as bridges, ways, fences, gates, etc. which a railroad is required to build and maintain for the benefit of the owners of land adjoining the right of way.

accompanied. Attended. Going with.

The word, as used in a statute, does not necessarily mean "simultaneously," but may mean "in relation to," "connected with," or "to follow." Tucker v Kerner (CA7 Ill) 186 F2d 79, 23 ALR2d 1027. Anno: 143 ALR 1457.

accompanied by licensed driver. See **riding with or accompanied by licensed driver.**

accomplice. One who knowingly, voluntarily, and with a common interest with others participates in the commission of a crime as a principal, accessory, or aider and abettor.

So far as his criminal liability is concerned, the question is whether he participated as a principal or as an accessory, aider or abettor; the term "accomplice" has no legal significance in deciding the question of his own guilt. Such term becomes significant if he is called as a witness and testifies upon the trial of another person and it is contended that, since he is an accomplice, his testimony is insufficient to support a conviction. 21 Am J2d Crim L § 118; 26 Am J1st Homi § 458.

accomplish. To complete performance; to fulfil one's obligation. Anno: 38 ALR 890.

accompt. Same as **account**.

accord. Literally, an agreement; in law, an agreement by one party to give or perform, and by the other to accept, in settlement of an existing claim, something other than that which is claimed to be due. 1 Am J2d Accord § 1.

accordance. Agreement; harmony in purpose.

accord and satisfaction. An executed agreement of accord. 1 Am J2d Accord § 1.

In order to be a satisfaction there must be an accord or agreement to accept in extinction of the obligation something different from or less than that which the creditor is claiming or is entitled to. The acceptance of the consideration of an accord satisfies the obligation. Homewood Dairy Products Co. v Robinson, 254 Ala 197, 48 So 2d 28, 22 ALR2d 1059.

accord executory. See **executory accord.**

according to law. Legal.

Administering an estate according to law means to administer it according to the will of the decedent in case the estate is testate. 31 Am J2d Ex & Ad § 127.

according to the tenor. According to the meaning or purport.

The words "according to the tenor" of a specified policy, inserted in a renewal receipt for accident insurance, import the policy and all contained therein or thereon, so that the policy and the receipt together constitute the insurance contract. 29 Am J Rev ed Ins § 363.

account. An unsettled demand or claim by one person against another, based upon a transaction or transactions creating a debtor and creditor relation between the parties, which is usually but not necessarily represented by an ex parte record kept by one or both of them. 1 Am J2d Acctg § 1.

The term is less frequently used in designating the action at law to obtain an accounting from the defendant and a judgment against him as for money had and received for whatever sum it appears is owing by the defendant to the plaintiff. 1 Am J2d Acctg § 44. Such action has been superseded in many jurisdictions by other actions, particularly the action in equity for an accounting.

See **accounting; mutual account; open account.**

accountable. Responsible. Liable to be called to account.

See **responsible.**

accountable receipt. A receipt in writing in which the receiptor not only admits receiving the money paid or goods delivered to him, but also acknowledges his undertaking to make payment or delivery thereof, or a part thereof, to a third party.

account acknowledged. See **account stated.**

accountant. One who makes the keeping or examination of accounts his profession or one who is skilled in keeping or adjusting accounts; one competent to design and control the systems of accounts required for records of multifarious transactions of business, trade, and finance. 1 Am J2d Acctg § 1.

See **certified public accountant; public accountant.**

accountant's lien. The statutory lien of a public or certified public accountant on such books and records of his client as he has worked upon, and improved or extended. Anno: 76 ALR2d 1322.

account book. A book in which accounts are kept.
See **book of account; book of original entry.**

account current. Same as **current account.**

account for. To render an account in respect of a specific transaction or transactions; to explain.

accounting. The act or system of making up or stating accounts. Frazer v Shelton, 320 Ill 253, 150 NE 696, 43 ALR 1086, 1093. An action, usually on the equity side, to secure an adjustment of complicated accounts. 1 Am J2d Acctg § 44. Making amends or restitution.

accounting office. See **general accounting office.**

account number. The social security number of a person which must be used as an identifying number, not only in reference to social security benefits, but in other instances also, such as preparing a tax return.

account of whom it may concern. See **on account of whom it may concern.**

account receivable. An account owing on an open account. 1 Am J2d Acctg § 2.
See **bills receivable.**

account render. The common-law action which served the same purpose as an equity action for an accounting under modern practice. 1 Am J2d Acctg § 44.

account rendered. A statement of his charges submitted by a creditor to his debtor.

account sales. An account rendered by a factor or broker to his constituent, listing the goods sold with the prices secured and the net yield.

account stated. An agreement concerning prior transactions between the parties with respect to the correctness of the separate items composing the account and the balance, if any, in favor of one or the other of the parties. 1 Am J2d Acctg § 21. An agreement between persons who have had previous transactions of a monetary character, fixing the amount due in respect to such transactions and promising payment. State ex rel. Kaser v Leonard, 164 Or 587, 102 P2d 197, 129 ALR 1125.

accouple (a-kup'l). To tie or join; to unite by marriage.

accredit (a-kred'it). To receive an envoy of a foreign country and acknowledge his authority as such; to give credentials to an envoy. To recognize as worthy of merit or rank, as to accredit a college.

accredulitare (a-krē-du″li-tā′re). To clear a person of an accusation of crime by an oath.

accrescere (a-krē′se-re). To grow.

accretion. The increase of riparian land by the gradual deposit by water of solid material, whether mud, sand, or sediment, so as to cause that to become dry land which was before covered by water. 56 Am J1st Wat § 476. Accumulation. Growth in size. Increment and addition. 15 Am J2d Chat Mtg § 68.

The meaning of the term as used in relation to shares of stock not being clearly defined in the law as comprehending either income or principal or both, may be resolved differently under varying circumstances and actual situations. Re Ferguson, 354 Pa 367, 47 A2d 245, 165 ALR 772.

accroach (a-krōch'). An obsolete term for encroach, particularly encroaching upon the authority of another. See 4 Bl Comm 75.

accrual. That which accrues; something growing or developing to be added or attached to something else, as interest to principal. See **clause of accrual**.

accrual basis. A term characterizing the keeping of records and the reporting of income for taxation according to the time of the accrual of the right to receive, rather than the actual receipt of, an item or amount. Enright's Estate v Commissioner (CA 3) 112 F2d 919.

But "accruing" within a specified period may be construed to mean received during the period for income tax purposes. Maryland Casualty Co. v United States, 251 US 342, 64 L Ed 297, 40 S Ct 155.

accrual of cause of action. The event whereby a cause of action becomes complete so that the aggrieved party can begin and maintain his cause of action.

A cause may accrue at the moment of the wrong, default, or delict by the defendant and the injury to the plaintiff, although the actual damage resulting therefrom may not be discovered until some time afterward, if the injury, however slight, is complete at the time of the act. Eising v Andrews, 66 Conn 58, 1 Am J2d Actions § 88. As a general proposition, a cause of action accrues the moment it comes into existence. 34 Am J1st Lim Ac § 113.

accrue. To develop and be added to something else, as interest to principal. Johnson v Humboldt Ins. Co. 91 Ill 92. To become complete by development. See **accrual of cause of action**.

accrued and unpaid taxes. Taxes assessed but unpaid, including those not payable until a later date. Cochran v Commonwealth, 241 Ky 656, 44 SW2d 603, 78 ALR 710.

accrued dividend. A dividend which became due and has either been paid or not paid. 19 Am J2d Corp § 809.

accrued water rights. Rights in waters which have vested prior to the adoption or enactment of a constitutional or statutory provision affecting the right of appropriation. 56 Am J1st Wat § 295.

accruer (a-krö′ẽr). Accrual; the fact of accruing.

acct. Abbreviation of account.

acct. curt. An abbreviation of account current, which is the same as **current account**.

accumulate. See **accrue**; **accumulation**.

accumulated surplus. See **surplus**.

accumulation. Increase by growth or addition. Rents and profits accumulating under directions in deed or will, such as prompted the enactment of statutes like the Thellusson Act. 41 Am J1st Perp § 44.

As the word appears in a community property statute which provides that the earnings and "accumulations" of the wife, while she is living separate from her husband, shall be her separate property, it means any property acquired and retained by her without regard to the means by which it was obtained. 15 Am J2d Community Prop § 37.

"When an executor or other trustee masses the rents, dividends, or other income which he receives, treats it as capital, invests it, makes new capital of the income therefrom, invests that, and so on, he is said to accumulate the fund, and the capital and accrued income procured constitute accumulations." See Webb v Webb, 340 Ill 407, 172 NE 730, 71 ALR 404.

See **accretion**; **cumulative**; **rule against accumulations**.

accumulative. See **cumulative**.

accumulative dividends. See **cumulative dividends**.

accumulative judgment. See **cumulative judgment**.

accumulative sentences. See **consecutive sentences**.

accuracy. Freedom from mistake or error. Globe Indemnity Co. v. Cohen (CA3 Pa) 106 F2d 687.

accurately. With accuracy.

accusare nemo se debet, nisi coram Deo (a-kū-zā′re nē′mo sē de′bet, nī′sī kō′ram De′ō). No one is bound to accuse himself, unless before God.

accusation. A declaration or statement that another person is guilty of some offense or misconduct. A formal charge of the commission of a crime, such as a complaint, information, or affidavit. Informing accused of nature and contents of charge. 21 Am J2d Crim L § 324.

accusatio suspecti tutoris (a-ku-zā′she-ō sus-pek′tī tu-tō′ris). A Roman law proceeding for the removal of a suspected guardian, which anyone might institute, although it was the duty of his fellow guardian to do so.

accusator post rationabile tempus non est audiendus, nisi se bene de omissione excusaverit (a-kū-zā′tor post ra-she-ō-nā′bi-le tem′pus non est â-di-en′dus, nī′sī sē be′ne dē o-mi-she-ō′ne ex-kū-zā′ve-rit). After the lapse of a reasonable time, an accuser should not be heard, unless he shall have well explained his delay.

accuse. To charge a person with the commission of an offense; it may be informal, as in a conversation, or formal, as where it is by way of an indictment, information, or complaint whereby a prosecution is started.

accused. A person charged with having committed a crime or misdemeanor; a defendant in a criminal proceeding.

The word is held to be inapplicable to a defendant in a civil action. Castle v Houston, 19 Kan 417.

accuser. A person who makes a formal charge of crime against another before a magistrate or judge.

accustomed. By habit or established course of conduct.
See **customary.**

accustomed rent. See **customary rent.**

acephalous (a-sef'a-lus). Without leadership.

acequia (ä-sä'kē̯ä). A ditch.

ac etiam (ak e'she-am). Literally, "and also," but its legal significance appears in the old practice in England of adding a fictitious cause of action to enable the court to take jurisdiction, that is, the adding of a count in trespass to one for debt, where the jurisdiction of the court was limited to civil injuries by force. The fictitious cause gave jurisdiction; the real cause for debt authorized an arrest. See 2 Bl Comm 288.

achat or achate (ak'ät). A purchase; a bargain; a contract.

acherset (a-cher'set). An old English corn measure, probably equivalent to about eight bushels.

acia. Same as **atia.**

acknowledge. To admit; to confirm; to concede; to recognize; to authenticate a signature under oath. Blythe v Ayres, 96 Cal 532, 31 P 916.

acknowledged to me. The equivalent of acknowledged before me. 1 Am J2d Ack § 73.

acknowledgment. An admission, confirmation, concession, or recognition of the existence of a fact. An authentication of an instrument or writing by a declaration or statement under oath by the person whose name appears as a signer that he executed the instrument or writing; also the certificate of the officer who administered the oath under which such declaration or statement was made. 1 Am J2d Ack § 1.

An instrument is acknowledged when an acknowledgment of it is made to the proper officer in the manner and under the circumstances prescribed by law. Hayden v Moffat, 74 Tex 647.
See **conditional acknowledgment,** infra.

Acknowledgment Act. One of the Uniform Laws.

acknowledgment money. Money paid to the new lord by a copyhold tenant, on the death of the old lord.

acknowledgment of child born out of wedlock. See **acknowledgment of paternity.**

acknowledgment of debt. Any remark by a debtor to the creditor, by which the former clearly admits the debt and expressly or by clear implication shows an intention to pay it. 34 Am J1st Lim Ac § 297.

acknowledgment of paternity. The recognition by admission, confirmation, or concession of the putative father that the child is his. 10 Am J2d Bast § 29.

acknowledgment of will. Sometimes a formal authentication by the testator under oath, although such is required only by force of special statutory provisions; usually, an informal recognition by the testator to attesting witnesses who did not see him sign the instrument, that the signature is his. 57 Am J1st Wills § 298.

a coelo usque ad centrum (ā sē'lō us'kwe ad sen'-trum). From the sky to the center of the earth.

acolyte (ak'ō-līt). A person, usually an adolescent, who assists in a commonplace way in a religious service, as by carrying the wine and bread for communion.
See **altar boy.**

a communi observantia non est recedendum (ā kom-mū'nī ob-zer-van'she-a non est rē-sē-den'dum). From common usage there should be no departure.

a consiliis (ā kon-sil'ī-is). Of counsel.

acquaintance. A person whom one has met often enough or under such circumstances to acquire at least a fair degree of knowledge concerning him.

A mere introduction does not make one an acquaintance. Wyllis v. Haun, 47 Iowa 614, 621.

acquainted. Familiarly known; as, acquainted with the contents of an instrument or with a person. Chauvin v Wagner, 18 Mo 531, 544.

acquest (a-kwest'). A civil law term for property acquired by purchase.

acquets (ah-kay'). (Civil law.) Property acquired during matrimony by either husband or wife, otherwise than by succession.

acquets and conquets (ah-kay', côn-kay'). The property jointly or severally acquired by husband and wife by industry or good fortune. With respect to such property the French law is the same as the Spanish, except that the personal property, only, possessed by the parties at the time of marriage, enters into the partnership, as also acquets and conquets acquired during coverture, whether real or personal. But real property, held by either party at the time of the marriage, continues to be held separately, unless the contrary is stipulated. The result of this community or partnership, both at the Spanish and French law is this: that on the dissolution of the partnership, the surviving party and the representative of the deceased each take back what was brought on his or her side into the partnership, and what remains, being considered as gains or profits, is equally divided as between partners. See Picotte v Cooley, 10 Mo 312, 318.

acquiesce. To consent quietly. To consent without enthusiasm, even without approval. Scott v Jackson, 89 Cal 258, 26 P 898.

acquiescence (ak-wi-es'ens). A tacit approval or at least an indication of lack of disapproval. Acceptance, perhaps without approval, as acquiescence in a decision. Stockstrom v Commissioner, 88 App DC 286, 190 F2d 283, 30 ALR2d 443, disapproved on the grounds in Automobile Club of Michigan v Commissioner, 353 US 180, 1 L Ed 2d 746, 77 S Ct 707. Conduct from which may be inferred assent with a consequent estoppel or quasi estoppel. Uccello v Gold'n Foods, 325 Mass 319, 90 NE2d 530, 16 ALR2d 459. The position of one who knows that he is entitled to impeach a transaction or to enforce a right and who neglects to do so for such a length of time that under the circumstances of the case the other party may fairly infer that he has waived or abandoned his right. Scott v Jackson,

89 Cal 258, 26 P 898, quoting Rapalje and Lawrence's Law Dictionary. See also, Lux v Haggin, 69 Cal 255, 10 P 674.

acquiescence for detection. The lending of either active or passive assistance to a person engaged in the commission of criminal offense, either as a feigned accomplice or otherwise, for the purpose of detecting and apprehending him.

The distinction between acquiescence for detection and entrapment which is a defense to a criminal prosecution is that between merely testing a suspect by giving him opportunity to commit the offense and actually inducing him to commit a violation of law which otherwise he would not have committed. 21 Am J2d Crim L § 143.

acquiescence in custom. Essential of a custom binding upon the parties to a contract. A peaceable, unprotesting, and fairly uniform assent to a custom by those whose rights would naturally be affected by it, for such a length of time that it is safe to say that the custom must have entered into the minds of the parties at the time of their negotiations or transactions and therefore formed a part thereof, if nothing was said to the contrary. 21 Am J2d Cust § 8.

acquietandis plegiis (ak-qui″ē-tan′dis plē′ji-is). A writ by which a surety could compel a creditor to release him when the debt of the principal had been paid.

acquietantia (ak-qui-ē-tan′she-a). Acquittance; discharge.

acquietare (ak-qui-ē-tā′re). To acquit; to pay.

acquietatus (ak-qui″ē-tā′tus). Acquitted.

acquire. To become the owner of property; to make property one's own. Wulzen v Board of Supervisors, 101 Cal 15, 35 P 353. To make property one's own for the purpose of using it, as in taking it under a lease. State ex rel. Cole v District Court, 79 Mont 1, 254 P 863.

acquired. Having purchased or otherwise obtained title, ownership, or possession, including, in the absence of a statutory restriction upon the meaning, a taking by descent. 3 Am J2d Aliens § 31. Having obtained possession under a lease. State ex rel. Cole v District Court, 79 Mont 1, 254 P 863.

The status of property as separate or community property is fixed as of the time when it is "acquired," the word contemplating the inception of the title and not its subsequent perfection. 15 Am J2d Community Prop § 22.

In a statute providing that all property acquired after marriage by either husband or wife, with specified exceptions, shall be community property, the word "acquired" was not used in an all-comprehensive sense, but in a more restricted sense embracing wages, salaries, earnings, or other property acquired through the toil, talent, or other productive faculty of either spouse, and did not include compensation for injuries to the person arising from violation of right of personal security. Nelson v American Employers' Ins. Co. 258 Wis 252, 45 NW2d 681, 22 ALR2d 1244.

acquired allegiance. The allegiance of a naturalized alien.

acquisitio hereditatis (ak-qui-zi′she-ō he-re-di-tā′tis). (Roman Law.) The acquisition or vesting of an inheritance.

acquisition. That which is purchased or otherwise brought into one's ownership, literally that which is acquired.

See **acquired.**

acquisition by conquest. See **conquest.**

acquisition by discovery and occupation. See **discovery and occupation.**

acquisitiones civiles (ak-qui-zi″she-ō′nēz si′vi-lēz). The modes of the acquisition of property which were recognized by the Roman Law.

acquisitiones naturales (ak-qui-zi″she-ō′nēz na-tū-rā′lēz). (Civil Law.) The modes of the acquisition of ownership of property which were peculiar to the jus gentium.

acquit. Judicially to set free or discharge from an accusation of guilt of a crime or even a civil liability. Dolloway v Turrill (NY) 26 Wend 383, 400.

acquittal. A verdict of not guilty. 21 Am J2d Crim L § 525. Not a matter of formal judgment, where the record in the case against the defendant ends with the verdict of acquittal. Arnold v State, 76 Wyo 445, 306 P2d 368, 65 ALR2d 839.

Ordinarily, in criminal jurisprudence, the word means a discharge after a trial, or an attempt to have one, upon its merits; but under statutes it may refer to a discharge for other reasons. Junction City v Keefe, 40 Kan 275, 19 P 735. Where a *nolle prosequi* is entered and a defendant discharged, he is acquitted of the criminal prosecution. Board of Commissioners v Johnson, 31 Ind 463, 466.

In the broad sense of the term, "acquittal" includes a discharge from civil liability.

See **acquit.**

acquittance (a-kwit-ans). A release; a receipt.

While the word is not strictly synonymous with the word receipt, it includes receipt. A receipt is one form of acquittance; a discharge is another form. A receipt in full is an acquittance. It has been held that a receipt for part of a demand or obligation is an acquittance pro tanto, but the authorities are not unanimous on this point. State v Shelters, 51 Vt 102.

acquittance pro tanto. See **acquittance.**

acre. A measure of land equal to 160 square rods, or 4,840 square yards, or 43,560 square feet.

acreage. The number of acres in a tract of land. A stated number of acres constituting the subject matter of a conveyance. A term occasionally used to denote a relatively small area near a city or village.

acre-dale (ā′kėr dāl). A field composed of parts which are each owned by different persons.

acrefight. A duel.

acre-foot. The volume of water covering an acre to a depth of one foot.

acre right. A share in the common lands of a town.

acre-shot (ā′kėr shot). A local tax on land.

acromion (a-krō′mion). Pertaining to the shoulder blade.

across. Laterally; from side to side.

ac si (ak sī). As if.

act. Verb: To perform; to fulfill a function; to put forth energy; to move, as opposed to remaining at rest; to carry into effect a determination of the will. Holt v Middlebrook (CA4 Va) 214 F2d 187, 52 ALR2d 1043. To simulate; to perform on stage, screen or television.

Noun: A thing done or established; a part of a

play or musical comedy; a deed or other written instrument evidencing a contract or an obligation. A statute; a bill which has been enacted by the legislature into a law, as distinguished from a bill which is in the form of a law presented to the legislature for enactment. Anno: 5 ALR 1422.

See **statute** and also various acts under the distinguishing or popular name, such as **Safety Appliance Act; betterment acts; curative acts; occupying claimant acts.**

acta (ak'tä). The minutes of court proceedings; the recorded proceedings of a legislative assembly.

acta diurna (ak'ta dī-ur'na). Done on this day; daily records of transactions.

Acta Martyrum (ak'ta mar'te-rum). Accounts of the early Christian martyrs taken from court registers or reports of witnesses, or prepared by ecclesiastical notaries.

acta publica (ak'ta pūb'li-ka). Matters of public concern.

Acta Sanctorum (ak'ta sangk-to'rum). Accounts of the Christian saints and martyrs, published by Jesuits.

act colore officii (ko-lō're of-fi'she-ī). An act done under the color of an office rather than under authority inherent in the office.

acting. Adjective: Performing as opposed to remaining inert. Substituting or taking the place of another officer temporarily, for example, an acting judge or acting treasurer. Participle: See **act.**

acting as agent. An allegation in pleading generally sufficient in attributing a contract made by an agent to his principal. 3 Am J2d Ag § 344.

acting within the scope of his office or employment. Acting with authority so as to bind a principal. Acting in line of duty as a member of the Armed Forces. Anno: 1 ALR2d 226.

act in pais (pah-ēs'). An act performed out of court.

actio (ak'she-ō). (Roman law.) A right of action by which a person who has acquired a right may prosecute and enforce it by process of law, if it is contested. See Mackeldey's Roman Law, § 17.

actio ad exhibendum (ak'she-ō ad ex-hi-ben'dum). An action of Roman law origin to compel the defendant to produce personalty or evidence of title to real estate in his control.

actio adjecticiae qualitatis (ak'she-ō ad'kek-ti'she-ē qua-li-tā'tis). A civil law action on a contract made for plaintiff by his agent.

actio ad supplendam legitimam (ak'she-ō ad supplen'dam le-ji'ti-man). A civil law action brought by a person claiming a statutory share of a decedent's estate to compel the beneficiaries under the will to contribute to furnish his statutory share.

actio aedilicia (ak'she-ō ē-di-li'she-a). A civil law action on an implied warranty of quality.

actio arbitraria (ak'she-ō ar-bi-trā'ri-a). A Roman law action in which the judex was permitted to order payment of money or to order restitution in kind, taking all the circumstances of the case into consideration.

actio auctoritatis (ak'she-ō âk-tō-ri-tā'tis). A civil law action for breach of warranty wherein the vendee was permitted to recover twice the amount of the purchase price.

actio bonae fidei (ak'she-ō bo'nē fī-dē'ī). (Civil law.) An action in good faith; an action in which the judge was authorized to take cognizance of equitable considerations in rendering his decision.

actio calumniae (ak'she-ō ka-lum'niē). Action for or to restrain a malicious prosecution. (Civil law.)

actio certae creditae pecuniae (ak'she-ō ser'tē kre'di-tē pe-kū'ni-ē). A Roman law action for the recovery of a certain fixed sum of money.

actio civilis (ak'she-ō si'vi-lis). An action based upon the civil law; also a civil as distinguished from a criminal prosecution.

actio commodati contraria (ak'she-ō kom-mo-dā'tī kon-trā'ri-a). (Civil law.) An action by a borrower against a lender to enforce their contract.

actio commodati directa (ak'she-ō kom-mo-dā'ti dī-rek'ta). Civil law action by lender against borrower for reimbursement.

actio communi dividendo (ak'she-ō kom-mū'-ni di-viden'dō). A civil law action seeking the division of common property.

actio condictio indebitati (ak'she-ō kon-dik'she-ō inde-bi-tā'tī). A civil law action to recover a payment made under mistake.

actio confessoria (ak'she-ō kon-fes-sō'ri-a). A civil law action wherein the plaintiff sought to establish his right to a servitude as against the owner of the land or any other adverse claimant, and also to compel acknowledgment of his right.

actio contrario (ak'she-ō kon-tra'ri-o). Literally, an action in the opposite direction; a cross action.

actio criminalis (ak'she-ō kri-mi-nā'lis). Criminal action; an action at law based upon a wrong of the defendant which constitutes an offense under the criminal law.

actio damni injuria (ak'she-ō dam'nī in-jū'ri-a). Civil law action for tort.

actio de dolo (ak'she-ō dē dō'lō). A civil law action for deceit.

actio de eo quod certo loco (ak'she-ō dē e'ō quod ser'tō lō'kō). A civil law action to enforce an obligation which by its terms is to be met by the defendant at a certain place.

actio de pauperie (ak'she-ō dē pâ-pe'ri-e). A civil law action for damage done by an animal.

actio de peculio (ak'shē-ō de pē-kū'li-ō). A civil law action involving the private property of a son or a slave.

actio de pecunia constituta (ak'she-ō dē pe-kū'ni-a kon-sti-tū'ta). A civil law action on a promise to pay one's own pre-existing debt or that of another. The action would lie even in the absence of a formal engagement to pay.

actio depositi contraria (ak'she-ō dē-po'zi-tī kon-trā'ri-a). A civil law action by a depositary against a depositor to enforce their contract.

actio depositi directa (ak'she-ō dē-po-zi'tī dī-rek'ta). A civil law action by a depositor to recover the subject of the bailment from the depositary.

actio de posito vel suspenso (ak'she-ō dē po'zi-tō vel sus-pen'sō). A praetorian action under Roman Law against one who had endangered a public way by suspending or placing something over it.

actio de recepto (ak'she-ō dē re-sep'tō). A civil law action against a shipowner, innkeeper, or stablekeeper for the loss of a traveler's goods.

actio de statu defuncti (ak'she-ō dē sta'tū de-fŭnk'tī). A civil law action to determine the testamentary capacity of a decedent.

actio de tigno juncto (ak'she-ō dē tig'no junk'tō). Civil law action to recover for material incorporated by another into his building.

actio directa (ak'she-ō di-rek'ta). A direct action, that is, an action against the person who transacted the business, whether an agent or representative; an action, the form of which is prescribed.

actio emti (ak'she-ō em'tī). A civil law action by the vendee against the vendor to recover the thing sold upon payment of the price.

actio ex conducto (ak'she-ō ex kon-duk'tō). A civil law action by a bailor against a bailee to recover goods hired.

actio ex contractu (ak'she-ō ex kon-trak'tū). A civil law action founded upon a contract.

actio ex delicto (ak'she-ō ex dē-lik'tō). A civil law action founded upon a tort.

actio exercitoria (ak'she-ō ex"er-si-tō'ri-a). A civil law action against a shipowner on a contract for freightage made by the owner's slave as captain of the ship.

actio ex interdicto (ak'she-ō ex in-ter-dik'tō). An action commenced as an ordinary civil law action, but prosecuted under "procedure extra ordinem."

actio ex locatio (ak'she-ō ex lō-kā'shē-ō). Civil law action against a bailee for hire.

actio ex stipulatu (ak'she-ō ex sti-pū-lā'tū). A civil-law action founded upon a stipulatio, which was a solemn, formal promise.

actio familiae erciscundae (ak'she-ō fa-mi'li-ē er-sis-kun'dē). A civil law action to effect the division of a common inheritance.

actio famosa (ak'she-ō fa-mō'sa). A civil law action wherein the judgment carried disgrace or infamy to the defendant.

actio ficticia (ak'she-ō fik-ti'she-a). (Civil law.) A fictitious action in which the judgment was based upon assumptions of nonexisting facts.

actio fiduciae (ak'she-ō fi-dū'she-ē). A civil law action by a debtor against his creditor to recover compensation for the latter's failure to return the security after the debt had been paid. No action lay for the recovery of the pledged property.

actio finium regundorum (ak'she-ō fi'ni-um re-gun-dō'rum). A civil law suit for the partition of real property.

actio furti (ak'she-ō fer'tī). A civil law action to recover a penalty for stealing goods; that is, four times the value if the thief was caught in the act; otherwise twice the value.

actio honorarium (ak'she-ō ho-nō-rā'ri-um). A Roman action based on the jus honorarium, that is, the praetorian law, the law made by the Roman officers, and not the civil law, which was the law made by the people.

actio in bonum et aequum concepta (ak'she-ō in bō'num et ē'quum kon-sep'ta). A praetorian action in which the praetor directed the judge to decide according to what he conceived to be fair.

actio in factum (ak'she-ō in fak'tum). A civil law action similar to an action on the case at common law.

actio in factum praescriptis verbis (ak'she-ō in fak'-tum prē-skrip'tis ver'bis). A civil law action in which the plaintiff demanded performance by the defendant by reason of having fully performed his own part of the contract.

actio injuriarum (ak'she-ō in-jū-ri-ā'rum). A personal, penal civil law action which lay for any vexatious violation of the rights of another person.

actio in personam (ak'she-ō in per-sō'nam). A personal action under the civil law.

actio in rem (ak'she-ō in rem). A civil law action against a thing; an action for the recovery of a thing or the establishment of a right to or in a thing independent of contract.

actio in rem hypothecaria (ak'she-ō in rem hi-po"the-kā'ri-a). A praetorian action under the Roman Law whereby a creditor, with whom a debtor had agreed that certain chattels should be security for the debt, could obtain possession of the chattels.

actio institoria (ak'she-ō in-sti-tō'ri-a). A civil law action against a master on a contract made by his slave, acting as his business manager.

actio interrogatoria (ak'shē-o in-ter-ro-gȧ-tȯr'i-a) (Roman law.) An action by which the defendant was obliged to make answer under oath to questions propounded. See 1 Pomeroy's Equity Jurisprudence, § 192.

actio judicati (ak'she-ō jū-di-kā'tī). A civil law action to determine whether a judgment had been rendered.

actio legati (ak'she-ō lē-gā'tī). A civil law action by a legatee to enforce an obligation against the person charged by the legacy with the obligation.

actio locati (ak'she-ō lō-kā'tī). A civil law action for damages by the bailor under a bailment for hire against the bailee.

actio mandati (ak'she-ō man-dā'tī). (Civil law.) An action by a person to whom another (the mandatory) has promised to execute a commission (mandate) for damages caused by the mandatory's negligence.

actio metus. Same as **actio quod metus causa.**

actio mixta (ak'she-ō mīx'ta). A mixed action under the civil law in the sense that the relief sought is both penal and reparatory.

actio mixtae persequendae causa comparata (ak'she-ō mix'te per-se-quen'dē kâ'sa kom-pa-rā'ta). A mixed action under the civil law for the recovery of a penalty and also for the recovery of compensation.

action. A judicial proceeding, either in law or in equity, to obtain relief at the hands of a court. A judicial remedy for the enforcement or protection of a right, or a legal proceeding in which a plaintiff claims against a defendant or fund the enforcement of some obligation toward the plaintiff which is binding upon the defendant or the fund. A prosecution in a court by one party against another party for the enforcement or protection of a right, the redress or prevention of a wrong, or the punishment of a public offense, without regard to the particular form of the procedure. 1 Am J2d Actions § 4.

The term is inclusive of cause of action or right of action, as well as a pending action, in a statute providing for the survival of an action. 1 Am J2d, Abat & R § 1.

In several jurisdictions, for example, New York, an action, which is commenced by the service of summons, is distinct under statute from a proceeding which is commenced by petition and notice. In some jurisdictions it is expressly provided by statute that the word "action," as used in the statute of limitations, shall include a special proceeding of a civil nature. 34 Am J1st Lim Ac § 112.

A distinction has been drawn between the word "action," as importing the right or power to enforce an obligation, and the word "suit" which imports the pursuit of the remedy by which the right is enforced. 1 Am J2d Actions § 4.

The word "action" standing alone might reasonably be held not to include a criminal prosecution, but when the word "proceeding" is added, a combination is presented which is well near inclusive of all forms of litigation. United States v P. F. Collier & Son Corp. (CA7 Ind) 208 F2d 936, 40 ALR2d 1389.

The view has been taken that where the reference in a statute concerning corporate existence following dissolution is for the purpose of permitting "suits" or "actions" to be instituted or maintained against the dissolved corporation, such words are to be construed as applying only to civil litigation and not to criminal prosecutions. Anno: 40 ALR2d 1397.

In French, the term "action" includes a share of stock in a corporation or joint stock company and the certificate representing the ownership thereof.

actionable (ak'shon-a- bl). Remediable by an action at law or a suit in equity.

actionable defamation. See **actionable per quod; actionable per se; libel; slander.**

actionable negligence. See **negligence.**

actionable per quod. Words or epithets spoken of or concerning the plaintiff which are not so defamatory in a legal aspect that damage will be presumed from their utterance or publication, so that an action will not lie upon the words in the absence of pleading and proof of special damage. 33 Am J1st L & S § 5.

actionable per se. Words actionable as defamatory, without allegation and proof of special damage, because their character as injurious to reputation is a matter of common knowledge. 33 Am J1st L & S § 5.

According to some authorities, written or printed words may be actionable per se where, if merely spoken or uttered, they would not be actionable in the absence of pleading and proof of special damages. 33 Am J1st L & S § 6.

See **negligence per se.**

actionable wrong. One for which an action will lie.

As to particular wrongs for which an action will lie, see specific terms, such as **negligence; nuisance;** etc.

actionably (ak'shọn-ạ-bli). In a manner which may render a person liable to be sued.

action against the state. An action which, because of the immunity of a state from suit under the 11th Amendment to the Constitution of the United States and established principles of jurisprudence, can be had only with the consent of the state. 49 Am J1st States § 91.

A suit to restrain state officers from taking steps by means of a judicial proceeding in execution of a state statute to which they do not hold any special relation, is a suit against the state within the meaning of the prohibition of the 11th Amendment. State v Southern Railway Co. 145 NC 495, 59 SE 570.

action against the United States. An action which can be maintained only with the consent of the United States clearly given by an Act of Congress and subject to such restrictions as Congress may impose. Jones v Tower Production Co. (CA10 Okla) 120 F2d 779 (holding an action to remove a federal tax lien to be an action against the United States.)

actional (ak'shon-al). Pertaining to actions.

actionare (ak"she-ō-nā're). To sue; to prosecute.

action at common law. An action for the determination of legal, as distinguished from equitable, rights. 34 Am J1st Lim Ac § 58. An action governed by the common law rather than the civil or continental law.

action at law (ak'shon). An action prosecuted in a law court, as distinguished from a suit in equity. An action, the purpose of which is the recovery of a sum of money or damages, or an action wherein the only relief obtainable or appropriate is a money judgment for damages. Royal Indem. Co. v Sangor, 166 Wis 148, 164 NW 821, 9 ALR 397.

Notwithstanding the abolition of the distinction between actions at law and suits in equity, it is still important to determine whether the case is at law or in equity. The method of review, the right to a jury trial, etc. may depend upon whether the case is to be regarded as at law or in equity. 1 Am J2d Actions § 7.

action brought. An action commenced. Goldenberg v Murphy, 108 US 162, 27 L Ed 686, 2 S Ct 388; Anno: 27 ALR2d 236, 253. A pending action; the status of an action wherein the defendant is subject to judicial orders rendered in the cause. 32 Am J2d Fed Prac § 424.

actio negatoria (ak'she-ō ne-gā-tō'ri-a). A civil law action by a property owner against one who has disturbed his possession, to compel him to pay damages and to discontinue the disturbance.

actio negotiorum gestorum (ak'she-ō ne-gō-she-ō'rum jes-tō'rum). A civil law action against one who has transacted business for the plaintiff in his absence or without his authority.

actionem constituere (ak-she-ō"nem kon-sti-tū'e-re). To bring an action; to sue.

actionem instituere (ak'she-ō"nem in-sti-tū'e-re). To bring an action; to sue.

action en declaration d'hypothèque (äk'si-ôn ôn dā-clär-ä'si-ôn dē'po-thĕk'). An action by a creditor to subject real property in possession of a third party to a lien held by the plaintiff.

action en interruption (äk'si-ôn ôn an-ter-rŭp'si-ôn). An action brought to stop the running of the statute of limitations against the plaintiff's claim.

action ex contractu (ex kon-trak'tū). An action based upon a contract. 1 Am J2d Actions § 8.

action ex delicto (ex dē-lik'tō). An action arising out of the violation of a duty or obligation created by positive law independent of contract. 1 Am J2d Actions § 8.

There may be a duty imposed by law by the relation of the parties, although the relation was created by contract, and when this is so, a neglect to perform this duty gives the injured person a right of action, and he may elect to sue upon the contract, or treat the wrong as a tort, and bring an action ex delicto. For example, a common carrier who wrongfully ejects a passenger who has paid his fare from a train commits a tortious act, although the relation of the parties had its origin in contract, and an action ex delicto may be maintained. 38 Am J1st Negl § 20.

action for conspiracy. See **conspiracy.**

action for death. See **wrongful death.**

action for determination of adverse claims. See **determination of adverse claims.**

action for divorce. See **divorce.**

action for mesne profits (ak'shǫn fôr mēn prof'its). See **mesne profits.**

action for partition. A suit in equity, the object of which is to enable those who own property as joint tenants, tenants in common, or coparceners to put an end to such tenancy so as to vest in each tenant a sole estate in specific property or a share of the proceeds of sale of the entire tract. 40 Am J1st Partit § 2.

action for restitution. See **restitution.**

action for separate maintenance. See **separate maintenance.**

action in equity. Same as **suit in equity.** 27 Am J2d Eq § 177.

action in personam. See **in personam.**

action in rem. See **in rem.**

actionize. Same as **actionary.**

actionnaire (äk-syo-när). A stockholder under French law.

action negatoire (äk'si-ôn ne'ga-tuär). An action by the owner of real property to establish the nonexistence of an easement or servitude on the property.

actionner. (French) To bring an action.

action not otherwise provided for. An omnibus provision intended to extend the application of a statute, such as a statute of limitations. 34 Am J1st Lim Ac § 70.

action of a local nature. An action in the federal court the subject matter of which, as appears from the allegations of the complaint, bill, or declaration, is situated wholly within the district in which the suit is brought. East Tennessee, Virginia & Georgia Railroad Co. v Atlanta & Florida Railroad Co. (CC Ga) 49 F 608.

action of assize. See **assize.**

action of book account or book debt. See **book debt.**

action of covenant. See **covenant.**

action of debt. See **debt.**

action of forcible entry. See **forcible entry and detainer.**

action of trespass. See **trespass.**

actio nominata (ak'she-ō nō-mi-nā'ta). An action with a name, as distinguished from an action on the case.

actio non (ak'she-ō non). A statement in a special plea that the plaintiff has no action.

Actio non accrevit infra sex annos (ak'she-ō non a-krē'vit īn'frā sex an'nōs). The plea that the action has not accrued within six years.

Actio non datur non damnificato (ak'she-o non da'ter non dam-ni-fi-kā'to). No action is given to a person who is not injured.

action on the case. See **trespass on the case.**

Actio non ulterius (ak'she-ō non ŭl-te'ri-us). A plea addressed to the further maintenance of the action.

actio noxalis (ak'she-ō nox-ā'lis). A civil law action to recover for an injury sustained from the act of the child, wife, or slave of the defendant.

action pending. The status of an action between the time of the commencement thereof and its final determination by a judgment.

An action is no longer pending after a judgment of dismissal has been made and entered, although third parties, who had secured an ex parte order permitting them to intervene, are about to do so. Minshull v McDougal, 143 Wash 599, 255 P 655. See **plea of another action pending.**

action populaire (äk-si-ôn pō'pū-lār). An action brought in the public interest.

action quasi in rem. See **quasi in rem action.**

action sur le case. Same as **action on the case.** See **trespass on the case.**

action to quiet title. See **quieting title.**

actio perpetua (ak'she-ō per-pe'tu-a). A civil law action as to which there is no limitation period.

actio personalis (ak'she-ō per-sō-nā'lis). A personal action.

Actio personalis moritur cum persona (ak'she-ō per-sō-nā'lis mo'ri-ter kum per-sō'nā). A personal action dies with the person. 1 Am J2d, Abat & R § 51.

Such principle of the common law is in modern times of little more than historical interest, since it has been abrogated by statute in most, if not all, American jurisdictions. 1 Am J2d Abat & R § 47. See **survival acts.**

Actio personalis quae oritur ex delicto moritur cum persona (ak'she-ō per-so-nā'lis kwē o'ri-ter ex dē-lik'to mo'ri-ter kum per-sō'na). A personal action which arises out of a tort dies with the person.

actio pignoraticia (ak'she-ō pig-nō"rā-ti'she-a). A civil law action founded upon a pledge.

actio poenalis (ak'she-ō pē-nā'lis). A civil law action brought by the injured party for the recovery of a penalty.

actio poena persequendae causa comparata (ak'she-ō pē'na per-se-quen'dē kâ'sa kom-pa-rā'ta). A civil law action for the recovery of a penalty; a penal action.

actio popularis (ak'she-ō po-pu-lā'ris). A civil law action by the people or any one of the people to recover a penalty.

actio praejudicialis (ak'shē-o pre-ju-di-she-ā'lis). A suit under the civil law preliminary to the principal action.

actio praescriptis verbis (ak'she-ō prē-skrīp'-tīs ver'-bis). A civil law action founded upon usage or precedent.

actio praetoria (ak'she-ō prē'tor-iạ). An action under the Roman law brought by the praetor.

actio pro socio (ak'she-ō prō so'she-ō). A civil law action by one partner against another to compel performance of the agreement of partnership.

actio protutelae (ak'she-ō prō-tū-tē'lē). A civil law action against one who had acted as a guardian when he was not one, or who was really a guardian and acted as one without knowing it.

actio Publiciana (ak'she-ō Pub-li-she-ā'na). A Roman-law action granted by the praetor to the possessor of lost property for the protection of his rights.

actio Publiciana confessoria in rem (ak'she-ō Pub-li-she-ā'na kon-fes-sō'ri-a in rem). A civil law action for the protection of servitudes not fully perfected.

actio Publiciana negatoria (ak'she-ō Pub-li-she-ā'na ne-gā-tō'ri-a). A civil law action for the disturbance of one's possession.

actio quanti minoris (ak'she-ō quan'tī mi-nō'ris). A civil law action by the vendee on an implied warranty of quality wherein he claimed a reduction in the price corresponding with the lower value caused by the defect.

actio quasi institoria (ak'she-ō quā'sī in-sti-tō'ri-a). A civil law action which would lie in every case where, if the representative were a free person, the *actio quod jussu* would lie.

actio quod jusso (ak'she-ō quod jus'sō). A civil law action by the creditor against the master on a contract made by a slave by the authority of the master.

actio quod metus causa (ak'she-ō quod me'-tus kā'za). An action allowed by the Roman praetor whereby one might recover property with which he had parted under fear arising out of threats.

actio rationibus distrahendis (ak'she-ō rā-she-ō'ni-bus dis-tra-hen'dis). A civil law action by a ward against his guardian for converting property of the ward to his own use. The ward could recover both damages and a penalty.

actio redhibitoria (ak'she-ō red-hi-bi-tō'ri-a). A civil law action by the vendee to rescind a sale.

actio rerum amotarum (ak'she-ō re'rum ā-mō-tā'rum). A special compensatory action granted by the injured party if either spouse stole from the other on the eve of a divorce.

actio rescissoria (ak'she-ō re-si-zō'ri-a). A civil law action to recover property lost by prescription.

actio re uxoriae (ak'she-ō rē ux-ō'ri-ē). A civil law action on the dissolution of a marriage for the restoration of the dowry given to the couple at the time of their marriage.

actio serviana (ak'she-ō ser-vi-ā'na). A civil law action in rem whereby the locator of a rural estate sued a farmer to recover the property of the farmer which had been pledged to secure payment of the rent.

actio stricti juris (ak'she-ō strik'tī jū'ris). A civil law action in which the court followed the letter of the law.

actio temporalis (ak'she-ō tem-pō-rā'lis). A Roman law action in respect to which the praetor had limited the time within which it could be brought.

actio tutelae (ak'she-ō tū-tē'lē). A civil law action of a ward against his guardian for failure to use that degree of care in the management of the guardianship which he was accustomed to exercise in the management of his own affairs.

actio utilis (ak'she-ō ū'ti-lis). A civil law action brought by the holder of the legal title in behalf of the person beneficially entitled.

actio venditi (ak'she-ō vēn'di-tī). A civil law action for the enforcement of a contract of sale.

actio vi bonorum raptorum (ak'she-ō vī bō-nō'rum rap-tō'rum). A civil law action for injury done by means of a robbery.

actio vindictam spirans (ak'she-ō vin-dik'tam spī'ranz). A civil law action brought by the plaintiff to secure personal satisfaction.

actio vulgaris (ak'she-ō vul-gā'ris). A Roman law term for a common action.

active bond (ak'tiv). A bond which bears interest from its date at a fixed rate.

active cause. That which produces an effect or result by active means; the efficient or proximate cause. 38 Am J1st Negl § 50.

active commerce. Commerce carried on in ships of the country's own register and not in ships of other countries.

active concealment. Conduct whereby concealment is effected by misleading and deceptive talk, acts, or conduct.

Active concealment produces the same result in law as positive misrepresentation. 23 Am J2d Fraud § 93.

active member. One who takes part in a movement by lending his aid, supporting it by activities in its behalf. Scales v United States, 367 US 203, 6 L Ed 2d 782, 81 S Ct 1469.

active militia. An organization of armed men from the body of the militia, engaging at stated periods in military drill or other military exercises, returning to their usual vocations after such drilling and exercising, but subject to call when public exigencies demand their services. 36 Am J1st Mil § 42.

active negligence. Want of care in performing an act, as distinguished from inaction which in a proper case may be negligence. 38 Am J1st Negl § 3.

active progress. A redundancy, but nevertheless found in certain statutes.

A labor dispute in a seasonal industry may permissibly be deemed in "active progress" subsequently to the reaching of a dead line fixed for negotiating a colwective bargaining agreement for the ensuing season, within the meaning of a provision of the Alaska Unemployment Compensation Act, where conferences between the union and employees continued after such date. Unemployment Com. v Aragon, 329 US 143, 91 L Ed 136, 67 S Ct 245.

active receivership. A receivership in which the receiver is charged with the duty of running a business or industry. 44 Am J1st Rec § 3.

active service. One in the Armed Forces who faces the enemy at the front and also one serving as a soldier, sailor, or airman in garrison, military camp, fort, or cantonment in support of forces at the front or in the performance of duty, even in time of peace. Anno: 4 ALR 850. Service in the Armed Forces, not necessarily in combat or in the movement of troops preparatory to an engagement. 57 Am J1st Wills § 663.

The distinguishing feature of active service is not exposure to the assaults of the enemy; it is service by one called to perform duty in contrast to readiness to serve or training for duty prior to the time that one is called from civilian life or from the reserve. 29A Am J Rev ed Ins § 1204.

active trust. A trust which maintains the legal estate in the trustee, to enable him to perform the duties devolved on him by the donor, and gives the cestui que trust only a right in equity to enforce the performance of the trust. 54 Am J1st Trusts § 13. A trust in which active duties are to be performed by the trustee with reference to the administration of the trust property, and in which the primary use of the property is to be expressly or impliedly, by reason of such active duty, vested in the trustee. Holmes v Walter, 118 Wis 409, 95 NW 380.

active use. A use in which active duties were to be performed by the feoffee to uses with reference to the administration of the property conveyed to him. 54 Am J1st Trusts § 11.

activity. A state of movement or performance as contrasted with inertness.
See concerted activity.

act malum in se. See **mala in se.**

act malum prohibitum. See **mala prohibita.**

act of adjournal. An order of the Scotch court of judiciary, entered in its minutes; a record of a criminal sentence.

act of bankruptcy. An act for which the person who performed it may be adjudicated a bankrupt, provided timely proceedings for an adjudication are invoked and the person is not within the class of persons excepted from an involuntary adjudication. 9 Am J2d Bankr § 141.

act of commission. A positive act, as distinguished from an omission.

Act of Congress. A statute enacted by Congress. See various federal acts under popular or distinguishing name, such as **Safety Appliance Act; Civil Rights Act,** etc.

act of curatory. Qualifying as a curator or guardian. 25 Am J1st G & W § 47.

act of dominion (ȧkt ov dọ-min′yọn). An act evidencing an assumption of ownership.

act of God. An unusual, extraordinary, sudden, and unexpected manifestation of the forces of nature which man cannot resist. 32 Am J1st L & T § 795. An act beyond the intervention of man, such as a storm, a bolt of lightning, or a tempest. 1 Am J2d Act of God § 2.

An exception to the liability of a tenant from liability for injuries caused by an "act of God" will not include an injury caused by a fire set by human agency, since an act of God refers to some irresistible disaster such as results from natural causes in no sense attributable to human agency. 32 Am J1st L & T § 811.

An extraordinary flood may constitute, and is frequently treated as constituting, an "act of God." Whether it does or does not do so has been held to be a mixed question of law and fact. The defining and limitation of the term are questions of law for the court; but the existence or nonexistence of the facts on which it is predicated is a question for the jury where the evidence is such as to admit of more than one conclusion. 56 Am J1st Wat § 91.

act of grace. A grant of general pardon or amnesty by a new king or queen in honor of some important royal event.
See **grace.**

act of indemnity. A statute in aid of officers who have failed to qualify for their offices.

act of insolvency. An act or omissions of a debtor which justifies the filing of a petition in insolvency against him, such as making a general assignment for the benefit of creditors, failure to procure the dissolution of an attachment of his property, preferential transfers, fraudulent conveyances, etc. 29 Am J Rev ed Insolv § 14.
See **act of bankruptcy.**

act of law. Anything which proceeds by operation of law or under judicial authority.

act of legislature. See **statute,** also various acts under popular or distinguishing name, such as **nonclaim statute; statute of frauds; moratory statute,** etc.

act of oblivion. See **oblivion.**

Act of Parliament. A statute enacted by the Parliament of the United Kingdom.

Act of Settlement. The English statute 12 and 13 Wm. III., c. 2, "whereby the crown was limited to his present majesty's illustrious house: and some new provisions were added, at the same fortunate era, for better securing our religion, laws, and liberties; which the statute declares to be 'the birthright of the people of England,' according to the ancient doctrine of the common law." See 1 Bl Comm 128.

act of state doctrine. The principle which precludes American courts from inquiring into the validity of the public acts of a recognized foreign sovereign power within its own territory. Banco Nacional De Cuba v Sabbatino, 376 US 398, 11 L Ed 2d 804, 84 S Ct 923.

Act of Supremacy. An English statute establishing the supremacy of the king over the church.

Act of Uniformity. A statute establishing uniform services in the Church of England.
See **uniform statutes.**

Act of Union. Often referred to as the Articles of Union, being the agreement, containing twenty-five articles, which in 1707 was entered into between the kingdoms of England and Scotland, whereby these two kingdoms were united into one kingdom by the name of Great Britain. These articles were ratified and confirmed by statute 5 Anne, c. 8. See 1 Bl Comm 96.

Acton Burnel (ak′ton). An English statute (1285) named from the place where it was passed and providing a procedure for the collection of debts.

act on petition. An English summary proceeding in admiralty cases.

actor. A performer on stage, screen, television, or radio. In the civil law, a plaintiff in an action, also one who acts for another, such as the manager of a business.

Actore non probante reus absolvitur (ak-tō′re non pro-ban′te re′us ab-sol′vi-ter). A defendant is exonerated by the failure of the prosecution to prove its case. Anno: 31 LRA (NS) 1169.

actores fabulae (ak-tō′rēz fa′bu-lē). Fictitious parties. Since common recoveries were themselves fabulous and fictitious proceedings, it was essential that there should be fictitious parties to them. See 2 Bl Comm 362.

Actori incumbit onus probandi (ak-tō′rī in-kum′bit ō′nus pro-ban′dī). Upon the plaintiff lies the burden of proof.

actor in rem suam (ak′tōr in rem su′am). One who acts for himself, not through another.

Actor qui contra regulam quid adduxit non est audiendus (ak′tor qui kon′trä rē′gu-lam quid ad-dūx′it non est â-di-en′dus). An advocate should not be heard who argues contrary to law.

Actor sequitur forum rei (ak'tor se'qui-ter fō'rum rē'ī). The plaintiff must invoke jurisdiction in the forum in which the defendant resides or in which the property involved in the litigation is located. Fisher, Brown, & Co. v Fielding, 67 Conn 91, 34 A 714.

actrix (ak'trix). The feminine of **actor**.

acts mala in se (aks ma'la in sē). See **mala in se**.

acts mala prohibita (aks ma'la prō-hi'bi-ta). See **mala prohibita**.

acts of possession. See **adverse possession**.

acts of preparation. See **preparation**.

acts of sederunt (akts of sē-dē'runt). Certain rules of court made by judges of the Scotch court of session.

Acts of the martyrs. See **Acta Martyrum**.

act through. To act by another who is one's agent.
To "act through" a subordinate, may well be synonymous with "to vest" such subordinate with power to act. See United States v Chemical Foundation, 272 US 1, 71 L ed 131, 47 S Ct 1.

actual (ak'tū-al). Something real, or actually existing, as opposed to something merely possible, presumptive, implied, or constructive. Steen v Modern Woodmen of America, 296 Ill 104, 129 NE 546, 17 ALR 406, 412; Jones v State, 144 Miss 52, 109 So 265, 59 ALR 1146.

actual authority. Such authority as a principal intentionally confers upon his agent, or intentionally or by want of ordinary care allows the agent to believe himself to possess. McIntosh v Dakota Trust Co., 52 ND 1021, 204 NW 818, 40 ALR 1021.
Actual authority, if conferred expressly or impliedly, empowers an agent to bind his principal, even in violation of private instructions, where the person dealing with him has no notice of the limitation upon authority. 29 Am J Rev ed Ins § 147.

actual bias. The existence of a state of mind, on the part of a juror, which leads to a just inference in reference to the case that he will not act with entire impartiality.
Literally, it is a leaning of the mind—a prepossession, something more than sympathy which can be set aside. 31 Am J Rev ed J § 172.

actual bona fide resident. See **bona fide resident**.

actual cash value. The price in cash obtainable in a fair market. The fair cash value. Birmingham Fire Ins. Co. v Pulver, 126 Ill 329, 18 NE 804.
Cost of reproduction less depreciation, although important evidence of value, is not an exclusive test of "actual cash value" within the meaning of an appraisal clause of an insurance policy. Schreiber v Pacific Coast Fire Ins. Co. 195 Md 639, 75 A2d 108, 20 ALR2d 951. Neither market value nor replacement cost is an exclusive test; all facts and circumstances which tend logically to assist in arriving at a correct estimate of actual cash value are to be considered. 29A Am J Rev ed Ins § 1545.

actual change of possession. A real, as distinguished from a scrambling, litigious, or constructive change of possession, is what is comprehended in speaking of part performance sufficient to take a case out of the statute of frauds by a change of possession. 49 Am J1st Stat of F § 439.

actual competition. See **competition**.

actual compulsion. Real compulsion, as distinguished from a presumed compulsion because of the relationship between the parties as husband and wife, parent and child, etc.

actual controversy. A justiciable controversy, one that is not merely moot or amounting merely to a difference of opinion, but involving persons adversely interested in matters as to which the determination of the court is sought. 22 Am J2d Dec J § 11.

actual damages. Damages in compensation for the loss or injury suffered rather than those allowed by way of punishment of the defendant or deterring others. 22 Am J2d Damg § 11.

actual delivery. Within the rule as to passing title under a sale, the term means a formal immediate tradition of the property to the vendee. Bridgham v Hinds, 120 Me 444, 115 A 197, 21 ALR 1024.
But an actual delivery of an insurance policy may be completed without a manual tradition of the instrument to the insured. Any disposition of the policy by the insurer which evidences an intention to put the policy out of its control and in the control of the applicant is sufficient to amount to a delivery or actual delivery of the policy. 29 Am JRev ed Ins § 216.
See **actual change of possession; delivery**.

actual doubt. A reasonable doubt, a doubt beyond the realm of vague apprehension. Anno: 147 ALR 1046.

actual escape. An escape which takes place when a prisoner gets out of prison or any place in which he may be confined, or from out of the authority in whose custody he is, and unlawfully regains his liberty, free from the authority and control of the power entitled to restrain him. 27 Am J2d Escape § 1.

actual eviction. A physical dispossession of a tenant as distinguished from a constructive eviction. 32 Am J1st L & T § 246.
See **actual ouster**

actual force. Real force, as distinguished from mere persuasion.
In robbery, the term implies personal violence, but the degree of force is immaterial so long as it is sufficient to compel one to part with his property. It is to be distinguished from constructive force in that it includes all force inflicted directly on the person robbed, while constructive force includes all demonstrations of force, menaces, and means by which the victim is put in fear sufficient to suspend the free exercise of the will, or prevent resistance to the taking. See 46 Am J1st Rob § 15.

actual fraud. Intentional and successful employment of cunning, deception, or artifice to circumvent, cheat, or deceive another. 23 Am J1st Fraud § 4.

actual immunity. See **immunity; self-incrimination**.

actual induction. The reception of a person into the Armed Forces of the United States which makes him a member thereof and responsible for the performance of the duties of a soldier, sailor, marine, etc.
It does not take place, under the Army and Selective Service regulations, until the selectee has taken the oath of induction, and where he refuses to take it it is not enough that he has been accepted after physical examination, or that the oath was read to him and that he was thereupon informed that he was in the Army, to subject him to a court-martial for disobeying an order. Billings v Truesdell, 321 US 542, 88 L Ed 917, 64 S Ct 737.

actual knowledge. Real knowledge as distinguished from presumed knowledge or knowledge imputed to one because of his having had information which should have put him on inquiry that would have led to real knowledge. In some cases, as where it is an element of wrongdoing, the equivalent of guilty knowledge.

Under the generally accepted doctrine that a bank director is not personally liable to a depositor of the bank for damages sustained by reason of the insolvency of the bank, unless the director had actual knowledge of the bank's insolvency, the term "actual knowledge" means a guilty knowledge, not an innocent bona fide ignorance arising from neglect on his part to inquire into the financial condition of the bank. 10 Am J2d Banks § 199.

One insured against loss by "robbery", defined by the policy to include the felonious and forcible taking of insured property ... by any other overt felonious act committed in his presence and of which he was "actually cognizant," is not thereby covered as to a loss of money which he had in his pocket, and which he discovered to be missing after he returned to his store from the street where two men, in helping him stop a dogfight, had jostled him. Ashcraft v United States Fidelity & Guaranty Co. (Ky) 255 SW2d 485, 37 ALR2d 1078.

actual loss. From breach of contract:—the loss of what the promisee would have made if the contract had been performed, less the proper deductions. 22 Am J2d Damg § 47.

Extent of insurer's liability under insurance on property:—the real loss is the measure of indemnity to which the insured is entitled without distinction between a total and partial loss. 29A Am J Rev ed Ins § 1538.

See **actual cash value.**

actually. Really. In fact. State v Ritschel, 220 Minn 578, 20 NW2d 673, 168 ALR 274.

actually cognizant. See **actual knowledge.**

actually collected. Actually received in funds. In some connections, the net amount received, that is, an amount received less costs of collection. Curtin v New York, 287 NY 166, 39 NE2d 903, 142 ALR 166.

actually paid. Really paid. Paid in cash, not by the giving of a note or other obligation of the debtor. Sometimes construed as "actually payable," as in the case of an insolvent reinsured under a contract of reinsurance. 29A Am J Rev ed Ins § 1756.

actual malice. Real as distinguished from legal or technical malice. 30 Am J Rev ed Interf § 45. Hatred, ill will, or hostility entertained by one person toward another. 34 Am J1st Mal §§ 2, 3.

Although the cases are not entirely in accord, it would appear that the better view is that wantonness may amount to actual malice. Crane v New York World Tel. Corp. 308 NY 470, 126 NE2d 753, 52 ALR2d 1169. Compare 34 Am J1st Mal § 3.

actual military service. See **active service.**

actual necessity. The existence of a genuine necessity, the most common use of the term being in reference to a taking of property under the power of eminent domain. See 26 Am J2d Em D §§ 111 et seq.

actual notice. Express information of a fact, as well as circumstances from which an inference of notice is clearly justified. 39 Am J1st Notice § 4.

"However closely actual notice may in many instances approximate knowledge, there may be actual notice without knowledge." Dunlap v Gibson, 83 Kan 757, 112 P 598.

The words do not always mean in law what in metaphysical strictness they import; they more often mean knowledge of facts and circumstances sufficiently pertinent in character to enable reasonably cautious and prudent persons to investigate and ascertain as to the ultimate facts. Texas Co. v Aycock, 190 Tenn 16, 227 SW2d 41, 17 ALR2d 322.

See **actual knowledge.**

actual notice in the second degree. An overly-refined expression for implied or constructive notice. Texas Co. v Aycock, 190 Tenn 16, 227 SW2d 41, 17 ALR2d 322.

actual occupation. Making use of, or living upon, premises either personally or through a tenant. Cox v Richerson, 186 Miss 576, 191 So 99, 124 ALR 1138.

See **actual possession.**

actual occupation test. A test to determine whether there has been a change of occupation of the insured under a policy of life insurance so as to diminish the recovery under the policy in accordance with a provision in the policy. 29 Am J Rev ed Ins § 769.

actual ouster. The actual expulsion of a tenant from the demised premises.

If a lessee, to avoid actual expulsion, yields possession and attorns in good faith to one having a title paramount to that of his landlord, and a right to immediate possession, it is equivalent to an actual ouster, since the tenant is not bound to hold unlawfully and subject himself to an action, and is not under any duty to resist such an entry. See 32 Am J1st L & T § 111.

See **actual eviction.**

actual pecuniary injury. An injury, the result of which can be actually measured in money. Drury v Franke, 247 Ky 758, 57 SW2d 969, 88 ALR 917.

actual possession. Substantial possession, possession in fact, sometimes referred to as by the foot or pedis possession. The term is also used by some authorities in referring to the possession of one part of a larger tract by possession in fact of the other part, where the occupant claims the whole as of right and there is substantial evidence of the boundaries of the entire larger tract, although other authorities refer to this type of possession by actual occupancy of another part as constructive possession. 42 Am J1st Prop § 42.

Actual possession is an essential of adverse possession. As such it means possession in fact, effected by actual entry upon the premises, and actual occupancy such as to indicate his exclusive ownership. 3 Am J2d Adv P § 13.

actual residence. A person's actual place of abode, the place where he actually lives, which is not necessarily his legal residence. Fitzgerald v Arel, 63 Iowa 104. See also 25 Am J2d Dom §§ 6, 9.

actual sale. A completed sale as distinguished from a contract to sell.

actual seizin. Seizin in fact, or seizin in deed, as distinguished from seizin in law, which is merely the right of an heir to the possession of the land descended when there is no adverse possession. See 23 Am J2d Desc & D § 23.

actual seizure. A seizure which is accomplished by

the manucaption of the thing intended to be seized. 6 Am J2d Attach § 296.

actual service. Personal service, as distinguished from service by publication or some other form of constructive service of process. 42 Am J1st Proc § 46.

The typical example of actual or personal service is that of reading the process to the person to be served or handing him a true copy upon his waiver of a reading.

See **active service.**

actual settler. As applied to settlers upon the public lands of the United States, a settlement completed by the settler and not a contemplated or possible settlement of an applicant for settlement.

The term implies an actual habitation established on some specific parcel of the land. Oregon & C. R. Co. v United States, 238 US 393, 432, 434, 59 L Ed 1360, 1395, 35 S Ct 908.

The residence required in order to qualify one as an actual settler must be continuous and personal. 42 Am J1st Pub L § 22.

actual total loss. This term as used in marine insurance means just what it implies, a total and actual loss to the insured of the subject matter of the insurance. To enable the insured to recover for a total loss, there must be a total destruction of value. It is not necessary to a total loss that there be an absolute destruction of the thing insured, so that nothing of it can be delivered at the point of destination, but there is a total loss if the thing is destroyed in specie, that is in the character or specie in which it was insured, even though some of its elements or parts may remain. 29A Am J Rev ed Ins § 1570.

actual use. The particular and real use to which property is devoted at a particular time. 7 Am J2d Auto Ins § 109.

As to what constitutes an actual use of materials within the meaning of a statute providing a mechanic's lien, see Anno: 39 ALR2d 452.

See **in actual use.**

actual value. The actual cash value or, if that is not ascertainable for want of a market, the intrinsic value or the value to the owner. 22 Am J2d Damg § 149. Practically identical with market value, or cash value, for the purposes of a tax statute. Re Frank, 123 Or 286, 261 P 893, 57 ALR 1155; Anno: 57 ALR 1158, supplemented 83 ALR 939, and 117 ALR 143.

actual violence. Physical as distinguished from inchoate violence; the element which distinguishes a battery from an assault. 6 Am J2d Asslt & B § 7.

actual waste. Commissive waste; acts injurious to the substance of an estate in land, such as cutting down trees valuable as timber and destroying, altering, or removing buildings. 56 Am J1st Waste § 4.

actuarial solvency. The ability of an insurance company or benefit society to meet accrued obligations and the obligations represented by policies and certificates in force as such appears in funds on hand and the present worth of payments of premiums and assessments to be made in the future by those insured under policies and certificates. Jenkins v Talbot, 338 Ill 441, 170 NE 735, 80 ALR 638.

actuarius (ăk-tu-ā'ri-us). A notary public under the civil law, but having duties of much greater variety and more significance than a notary public in common-law jurisdictions. 39 Am J1st Notary P § 3.

Other designations of the officer in civil law jurisdictions are **registrarius,** and **scrivarius.**

actuary. One engaged in the work of calculating the cost of carrying a risk, the amount of insurance premiums, the value of future interests, life estates, and annuities.

In the civil law, the word was used to signify a clerk or registrar; and in the ecclesiastical law, it denoted a clerk in the lower house of convocation.

actum (ak'tum). A deed.

actus (ak'tus). In the civil law, an act, something performed or accomplished; also a right of way.

Lord Coke, adopting the civil law, divided private ways into three kinds: a footway, called "iter;" a footway and horseway, called "actus," and a cartway, which embraced both of the other two, called "via." To these was added a "driftway," a road over which cattle could be driven. Jones v Venable, 120 Ga 1, 47 NE 549.

Actus curiae neminem gravabit (ak'tus kū-ri-ē ne'mi-nem gra-vā'bit). The act of the court shall prejudice no one. The maxim was applied to support the entry of a judgment nunc pro tunc, where delay was the fault of the court. See Borer v Chapman, 119 US 587, 30 L Ed 532, 7 S Ct 342.

actus Dei (ak'tus Dē'ī). The term is used interchangeably with "act of God," "vis major" and "Vis Divina."

See **act of God.**

Actus Dei nemini est damnosus (ak'tūs Dē'ī ne'mi-nī est dam-nō'sus). The act of God does no legal damage to anyone.

Actus Dei nemini facit injuriam (ak'tus Dē'ī ne'mi-nī fa'sit in-jū'rī-am). An act of God does not violate the legal right of anyone. The loss from an injury caused thereby must be borne by the one who suffered it. 38 Am J1st Negl § 7.

Actus Dei vel legis nemini facit injuriam (ak'tus Dē'ī vel lē'jis ne'mi-nī fā'sit in-jū'rī-am). Neither the act of God nor that of the law works legal wrong to anyone.

actus fictus in fraudem legis (ak'tus fik'tus in frâ'dem lē'jis). A fictitious act in fraud of the law.

actus legis nemini facit injuriam (ak'tus lē'jis ne'mi-nī fā'sit in-jū'rī-am). The act of the law works prejudice to no one.

Actus legitimi non recipiunt modum (ak'tus lē-ji'ti-mī non re-si'pi-unt mo'dum). Acts required by law do not admit of qualification.

Actus me invito factus, non est meus actus (ak'tus mē in-vī'tō fak'tus, non est me'us ak'tus). An act done by me against my will is not my act.

Actus non facit reum, nisi mens sit rea (ak'tus non fa'sit re'um, ni'si menz sit re'a). An act does not render one guilty, unless the mind is guilty. At common law, a crime had two essential elements: an act and an evil intention. 21 Am J2d Crim L § 81.

Actus repugnans non potest in esse produci (ak'tus re-pūg'nanz non po'test in es'se prō'du-sī). A repugnant act is of no effect.

Actus servi in iis quibus opera ejus communiter adhibita est, actus domini habetur (ak'tus ser'vī in i'īs qui'bus o'pe-ra ē'jus kom-mū'ni-ter ad-hi'bi-ta est, ak'tus do'mi-nī hā-bē'ter). The act of a servant, in the sort of work in which he is generally employed, is that of the master.

ACUERDO [26] ADD

acuerdo (ä-kö-är′dō). (Spanish.) The decision of a court; the resolution of a council or other board.

acute cholecystitis (ak-ūt′ kol-i-sis-tī′tis). A serious infection of the gall bladder. Home Life Ins Co. v Madere (CA5 Miss) 101 F2d 292.

acute disease. The antithesis of chronic disease; one which is severe, perhaps critical, as of the moment. Home Life Ins. Co. v Madere (CA5 Miss) 101 Fed 2d 292.

acya. Hate; malice.

ad (ad). Latin preposition: To; toward; for; until; about.

A. D. An abbreviation of Anno Domini, in the year of our Lord; since the birth of Christ.

ad abundantiorem cautelam (ad ab-un-dan-she-ō′rem kâ-tē′lam). For greater caution.

ad admittendum clericum (ad ad-mit-ten′dum kle′rī-kum). For admitting the clerk; a writ directing a bishop to admit and institute a clerk, that is, one of the clergy.

adaequatio (ad-e-quā′she-ō). An equivalent; a making equal.

adaerere (ad-ē′re-re). To value in money.

ad aliud examen (ad a′li-ud ex-ā′men). To another examination or trial. See 3 Bl Comm 113.

ad alium diem (ad a′li-um dī′em). At another day.

adam (ad′am). A bailiff or jailer.

Adamson Act. A federal statute declaring that eight hours shall be deemed a day's work for the purpose of reckoning the compensation of employees of common carriers by railroad. 45 USC §§ 65, 66; 31 Am J Rev ed Lab § 799.

ad annum vigesimum primum; et eo usque juvenes sub tutelam reponent (ad an′num vi-je′si-mum prī′mum; et e′ō us′kwe ju′ve-nēz sub tū-tē′lam rē-pō′nent). To the twenty-first year; and until then they place their young men under guardianship. See 1 Bl Comm 464.

adapted. Fit for use, sometimes after alteration or change.

ad assisas capiendas (ad as-sī′sas ka-pi-en′-dās). The word "assize" is derived, according to Sir Edward Coke, from the Latin assideo, to sit together, and originally it signifies the jury who try the cause and sit together for that purpose. By a figure it is now made to signify the court or jurisdiction which summons this jury together by a commission of assize, or "ad assisas capiendas," which means, literally, at the summoning of the assizes. See 3 Bl Comm 185.

a datu (ā dā′tū). From the date.

ad audiendum considerationem curiae (ad â-di-en′dum kon-si-de-rā″she-ō′nem kū′ri-ē). To hear the decision of the court.

ad audiendum errores (ad â-di-en′dum er-rō′rēz). To hear errors.

ad audiendum et determinandum (ad â-di-en′dum et de-ter″mi-nan′dum). For hearing and determining.

ad audiendum judicium. See **capias ad audiendum**, etc.

adavaunt. Before.

adayement (ä-dī′môn). Provocation.

adayer (ä-dä′yā). To provoke.

ad bancum (ad ban′kum). At the bench; to the bench.

ad barram (ad bar′ram). At the bar.

ad barram evocatus (ad bar′ram ē′vo-kā′tus). Called to the bar, admitted to practice law.

A.D.C. Abbreviation of **aide-de-camp**.

ad campi partem (ad kam′pi par′tem). For a share.

ad captandum (ad kap-tan′dum). For the purpose of catching or capturing.

ad captum vulgi (ad kap′tum vul′gī). By common understanding.

ad cautelam ex superabundanti (ad kâ-tē′lam ex sū-per-a-bun-dan′tī). For excessive caution.

ad colligendum. For temporary collection and preservation of assets.

ad colligendum bona defuncti (ad kol-li-jen′dum bo′na dē-fŭnk′tī). For collecting the goods of the decedent.
See **letters ad colligendum bona defuncti**.

ad communem legem (ad kom-mū′nem lē′jem). The name of a common-law form of writ of entry which lay for a reversioner, after the alienation and death of the particular tenant for life.

ad commune nocumentum (ad kom-mū′ne no-ku-men′tum). For the common nuisance.

ad comparendum (ad kom-pa-ren′dum). To appear.

ad comparendum et ad standum juri (ad kom-pa-ren′dum et ad stan′dum jū′rī). To appear and stand to the law, to appear in court and abide by the court's decision.

ad compotum reddendum (ad kom-pō′tum red-den′-dum). To render an account.

ad computandum. See **capias ad computandum**.

ad concordiam publicam promovendam (ad kon-kor′-di-am pub′li-kam prō-mō-ven′dam). To promote the public peace. See 4 Bl Comm 425.

ad consentiendum (ad kon-sen-she-en′dum). In consequence of consent. See 1 Bl Comm 168.

ad consulendum (ad kon-su-len′dum). To consult.

ad consulendum, ad defendendum regem (ad kon-su-len′dum, ad de-fen-den′dum rē′jem). For counselling and for defending the king. See 1 Bl Comm 227.

ad credulitare (ad kre-dū-li-tā′re). To clear one's self of a criminal charge by denial under oath.
See **purgation**.

ad crumenam (ad krū′men-am). To the purse.
See **argumentum ad crumenam**.

ad culpa (kul′pa). Until misconduct.

ad curiam (ad kū′ri-am). Before the court; to the court.

ad custagium (ad kus-tā′ji-um). For the costs.

ad custantia (ad kus-tan′she-a). For costs.

ad custum (ad kus′tum). At the cost.

ad damnum (ad dam′num). To the damage; formal claim for damages in a pleading.

ad damnum clause (ad dam′num klâz). That clause in a declaration or complaint which sets forth the plaintiff's demand for damages and the amount thereof.

add. Calculating a total; joining with something to increase the quantity.
See **advertisement**.

ad decisionem litis (ad de-si-zhe-ō'nem li'-tis). By the decision in the action.

added damages. Punitive or exemplary damages, sometimes called smart money. 22 Am J2d Damg § 236.

ad defendendum (ad dē-fen-den'dum). To defend; for defending.

ad deliberandum (ad dē-li-be-ran'dum). To deliberate; a writ for the removal of a prisoner for trial to the proper jurisdiction, usually called **habeas corpus ad deliberandum et recipiendum.**

ad deliberandum et recipiendum. See **habeas corpus ad deliberandum et recipiendum.**

ad delinquendum (ad dē-lin-quen'dum). To become delinquent.

addendum (a-den'dum). An appendix to an instrument or other writing.

addendum circle. A circle on a gear wheel which touches the points of the teeth of the wheel.

addicere (ad-di'se-re). To condemn; also to deliver.

addict (a-dikt', a'dikt). In the civil law, a commitment as a prisoner. In common usage today, one who becomes an habitual user of narcotics.

addictio (ad-dik'she-ō). (Civil law.) A judicial award under which ownership of property was acquired. The commitment of a debtor.

addictio in diem (ad-dik'she-ō in dī'em). A civil law sale contract with a proviso that the seller shall be released if a better offer is made to him on or before a certain day.

addiction (a-dik'shon). See **addict.**

ad diem (ad dī'em). At the day; at a day.

additio. Same as **addition.**

addition. The arithmetical process of computing a sum. A descriptio personae; that is, some title or description written after a person's name for certainty of identification; as, Jane Lewis, wife of A. V. Lewis. Commonwealth v. Lewis, 42 Mass (1 Met) 148, 152. Something added to an instrument which, in the case of a will, is an alteration that must be executed and attested as a will if it is to be effective. 57 Am J1st Wills § 508. A structure built on to another structure to produce an enlarged building.

As used in a fire insurance policy covering buildings and additions or personal property located in buildings and additions, the terms "additions" or "additions attached" are given a liberal construction in favor of the insured consistent with the intention of the parties. Effect is to be given to them by applying the terms to any building reasonably answering the description, provided such application is not inconsistent with other terms of the policy or clearly excluded by the facts and circumstances surrounding the parties at the time of the execution of the contract. 29 Am J Rev ed Ins § 294.

In a lease of premises already equipped for operating an oil refinery, a provision giving the lessee the right to erect and remove "additions" was held to cover new equipment installed to increase the capacity, and meet increased demands for the product. Anno: 91 ALR 540.

See **paid-up addition.**

additional (a-dish'on-al). Added; supplemental; coming by way of addition.

Matter which is additional is to be distinguished from that which is amendatory in a statute. Collier v Smaltz, 149 Iowa 230, 128 NW 396.

additional abstract. An appellee's abstract of the record; an amendatory abstract on appeal. 4 Am J2d A & E § 410.

additional allowances. Discretionary allowances of costs, in addition to the regular statutory costs, authorized in difficult and extraordinary cases. 20 Am J2d Costs § 71. Attorneys' or referee's fees, taxed as costs. 4 Am J2d A & E § 128.

additional arbitrator. See **third arbitrator.**

additional assessment. A redetermination of liability for a tax. A further assessment for a tax of the same character previously paid in part. Girard Trust Co. v United States, 270 US 163, 70 L Ed 524, 46 S Ct 229.

additional burden. See **additional servitude.**

A structure may be an "addition" within the meaning of a fire insurance policy, notwithstanding there is no physical connection between it and the main building insured by the policy. Also, a building may be considered to come within the policy as an addition, even though it is larger and more costly than the original building. The term additions is not confined to structures in existence at the time the contract of insurance was made. 29 Am J Rev ed Ins § 294.

additional entry. An entry made by a settler on public lands of the United States after he has made a previous entry.

additional instructions. Instructions given to the jury by the court after they have retired to deliberate.

The court may exercise a wide discretion in the matter of charging the jury, and may bring them in at any time and give them additional instructions, whether requested or not. 53 Am J1st Tr § 941.

additional insurance. See **contribution between insurers; double insurance; excess insurance; other insurance clause.**

additional insured. One other than the person named as the insured under an automobile liability policy, while using the motor vehicle with the permission of the named insured for the purposes for which it is insured and within the scope of the permission granted. 7 Am J2d Auto Ins § 110.

additional liability. See **superadded liability.**

additional premium. An additional payment required of a mortgagor for the privilege of paying the principal in advance, thereby stopping the accumulation of interest. Anno: 70 ALR2d 1334.

The term is also used to designate the increase in premium payable under an insurance policy when additional coverage is given, such as an additional premium where coverage for loss by hail is added to a policy otherwise insuring only against loss from fire and windstorm.

additional servitude. A use of a different character from that for which the land was originally taken under eminent domain proceedings, amounting to the imposition of a new and additional easement on the land and requiring a new condemnation to justify its taking. 26 Am J2d Em D § 207.

additional work. Work performed by the builder under a construction contract pursuant to a modification of the terms of the contract. 13 Am J2d Bldg Contr § 4.

additions. Plural of **addition.**

additio probat minoritatem (ad-di'she-o pro'bat mi-nō'ri-tā'tem). To add a word may indicate a lesser, as by changing "Colonel" to "Lieutenant Colonel."

additur (ad-di'tūr). An increase by the court in the amount of damages awarded by the jury. 22 Am J2d Damg §§ 398 et seq.

addone (ad-dō'nē). Given to.

addoubeur (äd'doo-bur). A promoter; one who aids in organizing an enterprise or business.

address. Verb: To speak or to write to a person or a body; to indicate the destination of mail. Noun: The direction given on a letter or other piece of mail as to the destination. A speech or a writing. A request of an executive by a legislative body for the removal of a judge or other officer. The technical description in a bill in equity of the court to which the bill is presented, including, if desired, but not as a requirement, the name of the chancellor or judge. 27 Am J2d Equity § 180.

To call the words which one minister speaks to his congregation a "sermon," immune from regulation, and the words of another minister an "address," subject to regulation, is merely an indirect way of preferring one religion over another, in violation of the constitutional guaranties of freedom of religion. Fowler v Rhode Island, 345 US 67, 97 L Ed 828, 73 S Ct 526.

addressare. Same as **adrectare.**

addresser (a-dres'ėr). To raise up; to hold up; to prepare.

adduce (a-dūs'). To bring forward; to present; to offer; to introduce.

It is apparent that the word may have widely different meanings in connection with evidence adduced, for evidence offered is very different from evidence introduced. Introduced evidence is evidence received. Offered evidence may or may not be received. Tuttle v Story County, 56 Iowa 316, 317, 9 NW 292.

ad ea quae frequentius accidunt jura adaptantur (ad e'a kwē fre-quen'she-us ak'si-dunt ju'ra ad-aptan'ter). Laws are adapted to those cases which more commonly occur.

adeem (a-dēm'). Taking away; to effect an ademption.
See **ademption.**

ad effectum (ad ef-fek'tum). To the purpose.

ad effectum sequentem (ad ef-fek'tum se-quen'tem). To the following effect.

adeling. Same as **atheling.**

ad emendum et vendendum sine onmibus malis tolnetis, per antiquas et rectas consuetudines (ad e-men'-dum et ven-den'dum sī'ne om'ni-bus ma'lis tol-ne'tis per an-tī'-quas et rek'tas kon"su-e-tū'di-nēz). For buying and selling without any improper tolls, according to old and proper customs.

ademptio. Same as **ademption.**

ademption. (a-demp'shon). The extinction or satisfaction of a legacy by some act of the testator, which indicates either a revocation of or an intention to revoke the bequest. American Trust & Banking Co. v Balfour, 138 Tenn 385, 198 SW 70, 57 Am J1st Wills § 1580. The practical nullification of a general legacy by the act of the testator, subsequent to the will, in paying money or transferring property to the legatee with the intent that the benefit conferred shall be applied on or substituted for the legacy. Anno: 26 ALR2d 14.

The foregoing definitions are subject to extension, since it is clear that an ademption of a testamentary bequest may occur by reason of the destruction or extinction of the subject matter without the agency of the testator, as by the death of an animal bequeathed by the will, in which case an ademption may occur without testatorial intention. 57 Am J1st Wills § 1580.

Where a legacy of stocks, bonds, or other corporate securities are not in the estate of the testator at the time of his death, the general rule is that the bequest is adeemed. Anno: 117 ALR 811.

adeo (ad'e-ō). To that point; so far.

adeo plene et integre (ad'e-ō plē'ne et in'te-gre). As fully and completely.

ad eosdem terminos (ad e-ōs'dem ter'mi-nos). At or on the same terms.

adeprimes (ad-prem). First; in the first place.

adequacy. Sufficiency; sufficiency for a particular purpose. Penn. & N. Y. C. & R. Co. v Mason, 109 Pa 296.

adequacy of consideration. See **adequate consideration.**

adequate. Fully sufficient; equal to what is required; lawfully and reasonably sufficient. Standard Dict. See Nagle v Billings, 77 Mont 205, 250 P 445.

adequate care. The standard of reasonable care under the circumstances of the case. 38 Am J1st Negl § 29.

adequate cause. As the term is used in the definition of manslaughter committed under sudden passion arising from an adequate cause, such cause as would commonly produce a degree of anger, rage, resentment, or terror, in a person of ordinary temper, sufficient to render the mind incapable of cool reflection. Boyett v State, 2 Tex App 93, 100.
See **adequate provocation.**

adequate compensation. The just and reasonable compensation to which an owner of property taken in an eminent domain proceeding is entitled. 27 Am J2d Em D § 266.

adequate consideration (ad'ē-kwąt kǫn-sid-ė-rā'shǫn). A fair and reasonable price for the subject-matter of the contract; a consideration not so greatly disproportionate to the value as to offend against fair business dealing. Anno: 65 ALR 85.

adequate facilities. See **adequate or reasonable facilities.**

adequate legal remedy. See **adequate remedy at law.**

adequately safe (ad'ē-kwāt-li). Sufficiently safe; sufficiently safe for a particular purpose. Pennsylvania & N. Y. C. & R. Co. v Mason, 109 Pa 296.

adequate or reasonable facilities. A relative expression, calling for such facilities as may be fairly demanded of a carrier, regard being had, among other things, to the size of the place, the extent of the demand for transportation, the cost of furnishing the additional accommodations asked for, and other circumstances which have a bearing upon convenience and cost. 13 Am J2d Car § 142.

adequate provocation. Provocation which is sufficient to reduce an intentional killing from murder to manslaughter and consisting of conduct on the part of the deceased which so excited the assailant

as practically to enthrall his reason. State v Grugin, 147 Mo 39.
See **reasonable provocation**.

adequate remedy at law. A remedy at law which defeats by its existence the jurisdiction of equity, being a remedy which is plain, clear and certain, prompt or speedy, sufficient, full, or complete, practical, and efficient to the attainment of the ends of justice. 27 Am J2d Equity § 94. A term impossible of complete and accurate definition, but meaning generally relief as certain, prompt, practicable, and efficient as an injunction would be. 28 Am J Rev ed Inj § 39.

aderere (ad-e-rē're). In arrears.

ad escambium ad valentiam (ad es-kam'bi-um ad va-len'she-am). For exchange to the value.

adesouth. Underneath.

ad essendum (ad es-sen'dum). To be.

ad essendum coram justiciariis (ad es-sen'-dum kō'ram jus-ti"she-ā'ri-is). To be before the justices.

ad essendum de consilio suo (ad es-sen'dum dē kon-si'li-ō su'ō). To be of his counsel.

ad estimationem pretii, damni, lucri, etc. (ad es-ti-mā-she-ō'nem pre'she-ī, dam'nī, lu'krī, etc). To estimate the price, damage, gain, etc. See 3 Bl Comm 397.

adeu (ä'de-oo). Without day, without appointing a future day, sine die.

adevant (ä'de-vôn). Before.

ad eversionem juris nostri (ad e-ver"zi-ō'nem jur'is nos'trī). To the upsetting of our rights under the law.

ad excambium. See **excambium**.

ad executionem decretorum judicii, ad estimationem pretii, damni, lucri, etc. (ad ex-e-kū-she-ō'nem de-kre-tō'rum jū'di-she-ī, ad es-ti-mā-she-ō'nem pre'-she-ī, dam'nī, lu'krī). To execute the decrees of the court, to estimate the price, damage, gain, etc. See 3 Bl Comm 397.

ad exhaeredationem (ad ex-hē-rē-dā"she-ō'nem). To disinherit; to disherison.

ad exhaeredationem ecclesia (ad ex-hē-rē-dā"she-ō'nem ē-klē'si-ē). To the disinherison of the church.

ad exhaeredationem ipsius (ad ex-hē-rē-dā"she-ō'nem ip-sī'us). To his own disinheritance.

ad exitum (ad ex-i'tum). At the end of pleading; at issue.

ad extremum (ad eks-trē'mum). At the end; finally.

ad faciendum (ad fā-she-en'dum). To do; to make; for doing; for making.

ad faciendum et recipiendum (ad fā-she-en'dum et re-si-pi-en'dum). See **habeas corpus ad faciendum et recipiendum**.

ad factum praestandum (ad fak'tum prē-stan'dum). A Scotch law obligation of a very binding nature.

adficio (ad'fi-cio). To strive for; to intend to accomplish.

ad fidem (ad fī'dem). Of allegiance.

ad fidem regis (ad fī'dem rē'jis). Under the allegiance of the king.

ad fidem utriusque regis (ad fī'dem u-trī'us-kwe rē'jis). Under allegiance to each king.

ad filum aquae (ad fī'lum a'quē). To the thread or center of the stream.

ad filum viae (ad fī'lum vī'ē). To the middle of the way. Parker v Inhabitants of Framingham, 49 Mass (8 Met) 260, 267.

ad fin. An abbreviation of **ad finem**.

ad finem (ad fī'nem). To the end; at the end.

ad finem litis (ad fī'nem lī'tis). At the end or to the end of the litigation.

adfines. Same as **affines**.

ad firmam (ad fir'mam). To farm.
See **fee farm**.

ad firmam ponere (ad fir'mam pō'ne-re). To put to farm.

adfixus. Same as **affixus**.

ad foedi firmam (ad fē'dī fir'mam). To fee farm.
See **fee farm**.

ad fundamen jurisdictionem (ad fun-dā'men jur-is-dik'shē-ōn'em). To the basic principles of jurisdiction.

ad gaolam deliberandam (ad ga'o-lam de-li"be-ran'-dam). For jail delivery.

ad gaolas deliberandas (ad gā'o-las dē-li-be-ran'das). To make a jail delivery.

adgisant (äd'gi-sänt). Adjacent.

adgisantz (äd'gē-sâns). Adjacent.

adgnoscere (ad-gnos'ce-re). To admit; to accept.

ad gravamen (ad gra-vā'men). To the grievance or damage.

ad gravamen tenetis sui (ad gra-vā'men te-nē'tis su'ī). To the grievance of his tenant.

ad grave damnum (ad gra've dam'num). To the great damage.

ad gustum (ad gus'tum). To the taste; to one's liking.

adherence (ad-hēr'ens). A Scotch action to restore marital rights. Supporting a person or a cause.

adhering. Cleaving to or supporting.

adhesion. Adherence. The uniting of tissues of the body which normally are separate, sometimes occurring as the aftermath of surgery. Acquiring relations with another nation by treaty or compact. 52 Am J1st Treat § 3.

adhesion contract. A contract that is drafted unilaterally by the dominant party and then presented on a take it or leave it basis to the weaker party, who has no real opportunity to bargain about its terms. Restatement Second, Conflict of Laws § 332a, Comment e.

adhibere deligentiam (ad-hi'be-re di-li-jen'she-am). To exercise case.

adhibere vim (ad-hi'be-re vim). To use force.

ad hoc (ad hōk). To this only; respecting this particularly. For this case only.

ad hoc autem creatus est et electus, ut justitiam faciat universis (ad hōk â'tem kre-ā'tus est et ē-lek'-tus, ut jūs-ti-she-am fā'si-at u-ni-ver'sis). He is created and chosen for the purpose of bestowing justice upon all.

Ad hoc facit (ad hōk fā'sit). It makes to this; it goes to this effect.

ad hoc officer. An officer, such as a referee in partition, whose tenure continues only for the duration of the case or the performance of his duties therein, ending when his work in the case has been performed and approved by the court. Saxe v Shea (CA2 NY) 98 F2d 83.

ad hominem (ad hom′i-nem). To the man; personal. See **argumentum ad hominem**.

Adhuc existit (ad′hŭk eg-sis′tit). It exists even now.

Adhuc remanet (ad′hŭk rē-mā′net). It remains at the present time.

Adhuc sub judice lis est (ad′hŭk sub jū′di-se lis est). The cause is still before the court.

Adhuc detinet (ad′hŭk dē′ti-net). He detains up to this time.

adhuc diem (ad′hŭk dī′em). At this day.

Adhuc possunt partes resilero (ad′hŭk pos′sunt par′tēz rē-si′le-re). The parties may withdraw at this time.

A dicto secundum quid ad dictum simpliciter (ā dik′tō se-kun′dum quid ad dik′tum sim-pli′si-ter). From what has been said to that which has been said plainly. An error of logic in concluding the existence of collateral facts from a presumption. Hyde v United States, 225 US 347, 385, 56 L Ed 1114, 1133, 32 S Ct 793.

ad idem (ad ī′dem). To the same effect. See **consensus ad idem**.

Ad idem facit (ad ī′dem fā-sit). It goes to the same effect.

adieu (a-dū′). Farewell. In old English, a dismissal without opportunity for another day in court.

A digniori fieri debet denominatio (ā dig-ni-ō′rī fī′e-rī de′bet dē-nō-mi-nā′she-ō). A designation should be made from the more fitting.

ad ignorantiam (ad ig-no-ran′she-am). To ignorance. See **argumentum ad ignorantiam**.

ad illud (ad il′lud). To that.

adimere (ad-i′me-re). To take away; to remove.

Ad impossibilia lex non cogit (ad im-pos″si-bi′li-a lex non cō′jit). The law does not compel impossible things. A streetcar violates no law in failing to turn out for a truck. Commonwealth v Temple, 80 Mass (14 Gray) 69, 78.

ad indefinitum (ad in-def-i-nī′tum). To the indefinite; indefinitely; without end.

ad inde requisitus (ad in′de re-qui-sī′tus). From thence required.

ad infinitum (ad in-fi-nī′tum). Without end; to any extent.

ad informandum conscientiam judicis (ad in-for-man′dum con-she-en′she-am jū′di-sis). To inform the mind of the judge.

ad inopiam (ad in-o′pi-am). Toward poverty.

ad inquirendum (ad in-qui-ren′dum). A common-law writ commanding an inquiry or investigation.

ad instantiam (ad in-stan′she-am). At the instance.

ad instantiam partio (ad in-stan′she-am par′she-ō). At the instance of a party.

Ad instructiones reparationesque itinerum et pontium, nullum genus hominum, nulliusque dignitatis ac venerationis meritis, cessare oportet (ad in-struk-she-ō′nēz re-pa-ra-she-ō-nez′kwe i-ti′ne-rum et pon′she-um, nul′lum jē′nus ho′mi-num, nul-lī-us′kwe dig-ni-tā′tis ak ve-ne-ra-she-ō′nis me′ri-tis, ses-sā′re o-por′tet). Respecting the construction and repair of roads and bridges no class of men of whatever rank or dignity ought to be exempt. See 1 Bl Comm 357.

ad int. An abbreviation of **ad interim**.

ad interim (ad in′te-rim). In the meantime; for the time, as an officer ad interim; temporary.

ad interim alimony. Same as **alimony pendente lite**.

ad interim copyright (ad in′te-rim). A copyright obtainable under particular circumstances and enduring for a limited time.

Where a book or periodical is first published abroad in the English language, the deposit of one complete copy of such foreign edition in the copyright office, not later than six months after its publication abroad, with a request for the reservation of the copyright and a statement of the name and nationality of the author and copyright proprietor and of the date of publication, secures to the author or proprietor an ad interim copyright having all the force and effect given to copyright by the Federal Copyright Law, which will endure until the expiration of 5 years after the date of the first publication abroad. 17 USC § 22.

ad invidiam (ad in-vid′i-am). To hatred or prejudice. See **argumentum ad invidiam**.

adiratus (ad-i-rā′tus). Lost; strayed.

adire in jus (ad-ī′re in jūs). To go to law.

adire in praetorem in jus (ad-ī′re in pre′tō′rem in jūs). To go to law.

adit (ad′it). A tunnel in a mine.

ad itinerandum (ad i-ti″ne-ran′dum). For the journey; for the voyage.

aditio haereditatis (ad-i′she-ō hē-rē-di-tā′tis). (Civil law.) The heir's formal entry upon land inherited from his ancestor.

Aditio haereditatis pro solutione cedit (ad-i′she-ō hē-rē-di-tā′tis prō sō-lū-she-ō′ne sē′dit). (Civil law.) Entering upon an inheritance suffices for payment.

aditus (ad′i-tus). A right of entrance.

a divisione (a di-vi-zhe-ō′ne). From a division or separation into parts. See **argumentum a divisione**.

adjacent. Near or close to. A somewhat relative term, sometimes meaning touching or contiguous. Clark v Coburn, 108 Me 26, 78 A 1107. But clearly not the equivalent of "abutting" in all cases. 23 Am J2d Deeds § 242.

adjacent land. A relative term, sometimes meaning adjacent land, at other times land in the neighborhood.

In a statute authorizing a special assessment on adjacent property, the term "adjacent" includes property in the neighborhood not actually touching the improvement, at least where the improvement is such that its benefits extend to property in the vicinity which does not lie contiguous to the improvement. 48 Am J1st Spec § 119.

As it appears in a statute conferring power to condemn "land adjacent" to that occupied by a public service corporation, the term "adjacent" may in view of the context of the statute and the purpose for which the land is taken refer to neighboring land not necessarily in contact. If a strict construction of the statute is required, as it is where the statute is in derogation of private rights, the

ADJACENT [31] **ADJUDICATION**

term may be confined to lands that are adjoining or contiguous. 26 Am J2d Em D § 114.

adjacent territory. The suburbs of a city which are not within the limits of another municipality. Johnson City v Weeks, 133 Tenn 277, 180 SW 327, 3 ALR 1431, 1432.

As the expression is used in an application to appropriate water for municipal use in adjacent territory, it is held to refer to built-up territory outside of but immediately adjacent to, the respective incorporated cities named in the application. Rich v McClure, 78 Cal App 209, 248 P 275.

adjection (a-jek'shon). A thing added.
See **addition**.

adjectire (ad-jek-tī're). To summon to court.

adjective law. Remedial law, that which prescribes how rights are presented for adjudication and enforced and defenses maintained, as distinguished from the law known as substantive law which creates rights and supports defenses. Mix v Board of County Commrs. 18 Idaho 695, 112 P 215.

adjectivus (ad-jek-tī'vus). Summoned to court.

adjicere (ad-ji'se-re). To add to; to annex; to join.

adjoining. In its etymological sense, touching or contiguous, as distinguished from lying near or adjacent. Re Ward, 52 NY 395, 397. In certain contexts, close or near to. Matthews v Kimball, 70 Ark 451, 464, 69 SW 547.

So, lands separated by a public way may nevertheless adjoin. 1 Am J2d Adj L § 1.

In a lease of the fourth store in a row of six, containing a covenant by the lessor not to let any of the adjoining shops for the purpose of a specified trade in which the lessee intends to engage, the word "adjoining" is not confined to the shop on either side of the one demised, but extends to any shop in the row, although, in the absence of the use of the word "any," as modifying the word "adjoining," the latter word may be interpreted to refer only to premises next door or physically "adjoining." Anno: 90 ALR 1461.

As the word appears in a deed which describes the subject matter by reference to the properties adjoining it, the word "adjoining" does not necessarily import that the boundary of the land conveyed is coterminous with the boundary of the adjoining land, for all that the word implies is contiguity, and hence it is equally applicable where one boundary is shorter than the other. 23 Am J2d Deeds § 242.

adjoining and communicating additions. Buildings or structures having some form of physical connection. 29 Am J Rev ed Ins § 294.

adjoining county. A contiguous county. For some purposes, a county which is near and readily accessible, as in a statute respecting the issuance of a writ of habeas corpus. 25 Am J1st Hab C § 106.

adjoining land. See **adjoining**.

adjoining landowners. The owners of lands that are separated by a common boundary line. 1 Am J2d Adj L § 1.
But see **adjoining**.

adjoining premises. See **adjoining**.

adjourn (a-jėrn'). To postpone or put over to a future time: as, to adjourn a meeting.

adjournal (a-jėr'nal). The proceedings of a day or session of the Scotch Court of Justiciary.
See **act of adjournal**; **book of adjournal**.

adjournamentum (ad-jour-nā-men'tum). Adjournment.

adjournare (ad-jour-nā're). To adjourn.

adjournatur (ad-jour-nā'ter). It is adjourned.

adjournatus (ad-jour-nā'tus). Adjourned.

adjourned term. A period or session of court which is merely the continuance or prolongation of a regular term, so that in reality there is no more than one term. Harris v Gest, 4 Ohio St 469, 473.

adjournent assisas (äd-jour'nent äs'sēs-säs). They shall adjourn the assizes.

adjourner (ad-jour-ne'). To adjourn.

adjournment. The suspension of business or sessions, either for a fixed time, indefinitely, or until the opening of another term.

As used in constitutional provision that a bill shall become a law if not returned by the executive within a specified time unless "adjournment" prevents its return, the word may signify either an adjournment which is temporary or one which is final in character, and resort must be had to the context to ascertain the true sense. Anno: 64 ALR 1446.

adjournment day. The day upon which a court or legislature adjourns. The day to which a session or meeting is adjourned.

adjournment in eyre (ad-jern'ment in år). An adjournment of court by the judges on circuit to a future session or day.

adjournment sine die (ad-jern'ment sī'ne dī'e). An adjournment without setting a time for another meeting or session. An adjournment which closes a term of court. 20 Am J2d Cts § 47. An adjournment which closes a session of a legislative body or a convention.

adjournment subject to call. Same as **adjournment sine die**.

adjournment without day. Same as **adjournment sine die**.

adjudge (a-juj'). To give judgment; to decide; to sentence.

adjudgeable (a-juj'a-bl). Capable of being adjudicated.

adjudged. Decided. Determined by the judgment of the court. Drinkhouse v Van Ness, 202 Cal 359, 260 P 869, 874.

adjudicataire (ad-ju-di-ka-tėr'). (A Canadian term from the French language.) The purchaser at a judicial sale.

adjudicate (a-jö'di-kāt). To give judgment; to render or award judgment.

adjudicated liability. A liability determined and fixed by judgment.

adjudicatio (ad-jū-di-kā'she-ō). An adjudication; the determination of title by means of a judgment.

adjudication. The determination of the issues in an action according to which judgment is rendered; a solemn, final, and deliberate determination of an issue by the judicial power, after a hearing in respect to the matters determined. Sans v New York, 31 NY Misc 559, 560, 64 NYS 681.
See **articulate adjudication**; **prior adjudication**.

adjudication in bankruptcy. The determination, whether by decree or by operation of law, that a

ADJUDICATIVE [32] ADMEASUREMENT

person is a bankrupt. Bankruptcy Act § 1(2) (11 USC 1(2)); 9 Am J2d Bankr § 264.

adjudicative power. Judicial power; the power of a court to hear and determine a controversy. 20 Am J2d Cts § 80.

adjudicatory. A term employed in speaking of the quasi-judicial functions of an administrative agency. 1 Am J2d Adm L § 138.

adjudicatory process. A process of courts and administrative agencies. 1 Am J2d Adm L § 15.

adjudicature (a-jö′di-ką-tụr″). The act of making an adjudication; an adjudication.

ad judicium (ad jū-di′she-um). To the judgment.

ad judicium provocare (ad ju-di′she-um prō-vo-kā′re). To invoke judicial functions; to bring an action.

adjunctio (ad-junk′she-ō). Adjunction; the acquisition of property by its annexation to other property.

adjunction (a-jungk′shon). The uniting of one article or material with another by which the lesser thing becomes a part of the greater. A synonym of accession. 1 Am J2d Access § 1.

adjunctum (ad-junk′tum). An adjunct; something united or connected with another thing.

ad jungendum auxilium (ad jū-jen′dum âk-zi′li-um). To join in aid.

ad jura legis (ad jū′ra lē′jis). For the rights of the law.

adjurare (ad-jū-rā′re). To bind one's self by oath.

ad jura regis (ad jö′rä rē′jis). A writ at the suit of a person holding a living from the king directed against those seeking to deprive him of it.

adjuration (a-ju-rā′shun). Advice most solemnly given; entreaty.

adjure (a-jör′). To command or require performance under oath; to entreat.

adjurnamentum (ad-jur-nā-men′tum). An adjournment.

adjurnare (ad-jur-nā′re). To adjourn.

adjust (a-just′). To settle or to bring to a satisfactory state, so that the parties are agreed in the result; as, to adjust accounts. State ex rel. Sayre v Moore, 40 Neb 854, 59 NW 755.

When applied to a liquidated demand, the verb "adjust" has the same meaning as the word "settle" in the same connection, and means to pay the demand. When applied to an unliquidated demand it means to ascertain the amount due or to settle. In the latter connection, to settle means to effect a mutual adjustment between the parties and to agree upon the balance. State v Staub, 61 Conn 553, 568.

adjusted basis. For income tax purposes, the original cost or other original basis adjusted for such things as casualty losses, improvements, and depreciation, when appropriate.

adjusted gross income. A tax-law term for gross income less the deductions permitted by law.

adjusted service bonds. Nontransferrable bonds bestowed in recognition of military service. Marshall v Felker, 156 Fla 476, 23 So 2d 555, 161 ALR 167

adjuster. A person who makes a determination of a claim, especially a claim against an insurance company, and objections made thereto by the debtor or insurance company, for the purpose of arriving at an amount for which the claim will be settled.

First National Bank v Manchester Fire Assur. Co. 64 Minn 96, 98, 66 NW 136. Sometimes acting as the agent of the insurance company or debtor, at other times as the agent of the claimant. Aetna Ins. Co. v Shryer, 85 Ind 362, 363; 7 Am J2d Attys § 86.

adjusting agency. In one sense, a collection agency; in another sense, an agency representing a debtor in making an arrangement with his creditors for the settlement of his obligations by modification of the indebtedness. 15 Am J2d Collect §§ 1, 2.

adjustment. The determination for the purposes of a settlement of the amount of a claim, particularly a claim against an insurance company, giving consideration to objections made by the debtor or insurance company, as well as the allegations of the claimant in support of his claim. 29A Am J Rev ed Ins § 1604.

Adjustment of claims is not confined to claims against insurance companies. An allowance made by a creditor, particularly a storekeeper, in response to a complaint by the debtor respecting the accuracy of the account or other claim, or a reduction in the claim or account made to induce a prompt payment, is in a proper sense an adjustment.
See **adjust.**

adjustment clause. A clause in a fire insurance policy, also known as a burned and unburned clause, providing that in the event of loss or damage at any location mentioned in the policy, the amount of insurance in force at that location shall be prorated to the burned and unburned portions of the property. Indiana Lumbermen's Mutual Ins. Co. v Fair (CA5 Miss) 109 F2d 607.

adjutant general. A state officer having duties in respect of the National Guard or active militia. See 36 Am J1st Mil §§ 42 et seq.

adjutor (a-ju′tor). A helper; an assistant; a deputy.

ad largum (ad lar′gum). At large.
See **ire ad largum.**

ad legem. (ad lē′gem). At the law.

adlegiare (ad-lē-ji-ā′re). To purge of an accusation of crime by means of an oath.

ad lib. An abbreviation of **ad libitum;** colloquially, to speak extemporaneously.

ad libitum (ad lib′i-tum). At pleasure; at will.

ad litem (ad lī′tem). For the purposes of the suit. During the pendency of the action or proceedings.

ad litis decisionem (ad lī′tis de-si-zhe-ō′nem). To the decision of the case.

ad litis ordinationem (ad li′tis or-di-na″she-ō-nem). To the regulation of the action.

ad lucrandum vel perdendum (ad lu-kran′dum vel per-den′dum). For profit or loss.

Adm. Abbreviation of **admiral;** also of **admiralty.** Abbreviation of **administrator.**

ad majoram cautelam (ad mā-jō′ram kâ-tē′lam). For greater caution.

ad majus (ad mā′jus). For the greater.

admanuensis (ad-man-ū-en′sis). A person who took oath with his hand on the Bible.

ad manum (ad mă′num). At hand.

admeasure (ad-mezh′ūr). To measure; to parcel out shares in land.

admeasurement (ad-mezh′ūr-ment). A measuring; an allotment; an assignment of one's share; a division.

ADMEASUREMENT [33] ADMINISTRATION

admeasurement of dower. Setting off to a widow the land to which she is entitled by right of dower. 25 Am J2d Dow § 156. A writ which lay against a widow to whom the heir, while under age, or his guardian, had assigned as dower more than that to which she was entitled. See 2 Bl Comm 136.

admeasurement of homestead. A preliminary to an execution sale of property of a judgment debtor who is entitled to a homestead exemption in a part of the tract sought to be subjected to execution and sale. 26 Am J1st Home § 96.

admeasurement of pasture. A writ for the proper division of rights of common.

ad medium filum aquae (ad mē'di-um fī'lum a'kwē). To the center or thread of the stream.

ad medium filum viae (ad mē'di-um fī'lum vī'e). To the center or thread of the way.

ad melius inquirendum (ad me'li-us in-qui-ren'dum). A writ ordering a further inquest.

admensurare (ad-mën'sū-rā-re). To make an admeasurement.

admensuratio (ad-men"sū-rā'she-ō). Same as **admeasurement**.

admensuratione dotis (ad-men-sū-rā'she-ō'ne dō'tis). See **de admensuratione dotis**.

admensuratio nihil aliud est quam reductio admensuram (ad-men-sū-ra'she-o' ni'hil a'li-ud est quam re-duc'she-o ad-men-sū'ram). A measurement is nothing more than a reduction to measure.

adminicle (ad-min'i-kl). Confirmatory evidence; corroboration.

adminicular (ad-mi-nik'ū-lär). Auxiliary; corroborative; confirmatory.

administer. To apply or enforce the law. To dispense justice. To dispense or apply medicine. To take charge; to manage, as in administering the estate of a decedent.
A board is said to administer a law while performing any ministerial act or acts which the law requires it to perform, but it does not so administer the law in the institution or defense of an action, because such latter act is done in the enforcement or resistance of the law and not in the administration of it. In re Winborne, 34 Wyo 349, 244 P 135.

administered estate. An estate of a decedent which has been completely managed and handled by executor or administrator, so that no assets remain in his possession or custody, all debts of the decedent and expenses of administration having been paid and the remaining assets distributed to the persons entitled thereto. As applied to determine the right of an administrator de bonis non to assets not "administered," goods, chattels, or credits of the decedent changed, altered, or converted by the prior executor or administrator. Chamberlin's Appeal, 70 Conn 363, 39 A 734.

administrare (ad-mi-ni-strā're). To administer; to take charge of.

administratio (ad-mi-nis-trā'she-ō). Same as **administration**.

administration. The execution of a law by putting it in effect, applying to the affairs of men. The management, care, or control of anything; an executor's or administrator's management of the estate of a decedent; an officer's management of his office.
See **administer**.

administration ad colligendum (ad-min-is-trā'shun ad kol-li-jen'dum). An administration for the temporary preservation of the estate of a decedent.
See **temporary administrator**.

administration cum testamento annexo (kum tes-ta-men'tō an-ne'xō). The administration of the estate of a decedent who left a will which did not name an executor, or which named one or more who will not or cannot qualify. Fidelity & C. Co. v Freeman (CA6 Tenn) 109 F 847.

administration de bonis non (dē bō'nis non). The administration of a decedent's estate by an administrator de bonis non.

administration durante absentia (du-ran'te ab-sen'-she-a). Administration upon the estate of a decedent during the absence of the person first entitled to letters of administration.
Concerning an appointment durante absentia, it has been ruled that such administration of the office is at an end the moment the absentee returns. See State ex rel. Hamilton v Guinotte, 156 Mo 513, 57 SW 281.
See **administrator of absentee**.

administration durante animo vitio. See **administrator durante animo vitio**.

administration durante minoritate administratoris. See **administrator durante minoritate administratoris**.

administration expenses. Items such as court costs, premium for surety bond, payments made for the preservation of the property of the estate while administration is pending, insurance premiums, attorney's fees incurred in litigation necessary in the preservation of the estate, burial expenses, allowances to widow and children, etc., for which the executor or administration may claim credit in the settlement of his accounts. 31 Am J2d Ex & Ad § 527. The expenses incurred in reducing the assets of the decedent's estate to possession, in holding them or disposing of them in accordance with the laws on succession and distribution and the decrees of the probate court. Hazard v Bliss, 43 RI 431, 113 A 469, 23 ALR 826. Rent paid by a receiver or trustee in bankruptcy for premises occupied by them during the administration of the estate in bankruptcy. In Re C. J. Rowe & Bros. (DC Pa) 18 F2d 658. Wages paid by a receiver to laborers hired by him pursuant to an order of court. Anno: 27 ALR2d 709.

administration minori aetate (mi-nō'rī ē-tā'te). The administration of a decedent's estate by an administrator appointed by the court because of the minority of the executor appointed by the will.

administration of estate. The management by a fiduciary, such as an executor, administrator, receiver, trustee, guardian, etc. of the estate which comes into his custody and possession by virtue of his office, including, as the fiduciary may be authorized by law, the collection of assets, the conservation and sale of property, instituting and defending actions on behalf of the estate, distribution of assets, and reporting to the court.
See **ancillary administration; assets; auxiliary administration; cost of administration; final distribution; foreign administration; letters of administration; not administered; plene administravit; special administration; special letters of administration**.

administration pendente absentia. See **administration durante absentia**.

administration pendente lite (pen-den'te li'te). The administration of a decedent's estate during the contest of the decedent's will.

administration pendente minoritate executoris. See **administrator pendente minoritate executoris.**

administration pro tem. See **administrator pro tem.**

administration suit. In English practice, an action by a creditor to subject a decedent's estate to the payment of his claim.

administration without probate. See **executor de son tort; independent executor.**

administrative act. A ministerial act. In another sense of the term, an act in the routine rather than one performed by one empowered to determine a course of action, for example, the act of a physician employed by a hospital, which is nonmedical and for which the hospital may be held liable in damages if it results in injury to a patient. Anno: 72 ALR2d 424.

administrative agency. A functionary concerned with administrative law. 1 Am J2d, Adm L § 49. A single officer, board, commission, office, or department exercising administrative authority. 1 Am J2d Adm L § 8.

administrative appeal. An appeal from the decision or determination of an administrative board to a higher officer or authority in the administrative system, 2 Am J2d Adm L § 539; an appeal from the decision or determination of an administrative agency to a court. 2 Am J2d Adm L § 553.

administrative assistants. Personnel of National Guard units. Anno: 57 ALR2d 1455.

administrative board. See **administrative agency.**

administrative capacity. See **administrative act; administrative discretion; administrative employee.**

administrative commission. See **administrative agency.**

administrative discretion. The power to choose between courses of conduct in the administration of an office or a duty pertaining thereto.

From their nature, the functions, powers, and duties of administrative agencies are classified as ministerial or discretionary, that is, according to the degree of subjective choice involved in their exercise, as discretionary, judgment-passing, fact-finding, or ministerial, the four classes representing degrees of progression from a theoretically absolute subjective choice in a matter of discretion to a theoretical absence of choice in a ministerial matter. 1 Am J2d Adm L § 83.

administrative employee. An employee who performs a variety of important functions of the business but has no managerial authority. Anno: 40 ALR2d 340.

As to who is employed in "administrative capacity" within exemptions from minimum wage and maximum hours provisions of Fair Labor Standards Act, see Anno: 40 ALR2d 332.

administrative law. The law that controls, or is intended to control, the administrative operations of government. 1 Am J2d Adm L § 1.

administrative officer. An officer of the executive department of government as distinguished from a judicial officer or a member of a legislative body. See **administrative agency.**

administrative offices of court. See **court administrative offices.**

administrative order. An order rendered by an administrative agency after a hearing and decision. 2 Am J2d Adm L §§ 434 et seq.

administrative ordinance. See **executive ordinance.**

administrative police. Officers of the police department whose function it is to maintain public order constantly in every part of their jurisdiction. State ex rel. Walsh v Hine, 59 Conn 50, 21 A 1024.

administrative power. The power of carrying laws into effect, giving them practical application to current affairs by way of management, oversight, investigation, regulation, and control, in accordance with and in execution of the principles prescribed by the lawmaker. 1 Am J2d Adm L § 81.

administrative practice. The practice prescribed by statute, which, in the case of a federal agency, is the Federal Administrative Procedure Act, for the presentation, hearing, and determination of issues by an administrative board or agency. 2 Am J2d Adm L §§ 340 et seq.

Administrative Procedure Act. A federal statute enacted in 1946 which provides a basic and comprehensive regulation of procedures in federal agencies. 2 Am J2d Adm L § 201. One of the uniform statutes.

administrative proceeding. A proceeding in or before an administrative body, as distinguished from a proceeding in a court. 1 Am J2d Adm L § 158. Any proceeding before an administrative agency which is not of such specific nature as to give it a more particular designation. 2 Am J2d Adm L § 317.

administrative remedy. A remedy which an administrative agency is empowered by statutory authority to grant. A remedy granted by a court upon review of an order rendered by an administrative agency, where the court is empowered by statute to substitute such order for the one under review as in its opinion the administrative agency should have rendered. 2 Am J2d Adm L 606.

administrative reports. Published opinions or orders in the adjudication of cases before administrative agencies. 2 Am J2d Adm L § 518.

administrative review. A review of the decision or determination of an administrative agency by a higher officer or authority in the administrative system. 2 Am J2d Adm L § 539. A judicial review of the decision or determination of an administrative agency. 2 Am J2d Adm L § 553.

administrative system. A plan adopted by statute as a broad general policy or objective to be attained by an administrative agency in the exercise of its power to make binding rules and regulations. 1 Am J2d Adm L § 16.

administrative tribunal. An administrative agency having an adjudicative function. 1 Am J2d Adm L § 49.

administrator. Broadly, one who administers. In the most common usage, the personal representative of a decedent's estate. Sometimes meaning an administrative agency. 1 Am J2d Adm L § 49.

See **administrator of decedent's estate.**

administrator ad colligendum (ad-min-is-trā'tor ad kol-li-jen'dum). One appointed by the court to act in an **administration ad colligendum.**

administrator ad litem (ad-min-is-trā'tor ad li'tem). An administrator appointed for the particular proceeding, under statutory authority, by the court of probate or the court of chancery, when an estate of a deceased person must be represented, and there is no executor or administrator of such estate, or the executor or administrator is adversely interested. Clark v Knox, 70 Ala 607.

administrator C. T. A. An abbreviation of **administrator cum testamento annexo.**

administrator cum testamento annexo (ad-min-is-trā'tor kum tes-ta-men'tō an-ne'xō). An administrator with the will annexed, that is, the administrator of a decedent whose will named no executor, or named an executor who cannot or will not act. Fidelity & Casualty Co. v Freeman (CA6 Tenn) 109 F 847.

administrator d. b. n. See **administrator de bonis non.**

administrator de bonis non (ad-min-is-trā'tor dē bō'nis non). An administrator appointed by the court upon the refusal of the executor to act, or upon the occurrence for any other reason, of a vacancy in the office of an executor or administrator. 31 Am J2d Ex & Ad § 603.

administrator de bonis non cum testamento annexo (ad-min-is-trā'tor dē bō'nis non kum tes-ta-men'tō an-nex'ō). An administrator who succeeds an executor. 31 Am. J2d Ex & Ad § 603.

administrator durante animi vitio. (ad-min-is-trā'tor du-ran'te a'ni-mī vi'she-ō). An administrator of a decedent's estate, appointed for the use and benefit of the next of kin who is of unsound mind but otherwise entitled to the appointment.

administrator durante minoritate administratoris. An administrator upon the estate of a decedent during the minority of the executor or the person entitled to general letters of administration. 31 Am J2d Ex & Ad § 649.

administrator of absentee. The administrator of the estate of a person who is presumed to be dead by reason of his absence for the statutory period. Estate of Kite, 194 Iowa 129, 187 NW 585, 24 ALR 850, 851.

See **administration durante absentia.**

administrator of decedent's estate. A person appointed by the probate court, in accordance with the governing statutes, to administer and settle intestate estates and such testate estates as have no competent executor designated by the testator. 31 Am J2d Ex & Ad § 1.

Although the position which he holds is frequently referred to as an office, he is not a public officer within the commonly accepted meaning of that term. It has been better said that the position of an administrator merely resembles an office, and that more strictly speaking it is a trust. 31 Am J2d Ex & Ad § 2.

See **ancillary administrator; coadministrator; domiciliary administrator; foreign administration; general administrator; letters of administration; plene administravit; public administrator; revocation of letters testamentary; special administrator; special letters of administration; temporary administrator.**

administrator pendente absentia. See **administration durante absentia.**

administrator pendente lite. See **special administrator.**

administrator pendente minoritate executoris (ad-min-is-trā'tor pen-den'te mi-nō''ri-ta'te ex-e-kū-tō'ris). An administrator to whom letters were formerly granted when the executor was under seventeen years.

It is now the prevailing practice in the United States to pass over a minor and grant general letters of administration to a competent person who has the best right, or as good a right as anyone else, to be appointed.

administrator's right of retainer. See **retainer.**

administrator with the will annexed. See **administrator cum testamento annexo.**

administratress. Same as **administratrix.**

administratrix (ad-min-is-trā'triks). A woman appointed by the court to administer the estate of a deceased person.

admiral (ad'mi-ral). An officer of the Navy of the highest rank, the typical command being the entire Navy or a fleet.

See **rear admiral; vice admiral.**

admiralty (ad'mi-ral-ti). The law of the sea and the practice pertaining thereto. Courts with jurisdiction in admiralty cases.

See **bottomry bond; court of admiralty; droits of admiralty; general average; high court of admiralty; high seas; libel; lord high admiral; maritime law; navigable, et seq.; prize court; proceeding in admiralty; proctor; respondentia bond; salvage; sea laws; towage; vice-admiralty courts.**

admiralty court. A court having admiralty jurisdiction.

admiralty jurisdiction. A special jurisdiction of maritime cases vested exclusively in the federal courts.

The limits of admiralty jurisdiction are not prescribed by the Constitution or statute; they have been prescribed as the occasion arose by judicial interpretation. 2 Am J2d Adm §§ 1-8.

admiralty law. Comprehended in term **admiralty.**

admiralty lien. A lien on a vessel enforceable by a suit in rem in admiralty for repairs, supplies, towage, use of dry dock or marine railway, or other necessaries furnished to the vessel. 2 Am J2d Adm § 124.

admissible evidence. Evidence which a court or other tribunal exercising judicial functions may properly receive and consider in a cause or matter which has been submitted to it.

admission. A statement of a party to an action inconsistent with his claim or position in the action and amounting therefore to proof against him. 29 Am J2d Ev § 597. Also, a statement in a pleading which admits an allegation in the pleading of his adversary, either expressly or impliedly by failure to deny the allegation. 41 Am J1st Pl § 197.

A denial coupled with a general exception of doubtful import, or a refusal to admit without specific denial or detailed reasons why an admission or denial cannot truthfully be made, constitutes an admission. Southern R. Co. v Crosby (CA4 SC) 201 F2d 878, 36 ALR2d 1186.

admission by demurrer. An admission for the purposes of the demurrer only.

A demurrer admits the facts well pleaded in the pleading attacked, and inferences of fact arising from the facts pleaded, for the purpose of testing the legal sufficiency of the pleading, not for the purpose of evidence in the case; once the demurrer is overruled, the admission by demurrer has served its purpose and is not to be considered evidence in the case. 41 Am J1st Pl §§ 238, 239.

admission of alien. A privilege granted to an alien upon terms prescribed by federal statute, the most important of which is the requirement of a visa. 3 Am J2d Aliens §§ 54, 55.

admission of new state into Union. The reception into the United States, under authority of an act of Congress for that purpose enacted, of a new state clothed with all the powers of sovereignty and jurisdiction which pertained to the original states and upon an equal footing with them. 49 Am J1st States § 9.

admissions tax. An excise tax upon the sale of a ticket or other means of admission to a theater or other place of entertainment.

admission ticket. See **theater ticket.**

admission to bail. The requiring of security by bond or deposit, known as bail, under which one charged with the commission of an offense or held to require the satisfaction of an indebtedness is released under the conditions of the bond or other security for his future attendance in court and his remaining within the jurisdiction of the court. 8 Am J2d Bail § 1.

admission to membership. The reception of a member by a club or society upon application made therefor and pursuant to the bylaws, rules, and regulations of the body and the conditions imposed thereby.
The granting of membership is a matter within the control of the body and the courts are without power to compel an admission to membership. 6 Am J2d Asso & C §§ 18-18.

admission to probate. A judicial determination in the form of a judgment of the court or a formal order declaring that an instrument propounded for probate is the will of the decedent who executed it.
Such determination is official evidence of the validity of the instrument until the judgment or order is reversed on appeal or revoked or set aside in a direct attack thereon. 57 Am J1st Wills § 934.

admission to the bar. The conferring of the privilege, license, or franchise to practice law within the jurisdiction by order or judgment of the court which declares the existence in the applicant of the requisite qualifications of residence, citizenship, education, and moral character. 7 Am J2d Attys § 8.

admittance (ad-mit'ans). The last stage, or perfection, of copyhold assurances. And this is of three sorts: first, an admittance upon a voluntary grant from the lord; secondly, an admittance upon surrender by the former tenant; and, thirdly, an admittance upon a descent from the ancestor. See 2 Bl Comm 370.
See **admission.**

admitted assets. A technical term of the insurance business, meaning assets of an insurance company so approved by state regulatory agencies as to permit their being taken into account in setting forth the financial condition of the company.

admitted set-off. A setoff admitted by the plaintiff is his summons or complaint.

admittendo clerico (ad-mi-ten'do kler'i-kō). A writ to enforce a judgment determining the king's right of making a presentation to a benefice.

admittendo in socium (ad-mi-ten'dō in sō'-shi-um). A writ associating certain persons to justices of assize.

admittere (ad-mit'te-re). To admit; to accept; to allow; to receive; to commit.

See **admission.**

admixture (ad-miks'tūr). A mingling. A substance formed by mixing two or more substances.

ad modum (ad mō'dum). In such a way or manner; after the manner.

admonitio trina (ad-mo-ni'she-ō trī'na). A warning which was given to a prisoner standing mute.

ad mordendum (mor-den'dum). To bite; a necessary averment in a civil law action for injury by a dog.

ad mordendum assuetus (ad mor-den'dum as-su-ē'tus). Accustomed to bite.

admortization. See mortmain; mortmain statutes.

admr. An abbreviation of **administrator.**

admx. An abbreviation of **administratrix.**

ad nauseam (ad nâ'sē-am). To a disgusting extent.

adnepos (ad'ne-pŏs). The son of a great-great-grandson.

adneptis (ad-nep'tis). The daughter of a great-great-granddaughter.

adnichelled (äd-nik'ell-ed). Avoided; made null.

ad nigrum. See **a rubro ad nigrum.**

adnihilare (ad-ni-hi-lā're). To annul.

ad nocumentum (ad no-ku-men'tum). To the damage or nuisance of.

ad nocumentum liberi tenementi ipsorum (ad no-ku-men'tum li'be-rī te-ne-men'tī ip-sō'rum). To the nuisance of their own freehold.

ad nocumentum liberi tenementi sui (ad-no-kū-men'-tum li'be-rī te-ne-men'tī su'ī). To the nuisance of his freehold tenement. Formal words used in an assize of nuisance. See 3 Bl Comm 221.

adnotare (ad-no-tā're). To sign.

adnotatio (ad-no-tā'she-ō). (Civil law.) One's subscription of his name.

adnullare. Same as **adnihilare.**

ad nullius sectam (ad nul-lī'us sek'tam). At the suit of no one.

adolescence (ad-ō-les'ens). The age between the beginning of the age of puberty and the beginning of lawful age.

adolescentia (ad-o-le-sen'she-a). Same as **adolescence.**

adopt. To approve, as to adopt a regulation. To take as one's own that which was not so before. Dallas v Beeman, 18 Tex Civ App 335, 339, 45 SW 626.

adopted child. One having by virtue of an adoption proceeding in conformity with the statutes the legal incidents of the natural relation of parent and child. 2 Am J2d Adopt § 88. Sometimes, but not always, considered a lawful heir or legal heir. 2 Am J2d Adopt § 99. Sometimes, but not always considered lawful issue of the adoptive parent. 2 Am J2d Adopt § 98.
Whether or not an adopted child is within the meaning of the word "heirs" as it appears in a deed, a trust indenture, a will or other instrument depends upon many diverse factors, especially the content and phraseology of the particular instrument involved. The express term of the statute under which the adoption took place or which fixes rights of adopted children in the distribution of intestate property or the construction placed upon the statute, may be a factor, although generally

such statutes are not determinative of the right of adopted children to take under an instrument which does not expressly include adopted children as grantees or beneficiaries, but are considered merely as aids in construction. Variations in interpretation may turn upon whether the grantor or testator was, himself, the adopting parent or whether the issue involved adopted children of persons other than the testator or grantor. Fiduciary Trust Co. v Brown, 152 Me 360, 131 A2d 191.

An adopted child is not considered to be an "heir of the body" in reference to the adopting parent, within the meaning of such term in a will, deed, or indenture of trust, unless the context of the instrument considered in its entirety demands such construction. 2 Am J2d Adopt § 92.

Adopted children, for whom adoption statutes create the same rights of heirship as children of the body, come within the meaning of the term "lineal descendants," as used in a statute providing for the non-lapse of a devise where the devisee predeceases the testator but leaves lineal descendants. Hoellinger v Molzohn, 77 ND 108, 41 NW2d 217, 19 ALR2d 1147.

adoptio (ad-op'she-ō). Same as **adoption**.

adoption. Approval, as the adoption of a statute Anno: 132 ALR 1061. Selecting and taking as one's own that which was not so before.

adoption arrogatio (ar-ro-gā'she-o'). An adoption in which the person adopted submits in his own right.

adoption by acknowledgment. A term used in some statutes which provide for legitimation by the acknowledgment by the father of his child born out of wedlock. There is, of course, a distinction between adoption and legitimation. 10 Am J2d Bast § 51.

adoption by deed or agreement. A statutory method whereby a child may be adopted by deed or contract duly executed, or duly executed and recorded. 2 Am J2d Adopt § 8.

adoption of child. The means by which the legal relationship of parent and child between persons who are not so related by nature is established or created; the taking into one's family of the child of another as son or daughter and heir, and conferring upon it a title to the rights and privileges of such. 2 Am J2d Adopt § 1.

Adoption signifies the means by which one may become the child and heir of another. Re Holibaugh's Will, 18 NJ 229, 113 A2d 654, 52 ALR2d 1222.

Compliance with the statutes is essential. As the term is used in inheritance tax statutes imposing a higher rate of taxation as to bequests to strangers of the blood than as to bequests to adopted children, an executory contract of adoption does not constitute the child a "child adopted as such in conformity with law," within the meaning of the statutes. Re Clark, 105 Mont 401, 74 P2d 401, 114 ALR 496.

See **foreign adoption.**

adoption of foreign corporation. The domestication of a foreign corporation by granting it a charter. 36 Am J2d For Corp § 382.

adoption of judgment. The waiver of the right to appeal from a judgment by some act on the part of the party who would so appeal amounting to a ratification of the judgment.

In order to effect such a waiver, there must be some intent to enjoy a benefit from, or base some interest on, the judgment. See Oatman v Hampton, 43 Idaho 675, 256 P 529. See also 5 Am J2d A & E § 709.

adoption of statute. The participation of the legislature in the making of the law, so that the law is "adopted" when it receives the approval of both branches of the legislature. Anno: 132 ALR 1061.

In other cases, the term has been construed to mean the date when the act takes effect. 50 Am J1st Stat § 503.

adoptive parent (a-dop'tiv). One who adopts a child under adoption proceedings.

adoptivus (ad-op-tī'vus). Adoptive, whether parent or child.

ad opus (ad ō'pus). For the work; for the benefit or use.

ad ordinationem litis (ad or-di-nā-she-ō'nem lī'tis). For the regulation of the action.

ad ostendendum (ad os-ten-den'dum). To show.

ad ostium ecclesiae (ad ōs'ti-um e-klē'si-ē). At the door of the church. That is, at one's marriage. At one time in England all marriages were solemnized at the church door. See 2 Bl Comm 132.

See **dower ad ostium ecclesiae.**

ad patria (ad pa'tri-a). To the country; to the jury.

ad perpetuam (ad per-pe'tu-am). In perpetuity; permanently.

ad perpetuam rei memoriam (ad per-pe'tu-am re'ī me-mō'ri-am). In perpetual memory of the matter.

ad perpetuam remanentiam (ad per-pe'tu-am rē-ma-nen'she-am). To remain perpetually.

ad primam diem litigii (ad prī'mam dī'em lī-ti'ji-ī). At the first day of the litigation.

ad probandum aliquid per credentiam duodecim hominum vicinorum (ad prō-ban'dum a'li-quid per krē-den'she-am du-ō'de-sim ho'mi-num vī-si-nō'rum). To prove a thing by the testimony of twelve men of the neighborhood.

adpromissor (ad-prō'mi-sor). A surety; one who binds himself to perform the same act as another.

ad propinquiorem consanguineum (ad prō-pin-qui-ō'rem kon-san-gwi'ne-um). To the nearest in blood relationship.

ad prosequendum (ad prō-se-quen'dum). To prosecute; for prosecuting.

See **habeas corpus ad prosequendum.**

Ad proximum antecedens fiat relatio, nisi impediatur sententia (ad prox'i-mum an-te-sē'denz fī'at re-lā'-she-ō, nī'sī im-pe-di-ā'ter sen-ten'she-a). Reference should be made to the matter next preceding, unless the meaning is thereby destroyed.

ad publicam vindicatam (ad pub'li-kam vin-di-kā'tam). For the vindication of the public.

ad punctum temporis (ad punk'tum tem'po-ris). At the point of time.

Ad quaestionem facti non respondent judices (ad quēst-she-ō'nem fak'tī non rē-spon'dent jū'di-cēz). Judges do not pass upon questions of fact. First Nat. Bank v Northwestern Nat. Bank, 152 Ill 296, 38 NE 739.

ad quaestionem juris non respondent juratores (ad quēst-she-ō'nem jū'ris non rē-spon'dent jū-rā-tō'rēz). Jurors do not pass upon questions of law. State v Burbee, 65 Vt 1, 25 A 964.

ad quaestionem legis respondent judices (ad quĕst-she-ō′nem lē′jis rē-spon′dent jū′-di-sēz). The judges answer a question of law.

ad quaestiones facti non respondent judices; ad quaestiones legis non respondent juratores (ad quĕst-she-ō′nez fak′tī non rē-spon′dent jū′di-sēz; ad quĕst-she-ō′nēz lē′jis non rē-spon′dent jū-rā-tō′rēz). Judges do not answer questions of fact; jurors do not answer questions of law.

ad quaestiones juris respondent judices; ad quaestiones facti respondent juratores (ad quĕst-she-ō′nēz jū′ris rē-spon′dent jū′di-sēz; ad quĕst-she-ō′nēz fak′tī rē-spon′dent jū-rā-tō′rez). Judges answer questions of law; jurors answer questions of fact.

ad quem (ad quem). To which.
See **a quo**.

ad querimoniam (ad kwe-ri-mō′ni-am). At the complaint.

adquieto (ad-qui-ē′to). To put to rest; to satisfy by payment.

adquirere (ad-qui′re-re). To acquire; to gain.

adquiritur possessio (ad-qui′ri-ter po-ze′she-ō). Possession is acquired.

ad quod curia concordavit (ad quod kū′ri-a kon-kor-dā′vit). To which the court agreed.

ad quod damnum (ad kwod dam′num). At what loss.

ad quod non fuit responsum (ad quod non fu′it re-spon′sum). To which there was no answer.

ad rationem ponere (ad ra-she-ō′nem po′ne-re). To cite to appear.

ad recipiendum (ad re-si-pi-en′dum). See **habeas corpus ad deliberandum et recipiendum; habeas corpus ad faciendum et recipiendum**.

ad recognoscendum (ad re-kog-no-sen′dum). To recognize.

adrectare (ad-rek-tā′re). To correct; to make amends.

ad referendum (ad ref-e-ren′dum). To be referred; to be deferred for subsequent attention.

ad rem (ad rem). To the thing; to the point.
See **right ad rem**.

ad remanentiam (ad rē-ma-nen′she-am). In fee.

ad reparationem et sustentationem (ad re-pa-rā-she-ō′nem et sus-ten-tā′she-ō-nem). For repair and keeping in order.

ad respondendum (ad re-spon-den′dum). To answer.
See **capias ad respondendum; habeas corpus ad respondendum**.

adrift. Floating without power and not anchored.
See **flotsam**.

adrogation (ad-rō-gā′shon). A civil law adoption of a child who has not reached the age of puberty.

ads. An abbreviation of **ad sectam**.

ad satisfaciendum (ad sa-tis-fa-she-en′-dum). In discharge or satisfaction.
See **capias ad faciendum; habeas corpus ad satisfaciendum**.

adscendentes (ad-sen-den′tēz). Ascendants; ancestors.

adscribere (ad-skrī′be-re). Same as **adnotare**.

adscripticius (ad-skrip-ti′she-us). Same as **adscriptus**.

adscripti glebae (ad-skrip′tī glē′bē). Plural of **adscriptus glebae**.

adscriptitii (ad-skrip-ti′she-ī). (Civil law.) Serfs.

adscriptus (ad-skrip′tus). Added or annexed by writing; bound to.

adscriptus glebae (ad-skrip′tus glē′bē). A term applied in the Roman law to laborer slaves who were permanently annexed to the land and went with a transfer of it.

ad sectam (ad sek′tam). At the suit of. Abbreviated, "ads."

adsecurare (ad-sē-kū-rā′re). To assure; to insure.

adsecuratio (ad-sē-kū-rā′she-ō). Assurance; insurance.

adsessores (ad-ses-sō′rēz). Special judges appointed to sit with or for the regular judges.

adsignare (ad-sig-nā′re). To assign; to allot.

adsm. An abbreviation of **ad sectam**.

ad standum rectum (ad stan′dum rek′tum). To stand for the right.

adstipulator (ad-stip′ū-lā-tor). A co-promisee having the same right as his associate to demand performance.

ad studendum et orandum (ad stu-den′dum et ō-ran′-dum). For study and prayer.

ad subeundum legem (ad sub-e-un′dum lē′jem). To submit to the law.

ad subjiciendum. See **habeas corpus ad subjiciendum**.

ad terminum annorum (ad ter′mi-num an-nō′rum). For a term of years.

ad terminum ponere (ad ter′mi-num pō′-ne-re). To postpone to another term.

ad terminum qui praeteriit (ad ter′mi-num quī prē-te′ri-it). For the term which has passed.
See entry **ad terminum qui praeteriit**.

ad terminum vel ad firmam (ad ter′mi-num vel ad fir′mam). For a term or to farm.

ad terminum vel ad tempus (ad ter′mi-num vel ad tem′pus). For a term or for a time.

ad terminum vitae vel annorum (ad ter′mi-num vi′tē vel an-nō′rum). For a term, for life, or for years.

ad testari (ad tes-ta′rī). To attest; to witness.

ad testificandum (ad tes-ti-fi-kan′dum). For giving testimony.
See **habeas corpus ad testificandum**.

ad tractandum et consilium impendendum (ad trak-tan′dum et kon-si′li-um im-pen-den′dum). For attending and valuable advice. Writs of summons ad tractandum et consilium impendendum were issued at the beginning of every parliament to require the judges and other high officials to attend the house of lords. See 1 Bl Comm 168.

ad tunc (ad′tunk). Then.

ad tunc et ibidem (ad′tunk et i-bī′dem). Then and there.

ad tunc existens (ad′tunk eg-zis′tenz). Then existing or being.

adult. A grown person. One no longer a child.
See **age of majority**.

adult children. Sons or daughters who have reached the age of majority.

adulter (a-dul′tėr). An adulterer; one who has carnal intercourse with the wife of another.

adultera (ad-ul'te-ra). An adulteress; one who has carnal intercourse with the husband of another.

adulterant (a-dul'ter-ant). An impure, debased, or cheaper substance put into or mixed with another substance.
    A substance used as a preservative may be an adulterant within the prohibition of a statute or ordinance in relation to pure food. Anno: 50 ALR 76.

adulterare (ad-ul"te-ra're). To commit adultery; to adulterate; to forge; to falsify.

adulterare rationes (ad-ul-te-ra're ra-she-o'nez). To falsify accounts.

adulterated. Impure; mingled with or deteriorated by a foreign substance in imitation of the genuine article.

adulterated butter. Butter with which there is mixed any substance foreign to butter with the effect of cheapening the product in cost, and any butter in the manufacture or manipulation of which any process or material is used with the intent or effect of causing the absorption of abnormal quantities of water. Schick v United States, 195 US 65, 49 L Ed 99, 24 S Ct 826.

adulterated coin. Coin made of gold or silver intermixed or "adulterated," with base metal. The term is sometimes erroneously used for "base coin." Gabe v State, 6 Ark 540, 542.
    See **base coin.**

adulterated drug. Within the meaning of the Federal Food, Drug, and Cosmetic Act, a drug which consists in whole or in part of any filthy, putrid, or decomposed substance; or which has been prepared, packed, or held under unsanitary conditions whereby it may have been contaminated or rendered injurious to health; or which is in a container of a poisonous substance which renders it injurious to health; or which is colored by a coal-tar preparation that has not been certified in accordance with the statute; or is represented to be a drug recognized in an official compendium and it falls below the standard of purity or quality set by the compendium; or if it is not of the quality and purity represented; or if any substance has been mixed therewith so as to reduce its quality and strength. 21 USC § 351.

adulterated food. Food that is diluted or depreciated in quality, which fails to come to the standards set by law as to ingredients, or to which any foreign substance, wholesome or unwholesome, is added. 22 Am J2d Food § 32.

adulteration. The process of putting an impure, debased, or cheaper substance into another substance.

adulteratores monetae (ad-ul-te-ra-to'rez mo-ne'te). Plural of **adulterator monetae.**

adulterator monetae (a-dul'ter-a'tor). A counterfeiter; a forger.

adulterer (a-dul'ter-er). A man who commits adultery.

adulteress (a-dul'ter-es). A woman who commits adultery.

adulterina moneta (ad-ul-te-ri'na mo-ne'ta). Counterfeit money.

adulterine (a-dul'ter-in). (Civil law.) A child born of adulterous intercourse.

adulterine bastard. The child of a married woman by a man not her husband. 10 Am J2d Bast § 1.

adulterinum signum (ad-ul-te-ri'num sig'num). A forged seal.

adulterinum testamentum (ad-ul-te-ri'num tes-ta-men'tum). A forged will.

adulterinus (ad-ul-te-ri'nus). Forged; counterfeit.

adulterium (ad-ul-te'ri-um). A fine imposed for adultery.

adulterous bastard. The child of a married woman by a man not her husband. 10 Am J2d Bast § 1.

adultery (a-dul'ter-e). At common law, sexual intercourse by a man, married or single, with a married woman not his wife. By statute in most jurisdictions, sexual intercourse by a married person with some person not his or her husband or wife. 2 Am J2d Adult § 1. As ground for divorce:—sexual intercourse between a husband and a woman other than his wife or between a wife and a man other than her husband. 24 Am J2d Div & S § 24.
    See **criminal conversation; incestuous adultery; living in adultery.**
    The term "adultery" was used in ecclesiastical law to denote intrusion into a bishopric.

ad ultimam vim terminorum (ad ul'ti-mam vim ter-mi-no'rum). To the extreme limit of the terms.

adult owner. An owner not under the disability of infancy.
    A corporate owner of land is held to be within a statute permitting adult owners to petition for the organization of a drainage district. Jordan Land Co. v Freeborn, 149 Wis 159, 135 NW 751.

ad usum et commodum (ad u'sum et kom'mo-dum). For use and benefit.

ad val. Abbreviation of **ad valorem.**

ad valentiam (ad va-len'she-am). At or of the value.

ad valentiam veri valoris (ad va-len'she-am ve'ri va-lo'ris). To the true value.

ad valorem (ad va-lo'rem). According to the value.

ad valorem contractus (ad va-lo'rem kon-trak'tus). To the value of the contract.

ad valorem duty. A customs duty calculated according to value of the import. 21 Am J2d Cust D § 82.

ad valorem tax (ad val-o'rum tax). A tax of a fixed proportion of the value of the property to be charged, an appraisement being a prerequisite to the determination of the amount of the tax. 51 Am J1st Tax § 26.

advance. Noun: A payment made before it is due or by way of a loan. Something supplied as an aid in the performance of a contract or an undertaking such as the growing of crops on leased premises. 32 Am J1st L & T § 578. An approach to win favor; an overture. Verb: To move ahead. To pay before the maturity of the obligation. To make a loan. To supply with goods.
    To advance is to supply beforehand; to loan before the work is done or the goods made. Laflin & Rand Powder Co. v Burkhardt, 97 US 110, 24 L Ed 973; 17 Am J2d Contr § 281.
    As used in statutes giving a landlord a lien on crops for supplies or money advanced to his tenant to aid him in raising the crops, an advance is anything of value for use directly or indirectly in making and saving crops, supplied in good faith to the lessee by the landlord. But generally, in order that

a landlord may have a lien for supplies furnished or money advanced, under such a statute, he must furnish or advance the same himself; and if he merely becomes a surety or guarantor for money advanced or supplies furnished by a third person, he is not entitled to a lien. If, however, the supplies are furnished the tenant by a third person solely on the credit of the landlord, they are in effect furnished by the landlord and he may claim a lien therefor. To fall within the statute the advances or supplies must be of some one or more of the articles enumerated in the statute, and for some one or more of the purposes mentioned therein. Otherwise there is no lien. 32 Am J1st L & T § 578.

advance bid. A bid made after a judicial sale at an advance of at least ten per cent over the bid received at the sale, such advance bid being made as a condition of re-opening the bidding. 30A Am J Rev ed Jud S § 106.

advance-bill. Same as **advance-note.**

advanced age. Old age.

Advanced Research Projects Agency. A research agency of the Department of Defense, headed by a Director. Am J2d Desk, Document No. 59.

advancement. A gift by a parent to a child which the parent intends to be charged against the donee's share of the parental estate if the donor should die intestate. Clement v Blythe, 220 Ark 551, 248 SW2d 883, 31 ALR2d 1033.

Basically and subject to changes made in the elements by statute, an advancement is a perfect and irrevocable gift, not required by law, made by a parent, during his lifetime, to his child, with the intention on the part of the donor that such gift shall represent a part or the whole of the donor's estate that the donee would be entitled to on the death of the donor intestate. 3 Am J2d Advancem § 1.

The doctrine of advancements applies to a testate estate only as the will so provides and then by analogy only, since strictly speaking the doctrine has application to intestate estates only. 3 Am J2d Advancem § 10.

advance-note. A shipmaster's written order on the owner given as an advance on account of wages to a sailor upon his signing the ship's articles.

advance payment. See **advance.**

advances. Forward movements. Promoting acquaintanceship with the idea of obtaining favors. Payments.
See **advance.**

advantage, concession, and discrimination. A combination of terms which bespeaks a violation of law.

These words as used in the Elkins Act of February 19, 1903 (49 USCA § 41) denouncing certain agreements between common carriers and shippers, must be construed to mean unlawful advantage, unlawful concession, unlawful discrimination. United States v P. Koenig Coal Co. 270 US 512, 70 L Ed 709, 46 S Ct 392. See also 13 Am J2d Car § 185.

advantagium (ad-van-tā'ji-um). An advantage.

advena (ad've-na). An unnaturalized alien.

advenir (äd've-ner). To come to; to happen.

advent (ad'vent). The period from the Sunday nearest November 30th until Christmas following.

adventicius (ad-ven-ti'she-us). Coming from without.

adventicius pecunia (ad-ven-ti'she-us pe-kū'ni-a). Money coming from an unusual source; not inherited or earned.

adventitius (ad-ven-ti'she-us). Adventitious.

adventitious. Accidental, not inherent; coming from an external source.

ad ventrem inspiciendum (ad ven'trem īn-spi-she-en'dum). A writ for the examination of a woman to determine whether or not she is pregnant.

adventura (ad-ven-tū'ra). Same as **adventure.**

adventurae maris (ad-ven-tū're' ma'ris). Adventures of the sea.

adventure. An undertaking with an element of risk. A shipment of goods in charge of an agent to be sold by him for the shipper at the best price obtainable.

As the word "adventure" is used in marine policies, it is everywhere employed as synonymous with "peril." The word is often used by the writers to describe the enterprise or voyage as a "marine adventure" insured against. Moores v Louisville Underwriters (CC Tenn) 14 F 226, 233.

See **gross adventure; joint adventure.**

adventurer (ad-ven'tūr-ėr). A shareowner in a mine; a mine promoter. One who takes a risk; one who casts his lot with others in an undertaking involving risk.

ad verecundiam (ad ve-re-kun'di-am). To a sense of decency. See **argumentum ad verecundiam.**

adversa fortuna (ad-ver'sa for-tū'na). Ill fortune.

adversary. The opposite party in a contest or an action.

adversary evidence (ad'ver-sạ-ri). Evidence otherwise inadmissible which one of the parties is permitted to introduce by reason of similar or related evidence which has been tendered by his opponent. 29 Am J2d Ev § 267.

adversary proceeding. A contested action or proceeding; one having parties, as distinguished from a proceeding on ex parte application.

adversary trial (ad'vėr-sā-ri). A trial in which there are adversary parties before the court, who have had full opportunity to present and establish their opposing contentions, if any they have. Bolden v Sloss-Sheffield Steel & Iron Co. 215 Ala 334, 110 So 574, 49 ALR 1206, 1214.

Adversa valetudo excusat (ad-ver'sa va-le-tū'dō ex-kū'zat). Bad health excuses, as, in a contract for personal services.

adverse (ad'vėrs). As an adjective, in legal signification the word involves the element of hostility under a claim or color of title. Eastern Oregon Land Co. v Cole (CA9 Or) 92 F 949, 952. The adjective also expresses the position of persons in litigation with conflicting interests, as **adverse parties.**

As a verb, in mining law, to file an adverse claim.

adverse claim. As respects adverse possession, a claim to possession which is hostile to the true owner. In mining law, a formal assertion of an adverse claimant made under oath and filed in the United States land office pending an application for a patent. Lightner Mining Co. v Superior Court, 14 Cal App 642, 112 P 909. A claim to property by one in possession thereof asserted against a trustee or receiver in bankruptcy. 9 Am J2d Bankr §§ 50-52.

See **adverse possession; quieting title.**

adverse enjoyment. The use of an easement under a claim of right.
See **adverse possession**.

adverse interest. An interest which displaces one's own interest in whole or in part.
As used in a statute permitting a litigant to call and cross examine any person having an adverse interest in the outcome of the litigation, the term "adverse interest" is to be construed according to its common and accepted meaning, not as synonymous with "adverse testimony." 58 Am J1st Witn § 560. Under a statute which prohibits a party from testifying where the adverse party is a guardian, trustee, executor, or administrator, it is adverse interest which disqualifies a person as a witness, not merely his nominal status as plaintiff or defendant. 58 Am J1st Witn § 285.
As used in a statute providing that accounts of executors and administrators settled in the absence of any person "adversely interested" and without notice to him may be opened upon his application, the term has been defined as meaning the situation of one who has some interest in the estate, that is, someone having such an interest as would entitle him to notice of the filing by the executor or administrator of a final report, together with a prayer for discharge. Re Holman, 216 Iowa 1186, 250 NW 498, 98 ALR 1363.

adversely interested. See **adverse interest**.

adverse parties. Persons who stand in relation to another person as being on the opposite side in an action or proceeding or whose interests are adverse to such person.
Within the meaning of the rule requiring a notice of appeal to be served upon all adverse parties, such parties include every party to the action or proceeding whose interest in the subject-matter of the appeal is adverse to, or will be affected by, the reversal or modification of the judgment, decree, or order from which the appeal is taken. Co-parties to an action who do not join in the appeal should, as a general rule, be served with notice of appeal where their interests are adverse to that of the appellant. 4 Am J2d A & E § 318.

adverse possession. An actual and visible appropriation of property commenced and continued under a claim of right inconsistent with and hostile to the claim of another. An open and notorious possession and occupation of real property under an evident claim or color of right; a possession in opposition to the true title and real owner—a possession which is commenced in wrong and maintained in right. 3 Am J2d Adv P § 1.
The term applied in matters concerning title to lands as distinguished from incorporeal hereditaments. Anno: 27 ALR2d 325.
A title acquired by adverse possession is a title in fee simple, and is as perfect a title as one by deed from the original owner or by patent or grant from the government. Thornely v Andrews, 40 Wash 580, 82 P 899.
See **constructive possession**.

adverse use. See **adverse user**.

adverse user. A continuous and exclusive user as of right for as long as the prescriptive period. 25 Am J1st High § 12. A use against the owner of the servient tenement as distinguished from a use under such owner. Zollinger v Frank, 110 Utah 514, 175 P2d 714, 170 ALR 770. One who uses property as his own under a claim of dominion or right existing in himself to the exclusion of all other claimants.

Use may be open and notorious and still not be adverse. Northern Pacific Ry. Co. v Cash, 67 Mont 585, 216 P 782. An adverse user which will ripen into an easement by prescription is an exclusive, open, visible, or notorious use without license or permission of the true owner of the premises, but with his knowledge and hostile to him, under a claim to a definite right which can be the subject of a grant, that continues without interruption for the length of the prescriptive period. 17A Am J Rev ed Ease §§ 74 et seq.

adverse witness. A witness who, in the opinion of the presiding judge, is hostile.

adverso. See **adversus**.

adversus. Opposed to; aligned against.

adversus bonos mores (ad-ver'sus bō'nos mō'rēz). Contrary to good morals.

advertise (ad'vėr-tīz or ad-vėr-tīz'). To give public notice of; to announce publicly; especially by a printed notice. Montford v Allen, 111 Ga 18, 19. To make known to the public through a medium of publicity that one's goods or services are available for sale or engagement.

advertisement (ad-vėr'tiz-ment or ad-vėr-tīz'ment). A notice published in handbills or a newspaper.
The word also includes notice by posting or display on signboards. The idea underlying the word has reference not so much to the vehicle or instrumentality used for getting the notice before the public, as to the diffusion, or bringing home to the public, of the information or matter contained in the notice. People v McKean, 76 Cal App 114, 243 P 898.

advertising lottery (ad'vėr-tī-zing or ad-vėr-tī'zing). The statutory offense provided for in nearly all jurisdictions of advertising in any manner whatsoever, either directly or indirectly, any lottery or the place or manner of conducting the same, or any offer or proposition to insure those participating therein from loss. In many instances the statutes are applicable to all forms of advertising, whether the lottery is to be drawn or conducted within the state or not. 34 Am J1st Lot § 27.

advice. View or opinion communicated to another, for example, a lawyer's advice to his client. In commercial law, information given as to shipments of goods, delays, the drawing of paper for acceptance, etc.

advisamento consilii nostri. See **de advisamento consilii nostri**.

advisamentum (ad-vi-sā-men'tum). Advisement.

advisare (ad-vi-sā're). To advise; to take under advisement; to consider; to be advised.

advisare vult. See **curia advisare vult**.

advisari (ad-vi-sā'rī). Same as **advisare**.

advise (ad-vīz'). To give advice; to offer an opinion as worthy or expedient to be followed; to counsel. Long v State, 23 Neb 33, 45, 36 NW 310.

advised. Armed with the facts or knowledge.

advisedly. Acting with a prepared mind, not on the spur of the moment.

advisement (ad-vīz'ment). Consideration. A court takes a case under "advisement" when, following a trial or argument on a motion, it delays rendering judgment or decision until it has examined and considered the questions involved. See Clark v Read, 5 NJL 571, 573.

adviser. One who gives advice, particularly one who advises in a consultation, such as a lawyer, an investment counselor, a physician, or a marriage counselor.

advisory (ad-vī'zō-ri). Informative; by way of suggestion; not conclusive. Watt v Starke, 101 US 247, 25 L Ed 826.
See **advisory instruction.**

Advisory Council. A federal agency composed of one delegate from each federal reserve bank, authorized to confer with the Federal Reserve Board on general business conditions, to make oral or written representations concerning matters within the jurisdiction of the board, and to call for information and to make recommendations with regard to discount rates, rediscount business, note issues, reserve conditions in the various districts, the purchase and sale of gold and securities by reserve banks, open market operations by those banks, and the general affairs of the reserve banking system. 10 Am J2d Banks § 5.

advisory instruction. An instruction given by the court as to the law applicable in a criminal case in a jurisdiction where by constitution or statute the jury are the judges of the law as well as the facts. 53 Am J1st Trial § 847.

advisory judgment. One which decides a mere difference of opinions, settling no actual controversy. 22 Am J2d Dec J § 10.

advisory opinion. The opinion of a higher court upon a point before a lower one; an opinion rendered by a court, in some jurisdictions, at the request of the legislature.

advisory verdict. A verdict of a jury which the court may or may not regard, as a jury's verdict in certain admiralty cases. 2 Am J2d Adm § 141. Also, the verdict in an equity case upon an issue submitted to a jury. 27 Am J2d Equity 241.

ad vitam (ad vī'tam). For life.

ad vitam aut culpam (ad vī'tam ât kul'pam). For life or until guilty of misbehavior, that is, during good behavior.

advocacy (ad'vō-kạ-si). The act of pleading for, supporting, or recommending; active espousal; advising or teaching: as, the advocacy of the doctrine of anarchy. Gitlow v People of New York, 268 US 652, 69 L Ed 1138, 45 S Ct 625. Involving active conduct, something more than adherence to an abstract doctrine. Yates v United States, 354 US 298, 1 L Ed 2d 1356, 77 S Ct 1064.

advocare (ad-vo-kā're). To call to; to summon counsel; to consult for legal advice. (Eccles.) To avow; to admit a clerk to a benefice.

advocassie (äd'vō-käs-sē). Advocacy; the functions of an advocate.

advocata (ad-vō-kā'ta). (Eccles.) A female patron having the right of presentation to a benefice; a patroness.

advocate (ad'vō-kāt). A barrister; one who may plead causes in court for another.
See **judge advocate; king's advocate.**

advocati (ad-vō-kā'tī). Advocates, persons who speak in behalf of a cause or a person; (Eccles.) Patrons; persons having the right of the presentation of a clerk or parson to a benefice.

advocatia (ad-vō-kā'she-a). Patrons; protectors; privilege of advocacy.

See **advowson.**

advocati fisci (ad-vō-kā'tī fi'sī). Fiscal advocates under the civil law. These advocates of the revenue somewhat resembled the king's counsel in England and could not be employed in any cause against the sovereign without special license, nor could they be employed or concerned in any private suits between subject and subject. See 3 Bl Comm 27.

advocatio (ad-vō-kā'she-ō). Legal advice or assistance.

advocation (ad-vō-kā'shon). A Scotch method of appeal.
See **bill of advocation.**

advocatione decimarum (ad-vō-kā-she-ō'ne de-si-mā'rum). An ecclesiastical writ for the recovery of tithes.

advocator (ad'vō-kā-tor). The warrantor of a title. In old Scotch law, an appellant.

advocatus (ad-vō-kā'tus). One who is called upon to assist in litigation either as an advocate or a witness; an advocate; a pleader; a patron.

advocatus fisci (ad-vō-kā'tus fi'sī). Singular of **advocati fisci.**

advocatus of the church. A term applied to a king or great nobleman when land is "loaned" to him in consideration of his patronage and protection.

ad voluntatem (ad vo-lun-tā'tem). At will.

ad voluntatem domini (ad vo-lun-tā'tem do'mi-nī). At the will of the master.

advouter (ad-vou'tėr). Same as **adulterer.**

advoutrer (ad-vou'trėr). Same as **adulterer.**

advoutress (ad-vou'tres). Same as **adulteress.**

advoutry (ad-vou'tri). Same as **adultery.**

advove (ad-vow'ē—English) (äd'voo-ā—French). An advocate.

advover (ad'voo-ā). Same as **avow.**

advow. Same as **avow.**

advowee (ad-vou-ē'). The holder of an advowson; a patron.

advowee paramount (ad-vow-ē' par'ạ-mount). The highest in patronage, the sovereign.

advowry. Same as **avowry.**

advowson (ad-vou'zn). The right of presentation of a clergyman to a church or ecclesiastical benefice. A right of patronage. See 2 Bl Comm 21.
See **collative advowson; medietas advocationis; patronage.**

advowson appendant. An advowson annexed to the possession of a manor.

advowson collative. Same as **collative advowson.**

advowson donative. An advowson whereby the patron may give a church or a chapel without presentation, institution or induction.

advowson in gross. An advowson annexed to the person of the owner and not to his manor or lands.

advowson of the moiety. The right of two patrons each to present a clerk or parson to the same church.

advowson presentative. An advowson whereby the patron has a right of presentation to the bishop or ordinary.

advowterer. An adulterer.

advowtress. An adulteress.

advowtry. Adultery.

ad warectum (ad wa-rek′tum). See **warectare.**

adyre. To say.

aedes (ē′dēz). A dwelling house; a residence.

Aedes alienas combussit (ē′dēz a-li-ē′nās kom-bus′-sit). He burned the dwelling of another.

aedificare (ē-di-fi-kā′re). To build a house.

aedificare in tuo proprio solo non licet quod alteri noceat (ē-di-fi-kā′re in tu′ō prō′pri-ō sō′lō non lī′set quod al′te-rī nō′se-at). It is not lawful to build on your own land that which may harm another.

aedificator (ē-di-fi-kā′tor). A builder.

Aedificia solo cedunt (ē-di-fi′she-a sō′lō sē′-dunt). Buildings go with the soil; that is, they pass with the title to the land.

aedificium (ē-di-fi′she-um). A building.

aedile (ē′dīl). A Roman officer who superintended the care of public buildings, streets, weights and measures, funerals, games, and the prices of provisions.

aeditus. Same as **editus.**

aeger (ē-ger). Sick in mind or body.

ael. A grandfather.

aenne (ān). Corrupted Latin for year.

Aequior est dispositio legis quam hominis (ē′qui-or est dis-pō-zi′she-ō lē′jis quam hŏ′mi-nis). The law's disposition of a matter is more just than that of a man.

aequitas (ē′qui-tas). Equity; good conscience.
For words, phrases, clauses, and maxims beginning with the word "aequitas" or "equity" see **equity** and phrases which follow such word.

aequo (ē′quō). To make equal. To make for justice and equity.

aequo et bono. See **ex aequo et bono.**

Aequum et bonum est lex legum (ē′qu-um et bō′num est lex lē′gum). That which is just and good is the law of laws.

aequum est neminem cum alterius detrimento fieri locupletiorem (ē′qu-um est ne′mi-nem kum al-te′ri-us de-tri-men′to fi′er-i lo-ku-plē-she-ō′rem). It is just that no one should be enriched by the suffering of another.

aequus (ē′qu-us). Equal; just.

aequus et bonus (ē′qu-us et bō′nus). Justice and right.

aera (ē′ra). Same as **era.**

aerarium (ē-rā′ri-um). The Roman treasury.

aerer (er′er). (A vernacular of the Latin "arare.") To plough.

aerial (ār′i-al). See **antenna.**

aerial navigation. See **aeronaut; aeronautics.**

aerial flight. A flight in an airplane. Anno: 17 ALR2d 1059.

aerial geology (ār′i-al jē-ol′ō-ji). A branch of the science of geology, pertaining to the making of maps of areas of the earth's surface occupied by peculiar rock formations. Lewis v Carr, 49 Nev 366, 246 P 695.

aerial photograph. A photograph taken from an airplane, usually by a camera which operates automatically or semi-automatically; admissible in evidence on the same basis as an ordinary photograph. Anno: 57 ALR2d 1352.

aerodrome (ā′ę-rō-drōm″). Same as **airdrome.**

aeronaut (ā′er-o-nôt′). One trained and skilled in the art or practice of managing and manipulating aircraft and navigating in the airspace above the earth. 8 Am J2d Avi § 2.

aeronautic expedition (ā″ęr-ō-nâ′tic). An expedition by aircraft.
Something more than riding as a fare-paying passenger would seem to be required to render one a participant in an aeronautic expedition, but the term in an exception to the risk in a life or accident policy has been construed with a contrary result at times, particularly where such construction is favored by other phrases of the exception. Anno: 155 ALR 1038; 29A Am J Rev ed Ins § 1270.

aeronautic operation. The act of operating an aircraft thru the air. Anno: 83 ALR 389; 99 ALR 202.
Usually understood, when appearing in an exception to the risk in a life or accident policy, purporting to exclude coverage while participating in an aeronautic operation, as not applicable to a fare-paying passenger, but a contrary result has been reached in some cases where other terms of the exclusion are considered with the expression in question. 29 Am J Rev ed Ins § 1270.

aeronautics (ā″e-rō-nâ′tiks). The art or practice of sailing in or navigating the air. Bew v Travelers' Ins. Co. 95 NJL 533, 112 A 859, 14 ALR 983; 8 Am J2d Avi § 2.

Aeronautics Act. A uniform statute, withdrawn by the commissioners in 1943 as obsolete. Boyd v Whitem, 128 Cal App 2d 641, 276 P2d 92.
See **Aircraft Financial Responsibility Act.**

Aeronautics and Space Act. A federal statute which makes provision for a national space program, declaring that it is the policy of the United States that activities in space should be devoted to peaceful purposes for the benefit of all mankind; a federal statute establishing and providing for the organization and functions of the National Aeronautics and Space Council, the National Aeronautics and Space Administration, and the Civilian-Military Liaison Committee. 42 USC §§ 2451-2476.

Aeronautics and Space Administration. A federal agency provided by the National Aeronautics and Space Act. 42 USC §§ 2472, 2473.

Aeronautics and Space Council. A federal agency provided by the Aeronautics and Space Act.

aeroplane (ā′ę-rō-plăn″, also ār′ō-plăn). See **airplane.**

aerostatics (ā′er-o-stat′iks). A branch of physical science dealing with the support which the air gives to objects therein.

aes (ēz). Money.

aes alienum (ēs a-li-ē′num). The money of another; a debt due to another.

aesnecia (ēs-nē′she-a). Same as **esnecy.**

aesneciae. See **jus aesneciae.**

aesnetia (ēs-nē′she-a). Same as **esnecy.**

aes suum (ēs su′um). His own money; a debt due from another.

aesthetic (es-thet′ik). That which is beautiful or in good taste. People v Wolf, 127 NY Misc 382, 386, 216 NYS 741, 744.

aestimare (ĕs-ti-mā're). To assess; to appraise; to value.

aestimatio capitis (ĕs-ti-mā'she-ō ka'pi-tis). The value of the head;—the fine imposed for committing a murder.

aestimatio litis (ĕs-ti-mā'she-ō lī'tis). The assessment of damages in a law suit.

aetas (ē'tas). Age.

aetas infantiae proxima (ē'tas in-fan'she-ē prox'i-ma). (Civil law.) The age nearest infancy. This was that part of the period of puerita, or childhood, from the age of seven years to ten and a half. From the time of his birth to the end of this period a child could not be punished for any crime. See 4 Bl Comm 22.

aetas legitima (ē'tas le-ji'ti-ma). Lawful age under the civil law; twenty-five years.

aetas perfecta (ē'tas per-fek'ta). Finished age, full age. Same as **aetas legitima**.

aetas prima (ē'tas prī'ma). The first age; infancy; a child's age up to seven years under the civil law.

aetas pubertati proxima (ē'tas pū-ber-tā'tī prox'i-ma). (Civil law.) The age next to, or approaching, puberty. This was that part of the period of puerita, or childhood, from the age of ten and a half years to fourteen. During this period a child was punishable for crime if found to be doli capax, that is, capable of mischief, but the punishment was with many mitigations and was not imposed with the utmost rigor. After this period minors were liable to punishment, even capitally. See 4 Bl Comm 22.

aetate probanda. See **de aetate probanda**.

aetheling (ē-thel-ing). A noble in Saxon times.

afeer (a-fēr'). To appraise; to assess; to assess a fine or amercement.

afeerer or **afeeror** (a-fēr'er or a-fēr'or). One appointed to tax an amercement. See 4 Bl Comm 380.

affair. A matter at hand; a matter of concern. State v Mitchell, 210 Wis 381, 245 NW 640, 86 ALR 1361. A word of broad meaning, including a business transaction, almost anything which engages the attention of a person, even a meretricious relation with one of the opposite sex.
The French "affaire" from which the English word derived is equally broad, including business, troubles, actions in court, etc.
See **public affair**

affaire (a-fĕ-r). The equivalent in French of **affair**.

affaires. See **affair; charge d'affaires**.

affearment (af-fēr'ment). Same as **affeerement**.

affect. To act upon; to produce an effect. Gaunt v Alabama Bound Oil & Gas Co. (CA5) 281 F 1279, 1282; NLRB v Suburban Lumber Co. (CA3) 121 F2d 829. To weaken, debilitate, or injure a person or thing. Ryan v Carter, 112 US 78, 23 L Ed 807.

affected. Influenced, involved, changed, weakened, touched.

affected by intoxicants. In a state of intoxication. Anno: 13 ALR2d 1003. Intoxicated. 29A Am J Rev ed Ins § 1230.

affected by plan. The status of a creditor or stockholder of a corporation in reference to the effect of a plan of reorganization upon his interest or interests.
A creditor or stockholder of a corporation in reorganization under the Bankruptcy Act is affected by a plan of reorganization only if his interest is materially affected. 9 Am J2d Bankr § 1598

affected with a public interest. Something of public consequence and affecting the community at large. 16 Am J2d Const L § 317.
See **business affected with a public interest**.

affecting (a-fek'ting). See **affect**.

affecting commerce. In commerce. Burdening or obstructing commerce. Anno: 8 ALR2d 739 (involving definition in federal labor law) 29 USC § 152(7).

affection. Tender feelings. In the medical sense, an ailment or disease, such as an affection of the liver, deranging the functions of the organ involved. Conn. Mut. Life Ins. Co. v Union Trust Co. 112 US 250, 257, 28 L Ed 708, 711, 5 S Ct 119.
See **alienation of affections; natural affection**.

affectus (af-fek'tus). Intent; disposition; attempt.

affectus punitur, licet non sequatur effectus (af-fek'-tus pu-nī'ter, lī'set non se-quā'ter ef-fek'tus). The attempt is punishable although the result intended does not follow.

affeere (a-fēr'). Same as **afeer**.

affer (a-fēr'). Cattle; horses.

afferatores (af-fe-rā-tō'rēz). Same as **afeerors**.

afferatus (af-fe-rā'tus). Assessed.

affere (a-fēr'). Same as **afeer**.

affermer (af'fer-mā). To let to farm; to confirm, make strong.

affiance (a-fī'ans). To pledge; to engage to marry.

affiant (a-fī'ant). A person who has made an affidavit. People ex rel Livingston v Wyatt, 186 NY 383, 79 NE 330.

affidare (af-fi-dā're). To swear one's faith; to make an oath of fealty or fidelity; to take the soldier's oath.

affidata (af-fī-dā'ta). An affianced woman.

affidatio (af-fi-dā'she-ō). A pledge of fealty.

affidatio dominorum (af-fī-dā'she-ō do-mi-nō'rum). The oath taken by the members of the House of Lords.

affidatus (af-fi-dā'tus). An ally, under the feudal system.

affidavit (af-i-dā'vit). Any voluntary ex parte statement reduced to writing, and sworn to or affirmed before some person legally authorized to administer an oath or affirmation. 3 Am J2d Affi § 1.
See **caption; deposition; jurat; venue; verification**.

affidavit for attachment. An affidavit made by or on behalf of the plaintiff and filed by him in the action in which the attachment is sought, as a prerequisite, in most jurisdictions to the issuance of the writ of attachment. 6 Am J2d Attach § 254.

affidavit in criminal prosecution. An affidavit charging the commission of a criminal offense upon which a warrant is issued for the arrest of the accused; the equivalent of a complaint or preliminary information. 21 Am J2d Crim L § 441.

affidavit of circulation. See **Newspaper Publicity Law**.

affidavit of copyright claimant. An affidavit, required upon deposit of copies of book with the Register of Copyrights, that the copies were made from type set, or from plates made from type set, within the limits of the United States. If the text was produced by lithographic or photo-engraving process, the affidavit must state that the process was wholly performed within the United States and that the printing and binding have also been performed within the United States. The affidavit must also state the place where the type was set or the plates were made or the other processes performed, the place of printing and binding, the date of completion of the printing or the date of publication. The affidavit may be made by the copyright claimant, his duly authorized agent or representative residing in the United States, or the printer who printed the books deposited. 18 Am J2d Copyr § 64.

affidavit of defense. The same in most jurisdictions as an **affidavit of merits.** In at least one jurisdiction, however, an affidavit of defense has been the equivalent of a plea or answer. 41 Am J1st Pl § 171, note.

affidavit of good cause. An affidavit required of the government in a denaturalization proceeding. 8 USC § 1451(a).

affidavit of good faith. Requirement on appeal:—an affidavit required by statute in some jurisdictions to be made by or on behalf of an appellant, stating that the appeal is not taken for delay. Even where such an affidavit is required to properly perfect an appeal, it will not be held insufficient on technical grounds. 4 Am J2d A & E § 313. The requirement of an affidavit of good faith applies in some jurisdictions to appeals from a justice of the peace. Prerequisite to filing or recording of chattel mortgage:—a requirement by statute in some jurisdictions made as a condition of the filing or recording of a chattel mortgage is the making of an affidavit by the mortgagor or, in some jurisdictions, his agent or attorney, that the mortgage is given in good faith without design to defeat, defraud, hinder, or delay creditors, and the filing or recording of the affidavit with the mortgage. Under the Uniform Security Code, neither a security agreement nor a financing statement need be accompanied by affidavits. 15 Am J2d Chat Mtg § 49.

affidavit of merits. (sometimes called affidavit of defense). An affidavit stating the foundation of the defendant's defense and denying the right of the plaintiff to recover in the action. 41 Am J1st Pl § 172.
Such affidavit is required on a motion to set aside a default. 30A Am J Rev ed Judgm § 719. It is also required under the practice in some jurisdictions to avoid the taking of a summary judgment against the defendant. 41 Am J1st Pl § 171.

affidavit of no collusion. An affidavit required of the plaintiff in a bill of interpleader stating that his bill is not filed in collusion with either of the defendants named therein, but merely of his own accord, to obtain the relief sought. Under modern practice, the affidavit is not required if the plaintiff's bill of complaint, duly verified, effectively alleges the absence of collusion. 30 Am J Rev ed Interpl § 24.

affidavit on demurrer. An affidavit required by statute or by the rules of the court in some jurisdictions to be made by the attorney filing a demurrer, stating that the demurrer is not interposed for purposes of delay and that it is in the opinion of the attorney well taken in point of law.

affidavit to hold to bail. An affidavit prerequisite to an arrest in a civil action.

affidavit upon information and belief. One which is little more than a statement of opinion and lacks the essential of a positive statement required to support a prosecution for perjury. 41 Am J1st Perj § 26.

affilare (af-fil-ā′re). To file.

affile (af-fīl′). To file; to deliver for filing. See **file.**

affiliate. To join or to become connected with, as to affiliate with a lodge or club. To trace connections, as in **affiliation proceedings.**

affiliated. Joined or connected.
Mere control of two or more corporations by the same persons, without control of substantially all of the stock, or the mere carrying on of a business unit by two or more corporations, is not enough to make them "affiliated" within the meaning of the Income Tax Law. Handy & Harmon v Burnet, 284 US 136, 76 L Ed 207, 52 S Ct 51.
For discussion of affiliated corporations, see Anno: 69 ALR 1271; 85 ALR 153.

affiliated corporations. See **affiliated.**

affiliated group. A tax-law term for a chain of corporations permitted to file a consolidated return because of a common parentage based upon stock ownership.

affiliation. Connection or close association. The act of joining a lodge or club.
"Affiliation" with an organization advocating the overthrow of the government by force and violence within the federal deportation statute means something more than mere co-operation with such an organization, even where the co-operation indicates a consistent course of conduct; the acts complained of must be of such quality as to indicate an adherence to or a furtherance of the purposes of objectives of the organization and a working alliance to bring them to fruition. Bridges v Wixon, 326 US 135, 89 L Ed 2103, 65 S Ct 1443.

affiliation proceedings. Judicial proceedings, otherwise known in some jurisdictions as bastardy proceedings, to establish the paternity of a child born out of wedlock and to compel the father to contribute to its support. 10 Am J2d Bast § 74.
See **affiliated.**

affinage. (äf′fin-āg) A word taken from the French which means refining, as of metals or sugar.

affiner (äf′fin-ā). To refine; to finish.

affines (af-fī′nēz). Relatives by marriage.

affinis (af-fi′nis). Singular of **affines.**

Affinis mei affinis non est mihi affinis (af-fī′nis me′ī af-fī′nis non est mi′hi af-fī′nis). A relative of my relative by marriage is not my relative.

affinitas (af-fī′ni-tās). Related by marriage. See **affinity.**

affinity (a-fin′i-ti). The connection existing in consequence of marriage between each of the married persons and the kindred of the other. Re Bordeau's Estate, 37 Wash 2d 561, 225 P2d 433, 26 ALR2d 249. The tie between one spouse and the blood relations of the other.
It is contrasted with consanguinity; it is no real kinship. Under the concept of affinity, a husband and wife are each related to the blood relations of the other spouse in the same degree as the latter, but the blood relations of one spouse are not regarded as related, by reason of the marriage, to the

blood relations of the other spouse, and the husband is not related by affinity to the wife. Re Bordeau's Estate, 37 Wash 2d 561, 225 P2d 433, 26 ALR2d 249; 23 Am J2d Desc & D § 45; 26 Am J1st H & W § 2; 27 Am J1st Incest § 4; 30A Am J Rev ed Judges § 144.

Under constitutional or statutory provisions, in practically all of the states, a judge is disqualified to act in any cause wherein he may be related to one of the parties within certain specific degrees of "affinity" or "consanguinity." 30A Am J Rev ed Judges § 142.

affirm (ạ-fẽrm'). To declare solemnly instead of making a statement under oath. 58 Am J1st Witn § 549; also, to confirm or ratify a statement, belief, opinion, decision or judgment, for example to affirm a judgment after appeal or review proceeding.

affirmance (ạ-fẽr'mans). The confirmation of a judgment or order of court. A final determination upon appeal that the proceeding under review is free from prejudicial error. 5 Am J2d A & E § 934. A positive declaration. The adoption by a person of the prior act of another which did not bind him at the time, but which was done or professed to be done on his account. 3 Am J2d Ag § 160.

affirmance-day-general. A day appointed for the general affirmance or reversal of judgments in the court of exchequer.

affirmance of judgment. A determination that the action or proceeding under review is free from prejudicial error and that the judgment appealed from shall stand. 5 Am J2d A & E § 934.

The dismissal of an appeal for want of prosecution is clearly *not* an affirmance of the judgment. Drummond v Husson, 14 NY 60, 61. Affirmance implies a consideration on the merits, while a dismissal may be very summary. 5 Am J2d A & E § 905

affirmant (ạ-fẽr'mant). A person who affirms in lieu of taking an oath.

Affirmanti, non neganti, incumbit probatio (af-fir-man'tī, non ne-gan'ti, in-kum'bit pro-bā'she-o). The burden of proof is on the party who affirms, not on him who denies. Anno: 23 ALR2d 1254.

affirmare (af-fir-mā're). To affirm; to assert.

affirmation. A positive statement. A solemn statement or declaration, made as a substitute for a sworn statement by a person whose conscience will not permit him to swear. 39 Am J1st Oath § 13.

An affirmation of fact constituting a representation is a warranty and not merely evidence of a warranty if its natural tendency is to induce the buyer to purchase the goods and the buyer thus induced does purchase them. Park v Moorman Mfg. Co. 40 Utah 273, 241 P2d 914, 40 ALR2d 273.

affirmative. An answer "yes"; something beyond passive tolerance or acceptance. The side supporting a proposition; bearing the burden of proof.

affirmative action. Constructive action rather than mere negation.

As the term is used in the National Labor Relations Act in authorizing "affirmative action" by the Labor Relations Board in ordering the reinstatement of an employee who was discharged for union activities, the statute contemplates remedial, and not punitive or disciplinary action, and the order must therefore be confined to restitution for the wrong done, however widely that should be conceived. NLRB v Leviton Mfg. Co. (CA2) 111 F2d 619.

affirmative authorization. A positive declaration of authority rather than authorization by implication.

A boom in a river authorized and constructed in the manner required by statute is within the exception of a Federal act prohibiting obstructions in navigable streams except those affirmatively authorized by law. Pickens v Coal River Boom Co. 66 W Va 10, 65 SE 865.

affirmative charge. An instruction to the jury which removes an issue from consideration by the jury.

affirmative defense. A defense which amounts to something more than a mere denial of the plaintiff's allegations; a defense which sets up new matter not embraced within the ordinary scope of a denial of the material averments of the complaint.

Among such defenses are accord and satisfaction, release, estoppel, fraud when set up as a matter in avoidance, mistake, alteration of contract, excuse for nonperformance of a covenant, act of God, the statute of limitations, title by prescription, and justification of an alleged tort. 41 Am J1st Pl § 144. See also 27 Am J2d Eq § 204.

affirmative easement. An easement which entitles the owner of the dominant tenement to use the servient tenement, or which clothes him with authority to do some act on the servient tenement which would otherwise be unlawful.

Rights of way, and rights of discharge of matter over the land of another, are illustrations of affirmative easements. 17A Am J Rev ed Ease § 13.

affirmative order. A rejected term of art.

In a seemingly technical distinction between "negative" and "affirmative" orders of the Interstate Commerce Commission, the opinion in Procter & Gamble v United States, 225 US 282, 56 L Ed 1091, 32 S Ct 761, gave authority to a doctrine which harmonizes neither with the considerations which induced it nor with the decisions which have purported to follow it. Later cases have made it clearer that "negative order" and "affirmative order" are not appropriate terms of art. Thus, the Supreme Court has had occasion to find that while an order was negative in form, it was affirmative in fact. Rochester Tel. Corp. v United States, 307 US 125, 83 L Ed 1147, 59 S Ct 754.

affirmative plea. In equity: a plea which alleges new matter of defense, proceeding on the theory that, admitting the case stated in the bill to be true, the matter pleaded by the plea affords a sufficient reason why the plaintiff should be denied relief. 27 Am J2d Eq § 204. At Law: a special plea of matters not provable under the general issue. 41 Am J1st Pl § 144.

affirmative pregnant. An allegation in the affirmative form implying a negative in favor of the adverse party.

Such allegations are denounced as bad pleading because they are ambiguous. See Fields v State, 134 Ind 46, 32 NE 780.

affirmative proof. Such evidence of the truth of the matters asserted as tends to establish them, and this regardless of the character of the evidence offered. Jenkins v Hawkeye Commercial Men's Asso. 147 Iowa, 113, 124 NW 199.

affirmative proof of loss. Evidence in such form as is usual and customary in such cases, or as is recognized by law, and such as is calculated to convince or persuade the mind of the truth of the facts alleged; clearly, something more than the unverified declaration of the party in interest. 29A Am J Rev ed Ins § 1404.

affirmative relief. Relief granted to a defendant in an action upon his demand therefor and proof of his right thereto.

affirmative representation. A positive allegation of a fact as presently existing. 29 Am J Rev ed Ins § 698.

affirmative statute. A statute commanding a positive act or duty, as distinguished from a prohibition.

affirmative warranty. A warranty by an insured which asserts the existence of a fact or condition, and appears on the face of the policy, or is attached thereto and made a part thereof. 29 Am J Rev ed Ins § 709.

affix. To attach in a degree of permanence.

affixed. Securely attached.

affixed to the freehold. So fastened to the land or to a fixture as to pass with the land; imbedded in the land, as in the case of walls; or permanently resting upon it as in the case of buildings. Miller v Waddingham, 3 Cal Unrep 375, 25 P 688.
See **fixture.**

affixus (af-fi'xus). Affixed to; fastened; annexed.

afflatus divinus (a-flā'tus di-vī'nus). Divine afflatus; inspired by divinity.

affliction. A cause of pain or distress.

afforare (af-fo-rā're). Same as **afere.**

afforatus (af-fo-rā'tus). Assessed.

afforce (a-fōrs'). To add force; to add to; to increase.

afforcer (äf'for-sā). Same as **afforciare.**

afforce the assize. To compel jurors to agree to a verdict by starving them, or by adding jurors until twelve agreed.

afforciamentum (af-for-she-ā-men'tum). The convening of a court in extraordinary session.

afforciamentum districtionis (af-for-she-ā-men'tum dis-trik"she-ō'nis). The afforcement or increase of a distress.

afforciamentum plegiorum (af-for-she-ā-men'tum ple-ji-ō'rum). The afforcement or increase of pledges.

afforciare (af-for-she-ā're). To increase or strengthen.
See **a fortiorari.**

afforer (äf'for-ā). To assess; to appraise.

afforest (af-for'est). To make into a forest.

afforestare (af-fo-res-tā're). To afforest.

afforestation (a-for-es-tā'shun). Same as **afforestment.**

afforestment (af-for'est-ment). The turning of land barren of trees into a forest.

affortiare (af-for-she-ā're). Same as **afforciare.**

affranchir (ä"fran-shēr'). To affranchise; to free.

affray (a-frā'). Fighting by two or more persons in a public place, to the terror of the people and the disturbance of public tranquility.
Words alone do not constitute an affray as so defined, but if words uttered in a public place are accompanied by threats, drawing weapons, and attempting to use them, thus terrifying the people and disturbing the public tranquility, the offense is committed. 12 Am J2d Breach P etc § 18.

affrayer (a-frā'ėr). One who indulges in affrays; a public disturber.

affrectamentum (af-frek-ta-men'tum). An affreightment.

affreighter (a-frā'tėr). The charterer of a ship, the party to a contract of affreightment who hires the vessel.
Such definition derives from the French and is not accepted in common-law jurisdictions without some dissent. At times, the owner of the vessel who lets it is called an "affreighter."

affreightment (a-frāt'ment). A contract for the hiring of a vessel. An agreement by the owner of a vessel to employ the vessel for the carriage of specific goods belonging to one person or many persons. 48 Am J1st Ship § 296.

affretamentum (af-fre-ta-men'tum). An affreightment, the hiring of a vessel.

affretement (äf-fret'môn). A contract for the hiring of a vessel.

affreter (a-frā'ter). To charter a vessel under a contract of affreightment.

affreteur (äf-fre-tur'). (French.) One to whom a vessel is let under a contract of affreightment. The owner of a vessel who lets it to another under such a contract is a freteur or freighter. These terms are not exactly parallel in the English translation. See **affreighter.**

affri carectae (af-fri ka-rek'tē). Plow horses or cattle.

affri carucae (af-frī ka-ru'sē). Beasts of the cart; draft horses or cattle.

affront. An insult or indignity by word or deed.

affurare (af-fu-rā're). Same as **afeer.**

afiert (a-fērt'). Belongs to; is a part of.

AFL. Abbreviation for American Federation of Labor, which organization is now joined with the Congress of Industrial Organizations, the new title being AFL-CIO.

aforce. Same as **afforce.**

aforcer. Same as **afforciare.**

aforciamentum. Same as **afforciamentum.**

aforesaid (a-fōr'sed). Written in an earlier part of the same article or document.

aforestare. To make into a forest.

aforethought. A thought had before; premeditation; prepense.
The words "premeditated," "aforethought," and "prepense," possess etymologically the same meaning. They are the Latin and Saxon synonyms, expressing a single idea, and may possess in law precisely the same force. Sullivan v State, 100 Wis 283, 293.
See **malice aforethought; prepense.**

a fortiori (ā fôr-shi-ō'ri). By the stronger reason; all the more.

African. See **negro.**

afri carectae. Same as **affri carectae.**

afri carucae. See **affri carucae.**

after. Behind; later in point of time. A word of futurity in a limitation of an estate in real property which in the absence of words of survivorship relates to the time of enjoyment of the estate limited and not the time of vesting. 28 Am J2d Est § 257. A word, which, as it appears in a contract, indicates a condition of performance. 17 Am J2d Contr § 320

Where an act is to be performed within a specified period "after" a day named, the general rule is to exclude the day designated and to include the last day of the specified period. 52 Am J1st Time § 27. But the word may have either an inclusive or an exclusive meaning, according to the subject-matter, context and purpose. See Halbert v San Saba Land & Live Stock Asso. 89 Tex 230, 34 SW 639.

after-acquired. Acquired at a time subsequent to a definite date.

after-acquired property. A term commonly employed in mortgages and for the double purpose of subjecting added security to the lien of the mortgage and of removing—in many cases—doubts which may arise as to whether improvements, repairs, and additions made since the mortgage was executed are included in it. Shaw v Bill, 95 US 10, 24 L Ed 333, 36 Am J1st Mtg § 33. Property acquired by the mortgagor after the date of a chattel mortgage. 15 Am J2d Chat Mtg § 24.

after-acquired title. The interest or estate in land which a grantor acquires after he has conveyed the same land to another person.

As a general rule, when a person conveys, by a deed which contains a warranty of title or which recites or imports that the grantor has title, land in which he has no interest at the time, but afterwards acquires a title to the same land, he will not be permitted to claim in opposition to his deed, from the grantee, or any person claiming title from the grantee. 23 Am J2d Deeds § 294.

afterbirth (àf'tėr-bėrth). The placenta and fetal membranes expelled from the womb after delivery of a child; a birth after the death of the father or after the making of a will by either parent.

after-born. Born afterward; born posthumously.

after-born child. A child born after the death of the father. A child born to a testator after the making of the will. 57 Am J1st Wills § 1367. A child born to the grantor in a deed after the execution and delivery of the instrument. 23 Am J2d Deeds § 214.
See **posthumous child.**

after completion of the operation. A phrase often appearing in policies of products liability insurance in clauses which exclude coverage. 29A Am J Rev ed Ins § 1360.

after dark. See **dark.**

after date. A familiar phrase in certain promissory notes employed in indicating the maturity of the instrument.

An instrument payable a certain number of days, months, or years "after date" matures on the last day of the time specified. 11 Am J2d B & N § 285. A note with time of payment specified only as "after date" is payable immediately or at any rate, within a reasonable time, in the absence of a contrary intent expressed in the instrument. Where a note payable "after date" was executed with a paper attached thereto stating that the payee has agreed that she will not attempt to collect the note until the maker's death, the note was held to become due on the date of death. 11 Am J2d B & N § 285.
See **on demand after date.**

after demand. A condition in an instrument for the payment of money which renders the same payable only upon or after the making of a demand for payment. 11 Am J2d B & N § 286.

after-discovered. Discovered after a specific time or event.

after-discovered evidence. Evidence discovered after trial. Weiss v United States (CA5 La) 120 F2d 472.
A more common term is newly discovered evidence.

aftermath (àf'tėr-màth). A second crop of grass the same season; the right to such a crop.

after maturity. See **indorsement after maturity.**

after nightfall. See **dark.**

afternoon. The part of the day between noon and evening.

after paying the preceding legacies and bequests. An expression used in a will which is generally held to have reference to the residue for distribution under a residuary clause and not to alter the application of the principle that lapsed legacies and devises pass under such a clause. 57 Am J1st Wills § 1449.

after possibility of issue extinct. See **fee tail after possibility of issue extinct.**

Presentment of a bill of exchange for acceptance is required in any case where the bill is payable "after sight." 11 Am J2d B & N § 730.

after sight. After presentment for acceptance.

after the death. Words of futurity in a limitation of an estate in real property, which, in the absence of words of survivorship, relate to the time of enjoyment of the estate limited and not to the time of vesting of the estate. 28 Am J2d Est § 257.

after the fact. See **accessory after the fact.**

after the passage of this act. Construed, as the expression appears in local option legislation which provides that liquor licenses issued "after the passage of this act" shall be void a specified time after the holding of an election at which the sale of intoxicating liquors shall be prohibited, to mean the time when the act takes effect. 30 Am J Rev ed Intox L § 111.

afterthought. A thought had after an event.

afterward. Subsequent to a definite happening.

againbuy (a-gen'bī). To buy back; to redeem.

against. In opposition; contrary to.
See **versus.**

against evidence. See **verdict against evidence.**

against her will. Essential allegation in indictment for rape. 44 Am J1st Rape § 56.
The words "against her will" mean exactly the same thing as "without her consent," since the crime may be committed when, strictly speaking, the woman exhibits no will at all in the transaction, as where she has been drugged, or is non compos mentis. 44 Am J1st Rape § 2.
See **against the will.**

against interest. See **declaration against interest.**

against my estate. Having reference, as a direction to charge taxes, to the general or the residuary estate. Anno: 37 ALR2d 111.

against public policy. See **public policy.**

against the form of the statute. A technical expression, the use of which is to be approved, if not declared a necessity, in an indictment founded on a statute which creates the offense charged. 27 Am J1st Indict § 39.

against the peace and dignity of the state. The conclusion of an indictment which is deemed essential to the validity of the indictment, except as words of like import are prescribed and used. 27 Am J1st Indict § 38.

The allegation of a prior conviction in an indictment seeking enhanced punishment of the accused as an habitual criminal need not conclude with the expression "against the peace and dignity of the state."

against the weight of the evidence. See **verdict against the evidence.**

against the will. Element of robbery.

As the phrase is used in the definition of the crime of robbery, which includes a taking against the will, it must be construed not only as to be evidenced by resistance, but also as meaning that resistance would have been offered, but was quelled either by actual force or violence, which was of itself sufficient to prevent resistance by disabling the victim, or by threat sufficient to frighten the victim into compliance. 46 Am J1st Rob § 22.

Against the will of prosecutrix in rape case, see **against her will.**

agalma (a-gal'mä). The impress of a design or figure on a seal.

agard (a-gard'). Award
See **nul fait agard.**

agatis. See **circumspecte agatis.**

age. The length of time that a person has lived, a thing has existed, or a structure has stood.

The word has several connotations, some of them inconsistent. Thus, a minor comes of "age," meaning that he has acquired discretion and can transact business without a guardian, while an older person acquires "age" at the peril of having his capacity questioned.

aged (ājd). Denoting the attainment of years, as "a boy, aged five."

(ā-jid) Denoting that a person has grown old or has been made old by events in his life.

While the term, as applied to human beings, is not for all purposes, susceptible of precise definition, and while it is not practicable arbitrarily to fix a period of life at which the condition of being "aged" can be said to have begun, it has been held in an English case that persons fifty years of age are "aged." Pomeroy v Willway, L R Ch Div 510, and an American case holds that a man of sixty-six, though hale and hearty maybe termed "aged." Allen v Pearce, 101 Ga 316, 28 SE 859. The span of life having been materially lengthened in the late decades, it is submitted that courts will be reluctant to accept the statements in the foregoing cases.

A statute which declares an assault aggravated when committed by a person in robust health upon one who is "aged" or decrepit, which fails to define the word "aged," does not sufficiently comply with the legal requirement that an offense be definitely defined before a conviction under it can be sustained. Anno: 83 L Ed 921.

agency. A fiduciary relationship by which a person confides to another the management of some business to be transacted in the former's name or on his account, and by which such other person assumes to do the business and render an account of it.

In its legal sense, the term always imports commercial or contractual dealings between two parties by and through the medium of another. 3 Am J2d Ag § 1.

See **administrative agency; exclusive agency.**

agency action. The whole or part of every administrative agency rule, order, license, sanction, relief, or the equivalent or denial thereof, or failure to act. 2 Am J2d Adm L § 204.

agency by estoppel. An agency created so far as third persons are concerned by acts and appearances which lead third persons to believe that it exists. 3 Am J2d Ag § 19.

It arises in those cases where the principal, by his culpable negligence, permits his agent to exercise powers not granted to him, even though the principal have no notice or knowledge of the conduct of the agent. It is sufficient to estop the principal from disputing the authority, in such cases, that the course of dealing in the transaction of the principal's business, between the agent and the third persons, was such as to justify them in believing that he possessed the requisite authority, and to make it the duty of the principal to know the manner in which the agent was conducting his affairs. Anno: 12 ALR 113.

agency by necessity. An agency created by necessity, that is, by an emergency arising from a particular situation making it necessary or proper for the agent to act without receiving the sanction or authorization of the principal in the matter, for example, the emergency which arises where one deserts his children, leaving them destitute. 3 Am J2d Ag § 19.

agency by operation of law. An agency which exists by force of law rather than by the mutual consent of principal and agent. 3 Am J2d Ag § 19.

agency coupled with an interest. See **power coupled with an interest.**

agency in fact. An agency created by the mutual consent of the principal and agent, as distinguished from an agency existing from necessity, by estoppel, or by operation of law.

agency of auctioneer. See **auctioneer.**

agency of the United States. A body which has the power to act as, not merely for, the highest administrative authority of the governmental establishment. Anno: 3 ALR2d 1200.

The Interstate Commerce Commission and National War Labor Board are agencies of the United States within the meaning of section 9 of the Portal-to-Portal Act. Rogers Cartage Co. v Reynolds (CA6 Ky) 166 F2d 317, 3 ALR2d 1090.

See **administrative agency.**

agency proceeding. Any process of a federal administrative agency. 2 Am J2d Adm L § 204

agency rule on expirations. An insurance agent's right to expirations on termination of the agency. 29 Am J Rev ed Ins § 174.

agency-shop agreement. A form of union-security agreement under which union membership remains optional with the employee in the sense that membership is neither compulsory nor unavailable, but the employee as a condition of employment is under a duty to pay the union initiation fees and regular dues.

Such an arrangement is valid as union-security, except where prohibited by state right to work laws. Anno: 11 L Ed 2d 1001.

agency to sell. Personal property:—an agency arising from express authorization, or implied from authorization to conduct another transaction for the principal where a sale is usually incidental to such transaction, usually accompanies it, or is reasonably necessary in accomplishing it. 3 Am J2d Ag § 99. See **exclusive agency to sell.**

Real property:—usually an agent authorized to sell real property is a special agent acting under a limited power rather than a general agent. See **power of attorney; real estate broker.**

agenda (ā-jen'da). Things to be done, matters to be attended to, at a meeting.

agens (ā'jenz). A manager; a plaintiff.

agent. One of the parties to an agency relationship, the one who acts for and represents the other party who is known as the principal, being a substitute or deputy appointed by the principal with power to do certain things which the principal may or can do. 3 Am J2d Ag § 1. One employed to represent the employer in contractual negotiations. American Nat Ins Co. v Denke, 128 Tex 229, 95 SW2d 370, 107 ALR 409.

The word imports the correlative idea of a principal, and implies employment, service, delegated authority—to do something in the name or stead of the principal. Brewer v State, 83 Ala 113.

As used in embezzlement statutes, the term is construed in its popular sense as meaning a person who undertakes to transact some business or to manage some affair for another by the latter's authority and to render an account of such business or affair. It imports a principal and implies employment, service, and delegated authority to do something in the name and stead of the principal—an employment by virtue of which the money or property embezzled came into the agent's possession. 26 Am J2d Embez § 26.

agent and patient. A peculiar situation which arises where one is appointed by another to do or perform a thing for his own benefit, as where A appoints his creditor B to be his executor and A dies, whereupon B, acting in his capacity as executor, is authorized to pay the debt owing by A to him and acting in his own right, to receive it.

agent entrusted with goods. A commercial agent. 22 Am J2d Fact § 55.

agentes et consentientes pari poena plectantur (a-jen'tez et kon-sen-she-en'tez pa'ri pē'na plek-tan'ter). Both actors and those consenting are liable to the same punishment.

agent for. Words of descriptio personae which are not so expressive of an agency relationship in the execution as to relieve the agent of personal liability, the question being resolved according to what is added to the words or what appears upon the face of the instrument. 3 Am J2d Ag § 193.

agential (ā-jen'shạl). Pertaining to agency or to an agent.

agent intrusted. See **agent entrusted with goods.**

agent not authorized to collect. Appearing in large print on the face of an invoice of merchandise, the words constitute conclusive notice to the purchaser not to pay the agent who sold the goods. McKindly v Dunhan, 55 Wis 515, 13 NW 485.

agent of. Words of descriptio personae.

Thus, "agent of" or "president of" a designated corporation merely identifies the person by indicating a personal relationship which he has. Tucker Mfg. Co. v Fairbanks, 98 Mass 101.

See **agent for.**

agent of insured. See **insurance agent.**

agent of insurer. See **insurance agent.**

agent's actual authority. Such authority as a principal intentionally confers upon the agent, or intentionally or by want of ordinary care allows the agent to believe himself to possess. 3 Am J2d Ag § 69.

agent's apparent authority. That authority of an agent which, though not actually granted, the principal knowingly permits the agent to exercise, or which the principal holds him out as possessing.

In effect, an agent's apparent authority is, as to third persons dealing in good faith with the subject of his agency and entitled to rely upon such appearance, his real authority, and it may apply to a single transaction or a series of transactions. 3 Am J2d Ag § 73.

agent's express authority. An authorization by words given orally or in writing to do or perform a certain act or series of acts. 3 Am J2d Ag § 69.

agent's implied authority. Actual authority, circumstantially proved, which the principal is deemed to have actually intended the agent to possess. 3 Am J2d Ag § 71.

agent's incidental authority. Implied authority to perform those acts which are of like kind with the acts which the agent is expressly empowered to perform and from which the authority is implied. 3 Am J2d Ag § 71.

agent's lien. The lien of an agent on property or funds of the principal in his possession for necessary expenditures, advances, or liabilities incurred under the authority conferred upon him, and for his commissions or other compensation for his services. 3 Am J2d Ag § 242.

agent to receive service of process. An "agent authorized by appointment to receive service of process" is one actually and expressly appointed as an agent to receive service, not one whose appointment is by implication only. 26 ALR2d 1087.

An agent actually appointed to receive process on behalf of his principal. Anno: 26 ALR2d 1087. An agent of a foreign corporation upon whom, by force of statute, service of process may be made so as to bind the corporation. 36 Am J2d For Corp §§ 540 et seq.

age of choice. See **age of discretion.**

age of consent. An arbitrary age fixed by statute without reference to physical development, varying in American jurisdictions from ten to eighteen years, to denote the time of her life at which a female may consent to sexual intercourse. 44 Am J1st Rape § 19. The age which qualifies one to enter into a marriage contract. 35 Am J1st Mar § 16.

age of discretion. The age, usually fourteen, at which, under statute, a minor is entitled to choose, or at least be consulted in the selection of, a guardian. 25 Am J1st Guar § 28.

age of election. Same as **age of discretion.**

age of majority. The age, usually twenty-one, at which the disability of infancy terminates. 27 Am J1st Inf § 5.

age of nurture. The age of a child under seven.

age of reason. See **age of discretion; Paine's Age of Reason.**

age prayer. A request of an infant party to a real action for a stay of proceedings until his majority.

age prier (äzh prē'ā). Same as **age prayer.**

ager (ā'jėr). An old English term meaning acre, derived from the Latin for land or field.

agere injuriam (ā'je-re in-jū'ri-am). To sue for damages.

agere non potest (ā'je-re non po'test). He cannot maintain an action.

agger (aj'ėr). A mound; a dam; a dike; a bank; a Roman road, raised in the center to shed water.

aggravated arson. The intentional damaging by an explosive substance, or setting fire to any structure, watercraft, or movable, wherein it is foreseeable that human life may be endangered. State v Murphy, 214 La 600, 38 So 2d 254.

aggravated assault. An offense variously defined in state statutes, sometimes referring to an assault with intent to commit murder, assault with intent to commit rape, assault with intent to commit robbery etc., at other times referring to a degree of the specific crime of assault. 6 Am J2d Asslt & B § 48.

aggravated damages. See **aggravation of damages.**

aggravated larceny. The offense in particular forms defined by statute, such as larceny from the person, larceny from a dwellinghouse, larceny from a railroad car, larceny of Federal property, larceny of commodity supplied by a public utility, etc. 32 Am J1st Larc §§ 43 et seq.

aggravated rape. The offense of rape under circumstances which render the offense more heinous, such as tender age of the victim or a blood relationship between the accused and the victim. State v Daniels, 169 Ohio St 87, 8 Ohio 56, 157 NE2d 736, 76 ALR2d 468.

aggravation (ag-ra-vā'shon). That which enhances the gravity of a criminal or tortious act; allegations in a declaration or complaint which tend to enhance damages. An enhancement of a wrong or injury.

In some jurisdictions, an offense is aggravated by the circumstance of a previous conviction of the same offense. State v Bruno, 69 Utah 444, 256 P 109.

aggravation of damages. A phrase of several connotations: (1) an increase in compensable damages because of the circumstances which surrounded the injury; (2) an increase in the damages suffered resulting from the failure of the injured party to seek medical relief or the unskilful treatment given by the physician whom he selected and employed, which category comes within the doctrine of avoidable consequences; (3) increasing the severity of a pre-existing physical or mental condition by committing a tort against the afflicted person; and (4) an increase in exemplary or punitive damages because of the high degree of malice in the acts of the defendant which injured the plaintiff. 22 Am J2d Damg § 199.

Matter of aggravation does not consist in acts of the same kind and description as those constituting the gist of the action, but in something done by the defendant, on the occasion of committing the trespass, which is, to some extent, of a different legal character from the principal act complained of.

A very graphic illustration of matter in aggravation appears where the plaintiff declares in trespass for breaking and entering his house, and alleges in addition, that the defendant also destroyed goods in the house and debauched his daughter. Hathaway v Rice, 19 Vt 102, 107.

aggregate. A mass; an assemblage of a sum of particulars, all taken together in one number. See Anno: to O'Brien v Chicago City Railway Co. 27 ALR 506.

See **corporation aggregate.**

aggregate damage. This term, as used in a liability insurance policy limiting the liability of the insurance company to a certain sum for each accident and to another stated sum for "aggregate damage", was meant to serve as a total limit of damage to property of different persons from a closely related series of events. Anchor Casualty Co. v McCaleb (CA5 Tex) 178 F2d 322.

aggregate liability restriction. A clause in a contract for the renewal of a bond which limits the extent of the liability of the surety. 12 Am J2d Bonds § 46.

aggregatio mentium (ag-re-gā'she-ō men'she-um). See **meeting of the minds.**

aggressor (a-gres'or). A person who willingly or knowingly after meeting his antagonist begins and brings about an affray or deadly conflict by using threatening language or doing some act reasonably calculated to lead to such an affray or conflict. Wilkie v State, 33 Okla Crim 225, 242 P 1057.

In order to make a man guilty of murder as the "aggressor," the one "in fault," or the one who "provokes a difficulty" in which his adversary is killed, he must have provoked it with the intent to kill his adversary or do him great bodily harm, or to afford him a pretext for wreaking his malice upon his adversary. Foutch v State, 95 Tenn 711, 34 SW 423.

aggrieved. Deprived of one's legal rights or having suffered an invasion of one's legal rights. Denied one's personal or property right. Gloss v People, 259 Ill 332, 102 NE 763.

aggrieved party. One who is injuriously affected by the act or omission of another. Anno: 13 ALR 301. One whose personal interests are or may be affected adversely. Anno: 74 ALR 1221 (review of refusal to abate a tax.) One, within the meaning of the statute governing appeals, who has an interest recognized by law in the subject matter which is injuriously affected by the judgment, or one whose property rights or personal interests are directly affected by the operation of the judgment or decree. 4 Am J2d A & E § 183.

agild (ā'gild). Released or exempt from fine.

agiler (a-gī'ler). A spy; an informer.

agillarius (a-jil-lā'ri-us). A cowherd.

agio (a-gi'ō). (French.) The rate of exchange between one currency and another.

agiotage (a-gi-ō'täg). (French.) Speculation.

agisant (ä'zhē-sôn). Lying.

agiser (ä"zhē-sä'). To lie.

agist (a-jist'). To agist is to feed or pasture the cattle of another on one's land, for hire.

agistamentum (a-jis"ta-men'tum). An agistment.

agistare (a-jis-tā're). To agist.

agistator (a-jis-tā'tor). An agister.

agister (a-jis'ter). A person who takes cattle for hire to pasture or to care for.

The agister's possession is that of a bailee for hire. Atwater v Lowe (NY) 39 Hun 150, 152; 4 Am J2d Ani § 72.

agister's lien (a-jis'terz lē'en or lēn). A lien upon an animal provided by contract or statute for the benefit of a person who has fed or cared for the animal. 4 Am J2d Ani § 74.

agistment (a-jist'ment). The particular kind of bailment under which a man, for a consideration, takes cattle to graze and pasture on his land. 4 Am J2d Ani § 72.

agistor (a-jis'tor, -tėr). Same as **agister**.

agitator. One who stirs up discontent with prevailing social, economic, or political conditions.
See **labor agitator**; **seditious agitator**.

agitur (ā'ji-ter). An action has been brought.

agnates (ag-nā'tēz). Blood relatives who trace their kinship through males.

agnati (ag-nā'tī). Romans who traced their name and lineage through the male line to a common deceased ancestor.

agnatic (ag-nat'ik). Deraigned through males or from a male.

agnatio (ag-nā'she-ō). Agnation; relationship upon the father's side.

agnation (ag-nā'shon). Relationship through males, or to a male.

agnats (ag'nāts). Same as **agnates**.

agnise (ag-nīz'). To acknowledge; to admit.

agnize (ag-nīz'). Same as **agnise**.

agnomen (ag-nō'men). A popular appellation appended to a person's true name, for example, "Louie, the short."

agony. Violent pain of body or mind. Chicago v McLean, 133 Ill 148, 24 NE 527.

agraphia (a-graf'i-a). A disorder of the brain affecting the ability to write.

agrarian (a̱-grā'ri-an). Pertaining to land.

agrarianism (a-grā'ri-a̱n-izm). A socialistic plan for an equal distribution of lands; any plan for a radical change in land tenure. A movement to promote the interests of farmers as a class.

agrarian laws. Laws of ancient Rome regulating the disposition of public lands.

agrarian murder. A murder committed in a dispute over lands, boundaries or tenancy.

agrarii (a-grā'ri-ī). The agrarians, who were the members of the Roman political party which stood for the distribution of the public lands among the people.

agrarium (a grā'ri-um). A tax upon land.

a gratia (ā grā'she-a). By favor; by indulgence.

agreamentum (ag-re''a-men'tum). Old English term meaning agreement.

agreare (ag-rē-ā're). To agree.

agreavit (ag-re-ā'vit). He agreed.

agree. To unite upon the terms of a contract or agreement; to make an agreement; to assume a harmonious relation.
The word "agree" may be read "grant" and an "agreement under seal" construed to be a grant. Bailey v Agawam Nat. Bank, 190 Mass 20, 76 NE 449. This does not mean that a defective grant is always to be considered an agreement to make a grant. Bailey v Agawam Nat. Bank, supra.

agree. (French.) A solicitor or attorney in the tribunals of commerce.

agreeance (ä-grā-ôns'). An agreement.

agreed. Having come to an agreement; having settled by mutual assent upon a course of action.
See **dismissed agreed**.

agreed case. A special proceeding, the chief characteristic of which is that the parties submit to the court an agreed statement of the ultimate facts essential to a determination of the particular litigation, so that the court will not be concerned with matters of fact, but will consider and determine openly matters of law. 3 Am J2d Agr C § 1.
The term is not an exclusive designation of the proceeding but is used interchangeably with other terms such as "case stated" and "case agreed." 3 Am J2d Agr C § 1. There is a distinction, however, between an agreed case and an **agreed statement of facts**.

agreed order. An order of court made upon the agreement of the parties rather than after a trial.

agreed price. The price agreed upon by the parties in their contract of employment or of purchase. Fyfe v Sound Development Co. 235 NY 266, 139 NE 263, 26 ALR 1325, 1327.

agreed statement of facts. A statement agreed or stipulated by respective counsel as being the facts of the case.
It is but a substitute for the evidence of those facts and in this respect an agreed statement of fact differs from an agreed case, which may be submitted for decison without any pleadings. Towle v Sweeney, 2 Cal App 29, 83 P 74.
According to some authorities, signatures of the parties or their attorneys is unnecessary to an agreed statement of facts admitted by the parties to be true in open court. Le Barron v Harvard, 129 Neb 460, 262 NW 26, 100 ALR 767.

agreed value. A value stipulated by the parties to a contract; the value of the insured property stated in an insurance policy known as a valued policy.
In a certificate of formation of a partnership, a statement that a limited partner had contributed property of the "agreed value" of a certain sum, the words "agreed value" had the same meaning as actual value so far as concerned the rights of third parties relying upon the certificate to their detriment. Walrath v Ramsay, 335 Mich 331, 55 NW2d 853, 34 ALR2d 1449.

agreement (a̱-grē'ment). The union of two or more minds in a thing done or to be done; a coming together of parties in opinion or determination; the union of two or more minds in a thing done or to be done. Woodworth v State, 20 Tex App 375, 380. A contract where made upon a sufficient consideration to do, or refrain from doing, a particular lawful thing. 17 Am J2d Contr § 1.
The legal import of the word includes not only a promise, but also the consideration for which the promise was made. Hunt v Adams, 5 Mass 358.
See **articles of agreement**; **compact**; **contract**.

agreement against public policy. See **contract against public policy**.

agreement by specialty. See **specialty**.

agreement for arbitration. A contract between parties to a dispute involving their respective legal rights and duties that the disputed matters shall be referred to the decision of others and that the parties shall be bound by the decision reached by such persons. 5 Am J2d Arb & A § 24. A contract constituting the first step in submission of a controversy to arbitration.

It may be either an agreement to submit a present controversy or part of the issues thereof or an agreement to arbitrate future controversies. In any event the rights and liabilities of the parties are controlled by the law of contracts and a valid contract is essential if a submission is to be required of a party. 5 Am J2d Arb & A § 1.

agreement for insurance. A form of temporary insurance, 29 Am J Rev ed Ins § 205; an agreement by an insurer to cover the insured pending the execution and delivery of the formal policy of insurance. Trustees of the First Baptist Church v Brooklyn Fire Ins. Co. 19 NY 305, 308.

agreement for lease. An agreement by a landowner to enter into a lease of the premises, as distinguished from a lease itself, the agreement being executory, vesting no interest in the land in the other party, and creating no liability for rent as such. In determining whether an instrument is a lease or a mere agreement for one, the intention of the parties, as manifested by the writing controls. As a rule, where the agreement contemplates the execution of a formal lease at a future time, especially where its future execution is conditional, the agreement is one for a lease and not a lease itself; but where the instrument contains apt words of present demise, and the estate granted and terms of the demise are definite and explicit, it is often held to be a present lease and not a mere agreement for one, although it also contains a provision or covenant for the execution of a more formal lease at a future time. 32 Am J1st L & T § 28.

agreement for submission. An **agreement for arbitration.**

agreement not to be performed within a year. Within the meaning of the Statute of Frauds, the expression includes only such agreements as, fairly and reasonably interpreted, do not admit of a valid execution within the space of one year.

The expression does not refer to a natural or physical impossibility, but an impossibility by the terms of the contract itself, or by the understanding and intention of the parties as shown by the contract. 49 Am J1st Stat of F § 23.

If an agreement may consistently with its terms be entirely performed within the year, although it may not be probable or expected that it will be performed within that time, it is not within the condemnation of the statute of frauds. Kent v Kent, 62 NY 560.

agreement of conveyance. Any agreement whereby one person conveys or agrees to convey to another real property or some interest therein. Larsen v Larsen, 44 Idaho 211, 256 P 369.
See **conveyance**; **deed.**

agreement of sale. A completed sale as distinguished from an agreement to sell.

agreements mala in se (ma'la in sē). See **contracts mala in se.**

agreements mala prohibita (ma'la prō-hi'bi-ta). See **contracts mala prohibita.**

agreement to receive a bribe. A statutory offense consisting of an agreement between two persons which necessarily carries with it the essential concept of a criminal and corrupt bargain to give on the one part, and to receive on the other. A meeting of the minds for such corrupt bargain. People v Coffey, 161 Cal 433, 119 P 901.

agreement to sell. An executory contract, as distinguished from a completed sale under an agreement of sale. Keogh v Peck, 316 Ill 318, 147 NE 266, 38 ALR 115.

agreement under seal. See **contract under seal.**

agreer. (French.) To approve; to allow; to accept. To rig or equip a ship.

agrees. See **agree.**

agrees to pay mortgage debt. Assumes the mortgage. 37 Am J1st Mtg § 997.

agres (agrès). Rigging on a vessel, as known under the French law of the sea.

agri (ag'rī). Fields; arable lands worked in common.

agricultural (ag-ri-kul'tūr-al). Pertaining to, connected with, or engaged in agriculture. Slycord v Horn, 179 Iowa 936, 162 NW 294, 7 ALR 1285, 1290.

Agricultural Adjustment Acts. Statutes providing for direct payment of public funds to farmers in connection with the regulation by the government of the production and marketing of agricultural products. 3 Am J2d Agri § 28.

Agricultural Adjustment Administration. A federal agency under an agricultural adjustment act. 7 USC 601-659 (Act of 1933); 3 Am J2d Agri § 28.

agricultural chemistry. The application of science to assist in the production of food crops and the improvement of such crops from the standpoint of nutrition.

Agricultural Children Act. An English statute (1873) regulating child labor on farms and education for child laborers. (36 and 37 Vict c 67.)

agricultural commodities. Products produced by labor upon land in an agricultural pursuit, as distinguished from lime and commercial fertilizer which are produced for the farm.

Agricultural Commodities Act. See **Perishable Agricultural Commodities Act.**

agricultural compositions and extensions. Proceedings under the Bankruptcy Act, provided as a temporary measure in 1933, but continued in effect until March 1, 1949, when the statute was allowed to expire, the objective of the legislation being to enable a farm debtor to hold onto his property and keep operating under extensions of time for payment or redemption. 9 Am J2d Bankr § 1625.

agricultural employment. See **farm labor.**

agricultural enterprises. Processes in the preparation and marketing of agricultural or horticultural commodities. Puerto Rico Tobacco Marketing Co-op. Asso. v McComb (CA1 Puerto Rico) 181 F2d 697,

agricultural fair. A fair or exhibition, conducted by a state or county board of agriculture or by an agricultural society, which is intended to promote agriculture by including exhibits of livestock, agricultural products, farm machinery, and other products and items of interest to farmers and their families, as well as to provide amusement and entertainment for its patrons. 4 Am J2d Amuse § 19.

Agricultural Gangs Act. An English statute (1867) regulating child and female labor on farms. (30 and 31 Vict 130.)

agricultural labor. See **farm labor**.

agricultural lands. A term of variable meaning in use, meaning, on the one hand, crop or grazing lands, and on the other hand, lands outside a city or village.

agricultural leases. Leases of farm lands. Bookout v White, 123 Mont 459, 214 P2d 861, 17 ALR2d 562; Anno: 17 ALR2d 566.

agricultural liens. Liens given by statute or special contract upon agricultural property, such as crops and domestic animals, to secure farm laborers and the vendors of seed grain, stock feed, and other products furnished for agricultural purposes. 3 Am J2d Agri § 10.

agricultural occupation. See **farming**.

agricultural products. See **farm products**.

agricultural pursuit. Every process and step taken and necessary to the completion of a finished farm product. 3 Am J2d Agri § 1; 58 Am J1st Workm Comp § 97.
See **farming**.

agricultural society. An association, which may be of a voluntary character or incorporated, organized and acting to further and advance the interests of agriculture through promoting educational activities, the holding of agricultural fairs, the collection and dissemination of information helpful directly and indirectly to farmers and stockraisers, and developing other measures intended to stimulate agriculture and promote its imporvement. Downing v Indiana State Board of Agriculture, 129 Ind 443, 28 NE Rep 123; 3 Am J2d Agri § 54.

agricultural workers. See **farm labor**.

agriculture. The science or art of cultivating the soil and its fruits, especially in large areas or fields, and the rearing, feeding, and management of livestock thereon, including every process and step necessary and incident to the completion of products therefrom for consumption or market and the incidental turning of them to account.

It is broader in meaning than "farming," since it includes activities deemed extraneous to farming, such as viticulture, dairying, poultry, bee raising, and ranching. 3 Am J2d Agri § 1; 58 Am J1st Workm Comp § 97.

The word refers to the field, or farm, with all its wants, appointments, and products, as horticulture refers to the garden with its less important, though varied, products. Slycord v Horn, 179 Iowa 936, 162 NW 249, 7 ALR 1285, 1290. For some purposes, however, the word "agriculture" includes horticulture, as well as forestry, and the use of land for any purpose of husbandry, inclusive of the keeping and breeding of livestock, poultry or bees, and the growing of fruit or vegetables. 58 Am J1st Workm Comp § 97.

agriculturist (ag-ri-kul′tu̇r-ist). A student of the science of agriculture. Downing v Indiana State Board of Agriculture, 129 Ind 443, 28 NE Rep 123. An expert in farming; a farmer.

agri limitati (ag′ri li-mi-tā′ti). (Roman law.) The territory acquired by conquest and assigned to the veteran soldiers.

agri mensuram (ag′ri men-sū′ram). To measure land.

agt. An abbreviation of **agent**.

ahteid (ä′tīd). Bound by oath.

aid. Verb: To support by furnishing strength or means. Anno: 22 ALR 1320. Noun: Money or substance given by way of assistance, for example, appropriations for foreign countries economically distressed.
See **aids**; **federal aid**; **state aid**; **welfare**.

aid and abet. See **aiding and abetting**

aid and assist. Implying knowledge of the illegal transportation, where the term is used in statutory provisions authorizing the seizure and confiscation of vehicles of persons who aided and assisted in the illegal transportation of intoxicating liquors. 30 Am J Rev ed Intox L § 481.

aid and comfort. Help; assistance; encouragement; counsel. An element of the crime of treason.

One gives aid and comfort to the enemy where he commits an overt act which, in its natural consequence, if successful, would encourage and advance the interests of the enemy. Young v United States, 97 US 39, 24 L Ed 992; 52 Am J1st Treas § 9. The term "aid and comfort" contemplates some kind of affirmative action, deed, or physical activity tending to strengthen the enemy or weaken the power to resist him, and is not satisfied by a mere mental operation. Cramer v United States, 325 US 1, 89 L Ed 1441, 65 S Ct 918, Kawakita v United States, 343 US 717, 96 L Ed 1249, 72 S Ct 950.

aid bonds. County or municipal bonds issued in aid of a private enterprise, such as a railroad, in the interest of the public. People ex rel. Danville, Olney & Ohio River Railroad Co. v Granville, 104 Ill 285, 288.
See **railroad aid bonds**.

aide. In one sense the same as **aid**; in another sense an officer in the armed forces who is an assistant to a superior.

aide de camp (ād′dē-kamp′). An officer of the armed forces serving as an assistant to an officer of higher rank.

aider. One who aids or abets; one who advises, counsels, procures, or encourages another to commit a crime. 21 Am J2d Crim L § 119.
See **aiding and abetting**.

aider by verdict. The cure of defects in a pleading by verdict, under the rule that any defect, imperfection, or omission in any pleading, whether in substance or form, is cured by verdict if the issue joined is such as necessarily requires proof on the trial of the facts so defectively or imperfectly stated or omitted, and without which it is not to be presumed that either the judge would direct the jury to give, or the jury would have given, the verdict. 41 Am J1st Pl § 404.

aiding and abetting. A familiar term in criminal law, meaning the advising, counseling, procuring, or encouraging another to commit a crime.

One accused of such acts cannot be guilty thereof unless the person aided committed a crime. 21 Am J2d Crim L § 119. If guilty, the one aiding and abetting is himself liable as a principal. 21 Am J2d Crim L § 122.

aiding an escape. Offense of rescue. 27 Am J2d Escape § 3.

aidoiomania (ā-doi-ō-mā′ni-a). A species of insanity in which the person afflicted longs for every woman he sees, whether she is married or not.

A deed procured by a husband to be made by the aidoiomaniac to his wife, would be set aside, for it runs to the subject of his mania. Ekin v McCracken (Pa) 11 Phila 534, 539.

aid-prayer (ād'prâr). A prayer or demand that other parties shall be joined in the action and help defend his title, which a defendant tenant may make in a real action as a preliminary step before putting in his plea. He may thus call for assistance because of the feebleness of his own estate. For example, a tenant for life may pray in aid, that is, call for assistance, on the remainderman or reversioner and an incumbent parson may thus call on the patron and the ordinary. See 3 Bl Comm 300.

aidre. Same as **aider.**

aids. Services or payments rendered to the lord by a tenant in chivalry on certain occasions. First there were payments called "aids;" in the theory of our earlier authors, they were offered of the tenant's free will, to meet the costs incurred by the lord on particular occasions; but they settled into a fixed custom afterwards, if they had not really done so when those authors wrote. See F. Pollock, Land Laws, iii.
See **fifteenths; tenths.**

aid societies. Organizations of women members of churches, having the purpose of aiding and promoting the work of the church, often engaging in money-raising activities.
See **benevolent associations; mutual benefit society.**

aiel (ī'el). A grandfather; a writ under which a grandchild could oust a stranger who dispossessed him on the day of the death of his grandfather, who was seised. See 3 Bl Comm 186.

aielesse (ī-el-es'). A grandmother.

aieul (ä-eul'). French for grandfather.

aieule (ä-eul'e). French for grandmother.

ail (āl). Noun: a corrupted French form of aiel, meaning grandfather. Verb: to become sick or suffer failing health.

ailment. A disease; sickness, indisposition; morbid affection of the body; not ordinarily applied to acute diseases. McDermott v Modern Woodmen of America, 97 Mo App 636, 654, 71 SW 833.
See **personal ailment.**

ailours (à-loor'). Otherwise; elsewhere.

aim. Verb: To act with a purpose; to direct a blow, to bring a firearm into position on target. Noun: Intention or purpose.

ainesse (ā-nes'). French for primogeniture.
See **esnecy.**

ainsi (an'sē). From the French, meaning so; thus.

aio (ā'ō). I say. The opening words of the statement of a Roman cause of action.

air. Noun: the combination of gases with which the earth is surrounded. Appearance or impression. A melody. Verb: To make known one's thoughts or grievances. To expose to the air.

air base. A center maintained by the armed services in support of activities in aviation.

airborne radioactive material. Any radioactive material disbursed in the air in the form of dust, fumes, mess, vapors, or gases. 10 CFR Cum Supp § 20.3(a)(2).

air-brake provisions. Federal regulations of appliances on trains. 44 Am J1st RR § 274.

air carrier. Any citizen of the United States who undertakes, whether directly or indirectly or by a lease or other arrangement, to engage in air transportation. 49 USC § 1301(10).

air chamber. Equipment of a motorboat to insure buoyancy in the event of capsizing. 12 Am J2d Boats § 12.

air-condition. To clean or temper the air in a building for the purpose of making the building more comfortable for habitation or work.

air-conditioning equipment. Appliances used in cleaning or cooling the air in a building.
Whether or not the equipment is a fixture, thereby constituting a part of the real estate, is a question to be answered according to the particular circumstances involved, such as the degree of attachment to the realty and the degree to which it is especially adapted to the premises involved. Anno: 43 ALR2d 1378.

air course. A passage for ventilation of a mine, now required by statute in mining states. 36 Am J1st Min & M § 147.

aircraft. Any contrivance now known or hereafter invented which is used, or designed for navigation of or flight in the air. 49 USC § 1301(5); 8 Am J2d Avi § 20.
The term "aircraft" in an aviation exclusion clause in a life or accident policy of insurance includes a glider and a seaplane. Anno: 54 ALR2d 414.
See **airplane; powered aircraft: public aircraft.**

Aircraft Financial Responsibility Act. A uniform statute, prepared by the National Conference of Commissioners on Uniform State Laws, which, by 1965, had been adopted in Massachusetts, Michigan, New Hampshire, and Connecticut. Am J2d Desk Book, Document No. 129.

airdrome (âr'drōm). An **airport.**

aire (ī're). A court conducted by justices on circuit.

airer (âr'ėr). To plow.

airline. A carrier by air, whether of persons, property, or both.

airman. Any individual who engages, as the person in command or a pilot, mechanic, or member of the crew, in the navigation of aircraft while underway; and (except to the extent that the Administrator of the Federal Aviation Agency may otherwise provide with respect to individuals employed outside the United States) any individual who is directly in charge of the inspection, maintenance, overhauling, or repair of aircraft, aircraft engines, propellors, or appliances, and any individual who serves in the capacity of aircraft dispatcher, or air-traffic control-tower operator. 49 USC § 1301(7).

air navigation facility. Any facility used in, available for use in, or designed for use in, aid of air navigation, including landing areas, lights, any apparatus or equipment for disseminating weather information, for signalling, for radio-directional finding, or for radio or other electrical communication, and any other structure or mechanism having a similar purpose for guiding or controlling flight in the air or the landing or takeoff of aircraft. 49 USC § 401(7); Hillsborough County Aviation Authority v National Airlines, Inc. (Fla) 63 So 2d 61, 40 ALR2d 1056.

air piracy. As defined by federal statute, any seizure or exercise of control, by force or violence or by threat of force or violence and with wrongful intent, of an aircraft in flight in air commerce. 49 USC 1472(i) (2), as amended Sept. 5, 1961.

airplane. An aircraft. Not a motor-driven car or vehicle. McBoyle v United States, 283 US 25, 75 L Ed 816, 51 S Ct 340; Re Hayden's Estate, 174 Kan 140, 254 P2d 813, 36 ALR2d 1278; 8 Am J2d Avi § 20.
See **aircraft.**

air pollution. The pollution of the air by noxious fumes produced and arising from industrial operations, the burning of waste and rubbish, the exhausts on the engines of motor vehicles, etc. Anno: 54 ALR2d 795; 26 Am J2d Electr § 264.

airport (ăr'pōrt). A field with improvements for the taking off and landing of aircraft, the loading and unloading of passengers and cargo, and the accomodation of airlines and their personnel.
The maintenance of airports comes legitimately within the scope of a municipal power in much the same manner as docks and harbor facilities for marine shipping. Municipalities are studying local conditions and commercial organizations are ever pressing the importance of establishing or improving terminal airports and of providing proper lighting for landing fields and facilities such as hangars, garages, and repair shops. Wichita v Clapp, 125 Kan 100, 263 P 12, 15.
See **federal airports.**

airport of entry. An airport designated as one of entry for purpose of collecting customs duties. 21 Am J2d Cust D § 60.

airship. See **aircraft.**

air show. A business use of an insured aircraft by an insured corporation engaged in flying services. 29A Am J Rev ed Ins § 1348.

airspace. That part of space extending upward from the surface of land which is necessary for the full use of the land and enjoyment of the incidents of its ownership. 8 Am J2d Avi § 3.
See **navigable airspace.**

airt and pairt (ārt). (Scotch.) Same as **art and part.**

air traffic rules. Statutes, rules and regulations prescribed by federal and state authority, or developed by way of application of common-law principles, which govern the operation of aircraft in the air or in landing and takeoff. 8 Am J2d Avi §§ 8 et seq.

Air Transport Adjustment Board. A federal agency for the adjustment of disputes between an employer operating an airline and its employees. 31 Am J Rev ed Lab § 348.

air transportation. Interstate, overseas, or foreign transportation of goods, other items of personal property, or the mail by aircraft. 49 USC § 1301(10).

airway. A route for aircraft in the air, open to all qualified aircraft other than those of the enemy, but subject to regulation and control under governmental authority in the interest of public safety and welfare. 8 Am J2d Avi §§ 9 et seq.
See **federal airway.**

aisement (ez'môn). Same as **easement.**

aisiamentum (ai-she-ā-men'tum). Same as easement.

aisne (ān). Eldest or first born.
See **aisne file; aisne fitz.**

aisneesse (ā-nēs'). Rule of primogeniture in descent.

aisne file (ān fē). The eldest daughter.

aisne fitz (ān fitz). The eldest son.

ajournement (a-jŭrn'e-ment). In French law, a summons, that is process for the commencement of an action; also, adjournment or postponement.

ajourner (ä'zhoor-nā''). To adjourn.

ajuger (ä'zhoo-zhā''). To adjudge.

ajutage (a-ju'tag). A tube or pipe used in waterworks.

ajutoir (a-ju'twär). Same as **ajutage.**

akin (a-kin'). Related by blood; similar.

al. An abbreviation of alius. French form of preposition "at" or "with" as in **al armes; al barre.**
See **et al.**

Alabama Claims. Claims for compensation from Great Britain for damages inflicted upon American shipping and property by the Alabama, a ship of the Confederate States, which was built in Great Britain. The claims were heard by a tribunal of arbitrators and allowed in a sum somewhat in excess of $16,000,000. The award is known as the Geneva Award and the board of arbitrators as the Geneva Convention. Similar claims for damages from depredations by the ships, Florida and Shenandoah, were also arbitrated.

al aid de Dieu (äl ed de Dyuh). With God's help.

alae ecclesia (a'lē e-kle'si-a). Architectural designation for wing aisles in a church.

Alaric. See **Law of Alaric.**

al armes (al ärm). With arms.

alarm. Literally, to arms, but in modern usage a warning of danger from fire, water, an enemy, or other source of peril.

alarm list. A listing of persons under obligation to act as watchers.

alarm system. An apparatus consisting of wire and bell or horn constructed so as to be actuated by electricity, placed with more or less permanency at the entrance of a house or place of business, or at the door of a vault, and so set that any movement of the door of the house or vault, sometimes even any movement of a person in the immediate vicinity, will sound an alarm. Anno: 133 ALR 428.

Alaska. The largest state of the Union, admitted as the 50th state on January 3, 1959, having an area of 586,400 square miles, which is the territory to which the United States acceded by purchase from Russia in 1867 conducted by Honorable William H. Seward, Secretary of State under President Andrew Johnson. The name "Alaska" is of Russian origin, having reference to the Aleutians, inhabitants of islands lying off the coast, who were the first natives contacted by Russian explorers.

a latere (ā lat'e-rē). From the side; collaterally.

alba. See **firma alba.**

albacea (al-bah-thee'a). An executor.

alba firma (al'ba fir'ma). Rent payable in silver.

albanagii jus (al-ba-nā'ji-ī jūs). Same as **albinatus jus.**

albanus (al-bā'nus). A foreigner; an alien.

al barre (al-bär). At the bar.

albinatus (al-bi-nā'tus). A foreigner; an alien. The word is doubtless derived from the Latin "alibi," meaning elsewhere, and natus, meaning born. See 1 Bl Comm 372.

albinatus jus (al-bi-nā'tus jūs). A French law, repealed in 1790, whereby all of the property of a deceased alien escheated to the king.

albino (al-bī'nō or al-bē'nō). A person, even any animal, lacking normal coloration, appearing therefore in extreme whiteness of skin.

albinus (al-bī'nus). Same as **albanus**.

album (al'bum). A book with blank pages for autographs or for mounting photographs or clippings from newspapers and magazines. (Roman law.) The white tablet upon which the praetor published his edicts; white; without writing; blank.

album argentum (al'bum ar-jen'tum). White silver; uncoined silver.

album judicum (al'bum jū'di-kum). (Roman law.) A tablet for making up a jury list.

albus liber (al'bus lī'bėr). A compilation of the laws of old London.

alcalde (al-kahl'de). A Spanish officer possessing judicial powers and jurisdiction similar to those of a justice of the peace. See Castillero v United States (US) 2 Black 17, 17 L Ed 360.

alcalde mayor (al-kahl'day mah-yor'). The chief officer of government in one of the less important jurisdictions of the Spanish empire of the Indies and southwestern America. See Strother v Lucas (US) 12 Peters 410, 443, note, 9 L Ed 1137, 1149, note.

alcaldes ordinarios (al-kahl'des or-de-nah're-ōs). In places in which no governor resided, the regidores chose for two years, one or two persons who were not in the employ of the government as alcaldes ordinarios, or magistrates who held their courts and administered justice in all the cases in which a government could decide. They had seats and votes in the ayuntamiento or council, except when a governor or corregidor happened to be present. See Strother v Lucas (US) 12 Peters 410, 445, note, 9 L Ed 1150, note.

alcohol (al'kō-hol). A volatile, organic, limpid, colorless liquid, hot and pungent to the taste, having a slight, but not offensive scent. It has only one source, fermentation, and is extracted from its by-products by distillation, its purity and strength depend on the degree of perfection or completeness of distillation and aging processes.

It is the intoxicating element in spiritous, vinous, malt, and other intoxicating liquors, but pure alcohol is rarely used as a beverage, and some, but not all authorities, declare that pure alcohol is not an ardent or vinous spirit, or liquor of any kind, but a distinct thing used as an intoxicating basis of strong liquors. 30 Am J Rev ed Intox L § 12.

Alcohol Administration Act. A statute containing various provisions with respect to trade practices in connection with the marketing of intoxicating liquors. 27 USC § 205; Anno: 123 ALR 748.

alcoholic. Containing or pertaining to alcohol. One addicted to excessive use of intoxicating liquor.

alcoholic beverage. A potable liquid which contains an appreciable amount of alcohol, yet not necessarily enough of that product to be intoxicating. 30 Am J Rev ed Intox L § 4.
See **alcoholic content**.

alcoholic content. The percentage of alcohol in a liquor, determined according to volume in the United States, but according to weight in some countries.

Frequently, liquor laws provide that the term "intoxicating liquors" includes liquors which contain a specified percentage of alcohol, so that liquors containing such amounts of alcohol are subject to such laws irrespective of their intoxicating qualities. 30 Am J Rev ed Intox L § 6.

alcoholic hallucinosis. A mental derangement brought on by excessive use of alcoholic beverages. 21 Am J2d Crim L.

alcoholic liquor. Any liquor, beer, beverage or compound, whether distilled, fermented, or otherwise, by whatsoever known or called, which will produce intoxication, or which contains in excess of one per centum of alcohol and is used as a beverage. State v Glover, 133 SC 124, 125, 130 SE 213.

The latter clause of the foregoing definition is akin to the view in some jurisdictions, usually by force of statute, that "alcoholic liquors" and "intoxicating liquors" are interchangeable terms. 30 Am J Rev ed Intox L § 4. Other authorities refuse to call all liquors which contain some alcohol "intoxicating liquors," without giving consideration to the percentage of alcohol contained therein. 30 Am J Rev ed Intox L § 6.

alcoholic principle. The concept that any beverage containing alcohol will produce intoxication if a quantity sufficient for the purpose is taken. State v Fargo Bottling Works Co. 19 ND 396, 124 NW 387.

alcoholism. A state of being poisoned by alcohol or diseased from excessive use of alcoholic liquors.

al common ley (al cŏm-mŏn' lā). At common law. See 4 Bl Comm 327, footnote.

al contrary (al cŏn-trā'ri). To the contrary.

alcove. A recessed part of a room.

alder-best (äl'der-best). The best of all.

alder-first (äl'der-first). The first of all.

alderman. In the United States, a municipal officer, often called a councilman, who is a member of the common council, the legislative body of the municipality. In the older England, an alderman had significant judicial power. Purdy v People NY 4 Hill 384, 409.

aldermannus civitatis vel burgi (al-der-man'nus si-vi-tā'tis vel bur'jī). An alderman of a city or borough.

aldermannus comitatus (al-der-man'nus ko-mi-tā'tus). A county alderman.

aldermannus totius Angliae (al-der-man'nus tō-she'us Ang'li-ē). Alderman of all England.

ale. A malt liquor, that is, one of the beverages produced by the fermentation of malt, being the product of a process by which grain is steeped in water to the point of germination, the starch of the grain being thus converted into saccharine matter, is kiln-dried, then mixed with hops, and, by a further process of brewing, made into a beverage.

It may be intoxicating, but is not a spirituous liquor, the latter being a product of distillation. 30 Am J Rev ed Intox L § 9.

Ale was in common use in Germany in the time of Tacitus. It was provided for royal banquets in England in the reign of Edward the Confessor. Nevin v Ladue NY 3 Denio 43, 44.

alea (a'le-a). A game of chance.

aleator (ā-le-ā'tor). A gambler.

aleatoribus. See **de aleatoribus**.

aleatory (ā'lē-a-tō'ri). Uncertain; dependent on chance; involving risk or hazard.

aleatory contract. A contract, the performance of which depends on an uncertain event, such as a fire insurance contract. Losecco v Gregory, 108 La 648, 651, 32 So 985.
  Although an agreement must be certain if it is to be enforceable as a contract, an agreement can be certain notwithstanding performance depends on an uncertain event, provided the contract is certain in respect of the assumption of the risk appertaining to such event. Moore v Johnston, 8 La Ann 488, 489.

aleatory sale. A sale the consummation of which rests upon an uncertainty.

ale conner (āl' kon"ėr). An ale taster,—an officer whose duty it was to see to the quality of the ale used within the leet.

aleger (ä-le'zhā). To redress.

a lege suae dignitatis (ā lē'je su'ē dig-ni-tā'tis). From the law of his dignity. This was said by the Saxons to be the source of the king's power to pardon. See 4 Bl Comm 397.

aleier (ä-lā'ā). Same as **adlegiare**.

alenage (ä"len-äzh'). Same as **alnage**.

aler (ä'lā). Same as **aller**.

ale-silver (āl'sil"vėr). A tax anciently imposed upon ale sellers in London.

ale-stake. Sign for a place where ale is sold.

aletaster (āl'tās"tėr). A conner or taster of ale.

aleu. Same as **alleu**.

a l'evesque. See **brief a l'evesque**.

alfalfa weevil. See **weevil**.

alfet (al'fet). A container for hot water used in the ordeal by water.

Alfred's Code. A code of laws compiled under Alfred the Great, about 877 A. D.

Alfred's Dome Book. The Liber Judicialis, or Dome Book which was said to have been compiled by King Alfred. See 1 Bl Comm 65.

algarum maris (al-ga'rum mar-is). See **ligan**.

algo (al-gō). (Spanish.) Something owned; property.

algor (al-gôr). (French.) Medicine.

al huis d'esglise (al hwee d'es-glēs'). At the church door. This was the customary place for the marriage ceremony.

alia (a'li-a). Other things.
  See **inter alia**.

alia enormia (a'li-a ē-nor'mi-a). Other wrongs. A formal, general allegation usually at the end of a declaration or complaint in an action of trespass, under which circumstances of aggravation accompanying the act complained of may be proved, without further specification in the pleading, when such acts do not afford a substantial ground of action in themselves. They give character and quality to the act complained of, and show the degree of the injury, and could not be redressed at all if not alleged to be proved as incidents of the trespass. 22 Am J2d Damg § 278.

alia generis (a'li-a je'ne-ris). Another kind.

alia juris (a'li-a jū-ris). Under the authority of another, such as parent or guardian; not acting sui juris.

aliamentia (a'lia-men"shä). Ways for the accommodation of a tenant.

aliance. Same as **alliance**.

alias (ā'li-as). Otherwise; also known as; at another time; as formerly.
  Where, in an indictment or information, the name of the accused is given, followed by "alias" and another name, "alias" stands for "alias dictus," and indicates, not that the person referred to bears both names, but that he is called by one or the other, and hence the use of either one of said names identifies the accused as the person referred to. See State v Melson, 161 La 423, 426, 108 So 794.

alias dictus. Also called.
  "The true name is that which precedes an alias dictus. An alias dictus, as one of the old cases says, is only reputation, and is not the truth." Reid v Lord (NY) 4 Johns 118.

alias execution. See **alias writ of execution**.

alias summons. A new summons issued in the same form and to serve the same purpose as one previously issued, and usually issued where the original summons has been returned, and hence has become functus officio, without having been served on any or all of the defendants. Hill v Morgan, 9 Idaho 718, 76 P 323.

alias warrant. A second warrant, for example, a second warrant for the collection of taxes or a distraint, issued after the first one has failed to produce.

alias writ. A writ issued to take the place of a similar writ which has been lost or returned or for some other reason has not taken effect or has become functus officio. See 3 Bl Comm 283.

alias writ of execution. A second writ of execution issued in the same cause, where a former writ of the same kind has been issued without effect or without complete effect in satisfying the judgment upon which the writ was issued. 30 Am J2d Exec § 84.

alibi. A rebuttal of evidence of the prosecution by evidence that the accused was elsewhere than at the alleged scene of the offense at the time of the offense. 21 Am J2d Crim L § 136.

alibi natus (al'i-bī nā'tus). Born in another place.

alien (āl'yen). Noun: A person born in another country of parents who are not citizens of the United States, and who has not been naturalized here, or, one who, having been a citizen of the United States, has expatriated himself. 3 Am J2d Aliens § 1. Verb: To transfer property to another. Same as **alienate**.
  See **deportation; immigrant**.

alienable (āl'yen-a-bl). Lawfully transferable.

alienage (āl'yen-āj). The state or condition of an alien. It carries some disabilities (3 Am J2d Aliens §§ 11-35), but on the whole is not an unpleasant or uncomfortable status in the United States.

alien amy. An alien whose nation is at peace with our own. 3 Am J2d Aliens § 2.

Aliena negotia exacto officio geruntur (ā"li-ē'na ne-gō'she-a egs-ak'to of-fi'she-ō je-run'ter). The business of another should be carried out with particular care.

alienare (ā-li-ē-nā're). To alienate.

aliena res (ā-li-ē'na rēz). The property of another.

alienate (āl'yen-āt). The voluntary transfer of property to another by bargain and sale, deed, will, gift, or other method effective to pass title. Butler v Fitzgerald, 43 Neb 192.

As used in statutes imposing liability for double the value of property of decedent alienated before granting of administration of letters testamentary, the term means wrongfully to transfer property of decedent to another, and that such alienation was a wrongful conversion of the property for which an action of trover was maintainable at common law. Anno: 29 ALR2d 256.

Another meaning of significance in the law is that of estranging or making unfriendly. See **alienation of affections.**

alienated (āl'yen-ā-ted). Conveyed so as to transfer title. Insane; mentally unbalanced. Having been made unfriendly.

alienatio (ā''li-ē-nā'she-ō). Alienation.

Alienatio licet prohibeatur, consensu tamen omnium in quorum favorem prohibita est, potest fieri (ā''li-ē-nā'she-ō lī'set prō-hi-be-ā'ter, kon-sen'sū ta'men om'ni-um in quō'rum fa-vō'rem pro-hi'bi-ta est, po'test fī'e-rī). While alienation may be restrained, yet it may be made with the consent of all those in whose favor it was restrained. The maxim is one of the common law, and the principle of it is no less applicable in equity. See Seip's Estate, 1 Pa Dist 26.

alienation. An estrangement, as in alienation of affections; also a mental derangement. A transfer of property in such manner as to transfer title. Butler v Fitzgerald, 43 Neb 192.

Within the meaning of a statute requiring the concurrence of both spouses to an alienation of homestead property, a lease has been held to be an alienation. 26 Am J1st Home § 136. Such view is consistent with the view that a lease is a conveyance. See 32 Am J1st L & T §§ 3, 4, 817.

See **inverse order of alienation; restraint on alienation; rule against suspension of power of alienation.**

alienation clause. The condition, stated in a policy insuring against loss of property by fire, windstorm, etc., that the policy shall become void in case of the sale or conveyance of the property, or a change in interest or title to the insured property, without the consent of the insurer. 29A Am J Rev ed Ins § 825.

alienation in mortmain. See **mortmain.**

alienation of affections. The actionable wrong committed against a husband by one who wrongfully alienates the affections of his wife, depriving him of his conjugal right to her consortium, that is, her society, affections, and assistance.

In some American jurisdictions, under Married Women's Acts, a wife is given the same cause of action for alienation of affections that a husband had at common law for the wrong stated above. The action, whether by the husband or the wife, has been modified by statute in recent years, and in some jurisdictions, such as New York, the right of action has been abrogated. 27 Am J1st H & W §§ 519 et seq.

See **criminal conversation.**

alienation office. The public office in London where the fees called the primer fine and the post fine were collected from those who employed the procedure of fine and recovery to effect transfers of land titles.

Alienatio rei praefertur juri accrescendi (ā''li-ēn-ā'she-ō rē'ī prē-fer'ter jū'rī ak-kre-sen'dī). The law prefers the alienation of property to the accumulation thereof.

alien declarant. An alien resident of the United States who has declared his intention in the manner provided by law, of becoming a citizen of the United States. Terrace v Thompson, 263 US 197, 68 L Ed 255, 44 S Ct 15; 3 Am J2d Aliens § 147.

aliene. Same as **alien.**

alienee (āl-yen-ē'). One to whom title is transferred.

aliener (āl'yen-ėr). To alienate.

alien friend. A citizen or subject of a nation with which the United States is at peace. 3 Am J2d Aliens § 2.

alienigena (ā-li-e-nī'je-na). An alien.

alieni generis (ā''li-ē'nī jē'ne-ris). Same as **alia generis.**

alieni juris (ā''li-ē'nī jū'ris). Same as **alia juris.**

alien immigrants. Aliens arriving in the United States from foreign countries, whether or not they had been previously domiciled in the United States and had temporarily gone abroad with the intention of returning here. Lapina v Williams, 232 US 78, 86, 58 L Ed 515, 517, 34 S Ct 196.

alienism (āl'yen-izm). Alienage, that is the condition of being an alien; also, the field in which an alienist practices.

alienist (āl'yen-ist). A doctor of medicine who has made mental diseases, those affecting the mind intellectually, and the moral or spiritual faculties, his special study and practice. State v Reidell, 14 Del (9 Houst) 470, 474, 14 A 550. A doctor of medicine qualified by reason of experience, knowledge, and previous opportunities to examine and give his opinion as to the mental condition of a person at a particular time. People v Norton, 138 Cal App 70, 31 P2d 809.

alien né (āl'yen nā). One born an alien.

alien nondeclarant. An alien resident of the United States who has not declared his intention of becoming a citizen, in the manner provided by law. Terrace v Thompson, 263 US 197, 68 L Ed 255, 44 S Ct 15.

alieno loco. Another place.

alienor (āl'yen-or). The grantor in a conveyance, one who alienates, that is, transfers ownership to another.

Alien Property Custodian. An officer, appointed pursuant to the Trading with the Enemy Act of 1917 and amendments thereto, to take custody, at the direction of the President of the United States, of the property, corporeal and incorporeal, of an enemy alien not licensed to retain control of his property. 56 Am J1st War § 85.

Alien Registration Act. A federal statute constituting a part of the comprehensive scheme for the regulation of aliens, requiring the registration and fingerprinting of all aliens in the country, those over 14 years of age on their own application and those under 14 years of age on the application of parent or guardian. 8 USC §§ 1301, 1302; 3 Am J2d Aliens § 112.

alien resident. A person who is a citizen of another country but residing in the United States.

See **expatriate.**

alien's duty. Imposts imposed on alien merchants in England.

alien seamen. Seamen who are aliens, whether serving on foreign or American ships. United States v

New York & Cuba S. S. Co. 269 US 304, 70 L Ed 281, 46 S Ct 114.

alienus (ā-li-ē′nus). Belonging to another; belonging to another country, an alien.

alienus homo (ā-li-ē′nus hō′mō). Another's man, a slave.

alieu (ä-lyuh′). Same as **alleu**.

alighting. The act of a passenger in leaving the conveyance of the carrier. 14 Am J2d Car § 982.

alighting from. A familiar clause in accident insurance policies extending coverage to injuries sustained in accidents occuring in and around motor vehicles. 29A Am J Rev ed Ins § 1247.

alignment. An arrangement in a line; technically, a plan for a highway or railroad.

alii (a′li-ī). Others; other persons.
See **et alii**.

alii e contra. See **et alii e contra**.

aliment (al′i-ment). (French and Scottish law.) Support, supply of necessaries; allowance for support. To support.

alimenta (a-li-men′ta). Items of support and maintenance.

alimented (al′i-men-ted). Having obtained a decree or order for one's support, as in the case of a divorced woman. Edgerton v Edgerton, 12 Mont 122, 29 P 966.

alimentum (al′i-men-tum). Support; alimony.

alimony. An allowance for the support and maintenance of one's spouse, or divorced spouse, made as a substitute for marital support. 24 Am J2d Div & S § 514.
  A suit for support of the complaining spouse is one for alimony even though an absolute divorce is not sought in the action. 27 Am J1st H & W §§ 401-403.
  Although in the usual sense of the term, alimony does not include support of children, there are instances in which a statutory reference to "alimony" has been held to include the support of a child. 17A Am J Rev ed Div & S § 851. An allowance of $150 for the support of a wife and two children is alimony payable to the wife and is not to be construed as an award of $50 to her and $50 to each of the children. Miller v Miller, 74 App DC 216, 122 F2d 209.
  By statute and in some jurisdictions as a matter of equity, alimony is awarded the wife as a successful plaintiff in an action for the annulment of a marriage. 4 Am J2d Annul § 102. In an annulment action, the allowance is of such a sum of money in gross or in instalments as will fairly reasonably compensate a divorced wife for the loss of her support by annulment of the marriage contract. Anno: 20 ALR2d 1412.
  A husband may be entitled to alimony in some jurisdictions, but it is only by force of that statute which clearly provides for an allowance to the husband, that he is entitled to an award. 17 Am J Rev ed Div & S § 574.
  See **permanent alimony; suit money; temporary alimony**.

alimony ad interim (ad in′te-rim). Same as **temporary alimony**.

alimony in general. An award of alimony to be satisfied by periodic payments of a definite sum for the indefinite future. 24 Am J2d Div & S § 614.

alimony in gross. An award of alimony in one definite sum, whether payable in instalments or in one payment. 24 Am J2d Div & S § 614.

alimony pendente lite. See **temporary alimony**.

A l'impossible nŭl n'est tenu (à l'ĭm-po-si′bl nŭl n'ā te′nŭ). No one is bound to perform that which is impossible.

alinement. Same as **alignment**.

alio (a′li-ō). Another form of the Latin **alius**, meaning another, other.

alio intuitu (a′li-ō in-tu′i-tu). From another point of view.

alio loco (a′li-ō lō′kō). In another place.

alios (a′li-ōs). Others.
  See **inter alios**.

alios acta (a′li-ōs ak′ta). Acts or transactions of others.
  See **inter alios acta**.

aliqualiter (a′li-qua′li-ter). In any way.

aliquid (a′li-quid). Something; somewhat.

aliquid conceditur (a′li-quid kon-se′di-ter). Something conceded.

aliquid possessionis et nihil juris (a′li-quid po-ze′′she-ō′nis et ni′hil jū′ris). Somewhat of possession, but nothing of right.

aliquis (a′li-quis). Someone; anyone.

Aliquis non potest esse judex in propria causa (a′li-quis non po′test es′se ju′dex in prō′pri-a kâ′za). One cannot be a judge in his own cause.

aliquot (al′i-kwot). Deriving from the Latin for several, and meaning in modern usage a several part of a larger number, that is, a number which divides a larger number evenly.

alis (al′is). An older Latin form of **alius**.

aliter (a′li-ter). Otherwise.

aliud (a′li-ud). The Latin neuter of **alius**; another thing.

Aliud est possidere, aliud esse in possessione (a′li-ud est pos-si-dē′re, a′li-ud es′se in po-ze′′she-ō′ne). To possess is one thing, to be in possession another.

Aliud est tacere, aliud celare (a′li-ud est ta-sē′re, a′li-ud sē-lā′re). It is one thing to keep silent, another to conceal. Stewart v Wyoming Cattle Ranch Co. 128 US 383, 32 L Ed 439, 9 S Ct 101.

Aliud est vendere, aliud vendenti consentire (a′li-ud est ven′de-re, a′li-ud ven-den′ti kon-sen-tī′re). It is one thing to sell and another to consent to selling or to agree to sell.

aliud examen (a′li-ud ex-ā′men). Another method of trial.

aliunde (ā-li-un′dē). From another place or source; independent of.
  See **evidence aliunde; extrinsic evidence**.

aliunde rule. The rule that a foundation must be laid by testimony aliunde of the misconduct of a juror or jurors before testimony of the jurors themselves will be received to impeach the verdict. 53 Am J1st Trial § 1105.

alius (a′li-us). Another; another person; different.

alive. Having life; existing as a living person.
  Although it is ordinarily said that life begins at birth, once a child is born, the law may look back to the time that he was in the mother's womb for

the purpose of determining his rights. See **in utero matris**.

See words and phrases beginning "live."

all. Sometimes said, where it appears in a statute, to be the most comprehensive word in the language, but said in other cases involving the construction of a statute to be a general, rather than a universal term, to be understood in one sense or another according to the demands of sound reason. 50 Am J1st Stat § 286.

all aboard. A direction to prospective passengers to board a train. Anno: 31 ALR2d 963.

all actions not otherwise provided for. A common provision in limitation statutes which is usually considered to be comprehensive of every form of action, whether real or personal, but held in some jurisdictions not to include special proceedings, probate proceedings, or proceedings for the revocation of licenses. 34 Am J1st Lim Ac § 70.

all-addendum. See **addendum circle**.

all and singular. Each one and all; with no exception.

all cases at law. For the purposes of a guaranty of right to a jury trial, this term means actions and proceedings peculiarly at law, involving predominantly rights and remedies peculiarly legal in character, as distinguished from suits in equity, divorce cases, probate proceedings, admiralty cases, trials by court-martial, special and summary proceedings, whether in regular or special courts, and minor cases in minor courts. 31 Am J Rev ed Jur § 21.

all costs. Including, where the term appears as a condition of an appeal bond, both costs on the appeal and costs in the trial court. 5 Am J2d A & E § 1056.

all damages. The provision in an appeal bond purporting to cover "all damages caused by wrongfully suing out said injunction," the appeal being from an order dissolving an injunction, does not bind the surety for damages sustained in consequence of the injunction being kept in force by the appeal. 5 Am J2d A & E § 1058.

allegans (al'e-ganz). Alleging.

Allegans contraria non est audiendus (al'le-ganz kon-trā'ri-a non est â-di-en'dus). Contradictory statements will not be listened to. Galbraith v Tracy, 153 Ill 54, 38 NE 937.

allegare (al-le-gā're). To allege; to assert.

Allegari non debuit quod probatum non relevat (al-le-gā'rī non de'bu-it quod pro-bā'tum non re'le-vat). Matters which are not relevant, if proved, ought not to be alleged.

allegata (al-lē-gā'ta). Pleaded matters.

allegata et probata (al-le-gā'ta et pro-bā'ta). Matters alleged and matters proved; pleadings and proof.

allegatio contra interpretationem verborum (al-lē-gā'she-ō kon'tra in-ter-pre-tā'she-o'nem ver-bō'rum). An allegation against the meaning of the words.

allegation (al-ē-gā'shon). An assertion; a statement of fact in a pleading; a statement of what one can prove; the positive assertion of a fact. Merrill v Pepperdine, 9 Ind App 416, 36 NE 921.

The technical name for a pleading in an ecclesiastical court.

allegation of faculties. A wife's statement in a divorce case in ecclesiastical court in which the estate of the husband is set forth as a basis for the allowance of alimony. Lovett v Lovett, 11 Ala 763, 771.

allegations upon information and belief. Allegations in an affidavit in the form of statements to the best of the affiant's information and belief, not as of a certainty. 3 Am J2d Affi § 22.

allegatum (al-lē-gā'tum). That which is alleged.

allege (a-lej'). To make an allegation; to state, recite, or charge; to plead.

alleged. Charged; claimed; described; asserted; set forth.

allegiance (a-lē'jans). The obligation of fidelity and obedience which the individual owes to the government under which he lives, or to his sovereign in return for the protection he receives. 30 Am Jur Internat L § 18.

See **oath of allegiance**.

allegiare (al-le-ji-ā're). To defend one's own cause; to justify one's own conduct and position by due course of law.

alleging diminution. The designation on appeal of a diminution or lack of completeness in the record. Hooper v Royster, 15 Va (1 Munf) 119, 130.

alleguer (al-le'ger). To plead.

all elections. A phrase in a constitution or statute, sometimes referring only to elections at which officers are to be elected, at other times to elections at which officers are to be elected or at which propositions, questions, or amendments to the constitution are to be submitted. 25 Am J2d Elect § 2.

Allen charge. The charge in an instruction approved in Allen v United States, 164 US 492, 41 L Ed 528, 17 S Ct 154, that the jurors should examine the questions submitted with candor and with a proper regard and deference to the opinions of each other.

Allen v. Flood. A celebrated English case decided in 1898, and frequently cited as laying down the rule that the malicious exercise of a definite legal right is not actionable although it results in damage to another person. [1898] A. C. 1.

aller (äl-lā). (French.) To go.

aller a dieu (äl-lā a diē). A term of dismissal.

aller a large (äl-lā'). To go at large.

aller al eau (al-lā'al ū). Let him go to the water.
See **hot-water ordeal**.

allergy. Sensitivity of a person in an usually high degree to certain foods, medicines, or particular elements thereof, pollens, or other minute particles carried by the air, reacting with disagreeable, even disastrous consequences.

aller sans jour (äl-lā' sanz jör). To go without day; to adjourn without day. See **adjournment sine die**.

alleu (äl-luh'). An allodial estate.

all events test. The test for determining the year in which an item of deduction for income tax purposes accrues, under which a tax is held to accrue when all events have occurred which fix the amount of the tax and determines the liability of the taxpayer to pay it. United States v Consolidated Edison Co. 366 US 380, 6 L Ed 2d 356, 81 S Ct 1326.

alleviare (al-lē-vi-ā're). To redeem by the payment of a fine.

alley (al'ĭ). A narrow way in a town or city for the convenience of the owner of property abutting thereon and of the persons who visit him. 25 Am

J1st High § 8. At times, a highway. Chicago Motor Coach Co. v Chicago, 337 Ill 200, 169 NE 22, 66 ALR 834. At other times, a private way.
See **bowling alley**; **private alley**.

alleynour (äl-lā-noor'). Same as **eloigner**.

alleyway (al'i-wā). Same as **alley**.

all faults. Disclaimer of warranty by making sale with "all faults."

all fours. See **on all fours**.

alliance (a-lī'ans). A banding together; a confederacy; an association between nations, such as The Triple Entente and the Triple Alliance, both being between European nations, which existed prior to World War I.
Alliances between families are created by intermarriages.

allies. Nations engaged on the same side in a war. Persons united in the pursuit of a purpose or undertaking.

allieu. Same as **alleu**.

alligner (äl-lē'nyā). Same as **alloigner**.

all inheritance taxes. Including succession and legacy taxes, as well as inheritance taxes in the narrow sense, where the term appears in a direction in a will for payment of taxes. Anno: 37 ALR2d 85.

allision (a-lizh'on). The running of one vessel into another vessel which is not under way; technically, to be distinguished from a collision between vessels, both of which are under way.

all matters in difference. Appearing in an arbitration agreement, the phrase refers to nothing beyond matters in relation to the subject referred for arbitration. Hemingway v Stansell, 106 US 399, 27 L Ed 245, 1 S Ct 473.

all my money. A comprehensive term standing alone, which may be tempered where it appears in a will by other testamentary language.
So the results upon the question whether it includes bank deposits, where it appears in a will, are conflicting. 57 Am J1st Wills § 1354.
See **ally**.

all my property. A very comprehensive term in a will which is construed in the absence of contrary context to include after-acquired property. 57 Am J1st Wills § 1213.
A bequest in such a form is general rather than specific. 57 Am J1st Wills § 1409.

all my worldly goods. A very comprehensive term of bequest which has been construed at times to include real property. Farish v Cook, 78 Mo 212.

alloc. An abbreviation of allocatur.

allocable (al'ō-kābl). Distributable. In analyzing accounts, the breaking down of a lump sum charged or credited to one account into several parts to be charged or credited to other accounts. Fleming v Commissioner (CA5) 121 F2d 7.

allocare (al-lō-kā're). To allow.

allocate (al'ō-kāt). To allow an appropriate proportion; to apportion; to assign; to allot.

allocatio (al-lō-kā'she-o). An allocation.

allocation (al-ō-kā'shon). An allowance upon an account in the English exchequer; in more familiar modern usage, an allotment.

allocatione facienda (al-lō-kā-she-ō'ne fa-she-en'da).
A writ by which an accountant secured an allowance due him from the English exchequer.

allocato comitatu (al-lō-kā'tō ko-mi-tā'tu). An old writ used in outlawry proceedings.

allocatur (al-ō-kā'tėr). Let it be allowed,—an order of a court or judge, allowing or granting something; as, an allocatur allowing a writ of certiorari. State v Vanderveer, 7 NJL 38.

allocatur exigent (al-ō-kā'tėr). A writ issued in the process of outlawry.

allocution (al-ō-kū'shon). The traditional formal inquiry under the common law, which exists by force of statute in American jurisdictions with some variations, to be directed by the court to one convicted of a felony before sentence:—whether the one convicted has anything to say why sentence should not be pronounced against him. 21 Am J2d Crim L § 530. The reason given for the importance attached to this form in England is, that the appellate court may see that the prisoner had an opportunity of moving in arrest, or of pleading a pardon. State v Ball, 27 Mo 324, 326.

allod (al'od). Same as **allodium**.

allodia (al-lō'di-a). Free lands, that is, lands not held in subordination to a feudal lord.

allodial (a-lō'di-al). The tenure of an estate by an owner in fee simple under the state as sovereign, as opposed to feudal tenure. The dominion is absolute and direct, subject only to escheat in the event of failure of successors in ownership. Allodial tenure is characteristic of the ownership of land in the United States. 28 Am J2d Est § 4.

allodium (a-lō'di-um). An allodial estate; an estate not held under a superior.

allograph (al'ō-gråf). A signature or other writing made for one person by another person; contrasting with authograph.

alloign. Same as **eloigne**.

allonge (a-lunj). A paper attached to a bill or note, or so firmly affixed, as to be a part thereof, upon which an indorsement of the instrument is written. 11 Am J2d B & N § 353.

allopathic practice. The old school and still the most prominent branch of the practice of medicine. The term distinguishes physicians of this school from homeopaths, osteopaths, eclectics, and chiropractors. Bradbury v Bardin, 34 Conn 452; 41 Am Jur Phys & S § 85.

allot (a-lot'). To make an allotment.

all other cases not expressly provided for. A common provision in limitation statutes which is usually deemed comprehensive of every action or proceeding in a court of justice wherein a contested question may arise, but sometimes limited to actions as distinguished from special proceedings. 34 Am J1st Lim Ac § 70.

all others not otherwise herein provided for. Not otherwise provided for in the statute of which the words are a part. 21 Am J2d Cust D § 38.

allotment (a-lot'ment). A division; a distribution.
See **Indian allotments**.

allotment certificate. A certificate issued to an applicant for shares in a corporation stating the number of shares allotted to him and the due dates and amounts of payments required of him.

allotment note. A written order drawn by a seaman upon his employer, accepted by the latter, and directing the payment of the seaman's wages in sums, to persons, and at times, specified in the order.

allotment of goods. The assignment by lot of the share of a ship's cargo which each purchaser is to buy.

allotment system. That system or practice under which lands are by treaty allotted to Indian tribes for use as hunting grounds and other purposes. The word allotted is not to be construed or understood in the sense of being parcelled out to the Indians as a favor, but rather in the sense of acknowledging their right to have the lands thus set out to them. Worcester v State of Georgia (US) 6 Pet 582, 8 L Ed 508.

allotment ticket. Same as **allotment note.**

allottee (al-o-tē'). One to whom an allotment is made.

allouer (a-lū'ā). (French law.) To allow; to grant.

allow. To approve, as to allow a cost bill or claim; to permit or acquiesce in; as to allow animals to run at large. 4 Am J2d Ani § 116.
  The words "allowed," "acquiesced," and "permitted" imply no inducement or enticement, and should be construed as creating a license. See Karns v Trostel, 44 Ohio App 488, 186 NE 405.

allowance. A word of broad and various meanings, ranging from the amount ordered paid to a successful litigant in addition to the stated costs, because of extraordinary difficulty in the litigation, to the amount paid by a parent to a child per week as an encouragement to good conduct and the promotion of thrift in the child. Something granted, as in the rendition of judgment. The recognition of a deduction or an exemption in the assessment of a tax. Virginia Hotel Corp. v Helvering, 319 US 523, 87 L Ed 1561, 63 S Ct 1260, 152 ALR 871.
  As used typically with respect to the armed forces and veterans, the word refers to benefits of one kind or another in addition to regular pay, such as subsistence, quarters, uniforms, and pensions. Walker v United States, 86 App DC 93, 180 F2d 194, 16 ALR2d 1328.

allowance of alimony. See **alimony; temporary alimony.**

allowance of owelty. See **owelty.**

allowance pendente lite. An order for payment or distribution made prior to the termination of litigation, such as an order for temporary alimony or an order for payment of the income from the sum constituting the res in the proceeding, or even a division of a part of the res itself, where it is apparent that enforcement of the judgment or order ultimately rendered will not be jeopardized by such an allowance.

allowance to member of armed forces. A benefit of one kind or another in addition to regular pay, such as subsistence, quarters, uniforms, and pensions. Waller v United States, 86 App DC 93, 180 F2d 194, 16 ALR2d 1328.
  It is sometimes in the nature of compensation, sometimes akin to reimbursement, but may at other times be entirely unearned; it is affirmative in nature and has no similarity to a statutory exemption. Waller v United States, supra.

allowance to widow. See **widow's allowance.**

allowed by law. See **fixed by law.**

alloy (a-loi'). An inferior or cheaper metal mixed with another in the coinage of money.

alloynour (äl-luä'noor). Same as **eloigner.**

all prior indorsements guaranteed. A phrase customarily added to the indorsement of the collecting bank.
  It is questionable whether the phrase adds anything to the liability of the bank as an indorser. Some authorities limit its meaning to the fact that the payee named actually indorsed the instrument. 11 Am J2d B & N §§ 616, 624.

all property of mortgagor. A term used in defining the property covered by a chattel mortgage, which is sufficient as a description, if accompanied by a designation of the location of the property. 15 Am J2d Chat Mtg § 56.

all-pul mill (âl pul mil). A steel rolling mill where the strip is pulled through the rolls and where if the pulling stopped, the power exerted on the strip by the rolls alone would not be sufficient to move the strip through. Cold Metal Process Co. v McLouth Steel Corporation (D. C. Mich.) 41 F Supp 487.

all right, title, and interest. Words in a conveyance operative to express whatever title the grantor has, whether an entirety of ownership or an undivided interest. 23 Am J2d Deeds § 289.
  "All the right, title, and interest" of a grantor pass under a deed granting the same, even though the phrase is followed by the expression "the same being one half undivided interest in and to the described property," because the words last quoted do not limit the extent of the previous term of conveyance or except out any interest conveyed by such previous term. 23 Am J2d Deeds § 197.
  An assignment of patent rights in such terms of designation of the subject matter does not, in the absence of an express agreement or of special circumstances from which a warranty may be implied, carry with it a warranty of validity of the patent. 40 Am J1st Pat § 133.
  A court may not read exceptions into a law referring to "all rights." Wailes v Curators of Cent. College, 363 Mo 932, 254 SW2d 645, 37 ALR2d 326.

All Saints Day. November 1st, when an annual festival honoring all the saints is celebrated.

all taxes. An expression comprehensive in form, but to be construed in connection with the context in which it appears. Anno: 37 ALR2d 88 et seq.
  An exemption from "all taxation," has been held inapplicable to an inheritance, succession, or estate tax. Anno: 47 ALR2d 1003-1005.

all that remains. Such term in a residuary bequest of the subject matter of the bequest is presumptive of an intention of the testator that lapsed legacies and devises shall pass under the residuary bequest. 57 Am J1st Wills § 1449.

all the green, pine timber. A sufficient description of the timber, in a deed of growing timber, where the location upon land is designated. 34 Am J1st Logs § 29.

all the members. A provision of the constitution of a religious society that its affairs shall be managed by the whole congregation, that is, "all the members," does not require the assent of each member to action taken; those members who do not attend a meeting or, if attending, do not vote, must be understood to be willing to be bound by the action taken by the members who do attend and vote. 45 Am J1st Reli Soc § 22.

all the real estate. An apt descriptive phrase in a deed where connected with the grantor, e.g. "all the real estate of the grantor in" etc. Anno: 55 ALR 162.

all the rest, residue, and remainder. See **residuary clause.**

all the timber and growth of timber. A sufficient description of the timber, in a deed of growing timber, where location upon the land is specified. 34 Am J1st Logs § 29.

all title and interest. See **all right, title, and interest.**

allure. See **inveigle.**

allurement. An enticement; an attraction which, as in the case of an attractive nuisance, may constitute in law an implied invitation to a child to enter upon the premises. See 38 Am J1st Negl § 144.

allusion (a-lū′zhọn). A passing, casual, slight or incidental reference; a hint; a suggestion; an insinuation. Atchison, T. & S. F. Ry. Co. v Vanordstrand, 67 Kan 386, 73 P 113.

alluvio (ạ-lū′vi-ō). Alluvion.

alluvio maris (al-lū′vi-ō ma′ris). Alluvion from the sea.

alluvion (ạ-lū′vi-ọn). The solid material which is added to land by accretion, that is, by the gradual deposit of such material by water.
Accretion denotes the gradual process which makes the deposit, while alluvion is the term applied to the deposit itself. 56 Am J1st Wat § 476. That which is added to a man's land by alluvion, belongs to him. St. Louis, I. M. & S. Ry. Co. v Ramsey, 53 Ark 314, 56 Am J1st Wat § 477. Conversely, that which is washed or worn away by the gradual process of alluvion is lost to the owner of the washed or worn parcel or tract. 56 Am J1st Wat § 477.

ally (a-lī). Verb: To associate with another person for a common purpose; to make a treaty with another nation calling for joinder in an enterprise or in defense against a common enemy. Noun: A person with whom one is associated for a common purpose; a nation with which another nation has by compact or treaty agreed to act. A nation which has joined with the United States in waging a war against another nation or nations.

ally of enemy. As it appears in the Trading with the Enemy Act, the term means nonresidents of the United States who are subjects of an enemy country. 3 Am J2d Aliens § 190.

alm (älm). Old English for soul, apparently a contraction of the Latin anima.
See **alms.**

almanac. A compilation of useful data, including a calendar of days, months, and years, astronomical events, weather predictions, geographical, political, governmental, and social facts, and a variety of other useful information. The term is also used for the appendix to the common service book of a church in which the days upon which Sundays or feast days fall are noted in a convenient and readable form.

alme (al′me). Same as **alm.**

almesfeoh. See **Peter's pence.**

almner (äm′ner). Same as **almoner.**

almoign (al-moin′). Alms.

almoigne. Same as **almoign.**

almoin (al-moin′). Same as **almoign.**

almoin tenure (al-moin′ ten′ūr). Same as **frankalmoigne.**

almoner (al′mọn-ėr). An officer charged with the duty of distributing alms.
See **overseers of the power.**

almost wholly of. A tariff statute term meaning that the essential character of the article is imparted by the named material, notwithstanding significant quantities of other material may be present. 21 Am J2d Cust, D etc. § 33.

alms (ämz). Donations to relieve the poor.
See **alm.**

alms fee. Same as **Peter's pence.**

almshouse (ämz′hous). A house provided by a city, town, or county for the reception and support of the poor; a house appropriated for the poor. Association for Colored Orphans v City of New York, 104 NY 581, 12 NE 279, 281.
See **county farm.**

alnage (al′nāj). Ell-measure; a duty on woolen cloth.

alnager (al′nę̄-jėr). An officer who measured woolen cloth and collected the duties thereon.

alnetum (al-nē′tum). An alder grove.

aloarius (a-lo-ā′ri-us). The holder of an allodium.

alod (a′lōd). Same as **allodium.**

alodarius (a-lō-da′ri-us). Same as **aloarius.**

alode (a′lōd). Same as **allodium.**

alodes (a-lō′dēz). Same as **allodium.**

alodial (a-lō′di-al). Same as **allodium.**

alodiarius (a-lō-di-ā′ri-us). Same as **aloarius.**

alodium (a-lō′di-um). Same as **allodum.**

alodum (a′lō-dum). Same as **allodium.**

alone. By one's self; sole.

along a highway. A phrase of frequent appearance in descriptions of real estate.
In the absence of other words or language in a conveyance which indicate a contrary intent, a description of the subject matter of the deed as "along" a highway is sufficient to fix the boundary at the center line of the highway. 12 Am J2d Bound § 51.

alongside (ạ-lông′sīd). A nautical term, common in charter-parties, meaning that the charterer is to bring the cargo as near the ship as practicable.

along the bank. See **along the shore.**

along the shore. A designation in the description of a boundary line which usually has the effect of excluding the stream itself from the tract bounded. 12 Am J2d Bound § 26.

A.L.P. Abbreviation of **American Labor Party.**

ALR. Abbreviation of **American Law Reports.**

ALR2d. Abbreviation of American Law Reports, Second Series.
See **American Law Reports.**

ALR3d. Abbreviation of American Law Reports, Third Series.
See **American Law Reports.**

already. By or before a time stated or implied. Messick v Powell, 314 Ky 805, 236 SW2d 897, 27 ALR2d 1341.

als. An abbreviation of **alius**, another, and **alios**, others.
See **et als.**

also. In addition; this too.

alt. An abbreviation of **alter**.

alta proditio (al'ta pro-di'she-ō). High treason.

altar. A raised platform or table used in religious services, especially in the portrayal of sacraments.

altarage (âl'tăr-ăj). The profits of a priest.

altaragium (al-ta-rā'ji-um). Same as **altarage**.

altar boy. A boy who assists the priest in a church service, especially at mass.
See **acolyte**.

alta via (al'ta vī'a). A highway.

alta via regia (al'tā vī'a rē'ji-a). The king's highway.

alta via regina (al'tā vī'a rē ji'na). The queen's highway.

altenheim (al'ten-hīm). The word is a German one, and means a home for old people. German Pioneer Verein v Meyer, 70 NJ Eq 192, 193, 63 A 835.

alter (âl'tėr). Noun: Other; another; the other party. Verb: To change in some respect. Sessions v State, 115 Ga 18, 20, 41 SE 259. To make different, as in changing an assessment. Adams v Shelbyville, 154 Ind 467, 57 NE 114.
The word, when applied to numbers, may well include "to increase," or "to diminish," for an increase or a diminution is certainly a change. See People v Sassovich, 29 Cal 480.
See **alteration**.

alteram partem. See **audi alteram partem**.

altera parte. See **ex altera parte**.

alteration. A change of a thing from one form or state to another—that is, making a thing different from what it was, but without destroying its identity. 4 Am J2d Alt of Inst § 1.
The term "alterations" in a lease, which expressly prohibits alterations to be made by the tenant in the buildings demised, means a substantial change; boring a small hole in a wall to permit the passage of electrical wires is not a change within the meaning of the prohibition. 32 Am J1st L & T § 208.

alteration of brand. Changing, defacing, or obliterating the brand on an animal, a criminal offense in states in the large cattle-raising areas of the country. 4 Am J2d Ani § 8.
The statutory offense of changing the brand or mark on an animal to a different brand or mark from what it was before. It is held that altering is to be distinguished from "defacing," which is the obliteration of the mark or brand, and that putting an additional brand to the one already on the animal is an alteration, although the latter brand may not interfere with or change the figure of the first one. Linney v State, 6 Tex 1.

alteration of contract. A modification of the terms of a contract with the assent of both parties, in effect a new contract to be supported by a good consideration, except as consideration is made unnecessary by the circumstances of the case. 17 Am J2d Cont § 465.
To alter or amend a contract is to change it as between the original parties and such others only, as have been permitted, by the mutual consent of the parties, to come into the enjoyment of its benefits and privileges; not to compel one of the parties to operate in conjunction with others, and share with them the privileges and benefits of the contract. Sage v Dillard, 54 Ky (15 B Mon) 340, 360.

alteration of highway. Widening or narrowing the way or effecting a change of location or route. 25 Am J1st High §§ 106, 107. To be distinguished from a discontinuance whereby a highway is abolished altogether. 25 Am J1st High § 127.

alteration of instrument. A change in the sense or language of the instrument effected by an intentional act performed on the instrument by a party entitled to the instrument.
In the legal sense of the term "alteration of instrument" it does not include an act performed on the instrument by a stranger thereof. 4 Am J2d Alt of Inst § 1.
In order to constitute a forgery, an alteration must be such as to make the instrument speak a language different in legal effect from that which it originally spoke, or which carries with it some change in the rights, interest, or obligations of the parties to the writing. 23 Am J2d 683 Forg § 16.
As to what constitutes an alteration of a will, see Anno: 34 ALR2d 626.
See **erasure**; **obliteration**; **spoilation**.

altercation (al-tėr-kā'shọn). A civil law term for trial by examination of witnesses; in English, a controversy, dispute, or quarrel waged in anger.

alter ego (al'tėr ē'gȯ). Literally, the other I, the other self.
For example, during the voyage of a ship, the shipmaster is said to be the alter ego of his principal. See 47 L Ed 773.

alter ego doctrine. Disregarding the corporate entity in furtherance of the ends of justice and treating the corporation and the individual or individuals owning all the stock and assets of the corporation as identical. 18 Am J2d Corp § 14.

alterfoits (äl'tėr-fwä). Same as **autrefois**.

alter-idem (al'tėr-ī'dem). Another the same; a counterpart.

altering. See **alteration**.

alternat (âl-tėr-nat). Rotation, as of the signatures of envoys to copies of a treaty.

alternate. A person appointed to substitute for another in a political convention. State v Young, 160 Mo 320, 323, 60 SW 1086.

alternate juror. An extra trial juror selected to attend the trial and to take the place of any one of the jury in case of the latter's illness or other disability during the trial. 31 Am J1st Jury § 128.

alternate valuation method. The valuation of the gross estate of a decedent for estate tax purposes as of a date other than that of his death, usually one year after the date of his death. IRC § 2032(c).

alternatim (al-ter-nā'tim). Interchangeably.

alternating custody. A division of the custody of a child between divorced parents. 24 Am J2d Div & S § 799.

alternative. The choice of one of two things, courses, or propositions which is excluded by the choice of the other. Malone v Meres, (Fla) 109 So 677, 693.

alternative allegations. See **disjunctive allegations**.

alternative contract. A contract which by its terms may be performed by doing either of several acts at the election of the party from whom performance is due. Crane v Peer, 43 NJ Eq 553, 563, 4 A 72, 17 Am J2d Contr § 363.

alternative damages. Contractual provision permitting choice as between stipulated damages and an assessment. 22 Am J2d Damg § 233.

alternative judgment. A judgment which gives an election to the party against whom rendered in respect of the obligation imposed upon and to be satisfied by him. Such a judgment is usually deemed void for want of certainty in determination of rights of the parties. 30A Am J1st Judgm § 57. A true and valid alternative judgment is provided by statutes for replevin actions, the provision being for a judgment in the alternative for the possession of the property or the value thereof. 46 Am J1st Replev § 122.

alternative owners. See **alternative payees; alternative remainders.**

alternative payees. Two or more persons designated in the alternative as payees of a bill of exchange, a promissory note, or United States Savings Bond. 11 Am J2d B & N § 117.

alternative punishment. Fine or imprisonment, not both. 21 Am J2d Crim L § 536. See **alternative sentence.**

alternative relief. See **prayer for alternative relief.**

alternative remainders. A limitation of more than one estate in remainder after a single precedent estate but under such terms that one takes effect only as the other one does not. 28 Am J2d Est § 216.

alternative remedy. A choice of remedy left open by statute where a new remedy is created by statute without supplanting a remedy previously existing.

alternative sentence. A sentence giving the defendant a choice, such as one in a traffic case giving an option to purchase a liability policy or to have license suspended; such a sentence is void for uncertainty. 21 Am J2d Crim L § 541. See **indeterminate sentence.**

alternative will. One of two different wills which on the happening of a contingency provided by the testator, is the one which is to come into force as his last will and testament. 57 Am J1st Wills, § 671.

alternative writ. See **alternative writ of mandamus; praecipe.**

alternative writ of mandamus. A writ, issued by the court in the beginning of a mandamus proceeding under older practice, which corresponds to a common-law declaration or to a complaint or petition in an ordinary action and usually deemed to be the first pleading in the cause.

In it all the material facts on which the relator relies must be distinctly set forth, so that they may be admitted or traversed, and by the writ the defendant is called on to perform the particular act sought to be enforced, or, by a return, to deny the facts alleged therein, or to state other matters sufficient to defeat the relator's application. 35 Am J1st Mand § 348.

The more modern practice makes use of an order to show cause, permitting this to be in the alternative of performing the act sought to be commanded or showing cause why it should not be commanded. 35 Am J1st Mand § 347.

alternative writ of quo warranto. A writ used in the commencement of an action in quo warranto under the older practice, one of little use in the modern practice. 44 Am J1st Quo Warranto § 70.

alternis vicibus (al-ter′nis vī′si-bus). Alternately.

alterum non laedere (al′te-rum non lē′-de-re). Not to injure another.

alteruter (al-ter-u′ter). One of two.

alteruter et quilibet (al-ter-u′ter et quī′li-bet). Each and every.

altius non tollendi (al′ti-us non tol-len′dī). (Civil law.) An easement restraining the height of one's buildings.

altius tollendi (al′ti-us tol-len′dī). (Civil law.) An easement by which the height of one's buildings was unlimited.

alto et basso (al′tō et bäs′sō). High and low; the whole matter.
See **de alto et basso.**

altum mare (al′tum ma′re). The high sea.

altus (al′tus). High; deep.

aluminum (a-lū′mi-num). A pliable metal which resists corrosion. As a commercial article, aluminum made from an ore called bauxite is little more than seventy-five years (in 1966) of age in the United States. There are also other ores in the United States from which aluminum can be made. Alunite which exists in Utah is one of them. It is said to exist elsewhere in this country. Leucite is another ore from which aluminum can be made. By a more expensive process experts say that aluminum can be made of common clay. United States v Aluminum Co. of America (DC NY) 44 F. Supp. 97.

alumna. A female graduate of a school, college, or other institution of learning.

alumnus. A male graduate of a school, college, or other institution of learning.

alunite. See **aluminum.**

a luy et a ses heires a touts jours (ä lu-ē′ä ä säz ärs ä tö jörs). To him and to his heirs forever.

alveus (al′vē-us). The bed of a stream or river.

alveus derelictus (al′vē-us de-re-lik′tus). (Roman law.) The bed of a stream which has dried up. The owners of the adjacent lands on such a stream divided the old bed of the stream, as in the case of a newly arisen island. See § 274 Dropsie's Mackeldey's Roman Law.

alyener (äl-i-ā′nä). Same as **alloigner.**

a. m. An abbreviation of "ante meridiem," before noon.

a majori ad minus (ä mä-jō′rī ad mī′nus). From the greater to the less. See **argumentum a majori ad minus.**

amalgamation. See **consolidation.**

Amalphitan Code. A compilation of marine laws of countries surrounding the Mediterranean Sea, made in the eleventh century, A. D.

a manendo (ä ma-nen′dō). From remaining.

amanuensis (a-man-ū-en′sis). One who copies a written document; one who writes a document from dictation; one who signs the name of another person who is present in the same room, at the direction of the latter. White Eagle Laundry Co. v Slowek, 296 Ill 240, 129 NE 753.

ambactus (am-bak'tus). A vassal; a client.

ambages (am-bā'jēz). Evasions.

ambassador. An envoy; a diplomatic representative of the highest rank.
The words "ambassadors and other public ministers" describe a class existing by the law of nations, and apply to diplomatic agents, whether accredited by the United States to a foreign power or by a foreign power to the United States, and the words are so used in section 2 of art. II and in section 2 of art. III of the United States Constitution. These agents may be called ambassadors, envoys, ministers, commissioners, chargés d'affaires, agents, or otherwise, but they possess in substance the same functions, rights and privileges as agents of their respective governments for the transaction of its diplomatic business abroad. Their designations are chiefly significant in the relation of rank, precedence or dignity. See Ex parte Baiz, 135 US 403, 34 L Ed 222, 10 S Ct 854.

amber (am'bėr). An old English measure equal to four bushels. A fossil resin substance which is easily polished.

ambidexter (am-bi-deks'tėr). An attorney who has received compensation from both sides; a bribed juror.

ambiguitas (am-bi-gu'i-tās). Ambiguity.

Ambiguitas contra stipulatorem est (am-bi-gu'i-tās kon'tra sti-pu-lā-tō'rem est). An ambiguity is resolved against the stipulator.

ambiguitas latens (am-bi-gu'i-tās lā'tenz). A **latent ambiguity.**

ambiguitas patens (am-bi-gu'i-tās pā'tēnz). A **patent ambiguity.**

ambiguity. Doubtfulness or uncertainty, especially in the meaning of language arising from its admitting of more than one meaning; duplicity in meaning. Kraney v Halsey, 82 Cal 209, 22 P 1137.
A word or phrase is "ambiguous" within the meaning of the parol evidence rule only when it is of uncertain meaning and may be fairly understood in more ways than one. 30 Am J2d Ev § 1069.
See **latent ambiguity**; **patent ambiguity**.

ambiguity on the factum. An ambiguity, not upon the construction, as whether a particular clause shall have a particular effect, but an ambiguity as to the foundation of the instrument, or a particular part of it, for example, whether a testator meant a particular clause to be part of the instrument, or whether it was introduced with his knowledge, or, again, whether a codicil was meant to republish a former or a subsequent will, or whether the residuary clause, or any other passage, was accidentally omitted. 57 Am J1st Wills § 873.

ambiguus (am-bi'gu-us). Ambiguous.

ambit (am'bit). An enclosing line or limit; a boundary line.

ambitus (am'bi-tus). A going around; an illegal canvassing for office; bribery. In the Roman law, the word signified the practice of trading in government offices.

amblotic (am-blot'ik). An abortifacient; something used to produce an abortion.

ambodexter (am-bō-deks'tėr). Same as **ambidexter.**

ambulance chaser. A derogatory term applied to an attorney at law who solicits business, particularly accident cases. 7 Am J2d Attys § 42.

ambulatoria (am-bu-la-tō'ri-a). Ambulatory; revocable.

ambulatoria est voluntas defuncti usque ad vitae supremum exitum (am-bu-la-tō'ri-a est vo-lun'tas de-funk'tī us'kwe ad vī'tē su-prē'mum ex-i'tum). A will is revocable until the last moment.

ambulatory. Mutable; capable of alteration; not fixed.
A will, being ambulatory, confers no right at the time of its execution, and nothing vests thereunder during the life of the testator. Until the death of the testator it is revocable. 57 Am J1st Wills § 15.

ambulatory jurisdiction. A jurisdiction which is transitory, having no fixed situs. State v Carter, 27 NJL 499.

ambush. Noun: 1st, the act of attacking an enemy unexpectedly from a concealed station; 2nd, a concealed station, where troops or enemies lie in wait to attack by surprise; an ambuscade; 3rd, troops posted in a concealed place for attacking by surprise. Verb: To lie in wait; to surprise; to place in ambush. Darneal v State, 14 Okla Crim 540, 1 ALR 638, 641, 174 P 290.

Am. Dec. An abbreviation of **American Decisions.**

ameasurement. Same as **admeasurement.**

ameliorating waste. See **meliorating waste.**

ameliorations. Betterments; improvements.

amenable (a-mē'na-bl). Obedient; responsible; answerable; liable to be called to account. Miller v Commonwealth, 62 Ky (1 Duv) 14, 17.
See **obedient.**

amend. To improve; to make better by change or modification. Sessions v State, 115 Ga 18, 20, 41 SE 259.

amendable. That which is not so defective that the law will not permit it to be amended.

amendable process. Process which is defective but amendable; voidable rather than void, that is, process which, although defective, will support a judgment, once the defect is remedied. 42 Am J1st Proc § 20.

amendatory statute. One which amends an existing statute; not to be confused with a statute which repeals an existing statute.
See **amendment of statute.**

amended pleading. See **amendment of pleading.**

amended statute. See **amendment of statute.**

amende honorable (a-mond' o-no-ra-bl'). An apology; also disgrace or infamy imposed by way of punishment, such as appearing in public with hair sprinkled with ashes.

amender (a-men'dėr). To amend.

amendment. A correction or revision of a writing to correct errors or better to state its intended purpose.
See **modification.**

amendment as of course. An amendment of a pleading made within such time, and in such compliance with conditions imposed by statute or rule of court, that leave of court is unnecessary. 41 Am J1st Pl § 289.

amendment by compulsion. An amendment of a pleading compelled by the court where the original pleading is so framed as to prejudice, embarrass, or delay the trial of the action. 41 Am J1st Pl § 290.

AMENDMENT / AMERICAN

amendment of constitution. A process of proposing, passing, and ratifying amendments to the United States Constitution or a state constitution.

amendment of income tax return. Filling omissions and correcting inaccuracies in a return which evinces an honest and genuine endeavor to satisfy the law. Zellerback Paper Co. v Helvering, 293 US 172, 79 L Ed 264, 55 S Ct 127.

amendment of judgment. See **modification of judgment.**

amendment of pleading. Correcting errors and omissions in a pleading, changing and supplying allegations, so that the case, so far as possible, may be determined on its real facts. 41 Am J1st Pl § 288.

See **amendment as of course; amendment by compulsion; amendment on court's own motion; amendment to conform to proofs; departure in amended pleading.**

amendment of statute. An alteration or change in an existing statute to make it more complete or perfect, or to fit it better to accomplish the object or purpose for which it was enacted, without disturbing the general framework of the statute. 50 Am J1st Stat § 3. The process of proposing and enacting a statute which effects a change or alteration of a prior act, and, if need be, the obtaining of a successful test of the change or alteration upon submission to the people through referendum.

A constitutional provision, that no bill shall be so altered or amended on its passage through either house as to change its original purpose, prohibits only changes during its passage through the legislature, and does not refer to earlier or later statutes. Anno: 158 ALR 423.

amendment on court's own motion. An amendment of a pleading permitted or required by the court without application made therefor. 41 Am J1st Pl § 290.

amendment to conform to proof. An amendment of a pleading permitted where the evidence introduced on trial was not admissible under the pleading in its original form and the amendment does not substantially change the cause of action or defense, sometimes known as an amendment to prevent a variance. 41 Am J1st Pl § 309.

amends (a-mendz'). Satisfaction for an injury. See **damages.**

amenity (a-men'i-ti). Something on the attractive, pleasant or desirable side of life. As a legal term in particular, the location, view, access to water courses or lakes, etc. which add to the desirability of a tract of real estate. A negative easement. Chapman v Sheridan-Wyoming Coal Co. 338 US 621, 94 L Ed 393, 70 S Ct 492.

amens (ā'menz). A person with no mind; an idiot.

a mensa et thoro (ā men'sa̧ et thō'rō). From bed and board.

See **divorce a mensa et thoro.**

amensuratio (a-mĕn-sū-rā'she-ō). Same as **admeasurement.**

amerce (a̧-mĕrs'). To fine or impose a penalty.

amercement (a̧-mĕrs'ment). A money penalty in the nature of a fine imposed by statute upon a sheriff or like officer for misconduct or neglect of duty, the object of the statute being to insure promptness and fidelity to duty and to furnish the plaintiff an opportunity to collect in a speedy manner his debt, damages, and costs. 47 Am J1st Sher § 187. A pecuniary penalty prescribed by a court as a punishment for a public offense.

See 4 Bl Comm 379. A fine imposed by the court upon an unsuccessful plaintiff for making a false claim. See 3 Bl Comm 376.

amerciament (a̧-mĕr'si-a̧-ment). Same as **amercement.**

amerciamenta hominum (a-mer-she-ā-men'ta ho'minum). An unusual franchise whereby a lord whose men had been amerced in the king's court could petition to have the amercements paid out of the exchequer to him.

amerciamentum (a-mer-she-ā-men'tum). Same as **amercement.**

American. Of the western hemisphere or, more particularly, the United States.

American Airlines. A trade name subject to misuse in unfair methods of competition. American Airlines v North American Air Lines, 351 US 79, 100 L Ed 953, 76 S Ct 600.

American and English Annotated Cases. A set of reports of cases with annotations, abbreviated "Ann. Cas."

See **annotation.**

American Arbitration Association. A nonprofit organization maintaining panels of qualified arbitrators and providing administrative services for the arbitration of both commercial and labor disputes.

American Bar Association. See **bar association.**

American clause. Double insurance clause in marine policies. 29A Am J1st Ins § 1563.

American Decisions. An older set of reports of leading cases with annotations, abbreviated "Am. Dec."

American Empire. The whole of the United States, composed of states and territories. Downes v Bidwell, 182 US 244, 261, 45 L Ed 1088, 1096, 21 S Ct 770.

American experience tables. See **mortality tables.**

American Federation of Labor. An affiliation of labor unions, now combined with the former Congress of Industrial Organizations under the abbreviated heading AF of L-CIO.

American Gold Star Mothers. See **Gold Star Mothers.**

American Indians. See **Indians.**

American Jurisprudence. A comprehensive and authoritative modern text statement of American law, state and federal, procedural as well as substantive, under approximately four-hundred-fifty titles, arranged alphabetically, now in part in a second edition, with work continuing on the remaining volumes; known to bench and bar under the familiar abbreviations "Am. Jur." and "Am. J2d."

American Labor Party. A political party organized in 1936, the activities of which were confined to the state of New York.

American Law Institute. An organization of an eleemosynary nature, its primary activity being the clarification of common-law principles, and its most celebrated projects The Restatement of the Law, and the Uniform Commercial Code prepared jointly with the National Conference of Commissioners on Uniform State Laws.

American Law Reports. Reports of selected leading cases decided by state and federal appellate courts, cited under the familiar abbreviations "ALR," "ALR2d," and "ALR3d," beginning with cases decided in 1918, continuing with the publication of current cases through the first and second series, published at the present time as the third series, with annotations appended to the reported cases which are exhaustive of authorities on the points annotated and facets of such points.

American Lloyd's. See **Lloyd's association.**

American mortality tables. See **mortality tables.**

American plan. That plan or system for operating a hotel under which meals are provided at regular hours for its patrons, who pay a stipulated sum per day, which includes both meals and room rent. New Galt House Co. v Louisville, 129 Ky 341, 11 SW 351. A term once applied to the open shop system in industry. See Industrial Asso. of San Francisco v United States, 268 US 64, 75, 69 L Ed 849, 852, 45 S Ct 403.

American Red Cross. See **Red Cross.**

American Reports. An older set of reports of leading cases with annotations.

American State Reports. An earlier set of reports of leading cases with annotations, abbreviated "Am. St. Rep." Sometimes "A.S.R."

American Theory. The fundamental conception of the supreme law, expressed in written form, in accordance with which all private rights must be determined and all public authority administered.

amesnable. Same as **amenable.**

amesner son hoste (ä-mes'nä sôn hōst). To lead his army.

ami (ä-mē'). Diminutive for the Latin "amicus." A friend.
See **prochein ami.**

amiables compositeurs (ä-mi-ä'ble cōm-pō'si-tur). (Canada.) Arbitrators who are so designated in their appointment and are permitted to dispense with the strict observance of those rules of law the nonobservance of which, as applied to awards, results in no more than irregularity.

amicable. Friendly.

amicable compounder. In Louisiana,—an arbitrator whose decision is binding on the parties.

amicable scire facias (a'mi-kạ-ble sī're fā'she-as). The revival of a judgment with the consent of the judgment debtor and without the issuance of a writ. Lyon v Cleveland, 170 Pa 611, 33 A 143.

amicable suit (am'i-kạ-bl sūt). A suit in which all the facts are admitted by the parties, leaving only one or more questions of law for the court to decide. Belloc v Rogers, 9 Cal 123. A suit in which, pursuant to prior agreement between the parties, needless expense and delay are eliminated by forgoing insistence upon technicalities and by the admission of facts on the part of either party knowing them to be true. Lord v Veazie (US) 3 How 251, 12 L Ed 1067.

amicitia (a-mi-sī'she-a). Friendship between persons or states.

amicus (a-mī'kus). A friend.

amicus curiae (a-mī'kus kū'ri-ē). Friend of the court. One who gives information to the court on some matter of law in respect to which the court is doubtful, the term implying the friendly intervention of counsel to call the court's attention to a legal matter which has escaped or might escape the court's consideration. 4 Am J2d Am Cur § 1. One who interposes in a judicial proceeding to assist the court by giving information, or otherwise, or who conducts an investigation or other proceeding on request of appointment therefore by the court. Re Ohlhauser's Estate, 78 SD 319, 101 NW2d 827.

amidships. A nautical term meaning the middle of the length of the load water-line, as measured from the fore side of the stem to the aft side of the sternpost.

amission (ạ-mish'ọn). A parting with possession; an involuntary loss rather than an abandonment. Rhodes v Whitehead, 27 Tex 304.

Amistad Case. A famous admiralty case involving the capture in 1839 by a United States brig of a Spanish vessel aboard which were a large number of negroes who had been kidnapped and enslaved in Africa by Spaniards in violation of the laws of Spain. The negroes mutinied near Cuba, killed the captain, and spared the lives of their captors on condition that the ship should return them to Africa forthwith. Their captors deceived them and brought the ship to New York where it was seized by United States naval authorities. In the libel suit which ensued, the negroes were held to be free and not to be pirates. United States v The Amistad (US) 15 Pet 518, 10 L Ed 826.

amita (a'mi-ta). A paternal aunt.

amita magna (a'mi-ta mag'na). A paternal great-aunt.

amitinus (a-mi-tī'nus). A cousin.

amittere (a-mit'te-re). To lose.

amittere curiam (a-mit'te-re kū'rī-am). To be deprived of the right of coming into court.

amittere liberam legem (a-mit'te-re li'be-ram lē'jem). To lose his free law; to lose the privilege of a court; to lose the right to testify; to become outlawed. See 3 Bl Comm 340.

amity. Friendship; peaceful relations between persons or nations.
As used in the Federal statute rendering the government liable for depredations committed by Indians whose tribe or nation has been in "amity" with the United States, the word is not a technical term, but must be given its ordinary meaning and signifies friendship, actual peace. Hostility for a single purpose only, as for example, resisting the opening of a military road, may not prevent a tribe from being in amity. See Leighton v United States, 161 US 291, 40 L Ed 703, 46 S Ct 495.

Am Jur. Abbreviation of **American Jurisprudence.**

Am. Jur. 2d. Abbreviation of **American Jurisprudence,** Second Edition.

amnesia (am-nē'si-ạ). Loss of memory.

amnesty (am'nes-ti). An act of the sovereign power granting oblivion, or a general pardon for a past offense, which is rarely, if ever, exercised in favor of single individuals, but is usually exerted in behalf of certain classes of persons, who are subject to trial, but have not yet been convicted. 39 Am J1st Pard § 6.
See **pardon; reprieve.**

among. Mingled with other things. Gibbons v Ogden (US) 9 Wheat 1, 6 L Ed 1. A good indication, when the word appears in a will, of an intent that the beneficiaries shall take in equal shares. 57 Am J1st

Wills § 1296. Some evidence, in the absence of a contrary showing, that a per capita distribution was intended. Anno: 13 ALR2d 1038.

among the several states. A phrase used to distinguish between commerce which concerns more states than one and commerce confined within one state and not affecting other states. Such distinction pertains to the power of Congress to regulate commerce, it having the power under the commerce clause only as to commerce between the states. 15 Am J2d Com § 3. Commerce in the District of Columbia and the territories of the United States, although within the power of Congress to regulate by virtue of its authority over such areas, is not commerce among the several states. 15 Am J2d Com § 3.

The business of producing stage attractions, including plays, musicals, and operettas, on a multistate basis, constitutes commerce among the several states. United States v. Shubert, 348 US 222, 99 L Ed 279, 75 S Ct 277.

amortisement (a-môr′tiz-mẹnt). Same as **amortization.**

amortizable premium. The premium paid for a bond, debenture, note, certificate, or other evidence of indebtedness which bears interest and is issued by a corporation, government, or political subdivision, including both registered and unregistered bonds. IRC § 171(d).

Where bonds are purchased by a trustee at a premium, the amount paid as premium is commonly amortized by deducting from each interest or coupon payment on the bonds equal instalments sufficient in amount in the aggregate to bring the purchase price of the bonds to par at maturity, paying only the balance of each such payment to the cestui que trust. Such amortization has been held to be a proper method of accounting for trustees in Massachusetts. Old Colony Trust Co. v Comstock, 290 Mass 377, 195 NE 389, 101 ALR 1.

amortizatio (a-mor-ti-zā′she-ō). Same as **amortization.**

amortization (a-môr-ti-zā′shon). Legally, destruction, killing, or deadening, the original use of the term in the law being to place lands in mortmain.

As the term is presently used, it has reference to the gradual extinction of a liability, usually one represented by a bond issue, by regular payments from a fund provided, known as a sinking fund.

amortize. See **amortization.**

amotibilis (a-mō-ti′bi-lis). Movable.

amotion (a-mō′shọn). A removal, such as the eviction of a tenant or a removal from office.

The term relates to *officers* of a corporation, not to *members,* and is the removal of such an officer from his office, still leaving him a *member* of the corporation. It is distinguishable from "disfranchisement" which only applies to *members* and which destroys or takes away their right of being a member. See Richards v Clarksburg, 30 W Va 491, 496, 4 SE 774.

See **eviction; removal from office.**

amount. Quantity. The sum total of two or more particular sums or quantities; the aggregate; the whole quantity; a totality. Connelly v Western Union Telegraph Company, 100 Va 51, 669, 40 SE 618. The aggregate of principal and interest.

The value of property for which stock may be issued by a corporation under a statute authorizing the issue of stock for property to "the amount of the value" of the property, is the actual or the fairly estimated value of the property exchanged for the shares of stock delivered in payment. Kelly v Fourth of July Mining Co. 21 Mont 291, 53 P 959.

amountant (ä-moon′tôn). Ascending.

amount in controversy. The amount or value of the subject matter in litigation according to which the jurisdiction of a court may be limited. 20 Am J2d Cts § 154. A term involved in determining the jurisdiction of a court, either from the standpoint of the minimum amount with which the court can be concerned or a maximum amount which represents the limit of an inferior court's jurisdiction

As so used, amount in controversy, is determined according to the amount claimed by the plaintiff in his complaint, declaration, or petition, not by the amount as it later appears according to the evidence or as finally recovered by the plaintiff in the verdict, decision, or judgment. 20 Am J2d Cts § 155.

If the demand of the plaintiff is for specific property, rather than a sum of money, the amount in controversy is determined according to the value of the property involved at or near the commencement of the suit. 54 Am J1st US Cts § 105.

amount in dispute. See **amount in controversy.**

amount of loss. In general, the amount for which compensatory damages are awarded. 22 Am J2d Damg § 11. In insurance, the amount of loss suffered by the insured in the destruction of or injury to the insured property.

The amount of the loss is not necessarily the amount for which the insured may recover, since the coverage as to amount may be only partial.

amount of the value. See **amount.**

amount per unit. See **rate.**

amount realized. The sum of money received for property plus the fair market value of goods, merchandise, or other property received in addition to the money. Crane v Commissioner, 331 US 1, 91 L Ed 1301, 67 S Ct 1047.

amove (a-möv′). To remove; to take away.

amoveas manus (ā-mo′ve-as ma′nus). A writ to restore lands forfeited to the crown.

amparo (äm-pä′rō). A term taken from Spanish law in some American jurisdictions, meaning a temporary patent to public lands. Trimble v Smithers, 1 Tex 790.

ampliare (am-pli-ā′re). See **amplificatio.**

ampliare jurisdictionem (am-pli-ā′re jū-ris-dik″she-ō′nem). To enlarge the jurisdiction.

ampliation (am-pli-ā′shọn). A deferment of the rendition of a judgment pending further consideration.

amplication. Same as **ampliation.**

amplificatio (am-pli-fi-ca′she-o). An enlarging; a deferring; an adjournment.

amplifier. A device, familiar in broadcasting, whereby sound is amplified so as to be more audible.

amplius (am′pli-us). Among the Roman lawyers, giving more time for the hearing of a case, deferring the case.

amputation. To cut off a member; by surgery.

Am St Rep. Abbreviation of American State Reports, an earlier set of reports of selected cases with annotations.

amtrustio (am-trus′ti-ō). A confidential vassal.

amusement. Pleasure or diversion.
See **place of amusement.**

amy (ami′). Same as **ami.**

an. The indefinite article used in place of "a" where a vowel follows.
See **a.**

an (ān). (French.) Year.

anacrisis (anạ-crī′sis). (Civil law.) An inquiry; an investigation.

anaesthesia. See **anesthesia.**

anaesthetic. See **anesthetic.**

anaesthetist. See **anesthetist.**

anagram. The rearrangement of the letters of a word, thereby making another word, for example, making "pat" from "tap."

anagraph. A register or inventory.

analogous. Having relation to. Comparable in some respects.

analogous arts and uses. (Patent law.) Whether arts or uses are analogous depends upon the similarity of their elements and purposes. If the elements and purposes in one art are related and similar to those in another art, and because and by reason of that relation and similarity make an appeal to the mind of a person having mechanical skill and knowledge of the purposes of the other art, such arts are analogous, and if the converse is true, they are nonanalogous arts. A. J. Deer Co. v U.S. Slicing Machine Co. (CA6 Mich) 21 F2d 812.

analogous cases. Cases which are not in point with one another but are closely related so that the reasoning in one may be accepted in the other.

analytical jurisprudence (an-ạ-lit′i-kal). The school or system of jurisprudence headed by John Austin and Jeremy Bentham depending wholly on analysis, comparison and classification of existing theories rather than upon principles of right and equity.

anaphrodisiac (an-af-rō-diz′i-ak). Something which lessens sexual power.

anarchist. A person who believes in or advocates the overthrow by force or violence of the government of the United States, or of all government or of all forms of law, or the assassination of public officials. United States ex rel. Turner v Williams, 194 US 279, 293, 48 L Ed 979, 985, 24 S Ct 719.

anarchy (an′ạr-ki). The absence of government; a state of society where there is no law or supreme power. Political disorder coupled with violence. Spies v People, 122 Ill 1, 12 NE 865, 17 NE 898.

anathema (a-nath′e-ma). A person or thing cursed; a curse.

a nativitate (ā nā-ti-vi-tā′te). From birth.
See **idiot a nativitate.**

anatocism (a-nat′ọ-sizm). Compound interest; the charging of such interest.

anatocismus (a-na-to-sis′mus). Compound interest.

Anatomy Act. An English statute authorizing and regulating the study of anatomy and the disposition of dead bodies.

an bellare unquam justum sit (an bel-lā′re un′quam jus′tum sit). Whether it is ever right to go to war.

ancestor. A predecessor in the family line.
In statutes which provide for descent and distribution, the term embraces both lineals and collaterals. 23 Am J2d Desc & D § 77. Also, for the purposes of an ancestral estate statute, the term "ancestor" usually embraces both lineals and collaterals. 23 Am J2d Desc & D § 77.

ancestral (an-ses′trạl). Pertaining to ancestors.

ancestral action. An action to recover land based upon the seisin or possession of the plaintiff's ancestor.

ancestral estate. An estate the title to which has been acquired by descent, and which, under the common-law rule, at least the common-law rule in England, should be kept in the line of the ancestor by whom it was brought into the family, so that descent of the same is limited to descent to lineal descendants of the intestate or, upon the failure of lineal descendants, to collateral relatives who were of the blood of the first purchaser. 23 Am J2d Desc & Dist § 75.
"There are but two characters of estate known to our jurisprudence. An estate is either ancestral or nonancestral. In some jurisdictions, the latter is termed 'new acquisition' or 'purchase.' " Gray v Chapman, 114 Okla 66, 243 P 522.

ancestral property. Property acquired by descent. Gray v Chapman, 114 Okla 66, 243 P 522.
See **ancestral estate.**

ancestrel. Same as **ancestral.**

anchor (ang′kọr). A measure equivalent to ten gallons; the instrumentality by which a ship is tied to the bottom of the sea.

anchorage (ang′kọr-ạj). A toll paid for casting a ship's anchor in port. A place where ships may be anchored.

anchor watch. A ship's lookout comprising either one or two men designated to perform that duty while the ship is at anchor. See O'Hara v Luckenbach S.S. Co. 269 US 364, 371, 70 L Ed 313, 317, 46 S Ct 157.

ancient. In the ordinary meaning of the term, very old, something that has existed for a long time; pertaining to the ancient world, that is, the world as it existed prior to the end of the Roman Empire.
In law, the term "ancient" is not limited to what is generally regarded as very old. Thus, a judgment which is 20 years old is an **ancient judgment.**

ancient boundaries. Trees, stone, and other markers which have been in existence since a time beyond the memory of living man and hence must be established as boundaries by evidence of reputation. 12 Am J2d Bound § 106.

ancient deeds. See **ancient documents.**

ancient documents. An ancient document, within the rule which excepts ancient documents from the requirement of authentication by the testimony of subscribing witnesses or otherwise, applies to documents purporting to be 30 years or more old, which are produced from proper custody and are, on their face, free from suspicion. 20 Am J2d Evi § 932.

ancient enclosure. See **ancient inclosure.**

ancient fence. A fence which has stood for so many years that it is to be taken as a practical location of a boundary, the monuments of the original survey having disappeared. 12 Am J2d Bound § 71.

ancient feud. See **feudum antiquum.**

ancient inclosure. Lands which have been inclosed from the open fields for more than twenty years. See **ancient boundaries.**

ancient judgment. A judgment which is 20 or more years old, so that there is a strong presumption in favor of its regularity. 30A Am J Rev ed Judgm § 38.

ancient lights. The doctrine that an owner of land acquires a right of action against an adjoining landowner for the stopping of ancient windows by the erection of a structure on his own land applies where the first owner has had an uninterrupted enjoyment of the window for 20 years. 1 Am J2d Adj L § 89.

ancient map. An original map, over 30 years old, found in proper custody, authorized or recognized as an official document, and free on its face of suspicion, is an ancient map admissible to prove the location of a boundary line. 12 Am J2d Bound § 115.

ancient matters. Historical facts of general or public notoriety which date so far in the past that proof thereof other than by reputation is unavailable. 20 Am J2d Evi § 467.

ancient meadow. A meadow which has not been plowed up for twenty years or more.

ancient pasture. Same as **ancient meadow.**

ancient readings. Essays on ancient English statutes.

ancients. The historical characters and other persons who inhabited ancient Egypt, Babylon, Assyria, Greece, Rome, etc. English attorneys who have attained peculiar seniority at the Inns of Court.

ancient serjeant. The eldest of the queen's serjeants.

ancient survey. A survey made by competent authority, recorded or accepted as a public document, produced from proper custody, and of the age of at least 30 years is admissible in evidence as an ancient survey without further verification. 12 Am J2d Bound § 113.

ancient wall. A party wall in use for twenty years or over. 40 Am J1st Part W § 5.

ancient will. A will so old, that is 30 years or more, calculated from the death of the testator, that it is not necessary to call the attesting witnesses to prove the will. 57 Am J1st Wills § 921.

ancient windows. Same as **ancient lights.**

ancient writings. See **ancient documents.**

ancienty (ān'shen-ti). Seniority.

ancilla (an-sil'ā). (Latin.) A maid servant.

ancillary (an'si-lā-ri). Subordinate. Complementing. Auxiliary.

ancillary action. A suit maintainable in a court of equity on the ground that it is ancillary to an action in another court and in aid of the enforcement of rights involved in such action.

The remedies of injunction, receivership, discovery, and perpetuation of testimony are examples of ancillary jurisdiction in equity. 19 Am J2d Equity § 16.

See **ancillary proceeding.**

ancillary administration. Administration on a decedent's estate, granted in pursuance of the laws of a government other than that of the decedent's domicil, for the due collection and disposition of property left by the decedent within the jurisdiction. Re Mitchell's Estate, 97 Ohio App 443, 56 Ohio Ops 357, 127 NE2d 39, 51 ALR2d 1020; 31 Am J2d Ex & Ad § 680.

There being an ancillary administration, the administration at the domicil of the decedent is called the principal administration. 21 Am J2d Ex & Adm § 850.

ancillary administrator. The administrator appointed in an ancillary administration. 21 Am J2d Ex & Ad § 850.

ancillary attachment. The ordinary remedy by attachment invoked in aid of the collection of plaintiff's demand in an action.

In some jurisdictions the execution of a writ of attachment is in effect the commencement of an action, in which case, of course, the attachment is a principal action rather than an ancillary action or proceeding. 6 Am J2d Attach § 11.

ancillary garnishment. The usual remedy of garnishment invoked in aid of the collection of plaintiff's demand in an action.

In some jurisdictions, garnishment is a principal action, the execution of the garnishment being the method by which the action is commenced. 6 Am J2d Attach § 11.

ancillary jurisdiction. The power of a court to hear, adjudicate and determine matters incidental to the exercise of its primary jurisdiction in an action. 20 Am J2d Cts § 100. A distinct department of equity jurisdiction which arose at an early day from the imperfection of the legal procedure, exercised, not to obtain any equitable remedy, nor to establish any equitable right or estate, but to aid in maintaining a legal right, and in prosecuting actions pending or to be brought in a court of law. 1 Pomeroy's Equity Jurisprudence, § 82.

In the federal courts it is invoked (1) to aid, enjoin, or regulate the original suit; (2) to restrain, avoid, explain, or enforce the judgment or decree therein; (3) to enforce or obtain an adjudication of liens upon, or claims to, property in the custody of the court in the original suit. Raftery v Senter (DC Pa) 41 F Supp 807.

The term "ancillary jurisdiction" is also used in referring to jurisdiction exercised by a court of bankruptcy other than that in which the main proceeding is pending. The Bankruptcy Act, expressly confers upon courts of bankruptcy ancillary jurisdiction over persons or property within their respective territorial limits in aid of a receiver or trustee appointed in any bankruptcy proceeding pending in any other court of bankruptcy. Bankruptcy Act § 2 (a) (20); 11 USC 11 (a) (20); 9 Am J2d Bankr § 77. In this connection, the term "ancillary jurisdiction", refers, not to plenary suits which follow the usual procedure of the forum, but to special proceedings in the exercise of summary jurisdiction. 9 Am J2d Bankr § 77.

ancillary letters. Letters of administration issued to an ancillary administrator.

ancillary proceeding. A proceeding which is ancillary to an action in another jurisdiction.

See **ancillary jurisdiction**; **ancillary proceeding in bankruptcy.**

ancillary proceeding in bankruptcy. A proceeding in a court of bankruptcy entertained in the exercise of the ancillary jurisdiction of such court. 9 Am J2d Bankr § 77.

See **ancillary jurisdiction.**

ancillary receiver. A receiver who has been appointed in aid of, and in subordination to, a foreign receiver for the purpose of collecting and taking charge of the assets of the insolvent corporation in the jurisdiction where he is appointed. Re Stoddard, 242 NY 148, 151 NE 159, 45 ALR 622, 630; 45 Am J1st Rec § 420. To be distinguished from a receiver in a provisional or pendente lite receivership which is in aid of a main or principal action. United States v Kensington, S. & D. Corp. (CA3 Pa) 187 F2d 709, 27 ALR2d 708.

ancillary receivership (an'si-lā-ri re-ceiv'er-ship). A receivership in aid of another receivership, usually one in another jurisdiction. 45 Am J1st Rec § 3.
See **ancillary receiver.**

ancillary suit. See **ancillary action.**

ancipitis usus (an-si'pi-tis ū'sus). A term familiar in the writings of Grotius in international law, meaning of uncertain use from the standpoint of promoting peaceful relations.

and. A conjunction which, taken by itself, calls for the things or matters conjoined to be considered jointly. 50 Am J1st Stat § 281. A word ordinarily to be interpreted in the copulative, rather than the disjunctive, sense, but which will be interpreted in the disjunctive when necessary to the spirit and intent of the entire contract in which it appears. 17 Am J2d Contr § 283.

In the construction of a statute, the word "and" is construed to mean "or," where such construction is required by the context or is necessary to harmonize the provisions of the statute and give effect to all provisions, to save the statute from unconstitutionality, or to effectuate the obvious intention of the legislature. 50 Am J1st Stat § 282. A similar rule prevails in the construction of municipal ordinances. 37 Am J1st Mun Corp § 187. Also, in construing a will, the court will construe "and" as "or" in order to give effect to what appears to have been the clear intent of the testator. 57 Am J1st Wills § 1154. Similarly, the word "and" in a deed will be construed as "or", where the obvious intention so requires. 23 Am J2d Deeds § 218.

When, in the listing of persons or things in a statute, the conjunction "and" is placed immediately before the last of the series, the same connective is understood to have been placed, in effect, between the persons or things previously listed in the series. 50 Am J1st Stat § 281.

The use of the word "and" or & in joining the surnames of partners in a partnership name without using their initials or Christian names does not create an assumed or fictitious name. 38 Am J1st Name § 24.

and by it. See **whereby.**

and company. An expression frequently appearing at the end of the name of a firm.

These words added to a surname or two or more surnames in sequence in adopting a name for a mercantile establishment or other business does not render the adopted name an assumed or fictitious name. 38 Am J1st Name § 24.

and family. Designating the wife and children of the testator where it appears in a will. 26 Am J1st H & W 74.

and his heirs. Words of limitation when used following the name of a devisee, for example, to A and his heirs. 57 Am J1st Wills § 1430.

The same is true of the words when used in a deed, although such a technical meaning will give way to a practical construction where justice and reason so require. 23 Am J2d Deeds § 215.

and/or. A concocted ambiguity. 17 Am J2d Contr § 283. Something of a monstrosity in the English language, used by draftsmen out of an over-abundance of caution. So indefinite as to render an administrative order inoperative or unenforceable for lack of certainty. 2 Am J2d Adm L § 462.

The expression "and/or" has no proper place in a judgment. 30A Am J Rev ed Judgm § 58. Appearing in a pleading "and/or" has been characterized as an equivocal connective, being neither positively conjunctive nor positively disjunctive. 41 Am J1st Pl § 43. Again, the use of the expression "and/or" in an indictment or information is condemned as destructive of the certainty, definiteness, and precision required in criminal pleading. 27 Am J1st Indic § 104. In statutes, however, the use of the expression "and/or" has been considered to have a significance, the view being that the intention of the legislature in using the expression is that the word "and" and the word "or" are to be construed as used interchangeably. 50 Am J1st Stat § 283.

Such usefulness as there is in the use of the expression in a contract lies in its self-evident equivocality. The intention is that the one word or the other may be taken according as the one or the other will best effect the purpose of the parties as gathered from the contract taken as a whole. The term is used to avoid a construction which, by the use of a disjunctive "or" alone, would exclude the combination of several of the alternatives, or, by the use of the conjunctive "and" alone, would exclude the efficacy of any of the alternatives standing alone. 17 Am J2d Contr § 283. In an insurance policy, the expression "and/or" is to receive a liberal construction in favor of the insured, as is the rule in respect to any ambiguity. 29 Am J Rev ed Ins § 262. A negotiable instrument payable to "A and/or B" is payable in the alternative to A, or to B, or to A and B together. 11 Am J2d B & N § 117.

androchia (an-drō'ki-a). A dairy woman.

androgyne (an'drō-jin). A hermaphrodite.

androgynous (an-droj'i-nus). Partaking of both male and female sexes.

androgynus. A hermaphrodite.

androlepsia (an-drō-lep'si-a). Same as **androlepsy.**

androlepsy (an-drō-lep'si). The practice of holding aliens as hostages in order to compel their nation to do justice.

andromania (an-drō-mā'ni-ą). Same as **nymphomania.**

androphonomania (an"drō-fon-ọ-mā'ni-ą). A mania for killing men; homicidal insanity.

and so forth. Other things and units of a like kind. 57 Am J1st Wills § 1335. A term obviously having reference to other things, other events, or other persons, but of so little significance in itself that construction must depend upon the context of the instrument, the enumeration and description of matters and things preceding it, and the subject matter to which it is applied. Muir v Kay, 66 Utah 550, 244 P 901.

and son. An expression frequently appearing at the end of the name of a firm.

The addition of the words "and son" to a surname in formulating a partnership name does not have the effect of creating an assumed name within the meaning of the statutes which regulate doing business under an assumed or fictitious name. 38 Am J1st Name § 13.

ane (ān). Same as **an.**

anecius (a-nē'shus). The first-born; the eldest.

anesthesia (an'es-thē''zhä). A dulling or complete loss of the sense of pain, caused occasionally by disease but normally produced by an anesthetic for the purpose of performing surgery.

anesthesiology (an'es-thē''zi-ol'o-ji). The science concerned with anesthetics and the producing of the state of anesthesia.

anesthetic (an-es-thet'ik). A drug which produces insensibility to pain, such as ether, chloroform, sodium pentothal.

anesthetist (a-nes'the-tist). One trained to administer anesthetics.

an et jour (ôn ā jör). A year and a day.

aneurism (an'ū-rizm). A soft pulsating sac or tumor arising from the preternatural dilation or rupture of the coats of an artery. Lewis v New York Life Ins. Co. 4 Hawaii 370, 374.

anew (a̯-nū'). Over again; de novo.

anfractus judicium (an-frak'tus ju-di'she-um). Legal intricacies.

angaria (an-gā'ri-a). Compulsory service for the government exacted as a punishment.
See **jus angarie.**

angary (an'gȧ-ri). Right of a belligerent to take the property of a neutral for use.

angel (ān'jėl). An ancient English coin of the value of ten shillings.

anger. A strong passion or emotion of displeasure or antagonism, excited by a real or supposed injury or insult to one's self or others; wrath, rage, fury, passion, ire, gall, choler, indignation, displeasure, vexation, grudge, spleen. Morris v Territory, 1 Okla Crim 617, 99 P 760, 768.
See **passion.**

angild. The legal estimated value of a man or a chattel.

angina pectoris (an-jī'na̯). A disease of the heart, so named from a sense of suffocating contraction or tightening of the chest over the sternum, which causes anguish and fear of sudden death. The disease is marked by severe pain and fainting sensations. The paroxysms come on unexpectedly after irregular intervals. See Estate of Lee, 46 NJ Eq 193, 18 A 525, 528.

Anglescheria (an gle she ri a). The fact of being an Englishman.

Angleterre (ān-glê-tär). England.

Anglia (An-gli-a). England.

Angliae jura in omni casu libertati dant favorem (An'gli-e jū'ra in ōm'ni kā'su li-ber-tā'ti dant fa-vō'rem). In every case the English laws are favorable to liberty.

Anglican (ang'gli-ka̯n). Pertaining to the Church of England; a member of that church.

Anglican Church. The Church of England.

Anglice (Ang'gli-sē). English.

angling. Fishing; slang expression for seeking to gain a favored position.

anguilde. See angild.

anguish (ang'gwish). Intense pain of body or mind. Hancock v Western Union Tel. Co. 137 NC 497, 49 SE 952.
See **mental anguish.**

anhlote. A tax or tribute paid as a prerequisite to the right to vote.

aniens (ä-ni-ĕn'). Null; void.

anient (ā'ni-ent). To make nil; to nullify.

anienter (ä-ni-en'tā). See **anient.**

anientisement. Waste.

aniline (an'i-lin). An oily liquid used in the making of dyes.

aniline dyes and colors, by whatever name known. A designation familiar in tariff laws, meaning articles commercially known as aniline dyes and colors. Pickhardt v Merritt, 132 US 252, 33 L Ed 353, 10 S Ct 80.

anima (an'i-ma). (Latin.) Soul.

animal. In law, all animal life other than man. An inferior or irrational sentient being, generally, though not necessarily, possessed of the power of locomotion. In etymology, comprehending all living creatures, whether brutish or human. 4 Am J2d Ani § 1.

animal husbandry. The breeding, raising, feeding and the marketing of animals; a course in agricultural schools.

animalia vagantia (a-ni-mā'li-a va-gan'she-a). Roving animals.

Animal Industry Act. An act of Congress approved May 29, 1884, which prohibits the transportation from one state or territory to another of livestock suffering from contagious diseases. The act also created the United States bureau of animal industry, whose duty it is to collect data on the general subject of communicable diseases and also to adopt such rules and regulations as may be deemed necessary for the speedy and effectual suppression thereof. See 4 Am J2d Ani § 31.

animal of a base nature. A term of the law of property, deriving from the nature of certain animals, such as dogs and cats, as property of a base nature. 4 Am J2d Ani §§ 6, 7.

animals domitae naturae (do'mi-tē na-tu'rē). Those animals which are naturally tame and gentle or which by long continued association with man have become thoroughly domesticated and are now reduced to such a state of subjection to his will that they no longer possess the disposition or inclination to escape. 4 Am J2d Ani § 2.

animals ferae naturae (fe'rē na-tu'rē). Such animals as are of a wild nature or disposition and so require to be reclaimed and made tame by art, industry or education, or else must be kept in confinement to be brought within the immediate power of the owner. 4 Am J2d Ani § 2.

animals mansuetae naturae (man-su-ē'tē na-tū'rē). Animals such as a common house pet, once of a wild nature but since tamed. 4 Am J2d Ani § 2.

animo (a'ni-mō). With a purpose; with intent.

animo cancellandi (a'ni-mō kan-sel-lan'dī). With intent to repudiate or cancel.

animo capiendi (a'ni-mō ka'pi-en'dī). With intent to take.

animo custodiendi (a'ni-mō kus-to-di-en'dī). With intent to take care of.

animo defamandi (a'ni-mō de-fa-man'dī). With intent to defame.

animo derelinquendi (a'ni-mō de-re-lin-quen'dī). With intent to abandon.

animo differendi (a'ni-mō dif-fe-ren'dī). With intent to delay.

animo dominandi. (Roman law.) An intention to control. Rhodes v Whitehead, 27 Tex 304.

animo donandi (a'ni-mō do-nan'dī). With intent to make a gift.

animo et acto (a'ni-mō et ak'tō). By intent and act.

animo et corpore (a'ni-mō et kor'po-re). In mind and body; with mind and body.

animo et facto (an'i-mō et fac'tō). The intent coupled with the fact, as in a change of domicil.

animo felonico (a'ni-mō fe-lo'ni-kō). With felonious intent.

animo furandi (a'ni-mō fu-ran'dī). With intent to steal. The specific intent which is always an essential in larceny. 32 Am J1st Larc §§ 36 et seq.

animo lucrandi (a'ni-mō lu-kran'dī). With intent to profit.

animo manendi (a'ni-mō ma-nen'dī). With intent to remain.

animo morandi (a'ni-mō mo-ran'dī). With intent to delay.

animo non revertendi (a'ni-mō non re-ver-ten'di). With no intention of returning.

animo possidendi (a'ni-mō pos-si-den'dī). With intent to take possession.

animo recipiendi (a'ni-mo re-si-pi-en'dī). With intent to receive.

animo remanendi (a'ni-mō re-ma-nen'dī). With intent to stay away.

animo republicandi (a'ni-mō re-pub-li-kan'dī). With the intention of republishing.

animo revertendi (a'ni-mō re-ver-ten'dī). The intention of returning.

animo revocandi (a'ni-mō re-vo-kan'dī). With intent to revoke. 57 Am J1st Wills § 459.

animo testandi (a'ni-mō tes-tan'dī). With the intention of making a will; with testamentary intent. 57 Am J1st Wills §§ 8 et seq.

animus (an'i-mus). The soul. The seat of the spiritual in man.

animus ad se omne jus dicit (a'ni-mus ad sē om'ne jūs di'sit). Every law is addressed to the spirit of the matter.

animus quo (a'ni-mus kuō). The intent with which an act was performed.

animus recipiendi (a'ni-mus re-si-pi-en'dī). The intention of receiving.

animus recuperandi (a'ni-mus re-ku-pe-ran'-dī). The intention of recovering.

animus republicandi (a'ni-mus rē-pu-bli-kan'dī). The intention of republishing.

animus restituendi (a'ni-mus res-ti-tu-en'-dī). The intention of restoring.

animus revertendi (a'ni-mus re-ver-ten'dī). The intention of returning. 17A Am J Rev ed Dom §§ 26, 27.

The owner of a dwelling house from which he and his family are temporarily absent, must have quitted the house "animo revertendi" to make unlawful breaking burglary. 13 Am J2d Burgl § 4.

A different rule prevails and a distinction is made between animals ferae naturae and such animals as have animum revertendi. As to them a temporary departure from the immediate control of their owner does not determine his property rights in them. Whether or not they possess animum revertendi depends upon whether or not they are usually in the habit of returning whence they have escaped, as carrier pigeons or hawks in pursuit of prey. 4 Am J2d Ani § 19.

animus revocandi (a'ni-mus re-vo-kan'dī). The intention to revoke. Some courts hold that where the revocation of a will has been prevented by the fraud of a person interested therein, and the acts of the testator indicating the animus revocandi have been shown by parol, the instrument will be held to be revoked. 57 Am J1st Wills § 459.

animus signandi (a'ni mus sig'nan-di). Intention to sign.

animus testandi (a'ni-mus tes-tan'dī). The intention of making a will. Whether or not an instrument is testamentary in character depends upon the intention of the maker. It is the animus testandi that makes an instrument a will. When the animus testandi is established, the character of the instrument is fixed and it is a will if the other requirements as to form and execution have been complied with. 57 Am J1st Wills §§ 8 et seq.

anker. A ten gallon measure.

ann. Abbreviation for annual, sometimes for annuity; the amount of a minister's stipend due his heir upon his death.

annales (an-nāl'ēz). Same as annals.

annals (an'alz). The year-books; writings of past events; masses conducted during a year for a person deceased.

annatto (a-nat'ō). An artificial coloring matter sometimes used in the adulteration of milk. St. Louis v Schuler, 190 Mo 524, 89 SW 621.

Ann. Cas. An abbreviation of **American and English Annotated Cases.**

Anne. Queen of England from 1703 to 1714; Princess Anne of England born to Queen Elizabeth and Prince Philip, August 15,1950; sometimes used in old works for year. See **Statute of Anne.**

annex (a-neks'). Verb: To attach to; to join on; to affix. Noun: A smaller building attached to another building.

annexation. The acquisition of territory by a nation, state, or municipal corporation; the fastening or affixing of one thing to another, the legal significance being primarily concerned with the law of fixtures. 22 Am J2d Fixt § 4.

In order to constitute a thing a fixture, there must be actual or constructive annexation, to the freehold, that is, the land, but regard must also be had to the object, the effect, and the mode of annexation; physical annexation is not alone sufficient. The extent and mode of actual annexation no longer carries much weight except insofar as they relate to the nature of the article itself, the use to which the article is applied, and other attending circumstances as indicating the intention of the party making the annexation, for which latter purpose the mode of annexation is an important factor for consideration. The fact that chattels may be removed and sold for other uses, or that they were not made

for special adaptation to the building in which they are placed, is not conclusive of the question whether they have become fixtures; nor is the fact that they can be removed without injury to themselves or to the freehold conclusive of the question. 22 Am J2d Fixt § 4.
See **consolidation; constructive annexation, fixture.**

annexation by reference. See **incorporation by reference.**

annexation de facto. An annexation of territory to a municipal corporation under proceedings which are defective as distinguished from wholly unauthorized. 37 Am J1st Mun Corp § 32.
Even an unauthorized annexation, as one under an unconstitutional statute, may by lapse of time ripen into a de facto annexation, the right of a private citizen or taxpayer to complain having been barred by laches. 37 Am J1st Mun Corp § 32.

annexed to the freehold. Fastened to the land.
See **annexation.**

annez (än'nā). Years.

anniculus (an-ni'ku-lus). A one year old child.

anniented (an'ni-ent-ed). Abrogated; set at naught; annulled.

Anni et Tempora (an'nī et tem'po-ra). Years and terms, an old name for the Year Books.

anni nubiles (an'nī nū'bi-lēz). The marriageable age of a girl.

anni spatium (an'nī spā'she-um). Space of a year.

anniversary. A day which recurs annually.

Anno Domini (an'ō dom'i-nī). In the year of our Lord; since the birth of Christ.

annona (an-nō'na). Yearly contributions of food for a person's support.

Annotated Cases. A set of reports of American and English cases with annotations, abbreviated "Ann. Cas."
See **annotation.**

annotation. A concise statement of the holding of a case, appended to a section of constitution or code of statutes, showing the application of such or a similar section in an actual case. A term sometimes applied to the several propositions of law appearing in a section of a digest of case law. A word of art and of the profession for one of the articles in an annotated series of law reports which follows the report of a case of interest and importance and treats a point or points of the case exhaustively on the case authorities.
The best illustration of the meaning of the word in the latter aspect is found in the annotations in **American Law Reports.**

annotatione principis (an-nō-tā-she-ō'nē prin'si-pis). With the signature of the prince.

announcement of decision. The court's peremptory declaration that he has decided thus and so. The court's expression of his mere intention or opinion as to what the decision shall be is not an announcement of his decision within the rule that a nonsuit cannot be taken after an announcement of decision. 17 Am J Rev ed Dism § 40.

anno Urbis Conditae (an'nō ur'bis kon'di-tē). In the year (753 B. C.) of the founding of the city (Rome), the beginning of the Roman calendar.

annoyance. A discomfort; a nuisance.

annua (an'nu-a). A yearly salary; a pension; an annuity.

annual (an'ū-al). Of or pertaining to a year; returning every year; coming or happening yearly. Payne v Gypsy Oil Co. 129 Okla 18, 263 P 138, 140.

annual assay. A yearly test officially made to determine whether gold and silver coins have been kept up to standard.

annual assessment labor. See **annual labor.**

annual crop. A crop which requires an annual planting or sowing. 21 Am J2d Crops § 2

annual depreciation. A theoretical depreciation of public utility property based upon estimated life of the property. 43 Am J1st Public Util § 129.

annual dividend. Normally, corporate dividends are paid quarterly but in the infrequent case where they are paid annually, the dividend received is known as an annual dividend.
The expression "annual dividend" is most frequently used in reference to dividends on insurance policies. See dividend on insurance policy.

annual dividend policy. A policy of life insurance upon which there is an annual distribution of dividend. 29 Am J Rev ed Ins § 111.

annual dues. Amounts paid annually to a fraternal organization or benefit society to keep in good standing; yearly premiums collected by old-line life insurance company under name "annual dues." Filley v Illinois Life Ins. Co. 91 Kan 220, 137 P 793.

annual fee. The periodical fee paid an attorney at law under a general retainer. 7 Am J2d Attys § 230.

annual interest. Interest payable annually. 30 Am J Rev ed Int § 11.

annual labor. A term of the mining law otherwise known as annual assessment labor. Union Oil Co. v Smith, 249 US 337, 350, 63 L Ed 635, 641, 39 S Ct 308. 36 Am J1st Min & M § 115. The labor performed under a statute requiring the annual expenditure of a prescribed amount of money on each mining claim for labor and improvements. Labor and improvements within the meaning of the statute are deemed to have been had on a mining claim, whether it consists of one location or several, when the labor is performed, or improvements are made, for its development; that is, to facilitate the extraction of the metals it may contain; though in fact such labor and improvements may be on ground which originally constituted only one of the locations, as in sinking a shaft, or be at a distance from the claim itself, as where the labor is performed for the turning of a stream, or the introduction of water, or where the improvement consists in the construction of a flume to carry off the débris or waste material. De Noon v Morrison, 83 Cal 165.

annually. See **per year;** happening every year.

annual meeting. Meeting of stockholders of a corporation. 19 Am J2d Corp § 600.

annual pension. See **pension.**

annual rent. The rent payable for a year's occupancy, usually of farm lands.

annual rest. Apart from a yearly vacation, the expression "annual rest" has a meaning in the law of interest. In charging compound interest to a fiduciary who otherwise will make a profit which a court of equity will not permit, the interest is computed

annually at periods designated as annual rests, at which time the fiduciary is charged with interest and credited with his commissions as well as lawful disbursements during the year. 30 Am J Rev ed Int § 60.

annual revenue. The amount produced in a year by the employment of capital without any impairment of capital. Re Tutorship of the Minors of George M. Ratcliffe, 139 La Ann 996, 72 So 713.

annual turnover. See **turnover**.

annual value. The net annual rental or income which the property ought reasonably to yield.

annual work. See **annual labor**.

annuell. (an'nu-ell). A Scottish term for annual value.

annuelte (an-nū'el-tē). Same as **annuity**.

annuity. In the older sense of the term, a yearly payment of a certain sum of money granted to another in fee, for life, or for years. In the modern sense, a right, bequeathed, donated, or purchased, to receive fixed or certain periodical payments, without contingency, either perpetually or for life or a stated period of time, but not including any interest of the annuitant in the principal fund or source from which the payments derive, his interest being only in the payments themselves. Commonwealth v. Beisel, 338 Pa 519, 13 A2d 419, 128 ALR 978; 4 Am J2d Annui § 1.

Typical modern annuities are those payable by insurance companies. 4 Am J2d Annui § 1. The annuity itself is the totality of the payments to be made under the contract. Where the payments are to be made to the annuitant until his death, the annuity is a life annuity. Where the payments are terminable by the voluntary act of the annuitant, the annuity is a term annuity. Bodine v Commissioner (CA3) 103 F2d 982.

Many of the payments called for by retirement plans of businesses and industries are annuities, although referred to as pensions. Annuities payable under retirement plans are not gratuities in the same sense as pensions paid to retired members of the armed forces, since such annuities are, in part, payable by contributions made by the annuitants themselves. Even where the annuitant makes no contribution in specie, the annuity is nevertheless not a gratuity, since it is in a proper sense provided for him as consideration for his services performed. 40 Am J1st Pens § 3.

An annuity contract is a security within the meaning of the Federal Securities Act. Securities & Exchange Com. v Variable Annuity Life Ins. Co. 359 US 65, 3 L Ed 2d 640, 79 S Ct 618.

See **simple annuity; straight annuity; refund annuity**.

annuity contract. See **annuity**.

annuity for education. An annuity provided for the education of a particular person. 4 Am J2d Annui § 9.

annuity for maintenance. An annual charge given for the maintenance of a particular person, without more, and ceasing with the life of the person to be maintained. 4 Am J2d Annui § 8.

annuity policy. A contract of an insurance company for the payment of an annuity beginning at a certain age of the annuitant stated in the policy, in consideration of a single premium or annual premiums payable by the annuitant. 4 Am J2d Annui § 1.

annuity tax. An annual tax levied in Scotland for the support of ministers of the gospel.

annul (a-nul'). To nullify; to set at naught; to make void; to reduce to nothing.

"The word is not a technical word and there is nothing which prevents the idea conveyed by it from being expressed in equivalent words." Woodson v Skinner, 22 Mo 13, 24.

annulment (a-nul'ment). The act of annulling or making void.

annulment of marriage. The judicial determination of the nullity of a marriage for causes existing at the time of the marriage solemnization. 4 Am J2d Annul § 1.

Annulment differs from a divorce in that it is not a dissolution of the marriage but a judicial declaration that no marriage has ever existed. Callow v Thomas, 332 Mass 550, 78 NE2d 637, 2 ALR2d 632.

annuo reditu (an'nu-a re'di-tū). A writ under old English practice for the recovery of an annuity.

annus (an'us). A year.

annus deliberandi (an'us dē-lib-e-ran'dī). The year which the law of Scotland gives to the heir to determine whether or not he will take his inheritance.

annus, dies et vastum (an'nus, di'ēs et vas'-tum). Year, day and waste.

annus inceptus (an'nus in-sep'tus). The beginning of a year; the same as the completion in computing age.

annus inceptus pro completo habetur (an'nus in-sep'-tus prō kom-ple'tō ha-bē-ter). The beginning of the year is considered to be the completion of it.

annus luctus (an'nus lūk'tus). (Civil law.) The year of mourning, during which the widow could not lawfully remarry. See 1 Bl Comm 457.

annus utilis (an'nus u'ti-lis). A year of advantage.

annuum (a'nu-um). (Roman law.) An annuity; a yearly pension or salary.

annuus reditus (an'nu-us re'di-tus). An annuity; an annual rent.

anomalous. Something very unusual; something which cannot be related to anything in the ordinary course of events.

anomalous plea. Equity terminology for a plea which combines affirmative and negative elements. 27 Am J2d Eq § 204.

anon. Abbreviation of **anonymous**. Adverb: In a short time.

anonymous (a-non'i-mus). Without a name.

anonymous case. A reported case in which the names of the parties are omitted.

another action pending. See **action pending; plea of another action pending**.

anoyer (a-noi-e'). To annoy.

anoysance. Same as **annoyance**.

ansel. See **auncel weight**.

ansement (äns'môn). Similarly; likewise.

answer. Verb: To reply; to assume liability, as to answer for the debt of another; in pleading, to make defense by negativing the allegations of the plaintiff or interposing affirmative defenses. Noun: The reply to a question, as in answering interrogatories in a deposition; the pleading in response to a complaint, declaration or petition, otherwise known in many jurisdictions as a plea, which either denies the allegations of the complaint, declaration, or petition or interposes affirmative matter intended to defeat the action or delay it. 41 Am J1st Pl § 115.

Under older concepts of equity pleading, now almost entirely abrogated by statute, an answer, in addition to being a pleading, served as a discovery and constituted evidence of the facts stated therein. 19 Am J2d Eq § 264.

In admiralty proceedings, the answer is that pleading of a defendant which corresponds with the plea in an action at common law; it must make response to the matters alleged in the libel in the same consecutive order. 4 Am Jur 2d Adm § 179.

See **counterclaim; cross-action; cross-complaint; general denial; sham answer; supplemental answer.** 4 Am J2d Adm § 179.

answerable (an'ser-a-bl). Liable to pay damages.

answer in bar. A defensive pleading interposing affirmative matter intended to defeat the action, as distinguished from a plea intended to delay the action. 41 Am J1st Pl § 115.

answering service. See **telephone answering service.**

answer over. See **pleading over; respondeat ouster.**

answer to writ. See **return to writ.**

antagonistic (an-tag-ọ-nis'tik). Combating; contending, or acting against. State v Brannon, 86 Mont 200, 283 P 202, 67 ALR 1020.

antapocha (an-ta'po-ka). A signed acknowledgment of a debt, by which the debtor is bound.

ante (an'tē). Before.

ante bellum (an'tē bel'um). Before the war.

antecedens (an-te-sē'denz). Antecedent.

antecedent. Preceding; going before.
See words and phrases beginning "**pre-existing.**"

antecedent debt. A debt previously contracted, whether or not due. Fletcher, Appellant, 136 Mass 340, 342. A debt once binding which has become unenforceable by operation of law, without release or discharge by the obligee. 17 Am J2d Contr § 130.

antecessor (an-tẹ-ses'ọr). An ancestor; a predecessor in title.

ante-date. To date an instrument as of a day prior to its actual execution; to precede in point of time.

ante exibitionem billae (an'te ex-hi-bi-she-ō'nem bil'lē). Before suit is filed.

ante-factum (an'te-fak'tum). Something done previously; a former act.

antejuramentum (an"tẹ-jū-ra-men'tum). An oath required of the plaintiff that he would prosecute, and of the defendant, that he was innocent.

ante litem (an'te lī'tem). Before suit.

ante litem contestatam (an'te lī'tem kon-tes-tā'tam). Before the trial of the case.

ante litem motam (an'tē lī'tem mō-tam). Before the commencement of the suit, such being a test of admissibility of declarations on the theory that at such time the declarant had no motive to distort truth. 29 Am J2d Evid § 605.

ante meridiem (an"tẹ mẹ-rid'i-em). Before noon.

ante-mortem (an'tē-môr'tem). Before death; immediately before death, as an ante-mortem statement.

antenatal (an-tẹ-nā'tal). Before birth.

antenatus (an-te-na'tus). A person born prior to a great event; a person born in the American colonies prior to the revolutionary war. Dawson's Lessee v Godfrey (US) 4 Cranch 321, 2 L Ed 634.

ante-Nicene (an-tẹ-Nī'sēn). Prior to the year 325 A. D. when the first general council met at Nicea in Asia Minor and promulgated the Nicene creed.

antenna (an-ten'a). Wires used to receive electromagnetic waves for conversion into sounds or pictures, by means of which communication by radio and television has been made practical.

While judicial notice has been taken of the custom of householders to use outside antennae for radio reception (St. Louis Park v Casey, 218 Minn 394, 16 NW2d 459, 155 ALR 1020), it should be equally well known that many radios and television sets have built-in antennae.

antenuptial (an-tẹ-nup'shal). Before marriage.

antenuptial agreement. See **antenuptial contract; antenuptial settlement.**

antenuptial conception. Conception resulting from coition prior to marriage. 10 Am J2d Bast § 13.
See **antenuptial pregnancy.**

antenuptial contract. A contract made between a man and a woman in contemplation of their marriage to one another.
See **antenuptial settlement; companionate marriage.**

antenuptial conveyance. A conveyance made by husband or wife before marriage. 25 Am J2d Dow § 60.

antenuptial pregnancy. Pregnancy prior to marriage, a ground for annulment where the pregnancy existed at the time of the marriage and was caused by one other than the husband; also a ground for divorce in some jurisdictions. 17 Am J Rev ed Div & S § 145.
See **antenuptial conception.**

antenuptial settlement. A contract or agreement between a man and woman in anticipation of their marriage by which they make an arrangement as to property then owned by one or both, sometimes varying substantially property rights which otherwise would arise upon the marriage by operation of law, even superseding the effect of statutes on property rights. 26 Am J1st H & W § 275.

ante occasum solis (an'te o-kā'sum sō'lis). Before sunset.

ante omnia (an'te om'ni-a). Before all other things.

antestari (an-te-sta'rī). To subpoena a witness.

anthracnose (an-thrak'nōs). A deleterious fungus.

anthracosis (an'thra-cō'sis). See **pneumoconiosis.**

anthrax (an'thraks). An infectious and usually fatal disease of animals, especially sheep and cattle, and occasionally man. Men who become its victims are usually those engaged in handling wool, hides or animals that were infected. The disease may be acquired either by inhaling the bacteria or by inoculation through an abrasion of the skin. The latter is the most usual way. Anno: 20 ALR 7.

anthropometry (an'thrọ-pom'e-try). Measurement of the human body, such being an important feature of anthropology and was at one time advanced as a means of identifying persons or the bodies of deceased persons. The latter aspect of the science has been largely supplanted by fingerprinting.

antichresis (an-ti-krē'sis). A pledge of immovable property, comparable to a mortgage. 41 Am J1st Pldg & Col § 2; 36 Am J1st Mtg § 12.

anticipate. To expect; to foresee; also to forestall. In pleading, to negative matters which the pleader's adversary may set up.

anticipatio (an-ti-si-pā'she-ō). Anticipation.

anticipation. Expectation; foreknowledge. The principle by which negligence is determined on the basis that an ordinary, careful, and prudent man would have foreseen the occurrence of injury. Bell Lumber Co. v Bayfield Transfer R. Co. 169 Wis 357, 172 NW 955, Prematurity.

anticipation of children. Anticipation of birth of child.
An essential condition of liability under the doctrine of attractive nuisance is that there must have been ground for anticipating the presence of the injured child, since, unless the presence of the child is reasonably to be anticipated, the duty of taking precautions for its safety does not arise. 38 Am J1st Negl § 145.

anticipation of defense. Allegations in the complaint, declaration, or petition of the plaintiff which are addressed to matters which it is anticipated the defendant will allege as a defense. 41 Am J1st Pl § 87.

anticipation of device. In the law of patents, the essential element of novelty of invention is lacking where the invention was anticipated. Anticipation is established where it appears that at the time of the invention in dispute there was in use a process or instrumentality which was the equivalent thereof, similar thereto, or of substantially the same character. 40 Am J1st Pat § 26. To constitute an anticipation, the prior device must be sufficiently full, clear, and exact to enable persons skilled in the art to construct or practice, without the exercise of further inventive skill or experiment, the invention described in the subsequent patent. See General Electric Co. v De Forest Radio Co. (DC Del) 17 F2d 90.

anticipation of income. Pledging income or revenue to accrue. 41 Am J1st Pldg & Col Security § 8. Certificates, bonds, or other instruments of indebtedness to be paid by appropriation of revenues and taxes to accrue in the future. 38 Am J1st Mun Corp § 441.

anticipation of injury. See **anticipation**; **apprehension of injury**.

anticipatory breach. A breach of contract committed before the time for performance has arrived, being the outcome of words or acts evincing an intention to refuse performance in the future, that is words or acts in repudiation or renunciation of the contract. 17 Am J2d Cont §§ 448, 449.
A good illustration of the application of the doctrine appears in the law of sales and contracts to sell. 46 Am J1st Sales § 194.

anticipatory nuisance. A nuisance which will necessarily result from an act or thing, although no injurious consequences are presently apparent. 39 Am J1st Nuis § 151.

anticipatory repudiation. A positive statement to the promisee or other person having a right under a contract, indicating that the promisor will not or cannot substantially perform his contractual duties. Restatement, Contracts, § 318; Hawkinson v Johnston (CA8 Mo) 122 F2d 724, 137 ALR 420.

anti-communist affidavit. An affidavit required by statute of a public officer, schoolteacher, or police officer, negativing membership in the Communist Party or adherence to the principles of such party.

anticonstitutional. Unconstitutional; in violation of the constitution.

Anti-Dumping Act. A federal statute intended to prevent sale of foreign merchandise at less than fair value. 21 Am J2d Cust D etc. § 15.

antient (ān'shent). Same as **ancient**.

anti-featherbedding laws. Statutes directed against the exaction of compensation for services not to be performed. 31 Am J Rev ed Lab § 261.

antigraph (an'ti-gráf). A copy of a written instrument.

anti-injunction acts. Statutes prohibiting injunctions in labor disputes.

anti-lapse statute. A statute intended to prevent the lapse of a legacy or devise by providing, in effect, that, in the event of the death of the legatee or devisee prior to the testator, the legacy or devise shall not lapse but shall take effect as if the death of the legatee or devisee had occurred immediately after the death of the testator, unless a contrary intention shall appear by the will. 57 Am J1st Wills § 1433.

anti-molestation clause. See **molestation clause**.

antinomia (an-ti-no'mi-a). A real or apparent contradiction in a statute.

Anti-Okie Law (an"ti-ō'ki lâ). A California statute which prohibited anyone from assisting non-resident indigent persons to enter the state.
The statute was held unconstitutional as imposing an unconstitutional burden upon interstate commerce. Edwards v People of State of California, 314 US 160, 86 L Ed 119, 62 S Ct 164.

Anti-polygamy Law. The Edmunds Anti-polygamy Law passed by Congress in 1882 providing for the punishment of polygamy and also the act of cohabitation with more than one woman at the same time. 10 Am J2d Big § 5.

antiqua custuma (an-tī'qua kus'tu-ma). Ancient custom; statutory duties on wool and leather.
See **antiquity of custom**.

antiquare (an-ti-quā're). (Roman law.) To restore or preserve the old law.

Antiqua Statuta (an-tī'qua sta-tū'ta). English statutes from 1189 to 1327.

antiquation (an-ti-kwā'shọn). (Roman law.) The repeal of a law.

antiquity. The remote past.

antiquity of custom. Under the English rule, a custom existing since 1189, the commencement of the reign of Richard I, which is accepted as the beginning of time of legal memory; in the United States, the element of antiquity exists if it shall have existed from time immemorial. The element of antiquity, however is no longer essential in establishing a custom with the force and effect of law, the modern view being to accept the custom as binding if it shall have existed a sufficient length of time to have become generally known and to warrant the conclusion that the contract or other transaction in question was made in reference to the custom. 55 Am J1st Usage & C § 5.

antiquum dominicum (an-ti'qu-um do-mī'ni-kum). Ancient demesne.

Anti-racketeering Act. A statute to prevent and punish racketeering, that is protecting trade and commerce against interference by violence and threats and checking the levy of blackmail upon business, particularly upon small shops where racketeering appears under the guise of collecting pay for services rendered. 18 USC § 420a-e; Anno: 138 ALR 812.

antithetarius (an-ti-the-tā'ri-us). A person seeking to escape punishment for a crime by charging his accuser with having committed it himself.

antitrust acts. Statutes, a prime example of which is the Federal Antitrust Act, which prohibit all contracts, combinations, and arrangements in the form of trusts, pools, or otherwise, among individuals, partnerships, and corporations, which operate to establish or maintain a monopoly in the manufacture or production, or sale of any commodity of general use in the jurisdiction, or which are in restraint of trade. 36 Am J1st Monop etc. § 119.
See **Clayton Act; Sherman Antitrust Act.**

antitrust affidavit. A verified statement required by statute in some states of corporations doing business in the state. Such statement must be filed annually with the secretary of state and must disclose any connection of the corporation with combinations, pools, trusts and like combinations in restraint of trade or commerce. 36 Am J1st Monop etc. § 123.

anti-vivisection society. An organization, qualifying as a charitable organization, the purpose of which is to oppose the conducting of experimental surgical operations upon living animals. 15 Am J2d Char § 88.

antrustio (an-trus'ti-ō). A confidential vassal.

a nubendo (ā nū-ben'dō). From covering.

anuels livres (än-ū-el' lē'vruh). The Year Books.

anus (ā'nus). The opening at the lower extremity of the alimentary canal.

anute. Same as **annuity.**

any. A flexible word.
In its broad, distributive sense, the sense in which the word is frequently used, it may have the meaning of "all," "every," or "each one of all." Its meaning is often restrained, limited, or influenced by the subject matter or manner in which it is used. It may mean "one indefinitely out of an indefinite number." When used in a statute, it should be so construed as to make its meaning comport with the general scheme of the statute in which it is used. Anno: 143 ALR 1054.
The word has been construed by some authorities to mean an indefinite number, as in the case of a stipulation in a promissory note that an indorser shall not be released by any extension of time. 11 Am J2d B & N § 943.
The word "any", used in a will, should be given a construction in context with other words used in the bequest, rather than a precise meaning doing violence to the testator's intention. Re Scheyer's Estate, 336 Mich 645, 59 NW2d 33, 38 ALR2d 835, construing devise of "any home in which we are residing at the time of my death".

any bank, banker or trust company. A sufficient designation of a person to constitute a special indorsement on a negotiable instrument. 11 Am J2d B & N § 361.

any corporation. Either a domestic or a foreign corporation. 23 Am J2d For Corp § 189 (involving terms of statute conferring power of eminent domain).

any covenant. Either an express or an implied covenant. Cole Petroleum Co. v United States Gas & Oil Co., 121 Tex 59, 41 SW2d 414, 86 ALR 719.

any degree under the influence of intoxicating liquor. Intoxication in some substantial degree. Anno: 13 ALR2d 1003 (construction of clause in accident insurance policy.)

any election. Comprehensive of all elections, primary elections as well as general elections. 30 Am J Rev ed Intox L § 249 (construction of statute prohibiting the sale of intoxicating liquors during the hours of a day when an election is being held.)

anyent. Same as **anient.**

anyer. Same as **annoyer.**

any person interested in the event of a suit. Having reference to a present, certain, and direct interest, so that the person will either gain or lose by the direct, legal operation and effect of the judgment of the court, or the record of the case be legal evidence for or against him in another action. 58 Am J1st Witn § 288.

any time. From time to time; an indefinite time; a reasonable time. On demand. 52 Am J1st Time § 32.
See **at any time.**

any vessel. Every description of watercraft used, or capable of being used, as a means of transportation on water. 12 Am J2d Boats § 16.

anz. Same as **annez.**

A. P. Abbreviation of **Associated Press.**

ap. A prefix used in certain ancient Welsh surnames, such as David ap Thomas (Bibithe's Case, 4 Coke, 43) signifying "son of;" sometimes abbreviated "a," as in John a Gaunt, and having the same significance as "o" in certain Irish surnames, as in O'Neill.

a palatio (ā pa-lā'she-ō). From palace. The word palatine was thus derived because the owners of counties palatine had regal rights as fully as the king had in his royal court. See 1 Bl Comm 117.

apanage (ap'an-āj). Same as **appenage.**

apares (a-pā'rēz). Peers.

apartment. A suite in an apartment house of which the occupant acquires exclusive possession. 29 Am J Rev ed Innk § 8.

apartment hotel. A building which contains apartments not furnished with cooking facilities, the proprietor usually maintaining a restaurant for the convenience of his guests and furnishing other services to them. 29 Am J Rev ed Innk § 8.

apartment house. A multiple dwelling, divided so as to make independent suites for occupancy by a single person, two or more persons, or even a family of some size. 29 Am J Rev ed Innk § 8. A building arranged in several suites of connecting rooms, each suite designed for independent housekeeping, but with certain mechanical conveniences such as heat, light, or elevator service furnished in common to all the occupants of the building. Konick v Champneys, 108 Wash 35, 183 P 75, 6 ALR 459, 463.

apasatio (a-pa-sā'she-ō). A contract.

a patre (ā pa'trē). From his father.

apeaus. Same as **appeaux.**

apennage (ap'en-nāj). Same as **appenage.**

aperire (a-pe-rī're). To open; to unseal.

aperta brevia (a-per'ta brē'vi-a). Open or unsealed writs, as distinguished from sealed writs, which were called close writs.

aperta luce. See **in aperta luce.**

aperte (a-per'tē). Same as **apertus.**

apertment (a-pert'ment). Openly; unsealed.

apertum. See **feudum apertum.**

apertum factum (a-per'tum fak'tum). An overt act.

apertus (a-per'tus). Open; patent; unsealed; not close.

apex juris (ā'pex jū'ris). An extremity or subtlety of the law. Hinsdale v Miles, 5 Conn 331, 334.
The plural is **apices juris.**

apex of vein. A mining-law term for the uppermost edge of the vein, or the course thereof, in place, at or near the surface of the earth.
This edge or apex is, of course, irregular. It may be higher at one place within the boundaries than it is at another; but mere elevation of the upper edge of the vein at different points within the location is of no moment. Anno: 1 ALR 418.

aphasia (a-fā'ziạ). A mental infirmity which may exist while the mental faculties of judgment, memory and understanding remain unimpaired, and which is marked by the inability of the victim to select and use proper words to express his ideas. A person suffering from the malady is not necessarily a person of unsound mind. Re Comfort, 63 NJ Eq 377, 380.

aphonia (a-fō'ni-ä). Loss of voice.

apices juris (a'pi-sēz jū'ris). Extremes; such can not be considered to be the law. State ex rel. Spillers v Johnston, 214 Mo 656, 113 SW 1083.
The extremity of justice is injustice; right too rigid hardens into wrong. Caldwell v Ryan, 210 Mo 17, 108 SW 533.

apices litigandi (a'pi-sēz li-ti-gan'dī). Extremes of the law.

apocae (a'po-sē). A receipt for payment.

apochae oneratoriae (a'po-kē o-ne-rä-tō'ri-ē). Bills of lading.

apocrisarius. A messenger; an ambassador.

apocrisiarius (a-pō-kri-sä'ri-us). Same as apocrisarius.

apograph (ap'ō-gråf). A copy.

apographa (a-po'gra-fa). An inventory.

apoincter (ä-pwank'tā). To appoint.

apostare (a-pos-tā're). To break; to violate.

apostare leges (a-pos-tā're lē'jēz). To break the laws.

apostasy (ạ pos'tạ-si). A break with, or an abandonment of, a faith previously held, especially a religious faith, and even more particularly, the Christian faith.

apostata capiendo (a-pos'ta-ta ka-pi-en'do). A writ for the seizure of an apostate.

apostate (ạ-pos'tāt). A person guilty of apostasy.

a posteriori (ā pos-tē-ri-ō'rī). From a later or subsequent aspect or point of view.

apostil (a-pos'til). A marginal note on a document.

apostiler (ä-pos'ti-lä). To make marginal notes.

apostille (a-pos'tēl). Same as **apostil.**

apostle (a-pos'l). A condensed statement of a case transmitted by a lower court to a higher one.
See **apostles.**

apostles. Letters granted to an appellant in admiralty stating that the record will be transmitted from the lower court to the higher one; the twelve disciples and other early, valiant, and faithful believers and teachers of Christianity; a preacher or missionary; the 12 high officials of the Mormon Church.

Apostles' Creed. The creed universally adopted by Christians about 500 A. D.

apostoli (a-pos'to-lī). Same as **apostles.**

apostolical notary (ap-ọs-tol'i-kal). An ecclesiastical officer charged with the duty of transmitting the orders of the papal see.

apothecary. A druggist or pharmacist. 25 Am J2d Drugs § 4.

app. An abbreviation of **appellate.**

appanage (ap'ạ-nāj). Same as **appenage.**

apparage (ap'par-ạj). Rank; nobility; quality.

apparance (ap-pār'ans). Same as **appearance.**

apparator (ap-pa-rā'tor). Same as **apparitor.**

apparatus. A generic word of most comprehensive signification, implying a full collection or set of implements or utensils for a given duty, but hardly extending to include complicated pieces of machinery. 31 Am J2d Exemp § 63.
See **implements.**

apparel. See **wearing apparel.**

apparent. Clear, or manifest to the understanding; plain; evident, obvious; appearing to the eye or mind. Milliken v McKenzie (Tex Civ App) 285 SW 1110, 1111.

apparent agent. One who, with or without authority, reasonably appears to third persons, as a result of statements, conduct, lack of ordinary care, or other manifestations of the principal's consent, to be acting with authority. Restatement, Agency 2d ed § 8.

apparent authority. That authority which, though not actually granted, the principal knowingly permits his agent to exercise, or which he holds him out as possessing. Ulen v Kneettle, 50 Wyo 94, 59 P2d 446, 111 ALR 565.

apparent authority of insurance agent. Authority which, although not actually granted, the insurance company knowingly permits the agent to exercise, or which it holds him out to the public as possessing. 29 Am J Rev ed Ins § 146.

apparent danger. A danger which is capable of being seen or otherwise comprehended through the medium of the senses; one as well known to a person injured thereby as to the owner of the premises upon which it exists. Martin v Brown, 56 Idaho 379, 54 P2d 1157.

apparent easement. An easement that is open and visible, such as a pathway or road, or one that is readily ascertainable, even though not visible, such as a drainpipe under the surface into which water is conducted from a roof. 25 Am J2d Ease § 8.

apparent error. See **error apparent.**

apparent good order and condition. A term in a bill of lading descriptive of the goods upon delivery to the carrier. 13 Am J2d Car § 285.

The issuance by a carrier of a bill of lading or shipping receipt which acknowledges receipt of the goods in "apparent good order" generally creates a presumption or prima facie case in favor of the shipper or consignee although the form and limits of this presumption or prima facie case are difficult to define with precision. Anno: 33 ALR2d 872.

apparent heir. See **heir apparent.**

apparent jeopardy (a-păr'ent jep'är-di). The status of the defendant in a criminal case on trial before a competent court and a jury duly empaneled and sworn.

His jeopardy is real unless it shall subsequently appear that a verdict could never have been rendered, by reason of the death or illness of the judge or a juryman, or that after due deliberation the jury could not agree, or by reason of some other like overruling necessity which compels their discharge without the consent of the defendant. Cardenas v Superior Court of Los Angeles County, 56 Cal 2d 273, 14 Cal 657, 363 P2d 889, 100 ALR2d 371.

apparent law. See **lex apparens.**

apparent maturity. The time when a negotiable instrument on its face appears to be due.

apparent servitude. See **apparent easement.**

apparere (ap-pă-rē're). To appear.

appares. Peers.

apparitio (ap-pa-ri'she-ō). An appearance.

apparitio in judicio (ap-par-i'she-ō in jū-di'she-ō). An appearance in court.

apparlement (ap-parl'ment). Resemblance; probability.

apparura (ap-pa-ru'ra). Furniture; implements.

app. ct. Abbreviation of **appellate court.**

appeach (a-pēch'). Same as **impeach.**

appeacher (a-pē'chėr). An accuser.

appeachment (a-pēch'ment). Same as **impeachment.**

appeal. Any form of appellate review other than by one of the extraordinary writs. 4 Am J2d A & E § 2. Generally regarded as a continuation of the original suit rather than as the inception of a new action, confined normally to consideration of the record which comes from the court below, with no new testimony taken or issue raised in the appellate court. 4 Am J2d A & E § 2.

To revert to a terminology arising from distinctions that are rarely recognized in modern practice, an appeal brings up questions of fact as well as of law, but upon a writ of error only questions of law apparent on the record can be considered, and there can be no inquiry whether there was error in dealing with questions of fact. Behn, Meyer, & Co. v Campbell & Go Tauco, 205 US 403, 407, 51 L Ed 858.

In the Roman law, to appeal (ap-pe-lā're) is to resort to court; to sue.

appealability. The question whether a case is procedurally apt, that is ripe, for appeal. 4 Am J2d A & E § 47.

appealable. That which may be taken before a higher court for review, as an appealable order; capable of being subjected to an appeal of felony.

"Appealable" in its proper sense denotes susceptibility to direct appeal, as distinguished (1) from "reviewable—that is, open to consideration by the appellate court on the record as made up for appeal from the judgment—and (2) from being appealable in the discretion of the trial judge. Collins v Miller, 91 App DC 143, 198 F2d 948, 37 ALR2d 746. Anno: 37 ALR2d 753.

appealable interest. An interest in a judgment or order which is direct, immediate, pecuniary, and substantial.

More specifically, a party has an appealable interest only when his property may be diminished, his burdens increased or his rights detrimentally affected by the order sought to be reviewed. If his interest or right in and to the subject matter ceases pendente lite, by conveyance, assignment, or otherwise his appealable interest thereby expires, however prejudicial the judgment may be to another. Furthermore, the right invaded or the injury sustained must be subsisting and immediate, not one arising as some possible, remote, unforeseen consequence. Re Michigan-Ohio Building Corp. (CA7 Ill.) 117 F2d 191.

appealable judgment or order. A judgment or order subject to review in appellate proceedings.

Ordinarily, but not universally, the term refers to a judgment or order of court rather than an order rendered in chambers. 4 Am J2d A & E § 19.

appeal bond. Security furnished in perfecting an appeal for the benefit of other parties to be affected. 4 Am J2d A & E § 323.

appeal in forma pauperis (for'ma pâ'pe-ris). See **in forma pauperis.**

appeal of death. See **year and a day.**

appeal of felony. In older times in England, an accusation by a private subject against another, for some heinous crime, demanding punishment on account of the particular injury suffered rather than for the offense against the public. The proceeding never obtained in the United States, and was abolished by act of Parliament in England in 1819.

appeal of mayhem. An ancient common-law action which combined the injured parties private action and a criminal prosecution. 36 Am J1st May § 7.

appear. To enter a formal appearance in an action or to appear by taking some step in contesting the action. To be manifest or evident. McClurg v Powell, 77 Miss 543, 27 So 927; R. S. Oglesby Co. v Lindsey, 112 Va 767. To seem to be of a certain kind or nature.

See **appearance.**

appearance. An outward manifestation. The first act of a defendant in court, being the overt act by which he submits himself to the court's jurisdiction. A formal or informal, direct or implied, written or oral submission by the defendant to the jurisdiction of the court in an action. 5 Am J2d Appear § 14. In a broader sense, a coming into court and submission to jurisdiction by either plaintiff or defendant. 5 Am J2d Appear § 1.

A defendant makes his appearance by entering a formal appearance or by taking some step in response to the action against him, such as filing or serving an answer or attacking the complaint, bill, or petition of the plaintiff by demurrer or motion. 5 Am J2d Appear §§ 14 et seq.

See **general appearance; special appearance.**

appearance bail. See **bail.**

appearance day. The last day upon which a defendant served with process may plead, submit a motion, or, in some jurisdictions, enter his appearance, thereby avoiding a default. Cruger v McCracken, (Tex. Civ. App.) 26 SW 282, 283. Sometimes called default day, although the former practice in many jurisdictions of having all actions returnable on the second day of the next term of court is fast becoming obsolete, the common provision being for the requirement of an appearance under pain of default a prescribed period of time after service of process, irrespective of the date of the opening of the term of court.

appearance docket. A docket kept by the clerk of court wherein appearances are entered.
It is often a part of a general docket wherein the various steps in a case from the service of process to the entry of judgment and the issuance of execution are registered.

appearance fee. The fee charged by a clerk of court for entering an appearance. 15 Am J2d Clk Ct § 14.

appearance term. The term of court at which the defendant in a civil case or the accused in a criminal case is cited to appear. The term of court at which it first becomes apparent that there is for trial and determination any issue of fact.

appearand heir (ap-pēr'and ār). (Scotch.) One who is entitled to inherit, but who has not yet made entry upon the land.

appearer. One who enters a formal appearance in court as or for a defendant.

appear generally. See **general appearance.**

appear gratis (a-pēr' gra'tis). To enter an appearance in an action without requiring or awaiting the service of summons or other process.

appears. See **appear; appearance.**

appear specially. To appear in an action without submitting to the jurisdiction of the court, as where the defendant challenges the sufficiency of the service of process. 5 Am J2d Appear § 2.
See **special appearance.**

appeaux (ap-pō'). Appeals.

appel (a-pel'). Appeal; appealed; accused.

appelans (äp'pe-lôn). An appellant; the accuser in an appeal of felony.

appele. Same as **appellee.**

appellant. A person who appeals from the judgment of a court; the complaining party in an appeal of felony.

appellare (ap-pel-lā're). To appeal; to prosecute an appeal of felony. (Roman law.) To appeal to; to demand; to sue.

appellare adversus sententiam (ap-pel-lā're ad-ver'-sus sen-ten'she-am). To appeal from a sentence.

appellate. Pertaining to the taking of an appeal, as appellate court, appellate procedure; of a higher jurisdiction. In its broadest sense the word denotes nothing more than the power of one tribunal to review the proceedings of another, either as to law or fact, or both. Marbury v Madison 5 US (1 Cranch) 137, 147, 2 L Ed 60, 64.

Appellate Division Conference. An agency of the United States for the settlement of a taxpayer's case not settled with the office of the District Director of Internal Revenue.

Appellate Division of the Supreme Court. An intermediate appellate court in New York.

appellate jurisdiction. The jurisdiction of appeal or review proceedings, as distinguished from trial court or nisi prius jurisdiction, being contingent on timely compliance with constitutional or statutory methods of appeal. Barney v Platte Valley Public Power & Irrig. Dist. 144 Neb 230, 13 NW2d 120.

appellatio (ap-pel-lā'she-ō). An appellation; a name; an appeal.

appellation. See **name.**

appellatione. Name.

appellator (ap-pel-lā'tor). Same as **appellant.**

appellee. A party against whom a cause is appealed from a lower court to a higher one.
In some jurisdictions, he is called the "respondent." The term "appellee" is also applied to the defendant in an appeal of felony. And, also, to a person who is "appealed" by an approver. See **approver.**

appello (ap-pel'lō). I appeal,—the formal word by which an appeal was taken under the Roman law.

appellor (a-pel'or). An appellant, a person who prosecutes an appeal from a lower court; an approver, who accuses his confederates in crime; a party who challenges a jury.

appellour (a-pel-lour'). Same as **appellant.**

appellum (ap-pel'lum). An appeal.

appenage (ap'pen-aj). Under French feudal law, the portion which was given to the sons of the king for their support. It reverted to the king on failure of male heirs.

append (a-pend'). Pending.

appendage (a-pen'dāj). An accessory of a more important thing, something connected with it, and either essential to its completion or to its advantageous and convenient operation. State Treasurer v Somerville & Easton Railroad Co. 28 NJL 21, 26, 27; Anno: 7 ALR 795.
Under a statute authorizing a school board to provide the necessary "appendages" for a schoolhouse, it may bind the district to pay for the drilling of a well in the school yard for the purpose of supplying drinking water, although no suitable water is found, and the well is on that account entirely useless. Schofield v School Dist. 105 Kan 343, 184 P 480, 7 ALR 788.

appendant. Appurtenant; belonging to another more important thing.
At common law, things incidental to a fee in land were classified as things "regardant," "appendant," and "appurtenant," marking distinctions which are now obsolete. New-Ipswich W. L. Factory v Batchelder, 3 NH 190.

appendant power. See **power appendant.**

appender (a-pen'dėr). To append; to affix; to annex.

appenditia (ap-pen-di'she-a). Appurtenances.

appendix. An addition to a book, placed at the end of the text, for convenient reference to supplemental and explanatory material contained therein; in appeals in the House of Lords and the Privy Council, a printed volume containing the material documents or other evidence used in the courts below and referred to in the cases of the parties.

appensura (ap-pen-su'ra). Payment in money by weight.

appent (ap-pent'). Same as **appendant.**

appertaining. Relating to.
See **appurtenant.**

appertinances (ap-per′tin-an-ses). Same as **appurtenances.**

appliance. A tool, an instrumentality of convenient use, especially in the use of a larger instrumentality, for example, appliances for use with a vacuum cleaner. Appliances are usually personal property, becoming real estate only as they may be so adapted to the use and enjoyment of real estate as to lose their identity as personalty. Doll v Guthrie, 233 Ky 77, 25 SW2d 947.

appliances of transportation. The roadbed, tracks, cars, engines, and all other machinery and equipment furnished by the carrier and used in connection with the conduct and management of its business, but not property belonging to the passenger which he takes into the car with him. See Burns v Pennsylvania R. Co. 233 Pa 304, 82 A 246.

applicable (ap′li-ka-bl). Appropriate; such as can be applied.
In determining the effect of a statutory adoption of the common law so far as it may be "applicable," the word is to be construed as meaning applicable to local conditions and habits and in harmony with the genius, spirit, and objects of local institutions. Fuchs v Goe, 62 Wyo 134, 163 P2d 783, 166 ALR 1329.

applicant. One who files an application or petition; a petitioner.

applicare (ap-pli-kā′re). To fasten; to moor a ship.

applicatio est vita regulae (ap-pli-kā′she-o est vī′ta re′gū-lē). The application is the life of the rule.

application. Use, as the application of a drug; devoting to a purpose, as the **application of payments.** A request; a seeking, usually in the form of writing; a petition.
One of the most frequent uses of the term is in the law of insurance, it referring in that connection to the first step in negotiating a contract or policy of insurance, being a signed statement by the prospective insured wherein he requests the insurance and fills in such details concerning the risk as the insurer seeks by way of information upon which it will decide whether or not to accept the risk and issue a policy. Dickinson v Bankers Life & Cas. Co. (Mo App) 283 SW2d 658.

application for incorporation. A formal application required by the statutes of some of the states to be made to some designated court for the approval of the court of the right of the applicants named therein to form a corporation. 18 Am J2d Corp § 42.

application for insurance. See **application.**

application of payments. The use or account to which a payment is applied or credited where a single creditor has two or more demands, and other creditors, as well as the debtor, will be affected by the particular application made. 40 Am J1st Paym §§ 108 et seq.

apply. See **application.**

appoint. To designate a person for a purpose, such as holding office; to fix a time.
See **appointment.**

appointee. A person who has been appointed to an office or trust.

appointing power. The power or authority to appoint public officers. Walker v Cincinnati, 21 Ohio St. 14.
See **power of appointment.**

appointment. The designation of a person to occupy a public office, including appointments under the Civil Service. 15 Am J2d Civ S § 1; 42 Am J1st Pub Of § 90. More broadly defined to include the selection of corporate officers and other officers of a private nature. Sometimes construed to include the result of a popular election. 25 Am J2d Elect § 1. An engagement to meet another at a specified time.
See **power of appointment.**

appointment of administrator. The issuance of letters of administration upon application therefor.
A proceeding for the appointment of an administrator is to be considered as an "action" within the meaning of that word as used in a general statute of limitations. 31 Am J2d Ex & Ad § 84.
See **letters of administration.**

appointment of appraiser. An appointment of a person to act in ascertaining a specific fact, to wit: the value of a certain property, piece of property or the loss incurred in its destruction in whole or in part. 5 Am J2d Arb & A § 3.
Under the arbitration clause of a fire insurance policy, the naming of a person to act as appraiser by one of the parties is not a "selection" until the other party has agreed to accept him. American Macaroni Mg. Co. v Niagara Fire Ins. Co. (DC Ala) 43 F Supp 933.

appointment of arbitrators. The selection of arbitrators under an agreement for arbitration of a dispute, the usual method being for each party to choose one and for the two thus chosen to select a third to serve with them. 5 Am J2d Arb & A §§ 86, 88.

appointment of counsel. Same as **assignment of counsel.**

appointment of executor. The designation of a person to act as executor appearing in a will. The issuance of letters testamentary upon application made therefor.
See **letters testamentary.**

appointment of shipmaster. The selection of the master of a ship by the owner or by the owners of a majority of the part interests. See 48 Am J1st Shipping § 114.

appointment of trustee. The designation of a person as trustee made by will, deed of trust, or other trust instrument, or the naming by a court of a person to act as trustee.

appointment to office. See **appointment.**

appointor (a-poin′tor). The person appointed by a donor, under the statute of uses, to execute a power.

apport (a-pōrt′). A tax or other tribute paid to the government. In French law, personal property or documents brought in or contributed.
See **apportum.**

apport en nature. (French law.) Payment in kind.

apportion. To divide and assign in proportion; to distribute among two or more a part or share to each.
See **apportionment.**

apportionamentum (ap-por-she-ō-na-men′tum). An apportionment.

apportionment. A division of property; also a determination of the liability of co-obligors in enforcing contribution. 18 Am J2d Contrib § 19.

APPORTIONMENT / APPROACH

See **partition; pro rata;** also terms beginning with word **prorating.**

apportionment of accretion. The division of accretion between adjoining riparian proprietors along the shore of a body of water. See 56 Am J1st Wat § 494.

apportionment of direct taxes. The requirement in reference to federal taxes under paragraph 4 of section 9 of Article I of the Constitution of the United States; apportionment according to the census.

apportionment of freight. See **freight pro rata itineris.**

apportionment of local assessment. The legislative act of determining the mode of distributing the burden of an assessment for a local improvement, designating the property out of which the tax is to be made, and establishing some certain standard of assessments. When not constitutionally restricted, the legislature may prescribe any method of apportionment which it deems equitable, unless it is palpably arbitrary and constitutes a plain abuse. See 48 Am J1st Spec A § 57.

apportionment of representatives. The determination of the number of representatives to which a state is entitled in the House of Representatives of the Congress of the United States or to which a county is entitled in a state legislature; the drawing of district lines to create election units.
See **reapportionment.**

apportionment statutes. Statutes providing in effect that the amount of an estate tax, state or federal, shall be paid out of the state before its distribution and shall be equitably prorated among the persons interested in the estate to whom benefit accrues, except as the decedent has directed otherwise in his will. Annos: 26 ALR2d 927; 37 ALR2d 203.
See **apportionment of direct taxes.**

apportum (ap-por'tum). The revenue derived from a right such as an incorporeal hereditament or a pension.

apposal of sheriffs. The charging of the sheriffs with money received by them on account of the exchequer.

appose (a-pōz'). To examine an officer with reference to his accounts.

appostille (ap-pos-tēl'). Same as **apostil.**

appraisal. A determination of worth or value, as the appraisal of a dwelling house, a manuscript, or a literary product.
See **appraise; appraisement.**

appraise (a-prāz'). To estimate value; to determine the amount of a loss according to the value of the property injured or destroyed. Vincent v German Ins. Co., 120 Iowa 272, 278, 94 NW 458. 29A Am J Rev ed Ins § 1610.

appraisement. The act of appraising; the amount determined as the value by an appraisement; another meaning sometimes confused with arbitration but essentially different, being a method of determining the value of a thing, agreed upon and provided in advance for the purpose of avoiding a dispute in the future. Sanitary Farm Dairies, Inc. v Gammel (CA8 Minn) 195 F2d 106; 5 Am J2d Arb & A § 3.

appraiser. A person selected to value property, for example, an appraiser of a decedent's property for inheritance tax purposes, or an appraiser of imported goods. See **customs appraiser.**

appreciare (ap-prē-she-ā're). To appraise.

appreciate. To rise in value; to understand; to recognize the value in a person or a thing.

appreciation of risk. See **apprehension of injury.**

apprehend. To make lawful arrest; to capture; to place in custody; to seize; to have knowledge of something.

apprehendere (ap-prē-hen'de-re). Same as **apprehend.**

apprehensio (ap-prē-hen'she-ō). Same as **apprehension.**

apprehension. The seizure, taking, or arrest of a person on a criminal charge. Hogan v Stophlet, 179 Ill 150, 53 NE 604. Another meaning relevant to the law is that of knowledge or perception.

apprehension of injury. The basis of a duty to avoid injury, an essential element of negligence. 38 Am J1st Negl § 24. Also, an essential of the defense of assumption of risk. Edwards v Kirk, 227 Iowa 684, 288 NW 875.

apprentice. In the broad sense, a learner; one who by labor seeks to acquire the art or mystery of the craft at which he is employed. Anno: 36 ALR 1348. In a technical and almost anachronistic sense, a minor who is bound in the form of law to a master for a specified length of time, terminable at his majority or prior thereto, to learn the art or mystery of some trade, craft, profession, or business in which his master is bound to instruct him, and to serve his master during the term of his apprenticeship.
See **articles of apprenticeship.**

apprentice en la ley (ôn lä lä). An apprentice at law. See **apprenticii ad legem.**

apprenticeship. See **apprentice; articles of apprenticeship.**

apprenticeship deed. Same as **articles of apprenticeship.**

apprenticii. Apprentices.

apprenticii ad legem (ap-pren-ti'she-i ad le'jem). Apprentices at the law; students at the inns of court.

apprenticius (ap-pren-ti'she-us). Same as **apprentice.**

apprenticius ad barras (ap-pren-ti'she-ùs ad bar'ras). A student preparing for the profession of barrister.

apprenticius ad legem (ap-pren-ti'she-ùs ad lē'jem). An apprentice at law; a law student.

apprentise (ap-pren'tis). Same as **apprentice.**

apprentise en la ley (ap-pren'tis ôn lä lä). Same as **apprentice en la ley.**

apprentissage (ap-pren'ti-sāj). Apprenticeship.

apprentitius (ap-pren-ti'she-us). Same as **apprentice.**

apprest (a-prest'). Ready; prepared; preparation for war by the enlistment of soldiers.

appresster (ap-pres'tā). To prepare.

apprimes (ap-prim'ēz). First.

appris (ap-prē'). Informed; learned.

apprise (a-prīz'). To teach; to give notice; to appraise.

apprises en la ley (ap-prēs' ôn lä lä). Learned in the law.

apprising (ap-prīz'ing). Teaching or informing; an ancient Scotch procedure whereby a debtor's land was conveyed to the creditor to settle the debt.

approach. To come near or in proximity. Wadsworth v Marshall, 88 Me 263, 34 A 30.

See **right of approach**.

approach of a bridge. The passage connecting the highway with a bridge, making the bridge accessible. For a reasonable limit, the approach is regarded by law as part of the bridge itself.

approbare (ap-pro-bā′re). To approve.

approbate and reprobate. To accept one part and reject another.

approbation. Approval; a technical term in use at one time in England and France for the official approval of publication of a book.

approbator (ap′rō-bā-tǫr). Same as **approver**.

approbatory articles. See **articles approbatory**.

approbo non reprobo (ap-prō′bō non re-prō′bo). I approve what I do not disapprove.

approcher (ap-pro-shā′). To approach.

approper (ap-pro-pā′). To appropriate.

appropriare (ap-prō-pri-ā′re). To appropriate.

appropriare communiam (ap-prō-pri-ā′re kom-mū′ni-am). To remove a piece of land from a common by enclosing or appropriating it.

appropriare et includere communiam (ap-prō-pri-ā′re et in-klū′de-re kom-mū′ni-am). To appropriate and enclose a common; to discommon.

appropriate (a-prō′pri-āt). Adjective: Fit; adapted to; designed; suitable. Thomas v State (Okla) 244 P 816.

appropriate (a-prō′pri-āt). A verb derived from the Latin "ad" and "proprius". To allot, assign, set apart, or apply to a particular use or purpose. State v La Grave, 23 Nev 25, 41 P 1075. To take to one's self to the exclusion of others; to set apart for a use in exclusion of all others. Newhouse v First Nat. Bank, (DC Ill) 13 F2d 887.

appropriate speed. A variable term to be resolved according to the surrounding circumstances. 8 Am J2d Auto § 687.

appropriation. A taking to the exclusion of others; a conversion of property where performed without right. 18 Am J2d Conv § 1. A taking of private property for public use under the power of eminent domain. Cushing v Gillespie, 208 Okla 359, 256 P2d 418, 36 ALR2d 1420.

appropriation bill. A proposed statute authorizing the appropriation of public funds for particular objects or purposes. 42 Am J1st Pub F § 43.

appropriation for war. The taking and use of property by the army or navy, in the course of war, not authorized by contract with the government. Filor v United States, 76 US (9 Wall) 45, 19 L Ed 549.

appropriation of fund. Legislative authority, given at the proper time and in legal form to the proper officers, to apply a distinctly specified sum from a designated fund out of the treasury, in a given year, for a specified object or demand against the appropriating body. 42 Am J1st Pub F § 43.
See **appropriation bill**.

appropriation of ice. Such exercise of dominion over ice on public waters, for example, cutting the ice into cakes, as will vest the exclusive right to the ice in the person so acting, provided he has the present ability and intention to proceed to a harvest of the ice. 27 Am J1st Ice § 5.

appropriation of payments. See **application of payments**.

appropriation of water. Application of water to some beneficial use. Farmers High Line Canal Co. v Southworth, 13 Colo 111, 21 P 1028.
See **prior appropriation**.

appropriation to capital. The application of net income of a corporation to an increase in the capital of the company, as by expanding the plant or making permanent improvements. Davis v Jackson, 152 Mass 58, 25 NE 21.

appropriator. See **appropriation; prior appropriation**.

approval. A sanction; expression of satisfaction.
In the law of agency, approval, ratification and acquiescence in an act all presuppose the existence of some actual knowledge of the act and what amounts to a purpose to abide by it. Williams v Vreeland, 250 US 295, 299, 63 L Ed 989, 992, 39 S Ct 438.

approval of performance. A determination, which, as called for by a provision in a building and construction contract, is to be made according to objective criteria. 13 Am J2d Bldg Contr § 30.
See **certificate of architect or engineer**.

approval sale. A sal on approval. 46 Am J1st Sales § 492.

approve. To confirm, ratify, sanction, or consent to, some act or thing done by another. Board of Education v Reno Community High School, 124 Kan 175, 257 P 957.
As used in a statute giving an officer power to "approve" an application, it is not ordinarily limited to a mere verification of the facts as stated in the application, but involves a grant of discretionary power, complete unless limited by the statute, and implies knowledge, the exercise of discretion after knowledge, and the act of passing judgment. McCarten v Sanderson, 111 Mont 407, 109 P2d 1108, 132 ALR 1229. "To approve," especially where it is a public officer who is to give sanction, is to go beyond an unexpressed mental acquiescence; his sanction should be given with certainty and by an unmistakable sign or declaration. People v Hall, 140 Cal App 745, 31 P2d 831. Approval by a finance committee of a municipality means that the members of the committee, acting upon their official responsibilities and having in view the public welfare, are to investigate and sanction according to their own independent judgment each separate item. It is not a ministerial function but implies active and important prudential obligations. Brown v Newburyport, 209 Mass 259, 95 NE 504.
A sense of the term much less familiar is that of accusing. A person who is indicted for crime is said to approve another person when he, the approver, before plea, confesses and accuses the other of the offense. In a sense that seems to have become obsolete; to "approve" land means to improve it by cultivation and reclamation.

approveamentum (ap-prō-vē-a-men′tum). Same as **approvement**.

approved bill. A bill of exchange drawn by one whose financial credit is good. Mills v Hunt, 20 Wend (NY) 431, 435.

approved note. A promissory note made or indorsed by one whose financial credit is good.

approved security. A term having particular reference to the security required of the purchaser at an auction sale, meaning such security as ought to be approved by the auctioneer. 7 Am J2d Auct § 47.

approvement (a-pröv'ment). The old English practice of encouraging accomplices to become crown witnesses by holding out the hope of pardon on a full disclosure of their own guilt and that of their accomplices. The word was also used in the past, in a sense that appears now to have become obsolete, to signify an improvement; an enclosure or fencing for the improvement or cultivation of the land.

approve of. See **approve; consent to.**

approver (a-pröv'ver). Also called a "prover" or "probator,"—a person who, after having been indicted for treason or other felony and arraigned for it, confesses his guilt before pleading guilty or not guilty and accuses the persons who were his accomplices, of the same crime, in order to obtain a pardon for himself. See 4 Bl Comm 330.

approximately. A word used in describing a course or distance, which usually is disregarded where not controlled or explained by a monument or other marker, and may be given meaning and effect where so controlled and explained. 12 Am J2d Bound § 57. An inconclusive term, standing alone, where used as a designation of the quantity of goods covered by a contract of sale. Annos: 7 ALR 511; 26 ALR2d 1120; 46 Am J1st Sales § 159.

This word has been given the same interpretation as "more or less" with respect to relief by way of rescission or adjustment of purchase price for mutual mistake as to quantity of land where the sale is in gross. Anno: 1 ALR2d 50, 96.

approximation doctrine. See **cy pres; equitable approximation doctrine.**

appruamentum (ap-prū-a-men'tum). Same as **approvement.**

appruare (ap-pru-ā're). Same as **approve.**

appulsus (ap-pul'sus). A driving toward; an impelling.

appunctuare (ap-punk-tu-ā're). To appoint.

appurtenance (a-pér'te-nans). A thing belonging to another or principal thing and which passes as an incident to the principal thing. Anno: 39 ALR2d 872; 23 Am J2d Deeds § 256. Such a thing as belongs to the land and is a part thereof. 55 Am J1st V & P § 124. An easement or servitude to be used or enjoyed with demised premises. 32 Am J1st L & T § 169. As the word appears in a sale of personal property:—accessories; possibly including, when fairly construed in the light of the entire context, articles and subjects not comprehended by the word as it appears in a conveyance of land. 46 Am J1st Sales § 146. As the word appears in a chattel mortgage:—personal property intimately connected with the operation of the principal thing which is mortgaged. 15 Am J2d Chat Mtg § 77.

Of a vessel: Everything that belongs to the ship, such as sails and rigging, rudder and cordage, compasses, chronometers, lights, tackle and apparel, even though such may not be on board, and also such special equipment as may be necessary in the employment of the vessel for a particular purpose. 48 Am J1st Ship § 71.

appurtenant. Pertaining; belonging to something else.
See **appurtenance.**

appurtenant easement. See **easement appurtenant.**

appurtenant power. See **power appendant.**

appurtenant rights. Everything essential or reasonably necessary to the full beneficial use and enjoyment of property. 23 Am J2d Deeds § 256. An incorporeal right attached to, and belonging with, some greater or superior right; something annexed to another more worthy thing with which it passes as an incident, being incapable of existence separate and apart from the particular property to which it is annexed and to which it bears a relationship connected with the use of such property. 25 Am J2d Ease § 11.

appurtenant way. A right of way which is incident to an estate, which inheres in the land, concerns the premises, pertains to its enjoyment and passes with it. 25 Am J2d Ease § 11.

apree (ä-pree'). Same as **aprés.**

a prendre (a prän'dr). To take.

aprés (a'prā). After.
See **en aprés.**

aprés le fait (a'prā le fā). After the deed.

aprés midi (a'prā mē'di). Afternoon.

aprés que (a'prā kě). After that.

a priori (ā prī-ō'rī). From the past; from what has previously transpired.

To argue or reason "a priori" is to conclude by deduction that because certain facts exist, certain other facts will necessarily follow as a consequence. See 1 Bl Comm 32.

apris (a-prē'). Same as **appris.**

apris de la leie (a-prē' de lä lā). Learned in the law.

aprovechamiento (ä-pro-ve-cha-mi-en'to). A right in the commons where pueblo lands are involved. Hart v Burnett, 15 Cal 530, 566.

apt. Fit; suitable; proper.

apta viro (ap'ta vi'rō). A girl of marriageable age.

apud (a'pud). With; at the house of; among.

apud acta (a'pud ak'ta). Among the recorded acts.

apud London videlicet, in parochia Beatae Mariae de arcubus, in ward de Cheap (a'pud Lon'don vi-dē'li-set, in pā-rō'ki-a Be-ā'tē mä-rē de är'ku-bus, in ward de Chēp). At London, that is to say, in the parish of St. Mary-le-bow, in the ward of Cheap. An old form for designating the venue.
See **SS.**

apud pares (a'pud pá'rēz). Before his peers.

apurtenaunces. Same as **appurtenances.**

aqua (ā'kwa). Water.

aqua aestiva (a'qua ēs'ti-va). Water used only in summer.

aqua ammoniae. A solution of nitrogen and hydrogen.

Aqua cedit solo (a'qua sē'dit sō'lo). The water goes with the land. Wholey v Caldwell, 108 Cal 95, 41 P 31.

aqua cooperta (a'qua kō-o-per'ta). Covered by water.

aqua currens (a'qua ker'renz). Running water.

Aqua currit et debere currere ut currere solebat (a'-qua ker'rit et dē-bē're ker're-re ut ker're-re sō-lē'bat). Water runs and ought to run as it is accustomed to run. San Gabriel Valley Country Club v Los Angeles County, 182 Cal 392, 188 P 554, 9 ALR 1200, 1207.

aqua ductus (a'qua duk'tus). The right to run water through the land of another.

aqua dulcis (a'qua dul'sis). Fresh water.

aquae (a'kwē). Waters; streams.
See **fullum aquae; judicium aquae.**

aquae haustus (a'kwē hâs'tus). The right to draw water from the land of another.

aquae immittendae (a'kwē im-mit-ten'dē). Easement of dripping water.

aqua fontanea (a'qua fon-tā'ne-a). Spring water.

aqua frisca (a'qua fris'ka). Fresh water.

aquagangium (a-qua-gan'ji-um). A waterway; a trench; a ditch.

aquagaugium (a-qua-gâ'ji-um). A water gauge; a mark on the bank to gauge the rising of the water.

aquage (ā'kwąj). A waterway; a toll paid for passage over water.

aquagium (ā-quā'ji-um). A waterway.

aquam ducendi. See **jus aquam ducendi.**

A qua non deliberentur sine speciali praecepto domini regis (a quā non dē-li-be-ren'ter si'ne spē-she-ā'li prē-sep'tō do'mi-ni rē'jis). From which they are not to be released without a special order from the king.

aqua pluvia (a'qua plū'vi-a). Rain water.

aqua profluens (a'qua pro-flu'ēnz). Flowing water.

aqua quotidiana (a'qua quo-ti-di-ā'na). Water available at all times.

aquarum cursus (a-quā'rum ker'sus). Watercourses.

aqua salsa (a'qua sal'sa). Salt water.

aquatic rights (ą-kwat'ik). Rights of fishing and navigation and in the soil under the sea and the rivers.

aquatiles (a-quā'ti-lēz). Waterfowl, such as mallards and heron.

aqua trestornata (a'qua tres-tor-nā'ta). Water or a stream turned out of its natural course.

aqua viva (a'qua vī'va). Flowing water.

a quo (ā quō). From which; from whom.

arabant (a-rā'bant). Holding by tenure of ploughing and tilling.

Arabant et herciabant ad curiam domini (a-rā'bant et her-she-ā'bant ad kū'ri-am do'mi-ni). They ploughed and harrowed at the lord's court.

arable land (ar'ą-bl). Land suitable for ploughing; land other than pasture, woodland and wasteland

arace (ä-räs'). To raze; to tear out; to uproot.

aracher (ä-rä-shā'). To uproot.

aracine (ä-ra-sēn'). Rooted; with growing roots.

araer (ä-rä'ā). Same as **arayer.**

aralia (a-rā'li-ą). Arable land.

arare (a-rā're). To plough.

aratia (a-rā'she-a). Same as **aralia.**

arationes (a-rā-she-ō'nēz). (Roman law.) Public lands leased at a yearly rental of one-tenth of the yield.

arator (a-rā-tō're). A ploughman.

aratores (a-rā-tō'rēz). (Roman law.) Tenants of public lands.

aratrum terrae (a-rā'trum ter'rē). Service rendered by a tenant by ploughing the land.

aratura terrae (a-rā-tū'ra ter'rē). The ploughing of the land; feudal service by ploughing.

araturia (a-rā-tū'ri-a). Same as **aralia.**

arayer (ä-rä'yā). To array; to arrange; to fix.

arbiter (är'bi-tėr). An arbitrator; formerly, a person who was governed in his decisions by law and equity, rather than by his own judgment.

arbitrable (är'bi-trą-bl). Capable of being submitted to arbitration; a matter constituting a controversy which may be the subject of an action. 5 Am J2d Arb & A § 54.

arbitrage (är'bi-trąj). The computation of differences in rates of money exchange and in the market values of securities for the purpose of profiting by sales and purchases in different places. A simultaneous matched purchase and sale of identical or equivalent securities. Falco v Donner Foundation, Inc. (CA2 NY) 208 F2d 600, 40 ALR2d 1340. A transaction sometimes employed to profit by differences in the rate of exchange; sometimes to capitalize dividends and prevent their receipt as income. Falco v Donner Foundation, Inc. supra.

arbitral (är'bi-trąl). Pertaining to arbitration.

arbitrament (är-bit'rą-męnt). The award of arbitrators.

Arbitramentum aequum tribuit cuique suum (ar-bi'-tra-men-tum ē'qu-um tri'bu-it kī'kwē su'um). A just arbitration renders to each party what is his.

arbitranda (ar-bi-tran'da). To be judged.

arbitrar (ar'bi-trar). (Spanish.) To adjudge or award; to strike out means or expedients. Sheldon v Milmo, 90 Tex 1, 15.

arbitrarily (är'bi-trą-ri-li). Acting in an unreasonable or arbitrary manner.

arbitrary. According to notion or whim rather than according to law. Despotic; without reason. Fixed or arrived at through an exercise of will or by caprice, without consideration or adjustment with reference to principles, circumstances or significance. United States v Carmack, 329 US 230, 91 L Ed 209, 67 S Ct 252.

A legislative classification of a group of persons is not arbitrary if it is based on a substantial difference between that group of persons and all other persons and such difference bears a proper relation to the purposes of the statute. Krebs v Board of Trustees, 410 Ill 435, 102 NE2d 321, 27 ALR2d 1434.

arbitrary decision. A decision rendered by a court, or judge, or other officer exercising judicial functions which is based upon the will of the officer alone, and not upon any course of reasoning and exercise of judgment. Mutual Ben. Life Ins. Co. v Welch, 71 Okla 59, 175 P 45, 49.

arbitrary discretion. Unsound discretion; deciding by whim or caprice; discretion exercised for an erroneous reason. National Ben. Life Ins. Co. v Shaw-Walker Co. 71 App DC 276, 111 F2d 497.

arbitrary government. An absolute monarchy or, as in modern times, a totalitarian government.

arbitrary punishment. A sentence that is not supported by law. Ex parte Lamar (CJ2) 274 F 160, 24 ALR 864, affd 260 US 711, 67 L Ed 476, 43 S Ct 251.

arbitrary test. An unreasonable test; a test imposed without reference to the purpose professed to be accomplished; discrimination.

arbitrate (är'bi-trāt). To submit to arbitration; to settle a controversy by arbitration.

arbitration. A mode of settling differences through the investigation and determination, by one or more persons selected for the purpose, of some disputed matter submitted to them by the contending parties for decision and award, in lieu of a judicial proceeding. Crosby v State Board of Hail Ins. 113 Mont 470, 129 P2d 99.
See **board of arbitration.**

Arbitration Act. A federal statute providing for the arbitration of disputes involved in maritime transactions or commerce. 9 USC §§ 1-14; Annos: 64 ALR2d 1338, §§ 2,3[a]; 100 L Ed 211. One of the uniform laws. 5 Am J2d Arb & A § 10.
The federal statute on arbitration is strictly limited to maritime transactions and commerce, but it is sufficient for the application of the statute that the matter involved is either a maritime transaction or commerce; it is not necessary that it be both. 5 Am J2d Arb & A § 6.

arbitration agreement. A contract to submit a dispute or disputes to arbitration, either present controversies or disputes which may arise in the future. 5 Am J2d Arb & A § 11.

arbitration and award. A plea raising the defense that the matter in suit has been previously settled by an arbitration.

arbitration association. See **American Arbitration Association.**

arbitration board. See **board of arbitration.**

arbitration bond. A bond of one of the parties to an arbitration given to secure his submission to the award.

arbitration clause. A clause in a contract providing for arbitration of any controversy arising out of the contract and its performance.
Sometimes such clause is incorporated by reference to the rules of a trade association or other organization. Anno: 41 ALR2d 872.

arbitration court. The International Court of Arbitration, known as the Hague Tribunal, established by the International Peace Conference in 1899.
This tribunal was succeeded by the Permanent Court of International Justice, established in 1920 under the auspices of the League of Nations, which in turn was succeeded by the International Court of Justice, established as the judicial branch of the United Nations organization. 30 Am J Rev ed Internat L § 54.

arbitratione facta. See **de arbitratione facta.**

arbitration of exchange. The payment in one country by a bill of exchange drawn upon a party in another country.

arbitration of labor dispute. The hearing, determination, decision, and award by a board of arbitrators of the issues involved in a labor dispute.

arbitrators. Private, extraordinary judges of a domestic tribunal chosen by parties by whose agreement they are invested with quasi-judicial power to decide, finally, and without appeal, matters in dispute between the parties. 5 Am J2d Arb & A § 84.
See **arbitrators; board of arbitration.**

arbitratus (ar-bi-trā′tus). Awarded.

arbitrement (ar-bi′tre-môn). Same as arbitrament.

arbitrios (ar-bē′trē-ōs). (Spanish.) The taxes which, in default of other means of revenue, a town imposes with competent authority upon certain articles of merchandise. As indicating the sources of revenue of a municipality, the words "proprios" and "arbitrios" are usually found linked together and when so connected, they are sometimes used as meaning "ways and means." Sheldon v Milmo, 90 Tex 1, 15.

arbitrium (ar-bi′tri-um). A Roman law judgment in which the judge was governed largely by his conscience; an award of arbitrators.

arbitrium alieno. See **in arbitrium alieno.**

arbitrium boni viri (ar-bi′tri-um bō′nī vi′rī) (Roman law.) The award or decision of a good man.
Freely translated, the decision upon the facts and circumstances of a case which would be made by a man of intelligence and high moral principle. 1 Pomeroy's Equity Jurisprudence, § 43.

Arbitrium est judicium (ar-bi′tri-um est jū-di′she-um). An award is a judgment.

Arbitrium est judicium boni viri, secundum aequum et bonum (ar-bi′tri-um est jū-di′she-um bō′nī vi′rī, se-kun′dum ē′qu-um et bō′num). An award is a judgment of a good man according to equity and good conscience.

arbitrium judicis. See **in arbitrium judicis.**

arbor (är′bor). A tree; a bower; a place shaded by trees or shrubbery.

arbor civilis consanguinitatis (ar′bor si′vi-lis kon-san-gwi-ni-tā′tis). A family tree.

Arbor dum crescit, lignum dum crescere nescit (ar′-bor dum kre′sit, lig′num dum kre′se-re ne′sit). It is a tree while it grows, but it is wood when it is not growing. Dexter v Taber, 12 Johns (NY) 239, 241.

arbor finalis (ar′bor fi-nā′lis). A boundary line tree.

arca (är′kạ). A money chest.

arca chirographica (ar′ka kī-ro-gra′fi-ka). A chest in which money lenders kept evidences of indebtedness.

arcana imperii (ar″kā′na im-pe′ri-ī). Imperial secrets.

arcarius (ar-kā′ri-us). A treasurer.

arceevesque (ar-sē-vesk′). A bishop.

arcessere (ar-ses′se-re). (Roman law.) To summon to court; to bring before a judge.

arcewesche. An archbishop.

archabbot (ärch″ab′ọt). The chief abbot of a monastery.

Archaionomia, sive de priscis Anglorum legis (ar-cha-i-o-nom′i-a, si′ve dē pri′sis An-glō′rum lē′jis). A compilation of Saxon law published in the reign of Elizabeth, about 1600.

archbishop (ärch″bish′up). A metropolitan bishop; a prelate; one in the hierarchy of the church who has supervision over the bishops in a church province.

archbishopric (ärch″bish′up-rik). The diocese or jurisdiction of an archbishop.

archdeacon (ärch″dē′kn). An ecclesiastical officer, with jurisdiction immediately subordinate to the bishop, throughout the whole of the diocese, or in some particular part of it.

archdeacon's court. An English ecclesiastical court with jurisdiction in probate, administration and ecclesiastical matters within the archdeanery; and, later, in the twelfth century, acquiring a customary

ARCHDEANERY [90] ARER

jurisdiction. An appeal lay from the archdeacon's court to the consistory court.

archdeanery (ärch'dē-nẹ-ri). One of the divisions or parts of a diocese, in charge of an archdeacon, under the English ecclesiastical system.

archery (är'chėr-i). The feudal service of maintaining a bow for the defense of the castle; the sport, skill, or pasttime of shooting with bow and arrow.

arches. See **dean of the arches.**

arches court. An ecclesiastical court of appeal and of original jurisdiction. It was the court of appeal from all the diocesan courts, and its original jurisdiction, which had been universal in ecclesiastical cases, was greatly curtailed by the Statute of Citations, in 1529.

archetype (är'kẹ-tīp). An original document.

archidiaconus (ar-ki-di-ā'ko-nus). An archdeacon.

archiepiscopal (är"ki-ẹ-pis'kō-pạl). Pertaining to an archbishop.

archiepiscopus (ar-ki-ē-pis'kō-pus). An archbishop.

Archiepiscopus Cantaur (ar-ki-ē-pis'ko-pus Kan'tar). The Archbishop of Canterbury.

Archiepiscopus Ebor (ar-ki-ē-pis'ko-pus e'bor). The Archbishop of York.

archievesque (ar-ki-e-vesk'). An archbishop.

architect. One whose profession it is to form and devise plans and designs, and draw up specifications, for buildings or structures, and to superintend their construction. Arkansas State Board of Architects v Bank Bldg. & Equipment Corp. 225 Ark 889, 286 SW2d 323, 56 ALR2d 720. 5 Am J2d Arch § 1.

architect's certificate. See **certificate of architect or engineer.**

architect's lien. A statutory lien upon the real estate for compensation for preparing plans and specifications or for superintendence, or for both plans and superintendence. 5 Am J2d Arch §§ 20-22.

architectural design. A design drawn for the purpose of construction according to architectural detail, in scale, and in accordance with the principles of mathematics, aesthetics, and the physical sciences. Hecht v Commuter's Cafe, 193 Misc 170, 80 NYS2d 861.

archium (ar'ki-um). Same as **archives.**

archives (ar'kīves). Public records and papers required or permitted by law to be filed in public places of deposit for preservation and use as evidence of facts or because of historical interest.

archivum (ar-kī'vum). Same as **archive.**

archon (är'kon). An Athenian magistrate.

archpriest (ärch'prēst'). (Eccles.) The dean of a cathedral.

arch-see (ärch'sē'). The see or diocese of an archbishop.

arcifinies (ar-si-fin'i-ēz). Those landed estates which have natural boundaries, such as rivers, mountains or woods. The right of alluvion belongs to those whose estates are arcifinies, and not to others. Smith v St. Louis Public Schools, 30 Mo 290, 303.

arcifinious (ä-si-fin'i-us). Possessing a frontier which forms a natural defense.

arcium constructio (ar'she-um kon-struk'she-ō). The building of forts or defensive works. This was a part of the trinoda necessitas, to which every man's estate was subject under the ancient law of England. Butler v Perry, 240 US 328, 331, 60 L Ed 672, 674, 36 S Ct 258.

arct (ärkt). Forced; compelled; constrained.

arcta (ark'tạ). Same as **arct.**

arctable (ark'tạ-bl). Forcible.

arcta et salva custodia (ark'ta et sal'va kus-to'di-a). In close and safe custody.

arctare (ark-tā're). To bind; to force; to constrain.

ardent spirits (är'dẹnt). Distilled liquors. Sarlls v United States, 152 US 571, 38 L Ed 556, 14 S Ct 721.

arder (är'dėr). To burn.

ardhel (ard'hel). Same as **arthel.**

ardour (är'dọr). An incendiary.

ardours de mesons (ar-door' de me-sôn'). Burners of houses.

Ardours sont qui ardent cite, ville, maison, beast, ou autres chateux (ar-door' sôn kē ar'dôn sēt, vēl, mā'son, best, oo ō-tre cha-tō'). Ardours are those who burn a city, a village, a house, a beast or other chattels.

are (âr). A French measure of area, being the equivalent of 119.6046 square yards.

area (ā-rẹ-ạ). An open space within a house or an adjoining inclosure.

area concept. The scheme in public housing projects whereby whole areas are selected for redevelopment, notwithstanding some of the properties may not be substandard or blighted. Berman v Parker 348 US 26, 99 L Ed 27, 75 S Ct 98.

area of production. A technical term employed in determining exemptions from the application of the Fair Labor Standards Act; a zone within which economic influences operate and outside of which they lose their force. Addison v Holly Hill Fruit Products, 322 US 607, 88 L Ed 1488, 64 S Ct 1215, 153 ALR 1007, reh den 323 US 809, 89 L Ed 645, 65 S Ct 27. A territorial area, wherein it is farm labor involved in the production of agricultural commodities, as distinguished from industrial labor required before such commodities are offered for sale to the consumer. 31 Am J Rev ed Lab § 690.

area-sneak. A thief who sneaks around dwellings in order to steal.

areaway. A cellar or room under the sidewalk on a street. 25 Am J1st Highways § 263.

areister (a-rā'stā). Same as **arester.**

arenales (a-re-na'lēz). Sandy beaches.

a rendre (à rän'dr). To render.

arenes (ä-ren'). Same as **arraigned.**

arenifodina (a-rē"ni-fo-dī'na). In Roman law,—a sandpit.

arentare (a-ren-tā're). To rent.

areopagus (ar-ẹ-op'ạ-gus). The seat of religious, political and judicial government in ancient Athens.

arer (ä'rā). Same as **arrer.**

arere (ä-rēr'). In arrear; back.

areremain (ä-rē're-man). Back again.

arer et semer. To plough and sow.

arerissement (ä-re-rēs'môn). Delay; hindrance.

A rescriptio argumentum (ā rē-skrip'she-ȯ ar-gū-men'tum). An argument based upon original writs in the record.

aresenez (ä-res-nā'). Same as **arraigned**.

aresnes (ä-res'nes). Same as **arraigned**.

arestare (a-res-tā're). Same as **arrestare**.

arester (ä-res'tā). To arrest; to stop.

arester (ä-res'ter). The creditor in an arrestment.

aret (ä-ret'). Same as **arret**.

a retro (ā rē'trō). In arrears.

aretro (a-rē'trō). Same as **a retro**.

arg. An abbreviation of **arguendo**.

argentaria (ar-jen-tā'ri-a). Dealing in money.

argentarii (ar-jen-tā'ri-ī). Money lenders.

argentarius (ar-jen-tā'ri-us). A money lender; a banker.

argentarius miles (ar-jen-tā'ri-us mī'les). A porter who carried money in the exchequer.

argenteus (är-jen'tē-us). A Roman coin worth about a denarius and a half.

argentifodina (ar-jen-ti-fo-dī'na). A silver mine.

argentum (är-jen'tum). Silver.

argentum album (är-jen'tum al'bum). Uncoined silver; silver coin; white rent.

argentum Dei (är-jen'tum De'ī). God's money; an earnest given to bind a bargain.

argentum factum (är-jen'tum fak'tum). Silver which has been wrought into some article.

argentum infectum (är-jen'tum in-fek'tum). Silver which has not been wrought into anything.

arguendo (ar-gu-en'dō). In argument; by way of argument.

argument. A reason offered to induce belief and convince the mind. Rahles v J. Thompson & Sons Mfg. Co. 137 Wis 506, 118 NW 350.

argumentative (är-gū-men'ta-tiv). Inferential; contentious.

argumentative denial. A denial in an argumentative or reasoning manner and not in direct, positive form of proper pleading. 41 Am J1st Pl § 134.

argumentative instruction. An instruction given by the court in its charge to the jury which directs the jury to look to certain facts as tending toward certain conclusions.

Such an instruction is objectionable but not reversible error, unless it appears to be prejudicial. 53 Am J1st Trial § 552.

argumentative pleading. A pleading which makes its allegations in the manner of reasoning rather than by direct and positive statements. 41 Am J1st Pl § 134.

argumentative traverse. An argumentative plea or answer. 41 Am J1st Pl § 134.

argument of counsel. The discussion by counsel for the respective parties of their contentions on the law and the facts of the case in hand in order to aid the jury in arriving at a correct and just conclusion. 53 Am J1st Trial § 452.

See **opening statement**; **summing up**.

argument on appeal. A written or printed legal argument, sometimes supplemented by an oral presentation, intended to assist the court in arriving at a just and proper conclusion by presenting the side of a party as supported by points of law and facts in evidence. 5 Am J2d A & E § 684.

See **brief**.

argumentum (ar-gu-men'tum). Argument.

Argumentum ab auctoritate (ar-gu-men'tum ab âk-tor-i-tā'te). Argument based on authority.

Argumentum ab impossibili (ar-gu-men'tum ab im-pos-si'bi-lī). An argument drawn from an impossibility.

Argumentum ab inconvenienti (ar-gu-men'tum ab in-kon-ve-ni-en'tī). An argument drawn from the inconvenience of a thing. Park v Candler, 114 Ga 466, 503.

Argumentum ab inconvenienti plurimum valet in lege (ar-gu-men'tum ab in-kon-ve-ni-en'tī plu'ri-mum va'let in lē'je). An argument drawn from the inconvenience of the thing is very forcible in law. See Broom's Legal Maxims, 184.

Argumentum a communiter accidentibus (ar-gu-men'tum ā kom-mu'ni-ter ak-si-den'ti-bus). An argument from ordinary occurrences.

argumentum ad crumenam (ar-gu-men'tum ad kru-mē'nam). An argument addressed to the purse.

argumentum ad hominem (ar-gu-men'tum ad ho'mi-nem). An argument addressed to the man, that is, a personal argument.

argumentum ad ignorantiam (ar-gu-men'tum ad ig-nō-ran'she-am). An argument addressed to ignorance, that is, one based upon the ignorance of the audience.

argumentum ad invidiam (ar-gū-men'tum ad in-vi'di-am). An argument resting in hatred or prejudice.

Argumentum a divisione. (ar-gu-men'tum ā di-vi-zhe-ō'ne). An argument from a division of the matter.

argumentum ad judicium (ar-gū-men'tum ad jū-di'-she-um). An argument appealing to one's judgment.

argumentum ad verecundiam (ar-gu-men'tum ad ve-re-kun'di-am). An argument addressed to the sense of decency.

Argumentum a majori ad minus (ar-gu-men'tum ā mā-jō'rī ad mī'nus). An argument from the greater to the less.

Argumentum a simili (ar-gu-men'tum ā si'mi-li). Argument from analogy.

argumentum baculinum (ar-gu-men'tum ba-ku-li'-num). An argument appealing to the club, to violence.

argumentum ex concesso (ar-gu-men'tum ex kon-ses'sō). An argument based upon what has been conceded or admitted.

aribannum (a-ri-ban'num). A feudal penalty imposed for disobedience of the king's order to take up arms.

arid lands. Lands of western states in need of reclamation by irrigation. 30 Am J Rev ed Irrig §§ 92—112.

A district is "arid" where rainfall is insufficient for agricultural purposes. Hall v Carter, 33 Tex Civ App 230, 233, 77 SW 19.

arier ban (ä'ri-ā ban). Same as **arrier ban**.

ariere. See **en ariere**.

arimanni (ä-ri-män′ni). Freemen who were employed on farms.

aripenna (a-ri-pen′na). Same as **arpennus**.

aripennum (a-ri-pen′num). Same as **arpennus**.

arise. To come into being or notice, as a cause of action arising at a particular time and place. Sherman v Droubay, 27 Utah 47, 74 P 348.

arisen. Generally understood to be the equivalent of "accrues", where it pertains to a cause of action. 34 Am J1st Lim Ac §46.

arising in another state. The accrual of a cause of action in a foreign jurisdiction in which the obligation was to be paid or discharged. 34 Am J1st Lim Ac § 224.

arising out of and in the course of the employment. Imposing double conditions, both of which must be satisfied before liability for workmen's compensation arises. 58 Am J1st Workm Comp § 209.

arising out of or in the course of the employment. Conditions imposed in the disjunctive, the fulfillment of either of which is sufficient in respect of liability for workmen's compensation. 58 Am J1st Workm Comp § 209.

arising out of the employment. Implying a causal connection between an injury to an employee and the performance of work required of him. 38 Am J1st Workm Comp § 211.

aristarchy (ar′is-tär-ki). Government by the best men of the country.

aristocracy (ar-is-tok′rạ-si). A government ruled by a class; an elite class; those who excel in a group, as the aristocracy of football coaches.

aristodemocracy (ar″is-tō-dẹ-mok′rạ-si). Government by a combination of the nobility and the common people.

arles (ärlz). Money given as an earnest to bind a bargain.

arm. Noun: A limb of the human and ape body; a weapon. Verb: To furnish with weapons.

arma (ar′ma). Arms; weapons.

arma capere (ar′ma ka′pe-re). To take arms; to assume knighthood.

arma dare (ar′ma da′re). To give arms; to knight.

Arma in armatos jura sinunt (ar′ma in ar-mā′tos jū′ra sī′nunt). The laws permit the use of arms against those who are armed.

arma libera (ar′ma li′be-ra). Free arms; the sword and lance given to a servant upon his manumission.

armamenta navis (ar-ma-men′ta nā′vis). The paraphernalia of a ship.

arma moluta (ar′ma mo-lū′ta). Cutting weapons.

arma pacis et justitiae (ar′ma pā′sis et jus-ti′she-ē). The arms of peace and justice.

arma perturbationis pacis et injuriae (ar′ma per-ter-bā-she-ō′nis pā′sis et in-jū′ri-ē). Arms of broken peace and injustice.

arma reversata (ar′ma re-ver-sā′ta). Reversed arms, an ancient punishment for treason and felony.

arma suscipere (ar′ma su-si′pe-re). To assume knighthood.

armata vis (ar-mā′ta vis). Armed force; armed services.

armatura (ar-ma-tū′ra). Armor.

armature (är′mạ-tụr). Armor; the revolving part of a dynamo or motor.

arme (arm). A weapon.

armed (ärmd). Furnished, equipped, or carrying weapons of offense or defense. State v Lynch, 88 Me 195, 198, 33 A 978. Carrying weapons for offensive or defensive combat. 56 Am J1st Weap § 2.

armed country. A nation prepared for war.

armed force. A posse of citizens called to duty to help maintain order or arrest a person charged with crime. Chapin v Ferry, 3 Wash 386, 28 P 754.

Armed Forces. The entire military establishment of the United States; Army, Navy, Air Force, Coast Guard, etc.

armed neutrality. The state of a country which is neutral as to the belligerents but arms to resist attack or invasion.

armed peace. The state of a country which in time of peace is ready for war; in the terminology of the day, a cold war.

armed services. The entire body of officers, noncommissioned officers, and enlisted men which stands ready for defense of the country, whether by land, sea, or in the air, perhaps, some day in space.

armed ship. A merchantman which has been equipped for fighting.

armig. Same as **armiger**.

armiger (är′mi-jėr). A squire; a knight's armor bearer; one entitled to bear heraldic arms.

armigeri natalitii (ar-mi′je-ri nā-ta-li′she-ī). Armor bearers or esquires by birth. Such were the eldest sons of younger sons of peers, and their eldest sons. See 1 Bl Comm 406.

armistice (är′mis-tis). An agreed interruption of hostilities between belligerent nations; a truce.

arm of the sea. A bay or river where the tide of the sea ebbs and flows.

armor bearer (är′mọr bār′ėr). One who carried the equipment of a knight or other fighting man; a squire.

Armorum appelatione, non solum scuta et gladii et fustes et lapides continentur (ar-mō′rum ap-pel-lā′she-ō-ne, non sō′lum sku′ta et gla′di-ī et fus′tēz et la′pi-dēz kon-ti-nen′ter). Under the term "arms" are included, not only shields and swords, but also clubs and stones.

arms. See **bearing arms**; **weapons**; **insignia**.

arms-bearing. See **bearing arms**.

arm's length. See **at arm's length**.

arms of the United States. The armed forces and armaments of all kinds of the United States. 22 USC § 2552(a).

armum molutum (ar′mum mo-lū′tum). A cutting weapon.

army. A body of armed men, or a body of men part of whom are armed and part of whom bear or work with other equipment compatible with their duties, so organized and disciplined as to act together, be mutually reliant, and perform in unison the evolutions of the march and the battlefield upon command given therefor. 36 Am J1st Mil § 3.

Army. The land forces of the United States Armed Services.

arnica (är'ni-kä). A drug. State Board of Pharmacy v Matthews, 197 NY 353, 90 NE 966.

aromatarius (a-ro-mȧ-tā'ri-us). A grocer.

arpen. Same as **arpent**.
In Louisiana, the word is infrequently and incorrectly used when the word "acre" is meant. Randolph v Sentilles, 110 La 419, 34 So 587.

arpent (är'pent). An ancient French land measure containing 100 perches, the equivalent of 100 square rods.

arpentator (är'pen-tā-tor). A land surveyor.

arpentum (ar-pen'tum). Same as **arpent**.

arpine (är'pin). Same as **arpent**.

arra (ar'ra). An earnest payment to bind a bargain.

arrage (ar'āj). Insane; demented.

arraign an assign. To sue; to arrange or prepare for an action or a trial.

arraigner (a̧-rā'nėr). To arraign.

arraignment. The act of bringing an accused before a court to answer the charge made against him by indictment, information, or complaint. It consists of bringing the accused into court, reading the charge to him then and there, and then calling upon him to plead thereto as "guilty" or "not guilty."

arraigns. See **clerk of arraigns**.

arrainare (ar-rā'nar're). To arraign.

arrameur (ar'rā-meur). A port officer who directed the proper loading and stowing of cargoes.

arranare (ar-ra-nā're). Same as **arrainare**.

arrangement. A term for what was formerly called a composition; a word with a dual meaning, one being the proceeding by which a debtor, in failing circumstances but not hopelessly insolvent, may have his financial affairs adjusted in the bankruptcy court and be rehabilitated; the other being the plan worked out in the proceeding whereby rehabilitation may be accomplished.
See **deed of arrangement**; **family arrangement**.

arrangement of music. An adaptation of a musical composition to instruments or voices other than those for which it was originally produced, such being a protected right under a copyright of the original composition. 18 Am J2d Copyr § 22.

arrangement of words. An author's intellectual production; the subject of copyright. 18 Am J2d Copyr § 4.

arras (ar'a̧s). A civil law term for property which the husband gives the wife on account of marriage. Cutter v Waddingham, 22 Mo 206, 254.

array (a-rā'). Noun: The list of names attached to the writ of venire which indicates the names of persons to be summoned as jurors. 31 Am J Rev ed Jury § 74. Also, the whole body of men and women summoned for jury duty. Durrah v State, 44 Miss 789, 796. An impanelled jury. Verb: To select jurors.

arrearages. Same as **arrears**.

arrears. Payments past-due, as arrears in alimony. Passed dividends on preferred stock. Anno: 25 ALR2d 802.

arrect (a-rekt'). To charge or accuse; charged or accused.

arrectatus (ar-rek-tā'tus). One accused or suspected of a crime.

arreist (ar-rāst'). (Scotch.) An arrest.

arrenatus (ar-re-nā'tus). Arraigned; accused.

arrendamiento. (Spanish.) A lease of realty.

arrent (a-rent'). To lease; to let at a rental.

arrentatio (ar-ren-tā'she-ō). Same as **arrentation**.

arrentation (ar-en-tā'shon). The right or privilege of leasing; the privilege granted to a tenant of forest land to enclose it on paying rent.

arrer (âr-rer). To plough.

arrerages (ar-re-rā-jez). Same as **arrears**.

arreragium (ar-re-rā'ji-um). Arrears; the balance due on an account.

arrere (âr-rer). To plough.

arrer le prees (ar'rā le prā). To plough the meadows.

arrest. The taking, seizing or detaining of the person of another, accomplished by (1) touching or putting hands on the person to be detained; (2) or by any act that indicates an intention to take him into custody and that subjects him to the actual control and will of the person making the arrest; or (3) by the consent of the person to be arrested. 5 Am J2d Arr § 1. In military law, the detention of a member of the armed forces resulting from the preferring of charges and the convening of a court-martial. United States v Smith, 197 US 386, 49 L Ed 801, 25 S Ct 489.
See **false arrest**; **malicious arrest**; **posse comitatus**; **rearrest**; **rescue**; **return of warrant of arrest**; **warrant of arrest**.

arrestandis bonis ne dissipentur (ar-res-tan'dis bō'nis nē dis-si-pen'ter). A writ which, pending litigation, prevented an irresponsible party to the action from making away with chattels involved in the action.

arrestando ipsum qui pecuniam recepit (ar-res-tan'dō ip'sum quī pē-ku'ni-am re-sē'pit). For arresting one who received money,—a writ for the arrest of a man who had received money for enlistment in the army and had then disappeared.

arrestare (ar-res-tā're). To make an arrest.

arrestari et imprisonari (ar-res-tā'ri et im-pri-zo-nā'ri). To be arrested and imprisoned.

arrestatio (ar-res-tā'she-ō). Same as **arrestment**.

arrestation (ar-es-tā'shon). The act of arresting or of making an arrest.

arrestatio navium (ar-res-tā'she-ō nā'vi-um). The arrestment of ships.

arrestee (a̧-rest-ē'). The person in whose possession goods are held under an arrestment; a garnishee in Scotch law.

Arrestentur corpora eorum (ar-res-ten'ter kor'por-a e-ō'rum). Their bodies shall be arrested.

arrester (a-rest'er). The party who sues out an arrestment.

arrest for debt. See **imprisonment for debt**.

arrest in civil action. See **civil arrest**.

arrestment (a̧-rest'ment). An old English and Scottish term for what is better known today as foreign attachment or garnishment, but applying only to the provisional remedy, not to any proceeding under or in aid of an execution. Wilder v Inter-Island Steam Navigation Co. 211 US 239, 246, 53 L Ed 164, 167, 29 S Ct 58.

arrestment jurisdictionis fundandae causa (a-rest'-

ment jū'ris-dik-she-ō"nis fun-dan'dē kâ'zä). An arrestment for the purpose of founding jurisdiction, a Scotch writ whereby a defendant was brought within the jurisdiction by attaching his goods.

arresto facto super bonis mercatorum alienigenorum (ar-res'tō fak'tō sū'per bō'nis mer-kā-tō'rum ā-li-ē"nī-je-nō'rum). A writ against the goods of aliens found in England to obtain recompense for goods taken from a denizen in a foreign country.

arrest of judgment. A remedy by motion for a party against whom a verdict has been rendered. A remedy solely for the defendant under the earlier practice where a judgment non obstante veredicto was available only for a plaintiff. 30A Am J Rev ed Judgm § 292. Preventing entry of judgment upon the verdict in a criminal case. 21 Am J2d Crim L § 520.

arrest of ship. A temporary detention, without design of depriving the owner of the vessel, but to liberate or restore the ship or goods detained, or to pay the value thereof. 29A Am J Rev ed Ins § 1323.

arrest on mesne process. Provisional relief by an attachment of the person of the defendant in a civil action.

arrests of princes. See **restraints of princes.**

arrestum (ar-res'tum). An arrest.

arrest without warrant. An arrest by a peace officer, or even by a private person in some instances, which is legal, notwithstanding the absence of a warrant of arrest, because of the existence of justification under the law, as where the officer has reasonable cause to believe that a felony has been committed and that the person arrested is the person guilty of the crime, and where an arrest made by a private person was that of a person who had committed an offense in his presence. 5 Am J2d Crim L §§ 22 et seq.

arret (a-rā' or a-ret'). The decision of a court; a published decree.

arretted (a-ret'ed). Arraigned; accused.

arrha (ar'ä). Same as **arra.**

arrhabo (arr-hā'bō). An earnest paid to bind a bargain.

arrhae sponsalitiae (ar'hē spōn-sā-li'she-ē). (Roman law.) Betrothal gifts of either of the betrothed to the other.

arrhes (arr'hes). Earnest money.

arriage and carriage. Indefinite and unlawful services formerly demanded of servants.

arriere fee (a-rēr' fē). A fee dependent upon a superior fee.

arriere fief (a-rēr' fēf). Same as **arriere fee.**

arriere vassal (a-rēr' vas'äl). The vassal of a vassal.

arrivagium (ar-ri-va'ji-um). An arrival.

arrival of ship. A term of various meanings, depending on the context in which it appears.

An American ship does not arrive at a foreign port, so as to require the master to deposit his papers with the American consul or commercial agent, unless the ship comes in on business which requires an entry, stay, and clearance, something more than coming in to escape a storm, to receive advice about the market, or ascertain the state of the weather. 48 Am J1st Ship § 222. For the purpose of marine insurance a ship ordinarily has not arrived until she has dropped anchor or moored; in the case where a voyage policy is involved, not until she has been moored in safety for 24 hours. 29 Am J Rev ed Ins § 328.

Within the meaning of the Federal Tariff Act of September 21, 1922, dealing with the unlawful unloading of ships, a ship was held to have "arrived" when she cast anchor seven or eight miles off the seacoast for the purpose of there disposing of her cargo. The Cherie (CA1 Me) 13 F2d 992.

arrogate (ar'ọ-gāt). To assert a claim to, or take, something without right; to exercise authority which one does not have.

arrogatio (ar-ro-gā'she-ō). An adoption wherein the person adopted submits in his own right.
See **arrogation.**

arrogation (ar-ọ'gā'shọn). Claiming or taking more than is lawfully due; taking or asserting without right.

arrogator. The adopting parent in an adoption arrogatio.

arrondissement (a-rôṅ-dēs'mon). (French.) A department subdivision.

arroyo (a-roi'ō). (Spanish origin) A stream or watercourse; a natural channel through which surface or flood waters flow. Kroeger v Twin Buttes R. Co. 13 Ariz 348, 114 P 553.

arrura (ar-rū'ra). Same as **arura.**

ars (ärs). Burnt; consumed by fire.

arsae et pensatae (ar'sē et pen-sā'tē). Burnt and weighed; used of coins to be minted.

arse. A good old English word for buttocks.

arsenic (är'se-nik). A poison used in many murders.

arser in le main (är'sā in le män). Branding by burning on the hand.

arseun (ar'sen). Same as **arson.**

arsine (är'sin). Same as **arson.**

arsion (ar'si-on). Same as **arson.**

arson. At common law, the malicious and voluntary or wilful burning of another's house, or dwelling house, or outhouse appurtenant to or a parcel of the dwelling house or within the curtilage.

By statute, the common law definition has been enlarged to make it applicable to the burning of buildings and property other than dwelling houses or other houses within the curtilage. 5 Am J2d Arson § 1.
See **attempt to commit arson.**

arsure in le main (ar-soor' in le män). Same as **arser in le main.**

art. A creation of form and beauty; the ability to create; cunning or craft.

"Art," within the meaning of the law of patents, is the mode or process of treating materials so as to produce a given result. Expanded Metal Co. v Bradford, 214 US 366, 53 L Ed 1034, 29 S Ct 652.

art and part. A Scotch term for abetting or instigating a crime; that is, for "arting" or instigating and participating.

arte. Forced; compelled; constrained.

arteriosclerosis (ar-tē'ri-ō-skle-rō'sis). Hardening of the arteries. A diseased condition so serious that it should be revealed in answer to an interrogatory in an application for life insurance as to consultation with a physician. Pacific Mut. Life Ins. Co. v Manley (DC Ga) 27 F2d 915, affd (CA5) 35 F2d 337.

artesian. The water contained or carried in a stratum of rock imprisoned between two impervious strata, the water-bearing stratum being inclined, and coming to the surface at some distant and higher point, called the "intake," where it receives the water, which percolates with greater or less rapidity along and through the inclined stratum, obedient to the law of gravity, until it reaches some obstruction so as to be imprisoned, in which event, if the stratum is pierced, water will rise in a tube or well by hydrostatic pressure, due to the greater height of the intake. 56 Am J1st Waters § 111.

The word "artesian" is often used to refer to underground water, notwithstanding it does not rise to the surface upon the piercing of the stratum. 56 Am J1st Waters § 112.

artesian well. A well in which water rises from a lower stratum under its own pressure and flows continuously above the surface of the ground. 56 Am J1st Waters § 111.

arthel (är-thel). To avouch.

article. Noun: A division of a constitution, statute, contract, charter, or of any other written or printed statement of principles, terms or conditions. A material or substance, natural artificial or manufactured in whole or in part. Junge v Hedden, 146 US 233, 238, 36 L Ed 953, 956, 13 S Ct 88. The adjective "a" or "an," known as the indefinite article. Verb: To bind by contract or agreement; to enter into a written contract containing several clauses or divisions.

articled clerk. A lawyer's clerk bound to him by a contract (articles) for his services and for his instruction in law.

articles approbatory. (Scotch.) A reply corresponding to an answer to a bill in equity.

articles improbatory. (Scotch.) A proceeding corresponding to the bill or complaint in an equity suit.

articles of agreement. A contract in writing, or a signed memorandum of a contract.

articles of apprenticeship. An instrument consisting of a contract or indenture whereby a minor was bound out to a master for a fixed period to learn a trade.

articles of association. The agreement entered into by and between the members on forming an unincorporated association. 6 Am J2d Asso & C § 5.

articles of commerce. Articles which are the subject of trade and barter, offered in the market as something having an existence and value independent of the parties to them; commodities to be shipped or forwarded from one state to another and then put up for sale.

An article becomes an article of interstate commerce when it becomes an article of trade from one state to another, and this does not occur until it begins to move, and this movement does not begin until the article is shipped, or is started for transportation from the one state to the other. Ware v Mobile County, 146 Ala 163, 41 So 153.

Articles of Confederation. The instrument forming the Confederation of the original thirteen states of the Union which was in force from March 1, 1781, to March 4, 1789. Owings v Speed, 18 US (5 Wheat) 420, 5 L Ed 124.

It formed a mere league of states, not a union of states in a nation, as did the Constitution which superseded it.

Articles of Faith. The creed of the Church of England known as the thirty-nine articles.

articles of impeachment. The formal written charge against the defendant in an impeachment proceeding.

articles of incorporation. The instrument, otherwise known as certificate of incorporation, which states the purpose or purposes for which the corporation is being organized, the place of business, the amount of authorized capital stock and a description of the classes of shares if the shares are to be classified, the amount of paid in capital with which it will begin business, the number of directors, the names and addresses of the directors for the first year, and the names and addresses of the incorporators. 18 Am J2d Corp § 36. The charter, in other words, the organic law of a corporation. 18 Am J2d Corp § 81.

articles of partnership. The agreement signed by the members of a partnership by which they are bound together as partners.

Articles of Religion. Same as **Articles of Faith.**

articles of roup. (Scotch.) The memorandum of the conditions governing a public auction sale.

articles of set. (Scotch.) A leasehold agreement.

articles of the clergy. An English statute, passed in 1315, concerning clergymen. 9 Edward II, ch 3.

articles of the navy. Statutory regulations governing the United States Navy.

articles of the peace. The complaint in a proceeding to compel a person to give bond to keep the peace.

Articles of Union. The compact of 1707 uniting the kingdoms of England and Scotland.

Articles of War. See **Code of Military Justice.**

articulate (är-tik′ū-lāt). To prepare a writing under separate clauses or provisions; to express one's thoughts clearly. The word is also an adjective, meaning ability to express; a clear method of expression.

articulate adjudication. (Scotch.) The practice of ascertaining the amount of each debt by itself where several different debts are due one creditor.

articulated pleading. A pleading in separate counts.

articuli (ar-ti′ku-lī). Articles.

Articuli Cleri (ar-ti′ku-lī kle′rī). Articles of the clergy,—the title of the statute 9 Edward II, C. 3, passed in 1315 concerning clergymen. See 4 Bl Comm 217.

articuli de moneta (ar-ti′ku-lī dē mo-nē′ta). Statutes concerning the English public currency.

Articuli Magnae Chartae (ar-ti′ku-lī mag′nē kar′tē). The preliminary forty-nine articles forming the basis for the Magna Charta.

Articuli Super Cartas. Same as **Articuli Super Chartas.**

Articuli Super Chartas (ar-ti′ku-lī sū′per kar′tas). Articles upon the charters,—the title of the statute 28 Edward I, c. 3, the purpose of which was to carry out and enforce the provisions of Magna Charta and Charta de Foresta. See 3 Bl Comm 45.

articulo (ar-ti′ku-lō). To speak distinctly; sometimes loosely used for **"articulus."**

articulo mortis (ar-ti′ku-lō mor′tis). At the moment or point of death.

articulus (är-tik'ū-lus). An article; a part of a discourse. A moment; a point of time.

artifice (är'ti-fis). Cunning; deception; a trick; a fraud. State v Hemm, 82 Iowa 609, 617, 48 NW 971.

artificer (är-tif'i-sėr). A workman or mechanic, as distinguished from an employer of such persons.

artificial (är-ti-fish'ạl). Created by man, not by nature. Having an existence presumed in law only, as a corporation.

artificial boundary. A boundary erected by man, as distinguished from a natural boundary, such as a stream.

artificial force. Natural force captured and channeled by the ingenuity of man.

artificial gas. Gas produced for household and industrial use by the burning of coal.

artificial insemination. The means of impregnating a female other than by sexual intercourse. 10 Am J2d, Bast § 1.

artifical limb. A limb of cork, wood, or other composition fitted and attached to the body in place of an amputated arm or leg.

artificial member. An artificial limb.

artificial person. A person created by law or by authority of law, such as a corporation, as distinguished from a natural person, that is, a human being. See 18 Am J2d Corp § 20.

artificial presumption. A presumption arising by force of the law of the jurisdiction, rather than from logic or probability alone. People v Hildebrandt, 308 NY 397, Holley v Purity Baking Co. 128 W Va 531, 37 SE2d 729, 167 ALR 648.

artificial succession. See **perpetual succession.**

artificial teeth. See **false teeth.**

artificial watercourse. A watercourse made by the hand of man.

In determining the nature of an artificial watercourse, three things seem generally to be taken into consideration by the courts: first, whether it is temporary or permanent; secondly, the circumstances under which it was created; and, thirdly, the mode in which it has been enjoyed and used. Where the way is of a permanent character, and is created under circumstances indicating that it shall become permanent, and it has been used consistently with such intention for a considerable period, it is generally regarded as stamped with the character of a natural watercourse. See 56 Am J1st Waters § 151.

artisan (är'ti-zan). A mechanic. A skilled worker in a trade involving work with the hands. McErlain v Taylor, 207 Ind 240, 192 NE 260, 94 ALR 1284.

artisan's lien. A lien for services in repairing an article. 33 Am J1st Liens § 16.

artist (är'tist). A person who produces art, that is something of form and beauty; a performer of ability.

art or process. A term familiar in patent law, meaning the method whereby materials are treated so as to produce a given result. Expanded Metal Co. v Bradford, 214 US 366, 53 L Ed 1034, 29 S Ct 652.

arts and uses. See **analogous arts and uses.**

a rubro ad nigrum (ā ru'brō ad ni'grum). From the red to the black,—from the title of a statute in red ink, to the body of it in black ink.

arura (a-rö'rạ). A ploughing; a day's ploughing.

arva (ar'va). Plough lands; arable lands.

arx (arks). A fortress or castle.
See **arcium constructio.**

as. For instance; to give an example; to the same amount or degree; equally.

The "as," or Roman pound, was commonly used to express any integral sum, and was divisible into twelve parts or unciae. Hence, twelve monthly payments or unciae were held to amount annually to one pound or as usurarius; and so the usurae asses were synonymous with the usurae centesimae; that is interest at the rate of one per cent per month, or twelve per cent per annum. See 2 Bl Comm 462.

as agent. An identification in signing a contract which relieves the person signing from personal liability. 3 Am J2d Contr § 190.

as a matter of course. See **of course.**

as a result of. A form of exception in a life or accident policy excluding injuries or death in connection with aviation or aeronautics. 29A Am J Rev ed Ins § 1262.

asaver (ä'sä-vä). That is to say; to wit.

as cash. A designation of the status in which commercial paper is taken by a bank. The equivalent of saying that title to the paper passes to the bank. 10 Am J2d Banks § 402.

ascaventer (äs-cä-ven'tā). To publish; to certify.

ascavoir (äs-cä-vwor'). To be understood; that is; to wit.

ascend (ạ-send'). To follow an ascending line of ancestors.

ascendent. One in the ascending line of relationship. father or mother, grandfather or grandmother, great grandfather or great grandmother, etc.

ascendentes (a-sen-den'tēz). Ascendants.

ascendientes (a-sen-di-en'tēz). Ascendants.

ascending line of descent. See **direct ascending line.**

ascent. Climbing; rising; the extension of a genealogical line to the past.

ascertain. To make certain; to fix; to establish with certainty; to establish judicially, that is by the finding and judgment or decree of the court. See Globe Publishing Co. v State Bank of Nebraska, 41 Neb 175, 59 NW 683.

ascerte (as-sert'). Certified as to the fact.

asceverer (äs-se've-rā). To assert; to affirm.

as check. Indicating acceptance of commercial paper by a bank for collection only. 10 Am J2d Banks § 402.

ascient (ä'sē-ent). Knowing; with knowledge; with scienter.

ascribere (as-krī'be-re). Same as **adscribere.**

ascriptitii. See **glebae ascriptitii.**

ascriptus (a-skrip'tus). Same as **adscriptus.**

ascun (äs-cun'). Someone; anyone.

ascunement (äs-cūn'e-môn). In any manner.

as designated on. Words in a deed, contract to sell, or other instrument concerning real estate, having reference to a map or plat, which, in effect, incorporate the map or plat into the description of the real estate, thereby making the description intelligible. Mitchell v Moore, 152 Fla 843, 13 So 2d 314.

aseir (ä-se-ēr'). To sit.

aselees (ä-se-lā'). Sealed.

a sequendo (ā se-quen'dō). From the following.

ases (ās'es). Assessed.

asexualization (ā-sex-u-al-i-zā'shọn). Sterilization of a person; an operation performed upon a person for the purpose of preventing procreation.
See **castration; vasectomy.**

as his interest may appear. See **as interest may appear.**

aside. See **set aside.**

a simile (ā si'mi-lē). From analogy.

as interest may appear. A conventional interest in insurance policies intended to protect, not only the named insured, but a mortgagee, lienor, or other person to the extent of whatever interest such person may have in the insured property at the time of the loss.
The phrase appears most often in loss payable or mortgagee clauses of fire insurance policies. 29 Am J Rev ed Ins § 435.
A stipulation in an assignment of a life insurance policy that the policy is payable as the interest of the assignee may appear means the interest as of the date of the death of the insured, when the policy is to be paid. An assignment of life insurance policies as the assignee's interest in a certain company may appear includes the interest of the assignee as a creditor of such company, and the rights of the assignee are not affected by the bankruptcy of the company except as the amount of the indebtedness is reduced by dividends on the assignee's claim filed in the bankruptcy proceedings; nor are such rights affected by the bankruptcy of the company. 29 Am J Rev ed Ins § 682.

as is. See **sale as is.**

ask. To petition; to include in a prayer for relief.

asking price. The price at which a landowner lists his property for sale with a real estate broker. 12 Am J2d Brok § 111.

A societate nomen sumpserunt, reges enim tales sibi associant (ā sō-si-e-tā'te nō'men sump-sē'runt, rē'jēz e'nim tā'lēz si'bi as-sō'she-ant). They took their name from the society, for they were the associates of the king. See 1 Bl Comm 398.

as of course. As a matter of course; as a matter of right; without the interposition of the court. Stoddard v Treadwell, 29 Cal 281.
See **amendment as of course; motion of course.**

asoyne (ä-soin'). Same as **essoign.**

as paper. Indicating acceptance of commercial paper by a bank for collection only. 10 Am J2d Banks § 402.

aspect. View; possibility.
See **contingency with a double aspect.**

as per. In accordance with. 17 Am J2d Contr § 281.
Thus, a merchant shipping goods in compliance with a letter of instructions to that effect, may write, "I have this day shipped goods as per instructions contained in your letter," meaning in accordance with the instructions; and one who draws bills upon another by agreement may write, "as per agreement, I have drawn," etc., meaning in accordance with, or subject to our agreement, or as by agreement authorized, I have drawn, etc. Continental Bank & Trust Co. v Times Publishing Co. 142 La 209, 76 So 612.

as per contract. In accordance with the contract. Words which destroy the negotiability of a bill or note when incorporated in the terms thereof. 11 Am J2d B & N § 143.

asperse (as-pėrs'). To defame; to slander or libel.

aspersive (as-pėr'siv). Defamatory; slanderous; libellous.

asphalt. A bitumen, a constituent of a mixture used in paving streets and highways, found in a natural state or obtained by the processing of crude oil.

asphyxia (as-fik'si-ạ). A condition of unconsciousness resulting from want of oxygen or too much carbon dioxide in the blood; a stopping of the pulse from the same cause. State v Baldwin, 36 Kan 1, 12 P 318. A condition caused as well by carbon monoxide in the blood. Davey v Turner, 55 Ga App 786, 191 SE 383; 29A Am J Rev ed Ins § 1279.

asphyxiation (as-fik'si-ā'shọn). A state of asphyxia. Suffering asphyxia.
See **asphyxia.**

aspirin. Acetylsalicylic acid; much used in tablet form for relieving headache.

asport (as-pōrt'). To carry away in the commission of larceny.

asportare (as-por-tā're). To carry away.

asportation (as-por-tā'shọn). The act of carrying away.
In larceny it is the carrying away of the goods following the caption or taking possession of them; it is the very first act of removal of the property and may consist of the least removing of the thing taken. See 32 Am J1st Larc § 17. Asportation is also an essential element of the crime of robbery. The taking of absolute control of the property, even for an instant, constitutes asportation. 46 Am J1st Rob § 6.

asportator (as-por-tā'tor). One who carries away stolen goods.

asportatus (as-por-tā'tus). Carried away.

asportavit (as-por-tā'vit). He carried away.

Aspris facetiis inlusus, quae ubi multum ex vero traxere, acrem sui memoriam relinquunt (as'pris fasē'she-is in-lū'sus, kwē ū'bi mul'tum ex vē'ro traxē're, ā'krem sū'i me-mō'ri-am re-lin'qu-unt). Being teased with cutting jests which when they are almost true leave a bitter remembrance. 4 Bl Comm 151.

A. S. R. See **Am. St. Rep.**

as result of pregnancy. Resulting from pregnancy. Anno: 97 ALR2d 1068.

ass. A donkey, a dull or incompetent person; a very common and unrefined expression for buttocks. An abbreviation of **assize.**

assach (Welsh.) An oath made by compurgators.

assaia (as-sai'a). Same as **assay.**

assaia mensurarum et ponderum (as-sai'a mēn-surā'rum et pon'de-rum). The assay of measures and weights.

assailant (ạ-sā'lạnt). A person who assails, or who assaults another; the aggressor. Scales v State, 96 Ala 69, 75, 11 So 121.

assaith (as-saith'). Same as **assath.**

assallire (as-sa-lī're). To assault.

assaltus (as-sal'tus). An assault.

assart (a-särt'). To root up trees; to deforest land; the land so deforested.

assartare (as-sar-tā're). To assart.

assartments (as-sart'ments). Same as **assart rent.**

assart rent. Rent paid for land which had been deforested.

assassin (ạ-sas'in). One who murders, striking suddenly and without warning, often for pay, sometimes from misguided motives, and usually making an important personage a victim.

assassination (ạ-sas-i-nā'shọn). The commission of a murder treacherously, with violence, for hire or as a member of a group devoted to killing.

assassinator (ạ-sas'i-nā-tọr). An assassin.

assath. Same as **assach.**

assault. A demonstration of an unlawful intent by one person to inflict immediate injury on the person of another then present; an intentional attempt by a person, by force or violence, to do an injury to the person of another; an attempt to commit a battery, or any threatening gesture showing in itself or by words accompanying it an immediate intention, coupled with the present ability, to commit a battery. 6 Am J2d Asslt & B § 3. An act, other than the mere speaking of words, which directly or indirectly is the legal cause of putting another in apprehension of an immediate and harmful or offensive contact, rendering the actor civilly liable, if he intends thereby to inflict a harmful or offensive contact upon the other or a third person or to put the other or a third person in apprehension thereof, and the act is not consented to by the other, or otherwise privileged. Restatement, Torts § 21(1).

The prolonged, excessive, and emotionally distressing interrogation of a civilian by a sergeant assigned to the Army's Criminal Investigation Division, which interrogation results in the temporary insanity of the civilian, constitutes an "assault" which is expressly excepted from the coverage of the Federal Tort Claims Act. United States v Hambleton (CA9 Wash) 185 F2d 564, 23 ALR2d 568. As the term "assault" appears in an exception, in a life or accident insurance policy, which relieves the insurer from liability for injuries or death sustained in such an altercation, it imports fault on the part of the insured. 29A Am J Rev ed Ins § 1201.

See **aggravated assault; civil assault; criminal assault.**

assault and battery. An assault upon a person carried into effect by striking him, throwing him down, or otherwise doing some violence to him. Rell v State, 136 Me 322, 9 A2d 129, 125 ALR 602.

assault with a dangerous or deadly weapon. An assault aggravated by the means used, a weapon inherently dangerous or capable of use in a deadly or dangerous manner. 6 Am J2d Asslt & B § 53.

assault with intent to kill. A criminal offense constituting a felony in some jurisdictions, a great, aggravated, or serious misdemeanor in others, and a mere misdemeanor in still other jurisdictions. 26 Am J1st Homi § 597.

assault with intent to rape. An aggravated assault. 6 Am J2d Asslt & B § 55.

To constitute this crime, two essential ingredients must coexist, and must be established by the evidence beyond a reasonable doubt; first, an assault, and, second, an intent to commit rape. It must appear, not only that the defendant intended to have carnal knowledge of the woman alleged to have been assaulted, forcibly and against her will, but that he did some overt act towards the accomplishment of his purpose, which amounted in law to an assault upon her. See 44 Am J1st Rape § 21.

assaut (as-sō'). An old spelling of **assault.**

assay (ạ-sā'). An examination or test; a trial or test by analysis of ore, especially to determine gold or silver content; a comparison of weights or measures with the standards for them.

assaya (as'sä-yä). Same as **assay.**

assayator regis (as-sa-yā'tor rē'jis). The assayer of the king.

assayer of the king (ạ-sā'ėr). A government officer of the king's mint having the duty of testing coins and bullion.

assayer of the mint. A government officer having the duty of testing coins and uncoined gold and silver.

asseal. To seal; to affix a seal.

assecurare (as-sē-kū-rā're). To make secure; to give security.

assecuratio (as-sē-kū-rā'she-ō). Assecuration.

assecuration (as''ẹ-kụ-rā'shọn). Assurance; marine insurance.

assecurator (as-sē-kū-rā'tōr). An insurer.

assembly (ạ-sem'bli). A meeting of several persons; the name given to the lower house of the legislature in some states. A constitutional right under the First Amendment to the Constitution of the United States. A constitutional guaranty cognate to the rights of free speech and free press. 16 Am J2d Const L § 354. The right of the people to meet for the purpose of petitioning the legislative body for a redress of grievances, for any purpose connected with the powers or duties of government, or for the purpose of advancing ideas and airing grievances. Bates v Little Rock, 361 US 516, 4 L Ed 2d 480, 80 S Ct 412.

See **General Assembly; unlawful assembly.**

assembly general. The highest Scotch ecclesiastical court.

assensu curiae. See **ex assensu curiae.**

assensu suo. See **ex assensu suo.**

assent. Consent by one person to what another person has done or what he agrees to do. An element of a contract, but objective in its manifestation, a matter of overt acts, not of inward motives, design, or interpretation of words. Sokoloff v National City Bank, 239 NY 158, 145 NE 917, 37 ALR 712, 719.

See **consent; mutual assent.**

assenter (ạ-sen'tėr). To assent.

assert. To declare; to allege positively.

assertare (as-ser-tā're). Same as **assartare.**

asserte (as-sert'). Same as **assart.**

assertory covenants. Affirmative covenants.

assertory oath. An oath which asserts a statement of fact, as in an affidavit, in distinction to an oath which pledges future conduct, as in the oath of a public officer taken in assuming the office. 39 Am J1st Oath § 4.

asses (ass'es). Sufficient; satisfaction.

assess. To list and value properties for the purpose of taxation. 51 Am J1st Tax § 647. To call upon the

ASSESSED [99] ASSEWIARE

members of an association or other organization for contributions, as in the case of a mutual benefit socity or beneficial order. To make an estimate.

assessed valuation. A listing and valuation of property as a basis upon which taxes are to be collected. Anno: 156 ALR 594.

assessed value. The value of property as estimated and fixed by the proper authorities for purposes of taxation. Baisden v Greenville, 215 Ala 512, 515, 111 So 2.

assessment. In the most common sense, the imposing of a tax by a listing of the persons and property to be taxed and a valuation of the property of each person as a basis of apportionment and levy, such acts usually being performed by administrative officers but sometimes by the legislature. State v Clement Nat. Bank, 84 Vt 167, 78 A 944. A special assessment, one imposed upon property within a limited area for the payment of a local improvement supposed to enhance the value of all property within that area. 48 Am J1st Spec A § 3. A call upon subscribers to corporate stock for payment of their subscriptions, or, if the subscriptions have been paid, a levy upon the stock for the purpose of correcting an impairment of capital. 18 Am J2d Corp § 346. Substantially, the equivalent of a premium collected by an insurance company, being the sum specifically levied by a mutual insurance company or association operating upon a fixed and definite plan, to pay losses and expenses, the sum being the consideration for the insurance provided. 29 Am J Rev ed Ins § 501. The levy against a member of a mutual benefit society or a fraternal benefit society as his share of the amount to be paid for the benefits extended by the society under the terms of his contract. 38 Am J2d Frat O § 88.

The word comes from the Latin words "ad," meaning "to," and "sedere," meaning "sit," through the Middle Latin "assessare," to "fix a rate" or "impose a tax." Thus, within limitations, the word "assessment" and "tax" can be employed synonymously. 48 Am J1st Spec A § 3.

In construing the expression "all taxes levied and assessed," as used in a statute governing adverse possession, it was held that the word "levied" referred to the act of the county board in making the levy, and that the word "assessed" referred to the act of the assessor in making the assessment. Allen v McKay & Co. 120 Cal 332, 52 P 828.

assessment association. See **benevolent association**; **mutual benefit society.**

assessment contract. See **assessment plan**; **assessment policy.**

assessment district. A unit of territory for the assessment of property for taxation; a district specially benefited by a local public improvement with the consequence that a special or local assessment is made against the property in the district to finance the improvement. 48 Am J1st Spec A § 114.

assessment for benefits. See **special assessment.**

assessment fund. See **assessment policy.**

assessment labor. See **assessment work.**

assessment list. A schedule of the taxable persons and properties in a political subdivision. Wilson v Wheeler, 55 Vt 446.

assessment of corporate stock. See **stock assessment.**

assessment of damages. Measuring and fixing the amount of compensatory damages. 22 Am J2d Damg §§ 45 et seq.

assessment plan. A plan of insurance whereby the payment of the benefit is in some manner or degree dependent upon the collection of an assessment upon persons holding similar policies. 29 Am J Rev ed Ins § 501. A form of insurance, also called the "natural premium plan," wherein the insurance company limited its assessments or premiums to such a sum as was necessary to cover the actual cost of insurance from one renewal period to another. Westerman v Supreme Lodge, Knights of Pythias, 196 Mo 670, 94 SW 470.

assessment policy. A policy issued by a mutual benefit society which contains the provision that on the death of a member, an equal or flat assessment shall be levied on all members, irrespective of age, for the purpose of creating a fund to be paid the beneficiary of a deceased member. Allin v Motorists Alliance of America, 234 Ky 714, 29 SW2d 19, 71 ALR 688. See **assessment plan.**

assessment work. A mining law term, meaning work required to be performed on a mining claim each year.
See **annual assessment labor.**

assessments of mutual benefit society. The amounts levied against members for the purpose of the payment of benefits extended by the society under the terms of their contracts or certificates of membership. 38 Am J2d Frat O § 88.

assessor (ą-ses'or). An officer whose duty it is to make an assessment of property, usually for the purpose of levying and collecting a tax. 51 Am J1st Tax § 662.

assessores (as-ses-sō'rēz). Assessors; masters in chancery. In civil law, advisors of magistrates.

assessors in admiralty. See **nautical assessors.**

assessus (as-ses'sus). Assessed.

assets. The property of a natural person or a corporation, real or personal, corporeal or incorporeal, especially property which is subject to seizure under and sale under process for payment of debts.
See **admitted assets; assets of a debtor; assets of a decedent's estate; marshaling assets; partnership assets.**

assets entre mains (ą'sets än'tr măn). Assets in hand.

assets in futuro. See **expectancy; judgment of assets in futuro.**

assets of a debtor. Any property which is in the debtor's name, or the title to which would be vested in him if a fraudulent conveyance were to be set aside. Dorrington v Jacobs, 213 Wis 521, 252 NW 307, 91 ALR 737.

assets of a decedent's estate. Property subject to the payment of the debts of the decedent, including real and personal, corporeal and incorporeal, property, but not homestead and other exemptions. 31 Am J2d Ex & Ad § 193.

The term has also been defined as being whatever property or money is lawfully recovered or received by an executor or administrator in virtue of his representative character. De Valengin's Admr. v Duffy, 14 Pet (US) 282, 10 L Ed 457.

assets per descent. Property which descends to the heir and not to the executor.

asseveration (ą-sev-ę-rā'shǫn). The solemn affirmation of the truth of a statement.

assewiare (as-se-wi-ā're). To draw or drain water from marshy land.

assez (as'sā). Same as **asses.**

assidenda (as-si-den'da). To be assessed.

assidere (as-si'de-re). To assess; to make an assessment for taxation.

assidere, taxare et levare (as-si'de-re, ta-xā're et lē-vā're). To assess, tax, and levy.

Assiderunt et taxarunt (as-si-dē'runt et ta-xā'runt). Assessed and taxed.

assiento (as-ē-en'tō). One of many contracts of the Spanish government with other countries and with traders for furnishing negro slaves to Spanish America prior to 1750.

assiete (as-si-et'). An assignment.

assign. Verb: To transfer, set over or grant, especially choses in action; to designate or point out. Noun: One to whom a right is assigned. An assignee.
See **assignee; assignment.**

assignable (a-sī'na-bl). Capable of being lawfully assigned or transferred; capable of being specified or pointed out; as an assignable error; transferable.

assignable chose in action. A chose in action which is of such nature as to be subject to transfer to another, so as to give ownership to the latter.
The assignability of things in action is now the rule and non-assignability the exception. 6 Am J2d Assign § 7.

assignable error. An error occurring at the trial of a cause capable of being pointed out or specified on appeal.

assignable lease. A lease which can be sold, transferred, and assigned by the lessee without permission from, or consent of, the lessor. Stillman v Lynch, 56 Utah 540, 192 P 272, 12 ALR 552, 560.

assignando (as-sig-nan'dō). See **dote assignando.**

assignare (as-sig-nā're). To assign; to seal.

assignati (as-sig-nā'tī). Assignees; assigns.

assignatio (as-sig-nā'she-ō). An assignment.

assignation. An assigning; a tryst or secret place of meeting of lovers, particularly lovers having meretricious relations.
See **house of assignation.**

assignator (as-sig-nā'tor). An assignor.

assignatus (as-sig-nā'tus). An assignee; an assign.

Assignavimus ad itinerandum (as-sig-nā'vi-mus ad i-ti-ne-ran'dum). Assigned for the circuit.
See **assizes.**

Assignavimus vos justitiarios nostros, ad inquirendum (as-sig-nā'vi-mus vōs, jūs-ti-she-ā'ri-os nos'trōs ad in-quī-ren'dum). Assigned to make inquiry.
See **assizes.**

assignay, or assigney. (Scotch.) An assignee.

assigned risk plan. An arrangement, in a state where automobile liability insurance is compulsory, whereby risks, which otherwise insurers would decline, are imposed by law upon particular insurers, so that all drivers and vehicles residing or located in the state are covered.

assignee. A person to whom a right is assigned, that is, the one to whom an assignment is made. 6 Am J2d Assign § 2. A person who becomes invested with the right of another person through some voluntary act of that other person. United States v Colorado Anthracite Coal Co., 225 US 219, 56 L Ed 1063, 32 S Ct 617. **More broadly defined as** including all those who take either immediately or remotely from or under the assignor, whether by conveyance, devise, descent, or act of law. Hoffeld v United States, 186 US 273, 46 L Ed 1160, 22 S Ct 927.
Where there are no qualifying words, the term in its usual meaning refers to an assignee in fact and does not comprehend an assignee by mere operation of law, such as a surviving partner. Burlington Nat. Bank v Beard, 55 Kan 773, 42 P 320. The words "assignee of such deceased person" in a statute disqualifying an adverse party as a witness is limited to an assignee in fact, and does not include an assignee by mere operation of law. So construed, the word does not include a legatee, a purchaser at an execution sale, or a trustee appointed on the death of a testamentary trustee. 58 Am J1st Witn § 335.

assignee at law. A person who merely by operation of law succeeds to the right, title, or interest of another. Burlington Nat. Bank v Beard, 55 Kan 773, 42 P 320.

assignee for the benefit of creditors. The person, firm or corporation to whom or to which an assignment for creditors is made. 6 Am J2d Assign for Crs § 89.

assignee in bankruptcy. See **trustee in bankruptcy.**

assignee in fact. An assignee to whom his assignor makes an actual transfer of that which is assigned, as distinguished from a transfer by mere operation of law. Burlington Nat. Bank v Beard, 55 Kan 773, 42 P 320.

assignee in insolvency. The person to whom an insolvent debtor makes an assignment for the benefit of his creditors.
See **trustee in bankruptcy.**

assignee in law. Same as **assignee at law.**

assignee in trust for the benefit of creditors. An assignee in insolvency. Anno: 113 ALR 745.

assignee of patent. A person who holds, by a valid assignment in writing, the whole interest of a patent, or any undivided part of such whole interest, throughout the United States. Moore v Marsh, 74 US (7 Wall) 515, 19 L Ed 37.

assignee's fees. The compensation of an assignee under an assignment for the benefit of creditors. 6 Am J2d Assigns for Crs § 91.

assignment. A transfer or setting over of property, or of some right or interest therein, from one person to another, and unless in some way qualified, the transfer of one's whole interest in an estate, chattel, or other thing. 6 Am J2d Assign § 1.
The word is ordinarily used in reference to choses in action.
See **equitable assignment; general assignment; preferential assignment; reassignment; voluntary assignment.**

assignment by delivery. The transfer of title to a chose in action by handing over to the assignee the evidence or symbol of title or ownership, such as a negotiable note, warehouse receipt, etc. 6 Am J2d Assign § 92.

assignment for the benefit of creditors. An assignment and transfer by a debtor, without consideration paid by the grantee, of substantially all the assignor's property, corporeal and incorporeal, to a person in trust to collect the amounts owing on obligations due the assignor, to sell and convey the property, to distribute the net proceeds of all the collections, sales, and conveyances among the creditors of the assignor, and to return the surplus, if any, to the assignor. 6 Am J2d Assign for Crs § 1.

assignment in bankruptcy. See **bankruptcy; trustee in bankruptcy.**

assignment in fact. See **assignee in fact.**

assignment in law. See **assignee in law.**

assignment of contract. The transfer by a party to a contract of his right and interest therein, subject to the performance of terms and conditions to which the other party to the contract is entitled.

A provision against assignment of contract is sometimes construed as one against the assignment of money payable or due thereunder. Anno: 37 ALR2d 1260.

See **assignee at law; assignment by delivery.**

assignment of copyright. The transfer or setting over to another by the owner of a copyright of his entire interest or a part of his interest in the copyright. 18 Am J2d Copyr § 89.

assignment of counsel. The appointment by the court of attorneys to defend indigent persons accused of crime, who are without counsel, and without the means of employing legal assistance. 21 Am J2d Crim L § 318.

assignment of dower. The remedy for segregating from the estate of a decedent the part to which the surviving spouse is entitled to by right of dower; the actual setting off or designation of that to which the surviving spouse is entitled by right of dower. 25 Am J2d Dow §§ 178 et seq.

assignment of errors. A specification of the alleged errors committed by the lower court and designated by the party complaining of them as grounds for reversal. 5 Am J2d A & E § 648.

assignment of insurance. A transfer by the insured of an insurance policy without the consent of the insurer or with the consent of the insurer where such consent is required on account of the nature of the policy. 29 Am J Rev ed Ins § 652.

assignment of lease. A transaction whereby a lessee transfers his entire interest in the demised premises or a part thereof for the unexpired term of the original lease. 32 Am J1st L & T § 313. A lease by the lessee of the whole of his unexpired term. Bedford v Terhune, 30 NY 453.

assignment of patent. The transfer by a patentee to another person of the whole of his interest in a patent for an invention issued to him by the United States, or of any undivided portion of, or rights in, such patent; a similar transfer by an assignee of a patent. 40 Am J1st Pat § 133.

assignment of policy. See **assignment of insurance.**

assignor. A person who assigns a right, whether he be an original owner or an assignee. 6 Am J2d Assign § 1.

assigns. Assignees, particularly assignees by voluntary act, that is assignees in fact, as distinguished from assignees by operation of law. United States v Colorado Anthracite Coal Co. 225 US 219, 56 L Ed 1063, 32 S Ct 617.

The word is often used in drafting legal instruments to denote the assignable nature of the interest or right created. The use of the word "assigns" indicates the intention of the parties to a contract that the contract is assignable, although it is not conclusive upon the question of assignability. 6 Am J2d Assign § 10. Some of older authorities adhere to the strict rule that the use of the word "assigns" is essential in impressing upon a covenant the character of running with the land, but the better view seems to be that although covenants intended to charge the land may be shown by the employment of the word "assigns," such intention may be quite as strongly indicated by other language contained in the deed. 20 Am J2d Cov § 32.

assigns forever. See **successors and assigns forever.**

assilire (as-si-lī're). To assault.

Assimilative Crimes Act. A federal statute which provides for punishment in the federal courts of a person guilty of conduct on a federal enclave which is punishable as a crime under the law of the state in which the enclave is situated. Anno: 2 L Ed 2d 1686, § 1 [a].

assimilative pay (a-sim'i-lā-tiv). Similar compensation for officers of the army and navy of the same rank. 36 Am J1st Mil § 69.

assisa (as-sī'sa). Same as **assize.**

assisa armorum (as-sī'sa ar-mō'rum). An English statute ordering the keeping of arms.

assisa cadere (as-sī'sa kā'de-re). To be nonsuit. See **judgment of nonsuit.**

assisa continuanda (as-sī'sa kon-ti-nu-an'da). A writ granting a continuance of the assize to allow the production of papers.

Assisa de Clarendon (as-sī'sa dē kla'ren-don). A statute passed in 1164 staying the exile of felons for forty days within which time they might get contributions for their support.

assisa de foresta (as-sī'sa dē fo-res'ta). See **assize of the forest.**

Assisa de Mensuris (as-sī'sa dē men-sū'ris). An English statute passed in 1198, regulating weights and measures.

assisa de nocumento (as-sī'sa dē no-kū-men'tō). A writ to abate a nuisance.

assisa de nova disseisima (as-sī'sa dē nō'va dis-sē-zī'na). Same as **assize of novel disseisin.**

assisa de ultima presentatione (as-sī'sa dē ūl'ti-ma prē-sen-tā-she-ō'ne). Same as **assize of darrein presentment.**

assisae statutae et juratae (as-sī'sē sta-tū'tē et jū-rā'tē). Assizes established and sworn.

assisae statutae panis (as-sī'sē sta-tū'tē pā'nis. The assize and assay of bread, i. e. a governmental examination into the quality of bakers' bread.

assisa forestae (as-sī'sa fo-res'tē). Same as **Assize of the Forest.**

assisa friscae fortiae (as-sī'sa fris'kē for'ti-ē). Same as **assize of fresh force.**

assisa generalis (as-sī'sa je-ne-rā'lis). The general assize, an old name for Parliament.

assisa juris utrum (as-sī'sa jū'ris u'trum). Same as **assize of utrum.**

assisa mortis antecessoris (as-sī'sa mor'tis d'an-ses-sō'ris). Same as **assize of mort d'ancestor.**

assisa novae disseysinae (as-sī'sa nō'vē dis-sā'si-nē). Same as **assize of novel disseisin.**

assisa panis et cerevisiae (as-sī'sa pa'nis et se-re-vi'-

she-ē). A statute regulating measures of bread and ale.

assisa proroganda (as-sī'sa prō-rō-gan'da). A writ to stay proceedings where one of the parties to the action is engaged on the business of the king.
See **de assissa proroganda.**

assisa ultimae presentationis (as-sī'sa ul'ti-mē prē-zen-tā-she-ō'nis). Same as **assize of darrien presentment.**

assisa venit ad recognoscendum (as-sī-sa vē'nit ad re-kog-no-sen'dum). The assize came to recognize.

assise. Same as **assize.**

assisers (as-sīs'ers). (Scotch.) A body which performed similar functions to those of the modern grand jury.

assistance of counsel. The right of one accused of crime to have legal counsel for his defense as provided by the Sixth Amendment to the United States Constitution or by a state constitution. 21 Am J2d Crim L §§ 309 et seq.

assistance writ. See **writ of assistance.**

assistant. One who aids, helps, or assists. 37 Am J1st Mun Corp § 273.
In the absence of a statute to the contrary, his capacity is more clerical than otherwise. The word is far from being synonymous with "deputy" which is the designation of a person who is appointed to act for another. Naill v State, 59 Tex Crim 484, 129 SW 630.

assistant bishop. (Eccles.) The assistant of the bishop of a diocese; a bishop coadjutor.

assistant rector. See **deacon.**

assisus reditus (as-sī'sus re'di-tus). Fixed or certain rent.

assith (as'sith). To indemnify.

assithment. A Scottish action to obtain damages for murder.

assize (a-sīz'). A word of such meanings and nuances in the law of England, especially the earlier law, that accurate and comprehensive definition is impossible. Noun: A court; a statute; a tax; the verdict of a jury in a court of assize; a writ; a jury summoned by a writ of assize; an action to recover land of which plaintiff's ancestor had been disseised. Verb: To fix; to regulate.

Assize of Arms. The statute (27 Hen II) requiring all freemen to furnish arms according to their wealth and station.

Assize of Clarendon (a-sīz' ov klar'ę-don). An English statute of 1166 which provided that persons of bad character should depart from the kingdom, although they had been acquitted on a trial by compurgation.

assize of fresh force. A writ to recover lands of which the demandant had been disseised within forty days.

assize of mort d'ancestor (a-sīz ov môr d'an-ses'tor). Assize of the death of the ancestor; a writ of assize to recover land from an abator of which the demandant's father or mother, brother or sister, uncle or aunt, nephew or niece had died seised. See 3 Bl Comm 185.

assize of novel disseisin (a-sīz ov nov'el dis-sē'zin). An assize of new disseisin,—a writ of assize to recover land of which the demandant had been recently seised. See 3 Bl Comm 187.

assize of nuisance. A common-law writ for nuisance with the two-fold purpose of abatement and the recovery of damages.
At common law this writ did not lie against the alienee of a wrongdoer, for the purchaser was to take the land in the same condition it was conveyed to him, but it lay against the wrongdoer himself, who levied or did the nuisance. This was changed by the statute of Westminster 2, 13 Edw. I, c. 24, which gave a remedy against either vendor or vendee. 39 Am J1st Nuis § 117, note.

Assize of The Forest. A statute passed under Edward I, concerning the king's forests.

assize of utrum (a-sīz ov u'trum). A writ by which a parson recovered lands which had been disposed of by his predecessor.

assizer (a-sī'zer). A member of the **grand assize.**

assize rent. Fixed rentals of freeholders and copyholders of a manor.

assizes. Sessions of the judges; more specifically, the sessions of the two or more judges who were sent out as commissioners of the king semiannually by the king's commission from Westminster on circuits covering the kingdom to try before a jury of the appropriate county any cases which were assigned to them.
These judges were called judges of assize or judges of assize and nisi prius.

Assizes of Jerusalem. A compilation of the feudal law made under Godfrey of Bouillon after the conquest of Jerusalem in 1099.

ass. mor. ant. Abbreviation of **assize of mort d'ancestor.**

ass. no. diss. An abbreviation of **assize of novel disseisin.**

associate. One engaged in the practice of law with another attorney at law or firm of attorneys at law but not as a partner or member of the firm. A member of an association. In the broad sense, one joined with another or others in the pursuit of a common purpose or design whether such be good or bad. Weir v United States (CA7 Ind) 92 F2d 634, 114 ALR 481.

associate counsel. An attorney at law associated in the prosecution or defense of a civil action or criminal prosecution with the attorney of record.

Associated Press. A well-known private organization for the gathering and dissemination of news, serving newspapers in its membership throughout the world.

associate justice. A justice of an appellate court who sits and decides with a chief justice and one or more other associate justices.
In a case at bar, his opinion is as conclusive as that of the chief justice, although the latter is in charge of the administration of the court business.

association. A collection of persons who have joined for the pursuit of a common purpose or design.
In the absence of a statute so providing, it is not an entity, having no status distinct from the persons composing it, but is rather a body of individuals acting together for the prosecution of a common enterprise without a corporate charter but sometimes assuming to exercise methods and forms used by corporations. Hecht v Malley, 265 US 144, 157, 68 L Ed 949, 957, 44 S Ct 462; Venus Lodge No. 62 v Acme Benev. Asso. 231 NC 522, 58 SE2d 109, 15 ALR2d 1446, 6 Am J2d Asso & C § 1.

At times, nonprofit corporations are referred to as "associations." Conversely, nonprofit associations are often regarded as so closely akin to corporate entities that the associates are not liable as partners for the debts of the body. 6 Am J2d Asso & C § 2.

In reference to the federal income tax, an association is ordinarily taxable as a corporation. Internal Revenue Code § 7701(a)(3).

See **articles of association; joint stock company; partnership; voluntary association; writ of association.**

association placer claim. A placer mining claim located under statute by an association of eight or more persons and including a maximum of 160 acres. 36 Am J1st Min & M § 91.

association theory. A doctrine of the law of master and servant that the master will not be excused for negligence resulting in injury to one servant which is inflicted by a fellow-servant, unless the servants are so engaged and situated as that each by carefulness and attention in the performance of his duties may protect himself from injury caused by the negligence of the person with whom he is working. Chesapeake & Ohio Railroad Co. v Brown, 152 Ky 479, 484, 153 SW 753.

Such doctrine, while salutary in its day, has become of little more than historical interest since the enactment of employers' liability acts which nullify the fellow-servant rule.

associe en nom. (French law.) A member of a limited liability company who is liable for the debts of the company, his name appearing in the firm name.

assoigne (as-soi'nyah). Same as **essoign.**

assoil (a-soil'). (Eccles.) To forgive or discharge one from an excommunication; to acquit; to set free.

assoilzie. Same as **assoil.**

assoinzie (as-soin-zē'). Same as **essoign.**

as soon as. A qualifying phrase in a contract which indicates a condition of performance. 17 Am J2d Contr § 320.

as soon as possible. Within a reasonable time, for the purposes of a condition as to time of payment of goods bought in credit. 46 Am J1st Sales § 190. Implying something other than immediacy, whether used in a contract of sale, 46 Am J1st Sales § 164; or in an application made to a carrier for a car. 13 Am J2d Car § 153.

Appearing in an insurance policy provision for notice of loss, the phrase means notice within a reasonable time under the circumstances of the case. Anno: 23 ALR2d 1083; 29A Am J Rev ed Ins § 1379.

as soon as practicable. See **notice as soon as practicable.**

assoyl. Same as **assoil.**

assultus (as-sul'tus). An assault.

assume. In ordinary parlance, to assume means to undertake; to engage; to promise. In matters of law, to take upon one's self. Springer v De Wolf, 194 Ill 218, 62 NW 542.

See **assumption of charge on land; assumption of mortgage; assumption of obligation.**

assumed name. See **ficticious name.**

assumed risk. See **assumption of risk.**

assumpserunt super se (as-sump-sē'runt sū'per sē). They undertook.

assumpsit. A common law action by which compensation in damages may be recovered for the nonperformance of a contract express or implied, written or verbal, but not under seal and not of record. Board of Highway Comrs. v Bloomington, 253 Ill 164, 97 NE 280; 1 Am J2d Actions § 11.

See **common counts; express assumpsit; indebitatus assumpsit; money counts; money had and received; money lent; money paid; nonassumpsit; nunquam indebitatus.**

assumpsit pro rata (a-sump'sit prō rā'ta). He undertook according to the proportion.

assumption clause. A clause in a deed, lease, or other transfer of property whereby the transferee assumes some obligation of the transferrer chargeable against the property. See 37 Am J1st Mtg §§ 994, 997.

assumption of charge on land. The agreement of the transferee of property to pay obligations of the transferrer which are chargeable on it. Springer v De Wolf, 194 Ill 218, 62 NW 542.

assumption of debt. See **assumption of obligation.**

assumption of employer's knowledge. An assumption, arising upon employer's assurance of the safety of an operation to be undertaken by an employee, the effect of which is to overcome the defense of assumption of risk. 35 Am J1st M & S § 321.

assumption of mortgage. An agrement by the grantee of mortgaged premises to pay the debt secured by the mortgage. 37 Am J1st Mtg § 997.

There is a broad and obvious distinction in the effect thereof upon the rights of the parties, between the taking of mortgaged property subject to a mortgage subsisting thereon at the time of such taking, and the assumption or agreement by the grantee to pay the debt secured by such mortgage, in that, where the purchaser or grantee of the mortgaged property takes it subject to the mortgage only, there being no express or implied agreement to assume the mortgage debt, he is bound only to the extent of the property, but if the debt be assumed by the grantee, he becomes the principal debtor, while the mortgagor becomes the surety. Brichetto v Raney, 76 Cal App 232, 245 P 235; 37 Am J1st Mtg § 982.

assumption of obligation. Undertaking to substitute one's self in the place and stead of the obligor; agreeing to discharge the obligation by payment. Stout v Folger, 34 Iowa 71.

assumption of risk. A defense against liability for negligence which is based upon the principle that one who knows, appreciates, and deliberately exposes himself to a danger assumes the risk thereof. 38 Am J1st Negl § 171.

An employee by his very act of entering the service of the employer—by his very contract of employment—assumes the ordinary risk of the service or such as usually are incident thereto, and accordingly has no common-law right of action against the employer for an injury sustained solely by reason of such a risk. 35 Am J1st M & S § 293. The doctrine of assumption of the risk, as applied in the master and servant cases, has been abolished as a defense in most American jurisdictions. 35 Am J1st M & S § 297. There is still scope for the application of the defense in other cases, however, since the better view is that it is not limited to cases where there was a contract relationship between the injured party and the defendant. 38 Am J1st Negl § 171.

assurable (a-shör'a-bl). Insurable; constituting a valid insurance risk.

assurance (a-shör'ans). Any written instrument evidencing title to real property; insurance.
See **collateral assurance; common assurances; covenant for further assurance; insurance.**

assurance fund. A fund provided in states which have the system of registration of land titles for the indemnification of those who lose their property through fraud or error, and who are without other means of redress. 45 Am J1st Reg L T § 8.

assure (a-shör'). To insure; to issue or to take out insurance.

assured. Ordinarily, synonymous with "insured." 29 Am J Rev ed Ins § 239. In some contexts, the person for whose benefit a policy of life insurance was made or taken, especially where he is the person who applied for the policy and pays the premiums. Conn. Mut. Life Ins. Co. v Luchs, 108 US 498, 27 L Ed 800, 2 S Ct 949; 29 Am J Rev ed Ins § 239.
See **insured.**

assured clear distance. The distance from which discernible objects, reasonably expected or anticipated to be upon the highway, may be observed. Snook v Long, 241 Iowa 665, 42 NW2d 76, 21 ALR2d 1; Anno: 31 ALR2d 1424.
The "assured clear distance ahead" of a motorist traveling at night, under a statute prohibiting a speed greater than will permit a motorist to stop within such distance, is the limit of his vision ahead afforded by the lights of his car, in the absence of any intermediate discernible obstruction. Erdman v Mestrovich, 155 Ohio St 85, 97 NE2d 674, 31 ALR2d 1417.

assured clear distance ahead. The limit of a motorist's vision of the highway ahead. Erdman v Mestrovich, 155 Ohio St 85, 97 NE2d 674, 31 ALR2d 1417. A variable distance, since it constantly changes as the motorist proceeds, being measured at any moment by the distance between the motorist's vehicle and the limit of his vision ahead, or by the distance between the motorist's vehicle and any intermediate discernible static or forward-moving object in the highway ahead constituting an obstruction in the motorist's lane of travel. 7 Am J2d Auto and H T § 188.

assurer (a-shör'ẻr). An insurer; an underwriter.

assysers (as'sē-sa). Same as **assisers.**

assythement (a-sīth'ment). A Scotch law action for damages for murder.

astigmatism (as-tig'ma-tizm). A common impairment of eyesight; one that is easily corrected by eye glasses. Baker v State, 91 Tex Crim 521, 240 SW 924, 22 ALR 1163, 1165.

astipulate (as-tip'ū-lāt). To stipulate; to agree.

astitution. See **astution.**

astrarius haeres (as-trā'rī-us hē'rēs). An heir whom an ancestor has placed in the house which is to be his inheritance.

astrer (as'trer). A householder.

astrict (as-trikt'). To restrict; to bind; to impose an astriction.

astriction (as-trik'shon). A servitude which "astricts" or binds a tenant, as where it binds him to have the corn raised upon the land to be ground at a certain mill.

astrihiltet. An ancient Saxon penalty of double damages for a wrong done.

astrology. The craft whereby fortunes are told ostensibly by reference to the positions and courses of the stars and other heavenly bodies.

astronomical day (as-tro-nom'i-kal). From noon of one day until noon of the next.

astrum (as'trum). A house; a hearth.

as trustee. A designation made in the execution of a contract by a trustee, which, in itself, is not sufficient to save the trustee against personal liability on a contract. 54 Am J1st Trusts § 352.

as trustee but not individually. An expression used by a trustee in the execution of a contract which should protect him against individual liability on the obligation. 54 Am J1st Trusts § 352.

astuti (as-to'tī). Cunning; crafty; acute.

astution (as-tū'shun). An arraignment.

A summo remedio ad inferiorem actionem non habetur regressus neque auxilium (ā sum'mō re-mē'di-o ad in-fer-i-o'rem ak-ti-ō'nem non ha-bē'tur re-gres'sus, ne'que âk-zi'li-um). A person cannot resort to an inferior remedy after having pursued a higher one.

as well as. And also.

asylum (a-sī'lum). A sanctuary; place where a person is immune from arrest; a state or country to which a person flees to escape arrest in another state or country. An institution for receiving, maintaining, and, as far as possible, ameliorating the condition of persons suffering from bodily defects, mental maladies, or other misfortunes, such as an asylum for the blind, an institution for the insane, and an orphan asylum. 26 Am J1st Hospit § 2.
Under a statute providing that no divorce shall be granted because of incurable insanity unless such person shall have been duly and regularly committed to and confined in a hospital or asylum for the insane, the words "hospital or asylum" mean an institution which under the law is authorized to accept insane persons for care and treatment. Anno: 15 ALR2d 1137.

asylum state: A state to which a person has fled after having committed a crime in another state. The term is one commonly used in extradition matters. 31 Am J2d Extrad § 18.

at. A word the significance of which is usually controlled by the entire context. Johnson v Cunningham, 107 Miss 140, 65 So 115. A relative term, signifying nearness when applied to a place. Rogers v Galloway Female College, 64 Ark 627, 44 SW 454; Los Angeles County v Hannon, 159 Cal 37, 43, 112 P 878; 23 Am J2d Deeds § 243. As a designation of time, sometimes denoting a fixed and definite point of time, as where the court admonishes the jury, "be back at 2 P.M.," and, at other times, meaning from or after, as where the provision in a will is that the property of the decedent shall be sold "at the death" of the life tenant named by him. 52 Am J1st Time § 31.

atamita (a-ta'mi-ta). A sister of a great-great-great-grandfather.

at and from. A phrase determinative of the attachment of the risk under a marine insurance policy, the same being effective only as a specified place or port is designated. 29 Am J Rev ed Ins § 326.

at any bank. A phrase which, as the place of payment of a promissory note, is indefinite, so that the maker has the right to require the holder to make an election as to which bank shall be the place of payment, and, in default of such election being made by the holder, to make his own election and give notice thereof to the holder. 11 Am J2d B & N § 972.

at any time. A phrase of relative meaning to be construed according to the particular context in which it appears.

Under a statute providing that anyone claiming an interest in the litigation may "at any time" be permitted to assert his right by intervention, it has been held that intervention may be allowed while the suit is pending in court, but not after the entry of final judgment. Anno: 37 ALR2d 1327.

As used in a statute authorizing a state bond issue and providing that the bonds shall be payable in not less than ten years or more than thirty, but that at the option of the Industrial Commission they shall be payable "at any time" after five years from the date of their issue, the phrase "at any time" does not mean that the bonds may be called only at the expiration of five years or within a reasonable time thereafter, but it means any time after five years from the date of issue and before the date of their stated maturities. Catholic Order of Foresters v State, 67 ND 228, 271 NW 670, 190 ALR 979.

at arm's length. With care, to avoid being overreached or imposed upon.

atavia (a'ta-vi'a). The mother of a great-great-grandmother or great-great-grandfather.

atavus (a'ta-vus). The father of a great-great-grandfather or great-great grandmother.

at bar. Before the bar, before the court.
See **plea at bar.**

at earliest convenience. As limiting a promise to pay: —when the promisor is able to pay or has the means of doing so. 34 Am J1st Lim Ac § 140.

a tegendo (ā te-jen'dō). From covering.

a tempore cujus contrarii memoria non existet (ā tem'po-re kū'jus kon-trā'ri-ī me-mo'ri'a nōn eg-zis'-tet). From a time when there is no memory to the contrary.

atha (ā'thā). In Saxon law, an oath.

athe (ā'the). Same as **atha.**

atheist (ā'thē-ist). A person who rejects all religious belief and denies the existence of God. Hale v Everett, 53 NH 9.

atheling (ath'el-ing). A member of the royal family; a nobleman.

at his earliest possible convenience. When the promisor is able to pay or otherwise perform his obligation. Anno: 28 ALR2d 792.

athletic club. As an organization exempt from federal income tax, a club not organized for profit or for the benefit of private shareholders. Internal Revenue Code § 501(c)(7). A club which maintains a gymnasium and outdoor courts wherein and whereon the members may engage in games and sports. Often a social club one of the activities of which is the sponsorship of athletic games. Sometimes a cover for a gambling house. 24 Am J1st Gaming § 29.

athletics. Sports, games, and exercises.

atia (ā'she-a). Hate; malice.

atilio decenti (a-ti'li-ō de-sen'tī). With proper tackle.

atilium (a-ti'li-um). Tackle; a ship's rigging.

atinian law. See **lex atinia.**

at interest. Bearing interest either at the legal rate or at the rate provided by the contract.

at issue. The status of a case at bar, in reference to the pleadings, where the issues of fact are completely drawn, so that the case can come before the trier of fact, whether court or jury.

Atlantic Charter. The statement of principles, made jointly by President Franklin D. Roosevelt, representing the United States, and Prime Minister Winston Churchill, representing the United Kingdom, on August 14, 1941, in the desire to make known to the world the national policies of the two countries in a world then beset by aggression which, if successful, would have struck a disabling blow against the great democracies of the world. Am J2d Desk Book, Document 14.

at large. An animal wandering, roving, or rambling at will and unrestrained. 4 Am J2d Ani § 42.
See **common at large; creditor at large; damages at large; in gross; running at large.**

at law. In law. Involving the law. Involving the rules of law rather than the rules of equity. By operation of law.

at law and in equity. A phrase inclusive of jurisdiction for the exercise of powers conferred by both law and equity and by statute as well. Wisconsin River Improv. Co. v Pier, 137 Wis 325, 118 NW 857. Exclusive in certain applications of jurisdiction in criminal, penal, ecclesiastical, admiralty, or military cases and proceedings. Gaines v Fuentes, 92 US 10, 23 L Ed 524 (statute relative to removal of causes to federal courts.

at least. A phrase which, as a designation of a period of time by days running after a stated date or event, may mean so many clear days. Boring v Boring, 155 Kan 99, 122 P2d 743.

Such meaning may be negatived by statute. 52 Am J1st Time § 26.

at least once a week for four successive weeks. A requirement for publication of notice of judicial sale, meaning a publication so that not more than a seven-days' interval shall occur between any two successive publications. 30A Am J Rev ed Jud S § 55.

atmatertera (at-mā-ter'te-ra). The sister of a great-great-great-grandmother.

at maturity. At the due date; at the time when payment or other performance falls due.

at my death. A phrase usually testamentary in character, but subject to construction in a proper context as not precluding the passing of a present interest. Burks v Burks, 222 Ark 97, 257 SW2d 369, 38 ALR2d 589; Anno: 11 ALR 51, 88.

atomic energy. All forms of energy released in the course of nuclear fission or nuclear transformation. 42 USC § 2014(c); 6 Am J2d Atomic E § 2.

Atomic Energy Act of 1954. A comprehensive federal statute covering the very modern subject of atomic energy. 42 USC §§ 2011 et seq.

Atomic Energy Commission. The governmental agency established by the Atomic Energy Act of 1954 to administer and carry out the provisions of the statute. 42 USC §§ 2031, 2032.

atomize. To separate into atoms.
See **atomic energy.**

at once. A phrase, variable with the context in which it appears, connoting immediacy, 13 Am J2d Car § 152; reasonable haste, 46 Am J1st Sales § 163; or within a time which is reasonable under the circumstances. 29A Am J Rev ed Ins § 1379.

atonement. The wiping out of bad conduct by subsequent sacrificial or otherwise good conduct. Allen v Allen 73 Conn 54, 46 A 242. The privilege under which, according to some authority, a defendant who has given cause for divorce, may by his subsequent conduct, deprive the other spouse of the right to a divorce for such cause. Allen v Allen, supra.

at or before. The equivalent of on or before a day specified. 52 Am J1st Time § 31.

at or upon. A designation or time in reference to a specific date, but to be construed according to the entire context. 52 Am J1st Time § 31.

at outside. A warranty in marine insurance in reference to storage of the insured watercraft; outside the shore. Macatawa Transportation Co. v Fireman's Fund Ins. Co. 168 Mich 365, 134 NW 193.

at owner's risk. Condition against liability in accepting paper for collection. 10 Am J2d Banks § 702.

at par. See **par.**

atramentum (ă-tra-men'tum). Ink, for writing.

at random. At hazard. Without any settled aim, purpose, or direction; left to chance; casual, or haphazard. Commonwealth v Bynum, 20 Ky LR 1982, 50 SW 843.

atriamentum (ă-tri-a-men'tum). A courtyard.

atrium (ā'tri-um). The open court in a Roman dwelling house.

atrocious assault. An assault aggravated by cruelty and brutality. 6 Am J2d Asslt & B § 48.

atropine (at'rō-pin). A drug derived from belladonna; used principally to dilate the pupil of the eye, thereby facilitating an eye examination.

ats. An abbreviation of **ad sectam.**

at sea. On the ocean; on the water. Slang for confused. A marine insurance term meaning absent on a voyage which was commenced within the time of the original risk, both going and returning, and although during part of the time the vessel may be necessarily in some port, in the prosecution of her voyage. Wood v New England Ins. Co., 14 Mass 31.

For the purpose of sea pay of a naval officer, a vessel is at sea where it is waterborne, even if at anchor in a bay, port, or harbor and not in condition presently to go to sea. 36 Am J1st Mil § 71.

at sight. On presentment; on being shown the instrument.
See **sight draft.**

atta (at'ă). Same as **atha.**

attach. To seize property under a writ of attachment and take it into custody to await the rendition of judgment or termination of the action in which the writ issued. Buckeye Pipe Line Co. v Fee, 62 Ohio St 543, 57 NE 446. Broadly, to seize property for the purpose of bringing it into the custody of the court. Anno: 4 ALR 340.
See **attachment.**

attachable (a-tach'a-bl). Subject to attachment levy.

attaché (a-ta'shā). A member of the staff of a foreign ambassador or other diplomatic officer. 4 Am J2d Ambas § 9.

attached. Connected, for example, attached buildings; seized under a writ of attachment. Tefft v Providence Washington Ins. Co., 19 RI 185. Having become an incident of, as where dower has attached upon the marriage of a landowner, or where a homestead right in public lands has attached upon a proper filing in the land office of the government. Kansas Pacific Railway Co. v Dunmeyer, 113 US 629, 644, 28 L Ed 1122, 1127, 5 S Ct 566.

attachiamenta bonorum (at-ta-chi-a-men'ta bō-nō'rum). An old form of attachment of chattels to recover a personal debt.

attachiamenta de spinis et boscis (at-ta-chi-ā-men'ta dē spī'nis et bos'kis). The right of forest officers to appropriate thorns and brushwood to their own use.

attachiamentum (at-ta-chi-ā-men'tum). Same as **attachment.**

attachiamentum forestae (at-ta-chi-a-men'tum fo-res'tē). Same as **attachment of the forest.**

attachiare (at-tà-chi-ā're). To attach; to levy an attachment.

attachment. A provisional remedy for the collection of a debt, which is incidental to an action against the debtor, proceeding by a seizure, under legal process called a writ of attachment issued in the action, of property of the debtor for the purpose of having the property available in satisfaction under execution and sale upon a judgment obtained against the debtor in the action. 6 Am J2d Attach § 1. The actual attaching, that is, the seizure and disposition of the debtor's property under a writ of attachment.
See **foreign attachment; pluries writs; writ of attachment; wrongful attachment.**

attachment bond. A bond required of a plaintiff seeking an attachment, conditioned to pay the costs and damages which the defendant may sustain if the writ has been sued out wrongfully. 6 Am J2d Attach § 518.

attachment execution. Garnishment, or a proceeding akin thereto, in the enforcement of a judgment. Patterson v Caldwell, 124 Pa 455, 17 A 18. A proceeding for the enforcement of a judgment for the payment of money where levy and sale of property of the debtor are inadequate for the purpose of enforcement. 30 Am J2d Exec § 774.

attachment garnishment. See **attachment execution.**

attachment lien. The lien, or quasi lien, obtained by the levy of a writ of attachment. Desiderio v D'Agostino, 127 Fla 377, 173 So 682; Hanly v. Davis, 170 Mass 517, 49 NE 914.

The authorities differ as to whether an attachment creates a lien or a mere right to legal custody of the property seized. Whatever lien or right is obtained is obtained by virtue of statute. 6 Am J2d Attach § 454.

attachment of risk. The inception of liability under a contract of insurance to answer for any loss or damage that may result from a risk insured against during the term of the insurance in an amount not exceeding the amount stipulated in the contract.

This involves both time and subject matter; that is, the question when the risk attaches, as well as the question to what it attaches or under what circumstances it will attach. In order that a risk insured against shall attach and become an existing obligation under which the insurer may become liable, it is first necessary, of course, that there should be a completed contract of insurance. Conditions of the policy fixing an earlier or later date for the risk to attach or purporting to cover property not yet owned or in existence at the time the contract of insurance is completed, also enter into the broad question of when the insurer's risk under a policy of insurance attaches and has its inception. 29 Am J Rev ed Ins § 309.

attachment of the forest. The least important of the forest courts.
It had jurisdiction to inquire into offenses against vert and venison and over attachments of the persons of the offenders. See 3 Bl Comm 71.

attachments. See **attachment; court of attachments.**

attack. To fall upon with force; to assault, as with force of arms; to assault. Phipps v State, 34 Tex Crim 560, 565, 31 SW 397. To question validity or sufficiency, as to attack a statute on constitutional grounds or to attack a pleading for want or insufficiency of allegations.
See **collateral attack; direct attack.**

attain de disseisin (at-tan' de dis-sā'san). Convicted of disseisin.

attainder (a-tān'dėr). The state into which the offender was placed by operation of law when sentence was pronounced against him for a capital offense, by the ancient common law.
The three principal incidents of attainder were forfeiture of property, corruption of blood, and civil death. 21 Am J2d Crim § 616.
See **bill of attainder; civil death; corruption of blood; forfeiture.**

attainder by confession. Pleading guilty before a court or abjuring the realm before a coroner.

attainder by process of outlawry. Adjudging a person who has fled to be an outlaw.

attainder by verdict. A finding of guilty by a jury.

attaint (a-tānt'). Verb: To pass sentence of attainder. Adjective: Under sentence of attainder. Convicted of high treason or felony; stained and degraded by conviction of a capital offense; deprived of all civil rights and capacities. Noun: An ancient writ employed to reverse a verdict.

attainted. See **attaint.**

attaintes pur serfs (ät-tant' pūr serfs). Convicted of being villeins.

atte (at'te). Same as **atha.**

attempt. Any overt act done with the intent to commit a crime and which, but for the interference of some cause preventing the carrying out of the intent, would have resulted in the commission of the crime.
It consists of two important elements: first, an intent to commit the crime; and second, a direct ineffectual act done towards its commission. 21 Am J2d Crim L § 110.
No definite line can be drawn between an "attempt" and "preparations" to commit a crime; the question is one of degree. United States v Coplon, (CA2 NY) 185 F2d 629, 28 ALR2d 1041.

attempt to commit arson. An intent to commit arson and a direct, ineffectual act done toward the completion of the offense.
An intent to commit the offense, plus preparations for commission, as by gathering combustible materials for kindling a fire, is not sufficient; there must be an act directed toward completion of the offense. State v Taylor, 47 Or 455, 84 P 82; 5 Am J2d Arson § 15.

attempt to commit burglary. An act performed with the intent to effectuate a burglary, carried beyond mere preparation but falling short of the actual commission of a burglary. 13 Am J2d Burgl § 29.

attempt to commit suicide. See **suicide.**

attempt to evade or defeat tax. A wilful attempt by any person in any manner to evade or defeat any internal revenue tax. IRC 1954 § 7201; 26 USC § 7201.

attempt to operate. Something less than the actual putting of the vehicle in motion. 7 Am J2d Auto § 256.

attendance. Physical presence plus freedom to perform the duties of an attendant. Fidelity-Phenix Fire Ins. Co. v Pilot Freight Carriers, Inc. (CA4 NC) 193 F2d 812, 31 ALR2d 839.

attendance by physician. Care and treatment by physician for a complaint, whether at the physician's office or in his own home. White v Providence Sav. Life Assur. Soc. 163 Mass 108, 108 NE 771.
Some authorities impose the qualification that the complaint for which treatment is given be of a serious nature or of more concern than a slight illness or temporary indisposition. Brown v Metropolitan Life Ins. Co. 65 Mich 306; 29 Am J Rev ed Ins § 758.
A physician attends a patient to treat, prescribe for, or act for him, to prevent, palliate or cure an ailment. If the person examined is not a patient there is no physician-patient relationship and therefore no physician-patient privilege. San Francisco v Superior Court, 37 Cal2d 227, 231 P2d 26, 25 ALR2d 1418.
See **medical attendance.**

attendance officer. A school officer, appointed by the school board, to ascertain the reason for absences of pupils, to visit the homes of the absentees, to take reasonable steps to require attendance, and in some jurisdictions, in a proper case, to take an absentee into custody for the purpose of taking him or her to school.

attendant. A person owing a duty of service to another or in some manner dependent upon him. A person in attendance.
See **attendance.**

attendant term. A lease or mortgage, the term of which has really expired, whose duration has been prolonged for the purpose of protecting the inheritance from incumbrance.

attended. See **attendance.**

attending circumstances upon execution of will. Family status, fiscal and mental condition of the testator, and the imminence of death, as well as the testator's declarations and instructions to the draftsman. Anno: 21 ALR2d 353-359.

attending physician. See **attendance by physician.**

attentare (at-ten-tā're). To attempt.

attentat (at-tĕn'tat). Any improper act done by a judge in an action, pending an appeal from his decision.

attentate (at-ten'tāt). Same as **attentat.**

atterminare (at-ter-mi-nā′re). To delay; to postpone.

atterminata,—posita ad talem terminum (at-ter-min-ā′ta,—po′si-ta ad tā′lem ter′mi-num). Adjourned, —put over to such a term.

atterminent querentes (at-ter′mi-nent kwe-ren′tēs). The plaintiffs may adjourn.

atterminer (at-ter′min-ā). To adjourn; to extend time for payment.

attermining. Extending the time for payment.

attest. Noun: A witness. Personal acts of authentication of genuineness. First Nat. Bank v Laperle, 117 Vt 144, 86 A2d 635, 30 ALR2d 958; 17 Am J2d Contr § 281. Verb: To bear witness to; to affirm to be true or genuine. Lorch v Page, 97 Conn 66, 115 A 681, 24 ALR 1204, 1207.

attestation. The act of witnessing the actual execution of a paper and signing one's name as a witness to that fact. 23 Am J2d Deeds § 28; 57 Am J1st Wills § 283. It incurs the manual act of subscription as well as the mental act of observation. 57 Am J1st Wills § 283.

Some authority draws a fine distinction between attestation and subscription, saying that attestation is the act of the senses, subscription is the act of the hand; that one is mental, the other mechanical. Swift v Wiley, 40 Ky (1 B Mon) 114, 117.

attestation clause. A writing at the end of a will but preceding the signature of the witnesses which sets forth with more or less completeness the performance of the statutory requisites to due execution and witnessing of the instrument, the purpose of the clause being to preserve a memorandum of the facts attending the execution of the instrument, so that in the event of the death, absence, or failure of memory on the part of the attesting witnesses, the due execution of the instrument may nevertheless be proved. Re Johnson (ND) 75 NW2d 313, 55 ALR2d 1049; 57 Am J1st Wills § 296. The clause in a deed, usually at the conclusion of it, sometimes called the hiis testibus (with these witnesses) clause, denoting that the persons signing are witnesses.

Usual forms of the clause in a deed are: "signed, sealed, and delivered in the presence of," "signed and sealed in the presence of us," "in witness whereof we hereto set our hands and seals," "sealed and delivered in the presence of," or even the word "teste." 23 Am J2d Deeds § 30.

attested. See **attest**; **attestation**.

attesting witness. A person who attests; one who witnesses the signing of a document by another person and signs his own name as a witness to that fact. Jenkins v Dawes, 115 Mass 599, 600. A credible or competent person who observes the execution of a will by the testator and signs his name as a witness to that fact, normally following an attestation clause. 57 Am J1st Wills § 308.

attestor of a cautioner (a-tes′tọr). (Scotch.) A guarantor of a debt.

atteynte (at-tent′). Same as **attaint**.

at the base. At the ground, when referring to a measurement of standing timber. 34 Am J1st Logs § 23.

at the courthouse door. A familiar phrase in posted and published notices of judicial sales, indicating the place where the sale is to be held and conducted. 30A Am J1st Jud S § 76.

at the date. A designation of time in reference to a specific day; subject to construction in some contexts as indicating a period of time up to the day designated. 52 Am J1st Time § 31.

at the death. Words of futurity which ordinarily have reference to the time when the devisee shall come into a right of possession, but do not prevent the vesting of title immediately upon the death of the testator. 28 Am J2d Est § 255.

at the earliest practicable moment. As soon as practicable; or as soon as possible; within a reasonable time under all the circumstances. Anno: 23 ALR2d 1083.

at the end of the will. A phrase used in stating the rule as to the place where a will must be signed, which is deceptive in the appearance of simplicity.

Is it the physical end, that is, the point most removed in space from the beginning of the instrument, or the logical end, that is, the point where the draftsman stopped writing in the consecutive order of composition? Either position has support in the authorities. 57 Am J1st Wills § 268.

at the ground. See **at the base**; **at the stump**.

at the king's pleasure. As applied to a punishment, in the king's courts and by his judges.

at the market. A direction to a stockbroker which means to buy or sell immediately, irrespective of price and prospects. 12 Am J2d Brok § 125.

at the next term. A condition of a bail bond, meaning at the first term to follow the execution of the bond.

As to whether the sureties are bound for the appearance of the prisoner at a term subsequent to the first term, see 8 Am J2d Bail § 101.

at the stump. An expression peculiar to the timber business, indicating that the measurement of a tree's circumference is to be taken at the point above ground where such timber is usually cut according to the custom of the locality. 34 Am J1st Logs § 23.

at the time. As of a certain time; also, forthwith, immediately, or during. 52 Am J1st Time § 31.

attic. The loft of a dwelling house; the space next to the roof.

attilamentum (at-ti-la-men′tum). Same as **attile**.

attile. Tackle; the rigging of a ship.

attilium (at-ti′li-um). Same as **attile**.

at time of passage. See **passage of statute**.

attincta (at-tink′ta). An attaint.

attinctus (at-tink′tus). Attainted.

attingere (at-tin′je-re). To touch; to amount to.

attorn (a-tẽrn′). To attorn is to make an attornment; to shift homage and fealty to a new lord; to accept and acknowledge a new landlord; to appoint an attorney or substitute.

attornamentum (at-tor-na-men′tum). Same as **attornment**.

attornare (at-tor-nā′re). To attorn.

attornare rem (at-tor-nā′re rem). To turn over a thing.

attornati et apprenticii (at-tor-nā′tī et ap-pren-ti′si-ī). Attorneys and law students.

attornato recipiendo. See **de attornato recipiendo**.

attornatus (at-tor-nā′tus). A person who attorned or who is substituted for another; an attorney.

attornatus vel procurator (at-tor-nā′tus vel pro-ku-rā′tor). An attorney or proctor.

attorne. An attorney.

attorney. An **attorney at law** or an **attorney in fact.**
The word, unless clearly indicated otherwise, is construed as meaning attorney at law. Re Morse, 98 Vt 85, 126 A 550, 36 ALR 527, 530.

attorney at law. One of a class of persons who are by license constituted officers of courts of justice, and who are empowered to appear and prosecute and defend, and on whom peculiar duties, responsibilities, and liabilities are devolved in consequence. 7 Am J2d Attys § 1. A quasi-judicial officer. 7 Am J2d Attys § 3.
Of course, the work of an attorney is not confined to appearances in court for prosecutions and defenses. A person acting professionally in legal formalities, negotiations, or proceedings, by the warranty or authority of his clients is an attorney at law within the usual meaning of the term. The distinction between attorneys or solicitors and counsel or barristers is practically abolished in nearly all the states. 7 Am J2d Attys § 1. While some men of the profession devote their time and talents to the trial of cases and others appear in court only rarely, the law imposes the same requirements for admission and the same standards of ethics for both classes.
See **barrister; of counsel; solicitor.**

attorney general. Chief law officer of the nation or a state, to whom is usually entrusted not only the duty of prosecuting all suits or proceedings wherein the government, national or state as it may be, is concerned, but also the task of advising the chief executive and other administrative heads of the government in all legal matters on which they may desire his opinion. 7 Am J2d Atty Gen § 1.

Attorney General of the United States. The head of the Department of Justice; a member of the President's Cabinet.
See **attorney general.**

attorney general's opinion. See **opinion of the attorney general.**

attorney in fact. An agent or representative authorized by a power of attorney to act for his principal in certain matters. 3 Am J2d Agency § 23. An agent, sometimes referred to as a private attorney who is authorized by his principal, either for some particular purpose, or to do a particular act, not of a legal character.
Such an agent is often designated by the word "attorney" after his name. Hall v Sawyer, 47 Barb (NY) 116, 119.

attorney of record. The attorney for a party to an action who has appeared for him by a formal appearance, by pleading or making a motion for him, or by an oral statement of appearance in open court, and is in charge of the party's business and interests in the action.
It is a common practice to refer to associate attorneys as "of counsel," to distinguish them from attorneys of record in a cause.

attorney of the wards and liveries. The third officer of the duchy court.

attorney's certificate. An English revenue receipt showing the payment of the annual duty exacted of any attorney at law.

attorney's charging lien. See **charging lien.**

attorney's fee. An allowance made by the court as costs in addition to the ordinary statutory costs. 20 Am J2d Costs § 72. Compensation to which an attorney at law is entitled for his services and, unless restricted by a contingent fee contract, payable to the attorney without reference to benefits accruing to his client. 7 Am J2d Attys § 203.
In some instances, the amount of an attorney's fee is fixed by contract, as in the case of an attorney's fee provision in a promissory note, and in other cases, by the court, as where the client is a fiduciary and must seek credit in his account for fees paid attorneys.
See **contingent fee; costs of collection.**

attorney's general lien. See **retaining lien.**

attorney's implied authority. The authority which an attorney has, by virtue of his employment as an attorney, to do all acts necessary and proper to the regular and orderly conduct of the case; being such acts as affect the remedy only and not the cause of action. Such acts of the attorney are binding on his client, though done without consulting him. 7 Am J2d Attys § 120.
An attorney employed to conduct a transaction not involving an appearance in court also has a measure of implied authority, although not in the broad scope accorded that of a counsel in litigation. For example an attorney employed to collect a claim has no implied authority to accept anything except lawful money in payment. Anno: 66 ALR 116, s. 30 ALR2d 949, § 5.

attorney's license. The leave or license of the court which the court grants to an attorney by its judgment of admission to the bar, and without which a person cannot practice as an attorney, even in the absence of any statute on the subject of admission to practice.
Such a license may be revoked by the court whenever misconduct renders the attorney holding it unfit to be intrusted with the powers and duties of his office. 7 Am J2d Attys § 12.

attorney's lien. General or retaining lien upon money or property of his client in his possession as security for the general balance due the attorney from the client for professional services rendered the client. 7 Am J2d Attys §§ 272 et seq. A special or charging lien upon a judgment, decree, or award obtained for his client as security for payment of the compensation due him for his services in obtaining such judgment, decree or award. 7 Am J2d Attys § 281.
See **charging lien; retaining lien.**

attorney's oath. An oath usually required by statute as a condition precedent to an attorney's admission to practice, and sometimes to his continuance in practice.

attorney special. An attorney appointed for certain cases or a certain case; an attorney attached to some particular court.

attorney's possessory lien. See **retaining lien.**

attorney's privilege or immunity. The immunity or privilege of an attorney at law against being subjected to arrest or the service of process in a civil action while going to the place of trial of an action in which he appears in his professional capacity, during the trial, and while returning to his office or residence. 42 Am J1st Proc § 140.

attorney's retainer. See **retainer.**

attorney's retaining lien. See **retaining lien.**

attorney's special lien. See **charging lien.**

attornment. The act or agreement of a tenant accepting one person in place of another as his landlord. 32 Am J1st L & T § 99.
In feudal times, the word meant the shifting of homage and fealty to a new lord.

attorn servitium tenentis (at'torn ser-vi'she-um te-nen'tis). To attorn the service of a tenant.

attractive agency. See **attractive nuisance; attractive nuisance doctrine.**

attractive nuisance. An unusual condition, instrumentality, machine, or other agency on premises which is dangerous to children of tender years but so interesting and luring to them as to attract them to the premises. Hayko v Colorado & Utah Coal Co., 77 Colo 143, 235 P 373, 39 ALR 482; 38 Am J1st Negl § 142.
See **attractive nuisance doctrine.**

attractive nuisance doctrine. The principle followed in many jurisdictions, but with some diversity of opinion as to the requisite conditions for its application, that one who maintains or permits upon his premises a condition, instrumentality, machine, or other agency which is dangerous to children of tender years by reason of their inability to appreciate the peril therein, and which may reasonably be expected to attract children of tender years to the premises, is under duty to exercise reasonable care to protect them against the dangers of the attraction.
The doctrine, within limitations, is for the benefit of the meddling, as well as of a trespassing child. Brittain v. Cubbon, 190 Kan 641, 378 P2d 141; Teagarden v. Russell, 306 Ky 528, 207 SW2d 18; Nichols v Consolidated Dairies, 125 Mont 460, 239 P2d 740, 28 ALR2d 1216; 38 Am J1st Negl § 141.
The principle is otherwise known as the **turntable doctrine.**

attrition (a-trish'on). (Eccles.) Regret or penitence for the consequences of wickedness. Cf. **contrition.**

atturn. Same as **attorn.**

atturne (at-turn'). An attorney.

attorney. The ancient English word from which the word "attorney" has derived, signifying a person that stands in the turn, place, or stead of another. Coke's First Institute, 51b.

at wharf. Delivery by the seller to the buyer on the wharf, free from charges to the buyer for unloading, etc. 46 Am J1st Sales § 189.

at will. See **estate at will.**

atya (at'i-a). Same as **atia.**

au (ō). At; in; to; until.

au aumone (ō ō-mōn'). For alms.

aubaine (ō-ban'). A stranger; an unnaturalized alien.

au besoin (ô bē-zoin). In case of need,—a designation in a bill of exchange of a person of whom payment may be required upon the refusal of the drawee to pay.

au bout de compte (ō boo de cômpt). At the end of the account; finally.

A. U. C. Anno urbis conditae; in the year (753 B. C.) of the founding of the city (Rome), the beginning of the Roman calendar.

au ceo temps (ō se tôm). At this time.

auceps syllabarum (â'seps syl-la-bā'rum). A snatcher of syllables; a caviler; a hairsplitter.

au ce temps (ō se tôm). At that time.

auctio (auk'she-ō). An auction.

auction. A public sale of property to the highest bidder. 7 Am J2d Auct § 1.
See **by-bidder; by-bidding; chilling bids; Dutch auction; knocked down; puffer; puffing; stifling bids; struck off; sub hastio; white-bonnet.**

auctionarii, quos Angli brokers decimus (âk-she-ō-nā'ri-ī, quōs Ang'li brō'kers de'si-mus). Vendors, whom we Englishmen call brokers.

auctionarius (âk-she-ō-nā'ri-us). A vendor; an auctioneer; a dealer in second-hand goods; a retailer.

auction business. The business of conducting auction sales; something more than the sale at acution by an individual or merchant of his own goods. 7 Am J2d Auct § 4.

auction by inch of candle. An auction at which the successful bidder is he who bids highest up to the time of the falling of the wick of a short candle lighted when the bidding began.

auctioneer (ak-son-ēr'). A person who conducts an auction sale for another on commission or for recompense, and who is deemed primarily the agent of the seller of the property, though for some purposes he is also deemed to be the agent of the purchaser.
Upon the fall of the hammer he becomes the agent of the buyer as well as the seller, and from that time to the consummation of the sale he is the agent of both for the purpose of drawing up and signing the memorandum of the transaction which takes the case out of the operation of the statute of frauds. 7 Am J2d Auct § 10.

auctioneer's lien. The lien of an auctioneer, for his charges and commissions, upon the property entrusted to him and the sums coming into his hands. 7 Am J2d Auct § 61.

auction pool. A system of placing wagers on horse races which for a time was successfully operated as an evasion of gaming laws. James v State, 63 Md 242, 248.

auction sale. See **auction.**

auction without reserve. See **without reserve.**

auctor (auk'tor). A plaintiff; an agent's principal; an auctioneer.

auctoritas (auk-tō'ri-tās). Authority.

Auctoritates philosophorum, medicorum, et poetarum, sunt in causis allegandae et tenendae (auk-tō-ri-tā'tēs phi-lo-so-phō'rum, me-di-kō'rum, et po-e-tā'rum, sunt in kau'sis al-le-gan'dae et te-nen'-dae). The opinions of philosophers, physicians and poets are to be alleged and received in causes.

auctour (ōk'toor). Same as **auctor.**

aucune foits (ô'ku-n fwa). Sometimes.

aucunement (ô'ku-n-mān). Somewhat.

Aucupia verborum sunt judice indigna (au-kū'pi-a ver-bō'rum sunt jū'di-sē in-dig'na). Caviling is unworthy of a judge's dignity.

audencia. A high court of justice in the Spanish empire, which sometimes was presided over by the administrator in chief of the law and police. Strother v Lucas, 12 Pet (US) 410, 442.

au dernier (ô dèr-nie'). At last.

Audi alteram partem (au-dī al'te-ram par'-tem). Hear the other side. A principle of the common law. Smith v Moore, 142 NC 277, 55 SE 275.

audience. A hearing; a body of people assembled to hear.

audience court. An ecclesiastical court with jurisdiction inferior to that of the court of arches, and in which the archbishop probably exercised a considerable part of his jurisdiction.

audiendo et terminando (â-di-en'dō et tèr-mi-nan'dō). To hear and determine.

audit. Noun: A formal or official examination and verification of accounts, vouchers and other records; an account as adjusted by auditors. Aron v Gillman, 309 NY 157, 128 NE2d 284, 51 ALR2d 598. The word is sometimes used in the sense of a verification of figures and computations by a mere accountant, but ordinarily it implies an exercise of discretion. Etzold v Board of Comrs. 82 Ind App 655, 146 NE 842.

Verb: To adjust; to allow or reject; to ascertain; to determine; to decide; to pass upon; to settle; to hear, examine, and determine a claim by its allowance or rejection in whole or in part.

The word applies only to claims ex contractu. Shields v Durham, 118 NC 450, 24 SE 794.

audita querela (â-dī'ta kwe-rē'la). A remedy granted in favor of one against whom execution has issued or is about to issue on a judgment the enforcement of which would be contrary to justice, either because of matters arising subsequent to its rendition, or because of prior existing defenses that were not available to the judgment debtor in the original action because of the judgment creditor's fraudulent conduct or circumstances over which the judgment debtor had no control. 7 Am J2d Aud Q § 1.

audito. See **ex audito.**

auditor. An officer of the government, whose duty it is to examine the acts of officers who have received and disbursed public moneys by lawful authority. Fajardo Sugar Co. v Holcomb (CA1 Puerto Rico), 16 F2d 92. An officer of the court who examines accounts for the court, preparing a report from which the court obtains the information necessary to the rendition of a decree. Re Walter Peterson, 253 US 300, 64 L Ed 919, 40 S Ct 543. An officer of court to whom references are made.

auditorium. A commodious room for audiences at lectures, theatrical performances, and political meetings or conventions; the building which contains such a room.

auditors of the imprest. Officers who formerly audited certain accounts of the exchequer.

auditory (â'di-tō-ri). A judge's seat in a court.

auditu. See **in auditu.**

auditum (â'di-tum). That which is heard; hearsay.

auditus (â'dī-tus). A hearing.

au fond (ō fôn). At the fount; substantially; essentially.

au fond en droit (ō fônt ôn druä). Essentially in point of law.

au fond en fait (ō fônt ôn fā). Essentially in point of fact.

augmentation (âg-men-tā'shon). The act of increasing or making larger by addition, expansion, or dilation; the act of adding to or enlarging; the augmentation of territory is the act of adding other territory to it. Vejar v Mound City L & W. Asso, 97 Cal 659, 32 P 713.

augmentation court. A court set up by Henry VIII to increase the royal revenue by putting down monasteries.

Augusta legibus soluta non est (â-gus'ta lē'ji-bus so-lū'ta non est). The queen is not exempt from the law. See 1 Bl Comm 219.

aujourd'huy. (ô-jour-dui). To-day.

aula (â'lä). A hall; a court; a court-baron.

aula ecclesiae (â'la e-klē'si-ē). The nave or body of a church.

aula regia (â'la rē'ji-a). William the Conqueror established a constant court in his own hall (aula), thence called by Bracton and other ancient authors "aula regia" or "aula regis" (the king's bench). This court was composed of the king's great officers of state resident in the palace, and usually attendant on his person. See 3 Bl Comm 37.

aula regis (â'la rē'jis). Same as **aula regia.**

aulnage. Same as **alnage.**

aumone (â'mōn). Alms.

auncel weight. Weighing with a balance or steelyard.

aunt. The sister of one's parent; a relative in the third degree according to the civil law method a computing degrees of kinship which prevails in most American jurisdictions. Anno: 55 ALR2d 645, § 1 [b]; 23 Am J2d Desc & D § 48.

au plus (ô plû). At most.

aupres (ô-prê). Near; high; about.

au quel (ô kèl). To which; to whom.

aura (â'rä). A medical term for the sensation, as of a wave of cold air hitting the head, prior to an epileptic seizure.

aures (au'rēs). (Saxon.) The cutting off of a thief's ears as a punishment for larceny.

auricularum scissio (â-ri-ku-lā'rum scis'-si-ō). The cropping of the ears.

aurum reginae (â'rum rē-jī'nē). Queen gold, a royal revenue belonging to the queen consort during her marriage with the king. See 1 Bl Comm 220.

aussi (ô-si). Also.

austercus. See **ostercus.**

Australian ballot. See **Australian ballot system.**

Australian ballot system. The term applied to the ballot used and the method and regulation of voting in American elections.

The system is not exactly the same as that used in Australia. It also varies between the states, but the statutes which impose the system of voting in the different states have enough in common with each other and with the Australian plan to warrant the use of the terms "Australian ballot" and Australian ballot system. The cardinal features of the statutes are: (1) an arrangement for polling by which compulsory secrecy of voting is secured, and (2) an official ballot containing the names of all candidates, printed and distributed under state or municipal authority. Allen v Glynn, 17 Colo 338, 29 P 670; State ex rel Gipe v Nelson, 358 Mo 164, 213 SW2d 905; 26 Am J2d Elect § 204.

austringer (ås'trin-jĕr). A falconer who kept goshawks.

austurcus (ås-ter'kus). A goshawk used by falconers in hunting fowl; the modern chicken hawk.

aut (åt). Either; or.

autarchy (å'tạr-ki). Same as **autocracy**.

au temps (ō tôn). At the time.

aut eo circiter (aut e'ō sir'si-ter). Or thereabouts.

auter (ō'tĕr). See **autre**.

auterfoits (ō'tĕr-fwo' or -foi'). Same as **autrefois**.

auterment (ō'ter-môn). Otherwise.

authentic (å-then'tik). Properly attested; executed according to law; genuine.

authenticate. To render authentic; to give authority to by proof, attestation, or formalities required by law; to prove authenticity.
See **acknowledge; attest**.

authentication. Such official attestation of a written instrument as will render it legally admissible in evidence. Mayfield v Sears, 133 Ind 86, 88, 32 NE 816. The act or mode of giving legal authority to a statute, record or other written instrument, or a certified copy thereof, so as to render it legally admissible in evidence.
See **authenticate; certificate of authentication**.

authentics. A collection of the novels, or new laws, of Justinian.

authenticum (å-then'ti-kum). (Civil law.) An original document, as distinguished from a copy.

author. One to whom anything owes its origin; an originator; a maker; one who completes a work of science or literature. 18 Am J2d Copyr § 37.
One may be an author without producing any original matter, provided he does something beyond a mere copying, such as compiling or editing. 18 Am J2d Copyr § 37.
See **authorship**.

authority. Judicial or legislative precedent; power; warrant; a duly constituted administrative agency, such as a port authority.
See **civil authority; color of authority; public authority; scope of authority**.

authority by estoppel. Essentially, authority under doctrine of apparent authority. 3 Am J2d Agency § 76.
See **agency by estoppel**.

authority of agent. The power of the agent to affect the legal relations of the principal by acts done in accord with the principal's manifestations of consent to him. See **agent's actual authority; agent's apparent authority; agent's express authority; agent's implied authority; agent's incidental authority**.

authority of law. See **warrant of law**.

authority of officer. The authority which inheres by force of statute or under the common law in an office, whether public or private.

authorize. To empower; to give a right to act, the connotation being permissive rather than mandatory.
While it is true that in many statutes the word may imply a command if it does so it is because other words have been used to express that intention. A mandatory construction has prevailed only in cases where the statute under consideration, when taken as a whole and viewed in the light of surrounding circumstances indicated a legislative purpose of enacting a law mandatory in its character. 121 Kan 109, 245 P 1019; 50 Am J1st Stat § 28.
The phrase as used in the Bankruptcy Act making it a condition of confirmation of a plan of composition of the indebtedness of a governmental unit on the petition of such unit that it must appear that the petitioner is "authorized by law to take all action necessary to be taken by it to carry out the plan" manifestly refers to state law. United States v Behins, 304 US 27, 82 L Ed 1137, 58 S Ct 811.

authorized. A word of permission. 17 Am J2d Contr § 281.
See **authorize**.

authorized by appointment to receive service of process. An actual appointment of an agent for the purpose of receiving service. Anno: 11 L Ed 2d 1038.

authorized by law. See **authorized**.

authorized capital stock. The maximum amount of stock which a corporation is authorized to issue under its charter or articles of incorporation. McLaren v Wold, 168 Minn 234, 237, 210 NW 29, 30; 18 Am J2d Corp § 208.

Authorized Version. Same as **King James Bible**.

authorship. A putting into production of something meritorious from the author's own mind, something which embodies thought of the author, perhaps the thought of others, and that would not have found existence in the form presented except for the distinctive individuality of mind from which it sprang. 18 Am J2d Copyr § 37.

au tiel forme (ō tēl for-m). In such manner.

autocracy (å'tok'rạ-si). Self-government; self-rule; a government whose monarch's power is unlimited.

auto da fe (ou'to dā fā). Same as **auto de fe**.

auto de fe (ou'tō dā fā). The publication of sentences of persons tried by the courts of the Spanish Inquisition; the execution of the sentence.

autograph (å'tō-gråf). A document written wholly in one's own handwriting; a person's signature.

auto livery. Taxicab service.

automatic continuance. An adjournment of a case by operation of law, as where it is not disposed of at the end of the term and necessarily must go over to the next term. 17 Am J2d Contin § 1.

automatic elevator. An elevator, particularly one for the carriage of passengers, which does not require an attendant in operation, responding to the push of a button. Anno: 6 ALR2d 391.

automatic insurance. Protection under a clause in standard automobile liability policies which extends the coverage to the operation by the insured of cars acquired during the life of the policy by replacement and purchase. 7 Am J2d Auto Ins § 100. Insurance provided by nonforfeiture clauses in life insurance policies. 29 Am J Rev ed Ins § 633.
Insurance which can be extended by a mere notice from the insured and without any new contract can be fairly called automatic insurance, though perhaps renewable insurance would be a better term. Continental Casualty Co. v Trenner (DC Pa) 35 F Supp 643.

automatic revocation of trust. The death of the beneficiary of a tentative trust of a savings deposit prior to the death of the depositor. Anno: 38 ALR2d 1246.

automatism. Action uncontrolled by thought.

automobile. A vehicle propelled by a motor, capable of standing erect when stationery, designed for carrying persons or property, and which does not run upon fixed rails or tracks. 7 Am J2d Auto § 1. The "car" to millions of Americans. Ordinarily, although not absolutely, to be distinguished from carriage, cart, or wagon. 7 Am J2d Auto § 3. In the ordinary sense of the term, something different from a farm tractor. 7 Am J2d Auto Ins § 43. An "effect" within the constitutional protection of the right of the people to be secure in their effects against unreasonable search and seizure. Dalton v State, 230 Ind 626, 105 NE2d 509, 31 ALR2d 1071.

In the ordinary sense of the term, as the word is to be understood where it appears in an automobile liability policy, automobile is equivalent to motor vehicle and is inclusive of trucks and tractors. 7 Am J2d Auto Ins § 99.

Although the generic word "automobile" is broad enough to include all forms of self-propelling vehicles, the word is to be defined in a particular case from its association in the context and by considering the purpose of the instrument in which it is used. Modern usage assigns to the word "automobile" the restricted meaning of a motor-driven vehicle suitable and intended for conveyance of persons. Washington Nat. Ins. Co. v Burke (Ky) 258 SW2d 709, 38 ALR2d 861.

As to what is an "automobile" or a "car" within coverage of accident policy, see Anno: 38 ALR2d 867.

automobile accessories. Articles and instrumentalities placed in the mechanism or structure of an automobile for use in the operation of the vehicle, either as a matter of necessity or for convenience, pleasure, and comfort, in operation.

automobile accident. See **accident**.

automobile association. An association or club which provides towing or emergency road service, map and touring service, bail-bond service, etc., and often engages in activities for the promotion of driver training and the enactment of statutes and ordinances in the interest of safety in driving. Anno: 89 ALR 930.

automobile club. See **automobile association**.

automobile collision insurance. See **collision insurance**.

automobile comprehensive insurance. A policy of insurance which, in addition to coverage of loss by fire, theft, collision, and upset, protects against loss from practically every other occurrence, manifestation of nature, and event causing injury to an automobile, such as windstorm, hail, lightning, malicious mischief, vandalism, pilferage, civil riot or commotion, etc. 7 Am J2d Auto Ins § 74.

Automobile Dealers' Day in Court Act. Another term for Federal Automobile Dealers Franchise Act which is intended to establish a balance of power as between manufacturers and dealers in the automobile industry by curtailing the economic advantages of the larger manufacturers and increasing those of the dealers. 7 Am J2d Auto § 348.

automobile fire insurance. Protection against fire given by the ordinary automobile insurance policy. See **automobile insurance**.

automobile guest. One who is invited, either directly or by implication, to enjoy the hospitality of the owner or operator of an automobile, and who accepts such hospitality and takes a ride either for his own pleasure or on his own business, without making any return to or conferring any benefit upon the owner or operator of the motor vehicle other than the mere pleasure of his company. 8 Am J2d Auto § 475.

automobile indemnity insurance. A policy of insurance for the protection of an owner or operator of a motor vehicle having the same purpose in general as an automobile liability policy but distinct from the latter in the respect that the liability of the insurer under the policy does not attach until the insured has sustained an actual loss in the discharge of a liability incurred by him in the operation of the vehicle causing injury to the person or property of another. 7 Am J2d Auto Ins § 81.

automobile insurance. A generic term inclusive of the several kinds of contracts and policies which affor protection against risks involving the ownership and operation of automobiles, such as collision, fire, flood, theft, transportation, and, perhaps most important of all, insurance against liability for death, personal injury, or damage to property, occurring from the operation of a motor vehicle. 7 Am J2d Auto Ins § 1.

automobile liability insurance. A policy of insurance under which the insurer agrees to pay, on behalf of the insured and within specified limits, all sums which the insured shall become legally obligated to pay as damages because of personal injury to or the death of any person, or because of injury to or the destruction of property, caused by accident and arising out of the ownership, maintenance, and use of the vehicle or vehicles insured. 7 Am J2d Auto Ins § 80.

automobile lights. See **clearance lights; headlights; side lights; taillight**.

automobile theft insurance. Insurance against loss from the theft of a motor vehicle or articles carried therein, provided by a separate policy or, as is usually the case at the present time, in a comprehensive policy. 7 Am J2d Auto Ins § 46.

As to whether automobile theft insurance covers a loss where the taking of the car amounts to larceny by trick or the offense of obtaining property by false pretenses, see Anno: 48 ALR2d 20.

autonomy (â-ton'ọ-mi). Independence; self-government; the negation of a state of political influence from without or from foreign powers. Green v Obergfell, 73 App DC 298, 121 F2d 46, 138 ALR 258. A self-governed community.

autopsy. A method of discovery. 23 Am J2d Dep §§ 209, 322, 323. Opening, examination, and dissection of a dead body to determine cause of death. 22 Am J2d Dead B § 32.

autoptic proference. Real or demonstrative evidence. 29 Am J2d Evid § 769.

auto stage (ou'tō stāj). A motor vehicle used for the purpose of carrying passengers, baggage, or freight on a regular schedule of time and rates. State v Ferry Line Auto Bus Co. 99 Wash 64, 168 P 893.

auto transportation company. Every corporation or person operating or managing any motor-propelled vehicle, not usually operated on or over rails, in the business of transporting persons and property over a public highway for compensation. Strickler v Schaaf, 199 Wash 372, 91 P 1007, 123 ALR 226.

autre (ô-tr). Other; another.

autre action pendant (ô-tr ak-siōn pān-dān). Another action pending.

autre droit (ō'tre druä'). The right of another.

autrefois (ô-tr-foa). Formerly; hertofore; previously.

autrefois acquit (ô-tr-foa a-ki). Formerly acquitted; a plea of one accused of crime setting up his previous acquittal of the same offense as a bar to further prosecution. Potter v State, 91 Fla 938, 109 So 91, 92.
See **prior jeopardy.**

autrefois attaint (ô-tr-foa a-tānt). An older doctrine that a person already convicted and serving a term of imprisonment for the offense is not to be held for another offense while in confinement. 21 Am J2d Crim L § 140.

autrefois convict. Previously convicted; a plea setting up a prior conviction for the same offense as a defense.
See **prior jeopardy.**

autre soile. See **en autre soile.**

autres sages come leur semblera. (ō'tre säzh côm ler sôm'ble-rä). Such other skilled men as to them shall seem fit.

autre vie (ō'tre vē). The life of another.

autri (ô-tri'). Other; another.

autry. Same as **autri.**

auxiliary (âg-zil'iär-ē). Collateral; incidental; conducive; assisting.
See **ancillary.**

auxiliary administration. See **ancillary administration.**

auxiliary chaplain. A parish priest's assistant.

auxiliary jurisdiction. See **ancillary jurisdiction.**

auxiliary proceeding. See **ancillary proceeding.**

auxiliary to or supplemental of. An expression in the Federal Motor Carrier Act which is determinative of the relation of motor carrier service to train service in reference to the legality of acquisition of the motor carrier by the rail carrier. 13 Am J2d Car § 89.

auxilium (âk-zi'li-um). Aid.

auxilium curiae (āk-zi'li-um kū'ri-ē). An order of court citing a person, at the suit of another to appear and warrant something.

auxilium petere (âk-zi'li-um pe'te-re''). To seek aid.

auxilium regis (âk-zi'li-um rē'jis). A subsidy paid to the king.

auxilium vice comiti (âk-zi'li-um vī'sē ko'mi-tī). An ancient duty paid to sheriffs.

auxionarii et auxionatrices panis, cervisiae, et aliarum rerum (âk-she-ō-nā'ri-i et âk-she-ō-nā'tri-sēs pā'nis, ker-vi'si-ē et a-li-ā'rum rē'rum). Male and female vendors of bread, beer and other things.

auxionarius (âk-she-ō-nā'ri-us). Same as **auctionarius.**

auxy icy (ō'xe ē'sē). So here.

auxy pleinment (ō'xē plen'môn). As fully.

auxy sovent que (ō'xē sō-vôn' ke). As often as.

A.V. Abbreviation of **Authorized Version,** which is the **King James Bible.**

availability for work. Readiness and willingness to accept suitable work at a point where there is an available labor market, which work one does not have good cause to refuse. A willingness to accept any suitable work which may be offered without attaching thereto conditions not usual and customary in the occupation but which the individual may desire because of his particular needs or circumstances. Unemployment Compensation Com. v Tomko, 192 Va 463, 65 SE2d 524, 25 ALR2d 1071; Anno: 25 ALR2d 1077.

available market. A place where goods can be bought or sold; from the standpoint of a buyer of goods which the seller wrongfully refuses to deliver, a place where the buyer can purchase similar goods. Buyer v Mercury Technical Cloth & Felt Corp. 301 NY 74, 92 NE2d 896, 20 ALR2d 815.

available means. A mercantile term for anything which is readily convertible to money, such as negotiable promissory notes and bills of exchange, stocks and bonds. Brigham v Tillinghast, 13 NY 215, 218, 219.

avail of marriage (a̱-vāl'). The value of the marriage; that is, the amount which the suitor would give.

avails. The proceeds of the sale of property. McNaughton v McNaughton, 34 NY 201, 205. The proceeds of an insurance policy. Le Blanc's Succession, 142 La 27, 76 So 223.

aval (a-val'). A guaranty of a negotiable instrument.

avalanche (av'a-lanch). A slide of snow from the top or side of a mountain, often destructive of life and property; an Act of God. Anno: 34 ALR2d 834, § 3.

avant. See **en avant.**

avantagium (a-van-tā'ji-um). Advantage; profit.

avanture. An adventure; chance; misadventure; an accident causing death.

avaria (a-vā'ri-a). Average; loss to a ship or cargo at sea.

aveigner (ä-vā'nyä). Same as **advenir.**

avenage (av'ē-nāj). A feudal tenant's payment of rent in oats.

avener (av'ē-nėr). Same as **advenir.**

aventure. Same as **adventure.**

avenue. A thoroughfare in a city or populated area; usually a wide street, sometimes with trees.

aver (a̱-vėr'). To allege; to plead; to assert; to state.

aver (ā-vėr'). Verb: To have. Noun: Property; substance.

average. The mean between extremes or between two or more quantities, measurements, distances, weights, etc. Feudal service performed by tenants consisting of hauling and carrying with wagons and work animals. Sometimes used as the equivalent of **general average.**
See **free from average unless general; free from particular average; general average; particular average; petty average.**

average agreement. A rule or regulation for calculating demurrage, whereby the shipper or consignee is allowed a credit for cars released prior to the expiration of the free time. 13 Am J2d Car § 488.

average bond. See **general average bond.**

average clause. A clause in a blanket fire insurance policy providing that in case of loss the policy shall attach on each building in such proportion as the value of each building bears to the aggregate value of the entire property insured.

Such provision is in no sense a coinsurance clause. 29A Am J Rev ed Ins § 1540.
See **free from average unless general; free from particular average.**

average earnings. Average over recent years; a measurement of value of lost time. 22 Am J2d Damg § 91.
In applying workmen's compensation statutes, the words "average weekly earnings" are to be taken in their common and ordinary sense. 58 Am J1st Workm Comp § 309.

average profits. Net profits over a reasonable period of time dating back from time of injury to business. 22 Am J2d Damg § 329.

average-taker. An expert employed to adjust general average in a marine loss.
See **general average.**

average unless general. See **free from average unless general.**

average value. See **fair average value.**

average weekly earnings. See **average earnings.**

a verbis legis non est recedendum (ā ver'bis lē'jis nōn est re-sē-den'dum). From the words of the law there should be no departure.

avercorn. Rent in corn.

aver de pois (ā'vå de pwä). True weight; full weight.
See **avoirdupois weight.**

aver et tenir (ā'-vĕr ā te'nĕr). To have and to hold.

averia (a-ve'ri-a). Plural of **averium.**

averia carucae (ā-ve'ri-a ka-rū'kē). Beasts of the plough.

averia elongata (ā-ve'ri-a ē-lon-gā'ta). Cattle which have been taken away.

averiis captis in withernam (ā-ve'ri-is kap'tis in with'-er-nam). A writ by which a person whose cattle had been taken away could have cattle of the taker.

averiis retornandis. See **de averiis retornandis.**

averium (a-ve'ri-um). A work animal.
See **heriot.**

averium ponderis (a-ve'ri-um pon'de-ris). True weight; full weight.

averland (ā'vėr-land). Land which was subject to the feudal service of average.

averment. An allegation.

averment on information and belief. An allegation in a pleading which states that the pleader is informed and believes the facts stated to be true, instead of making a direct statement of such facts. 41 Am J1st Plead § 40.

a vero domino (ā vē'rō do'mi-nō). From the true owner. Rhodes v Whitehead, 27 Tex 304.

averpenny (ā'vėr-pen"i). A feudal tenant's payment of money in lieu of average.

averrare (a-ver-rā-re). A feudal service of carrying goods in a wagon or on horses.

aver silver. A feudal tenant's payment of money in lieu of average.

aversio (ā-ver'si-ō). An averting or turning away; a sale or lease of property as a whole.

aversio periculi (ā-ver'si-ō pe-ri'ku-lī). The averting of peril or danger.

averum (a've-rum). Property.

avet. To abet; to aid or assist.

avia (a-vi-a). A grandmother.

aviation (ā'vi-ā'shon). The art of flying; the management of aircraft, particularly aircraft heavier than air. Masonic Acci. Ins. Co. v Jackson, 200 Ind 472, 164 NE 628, 61 ALR 840. The science and the business of flight as practiced by man.
See **aeronautics; aircraft; airport; engaged in aviation.**

Aviation Act. The federal statute which provides in detail for a federal aviation program, continues the Civil Aeronautics Board as an agency of the United States, and also establishes a Federal Aviation Agency which is headed by an Administrator. 8 Am J2d Avi § 10.

Aviation Administrator. The head of the Federal Aviation Agency. 8 Am J2d Avi § 10.

Aviation Agency. An agency of the United States created by statute for the regulation of aviation, including such matters as the certification, identification, and marking of aircraft; airplane and aircraft air worthiness; the maintenance, repair, and alteration of aircraft; the transportation of dangerous articles, air-traffic rules, etc. 8 Am J2d Avi § 12.

aviation liability insurance. An insurance contract which insures the owner of an aircraft against loss sustained on account of having to pay damages for injuries to persons or property inflicted by or in the operation of such aircraft. 29A Am J Rev ed Ins § 1348.

a villa (ā vil'la). From a village.

a vinculo matrimonii (ā vin'ku-lō mā-tri-mō'ni-ī). From the bonds of matrimony.

avis (a'vis). Advice; counsel.

avisamentum (a-vī-sa-men'tum). Same as avis.

avizandum (a-vi-zan'dum). A Scotch practice of submitting a matter privately to a judge.

avo. See **de avo.**

avocat (av-ō-kä'). (French.) An advocate; a lawyer.

avocation (av-ọ-kā'shọn). That which is outside a person's regular calling; a minor occupation. Anno: 11 ALR 503.

avocatory. See **letters avocatory.**

avoid (ạ-void'). To annul; to make void; to declare void that which is voidable; to keep away from.

avoidable. See **voidable.**

avoidable consequences doctrine. Precluding recovery of damages flowing from consequences reasonably avoidable by plaintiff. 22 Am J2d Damg § 30.

avoidance. Nullifying; rendering void.
See **confession and avoidance; plea in confession and avoidance.**

avoidance of taxes. Permissable acts and conduct, as distinguished from the reprehensible "evasion" of taxes.

avoirdupois weight (av"ọr-dū-poiz'). A measure characterized by a sixteen-ounce pound, as distinguished from troy weight of twelve ounces to the pound.

avoucher (ạ-vou'cher). To call a warrantor of land to come in and defend the title for the warrantee.

avoue (a-vö-ā'). (French.) Attorney; solicitor in Canada.

avow. To declare solemnly; to make avowry. See **avowry**.

avowal. A direct statement or declaration. A formal offer of proof made to preserve an exception to a ruling of the trial court excluding evidence as inadmissible or holding the witness to be incompetent. Murphy v Phelps, 241 Ky 339, 43 SW2d 1010; Huff v Commonwealth, 248 Ky 700, 59 SW2d 985; 53 Am J1st Trial §§ 99-103.

avowant (a-vou'ant). A person who avows; a person who makes an avowry. One who makes an avowal.

avowee (a-vou'ē). An advocate of a church living.

avowry. A landlord's common-law pleading justifying the distraint of property. 32 Am J1st L & T § 647.

avowterer (a-vou'tā-rā). An adulterer.

avowtry (a-vou'tri). Adultery.

avulsion. A sudden and perceptible loss or addition to land by the action of water, or a sudden change in the bed or course of a stream. 56 Am J1st Water § 477.

avunculus (a-vun'ku-lus). A mother's brother; a maternal uncle. See 2 Bl Comm 230.

avunculus magnus (a-vun'ku-lus mag'nus). A grandmother's brother, a great uncle.

avus (a'vus). A grandfather. See 2 Bl Comm 207.

await (a-wāt'). To delay; to wait for an event; to waylay.

await further conveyance. A clause in a bill of lading relieving the carrier from liability other than as warehousemen respecting property at its depot or pier to be accepted by a succeeding carrier. Texas & Pacific R. Co. v Reiss, 183 US 621, 46 L Ed 358, 22 S Ct 252.

award. The decision, decree, or judgment of arbitrators determining the disputed matter submitted to them. 5 Am J2d Arb & A § 124. In effect, a judgment, where workmens' compensation is awarded. 38 Am J1st Workm Comp § 484. A judgment or order for the payment of costs. 20 Am J2d Costs § 87. A judgment or decree of an admiralty court for salvage. 47 Am J1st Salv §§ 31 et seq. The amount of a judgment or verdict.

award in gross. A final property settlement between the parties which, when legally brought about, is as binding, conclusive, and final as the decree of divorce itself, its purpose being to finally adjust and determine the financial relations as well as the marital rights at one and the same time. Anno: 127 ALR 744.
See **alimony in gross**.

aware of. Informed or having knowledge of something.
See **become aware of**.

away-going crops. Annual crops which mature after the termination of a tenancy but are nevertheless removable by the tenant. 21 Am J2d Crops § 25.

awm. A wine measure.

axiom. A principle that is not disputed; a maxim.

ayant cause. (French law.) An assignee.

ayant droit. (French law.) Person entitled.

ayde (ed). Same as **aid**.

ayd pryer (ed prē'ā). Same as **aid prayer**.

ay (āi or ī). Yes; an affirmative vote.

ayel (ä-yel). Same as **aiel**.

ayle (ail). A grandfather.

ayre (ār). (Scotch.) An eyre; a circuit.

ayuntamiento (ä-yön"tä-mi-en'tō). The council or cabildo of the capital of a Spanish-American jurisdiction.

The seats of administration or capitals of provinces or other lesser divisions were generally the largest towns from which the section usually took its name. In every such capital there was an ayuntamiento. Strother v Lucas, 12 Pet (US) 410, 442, note, 9 L Ed 1137, 1149, note.

Azo (äd'zō). An ancient teacher of law who lived at Bologna.

B

B. A. Abbreviation for **Bachelor of Arts.**

baby act. Conduct in seeking sympathy. A plea of infancy as a defense to an action.

baby sitter. One who cares for a baby, or parents are otherwise engaged.

baccalaureate (bak-a-lå′rē-āt). The degree of bachelor of arts or science. The address given to a graduation class.

baccarat. A game of chance which is prohibited as gambling, where played for a stake. 24 Am J1st Gaming § 20.

bacheleria (ba-che-le′ri-a). Commonalty or yeomanry.

bachelor (bach′e-lor). A male unmarried, although old enough to wed; an inferior knight; a squire.

Bachelor of Arts. The first degree given in a liberal arts college; the holder of a bachelor of arts degree.

Bachelor of Civil Law. A degree held by one learned in the civil law of the European continent and of nations which have derived their legal systems from Europe.

Bachelor of Education. The degree awarded on graduation from a teachers' college.

Bachelor of Engineering. The degree awarded upon graduation from some colleges of engineering.
In other such colleges, the degree awarded is bachelor of science.

Bachelor of Finance. A degree given by some universities or colleges to a graduate of the college or school of commerce.

Bachelor of Fine Arts. A degree given upon graduation from a college or school of instruction in the aesthetic arts.

Bachelor of Forestry. The degree given upon graduation from a college of forestry.

Bachelor of Law. A degree given upon graduation from law school.
It has been supplanted to a great extent by the degree doctor of jurisprudence, but may still be given to one who has completed the law school course successfully but does not have an academic or liberal arts degree which is necessary to qualify for the doctor of jurisprudence degree.

Bachelor of Letters. A degree infrequently given to graduates of liberal arts colleges.

Bachelor of Library Science. A degree given in some colleges and universities to graduates of the school of library science.

Bachelor of Pharmacy. The degree granted to a graduate of a college of pharmacy.

Bachelor of Philosophy. The degree granted by some colleges to a graduate with a major in philosophy.

Bachelor of Science. The first degree given in a college of science; the holder of a bachelor of science degree.

Bachelor of Theology. The degree conferred upon graduation from a divinity school.

back. To support; to indorse; to reverse.
See **backing.**

backadation. A sum paid by the seller of shares of stock to postpone the date of their delivery.

backbear. To carry away game wrongfully killed.

backberend. The carrying away of goods which he has stolen, on his back, by a thief.

back-bond (bak′bond). An indemnity bond; a Scotch term for a deed which had the force and effect of an English deed of declaration of trust.

back-deed. Same as **back-bond.**

back dues. Dues owing by a member of a labor union, fraternal order, mutual benefit society, or club for such a length of time as to render the member delinquent in status.

back fill. A term of the construction business for filling an excavation with the same material as that removed in the excavating. Leo F. Piazza Paving Co. v Montrose, 141 Cal App 2d 226, 296 P2d 369.

backgammon. A game of chance which is prohibited as gambling, where played for a stake. Anno: 135 ALR 120.

backing. Reversing in direction. The indorsement of a negotiable instrument. The indorsement of an entry or memorandum on the back of a writ, warrant, subpoena, or other process. Gondas v Gondas, 99 NJ Eq 473, 477, 134 A 615, 617. The last sheet of a pleading or motion, or of a document prepared by an attorney, usually of heavier paper than the body of the instrument, which, when the instrument is folded, appears on the outside and carries notations, such as the name of the court, the title of the cause, the kind of pleading or motion, if the paper is one connected with an action or proceeding; the kind of instrument and the names of the parties, if it is a private document; and, in any event, the name and address of the attorney who drafted or prepared the paper.

back lines. Lines established on building lots, sometimes by municipal regulation, but more often by restrictive covenants, to mark the limits of construction in the direction of the back or rear line of the lot. 20 Am J2d Cov § 240.

back pay. Unpaid or uncollected salary or wage to which an employee is entitled.

back pay orders. Orders that employees be given their back pay, such being rendered in connection with the reinstatement of the employees. 31 Am J1st Lab § 309.

backside (bak′sīd′). The buttocks. The backyard of a dwelling house.

back taxes. Those taxes on which the ordinary processes provided by law for collection have been exhausted; taxes in arrears; Commonwealth v Louisville Water Co., 132 Ky 305, 309, 116 SW 712.

backwardation. See **backadation.**

backwards. Moving with the back foremost; moving in the opposite of the previous course followed.
See **forwards and backwards at sea.**

back-water. Water backed up by an obstruction in a stream.

baco (bah′co). A hog yielding bacon.

bacterial infection. An infection produced by bacteria; a term to be construed in the popular or commonly accepted meaning. Anno: 131 ALR 1063.

baculus (bak'ū-lus). A divining rod; a rod used in making livery of seisin.

baculus nuntiatorius (ba'ku-lus nun"she-ā-tō'ri-us). The announcing rod or staff,—the white stick or wand which was erected on the defendant's land to give him warning or notice that he had been sued in a real action. See 3 Bl Comm 279.

bad. Immoral; unworthy; unfit; of inferior quality.
Good and bad are both terms of comparison. The same article may be called, not inaccurately, good when compared with one of the same kind of a much inferior quality; and it may, with equal correctness, be characterized as bad when spoken of with reference to the most perfect article of the kind. Tobias v Harland (NY) 4 Wend 537, 541.

bad debt. An uncollectible debt. A debt which may be deducted from gross income in determining income subject to tax. Anno: 39 ALR2d 898. A debt which is worthless because, in the exercise of sound business judgment, there is no likelihood of recovery thereon at any time in the future. O'Bryan Bros., Inc. v Commissioner (CA6) 127 F2d 645, cert den 317 US 647, 87 L Ed 521, 63 S Ct 41. A business debt which in the opinion of the Treasury is recoverable only in part at best. IRC § 166(a)(2).
A debt which results from an unpaid loan of money is a "bad debt" and therefore deductible in the computation of income taxes only where there was an expectation of repayment. Such advances made with the belief that they would not be repaid are in the nature of gifts, and are not deductible as bad debts. American Cigar Co. v Commissioner (CA2) 66 F2d 425.

bad debtor. A person who is not in the habit of paying his honest debts; a person unworthy of credit. State v Armstrong, 106 Mo 395.

bad faith. The antithesis of good faith; a state of mind affirmatively operating with a furtive design, with a motive of self interest or ill will, or for an ulterior purpose. 37 Am J2d Fraud § 1.
Though an indefinite term, it differs from and is stronger than the idea of negligence in that it contemplates a state of mind affirmatively operating with a furtive design or with some motive of self-interest or ill will, or for an ulterior purpose. Warfield Natural Gas Co. v Allen, 248 Ky 646, 59 SW2d 534, 91 ALR 890.
If a man makes a statement in the honest belief of its truth, he does not make it in bad faith, even if honest ignorance of the truth is the result of the grossest carelessness. Penn. Mut. Life Ins. Co. v Mechanics Sav. Bank & Trust Co. (CA6 Tenn) 73 F 653.

badge (baj). Something noticeable worn on the person to indicate his connection with some enterprise, person, lodge, club, society, or matter. A sign of authority, such as the star of a policeman or other law-enforcement officer.

badge of fraud. Suspicious circumstances that overhang a transaction, or appear on the face of the appurtenant papers, having evidentiary force unless the suspicion is dispelled by a satisfactory explanation. Royal Indem. Co. v McLendon, 64 NM 46, 323 P2d 1090.
There are many badges of fraud; to enumerate a few, insolvency of a grantor, lack of consideration for a conveyance, secrecy or concealment, etc. 37 Am J2d Frd Conv § 10.

badger. Noun: A hawker or huckster. A burrowing animal, the name of which has been given to residents of Wisconsin and the University of Wisconsin athletic teams. Verb: To torment.

badger game. A blackmailing trick; a method of artifice in obtaining money.

bad girl. A naughty girl, if she is of tender years; an immoral or wayward girl, if of an age to distinguish between right and wrong.
The imputation is not necessarily that of unchastity. 33 Am J1st L & S § 39.

bad law. A decision, ruling, or opinion which does not accord with law.

bad moral character. Any and every trait involving moral turpitude; lechery; habitual drunkenness. State v Scott, 332 NM 235, 58 SW2d 275, 90 ALR 860. In days gone by, even profanity coupled with Sabbath-breaking. Wieman v Mabee, 45 Mich 484.

bad weather. Rainy, stormy, or inclement weather. As the term appears in a charter party, not merely weather during which cargo cannot, by any possibility, be loaded, on a ship but such weather as is not reasonably fit and proper for loading; weather in which it is not reasonably safe to attempt loading with the appliances at hand, such as lighters.
The term has also been held to include weather unfit for loading by reason of the state of the sea as well as that of the atmosphere. Anno: 26 ALR 1440.

bag. A piece of luggage; a large purse carried by a woman; a sack or pouch for carrying dry products. A slang term of derision applied to a person, usually a woman.

baga (ba'ga). A bag or purse.

baggage. Articles which one usually carries with him for his personal use, convenience, instruction or amusement, 29 Am J Rev ed Innk § 100. Articles which a passenger of a carrier usually takes with him for his own personal use, comfort and convenience during the journey, taking into consideration his tastes, habits, and station in life, and having some regard for the object and length of the journey. 14 Am J2d Car § 1223.
Baggage does not include merchandise or valuables not designed for personal use or personal convenience. 29 Am J Rev ed Innk § 100. Articles carried for the purpose of business, such as merchandise or samples, constitute baggage only as they are accepted as such by the carrier. The same is true of articles of extraordinary value. 14 Am J2d Car § 1223.

baggage car. The car of a passenger train in which baggage checked by passengers is carried.

baggage insurance. See **tourists' policy**

baggage lien. The lien which a carrier of passengers has on the baggage that a passenger carries with him for pleasure of convenience for all unpaid charges for transportation which the passenger incurs during the journey.
This lien does not extend to the clothing or other personal furnishings or conveniences of the passenger in immediate use. Roberts v Koehler (CC Or) 30 F 94, 96, 97.

baggage master. An employee of a carrier in charge of the baggage room.

baggage room. The room devoted by a carrier at its station to the reception and delivery of the baggage of its customers.

bahadum (ba-hā'dum). A chest or coffer.

bail (bāl). Noun: The means of procuring the release from custody of a person charged with a criminal offense or with debt by assuring his future appearance in court and compelling him to remain within the jurisdiction. Manning v State, 190 Okla 65, 120 P2d 980. The security given for a defendant's appearance in court in cash, bond, or undertaking. Sawyer v Barbour, 142 Cal App 2d 827, 300 P2d 187. The surety on a bail bond. (French.) A lease of real estate. Verb: To deliver from custody on the security of bail. 8 Am J2d Bail § 1 (French.) To prepare a lease.
See **bail above; bail below.**

baila (bai'la). Bail.

bailable (bā'la-bl). Admitting of bail, as, a bailable offense; entitled to be released on bail, as, a bailable prisoner.

bailable action. An action in which a defendant must find bail or suffer imprisonment until the plaintiff's demand is satisfied or until discharged by the court.

bailable offense. An offense a defendant charged with which may be released on bail.

bailable person. One under arrest for a bailable offense.

bailable process. Process under which an officer may take bail and release a person arrested from custody.

bail above. Bail on the mesne process of civil arrest, otherwise known as bail to the action, put into the court on the return day of the writ, wherein the undertaking of the surety, in the event of judgment against the principal, was either to pay the judgment debt and costs or surrender the principal into custody. 8 Am J2d Bail § 1.

bail below. Bail on the mesne process of civil arrest, otherwise known as special bail, for the appearance of the principal in court on the return day of the writ. 8 Am J2d Bail § 1.

bail bond. A bond given as security for the purpose of obtaining release of a person in custody.
See **bail.**

bail court. A court auxiliary to the queen's bench having cognizance particularly of matters of procedure.

bail de la seisine (bahl de la sē'sin). Livery of seisin.

bailee. The person to whom a bailment is made. 8 Am J2d Bailm § 2.

bailee for hire. A person who takes personal property into his care and custody for a compensation. 8 Am J2d Bailm § 7.

bailee's lien. The lien of a bailee entitled to compensation or reimbursement as security for the payment thereof. 8 Am J2d Bailm § 227.

bailie. A Scotch alderman, bailiff, or magistrate.

bailiff (bā'lif). A court attendant; a sheriff's deputy; a keeper; a servant that has the administration and charge of lands, goods and chattels, to make the best benefit for the owner, against whom an action of account lies, for the profits which he has raised or made, or might by his industry or care have raised or made. Barnum v Landon, 25 Conn 137, 149.

bailiff errant. A deputy appointed by the sheriff to go about serving writs and process.

bailiffs of franchises. Officers acting as sheriffs within privileged jurisdictions where the king's writ could at that time not be executed by the sheriff.

bailiffs of hundreds. Officers appointed by sheriffs in their respective hundreds to collect fines therein, to summon juries, to attend the judges at assizes and quarter sessions and to execute writs and process. See 1 Bl Comm 345.

bailiffs of manors. Stewards who were appointed by lords of manors.

bail in error. Bail procured by a plaintiff in error as security for his prosecution of his writ of error with effect, that in case of affirmance he will pay the judgment of the lower court and all costs and damages assessed and whatever damages shall be awarded for the delay of execution of the affirmed judgment.

bailing. See **bail.**

bailivia (bai-li'vi-a). An old form of **bailiwick.**

bailiwick. The jurisdiction of a sheriff or bailiff; a word introduced by the princes of the Norman line, in imitation of the French, whose territory is divided into bailiwicks, as that of England into counties. See 1 Bl Comm 344.

bailleur. (French.) A lessor.

bailleur de fonds. (French; French Canadian.) An unpaid lender; an unpaid vendor.

bailli. A person to whom judicial authority is delegated.

baillie. A bailiwick.

bailment. The delivery of personal property by one person to another in trust for a specific purpose, with a contract, express or implied, that the trust shall be faithfully executed, and the property returned or duly accounted for when the special purpose is accomplished, or kept until the bailor reclaims it. 8 Am J2d Bailm § 2.

bailment for compensation. See **bailment for hire.**

bailment for hire. A bailment in which the bailee is compensated; a bailment for the benefit of both parties. 8 Am J2d Bailm § 7.

bailment for sale. A consignment contract. 8 Am J2d Bailm § 34.

bailment-lease. A form of contract calling for instalment payments, but without a debtor-creditor relationship expressly created. Re Robinson (DC Pa) 40 F Supp 320.

bail money. A deposit of money in lieu of a bail bond or undertaking. Sawyer v Barbour, 142 Cal App 2d 827, 300 P2d 187.

bailor. One who makes a bailment of property. Watson v State, 70 Ala 13.
He need not have in himself absolute title to the thing bailed, provided he is invested with such possessory interest as will entitle him to hold it against all the world except the rightful owner. 8 Am J2d Bailm § 44.

bailout stock. Preferred stock issued as a nontaxable stock dividend. IRC § 305.

bailpiece. A written memorial that a person has become bail; evidence of authority of the sureties on a bail bond to make an arrest of the principal. Worthen v Prescott, 60 Vt 68, 11 A 690.

bail to the action. Same as **bail above.**

baily (bā'li). Same as **bailie.**

Baine's Act. An English statute passed in 1848, placing accessories before the fact and principals on equal footing and providing for separate trials for accessories after the fact.

bair-man (Scotch.) A man who has been stripped bare by his creditors; a bankrupt.

bairns. (Scotch.) Children.

bairns' part. (Scotch.) A third of a decedent's estate, if there was a widow, a half, if there was not, to go to his child or children.

bait. Noun: Something offered to entice. Verb: To harass.

baker. One who follows the occupation of baking bread and pastries in a bakery or a restaurant.

baker's dozen. Thirteen.

bakery. A place where bread and pastries are baked and sold or baked for delivery in commerce.

baking powder. A leavening agent used to raise dough before baking.

balaena (ba-lē'nä). A whale.
See **fish royal**.

balance. A word which had its origin in the field of weights, but has a present meaning of that which remains after the taking away or deduction of a part, such as the balance of an account.
The entry of a "balance" is not an original entry within rule of admissibility of books of account. Anno: 17 ALR2d 235.
The word, when used in a residuary clause of a will, will be regarded as presumptively indicating an intention that lapsed or ineffectual gifts should pass thereunder. When used with reference to some specific fund, it is given a restricted construction and held not to pass a lapsed legacy or devise outside of such fund. 57 Am J1st Wills § 1449.

balance due. The amount owing on a debt after a partial payment or payments.
The "balance due" on a general account by a correspondent is, in mercantile language, the fund found in his hands. Parsons v Armor (US) 3 Pet 413, 430, 7 L Ed 724.

balance of convenience. The importance of granting relief by injunction to the plaintiff, measured against the injury, hardship, or inconvenience which the defendant is likely to suffer from such relief. 28 Am J Rev ed Inj § 52.

balance of power. The doctrine that there will be no great wars if the possible belligerents are kept in equal strength by armament and alliances, so that the one side seems to have no advantage over the other and therefore no good reason for starting a war.

balance sheet. As the term is uniformly used by bookkeepers and businessmen, a summation or general balance of all accounts, but not showing the particular items going to make up the several accounts. Eyre v Harmon, 92 Cal 580, 28 P 779.

balance sheet test. The test of insolvency under the bankruptcy definition of insolvency. 9 Am J2d Bankr § 1065. Considering the aggregate of liability against the aggregate value of assets; the relation of the aggregate of liabilities to assets. 9 Am J2d Bankr § 160.

balcony. The upper section of a conventional theater; a platform extending out from a building and enclosed by a railing.

baldio (bal-dee'o). (Spanish.) Abandoned public land.

bale. A large package or bundle; sorrow.

baleine (ba-lēn). (French.) Whale or whalebone.

baling band. Bands upon bulky bales of cargo, necessary to keep the bales tight and in workable dimensions. 48 Am J1st Ship § 212. Wire or cord bands used in baling hay.

balise. In French maritime law, a buoy or beacon.

balius (ba'li'us). A tutor; a guardian; a teacher.

baliva, or balliva (ba-lī'va). A bailiwick or county.

balivo amovendo (ba'li-vō ā-mo-ven'dō). A writ to oust a bailiff from his office.

ballast. A word somewhat analogous to "dunnage" and applied to matter such as coal, iron, ore or stone, placed in a ship's hold for trimming the ship, and bringing her down to a draft of water proper and safe for sailing. Great Western Ins. Co. v Thwing (US) 13 Wall 674, 20 L Ed 607.

ballastage (bal'as-tāj). A toll imposed upon ships for the privilege of taking on as ballast soil from the bottom of a seaport.

ballistics. The science of projectiles, by the application of which, at the hands of an expert, it is possible to show that a bullet found in the body of a victim of a homicide was fired from a particular pistol or rifle. 26 Am J1st Homi § 440.

balloon. An aircraft which will rise from the earth because it is inflated with a gas which is lighter than air.

balloonist. The pilot of a balloon. 8 Am J2d Avi § 33.

ballot. Deriving from the Greek "ballo". Noun: The implement of voting, whether a paper to be marked by an elector or the face of a voting machine prepared for an election. 26 Am J2d Elect § 202.
See **Australian ballot system**.

ballot box. A box or receptacle for the deposit of ballots cast by electors at an election. The box in which the names of jurors on the panel for the trial term are deposited preparatory to drawing jurors for a case on trial. 31 Am J Rev ed Jury § 76.

ballottement (bà-lot-mon'). (French.) Balloting in an election. Tossing. A test of pregnancy by palpitation.

balnearii (bal-ne-ā'ri-ī). (Roman law.) Thieves who stole the clothes of persons who were bathing in the public baths.

balustrade (bal-us-trād). A railing with supporting posts.
See **bannister**.

ban (ban). A public edict or proclamation; a sentence of excommunication in an ecclesiastical court. A prohibition.
See **banning; banns of matrimony**.

banality (ba-nal'i̧-ti). A platitude. The right by which the lord made his vassals grind at his mill and bake at his oven.

banc (bangk). A bench; a meeting of all the judges of the court.

banci narratores (ban'si nav-vā-to'rēz). Pleaders at the bench. Sergeants and advocates of the law. See 1 Bl Comm 24, note.

banc le roi. The king's bench.

banco (bang′kō). See **banc; in banco.**

bancus reginae (ban′kus re-jī′nē). The court of queen's bench.

bancus regis (ban′kus rē′jis). The court of king's bench.

bancus superior (ban′kus su-pe′ri-or). The upper bench,—at one time the name of the court of king's bench.

band. Something that binds. A company of persons; a group of musicians who play together, especially upon wind and percussion instruments. In the Scottish, a call to arms.
See **Indian band.**

band and tribe. See **Indian band.**

bandit. An outlaw.

bane (bān). A malefactor; a slayer; the cause of harm or trouble.

baneret. Same as **banneret.**

bani. Same as **deodand.**

banishment. The removal, expulsion, or deportation of a person from a country by the political authority thereof on the ground of expediency.
The better use of the word appears to exclude its employment in the sense of transportation or exile by way of punishment for crime. Fong Yue Ting v United States, 149 US 698, 709, 37 L Ed 905, 911, 13 S Ct 1016. It has, however, been used in the latter sense by some authority. Ex parte Scarborough, 76 Cal App 2d 648, 173 P2d 825.

banister. See **bannister.**

bank. An institution, usually incorporated, the business of which is primarily receiving deposits of money, the collection of commercial paper, discounting commercial paper, lending money, issuing, purchasing, and accepting bills of exchange or drafts, and issuing its own notes and certificates of deposit. Bank of Augusta v Earle (US) 13 Pet 519, 593, 10 L Ed 274, 310; Oulton v German Sav. & Loan Soc. (US) 7 Wall 109, 21 L Ed 618.
See **banc; bank of river; commercial bank; savings bank.**

bankable note. A note which will be taken by a bank as cash or subject to a discount. Pasha v Bohart, 45 Mont 76, 122 P 284. The condition that a buyer must pay by cash or a "bankable note" was at one time a familiar one in auction sales. The courts are split as to whether a note is bankable when banks refuse to discount it because of the general stringency of the money market, and not because of the financial irresponsibility of the parties. 46 Am J1st Sales § 179.

bank account. The deposits made by a customer less his withdrawals plus the other charges which the bank is entitled to make.
The difference remains to be withdrawn; if the withdrawals and charges exceed the aggregate of the deposits, the account is in the state of an **overdraft.**

bank a deal. To advance money, usually by way of a loan bearing interest and secured, to one with whom the lender desires to consummate a contract, under such terms that he does not become a partner of the borrower, but a secured creditor. Cray, McFawn & Co. v Hegarty, Conroy & Co. (DC NY) 27 F Supp 93.

bank bills. See **bank notes.**

bank board. The directors of the bank acting as a body.

bank book. A book in which a customer of a bank keeps account of his deposits, withdrawals, and balance.

bank cashier. See **cashier.**

bank chairman. The chairman of the board of directors of a bank, who is in some institutions the chief executive officer, but usually exercises no functions except those of presiding at board meetings and acting with the board.

bank check. A check in the ordinary sense of the term, that is, a check drawn on a bank.
See **cashier's check; check.**

bank collections. A long established function of banks, the collection of commercial paper for its patrons. 10 Am J2d Banks § 694.

bank commissioner. A state officer appointed and invested with power to license banks, supervise the conduct of the banking business within the jurisdiction, and liquidate failed banks. 10 Am J2d Banks § 17.

Bank Conservation Act. A federal statute which provides for the appointment by the Comptroller of the Currency of a conservator of a national bank found by the comptroller to be in failing circumstances, not for liquidation of the bank but for conservation of assets, there being prospect that the bank later may be in position to reopen and resume its corporate functions. 12 USC §§ 201-211; Davis Trust Co. v Hardee, 66 App DC 168, 85 F2d 571, 107 ALR 1425.

bank conservator. See **Bank Conservation Act.**

bank credit. The rating of a borrower at a particular bank as to the maximum loan to be made to him and the maximum amount of his drawings upon the bank in the aggregate which will be accepted.

bank deposit. A contractual relationship ensuing from the delivery, by one known as the depositor, of money, funds, or even things into the possession of the bank, which receives the same upon the agreement to pay, repay, or return, upon the order or demand of the depositor, the money, funds, or equivalent amount.
This agreement on the part of the bank is usually a tacit one and implied, and it may include an implied promise to pay interest upon the deposit, depending upon the nature of the deposit and the account into which it is placed. 10 Am J2d Banks § 337.
Where the terms of the law provide for the safeguarding of deposits in banks, it extends only to such deposits as are general deposits; money or the equivalent of money must in intention and effect be placed in, or at the command of, the bank so that the relation of debtor and creditor is created. Re Farmers State Bank, 67 SD 51, 289 NW 75, 126 ALR 619.
See **safe-deposit box; savings account.**

bank deposits tax. A tax upon the franchise of the bank measured by the amount of deposits. 51 Am J1st Tax § 931. A tax upon a deposit as moneys or credits of the depositor.

bank directors. The members of the board of directors of a banking corporation who, acting as a board, appoint the officers and agents necessary to carry on the business of the bank and who are responsible for proper and prudent management of the bank. 10 Am J2d Banks §§ 77, 178.

banke. See **en banke.**

banker. A dealer in capital, that is, an intermediary between the borrower and the lender, who borrows from one party and lends to another; every person, firm, or company having a place of business where credits are opened by the deposit or collection of money or currency, subject to be paid or remitted upon draft, check or order, or where money is advanced or loaned on stocks, bonds, bullion, bills of exchange, or promissory notes, and commercial paper is received for discount or for sale. 10 Am J2d Banks § 2. One who accepts and holds the stake or stakes in a gambling game or wager. 24 Am J1st Gaming, etc. § 26.

bankerout. A bankrupt.

banker's acceptances. In the broad sense, acceptances of bills of exchange by banks; in the technical and peculiar sense of the banking business, extensions of credit by acceptances of bills of exchange. Atterbury v Bank of Washington Heights, 241 NY 231, 239.

bankers' blanket bond. A fidelity bond protecting a bank against loss through the fraud or dishonesty of employees. Anno: 74 ALR 284.

bankers' cash notes. Formerly called goldsmiths' notes; promissory notes issued by bankers, payable to bearer on demand and used as money.

banker's lien. The lien that a banker has on all moneys and funds of his depositor or customer in his possession for the balance of the general account; and upon all securities of the customer in his hands unless such securities have been delivered to him under a particular agreement limiting their application, or unless there are other circumstances which would make such a lien inconsistent with the actual or presumed intention of the parties. Anno: 22 ALR2d 478; 10 Am J2d Banks § 660.

banker's note. A bank note issued by a private, unincorporated bank.

bank examiner. A federal or state officer authorized to conduct an investigation of the accounts of a bank and determine the state of solvency of the institution. 10 Am J2d Banks § 18.

In some jurisdictions, examiners act on behalf of the commissioner or superintendent of banks in the liquidation of insolvent banks.

bank failure. See **failed bank.**

bank for co-operatives. See **Central Bank; regional banks.**

bank guaranty law. A statute which has for its purpose the guaranty of payment of bank deposits in whole or in a stated percentage, subject to limitations upon the amount of the deposit.
See **Deposit Insurance Corporation.**

bank holiday. Known to some as a day, such as Christmas, Memorial Day, or other national or state holiday, when banks are closed; known also to people of an older generation as the trying period in 1933 during which all banks in the United States were closed by the proclamation of newly-inaugurated President Franklin D. Roosevelt or the orders of governors of states and banking authorities rendered and declared in keeping with the presidential proclamation.

The purpose of the holiday was to prevent the drain of currency from the banks by withdrawals by frightened depositors and give the people a chance to reassess the situation and recover from their fears of an impending collapse of the entire financial structure of the nation.

banking. Receiving deposits payable on demand; making collections; discounting commercial paper; making loans of money, often on collateral security; accepting, buying, and selling bills of exchange, negotiating loans; and dealing in negotiable securities issued by the government, state, national, or municipal, and other corporations. 10 Am J2d Banks § 3.

The safe-deposit business must be a "banking function" authorized by Congress. The obvious fact, known to all, is that national banks do and for many years have carried on a safe-deposit business. State banks quite usually are given the power to do so. Colorado Nat. Bank v Bedford, 310 US 41, 84 L Ed 1067, 60 S Ct 800.

banking business. See **banking.**

banking corporation. Essentially, a corporation engaged in the banking business or in some features of the banking business. For the purposes of an exception from adjudication in bankruptcy, an organization, other than a private bank, banking partnership, or other form of unincorporated association, which is engaged in the banking business or having authority to engage in such business. 9 Am J2d Bankr §§ 129, 130.

banking game. A slang expression for the banking business; gambling games, such as faro or craps, in which one person takes all the bets, and the running of slot machines. 24 Am J1st Gaming, etc. § 26.

Any game of chance is a banking game if it is a game wherein the chances are unequal and in favor of the exhibitor of the table. The advantages or chances in favor of the player or exhibitor of the table are not the same in each case, but in each case the chances are in his favor, and this is the distinctive characteristic of this class of gambling games. Territory v Jones, 14 NM 579, 99 P 338.

banking hours. The hours in which banks are open for business.
See **bank night.**

banking institution. See **bank, banking, banking corporation.**

banking powers. The powers of engaging in the ordinary banking business of receiving deposits, making collections, accepting bills of exchange, making loans, etc. and, in addition the powers in carrying on other functions, which may or may not be incidental to the business of banking, but are such as can be exercised advantageously in connection with the banking business. 10 Am J2d Banks § 270.

bank lien. See **banker's lien.**

bank money order. An instrument issued by an authorized officer of a bank and directed to another bank, evidencing the fact that the payee may demand and receive upon indorsement and presentation to the other bank the amount stated on the face of the instrument, liability for ultimate payment resting solely on the issuing bank. 10 Am J2d Banks § 545.

bank night. An evening upon which banks remain open for the convenience of working people; a scheme once fairly common in theaters which led to prosecutions for conducting a lottery.

The scheme usually provides for registration by the individual in a book, provided by the theater or other place conducting the scheme, which gives him a registration number. On certain specified nights numbers are drawn from among those registered entitling the one holding such number to a prize. Theoretically, at least, everyone may register free of charge and need not attend the performance, but he must be nearby at the time of the drawing in order to present himself within the short time allotted to claim the prize. Some courts hold that the scheme is not a lottery because no consideration is involved, but others hold that the free registration is only a subterfuge and that there is a consideration involved. Still others hold that whether there is a consideration or not is a question in each case for the jury. 34 Am J1st Lot § 9.

bank notes. Notes or bills issued by banks and passing as money or common currency. 10 Am J2d Banks § 320.
See **bank of issue.**

bank of circulation. See **bank of issue.**

bank of discount. See **discount.**

bank of issue. A bank authorized to issue notes intended to circulate as money.
For many years, national banks were authorized and did issue notes which passed as currency. This power has since been withdrawn from national banks. The only banks of issue at the present time are the federal reserve banks.

bank of river. The water-washed and relatively permanent elevation or acclivity at the outer edge of the river bed which separates the bed from the adjacent upland, and serves to confine the waters within the bed and to preserve the course of the river. 56 Am J1st Wat § 448.

bank president. Normally, the chief executive officer of a bank, but in some banks, giving way in this respect to the chairman of the board, and in a few small-town banks, even to the cashier.

bank receiver. A bank acting in the capacity of a receiver. 10 Am J2d Banks § 304. A person designated by statute or appointed to take charge of the assets of an insolvent bank and conserve them for liquidation or reorganization of the bank. 10 Am J2d Banks §§ 763 et seq.
The receiver of an insolvent national bank is an officer of the United States. Pufahl v Park's Estate, 299 US 217, 81 L Ed 133, 57 S Ct 151.

bank receivership. See **bank receiver.**

bank reorganization. Broadly, a change in the corporate structure of a bank. In a narrower but usual sense of the term, the rehabilitation of a failing or financially embarrassed bank by freezing the assets through the suspension of payment to depositors and creditors, followed by the adoption of a plan of reorganization affecting the rights of depositors, creditors, and stockholders whereunder the bank reopens for business as a bank. 10 Am J2d Banks § 821.

bank reserve. See **reserve.**

Bank Robbery Act. A federal statute intended to state comprehensively criminal offenses committed against a national or federal bank, or a federal savings and loan association, in entering the institution with intent to commit a felony therein, in the taking of property of the institution with force or violence, in carrying away property of the institution with intent to steal or purloin, and the receiving of property stolen from the institution. 18 USC § 2113; Anno: 59 ALR2d 954.

bankrupt. A person, corporation, partnership, or unincorporated association which has been adjudicated bankrupt by a court of bankruptcy.
The word is derived from the terms "banque" and "rupt," which had reference to the broken bench or table of a failed trader, symbolizing his failure.

bankruptcy. A system of jurisprudence, which, while statutory, is comparable to equity or admiralty. The law whereunder an insolvent debtor may bring all his assets not exempt from execution into court and have them administered and sold for the benefit of his creditors, and be discharged from all of his debts not excepted from discharge; or bring all of his assets into court, not for their liquidation and his discharge from his debts, but for his financial rehabilitation. 9 Am J2d Bankr § 2.

Bankruptcy Act. A national bankruptcy act.
There have been four of such acts in the United States, effective respectively in 1800, 1841, 1867, and 1898. The last of these is the present Bankruptcy Act, although some have regarded the Amendatory Act of 1938, known as the Chandler Act, as a new bankruptcy act because of the very extensive revision which it made of the Act of 1898. There have, of course, been amendments since 1938, but none of them so extensive by any means as the Chandler Act.

bankruptcy proceeding. See **proceeding in bankruptcy.**

bankruptcy trustee. See **trustee in bankruptcy.**

bankrupt's estate. See **estate in bankruptcy.**

bank stock. Stock in a banking corporation.

bank stock lien. The lien which a bank has on shares of its stock to secure the payment of indebtedness due the bank from its stockholder.
Such lien exists by force of statute, by charter, by bylaw, or by contract. 10 Am J2d Banks §§ 55 et seq.

bank teller. See **teller.**

banleuca (ban-lū′ka). The territory without the walls, but within the town or city limits.

banlieu (ban′lū). Same as **banleuca.**

banner. A flag; a cloth carrying the names of candidates for election, or of products for sale, sometimes hung for display to passers-by, sometimes carried on the streets, and sometimes trailed by an airplane.

banneret (ban′ĕr-et). A rank of knighthood.
See **knights banneret.**

banning. Excluding; outlawing; swearing at or berating a person.

banni nuptiarum (ban′nī nup-she-ā′rum). The banns of matrimony.

bannister. The railing on stairs or around the well of a stairway.

bannition (ba-nish′ǫn). Same as **banning.**

bannitus (ban′ni-tus). An outlaw; a person who has been banished.

banns of matrimony. Notice given of an intended marriage, usually given by proclamation in church.

bannum (ban′num). A ban; the boundaries of a manor or a town.

bannus (ban′nus). A proclamation.

bannus regis (ban'nus rē'jis). A proclamation of the king forbidding interference at a trail by combat.

banque (bank). A bench or counter of a trader.

baptismal register. A church record of baptisms.

Baptist Church. A protestant church of strength in the United States. Park v Champlin, 96 Iowa 55, 64 NW 674.
See **Free Baptists.**

bar. Noun: A rail inclosing the officers of a court; the place in a court occupied by a prisoner on his trial. The court itself, as where one speaks of the case at bar. The attorneys at law taken collectively in a municipality, county, state, or the nation. A defense defeating an action; a kind of answer or plea. A molded chunk or piece of metal, such as a gold bar; a lever or pry of wood or metal. A room or place where alcoholic beverages are sold and drunk, sometimes with, but more commonly without, meals. 30 Am J Rev ed Intox L § 20. A place where coffee, tea, grape juice, orange juice, or other nonintoxicating beverage is sold. The counter at which beverages are served. Verb: To prevent; to keep persons or animals out of a building or area.
See **barroom; integrated bar; plea in bar; state bar.**

bar association. An organization of members of the bar of the United States or of a state, county, or municipality, the primary function of which is the improvement of the profession which will result in improvement in the administration of justice.

barat. To quarrel.

barator. An old form of **barrator.**

Baratriam committit qui propter pecuniam justitiam baractat (ba-rā'tri-am kom-mit'tit quī prop'ter pē-kū'ni-am jūs-ti'shē-am ba-rak'tat). Barratry in selling justice for money.

barbarous. Strange, rude, and uncivilized.

barber. A tonsorial artisan; one who performs work in cutting hair, shaving, shampooing, massaging, singeing hair, and other functions intended to promote cleanliness and personal attractiveness.
In ancient times, barbers performed some of the services now performed by physicians and surgeons, such as lancing and draining boils, and stopping nosebleed, and hiccups.

barbican (bär'bi-kan). A watchtower.

barbicanage (bar'bi-kan-age). Financial support for a watchtower.

barbiturate (bär-bi'tū-rāt). A drug employed as a sedative. People v Wittpen, 190 Misc 565, 75 NYS2d 670.

bare. Mere; unaccompanied; naked; nude; nothing more.

bareboat charter. A charter under which full possession and control of the stripped vessel is delivered to the charterer for a period of time, making him for most purposes the owner or, as he is generally called, owner pro hac vice. Reed v The Yaka, 373 US 410, 10 L Ed 2d 448, 83 S Ct 1349.

bare contract. The essential conditions.

bare licensee. One whose presence on premises is not invited, but not resisted, merely tolerated.
See **licensee.**

bare possibility. An expectancy; something that may but is not likely to happen.

baret (bar'et). A quarrelsome litigation; a fraud; a deceit.

bare trustee. A trustee whose sole function is to hold the title to the trust property.
See **dry trust; passive trust.**

bare wires. Uninsulated wires. New England Tel & Tel. Co. v Butler (CA1 Mass) 156 F 321.

bar fee (bär' fē). A sheriff's fee which is due him on the acquittal of a prisoner in his custody.

bargain. An agreement of two or more persons to exchange promises or to exchange a promise for a performance. 17 Am J2d Contr § 1. As the terms upon which persons contract with one another. Salmon Falls Mfg. Co. v Goddard (US) 14 How 446, 14 L Ed 493.

bargain and sale. A deed in the form of a contract which became effective to transfer legal title by virtue of the Statute of Uses. 23 Am J2d Deeds § 13. A sale of personal property which vests title in the buyer, 46 Am J1st Sales § 2. A contract within the meaning of statutes taxing transfers by bargain and sale. Schroeder v Zink, 4 NJ 1, 71 A2d 321.

bargain and sale deed. See **bargain and sale.**

bargain collectively. See **collective bargaining.**

bargainee (bär-ga-nē'). The grantee or vendee in a bargain and sale.

bargaining unit. A labor union or other body participating on behalf of labor in collective bargaining.

bargain money. Money paid to bind a bargain; earnest money.

bargainor (bä'gan-or). The grantor or vendor in a bargain and sale.

barganizare (bar-ga-ni-zā're). To bargain; to agree.

barganizavit et vendidit (bar"ga-ni-zā'vit et ven'di-dit). He has bargained and sold.

barge. Noun: Watercraft; a ship or boat of state used in the transportation of rulers and dignitaries; a flat bottomed boat used in the loading and unloading of ships which cannot dock; a towed boat on rivers and canals, carrying oil, coal, grain, and various heavy cargoes. Verb: A colloquial expression meaning to enter abruptly and somewhat heavily.

bar integration. See **integration of the bar.**

bark. The covering of the trunk and branches of a tree; superficial appearance, as distinguished from heart or substance.

barley. A food grain; a crop.

barleycorn (bär'li-kôrn). A lineal measure equal to a third of an inch.

barmote courts (bär'mōt). Courts established in the reign of Edward the Third, and held twice a year in Derbyshire, in which matters connected with mining are considered.

barn. A building, found on farms and in some villages and hamlets, for sheltering livestock and affording a storage place for livestock feed.

barnard (bär'nard). A swindler who acts as a decoy for other swindlers.

Barnard's Inn. One of the inns of the English chancery.

baro (bar'ō). A baron; a knight; a freeman.

baron (bar'on). A person having the most general and universal title of the English nobility; a judge

BARONAGE [125] **BASE**

or officer of the court of exchequer; a husband; a vassal of the king.

baronage (bär'ọn-āj). The rank of a baron; a barony.

baron court (bar'ọn kōrt). See **court baron**.

baronet (bar'ọn-et). An English title of lower rank than the nobility and which is a dignity of inheritance created by letters patent and usually descendible to male issue. See 1 Bl Comm 403.

baron et feme (ba-ron et fem). Husband and wife.

barons of the cinque ports (singk). The members of parliament from the five English ports nearest France: Hastings, Romney, Hythe, Dover, and Sandwich. At one time, these ports were considered the most important in England.

barons of the exchequer. The judges of the court of exchequer. They are always referred to as barons and not as judges.

barony (bar'ọn-i). The rank of a baron; the lands held by a baron; the tenure by the service of attending the king in his courts as a baron.

barony of land. An old term for an area of land, perhaps fifteen acres.

barra (bar'ạ). Same as **bar**.

barrasterius (bar-ras-ter'i-us). A barrister. See **barratry**.

barrator (bar'a-tor). A person guilty of barratry. 14 Am J2d Champ § 19.

barratrous (bar'ạ-trus). Tainted with barratry; fraudulent.

barratry (bar'ra-try). The offense of frequently exciting or stirring up suits and quarrels between others. 14 Am J2d Champ § 19. A marine term meaning acts or conduct of master or mariners in their character as such, committed for some unlawful or fraudulent purpose, contrary to their duty to the owners of the ship or cargo, whereby the owners sustain injury. 29A Am J Rev ed Ins § 1320; 48 Am J1st Ship § 652.

barre (ba-rā'). Same as **bar**. See **en barre**.

barred. See **bar**.

barrel. A liquid measure of thirty-six gallons. Gardner v Lane, 91 Mass (9 Allen) 492. A container for transportation or storage of liquids, grain, flour, whiskey, etc., sometimes of a specific capacity, for example a barrel of flour, 192 pounds, the equivalent of four 48 pound bags.

barren money (bar'en). A debt bearing no interest.

barrenness. Inability to bear children.
The word is in no sense a synonym of "impotency." Anonymous, 89 Ala 291, 7 So 100.

barretor. Same as **barrator**.

barretry. Same as **barratry**.

barricade. A barrier against the onslaught of enemies or rioters; a hastily-constructed fence or wall in the street to prevent travelers from driving or stepping into excavations, in which case, the word imports an obstruction, not merely a warning, but an actual impediment to travel. American Water-Works Co. v Dougherty, 37 Neb 373, 376, 55 NW 1070.

barrier. See **barricade**.

barring. Closing and locking up; keeping people or animals out of a building or area; a technical term in railroading; the shifting of freight cars for short distances by means of crowbars applied to the wheels in order to make the cars more accessible for loading and unloading. Jarka Corp. v Pennsylvania R. Co. (DC Md) 42 F Supp 371.

barring the entail. Defeating an estate tail and the onerous effect of the Statute de Donis by common recovery or fine. 19 Am J1st Est § 50.
See **common recovery; fine**.

barrister (bar'is-tèr). A person learned in the law and who is permitted to plead at the bar of the courts in England.
The nearest American term in counterpart is "trial lawyer," the most essential difference being that the barrister's professional work is confined exclusively to the trial of cases, while an American trial lawyer often performs the professional work of ordinary office practice.

barroom. A room or place where intoxicating liquors are sold and drunk, usually without meals. 30 Am J Rev ed Intox § 20.
See **bar**.

bar sinister. Bastardy in the family line.

bartender. A person, usually an employee rather than an owner of a bar, who draws, pours, mixes and dispenses alcoholic beverages.

barter. Noun: The exchange of one commodity or article of property for another. 30 Am J2d Exch P § 1. Verb: To negotiate for the acquisition of a thing. Homan v Board of Dental Examiners (Cal App) 254 P 907; Clark v State, 167 Ala 101, 52 So 893.
Broadly defined, "barter" includes a sale as well as a trade.

barton (bär'tọn). The unrented lands of a manor; the demesne lands of a manor; the manor house itself.

bas (ba'). Base; humble; inferior.

bas chevaliers (bâ shev-a-lēr'). Minor knights.

base. Noun: A foundation; a starting point. Adjective: Low, vile, corrupt.

base animal. See **animal of a base nature**.

baseball. A game played with a ball and a wooden bat by opposing teams of nine men each; a sport, amateur in origin, which has become professional to a great extent, leading to complex organization as an enterprise in entertaining people.
See **professional baseball**.

base coin. Coin made of base metal altogether, colored by artificial means.
Base is not to be confounded with "adulterated" coin, which is a distinct species. Gabe v State, 6 Ark 540, 542.

base court. An inferior English court, not a court of record, as the court baron.

base estate. An estate held by a base tenant. See **base fee**.

base fee. An estate in real property which has the possibility of enduring forever but which may be determined and put to an end without the aid of a conveyance by some act or event circumscribing its continuance or extent. An estate limited to a person and his heirs, with a qualification annexed to it providing that such estate must determine whenever that qualification is at an end. 28 Am J2d Est § 22.

base infeftment. (Scotch.) A disposition of lands by a vassal, to be held of himself.—Black's Law Dict.

base line. An east and west line, parallel to the equator, established as a means whereby townships created in the government survey of public lands are described as such by the number of the tier of townships in which it appears north or south of such line, the description, operating with a similar description in terms of a north and south line or principal meridian, to give the location of the township. Meas v Whitener-London Realty Co. 119 Ark 301, 178 SW 390.

See **range**.

basement. The lowest story of a building; the story which is wholly or partially lower than the surface of the ground.

base nature. See **animal of a base nature**.

base of operations. A place where activities are centered; one may have more than one base of operations, working out of one in one state and out of another in another state. Re Mallia, 299 NY 232, 86 NE2d 577, 9 ALR2d 636.

base property. An older concept of the common law, which has been changed to a great extent, if not entirely, by statute or evolution in the common law, that certain things, such as dogs and cats, were property of an inferior nature, so that they were not subjects of larceny. 32 Am J1st Larc § 79. The inferior nature of the property in such animals did not prevent the maintenance of an action for their conversion. Columbus Railroad Co. v Woolfolk, 128 Ga 631, 58 SE 152; Commonwealth v Flynn, 285 Mass 136, 188 NE 627, 92 ALR 206.

See **base fee**.

base right. (Scotch.) A subordinate right.

base services. Services annexed to feudal tenure of villeinage; such services were of a base or servile nature.

base tenants. Tenants rendering services of a base or servile nature.

base tenure. Villeinage.

basileus (ba'si-leus). A Greek word meaning king, in use in England prior to the Norman Conquest.

basilica. A rectangular building in use in ancient times as a courtroom or public hall; a church in the architectural form of a basilica.

Basilica (ba-sil'i-kạ). The Byzantine Code adopted from the Code of Justinian and published in the early part of the tenth century.

basin. A part of the sea inclosed in rocks, the area drained by a river; a bowl.

basis. The foundation of a principle; a technical term in the law of income taxes for the cost of property, or the value of investment in property, as of a certain date, upon which depreciation can be computed. Anno: 40 ALR2d 446.

basis of keeping accounts. For income tax purposes, the bookkeeping system followed by the taxpayer, not the items or entries upon his books. United States v American Can Co. 280 US 412, 74 L Ed 518.

basis of tax. The ground or foundation on which the tax is computed; the rate is the percentage fixed by the statute applied to the basis in making the calculation. The result is the amount of the tax to be paid. Pacific Mut Life Ins. Co. v Lowe, 354 Ill 398, 188 NE 436.

basis patent. A patent in a virgin field; a pioneer patent. A patent following a discovery in a field theretofore unknown to the discoverer, or if once known, had since become unknown, to him, which appears to the scientific world or the industry to which it pertains as a startling, unexpected, unprophesied, and unheralded innovation. Northwest Engineering Corp. v Keystone Driller Co. (CA7 Wis) 70 F2d 13.

basket tenure. Tenure by the service of basket-making.

basse justice (bās jus'tis). Low justice; the right of a feudal lord to try petty offenders.

basset. An unlawful game.

bastard. A person begotten and born out of wedlock, otherwise known in common parlance as an illegitimate child or natural child. 10 Am J2d Bast § 1.

The word "bastard" shall not be used in any local law, ordinance, or resolution, or in any public or judicial proceeding, or in any process, notice, order, decree, judgment, record, or other public document or paper, but there shall be used in place of such word the term "child born out of wedlock." NY General Construction Law § 59.

See **adulterine bastard; delivery of bastard child; illegitimate child; incestuous bastard**.

bastarda. A female bastard.

bastard eigne. (bas'tärd ain). The elder son of parents who were married to each other after his birth as a bastard. 2 Bl Comm 248.

bastardize. To prove a person to be a bastard.

Bastardus non potest habere haeredem nisi de corpore suo legitime procreatum (bas-tar'dus non po'-test ha'be-re hē're-dem ni'si de kor'po-re su'ō lē-ji'ti-me prō-kre-ā'tum). A bastard cannot have an heir unless he is one lawfully begotten of his own body.

Bastardus nullius est filius; aut filius populi (bas-tar'dus nul-lī'us est fī'li-us; ât fī'li-us po'pu-lī). A bastard is the son of no one, or a son of the people.

bastardy. The state of being a bastard; a man's illicit carnal connection with a woman causing the birth of an illegitimate child. Dinkey v Commonwealth, 17 Pa 126.

bastardy bond. A bond given by the father of a bastard to insure his support and maintenance.

bastardy proceeding. A proceeding, otherwise known as a filiation proceeding, of a civil nature to compel a bastard's father to support him or her. 10 Am J2d Bast §§ 74 et seq.

bastardy process. Same as **bastardy proceeding**.

bastart. Same as **bastard**.

bastinado (bas-ti-nā'dō). The beating of the soles of a man's feet with a club as a punishment for an offense; a cudgel.

baston (bas'ton). A baton; a club; a servant of a warden of the Fleet Prison.

bas-ville (ba'vēl). The suburbs of a town or city.

batable (bā'tạ-bl). Debatable; Questioned; disputed.

batable ground (bā'tạ-bl). Land the title to which is in dispute; land lying between England and Scotland, claimed by each; an area of principle subject to be questioned or disputed.

bataille (bat-āl'). Same as **battel**.

batiment. (French.) A building, structure, vessel, or ship.

batonnier. (French.) The president of an organized bar of attorneys at law.

battel (bat'l). A duel; a combat which was sanctioned by law in ancient times as a form of trial, under the superstition that the right would triumph. The last trial by battel on record was in 1638. See 3 Bl Comm 337 et seq.

battery. The unlawful touching or striking of the person of another by the aggressor himself, or by any substance put in motion by him, with the intention of bringing about a harmful or offensive contact or apprehension thereof which is not legally consented to by the other and not otherwise privileged. 6 Am J2d Asslt & B § 5.
As defined in the American Law Institute's Restatement of the Law of Torts, a battery is an act which, directly or indirectly, is the legal cause of a harmful contact with another's person; such act makes the actor liable to the other, if the act is done with the intention of bringing about a harmful or offensive contact or an imminent apprehension thereof to the other or a third person, and the contact is not consented to by the other or the other's consent thereto is procured by fraud or duress, and the contact is not otherwise privileged. Restatement, Torts 2d § 13.
See **assault and battery.**

battle. A fight between the armed forces of nations. See **battel; war.**

batture (ba-tūr'). An accumulation or deposit of sand, stone, or rock mixed together on the bed of a stream or other body of water and rising toward the surface by the process of accumulation. 56 Am J1st Water § 499. When it ceases to be covered at the time of ordinary high water, it ceases to be batture and becomes the bank of the river. Boyce Cottonseed Oil Mfg. Co. v Board of Comrs. 160 La 727, 734, 107 So 506.

Baume gravity. See **gravity.**

bauxite (bō'zīt). Earth that contains aluminum in sufficient quantities to make it worth working for the extraction of aluminum. Carson v Missouri P. R. Co. 212 Ark 963, 209 SW2d 97, 1 ALR2d 784.

bawd. A madam of a house of prostitution; a procuress; a prostitute. Dyer v Morris, 3 Mo 214, 216.

bawdy house. A house of prostitution, most frequently called a whorehouse. 42 Am J1st Prost § 3.

bay. An arm of the sea or of a lake; a body of water around which the land forms a curve; a recess or inlet between capes or headlands. Ocean Industries, Inc. v Superior Court, 200 Cal 235, 252 P 722.

bayley. A bailiff.

bayou (bī'ō). A slow-moving stream, sometimes with an imperceptible current, connecting a swamp or lagoon with a river or with the sea; in the lower Mississippi valley, streams that lead out of a main stream to swamp and marsh.

bay rum (bā'rum'). A fragrant spirit obtained by distilling rum with leaves of the bayberry, or by mixing various oils with alcohol. Jordan v Roche, 228 US 436, 442, 57 L Ed 908, 910, 33 S Ct 573.

bay window. A window in an alcove or projection from the wall of a house; a slang term for a fat belly.

bazaar. A market or market place.

B.C. Abbreviation for "before Christ"; "bachelor of chemistry"; "bachelor of commerce"; "British Columbia."

B. C. L. An abbreviation of the law degree "bachelor of civil law."

B. E. Abbreviation for **board of education; Bachelor of Engineering; Bachelor of Education; bill of exchange.**

beach. Land on the margin of the sea, lake or river. 56 Am J1st Water § 448; the land lying between the lines of high water and low water, land over which, if a tidal stream or body of water is involved, the tide ebbs and flows. 12 Am J2d Bound § 13.
See **shore.**

beach for driftwood and timber. That line of shore to which seaweed and driftwood are usually carried in ordinary seasons by the highest winter floods, and which in fact is usually marked on the beach by a line of seadrift. Brown v Lakeman, 34 Mass (17 Pick) 444.

beaching. The voluntary stranding of a ship to save it from the greater loss from sinking. Fowler v Rathbone (US) 12 Wall 102, 20 L Ed 281.

beacon. A sign, signal, light, or other contrivance to guide or warn a traveler or ships; a lighthouse or other fixed marine signal formerly used to warn the inhabitants of the approach of an enemy, but later to indicate dangers to ships.

beaconage. Money paid as expenses to maintain beacons or signal lights.

beadle (bē'dl). A court crier; a parish officer whose duties resembled those of a constable; in addition to which he was required to attend and serve the vestry of the parish church.

beam. Noun: A long and sturdy piece of wood or metal; the width of a ship at its widest; a shaft of light; a radiance. Verb: To shine; to be radiant.

beam and balance. A weighing scales.

beans. Vegetables rather than seeds, for tariff purposes. Sonn v Magone, 159 US 417, 40 L Ed 203, 16 S Ct 67.

bear. Noun: A large mammal of the temperate and arctic zones, having a heavy coat of shaggy hair, varying in color, according to species, from black to brown, to gray, to white. Verb: To carry, as to bear arms.

bear arms. See **right to bear arms.**

bearer. One who is carrying some article, particularly a letter, message, of other writing; one who has information to impart orally; a word used in designating the payee of a negotiable instrument; the holder of a negotiable instrument not payable to a named person, for example, one payable to "cash" to "bills payable;" or just "to bearer." 11 Am J2d B & N § 124; the holder of an instrument indorsed in blank. 11 Am J2d B & N § 106; the person in possession of an instrument, document of title, or security payable to bearer or indorsed in blank. UCC § 1—201(5). A person guilty of the offense of maintenance; an oppressor.

bearer form. A security which runs to bearer according to its terms, not by reason of any indorsement. UCC § 8—102(1).

bearer paper. Commercial paper payable to bearer or the order of bearer; to a specified person or bearer; to cash or the order of cash, or payable according to any other indication which does not purport to designate a specific payee or indorsee. UCC § 3-111(a)(b); 11 Am J1st B & N § 106.

bearer security. A security which runs to bearer according to its terms and not by reason of any indorsement. UCC § 8—102(1)(d).

bearing. The posture or demeanor of a person; a support; the part of a machine which lends support to a moving shaft or sliding part; position; relevancy; producing.

bearing arms. See **right to bear arms.**

bearing child. Giving birth.

bearing date. Dated, as an instrument dated March 4, 1966.

bearing interest. Running at interest.

bearing the burden. Should mean lead to reaping the benefits. Pennington v Todd, 47 NJ Eq 569, 21 A 297.

beast. Any animal with four feet; a brutish, vile, or lecherous person.

beasts of the chase. Wild animals, especially the fox, wolf, and deer.

beasts of the forest. See **beasts of the chase.**

beasts of the park. An old expression meaning about the same as beasts of the chase.

beasts of the plow. Work animals.

beasts of the warren. Hares, conies and roes. See **free warren.**

beat. Verb: To strike with hand or weapon, or cudgel of any description; to commit battery upon a person; Goodrum v State, 60 Ga 509, 511. To win over another in a contest; to obtain the better deal in a transaction with another person. Noun: The territory which an officer of the law is assigned to cover; a colloquial for a subdivision of a county. Williams v Pearson, 38 Ala 299, 308. Adjective: Slang for beaten or exhausted.

beaten. Having suffered blows; having been the victim of an assault and battery.

beat hand. A disease of the hands commonly contracted by steel riveters from the constant shock of the riveting hammer causing chronic soreness. Anno: 20 ALR 13.

beaupleader (bō'plē-der). A writ which prohibited the taking of a fine for ill-pleading or bad pleading.

beautician. One whose business it is to take care of and beautify a client's hair, hands, or complexion. Anno: 56 ALR2d 883.

beauty parlor. A place for the performance for women of various services in the interest of personal attractiveness, such as cutting, dressing, waving, and setting hair, shampooing, the application of refined cosmetics, etc.

beauty shop. See **beauty parlor.**

because. For the reason or cause that; on account of.

because of employment. As the phrase appears in a provision of a workmen's compensation statute relieving the employer from liability for injuries inflicted upon an employee by the wilful act of a third person directed against an employee "because of his employment," it means, not that the employer is relieved from liability where the employee was injured merely because he was in employment in the general sense of that term, but rather where it was apparent that the injury was inflicted because the assailant of the employee wished to prevent him from serving that particular employer. Pinkerton Nat. Detective Agency v Walker, 157 Ga 548, 122 SE 202, 35 ALR 557.

because of vicinage. See **common because of vicinage.**

become a member. To join a fraternal order, a church, or a service organization.

become aware of. The equivalent of actual knowledge. Anno: 23 ALR2d 1076.

become void. A term which comprehends every manner of bringing something to an end and complete nullification. Sharp v Curds, 7 Ky (4 Bibb) 547, 548.

be complied with. An expression which calls for performance in the future, having reference to subsequent, not past, performance. United States v Bank of Metropolis (US) 15 Pet 377, 10 L Ed 774.

bed. A layer, a stratum, an extended mass of anything, whether upon the earth or within it, as a bed of sulphur, a bed of sand or clay. State v Willis, 104 NC 764, 769, 10 SE 764. A foundation; a place of repose.

bed and board. See **divorce a mensa et thoro.**

bedding. A base or foundation; materials of any description which go to make a bed for rest or sleep.

bedel (bē'dl). Same as **beadle.**

bedelary (bē'dl-ary). The jurisdiction of a beadle.

bederepe. The service binding the tenant to reap the landlord's corn.

bedeweri (be-de'we-rī). Bandits.

bedlam (bed'lạm). Great confusion with much noise; a hospital for the mentally ill.

bed of justice. The sitting of the king in the French parliament.

beef. Meat from the carcasses of cattle; an animal fit for use as beef, a steer, a heifer, an ox, or a cow. Davis v State, 40 Tex 135.

beer. A fermented beverage made from any malted grain, with hops or other bitter flavoring matter added; an alcoholic and an intoxicating beverage. 30 Am J Rev ed Intox L § 10; any beverage obtained by alcoholic fermentation of an infusion or decoction of barley, malt and hops, or of any other similar products in drinkable water. Fletcher v Paige, 124 Mont 114, 220 P2d 84, 19 ALR2d 1108.

before. A word of time meaning prior to, but subject to construction in connection with the context in which it appears. 32 Am J1st Time § 26.

Generally, where an act is required to be done a specified number of days before an event, the required number of days is to be computed by excluding the day on which the act is done and including the day on which the event is to occur. 52 Am J1st Time § 26.

Some authorities hold that such computation does not apply to a designation of time in terms of so many days before a given day. 52 Am J1st Time § 26.

before due. Before the maturity of a note, mortgage, or other instrument.
See **indorsement before due.**

before the fact. See **accessory before the fact.**

before trial. Literally, before the commencement of the step in an action where the issues of law or fact are determined. For some purposes, before final submission of the issues to court or jury for determination. Anno: 126 ALR 285.

beg. To ask for something with an appeal to charitable instincts made by words, signs, demeanor, or conduct. Re Haller (NY) 12 Hun 131, 132.

bega (bē'gä). A land measure of about a third of an acre.

beget. To procreate, as a father or sire; to generate; usually applied to the male, but sometimes to both male and female, and infrequently used with reference to the female only. Grainger v Grainger, 147 Ind 95, 46 NE 80.

beggars. Persons who beg or solicit alms.

begging the question. An argument which assumes as proved the very thing in issue.

begin. To start; to institute; to initiate; to commence. Bates Mfg. Co. v United States, 303 US 567, 82 L Ed 1020, 58 S Ct 694.

begin action. See **commencement of action.**

beginning of life. Biologically speaking, the moment of conception in the mother's womb. In law, for the purposes of inheritance or of taking under a will, the biological concept of the beginning of life in the womb. 27 Am J Rev ed Inf § 3.
  The beginning of life has been more narrowly defined when the question was of the capacity of an unborn child to acquire a right of action for a personal injury, on which it could sue after birth. The authorities are divided upon the question whether a child or its personal representative may, in the absence of statute, maintain an action in damages for prenatal injury. 27 Am J Rev ed Inf § 3.

begotten. The words "begotten" and "to be begotten," "procreatis" and "procreandis" have always been held to have the same import, unless a contrary intent plainly appears. Wager v Wager (Pa) 1 Serg & R 374, 378.
  See **beget.**

behalf. In the name of; on account of; for the benefit, advantage, interest, profit, or vindication of. State v Eggerman & Co. 81 Tex 569, 572.
  See **on his behalf.**

behavior (bē-hāv'yor). Conduct; manners.

behavior as heir. Acts or conduct indicating one's acceptance of an inheritance.

behetria (bay-ay-tree'ah). (Spanish.) Lands in districts and manors in which the inhabitants could select their own lords.—Bouvier's Law Dict.

behoof (bē-hōf'). Same as **behalf.**

Behring Sea Arbitration. See **Bering Sea Arbitration.**

being. Noun: A person; a living thing. The present participle of the verb "to be;" equivalent in a pleading to the words "which is." Porter v Ritchie, 32 Utah 381, 91 P 24, 27.
  The word has been held to be sufficient as an averment of an existing fact. State v Boncher, 59 Wis 477, 18 NW 335.
  See **in being.**

being in control of motor vehicle. Steering the vehicle under way or even while it is being towed or pushed by another vehicle. 7 Am J2d Auto § 256.

being operated. See **operate.**

being understood. See **it being understood.**

belief. The conviction of the mind, founded on evidence that a fact exists, that an act was done, that a statement is true. When one says, I believe that a fact exists, or that an act was done by another, he must be understood to assert that there is present to his mind evidence sufficient to convince him, that the fact does in reality exist, or that the act was done. Giddens v Mirk, 4 Ga 364, 369.
  See **information and belief; reasonable belief; religion; religious principles.**

believe. To have a belief or an opinion.

bell. See **curfew.**

belladonna (bel-a-don'ä). A drug.
  See **atropine.**

belligerency. See **belligerent; recognition of belligerency.**

belligerent (be-lij'e-rent). A nation, power, or state carrying on war against another nation, power, or state; or a portion of one nation carrying on war against the nation, which has been recognized by other nations as a belligerent. 30 Am J Rev ed Internat L § 11; 56 Am J1st War § 3.

belligerent rights. Those peculiar rights recognized and sanctioned by the laws of war, which are exercised by a nation, power, or state as a means for carrying on a war. These are not unlimited under the law. It is not with the authority of law that a belligerent runs rampant in the world, killing both combatants and noncombatants, old men, women, and children. There are conventions, treaties, and unwritten principles of international law limiting the rights of belligerents by defining the laws and customs of war on land, sea, and in the air in the interest of humanity. 56 Am J1st War § 12.

bello. Waging war.

Bello parta (bel'lō par'ta). Spoils of war.

bellum (bel'lum). War.

belong. The primary meaning of the verb to belong is to be the property of. The word is aptly used to express ownership and may properly be so used in a pleading. State v Fox, 80 Iowa 312.

belongings. Personal effects; a word often involved in the ejusdem generis rule of construction. 57 Am J1st Wills § 1130; under a broad construction, including personal property of every nature, even real property. 57 Am J1st Wills § 1343.

belonging to (bē-lông'ing). Being the property of. Ownership under either legal or equitable title. 51 Am J1st Supp Tax § 544.

below. Inferior, as the court below; under; in a position of lower rank; physically lower.
  See **bail below.**

belt. See **maritime belt.**

bench. A court; the judges of a court; the seat upon which the judges of a court are accustomed to sit while the court is in session; all the judges and justices of a state or subdivision, as in a reference to "bench and bar."

bencher (ben'chėr). One of the senior or governing members of one of the English Inns of Court. As soon as a member has been appointed king's counsel or queen's counsel, it is customary for his fellow members to elect him as a bencher.

bench law. A term of derision for a decision against precedent.
  See **bench legislation.**

bench legislation. Also called "judicial legislation," —a term of opprobrium applied to decisions which are criticised as being clearly contrary to law and which therefore infringe upon the legislative department of the government. State ex rel. Ragan v Junkin, 85 Neb 1, 122 NW 473.

bench warrant. A warrant issued by a judge for the apprehension of a person on a charge of contempt; a warrant for arrest issued by a judge of a court of general jurisdiction for the apprehension of a person who has been indicted for a criminal offense; a warrant for the arrest of an accused under bail who has failed to appear, the warrant being issued and signed by the judge. 5 Am J2d Arr § 78; the equivalent of a summons in a support proceeding. Commonwealth ex rel. Schaffer v Schaffer, 175 Pa Super 100, 103 A2d 430, 42 ALR2d 761 (proceeding in case certified to a Pennsylvania court by a Florida court).

bends. Same as **caisson disease.**

bene (be'ne). Well; properly.

beneath. A designation of a position, physical or graphical, as a stratum of limestone beneath a layer of sandstone, and a corporal beneath a sergeant. Truman v Deere Implement Co. (CC Cal) 80 F 109.

benedicta (be-ne-dīk'ta). Blessed.

bene esse. See **de bene esse.**

benefice (ben'ē-fis). A church living or preferment. In feudal times, an estate held by the Church of Rome in feudal tenure.

benefice de discussion (be'ne'fi-s de dis-ku-siōn). (French.) A guarantor's right to have his principal's property first applied on the debt which he has guaranteed to see paid.

benefice de division (be'ne'fi-s de di-vi-ziōn). (French.) A cosurety's right to contribution.

benefice d'inventaire (bē-ne'fi-s d'īn-vän-tè-r). Same as **benefit of inventory.**

beneficence. Charity; good will; kindness.
See **contract of beneficence.**

beneficia (ben-ē-fish'i-a). Estates held by feudal tenure, being originally gratuitous donations, were at one time called beneficia. See 4 Bl Comm 107.

beneficial. Of benefit; profitable; advantageous; enjoying; gaining.

beneficial association. See **benevolent association.**

beneficial devise. A devise which bequeaths a beneficial interest; a devise under which the devisee is intended by the testator to receive a direct interest under the will in the property of the testator. When an interest arises consequentially from a devise, as in the case of a dower right arising out of a devise to the husband, the devise is not a beneficial devise to the person thus incidentally benefited. Sullivan v Sullivan, 106 Mass 474.

beneficial enjoyment. The advantages of the ownership of property, sometimes had without possessing the legal title.

beneficial interest. An expression with variable meaning, dependent on the context in which it appears; that which remains of the estate of a decedent after the payment of debts and the expenses of administration. 28 Am J Rev ed Inher T § 388; such an interest as a devisee takes solely for his own use or benefit, and not as the mere holder of the title for the use of another. People v McCormick, 208 Ill 437, 70 NE 350; the right of one having a power of appointment to appoint himself. 41 Am J1st Pow § 3; the interest in a tract of land, the title to which is in the government, of one who has done everything to entitle him to a patent not yet issued by the government to him. Montana Catholic Missions v Missoula County, 200 US 118, 127, 50 L Ed 398, 402, 26 S Ct 197; an interest that will result in an appreciable gain to the holder. Cox's Appeal, 126 Me 256, 137 A 771, 53 ALR 208; an interest of value, worth, advantage, or use. Re Duffy, 228 Iowa 426, 292 NW 165, 128 ALR 943.

beneficially entitled. Having title legally or having it equitably, so as to reap the benefits of ownership. People v McCormick, 208 Ill 437, 70 NE 350.

beneficial ownership. See **beneficial interest; beneficial use.**

beneficial power. A power which has for its object the grantee of the power, and which is executed solely for his benefit. Tilden v Green, 130 NY 29, 28 NE 880.

beneficial society. See **benevolent association; mutual benefit society.**

beneficial use. See **beneficial interest; use.**

beneficiary. A person who receives a benefit or advantage. State v Willett, 17 Ind 296, 86 NE 68; a person receiving or entitled to receive a gift, a devise, or legacy; a cestui que trust; a person who is entitled to receive or who is receiving profit, benefit, or advantage from a contract or from an estate; one entitled by the terms of a life insurance policy to receive the proceeds of the policy upon the death of the insured. 29A Am J Rev ed Ins § 1631; a person named by statute as entitled to the proceeds, or a share of the proceeds, of a statutory action, such as an action for wrongful death. 22 Am J2d Dth §§ 47–59.

beneficiary heir. A term of significance in Louisiana. One taking according to inventory.
See **beneficium inventari.**

beneficiary privileges. Patent rights; copyrights.

beneficio cedendarum actionum (be-ne-fi'shē-ó sē-den-dā'rum ak-shē-ō'num). The right of assigned or transferred actions,—the civil law right which a surety had, even before paying the creditor, to an assignment by the creditor to him of the claims which the creditor held against the principal debtor.

beneficio primo ecclesiastico habendo (be-ne-fi'shē-ō pri'mō ēc-klē-si-as'ti-kō hā-ben'dō). A writ emanating from the king directing the chancellor or lord keeper to appoint a certain man to the first vacant benefice.

beneficium (be-ne-fi'shē-um). A benefice; an advantage; a profit; a privilege; a right.

beneficium abstinendi (be-ne-fi'shē-um ab-stin-en'dī). The privilege of abstaining,—the right or privilege of an heir to reject an inheritance.

beneficium cedendarum actionum (be-ne-fi'shē-um sē-den-dā'rum ak-shē-ō'num). A Roman law right of subrogation by the surety to the claims of the creditor against the principal debtor.

beneficium clericale (be-ne-fi'shē-um kle-ri-kā'le). Benefit of clergy.

beneficium competentiae (be-ne-fi'shē-um kom-pe-ten'shē-ē). The privilege of a competency,—the civil law exemption of enough property to live upon by one making an assignment to his creditors.

beneficium divisionis (be-ne-fi'shē-um di-vi-zhe-ō'nis). The right of division,—the civil law right of a surety who had been compelled to pay to exact pro rata contribution from his cosureties.

beneficium inventari (be-ne-fi'shē-um in-ven-tā'rī). (Civil law.) The benefit of inventory, the limitation of an heir's liability for debts of the estate to the value of his inheritance.

beneficium non datum nisi propter officium (be-ne-fi'shē-um non da'tum ni'si prop'ter of-fi'shē-um). A benefit not conferred unless in recognition of an obligation.

beneficium ordinis (be-ne-fi'shē-um or'di-nis). (Civil law.) The privilege of order,—the right of a surety to have all remedies against his principal first exhausted before resorting to the surety.

beneficium separationis (be-ne-fi'shē'um se-pa-rā'shē-ō'nis). (Civil law.) The right of separation,— a creditor's right to have a decedent's goods separated from those of the heirs.

benefit. A contribution to prosperity; whatever adds value to property; advantage; profit; whatever promotes our prosperity, happiness, or enhances the value of our property rights, or rights as citizens, as contradistinguished from what is injurious. National Surety Co. v Jarrett, 95 W Va 420; 121 SE 291; 36 ALR 1171, 1176; the acquisition of a legal or equitable right to which one otherwise would not be entitled. 17 Am J2d Contr § 96; goods, services, the payment of a debt for another, anything which adds to the advantage or security of another. Heitfield v Benevolent & Protective Order of Keglers, 36 Wash 2d 685, 220 P2d 655, 18 ALR2d 983.
See **hope of benefit**.

benefit association. See **benevolent associations; mutual benefit society**.

benefit building society. A building and loan association.

benefit insurance. See **benevolent association; mutual benefit society**.

benefit of bargain rule. The rule of damages that a person who purchases in reliance upon fraudulent representations of the seller is entitled, in an action against the seller for the fraud, to recover as damages the difference between the real and the represented value of the property. Anno: 124 ALR 34.

benefit of cession. (Civil law.) Immunity from imprisonment for debt of a debtor who has assigned all his property to his creditors.

benefit of clergy. The exemption of clergymen from trial or punishment for crime in or at the hands of the secular courts.

benefit of counsel. See **right to counsel**.

benefit of discussion. (Civil law.) The right of a surety to have his principal's property first subjected to the payment of the obligation.

benefit of division. (Civil law.) The right of a surety to enforce contribution from his co-sureties.

benefit of inventory. (Civil law.) The limitation of an heir's liability for the debts of the estate to the value of his inheritance.

benefit of order. See **ordinis beneficium**.

benefit society. See **mutual benefit society**.

benefit theory. The principle that one who wishes to rescind a contract must place the opposite party in statu quo by restoring to him the benefits received from him. 17 Am J2d Contr § 512.

bene placitum (be'ne plà-sī'tum). While it well pleases; at pleasure.

benerth. A feudal service rendered by the tenant to his lord with plough and cart.

bene se gesseret. See **dum bene se gesseret**.

benevolence. Acts or gifts prompted by good will or kind feelings; essentially philanthropy. 15 Am J2d Char § 4.
The term is inclusive of charity, but not limited to charity. A gift may be from benevolence, even though the recipient is in no need of charity.

benevolent. Charitable. 51 Am J1st Tax § 601; philanthropic, Anno: 115 ALR 1138; but at times something different from what such terms suggest. A word descriptive of a gift, too broad in scope for the gift to qualify as a charitable trust. 15 Am J2d Char § 9.
Acts dictated by kindness, good will, or a disposition to do good, the objects of which have no relation to the promotion of education, learning, or religion, the relief of the needy, the support of public works, or the relief of public burdens, and so cannot be deemed "charitable" in the legal sense, may nevertheless be "benevolent." 51 Am J1st Tax § 601.

Benevolent and Protective Order of Elks. A fraternal order.

benevolent associations. Benevolent and beneficial associations are either purely voluntary aggregations of individuals or bodies corporate, formed and organized, not with a view to the accumulation of wealth and the making of profit, but, aside from fraternal objects, solely for the purpose of rendering financial aid or other assistance to their members, or certain designated beneficiaries of the latter, when visited by sickness, death, or other misfortunes specifically agreed upon. 38 Am J2d Frat O § 1.
See **mutual benefit society**.

benevolent corporation. A nonprofit corporation; an eleemosynary corporation; a corporation created by charitable rather than for business purposes.

benevolent insurance company. Benevolent associations, formed primarily for social and charitable purposes and for securing efficient mutual aid for their members are sometimes referred to as insurance companies, because they issue death certificates which are, in effect, policies of life insurance. Penn. Mut. L. Ins. Co. v Mechanics' Sav. Bank & T. Co. (CA6 Tenn) 72 F 413.
See **mutual benefit societies**.

Benigne faciendae sunt interpretationes chartarum propter simplicitatem laicorum (be-nig'nē fa-shē-en'dē sunt in-ter-pre-ta"shē-ō'nēz kar-tā'rum prop'ter sim-pli-si-tā-tem lai-kō'rum). The construction of written instruments must be liberal because of the artlessness of laymen. Edgerly v Barker, 66 NH 434, 31 A 900.

Benigne faciendae sunt interpretationes chartarum, ut res magis valeat quam pereat (be-nig'nē fa-shē-en'dē sunt in-ter-pre-ta"shē-ō'nēz kar-tā'rum, ut rēz ma'jis va'le-at quam per'e-at). Liberal construction should be given to an instrument so that it may stand rather than fall.

Benignius leges interpretandae sunt quo voluntas earum conservetur (be-nig'ni-us lē'jēz in-ter-pre-tan'dē sunt quō vo-lun'tas e-a'rum kon-ser-vē-ter). Laws should be construed more liberally in order that their intent may be preserved.

benzene (ben'zēn). A highly inflammable liquid obtained by distillation of coal tar, used as a solvent in making lacquers, varnishes, and some other products.

bequeath. A legacy, that is, a disposition of personal property by will. Hoellinger v Molzhon 77 ND 108, 41 NW 2d 217, 19 ALR2d 747; often considered to include either a legacy of personality or a devise of real estate. 57 Am J1st Wills § 1400. To make a bequest.
See **bequest.**
To bequeath has been judicially construed by many of the ablest courts of this country to be synonymous with "to devise," when used with reference to a testamentary gift of real estate. Gannon v Albright, 183 Mo 238, 81 SW 1162; Jacobsen v Farnham, 155 Neb 776, 53 NW2d 751, 33 ALR2d 543.
See **devise; legacy; residuary bequest.**

bequeathment (bē-kwēth'męnt). A bequest.

berbiage (ber'bi-ā-ge). Rental for sheep pasture.

bercaria (ber-kā'ri-a). A sheepfold.

bercarius. A shepherd.

bercator (ber-kā'tor). A shepherd.

bereft. Deprived; especially, deprived of a loved one.

bereft of reason. mental incompetency; want of capacity to reason.

berenica (be-ren'i-ka). A manor; a town.

berewick. Same as **barton.**

berg (berg). A plain; a field; a manor; an iceberg.

bergmote (ber'ga-mot). Same as **barmote.**

beria (be-rī'a). A plain; a field.

Bering Sea Arbitration. An arbitration held under a treaty between England and the United States in 1893, the award of which was later confirmed by an act of Congress and finally settled the rights of the United States in the waters of Alaska and of Bering Sea, and all questions concerning the rights of its own citizens and subjects therein, as well as those of the citizens and subjects of other countries. La Ninfa (CA9 Alaska) 75 F 513, 517.

berm (berm). The shoulder of a highway or canal.

berme-bank (berm). The side of a canal which has no towpath.

Berne Convention. Copyright Treaty of 1886, not ratified by the United States. 18 Am J2d Copyr § 76.

bernet (ber'net). The crime of burning a dwelling house, corresponding to the modern crime of arson.

Bernstein test. A blood test devised to assist in the determination of the parentage of children, postulated upon the existence of four types of blood and the inheritability of blood type. 29 Am J2d Ev § 370.

berra (ber'ra). A plain, open heath.

berry. A fruit, such as a raspberry or strawberry; the dried coffee bean. An older meaning is that of a mansion house.

Bertillon System (ber-tē-yôn' sĭs'tĕm). A system for the identification of criminals by measurement and description, the employment of which in state prisons is prescribed by statute in some states. Re Molineux, 177 NY 395, 69 NE 727.

berton (ber'ton). A large farm; the barnyard of a large farm.

berwick. Same as **barton.**

bes (bēs). (Latin.) Two thirds of the Roman as or pound weight.

besayl. Derived from the French "bisaïeul." A writ by which a great-grandchild secured his right to his ancestor's property; a great-grandfather.

besides. Also; furthermore; in addition to.

besoin (be-soa'). Need; necessity. See **au besoin.**

besot (bę-sot'). To stupefy; to make dull or senseless; to make delirious, silly, or insane. Gates v Meredith, 7 Ind 440, 441.

besotted. Silly, foolish, confused by alcoholic liquor.

Bessemer. The process of making steel in a blast furnace, the name being that of the inventor of the process, Sir Henry Bessemer.

best. The superlative in quality.

best bid. In an auction, the highest bid; in the letting of a contract for public works, the lowest bid by a responsible bidder. 43 Am J1st Pub Wks § 42.

bestes. Beasts; cattle.

best evidence. The best proof obtainable under existing circumstances; the most superior, as contrasted with any other form of, proof that the party can offer. 29 Am J2d Ev § 448.

best evidence rule. The rule of evidence that the best evidence of which the case in its nature is susceptible and which is within the power of the party to produce, or is capable of being produced, must be adduced in proof of every disputed fact. Lego v Olson, 110 Colo 508, 136 P2d 277; Roddy v State, 65 Idaho 137, 139 P2d 1055.

bestiales (bes-ti-ā'lēz). Beasts; cattle.

bestiality. Sexual intercourse with an animal; a criminal offense. 48 Am J1st Sod § 1.

best of his knowledge and belief. An expression somewhat less than positive statement. 3 Am J2d Affi § 21.

bestow. See **bequeath, gift, grant.**

bet. Verb: To hazard money or property upon an incident by which one or both parties stand to win or lose by chance. 24 Am J1st Gaming § 2. The hazard may be the result of a game or another incident of chance. 24 Am J1st Gaming § 2. Noun: The arrangement by which money or property is placed at the incident of chance. It may involve the putting up of money or property by the parties, called stakes, to be held by a third party pending the occurrence of the event which constitutes the hazard.
See **gaming; gambling.**

Bethlehem (beth'lę-ęm). The birthplace of Jesus Christ, now in Jordan, under the spelling Bayt Lahm; the name of an ancient lunatic asylum in London; a lunatic asylum; a bedlam.

betrayal. A breach of confidence; disloyalty to friend or country. The disclosure of a professional secret by a physician. Simonsen v Swenson, 104 Neb 224, 177 NW 831, 9 ALR 1250, 1252.

betrothal (bę-trōth' or bę-trōth'ąl). An engagement to wed.

betrothment (bę-trōth'męnt). Same as **betrothal.**

better equity (bet′ẽr). The superior or prevailing one of two equitable interests.

betterment. An improvement to realty which is more extensive than an ordinary repair, and which increases in some substantial degree the value of the property.
See **occupying claimant acts**.

betterment acts. See **occupying claimant acts**.

betting. See **bet; gambling; gaming**.

betting book. The book wherein a bookmaker registers the wagers which he receives from his customers.
See **bookmaking**.

betting on election. See **election bet**.

between. Intermediate, when used in designating time, implying the exclusion of both first and last terminal days. Anno: 98 ALR2d 1369.
When predicable of persons, in a strict and correct use of the word it implies that there are but two persons, as where a division is made between A and B, but courts will notice judicially that uneducated persons frequently use the word as referring to more than two persons and as meaning "among," and when thus used, it is so construed. Rogers v Morrell, 82 SC 402, 404, 64 SE 143. Similarly, while "between" calls for a per stirpes distribution in a strict and correct sense of the word, if it appears to have been used in the sense "among," a per capita distribution will be decreed. Anno: 13 ALR2d 1037; 57 Am J1st Wills § 1296.

between eight and 14 years. A period which ends upon the child's passing the anniversary of the higher age. 27 Am J1st Inf § 3.

between Scylla and Charybdis (Sil′ä & Ka̧-rib′dis). In a grave dilemma; facing danger on either side.

beverage. A liquid which is taken by a person to satisfy thirst or for the pleasure of the taste or effect, rather than to have the advantage of medicinal qualities. Commonwealth v Sookey, 236 Mass 448, 128 NE 788, 11 ALR 1230; McLean v People, 66 Colo 486, 180 P 676. The term is inclusive of, but not confined to, a drink with alcoholic content. Tea and coffee are both beverages.
See **alcoholic beverage**.

beverches. Customary services rendered the lord at his request by inferior tenants.

bevo. A nonalcoholic imitation of malt liquor. State ex rel. Springer v Bliss, 199 Okla 198, 185 P2d 220.

beyond a reasonable doubt. The degree of proof required of the state in a criminal prosecution; a fair doubt based upon reason and common sense, growing out of the evidence in the case; not an imaginary, captious, or possible doubt. 20 Am J1st Ev § 1257.

beyond the four seas (be̞-yond′). Beyond the British Isles.
See **beyond the seas**.

beyond the jurisdiction. Beyond the reach of the process of the court. New York Cent. R. Co. v Stevens, 126 Ohio St 395, 185 NE 542, 87 ALR 884.

beyond the seas. Beyond the limits of the United States. For the purposes of a statute of limitation, beyond the limits of the state. 34 Am J1st Lim Ac § 215.
See **beyond the four seas**.

b. f. An abbreviation of "bonum factum," meaning, a good deed; a valid decree; also an abbreviation for the printing term "boldface."

B. F. Abbreviation for the bookkeeping term "brought forward"; also for Bachelor of Finance and Bachelor of Forestry.

B. F. A. An abbreviation for Bachelor of Fine Arts.

bias. Propension; something that turns the mind and sways the judgment, Anno: 16 ALR2d 19. A hostile feeling or spirit of ill will toward one of the litigants, or undue friendship or favoritism toward one; involving a mental attitude toward a litigant, not toward the subject matter of the litigation. 30A Am J Rev ed Judges § 170.

bias of juror. A propensity or prepossession which does not leave the mind indifferent; it may be actual or implied—that is, bias in fact or bias presumed as a matter of law, as where the juror is a close relative of a party. 31 Am J Rev ed Jury § 172.
Among the various matters which, at common law, were held to be principal cause for challenge, —that is, cause from which bias or partiality would be inferred as a legal conclusion,—were these: Consanguinity or affinity of the juror with either of the parties within the ninth degree; that the juror was godfather to the child of either of the parties; that the juror was of the same society or corporation with either party; or was tenant or "within the distress" of either party; or had an action implying malice between him and either party; or was master, servant, counsellor, steward, or attorney for either party; or, after he was returned, he ate and drank at the expense of either party, or had been chosen as arbitrator by either party. Most authorities also held it to be ground for principal challenge that the juror had formed and declared his opinion touching the matter in controversy. Coughlin v People, 144 Ill 140, 33 NE 1.

bias of witness. A ground of impeachment; near relationship, sympathy, hostility or prejudice. Bessemer Land & Improv. Co. v Jenkins 111 Ala 135, 18 So 565.

biathanatoi (bī′′a-tha′na-toi). Persons dying by violence or suicide.

Bible. A book of Divine instruction as to the creation of man, his relation to, dependence on, and accountability to God. People ex rel. Ring v Board of Education, 245 Ill 334, 92 NE 251.

Bible reading. See **sectarian purpose**.

bicameral. Two-chambered, the term having reference to the usual division of a legislature into two houses.

bicycle. A two-wheeled vehicle, self-propelled by pushing pedals, the movement of which actuates a gear; a vehicle within the meaning of regulations concerning the use of highways. 7 Am J2d Auto § 4; a vehicle within the meaning of an accident insurance policy. 29A Am J Rev ed Ins § 1237; a vehicle but not a wagon within the meaning of an exemption statute. 31 Am J2d Exemp § 64.

bicycle paths. Paths which are set apart and maintained by cities and towns under statutory authority for the exclusive use of bicyclists.

bicyclist's stop. Riding in a circle instead of coming to a full stop as required by stop signals or by law.

bid. Verb: To invite; to make an offer, particularly, at a contract letting, an auction or judicial sale, by the spoken or written word, by a sign, such as a

lifting of the hand, sometimes only a nod or a wink, anything by which the bidder signifies his willingness and intention to pay a particular price. 7 Am J2d Auct § 25; 30A Am J1st Jud S § 91. Noun: An offer, especially an offer made at a contract letting, an auction sale, or a judicial sale.

See **by-bidding; opening the biddings.**

bid bond. A bond required of one who bids in the letting of a contract for the construction of a public improvement, the purpose of the bond being to indemnify the public body against loss resulting from the withdrawal of the bid or the refusal of the bidder, upon the award of the contract to him, to enter into a contract. 43 Am J1st Pub Wks §§ 62, 63.

See **responsible bidder.**

bidder (bid'ẽr). A person who makes an offer at auction, judicial sale, contract letting; an offeror.

bid in. The act of the owner of property put up at an auction sale in taking the property out of the auction by a protective bid, that is, a bid made to prevent a sacrifice of the property at a sale less than its real value; the act of a mortgagee or lienholder in purchasing the property covered by the mortgage or lien at an auction sale.

bid off. To purchase by bid at auction or judicial sale.

bid security. The expression is not a phrase of art having a precise meaning in the law of contracts, but its natural meaning in a proposal for public work is that a deposit is required of the bidder in order to assure the government of the seriousness of the bid, the deposit to be forfeited if the bidder should●ithdraw his bid before the government had accepted it. United States v Conti (CA1 Mass) 119 F2d 652.

bielbrief. A particular and detailed description of a ship, furnished by the builder.

bien (bē-an'). Well; lawfully.

bienes gananciales (bi'ens ga-nan'she-als). See **ganancial property; ganancias.**

biennial. The word is derived from the Latin word "bis," twice, and "annus," year, meaning the happening or taking place of anything once in two years. State v Smith, 42 Mo 506, 507.

biennium (bī-en'ni-um). A period of two years.

biens (bē-an). A term of the French law covering all kinds of property, real and personal. Biens are divided into biens meubles, movable property, and biens immeubles, immovable property. Lindsay v Wilson, 103 Md 252, 63 A 566.

biens meubles et immeubles (b-ēän' mēbl'ȧ immēbl'). Movable and immovable goods.

bifurcated trial. Separate trial of a particular issue, such as insanity in a criminal case. 21 Am J2d Crim L § 47.

biga (bī'gä). A two-horse chariot.

bigamia (bi-gā'mi-a). Bigamy.

bigamist. A person who has committed the crime of bigamy; a man who, having contracted a bigamous marriage, and become the husband, at one time, of two wives, continues to maintain that relation and status. Murphy v Ramsey, 114 US 16, 29 L Ed 16, 5 S Ct 747.

bigamus (bi'ga-mus). A bigamist.

bigamy. The crime committed by the act of marrying while the spouse of a former marriage is still alive and former marriage is still in force. 10 Am J2d Big § 1. In some jurisdictions, the act of cohabitation with the second spouse is made an offense. See 10 Am J2d Big § 1.

bigotry. Intolerance; an intrusion upon our traditional concept of religious liberty. United States Nat. Bank v Snodgrass, 202 Or 530, 275 P2d 860, 50 ALR2d 725.

big with child. Pregnant.

bilagae (bī-lā'gae). Bylaws; ordinances.

bilagines (bī-lā'gi-nēs). Bylaws; ordinances.

bilan (be-lȯn'). A balance sheet. Dauphin v Soulie (La) 3 Mart NS 446.

bilanciae (bī-lan'shē-ē). Balances; weighing scales.

bilanciis deferendis (bī-lan'shē-is dē-fe-ren'dis). An ancient writ commanding a corporation to carry weights to a given place to weigh wool, the transportation of which had been licensed.

bilateral agreement. See **bilateral contract.**

bilateral contract. A contract under which each party promises or undertakes performance, the promise or the undertaking by the one furnishing the consideration for the promise or undertaking of the other, Christensen v Pugh, 84 Utah 440, 36 P2d 100, 95 ALR 608; a transaction in which each party promises performance, each party thereby binding himself to the other and each party reciprocally acquiring a right to what is promised by the other. 17 Am J2d Contr § 1.

bilboes (bil'bōz). A contrivance for the discipline and punishment of unruly sailors on shipboard, consisting of a board with holes in it through which the man's feet and arms protruded.

bilge. Bulge; the lower part of a ship, barge, or other watercraft, in which water accumulates; the dirty water that collects at the bottom of a ship; slang for nonsensical talk, wild rumors, or scandal.

bilge ventilator. Required equipment under Motor Boat Act of 1940. 46 USC § 526j.

bilging. As applied to a ship, to constitute "bilging" there must be a breach in the vessel, though the authorities differ as to the particular place which must be fractured. There is no bilging because a plank is almost worn through, if there is no actual breach. Nor will a bad straining which opens seams and lets in water constitute a bilging, although water thus injures the cargo. Ellery v Merchant's Ins. Co. 20 Mass (3 Pick) 46, 48.

biline. Collateral relatives.

bilingual. Double-tongued, speaking two languages.

bilinguis (bī-lin'gu-is). Bilingual.

bill. A complaint in suit in equity; a document in the form of a law, presented to the legislature for enactment; a denomination of paper money; a bank note; a handbill given to pedestrians on the street or passed out door-to-door in residential sections, advertising goods, giving notice of a coming event, or extolling a candidate for office; a listing of things offered to patrons or customers, as at a theater or in a restaurant; the amount owing on an account; the charge for a purchase; an indictment or the charge made against the accused in an indictment; the statement of an account presented to the debtor for payment. Verb: To present an account for payment, usually by mail; to advertise by posters or handbills.

billa (bil'la). A bill.

billa cassetur (bil'la kas-sē'tėr). That the bill may be quashed, made void or abated. See 3 Bl Comm 303.

billa excambii (bil'la ex-kam'bi-ī). A bill of exchange.

billa exonerationis (bil'la ex-o-ne-rā-shē-ō-nis). A bill of lading.

bill and note broker. A broker who negotiates the purchase and sale of bills of exchange and promissory notes. Little Rock v Barton, 33 Ark 436, 446.

billa vera (bil'la vē'ra). Same as **true bill.**

billboard. A signboard; a building within the meaning of building line regulations. 13 Am J2d Bldgs § 2.

bill-book (bil'bůk). An account book in which bills and notes are entered, showing their dates, due dates and the names of the parties.

bill chamber (bil' chăm"bėr). A department of the Scotch court of session.

billet. A place of lodging, especially of military personnel.

billeta (bil'le-ta). A bill or petition exhibited in parliament.

billet de change (bi-lè de shān-j). (French.) A contract to furnish a bill of exchange; a bill of exchange.

bill for a new trial. A bill in equity to enjoin the enforcement of a judgment of a court of law where such enforcement would be against conscience by reason of facts of which the party seeking relief could not have availed himself in the law court, or could have done so but was prevented by fraud or unavoidable accident, with no fault or negligence on his part. Spokane Co-operative Mining Co. v Pearson, 28 Wash 118, 68 P 165.

bill for appropriation. See **appropriation bill.**

bill for cancellation. A bill in equity for the cancellation of a written instrument.

bill for foreclosure. A bill in equity in a suit to foreclose a lien, a mortgage or a pledge.

bill for raising revenue. See **revenue bill.**

bill for reformation. A bill in equity in a suit for the correction of an error in a deed or other written instrument.

bill for revenue. See **bill for raising revenue.**

bill for specific performance. A bill in equity to compel the actual accomplishment of a contract by the party bound to fulfil it, a means of compelling the party to do precisely what he ought to have done without being coerced by a court. See 49 Am J1st Spec Per §§ 2, 159.

bill-head. A sheet of paper with name and address of a place of business, sometimes ruled, being used in billing a customer.

billiards. A refinement upon the game of pool, being played on a pool table but with only three balls. In broad usage, any game of pool.

bill in chancery. Same as **bill in equity.**

bill in equity. The declaration or complaint of the plaintiff where the relief demanded is such as is granted by a court of equity; a petition for relief addressed to a court of equity which states the facts on which the claim for relief is based. 27 Am J2d Eq § 179.

See **complaint; original bill.**

bill in perpetuam rei memoriam (bill in per-pe'tu-am rē-ī me-mō'ri-am).

See **bill to perpetuate testimony.**

bill in the nature of a bill of review. Where a decree is final, the bill of review is not regarded as a part of the cause in which the decree was rendered, but as a new suit, having for its object the correction of the decree in the former suit. But where a decree is only interlocutory, but liable to the same objection, the party injured must seek his redress, not by a bill of review, as such, but by petition or supplemental bill in the nature of a bill of review. Such petition or supplemental bill is regarded as a part of the very cause the decree in which is sought to be corrected, and any order or decree of the court on the petition or bill is only interlocutory. Zegura v United States (CA5 La) 104 F2d 34.

bill in the nature of interpleader. A bill seeking affirmative relief independent of the conflicting claims of the several defendants, which a party may often be allowed to file when he asserts a substantial interest in the fund or property in controversy and hence cannot file a bill to compel other claimants to interplead concerning the same. 30 Am J Rev ed Interpl § 16.

bill in trade. A tradesman's bill; an itemized account of goods sold or services rendered, or both.

bill not original. A bill in equity relating to some matter already litigated in the court by the same parties, and depending on the prior suit, that is, supplementing or continuing the former suit, or seeking relief in respect to some matter growing out of that suit and connected with it. 27 Am J2d Eq § 179.

bill obligatory. A bond without a condition; differing from a promissory note in nothing but the seal which is affixed to it. Farmers' & Mechanics' Bank v Greiner (Pa) 2 Serg & R 114, 115. Often called a single bill. A written acknowledgment of indebtedness in a certain sum to be paid on a certain day, and having a seal affixed to it. Osborne & Co. v Hubbard, 20 Or 318, 25 P 1021.

bill of adventure. A statement signed by a shipper declaring that the goods shipped are those of another person and that they are shipped at the owner's risk.

bill of advocation. (Scotch.) A petition praying the supreme court to transfer to itself a cause pending in a lower court.

bill of appeal. A writ of appeal; the complaint in an appeal of felony.

bill of attainder. A legislative act which inflicts punishment without a judicial trial. Inland Steel Co. v NLRB (CA7) 170 F2d 247, 12 ALR2d 240. Congress is prohibited from passing such an act by Art I § 9, clause 3, of the United States Constitution. The same prohibition applies to the states. Art I § 10, of the Constitution of the United States.

bill of certiorari (bill of ser-shē-ō-rā'rī). A bill in equity for the removal of a suit to a higher court.

bill of conformity. A bill in equity by which an executor or administrator seeks to secure the aid of the court in the administration of an involved estate.

bill of costs. An itemized statement of costs and disbursements to be filed by the party entitled to costs and a copy thereof served upon the adverse party. 20 Am J1st Costs § 91.

bill of credit. A paper issued by a state, intended to circulate as money or to answer the ordinary purposes of money. 36 Am J1st Money § 17.

bill of debt. An old term including promissory notes and bonds for the payment of money. It was also called a "bill obligatory" and was both sealed and unsealed.

bill of discovery. A bill filed for the sole purpose of compelling the defendant to answer its allegations and interrogatories, and thereby to disclose facts within his own knowledge, information, or belief, or to disclose and produce documents, books and other things within his possession, custody or control, and it is usually employed to enable a party to prosecute or defend an action. Peyton v Werhane, 126 Conn 382, 11 A2d 800.

bill of divorcement. Under the Mosaic law, a husband could divorce his wife by giving her a "bill of divorcement" and sending her out of his house.

bill of entry. A written description of imported goods filed with the customs officials.

bill of evidence. A transcript of testimony.

bill of exceptions. The means provided by law for importing into the judgment roll or decision matters dehors the record which are dependent for their authenticity on the signature of the trial court or on a prescribed procedure.
It is intended to complete the record to be filed in the appellate court. Its function is to present to the appellate court exceptions taken during the progress of the trial to rulings and decisions of the trial court in matters which otherwise would remain in pais, and to provide for the appellate court a succinct and intelligible statement of the errors about which complaint is made on the appeal. 4 Am J2d A & E §§ 417, 418.

bill of exchange. A written order of one party upon another for absolute payment of money to a third or designated person, or to his order or to bearer, upon demand or at a specified or determinable future time. 11 Am J2d B & N § 13. The term is equated with "draft" by the Uniform Commercial Code and is completely synonymous with "draft," even apart from the Code. 11 Am J2d B & N § 13.
See **check**.

bill of goods. A list of articles purchased; a slang expression of one who feels that he has suffered some imposition or been induced to take some action that he regrets, and says accordingly, "he sold me a bill of goods."
See **bill of parcels; bill of sale**.

bill of gross adventure. (French.) A written contract of bottomry, respondentia, or other maritime loan.

bill of health. A statement of a proper official certifying the healthful condition of a ship, its cargo and crew; a physician's statement certifying to the good health of a person.

bill of indemnity. A statute relieving officers from their failure to take their official oaths.

bill of indictment. The name properly applied to that paper which contains a criminal charge, before the paper is handed out to the grand jury. After it is found and all the blanks are filled in, it is called an "indictment." When it is thus made perfect, it must be decided to be valid or invalid, according to the requirements of the law. State v Ray, 24 SCL (Rice L) 1.

bill of information. An information.
See **information**.

bill of interpleader. See **interpleader**.

bill of lading. A written acknowledgment by a carrier of the receipt of goods described therein and an agreement to transport them to the place specified therein and deliver them there to the person named therein or his order. Griggs v Stoker Service Co. 229 NC 572, 50 SE2d 914, 15 ALR2d 798; a written acknowledgment, signed by the master of a vessel, that he has received the goods therein described, from the shipper, to be transported on the terms therein expressed, to the described place of destination, and there to be delivered to the consignee or parties therein designated. 48 AJ1st Ship § 386.
See **clean bill of lading; order bill of lading; straight bill of lading**.

bill of lading with draft attached. See **document bill**.

bill of Middlesex. An old form of writ by which actions in the king's bench were commenced. The name was adopted because the court out of which it was issued usually sat in Middlesex.

bill of mortality. A copy of a public record of deaths in a given community.

bill of pains and penalties. A form of legislative sentence for crime, in all respects identical with a bill of attainder, except that it prescribes the infliction of a punishment less than capital. Cummings v Missouri (US) 4 Wall 277, 18 L Ed 356. It is within the constitutional prohibition of bills of attainder.
See **bill of attainder**.

bill of parcels. An informal memorandum of the items of a sale of goods, given to the buyer by the seller, not purporting to state the terms of the contract of sale, and hence not of sufficient dignity to constitute a written contract which cannot be varied by parol. Leavitt v Fiberloid Co. 196 Mass 440, 445, 82 NE 682. But regarded by some courts as a bill of sale. Anno: 33 ALR2d 364, 367, 393.

bill of particulars. In civil actions: An amplification or more particular specification of the matter set forth in a pleading, which may be ordered on motion therefor by the adverse party, the purpose of which is to inform the adverse party of the precise nature of the cause of action or defense which the pleader has attempted to set forth and thereby to guide his adversary in his preparations for trial, and reasonably to protect him against surprise at the trial. 41 Am J1st Tr § 268. Criminal prosecutions: A more specific and detailed statement of the offense charged in an indictment or information which is generally good but does not allege the nature and extent of the offense charged so precisely as to enable the defendant properly to prepare his defense. 27 Am J1st Indict § 111.
See **motion for more specific statement**.

bill of peace. A bill filed to procure repose from repeated litigation and one of the earliest instances in which chancery courts entertained jurisdiction on the ground of preventing a multiplicity of suits. 19 Am J1st Eq § 81.
See **quieting title**.

bill of privilege. A special form of action employed at common law when suing an attorney, clerk or other person attending a court of justice. This special form of procedure was deemed necessary because these persons were not liable to arrest by the ordinary process of the court. Greenleaf v People's Bank, 133 NC 292, 45 SE 638.

bill of proof. A claim asserted by a third party to the subject-matter of a suit.
See **intervention.**

bill of review. A bill in equity for the purpose causing the court to review and reverse or revise its own decree. 19 Am J1st Eq § 423.
See **bill in the nature of a bill of review.**

bill of review for error apparent. A bill in equity which sets up no new facts or newly discovered matter, the sole purpose being to obtain a review and reversal of the decree for some error or defect on the face of the proceedings. 19 Am J1st Eq § 429.

bill of revivor. A special form of bill in equity for reviving a suit where the defect supervening on the proceeding is of such a nature as to cause an abatement, as where a plaintiff or defendant, suing or being sued in his own right, dies pending the suit. 19 Am J1st Eq § 355.

bill of revivor and supplement. A bill in equity to revive an abated suit and to introduce and plead new matters which could not be supplied by amendment. Westcott v Cady (NY) 5 Johns Ch 334.

bill of rights. A guaranty of rights by constitution; that portion of the Federal Constitution and the constitution of each state which consists of the guaranties of such rights as are to a large extent declaratory of fundamental principles and the foundation of citizenship, such as those providing against the exaction of excessive fines or the infliction of cruel and unusual punishments. The first ten amendments comprise the bill of rights of the United States Constitution. 16 Am J2d Const L §§ 329, 332.

bill of sale. A written instrument evidencing the transfer of title to personal property described therein from a seller to a purchaser. State v Blizzard, 70 Md 385.
See **grand bill of sale; invoice.**

bill of sight. A custom-house entry of goods by an importer who, for want of knowledge of the quality or quantity of the merchandise, must report according to his best information and belief.

bill of store. A custom-house license exempting a ship's stores and supplies from the payment of duties.

bill of sufferance. A license exempting from the payment of duties a merchant trading between English ports.

bill of supply. An appropriation bill to provide for the expenses of the government.

bill original. A bill or complaint in equity which begins an independent suit unconnected with any other previous or pending suit in the same court. 19 Am J1st Eq § 212.

bill penal. A written promise to pay a larger sum than the promisor owes.

bill pro confesso. See **pro confesso.**

bill quia timet (bill qüi′a ti′met). Literally, an application for equitable relief because the plaintiff fears, such relief being intended to prevent the harassment of a plaintiff by repeated suits brought by the defendant concerning a subject matter of such nature that equity can for once and for all determine conclusively and finally the rights of the plaintiff and the defendant thereto.
See **bill of peace; quieting title.**

bill rendered. A statement of account.

bills and notes. Commercial paper; negotiable and nonnegotiable instruments.
See **bill of exchange; drafts; promissory notes.**

bills in a set. A bill of lading drawn in a set of parts, each of which is numbered and expressed to be valid only if the goods have not been delivered against any other part, the whole of the parts constituting one bill. 13 Am J2d Car § 268. One bill of exchange, usually a foreign bill, drawn in a set of identical instruments, each one duly executed by the drawer, and numbered, and containing a direction to pay it, with the notation that number 2, number 3, or whatever other numbers are in the set, are unpaid.

The purpose is to prevent delays and inconveniences resulting from the loss of a bill in transmission to the drawee, the separate but identical instruments being transmitted in different mails. 11 Am J2d B & N § 59.

There is nothing in the purpose or effect of such practice which should render it inapplicable, under all circumstances, to checks. 11 Am J2d B & N § 59.

bill single. A written promise to pay, executed under the seal of the maker. 11 Am J2d B & N § 38.

bills in parts. See **bills in a set.**

Bills of Exchange Act. A Canadian statute passed in 1882 and modified in 1906, which in all essential particulars is an adoption of the negotiable instruments law adopted by most of the states of the Union.

Bills of Lading Act. A federal statute, which became effective on January 1, 1917, following closely the provisions of the Uniform Bills of Lading Act, but with a number of important changes evidently designed to adapt the latter Act to interstate commerce. 49 USC §§ 81-124.

bills payable. An accounting term used in financial statements to indicate the obligations of a business remaining unpaid; a form of designation of payee which renders the instrument a bearer instrument. 11 Am J2d B & N § 124.

An ordinary promissory note is a "bill payable" within a statute prohibiting bank cashiers from issuing "bills payable" without consent of the directors. W. J. Howey Co. v Cole, 219 Mo App 34, 269 SW 955.
See **payable to bills payable.**

bills receivable. An accounting term used in financial statements, promissory notes, bills of exchange or other written instruments for the payment of money at a future date. Miami Coal Co. v Fox, 203 Ind 99, 176 NE 11, 79 ALR 333; demands generally. State use of Dittman v Robinson, 57 Md 486, 501.
See **accounts receivable.**

bill to carry a decree into execution. A bill in equity which a party may maintain in aid of the execution of a decree which has been rendered in his favor. 19 Am J1st Eq § 213.

bill to examine witnesses de bene esse. Same as **bill to take testimony de bene esse.**

bill to marshal assets. See **marshaling assets.**

bill to perpetuate testimony. A bill in equity. Whenever there is reasonable cause to apprehend future litigation in regard to a particular subject or matter and the person threatened with or exposed to suit is himself unable to bring the issue to an immediate judicial determination, or when he himself proposes or intends to institute an action for the purpose of establishing his rights with respect to a particular matter or subject, but is unable, by reason of some legal impediment, to do so immediately, a court of equity will entertain a bill or petition to perpetuate, by the taking and filing of their depositions, the testimony of witnesses for the plaintiff in the bill or petition, who, because of his peculiar position, cannot avail himself of such testimony in an immediate judicial trial and decision of such controversy. 23 Am J2d Dep § 8.

bill to remove cloud on title. See **cloud on title.**

bill to suspend a decree. A bill in equity in a suit to set aside or suspend a decree.

bill to take testimony de bene esse (bill to take testimony dē be'ne es'se). A bill in equity which a party may maintain to secure the testimony for use in a pending action of a witness whose testimony cannot be taken in court. 23 Am J2d Dep § 6.

billy. A term used to denote masculine gender, as in billy goat; a club carried by a policeman.

billy-club. See **billy.**

bimetallism. A word made commonplace for the earlier part of the political career of the Honorable William Jennings Bryan, being the doctrine which favored the use of both gold and silver as monetary standards.

bind (bīnd). To create a definite legal obligation upon one's self or upon another. Such an obligation may be created by contract, by statute, by common law, by a judgment or decree, by the act of an agent, wife, child, etc.

binder. Said to be synonymous with insurance policy. Red Cab Co. v St. Paul Mercury Indem. Co. (CA7 Ind) 98 F2d 189; but better defined as a written instrument, sometimes called a binding slip or interim receipt, used when an insurance policy cannot be issued immediately; to evidence that the insurance coverage attaches at a specified time and continues until the policy is issued or the risk is declined and notice thereof given; a written memorandum of the most important terms of a preliminary contract of insurance intended to give temporary protection to the owner pending the investigation by the company or until the issuance of a formal policy. Sherri v National Surety Co. 243 NY 266, 270, 153 NE 70.

Life, health, and accident insurance companies have devised and used a form of binder, called a binding receipt or conditional receipt, which actually does not bind the insurance company absolutely to protect the risk pending the issuance of a policy, but is conditioned upon the approval of the application, the issuance and delivery of a policy, or similar condition. 29 Am J Rev ed Ins § 208.

binding instruction. An instruction which the jury are bound to follow by virtue of the rule that it is their duty to take the law from the court and apply it to the facts as they find the facts to be. 53 Am J1st Tr § 845.

binding over. Accepting bail from accused binding him to appear for trial. 21 Am J2d Crim L § 450; or other subsequent proceeding in the case, putting a person under a peace bond, a recognizance conditioned upon the keeping of the peace by the principal. 12 Am J2d Breach P § 41.

See **affidavit to hold to bail.**

binding slip. See **binder.**

bind out. To apprentice.

bingo. A game of chance which is played by each player buying from the keeper at a fixed price one or more checkered cards, 15 of the checkered spaces on each card bearing numbers, the keeper or his agent drawing a number from a bag or other receptacle, which is announced, and each player covering that number on his card if he has it, and the game proceeding until some player first gets all the numbers on a card or in a row of a card, according to the rule adopted, whereupon he calls, "bingo," and, on verification, the stakes of all the players less the keepers percentage go to him as a winner. Anno: 96 L Ed 315.

binocular. Seeing with both eyes at the same time.

binoculars. Field glasses.

bipartisan board. A municipal board composed of an even number of officers selected equally from the two leading political parties. 37 Am J1st Mun Corp § 86. Such boards are not confined to municipalities. Boards or commissions of the state or national government may be created by statutes which provide for equal representation of the two leading political parties in the personnel of the board in order to prevent the evil of partisan politics in the performance of the functions of the board.

bipartite. In two parts; in duplicate.

birretum (bĭr-re'tum). The cap or coif of a judge or a sergeant-at-law.

birth. Delivery from the womb; a beginning, as a birth of a nation.

See **abortion; born; Caesarean operation; deadborn; en ventre sa mere; foetus; possibility of issue extinct; still-born; vital statistics.**

birth certificate. A certification of the date and place of a person's birth, with a notation of his parentage, according to the facts as registered in the record of vital statistics kept in the county, municipality, town, or township of birth.

birth control. The prevention of conception by chemical or mechanical means, sometimes called planned parenthood. 12 Am J2d Birth C § 1.

bis (bis). Twice.

bisaile. See **besayl.**

bi-scot. A fine imposed for neglect to keep banks, ditches and causeways in repair.

bis dat qui cito dat (bis dat quī si'tō dat). He gives twice who gives quickly.

bishop. The chief ecclesiastical officer of a diocese in the Church of England and the Roman Catholic Church in the United States; a high-ranking clergyman in other American denominations. A sole corporation in his character as the embodiment of the Church in transacting business and holding property. 18 Am J2d Corp § 7.

bishopric (bish'up-rik). The jurisdiction of a bishop; a bishop's diocese.

bishop's court. An ecclesiastical court in a diocese.

bis petitum (bis pe'ti-tum). Twice demanded.

bissextile (bi-seks'til). Containing the extra day—the

bissextile day, February 29th—added in leap years in the Julian calendar. Anno: 5 ALR2d 1146.

bissextus (bi-seks'tus). February 29th, the day added in leap years in the Julian calendar.

bitch. A female dog; a coarse word of derision or contempt applied to an older girl or woman; not synonymous with "whore." Schurick v Kollman, 50 Ind 336, 337.

Biting rule. The principle that a provision in a deed or will to be inoperative where it attempts to cut down, modify, or qualify an apparent fee theretofore granted in the instrument. Hanks v McDanell, 307 Ky 243, 210 SW2d 784, 17 ALR2d 1.

bitters. A preparation of alcohol and other ingredients, principally herbs, sometimes used as medicine, but far more often in mixing alcoholic beverages, especially cocktails. 30 Am J Rev ed Intox L § 16.

bitulithic. See **asphalt; bitumen.**

bitumen. Asphalt; a residual material obtained in the distillation of crude oil.

bituminous coal. Soft coal; coal which burns readily on account of the content of pitch.

bituminous macadam. See **macadam.**

bk. An abbreviation of "bank," "block," and "book."

bkpt. Abbreviation of bankrupt.

bl. Abbreviation of bale and barrel, for both singular and plural.

B. L. An abbreviation of the law school degree of "bachelor of laws" and of the degree in liberal arts, called Bachelor of Letters; also of bill of lading.

B. L. A. An abbreviation of the degree Bachelor of Liberal Arts.

black. A negro. People v Hall, 4 Cal 397, 400. Adjective: Without light; dark-complexioned.

Blackacre. The name of a suppositious parcel or tract of land, often used in moot cases or in argument.

Black Act (blak akt). An English statute passed in 1722 to suppress bands known as "the blacks," who were ruffians who went about committing outrages with their faces blackened.

black acts. Scotch statutes enacted in the sixteenth century and written in black-letter.

Black Bass Act. A federal statute making it a criminal offense to deliver black bass or other fish for transportation from a state, if such transportation is contrary to the law of the state. 16 USC § 852.

Black Book of the Admiralty. The title of an ancient English commentary on admiralty law.

Black Book of the Exchequer. A book in the English exchequer containing treaties, conventions, and charters.

black cap. A cap worn by the judge in England when passing a death sentence; a cap or bag pulled down over the head of a convict about to be hanged.

black code. The laws providing for the segregation of the races in public places.

black damp. A noxious gas encountered in coal mines, commonly known as carbonic acid gas, or dead air, with the properties of oxygen exhausted, and causing suffocation by excluding oxygen from the lungs. Jellico Coal Mining Co. v Walls, 160 Ky 730, 732, 170 SW 19.

black game (blak'gām). Heath fowl, as distinguished from red game, such as the grouse.

blackjack. A weapon made by covering a piece of lead or other metal with leather and extending the leather covering over a handle that is flexible; used by thugs and sometimes by police officers. People v Brown, 253 Mich 537, 235 NW 245, 82 ALR 341. A card game, often played for money.

blackleg. A disease of cattle; a term of opprobrium applied to a dishonest gambler, a strikebreaker, and sometimes to any man who is untrustworthy. United Mine Workers v Cromer, 159 Ky 605, 608, 167 SW 891.

black-letter (blak'let"ėr). The name given to the Old English or Gothic letter which was used in the old English manuscripts and in the first printed books; sometimes used by persons not familiar with printing in speaking of boldface.

black liquor. A trade term of the paper pulp industry; the residual liquor coming from the digesters in which wood in the form of chips is cooked under heat and pressure in a solution of chemicals. The organic matter binding the cellulose fibers in the wood is dissolved out. After the cooking is completed, the wood pulp is removed from the solution and goes to the pulp treating section of the plant. Babcock & Wilcox v North Carolina Pulp Co. (DC Del) 35 F Supp 215.

blacklist. A generic term that may be defined as a list of persons marked out for special avoidance on the part of those among whom the list is intended to circulate, but which, as the term is now most generally understood, refers to lists of discharged employees sent by the discharging employer to other employers. 31 Am J Rev ed Lab § 83; and to the listing of names with information transmitted by a union member or agent to others with the intention that the result will be to prevent or terminate the employment of the workmen against whom the information is directed, and to make it impossible for them to obtain other employment within the jurisdiction of the union. Anno: 46 ALR2d 1125.

blacklisting. Putting a person's name upon a blacklist.
See **blacklist.**

blackmail. A criminal offense as a form of extortion; usually, extortion by threat of exposure of a criminal offense by, or of some conduct or act of, the victim which, if made public, will operate to his disadvantage; occasionally applied to extortion by threat of violence to the victim or members of his family. 31 Am J2d Extor § 18.
Another meaning of the term is **black rents.**

Black Maria (blak ma-rī'a). A covered vehicle, commonly black, used to transfer prisoners to and from a prison or jail.

blackout. An incident of modern warfare and drilling for civil defense, consisting in an enforced extinguishment at night of all street and highway lights and the obscuring of all lights in business places, offices, and dwelling houses against being seen from outside the building, such precautions being deemed necessary in time of war to prevent bombing of a city by airmen who otherwise would be aided in navigation by city lights; a temporary loss of consciousness.

black rents. Rents, also called "reditus nigri" and "blackmail," payable in work, grain, or money baser than silver, as distinguished from white rent, which was payable in silver or white money. See 2 Bl Comm 42.

black rod (blak' rod). An official messenger in the English house of lords.

blacksmith. An artisan who shapes iron by heating and pounding it, and shoes horses.

black ward. A feudal subvassal who held ward of the king's vassal.

blada (blā'da). Corn; grain; crops.

blada a solo separata (blā'da ā sō'lō se-pa-rā'ta). Grain severed from the soil.

blada crescentia (blā'da kres-sen'she-a). Growing corn, grain, or other crop.

blada nondum a solo separata (blā'da non'dum ā sō'lō se-pa-rā'ta). Grain not yet severed from the soil.

bladarius (bla-da'ri-us). A corn dealer; a grain dealer.

blada vel alia catalla (blā'da vel a'li-a ka-tal'la). Grain or other chattels.

blade. A sword or knife.
See **blada.**

blanc (blangk). White; plain; bearing no marks or writing.

blanc bar. Same as **blank bar.**

blanch. To whiten.

blanche. See **carte blanche.**

blanch-farms. White-rents, also called "reditus albi," which were rents payable in silver or white money. See 2 Bl Comm 42.

blanch-holding (blánch'hōl"ding). An ancient Scotch land tenure.

blanc seing. Same as **blank seing.**

blancus (blan'kus). Same as **blanc.**

blank. Plain; bearing no marks or writing; a space in a document intended to be filled to complete the meaning.
See **acceptance in blank; indorsement in blank.**

blank bar. A plea in an action of trespass quare clausum fregit, the object of which was to compel the plaintiff to name the place of the alleged trespass.

blank bonds. (Scotch.) Securities made payable to any payee who wrote his name in the blank space provided for it. They were declared void by statute in 1696.

blank deed. A blank paper signed, sealed, and delivered, the operative effect of which when finally filled in depends upon authorization by the grantor. 23 Am J2d Deeds § 138.

blanket ballot. A ballot for use at an election on which appear all of the names of the candidates for all the offices to be filled at the election.

blanket patent. Letters patent covering several devices each of which would be patentable separately.

blanket policy. The name given to a contract of insurance because of the manner in which the subject matter, that is the insured property or the risk is described, typically illustrated by a policy covering a stock of merchandise, which, because of the changing character of the property insured from day to day as articles are sold and replaced in the course of business, can be described only in general terms describing the nature of the stock and its location.
Another typical illustration is that of a policy covering a warehouse risk, which, of course, varies from day to day as new customers bring in their property and old customers remove their property from the warehouse. 29 Am J Rev ed Ins § 306.
Blanket or float policies are sometimes issued to factors or to warehousemen, intended only to cover margins uninsured by other policies, or to cover nothing more than the limited interest which the factor or warehouseman may have in the property which he has in charge. Home Ins. Co. v Baltimore Warehouse Co. 93 US 527, 541, 23 L Ed 868, 869.

blanket rate. See **blanket territory.**

blanket search warrant. A single warrant which describes two or more separate premises to be searched. Williams v State, 95 Okla Crim 131, 240 P2d 1132, 31 ALR2d 851.

blanket territory. A term employed in rate-making for carriers, so called because a "blanket" rate on logs and lumber is made from all shipping points within the territory to points beyond. That is, the rate is the same regardless of the distance hauled *within* the territory.

blanket vein. (Mining.) A horizontal vein or deposit of mineral. Iron Silver Mining Co. v Mike & Starr Gold & Silver Mining Co. 143 US 394, 400, 36 L Ed 201, 203, 12 S Ct 543.

blank indorsement. An indorsement of a negotiable instrument by the payee or subsequent holder which specifies no indorsee. 11 Am J2d B & N § 360; an indorsement of a security in registered form which specifies no one as indorsee, the effect being an indorsement to bearer. 15 Am J2d Com C § 32.

blank seing (blank säng). A paper signed at the bottom by him who intends to bind himself, give acquittance, or compromise, at the discretion of the person whom he intrusts with such paper, giving him power to fill it with what he may think proper, according to agreement. Musson v Bank of United States (La) 6 Mart 707, 718.

blasarius (bla-sā'ri-us). An incendiary.

blasphemous libel (blàs'fę-mus). A libel of God or Christianity published with intent to insult or subvert religious belief.
See **Paine's Age of Reason.**

blasphemy. A crime in maliciously reviling God or religion, or maliciously reviling the founder of Christianity. 12 Am J2d Blas § 2.
See **blasphemous libel; Paine's Age of Reason; profane; profanity.**

blast furnance. A furnace which takes its name from the feeding of a blast of air to produce intense heat; used to burn out the impurities in ore.

blasting. Tearing apart the layers of earth and rock by the use of high explosives; destroying; blighting.

bleachers. Uncovered seats in a grandstand or stadium.

blees (blēz). Grain.

blees scies. Grain which has been cut.

blench holding (blench). Same as **blanch-holding.**

blended fund. A fund consisting of the proceeds of an executor's sale of all his testator's real and personal estate under the will.

bleta (blē'ta). An old name for peat, a dried earth used for fuel.

blighted area. An unaesthetic and uneconomic section; an area of such kind that razing all the buildings will serve a public purpose, even though a few of them may not be substandard or blighted. Velishka v Nashua, 99 NH 161, 106 A2d 571, 44 ALR2d 1406.

blind. See **blindness**.

blind alley. A way from which exit can be made only by retreat to the place of entrance; a dilemma; a position from which no progress can be made.

blind corner. An intersection of streets or roads at which a driver's view of vehicles approaching on the intersecting highway is obscured by natural formations or artificial structures.

blindcraft. Useful and artistic articles produced by blind persons.

blind head. A bed or seam or soft rock which would prevent an upward explosion from blasting operations and would cause the gases to spread laterally. Anno: 20 ALR2d 1396.

blinding lights. Any lights which blind a person beyond the possibility of good vision but applied mostly to the headlights of motor vehicles.

blindness. Without sight in whole or in part.
See **color blindness**.

blind station. A railroad station at which there is no station house, agent, or telegraph operator. Mobile & Ohio Railroad Co. v Massey, 52 Ill App 556, 557.

blind tiger. A term, of frequent use during the period of national prohibition, meaning a place where intoxicating liquor is sold in violation of law. State v Tabler, 34 Ind App 393, 72 NE 1039.

blinks (blingks). Broken boughs thrown where deer are likely to pass.

bloc. A group of persons who support a legislative measure as a body, even though they are of different political persuasions, as the "farm bloc" in Congress.
See **en bloc**.

block. A square or rectangular, sometimes an irregular, portion of a city or village which is enclosed by streets. Anno: 6 ALR 1167; the portion of a street, including both sides, measured from one intersecting street to the next intersecting street. Chamberlain v Roberts, 81 Colo 23, 253 P 27; a section of a railroad line set up in the installation of automatic signals regulating traffic, the purpose being to prevent the presence of more than one train in one block at one time.

blockade. An interdiction of commerce with a nation or people in that nation. 30 Am J Rev ed Internat L § 53. Blockades are maritime blockades, or blockades by both sea and land; and they may be either military or commercial, or may partake of the nature of both. A blockade of either kind is a sort of circumvallation round a place, by which all foreign connection and correspondence are, so far as human force can effect it, to be entirely cut off. Vattel says: "All commerce is entirely prohibited with a besieged town. If I lay siege to a place, or only form a blockade, I have a right to hinder any one from entering, and to treat as an enemy whoever attempts to enter the place, or carry anything to the besieged, without my leave." 56 Am J1st War § 171.
See **commercial blockade; effective blockade; paper blockade; simple blockade; violation of blockade**.

blockade de facto. See **de facto blockade**.

blockage rule. A recognition of the principle that a large block of corporate stock is not as readily marketable, or marketable as advantageously, as a few shares. Phipps v Commissioner (CA10) 127 F2d 214.

block and tackle. Rope and pulley used in lifting weights.

block booking. The booking of moving pictures in a theater by the job lot, without selection of particular pictures by the proprietor of the theater.

blocked frog. A term of railroad parlance which signifies that the space between the rails of a track, at the point where a car or a train is switched from one track to another, is filled with wood or other material, so as to prevent the catching and holding of a person's foot. Southern Pacific Railroad Co. v Seley, 152 US 145, 150, 38 L Ed 391, 14 S Ct 530.

block to block rule. A rule which purports to carry out the principle of special assessment according to benefit by assessing against the property in a city block the cost and expenses of the acquisition of land for opening a street which runs through the block.

blodwita (blō'wi-ta). Same as **bloodwit**.

blood. The sustenance of life that flows through the body of a person and of many animals; the relationship between persons derived from having the blood of a common ancestor.
See **consanguinity; corruption of blood; full blood; half blood; heirs by blood; inheritable blood; nearest of blood; whole blood**.

blood brother. A brother by birth.

blood clot. See **pulmonary embolism**.

blood feud. A state of hostility between families, leading to a series of attacks and counterattacks by arms.

blood-frenzy. An irresistible impulse for bloodshed.

blood heirs. See **heirs by blood**.

bloodhound. A dog adaptable by breeding and care to training and successful performance in the tracking of a man.

bloodhound trailing. Evidence in the identification of an accused. 13 Am J2d Burgl § 44.

blood kin. See **relatives by blood**.

blood money. The price paid for causing a person's death.

blood poisoning. A toxic condition of the blood caused either from or through a surface wound or some internal lesion, or from the breaking down of tissue incident to an existent or precedent disease, and thereby producing suppuration; not a primary or idiopathic disease. Jones v Pennsylvania Casualty Co. 140 NC 262, 52 SE 578.

blood pressure. See **systolic pressure**.

blood relationship. See **relatives by blood**.

blood relatives. See **relatives by blood**.

blood stains. Evidence of homicide where found on

the accused and properly identified. People v Gonzalez, 35 NY 49, 60.

blood test. A test to determine physical condition. A test of paternity; a test of special value in a case of disputed paternity because, although it cannot indicate with precision that a particular person is the father of the child whose paternity is in issue, in many instances it can establish that an alleged father could not have been the sire. Anno: 46 ALR2d 1003 § 1(b).
See **microspectroscopic blood test.**

bloodwit. An amercement for bloodshed; (Scotch.) A bloody riot.

bloody hand. A hand stained with deer's blood,— evidence of poaching.

blotter. A police record, kept at the station, of arrests.
See **rough minutes.**

blown upon. A metaphor, with little to recommend its use, meaning doubted or cast in doubt. Luckett v Delpark, 270 US 496, 504, 70 L Ed 703, 706, 46 S Ct 397.

blowout. A sudden rupture of the tube of an automobile tire.

B. L. S. Abbreviation for Bachelor of Library Science.

bludgeon (bluj'ọn). Noun: A weapon; a stick or club that is heavy by nature or loaded with metal. Verb: To strike with a club. State v Phillips 104 NC 786, 789.

blue book. A publication listing the value of used automobiles by make, type, and year; a register of the socially prominent; a listing of public officers.

blue chips. A term characterizing first-class investments.
See **first-class investments.**

Blue Cross. A comprehensive plan or system of providing hospital service and care for participants in consideration of regular payments, often called premiums, by the participants. 29 Am J Rev ed Ins § 12.

Blue Cross contract. A contract issued under a Blue Cross plan for providing payment of the expense of hospitalization of members participating in the plan and members of their families. Michigan Hospital Service v Sharpe, 339 Mich 357, 63 NW2d 638, 43 ALR2d 1167.

blue discharge. A discharge from military service which is neither honorable nor dishonorable. Longernecker v Highley, 97 App DC 144, 229 F2d 27.

blue laws (blö lâz). Strict statutes or ordinances, particularly those which affected observance of the Sabbath.

blue nose. A colloquial expression for one who is illiberal in his views as to activities which most persons regard as joys of living, such as dancing, card-playing, drinking alcoholic beverages, attending theatrical performances, etc.

blue note. A promissory note given for the initial premium on a life insurance policy. A melancholy air in music.

blue ribbon jury. A jury made up of particularly qualified persons; a jury selected by a sifting procedure which reduces the general panel to one of a much lesser number of persons. 31 J Rev ed Am Jur § 72.

Blue Shield. A comprehensive plan or system for providing surgical and medical services for participants in consideration of regular payments, often called premiums, by the participants. 29 Am J Rev ed Ins § 12.

blue sky laws. An appellation for a type of statutes, which apparently originated in the expression concerning the credulous as "dumb enough to buy blue sky, if it is offered to him"; statutes intended, by the requirements which they impose, to prevent fraud in the sale of securities. Hall v Geiger-Jones Co. 242 US 538, 61 L Ed 480, 37 S Ct 217.
See **securities acts.**

bluff. A steep bank of considerable height; a bold front assumed for the purpose of misleading another.

blunderbus. An old time firearm good only at short range, since its effectiveness depended upon the scattering of the shot, rather than marksmanship; a derisory term applied to a complaint or petition in many counts, also to an argument of counsel which covers the case too minutely to be effective.

blunt instrument. An instrument which, when used as a weapon, injures by pounding rather than by piercing or slashing; stick, butt of a gun, gas pipe, hammer, or something similar. People v Lukoszus, 242 Ill 101, 89 NE 749.

b.n. Abbreviation of bank note.

B/O. Abbreviation of **brought over;** used in bookkeeping.

boar. A male hog; a sire.

board. A convenient term in referring to the board of directors of a corporation, the reference being in the individual as well as the collective sense. State ex rel. Keller v Grimes, 65 W Va 451, 64 SE 728.
The term implies agency—a committee of managers,—official servants charged with executive duties, and acting for and in the interest of others. See People v North River Sugar Refining Co. 121 NY 582, 24 NE 834. An organization, although called a board, may be an association. 6 Am J2d Asso & C § 1.
Meals, usually in the sense of all, or nearly all, the meals for the period, as board by the day or week. While the word is sometimes given a meaning sufficiently broad to include both lodgings and meals, Heron v Webber, 103 Me 178, 68 A 744, where it is used in a statute, the context may show that is was intended to apply to meals alone. Pacific Coal Co. v Silver Bow County, 79 Mont 323, 256 P 386. Verb: To supply with meals; to take in a boarder or boarders.

boarder. One who takes his meals regularly at a single, definite place, the term sometimes carrying with it the idea of residence. 29 Am J Rev ed Innk § 12. He usually pays by the week, occasionally, by the month.

board foot. A unit of measure in the lumber trade, meaning a board one foot square and one inch thick.
See **board measure.**

boarding. The act of a prospective passenger in getting on a conveyance of the carrier. 14 Am J2d Car § 982; furnishing board; taking board.

boardinghouse. A quasi-public house, where boarders are generally and habitually kept, and which is held out and known as a place of refreshment of that kind. Anno: 19 ALR 538; 29 Am J Rev ed Innk § 11.

boardinghouse keeper's lien. The statutory lien of the keeper of a boarding house upon the goods of a boarder or lodger brought upon the premises for the former's charges against the latter for services and things furnished for the accommodation, comfort, and entertainment of the boarder or lodger, the lien sometimes being extended by statute to goods of a third person brought upon the premises by the boarder or lodger. 29 Am J Rev ed Innk §§ 145 et seq.

board measure. The number of feet of board which a log will produce when sawed. Destrehan v Louisiana Cypress Lumber Co. 45 La Ann 920.
See **board foot.**

boarding school. An educational institution, lower than college rank, wherein the students are boarded and lodged.

board of aldermen. The common council of a city or other municipality.

board of arbitration. A quasi-court, appointed to act in a judicial and impartial manner, under the rules of arbitration, in hearing the parties to a dispute and settling the controversy by an award. Anno: 104 ALR 563.

board of audit. A board authorized to audit or pass upon the accounts of a public officer. 43 Am J1st Pub Of § 324.

board of directors. The directors of a corporation acting as a unit in representing the corporate body and conducting the business of the corporation. 19 Am J2d Corp § 1145.
See **bank directors; directors.**

board of education. A public corporation created by statute for the purposes of public education; the directors or trustees of a municipality or school district, who, acting as a body, administer the law governing the public schools in the municipality or school district. 47 Am J1st Sch § 29.

board of equalization. A board having a function or functions in reference to taxation, such as spreading the tax burden evenly over all the taxable property in a tax district, so that, taking account of difference in values of the assessed properties, one part of the district is neither unduly burdened nor unduly favored; equalizing the burden of taxes as between tax districts or as between the counties or towns of a state; and even the reducing or increasing of assessments on individual properties. 51 Am J1st Tax § 742.

board of examiners. A state board vested with the power to examine an applicant for a license to practice a profession or an occupation in which special learning is required.

board of fire underwriters. A board composed exclusively of fire insurers; that is, of persons engaged in the business of insuring others, on property, against loss by fire.
Prior to any legislation on the subject, associations called boards of underwriters (either fire or marine) existed in various cities. These were voluntary associations, composed exclusively of those engaged in that particular line of business. Their general object was to consult and co-operate in matters affecting their business and they often established salvage corps at their own expense. These associations were the forerunners of incorporated associations or boards formed under statutory authority and clothed with power to exercise these and similar functions. Childs, ex rel. Smith v Firemen's Ins. Co. 66 Minn 393, 69 NW 141.
See **underwriters' association.**

board of health. A public body, municipal or state, in charge of the sanitary and hygienic affairs of a community or the state. An administrative agency created by legislative act, acting as an arm of the state or municipal government, according to the authority vested in it upon its creation or thereafter conferred, for the essential purpose of protecting the public health. 25 Am J1st Hlth § 5.

board of pardons. A state board composed of several persons, of which the governor is usually a member, a majority of whom are generally authorized to grant pardons and to grant clemency to convicted prisoners as a branch of the executive department of the state government. 39 Am J1st Pard § 20.

board of parole. A state board authorized and directed to consider the cases of inmates of state prisons and reformatories with reference to the parole of such prisoners, and to release prisoners on parole under such conditions as may be prescribed by law or, as the board, acting under powers vested in the board, may prescribe.

board of regents. See **regents.**

board of review. A board authorized to hear complaints alleging errors in assessing property for taxation; in a few cities, a board authorized to hear complaints as to brutality or excessive force exercised by police in making an arrest or interrogating a prisoner.

board of supervisors. The county board, sometimes called the county court; the governing body of a county.

board of tax appeals. See **tax court.**

board of trade. A body of men organized for the advancement and protection of business interests, Retailers Credit Asso. v Commissioner, 90 F2d 47, 111 ALR 152. Sometimes business interests in one particular line of commercial activity, even in one particular line in a specific municipality or other geographical location. Retailers Credit Asso. v Commissioner, 90 F2d 47, 111 ALR 152; narrowly defined as any exchange or association, whether incorporated or unincorporated, of persons who shall be engaged in the business of buying or selling grain or receiving the same for sale on consignment. Trusler v Crooks, 269 US 475, 479, 70 L Ed 365, 366, 46 S Ct 165.

board of works. A public body having charge of public works.

boards of underwriters. Organizations of insurance companies or insurance agents which have the purpose of promoting the insurance business and securing uniformity in the business. 29 Am J Rev ed Ins § 109.
See **board of fire underwriters; rating bureaus.**

boardwalk. A sidewalk constructed of boards; the promenade at a seaside resort.

boast. To brag; a brag; a braggart.

boat. Preferably a watercraft, small in size but, as used in common parlance, it is a generic term for watercraft of different sizes, sometimes inclusive, but erroneously, according to mariners, of ships. Sometimes regarded in the more limited sense of watercraft for use upon inland waters. State v Hutchins, 79 NH 132, 105 A 519, 2 ALR 1685, 1691.

boatable waters. Waters within a state which are of common passage, as highways; that is, waters which can be used in their ordinary condition as highways for commerce conducted in the customary mode of trade and travel on water. New England Trout & Salmon Club v Mather, 68 Vt 338, 35 A 323. But waters which are private property are not boatable, notwithstanding otherwise they are boatable in fact. 56 Am J1st Wat § 3.
See **navigable waters**.

boating. A conveyance of persons or freight by boat and also the use of a boat for amusement. 12 Am J2d Boats § 1.

Boating Act. A federal statute governing the operation of pleasure craft upon navigable waters. 46 USC § 527.

boat livery. A business or enterprise having boats for rent. 12 Am J2d Boats § 81.

boatswain. A petty officer in charge of the deck crew on watch, including operations in loading or unloading cargo. Larson v Alaska S. S. Co. 96 Wash 665, 165 P 880.

bobtail. A horse having a docked or shortened tail.

boc (bok). A book; a written instrument; a charter.

boc horde (bok hōrd). Same as **book hoard**.

bock hord. Same as **book hoard**.

bock land. Same as **book land**.

boc land (bok land). Same as **book land**

boddemerey (bŏd'o-mē-rey). Bottomry.

bodemerie (bŏd'mē-re). Bottomry.

bodily. Pertaining to or concerning the body; of or belonging to the body or to the physical constitution; not mental, but corporeal. Terre Haute Electric Railway Co. v Lauer, 21 Ind App 466, 475, 52 NE 703.

bodily harm. Physical injury to the person, especially injury by violent, hostile, and aggressive means. People v Moore (NY) 50 Hun 356, 358.

bodily heirs. Heirs of the body. Watson v Wolff-Goldman Realty Co. 95 Ark 18, 128 SW 581; children. 28 Am J Rev ed Est § 42; heirs of the body as distinguished from heirs by adoption. 2 Am J2d Adopt § 98.
See **heirs of the body**.

bodily hurt. Personal injury. Murray v Allen, 103 Vt 373, 154 A 678.
See **bodily harm; bodily injuries**.

bodily infirmity. Something of a permanent, established, or settled character, that materially impairs, weakens, or undermines the constitution of a person, tends to reduce his powers of resistance, and thereby enhances the risk of death in case of injury. 29A Am J Rev ed Ins § 1211.
See **physical infirmity**.

bodily injuries. Personal injuries. Cormier v Hudson, 284 Mass 231, 187 NE 625, in various degrees of harm, Anno: 37 ALR2d 1087, resulting from an external cause, 29A Am J Rev ed Ins § 1168; but including, according to some authority, distress from a cause other than one involving force, for example, injury by seduction or malpractice, 34 Am J1st Lim Ac § 105, sunstroke; freezing, causing death; ulcerations upon the insured's fingers, caused by exposure to an X-ray used in his business; and contact, resulting in death of a professional nurse, with germs of a communicable disease while attending a patient, 29A Am J Rev ed Ins § 1168, but excluding, according to other authority, anything not resulting from force or violence, such as loss of consortium, 7 Am J2d Auto Ins § 212, or disease. 29A Am J Rev ed Ins § 1168.
See **personal injury**.

bodily issue. Ordinarily words of limitation in a grant or devise, but they may be words of purchase, as where the grantor or testator had children living at the time of the grant and the context shows that the words were not used in a technical sense, but referred especially to children. 28 Am J Rev ed Est § 42.

bodmerie. Bottomry.

body. The corporeal or physical person or being; the trunk, as distinguished from the head and limbs, that part of the human being between the upper part of his thighs or hips and his neck, excluding his arms. Walker v State, 34 Fla 167, 173; the substantial part, as the body of a building in distinction to the accessory or auxiliary parts; the hull of vessel. 29 Am J Rev ed Ins § 304; a corporation; an unincorporated association; a board; a code of laws.

body corporate. A corporation.

body execution. An execution against the person; a writ of execution for the satisfaction of a judgment to be served by arresting the judgment debtor. 30 Am J2d Exec § 865.
See **execution against the person**.

body heirs. See **bodily heirs**.

body of a county. The county as a whole.

body of an instrument. The meat or substance of the instrument.

body of ship. The hull. 29 Am J Rev ed Ins § 304.

body of the crime. See **corpus delicti**.

body politic. A social compact by which the whole people covenants with each citizen, and each citizen with the whole people, that all shall be governed by laws for the common good. Munn v Illinois, 94 US 113, 124, 24 L Ed 77, 84.

body politic and corporate. A term often applied to a municipal corporation. A county is such a body. Waterbury v Board of Comrs. 10 Mont 515, 26 P 1002.

body snatching. Stealing a corpse. The taking of a corpse from the grave secretly and without authority; a criminal offense, as violation of sepulture. 22 Am J2d Dead B § 50.

body stealing. See **body snatching**.

bog grass. A kind of hay but constituting a part of the freehold, so that it is waste for a life tenant to take it as fodder. Sarles v Sarles (NY) 3 Sandf Ch 601.

bogus (bō'gus). Spurious; fictitious; sham. Williams v Territory, 13 Ariz 27, 108 P 243.

bogus check. A check given by a person upon a bank in which he has no funds, or funds less than the amount of the check, which he has no reason to suppose will be honored, and which is not honored. Williams v Territory, 13 Ariz 27, 108 P 243.

Bohemian oats. A characterization of a contract whereby seed grain of a variety of oats known as Bohemian oats is sold at a very high price under representation that the seller will sell for the purchaser a much larger quantity of the grain at an equally exorbitant price. A characterization of similar contracts involving other grains. 46 Am J1st Sales § 122.

boil. A swelling on the skin, pus-filled and very painful. Beck v State, 29 Ala App 410, 197 So 42. Verb: To come to the boiling point, e.g., water at 212 degrees Fahrenheit; a slang expression for becoming angry.

boilary (boi'lėr-i). Salt water taken from a well belonging to a person who does not own the land.

boiler. A metal container in which food, such as potatoes or ears of sweet corn, may be heated and boiled; a large and tight container of heavy metal in which water may be turned into steam for commercial or household use for the purposes of power or heating.

Boiler Inspection Act. A federal statute intended for the protection of railroad employees, perhaps also of passengers and the public at large, from injury due to industrial accident. Urie v Thompson, 327 US 163, 93 L Ed 1282, 69 S Ct 1018, 11 ALR2d 252. A statute regulating railroads in respect of the safety of certain equipment. 44 Am J1st RR § 274.

boiler insurance. A type of casualty insurance covering damage to property of the insured or of others for which the insured may be liable, including damage to the boiler itself, as well as loss to the insured for damages on account of the death or personal injury of any person caused by the explosion or collapse of a boiler. 29A Am J Rev ed Ins § 1365.

boiler plate material. A term of the trade for stereotype matter in a newspaper. 39 Am J1st Newsp § 8.

bois (bwo). A wood.

boldagium (bol-dā'gi-um). Same as **bolhagium**.

Bold Buccleugh. See **The Bold Buccleugh.**

bolhagium (bol-hā'gi-um). A small dwelling house.

boll of land (bōl). (Scotch.) About an acre.

boll weevil. A beetle, the larvae of which are destructive to cotton plants; an agricultural pest. 3 Am J2d Agri §§ 38 et seq.

bolter (bōl'tėr). Bran; a horse that breaks away and runs uncontrolled by rider or driver; a person who leaves his political party, or supports a candidate of another party, usually for a single election.

bolt. A roll of cloth, such as a bolt of silk; a metal rod or pin, usually threaded to permit staying by a nut.
See **bolter; bolting.**

bolting. The holding of moot arguments at the inns of court; sifting ground wheat to remove the chaff from the edible flour.

bomb scare. The criminal offense of conveying, or causing to be conveyed, false information that a bomb or other explosive has been or is to be planted in an airplane, bus, other vehicle, building, or the like. Smith v United States (CA6 Ohio) 283 F2d 16, 87 ALR2d 394, cert den 365 US 847, 5 L Ed 2d 811, 81 S Ct 908.

bon (bōn). Good.

bona (bō'nạ). Adjective: Good. Noun: Goods and chattels.

bona confiscata (bō'na kon-fis-kā'ta). Property confiscated by, or forfeited to, the crown.

bona dea (bō'na dē'a). The good goddess.

bonae fidei (bō'ne fī'dē-ī). Of good faith.

bonae fidei emptor (bō'ne fī'dē-ī emp'tor). A purchaser in good faith.

bonae fidei possessor (bō'ne fī'dē-ī). A possessor in good faith,—one who believes his right of possession to be better than that of anyone else.

bona felonum (bō'na fe'lo-num). The goods of felons.

bona fide. Acting in good faith.
See **good faith.**

bona fide debt. A debt incurred without fraud or deceit. Ware v Jones (US) 3 Dall 199, 241, 1 L Ed 568, 586.

bona fide holder. See **holder in due course.**

bona fide holder for value without notice. A holder in due course. 11 Am J2d B & N § 397.
See **holder in due course.**

bona fide operation. Real and substantial operation, not something of pretense or sham. 13 Am J2d Car § 85.

bona fide possessor. A person who is in possession of property and is ignorant of all the facts and circumstances relating to his adversary's title. Henderson v Pickett's Heirs, 20 Ky (4 TB Mon) 54, 60; actual rather than potential or simulated service, and substantial as distinguished from incidental, sporadic, or infrequent service. Anno: 4 ALR2d 705. (Civil law.) A possessor who believes that no other person has a better right to the possession than himself. See Mackeldey's Roman Law § 243.

bona fide purchaser. One who purchases a chattel for value, without notice of a defect in the title of the person from whom he purchased or of the right of a seller in the chain of title to avoid or rescind the sale which he made. 46 Am J1st Sales § 465. One who purchases real estate with an honest purpose and for a valuable consideration, without knowledge or notice of outstanding interests or of facts or circumstances from which his knowledge of outstanding interests should be implied. 55 Am J1st V & P § 687.

Possession of realty by one other than the grantor is sufficient to require the purchaser to make inquiry as to the rights of such other person in possession. Holgerson v Gard, 257 Ala 579, 60 So 2d 427, 33 ALR2d 1315.

To constitute one a bona fide purchaser entitled to priority over one claiming under a prior equity or conveyance, he must be the purchaser of the legal title, as distinguished from the equitable title, in good faith, for value, without notice, at or before the time of parting with the consideration of such other's equity or conveyance. Larkins v Howard, 252 Ala 9, 39 So 2d 224, 7 ALR2d 541.
See **holder in due course.**

bona fide residence. A residence which amounts to a domicil, that is, a place where a person lives or has his home, to which, when absent, he intends to return and from which he has no present purpose to depart permanently. 17 Am J2d Div & S § 247.

bona fides (bō'na fī'dēz). Good faith.

bona forisfacta (bō'na fō"ris-fak'ta). Same as **bona confiscata**.

bona fugitivorum (bō'na fū-ji-ti-vō'rum). The goods of fugitives.

bona gestura (bō'na jes'tū-ra). Good behavior.

bona gratia (bō'na grā'she-a). With good grace; freely; with full consent.

Bona gratia matrimonium dissolvitur (bō'na grā'shea ma"tri-mō'ni-um dis-sol'vi-ter). Full consent to the dissolution of a marriage.

bona immobilia (bō'na im-mō'bi-li-a). (Civil law.) Immovable property; land; buildings; any corporeal real property.

bona memoria (bō'na me-mō'ri-a). With good memory.

bona mobilia (bō'na mō-bi'li-a). Chattels; personal property; articles which move under their own power or are moved by external force applied to them. 42 Am J1st Prop § 24.

bona notabilia (bō'nạ nō-tạ-bil'i-ạ). Goods and chattels of some value, of sufficient value to require administration of the estate of a deceased owner.

bonanza. A term originally applied to a rich vein of ore or a highly productive mine, especially a gold or silver mine, and now applied to any business or commercial activity which is very rewarding financially, particularly a new enterprise which produces a big profit quickly.

bona patria (bō'na pā'tri-a). (Scotch.) A jury of countrymen or good neighbors.

bona peritura (bō'nạ per-i-tū'rạ). Perishable goods.

bona utlagatorum (bō'na ut-la-ga-tō'rum). The goods of outlaws.

bona vacantia (bō'na vā-kan'she-a). Property without an owner. Personal property which went to the Crown, under the common law, for want of an owner. 27 Am J2d Esch § 1.

bona waviata (bō'na wā-vi-ā'ta). Goods stolen, and waived or thrown away by the thief in his flight, for fear of being apprehended.

bond. Noun: The obligation secured by a mortgage or deed of trust; a corporate obligation. 19 Am J2d Corp § 1059; at common law, a sealed instrument or specialty. 34 Am J1st Lim Ac § 82; an obligation in writing which binds a signatory to pay a sum certain upon the happening of an event and carries a seal, except where controlled by a statute which dispenses with the necessity of a seal. 12 Am J2d Bonds § 1. So defined, the term is generic, embracing investment bonds, penal bonds, indemnity, fidelity, and surety bonds. 12 Am J2d Bonds § 1. Less frequently, the term is used for a bail or a surety. Verb: To give a bond as security.
See **undertaking**.

bonda (bon'da). A boundary.

bondage (bon'dạj). Involuntary personal servitude; slavery.

bond and disposition in security. (Scotch.) A mortgage of real property.

bond broker. See **broker; underwriting contract**.

bond-creditor (bond'kred"i-tọr). A creditor who has taken a bond to secure his debt.

bonded debt. An indebtedness secured by a bond issue; written obligations contracted for corporate purposes pursuant to law and to be paid out of taxes to be levied upon all property within the corporate boundaries. Bolton v Wharton, 163 SC 242, 161 SE 454, 86 ALR 1101.

bonded goods. Goods in respect to which a bond has been given to secure the payment of the excise or duty on them.

bonded indebtedness. See **bonded debt**.

bonded liquor. See **bonded goods**.

bonded warehouse. A building or part of a building, usually at a port of entry, designated by the Secretary of the Treasury as a bonded warehouse for the storage of imported merchandise entered for warehousing, for the manufacture of merchandise in bond, or for the repacking, sorting, or cleaning of imported merchandise.

The owner or lessee of such premises is required to give bond in such sum and with such sureties as may be approved by the Secretary of the Treasury, to secure the government against loss or expense connected with or arising from the deposit, storage, or manipulation of merchandise in such warehouse. 19 USC § 1555.

See **private bonded warehouse; public bonded warehouse**.

bond for costs. See **security for costs**.

bond for support. A bond conditioned upon furnishing support for a child, furnished in a prosecution for abandonment or nonsupport of the child. 23 Am J2d Desert § 118.

bond for title. See **title bond**.

bondholder. A person who is the holder or owner of a government bond, mortgage bond, debenture, or other investment bond.

bond issue. The entire process of executing and delivering the instruments, known as bonds, and having the effect of obligations of indebtedness of the corporation or public body which issues them, to the purchasers, holders, or owners, Vans Agnew v Ft. Myers Drainage Dist. (CA5 Fla) 69 F2d 244; Turner v Roseberry Irrig Dist. 33 Idaho 746, 198 P 465; Joint School Dist. v Dabney, 127 Okla 234, 260 P 486; the aggregate of bonds issued by a corporation or public body under one authorization.

bondman (bond'màn). A slave; a person bound to serve without pay; a bond-tenant.

bond on appeal. Security furnished in perfecting an appeal for the benefit of other parties to be affected. 4 Am J2d A & E § 323.

bond post obit (bond post ob'it). Bond after he has died,—a bond given to secure the performance of some act or acts after a certain person shall have died. A kind of bond whereby the obligor agrees that in consideration of the payment to him of a sum of money by the obligee, he, the obligor, will upon receipt thereof from the estate of a person now living from whom he expects to inherit, pay a larger sum, exceeding the legal rate of interest. Boynton v Hubbard, 7 Mass 112, 120.

bond premium. The amount paid for a bond by the holder thereof in excess of the face value of the instrument.

bond single. A bond without a condition; in effect, a promissory note under seal.

bondsman (bondz'mạn). A surety on a bond, especially a bail.

bond-tenants. Copyhold tenants; customary tenants. See **bondman**.

bond to keep the peace. A bond or undertaking required by a magistrate to be given by a person who has threatened to commit a breach of the peace. A bond or undertaking given as security against the commission of a breach of peace by the obligor. 12 Am J2d Breach P etc. §§ 41—51.

bone boiling plant. A place where bones are reduced to constituents by boiling.

bone marrow biopsy. A part of a physical examination to which the plaintiff in a personal injury action may be required to submit. 23 Am J2d Dep § 216.

bones gents (bōn jān). Good men; competent or qualified persons.

boni et legales homines (bō'nī et lē-gā'lēz ho'mi-nēz). Good and lawful men; qualified jurors.

bonification of tax. The remission of taxes, particularly taxes on goods to be exported. United States v Passavant, 169 US 16, 42 L Ed 644, 18 S Ct 219.

boni homines (bō'nī ho'mi-nēz). Good men.

Boni judicis est ampliare justitiam (bō'nī jū'di-sis est am-pli-ā're jūs-ti'shē-am). The duty of a good judge to make precedents in the amplification of justice. Koerber v Patek, 123 Wis 453, 102 NW 40.

boni judicis est litis dirimere; et interest reipublicae ut sint fines litium (bō'nī jū'di-sis est lī'tis di-ri'mere; et in'ter-est re''ī-pub'li-se ut sint fi'nez lī'shē-um). A good judge should end litigation; and it is of interest to the state that litigation should end.

bonis. See **in bonis; in bonis defuncti.**

bonis maternis. See **ex bonis maternis.**

bonis non amovendis (bō'nīs non ā-mo-ven'dīs). For not removing the goods,—a writ to restrain a judgment debtor from removing his goods pending a writ of error.

bonne (bon). Good.

bonne foy. See **en bonne foy.**

bono et malo (bō'nō et ma'lo). See **de bono et malo.**

bono gestu. See **de bono gestu.**

bonorum. See **cessio bonorum; collatio bonorum.**

bonorum possessio (bō-nō'rum po-ze'she-ō). (Civil law.) The possession of goods.

bonos mores. See **contra bonos mores.**

bonum (bō'num). Goodness; welfare; advantage; benefit.

bonum vacans (bō'num va'kans). Singular of **bona vacantia.**

bonus. A payment made by a borrower in advance, sometimes called a commission. 55 Am J1st Usury § 41; a sum paid by a mortgagor as a condition of prepayment of the mortgage debt. Anno: 70 ALR2d 1334; a payment of something extra, Kenicott v Supervisors of Wayne County (US) 16 Wall 452, 21 L Ed 319; something paid an employee above stipulated wages. Anno: 28 ALR 332; 35 Am J1st M & S § 71; an extra dividend; a payment made for expeditious service; a payment in appreciation of a privilege granted. Kenicott v Supervisors of Wayne County (US) 16 Wall 452, 21 L Ed 319; the payment of a share of earnings required of a public utility in consideration of the grant of a charter. Baltimore & Ohio R. R. Co. v Maryland (US) 21 Wall 456, 22 L Ed 678; a reward for military services. 40 Am J1st Pens § 3; a drawback of taxes. United States v Passavant, 169 US 16, 42 L Ed 644, 18 S Ct 219.

An adjective in the Latin; good; advantageous; profitable.

bonus homo (bō'nus hŏ'mō). A good man.

bonus judex (bō'nus jū-dex). Good judge.

bonus plan. An established plan, followed by a corporation, for the remuneration of officers and employees, in addition to regular salaries or wages, as an incentive to additional effort and use of skill on behalf of the company. See 19 Am J2d Corp § 1413.

bonus stock. Corporate stock issued without payment made therefor or issued for property or services at an inflated and unrealistic value. 19 Am J2d Corp § 764.

bony. Adjective: Thin; having bones with prominent protrusions; having many bones, as applied to fish in reference to serving them as food. Noun: Refuse, especially refuse from a mine.

boodle. Money given or received as a bribe. 33 Am J1st L & S § 22; money or property gained in an illegal enterprise, theft, or fraudulent scheme. Money fraudulently obtained in public service; especially, money given to or received by officials in bribery, or gained by collusive contracts, appointments, etc.; by extension, gain from public cheating of any kind; often used attributively. Boehmer v Detroit Free Press, 94 Mich 7.

book. A generic term inclusive of a bound volume, even a very loosely bound volume, sometimes sheets held together by a ring or loop of wire, of such a variety of content as to embrace a body of blank pages on the one hand or the world's greatest literary masterpiece on the other. Any species of publication which an author selects to embody his literary product and for which he seeks the protection of a copyright. 18 Am J2d Copyr § 38. In the ancient concept, a term including any volume, whether of paper, of parchment, or of some other material.

book account. An account based upon transactions creating a debtor and creditor relation, evidenced by entries made in a book regularly kept and used for that purpose. Plunkett-Jarrell Grocery Co. v Terry, 222 Ark 784, 263 SW2d 229, 44 ALR2d 917.
See **book of account.**

book-case. A set of shelves for books.

book cases. Published reports of cases which have been decided.

book debt. A common-law form of action to recover for such items as are the proper subjects of book charge, that is, proper for entry or charge in a book of account. Newton v Higgins, 2 Vt 366, 369.
See **book of account.**

booked. See **booking.**

booker. See **bookmaker; booking agency; motion picture booker.**

book hoard (buk hord). A place where books or written instruments were kept.

bookie. See **bookmaker.**

booking. Entering an event or a transaction in a book; a police-station term for the entry of an arrest and the charge for which the arrest was made; the engagement of talent for a theater, a night club or other place of entertainment. The system or practice of steamship companies in making specific engagements with shippers for a reservation of space for commodities to be shipped on a particular vessel in advance of its sailing day. Any certain commodity for which space has been thus arranged is referred to as "booked." Ocean Co. v Savannah Locomotive S.S. Works & Supply Co. 131 Ga 831, 63 SE 577.
See **freight booking.**

booking agency. An agency, otherwise known as a theatrical agency, which represents actors, or other entertainers, and lecturers, in obtaining engagements for them.

booking contract. A contract for the employment of an actor or other entertainer. Hart v B. F. Keith Vaudeville Exchange (CA2 NY) 12 F2d 341.

bookkeeper. See **bookkeeping; bookmaking.**

bookkeeping. Keeping the accounts of an individual or a business, in other words, accounting. 1 Am J2d Accts § 2. The art of recording, in a systematic manner, the transactions of merchants, traders and other persons engaged in pursuits connected with money; the art of keeping accounts. In the commercial world, bookkeeping is a distinct profession requiring peculiar adaptation and thorough training. Western Assur. Co. v Altheimer, 58 Ark 565, 573.

book-land (bŭk′land). Land which was held by deed under certain rents and free services, otherwise known as charterland, and which, in effect, did not differ from the free socage-lands. See 2 Bl Comm 90.

bookmaker. A binder of books; a person who is engaged in bookmaking. Anno: 153 ALR 464.
See **bookmaking.**

bookmaking. The receiving from several persons of wagers on the same sporting event, more often than not a horse race, the odds having been calculated beforehand by the bookmaker, and the total sum received by way of the wagers to be given to the winner, subject to a deduction of the bookmaker's commission. Anno: 96 L Ed 317.

Tickets are given the persons who make the wagers in evidence of their selections and of their interest in the total sum or pool received from all persons betting on the particular event, according to whether they win or lose. 24 Am J1st Gaming § 24. Bookmaking is a form of gambling and, as such, illegal under the statutes of most jurisdictions, except as legalized in reference to particular events, such as horse racing and dog racing.

book-oath (bŭk ōth). An oath made by swearing on the Bible.

book of account. Otherwise known as a shop-book; a book of original entry of transactions with customers in a store or shop, which is admissible in evidence in an action by the storekeeper or shopkeeper to recover on the account of a customer, where properly authenticated as to the person or persons who made the entries, the time, the occasion, and accuracy of the entries. 30 Am J2d Ev § 918.

See **book of original entry; journal; shop-book rule; waste-book.**

book of acts. The records of a surrogate court.

book of adjournal. (Scotch.) The book of the records of the court of justiciary.

Book of Fiefs or Feuds. A compilation of the feudal law made in Lombardy in the 12th century.
See **liber feudorum.**

book of original entry. The first permanent record of a transaction made by a shopkeeper or storekeeper, as a creditor of a customer, in the usual course of business and within a reasonably short time after the transaction itself, although the items may have been first entered as a temporary assistance to the memory upon some slate, book, paper, or other substance; it is of no consequence what the latter material was, or the size or shape, so long as the notation thereon was a mere minute, not intended to be preserved as evidence, but to be used in the preparation of a book of account to be preserved. 30 Am J2d Ev § 941.

An original entry within rule admitting in evidence books of account consisting of such entries must have been made in the regular course of business; must, as a rule, have been a part of the series; must be fairly contemporaneous with the items entered; and must be the first permanent record of a transaction recorded. Anno: 17 ALR2d 239.

book of rates. A list of duties and tariffs authorized by the English Parliament.

book of responses. An account book kept by the director of the Scotch exchequer.

Book of The Assizes. The fourth volume of decisions reported in the reign of Edward the Third.

books of account. See **book of account.**

books of exact science. A term in the law of evidence for books admitted in evidence, subject to authentication, as publications containing statements of ascertained scientific facts rather than of opinions, or which, by long use in the practical affairs of life, have come to be accepted as standard and unvarying authority in determining the acts of persons who use them, eg. mortality tables, almanacs, tables of weights and measures, and similar compilations. 29 Am J2d Ev § 889.

book value. A value, which, in its application to corporate stock, is theoretical only, unless there is stated with it the accounting procedure and formula by which it is determined. Anno: 51 ALR2d 606. By a mere rule of thumb, the book value of corporate stock is the figure obtained upon dividing the amount of the difference between assets and liabilities by the total number of outstanding shares, in other words, the value shown by the balance sheets of the company. Early v Moor, 249 Mass 223, 144 NE 108; 33 ALR 362. The term contemplates a theoretical value resulting from depreciation or appreciation as computed upon an originally determined base, which is supplied by some form of stipulation or acquiescence or through acceptance of particular accounting procedures previously applied. 18 Am J2d Corp § 219.

The book value of a partner's interest is the money value of that interest arrived at by taking the total value of the assets of the partnership, as shown on the general ledger and other books of account, and deducting therefrom the total liabilities of the partnership. Rubel v Rubel, 221 Miss 848, 75 So 2d 59, 47 ALR2d 1410.

An expression used in the automobile used car market, meaning an established, arbitrary value for every make, model, and year. 8 Am J2d Auto § 1042.

book warranty. A warranty in an insurance policy covering a stock of goods and merchandise against loss by fire, windstorm, burglary, or theft, that the insured shall make and keep inventories and books of account, which shall be kept in a fireproof safe or other secure place, and that the insured shall, upon demand, produce such books and inventories for the inspection of the insurer. 29A Am J Rev ed Ins § 939. Such a provision is often referred to as an iron safe clause. Anno: 33 ALR2d 619; 29A Am J Rev ed Ins § 939.

boom. A structure erected in a stream or river for the purpose of catching and collecting logs floating down stream and forming an artificial harbor for

boomage. A charge imposed by the proprietor of a canal for the use of a terminal as an anchorage. Watts v Savannah & O. Canal Co. 64 Ga 88; a charge made by a booming company for collecting and distributing logs which have accumulated at its boom. 34 Am J1st Logs § 89.

the logs, of which harbor one side is furnished ordinarily by the natural bank of the stream, and the other is provided by piers and the timber or other obstruction to the passage of logs which connect the piers together. 34 Am J1st Logs § 78.

boom company. A company formed for the purpose of constructing and maintaining booms and for running, driving, booming, and rafting logs. Watts v Tittabawassee Boom Co. 52 Mich 203, 206.

boom value. Speculative or fanciful value, as distinguished from reasonable market, salable value. Blincoe v Choctaw, Oklahoma & Western Railroad Co. 16 Okla 286, 83 P 903.

boon days (bön). Days appointed for base services of copyhold tenants.

boosted fire. A fire rendered impossible of extinguishment because of inflammables or combustibles stored or kept in the building. Anderson v Miller, 96 Tenn 35, 33 SW 615.

boot (böt). A covering for the foot; a patch for an automobile tire. Something paid by one of the parties to a trade or exchange to the other.

bootblacking stand. A place for obtaining a shoeshine, which, according to some but not all authority, is a place of public accommodation. 15 Am J2d Civ R § 20.

booth. A small structure, usually for occupancy by one or two persons, open at one end, except for railing, bar, or counter, in use for the most part in selling admission tickets or soliciting business at exhibitions, fairs, markets, games, etc. Also, a partial enclosure in a lobby of a place of entertainment for the sale of tickets. Also, a house or shed built of boards or other slight materials for temporary occupation. People v Hagen, 60 Hun 577, 14 NYS 233.

boothage (bö'thāj). Money paid for the privilege of maintaining a market booth or stall.

booting-corn (bö'ting-kôrn). Rent paid in corn.

bootlegger. One who sells alcoholic beverages in violation of law; one who keeps alcoholic beverages for the purpose of making sales in violation of law. State v Vanderpool, 195 Iowa 43, 44, 191 NW 357.

bootleg whisky. Whisky manufactured, sold, or kept for sale, in violation of law. State v Tillery, 243 NC 706, 92 SE 2d 65.

bootstrap sale. A tax-saving device whereby the seller in effect converts ordinary income from his business into capital gain from the sale of corporate stock. Commissioner v Brown, 380 US 563, 14 L Ed 2d 75, 85 S Ct 1162.

booty (bö'ti). Goods captured in war on land by land forces. Property taken by theft, robbery, or larceny. See **boodle.**

booze. Verb: To drink heavily of alcoholic beverages. Noun: Alcoholic beverages.

bord (bôrd). (Saxon.) A dwelling house; a cottage.

bordage (bôr'dāj). A feudal tenure under the Norman kings by which the tenant held his cot in return for menial service. Such a tenant was called a bordar.

bordagium (bor-dā'gi-um). Bordage.

bordar (bôr'dar). See **bordage.**

bordaria (bor-dā'ri-a). A cottage.

bordarii (bor-dā'ri-ī). Tenants in bordage; bordars; cottagers.

bord-brigch (bord-brīk'). Same as **borghbrech.**

border-crossing. An identification card given to a Canadian crossing the border into the United States. 8 USC § 1303(a).

bordereau (bôr-dro'). (French.) A note or memorandum; a list of documents or contracts more or less in detail. An account.

border warrant (bôr'dėr wor"ạnt). (Scotch.) A warrant for the arrest of a debtor on the English side of the border between England and Scotland.

bord-halfpenny. Money paid for the liberty of setting up and maintaining a market stall at fairs and markets.

bord-land. Land held by a tenant in bordage.

bordlode (bord'lōd). Rent service rendered by bordarii.

bord-service (bôrd'sėr"vis). Bordage.

borel (bur'el). Pertaining to the laity.

borel folk. Laymen, as distinguished from the clergy; country people.

borg (borg). Same as **borgh.**

borgesmon (borg'es-mon). (Saxon.) The head of a family.

borgh (borg). A suretyship; a pledge; a surety.

borghbrech (borgbreech). Pledge-breach; the breach of a pledge or suretyship; the violation of the pledge given by every inhabitant of a tithing to keep the peace.

born. Brought forth, delivered, or expelled from the womb; contrasted with adopted within the meaning of provisions in wills intended to confine legacies and devices to relatives by blood. 57 Am J1st Wills § 1174.
See **birth.**

born alive. Completely delivered from the womb, and breathing or attempting to breath, without reference to the fact that the child is dead before the umbilical cord is severed. Goff v Anderson, 91 Ky 303, 15 SW 866. Some authority insists that "not to have breathed is not to have lived." State v Winthrop, 43 Iowa 519.

born dead. See **dead-born.**

born deaf, dumb and blind. See **deaf, dumb and blind.**

borne. Carried.

born out of wedlock. Born to an unmarried female; born to a married female but begotten during the continuance of the marriage status by one other than her husband. State v Coliton, 73 ND 582, 17 NW2d 546, 156 ALR 1403. Anno: 156 ALR 1411.

borough. In the American sense of the term, a unit of a large city, as the borough of Brooklyn in New York City; an incorporated town or township with powers of self-government, sometimes including a village within its limits. In England, there is the additional meaning of a town which sends a member to Parliament. Atherton v Essex Junction, 83 Vt 218, 74 A 1118.
See **burgess; rotten boroughs.**

borough council. The managing board elected by the voters of the borough.

borough courts (bur'ō kortz). Courts of limited jurisdiction held within boroughs by prescription, by charter or by act of parliament. See 3 Bl Comm 81.

borough-English (bur'ō-ing'glish). A custom attached to burgage tenure whereby the youngest and not the eldest son succeeded to the tenement on the death of his father. It was so named in contradistinction to the Norman rule of primogeniture.

borough-head. The head man or chief of an English borough, tithing or frank-pledge.

borough-holder (bur'ō-hōl''dėr). Same as **borough-head.**

borough reeve (bur'ō rēv). The governor of a borough.

borough sessions (bur'ō sesh''ǫnz). The sessions of a borough court.

borrow. To obtain upon loan from the owner or other person having the right of disposition; to engage the use of money by contract. State ex rel. Kimball v School Dist. 13 Neb 82, 88.
The renewal of an existing indebtedness is not "borrowing money" or "effecting a loan." State v Love, 170 Miss 666, 150 So 196, 90 ALR 506.
See **loan.**

borrowe. (Scotch.) A pledge.

borrower. One who borrows.
See **usury.**

borrowing member. A member of a building and loan association who has borrowed from the association. 13 Am J2d B & L Assoc § 19.

borrowing money. See **borrow; borrower; loan.**

borrowings. A local banking term for overdrafts.

borrow pit. A term familiar in cases pertaining to the construction of highways and railroads, meaning land used for excavation to obtain dirt for making fills. Arkansas Valley & Western Railway Co. v Witt, 19 Okla 262, 91 P 897. Often it is necessary to condemn land in order to obtain a borrow pit.

borsholder (bôrs'hōl-dėr). Same as **borough-head.**

boscage (bos'kāj). Tree leaves and bushes used as cattle feed.

boscaria (bos-kā'ri-a). Cattle-sheds.

boscus (bos'kus). Growing wood.

bosom of the country. See **in the bosom of the country.**

bosom of the court. See **breast of the court.**

botable waters. Waters that are of common passage as highways for business or pleasure. 56 Am J1st Wat § 3.

bote (bōt). Estovers; compensation; satisfaction.

boteless (bōt'les). Without a remedy; without relief.

botellaria (bo-tel-lā'ri-a). A wine or liquor cellar.

both. The two of them, whether persons or things; taking two together; as well.

botha (bō'tha). A market stall or booth.

bothagium (bo-thā'gi-um). Same as **boothage.**

both legal and equitable. A phrase elaborating the sole and unconditional ownership clause of a fire insurance policy, meaning, according to some authorities, a vested legal, as well as an equitable, title, but, according to other authorities, no more than an equitable title with the right to the conveyance of the legal title. 29A Am J Rev ed Ins § 791.

bothna. (Scotch.) A pasture.

both-to-blame. The admiralty doctrine whereby the full burden of losses sustained by both ships in a collision should be shared equally. 2 Am J2d Adm § 187.
See **contributory negligence.**

botiler of the king (bŭt'lẽr). A king's officer whose duty it was to select one cask before the mast and one behind it from every ship freighted with wine which was to be sold.

boting corn (bō'ting korn). Same as **booting corn.**

botless. Same as **boteless.**

bottled gas. Gas for household use, furnished, not in the conventional manner by mains and service pipes but by supplying the product in containers, called bottles, which have outlets for connection with the pipes of the house.
See **liquid gas.**

bottom (bot'um). The national registry of a vessel.

bottomage. Same as **bottomry.**

bottom land. Land in the flood plain of a river; land which is overflown by a river unless protected by flood control constructions.

bottomry. A contract, usually executed in a foreign port by the master of a vessel, for repayment of advances made to supply the necessities of the ship, together with such interest as may be agreed upon, the performance whereof is secured by a pledge of the keel or bottom of the ship, which, of course, is actually a pledge of the ship itself, but under the characteristic provision that payment of principal and interest are at the risk of the lender during the voyage, so that repayment depends upon its successful termination. 48 Am J1st Ship § 593.

bottomry bond. An instrument which sets forth a contract of bottomry.
See **bottomry bond.**

bottomry lien. The lien upon a vessel created by a bottomry bond. See 48 Am J1st Ship § 605.

bottoms. Keels or the parts of vessels below water; a term of the shipping business, used at times for freighters; for instance, the expression, "50 bottoms available," meaning 50 ships in port and ready to take on cargo; a slang term used by persons who deal in forged notes to denote paper for making the notes. Rex v Dade (Eng) 1 Moody CC 307.

botulism. A form of food poisoning which results from imperfect canning or preserving.

bouche (bōsh). A feudal allowance for food supplies during active military service; mouth.

bouche of court. The king's allowance to his knights and personal servants for food supply during active military service.

bought. Purchased, either for cash or upon terms of credit.

bought and sold notes. Two memoranda of a transaction by a broker, one going to the purchaser and the other to the seller, the former being the bought note and the latter the sold note.

boulder. A rock, as known to geologists, but not necessarily to all persons, so that where the term appears in a contract, it is to be construed with the entire context, perhaps contrary to geology.

Chicago v Duffy, 117 Ill App 261, affd 218 Ill 242, 75 NE 912.

Boulder Canyon Project Act. The federal statute providing for the construction of the Boulder Dam, otherwise known as the President Hoover Dam, in the canyon of the Colorado River known as Boulder Canyon. 43 USC § 617.

boulevard. A street or highway more elaborate than the ordinary highway or street in respect both of width, style, and manner of construction. 25 Am J Rev ed High § 6. It may be given a parklike appearance by reserving spaces at the sides or center for shade trees, flowers, seats, and the like, and be set apart for pleasure driving rather than the general purposes of traffic. Haller Sign Works v Physical Culture Training School, 249 Ill 436, 94 NE 920.

boulter (bōl'tėr). Same as **bulter**.

bouncer. A man, often an ex-pugilist, employed in a restaurant or other place of public entertainment to maintain order and eject riotous or quarrelsome persons.

bouncing check. See **bogus check**.

bound (bound). Noun: A **boundary**.
 In an indorser's waiver of protest of a note, in which he stipulates to be bound as if protest had been made, the word bound has been held to amount to a waiver of both demand and notice, since otherwise the stipulation would be without effect. Union Bank v Hyde (US) 6 Wheat 572, 5 L Ed 333.
 Adjective: Tied, fastened securely to something else; deprived of movement by cord or fetters; under contract, obligated.

boundary. The marking or dividing line between two parcels of real estate. 12 Am J2d Bound § 1.

boundary action or suit. An action at law or a suit in equity, sometimes a special statutory proceeding, for the determination of a boundary as between adjoining landowners. 12 Am J2d Bound § 91.

boundary point. The extremity of a boundary line, being indicated by a monument or marker, a course or a distance as it appears on a map or plat, the adjoining land, or by a combination of such things. 12 Am J2d Bound § 1.

boundary trees. Trees, standing on the boundary between adjoining tracts of land in different ownership, so that the boundary line passes through them. The trees are the common property of the proprietors of the adjoining tracts as tenants in common. 1 Am J2d Adj L § 22.
See **bounded tree**.

boundary waters. Rivers, lakes, or other bodies of water which delimit a nation, state, or political subdivision.

bound-bailiff (bound'bā"lif). Also known as hound-bailiff,—a deputy sheriff who was under bond for the faithful performance of his duties and was employed only on account of his adroitness and dexterity in hunting. 1 Bl Comm 345.

bounded by a highway. A designation in the description of a boundary that will carry title to the center of the highway, in the absence of other words in the conveyance which indicates a contrary intent. 12 Am J2d Bound § 51.

bounded tree (boun'ded). A tree marking a corner of a tract of land.
See **boundary trees**.

bounden. Same as **bound**.

bounders. Visible marks showing courses and distances in a land survey; rude, ill-mannered, or unprincipled persons.

bounds. Boundaries.
See **metes and bounds**.

bounty. In common parlance, a gift or favor bestowed as an expression of liberality or kindliness; in a narrower and more precise legal sense, it is money paid, or a premium offered, to encourage or promote an object, or to procure a particular act or thing to be done. 12 Am J2d Bount § 1; an amount offered for services performed or to be performed. 46 Am J1st Rew § 2; a payment made to induce enlistments in the armed forces or as a reward for industrial activities in the national defense. 12 Am J2d Bount § 2.

bounty lands. Lands donated by the government as a bounty.

Bounty of Queen Anne. A fund provided by statute to aid the smaller church livings.

bourbon (bör'bon). Adjective: Reactionary. Noun: Whisky made from corn.

Bourdon tube (bour'don tūb). A well-known pressure-responsive device, commonly used in pressure gauges of steam boilers. James P. Marsh Corp. v United States Gauge Co. (DC Ill) 42 F Supp 998.

bourg (börg). A fortified town.

bourgeois (bör-zhwa'). An inhabitant of a town; a burgess; one of a middle class, usually having at least some property of value. Adjective: Smug; conservative.

bourgeoisie (bör-zhwa-zē'). Plural of **bourgeois**.

bourse (börs). A stock exchange.

boussole. (French). A compass for use in navigation.

bout (bout). A butt; an end; an end boundary; a contest, such as a boxing bout.

bouter (bu-tê'). To put or place.

bouter avant (bu-tê' a-vân'). To place or put before; to exhibit.

bouts et cotes (bout a kôt). Butts and bounds; metes and bounds; end and side boundaries.

bouwerye (bow'er-y). (Dutch.) A farm.

bouwmeester (bouw-mees-ter). (Dutch.) A farmer.

bovarius (bo-vā'ri-us). An ox-team driver.

bovata terrae (bō-vā'ta ter'rē). A parcel of land which could be tilled by one ox.

bovettus (bo-vet'tus). A young steer.

bovicula (bo-vi'ku-la). A heifer.

Bovill's Act. An English statute (1865) whereby one was not liable as a partner simply because he shared in the profits of the business; an English statute regulating procedure in petitions of right.

bovine. Pertaining to the cow or ox; patient, slow, and stupid.

bow-bearer (bō'bär"ėr). A kind of forest police with the duty of enforcing the forest laws.

bowery. Same as **bouwerye**.

bowie-knife (bō'ę̄-nīf). A knife with a strong blade from ten to fifteen inches long, double edged near the point; used as a hunting knife and formerly as a weapon in the southwestern part of the United

States. Phoenix v State, 103 Tex Crim 441, 444, 281 SW 567; a deadly weapon. 56 Am J1st Weap § 3.

bowling alley. A lane, having a smooth, wooden floor, used in the game of bowling, pins being set up at one end and the player, called a bowler, throwing a heavy ball, with underhand motion, from the other end, his purpose being to strike down the pins or as many of them as possible; a building having bowling alleys in it. Williams v Vincent, 70 Kan 595, 79 P 121.

bow window (bō' win'dō). See **bay window**.

bowyers (bō'yėrs). Makers of archery supplies.

box. See **ballot-box; jury box**.

box car (boks' kär). A railroad freight car which is inclosed. State v Green, 15 Mont 424, 39 P 322.

boxed weight. A mercantile term, of special significance in the meat business, meaning weight after the necessary packaging.

boxing. A sport, often called fighting, in which the participants, wearing so-called boxing gloves, which are padded, seek to deliver blows by the hand, left or right, to the face and the upper part of the torso of his opponent. The sport is both amateur and professional.

boxing match (bok'sing mach). A boxing contest, a mere exhibition of skill in sparring with gloves, not calculated to do great bodily injury. State v Olympic Club, 46 La Ann 935, 15 So 190.

box-step. A step on a railroad passenger car by which a passenger moves from the station platform to the vestibule of the car or vice versa.

box strap. A strip of leather, plastic, or thin metal used to reinforce the ends, sometimes the tops and bottoms, of shipping cases made of wood or card board.

boy (boi). A male under the age of puberty. Central of Georgia Railroad Co. v Robins, 209 Ala 6, 95 So 367, 36 ALR 10, 13.

boycott. A species of ostracism, a combination in refusing to have business dealings with another until he removes or ameliorates conditions deemed inimical to the members of the combination, or some of them, or grants concessions which are deemed to make for the removal or amelioration of such conditions. 31 Am J Rev ed Lab § 461. The word is derived from the name of Captain Boycott who, in 1880, as an Irish land agent gave offense to the populace and was treated to this sort of social interdiction. As applied to labor unions, a boycott is an attempt, by arousing a fear of loss, to coerce others, against their will, to withhold, from one denominated "unfriendly to labor," their beneficial business intercourse. 31 Am J Rev ed Lab § 461.

As defined above, the influence brought is persuasion by causing fear of loss of business; at times, boycotts have been accompanied by intimidation and threats causing fear of bodily injury. Gray v Building Trades Council, 91 Minn 171, 97 NW 663.

See **primary boycott; secondary boycott**.

boys (boiz). Males under the age of puberty; a wood.

Boy Scouts. A worldwide organization for training in leadership, patriotism, and good citizenship, which qualifies easily as having a charitable purpose. 15 Am J2d Char § 68.

bozero (bo-the'rho). (Spanish.) An advocate.

bozo (bō'zō). A slang term applied to a man in derision or contempt, especially to a strikebreaker in a labor dispute; occasionally used without rancor in speaking familiarly and humorously to persons on one's own level. State v Christie, 97 Vt 461, 123 A 849, 34 ALR 577, 579.

b.p. Abbreviation for **boiling point**.

B. P. Abbreviation for **Bachelor of Philosophy** and for **Bachelor of Pharmacy**.

B/P. Abbreviation for **bills payable**.

B. P. O. E. Abbreviation for the **Benevolent and Protective Order of Elks**.

B.R. Abbreviation for **bills receivable**; an abbreviation of "bancus regis" and also "bancus reginae,"—king's bench and queen's bench. K. B. and Q. B. are also used.

brabant (bra-bant'). An English coin current in the thirteenth century.

brace de la mer (brās). An arm of the sea.

bracelets (bras'lets). Undersized hounds or beagles.

bracery (brā'se-ri). The name of an offense created by the statute 32 of Henry the Eighth directed against the evil of buying and selling of titles and pretended rights of persons not being in possession. Webb v Camp, 26 Ga 354, 357; Cain v Monroe, 23 Ga 82, 94.

See **embracery**.

bracetus (bra-sē'tus). A hound.

brachium maris (brā'ki-um ma'ris). An arm of the sea.

bracket. Marks used to set off a parenthetical clause or expression.

See **parenthesis; tax bracket**.

Bradlaugh's Case. A celebrated case involving the form of oath required of members of the English house of commons.

Brahmin. A Hindu priest; an ultra-conservative person; a snob.

brain. The seat of physical control of the body and also of intelligence; a slang term applied by students to a superior student.

See **water on the brain**.

brake. A mechanical device for stopping or slowing a vehicle in motion or a moving part of a machine.

braking distance. The distance traveled by a motor vehicle from the time that brake pressure is applied until the vehicle comes to a full stop.

For a chart of braking distance in terms of percentages of braking efficiency with formulas and separate chart of reaction time distance, see Am J2d Desk Book, Document 175.

branch. A line of descent from a common ancestor; one of the divisions of a legislative body; a creek or small stream tributary to a larger stream or river; a subordinate part.

A will establishing a trust and providing "If, at the time of the termination of said trust, any of the three branches of my family as represented by my three children, should have become extinct, then the branches of my family represented by issue or descendants shall take the said estate in equal proportions" will be interpreted to mean direct branches or surviving issue or descendants of his children, rather than collateral branches not mentioned in the will, where such provision appears to have been inserted merely to amplify and reaffirm such an intention clearly disclosed by prior privisions. Dennis v Omaha Nat. Bank, 153 Neb 865, 46 NW2d 606, 27 ALR2d 674.

branch bank. A bank established by another bank, known as the principal or main bank, at a location in a city, village, or town other than that in which the main bank is located, for transacting a banking business; sometimes to be regarded as a separate institution, at other times as an agent of the main bank. 10 Am J2d Bks § 326. There is a distinction between a branch bank and an additional office of a bank for the receipt of deposits and the payment of checks. Marvin v Kentucky Title & Trust Co. 218 Ky 135, 291 SW 17, 50 ALR 1337.

branch postoffice. A place established, usually in a store or other place of business, for the transaction of postal business or a part of the functions of a postoffice.

The term includes every place within such a branch office where letters are kept in the regular course of business, for reception, stamping, assorting, or delivery. Goode v United States, 159 US 663, 671, 40 L Ed 297, 301, 16 S Ct 136.

branch railroad. See **lateral.**

brand. Noun: A kind of commodity, usually designated by name given by the producer, as "twenty mule team borax;" an identifying label on merchandise; a mark on the hide of a cow or steer made with a hot iron; a stick on fire at one end, carried for the purpose of setting fire. Verb: To mark with a brand; to bring a person into disgrace by speech or writing. See **label.**

branding. See **brand.**

branding-helmet. A helmet used for branding on the cheek a person who pleaded benefit of clergy as a defense in a criminal prosecution.

brandy. A spirituous and intoxicating liquor, generally distilled from wine, although the name is sometimes given to distillations from other liquors. 30 Am J Rev ed Intox L § 12.

brank (brangk). Buckwheat was so called in Essex.

branks (brangks). A bridle which was used as a punishment for a common scold.

brasiator (bra-si-ā′tor). A brewer.

brasium (bra′si-um). Malt.

brass knuckles. A weapon used for offense and defense, worn upon the hand to strike with as if striking with the fist. When first known and used, the weapon was commonly made of brass, but it is now made of steel, platinum or other heavy metal, as well as of brass, but it retains the name of brass knuckles, no matter of what material it is made. Harris v State, 22 Tex App 677, 38 SW 477.

brawl (brâl). A noisy quarrel.

brawling (brâ′ling). The offense of quarreling noisily in or about a church, which was punished under a statute of Edw. VI.

breach. A break; a breaking; a violation; the violation of an obligation, engagement or duty; a hernia.

breach of arrestment. (Scotch.) The unlawful delivery of arrested or seized goods to the debtor.

breach of close. A trespass, that is, wrongful entry on the soil of another.

breach of contract. A failure without legal excuse to perform any promise which forms a whole or a part of a contract, including the refusal of a party to recognize the existence of the contract or the doing of something inconsistent with its existence. National City Bank v Erskine & Sons, 158 Ohio St 450, 49 Ohio Ops 395, 110 NE2d 598; a nonperformance of any contractual duty of immediate performance; the breach may be total or partial, and may take place by failure to perform acts promised, by prevention, or hindrance, or by repudiation. Restatement, Contracts § 312.

breach of covenant. The violation of a covenant by an act or omission, depending upon whether the duty prescribed by the covenant is one of action or refraining from an act.

breach of duty. The failure or omission to do that which a person is bound by law to do, or the doing of it in an unlawful manner.

See **breach of contract; breach of covenant; negligence.**

breach of peace. Such a violation of the public order as amounts to a disturbance of the public tranquility, by act or conduct either directly having this effect, or by inciting or tending to incite such a disturbance of the public tranquility. 12 Am J2d Breach P § 4.

breach of pound. The breaking of a pound by the owner of goods or animals placed in the pound under a warrant of distraint and the removal or release by him of such goods or animals from the pound.

breach of prison or jail. See **prison breaking; jail breaking.**

breach of privilege. An excess or abuse of the privilege of a member of the legislature, as determined by the legislature; excess or abuse of the privilege of communication, whereby the privilege is lost and liability for defamation ensues, as by violent and intemperate language. 33 Am J1st L & S § 186.

breach of promise. Literally the failure to perform a promise, but known to the law and also to laymen as breach of promise of marriage. 12 Am J2d Breach P § 1.

breach of trust. A term susceptible of wide application, comprehending derelictions by persons in all confidential and fiduciary relationships, but applicable particularly to a violation of duty by a trustee, whether it be willful or fraudulent, occurring by negligence, or arising from mere oversight or forgetfulness. 54 Am J1st Trusts § 300.

breach of warranty. The violation of an express or implied contract of warranty.

See **breach of covenant.**

breachy animal. A colloquial term for a domestic animal in the habit of escaping from the place of confinement, particularly by breaking through or jumping over a fence.

bread. The staff of life, baked from flour, usually wheat flour, but may be flour from almost any food grain.

bread and cheese. Food which is not to be abhorred by any means, but which has little significance in the law beyond its use in the earlier period of English history as a morsel of execration.

bread and water. A diet constituting a special condition of imprisonment for crime. 21 Am J2d Crim L § 615.

break (brāk). To separate; to divide; to violate; a breach; a breaking.

As applied to machinery, in a limited sense, the

word signifies a separation into parts or fragments as a result of stress or force. In a broader sense, it indicates a weakness, impairment, or destruction of parts, however caused. American Locomotive Co. v National Wholesale Grocery Co. 226 Mass 314, 115 NE 404.

breakage. An item of loss or damages, as breakage in transit; an inevitable loss over a period of time in some lines of business, such as hotels, restaurants, electric companies, etc. As the word is used in a bill of lading exempting the carrier for loss by breaking, it refers to the breakage of goods, wares, and merchandise, other than living animals, and does not include the breaking of a horse's leg. Coupland v Housatonic Railroad Co. 61 Conn 531, 23 A 870.

As the term is used in connection with pari-mutuel betting, it means the odd cents of all redistributions exceeding a sum equal to the next lowest multiple of five. Wise v Delaware Steeplechase & Race Asso. 28 Del Ch 532, 45 A2d 547, 165 ALR 830.

See **broken.**

breakdown. A cogent analysis; a deterioration in the health of a person amounting to a collapse; a machine out of condition so as to be inoperable.

See **breakdown clause.**

breakdown clause. A clause in a charter party, providing for a deduction from the hire of the vessel for delay and expense caused by accidents or eventualities named in such clause; such as deficiency of men or stores, fire, breaking down of hull, machinery, detention by accidents to cargo, etc., Dampskibs Aktieselskabet Jeannette Skinner v Munson Steamship Line (CA2 NY) 20 F2d 345; a term for a condition in the substituted automobile provision of an automobile liability policy, whereunder, in order for the provision to apply, it must appear that the vehicle described in the policy had been withdrawn from normal use because of its "breakdown". Anno: 34 ALR2d 949.

breakdown service. The maintenance of a hook-up between a public utility furnishing electricity and a manufacturing plant for service only in the emergency which results when the power plant of the manufacturing plant fails.

breakers. Machinery employed in breaking chunks of coal to small pieces; the waves of lake or sea as they come upon rock or shore with such force as to be broken in part into foam.

breaking. A breakage; the removal of any protection against intrusion for the purpose of effecting an unlawful entry; a substantial and forcible act within the meaning of the offense of burglary, 13 Am J2d Burg § 8, although pushing open a door entirely closed will suffice. Anno: 23 ALR 112. What would be a breaking in burglary, it has been held, is equally a breaking by the sheriff to serve process and the right even to lift a door latch has been denied. Other cases hold that the door may be opened in the ordinary or usual manner, as by lifting the latch, turning the knob or turning a key left in the lock. See 42 Am J1st Proc § 44.

See **constructive breaking; forcibly; housebreaking; jail breaking; prison breaking.**

breaking a case. The informal expressions of opinion between judges prior to their formal decision of the case before them; detectives, police, and other law enforcement officers coming to the point of solving the question of who committed a particular crime.

breaking a close. A trespass upon real estate.

breaking and entry. Elements of the offense of burglary. 13 Am J2d Burgl §§ 8 et seq. Some courts take the view that the use of the conjunctive "or" in a statute eliminates the necessity for both a breaking and an entering. Others, however, take the view that the word "or" must be read as the equivalent of "and", thus requiring both a breaking and an entering to constitute burglary. Anno: 23 ALR 288, 290.

See **breaking; entry.**

breaking a will. Rendering a judgment against the validity of a will upon a contest thereof.

breaking bulk. The division or separation of the contents of a package or container. Lord Coke says, "If a bale or pack of merchandise be delivered to carry to one at a certain place, and he goeth away with the whole pack, this is no felony; but if he open the pack and take anything out animo furandi, this is larceny." State v Fairclough, 29 Conn 47. The reasons given in the cases for this settled doctrine of the common law are not satisfactory nor in accord and Kelyng at page 83 of his reports observes, possibly with sly humor: "But I marvel at the case put, 13 Edw. IV, 9 (1473): That if a carrier have a tun of wine delivered to him to carry to such a place, and he never carry it, but sell it all, this is no felony, but if he draw part of it out above the value of twelvepence, this is felony. I do not see why the disposing of the whole should not be felony also." Such refinements in the offense of larceny disappear with the enactment of statutes which provide that conversion of the bailed property by the bailee is larceny. 32 Am J1st Larc § 32.

breaking ground. The beginning of a voyage by a vessel. See 48 Am J1st Ship § 425; the commencement of work upon a building or other structure; the act of taking a shovelful of dirt from the ground, symbolizing the commencement of work upon a building, in the construction of which, the public is interested, such as a church, a postoffice, a memorial building, a courthouse, etc.

breaking land. Plowing virgin soil. Not an improvement for the purposes of a mechanic's lien. Brown v Wyman, 56 Iowa 452, 9 NW 344.

breaking of arrestment. Same as **breach of arrestment.**

breaking of breakable goods and machines. See **breakage; breakdown; breakdown clause.**

breaking out. A rash on the skin; criminal offense in breaking out of a building after entry with intent to commit a felony. 13 Am J2d Burgl. § 14.

See **prison breaking; jail breaking.**

breaking point. Colloquially, an emotional state; technically, the Mississippi River which marks a material line in the establishment of joint rates for carriers. Beaumont, S. L. & W. R. Co. v United States, 282 US 74, 75 L Ed 221, 51 S Ct 1.

breaking prison or jail. See **prison breaking; jail breaking.**

break or enter.
See **breaking and entering.**

breast of the court (brest). The judgment or mind of the court. A decision in a case that has been tried and submitted to the court is in the breast or bosom of the court until it is handed down.

breathing test. Part of a physical examination sometimes sought to be required of a plaintiff in a personal injury action. 23 Am J2d Dep § 216.

breath test. A test of the alcoholic content of the breath, employed in determining intoxication or degree of intoxication of a motor vehicle driver. 7 Am J2d Auto § 259.

brebis. Sheep; flock of sheep.

bredwite (bred'wit). (Saxon.) An amercement, fine, or penalty.

brehon (bre'hon). (Irish.) A judge.

brehon law (bre'hon). An old system of Irish law.

brenagium (bre-nā'ji-um). Same as **brennage.**

brennage (bren'ąj). A kind of land tenure by the service of furnishing bran for the lord's hounds.

brephotrophi (bre-pho-trō'phī). (Roman law.) Caretakers of foundling asylums.

brethren. An older word for brothers, used presently in speaking of fellow members of a religious society or fraternal order.

brethwalda (bret'wol-dą). An Anglo-Saxon king.

Bretts and Scotts. See **Laws of the Bretts and Scotts.**

breva (brē'va). Same as **breve.**

breve (brēv). A writ; a brief.
See **brief; writ.**

breve de recto (bre've de rek'tō). A writ of right.

breve domini regis non currit (brē've do'mi-nī rē'jis non kur'rit). The king's writ does not run.

breve innominatum (bre've in-nō-mi-nā'tum). A writ reciting the cause of action in general terms.

Breve ita dicitur, quia rem de qua agitur, et intentionem petentis, paucis verbis breviter enarrat (brē've i'ta di'si-ter quī'a rem dē qua ā'ji-ter, et in-ten-shē-ō'nem po-ten'tis, pâ'sis ver'bis brē'vi-ter ē-nor'rat). A writ is so called, because it states the controversy and the purpose of the plaintiff briefly in a few words.

Breve judiciale debet sequi suum originale, et accessorium suum principale (brē've jū-di-shē-ā'le de'bet se'quī su'um o-ri-ji-nā'le, et ak-ses-sō'ri-um su'um prin-si-pā'lē). A judicial writ ought to follow its original, and an accessory its principal.

Breve judiciale non cadit pro defectu formae (brē've jū-di-shē-ā'le non ka'dit prō dē-fek'tū for'mē). A judicial writ does not fall by reason of a defect of form.

breve nominatum (brē've nō-mi-nā'tum). A writ which recites the cause of action of the plaintiff with particularity.

breve originale (brē've o-ri-ji-nā'le). An original writ.

breve perquirere (brē've per-quī're-re). To purchase a writ,—to purchase a writ of license of trial in the king's court by the plaintiff.

brevet (brę-vet'). Letters patent; a term of the military meaning higher rank without higher pay, sometimes without a higher command. United States v Hunt (US) 14 Wall 550, 20 L Ed 739.

breve testatum (brē've tes-tā'tum). See the plural **brevia testata.**

brevia (brē'vi-ą). Writs, plural of **breve.**

brevia adversaria (brē'vi-a ad-ver-sā'ri-a). Adversary writs to recover land.

brevia amicabilia (brē'vi-a a-mī-ka-bi'li-a). Writs obtained by the consent of the opposing party in the action.

brevia anticipantia (brē'vi-a an-ti-si-pan'she-a). Writs of prevention.

brevia de cursu (brē'vi-a dē ker'sū). Writs of course, —writs issued as a matter of right without showing cause.

brevia formata (brē'vi-a for-mā'ta). Writs of established form.

brevia judicialia (brē'vi-a jū-di-shē-ā'li-a). Judicial writs.

brevia magistralia (brē'vi-a ma-jis-trā'li-a). Writs drawn by masters in chancery.

Breviarium Alaricianum (Bre-vi-ā'ri-um A-la-ri'si-ā'num). The abridgment or breviary of Alaric,—a code of Roman law compiled under Alaric II, king of the Visigoths, published in 506 A. D.

brevia selecta (brē'vi-a se-lek'ta). Selected writs.

Brevia, tam originalia quam judicialia, patiuntur Anglica nomina (brē'vi-a, tam o-ri-ji-nā'li-a quam jū-di-she-ā'lia, pa-she-un'ter an'gli-ka nō'mi-na). Some original, as well as judicial writs, bear English names.

breviate. An abstract or synopsis.

brevia testata (brē'vi-a tes-tā'ta). Written memorandums or attestations introduced in feudal times to perpetuate the tenor of the conveyance and investiture, when grants by parol became subjects of dispute and uncertainty. The witnesses did not sign their names, but after they had heard it read, the clerk or scribe inserted their names as witnesses to its execution in the memorandum which was registered in the deed. See 2 Bl Comm 307.

brevibus et rotulis liberandis (brē'vi-bus et ro'tu-lis li-be-ran'dis). A writ ordering a sheriff to turn over all the paraphernalia of his office to his successor.

brew. See **ale; beer; small brew.**

brewer. One who follows the occupation of brewing ale or beer.

bribe. Noun: To influence official action by bribery. Verb: The payment or gift made or promised in accomplishing bribery. Randall v Evening News Asso., 97 Mich 136, 143, 56 NW 361.
See **boodle; bribery.**

bribery. A crime; the voluntary giving or receiving of anything of value in corrupt payment for an official act done or to be done or with the corrupt intent to influence the action of a public official or of any other person professionally concerned with the administration of public affairs, whether that public official or other person be in the legislative, executive, or judicial department of government. 12 Am J2d Brib § 2. For comparable definition by federal statute, see 18 USC § 201. The offense has been extended by state statute beyond corrupt influence upon public officials to include the corrupting of candidates for office, jurors, witnesses, voters, labor representatives, agents, even participants in sport. Glickfield v State, 203 Md 400, 101 A2d 229.
See **commercial bribery; receiving a bribe; soliciting a bribe.**

bribery at election. The purchase of a vote by corrupting the voter in paying him money or giving him goods or merchandise, often alcoholic beverages, to obtain his vote for a certain candidate or candidates. 26 Am J2d Elect § 377.

bribour (brī'ber). A thief; a robber.

brick. Building material, made from clay and shale, molded and baked in a kiln in oblong blocks, 4 inches wide, 8 inches long, and 2-1/2 inches high.

brick kiln. A plant for the manufacture of brick and tile. Windfall Mg. Co. v Patterson, 148 Ind 414, 47 NE 2.

brick mason. See **mason**.

bridewell (brīd'wel). A house of correction.

bridge. A structure, formerly constructed of wood, iron, brick, or stone, but, in modern times, usually built of concrete and steel, which carries pedestrians, vehicles, or both, over a river, creek, or smaller stream of water, a bay, a lake, arm of the sea, a valley, a railroad, even a highway; false work made by a dentist and anchored to sound teeth; a connection, as in the words of the late President Franklin D. Roosevelt, "a bridge of ships between the United States and the United Kingdom."

bridge-masters. Officers in charge of public bridges.

bridle. An instrument of punishment for common scolds; the harness placed on the head of a horse for guiding and controlling him while he is being driven or ridden.

bridle road. A road used by riders on horseback, but not necessarily confined to that kind of traffic.

brief. A concise and brief statement of authorities in various forms suitable to the purpose of counsel or the court, but, in a case on appeal, a more formal and conventional, but nevertheless concise presentation, in printing, typewriting, or writing, as the rules of the court require or permit, of the points and questions involved, as they appear from the pleadings, brief abstracts of which are included, and the record of the case, together with the authorities relied upon, all for the assistance of the court, and the edification of opposing counsel, in arriving at a just and proper decision in the case. 5 Am J2d A & E § 684. The form of briefs on appeal is by no means uniform throughout the United States. In some jurisdictions there is appended to the brief proper an argument of counsel expounding on the legal issues and the authorities cited by him as well as those cited by the opposing counsel.

briefe de recto claus (brēf de rek'to klôz). Writ of right close; a writ which lay for the king's tenants in ancient demesne, and others of a similar nature, to try the right of their lands and tenements in the court of the lord exclusively. See 3 Bl Comm 195.

brief of title. Same as **abstract of title**.

brief on appeal. See **brief**.

brieve (brēv). (Scotch.) A writ.

brieve of richt (breeve of rīcht). (Scotch.) A writ of right.

briga (brī'ga). Strife; contention; litigation.

brigbote (brig'bōt). (Saxon.) A contribution for the repair of a bridge.

brine. A solution of salt; the sea.

bring about. To accomplish. See **commit**.

bringing action. See **action brought**; **commencement of an action**.

bringing action to trial. Serving note of issue or taking any other step necessary and proper for the purpose of placing the case on the trial calendar and having it tried before court or jury, as the case may be.

bringing money into court. See **payment into court**.

bringing up. Rearing a child; referring to something by way of starting a discussion.

bris (bris). A wreck; wreckage.

Bristol bargain (bris'tol). A contract by which A lends B £1000, on good security, and it is agreed that £500, together with interest, shall be paid at a time stated, and, as to the other £500, that B, in consideration thereof, shall pay to A £100 per annum for seven years.—Wharton.

British. The people of the United Kingdom, or, as the term is sometimes used, the people of the British Commonwealth of Nations; pertaining to the United Kingdom or the British Commonwealth of Nations.

British Commonwealth. See **Commonwealth**.

British Constitution. See **British Theory of Constitutional Law**.

British Commonwealth of Nations. Often called shortly, the British Commonwealth; a political aggregate comprising the United Kingdom, that is, Great Britain and Northern Ireland; the Dominions beyond the seas; and such colonies, protectorates, dependencies, or independent nations, as remain attached by political ties to Great Britain.

British Ruling Cases. A set of annotated reports of cases from the United Kingdom and countries of the British Empire.

British sovereigns. See **regnal years of British sovereigns**.

British Theory of Constitutional Law. The existence of an absolute power in the British Parliament, which is at once a legislative and a constitutional convention, with power so transcended that it is not to be confined within any bounds either for causes or persons. 16 Am J2d Const L § 9.

British Thermal Unit. The heat required to raise the temperature of one pound of water from 62 degrees Fahrenheit to 63 degrees Fahrenheit.

Brit. Rul. Cas. An abbreviation of "**British Ruling Cases.**"

bro. Abbreviation for **brother**.

broach (brōach). To tap a keg or barrel.

broad. Spacious; liberal, tolerant; a vulgar term for woman or girl.

broadcasting. The dissemination of radio communications intended to be received by the public, directly or by the intermediary of relay stations. 47 USC § 153; a kind of wireless telephony, in the operation of which the microphone is the transmitter and the "radio set" the receiver. Dunbar v Spratt-Snyder Co. 208 Iowa 490, 226 NW 22, 63 ALR 1016; a public performance of a musical composition, even though there is no audience at the place where the music is made audible, so that it can be picked up and broadcast. 18 Am J2d Copyr § 111.

Broadcasting is distinct from televising. Norman v Century Athletic Club, 193 Md 584, 69 A2d 466, 15 ALR2d 777. The communications are by sound only, but available to bring music and speech to persons who have appropriate receivers.

broad construction. An interpretation which, brushing aside minor objections and trivial technicalities, effectuates the intent of the statute or other writing involved. Re Senate Resolution No. 2, 94 Colo 101, 31 P2d 325.

See **liberal construction**.

broad evidence rule. A term peculiar to the law of insurance, under which the trier of facts may consider any evidence logically tending to the formation of a correct estimate of the value of the insured property at the time of loss. 29A Am J Rev ed Ins § 1545.

broad-halfpenny (brâd). Same as **bord-halfpenny**.

broadside objection. An objection to evidence on the general grounds of incompetency, immateriality, and irrelevancy, without specifying the grounds particularly. 23 Am J2d Dep § 136.

brocage (brō'kăj). Brokerage.

brocard (brok'ärd). A legal maxim.

brocarius (brō-kā'ri-us). A broker.

brocator (brō-kā'tor). A broker.

brocella (brō-sel'la). A copse; a thicket.

brode-halfpenny (brōd-halfpenny). Same as **bord-halfpenny**.

broken. Separated forcibly into parts; fractured; shattered; ruptured; as broken reeds; a broken limb; broken skin; broken waves.
See **breakage**.

broken financially. See **bankrupt**.

broken stowage. Room on shipboard for more cargo; space for cargo other than the hold.

broker. A person whose business is to bring buyer and seller together. Moore v Turner, 137 W Va 299, 71 SE2d 342, 32 ALR2d 713. More precisely defined as an agent who, for a commission or brokerage fee, bargains or carries on negotiations in behalf of his principal as an intermediary between the latter and third persons in transacting business relative to the acquisition of contractual rights, or to the sale or purchase of any form of property, real or personal, the custody of which is not entrusted to him for the purpose of discharging his agency. 12 Am J2d Brok § 1. Other definitions differentiate between **real estate broker** and **stockbroker**.
See **bill and note broker**; **exchange broker**; **grain broker**; **insurance broker**; **investment broker**; **marriage brokerage**; **pawnbroker**; **ship broker**; **stockbroker**.

brokerage. The business of a broker; the compensation or commission of a broker. Little Rock v Barton, 33 Ark 436, 447. The very essence of a brokerage commission is its dependence upon success, and its independence of the amount of work done by the broker. It is earned if the broker, without devoting much or any time to finding a customer, succeeds in procuring one. No commission is earned if a broker is not successful, and he is not entitled to any compensation, no matter how much time he has spent in finding a customer, if no customer is found. Cadigan v Crabtree, 179 Mass 474, 61 NE 37.

brokerage contract. A contract of agency whereby the broker is employed to make contracts of the kind agreed upon in the name and on behalf of his principal and for which he is paid an agreed commission. Nolen's Adm. v Robinson, 213 Ky 752, 755, 281 SW 1034.

brokers' blanket bond. A fidelity bond protecting a broker against loss through the fraud or dishonesty of employees. Anno: 74 ALR 284.

broker's lien. The lien of a broker upon the proceeds of a sale made by him, or upon property purchased by him, for a customer, for his commissions or for an advance made by him to complete the purchase. 12 Am J2d Brok § 241.
See **custom broker's lien**; **insurance broker's lien**; **real estate broker's lien**.

bronchitis. As the word appears in an application for life insurance, it means chronic disease which will not readily yield to treatment, not an acute attack followed quickly by complete recovery. 29 Am J Rev ed Ins § 747.

bronze. An alloy of copper and tin.

Bros. Abbreviation for **brothers**. Anno: 42 ALR2d 564.

brossus (bros'sus). Wounded or bruised.

brothel (broth'el). A bawdyhouse; a house of prostitution; a house of ill fame, kept for the resort and convenience of lewd people of both sexes.

brothel house (broth'el hous). Same as **brothel**.

brother. A male related collaterally to one by common parentage, that is, a person having the same parent or parents as another; one who may take as heir or next of kin, where a direct heir is wanting. 23 Am J2d Desc & D § 58.

brother-in-law. The brother of one's spouse or the husband of one's sister; sometimes, the husband of a wife's sister or the husband of a husband's sister, but this is not common usage throughout the United States.

brothers and sisters. In most, although not all, statutes of descent "brothers and sisters" include brothers and sisters of the half, as well as the full, blood. 23 Am J2d Desc & D § 58. In a number of cases, the courts, in construing the will to arrive at the testator's intention, have held that a gift to brothers and sisters, in the absence of any indication of intent to the contrary, included brothers and sisters of the half blood. Anno: 49 ALR2d 1373.
See **brothers**; **sisters**.

Brougham's Act. See **Lord Brougham's Act**.

brought. Fetched; carried; produced.
See **action brought**.

bruarium (bru-ā'ri-um). A place where heath grows.

brudhote. Same as **brigbote**.

brugbote (brŭg-bote). Same as **brigbote**.

bruillus (bru-il'lus). A thicket or copse.

bruise. An injury on the surface with effect confined to discoloration of the skin and pain no deeper or little deeper than the skin; an injury, which, in contrast with a wound, includes no breaking or cutting of the skin. Montgomery v Lansing City Electric Co. 103 Mich 46, 61 NW 543.

brukbarn (brŭk-barn). (Swedish.) A legitimized child conceived in rape.

brush. Noun: A thicket. Verb: To smooth; to clear the dust from an article, especially an article of clothing.

brush discharge. A charge of electricity, also called a "disruptive discharge" which is sometimes thrown off by uninsulated wires in sufficient force to cause the death of a person in close proximity thereto, without his actual contact with the wire. The fact is well known to electricians and those familiar with this generally unknown, powerful, and destructive agency. Hoppe v Winona, 113 Minn 252, 129 NW 577.

brutum fulmen (brö'tum ful'men). Empty or harmless thunder.
"That the national will, thus declared, may not be a mere brutum fulmen, the last section of the amendment (the Fourteenth) invests Congress with power to enforce it by appropriate legislation." See Civil Rights Cases, 109 US 3, 11, 27 L Ed 835, 839, 3 S Ct 18.

b. s. Abbreviation for **balance sheet,** also for **bill of sale, bags,** and **bales.**

B. S. Abbreviation for the degree **Bachelor of Science;** a basic substance known by these initials, consisting of the impurities in crude oil, which accumulates in the bottom of storage tanks and which it becomes necessary at times to remove. Crude Oil Contracting Co. v Insurance Co. of North America (CA10 Okla) 118 F2d 476.

B. S. Ed. Abbreviation for **Bachelor of Science in Education.**

Bs/L. Abbreviation for **bills of lading.**

B. Th. Abbreviation for **Bachelor of Theology.**

B. T. U. Abbreviation for **British Thermal Unit.**

bubble. A dishonest investment or speculation scheme projected by dishonest persons to defraud the investors.

Bubble Act. An English statute passed to prevent corporate frauds such as the South Sea Bubble. See **South Sea Bubble.**
An early English statute which provided that any company formed without authority of Parliament and asserting powers and privileges not possessed by individuals or partnerships should be deemed a public nuisance. 6 Geo I Ch 18.

bubonic plague. A disease, accompanied by intermittent chills and fever, which easily becomes of epidemic proportions and in fear of which sanitary regulations are imposed. 13 Am J2d Bldgs § 29.

Buck Act. A statute which relieves an instrumentality of the United States from taxation by a state. Maynard & Child v Shearer (Ky) 290 SW2d 790.

bucketing. Running a bucket shop. See **bucket shop.**

bucket shop. An establishment conducted ostensibly for conducting, as brokers, transactions in securities listed on a stock, produce, or grain exchange, but really for the registration of bets or wagers, usually for small amounts, on the rise or fall of the prices of stocks, grain, oil, etc.; there being no transfer or delivery of the stocks or commodities nominally dealt in. Western Union Tel. Co. v State, 165 Ind 492, 76 NE 100.

Buck's extension (buks'). A surgical term meaning some uniform continuous force or pull applied to the leg or foot below the break to overcome the natural contraction of the muscles of the thigh, which have a strong tendency to pull the broken ends together and cause them to slip by each other and overlap, especially when the break is oblique in its course across the bone. Sweet v Douge, 145 Wash 142, 259 P 25.

buckstall (buk'stâl). A net used to trap deer.

buddy. A term employed by coal miners to designate a miner who is working with a fellow miner. Continental Coal Corp. v York's Adm. 159 Ky 334, 335. The term is also applied by a railroad section hand to the one who works with him, and by a soldier to a comrade with whom he is particularly friendly and closely associated.

budge of court (buj). Same as **bouche of court.**

budget. A plan officially laid out showing how much money will be required to meet the various departments of the national government, a state, county, city or other government for the year ensuing.

Budget Bureau. A bureau, headed by a Director, to assist the President in planning the budget to be submitted to Congress.

budget planning. The preparation of a budget for the national government, a state, a county, a town, a city, or other municipality; a part of the functions of personal debt adjusting. 15 Am Jur 2d Collect § 2.

Buenos Aires Convention. A copyright treaty to which the United States became a party. 18 Am J2d Copyr § 76.

buffer. A polisher of metal or wood; a stiff brush for polishing metal or wood; shock absorbers, called dead woods, in use at one time on railroad freight cars to take up and arrest the force of the blow resulting from the coupling of cars, but eliminated apparently as a safety measure, since they rendered the job of coupling dangerous, resulting in many injuries to the hands and fingers of brakemen. Louisville & Nashville Railroad Co. v Boland, 96 Ala 626, 11 So 667.

buffet (buf'it). Verb: To belabor with blows. Noun: Blows, sometimes figuratively, as the buffets of fate.

buffet (bu-fā'). Refreshment or even a meal at which the guests, whether social or business, serve themselves from a table or counter.

bug. An insect that crawls; a slang term for a defect in a machine, also for a sending device in telegraphy which makes use of a movable, horizontal bar instead of the conventional Morse key. Verb: A slang term for torment, irritate, or worry.

buggery. Another term for the criminal offense of sodomy, also including the offense of bestiality. Ausman v Veal, 10 Ind 355.
See **bestiality; sodomy.**

buggy. A one-seated, light, four-wheeled vehicle, drawn by one or two horses, now, a relic of past generations; a small carriage for a baby, usually one to be pushed rather than pulled.

build. To construct something, literally, as erecting an office building, or, symbolically, as building a fortune or building respect.

builder. The party to a building and construction contract who undertakes to perform the work required by the contract; one who builds, or whose occupation is that of building; specifically, one who controls or directs the work of construction in any capacity. In the practice of civil architecture, the builder comes between the architect who designs the work and the artisans who execute it. Wortman v Kleinschmidt, 12 Mont 316, 345, 30 P 280, 290.

builder's risk insurance. A policy of fire or other property insurance covering the interest of a contractor, as such, in a building under construction by him; a liability policy insuring a contractor against liability for damages or injuries occurring in connection with the performance of his contracts. 29A Am J Rev ed Ins § 1349.

building. A structure designed and suitable for habitation or sheltering human beings and animals, sheltering or storing property, or for use and occupation for private and public business, trade, or manufacture. 13 Am J2d Bldgs § 1; 13 Am J2d Burgl § 6; in the broad sense, any structure erected and fixed upon or in the soil, composed of different pieces connected together and designed for permanent use in the position in which it is so fixed, provided the purpose of use is that of habitation, trade, manufacture, religion, education, entertainment, or ornament. 20 Am J2d Cov § 194. Still more broadly defined as any structure with walls and a roof. 29 Am J Rev ed Ins § 293.

In contracts, the term "building" is variable, depending for interpretation upon the purpose and context of the contract. So, an incomplete structure is a "building" within the meaning of an insurance contract. 29 Am J Rev ed Ins § 293; and a foundation without more is a building within the meaning of a mechanic's lien law, where the failure to complete the building was due to the owner of the premises. 36 Am J1st Mech L § 42. A wall, or even a fence, is sometimes deemed a building for the purposes of a restrictive covenant. Anno: 23 ALR2d 946.

Of course, the foundation is a part of a building. Davison v Walla Walla, 52 Wash 453, 100 P 981.

building and loan association. An organization of people entitled to equal privileges, cooperating by established periodic and equal payments per share in the creation of a common fund which may be loaned to any member for the purpose of building on property purchased therewith or on other property on which the association obtains a lien, and sharing the profits and losses of the association according to their respective interest. 13 Am J2d B & L Assoc § 1.

Building and loan associations are not commercial banks, and, in most jurisdictions, they are not classed as either savings banks or savings institutions. In a few states, they are permitted to perform functions in the nature of banking. 13 Am J2d B & L Assoc § 3.

See **savings and loan association**.

building association. Same as **building and loan association**.

building contract. See **construction contract**.

building inspector. A municipal officer charged with the duty of inspecting buildings as to construction and maintenance in reference to safety and sanitation.

building is covered. A phrase in a binder or contract of temporary insurance which means that the building is covered pending the issuance of a complete policy of insurance, or the rejection of the application for insurance, as it would be by an insurance policy in the standard form. 29 Am J Rev ed Ins § 205.

building lease. A lease of land wherein the lessee undertakes to erect buildings on the land.

building lien. See **mechanic's lien**.

building lines. Otherwise known as setback lines or front lines; lines established by statute or ordinance in the interest of public health, public safety, and aesthetics, and sometimes designated by restrictive covenants, which, for the purpose of providing an open space between the buildings on a street and the street, prohibit the building of any structure between the line as established or designated and the street. 13 Am J2d Bldgs § 14; 20 Am J2d Cov § 237; 58 Am J1st Zon § 51.

See **back lines**; **side lines**.

building loan agreement. An agreement for a loan to be used in making payments to a contractor engaged in the construction of a building or other structure for the borrower, or to materialmen who furnish supplies for the construction of a building or other structure for the borrower, the arrangement normally providing for the security of the lender, in the form of a mortgage on the property under improvement, which covers both present advances and advances to be made in the future during the course of the work and its completion by the contractor.

building loan mortgage. A mortgage on premises under improvement or to be improved, covering advances made or to be made to or on behalf of the borrower for payment of contractor or materialmen rendering services or furnishing materials in the construction of a building or other structure for the borrower.

building material. Material used in the construction of a building or other structure. In order to be lienable under the mechanics' lien law, the material must be such, both as to quantity and quality, and of a kind, that would induce a careful, prudent, and skilful man, acquainted with the building or other structure, to believe that it could be used in its erection, unless the material is furnished upon the order of the owner of the property under improvement, since he, of course, may pledge his own property for any kind of material. 36 Am J1st Mech L § 60.

building permit. A permit for the construction of a building granted by a municipal officer or board, which is required by statute or municipal ordinance of any person who proposes to erect a building within the limits of a municipality. 13 Am J2d Bldgs § 8.

building regulation. A restriction or regulation upon the manner in which a property owner may use his property in respect of constructing a building or other structure thereon. 13 Am J2d Bldgs § 2. Such a regulation or restriction is created by statute or municipal regulation under the police power and also by contractual stipulations in the form of restrictive covenants.

See **planning**; **restrictive covenants**; **zoning**.

building site. A lot or tract of land suitable for the erection of a dwelling house or other building; the term, at least in reference to a lot in a city, means the whole of the lot, not just the part upon which the structure is to rest.

building society. Synonymous with **building and loan association** and used principally in England.

building standard. A standard prescribed by law as one to be followed in the construction of a building, particularly in reference to features involving health and safety.

building-type restriction. See **type restriction**.

built-up district. A zoning term which refers to an area having few, if any, vacant lots. 58 Am J1st Zon § 36.

bulk. The main mass of the body; the largest or principal portion; the majority, as the bulk of a debt. When we speak of the bulk of anything, the other two words are an appositional genitive of the word bulk and mean the same thing. For example, "the bulk of the goods sold," means the goods themselves. F. A. D. Andrea, Inc. v Dodge (CA3 Pa) 15 F2d 1003.

See **breaking bulk; laden in bulk; open bulk.**

bulkhead. A partition in the hold of a ship, airplane, or freight car, separating the cargo space, and in some instances, cargo space from passenger space.

bulk mortgage. Literally, a chattel mortgage on property in bulk, that is, articles, goods, or merchandise in a job lot, not counted, measured, or listed by specific articles, but described merely in the terms of the building or container which holds the property; in legal significance, a chattel mortgage on stock of goods or merchandise in a store, shop, or other place of business. 15 Am J2d Chat Mtg § 76. In many jurisdictions, a chattel mortgage on a stock of goods is void where the mortgagor retains possession with the power to sell the property. 15 Am J2d Chat Mtg § 130.

bulk sale. Literally, any sale of articles, goods, or merchandise in a job lot, without count or measure, but, in legal significance, the sale of all or any portion of a stock of merchandise other than in the ordinary course of trade. 37 Am J2d Fed Conv § 238.

Bulk Sales Acts. Statutes intended for the protection of creditors of merchants, providing that the sale of all or any portion of a stock of merchandise otherwise than in the ordinary course of trade shall be fraudulent and void against creditors of the seller, unless the seller delivers to the purchaser a list of his creditors and the purchaser in turn notifies such creditors of the proposed sale a stipulated time in advance. Under some statutes, the seller is required to furnish the purchaser with an inventory of the goods in the stock. 37 Am J2d Fed Conv § 238.

bulk sales station. A place wherein gasoline and oil is stored pending distribution to retail dealers. Louisiana Oil Co. v Renno, 173 Miss 609, 157 So 705, 98 ALR 1296.

bulky property. Personal property of such a bulky or cumbersome nature that seizure and removal thereof under a levy of an attachment will be attended with great expense or difficulty. 6 Am J2d Attach § 298.

bull. A male bovine, also the male of certain other large animals, such as elephants, walrus, and whale; a papal edict; a sealed proclamation or mandate of either the pope or the bishop of Rome.

bulla (bul′ạ). Seals used by the Roman emperors.

bulldozer. A self-propelled heavy vehicle with blade used for pushing dirt or debris; for some purposes, a motor vehicle. Anno: 77 ALR2d 946.

bullet. The shot or lethal part of the discharge of a pistol, rifle, or even heavier arm; the shot and the propellant of powder encased in a cartridge.

bulletin. A published official report of a matter or fact of public interest; sometimes a short statement from a private source concerning an occurrence of public interest.

bulletin des lois. (French.) The official notice of a law or decree.

bullheaded. Very stubborn, not inclined to listen to argument or reason.

bullion (bùl′yọn). Uncoined gold or silver.

bullio salis (bul′li-ō sa′lis). A salt measure of twelve gallons.

bull pen. A name given at some of the state penitentiaries to that part of the prison where prisoners are kept in close confinement. State v Kelley, 118 Or 397, 247 P 146. The name is also given facetiously to the common room in a men's dormitory, the student room in a law school, and other various places where men gather socially.

bulter (bōl′ter). Bran.

bum-bailiff (bum-bā′lif). A bailiff's deputy.

Bumboat Act. An English statute passed in 1761 for the suppression of harbor thieves.

bummaree bond (bum′ạ-rē bond). Same as **bottomry bond.**

bunching. An accumulation of freight cars due to the carrier's fault and operating to relieve a shipper from liability for demurrage. 13 Am J2d Car § 487.

bunco. A swindle or fraud.

bunda (bun′da). A boundary.

bundae et metae et rationabiles divisae (bun′dē et me′tē et ra″she-ō-nā′bi-lēz di-vī′sē). Metes and bounds and rational limits.

bundle. Noun: A pack of articles, usually tied with string or cord. Verb: To make a pack of articles. The word has another meaning in the peculiar sense of a courting couple being in bed together without undressing, thus accomplishing rest, sleep, or no more than pleasant companionship, without a blemish upon virtue, especially where the mother of the female has guarded virtue by good, solid stitches in her clothing. This is doubtless the practice referred to in Sengar v Slingerland (NY) 2 Caines 219, where the court says: "We lay out of view the custom which it is agreed prevails in that part of the country, for young people, who are courting, to sleep together."

bungalow. A residential structure, usually consisting of not more than one and a half stores.

bungalow court. A motel.

bunk car. A railroad car, often an old passenger or Pullman car, placed on a siding, and used by railroad employees who work in gangs for lodging and sometimes for boarding. 35 Am J1st M & S § 440.

buoy. A navigation marker which floats, indicating the channel to be followed and warning of shoals or rocks; a float which is an aid to one learning to swim and also a life preserver for one who is not a swimmer for want of learning to swim or from temporary disablement.

bur. A dental instrument. Anno: 83 ALR2d 163; a pest among plants, the cocklebur.

burden. A weight to be carried literally; or figuratively, as a burden of sorrow or sin.

burdened vessel. Of two vessels approaching each other the "burdened vessel" is the one which is required by the rules of navigation to keep out of the way of the other vessel. The Knoxville City (CA 9 Cal) 112 F2d 223.

burden of evidence. The duty of a party to proceed with evidence at the beginning, or at any subsequent stage, of the trial, in order to make or meet a prima facie case. 29 Am J2d Ev § 123.

This duty, otherwise, and perhaps more appropriately, called the burden of producing evidence, may arise at different stages of the trial, even be borne successfully once, only to arise again at a later stage, thereby being distinguished from the "burden of proof" which is one to be carried during the entire trial, that is, ultimately.

The term "burden of evidence" has been defined as meaning the burden of "getting by" the judge to the jury, by making a prima facie showing as to each factual ingredient necessary to establish a prima facie case. Having done this, a plaintiff has discharged his burden of evidence, and the burden shifts to the defendant to produce, if he desires, competent controverting evidence, which, if believed, will offset the plaintiff's prima facie case. If the defendant has thus met the burden of evidence and made a prima facie defense the burden thereupon swings back to the plaintiff to bring forward evidence in rebuttal, and so on. McCloskey v Koplar, 329 Mo 527, 46 SW2d 557, 92 ALR 641.
See **burden of proof.**

burden of going forward with evidence. See **burden of evidence.**

burden of persuasion. The burden of convincing the jury or the court as the trier of the issue or issues of fact; the ultimate burden of proof.
See **burden of proof.**

burden of producing evidence. See **burden of evidence.**

burden of proof. The duty of establishing ultimately in the trial the truth of a given proposition or issue by such a quantum of evidence as the law demands in the case in which the issue arises. 29 Am J2d Ev § 123.
See **burden of evidence.**

burden on interstate commerce. Interference with interstate commerce.
See **interstate commerce.**

bureau (bū′rō). A department of a municipal or state government; in the federal government, usually a department within a department, a subdivision of a department.
Note that many particular bureaus are to be found herein under the specific designating term, such as Census Bureau; Internal Revenue Bureau etc.

bureaucracy (bū-rō′kra̧-si). A government by bureaus or departments.

Bureau of Investigation. The Federal Bureau of Investigation, popularly known as the FBI, the investigative arm of the Department of Justice, elaborately organized for the detection of crimes, particularly federal offenses; maintaining an identification division and a clearinghouse for identification data, particularly fingerprints; collaborating with state and local law-enforcement agencies; and carrying out the duty delegated to it of protecting the internal security of the United States.

burg (bėrg). In origin, a fortified place on a hilltop; a borough; a slang term for municipality.

burgage-holding (bėr′gāj). A Scotch tenure under which land was held of the crown by the service of watch and ward.

burgage-tenement (bėr′gāj-ten″ẹ-ment). A tenement held by burgage tenure.

burgage tenure. A form of socage tenure wherein the king or other person was lord of an ancient borough in which the tenements were held by a rent certain.
See 2 Bl Comm 82.

burgator (bur-gā′tor). A burglar.

burgbote (burg-bote). Contributions for the maintenance of town walls and their defenses.

burgenses (bur-jen′sēz). Inhabitants of a borough; burgesses.

burgess (bėr′jes). An inhabitant of a borough or town; a borough magistrate; a representative of a town, borough, or university in the Parliament of Great Britain; A member of the colonial Virginia House of Burgesses, the lower house of the colonial legislature which, after the Revolution was called the House of Delegates.

burgh (bėrg or bur′ō). A borough; slang for a municipality; the Saxon word for house.
See **burg.**

burgh-brech (burgh-brech). The offense of violating the pledge given by every inhabitant of a tithing to keep the peace.

burgh-English. Same as **borough-English.**

burgh-Engloys. Same as **borough-English.**

burgh-halfpenny. Same as **bord-halfpenny.**

burglar. One guilty of the offense of burglary.
See **burglary.**

burglar alarm. See **alarm system.**

burglariously. With intent to commit burglary. 13 Am J2d Burgl § 69.

burglarized. The condition of premises upon which the offense of burglary has been committed. Having committed burglary upon certain premises. State v Mares, 61 NM 46, 294 P2d 287.

burglars' tools. Tools or implements of such design and construction as to be adaptable for use in cutting through, or breaking open any building, room, vault, safe, or other depository. 13 Am J2d Burgl § 74.
See **possession of burglars' tools.**

burglary. A compound of the Saxon word "burgh," a house, and "laron," theft , meaning, at common law, the breaking and entering, in the nighttime, of the dwelling of another with intent to commit a felony therein. Clum v New Amsterdam Casualty Co. 281 Pa 464, 126 A 810; 36 ALR 1122.

The offense of burglary has been materially broadened by statute to include the acts of breaking and entering structures other than a dwelling. 13 Am J2d Burgl §§ 3 et seq. retaining, however, the element of intent to commit a felony.
See **second degree burglary.**

burgle (bėr′gl). An ancient word meaning to burglarize; to commit burglary. Wulward of Wadebridge was burgled. Rex v Hay, Selden Soc. Select Pleas of the Crown Vol I p 5.

burgmote (burg-mōt). A court of a borough.

burgomaster (bėr′gō̧-mȧs″tėr). The chief magistrate of a German or Dutch town.

burgwharl (burg-whar). A burgess; a citizen.

burh. Same as **burgh.**

burial. Disposition of dead body by interment.
See **interference with burial; right of burial.**

burial at sea. Interment at sea under exigency or at direction of person having right of burial. 22 Am J2d Dead B § 13.

burial expenses. See **funeral expenses.**

burial ground. See **cemetery.**

burial insurance. A contract for the payment of burial or funeral expenses at the death of the holder, usually an older person of limited, financial means. 29 Am J Rev ed Ins § 8. In its ordinary form, it is a contract issued by an association whose declared object is to secure, or make certain, by a system of mutual contribution, to each member of the association, at death, the specific benefit of a specified sum of money for application to his burial service. State v Willett, 171 Ind 296, 303, 86 NE 68.

burial lot. A place of burial. A lot in a cemetery, the purchaser of which acquires a right of burial therein. 14 Am J2d Cem § 25.

burial place. See **burial; burial lot; cemetery.**

buried in price. Absorbed in the purchase price, for example a sales tax included in the general purchase price. 46 Am J1st Sales § 184.

burke (bėrk). To murder by smothering; to murder for the purpose of selling the corpse for purposes of dissection.

burkism. The crime of committing murder by smothering the victim; the crime of killing a person for the purpose of selling his corpse for dissection.

burlaw. An old Scotch system of the appointment of judges by neighbors.

burlaw courts. Scotch courts in which the judges were appointed by neighbors.

burlaw-men. The judges in burlaw courts.

burlesque. Descriptive of two very different kinds of shows:—(1) a series of unrelated episodes and dances making up a show that is completely sex-centered; and (2) a type of show characterized by broad humor and slapstick comedy and consisting of songs, ballet dancing, and caricatures of well known actors and plays. Adams Theater Co. v Keenan, 12 NJ 267, 96 A2d 519. A parody of a literary or dramatic work, usually presented as a comedy. 18 Am J2d Copyr § 105.

burn. Verb: To consume something by fire. For the purposes of the law of arson, it is usually deemed synonymous with "set fire to," both expressions meaning that there must be some actual consumption by fire. 5 Am J2d Arson § 8. Noun: A mark made by burning or branding; a little stream; slang for death by electrocution.

burned and unburned clause. See **adjustment clause.**

burned out of sight. Completely destroyed or reduced to ashes.

Burnel. See **Acton Burnel.**

burning. See **burn.**

burning fluid. A highly combustible liquid used in cigarette lighters and in igniting charcoal or other fuel in outdoor cookers.

burning in the hand. The practice of burning with a hot iron in the brawn of the left thumb all laymen admitted to the benefit of clergy to guard against their admission thereto a second time. The statute directed that no person once admitted should be entitled to be admitted to benefit of clergy a second time, unless he produced his credentials as a clergyman. See 4 Bl Comm 267.

burning to defraud insurer. The criminal offense of burning with intent to injure or defraud an insurer. An offense related to arson but distinct in the fact that the property destroyed is that of the accused. 5 Am J2d Arson § 2.

burro. A donkey; a game of chance popular among Filipinos. Anno: 135 ALR 126.

burrochium (bur-rō'ki-um). A dam or a fish-trap weir.

Burr's Case. The prosecution of Aaron Burr for treason against the United States.

bursa (bėr'sạ). A purse or bag.

bursar (bėr'sạr). A purser; the treasurer of a college.

bursarum scissores (bur-sā'rum scis-sō'rēz). Cutpurses, thieves who made a practice of cutting purses to steal the contents.

bursary (bėr'sạ-ri). The treasury of a college.

burse (bėrs). A bourse; a purse.

bury. Noun: A borough; a castle; a manor house. Verb: To cover; to place in the ground and cover with dirt; to inter a dead body.
See ¹Iri☑l.

burying alive. An ancient punishment for sodomy and also for dealing with Jews.

burying-ground. See **cemetery.**

bus. A self-propelled vehicle for carrying passengers in number exceeding the capacity of an ordinary automobile, most often in use as the vehicle of a common carrier transporting passengers on prescribed routes, but also in use in carrying employees, pupils of public and parochial schools, servicemen, etc. A bus is usually a motor vehicle. Northern Indiana Transit, Inc. v Burk, 228 Ind 162, 89 NE2d 905, 17 ALR2d 572. At times, called trolley busses, they are electrically propelled, receiving power through overhead electric lines.

bushel. A unit of dry measure, consisting of 4 pecks or 32 quarts and having volume of 2150.42 cubic inches.

bushelman. A tailor.

bushwhacker (bùsh'hwak''ėr). A term applied to a class of persons who are not a part of any regular army, and are not answerable to any military discipline, but who are mere lawless banditti, engaged in plundering, robbery, murder, and all conceivable crimes while a war is being waged. Curry v Collins, 37 Mo 324, 329.

business. The work in which one is regularly or usually engaged, the activity in which he spends the major portion of his time, and from which he makes a living. La Belle v Hennepin County Bar Asso. 206 Minn 290, 288 NW 788, 125 ALR 1023; a commercial enterprise, conducted for monetary reward, as distinguished from a religious or charitable enterprise. Anno: 42 ALR2d 538. As used in the immigration laws, intercourse of a commercial character, not including temporary visits for the purpose of performing labor for hire. Karnuth v United States, 279 US 231, 73 L Ed 677, 49 S Ct 274. That which occupies one's time and engages his efforts in fulfilling his responsibilities; commerce and trade; an establishment where trade or commerce is conducted; commercial policy; activities in a dramatic production which round out the representation by supplementing the reading of the lines by the actors.

The term "business" means "busyness"; it implies that one is kept more or less busy, that the activity is an occupation. Generally, carrying on a business implies an occupational undertaking to which one habitually devotes time, attention, and effort, with substantial regularity. Anno: 46 ALR2d 656.

The practice of law is included within a statute granting cities authority to raise revenue by levying a license fee or tax "on any business" within the limits of the city, notwithstanding previous construction of the statute not to include the practice of law because of another statute enumerating the businesses subject to municipal license, tax, and regulation and not including in its enumeration the practice of law, and because of the repeal of another statute permitting cities to license and tax lawyers, where a subsequent amendment provides that no enumeration of municipal power shall be deemed to limit or restrict the general grant of authority. Davis v Ogden City, 117 Utah 315, 215 P2d 616, 223 P2d 412, 16 ALR2d 1208.

A restrictive covenant against the use of property for any "business purpose" is not violated by the erection of a church building. Wiggins v Young, 206 Ga 440, 57 SE2d 486, 13 ALR2d 1237.

business affected with a public interest. A phrase difficult, if not incapable, of exact definition, but most broadly defined by Mr. Justice Roberts of the United States Supreme Court, in reference to the constitutionality of statutes regulating a business, as an industry which, for adequate reason, is subject to public control. Nebbia v New York, 291 US 502, 78 L Ed 940, 54 S Ct 505, 89 ALR 1469. Otherwise defined, of the public demands that it be reasonably regulated to conserve the rights of the public. 16 Am J2d Const L § 317. As a business, which may be regulated by statute, because it has reached such proportions that the interest of the public demands that it be reasonably regulated to conserve the rights of the public; a business which, in operation, affects the health, safety, and welfare of the people, so that reasonable regulation is permissible. 16 Am J2d Const L § 317. Tyson & Bro. —United Theatre Ticket Offices v Banton 273 US 418, 71 L Ed 718, 47 S Ct 426, 58 ALR 1236.

See **corporation affected with a public interest.**

business agent. A representative of a labor union; an agent managing the business of his principal. Denver & R.G.R. Co. v Roller (CA9 Cal) 100 F 738.

business and closely built-up. See **business section.**

Business and Defense Services Administration. A federal administrative agency in the Department of Commerce.

business broker. One engaged in selling going concerns for clients, where not only the physical property, including the real estate, is sold, but personal property, such as machinery, stock in trade, and sometimes the good will of the business. 12 Am J2d Brok § 15.

business capacity. A city or other municipal corporation is said to act in its business capacity, as distinguished from its governmental capacity when it engages in the operation of a business which is distinct from the government of the city or other municipal corporation. The operation of a municipally owned gas plant is an instance. Baily v Philadelphia, 184 Pa 594, 39 A 494.

business club. See **commercial club; social club.**

business compulsion. Duress, clothed in modern dress, arising from business necessity or economic compulsion, as where the owner of a business yields to an unlawful demand out of fear of a serious loss of trade, unless he complies. 25 Am J2d Dur §§ 6, 7.

One cannot be said to be intimidated or coerced, in the sense of unlawful compulsion, by being induced to forego business relations with A, rather than lose the benefit of more profitable relations with B. Ex parte Lyons, 27 Cal App 2d 293, 81 P2d 190.

business contract. A contract made between businessmen in the regular course of business. 17 Am J2d Contr § 287.

business corporation. The ordinary corporation, a commercial corporation; a corporation organized to engage in some business for profit; as the term is used in the Bankruptcy Act, a corporation the sole motive of which is pecuniary gain and the chief purpose of which is to carry on trade or commerce in an established field and to do this primarily for the financial benefit of those who have joined in its organization and in the conduct of its affairs. Wisconsin Coop. Milk Pool (CA7 Wis) 119 F2d 999.

When a corporation is doing the very things it was organized to do, and it is not a charitable, benevolent, or social corporation, it is a business corporation within the meaning of the state and Federal franchise tax statutes. Union Oil Associates v Johnson, 2 Cal 2d 727, 43 P2d 291, 98 ALR 1499.

Business Corporation Model Act. A statute, prepared as a model act by the National Conference of Commissioners of Uniform State Laws, which has been adopted in Alaska, Idaho, Kentucky, Louisiana, Tennessee, and Washington. Am J2d Desk Book, Document 129.

business day. A day other than Sunday. A day for the transaction of business generally. State v Duncan, 118 La 702, 43 So 283.

business district. See **business section.**

business enterprise. Adaptability, skill, and zeal in engaging in business; a commercial enterprise, as distinguished from a charitable enterprise.

Although an employee uses his automobile for the purpose of returning two of his employer's trailers to their station by attaching one to his automobile and loading the second trailer onto the first one, he is not engaged in a "business enterprise" within the meaning of a clause in an automobile liability insurance policy exempting from coverage the towing of a trailer used to transport goods or materials "in any business enterprise," where the employee engages in the undertaking on a trip made on his day off solely for his own pleasure and he acts of his own volition without authorization by the employer, neither expecting nor receiving any compensation therefor. Lintern v Zentz, 327 Mich 595, 42 NW2d 753, 18 ALR2d 713.

business entries. See **book of original entry; shopbook rule.**

business entry statute. A federal statute governing the admissibility of business entries in evidence. 28 USC § 1732.

See **Business Records Act.**

business expense. As a deduction in income tax return, any of the various expenses incurred in carrying on a trade or business, provided it is both ordinary and necessary in relation to the trade or business. IRC § 162(a).

business guest. Same as **business visitor.**

business hours. That period or portion of the day during which the business of the community gener-

ally is ordinarily transacted. Casalduc v Diaz (CA 1 Puerto Rico) 117 F2d 915.
See **banking hours; usual business hours**.

business indemnity insurance. See **business interruption insurance**.

business insurance. Life insurance through which a corporation or firm protects itself from the loss of human assets by taking out policies on the lives of the officers and key men in management and production.

business interruption insurance. Insurance protecting against loss from the interruption of business as a whole, as distinguished from coverage upon the merchandise or other property owned, held, or used in the business. 29A Am J Rev ed Ins § 1366.

business invitee. See **business visitor**.

business league. An association or club of businessmen; a commercial club organized for purposes similar to those of a chamber of commerce. Northwestern Municipal Asso. v United States (CA8 Minn) 99 F2d 460.

business month. A month of thirty days, as distinguished from the calendar month.

business name. The name under which a business is operated. In the case of an individual, it may be his real name or an assumed or ficticious name. In the case of a partnership, the business name may be a combination of the names of the partners or an assumed or business name. In the case of a business corporation, the name is provided by the articles of incorporation.
See **trade name**.

business of banking. See **banking**.

business or closely built-up sections. See **business section**.

business or commercial corporation. See **business corporation**.

business purpose. See **business**.

business records. See **back of original entry; business entry statute; Business Records Act; shop-book rule**.

Business Records Act. A federal statute creating an exception to the hearsay rule in respect of business records. 28 USC § 1732; Matthews v United States (CA5 Ga) 217 F2d 409, 50 ALR2d 1187; a statute, drafted by the National Conference of Commissioners on Uniform State Laws, which has been adopted in 26 states. Am J2d Desk Book, Document 129.

business requirements. See **requirements of the business**.

business section. That part of a city which is occupied by places of retail business, shops, and offices, to the exclusion generally of residences and factories.
The phrase "business and closely built-up" sections has been held to apply only to sections which are both "business" and "closely built-up"; whereas the phrase "business or closely built-up" has been held to apply to closely built-up sections which are not necessarily "business". Anno: 50 ALR2d 348.

business situs. A term of application in the law of taxation of intangibles, meaning a situs in a place other than the domicil of the owner, where such owner, through an agent, manager, or the like, is conducting a business out of which credits or open accounts grow and are used as a part of the business of the agency. 51 Am J1st Tax § 469.

business time. See **loss of business time**.

business trust. Otherwise known as a Massachusetts trust or common-law trust. A form of business organization consisting essentially of an arrangement whereby property is conveyed to trustees, in accordance with the terms of an instrument of trust, to be held and managed for the benefit of such persons as may from time to time be the holders of transferable certificates issued by the trustees showing the shares into which the beneficial interest in the property is divided. Hecht v Malley, 265 US 144, 68 L Ed 949, 44 S Ct 462; an unincorporated business organization created by an instrument, by which property is to be held and managed by trustees for the benefit and profit of such persons as may be or may become the holders of transferable certificates evidencing the beneficial interests in the trust estate. 13 Am J2d Bus Tr § 1; a convenient method by which persons become associated for dealings in real estate, the development of tracts of land, the construction of improvements and the purchase, management and sale of properties. Morrissey v Commissioner, 296 US 344, 80 L Ed 263, 56 S Ct 289.
An organization within the meaning of the Uniform Commercial Code; an association, for the purpose of taxation under the Internal Revenue Code, where created for the transaction of business. 13 Am J2d Bus Tr § 89.

business use. The use of real property for the purpose of obtaining profit or additional income therefrom. Anno: 14 ALR2d 1428.
See **business**.

business visitor. One who comes upon premises for the purpose of trade, commerce, or a business or commercial transaction, with one who keeps open upon the premises a store, shop, or office for the transaction of business with the public generally. 38 Am J1st Negl § 98; a person who is invited or permitted to enter or remain on land in the possession of another for a purpose directly or indirectly connected with business dealings between them. Yeager v Chapman, 233 Minn 1, 45 NW2d 776, 22 ALR2d 1260; a person who comes upon premises, not as an invited or uninvited guest, a volunteer, licensee, or employee of the occupant, or as anyone so connected with the occupant, that he must be deemed to accept the premises, dangers and all, as he finds them, but as one who has business to transact with the occupant, and upon the invitation of the occupant, express or implied. Indermaur v Dames (Eng) LR 1 CP 274.
The status of an invitee on business premises may arise from a visit by one not on the premises for the purpose of the proprietor's business, but for the convenience of others on the premises for such purpose. Murphy v Kelly, 15 NJ 608, 105 A2d 841, 44 ALR2d 1316.

bussa (bus′sa). (Old English.) A ship of large size and clumsy construction.—Spelman.

bus station. See **bus terminal**.

bus terminal. The end of a bus line; a bus depot; a place on the line of a motor carrier where passengers may board or leave the busses and where some goods may be accepted for shipment or delivered to consignees.

but. A word, originally a conjunction, which has developed into additional use as a preposition and an adverb: yet, still, however, except, provided, merely.

butane. A gaseous hydrocarbon, which, in the liquid form, is adaptable for, and is used in, the engines of motor vehicles, as fuel, particularly truck engines.

butcher. A person who kills or slaughters animals to procure their meat. A person who buys the carcasses of animals that have been slaughtered (by a butcher) for meat, and cuts them up and retails them, without more, is neither a butcher nor engaged in the butcher business. Henback v State, 53 Ala 523; more broadly defined, in accord with modern usage, one who keeps a shop for the sale of meat, but hardly a mere clerk in the meat department of a supermarket.

butcher knife. A knife with a long blade for cutting meat; a domestic and household instrument but nevertheless a deadly weapon. 56 Am J1st Weap § 3.

butcher shop. A place for the sale of meat at retail.

but-for rule. A name which has sometimes been applied to the generally discarded rule for determining the proximate cause of an accident as being that act or omission "but for" which the accident would not have occurred. So many elements, however, may enter into the determination of what is the efficient cause, and so long a train of antecedents may come under consideration, "but for" the happening of any one of which the result complained of would not have occurred, that we may still be involved in the difficulties of selecting from the train of antecedents the one to which should attach the legal liability sought to be imposed. Causes of injury which are mere incidents of the operating cause, while in a sense factors, are so insignificant that the law cannot fasten responsibility upon one who may have set them in motion. 38 Am J1st Negli § 54.

butler. The head of the servants in a household; the man in charge of the pantry and wine cellar.
See **botiler of the king**.

butt (but). A ridge left in ploughing; an archery target; a liquid measure of one hundred and ten gallons; a barrel; the thicker end, as the butt of a log.

buttals (but'als). End boundary lines.

butte. A term used in the western part of the United States for a hill, usually a hill which is prominent because it is surrounded by a plain.

butted and bounded. Abutting and bounded; bounded.

butter. A dairy product used in cooking and as a spread for bread.
See **adulterated butter**.

butterfat. The fat in milk from which butter is made and by the amount of which milk is graded.

butts. See **butt**.

butts and bounds. Boundaries.

butty (but'i). A coal mining contractor.

buy. Verb: To purchase; to acquire a right or title to property by paying money or some other consideration for it. Noun: A purchase.

buy and sell. A constitutional right under the guaranty of life, liberty, and property. 16 Am J2d Const L § 357.

buyer. One who makes a purchase.
See **able buyer; ready, able, and willing buyer; purchaser; vendee**.

buyer's option. Literally, any option which a purchaser may be entitled to under the contract of purchase; technically, the right of the buyer of securities on margin to pay or tender the amount owing to the broker and receive the securities. 12 Am J2d Brok § 133.

buyer's risk. In sales, the risk follows the title and if the title to the goods vests in the buyer at the moment of the sale or upon delivery to the carrier, then the risk of loss or damage to the goods during transportation is upon the buyer. 46 Am J1st Sales § 279.
See **caveat emptor; resale at purchaser's risk**.

buy in. To become a partner in a firm by purchasing an interest.
See **bid in**.

buying and selling dormant titles. A particular form of maintenance which was prohibited by an English statute in 1541. In some jurisdictions such transactions are prohibited by the common law. In others, statutes forbid the transfer to a stranger of the title to land in adverse possession of another. 14 Am J2d Champ § 11.

buying long. A stock market term for one who is a purchaser rather than a seller of stocks. The term is redundant, since every buyer becomes long, at least for the moment.
See **long**.

buying of pleas. An inept term for purchase of a chose in action, a form of maintenance at common law. 14 Am J2d Champ § 10.

buying titles. See **buying and selling dormant titles; bracery**.

by. At or near a designated place; at the hand of; through the means, act, or instrumentality of. Thus, "an injury by accident" is synonymous with "an injury caused by accident." Carroll v Industrial Com. 69 Colo 473, 195 P 1097; 19 ALR 107, 109. Executing a bill, note, or contract in the name of the principal, followed by that of the agent, separated by the word "by," is a method of executing an agency so as to impose liability upon the principal and, conversely, no personal liability upon the agent. 3 Am J2d Agency § 190; 11 Am J2d B & N § 559.

In designating a terminal point of time, the word is variously construed as meaning "as soon as," "as early as," "before," "on or before," or "not later than," but in some cases as exclusive of the day named. 52 Am J1st Time § 29.

by a moiety and not by all. A phrase descriptive of the nature of possession of tenant in common. 20 Am J2d Coten § 26.

by-bidder. See **by-bidding**.

by-bidding. The making of sham or fictitious bids at an auction sale for the purpose of inflating the ultimate and highest bid. Osborn v Apperson Lodge, 213 Ky 533, 281 SW 500, 46 ALR 117, 121.
See **puffing**.

by bill. By original bill. Some suits were commenced by original bill, others by original writ.

by bill without writ. Same as **by bill**.

by color of office. See **colore officii**.

by due course of law. An open court and an available remedy under the law for all injuries or wrongs. 16 Am J2d Const L § 384.

by due process of law. According to the settled course of judicial proceedings or in accordance with natural, inherent, and fundamental principles of justice, enforceable in the usual modes established in the administration of government with respect to kindred matters. 16 Am J2d Const L § 546.
See **due process of law.**

bye. See **by the bye.**

by estimation. An expression used in conveyancing, signifying "more or less."

by God and my country. The most formal answer of a defendant upon arraignment in reply to a question as to how he will be tried.

by her own labor. The avails of manual labor and the proceeds of a business conducted through agents. 27 Am J1st H & W § 466.

by inch of candle. See **auction by inch of candle; sale by the candle.**

by law. In accord with law, whether the common law, a constitution, or a statute or ordinance which is constitutional.

by-laws. Rules and regulations adopted for their government by corporations, unincorporated associations, business trusts, fraternal orders and benefit societies, and benevolent associations, clubs, and societies, which, if not in violation of statute or the charter of the body, must be applied within the body in determining the manner of conduct of the business and the rights and liabilities of members.
See **municipal by-law.**

by my estate. A common phrase in a direction for the payment of estate tax, having reference to the general estate or residuary estate. 28 Am J Rev ed Inher T § 515.

by operation of law. See **operation of law.**

by-pass. Noun: A way that misses or avoids something in or along a highway, applied most frequently at the present to alternate ways which miss the congested part of cities. Verb: To detour; to avoid.

by-product. A secondary or additional product of value; something produced in the course of an industry in addition to the principal product. It is well known that packing houses, oil refineries, and some other kinds of manufactories, make by-products amounting in value to a material part of their gross income. The right so to do is a private property right which should be encouraged rather than prohibited. Bishop v Tulsa, 21 Okla Crim 457, 209 P 228, 27 ALR 1008, 1012.

by-product material. Radioactive material, with the exception of special nuclear material, yielded in or made radioactive by exposure to radiation incident to the process or producing or utilizing special nuclear material. 42 USC § 2014(e).

by reason of. By virtue of. See United States v William Cramp & Sons Ship & E. Bldg. Co. 206 US 118, 51 L Ed 983, 27 S Ct 676.
See **proximate cause.**

byrlaw (bir'lâ). Same as **burlaw.**

by-road. A public road, but not heavily traveled; a road out of the main stream of traffic. Wood v Hurd, 34 NJ L 87 89.

bystander. A person who stands near; a person who has no concern with the business which is being transacted. State v Jones, 102 Mo 305, 307. A person present in court but not participating in or connected with the proceedings. A witness, being a participant in the proceedings, is not a bystander. McConnell v McCord, 170 Ark 839, 840, 281 SW 384. A person close by when an accident occurs.
See **talesmen.**

by the acre. See **sale by the acre.**

by the bye. Declaring against a defendant without the issuance of process to secure his appearance. This was permitted when the defendant was already before the court as defendant in some other action.

by the candle. See **sale by the candle.**

by the law of the land. By due process of law; by a law that gives a man an opportunity to be heard, before depriving him of his life, liberty, or property; by a law which hears before it condemns; which proceeds upon inquiry, and renders judgment only after trial.
See **by due course of law; by due process of law.**

by the moiety or half and by the whole. A phrase descriptive of the nature of possession of joint tenant. 20 Am J2d Coten § 7.

by the shore. A phrase in the description of a boundary, meaning to low-water mark. Stevens v King, 76 Me 197.

by various courses. The expression is sometimes employed in descriptions of land bounded by a stream or river, as "extending down Potomack river by various courses 3152 po.," and implies that the grant described follows the line of the stream. Such meaning is held not to be changed by the words "including several small creeks or inlets." Marine Railway & Coal Co. v United States, 257 US 47, 63, 66 L Ed 124, 130, 42 S Ct 32.

by virtue of. The term means literally by force of, or by authority of; but it is not too great a stretch to make it equivalent to "by reason of." The two expressions were regarded as equivalents in a certain connection in United States v Wm. Cramp & Sons Co. 206 US 118, 51 L Ed 983, 27 S Ct 676. Phillips v Houston Nat. Bank (CA5 Tex) 108 F2d 934.

by warrant of law. See **warrant of law.**

Byzantine Code. See **Basilica.**

C

C. Roman numeral for 100.
At one time, the letter "C" was branded on the forehead as a punishment for counterfeiting, in Rhode Island.

c. Abbreviation for cent or cents; capacity; centimeter; century; chapter; chancellor; cubic; hundredweight; and, in rare instances, court; a symbol for "copyright," in a notice of copyright, where inclosed within a circle, thus ©. 18 Am J2d Copyr § 58; a brand mark placed upon chattels belonging to the United States, previously branded US, where they are offered for sale, which is usually after they have been inspected and condemned for government use. 46 Am J1st Sales § 311.

C. An abbreviation, infrequently used, for Corps; Court; or Chancellor.

ca. An abbreviation of the Latin word "circa," meaning "about." It is often used with dates, as circa 1492, or ca. 1492.

C.A. Abbreviation for Court of Appeals.

C/A. Abbreviation for **current account.**

CAA. Abbreviation for Civil Aeronautics Authority.

cab. See **taxicab.**

cabal (ka-bal'). A junto; a small political faction.

caballeria (kä-bä-lyä-rē'ạ). A Mexican term for the measure of a tract containing 105.75 acres. Ainsa v United States, 161 US 219, 40 L Ed 677, 16 S Ct 544.

caballero (kä-bäl-yā'rō). Gentleman.

cabaret. A restaurant wherein alcoholic beverages are served; a restaurant with instrumental music and singing.

cabinet. A body of officials forming an advisory council, the most illustrious of which is the Cabinet of the President of the United States, consisting of the heads of the Departments of Government.

cabinet council. A council of cabinet members held privately to consider public matters.

cable. Noun: A heavy rope, often made of wire; an underground or underseas bundle of wires in insulation used for the transmission of messages by telegraph or telephone. Verb: To send a message by undersea cable.

Cable Act. A federal statute of Sept. 22, 1922, repealing the rule by which the naturalization of a female was effected by her marriage to a citizen.

cablegram. A message transmitted by undersea cable.

cable system. A system of operating street railway cars by means of an underground cable set in motion by a stationary engine at the power house of the system. Hooper v Baltimore City Passenger Railway Co. 85 Md 509, 37 A 359.

cable transfer of exchange. An arrangement whereby the person contracting to deliver exchange contracts that he will make available by cable to the person contracting to take such exchange, a credit of the amount specified, at the point specified, and at the time specified. In such an agreement there is no guaranty or necessary implication that the contractor has any credit which he is selling, or agreeing to sell, or that he will place the credit through a third party as correspondent. Equitable Trust Co. v Keene, 232 NY 290, 133 NE 894, 19 ALR 1137, 1139.

cablish (kab'lish). Brushwood; wood or brush blown down by the wind.

caboose car (kạ-bös'). A car which is coupled at the rear end of a freight train and which is intended primarily for the accommodation of the men connected with the train. Shoemaker v Kingsbury (US) 12 Wall 369, 20 L Ed 432. It is, however, the car in which drovers accompanying shipments of livestock are accommodated. 14 Am J2d Car § 756. Occasionally, passengers for hire are carried on freight trains, in which case, they ride in the caboose. 14 Am J2d Car § 860.

cache (kash). A place, usually in wilderness or an unfrequented region, where supplies are stored. The word implies concealment. Lane v Washington Daily News, 66 App DC 245, 85 F2d 822.

cachepolus (ka"che-pō-lus'). A catchpoll; a bailiff; a constable.

cacicazgos (ka-thi-kath'gos). Lands held in entail by the caciques in Indian villages in Spanish-America. —Bouvier's Law Dict.

cadaster (ka-das'tẻr). Same as **cadastre.**

cadastral survey. An original survey of a large area of public lands made by the government.

cadastre (ka-das'tẻr). An official statement of the quantity and value of real property in any district, made for the purpose of justly apportioning the taxes payable on such property. Strother v Lucas (US) 12 Pet 410, 428 note, 9 L Ed 1137, 1144 note.

Cadat a causa sua (ka'dat ā kâ'za su'ā). He shall fail in, or lose, his case.

cadaver (ka-da'ver). A corpse.
See **dead body.**

cadere (ka'de-re). To fall; to fail; to end; to abate.

cadere assisa (ka'de-re as-sī'sa). To be nonsuit.

cadere causa (ka'de-re kâ'za). To fail or lose a cause or case.

cadet (kạ-det'). A youth under tuition and drill with a view to his becoming an army or navy officer.

cadi (kā'dī). A Turkish civil magistrate.

Cadit a causa (ka'dit ā kâ'za). He loses his case.

Cadit actio (ka'dit ak'she-ō). The action fails.

Cadit warrantia (ka'dit war-ran'she-a). The warranty fails.

caduca (ka-dū'ka). That which is inherited; also a testamentary gift which lapses and an escheat.

caducary (ka-dū'ka-ri). Relating to or subject to escheat or forfeiture of property.

caducus (ka-dū'kus). Falling.

caedua (kae'du-a). Preserved for cutting, as wood.

Caesarean operation (sẹ-zā'rẹ-ạn). The delivery of a child by surgery, the term deriving from the fact or legend respecting the birth of Julius Caesar.

Caesarean section. A more professional term for **Caesarean operation.**

Caetera desunt (sē'te-ra dē'sunt). Other things are wanting or lacking.

caeteris paribus (sē'te-ris pa'ri-bus). Other things being equal.

caeteris tacentibus (sē'te-ris ta-sen'ti-bus). The others being silent, not voting, not expressing opinions.

caeteros. See **inter caeteros**.

caetororum (sē-te-rō'rum). Of the rest or residue,— a term applied to the residuum of an estate.

c. a. f. An abbreviation for "cost, freight and assurance," sometimes used in mercantile transactions, especially in England. The letters in such form have also been used in mercantile transactions as an abbreviation of "cost and freight." 46 Am J1st Sales § 136.
See **cost and freight; cost, insurance, and freight**.

cafe (ka-fā'). A restaurant. 29 Am J Rev ed Innk § 9. As used in a Sunday law, either by way of prohibition or of exception to a prohibition, the terms café, restaurant and victualing house, seem to have the same meaning, and to intend an establishment where food is sold to the public for consumption on the premises. Anno: 9 ALR 428.
A cafe is not an inn. 29 Am J Rev ed Innk § 9.

cahier (ka-iā'). A memorial; a petition; a report; a section of a book.

caisson disease (kā'son di-zēz"). Caisson disease, or "the bends," as the most prevalent and dangerous ailment of divers or men who work in a compressed-air atmosphere is known, results when a diver who has been working under great pressure is too quickly brought to the surface and normal pressures. Nitrogen in the air goes into and out of solution in the blood slowly. When pressure is too quickly reduced, this slow change causes bubbles in the blood and the attacks are frequently fatal.

calaboose (kal-a-bös'). A jail.

calami diversitas vel atramenti (ka'la-mī dī-ver'si-tās vel a-tra-men'tī). A difference in penmanship or ink.

calamity. A cause of general distress in the nation, a state, or a subdivision of the state, which arises from natural forces and also from adversities such as widespread unemployment. Muskegon Heights v Danigelis, 253 Mich 260, 235 NW 83, 73 ALR 696. The devastation of a country by hurricanes or earthquakes, and the desolation of its inhabitants by famine or plague, are great calamities. Jones v Williams, 121 Tex 94, 45 SW2d 130, 79 ALR 983.

calamus (kal'a-mus). A writing pen made of a reed; handwriting with a pen.

calangium (ka-lan'ji-um). A disputed claim.

calcea (kal'sē-a). A causeway.

calceto reparendo. See **de calceto reparendo**.

calcetum (kal-sē-tum). A causeway

calculated. Computed; reckoned; intended. State v Wyman, 56 Mont 600, 186 P 1; fitted, adapted, or suited by design. Smallwood v Commonwealth (Ky) 40 SW 248; Gerrish v Norris, 63 Mass (9 Cush) 167, 170.

calefagium (ka-le-fā'gi-um). The right to take fuel annually.

calendar. The mode of adjusting the natural divisions of time with respect to each other for the purposes of civil life. 52 Am J1st Time § 9; a tabulation of time by days and weeks in the succession of the months; a system of measuring time as in years, months and days.
See **court calendar; Gregorian calendar; intercalary month; judge's calendar; Julian calendar; tax calendar**.

Calendar Amendment Act. An English statute passed in 1751, adopting the Gregorian calendar.

calendar call. The reading of the trial calendar, that is, the list of cases for trial during the term or a week of the term, ordinarily on a stated day of the week, for which attorneys attend and respond, when their cases are called, to indicate whether a case is ready for trial.

calendar days. Consecutive days, including Sundays and holidays. Okanogan Indians v United States, 279 US 671, 73 L Ed 894, 49 S Ct 463, 64 ALR 1434.

calendar month. A month by the calendar, that is, a month computed, not by counting the days intervening, but by referring to the calendar for a month as it appears therein, without regard to the number of days it may contain. 11 Am J2d B & N § 291; a month according to the calendar rather than a lunar month. Simmons v Hanne, 50 Fla 267, 39 So 77.

calendar of causes. See **court calendar**.

calendar of prisoners. A sheriff's list of prisoners with their sentences or commitments.

calendar week. A period of seven days, usually reckoned from one Sabbath or Sunday to the next. 52 Am J1st Time § 12.

calendar year. The period from January 1st to December 31st, inclusive, of any year.

calends (ka-lendz). The first day of the month in the Roman calendar.

calf. The offspring of a cow, so called until it has shed its two front milk teeth; a colloquial term for an awkward youth, also for a person who complains unduly.

call. A reference made in a description of real estate to a course, distance, marker, monument, or a natural object such as a tree, stream, rock, etc., by which a boundary is to be determined; stopping at a place for a social visit, or, in the case of a physician, a professional visit; a notice by an obligor that its securities are being redeemed; a notice of a meeting to be held by the stockholders or board of directors of a corporation; an assessment made upon the members of an association, club, or society; a demand on a subscriber to stock in a corporation for an additional contribution to the capital of the corporation; an option to purchase property, particularly corporate stock, securities, or commodities, at a stipulated price, on or before a specific future date or within a specified future period of time, say, 30, 60, or 90 days.
See **on call; port of call**.

callable bonds. See **redeemable bonds**.

call-board contract. A contract between members of a stock exchange representing a specified quantity of a commodity, which a seller might produce and deliver to the buyer instead of the commodity itself. Berry v Kowalsky, 95 Cal 134, 30 P 202.

called meeting. A special meeting of an organized group held upon notice.

called upon to pay. Compelled or required to pay by law. H. Koehler & Co. v Reinheimer, 20 Misc 62, 45 NYS 337.

call girl. A prostitute whose appointments are made by telephone.

calling. Business, occupation, profession, trade, or vocation.

calling the plaintiff. An old and abandoned procedure followed in a stratagem by a losing plaintiff to avoid an adjudication. Blackstone has stated that before a verdict is delivered by the jury, if the plaintiff is not present or represented by counsel, it is the common-law practice for the crier to call the plaintiff, after which the plaintiff is nonsuited if he or his counsel stay away. The plaintiff adopts this course if it appears that the verdict will be against him, in order to avoid an adverse verdict which would be a bar to a renewal of the same litigation, while a nonsuit would not be such a bar. See 3 Bl Comm 376.

calling to the bar. Admitting a law student to the privilege of practicing law before the courts.

call of nature. The prompting of a visit to the bathroom, toilet, or lavatory.

call patent. A land patent in which the corners in the description of the land are all stakes, or all but one, or whose lines were not run out and marked at the time of the issuance of the patent. Hall v Pratt, 142 Ky 561, 563, 134 SW 900.

calls. See **call**.

call to arms. An ancient expression, meaning to call on a man to put on his armor and take up his weapons.

calpe (kal'pē). Tribute paid by a clansman to his chief for personal protection.

calumnia (ka-lum'ni-a). A false charge; a calumny; a claim; a demand.

calumniae juramentum (ka-lum'ni-ē jū-ra-men'tum). The oath against calumny; an oath of good faith.

calumniare (ka-lum-ni-ā're). To claim; to calumniate.

calumniators (ka-lum'ni-ā-tọrs). Persons who make false accusations maliciously.

calumniatrix (ka-lum''ni-ā'trix). A female slanderer.

calumny (kal'um-ni). Libel; slander; defamation.
"There was a word called '*calumny*' in the civil law, which signified an unjust prosecution or defense of a suit, and the phrase is still said to be used in the courts of Scotland and the ecclesiastical and admiralty courts of England, though we do not find cases of the kind in the reports." See Lanning v Christy, 30 Ohio St 115, 117.
See **oath of calumny**.

Calvinism (kal'vin-izm). The theological doctrine of the Presbyterian church, of which doctrine John Calvin was the first expounder. Its polity consists in self-government through chosen representatives, rejecting alike the rule of one man, and the rule of the extemporized and irresponsible assembly. Ramsey v Hicks, 174 Ind 428, 91 NE 344.

Calvin's Case. An action in which it was held that Calvin, though born in Scotland after the English crown descended to James the First, who was also king of Scotland, was entitled to hold land.

camara (kam-a̱-rā). A chamber; a vault; a treasury.

camarage (kam'a̱-rāj). Rent paid for storage.

cambellanus (kam''bel-lā'nus). A chamberlain.

cambiator (kam-bi-ā'tor). A cambist.

cambio (kam'bi-ō). An exchange; a bourse.

cambipartia (kam''bi-par'she-a). Champerty.

cambiparticeps (kam''bi-par'ti-seps). A person who is a party to the offense of champerty.

cambist (kam'bist). A dealer in negotiable paper.

cambium (kam'bi-um). (Civil law.) An exchange; an exchange of lands.

camera (kam'ẹ-rạ̈). Same as **camara**.
See **in camera**.

cameralistics. The science of finance.

camera regis (ka'me-ra rē'jis). A harbor.

camerarius (ka-me-rā'ri-us). A treasurer; a chamberlain.

camera scaccarii (ka'me-ra ska-kā'ri-ī). The exchequer chamber.

camera stellata (ka'me-ra stel-lā'ta). The star-chamber.

camino (ka-mē'no). A highway.

camorra (ka-mor'ạ̈). An Italian secret society.

camouflage. The art of disguising or concealing the nature of objects. Palmer v Commonwealth, 240 Ky 175, 41 SW2d 936; deception, particularly by concealing ultimate purpose.

campana (kam-pā'na). A church-bell; a bell.

campana bajula (kam-pā'na ba-jū'la). A hand-bell used by court criers.

campanile (kam-pạ-nē'le). A bell tower.

campartum (kam-par'tum). A part of a field.

Campbell's Act. An English statute giving a remedy for death by wrongful act, 9 & 10 Victoria c 93.

campers (kam'pẹrs). A share, particularly a share by a champertous division.

campertum (kam-per'tum). A grain or corn field.

campfight (kamp'fīt). A duel; a battle.

camphor. See **spirits of camphor**.

campias in withernam (kam'pi-as in wi-ther-nam'). A writ to seize other goods of equal value when the plaintiff's goods have been taken out of the county.

campi-partitio (kam'pī par-ti'she-ō). A champertous division of the land.

campus. A field; the grounds of a school, college, or university.

campus maii (kam'pus mā'ī). May day—a Saxon anniversary.

can. Verb: To have ability or power to accomplish. Sometimes confused with "may." As used in an oil lease for a stated number of years and as much longer as oil and gas "can" be found in paying quantities, the word has the same meaning as "is". Lowther Oil Co. v Miller-Sibley Oil Co. 53 W Va 501, 44 SE 433.
Noun: A container, especially for liquids and soft substances. A slang term for jail, also for lavatory.

Canada. The great nation, an independent nation of the British Commonwealth of Nations, on the northern boundary of the United States.

Canadian money. Legal currency in Canada. Thompson v Sloan (NY) 23 Wend 71.
The words "Canada money" in which a note is expressed to be payable may be shown to mean Canadian bank bills and not specie, by proof of a custom. Thompson v Sloan (NY) 23 Wend 71.

canal. An artificial waterway, public or private in character, which is usually, although not necessarily, used for navigation. If a canal is navigable and its situation is such as to form a continuous waterway for interstate or foreign commerce, it constitutes navigable water of the United States to which the admiralty jurisdiction of the Federal courts attaches. 13 Am J2d Can § 3.

canalized river. A natural stream which is a part of a canal or system of canals, for example the Genesee river in New York. In the language of engineers, rivers are "canalized" when dams or locks are so constructed and operated in them as to raise their water level along certain stretches by means of backwater, so as to render them, to the extent of the raising, artificial canals instead of natural waterways. United States v Cress, 243 US 316, 61 L Ed 746, 37 S Ct 380.

Canal Zone. A reservation of the United States Government on the Isthmus of Panama, under a treaty with the Republic of Panama, consisting of a strip of land which contains the Panama Canal.

cancel. To annul or strike out; to set aside. Otterbein v Babor & C. Co. 272 NY 149, 5 NE2d 71, 107 ALR 510. As applied to a contract, the words cancel and terminate are not synonymous, but the infinitive "to cancel" is embraced by the infinitive "to terminate." A contract cannot be cancelled without being terminated, although it may be terminated in any of several methods, one of which is by cancellation. A claim that a contract has been cancelled is an admission that it was terminated. Acme Mills v Tanner-Brice Co. (CA5 Ga)112 F2d 910.
See **cancellation.**

cancellaria (kan-se-lā'ri-ą). Chancery. The high court of chancery, says Blackstone, has its name from the judge, the lord chancellor or cancellarious who presides there and who was so termed from cancelling the king's letters patent when granted contrary to law, which is the highest point of his jurisdiction. See 3 Bl Comm 46.

cancellarius (kan"sel-lā'ri-us). A chancellor.

cancellation. An erasure, blotting out, striking out, or crossing out of some portion of a written instrument. Dowling v Gilliland, 286 Ill 530, 122 NE 70, 3 ALR 829; the nullification of a contract by agreement of the parties or by one of the parties under a cancellation clause contained in the contract; a remedy whereby a court of equity in exceptional cases exercises its jurisdiction to decree the surrender and cancellation of written instruments. 13 Am J2d Canc Inst § 2.
See **rescission.**

cancellation clause. The provision in a contract for the termination thereof by one of the parties, as illustrated in contracts of insurance; a clause in a charter-party whereby the charterer reserves the right to cancel the charter-party if the ship shall fail to arrive on a specified day at a named port ready for cargo. Disney v Furness, Withy & Co. (DC Md) 78 F 810, 814.

cancellation of insurance. The rescission or nullification of a contract of insurance under statutory provisions or stipulations of the insurance contract itself, including provisions for cancellation upon notice or request; by the mutual consent or acquiescence of the parties; or because of fraud, misrepresentation, mistake, an adjudication of insolvency of the insurer, or the making of an assignment for the benefit of creditors by the insurer. Otterbein v Babor & C. Co. 272 NY 149, 5 NE2d 71, 107 ALR 1510.

cancellatura (kan"sel-lā'tu-ra). A cancellation.

cancelled check. A check paid by the bank upon which it is drawn and delivered to the drawer with his monthly statement.

cancelli (kan-sel'i). The railing inclosing the bar of a court; cancellation marks.

candidate. A person who seeks office and who, in the case of a public office to be filled by election, has taken the steps required by the election law to have his name presented at the election so that the voters may vote for him. 25 Am J2d Elect §§ 128 et seq. A person who, after having been nominated as a candidate, is presented in that capacity to the voters at an election. State v Hirsch, 125 Ind 207, 24 NE 1062. A person who seeks a nomination for public office at a primary election.
A man is a candidate for an office when he is seeking such office. It is begging the question to say that he is only a candidate after nomination, for many persons have been elected to office who were never nominated at all. Leonard v Commonwealth, 112 Pa 607, 624, 4a 220.
See **independent candidate; party candidate.**
Another meaning of the term "candidate" is that of a person proposed for an award or for initiation into a fraternal order.

candle. See **auction by inch of candle; sale by the candle.**

Candlemas Day (kan'dl-mąs). February second.

cane. The plant from the stalk of which juice is taken for the manufacture of sugar or molasses; the stem of a plant; (Scotch.) a tax; rent paid in produce.

canem et lupum. See **inter canem et lupum.**

cannabis. A narcotic drug derived from the marijuana plant. People v Yeargin, 3 Ill 2d 25, 119 NE2d 753. As defined in the Uniform Narcotic Drug Act, it includes (a) The dried flowering or fruiting tops of the pistillate plant Cannabis Sativa Linne from which the resin has not been extracted, (b) the resin extracted from such tops, and (c) every compound, manufacture, salt, derivative, mixture, or preparation of such resin, or of such tops from which the resin has not been extracted. Anno: 119 ALR 1402.

canning barge. A fishing vessel equipped for canning the catch.

cannot. A word so mandatory in a statute as to preclude a choice. Burtnett v King, 33 Cal 2d 805, 205 P2d 657, 12 ALR2d 333.

canon (kan'ǫn). A law; a church officer who took revenue for conducting service.

canonic (kạ-non'ik). Pertaining to a canon or church law.

canonical (kạ-non'i-kạl). Same as **canonic.**

canonical impediments (kạ-non'i-kạl). The personal relationships or defects which under the ecclesiastical law rendered voidable a marriage of one who possessed them. Among these impediments were consanguinity, affinity and impotence, while the so-called civil disabilities, such as want of age, idiocy, lunacy, and the like, made a marriage void ab initio. 35 Am J1st Mar § 85.

canonical purgation. An ancient proceeding wherein a defendant charged with crime was permitted to

CANONICATE [171] CAPIAS

clear himself by denying the charge under oath. See 4 Bl Comm 342.

canonicate (ka-non'i-kāt). The office of a canon.

canonicus (ka-no'ni-kus). A canon.

canon law (kan'on-lâ). A body of Roman ecclesiastical law, relative to such matters as the church of Rome either had, or pretended to have jurisdiction over. See 1 Bl Comm 82.

canon law of England. A kind of national canon law composed of legatine and provincial constitutions, and adapted only to the exigencies of the church and kingdom of England. See 1 Bl Comm 82.

canonry (kan'on-ri). The office or benefice of a canon.

canons of descent. The rules of descent; the English rules of descent during the feudal period. 23 Am J2d Desc & D § 7.

canons of inheritance. Same as **canons of descent.**

Canons of Judicial Ethics. A concise statement, in numbered canons or paragraphs, by the American Bar Association, of its views in reference to the principles and ethical standards which should govern the personal practice of members of the judiciary in the administration of their office, offered as a proper guide and reminder for judges, and as indicating what the people have a right to expect from them. Am J2d Desk Book, Document 67.

Canons of Professional Ethics. The rules and principles adopted by the American Bar Association for the guidance of lawyers in reference to their duties and standard of conduct in litigation and all the relations of professional life. Am J2d Desk Book, Document 91; rules and principles prescribing ethical standards for lawyers adopted by local or state bar associations.

cant. Jargon; insincerity. (Civil law.) Also called "licitation,"—a mode of dividing property held in common by two or more persons; which may be avoided by the consent of all those who are interested, in the same manner that any other contract may be avoided, which is entered into by consent of the parties. Hayes v Cuny (La) 9 Mart 87, 89.

Cantaur (kan'tor). Latin for "Canterbury."

cantel (kan'tel). The excess over full measure.

canton (kan'ton). A hundred; district.

cantred (kan'tred). (Welsh.) A district; a hundred.

canum (ka'num). A Scotch duty paid in produce.

canvass. An examination. The solicitation of votes, orders for goods, etc., by going from house to house or from place of business to place of business; the tabulation prior to an election of probable votes for the purpose of predicting the outcome of the election; the opening and examination of election returns and the compiling of a summarized statement of the several returns, showing the result of the election within the territorial unit composed of the smaller units from which the returns are made. 26 Am J2d Elect § 298. "To canvass the votes" cast at an election is an expression used in the election statutes which frequently has the same meaning as "to canvass the returns" of the election, and does not necessarily include the counting of the ballots cast at the election. People v Sausalito, 106 Cal 500, 40 P 11.

canvasser (kan'vas-ėr). One of a class of persons who, in a given town or city or county, go from house to house in their efforts to take orders for goods. They are not to be confused with "traveling salesmen." Price Co. v Atlanta, 105 Ga 358, 367. One who goes from house to house seeking votes, signatures on a petition, contributions, or support for a religious society.
See **canvass.**

canvass of election returns.
See **canvass.**

CAP. Abbreviation of **Civil Air Patrol.**

cap. See **black cap.**

capable. Susceptible; competent; qualified; fitting; possessing legal power or capacity. United States v Sischo (DC Wash) 262 F 1001.

capable of being used as a beverage. A term familiar in liquor legislation which includes within its scope those liquids which, although not generally considered as beverages, are yet capable of being so used, such as fruits preserved in alcohol, but not liquors which are so compounded with other substances or ingredients as to lose their character as intoxicating liquors. 30 Am J Rev ed Intox L § 7.

capable of producing intoxication. A beverage having intoxicating quality. 30 Am J Rev ed Intox L § 5.

capacity. Holding space, as the capacity of a ship or freight car; ability; legal competency; a person's ability to understand the nature and effect of the act in which he is engaged and the business which he is transacting. Tiger v Lozier, 124 Okla 260, 267, 256 P 727; the status in which one acts, for example, as an agent or an attorney.
See **business capacity; competency; criminal capacity; legal capacity; mental capacity; representative capacity; testamentary capacity.**

capacity of corporation. The capacity to act, akin to that of the capacity of a person, not the authority to perform an act. 19 Am J2d Corp § 952.

capacity of testator. See **testamentary capacity.**

capacity to labor. See **physical inability to work.**

capacity to sue or be sued. The status of a person which permits him to be a party to an action.

capax (ka'pāx). A holder; capable.

capax doli (ka'pāx do'lī). Capable of committing crime.

capax negotii (ka'pāx ne-gō'she-ī). Capable of transacting business; capable of contracting.

cape (kāp). A judicial writ to recover land on the tenant's default.

Capehart Act. A federal statute designed to provide urgently needed housing for military personnel on government property. 42 USC § 1594.

cape magnum (kā'pe mag'num). A judicial writ which lay to recover the possession of land when the tenant defaulted in a real action.

cape parvum (kā'pe par'vum). A judicial writ to recover the possession of the land in a real action in which the defendant had appeared.

caper (kā'pėr). A Dutch privateer.

capias (kā'pi-as). A writ to be executed by seizing, in some instances, the property, in other instances, the person of the defendant.

capias ad audiendum judicium (kā'pi-as ad â-di-en'dum jū-di'she-um). A writ issued to bring a defendant found guilty of a misdemeanor before the court to receive sentence. See 4 Bl Comm 375.

capias ad computandum (kā'pi-as ad kom-pu-tan'-dum). A writ commanding a defendant to account, upon his refusal to do so.

capias ad respondendum (kā'pi-as ad res-pon-den'-dum). A writ directing the arrest of the defendant in a civil action and his production in court on a day certain. 5 Am J2d Arr § 52.

capias ad satisfaciendum (kā'pi-as ad sa-tis-fā"she-en'dum). A writ for the arrest and imprisonment of a judgment debtor until the claim against him shall be satisfied or otherwise discharged according to law. 30 Am J2d Exec § 28.

capias in withernam (kā'pi-ăs in with'er-nam). A writ which issued against the goods or beasts of a distrainor who had eloigned—unlawfully removed out of the county, or concealed—the goods or beasts which he had distrained. Thus, there was a distress against a distress by way of reprisal for the eloignment, and the goods or beasts seized under the writ could not be replevied by their owner until the original distress was forthcoming. See 3 Bl Comm 148.

capias nomine districtionis (kā'pi-as nō'mi-ne dis-trik-shē-o'nis). "If an accountant failed to render his accounts, a process was issued, termed a *capias nomine districtionis*, against the body, goods, and lands of the accountant." Murray v Hoboken Land Co. (US) 18 How 272, 15 L Ed 372.

capias pro fine (kā'pi-as prō fī'ne). A writ for the arrest of a person who had not paid a fine which had been imposed upon him.

capias utlagatum (kā'pi-as ut-la-gā'tum). A writ which issued in a civil action for the arrest of a defendant who had absconded and had been outlawed and under which he could be committed until the outlawry was reversed. The purpose of the process being to secure the appearance of the defendant, such a reversal was usually secured as a mere formality. See 3 Bl Comm 284.

capita (ka'pi-ta). Heads; persons; persons regarded as individuals and not as belonging to an ancestral root or stock. See 2 Bl Comm 218. The word is the plural of "caput."

See **in capita; per capita; per stirpes or per capita.**

capital. In economics, money or property used for the production of wealth; used broadly, the entire assets of a corporation; ordinarily, that portion of the assets of the corporation, regardless of their source, which is utilized for the conduct of the corporate business and for the purpose of deriving therefrom gains and profits. Sohland v Baker, 15 Del Ch 431, 141 A 277, 58 ALR 693; Parkinson v State Bank, 84 Utah 278, 35 P2d 814, 94 ALR 1112; a fund so set apart and devoted to the corporate uses and the security of creditors that the law jealously guards it from the encroachment of directors in the declaration of dividends; it is in no way open to the directors to return it to the stockholders. 33 Am J1st Life Est § 405.

See **floating capital; invested capital; moneyed capital; nominal capital.**

capital asset. For income tax purposes, all the assets held by the taxpayer, whether or not connected with his trade or business except for certain assets listed in the statute. IRC § 1221.

capital crime. Same as **capital offense.**

capital expenditures. An unlawful encroachment upon the capital of a corporation by declaring a distribution or dividend of capital to stockholders; an income tax term for certain unusual expenditures, not deductible as ordinary and necessary business expenses, such as expenditures by a lessee for permanent improvements. 34 Am J2d Fed Tax ¶ 6061.

capitale (ka-pi-tā'le). A thing which is stolen, or its value.—Blount.

Expenditures made in defense of title to property, or to remove claims of others against property, or to perfect title to property are capital expenditures and not deductible, for income tax purposes, from gross income as expenses. Addison v Commissioner (CA8) 177 F2d 521, 23 ALR2d 897.

For income tax purposes, amounts paid out for new buildings, permanent improvements, or betterments, made to increase the value of property, or an amount spent to restore property or to make good the exhaustion of the property for which a deduction is or has been made for depreciation, amortization or depletion. IRC § 263.

capital gain. For income tax purposes, a gain realized only from sale or exchange of capital assets.

A taxable gain is conditioned upon the presence of a claim of right to the alleged gain and the absence of definite obligation to repay or return that which would otherwise constitute a gain, and does not accrue from the mere receipt of property or money which one is obliged to return or repay to the rightful owner. Commissioner v Wilcox, 327 US 404, 90 L Ed 752, 66 S Ct 546, 166 ALR 884, 887.

See **capital asset; gain derived from capital.**

capital improvement. An expense to be charged against principal, not income, of a trust. NY EPTL § 11-2.1, 1 (4)(B).

capitalis (ka-pi-tā'lis). Capital.

capitalis baro (ka-pi-tā'lis ba'ro). Chief baron.

capitalis custos (ka-pi-tā'lis kus'tōs). Chief magistrate or warden.

capitalis debitor (ka-pi-tā'lis de'bi-tor). The principal debtor.

capitalis dominus (ka-pi-tā'lis do'mi-nus). The chief lord.

capitalis justiciarius (ka-pi-tā'lis jūs"ti-she-ā'ri-us). The chief justice.

capitalis justiciarius banci (ka-pi-tā-lis jūs-ti-she-ā'ri-us ban'sī). Chief justice of the bench.

capitalis justiciarius totius Angliae (ka-pi-tā'lis jūs-ti-she-ā-ri-us to-she'us an'gli-ē). The chief justiciar of all England, a special magistrate who presided over the aula regia, was the principal minister of state and guardian of the realm in the absence of the king. His great power was considerably weakened by Magna Charta and was further curtailed under Henry III. See 3 Bl Comm 39.

capitalis plegius (ka-pi-tā'lis ple'ji-us). A chief surety.

capitalis redditus (ka-pi-tā'lis red'di-tus). Chief rent.

capitalization. The structure of a corporation in reference to the stock and bonds issued by it; the term is often applied in corporate reorganization cases, one aspect being the fairness of the allocation of securities under a plan of reorganization, the other being the feasibility of the new capital structure. 9 Am J2d Bankr § 1590.

capitalize. To compute periodical payments by reckoning their value as a sum in hand, as where earnings are capitalized for the purpose of ascertaining value for inheritance tax purposes. 28 Am J Rev ed Inher Tax § 373.

capital loss. For income tax purposes, a loss resulting only from a sale or exchange of capital assets. See **capital assets.**

capital of a corporation. See **capital.**

capital offense. An offense which may be punished capitally, that is, by the execution of the death penalty. The test of a "capital crime" is not the punishment which is imposed, but that which may be imposed. 21 Am J2d Crim L § 18.

capital punishment. A punishment for crime by the infliction of the death penalty. 21 Am J2d Crim L § 595.

capital stock. In common parlance, the shares of stock issued by a corporation and outstanding. Precisely, the amount of money, property or other means authorized by the charter of the corporation and contributed, or agreed to be contributed, by the shareholders as the financial basis for the prosecution of the business of the corporation, such contribution being made either directly through stock subscription or indirectly through the declaration of stock dividends. Dodge v Ford Motor Co. 204 Mich 459, 170 NW 668, 3 ALR 413; the total of all the corporate wealth, subject to all corporate liabilities and obligations. Anno: 45 ALR 1505; 51 Am J1st Tax § 826.
See **authorized capital stock; net capital stock; stock.**

capital stock tax. A term applied to two taxes of different kinds: one a tax on the property represented by stock in the hands of an individual stockholder, the other a tax on the privilege of existing or doing business in the corporate form which is measured for the purpose of the exaction by the amount of capital stock. 51 Am J1st Tax § 825.

capitaneus (ka-pi-ta′ne-us). One holding land in capite.

capitas diminutio (kā′pi-tās di-mi-nū′she-ō). Civil death.

capitatim (kap-i-tā′tim). By heads; per head.

capitation grant (kap-i-tā′shǫn grant). A grant of a certain quantity of land per head or person.

capitation tax. A poll tax; a direct tax imposed without regard to property, profession, or any other external circumstance of the taxpayer. 51 Am J1st Tax § 412.

capite (ka′pi-te). See **in capite.**

capite doli. See **ex capite doli.**

capite fraudis. See **ex capite fraudis.**

capite minutus (ka′pi-te mi-nū′tus). A person who is undergoing civil death.

capitis diminutio maxima (ka′pi-tis di-mi-nū′she-ō max′i-ma). A complete loss of civil status.

capitis diminutio media (ka′pi-tis di-mi-nū′she-ō me′-di-a). A partial loss of civil status.

capitis diminutio minima (ka′pi-tis di-mi-nū′she-ō mi′ni-ma). A slight loss of civil status.

capitula (ka-pi′tu-la). Laws and ordinances collected under appropriate headings or divisions.

capitula coronis (ka-pi′tu-la ko-rō′nis). Detailed schedules.

Capitula de Judaeis (ka-pi′tu-la dē jū-dē′is). An embodiment of political decrees concerning the Jews which was compiled during the reign of Richard I, and a copy of which was preserved by Roger of Hoveden. See 2 Bl Comm 342.

capitular (ka-pit′ū-lạr). A law or canon passed by an ecclesiastical chapter; a chapter member.

capitulary (ka-pit′ū-lạ-ri). Same as **capitular.**

capitulate. To make heads for divisions of an article; to give brief sketches of a discussion; to surrender to an enemy under terms.

capitulum (ka-pit′ū-lum). A chapter or section of a book.

capitur pro fine (kā′pi-ter prō fī′ne). Same as **capias pro fine.**

capper (kap′ėr). A person employed by an attorney to solicit business for him; a sham bidder at an auction sale. McMillan v Harris, 110 Ga 72, 35 SE 334.

Capper-Volstead Act. A federal statute which authorizes producers of agricultural products to act together in collectively processing, preparing for market, handling, and marketing their products in interstate commerce, to have marketing agencies in common, and to make the necessary contracts and agreements to effect such purposes, and gives to the Secretary of Agriculture the powers of regulation and visitation where he has reason to believe that any such enterprise in co-operation has monopolized or restrained trade to the extent that the price of an agricultural commodity has been unduly enhanced. 7 USC §§ 291 et seq.

caprice. A turn of mind without substantial cause, implying wilfulness or wantonness in some degree. Waller v Skelton, 186 Tenn 433, 211 SW2d 445.

capricious. Changeable in purpose or view; freakish; whimsical. United States v Carmack, 329 US 245, 91 L Ed 209, 67 S Ct 252.

capsizing. Overturning, especially the overturning of watercraft.

captain (kap′tān). The officer in command of a company or troop of soldiers; a naval officer who commands a ship; the chief in command of a merchant vessel.

captation (kap-tā′shǫn). A term adopted in the laws of Louisiana from the Code Napoleon and having a meaning practically synonymous with "undue influence." Zerega v Percival, 46 La Ann 590, 606, 15 So 476.

captator (kap-tā′tor). A person who exercises undue influence over another.

captio (kap′she-ō). A caption.

caption (kap′shǫn). A taking; a seizure; literally, a heading, but of variable meaning in the law of practice. In some jurisdictions, the title of the court and the style of the cause as formed from the names of the plaintiff and defendant, their relation on the record being indicated by the familiar "vs." or the equivalent "against." Jackson v Ashton (US) 8 Pet 148, 8 L Ed 898; in other jurisdictions, all that appears at the head of a pleading or order of court, including the title of the court, the names of the parties, the docket number, and such other entries respecting the nature of the suit and the process under which it is maintained as may be required by statute or rule of court; in still other jurisdictions, the phrasing at the head of an order showing how, when, and where the cause arose came on for trial or hearing, the name of the judge or justice presiding, and the presence of the officers of the court; the statement of venue in a certificate of acknowledgment. 1 Am J2d Ack § 46; the heading of an affidavit which states the title of the court and the cause in which it is to be used and the names of the parties. 3 Am J2d Affi § 13; the heading of a deposition which usually contains the authority under which the deposition is taken, the name and description of the supervising officer, the court in the case in which it is intended to be used, the name of the deponent and the fact that he was sworn, the time and place of the taking, and the names of the parties and attorneys present, such being the matters to which the supervising officer must certify. 23 Am J2d Dep § 69; the history or record of a criminal case up to the finding of an indictment, appearing as a preamble to the indictment. 27 Am J1st Indict § 36; the designation of court and parties in an assignment of errors. 5 Am J2d A & E § 659; in a deed, the part of the instrument, otherwise known as "the premises," which precedes the habendum clause, in effect, the part of the instrument in which the property is really granted. 23 Am J2d Deeds § 33.

captive mine (kap'tiv mīn). A mine in which coal rights are held under lease and the coal is extracted directly by the lessee. Powell v Gray (CA4) 114 F2d 752.

captor. One who takes or seizes property in time of war; in a stricter sense, the one who takes a prize at sea. Oakes v United States, 174 US 778, 43 L Ed 1169, 19 S Ct 864.

capture. A taking; that which is taken; booty; the seizure of property or soldiers of an enemy in time of war; a prize of war where the taking meets the condition imposed by law. Manila Prize Cases, 188 US 254, 47 L Ed 463, 23 S Ct 415; the seizure of an enemy vessel accompanied by acts indicative of an intention to seize and to retain her as a prize. The Grotius, 9 Cranch 368, 3 L Ed 762; a taking by the enemy of a vessel or cargo as prize in time of war or by way of reprisal with intent to deprive the owner of it, also the taking of a neutral ship and cargo by a belligerent, and also the taking forcibly by a friendly power in time of peace, and even by the government itself to which the insured belongs. 29A Am J Rev ed Ins § 1327.

In Texas, according to conventional doctrine, the holder of an oil lease "owns" the oil in place beneath the surface. But equally recognized is the "rule of capture" which subjects the lessee's interest to his neighbors' power to drain his oil away. Therefore, to speak of ownership in its relation to oil, is to imply a contingency of control not applicable to ordinary interests in realty. Railroad Com. v Rowan & Nichols Oil Co. 310 US 573, 84 L Ed 1368, 60 S Ct 1021.

capus lupus (kā'pus lū'pus). A wolf's head,—an outlaw.

caput (kap'ut). A head; a chief; a principal. Latin: Life; existence. Top; summit.

Strangely enough, this word has become slang for finished or dead.

caputagium (ka-pu-tā'ji-um). Head, money.

caput baroniae (ka'put ba-rō'ni-ē). A nobleman's mansion-house.

caput genere lupinum (ka'put je'ne-re lu'pi-num). To bear the head of a wolf. The expression was anciently applied to an outlaw, and its meaning was that anyone might knock him on the head as a wolf, in case he would not peaceably surrender himself when taken. Drew v Drew, 37 Me 389, 391.

caputium (ka-pu'she-um). A headland.

caput lupinum (ka'put lū'pi-num). Same as **capus lupus**.

caput mortuum (ka'put mor'tu-um). A deadhead; a nullity.

caput portus (ka'put por'tus). The chief town of a port, from which the port takes its name.

caput, principium, et finis (ka'put, prin-si'pi-um et fi-nis). The head, the beginning, and the end. The king was said to bear this relation toward the body politic of the kingdom. See 1 Bl Comm 153.

CAR. Abbreviation of **Civil Air Regulations**.

car. Any vehicle adapted to the rails of a railroad or railway, including freight cars, passenger cars, locomotives, construction cars, terminal cars, hand cars, and street cars. 44 Am J1st RR § 272.

The Federal Safety Appliance Act (45 USC § 11) requiring "all cars" to be equipped with efficient hand brakes uses the term in its generic sense to mean all kinds of cars running on the rails and applies to a track motorcar used by railroad maintenance employees, even though such car is not attached to a train or used as a part of a train movement. Martin v Johnston (Fla) 79 So 2d 419, 49 ALR2d 1297.

In modern times, the word "car" is correctly and most frequently used for "automobile." So used, it is a generic term embracing a number of different types of vehicles with certain basic similarities. 29A Am J Rev ed Ins § 1239.

See **cars**.

carack (kar'ak). A bulky ship for both commerce and war.

carat (kar'at). A weight of four grains.

caravan. A motor vehicle in tow of another motor vehicle, usually for transporting the towed vehicle to a place where it is to be sold or offered for sale. 7 Am J2d Auto § 134.

See **trailer**.

caravaning. A technical term in many modern statutes, meaning the transportation of any motor vehicle operating on its own wheels, or in tow of another motor vehicle, for the purpose of selling the same or offering the same for sale. 7 Am J2d Auto § 134.

A typical statute provides that caravaning shall mean the transportation from without the state of any motor vehicle operating on its own wheels, or in tow of another motor vehicle, for the purpose of selling or offering the same for sale to or by any agent, dealer, manufacturer, representative, purchaser, or prospective purchaser, whether such agent, etc., be located within or without the state. Wallace v Pfost, 57 Idaho 279, 65 P2d 725, 110 ALR 613.

carbolic acid. A poisonous acid, obtained from coal tar, and used as an antiseptic, although not as much as formerly.

carbon copy. A copy of a letter, document, or other paper made at the same time as the original by impression upon carbon paper.

carbon monoxide. A gas which is highly dangerous to life because of its asphyxiating quality; the type of gas which comes from the exhaust of an automobile engine. 29A Am J Rev ed Ins § 1279.

carcan (kär'kạn). A kind of collar worn as a punishment for crime.

carcare (kar-kā're). To load.

carcata (kar-kā'ta). Freighted or loaded.

carcelage (kär'se-lạj). Prison fees.

carcer (kar'ser). A jail.

Carcer ad homines custodiendos, non ad puniendos, dari debet (kar'ser ad ho'mi-nēz kus"tō-di-en'dos, non ad pu-ni-en'dōs, da'rī de'bet). A jail ought to be devoted to the custody of men, and not to their punishment.

card. A token of membership in a labor union, political party, fraternal order, or a credit-guaranty organization.

card games. Games, such as bridge, poker, pitch, pinochle, etc., played with a deck, or part of a deck, of cards, and which come within the prohibition of statutes which penalize gambling, where the play is for a stake. 24 Am J1st Gaming § 20.

cardinal. A high officer in the church of Rome.

card-playing. See **card games**.

care. A word of most variable meaning, but usually to be interpreted easily in the context. Noun: Custody; safekeeping, charge, Ker v People, 110 Ill 627, 649; support and maintenance, Kelly v Jefferis Del (3 Penn) 286, 50 A 215; professional attendance, as by a physician or in a hospital, Re Swinson's Estate, 167 Pa Super 293, 74 A2d 485, 18 ALR2d 1231; caution; heed; watchfulness. Verb: To have a liking or affection for something or someone; to furnish support and maintenance; to be watchful and diligent for protection and well-being of one's self or another.

See **degrees of care; maintenance and cure**.

carecta (ka-rek'ta). A cart.

careless. A word of broad significance, including negligence, wantonness, and recklessness. The word is synonymous with the word "negligent," but "negligent" is probably the preferable word when used in legal pleadings and proceedings. Delmore v Kansas City Hardwood Flooring Co. 90 Kan 29, 133 P 151.

careless driving. Negligent driving. 7 Am J2d Auto § 272.

See **reckless driving**.

carelessly and wantonly (kār'les-li). Without that degree of care an ordinarily prudent person would use under like and similar circumstances, and in reckless disregard of the consequences thereof, or of the effect of the act done upon the person or life of another. Hollingsworth v Warnock, 112 Ky 96, 104, 65 SW 163.

carelessness. See **careless; negligence**.

carena (ka-rē'na). A quarantine.

care of physician or surgeon. Charge, oversight, watchful regard, and attention. Lustenberger v Boston Casualty Co. 300 Mass 130, 14 NE2d 148, 115 ALR 1055.

ca. resp. An abbreviation of **capias ad respondendum**.

careta (ka-rē'ta). A cart.

Carey Act. The popular name for the Federal Desert Lands Act which sets forth a plan for aiding the reclamation of arid lands in the public land states. 30 Am J Rev ed Irrig § 101.

car float. A vessel for transporting railroad cars, used as an adjunct to railroad transportation. 2 Am J2d Adm § 33.

cargo. The load or lading of a ship or other vessel, having no more than a transitory connection with the vessel, the intent being to unload it at the destination or port of call of the vessel. 48 Am J1st Ship § 2. In marine insurance, the word cargo signifies the "contained," whereas the word body or hull signifies the "container." Therefore, insurance upon cargo does not insure the ship, and conversely, insurance upon a vessel does not cover its cargo. In America, separate forms of marine policies usually are provided for ship and cargo. 29 Am J Rev ed Ins § 304.

cargo lien. A lien on account of salvage, demurrage, general average, freight, or other maritime service or obligation.

While the lien on cargo is frequently spoken of as a maritime lien, the prevailing view is that it has not such quality but is no different from a common-law lien, continuing only while the goods are in the possession of the person having the demand or performing the service. 48 Am J1st Ship § 562.

See **carrier's lien; demurrage lien; salvage lien**.

carl (kärl). Same as **churl**.

car lease. See **drive-it-yourself system; freight line company**.

Carlisle tables. Tables of life expectancy compiled at Carlisle, England, in 1870.

Carmack Amendment. An amendement to the Interstate Commerce Act, applicable to railroad carriers and other common carriers, including motor carriers and freight forwarders, which prescribes the liability of the carrier for loss, damage, or injury caused to the property carried, where the shipment is interstate, to the District of Columbia, or to an adjacent foreign country. 14 Am J2d Car § 518.

carnal (kär'nạl). Sensual; lustful.

carnal abuse. The term has been held to be synonymous with "carnal knowledge." State v Sebastian, 81 Conn 1, 69 A 1054. Other authority draws a distinction between the two terms, saying "carnal abuse" is an act which does not amount to penetration, while "carnal knowledge" constitutes penetration, the offense commonly called statutory rape consisting of "carnal abuse" and not of "carnal knowledge." State v Huggins, 84 NJL 254, 87 A 630.

carnaliter (kar-nā'li-ter). Carnally; sensually; lustfully.

carnaliter cognovit (kar-nā'li-ter kog-nō'vit). He carnally knew; he had sexual intercourse with.

carnal knowledge. Sexual intercourse, Noble v State, 22 Ohio St 541, 545; synonymous with "carnal abuse," according to some authority, State v Sebastian, 81 Conn 1, 69 A 1054; but distinguished from that term by other authority on the ground that while penetration is an essential element of "carnal knowledge," "carnal abuse" may be inflicted without penetration. State v Huggins, 84 NJL 254, 87 A 630.

carnet. A notebook. A check book. A book containing memorandums authenticating the ownership of an automobile and the existence of insurance thereon which may be used severally at international borders by the owner or driver of the automobile in obtaining permission to enter a country.

carno (kar'nō). An immunity or privilege.

Carn's Act. An English statute authorizing the award of damages in equity suits.

carpenter. An artisan who works in wood, constructing and repairing buildings and wooden articles.

carpenter's lien. An artisan's lien. 8 Am J2d Bailm § 229; a maritime lien. 12 Am J2d Boats § 30.

car pool. An arrangement whereby two or more persons ride to work in a single car, usually rotating from the car of one to the car of another, but on a share-the-expense agreement if only the car of one is used.

car port. A structure attached to a dwelling house, often consisting of no more than a roof and supports therefor, wherein an automobile or automobiles may be sheltered. 20 Am J2d Cov § 222.

carriage. A horse drawn vehicle, normally for four passengers; but the term, appearing in a statute, is sufficiently elastic to cover an automobile so as to give to the statute the meaning which its context demands. Anno: 37 ALR2d 717, 726; 7 Am J2d Auto § 3. Transportation of freight or passengers; the service of a horse and cart. The posture of a person, even of a horse in movement. A term peculiar to equity, meaning the right to conduct or control a suit where other persons are involved on the same side.

Carriage of Goods by Sea Act. A federal statute relieving an owner of a vessel of liability for loss or damage to merchandise on board the vessel by means of a fire not due to the design or neglect of the owner. 46 USC § 1406.

carrier. A transporter of passengers or freight; one who undertakes to transport persons or property from place to place. 13 Am J2d Car § 1.
See **common carrier; express company; ferry; forwarder; motor carrier; pick-up service; private carrier; railroad; sleeping car company; shipping; street railway.**

carrier by air. One who engages, whether directly or indirectly by a lease or any other arrangement, in air transportation. 49 USC § 1301(3).

carrier by railroad. A railroad company acting as a common carrier. Chicago, M.Y. & B. Refrigerator Co. v Interstate Commerce Com. 265 US 425, 68 L Ed 1087, 44 S Ct 560.
See **railroad.**

carrier for hire. Either a private or a common carrier receiving or charging compensation in some form for transportation. Huron Portland Cement Co. v Woodworth (DC Mich) 19 F2d 530. Under an exclusion clause in an automobile liability policy prohibiting the carrying of passengers for a consideration, a few cases have held that the word "passenger" as so used includes only passengers transported by a public carrier, but more cases have held to the contrary. Myers v Ocean Acci. & Guarantee Corp. (CA4 NC) 99 F2d 485. Where the arrangement for compensation under which the person is carrying his passengers is more than a reimbursement for the gas and oil used by all in common on the trip, but goes to the additional extent of compensating him for the use of the car, he is carrying passengers for hire. Gross v Kubel, 315 Pa 396, 172 A 649, 95 ALR 146.

carrier of goods. A common carrier engaged in transporting commodities, as distinguished from one carrying livestock or passengers.

carrier of livestock. A common carrier of goods which transports livestock is as to the latter property also a common carrier, but in some states carriers of livestock are not regarded as common carriers unless they have expressly assumed the responsibilities of common carriers by special contract. 13 Am J2d Car § 346.

carrier of passengers. See **carrier; carrier for hire.**

carrier's acceptance. See **delivery to carrier.**

carrier's demurrage lien. See **demurrage lien.**

carrier's lien. The lien of a carrier upon the goods in a shipment for the charges of transportation and such storage charges as it may be entitled to collect. 13 Am J2d Car § 497. The lien of a carrier by water upon the cargo for freight and all lawful charges, whether the vessel is operated under charter of affreightment or a general ship. 48 Am J1st Ship § 436.
See **baggage lien; common carrier's lien; demurrage lien.**

carrier's receipt. A bill of lading for goods to be transported by land. Dodge v Meyer, 61 Cal 405, 418.
See **delivery to carrier.**

carry. To transport, as to carry a passenger; to hold or possess, as to carry insurance, Metropolitan Life Ins. Co. v Dimick, 69 NJL 384, 55 A 291; to extend credit; to extend one's credit to another. State v Capital City Bank, 32 NM 369, 257 P 993.

carryback. An income tax law term for applying a net operating loss for one year in the recomputation of tax for an earlier year. 9 ALR2d 352, Later Case Service.

carryers (kar'i-ėrs). Men who "in ancient times of corrupt politics" undertook from money to get titles and honors for those who agreed to pay them for their influence. Montefiore v Menday Co. (Eng) 2 KB 241.

carrying a debtor. Extending credit; liberality in extensions of time for payment.

carrying away. The asportation or complete removal of goods.

carrying capacity. The number of passengers who may be carried in a particular automobile without crowding; sitting capacity. 7 Am J2d Auto § 66.

carrying charges. Charges for interest, insurance, filing fee, and attorney's fee included in an a conditional sale or instalment sale contract, chattel mortgage, or trust receipt.

carrying concealed weapon. See **carrying weapon; concealed weapon.**

carrying costs. Awarding costs; a judgment which includes the costs as a part thereof.
See **carrying charges.**

carrying goods. See **carrier; carrier of goods.**

carrying on business. A term with a meaning variable according to the context within which it appears and the circumstances under which it is used, but in any event it is something more than isolated transactions. Kirkwood v Gadd (Eng) [1910] A.C. 422, 432. It is the pursuing of business as an enterprise embracing many transactions and to which one usually devotes both time and skill. 27 Am J1st H & W § 474. The carrying on of a liquor business involves transactions extending over a considerable period of time, except where one has made all

carrying [...]

preparations, holds himself out as a dealer, and has solicited trade. 30 Am J Rev ed Intox L § 217.
See **doing business; doing business in state.**

carrying on liquor business. See **carrying on business.**

carrying passengers. See **carrier; carrier for hire.**

carrying passengers for a consideration. See **carrier for hire.**

carrying sail. See **under sail.**

carrying weapon. Any method of carrying which renders the weapon readily accessible and available for use, irrespective of whether the person moves from place to place while having the weapon in possession. 56 Am J1st Weap § 10. A statute against carrying a pistol was held not to be violated if one finds or buys a pistol and takes it home or to his place of business, or if he takes it to and from a shop for repairs, whether loaded or not, and even though he fires it off on the way. Pressler v State, 19 Tex Crim 52.
See **concealed weapon.**

carryover. An income tax term for using a loss occurring in one year as a deduction in a later year. An item of an inventory, or of the accounts of a business for one year which is transferred to the inventory or accounts of the following year.

carry the iron. To carry a piece of red-hot iron of from one to three pounds weight in the hand, in a trial by fire-ordeal. See 4 Bl Comm 342.

cars. A generic term for some purposes, including even locomotives. Baltimore & Ohio R. Co. v Jackson, 353 US 325, 1 L Ed 2d 862, 77 S Ct 842.
See **car.**

car service. The use, control, supply, movement, distribution, exchange, interchange, and return of locomotives, cars, and other vehicles used in the transportation of property, including special types of equipment, and the supply of trains. 49 USC § 1(10). The term imports the instrumentalities of the service of transportation, not transportation itself. Cars and locomotives, like tracks and terminals, are the instrumentalities. The Esch car service act made these instrumentalities available in emergencies to a carrier other than the owner, making provision for the movement, distribution, exchange, interchange, and return of locomotives, cars, and other vehicles used in the transportation of property. Peoria & Pekin Union Railway Co. v United States, 263 US 528, 533, 68 L Ed 427, 430, 44 S Ct 194.

Car Service Act. See **car service.**

car service association. An association of railroad companies formed to facilitate the collection of charges for demurrage and to make such charges uniform throughout the United States. 13 Am J2d Car § 481.

car spotting. See **"spotting service."**

cart. A small horse drawn vehicle, carrying not more than two passengers; the term is also applied to a two-wheeled, horse-drawn vehicle suitable for carrying no person other than the driver; sometimes construed to include a four-wheeled vehicle. Favers v Glass, 22 Ala 621; even a motor vehicle. Anno: 37 ALR2d 717; a small vehicle, two-wheeled or four-wheeled, to be pushed or pulled by manpower.

carta (kar'ta). A deed or charter.

carta de foresta (kar'ta dē fo-res'ta). Laws of the forest.

cartage. Services in transporting property by truck; the charges for transportation of property.

cart-bote (kart-bōte). The right of a tenant to take from the premises an amount of wood reasonably necessary for the making and repair of his farming tools. See 2 Bl Comm 35.

carte blanche (kärt blonsh). A blank card; a signed blank instrument intended by the signer to be filled in and used by another person, without restriction; freedom to act in a situation as one thinks best.

cartel. An association of industrialists or financiers for a purpose, usually secret, and sometimes ulterior, such as fixing prices, creating a monopoly, or cornering the market; a challenge to combat.

carter. One who hauls or transports property for another.

cartis reddendis. See **de cartis reddendis.**

cartman. See **carter; drayman.**

carton. A container for cigarettes and other merchandise.

cartoon (kär-tön'). A caricature, often uncomplimentary, sometimes derogatory, and occasionally libelous. 33 Am J1st L & S § 55.

car trust. A partnership association formed by a number of persons for the purpose of buying, selling and leasing railroad rolling stock to be leased to a railroad company. Ricker v American Loan & Trust Co. 140 Mass 346, 347.

cartway (kärt'wā). A way for the free passage of all persons on foot or horseback, carts and wagons. Cozad v Kanawha Hardwood Co. 139 NC 283, 51 SE 932.
See **iter.**

caruca (ka-rö'kā). A plough.

carucae. See **affri carucae; averia carucae.**

carucage (kar'ö-kāj). A tax on land ploughable with one plough.

carucata (ka-rū-kā'ta). A plough.

carve (kärv). To carve is to segregate; to cut out, as a smaller estate or parcel from a larger one. As used in criminal cases involving former conviction or acquittal, the verb to carve seems to import the selection from the facts of the transaction any one or more of such facts as may, taken singly or together, constitute a criminal offense, for the purpose of embodying such fact or facts in an indictment or information. "Although, when a man has done a criminal act, the prosecutor may carve as large an offense out of the transaction as he can, yet he is not at liberty to cut but once." People v Stephens, 79 Cal 428, 21 P 856.

cas. An abbreviation of "case"; also of **cas fortuits.**

ca. sa. An abbreviation of **capias ad satisfaciendum.**

case (kās). A contested question in a court of justice. See 34 Am J1st Lim Ac § 64; an action variously known as "case," "action on the case" and "trespass on the case," 52 Am J1st Tresp § 2; a controversy presented according to the regular course of judicial proceedings, so that the judicial power is capable of acting upon it to determine and decide the issues presented by the allegations of the parties. Muskrat v United States, 219 US 346, 356, 357, 55 L Ed 246, 250, 31 S Ct 250. The term includes a habeas corpus proceeding. King v

McLean Asylum of the Massachusetts General Hospital (CA1 Mass) 64 F 331; but, as used in a statute respecting the right to a jury trial, not a special proceeding. Anno: 21 Ann Cas 670.

case agreed. See **agreed case.**

case and controversy. See **case; case or controversy; controversy.**

case certified. A distinct point or question of law certified by a lower court and submitted to a higher court for decision. Fire Assur. Asso. v Wickham, 128 US 426, 32 L Ed 563, 9 S Ct 113.

case in law or equity. A judicial proceeding at law or in equity presenting a question in such form that relief at the hands of the court is obtainable. 1 Am J2d Actions § 4; but not embracing a case within the jurisdiction of admiralty. 2 Am J2d Adm § 5.

case in point. A precedent.

case law. The law as laid down in the decisions of the courts; that is, in the cases which have been decided.

case made. See **bill of exceptions; case reserved.**

case of first impression. See **first impression.**

case of novel impression. See **res integra.**

Case of the Seven Bishops. An English case decided in 1688, wherein the primate and six bishops were charged with libel for petitioning against the king's order that "his declarations for liberty of conscience" be read in the churches.

case or controversy. An actual controversy over an issue, not merely a desire for an abstract declaration of the law. Re Summers, 325 US 561, 89 L Ed 1795, 65 S Ct 1307.

A "case" was defined by Chief Justice Marshall to be a suit instituted according to the regular course of judicial procedure and in the jurisdiction clause of the Federal Constitution the word "controversy" is held to have the same meaning. If the two words as there used are distinguishable at all, it is possibly because "controversies" are confined to suits of a civil nature. Muskrat v United States, 219 US 346, 55 L Ed 246, 31 S Ct 250.

case primae impressionis (case prī'mē im-pres-she-ō'nis). A case of first impression; a case for the determination of which no precedent can be found. Vaughan v Menlove, 3 Bingham's New Cases 468.

case reserved. A decision rendered pro forma for the purpose of obtaining the opinion of the same court in bank or that of a higher court.

cases. See **case; case in law or equity; case or controversy.**

case stated. Another term for agreed case. 3 Am J2d Agr C § 1.

case system. The method of the study of law, now prevailing in the United States, by the analysis of actual cases in court and the opinions rendered therein by the justices.

case to move for a new trial. The losing party's statement of the case prepared for use on his motion for a new trial.

cas fortuit (kä for-twe'). A fortuitous event; an event caused by a force that one cannot resist; an unforeseen accident; an irresistible force; an inevitable accident. Viterbo v Friedlander, 120 US 707, 30 L Ed 776, 7 S Ct 962.

cash. Coin; money; ready money or money in hand, either in current coin or other legal tender, or in bank bills paid and received as money. Palliser v United States, 136 US 257, 34 L Ed 514, 10 S Ct 1034; the antonym of credit; it includes coins, currency, a cashier's check, and a certified check. Greenberg v Alter Co. 255 Iowa 899, 124 NW2d 438. Under provisions of statutes or corporation charters requiring stock subscriptions to be paid in cash or in money, the general American rule is that payment cannot be made in services or property. Whether a check constitutes cash payment under such provisions is disputed, although a certified check is generally considered cash. 18 Am J2d Corp §§ 257, 265.

cash account. An account in a bank subject to draft or check.

cash basis. Reporting income for taxation when cash or property is actually or constructively received and taking deductions in the year cash or property is paid or transferred. IRC § 451(a).

cash-book. A book of account of money received and paid out.

cash customer. A customer who pays when the purchase is made, so is not billed; a customer of a broker who has paid the full price for identifiable securities left in the hands of the broker but to which the customer is entitled upon the bankruptcy of the broker. 9 Am J2d Bankr § 1099.

cash dividend. A distribution to the stockholders of a corporation, as the reward of the corporate enterprise, of the profits or surplus assets of the corporation, usually, but not necessarily in cash; it may be in other property, in which event, the terminology is appropriate nevertheless to indicate a distinction from a stock dividend. 19 Am J2d Corp § 809.

See **dividends; stock dividend.**

cash flow. A modern term in accounting, being the aggregate of net income plus the amounts allowed for depreciation of plant and equipment and amortization of patents and licenses for the use of patents.

cashier. An employee of a restaurant, store, or other place of business, whose duty it is to have charge of the cash register and take payments from the customers, ordinarily at a position near the exit from the place of business; the chief executive officer of a bank, who transacts the bank's business under the orders and supervision of its board of directors. Martin v Webb, 110 US 7, 28 L Ed 49, 3 S Ct 428. The cashier of a bank is at least an executive officer rather than a mere employee. Blanc v Paymaster Mining Co. 95 Cal 524, 531, 30 P 765; of course, the authority actually exercised by a bank cashier depends upon the plan of operation of the particular bank. In some banks, the cashier follows closely the directions of the president or chairman of the board, looking to one or the other for advice in important transactions.

cashier's check. A bill of exchange, drawn by a bank upon itself, and accepted by the act of issuance.

The bank is the debtor and its obligation to pay the check is like that of the maker of any other negotiable instrument payable on demand. 10 Am J2d Banks § 308.

cash note. A promissory note payable in cash.

cash on hand. Money on hand or a deposit in a solvent bank subject to check. Re Banfield, 137 Or 282, 3 P 116.

cash or its equivalent. Money or that which is convertible into money on presentation for payment,

cash or order. See **pay cash or order.**

cash sale. A sale by the terms of which payment of the purchase price and delivery of the goods sold are to be concurrent. Western Seed Marketing Co. v Pfost, 45 Idaho 340, 262 P 514; a sale for the money in hand.
Upon such a sale the owner is not bound to deliver the goods until the price is paid. If the price cannot be ascertained until the goods are weighed or measured, ordinarily no property passes to the purchaser until that is done. Steward v Scudder, 24 NJL 96, 101.

cash surrender value. The cash value of a life insurance policy as ascertainable by established rules, where the policy has been abandoned and given up for cancellation to the insurer by the person having a contractual right to do so. 29 Am J Rev ed Ins § 620; the reserve, less a surrender charge. And in case of a single-premium policy, the reserve is the face amount of the contract discounted at a specified rate of interest on the basis of the insured's expected life. Guggenheim v Rasquin, 312 US 254, 85 L Ed 813, 61 S Ct 507.
A life insurance policy having a cash surrender value is property within the meaning of the Bankruptcy Act provision that title to property of the bankrupt vests in the trustee in bankruptcy. 9 Am J2d Bankr § 914. In bankruptcy proceedings the term "cash surrender value" has been regarded as covering any and every insurance policy under which the insured, by his own efforts and unassisted by any beneficiary or assignee, can obtain a sum from the insurer in cash, on cancellation of the policy at the date of the filing of the petition in bankruptcy, the amount being determined in accordance with a fixed and definite method of compensation, uniform in all cases; and it is immaterial whether the amount which the insured can obtain is secured to him by statute or rests upon the mere willingness of the insurance company to purchase the policy at the particular time, the material and important fact being that at the time of the adjudication the policy has a value which the company is willing to pay and which the bankrupt by his own act can obtain. 9 Am J2d Bankr § 916.

cash value. The amount for which an article or piece of property may be sold at a sale which is not forced or compelled upon the seller where the terms of sale call for cash, no credit being extended to the purchaser; market value, fair market value, or clear market value. 28 Am J Rev ed Inher T § 359.
See **actual cash value; fair cash value; full cash value; true cash value.**

casing head gas. Natural gas from an oil well. The term does not include gasoline or gas manufactured artificially from the natural product of the well. See Wilson v King-Smith Refining Co. 119 Okla 256, 250 P 90.

cassare (kas-sā're). To nullify; to annul; to dismiss.

cassation (ka-sā'shon). Annulment; abatement; dismissal.
See **court of cassation.**

cassetur billa (kas-sē'ter bil'la). That the bill be quashed. See 3 Bl Comm 303.
See **judgment of cassetur billa.**

cassetur breve (ka-sē'tėr brē'vē). Same as **cassetur billa.**

cast. Verb: To decide against; to convict; to allege; to proffer; to deposit, as a ballot; to form a solid piece, such as iron, from molten metal; to devolve by operation of law, as in the descent of an estate to the heirs. Estate of Donahue, 36 Cal 332. Noun: A solid piece, such as iron, made from molten metal in a form; a covering of a limb which has been fractured, applied, for the purpose of keeping the severed bone pieces of the broken bone in proper alignment, in a soft plaster which hardens after application.

castaway. A shipwrecked person; a thing thrown away; a person abandoned; an outcast.

cast away (kȧst'ạ-wā). To throw away; to abandon.

castellan (kas'te-lạn). The governor of a castle.

castellarium (kas''tel-lā'ri-um). Same as **castlewick.**

castellorum operatio (kas-tel-lō'rum o-pe-rā'she-ō). The maintenance of castles.

castigation (kas-ti-gā'shọn). Chastisement.

castigatory (kas'ti-gā-tọ-ri). A contrivance for punishing common scolds.
See **cucking-stool.**

casting descent. See **descent case.**

casting lots. Determining something by chance, as by a throw of dice or the drawing of straws.

casting vote. Literally, the act of depositing a paper ballot or voting upon a voting machine, but in modern usage, the term means the expression of a choice in any election to choose officers or determine policies and by any means appropriate for the occasion. By the common law, the term sometimes signifies the single vote of a person who never votes, as where the presiding officer is given the casting vote; but in the case of an equality, sometimes the double vote of a person who first votes with the rest, and then, upon an equality, creates a majority by giving a second vote. People v Rector, etc., of Church of the Atonement (NY) 48 Barb 603, 606.

castle (kȧs'l). A fortified building; a fortress; the dwelling place of a king, prince, or nobleman.

castleguard (kȧs'l-gärd). Feudal services or payments toward the maintenance of the lord's castle.

castlery (kȧs'l-ri). The government or tenure of a castle.

castleward (kas'l-wȧrd). Same as **castleguard.**

castlewick (kȧs'l-wik). The district under the jurisdiction of a castle.

castration. The severance of the testicles by accident or surgery; a necessary operation in animal husbandry but constituting cruelty where performed unnecessarily or with unnecessary cruelty. 4 Am J2d Ani § 28.

casual. Occasional; irregular, or incidental, in contradistinction from stated or regular. Anno: 33 ALR 1452.

casual ejector. A fiction whereby the old common law action of ejectment was utilized for the purpose of determining title to real estate. 25 Am J2d Eject § 2.

casual employee. A person employed temporarily, occasionally, intermittently, seasonally, not regularly. Mitchell v Main Feldspar Co. 121 Me 455, 118 A 287, 33 ALR 1447; Anno: 33 ALR 1452.
For some purposes, particularly that of the ap-

plication of a workmen's compensation act, a "casual employee" is one working for an employer but not in the usual and normal course of the business or industry regularly pursued by the employer. This distinct meaning of the term in compensation cases is based upon definitions of "casual employment" in compensation acts.
See **casual employment**.

casual employment. Literally, employment which is temporary, seasonal, sometimes fortuitous, in any event, not employment which is to continue for a fixed period of time of considerable duration. Blake v Wilson, 268 Pa 468, 112 A 126, 15 ALR 726. The meaning of the term in workmen's compensation statutes is variable because of the variance in statutory definitions. Under some statutes, casual employment is employment for something other than trade or business. Thompson v Twiss, 90 Conn 444, 97 A 328; under other statutes, it is employment not in the usual course of the employer's trade or business. Cardillo v Mockabee, 70 App DC 16, 102 F2d 620; Oliphant v Hawkinson, 192 Iowa 1259, 183 NW 805, 33 ALR 1433, 1436; and under still other statutes, it is employment at work of a duration of not more than a specified number of days, such as ten, fifteen, or twenty days, or at work, the cost of which is not more than a specified amount, such as one hundred, two hundred, or even five hundred dollars. Moody v Industrial Acc. Com. (Cal App) 260 P 967, 969.

casual fence. A temporary fence.

casualis (ka-zū-ā'lis). Casual.

casualiter (ka-zū-ā'li-ter). Casually; accidentally.

casualiter et per infortuniam, et contra voluntatem suam (ka-zū-ā'li-ter et per in-for-tu'ni-am et kon'trạ vo-lun-tā'te su'am). Accidentally and involuntarily. Stanley v Powell (Eng) LR 1 QB Div 86.

casual negligence. Slight negligence or, at most, no more than ordinary negligence.

casual pauper. A pauper who receives aid outside the jurisdiction of his domicil or residence.

casualties. Sums due from a vassal to his superior on the happening of certain events, the plural of "casualty."
See **casualty**.

casualty. A disastrous occurrence by chance or accident; a serious mishap or misfortune; an accidental death or disablement. Morris & Co. v Industrial Board of Illinois, 284 Ill 67, 119 NE 944. For the purpose of the Federal Hours of Service Act, an occurrence which proceeds from an unknown cause, or is an unusual effect of a known cause. 31 Am J Rev ed Lab § 803. For the purpose of a deduction in computing net income subject to federal income tax, a complete or partial destruction of property resulting from an identifiable event of a sudden, unexpected, or unusual nature. 34 Am J2d Fed Tax ¶6605.
See **inevitable casualty; unavoidable casualty**.

casualty insurance. Literally, this term is inclusive of insurance of all kinds except life insurance. In the insurance business, however, it has been a trade term applied with considerable variation as between insurance companies, often as a catch-all for new types of insurance as they are developed, such as plate glass insurance, hail insurance, boiler insurance, and insurance on domestic animals, Employers' Liability Assur. Corp. v Merrill, 155 Mass 404, 29 NE 529; and in more recent years to various forms of liability or indemnity insurance.

casualty loss. A deduction in an income tax return for a loss arising from fire, storm, shipwreck or other casualty to property owned by the taxpayer. IRC § 165(c)(3).

casualty of war. One killed or wounded in combat, or taken as a prisoner of war. As the term was used in a life insurance policy exempting the insurer from liability for death caused by the casualties or consequences of war or rebellion, such exemption included only death from casualties or consequences of war or rebellion, carried on or waged by authority of some government which was at least de facto. Welts v Connecticut Mut. Life Ins. Co. 48 NY 34.

casual worker. See **casual employee**.

casu consimili (kā'sū kon-si'mi-lī). In a similar case; a writ of entry to recover a reversion in land alienated by the tenant.
See **in casu consimili**.

casu proviso (kā'sū prō-vī'zō). A writ of entry to recover a reversion against a tenant in dower.
See **in casu proviso**.

casus (kā'sus). A case; an event; a happening.

casus belli (kā'sus bel'ī). An occasion of war.

casus foederis (kā'sus fē'de-ris). A case falling within the provisions of a treaty.

casus fortuitus (kā'sus for-tū'i-tus). Same as **cas fortuit**.

Casus fortuitus non est sperandus, et nemo tenetur divinare (kā-sus for-tū'i-tus non est spe-ran'dus, et nē'mō te-nē'ter di-vī-nā're). A chance happening is not to be expected, and no one is held to foresee it.

Casus fortuitus non est supponendus (kā-sus for-tū'i-tus non est sup-pō-nen'dus). A chance happening is not to be expected.

casus major (kā'sus mā'jor). An unusual event.
See **vis major**.

casus omissi (kā'sus ō-mis'sī). Plural of **casus omissus**. See 4 Bl Comm 85.

casus omissus (kā'sus ō-mis'sus). A case omitted. Where a statute attempts to cover a subject and a case arises which the statute should have provided for, the case is sometimes spoken of as a "casus omissus." See 2 Bl Comm 260.

Casus omissus et oblivioni datus dispositioni communis juris relinquitur (kā'sus ō-mis'sus et ob-li-vi-ō'nī dā'tus dis-pō-zi-she-ō'nī kom-mū'nis jū'ris re-lin'-qui-ter). An omitted and forgotten case is left to the disposal of the common law. See Broom's Legal Maxims 46.

cat. A small domesticated animal with soft fur, white, black, gray, colored, stripped or multi-colored, which is a household or barnyard pet; any of the carnivorous mammals related to the household cat, such as lion, tiger, leopard, or puma; a sharp-tongued or gossip-peddling woman; a whip, otherwise known as a cat-o-nine tails. Slang for a caterpillar tractor. Teenage slang for a clever person. In the slang of an older day, a woman who makes trouble.

A cat is a domestic animal which if kept as a household pet is a thing of value which ministers to the pleasure of its owner. As such it is the proper subject of a civil action, such as trover; it is property subject to taxation and is such an animal as is included in statutes against cruelty, although it was not the subject of larceny at common law. Thurston v Carter, 112 Me 361, 92 A 295.

catalla (ka-tal'la). Chattels.

Catalla juste possessa amitti non possunt (ka-tal'la jūs'tē po-ze'sa ā-mit'tī non pos'sunt). Chattels lawfully possessed cannot be lost.

catalla otiosa (ka-tal'la ō-she-ō'sa). Idle cattle or beasts.

Catalla reputantur inter minima in lege (ka-tal'la re-pu-tan'ter in'ter mi'ni-ma in lē'je). Chattels are regarded in law among things of lesser importance (than land).

catallis captis nomine districtionis (ka-tal'lis kap'tis no'mi-ne dis-trik"she-ō'nis). A writ to distrain doors, windows or gates of a house for rent.

catallis reddendis (ka-tal'lis red-den'dis). For the return of the chattels.

catallum (ka-tal'lum). A chattel.

catalog. A list of the articles to be offered for sale at auction, including representations as to the character of particular articles. 7 Am J2d Auct § 16. A listing of merchandise for sale, sometimes with a secret code or system of letters, figures, and characters which show the cost and selling price. 18 Am J2d Copyr § 16.

cataneus (ka-tā'ne-us). A tenant in capite, that is, on holding directly under the king.

catchall. A clause in a contract, will, or statute, intended to broaden the application of the instrument or statute; a provision in a statute, following an enumeration of various things and contingencies, intended to broaden the application of the statute beyond dispute, such as a provision in a statute fixing venue, following an enumeration of specific cases, that in all other cases the action shall be tried in the county in which the defendant, the defendants, or any of them reside.

catching bargain. A bargain or agreement of an expectant heir, remainderman or reversioner for the sale of his expectancy at a grossly inadequate price and under circumstances rendering the transaction an unconscionable one. 41 Am Rep 713, note.

catchland (kach'land). Land, the tithes from which went as a right to the first of two parsons who claimed them.

catch point (kach point). A derailing switch on a railroad siding used to prevent cars on the siding from running downgrade into the main line. See McDowall v Great Western Railway Co. (Eng) [1903] 2 KB 331.

catchpole or catchpoll (kách'pōl). A bailiff; a constable.

catch time charter. A term which relates simply to the amount of compensation to be paid by the charterer of a boat. Ordinarily, when a boat is hired, the rent is so much a day. When "catch time" is followed, it is paid for when and as actually used, accounting being at some subsequent period. Under such a charter, however, the custody of the charterer commences at once whether the boat is actually being used by him or not, and the owner ceases to have any control over it. Schoonmaker-Conners Co. v New York Cent. R. Co. (DC NY) 12 F2d 314.

catena (ka-tē'nạ). A chain; a connected series; as, a catena of authorities cited to sustain a point of law.

cater-cornered. From corner to corner; diagonal.

cater-cousin (kā'tèr). A fourth cousin.

cathedral (kạ-thē'drạl). The church of a bishop; in common parlance, any large and imposing church.

catheter (kath'e-eter). A tube used to withdraw fluid from a cavity of the body, especially urine from the bladder, by way of relieving a stoppage of flow or of obtaining a sample for analysis in conducting a physical examination. O'Brien v La Crosse, 99 Wis 421, 75 NW 81.

catholic. Universal; broad-minded and liberal in understanding and sympathies.
See **Roman Catholic**.

Catholic Bible. The Bible of the Roman Catholic Church.
See **Douay Bible**.

catholic creditor. A creditor whose debt is secured by more than one property of the debtor.

Catholic Emancipation Act. An English statute, enacted in 1829, by which Roman Catholics were assured of all civil rights with the exception of appointment to ecclesiastical offices and certain high public offices.

Catoniana regula (ka-tō-ni-ā'na re'gu-la). A Roman law rule that lapse of time will not cure that which was invalid at the outset.

cats. See **cat**; **custos horrei regii**.

cattery (cat'èr-i). A place for the care of homeless animals. Re Graves, 242 Ill 23, 89 NE 672.

cattle. Domestic bovine animals; cows, bulls, steers or oxen, including heifers and in the generic sense of the term even calves; farm animals collectively, that is livestock, although even in this broad sense not including poultry. First Nat. Bank v Home Sav. Bank, 88 US (21 Wall) 294, 22 L Ed 560. Some authority, especially older authority, confines the term to neat cattle, that is, cattle of the bovine species, thereby excluding horses, mules, etc. Brown v Bailey, 4 Ala 413.
See **neat cattle**.

cattle-gate. A right to pasture animals on the land of another.

cattle guard. Such an appliance as will prevent cattle and other farm animals from going from a highway or private way crossed by a railroad track onto the track or right of way of the railroad. Ford v Chicago Rock Island & Pacific Railway Co. 91 Iowa 179, 59 NW 5.

cattle range. A large area where cattle may roam and pasture; a large stretch of country, consisting generally of many square miles, which is usually uninclosed, and has no definite or fixed boundaries, on which cattle are permitted to run at large during the entire year. Big Butte Horse & Cattle Asso. v Anderson, 133 Or 171, 289 P 503, 70 ALR 399.

Caucasian. A person of the white race; the white race.

caucus (kâ'kus). A local political meeting; a meeting of persons of the same political party or of the same views in general, called and conducted for the purpose of determining a course of action which the participants should follow as a group in a larger meeting to be held later.

causa (kâ'zạ). A cause; an action; a reason; a consideration.

causa adulteri (kâ′za a-dul′te-rī). By reason of adultery.

causa belli (kâ′za bel′lī). A cause of war.

causa causae est causa causati (kâ′za kā′zē est kâ′za kâ-za′tī). A cause of a cause is the cause of the effect.

causa causans (kâ′za kâ′zanz). The causing cause; the efficient cause.

causa causantis causa est causati (kâ′za kâ-zan′tis kâ′za est kâ-zā′ti). The cause of the thing causing is the cause of the effect; a maxim which obviously leads to "a labyrinth of refined and bewildering speculation." Gilman v Noyes, 57 NH 627.

causa data et non secuta (kâ′za dā′ta et non se-kū′ta). Consideration given and not followed.

Causa ecclesiae publicis aequiparatur; et summa et ratio quae pro religione facit (kâ′za e-kle′si-ē pub′li-sis ē-qui-pa-rā′ter; et sum′ma et rā′she-ō kwē pro re-li-ji-ō′ne fā′sit). The cause of the church is equal to that of the public; and most important of all is the reason which makes for religion.

Causae dotis, vitae, libertatis, fisci sunt inter favorabilia in lege (kâ′zē dō′tis, vī′tē, li-ber-tā′tis, fis′kī sunt in′ter fa-vō-ra-bi′li-a in lē′jē). The cases of dower, life, liberty and public moneys are among those favored in law.

Causa et origo est materia negotii (kâ′za et ō′ri-gō est ma-te′ri-a ne-gō′she-ī). The cause and its origin are the gist of the transaction.

causa honoris. See **honoris causa.**

causa hospitandi (kâ′za hos-pi-tan′dī). For the purpose of being received as a guest.

causa impotentiae (kâ′za im-pō-ten′she-ē). By reason of impotence.

causa jactitationis matrimonii (kâ′za jak-ti-tā-she-ō′nis ma-tri-mō′ni-ī). An action which a person might maintain in the ecclesiastical court to enjoin another of opposite sex from continuing to boast or give out that he or she is married to the plaintiff, contrary to the fact. See 3 Bl Comm 93.

causal relation. See **compensable injury; proximate cause.**

causa lucrativa. See **ex causa lucrativa.**

causa matrimonii praelocuti (kâ′za ma-tri-mō′ni-ī prē-lo-kū′tī). An ancient writ which a woman had when she had given land in fee or for life to her affianced suitor who refused to marry her. See 3 Bl Comm 183, note.

causam nobis significes quare (kâ′zam nō′bis sig-ni′fi-sēs quā′rē). A writ against a town mayor directing him to give seisin to a grantee of the king.

causa mortis (kâ′za mor′tis). In expectation of death. See **gift causa mortis.**

causa patet (kâ′za pa′tet). The cause or reason is apparent.

causa praeallegata (kâ′za prē′al-ė-gá-ta). For the aforesaid reasons.

Causa propinqua, non remota spectatur (kâ′za pro-pin′qua, non re-mō′ta spek-tā′ter). The proximate, and not the remote, cause is regarded. Wood v New England Ins. Co. 14 Mass 31.

causa proxima (kâ′za pro′xi-ma). The proximate cause.

causa proxima, non remota spectatur (kâ′za pro′xi-ma, non re-mō′ta spek-tā′ter). The proximate, and not the remote cause, is regarded.

No court is bound to "stick in the bark" of the maxim. Proximate cause should be determined upon mixed considerations of logic, common sense, policy, and precedent. 38 Am J1st Negl § 53.

causa qua supra (kâ′za qua su′pra). For the reason above stated.

causare (kâ-zā′re). To litigate.

causa rei (kâ′za rē′ī). The accessions, appurtenances, or fruits of a thing.

causa remota (kâ′za re-mō′ta). A remote cause. See **causa proxima, non remota spectatur.**

causa scientiae patet (kâ′za sī-en′ti-ē pa′tet). The reason of the knowledge is apparent.

causa sine qua non (kâ′za sī′ne quā non). A cause without which the thing would not have happened; a cause which if it had not existed, the injury would not have been sustained. 38 Am J1st Negl §§ 53, 166.

causation. A matter of being the cause of an occurrence, the producing of a result. Derosier v New England Tel. & Tel. Co. 81 NH 451, 130 A 145, 61 ALR 1178.

See **chain of causation; proximate cause.**

causator (kâ-zā′tor). A party to an action.

causa turpis (kâ′za ter′pis). For a base or evil cause or reason.

Causa vaga et incerta non est causa rationabilis (kâ′za va′ga et in-ser′ta non est kâ′za rā-she-ō-nā′bi-lis). A vague and uncertain cause is not a reasonable one.

cause. An action or suit. 1 Am J2d Actions § 4; including a criminal prosectuion. Anno: 20 ALR 606; a cause of action; a consideration; motive; origin; that which produces or effects a result, even though unintended. United States v Weisman, (CA2 NY) 83 F2d 470, 107 ALR 293; that from which anything proceeds, and without which it would not exist; that which supplies a motive; that which decides action or constitutes the reason why anything is done.

The word "cause" and the word "case" are frequently used synonymously. Ward v Town Tavern, 191 Or 1, 228 P2d 216, 42 ALR2d 662. In any legal sense, "action," "suit," and "cause" are convertible terms. Ex parte Milligan (US) 4 Wall 2, 112, 18 L Ed 281, 293. Even an ex parte proceeding constitutes a cause for some purposes, as in the case of a statute disqualifying a judge from sitting in any "cause," under circumstances specified in the statute. 30A Am J Rev ed Judges § 93.

See **good cause; procuring cause; proximate cause; reasonable cause.**

cause célèbre. (French.) A celebrated case.

cause list. A court calendar or docket.

cause of a cause. See **causa causantis causa est causati.**

cause of action. A term difficult of precise definition, perhaps best defined as the fact or facts which establish or give rise to a right of action, in other words, give to a person a right to judicial relief. Fielder v Ohio Edison Co. 158 Ohio St 375, 109 NE2d 855, 35 ALR2d 1365. More summarily defined, a cause of action is the right which a party has to institute a judicial proceeding. 1 Am J2d Actions § 1. A cause of action is to be distinguished from right of action. A right of action is the right to enforce presently a cause of action, that is, a remedial right; a cause of action, on the other hand, is the operative fact or facts which give rise to a right of action. 1 Am J2d Actions § 2. A cause of action is a matter of substance concerned with the violation of a right, not a matter of remedy. 34 Am J1st Lim Ac § 45. But "cause of action" is synonymous with "action" in the sense that the survival of an "action" is the survival of a "cause of action." 1 Am J2d Abat & R § 1.

See accrual of cause of action; identity of causes of action; joinder of causes of action; misjoinder of causes of action; separate cause of action; splitting a cause of action.

cause of loss. See proximate cause; risks and causes of loss.

causeway. Webster defines the word as a way raised above the natural level of the ground by stones, earth, timber, fascines, etc., serving as a dry passage over wet or marshy ground, or as a mole to confine water to a pond or restrain it from overflowing lower ground. O. & R. V. R. Co. v Severin, 30 Neb 318, 322.

causidical (kâ-sid'i-kal). Relating to pleading.

causidicus (kâ-si'di-kus). An advocate; a pleader.

cautela (kâ'te-la). Caution; vigilance.

cauti juratoria (kâ'tī jū-ra-to'ri-a). Caution juratory.

cautio (kâ'she-ō). Caution; care; security.

cautio fidejussoria (kâ'she-ō fī''de-jūs-sō'ri-a). Security by way of a surety bond.

caution. Care; prudence; regard for danger; a written notice filed in the office of the registrar of land titles warning against dealing with the land without giving notice to the person filing the caution.

cautionary (kâ'shon-a-ri). By way of pledge or security; admonishing or warning.

cautionary instruction. An instruction to the jury in which the court admonishes the jury to be vigilant against external influence; to refrain from conversing with anyone about the case while the trial is in progress; etc.

cautionary judgment. A judgment entered against a defendant as a lien against his property, in order to secure the plaintiff for the amount which may become due him on the final disposition of the case, where it appears that the defendant is about to remove or fraudulently transfer his property. Seisner v Blake, 13 Pa 333.

cautione admittenda. See de cautione admittenda.

cautioner (kâ'shon-ėr). A surety.

caution juratory. Security by means of an oath.

caution-money (kâ'shon mun'i). Money paid as security for the performance of an obligation or contract.

cautionry (kâ'shon-ri). Suretyship; becoming surety.

cautio pignoratitia (kâ'she-ō pig''nō-rā-ti'she-a). Security by way of pledge.

cautio pro expensis (kâ'she-ō prō ex-pen'sis). Security for expenses.

cautious. Prudent; in a secondary sense, the term, standing without the qualification of "reasonably," implies, to some people at least, the idea of being fearful, timorous, or overly prudent. Jenkins v Gilligan, 131 Iowa 176, 108 NW 237.

There may be an infinitesimal shade of difference between "cautious" and "prudent," but a reasonably prudent person and a reasonably cautious person are substantially the same, and possess identical significance for all practical purposes. Certainly the words "cautious" and "prudent" are used interchangeably in defining negligence. Malcolm v Mooresville Cotton Mills, 191 NC 727, 730, 133 SE 7.

cautio usufructuaria (kâ'she-ō ū-su-fruk''tu-ā'ri-a). Security against a tenant's waste.

cav. An abbreviation of **cavalry**.

c. a. v. An abbreviation of "curia advisare vult," the court wishes to deliberate.

cavalry. Soldiers mounted on horses or, in modern times, on motorized vehicles.

caveat. Literally, a notice to beware; a notice given or placed on file to prevent action until the caveator can be heard; a statement of opposition to the probate of a will, or against its probate in a particular form, filed at any time prior to the hearing of proof of the will. 57 Am J1st Wills § 842. A notice filed by an inventor in the United States patent office, describing the invention and praying the protection of his right to a patent until he shall have matured his invention. The purpose of a caveat is to secure an opportunity to have questions of priority between rival inventors determined before the issue of a patent. Electric Railway Co. v Jamaica & Brooklyn Railroad Co. (CC NY) 61 F 655, 671.

(Ecclesiastical law) A notice usually entered with the bishop by a party of his intended opposition to prevent the institution of his antagonist's clerk in a living. By the ecclesiastical law, an institution after a caveat entered is void. See 3 Bl Comm 246.

Caveat actor (kā've-at ak'tor). Let the doer beware.

caveatee. The person propounding an instrument for probate as a will. 57 Am J1st Wills § 793; more broadly defined as a person bound by the caveat of another.

Caveat emptor (kā've-at emp'tor). Let the buyer beware, a maxim of the common law expressing the rule that the buyer purchases at his peril. Implied warranties in the sale of personal property are exceptions to the rule thus expressed. 46 Am J1st Sales § 337. The maxim is applicable to sales of real estate in respect of conditions of the premises open to observation. 55 Am J1st V & P § 79. The doctrine of the maxim applies in its utmost vigor and strictness to judicial sales, so that the purchaser takes upon himself the risk of finding outstanding rights that could have been asserted against the parties to the proceedings and which necessarily affect the title conveyed to him. 30A Am J Rev ed Jud S § 180.

Caveat emptor; qui ignorare non debuit quod jus alienum emit (kā've-at emp'tor; qui ig-no-rā're non de'bu-it quod jūs ā-li-ē'num e'mit). Let the buyer beware; he who should not ignore the fact that he is purchasing the right of another.

caveator (kā'vē-ā-tor). (Patent law.) A person who files a caveat; a person who opposes the probate of an instrument propounded for probate as a will. 57 Am J1st Wills § 793.

Caveat venditor (kā've-at ven'di-tor). Let the seller beware. Caveat venditor is not the law if by it is intended anything more than that it is the seller's duty to do what the ordinary man would do in a similar situation. Pantebakos v Rockingham Light

& Power Co. 81 NH 441, 128 A 534, 38 ALR 1063, 1065.

Caveat viator (kā′ve-at vi-ā′tor). Let the traveler beware.

Cavendum est a fragmentis (ka-ven′dum est ā fragmen′tis). Beware of fragments.

caver (kāv′ėr). In Derbyshire, a thief who stole ore from a mine.

cavere (ka-vē′re). To beware; to take care; to be cautious.

cay (kā). A quay or wharf; a sandbank or reef off a shore.

cayagium (ka-yā′ji-um). Wharfage duties.

C. B. An abbreviation of "common bench"; "chief baron."

cc. Abbreviation for cubic centimeters.

C. C. An abbreviation of "county commissioner," "county court," "cepi corpus," "civil code," "criminal cases," "civil cases," "crown cases," "circuit court."

C. C. A. Abbreviation for Circuit Court of Appeals.

CCC. Abbreviation for Commodity Credit Corporation, also for Civilian Conservation Corps.

ccm. Abbreviation for centimeter.

C. C. P. An abbreviation of "court of common pleas;" "code of civil procedure."

c.d. Abbreviatior of discount for cash.

ce. See **en ce.**

ceapgild (kē′ăp-gĭld). The payment of an animal.

cease. To stop; to discontinue; to go out of existence. Oakland Paving Co. v Hilton, 69 Cal 479, 11 P 3.

cease and desist order. An order by an administrative agency which requires that certain practices specified be stopped. 2 Am J2d Admin L § 467. Thus, an order of a National Labor Relations Board restraining an employer from an unfair labor practice. 31 Am J Rev ed Lab § 301.

cede. The precise meaning of the word depends somewhat on the subject matter with which it is connected. In some instances, it is used in the sense of "grant," but ordinarily it means to yield; to surrender; to give up. Mayor & City Council v Turnpike Road, 80 Md 535, 542. Thus, a person grants, conveys, or deeds land, whereas a nation transfers territory by "ceding it." The word is also familiar in the law of reinsurance, expressing the act whereby an insurer, by contract known as a "treaty," transfers its risks or some of its risks to, or reinsures them with, another insurer.
See **cession.**

cedent (sē′dęnt). An assignor.

cedo (sē′dō). The word of grant in a Mexican conveyance. Mulford v Le Franc, 26 Cal 88, 108.

cedula (sed′ṵ-lạ). (Spanish.) A promissory note.

Cedunt arma togae (sē′dunt ăr′ma to′gē). Let arms yield to the toga, that is, let war yield to peace.

ceiling. The top part of a room, opposite the floor. A top or limit, as a ceiling on the price of a specific article.

celation (sel-a′shun). The concealment by a woman of her pregnancy.

celebrate (sel′ę̄-brăt). To solemnize; to give due publicity to an event.

celebration of marriage. The performance of the ritual of a marriage publicly and solemnly; in the modern terminology of the law, the taking of the marriage vows before a person authorized to perform marriage ceremonies; the performance of the formal act or ceremony by which a man and woman contract marriage and assume the status of husband and wife. 35 Am J1st Mar § 25; giving utterance to and public evidence of the contract of marriage. Howard v Kelly, 111 Miss 285, 71 So 391.

celibacy (sel′i-bạ-si). The state of being unmarried, particularly of one under vow to remain unmarried.

cellar. A storeroom; an underground space, usually but not necessarily below a building.

cemetery. A place or area set apart, either by governmental authority or private enterprise, for the interment of the dead. 14 Am J2d Cem § 1. The term is used interchangeably with "graveyard", "burial ground", and "place of burial". Anno: 50 ALR2d 907. It includes not only lots for depositing the bodies of the dead, but also avenues, walks, and grounds for shrubbery and ornamental purposes. The controlling circumstance in the creation of a cemetery is not the burial of the dead, but the act of setting the ground apart for burial and distinguishing it from the surrounding territory as a place of burial. Villa Park v Wanderer's Rest Cemetery Co. 316 Ill 226, 147 NE 104.

cemetery lot. See **burial lot.**

cemetery purposes. Use for a cemetery in the conventional sense, also use for a crematory for the reduction of dead bodies to ashes and a columbarium for the preservation of the ashes. Moore v United States Cremation Co. 275 NY 105, 544, 9 NE2d 795, 11 NE2d 743, 113 ALR 1124.

cenegild. A fine paid by a murderer to his victim's relatives.

cenninga (sen-nin′ga). A notice given by a vendee to his vendor that the goods sold have been claimed by a third person.

cens (sóns). An annual payment to a superior lord made as a tribute to his superiority.

censaria (sen-sā′ri-a). A farm, or house and land, let at a standing rent.—Cowell.

censarii (sen-sā′ri-ī). Farmers.

cense (sens). An assessment; a tax; a census.

censitaire (sоn-si-tār). A tenant who paid "cens."

censive (sen′siv). The land the tenant of which paid a "cens."

censo (sen′sō). Spanish for ground rent. Trevino v Fernandez, 13 Tex 630, 655.

censor (sen′sǫr). Noun: A high Roman officer who with his co-censor kept the census, attended to matters involving public manners and morals, and administered public finances; in modern usage, a person authorized to view a picture, read a book or article, or see a musical play or dramatic production, and determine whether or not such picture, book, article, or production is objectionable as indecent, obscene, or immoral; also, an officer of the armed forces authorized to read letters written by servicemen for the purpose of deleting portions from which the enemy might gain intelligence. Verb: To strike out as objectionable.

censo reservativo (sen′sō re-ser-vă-ti′vō). In Spanish-American grants,—the right to receive from an-

censorship. An examination of a picture, article, book, motion picture, or play for the purpose of appraising its decency and prohibiting publication or production where the same is found objectionable as indecent, obscene, or immoral; striking from letters of men in the armed services portions which might give intelligence to the enemy.

other an annual pension by virtue of having transferred land to him by full and perfect title. Trevino v Fernandez, 13 Tex 630, 656.

censuere (sen-su'e-re). A judgment or decree of the Roman senate.

censumethidus (sen-su-me'thi-dus). In the dead hand.
See **mortmain.**

censure. Severe criticism; condemnation; obloquy Bettner v Holt, 70 Cal 270, 275, 11 P 713.

census. An official enumeration of the population of inhabitants of a country, state, county, city, or other political subdivision or administrative district. 14 Am J2d Census § 1; a decennial official count by the government of the United States of the inhabitants and wealth of the country and the taking of other statistics.

Census Bureau. An agency within, and under, the jurisdiction of the Department of Commerce, having the function of administering the federal census laws. 14 Am J2d Census § 3.

census regalis (sen'sus rē-gā'lis). The royal revenue, including forfeitures to the Crown.

cent. A penny; an abbreviation of "centum," one hundred; **centime, centigrade.**

cental (sen-tal). An English weight measure of one hundred pounds.

centena (sen'te-nä). A hundred.

centenarii (sen-te-nā'ri-ī). Plural of **centenarius.**

centenarius (sen-te-nā'ri-us). A term of early France, later introduced to England, meaning the head of a "hundred," that is, a military force of one hundred freemen.

centeni (sen-tē'nī). The principal inhabitants of a district composed of different villages, originally in number a hundred, but afterwards only called by that name; and who probably gave the same denomination to the district out of which they were chosen. See 3 Bl Comm 34.

center of gravity theory. A theory in the subject of conflict of laws, that the execution, validity, construction, and performance of a contract should be governed by the law of the place with which the matter in dispute has the most significant contacts, instead of looking to the place of execution or of performance, or to the intention of the parties, to determine which law shall govern. 16 Am J2d Confl L § 42.

center of intersection. The point where the center line of one street or road meets the center line of the other, both lines being drawn parallel to and halfway between the curbs and projected to the point of meeting. Stewart v Olson, 188 Wis 487, 206 NW 909, 44 ALR 1292.

center of road. A point in the middle of the road equidistant from the termini. If the road has not been surveyed it is impossible to locate the point with exactness. Rice v Douglas County, 93 Or 551, 183 P 768.

centesima (sen-te'si-ma). One one-hundredth part; one per cent.

centime (soṅ-tēm). A coin representing the one hundredth part of a franc.

centimeter. A linear measure of the metric system, equivalent to 0.3937 inches.

centner (sent'nėr). A hundredweight.

Central Bank. A bank in a foreign country which is the fiscal agent of the foreign country. Bank of China v Wells Fargo Bank & Union Trust Co. (Two Cases) (CA9 Cal) 209 F2d 467, 48 ALR2d 172; a bank established by statute in 1933, with 12 regional banks to provide a source of credit for farm co-operatives, operating under the Farm Credit Administration. 12 USC §§ 1134 et seq.
See **International Bank for Reconstruction and Development.**

Central Intelligence Agency. A federal agency operating to coordinate all intelligence activities of the United States, to obtain information vital to the security of the country from military and diplomatic sources, and also from its own field agents, to sift and analyze the reports obtained from the various sources, draw conclusions therefrom, and present such conclusions to the National Security Council.

centralization of schools. A modern movement in the interest of economy, more efficient administration, and improvement in education, whereby all the schools of an entire area, such as a township, a part of a county, two or more townships, or part of one township and part of another township, sometimes part of one county and part of another county, are brought together into one centralized district, in which one or more, usually several, public schools shall be maintained, the most common system being to have one high school and a number of separate schools, each of which is equipped for the education of one or two grades, from kindergarten or first grade through the eighth grade, transportation of pupils in busses being provided all pupils.

centralized district. A school district established in the centralization of schools.
See **centralization of schools.**

central time. See **standard time.**

centum (sen'tum). One hundred.

centumviri (sen-tum'vi-rī). The one hundred and five Roman judges who were appointed to decide common causes among the people. See 3 Bl Comm 515.

century (sen'tụ-ri). The Roman hundred; a period of one hundred years; the twentieth century.

ceorlus (kur'lus). A churl.

cepi (sē'pī). I have taken.

Cepi corpus (sē'pī kor'pus). I have taken the body; a form of return of a warrant for the arrest of a debtor.

Cepi corpus et est in custodia (sē'pī kor'pus et est in kus-tō'di-a). I have taken the body and it is in custody;—a form of return of an officer upon executing a writ for the seizure of a person.

Cepi corpus et paratum habeo (sē'pī kor'pus et parā'tum hā'be-ō). I have the body and I have it ready; formal words used in the return on a writ for the arrest of a person.

Cepit (sē'pit). He took.

CEPIT [186] CERTIFICATE

Cepit et abduxit (sē'pit et ab-du'xit). He took and led away.

Cepit et asportavit (sē'pit et as-por-tā'vit). He took and carried away.

Cepit in alio loco (sē'pit in a'li-ō lō'kō). He took in another place; a form of plea in a replevin action.

ceppagium (sep-pā'ji-um). The stumps of felled trees.

ceps (seps). The stocks in which offenders were confined.

cere (sēr). Wax; a wax seal.

cerebral embolism A blood clot in a blood vessel of the brain. Anno: 20 ALR 81.

cerebral hemorrhage. A flooding of the brain by blood, resulting from the breaking of a blood vessel.

cerebral palsy. A most pitiful affliction, suffered at birth usually, arising from an injury to the brain, and causing paralysis.

cerebral vascular disability. See **cerebral hemorrhage.**

ceremony. See **celebration of marriage.**

Certa debet esse intentio, et narratio et certum fundamentum, et certa res quae deducitur in judicium (ser'ta dē'bet es'se in-ten'she-ō, et nar-rā'she-ō et ser'tum fun-da-men'tum, et ser'ta rēz kwē de-du'si-ter in jū-di'she-um). The intention, declaration, foundation, and matter brought to judgment ought to be certain.

certain (sēr'tan). Free from doubt.

certain information that a felony has been committed. Information of circumstances sufficiently strong to warrant a cautious man in the belief that the person arrested has committed a felony were held sufficient. Burton v McNeill, 196 SC 250, 13 SE2d 10, 133 ALR 603.

certain is that which can be rendered certain. Leaving no scope for application of rule of construction against the grantor. Elterich v Leicht, Real Estate Co. 130 Va 224, 107 SE 735, 18 ALR 441.

certain services. Base services, stinted in quantity and not to be exceeded. See 2 Bl Comm 61.

certainty (sēr'tan-ti). Clarity; accuracy; precision; particularity.
See **definiteness.**

certainty of allegation. Precision and particularity, as opposed to ambiguity and generality, but reasonable certainty is all that can be demanded of the pleader. David v David's Admr. 66 Ala 139, 148.

certainty of damages. Having a basis for a reasoned conclusion; a reasonable basis for computation; absolute exactness of calculation is not a requisite. Palmer v Connecticut Railway & Lighting Co. 311 US 544, 85 L Ed 336, 61 S Ct 379.

certa res (ser'ta rēz). A certain matter or thing.

certa scientia. See **ex certa scientia.**

certifiable questions. Single or particular questions, as to distinct propositions of law actually presented in the case, and which are material, and will aid the lower court in determining the case before it. 5 Am J2d A & E § 1026.

certificando. See **de certificando.**

certificate. A formal statement intended as an authentication of the fact asserted and set forth, usually under seal where made by a public officer.
See **license.**

certificate into chancery. The decision of a court of law on a matter submitted for such decision by a court of chancery.

certificate of abstracter. A statement appended by an abstracter of titles at the end of an abstract prepared by him, showing the records of title covered by the search, and, in addition, the date from which the search made by him ran and the day and hour at which it terminated. 1 Am J2d Abstr T § 5.

certificate of accountant. An accountant's license to practice as a certified public accountant. 1 Am J2d Accts § 2; the statement by a certified public accountant, or other accountant, employed to examine the books of a corporation, partnership, or individual engaged in business, or of a charitable corporation, appended to the financial statement of the corporation, partnership, or individual, that he has examined the books and accounts of the corporation, partnership, or individual, and that the financial statement is a true representation of the financial condition of the business conducted or the charity administered.

certificate of acknowledgment. The written evidence of an acknowledgment by the officer who takes the acknowledgment, which states in substance that the person named therein was known to and appeared before him and acknowledged the instrument to be his act and deed. 1 Am J2d Ack § 1. The certificate is to be signed by the officer taking the acknowledgment. 1 Am J2d Ack §48. Whether or not a seal is required depends upon the provisions of local statute. If the statute does not in express terms or by clear implication require a seal, the want of a seal does not invalidate the certificate, even when it is executed by a notary public or commissioner of deeds. But if the attributable statute requires that the certificate bear the seal of the officer or requires that the officer taking the acknowledgment authenticate his acts by the use of his seal, the omission of the seal from the certificate is fatal. 1 Am J2d Ack § 50.

certificate of architect or engineer. A formal approval in writing by architect or engineer of the performance by the contractor under a building contract, usually required under the terms of a building or construction contract as a condition of the contractor's right to compensation. 13 Am J2d Bldg Contr § 32. The certificate is either one of completion or of progress, the latter being one given during the progress of the work, certifying as to the extent or value of the work done or materials furnished, its purpose being to enable the contractor to collect, under the terms of the contract, the portion or instalment of the contract price for work performed or materials furnished to date. 13 Am J2d Bldg Contr §§ 32 et seq.

certificate of arrival. A certificate which, under a former statute, was required of an alien seeking citizenship, the requirement being that the certificate be filed with the petition for citizenship. 3 Am J2d Aliens § 148.

certificate of assize. A writ under which a second trial of the same cause by the same jury was had because of a failure of justice through an error of the court. See 3 Bl Comm 389.

certificate of authentication. The certificate of an officer of a court of record, or like official, to the effect that the officer taking an acknowledgment or proof by affidavit was, at the date thereof, such officer as he claimed to be, and authorized to take the acknowledgment or proof, and that signature appended to the acknowledgment or proof is the genuine signature of the officer. Such certificate is sometimes known as a county clerk's certificate. 1 Am J2d Ack § 78; the authentication of a document or copy by the officer, such as a clerk of court, who has custody of the document. 30 Am J2d Ev § 997.

certificate of birth. See **birth certificate.**

certificate of citizenship. A certificate issued by a court of naturalization that a person has been admitted to citizenship on application made and proceedings had thereon; a certificate by the Attorney General of the United States that a person has acquired citizenship by the naturalization of his parents, or circumstances other than by application and proceedings for naturalization, and the taking of an oath of allegiance. 3 Am J2d Aliens § 156.

certificate of completion. See **certificate of architect or engineer.**

certificate of conformity. A certificate by an officer of a court, usually the clerk of court, or other proper officer, that an acknowledgment or proof by affidavit is in conformity with law. Such certificate is often combined with a certificate of authenticity. 1 Am J2d Ack § 78.

certificate of corporate stock. See **stock certificate.**

certificate of costs. A certificate of the trial judge in an action of trespass attesting the fact that the trespass complained of was wilful and malicious. When such a certificate was made, the plaintiff became entitled to full costs, whether they exceeded his damages or not. See 3 Bl Comm 214.

certificate of death. See **death certificate.**

certificate of deposit. A written acknowledgment by a bank or banker on the receipt of a sum of money on deposit which the bank or banker promises to pay to the depositor, to the order of the depositor, or to some other person or to his order, whereby the relation of debtor and creditor between the bank and the depositor is created. 10 Am J2d Banks § 455; a writing having the requisites of negotiability and consisting of an acknowledgment by a bank of receipt of money with an engagement to repay it. UCC § 3-104(2).

Certificates of deposit are divided into two classes as regards time of payment, that is, demand certificates and time certificates. 10 Am J2d Banks § 455.

certificate of engineer. See **certificate of architect or engineer.**

certificate of entry. A certificate issued by the government upon the making of an entry of public land. 42 Am J1st Pub L § 34.

certificate of graduation. A certificate given upon graduation from a school.

certificate of identity. A certificate, otherwise known as a certificate of alien registration, which an alien obtains upon registration. 3 Am J2d Aliens § 112.

certificate of incorporation. Same as **articles of incorporation.**

certificate of indebtedness. An instrument issued by a building and loan association for borrowed money. 13 Am J2d B & L Assoc § 10; an obligation issued by a receiver, trustee, or debtor in possession, for money borrowed for the purpose of continuing the operation of the bankrupt's or debtor's business while bankruptcy proceedings or reorganization proceedings continue. 9 Am J2d Bankr §§ 1308, 1357, 1555; one of an issue of instruments by a public body to obtain funds for carrying on the administration of government, being similar to a bond in the respect that both are promises to pay a sum certain at a definite time or times. 43 Am J1st Pub Sec § 12. For many years the form of obligation used to raise money for municipal improvements when the loan was for a large sum and intended to cover a long term of years was an instrument under seal known as a "certificate of loan," with certificates of interest attached, payable to the bearer at particular times within the year, at some particular place, being a part of the contract from which they must be cut off to be presented for payment. These certificates of loan are now known as coupon bonds. Amey v Allegheny City (US) 24 How 364, 16 L Ed 614.

certificate of loan. See **certificate of indebtedness.**

certificate of membership. Sometimes called a benefit certificate, issued to a member of a mutual benefit society, constituting the contract between him and the corporation, but construed and governed by its charter constitution, and bylaws.

The certificate is in effect a policy of life insurance, albeit of a distinctive character. Supreme Council Catholic Knights of America v Densford, 21 Ky LR 1574, 56 SW 172. Certificates are also used to represent membership in fraternal orders, social clubs, and various societies organized for charitable purposes.

certificate of mutual benefit society. See **certificate of membership.**

certificate of naturalization. See **certificate of citizenship.**

certificate of notary public. See **notary's certificate.**

certificate of partnership. A certificate showing the names of all of the members of the partnership, the filing of which is required by law in a number of states, under penalty of not being entitled to maintain or defend actions in the courts unless the statutes are complied with. See 40 Am J1st Partn § 431.

certificate of progress. See **certificate of architect or engineer.**

certificate of protest. See **protest.**

certificate of public convenience and necessity. A certificate from a public service commission as a prerequisite to the construction or extension of a public utility plant or system. 43 Am J1st Pub Util § 198; a certificate, issued by the appropriate regulatory commission to a common carrier by motor vehicle, which confers the privilege of operating upon the public highway, sometimes regarded as a rebuttable license, but in other states deemed to be a definite economic asset, and a franchise. 13 Am J2d Car § 78; a certificate issued by the Interstate Commerce Commission evidencing its permission to the holder thereof to operate as a common carrier between named points in different states upon the conditions and in the manner set forth in the certificate. Inland Motor Freight v United States (DC Idaho) 36 F Supp 885.

certificate of qualification. See **license.**

certificate of receiver. See **certificate of indebtedness.**

certificate of registration. The certificate obtained by an alien upon registration. 3 Am J2d Aliens § 112; an authorization, otherwise known as a license, to use a designated motor vehicle upon the highways of the state. 7 Am J2d Auto § 53.

certificate of sale. A certificate given by the sheriff or other officer conducting a sale under execution, in a jurisdiction where such a sale is subject to redemption by the owner or execution defendant for a fixed period of time, which declares the making of a sale to a designated purchaser and the right of the purchaser to receive a deed from the sheriff or other officer upon presentation of the certificate after the expiration of the redemption period. 30 Am J2d Exec § 393 et seq.

certificate of sale for taxes. See **tax certificate of sale.**

certificate of stock. See **stock certificate.**

certificate of teacher. See **teacher's certificate.**

certificate of title. An instrument, issued by a registrar or other public officer, intended to show who is the owner of the motor vehicle described in the instrument. 7 Am J2d Auto § 24; the certificate issued by the registrar of titles, in a jurisdiction where titles to real estate are registered under the Torrens or a similar system, after a proceeding for registration or, in a case of the transfer of a registered title, upon the filing of a transfer of title by a grantee or purchaser.

certificate of trustee. See **certificate of indebtedness.**

certification. The return of a writ; a formal attestation of a matter of fact, that is, the making of a certificate of any kind.

certification of bond. The identification of a bond by a mortgage trustee as one of the series of bonds mentioned and described in the mortgage. Bauernschmidt v Maryland Trust Co. 89 Md 507, 43 A 790.

certification of check. See **certified check.**

certification of question. A practice, based on a procedure first developed in the federal courts, under which an entire case or a specific question of law involved in a case, may be sent from a lower to a higher court for decision. 5 Am J2d A & E § 1025.

certification of record on appeal. The signature by the judge to the bill of exceptions and attestation by the clerk of court, under the seal of the court, to the signature. 4 Am J2d A & E §§ 466, 467.

certification proceeding. A proceeding of a nonadversary, fact-finding character in which the National Labor Relations Board acts the part of disinterested investigator seeking merely to ascertain the desires of the employees as to their representation. Southern S. S. Co. v NLRB (CA3) 120 F2d 505.

certified case. See **case certified; certification of question.**

certified check. A check upon which the drawee bank has stamped or written the words "certified," "good," "accepted," or an equivalent expression, with the signature of the certifying officer, the effect of which stamp is equivalent to an acceptance of a bill of exchange by the drawee. 10 Am J2d Banks § 587.

The certification of a check by a bank that it is *good,* is similar to the accepting of a bill, for the banker thereby admits assets, and makes himself liable to pay. By the law merchant such certification is equivalent to acceptance. It implies that the check is drawn upon sufficient funds in the hands of the drawee, that they have been set apart for its satisfaction, and that they shall be so applied whenever the check is presented for payment. It is an undertaking that the check is good then, and shall continue good; and this agreement is as binding on the bank as its notes of circulation, a certificate of deposit payable to the order of the depositor, or any other obligation it can assume. First Nat. Bank v Currie, 147 Mich 72, 110 NW 499.

certified copy. A copy certified as true by the officer to whose custody the original is entrusted. 29 Am J2d Ev § 910.
See **certificate of authentication.**

certified public accountant. One who has received from a commission, board, or proper officer a certificate qualifying him to practice as a certified public accountant. Frazer v Shelton, 320 Ill 253, 150 NE 696, 43 ALR 1086.

certified question. See **certification of question.**

certify. To authenticate by a certificate; to vouch for a thing in writing; a certificate is an authoritative attestation, and any form which affirms the fact in writing is sufficient. Re Kostohris' Estate, 96 Mont 226, 29 P2d 829; to assert in writing the correctness of identity of an instrument. Sawyer v Lorenzen, 149 Iowa 87, 127 NW 1091.

certiorando. See **de certiorando.**

certiorari. A method of review of the action taken by an administrative agency. 2 Am J2d Admin L § 625; a writ issued by a superior to an inferior court of record, or to some other tribunal or officer exercising a judicial function, requiring the certification and return of the record and proceedings in order that the record may be revised and corrected in matters of law. It is a common law writ, but usually provided for by statute. 14 Am J2d Cert § 1.

cert money (sėrt' mun"i). Yearly payments made to the lord of the manor for the keeping of the leet.

Certum est quod certum reddi potest (ser'tum est quod ser'tum red'dī po'test). That is certain which is capable of being rendered certain. Wells v Alexandre, 130 NY 642, 29 NE 142.

cervisia (sėr-vis'i-ạ). Beer.

cervus (sėr'vus). A stag.

cesionario (se"se-o-nah're-o). An assignee.

cess (ses). To neglect a legal duty; a tax.

Cessante causa, cessat effectus (ses-san'te kâ'za, ses'-sat ef-fek'tus). The cause ceasing, the effect ceases.

Cessante ratione cessat, et ipsa lex (ses-san'te rā-she-ō'ne ses'sat, et ip'sa lex). The reason for the law having ceased, the law itself ceases.

Cessante ratione legis cessat, et ipsa lex (ses-san'te rā-she-ō'ne lē'jis ses'sat, et ip'sa lex). Where the reason for the existence of a law ceases, the law itself should also cease. The maxim means that no common-law rule can survive the reasons on which it is founded. It needs no statute to change it; it abrogates itself. If the reasons on which a law rests are overborne by opposing reasons, which, in the progress of society, gain controlling force, the old law, though still good as an abstract principle, and good in its application to some circumstances, must cease to apply or to be a controlling principle to the new circumstances. Beardsley v Hartford, 50 Conn 542.

Cessante statu primitivo, cessat derivatus (ses-san'te sta'tū prī-mī-tī'vō, ses'sat dē-ri-va'tus). The primary state ceasing, the derivative ceases also.

cessare (ses-sā're). To cease; to stop.

Cessa regnare, si non vis judicare (ses'sa reg-nā're, sī non vis jū-di-kā're). Cease to rule, if you do not wish to judge.

cessavit per biennium (ses-sā'vit per bi-en'ni-um). He ceased for two years,—a writ, also called a "cessavit" which lay by statute for a landlord to recover land from his tenant after two years of failure to pay rent or to render the prescribed services. The writ also lay for the donor of land to a religious house on condition of performing some religious service, after neglect of such service for two years. See 3 Bl Comm 232.

cesse. Same as **cess**.

cesser (ses'ėr). A ceasing or stopping.

cesser clause. A stipulation in a charter party that the charterer's liability thereunder shall cease when the vessel is loaded and the bills of lading are signed, the owner agreeing to settle with the consignees of the cargo all questions regarding freight, demurrage, and other liabilities, under the protection of his lien for charges. It is intended to free the charter, on his furnishing a full cargo, from possible liabilities cast upon him by the terms of the charter party, which, by its terms, he might otherwise personally be called on to discharge after the full cargo had been shipped on board. 48 Am J1st Ship § 325.

cesset executio (ses'set ex-e-kū'she-ō). An order directing a stay of execution.

cesset processus (ses'set pro-ses'sus). An order directing a stay of proceedings in the action.

cessio (sesh'i ō). A cession.

cessio bonorum (sesh'i ō bō-nō'rum). (Roman law.) The right of an impoverished debtor to anticipate his creditors by voluntarily ceding his estate to them and thereby exempt himself from imprisonment and from infamy. It was doubtless the ancestor of our modern bankruptcy law. Sturges v Crowninshield (US) 4 Wheat 122, 4 L Ed 529.

cession (sesh'ọn). A surrender; a giving up; a relinquishment of jurisdiction by a board in favor of another agency. 31 Am J Rev ed Lab § 213; the transfer of territory by one nation to another. See **cede**.

cessionary (sesh'ọn-ạ-ri). An assignee.

cessionary bankrupt. An assignor for the benefit of his creditors.

cession des biens (sè-sion dê bi-īn'). An assignment for the benefit of one's creditors.

cessment (ses'mẹnt). An assessment or tax.

cessor (ses'ọr). A tenant who by neglect to pay rent was liable to a writ of cessavit.

cessure. Same as **cesser**.

c'est ascavoir (sā äs-sä-voa'). (French.) That is to say.

C'est le crime qui fait la honte, et non pas l'echafaud (sā le crīm kē fā la hônt, ā non pä' l'esha-fô'). It is the crime which brings disgrace, not the scaffold.

cestui (ses'twē). A short form for cestui que trust; the beneficiary of a trust.

cestui que trust (ses'twē kē trust). The beneficiary of a trust; the person for whose benefit property is held in trust by a trustee. See 54 Am J1st Trusts § 136.

cestui que use (ses'twē kē ūz). Also spelled cestuy que use.—A person for whose use land was granted to another. See 2 Bl Comm 328.

cestui que vie (ses'twē kē vē). A person for the duration of whose lifetime an estate has been granted.

cestuis que trustent (ses'twē kē trust'tent). Plural of **cestui que trust**.

cestuy (ses'twē). Same as **cestui**.

Cestuy, que doit inheriter al pere, doit inheriter al fils (se-twi' ke doa in-her'i-te' al pèr, doa in-her'i-te al fi). He who should inherit from the father, should inherit from the son.

cet (set). That.

cetera. See **et cetera**.

ceux (sō). Those.

cf. An abbreviation of "confer," "compare."

c/f. Bookkeeping abbreviation for carried forward.

C. F. Abbreviation for cost and freight.

C. F. I. Abbreviation for cost, freight, and insurance.

CFR. Abbreviation of **Code of Federal Regulations**.

cg. Abbreviation for centigram.

C. G. Abbreviation of Coast Guard, also of Consul General.

c.h. Abbreviation for custom house.

Ch. Abbreviation for chapter.

c. h. An abbreviation of "courthouse."

chace (chās). A chase; a hunting preserve.

chacea (cha-sē'a). A chase; a hunting preserve.

chaceable (chās'ābl). Subject to the sport of hunting, as chaceable animals.

chacea est ad communem legem (cha-sē'a est ad kommū'nem lē'jem). A chase exists by the common law.

chafewax (chāf'waks). A chancery officer who attended to the wax used in sealing writs.

chaffer (chåf'ėr). Goods; wares; merchandise.

chain (chān). A series of metal links or rings, connected or fitted into one another, used as a hitch or as a secure binding of a load otherwise not stable, for example, the binding of a truckload of logs; a watch chain; a gold or silver chain on a locket; a linear measure of 100 links, each 7.92 inches long, or 66 feet in all. This, known as Gunter's chain, is in common use and is used in public land surveys. Another much less common chain is the engineer's chain of 100 links each one foot long.

chain-gang. A number of convicts chained together, usually for labor; a work gang of convicts or jail prisoners working on a highway, canal, or other public improvement.

chain of causation. Such a succession of events as link an act or legal cause with a result or damage; an element of proximate cause. 38 Am J1st Negl § 56.

chain of title. The successive conveyances and devolutions of title, commencing with the patent from the government or some other source and ending with the conveyance or devolution to the person claiming title presently. Capper v Poulsen, 321 Ill 480, 482, 152 NE 587, 588.

chain reaction. A series of events, each of which is productive of or influential upon the succeeding event; a term applied especially to nuclear reaction.

chairman (chār'mạn). The presiding officer of a deliberative body.

chairman of the board. The person in the chair, that is, the person who presides at the meeting of the board of a corporation of any kind. Although the nature and the duties of this office varies as between corporations, usually the top executive is the president rather than the chairman of the board.

chaldron (châl'dron). A coal measure of thirty-six bushels.

challenge (chal'enj). Noun: An objection; an exception. Verb: To object; to take exception to.

challenge for actual bias. Same as **challenge to the favor.**

challenge for cause. An objection to a juror, made on voir dire for cause stated, that is, pointing out the ground upon which the juror is disqualified.
See **challenge for principal cause; challenge to the favor.**

challenge for favor. Same as **challenge to the favor.**

challenge for principal cause. An objection lodged against a juror on voir dire on the ground of an absolute disqualification, such as consanguinity or relationship within the prohibited degree, leaving nothing to the discretion of the court in reference to the determination of the likelihood of actual bias. 31 Am J Rev ed Jur § 147.

challenge of judge. See **rescusation.**

challenge propter affectum (prop'ter af-fek'tum). A challenge to a juror on the ground of bias or partiality. 31 Am J Rev ed Jur § 157.

challenge propter defectum (prop'ter dē-fek'tum). A challenge to a juror for cause on account of some deficiency in the man himself, as that he is an alien or an ex-convict. 31 Am J Rev ed Jur § 157.

challenge propter delictum (prop'ter dē-lik'tum). The challenge to a juror on the ground of infamous crime. 31 Am J Rev ed Jur § 157.

challenge propter honoris respectum (prop'ter honō'ris res-pek'tum). A challenge to a lord of Parliament on the jury panel. 31 Am J Rev ed Jur § 157.

challenge to duel. See **challenge to fight.**

challenge to fight. To confront a person, either directly or through another known as a second, with writing, spoken words, or conduct which conveys the intention, at least somewhat formally, to duel or fight with him. 25 Am J2d Duel § 2.

Challenge to juror. An objection to a juror made on voir dire.
See **challenge for cause; peremptory challenge.**

challenge to the array. See **challenge to the panel.**

challenge to the favor. An objection lodged against an individual juror for bias, such to be determined by the trial court acting in the exercise of a sound discretion. 31 Am J Rev ed Jur § 147.

challenge to the panel. An objection lodged against the entire panel from which the trial jury in a particular case is to be selected, based on some legal defect, partiality, or other misconduct of an officer in summoning the panel. 31 Am J Rev ed Jur § 147.

challenge to the poll. A challenge to an individual juryman. 31 Am J Rev ed Jur § 147.

chamber. See **bill chamber; coal chamber.**

chamber business (chām'bėr biz'-nes). A term applied to all such judicial business as may properly be transacted by a judge in his chambers or elsewhere, as distinguished from such as must be done by the court in session; all business done out of court by the judge. Atchison, T. & S. F. Ry. Co. v Long, 122 Okla 86, 251 P 486.

chamber-counselor (chām'bėr-koun"sel-or). A lawyer who counsels and advises, but does not appear in court.

chamberlain (chām'bėr-lạn). A treasurer.

chamberlaria (cham-ber-lā'ri-a). A chamberlain.

chamber of accounts. A French court corresponding to the English court of exchequer.

chamber of commerce. A board of trade; an association of business men or industrialists of a city and its environs, organized and operating to promote and safeguard the commercial interests of the city and surrounding territory.

Chamber of Commerce Arbitration Court. See **Court of Arbitration of the Chamber of Commerce.**

chamber of deputies. The popular house of the English parliament; the assembly, in France, Italy and Spain.

chambers. The place, other than the courtroom, where a judge transacts the business of the court. 30A Am J Rev ed Judges § 35; a judge's private office, usually near, but not a part of, the courtroom; the private room or office of a judge where, for the convenience of parties, he hears such matters and transacts such business as a judge in vacation is authorized to hear, and which do not require a hearing by the judge sitting as a court; the office or private rooms of a judge, where parties are heard and orders made in matters not required to be brought before the full court. Atchison, Topeka & Santa Fe Ry. Co. v Long, 122 Okla 86, 251 P 486.

chambers decision. A decision rendered by a judge acting in vacation. Floyd v Smith, 63 Ga App 524, 11 SE2d 719.

chambers judgment. A judgment rendered by a judge in a proceeding at chambers. 30A Am J Rev ed Judgm § 53.
The proceedings of a session are properly part of the record on appeal, although the session was held in chambers. Gibson v Southern Pacific Co. 137 Cal App 2d 337, 290 P2d 347, 63 ALR2d 1205 (motion for directed verdict, heard outside presence of jury).

chambers of the king. The harbors of England.

chambers order. An order rendered by a judge sitting in chambers.

champart (shām-pâr). A French law term signifying a division of profits, being a part of the crop annually due the landlord by bargain or custom. See 4 Bl Comm 135.

champarty. Same as **champerty.**

champertia. See **de champertia.**

champertor (cham'pėr-tor). A person who commits champerty; the person who makes champertous agreement with a plaintiff or defendant. 14 Am J2d Champ § 3.

champertous (cham'pėr-tus). Partaking of or tainted with champerty.

champertous assignment. An assignment of a chose in action with the sole intent and purpose of having the assignee bring a suit thereon. 14 Am J2d Champ § 10.

champertous contract. A contract having a tendency to foment or protract litigation, or transferring the control and management of a suit to one having no right or interest in the subject of the action other than such as was derived from the litigious agreement, especially a contract by an attorney at law for a contingent fee in the proceeds of an action, whereby the attorney agreed to save the client harmless from costs and expenses of the proposed litigation. 14 Am J2d Champ § 4.

champerty (cham'pėr-ti). A species of maintenance, being a bargain made by one called the champertor with a plaintiff or defendant for a portion of the matter involved in a suit in case of a successful termination of the action, which the champertor undertakes to maintain or carry on at his own expense. 14 Am J2d Champ § 3.

chance. Hazard, risk, or the result or issue of uncertain and unknown conditions or forces, Dixon v Pluns, 98 Cal 384, 33 P 268; the possibility of something occurring without design or effort to make it occur. 34 Am J1st Lot § 6.
See **game of chance.**

chancellor (chản'sel-ọr). A judge of a court of chancery; in Scotland,—the foreman of a jury.

chancellor of a diocese. An ecclesiastical officer appointed by a bishop to hold his courts for him and to assist him in matters of ecclesiastical law. See 1 Bl Comm 382.

chancellor of the exchequer. The chief financial minister of England.

chance-medley (chảns'med"li). A casual affray; such killing as happens in self-defense upon a sudden encounter. See 4 Bl Comm 184.

chancery. See **court of chancery; equity; master in chancery.**

chance verdict. A verdict reached by tossing a coin, drawing lots, or any method wherein the reasoning and understanding of the individual jurors plays no part in determining the result. 53 Am J1st Trial § 1029.

chandler (chan'dlẻr). A retailer of groceries and other merchandise.

Chandler Act. An amendatory act approved by the President on June 22, 1938 and effective September 22, 1938, intended to modernize the law of bankruptcy, especially by adding provisions whereby debtors might be rehabilitated in their fortunes without the necessity of a complete liquidation of their assets. 9 Am J2d Bankr § 2.

change. Noun: Coin; another term for "exchange," a place for the transaction of business. Verb: To mean to put one thing in the place of another; to exchange; to alter or make different; to cause to pass from one state or place to another. Territory ex rel. Smith v Scott, 3 Dak 357, 432.
See **exchange; vary.**

changed conditions. Appearing in a contract for the construction of a public improvement, the term means conditions differing materially from those stated in the contract, and also unknown conditions of an unusual nature not ordinarily encountered in the kind of work provided for in the contract. Anno: 85 ALR2d 213.

change in title. See **change of title.**

change of abode. See **change of domicil.**

change of beneficiary. A clause in a life insurance policy which changes the interest of the beneficiary named from a vested to a contingent interest by reserving to the insured the right to change the beneficiary in accordance with requirements prescribed in the policy. 29A Am J Rev ed Ins § 1675; the effecting of a change of beneficiary of a life insurance policy, such being dependent upon the capacity of the insured and the observance of the conditions for a change prescribed by statute or terms of the policy. 29A Am J Rev ed Ins §§ 1677–1689.

change of county seat. The transfer of the seat of government of a county from one place to another in the county, usually after an election on the question of change.

change of domicil. The physical abandonment of a domicil together with an intent not to return to it as a domicil, and the acquisition of a new domicil in another place by actual residence in such place with the intention of making it a permanent home. 25 Am J2d Dom § 16.

change of grade. The lowering or elevating of the degree in which a highway inclines or declines by excavating, filling, or grading. 25 Am J1st High § 39; a change in the inclination or declination of an area, such as a city lot, by excavating or filling, often made for purpose of drainage, sometimes resulting in controversies with adjoining owners in reference to the obstruction of the flow of surface waters. 56 Am J1st Wat §§ 67 et seq.

change of identity. An intermingling or intermixture of goods owned by different persons so that the property of each can no longer be distinguished; a change made in the form of an article, a transmutation in the species; the combining or uniting of materials into one single, joint product. 1 Am J2d Access § 1.

change of interest. See **change of title.**

change of name. The taking and adoption of a new name by a person or a business, which, in either case is usually regulated rather closely by statute. 38 Am J1st Name §§ 28-35. A change of name of a corporation requires resort to formal proceedings. 18 Am J2d Corp § 145.

change of occupation. A familiar condition in a life or accident insurance policy, normally being a condition against a change in insured's occupation to one of more hazards to life or limb, the condition having reference to the nature of duties performed, not the precise designation given to an employment. 29 Am J Rev ed Ins § 766.

change of possession. A conventional clause or condition of a contract for the sale of real estate. 55 Am J1st V & P § 323; a clause, in a policy insuring property against loss by fire, windstorm, etc., which provides that the policy shall become void in the event of a change in the possession of the property without the consent of the insurer. 29A Am J Rev ed Ins § 825.
See **change of title; delivery.**

change of residence. See **change of domicil.**

change of title. That which takes place where there is a change in ownership which carries the legal right of possession and property. 42 Am J1st Prop § 37; an instrument, filed by requirement of law, by a personal representative of a decedent's estate upon the completion of the administration, for the purpose, among other things, to show the new ownership of the estate property resulting from the death of the former owner and the devolution of the property under his will or by the laws of descent, so that the new ownership will appear in the tax records; a clause, usually appearing in policies of fire insurance or the other insurance on property to the effect that the policy shall become void in case of a sale, conveyance, or a change in the interest, title, or possession of the property insured, without the insurer's consent. 29A Am J Rev ed Ins § 825; a breach of the foregoing clause or condition, that is, a change of title or interest by sale or conveyance which places the risk of loss of the property upon the buyer or grantee, creates a motive for the destruction of the property, or lessens the interest of the insured in protecting it. Mackintosh v Agricultural Fire Ins. Co. 150 Cal 440; 89 P 102.

change of venue. The removal of a cause for trial from one county to another county. See 56 Am J1st Ven § 42.

change of voyage. A common term in marine insurance policies, meaning a voluntary departure, without necessity or justifiable cause, from the regular and usual course of the voyage. 29A Am J Rev ed Ins § 1000.

channel. The bed of a stream, with well defined banks, cut through the turf and into the soil by the flowing of water, presenting on a casual glance the evidences of the frequent action of running water, and not a mere depression. 56 Am J1st Wat § 76; the part of a navigable waterway which is traversed by the traffic thereon. The Arlington (CA2 NY) 19 F2d 285.

chantry (chán'tri). A church endowed with land for the support of priests who prayed and sang for the welfare of the soul of the person named in the gift.

chapel (chap'el). A small church.

chapel of ease. A secondary church for the use of parishioners living at a distance from the principal one.

chapelry (chap'el-ri). The legal precincts of a chapel.

chapitre (sha-pi-tr). The summary of matters to be inquired of by, or presented before, justices in eyre, justices of assize, or justices of the peace; articles delivered orally or in writing by the justice to the inquest.—Wharton.

chaplain (chap'lăn). The person who officiated in a chapel.

chaplaincy (chap'lăn-si). The office of a chaplain.
In the Roman Catholic Church it is an institution founded by an individual for the purpose of celebrating or causing to be celebrated annually a certain number of masses conforming to the will of the founder. They are commonly divided into two classes—lay and ecclesiastical. Gonzalez v Roman Catholic Archbishop, 280 US 1, 74 L Ed 131, 50 S Ct 5.

chapman (chap'măn). An itinerant merchant. See **petty chapmen.**

chap-money (chap'mun″i). Money repaid by a seller to a buyer upon full payment of the purchase price.

chappelage. The vicinity or precinct of a chapel.

chapter (chap'ter). A bishop's council. See **dean and chapter.**

chap-woman (chap'wŭm″ạn). A female trader.

char (chär). To reduce wood to coal by burning. Anno: 1 ALR 1169, note.

character. That which a person is as demonstrated by his acts and utterances, whether good or bad from the standpoint of morals; reputation. Michelson v United States, 335 US 469, 93 L Ed 168, 69 S Ct 213.

Character consists of the qualities which constitute the individual, while reputation is the sum of opinions entertained concerning him. The former is interior; the latter external. The one is the substance; the other the shadow. Character is what a person is. Reputation is what people say of him. But notwithstanding this distinction which is everywhere agreed upon, the two words are sometimes used, even by judges, as synonymous. United States v Hrasky, 240 Ill 560, 88 NE 1031.

"Character" is frequently used interchangeably with "reputation." In a legal sense, it means reputation as distinguished from "disposition." Character grows out of particular acts, but is not proved by them, since a person may, under the stress of special circumstances, do a thing which is contrary to his ordinary disposition and practice. The method of proving character is by showing the general reputation of the person in the neighborhood in which he lives. What is thus proved, therefore, is not a person's real character, but his character as reputed among his neighbors, or what the consensus of opinion of the neighbors is as to his character. Anno: 10 ALR 9.

Another and distinct meaning of the term "character" is that of a recommendation given an employee upon his leaving service. 35 Am J1st M & S § 39.

character evidence. Testimony relating and confined to the general reputation which the person who is subject of the inquiry sustains in the community or neighborhood in which he lives or has lived. 29 Am J2d Ev § 347.

characterization. A statement of the distinguishing characteristics of a person by way of representing him to others. A technical term for determining the nature of the question before the court, as one of tort, contract, etc. in order to determine the law applicable as between the laws of two or more jurisdictions. 16 Am J2d Contr § 3.

charbon (shär'bon). Another name for the disease of anthrax. Stedman v United States Mut. Acci. Asso. 123 NY 304, 25 NE 399.

charge. Noun: An obligation or indebtedness to be paid, as a charge for merchandise or services. Merchants Exchange Nat. Bank v Commercial Warehouse Co. 49 NY 635, 639; a form under which interest taken in advance. 55 Am J1st Supp Usury § 41; Houchard v Berman, 79 Ariz 381, 290 P2d 735, 57 ALR2d 627; an expense incurred in an enterprise; an item of costs or expenses in litigation; an accusation of the commission of a crime or offense, as in an information or indictment. Hale v Henkel, 201 US 43, 59, 50 L Ed 652, 659, 26 S Ct 370; Rhodes v McWilson, 202 Ala 68, 79 So 462, 1 ALR 568, 577; People v Ross, 235 Mich 433, 444, 209 NW 663, 666; the technical term for the mere statement of the offense for which one is brought before a court-martial for trial, as distinguished from the "specifications" which set forth the specific acts or omissions of the accused constituting the offense. 36 Am J1st Mil § 98; a pleading in an administrative proceeding corresponding to the complaint in an action. 2 Am J2d Admin L § 371; a provision in a will which subjects real estate of the testator to the payment of debts of the testator or of legacies under the will. 57 Am J1st Wills §§ 1470, 1484; sometimes to the payment of annuities. 4 Am J2d Annui § 12; sometimes to the payment of taxes. Anno: 37 ALR2d 135; a lien or encumbrance upon land. First Nat. Bank v Elliott, 125 Ala 646, 27 So 7; an instruction to the jury to aid them in their deliberations and assist them in arriving at a proper verdict. Gardner v State, 27 Wyo 316, 196 P 750, 15 ALR 1040, 1046; an admonition directing the jury in respect of proper conduct in their deliberations. Verb: To impose an obligation; to enter the charge made for goods or services in an account book or by any method used in keeping the accounts of customers; to accuse one of the commission of a crime or offense; to impose against a devise the obligation of paying debts of the testator or legacies provided by his will. To instruct or advise, particularly to instruct the jury.

chargeable. Capable of being charged, subject to be charged, liable to be charged, proper to be charged, or legally liable to be charged. Walbridge v Walbridge, 46 Vt 617, 625.

charge and discharge. The complainant's delivery of his account to the master in chancery and the defendant's filing of his defense thereto.

charge and specifications. The general allegation of the commission of the crime by the defendant, and the detailed facts thereof; the statement of the offense for which one is brought before a court-martial for trial, followed by a statement of the specific acts or omissions constituting the offense. 36 Am J1st Mil § 98.

charge-back. A setting off of one debt against another.

chargé d'affaires (shär-zhā dȧ-făr). A diplomatic representative, either a chargé d'affaires ad hoc, an officer originally sent by his government, or a chargé d'affaires per interim, an officer substituted in the place of the ambassador or minister to represent the nation during the latter's absence. 4 Am J2d Ambass § 1.
A consul may be appointed chargé d'affaires and thus occupy a double political capacity. Ex parte Baiz, 135 US 403, 34 L Ed 222, 10 S Ct 854.

chargé d'affaires ad hoc. A diplomatic representative originally sent in such status by his government. 4 Am J2d Ambass § 1.

chargé d'affaires ad interim. See **chargé d'affaires**.

charged with crime. Accused of the commission of a crime, either formally, as by indictment, information, or affidavit, or informally, as by the statement in writing or by word of mouth that a person is guilty of a specified crime. In an extradition proceeding, the question, whether an accused is "charged with crime" in the demanding state or country, is one of law and open to judicial inquiry. 31 Am J2d Extrad § 54. As the expression is used in the Federal extradition statutes, a person is charged with crime when an affidavit is filed, alleging the commission of the offense, and a warrant is issued for his arrest; and this is true whether a final trial may or may not be had upon such charge. Re Strauss, 197 US 324, 331, 49 L Ed 774, 778.

charged with notice. The condition of a person who has information which should have put him upon inquiry, if, by following up such information, with diligence and understanding, the truth could have been ascertained. 39 Am J1st Notice § 6.

charge off. An accounting term for the elimination from assets of an item of corporeal property or of an account receivable, because of loss of value rendering the corporeal property worthless or the insolvency of the person indebted upon the account rendering it uncollectible. Rubinkam v Commissioner (CA7 Ill) 118 F2d 149; a bad debt deduction for income tax purposes. 34 Am J2d Fed Tax ¶ 6450.

charge of indictment. That part of an indictment which states the facts constituting the offense of which the defendant is accused. See 27 Am J1st Indict § 54.

charge on. An income tax term, applying in accrual accounting for taxpayer's business to accrued tax exempt interest, such interest not being permitted to be accrued for any taxing purpose. District Bond Co. v Commissioner (CA9 Cal) 113 F2d 347.

charges. See **charge**.

charge-sheet (chärj'shēt). A police station blotter upon which are entered the names of and charges against prisoners, and the names of their accusers; a day book upon which charges are entered, later to be entered in journal or ledger.

charges upon land. See **charge**.

charge to enter heir. (Scotch.) A writ summoning an heir to take possession of his inheritance upon the death of his ancestor.

charge to jury. See **instructions to jury**.

charging lien. The lien of an attorney at law, upon a judgment, decree, or award obtained for his client in an action or proceeding, to secure the attorney for his disbursements, and his compensation for services on behalf of the client, in the action or proceeding. 7 Am J2d Attys § 281.
An attorney's special or charging lien is one which arises in favor of the attorney for his bill of costs as compensation for his services for procuring judgment, decree, or award to which it attaches. Norrell v Chasan, 125 NJ Eq 230, 4 A2d 88, 120 ALR 1238.

charging order. A term of the English practice for a court order subjecting the stock or funds in a public company, belonging to the judgment debtor, to the satisfaction of the judgment.

charging part. The part of a bill in equity following the confederating clause, under the old chancery practice, in which is a statement of all matters of evidence in regard to which discovery is desired. 27 Am J2d Eq § 181.

chariot (char'i-ot). A half coach with four wheels, used for convenience and pleasure. Cincinnati, Lebanon, & Springfield Turnpike Co. v Neil, 9 Ohio 11, 13; a vehicle of the ancients used in war, in races, and in parades.

charitable. Having the inclination to relieve others from the burden of pain, poverty, or ignorance, and to promote the betterment of the public.
See **charity**.

charitable corporation. A corporation not for profit; a corporation organized for a charitable purpose, such as the relief of the poor, the care of the sick, maimed or injured, and the education of children, and adults as well, who do not have the means to educate themselves. 18 Am J2d Corp § 10.

charitable gift. A gift for a charitable purpose; something given from the love of God or of fellowmen, free from consideration of self or of gain or profit to self. Hoeffer v Clogan, 63 Am St Rep 249 and note; in its broadest meaning, something done or given for the benefit of fellowmen or the public. Taylor v Hoag, 273 Pa 194, 116 A 826, 21 ALR 946.

charitable immunity doctrine. The principle that relieves a charitable organization or trust from tort liability. 15 Am J2d Char § 152.

charitable institution. An institution organized for benevolent and charitable purposes, free from any element of private or corporate gain, and which devotes its entire revenue to the payment of current expenses and the relief of the poor and needy, albeit it may confine its benefits primarily to its own needy members and their families. Hibernian Benevolent Soc. v Kelly, 28 Or 173, 192, 42 P 3.
See **charitable corporation; charity.**

charitable purpose. A purpose in making a gift which comes within the definition of the term "charity"; a purpose evidenced by concrete, practical, objective charity, manifested in things actually done for the relief of the unfortunate and the alleviation of suffering, or in some work of practical philanthropy, as contrasted with the sentimental or ethical viewpoint. Scottish Rite Bldg. Co. v Lancaster County, 106 Neb 95, 182 NW 574, 17 ALR 1020, 1023.
See **charity.**

charitable trust. A trust for the benefit of an indefinite class of persons constituting some portion or class of the public or, more broadly defined, a trust limiting property to some public use; a gift in some manner dedicated to the ultimate benefit or betterment of the public, or some significant portion thereof, not necessarily involving illegal activities or a use contrary to public policy, for promotion of something within a recognized field of general welfare. 15 Am J2d Char § 5; a gift for the benefit of persons, either by bringing their hearts and minds under the influence of education or religion, by relieving their bodies of disease, suffering, or constraint, by assisting to establish them for life, by erecting or maintaining public buildings, or in other ways lessening the burdens or making better the condition of the general public, or some class of the general public, indefinite as to names and numbers, or, in short, a gift to a general public purpose. State ex rel. Emmert v Union Trust Co. 227 Ind 571, 86 NE2d 450, 12 ALR2d 836.

charitable trusts acts. Statutes regulating the administration of charities by the trustees thereof.

charitable use. A use for the benevolent, educational, or religious purposes or for the ultimate benefit or betterment of the public or some significant portion thereof. 15 Am J2d Char §§ 5, 6.
The Statute of Uses, 43 Elizabeth, Chapter 4, in its preamble, names twenty-one distinct charitable uses, "but upon examining the earlier English statutes and decisions, Mr. Justice Baldwin found forty-six, including all that are enumerated in the statute." A list of the twenty-one uses and also of the forty-six is to be found in note to Hoeffer v Clogan, 63 Am St Rep 252, 253.
See **charitable trust.**

Charitable Uses Act. An English statute of 1861, favoring conveyances for charitable uses. Am J2d Desk Book, Document 113.

charity. One of the three great virtues preached by the Apostle Paul. In law, a gift, to be applied consistently with existing laws, for the benefit of an indefinite number of persons, by bringing their hearts under the influence of education or religion, by relieving their bodies from disease, suffering, or constraint, by assisting them to establish themselves for life, or by erecting or maintaining public buildings or works, or otherwise lessening the burdens of government. 13 Am J2d Char § 3.
The scope of the word "charity" changes and enlarges with the needs of men and must advance with the progress of civilization so as to encompass varying wants of humanity properly coming within its spirit. Re Tarrant, 38 Cal 2d 42, 237 P2d 505, 28 ALR2d 419.
See **works of charity.**

charity child (char'i-ti chīld). A child reared by a charity.

charity school. A school operating on a charitable basis in giving instruction in the useful branches of learning by methods common to schools and institutions of learning, as distinguished from schools conducted primarily for teaching dancing, riding, deportment, etc. Anno: 95 ALR 63.

charivari (shä-ri-vä'ri). A mock serenade in which the "musicians" play on tin pans and kettles, old buckets, and the like for the purpose of calling persons out from their homes, particularly young married couples. Cherryvale v Hawman, 80 Kan 170, 101 P 994.

charlatan (shär'la-tan). A cheat; an impostor; a quack.

charnel (chär'nel). A charnel-house —a place where dead bodies are deposited.

charnel-house (chär'nel-hous). See **charnel.**

chart. A map used by mariners, showing the seas, lakes, or rivers to be traversed on a voyage, the harbors, shoals, courses, and distances; a representation by lines and figures of developments in production and prices.

charta (kär'ta). A charter; a deed; a writing.

charta communis (kar'ta kom-mū'nis). A common deed,—an indenture.

charta cyrographata (kar'ta cy"rō-gra'pha-ta). A deed executed in two parts and divided in the middle.

Charta de feoffamento (kar'ta de fef-a-men'to). A deed or charter of feoffment. See 2 Bl Comm 313.

Charta de Foresta (kar'ta de fo-res'ta). One of the two famous charters of English liberties—the other of which was Magna Charta—to which King John, and afterward his son, Henry the Third, consented. Its purpose was to redress many grievances and encroachments of the crown in the enforcement of the forest laws. See 4 Bl Comm 423.

Charta de non ente non valet (kar'ta dē non en'te non va'let). A deed of a thing not in being is void.

chartae libertatum (kar'tē li-ber-tā'tum). The charters of liberties,—the Magna Charta and the Charta de Foresta. See 4 Bl Comm 423.

charta partita (kar'ta par-tē'ta). A charter-party.

Chartarum super fidem, mortuis testibus, ad patriam de necessitudine, recurrendum est (kar-tā'rum su'per fī'dem, mor'tu-is tes'ti-bus, ad pa'tri-am dē ne-ses"si-tū-di-ne, re-kur-ren'dum est). If the witnesses are dead, the credibility of deeds must of necessity be referred to the country.

chartel (kär'tel). A challenge to single combat.

charte partie (shar-t-par-tî). (French.) A charter-party.

charter. A grant of power to act as a corporation under a special act of the legislature, Humphrey v Pegues, (US) 16 Wall 244, 21 L Ed 326; a grant of power to act as a corporation given by Congress; articles of incorporation, considered together with the statutes and laws respecting corporate powers. 18 Am J2d Corp §§ 26 et seq; the organic law of a mutual or fraternal benefit society; the organic law of a city or town, and representing a portion of the statute law of the state, C. J. Kubach Co. v McGuire, 199 Cal 215, 248 P 676. The demise of a vessel. 48 Am J1st Ship § 296.

See **charter of affreightment; charter party.**

chartered by law. Corporations organized under either a general or special law. 34 Am J1st Logs § 114.

charterer. A person who in his own right, is entitled to possess, use, and have the benefits resulting from the use of the thing hired or chartered, and those rights must be acquired by contract with persons having such dominion over the thing hired or chartered as enables them to confer on the hirer or charterer the right to use the thing hired or chartered, and to have the benefits resulting therefrom. Turner v Cross, 83 Tex 218, 18 SW 578.

A person who by contract acquires the right to use a vessel belonging to another person, in other words the lessee or grantee of a vessel under a charter or charter party of the vessel.

See **charter party.**

charter governments. English colonial governments in the nature of civil corporations, having power to make by-laws for their own internal regulation, not contrary to the laws of England and with such rights and authority as are specially granted to them by their charters of incorporation. Their form of government was generally borrowed from that of England. See 1 Bl Comm 108.

charter-land (chär'tėr-land). Also called "book land,"—land which was held by deed under certain rents and free services and which in effect did not differ from the free socage-lands. See 2 Bl Comm 90.

charter-master (chär'tėr-màs"tėr). A coal mining contractor.

charter money. The compensation to be paid for the use of a vessel which is generally specified in the charter party and which may be a fixed sum, or made ascertainable by a defined rule of calculation, or it may be left dependent on the profits of the adventure. 48 Am J1st Ship § 320.

charter of affreightment. An agreement, contract, lease or commitment by which the possession or services of a vessel are secured for a period of time, or for one or more voyages, whether or not a demise of the vessel. 48 Am J1st Ship § 296. Contracts of affreightment are of two kinds which differ widely in their nature and legal effect. Charterers or freighters may become the owners for the voyage without any sale or purchase of the ship, as in cases where they hire the ship and have by the terms of the contract, and assume in fact, the exclusive possession, command and navigation of the ship, and contracts for a specified voyage, as, for example to carry a cargo from one port to another, the arrangement in contemplation of law is a mere affreightment sounding in contract, and not a demise of the vessel, and the charterer or freighter is not clothed with the character or legal responsibility of ownership. Reed v United States (US) 11 Wall 591, 20 L Ed 220.

charter of bank. The general laws under which banks are created, taken together with their articles of incorporation or, where a former general practice still prevails, a special charter which authorizes the bank to do business, prescribes its powers, and regulates the manner of doing business. 10 Am J2d Banks § 20.

charter of demise. The charter of a vessel wherein the vessel is hired or rented out for a specific period or voyage without a crew, or with a crew paid by and responsible to the charterer. A demise charter is often called a "bare boat charter," notwithstanding the fact that the demised vessel may be hired with a complete staff of servants and employees on board. The Steel Inventor (DC Md) 35 F Supp 986.

Charter of Liberties. See **Magna Charta.**

charter of pardon. A charter granting a pardon to a person convicted of a criminal offense. Such a charter has been likened to a deed, in the sense that it is of no force and effect until it has been delivered and accepted. See 39 Am J1st Par § 13.

Charter of the Forest. See **Charta de Foresta.**

charter party. A maritime contract within admiralty jurisdiction. 2 Am J2d Adm § 67; a contract by which an entire ship, or some principal part thereof, is let by the owner to another person for a specified time or use. 48 Am J1st Ship § 296.

See **charter of affreightment; charter of demise.**

charter party representation. A stipulation in a charter party which does not go to the whole consideration on either side and is not such an essential condition that nonperformance thereof will permit the other party to declare the contract at an end. See 48 Am J1st Ship § 303.

charter party warranty. A covenant in a charter party that goes to the whole consideration on either side, on the failure or nonperformance of which the party aggrieved may repudiate the whole contract, and the plaintiff must perform the condition before he can maintain an action to enforce the liability of the other party. 48 Am J1st Ship § 303.

charter rolls. Old records of charters.

chartis reddendis (kar'tis red-den'dis). A writ to secure the return of deeds.

chartophlyax (char-tō'phly-ax). A keeper of records or public instruments.—Spelman.

chase. Verb: To pursue. Noun: The pursuit of beasts of the chase; a hunting ground.

See **beasts of the chase.**

chase women. See **woman chaser.**

chasm (kasm). A gorge; an abyss; as a figure of speech, an omission, an event or condition which has been omitted or left unprovided for in a contract or statute.

chaste. One in a state of chastity.

See **chastity.**

chaste character. Actual virtue, not mere reputation for virtue. 47 Am J1st Seduc § 12.

See **chastity.**

chaste female. See **chaste.**

chastise (chas-tīz'). To punish corporally, as by whipping. People v Kehoe, 123 Cal 224, 229, 55 P 911.

chastisement. See **corporal punishment.**

chastity. As applied to an unmarried person, undefiled, which, in the case of a female, means one who has retained her virginity. State v Dacke, 59 Wash 238, 109 P 1050. Purity of body in the sense of never having had meretricious relations. State v Holter, 32 SD 43, 142 NW 657. Some authority applies the additional condition in respect of the unmarried female that she never have indulged in obscenity of language, indecency of conduct, or undue familiarity with men. 47 Am J1st Seduc § 13. Other authority takes the contrary view that so long as the unmarried female is a virgin, she is to be considered chaste, notwithstanding her conduct, permitting familiarities and liberties to be taken with her by men, at the thought of which, some women blush.

Married persons are chaste where faithful to the marriage vows. State v Carron, 18 Iowa 372, 375. So, a widow or divorcee may be chaste, notwithstanding she is no virgin. 47 Am J1st Seduc § 14.

chattel. See **chattels.**

chattel fixture. A chattel affixed to land with no express or implied intention on the part of the annexor that the chattel is to become a part of the land.

chattel interest. Any interest in land of less dignity than a freehold estate.

chattel mortgage. An instrument whereby an owner transfers title to, or creates a lien upon, personal property as security for the performance of an act, which is usually the payment of money, with the title or lien subject to defeasance upon performance. 15 Am J2d Chat Mtg § 1; more summarily defined, with accuracy, under the law of some jurisdictions, as a bill of sale with a defeasance clause. 15 Am J2d Chat Mtg § 1. Constituting an interest in the mortgaged property. Moody v Shuffleton, 203 Cal 100, 262 P 1095.

chattel paper. A writing or writings which evidence both a monetary obligation and a security interest in or a lease of specific goods. UCC § 9—105(1)(b).

chattels. Property which is movable and not so connected with the ground as to become a part of the real estate. State v Donahue, 75 Or 409, 144 P 755, 147 P 548, 5 ALR 1121; visible, tangible, movable, personal property. 42 Am J1st Prop § 24.

chattels personal. Things which have no concern with land, such as mere movables and rights connected with them, the term being used in distinction to "chattels real." 42 Am J1st Prop § 24.

chattels real. Interests in real estate less than freehold, such as estates for years, at will and by sufferance, which are personalty except as modified by statute. 42 Am J1st Prop § 25.

A lease of real estate for a term of years constituting an estate less than a freehold estate is a chattel real which passes a present interest in real property. Abraham v Fioramonte, 158 Ohio St 213, 107 NE2d 321, 33 ALR2d 1267.

chaud-medley (shŏd′med″li). An affray in the heat of blood or passion. See 4 Bl Comm 184.

chauffeur (shō-fēr′). A person whose business or calling it is to operate and propel an automobile along the public highway. Christy v Elliott, 216 Ill 31, 74 NE 1035; State v Swagerty, 203 Mo 517, 603, 102 SW 483. Better defined, according to modern usage, as a person who drives a motor vehicle for another as an occupation. 7 Am J2d Auto § 103.

chauntry (chản′tri). Same as **chantry.**

chaussée (shō-sā′). A levee of earth, which is made along the stream to retain the water of a river or pond; a levee which is made in low, wet and swampy places to serve as a road or way. De Armas v Mayor, etc. of New Orleans, 5 La 132, 152.

Chautauqua. Meetings of an educational and entertaining character, from a sophisticated viewpoint, conducted by a literary and scientific circle or assembly at Chautauqua Lake in the southwestern part of New York State; meetings conducted elsewhere in the United States in imitation of the meetings at Chautauqua Lake. Radcliffe v Query, 153 SC 76, 150 SE 352.

cheat. See **cheating; cheating or swindling.**

cheating. Defrauding; obtaining an advantage by deception; a common law offense, otherwise known as "cheat," less than a felony, effected by means of some token or device having the semblance of public authenticity, such as spurious money of the realm or bank notes circulating throughout the country as a medium of exchange, fake weights and measures, or false impersonation, to the injury of one in some pecuniary interest. 22 Am J2d § 3; a slang term for being unfaithful to the marriage vows in reference to fidelity.

cheating or swindling (chēting). As the words are ordinarily used, they relate to the fraudulent causing of pecuniary or property loss. United States v Cohn, 270 US 339, 346, 70 L Ed 606, 619, 46 S Ct 251.

check. An order directed to a bank in writing for the payment of money to a person named in the instrument. Brown v Eastman Nat. Bank (Okla) 291 P2d 828, 55 ALR2d 971; a draft drawn on a bank and payable on demand. UCC § 3-104(2)(b); 10 Am J2d Banks § 538. A simple contract in writing. 34 Am J1st Lim Ac § 84.

As between the drawer and the payee, it is an evidence of indebtedness. Usually a check is given for money borrowed or a debt contracted, and, in commercial transactions, as well as in law, it is equivalent to the drawer's promise to pay, and an action may be brought against him thereon as on a promissory note. Camas Prairie State Bank v Newman, 15 Idaho 719, 99 P 833.

The verb "check means to examine for accuracy for example, the addition in an account, or for defects in a manufactured article; to draw on funds in a bank.

See **cashier's check.**

checkbook (chek′bu̇k). A book of blank bank checks.

check cashing exchange. A business, usually located near a large industrial plant, which cashes checks for a fee.

checker (chek′ẽr). Exchequer; an American term for one whose duty it is to examine a manufactured article for possible defects.

See **plant checker.**

checking out. Termination of the status of a person as guest in a hotel. 29 Am J Rev ed Innk § 25; the operation in a supermarket whereby the customer's purchases are totaled, payment made by him, and the merchandise placed in bags for convenience in transporting it.

checkoff. The deduction of union dues and assessments by the employer from the wages of the employee and the turning over of the amounts so deducted to the labor union. Anno: 14 ALR2d 177.

check-out. See **checking out.**

checkroom. A place in a hotel, restaurant, depot or other place of public accommodation where patrons may leave their luggage, articles of wearing apparel, or small items of personalty for safekeeping.

chef (shef). A head or chief; a cook.

chemical test. A term of general application but most significant in the law respecting the method of determining intoxication. 7 Am J2d Auto § 259.

chemin (shė-man'). A road; a highway.
See **en chemin**.

chemin de fer (shė-man' dė fār). Railway; railroad; a game of chance which is prohibited as gambling where played for a stake. 24 Am J2d Gaming § 20.

cheque (chek). A check; a bank check.

cherif (sherif). A sheriff.

Cherokee. The name of an Indian nation or tribe; a member of the Cherokee nation or tribe. Ephraim v Garlick, 10 Kan 280.

Chesterfield. See **Lord Chesterfield's Act.**

chevage. Same as **chiefage**.

chevaliers. See **bas chevaliers**.

chevantia (che-van'she-a). A loan of money.

chevisance. An agreement; an unlawful or usurious contract.

chicane (shi-kān'). Trickery; fraud.

chicanery (shi-kān'nėr-ė). Trickery; fraud of which the law takes cognizance where damage caused thereby to another.

Chickasaw. The name of an Indian nation or tribe; a member of the Chickasaw nation or tribe.

chicken hawk. A species of hawk which preys on chickens.

chicory (chik'ō-ri). A plant noted for the root which is dried and ground to produce a substance, also known as "chicory," which is sometimes, particularly in some of the southern states, mixed with coffee; sometimes used as a substitute for coffee, and occasionally as an adulteration of coffee. Arthur v Herold, 100 US (10 Otto) 104, 25 L Ed 568.

chief. Noun: An officer of the highest rank or authority; a principal; a head; a leader of an Indian nation or tribe. Adjective: Primary; main; most important.

chiefage (chē'fāj). An annual payment by villeins to their lord; a poll tax.

chief baron. The presiding judicial officer of the court of exchequer. See 3 Bl Comm 44.

chiefe. See **en chiefe**.

chief judge. The judge who directs the work of the court in assigning cases, instructing the officers of the court, and making the physical arrangements necessary for holding court, in a district or circuit where there is more than one judge.
See **chief justice; chief magistrate.**

chief justice (chēf' jus'tis). The presiding justice of a court with three or more justices or judges who sit together.

chief justiciar. A special magistrate or justice who presided over the Norman aula regis, being the principal minister of state and the second man in the kingdom. See 3 Bl Comm 38.

chief lord. The highest lord of the fee in the feudal system.

chief magistrate. As an executive officer, the highest officer, as the President of the United States or the governor of a state. State ex rel. McNichols v Justus, 84 Minn 237, 87 NW 770; as a judicial officer, the chief judge among police court judges.

chief petty officer. A noncommissioned officer of the Navy, ranking immediately above petty officer, 1st class, and immediately below senior chief petty officer.

chief place of business. As the term is used in a statute providing for the service of process on a corporation at its chief place of business, it means that service can be made either where the office of the corporation is located, or in the county where the corporation is located and has its being. Loraine v Pittsburg, Johnstown, Ebensburg & Eastern Railroad Co. 205 Pa 132, 54 A 580.
See **principal place of business.**

chief pledge. The borsholder or chief of the borough. —Spelman.

chief rents (chēf'rents). Rent which was paid by a freeholder to his landlord in full discharge of all service. See 2 Bl Comm 42.

chiefry (chēf'ri). Rent paid to the lord paramount.

child. A juvenile subject to parental control or guardianship. State v Gonzales, 241 La 619, 129 So 2d 796, 84 ALR2d 1248; one under the age of puberty, or not old enough to dispense with parental aid or care. Central of Georgia R. Co. v Robins, 209 Ala 6, 95 So 367, 36 ALR 10; a person of tender years, as distinguished from a youth, who, although legally an infant, possesses the size and strength of a man. 27 Am J1st Inf § 112; a son or daughter of a person, whether infant or adult. 2 Am J2d Adopt § 11; 39 Am J1st P & C § 2; a natural child, as distinguished from a child by adoption, unless the context of an instrument in question indicates an intention to include an adopted child or to use the term child in a more extensive sense than its natural import, or such intention is to be inferred from the attendant circumstances, or such a construction is required by a statutory definition. 2 Am J2d Adopt § 96; a word which is not a technical legal term having a fixed and definite meaning, but one which is flexible and subject to construction to give effect to the intention of the maker of the instrument in which it appears. Conner v Gardner, 230 Ill 258, 82 NE 640.
See **children; emancipation; grandchild; infant; in loco parentis; minor; parent.**

childbirth. See **birth.**

Childermas (chil'dėr-mas). Holy Innocents' Day, December twenty-eighth.

childishness. A mark of senility; a mature person acting in the manner of a child.

child labor. The employment of children, the legal significance of which is the prohibition of such employment in dangerous occupations, in places where they may be corrupted by the surroundings, at work which is of such nature as to tax the strength of the child and undermine his health, and for hours so long as to tire a child to the point of exhaustion and sickness.

Child Labor Amendment. A proposed amendment to the United States Constitution, granting to Congress the power to limit, regulate, and prohibit the labor of persons under 18 years of age; submitted to the states for ratification by Congress in 1924, but failing of ratification, being ratified by only 28 states.

childnit (chīld-nit). The customary fine paid by a bastard's reputed father to the lord.—Cowell.

child of fourteen. The criterion at common law of presumptive capacity for the commission of a crime. 21 Am J2d Crim L § 27.

child of tender years. A child whose imprudences are usually due to the play of childish instincts, unenlightened by experience, and unrestrained by reason; hence, a child too young to be chargeable with contributory negligence. Central of Georgia Railroad Co. v Robins, 209 Ala 6, 95 So 367, 36 ALR 10, 12.
Even a child of tender years is held to liability in tort. 27 Am J1st Inf § 90.
See **minor of tender years.**

children. Persons of tender years; the sons or daughters of one, whether adults or infants; a word which is not a technical legal term having a fixed and definite meaning, but one which is flexible and subject to construction to give effect to the intention of the maker of the instrument in which it appears. Conner v Gardner, 230 Ill 258, 82 NE 640.
Not being the equivalent of "heirs," "children" usually is a word of purchase rather than a word of limitation in a deed, but becoming a word of limitation where the limitation in the instrument is to children of the grantee, and the grantee has no children in being at the time of the execution of the deed. 28 Am J2d Est § 43. It is also a word of purchase in a will, except as the context of the instrument or the force of surrounding circumstances, such as there being no children in existence at the death of the testator, may make it a word of limitation. 19 Am J1st Est § 44; 57 Am J1st Wills § 1364.
The word "children" appearing in a deed, trust indenture, or will, may, but does not necessarily, include an adopted child, the question being one of construction. 2 Am J2d Adopt §§ 92 et seq. It means, prima facie, legitimate offspring. Anno: 34 ALR2d 19; 10 Am J2d Bast § 137.
It has been held that an illegitimate child is a "child" within the provisions of inheritance, succession, or estate tax statutes respecting exemption and tax rates. Whorff v Johnson, 143 Me 198, 58 A2d 553, 3 ALR2d 160. But it has also been held to the contrary under some of such statutes. Anno: 3 ALR2d 166.
As a designation of beneficiaries in an insurance policy, the term "children" ordinarily means descendants of the first degree, not including grandchildren, but including an after-born child, even an adopted child. 29A Am J Rev ed Ins § 1658.
See **after-born child; child; grandchild; wife and children.**

children of full blood. See **full blood.**

children of her body. Words of purchase rather than of limitation, except as the entire context of the instrument applied to the circumstances of the case, makes it a word of limitation. 28 Am J2d Est § 43.

children's courts. Same as **juvenile courts.**

chilling bids. Any word or act preventing free competition among bidders at an auction sale. 7 Am J2d Auct § 25; controlling competition in bidding at an execution sale. 30 Am J2d Exec § 365; any act or word which stifles the bidding at a judicial sale, thereby preventing a free, fair and open sale. 30A Am J Rev ed Jud S § 98.

chiltern hundreds. See **steward of chiltern hundreds.**

chimin. Same as **chemin.**

chiminage. A toll paid on a forest road.

chimino. See **de chimino.**

chiminus (chi'mi-nus). A private or other road over which the king, his subjects and persons who were under his protection might pass.

chimney-corner survey. A survey made by a land surveyor in his office, without planting his instrument or stretching a chain upon the ground. Smith v Chapman, 51 Va (10 Gratt) 445, 457.

chimney-money. An ancient English tax which was laid on chimneys.

China Trade Corporation. A corporation chartered under the provisions of Chapter 4 of Title 15 of the United States Code. 15 USC § 142(c).

Chinese Exclusion Act. A former statute, enacted in 1882, amended in 1884, in pursuance of a policy since abandoned of forbidding the emigration of Chinese to the United States, except as the purpose of their coming, such as education, might provide a reason for relaxing the prohibition.

Chinese tong. See **highbinder.**

chippingavel. A toll paid for the privilege of buying and selling.

chirgemote (chur'ge-mōte). An ecclesiastical court.

chirograph (kī'rọ-gråf). An instrument in pen; an indenture; a deed in two parts, cut from one parchment, the corresponding edges of which must fit.
Formerly, when deeds were more concise, it was usual to write both parts on the same piece of parchment, with some word or letters of the alphabet written between them, through which the parchment was cut, either in a straight line or an indented one, so as to leave half of the word or letters on one part and half on the other. Such deeds were called "syngrapha" by the canonists and by lawyers "chirographa" or handwritings, the word "cirographum" or "cyrographum" being the word customarily written and divided as above described. See 2 Bl Comm 295.
See **indenture.**

chirographa. See **chirograph.**

chirographer of fines (kī-rog'ra-fėr). An officer in the court of common pleas who engrossed fines of land.

chirographum (kī-rog'ra-fum). A writing evidencing an indebtedness; a written obligation.

Chirographum apud debitorem repertum presumitur solutum (kī-ro'gra-fum a'pud de-bi-tō'rem re-per'-tum prē-sū'mi-ter so-lū'tum). A written obligation found in the hands of the debtor is presumed to have been paid.

Chirographum non extans presumitur solutum (kī-ro'gra-fum non ex'tans prē-sū'mi-ter so-lū'tum). A written obligation which does not exist is presumed to have been paid.

chirography (kī-rog'ra-fi). See **handwriting.**

chiropodist. One who treats diseases or malformations of the hands or feet, especially a surgeon for the feet, hands, or nails—a cutter or extractor of corns and callosities. State v Armstrong, 38 Idaho 493, 255 P 491, 33 ALR 835.

chiropody. A limited branch of medicine or surgery; medicine or surgery as practiced by a chiropodist. American Policyholders Ins. Co. v Michota, 156 Ohio St 578, 103 NE2d 817, 35 ALR2d 448.
See **chiropodist.**

chiropractic (kī-rō-prak'tik). Derived from the Greek; manipulation by hand; a drugless method of treating human ailments. State v Hopkins, 54 Mont 52, 166 P 304; a system of healing that treats disease by manipulation of a spinal column. State v Gallagher, 101 Ark 593, 143 SW 98. It is the practice of medicine in a restricted form. Lowman v Kuecher, 246 Iowa 1227, 71 NW2d 586, 52 ALR2d 1380; the practice of medicine in the very broad aspect of the term "medicine." State v Johnson, 84 Kan 411, 114 P 390; not the practice of medicine in the more limited sense of prescribing and administering drugs. State v Gallagher, 101 Ark 593, 143 SW 98.

chiropractor (kī-ro'prak'tor). A person engaged in chiropractic.

chirurgeon (kī-rėr'jon). A surgeon.

chit (chit). A promissory note; a voucher for a small sum of money, for example, the charge for a drink at a bar; a short letter or memorandum.

chivalry (shiv'al-ri). Knight service; the medieval system of knighthood.

chloroform (klō'rō-fôrm). An oily liquid of an aromatic etheral odor, consisting of carbon, hydrogen and chlorine; formerly much used as an anesthetic in surgery; not an intoxicant. Anno: 13 ALR2d 998.
In common parlance it is classed among the poisons and statutes have been passed requiring it to be labeled as poison. State v Baldwin, 36 Kan 1, 12 P 318.

Choctaw. An Indian tribe or nation; a member of the Choctaw nation or tribe.

choice. Noun: The opportunity or power to determine or select between alternatives. People v Mosher, 45 App Div 68, 61 NYS 452. Adjective: Meriting preference; of exceptional grade; fine. Brophy v Idaho Produce & Provision Co. 31 Mont 279, 78 P 493. A term applied to beef cattle of superior quality.
See **domicil of choice; election.**

choke-bail (chōk'bāl). Nonbailable.

cholicystitis. See **acute cholicystitis.**

choose. To make a choice as between alternatives. See **choice; elect.**

choosing-stick. A divining rod.

chop. Noun: A slice of pork, mutton, or veal; an oriental term for a license or permit; a shift in the wind. Verb: To cut into pieces; to shift or veer.

chop-church. A derogatory term for a person who sold his benefice or exchanged it for another.

chops. The mouth and cheeks of a person; the mouth of a harbor.
See **chop.**

chorepiscopi (kō-rẹ-pis'kō-pi). Bishops whose powers were limited or restricted.

chose (shōz). A thing; a chattel; a personal right; a chose in action; a cause of action.

chose ex delicto (shōs ex de-lik'tō). A right or cause of action arising out of the commission of a tort.

chose in action. An incorporeal right; the right of a creditor to be paid; a right not reduced to possession but recoverable by bringing and maintaining an action. 42 Am J1st Prop § 26.

chose in possession. A thing which a person has the right to enjoy or occupy and of which he has also the actual enjoyment or occupation. See 2 Bl Comm 396, 408, 443.

chose local. A chattel which is in a fixed location, annexed to a place, such as a mill.

chosen freeholders (chō'zn). A local term for a county or township board.

chose transitory. A movable chattel which may be taken or carried from one place to another.

Christian (kris'tian). A person who believes in the teachings of Christ.

Christian calendar. Another name for the Gregorian calendar, now in use in the United States and most of the world, which numbers the years from the birth of Christ, either before, by B. C., or after, by A. D.

Christian Era. The period from the birth of Christ to the present.

Christianitatis curia (kris-ti-a"ni-tā'tis kū'ri-a). A court Christian; an ecclesiastical court.

Christianity. The religion of those who believe that Jesus Christ is the true Messiah and the Savior of men, and who receive the Holy Scriptures of the Old and New Testaments as the word of God. Hale v Everett, 53 NH 9.

Christian name. The name given a person at his birth or formal christening, sometimes referred to as a first name in distinction from the surname or family name which comes last. 38 Am J1st Name § 4.

Christian Science. A comparatively new religion, best known to the world for the system of healing which is a part of the faith, the great principle of the religion being that all cause and effect in sickness, as well as sin, is mental, Eggleston v Landrum, 210 Miss 645, 50 So 2d 364, 23 ALR2d 696; that disease will disappear and physical perfection be attained as a result of prayer, or that humanity will be brought into harmony with God by right thinking and a fixed determination to look on the bright side of life. State v Mylod, 20 RI 632, 637.

Christian Science healer. One who treats disease by prayer. Re First Church of Christ, 205 Pa 543, 55 A 536; one who treats disease by prayer and mental suggestion, perhaps better stated as mental adaption, pursuant to the principles of the Christian Science religion. 41 Am J1st Phys & S § 30.
Some authorities hold that such a healer practices medicine within the meaning of statutes which provide for the licensing of such practicing physicians, but other authorities hold that the practice of medicine is not involved in healing or endeavoring to heal by Christian Science. 41 Am J1st Phys & S § 30.

Christian Scientists. Believers in Christian Science.

Christmas. The birthday of Christ, December 25th.

Christmas club deposit. A type of bank deposit made in accordance with a plan which provides for the making of regular deposits during the year and withdrawal of the money for use at Christmas.

chronic. Long continued.

chronic dementia (kron'ik de-men'she-a). A type of insanity, usually of slow progress, marked in its early stages by general impairment and feebleement of the intellectual faculties, and ending in mental decay and idiocy. Re Will of Blakely, 48 Wis 294, 297.

chronic disease. A disease of long standing, deep-

chronic rooted, obstinate, persistent, and unyielding to treatment. State Medical Board v McCrary, 95 Ark 511, 130 SW 544. A disease is not to be held chronic for the fact alone that it continued for a period of four months immediately preceding the death of the afflicted. Williams v Southern Surety Co. 211 Mich 444, 179 NW 272, 15 ALR 1239.

chronic hemiplegy (kron'ik hem'i-plē-ji). See **hemiplegy**.

church. A religious society; an organization consisting of an indefinite number of persons, of one or both sexes, who have made a public confession of religion, and who are associated together by a covenant of church fellowship, for the purpose of celebrating the sacrament, and watching over the spiritual welfare of each other, 45 Am J1st Reli Soc § 2; a society of persons who unite in the profession of the Christian faith, Josey v Union Loan & Trust Co. 106 Ga 608, 611, 32 SE 628; Wiggins v Young, 206 Ga 440, 57 SE2d 486, 13 ALR2d 1237; any structure used principally for religious worship or bible study. 30 Am J Rev ed Intox L § 267; a building for religious worship and related activities, such as men's and women's social groups, religious teaching, boy and girl scouts, Sunday school, sleeping quarters for retreatants, and parking accommodations. Anno: 74 ALR2d 403.
See **religious society**.

church building acts. English statutes enacted for the promotion and extension of the Church of England.

church court. See **church judicatory**.

church door. See **ostium ecclesiae**.

churchesset (church-es-set). A certain measure of grain paid to the church on St. Martin's day.

church judicatory (chẻrch jö'di-kā-tō-ri). An ecclesiastical court with judicial powers. A court of a church or religious society for the adjudication of questions relating to the faith and practice of the church over which legal or temporal tribunals do not have jurisdiction. 45 Am J1st Reli Soc § 40.

church land. Land belonging to the church or to an ecclesiastical corporation or body; more narrowly defined, for the purpose of a statutory exemption from taxation, as land upon which a church building stands and such land around the building as is required reasonably for convenient ingress and egress, light, air, parking for vehicles, and appropriate and decent ornamentation, but not lots adjacent to the church building, not reasonably needed for the convenient enjoyment of the building as a church, and leased for other purposes, or not used for any purpose. 51 Am J1st Tax § 615.
See **church property**.

church living (chẻrch liv'ing). A benefice in an established church.

church meeting. The annual or other periodical meeting of a religious society for consideration of, and action upon, the affairs of the society and the church which it maintains; a special meeting called for the consideration of business of the church. 45 Am J1st Reli Soc § 20.

Church of England. The national church of England; the Episcopal Church in England.

church property. Property which is primarily—that is, principally and generally—used for religious purposes. It will not lose its character as church property by some part of it being incidentally used for some secular purpose connected with the church. Ramsey County v Church of the Good Shepherd, 45 Minn 229, 47 NW 783.
See **church land**.

church rate. A tax imposed upon a parish by a vote of a majority of the parishioners for the upkeep and maintenance of the parish church.

church reeve (chẻrch' rēv). A church warden.

church-scot (chẻrch' skot). Customary obligations paid to the parson of a parish; services rendered by a tenant of church lands.

church society. A religious society; a society within an individual church, such as a ladies aid society or a sodality.
See **religious society**.

church tribunal. See **church judicatory**.

church wardens. The guardians or keepers of a church who are also the representatives of the body of the parish. Sometimes they are appointed by the minister, and sometimes by the parish, or by both. For some purposes they are the growth and efficiency of the work of corporation; they may by that name have property in goods and chattels, and sue for the use and profit of the parish. See 1 Bl Comm 394.

church-writ. A writ which issued out of an ecclesiastical court.

churl (chẻrl). A freeman of one of the lowest classes.
See **karl**.

chute. A conveyor using the force of gravity, such as a coal-chute from surface of the ground to basement or a hay chute from mow of a barn to the manger below; a device in amusement parks upon which children slide. 4 Am J2d Amuse § 93.

ci (si). So; as.

CIA. Abbreviation for Central Intelligence Agency.

cibaria (si-bā'ri-ạ). (Civil law.) Food.

ci bien (si bi-īn'). As well.

cider. The expressed juice of apples, either fermented or unfermented, that is, graphically stated, either hard or sweet. 30 Am J Rev ed Intox L § 17.

ci devant (sē dē-von'). Formerly.

C. I. F. An abbreviation for cost, insurance and freight. 1 Am J2d Abbr § 7.
See **cost, insurance, and freight**.

cigarette. A small cylinder of tobacco wrapped in paper. Some authorities regard fine tobacco rolled in tobacco leaves as cigarettes but there is a difference of opinion on such classification. Such creations are sometimes classed as little cigars, rather than cigarettes. Goodrich v State, 133 Wis 242, 246, note.

cigarette tax. An excise tax on cigarettes, one that seems to be ever-increasing both in the scope of its application and in amount.

cigar factory. A place where cigars are made. Ludloff v United States, 108 US 176, 27 L Ed 693.

cinerary urn. A receptacle for the ashes from a cremation.

cinque ports (singk port). The five seaports on the southern coast of England, which were formerly the most important. They were those of Hastings, Romney, Hythe, Dover and Sandwich.

CIO. An abbreviation for Congress of Industrial Organizations, an affiliation of labor unions. Such affiliation is now joined to the American Federa-

tion of Labor, the abbreviation for the consolidated group being AFL-CIO.

cippi (sīp′pī). The stocks, a contrivance for discipline and punishment.
See **stocks**.

circa (sër′kạ). About; around; concerning; in respect to; in the neighborhood of.

circa ardua regni (sër′kạ ar′du-a reg′nī). In respect to the arduous affairs of the kingdom. See 1 Bl Comm 219.

circle. See **traffic circle**.

circuit. The area within the jurisdiction of a particular court, the word deriving from the route or journey which a judge makes in holding court at the several places within his jurisdiction wherein court is held; any one of the eleven judicial circuits in which the United States is divided and in which there is a United States Court of Appeals. 20 Am J2d Cts § 10.

circuit breaker. A device, operating automatically, to cut off the electric current flowing through a line or wire when the current becomes excessive for the line or wire; a mechanical device for cutting an electric current intermittently by means of a movable contact moving to and from a stationary contact for such time as the machine which utilizes the device is being operated. Re Frank, 29 Cust & Pat App (Pat) 713, 123 F2d 820.

circuit court. A court presided over by a judge or by judges at different places in the same district; a name given to certain courts of general jurisdiction by constitution or statute. 20 Am J2d Cts § 16.

Circuit Courts of Appeals. The former designation of the intermediate federal appellate courts, such name having been changed to the present designation, Courts of Appeals. 20 Am J2d Cts § 6.

Circuitus est evitandus (sër-kū′i-tus est ē-vi-tan′dus). Circuity is to be avoided.

circuity of action. Indirectness of remedy to be attained by unnecessary litigation.

circuity of liens. A legal situation difficult of analysis, often presented in the examination of law students to puzzle and harass them, illustrated by the following: the lien of A has priority over the lien of B; the lien of B has priority over the lien of C; but the lien of C is prior, or at least equal in priority, to the lien of A. 30A Am J Rev ed Judgm § 529.

circular. A printed sheet used for the purpose of advertising or for the advocacy of political principles; a listing of articles to be offered for sale at auction, with representations as to the character and worth of the respective articles. 7 Am J2d Auct § 16.

circular notes (sër′kụ-lạr). Letters of credit.

circulating notes. The terms "circulating notes," "notes used in circulation," and "circulation," as they are used in relation to the instrumentalities of banking operations, are equivalent and synonymous terms. The word "circulation" in this connection is defined by the lexicographers as "currency; or circulating notes or bills current for coin." United States v White (CC NY) 19 F 723, 724.

circulation affidavit. See **newspaper publicity law**.

circulation of bank. Certified checks and all notes and other obligations calculated or intended to circulate or to be used as money, but not including such money or other items as are in the vault of the bank or redeemed and on deposit for the bank. 26 USC § 4881(a)(1).
See **circulating notes**.

circulation of newspaper. See **newspaper of general circulation**.

circumduct (sër-kum-dukt′). To make void; to nullify.

circumduction (sër-kum-duk′shọn). Annulment; avoidance; cancellation.

Circumspecte Agatis (sir-kum-spek′te a-gā′tis). An English statute of an early period which conferred jurisdiction of suits for breach of faith upon the ecclesiastical courts. See 3 Bl Comm 52, note.

circumstantial evidence. Facts and circumstances surrounding a transaction from which the jury or trier of the fact may infer other connected facts which reasonably follow, according to the common experience of mankind. 29 Am J2d Ev § 264.

circumstantibus (sir-kum-stan′ti-bus). Bystanders, present in the courtroom.

circumvention. Trickery; outwitting; fraud or deceit.

cirliscus (sir-lis′cus). A churl; a lout.

cirographum (sī-ro-gra′phum). See **chirograph**.

citacion (the-tah-the-on′). (Spanish.) An order of the court commanding the defendant in an action to appear and defend.

citatio (sī-tā′shē-o). A citation.

citatio ad reassumendam causam (sī-tā′shē-o ad re-as-su-men′dam kâ′zam). A citation directed to the heir of a plaintiff who has died pending the action.

citatio est de jure naturali (si-tā′shē-o est dē jū′rī na-tu-rā′lī). A summons or citation is of natural right.

citation. A writ commanding a person to appear for some purpose specified. Sheldon v Sheldon, 100 NJ Eq 24, 30, 134 A 904, 907; a notice of a proceeding, especially a proceeding in a probate or surrogate's court; process in admiralty whereby notice is given of the institution of a suit in personam. 2 Am J2d Adm § 153; specifying a particular authority for a point of law, as a case by title, volume, and page of the report or reports in which the opinion appears, or an encyclopedic work, such as American Jurisprudence, by volume, title and section of article.

Citationes non concedantur priusquam exprimatur super qua re fieri debet citatio (sī-tā-shē-ō′nēz non kon-se-dan′ter pri-us′quam ex-pri-mā′tur su′per qua rē fī′e-rī de′bet sī-tā′shē-o). Citations are not to be granted until it is shown concerning what matter the citation ought to be made.

cite (sīt). To summon or notify to appear in court, often by means of a citation served upon the party cited; to refer to as an authority or precedent, or case in point; to quote.

citizen. One who has acquired citizenship by birth, naturalization, or other lawful means; in a popular but nonetheless appropriate sense of the term, one, who by birth, naturalization, or other means, is a member of an independent political society. 3 Am J2d Aliens § 1.
See **corporate citizenship**; **denizen**; **expatriation**; **natural-born citizen**; **naturalization**; **naturalized citizen**; **oath of abjuration**; **United States citizen**.

citizen by naturalization. See **naturalized citizen.**

citizen of a state. A citizen of the United States, residing in any state of the Union; Fourteenth Amendment to the Constitution of the United States.
See **citizens resident in the state.**

citizen of the United States. A person born or naturalized in the United States and subject to the jurisdiction. 3 Am J2d Aliens § 116.
See **corporate citizenship; United States citizen.**

citizen's appeal. An appeal taken by a citizen which will be heard, not because of his status merely as a citizen, but because he shows a direct pecuniary interest in the proceeding. 4 Am J2d A & E § 202.

citizenship. The privilege of membership in a political society, implying a duty of allegiance on the part of the member and a duty of protection on the part of the society; the status of a citizen with its respective rights and duties. 3 Am J2d Aliens § 115.

citizens of different states. See **diversity of citizenship.**

citizens resident in the state. Natural persons who are citizens and residents and corporations chartered in the state. 30 Am J Rev ed Intox L § 126.

city. A municipal corporation of the largest and highest class, usually under a government in three branches, one the executive, headed by a mayor, the second a legislative body called a council or board of aldermen, and a third called the municipal court or city court, operating under a charter which gives it at least a measure of home rule, sometimes almost complete home rule, such organization having been altered in some instances under constitutional provision or statute to provide a city manager or commission form of government. 37 Am J1st Mun Corp § 5.
A city is a town in the broad sense and popular sense of the latter term. 37 Am J1st Mun Corp § 5.
See **municipal corporation** and other expressions beginning **municipal.**

city block. See **block.**

city court (sit'i kort). A court the jurisdiction of which is confined to the limits of the city.

city directory. See **directory.**

city election. An election wherein officers of a city are elected; an election held in a city. Wing v Ryan, 255 App Div 163, 6 NYS2d 825.

city employee. An employee of a city; a person employed in city service, such as a person working on a municipal subway. Colbert v Delaney, 249 App Div 209, 291 NYS 801.

city lot. See **lot.**

city manager. The chief administrative officer of a city under a comparatively modern form of municipal government known as the city manager plan. 37 Am J1st Mun Corp §§ 72 et seq.

city officer. See **municipal officer.**

city purpose. A familiar expression in contracts between a city and a public utility which means a purpose primarily for the benefit, use, or convenience of the city as distinguished from that of the public outside the city. 43 Am J1st Pub Util § 184.

city service. See **city employee.**

civic. Pertaining to the city or body politic, or to the citizen, or to citizenship. Cleveland Grand Opera Co. v Cleveland Civic Opera Asso. 22 Ohio St 400, 405, 154 NE 352, 353.

civics. A course of study better known at present as "political science" or "government."

civil. Pertaining to the citizen or to the community, for example, civil responsibility; pertaining to the ordinary status of an ordinary citizen, as distinguished from one in military service; pertaining to the remedies for enforcement of private rights, as distinguished from criminal prosecutions. Brown & Allen v Jacobs Pharmacy Co. 115 Ga 429, 41 SE 553.

civil action. An action brought to enforce a civil right; an ordinary action as distinguished from a criminal action, or a special proceeding. Wurth v Affeldt, 265 Wis 119, 60 NW2d 708, 40 ALR2d 1376; the ordinary proceeding in a court of justice by one party against another for the redress or prevention of a legal wrong or for the enforcement or protection of a private right. 1 Am J2d Actions § 43; more broadly defined as any proceeding in a court of justice by which an individual pursues that remedy which the law affords him. Stoll v Hawkeye Casualty Co. (CA8 SD) 185 F2d 96, 22 ALR2d 899; comprehending every conceivable cause of action, whether legal or equitable, except such as are criminal in the usual sense that the judgment against the defendant may be a fine or imprisonment, or both. 1 Am J2d Actions § 44.

Civil Aeronautics Act. A statute which preceded the Federal Aviation Act of 1958. 8 Am J2d Avi § 10.

Civil Aeronautics Authority. A federal agency with administrative functions respecting the operation of aircraft, since replaced by the Civil Aeronautics Board.

Civil Aeronautics Board. The federal agency with administrative functions respecting the operation of aircraft. 49 USC § 1321(a)(1).

civil aircraft. As defined by the Federal aviation Act, any aircraft other than a public aircraft. 49 USC § 1301(14).
See **public aircraft.**

civil aircraft of the United States. Any aircraft registered as provided in the Federal Aviation Act. 49 USC § 1301(15).

Civil Air Patrol. A corporation created by federal statute, the purposes of which are encouragement and aid to citizens in the contribution of their efforts, services, and resources in the development of aviation and the maintenance of air supremacy, and the making of provision for aviation education and training of senior and cadet members. 36 USC §§ 201, 202.

Civil Air Regulations. The detailed regulations for civil aviation adopted, written, and published by the Civil Aeronautics Board.

civil airway. See **airway.**

civil and criminal business arising in a county. All civil and criminal matters arising in a county which occupy the attention of men engaged in legal affairs. Sherman v Droubay, 27 Utah 47, 74 P 348.

civil arrest. A provisional or auxiliary remedy intended to secure the presence of the defendant in a civil action until final judgment. 5 Am J2d Arr § 52.

civil assault. An assault for which the assailant is liable in a civil action; an assault for which an action for damages may be maintained.

civil authority. The authority vested in civil, as distinguished from military, officers. As used in a fire policy exempting the insurer from liability for loss or damage by fire caused by order of any civil authority, the term includes civil officers in whom a portion of the sovereignty is vested and in whom the enforcement of municipal regulations or the control of the general interest of society is confided for the prevention of destruction by fire. Policemen and firemen are civil authorities within the meaning of the term thus employed. Princess Garment Co. v Fireman's Fund Ins.Co. (CA6 Ohio) 115 F2d 380.

civil bail. A bond or deposit, given or made to secure the release of a person under civil arrest, the purpose of which is either directly or indirectly to secure the payment of a debt or the performance of some other civil duty. 8 Am J2d Bail § 3.

civil bill court. An Irish court the jurisdiction of which is similar to that of the county courts in England.

civil case. The legal means by which the rights and remedies of private individuals are enforced or protected, in contradistinction to the expression "criminal case" which refers to public wrongs and their punishment. State ex rel. Kochtitzky v Riley, 203 Mo 175, 101 SW 567
See **civil action; civil suit.**

civil commitment. The jailing of a person for debt or nonpayment of alimony; the confinement of an insane person, alcoholic, or drug addict for treatment or protection; the commitment of a person under civil arrest.

civil commotion. An uprising of citizens; an insurrection; interference with the powers of government by violent action. 29A Am J Rev ed Ins § 1368.

civil conspiracy. A combination of two or more persons by concerted action to accomplish an unlawful purpose, or a lawful purpose by criminal or unlawful means, to the injury of another. 16 Am J2d Consp § 43. To sustain an action, damage must have resulted from the combination. To warrant an injunction, damage must be threatened. National Fireproofing Co. v Mason Builders' Asso. (CA2 NY) 169 F 259.

civil contempt. The dividing line between civil and criminal contempt is indistinct. It can be said with some assurance, however, that where the primary purpose of a contempt proceeding is to provide a remedy for an injured suitor and to coerce compliance with an order, the contempt is civil. 17 Am J2d Contpt § 4. A civil contempt differs from a criminal contempt, the sentence for which is punitive in the public interest to vindicate the authority of the court and to deter other like derelictions. Ex parte Grossman, 267 US 87, 69 L Ed 527, 45 S Ct 332, 38 ALR 131.

civil contempt proceeding. A proceeding, summary in nature and sui generis in character, by which a party to an action is enabled to compel obedience to orders, judgments, and decrees rendered in the action which declare the rights to which he is entitled. In some jurisdictions, such proceeding is regarded as an independent proceeding, in others, it operates as a part of the suit in which the judgment, decree, or order to be enforced by the proceeding was rendered. 17 Am J Rev ed Contpt § 77.

civil corporation. A public corporation, such as a county, township, school district, or road district, otherwise known as a quasi corporation, of an involuntary character, being created by the state without the intervention of the people within its boundaries as an arm and instrumentality of the state for the administration of government locally. Dunn v Brown County Agricultural Soc. 46 Ohio St 93, 18 NE 496; Herald v Board of Education, 65 W Va 765, 65 SE 102.

Civil Damage Acts. Statutes which grant a right of action to persons injured in person, property, or means of support, by an intoxicated person, or in consequence of the intoxication of any person, against the person selling or furnishing the liquor which caused the intoxication in whole or in part. 30 Am J Rev ed Intox L § 525.

civil day. A period of twenty-four consecutive hours, beginning at midnight. Re Ten-Hour Law for Street Railway Corporations, 24 RI 603, 54 A 602.

civil death. The extinction of all civil rights, such as occurred at common law upon a person being banished, abjuring the realm, or entering a religious order, and to a certain extent upon conviction of any felony.
It has been held in the United States that the doctrine of civil death does not apply unless provided for by statute, but it has also been held that the common-law consequences of a conviction, including civil death, continue until abrogated by statute. 21 Am J2d Crim L § 626.

civil defense. Concerted activities for the protection of civilians in time of war, particularly nuclear war, and emergencies fraught with danger to human life.

civil disability. See **disability.**

civil embargo. See **embargo.**

civilian. A scholar who is versed in the Roman law and the civil law; a person who is not in the armed forces. Discharged military prisoners, discharged enlisted men, and rejected applicants for enlistment in the army, all have the status of the civilian. United States v Union Pacific Railroad Co. 249 US 354, 358, 63 L Ed 643, 645.

civil injury. The infringement or privation of the civil rights which belong to the individual, considered merely as an individual. Anno: 23 ALR 529; in the broader sense of the term, a wrong for which redress may be had by a civil action.

civil interruption. Under the civil law—an interruption of a period of prescription by making a lawful claim of right thereto in a court of justice. Innerarity v Heirs of Mims, 1 Ala 660, 674.

civilis (si'vi-lis). Civil.

civilis possessio. See **possessio civilis.**

civiliter (si-vi'li-ter). Civilly, in a civil aspect.

civiliter mortuus (si-vi'li-ter mor'tu-us). Civilly dead. See **civil death.**

civil law. The body of law, sometimes called municipal law, adopted in a country or a state, as distinguished from the so-called natural law and international law; the body of law which determines private rights and liabilities, as distinguished from criminal law; a rule of civil conduct prescribed by the supreme power of a state. Merchants' Exchange v Knott, 212 Mo 616, 111 SW 565; the civil or municipal law of the Roman empire, as comprised in the institutes, the code and the digest of the Emperor Justinian, and the novel constitutions of himself and some of his successors. These form the body of Roman law, the corpus juris civilis (the body of civil law), as published about the time of

Justinian. It was under his auspices that the present body of civil law was compiled and finished by Tribonian and other lawyers, about 533 A. D. See 1 Bl Comm 80, 81.

civil liability. Liability to be sued in a civil action, as distinguished from criminal liability which is the liability to a criminal prosecution.

Civil Liability for Support Act. One of the uniform laws. 23 Am J2d Desert § 125.

civil liberties. Political liberties; the liberties of a member of society; the natural liberties of a person so far restrained by human laws as is necessary and expedient for the general welfare. Dennis v Moses, 18 Wash 537, 52 P 333; civil liberties, as guaranteed by the Constitution, imply the existence of an organized society maintaining public order without which liberty itself would be lost in the excesses of unrestrained abuses. Cox v New Hampshire, 312 US 569, 85 L Ed 1049, 61 S Ct 762. The concept of personal rights of liberty, equality etc., protected from abridgment by constitutional guaranties. 28 Am J Rev ed Inj § 80.

civil list. In England it is the fiscal appropriation for the maintenance and support of the royal family. In the United States, it is general governmental expense, not including the army and navy.

civil maintenance. An action for damages for maintenance. Such an action lies at common law at the instance of the party aggrieved, but such actions have rarely been brought and few modern examples are to be found. 14 Am J2d Champ § 17. See **maintenance.**

civil nature. See suits of a civil nature.
See all expressions beginning **civil.**

civil obligation. An obligation which is enforceable through the means of a civil action.

civil office. A public office as distinguished from an office in the armed services; State ex rel. Barney v Hawkins, 79 Mont 506, 257 P 411, 53 ALR 583; any kind of a public office, whether legislative, executive, or judicial. 42 Am J1st Pub Of § 22.

civil officer. The incumbent of a civil office; any officer in the administration of government, except an officer of the armed forces.
See **civil office.**

civil officers of the United States. All officers of the United States, with the exception of officers in the armed services are civil officers. State ex rel. Summerfield v Clarke, 21 Nev 333, 31 P 545.

civil or municipal law. See **civil law.**

civil possession. A Roman law term for the possession under a claim of ownership which is requisite to the acquisition of title by prescription.

civil proceeding. See **civil action; special proceeding.**

civil remedy. A remedy sought in the prosecution of a suit or action by or at the instance of a private person for the assertion of a private right. People ex rel. Raster v Healy, 230 Ill 280, 82 NE 599.

civil responsibility. Same as **civil liability.**

civil rights. Broadly defined, such rights as the law will enforce, or as all those rights which the law gives a person. In the more restricted sense, however, in which the term is used most often, "civil rights" means the enjoyment of the guaranties contained in constitutional or statutory provisions designed to prevent discrimination in the treatment of a person by reason of his race, color, religion, or previous condition of servitude. 15 Am J2d Civ R § 1.

Civil Rights Acts. Statutes adopted by Congress in the aftermath of the Civil War and in the more recent years of 1957 and 1964, primarily intended to implement the constitutional guaranties against denial of due process and equal protection of the laws to all persons irrespective of race or color. 15 Am J2d Civ R §§ 11 et seq. Guaranties in constitutions and statutes against denial of the rights of a person by reason of his or her race, color, religion, or previous condition of servitude. 15 Am J2d Civ R §§ 3, 4; statutes which prohibit discrimination against a person by reason of his race or color in denying him access to places of public accommodation, such as hotels, restaurants, and lunch counters; places of amusement and recreation, such as parks, theaters, and public resorts; the cars and vehicles of common carriers; and educational facilities maintained by public funds; and provide an aggrieved party the right to recover a penalty for violations. 15 Am J2d Civ R §§ 18 et seq.

civil rights amendments. The Thirteenth, Fourteenth and Fifteenth amendments to the United States Constitution are often so referred to, because they constitute a substantial departure in the character of the constitutional protection accorded fundamental rights.

Civil Rights Bill. An act of Congress passed at the close of the Civil War in 1866, granting citizenship to persons born in the United States, including those who had been slaves.
See **Civil Rights Acts.**

Civil Rights Cases. These were five cases which originated in Federal Courts in Kansas, District of Columbia, Missouri, New York, and Tennessee, respectively, and which were heard and disposed of together in the Supreme Court, since each of them involved the rights of freedmen under the Civil Rights Act of March 1, 1875, providing for full and equal accommodations for all persons at hotels, theaters, public conveyances and places of amusement, without regard to race, color, or previous condition of servitude. The court held the statute to be unconstitutional and not to be within the scope of either the Thirteenth or the Fourteenth Amendment. See Civil Rights Cases, 109 US 3, 27 L Ed 836, 3 S Ct 18.

To the foregoing, there is to be added Brown v Board of Education, 347 US 483, 98 L Ed 873, 74 S Ct 686, 38 ALR2d 1180, supp op 349 US 294, 99 L Ed 1093, 75 S Ct 753, which, in holding that the denial to negro children of admission to public schools attended by white children, under state laws requiring or permitting segregation according to race, deprives them of the equal protection of the laws guaranteed by the Fourteenth Amendment to the United States Constitution, established a precedent for numerous later cases involving segregation of the races.

Civil Rights Commission. A commission in the nature of a fact finding agency established by federal statute. 42 USC §§ 1975—1975e; Hannah v Larche, 363 US 420, 4 L Ed 2d 1307, 80 S Ct 1502, reh den 364 US 855, 5 L Ed 2d 79, 81 S Ct 33.

Civil Rights Division of Department of Justice. A division of the justice department headed by an Assistant Attorney General. 5 USC § 295—1.

civil service. In the broad sense, civil service includes all civilian officers and personnel in the employment of the state or federal government. The term, in a practical parlance, means the civil service system under which appointments to and tenure of, public office are determined by the merit system instead of the spoils system formerly operative under which appointment to public office was usually gained as a reward for political work, with the resulting evils of inefficiency, extravagance, interruption of public business by job hunters, corruption of the electoral franchise, and political assessments. 15 Am J2d Civ S § 1.

Civil Service Act. The act of Congress approved January 16, 1883, providing for the creation of the Civil Service Commission of the United States.

Civil Service Commission. A federal or state commission empowered to administer the rules and regulations embraced in the civil service system. 15 Am J2d Civ S § 6. The United States Civil Service Commission composed of three members appointed by the President by and with the advice and consent of the Senate. 15 Am J2d Civ S § 4.

civil service examination. An examination to fill a civil service position which, in some instances, may be open, and, in other instances, promotional, as where persons already in the service compete with one another for promotion to a more desirable office. 15 Am J2d Civ S § 10.
See **competitive examination.**

civil side. The civil department or calendar of a court having also a criminal department or calendar.

civil suit. A civil action; for the purposes of a venue statute, proceeding, action, or suit by which private rights are protected or enforced or their violation redressed. 56 Am J1st Ven § 52.

civil war. An armed struggle between opposing and contending forces of the same nation for the control of the government. 56 Am J1st War § 2. While protection of the law of war is not accorded to those engaging in an insurrection or rebellion against the constituted authority, unless a state of belligerency is recognized by the existing government, when hostilities attain dimensions which interfere with the exercise of the jurisdiction of the existing government in some of its territorial districts, a state of war exists. The War between the Federal government of the United States and the seceding Confederate States, although referred to as the "Civil War," sometimes as the "War of Rebellion" or "The Great Rebellion," was accompanied by the general incidents of an international war, and the rules of war, as recognized by the public law of civilized nations, were applied, even though the general principles and purposes of the Federal government were the re-establishment of national authority and the ultimate restoration of the seceding states and their citizens to their national relations without any view of subjugation by conquest. 56 Am J1st War § 3.

Civil War Claims. Claims arising under the captured and abandoned property act of 1863, which provided that property when captured should be sold and the proceeds paid into the United States treasury, and that any person claiming to be the owner of property thus captured and sold might at any time within two years after the close of the civil war bring suit in the court of claims for the proceeds and on satisfactory proof of certain facts recover its value, less some specified deductions. 54 Am J1st US § 109.

civil year. Same as **solar year.**

civis (si'vis). (Roman law.) A citizen.

civitas (si'vi-tās). A state or government.

civitatus. See **defensor civitatus.**

C. J. An abbreviation of **chief justice**; also of **Corpus Juris.**

claim. A demand for money or property; the assertion of a demand, or the challenge of something, as a matter of right; a demand of some matter, as of right, made by one person upon another to do or to forbear to do some act or thing, as a matter of duty, Vulcan Iron Works v Edwards, 27 Or 563, 36 P 22; a challenge by a man of the propriety or ownership of a thing, which he has not in his possession, but which is wrongfully detained from him, Prigg v Commonwealth of Pennsylvania (US) 16 Pet 539, 10 L Ed 1060; a demand made by the owner, or on behalf of the owner, of a vessel for its return after a seizure of the vessel by way of perfecting a forfeiture thereof by a proceeding in admiralty. 48 Am J1st Ship § 30; a demand against an insurance company for payment of a loss; a writing which uses words showing an intention to claim benefits under veteran's insurance. 29A Am J Rev ed Ins § 1989; an assertion of ownership to a portion of the unappropriated soil of the public domain, protected by an entry in accordance with the federal statutes. 42 Am J1st Pub L § 19; a precise assertion of rights by an inventor respecting his discovery or invention. 40 Am J1st Pat § 92; a cause of action for some purposes. As used in a statute concerning claims against the state and providing for their enforcement by suit, the term is equivalent to "cause of action." Northwestern & Pacific Hypotheek Bank v State of Washington, 18 Wash 73, 50 P 586.

The term does not include causes of action purely equitable and in which purely equitable relief is sought. Ashbauth v Davis, 71 Idaho 150, 227 P2d 954, 32 ALR2d 361.
See **adverse claim; mining claim.**

claim adjuster. See **adjuster; claimant adjuster.**

claim against decedent's estate. A debt or demand of a pecuniary nature which could have been enforced in law or equity against the decedent in his lifetime and could have been reduced to a simple money judgment. 31 Am J2d Ex & Ad § 276.

Most courts have held that the term as used in a statute relating to the competency of interested witnesses in the prosecution of a "claim or demand" against an estate, refers to the assertion of any right against an estate. According to this view the words are not restricted to a money claim, but apply also to any other demand which would tend to deplete the estate. Other courts have limited these terms to such claims as can give rise to a suit calling for a money judgment. Anno: 41 ALR 1044.

claim against the United States. A right to demand money from the United States. 54 Am J1st US § 102.

claim agent. An employee of a railroad company, a business, or an industry, whose duty it is to investigate claims made against his employer and report to the employer whether a claim should be paid, denied, or adjusted.

claim and delivery. A statutory action in some jurisdictions, partaking of the nature of common-law replevin in contemplating the recovery of the specific property claimed, where such is possible, but resembling trover in permitting the recovery of the value where delivery of the specific property is impossible. 46 Am J1st Replev § 6.

claimant. One who claims; a voluntary applicant for justice; the libelant in a proceeding in rem in admiralty or one who appears in such a proceeding to claim the res or an interest therein. 2 Am J2d Adm § 142.
See **claim**.

claim check. A receipt for goods bailed, especially for baggage delivered by a passenger to a carrier.

claim in arrangement proceeding under the Bankruptcy Act. A proof of claim against the debtor or a claim scheduled by the debtor. 9 Am J2d Bankr § 1310.

claim in a service. A petition by an heir to be served as heir of the decedent.

claim in bankruptcy. A proof of claim against the bankrupt.
See **proof of claim; provable debt**.

claim in corporate reorganization. A claim of whatever character against a debtor or its property, except stock, whether or not such claim is provable in an ordinary bankruptcy proceeding and whether secured or unsecured, liquidated or unliquidated, fixed or contingent. Bankr Act § 106(1); 11 USC § 506(1).

claim in proceeding for readjustment of public debt under the Bankruptcy Act. The claim of a creditor holding securities in the technical or nontechnical sense, even a holder of an unliquidated claim against the municipality or other public body. 9 Am J2d Bankr § 1423.

claim in proceeding for wage earner's plan. A claim of whatever character against the debtor or his property, whether or not provable as a debt in ordinary bankruptcy, and whether secured or unsecured, liquidated or unliquidated, fixed or contingent, but not a claim secured by an estate in real property or chattels real. Bankr Act § 606(1); 11 USC § 1006(1).

claim in real property arrangement. A claim of whatever character against the debtor or his property, whether or not such is provable in ordinary bankruptcy and whether secured or unsecured, liquidated or unliquidated, fixed or contingent. 9 Am J2d Bankr § 1359.

claim jumping. Taking advantage of the failure of one, who has settled on public lands or has begun a mining operation on such lands, to perfect his claim in the manner required by law, by locating a claim to the same area in the manner required by law, for the purpose of obtaining the same area irrespective of the work performed by the first occupant or claimant or of any right he may have by virtue of prior possession or occupation. Nelson v Smith, 42 Nev 302, 176 P 261, 178 P 625.

claim-notice (klăm'nō"tis). A notice posted on his mining claim by a miner or prospector setting forth his claim to mining rights in the land.

claim of cognizance (cog'ni-zans). A claim of the right or privilege of taking jurisdiction of a cause. See 2 Bl Comm 298.

claim of conusance. Same as **claim of cognizance**.

claim of exemption. The assertion of a right given by law to a debtor to retain a portion of his personal property free from seizure and sale by his creditors under judicial process. 31 Am J2d Exemp § 1.

See **notice of exemption**.

claim of liberty. A suit or petition to the crown, in the court of exchequer, to have liberties and franchises confirmed there by the attorney general.— Wharton's Law Dict.

claim of lien. The assertion of the existence of a lien in claimant's favor; the filing of a verified statement of a mechanic's lien for record, required in perfecting such a lien. 36 Am J1st Mech L § 131.

claim of ownership. See **claim of right**.

claim of right. An entry upon land with the intent to claim the land and to hold it; the intention of a disseisor to appropriate and use land as his own to the exclusion of all others, irrespective of any semblance or shadow of actual title or right. Guaranty Title & Trust Corp v United States, 264 US 200, 204, 68 L Ed 636, 638, 44 S Ct 252.

claim of title. The entry and occupation of land with the intent to hold it as the claimant's own against the world, irrespective of any shadow or color or right or title as a foundation of his claim. Anno: 2 ALR 1457.
See **claim of right**.

claim or demand. See **claim; claim against decedent's estate**.

claims and controversies. See **controversy**.

claim to property within jurisdiction. A prequisite to jurisdiction. Kohagen v Harwood (CA7 Wis) 185 F2d 276, 30 ALR2d 201.

claim, vi, furto aut precario (klăm, vī, fur'tō ât pre-ka're-o). A claim accompanied by force, stealth or supplication.

clairvoyance. Keen perception; the ability to perceive occurrences out of sight.

clam. Noun: A bivalve mollusk, the soft part of which in some species is edible. Adverb: Secretly; furtively. Verb: A slang term of the underworld for remaining silent.
See **shellfish**.

clam bed. An area along the shore of the sea between high and low watermark from which clams are dug. Allen v Allen, 19 RI 114, 32 A 166. The bed may be a work of nature or of artificial cultivation, and subject to limitations, property rights may be acquired therein. 35 Am J2d Fish § 13.

clam delinquentes magis puniuntur quam palam (klam de-lin-quen'tĕz mā'jis pū-ni-un'ter quam pa'-lam). Those who offend in secret should be more severely punished than those who do so openly.

clamea admittenda in itinere per attornatum (klā'me-a ad-mit-ten'da in ī-ti'ne-re per at-tor-nā'tum). A writ commanding the admission of an attorney to represent a claimant who was abroad.

clamor (klam'or). A complaint; an outcry; a claim.

clandestine (klan-des'tin). Surreptitious; hidden or, at least, unpublicized, usually for an illegal or unworthy purpose.

clandestine introduction. An offense also known as smuggling and embracing all unlawful acts of concealment or other illegal conduct tending to show a fixed intent to evade the customs duty by subsequently passing the goods through the jurisdiction of the customs officials without paying the duties imposed thereon by law. Keck v United States, 172 US 434, 43 L Ed 505, 509, 19 S Ct 254.

clandestine marriage. A form of marriage, valid at common law, entered into before witnesses, usually with an irregular ceremony,—without the publication of banns, and lacking other requisites of the ecclesiastical law. Sharon v Sharon, 75 Cal 1, 16 P 345.

clap-stick (klap-stik). A watchman's alarm rattle.

clare constat (klā'rē kon'stat). It clearly appears.

claremethen. A warranty of the title of goods which had been stolen.

Clarendon. See **Constitutions of Clarendon.**

Clarification Act. A federal statute pertaining to the rights and remedies of a seaman injured in the service of the ship. 50 USC Appx § 1291.

class. A large number of persons who may be designated collectively, irrespective of geographical limitation, political division, place of abode, or any similar restriction. Anno: 97 ALR 281.

class action. An action brought by one or more nominal plaintiffs on behalf of a class of persons. An action maintained in the Federal courts by authority of Rule 23 of the Federal Rules of Procedure where several persons jointly act to the injury of many persons so numerous that their voluntarily, unanimously joining in a suit is concededly improbable and impracticable. In such situation the injured parties who are so minded may sue on behalf of all, and the remaining members of the class may join as they see fit. Weeks v Bareco Oil Co. (CA 7 Ill) 125 F2d 84.
See **class suit.**

class gift. See **gift to a class.**

classification. Dividing into class; in a more sophisticated statement, the grouping of things in speculation or practice because they "agree with one another in certain particulars and differ from other things in those same particulars." Billings v Illinois, 188 US 97, 47 L Ed 400, 23 S Ct 272. "Classification is the most inveterate of our reasoning processes. We can scarcely think or speak without consciously or unconsciously exercising it. It must therefore obtain in and determine legislation; but it must regard real resemblances and real differences between things and persons, and class them in accordance with their pertinence to the purpose in hand." Truax v Corrigan, 257 US 312, 66 L Ed 254, 42 S Ct 124, 27 ALR 375, 388.
"Classification" is a technical term for the practice in the English chancery courts of assigning litigants having similar interests in the same cause to one solicitor, to save expense.

classification of cities. The classification of cities within a state, usually on the basis of population, so as to make possible and legal difference in charter, powers, and form of municipal government as between the several or many cities of the state. 37 Am J1st Mun Corp § 98.

classification of counties. The practice of grouping or classifying counties by population, authorized in some states, for the purpose of fixing the compensation of county officers, the purpose of regulating the registration of voters and the conduct of elections, or the selection and impanelment of jurors, or in relation to the establishment, jurisdiction, and procedure of courts.

classified service. Classified and graded positions in the civil service. 15 Am J2d Civ S § 16.

classis (klas'is). A synod. See 45 Am J1st Reli Soc § 29.

class legislation. All legislation involves classification. Prohibited class legislation, which is what the term implies, is nothing more than the other side of the shield of the guaranty of equal protection of the laws; it is legislation which discriminates against some and favors others. 16 Am J2d Const L § 494; legislation which denies to one rights which are accorded to others, or inflicts upon one individual a more severe penalty than is imposed upon another in like case offending. People v Bellet, 99 Mich 151, 57 NW 1094.

class of creditors. A class created by the Bankruptcy Act for the purpose of priority in distribution of a bankrupt's assets. 9 Am J2d Bankr § 1080.

class rate. A freight rate applying to a number of articles of the same general character.

class suit. An invention of equity to enable it to proceed to a decree in suits where the number of those interested in the subject of the litigation is so great that their joinder as parties in conformity with the usual rules of procedure is impracticable. Hansberry v Lee, 311 US 32, 85 L Ed 22, 61 S Ct 115. A salvage suit in admiralty brought by the master on behalf of himself and the members of his crew. 2 Am J2d Adm § 152.
See **class action.**

clause. As a grammatical form, a division of a compound or complex sentence, with a subject and a verb; in the language of the law, a sentence, a part of a sentence, sometimes a clause in the grammatical form, or a paragraph, such as in a will where division of the instrument into parts is made according to the rank of property or class of beneficiaries. Eschbach v Collins, 61 Md 478, 499.

clause irritant. A clause in a deed which limited the right of an absolute proprietor in entails.

clause of accrual. A clause in a will or deed directing to whom the property shall go in the event of the death of the devisee or grantee.

clause of accruer. Same as **clause of accrual.**

clause of ac etiam. See **ac etiam.**

clause of devolution. A clause imposing some obligation contingent upon an event.

clause of hiis testibus. See **hiis testibus clause.**

clause of return. A clause in a deed providing that a right shall upon certain specified contingencies revert to the grantor.

clause rolls (klâz'rōlz). Same as **close rolls.**

clausula (klâ'zu-la). A clause or distinct part of a sentence.

clausula derogatoria (klâ-sū'lä de-ro'ga-tōr-i-ä). A derogatory clause; a clause which impinges upon authority not to be denied.

Clausulae inconsuetae semper inducunt suspicionem (klâ'sū-lē in-kon-sū-ē'tē sem'per in-dū'kunt sus-pi-shi-ō'nem). Unaccustomed or unusual clauses always arouse suspicion.

Clausula generalis de residuo non ea complectitur quae non ejusdem sint generis cum iis quae speciatim dicta fuerant (klâ'zu-la je-ne-rā'lis de re-si'du-ō non ē'a kom-plek'ti-ter kwē non ē-jus'dem sint je'ne-ris kum ī'is kwē spe-she-ā'tim dik'ta fu'e-rant). A general clause of remainder does not include matters not of the same kind with those specially mentioned.

Clausula generalis non refertur ad expressa (klâ'zu-la je-ne-rā'lis non re-fer'ter ad ex-pres'sa). A general clause does not refer to matters expressly mentioned.

Clausula quae abrogationem excludit ab initio non valet (klâ'zu-la kwē ab-rō-gā-shē-ō'nem ex-klū'dit ab i-ni'she-ō non va'let). A clause which forbids repeal is void from the beginning.

Clausula vel dispositio inutilis per praesumptionem remotam vel causam, ex post facto non fulcitur (klâ'zu-la vel dis-po-si'she-ō in-u'ti-lis per prē-sump-she-ō'nem re-mō'tam vel kâ'zam, ex post fak'tō non ful'si-ter). A useless clause or disposition is not supported by a remote presumption or by a fact which occurs subsequently.

clausum (klâ'zum). A close; a piece of land enclosed by a visible, material fence, or by an ideal, invisible boundary.

clausum fregit (klâ'zum frē'jit). He broke the close by a literal or figurative trespass, breaking a fence or walking across a boundary line.

clausura (klâ'zūr-a). An inclosure; a close.

claves curiae (klā'vēz kū'ri-ē). The keys of the court.

clayme (klām). An old form of the word "claim."

Clayton Act. A federal statute, approved by the President on October 15, 1914, having the purpose of protecting the public against the evils resulting from a lessening of competition, and forbidding certain practices in business which reduce competition and price discriminations. 15 USC §§ 12-27; 36 Am J1st Monop etc §§ 141, 142.

clean bill of lading. A bill of lading which contains nothing in the margin qualifying the words in the bill itself. 13 Am J2d Car § 265; a bill of lading for carriage by vessel which imports stowage below deck. 48 Am J1st Ship § 382.

clean hands doctrine. The equitable principle which requires a denial of relief to a complainant who is himself guilty of inequitable conduct in reference to the matter in controversy. 27 Am J2d Eq § 136; 28 Am J Rev ed Inj § 33.

Within the meaning of the maxim of equity requiring one who comes to it for relief to come with clean hands and an apparently clear conscience, the term unclean hands is a figurative description of a class of suitors to whom a court of equity as a court of conscience will not even listen, because the conduct of such suitors is itself unconscionable, that is, morally reprehensible as to known facts. 27 Am J2d Eq § 137.

See **improper use doctrine**.

clean paper. A banking term which is applied to such documents as bills, drafts and promissory notes, as distinguished from special paper such as bills of lading with sight drafts attached. Bunge v First Nat. Bank (DC Pa) 34 F Supp 119.

clear. Verb: To acquit; to justify; to excuse; to exonerate; to depart from port. Adjective: Certain; not clouded or obscured; not impinged upon. Ford v Ruxton, 1 Colly Ch Cas 403, 63 Eng Reprint 474.

clearance. A certificate which evidences the right of the vessel to depart the port on a voyage, operating as a permission to sail; the act of departing from a port. 48 Am J1st Ship § 19; the space permitted by the physical circumstances for a movement, as the distance between a turning car and a parked car, or the distance between a railroad car in movement on one track and a building or other railroad car, the latter distance being important in reference to the question whether a brakeman is in peril in a position on the moving car. Anno: 50 ALR2d 699; a term used in the motion picture business, meaning the interval of time which must elapse under the contract after the conclusion of the exhibition of a picture at one theater before it can be exhibited in any other theater in which it has not been exhibited. Waxmann v Columbia Pictures Corp. (DC Pa) 40 F Supp 108.

clearance card. A letter given an employee upon his leaving service, setting forth the nature and duration of the services rendered and the cause of leaving, not necessarily so complimentary of the services as to constitute a recommendation. Cleveland, Cincinnati, Chicago & St. Louis Railway Co. v Jenkins, 174 Ill 398, 402, 51 NE 811.

clearance lights. Side lights on a motor vehicle. 8 Am J2d Auto § 712.

See **side lights**.

clear and convincing evidence. A degree of proof higher than that of preponderance of the evidence. 20 Am J2d Ev § 1253.

clear and present danger. The test of whether words spoken or written are capable of producing such a substantial evil that they are not within the protection of the constitutional guaranty of freedom of speech and press. 16 Am J2d Const L § 347.

clear days. Entire days; intervening days of which the first and last are excluded. Thus, the clear days between the first and the fourth, would be the second and the third.

clear distance ahead. See **assured clear distance ahead**.

clear, distinct, and unequivocal possession. A characterization of adverse possession. 3 Am J2d Adv P § 34.

clearinghouse. A voluntary association composed of banks, the purpose of which is to effect at one place in a city a daily exchange of checks, drafts, and other evidences of indebtedness held by one member and due from another. 10 Am J2d Banks § 838; an organization within a stock or commodity exchange which acts as a universal go-between or clearinghouse, for the debits and credits of its members with one another. At the close of each day's business all of these transactions are reported to the association, which then becomes the opposite party to the transactions of each member for the purpose of offsetting the same. 50 Am J1st Stock Ex § 20.

clearinghouse association. An association between banks or members of a stock or commodity exchange for maintaining a clearinghouse.

clearing land. Removing bushes, sprouts, and trees; an act of ownership. 3 Am J2d Adv P § 21.

clearly erroneous rule. A standard followed in reviewing a determination of an administrative agency. 2 Am J2d Admin L § 619.

clearly reflecting income. An income tax law term applied to a method of accounting, meaning a method which is plain, honest, straightforward, and frank, but not necessarily accurate and precise, without error or defect. Huntington Secur. Corp. v Busey (CA6 Ohio) 112 F2d 368.

clear market value. The sum which property will bring on a fair sale when sold by willing seller not obliged to sell to a willing buyer not obliged to buy. 28 Am J Rev ed Inher T § 359.

clear of all deductions. A clause intended to indicate a gift or legacy of a sum which shall remain in the complete amount in which it is designated, without deduction for expenses, inheritance taxes, or estate taxes. Marris v Burton, 11 Sim 161, 59 Eng Reprint 836.

clear proof. That which may be seen; that which is discernible; that which may be appreciated and understood. In such sense, it may not really mean any more than a fair preponderance. It may, however, under emphasis, convey the idea of certainty, and it probably would to the common mind. Aubin v Duluth Street Railway Co. 169 Minn 342, 348, 211 NW 580.

clear, strong, and convincing. A degree of proof higher than that of preponderance of the evidence. 30 Am J2d Ev § 1167.

clear title. Good title; a legal and equitable title to land free from litigation, grave doubts, and palpable defects. Veselka v Forres (Tex Civ App) 283 SW 303, 306; a title free from material defects; a merchantable or marketable title. 30 Am J2d Exch § 23.

clear value. Net value after deductions. Bouse v Hutzler, 180 Md 682, 26 A2d 767, 141 ALR 843.
See **clear market value.**

clemency. Mildness; a disposition to forgive or to be lenient in punishment; the granting of a pardon or commutation of sentence.

Clementines (klem'en-teenz). The collections of canon law made by Pope Clement in 1311.

cleofan. (Anglo-Saxon.) Uniting to divide. Merion Cricket Club v United States (CA3) 119 F2d 578, affd 315 US 42, 86 L Ed 656, 62 S Ct 430; a term expressive of the theory of association in club or society.
Graphically expressed, the glutton and toper eat and drink at the expense of their more abstemious brethren and the more athletic or more enthusiastic golfer lives off his weaker or less zealous colleagues. Merion Cricket Club v United States, supra.

cleptomania (klep-tō-mā'ni-ạ). Same as **kleptomania.**

cleremonia (kle-re-mō'ni-a). The clergy.

clergy. In olden times, a word for a clerk or educated man; in modern times, the pastors or priests of churches and the persons above them in the organization or hierarchy of the church.

clergyable (klėr'ji-ạ-bl). Entitled to benefit of clergy, as a clerk or clergyman. The adjective was also applied to those felonies and misdemeanors in respect to which benefit of clergy could be claimed.
See **benefit of clergy.**

clergyman (klėr'ji-mạn). One of the clergy.
See **clergy.**

clerical (kler'i-kạl). Pertaining to a clerk or to the functions of a clerk.

clericale privilegium (kle-ri-kā'le pri-vi-lē'ji-um). Benefit of clergy.

clerical error. An error in technique rather than in substance of thought; the misprision of a clerk or other officer of the court, causing a defect or omission in the record. As the phrase applies to the record of a judgment, it means the failure to preserve or correctly represent in the record, in all respects, the actual decision of the court. Annos: 10 ALR 589, s. 67 ALR 842 and 126 ALR 977; 14 ALR2d 234. An error of a judge is a clerical error where it is one which cannot reasonably be attributed to exercise of judicial consideration or discretion. Anno: 14 ALR2d 234.

clerici de cancellaria (kle'ri-sī dē kan-sel-lā'ri-a). Clerks of the court of chancery.

clerici praenotarii (kle'ri-sī prē-nō-tā'ri-ī). The six clerks in chancery. They were the clerks who filed pleadings and other papers.

clerico admittendo (kle'ri-kō ad-mit-ten'dō). A writ commanding a bishop to admit a clergyman to a living.

clerico capto, etc. See **de clerico capto, etc.**

clerico convicto, etc. See **de clerico convicto, etc.**

clericus (kle'ri-kus). A clergyman; a clerk.
See **clergy.**

Clericus et agricola et mercator, tempore belli, ut oret, colat, et commutet pace fruuntur (kle'ri-kus et a-gri'kō-la et mer-kā'tor tem'pō-re bel'lī, ut ō'ret, ko'lat, et kom-mū'tet, pa'sē fru-un'ter). Clergymen, farmers and merchants enjoy peace in time of war, so that they may preach, cultivate the soil, and trade.

clericus mercati (kle'ri-kus mer-kā'tī). Clerk of the market.

Clericus non connumeretur in duabus ecclesiis (kle'ri-kus non kon-nu-me-rē'ter in du-ā'bus ec-klē'si-īs). A clergyman should not be appointed by two churches.

clericus parochialis (kle'ri-kus pa-rō-ki-ā'lis). A parish clerk.

clerigos (clay're-gos). (Spanish.) Clergymen.

clerk. In the earlier days of the common law, a word for an educated person, that is to say, as of that period, a clergyman, one of the clergy who for want of education of other classes, became judicial officers and were known to be such from their status as clerks or clergymen; in modern times, one who keeps accounts for another; an accountant; a scribe; a public officer who keeps the accounts of the political subdivision which he serves; also one employed in a store to sell goods and transact other business of a perfunctory character for the owner, but not to act only as a cashier. Miller v State, 88 Tex Crim 69, 225 SW 379, 12 ALR 597, 601.
See **law clerk; law office clerk.**

clerk of arraigns. The clerk of the central criminal court in England; a deputy of the clerk of assize.

clerk of assize. The clerk who attended the justices of assize in their circuits.

clerk of court. Primarily a ministerial officer, the assistant or official scribe of the court, whose principal duty is to make a correct memorial of the proceedings of the court, and who has custody of the court's records and seal, with authority to certify to the correctness of transcripts from such records, and to perform certain acts of a judicial nature incidental to his ministerial duties. 15 Am J2d Cl C § 1. In some jurisdictions, by force of statute, the clerk of court has the function of a county recorder of instruments affecting title to real estate.

clerk of enrollments. At one time the chief officer of the English enrollment office.

Clerk of the House of Commons. An officer appointed by the crown who has the custody of the memorials and journals of the acts of the house of commons.

clerk of the peace. An officer whose function was to assist the justices of the peace in their quarter sessions.

clerk of the petty bag. An officer of the English chancery court who enrolled the admission of solicitors and other officers of the court.

clerk of the privy seal. An officer who formerly attended the lord privy seal.

clerk of the signet. An officer who attends the principal secretary of the king.

clerkship (klėrk'ship). The service of an attorney's clerk during his preparation for admission to the bar.

clerks of indictments. Clerks in the English central criminal court whose chief duty was to prepare indictments.

clerks of seats. Officers who attend to the clerical work in the principal registry of the probate division of the English high court.

clerks of the general sessions of the peace. Clerks of the courts of common pleas, known as county clerks, in England and in the American colonies, who were also ex-officio clerks of the general sessions of the peace and registers of deeds in their respective counties.

clerus (klē'rus). The clergy.

client. A person who applies to a lawyer or counsellor for advice and direction on a question of law, or commits his cause to his management in prosecuting a claim or defending against a suit, in a court of justice. McCreary v Hoopes, 25 Miss 428, 429; a patron or employer of an attorney or solicitor; a person who applies to an advocate for counsel and defense; one who retains an attorney, who is responsible to him for his fees, and to whom the attorney is responsible for his management of the suit. McFarland v Crary (NY) 6 Wend 297, 312.
In recent times, the term has been extended to cover the employer or customer of persons engaged in activities other than the practice of law. So, a broker in stocks, insurance, or real estate, speaks of his "clients," as does a dressmaker, even a barber.

Clifford's Inn. One of the inns of the English court of chancery.

climacteric insanity (klī-mak-ter'ik). A form of temporary insanity arising from some peculiar transitional condition of the system. Leache v State, 22 Tex Crim 279.

climbing spurs. See **spurs.**

clinic. The outpatient department of a hospital; a place wherein physicians practice in close association with one another, particularly physicians with specialities in the practice.

clinical. Pertaining to a clinic; study or practice in medicine by full and complete observation.

clinical examination. The acts of a physician in examining a patient for objective symptoms, interviewing the patient to obtain at least a partial history of the case, and supplementing the history thus obtained from other possible sources. Peterson v Widule, 157 Wis 641, 147 NW 966.

clocking. Ascertaining the rate of speed, particularly of motor vehicles. 7 Am J2d Auto §§ 326–329.

clogging (klog'ing). Cheating with cogged or loaded dice.

clogging equity of redemption. Imposing upon a mortgage an agreement whereby the mortgagor forfeits, clogs, or fetters his equity of redemption. 15 Am J2d Chat Mtg § 241; 36 Am J1st Mtg § 184.

close (klōz). Noun: A tract or parcel of land enclosed by a fence or an invisible boundary; the end. Verb: To finish, as to close one's argument or case; to make an enclosure. Adjective: Wrapped up; sealed.

close. Attached by bonds of affection and regard; near together.

close clearance. See **clearance.**

close confinement. Such custody of a prisoner as will safely secure him. Rooney v North Dakota, 196 US 319, 49 L Ed 494, 25 S Ct 264.
See **solitary confinement.**

close copies. Copies which may be written with any number of words on a sheet.

close corporation. A corporation in which the officers and directors have the power to fill vacancies in office without submitting the choice to the stockholders; another term for a "family corporation," in which the most of the stock is held by members of one family. 18 Am J2d Corp § 13.

closed. Terminated; being at an end. The term is of somewhat variable meaning as relating to a business transaction, one meaning being that of reaching an agreement, the other being that of putting an agreement into effect, as where the parties to a real estate contract say the deal is "closed" when the parties meet and perform their engagements, the one delivering a deed and the other making payment of the consideration promised. Tahir Erk v Glenn L. Martin Co. (DC Md) 32 F Supp 722.

closed bank. Literally a bank not open for business at the time, but for most purposes, such as the necessity for presentment at a bank of an instrument payable at the bank, a closed bank is a failed bank, an insolvent bank, or a bank which has ceased to exist. 11 Am J2d B & N § 760.
See **failed bank.**

closed car. A private car on a railroad. 14 Am J2d Car § 860; an automobile with body and top for the protection of driver and passengers.

closed investigations. Private investigations. 2 Am J2d Admin L § 258; completed or terminated investigations by detectives or police officers.

closed season. A restriction or absolute prohibition imposed by law upon fishing or hunting during a specified period of the year. 35 Am J2d Fish § 46. The restriction, which is imposed by statute or administrative regulation in the interest of conservation of fish and wild life, may apply to all kinds of fish and all species of game birds and animals during the specified period or, as it usually does, to designated kinds of fish and particular game birds and animals, with variations from season to season in the scope of the coverage.

closed shop. A place of employment in which all employees are required by contract between the employer and a labor union to be members of the union. 31 Am J Rev ed Lab § 95; more broadly defined, a place of employment where either unionism or nonunionism excludes an applicant from employment. Anno: 95 ALR 11.

closed shop basis. An arrangement wherein an employer agrees to employ no workmen who do not belong to a union. Fenske Bros. v Upholsterers'

International Union, 358 Ill 239, 193 NE 112, 97 ALR 1318.
See **closed shop.**

closed trial or hearing. A trial conducted in private, not in open court. 53 Am J1st Trial § 36; an investigation by an administrative body which is closed to the public. 2 Am J2d Admin L §§ 258, 412.

closed union. A labor union whose membership is limited in number. 31 Am J Rev ed Lab § 57.

closed venire. A list of names of persons to be summoned for jury duty which is complete in the sense that the names of the prospective jurors are listed and there shall be no further selection for such venire. 31 Am J Rev ed Jur § 91.

close letters. See **close writs; literae clausae.**

closely built up. A term for a heavily populated area. 7 Am J2d Auto § 191.

closely related occupation. See **directly essential to production.**

close port. An inland port, situated on a river.

close rolls. English public records of close writs. See 2 Bl Comm 346.

close-time. Same as **closed season.**

close writs. Letters or grants from the king, sealed with his great seal, but directed to particular persons, and for particular purposes, and which, not being proper for public inspection, were closed up and sealed on the outside. They were also called literae clausae. See 2 Bl Comm 346.

closing. Making the final argument; summing up. Completing a transaction, particularly a contract for the sale of real estate, in execution of the contract.
See **rest.**

closing agreement. The rarely used formal agreement for determining liability for federal taxes with a degree of finality otherwise achieved only through a court decision; in effect, a mutual release which binds both parties. IRC § 7121; Proctor v White [DC Mass] 28 F Supp 161.

closing statement. The closing argument or summation by counsel in a trial.

cloth (klôth). The clergy; woven material used primarily for wearing apparel.

clothed with a public interest. Something of public consequence and affecting the community at large. 16 Am J2d Const L § 317.
   A business is clothed with a public interest where the circumstances are such as to create a close relation between the public and the persons engaged in the business and raise implications of an affirmative obligation on the latter to be reasonable in dealing with the public. Charles Wolfe Packing Co. v Court of Industrial Relations, 262 US 522, 67 L Ed 1103, 43 S Ct 630, 27 ALR 1280.

clothing. See **wearing apparel.**

cloud on title. An outstanding instrument, record, claim, unreleased encumbrance, or defectively executed deed in the chain of title, which superficially renders the title doubtful but is actually illegal or unenforceable for want of equity in enforcement and of which equity will take cognizance in a suit for cancelation of the offending instrument or the quieting of the title against the defect or imperfection. 13 Am J2d Canc Inst § 50; 44 Am J1st Quiet T § 11; a semblance of title, either legal or equitable, or a claim of a right in lands, appearing in some legal form, but which is, in fact, invalid, or which it would be inequitable to enforce. 44 Am J1st Quiet T § 11.

cloud seeding. An attempt to control natural phenomena by artificial means, that is, by scattering certain chemical substances in a cloud from an airplane.
   The purpose is usually to promote rainfall, but, at times, to suppress hail and lightning. 1 Am J2d Adj L § 40; 3 Am J2d Agri § 6.

clough (kluf or klou). A valley.

cloven hoof. See **neat cattle.**

club. An organization or association of persons who meet together for the purpose of social intercourse or some common object such as the pursuit of literature, science, politics, art, and athletic pursuits or sports, such as swimming, tennis, and golf. United Cerebral Palsy Asso. v Zoning Board of Adjustment, 382 Pa 67, 114 A2d 331, 52 ALR2d 1093.

clubhouse. A building, plain or elaborate, used for the indoor activities, entertainment, and refreshment of the members of a club and their guests. Anno: 52 ALR2d 1098.

Co. Abbreviation for company, also for county.

C. O. Abbreviation for commanding officer, also for conscientious objector.

c/o. Abbreviation for care of, also for carried over.

coach (kōch). A word of variable meaning, applied originally to a commodious horse-drawn vehicle, now applied to some motor vehicles, particularly large vehicles which carry passengers for hire; a car on a passenger train where passengers paying regular fare are accommodated; an airplane, or section of an airplane, operated by an airline for the accommodation of passengers carried at an economy rate.
See **coaching.**

coaching. Instructing a witness before he takes the stand, an unobjectionable practice so long as it is confined to instruction calculated to lessen the ordeal of testifying, explaining what is expected in the demeanor of a witness, but becoming highly objectionable when it comes to the point of telling the witness what his testimony shall be; whispering or signaling to a witness on the stand for the purpose of influencing his testimony.

coadjutor (kō-a-jö′tọr). An assistant, particularly the assistant of a bishop or other prelate of the church of England.

coadministrator. One of two or more administrators appointed by the court to act jointly in the administration of the estate of a decedent.

coadunatio (kō-ad-ū-nā′she-ō). A conspiracy.

coadventure. See **joint adventure.**

coafforest (kō-a-for′est). To convert clear land into a forest, or to increase a forest.

coagent (ko-ā′jẹnt). An agent acting jointly with another agent; an accomplice.

coal and minerals. A broad term, sometimes held to include oil and gas, where appearing in a deed or reservation in a deed. Gibson v Sellars (Ky) 252 SW2d 911, 37 ALR2d 1435.
   For practical purposes, the right to coal consists in the right to mine it. What makes the right to mine coal valuable is that it can be exercised with profit. A statute making it commercially impracticable to

mine certain coal has very nearly the same effect for constitutional purposes as appropriating or destroying it. Pennsylvania Coal Co. v Mahon, 260 US 393, 67 L Ed 322, 43 S Ct 158, 28 ALR 1321.

coal chamber. An underground space or room created in mining coal. 36 Am J1st Min & M § 181.

coal hole. An aperture in a sidewalk, close to a building, through which, coal or other dry product in grains or chunks may be shoveled so as to reach the basement of the building.

coal mine. See **mine.**

coal mining. See **mining.**

coal mining lease. See **mining lease.**

coal note (kōl'nōt). A kind of promissory note used at the port of London.

coal oil. See **kerosene.**

coal tar colors. Food coloring made from coal tar, the use of which in food renders the food adulterated within the meaning of the Federal Food, Drug, and Cosmetic Act, unless the coloring is from a batch duly certified and listed as a product harmless and suitable for use in food. 21 USC § 342(c).

coal tipple. A devise whereby railroad cars loaded with coal are unloaded by shaking them; an elevated structure in railroad yards or in coal mines to which coal is elevated and stored temporarily, to be released into railroad cars, aided by the force of gravity.

coassignee. One of two or more persons to whom an assignment has been made.

coast. The seaboard. Pacific Milling & Elevator Co. v Portland, 65 Or 349, 133 P 72.
See **coasting.**

coast and geodetic survey. An operation of the Department of Commerce for the benefit of mariners, pilots, aircraft pilots, land surveyors, radio engineers, scientists, and others, its major activities being the surveying and charting of the coasts of the United States and its possessions to insure the safe navigation of coastal and intracoastal waters; the surveying of lakes, rivers, and other inland waters by hydrographic and topographic methods; the fixing of geographical positions and elevations in the interior of the country, thereby providing a framework for mapping and other engineering work; studying tides and currents and making tables thereof; compiling aeronautical charts, making seismological, gravitational, and astronomical observations and compiling the data obtained thereby to assist in designing structures resistant to earthquakes and providing data for scientific investigation of the crust of the earth.

coaster. A vehicle without power used by children in riding on a hill; a sled.
See **coasting vessel.**

coasting. Operating a motor vehicle on a grade with the motor disengaged. 8 Am J2d Auto § 687; the sport of traveling downhill on snow in a sled; engaging in the coasting trade.
See **coasting trade.**

coasting license. The license of a ship or vessel to engage in the coasting trade. See 48 Am J1st Ship § 48.

coasting trade. Domestic trade as distinguished from foreign trade; commerce between ports of the United States, including trade on interior rivers or lakes, along the coasts, Alaska and with the outlying territories and insular possessions of the United States. 48 Am J1st Ship § 50.

coasting vessel. A ship often called a "coaster," plying exclusively between domestic ports; a ship engaged in coasting or domestic trade, as distinguished from foreign trade. 48 Am J1st Ship § 50; a vessel on a course near to and following the coast. 12 Am J2d Boats § 1.

The fact that an ocean going steamer may touch at some other port of the United States, after leaving her port of departure does not make her a coaster. See Belden v Chase, 150 US 674, 696, 37 L Ed 1218, 1226, 14 S Ct 264.
See **coasting trade.**

coat of arms. See **arms; insignia.**

cobelligerent (kō-be-lij'ẹ-rẹnt). Allied in war.

coca leaves. A material containing the substance of a narcotic drug. 25 Am J2d Drugs § 34.

cocket (kok'et). A custom house seal; a certificate issued by a customs officer showing the payment of duties.

cockfight. A contest, usually to the death of a participant, in which gamecocks are pitted in combat. Anno: 82 ALR2d 821 § 6.

cock-loft (kok'loft). A nickname for the English Court of the Vice-Chancellor.

cockpit. The meeting-room of the English privy council at Westminister, the place from which small watercraft and small airplanes are controlled; a region where many battles have been fought; the space in which cockfights are held.

cocktail. A drink, strong, stimulating, and cold, made of spirits, bitters, and a little sugar, with various aromatic or stimulating additions or substitutions. The two most popular cocktails are the martini and the manhattan, the basis of which respectively is gin and whiskey. The daiquiri, which is made from rum, is also a popular drink. 30 Am J Rev ed Intox L § 15.

cocoa leaves. See **coca leaves.**

C. O. D. Abbreviation for collect on delivery. 1 Am J2d Abbr § 7.
See **collect on delivery.**

code. The published statutes of a jurisdiction, arranged in a systematic form by chapters and sections; a part of the statutes of a jurisdiction, such as a Commercial Code, or Practice Code; the official or authenticated book or books of statutes; a systematic and complete body of law, Johnson v Harrison, 47 Minn 575, 578; a codification of the entire body of law, or of the entire body of law on a distinct subject, compiled by a selective process, including some modifications of, and additions to, pre-existing law, and made official through legislative adoption, Central of Georgia Railway Co. v State, 104 Ga 831, 31 SE 531; Litchfield v Roper 192 NC 202, 205, 134 SE 651; a set of signs or symbols used in sending messages for the purpose of secrecy.

Code Civil (kōd siv'il). Same as **Code Napoleon.**

Code Napoleon. A codification of French law made during the reign of Napoleon I and at his direction.

Code of Federal Regulations. An orderly arrangement of the general and permanent rules promulgated by the executive departments and agencies of the United States and published in the Federal Register, the code itself being published as a special edition of the register.

Code of Military Justice. A code which embraces, unifies, consolidates, and codifies the disciplinary laws governing the Armed Forces of the United States, replacing the Articles of War. 10 USC §§ 801-940.

codex (kō'deks). A code.

codicil (kod'i-sil). Some addition to or qualification of one's last will and testament. Codicils were formerly actually attached to the will, but now if the codicil is a separate document referring to and ratifying the will it may be said to incorporate the will by reference. 57 Am J1st Wills § 605.

codification. A code; the process of making a code covering the whole law or particular subject of the law.
See **code.**

Coe Case. An important decision by the United States Supreme Court on the effect of a foreign judgment of divorce as res judicata on the issue of jurisdiction where the defendant, a nonresident, appeared in the action but did not raise the issue of jurisdiction. Coe v Coe, 334 US 378, 92 L Ed 1451, 68 S Ct 1094, 1 ALR2d 1376.

coemployee. A fellow servant. Shank v Edison Electric Illuminating Co. 225 Pa 393, 74 A 210.

coemptio (cǫ-emp'shi-ō). A fictitious sale of an estate to relieve it of sacrificial duties attached to it; a marriage ceremony depicting the sale of bride and groom to one another.
See the derivative term **coemption.**

coemption (kō-emp'shǫn). The buying up of a commodity for the purpose of obtaining a monopoly and controlling the price; under the Roman law, a civil marriage contract in which both parties contributed money.

coercion. Compulsion by the application of physical or mental force or persuasion. A word descriptive of the result of an act rather than a designation of an act. NLRB v Grower-Shipper Vegetable Asso. (CA9) 122 F2d 368. A form of abuse of process. 1 Am J2d Abuse P § 9. The compulsion, presumed by some, especially older, authorities, to have been exercised by a husband upon the wife for the commission of a crime which was committed by her in his presence. 21 Am J2d Crim L § 102; As a defense to an action upon a written instrument:—importunity which destroys the free agency of person subjected and substitutes the will of another in place of his own, Gomillion v Forsythe, 218 SC 211, 62 SE2d 297, 53 ALR2d 169; As an unfair labor practice:—physical or mental persuasion by affirmative conduct. 31 Am J Rev ed Lab § 226; As an excuse for the commission of an act, otherwise criminal a present, imminent, and impending physical or mental force of such a nature as to induce a well-grounded apprehension of death or serious bodily injury if the act is not done. State v St. Clair (Mo) 262 SW2d 25, 40 ALR2d 903.
See **duress.**

coercion in fact (kō-ėr'shon in fakt). That duress of person or goods, where the present liberty of person or immediate possession of goods is so needful and desirable, as that an action or proceedings at law to recover them will not at all answer the pressing purpose. Adrico Realty Corp. v New York, 250 NY 29, 164 NE 732, 64 ALR 1.

coexecutors. Two or more persons appointed to act jointly in the administration of a testator's estate.

coffee agreement. See **Inter-American Coffee Agreement.**

coffee break. A short rest period, now generally accepted as a condition of employment. Mitchell v Greinetz (CA10 Colo) 235 F2d 621, 61 ALR2d 956.

cofferer of the queen's household (kof'ėr-ėr). A principal officer of the royal court, being a paymaster.

cogger (kog'ėr). Slang for a cheat or swindler.

cogging (kog'ing). Slang for cheating by means of cogged or loaded dice.

Cogitationis poenam nemo patitur (ko-ji-tā-she-ō'nis pē'nam nē'mō pā'ti-ter). No one suffers punishment for mere intent. State v Taylor, 47 Or 455, 84 P 82.

Cogito ergo sum (koj'i-tō ėr'gō sum). I think, therefore I am. The fundamental maxim of the philosophy of Descartes.

cognac (kō'nyak). A brandy named for a region of France. Benson v United States (CA5 Tex) 10 F2d 309.

cognates (kog'nāts). Relatives on the mother's side or by females. See 2 Bl Comm 235.

cognati (kog-nā'tī). Blood relatives traced through the mother or other females. See 2 Bl Comm 235.

cognatio (kog-nā'she-ō). (Roman law.) Relationship; blood relationship.

cognation (kog-nā'shǫn). Relationship by ties of blood or family.

cognisance. Same as **cognizance.**

cognitio (kog-ni'she-ō). Same as **cognizance.**

cognitionibus admittendis (kog-nish-i-on'i-bus ad-mi-ten'dis). A writ requiring an officer to certify to the court of common pleas a list of the fines which had been paid, the payment of which had not been reported.

cognizable (kog'ni or kon'i-zạ-bl). Within the jurisdiction of a specific court or tribunal.

cognizance (kog'ni or kon'i-zạns). Acknowledgment; recognition; jurisdiction. Precisely, the assumption of jurisdiction. Kendall v United States (US) 12 Pet 524, 622, 9 L Ed 1181, 1220.

cognizance of pleas. The exclusive right or franchise of trying cases within a particular limited jurisdiction. See 3 Bl Comm 298.

cognizance of the cause. A term often invoked in determining priority of jurisdiction as between courts having concurrent jurisdiction, signifying that some step has been taken in a court in reference to a cause, such as the issuance of process, entertaining a motion, etc., so that the cause is pending. 20 Am J2d Cts § 136.

cognizant (kog'ni or kon'i-zạnt). Legally qualified to take jurisdiction.

cognizee (kog-ni' or kon-i-zē'). The person to whom a fine of land was levied. See 2 Bl Comm 351.

cognizor (kog'ni or kon'i-zôr). A party levying a fine of land. He was thus designated from his acknowledgment or recognition of the right of the complainant to recover the land in question. See 2 Bl Comm 350.

cognomen (kog-nō'men). A name, especially the family name of a person; a nickname.

COGNOSCE [214] COLIBERTUS

cognosce (kog-nos'). To give judgment; to adjudge; to adjudicate.

cognoscere (kog-nos'se-re). To acknowledge.

cognovit (kog-nō'vit). See **cognovit actionem; cognovit note.**

cognovit actionem (kog-nō'vit ak-she-ō'nem). Confession of judgment after service of process; instead of entering a plea, acknowledging and confessing that the plaintiff's cause of action is just and right. 30A Am J Rev ed Judgm § 156.

Cognovit actionem relicta verificatione (kog-nō'vit ak-she-ō'nem re-lik'ta ve-ri-fi-kā"she-ō'ne). The defendant's abandonment of his defense or plea which he has interposed in the action. 30A Am J Rev ed Judgm § 156.

cognovit note. A promissory note which contains a provision authorizing an attorney, agent, or other representative to confess judgment on the instrument and direct entry of such judgment. 11 Am J2d B & N § 199.

cognustre. To acknowledge.

coguardian. One of two or more joint guardians.

cohabit. To live together as man and wife; to live together as though the conjugal relation existed. 2 Am J2d Adult § 1; to have sexual intercourse illegally. Martin v Commonwealth, 195 Va 1107, 87 SE2d 574.

cohabitation. A dwelling together of man and woman in the same place in the manner of husband and wife. 2 Am J2d Adult § 1. The word does not necessarily imply sexual intercourse but may mean simply that a man holds out to the world as his wife more than one woman, and that he provides homes for them, supports them, and acknowledges them as his wives. 10 Am J2d Big § 5.
See **matrimonial cohabitation.**

cohabiting. See **cohabit; cohabitation.**

cohaeredes (kō-hē're-dēz). Coheirs; joint heirs.

Cohaeredes una persona censentur, propter unitatem juris quod habent (kō-hē're-dēz ū'na per-sō'na sen-sen'ter, prop'ter ū-ni-tā'tem jū'ris quod hā'bent). Coheirs are regarded as one person because they hold under unity of right.

cohaeres (kō-he'res). Same as **coheir.**

coheir. A joint heir; a person who succeeds or inherits jointly with another, or with other, heirs; an heir who takes as joint tenant with another, or with other, heirs.

coif (koif). A cap worn by sergeants-at-law in the English courts.
See **Order of the Coif.**

coin. Noun: A piece of metal, made, stamped as of a certain value, and declared by law to be money; the die used in stamping money. Verb: To stamp metal and convert it to a piece of money. Borie v Trott (Pa) 5 Phila 366, 403. To coin money means to mould into form a metallic substance of intrinsic value, and stamp on it its legal value, so as to encourage and facilitate its free circulation and assure stability in the currency. Griswold v Hepburn, 63 Ky (2 Duv) 20, 29. To coin money means to make money out of coin and nothing else. To coin money cannot mean to coin it out of paper. Thayer v Hedges, 22 Ind 282, 306.

See **adulterated coin; base coin; counterfeit coin; current coin; gold coinage; hard money; imbasing of money; money; silver coinage; specie.**

coinage. The process of coining money; the system and the principles regulating and governing the production of the metal currency of the country.

coiner (koi'nėr). One who coins money; a counterfeiter.

coinheritance (kō-in-her'i-tans). A joint inheritance.

coin money. See **coin.**

coin operated amusement or gaming device. A slot machine. United States v Korpan, 345 US 271, 1 L Ed 2d 1337, 77 S Ct 1099.
See **silver coinage.**

coinsurance. Literally, two or more policies of insurance issued by different insurers covering the same risk; in modern insurance parlance, a relative division of the risk between insurer and the insured, dependent upon the relative amount of the policy and the actual value of the property insured thereby. 29A Am J Rev ed Ins § 1548.
See **coinsurance clause.**

coinsurance clause. A clause in a contract of insurance which in substance requires the insured to maintain insurance on the property covered by the policy in a certain amount, and stipulates that upon his failure to do so, the insured shall be a coinsurer and bear his proportionate part of the loss on the deficit in the coverage. 29A Am J Rev ed Ins § 1548.

coinsurer. One of two or more insurers who have issued policies covering the same risk, and who contribute ratably in case of loss. Chesbrough v Home Ins. Co. 61 Mich 333, 335; the position or status of the insured under a coinsurance clause.
See **coinsurance clause.**

coition (kō-ish'on). Copulation; sexual intercourse; the consummation of marriage. Anonymous, 89 Ala 291, 7 So 100.

coitus (kō'i-tus). Copulation; sexual intercourse.

coitus interruptus. Withdrawal before emission. 4 Am J2d Annul § 6.

cojudices (kō-jū'di-sēz). Associate judges.

Coke. A renowned English jurist who served as Lord Chief Justice of England and contributed notably in opinions and legal articles to the development of the common law.
See **Institutes of Coke; Littleton.**

col. (kol). An abbreviation of the word "colored," used with reference to a person. Collins v Oklahoma State Hospital, 76 Okla 229, 184 P 946, 7 ALR 895, 899.

cold storage. The preservation of food by storage in a room where the temperature is kept at a low degree, sometimes in a refrigerating vault or chamber, yet not necessarily at a temperature below freezing for all foods in the place. Allen v Somers, 73 Conn 355, 47 A 653.

cold-wall method. A term descriptive of a method of handling milk in the dairyman's barn. Southside Co-op. Milk, etc. Asso. 198 Va 108, 92 SE2d 353.

cold-water ordeal. A trial by ordeal in which the defendant was thrown into cold water; if he sank, he was deemed innocent; if he floated, he was found guilty.

colessee (kō-le-sē'). One of two or more joint lessees.

colessor (kō-les'or). One of two or more joint lessors.

colibertus (kō-li-ber'tus). A tenant in free socage who was nevertheless under a duty of rendering some service to the lord.

Co. Litt. An abbreviation of Coke's Littleton.
See **Institutes of Coke; Littleton.**

collapse. Falling in or falling together; shrinking so that sides meet; the antithesis of "explosion." Louisville Underwriters v Durland, 123 Ind 544, 24 NE 221.

collapse of building. A falling in, loss of shape, or flattening of a building, or some other disastrous occurrence which causes a building to lose its distinctive character as a building. Central Mut. Ins. Co. v Royal, 269 Ala 372, 113 So 2d 680, 72 ALR2d 1283.

collapsible corporation. A corporation organized under a prearranged plan for its liquidation before there is opportunity for it to realize any or any substantial taxable income. IRC § 341.

collat. Abbreviation for **collateral.**

collateral. Noun: Stocks or bonds accompanying an obligation as security therefor; a collateral relative. Adjective: Accompanying in the sense of going side by side, as security accompanying the principal obligation.

collateral act. An act the performance of which is secured by a bond.

collateral agreement. See **collateral contract.**

collateral ancestors. A paradoxical term, since ancestors are those persons from whom one is lineally or directly descended, but occasionally used for aunts, uncles, and other collateral relatives of older generations. Banks v Walker (NY) 3 Barb Ch 438, 446.

collateral assurance. A deed or conveyance made subsequently to the original one for the purpose of perfecting the grantee's title.
See **covenant for further assurance.**

collateral attack. Attempting to impeach or challenging the integrity of a judgment, decree, or order in an action or proceeding other than that in which the judgment, decree, or order was rendered, other than by appeal from, or review of, the judgment, decree, or order, and other than an action or proceeding instituted for the express purpose of annulling, correcting, or modifying the judgment, decree, or order, or enjoining its execution. Morrill v Morrill, 20 Or 96, 25 P 362; an attack upon a judgment, decree, or order offered, in an action or proceeding other than that in which it was obtained, in support of the allegations or contentions of an adversary in the action or proceeding, as where the judgment is offered in support of a title or as a foundation for applying the doctrine of res judicata. 30A Am J Rev ed Judgm § 851.
    An attack is collateral if made upon a judgment in an action that has an independent purpose other than impeaching a judgment, even though impeaching the particular judgment may be essential to the success of the action. Hoverstad v First Nat. Bank & Trust Co. 76 SD 119, 74 NW2d 48, 56 ALR2d 938.

collateral attack on judgment. See **collateral attack.**

collateral consanguinity. A blood relationship between persons under a descent from a common ancestor but by different lines; the relationship between persons who descend from the same stirps or root but who do not lineally descend from each other. One's brothers and cousins are his collateral relatives, that is, in collateral consanguinity with him. 23 Am J2d Desc & D § 42.

collateral contract. A contract prior to, or contemporaneous with, a deed, which, if not incorporated in the deed, is not effective to limit the estate conveyed or bind directly the use of the property included in the grant, but may be given effect as a personal covenant binding upon the parties and persons in privity of estate and having notice. 28 Am J2d Est § 137.
See **collateral contract doctrine.**

collateral contract doctrine. An exception to the parol evidence rule, similar in many respects to the doctrine of partial integration, which permits proof by parol of a separate and independent verbal contract between the parties to a written contract under the principle that the parol evidence rule does not affect a purely collateral contract distinct from, and independent of, the written agreement. 36 Am J2d Ev § 1016.

collateral covenant. A covenant in a deed which does not relate to the grant.
See **collateral contract.**

collateral descent. Descent to collateral relatives, as from brother to brother, cousin to cousin, etc. Anno: 54 ALR2d 1009.

collaterales et socii (kol-la-te-rā′les et sō′she-ī). Masters in chancery.

collateral estoppel. Another expression for the doctrine of estoppel by judgment or, as used in some instances, for the doctrine of res judicata. 30A Am J Rev ed Judgm § 328; the doctrine of res judicata in relation to administrative agencies. 2 Am J2d Admin L § 324.
See **estoppel by judgment; res judicata.**

collateral facts. Facts which are inadmissible in evidence because they are incapable of affording any reasonable presumption or inference as to the principal fact or matter in dispute. Darling v Westmoreland, 52 NH 401.

collateral fraud. Same as **extrinsic fraud.**

collateral guaranty. An anomalous expression, since a guaranty is inherently collateral, being collateral to the principal obligation, but used by way of emphasizing the existence of a guaranty in the strict sense of the term, in which the obligation of the guarantor is to pay if the principal shall fail to pay or perform, as distinguished from a suretyship, in which the surety is obligated under a direct promise or undertaking to pay or perform. Nading v McGregor, 121 Ind 465, 23 NE 283.

collateral heir. An heir by collateral descent, such as a brother or cousin. Anno: 54 ALR2d 1009.

collateral impeachment. A collateral attack. Racey v Racey, 12 Okla 650, 73 P 305.
See **collateral attack.**

collateral inheritance tax. An inheritance or succession tax on the devolution of property under the laws of descent or under a will to the collateral relatives of the decedent or persons other than the spouse, descendants, or parents of the decedent. 28 Am J Rev ed Inher T § 11.

collateral issues. Issues arising in a case which do not involve the merits of the controversy.
See **collateral facts.**

collateral kinsmen. Blood relatives of a person other than his lineal relatives.
See **collateral consanguinity.**

collateral limitation. A limitation provided for in a conveyance which gives an interest for a prescribed period, but makes the right to possess or enjoy the thing conveyed to depend upon some collateral event. Templeman v Gibbs, 86 Tex 358, 362, 24 SW 792.

collateral matter. See **collateral facts.**

collateral power. A power, otherwise known as a "naked power" or "power without interest," to dispose of property, given to a stranger, that is, one having no interest or estate in the property. Columbia Trust Co. v Christopher, 133 Ky 335, 344, 117 SW 943.

collateral proceeding. An action or proceeding wherein a judgment is attacked collaterally, that is, without seeking directly the overturning of the judgment. Alford v Guffy (Ky) 115 SW 216, 217. See **collateral attack.**

collateral promise to answer for the debt of another. An undertaking which renders the promisor a guarantor or surety upon a debt owing by a third person who is primarily liable; a promise to pay the debt of another person made under such circumstances that, as between the debtor and the promisor, the former should pay. 49 Am J1st Stat of F § 61; an undertaking by a person not before liable for the purpose of securing or performing the same duties for which the party for whom the undertaking is made continues liable. Goldsmith v Erwin (CA4 NC) 183 F2d 432, 20 ALR2d 240.

collateral relative. See **collateral consanguinity.**

collateral security. An additional security, in the form of an article of value or an evidence of indebtedness, for the payment of a debt, or the performance of an obligation, whether the debt or obligation be antecedent or newly created, designed to increase the means of the creditor or obligee to realize upon the debt or obligation, and given to the creditor or obligee to be held by him as subsidiary to the principal debt or obligation and as running parallel with such debt or obligation, so that when it is collected by the creditor or obligee, the proceeds are to go to the credit of the principal debt or obligation, or, if the principal debt or obligation be paid, satisfied, or performed without realizing upon the collateral, the latter shall be returned to the debtor or obligor. Seanor & Bierer v McLaughlin, 165 P 150, 30 A 717.

collateral source rule. The rule of damages that benefits received by the plaintiff from a source wholly independent of and collateral to the wrongdoer will not diminish the damages otherwise recoverable. 22 Am J2d Damg § 206.

collateral succession tax. See **collateral inheritance tax.**

collateral undertaking. See **collateral contract; collateral promise to answer for the debt of another.**

collateral warranty. A warranty of a title made by a person who is a stranger to the title. As a general rule, the covenant of a stranger to the title is personal to the covenantee and is incapable of transmission by a mere conveyance of the land. 20 Am J2d Cov § 36.

collatio bonorum (kol-lā'she-ō bo-nō'rum). Collation of advancements or hotchpot.

collation (ko-lā'shon). The comparison of a copy with the original document.

See **collation of advancements; collation of seals; collation to a benefice.**

collatione facta uni post mortem alterius (kol-lā-shē-ō'ne fak'ta ū'nī post mor'tem al-tē'ri-us). A writ commanding the justices to issue their writ to the bishop to admit a clerk instead of one who has died since he was appointed by the king.

collation of advancements. The grouping with the assets of a decedent's estate of an intestate's estate of the value of property given by him by way of advancement to heirs or distributees during his lifetime, so that the whole may be divided so far as possible in accordance with the statutes of descent and distribution, each share being charged with what has already been received.

collation of seals. A comparison of seals.

collation to a benefice. The conferring of a benefice by a bishop who holds the patronage.

collatio signorum (kol-lā'she-ō sig-nō'rum). A comparison of seals.

collect. To receive payment; to do that which may be lawfully done by the holder of the obligation to secure its payment or liquidation after its maturity. Hutson v Rankin, 36 Idaho 169, 213 P 345, 33 ALR 91, 95. As used in a statute allowing an employer of an injured employee to "collect" indemnity from the wrongdoer, the word imports an act of payment without reference to the legal grounds on which payment may be demanded. The word is not usually employed in a statute creating legal liability. Walters v Eagle Indem. Co. 166 Tenn 383, 61 SW2d 666, 88 ALR 654.

collecting agent. An agent of an insurance company who is authorized to accept payment of the premium. 29 Am J Rev ed Ins § 560.

collect in the ordinary way. A direction which authorizes the employment of a bank as a subagent for the purpose of collecting. 3 Am J2d Agency § 137.

collection. A group of things assembled, as a collection of rocks; an item of business of a collection agency or, as the term is sometimes used, of a lawyer in the commercial line; the act of receiving payment of a debt, whether payment be voluntary or compelled by legal action or process.

See **costs of collection; deposit for collection.**

collection agency. A person or firm engaged in the business of collecting or receiving for payment claims of all kinds on behalf of others. 15 Am J2d Collect § 1.

See **collection service.**

collection district. One of the districts into which the United States is divided for the purpose of the collection of customs duties. 21 Am J2d Cust D § 60.

collection service. A collection agency; a business, otherwise known as a skip-tracing agency, which provides creditors with mailing materials and other services to assist them in the collection of accounts by helping them locate delinquent debtors and by uncovering financial and other information about such debtors. 15 Am J2d Collect § 1.

collective bargaining. A course of conduct or process calculated to insure freedom of negotiation in the settlement of issues involved in labor disputes and to facilitate an arrival at equitable understandings respecting hours of employment, wages, working conditions, and other matters of concern in employer-employee relationships. The negotiation of terms and conditions of employment between an organization acting on behalf of the employed, and an employer, or association of employers, in contradistinction to bargaining between an employer and an individual employee. Anno: 95 ALR 11. The right of a labor union to bargain collectively on behalf of its members, including by implication that which is reasonably necessary to protect that right. Art Metals Constr. Co. v NLRB (CA2) 110 F2d 148. Whatever may have been the law of earlier times, it is now crystal clear that the rights of workingmen to organize and to designate their representatives for purposes of collective bargaining are clearly recognized both by the courts and statutes. No longer can there be doubt that a labor union when authorized by its members may make contracts in their behalf. 31 Am J Rev ed Lab § 86. As contemplated by the National Labor Relations Act, collective bargaining is a procedure looking toward the making of a collective agreement between the employer and the accredited representative of his employees concerning wages, hours and other conditions of employment. It requires that the parties involved deal with each other with an open and fair mind and sincerely endeavor to overcome obstacles or difficulties existing between the employer and the employees to the end that employment relations may be stabilized and obstruction to the free flow of commerce prevented. NLRB v Boss Mfg. Co. (CA7) 118 F2d 187.

collective bargaining agreement. See **collective labor agreement.**

collective bargaining unit. As defined by statute, the term means all of the employees of one employer except where a majority of such employees engaged in a single craft, division, department, or plant, shall have voted to constitute such group a separate bargaining unit. Re International Asso. of Machinists, 249 Wis 112, 23 NW2d 489; 174 ALR 1267.

collective examination. A form of examination of jurors whereby questions are put to the jurors in the box collectively, each juror answering as answers are required. Ordinarily, this form of examination is used for statutory or routine questions, after which counsel interrogates each juror individually. 31 Am J Rev ed Jur § 137.

collective facts rule. See **composite facts rule.**

collective labor agreement. An agreement, sometimes known as a "collective bargaining agreement" or "trade agreement," reached by bargaining as to wages and conditions of work, entered into by groups of employees, usually organized into a union or brotherhood, on one side, and an employer or groups of employers on the other side. Anno: 88 L Ed 776; 31 Am J Rev ed Lab § 90. A contract between the employer and the employees acting through the agency of the representative organization or group. 31 Am J Rev ed Lab § 91.

It is not the equivalent of an individual contract of employment between the employer and each employee, but an agreement between the representative organization and employer laying down certain conditions of employment which, it is contemplated, are to be incorporated in the separate contracts of hiring with each employee. MacKay v Loew's, Inc. (CA9 Cal) 182 F2d 170, 18 ALR2d 348.

Such an agreement may be a brief statement of labor and wages, or, on the other hand, it may take the form of a book or an exhaustive pamphlet regulating, in greatest minuteness, every condition under which labor is to be performed, and touching upon such subjects as strikes, lockouts, walkouts, seniority, apprentices, shop conditions, safety devices, and group insurance. Rentschler v Missouri Pacific R. R. Co. 126 Neb 493, 253 NW 694, 95 ALR 1.

collective naturalization. The admission to citizenship of considerable bodies of persons by treaty or by act of Congress. 3 Am J2d Aliens § 131.

collective trademark. A device, mark, label, or symbol used to identify a fraternal benefit society, insurance company, or trade association. R. M. Hollingshead Corp. v Davies-Young Soap Co. 28 Cust & Pat App (Pat) 1286, 121 F2d 500.

collect on delivery. A provision, usually abbreviated to c.o.d., in a contract of shipment, whereby the carrier undertakes to collect from the consignee, upon delivery, a specified amount for and on behalf of the consignor, in addition to the carrier's own charges. 13 Am J2d Car § 454.

collector. A special administrator appointed by the court to collect and preserve a decedent's estate pending the appointment of an executor or administrator; one who collects accounts receivable for another person or business; one who collects taxes or duties due the United States, a state, or public body, such as a **collector of customs** or **tax collector.**

collector of births and burials. An English officer whose duty it is to make weekly reports of the births and burials to the magistrates.

collector of customs. An officer of the United States for the collection of customs duties and the performance of such other duties as the Secretary of the Treasury may prescribe. 5 USC § 281; 21 Am J2d Cust D § 64.

For some purposes, the term "collector" means collector of customs and includes assistant collector of customs, deputy collector of customs, and any person authorized by law or by regulations of the Secretary of the Treasury to perform the duties of a collector of customs. 19 USC § 1401(h).

collector of the port. A collector of customs. See **collector of customs.**

collega (ko-leg'ạ). A co-officer or appointee.

collegatarius (ko-leg'ạ-tā-rius). A co-legatee, a beneficiary named with another or with others in a will.

college. An institution of learning, having corporate powers, and possessing the right to confer degrees, and which, with reference to its educational work, consists of the trustees, teachers, and scholars or students, all of whom make up the membership of the college and represent its active work. 15 Am J2d Colleges § 1; an institution of higher learning, usually incorporated, admitting graduates of approved high schools and preparatory schools, and offering them instruction in arts, letters, and sciences, leading to a bachelor's degree; a building or group of buildings in which students are housed, fed, instructed, and governed while qualifying for university degrees, whether the university includes a number of colleges or a single college. Yale University v New Haven, 71 Conn 316, 42 A 87.

See **electoral college.**

college education. The education attained by attending college. The term "completion of a college education" ordinarily means the completion of the four-year undergraduate course culminating in a bachelor of arts degree, but not post graduate work. Epstein v Juvin, 25 NJ Super 210, 95 A2d 753, 36 ALR2d 1320. The term "college education," appearing in a decree requiring a parent to provide for the education of a child includes maintenance of the child for four years in college and the incidents thereto, such as board, lodging and laundry, for the full twelve months of each of the four years, but to be confined to a four-year undergraduate course leading to a bachelor's degree, and not to include post graduate work. Anno: 36 ALR2d 1325-1329.

college fraternities. See **fraternities.**

college graduate. See **graduate.**

collegia (ko-lē'ji-a). Corporations.

collegialiter (ko-lē'ji-al-i-ter). As a corporation.

collegiate church. An English church which has a chapter consisting of a dean, canons and prebends, but which has no bishop's see.

collegium (ko-lē'ji-um). A corporation; a college; an ecclesiastical body which is not controlled by the state. See 1 Bl Comm 469.
See **universitas.**

Collegium est societas plurium corporum simul habitantium (kol-lē'ji-um est sō-si'e-tās plū'ri-um kor'-pō-rum si'mul ha-bi-tan'she-um). A college is a society composed of many persons living together.

collide. To strike or dash against each other; to come into collision. Carey v Pacific Gas & Electric Co. 75 Cal App 129, 242 P 97.
See **collision.**

colliery (kol'yėr-i). A coal mine.

colligendum bona defuncti (kol-li-jen'dum bo'na dē-funk'tī). The collection of the goods of a decedent.
See **collector.**

collision. The act of striking or dashing together of two bodies, the meeting and mutual striking or clashing of two or more moving bodies or of a moving body with a stationary body. Great American Mut. Indem. Co. v Jones, 111 Ohio St 84, 144 NE 596, 35 ALR 1023. A risk of loss covered by an automobile insurance policy. 7 Am J2d Auto Ins § 57.
See **collision of aircraft; collision of automobiles; collision of vessels.**

collision insurance. A kind of automobile insurance which, under customary practices of the business of insurance, appears as one of the risks covered by a more comprehensive policy. 7 Am J2d Auto Ins § 57. The coverage of collision insurance naturally depends upon the meaning attributable to the term "collision."
See **collision; collision of automobiles.**

collision of aircraft. Mid air collisions and ground collisions between aircraft; a collision between an aircraft and another vehicle. 8 Am J2d Avi § 92.

collision of automobiles. The impact of two or more motor vehicles. If unlimited by other provisions of the policy, the term "collision," in an automobile insurance policy covering the risk of collision, means coming in contact with anything that could be described as an object, irrespective of whether it is moving or stationary or whether it is on the same plane or level as the motor vehicle which hit it. Anno: 23 ALR2d 398; 7 Am J2d Auto Ins § 59. The term "collision" in a motor carrier liability policy has been held to include contact between the load on a truck with an object, such as an overhead bridge, but it is not to be said under the present state of the authorities, that this is a view which is certain to be followed in all jurisdictions. 29A Am J Rev ed Ins § 1357.

collision of motor vehicles. See **collision of automobiles.**

collision of vessels. The coming together with force of two navigating vessels. 2 Am J2d Adm § 56; the impact of a vessel with another vessel or other floating object. 29A Am J Rev ed Ins § 1317; a peril of the sea within the meaning of a marine insurance policy. 29A Am J Rev ed Ins § 1316.

Within the meaning of a marine insurance policy, a ship is in collision when the circumstances can be fairly described, within the ordinary use of language, as amounting to a collision. An impairment of seaworthiness of a vessel caused by contact with another is not essential to a collision, and vessels may be in collision although one is temporarily aground, at anchor, or at her dock. In this country the term has in time and by common usage been extended to include the impact of the vessel with other floating objects. But the English cases hold that the term applies only to the striking together of two navigable vessels, and that it does not apply to a case where a vessel runs into a sunken object, or a stationary or permanent obstruction; and in the United States it has been held no collision where a vessel strikes some sunken obstruction in the water. 29A Am J Rev ed Ins § 1317.

collistrigium (kol-li-stri'ji-um). The pillory.

collitigant (ko-lit'i-gant). A person who litigates with another or against another.

collocation (kol-ō-kā'shon). A classification of the creditors of an estate made for the purpose of paying them off in proper order.

colloquium (ko-lō'kwi-um). The allegations in a complaint, declaration, or petition in an action for libel or slander which point to the plaintiff as the person defamed, allegations of specific facts being required by the common law, general allegations that the defamatory matter was published or spoken of the plaintiff being sufficient under the statutes of many jurisdictions. 33 Am J1st L & S § 240.

collude (ko-lūd'). To enter into a collusion.

collusion. An agreement between two or more persons to defraud another of his rights by the forms of law or to secure an object forbidden by law. Warren v Union Bank, 157 NY 259, 51 NE 1056. An agreement, between persons interested in bidding in the letting of a contract for construction of a public improvement, which has for its purpose the suppression or diminishing of competition between bidders. 43 Am J1st Pub Wks § 15. As a defense in a divorce case: an agreement between a husband and wife to obtain or facilitate the obtaining of a divorce by having the accused spouse commit, or appear to commit, or be falsely represented in court as having committed, an act which constitutes a ground for divorce, or to suppress or refrain from presenting evidence which would prove or tend to prove a defense to an action for divorce. 24 Am J2d Div & S § 190.

collusive. Resulting from or tainted with collusion.
See **collusion.**

collusive action. See **collusive suit.**

collusive bids. See **collusion.**

collusive divorce. A divorce obtained by collusion between the parties.
See **collusion.**

collusive spoliation. The damaging of a vessel, which is a tort within admiralty jurisdiction. 2 Am J2d Adm § 78.

collusive suit. An action brought by collusion, without any real controversy to adjudicate. Haley v Eureka County Bank, 21 Nev 127, 26 P 64; an action intended to obtain a judicial opinion rather than to decide and determine an actual and existing controversy. 1 Am J2d Actions § 56.

collybist (kol'i-bist). A money changer.

collybum (kol'i-bum). (Civil law.) Exchange; the rate of exchánge.

Colonel. An officer of the army, usually in command of a regiment, and ranking just below a brigadier general, an honorary title conferred formally or informally upon a person worthy of respect.

colonial. Pertaining to the colonies of the English government, known as the American colonies; pertaining to colonies; subservient rather than free and independent.

colonial court. Any of the courts held in the colonies before Independence.

colonial laws (kǫ-lō'ni-ạl lâs). The laws enacted by the legislatures of the American colonies of England, prior to the Revolutionary War; laws enacted in the colonies of Great Britain.

colonna. See **di colonna**.

colonus (ko-lō'nus). A serf; a husbandman.

colony (kol'ǫ-ni). A body of emigrants who settle abroad, but who remain loyal to their mother country; a dependency; territory attached to a nation, known as the mother country, by ties of allegiance and usually by economic and political compacts or arrangements.

color. Mere semblance of a legal right. State ex rel. West v Des Moines, 96 Iowa 521, 65 NW 818; a characteristic of some races of men, but of primary legal significance in reference to Negroes; a personal characteristic of vivid quality, usually with some measure of flamboyance.
See **colored; colored person; color of title**.

colorable case. See **colorable cause**.

colorable cause. A case which upon the facts stated in a complaint or accusation is sufficient to invoke the jurisdiction of an inferior court to issue process. Broom v Douglass, 175 Ala 268, 57 So 860.

colorable claim. A claim which superficially is proper and well-founded, but may actually be invalid; a claim to property by a person in possession against the demand of a trustee in bankruptcy for possession, made in bad faith and without legal justification or so lacking in substance and merit as to amount to a mere pretense. 9 Am J2d Bankr § 52.

colorable imitation. An imitation calculated to deceive.

colorable invocation of jurisdiction. See **colorable cause**.

colorable transaction. A transaction which presents an appearance which does not correspond with the reality and is intended to conceal or to deceive. Osborn v Osborn, 102 Kan 890, 172 P 23.
See **fraudulent conveyance**.

color blindness. An absence or great weakness of the sensations upon which the power of distinguishing colors must be founded. It is not a mere incapacity for distinguishing colors, for this might be due to lack of training. Kane v Chicago, Burlington & Quincy Railroad Co. 90 Neb 112, 114, 132 NW 920.

colore. See **ex colore**.

colored. As applied to a person, one of a colored race, which ordinarily means a Negro. Collins v Oklahoma State Hospital, 76 Okla 229, 184 P 946, 7 ALR 895, 899.

colored person. Literally, one of a race other than the white race, but generally understood, in the absence of a statutory definition to the contrary, to mean persons of Negro blood, the black people of Africa, known as Negroes, and their descendants of mixed or unmixed blood, at least those with a predominance of Negro blood. 35 Am J1st Mar § 146; 47 Am J1st Sch § 216.
See **Negro**.

colore officii (ko-lō're of-fi'si-ī). Color of office.

color of authority. Authority derived from an election or appointment, however irregular or informal, so that the incumbent is not a mere volunteer. State ex rel. Brockmeier v Ely, 16 ND 569, 113 NW 711.

color of law. Mere semblance of a legal right. State ex rel. West v Des Moines, 96 Iowa 521, 65 NW 818.

color of office. An expression for acts performed by an officer which are entirely outside of or beyond the authority conferred by the office. Haffner v United States Fidelity & Guaranty Co. 35 Idaho 517, 207 P 716; Wilson v Fowler, 88 Md 601, 42 A 201.

color of title. The appearance but not the reality in title. 27 Am J1st Improv § 11; that which gives the semblance or appearance of title, but is not title in fact—that which, on its face, professes to pass title, but fails to do so because of a want of title in the person from whom it comes or the employment of an ineffective means of conveyance. 3 Am J2d Adv P § 96.

colorogal. A liquid used in taking an X-ray picture of an organ of the body by injecting it so as to render the organ opaque. United States Fidelity & G. Co. v Wickline, 103 Neb 681, 173 NW 689.

colportage (kol'pōr-tǎj). The sending forth of persons to labor for the spread of the Gospel by distributing religious books and tracts. Anno: 17 ALR 1052.

colporteur (kol'pōr-tẻr). A person who travels for the sale and distribution of religious tracts and books; a hawker and peddler, especially, in modern usage, a peddler of religious books. Will of Fuller, 75 Wis 431, 436.

colt. An animal of the horse family, not more than three years old, or even younger, depending upon local terminology; a young person with little experience.

columbarium (kol-um-bā'ri-um). A building containing niches in which are placed urns containing the ashes of the deceased after cremation. 14 Am J2d Cem § 1.

comaker. A joint maker.
See **joint maker**.

combat. Noun: A fight or battle. Verb: To fight; to engage in battle. As the word appears in a clause excepting injuries received in combat, the term imports causation, aggression or fault on the part of the insured. 29A Am J Rev ed Ins § 1201.
See **mutual combat**.

combe (kōm). A narrow valley.

combination. An object produced by uniting two or more objects; a combine in the sense of something creating a monopoly; an invention, that is, an instrument created by bringing elements in composition. 40 Am J1st Pat § 19.
See **combine.**

combine. An agreement or arrangement which is illegal under anti-trust statutes or statutes intended to prevent monopolies in that it tends to create a monopoly or is in restraint of trade, or involves a delegation of corporate powers and is inimical to the public welfare. 36 Am J1st Monop etc § 132; a farm implement by which the cutting and threshing of grain is performed in one operation.

combined bill. A bill in equity combining a supplemental bill and a bill of revivor. See 27 Am J2d Eq § 179.

comburgess (kom-bėr′jes). An inhabitant of the same borough as another.

combustio (kom-bust′she-ō). A burning.

combustio domorum (kom-bust′she-ō do-mō′rum). The burning of houses,—arson.

combustio pecuniae (kom-bust-she-ō pe-kū′ni-ē). The testing of money by melting it.

come. To appear in court.

comes (kums). An introductory word in a formalized pleading, indicating an appearance to plead, for example, "Now comes the defendant, and answering the complaint of the plaintiff, states as follows," etc. (Latin). A comrade or associate.

come semble (ko-m′ sän-bl). As it seems.

comes stabuli (ko′mēz sta′bu-lī). Count of the stable; a constable. See 1 Bl Comm 355.

comfort. Consolation; freedom from want; pleasure; satisfaction; reasonable physical, spiritual, and mental enjoyment. Everett v Paschall, 61 Wash 47, 111 P 879; National Surety Co. v Jarrett, 95 W Va 420, 121 SE 291, 36 ALR 1171, 1176.

comfortable enjoyment. Mental quiet and physical comfort. Everett v Paschall, 61 Wash 47, 111 P 879.

coming to a nuisance. The doctrine, which is now against the weight of authority, that one who moves into the neighborhood of an existing nuisance cannot complain of it. 39 Am J1st Nuis § 197.

coming to rest. A doctrine, applied to the loading and unloading clause of a truck liability policy, which limits the coverage in unloading to the period of the actual removing or lifting of the article from the motor vehicle, which is deemed to terminate the moment when the article which was taken off the vehicle has actually come to rest and every connection of the motor vehicle with the process of unloading has ceased. Stammer v Kitzmiller, 226 Wis 348, 276 NW 629.

cominus (ko′mi-nus). Hand to hand; in close combat.

comitas (kom′i-tas). Comity; courtesy.

comitas inter communitates (kom′i-tas in′tėr kom-mū-ni-tā′tēz). Comity between states. Re Perkins, 2 Cal 424, 448.

comitate. Comity; courtesy.

comitatus (kom-i-tā′tus). A county. The word is probably derived from the Frankish word "count," meaning an earl or alderman of a shire, to whom the government of it was intrusted. This he usually exercised by his deputy, still called in Latin "vice-comes," and in English, the "sheriff," "shrieve," or "shire-reeve," signifying the officer of the shire upon whom, in course of time, the civil administration of it totally devolved. See 1 Bl Comm 116.
See **posse comitatus.**

comites (kom′i-tēs). Plural of comes; attendants; companions.

comitia (kō-mish′iạ). (Roman law.) Assemblies of the people.

comitia centuriata (kō-mish′i-a sen-tu-ri-ā′ta). An assembly of the Romans in which they voted by centuries or hundreds.

comitia curiata (kō-mish′i-a kū-ri-a-ta). A Roman assembly which was composed of thirty patricians.

comitia tributa (kō-mish′i-a tri-bū′ta). An assembly of the Romans in which they voted by tribes or neighborhoods.

comitissa (ko-mi-tis′sa). A countess.

comitiva (ko-mi-tī′va). The office of an earl or count.

comity. Literally, courtesy or civility, to which the law adds some refinements in defining the term for the purposes of conflicts of laws and international law:—Neither a matter of absolute obligation on the one hand nor a mere courtesy and good will on the other, but the recognition which one nation or state allows within its territory to the legislative, executive, or judicial acts of another nation or state, having due regard both to international duty and convenience and to the rights of its own citizens or of other persons who are under the protection of its laws. 16 Am J2d Confl L § 4; 30 Am J Rev ed Internat L § 6.

comity inter gentes (in′tėr jen′tēz). The comity of or between nations.

comity of nations. The extent to which the law of one state or nation is allowed to operate within the dominion of another. 16 Am J2d Confl L § 4.
See **comity.**

comma. A punctuation mark. The comma and semicolon are both used for the same purpose, namely, to divide sentences and parts of sentences, the only difference being that the semicolon makes the division a little more pronounced than the comma; but at the last it is the sense of the words, taken together, that dictates where the punctuation marks are to be placed, and what they shall be. Holmes v Phenix Ins. Co. (CA8 Mo) 98 F 240.

command. See **request; require; required.**

commander-in-chief. See **President of the United States.**

commanditaire (kom-mon-di-tãr′). A silent partner.

commandite (kom-mon-dēt′). A special partnership.

commandment. An ancient English offense consisting of directing or commanding a person to do an unlawful act.

commark (kom′ärk). A frontier; a boundary.

comme (kom). (French.) As, since, because; whereas.

commencement of action. Demanding something by the institution of process in a court of justice. Cohen v Virginia (US) 6 Wheat 408, 5 L Ed 257. In some jurisdictions, the issuance of process is the commencement of an action; in other jurisdictions an action is not commenced until the process is delivered to the sheriff or other officer for the purpose of having him serve it upon the defendant; in still other jurisdictions, an action is not commenced until the process is actually served. 1 Am J2d Actions § 86. An attempt to commence an action is sometimes deemed the equivalent of the commencement of an action. Goldenberg v Murphy, 108 US 162, 27 L Ed 686, 2 S Ct 388.

commencement of action at law. At common law, an action was commenced and pending from the first moment of the day on which the writ was issued and bore teste. Newman v Chapman, 23 Va (2 Rand) 93.

For definition in accord with modern practice, see **commencement of action.**

commencement of a prosecution. See **commencement of criminal proceeding.**

commencement of criminal proceeding. A phrase variously defined, some authorities saying that a criminal proceeding is commenced on the filing of a complaint, preliminary information, or affidavit, others saying that the issuance of a warrant for arrest and the placing of it in the hands of an officer for service is the commencement of a criminal proceeding, and still others insisting that the arrest is the commencement of such a proceeding.

There is, moreover, authority for the view that a prosecution for a felony is not commenced before the return of an indictment or information, notwithstanding the prior arrest of the accused and his commitment, such view being that all proceedings prior to indictment or information are only preliminary to a prosecution. 21 Am J2d Crim L § 3.

commencement of suit in equity. The filing of a bill or complaint in the office of the clerk of the court. 27 Am J2d Eq § 177.

For more modern view as to the commencement of an action, see **commencement of action.**

commencement of risk. See **inception of risk.**

commencement of work. According to some authority, the time at which a mechanic's lien, at least an inchoate lien, attaches to the property under improvement. 36 Am J1st Mech L § 167. The term means some work and labor on the ground, the effects of which are apparent—easily seen by everybody—such as beginning to dig the foundation, or work of like description, which everyone can readily see and recognize as the commencement of a building. English v Olympic Auditorium, 217 Cal 631, 20 P2d 946, 87 ALR 1281.

commend (kọ-mend'). To praise; to recommend; to place under the care of another.

commenda (kọ-mend'ạ). An association in which the management of the property of the association was entrusted to individuals. The delivery of a benefice to one not of a status to permit him to hold legal title.

commendam (ko-men'dam). The appointment of a temporary clergyman to hold a living pending the appointment of a regular parson.

commenda recipere (kom-men'da re-si'pe-re). To receive a commended living.

commenda retinere (kom-men'da re-ti-nē're). To retain a commended living.

commendatio (kom-men-dā'she-ō). A recommendation; praise.

commendation (kom-en-dā'shon). Praise; recommendation; the voluntary subjection of a freeman to a lord in order that he might secure the lord's protection.

commendator (kom'en-dā-tọr). A person holding a benefice in commendam, that is, pending the appointment of a regular parson.

commendatory letters (kọ-men'dạ-tō-ri). Letters of recommendation; letters of credence from a bishop in behalf of travelers from his diocese.

commendatus (kom-men-dā'tus). Voluntary service rendered to a superior.

comment. Remarks, observation, or criticism; gossip, discourse, talk; a note or observation intended to explain, illustrate, or criticise the meaning of a writing, book, etc.; explanation; annotation; exposition. United States v Dorr (Philippine Sup Ct) Appx, 47 L Ed 1187, 23 S Ct 859.

See **fair comment; unfair comment.**

commentary. Comment on one's observations in the form of notes; annotations or notes appended to the literary product of another. 18 Am J2d Copyr § 12.

Coke's commentaries on Littleton. See **Institutes of Coke.**

commerce. A term of broader significance than trade. 36 Am J1st Monop etc. § 157; buying and selling, traffic, intercourse for the purpose of trade, comprising every species of commercial intercourse. 15 Am J2d Com § 2; including the purchase, sale, exchanging, leasing, and distribution of commodities. Binderup v Pathe Exchange, 263 US 291, 68 L Ed 308, 44 S Ct 96; navigation and the transit of persons and property into the ports of the United States, navigation and the transit of persons and property. Mobile County v Kimball, 102 US 702, 26 L Ed 241; the transportation of persons and property as a business. Guinness v King County, 32 Wash 2d 503, 202 P2d 737, 6 ALR2d 1361; as the term appears in the Fair Labor Standards Act: —trade, commerce, transportation, transmission, or communication among the several states or between any state and any place outside thereof. 29 USC § 203(b); 31 Am J Rev ed Lab § 642.

The original definition of commerce connoting the exchange of merchandise on a large scale between different places or communities has been greatly enlarged, but the term still suggests that the transaction must be something other than trivial or incidental to a person's real purpose. Chauncey v Kinnaird (Ky) 279 SW2d 27, 51 ALR2d 1190.

See **foreign commerce; interstate commerce.**

commerce among the several states. See **among the several states; interstate commerce.**

commerce and trade. Business enterprises, not necessarily involving trading in merchandise. Frick v Webb, 263 US 326, 68 L Ed 323, 44 S Ct 115.

See **commerce.**

commerce clause. The third clause of the eighth section of the first article of the United States Constitution providing that Congress shall have power to regulate commerce with foreign nations, and among the several states, and with the Indian tribes.

Commerce Court. A court established by act of Congress of June 18, 1910, part of which was superseded by chapter 9 of the Judicial Code, and was abolished by act of October 3, 1913. Its jurisdiction embraced only complaints of affirmative action by the Interstate Commerce Commission.

commerce with foreign nations. See **commerce; foreign commerce.**

commerce with the Indian tribes. Commerce with the Indian tribes and with the Indians of the Indian tribes. 27 Am J1st Indians § 54.

commercia belli (kom-mer'she-a bel'lī). Contracts between citizens of belligerent countries.

commercial. Pertaining to the purchase and sale or exchange of goods and commodities and connoting as well forms of, and occupations in, business enterprises not involved in trading in merchandise; in a broad sense, embracing every phase of commercial and business activity and intercourse. Jordan v Tashiro, 278 US 123, 73 L Ed 214, 49 S Ct 47.

commercial agency. Literally, the agency of a commercial agent; a collection agency; in a more refined sense, an agency for the collection of past due accounts arising out of commercial transactions, that is, transactions not involving consumers. 15 Am J2d Collect § 1; a person, firm, or corporation engaged in the business of collecting information relating to the financial standing, credit, character, responsibility, and general reputation of persons, firms, and corporations engaged in business, and furnishing this information to subscribers for a consideration. 15 Am J2d Collect § 3.

commercial agent. Another term for a broker in merchandise; one who sells merchandise by sample, catalogue, or otherwise, without having possession of the goods. Re Orville S. Wilson (Dist Col) 8 Mackey 341. The term is also used to designate a consular officer in charge of the commercial interests of his country at a foreign port.

See **commercial agency.**

commercial airline. A carrier of freight and passengers by air. 8 Am J2d Avi § 38.

commercial bank. The ordinary bank of deposit and discount, with checking accounts, as distinguished from a savings bank operating on the mutual system in which the depositors are entitled to receive the profits of the business as dividends and in which withdrawal of a deposit is made only by presentation of the customer's passbook by him at the bank, no provision being made for checking against an account. 10 Am J2d Banks § 4.

commercial blockade. An instrumentality of naval warfare by which the forces of one belligerent interdict commerce between the other belligerent and neutral nations by investing the ports of the other belligerent with such forces as effectively to prevent ingress and egress. 56 Am J1st War § 171.

commercial bribery. Giving or receiving a gift for the purpose of influencing any agent to discharge improperly a duty entrusted to him by a private individual or corporation. 12 Am J2d Brib § 17. As an unfair trade practice this vice of commercial bribery is the advantage which one competitor secures over his fellow competitors by his secret and corrupt dealing with employees or agents of prospective purchasers. American Distilling Co. v Wisconsin Liquor Co. (CA7 Wis) 104 F2d 582, 123 ALR 739.

commercial broker. A broker in merchandise who negotiates sales without having possession or control of the goods. Adkins v Richmond, 98 Va 91, 34 SE 967.

See **commission merchant.**

commercial club. An organization of merchants and other businessmen of a village or small city which performs on a lesser scale the functions of a chamber of commerce in a larger city, promoting business in general, lending encouragement to new businesses, seeking new industries, working for improvement in highway traffic, better schools, more efficient public offices, and a fair tax structure, and sometimes promoting social relations between the members, at least to the extent of having semi-weekly luncheons.

Commercial Code. One of the uniform laws; a compilation of principles formulated through the joint efforts of the National Conference of Commissioners on Uniform State Laws and the American Law Institute dealing with most aspects of commercial transactions. 15 Am J2d Com C § 1.

commercial commodity. Any commodity which may be transported and which is an article which may be bought and sold in the markets of the country. Gas in the earth may not be a commercial commodity, but when brought to the surface and placed in pipes for transportation it must assume that character as completely as coal in the cars. State of Indiana ex rel. Corwin v Indiana & Ohio, Oil, Gas & Mining Co. 120 Ind 575, 22 NE 778.

commercial corporation. A corporation engaged in a business, the business which it is chartered to conduct and which it pursues for profit, not for charitable, benevolent, or social purposes. Union Oil Associates v Johnson, 2 Cal 2d 727, 43 P2d 291, 98 ALR 1499.

commercial domicil. A domicil acquired by residence in a country for the purposes of trading. 25 Am J2d Dom § 12.

A corporation is domiciled and has its residence in the state of its creation, although it engages in business elsewhere under local authority and has a "business situs" or "commercial domicil" there for taxation and other purposes. State v Garford Trucking, 4 NJ 346, 72 A2d 851, 16 ALR2d 1407.

commercial fertilizer. See **fertilizer.**

commercial frustration. An event which excuses nonperformance of a contract because it substantially frustrates the objects contemplated by the parties when they made the contract; an event which robs the contract of a foundation. 17 Am J2d Contr § 401. A prime example of commercial frustration is the situation where the subject matter of an executory contract is, because of wartime conditions, put under government control or requisitioned. 17 Am J2d Contr § 435.

commercial impracticable. Words which depict a situation involved in the performance of a contract which could not have been within the contemplation of the parties at the time the contract was made. Naylor, B. & Co. v Krainische Industrie Gesellschaft (Eng) 118 LT NS 442.

See **commercial frustration.**

commercial law. The law which relates to shipping, insurance, exchange of money, brokerage, bills of exchange, promissory notes, and other matters of concern to merchants and traders throughout the world, being, on account of the world wide extent of the operations which it governs, the least localized of legal systems with the exception only of international law. Brooklyn City & Newton R. R. Co. v National Bank of the Republic, 102 US (12 Otto) 14, 55, 26 L Ed 61, 76.

commercial letter of credit. See **letter of credit.**

commercially marketable mineral product. The salable product of a mine, not necessarily salable at a profit. United States v Cannelton Sewer Pipe Co. 364 US 76, 4 L Ed 2d 1581, 80 S Ct 1581.

commercial paper. Negotiable instruments, drafts, checks, certificates of deposit, and promissory notes. The term also includes bearer bonds where such are not specifically excluded from the classification by statute. 11 Am J2d B & N § 8.

The Uniform Commercial Code classifies paper in commercial transactions as "money paper," which is "commercial paper," "investment paper," and "commodity paper." Comment to UCC §§ 3-104, 7-104, 8-101.

See **bills of exchange; checks; promissory notes.**

commercial partnerships. Partnerships organized for the purpose of conducting trade or commerce; a more refined classification, made by statute in some jurisdictions, of partnerships formed for the purchase and sale of personal property as principals, or as factors or brokers, or for the carriage of personal property for hire in ships or other vessels. 40 Am J1st Partn § 11.

commercial railroad. A term applied to the former "interurbans," which operated between cities but ran part of their tracks on the streets or used the tracks of street car lines, carrying both passengers and freight. Anhalt v Waterloo, C. F. & N. Ry. Co. 166 Iowa 479, 147 NW 928; McClintock v Richlands Brick Corp. 152 Va 1, 145 SE 425, 61 ALR 1033.

commercial services by railroads. Services furnished by railroads not essential to the actual transportation of the goods. Baltimore & O. R. Co. v United States (DC NY) 20 F Supp 273.

commercial situs. See **business situs.**

commercial traveler. See **traveling salesmen.**

commercial use. Use in a business in which one is engaged for profit. Lintern v Zentz, 327 Mich 595, 42 NW2d 753, 18 ALR2d 713 (defining term as used in exception from coverage of an automobile liability policy); not necessarily exclusive of "use for business or pleasure." Anno: 18 ALR2d 721.

See **business use.**

commercial vehicle. A motor vehicle used other than for pleasure or private convenience of the owner. 7 Am J2d Auto § 69.

commercium (kom-mer'she-um). Commerce.

Commercium jure gentium commune esse debet et non in monopolium et privatum paucorum quaestum convertendum (kom-mer'she-um jū're jen'she-um kom-mū'ne es'se de'bet et non in mo-nō-pō'li-um et pri-vā'tum pau-kō'rum kwēs'tum kon-ver-ten'-dum). By the law of nations, commerce ought to be common and not converted into a monopoly and the private profit of a few persons.

comminatorium (ko-min-a-tō'ri-um). An admonition inserted in a writ, cautioning the sheriff to exercise diligence.

comminatory (ko-min'a-tō-ri). Threatening; coercive.

commingling of funds. A term often applied to the act of an agent, broker, attorney at law, or trustee in mingling the funds of his client, customer, or cestui with his own funds; the act of a fiduciary in mingling funds of different trusts. 54 Am J1st Trusts § 320; the act of a trustee in combining a trust fund with other funds in making an investment. 54 Am J1st Trusts § 396; the act of a guardian in mingling the funds of the ward with his own funds. 25 Am J1st G & W § 94.

commingling of goods. Confusion of goods. 1 Am J2d Access § 1.

comminute (kom'i-nūt). To macerate; to tear up; to reduce to minute particles; to crush or pulverize. Nordell v International Filter Co. (CA7 Ill) 119 F2d 948.

commis (ko-mē'). (French.) An agent.

commissari lex (kom-mis-sā'rī lex). (Roman law.) The right of a seller who extends credit to rescind the sale upon the buyer's default in payment.

commissariat (kom-i-sā'ri-at). The branch of the service in an army responsible for furnishing food and supplies. The jurisdiction of a commissary.

commissary (kom'i-sa-ri). An ecclesiastical officer whose functions were similar to those of an archdeacon. An older title for the officer of an army in command of the commissariat.

See **commissariat.**

commissary court (kom'i-sa-ri kōrt). A supreme court having a jurisdiction which was formerly exercised by the bishop's commissaries.

commission. A word of various meanings, one of the most common of which is that of a public board, usually an adminstrative body, such as a tax commission or civil service commission. 2 Am J2d Admin L § 8; an authority; a writ; an authorization; a written authority from a competent source given to a public officer as the warrant for the exercise of the powers and duties of the office which he occupies. 42 Am J1st Pub Of § 115; the authority under which a deposition is taken. 23 Am J2d Dep § 22; a fee or compensation calculated on a percentage basis, particularly the compensation of a sales agent; a form under which interest is charged in advance. Anno: 57 ALR2d 649-651.

commission-agent. An agent who buys or sells on commission.

See **commission merchant.**

commission day. The opening day of the assizes.

commission del credere (ko-mish'on del kre'de-re). See **del credere commission.**

commission de lunatico inquirendo (dē lū-nā'ti-kō in-que-ren'dō). Same as **commission of lunacy.**

commissioned officer. One who holds as evidence of right to office a commission signed by the president. Stephens v Civil Service Comm. 101 NJL 192, 127 A 808; any civil officer who has a written commission as evidence of his authority to hold and execute the authority of an office; one who holds rank in the military service under a commission issued by the proper authority.

commissioner. A person having a commission, letters patent, or other lawful warrant, to examine any matters, or to execute any public office, such as a commissioner of public safety in a city. Morris Canal & Banking Co. v State, 14 NJL 411, 428; one of the members of an administrative board or commission, 2 Am J2d Admin L § 8.

commissioner of banks. See **bank commissioner.**

commissioner of court. An officer of an admiralty court to whom certain matters in controversy are referred. 2 Am J2d Adm § 195; a person appointed to conduct a judicial sale. 30A Am J Rev ed Jud S § 37; a lawyer appointed to act as a court in hearing cases in order to clear a congested calendar.

See **commission of appeals.**

commissioner of deeds. An officer authorized to take acknowledgments and to perform other acts of the same nature as those performed by a notary public;

an officer authorized to take outside the state an acknowledgment of a deed or other instrument to be used within the state.

Commissioner of Internal Revenue. The head of the Internal Revenue Service, provision for the office being made by the Internal Revenue Code. 26 USC § 7801.

commissioner of jury. See **jury commissioner**.

Commissioner of Patents. The head of the bureau operating under the Secretary of the Interior, known as the Patent Office, whose primary duty is that of passing upon the merit of applications for letters patent. 40 Am J1st Pats §§ 10, 11.

Commissioner of United States. See **United States Commissioner**.

commissioners in partition. See **partition commissioners**.

commissioners of bail (kọ-mish'ọn-ėrs of bāl). Officers appointed by the court to take bail in cases of arrest on civil process.

commissioners of bankrupt. Persons who were appointed by the lord chancellor to act as a body to inquire and examine into the affairs of a bankrupt. 2 Bl Comm 480.

commissioners of highways. Local officers clothed with the duty of laying out and maintaining the public highways within their districts.
State highway commissioners. See **Highway Commission**.

commissioners of municipality. Officers forming the commission of a municipality, usually with the mayor, under the commission form of government. 37 Am J1st Mun Corp §§ 72 et seq.

commissioners of oyer and terminer. See **oyer and terminer**.

commissioners of sewers. Members of a sewer commission in a city having such a commission separate from a street commission; a one-time temporary tribunal in England having jurisdiction over repairs of sea banks and sea walls, the cleansing of rivers, public streams, ditches and other conduits by which any waters are carried off. This jurisdiction was limited to the particular county or district specified in the appointment of the body. 3 Bl Comm 73.

commission form of government. A system of municipal government, the details of which differ in different states but whose characteristic feature is the delegation of all executive and legislative powers to a single board consisting of a mayor and a very limited number of other officers, generally not more than four, known as commissioners. See 37 Am J1st Mun Corp § 72.

commission merchant. A term nearly, if not exactly, synonymous to factor, the term "factor" being more common in the language of the law, and the term "commission merchant" more familiar in the language of commerce. I. J. Cooper Rubber Co. v Johnson, 133 Tenn 562, 182 SW 593.
Some authorities, however, distinguish between commission merchants and factors in defining the former on the point of possession of the goods or merchandise sold, stating that a commission merchant is a person who sells goods in his own name at his own store, and on commission, although from samples, not having the goods in his possession, but obtaining possession as soon as sales are made, and delivering or shipping them to his customers. Slack v Tucker (US) 23 Wall 321, 23 L Ed 143. A commission merchant differs from a broker in that he may buy and sell in his own name without disclosing his principal, while a broker can only buy and sell in the name of his principal.

commission of appeals. A tribunal appointed to relieve an appellate court the calendar of which is overcrowded.

commission of array. A royal command for the drafting of soldiers for the army. See 1 Bl Comm 411.

commission of assize. A commission or authority appointing the justices and serjeants named therein to sit as judges of assize in those years when the justices in eyre did not. See 3 Bl Comm 59.

commission of delegates. Same as **court of delegates**.

commission of gaol delivery. A commission appointed by the court to try all of the prisoners who are confined in a jail.

commission of lunacy. A commission, usually having at least one physician in its membership, appointed to determine whether a person charged with lunacy is in fact a lunatic or of unsound mind, so that provision should be made for safeguarding his person and such property as he may have. Misselwitz's Lunacy, 177 Pa 359, 362, 35 A 722.

commission of nisi prius (ni'si pri'us). An authority or commission which was a consequence of the commission of assize, since it was annexed to the office of the justices of assize by the statute which authorized the commissioners to try all questions of fact issuing out of the courts of Westminster by a jury from the county where the action arose, unless before the day appointed the judges of assize should come into the county in question. See 3 Bl Comm 59.

commission of oyer and terminer. See **oyer and terminer**.

commission of partition. A commission appointed by the court in a suit for the partition of real estate, usually after an interlocutory judgment or decree of partition, to examine the premises, make a preliminary partition thereof, and report back to the court. 40 Am J1st Partit § 76.

commission of rebellion. A commission appointing four commissioners to find and seize the person of a defendant in equity who was in contempt for his failure to appear and plead as required by the subpoena which had been served upon him, and after the sheriff had failed to find him. Matters of equity were at one time determined by the king in person and the contempt in question was in the nature of a rebellion against the king's command. See 3 Bl Comm 444.

commission of review. A commission sometimes granted in extraordinary ecclesiastical cases to revise the sentence of the court of delegates, when it is believed that they have been led into a material error. See 3 Bl Comm 67.

commission of the peace. A commission which issued under the king's great seal appointing justices of the peace. See 1 Bl Comm 351.

Commission of Uniform Laws. See **uniform statutes**.

commission pro aetate probanda (prō ē-tā'te prō-ban'da). A commission appointed to determine whether one who was a tenant of the king and who held in chief by chivalry was of full age to receive his lands.

commission rogatoire (ro-ga-to-ar'). Letters rogatory.

commissions. See **commission**.

commission to examine witnesses. See **commission to take testimony**.

commission to take testimony. The authority under which a deposition is taken. 23 Am J2d Dep § 22.

commissive waste. Voluntary waste, often called actual waste, consisting in such acts as destroying, altering, or removing buildings, or cutting trees. 56 Am J1st Waste § 4. The term contemplates participation, at least to some extent, by the tenant or occupant of the premises. Anno: 84 ALR 394.

commit. To make a commitment; to perpetrate, as to commit burglary.
   Under the statute making it an offense to conspire to "commit" an offense against the United States, the word means no more than "bring about." It is not necessary that the conspiracy contemplate that the conspirators or some of them shall themselves directly break the law. It is quite sufficient if the conspiracy contemplates that that shall be done which does violate the law. United States v Hipsch (DC Mo) 34 F Supp 270.
   See **commitment**.

commitment. A warrant of authority, otherwise known as a mittimus, for confining a person to prison or jail; the delivery to jail, for want of bail, for detention pending action by the grand jury or trial, of one accused of crime. 21 Am J2d Crim L § 450; the delivery of a person under sentence of confinement to a jail or prison to the institution and the placing of him under confinement therein. People v Rutan, 3 Mich 42, 49; the confinement of an insane person. 29 Am J Rev ed Ins Per § 34.

commitment by lawful warrant in deed. A commitment by a warrant in writing. State v Shaw, 73 Vt 149, 168, 50 A 863.

commitment by lawful warrant in law. A commitment by lawful warrant in writing or by authority of law without a writing. State v Shaw, 73 Vt 149, 50 A 863.

committed in his presence. See **presence**.

committee. A body of persons who have been selected and appointed with authority to perform some public service or duty; the guardian of the person or the property of an insane person.
   See **political committee**.

Committee for Industrial Organization. A combination of labor unions, succeeded by the Congress of Industrial Organizations.

Committee of Arbitration. A body created by the Chamber of Commerce in New York City for the arbitration of disputes between merchants and other persons in business and industry, still in existence but inactive for the most part, its field of activity having been taken over by the American Arbitration Association.

committing magistrate. A justice of the peace, mayor, police judge, or other judicial officer authorized to commit a person arrested for crime pending preliminary examination and trial, sometimes trial by a higher court. State v Rogers, 31 NM 485, 247 P 828.

committitur (kom-mit'ti-ter). A record entry of a defendant's commitment.

committitur piece. An instrument in writing, charging on execution under a judgment the person of one already in prison. Bouvier's Law Dict.

commixtion (ko-mik'shon). The mingling of dry or solid substances belonging to different owners.

commodate (kom'ō-dāt). Same as **commodatum**.

commodato (ko-mo-dah'to). (Spanish.) An agreement for the gratuitous loan of a chattel.

commodatum (kom'ō-dāt-um). The gratuitous loaning of personal property to be used by the bailee and returned in specie. 8 Am J2d Bailm § 5.

commodatum bailment (kom'ō-dat-um bāl'ment). The gratuitous loaning of personal property to be used by the bailee and returned in specie. Lowney v Knott, 85 RI 505, 120 A2d 552, 57 ALR2d 1036.

commodities clause. An important provision of the Hepburn Act of June 29, 1906, regulating interstate commerce, intended to prohibit the transportation in interstate commerce by any railroad company of commodities produced or mined by such company or under its authority, or which it may own in whole or in part, or in which it may have an interest, direct or indirect, except timber and products manufactured from timber and such articles or commodities as may be necessary and intended for use in the business of the railroad company. United States ex rel. Atty. Gen. v Delaware & Hudson Co. 213 US 366, 53 L Ed 836, 29 S Ct 527.

commodity. A useful thing; an article of commerce; a moveable and tangible thing produced or used as the subject of barter or sale. State ex rel. Moose v Frank, 114 Ark 47, 169 SW 333.
   See **commercial commodity**.

Commodity Credit Corporation. An agency of the United States operating under a federal charter in supporting prices of agricultural commodities through loans, purchases, and payments; disposing of surplus agricultural commodities; promoting the marketing of agricultural commodities in both domestic and foreign markets; and procuring agricultural commodities in the country for sale to foreign governments, relief agencies, and other government agencies.

commodity rate. A freight rate which applies to one specific commodity alone, as distinguished from a class rate which applies to a number of articles of the same general character. Norfolk Southern Railroad Co. 145 Va 207, 133 SE 817.

commodum (ko-mod'um). Profit; gain; advantage.

Commodum ejus esse debet cujus periculum est (kom-mō'dum ē'jus es'se de'bet kū'jus pe-ri'ku-lum est). He who takes the risk should have the profit.

Commodum ex injuria non oritur (ko-mod'um ex in-jū'ri-a non or'i-tėr). An advantage or profit cannot arise from the violation of a legal right. Bird v Holbrook (Eng) 4 Bing 628.

Commodum ex injuria sua non habere debet (kom-mō'dum ex in-jū'ri-a su'a non hā-bē're de'bet). One ought not to profit by his own wrong.

common. A right, otherwise known as a "profit a prendre," to be exercised in the land of another, accompanied with participation in the profits of the soil, or a right to take a part of the soil or produce of the land. 25 Am J2d Ease § 4; better known in the popular sense as an area left open for common and public use, for the convenience, accommodation and pleasure of the inhabitants of a municipality. 39 Am J Rev ed Pks & S § 2. In earlier days of this country, the common was a place of pasturage for the benefit of the inhabitants of the town or municipality.

commonable beasts. Beasts of the plough or such as manure the ground. See 2 Bl Comm 33.

commonage (kom'on-aj). The use of a thing by one person in common with other persons.

commonalty (kom'on-al-ti). The common people, as distinguished from the peers. See 1 Bl Comm 403.

commonance (kom'on-ans). Persons who have the right of common in an open field.

common ancestor. The same ancestor of two or more persons.

common ancestry. One to whom the ancestry of two or more persons is traced.

common appendant. The prescriptive right of a tenant to feed cattle on land which he does not hold, but which is situate in the same manor.

common appurtenant. The right of a land owner to feed cattle on the land of another.

common assurances. Title deeds.
See **covenant for further assurance.**

common at large. Same as **common in gross.**

common bail. An old form of "bail" given by a defendant in a civil action, intended to serve as an appearance in the action, the sureties being fictitious.

common bar (kom'on bar). Also called "blank bar," —a plea interposed in an action of trespass to compel the plaintiff to specify the place of the alleged trespass.

common barrator. See **common barratry.**

common barratry. The offense of frequently exciting or stirring up quarrels between others, several, at least three, acts being required to constitute the offense. 14 Am J2d Champ § 19.

common barretor. See **common barratry.**

common because of vicinage. The mutual licenses of adjoining landowners whereby each of them might feed cattle on the land of the other.

common belief. An opinion of which the legislature may take cognizance, because it is entertained by most of the people of the community, notwithstanding it is not universally accepted and actually may ultimately be shown to be wrong by scientific observations and developments. Jacobson v Massachusetts, 197 US 11, 49 L Ed 643, 25 S Ct 358.

common bench (kom'on bench). The English court of common pleas.

common carrier. One who holds himself out to the public as engaged in the business of transporting persons or property from place to place, for compensation, offering his services to the public generally. 13 Am J2d Car § 2. A status dependent upon the activities of the person alleged to be a common carrier and the circumstances under which his services were rendered. 29A Am J Rev ed Ins § 1251. The dominant and controlling factor in determining the status of one as a common carrier is his public profession or holding out by words or by a course of conduct, as to the service offered or performed. Ace-High Dresses v J. C. Trucking Co. 122 Conn 578, 191 A 536, 112 ALR 86. For the purposes of the Federal Powers of Service Act, the status of a company as a common carrier depends upon what it does, not upon the purpose declared by the charter of the company, or how the company is regarded in the state of incorporation. United States v Brooklyn Eastern Dist. Terminal, 249 US 296, 63 L Ed 613, 39 S Ct 283, 16 ALR 527. The determination of the question, whether one engaged in furnishing transportation, or the means of transportation, is to be considered a "common carrier" within the meaning of an insurance contract providing for indemnity or increased payments where injury or death results from an accident while on a conveyance operated by a common carrier, depends upon the activities of the one alleged to be the common carrier and upon the circumstances under which his services were rendered to the insured. Anno: 149 ALR 1293.

common carrier by air. An airplane company or operator of airplanes, catering to the public generally, and undertaking to transport for hire all persons and goods of persons indifferently who apply for passage or transportation. 8 Am J2d Avi § 38.

common carrier by motor vehicle. A carrier having the status of a common carrier who uses busses, taxicabs, trucks, or other motor vehicles as the means of transportation. 13 Am J2d Car §§ 14, 17. As defined by section 303(a) of the Motor Carrier Act of 1935, "any person who or which undertakes, whether directly or by a lease or any other arrangement, to transport passengers or property, or any class or classes of property, for the general public in interstate or foreign commerce by motor vehicle for compensation, whether over regular or irregular routes, including such motor vehicle operations of carriers by rail or water, and of express or forwarding companies, except to the extent that these operations are subject to the provisions of chapter 1 of this title." Interstate Commerce Com v A. W. Stickle & Co. (DC Okla) 41 F Supp 268.
See **common carrier.**

common carrier by railroad. One who operates a railroad as a means of carrying for the public. Thornhill v Davis, 121 SC 49, 113 SE 370, 24 ALR 617.
See **common carrier.**

common carrier of livestock. A common carrier of goods, which transports livestock, is as to the livestock also a common carrier. Central of Georgia Railway Co. v Hall, 124 Ga 322, 32 SE 679.

common carrier of passengers. See **common carrier.**

common carrier of property. See **common carrier.**

common carrier's lien. A lien existing independently of contract on goods delivered to a common carrier for carriage, which attaches as soon as the carrier's liability as such begins, and continues until the freight charges, including storage charges, are paid. 13 Am J2d Car § 497.

common chase. A place where all persons might lawfully hunt wild game.

common conspiracy clause. Same as **confederating clause.**

common council. The legislative body of a city or other municipal corporation, except in jurisdictions where the traditional form of municipal government has given way under statute to a commission or manager form. 37 Am J1st Mun Corp § 46.

common counts. The various forms of an action of assumpsit. 1 Am J2d Actions § 13.
See **assumpsit; indebitatus assumpsit; insimul computassent; money counts; money had and re-**

ceived; money lent; money paid; quantum meruit; quantum valebant.

common day (kom'ọn dā). The period of time elapsing between midnight of one day and that of the next.

common debtor. (Scotch.) A debtor whose chattels have been seized by several creditors.

common disaster. A calamitous occurrence causing the death of two or more persons allied in interest as husband and wife, heirs of a common ancestor, or devisees of a common testator, the pertinency of the term in the law involving the succession to property where it is impossible to determine which of the two or more persons who suffered death survived the longest. The disaster which results in the death of two or more persons whose relationship to one another by contract, such as an insurance contract in which one is named as the beneficiary of a policy upon the life of the other, makes the time of death material. 29A Am J Rev ed Ins § 1653.

common drunkard. A person who drinks intoxicating liquors to excess, with habitual frequency. State ex rel. Atty. Gen. v Savage, 89 Ala 1, 7 So 183.

common enemy doctrine. The name applied to the rule of some jurisdictions that there is no wrong in any act undertaken by a landowner for the purpose of repelling surface water. 56 Am J1st Wat § 69.

common enterprise. See **joint enterprise**.

commoner (kom'ọn-ėr). A member of the house of commons, the lower house of the British parliament; a person belonging to the "commonalty;" a person owing a right of common in the lands of another. See 3 Bl Comm 238.

common error makes law. A maxim to be applied with caution where there has been a long-continued and general error in the observance, construction, or interpretation of the law, and injurious consequences will flow from a contrary construction, interpretation, or method of observance, but not to be applied so as to, in effect, repeal a positive statute. O'Donnell v Glenn, 9 Mont 452, 23 P 1018.

common field (kom'ọn fēld). A term of American invention adopted by Congress to designate small tracts of land of a peculiar shape usually from one to three arpents in front by forty arpents in depth, used by the occupants of the French villages for the purposes of cultivation, and protected from the inroads of cattle by a common fence. The peculiar shape of the lot, its contiguity to others of similar shape, and the purposes to which it was applied, constituted it a common field lot. It could not be confounded with lots or tracts of land of any other character. Glasgow v Hortiz, (US) 1 Black 595, 600, 17 L Ed 110, 113.

common fine (kom'ọn fīn). A fine imposed upon all the inhabitants of a district.

common fishery. A fishery open to a number of persons, sometimes to the public; a free fishery and a common fishery are usually and properly considered equivalent rights. 35 Am J2d Fish § 6.

common form of probate. See **probate in common form**.

common gambler. One who supports himself chiefly by gaming or who frequently or habitually engages in gambling in violation of law. 24 Am J1st Gaming § 46.

common gaming house. A house kept for the purpose of permitting persons to resort to it and gamble therein in violation of law. 24 Am J2d Disord H § 3.

common highway (kom'ọn hī'wā). A public highway on land or navigable water. As used in Art 9 § 1, of the Constitution that navigable waters "shall be common highways and forever free" the term does not refer to physical obstructions of the waters, but refers to political regulations which would hamper the freedom of commerce. Re Southern Wisconsin Power Co. 140 Wis 245, 122 NW 801.

common humanity rule. See **humanitarian rule**.

commonia turbariae (kom-mō'ni-a ter-bā'ri-ē). Same as **common of turbary**.

common informer. Another term for "informer." See **informer**.

common in gross. An easement in gross, that is, a right not supported by a dominant estate but attached to, and vested in, the person to whom it is granted.
See **easement in gross**.

common injunction. A term of the early English practice for an injunction in aid of or as secondary to another equity, as in the case of an injunction to restrain proceedings at law, in order to protect and enforce an equity which could not be pleaded in the action at law. 28 Am J Rev ed Inj § 10.

common injury. An injury of the same kind and character, and such as naturally and necessarily arises from a given cause, but not necessarily similar in degree or equal in amount. If the injury is the same in kind to all, it is a common injury, although one may actually be injured or damaged more than another. Anthony Wilkinson Live Stock Co. v McIlquham, 14 Wyo 209, 83 P 364.

common intendment. According to the ordinary meaning.

common intent. The intent of two or more persons acting in concert to commit a specific crime, or to commit acts from which the law will infer a community of intention. Regina v Doddridge (Eng) 8 Cox CC 335. The corrupt intent existing in the minds of the parties to a conspiracy. 16 Am J2d Consp § 9.

common in the soil. The right of a person to mine or quarry on the land of another.

common jail. The building provided by a county or municipality for the custody of persons committed by legal process. 41 Am J1st Pris & P § 2.

common jury. An ordinary trial jury, as distinguished from a grand jury, a special jury, or a coroner's jury; a petit jury.

common labor. As the term is used in statutes prohibiting common labor on Sunday, it cannot in the nature of things be given an exact definition. Courts can only determine whether each case, as it arises, falls within the legislative intention. The term is not restricted to mere manual labor. The execution of ordinary contracts and the transactions to which they relate are within the meaning of the term. Such transactions belong to the ordinary business affairs of life and are as well within the meaning of the term as the work of the farmer in his field, of the mechanic in his shop, or the common laborer upon a public improvement, but the making of a subscription toward a charitable enterprise, such as a church debt, is not common labor. Bryan v Watson, 127 Ind 42, 26 NE 666. Neither holding courts nor transacting public business is common labor. State v Thomas, 61 Ohio St 444, 56 NE 276.

common knowledge. A matter is of common knowledge where it is so generally, even if not universally, accepted by the public without qualification or contention, that the courts will accept it without proof. 29 Am J2d Ev § 22.

common law. Those principles, usages and rules of action applicable to the government and security of persons and property which do not rest for their authority upon any express or positive statute or other written declaration, but upon statements of principles found in the decisions of the courts. 15 Am J2d Com L § 1. In a broader sense the common law is the system of rules and declarations of principles from which our judicial ideas and legal definitions are derived, and which are continually expanding; the system being capable of growth and development at the hands of judges. Linkins v Protestant Episcopal Cathedral, 87 App DC 351, 187 F2d 357, 28 ALR2d 521; Ney v Yellow Cab Co. 2 Ill 2d 74, 117 NE2d 74, 51 ALR2d 624.

In its broadest aspect, the common law may be said to be the general Anglo-American system of legal concepts and the traditional technique which forms the basis of the law of the states which have adopted it. 15 Am J2d Com L § 1. The common law of England, in its broadest significance, is the basic component of the common law as adopted by American courts. 15 Am J2d Com L § 6. English statutes enacted before the emigration of the American colonists constituted a part of the common law on its adoption in this country, so far as they were not merely local in character or inapplicable to American institutions and conditions; if such statutes are so far removed in point of time that one must be hesitant in declaring that they are a part of the common law for the purposes of the present, they are nevertheless part of our judicial heritage and should be interpreted and applied accordingly. 15 Am J2d Com L § 7.

As the words are used in the seventh amendment to the United States Constitution providing that "no fact tried by a jury, shall be otherwise re-examined in any court of the United States, than according to the rules of the common law," the common law referred to is not the common law of any individual state (for it probably differs in all), but it is the common law of England, the grand reservoir of all our jurisprudence. Under that law, the facts once tried by a jury are never re-examined, unless a new trial is granted; or unless the judgment of the trial court is reversed by a superior tribunal, on a writ of error, and a venire facias de novo is awarded. Capital Traction Co. v Hof, 174 US 1, 8, 43 L Ed 873, 876, 18 S Ct 580.

See **federal common law**; **proceeding according to the course of the common law**; **unwritten law.**

common-law action. See **action at common law.**

common-law actionable negligence. The failure of one owing a duty to another to do what a reasonable and prudent person would ordinarily have done under the circumstances, or doing what such a person would not have done. Pratt v Daly, 55 Ariz 535, 104 P2d 147, 130 ALR 341.

See **negligence.**

common-law actions. Forms of actions as they existed under the common law, being the ex contractu forms of account, assumpsit, covenant, and debt, and the ex delicto forms of detinue, replevin, trover, trespass on the case, ejectment, forcible entry, and trespass. There are also the common-law actions of dower, waste, the writ of right, and the writ of entry. 1 Am J2d Actions § 10.

common-law arbitration. A matter of the law of remedies, rather than of the substantive law; arbitration by agreement which designates a specific issue to be decided and includes a provision binding the parties to abide by the award. Carey v Herrick, 146 Wash 283, 263 P 190, 193.

See **arbitration.**

common-law bond. An obligation in writing and under seal. 12 Am J2d Bonds § 1; a bond voluntarily executed by a public officer in the absence of any constitutional or statutory provision requiring him to furnish a bond. 43 Am J1st Pub Of § 411.

common-law jurisdiction. Jurisdiction to try and decide cases which were cognizable by the courts of law under what is known as the common law of England. Re Dean, 83 Me 489, 22 A 385.

common-law jury. A jury of 12 persons, no more and no less, summoned from the vicinity, duly examined, and sworn to try the case on the facts presented by the evidence introduced at the trial. State v James, 96 NJL 132, 114 A 553, 16 ALR 1141.

common-law lien. A lien arising by implication of law, not by contract, which entitles the lienor to retain possession of an article in his possession which belongs to another until certain demands against such other person are satisfied. 33 Am J1st Liens § 16.

common-law marriage. A marriage entered into without ceremony, the parties assuming the relationship of husband and wife inter se by agreement in words of the present tense to be husband and wife, followed, as required in some, but not all jurisdictions, by cohabitation and reputation or repute of marriage. 35 Am J1st Mar § 28.

A common-law marriage depends upon facts and circumstances evidencing a mutual agreement to live together as husband and wife, and not in concubinage. Rodgers v Herron, 226 SC 317, 85 SE2d 104, 48 ALR2d 1241.

common-law meaning. The meaning of a word or expression as known and understood by the common law.

If the legislature makes use of a term without defining it, and it has by the common law received a settled meaning, it will be presumed that it is used in the common-law sense. Hillhouse v Chester (Conn) 3 Day 166.

common-law mortgage. A feoffment on the condition that the feoffer might re-enter if he performed the condition of paying a certain sum of money on a certain date to the feoffee, the transaction also being known as dead pledge, because, upon nonperformance of the condition, the land was lost to the feoffer forever. Anno: 27 L Ed 910.

common law of England. The system of law which prevails in England, and in the United States by adoption, as distinguished from the Roman or civil-law system. 15 Am J2d Com L § 1.

See **common law.**

common-law procedure acts. English statutes enacted in 1852, 1854, and 1860, simplifying the forms of pleading and practice.

common-law receiver. A receiver appointed by a

court of equity without reference to statutory authority. 45 Am J1st Rec § 3.

common-law trademark. A right, recognized by the common law in the absence of statute, as existing in a trademark by virtue of prior appropriation and use. 52 Am J1st Tradem § 26.

common-law trust. See **business trust.**

common lawyer (kom'ọn lâ'yėr). A lawyer who is learned in the common law.

commonly. In a manner that is common; usually; generally; ordinarily; frequently; for the most part; familiarly. Webb v New Mexico Pub. Co. 47 NM 279, 141 P2d 333, 148 ALR 1002.

common nightwalker. A person having the habit of being abroad at night for the purpose of committing some crime, of disturbing the peace, or of doing some wrongful or wicked act. State v Dowers, 45 NH 543, 544.

common nuisance. A public nuisance, that is a condition of things which is prejudicial to the health, comfort, safety, property, sense of decency or morals of the citizens at large, resulting either from an act not warranted by law, or from neglect of a duty imposed by law. Nuchols v Commonwealth, 312 Ky 171, 226 SW2d 796, 13 ALR2d 1478; Powell v Bentley & Gerwig Furniture Co. 34 W Va 804, 12 SE 1085.
See **public nuisance.**

common occupant. Where land was granted to a man for the life of another, and the grantee died before the cestui que vie, the land belonged to nobody during the remainder of the life of the cestui que vie, and any man who entered and occupied the land for that period was called common occupant. See 2 Bl Comm 259.

common of estovers. The right a tenant has of taking necessary wood and timber from the woods of the landlord, for fuel, fencing, etc. See 32 Am J1st L & T § 219.

common of fishery. The right that a tenant has of taking fish in the water of the landlord. Van Rensselaer v Radcliffe (NY) 10 Wend 639.
See **common fishery.**

common of pasture. A right of feeding the beasts of one person on the lands of another. Van Rensselaer v Radcliffe (NY) 10 Wend 639.

common of piscary (kom'on of pis'kạ-ri). The right that a tenant has of taking fish in the waters of the landlord. Van Rensselaer v Radcliffe (NY) 10 Wend 639.
See **common fishery.**

common of turbary (kom'on of tėr'bạ-ri). The right that a tenant has of cutting turf in the grounds of his landlord. See Van Rensselaer v Radcliffe (NY) 10 Wend 639.

common order. The usual order under the practice of some jurisdictions, in the nature of a conditional judgment, directed to a defendant in default for want of an appearance and threatening him with the rendition of an actual judgment against him unless he appear and plead. Mahoney v New South Bldg. & Loan Asso. (CC Va) 70 F 513.

common passageway. A hall or stairway in an apartment house which is open to use and used by all tenants, or all tenants on one floor or in one section of the building.

common people. See **commonalty.**

common pleas. A term for civil actions as distinguished from criminal prosecutions.
See **Court of Common Pleas.**

common pleas court. See **Court of Common Pleas.**

common probate. See **probate in common form.**

common prostitute. A female who submits indiscriminately to sexual intercourse, irrespective of financial gain. People v Ward, 95 Misc 508, 160 NYS 763.

common pur cause de vicinage (pour kâz dē vis'i-nāj). Same as **common because of vicinage.**

common purgation. See **judicium Dei.**

common purpose. See **common intent; prosecution of a common purpose.**

common recovery. A fictitious suit brought by a third person against the holder of an estate in tail with the ultimate object of barring the estate in tail and giving the tenant in tail the power of disposing of the property in fee simple. Dutton v Donahue, 44 Wyo 52, 8 P2d 90, 79 ALR 1355.
See **Fine and Recoveries Act.**

common return days. Fixed days for appearance of defendants in court.

common right. A right supported by common law; for some purposes, the common law itself. Coral Gables v Christopher, 108 Vt 414, 189 A 147, 109 ALR 474; a right that is not absolute in the sense that an absolute right is not to be denied, but is nevertheless entitled to protection against malicious interference. 30 Am J Rev ed Interf § 44; a qualified right which may be exercised only where there is justification therefor, as distinguished from an absolute right which may be exercised without reference to one's motive or to any injury directly resulting therefrom. 30 Am J Rev ed Interf § 51.

common river boundary. See **river boundary.**

common rule. See **entering the common rule.**

commons. In reference to land, the plural of **common;** the House of Commons, the popular and more powerful body of the British Parliament; freeholders not of the peerage; commoners, that is persons of the **commonalty.**

common sans nombre (kommon sān nōn-br). Common without number.

common schools. The public schools as established in the United States: grade schools, grammar schools, and high schools. 47 Am J1st Sch § 3.

common-school system. The system of public schools in the United States that is, the graded, grammar, and high schools. 47 Am J1st Sch § 3.

common scold. A troublesome and angry woman who, by brawling and wrangling among her neighbors, commits a breach of the public peace, increases discord, and becomes a nuisance in the neighborhood. 15 Am J2d Com S § 2.

common seal (kom'ọn sēl). The seal of a corporation.

common serjeant (kom'on sär'gent). An assistant to the recorder of the City of London.

common socage (kom'on sok'ạj). Same as **free socage.**

common stock. The kind of stock ordinarily and usually issued by a corporation, without extraordinary rights or privileges, and the kind of stock which, in the absence of other classes of stock having superior rights, represents the complete interest in a corporation. 18 Am J2d Corp § 212.

common thief. A person who persists in the offense of larceny.

common trust fund. A trust fund, held by a bank or trust company as trustee, which is actually a combination of several, sometimes many, trust funds in limited amounts, the funds being mingled for the purpose of efficiency and economy in administration and investment by the trustee.

commonty (kom'ǫn-ti). The commonalty; land which is owned in common and which usually is subject to certain servitudes.

common vouchee (kom'on vow-chē'). The fictitious party in an action of common recovery who was named by the tenant as his warrantor and grantor. It was the common practice in such a proceeding to name the crier of the court as the common vouchee. 2 Bl Comm 358.

common wall. See **party wall**.

commonweal (kom'ǫn-wēl'). Common welfare; the public welfare.

commonwealth (kom'ǫn-welth'). The public; the state; the body politic; the English government under Cromwell.

Commonwealth. The association, sometimes called the British Commonwealth, of the United Kingdom with independent nations, dominions, dependencies, protectorates, and trust territories beyond the seas.

common without stint. A frequently used, but erroneous name for the unmeasured right of common; that is a right of common which has not yet been admeasured or apportioned. See 3 Bl Comm 239. It was also called "common sans nombre."

commorancy (kom'ō-ran-si). In American law, residence for a short time; temporary residence; in English law, dwelling as an inhabitant of a place, which means usually lying there. 4 Bl Comm 273.

commorant (kom'ō-rạnt). See **commorancy**.

commorientes (kom-mō-ri-en'tēz). Persons who die at the same time.

commote (ko-mōt'). (Welsh.) Half a hundred.

commotion. A disturbance; turmoil.
See **civil commotion**.

commun. See **droit commun**.

commune. Verb: To engage in intimate conversation; to take communion. (French.) Noun: A community; the common people; a small administrative unit of government; the name given to revolutionary governments; (Latin.) common.

commune bonum (ko-mū'nē bō'num). Common good, public welfare.

commune concilium regni (kom-mū'ne kon-si'li-um reg'ni). The common council of the realm,—an ancient name of the general assembly which came to be known as parliament. See 1 Bl Comm 148.

commune placitum (kom-mū'ne pla'si-tum). A common plea; a civil action.

commune socagium (kom-mū'ne so-kā'ji-um). Common socage. Same as **free socage**.

commune vinculum (kom-mū'ne vin'ku-lum). The common bond or tie. The common stock of consanguinity. See 2 Bl Comm 250.

communia (kom-mū'ni-a). Common; ordinary.

communia pasturae (kom-mū'ni-a pas'tu-rē). Same as **common of pasture**.

communia piscariae (kom-mū'ni-a pis-kā'ri-ē). Same as **common of piscary**.

communia placita (kom-mū'ni-a pla'si-ta). Same as **common pleas**.

Communia placita non sequantur curiam regis, sed teneantur in aliquo loco certo (kom-mū'ni-a pla'si-ta non se-quan'ter kū'ri-am rē-jis, sed te-ne-an'ter in a'li-quō lō'kō ser'tō). The court of common pleas shall not follow the king's court, but shall be held in some fixed place. 3 Bl Comm 38.

communia turbariae (kom-mū'ni-a tur-bā'ri-ē). Common of turbary.

communibus annis (kom-mū'ni-bus an'nis). In common or ordinary years; one year with another; upon an average. See 2 Bl Comm 322.

communicable diseases. Infectious diseases.

communicare (kom-mū-ni-kā're). To commune.

communicate. To make known; to impart information; to give by way of information. Messages of the Senate were communicated to the President. Prevost v Morgenthau, 70 App DC 306, 106 F2d 330.
See **communication**.

communicating additions. An expression, common in fire insurance policies for the purpose of extending the coverage beyond the house or main building to other buildings on the premises used by the household, even though not physically attached to the main building. Frohlich v National Fire Ins. Co. 327 Mich 653, 42 NW2d 657, 19 ALR2d 604.

communication. A statement made in writing or by word of mouth by one person to another; the transfer of information by speech and by acts, signs, and appearances. People v Daghita, 299 NY 194, 86 NE2d 172, 10 ALR2d 1385.
See **privileged communications**.

Communications Act. The federal statute which provides the Federal Communications Commission and prescribes its powers and duties. 44 Am J1st Rad § 6.

By the Communications Act of 1934, jurisdiction over telephone and telegraph companies was transferred from the Interstate Commerce Commission to the Federal Communications Commission. 52 Am J1st Teleg & T § 42.

Communications Commission. The federal regulatory agency for radio and television, 44 Am J1st Radio § 6, also for telegraphs and telephones. 52 Am J1st Teleg & T § 42.

communidad. (Spanish.) A partnership for the purposes of the Bankruptcy Act. Benitez v Bank of Nova Scotia (CA1 Puerto Rico) 125 F2d 523.

communi dividendo (kom-mū'nī di-vi-den'dō). A Roman law action for the partition of property held in common.

communings (kǫ-mūn'ingz). Offers to deal with or contract.

communio bonorum (kom-mū'ni-ō bo-nō'rum). A community of goods.

Communi observantia non est recedendum (kom-mū'nī ob-ser-van'she-a non est re-sē-den'dum). There must not be a departure from common or general observation or practice. The probable origin of this maxim is traced in O'Donnell v Glenn, 9 Mont 452, 23 P 1018.

communis (kom-ū'nis). Common.

communis bancus (kom-mū'nis bangk'us). The common bench, the English court of common pleas.

Communis error facit jus (kom-mū'nis er'ror fā'sit jūs). See **common error makes law**.

Communis et recta sententia est, in rebus immobilibus servandum esse jus loci in quo bona sunt sita (kom-mu'nis et rek'ta sen-ten'she-a est, in rē'bus im-mō'-bi-li-bus ser-vān'dum es'se jūs lō'sī in quō bō'na sunt si'ta). It is common sense and proper that the law of the place in which the property is situated should control immovable property. Suydam v Williamson (US) 24 How 427, 434, 16 L Ed 742, 745.

communism. In the pristine sense, the ownership of the means of production by the community, each member of the community participating in production according to his ability and sharing in the products according to his need; in common usage of the present day, suggestive of the theories of Marx and Lenin and the politics and authoritarian rule of Stalin and his successors in Russia and the leaders in China since the People's Republic was proclaimed in 1949.

communis opinio (kom-mū'nis ō-pi'ni-ō). The common opinion. In Coke upon Littleton, the learned author often prefaces the announcement of a legal principle with the words: "It is commonly said." By these words is meant: "It is commonly the legal opinion." To the expression cited, Littleton adds: "That is, it is the common opinion, and communis opinio is good authority in law." O'Donnell v Glenn, 9 Mont 452, 23 P 1018.

communis pacis perturbatrix (kom-mū'nis pa'sis per-tur-bā'trix). A common disturber of the peace.

communis paries (kom-mū'nis pa'ri-ēz). A common wall, a party wall.

communis pugnatrix (kom-mū'nis pug-nā'trix). A common brawler.

communis rixatrix (kom-mū'nis ri'xa-trix). Same as **common scold**.

communis scriptura (kom-mū'nis scrip-tu'ra). A common writing; a deed.

communis stirpes (kom-mū'nis stir'pēz). People of a common stock; a stock of a common ancestry.

Communist. One who believes in communism; a member of the Communist Party.
See **communism**.

communistic tenure (kom-ū-nis'tik ten'yur). The tenure in which land is held by a religious or other incorporated or unincorporated society, where the members have surrendered to it their property to be held in common for the benefit of all. See 45 Am J1st Reli Soc § 52.

Communist Party. A political party, often the only political party, in various countries, supporting communism in theory, although not absolutely in practice, and upholding authoritarian forms of government; a political party in the United States, numerically weak, but now operating with legality.
See **communism**.

Communist Sympathizer. Essentially the same in the common mind as "Communist." Anno: 33 ALR2d 1212.

communitas regni Angliae (kom-mū'ni-tās reg'nī Ang'li-ē). The community of the realm of England, —one of the ancient names of the general council which finally became parliament. See 1 Bl Comm 148.

communiter usitata et approbata (kom-mū'ni-ter ū-si-tā'ta et ap-prō-bā'ta). Things which have been commonly used and approved.

community (kǫ-mū'ni-ti). A town; a municipality; a district; a neighborhood; an entity composed of a husband and his wife, which is quite distinct from that of either, considered separately and individually. As a community they hold property by a different title from that by which they hold title to their separate property. Stanton v Everett Trust & Sav. Bank, 145 Wash 165, 259 P 10.
See **community estate; community property**.

community center. A place where the people may meet in the pursuit of social, cultural, or recreational activities.
See **recreational center**.

community chest. A fund collected in a city for various charities maintained in the city, the purpose being to avoid the expenses and efforts otherwise required to solicit separately for each of the charities; the organization maintained to administer the collection of the fund and the disbursement thereof to the organizations entitled.

community church. One of the earliest manifestations of the ecumenical movement. The term does not signify a religious association which has distinctive doctrines and beliefs, but rather a federation of two or more churches, all retaining their separate identity and their distinctive doctrines. Christian Church of Vacaville v Crystal, 78 Cal App 1, 247 P 605.

community debt. See **community obligation**.

community estate. A marital estate, incapable of existing except between husband and wife during coverture. 15 Am J2d Community Prop § 6. The estate left by a decedent is called a community estate when it consists wholly of community property. Gump v Commissioner (CA9) 124 F2d 540.
See **community property**.

community house. See **community center; tenement house**.

community income. The income from community property and also the earnings of husband or wife or profits or rents realized by either one from his or her business transactions, or property, which become community property. 15 Am J2d Community Prop §§ 35-37.

community obligation. A liability incurred for the benefit, or arising out of the management, of the community. 15 Am J2d Community Prop § 82.

community of intention. See **common intent**.

community of interest. A joint or common interest.

community property. A system, derived by several states through adoption or succession from the Spanish, Mexican, or French law, relative to property rights of husband and wife, the essential principle of which is that the earnings of either spouse by his or her toil and the exercise of his or her productive faculties belong, not to the earning or producing spouse as his or her property, but to the "community," the entity of husband and wife. 15 Am J2d Community Prop §§ 1, 3; property acquired by either spouse during a marriage, otherwise than by gift, devise, legacy, or descent;

whatever is gained, during coverture, by the toil, talent, or other productive faculty of either spouse. 15 Am J2d Community Prop § 3.

The foregoing definition is not inclusive of all property rights. For example, the right to practice a profession, although not acquired by gift, devise, legacy, or descent, is not to be classed as community property. 15 Am J2d Community Prop § 3.

community recreational center. See **recreational center.**

commutation. A money compensation paid by the government to military officers when it cannot furnish them with quarters at stations. 36 Am J1st Mil § 79.

commutation of homestead entry. A cash payment by a homestead settler on public lands, in lieu of remaining in possession of the land for five years, made to obtain a patent for the land from the government. 42 Am J1st Pub Land § 28.

commutation of punishment. See **commutation of sentence.**

commutation of sentence. The changing of a sentence imposed for crime to less severe punishment; the substitution of a lesser punishment for a greater by authority of law. 39 Am J1st Pard § 8.

commutation of tax. An abatement of a tax; the payment of a designated sum for the privilege of exemption from taxation, or the selection in advance of a specific sum in lieu of an ad valorem tax. It has been held that either of these methods of commutation works an exemption pro tanto from taxation. Hogg v Mackay, 23 Or 339, 31 P 779.
See **abatement of taxes.**

commutation of tithes. The payment of tithes in money, instead of produce.

commutation of toll. The reduction or exoneration of payment of tolls for the use of a toll road. 54 Am J1st Turn & T R § 14.

commutation ticket. A ticket issued by a carrier of passengers, at a reduced rate per trip, for a specified number of trips between named stations or points. Pennsylvania R. Co. v Towers, 245 US 6, 62 L Ed 117, 38 S Ct 2.

commutative contract. A contract which involves mutual and reciprocal obligations, and wherein the acts to be done and performed on one side form the consideration for those to be done and performed on the other. Hyde & Gleises v Booraem & Co. 16 Pet 169, 10 L Ed 928. The use of the term appears to be confined to Louisiana.

commutative justice. Mutual justice; justice on the one side equal to that on the other.

commutator. See **dynamo.**

commuted value. The value of a gift of a future interest reduced to present worth. 28 Am J Rev ed Inher Tax §§ 619, 620.
See **present worth.**

commuting expense. The expense of transportation between residence and place of work located within the area of the residence, that is, near enough to be reached within a reasonable time, considering the nature of the work to be done.

compact. Noun: A contract, Green v Biddle (US) 8 Wheat 1, 92, 5 L Ed 547, 570; particularly, a contract of an important and serious nature, as a contract between states settling a boundary dispute. State of Virginia v State of Tennessee, 148 US 503, 509, 37 L Ed 537, 543, 13 S Ct 728. Adjective: Closely united. Anno: 2 ALR 1356.

compact territory. A district whereof the divisions not only touch each other but are closely united. Anno: 2 ALR 1356.

Companies Act (kọm'pạ-nies akt). An English statute passed in 1862, regulating non-partnership companies.

companionate marriage. Either an illicit relationship or a relationship based upon a marriage which the parties have, by antenuptial contract or arrangement, sought to control so as to render the marriage terminable at pleasure, with consent, or at some future time. 35 Am J1st Marr § 39.

company. Usually, but not necessarily, a corporation, since the word is inclusive of natural persons. 18 Am J2d Corp § 4; a union of two or more persons for the carrying on of a joint enterprise or business; a partnership; a corporation; an association; a joint stock company. An association of individuals operating under a declaration of trust, by the terms of which the capital contributed by them to a common enterprise is divided into units or interests, is a "company" within the meaning of the word as it is used in the blue sky law of California. Barrett v Gore, 88 Cal App 372, 263 P 564.

company car. A motor vehicle owned by an employing company and driven by an officer or employee.

company housing. Dwelling houses owned by an employer and rented to employees, usually under an arrangement for deducting the rent from wages.

company union. A labor union whose membership is confined to the employees of a single company or the employees of a company and its subsidiaries.

comparatio literarum (kom-pa-rā'she-ō li-te-rā'rum). A comparison of letters; that is, of handwritings.

comparative injury. A doctrine of equity which denies relief where the inconvenience and the injury to the plaintiff are not of a pressing character and the result of equitable relief by injunction will be to cause a large loss to the defendant. 28 Am J Rev ed Inj § 52; 39 Am J1st Nuis § 161.

comparative negligence. The negligence of the defendant in an action to recover damages for negligence as compared with that of the plaintiff, the comparison being made for the purpose of applying the rule of admiralty, which has been adopted by statute for negligence cases generally in some jurisdictions, that the more gross the negligence of the defendant appears, the less degree of care is required of the plaintiff to permit a recovery by him; that the negligence of the plaintiff operates, not to relieve the defendant entirely from liability, but merely to diminish the damages recoverable. 38 Am J1st Negl §§ 231-233.

comparative rectitude. The name given to the principle that where both parties to a marriage are guilty of misconduct for which a divorce may be granted, the court will grant a divorce to the one who is less at fault. 24 Am J2d Divorce § 228.

comparere (kom-pā-rē're). To appear, to submit to the jurisdiction of the court.

comparison. The act of bringing together for the purpose of observing not only likenesses, but differences as well. Succession of Baker, 129 La 74, 82, 55 So 714.
See **evidence by comparison.**

comparison of handwriting. The now generally accepted practice of determining the genuineness of a disputed writing or signature by comparison thereof with a specimen of the person's writing that is proved or admitted to be genuine. 29 Am J2d Ev § 806.

compartner (kọm-pärt′nėr). Same as **copartner**.

compascuum (kom-pas′ku-um). Same as **common of pasture**.

compass. Noun: An instrument for showing direction, particularly an instrument with a magnetic needle which swings freely and points to the north. Verb: To accomplish; to plot, scheme, or contrive harm to another.

compaternity (kom-pā-tėr′ni̯-ti). The relation of a godparent toward his godchild.

compatibility (kọm-pat-i-bil′i̯-ti). Such an absence of conflict in two or more offices that one person may with propriety fill each of them at the same time; a harmonious relationship between persons living together, especially husband and wife.

compear (kom-pēr′). (Scotch.) To enter an appearance in an action, either in person or by attorney.

compearance (kom-pēr′ạns). (Scotch.) An appearance in an action or proceeding.

compelled. Moved by force, which, in the law, may mean an unavoidable force. A witness is not "compelled" to testify if he makes no claim of privilege upon the ground that his testimony might incriminate him or upon any other ground. State v Whalen, 108 Wash 287, 183 P 130.

Compendia sunt dispendia (kom-pen′di-a sunt dispen′di-a). Short cuts are wasteful.

compensable injury. A personal injury to an employee for which he is entitled to compensation under a workmen's compensation act, which means that there is a causal relation between the employment and the injury. Trudenich v Marshall (DC Wash) 34 F Supp 486.

compensacion (com-pen-sah-the-on′). (Spanish.) A set-off or counterclaim.

compensate. To counterbalance; to make up for; to make amends for; to pay. Pacific Tel. & Tel. Co. v Henneford, 195 Wash 553, 81 P2d 786.

compensated surety. See **corporate surety**.

compensating tax. A state tax the primary purpose of which is to protect merchants of the state from discrimination resulting from the inability of the state, under Federal Law, to impose a tax upon sales made to residents of the state by competitive merchants in other states. Pacific Tel. & Tel. Co. v Henneford, 195 Wash 553, 81 P2d 786.
See **use tax**.

compensatio (kom-pen-sā′she-ō). The set-off of the Roman law. See 3 Bl Comm 305.

compensatio criminum (kom-pen-sā′she-ō kri′minum). Recrimination, a defense in an action for divorce. 24 Am J2d Div & S § 226.
See **recrimination**.

compensation. A return for a benefit conferred or promised, that is, a consideration. Searcy v Grow, 15 Cal 117; a remuneration for services, whether in the form of a fixed salary, fees, commissions, or perquisites of whatever character. 43 Am J1st Pub Of § 340; redress for property taken or injury caused by the taking of property under the power of eminent domain. Symonds v Cincinnati, 14 Ohio 147. A set-off in the Scottish law; redress in damages for injuries generally; the payment made to an injured employee by the employer under a workmen's compensation act. As the term is used in workmen's compensation acts, it means the money relief afforded according to the scale established and for the persons designated by the act, and it does not refer to the compensatory damages which may be recovered in an action at law for a wrong done or a contract broken. Mosely v Empire Gas & Fuel Co. 313 Mo 225, 281 SW 762, 45 ALR 1223, 1232.

A civil law term meaning the extinction of debts of which two persons are reciprocally debtors to one another, by the credits by which they are reciprocally creditors to one another. 20 Am J2d Countcl etc. § 5.
See **compensatory damages; unemployment compensation; workmen's compensation**.

compensation court. A workmen's compensation commission. 58 Am J1st Workm Comp § 370.

compensation, wages, or hire. As the term is used in a statute requiring a driver's license, the term means something more than the operation of a motor vehicle as a mere incident of the business of one's employer. Matthews v State, 85 Tex Crim 469, 214 SW 339.

compensatory damages. The damages recoverable in satisfaction of, or in recompense for, loss or injury sustained, including all damages except nominal damages, punitive, or exemplary damages. 22 Am J2d Damg § 11. Damages awarded not only as a recompense for actual injury to the person or property, including expenses, loss of time, bodily suffering, etc., occasioned by the defendant's wrongful act, but also such additional sum as in the opinion of the jury is warranted by the circumstances of contumely, anguish or oppression, including mental suffering and wounded sensibilities. Murphy v Hobbs, 7 Colo 541, 5 P 119.

compensatory fine. A fine which the court may impose in a civil contempt action as a remedial punishment, payable to an aggrieved litigant as compensation for the special damages which he may have sustained by reason of the contumacious conduct of the offender. Parker v United States (CA1 Mass) 126 F2d 370.

comperendinatio (kom-pe-ren-di-nā′she-ō). (Roman law.) The postponement of a trial to the third day.

compertorium (kom-per-tō′ri-um). (Civil law.) A judicial inquest by delegates or commissioners to find out and relate the truth of a cause.

comperuit ad diem (kom-pe′ru-it ad dī′em). He appeared at the day.

compester (kom-pes′ter). To apply manure to the soil.

competency. Capability; capacity; qualification for the performance of an act.

competency of evidence. The admissibility of evidence under the established rules of evidence. 29 Am J2d Ev §§ 257, 260.

competency of person. See **competent person**.

competency of testator. See **testamentary capacity**.

competency of witness. See **competent attesting witness; competent witness**.

competent attesting witness. One legally competent, as of the time of the attestation and as determined by the substantive law of wills, to testify in a court of justice to the facts which he attests by signing his name to the will as a subscribing witness, not being disqualified by mental incapacity, crime, or other cause such as interest. Gillis v Gillis, 143 Ga 1, 23 SE 107.

competent and omitted. The term is applied to a plea which might have been interposed, but was not.

competent arbitrator. Any disinterested person, whatever his or her legal status may be, except as qualifications are prescribed in the agreement for arbitration, in which case only persons who meet the prescribed qualifications are competent. 5 Am J2d Arb & A § 97. As used in insurance policy providing for the appointment of "competent arbitrators," the term means persons who are disinterested, and have the requisite ability to act in the matter. Aetna Ins. Co. v Stevens, 48 Ill 31.

competent court. A tribunal having jurisdiction. State ex rel. Degen v Freeman, 168 Minn 374, 375, 210 NW 14. A court legally constituted; a court the judgments and proceedings of which are not open to collateral attack. A court created without color of authority, or a mere usurper is not within the definition, but a de facto court is a competent court. State ex rel. Bales v Bailey, 106 Minn 138, 118 NW 676.

See **court of competent jurisdiction.**

competent evidence. Evidence which is legally admissible.

See **competency of evidence.**

competent jurisdiction. The power and authority of law, at the time of acting, to do the particular act. Re Justus, 3 Okla Crim 111, 104 P 933.

competent person. A capable person; a person legally qualified by age and mental capacity.

See **competent attesting witness; competent witness.**

competent tribunal. See **competent court.**

competent witness. A person qualified to testify under oath; a person who meets the test of age, mental power, religious belief, and capacity to understand the nature and obligation of an oath. Lenier v Bryan, 184 NC 282, 114 SE 6, 26 ALR 1488. A credible witness; that is, such a person as is not legally disqualified from testifying in courts of justice by reason of mental incapacity, interest, or the commission of a crime, or other cause excluding him from testifying generally, or rendering him incompetent in respect of the particular subject matter, or in the particular suit. Blythe v Ayres, 96 Cal 532, 586, 31 P 915. A person is competent to testify as a witness if he has sufficient understanding to receive, remember, and narrate impressions and is sensible of the obligation of an oath. 66 Va (25 Gratt) 865.

See **competent attesting witness.**

competere (kom-pe'te-re). To be available.

competing. In a state of competition; two or more businesses or industries producing or selling the same or essentially the same products or services without restraint of any kind upon their efforts to sell any or all of their products or services to any and all customers within practicable territorial limits.

competing lines. See **competing railroads.**

competing railroads. Two railroads which have each a through and separate line of communication between two given points, for which line each seeks the traffic between such points. As a general rule, whether lines of railroad are competitive depends upon the business of the companies, the conduct of the roads by their authorities, their channels of traffic, and generally upon whether the roads extend for transportation from and to the same points along their routes. See 44 Am J1st RR § 323.

competing unions. See **rival unions.**

competit assisa (kom-pe'tit as-sīs'a). An assize lies, an action lies.

competition. The activities of persons conducting a business, following a profession, or engaging in a sport, in an effort to succeed. The act of seeking or endeavoring to gain what another is endeavoring to gain at the same time; common contest or striving for the same object; strife for superiority; rivalry. The status of persons dealing in or furnishing goods or services of the same kind and soliciting trade or patronage from the same customers or class of customers in the same territory at the same time. 52 Am J1st Tradem § 94. (Scotch.) The contest between the creditors of a bankrupt to establish their respective ranks and preferences.

See **competing; unfair competition.**

competition with mails. The Federal offense of carrying mail in competition with the Post Office Department, so as to deprive the department of its monopoly in the business of receiving, transporting, and delivering mail matter. 41 Am J1st P O § 106.

competitive examination. A test by objective standards or measures. Where the standard or measure is wholly subjective, it differs, in effect, in no respect from an uncontrolled opinion of the examiners and cannot be termed "competitive." Fink v Finegan, 270 NY 356, 1 NE2d 462.

complain (kom'plān). To file a complaint; to make a formal charge or accusation of crime against a person; to make a charge.

complainant. The petitioner in a suit in a court of equity; a plaintiff; a prosecuting witness in a criminal proceeding; a person who files a formal charge or accusation of crime.

complaining witness. See **prosecuting witness.**

complaint. A bill in equity. 27 Am J2d Eq § 179; a pleading by which the plaintiff in a civil action, whether of a legal or equitable nature, sets out the cause of action and invokes the jurisdiction of the court. 41 Am J1st Pl § 73. In some instances and under some statutes, it comprehends oral as well as written allegations. Asbell v Edwards, 63 Kan 610, 66 P 641.

The formal charge, made under oath, of the commission of a crime or offense. 21 Am J2d Crim L § 441. If the offense charged is a minor one, the complaint, otherwise known as an affidavit or preliminary information, will stand as the pleading upon which the accused will be tried; if the offense is a felony, the accused is not put to trial upon the complaint, since he can be charged with felony only by an indictment or an information filed by the state's attorney. State v Hamilton, 133 W Va 394, 56 SE2d 544, 12 ALR2d 573.

See **bill; declaration; outcry; petition.**

complete. Finished; ready for the use or purpose for which it was intended. See Maxcy v Oshkosh, 144 Wis 238, 128 NW 899.

completed. Finished; the last operation on a job performed. Re Mt. Washington S. S. Co. (DC NH) 43 F Supp 176.

completed railroad. Fitted for use as a railroad; a railroad ready and in proper condition for the placing and running of regular trains upon it, or for operation as it is usually termed. Some authorities, however, take the view that the term means that the road is in condition to be operated for regular passenger and freight traffic and is actually in use. 44 Am J1st RR § 3.

complete enjoyment rule. A principle of the law of implied easements that the extent of the grantee's private right of user in streets and alleys shown on a map or plat, by reference to which his conveyance was made, is limited to such streets and alleys as are reasonably or materially beneficial to the grantee and of which the deprivation will reduce the value of his lot by preventing his complete enjoyment of the premises. Anno: 7 ALR2d 633; 25 Am J2d Ease § 26.

complete immunity. Immunity granted a defendant as a matter of law by virtue of the charitable nature of the defendant, irrespective of the status of the person damaged or injured in relation to the defendant and regardless of the negligence of the defendant in employing or retaining an incompetent employee. 13 Am J2d Char § 156.

complete jurisdiction. The power to hear and determine the cause, and the power to enforce the judgment. Cooper v Reynolds (US) 10 Wall 308, 19 L Ed 931.

complete loss of sight. The absence of sight for practical purposes, even though there is sufficient response in the eyes to distinguish between light and dark. 29A Am J Rev ed Ins § 1513.

complete manufacture. The ultimate product of prior successive manufactures or an intermediate product which may be used for different purposes. 21 Am J2d Cust D § 44.

complete operation doctrine. A principle, applied in reference to the loading and unloading clause of an automobile liability insurance policy, that the clause covers the entire process involved in the movement of goods from the moment when they are given into the insured's possession until they are turned over at the place of destination to the party to whom delivery is to be made. According to this doctrine, loading and unloading includes more than the mere placing of the goods on the truck or the removal of the goods from the truck, so that when they are taken directly from the truck and in one continuous operation, are carried into the customer's place of business, they are still in the process of being unloaded when set down therein. 7 Am J2d Auto Ins § 88.

complete remedy at law. See **adequate remedy at law.**

completing an abstract. The work of abstracters of title and title insurers. Anno: 80 ALR 772.

completion of public improvement. The finishing of the last work, not the acceptance of the work by the public body. Dickey v United States Fidelity & G. Co. 107 Kan 605, 193 P 346. The right of the surety on a contractor's bond. 17 Am J2d Cont Bond §§ 57, 111-113.

completion of record. The clerical function of a clerk of court in filling in blanks left by a judge in rendering a judgment. 30A Am J Rev ed Judgm § 105.

completion of the work. See **completion of public improvement.**

complicated accounts. A basis for seeking the remedy of an accounting. Scott v Caldwell, 160 Fla 861, 37 So2d 85. Accounts involving several issues for determination or requiring a discovery in determining the rights of the parties. 1 Am J2d Acctg § 53.

complice (kom'plis). An accomplice.

complicity. The state or condition of a person who is involved as an accomplice.

complot (kom-plot'). To plot with another or others; to conspire.

comply. To perfect or carry into effect; to complete; to perform or execute in accord with a previous contract or arrangement. Cleland v Waters, 16 Ga 496, 503.

composite facts rule. The rule of evidence which supports the admissibility of testimony, which is literally in the form of a conclusion of the witness, but actually is testimony to what the witness knows or has observed concerning circumstances of such nature that practicably they are best presented in the form of a composite rather than in detail, as where a witness is permitted to testify that he is dependent upon another for support, notwithstanding the superficial element of conclusion. See 31 Am J2d Ev § 6.

compositeurs. See **amiables compositeurs.**

Compositio Mensurarum (kom-po-zi'she-ō men-sū-rā'rum). The regulation of measures,—the name of the earliest English statute which established a standard of weight. This was originally taken from corns or grains of wheat, thirty-two of which, by the statute, made a pennyweight, twenty of these an ounce, and twelve ounces a pound. See 1 Bl Comm 275.

composition agreement. See **composition with creditors.**

composition in bankruptcy. See **composition with creditors.**

composition of tithes. An agreement made between a landowner and the parson of the parish whereby the former's land is discharged from liability for tithes.

See **real composition.**

composition with creditors. An agreement between an insolvent or embarrassed debtor and two or more of his creditors whereby the creditors, for some consideration, such as an immediate payment, agree to the discharge of their respective claims on the receipt of payment which is in a lesser amount than that actually owing on the claim. 15 Am J2d Comp Cred § 1. An agreement by a debtor made with his creditors which fixes a basis or plan whereby the debts may be paid, he being favored by a reduction of the claims, and extension of time for payment, or both; proceedings in the bankruptcy court for debt readjustment. 9 Am J2d Bankr §§ 1279 et seq.

compositio ulnarum et perticarum (kom-po-si'she-ō ul-nā'rum et per-ti-kā'rum). The regulation of yards and perches,—an ancient English statute establishing a standard of linear measure. It provided that an inch should be the length of three grains of barley, a foot should equal twelve inches, a yard, three feet, and five and a half yards, a perch. See 1 Bl Comm 275.

compos mentis (kom'pos men'tis). Of sound mind; sane.

compos sui (kom'pos su'ī). Possessing the control of one's self.

compotus (kom-pō'tus). An account.

compound. Noun: That which is compounded or formed by the union or mixture of elements, ingredients, or parts. United States v Brunett (DC Mo) 53 F2d 219. Verb: To create a product by mixing several products; the putting together by human agency of two or more substances, previously separated, to form a substance by union. Rutan v Johnson & Johnson (CA3 NJ) 231 F 369; to compromise; to effect a composition with a creditor; to obtain discharge from a debt by the payment of a smaller sum. First Nat. Bank v Malheur County, 30 Or 420, 45 P 781.

compounder. One who compounds.
See **amicable compounder.**

compounding a crime. The making by one directly injured by the commission of a crime of an agreement not to inform against or prosecute the offender in return for a reward, bribe, or reparation for the injury. 15 Am J2d Comp Cri § 1.

compounding elements. See **compound.**

compounding for differences. A form of gambling in stocks, securities, and commodities, wherein a fictitious sale is made for delivery at a future time with no intention to deliver and settlement is to be made on the difference between the contract price and the market price at such future time. 24 Am J1st Gaming §§ 66, 67.

compound interest. Interest charged on interest by adding accrued interest to principal and computing interest for the next interest period upon the new principal. 30 Am J Rev ed Int § 57.

compound larceny. The offense of larceny aggravated by the taking from one's house or person. State v Chambers, 22 W Va 779.

comprehensive insurance. A policy of insurance which provides coverage for various risks, each of which might form the subject matter of a policy.

compromise. An agreement to terminate, by means of mutual concessions, a controversy over a claim which is disputed in good faith or unliquidated. 15 Am J2d Compr § 1.

compromise and settlement. A compromise agreement followed by the performance of the promises contained in the agreement. 15 Am J2d Compr § 1.

compromise verdict. A verdict which is reached only by the surrender of conscientious convictions as to a material issue by some members of the jury in return for a relinquishment by other members of their like settled opinion on another issue, the result not commanding the approval of the whole panel. Such verdict is improper and should be set aside as subversive of trial by jury. 53 Am J1st Trial § 1033.

compte arrêté (kompt ä-rê-té). An account acknowledged; that is, an account stated in writing and acknowledged to be correct on its face by the party against whom it is stated. Chevalier v Hyams, 9 La Ann 484, 485.

compter (koun'tėr). To calculate; to intend; to expect.

comptroller (kǫn-trō'lėr). A corporate or public officer in charge of the financial affairs of the corporation or public body.

compulsion. The application of physical or mental force to compel the performance or the omission of performance, of an act. The word is frequently used as synonymous with the word "duress." Joannin v Ogilvie, 49 Minn 564, 52 NW 217.
See **coercion; commercial frustration; compulsion of wife; constraint.**

compulsory. Under compulsion; forced physically or morally.

compulsory arbitration. An arbitration proceeding to which the consent of at least one of the parties is enforced by statutory provisions. 5 Am J2d Arb & A § 9. Compulsory arbitration has attracted the most attention in labor disputes. Arbitration of such disputes may be compelled by statute where the industry is one affected by a public interest and the statute provides adequate standards for the guidance of the arbitrators. Anno: 55 ALR2d 447.

compulsory assignment. An assignment for the benefit of creditors made by operation of law or under legal compulsion. 6 Am J2d Assign for Crs § 3.

compulsory counterclaim. A demand of the defendant which must be pleaded in response to plaintiff's suit or be barred. 20 Am J2d Countcl § 13; any claim which, at the time of serving the pleading, the pleader has against any opposing party, growing out of the occurrence or transaction that is the subject matter of the opposing party's action, unless the counterclaim is already the subject of a pending action. Rule 13(a), Fed Rules of Civ Proc; 20 Am J2d Countcl § 4.

compulsory education. Such education as a parent or guardian of a child is required by law to provide for the child. 47 Am J1st Sch § 156.

compulsory insurance. Automobile liability insurance which is required as a condition of the right to operate an automobile. 7 Am J2d Auto Ins § 4.

compulsory integration. See **compulsory pooling; integration.**

compulsory liability insurance. See **compulsory insurance.**

compulsory military training. Required military training of students in universities accepting the benefits of the Federal Land-Grant Act. 15 Am J2d Colleges § 24; training compelled under the selective draft.
See **Selective Draft Law.**

compulsory nonsuit. See **nonsuit.**

compulsory novation. An unusual term for garnishment. Cole v Randall Park Holding Co. 201 Md 616, 95 A2d 273, 41 ALR2d 1084.

compulsory payment. A payment compelled by force of law either directly through process or by suasion through threat of process which is not to be resisted. Blanchard v Blanchard, 201 NY 134, 94 NE 630. To constitute a compulsory payment, it is not essential that the demand be made by an officer who is prepared to enforce it by process. There may be compulsion which justifies and virtually requires payment to be made of the illegal demands of a private person who has it in his power seriously to prejudice the property rights of another, and to impose upon the latter the risk of suffering great loss if there be no compliance with the demand. State ex rel. McCarty v Nelson, 41 Minn 25, 42 NW 548. To constitute "compulsion" which will be regarded as sufficient to make a payment involuntary, there must be some actual or threatened exercise of power possessed, or believed to be possessed, by the party exacting or receiving the payment over the person or property of another, for which the latter

has no means of immediate relief other than making the payment. 40 Am J1st Paym § 162.
See **involuntary payment.**

compulsory pilotage. The requirement imposed by law, in states with harbors, upon a vessel approaching or leaving a harbor, that it take on a pilot duly licensed under the local law, who shall conduct the vessel into or out of the harbor as the case may be. 48 Am J1st Ship § 204.

compulsory pooling. The combining of small or irregularly shaped tracks owned by different persons to develop their lands as a single oil drilling or gas drilling unit, the purpose being conservation. Superior Oil Co. v Foote, 214 Miss 857, 59 So 2d 85, 37 ALR2d 415.

compulsory process. Compulsory process for a witness signifies and means a process that will compel the attendance of such witness; a process that will bring a witness into court who refuses to come without it. Ex parte Marmaduke, 91 Mo 228, 238.
See **subpoena.**

compulsory sale. See **eminent domain; involuntary alienation.**

compulsory service. See **peonage; Selective Draft Act.**

compulsory unitization. A term, sometimes used interchangeably with "compulsory pooling," although it refers to joint operations on a large scale, comprehending a measure in the interest of conservation for combining oil drilling or gas drilling operations into single units. Superior Oil Co. v Foote, 214 Miss 857, 59 So 2d 85, 37 ALR2d 415.

compurgation (kom-pėr-gā'shọn). An ancient form of trial, which was also known as "wager of law," wherein the defendant could call eleven compurgators to swear to their belief in his innocence. 3 Bl Comm 343.

compurgator (kom'pėr-gā-tọr). One of a defendant's eleven neighbors who accompanied him at a trial by wager of law and avowed under oath that they believed in their consciences that he had spoken the truth in giving his testimony. 3 Bl Comm 343.

computation. Calculation.
See **interest; time.**

computo. See **de computo.**

Comstock Act. The federal statute relative to the use of the mails for the delivery of contraceptives or of written or printed matter advertising contraceptives or giving information concerning methods of preventing conception. 18 USC § 334; 41 Am J1st P O § 114.

comte (kônt). A count.

con. Slang: to swindle; to trick; to deceive.

conacre (ko'āk-ėr). A kind of tenancy under which wages are in whole or in part applied to rental.

conatus (kon-ā'tus). A bare attempt to commit an act, as distinguished from a complete accomplishment. 44 Am J1st Rape § 3.

conceal. To keep facts secret or withhold them from the knowledge of another; to hide or secrete physical objects from sight or observation. Gerry v Dunham, 57 Me 334, 339. As the word appears in a statute prescribing a ground for attachment, to "conceal" property is to hide it or put it where an officer of the law will be unable to find it. 6 Am J2d Attach § 236. As used in a statute against concealing stolen goods, knowing them to have been stolen, to "conceal" means to secrete with intent to deprive the owner of his property. Bailey v State, 115 Neb 77, 80, 211 NW 200. For the purposes of the Bankruptcy Act, to "conceal" means to secrete, falsify, and mutilate. Bankr Act § 1(7); 11 USC § 1(7). The criminal offense of concealment of property belonging to the estate of a bankrupt is not limited to physical secretion, but includes the preventing of discovery by the withholding of knowledge through refusing to divulge information as to the location of the property. 9 Am J2d Bankr § 1715. For some purposes, as in the case of executing process in a claim and delivery action, to refuse the demand of an officer holding process for the property in suit is to "conceal" it. State v Pope, 4 Wash 2d 394, 103 P2d 1089, 129 ALR 240.
See **concealment; secrete; treasure trove.**

concealed. See **conceal; concealed weapon; concealment.**

concealed weapon. A weapon so placed that it cannot be readily seen under ordinary observation, even though not absolutely invisible to other persons. 56 Am J1st Weap § 10.

concealer (kọn-sē'lėr). A person who was employed to discover lands which had been secretly kept from the king.

concealment. A suppression of or neglect to disclose facts which a person knows and which he ought to communicate; the nondisclosure of a fact which should be revealed. 37 Am J2d Fraud § 2; the designed and intentional withholding of any fact material to the risk which the insured in honesty and good faith ought to communicate to the insurer. 29 Am J Rev ed Ins § 689.
See **conceal; concealed weapon.**

concedere (kon-sē'de-re). To grant.

conception. An idea, as an idea for a patentable invention, which must include every essential attribute of the complete and practical invention. If anything remains to be completed or devised in order to enable the instrument or art to perform its functions in the manner proposed by the inventor, his conception of the invention is not finished, nor has he brought into existence any true idea of means. Zublin v Pickin, 21 Cust & Pat App (Pat) 1097, 70 F2d 732. Fertilization of the female ovum by the male germ cell. Am Jur Proof of Facts, Medical Glossary.
See **antenuptial conception.**

concerted action. See **concerted activity.**

concerted activity. Group action by several or more employees for the furtherance of their common interests as such. 31 Am J Rev ed Lab § 189; an element of a secondary boycott which constitutes an unfair labor practice. 31 Am J Rev ed Lab § 253.
A single spontaneous brief work stoppage by nonunion employees to present wage grievances to the employer is a "concerted activity" of a "labor organization" so as to protect participants therein from discharge under provisions of the National Labor Relations Act making it an unfair labor practice for an employer to discourage membership in any "labor organization" by discrimination in regard to tenure of employment, or to interfere with employees in the exercise of the right to engage in "concerted activities" for the purpose of collective bargaining or other mutual aid or protection. NLRB v Kennametal, Inc. (CA3) 182 F2d 817, 19 ALR2d 562.

concessi (kon-ses′sī). I have granted. The word is a technical one which was used in conveyancing. It had the same meaning and use as the word "demisi," I have demised, and if a grantor used it in a lease for years, it implied a covenant that if the assignee of the lessee be evicted, he should have a writ of covenant. Wiggins v Pender, 132 NC 628, 44 SE 362.

concessimus (kon-ses′si-mus). We have granted.

concessio (kon-sesh′i-ō). A grant; a concession.

concession. An acknowledgment of a point made by another; a rebate given by a carrier. 13 Am J2d Car § 203; the right to do business upon the premises of another, such right normally being granted to one for the sale of candy, drinks, programs, and merchandise at exhibitions and amusement places. Anno: 14 ALR 627. As the word is used in Spanish-American grants, it means "whatsoever is granted as favor or reward, as the privileges granted by the prince." De Haro v United States (US) 5 Wall 599, 18 L Ed 681, 688.
See **advantage, concession, and discrimination.**

concessionarie. A person holding a concession.

concessione. See **ex concessione.**

Concessio per regem fieri debet de certitudine (kon-sesh′i-ō per rē′jem fī′er-i de′bet dē ser-ti-tu′di-nē). A grant from the king ought to be of that which can be ascertained.

Concessio versus concedentem latam interpretationem habere debet (kon-sesh′i-ō ver′sus kon-se-den′tem la′tam in-ter-pre-tā-she-o′nem hā-bē′re de′bet). A grant ought to have a broad construction against the grantor.

concessis. See **ex concessis.**

concessor (kon-ses′or). A grantor.

conciliation. The adjustment of disputes in a friendly manner, or, if not in a friendly manner, at least without violence. One of the primary examples of conciliation is the adjustment of labor disputes without a strike or an extended strike. 31 Am J Rev ed Lab § 371.

conciliation board. A body established for the purpose of encouraging amicable adjustment of small claims. 20 Am J2d Courts § 31; an agency for the adjustment of labor disputes. 31 Am J Rev ed Lab § 371.
See **council of conciliation.**

conciliation commissioner. An officer of a court of bankruptcy under the now obsolescent § 75 of the Bankruptcy Act on agricultural compositions and extensions, his duties partaking of the nature of those of a referee but confined to proceedings under such section. Federal Land Bank v Castanien (CA6 Ohio) 116 F2d 589.

concilium (kon-sil′i-um). A council.

concisely. Comprehensively, but succinctly. Bertolet's Election, 13 Pa C 353, 355.

concise statement of decision. The conclusion without the reasoning. Schmid v Thorsen, 89 Or 575, 175 P 74.

conclude. To form a final judgment after consideration, consultation or advice. Dunbar v Fant, 170 SC 414, 170 SE 460, 90 ALR 1412. To come to an end, whether of a story or an argument.

concluding argument. See **closing argument.**

conclusion. A deduction; the result of reasoning; the end or last part of a discourse; matter in a declaration or complaint, following the statement of the plaintiff's cause of action; the formal closing of a plea, usually, under modern practice merely a demand for judgment. Pierson v Wallace, 7 Ark 282, 291.

conclusion of fact. A finding of fact; an ultimate fact, Caywood v Farrell, 175 Ill 480, 482; the result of reasoning from the evidentiary facts. Greenberg v Lee, 196 Or 157, 248 P2d 324, 35 ALR2d 567.
See **finding of fact.**

conclusion of indictment. The concluding words, "against the peace and dignity of the state," or other formula, often one prescribed by constitution or statute. 27 Am J1st Indict § 38.

conclusions of law. The conclusions drawn by the court, in a trial to the court, in the exercise of its legal judgment from the facts found by it, which, in connection with the findings of fact, constitute the basis of the decision in the case. 53 Am J1st Trial § 1132. The court's statement of what the law on a controverted point is, as distinguished from an order or judgment. 4 Am J2d A & E § 76. Statements in a pleading which depart from the objective of pleading the facts. 41 Am J1st Pl § 16.

conclusion to the contrary. The formal closing of a plea, tendering an issue of fact for the jury to decide.

conclusive. Final; decisive or, at least, convincing.

conclusive evidence. Facts in evidence which are, as a matter of law, determinative of the issue; facts in evidence which are so convincing as to support verdict or findings, but are not absolutely beyond contradiction. New York L. Ins. Co. v Kuhlenschnidt, 218 Ind 404, 33 NE2d 340, 135 ALR 397; Hoadley v Hammond, 63 Iowa 599, 602.

conclusiveness. A word of variable meaning, depending to a great extent on the context in which it appears. 2 Am J2d Admin L § 483; sometimes meaning finality, 2 Am J2d Admin L § 483; in other connections, as in its relation to evidence, meaning convincing, but not necessarily beyond contradiction.
See **conclusive evidence.**

conclusiveness of judgment. Verity, finality, and binding effect. 30A Am J Rev ed Judgm § 311. A judgment or an equivalent order is final and conclusive when it terminates a matter in such a way as to end it and to preclude all further inquiry concerning the truth thereof. Re Enger, 225 Minn 229, 30 NW2d 694, 1 ALR2d 1048. The conclusiveness of a judgment is an effect limited to collateral attack; a judgment does not import absolute verity, and is not regarded as conclusive, where it is being subjected to a direct attack by motion to vacate or an appeal. Capos v Clatsop County, 144 Or 510, 25 P2d 903, 90 ALR 289.

conclusive presumption. A presumption so peremptorily drawn from specific facts in evidence that the law will not permit it to be rebutted, Brandt v Morning Journal Asso. 81 App Div 183, 185, 80 NYS 1002; in effect, a rule of substantive law, to be applied by the court in its evaluation of the issues the same as any other fixed rule of law. Farnsworth v Hazelett, 197 Iowa 1367, 199 NW 410, 38 ALR 814; 29 Am J2d Ev § 164.

concord. A settlement; a compromise; peaceful relations.

The term "concord" was used to designate the third step in the levying of a fine to convey land. It was the agreement of the parties made with leave of court, consisting usually of an acknowledgment from the deforciants who were keeping the other out of possession that the lands in question were the right of the complainant. See 2 Bl Comm 350.

Concordare leges legibus est optimus interpretandi modus (kon-kor-dā´re lē´jēz lē´ji-bus est op´ti-mus in-ter-pre-tan´dī mo´dus). To reconcile laws with other laws constitutes the best method of interpreting them.

concordat (kon-kôr´dat). An agreement; a covenant. In the civil law, a composition deed.

Concordia Discordantium Canonum (kon-kor´di-a dis-kor-dan´she-um ka´no-num). The orderly arrangement of the confused canons—the title of a compilation made about 1151 by Gratian, an Italian monk, whereby he reduced the Roman ecclesiastical constitutions into three books, after the manner of Justinian's pandects. See 1 Bl Comm 82.

concourse. An open space. The space in an airport or railroad station between waiting room and place for boarding planes or cars. A concert of activity; co-operation.

concourse of actions (kong´kōrs). The maintenance of a civil action and a criminal prosecution for the same alleged wrong, at the same time.

concrimination (kon-krim-i-nā´shǫn). The accusation of two or more persons for the same criminal offense.

concubaria (kon-kụ-bā´ri-ạ). A cattle-pen.

concubeant (kon-ku´be-ant). Lying together.

concubina (kǫn-kū´bi-nạ). A concubine.

concubinage (kǫn-kū´bi-nāj). Cohabitation of a man and a concubine; the state of a woman who sustains a relation involving continuous and regular illicit intercourse with a man to whom she is not a wife. Such a relation need not exist for any considerable period of time to constitute concubinage, but the relation which gives rise to the disreputable state of a woman indicated by the term, may like that of marriage, be contracted or assumed in a day as easily as in a year. Henderson v People, 124 Ill 607, 17 NE 68.
See **concubine.**

concubinatus (kong-kụ-bīn-at´us). A legalized concubinage under the Roman law.

concubine (kong´kụ-bīn). A woman who habitually assumes and exercises toward a man not her husband the rights and privileges which belong to the matrimonial relation. Anon v Anon, 172 Ind 134.

The concubine must not be confounded with the courtezan, or even with what is ordinarily called a mistress. Concubinage is the act or practice of cohabiting in sexual intercourse without the authority of law or legal marriage. Gauff v Johnson, 161 La 975, 977, 109 So 782.

concubinus (kon-kū´bi-nus). A man living in a state of concubinage.

concubitu prohibere vago (kon-ku´bi-tū prō-hi-bē´re va´gō). To forbid promiscuous copulation. One of the ends of society and government. See 1 Bl Comm 438.

Conculcavit et consumpsit (kon-kul-kā´vit et konsump´sit). He trampled upon and destroyed.

concur. To agree with; to join with other creditors in making claim against the estate of their insolvent debtor; to happen at the same time.

concurrent causes. Two or more causes which run together and act contemporaneously to produce a given result or inflict an injury. Stacy v Williams, 253 Ky 353, 60 SW2d 697; Herr v Lebanon, 149 Pa 222, 24 A 207.
See **concurring cause.**

concurrent conditions. The conditions in a contract whereof performance by one party of his promises is conditioned upon performance by the other party of his promises; in other words, concurrent conditions are mutual conditions precedent to be performed simultaneously in the sense that when one party is ready to perform and offers to perform, the other party must perform or be in default. 17 Am J2d Contr § 321.

concurrent consideration. An act or a promise which a party to a contract does or makes as a consideration therefor, simultaneously with an act or a promise on the part of the other party which furnishes the consideration running from him; mutual promises mutually binding. 17 Am J2d Contr § 105.

concurrent covenants. Covenants in a bond, deed, or contract whereof performance by one party of his undertaking is conditioned upon performance by the other party of his undertakings, so that, performance on the two sides shall be simultaneous in the sense that when one party is ready to perform, and offers to perform, the other party must perform or be in default. Snow v Johnson, 1 Minn 48, 52; 20 Am J2d Cov § 8.

concurrent insurance. A term, according to some authority, which does not have a definite, precise, meaning in the law of insurance. Globe & Rutgers Fire Ins. Co. v Alaska-Portland Packers' Asso. (CA9 Or) 205 F 32; obviously, meaning "other insurance" on the same risk, in a "concurrent insurance permitted" clause. L'Engle v Scottish Union & Nat. Ins. Co. 48 Fla 82, 37 So 462.
See **coinsurance; other insurance.**

concurrent insurance permitted clause. See **concurrent insurance.**

concurrent jurisdiction. The jurisdiction conferred upon and existing in two, possibly more, courts over the same class of cases or matters. 20 Am J2d Cts § 106. Jurisdiction existing in a court and in an administrative agency over the same matter. 20 Am J2d Cts § 128. That jurisdiction which entitles one government to as much power—legislative, judicial, and executive—as that possessed by another government. Wedding v Meyler, 192 US 573, 48 L Ed 570, 24 S Ct 322. That authority commonly exercised concurrently upon water divided by the boundary line between two countries. It relates to matters at least in some way connected with the use of water for navigable purposes, to things afloat, or in some legitimate sense on the water—things difficult to deal with if it were necessary to determine in each instance of the exercise of jurisdiction the precise location of the particular act involved as regards the boundary line. 30 Am J Rev ed Internat L § 28.

concurrent lease. A second lease made by the owner of the reversion to a person other than the tenant under the first lease, covering all or part of the same premises as the first lease, the terms of the two leases including at least some time in common. 32 Am J1st L & T § 93.

concurrent liens. Liens which arise simultaneously, in consequence of their creation at the same time or by the same instrument and which are therefore of equal dignity and are entitled to equal rank in priority. 33 Am J1st Liens § 33.

concurrent negligence. The contributory negligence of the plaintiff in an action for negligence, it and the negligence of the defendant both contributing to produce the injury for which damages are claimed. Dyerson v Union Pacific Railroad Co. 74 Kan 528, 87 P 680. The negligence of a third person concurring with that of the defendant in an action for negligence. Alabama Power Co. v Bass, 218 Ala 586, 119 So 625, 63 ALR 1.
See **concurrent causes.**

concurrent powers. A term familiar in constitutional law, having reference to the class of powers, under a classification of the United States Supreme Court, which may be exercised concurrently and independently by both federal and state governments. 16 Am J2d Const L § 198.

concurrent promises. Mutual promises by the parties to a contract, to be performed simultaneously in the sense that when one party is ready to perform, and offers to perform, his promises, the other party must perform his promises or be in default. Dermott v Jones, (US) 23 How 220, 16 L Ed 442, 447; 17 Am J2d Contr § 321.

concurrent remedies. Two or more actions or proceedings available to a person in obtaining redress for a wrong inflicted upon him, although not necessarily co-extensive in respect of the relief obtainable. Sinnott v Feiock, 165 NY 444, 59 NE 265.

concurrent resolution. See **joint resolution.**

concurrent sentences. Sentences of imprisonment for crime in which the time of each is to run concurrently with the others, and not seriatim.

concurrent stipulations. See **concurrent conditions; concurrent covenants, concurrent promises.**

concurrent writs. Writs issued for the same purpose to be used or served in different places or in respect to different persons.

concurring cause. A cause which operates contemporaneously with the primary cause to produce the injury, so that the injury would not have happened in the absence of either. The phrase is contrasted with an intervening cause, a cause which succeeds or follows the primary cause. Horne v Southern R. Co. 186 SC 525, 197 SE 31, 116 ALR 745.
See **concurrent cause.**

concursu (kon-ker′sū). A remedy provided by the laws of Louisiana, to enable creditors to enforce their claims against a debtor. Schroeder's Syndics v Nicholson, 2 La 350, 355.

concursus (kon-kėr′sus). A special remedy under Louisiana statute afforded a certain class of creditors for the concurrent enforcement of their claims and to regulate their rights as between themselves and against a contractor doing public work, and the surety on his bond. Seal v Gano, 160 La 636, 107 So 473.

concuss (kọn-kus′). To use threats; to exercise duress.

concussio (kon-kush′i-ō). Concussion; extortion.

concussion (kọn-kush′ọn). A Civil Law term: —extortion; compulsion by threats and without force, as by threatening to expose a person to disgrace.

condemn. To declare a building unfit for use and order its destruction as a peril to health and public safety; to order the slaughter of diseased animals. 4 Am J2d Ani § 35. To adjudge guilty; to pass sentence upon a person convicted of crime. To appropriate property for public use. Wulzen v Board of Supervisors, 101 Cal 15, 35 P 353; Wescott v State Highway Com. 262 NC 522, 138 SE2d 133.

condemnation. The taking of private property for public use through the exercise of the power of eminent domain. Venable v Wabash Western Railroad Co. 112 Mo 103, 20 SW 493. A forfeiture of goods, as for the nonpayment of customs duties. The passing of sentence upon a person convicted of crime; an order made by competent authority adjudging a building or a ship unfit for use; an order for the slaughter of diseased animals. 4 Am J2d Ani § 35.
See **inspected and condemned.**

condemnation of felony. Conviction of felony. Davis v Davis, 102 Ky 440, 43 SW 168.

condemnation suit (kon-dem-nā′shọn sūt). A judicial proceeding for the purpose of having property taken by eminent domain for public use upon the payment of just compensation for such taking. 27 Am J2d Em D § 375.

condemnator. See **decree condemnator.**

condemned. See **condemn; condemnation.**

condere (kon′de-re). To make; to establish; to found.

condescendence (kon-dẹ-sen′dẹns). A plaintiff's written statement of his cause of action.

condictio (kon-dik′she-o). An action; a summons.

conditio (kon-di′she-ō). A condition.

Conditio beneficialis, quae statum construit, benigne, secundum verborum intentionem est interpretanda; odiosa autem, quae statum destruit, stricte, secundum verborum proprietam, accipienda (kon-di′she-ō be-ne-fi-she-ā′lis, kwe stā′tum kon-stru′it, be-nig′ne, se-kun′dum ver-bō′rum in-ten-she-ō′nem est in-ter-pre-tan′da; ō-di-ō′sa â′tem, kwe stā′tum de-stru′it, strik′te, se-kun′dum ver-bō′rum prō-pri-e-tā′tem, ak-si-pi-en′da). A beneficial condition which creates an estate, ought to be interpreted favorably, according to the intent of the language; but an odious condition which destroys an estate, should be construed strictly according to the letter.

Conditio dicitur, cum quid in casum incertum qui potest tendere ad esse aut non esse, confertur (kon-di′she-ō di′si-ter, cum quid in kā′sum in-ser′tum kwī po′test ten′de-re ad es′se ât non es′se, kon-fer′ter). It is called a condition when something is given on an uncertain event which may or may not happen.

Conditio illicita habetur pro non adjicta (kon-di′she-ō il-li′si-ta hā-bē′ter prō non ad-jik′ta). An unlawful condition is held not to be binding.

condition. Verb: To put in shape, as a horse for a race, a pugilist for a match. Noun: A provision in a contract creating no right or duty of and in itself but merely limiting or modifying rights and duties under the contract. 17 Am J2d Contr § 320; a clause in a contract or agreement which has for its object the suspension, rescission or modification of the principal obligation, or, in case of a will, to suspend, revoke or modify the devise or bequest. Pedro v Potter, 197 Cal 751, 759, 242 P 926, 42 ALR 1165, 1169. A qualification or restriction annexed to a conveyance of lands, whereby it is provided that in case a particular event does or does not happen, or in case the grantor or grantees do or omit to do a particular act, an estate shall commence, be enlarged, or be defeated. Pedro v Potter, 197 Cal 751, 759, 242 P 926, 42 ALR 1165, 1169; a provision in a grant or devise, under which an estate is made to vest, to be enlarged, or to be defeated, upon the happening or not happening of some event described therein. Raley v County of Umatilla, 15 Or 172, 13 P 890. The distinction between a condition and a covenant lies in the effect of a breach. Upon a breach of the condition upon which an estate is granted, the estate is forthwith forfeited, whereas a breach of covenant gives rise to an action at law to recover damages or a suit in equity for equitable relief. In the construction of deeds, courts will always incline to interpret the language as a covenant rather than a condition. See note to Woodruff v Woodruff, 1 LRA 381.

The expression "on condition" has frequently been used in written instruments so as to give to the word "condition" a looser and broader meaning than the law attaches to it. And it is often manifest from a perusal of the whole instrument that that which is called a condition is really but a covenant or agreement to be performed independently of the counter obligation with which it is associated, and in such case, the courts will give it that construction. Green County v Quinlan, 211 US 582, 594, 52 L Ed 335, 341, 29 S Ct 162.

The state of one's health, of his physical or mental being; the physical state of an animal.

See **concurrent conditions; condition precedent; condition subsequent; estate on condition; express condition; implied condition; negative condition; on condition.**

conditional. Subject to condition; contingent; not absolute. Loventhal v Home Ins. Co. 112 Ala 108, 20 So 419.

conditional acceptance. An acceptance of a bill of exchange containing some qualification, limitation, or condition, different from what is expressed on the face of the bill, or from what the law implies, upon a general acceptance. Todd v Bank of Kentucky, 66 Ky (3 Bush) 626, 628. It would appear, however, that a bill of exchange is dishonored by a conditional acceptance, since an acceptance is the drawee's engagement to honor the bill of exchange as presented to him. 11 Am J2d B & N § 500.

conditional acknowledgment. An acknowledgment by one alleged to be indebted to another which signifies his willingness to admit liability if the creditor will comply with conditions imposed upon him in the acknowledgment by the debtor, or if a certain condition which does not then exist thereafter comes into existence. Stone v Smoot, 191 Okla 512, 131 P2d 85, 143 ALR 1426.

conditional affirmance. An affirmance of the judgment rendered by the lower court, subject to remittitur or additur, depending upon whether the damages are found excessive or inadequate. 5 Am J2d A & E § 933.

conditional bequest. See **conditional legacy or devise.**

conditional binding receipt. A term familiar in the law of life insurance, which means temporary coverage upon condition of the ultimate approval of the application. 29 Am J Rev ed Ins §§ 208, 209.

conditional contract. Not just a contract with conditions, but a contract, the very existence of which depends upon the fulfillment or occurrence of a condition or contingency. Nashville & Northwestern Railroad Co. v Jones & Baker, 42 Tenn (2 Coldw) 574, 584.

conditional conveyance. A deed with a provision for a reconveyance or a defeasance of the estate on the performance of certain conditions; a mortgage. 36 Am J1st Mtg § 164.

conditional dedication. A dedication of land to the public whereunder the dedicator imposes reasonable terms and conditions which are not inconsistent with the terms of the grant or against public policy. 23 Am J2d Ded § 37.

conditional delivery. The delivery of an instrument for the payment of money, such as a promissory note, on a condition, such condition being binding as between the immediate parties and as regards a remote party other than a holder in due course, even though the condition is an oral one, if it is a condition precedent. 11 Am J2d B & N § 279; the delivery of a deed on a condition of effectiveness, such as one that the instrument is not effective until it has been signed by all grantors. 23 Am J2d Deeds § 84; the delivery of an insurance policy to the insured upon some condition affecting the commencement of the risk, such as the condition that the policy shall not take effect until the insurer has approved and accepted the risk. 29 Am J Rev ed Ins § 217.

conditional devise. See **conditional legacy or devise.**

conditional discharge. A probationary discharge of a person confined in a state hospital or asylum for the insane. 29 Am J Rev ed Ins Per § 50.

conditional dismissal. A dismissal on condition, for example, the dismissal of a suit for foreclosure of a mortgage on condition of payment of the amount of a tender which induced the dismissal. Thompson v Crains, 294 Ill 270, 128 NE 508, 12 ALR 931.

conditional dividend. A dividend declared by an insurance company but made conditional upon some such event as the payment of the next annual premium so as to continue the policy in force after its first anniversary. 29 Am J Rev ed Ins § 649.

conditional endorsement. See **conditional indorsement.**

conditional estate. See **conditional fee; conditional limitation; estate on condition.**

conditional fee. A common-law estate in land, otherwise known as a fee conditional or fee simple conditional, distinctive by reason of the limitation to particular heirs, exclusive of others, as a grant to a named person and "the heirs of his body," or, in the case of a special conditional fee, to a named person and "the male heirs of his body." 28 Am J2d Est § 38.

If the donee had no heirs of his body, or no male heirs of the body, as the case might be, the estate reverted to the donor; but if the condition as to heirs was fulfilled by birth of issue, this was such performance as rendered the estate of the donee absolute; at least he could alien, he might forfeit, he might charge the land with rents or other incumbrances which would bind the issue. To prevent a reversion to the donor it was usual for such tenants, as soon as they had performed the condition by having heirs, to alien the land and then repurchase, taking an absolute estate which would descend to their heirs general. It was to defeat this practice that the Statute de Donis Conditionalibus was passed. 28 Am J2d Est § 38.

See **de donis.**

conditional gift. A gift accompanied by a condition or qualification not inconsistent with the vesting of title in the donee. 24 Am J1st Gifts § 44.

conditional guaranty. A guaranty which imposes as a condition of the guarantor's liability, the happening of some contingent event other than the default of the principal debtor or the performance of some act on the part of the obligee. 24 Am J1st Guar § 16.

conditional indorsement. An indorsement of a negotiable instrument to which there is added to the signature of the indorser the words "without recourse," or words of similar import. Uniform Negotiable Instruments Law § 38; Anno: 91 ALR 399; 11 Am J2d B & N § 363.

conditional instruction. An erroneous form of instruction to a jury by which the court directly or in effect instructs the jury that a charge is to be considered by them if evidence has been given to sustain it, and otherwise to disregard it. 53 Am J1st Trial § 553.

conditional judgment. A judgment to which a condition upon which it is rendered is annexed. 30A Am J Rev ed Judgm § 120.

conditional legacy or devise. A legacy or devise, the operative effect of which, by the terms of the will, is made dependent or contingent upon the occurrence of some uncertain event. 57 Am J1st Wills § 1503.

See **conditional limitation; conditional will; estate on condition; contingent bequest.**

conditional limitation. An executory interest in real estate, created by conveyance, which divests and succeeds a preceding interest upon the happening of a particular contingency or stated event; an executory interest in real estate characterized by a condition and a limitation over, the former stating the effect of a breach in terminating an estate and the latter providing a succeeding estate in the holder of the next expectant interest, without any act on his part. 28 Am J2d Est § 335; a provision in a lease by virtue of which the lease terminates ipso facto upon a certain event happening or not happening or the performance or nonperformance of an act, irrespective of re-entry by the landlord or other act. 32 Am J1st L & T § 825.

conditionally necessary party. A person who should be a party to an action, so that complete relief may be obtained, but who is not an indispensable party. Anno: 28 ALR2d 417.

conditionally privileged communication. A communication made in good faith on a subject in which the person communicating has an interest, or in reference to which he has a duty, to a person having a corresponding interest or duty, even though it contains matter which, without privilege, would be actionable as defamatory, and even though the duty is not a legal one, but only a moral or social duty. Richardson v Gunby, 88 Kan 520, 127 P 533, quoting Townshend, Slander & Libel § 209; Mullens v Davidson, 133 W Va 557, 57 SE2d 1, 13 ALR2d 887.

A publication is conditionally or qualifiedly privileged where circumstances exist, or are reasonably believed by the defendant to exist, which cast on him the duty of making communications with certain other person to whom he makes such communication in the performance of such duty, or where the person is so situated that it becomes right in the interest of society that he should tell third persons certain facts, which he in good faith proceeds to do. Faber v Byrle, 171 Kan 38, 229 P2d 718, 25 ALR2d 1379.

This type of a communication is a defamatory communication made on what is called an occasion of privilege without actual malice and as to such communications there is no civil liability. Mullens v Davidson, 133 W Va 557, 57 SE2d 1, 13 ALR2d 887.

conditional obligation. An obligation which becomes binding only upon the fulfilment of a condition.

See **conditional contract.**

conditional pardon. A pardon granted either on a condition precedent, becoming operative when, and not until, the grantee has performed the designated act, or on a condition subsequent, in which case the pardon will take effect when it is delivered and accepted, but will become null and void upon the violation by the grantee of any of the specified terms or conditions. Anno: 60 ALR 1410.

conditional receipt. See **conditional binding receipt.**

conditional reversal. A reversal with conditions imposed upon the successful appellant, as where he is required to enter his assent that the original judgment shall stand as security for whatever damages may be found against him upon a second trial. 5 Am J2d A & E § 954.

conditional revocation. See **dependent relative revocation.**

conditional sale. A sale in which the vendee receives the possession and right of use of the goods or articles sold, but transfer of complete title to the vendee is made dependent upon the performance of some condition or the happening of some contingency, usually the full payment of the purchase price. 47 Am J1st Sales § 828.

A chattel mortgage is, in effect, a conditional sale of the mortgaged property. State Ins. Co. v Schreck, 27 Neb 527, 43 NW 340; Reinstein v Roberts, 34 Or 87, 55 P 90.

conditional sale contract. A contract for the sale of goods by the terms of which the goods are to be delivered to the buyer, but the seller is to retain or reserve the right of possession or property in the goods until certain conditions specified in the contract have been fulfilled. John Deere Plow Co. v Hamilton (CA7 Ill) 19 F2d 965.

See **conditional sale.**

Conditional Sales Act. A uniform act specifically repealed by the Uniform Commercial Code. 15 Am J2d Com C § 6.

conditional stipulation. A stipulation which is dependent upon a condition.

conditional subscription. A subscription in which the liability of the subscriber is dependent upon the performance of some act by the beneficiary or other person. 50 Am J1st Subscr § 19.

conditional will. A will which is dependent for its operation upon the happening of a specified condition or contingency. If the condition fails, the will is inoperative and void thereafter, unless it is republished. Kimmels Estate, 278 Pa 435, 123 A 405, 31 ALR 678.

conditioned. Subject to one or more conditions; made dependent on one or more conditions; good physical condition; ready for exertion; inured to the climate and one's surroundings.

Conditionem testium tunc inspicere debemus cum signarent, non mortis tempore (kon-di-she-o'nem tes'-ti-um tunk in-spi'se-re de-bē'mus kum sig-nā'rent, non mor'tis tem'pō-re). We ought to consider the condition of witnesses as of the time when they signed, not at the time of the testator's death.

Conditiones quaelibet odiosae; maxime autem contra matrimonium et commercium (kon-di-she-ō'nēz kwe'li-bet ō-di-ō'se; ma'xi-me â'tem kon'tra ma-tri-mō'ni-um et kom-mer'she-um). Any conditions are odious, especially those in restraint of marriage and trade.

condition implied in law. See **implied condition.**

condition in law. See **implied condition.**

condition in restraint of marriage. See **in terrorem; restraint of marriage.**

condition meritorious. A condition which exists where the event upon which an obligation becomes payable is in the power of the obligee, and is to be brought about by his doing or not doing a certain thing. Sterling v Sinnickson, 5 NJL 885, 892.

condition precedent. A condition which is precedent either to the existence of a contract (17 Am J2d Contr § 24) or to the inception of an obligation immediately to perform a contract previously made. 17 Am J2d Contr § 321; in the law of estates, a condition which must take place before an estate can vest or be enlarged. 28 Am J2d Est § 132. In the law of insurance, a condition without the performance of which a contract of insurance, although in form executed by the parties and delivered, does not spring into life. Chambers v Northwestern Mut. Life Ins. Co. 64 Minn 495, 67 NW 367; in a lease, a condition that must occur or be performed before the lease becomes binding and the tenancy comes into existence. 32 Am J1st L & T § 825.

condition resolutory. Same as **condition subsequent.**

conditions in terrorem (kon-dish'on in te-rō'rem). See **in terrorem.**

condition subsequent. A condition in a contract which follows liability upon the contract and operates to defeat or annul such liability upon the subsequent failure of the other party to comply with its terms. 17 Am J2d Contr § 323; in the law of estates, a condition which operates on an estate conveyed or devised so as to render it liable to be defeated for breach of the condition; the title passes to the grantee or devisee, subject to divestiture on failure of performance of the condition. 28 Am J2d Est § 132; in the law of insurance, a condition which presupposes an absolute obligation under the policy, and provides that the policy shall become void, or its operation be defeated or suspended, upon the happening of some event or the doing or omission of some act. 29 Am J Rev ed Ins § 718. In a lease, a condition which has no relation to the inception of the lease and the commencement of the tenancy, but, instead, gives the landlord, on its happening or not happening or its performance or nonperformance, a right to re-enter and terminate the lease. 32 Am J1st L & T § 825.

See **interest upon condition subsequent.**

condition suspensive. Same as **condition precedent.**

Conditio praecedens adimpleri debet priusquam, sequatur effectus (kon-di'she-ō prē-sē'dens ad-im-plē'rī de'bet pri'us-quam, se-quā'ter ef-fek'tus). A condition precedent is to be fulfilled before the effect can follow.

conditio sine qua non (kon-dish'i-ō sī'nē kwä non). A condition without which not, —an indispensable condition.

condom. A contraceptive and a prophylactic. State v Tracy, 29 NJ Super 145, 102 A2d 52.

condominium (kon-dō-min'i-um). Joint ownership; a multiunit dwelling, each of whose residents, known as unit owners, enjoys exclusive ownership of his individual apartment or unit, holding a fee simple title thereto, while retaining an undivided interest, as a tenant in common, in the common facilities and areas of the building and grounds which are used by all the residents. 15 Am J2d Cond Apt § 1.

condonable offense. A single act or series of acts of misconduct constituting a ground for divorce which in theory may be forgotten or forgiven, or a species of misconduct which considerate and affectionate treatment might serve to obliterate. 24 Am J2d Div & S § 204.

condonacion (kon-do-nah'the-on). The forgiveness or discharge of a debt.

condonation (kon-dō-nā'shon). The forgiveness, either express or implied, by a husband of his wife, or by a wife of her husband, of a breach of marital duty, with an implied condition that the offense shall not be repeated. 24 Am J2d Div & S § 204.

See **condonable offense.**

conduct. Noun: Behavior, as portrayed by that which one does or omits to do. Church of Christ v McDonald, 180 Tenn 86, 171 SW2d 817, 146 ALR 1173. Verb: To carry on, to manage; to regulate, to guide, as to conduct a group on tour. Harvey v Vandegrift, 89 Pa 346, 352.

conductio (kon-duk'she-ō). A hiring.

conduction. A transmitting or conveying; the flow of electricity through the medium of the earth, from one wire to another without actual contact. Phillippay v Pacific Power & Light Co. 120 Wash 581, 207 P 957, 211 P 872, 23 ALR 1251.

conduct-money. Money paid to a witness to reimburse him for expenses.

conductor. A railroad employee in charge of a train or, at least, such part of the operations as are not within the province of the engineer.

conduit (kon' or kun'dit). A channel or structure by which flowing water can be conducted from one point to another. Sefton v Prentice, 103 Cal 670, 37 P 641. A tube or trough in which telegraph, telephone, or electric wires may be strung.

See **underground conduit.**

cone and key (kōn and kē). Accounts and keys, a symbol of the fitness of a woman to assume the care of a house.

confarreatio (kon-far-re-ā'she-ō). An ancient Roman marriage ceremony.

confectio (kon-fek'she-ō). A Civil Law term for the execution of a written instrument.

confectionary. Candy, and other sweets; a place where sweets are sold.

confederacy. A union of people, groups of people, even nations, for a common purpose; a union of people for an unlawful purpose, a conspiracy. State v Crowley, 41 Wis 271, 284.

Confederacy. See **Confederate States of America.**

Confederate States. The eleven southern states which seceded from the Union in 1860 and 1861 and formed the Confederate States of America.

Confederate States of America. The confederacy formed by the eleven seceding southern states in 1861, which waged a war for four years against the United States, but never acquired the status of a government de jure or de facto as those terms are known and used in the law of nations. Thorington v Smith (US) 8 Wall 1, 19 L Ed 361.

confederating clause. A clause, also known as the common conspiracy clause, of a bill in equity under the old chancery practice, consisting of an allegation to the effect that the grievance complained of by the plaintiff was brought about by a conspiracy among the several defendants and others not made parties to the bill, and that they had all conspired to injure the plaintiff and co-operated in the perpetration of the wrong. 19 Am J2d Eq § 222.

confederation (kọn-fed-ẻr-ā'shọn). An agreement or compact between two or more governments.
See **Articles of Confederation**; **Confederate States of America.**

conference. See **Judicial Conference.**

Confessio facta in judicio omni probatione major est (kon-fes'si-ō fak'ta in jū-di'she-ō om'nī prō-bā-she-ō'ne mä'jor est). A confession made in court is more important than all proof.

confession. A voluntary admission, declaration or acknowledgment by one who has committed a felony or a misdemeanor that he committed the crime or offense or participated in its commission; a voluntary admission or declaration of one's agency or participation in a crime. 29 Am J2d Ev § 523.
A confession is voluntary when made of the free will and accord of the accused, without fear or threat of harm and without hope or promise of benefit, reward, or immunity. 29 Am J2d Ev § 529.
See **judicial confession; plea in confession and avoidance; third degree.**

confession and avoidance. See **plea in confession and avoidance.**

confession in open court. A plea of guilty in a criminal prosecution. State v Willis, 71 Conn 293, 308, 41 A 820.

confession of error. A party's admission, express or implied, made on appeal, that the court below committed an error in his favor, or prejudicial to the rights of an adverse party. Burgen v State, 32 Ariz 111, 256 P 111; Halpin v Scotti, 415 Ill 104, 112 NE2d 91.

confession of judgment. The entry of a judgment upon the admission or confession of the debtor, without the formality, time, or extent involved in an ordinary action or proceeding. Cuikendall v Doe, 129 Iowa 453, 105 NW 698.
See **cognovit actionem; cognovit note; confession relicta verificatione.**

confession relicta verificatione (kọn-fesh'on re-lik'ta ve-ri-fi-kä-she-ō'ne). Confession of judgment after pleading and before trial, the defendant confessing the plaintiff's cause of action and withdrawing or abandoning his defense or other procedures taken by him. 30A Am J Rev ed Judgm § 156.

confessor (kọn-fes'ọr). A priest who hears confessions; one who confesses.

Confessus in judicio pro judicato habetur et quodammodo sua sententia damnatur (kon-fes'sus in jū-di'-she-ō prō jū-di-kā'to hā-bē'tur et quō'dam-mō'dō su'a sen-ten'she-a dam-nā'ter). One who confesses in court is held to have been adjudged and in a manner is condemned by his own sentence.

confidence. Assurance; trust in one's own abilities; assurance of secrecy; reliance upon another. An obsolete technical term for an interest by way of trust or use. Jones v Jones, 223 Mo 424, 123 SW 29.
See **faith.**

confidence game. Essentially, a swindling operation in which advantage is taken of the confidence reposed by the victim in the swindler. State v Theriot, 139 La 741, 72 So 191.

confidence man (kon'fi-dẹns mạn). A swindler; a trickster.
See **confidence game.**

confidential communications. Communications made in confidence; communications made to such persons that the law regards them as privileged beyond forcing a disclosure thereof.
See **privileged communications.**

confidential position. A position in civil service involving secrecy, integrity, trust, confidence, skill, and competence. Klatt v Akers, 232 Iowa 1312, 5 NW2d 605, 146 ALR 808.

confidential relation. A technical fiduciary relation, such as trustee and beneficiary, and any informal relation between parties wherein one of them is in duty bound to act with the utmost good faith for the benefit of the other party, 57 Am J1st Wills § 390; a relation between two persons as a result of which there is confidence reposed on one side and a resulting superiority in position and influence on the other, 37 Am J2d Fraud §§ 15, 16; a relation in which confidence is reposed, and in which dominion and influence resulting from such confidence may be exercised by one person over another, Burgdorfer v Thielemann, 153 Or 354, 55 P2d 1122, 104 ALR 1407; State v Russell (Mo) 265 SW2d 379, 45 ALR2d 617; a peculiar relation which exists between attorney and client, principal and agent, principal and surety, landlord and tenant, parent and child, guardian and ward, ancestor and heir, husband and wife, trustee and cestui que trust, executor or administrator and creditors and in many other cases. Robins v Hope, 57 Cal 493.
Some courts, in dealing with the question of fraud, indiscriminately use the terms "fiducial relation" and "confidential relation," as being synonymous insofar as they affect the good-faith dealings between the parties to the relation. There is, however, a technical distinction between the two terms, the former being more correctly applicable to legal relationships between the parties, such as guardian and ward etc., while the latter includes them and also every other relationship wherein confidence is rightfully reposed and is exercised, among which is a situation involving superiority of knowledge on the part of the one seeking to uphold the contract and confidence reposed in him by the other. Roberts v Parsons, 195 Ky 274, 242 SW 594.

confine. Verb: To deprive one of his liberty; to place in prison or jail; to keep a person in bed; to require a person to remain at home; to keep animals within an enclosure. Walker v McAfee, 82 Kan 182, 107 P 637. Noun: A limit, end, or boundary.

confined. Imprisoned; required to remain in one place. As the word is used in a sick benefit insurance policy, a person is "confined," when his illness keeps him at home and totally disables him from following his vocation. The word does not import that he shall be confined to his bed. Home Protective Asso. v Williams, 150 Ky 134, 136, 150 SW 11.

See **close confinement; solitary confinement.**

confined to bed. A familiar term in the law of health and accident insurance, as to which there is divergence of opinion in interpretation, some cases holding that the term is satisfied only by an actual confinement to bed, while other cases hold that the term is intended to express a required degree of disability, not necessarily an actual confinement to bed. 29A Am J Rev ed Ins § 1531.

confined to house. See **house confinement clause.**

confined to institution. A term appearing in some statutes which prescribe grounds for divorce based on insanity of the defendant requiring his confinement for a specified continuous period. Under statutory provisions requiring that the insane spouse shall have been confined within an institution for a specified continuous period as a necessary condition to the granting of a divorce on the ground of insanity, there are conflicting decisions as to whether "confined" is to be taken in its literal sense, or merely in the sense of supervision by the authorities, so as to permit periods of absence, not amounting to discharges from the institution, to be considered as a part of a period of continuous confinement, rather than interruptions thereof. Anno: 24 ALR2d 878.

confinement. State of being confined; lying in for childbirth.

See **confined; confined to bed; confined to institution; house confinement clause.**

confinio comitatus. See **in confinio comitatus.**

confirm. To strengthen; to approve; to make certain, as to "confirm" a hotel reservation.

Confirmare est id quod prius infirmum fuit simul firmare (kon-fir-mā're est id quod prī'us in-fir'mum fu'it si'mul fir-mā're). To confirm is to make firm that which was previously infirm.

Confirmare nemo potest priusquam jus ei acciderit (kon-fir-mā're nē'mō po'test pri'us-quam jūs ē'ī ak-si-de'rit). No one can confirm a right before it has fallen to him.

confirmatio (kon-fir-mā'she-ō). A confirmation.

Confirmatio Cartarum (kon-fir-mā'she-ō kar-tā'rum). A famous statute enacted in the twenty-fifth year of the reign of Edward I, providing that Magna Charta should thereafter be taken as common law, that all judgments contrary to Magna Charta should be void, that copies should be sent to all cathedral churches and read to the people twice each year, and that any person who should offend against it should be excommunicated. 1 Bl Comm 128.

Confirmatio Chartarum. Same as **Confirmatio Cartarum.**

confirmatio crescens (kon-fir-mā'she-ō kre'senz). A confirmation increasing a rightful estate.

confirmatio diminuens (kon-fir-mā'she-ō di-mi'nu-enz). A confirmation the effect of which was to release a part of the services supporting a tenure.

Confirmatio est nulla, ubi donum praecedens est invalidum (kon-fir-mā'she-ō est nul'la, ū'bi dō'num pre-sē'denz est in-va'li-dum). A confirmation is a nullity, where the preceding gift is invalid.

confirmation. The affirmance or making certain of that which before was not certain; the removal of a doubt, Biddle Boggs v Merced Mining Co. 14 Cal 279, 306; an approval which gives purpose, effect, and finality, for example, the confirmation of an award by arbitrators. 5 Am J2d Arb & A § 152. A religious service in which boys and girls, having reached a certain age and having attained a desired proficiency in the catechism or other statement of principles of the church, are formally received into full membership.

Confirmation of Charter. See **Confirmatio Chartarum.**

confirmation of estate. The conveyance of an estate, or right, that one has in land, to another who has possession of it, or some estate in it, making valid a voidable estate, or increasing and enlarging a particular estate. Langdeau v Hanes, 21 Wall 521, 22 L Ed 606. Confirmation may make good a voidable or defeasible estate, but it cannot operate upon or aid an estate which is void in law. As to such an estate, a confirmation only confirms its infirmity. Branham v Mayor & Common Council of San Jose, 24 Cal 585, 605.

confirmation of executor. The formal clothing of the executor with title.

confirmation of sale. The formal approval of an executor's or administrator's sale of property of the estate of his decedent by the probate court, which, in some jurisdictions is made a condition precedent to the passing of a valid title to the property. Horton v Jack, 115 Cal 29, 46 P 920. The approval by the court of a judicial sale upon report thereof made by the officer conducting the sale. 30A Am J Rev ed Jud S § 114. A court's approval of the report made by an officer, usually a commissioner, of his sale on foreclosure. See 37 Am J1st Mtg § 637.

See **decree of confirmation.**

Confirmatio omnes supplet defectus, licet id quod actum est ab initio non valuit (kon-fir-mā'she-ō om'-nēz sup'plet de-fek'tus, lī'set id quod ak'tum est ab in'she-ō non va'lu-it). Confirmation supplies all defects, though what has been done was not valid at the beginning.

confirmatio perficiens (kon-fir-mā'she-ō per-fi'si-enz). A confirmation which makes valid a defeasible title.

Confirmat usum qui tollit abusum (kon-fir'mat ū'sum quī tol'lit ab-ū'sum). He confirms a use who removes an abuse.

confirmavi (kon-fir-mā'vi). I have confirmed or ratified.

confirmee (kon-fẽr-mē'). A person to whom a right is confirmed.

confirmor (kon-fir'mor). A person who makes a confirmation.

confiscare (kon-fis-kā're). To confiscate.

confiscata. See **bona confiscata.**

confiscate. To take property from a private person for the state; to appropriate property for the state as forfeited. Ware v Hylton (US) 3 Dall 199, 234, 1 L Ed 568, 583; to take property belonging to the enemy in time of war. 56 Am J1st War § 154.

confiscation. See **confiscate; incautacion.**

Confiscation Acts (kon-fis-kā'shon akts). The acts of Congress of August 6, 1861, and July 17, 1862, providing for the seizure and sale of property used to abet the Confederate cause. 56 Am J1st War § 78.

Confiscation Cases. Cases arising under the act of Congress of August 6, 1861, authorizing the confiscation of property used in aiding, abetting or promoting insurrection against the government of the United States. Confiscation Cases (US) 7 Wall 454, 19 L Ed 196; United States v Clarke (US) 20 Wall 92, 22 L Ed 320.

confiscation loss. A loss, deductible in an income tax return, resulting from the confiscation or nationalization of the taxpayer's property. Elek v Commissioner, 30 T CT 731(A).

confiscatory order or regulation. A rate order or regulation fixing the rate or rates of a common carrier or public utility so low that the carrier or utility is deprived of a fair return on its investment, or providing rates so low that they tend toward depriving the carrier or utility of a fair return. Pennsylvania Railroad Co. v Philadelphia County, 220 Pa 100, 68 A 676; Minneapolis, St. Paul & Sault Ste. Marie Railroad Co. v Railroad Com. of Wisconsin, 136 Wis 146, 116 NW 905.

confisk (kon'fisk). To confiscate.

confitens reus (kon-fi'tenz re'us). A person who confesses after being charged with the commission of a crime.

conflicting evidence. Evidence from different sources which cannot be reconciled; evidence for the plaintiff and evidence for the defendant, considered together and presenting at least a fair and reasonable ground for difference of view as to which should prevail. Lefrooth v Prentice, 202 Cal 215, 259 P 947.

conflicting grants. Deeds by the same grantor covering the same premises but running to different grantees.

conflicting interest. A term, the legal significance of which is confined to representation of the interest, as where a real estate broker is representing both buyer and seller, and an attorney at law attempts to act both for his client and for one whose interest is adverse to or conflicting with that of his client in the same general matter. 7 Am J2d Attys § 154.

conflicting presumptions. Presumptions arising from the same facts which are so opposed in the fact presumed that one of them must give way to the other and stronger of the two, for example, the presumption of identity of person from identity of name gives way to the presumption of regularity of official acts and proceedings. 29 Am J2d Ev § 167.

conflict of laws. A subject, otherwise known as private international law, which is that part of the law of each state or nation which determines whether, in dealing with a legal situation, the law of some other state or nation will be recognized, be given effect, or be applied. 16 Am J2d Confl L § 1.

conflicts in administration. Conflicts between administrative agencies. 2 Am J2d Admin L §§ 209 et seq.

conformably to the laws. In accordance with a recognized long established system of laws existing in states adopting constitutions, as well as in the prior political organizations from which the states were formed. McCoy v Kenosha County, 195 Wis 273, 218 NW 348, 57 ALR 412.

conformity. Correspondence in form and manner, resemblance, agreement, harmony. Westlake Mercantile Finance Corp. v Merritt (Cal App) 262 P 815, 817. (Ecclesiastical.) Adherence to the Church of England.

Conformity Act. The act of Congress of June 1, 1872, providing that the practice, pleadings, and forms and modes of proceeding in civil causes, other than equity and admiralty causes, in the Federal circuit and district courts, shall conform, as near as may be to the practice, pleadings, and forms and modes of proceeding existing at the time in like causes in courts of record of the state within which such circuit or district courts are held, any rule of court to the contrary notwithstanding.

conform to proofs. See **amendment to conform to proofs.**

confrairie (kon-fre'ri). A brotherhood.

confront. To come face to face with a person.

confrontation of witness. A constitutional right of an accused to face a witness in court so that the accused may make any objection he has to the witness, be present when the witness is examined, and have opportunity for cross-examination. Garcia v State, 151 Tex Crim 593, 210 SW2d 574. The act of placing an accused in such proximity to the witness that he may see him and hear his testimony. People v Elliott, 172 NY 146, 64 NE 837.

confrontment (kon-frunt'mėnt). A confrontation. See **confrontation of witness.**

confusio (kon-fū'she-ō). Same as **confusion.**

confusion of debts. Same as **confusion of rights and obligations.**

confusion of goods. An intermingling or intermixture of goods owned by different persons to such extent that the property of each person can no longer be distinguished. 1 Am J2d Access § 1. A confusion may be the result of a wilful and fraudulent intermixture, but may arise also from a mixture made by the consent of the owners, or by mistake, inevitable accident, or vis major. 1 Am J2d Access § 1.

The doctrine of confusion is that where an owner of goods wilfully and tortiously mixes and confuses his goods with the goods of another so that they are indistinguishable and not susceptible of division according to the rights of each owner, the one who mixed the goods must bear the whole loss, and the innocent party will take the whole property. 1 Am J2d Access § 15.

confusion of rights and obligations. A merger of the obligor and the obligee in one person; the concurrence of two adverse rights to the same thing in one and the same person; the concurrence of the character of the sole debtor and the sole creditor in the same person, thereby extinguishing the debt. Woods v Ridley, 30 Tenn (11 Humph) 195, 198.

congé (kôn-zhā'). Leave or permission.

congeable (kon'jē-a-bl). Lawful.

congé d'accorder (kŏn-zhā d'a-kor-de'). The licentia concordandi, or leave to agree the suit. This was the second step in the levying of a fine to convey land. As soon as the action was brought, the defendant, knowing himself to be in the wrong, was supposed to make overtures of peace to the plaintiff. The plaintiff then applied to the court for leave to ac-

CONGE [247] CONJUGES

cord or agree, lest he might lose the pledges he had given to prosecute the action. 2 Bl Comm 350.

congé d'appel (kōn-zhā' d'a-pel). (Civil law.) Leave to appeal.

congé de defaut (kōn-zha' dē dē'fô). The dismissal of an action by reason of the default of the plaintiff.

congé d'emparler (kōn-zhā' d'em-par-le'). The licentia loquendi, or leave to imparl, which was the leave of court which a defendant might demand before putting in his plea, for time in which to talk with the plaintiff for the purpose of ascertaining whether the action might be settled amicably. 3 Bl Comm 299.

congé d'eslire (kōn-zha' d'es-lî-r). Leave to elect or choose. The term was applied to the king's leave or license to a dean and chapter to proceed to elect a bishop. If the king refused such leave, the electors could proceed without it. 1 Bl Comm 379.

congested district. A district in which there is very heavy traffic upon the streets and highways. Craft v Stone, 74 Ind App 71, 124 NE 473.

congius (kon'ji-us). An old Roman liquid measure equal approximately to the modern gallon.

congregation. A collective word signifying the electors of a religious corporation and embracing the stated hearers or attendants on divine worship who are competent to vote for trustees. Robertson v Bullions (NY) 9 Barb 64, 93; an assemblage or union of persons in society for some religious purpose, to unite in the public worship of their God, in such manner as they deem most acceptable to Him. Runkel v Winemiller (Md) 4 Harr & McH 429, 452; the body of worshipers in attendance at a religious service.

congress. A formal gathering of delegates or representatives.

Congress (kong'gres). The national legislature of the United States, consisting of the Senate and the House of Representatives.

congressional authentication. A method of authentication of a public act, proceeding, or record for use as evidence in another state, provided by Act of Congress, the effect of which is to create a uniform method of authentication which all the courts in the United States are bound to respect. 30 Am J2d Ev § 989.

Congressional Cemetery. A burial ground on premises of Christ Church in Washington, D. C., established by the Vestry in the early days of the country, frequently used for some years as a place for the burial of Senators, Representatives, and Executive Officers who died in the city and whose homes were at a distance, and recognized as having a semiofficial status by an appropriation made by Congress in 1816 in order to make certain the reservation of part of the ground for the burial of officials of the government.

congressional court. Any federal court established by act of Congress under Section 1 of Article III of the Constitution of the United States.

congressional districts. The divisions of a state for representation in the House of Representatives of the Congress of the United States, each district being separately represented by a member of the House. 54 Am J1st US § 21.

congressional grant (kǫn-gresh'ǫn-al). A grant of public land of the United States made by an act of Congress. Such an act is both a law and a grant,

and the intent of Congress when ascertained is to control in the interpretation of the law. 42 Am J1st Pub L § 32.

congressional investigations. Investigations conducted by Congress though through committees into matters of concern to Congress in the exercise of its function of legislation. 54 Am J1st US § 32.

Congressional Library. See **Library of Congress.**

Congressional Record. The printed record of the proceedings of the Congress of the United States.

Congressional Survey. The method of survey first established by Congress for the lands in the Northwest Territory, since extended to public lands in the western and many other states of the Union, whereby the lands are surveyed and platted into square or rectangular tracts, known as townships, sections, and fractional parts of sections. 42 Am J1st Pub L § 40.

congressional township. An area six miles square under the survey of public lands made by the government. 52 Am J1st Towns § 2.
See **Congressional Survey.**

Congressman. Literally, a member of Congress, whether of the House of Representatives or the Senate, but usually confined to members of the House.

Congress of Industrial Organizations. An affiliation of labor unions established in 1938, since combined with the American Federation of Labor under the abbreviated heading CIO-AF of L.

congruere (con-grū'ēre). (Civil law.) To agree.

conjectio causae (kon-jek'she-ō kau'sē). A statement of the case.

conjectural evidence. Evidence not of a character to permit a reasoned conclusion; evidence so slight as to permit nothing better than a guess in respect of its application to an issue. 29 Am J2d Ev §§ 251-253, 256.

conjecture. A guess or, at best, a very slight inference; a vast field into which no jury is permitted to roam. Meidel v Anthis, 71 Ill 241, 245.

conjoints (kǫn-joints'). Persons owning property jointly; the term is sometimes applied to husband and wife.

conjoint will. A joint will bequeathing or devising property which the testators own in common. Anno: 169 ALR 12.
See **joint will.**

conjugal (kon'jö-gal). Pertaining to the marital relation.

conjugal duties. Marital duties; the duties of husband and wife as such. 26 Am J1st H & W § 5.

conjugal fellowship. See **consortium.**

conjugal kindness. The treatment which one spouse has the right to expect from the other; a condition of condonation of a ground of divorce. Anno: 32 ALR2d 163.

conjugal rights (kon'jö-gal rīts). Marital rights; the rights of husband and wife, as such. 26 Am J1st H & W § 5.

conjugal seducer. One who accomplishes a seduction under promise of marriage. Cropp v Tilney (Eng) 3 Salk 225.

conjuges. See **inter conjuges.**

conjugium (kọn-jō'ji-um). Marriage.

conjunct (kọn-jungkt'). Concurrent; joint.

conjuncta (kon-junk'ta). Joined; united.

conjunctim (kon-junk'tim). Jointly.

conjunctim et divisim (kon-junk'tim et di-vi'sim). Jointly and severally.

Conjunctio mariti et feminae est de jure naturae (kon-junk'she-ō ma'ri-tī et fe'mi-nē est de ju're nā-tū'rē). The union of husband and wife is according to the law of nature.

conjunction. A union; in grammar as a connective. See **conjunctive**.

conjunctive. Together; jointly; connecting the elements of a sentence, thereby imparting a meaning.

conjunct persons. Persons related to one another in some degree.

conjuratio (kon-jọ-rā'she-ō). A conspiracy.

conjuration. Appealing to supernatural forces in the spirit world for the accomplishment of extraordinary feats in allaying storms and healing sickness; the pretension of ability to secure the aid of supernatural and superior powers. Cooper v Livingston, 19 Fla 684, 694.

conjurator (kon'jọ-rā-tọr). A conspirator; a person combining with another or with others in a conjuration.
See **conjuration**.

conjurer (kọn-jör'ėr). See **conjuration**.

conjuror (kọn-jö'rọr). See **conjuration**.

Connally Act. A federal statute having the purpose of aiding the enforcement of state laws limiting the production of oil, in certain fields, by prohibiting the shipment in interstate commerce of oil, known as hot oil, produced in excess of the limit set by state statute. 15 USC §§ 715 et seq.; Bolling v Bowen (CA4 Va) 118 F2d 59.

connecting carrier. Any one of several common carriers whose lines or parts thereof together constitute the entire route over which a shipment of goods is transported. 14 Am J2d Car § 662.

connecting carrier's lien. The lien of a connecting carrier on the goods in the shipment for its charges, including the charges of preceding carriers in the succession of carriers paid by it, such lien being for the amount due it under the legal and fixed rate, notwithstanding the amount may be in excess of a through rate guaranteed by the initial carrier, the connecting carrier, however, not being entitled to a lien if it has accepted the shipment with knowledge that a through contract of shipment has been made with the initial carrier and the entire charge paid in advance. 14 Am J2d Car § 666.

conner. See **ale conner**.

connivance. A secret cooperation in an illegal or wrongful act. As a defense in an action for divorce on the ground of adultery:—a corrupt consent by one spouse that the other shall commit adultery. Giddings v Giddings, 167 Or 504, 114 P2d 1009.

A wife is guilty of connivance where, with corrupt intention, she behaves in such a way as to promote or encourage the continuation of an adulterous intercourse started by the husband without any fault on the part of the wife. Woodbury v Woodbury, [1949] Prob 154, [1948] 2 All Eng 684, 17 ALR2d 334.

connoissement (kon-i-noa-sē-män). (French.) A bill of lading.

connubial (kon-nū'bi-ạl). Pertaining to the married state; conjugal; marital.

connubium (kọ-nū'bi-um). Marriage.

conocimiento (co-no-the-me-en'to). (Spanish.) A bill of lading.

conpossessio (kon-po-zesh'i-o). A joint possession.

conquereur (kōn-ke'rer). The first purchaser of an estate.
See **first purchaser**.

conqueror (kong'kėr-ọr). William the Conqueror, king of England from 1066 to 1087; a purchaser.

conquest. A method by which a nation may acquire territory in the absence of treaties or conventions to the contrary. 30 Am J Rev ed Internat L § 41; 54 Am J1st US § 78. The acquisition of property otherwise than by inheritance or conveyance in manner permitted by law.

The Norman Conquest is often referred to as "The Conquest."

An island is "acquired" by the United States, so as to bring it within the scope of a workmen's compensation act covering employees at a military or air base acquired after a certain date, upon its capture from an enemy force. Anno: 2 L Ed 2d 1980.

conquestus (kon-kwest'us). Acquisition.

conquets (kong-kwets'). (Civil law.) Same as **acquest**.
See **acquets and conquets**.

conquisitio (kon-kwe-zish'i-o). Acquisition.

conquisitor (kong-kwi'zit-or). A conqueror; a purchaser.

consanguineos (kon-sang-gwin'ẹ-os). Blood relations, persons who have in their veins a portion of the blood of a common ancestor. 2 Bl Comm 205.
See **de consanguineo**.

consanguineus (kon-sang-gwin'ē-us). Related by blood.
See **frater consanguineus**.

Consanguineus est quasi eodem sanguine natus (kon-sang-gwin'ē-us est kwā'sī ē-ō'dem sang-gwi'ne nā'-tus). A person related by consanguinity is, as it were, one born of the same blood.

consanguineus frater (kon-sang-gwin'ē-us frā-ter). A brother by the father's side, that is, a brother born of the same father. 2 Bl Comm 232.

consanguinity (kon-sang-gwin'i-ti). Relationship by blood. Re Bordeaux Estate, 37 Wash 2d 561, 225 P2d 433, 26 ALR2d 249. The having of the blood of some common ancestor. Blodget v Brinsmaid, 9 Vt 27, 30.
See **collateral consanguinity**; **kin**; **kindred**; **lineal consanguinity**.

conscience. A person's natural judgment of right and wrong. "Principle" the result of judgment, is tested by reason, defended by argument, and yields to the decision of an intelligent mind. "Conscience" springs from some internal source of self-knowledge, which acknowledges no superior, bows to no authority, yields to no demonstration, and is governed by no law; it ignores reason, defies argument, and is unaccountable and irresponsible to all human tests and standards; it is a law unto itself, and its scruples and its teachings are not amenable to human tribunals, but rest alone with its possessor and his God. People v Stewart, 7 Cal 140. An element of equitable jurisdiction, not the private opinion of an individual court, but rather to be regarded as a metaphorical term designating the common standard of civil right and expediency combined, based upon general principles and limited by established doctrines, to which the court appeals and by which it tests the conduct and rights of suitors. National City Bank v Gelfert, 284 NY 13, 29 NE2d 449, 130 ALR 1472.

conscience money. Money paid in settlement of an obligation which the person paying has previously evaded or concealed.

Conscientia dicitur a con et scio, quasi scire cum Deo (kon-she-en'she-a di'si-ter a kon et sī'ō, quā'sī sī're cum dē'ō). Conscience is so called from "con" (meaning "with") and "scio" (meaning "I know"), as it were, I know with God.

conscientiae detrimentum (kon-she-en'she-ē de-tri-men'tum). Shipwreck of conscience.

conscientia rei alieni (kon-she-en'she-a rē'ī ā-li-ē'nī). Knowledge of another person's ownership.

conscientious objector. One seeking exemption from required military service as opposed on religious grounds to participation in war. United States v Seeger, 380 US 163, 13 L Ed 2d 733, 85 S Ct 850.

conscionable (kon'shon-a-bl). According to honesty.

conscious. Possessing sufficient power of mind to understand the real nature and true character of one's acts. Brown v Commonwealth, 78 Pa 122, 128.

conscription. Requiring the performance of military service. 36 Am J1st Mil § 22. Enforcing the employment of capital or labor in military service.
See **selective draft.**

Consecratio est periodus electionis; electio est praeambula consecrationis (kon-se-krā'she-ō est pe-ri-ō'dus e-lek-she-ō'nis; e-lek'she-ō est pre-am'bu-la kon-se-krā-she-ō'nis). Consecration is the termination of election; election is the preamble of consecration.

consecration. The act of devoting to religious use or making sacred.
See **parish church.**

consecutive sentences. Sentences succeeding one another in a regular order, with an uninterrupted course or succession, and without interval or break, State v Rider, 201 La 733, 10 So 2d 601; the opposite of concurrent sentences, Subas v Hudspeth (CA10 Kan) 122 F2d 85; sometimes called accumulative or cumulative sentences. 21 Am J2d Crim L § 547.

consedo. Same as **cedo.**

conseil (kōn-sè-ï). (French.) Counsel; advice; sanction.

conseil de famille (kōn-sè-ï dē fa-mi-i). (French.) The consent of the family.

conseil judiciare (kōn-sè-ï ju-di-si-è-r). (French.) A kind of guardian appointed by the court to protect the estate of a spendthrift.

consensual (kon-sen'sū-al). Depending upon consent; existing by consent.

consensual contract. (Civil law.) An agreement which was enforceable merely because the parties consented to it.

consensu regio (kon-sen'sū rē'ji-ō). By royal command. 3 Bl Comm 95.

consensus. Agreement, especially in a matter of opinion; a general opinion.

consensus ad idem (kon-sen'sus ad ī'dem). An agreement for the same thing; a meeting of the minds without which no contract can arise. Wheat v Cross, 31 Md 99.

Consensus est voluntas plurium ad quos res pertinet, simul juncta (kon-sen'sus est vo-lun'tās plū'ri-um ad quōs rēz per'ti-net, sī'mul junk'ta). Consent is the joint will of many persons to whom the thing belongs.

Consensus facit jus (kon-sen'sus fā'sit jus). Consent makes law. The parties make their own law by their agreement. Shields v Ohio, 95 US 319, 326, 24 L Ed 357, 359. The maxim probably means that it is the consent of the governed which causes law to come into being, and conversely that without such consent we would have no law. St. Louis & San Francisco R. Co. v Gill, 54 Ark 101, 15 SW 18. Taking account of the oft repeated axiom that "there is no law in a settlement," perhaps the real meaning of the maxim is that consent takes the place of law.

Consensus, non concubitus, facit matrimonium (kon-sen'sus, non kon-kū'bi-tus, fā'sit ma-tri-mō'ni-um). A meeting of the minds, and not cohabitation, constitutes a marriage. This was a maxim of the common law, the civil law and of the ecclesiastical law as well, and the sounder rule established by express decisions on the question is that mutual consent only is necessary. 35 Am J1st Mar § 29.

Consensus, non concubitus, facit nuptias vel matrimonium et consentire non possunt ante annos nubiles (kon-sen'sus, non kon-kū'bi-tus, fā'sit nup'she-ās vel ma-tri-mō'ni-um, et kon-sen-tī're non pos'sunt an'te an'nōs nū'bi-lēz). Consent, not cohabitation, makes nuptials or marriage, and those under marriageable age cannot consent.

Consensus tollit errorem (kon-sen'sus tol'lit er-rō'rem). Consent permits error. A person cannot object to that to which he has consented. Fuller v State, 100 Miss 811, 57 So 806.

Consensus voluntas multorum ad quos res pertinet, simul juncta (kon-sen'sus vo-lun'tās mul-tō'rum ad quōs rēz per'ti-net, si'mul junk'ta). Consent is the will of several persons joining simultaneously in one transaction.

consent. Verb: To agree or to give assent to something proposed or requested. Noun: Agreement; approval; acquiescence. Unity of opinion—accord of minds—to thinking alike—being of one mind. Consent involves the presence of two or more persons, for without at least two persons there cannot be a unity of opinion, or an accord of minds, or any thinking alike. Huntley v Holt, 58 Conn 445, 449. As a defense in a prosecution for rape:—an exercise of the intelligence, based upon knowledge of the significance of the act and the question of morality involved therein, in making a choice between resistance and assent. People v Palvino, 216 App Div 319, 321, 214 NY 577, 578.

consent decree. A decree entered in an equity suit on consent of the parties. Such a decree, when entered, is binding on the consenting parties, and it cannot be heard or reviewed except on a showing that consent was obtained by fraud or that the decree was based on mutual error. 27 Am J2d Eq § 246.

Consentientes et agentes pari poena plectentur (kon-sen'she-en'tēz et ā-gen'tēz pa'rī pē'na plek-ten'ter). Persons who consent and those who act are subject to the same penalties.

Consentire matrimonio non possunt infra annos nubiles (kon-sen-tī're ma-tri-mō'ni-ō non pos'sunt in'-fra an'nōs nū'bi-lēz). Persons who are under marriageable age cannot consent to marriage.

Consentire videtur qui tacet (kon-sen-tī're vi-dē'ter kwī ta'set). Those who are silent are deemed to have consented. Silence gives consent.

consent judgment. A judgment entered by consent of the parties for the purpose of executing a compromise and settlement of an action; in effect, an agreement or contract of the parties, acknowledged in court, and ordered to be recorded, with the sanction of the court. 30A Am J Rev ed Judgm § 144.

A consent judgment is a determination by the parties, rather than by the court, but it is equally immune to collateral attack as a judgment rendered after a determination by the court. 30A Am J Rev ed Judgm § 847.

consent of insured. An expression in the omnibus clause of an automobile liability insurance policy, meaning the permission of the insured owner for the use of the automobile by another. Didlake v Standard Ins. Co. (CA10 Okla) 195 F2d 247, 33 ALR2d 941.

consent reference. See **reference on consent.**

consent rule. A rule employed to facilitate the legal fiction whereby an ejectment suit is employed as a remedy for determination of title, the rule requiring the defendant to confess the fictitious lease, entry, and ouster, and to plead not guilty. 25 Am J2d Eject § 2.

consent to. The words "consent to" and "approve of" do not, singly or combined, express the idea of wilful contribution to or procurement of a felonious act, which is essential to guilt. A person may be present and heartily approve of an act after its commission, without being at all willing or capable of advising, aiding or procuring the act; or he may consent in the sense of offering no resistance, without the slightest contribution to it by his own will. True v Commonwealth, 90 Ky 651, 654, 14 SW 685.

consequence. That which follows as the result or effect of a cause. Tierney v Occidental L. Ins. Co. 89 Cal App 779, 265 P 400. When an event is followed in natural sequence by a result which it is adapted to produce, or aid in producing, that result is a consequence of the event. Landstrom v Thorpe (CA8 SD) 189 F2d 46, 26 ALR2d 1170.

See **natural and probable consequences; natural consequences; probable consequence.**

consequentiae non est consequentia (kon-se-kwen'-she-ē non est kon-se-kwen'she-a). A consequence is not the result of a consequence.

consequential damages. An equivocal expression, meaning both damages which are so remote as not to be actionable, and damages which are actionable, Eaton v Boston C. & M. R. Co. 51 NH 504; in one sense, the direct or proximate damages, 22 Am J2d Damg § 20; in another sense, indirect damages; damages which are not produced without the concurrence of some other event attributable to the same origin or cause. Loiseau v Arp, 21 SD 566, 114 NW 701.

A provision, in a contract for the installation of elevators, against liability of the elevator company for "consequential damages," provides against liability for damages that do not arise according to the usual course of things from the breach of the contract itself, that is, against liability for damages that are the consequence of special circumstances. Boylston Housing Corp. v O'Toole, 321 Mass 528, 74 NE2d 288, 172 ALR 1251.

See **compensatory damages.**

conservancy districts. Essentially the same as drainage districts, being organized under statutes enacted for the purpose of controlling floods and protecting life and property against their ravages. Re Proposed Middle Rio Grande Conservancy Dist. 31 NM 188, 242 P 683.

conservation. The protection of property against loss, misuse, or waste, particularly, in the modern sense of the term, natural resources, wildlife, and natural settings in mountains, rivers, lakes, prairies, etc., in which the people may find recreation.

conservator. One placed in charge of property by a court as a temporary guardian or custodian. Re Guardianship of Hampson's Estate, 190 Or 279, 223 P2d 1039, 21 ALR2d 873; one appointed to take custody of the property or estate of a missing person, 1 Am J2d Absent § 2; a person appointed for the custody and protection of property of an insane person. 29 Am J Rev ed Ins Per § 62.

conservatores pacis (kon-ser-va-tō'rēz pa'sis). Keepers of the peace,—peculiar officers appointed by the common law for the maintenance of the public peace. 1 Bl Comm 349.

conservatorship. The holding of property by a conservator.

See **conservator.**

conservators of the peace. Same as **conservatores pacis.**

conservators of truce and safe-conduct. Officers who were appointed in every port in England and who were empowered to hear and determine breaches of truce and safe-conduct. 4 Bl Comm 69.

conservatrix (kon'sėr-vā-triks). A female conservator.

consessimus (kon-ses'si-mus). We have granted or given.

considerable provocation. A term of reference in the law only to express an element reducing a homicide from murder to manslaughter, and so elusive of accurate definition that the most that can be said is that it means "legal provocation" or "adequate provocation," such being matters for determination by the court. McClurg v Commonwealth (Ky) 36 SW 14, 15.

consideratio curiae (kon-si-de-rā'she-ō kū'ri-ē). The consideration of the court.

consideration. An essential of a valid and enforceable contract. 17 Am J2d Contr § 86; a matter of contract, something within the contemplation of the parties to the contract. Van Houten v Van Houten, 202 Iowa 1085, 209 NW 293; the price bargained and paid for a promise, in other words, something given in exchange for the promise. 17 Am J2d Contr § 85; a benefit to the promisor or a loss or detriment to the promisee. Test v Heaberlin, 254 Iowa 521, 118 NW2d 73; 11 Am J2d B & N § 216; some right, interest, profit, or benefit accruing to one party to a contract, or some forbearance, detriment, loss, or responsibility given, suffered or undertaken by the other. 17 Am J2d

Contr § 85; 11 Am J2d B & N § 216; an act or a forbearance, the creation, modification, or destruction of a legal relation, or a return promise bargained for and given in exchange for a promise. 17 Am J2d Contr § 85.

See good consideration; failure of consideration; moral consideration; past consideration; valuable consideration.

considerátione legis. See in consideratione legis.

consideratione praemissorum. See in consideratione praemissorum.

consideration of a sale. The amount paid or to be paid for the articles furnished. See 46 Am J1st Sales § 60.

consideratum est per curiam (kon-si'de-rā'tum est per kū'ri-am). It is considered by the court. A judgment takes this form to show that it is the act of the law as interpreted by the court and so declared after due deliberation; for if a judgment recited "it is decreed, or resolved," by the court, it might appear to be the act of the court rather than the act of the law. 3 Bl Comm 396.

consideratur (kọn-sid'ĕr-ā-ter). It is considered.

considered. Thought about, brought into a process of reasoning, but not necessarily determining a decision. Schreiber v Pacific Coast Fire Ins. Co. 195 Md 639, 75 A2d 108, 20 ALR2d 951. In some connections, the word has been construed as meaning "reasonably regarded." Polsgrove v Moss, 154 Ky 408, 413, 157 SW 1133.

considered as a unit. As the phrase appears in an inheritance statute, it refers to the total of all transfers to one beneficiary. 28 Am J Rev ed Inher T § 298.

considered dictum. An expression of opinion on a point deliberately passed upon by the court, although not necessary to the disposition of the case. Scovill Mfg. Co. v Cassidy, 275 Ill 462, 114 NE 181.

consign. To commit or entrust goods to a person for care or sale by such person. Sturm v Boker, 150 US 319, 37 L Ed 1099, 14 S Ct 99; to send or transfer goods to a merchant or factor for sale. Wasey v Whitcomb, 167 Mich 58, 132 NW 572; to place goods in the hands of a carrier for transportation and delivery to a designated person.

consignatio (kon-sig-nā'she-o). A consignment.

consignation (kon-sig-nā'shọn). A deposit, under French law, which a debtor makes by authority of the court of the thing or sum which he owes, in the hands of a third person. Weld v Hadley, 1 NH 295, 304.

consignee. The person to whom a carrier is to deliver a shipment of goods; the person named in a bill of lading to whom or to whose order the bill promises delivery. 15 Am J2d Com C § 13; a factor or other person to whom goods are consigned, shipped, or otherwise transmitted, either for sale or for safekeeping. Powell v Wallace, 44 Kan 656, 25 P 42; Sturm v Boker, 150 US 319, 37 L Ed 1099, 14 S Ct 99; Anno: 53 ALR 364. The term itself implies an agency. Wasey v Whitcomb, 167 Mich 58, 132 NW 572.

consignment. The entrusting of goods to another, to a carrier for delivery to a consignee designated or to one who is to sell the goods for the consignor. A consignment is nothing more than a bailment for sale. Re Sachs (DC Md) 21 F2d 984, 986.

consignment contract. A consignment of goods to another with the understanding that the consignee shall either sell the property for the consignor and remit to him the price, or if he does not sell the property, return the goods to the consignor. 8 Am J2d Bailm § 34. Such a transaction is a bailment for sale. 8 Am J2d Bailm § 34.

consignor (kọn-sī'nọr or kon-si-nôr'). A person who sends goods to another on consignment; a shipper or transmitter of goods; the person named in a bill of lading as the person from whom the goods have been received for shipment. UCC § 7—102(1)(b)(c).

Consilia multorum requiruntur in magnis (kon-si'li-a mul-tō'rum re-qui-run'ter in mag'nis). The advice of many is required in affairs of magnitude.

consiliarius (kon-si-li-ā'ri-us). A counselor.

consilium (kon-si'li-um). A day set for an argument or hearing.

consimili casu (kon-si'mi-lī kā'sū). A writ by which a reversioner might recover land from the alienee of a life tenant or tenant by the curtesy. See 3 Bl Comm 183, note.

consistory (kọn-sis'tọ-ri or kon'sis-tọ-ri). An ecclesiastical court.

consistory court (kọn-sis'tọ-ri kõrt). Also called the bishop's court,—a court of every diocesan bishop which was held in their several cathedrals, for the trial of all ecclesiastical causes arising within their respective dioceses. The bishop's chancellor, or his commissary was the judge and from the sentence of this court an appeal lay to the archbishop of the province. 3 Bl Comm 64.

consolato del mare (kon-sō-lä'tọ del mä're). A maritime code which was at one time in effect on the Mediterranean Sea. It was compiled about 1000 A. D.

consolidate. To unite into one mass or body, as to consolidate the forces of an army, or various funds. In parliamentary usage, to consolidate two bills is to unite them into one. In law, to consolidate benefices is to combine them into one. Independent Dist. of Fairview v Durland, 45 Iowa 53, 56.

consolidated corporation. The single corporation that exists after a consolidation of two or more corporations. State ex rel. Nolan v Montana Railway Co. 21 Mont 221, 53 P 623.

consolidated fund. The combined revenue of Great Britain and Ireland.

consolidated income tax return. A return by the parent company for all the members of an affiliated group of corporations in place of a separate corporate income tax return by each member. IRC §§ 1501-1505.

Consolidated Orders. A compilation of the orders which regulated practice in the English chancery court, made in 1860.

consolidation. A bringing together of separate things to make one thing; uniting or bringing together the parts of a thing to make it more firm.

consolidation of actions. The joining of separate pending suits for trial as one suit, in the interest of justice or procedural convenience. 2 Am J2d Adm § 197; 53 Am J1st Tr § 66; the fusing by order of court of several pending actions which might have been brought as a single action or suit; the stay of some actions or proceedings pending before a court until it can be determined whether the disposition of another case may not dispose of all of them. 1 Am J2d Actions § 156.

consolidation of appeals. The joinder on motion to the reviewing court, or on the court's own motion, of appeals from a single judgment or from identical judgments, and from judgments which involve the same question and the same parties. 5 Am J2d A & E § 681; joining numerous appeals to the court from a single legislative order by an administrative agency, pursuant to an order of the court, thereby permitting the several appeals to be maintained as one appeal. 2 Am J2d Admin L § 730. Reviewing courts may, and frequently do, without formally consolidating cases, hear and determine two or more of them together for reasons of convenience or because of the similarity of the facts or questions involved. 5 Am J2d A & E § 681.

consolidation of corporations. A union, blending, or coalescence of two or more corporations in one corporate body whereby, in general, their properties, powers, rights, and privileges inure to, and their duties and obligations devolve upon, a new organization thus called into being; and whereby they cease to exist except constructively in certain cases, as, for example, where the jurisdiction of the courts and the power of the state to tax and regulate are concerned. 19 Am J2d Corp § 1491.

There can never be a consolidation of corporations except where all the constituent companies cease to exist as separate corporations and a new corporation, the consolidated corporation, comes into being. Anno: 27 ALR2d 777.

"Amalgamation" is the older English word for consolidation. State ex rel. Nolan v Montana R. Co. 21 Mont 221, 53 P 623.

For distinction between "consolidation" and "merger," see **merger of corporations.**

consolidation of hearings. A practice within the discretion usually reposed in an administrative agency. 2 Am J2d Admin L § 408.

consolidation of municipal corporations. The joining of existing municipal corporations, usually by creating a new corporation, whereby the original corporations cease to exist. 37 Am J1st Mun Corp § 21.

consolidation of railroads. In the most simple sense of the term, a consolidation of two or more railroad corporations, but in actual practice, a long and involved process, the success of which depends upon the approval of the consolidation by the Interstate Commerce Commission and sometimes by state regulatory commissions, the business of railroads touching the public interest so closely that the regulatory commissions are alert to the possibility that a proposed consolidation will eliminate competition, thereby resulting in higher rates, or be adverse to the public interest in point of service. State ex rel. Nolan v Montana Railway Co. 21 Mont 221, 63 P 926; 44 Am J1st RR §§ 319 et seq.

consolidation of school districts. The uniting of two or more school districts into one district. 47 Am J1st Sch § 22. The annexing of one school district to another is indistinguishable from the consolidation of one district with the other. Evans v Hurlburt, 117 Or 274, 243 P 553.

See **centralization of schools.**

consolidation of schools. See **centralization of schools.**

consolidation rule. A rule or order of court for the consolidation of two or more actions into one. Dunning v Bank of Auburn (NY) 19 Wend 23.

See **consolidation of actions.**

consols (kǫn-solz'). A word used for certain state bonds, but better known as annuities issued at one time by Great Britain in funding public debt. English consols are but annuities; the interest only is paid, the principal is never reimbursed, and the government can only redeem them by buying them in the market. Henry v Henderson, 81 Miss 743, 33 So 960.

consort. A husband or wife.

See **prince consort; queen consort.**

Consortio malorum me quoque malum facit (kon-sor'she-ō ma-lō'rum me kwō'kwe ma'lum fā'sit). The companionship of the wicked makes me wicked also.

consortium (kǫn-sôr'shi-um). At earlier common law, the status and rights of the husband arising from the marriage relationship, while "coverture" denoted the status and rights of the wife arising therefrom.

But "consortium" has now come to mean the rights and duties of both husband and wife, resulting from the marriage, in other words, the marital rights and duties of the spouses inter se, the reciprocal rights and duties of society, companionship, love, affection, aid, services, co-operation, sexual relations, and comfort, such being special rights and duties growing out of the marriage covenants. Hitaffer v Argonne Co. 87 App DC 57, 183 F2d 811, 23 ALR2d 1366. Loss of consortium is not a bodily injury. 7 Am J2d Auto Ins § 212.

consortium vicinorum (kǫn-sôr'she-um vi-si-nō'rum). The society of one's neighbors.

conspectu ejus. See **in conspectu ejus.**

conspicuous. Clearly visible; easily seen. In the case of a posted notice the place must be conspicuous and the notice must be conspicuous in the sense that it may be easily read. R. S. Oglesby Co. v Lindsey, 112 Va 767, 72 SE 672. In reference to a term or clause in an instrument, the words must be so written that a reasonable person against whom they are to operate ought to have noted them. 15 Am J2d Com C § 7.

conspiracy. An agreement between two or more persons to accomplish together a criminal or unlawful act or to achieve by criminal or unlawful means an act not in itself criminal or unlawful. 16 Am J2d Consp § 1. Conspiracy is a criminal offense, a misdemeanor in some jurisdictions, a felony in others. 16 Am J2d Consp §§ 2, 3. Conspiracy is also a wrong which will constitute a cause for a civil action. 16 Am J2d Consp § 43. The cause of action is the damage suffered. It is the civil wrong resulting in damage, and not the conspiracy which constitutes the cause of action. Mox, Inc. v Woods, 202 Cal 675, 262 P 302.

conspiracy clause. The clause of a bill in equity under the older practice, consisting of an allegation that the wrong complained of was brought about by a conspiracy between the several defendants, that they had all conspired to injure the plaintiff, and had co-operated in the perpetration of the wrong. 19 Am J2d Eq § 181.

conspiratione. See **de conspiratione.**

conspirators (kǫn-spir'ạ-tǫrs). Persons who participate in a conspiracy.

constable. A public officer, a peace officer, of a county or a town, whose special duty is the execution of process in and of the courts of justices of the peace. Formerly, the office was important in both England and France, a constable in those earlier days being one of the high officers of the crown, having military as well as judicial duties. 47 Am J1st Sher § 2.

constable of England. The lord high constable of England,—an officer of great and numerous functions and powers, both military and civil, which originated with the Normans and diminished to an ornamental rank for state occasions only during the reign of Henry the Eighth. See 1 Bl Comm 355.

constablery (kun'stạ-bl-ri). The jurisdiction of a constable.

constablewick (kun'stạ-bl-wik). The jurisdiction of a constable.

constabulary (kọn-stab'ụ-lạ-ri). A collective word denoting the constables of a district.

constant watch. A term, in a provision of a fire insurance policy relative to insured's duty in protection of the premises, construed as a representation rather than a warranty, imposing upon the insured the duty to use all reasonable care and to take all reasonable means to see that a constant watch was kept. King Brick Mfg. Co. v Phoenix Ins. Co. 164 Mass 291, 41 NE 277.

constat (kon'stat). It is clear; a certificate that certain matters appear of record.
See **clare constat.**

constat de persona (kon'stat dē per-sō'na). There is proof as to the person; certainty as to the person is established; the formal identification of the defendant in a criminal prosecution, by his holding up his hand upon his arraignment and thus acknowledging himself to be the person charged in the indictment. See 4 Bl Comm 323.

constate (kọn-stāt'). To verify or prove.

constating instruments. The charter, the organic law of a corporation, or the grant of powers to it. Ackerman v Halsey, 37 NJ Eq 356, 363.

constipation (kon-sti-pā'shọn). Infrequency in movement of waste matter from the bowels. United States v Ridgeway (CC Ga) 31 F 144, 147.

constituent. A person represented by another, as the principal in the relation of principal and agent, and an inhabitant of a state or district represented by a United States Senator, a Congressman, or a member of the state legislature; one of the corporations joining in a consolidation.

constituere (kon-sti-tu'e-re). To appoint; to establish; to ordain.

constitute (kon'sti-tût). To set up or establish, for example, a government or a body of law; to form the elements of something; to ordain or appoint a person to an office or position.

constituted authorities. The existing and lawfully appointed officers of the government

constitutio (kon-sti-tū'she-o). A constitution; a statute.

constitutio dotis (kon-sti-tū'she-o dō'tis). The establishment of dower.

constitution. A system of fundamental laws or principles for the government of a nation, state, society, corporation, or other aggregation of individuals. 16 Am J2d Const L § 1.

Although a constitution, in the broad sense of the term, may be written or unwritten, in the United States, the word as applied to the organization of the federal and state governments, always implies a writing. 16 Am J2d Const L § 1.
"A written constitution is not only the direct and basic expression of the sovereign will, but is the absolute rule of action and decision for all departments and offices of government in respect to all matters covered by it, and must control as it is written until it shall be changed by the authority that established it." Wright v Hart, 182 NY 330, 75 NE 404.

A constitution differs from a statute in that a statute must provide at least to a certain degree, the details of the subject of which it treats, whereas a constitution usually states general principles and builds the substantial foundation and general framework of the law and government. 16 Am J2d Const L § 3
See **state constitution; United States Constitution.**

constitutional (kon-sti-tū'shọn-ạl). Pertaining to a constitution; in accordance with, agreeably to, consonant with, not in conflict with, the constitution.

constitutional convention. A representative body meeting to form and adopt a constitution, such as the Federal Convention of 1787, meeting in Philadelphia to form and adopt the Constitution of the United States, or meeting to form, consider, and adopt amendments to an existing constitution.

constitutional courts. Courts which are directly established by the constitution, and therefore beyond the power of the legislature to abolish or alter. 20 Am J2d Cts § 17; Federal courts established by Congress pursuant to Article 3, section 1 of the Constitution of the United States. 20 Am J2d Cts § 8.

constitutional disease. A disease which has, at least, some bearing upon the general health. 29 Am J Rev ed Ins § 748.

constitutionality. The matter of being in accord with, or in conflict with, and opposed to, the provisions and principles of a constitution.
See **constitutional.**

constitutional law. A body of principles which apply in the interpretation and construction of constitutions and the application of the law of constitutions, that is, fundamental law, to statutes and other public acts. 16 Am J2d Const L § 1. In the form which it has taken in the United States, "constitutional law" is an American graft on English jurisprudence. Its principles and rules are mainly the outgrowth of the development of this country and the states. They rest upon the fundamental conception of a supreme law, expressed in written form, in accord with which all private rights must be determined and all public authority administered. State v Main, 69 Conn 123, 37 A 80.

constitutional liberty. The liberty guaranteed under the American system of constitutional government; a very broad and extensive concept, embracing not only freedom from physical restraint, but the right of man to be free in the enjoyment of the faculties with which he is endowed by the Creator, subject only to such restraints as are necessary for the common welfare. 16 Am J2d Const L §§ 358, 359.

constitutional limitations. Those provisions of a constitution which restrict or confine the power of the legislature to pass laws. 16 Am J2d Const L §§ 228 et seq.

constitutional office. A public office created by the United States Constitution or by a state constitution, as distinguished from an office created by statute, or from an office which, like that of notary public, has existed in nearly all countries for centuries. Opinion of Justices, 165 Mass 599, 43 NE 927.

constitutional right. A right guaranteed to a person by the Constitution of the United States or a state constitution, and so guaranteed as to prevent legislative interference with that right. 16 Am J2d Const L § 328.

constitutiones (kon-sti-tu-she-ō'nēz). The laws of the Roman emperors.

Constitutiones tempore posteriores potiores sunt his quae ipsas praecesserunt (kon-sti-tu-she-ō'nēz tem'-po-re pos-te-ri-ō'rēz po-she-ō'rēz sunt hīs kwē ip'sas prē-ses-sē'runt). (Civil law.) Later laws prevail over those which preceded them.

Constitution of the United States. The Constitution as it was adopted in the Convention of 1787, was ratified by the states, and went into effect on March 4, 1789, together with the Amendments to that constitution, duly adopted and ratified.

Constitutions of Clarendon. English statutes enacted in 1164, limiting the powers of the Church of England.

constitutor (kon'sti-tū-tor). (Civil law.) A person who promised to pay the debt of another.

constitutum (kon'sti-tū-tum). (Civil law.) An agreement to pay a pre-existing debt.

Constitutum esse eam domum unicuique nostrum debere existimari, ubi quisque sedes et tabulas haberet, suarumque rerum constitutionem fecisset (kon-sti-tū'tum es'se ē'am do'mum ū-ni-kwē'kwe nos'trum de-bē're eg-zis-ti-mā'rī, ū'bi kwis'kwe sē'-dēz et ta-bū'lās hā-bē'ret, su-ā-rum'kwe rē'rum kon-sti-tū-shē-ō'nem fē-sis'set). (Civil law.) It is established that the home of each of us is considered to be the place where he has his abode and his books and where he may have made an establishment of his business.

constraint (kon-strānt'). Duress; restraint; compulsion. Gates v Hester, 81 Ala 357, 360; an abridgment of liberty or hindrance of the will. Edmondson v Harris, 2 Tenn Ch 427, 433.

construct. To build; to erect; sometimes used in the sense of "to provide." Seymour v Tacoma, 6 Wash 138, 32 P 1077.

constructed value. A technical term in the law of customs duties which refers for calculation to cost of materials, expenses and profit, and cost of containers and packaging. 19 USC § 1401a(d).

constructio arcium. See **arcium constructio.**

Constructio legis non facit injuriam (kon-struk'she-ō lē'jis non fā'sit in-jū'ri-am). The interpretation of the law works no injury. See Broom's Legal Maxims 603.

construction. The erection of buildings; the creation of structures; something constructed; ascertaining the meaning of a constitution, statute, charter of a corporation, bylaws of a mutual benefit society, contract, will, or any other instrument in litigation or having a bearing upon litigation. There is an abstract distinction between "construction" and "interpretation," in that "construction" is the drawing of conclusions from elements known from, given in, and indicated by, the language used, while "interpretation" is the art of finding the true sense of the language itself, or of any form of words or symbols. In other words, "interpretation" is used with respect to language or symbols themselves, while "construction" is used to determine, not the sense of the words or symbols but the legal meaning of the entire contract. But, on the whole, it is doubtful whether anything is to be gained by attempting the difficult and unrewarding task of making a distinction between the two terms. 17 Am J2d Contr § 240.

See **broad construction; equitable construction; interpretation; liberal construction; narrow construction; original construction; practical construction; rational interpretation; strict construction.**

construction car. A car used in work on a railroad, carrying equipment, materials, even laborers.

construction contract. A contract for the construction of a building or other structure, the distinguishing characteristics of which are the plans and specifications, according to which the work is to be performed by the builder or contractor; the performance of a part, sometimes all the work required to be performed by subcontractors, and public regulation of the contracting business, which, of course, by imposing licensing requirements determines who are competent to contract as builders.

construction interest. That sum of money estimated for payment of interest accruing on special assessment warrants, sold to defray the cost of an improvement, from the time of such sale until special assessments become due and payable and begin to draw interest, such sum being added to the cost of the improvement and included in the total amount of the special assessment warrants issued and sold. Hoffman v Minot (ND) 77 NW2d 850, 58 ALR2d 1338.

construction work. Work in erecting buildings, providing other structures, such as bridges and viaducts, improving harbors, digging canals, making and repairing highways, etc. As used in workmen's compensation acts to describe a particular type of employment, the term includes reconstruction, and applies to the strengthening, by the addition of stays and supports, of a completed building found to be faulty. 58 Am J1st Workm Comp § 98.

construction workers. Persons engaged in the construction work.
See **construction work.**

constructive. Informative; helpful; inferred, deduced, or presumed from circumstances, sometimes by forced or strained conclusions.

constructive acceptance. An element of an implied relation of bailor and bailee, where the latter has acquired possession by chance, as by finding the property, or where wearing apparel or other article has been left in a store, office, or other place of business by a customer, client, or patient. 8 Am J2d Bailm § 60.

constructive admission. The effect of failure to respond, or a bad response, to a request for an admission under the federal rule which supports such request. 23 Am J2d Dep §§ 303, 306.

constructive adverse possession. See **constructive possession.**

constructive annexation. The assumption of the character of realty by movable things which have been fitted and adapted to realty, such as doors, mantels, casings, columns, etc., although not affixed to the realty. 35 Am J2d Fixt § 11.

constructive assignment. An assignment for the benefit of creditors arising by operation of law, as where a preferential or fraudulent transfer is converted by statute into an assignment for the benefit of creditors. 6 Am J2d Assign for Crs § 47.

constructive attachment. An attempt to perfect an attachment without seizure and removal of personal property. 6 Am J2d Attach §§ 296, 297.

constructive bailment. The holding of a chattel under such circumstances that the law imposes upon the person in possession the obligation to deliver the chattel to another. 8 Am J2d Bailm § 8.

constructive breaking. In the law of burglary, such a breaking as is effected where the entry is accomplished by means of fraud or threats, or by confederacy with the servants in the house. 13 Am J2d Burgl § 13.

constructive contempt. A contempt of court committed, not in the presence of the court, but at some distance away from it, usually consisting in disobeying or resisting process, intimidating a witness, or giving a false report of judicial proceeding while the same is pending before the court. 7 Am J2d Contpt § 6. Often referred to as indirect contempt.
See **indirect contempt.**

constructive contract. Same as **quasi contract.**

constructive conversion. A conversion which takes place when a person does such acts in reference to the goods of another as amount in law to appropriation of the property to himself. Laverty v Snethen, 68 NY 522, 524.
See **equitable conversion.**

constructive delivery. A symbolic delivery whereby the party to whom delivery is made is clothed with all the usual muniments of title and indicia of ownership, as in the case of the deposit of a warehouse receipt or bill of lading for goods in store or in transit. 46 Am J1st Sales § 434. By carrier:—the disposition of a shipment where the carrier agrees with the consignee or some person entitled under the latter to hold the goods for some purpose other than that of carriage to and delivery at the destination directed by the shipper. State v Intoxicating Liquors, 104 Me 463, 72 A 331. Of life insurance policy:—an unconditional acceptance of the terms of the contract by the insured, coupled with both insurer and insured treating the policy as in force, although the policy remains in the possession of the agent of the insurer. 29 Am J Rev ed Ins § 215.

constructive desertion. Misconduct by a spouse so serious as to compel the other spouse to leave or remain away from it. 24 Am J2d Div & S § 112.

constructive dividend. A division of profits of a corporation among the stockholders without a formal declaration of a dividend or an intent by the directors to declare a dividend. Morgan v Wisconsin Tax Com. 195 Wis 405, 217 NW 407, 218 NW 810, 61 ALR 357, error dismd 278 US 583, 73 L Ed 519, 49 S Ct 186, cert den 279 US 835, 73 L Ed 983, 49 S Ct 250.

constructive escape. The obtaining by a prisoner of more liberty than the law allows him, although he still remains confined. 27 Am J2d Escape § 23.

constructive eviction. As a breach of a covenant of title:—a yielding by the grantee to the hostile assertion of an adverse paramount title. 20 Am J2d Cov § 101. Any disturbance of a tenant's possession by the landlord, or someone acting under his authority, or an omission by the landlord to act or perform where it is his duty to act or perform, which renders the premises unfit for occupancy for the purposes for which they were demised or which deprives the tenant of the beneficial enjoyment of the premises, causing him to abandon them, amounts to a "constructive eviction," provided the tenant abandons the premises within a reasonable time. 32 Am J1st L & T §§ 246-248.

constructive flight. A fiction which has been adopted to secure the return, from a sister state as a fugitive from justice, of a person who has by his constructive presence committed a crime in the demanding state. 31 Am J2d Extrad § 5.

constructive force. In robbery, such force consists of any demonstration of force, menace, or means by which the person robbed is put in fear sufficient to suspend the free exercise of his will, or to prevent resistance to the taking. See 46 Am J1st Rob § 16.

constructive fraud. Legal fraud as distinguished from actual fraud, being presumed from the relation of the parties to a transaction or from the circumstances under which it takes place, not necessarily a matter of conscious wrongdoing. 37 Am J2d Fraud § 4.
In its generic sense, "constructive fraud" comprises all acts, omissions, and concealments involving a breach of legal or equitable duty, trust, or confidence which result in damage to another. Constructive fraud exists in cases in which conduct, although not actually fraudulent, ought to be so treated—that is, in which such conduct is a constructive or quasi fraud which has all the actual consequences and legal effects of actual fraud. Re Arbuckle's Estate, 98 Cal App 2d 562, 220 P2d 950, 23 ALR2d 372.

constructive levy. The act of an officer armed with a writ of attachment or execution in reference to property of the defendant which would render the officer liable for conversion or trespass if it were not for the protection given him by the writ. 6 Am J2d Attach § 296. A paper levy upon real estate, that is, a levy accomplished by the officer without actual entry upon the land. 6 Am J2d Attach § 312.

constructively received. For income tax purposes:—a dividend which, although not actually received by the stockholder, has been made unqualifiedly subject to his demand. Anno: 120 ALR 1282.
See **constructive delivery.**

constructive mortgage. An instrument in the form of an absolute deed of real estate but intended as a mortgage, being given as security for the payment of a debt. Plumner v Isle, 41 Wash 5, 82 P 1009.

constructive notice. Not actual notice; such circumstances as the law deems the equivalent of actual notice since they are such as, under the law, put a party upon inquiry. 55 Am J1st V & P § 697. The substitute in law for actual notice, being based upon a presumption of notice which is so strong that the law does not permit it to be controverted. 39 Am J1st Notice § 7. Sometimes confused with "implied notice" which is a matter of actual notice rather than legal inference. 39 Am J1st Notice § 6.
A recorded deed is an instance of notice. It is of no consequence whether the second purchaser has actual notice of the prior deed or not. He is bound to take, and is presumed to have the requisite notice. Legal notice is the same as constructive notice,

and cannot be controverted by proof. Cooper v Flesner, 24 Okla 47, 103 P 1016. Recording statutes are intended ordinarily to make a recorded instrument effective to give constructive notice to all with whom the person in possession may undertake to deal. But the protection is not entirely one-sided or absolute. The statute has another function, namely, to provide an opportunity for investigation of the title. The opportunity to investigate is the foundation of constructive notice. But the statute is a bulwark, not a trap, and such notice may be negatived by the fraud or misrepresentations of the party recording the instrument. Fogle v General Credit, 74 App DC 208, 122 F2d 45, 136 ALR 814.
See **implied notice.**

constructive placement of cars. An assumed placement where a carrier is prevented from making an actual placement by reason of conditions for which the shipper or consignee is responsible, and it is necessary under the rules and regulations of the carrier to have a point of time from which the period of detention of the cars for the purpose of imposing demurrage charges can be calculated. 13 Am J2d Car § 485.

constructive possession. That possession which the law annexes to the title; sometimes called legal possession, or possession in law, to distinguish it from possession in deed or in fact, which actual occupancy gives. 42 Am J1st Prop § 42. As applied to a disseisor:—a claim of ownership under color of title to a tract of land of which only a part is in the actual possession of the claimant. 3 Am J2d Adv P § 18.

By force a statute, payment of taxes, under color of title, is constructive possession of unimproved and uninclosed land. Such possession is constructive adverse possession as distinguished from actual adverse possession. Canaday v Miller, 102 Kan 577, 171 P 651.

constructive presence. A fiction of criminal law whereby a person who is physically elsewhere at the time of the commission of the crime, is regarded as being present at the scene of the crime committed through agencies set in motion by that person. Hyde v United States, 225 US 347, 362, 56 L Ed 1114, 1124, 32 S Ct 793.

In the eyes of the law a person may be present, although he is absent. If a person keeps away from the place where a crime is being committed for the purpose of facilitating the commission of the offense, he is considered as being constructively present as a principal to the crime, although he is not sufficiently near to give assistance if required. State v Poynier, 36 La Ann 572.

constructive repeal. See **implied repeal.**

constructive seizure. See **constructive levy.**

constructive service doctrine. The doctrine that an employee unlawfully dismissed from employment who holds himself ready and willing to perform the work for which he was employed shall be regarded in law as having actually performed it—that is, that readiness to perform is for all purposes equivalent to performance. 35 Am J1st M & S § 53. The doctrine that the right of a father to the services of his unmarried infant daughter is sufficient to support an action for her seduction, although it does not appear that she rendered any actual services for him. 47 Am J1st Seduc § 75.

constructive service of process. Service of process by publication, posting, mail, or any method of service other than personal. 42 Am J1st Proc § 57. The term is also applied in some jurisdictions to service by leaving a copy of the process at the usual place of abode of the person to be served, but in other jurisdictions such service is regarded as personal service. 42 Am J1st Proc § 60.

constructive taking. A taking by fraud, trick, or deception. 32 Am J1st Larc § 12.

constructive total loss. A loss of such a character as to authorize the insured to abandon the property and recover as for a total loss, although there is not an absolute extinction of the subject of the insurance. 29A Am J Rev ed Ins § 1571.

constructive trust. A trust by operation of law which arises contrary to intention and against the will, declared against one who, by fraud, actual or constructive, by duress or abuse of confidence, by commission of wrong, or by any form of unconscionable conduct, artifice, concealment, or questionable means, either has obtained or holds the legal right to property which he ought not, in equity and good conscience, hold and enjoy. 54 Am J1st Trusts § 218.

construe. To interpret; to read for the purpose of ascertaining the meaning of a writing or a statute. O'Donnell v Glenn, 9 Mont 452, 23 P 1018.
See **construction.**

constuprate (kon'stu-prāt). To violate; to debauch; to defile.

consuetudinary law (kon-swē-tū'di-nạ-ri lâ). The law which is established by custom.

consuetudines (kon-su-e-tū'di-nēz). Usages. See 1 Bl Comm 314.

consuetudinibus et servitiis. See **de consuetudinibus et servitiis.**

consuetudo (kon-su-ē-tū'dō). A custom or usage.

Consuetudo contra rationem introducta, potius usurpatio quam consuetudo appelari debet (kon-su-ē-tū'dō kon'tra rā-shē-ō'nem in-trō-duk'ta, pō'she-us ū-sur-pā'she-ō quam kon-su-ē-tū'dō ap-pel-lā'rī de'bet). A custom introduced which is contrary to reason ought rather to be called a usurpation than a custom.

consuetudo curiae (kon-su-ē-tū'dō ku'ri-ē). The custom or usage of the court.

Consuetudo debet esse certa (kon-su-ē-tū'dō de'bet es'se ser'ta). A custom ought to be certain.

Consuetudo debet esse certa; nam incerta pro nullis habentur (kon-su-ē-tū'dō de'bet es'se ser'ta; nam in-ser'ta prō nul'lis hā-ben'ter). A custom should be certain, for uncertain things are held as nothing.

Consuetudo est altera lex (kon-su-ē-tū'dō est al'te-ra lex). Custom is another kind of law.

Consuetudo est optimus interpres legum (kon-su-ē-tū'dō est op'ti-mus in-ter'prēz lē'gum). Custom is the best interpreter of the law. Boyd v United States, 116 US 616, 622, 29 L Ed 746, 748, 6 S Ct 524.

Consuetudo et communis assuetudo vincit legem non scriptam, si sit specialis, et interpretatur legem scriptam, si lex sit generalis (kon-su-ē-tū'dō et kom-mū'nis as-su-ē-tū'dō vin'sit lē'jem non skrip'-tam, sī sit spē-she-ā'lis, et in-ter-pre-tā'ter lē'jem skrip'tam, sī lex sit je-ne-rā'lis). Custom and common usage override the unwritten law, if it is special, and they explain the written law, if the law is general.

Consuetudo ex certa causa rationabili usitata privat communem legem (kon-su-ē-tū′dō ex ser′ta kâ′za rā-she-ō-nā′bi-lī ū-si-tā′ta pri′vat kom-mū′nem lē′jem). Custom adopted from certain reasonable cause, supersedes the common law. See Broom's Legal Maxims 919.

Consuetudo licet sit magnae auctoritatis, nunquam tamen praejudicat manifestae veritati (kon-su-ē-tū′dō li′set sit mag′nē âk-tō-ri-tā′tis, nun′quam ta′men pre-jū′di-kat ma-ni-fes′tē ve-ri-tā′tī). Custom, although it may be high authority, should never be prejudicial to plain truth.

Consuetudo loci observanda est (kon-su-ē-tū′dō lō′sī ob-zer-van′da est). The custom of the locality should be observed.

Consuetudo manerii et loci observanda est (kon-su-ē-tū′dō ma-ne′ri-ī et lō′sī ob-zer-van′da est). The custom of the manor and the locality should be observed.

consuetudo mercatorum (kon-su-ē-tū′dō mer-kā-tō′rum). The custom of merchants.

Consuetudo neque injuria oriti, neque tolli potest (kon-su-ē-tū′dō ne′kwe in-jū′ri-a ō′ri-tī, ne′kwe tol′-lī po′test). A custom can neither spring from, nor be overcome by, a wrongful act.

Consuetudo non habitur in consequentiam (kon-su-ē-tū′dō non hā′bi-ter in kon-se-quen′she-am). A custom should not be turned into a consequence.

Consuetudo non trahitur in consequentiam (kon-su-ē-tū′dō non tra′hi-ter in kon-se-quen′she-am). Custom should not be drawn into consequence.

Consuetudo praescripta et legitima vincit legem (kon-su-ē-tū′dō prē-skrip′ta et lē-ji′ti-ma vin′sit lē′jem). A prescriptive and lawful custom prevails over law.

Consuetudo regni Angliae est lex Angliae (kon-su-ē-tū′dō reg′ni ang′li-ē est lex ang′li-ē). The custom of the English kingdom is the law of England.

Consuetudo semel reprobata non potest amplius induci (kon-su-ē-tū′dō se′mel re-prō-bā′ta non po′test am′pli-us in-dū′sī). A custom once denied cannot be further invoked.

Consuetudo tollit communem legem (kon-su-ē-tū′dō tol′lit kom-mū′nem lē′jem). Custom supersedes the common law.

Consuetudo vincit communem legem (kon-su-ē-tū′dō vin′sit kom-mū′nem lē′jem). Custom supersedes the common law.

Consuetudo volentes ducit; lex nolentes trahit (kon-su-ē-tū′dō vo-len′tēz dū′sit; lex no-len′tez tra′hit). Custom leads those who are willing; the law drags those who are unwilling.

consul. An officer commissioned by a government to hold office and to represent it at a particular place in a foreign country for the purpose of promoting and protecting its interests and those of its citizens or subjects. He is not a diplomatic officer and as a rule he has no diplomatic powers. 4 Am J2d Ambss § 11.

consular agent. An officer whose functions are similar to those of a consul, but whose authority is more limited.

consular court. A court held by a consul, that is, a representative of a country other than that in which the court sits.

consulatory response. Same as **consultative opinion**.

consules a consulendo; reges enim tales sibi associant ad consulendum (kon′su-lēz ā kon-su-len′dō; rē-jēz e′nim tā′lēz si′bi as-sō′she-ant ad kon-su-len′dum). Advisors for consultation; for such the kings gather around them for consultation.

consult. To seek advice, as to consult a lawyer.

consultation. The deliberation of two or more persons on some matter; a council or conference to consider a special case. Dunbar v Fant, 170 SC 414, 170 SE 460, 90 ALR 1412; a writ awarded by the superior court upon its refusal to issue a writ of prohibition for the removal of a cause from the ecclesiastical court to the superior court. See 3 Bl Comm 114.

consultation with physician. An application by a person concerning some disease or ailment to a physician, for diagnosis, treatment, advice, or prescription; a term in an application for a policy of life insurance which has been construed as requiring the disclosure of a consultation with reference to even a slight and temporary illness, while in other cases the seriousness of the ailment is considered material. 29 Am J Rev ed Ins § 758.

consultative opinion. The opinion of a court on a point of law rendered, not in an actual case or controversy before the court, but at the request of a public officer or body.
See **advisory opinion**.

consulto. See **ex consulto**.

consume. To use up; to eat; to destroy, as by fire.

consumer. Literally, one who consumes; in economics and also in law, one of the great class affected by rising and falling prices, good and poor quality of merchandise, and public regulation of producers and middlemen.

consumer cooperative. A cooperative association of consumers of merchandise, dry goods, shoes, clothing, groceries and food products, for the purpose of obtaining such goods and articles at a reasonable price and of good quality, the function usually being carried out by the establishment and operation of a store. 18 Am J2d Co-op Asso § 1.

consumer goods. Articles used or bought for use primarily for personal, family, or household purposes. UCC § 9—109(1)

consummate (kọn-sum′āt or kon′sum-āt). To complete; to carry out, as, to consummate an agreement for the exchange of property. Connor v Riggins, 21 Cal App 756, 760, 132 P 849.

consummate dower. See **dower consummate**.

consummation of marriage. Cohabitation of the spouses. 4 Am J2d Annul § 1. The usual meaning of the term, in a common-law sense, is sexual intercourse between the parties after the marriage has been formally solemnized, or consent given, but statute has given the term a wider meaning in some jurisdictions. Sharon v Sharon, 75 Cal 1, 16 P 345.

consummation of offense. The completion of a criminal offense by the performance of acts requisite to the offense.

consumption. A consuming; destruction by use. Revzan v Nutelman, 370 Ill 180, 18 NE2d 219; use of a thing, sometimes, but not necessarily, to the complete extermination of the thing. 47 Am J1st Sales T § 25. The disease of **tuberculosis**.

consumption tax. See **use tax**.

contagious. Communicable; spreading by contact.

contagious abortion. A disease of cows, generally contracted through the digestive tract from infected food, which causes the premature birth of calves. Gesme v Potter, 118 Or 621, 247 P 765.

contagious disease. A disease communicable by contact, or by bodily exhalation. Grayson v Lynch, 163 US 468, 477, 41 L Ed 230, 233, 16 S Ct 1064.
See **infectious disease.**

container. A box, can, or jug; a wrapper. People v Harris, 135 Mich 136, 97 NW 402.

containing. A technical term of the law of customs duties, meaning that the imported article contains a significant quantity of the named material. 19 USC § 1202, headnote 9(f).

contamination. A condition of impurity resulting from mixture or contact with a foreign substance. Anno: 80 ALR2d 1289.

contango (kọn-tang′gō). A broker's charge for carrying over the account of a customer to the next settlement day.

contek (kọn-tek′). Strife; contention; contestation.

contemner (kọn-tem′nėr). A person who commits a contempt.

contemnor (kon-tem′nor). A person guilty of contempt of court.

contemplated. In expectation.

contemplated suicide. As the term appears in a statute relative to the defense of suicide in an action on a life insurance policy, it means an insured who intended or had resolved to commit suicide at the time he applied for the policy. Aetna Life Ins. Co. v Florida (CA8 Mo) 69 F 932, cert den 163 US 675, 41 L Ed 311, 16 S Ct 1198.

contemplation of bankruptcy. A phrase of some pertinence under former bankruptcy acts, having reference to an assignment, conveyance, or transfer made or given with bankruptcy proceedings, voluntary or involuntary in mind, and with the intent of removing the thing assigned or property conveyed from administration and distribution in bankruptcy.

It is to be observed that under the present Bankruptcy Act, actual intent is not an element of a voidable preference. 9 Am J2d Bankr § 1082; neither is it an element of a fraudulent preference under the Act. 9 Am J2d Bankr § 1115.

contemplation of death. That expectancy of death which actuates the mind of the person on doing the act in question. Anno: 4 ALR 1523; something more than the general expectation of death which all persons entertain; an apprehension of death arising from some existing infirmity or impending peril. Anno: 21 ALR 1336.

Within the meaning of the inheritance tax statutes, for a transfer of property to be "in contemplation of death," it is not necessary that the transferrer be in fear of immediate death from an existing malady, as a gift causa mortis, but, on the contrary it is conceivable that a person of comparative youth, enjoying perfect health and vigor, may, nevertheless, make a transfer of his property in contemplation of death. Chambers v Larronde, 196 Cal 100, 235 P 1024, 41 ALR 980, 989.

As the words are used in succession tax statutes dealing with gifts made "in contemplation of death," they refer to an expectation of death which arises from such a bodily or mental condition as prompts persons to dispose of their property, and bestow it on those whom they regard as entitled to their bounty. Re Dessert, 154 Wis 320, 142 NW 647.

contemplation of insolvency. The attitude of the officers of a bank when it becomes known, or reasonably should be apparent, to them that the bank presently will be unable to meet its obligations and will be obliged to suspend its ordinary operations. Smith v Baldwin, 63 App DC 72, 69 F2d 390.
See **contemplation of bankruptcy.**

contemplation of parties rule. The rule of damages applied in actions for breach of contract that the damages recoverable for the breach are such as may fairly and reasonably be considered as arising naturally—that is, according to the usual course of things—from the breach of contract itself, or such as reasonably may be supposed to have been in the contemplation of both parties at the time they made the contract, as the probable result of the breach. 22 Am J2d Damg § 56. In the great majority of cases the courts have refused to apply this rule in tort actions. Anno: 48 ALR 318.

Contemporanea expositio est fortissima in lege (kon-tem-po-rā′ne-a ex-po-zi′she-ō est for-tis′si-ma in lē′je). A contemporaneous interpretation is best in law. State v George, 134 La 177, 63 So 866.

Contemporanea expositio est optima et fortissima in lege (kon-tem-pō-rā′ne-a ex-pō-zi′she-ō est op′ti-ma et for-tis′si-ma in lē′je). A contemporaneous construction is best and most powerful in law. Boyd v United States, 116 US 616, 622, 29 L Ed 746, 748, 6 S Ct 524.

contemporaneous. Occurring at the same time as another occurrence or event; occurring at a time within a period during which another occurrence or event is occurring. Hilton Lumber Co. v Atlantic Coast Line Railroad Co. 141 NC 171, 53 SE 823.

contemporaneous construction. The doctrine of statutory interpretation that a statute under construction, because of ambiguity, should be viewed in the light of conditions surrounding at the time of the passage of the statute. Houghton v Payne, 194 US 88, 48 L Ed 888.

contemporaneously. In a statute prohibiting discrimination in freight rates, the word does not mean that the shipment must have been made the exact day and hour, or necessarily in the same month; but it means a period of time through which the shipments of goods or freight are made by the complaining party at one rate and by other shippers at another rate. Hilton Lumber Co. v Atlantic Coastline Railroad Co. 141 NC 171, 53 SE 823.

contemporaneous services. As the term is used in a statute forbidding discrimination by a carrier, it means services within a period of time through which shipments of goods are made by one shipper at one rate and by other shippers at another rate. Hilton Lumber Co. v Atlantic Coastline R. Co. 141 NC 171, 53 SE 823.

contempt. An exhibition of scorn or disrespect toward a court or legislative body.

contemptibiliter (kon-temp″ti-bī′li-ter). Contemptuously; with intent to commit a contempt.

contempt of Congress. Conduct against the dignity or in disrespect of Congress in its proceedings of a legislative character, or in the course of an inquiry within the legitimate scope of the legislative functions of Congress, where such conduct has the effect of obstructing the proceedings or inquiry. 17 Am J2d Contpt § 125.

contempt of court. Conduct tending to bring the authority and administration of the law into disrespect or disregard, interfering with or prejudicing parties or their witnesses during the litigation, or otherwise tending to impede, embarrass, or obstruct the court in the discharge of its duties. 17 Am J2d Contpt § 3.
See **civil contempt; criminal contempt**.

contempt of legislature. Conduct exhibiting such disrespect for a legislative body as to impair its usefulness or conduct impeding the body or a committee thereof in performing legislative functions. 17 Am J2d Contpt § 119.
See **contempt of Congress**.

contenement (kon-ten'ę-ment). Countenance; appearance; that which is necessarily appurtenant to a tenement. Lord Coke says "contenement signifieth his countenance, as the armour of a soldier is his countenance, the books of a scholar his countenance, and the like." See 4 Bl Comm 379.

contention (kon-ten'shon). That for which one contends; that which one claims, or asserts, or argues in support of.

contentious jurisdiction. That jurisdiction of the ecclesiastical courts which is concerned with administering redress to injuries, that is in the litigation of controversies between adverse parties. The term is employed in contradistinction to voluntary jurisdiction, which merely administers those routine affairs connected with the church in which there is no opposition, such as the granting of dispensations, which Blackstone refers to as "remnants of papal extortions." See 3 Bl Comm 66.

contents. All articles and things contained in a designated holder or place; a word of comprehensive meaning in the context of a will, except as a consideration of the will in its entire context reveals the testator's intent to use the word in a special and restricted sense. Old Colony Trust Co. v Hale, 302 Mass 68, 80 NE2d 432, 120 ALR 1207.

contents of a chose in action. The rights created by the chose in action in favor of the party in whose behalf stipulations are made in it which he has a right to enforce in a suit founded on the contract; and a suit to enforce such stipulations is a suit to recover such contents. Austin Corbin v Black Hawk County, 105 US 659, 26 L Ed 1136.

contents unknown. An expression used in filling out bills of lading importing that the carrier has received certain packages described as containing, or purporting to contain, certain specified articles, the actual contents of which were unknown to the carrier. A qualifying phrase in a bill of lading which permits the shipper to show that a quantity of goods greater than that shown by the bill of lading was delivered by him to the carrier. 13 Am J2d Car § 283.

conterminous (kon-tėr'mi-nus). Adjoining; a common boundary.

contest. Noun: An attempt to defeat the probate of an instrument offered as a will, being inclusive of resistance to probate and an action or proceeding to set aside probate. 57 Am J1st Wills § 743; a technical term for a proceeding to cancel or defeat an entry of public lands. 42 Am J1st Pub L § 31; within the meaning of an incontestable clause in an insurance policy:—some affirmative or defensive action taken in court to cancel the policy or prevent its enforcement, to which the insurer and the insured, or his representatives or beneficiaries, are parties. Anno: 36 ALR 1245, 64 ALR 959, 101 ALR 868; a proceeding by which a disagreement as to the result of an election of a public officer may be determined. 26 Am J2d Elect § 316.

The phrase "contested election" has no technical or legally defined meaning, but an election may be said to be contested whenever an objection is formally urged against it which, if found to be true in fact, would invalidate it. This must be true both as to objections founded upon some constitutional provision as well as upon any mere statutory enactment. Robertson v State ex rel. Smith, 109 Ind 79, 116.

Verb: To make a subject of dispute, contention, or litigation; to call in question; to controvert; to oppose; to dispute; to defend, as a suit or other judicial proceeding; to dispute or resist, as a claim, by course of law; to litigate. Robertson v State ex rel. Smith, 109 Ind 79, 116; Moran v Moran, 144 Iowa 451, 123 NW 202.

contestatio litis (kon-tes-tā'she-ō lī'tis). (Civil law.) The general assertion of the defendant in an action that the plaintiff has no ground of action, which assertion is afterwards extended and maintained in the defendant's plea. See 3 Bl Comm 296.

Contestatio litis eget terminos contradictarios (kon-tes-tā'she-ō lī'tis ē'jet ter-mi-nōs kon-tra-dik-tā'ri-ōs). An issue requires contradictory conclusions.

contested. Opposed; resisted; attacked through legal proceedings.
See **contest**.

contest of election. See **contest**.

contest of land entry. See **contest**.

contest of life insurance policy. See **contest**.

contest of will. See **contest**.

context. The words or language of a written instrument or a statute which accompany the part of the instrument or statute which is under construction.

contiguous. Literally, in actual contact, an actual touching. One parcel of land is "contiguous" to another parcel of land when the two parcels are not separated by outside land. See Vestal v Little Rock, 54 Ark 321, 15 SW 891. Appearing in statutes, the term is construed at times somewhat differently, depending upon the context and subject matter of the entire statute. 50 Am J1st Stat § 288. In its popular sense, and as used in local improvement acts, the word means in actual or close contact; touching; adjacent; or near. 48 Am J1st Spec A § 119. Within the meaning of homestead statutes, whether lands touching at a common corner only are contiguous is a question upon which the decisions are in conflict. Some decisions hold that they are. Others hold that the homestead law may not be invoked in respect to two parcels which only corner with each other. The view has also been expressed that under the strict definition of the term "contiguous," as meaning touching sides, adjoining, or adjacent, two tracts of land which touch only at one point are not contiguous. 26 Am J1st Home § 37. A building 25 feet from another building is not "contiguous" to it within the meaning of the provision in a fire insurance policy as to the erection of the building contiguous to that insured. 29A Am J Rev ed Ins § 878.
See **adjacent**.

contiguous territory. Touching, adjoining, and connecting territory, as distinguished from territory separated by other territory. 25 Am J2d Elect § 18.

continens (kon'ti-nęns). (Roman law.) Joined together.

Continental Shelf. See **Outer Continental Shelf.**

continenti. See **ex continenti.**

contingency. That which possesses the quality of being contingent or casual; the possibility of coming to pass; an event which may occur; a possibility. Anno: 41 ALR 146. A technical term in an inheritance tax statute which has reference to a contingent interest which might affect the duration of the interest to be enjoyed by the person receiving the transfer or succession. 28 Am J Rev ed Inher T § 561.

contingency on which the claim is founded. A term appearing in limitation provisions in a federal statute on veterans' insurance which means, in the case of death benefits, the death of the insured, and, in the case of disability benefits, the inception of total disability. 29A Am J Rev ed Ins § 1995.

contingency with a double aspect. See **remainders on a contingency with a double aspect.**

contingent. Possible, or liable, but not certain, to occur; incidental; casual; dependent on that which is undetermined or unknown; dependent for effect on something that may or may not occur. All anticipated future events which are not certain to occur are contingent events, and may be properly denominated mere possibilities, more or less remote, while anticipated events which are certain to occur, or must necessarily occur, are in no degree contingent. Anno: 41 ALR 146.

See expressions commencing "**conditional.**"

contingent beneficial interest. See **contingent interest.**

contingent bequest. A legacy which is intended by the testator to vest only in the event and upon condition of the happening of a contingency named therein. If the time of payment merely be postponed, and it appears to be the intention of the testator that his bounty should immediately attach, the legacy is of the vested kind; but if the time be annexed to the substance of the gift, as a condition precedent, it is contingent, and not transmissible. Furness v Fox, 55 Mass 1 Cush 134; Magoffin v Patton (Pa) 4 Rawle 113, 116.

See **conditional legacy or devise.**

contingent claim. A liability which depends upon some future event which may or may not happen, and which, therefore, makes it wholly uncertain whether ultimately there ever will be a liability. Re Ayeres, 123 Neb 453, 243 NE 274. A claim against an insolvent contingent upon the happening of some occurrence which has not happened at the time when claim is made. 29 Am J Rev ed Insolv § 35.

contingent delivery. Same as **conditional delivery.**

contingent estate. An estate limited so that the person to whom or the event upon which it is to take effect remains uncertain. 33 Am J1st Life Est § 97.

contingent fee. A fee of an attorney the amount of which or the payment of which depends upon the outcome of the litigation. 7 Am J2d Attys § 214.

contingent fee contract. A contract between an attorney at law and a client wherein the former agrees to represent the latter as the latter's attorney at law in the commencement and prosecution of a suit on behalf of the latter for a fee amounting to a certain percent of the amount of the judgment obtained in the action for the client, no charge to be made by the attorney against the client in the event the action is not successful on behalf of the client. In general, such contracts are valid, but they are made invalid by the inclusion of a condition whereby the attorney obligates himself to save the client harmless from costs and expenses of the litigation. 7 Am J2d Attys §§ 214 et seq.

contingent intent. An intent to act, subject to a contingency, as where one proposes to inflict violence upon the person of another, provided the latter does not comply with an order. 6 Am J2d Asslt & B § 30.

contingent interest. An interest which is uncertain either as to the person who will enjoy it in possession or as to the event on which it will arise. 57 Am J1st Wills § 1217. A future interest is contingent where the person to whom or the event upon which it is limited to take effect in possession or become a vested estate is uncertain. Caine v Payne, 86 App DC 404, 182 F2d 246, 20 ALR2d 823. If the condition upon which a future interest depends is precedent, the interest is contingent; if the condition is subsequent, the interest is vested, subject to defeasance. Anno: 131 ALR 712.

contingent legacy. See **contingent bequest.**

contingent liability. A liability arising out of contract, the duty to perform which is dependent as to when or whether the obligation shall become absolute, upon the occurrence of an event the happening of which is a matter of some uncertainty. Haywood v Shreve, 44 NJL 94, 104.

contingent remainder. An estate in remainder under a limitation which is uncertain as to the person who is to take or as to the event upon which the preceding estate is to terminate, so that the preceding estate may terminate and yet the remainder never take effect. Re Youngs Will, 248 Iowa 309, 79 NW2d 376.

A contingent remainder is only the possibility or prospect of an estate, which exists when what would otherwise be a vested remainder is subject to a condition precedent, or is created in favor of an uncertain person or persons. Sands v Fly, 200 Tenn 414, 292 SW2d 706, 57 ALR2d 188.

See **remainders on a contingency with a double aspect.**

contingent right. A right which depends on the performance of some condition or the happening of some event before some other event or condition happens or is performed. 16 Am J2d Const L § 421.

See **contingent interest.**

contingent use. A use, the vesting of which is conditioned upon the happening of some uncertain event. Haywood v Shreve, 44 NJL 94, 104.

contingent will. Same as **conditional will.**

continual claim. A formal claim of right to the possession of land made by a person entitled thereto who does not dare enter through fear of his life or bodily harm. The claimant thus effects a livery in law, if he makes such claim during the life of the feoffor. 2 Bl Comm 316.

continuance. An adjournment of a cause from one day to another, in the same or in a later term, or to a later hour of the same day. 17 Am J2d Contin § 1.

A continuance is usually thought of as an adjournment granted on an application by one of the parties, but it may result by the agreement of both parties, by an order made by the court on its own motion, or by operation of law, the latter result occurring where cases noted for trial are not disposed of at the end of a term of court; such cases necessarily must be continued to the next term and are so continued without any special order of court. 17 Am J2d Contin § 2.

continuance in good health. A condition in a life insurance policy construed by some authorities to mean that there have been no changes in the condition of the insured's health following the making of the application for insurance, but other authorities hold that the condition requires that the applicant be in good health at the time the policy is issued or delivered, irrespective of whether or not the condition was the same at delivery as it was at the application for the policy. 29 Am J Rev ed Ins § 224.

continuando (kon-ti-nū-an'dō). In trespasses of a permanent nature, where the injury is continually renewed—as by spoiling or consuming the herbage with the defendant's cattle,—the declaration may allege the injury to have been committed by continuation from one given day to another—which is called laying the action with a "continuando"—and the plaintiff shall not be compelled to bring separate actions for every day's separate offense. But where the trespass is by one or several acts, each of which terminates in itself, and being once done cannot be done again, it cannot be laid with a "continuando;" yet if there be repeated acts of trespass committed, as cutting down a certain number of trees, they may be laid to be done, not continually, but at divers days and times within a given period. 3 Bl Comm 212.

continuando assisam. See **de continuando assisam.**

continue. To endure; to remain, as to remain in office. State ex rel. Robert v Murphy, 32 Fla 138, 197. To grant a continuance.
See **continuance.**

continued drunkenness. Gross and confirmed habits of intoxication. Gourlay v Gourlay, 16 RI 705, 19 A 142.

continuing bail. A form of statutory bail which extends the obligation of the surety from term to term, until the accused is discharged or surrendered to the proper official. 8 Am J2d Bail § 99.

continuing consideration. A consideration partly executed and partly executory. Hargroves v Cooke, 15 Ga 321, 326.

continuing contempt. A failure or refusal to comply with the order of the court to deliver or pay money, or the like, or to purge the contempt. Tindall v Westcott, 113 Ga 1114, 39 SE 450.

continuing contract. An executory, as distinguished from an executed contract. 17 Am J2d Contr § 6. A contract calling for performance in several units over a period of time. Spaeth v Becktell, 150 Or 111, 41 P2d 1064, 97 ALR 771.

continuing crime. Same as **continuing offense.**

continuing damages. Intermittent or occasional damages, sometimes called temporary damages, for the recovery of which successive actions may be required. 22 Am J2d Damg § 28.

continuing guaranty. A guaranty which covers a series of transactions or a succession of credits extended to the principal debtor, its purpose being to give him a standing credit usable from time to time. 24 Am J1st Guar § 18.

continuing jurisdiction. An expression of variable meaning:—(1) the jurisdiction of a court, once invoked by the commencement of an action, from that time to the final termination of the action; (2) jurisdiction for relief after final judgment; (3) and the jurisdiction of a court to which a case has been sent in granting a motion for change of venue.

continuing offense. A continuous unlawful act or a series of acts set on foot by a single impulse and operated by an unintermittent force, however long a time it may occupy; a continuing offense is of such nature that it may be committed partly in one county or district and partly in another, or continuously in several. 21 Am J2d Crim L § 392.

continuing offer. An offer which is to be kept open for a certain time, or a proposal made to be accepted within a specified time. 17 Am J2d Contr § 32. If it is supported by a consideration, it is usually called an "option."
See **option.**

continuing recognizance. See **continuing bail.**

continuing trespass. A wrongful act involving a course of action which is a direct invasion of the rights of another. 52 Am J1st Tresp § 18. A trespass in the taking of goods, although without intent to appropriate them, followed by an appropriation, the original trespass being deemed to continue to the time of the appropriation, so that the subsequent appropriation is larceny. State v Coombs, 55 Me 477. But see People v Laurence, 137 NY 517, 33 NE 547.

continuing wrong. See **continuing trespass.**

continuous account. See **open account; running account.**

continuous adverse possession. See **continuous possession.**

continuous and uninterrupted use. A term of the law of prescription, meaning a use that is not interrupted by the act of the owner of the servient premises or by voluntary abandonment by the person claiming the easement. 25 Am J2d Ease §§ 56, 57.

continuous disability. A disability which continues without interruption. 29A Am J Rev ed Ins § 1528.

continuous easement. An easement, the enjoyment of which may continue without the necessity of any actual interference by man; an easement depending upon some artificial structure upon, or natural formation of, the servient tenement, obvious and permanent, and constituting a means of enjoying the easement, such as the bed of a running stream, an overhanging roof, a drain, or a sewer. 25 Am J2d Ease § 10.

continuous employment. See **continuously employed.**

continuously. Uninterruptedly, in an unbroken sequence, without intermission or cessation, without intervening time. Rocci v Massachusetts Acci. Co. 222 Mass 336, 110 NE 972. Regularly, protracted, enduringly, and without substantial interruption of sequence, as distinguished from irregularly, spasmodically, intermittently, or occasionally. 29A Am J Rev ed Ins § 1528.

continuously employed. As used in a provision of a group insurance policy requiring, as a condition of disability benefits, that claimants shall have been "continuously employed" for two full years, the term refers to employment that has not been terminated or interrupted during the prescribed period; a layoff does not, of itself, interrupt or terminate the employment. Transky v Metropolitan L. Ins. Co. 232 Wis 474, 287 NW 731, 124 ALR 1489; Anno: 124 ALR 1494.

continuously resided. Remaining in a place without a change of legal residence, which does not mean that there has not been a temporary absence, or even somewhat of an extended period of absence, so long as the intent to change residence was not present. Allan v Allan, 132 Conn 1, 42 A2d 347, 159 ALR 493. Under an immigration act providing for exemption from exclusion in cases of five years' continuous residence, such continuous residence cannot be made up by tacking together two or more visits to this country, each of which was less than five years, although continuous residence in a place does not always mean continually remaining in that place, "residence" not being synonymous with "immovability." See United States v Curran (CA2 NY) 11 F2d 468.

continuous possession. An element of adverse possession, being such continuity of possession as will furnish a cause of action for everyday during the whole period required to perfect title by adverse possession, 3 Am J2d Adv P § 54; that possession of a claimant from which, his acts and conduct, it is apparent to men of ordinary prudence that he is asserting and exercising ownership over the property, taking into consideration the nature, character and location of the property and the uses for which it is fitted or to which it has been put. 3 Am J2d Adv P § 54.

continuous quotations. Market reports on prices of commodities or stocks bought and sold which are collected and circulated at intervals of less than 10 or 15 minutes. 50 Am J1st Stock Ex § 16. The modern instrumentalities in brokers' offices give quotations almost immediately after the transactions from which they are taken.

continuous residence. See **continuously resided.**

continuous retraction of agreement. This can mean no more than breach of agreement. Hotel & Restaurant Employees & Bartenders Union v Boca Raton Club, Inc. (Fla) 73 So 2d 867, 48 ALR2d 986.

continuous service. As a condition of a right to holiday pay under a collective bargaining agreement, "continuous service" is service without deliberate stoppage of work for several days but not without breaks for personal reasons which would appeal to reasonable men to be excusable under the circumstances. Kennedy v Westinghouse Elec. Corp. 16 NJ 280, 108 A2d 409, 47 ALR2d 1025.

continuous servitude. See **continuous and uninterrupted use; continuous easement.**

contra. Otherwise; the other way; disagreeing with; contrary to.
See **e contra.**

contraband. Intoxicating liquor kept or transported in violation of law. 30 Am J Rev ed Intox L § 475; intoxicating liquors imported into the state without the certificate prescribed by law. 30 Am J Rev ed Intox L § 204.

contraband of war. All such articles as may serve a belligerent in the direct prosecution of his hostile purposes. 56 Am J1st War § 157. The term is applicable to goods only, not to persons. 29A Am J Rev ed Ins § 989.

contra bonos mores (kon-trạ bō'nōs mō'rēz). Contrary to good morals, having mischievous or pernicious consequences. Exchange Nat. Bank v Henderson, 139 Ga 260, 77 SE 36; against true principles of morality. State v Smith, 24 NC 402.

contracausator (kon-tra-kâ-zā'tor). A person who has committed a crime.

contraceptive. A drug or device used to prevent the fertilization of human ovum.

contraceptive method. A means or method of preventing pregnancy and the ultimate result, birth. 12 Am J2d Birth C § 1.

contract. Noun: A term which is simple in its superficial aspect but actually difficult of succinct definition, since nothing less than the whole body of applicable precedent will suffice for the purpose of definition. Williston, Contracts 3rd ed § 1; summarily defined as an agreement upon sufficient consideration to do, or refrain from doing, a particular lawful thing. 17 Am J2d Contr § 1. For the purposes of the Uniform Commercial Code, "contract" means the total legal obligation which results from the parties' agreement as affected by the code and other applicable rules of law. UCC § 1-201(11). In popular speech, the word "contract" is frequently used as meaning the work done under a contract. Independent Bridge Co. v Aetna Casualty & S. Co. 316 Pa 266, 175 A 644, 96 ALR 549; a work or improvement for the prosecution of which public authorities have entered into a contract. Independent Bridge Co. v Aetna Casualty & Surety Co. 316 Pa 266, 175 A 644, 96 ALR 549. Within the meaning of the obligation of contract clause of the Federal Constitution, the term "contract" includes not only contracts as the word is ordinarily understood, but all instruments, ordinances and measures, by whatever name known, which embody the inherent qualities or purposes of valid contracts and carry like them their reciprocal obligations of good faith. 16 Am J2d Const L §§ 438 et seq. Verb: To enter into a binding obligation of contract.

See **consideration; executed contract; executory contract; implied contract; parol contract; quasi contract.**

contract against public policy. See **public policy.**

contract by parol. See **parol contract.**

contract by specialty. See **specialty.**

contract carrier. A private carrier; a carrier which does not undertake to carry for all persons indiscriminately but transport only for those with whom they see fit to contract. 13 Am J2d Car § 8.
See **contract hauler; private carrier.**

contract carrier by motor vehicle. A private carrier by motor vehicle; a carrier which does not carry for all persons indiscriminately but only under individual contracts with the various customers whom it chooses to serve. Interstate Commerce Com. v A. W. Stickle & Co. (DC Okla) 41 F Supp 268; Motor Haulage Co. v Maltbie, 293 NY 338, 57 NE2d 41, 161 ALR 401. The question of who are contract carriers by motor vehicle under statutes relating to the use of highways by such carriers depends upon the particular operations of the carrier, as well as the individual statutory provisions, involved. Anno: 175 ALR 1342.

contract clause. That clause contained in the first paragraph of the tenth section of the first article of the Federal Constitution, providing that no state shall pass any law impairing the obligation of contract. Trustees of Dartmouth College v Woodward (US) 4 Wheat 518, 4 L Ed 629.

contract for hire. See **contract of hire.**

contract hauler. As defined by a state statute regulating motor carriers, the term means every person hauling, controlling or operating, or managing any motor vehicle used in the business of transporting property for compensation. State ex rel. Scott v Superior Court, 173 Wash 547, 24 P2d 87.
See **contract carrier.**

contract implied in fact or in law. See **implied contract; quasi contract.**

contract in restraint of trade. See **restraint of trade.**

contractions The shortening of a word or phrase, Eg. "don't" for do not; abbreviations.

Contractio rei alienae animo furandi, est furtum (kon-trak'she-ō rē'ī ā-li-ē'nē a'ni-mō fu-ran'dī, est fer'tum). Larceny is the taking and carrying away of a thing with intent to steal.

contract laborers. Emigrants who, without sufficient means in their own hands or in those of their friends, agree in consideration of the payment of their passage, to accept designated employment in the United States at stated wages, usually the lowest possible rate. Church of Holy Trinity v United States, 143 US 457, 36 L Ed 226, 12 S Ct 511.
See **convict labor.**

Contract Labor Law. The federal statute regulating and restricting the practice of inducing immigration by paying the expenses of travel to the United States for the purpose of obtaining cheap manual labor. 3 Am J2d Aliens § 62.
See **convict labor.**

contract lien. A security, charge, or claim in the nature of a lien on real or personal property whereof a party is the owner or in possession, which he may, by manifest intent and agreement create and which a court of equity will enforce against him, his heirs and personal representatives, and volunteers or claimants under him with notice of the agreement. See 33 Am J1st Liens § 19.

contract malam in se (kǫn-trakt' ma'lum in sē). See **contracts mala in se.**

contract mala prohibita (kǫn-trakt' ma'la pro-hi-bē-tâ). See **contracts mala prohibita.**

contract not to be performed within a year. See **agreement not to be performed within a year.**

contract of adhesion. See **adhesion contract.**

contract of affreightment. See **charter of affreightment.**

contract of agency. A contract between principal and agent which ordinarily is the basis of the relation between them. 3 Am J2d Agency §§ 2, 17, 18. The agency relationship is not necessarily based upon contract, since the relationship may be created by operation of law or by the agent's assuming his position gratuitously. 3 Am J2d Agency § 2.

contract of beneficence. A contract for the benefit of one of the parties only.

contract of carriage. The undertaking of a common carrier to transport goods to a particular destination, including the obligation of a safe delivery of them, within a reasonable time, to the consignee. Alabama Great Southern Railroad Co. v Couturie, 145 Ala 436, 40 So 120.
See **bill of lading; contract carrier; ticket.**

contract of employment. See **contract of hire; employment contract.**

contract of guaranty. See **guaranty.**

contract of hire. A contract whereby the use of a thing, or the services or labor of a person are stipulated to be given for a certain reward. Wingate v Wingate, 11 Tex 430, 437. As used in a state unemployment compensation law, the term means an agreement whereby one undertakes or obligates himself to render personal service for another for a remuneration to be paid because the service was rendered, regardless of the element of profit or loss resulting from the work. Fuller Brush Co. v Industrial Com. 99 Utah 97, 104 P2d 201, 129 ALR 511.

contract of indemnity. See **indemnity.**

contract of indorsement. See **indorsement.**

contract of insurance. See **insurance; insurance contract.**

contract of marriage. A contract between a man and a woman whereby they mutually agree to enter into a matrimonial relationship, and which becomes executed by their act of marriage. Lewis v Tapman, 90 Md 294, 45 A 459.
See **marriage articles.**

contract of mateship. A contract called "mating" entered into between the masters of two whaling ships, whereby they enter into a species of partnership in the business of taking whales and procuring oil; so that if the ships cruise together, they divide equally the oil procured by both, before they separate; or, if they cruise separately, upon their first meeting afterward, they make an equal division of their oil. If they are not then full, they proceed independently or enter into a new contract of mateship. If, after agreeing to mate, they accidentally separate and do not meet again until after the completion of the voyage, neither can claim of the other if either returns filled with oil. But when they do meet abroad after such mateship, the settlement and division of oil take place immediately, unless one has filled. Baxter v Rodman, 20 Mass (3 Pick) 435.

contract of record. A contract recorded pursuant to recording statutes, for example, a contract for the sale of real estate. 45 Am J1st Records § 38.

While a judgment is in no proper sense a contract, judgments have sometimes been classed as "contracts of record." O'Brien v Young, 95 NY 428, 436.

contract of sale. See **contract to sell; executed contract of sale; executory contract of sale; land contract.**

contract of sale or return. See **sale or return.**

contract of suretyship. See **suretyship.**

contractor. Literally, a person who has assumed obligations as a party to a contract, but in common usage, a person who pursues an occupation or business, wherein he contracts to render services for others, including public bodies, in building, painting, excavating, etc., the most significant feature of which is that while he may have an "employer" in the broad sense of that term, he is not under direction in respect of the means by which his work is accomplished. Storm v Thompson, 185 Iowa 309, 170 NW 403, 20 ALR 658, 660; Smith v Milwaukee Builders & Traders' Exchange, 91 Wis 360, 367. As used in a mechanic's lien statute, a "contractor" is a person who furnishes labor and appliances necessary for the work, and who pays therefor, but who

does not work or labor personally. Little Rock, H. S. & T. Railway v Spencer & Maney, 65 Ark 183, 47 SW 196. The word in a statutory provision giving his employee a right to claim compensation, under the Workmen's Compensation Act, from the principal where specific conditions are met, has the same significance as "independent contractor," and the test in determining whether the employer is a "contractor" is the same as that which determines whether a person who is himself claiming compensation is an employee or an independent contractor. United States Fidelity & G. Co. v Spring Brook, 135 Conn 294, 64 A2d 39, 13 ALR2d 769.
See **independent contractor; subcontractor.**

contractors' bonds. Bonds of two types:—(1) a performance bond which guarantees that the contractor will perform the contract and if he defaults and fails to complete the contract, the surety will complete the work or pay damages up to the limit of the bond; (2) a labor and materials payment bond which guarantees the owner that all bills for labor and materials contracted for and used by the contractor will be paid by the surety if the contractor defaults. 17 Am J2d Cont Bonds § 1.

contractor's lien. A lien which arises by operation of law, independently of the express terms of any contract, which a contractor has upon the premises upon which he has erected improvements. This lien springs out of the obligation of the owner to pay for the stipulated labor and the promised materials, when furnished, provided the contractor shall give the notice required by statute. Richmond & Irvine Constr. Co. v Richmond, N. I. & B. Railroad Co. (CA6 Ky) 68 F 105.
See **mechanic's lien.**

contract price. Literally, the amount to be paid under a contract of sale, a contract to render services, or a construction contract. In a contract for the construction of a building, the words "contract price" were held to mean not the abstract price or amount agreed to be paid by the owner to the builder, but the sum which the builder was actually entitled to receive for the whole of the work done by him. Doll v Young, 149 Ky 347, 350, 149 SW 854.
See **total contract price.**

contract right. Any right to payment under a contract not yet earned by performance and not evidenced by an instrument or chattel paper. 15 Am J2d Com C § 52.

contracts mala in se (kǫn-trakts' ma'la in sē). Contracts which are absolutely void because the acts to be performed thereunder are immoral, iniquitous, and contrary to a sound public policy, as well as in violation of statute. 17 Am J2d Contr § 167.

contracts mala prohibita (kon-trakts' ma'la pro-hi'-bē-tâ). Contracts which are not absolutely void in all instances because the acts to be performed thereunder are prohibited by statute, but are void or voidable according to the nature and effect of the act prohibited. 17 Am J2d Contr § 167. It is to be noted, however, that substantial authority supports the elimination of distinction based upon theories playing upon the terms "mala in se" and "mala prohibita." 17 Am J2d Contr § 167.

contract system. The system in vogue in the management of the prisons whereby the labor of prisoners is sold or farmed out by contract. People v Hawkins, 157 NY 1, 51 NE 257.

contract to adopt. A contract to adopt another as a child of the latter which is usually ineffective to complete a legal adoption in itself, but, even if not consummated and given legal effect by adoption proceedings during the lifetime of the adopting parent, may, upon the latter's death be enforced by declaring a right of inheritance in favor of the child. 2 Am J2d Adopt § 8.

contract to contract. A contract, upon a valid consideration, that the parties will at some specified time in the future, at the election of one of them, enter into a particular contract, specifying its terms. 17 Am J2d Contr § 26.

contract to repair. See **repair.**

contract to sell. A contract whereby the seller agrees to transfer the property in goods to the buyer for a consideration called the price. 46 Am J1st Sales § 2.
See **executed contract of sale; executory contract of sale; land contract; sale.**

contractu. See **ex contractu.**

contractual. Pertaining to a contract or to a relation between persons created by a contract, express or implied. A term often applied to the older concept of the assumption by an employee of the risks and dangers covered by the contract of employment. Ashton v Boston & Maine Railroad Co. 222 Mass 65, 109 NE 820.

contractual consideration. Literally, the consideration for a contract, but in a more technical sense, a consideration to be determined as to amount, manner, and means of payment according to a provision or provisions of the contract, such being distinguished from a consideration merely recited in the contract, as to which parol evidence in explanation is admissible.

contractual obligation. An obligation arising out of a contract, express or implied. Halsey v Minnesota-South Carolina Land & Timber Co. 174 SC 97, 177 SE 29, 100 ALR 1.

contract uberrimae fidei (kon'trakt u-ber-ri-mē fī'de-ī). A contract which calls for the utmost of good faith and fair dealing between the parties, of which an insurance contract is a good example. 29 Am J Rev ed Ins § 689.
See **uberrima fides.**

contract under seal. A specialty; a written promise signed by the promisor and sealed with his seal. Such obligations derived their force from their form and were enforceable before the evolution of the doctrine of consideration as applied to simple contracts. 17 Am J2d Contr § 85.
See **specialty.**

contractus (kǫn-trak'tus). A contract. See **forum contractus.**

contractus bonae fidei (kǫn-trak'tus bo'nē fī'de-ī). A Roman law contract which was subject to an equitable defense.

Contractus est quasi actus contra actum (kǫn-trak'-tus est quā'sī ak'tus kon'tra ak'tum). A contract is, as it were, "actus" (an act) "contra" (for) "actum" (an act).

Contractus ex turpi causa, vel contra bonos mores nullus est (kǫn-trak'tus ex tur'pī kâ'za, vel kon'tra bo'nōs mō'rēz nul'lus est). A contract with an evil consideration or one against good morals is void.

Contractus legem ex conventione accipiunt (kǫn-trak'tus lē'jem ex kon-ven-she-ō'ne ak-si'pi-unt).

(Civil law.) Contracts take their law from the agreement.

contradict. To say the contrary; to give evidence to disprove testimony which has been received.

contradiction in terms. An expression which contradicts itself.

contradiction of witness. The introduction of evidence contrary to the testimony of the witness. A method of impeachment where confined to matters material to the issue. 58 Am J1st Witn §§ 782, 783.

contradictory defenses. See **inconsistent defenses**.

contradictory instructions. Instructions given to the jury containing contradictory and conflicting rules without explanation, so that following one of them will lead to a result different from that which will obtain if another is followed. 53 Am J1st Trial § 557.

contraescritura (kon-trah-es-kre-too'rah). An instrument executed secretly by parties to a public contract, the effect of which is intended to change or modify the terms of the contract.

contrafactio (kon-tra-fak'she-ō). Counterfeiting.

Contra fictionem non admittitur probatio (kon'tra fik-she-ō'nem non ad-mit'ti-ter prō-bā'she-ō). Proof is not received to contradict a fiction of the law. See 3 Bl Comm 43, note.

contra formam collationis (kon'tra for'mam kol-lā-she-ō'nis). Against the form of the collation,—a writ by which a donor of lands to be held by religious service, could recover the lands after they had been wrongfully alienated.

contra formam doni (kon'tra for'mam dō'nī). Against the form of the gift or grant.

contra formam feoffamenti (kon'tra for'mam fe-of-fa-men'tī). Against the form of the feoffment,—a writ whereby a tenant could resist the demanded performance of more services than the charter of his ancestor required.

contra formam statuti (kon'tra for'mam sta-tū'tī). Against the form of the statute.

contra formam statuti in hoc casu nuper edict et provis (kon'tra for'mam sta-tū'tī in hōk kā'sū nū'per e-dikt' et pro'vis). Against the form of the statute in such case lately made and provided.

contra hostem. See **expeditio contra hostem**.

contrainte par corps (kôn-trant' pär kōr). An arrest of the body; an imprisonment for debt.

contra jus belli (kon'tra jūs bel'lī). Against the laws of war.

contra jus commune (kon'tra jūs kom-mū'ne). Against common right.

Contra legem facit qui id facit quod lex prohibet; in fraudem vero qui, salvis verbis legis, sententiam ejus circumvenit (kon'tra lē'jem fā'sit kwī id fā'sit quod lex prō-hi'bet; in frā'dem vē'rō kwī, sal'vis ver'bis lē'jis sen-ten'she-am ē'jus ser-kum-vē'nit). He who does what the law prohibits acts contrary to law; he who acts in fraud of it, the letter of the law being inviolate, cheats the spirit of it.

contra legem terrae (kon'tra lē'jem ter'rē). Against the law of the land.

contra leges et statuta (kön'trạ le'jēz et sta-tū'ta). Against the laws and the statutes.

contraligatio (kon-tra-li-gā'she-ō). A counter-obligation.

contramandatio placiti (kon-tra-man-dā'she-ō pla'si-tī). An extension of the time to plead.

Contra negantem principia non est disputandum (kon'tra ne-gan'tem prīn-si'pi-a non est dis-pū-tan'-dum). It is useless to dispute with one who denies principles.

Contra non valentem agere non currit praescriptio (kon'tra non va-len'tem ā'je-re non kur'rit prē-skrip'she-ō). Prescription does not run against a person who is under a legal disability to sue. The maxim is from the civil law, which held, as does our law, that there must not only be a right of action to support a cause of action, but also there must be some person in existence who may sue. Tynan v Walker, 35 Cal 634, 637.

Contra non valentem agere nulla currit praescriptio (kon'tra non va-len'tem ā'je-re nul'la kur'rit prē-skrip'she-ō). No prescription runs against a person who is unable to act. See Broom's Legal Maxims 903.

contra omnes gentes (kon'tra om'nēz jen'tēz). Against all the people.

Contra omnes homines fidelitatem fecit (kon'tra om'-nēz ho'mi-nēz fī-de"li-tā'tem fē'sit). He took oath of fealty against all men. See 1 Bl Comm 367.

contra pacem (kon'tra pa'sem). Against the peace.

contra pacem ballivorum (kon'tra pa'sem bal-li-vō'rum). Against the peace of the bailiffs. By the ancient law, in all peculiar jurisdictions, offenses were said to be committed against the peace of the court in which they were tried and if they were tried in the court of a corporation they were "contra pacem ballivorum." See 1 Bl Comm 117.

contra pacem domini (kon'tra pa'sem do'mi-nī). Against the peace of the king. At common law all crimes were treated as being against the king's peace. See 1 Bl Comm 166.

contra pacem regis (kon'tra pa'sem rē'jis). Against the peace of the king. Any public offense which was committed within the kingdom of England was said to be committed against the king's peace. Commonwealth v Macloon, 101 Mass 1.

contra pacem vice-comitis (kon'tra pa'sem vī"se-ko'-mi-tis). Against the peace of the sheriff. That is, against the peace of the sheriff's court in which the offense was tried. See 1 Bl Comm 117.

contraplacitum (kon-tra-pla'si-tum). A counter plea.

contrapositio (kon-tra-pō-zi'she-ō). A plea.

contra proferentem (kon'tra prō-fe-ren'tem). Against the offeror; against the party offering the evidence.

contra regiam proclamationem (kon'trạ rē'ji-am prok-la-mā-she-o'nem). Against the royal proclamation. See Proclamations, 12 Coke's Rep. (Eng) 74.

Contrariorum contraria est ratio (kon-trā-ri-ō'rum kon-trā'ri-a est rā'she-ō). The reason for contrary things is contrary.

contrarotulator (kon-trạ-rō'tụ-lā-tọr). (French.) A controller.

contrary to good morals. Immoral; having mischievous or pernicious consequences. Exchange Nat. Bank v Henderson, 139 Ga 260, 77 SE 36.

contrary to law. Illegal; contrary to any law. General Motors Acceptance Corp. v United States, 286 US 49, 76 L Ed 971, 52 S Ct 468, 82 ALR 600. If the term is used in a later statute dealing with the same subject, it may refer to an infraction of the earlier

statute. Callahan v United States, 285 US 515, 76 L Ed 914, 52 S Ct 454.
See **verdict contrary to law**.

contrat (kôn-trä'). (French.) A contract.

contra tabulas (kon'tra ta-bū'lās). (Civil law.) Contrary to the instrument.

contrat aléatoire. Same as **aleatory contract**.

contrat de vente (kôn-trä' dė vônt). (Civil law.) A contract of sale.

contratenere (kon-tra-te-nē're). To hold against; to withhold.

contravene. To go against; to violate: as, to contravene the constitution.

contravention. Violation; infraction.

Contra veritatem lex nunquam aliquid permittit (kon'tra ve-ri-tā'tem lex nun'quam a'li-quid per-mit'tit). The law never allows anything contrary to the truth.

contra voluntatem suam (kon'tra vo-lun-tā'tem su'am). Against his own will; involuntarily.

contrectare (kon-trek-tā're). To take; to deal with; to meddle with.

Contrectatio rei alienae animo furando, est furtum (kon-trek-tā'she-o rē'ī ā-li-ē'nē a'ni-mō fu-ran'dī, est fer'tum). The taking of the goods of another with intent to steal, is larceny.

contrefacon (kōn-trĕ-fa-sōn). (French.) An infraction or infringement of a copyright.

contribute. To make a gift with others, as to a community chest; to help to cause, or to furnish some aid in causing, the result. Broschart v Tuttle, 59 Conn 1, 21 A 925. In the ordinary signification of the word, one thing is understood "to contribute" to a given result when such thing has some share or agency in producing such result, and is not understood to convey the idea that such thing was the efficient cause of such result in the sense that without it such result would not have occurred; for it is possible that such result may have occurred, even in the absence of the thing which is supposed to have had some share or agency in producing such result. Wragge v South Carolina & Georgia Railroad Co. 47 SC 105, 25 SE 76.

contributing to delinquency. An act or omission causing or tending to cause juvenile delinquency. 31 Am J Rev ed Juv Ct § 95.

contribution. A gift made with others, as to the Cancer Fund; the money, property, skill, knowledge, or services, which a party to a joint enterprise puts into the venture. 30 Am J Rev ed Jnt Adv § 9. An aid in following an objective or reaching a result. As used in the law of negligence, the word necessarily connotes a share in causation. Snyder v Bicking, 115 NJL 549, 181 A 161, 102 ALR 409. A payment made by each person, or by any of several persons, having a common interest or liability, of his share in the loss suffered or in the money necessarily paid by one of the parties in behalf of the others. 18 Am J2d Contrib § 1. A joint tortfeasor's right of contribution, where it exists under the law of a particular jurisdiction, is a quasi-contractual right arising by reason of an implied engagement of each tortfeasor to help bear the common burden. Builders Supply Co. v McCabe, 366 Pa 322, 77 A2d 368, 24 ALR2d 319.
See **general average**.

contribution between beneficiaries. The right of a devisee or legatee, whose devise or legacy has been impaired by the payment of debts of the testator, by the payment of charges imposed against the devise or legacy, or by the exercise of the election of the surviving spouse in respect of the will, to have other devisees and legatees contribute in defraying the loss caused by such impairment. 57 Am J1st Wills §§ 1408, 1502, 1551.

contribution between cotenants. The principle that where one cotenant has paid a debt or obligation for the benefit of the common property, has discharged a lien or assessment imposed against it, or has purchased an outstanding title, with his own money, he is entitled to have his cotenant or cotenants refund to him their proportionate shares of the amount paid by him or else abandon their interests in the property. See 20 Am J2d Coten §§ 76, 77.

contribution between insurers. The obligation of an insurer who has issued a policy covering the same risk and loss as that insured by one or more other insurers to contribute ratably to the other insurer, or one of the other insurers, who has paid the entire loss. 29A Am J Rev ed Ins § 1717.

contributione facienda (kon-tri-bu-she-ō'ne fā-she-en'da). See **de contributione facienda**.

contributory. Additional; added to; supplementary; acting with something else. As a noun the word is applied to a person who is liable as a member of a company to contribute to the assets on the winding up of the company.

contributory cause. A cause aiding in the production of a result. Broschart v Tuttle, 59 Conn 1, 21 A 925.

contributory infringement. Any act or acts whereby one who is not himself in strict parlance an infringer of a patent may yet be held accountable for having aided or encouraged others to infringe. 40 Am J1st Pat § 151.

contributory negligence. A breach of duty on the part of the plaintiff in an action to recover damages for negligence to exercise the standard of care, which is ordinary care, the care that a reasonably prudent person would exercise, for his own safety, such breach constituting a defense, in the absence of legislation to the contrary, where it was a legally contributing cause of the accident. Brakensiek v Nickles, 216 Ark 889, 227 SW2d 948, 34 ALR2d 94, 28 NCCA NS 275; Wertz v Lincoln Liberty L. Ins. Co. 152 Neb 451, 41 NW2d 740, 17 ALR2d 629, 30 NCCA NS 133; Heinis v Lawrence, 160 Neb 652, 71 NW2d 127, 52 ALR2d 1428; 38 Am J1st Negl § 181.

Mutual contributory or co-operative negligence exists when the injury would not have happened but for the negligence or wrong of both parties. See Alexander v Missouri, Kansas & Texas Railroad Co. (Tex Civ App) 287 SW 153, 155.

The use of the expression "contributory negligence" is restricted to cases in which it appears that both of the parties to the injurious occurrence are responsible therefor. An employer having been negligent, it is appropriate to say that the employee was guilty of contributory negligence, provided, of course, his conduct is subject to such evaluation. 35 Am J1st M & S § 243.

contrition (kǫn-trish'ǫn). (Eccles.) Regret or penitence for wickedness.

contrivance. Something contrived or arranged, often to deceive; a device; a disguise. Maley v Heichemer,

81 Colo 379, 256 P 4. A tool, instrument, or other article, made with more or less ingenuity, to accomplish some mechanical purpose, perhaps the twirling of a wheel upon which wagers may be placed. 24 Am J1st Gaming § 57.

contrivance used for gambling. Any instrument whereby money or things of value are won or lost. Gilley v Commonwealth, 312 Ky 584, 229 SW2d 60, 19 ALR2d 1224.

control. Verb: To check, restrain, govern, have under command, and authority. Wolffe v Loeb, 98 Ala 426, 432. Noun: A position of authority in direction and management.

control group. The officers and agents of a corporation authorized to make decisions. Anno: 98 ALR2d 245.

controller (kọn-trō'lėr). An officer who has charge of the financial affairs of a public or private corporation; a state officer in some states.

controlling interest. A majority of the shares of stock of a corporation. 18 Am J2d Corp § 496.

controlment (kọn-trōl'mẹnt). The auditing or checking of an account.

control of bidding. See **chilling bids.**

control of car. See **control of vehicle.**

control of child. The exercise of guardianship, whether that existing by nature, as in the case of a parent, or by operation of law, as in the case of a guardian, over a child, directing him and imposing discipline as direction and discipline are required. A person to whom the control of a child is intrusted ordinarily has the care and the custody of the child, but the word may be so used as to convey the idea that the person may be intrusted with a legal power to direct and dispose of the child without having actual physical care and custody. Cowley v People, 83 NY 464.

control of corporation. Power to dictate the action of the corporation, not the mere management of a department of the operations. 36 Am J1st Monop etc § 132; the ownership or control of the stock of a corporation which has power to dominate the business, together with the voting strength to make that domination effective. Commissioner v Shillito Realty Co. (CA6) 39 F2d 830, 69 ALR 1266; ultimately, the control exercised by the owners of a majority of the shares of stock. 18 Am J2d Corp § 496.

In a legal sense, one corporation cannot be said to "control" another corporation because nearly all of the stock of the latter corporation is owned by the former. Under such circumstances, the corporation owning the shares can elect the board of directors, but there its power of management stops and the control is lodged in the board of directors. Pullman's Palace Car Co. v Missouri Pacific Railway Co. 115 US 587, 596, 29 L Ed 499, 6 S Ct 194.

control of prices. See **price control.**

control of vehicle. A term of variable meaning:— operating with due care; being ready to stop quickly; being attentive in anticipation of the necessity of a sudden turn or stop; having the ability to avoid collision with one using the highway and exercising proper caution on his own part. 7 Am J2d Auto § 354.

See **assured clear distance.**

control test. A criterion applied in determining whether an organization in the form of a business trust is, in legal effect, a true trust or a partnership. 13 Am J2d Bus Tr § 11.

See **loaned servant doctrine.**

control tower. A structure built and equipped for the management of air space, the guiding or controlling of aircraft in the air or landing and taking off at airports. 8 Am J2d Avi § 92.

controver (kon-trọ-vėr'). A person who invents false news.

controversy. A word used in delimiting judicial power meaning an issue appropriate for judicial determination, being definite and concrete, concerning legal relations among parties with adverse interests, and being so real and substantial as to be capable of a decision granting or denying specific relief. Aetna Life Ins. Co. v Haworth, 300 US 227, 81 L Ed 617, 57 S Ct 461, 108 ALR 1000, reh den 300 US 687, 81 L Ed 889, 57 S Ct 667. As used in Article III, Section 2, of the Constitution of the United States, the term "controversy" refers to the claims or contentions of litigants brought before the courts for adjudication by regular proceedings established for the protection or enforcement of rights, or the prevention, redress, or punishment of wrongs. Interstate Commerce Com. v Brimson, 154 US 447, 475, 38 L Ed 1047, 1057, 14 S Ct 1125. A "controversy" under the Civil Practice Act provision for bringing in other parties where a complete determination of the controversy cannot be had without their presence, is not confined to the claim originally asserted by the plaintiff against the defendant; it is sufficient that the controversy as delimited by the complaint and counterclaim relates to a single occurrence and presents common questions of law and fact. Johnson v Moon, 3 Ill 2d 561, 121 NE2d 774, 46 ALR2d 1246.

See **case**; **case or controversy.**

controverted facts. Facts in issue; a ground for trial and, conversely, for the denial of summary judgment. Associated Press v United States, 326 US 1, 89 L Ed 2013, 65 S Ct 1416.

contubernium (kon-tū'bėr-ni-um). A marriage of slaves.

contumace capiendo (kon-tu-mā'se kā-pi-en'dō). See **de contumace capiendo.**

contumacious (kon-tū-mā'shus). Stubborn; disobedient.

See **contempt.**

contumacious witness (kon-tū-mā'shus wit'nes). A witness who testifies in such a manner as to render him guilty of contempt of court. Re Blim, 5 F Supp 678; a witness who refuses to testify or testifies falsely. 17 Am J2d Contpt §§ 28-33.

contumacy (kon'tū-mạ-si). The contemptuous disobedience of an order of the court; refusal to submit to authority.

See **contempt.**

contumax. An outlaw.

contumely. Rudeness; indignity; in some jurisdictions, a ground for divorce. 24 Am J2d Div & S § 159.

contusion (kọn-tū'zhọn). A bruise; an injury without a breaking of the skin.

See **visible contusion.**

contutor (kon-tū'tor). A joint guardian.

conus (ko'nus). Known.

conusance (kŏn'ū-sans). Same as **cognizance**.

conusance of pleas (kŏn'ū-sans of plēz). Exclusive jurisdiction.

conusant (kon'ū-sant). Knowing; having notice or knowledge of anything.

conusee (kon-ū-sē'). A person to whom a recognizance is made.

conusor (kon'ū-sor'). A person who enters into a recognizance; an ancient form of the word **cognizor**.

convalescent. Recovering health.

convalescent home. See **nursing home**.

convalescere (kon-va-le'se-re). To become valid.

convenable (kọn-vē'nạ-bl). Suitable; proper.

convene. To assemble; to meet as a body; to call a meeting. (Civil law.) To file an action; to sue.

convenience. Whatever conduces to freedom from difficulty, from trouble, or from annoyance; whatever promotes one's ease or advantage or is fit for one's use or suitable for one's wants. Boston Safe Deposit & T. Co. v Stebbins, 309 Mass 282, 34 NE2d 616, 148 ALR 1036; Anno: 2 ALR2d 1390. An opportunity to purchase a thousand-mile ticket for less than the standard rate is not a "convenience," within the rule that the legislature may make regulations of the business of carriers to provide for the safety, health and convenience of the public. Lake Shore & M.S.R. Co. v Smith, 173 US 684, 43 L Ed 858, 19 S Ct 565.

convenience of employer rule. The rule that excludes the value of meals and lodging furnished an employee in calculating the gross income of the latter. Anno: 84 ALR2d 1217, 1219.

convenience of the maker. An expression used in a note in reference to the time of payment, which, in no event, entitles the maker to more than a reasonable time. 11 Am J2d B & N § 288.

convenient. Fit or adapted to an end; suitable; becoming; appropriate. Grand Island v Oberschulte, 36 Neb 696, 699.
    See **payable as convenient**.

convenient place of business. A suitable or proper place. Susquehanna Fertilizer Co. v Malone, 73 Md 268, 20 A 900.

convening order. A term, otherwise known as the placita, for the statement, usually appearing in the caption of an order of court, that the court was regularly held at a certain time and place.
    See **placita**.

convenire (kon-ve-nī're). To covenant; to sue.

convenit (kon-vē'nit). It is agreed.

conventicle (kọn-ven'ti-kl). A prayer meeting of dissenters.

conventio (kon-ven'she-ō). An agreement; a covenant; a writ for breach of covenant.

Conventio facit legem (kon-ven'she-ō fā'sit lē'jem). An agreement makes law. A maxim meaning that the law binds the parties to that to which they have consented. Newcomb v Wood, 97 US 581, 24 L Ed 1085.

convention. An organized assemblage of delegates representing a political party or a political principle. 18 Am J1st Elect § 135; a meeting of delegates or representatives of subordinate bodies of a national or state fraternal, social, or religious body; an agreement, particularly an agreement between nations.
    "The governors of North Carolina and Virginia then entered into a 'convention' upon the subject of the boundary between the two provinces. The king and council approved it." Virginia v Tennessee, 148 US 503, 507, 37 L Ed 537, 539, 13 S Ct 728.
    See **treaty**.

conventional (kọn-ven'shọn-ạl). Formal; conforming to rules; based or founded upon a contract or agreement; expressly created by acts of the parties. See 2 Bl Comm 120.

conventional estate. An estate in land created by agreement rather than by operation of law.

conventional heir. See **heir conventional**.

conventional interest. A charge, made pursuant to agreement between lender and borrower, by way of rental or compensation for the use of money. 30 Am J Rev ed Int § 2.

conventional life estate. A life estate created by the act of the parties, by deed, will, or contract. 28 Am J2d Est § 56. Conventional life estates are also frequently created, not by express words, but by general grant, not defining or limiting any specific estate. They are then truly created by the act of the parties, but recognized through construction or implication. They are not to be deemed as arising by operation of law, as do "legal life estates." 28 Am J2d Est § 56.

conventional obligation. An obligation arising out of a contract.

conventional subrogation. A contract right of subrogation; subrogation founded upon some understanding or agreement, express or implied, and not arising merely from the equities of the situation. New York Ins. Co. v Tice, 159 Kan 176, 152 P2d 836, 157 ALR 1233; a subrogation whereby the party paying does so at the request of either the debtor or the lienor, with the understanding that he, the party paying, shall be subrogated. Kocher v Kocher, 56 NJ Eq 547, 548, 39 A 536; a subrogation depending upon a lawful contract which occurs where one having no interest in or relation to the matter pays the debt of another, and by agreement is entitled to the securities and rights of the creditor so paid. 50 Am J1st Subro § 3.

convention candidate. A candidate at a primary election nominated at a preprimary convention.

conventione (kon-ven''she-ō'ne). See **de conventione**.

convention in unum (kon-ven' shun in ū'num). An agreement on one thing; a meeting of the minds.

Conventio privatorum non potest publico juri derogare (kon-ven'she-ō prī-vā-tō'rum non po'test pub'-li-kō jū'rī dē-rō-gā're). An agreement of private parties cannot derogate from public right.

Conventio vincit legem (kon-ven'she-ō vin'sit lē'jem). The contract controls the law. Winkley v Salisbury Mfg. Co. 80 Mass (14 Gray) 443, 446.

conventual church (kọn-ven'tū-ạl chėrch). A church which is attached to a convent.

conventus (kon-ven'tus). A contract; an agreement.

conventus juridicus (kon-ven'tus jū-ri'di-kus). A Roman civil court.

conventus magnatum vel procerum (kon-ven'tus mag-nā'tum vel prō-sē'rum). An assembly of the great men or the nobles,—an ancient name of the general council from which the British parliament was eventually developed. See 1 Bl Comm 148.

conversantes (kon-ver-san'tez). Persons who are conversant with or informed upon or versed in.

converse trusts. See **reciprocal trusts.**

conversion. A distinct act of dominion wrongfully exerted over another's personal property in denial of or inconsistent with his title or rights therein, or in derogation, exclusion, or defiance of such title or rights. 18 Am J2d Conversion § 1. It is an essentially tortious act, an unlawful act, an act which cannot be justified or excused in law. 18 Am J2d Conversion § 1; the act of placing absolute faith in a religion.
See **equitable conversion.**

conversion by bailee. Acts in derogation of the bailor's title or his possessory rights by a destruction of the property or some unlawful interference with his use and enjoyment of it, or dominion over it—an appropriation of it by the bailee to his own use, or to the use of a third person, in disregard of or defiance of the owner's right, or a withholding of possession under a claim of title inconsistent with the title of the bailor. 8 Am J2d Bailm § 106.

conversion by bailor. The act of the bailor in taking possession of the bailed property from the bailee in contravention of the latter's rights, or having received possession for a special purpose, after such purpose has been answered and before termination of the bailee's right to possession under the bailment, to refuse to restore possession to the bailee. 8 Am J2d Bailm § 102.

conversion insurance. See **theft insurance.**

conversion of insurance policy. The surrender of a life insurance policy to the insurer in exchange for another policy pursuant to a right or privilege provided the insured in the original policy. 29 Am J2d Ins § 367.
See **exchange of policy.**

converso. See **e converso.**

convert. To change or transform, as by making soap out of grease; to appropriate the property of another, thereby committing the tort of conversion.

converted term insurance. Term life insurance which has been changed to a policy providing surrender and paid-up values by virtue of a provision in the term policy.

convertible. An automobile with a top that can be withdrawn so as to have an open car; anything that can be changed to something else.

convertible bonds or debentures. Bonds or debentures issued with the privilege of converting them into other securities, usually the common stock of the issuing corporation. 19 Am J2d Corp § 1070.

convertible stock. Corporate stock which the stockholder is entitled to surrender for another class of stock or for other obligations of the corporation. 18 Am J2d Corp § 217.

convertible term insurance. Term insurance with a conversion privilege under which the insured may convert the policy to ordinary life, endowment, or other form of life insurance written by the insurer, without an additional medical examination.

convey. To carry; to transfer the title to property from one person to another by deed. When used in a deed the word shows an intent to transfer title presently by the instrument, as distinguished from a writing which contemplates transfer of title by a subsequent instrument. 23 Am J2d Deeds § 35.

To lease is not to "convey," and although the word is sometimes used with reference to a leasing, the preferable word in that connection is the word "transfer." Duff v Keaton, 33 Okla 92, 124 P 291.

conveyance. A means of transportation; in most common usage, a deed transferring the title to land from one person to another, both the term "deed" in the restricted sense and the term "conveyance" being an abbreviated form of the expression "deed of conveyance." 23 Am J2d Deeds § 2. The term "conveyance", however, is susceptible of a broader meaning. As used in some recording acts, a conveyance is a written paper or instrument signed and delivered by one person to another, transferring the title to or creating a lien on property, or giving a right to a debt or duty. Warnock v Harlow, 96 Cal 298, 31 P 166.

Some authority regards a contract or lease creating a term for years as a "conveyance." 32 Am J1st L & T § 3. In its broadest aspect, the term "conveyance" includes a transfer of personal property. As used in the Uniform Fraudulent Conveyance Act, the word "conveyance" includes every payment of money, assignment, release, transfer, lease, mortgage, or pledge of tangible or intangible property, and also the creation of any lien or incumbrance. Uniform Fraudulent Conveyance Act § 1.
See **deed.**

conveyance by lease and release. See **lease and release.**

conveyance by record. A conveyance evidenced by the order, judgment or decree of a court of record.

conveyance in fraud of dower. The conveying away of his real estate by a husband to be, before his marriage, without consideration, and without the consent or knowledge of his betrothed, with the purpose and result of unfairly depriving her of dower. 25 Am J2d Dow § 98.

conveyancer. A person who makes a business of conveyancing.
See **conveyancing; scrivener.**

conveyance to uses. A conveyance creating an executory interest known as a shifting or springing use. 28 Am J2d Est § 333.
See **shifting uses.**

conveyancing. Preparing documents for the transfer of real property, and investigating the title to such property.

convey and warrant. Words in a conveyance sufficient to convey a fee in some jurisdictions. Palmer v Cook, 159 Ill 300, 42 NE 796.

conveyor belt. An endless belt, sometimes constructed of steel webbing, moving under power capable of carrying somewhat of a load, and put to a variety of uses, such as carrying grain into an elevator, loading cargo upon ships or freight cars, and especially in factories to carry parts for assembly or completed articles for inspection.

Convicia si irascaris tua divulgas; spreta exolescunt (kon-vī'she-a si ī-rās-kā'ris tu'a dī-vul'gas; sprē'ta ex-ō-les'kunt). If you are angered by insults, you publish them; if despised they disappear.

convicium (kon-vī'she-um). An insult; a slander.

convict. Noun: A person who by reason of having been convicted of a crime has forfeited for a certain time his liberty or right of locomotion and who is by law subject to confinement and labor for a

specified time. 41 Am J1st Pris & P § 2. One who is under sentence as the result of a conviction for crime is a "convict" within the meaning of a statute requiring photographs for identification purposes, although an appeal from the conviction is pending. 41 Am J1st Pris & P § 2. Verb: To find a person guilty of a crime with which he is charged, upon either the verdict of a jury or a plea of guilty.
See **conviction**.

convicted. See **conviction**.

conviction. An adjudication that a person is guilty of a crime based upon a verdict or, in a proper case, the ascertainment of guilt by a plea of guilty or nolo contendere. 21 Am J2d Crim L § 617. Such is the primary and usual meaning of the term "conviction," but "it is possible that it may be used in such a connection and under such circumstances as to have a secondary or unusual meaning, which would include the final judgment of the court." United States v Watkinds (CC Or) 6 F 152, 158, 159; 39 Am J1st Pard § 38. There is no conviction, within the meaning of constitutional or statutory provisions disfranchising one convicted of crime, unless there is something in the nature of a final judgment upon the verdict of guilt declared by the jury; suspension of sentence or granting of probation is insufficient. Truchon v Toomey, 116 Cal App 2d 736, 254 P2d 638, 36 ALR2d 1230; Anno: 36 ALR2d 1238. The weight of authority is to the effect that the word "conviction" as used in statutes providing for increased punishment for persons formerly convicted of crime necessitates the pronouncement of sentence upon the verdict or plea of guilty in order to obtain a judgment that is final, so far as the trial court is concerned. Anno: 5 ALR2d 1104. In a few instances the view has been taken that a "conviction" results within the meaning of a habitual criminal statute even though no sentence was imposed. Anno: 5 ALR2d 1107.

convict labor. The performance of services by convicts hired out to employers of labor. 21 Am J2d Crim L § 615.
A statutory provision which forbids the hiring out of convicts, except under order of the court, embodied in the sentence, applies only to farming out convicts to individuals and corporations, and does not extend to labor employed upon public works, and under the supervision and control of public agents. State v Yandle, 119 NC 874, 25 SE 796.
See **convict labor contract**.

convict labor contract. A contract, such as the statutes of some states have authorized, under which convicts or persons imprisoned in jails under conviction of crime are hired out. 41 Am J1st Pris & P § 30.

convict lease. Another term for **convict labor contract**.

convincing evidence. Satisfactory and sufficient evidence. 30 Am J Rev ed Ev § 1080. To "convince" is primarily to overcome or subdue, and, in logic, to satisfy the mind by proof. If evidence is convincing, in any case it is sufficient, and to say it ought to be more convincing in one case than in another, is giving the word degrees of comparison which it does not possess, the word itself being superlative. Evans v Rogers, 57 Wis 623, 626.

convivium (kon-vi'vi-um). A kind of land tenure by the service of providing food and drink for the lord.

convocation (kon-vō-kā'shọn). An assembly of the English clergy.
See **court of convocation**.

convoy (kon'voi). An escort for a merchant ship, composed of one or more naval vessels.

cony. A rabbit, a beast of the warren.

co-obligor. See **joint obligor**.

cook. One who cooks; one who pursues the occupation of cooking; an employee whose services are maritime services within admiralty jurisdiction, where employed on a vessel. 2 Am J2d Adm § 72.

cooling system. The radiator with connecting hose and pipes through which water circulates for the purpose of preventing a motor vehicle engine from overheating; the system of pipes and ducts in a building whereby the structure is kept cool by the circulation of air cooled by water.

cooling time. A relative term, as it applies to a period for reflection between the provoking act or circumstance and the infliction of the fatal stroke by one charged therefor with homicide, depending for its meaning upon the nature of man and the laws of the human mind, as well as on the nature and circumstances of the provocation, the extent to which the passions have been aroused, and the nature of the act causing the provocation. 26 Am J1st Homi § 24; a familiar expression in labor cases, meaning a period provided by statute or collective labor agreements during which differences between labor and management may be composed. 31 Am J Rev ed Lab §§ 392, 510; a period provided by law, otherwise known as a "waiting period," between the commencement of an action for divorce and the trial of the case. 24 Am J2d Div & S § 331.

co-op (kō-op'). Abbreviation for **co-operative**.

cooper. A maker of barrels.

cooperage. The work or workshop of a cooper; a term applied in the brewing business to bottles, cases, and other containers. Falstaff Brewing Corp. v Iowa Fruit & Produce Co. (CA8 Neb) 112 F2d 101.

co-operation. See **co-operation and assistance clause**.

co-operation and assistance clause. Essentially the same as co-operation clause.
See **co-operation clause**.

co-operation clause. A clause in an automobile liability policy which provides in substance that the insured shall cooperate with the insurer, and, upon the insurer's request, shall attend hearings and trials and shall assist in effecting settlements, securing and giving evidence, obtaining the attendance of witnesses, and in the conduct of suits. 7 Am J2d Auto Ins § 176; 29A Am J Rev ed Ins § 1471. When persons "co-operate," they act jointly and concurrently toward a common end. In an insurance case they are governed by the contract. The common end is not that the assured, regardless of truth, shall establish nonliability for himself or for the company, but in this connection "co-operation" means that there shall be a fair and frank disclosure of information reasonably demanded by the insurer to enable it to determine whether there is a genuine defense. Ocean Acci. & Guaranty Corp. v Lucas (CA6 Ohio) 74 F2d 115, 98 ALR 1461.

co-operative. Noun: A co-operative association; a word, the use of which is restricted by law. 18 Am J2d Co-op Asso § 5. Adjective: Co-operating or ready to co-operate.

See **co-operation clause**; **co-operative association**.

co-operative apartment house. A multiunit dwelling in which each resident has (1) an interest in the entity owning the building and (2) a lease entitling him to occupy a particular apartment within the building. 15 Am J2d Con Apt § 2.

co-operative association. Any combination of the efforts of two or more persons for the achievement of a common purpose; a corporation created by a banding together of persons for their common advantage or advancement, financial or otherwise, and organized for the mutual benefit of its members. 18 Am J2d Co-op Asso § 1. A co-operation association organized and acting in furnishing gas or electricity to its members becomes a public utility where it serves or is willing to serve the public. 43 Am J1st Pub Util § 6.

co-operative business corporation. A corporation which is authorized to divide its profits with persons who hold no stock in the corporation.
    The word "co-operative" has been used in the names of ordinary business corporations. Such use is now restricted by statute in many jurisdictions. 18 Am J2d Co-op Asso § 5.

co-operative marketing association. A co-operative association of producers, particularly farmers, organized to secure for their members the advantages of co-operative bargaining in selling their products, and to perform certain functions at a lower cost per unit than can the individual acting alone. An additional feature of great importance is a marketing contract between members and the association which requires each member to sell all of his product to or through the association. 18 Am J2d Co-op Asso §§ 2-4.

co-operative negligence. See **contributory negligence**.

co-operative store. A store operated by a co-operative association.
    See **Rochdale store**.

co-operative utility. A utility which supplies service such as is furnished by a public utility but on a co-operative basis, not for profit. Anno: 172 ALR 1022.

co-opertus (kō-o-per'tus). Covered; covert.

co-ownership. Ownership by more than one person; ownership in which there is a plurality of tenants.
    See **cotenancy**; **joint tenancy**.

cop. Slang for policeman.

coparcenary. An estate arising in any case where the ownership is in heirs who take from the same ancestor, such heirs being regarded as one heir joined together by unity of interest, unity of title, and unity of possession.
    The estate is of little importance at the present time, since statutes have converted the estate to a tenancy in common. 20 Am J2d Coten § 1.

coparcener. One who, with others, holds an estate in coparcenary. Gibson v Johnson, 331 Mo 1198, 88 ALR 369, 56 SW2d 783.

coparticeps (ko-pàr'ti-seps). A coparcener.
    See **coparcenary**.

coparties. See **joint parties**.

copartner. One of two or more members of a partnership; a partner.

copartnership. A partnership.
    See **partnership**.

copartnery (kō-pärt'nėr-i). A partnership.

cope (kōp). A duty on lead exported from the mines of Derbyshire.

copeman (kōp'man). A chapman; a peddler.

copesmate (kōps'māt). A merchant.

copia (kō'pi̯ạ). (Latin.) Abundance; opportunity.

copie (kop'i). (French.) Copy.

copia libelli deliberanda (kō'pi-ạ̈ lī-bel'ī dẹ-lib-ẹ-ran'dạ̈). An ecclesiastical writ commanding the defendant to furnish the plaintiff with a copy of the complaint.

copia vera (kō'pi-a vē'ra). A true copy.

coppa (kop'pa). Crops which have been stacked for the reckoning of tithes.

copper. A base metal which has been known from the most ancient periods of which we have any historical account. Bronze which is made of copper with an alloy of tin is the first metallic compound which history records. It was known 3500 years before the time of Christ. United States v Aluminum Co. of America (DC NY) 144 F Supp 97.

coppice (kop'is). Same as **copse**.

copr. An abbreviation of **copyright**.

copse (kops). A thicket; a hedge.

copula (kop'ụ-lạ̈). Sexual intercourse; the term is sometimes spoken of as referring to the consummation of a marriage. Sharon v Sharon, 75 Cal 1, 16 P 345.

copulation. Coition; sexual intercourse.

Copulatio verborum indicat quod accipiantur in eodem sensu (ko-pu-lā'she-ō ver-bo'rum in'di-kat quod ak-si-pi-an'ter in e-ō'dem sen'sū). The coupling of words together shows that they are to be taken in the same sense. Saltonstall v Sanders, 93 Mass (11 Allen) 446, 470.
    When the meaning of any particular word is doubtful or obscure, or when the expression taken singly is inoperative, the intention of the parties using it may frequently be ascertained and carried into effect by looking at the adjoining words, or at expressions occurring in other parts of the same instrument. Breasted v Farmers' Loan & Trust Co., 8 NY 299.

copulative condition (kop'ụ-lạ̈-tiv). A condition which depends upon the happening of each one of several events.

copy. Noun: A reproduction of an original work. 18 Am Jur 2d Copyr § 1; Anno; 23 ALR2d 337; a reproduction or transcript of a writing; secondary evidence of a written instrument. 29 Am J2d Ev § 486.
    See **certified copy**; **close copies**; **duplicate**; **examined copy**; **exemplified copy**; **facsimile**; **model**; **office copy**; **sworn copy**; **tracing**; **transcript**.

copy fee. The fee allowed an attorney in some jurisdictions for preparing the copy of a pleading for the adverse party or the attorney of the adverse party; the expense incurred in obtaining a copy of a document for use in a case. 20 Am J2d Costs § 60.

copyhold. See **copyhold estate**.

copyholder. A tenant who held his estate by copyhold; the holder of a copyhold estate; one who reads manuscript to a proofreader.

copyhold estate. A form of English land tenure, unknown in this country, being an estate at will which was enrolled, thereby establishing the rights of the tenant and giving more permanency to his estate than an ordinary estate at will. Anno: 114 ALR 626.

copyhold tenure. See **copyhold estate.**

copyright. The exclusive privilege, by force of statute, of an author or proprietor to print or otherwise multiply, publish, and vend copies of his literary, artistic, or intellectual productions, and to license their production and sale by others during the term of its existence. 18 Am J2d Copyr § 1.
See **literary property; notice of copyright.**

copyright after publication. The right to multiply copies secured by statute. 18 Am J2d Copyr § 1.

copyright before publication. A term of loose usage for the common law right of first publication. See **first publication.**

copyrighted. Protecting a publication by a copyright. Solis Cigar Co. v Pozo, 16 Colo 388, 26 P 556.
See **copyright.**

copyright notice. See **notice of copyright.**

cor. An abbreviation of the word "corner," used in descriptions of real property, also of "coroner."

coram (kō'ram). Before; in the presence of.

coram domino rege ubicunque tunc fuerit Angliae (kō'ram do'mi-nō rē'je u-bi-kun'kwē tunk fu'e-rit ang'li-ē). Before our lord the king wherever he may then be in England.

coram ipso rege (kō'ram ip'sō rē'je). In the presence of the king himself. This was the style given to the court of king's bench from the fact that the king formerly sat there in person. See 3 Bl Comm 41.

coram judice (kō'ram jö'di-sē). Within the jurisdiction of the court. The United States v Arredondo (US) 6 Pet 691, 8 L Ed 547, 554.

coram me vel justiciariis meis (kō'ram mē vel jūs-ti-she-ā'ri-is mē'is). Before me or my justices.

coram nobis (kō'ram nō'bis). In our presence; before us. A writ used to obtain review of a judgment for the purpose of correcting errors of fact in criminal as well as in civil proceedings. 18 Am J2d Coram Nobis § 1.
For fine distinction between "coram nobis" and "coram vobis," see **coram vobis.**

coram non judice (kō'ram non jö'di-sē). Before one who is not the judge. That is, before a court which has not jurisdiction of the matter. A proceeding had and determined by a court without such jurisdiction is said to be "coram non judice," the situation being the same as if there were no court. Grumon v Raymond, 1 Conn 40.

coram paribus (kō'ram par'i-bus). In the presence of his peers. As was the custom with all other solemn transactions, the attestation of a deed was always coram paribus, and this was often done when they were assembled in the court-baron, hundred, or county court. See 2 Bl Comm 307.

coram paribus de vicineto (kō'ram pa'ri-bus dē vi-sī'ne-tō). In the presence of the peers or freeholders of the neighborhood.

coram rege (kō'ram rē'je). In the presence of the king. "For at first the words nisi per legale judicium parium (unless by the lawful judgment of his peers) had no reference to a jury: they applied only to the pares regni (the peers of the realm), who were the constitutional judges in the court of exchequer and coram rege. Hurtado v California, 110 US 516, 529, 28 L Ed 232, 236, 4 S Ct 111, 292.

coram sectatoribus (kō'ram sek-tā-tō'ri-bus). Before or in the presence of the suitors.

coram vobis (kō'ram vō'bis). Before you; in your presence. A writ for the correction of error which is essentially the same as a writ of coram nobis, the only distinction being that where the writ is directed by the reviewing court to another arm of the same court, it is called "coram nobis," while if it is directed by the reviewing to the trial court it is called "coram vobis." 18 Am J2d Coram Nobis § 1.

cord. A unit of wood-measure applied to wood cut for fuel, being a pile of wood eight feet long, four feet high and four feet wide, containing one hundred and twenty-eight cubic feet. Kennedy v Oswego & Syracuse Railroad Co. (NY) 67 Barb 169, 178.
See **umbilical cord.**

cordial. Noun: A liqueur. Adjective: Hearty; friendly with warmth of feeling exhibited.

corespondent. The third party in the triangle of persons presented in an action for divorce on the ground of adultery. The person who is accused by the plaintiff in a suit for divorce of having committed adultery with the defendant.

corf (kôrf). A box for carrying coal, used in coal mining.

corium forfisfacere (ko'ri-um for"fis-fā'ke-re). The forfeiture of skin,—a punishment for crime which was administered by flogging.

corn. In the very broad sense of the term, "corn" is grain, but in this country, "corn" means the grain or the plant of maize, often called Indian corn. A coarse spot on a toe caused by a thickening of the skin produced by pressure of ill-fitting shoes. A slang term for corn whiskey, also for banal or overly sentimental expressions.

cornage (kôr'nāj). Same as **cornage tenure.**

cornage tenure. A tenure by the service of blowing a horn when the Scots or other enemies entered the land, in order to warn the king's subjects. Like other services of the same nature, it was a species of grand serjeanty. See 2 Bl Comm 74.

Cornelian law. See **lex Cornelia,** et seq.

corner. The point at which converging lines meet; a point established by a survey and located by calls in a description of the boundaries of a tract of land. 12 Am J2d Bound § 72. The northeast, southeast, southwest, and northwest extremities of sections, quarter sections, and one-sixteenth sections of land as laid out by the government survey. The situation which exists where a person or a number of persons acting jointly have entered into contracts for future purchases of a given commodity in excess of the aggregate of the supply of such commodity in the market. Anno: 83 ALR 587. Acquiring control of all or a dominant quantity of a commodity with the purpose of artificially enhancing the price, executed by purchases and sales of the commodity and of options and futures therein, in such a way as to depress the market price, whereby the participants are enabled to purchase the commodity at satisfactory prices and withhold it from the market for a time, thereby inflating the price. United States v Patten, 226 US 525, 57 L Ed 333, 33 S Ct 141.

corner lot. A lot at a corner of intersecting streets.
See **frontage.**

cornice. A projecting top on the wall of a building. 1 Am J2d Adj L § 123.

corn laws. English statutes which regulated commerce in grain.

corn-rent. See **grain rent.**

corodium (ko-rō'di-um). Same as **corody.**

corody (kor'ọ-di). An incorporeal hereditament which allowed a means of sustenance to the holder.

corona (kọ-rō'nạ). The crown.

coronare (kō-rō-nā're). To crown; to make of a person a priest.

coronare filium (kō-rō-nā're fi'li-um). To make one's son a priest.

coronary. Pertaining to an artery which supplies blood to the tissues of the heart.

coronary occlusion. A blocking of the coronary artery, resulting in unconsciousness and death, unless medical aid is available and availing. Heart trouble within the meaning of a policy excepting from coverage disability caused by "heart trouble." Frank v United Ben. Life Ins. Co. (Mo App) 231 SW2d 234.

coronator. See **coroner.**

coronatore eligendo. See **de coronatore eligendo.**

coronatore exonerando. See **de coronatore exonerando.**

coroner. A judicial and ministerial officer of great importance in the middle ages and an office of great dignity under the earlier common law, but whose functions have gradually been diminished in importance by legislation, until today, where the office exists at all, the coroner has little, if anything to do except to serve some process in the absence of the sheriff and, in some jurisdictions, conduct an inquiry, sometimes with the aid of a jury, into the cause of death of persons who appear to have come to an end from other than natural causes. 18 Am J2d Corn § 1.

coroner's court. An English court of record presided over by the coroner of the county. Cox v Royal Tribe, 42 Or 365, 71 P 73.

coroner's inquest. See **inquest.**

coroner's jury. A jury summoned by a coroner to make an inquiry into the cause of the death of a person. 18 Am J2d Corn § 12.

corporal. Noun: A noncommissioned officer of the army. Adjective: Pertaining to the body; as a corporal injury.

corporale sacramentum (kōr-pō-rạ'le sak-ra-men'tum). Same as **corporal oath.**

Corporalis injuria non recipit aestimationem de futuro (kor-pō-rā'lis in-jū'ri-a non re'si-pit ēs-ti-mā-she-ō'nem dē fū-tū'rō). Bodily injury does not look to future proceedings for compensation. See Broom's Legal Maxims 278.

corporal oath. An oath in which the affiant lifts an arm or touches the Holy Bible with his hand. 39 Am J1st Oath § 3.

corporal punishment. Physical punishment; any kind of punishment inflicted on the body, such as whipping or slapping, but not the execution of the death penalty itself. Imprisonment may come within the term "corporal punishment," where such is construed with the context of the statute.

Within the meaning of the statute prohibiting "corporal punishment" aboard a vessel, the term implies that the punishment must have been inflicted by virtue of an authority to which the person punished was subject. Fights resulting from private differences and personal quarrels between officers and seamen have nothing to do with their employment on the vessel and do not come within the purview of the statute. Fowler v American Line (CA9 Cal) 69 F2d 905.

corporate. Pertaining to corporations, sometimes indicating a private as distinguished from a public body. Trustees of Academy v City Council of Augusta, 90 Ga 634, 17 SE 61.

In other uses, the term "corporate" is not limited to private corporations, for example, the "corporate limits" and "corporate authorities" of a municipality.

corporate act. The act of a corporation. The act of a municipal corporation in performance of a proprietary, as distinguished from a governmental, function. 37 Am J1st Mun Corp § 114.

corporate agents. The officers and employees of a corporation who have the authority to act for the corporation, at least in some capacity. Literally, persons authorized to act for a corporation in one or more matters; technically, persons under employment in an agency created by officers of a corporation. 19 Am J2d Corp § 1090.

corporate authorities. Those officers of cities and villages to whom is given the ordinance-making power; the legislative branch of a city government. State ex rel. Gerry v Edwards, 42 Mont 135, 111 P 734. The term has also been defined as referring to those municipal officers who are either directly elected by the people of the municipality, or appointed in some mode to which the people have given their assent. Booten v Pinson, 27 W Va 412, 89 SE 985; 51 Am J1st Tax § 137.

corporate body. See **body corporate.**

corporate bond. A bond which is issued by and becomes the obligation of a corporation.
See **bonds.**

corporate bylaws. See **bylaws.**

corporate charter. See **charter.**

corporate citizenship. Citizenship attributed to a corporation for some specific purpose, such as the obtaining of a liquor license. 30 Am J Rev ed Intox L § 126.

A corporation of a state is a "citizen of the United States," within the meaning of the Act of Congress providing for the adjudication of claims of citizens of the Unites States for property taken or destroyed by Indians. United States v Northwestern Express, Stage & Transp. Co. 164 US 686, 41 L Ed 599, 17 S Ct 206.

corporate conduct. The conduct of a corporation; that is, a corporation's act or omission, formal or informal, done or omitted by any agency through which the corporation is authorized to act. People v North River Sugar Refining Co. 121 NY 582, 24 NE 834.

corporate directors. See **directors.**

corporate domicil. The situs or residence of a corporation belonging exclusively to the state or sovereignty under whose laws it is created. 18 Am J2d Corp § 159. A corporation is domiciled and has its residence in the state of its creation, although it engages in business elsewhere under local authority and has a "business situs" or "commercial domi-

CORPORATE [274] CORPORATE

cil" there for taxation and other purposes. Unlike a natural person, a corporate entity cannot change its domicil at will. State v Garford Trucking, 4 NJ 346, 72 A2d 851, 16 ALR2d 1407. The domicil of a corporation within the state is the town or city in which the principal office or place of business of the corporation is located, and not where the principal labor of its employees is carried on. 51 Am J1st Tax § 805.

corporate entity. The status of a corporation distinct from its individual members or stockholders, who, for the purpose of the existence of the corporation, are merged in the corporate identity. 18 Am J2d Corp § 13.

See **disregarding corporate entity.**

corporate excess. In the language of a Massachusetts statute, "corporate excess employed within the commonwealth by a foreign corporation (shall mean) such proportion of the fair cash value of all the shares constituting the capital stock on the first day of April, when the return called for by the statute is due, as the value of the assets, both real and personal, employed in any business within the commonwealth on that date, bears to the value of the total assets of the corporation on that date." Alpha Portland Cement Co. v Massachusetts, 268 US 203, 208, 69 L Ed 916, 920, 45 S Ct 477.

corporate franchise. See **franchise.**

corporate function. See **corporate act.**

corporate limits. The territorial limits of a muncipal corporation. 37 Am J1st Mun Corp § 16.

corporate name. The name of a corporation, as fixed by its charter or the statute by which the corporation was created, such being an essential of existence as a corporation and a part of the franchise to be a corporation. 18 Am J2d Corp § 141.

corporate office. See **principal place of business.**

corporate officers. The officers of corporations, such as president, vice-president, secretary, treasurer or comptroller, and often a manager or general manager; technically, the persons filling offices created by the charter or bylaws of the corporation. 19 Am J2d Corp § 1080.

corporate pocketbook. A graphic expression of tax lawyers for the personal holding company.

corporate powers. The powers granted to a corporation in its charter, or by the statutes under which it is created, or such powers as are necessary for the purpose of carrying out its express powers and the object of its incorporation. 19 Am J2d Corp § 952.

See **capacity of corporation.**

corporate practice of law, medicine, etc. See **professional corporation.**

corporate purpose of a municipal corporation. See **municipal purposes.**

corporate purposes. The purposes for which corporations may be organized, as declared by statute, it now being usual for the general corporation laws of a state to provide for the formation of corporations for any lawful purpose, business purpose or purposes, other than the practice of a profession or the conducting of specified classes of business for the conduct of which corporations are to be formed under other statutory provisions. Uniform Business Corporation Act § 2; 18 Am J2d Corp § 31.

The word "unlawful", as it pertains to purposes for which a corporation may be organized, is not used exclusively in the sense of malum in se or malum prohibitum; it is also used to designate powers which corporations are not authorized to exercise, or contracts which they are not authorized to make, or acts which they are not authorized to do; or in other words, such acts, powers, and contracts as are ultra vires. People ex rel. Peabody v Chicago Gas Trust Co. 130 Ill 268, 22 NE 798.

See **ultra vires.**

corporate records. The transcript of charter and bylaws, the minutes of meetings of directors and stockholders, the books containing the accounts of official doings of the corporation, and the written evidence of its contracts and business transactions. United States v Louisville & N. R. Co. 236 US 318, 59 L Ed 598, 35 S Ct 363.

corporate reorganization. The act or process of organizing again or anew to effect a corporate readjustment of existing interests, almost invariably involving a corporation in financial distress or in a condition of inability to compete in the commercial world. 19 Am J2d Corp §§ 1515 et seq. A means whereby those variously interested financially in a distressed corporation seek, through continuance of the business as a going concern, to work out of the difficulty for themselves and thus gain more than they could by a sale of the assets or of the business to others. Warner Bros. Pictures, Inc. v Lawton-Byrne-Bruner Ins. Agency Co. (CA8 Mo) 79 F2d 804. Often accomplished by a judicial sale of the corporate property and franchises and the formation by the purchasers of a new corporation in which the property and franchises are thereupon vested, and the stock and bonds of which are divided among such of the parties interested in the old company as are parties to the plan of reorganization. 19 Am J2d Corp § 1515. A proceeding in the bankruptcy court to obtain a change in the capital structure, a reduction of indebtedness, and other permissible changes to rehabilitate a failing corporation and promote the prospects of creditors to obtain a full realization of their claims or a better realization than would occur through immediate realization. 9 Am J2d Bankr § 1496.

corporate report. See **report.**

corporate rights. See **rights.**

corporate seal. The seal of a corporation, no longer necessary to validate an act or a contract of a corporation which would not require a seal if it were the act or contract of a natural person, or which does not require the corporate seal by virtue of charter or statutory provision, and consisting of a seal of any character, even a variety of seals for different occasions. 18 Am J2d Corp § 154. A scroll, a printed impression, or the letters "L. S." inclosed in brackets is sufficient. Cannon v Gorham, 136 Ga 167, 71 SE 142.

corporate securities. Stock, bonds, debentures, certificates of indebtedness, notes, and other evidences of indebtedness issued by a corporation for the purpose of obtaining funds to use in the business of the corporation. Wilkinson v Mutual Bldg. & Sav. Asso. (CA7 Wis) 13 F2d 997; United States v American Trust & Banking Co. (CA6 Tenn) 125 F2d 113. Anno: 36 ALR2d 975.

See **securities.**

corporate stock. See **stock.**

corporate stockholder. See **stockholder.**

corporate stock rights. See **rights.**

corporate surety. Literally, a surety which is a corporation, but, in common usage, a corporation engaged in the business of acting as surety for a compensation. 12 Am J2d Bonds § 22; 50 Am J1st Suret § 312.
See **fidelity company**; **surety company**.

corporate trustee. An incorporated trustee, such as a bank or trust company empowered to act in the capacity of a trustee.

corporation. An artificial being, invisible, intangible, and existing only in contemplation of law; an association of persons to whom the sovereign has offered a franchise to become an artificial juridical person, with a name of its own, under which they can act and contract and sue and be sued, and who have either accepted the offer and effected a corporation in substantial conformity with its terms (in which case a corporation de jure has been constituted) or have done acts indicating a purpose to accept such offer and effected an organization designed to be, but, in fact not, in substantial conformity with its terms (in which case a corporation de jure de facto has been constituted). 18 Am J2d Corp § 1. For some purposes, as in a venue statute, the term "corporation" includes unincorporated associations or at least special forms of them, such as joint stock companies. 56 Am J1st Ven § 7. For the purposes of the Federal income tax, the term "corporation" includes associations, joint-stock companies, and insurance companies. 33 Am J2d Fed Tax ¶ 2005. As defined by the Bankruptcy Act the term "corporation" includes all bodies having any of the powers and privileges of private corporations not possessed by individuals or partnership and further includes partnership associations organized under laws making the capital subscribed alone responsible for the debts of the association, joint stock companies, unincorporated companies and associations, and any business conducted by a trustee or trustees wherein beneficial interest or ownership is evidenced by certificate or other written instrument. Bankr Act § 1(8); 11 USC § 1(8). Business trusts have frequently been held to be subject to statutory regulations of corporations and to provisions aimed primarily at corporations. Hemphill v Orloff, 277 US 537, 72 L Ed 978, 48 S Ct 577.
See **incorporation**; **municipal corporation**; **person**; **public corporation**.

corporation affected with a public interest. A public service corporation, otherwise known as a quasi public corporation. 18 Am J2d Corp § 9.
See **public service corporation**.

corporation aggregate. A collection of individuals united in one body under a special denomination, and vested by the policy of the law with the capacity of acting in several respects as an individual; a legal institution devised to confer upon the individuals of which it is composed powers, privileges, and immunities which they would not otherwise possess, the most important of which are continuous legal identity, and perpetual or indefinite succession under the corporate name, notwithstanding successive changes by death or otherwise in the corporation or members of the corporation. 18 Am J2d Corp § 1. An artificial body of men, composed of divers constituent members ad instar corporis humanis (after the manner of the human body), the ligaments of which body politic, or artificial body, are the franchises and liberties thereof, which bind and unite all its members together; and in which the whole frame and essence of the corporation consist. Louisville, Cincinnati & Charleston Railroad Co. v Letson (US) 2 How 497, 552, 11 L Ed 353, 375.

corporation de facto (kôr-pōr-rā'shọn dē fak'tō). See **de facto corporation**.

corporation de jure (kôr-pōr-rā'shọn de jū're). See **de jure corporation**.

corporation excise tax. A tax on the conduct of business in a corporate capacity, sometimes measured by the income of the corporation, but not becoming an income tax because of such feature. 34 Am J2d Fed Tax ¶ 8860 et seq.

corporation for profit. See **profit corporation**.

corporation franchise tax. See **franchise tax**.

corporation not for profit. A charitable corporation; a membership; corporation; an eleemosynary corporation.
A proposed corporation is not entitled to incorporation as a "corporation not for profit" where its clear purpose is to confer direct and indirect benefits on its members consisting of a saving of expense or obtaining a service at a cost lower than that which otherwise would be paid therefor, notwithstanding a provision of the articles of incorporation that each member agrees not to accept pecuniary gain or profit from any corporate surplus. The character of a proposed corporation warranting its incorporation as a "corporation not for profit" is determined, not by the authority that probably will actually be exercised by the corporation, but rather by the authority it actually possesses and may exercise under the articles recorded. State ex rel. Russell v Sweeney, 153 Ohio St 66, 91 NE2d 13, 16 ALR2d 1337.

corporation officers. See **corporate officers**.

corporation president. See **president of corporation**.

corporation sole. A corporation consisting of one person only and his successors. An older concept of the status of a king or a bishop as incorporated in order to give to them and their successors legal capacities and advantages, particularly that of perpetuity, which they could not have in their natural capacities. 18 Am J2d Corp § 7.

corporator. A person who joins in the formation of a corporation; a promoter; a stockholder; a shareholder; a member. 18 Am J2d Corp § 35.
See **promoter**.

corporeal (kôr-pō'rē-al). Possessing physical substance; tangible; perceptible to the senses.

corporeal hereditaments. Property and things of substance capable of being inherited.

corporeal property. Property which has corporeal tangible substance. See 42 Am J1st Prop § 12.

corpore comitatus. See **de corpore comitatus**.

corpore et animo (kor'po-re et a'ni-mō). In body and mind.

corps diplomatique (kōr di-plo-ma-ti'k). The diplomatic corps.

corpse (kôrps). The dead body of a human being.

corpus (kôr'pus). The body or substance of anything; the capital or res of an estate or fund, as distinguished from the income thereof.

corpus comitatus (kor'pus ko-mi-tā'tus). The body of a county, the inhabitants of a county considered collectively.

corpus corporatum (kor'pus kor-po-rā'tum). An incorporated body, a corporation.

corpus cum causa (kor'pus kum kâ-za). See **habeas corpus cum causa**.

corpus delicti (kor'pus dē-lik'ti). The body of the crime; the fact that a crime has actually been committed, that someone is criminally responsible. Hilyard v State, 90 Okla Crim 435, 214 P2d 953, 28 ALR2d 961; 29 Am J2d Ev § 149. In homicide cases, the facts of death and the criminal agency of another person as the cause thereof. 26 Am J1st Homi § 6. In larceny cases, the facts that the owner of property was deprived thereof and that he was deprived by a felonious taking. 32 Am J1st Larc § 121.

Corpus humanum non recipit estimationem (kor'pus hū-mā'num non re'si-pit es-ti-mā-she-ō'nem). A human body is not susceptible of valuation. Griffith v Charlotte, Columbia & Augusta Railroad Co. 23 SC 25.

corpus juris (kor'pus jū'ris). The body of the law.

Corpus Juris (kor'pus jū'ris). The title of an encyclopedic work on the law.

corpus juris canonici (kor'pus ju'ris ka-nō'ni-sī). The decrees of the Roman church. See 1 Bl Comm 82.

Corpus Juris Civilis (kor'pus ju'ris si'vi-lis). The whole body of the Roman law, being the Digest, the Institutes, and the Novellae of Justinian.

Corpus Juris Secundum (kor'pus jū'ris sē-kund'um). A successor of the encyclopedic work on the law published under the title "Corpus Juris."

correct. To eliminate error; to amend; to make to conform to law. Hutcheson v Storrie, 92 Tex 685, 51 SW 848.

correction. See **amendment**.

correctional institutions. See **house of correction; industrial school; reformatory**.

corregidor (ko-rej'i-dôr). The chief magistrate of a town.

Corregidor (ko-rej'i-dôr). A small island at the entrance to Manila Bay in the Philippines, most vividly brought to the attention of the American people by the valiant stand made there by American and Philippine troops against much larger Japanese forces.

correi credendi (kor're-ī kre-den'di). (Civil law.) Joint creditors.

correi debendi (kor're-ī de-ben'di). (Civil law.) Joint debtors.

correlative rights. Another term for the reasonable use doctrine in reference to percolating waters. 56 Am J1st Wat § 114.
See **reasonable use doctrine**.

correspondence course. See **correspondence school**.

correspondence school. A school in which the contact between teacher and student is by mail, the lessons being mailed to the student with written tests to be accomplished and returned to the teacher for grading.

corroborate. To state facts tending to produce confidence in the truth of a statement made by another person. People v Ranney, 153 Mich 293, 116 NW 999.

corroborating circumstances. Facts which tend to support the testimony of a witness, especially circumstances which tend to fix the transaction in the mind of the witness. 58 Am J1st Witn §§ 807, 808.

corroborating evidence. Additional evidence of a different character to the same point. People v Sternberg, 111 Cal 11, 43 P 201. Such evidence as tends to confirm and strengthen the testimony of the witness sought to be corroborated; that is, such as tends to show its truth, or the probability of its truth. Rosinski v Whiteford, 87 App DC 313, 184 F2d 700, 21 ALR2d 1009.
See **corroborating circumstances**.

corroboration. Producing corroborating evidence. As a requirement in a divorce action: evidence of such substantial facts and circumstances as will produce in a sound and prudently cautious mind a confident conclusion that the testimony of the complainant is true in all essentials. 24 Am J2d Div & S § 382. Corroboration is somewhat less than confirmation; evidence of corroboration need not be of such weight as is required to prove the alleged ground for divorce. Carter v Carter, 191 Kan 80, 379 P2d 311.

corroborative (kö-rob'ō-rā-tiv). Confirmatory; tending to support or uphold.

corroborative evidence. See **corroborating evidence**.

corrupt. Contaminated; spoiled; subverting the instrumentalities of government to personal profit; impeding justice and obstructing the administration of justice. United States v Polakoff (CA2 NY) 121 F2d 333.

corruption. A hard word, not always accurately understood; covering a multitude of official delinquencies, great and little; but it is strictly accurate to apply it to any color of influence, of mere relation of any kind, on the administration of justice. Wight v Rindskopf, 43 Wis 344, 351.
See **corrupt**.

corruption fund. A fund in hand to be used for the purpose of corruption.

corruption of blood. A doctrine, arising in feudal times but generally abrogated expressly by state constitutions, whereunder one was disqualified to inherit by conviction of a felony. 23 Am J2d Desc & D § 91.

Corruptio optimi est pessima (kor-rup'she-ō op'ti-mī est pes'si-ma). The corruption of the best is worst. So, the worst form of argument is that which draws erroneous conclusions from sound principles or premises. Jacobs v Beecham, 221 US 263, 55 L Ed 729, 31 S Ct 555.

corruptly (ko-rupt'li). Wrongfully; acting with the intent to obtain an improper advantage for self or someone else, inconsistent with official duty and the rights of others. State v Lehman, 182 Mo 424, 81 SW 1118; State v Johnson, 77 Ohio St 461, 83 NE 702.

corrupt practices acts. Statutes found in the laws of practically every state in the union and in federal legislation, featured by provisions regulating the expenditures of candidates for election by requiring the filing of statements of expenses, in some instances by limiting the amount of money that may be spent, and sometimes including regulations respecting the solicitation of campaign contributions, the treating of voters, and the making of charges against, and attacks on, candidates. 26 Am J2d Elect § 287.

corse (kôrs). A corpse.

corse-present. A mortuary, which was a customary gift claimed by and due to the minister in many parishes on the death of a parishioner, was called a corse-present when it was brought to the church along with the corpse at the burial of the deceased parishioner. At an earlier time, a corse-present had probably been, as its name would indicate, a voluntary donation. See 2 Bl Comm 425.

corsned (kôrs'ned). A form of trial by purgation which consisted in feeding the accused person a small piece of consecrated bread or cheese and at the same time praying for his ability to swallow it if innocent and for his choking if guilty. The term was also applied to the bread or cheese itself, the morsel of execration. See 4 Bl Comm 345.

cortes (kôr'tes). The national legislature of Portugal.

corvée (kôr-vā'). (French.) An exaction of labor imposed upon the inhabitants of a district for the upkeep and repair of public roads and bridges.

Corwin Amendment. A proposed amendment to the United States Constitution, providing against any amendment to the Constitution granting to Congress the power to abolish or interfere with the domestic institution of slavery; submitted by Congress for ratification in 1861, but failing of ratification by the requisite number of states.

cosa juzgada (kos huth-gä'da). (Spanish.) Res adjudicata.

cosalvor (ko-sal'vor). In admiralty law, a salvor who contributes with another salvor or with other salvors to the result. 47 Am J1st Salv § 26.

cosbering. The ancient right of the lord of the manor to sleep and eat in the house of his tenant.

cosduna (kos'du-na). A custom; a tribute.

cosen. Same as **cozen**.

cosenage (kŭz'nāj). Same as **cousinage**.

cosening (kuz'n-ing). Same as **cozening**.

co-servants. Same as **fellow servants**.

coshering (kosh'ėr-ing). A word of Irish origin for pampering.
See **cosbering**.

cosinage (kuz'n-āj). Same as **cousinage**.

cosmetologist. A person who follows the occupation of hairdressing and beautifying the human skin. 10 Am J2d Barbers § 2.

cost. The amount of money, services, or property required to obtain a thing or to build a structure.
See **costs**; **original cost**.

cost and freight. A mercantile term which, when used in connection with a contract for the sale of goods, shows that the price quoted to the purchaser includes the cost of the goods and freight charges to the place of destination. Pepper v Western Union Tel. Co. 87 Tenn 554, 11 SW 783.

cost depletion. A deduction for federal income tax allowed an owner of mineral or timber property. IRC § 612.

coste. See **en coste**.

cost, insurance, and freight. A mercantile term, abbreviated "c. i. f." or "c. a. f." which, when used in connection with a contract for the sale of goods, indicates that the price quoted to the purchaser includes the cost of the goods, the cost of insurance thereon, and freight charges to the place of destination. 46 Am J1st Sales § 136.

Under a c.i.f. contract the seller receives a purchase price payable as the parties agree and for that consideration is bound to arrange for the carriage of the goods to their agreed destination, for insurance upon them for the benefit of the buyer, and either to pay the cost of the carriage and insurance or allow it on the purchase price. When this has been done the seller has fully performed and is entitled to be paid upon delivery of the documents to the seller regardless of whether the goods themselves have arrived at their destination or ever will. It has been said that a c.i.f. contract is one for the sale of documents relating to goods rather than a sale of the goods but it seems more realistic to treat such a contract as one under which the title to the goods passes to the buyer upon delivery of the documents alone. Warner Bros. & Co. v Israel (CA2 NY) 101 F2d 59.

costipulator. A joint promisor.

cost of construction. The cost of labor and materials which have been combined to make the materials a part of the building. Washington Constr. Co. v Spinella, 8 NJ 212, 84 A2d 617, 28 ALR2d 863. The term also includes incidentals, such as premiums paid for workmen's compensation insurance.

cost plus contract. A building or construction contract under which the contractor is entitled to recover the cost of the work to him plus an agreed upon percentage. 13 Am J2d Bldg Contr § 20.

cost price. A mercantile term, the meaning of which is relative, depending upon the circumstances under which it is used and the situation of the parties, but which ordinarily would appear to mean merely that amount paid or promised to be paid for an article.

As applied to a stock of merchandise, it ordinarily will mean the wholesale price. Sylvester v Ammons, 126 Iowa 140, 101 NW 782.

cost restrictions. Provisions in a restrictive covenant which limit the dwellings to be constructed to buildings costing not less than a stated amount. 20 Am J2d Cov § 260.

cost rule of damages. A rule of damages for breach of a building contract by failure to complete performance, under which reconstruction cost is the measure of damages. Shell v Schmidt, 164 Cal App 2d 350, 330 P2d 817, 76 ALR2d 792, cert den 359 US 959, 3 L Ed 2d 766, 79 S Ct 799.

costs. Allowances made to a party to an action for his expenses incurred in the action; otherwise defined, "costs" are the sums prescribed by law as charges for the services enumerated in the fee bill. 20 Am J2d Costs § 1. The word "costs" is normally used in referring to those items which may be included in the taxable bill of costs established by applicable statute or court rule. Anno: 9 ALR2d 1146. Statutory authorization of recovery of "costs" against the losing party does not include attorneys' fees. Turner v Zip Motors, 245 Iowa 1091, 65 NW2d 427, 45 ALR2d 1174. With few exceptions, the courts in the cases in which the question has arisen have construed condemnation statutes which provided for payment of "costs," "expenses," "just compensation," and the like, without making any express stipulation as regards attorneys' fees, as not intending to provide for the payment of such fees, these not being part of the costs, expenses, or just compensation. Anno: 26 ALR2d 1296.

costs and disbursements. Full costs. 5 Am J2d Appear § 23.

costs bill. See **bill of costs.**

costs bond. See **security for costs.**

costs de incremento (dē in-kre-men'tō). Costs awarded by the court and added to the damages assessed by the jury. At first, by the common law, no costs were awarded to either party eo nomine. If the plaintiff failed to recover he was amerced pro falso clamore. If he recovered judgment, the defendant was in misericordia for his unjust detention of the plaintiff's debt, and was not therefore punished with the expensa litis under that title. But this being considered a great hardship, the Statute of Gloucester (6 Edw I., c 1) was passed, which gave costs in all cases when the plaintiff recovered damages. This was the origin of costs de incremento; for when the damages were found by the jury, the judges held themselves obliged to tax the moderate fees of counsel and attorneys that attended the cause. Day v Woodworth (US) 13 How 362, 14 L Ed 181.

costs of administration. The "costs of administration" which have priority of payment over claims of general creditors in receivership proceedings include not only compensation for the receiver but also all other obligations incurred by him in the discharge of his duties. Parks v Central Door & Lumber Co. 164 Or 363, 102 P2d 706, 128 ALR 375.

costs of collection. A provision in a promissory note which has reference to an attorney's fee for plaintiff's attorney in case the note is not paid at maturity and suit is instituted thereon and maintained successfully. 11 Am J2d B & N § 163.

costs of prosecution. The costs incurred by the plaintiff in an action.
A statute authorizing an award for "costs of prosecution" does not support an award of attorneys' fees. State v Raible (Ohio App) 117 NE2d 480, 40 ALR2d 950.

costs of the day. Costs which are taxed against a party to an action in a proceeding which is incidental to the main action; costs incurred in preparing for trial set for a day certain.

costs to abide the event. A term for a provision as to costs made by an appellate court in reversing a judgment and sending the case back for new trial, meaning that the costs in the appellate court shall be paid by the party who is unsuccessful in the further litigation on new trial. First Nat. Bank v Fourth Nat. Bank, 84 NY 469. The term does not necessarily import that the party finally prevailing must recover costs for all the proceedings in the cause. Full effect is given to the words by giving to the party finally prevailing his costs in the appellate court. Colgan v Dunne, 50 Hun 441, 443, 3 NYS 297.

cosureties. Joint sureties; two or more sureties on the same obligation. 50 Am J1st Surety § 4.

cota (kō'tạ). A cottage.

cotarius (ko-tā'ri-us). A cottager holding at the will of the lord.

cotenancy. The ownership of property by two or more persons in such manner that they have an undivided possession or right to possession, but several freeholds, the term including joint tenancies, tenancies in common, and tenancies by the entirety. 20 Am J2d Coten § 1.

cotenant. One of the owners in cotenancy.
See **cotenancy.**

coterellus. Same as **cotarius.**

cotes. See **bouts et cotes.**

coteswold. A place bare of wood.

cotland (kot'land). Land appendant to a cottage.

co-tortfeasors. See **joint tortfeasors.**

cotrespassers. See **joint trespassers.**

cotrustees. Two or more persons in whom the administration of a trust is vested, forming but one collective trustee and exercising jointly all the powers that call for their discretion and judgment. 54 Am J1st Trusts § 296.

cotset. A householder or tenant under an ancient service tenure of rendering personal labor.

cotsethland. Same as **cotland.**

cotsetus. Same as **cotset.**

Cots-wold. A breed of sheep, characterized by the long wool borne by them.

cottage (kot'ạj). The service to which a cotset was bound; a little house. A grant of a "cottage" will pass a little dwelling house that has no land belonging to it. Gibson v Brockway, 8 NH 465.

cottage residence. A restrictive term in a covenant in a deed which precludes the erection of a building such as a rooming house upon the premises, and, according to some, but not all, authorities, excludes multiple dwellings. Rosenblatt v Levin, 127 NJ Eq 207, 12 A2d 727.

cottagium (kot-tā'ji-um). Same as **cottage.**

cotton gin. The machine for separating the fiber of cotton from the seeds.

couchant (kou'chant). Lying down.
See **levant et couchant.**

coucher (kou'chèr). A banker; a factor.

coucher de soel. The setting of the sun; sunset.

could and should test. A test applied in determining the scope and extent of judicial review of an action of an administrative agency:—(1) whether the particular type of act was within the authority of the particular type of agency which acted and (2) whether the act should have been performed—that is, whether the conclusions of the agency were correct, whether its act was proper or justified, and whether the facts or evidence warranted it. 2 Am J2d Admin L § 611.

council. Broadly, an assembly, the derivation being from the Latin "consilium," but, in modern usage, the legislative department of a city or other municipal corporation. 37 Am J1st Mun Corp § 46.

council of censors. The name given in some states to a body elected or appointed to examine into the conduct of state officers and alleged violations of the constitution.

council of conciliation. An agency for the adjustment and settlement of labor disputes. 31 Am J Rev ed Lab § 371.

council of the north. A court established under Henry the Eighth in the northern counties of England.

counsel. A counselor; an attorney at law; one or more attorneys representing parties in an action. Ludlam v Broderick, 15 NJL 269, 270.
See **attorney at law; of counsel.**

counseling. Advising; deliberating with another to aid him in coming to a conclusion.

counselor. See **counselor at law; chamber-counselor.**

counselor at law. An attorney who has been duly admitted to the bar and presently qualified to practice law; an advising lawyer. 7 Am J2d Attys § 1.
See **chamber-counselor; of counsel; practicing law.**

count. The tally of votes cast at an election. 26 Am J2d Elect § 291; a division of a complaint, declaration, bill, or petition, wherein a separate cause of action is stated. 41 Am J1st Plead § 106; a separate part of an indictment or information wherein a separate and distinct offense is stated, division into counts being necessary where two or more distinct offenses are charged in a single indictment under one caption. 27 Am J1st Indict § 124.
See **common counts; election of counts; money counts; narratio; omnibus count; paragraph; tale.**

countee. An earl.

countenance (koun'tẹ-nạns). Face; credit; credibility; approval.

counter (koun'tẽr). Noun: A pleader; an attorney-at-law employed to defend in litigation. Verb: To oppose or defend against attack.
See **countors.**

counter-affidavit. An affidavit responding to and contradicting the affidavit produced by an adversary.

counter-appeal. See **cross-appeal.**

counter-bond. A bond given to indemnify a surety. See **redelivery bond.**

counterbranding. Branding domestic animals for identification. 4 Am J2d Ani § 8.

counterclaim. A claim which, if established, will defeat or in some way qualify the judgment or relief to which the plaintiff is otherwise entitled. 20 Am J2d Countcl § 3; a counter demand or a cause of action existing in favor of the defendant against the plaintiff, on which the defendant might have secured affirmative relief had he sued the plaintiff in a separate action. 20 Am J2d Countcl § 3. The statement, in a separate division of an answer, of defendant's cause of action against plaintiff is a counterclaim. Linscott v Linscott, 243 Iowa 335, 51 NW2d 428, 30 ALR2d 789.
See **cross-demand; recoupment; reconvention; setoff.**

counter demand. See **cross-demand; setoff.**

counterfeasance (koun-ter-fe'sanz). Counterfeiting.

counterfeit. Verb: To make a copy without authority or right and with the view to deceive or defraud by passing the copy as original or genuine; to fabricate a false image or representation. But as ordinarily understood in law, the term is confined to the making and uttering of false money, postage stamps, revenue stamps, bonds, etc. 20 Am J2d Counterf § 1. Noun: Something made in imitation of something else with a purpose to deceive. Adjective: Spurious; sham.

counterfeit coin. See **counterfeit money.**

counterfeiting. Making a counterfeit, especially counterfeit money; the federal offense of making counterfeit money. 20 Am J2d Counterf § 1.

counterfeit money. An imitation of real money, produced with the intent that it shall pass as money and be accepted in trade as money. 20 Am J2d Counterf § 2. As the term is used in the Federal statutes dealing with the crime of counterfeiting, the coin to be "counterfeit" must be in the resemblance or similitude of a genuine United States coin. It is not necessary that the resemblance should be exact in all respects. The resemblance is sufficient if the coins are so near alike that the counterfeit coin is calculated to deceive a person exercising ordinary caution and observation in the usual transactions of business. United States v Gellman (DC Minn) 44 F Supp 360.

counterfoil. A part of a document, torn off and retained by the maker of the document as a memorandum; as, a check stub.

counter-injunction. An injunction restraining the enforcement of an injunction. State v Nortoni, 331 Mo 764, 55 SW2d 272, 85 ALR 1345.

counter-letter. A separate instrument, executed simultaneously with a deed absolute on its face, whereby the grantee named in the deed undertakes to reconvey the property to the grantor, upon the fulfilment of the terms and conditions stated in the counter-letter. Livingston's Exr. v Story (US) 11 Pet 351, 9 L Ed 746.

countermand. To revoke an order previously given.

countermanding payment. See **stopping payment.**

countermotion. A motion, made after a motion for change of venue to the proper county, to retain the case in the county where it was commenced on the ground of the convenience of witnesses and the ends of justice. Anno: 74 ALR2d 50.

counteroffer. An offer made by one of two negotiating parties in response to an offer by the other party. Where an acceptance of an offer is conditional, or introduces a new term, or varies substantially in any way from the terms of the offer, it may be treated as a counteroffer. 17 Am J2d Contr § 40.

counterpart. A person or thing closely resembling another person or thing; an obsolete term for copy. 2 Bl Comm 296.

counterplea (koun'tẽr-plē). A replication; a plea interposed in reply to another plea.

counterplead. To interpose a counter-plea; to plead against; to plead the contrary; to deny.

counterroll (koun'tẽr-rōl). A duplicate record.

countersecurity. Security given to a surety to indemnify him against loss.

counter service. Service at a counter, a method of serving meals or lunches in a public eating place. 29 Am J Rev ed Innk § 9.

countersignature. A signature, often that of a subordinate, added to the signature of an officer or superior, by way of authentication; an additional signature required by the terms of a written contract, as in the case of the requirement for the signature of a particular officer or agent of an insurance company in addition to the regular signature appended upon the issuance of a policy. 29 Am J Rev ed Ins § 214.
See **countersign**

counterwills. Another term for reciprocal wills in which the testators name each other as beneficiaries under similar testamentary plans. 57 Am J1st Wills § 681.
See **mutual wills; reciprocal wills.**

countez (koun'tay). A word by which, when the jury are all sworn, the officer bids the court crier to number them. Blackstone facetiously remarks, "we now hear it pronounced in very good English 'count these'." See 4 Bl Comm 340, note.

counties. See **county.**

counties palatine. Certain counties of England, the owners of which enjoyed powers and privileges which were practically those of a king in his palace. Originally, there were three of these counties, Chester, owned by the earl of Chester, Durham, by the bishop of Durham, and Lancaster, by the duke of Lancaster. These privileges were probably extended to Chester and Durham because their counties bordered on Wales and Scotland which were hostile to England, and thus it was considered more feasible to protect them by a home government. See 1 Bl Comm 117.

counting upon a statute. In pleading,—making express reference to a statute; as by the words, against the form of the statute, or by force of the statute, in such case made and provided. Hart v Baltimore & Ohio Railroad Co. 6 W Va 336, 348.

countors (koun'torz). Persons who prepared counts or declarations at common law. See 1 Bl Comm 24, note.

country. A nation or land, also the people of a nation or state; any place out of court; the persons living in the district available for jury duty; a jury. A settlement in pais (in the country) is a settlement out of court.

As the word "country" is used in the revenue laws of the United States, it has always been construed to embrace all the possessions of a nation, however widely separated, which are subject to the same supreme executive and legislative control. Stairs v Peeslee (US) 18 How 521, 15 L Ed 474, 476. Adopting this definition, the Philippine Islands were held to be neither a foreign country nor another country within the meaning of the Cuban treaty. Faber v United States, 221 US 649, 659, 55 L Ed 897, 899, 31 S Ct 659.

See **jury of the country; trial by the country.**

country club. A social club, ordinarily located in the outskirts of a metropolitan area, and usually having spacious grounds surrounding a clubhouse, a golf course, and swimming pool, sometimes stables for riding horses, and a ring for exhibitions of horsemanship.

See **club.**

country road. Literally, a road outside a metropolitan area; sometimes defined in the bucolic aspect of a way unimproved by the hand of man beyond the traveled lane or path. Nelson v Spokane, 45 Wash 31, 87 P 1048.

county. A political subdivision of the state; a public or municipal corporation, established for the more convenient administration of government, its powers and importance varying throughout the nation, depending upon whether it or the town has been adopted by statute as the more important arm of government; an agency of the state. 6 Am J2d Attach § 80; a circuit or portion of the state established for the better government thereof. State ex rel. Milton v Dickenson, 44 Fla 623, 33 So 514.

county attorney. An attorney at law employed by a county to represent it in civil matters; in some jurisdictions, the prosecuting attorney.

county board. The body in which the government of a county, particularly the administrative part of the government, is vested; otherwise known as board of supervisors or board of commissioners.

county clerk. The clerk of court, the title having survived from the time when the colonial court of common pleas was known as a county court and the clerk thereof as a county clerk.

See **clerk of court.**

county clerk's certificate. See **certificate of authenticity; certificate of conformity.**

county commissioners. The members of the county board, the primary administrative board of a county often called supervisors.

See **county board.**

county coroner. See **coroner.**

county corporate. A term applied to certain cities and towns in England, including London, York, Bristol, Norwich and Coventry, and the territory annexed to them, to which out of special favor, the kings granted the privilege to be counties of themselves and not to be included in any other county, and to be governed by their own sheriffs and other officers, so that no officers of the county at large had any power to act therein. See 1 Bl Comm 120.

county court. A state court, sometimes of limited jurisdiction, sitting in one particular county, but in some states having the power to issue process effective in any part of the state. 20 Am J2d Cts § 17; in a few states, a fiscal court, that is, a court vested with responsibility for the conduct of fiscal affairs of the county, being an administrative body rather than a court in the ordinary sense of the term. Mitchell v Henry County, 124 Ky 833, 100 SW 220.

county court judge. The judge of a county court, having the status of a state officer where the court is granted general jurisdiction by constitution or statute. 30A Am J Rev ed Judges § 5.

county election. An election wherein county officers are elected.

See **votes polled.**

county engineer. A county officer, usually holding by appointment, qualified as a civil engineer, whose primary duties are making surveys preparatory to the construction of public improvements and the laying out of highways or in determination of boundaries of lands privately owned.

county farm. An institution located on a tract of farmland, in some states for the care of indigent, in other states for the detention of prisoners under sentence for crime, and in either case, ordinarily using the services of such inmates as are physically able to perform farm labor.

county home. See **almshouse; county farm.**

county manager. The chief administrative officer of a county under a comparatively modern form of county government.

county officer. One of several officers by whom a county performs its political or governmental functions, the sheriff, county clerk, county treasurer, coroner, etc.

county palatine. See **counties palatine; courts of the counties palatine.**

county prison. The building provided by the county for the custody of persons committed by legal process. 41 Am J1st Pris & P § 2.

county property. Public property held by a county in a governmental capacity as an agent of the state; any property acquired, owned, and held by a county under and pursuant to authority vested in it. State v Brown, 73 Mont 371, 236 P 548.

county rate (koun'ti rāt). A tax levy for county purposes.

county seat. The place in a county where the principal county offices are located, where the primary affairs and business of the county are conducted, and where court is held. 20 Am J2d Cts §§ 37 et seq.

county seat de facto. Same as **de facto county seat.**

county sessions. The general quarter sessions of the peace.
  See **court of quarter sessions of the peace.**

county site. The term is used interchangeably, in some jurisdictions, with the term county seat. Watts v State, 22 Tex App 572, 578.
  See **county seat.**

county warrants. Instruments, generally in the form of bills of exchange or orders, drawn by an officer of the county upon its treasurer, directing him to pay an amount of money specified to the person named therein, to the order of such person or to bearer.

county where the cause arose. The county where the act or omission creating the right to bring an action occurred; not the same as "county where the transaction in question occurred." 56 Am J1st Ven § 34.

county where the parties live. A venue provision applicable in actions for divorce, construed to mean the county in which the aggrieved party lives at the time of commencement of suit. Harteau v Harteau, 31 Mass (14 Pick) 181.

coupled with an interest. See **power coupled with an interest.**

coupon. An instrument payable in money or redeemable in merchandise; an instrument attached to another instrument but detachable for use by itself, as in the case of an interest coupon which evidences the interest payable on the instrument to which it is attached. 30 Am J Rev ed Int § 64. Coupons of such type are usually regarded as negotiable and as having all the qualities of commercial paper. 43 Am J1st Pub Sec § 14.

coupon bond. A bond in which the interest payable separately from the principal is represented by detachable coupons. Amey v Allegheny City (US) 24 How 364, 16 L Ed 614; Tennessee Bond Cases, 114 US 663, 29 L Ed 281, 5 S Ct 1098.
  See **coupon.**

coupon note. A promissory note with coupons attached, the coupons being notes for the interest, written at the bottom of the note and designed to be cut off when the notes are presented for payment or paid. Williams v Moody, 95 Ga 8, 11.
  See **coupon; coupon bond; coupon note; interest coupons.**

coupon ticket. A ticket for transportation in one trip over the lines of different carriers, made up of detachable portions or coupons, each one of which represents the part of the trip to be made over the line of one of the respective carriers. Louisville & Nashville Railroad Co. v Klyman, 108 Tenn 304, 67 SW 472.

cour de cassation. Same as **court of cassation.**

course. The direction of a line run with a compass or transit and with reference to a meridian. 12 Am J2d Bound § 10. Progression in order; a way in which something moves, as a race course.
  See **holder in due course.**

course of descent. The course of intestate property to the heirs and distributees who take and the proportion in which they take. 23 Am J2d Desc & D § 41.

course of employment. See **in the course of the employment.**

course of trade. The trend of business; that which is customary among merchants.

course of vessel. The direction taken by a vessel under way; her apparent course rather than her heading at a given moment. The Eastern Glade (CA2 NY) 101 F2d 4. The course of a vessel referred to in the International Regulations to Prevent Collisions is her actual course, and not the compass direction, of the heading of the vessel at the time the other vessel is sighted. Liverpool, Brazil & River Plate Steam Navigation Co. v United States (DC NY) 12 F2d 128.

courses and distances. See **course.**

court. An organ of the government, consisting of one person, or of several persons, called upon and authorized to administer justice; a place where justice is judicially administered. 20 Am J2d Cts § 1; judge and jury combined. Welch v Welch (Tex Civ App) 369 SW2d 434.
  The three elements essential to the conception of a court are: (1) a time when judicial functions may be exercised, (2) a place for the exercise of judicial functions, and (3) a person or persons exercising judicial functions. Hamblin v Superior Court, 195 Cal 364, 233 P 337, 43 ALR 1509. In many cases, the words "court" and "judge" are used interchangeably. 30A Am J Rev ed Judges § 4.
  See **jurisdiction;** see also words and phrases beginning **court** which follow.

court administrative offices. Nonjudicial offices created to perform administrative functions and details necessary to the performance of the duty of courts to administer justice, thereby relieving the judges or justices of such details and permitting them to concentrate on the purely judicial phases of court work. Am J2d Desk Book, Document 75.

court-baron (kōrt'bar″ǫn). A court within a manor in which the tenants litigated and were tried.

court calendar. A list of the cases for trial by the term, the week, or even the day, at which a particular case will come on for trial.
  There may be separate calendars for various steps in a proceeding, such as a motion calendar or a pretrial conference calendar. An appellate court calendar is a register of the actions and proceedings in the court, such usually determining the order in which the appeals will be heard. 5 Am J2d A & E § 678.
  See **docket.**

court commissioner. See **commissioner of court.**

court costs. See **costs.**

court days. Time of holding court. 20 Am J2d Cts § 42.

court en banc. See **full bench.**

court decision. See **decision.**

court docket. See **docket.**

courtesy. Polite and gracious behavior; consideration for others.
  See **curtesy.**

courtesy card. A card passed out by bus driver, motorman, or conductor to passengers for the purpose

of obtaining their names and addresses after the occurrence of an accident causing injury to person or property.
See **credit card**.

courtezan (kor'te-zan). See **concubine**.

court for crown cases reserved. Same as **court of criminal appeal**.

court for divorce and matrimonial causes. An English court established under the statute 20 & 21 Victoria, c. 85, having jurisdiction in suits for divorce and annulments of marriage.

court for the relief of insolvent debtors. A London bankruptcy court.

court hand. The style of handwriting which is peculiar to English court records.

courthouse. The place provided for holding court; a building occupied and appropriated according to law for the holding of the courts. Harris v State, 72 Miss 960, 18 S 387.

courthouse door. A designation as the place for conducting a judicial sale of real estate at auction. 30A Am J Rev ed Jud S § 76.

court interpreter. See **interpreter**.

court-lands. Lands which were retained by the lord for the use of his family.

court-leet (kōrt'lēt). An ancient English court presided over by the steward of the leet, with jurisdiction to try petty offenders and to hold preliminary examinations in felony cases.

court-martial. A court of the military, of one of the Armed Services, for the trial of offenses under the Code of Military Justice, which may be in the order of rank a **general court-martial**, a **special court-martial**, or a **summary court-martial**; a prosecution before one of such courts-martial.

court not of record. An inferior court, or court of limited or special jurisdiction, such as the court held by a justice of the peace, a mayor, or other magistrate, and some city courts. The term "court not of record" is inexact and indifferent, so that in the absence of a statute declaring a court as one of record or not of record, difficulty is experienced in classification. A justice of the peace does keep a record of his judicial acts and of judgments rendered by him, even though he does not enroll them in an extended form. 20 Am J2d Cts § 26. Usually, the term "court not of record" has reference to a court of limited jurisdiction, negativing the idea that the court so described is one of general jurisdiction. 20 Am J2d Cts § 103.
See **court of general jurisdiction**; **court of limited jurisdiction**.

court of admiralty. A court entitled to exercise admiralty jurisdiction, which is a federal district court, state courts having no admiralty jurisdiction. 2 Am J2d Adm § 10.

court of ancient demesne. A court held by the king's bailiff for tenants of the king's demesne. Some tenants in ancient demesne had special immunities and favors granted to them, such as to try the right of their property in the court of ancient demesne, by a peculiar process called the writ of right close. See 2 Bl Comm 99.

court of appeals. A court in which appeals from a lower court are heard and disposed of.

Court of Appeals. The highest appellate court of the State of New York and of some other states; an intermediate federal appellate court.
The United States is divided into eleven judicial circuits. In each circuit there is a United States Court of Appeals for the circuit, having appellate jurisdiction as set forth in the United States Code. 28 US §§ 1271-1294.

Court of Arbitration of the Chamber of Commerce. A court in New York City for the settlement by arbitration of disputes between merchants, created by special act of the legislature (Laws 1874 Ch 278, amended Laws 1875 Ch 495) but not continuing in existence after 1879.

court of archdeacon. See **archdeacon's court**.

court of arches. See **arches court**.

court of assize. A court of nisi prius was also called a court of assize and nisi prius.
See **assize**; **nisi prius**.

court of attachments. An ancient English forest court for inquiry into offenses against vert and venison, that is, against unlawfully killing deer or stealing wood in the king's forests, or preparing to do so. It was called the court of attachments because persons thus offending could be attached in their bodies if taken in the act, or else attached by their goods. See 3 Bl Comm 71.

court of augmentation. An old English court for the control of the funds and property of monasteries.

court of bankruptcy. A court having jurisdiction of proceedings in bankruptcy, which, in the terms of the Bankruptcy Act, is a United States District Court and a District Court of the territories and possessions to which the Act is or may hereafter be applicable. 9 Am J2d Bankr § 25. Unless the context of the Bankruptcy Act requires otherwise, the term "court," as used in the Act, means the judge or the referee of the court of bankruptcy in which the proceedings are pending. 9 Am J2d Bankr § 92.

court of cassation (kas-sā'shun). The highest court of appeal in France.

court of chancery. A court of equity, in England and some of the United States.
See **High Court of Chancery**.

court of chivalry (shi'val-ri). A court known also as the marshal court which was formerly held before the lord high constable and earl marshal of England jointly; but, since the extinguishment of the office of lord high constable, it has usually, with respect to civil matters been held before the earl marshal only, and takes cognizance of contracts and other matters touching deeds of arms and war, as well out of the realm as in it. The court had grown almost obsolete in Blackstone's time. See 3 Bl Comm 68.

Court of Claims. The federal court, created by statute, and vested with jurisdiction of claims against the United States. 28 USC §§ 1491 et seq.; United States v Sherwood, 312 US 584, 85 L Ed 1058, 61 S Ct 767; the designation given in some of the states to the court vested with jurisdiction of claims against the state. 20 Am J2d Cts § 33.

court of commerce. See **Commerce Court**.

court of common pleas. A nisi prius court of general jurisdiction, at least over civil cases. American colonial courts of common pleas were courts of justice presided over by judges appointed by the king and were known as county courts. "The court of common pleas is the general fountain of justice; and where the rights of a citizen, either derived from the common law or the statutes, are invaded, and the power to protect is conferred on no special jurisdiction, he may seek redress in that court." Moore v Barry, 30 SC 530, 9 SE 589.

Court of Common Pleas. The name given in several states to a court of general jurisdiction; the trial court of several states.

court of competent jurisdiction. See **competent jurisdiction.**

court of conscience. An English court for the collection of small debts; a court of equity. Harper v Clayton, 84 Md 346, 35 A 1083. A court of equity is a court of conscience, and whatever, therefore, is unconscionable is odious in its sight. Fraud is more odious than force, and one of the peculiar provinces of a court of equity is to relieve against wilful misrepresentation and fraud. Dowell v Goodwin, 22 RI 287, 47 A 693.

court of convocation (kon-vō-kā'shun). An ecclesiastical court having jurisdiction of the trial of offenses against the ecclesiastical law.

court of criminal appeal. A court composed of judges of the English superior courts which decided questions of law referred to it in pending criminal cases.

Court of Criminal Appeals. The name given in several states to an appellate court with jurisdiction of appeals in criminal cases.

Court of Customs and Patent Appeals. A court with jurisdictions of customs and patent matters created by federal statute. 28 USC § 211.

court of delegates. The great court of appeal in all ecclesiastical cases. The judices delegati or judges of the court were appointed by the king's commission issuing out of chancery to represent his royal person, and hear all appeals in ecclesiastical matters. The jurisdiction of this court was removed to the judicial committee of the privy council by statute in the reign of William the Fourth. 3 Bl Comm 66.

court of equity. A court having jurisdiction of suits in equity and in which equitable remedies are administered.
See **court of conscience; equity.**

court of exchequer (eks'chek-er). An English superior court with jurisdiction of matters of law and matters involving government revenue.

court of exchequer chamber. An English court of appeals for the correction of the errors of other jurisdictions. It also heard important matters of great difficulty which were suspended and submitted to it before any judgment was rendered in the court below. See 3 Bl Comm 56.

court of faculties. An English ecclesiastical court which had the granting of ecclesiastical licenses, pew rights and the like.

court of general jurisdiction. A term sometimes equated with "court of record"; a court of extensive, although not necessarily of unlimited, jurisdiction. 20 Am J2d Cts § 103; a superior court. Hahn v Kelly, 34 Cal 391; a court which is competent by its constitution to decide on its own jurisdiction, and to exercise it to a final judgment, without setting forth in its proceedings the facts and evidence on which it is rendered, whose record is absolute verity and behind which there can be no judicial inspection save by appellate power. Lessee of Grignon v Astor (US) 2 How 319, 341, 11 L Ed 283, 292.

Court of General Sessions. A local court of the Borough of Manhattan in New York City having a general criminal jurisdiction.

court of greatest convenience. A term involved in the transfer of cases in bankruptcy, meaning of greatest convenience from the standpoint of proximity to the bankrupt, creditors, and witnesses, the location of assets, and the economic and efficient administration of the estate. Re Triton Chemcial Corp. (DC Del) 46 F Supp 326.

court of hustings. See **hustings court.**

court of industrial relations. See **industrial relations court.**

court of inquiry. A court convened by the President of the United States for a preliminary investigation of charges preferred against a soldier or an officer of the armed services. 36 Am J1st Mil § 90.

court of justiciary (jus-tish'i-ary). The supreme criminal court of Scotland.

court of king's bench. A court which was formerly the supreme English common-law court, but later became a department of the high court of justice.
In a reign of a queen, the same court is called the court of queen's bench.

court of last resort. The highest court to which a case may be taken; a court from the judgments of which no appeal can be taken.

court of limited jurisdiction. A term which lacks precision as a description of a court, since there may be limitations upon the jurisdiction of a court properly classed as a court of general jurisdiction; a term sometimes used for an inferior court, a court not of record, one whose judgments do not carry the verity of those of a court of general jurisdiction and may be questioned unless jurisdiction appears upon the face of the proceedings. Lessee of Grignon v Astor (US) 2 How 319, 341, 11 L Ed 283, 292; Hahn v Kelly, 34 Cal 391; 20 Am J2d Courts § 103; a court of special jurisdiction, such as a juvenile court. 31 Am J Rev ed Juv Ct § 5.

court of magistrates and freeholders. A court formerly existing in North Carolina for the trial of colored persons on criminal charges.

Court of Military Appeals. A court with jurisdiction to hear appeals from the judgment in a court-martial, being established by federal statute. 10 USC § 867.

court of nisi prius (nī'sī prī'us). See **nisi prius.**

court of orphans. See **orphans' court.**

court of oyer and terminer (ōy'er and ter'min-er). Old courts presided over by commissioners of oyer and terminer appointed by the king. Among these commissioners were usually two common-law judges of the courts at Westminster. These courts were held twice each year in most of the counties of England and eight times in London and Middlesex. They had jurisdiction to hear and determine all cases of treason, felony and misdemeanor. See 4 Bl Comm 269. In the United States the higher criminal courts of some states have been given this name.

court of oyer and terminer and general gaol delivery. A nisi prius court of criminal jurisdiction in England.

court of passage. An inferior court of record held at Liverpool.

court of peculiars. An ecclesiastical court which was a branch of the court of arches to which it was annexed. It had jurisdiction over those parishes in the province of Canterbury which were situated in dioceses exempt from the ordinary's jurisdiction. All ecclesiastical causes arising within these "peculiar" or exempt jurisdictions were originally cognizable by this court. See 3 Bl Comm 65.

court of piepoudre (pī-pou-dr). See **pie-powder court.**

court of policies of insurance. An English court with jurisdiction in insurance cases, established about 1550 and abolished about 1863.

court of probate. See **probate court.**

court of quarter sessions of the peace. A minor English court held quarterly in each county and presided over therein by two justices of the peace.

court of queen's bench. See **king's bench.**

court of record. A term which seems to have originated in the practice of superior courts in extending the record of their proceedings, orders, and judgments, at length and as perpetual memorials, on sheets of parchment, but, in more recent times, to have been used as a designation of courts of general jurisdiction, the judgments of which import verity. 20 Am J2d Cts §§ 26, 103.

A court of record is a court presided over by a man of experience and learned in the law, assisted by counsel also of experience and learning who act as advisers of the court. Its proceedings are conducted with solemnity and deliberation, and in strict conformity with established modes, and they are taken down and made a matter of record at or about the time they transpire. Hahn v Kelly, 34 Cal 391.

court of regard (rē-gard'). A forest court held triennially for the lawing or expedition of mastiffs, that is, by cutting off the claws and ball of each fore-foot to prevent the dog from attacking deer. See 3 Bl Comm 72.

court of requests. Same as **court of conscience.**

court of sessions. The supreme civil court of Scotland.
See **Court of General Sessions.**

court of special jurisdiction. Same as **court of limited jurisdiction.**

court of star-chamber. A court which tried certain high crimes without the intervention of a jury. The court was abolished in the reign of Charles the First.

court of survey (ser'vāy). An English and Welsh court held under the Merchants' Shipping Act of 1894.

court of sweinmote (swīn'mōt). A forest court held three times in each year before the verderors of the forest as judges and with sweins or freeholders of the forest as jurors, to inquire into grievances committed by forest officers and to try presentments certified from the court of attachments. See 3 Bl Comm 72.

court of the clerk of the market. A court which was held at the place and time of a fair or market in England.

court of the coroner. A coroner's inquest.

court of the Duchy of Lancaster. A court of equity of special jurisdiction in cases relating to lands held of the king in right of the Duchy of Lancaster. It appears not to have been a court of record. See 3 Bl Comm 78.

court of the judiciary. A court of the state with supervisory powers over the administration of all the courts in the state, sometimes having jurisdiction of proceedings for removal of judges or disbarment of attorneys.

court of the lord high steward. A court where peers of England were tried for felony and certain other high crimes.

court of the lord high steward of the universities. A court for the trial of indictments of scholars and officers of the universities of Oxford and Cambridge.

court of the marshalsea (mar'shal-sē). An English court with jurisdiction of cases involving royal servants.

court of the ordinary. An English ecclesiastical court which was presided over by a bishop.

court of the steward and marshal. An English court for the trial of cases arising within twelve miles of the king's actual residence.

court of the steward of the king's household. An English court which tried persons for certain crimes committed near the king's residence.

court of upper bench. The court of king's bench, as it was called during the interregnum, 1649-1660.

court of wards and liveries. A court which was erected in the reign of Henry the Eighth for the conducting of inquiries into reliefs, wardships, primer seisins and other profits which accrued to the king. The court was abolished by statute in the reign of Charles the Second. See 2 Bl Comm 68, 77.

court opinion. See **opinion of court.**

court order. See **order of court.**

court receiver. A receiver appointed by a court under statutory authority or by virtue of its equity jurisdiction. 44 Am J1st Rec § 3.

court record. An official writeup or memorandum of what happened or occurred in court during the proceedings in a particular case. 20 Am J2d Cts § 52; any part of the record of a case in court, including pleadings, exhibits, examinations, writs and levies, etc. 20 Am J1st Ev §§ 994 et seq.

In a criminal case, after the caption stating the time and place of holding the court, the record should consist of the indictment properly indorsed, as found by the grand jury; the arraignment of the accused, his plea, the impaneling of the traverse jury, their verdict, and the judgment of the court. This, in general, is all that the record need state. United States v Taylor, 147 US 695, 37 L Ed 335, 13 S Ct 475.

Nothing which is not properly matter of record can be made such by inserting it therein. United States v Taylor, 147 US 695, 37 L Ed 335, 13 S Ct 475.

See **court of record.**

court reporter. A stenographer who takes down in shorthand during the trial of a case the testimony of witnesses by question and answer and the colloquy between counsel and between counsel and the court, and later prepares transcripts from such record as such may be needed and ordered for appeal or review proceedings; sometimes having the status of an officer of the court. 20 Am J2d Cts § 4; an officer of court in charge of the publication of the opinions of the court.

See **stenographically reported.**

court reports. Official or unofficial reports of cases decided by a court or by one or more courts, giving in full the opinions rendered in the cases, usually including concurring and dissenting opinions, and having headnotes or syllabi prepared officially by the court reporter or unofficially by an editor of the publisher's staff. 20 Am J2d Cts §§ 76, 77.

court-rolls. The rolls or records of a court.

court rules. See **rules of court.**

courts Christian. Ecclesiastical courts. Anderson v Commonwealth, 26 Va (5 Rand) 627.

court seal. See **seal of court.**

courts-martial. Plural of **court-martial.**

courts of the cinque ports (singk ports). Courts which were established at the cinque ports, which were the five most important havens on the English coast, to wit: Dover, Sandwich, Romney, Hastings and Hythe. To these five Winchelsea and Rye were added later. See 3 Bl Comm 79.

courts of the counties palatine (pal'a-tīn). Courts which were held in counties palatine. See **counties palatine.**

courts of the principality of Wales. Courts which were established in Wales during the reign of Henry the Eighth in which all pleas of real and personal actions were held in the same manner as in the court of common pleas at Westminster. They were courts of record and appeals lay from them to the court of king's bench. These courts were abolished in the reign of George the Fourth. See 3 Bl Comm 77.

courts of the two universities. Courts of local jurisdiction held at the universities of Oxford and Cambridge. See 3 Bl Comm 83.

courts of the United States. See **United States Courts.**

court's presence. See **presence of the court.**

court stenographer. See **court reporter.**

court vacation. See **vacation.**

cousin. The child of one's uncle or aunt; a relative in the fourth degree according to the method of computing kinship used in most jurisdictions. 23 Am J2d Desc & D § 48.

The children of brothers, sisters, or a brother and sister, respectively, are related as first cousins. Re O'Mara's Estate, 106 NJ Eq 311, 151 A 67; Re Oatley, 83 Misc 655, 146 NYS 796. The general rule is that a devise to "cousins", in the absence of testamentary qualification, express or implied, includes only first cousins. Bishop v Russell, 241 Mass 29, 134 NE 233, 19 ALR 1408.

In England, any peer of the degree or station of an earl or better is often addressed by king or queen as cousin.

See **cater-cousin; quater cousin; second cousin.**

cousinage (kuz'nāj). The relationship of cousins; collateral relationship.

cousin german. A first cousin, that is, a child of an uncle or an aunt. Anno: 99 ALR 672.

coustum (kous'tom). A toll; a tribute.

couthutlaugh (köth'ut-lâ). A person who harbored an outlaw.

cove. A nook, a small bay; a concave molding. Keller Products, Inc. v Rubber Linings Corp. (CA7 Ill) 213 F2d 382, 47 ALR2d 1108.

covenant. Words used in a deed whereby the grantor, the grantee, or each of them, binds himself to the other for the performance or nonperformance of a particular act or thing, or for the existence or nonexistence of a particular state of facts, and for the breach of which obligation the party bound should be answerable in damages. Mackenzie v Trustees of Presbytery, 67 NJ Eq 652, 61 A 1027; a term now used principally in connection with promises in conveyances or other instruments pertaining to real estate, although in the broadest sense of the term it indicates a contract. In a more specific application of the term, it imports an agreement reduced to writing and duly executed whereby one or more of the parties named therein engages that a named act is to be performed or is to be performed sometime in the future. 20 Am J2d Cov § 1. In a lease, the term usually means no more than a promise or agreement. 32 Am J1st L & T § 140. A seal was a requisite of a covenant at common law, but with the elimination of the requirement of a seal upon written contracts, as such has occurred in most jurisdictions, a mere written agreement may suffice as a covenant. 20 Am J2d Cov § 1.

A breach of covenant gives rise to an action at law to recover damages or an action for equitable relief, whereas, the breach of a condition upon which an estate is granted is a forfeiture of the estate forthwith.

The term "covenant" is the name of the common-law remedy for breach of a contract under seal. 1 Am J2d Actions § 19. It was the remedy at common law for the recovery of rent upon a lease under seal. 32 Am J1st L & T § 523.

See **restrictive covenants; title covenants.**

covenant against encumbrances. A title covenant in the form of a stipulation by the covenantor that there are no outstanding rights or interest to the estate conveyed or any part thereof which will diminish the value of the estate, but which are consistent with the passing of the estate. 20 Am J2d Cov § 81.

covenant appurtenant. Same as **covenant running with the land.**

covenant collateral. A covenant in a deed which does not relate to the grant.

covenantee. The person to whom the performance of the terms of a convenant is due.

covenanter. Same as **covenantor.**

covenant for further assurance. A covenant of title binding the grantor to perform all acts, deeds, conveyances and assurances which may be wanting to the confirmation of the grantee's title, or to secure the execution of such other deeds or instruments as shall be necessary to perfect or confirm the title. 20 Am J2d Cov § 108.

covenant for possession. Same as **covenant of quiet enjoyment.**

covenant for quiet enjoyment. See **covenant of quiet enjoyment.**

covenant for title. See **title covenants.**

covenant inherent. See **inherent covenant.**

covenant in law. A covenant which the law implies or intends from the nature of the transaction, although it is not expressed by words in the instrument which contains it. It is a rule that such a covenant is operative only when the parties have omitted to insert covenants in the instrument. 20 Am J2d Cov § 12.

See **implied covenant.**

covenant not to sue. A device most familiar in the law of torts, being used to prevent the release of a tortfeasor upon settling with his joint tortfeasor. 1 Am J2d Accord § 9.

A covenant not to sue recognizes that the obligation or liability continues but the injured party agrees not to assert any rights grounded thereon against a particular covenantee. Atlantic Coast Line R. Co. v Boone (Fla) 85 So 2d 834, 57 ALR2d 1189. Indicia of such a covenant are: No intention on the part of the injured person to give a discharge of the cause of action, or any part thereof, but merely to treat in respect of not suing thereon, and this seems to be the prime differentiating attribute; full compensation for his injuries not received, but only partial satisfaction; and a reservation of the right to sue the other wrongdoer. Smith v Dixie Park Co. 128 Tenn 112, 120 SW 900.

covenant of good right to convey. A synonym of covenant of seisin.
See **covenant of seisin.**

covenant of quiet enjoyment. A title covenant, an assurance that the grantee shall have legal, quiet, and peaceful possession. 20 Am J2d Cov § 97; an express or implied covenant in a lease that the lessee shall not be evicted or disturbed in his possession of the demised premises or any part thereof. 32 Am J1st L & T § 268.

The covenant of quiet enjoyment extends only to the possession, not to the title of the property transferred, and is sometimes referred to as a "covenant for possession." 20 Am J2d Cov § 97.

covenant of seisin. A covenant of title, otherwise known as a covenant of good right to convey, is a general covenant that the grantor is lawfully seised and has the right to convey the property at the time of the execution of the conveyance, extending to the land itself and to whatever is properly appurtenant to, and passing by, the conveyance of the land. 20 Am J2d Cov § 73.
See **seisin.**

covenant of special warranty. See **special warranty.**

covenant of title. See **title covenants.**

covenant of warranty. The principal title covenant, being an agreement by the grantor or warrantor that upon the failure of the title which the deed purports to convey, either for the whole estate or part only, he will make compensation in money for the loss sustained. It is an assurance or guaranty of title, or an agreement or assurance by the grantor of an estate that the grantee and his heirs and assigns shall enjoy it without interruption by virtue of a paramount title, and that they shall not, by force of a paramount title, be evicted from the land or deprived of its possession. 20 Am J2d Cov § 50.

covenantor. A person who covenants; the maker of a covenant.

covenant performed. A form of plea in actions of covenant, which admits the execution of the covenants, but pleads the performance of them. Roth v Miller (Pa) 15 Serg & R 100, 105.

covenant real. See **real covenant.**

covenant running with the land. A real covenant, a covenant under which either the liability for performance or the right to performance passes to a vendee or assignee. 20 Am J2d Cov § 29; a covenant of a lease, the burdens, as well as the benefits of which, are upon the assignee. 32 Am J1st L & T § 157.

See **real covenant.**

covenant to convey. A covenant by which the covenantor agrees to convey certain described property.

covenant to rebuild. A covenant by the lessor to rebuild the structures upon the demised premises after their destruction by fire or the elements. 32 Am J1st L & T § 709.

covenant to redeliver. An implied obligation or covenant on the part of a lessee to redeliver possession of the demised premises on the expiration of the lease. 32 Am J1st L & T § 841.

covenant to repair. An express agreement in a lease binding the lessee to surrender the premises upon the expiration of the lease in a designated condition of repair. 32 Am J1st L & T § 803; a covenant by the lessor to repair the premises after injury thereto by fire or the elements. 32 Am J1st L & T § 709.

covenant to stand seised to uses. A covenant by which a man, seised of land, covenants in consideration of blood or marriage that he will stand seised of the same to the use of his child, wife, or kinsman, for life, in tail, or in fee. In such case, the statute of uses executed the estate at once for the beneficiary having thus acquired the use, the statute clothed him with possession, "by a kind of parliamentary magic." See 2 Bl Comm 338.

Coventry Act (kuv'ęn-tri akt). An Act of Parliament, passed in 1683, making an assault with intent to maim or disfigure a person a felony.

cover. To overspread; as applied to insurance, it means to protect by means of insurance. A. Perley Fitch Co. v Phenix Ins. Co. 82 NH 318, 320, 133 A 340, 342.

coverage. The risk of loss covered by an insurance policy.
See **risks and causes of loss.**

covered wagon. A vehicle well known in history and romantic legends. The vehicle by which the pioneers traveled west. A large wagon having a canvas cover.

A covered wagon traveling from place to place, in which prostitution is carried on, may constitute a house of ill fame, within the meaning of the statute. State v Chauvet, 111 Iowa 687, 83 NW 717.

covert (kuv'ẽrt). Covered; protected; as, a feme covert, a married women.

covert-baron (kuv'ẽrt-bar"ǫn). A married woman.

coverture. The status and rights of the wife arising from the marriage relationship. 26 Am J1st H & W § 5.

covin (kuv'in). Fraud; deceit; collusion; a contrivance between two to cheat a third. Mix v Muzzy, 28 Conn 186, 191.

covinous (kuv'i-nus). Collusive; deceitful; fraudulent.

cow. The mature female of the ox family, also of elephants and whales, sometimes and for some purposes including the immature female of the ox family known as a heifer. Carruth v Grassie, 77 Mass (11 Gray) 211.

cowitch (kou'ich). A plant whose spines cause violent itching in contact with the skin of a person. Commonwealth v Cramer (Pa) 2 Pearson 441, 444.

Cox v Hickman. A celebrated English case (8 H. L. Cas. 268) in which the court established the principle, which has since become general, that persons who are not in fact partners are not liable to third persons as such merely because they have shared in the profits of a business unless there has been an estoppel or a holding out of such persons as partners.

cozen (kuz'n). To cheat.

cozening (kuz'n-ing). Cheating or defrauding a person by some deceitful practice, whether in a matter of business or not, as by a counterfeit letter, cogged dice or other false token. See 4 Bl Comm 158.

CPA. Abbreviation of **certified public account.** 1 Am J2d Accts § 1.

c. r. An abbreviation of **curia regis.**

crabs. A kind of shellfish; a sour-tempered person.

cracking. Breaking or splitting without complete separation of parts. A processs in refining crude oil into useful constituents, such as lubricating oil and gasoline. Universal Oil Products Co. v Globe Oil & Refining Co. (DC Ill) 40 F Supp 575.

craft. Trickery or deception; an occupation requiring skill; the members of a skilled trade. Re International Asso. of Machinists, 249 Wis 112, 23 NW2d 489, 174 ALR 1267. The members of a secret fraternal order which simulates a skilled trade in instructing its members in the principles of the order. Watercraft, especially small vessels. Owners of Steamboat Wenonah v Bragdon, 62 Va (21 Gratt) 685, 697.

craft union. A labor union, the membership of which is confined to persons of a single craft or closely related crafts. 31 Am J Rev ed Lab § 13.

cranage (krā'nąj). A license to use a wharf crane. The charge made for such license.

crane. A device with a movable arm for lifting heavy weights. A large bird with long legs, frequenting swamps.
See **mail crane.**

Cranworth. See **Lord Cranworth's Act.**

crap (krap). Buckwheat. The throw which loses in a game of craps.
A slang term for something worthless, especially idle talk.
See **craps.**

craps. A game played with dice.
See **dice.**

crassa (kras'ạ). Gross.

crassa negligentia (kras'sa neg-li-jen'she-a). Gross negligence; a gross breach of duty. See Briggs v Spaulding, 141 US 132, 171, 35 L Ed 662, 677, 11 S Ct 924.

crastinum or crastino (krās'ti-num or krās'ti-nō). Tomorrow; the next day.

cratering (krā'tėr-ing). The creation of a bowl-shaped depression around or in an oil well by the collapse of the earth's structure beneath the drilling unit or the eruption of oil, gas, water, or other material from the well. Midwestern Ins. Co. v Rapp (Okla) 296 P2d 770.

cravant (krā'vȧnt). Same as **craven.**

crave (krāv). To demand; to dun; to desire.

craven (krā'vn). Cowardly; a coward. A word employed in trial by battle which when uttered by either champion ended the combat with disgrace and defeat for him, and the punishment of infamy besides. See 3 Bl Comm 340.
See **recreant.**

cravent (krā'vėnt). Same as **craven.**

crave oyer. See **oyer.**

crazy. Insane or mentally deranged. Shaver v McCarthy, 110 Pa 339, 345; Thompson v State, 104 Tex Crim 637, 645, 285 SW 826, 830. A state of great enthusiasm for a person, a thing, or an idea; a thing or an idea that is fitting for a crazy person to have.

creamus (kre-ā'mus). We create.

Creamus, erigimus, fundamus, incorporamus (kre-a'mus ē-ri'ji-mus, fun-dā'mus, in-kor-po-rā'mus). We create, we erect, we found, we incorporate. See 1 Bl Comm 473.

creance (krē'ans). A collateral security; a pledge.

creancer (krē'ans-er). A creditor.

creansor. Same as **creancer.**

create. To bring into being; to cause to exist; to produce; to make, for example, a machine or a corporation. Bank of Commerce v Wiltsie, 153 Ind 460, 53 NE 950, 952.

creation. The act of producing or making. The universe and everything contained therein.

creature of reason. Man. State v Jones, 1 Miss (Walk) 83, 85.

credence. Belief in the statements of another.
See **letter of credence.**

credentials. Documents or evidences of a person's authority. Something which entitles a person to be believed. The letter of credence given to an ambassador or other foreign representative. 4 Am J2d Ambss § 2.

credere. See **del credere.**

credibility (kred-i-bil'ị-ti). Capacity for being believed or credited.

credible person. See **credibility; credible witness.**

credible witness. A competent witness who is worthy of belief. Hawes v Humphrey, 26 Mass (9 Pick) 481; Wilson v State, 27 Tex App 47, 10 SW 749.
See **competent witness.**

credit. Noun: The quality that attracts trust, particularly trust in one's disposition and capacity to pay. Dry Dock Bank v American Life Ins. & Trust Co. 3 NY 344, 356. The antonym of cash on delivery; the trust or confidence which is reposed by the seller in the buyer when the time of payment is extended without security. Parrish v American Ry. Employees' Pub. Corp. 83 Cal App 298, 256 P 590. An accounting term for what appears to be owing by one person to another upon an accounting between the two. Propper v Clark, 337 US 472, 93 L Ed 1480, 69 S Ct 1333, reh den 338 US 841, 94 L Ed 514, 70 S Ct 33. Most broadly defined as the obligation owing by the debtor to his creditor, including a promissory note. Davis v Mitchell, 34 Cal 81. But not a share of corporate stock. In some jurisdictions, for the purpose of garnishment, something belonging to the defendant but in the possession and under the control of the garnishee. 6 Am J2d Attach § 449.

As the term "credits" is defined by an Ohio tax statute, it means the excess of the sum of all legal claims and demands, whether for money or other valuable thing, or for labor or service due or to become due to the person liable to pay taxes thereon, over and above the sum of the legal bona fide debts owing by such person. Fayette County v People's & Drover's Bank, 47 Ohio St 503, 25 NE 697. The term "credit" also stands for the certification earned by a student upon the successful completion of a subject or course of study. Again, it represents a reward to a prisoner for good conduct, the ultimate effect of which may be the shortening of the time of his imprisonment. 41 Am J1st Pris & P § 44. Verb: To acknowledge a payment of or upon an obligation. To give credence to a statement.

See **letter of credit; tax credit.**

credit agency. See **commercial agency; mercantile agency.**

credit at bank. An arrangement or understanding with the bank upon which a check is drawn for the payment of such check. Berry v State, 153 Ga 169, 111 SE 669, 35 ALR 370.

crédit foncier (krā-dē′ fôn-syā′). An association which is engaged in lending money on real estate security.

credit insurance. A policy of insurance which protects the insured against loss resulting from the insolvency or inability of his customers to pay their accounts. Such policies usually provide that the insured shall bear an initial loss of an agreed upon amount before the insurer's liability shall attach. 29A Am J Rev ed Ins § 1367.

credit card. A card or plate issued by a department store to a person whose credit is acceptable to the merchant, to be used in making purchases at the store on credit, without further identification or investigation as to credit standing; a card or plate issued by an oil company for the purpose of enabling the holder to purchase gasoline, oil, and automobile accessories at stations of the company wherever the latter may be in the country or, under some cards, even abroad; a card or plate issued by a bank or guaranty company for the purpose of enabling the holder to obtain on credit hotel or motel accommodations, meals, and airline tickets at home, in this country, and even abroad. Anno: 158 ALR 762.

credit limit. See **margin of credit.**

creditor. An obligee, a person, natural or artificial, public or private, in whose favor an obligation exists by reason of which he is or may become entitled to the payment of money, at least if the obligation is one on a liquidated demand based upon an agreement. Henley v Myers, 76 Kan 723, 93 P 168; Lindstrom v Spicher, 53 ND 195, 205 NW 231, 41 ALR 968, 971. A general creditor, a secured creditor, a lien creditor, and any representative of creditors, including an assignee for the benefit of creditors, a trustee in bankruptcy, a receiver in equity, and an executor or administrator of an insolvent debtor's or assignor's estate. 15 Am J2d Com C § 7. As the term appears in an assignment for the benefit of creditors, "creditor" means one who has a definite demand against the assignor, or a cause of action capable of adjustment and liquidation at trial. 6 Am J2d Assign for Crs § 109. As the term appears in the Bankruptcy Act, unless inconsistent with the context, "creditor" includes anyone who owns a debt, demand or claim provable in bankruptcy, and may include his duly authorized agent, attorney, or proxy. 9 Am J2d Bankr § 389. Under the Uniform Fraudulent Conveyance Act, a creditor is a person having any claim, whether matured or unmatured, liquidated or unliquidated, absolute, fixed, or contingent. Uniform Fraudulent Conveyance Act § 1, applied in American Surety Co. v Conner, 251 NY 1, 166 NE 783, 65 ALR 244.

See **debtor and creditor relationship.**

creditor at large. Same as **general creditor.**

creditor-beneficiary. A third person designated to receive the benefit of performance by one of two contracting parties under the terms of the agreement with the other, who is to receive the benefit of performance because of a specific obligation owing to him by the promisee. Northern Nat. Bank v Northern Minnesota Nat. Bank, 244 Minn 202, 70 NW2d 118; Breaux v Banker (Tex Civ App) 107 SW2d 382.

creditor of decedent. A person to whom the decedent was indebted personally or a person who, by operation of law, becomes the legal owner of a claim against the decedent, as, for example, the administrator of a creditor. See 31 Am J2d Ex & Ad § 57.

See **claim against decedent's estate.**

creditors' bill. An action or suit brought by a creditor to enforce the payment of a debt out of property or an interest of his debtor which cannot be reached by ordinary legal process. 21 Am J2d Cred B § 1. The term is also used broadly to refer to certain other actions brought by creditors, such as a suit brought by the creditors of a decedent to obtain administration of his estate, a suit by junior lien creditors to secure a marshaling of a debtor's assets, and suits to set aside fraudulent conveyances.

See **marshaling assets; fraudulent conveyances.**

creditor's claim. See **claim.**

creditors in solido (so′li-dō). Joint creditors.

creditors' meeting. A meeting of creditors of a bankrupt required to activate the administration of an estate in bankruptcy. 9 Am J2d Bankr § 579. Also a meeting of the creditors of a debtor in the bankruptcy court for the purpose of obtaining an arrangement or reorganization which shall rehabilitate the business.

creditor's suit. See **creditors' bill.**

Creditorum appellatione non hi tantum accipiuntur qui pecuniam crediderunt, sed omnes quibus ex qualibet causa debetur (kre-di-tō′rum ap-pel-lā-she-ō′ne non hī tan′tum ak-si-pi-un′ter kwī pe-kū′ni-am kre-di-dē′runt, sed om′nēz quī′bus ex quā-li′bet kâ′za de-bē′ter). By the term "creditors" is understood not only those who have lent money, but all to whom a debt is owing from any cause.

credit plate. See **credit card.**

credit rating. An opinion as to the reliability of a person, natural or artificial, concerning ability and promptness in the payment of debts.

The opinion may be one merely of reputation in the community but is usually one given by a professional credit-rating agency.

credit report. A report made by a commercial or mercantile agency concerning the financial standing, credit, character, responsibility, and general reputation of a particular person, firm, or corporation engaged in business. 15 Am J2d Collect § 3.

credit-reporting agency. Another term for a commercial or mercantile agency.

credits. See **credit.**

credit standing. One's rating in respect of his trustworthiness and capacity to pay his bills as they become due.

See **credit rating.**

credit statement. A written and signed statement of assets, liabilities, and other personal information, given by a borrower to a bank or other money lending institution in obtaining a loan.

credit the drawer. Words which, when appearing on the face of a promissory note, signify that the note is for the maker's accommodation, and that the proceeds thereof are his, notwithstanding it is drawn payable to another. Merchants Nat. Bank v Raesly, 288 Pa 374, 136 A 238, 56 ALR 230. Written on the face of a promissory note, the words imply no promise or undertaking on the part of him who uses them, but are a direction to all persons to whom the note may be presented, to treat with the drawer as the owner, notwithstanding the apparent title of the indorsee. Temple v Baker, 125 Pa 634, 643, 17 A 517.

credit union. A corporation organized under special statutory provisions to promote thrift among, and provide credit for, its members. 13 Am J2d B & L Asso § 4. A cooperative association organized under the Federal Credit Union Act for the purpose of promoting thrift among its members and creating a source of credit for provident or productive purposes. 12 USC 1752.

Credit Union Act. An act of Congress providing for federal credit unions and the supervision thereof. 12 USC §§ 1751 et seq.

credo (krē'dō). I believe.

creed (krēd). A formal declaration of religious belief. The word has no reference, in its ordinary meaning, to benevolent, philanthropic, or fraternal organizations, secret or otherwise, even though of a moral character. Hammer v State, 173 Ind 199, 89 NE 850.

See **Apostles' Creed.**

creek (krēk). In its most common usage, a small river; occasionally it signifies a small bay, inlet, or cove. French v Carhart, 1 NY 96, 107. A small seacoast town having no customs office.

Creek (krēk). The name of an Indian tribe; a member of the Creek tribe.

See **five civilized tribes.**

cremation. The disposal of a dead body by burning it.

crematory. A place equipped and operated for the disposal of dead bodies by cremation.

creme de menthe. A liqueur, usually served after dinner.

crementum comitatus (kre-men'tum ko-mi-tā'tus). The increase of the county.

crepare oculum (kre-pā'rė ō-ku'lum). To put out an eye.

crepusculum (krẹ-pus'kụ-lum). (French.) Twilight, that is, the partial light of day which precedes sunrise and follows sunset.

Crescente malitia crescere debet et poena (kres-sen'tė ma-li'she-a kres'se-re de'bet et pē'na). Punishment ought to be increased as malice increases.

cressant. Growing.

cresser. To grow.

cretio (krē'she-o). The period immediately following the death of the ancestor during which the heir might decide whether to take or to reject his inheritance.

crew. The seamen manning a ship, including, for some purposes, the officers, even the master. 48 Am J1st Ship § 111. The word has a varying legal significance. In a general sense, it is equivalent to ship's company, which would embrace all of the officers as well as the common seamen. It is sometimes used to comprehend all persons composing the ship's company, including the master; sometimes to comprehend the officers and common seamen, excluding the master; and sometimes to comprehend the common seamen only. When, therefore, the word is used in a statute it is necessary to consider the context of the particular use of the term and the object to be accomplished by the enactment under consideration. South Chicago Coal & Dock Co. v Bassett, 303 US 251, 84 L Ed 732, 60 S Ct 544.

crew of aircraft. This term does not have an absolutely unvarying legal significance, but must always be considered in its context, whether used in connection with watercraft or aircraft. Le Breton v Penn Mut. Life Ins. Co. 223 La 984, 67 So 2d 565, 45 ALR2d 446. It may include the air crew assisting in the operation of the craft while in the air, and a landing or ground crew assisting in the handling of the plane on the ground; but the word has no unvarying significance and may consist of only one person. 8 Am J2d Avi § 33. The operator of an airport, complying with the request of the owner and operator of an airplane, stored on the former's grounds, when asked to assist the latter in pushing the plane from the hangar and in starting the plane by cranking the propeller, is a member of the crew within the coverage of an aviation accident policy. Miner v Western Casualty & Surety Co. 241 Iowa 530, 41 NW2d 557, 14 ALR2d 1358. As the term appears in an aviation exception clause of a life or accident insurance policy, the "crew" is not limited to persons who actually operate an airplane in flight, but is inclusive of attendants or stewards aboard a passenger plane in the regular course of their employment. 29A Am J Rev ed Ins § 1266. On the other hand, a provision of a life insurance policy excluding from full coverage an aircraft pilot, instructor, officer, or other member of the crew, appears from the context not to apply to all occupants notwithstanding permissible use of the term "crew" in its largest sense as a "company of people associated together." Le Breton v Penn Mut. Life Ins. Co. 223 La 984, 67 So 2d 565, 45 ALR2d 446.

crew of train. Conductor, engineer, fireman, flagmen, or brakemen.

See **Full Crew Law.**

cribler. To argue.

cribs. Buildings or parts of a barn used for the storage of grain, especially corn. Small rooms in a house. Pon v Wittman, 147 Cal 280, 284, 81 P 984.

cricket. A game played by teams of 11 men each, with a ball, bat, and wicket, popular in England and becoming more popular in the United States; fair play, good sportsmanship, and good conduct in general.

crie de pays (kri dē pè-i). Hue and cry.

crier. An auctioneer or a person employed by an auctioneer to make the outcry, at an auction sale, under his personal supervision and direction. 7 Am J2d Auct § 4. A person employed to announce sales of property at auction, such person going about the streets ringing a bell for the purpose of attracting attention, and then making proclamation of the

place where and of the kind of goods or property to be sold at auction. Rochester v Close (NY) 35 Hun 208, 210. Verb: To proclaim. (French.)

criez la peez. (French.) Rehearse the concord,—one of the formalities in the levying of a fine.

crim. con. (krim). An abbreviation of "criminal conversation," q. v.

crime. An offense against sovereignty; an act committed, or omitted, in violation of the public law which forbids or commands it. 21 Am J2d Crim L § 1. In some contexts, the term "crime" means any offense against the law, not excluding misdemeanors. 22 Am J2d Extrad § 21. On the other hand, the word is sometimes used in a more limited sense to embrace only the more serious offenses. 21 Am J2d Crim L § 1.
See **capital offense; continuing offense; convict; felony; misdemeanor; mala in se; mala prohibita; moral turpitude.**

crime against nature. Sodomy; sexual relations with a person of the same sex or with a beast; unnatural sexual relations between persons of the same sex. 48 Am J1st Sod § 1.

crime against spouse. For the purposes of rendering the wife competent as a witness, an offense amounting to personal violence, or a physical assault, upon an innocent spouse. 58 Am J1st Witn § 193.
See **uxoricide.**

crime involving moral turpitude. See **moral turpitude.**

crimen (krī'men). A crime.

crimen falsi. See **falsi crimen.**

Crimen falsi dicitur, cum quis illicitur, cui non fuerit ad haec data auctoritas, de sigillo regis rapto vel invento brevia, cartasve consignaverit (krī'men fal'sī di'si-ter, kum quis il-li'si-ter, kī non fu'e-rit ad hek dā'ta âk-tō'ri-tās, dē si-jil'lō rē'jis rap'tō vel in-ven'tō brē'vi-a, kar-tas've kon-sig-nā've-rit). The crime of falsifying applies to one to whom authority has not been given who has signed writs or charters with the king's seal, stolen or found.

crimen furti (krī'men fer'tī). Larceny. See **furti crimen.**

crimen incendii (krī'men in-sen'di-ī). See **incendi crimen.**

crimen laesae majestatis (krī'men lē'se ma-jes-tā'tis). The crime of injuring majesty,—high treason. See 4 Bl Comm 75.

Crimen laesae majestatis omnia alia crimina excedit quoad poenam (krī'men lē'se ma-jes-tā'tis om'ni-a a'li-a krī'mi-na ex-sē'dit quō'ad pē-nam). The punishment for high treason exceeds that for all other crimes.

crimen majestatis (krī'men ma-jes-tā'tis). Treason.

Crimen omnia ex se nata vitiat (krī'men om'ni-a ex sē nā'ta vi'she-at). Crime vitiates everything which springs from it. Parker v Hughes, 64 Kan 216, 67 P 537.

crimen raptus (krī'men rap'tus). Rape.

crimen roberiae (krī'men ro-be'ri-ē). Robbery.

Crimen trahit personam (krī'men tra'hit per-sō'nam). A crime draws the person with it. That is, if a criminal act has been committed within the territorial jurisdiction of the court, so that the court has jurisdiction of the crime, it follows that the court also has jurisdiction over the criminal. People v Adams (NY) 3 Denio 190.

crime of moral turpitude. See **moral turpitude.**

crime of omission. An offense in the form of failure to perform a required act, rather than the doing of a prohibited act. 21 Am J2d Crim L § 6.

crime of reputation. A crime predicated by statute on reputation, such as the offense of keeping, frequenting, or being an inmate of premises reputedly used for designated unlawful purposes. 21 Am J2d Crim L § 5.

crime of status. A crime, such as vagrancy, living in adultery, or living in fornication, predicated on a status, condition, or mode of life. 21 Am J2d Crim L § 5.

criminal (krim'i-nal). Adjective: Relating to or having the character of crime. People v Bradley, 60 Ill 390, 402. Noun: A person who has committed a crime, especially, if he is a recidivist or the crime is a serious or violent one. In the eyes of the law, a person is a criminal who has been adjudged guilty of a crime, and he continues to be a criminal so long as the judgment remains in force. Re Molineux, 177 NY 395, 69 NE 727.

criminal act. Any act which is punishable as a crime.

criminal action. An action by the sovereign, that is the state or the United States, or instituted on behalf of the sovereign, against one charged with the commission of a criminal act, for the enforcement of the penalty or punishment prescribed by law. 1 Am J2d Actions § 43.

criminal anarchy. The doctrine that organized government should be overthrown by force, violence, assassination of the executive head, or of other executives of the government, or by any unlawful means. 47 Am J1st Sedit etc. § 3.

criminal appeals. Appeals from judgments in criminal cases. 4 Am J2d A & E § 159.

criminal assault. An assault for which the assailant may be criminally prosecuted. 6 Am J2d Asslt & B § 8.
A statute which provides that whoever unlawfully attempts to strike, hit, touch, or do any violence to another, however small, in a wanton, wilful, angry, or insulting manner, having an intention and existing ability to do some violence to such person, is guilty of an assault, and that if such attempt is carried into effect, he is guilty of assault and battery, and upon conviction shall be subject to a penalty within maximum limits, and when the offense is of a high and aggravated nature, shall be subject to a greater penalty, is merely declaratory of the common law. Rell v State, 136 Me 322, 9 A2d 129, 125 ALR 602.

criminal attempt. See **attempt.**

criminal bail. Bail given in a criminal case. See **bail.**

criminal business. For the purposes of a venue statute, the term "criminal business" means the criminal matters occupying the attention and labor of men engaged in legal affairs, coming into being or notice in any county. Sherman v Droubay, 27 Utah 47, 74 P 348.

criminal capacity. The capacity to commit a crime, that is, legal mental capacity, whereunder responsibility for the commission of an act prohibited by law and susceptibility to punishment provided by law attaches to the wrongdoer. 21 Am J2d Crim L § 26. Substantial capacity either to appreciate the criminality of one's act and to conform to the re-

quirements of the law. American Law Institute's Model Penal Code.
See **right and wrong test.**

criminal case. The prosecution of a person for a criminal offense. Re Carter, 166 Mo 604, 57 LRA 654, 655, 66 SW 540. Criminal cases are those which refer to public wrongs and their punishment, as distinguished from civil cases and suits which refer to the legal means by which rights and remedies of private individuals are enforced or protected. State ex rel. Kochtitzky v Riley, 203 Mo 175, 101 SW 567.

criminal charge. An affidavit, complaint, indictment, or information which accuses the defendant or accused with the commission of a specified crime or offense and states the crime or offense in sufficient particulars to advise the defendant or accused of the acts or omissions for which he is being brought into court; a count in an indictment or information charging two or more crimes or offense. The popular understanding of the term "criminal charge" is "accusation," and it is freely so used in conversation and in the newspapers, but in legal phraseology it is properly limited to such accusations as have taken shape in a prosecution. In the eye of the law, a person is charged with crime only when he is called upon in a legal proceeding to answer to such a charge. United States v Patterson, 150 US 65, 68, 37 L Ed 999, 1000, 14 S Ct 20.

criminal conspiracy. See **conspiracy.**

criminal contempt. Some authorities are critical of the use of this expression, saying that it is as redundant as "criminal crime." It can be said with some assurance, however, that where the primary purpose of a contempt proceeding is to preserve the court's authority and to punish for disobedience of its orders, the contempt is criminal. 17 Am J2d Contpt § 4. A charge of procuring false testimony in a civil action is a charge of criminal contempt, as distinguished from civil contempt. Osborne v Purdome (Mo) 244 SW2d 1005, 29 ALR2d 1141. Courts have power to punish such contempts and, in such instance, the proceeding is punitive and the punishment operates in terrorem, and by that means has a tendency to prevent the repetition of the offense. State v Shepherd, 177 Mo 205, 76 SW 79.

Criminal contempts are "offenses against the United States" within the meaning of the Constitutional provision which gives to the President power to grant pardons for offenses against the United States. Ex parte Grossman, 267 US 87, 69 L Ed 527, 45 S Ct 332.

criminal conversation. The tortious invasion of the rights of husband and wife which occurs when a third person has adulterous intercourse with one of them and for which the innocent and offended spouse has a cause of action against the adulterer. At common law no action lay on behalf of a wife for the seduction of her husband, but statute has changed this rule in the great majority of American jurisdictions. 27 Am J1st H & W § 535.

criminal court. A court having jurisdiction of prosecutions for crimes. A juvenile court specially created by a statute providing for the disposition to be made of delinquent children is not a criminal court. 31 Am J Rev ed Juv Ct § 5.

Criminal Extradition Act. One of the uniform laws.

criminal homicide (hom'i-sīd). The unlawful taking by one human being of the life of another in such a manner that he dies within a year and a day from the time of the giving of the mortal wound. If committed with malice, express or implied by law, it is murder; if without malice, it is manslaughter. No personal injury, however grave, which does not destroy life, will constitute either of these crimes. The injury must continue to affect the body of the victim until his death. If it ceases to operate, and death ensues from another cause, no murder or manslaughter has been committed. Commonwealth v Macloon, 101 Mass 1.
See **manslaughter; murder.**

criminal information. See **information.**

criminal insanity. A want of mental capacity and moral freedom to do or abstain from doing a particular act. State v Schafer, 156 Wash 240, 286 P 833.
See **insanity; right and wrong test.**

criminal intent. A state of mind which operates jointly with an act or omission in the commission of a crime; a guilty or evil intent in performing an act prohibited by law and penalized as a crime. 21 Am J2d Crim L § 81.
See **mens rea.**

criminaliter (kri-mi-nā'li-ter). Criminally.

criminal law. That branch of jurisprudence which teaches of the nature, extent and degree of every crime and adjusts to it its adequate and necessary penalty. United States v Reisinger, 128 US 398, 32 L Ed 480, 9 S Ct 99.

criminal letters. A prosecution for crime by a procedure similar to that followed in a prosecution by information.

criminal liability. The penalty or forfeiture imposed as punishment for crime.

criminal libel. A libel punishable as a crime. 32 Am J1st L & S § 308.
See **libel.**

criminally intimate. See **intimate.**

criminal negligence. Negligence which is proscribed by law and for which punishment is provided as constituting a crime. 38 Am J1st Negl § 9.
See **negligent homicide.**

criminal offense. A crime by force of statute or the common law, whether a felony or misdemeanor, and including, according to some, but not all the authorities, the violation of a municipal ordinance. 5 Am J2d Crim L § 38.

As the term is used in statutes permitting the introduction of evidence of his commission of a criminal offense to affect the credibility of a witness, the term is usually held to include both felonies and misdemeanors, but not to include the violation of a municipal ordinance. Koch v State, 126 Wis 470, 106 NW 531.

Under a constitutional provision for the prosecution of all criminal offenses by presentment or indictment of a grand jury, acts of a militiaman which merely constituted a violation of the military code do not amount to a criminal offense. State ex rel. Madigan v Wagener, 74 Minn 518, 77 NW 424.

criminal procedure. Court practice connected with criminal prosecutions.

criminal proceeding. A proceeding in court in the prosecution of a person charged or to be charged with the commission of a crime, contemplating the conviction and punishment of the person charged or to be charged. State ex rel. Sweezer v Green, 360

Mo 1249, 232 SW2d 897, 24 ALR2d 340. A proceeding against a juvenile offender is in no sense a criminal proceeding, where it does not contemplate punishment for an offense, but prevention of an erring minor from becoming a criminal. State v Freeman, 81 Mont 132, 262 P 168, 171.
See **criminal prosecution.**

criminal process. Process which issues to compel a person to answer for a crime or misdemeanor. Mowlan v State, 197 Ind 517, 520, 151 NE 416, 417.

criminal prosecution. The use of the processes of the law to accuse or charge a person with the commission of a crime, to bring him before a court, to convict him of the offense, and to impose upon him such punishment as is provided by law for the offense. Although sometimes instituted by an individual, a criminal prosecution is not in any sense an action between the person instituting it and the prisoner. Anno: 46 ALR 463. A preliminary investigation is not a criminal prosecution within the Sixth Amendment to the Federal Constitution. Anno: 93 L Ed 992.

criminal registration act. A statute or municipal ordinance which requires a person previously convicted of crime to register with a designated official. Anno: 82 ALR2d 398.

criminal responsibility. See **criminal capacity.**

criminal statute. A statute providing that an act or omission described therein shall constitute a criminal offense. Langenberg v Decker, 131 Ind 471, 31 NE 190. Statutes creating courts having jurisdiction of juvenile offenders, are not intended to provide punishment, but to save the child from becoming a criminal, and are in no sense criminal statutes. 31 Am J Rev ed Juv Ct § 5.

criminal syndicalism. Any doctrine or precept advocating, teaching, or aiding and abetting the commission of crime, sabotage, or unlawful acts of force and violence or unlawful methods of terrorism, as a means of accomplishing a change in industrial ownership or control, or effecting any political change. 47 Am J1st Sedit etc. § 3.

Crimina morte extinguuntur (kri'mi-na mor'te ex-tin-gu-un'ter). Crimes are extinguished by death.

criminate (krim'i-nāt). To incriminate; to involve a person in the commission of a crime; to give evidence against a defendant in a criminal prosecution against him.

crimp (krimp). To kidnap or decoy a person aboard a ship for service as a sailor; a person who crimps.

criterion. A sole or controlling test; as a criterion of value. Kennebec Water Dist. v Waterville, 97 Me 185, 54 A 6.

criticism. A discussion, or, as applicable in libel cases, a censure, of the conduct or character, or utterances of the person criticized. Belknap v Ball, 83 Mich 583, 47 NW 674.
See **fair comment.**

cro. A compensation paid to one person for causing the death of another.

croft (krôft). A small farm.

croise. A crusader.

Cromwell. See **interregnum.**

crop. Noun: A product of the soil, anything produced from the earth by planting, cultivation and labor; either a gathered or a growing crop. 21 Am J2d Crops § 1; goods within the definition of the Uniform Commercial Code. UCC § 2—105(1).

The term "crop" has been defined as including fruit grown on trees, although the trees themselves are not included in that term. Story v Christin, 14 Cal 2d 592, 95 P2d 925, 125 ALR 1402. Even grass used for pasturage, not for hay or seed crop, is a crop. Superior Oil Co. v Griffin (Okla) 357 P2d 897, 87 ALR2d 224. Verb: To cut off; to reap.
See **away-going crops.**

crop dusting. See **dusting.**

crop insurance. A policy covering growing crops against loss from the elements, particularly hail; insurance on agricultural commodities against loss due to unavoidable causes, such as flood, hail, wind, hurricane, plant disease, etc., but not extending beyond the period that the insured crop is in the field, except in the case of tobacco. 7 USC § 1508(a).

Crop Insurance Act. A federal statute to promote the national welfare by improving the economic stability of agriculture through a sound system of crop insurance and providing the means for the research and experience helpful in devising and establishing such insurance. 7 USC § 1502; Anno: 175 ALR 1081.

Crop Insurance Corporation. A corporation created in carrying out the purposes of the Federal Crop Insurance Act, with capital stocks subscribed by the United States, the management vested in a board of directors, and having power to insure agricultural commodities against loss due to unavoidable causes, including drought, flood, hail, wind, tornado, insect infestation, plant disease, and such other unavoidable causes as may be determined by the board of directors of the corporation, but except, for tobacco, not extending beyond the period that the insured crop is in the field. 7 USC § 1508(a).

crop lien of landlord. See **landlord's lien.**

crop mortgage. A chattel mortgage upon growing crops or upon crops to be planted. 15 Am J2d Chat Mtg §§ 30, 31.

cropper. See **sharecropper.**

cropper's contract. Technically, the contract between an owner and a cropper or sharecropper, under which the latter agrees to farm the land and receive for his services a share of the grown crops, creating a relationship different from that of the conventional relationship of landlord and tenant. The term, loosely used, has been applied to a contract or lease of a farm, for rent payable in a share of the crops raised on the premises, which does create the relationship of landlord and tenant. 32 Am J1st L & T § 468.
See **sharecropper.**

crop rent. Rent payable in a share of the crops raised on the demised premises. 32 Am J1st L & T § 468.

crops. See **crop.**

croppy. An old word applied to a person punished for treason by having his ears cut off.

crop spray. See **spraying crops.**

crop-time. The period of the year during which the ground is prepared for a crop, the crop planted, and the ground cultivated, such period terminating when the crop, having reached the stage of maturity when no further work is required to produce it, is in the terminology of farmers, "laid by." Martin v Chapman (Ala) 6 Port 344, 351.

cross. The symbol of the Christian Faith; the mark which a voter uses in expressing his choice of a candidate whose name appears upon a written ballot, any kind of a cross being sufficient for this purpose, the only requirement being that two lines cross one another at a common center. Winn v Blackman, 229 Ill 198, 82 NE 215.

crossaction. An action under a cross complaint or cross bill; an independent action brought by a defendant in an action against the plaintiff or another defendant therein.

crossappeal. An appeal filed by the appellee or defendant in error as an incident of review proceedings instituted by the opposing party. 4 Am J2d A & E § 177.

cross-assignment of error. A procedure by which an appellee obtains a review of errors prejudicial to him, without filing a separate or cross appeal. 5 Am J2d A & E § 653.

cross bill. A bill of complaint by a defendant against a complainant, against a codefendant or codefendants, or against both a complainant and codefendant, upon a subject appearing in the complainant's bill. The pleading by cross bill is auxiliary to the original suit and dependent thereon, and the result of filing or serving a cross bill is that from this juncture and the suit comprises two interrelated and consolidated actions. 19 Am J2d Eq § 211.

crossclaim. See **crossdemand.**

cross complaint. A pleading by the defendant in an action wherein he seeks affirmative relief, relating to or depending upon the transaction on which the action is based or affecting property to which it relates, against the plaintiff or any other party to the action. 41 Am J1st Pl § 256.

crossdemand. A cause of action in favor of the defendant against the plaintiff, whether on contract or tort, and pleadable whether the plaintiff's cause of action pleaded be on contract or tort. Musselman v Galligher, 32 Iowa 383, 389.

See **counterclaim; recoupment; reconvention; setoff.**

cross easements. Reciprocal easements created by contract, the one being granted in favor of premises of one party in consideration of a grant by such party in favor of premises of the other party.

crossed check. A name given to a system long recognized as valid in England whereby there is stamped across a check the name of a certain banker through whom it must be presented for payment, and if presented by anyone else, payment must be refused. Farmers' Bank v Johnson, 134 Ga 486, 68 SE 85.

crosserrors. See **cross-assignment of error.**

cross-examination. The most effective art of the skilled trial lawyer; the interrogation of a witness for the opposing party by questions framed to test the accuracy and truthfulness of his testimony on direct examination and to bring out the truth of the matter in issue; an absolute right in actions and proceedings. 58 Am J1st Witn §§ 609 et seq.

crossing. The act of going over something, e. g., the Atlantic Ocean or the State of Iowa; a way for a pedestrian across a street or highway; the intersection of two ways.

See **farm crossing; grade crossing; intersection; railroad crossing.**

crossing courses. The established rule in the second circuit of the Federal courts that in a crossing situation the privileged vessel may "cross" the signal of the burdened vessel and hold her course and speed until it becomes evident that the burdened vessel either cannot or will not keep out of the way. The Eastern Glade (CA2 NY) 101 F2d 4.

See **course of vessel; burdened vessel; privileged vessel.**

crossing sign. A sign erected and maintained by a railroad company to warn travelers on the highway that they are approaching a railroad crossing. 44 Am J1st RR § 399.

cross-interrogatories. Interrogatories propounded in the cross-examination of a deponent.

cross libel. The pleading in admiralty whereby a defendant or respondent seeks an affirmative recovery. 2 Am J2d Adm § 182.

crossover. A way between the two parts of a divided highway where a motorist may reverse directions by crossing from the one part to the other. 7 Am J2d Auto § 218.

See **open primary.**

cross-question. To cross-examine.
See **cross-examination.**

cross remainders. Remainders limited after particular estates to two or more persons in several parcels of land, or in several undivided shares in the same parcel of land, in such way that on the determination of the particular estates in any of the several parcels or undivided shares, they remain over to the other grantees, and the reversioner or ulterior remainderman is not let in till the determination of all the particular estates. 33 Am J1st Life Est § 82. The ulterior estates are called cross remainders because each of the grantees has reciprocally a remainder in the share of the other.

cross rules. Rules nisi entered on behalf of both the plaintiff and the defendant.
See **rule nisi.**

cross the fall. A term used in stevedoring, meaning that one layer of the rope on the drum would be put across and on top of another so that the strain would jamb it against the drum, making the winch more safe to operate. It is customary to cross the fall, without regard to how the end of the rope is secured to the drum. Glover v Compagnie Generale Transatlantique (CA5 Tex) 103 F2d 557.

cross trade. The offsetting by a broker of the orders of one customer to purchase with the orders of another customer to sell. 12 Am J2d Brok § 127.

cross trusts. Reciprocal trusts between husband and wife or close members of the same family. 28 Am J Rev ed Inher T § 118.

crown. A term for the ruler or sovereign under a monarchial form of government, absolute or limited.

crown cases (kroun). English criminal cases.

crown cases reserved. Criminal cases reserved for the opinion of all the judges of the court on questions of law.
See **court for crown cases reserved.**

crown colony. A colony under the sole control of the crown, as distinguished from one having a government of its own.

crown debt. A debt owing to the crown.

crown demise. See **demise of the crown**.

crowner (krou'nėr). Same as **coroner**.

crowner's quest. A coroner's inquest.

crown grant. The grant by letters patent from the sovereign of rights or property which the sovereign held as proprietor and not including any right or property which the sovereign held as sovereign. Lewis Blue Point Oyster Cultivation Co. v Briggs, 198 NY 287, 91 NE 846.

crown lands (kroun' lands). Lands which belong to the sovereign.

crown law (kroun lâ). The common law applicable to crimes.

crown lawyer (kroun lâ'yėr). A criminal lawyer; a lawyer who defends criminal prosecutions.

crown office. A department of the court of king's bench which had jurisdiction of all criminal cases. On the crown side, or crown office, the king's bench court took cognizance of all criminal cases, from high treason down to the most trivial misdemeanor or breach of the peace. See 4 Bl Comm 265.

crown side (kroun sīd). See **crown office**.

crown solicitor. An English court officer who prepares the case for the prosecution of a crime.

cruce signati (krūs sig-nā'ti). Signed with the cross.

crude. The word usually means raw or unfinished, and is applied to products other than those which have been manufactured. Nortmann-Duffke Co. v Federal Crushed Stone Co. 167 Minn 333, 334, 209 NW 17, 18.

crude oil. The product of an oil well in the form in which it comes from the well.
An interesting and instructive dissertation on natural gasolene, straight-run gasolene, wet gas, natural gas, dry gas, and their relation to crude petroleum is to be found in Phillips Pipe Line Co. v United States, 94 Ct Cl 462, 40 F Supp 981.

crude petroleum. See **crude oil**.

cruel and inhuman treatment. A ground for divorce. See **cruelty**; **inhuman treatment**.

cruel and unusual punishment. Excessive, inhuman, or barbarous penalties. 21 Am J2d Crim L § 611.
As the words "unusual punishment" are used in the United States constitution, they include that class of punishments which never existed in the state, and any punishment which if ever employed at all, has become altogether obsolete. But they do not include fine or imprisonment. Hobbs v State, 133 Ind 404, 32 NE 1019.

cruel treatment. See **cruel and inhuman treatment**; **cruel and unusual punishment**; **cruelty**; **cruelty to animals**.

cruelty. The infliction of physical or mental pain or distress.
As a ground for divorce, "cruelty" means physical violence intentionally inflicted, threats of physical violence, or wilfully causing mental distress, which renders it impossible for the complaining party to continue in the marital relation. Mere austerity of temper, petulance of manners, rudeness of language, want of civil attention and accommodation, even occasional sallies of passion, if they do not threaten bodily harm, do not amount to cruelty which constitutes a ground for divorce. 24 Am J2d Div & S § 37. But as a ground for divorce, cruel and inhuman treatment may consist wholly of abusive and insulting words. Ekerson v Ekerson, 121 Or 405, 255 P 480.

cruelty to animals. Every act, omission, or neglect whereby unjustifiable pain or suffering, and, under some statutes, death, is caused an animal. 4 Am J2d Ani § 28.
See **fox hunt**; **pigeon shooting**; **societies for the prevention of cruelty**; **spaying**.

cruise. A naval expedition in search of ships of an enemy; the voyage of a commercial vessel.

cruising. In addition to the usual meaning of a ship under way, the term applies to a taxi driver seeking passengers by driving around the streets and police vehicles covering territory assigned to them.

cry. To make oral and public proclamation; to notify or advertise by outcry, especially things lost or found, goods to be sold; public advertisement by outcry, as by hawkers of their wares. Rochester v Close (NY) 35 Hun 208, 210. To weep; to sound the voice in pain or sorrow.
See **hue and cry**.

cry de pays or cry de pais. Same as **hue and cry**.

cryer (krī'ėr). Same as **crier**.

crypt (kript). A vault or chamber which is either wholly or partly beneath the surface of the earth and set apart for the interment of a dead body. 14 Am J2d Cem § 1.

ct. An abbreviation of "cent" or "cents."

c. t. a. An abbreviation of "cum testamento annexo," that is, with the will annexed.

cts. An abbreviation of "cents."

cucking-stool (kuk'ing-stöl). A contrivance, also called the trebucket or castigatory, formerly provided in England for the "correction" of common scolds. The word was said to have come from the Saxon language in which it signified a scolding stool. It was finally corrupted into "ducking" stool, because part of the punishment consisted in plunging the scold into water while fastened in the stool or chair. See 4 Bl Comm 168.
See **common scold**.

cuckold (kuk'ōld). A husband whose wife is unfaithful; the husband of an adulteress. To make a cuckold of a man is to seduce his wife. Hall v Huffman, 159 Ky 72, 73, 166 SW 770.

cui ante divortium (kī an'te di-vor'she-um). Whom before the divorce;—a writ of entry which a woman who was divorced had to recover lands which belonged to her and which her husband had aliened during their marriage. See 3 Bl Comm 183, note.
See **entry cui ante divortium**.

cui bono (kī bō'nō). For whose benefit or welfare.

Cuicunque aliquis quid concedit concedere videtur et id, sine quo res ipsa esse non potuit (kī-kun'kwē ā'li-quis quid kon-sē'-dit kon-sē'de-re vi-dē'ter et id, sī'ne quō rēz' ip'sa es'se non po'tu-it). One who grants something to another is held to grant also that without which the thing is worthless. See Broom's Legal Maxims 479.

cui in vita (kī in vī'ta). Whom in his lifetime;—a writ of entry which a widow had to recover lands which belonged to her and which had been aliened by her husband during his lifetime. See 3 Bl Comm 183, note.

cui in vita sua, vel cui ante divortium, ipsa contradicere non potuit (kī in vī'ta su'a, vel kī an'te di-vor'she-um, ip'sa kon'tra-di'se-re non po'tu-it). Whom she herself could not, in his lifetime nor before a divorce, contradict. See 3 Bl Comm 183, note.

Cui ipsa ante divortium contradicere non potuit (kī ip'sa an'te di-vor'she-um kon-tra-di'se-re non po'-tu-it). Whom before the divorce she could not deny. See **cui ante divortium.**

Cui jurisdictio data est, ea quoque concessa esse videntur sine quibus jurisdictio explicari non potest (kī jū-ris-dik'she-ō dā'ta est, ē'a kwō'kwe kon-ses'sa es'se vi-den'ter sī'ne quī'bus jū-ris-dik'she-ō ex-pli-kā'rī non po'test). Those things without which jurisdiction could not be exercised are held to be given to him to whom jurisdiction has been granted.

Cui jus est donandi, eidem et vendendi et concedendi jus est (kī jūs est dō-nan'dī, ē-ī'dem et ven-den'dī et kon-sē-den'dī jūs est). One who has a right to give has also a right to sell and to grant.

Cuilibet in arte sua perito est credendum (kī'li-bet in ar'te su'a pe-rī'tō est krē-den'dum). Any expert in his own art is credible therein.

Cuilibet in sua arte credendum est (kī'li-bet in su'a ar'te kre-den'dum est). Each man is to be believed or credited in reference to his own art or profession. See 1 Bl Comm 75.

Cuilibet licet juri pro se introducto renunciare (kī'li-bet lī'set jū'rī prō sē in-trō-duk'tō re-nun-she-ā're). One may waive a legal right existing in his favor.

Cui licet quod majus non debet quod minus est non licere (kī lī'set quod mā'jus non de'bet quod mi'nus est non lī-se're). One who has a greater power ought not to be denied a less one. See Broom's Legal Maxims 176.

Cui pater est populus non habet ille patrem (kī pā'ter est pō'pu-lus non hā'bet il'le pa'trem). One whose father is "the people," has no father.

Cuique enim in proprio fundo quamlibet feram quoque modo venari permissum (kī'kwe e'nim in prō'pri-ō fun'dō quam'li-bet fe'ram quō'kwe mō'dō ve-nā'rī per-mis'sum). For it is permissible to everyone to hunt any wild animals upon his own estate in whatever manner. See 2 Bl Comm 415.

Cuique in sua arte credendum est (ki'kwe in su'a ar'te krē-den'dum est). Anyone is entitled to credence in matters pertaining to his own craft. Winans v New York & E. R. Co. (US) 21 How 88, 16 L Ed 68.

Cujus est commodum ejus debet esse incommodum (kū'jus est kom'mo-dum ē'jus de'bet es'se in-kom'-mo-dum). One who enjoys a benefit should take the burden with it.

Cujus est commodum, ejus est onus (kū'jus est kom'-mo-dum, ē'jus est o'nus). He who enjoys the benefit must carry the burden. Oliver v Newburyport Ins. Co. 3 Mass 53.

Cujus est dare, ejus est disponere (kū'jus est da're, ē'jus est dis-pō'ne-re). He who has the gift of anything has the right to dispose of it. The law's protection of a spendthrift trust rests upon the principle of the maxim. It allows the donor to condition his bounty as he will, so long as he violates no law in so doing. Re Morgan, 223 Pa 228, 72 A 498.

Cujus est divisio, alterius est electio (kū'jus est di-vi'zhe-ō, al-tē'ri-us est ē-lek'she-ō). She who makes the division has the last choice. This was one of the common law rules in the partition of an estate held in coparcenary. See Bl Comm 189.

Cujus est dominium ejus est periculum (kū'jus est do-mi'ni-um ē'jus est pe-ri'ku-lum). He who has the ownership should have the risk.

Cujus est instituere ejus est abrogare (kū'jus est in-sti-tu'e-re ē'jus est ab-rō-gā're). Whoever may institute may abrogate. See Broom's Legal Maxims 878, note.

Cujus est solum ejus est usque ad coelum (kū'jus est so'lum ē'jus est us'kwē ad sē'lum). The owner of the soil owns to the sky. It has been held that this maxim is not strictly and absolutely applicable to all of the relations of the proprietors of adjoining lands. To apply it strictly in all cases would be to infringe upon that other maxim of the common law, "Sic utere tuo ut alienum non laedas." Stillwater Water Co. v Farmer, 89 Minn 58, 93 NW 907.

Cujus est solum, ejus est usque ad coelum et ad inferos (kū'jus est so'lum, ē'jus est us'kwe ad sē'lum et ad in'fe-rōs). The owner of the soil owns to the heavens and also to the lowest depths.

Cujus est solum, ejus est usque ad inferos (kū'jus est so'lum, ē'jus est us'kwē ad in'fe-ros). The owner of the soil owns to the lowest depths. This maxim of the common law is said to furnish a rule of easy application and to save a world of judicial worry in many cases, and one which is perhaps always applicable in England and in the eastern states of the Union, but it is one which would work great injustice if applied to percolating waters in the arid districts of the west where much irrigating water is pumped from wells. Katz v Walkinshaw, 141 Cal 116, 70 P 663, 74 P 766.

Cujus juris est principale, ejusdem juris erit accessorium (kū'jus jū'ris est prin-si-pā'le, ē-jus'dem ju'-ris e'rit ak-ses-sō'ri-um). He who has jurisdiction of the principal thing has jurisdiction of the accessory also.

Cujus per errorem dati repetitio est, ejus consulto dati, donatio est (kū'jus per er-rō'rem dā'tī re-pe-ti'she-ō est, ē'jus kon-sul'tō dā'tī, dō-nā'she-ō est). He who gives a thing by mistake may recover it, but if he gives deliberately, the gift is complete.

Cujusque rei potissima pars principium est (kū-jus'kwe rē'ī po-tis'si-ma parz prin-si'pi-um est). The most important part of anything is the first part of it.

cul (kul). Guilty; probably a contraction of "culpable."

cul de sac (kül' dė sak'). A way, street or alley open only at one end.

culpa (kul'pa). Guilt; fault; negligence.
See **diligentia; lata culpa.**

culpabilis (kul-pā'bi-lis). Guilty.

culpable (kul'pa̱-bl). Criminal; censurable.
Where the term is applied to the omission of a person to preserve the means of enforcing his own rights, "censurable" is more nearly an equivalent. Waltham Bank v Wright, 90 Mass (8 Allen) 121, 122.

culpable neglect. The neglect which exists where the loss or damage can fairly be ascribed to carelessness, improvidence or folly. Waltham Bank v Wright, 90 Mass (8 Allen) 121, 122. Under ordinary circumstances, the failure of the creditor to discover the death of his debtor is "culpable neglect" as a matter of law. Mulligan v Hilton, 305 Mass 5, 24 NE2d 676, 133 ALR 376.

culpable negligence. A term sometimes defined in a manner similar to definitions of ordinary negligence, it being said that "culpable negligence" is the omission to do something which a reasonable, prudent and honest man would do, or doing something which such a man would not do under all the circumstances surrounding each particular case. State v Emery, 78 Mo 77; Kent v State, 8 Okla Crim 188, 126 P 1040. Other authorities consider "culpable negligence" as something beyond ordinary negligence, defining it as the conscious and wanton disregard of the probabilities of fatal consequences to others as the result of the wilful creation of an unreasonable risk thereof; or a wanton disregard of, or indifference to, the safety of human life. Smith v State, 197 Miss 802, 20 So2d 701, 161 ALR 1. The term, as used in workmen's compensation acts excepting employees guilty of such negligence from the right to compensation, does not have the same meaning as the word "blamable," but means practically the same as "wilful and serious misconduct" which in turn means improper conduct of a grave and aggravated character, either intentional misconduct, or misconduct of such a character as to evince a reckless disregard of consequences to the one who is guilty of it. Fuhs v Swenson, 58 Wyo 393, 131 P2d 333; 58 Am J1st Workm Comp § 200. In most of the jurisdictions the term, as used in a manslaughter statute, has been construed as meaning negligence of a higher degree than ordinary negligence which suffices as a basis for liability in a civil action. However, in a few jurisdictions the term has been construed as denoting merely ordinary negligence when used in such a statute. Anno: 161 ALR 10.

See **negligent homicide**.

Culpa caret, qui scit sed prohibere non potest (kul′pa ka′ret, quī sit sed prō-hi-bē′re non po′test). (Civil law.) One who knows (the danger), but is unable to avert it, is without fault.

Culpae poena par esto (kul′pē pē′na par es′tō). Let the punishment fit the crime.

Culpa est immiscere se rei ad se non pertinenti (kul′pa est im-mis′se-re sē rē′ī ad sē non per-ti-nen′tī). A person is at fault who intermeddles in things which do not concern him.

Culpa lata dolo aequiparatur (kul′pa lā′ta do′lō ē-qui-pa-rā′ter). Gross negligence is equivalent to malice.

culpa levissima. See **ex culpa levissima.**

Culpa tenet suos auctores (kul′pa te′net su′ōs âk-tō′rēz). Guilt binds only its own originators.

Culpa tenet suos auctores tantum (kul′pa te′net su′ōs âk-tō′rez tan′tum). Guilt binds its own originators most.

cul. prit. (kul prit). See **culprit.**

culprit (kul′prit). A person brought into court as accused of crime. A formal word announced by the clerk of assize or clerk of arraigns as a replication viva voce on behalf of the king when a prisoner had pleaded not guilty, thus replying to this plea in the two syllables "cul" and "prit," the first one signifying "culpable," that is that the prisoner was guilty and the second, "prit" (derived from the Latin "paratus"), that the king was ready to prove him guilty. See 4 Bl Comm 339.

cultivate. To cultivate means to till, or husband the ground; to forward the product of the earth, by general industry. State v Allen, 35 NC (13 Ired L) 36, 37. To prepare land for grazing only is not to "cultivate" it within the meaning of the homestead law. United States v Niemeyer (DC Ark) 94 F 147.

cultivation. See **cultivate; fit for cultivation.**

culvert. An enclosed drain for carrying water under a road or railroad. Oursler v Baltimore & Ohio Railroad Co. 60 Md 358, 367.

culvertage (kul′vėr-tāj). A person's forfeiture of his status as a freeman.

cum (kum). With; together with. The word is also used for the word "quum," meaning "when"; "whereas."

Cum actio fuerit mere criminalis, institui poterit ab initio criminaliter vel civiliter (kum ak′she-ō fu′e-rit me′re kri-mi-nā′lis, in-sti′shu-ī po′te-rit ab in-ī′she-ō kri-mi-nā′li-ter vel si-vi′li-ter). When an action is merely criminal, it can be instituted either criminally or civilly at the beginning.

Cum adsunt testimonia rerum, quid opus est verbis? (kum ad′sunt tes-ti-mo′ni-a rē-rum, quid o′pus est ver′bis?). When there is evidence of the facts, what need is there of words?

Cum aliquis renunciaverit societati, solvitur societas (kum a′li-quis re-nun-she-ā′ve-rit so-si-e-tā′tī, sol′-vi-ter so-si′e-tās). When any one of the partners shall have renounced the partnership, it is dissolved.

cumbersome property. See **bulky property.**

cum causa. See **habeas corpus cum causa.**

cum certum est an et quantum debeatur (kum ser′-tum est an et quan′tum de-be-ā′ter). When it is certain whether (anything is due) and how much is due. Roberts v Prior, 20 Ga 561, 562.

Cum confitente sponte mitius est agendum (kum kon-fi-ten′te spon′te mi′she-us est ā-jen′dum). When a person makes a voluntary confession, he should be treated the more gently.

Cum de lucro duorum quaeritur melior est causa possidentis (kum dē lu′krō du-ō′rum kwē′ri-ter me′li-or est kâ′za pos-si-den′tis). (Civil law.) When two persons are striving over gain, the cause of the one in possession of it is the better.

Cum duo inter se repugnantia reperiuntur in testamento, ultimum ratum est (kum du′o in′ter sē re-pug-nan′she-a re-pe-ri-un′ter in tes-ta-men′tō, ul′ti-mum ra′tum est). When two repugnant matters are found in a will, the latter one will be confirmed. Jackson ex dem. Livingston v Robins (NY) 16 Johns 537, 547.

Cum duo jura concurrunt in una persona aequum est ac si essent in duobus (kum du′o jū′ra kon-kur′runt in ū′na per-sō′na e′qu-um est ak sī es′sent in du-ō′bus). When two rights come together in one person, it is the same as if they were in two persons.

cum grano salis (kum grā′nō sā′lis). With a grain of salt; that is, with reservations.

Cum in corpore dissentitur, apparet nullam esse acceptionem (kum in kor′po-re dis-sen′ti-ter, ap-pā′ret nul′lam es′se ak-sep-she-ō′nem). When there is a disagreement as to the substance of the thing, it appears that there is no acceptance. The maxim is one of the civil law, but holds good in the modern law of sales. Gardner v Lane, 94 Mass (12 Allen) 39, 44.

Cum in testamento ambigue aut etiam perperam scriptum, est benigne interpretari, et secundum id quod credibile est cogitatum credendum est (kum in tes-ta-men'tō am-bi'gu-ē ât e'she-am per'pe-ram skrip'tum, est be-nĭg'nē in-ter-pre-tā'rī, et se-kun'-dum id quod kre-di'bi-le est kō-ji-tā'tum krē-den'-dum est). When an ambiguous, or even an incorrectly written, clause is found in a will, it should be interpreted liberally and according to what is believed to be the intention (of the testator). Broom's Legal Maxims 568.

Cum legitimae nuptiae factae sunt patrem liberi sequuntur (kum lē-ji'ti-mē nup'she-ē fak'tē sunt pa'trem lĭ'be-rī se-kwu-un'ter). The children of lawful wedlock inherit from their father.

Cum lex abrogatur, illud ipsum abrogatur, quo non eam abrogari oporteat (kum lex ab-rō-gā'ter, il'lud ip'sum ab-rō-gā'ter, kwo non eam ab-rō-ga'ri ō-por'te-at). When a law is repealed the very part is repealed by which it is sought to prevent its repeal. See 1 Bl Comm 91.

Cummins Amendments. Amendments to the Interstate Commerce Act respecting a carrier's limitation of liability. 14 Am J2d Car § 539.

cum onere (kum ō'ne-re). With the burden; that is, with whatever disadvantages or incumbrances that may be connected with the enjoyment of the right. See Dugan v Bridge Co. 27 Pa 303.

Cum par delictum est duorum, semper oneratur petitor, et melior habetur possessoris causa (kum par dē-lik'tum est du-ō'rum, sem'per ō-ne-rā'ter pe'ti-tor, et me'li-or hā-bē'ter po-ze-sō'ris kâ'za). (Civil law.) When two parties are equally at fault, the claimant always has the burden, and the one in possession has the better cause.

cum pertinentiis (kum per-ti-nen'she-is). With the appurtenances. Morgan v Mason, 20 Ohio 401.

cum potestate regis et legis (kum po-tes-tā'te rē'jis et lē'jis). By the power of the king and the law.

Cum quod ago non valet ut ago, valeat quantum valere potest (kum quod ā'gō non va'let ut ā'go, va'le-at quan'tum va-lē're po'test). When what I do is void as I do it, it shall be as effective as it can (otherwise) be made.

cum quolibet et qualibet eorum (kum quō'li-bet et quā'li-bet ē-ō'rum). Taken in one sense or another.

cum testamento annexo (kum tes-ta-men'tō an-neks'ō). With the will annexed.
See **administration cum testamento annexo; administrator cum testamento annexo; administrator de bonis non cum testamento annexo.**

cumulative (kū'mū-lạ-tiv). Adding to or added to something else; by way of increase.

cumulative bequest. Same as **cumulative legacy.**

cumulative dividends. Dividends on preferred stock which accumulate under contract, charter, or bylaw provision, where a dividend or dividends are passed because of want of the requisite net earnings to permit the payment of a dividend, and which must be paid before any dividend whatever for any later year is paid to common stockholders or to preferred stockholders of a class not entitled to cumulation of dividends. See 19 Am J2d Corp § 878 et seq.

cumulative errors. Errors of the lower court, of such minor consequence that no single one is a ground for reversal in itself, operating in cumulation as such ground only as prejudice therefrom accumulates. 5 Am J2d A & E § 789.

cumulative evidence. Additional evidence of the same kind to the same point. 39 Am J1st New Tr § 173.
See **corroborating evidence.**

cumulative judgment. A second judgment to take effect after the expiration of the first one.
See **consecutive sentences.**

cumulative legacy. A legacy in addition to another legacy to the same person in the same will. Where the same beneficiary is given two monetary legacies of the same amount in different clauses of the same will, the presumption is that the testator intended the later bequest to be substitutional rather than cumulative, and the legatee is accordingly entitled to take only it. 57 Am J1st Wills § 1164.

cumulative offense. An offense which can be committed only by a repetition of acts of the same kind, which acts may be on different days. An apt illustration is the offense of being a common gambler. 24 Am J1st Gaming § 46.

cumulative penalties. Successive or continuing penalties for delay in payment of claims, or performance of a contract, or violation of statute. 36 Am J2d Forf & P §§ 55, 65.
See **cumulative punishment.**

cumulative punishment. The greater punishment imposed on an habitual or second offender; consecutive sentences rather than concurrent sentences.
See **habitual criminals; consecutive sentences.**

cumulative remedy. A new or further remedy in addition to a remedy or remedies already existing. Chicago & Northwestern Railway Co. v Chicago, 148 Ill 141, 35 NE 881, 886. An administrative remedy in addition to a judicial remedy. 2 Am J2d Admin L §§ 784, 785.

cumulative sentences. Sentences for different crimes to run consecutively.
See **consecutive sentences.**

cumulative voting. A system of voting at an election whereby an elector entitled to vote for several candidates for the same office may cast more than one vote for the same candidate, distributing among the candidates, as he chooses, a number of votes equal to the number of persons to be elected. 26 Am J2d Elect § 274. In corporate elections, the method of voting for corporate directors whereby each shareholder is entitled to cast a number of votes equal to the number of his shares multiplied by the number of directors, or the number of directors to be elected, with the option of giving all his votes to a single candidate or of distributing them among two or more as he sees fit. Wolfson v Avery, 6 Ill 2d 78, 126 NE2d 701. The right of cumulative voting in electing directors is, by its nature, exercisable only where more than one director is to be elected. Bridgers v Staton, 150 NC 216, 63 SE 892.

cuneator (ku'nẹ-ā-tọr). The custodian of the dies of a mint.

cunnilingus. An act committed with the mouth and female sex organ or an oral-genital contact.

cur. (kėr). An abbreviation of **curia.**

cura (kū'ra). Care; custody; charge; diligence.

cura animorum (kū'ra a-ni-mō'rum). The care of souls.

curacy. See **perpetual curacy.**

cur. ad. vult. An abbreviation of **curia advisare vult.**

curagulos (ku-rā'gu-los). A caretaker.

curate (kū'rāt). An assistant to the rector of a parish or to a vicar. A curate is the lowest degree in the church, being in the same state that a vicar was formerly, an officiating temporary minister, instead of the proper incumbent. See 1 Bl Comm 393.

curatio (ku-rā'she-ō). A guardian.

curative act. A form of retrospective legislation reaching back on past events to correct errors or irregularities and to render valid and effective attempted acts which otherwise would be ineffective for the purpose the parties intended, particularly irregularities in conveyancing; operating to complete a transaction which the parties intended to accomplish but carried out imperfectly. 16 Am J2d Const L § 430. A validation by statute of an imperfect or irregular deed. 23 Am J2d Deeds § 141.

curative medicine. A substance or preparation administered internally for the cure, removal, or healing of some disease or condition demanding medical treatment. State v Stoddard, 215 Iowa 534, 245 NW 273, 86 ALR 616.
See **internal medicine.**

curator (kū-rā'tor). The person in charge of a museum, art gallery, or library. A guardian. The guardian, at common law, performs the office of both the tutor and the "curator" of the Roman civil law, the former of whom had charge of the maintenance and education of the minor, and the latter the care of his fortune. Mercer v Watson (Pa) 1 Watts 330, 348.

curator ad hoc (ku-rā'tor ad hōk). (Civil law.) A curator appointed by the court to act for a minor in the absence of his under-tutor, or subrogated tutor, as he was formerly called. Welch v Baxter, 45 La Ann 1062, 1064, 13 So 629.

curator ad litem (ku-rā'tor ad lī'tem). Same as **guardian ad litem.**

curator bonis (ku-rā'tor bo'nis). The guardian of an estate.

curatores viarum (ku-rā-tō'rēz vī-ā'rum). Keepers of ways. Under the Roman law, curatores viarum were officers whose duty it was to superintend the making and mending of the roads. See 1 Bl Comm 357, footnote.

curatorship (kū-rā'tor-ship). A guardianship.

curatrix (kū-rā'triks). A female guardian.

curatus non habet titulum (ku-rā'tus non hā'bet ti'tulum). A curate has no title.

curb. Verb: To restrain. Noun: A strap attached to each end of the bit of a horse's bridle and passing around the half circle of his lower jaw. The raised edge of the pavement of a street or highway, next to sidewalk, shoulder of highway, or park strip. A term sometimes applied to the park strip itself.

curb market. An exchange wherein the transactions in stocks, bonds, or commodities are completed in whole or in part upon the street. A market in securities not listed on an exchange.

curb service. Selling merchandise, lunches, cigarettes, cigars, etc. to persons on the street in vehicles.
The use of the public streets by a person, firm or corporation engaged in business in any store, temporary or permanent stand or box, building, structure or the like, for the sale or solicitation of goods, wares or merchandise. People v Dmytro, 280 Mich 82, 273 NW 400, 111 ALR 128.

curb teller. A booth erected on the sidewalk in front of a bank close enough to the paved portion of the street to permit a customer to transact his business with a bank employee in the booth, without alighting from his automobile. Adams v Merchants & Planters Bank & Trust Co. 226 Ark 88, 288 SW2d 35.

cure by judgment, verdict, or findings. Error rendered harmless by subsequent proceedings in the case, as where the party against whom error was committed prevails by the verdict. 5 Am J2d A & E § 792. A verdict for a party will cure defects in his pleading where the substantial rights of the adverse party are not affected. 5 Am J2d A & E § 795.

cure of souls (kūr of sōls). The pastoral charge of a parish.

curfew (kėr'fū). A fixed point of time in the evening, after which persons not having duties to perform on the streets, particularly children, shall not be abroad. A restriction established by order against all persons of Japanese ancestry residing in the West Coast Military Area during the war between the United States and Japan. 56 Am J1st War § 29.
In England during the Middle Ages, the ringing of a bell at eight o'clock each night, in every city and town, as a signal that all company must disperse, and all fires and lights must be extinguished. These curfew regulations were established by the Normans following the Conquest. 4 Bl Comm 419.

curia (kū'ri-ạ). A court.

curia admiralitatis (kū'ri-a ad-mi-rā-li-tā'tis). A court of admiralty.

curia advisare vult (kū'ri-a ad-vi-sā're vult). The court wishes to consider. Judgments are not required to be entered immediately, and it is common in all courts to delay for the purpose of examination and advisement. Clark v Read, 5 NJL 571, 573.

curia baronis (kū'ri-a ba-rō'nis). A court-baron.

Curia cancellariae est officina justitiae (kū'-ri-a kan-sel-lā'ri-ē est of-fi-sī'na jūs-ti'she-e). The court of chancery is the workshop of justice.

curia claudenda (kū'ri-a klâ-den'da). An old English writ requiring a landowner to fence his land.

curia comitatus (kū'ri-a ko-mi-tā'tus). The county court.

curia consentiente. See **et curia consentiente.**

curia domini (kū'ri-a do'mi-nī). The lord's court.

curiae Christianitatis (kū'ri-a kris-che-a-ni-tā'tis). Courts Christian. The courts of the archbishops and bishops and their derivative officers. See 1 Bl Comm 83.

curiality (kū-ri-al'ị-ti). Same as **curtesy.**

curia magna (kū'ri-a mag'na). The great court, the English Parliament.

curia majoris (kū'ri-a mā-jō'ris). The mayor's court.

curia palatii (kū'ri-a pa-lā'she-ī). The palace court.

Curia parliamenti suis propriis legibus subsistit (kū'-ri-a par-li-a-men'ti su'is prō'pri-is lē'ji-bus sub-sis'-tit). Parliament is governed by its own laws.

curia pedis pulverizati (kū'ri-a pe'dis pul-ve-ri-zā'ti). The court of dusty foot; that is the court of piepoudre. It was instituted to administer justice at fairs and markets and was a court of record. See 3 Bl Comm 32.

curia regis (kū'ri-a rē'jis). The king's court.

curing error. Affidavits explaining discrepancies appearing in an abstract of title. Attebery v Blair, 244 Ill 363, 91 NE 475. Supplying an acknowledgment or correcting a defective acknowledgment. 1 Am J2d Ack § 107. Developments in a case which eliminate the prejudicial effect of an error by the court.
See **cure by judgment, verdict, or findings.**

Curiosa et captiosa interpretatio in lege reprobatur (ku-ri-ō'sa et kap-she-ō'sa in-ter-pre-tā'she-ō in lē'je re-pro-bā'ter). A curious and captious interpretation is disapproved in the law.

currency. Paper money which passes at par as a circulating medium in the business community; money, whether in coin or paper. 36 Am J1st Money § 8.

Currens test. A test of insanity which will constitute a defense in a criminal prosecution, requiring no more than that the jury must be satisfied that at the time of committing the prohibited act, the accused, as a result of mental disease or defect, lacked substantial capacity to conform his conduct to the requirements of the law which he is alleged to have violated. United States v Currens (CA3 Pa) 290 F2d 751.

current. Noun: The flow of a stream; the flow or rate of flow of an electric force. Adjective: Running, moving, flowing, passing; passing from one to another, especially widely circulated; publicly known; general; prevalent, as, the current ideas of the day; now passing; present in its course: as, the current month of the year. Shaffer v George, 64 Colo 47, 171 P 881; State v Bartley, 39 Neb 353, 360.

current account. An open account, a running account. Anno: 51 ALR2d 334. An account based upon running or concurrent dealing between the parties which has not been closed, settled, or stated, and which is kept unclosed with the expectation of further transactions. 1 Am J2d Acctg § 4.

current bank notes or bills. Bank notes or bills which pass as currency at their par value.

current coin. Coin which is in general circulation.

current coin of the realm. Money; legal tender. 52 Am J1st Ten § 2.

current cost rate. See **step rate method.**

current earnings. Present earnings; earnings of a corporation for the period during which a dividend normally is paid.

current funds. Money circulating without discount; whatever is receivable and current by law as money, whether in the form of notes or coins. 36 Am J1st Money § 8.
See **currency.**

current income. For income tax purposes, income for the current tax year. See Supplee v Magruder (DC Md) 36 F Supp 722.

current maintenance. The expense incurred in keeping a physical property in the condition required for continued use during the service life. Lindenheimer v Illinois Bell Tel. Co. 292 US 151, 78 L Ed 1182, 54 S Ct 658.

current market price. A commercial term, familiar in contracts for the sale of goods, meaning that the contract price shall run or flow with the market, following its fluctuations. Ford v Norton, 32 NM 518, 260 P 411, 55 ALR 261.

current money. Money which is in general circulation; currency.

See **currency.**

current salary. See **current wages.**

current wages. The present rate of wages for specific work or employment. Compensation for services continuing for some time and payable periodically as it accrues for a wage period, that is, a week, two weeks, or a month, or by the day as the work is performed. First Nat. Bank v Graham (Tex Crim App) 22 SW 1101.

The term "current wages" has the same meaning as current salary, and where wages are payable monthly, the term refers to wages for the current or present month. See Bell v Indian Live Stock Co. (Tex) 11 SW 344.
See **current yearly pay.**

current year. Ordinarily, the calendar year in progress. Sometimes construed, as in an exemption statute, as meaning from harvest to harvest, and not a calendar year. 31 Am J2d Exemp § 114.

current yearly pay. As used in a statute respecting the compensation of army officers, the term "current yearly pay" means the regular, ordinary pay which an officer may be entitled to for a year's service under the facts of his case. United States v Mills, 196 US 223, 49 L Ed 732, 25 S Ct 434.

currere (kur're-re). To run.

Currit quatuor pedibus (kur'rit qua'tu-or pe'di-bus). It runs on four feet. That is, it is on all fours, in precise accord.

Currit tempus contra desides et sui juris contemptores (kur'rit tem'pus kon'trā dē'si-dēz et su'ī jū'ris kon-temp-tō'rēz). Time runs against the slothful and those who ignore their rights.

cursing (kėr'sing). Profane swearing, sometimes a criminal offense. 12 Am J2d Blas § 10. A public or common nuisance where the profane words are uttered in a public place. 12 Am J2d Blas § 11.

cursitor (kėr'si-tor). A chancery clerk.

cursitor baron (ker'si-tor baron). An officer who had authority to administer oaths.

Cursus curiae est lex curiae (ker'sus kū'ri-ē est lex kū'ri-ē). The practice of the court is the law of the court.

curtesy. The common-law right of a husband in his wife's property which arises from the marriage. An estate by the curtesy is either curtesy initiate or curtesy consummate. 25 Am J2d Dow § 2.
See **curtesy consummate; curtesy initiate.**

curtesy consummate. A common law estate for life of a surviving husband in all of the lands of his wife, subject to the same conditions requisite to the existence of curtesy initiate and the additional condition of the death of the wife.

In other words, an estate by the curtesy initiate becomes an estate by the curtesy consummate upon the death of the wife. 25 Am J2d Dow § 2.

curtesy initiate. At common law, a life estate of the husband in the real property of which his wife is seised of an estate of inheritance during the duration of the marriage, the conditions under which such an estate arises being the marriage, seisin by the wife, and birth of issue capable of inheriting. 25 Am J2d Dow § 2.

As soon as a child was born, the father began to have a permanent interest in those lands of his wife in which she was seised of an estate of inheritance; he became one of the vassals of the lord's court, did homage to the lord, and was called tenant by the

curtesy initiate; and this estate being once vested in him by the birth of the child, was not suffered to determine by the subsequent death or coming of age of the child. See 2 Bl Comm 127.

curtilage (kėr'ti-lāj). The open space situated within a common enclosure belonging to a dwelling house. Anno: 38 ALR2d 848; 13 Am J2d Burgl § 5. Such space as is necessary and convenient, and is habitually used, for family purposes, and the carrying on of domestic employments, including a yard, a garden, or even a nearby field used in connection with the dwelling. 5 Am J2d Arson § 1. For the purpose of determining the existence of a right of self defense, the "curtilage" of the home will ordinarily be construed to include at least the yard around the dwelling house, as well as the area occupied by barns, cribs, and other outbuildings. State v Frizzelle, 243 NC 49, 89 SE2d 725, 52 ALR2d 1455.

curtillum (ker-til'lum). Same as **curtilage**.

curtis (ker'tis). A court; a yard; a curtilage. Blackstone refers to the word as a sample of law-Latin which "may raise a smile in the student as a flaming modern Anglicism." See 3 Bl Comm 320.

custa (kus'ta). Costs.

custagium (kus-ta'ji-um). Costs.

custantia (kus-tan'she-a). Costs.

custode admittendo. See **de custode admittendo.**

custode amovendo. See **de custode amovendo.**

custodes (kus-tō'dēz). Custodians; keepers; guardians; wardens.

custodes pacis (kus-tō'dēz pa'sis). Guardians of the peace;—conservators of the peace;—peculiar officers who anciently were appointed by the common law for the maintenance of the public peace. See 1 Bl Comm 349.

custodia (kus-tō'di-ạ). Also called ward, or guard,— one of the two chief duties of constables. It was a duty performed mainly in the daytime and looked chiefly to the apprehension of rioters and highway robbers. See 1 Bl Comm 356.
See **arca et salva custodia.**

custodia comitatus (kus-tō'di-a ko-mi-tā'tus). The custody of the county. This was committed to the sheriff by the king's letters patent. See 1 Bl Comm 339.

custodia legis (kus-tō'di-a lē'jis). The custody of the law. Gilman v Williams, 7 Wis 329, 334.
See **custody of the law.**

custodiam comitatus (kus-tō'di-am ko-mi-tā'tus). The custody of the county. See 1 Bl Comm 339.

custodian (kus-tō'di-ạn). A person whose duty it is to watch, guard, and account for that which is committed to his custody. State v Taylor, 7 SD 533, 544, 64 NW 548.

custodia terrae et haeredis. See **de custodia terrae et haeredis.**

custody. As applied to property, "custody" means control or care, not possession; the mere putting of one's property in the custody of another does not divest the possession of the owner. 42 Am J1st Prop § 42; 32 Am J1st Larc § 56. As applied to a person, "custody" means physical control of the person, sometimes by his imprisonment. For the purpose of habeas corpus:—such restraint of a person by another that the latter can produce the body of the former at a hearing as directed by writ or order. Palmer v State, 170 Ala 102, 54 So 271.

There is no such thing as custody of a person physically at large. State v Freauff, 117 Or 214, 243 P 87.
See **in custody.**

custody of child. The control, care, and maintenance of a child, whether at one's own expense or under an award, providing compensation to be paid by another.
See **guardianship; ward of the court.**

custody of the law. A lawful seizure and holding of property by an officer of the law acting pursuant to a lawful writ or process. Buck v Colbath (US) 3 Wall 334, 18 L Ed 257; 46 Am J1st Replev § 37. The custody of a depository of property delivered to it pursuant to an order of court, subject to the further order of the court. Bradley v Roe, 282 NY 525, 27 NE2d 35, 129 ALR 633.

custom. A practice which has by its universality and antiquity acquired the force and effect of law in a particular place or country, in respect of the subject matter to which it relates. 21 Am J2d Cust & U § 1.

customarily. Usually, habitually, according to the customs, general practice or usual order of things, regularly. Fuller Brush Co. v Industrial Com. 99 Utah 97, 104 P 201, 129 ALR 511.

customary acre. As much land as an ox team could plow in a day.

customary court. A court held within the manor by the lord or his steward.

customary court-baron. A customary court which appertained entirely to copyholders and in which their estates were transferred by surrender and admittance, and other matters transacted relative to their tenures only. See 3 Bl Comm 33.

customary despatch. As employed in a charter party requiring the loading of the ship with customary despatch, the words do not relate to the average or usual conditions surrounding such a loading, but they are to be read and understood in relation to the circumstances, ordinary or extraordinary which existed at the time when the loading was done. Parrish v Lederer (DC Del) 14 F2d 985.

customary estates. Lands of certain copyholders of free and privileged tenure, which were derived from the ancient tenants in villein-socage who did not hold at the will of the lord, but only according to the custom of the manor. The law did not regard the freehold of such lands as resting in the lord of whom the tenants held, but in the tenants themselves, who were sometimes called customary freeholders, being allowed to have a freehold interest, though not a freehold tenure. See 2 Bl Comm 149.

customary freehold. A tenancy by copyhold, not at the will of the lord of the manor. See 2 Bl Comm 149.

customary freeholders. See **customary estates.**

customary home occupation. An occupation carried on in a dwelling house by an occupant thereof without assistance other than such as may be rendered by other members of the family who are occupants of the same dwelling. Anno: 73 ALR2d 442.

customary interest. The rate of interest which is general and usual by custom, at a given time, in a given place. Fowler v Smith, 2 Cal 568, 570.
See **legal interest.**

customary rent. The amount payable according to old custom.

customary services. Definite and certain services due from the tenant according to the custom of the manor. See 2 Bl Comm 147.

customary tenants. Tenants holding customary estates. See **customary estates**.

customer. In common usage, a person who buys the merchandise or engages the services of another person. In some contexts, the term has the more extensive connotation of a person who comes to the place of business of another for any purpose of concern to the latter, such as a person who comes to perform mechanical services for the proprietor. Anno: 33 ALR 181; 43 ALR 866; 46 ALR 1111.

The term "customers of a stockbroker," as defined by the Bankruptcy Act, includes persons who have claims on account of securities received, acquired, or held by the stockbroker from or for the account of such persons (a) for safekeeping, or (b) with a view to sale, or (c) to cover consummated sales, or (d) pursuant to purchases, or (e) as collateral security, or (f) by way of loans or securities by such persons to the stockbroker, and it also includes persons who have claims against the stockbroker arising out of sales or conversions of such securities. Bankruptcy Act § 60(e) (1); 11 USC § 96(e)(1).

One obtaining jewelry from a jeweler on the pretext of showing it to certain persons for their approval with a view to a purchase by them is not a "customer" within an exception in a theft insurance policy of a loss by customers of goods intrusted to them by the insured. 29A Am J Rev ed Ins § 1333.

See **able customer**; **cash customer**; **invitee**.

customer's man. An agent or representative of a brokerage firm with limited authority, his primary duty being to solicit and take orders from customers. 12 Am J2d Brok § 117.

Custome serra prise stricte. A custom or usage should be strictly interpreted.

custom-house (kus′tum-hous). An office where customs duties are paid and where clearance is given to ships.

custom-house bushel. See **bushel**.

custom of London. The rule that where a married woman follows any craft in the city of London on her sole account, the husband having nothing to do with her trade, she shall be charged as a feme sole concerning everything that touches the craft. 27 Am J1st H & W § 464.

custom of merchants. The customary practices of merchants in respect to mercantile contracts; the law merchant. Adams v Pittsburgh Insurance Co. 95 Pa 348.

See **law merchant**.

custom of officers. The rule for construction of the statute in line with administrative interpretation. 28 Am J Rev ed Inher T § 54.

custom of York. The rule of descent peculiar to the province of York, whereby the estate of an intestate was divided into thirds, one third to the widow, one to the children and one to the administrator. See 2 Bl Comm 518.

customs. The custom-house; the duties payable on imports.

See **collector of customs**; **custom**; **customs duties**.

Customs and Patent Appeals. See **Court of Customs and Patent Appeals**.

customs appraiser. A revenue officer whose duty it is to examine and estimate the true value of imported goods subject to customs duties. 21 Am J2d Cust D § 86.

customs broker. A person to whom goods coming from abroad are consigned for the purpose of having him obtain clearance.

customs broker's lien. The lien of a customs broker for an advance made to procure the release of goods from the customs house for a customer. 12 Am J2d Brok § 241.

Customs Court. A federal court sitting at the port of New York with jurisdiction for review of decisions and findings of any collector of customs. 21 Am J2d Cust D §§ 96, 97.

customs districts. Collection districts established by dividing the United States for convenience in collecting customs duties and the administration of the customs laws. 21 Am J2d Cust D § 60.

customs duties. The tariff payable on imported merchandise; the levy or tax applied by the government on the importation of commodities into the country. 21 Am J2d Cust D § 1. Not merely a duty on the act of importation, but a duty on the thing imported; not confined to a duty levied while the article is entering the country, but extending to a duty levied after it has entered the country. Brown v Maryland (US) 12 Wheat 419, 6 L Ed 678.

customs entry. See **entry**.

customs inspection. See **inspection by customs**.

customs lien. The lien of the government for unpaid duties which attaches to imported articles from the moment of their importation. 21 Am J2d Cust D § 104.

customs officers. The collectors and other officers engaged in the collection of customs duties. 21 Am J2d Cust D § 64.

customs of London. A term applied to the many particular customs or usages within the city of London, with regard to trade, apprentices, widows, orphans, and a variety of other matters. All these are contrary to the general law of the land, and are good only by special usage, although they are also confirmed by act of parliament. See 1 Bl Comm 75.

customs territory of the United States. The states, the District of Columbia, and Puerto Rico. 19 USC § 120.

customs waters. A term of application particularly to a foreign vessel subject to a treaty or other arrangement between the nation of registry and the United States, signifying the waters within such distance of the coast of the United States as the customs authorities are enabled or permitted by such treaty or arrangement to board and examine the vessel. 21 Am J2d Cust D § 2.

custos (kus′tos). A custodian; a keeper; a guardian; a warden.

custos brevium (kus′tōs brē′vi-um). The clerk of the old English court of common pleas.

custos ferarum (kus′tōs fe-rā′rum). A game warden.

custos horrei regii (kus′tōs ho′re-ī rē′ji-ī). The guard of cats at the royal granary. See 2 Bl Comm 394.

custos morum (kus′tōs mō′rum). The guardian of morals. The court of king's bench is frequently thus described. See 4 Bl Comm 310.

custos placitorum coronae (kus'tōs pla-si-tō'rum ko-rō'ne). The keeper of pleas of the crown;—the keeper of the criminal records.

custos rotulorum (kus'tōs ro-tu-lō'rum). The keeper of the rolls or records of the county, who was the principal justice of the peace. See 1 Bl Comm 349. He was nominated by the king's sign manual and was the principal civil officer in the county. See 4 Id 272.

custos sigilli (kus'tōs si-jil'lī). The keeper of the seal.

custos spiritualium (kus'tōs spi-ri-tu-ā'li-um). An ecclesiastical officer who was appointed to officiate during the vacancy of a see.

Custos statum haeredis in custodia existentis meliorem non deteriorem, facere potest (kus'tōs stā'tum hē-rē'dis in kus-tō'di-a eg-zis-ten'tis me-li-ō'rem non de-te-ri-ō'rem, fā'se-re po'test). A guardian can make the estate of an heir which is in his custody better, but not worse.

custos temporalium (kus'tōs tem-po-rā'li-um). An ecclesiastical officer who was appointed to officiate in temporal matters during the vacancy of a see.

custos terrae (kus'tōs ter'rē). A warden or keeper of the land.

custum (kus'tum). Cost.

custuma (kus'tu-ma). The law-Latin word for customs for duties. This word has no connection with the word "customs," meaning usages, which was derived from the Latin word "consuetudo." See 1 Bl Comm 314.

custuma antiqua sive magna (kus'tu-ma an-tī'qua sī've mag'na). Ancient or great customs. These were the duties on wool, sheep-skins, or woolfells, or leather, exported, and were payable by all merchants, both native and strangers; but the aliens paid as duties half as much again as the native merchants. See 1 Bl Comm 314.

custuma parva et nova (kus'tu-ma par'va et nō'va). Small and new customs. These were an impost of three pence per pound due from alien merchants only, for all commodities exported or imported and were usually called the "alien's duty." See 1 Bl Comm 314.

cut. Noun: A wound with an instrument having an edge. State v Patza, 3 La Ann 512, 514. A lowering of the surface of the ground at one point to bring a highway or railroad line to a level. Verb: To sever with an edged instrument; to divide money or property, especially the loot of a crime; to reduce the strength of a substance by adding something, e. g. water to alcohol.

cuth. Customary.

cutoff date. The end of the period within which certain action may be taken, e.g. the period during which the holder of securities issued by a corporation presently undergoing reorganization in a proceeding in a court of bankruptcy may surrender such securities in exchange for securities of the reorganized corporation. Anno: 41 ALR2d 1008.

cutoff drainage. The drainage of seepy hillsides by tiles placed along the hillside to intercept the seep water and prevent its reaching the bottom land. United States v Warmsprings Irrig. Dist. (DC Or) 38 F Supp 239.

cut out. See **muffler.**

cutpurse. A thief who cut purses in order to secure their contents; hence, a pickpocket.

cutting back. The operation in driving a motor vehicle wherein the driver, after passing another vehicle, turns back onto the right hand side. 7 Am J2d Auto § 221.

cutting corners. A violation of a statute or ordinance requiring vehicles turning at street intersections to keep to the right of the center of the intersection. 8 Am J2d Auto § 802.

cutting out. Dividing a herd of cattle into separate herds according to the individual ownership of the animals; dividing a herd of cattle according to animals ready for market and animals requiring further growth or feeding to make them marketable most advantageously.

cwt. An abbreviation of "hundredweight."

cy-apres (sē-a-prê). (French.) Hereafter.

cyclone. A rotary storm or whirlwind of extended circuit. Queen Ins. Co. v Hudnut Co. 8 Ind App 22, 26, 35 NE 397. An atmospheric disturbance one of the characteristics of which is a circular or gyratory motion, evidenced by a twisting effect; sometimes becoming a tornado. Maryland Casualty Co. v Finch (CA8 Minn) 147 F 388. A risk insured against under a form of property insurance. 29A Am J1st Ins § 1329.
See **hurricane; tornado; windstorm.**

cyclotron. An instrumentality of the atomic age, a unique device for giving extremely high energy to particles known as protons and deuterons, causing them to move with increasing energy in a spiral path until they collide with an arranged target.

cy-devant (ci-dĕ-vān). (French.) Heretofore.

cy gist (sē jist). Here lies.

cynebote (kü'ne bot). Same as **kinebot.**

cyphonism (sī'fō-nizm). An ancient form of punishment by smearing the body of the person with honey and exposing him to the attacks of insects.

cy pres (sē prā'). As near as practicable; so near. The doctrine which permits a gift for a charitable purpose to be applied as nearly as may be to the fulfilment of the underlying charitable intent, where, for one reason or another, it cannot be carried out as directed by the donor. 15 Am J2d Char § 131.

cyrce (kir'ke). A church.

cyricbryce (kirk-brī-ke). Breaking into a church; church-breaking.

cyrographata. See **charta cyrographata.**

cyrographum (si-rō'gra-fum). Same as **chirograph.**

cystoma (sis'tō-mä). A disease common to both sexes, involving calcium formations in the bladder. Anno: 23 ALR2d 1023.

cystoscopic examination (sis'tō-skop'ik eg-zam-i-nā'shon). An examination of the bladder made with a cystoscope; sometimes sought to be had as part of an involuntary physical examination. 23 Am J2d Dep § 216.

D

D. Roman numeral for 500.

D. A. Abbreviation for district attorney.

d'accroisement. See **droit d'accroisement.**

dacion (dah-the-ón). (Spanish.) A delivery made in accordance with the terms of a contract.

dacker (dak'ėr). A dispute.

dacoity (da-koi'ti). (India.) A robbery committed by a band composed of five or more persons.

dactylography (dak-ti-log'graf-ē). The scientific study of fingerprints as a means of identification. State v Steffens, 210 Iowa 196, 230 NW 536, 78 ALR 748; State v Kuhl, 42 Nev 185, 175 P 190, 36 ALR 1694.

daemon. See **voluntarius daemon.**

dagger. A straight knife; a weapon for stabbing; a generic term covering the dirk, stiletto, and poniard. People v Ruiz, 88 Cal App 502, 263 P 836.

dagger-money. Payments of money which were made to the justices of assize on the northern circuit of England as a defense fund against robbers.

daily (dā'li). On every day; each day.

daily balance. An expression of moment in reference to an interest-bearing bank account, meaning the balance standing in favor of the depositor at the close of business on any day of the interest period, an average being taken of the daily balances for the period in computing the amount upon which interest is to be paid.

daily newspaper. A newspaper published customarily on every day of the week except one, for instance, Sunday or Monday; a newspaper published every day in the week except both Sunday and Monday. 39 Am J1st Newsp § 4.

d'ainesse. See **droit d'ainesse.**

daker (dā'kėr). Same as **dacker.**

dam. A structure, composed of wood, earth, or other material, erected in and usually extending across the entire channel of a stream at right angles to the thread of the stream, and intended to retard or retain the flow of water. Morton v Oregon Short Line Railway Co. 48 Or 444, 87 P 151; the female parent of an equine.

damage. The loss, hurt or harm which results from the injury consequent upon the illegal invasion of a legal right. 22 Am J2d Damg § 1.

Although the words, "damage," "damages," and "injury," are sometimes treated loosely as synonyms, there is a material distinction between them. Injury is the illegal invasion of a legal right; damage is the loss, hurt, or harm which results from the injury; and damages are the recompense or compensation awarded for the damage suffered. 22 Am J2d Damg § 1.

damage by rust. See **rust.**

damage by the elements. Such injuries as result from the operation of the most common destructive forces of nature against which property needs to be protected, the clause being exclusive of direct human agency. Pope v Farmers Union & Milling Co. 130 Cal 139, 62 P 384; injuries resulting from sudden, unusual, or unexpected action, as distinguished from gradual changes and decay. O'Neal v Bainbridge, 94 Kan 518, 146 P 1165 (damage by fire); Kirby v Wilie, 108 Md 501, 70 A 213. Some authorities construe the term as sufficiently broad to include all damage caused by the action of nature, including damage by gradual decay. 32 Am J1st L & T § 795.

damage-cleer. A fee paid into court on the recovery of damages.

damaged. Injured; the equivalent of "taken" under most eminent domain statutes. 26 Am J2d Em D § 158. As applied to property, the word "damaged" imports some disturbance to its intrinsic value; some damage to the property considered as property, and it does not include damages consequential from a wrong done in taking away property and thus rendering its owner unable to realize the real value of property not taken or damaged. Price v United States, 174 US 373, 378, 43 L Ed 1011, 1014, 19 S Ct 765. The insertion of the word "damaged," or a similar word in a constitutional provision for compensation has generally been considered necessary to justify an award of damages for the obstruction or diversion of, or other interference with, surface water by a public improvement. But in some cases the word "taking" alone has been construed to require the payment of compensation for damages resulting from such obstruction or interference. Anno: 128 ALR 1196.

damage feasant (fez'ant). Doing damage; the damage caused by trespassing animals.
See **distress damage feasant.**

damage in taking by eminent domain. Physical injury to property not taken caused by any act in the course of the construction of a public improvement which if done by a private individual would give rise to an action at law. Farnandis v Great Northern Railway Co. 41 Wash 486, 84 P 18, 21.

damages. The sum of money which the law awards or imposes as pecuniary compensation, recompense, or satisfaction for an injury done or a wrong sustained as a consequence either of a breach of a contractual obligation or a tortious act. 22 Am J2d Damg § 1. The pecuniary compensation or indemnity which may be recovered in the courts by any person who has suffered loss, detriment, or injury, whether to his person, property, or rights, through the unlawful act or omission or negligence of another. Aetna Casualty & Surety Co. v Hanna (CA5 Fla) 224 F2d 499, 53 ALR2d 1125.

See **actual damages; compensatory damages; damage; double damages; exemplary damages; liquidated damages; mitigation of damages; nominal damages; punitive damages; speculative damages.**

damages and costs. As the phrase appears in an appeal bond, it binds the appellant to answer for the judgment, including interest. 5 Am J2d A & E § 1060.

damages at large. An award for which there is no monetary standard of computation, such as damages for pain and suffering. Broughel v Southern New England Tel. Co. 73 Conn 614, 621.

damages for delay. As the term appears in a supersedeas bond, such damages arising from the delay caused by the appeal as may properly constitute legal damages to the party delayed. 5 Am J2d A & E § 1058; the damages recoverable for a carrier's delay in transporting and delivering goods. 13 Am J2d Car § 377; the damages recoverable for a contractor's delay in performance. 13 Am J2d Bldg Contr § 76; 22 Am J2d Damg § 49; interest allowed for delay in payment of compensation for property taken under power of eminent domain. 27 Am J2d Em D § 297.

damages for loss of use. See **usable value**.

damage to the person. Personal injury. There is a difference of opinion on the question whether a statute providing for the survival of an action for injury to the person, after the death of the injured person, includes an action for an injury to the feelings or sensibilities. 1 Am J2d Abat & R § 68.

damage without wrong. Loss or harm resulting to a person which is not the result of the violation of a legal duty. 22 Am J2d Damg § 1. The practical sense of the expression is that there is no cause of action. 1 Am J2d Actions § 70.

dame (dăm). The wife of a baronet.

damn (dam). To condemn; to deem, think or judge anyone to be guilty or to be criminal; to give judgment, or sentence, or doom of guilt; to adjudge, or declare the penalty or punishment. Blaufus v People, 69 NY 107, 111.

damna (dam'na). Damages.

damnatus (dam-nā'tus). Condemned; sentenced; declared to be guilty; illegal.

damned rascal. See **rascal**.

damnify (dam'ni-fī). To injure; to cause loss or damage.

damni injuriae actio (dam'nī in-jū'ri-ē ak'she-ō). (Roman law.) An action for intentional injury to the beast of another.

damno. See **in damno**.

damnosa haereditas (dam-nō'sa hē-rē'di-tās). An incumbered inheritance.

damnum (dam'num). A species of loss.
See **ad quod damnum; damage.**

damnum absque injuria (dam'num abs'kwē in-jū'ri-a). Damage without wrong, the sense of the expression being that there is no cause of action. 1 Am J2d Actions § 78.
The phrase applies where an accident occurs and no fault or negligence is chargeable to either of the parties to the occurrence, as where the accident was inevitable or is properly characterized as an act of God. 38 Am J1st Negl § 4. A legal right must be violated in order that an action of tort may be maintained. The mere fact that a complainant may have suffered damage of the kind which the law recognizes is not enough. There must also have been a violation of a duty recognized by law. "Damnum" is not enough; there must also be "injuria." The maxim comes from the civil law. West Virginia Transp. Co. v Standard Oil Co. 50 W Va 611, 40 SE 591.

Damnum absque injuria esse potest (dam'num abs'kwē in-jū'ri-a es'se po'test). There can be loss or damage without the violation of a legal right. One cannot always look to others to make compensation for injuries received, since many accidents occur, the consequences of which the sufferer must bear alone. To warrant the recovery of damages in any case, there must be a right of action for a wrong inflicted by the defendant, and damage resulting to the plaintiff therefrom. 1 Am J2d Actions § 70; 22 Am J2d Damg § 1.

damnum et injuria. Loss and wrong, the two elements which must exist in combination as essentials of a cause of action. 1 Am J2d Actions § 70.

damnum fatale (dam'num fā-tā'le). By the Roman law, an innkeeper was accountable for the value of property intrusted to his charge, though the loss occurred or the thing perished without his fault, unless it happened damno fatale, or by the act of God. Under the term damnum fatale, the civilians included all those accidents which are summed up in the common-law expressions "act of God," or "public enemies," though perhaps it embraced some more which would not now be admitted as occurring from an irresistible force. Thickstun v Howard (Ind) 8 Blackford 535, 536.

damnum infectum (dam'num in-fek'tum). Threatened damage or loss.

damnum rei amissae (dam'num rē'ī a-mis'sē). A loss suffered through making a payment by mistake of law.

damnum sine injuria (dam'num sī'ne in-jū'ri-a). Loss or damage without the violation or infringement of a legal right. Such damage or loss can impose no liability on a defendant. Kingsley v Delaware, Lackawanna & Western R. Co. 81 NJL 536, 80 A 327.
See **damage without wrong; damnum absque injuria.**

Damnum sine injuria esse potest (dam'num sī'ne in-jū'ri-a es'se po'test). There can be loss or damage without the violation of a legal right.

damp. See **black damp**.

dance. A recreation, also an art, in which the body, particularly the feet, sometimes the hands, move in rhythm and to music; a party at which the guests dance; a display of emotion, particularly of joy, sometimes of pain.

dance hall. A place for public dancing, that is a place to which the public is admitted for dancing. Bungalow Amusement Co. v Seattle, 148 Wash 485, 269 P 1043, 60 ALR 166; a public hall primarily and predominantly, although not necessarily, exclusively devoted to dancing. Anno: 48 ALR 147, s. 60 ALR 173.
Construed in accordance with ordinary usage of the term, a "dance hall" is a place maintained for promiscuous and public dancing, admission to which is not based upon personal selection or invitation. 4 Am J2d Amuse § 3.

dance house. Same as **dance hall**.

dancing school. A place for instruction in dancing and etiquette, particularly the etiquette of the dance.

dandy-note (dan'di-nōt). An English customs permit authorizing the removal of goods from a warehouse.

danegelt (dān'geld). Dane-gold,—an ancient annual tax levied in England to provide funds for warfare with the Danes.

danelage. Also written Dane-lage. The Danish law which was one of the three principal systems of laws at the beginning of the eleventh century. It was principally maintained in certain of the midland counties of England and also on the eastern coast, the part most exposed to the visits of pirates. See 1 Bl Comm 65.

danelaw (dān'lâ). Same as **danelage**.

danger. Peril; a likelihood of injury; a relative term, since all life is to some extent a surmounting of peril. In the general law of negligence it includes such contingent harm or injury as reasonable prudence ought to foresee and provide against, as probably in prospect. Drennen Co. v Jordan, 181 Ala 570, 983, 61 So 938, 23 ALR 981; an ancient duty which the tenant paid for leave to till the soil at certain seasons.

dangerous. Unsafe; perilous; having at least some element of danger.
See **imminently dangerous; inherently dangerous**.

dangerous agency. See **dangerous instrumentality**.

dangerous instrumentality. A basis for liability without fault in respect of injury to adjoining property or to persons upon adjoining property. 1 Am J2d Adj L § 11; a term of moment in reference to liability of an owner or possessor for negligence. 38 Am J1st Negl § 85; also, a term of practical application in considering the absolute liability of an employer for an injury inflicted upon a third person by an instrumentality in the hands of an employee. The term has reference to appliances or things dangerous in themselves, inherently dangerous. 35 Am J1st M & S § 547; 38 Am J1st Negl § 85. Only where a "dangerous agency" amounts to a nuisance, and is unnecessary under the existing social conditions, may the employer be held absolutely liable for injuries resulting from its use by an employee. 35 Am J1st M & S § 547.

dangerous per se. Instrumentality is "dangerous per se" if it may inflict injury without the immediate application of human aid. Southern Cotton Oil Co. v Anderson, 80 Fla 441, 86 So 629, 16 ALR 255.

dangerous premises. Grounds upon which there are pitfalls or hidden sources of danger to a pedestrian. 38 Am J1st Negl § 96.

dangerous weapon. An instrument which, when used in the ordinary manner contemplated by its design and construction, will, or is likely to, cause death or great bodily harm. Barboursville ex rel. Bates v Taylor, 115 W Va 4, 174 SE 485, 92 ALR 1093.
Whether an unloaded firearm is to be considered a dangerous weapon depends ordinarily upon the manner in which the instrument is used or attempted to be used, whether as a firearm or as a bludgeon. 56 Am J1st Weap § 4.

dangers of lake navigation. All the ordinary perils which attend navigation on the Great Lakes, and among such perils, that which arises from shallowness of the waters at the entrance of harbors formed from them. Tyler v Defrees (US) 11 Wall 129, 20 L Ed 160.

dangers of navigation. Those perils incident to a lawful course of navigation conforming to public regulations of which the vessel must take notice; natural accidents, peculiar to the sea, which do not happen by the intervention of man and are not preventable or avoidable by human prudence. The term is broader than acts of God and includes many accidents peculiar to navigation on the sea which would not come within that term. 48 Am J1st Ship § 454.
See **dangers of the sea; perils of the sea**.

dangers of the river. A term analogous to and of like import with "perils of the sea," including risks arising from natural accidents peculiar to the river, canal or lake, which do not happen by the intervention of man and are not to be prevented by human prudence, and has been extended to cover losses arising from some irresistible force or overwhelming power which no ordinary skill could anticipate or evade. 48 Am J1st Ship § 455.

dangers of the sea. Perils of the sea, denoting natural accidents peculiar to the sea which do not happen by the intervention of man and are not to be prevented by the prudence of man. 48 Am J1st Ship § 454. Capture and plundering by pirates have been deemed included within the term as an exception to the general limitation to natural occurrences. Jones v Pitcher (Ala) 3 Stew & P 135.
See **perils of the sea**.

danger trees. Trees standing adjacent to the right of way of an electric power transmission line which, by reason of their size or condition involve a concrete threat of injury to the line. 26 Am J2d Electr § 146.

danism (dā'nizm). A usurious loan.

dano (dah'nyo). (Spanish.) Damage.

dans (dān). In; within.

dans et retinens, nihil dat (danz et re'ti-nenz, ni'hil dat). A person who gives and retains possession, gives nothing.

dapifer (dap-i-fėr). A court officer whose functions were those of a steward.

darbies (dar'bēz). Handcuffs.

dare (dâre). To give; to transfer; to convey; to risk; to hazard.

dare ad remanentiam (da're ad re-ma-nen'she-am). To convey in fee simple.

dareyne. Same as **darrein**.

dark. Noun: The period of time after nightfall. Adjective: An absence or deficiency of light, as in the nighttime or after nightfall. Wichita Falls & NW Ry. Co. v Woodman, 64 Okla 326, 168 P 209.

Darnell's Case (där'nels kās). A celebrated English case, decided in 1627, which sustained the refusal of the defendant to subscribe to a forced loan.

darraign. Same as **deraign**.

darrein (dar'ān). Last.

darrein continuance (dar'ān kọn-tin'u-ạns). The last continuance.
See **puis darrein continuance**.

darrein presentment (dar'ān prē-zent'ment). Last presentment; this was a writ or assize which lay when a man, or his ancestor, under whom he claimed, had presented a clerk to a benefice, who was instituted, and later a stranger presented a clerk, and thereby disturbed the real patron. The writ directed the sheriff to summon an assize or jury to determine who was the last patron, and upon their finding, a writ issued to the bishop to institute the clerk of the proper patron. See 3 Bl Comm 245.

darrein seisin (dar'ān sē'zin). The name of a form of plea which might be interposed by the tenant in his defense against a writ of right, and whereby the tenant alleged title and seisin to be in himself as against the demandant. Hunt v Hunt, 44 Mass (3 Met) 184.

Dartmouth College Case. A very celebrated case— Dartmouth College v Woodward (US) 4 Wheat 518, 4 L Ed 629, decided by the United States Supreme Court in 1819, announcing the doctrine that a grant of corporate powers by the sovereign to an association of individuals for public use constitutes a contract within the meaning of the Federal Constitution prohibiting state legislatures from passing laws impairing obligations of contract. 36 Am J2d Franch § 6.

data (dā'ta). Collected information; known facts. Plural of **datum**.

date. The time of an occurrence or happening; an indication of time, as upon a coin or an instrument. The date of a written instrument means the year, month, and day of its execution. Estate of Carpenter, 172 Cal 268, 156 P 464. The word is frequently used to designate the actual time when an event takes place; but as applied to written instruments, its primary signification is the time specified therein. This is the meaning which its derivation from the Latin "datus," meaning "given," most naturally suggests. This primary meaning is not time in the abstract, nor time taken absolutely, but, as its derivation indicates, it is the time given or specified,—time in some way ascertained or fixed. The date of a deed is not the time when it was actually executed, but the time of its execution, as given or stated in the deed itself; the date of a charge in an account not necessarily the time when the article charged was actually furnished, but the time given or set down in the account in connection with such charge. Mutual Life Ins. Co. v Hurni Packing Co. 263 US 167, 174, 68 L Ed 235, 44 S Ct 90, 31 ALR 102, 107.

date certaine (da-t sèr-tīn). (French.) The date of the recording of an instrument.

date of adjudication in bankruptcy. The date of the filing of any petition which operates as an adjudication, or the date of entry of a decree of adjudication, or, if such decree is appealed from, then the date when such decree is finally confirmed or the appeal is dismissed. Bankr Act § 1(12); 11 USC 1(12); 9 Am J2d Bankr § 264.

date of issue. An arbitrary date fixed, as the beginning of the term for which notes and bonds of a series are to run, without reference to the precise time when convenience or the state of the market may permit of their sale or delivery. Yesler v Seattle, 1 Wash 308, 322, 25 P 1014, 1019; an arbitrary date noted in an insurance policy, rather than the date of execution or delivery. 29 Am J1st Ins § 518.

date of judgment. The date of rendition of the judgment which is the day when the judgment is signed by the judge and filed with the clerk of court. Bell v McDermoth, 198 Cal 594, 246 P 805. Such is the date of the judgment from the standpoint of the judicial act in the rendition of a judgment. Clerical acts in entry, docketing, and spreading the judgment upon the records of the court, requisite in giving a judgment full effect, are subsequent to the rendition. 30A Am J Rev ed Judgm §§ 91 et seq.

date of publication. For the purpose of determining the duration and expiration of a copyright, the "date of publication" is the earliest date when copies of the first authorized publication are placed on sale, sold, or publicly distributed by the proprietor of the copyright or under his authority. 17 USC § 26.

See **publication date**.

date wanted—as desired. A usual stipulation in mercantile agreements, the equivalent of on demand. Tampa Shipbuilding & Engineering Co. v General Constr. Co. (CA5 Fla) 43 F2d 309, 85 ALR 1178.

datio (dā'she-o). Same as **dation**.

datio in adoptionem (dā'she-ō in a-dop"she-ō'nem). (Roman law.) Given in adoption. Adoption is either arrogatio, when a man in his own right (homo sui juris) is adopted or datio in adoptionem, when a filius familias of him who has such person in his power is given to another for adoption. See Mackeldey's Roman Law § 592.

datio in solutum (dā'she-ō in so-lū'tum). An accord and satisfaction under the civil law, wherein the payment was made in property and not in money.

dation (dā'shọn). A giving or transfer in the fulfillment of a duty; an appointment, as to an office.

dation en paiement (än pè-i-mān). A proceeding under the law of Louisiana whereby a debtor conveys property to his creditor, and the creditor accepts the conveyance as payment of the debt. Bradley v Claflin, 132 US 379, 385, 33 L Ed 367, 370, 10 S Ct 125.

dative (dā'tiv). That which a person may give or appoint to at will, as an office; given or appointed. See **decree dative**.

dative curatorship. See **dative tutorship**.

dative tutorship. Also called "dative curatorship,"—a tutorship or curatorship which is conferred by a family meeting on a person having charge of a minor, or of an interdict. Interdiction of Bothick, 43 La Ann 547, 9 So 477.

Da tua dum tua sunt, post mortem tunc tua non sunt (da tu'a dum tu'a sunt, post mor'tem tunk tu'a non sunt). Give that which is yours while it is yours; after death it is not yours.

datum (dā'tum). That which is delivered; executed; a date.

datur digniori (dā'ter dig-ni-ō'rī). It is given to the more worthy.

d'aubaine. See **droit d'aubaine**.

daughter. A girl or woman who is the child in a parent and child relationship; a word which is not a technical legal term having a fixed and definite meaning, but one which is flexible and subject to construction to give effect to the intention of the maker of the instrument in which it appears. Coner v Gardner, 230 Ill 258, 82 NE 640. The designation "daughter" appearing in a will may serve to indicate the inclusion of an illegitimate child of the testator among his beneficiaries. 10 Am J2d Bast § 141.

dauphin (dâ'fin). The eldest son of the king of France was so called.

Davies v Mann. A celebrated English case reported in 10 Mees & W 546, 152 Eng Reprint 588, 19 ERC 190, to which the origin of the rule of last clear chance is traced. The case is often referred to as the Donkey Case because it was a donkey which was injured by the defendant's act.

Davis-Bacon Act. A federal statute with minimum wage provisions in reference to employees of contractors engaged in federal public works. 40 USC § 276a.

Davis Case. A leading case in reference to the validity of a foreign divorce. Davis v Davis, 305 US 32, 83 L Ed 26, 59 S Ct 3, 118 ALR 158.

day. A manifestation of the natural phenomena of the rotation of the earth. 29 Am J2d Ev § 100; a division of time, consisting of twenty-four hours, the period which elapses while the earth makes a complete revolution on its axis, running from midnight to midnight. State ex rel. State Pharmaceutical Association v Michel, 52 La Ann 936, 27 So 566.

See **calendar day; fraction of a day.**

day-book (dā-buk'). An account-book of original entry in which transactions are set down as they occur.

daybreak. The dawn or first appearance of light in the morning. Sullivan v Chicago City R. Co. 167 Ill App 152.

day burglary. A statutory offense sometimes called daytime burglary, the distinctive element being the commission of the offense in the daytime. 13 Am J2d Burgl § 23.

day in court. A phrase meaning nothing less than due process, that is, the right to, and opportunity for, a hearing. 16 Am J2d Const L § 569. A "day in court" means an opportunity to be heard after notice to appear, and is denied a corporation where no officer or agent bearing the duty to defend actions is given notice of the pending action until after judgment. Townsend v Carolina Coach Co. 231 NC 81, 56 SE2d 39, 20 ALR2d 1174.

It is sufficient if the record shows that the parties might have had their controversies determined according to their respective rights if they had presented all their evidence and the court had applied the law. Olsen v Muskegon Piston Ring Co. (CA6 Mich) 117 F2d 163.

day laborer. A person employed by the day to perform manual labor. Briscoe v Montgomery & Co. 93 Ga 602.

daylight. The natural light of daytime; dawn; daylight.

See **de die claro.**

daylight saving time. Time advanced for the purpose of taking advantage of the longer periods of daylight during the summer months. 52 Am J1st Time § 4; achieved by advancing clock or other timepiece one hour; prevailing from the last Sunday of April at 2 A. M. to the last Sunday of October at 2 A. M. under Act of Congress, for all states, the District of Columbia, and possessions of the United States, except as any state may exempt itself by statute from using such time.

day of 24 hours. A period designated for the purpose of expressing with certainty and precision the exact period during which the capacity of a distillery for production is to be ascertained or fixed for tax purposes. Chicago Distilling Co. v Stone, 140 US 647, 35 L Ed 532, 11 S Ct 862.

day-rule (dā'rōl). An order of court permitting a prisoner to spend a day out of prison.

days in bank (dāz in bangk). Days set by law for the return of writs or for the appearance in court of the parties served; default day.

daysman (dāz'man). An arbiter.

days of grace. An additional three days following the date specified for payment in a negotiable instrument, allowed the obligor under the rule of law merchant and perhaps in a very few states, although not in respect of checks. Bull v First Nat. Bank, 123 US 105, 31 L Ed 97, 8 S Ct 62; an allowance of three days to the debtor to make payment, beyond the time at which by the terms of the contract, it becomes due and payable. Bell v First Nat. Bank, 115 US 373, 29 L Ed 409, 6 S Ct 105; an extended period, usually 30 days, under statute or contractual provision, for the payment of premiums under a life insurance policy. 29 Am J Rev ed Ins § 519; additional opportunity to obey appellate court order. 4 Am J2d A & E § 238.

day's work. The number of hours, as prescribed by statute, constituting a lawful day's work, unless otherwise agreed by the parties. 31 Am J Rev ed Lab § 780.

Such statutes are to be distinguished from those which limit absolutely the length of a working day.

In underground metal mining, the workday starts when the miner reports for duty as required at or near the collar of the mine, and ends when he reaches the collar at the end of the shift. It also includes the aggregate of the time spent on the surface in obtaining and returning lamps, carbide and tools, and in checking in and out, but it does not include any fixed lunch period of one-half hour or more during which the miner is relieved of all duties, even though the lunch period is spent underground. McWhirter v Otis Elevator Co. (DC SC) 40 F Supp 11.

See **hours of labor; Portal to Portal Pay Act.**

daytime. The period of daylight, commencing before sunrise and continuing a while after sunset, during which it is possible to discern the face of a person or object by natural light. 13 Am J2d Burgl §§ 23, 24.

daytime burglary. See **day burglary.**

daywere. A quantity of land which could be ploughed in one day.

day-writ (dā-rit). Same as **day-rule.**

dazzling light. In reference to automobile headlights, high, as opposed to low, headlight beams. People v Meola, 7 NY2d 391, 198 NYS2d 276, 165 NE2d 851.

D. B. Abbreviation of **Domesday Book.**

d. b. e. An abbreviation of **de bene esse.**

d. b. n. An abbreviation of **de bonis non.**

See **administrator d. b. n.**

D. C. Abbreviation of district court, also of District of Columbia, and of Doctor of Chiropractic.

D. C. L. Letters representing the university degree of "doctor of civil law."

dd. Abbreviation of delivered.

d. d. An abbreviation of "days after date."

D. D. Abbreviation of demand draft and of Doctor of Divinity.

D. D. S. Abbreviation of Doctor of Dental Science.

D. E. Abbreviation of Doctor of Engineering.

de (dē). (French and Latin.) From; of; concerning; among.

deacon. The assistant of a priest or other clergyman. In some Protestant denominations, a member of the governing board of a church or congregation.

de acquirendo rerum dominio (dē ak-qui-ren'dō rē'rum do-mi'ni-ō). Of acquiring the control of things.

dead (ded). Without life; of no effect.

dead animal. A carcass which in some way endangers the public health or contributes to the discomfort of the populace. Anno: 121 ALR 743, 747.

dead beat. (Slang.) Noun: A person who does not pay his bills and has no property out of which the bills can be collected under process. Adjective: Exhausted.

dead body. The corpse of a human being. A dead animal.

dead-born. Born dead; stillborn.

dead freight. A shipping term used to denote the compensation payable to a shipowner when the charterer under a contract of affreightment has failed to ship a full cargo; that is, compensation for the loss sustained by the shipowner by reason of the charterer's failure to deliver the agreed quantity of cargo. California & Eastern S.S. Co. v 138,000 Feet of Lumber (DC Md) 23 F2d 95, 97.

dead hand. Control from the grave by a blind observance of principles and practices enunciated and developed by persons long since dead; holding property out of the channels of commerce and industry.
See **in mortua manu; mortmain.**

deadhead. A term applied to persons other than the president, directors, officers, agents or employees of a railroad company, who are permitted by the company to travel on the road without paying any fare therefor. Gardner v Hall, 61 NC 21, 22.

deadhead message. A telegram which is usually marked "d. h.," and is sent without charge. Connelly v Western Union Tel. Co. 100 Va 51, 40 SE 618.

dead letter. A law which is not enforced; an undelivered letter which has been sent to the dead letter office by the post office department to be destroyed.

deadline. A point of time, day, hour, or minute, as of which an act shall be performed, such as filing a claim or producing an article for publication in a specific issue of a newspaper or periodical; a line which a prisoner may not cross without exposing himself to gunfire.
See **midnight deadline.**

deadlock. An even division of the directors of a corporation in voting. 19 Am J2d Corp § 1129; an even division of members of an administrative agency on a particular question. 2 Am J2d Admin L § 198.
See **equally divided court.**

deadly. See **mortal.**

deadly weapon. An instrument which is likely to or which will cause or produce death or great bodily harm when used in the manner contemplated by its design and construction. Barboursville ex rel. Bates v Taylor, 115 W Va 4, 174 SE 485, 92 ALR 1093; 26 Am J1st Homi § 7; 56 Am J1st Weap § 2.
Whether an unloaded firearm is to be considered a deadly weapon depends ordinarily upon whether the manner in which the instrument is used or attempted to be used, whether as a firearm or a bludgeon. 56 Am J1st Weap § 4.

dead man's part (ded' manz part). That portion of the personal property of a married man of which he could lawfully dispose by will to the exclusion of his widow and his children.

de admensuratione (dē ad-men-su-rā-shē-ō'ne). For admeasurement; for adjustment or settlement.

de admensuratione dotis (dē ad-men-su-rā-shē-ō'ne dō'tis). A writ for the admeasurement of dower, which lay where more land had been assigned to a widow as dower than she ought legally to have. This might occur where a minor heir or his guardian had made the excessive assignment. See 2 Bl Comm 136.

de admittendo clerico (dē ad-mit-ten'dō kle'ri-kō). A writ commanding a bishop to admit to a living a clergyman who had been regularly appointed thereto.

dead pay (ded' pā). The pay or wages of dead soldiers and sailors which have been wrongfully collected from the government after their death.

dead pledge. A mortgage; the property mortgaged.
It was called a "dead" pledge because the rents and profits of it did not go toward the discharge or payment of it. Hence, it yielded nothing to the mortgagee and was, in that sense, dead.

dead rent (ded rent). A rent reserved in the lease of mining property in addition to royalties.

dead's part (dedz' pärt). Same as **dead man's part.**

dead storage. The storage of goods wherein they come to rest for safekeeping. Tipp v District of Columbia, 69 App DC 400, 102 F2d 264. In "dead storage" of a motor vehicle, the battery is removed, so that the vehicle can not be moved under its own power.

dead use (ded ūs). A future use.

dead vessel. A ship permanently withdrawn from use for navigation purposes. 2 Am J2d Adm § 31.

de advisamento consilii nostri (dē ad-vī-sa-men'to kon-si'li-ī nos'trī). By the advice of our counsel.

dead wall. A term common to building regulations, meaning a solid wall, that is a wall without openings. 13 Am J2d Bldgs § 28.

deadwoods (ded'wŭds). See **buffers.**

de aequitate (dē ē-qui-tā'te). In equity.

de aetate probanda (dē ē-tā'te prō-ban'da). For proving age,—a writ which lay to determine the time of the majority of the infant heir of a tenant in capite.

deaf, dumb, and blind. The common law regarded a man who was born deaf, dumb and blind as being in the same state with an idiot, because being deemed incapable of understanding, he was supposed to be lacking in all those senses which furnish the human mind with ideas. See 1 Bl Comm 304. Such concept is negatived absolutely by the remarkable achievements which have been accomplished in modern times by persons working under the handicap of the combination of such infirmities. 29 Am J Rev ed Ins Per § 4. One of our finest minds is that of Helen Keller.

deafforest (dē-a-for'est). To take from a forest its character as a forest, and thus to remove it from the operation of the forest laws.

deaf mute. A person who can neither hear nor speak.
See **deaf, dumb, and blind.**

deal. Verb: To transact business; to be concerned with a person or a thing. State v Morrow, 313 Mo 114, 125, 280 SW 697; to buy or to sell. Commonwealth v Silverman, 220 Mass 552, 108 NE 358; to distribute the cards to the players in a card game; Noun: A transaction; a bargain; an arrangement to attain a desired result. Reynolds v Pray, 148 Iowa 213, 127 NW 50; a secret arrangement, especially in politics, whereby support is given on promise of future favors. Oregon Home Builders v Montgomery Invest. Co. 94 Or 349, 184 P 487; the playing of one hand of cards around in a card game.

de aleatoribus (dē a-le-a-tō'ri-bus). Concerning gamblers.

dealer. One who buys and sells any commodity, such as grain, sugar, wheat etc. Gibson v Bolner, 165 Ohio St 357, 59 Ohio Ops 467, 135 NE2d 353; a person who buys and sells at a place of business rather than from house to house as a peddler. 40 Am J1st Ped § 3; one who sells goods substantially in the form in which they are bought, and who has not converted them into another form of property by his own skill and labor. 51 Am J1st Tax § 320.

dealer in lands. See **land jobber.**

dealer in liquor. A person who buys and sells liquor or buys it with the intention of selling it. 30 Am J Rev ed Intox L § 217.

dealer in narcotics. One who sells narcotics promiscuously, and who is ready or willing to sell to anyone who applies to purchase. Taylor v United States (CA8 Mo) 19 F2d 813.

dealer in securities. A merchant of securities with an established place of business, regularly engaged in the purchase of securities and their resale to customers. Internal Revenue Code § 1236(c); Helvering v Fried, 299 US 175, 81 L Ed 104, 57 S Ct 150; one who engages in repeated and continuous transactions in securities, as distinguished from a person who buys or sells only occasionally. 47 Am J1st Secur A § 21.

dealer's policy. An automobile insurance policy which covers the risk or risks of an automobile dealer. 7 Am J2d Auto Ins §§ 43, 73, 96, 97.

dealer's talk. See **puffing.**

dealing. Buying and selling. The word is often used as equivalent in meaning to the word "trading." Fleckner v Bank of United States (US) 8 Wheat 338, 352, 5 L Ed 631, 634; acting as dealer in a card game.
See **dealer; trading.**

dealing in futures. See **futures.**

dealing off the cuff. A slang term for acting without sufficient forethought.

de allocatione facienda (dē al-lō-kā-she-ō'ne fā-she-en'da). For making an allowance,—an old English writ to compel the lord treasurer and barons of the exchequer to make allowances to certain government officers for payments made by them.

de alto et basso (dē al'tō et bãs'sō). From top to bottom; fully; completely; in all particulars. The phrase may be compared with the nautical expressions "from stem to stern," "from stem to gudgeon."

de ambitu (dē am'bi-tū). Concerning bribery. Under the Julian law a person convicted of corruption at an election was fined and adjudged infamous, but if he thereafter convicted another offender, his credit was restored. See 1 Bl Comm 179, footnote.

dean (dēn). The title of an ecclesiastical officer; the president of a bar association; an honorary title given to the oldest member of a profession or trade in a particular place.

dean and chapter. The council of a bishop, to assist him with their advice in religious matters, and also in the temporal affairs of his see. See 1 Bl Comm 382.

deanery. See **Archdeanery.**

de annua pensione (dē an'nu-a pen-she-ō'ne). Of annual pension,—an old English writ to compel an abbot or prior to make payment of pension money due the king from the abbey or priory.

de annuo reditu (dē an'nu-ō re'di-tū). An old English writ which lay to recover an annuity.

dean of the arches. The chief judicial officer of the archbishop of Canterbury.

de apostata capiendo (dē a-pos-tā'ta kā-pi-en'dō). For taking an apostate,—an old English writ for the arrest of a religious officer who had abandoned his post.

de arbitratione facta (dē ar-bi-trā-she-ō'ne fak'ta). For making an arbitration,—an old English writ to restrain an action based on a claim which had been submitted to arbitration.

de arrestandis bonis ne dissipentur (dē ar-res-tan'dis bō'nis nē dis-si-pen'ter). For the seizure of goods lest they disappear,—an old English writ for the seizure of goods taken by a person who might leave the owner without a remedy.

de arrestando ipsum qui pecuniam recepit (dē ar-res-tan'dō ip'sum quī pe-kū'ni-am re'se-pit). For arresting him who had received money,— an old English writ for the arrest of a deserting soldier who had received his pay.

de arte et parte (dē ar'te et par'te). Of art and part.

De Asportatis Religiosorum (dē as-por-tā'tis rē-li-ji-ō-sō'rum). Concerning the asportations of religious persons,—the title of a statute of 35 Edward the First, the purpose of which was to curb the acquisitions of the church.

de assissa mortis antecessoris (dē as-sī'sa mor'tis ante-ses-sō'ris). Concerning the assize of the death of an ancestor.

de assissa proroganda (dē as-sī'sa prō-rō-gan'da). For postponing the assize,—a writ to postpone the issue of an assize during the absence in war of one of the parties to the action.

death. The end of life; the state of being dead.
See **civil death.**

death acts. Statutes permitting civil actions for death caused by wrongful act. 22 Am J2d Dth § 2.
See **wrongful death.**

deathbed expenses. The expenses of a person's last illness.

death by accident. See **accident.**

death by accidental means. See **accidental means.**

death by his own hand. A synonym of suicide. 29A Am J Rev ed Ins § 1145. The expression does not include death by accident; there must be an intent to commit suicide. Such an intent, however, may be present even while the assured is in a state of intoxication. Equitable Life Assur. Soc. v Paterson, 41 Ga 338.

death by natural cause. See **natural death.**

death by poison. See **poison; poisoning.**

death by wrongful act. See **wrongful death.**

death certificate. The official proof of death, issued on the showing made by an official registry kept pursuant to law. 22 Am J2d Dth § 302.

death duties. Another term for inheritance or estates taxes. 28 Am J Rev ed Inher T § 3; duties which are not a tax upon property eo nomine, but upon its passage by will or by descent in cases of intestacy, as distinguished from taxes imposed on property real or personal, as such, because of its ownership or possession. In other words, the public contribution which death duties exact is predicated on the passing of property as the result of death,

as distinct from a tax on property disassociated from its transmission or receipt by will, or as the result of intestacy. Knowlton v Moore, 178 US 41, 44 L Ed 969, 20 S Ct 747.
See **estate taxes; inheritance taxes.**

death from. See phrases beginning **death by.**

Death on High Seas Act. A federal statute which applies to death caused by wrongful act, including neglect or default, on the high seas more than a marine league from the United States, and authorizes suit for damages in an admiralty court, by the personal representatives of the decedent and for the personal benefit of the decedent's wife, husband, parent, child, or dependent relative. 46 USC § 761; 2 Am J2d Adm § 130.

death penalty. The extreme penalty for the commission of a crime, to be executed within the manner provided by statute, such as hanging, electrocution, or asphyxiation by gas. There is a definite legislative trend toward the abolition of the death penalty, either absolutely or subject to few exceptions.

death sentence. See **death penalty.**

deathsman (deths'man). An executioner; a person who executes the death penalty for a capital offense.

death's part (deths' pärt). Same as **dead man's part.**

death taxes. Another term for inheritance or estate taxes. 28 Am J Rev ed Inher T § 3.
See **death duties.**

deathwarrant. The warrant or order of a court commanding the execution of a sentence to death.

death without issue. See **die without issue.**

deathwound. A fatal wound.

de attornato recipiendo (dē at-tor-nā'tō re-si-pi-en'dō). For receiving an attorney,—a writ to compel the judges to receive an attorney of a party to an action pending before them.

de audiendo et terminando (dē â-di-en'dō et ter-mi-nan'dō). To hear and determine; a writ directing commissioners to try and decide certain cases assigned to them.

de averiis captis in withernam (dē a-ve'ri-is kap'tis in wi'th-er-nam). Same as **averiis captis in withernam.**

de averiis retornandis (dē a-ve'ri-is re-tor-nan'dis). For returning cattle,—a writ for the seizure of the cattle of a person in the place of other cattle which he has wrongfully driven away.

de avo (dē a'vō). From the grandfather,—a writ whereby an heir secured land entered by a stranger on the day of the death of the heir's grandfather, who had died seised of it. See 3 Bl Comm 186.

deawarren (dē-a-war'ren). To break up and discontinue or abandon a warren.

debar (dẹ-bär'). To cut off from entrance; to preclude; to hinder from approach, entry or enjoyment; to shut out or exclude. Printup v Alexander & Wright, 69 Ga 553, 556.

debas (de-bah'). Below.

debase (dẹ-bās'). To adulterate.

debasing coin. Reducing the standard of quality by increasing the percentage of alloy.

debatable land. Land lying near the boundary between England and Scotland which at one time was claimed by each of them.

debauched (dẹ-bâcht'). Carnally known. 47 Am J1st Seduc § 6.

debauchery (dẹ-bâ-chêr-i). An excessive indulgence of the body; licentiousness; drunkenness; corruption of innocence; taking up vicious habits; sometimes defined as sexual immorality, where appearing in a statute. Athanasaw v United States, 227 US 326, 57 L Ed 528.

debauchery and immoral purpose (dẹ-bâ'chêr-i and i-mor'ạl per'pọs). As these terms are used in the White Slave Traffic Act, by association with the term prostitution, they have been restricted in meaning to immorality consisting of sexual debauchery, and as thus limited by judicial decisions the language of the statute furnishes a sufficiently definite description of the condemned conduct. United States v Lewis (CA7 Ind) 110 F2d 460.

debauchment. A debauching or being debauched; sometimes defined as seduction. Reutkemeier v Nolte, 179 Iowa 342, 161 NW 290.

de bene esse (dē bē'nē es'ē). Of present, temporary validity; for what it is worth; conditionally; provisionally; subject to a defeasance of condition subsequent.
See **deposition de bene esse.**

debent (dẹ-bent). They owe.

debenture (dē-ben'tūr). A voucher for an indebtedness; a corporate bond, often unsecured, in other instances secured by a pledge of income only.
See **mortgage debentures.**

debet (de'bet). He owes; he ought.

debet esse finis litium (de'bet es'se fī'nis lī'she-um). There ought to be an end of a litigation.

debet et detinet (de'bet et de'ti-net). He is indebted and he withholds. A writ of debet was said to be brought in the debet and detinet, or in the detinet only; that is it alleged that the defendant owed the debt and withheld it, or simply that he withheld or detained it. If the original creditor sued the original debtor, or sued the original debtor's heirs upon an obligation binding on them, the writ was brought in debet and detinet, but otherwise only in detinet, for the reason that a simple duty to pay a debt was purely personal and died with the debtor unless his heirs were bound. See 3 Bl Comm 155.

debet et solet (de'bet et sō'let). He ought and has been accustomed.

Debet quis juri subjacere ubi delinquit (de'bet quis jū'rī sub-ja'se-re u'bi de-lin'quit). A person ought to be subject to the law of the place where he commits an offense.

Debet sua cuique domus esse perfugium tutissimum (de'bet su'a kī'kwe dō'mus es'se per-fu'ji-um tu-tis'si-mum). Each man's home should be a very safe refuge. "The law has a tender regard for the asylum of a private dwelling." Clason v Shotwell (NY) 12 Johns 31, 54.

de bien et de mal (de biēn et de mal). For good and evil.
See **de bono et malo.**

de biens le mort (de bien le mor). Of the goods of the deceased.

De Bigamis (dē bi'ga-mis). An English statute passed in 1276, declaring what should be the force and effect of certain words in a deed.

Debile fundamentum, fallit opus (de'bi-le fun-dā'men'tum, fal'lit ō'pus). When the foundation is weak, the structure falls. "Justice does not allow one to profit by his own iniquity." Anderson & Co. v Stapel, 80 Mo App 115, 122.

debit. Verb: To charge. Noun: Whatever is charged as due or owing.

debita (de′bi-ta). Debts.

debita fundi (de′bi-ta fun′dī). Debts which were secured by real property.

debita laicorum (de′bi-ta lā-i-cōr′um). Debts of the laity, as distinguished from debts of the clergy which were not recoverable in the civil courts.

Debita sequuntur personam debitoris (de′bi-ta se-qu-un′ter per-sō′nam de-bi-tō′ris). Debts follow the person of the debtor.

debito. See **de debito.**

debito justitiae. See **ex debito justitiae.**

debito naturali. See **ex debito naturali.**

debitor (deb′i-tor). One who owes; a debtor.

Debitor creditoris est debitor creditori creditoris (de′bi-tor kre-di-tō′ris est de′bi-tor kre-di-tō′rī kre-di-tō′ris). The debtor of the creditor is also the debtor of the creditor's creditor. "This process of attachment went not only against those in the actual possession of himself, his factors or agents, but also against those in the hands of his debtors, since the maxim taken from the Justinian code was 'Debitor creditoris,' " etc. Atkins v Fiber Disintegrating Co. (US) 18 Wall 272, 21 L Ed 841, 845.

debitores in solido (de-bi-tor′ez in sō′li-dō). Joint debtors.

Debitor non praesumitur donare (de′bitor non prē-zu′mi-ter do-nā′re). A debtor is not presumed to make gifts.

Debitorum pactionibus, creditorum petitio nec minui potest (de-bi-tō′rum pak-she-ō′ni-bus, kre-di-tō′rum pe-ti′she-ō nek mi′nu-i po′test). The rights of creditors to sue cannot be prejudiced by agreements between their debtors.

debitrix (de′bi-trix). A woman who owes money.

debitum (de′bi-tum). A debt.

debitum et contractus sunt nullius loci (de′bi-tum et kon-trak′tus sunt nul′li-us lō′sī). Debt and contract are of no place,—expressing a rule of the common law that actions arising out of contract are transitory in character regardless of the place where the contract was executed or was to be performed. 56 Am J1st Ven § 19.

debitum fundi (de′bi-tum fun′dī). A debt secured by real property.

debitum in presenti, solvendum in futuro (de′bi-tum in pre-zen′tī, sol-ven′dum in fu-tū′rō). A present indebtedness to be paid at a future time. "Although the duties thus accrue to the government as a personal debt of the importer, upon the arrival of the goods at the proper port of entry, yet it is but a debitum in presenti, solvendum in futuro, according to the Revenue Collection Act." Meredith & Ellicott v United States (US) 13 Pet 486, 493, 10 L Ed 258, 262.

debitum sine brevi (de′bi-tum sī′ne brē′vi). He owes without declaration filed. 30A Am J Rev ed Judgm § 156; an action of debt brought without a writ.
See **judgment debitum sine brevi.**

de bone memorie (dē bō′ne me′mor-e). Of good memory; of sound mind.

de bonis asportatis (dē bō′nis as-por-tā′tis). For carrying away goods.
See **trespass de bonis asportatis.**

de bonis defuncti (dē bō′nis de-funk′tī). From the goods of the deceased. See 2 Bl Comm 512.

de bonis ecclesiasticis (dē bō′nis e-klē-si-ās′ti-sis). Of ecclesiastical goods,—the name of a species of writ of execution which was only used against ecclesiastics. The writ was given even after the sheriff had made his return upon a common writ of execution stating that the defendant was a beneficed clerk, not having any lay fee. See 3 Bl Comm 418.

de bonis intestati (dē bō′nis in-tes-tā′tī). Out of or from the goods of the intestate.
See **judgment de bonis intestati.**

de bonis non (dē bō′nis non). See **de bonis non administratris.**

de bonis non administratis (dē bō′nis non ad-mi-nis-trā′tis). Of goods not administered.
See **administration de bonis non; administrator de bonis non; administrator de bonis non cum testamento annexo.**

de bonis non amovendis (dē bō′nis non ā-mō-ven′dis). For the nonremoval of goods,—a writ to prevent the removal of goods pending the court's decision on the defendant's writ of error.

de bonis propriis (dē bō′nis prō′pri-is). Out of, from, or concerning the property of a person who is an executor or administrator, belonging to himself, personally.

de bonis testatoris (dē bō′nis tes-tā-tō′ris). Out of, from, or concerning the property of the testator.

de bonis testatoris ac si (dē bō′nis tes-tā-tō′ris ak sī). Out of or from the goods of the testator, if there are any.

de bono et malo (dē bō′nō et ma′lō). For good and evil,—a formal expression of an appellee who was appealed for felony, when he rested his case with the jury; the name given to special writs of gaol delivery which it was anciently the course to issue for each particular prisoner. These writs being found inconvenient and oppressive, a general commission for all the prisoners was long ago established in their stead. See 4 Bl Comm 270.

de bono gestu (dē bō′nō jes′tū). For or during good behavior.

debruser (dē-bru′ser). To break; to break up.

debt. A common-law action for the recovery of a fixed and definite sum of money or for a sum of money which can be ascertained from fixed data by computation or is capable of being readily reduced to certainty. 1 Am J2d Actions § 20; that which is owing to a person under any form of obligation or promise, including obligations arising under contract, obligations imposed by law without contract, even judgments. Anno: 12 ALR2d 799. In the broad sense of the term, "debt" includes a claim for unliquidated damages. Anno: 69 L Ed 380.

In the ordinary sense, "debt" is not merely a promise to pay money but is an unconditional and legally enforceable obligation for the payment of money; it involves the relationship of debtor and creditor, or of borrower and lender. Evans v Kroh (Ky) 284 SW2d 329, 58 ALR2d 1446. In a narrower sense, a "debt" is an obligation arising out of contract, express or implied, which entitles the creditor unconditionally to receive from the debtor a sum of money which the debtor is under legal, equitable, or moral obligation to pay without regard to any future contingency. Evans v Kroh (Ky) 284 SW2d 329, 58 ALR2d 1446.

An action is one for a "debt," sufficient for the issuance of a writ of garnishment, where it is based on rescission of a contract because of fraud of the seller, and seeks recovery back of a specified sum paid under the contract, even though actual rescission of the contract before institution of the suit was prevented by absence of the defendant, and recovery of damages for fraud and deceit is requested in the alternative. Cleveland v San Antonio Bldg. & L. Asso. 148 Tex 211, 223 SW2d 226, 12 ALR2d 781.

The word "debt," appearing in a constitution or statute fixing a debt limit for municipalities, does not have a fixed legal signification but is used in different statutes and constitutions in senses varying from a very restricted to a very general signification. Its meaning, therefore, in any particular statute or constitution is to be determined by construction. 38 Am J1st Mun Corp § 410. Unless absolutely required, the words "debt" or "liability" in debt limitation provisions should not be so interpreted as to paralyze the legal functioning of municipal corporations which have reached or exceeded their existing debt limits. Moores v Springfield, 144 Me 54, 64 A2d 569, 16 ALR2d 502.

A sum of money which is payable is a debt, without regard to whether it be payable presently or at a future time. Hence, a debt may be a debt due or a debt not due. State ex rel. Rice v Wilkinson, 82 Mont 15, 264 P 679, 683.

debt by special contract. Same as **debt by specialty.**

debt by specialty. Also called a debt by special contract. It is a debt or contract whereby a sum of money becomes, or is acknowledged to be, due by deed or by an instrument under seal. Kerr v Lydecker, 51 Ohio St 240, 37 NE 267.
See **specialty**.

debt due. Literally, an obligation which is due, that is, mature. Within the meaning of a garnishment statute, a debt is "due" and therefore subject to a garnishment when there is an existing obligation to pay in the present or in the future. That is, the debt need not be presently payable, nor need it be liquidated. Calechman v Atlantic & Pacific Tea Co. 120 Conn 265, 180 A 450, 100 ALR 302.

debtee (de-tē'). One to whom a debt is due; a creditor.

debt limit. See **limitation of indebtedness.**

debt not due. See **debt due; maturity.**

debt of another. See **promise to pay the debt of another.**

debt of record. A sum of money which appears to be due by the evidence of a court of record; a debt evidenced by the judgment of a court of record. 2 Bl Comm 465; a debt or contract created of record, such as a statute staple, or statute merchant, and not one whose previous existence is only admitted of record. Bowie v Henderson (US) 6 Wheat 514, 518, 5 L Ed 319, 320.

debt of specialty. Same as **debt by specialty.**

debtor. A person who owes another anything, or who is under obligation, arising from express agreement or implication of law, to render and pay a sum of money to another. Stanly v Ogden (Conn) 2 Root 258, 262; the person obligated by a debt.
See **debt**.

debtor and creditor adjustment. See **balance**.

debtor and creditor relation. The relationship which exists between two persons when one of them, the debtor, owes money to the other, the creditor. Kansas City, St. L. & C. R. Co. v Alton R. Co. (CA7 Ill) 124 F2d 780. The relationship of debtor and creditor arises in tort cases the moment the cause of action accrued, within the meaning of a statute relating to conveyances fraudulent as to "creditors," so as to entitle one securing a judgment against the grantor to have set aside a fraudulent conveyance executed pending the action. Hansen v Cramer, 39 Cal 2d 321, 245 P2d 1059, 30 ALR2d 1204.

debtor in possession. The term applied to a debtor who continues in possession while proceedings are had in the bankruptcy court to perfect a reorganization or arrangement whereby his financial affairs may be rehabilitated.

debtor relief. The term applied to provisions of the Bankruptcy Act for compositions, debt readjustments, and reorganizations.

Debtors' Act of 1869. An English statute which abolished imprisonment for debt.

debtor's oath. See **poor debtor's oath.**

debtor's summons. A summons which issued out of an English Bankruptcy court, giving notice to a debtor to pay his creditor or become subject to bankruptcy proceedings.

debt owing. A debt which is unpaid. Such a debt is a debt owing, whether it is past due, presently due or due at a future time. State ex rel. Rice v Wilkinson, 82 Mont 15, 264 P 679, 683.

debts. See **debt; debts of decedent; debts of the United States.**

debts of decedent. All claims of creditors enforceable in law or equity. 31 Am J2d Ex & Ad § 276. As it appears in a will, the term means obligations of the decedent due or expected to become due in his lifetime. Nolte v Nolte, 247 Iowa 868, 76 NW2d 881, 56 ALR2d 854. Some authority has construed the term as including expenses of administration. Re Dickey, 87 Ohio App 255, 94 NE2d 223, 20 ALR2d 1220 (term appearing in a will). Some authority construes a widow's allowance as a "debt of the decedent." 31 Am J2d Ex & Ad § 324. But unanimity upon such construction is not to be expected.

debts of the United States. As these words are used in Art. 1, § 8 of the Constitution conferring upon Congress the power to pay debts of the United States, the debts are not limited to those which are evidenced by some written obligation, or to those which are otherwise of a strictly legal character. The term "debts" includes those debts or claims which rest upon a merely equitable or honorary obligation, and which would not be recoverable in a court of law if existing against an individual. The nation, speaking broadly, owes a "debt" to an individual when his claim grows out of general principles of right and justice,—when, in other words, it is based upon considerations of a moral or merely honorary nature, such as are binding upon the conscience or the honor of an individual, although the debt could gain no recognition in a court of law. The power of Congress extends at least as far as the recognition and payment of claims against the government which are thus founded. Cincinnati Soap

Co. v United States, 301 US 308, 81 L Ed 1122, 57 S Ct 764.

debuit (de'bu-it). He owed; he ought.

debuit repare (de'bu-it re-pa're). He ought to repair.

de caetero (dē se'te-rō). In future; henceforth; hereafter.

de calceto reparendo (dē kal'se-tō re-pa-ren'dō). A writ for the repair of a causeway.

decalogue (dek'ạ-log). The ten commandments.

decanatus (dē-kā-nā'tus). A deanery; the jurisdiction of a dean.

decania (de-kā'ni-a). Same as **decanatus**.

decanus (dē-kā'nus). A dean, an ecclesiastical officer who originally was probably appointed to superintend ten (decem) canons or prebendaries. See 1 Bl Comm 382.

de capitalibus dominis feodi (dē ka-pi-tā'li-bus do'mi-nis fe'o-dī). Of the chief lords of the fee. Ancient charters recited that the tenements granted should be so held. See 2 Bl Comm 299.

decapitation (dẹ-kap-i-tā'shọn). Severing the head from the body, at one time a method of capital punishment in England.

de capite minutis (dē ka'pi-te mi-nū'tis). Of those persons who have suffered loss of citizenship.

de cartis reddendis (dē kar'tis red-den'dis). An old English writ for the recovery of deeds.

de catallis reddendis (dē ka-tal'lis red-den'dis). An old English writ for the recovery of chattels.

de cautione admittenda (dē kâ-she-ō'ne ad-mit-ten'da). For admitting caution,—an old English writ to compel a bishop to admit an ecclesiastical prisoner to bail or caution.

decease (dẹ-sēs'). Death. As a verb, to die; to cease living; to depart this life.

deceased (dẹ-sēst'). A decedent; a dead person; a person who has died.

deceased person. A decedent; a person who has died. An absentee who has been absent for the statutory period and not heard from is neither a deceased person nor a decedent in the eyes of the law, although absentee administration has been had upon his estate. Estate of Kite, 194 Iowa 129, 187 NW 585, 24 ALR 850, 853.
See **estate of deceased person; personal representatives**.

Deceased Wife's Sister Bill. An English statute forbidding a widower's marriage with the sister of his deceased wife.

decedens (dē-sē'denz). A deceased person.

decedent. See **deceased person**.

decedent's estate. See **estate of deceased person**.

deceit. A species of fraud; any false representation or contrivance whereby one person overreaches and misleads another to the hurt of the latter. Walter v State, 208 Ind 231, 195 NE 268, 98 ALR 607.

decem tales (de'sem tā'lēz). A tales of ten. A writ of decem tales or octo tales (a tales of eight) was issued to the sheriff directing him to summon an additional number (eight or ten) of talesmen to make up a trial jury, when there was a deficiency. See 3 Bl Comm 364.

decemviri litibus judicandis (de-sem'vi-rī lī'ti-bus jū-di-kan'dis). (Roman law.) Ten persons or ten judges who were appointed to aid the praetor in deciding questions of law.

decenna (dẹ-sen'ạ). A tithing; a decennary.

decennarius (de-sen-nā'ri-us). One of the ten freeholders of a decennary or tithing.
See **decennary**.

decennary (dē-sen'ạ-ri). A tithing, consisting of ten freeholders of the neighborhood and their families.
See **frank pledges**.

decennial census. The United States census which is regularly taken every 10 years. 14 Am J2d Census § 1.

decent burial. A relative term, varying with the financial and social standing of the deceased and his relatives, and often affected by the community and the rules of religious, social, or political organizations with which the deceased was affiliated, as a member or otherwise.
What would be regarded as proper and appropriate by one might be regarded as wholly inadequate and unsuitable by another, and no rule or definition can well be formulated, but by common consent, a determination of these matters is left exclusively to the relatives or friends of the deceased. Seaton v Commonwealth, 149 Ky 498, 149 SW 871.

de ceo se mettent en le pays. See **et de ceo se mettent en le pays**.

deceptione. See **de deceptione**.

Deceptis non decipientibus, jura subveniunt (dē-sep'-tis non dē-si-pi-en'ti-bus, jū'ra sub-ve'ni-unt). The laws aid those who have been deceived, but not the deceivers.

decern (dẹ-sẻrn'). To decree.

de certificando (dē sẻr''ti-fi-kan'dō). A writ which lay to compel the certification of a document.

de certiorando (dē ser-she-ō-ran'dō). A writ which lay to compel a sheriff to give his certificate of a fact.

decessus (de-ses'sus). Decease; death.

decet (de'set). It is fitting; it is proper; it is becoming.

de cetero (dē sē'te-rō). In future; hereafter; henceforth.

Decet tamen principem, servare leges, quibus ipse solutus est (de'set ta'men prin'si-pem ser-vā're lē'jēz, qui'bus ip'se so-lū'tus est). Yet it becomes a prince to protect those laws from which he himself is exempt. This was a rule of the Roman law which "is at once laying down the principle of despotic power, and at the same time acknowledging its absurdity." See 1 Bl Comm 239.

de champertia (dē kam-per'she-a). An old writ which issued for the enforcement of the statutes against champerty.

de char et de sank. Of flesh and blood.

de chimino (dē ki'mi-nō). A writ to secure or enforce a right of way.

De Cibariis Utendis (dē si-bā'ri-is ū-ten'dis). Concerning things useful as food,—the title of a sumptuary law passed in the reign of Edward the Third.

decide. To determine an issue or issues. To "decide" includes the power and right to deliberate, to weigh the reasons for and against, to see which preponderate, and to be governed by that preponderance. Commonwealth v Anthes, 71 Mass (5 Gray) 185, 253.

decies tantum (desh′i-es tan′tum). Ten times as much,—an ancient writ or proceeding under which a juror who had been bribed was made to pay ten times the amount received by him for his vote.

decimae (de′si-me). Tenths; tithes; the tenth part of the annual profit of each clergyman's living. Originally these tithes went to the pope, but with the end of papal authority in the reign of Henry the Eighth, they were transferred to the king as the head of the church. See 1 Bl Comm 284.

Decimae debentur parocho (de′si-me de-ben′ter parō′kō). Tithes are due the parish parson.

Decimae de decimatis solvi non debent (de′si-me dē de-si-mā′tis sol′vī non de′bent). Tithes are not due from that which is paid as tithes.

Decimae non debent solvi, ubi non est annua renovatio, et ex annuatis renovantibus simul semel (de′si-me non de′bent sol′vī, u′bi non est an′nu-a re-nō-vā′she-o, et ex an-nu-ā′tis re-nō-van′ti-bus sī′mul se′mel). Tithes ought not be paid where there is not an annual renovation, and only once from annual renovations.

decimation. Selection by lot and the killing of every tenth one; the killing of a large part. A tithing.

deciner. Same as **decennarius**.

Decipi quam fallere est tutius (de′si-pī quam fal′le-re est tu′she-us). It is safer to be deceived than to mislead.

de circumstantibus (dē ser-kum-stan′ti-bus). From the bystanders. Whenever the general panel was exhausted and additional jurors were required to complete a trial jury, they were formerly summoned (de circumstantibus) from the bystanders by the sheriff. 31 Am J Rev ed Jury § 91.

decision. The report of a conclusion reached, especially the conclusion of a court in the adjudication of a case or the conclusion reached in an arbitration. Pierre Water-Works Co. v Hughes County, 5 Dak 145, 163, 37 NW 733; an adjudication by the court without formulating the result in a judgment. Anno: 73 ALR2d 288–291; 20 Am J2d Cts § 70; sometimes synonymous with judgment, as where both words are used in a statute requiring a liberal construction. 30A Am J Rev ed Judgm § 14; the application, by a court of competent jurisdiction, of the law to a state of facts proved, or admitted to be true, and a declaration of the consequences which follow. Le Blanc v Illinois Cent. Railroad Co. 73 Miss 463, 468, 19 So 211.
    See **opinion of court**.

decision at chambers. See **chambers decision**.

decision on appeal. The conclusion of an appellate court; an affirmance, reversal, modification, dismissal, remanding for further proceedings, a direction to the trial court to enter a particular judgment, or the entry of a final judgment. 5 Am J2d A & E § 897.

decisis. See **stare decisis**.

decisive oath. See **oath decisory**.

decisory oath. See **oath decisory**.

decitizenize (dē-sit′i-zn-īz). To deprive of citizenship.

de clamia admittenda in itinere per attornatum (dē kla′mi-a ad-mit-ten′da in ī-ti′-ne-re per at-tor-nā′tum). A writ to compel the justices to allow a person who was engaged in the service of the king to appear by attorney.

declarant. A person who makes a statement which may thereafter be offered as evidence.

declaration. The pleading, better known in modern practice as a complaint or petition, wherein the plaintiff sets forth his cause of action. 41 Am J1st Pl § 73; the listing by a person entering the United States of merchandise or other articles brought into the country by him. 21 Am J2d Cust D § 74; a written or oral statement, the significance of which in the law of evidence is connected with its hearsay character, that is, its effect as a statement of one other than a witness upon the stand. 29 Am J2d Ev § 597.

declaration against interest. Simply, as the term implies, a statement against the interest of the declarant. 29 Am J2d Ev § 617.

declaration of abandonment of homestead. A formal declaration of abandonment of a homestead, executed and acknowledged as required by statute and recorded in the office in which the homestead was recorded.

declaration of dividend. Action taken by the board of directors of a corporation which creates a dividend to be paid by the corporation and the right of a stockholder to demand and receive it. 19 Am J2d Corp § 839; involving the creation of a debt owing by the corporation to each stockholder and an appropriation of surplus to the payment of such debt. Maloney v Western Cooperage Co. (CA9 Or) 103 F2d 992.

declaration of homestead. A statement of the fact of claiming a homestead exemption describing the property selected and filed with the county recorder for the purpose of showing the world that the occupants claim their homestead exemption rights in the property. 26 Am J1st Home § 90.

Declaration of Independence. The formal public announcement by the Continental Congress on July 4, 1776, reciting the grievances of the American colonies against the British Government and declaring them to be free and independent states. While the statements in the document do not have the force of organic law, it is always safe to read the Constitution in the light of it. 16 Am J2d Const L § 15.

declaration of intention. A declaration by an alien of his intention to become a citizen. The filing of such a declaration is permissive under the present law. United States v Menasche, 348 US 529, 99 L Ed 615, 75 S Ct 513. Under the former law, the filing of a declaration of intention was a condition precedent to the filing of a petition for naturalization. 3 Am J2d Aliens § 147.

Declaration of London. A statement by the powers assembled at the London Naval Conference of 1909, concerning the laws of naval warfare.

Declaration of Paris. An international declaration on important points of maritime law made at Paris in 1856.

declaration of rights. That part of a state constitution containing a formal declaration enumerating somewhat in detail the rights of the citizen which the state government must respect; "not a mere enunciation of abstract principles, but a solemn enactment by the people themselves, guarded by a sufficient sanction." McMasters v West Chester Normal School, 13 Pa Co 481, 487.
    See **bill of rights**.

Declaration of Taking Act. A federal statute in respect of the taking of private property for public use upon a formal declaration of taking, the same to be followed by proceedings for the determination of the compensation to be paid for the property. United States v Miller, 317 US 369, 87 L Ed 336, 63 S Ct 276, 147 ALR 55, reh den 318 US 798, 87 L Ed 1162, 63 S Ct 557.

declaration of trust. A means whereby an owner of property may create a trust therein, consisting of his voluntary statement indicating or manifesting his intention to create a trust, which equity will regard as a transfer of title, notwithstanding there is no transfer of the subject matter, subject to the requirement of a writing where the nature of the property and the conditions of the transaction bring it within the statute of frauds. 54 Am J1st Trusts § 61; a judgment or decree declaring the existence of a trust. 54 Am J1st Trusts § 628.

declaration of uses. See **declaring a use; declaration of trust.**

declaration of war. A formal statement by a nation through its executive or legislative department announcing that a state of war exists with another nation. 56 Am J1st War § 5.

declarations. See **declaration** and terms beginning **declaration.**

declarative remedies. Those remedies in equity whose main and direct object is to declare, confirm, and establish the right, title, property, or estate of the plaintiff, whether it be legal or equitable. See 1 Pomeroy's Equity Jurisdiction § 112. See **declaratory judgment.**

declaratory. Explanatory; affirmative; tending to remove doubt.

declaratory judgment. A judgment which declares conclusively the rights and duties, or the status, of the parties but involves no executory or coercive relief following as of course. Clein v Kaplan, 201 Ga 396, 40 SE2d 133; Brindley v Meara, 209 Ind 144, 198 NE 301, 101 ALR 682; Savage v Howell, 45 NM 527, 118 P2d 1113.

An action for a declaratory judgment is the appropriate remedy for the determination of a justiciable controversy where the plaintiff is in doubt as to his legal rights and wishes to avoid the hazard of taking steps in advance of the determination of such rights. 22 Am J2d Dec J § 1.

Declaratory Judgment Act. A federal statute, enacted in 1934, providing that in cases of actual controversy the courts of the United States shall have power, upon petition, declaration, complaint, or other appropriate pleadings, to declare rights and other legal relations of any interested party petitioning for such declaration whether or not further relief is or could be prayed, and that such declaration shall have the force and effect of a final judgment or decree and be reviewable as such. 28 USC §§ 2201, 2202; the Uniform Declaratory Judgments Act, first proposed in 1922, which has been adopted by the great majority of states, in some instances with slight modifications. See 9A Uniform Laws Annotated, Declaratory Judgments.

declaratory part of a statute. That part which declares or states the need or requirement which the statute was framed to fulfil, often introduced by the word "whereas." 50 Am J1st Stat § 152.

declaratory relief. See **declaratory judgment; declaratory remedies.**

declaratory statute. A statute which is declaratory or expressive of the common law, Gray v Bennett, 44 Mass (3 Metcalf) 522, 527; a statute, the purpose of which is to declare or settle the law where its correct interpretation has been doubtful or uncertain.

declare. In common parlance, to state; to assert; to publish; to utter; to announce; to announce clearly some opinion or resolution. Knecht v Mutual Life Ins. Co. 90 Pa 118, 121; in pleading, to allege or set forth in a declaration or other affirmative pleading.

declared dividend. See **dividend declared.**

declared value capital stock tax. A former federal excise tax. Helvering v Lerner Stores Corp. 314 US 463, 86 L Ed 343, 62 S Ct 341.

declared war. A status which continues during the actual hostilities and thereafter during the postwar period where no treaty of peace has been signed and, according to the political branch of the government, a state of war still exists. 3 Am J2d Aliens § 183.

declaring a use. Making a deed to show the object or use after a fine or recovery. If fines or recoveries were levied or suffered without any good consideration, and without any uses declared, they enured only to the use of him who levied or suffered them, unless their force and effect were directed by other deeds expressing particular uses. If such deeds were made before the fine or recovery, they were called deeds to lead the uses. If they were made subsequently, they were called deeds to declare the uses. See 2 Bl Comm 363. See **declaration of trust.**

de claro die (dē klā'rō dī'ē). By the light of day.

de clauso fracto (dē klâ-sō frak'tō). Of breach of close.

de clerico admittendo (dē kle'ri-kō ad-mit-ten'dō). For admitting the clerk. A writ of execution which was directed to the bishop or archbishop, not to the sheriff, requiring the admission and institution of the clerk presented by the patron who had recovered in a quare impedit, or assize of darrien presentment. See 3 Bl Comm 412.

de clerico capto per statutum mercatorium deliberando (dē kle'ri-kō kap'tō per sta'tu-tum mer-ka-tō'ri-um de-li-be-ran'dō). A writ for the liberation of a clerk who was arrested or imprisoned for the violation of a statute merchant.

de clerico convicto commisso gaolae in defectu ordinarii deliberando (dē kle'ri-kō kon-vik'tō kommis'sō gā'o-le in de-fek'tū or-di-nā'ri-ī de-li''be-ran'dō). A writ for the liberation of a clergyman convicted and committed to jail in the absence of the ordinary.

De Clero (dē kle'rō). Concerning the clergy,—the title of the statute 25 Edward III, st. 3, c. 4 (1350), providing benefit of clergy for clerks convicted of any "treasons or felonies touching other persons than the king himself or his royal majesty." See 4 Bl Comm 373.

declination (dek-li-nā'shọn). A plea to the jurisdiction.

declinatory plea (dẹ-klī'nạ-tọ-ri plē). A plea which was at one time interposed before trial or conviction setting up the defendant's right to benefit of clergy. But later, when a defendant was allowed his clergy even after conviction, the plea was not used, for the reason that the prisoner had a chance of acquittal without using it and could pray for benefit of clergy after conviction and before judgment. A plea of sanctuary was also called a declinatory plea. See 4 Bl Comm 333.

declinature (dẹ-klī'nạ-tụr). Same as **declination**.

decline. To refuse in polite terms, as to decline appointment to an office or nomination as a candidate for office.

declined. Refused.

decollatio (de-kol-lā'she-o). Same as **decapitation**.

decollation (dē-ko-lā'shọn). Same as **decapitation**.

de combustione domorum (dē kom-bust-she-ō'ne domo'rum). An appeal of felony charging the crime of arson.

de common droit (dē ko'mon droa). Of common right.

de commorientibus (dē kom-mō-ri-en'ti-bus). Concerning those dying together.

de communi consilio super negotiis quibusdam arduis et urgentibus, regem, statum, et defensionem regni Angliae et ecclesiae Anglicanae concernentibus (dē kom-mū'nī kon-si'li-ō sū'per ne-gō'she-is qui-bus'-dam ar'du-is et ur-jen'ti-bus, rē-jem, stā'tum, et defen-she-ō'nem reg'nī Ang'li-ē et e-klē'si-ē Ang-li-kā'nē kon-ser-nen'ti-bus). Concerning the common council upon certain difficult and urgent affairs relating to the king, the state, the defense of the kingdom of England and of the English church. See 1 Bl Comm 159.

de communi dividendo (dē kom-mū'nī di-vi-den'dō). A writ for the partition of property held by tenants in common.

de comon droit. Same as **de common droit**.

decompose. To rot; to come apart by deterioration. Anno: 45 ALR2d 873 (food).

de computo (dē kom-pū'tō). A writ of account, to compel a person to render an account.

de concilio curiae (dē kon-si'li-ō kū'ri-ē). By the advice of the court.

de conflictu legum (dē kon-flik'tū lē'gum). Of or concerning the conflict of laws.

De Conjunctim Feoffatis (dē kon-junk'tim fe-of-fā'tis). Of or concerning joint feoffees,—the title of a statute passed in the reign of Edward the First.

de consanguineo (dē kon-san-gwi'nē-ō). A writ of cosinage.
See **cosinage**.

de consilio (dē kon-si'li-ō). Of counsel.

de consilio curiae (dē kon-si'li-ō kū'ri-ē). By the advice of the court.

de conspiratione (dē kon-spi-ra-she-ō'ne). A writ of conspiracy.

De Conspiratoribus (dē kon-spi-ra-tō'ri-bus). Concerning conspirators,—a famous statute of 33 Edw. I, often credited with originating the crime of conspiracy, but erroneously so, because the offense previously existed at common law. Commonwealth v Donoghue, 250 Ky 343, 63 SW2d 3, 89 ALR 819.

de consuetudine Angliae (dē kon-su-e-tū'di-ne Ang'-li-ē). By the custom of England. See 3 Bl Comm 95.

de consuetudinibus et servitiis (dē kon-su-ē-tū-di'ni-bus et ser-vi'she-is). Of customs and services,—the name of a writ which lay for the lord against his tenant who withheld rents and services due the landlord by custom or tenure. See 3 Bl Comm 232.

de continuando assisam (dē kon-ti-nu-an'dō as-sī'sam). A writ to continue the assize.

de contributione facienda (dē kon-tri-bū-she-ō'ne fā-she-en'da). A writ for making contribution,—a writ to compel coparceners or cotenants to contribute for services rendered.

de contumace capiendo (dē kon-tu-mā'se kā-pi-en'dō). A chancery writ for the arrest of a person who had committed a contempt.

de conventione (dē kon-ven-she-ō'ne). A writ of covenant.

de copia libelli deliberanda (dē kō'pi-a lī-bel'lī dē-li-be-ran'da). A writ for the delivery of a copy of a libel.

Decoration Day. See **Memorial Day**.

de cornes et de bouche (dē kōr-nè a dē bou-sh). With hue and cry.

de coronatore eligendo (dē ko-rō-nā-tō're e-li-jen'dō). For the election of a coroner,—a writ for the election of a coroner which was originally an elective office. After election, the writ was returned in chancery and was a judicial act of record. The office did not cease with the king's death, but continued until the coroner was removed.

de coronatore exonerando (dē ko-rō-nā-tō're ex-o-ne-ran'dō). For discharging a coroner,—a writ which lay for the removal of a coroner from his office for neglect of duty.

de corpore (dē kor'po-re). Of the body.

de corpore comitatus (dē kor'po-re ko-mi-tā'tus). From the body of the county. Since the statute 24 George II, c. 18 (1750), juries have been summoned from the county at large, and not de vicineto, from the particular neighborhood, as formerly. See 3 Bl Comm 360.

de corpore suo (dē kor'po-re su'ō). Of his body. 28 Am J2d Est § 49.

de coste (dē kost). On the side; from the side; collateral.

decoy. Verb: To entice; to tempt; to lure or allure. Eberling v State, 136 Ind 117, 120. Noun: A person or a thing which allures. The use of the police decoy is not necessarily an entrapment. 21 Am J2d Crim L § 144.

decoy duck. A sham bidder at an auction sale. 7 Am J2d Auct § 26.

decoying. A possible method of kidnapping. 1 Am J2d Abduct § 13.
See **decoy**.

decoy letter. An imitation of a genuine letter, usually marked and directed to a fictitious person, placed in the mails by postal inspectors or officers of the Department of Justice for the purpose of detecting a post office employee who is suspected of appropriating letters or their contents; or a letter sent through the mails by such officers to a person suspected of sending prohibited matter through the mails, for the purpose of detecting him in such violation of the law. Montgomery v United States, 162 US 410, 40 L Ed 1020, 16 S Ct 797; Goode v United States, 159 US 663, 40 L Ed 297, 16 S Ct 136.

decrease. Diminution.

de credulitate (dē kre-dū''li-tā'te). Upon belief, the form of oath made by compurgators in a wager of law. See 3 Bl Comm 343.

decree. The judgment of a court of chancery or equity. 27 Am J2d Eq § 245. A final determination of the rights of the parties in an action in equity.

In many states which have adopted code procedure or operate under a comprehensive set of rules of practice, the distinction between decrees and judgments are abolished for all practical purposes, relief in all actions and suits, whether of a legal or equitable character, being obtained by a judgment in a civil action. 30a am J Rev ed Judgm § 10.

While formerly there was a strict distinction between the terms "judgment" and "decree," the term "judgment" being applied to decisions in actions at law, and "decree" being applied to decisions in cases in equity, the modern tendency is to construe constitutional and statutory provisions dealing with appealability of "judgments" as also including "decrees." Jelm v Jelm, 155 Ohio St 226, 44 Ohio Ops 246, 98 NE2d 401, 22 ALR2d 1300.

decree absolvitor (decree ab-sol′vi-tor). A decree acquitting a defendant.

decree a mensa et thoro (decree ā men′sa et tho′rō). See **divorce a mensa et thoro.**

decree a vinculo matrimonii (decree ā vīn′ku-lō ma-tri-mō′ni-ī). See **divorce a vinculo matrimonii.**

decree by consent. See **consent decree.**

decree condemnator (decree kon-dem-nā′tor). A decree in favor of a plaintiff.

decree dative. A decree which appointed as executor a person who was not nominated in the will.

decree in absence. A decree rendered against a party by reason of his default.

decree nisi. A provisional judgment to be made absolute on motion unless cause is shown against it, the distinguishing characteristic being that further order is required to complete the rendition of a final judgment. 30A Am J1st Judgm § 119. The interlocutory judgment or decree in a divorce action. 24 Am J2d Div & S § 427.

decree nunc pro tunc. See **nunc pro tunc order.**

decree of confirmation. A judgment or decree of court confirming a sale by an administrator, executor, guardian, committee, receiver or other officer of court, usually a prerequisite to the passing of title.

decree of distribution. See **order for distribution.**

decree of divorce A judgment which grants a divorce, not to be distinguished from judgments rendered in cases other than divorce actions, in the absence of statutory provisions creating such distinction. Jelm v Jelm, 155 Ohio St 226, 98 NE2d 401, 22 ALR2d 1300.
See **divorce.**

decree of foreclosure. See **foreclosure.**

decree of interpleader. A decree in favor of the plaintiff in interpleader, discharging him and leaving the claimants interpleaded by him to litigate between themselves for the stake brought by him into court. 30 Am J Rev ed Interpl § 266.

decree of nullity. A judgment or decree annuling a marriage. 4 Am J2d Annul § 92.

decree pro confesso (decree prō kon-fes′sō). A judgment or decree in a suit in equity taken against a defendant in default. 27 Am J2d Eq § 221.

The method in equity of taking a bill pro confesso is consonant with the rule and practice of the courts of law, where, if the defendant makes default, judgment is given for the plaintiff. To take a bill pro confesso is to order it to stand as if its statements were confessed to be true. Thompson v Wooster, 114 US 104, 111, 29 L Ed 104, 107, 5 S Ct 788.

decree quasi in rem. See **proceeding quasi in rem.**

decreet (dẹ-krēt′). Same as decree.

decrementum maris (de-kre-men′tum ma′ris). Reliction; the receding of the sea.

decrepit (dẹ-krep′it). Worn out by illness, age, or hard work. A person may be decrepit without being old. Hall v State, 16 Tex App 6.

decreta (dē-krē′ta). Decrees, plural of **decretum.**

Decreta conciliorum non ligant reges nostros (dē-krē′ta kon-si-li-ō′rum non li′gant rē′jēz nos′tros). The decrees of councils do not bind our kings.

Decretalia Gregorii Noni (de-kre-tā′li-a Gre-gō′ri-ī nō′nī). The decretals of Pope Gregory the Ninth published about 1230. See 1 Bl Comm 82.

decretal order. An order in equity preliminary to the final decree or judgment in the case. See **interlocutory decree.**

decretals (de-krē′talz). Canonical opinions of the popes.

decretum (dēk′rē-tum). A decree; a law.

Decretum Gratiani (dēk-rē′tum grā-she-ā′nī). A compilation of canon law made by the Italian monk, Gratian, about 1151. See 1 Bl Comm 82.

decry (dẹ-krī′). To discredit; to cry down. Blackstone said that the king of England might at any time decry, or cry down, any coin of the kingdom, and thus make it no longer current. See 1 Bl Comm 278.

de curia claudenda (dē kū′ri-a klâ-den′da). A writ which lay at common law for the tenant of an adjoining close, whereby he could compel his neighbor to erect a fence and pay him damages, if he could show a prescriptive right to have the fence erected and maintained by the defendant. Rust v Low, 6 Mass (6 Tyng) 90, 94.

decurio (de-kū′ri-ō). An ancient Roman city manager; a Roman commander of ten soldiers.

de cursu (dē kėr′sū). Of course; as a matter of right.

de custode admittendo (dē kus-tō′de ad-mit-ten′dō). A writ for the admission of a guardian.

de custode amovendo (dē kus-tō′de ā-mō-ven′dō). A writ which lay for the removal of a guardian.

de custodia terrae et haeredis (dē kus-tō′di-a ter′rē et hē-rē′dis). For the custody of land and heir,—a writ whereby the guardian of a minor recovered possession and custody of the lands and person of his ward. See 3 Bl Comm 141.

de cy en avant (dē si an a-vän). From the present henceforth.

dedbaba. Homicide; the killing of a human being.

de debito (dē de′bi-tō). A writ of debt.

de debitore in partes secando (dē de-bi-tō′re in par′tēz se-kan′dō). For cutting a debtor into pieces. The ancient law of the twelve tables has been interpreted to mean that creditors might lawfully dessicate their debtor's body and divide the pieces proportionately to their claims. See 2 Bl Comm 472.

de deceptione (dē dē-sep-she-ō′ne). A writ of deceit.

de defaute de droit (dē dē-fōt dē droa). For failure of right.

de deoneranda pro rata portionis (dē de-ò-ne-ran′da prō rā′ta por-she-ō′nis). A writ which lay for a tenant whose goods had been distrained for rent to enforce contribution against others who were jointly liable with him.

de déshérence. See **droit de déshérence.**

dedi (de′dī). I have given. An apt word of conveyance used in ancient deeds. 2 Bl Comm 310.

dedicate. To make a dedication. See **dedication.**

dedication. The setting aside of land for a public use, in other words, the intentional appropriation or donation of land, or of an easement or interest therein, by its owner for some proper public use. Sioux City v Tott, 244 Iowa 1285, 60 NW2d 510.

dedication by deed. A common form of dedication, being a dedication made by a deed setting forth the exact purpose for which the land is conveyed, either with or without the use of the word "dedicate," and the recording of the instrument, together with a plat of the property. 23 Am J2d Ded § 22.

dedication by plat. A common method of dedicating property for streets, sidewalks, public parks, and squares by selling and conveying lots described with reference to a map or plat upon which areas are designated as used or to be used for streets, sidewalks, etc. 23 Am J2d Ded § 25. The making, signing and acknowledgment of a map or plat of land upon which areas appear as devoted to public use as streets, sidewalks, parks, and squares, at least if followed by a recording of the map or plat. 23 Am J2d Ded §§ 23, 24.

dedication of literary property. Publication without a copyright notice or without any step taken toward obtaining protection of the work by a copyright. Deward & Rich v Bristol Sav. & Loan Corp. (CA4 Va) 120 F2d 537.

dedication to public. Any dedication of property. The essence of dedication is that it shall be for the use of the public at large. 23 Am J2d Ded § 3.

dedicator. One who dedicates land to public use. Such a dedication must be made by the owner or with his consent. 23 Am J2d Ded § 8.

de die claro (dē dī′e kla′rō). By the light of day; by daylight.

de die in diem (dē dī′e in dī′em). From day to day.

dedi et concessi (de′dī et kon-ses′sī). I have given and granted. Words of conveyance used in ancient deeds.

dedimus (de′di-mus). We have given.

dedimus et concessimus (de′di-mus et kon-ses′si-mus). We have given and granted.

dedimus potestatem (de′di-mus po-tes-tā′tem). A commission directed to a judicial officer or an individual by name, authorizing him to take the deposition of the witness named therein. 23 Am J2d Dep § 22.

dedimus potestatem de attorno faciendo (de′di-mus po-tes-tā′tem dē at-tor′nō fā-she-en′dō). We have given the power of receiving an attorney,—a king's writ authorizing a court to permit a party to appear by attorney.

dedit et concessit (de′dit et kon-ses′sit). He has given and granted.

dedititii (dē-di′she-she-ī). Subjects of Rome who had no rights or had surrendered unconditionally.

de diversis regulis juris antiqui (dē di-ver′sis rē′gu-lis jū′ris an-tī′quī). From divers rules of ancient law.

de dolo malo (dē do′lō ma′lō). From evil or wicked design; of or concerning fraud.

de domo reparanda (dē dō′mō re-pa-ran′da). An old writ to compel a person to repair a house because it was dangerous to the community.

De Donis (dē dō′nis). See **Statute de Donis.**

De Donis Conditionalibus. See **Statute de Donis.**

de dote assignanda (dē dō′te as-sig-nan′da). For the assignment of dower,—a writ under which the widow of a tenant in capite compelled the assignment of her dower.

de dote unde nihil habet (dē dō′te un′de ni′hil hā′bet). Of dower whereof she has nothing,—a writ under which a tenant was compelled to assign to a widow her dower. See 3 Bl Comm 183.

de droit (dē droa). Of right.

deductible clause. A clause in an insurance policy, social security statute, or state plan for payment of medical or hospital expenses, expenses first incurred in a moderate amount are withdrawn from the protection of the policy or statute. A clause in an automobile collision policy whereby a stated sum, usually $50 or $100, is deductible from the amount for which the insurer would otherwise be liable. Under such a clause, a deduction for "each collision or upset" contemplates one deduction for each accident giving rise to a cause of action on the policy. 7 Am J2d Auto Ins § 192.

deductible losses. Losses resulting when a taxpayer's property is destroyed, damaged, confiscated, stolen, abandoned, taken by foreclosure, becomes entirely worthless or suffers other special losses, which a taxpayer is permitted to deduct in computing his net income for tax purposes providing the losses are not fully compensated for by insurance or otherwise. 34 Am J2d Fed Tax ¶ 6500.

deduction. Reasoning from a known principle; subtraction. An amount allowed a taxpayer in reduction of gross income to determine taxable income. An item to be deducted from the gross estate of a decedent in computing the taxable estate.

deduction for new. A deduction of one third from the whole amount of the cost of repairing a ship, in computing the amount to be paid the insured under a marine insurance policy. Orrok v Commonwealth Ins. Co. 38 Mass (21 Pick) 456, 469; 29A Am J Rev ed Ins § 1567.

deduction of a claim. The proof of a right by showing its origin either in law or in equity.

deed. Broadly defined, a writing sealed and delivered by the parties; in the modern sense, an instrument conveying real property or an interest therein. 23 Am J2d Deeds § 1.
 See **absolute deed; bargain and sale; quitclaim deed; release and quitclaim; release deed; warranty deed.**

deed absolute. Same as **absolute deed.**

deeded. Conveyed by deed.

deed indented. Same as **deed of indenture.**

deed inter partes. A deed executed by grantor and grantee. Smith v Emery, 12 NJL 53, 60. A deed executed by the persons named therein as grantor and grantee, as distinguished from a deed executed by the agent or attorney of one of the parties or by the agent of each of them, acting in their behalf. Abbey v Chase, 60 Mass (6 Cush) 54.

deed of arrangement. An assignment for the benefit of creditors.

deed of bargain and sale. See **deed of purchase.**

deed of gift. A voluntary deed, as distinguished from a conveyance of property based upon a consideration. See McWillie v Van Vacter, 35 Miss 428.

deed of indenture. See **indenture.**

deed of partition. A deed to one joint tenant from the others or to one tenant in common from his cotenants, whereby an estate in severalty is created in the grantee.

deed of purchase (pér'chās). A bargain and sale deed. See **bargain and sale.**

deed of quitclaim. See **quitclaim deed.**

deed of release. Formerly, the term seems to have been applied only to deeds conveying all the right, title, and interest of the grantor to a grantee who already had some estate in possession in the land released, but in modern usage it is not one of the essentials of a release deed that the grantee shall already have some right, title, or interest in the property released. The term is therefore now synonymous with the term quitclaim deed. Anno: 44 ALR 1269.
See **quitclaim deed.**

deed of separation. A separation agreement and conveyance between husband and wife whereby their respective properties are disposed of between themselves.

deed of trust. A conveyance creating a trust in real estate; a conveyance given as security for the performance of an obligation, which is generally regarded as containing the elements of a valid mortgage. 36 Am J1st Mtg § 16. A species of deed which is in the nature of a mortgage and is a conveyance in trust for the purpose of securing a debt, subject to a defeasance.
It differs from an assignment for creditors, which is more than a security for the payment of debts, being an absolute appropriation of money for their payment. Union Nat. Bank v Bank of Kansas City, 136 US 223, 232, 34 L Ed 341, 344, 10 S Ct 1013.
The difference between a deed of trust and a mortgage is essentially one of form, the former being executed in favor of a disinterested third person as trustee, while the latter is executed directly to the creditor to be secured.

deed poll (pōl). A deed made in one part and signed only by the grantor. It took its name from the fact that the edges were smooth and polled or shaven, as distinguished from a deed which was indented and in two parts. When such a deed is accepted by the grantee, it becomes the mutual act of the parties and therefore the grantee is bound by any covenants in it which are to be performed by him. Midland Railway Co. v Fisher, 125 Ind 19, 24 NE 756.

deed to declare uses. See **declaring a use; leading a use.**

deed to lead uses. See **declaring a use.**

deed to support. A deed made in consideration of the grantor's future support. 50 Am J1st Sup of Per § 2.

deed to timber land. A conveyance of forest land.

de ejectione custodiae (dē ē-jek-she-ō'ne kus-tō'di-ē). For the ejectment of a ward,—a writ which lay for a guardian to secure the person or land of his ward.

de ejectione firmae (dē ē-jek-she-ō'ne fir'mē). The writ of ejectment of farm. This writ lay to recover restitution and damages for ouster of possession from a term for years of the tenant against the lessor, reversioner, remainder-man, or any stranger who had turned him out during the continuance of his term. See 3 Bl Comm 199.

deem (dēm). To judge; to determine or conclude upon consideration; to form a judgment.
The word "deem," as used in the federal statutes, providing that personal property of a serviceman shall not be "deemed" to have a situs for taxation in a state in which he is required to be present by virtue of his service, does not imply a rebuttable presumption so as to permit taxation by the state of temporary presence in some cases. Dameron v Brodhead, 345 US 322, 97 L Ed 1041, 73 S Ct 721, 32 ALR2d 612.

deem advisable. Words which confer a discretion upon a trustee. 33 Am J1st Life Est § 287.

deemster (dēm'stėr). One of the two chief justices of the Isle of Man.

deeply indebted. The financial state of a person whose property is inadequate or barely sufficient for the payment of his debts. Winchester v Charter, 102 Mass 272, 274.

deer-fald (dēr'fōld). An inclosed tract or park for deer, sometimes referred to as a deer-fold.

deer-fold (dēr'fōld). See **deer-fald.**

de escambio monetae (dē es-kam'bi-ō mo-nē'tē). A writ to secure authority for drawing a bill of exchange.

de eschaeta (dē es-chē'ta). A writ for escheat, which lay for a lord to recover the land where the tenant died without heirs.

de esse in peregrinatione (dē es'se in pe-re-gri-na-she-ō'ne). Of being on a journey,—an excuse for not appearing at court.

de essendo quietum de theolonio (dē es-sen'dō quī-ē'tum dē the-ō-lō'ni-ō). Of being quit of toll,—a writ to secure an exemption from payment of toll.

de essonio de malo lecti (dē es-so'ni-ō dē ma'lō lek'tī). A writ to examine into an excuse of being sick in bed for failing to appear at court.

de estoveriis habendis (dē es-to-ve'ri-is ha-ben'dis). A writ for having estovers. The writ lay for a wife divorced a mensa et thoro, whose husband refused to pay her estovers or alimony which the court had allowed her out of her husband's estate for her support. See 1 Bl Comm 441.

de estrepamento (dē es-tre-pa-men'tō). A writ to restrain waste during the pendency of an action concerning the land.

de et super praemissis (dē et sū'per prē-mis'sis). Of and upon the premises.

de eve et de treve (dē ēv ă dē trĕv). From his grandfather and remote ancestors.

de excommunicato capiendo (dē ex-kom-mū-ni-kā'tō kā-pi-en'dō). An English chancery writ which issued to aid in carrying into effect a sentence of excommunication.
The writ has been said by some to be a writ grantable ex debito justitiae, and by others ex gratia. Smith v Nelson, 18 Vt 511, 555.

de excommunicato deliberando (dē ex-kom-mū-ni-kā'tō de-li-be-ran'dō). A writ which issued out of chancery to release a prisoner from the county jail after the bishop had certified the prisoner's reconciliation with the church, following his arrest and imprisonment under a writ de excommunicato capiendo. See 3 Bl Comm 102.

de excommunicato recapiendo (dē ex-kom-mū-ni-kā'tō re-kā-pi-en'dō). A writ for the retaking of a person who had been excommunicated from the church and who had failed to comply with the conditions of his reconciliation with the church after having been released from imprisonment.

de executione facienda in witherman (dē ex-e-ku"-she-ō'ne fā-she-en'da in wi'ther-nam). A writ of execution in witherman; that is in retaliation or by way of reprisal.

de executione judicii (dē ex-e-ku"she-ō'ne jū-di'she-ī). A writ ordering the sheriff to execute a judgment; a writ of execution.

de exemplificatione (dē eg-zem-pli-fi-kā"she-ō'ne). A writ for the exemplification of an original document.
See **exemplification**.

de exitibus terrae (dē ex-i'ti-bus ter'rē). From the issues or profits of the land.

de exoneratione sectae (dē ex-o-ne-rā"she-ō'ne sek'tē). For exemption from suit,—a writ for the exemption of a ward of the king from being sued.

de expensis civium et burgensium (dē ex-pen'sis si'vi-um et bur-jen'she-um). A writ for the levy of the expenses of citizens and burgesses of parliament.

defacing brand. The obliteration of the brand on an animal. 4 Am J2d Ani § 8.

de facto (dē fak'tō). In fact, as distinguished from "de jure," by right.

de facto annexation. See **annexation de facto**.

de facto blockade. A blockade, which may be established by a naval officer acting upon his own discretion or under direction of superiors, without governmental notification, as an adjunct to naval operations, merely by giving notice on the spot to ships coming from a distance. 56 Am J1st War § 172.

de facto contract of sale. A contract of sale which purports to pass the property from the owner to another person. Farmers & Merchants' Nat. Bank v Logan, 74 NY 568, 575.

de facto corporate officer. An officer of a corporation in possession of, and exercising the powers of, the office under the claim and color of an election or appointment, although he is not an officer de jure and may be removed by proper proceedings. 19 Am J2d Corp § 1100.

de facto corporation (dē fak'tō kôr-po-rā'shọn). A corporation in fact, an apparent corporate organization, asserted to be a corporation by its members, and actually acting as such, but lacking the creative fiat of the law—an organization with color of law, exercising corporate rights and franchises, the right of which to corporate functions and attributes is complete as against all the world, except the sovereign. 18 Am J2d Corp § 49.
See **de facto director**.

de facto county seat. A place occupied and recognized as the county seat under color and authority of law; that is, under color of its having been selected and established as such county seat in the mode provided by law. Watts v State, 22 Tex App 572, 578.

de facto court. A paradoxical expression, since the power to create courts is an attribute of sovereignty that can only be exercised by constitutional or statutory provisions. 20 Am J2d Cts § 19.

A de facto court is a competent court, or a "legally constituted court," because its judgments and proceedings are not open to collateral attack. This, of course, does not apply to a court created without color of authority, or to a mere usurper. State ex rel. Bales v Bailey, 106 Minn 138, 118 NW 676.

de facto custody. The custody by a divorced parent of a child, where custody has not been granted by the court to such parent, but he or she has assumed custody because of the abandonment of the child by the parent awarded custody or by the relinquishment of custody of the child by the other parent. 24 Am J2d Div & S § 872.

de facto director. A person who usurps the office of a member of a board of directors of a corporation, and exercises the functions of a member of the board, under color of an election or appointment in itself not legal. Hulings v Hulings Lumber Co. 38 W Va 351, 361, 18 SE 620.

de facto dissolution. That dissolution of a corporation which takes place, in substance and in fact, in the case of corporations organized for pecuniary gain, when the corporation, by reason of insolvency or for other reason, suspends all its operations and goes into liquidation. Youree v Home Town Mut. Ins. Co. 180 Mo 153, 164, 79 SW 175.

de facto government. A new government which exercises undisputed sway over the entire country, the former established government having been nullified by successful rebellion or having lost the support of the people.

A de facto government arises where the established government has been subverted by rebellion, so that the new government exercises undisputed sway for the time being over the entire country, or where the people of any portion of a country subject to the same government throw off their allegiance to that government and establish one of their own, and show not only that they have established a government, but also their ability to maintain it. 30 Am J Rev ed Internat L § 12.

de facto grand juror. A person who sits on a grand jury and acts under color of law in joining in the return of an indictment, although subject to removal upon direct attack by reason of a legal impediment, such as having once refused to qualify for such grand jury and having paid a fine imposed for such refusal. 24 Am J1st Grand J § 23.

de facto grand jury. A grand jury sitting under color of law and recognized by the court as lawful, although subject to a direct attack against the exercise of functions by it by reason of a legal impediment, as where it was impaneled for a term of court that has terminated and is holding over into the next succeeding term. 24 Am J1st Grand J § 6.

de facto guardian. One who intercedes to assume the management of the person and property of an infant left unprotected by the death of its parents, without waiting for a formal appointment as guardian, although so related to the infant as to be entitled to appointment. Maish v Valenzuela, 71 Ariz 426, 229 P2d 248, 25 ALR2d 747.

de facto judge. One who exercises the duties of the judicial office under color of an appointment or election thereto; one who exercises such duties, first, without a known appointment or election, but under such circumstances of reputation or acquiescence as are calculated to induce people, without inquiry, to submit to or invoke his action, supposing him to be the judge he assumed to be; or, second, under color of a known and valid appointment or election, but where the person appointed or elected judge has failed to conform to some precedent, requirement, or condition, such as to take an oath, give a bond, or the like; or, third, under color of a known election or appointment, void because the person appointed or elected judge was not eligible or because there was a want of power in the electing or appointing body or by reason of some defect or irregularity in its exercise, such ineligibility, want of power, or defect being unknown to the public; or, fourth, under color of an election or appointment by or pursuant to a public, unconstitutional law, before the same is adjudged to be unconstitutional. 30A Am J Rev ed Judges § 229.

de facto justice of the peace. An officer who has the possession of the office of justice of the peace and performs the duties of such office under color of right, without being actually qualified in law so to act, but is not in fact a mere usurper. 31 Am J Rev ed J P § 6.

de facto king. A usurper who has secured possession of the throne. Temporary allegiance is due such a king, for his administration of the government, and the temporary protection of the public. "Treasons committed against Henry the Sixth were punished under Edward the Fourth, though all the line of Lancaster had been previously declared usurpers by Act of Parliament." See 4 Bl Comm 77.

de facto municipal corporation. See **municipal corporation de facto.**

de facto officer. See **de facto corporate officer; de facto public officer.**

de facto official newspaper. A newspaper which has acted as an official newspaper without having been legally and regularly designated as such. 39 Am J1st Newsp § 12.

de facto public officer. Summarily defined as one who has the reputation of being the officer he assumes to be, and yet is not a good officer in point of law. Comprehensively defined as a person exercising the duties of the office (1) without a known appointment or election, but under such circumstances of reputation or acquiescence as were calculated to induce people, without inquiry, to submit to or invoke his action, supposing him to be the officer he assumed to be; (2) under color of a known and valid appointment or election, but where the officer had failed to conform to some precedent, requirement, or condition, as to take an oath, give a bond, or the like; (3) under color of a known election or appointment, void, because the one elected or appointed was not eligible, or because there was a want of power in the electing or appointing body, or by reason of some defect or irregularity in its exercise, such ineligibility, want of power, or defect being unknown to the public; (4) under color of an election or appointment by or pursuant to a public, unconstitutional law, before the same is adjudged to be such. 43 Am J1st Pub Of § 471.

de facto road. A road actually used by the public. Locke v First Div. St. Paul & Pacific Railroad Co. 15 Minn 350.

de facto school district. A school district acting under color of law. 47 Am J1st Sch § 24.

de facto segregation. Racial imbalance in the public schools resulting, not from a qualification of color, but from the concentration of persons of one race in the area of school attendance. 15 Am J2d Civ R § 39.

de faire echelle (de fe′r e-shel′). A clause commonly contained in French marine insurance policies which is the equivalent of a license to touch and trade at intermediate ports. American Insurance Co. v Griswold (NY) 14 Wend 399, 491.

defalcation. Including embezzlement and misappropriation but a broader term than either. Re Butts (DC NY) 120 F 966, 970. As used in the provision of the bankruptcy act excepting debts created by defalcation from the effect of a discharge, "defalcation" was intended to include defaults other than malversations implied by fraud, embezzlement and misappropriation, and does not necessarily denote moral deliction. First Citizens Bank v Parker, 225 NC 480, 35 SE 489, 163 ALR 1003.

Used in an unusual but proper sense, the term "defalcation" is synonymous with recoupment and counterclaim. 21 Am J2d Countcl § 12.

See **without defalcation.**

De Falso moneta (dē fal′sō mo-nē′ta). Of false money,—the title of a statute passed in the reign of Edward the First, making the importation of certain foreign coins a capital offense.

defalta (de-fal′ta). Default.

defamation. Libel or slander. The publication of anything which is injurious to the good name or reputation of another person, or which tends to bring him into disrepute. Hollenbeck v Hall, 103 Iowa 214, 72 NW 518. Words which produce any perceptible injury to the reputation of another; a false publication likely to bring another in disrepute. Mosnat v Snyder, 105 Iowa 500, 504, 75 NW 356.

See **defamatory; libel; malice; privileged communications; slander; unfair comment.**

defamatory. Slanderous; libelous; injurious to reputation. Hollenbeck v Hall, 103 Iowa 214, 72 NW 518. A publication is "defamatory" when it tends to injure one's reputation in the community and to expose him to hatred, ridicule, and contempt. Muchnick v Post Publishing Co. 332 Mass 304, 125 NE2d 137, 51 ALR2d 547.

See **defamation.**

defamatory advertising. An advertisement which is libelous or disparaging of a product. 3 Am J2d Advertg § 2.

defamatory per se. See **libelous per se; slanderous per se.**

defamer (dē-fā′mėr). A person who has published a defamation concerning another.

See **defamation; defamatory.**

default. Fault; neglect; omission; the failure to perform a duty or obligation; the failure of a person to pay money when due or when lawfully demanded. Docking v National Surety Co. 122 Kan 235, 252 P 201. The failure of a party to an action to appear in the action where he is under duty to appear, as where a defendant has been served with timely and legal process or to plead in an action where he is required to plead. 30A Am J Rev ed Judgm §§ 198 et seq.

In the law of mandamus a "default" is a failure of a public officer or a group of officers to perform a legal duty. Anno: 175 ALR 650.

See **default judgment; wilful default.**

default day. Same as appearance day,—the last day upon which a defendant may appear in order to avoid a default and the taking of a default judgment. Cruger v McCracken (Tex Civ App) 26 SW 282, 283. In an older day and under a practice which has been eliminated in most jurisdictions, a particular day of the term of court, usually the second day, was the "default day" for all actions commenced for the term irrespective of the time that had intervened between the service of process and the beginning of the term. Consequently "default day" was an occasion at which most of the lawyers of the county and many of the circuit outside the county gathered to take or prevent defaults. Liberality on the part of some judges, even at times in conflict with statute, permitted an appearance to be entered on behalf of a defendant when the case was called in the reading of the judge's calendar.

default final. See **judgment by default final.**

default inquiry. See **judgment by default and inquiry.**

default judgment. A judgment rendered upon an omission by the defendant to take a necessary step in the action within the proper time, for example, a failure to appear or a failure to plead, such omission being a default entitling the plaintiff to have judgment rendered in his favor, usually, but not invariably, without proof of his claim except as evidence is required to establish damages. 30A Am J Rev ed Judgm §§ 198 et seq.

defeasance (dē fē'zans). The clause of a mortgage intended to define the terms and conditions upon which the mortgage shall be satisfied, cease to be security for a debt, and become void. First Nat. Bank v Bain, 237 Ala 580, 188 So 64. More generally defined as a clause in a deed, lease, or other written instrument the legal effect of which is to defeat, cancel, or annul the instrument in whole or in part and thus wholly or partly to release the parties from obligations arising under it upon the happening or not happening of a condition subsequent. Escambia Land & Mfg. Co. v Ferry Pass Inspectors & Shippers Asso. 59 Fla 239, 52 So 715.

defeasible. Subject to defeasance.
See **defeasance.**

defeasible fee. See **determinable fee.**

defeat (dẹ-fēt'). To make void; to annul; to overcome.

defect. An insufficiency; an absence of something necessary for completeness or perfection. Boldt v Budwig, 19 Neb 739, 741.
See **hidden defect; physical defect.**

defect in ways, works, or machinery. Imperfections which render the ways, works or machinery less fit for the use for which they were intended, subsisting in some inherent condition of a permanent nature; some weakness of construction with reference to the proposed uses; some inadaptation to its purposes; some break or misplacement of the parts, or absence of some part; some innate abnormal quality of the thing which renders its use dangerous; some obstacle in the way of use or obstruction to use which is part of the thing itself, or of the condition of the thing itself. Hubbard v Central of Georgia Railway Co. 131 Ga 658, 63 SE 19.

defective. Having defect or flaw of any kind; imperfect; incomplete; lacking; faulty.

The word is not the antonym of the word efficient and yet there are cases in which it has been held to be synonymous with inefficient. Thayer v Denver & R. G. R. Co. 25 NM 559, 185 P 542.
See **mental defect; physical defect.**

defective highway. A highway which is not in such physical condition as to render it reasonably safe for travel by one exercising ordinary care, due to inadequacy of original construction or repairs, subsequent deterioration, obstacles in the way, structures extending or hanging above the way, even wires stretched across the way. 25 Am J1st High § 476.

defective or broken fixtures. An ordinance prohibiting the installation of "defective or broken plumbing fixtures" is invalid inasmuch as its ambiguous language is subject to application to defects not impairing the operating efficiency of the fixtures and therefore not endangering the public health. Thrift Hardware & Supply Co. v Phoenix, 71 Ariz 21, 222 P2d 994, 22 ALR2d 810.

defective record. A record of an instrument so defective for want of index or inaccuracy in copying that constructive notice of the instrument is not imputed to a third person. 45 Am J1st Recds § 113.

defective street. Same as **defective highway.**

defective title to instrument. The title of a person negotiating a negotiable instrument is defective when he obtained the instrument, or any signature thereto, by fraud, duress, force, fear, or for other unlawful means, or for an illegal consideration, or when he negotiates it in breach of faith or under such circumstances as to amount to a fraud. Uniform Negotiable Instruments Law § 55; Vincennes Sav. & Loan Asso. v Robinson, 107 Ind App 558, 23 NE2d 431, 24 NE2d 558.

defective title to real estate. A title which is not marketable.
See **marketable title.**

defect of form or substance. If the right of the party pleading sufficiently appears to the court, although the pleading does not conform to the established method of procedure, the pleading is said to be defective in matter of form. But if the right does not sufficiently appear to the court, the pleading is defective in matter of substance. Lake Shore & Michigan Southern Railway Co. v Kurtz, 10 Ind App 60, 75, 37 NE 303.

defect of heirs. The want of inheritable blood which, upon the death of the tenant, was one of the causes of escheat under feudal tenure. See 2 Bl Comm 245.

defect of parties. A matter of too few, not too many. The failure to join as plaintiffs or defendants persons whose presence in the action is necessary to the determination of the action. Baird v Meyer, 55 ND 930, 215 NW 542, 56 ALR 175.

defect of substance. See **defect of form or substance.**

defectu juris. See **ex defectu juris.**

defectum (de-fek'tum). A defect; an insufficiency.

defectu natalium. See **ex defectu natalium.**

defectu sanguinis. See **ex defectu sanguinis.**

defectus sanguinis (de-fek'tus san'gui-nis). The absence of blood-relationship; the lack or failure of heirs capable of inheriting.

defend. To oppose an attack; to oppose force by force; to oppose a claim or an action; to plead in defense of an action; to contest an action suit or proceeding; to deny. To fence in and shut against common use; as the banks of a river are said to be defended when they are thus closed to the public as a place to fish. Arnold v Mundy (NJ) 1 Halsted 1.

defendant. The person against whom an action or proceeding is brought. The respondent in an action in admiralty. 2 Am J2d Adm § 142. Any natural or artificial person who is sued or who is joined with another party or other parties who are sued. 39 Am J1st Parties § 23.

A party who appears in an action as an intervener, who prays to be made a party defendant, and whose prayer is allowed by the court, is a party defendant in the action. Real Estate Loan Co. v Brown (DC Ga) 23 F2d 331.
See **respondent.**

defendant in error. An appellee; a person in whose favor a judgment was rendered and who is named by the appellant or plaintiff in error as a party to an appeal or error proceeding. 4 Am J2d A & E § 278.

defendemus (de-fen-dē'mus). We will defend,—a formal word used in covenants of warranty.

defendendo. See **homicide se defendendo.**

defender. A defendant in an action, particularly in Scotland; a champion.
See **public defender.**

defendere (de-fen'de-re). To defend; to deny.

defendere se per corpus suum (de-fen'de-re sē per kor'pus su'um). To defend himself with his body,— to wage battle.

defendere se unica manu (de-fen'de-re sē ū'ni-ka ma'nū). To defend himself with one hand, probably by raising it to make oath; to wage his law.
See **compurgation.**

defender of the faith. One of the several titles of the King or Queen of England.

defendit vim et injuriam (de-fen'dit vim et in-jū'ri-am). He defends or denies the force and injury.

defendour (dé-fān-dour). A defender; a champion.

defendre (de'fān-dr). To defend; to deny.

defendress (dẹ-fen'dres). A female defender.

defeneration (dē-fen-er-ā'shon). Lending of money at a usurious rate of interest

defensa (dē-fen'sa). An inclosure; a place which is fenced; a park.

defense. Protection against attack; a matter pleaded by a defendant in an action either to delay the action without destroying the cause or right of action or to defeat the action for all time. 41 Am J1st Pl § 115.
See **national defense; plea; self-defense.**

defense au fond en droit (de'fān-s ô fōn än droa). A denial of the foundation of the (plaintiff's) right,— a denial that the plaintiff has a cause of action,— a general demurrer.

defense au fond en fait (de'fān-s ô fōn än fè). A denial of the foundation of the (plaintiff's) facts,—a general denial.

Defense Bases Compensation Act. A federal statute which, subject to certain exceptions, renders the workmen's compensation benefits of the Longshoremen's and Harbor Workers' Compensation Act available to any employee who is injured while employed outside the United States under a public work contract or while doing work which is preparatory and ancillary thereto. Anno: 2 L Ed 1979.

defense counsel. A trial lawyer; a lawyer conducting or assisting in conducting the defense in a civil action or criminal prosecution; the counsel for the accused in a general or special court-martial.

Defense Department. An executive department of the United States government created by National Security Act Amendments of 1949, inclusive of the Department of the Army, the Department of the Navy, and the Department of the Air Force, since reorganized by the Department of Defense Reorganization Act of 1958. 5 USC §§ 171 et seq.

defense en droit (de'fān-s än droa). Same as **defense au fond en droit.**

defense on the merits. See **meritorious defense.**

defensio (de-fen'she-ō). A defense; a prohibition.

defensive allegation. A kind of pleading in which a defendant in an ecclesiastical cause must propound any circumstances he had to offer in his defense. Thereupon the defendant was entitled to the plaintiff's sworn answer to this defensive allegation, and thence the parties proceeded with their proofs. See 3 Bl Comm 100.

defensive negative averments. See **negativing defenses.**

defensor (dẹ-fen'sor). A defendant; a guardian; a warrantor of title.

defensor civitatus (de-fen'sor si-vi-tā'tus). A Roman city officer who had charge of the public safety.

defensum (de-fen'sum). A place fenced in; a park; an inclosure.

de feodo (dē f'o-dō). In fee.

deferment. Putting off to a future time; postponement of vesting or enjoyment of an estate; the action of a selective service draft board in postponing the call of a person within the draft to service in the armed service.

deferred dividend policy. A policy of life insurance wherein it is stipulated that the insured is not entitled to any part of the surplus or dividend, otherwise accruing upon the policy annually, until the expiration of a dividend period, which may be 5 years, 10 years, 15 years, even 20 years, depending upon the stipulation, and if he dies, and his policy shall be paid within the period, the dividends accumulated on his policy are lost and go to augment the dividend fund to be applied to other policies of the same class which survive the dividend period. Maddox v Mutual Life Ins. Co. 193 Ky 38, 234 SW 949, 22 ALR 1276. Benefiting survivors, as it does, the stipulation has a tontine element.
See **tontine policy.**

deficiency. A characteristic term under tax laws for an additional amount owing by a taxpayer. The amount by which the federal estate tax imposed exceeds the amount shown as the tax by the executor upon his return. United States v Kelley (DC Cal) 24 F2d 234, 236; the amount by which the federal income tax owing by a taxpayer exceeds the amount shown to be owing by the return filed by him. Moore v Cleveland Ry. Co. (CA6 Ohio) 108 F2d 656.

deficiency assessment. An assessment of an additional income tax to cover a deficiency in income revealed upon an audit of the return made by the taxpayer. 34 Am J2d Fed Tax ¶¶ 9042, 9125.

deficiency judgment. A personal judgment, rendered against any person liable for the mortgage debt, in the event of a deficiency on foreclosure, for the amount of such deficiency. 37 Am J1st Mtg § 858. There are judicial, as well as legislative restrictions upon the rendition of such judgments, some of the latter constituting prohibitions in effect. 37 Am J1st Mtg § 864.

deficiency on foreclosure. The amount remaining due the creditor after the foreclosure of a mortgage or other security. 37 Am J1st Mtg § 857.

Deficiente uno sanguine non potest esse haeres (de-fī-she-en'te ū'nō san'gwi-ne non po'test es'se hē'rēz). Devoid of the same blood (as the alleged ancestor), he cannot be an heir (of that alleged ancestor).

De fide et officio judicis non recipitur quaestio sed de scientia, sive sit error juris, sive facti (dē fī'dē et of-fī'she-ō jū'di-sis non re-si'pi-ter quēst'she-ō sed dē sī-en'she-a, sī've sit er'ror jū'ris, sī've fak'tī). The good faith and honesty of a judge are not questioned, but his knowledge, whether it be in error of law or fact, may be.

de fidei laesione (dē fī'dē-ī lē-zhe-ō'ne). The form of oath made by the defendant in a wager of law. See 3 Bl Comm 343.

defile. To pollute; to corrupt the chastity; to debauch; to violate. State v Montgomery, 79 Iowa 737, 738, 45 NW 292.
See **forcibly to defile.**

de filio vel filia rapta vel abducta (dē fī'li-ō vel fī'li-a rap'ta vel ab-duk'ta). A writ for damages for the ravishment or abduction of a son or daughter. See 3 Bl Comm 141.

define. To state the meaning; to describe with exactness. When spoken of space, the word means to set or establish its boundaries authoritatively. Redlands Foothill Groves v Jacobs (DC Cal) 30 F Supp 995.

de fine capiendo pro terris (dē fī'ne kā-pi-en'dō prō ter'ris). Of taking a fine in lieu of the land,—a writ to secure the release of an attainted juror and his goods on his payment of a fine.

de fine force (dē fī'ne fors). Of pure necessity; of absolute necessity.

de fine non capiendo pro pulchre placitando (dē fī'ne non kā-pi-en'dō prō pul'kre pla-si-tan'dō). A writ to prevent the taking of a fine for beaupleader or ill pleading; that is, for not pleading fairly or aptly.

de fine pro redisseisina capiendo (dē fī'ne prō re-dis-sē'si-na kā-pi-en'dō). A writ to secure the release of a disseisor who had made a second disseisin of the same premises.

De Finibus Levatis (dē fī'ni-bus le-vā'tis). Of the fines levied,—the title of a statute of the reign of Edward the First providing that the levy of every fine should be read in court.

definienda (dē-fī''ni-en'da). To be declared.

definite and permanent source of supply of water. A term familiar in irrigation law, which simply means that a stream carries sufficient water at such intervals as to make irrigation from the stream practicable. 30 Am J Rev ed Irrig § 2.

definite failure of issue. A technical term of the law of estates in real property which applies where a precise time is fixed for the failure of issue, not in express terms, but inferable with reference to any particular time or event, as in the case of a devise to a designated person, but if he dies without lawful issue living at the time of his death, then over. McWilliams v Havely, 214 Ky 320, 283 SW 103.
See **die without issue.**

definitive. Complete and accurate; final; conclusive; effecting a termination of a controversy or a litigation.

definitive sentence. The final judgment of an ecclesiastical court.

deflation. An economic condition wherein money acquires more value, with the consequence that prices are lowered; a condition which more than once in the history of the United States has been followed by a grievous economic depression.

deflected lights. Motor vehicle headlights, the beams of which are deflected downward so as to avoid casting a glare into the eyes of an approaching driver. 8 Am J2d Auto § 707.

defloration (def-lō-rā'shon). Seduction; the deprivation of a woman's virginity.

deforce (dē-fōrs'). After having lawfully entered and taken possession of land, to withhold it from the true owner or from any other person who has a right to the possession of it. See 3 Bl Comm 172.
See **deforcement.**

deforcement (dē-fōrs'ment). An abatement, an intrusion, a disseisin, a discontinuance, or any other kind of wrong by which a person who has a right to the freehold is kept out of possession. See 3 Bl Comm 172; detention of dower from a widow. 25 Am J2d Dow § 1860.

deforceor (dē-fōr'sor). Same as **deforciant.**

deforcians (de-for'she-anz). Same as **deforciant.**

deforciant (dē-fōr'siant). In levying a fine of lands, the person against whom the fictitious action is brought upon a supposed breach of covenant, is called the deforciant. See 3 Bl Comm 174. See also 2 Bl Comm 350.

deforciare (de-for-she-ā're). To deforce.

de forisfactura maritagii (dē fo-ris-fak-tū'ra ma-ri-tā'ji-ī). A writ of forfeiture of marriage.

deformity. Any malformation of a person's body. As the word appears in an application for life insurance: an infirmity of a substantial character which in a material degree impairs the physical condition and health of the applicant, and increases the chance of death, sickness, or accident against which the insurance company is asked to issue a policy. 29 Am J Rev ed Ins § 749.

defossion (dē-fosh'on). An ancient punishment for crime by burying the person alive.

De Frangentibus Prisonam (dē fran-jen'ti-bus pri'sō-nam). Concerning those who break prison,—a statute (1 Edw. II, 2) providing that no one should suffer life or limb for prison breach unless committed for a capital offense. See 4 Bl Comm 130.

defraud. To commit acts, omissions or concealments, which involve a breach of legal or equitable duty, trust, or confidence justly reposed, and are

injurious to another, or by which an undue and unconscionable advantage is taken of another. Petrovitzky v Brigham, 14 Utah 472, 47 P 666. In other words, to defraud is to commit a fraud.
See **fraud**.

defraudacion (de-frau-da'the-on). (Spanish.) The fraudulent evasion of payment of taxes.

defunct (dẹ-fungkt'). Dead; a deceased person; a decedent.

de furto (dē fer'tō). Of larceny; an appeal of felony for larceny.

de futuro (dē fu-tū'rō). In the future; for the future; hereafter.

degaster. To commit waste.

de gestu et fama (de jes'tū et fā'ma). Of behavior and reputation,—a writ for the redress of an attack upon a person's conduct or reputation.

degradation. A state of disrepute; to the geologist, a process of erosion by the nibbling of a stream at its banks.

de gratia (dē grā'she-a). By favor; by grace.

De gratia speciali certa scientia et mero motu, talis clausula non valet in his in quibus praesumitur principem esse ignorantem (dē grā'she-a spe-she-ā'lī ser'ta sī-en'she-a et me'rō mō'tū, tā'lis klâ'zu-la non va'let in his in qui'bus prē-zu'mi-ter prin'si-pem es'se ig-nō-ran'tem). The clauses "of special favor," "of certain knowledge" and "of mere motion" are worthless (in those royal grants) in respect to which the prince is presumed to be ignorant.

degree. Estate or rank in life; an abstract measure of importance or seriousness, as the degree of a crime; an award of rank in having completed a course of study; a distance, as shown on a chart, of 60 nautical miles. Steamboat Co. v Fessenden, 79 Me 140.

degree of care. A relative standard by which conduct is tested to determine whether it constitutes negligence. 38 Am J1st Negl § 29.
See **due care; extraordinary care; great care; ordinary care; prudence; reasonable care; slight care; utmost care**.

degree of crime. The grade of a crime according to the gravity of the offense and the culpability of the guilty person, considered, from the practical standpoint, in determining the punishment. 21 Am J2d Crim L § 18.

degree of evidence. See **degree of proof**.

degree of proof. The measure of the evidence required in an action, suit, or proceeding, for the establishment of the truth of an allegation pleaded by verdict of the jury or the finding by the court in a trial to the court. In civil actions, the measure is ordinarily preponderance of the evidence. In criminal prosecutions, proof beyond a reasonable doubt is required to convict. 29 Am J2d Ev §§ 1163 et seq.

degrees of kinship. A classification necessitated where descent is to "next of kin" or "nearest of kin," degrees being determined by counting the generations upward from the intestate to the nearest common ancestor, then downward to the claimant, each generation representing one degree. Anno: 54 ALR2d 1012, § 1.
Such is the so-called civil-law method which prevails in most American jurisdictions. There is another method of computing degrees of kinship, known as the common-law or canon-law method. According to this method, degrees are determined by the number of generations from the nearest common ancestor to the intestate or to the claimant, taking the longer of the two lines where they are unequal. Anno: 54 ALR2d 1013, § 1[b].

degrees of negligence. The classes or grades of negligence into which it has been divided by statutes and judicial decisions, ranging from slight negligence to that which is gross, wilful, or wanton.
The majority of common-law authorities have disapproved the concept of dividing negligence according to degrees, but legislative action and even some judicial opinions have injected into the law of negligence the classification of negligence in cases involving certain acts and instrumentalities according to whether it is slight, simple, or gross or whether it amounts to wilful or wanton misconduct. 38 Am J1st Negl § 43.

degrees of offenses. See **degree of crime**.

degrees of relationship. See **degrees of kinship**.

De grossis arboribus decimae non dabuntur sed de sylvia caedua decimae dabuntur (dē gros'sis ar-bō'ri-bus de'si-mē non da-bun'ter sed dē sil'vi-a se'du-a de'si-mē da-bun'ter). Tithes are not given from entire trees, but they are given from cut wood.

de haerede deliberando alteri qui habet custodiam terrae (dē hē-rē'de de-li-be-ran'dō al'te-rī quī hā'bet kus-tō'di-am ter'rē). A writ for the delivery of the heir to another person who has the custody of the land.

de haerede deliberando illi qui habet custodiam terrae (dē hē-rē'de dē-li-be-ran'dō il'lī quī hā'bet kus-dō'di-am ter'rē). A writ to deliver the heir to the custodian of the land.

de haerede rapto et abducto (dē hē-rē'de rap'tō et ab-duk'tō). For seizing and abducting the heir,—a writ whereby a guardian recovered the custody of his female ward who had been abducted.

de haeretico comburendo (dē he-re'ti-kō kom-bu-ren'dō). For burning a heretic,—a writ issuing only by special direction of the king for causing one convicted of heresy to be burned to death. See 4 Bl Comm 46.

de haut en bas (dē hô an ba). Of high and low.

deherison. Disinheritance.

de hoc ponit se super patriam. See **et de hoc ponit se super patriam**.

de homagio respectuando (dē ho-mā'ji-ō rēs-pek-tu-an'dō'). A writ for the postponement of homage.

de homine capto in withernam (dē ho'mi-ne kap'tō in wi'ther-nam). For taking a man in withernam,—a writ for taking, by way of reprisal or retaliation, a person who had himself taken a bondman out of the country.

de homine replegiando (dē ho'mi-ne re-ple-ji-an'do). The writ for trying title to a feudal slave or to restore a slave to his master. Williamson's Case, 26 Pa 9.

dehors (dẹ-hôrz'). Outside of; disconnected with; unrelated to; extrinsic.

dehors the record (dē-hôrz'). Outside the record; matters outside the transcript of evidence produced at a hearing by an administrative agency. 2 Am J2d Admin L § 445; matters outside the records of title to realty. 1 Am J2d Abstr T § 6.

Dei. See **Dei gratia; judicium Dei.**

de identitate nominis (dē ī'den-ti-tā'te nō'mi-nis). Of identical name,—a writ to cause the release of a person of the same name as that of the true defendant.

de idiota inquirendo (dē i-di-ō'ta in-qui-ren'dō). Of inquisition concerning an idiot; an ancient common-law writ for inquiring whether or not a man was an idiot. See 1 Bl Comm 303.

d'eignesse. See **droit d'eignesse.**

Dei gratia (Dē'ī grā'she-ą). By the grace of God.

De Iis Qui ponendi Sunt in Assisis (dē ī'is quī pō-nen'dī sunt in as-sī'sis). Of those who are to be placed on the assizes,—the title of a statute of the reign of Edward the First.

Dei judicium (Dē'ī jö-dish'i-um). The judgment of God. The ancient trial by ordeal was so called.

de incremento (dē in-krē-men'tō). Of increase; added.

de infirmitate (dē in-fer-mi-tā'te). Of infirmity,—an essoin or excuse for failure to appear at court.

de ingressu (dē in-gres'sū). A writ of entry, which lay for a tenant who had been wrongfully dispossessed of his land.

de injuria (dē in-jū'ri-a). An abbreviation of **de injuria sua propria absque tali causa.**

de injuria sua, absque residuo causae (dē in-jū'ri-a su'a, abs'kwe re-zi'du-ō kâ-zē). By his own fault, without the rest of the alleged cause.

de injuria sua propria absque tali causa (dē in-jū'ri-a su'a prō'pri-a abs'kwe tā'lī kâ'za). By his own fault, without such cause; a formal common-law introduction for a defendant's plea in excuse.

de injuriis (dē in-jū'ri-is). Concerning personal injuries. See 3 Bl Comm 120.

de integro (dē in'te-grō). Anew; over again.

de intrusione (dē in-tru"zhe-ō'ne). A writ of intrusion to oust a person who entered unoccupied premises without color of right.

deists (dē'ists). Persons who entertain a religion which admits no divine revelation as its foundation. Hale v Everett, 53 NH 9.

deit (dē'it). He owes; he is indebted.

dejacion (day-hah-the-on'). (Spanish.) An insolvent's surrender of his property to his creditors.

de jactura evitanda (dē jack-tū'ra e-vi-tan'da). For the sake of avoiding loss; the position of a defendant in an action who is seeking no affirmative relief but merely seeks to bar the plaintiff's recovery. Jones v Sevier, 11 Ky (1 Litt) 50.

dejeration (dej-ę-rā'shǫn). An oath.

De Judaeis. See **Capitula de Judaeis.**

De Judaismo (dē ju-da-is'mō). Of Judaism,—the title of a usury law of the reign of Edward the First.

de judicato solvendo (dē jū-di-kā'tō sol-ven'dō). For the payment of the sum adjudged.

de judiciis (dē jū-di'she-is). Of or concerning judicial proceedings.

de judicio sisti (dē jū-di'she-ō sis'tī). For appearing in court.

de jure (dē jö'rē). By right; by lawful right; rightfully; complying with the law in all respects; valid in law.

de jure communi (dē jū're kom-mū'ni). At common law.

de jure corporation (dē jö'rē kôr'pō-rā'shǫn). A corporation which has been regularly created in compliance with all legal requirements, so that its right to exist as a corporation and exercise its franchise is invulnerable against attack by the state in quo warranto proceedings. 18 Am J2d Corp § 49.

De jure decimarum, originem ducens de jure patronatus, tunc cognitio spectat ad legem civilem, i.e., communem (dē jū're de-si-mā'rum, ō-ri'ji-nem dū'senz dē jū're pa-tro-nā'tus, tunk kog-ni'she-ō spek'tat ad lē'jem si'vi-lem, i. e., kom-mū'nem). As to the right of tithes, taking its origin from the right of the patron, then the civil law has jurisdiction of it, that is, the common law.

de jure director. A director of a corporation who has been duly elected or appointed in compliance with law and the charter and bylaws of the corporation. Hulings v Hulings Lumber Co. 38 W Va 351, 361, 18 SE 620.

de jure government. A government legally established and legally exercising its authority.

De jure judices, de facto juratores, respondent (dē jū're jū'di-sēz, dē fak'tō jū-rā-tō'rēz, re-spon'dent). The judges decide questions of law, the jurors, questions of fact.

de jure justice of the peace. An officer who has the lawful right or title to the office of justice of the peace, with or without the possession of the office. 31 Am J Rev ed J P § 6.

de jure king. A king by right, one who is the rightful heir of the crown. See 4 Bl Comm 77.

de jure officer. A public officer who is in all respects legally appointed and qualified to exercise the office. 43 Am J1st Pub Of § 472; a person who has a lawful right to the office, but who has either been ousted from or has never actually taken possession of the office. Hamlin v Kassafer, 15 Or 456, 15 P 778.

De jure respondent judices, de facto juratores (dē jū're rē-spon'dent jū-di-sēz, dē fak'tō jū-rā-tō'rēz). The judges decide questions of law, the jurors, questions of fact. Piles v Bouldin (US) 11 Wheat 325, 330, 6 L Ed 486, 487.

de la plus belle (de la plū bel). Of the fairest part,— a species of dower which was abolished along with the military tenures, of which it was a consequence. See 2 Bl Comm 132.

delate (dę-lāt'). To charge with crime; to accuse.

de latere (dē la'te-re). Collaterally.

delatio (de-lā'she-ō). An accusation; a charge of crime.

delator (dę-lā'tǫr). An accuser; a spy; an informer.

delatura (de-lā-tū'ra). A charge of accusation of crime; a reward for giving information concerning the commission of a crime.

delay. Verb: To obstruct movement; to detain; to put off to a time in the future; to postpone. Noun: An interference with performance; a detainment.
See **laches; postponement; unavoidable delay.**

delay days. See **lay-days.**

delaying creditors. Building obstructions to hold creditors where they cannot obtain their lawful demands from assets of the debtor. 37 Am J2d Frd Conv §§ 5 et seq; interposing something unjustifiably, before creditors can realize what is due them out of the debtor's property. Petrovitzky v Brigham, 14 Utah 472 47 P 666.

delay rentals. Rentals charged on leased gas wells pending delay in production during drilling and development operations. United Fuel & Gas Co. v Railroad Com. 278 US 300, 73 L Ed 390, 49 S Ct 150.

del bien estre (del bee-an ëstr). Same as **de bene esse**.

del credere (del kre'de-re). A term of Italian origin signifying guaranty or warranty.

del credere agent. An agent who guarantees his principal against the default of those with whom contracts are made.
See **del credere factor**.

del credere commission. An additional compensation paid to a factor for undertaking, in case of a sale, to guaranty to his principal the payment of the debt due from the buyer. Duguid v Edwards (NY) 50 Barb 288, 296.

del credere factor (del kre'de-re fak'tor). A factor who for an additional commission guaranties the solvency of the purchaser and his performance of the contract. Pocohontas Guano Co. v Smith, 122 Va 318, 94 SE 769.

delectus personae (dẹ-lek'tus pėr-sō'nē). A choice or selection of the person. Kingman v Spurr, 24 Mass (7 Pick) 235, 238. The doctrine of delectus personae applies to the selection of a natural person in whose integrity and confidence the donor of a power confides and has no application to a corporation which has been appointed as trustee. Adams v St. Clair, 185 Miss 416, 188 So 559.

delectus personarum (dē-lek'tus per-sō'nā'rum). A selection or choice of persons.
See **delectus personae**.

delegare (de-le-gā're). To delegate.

delegate (del'ẹ-gāt). Noun: A representative; an agent; a person who is substituted for another. Verb: To appoint; to depute; to relegate; to authorize.

delegated legislation. Rules or regulations made and promulgated by an administrative agency. 1 Am J2d Admin L § 93.

delegated power. Authority which has been delegated or bestowed upon a person or body by a superior or higher person or body.

delegates. Representatives; persons authorized to act for others, especially in political conventions and state or national conventions held by religious, fraternal, or social bodies.
See **court of delegates**.

delegatio (de-le-gā'she-o). (Civil law.) A substitution of debtors.

delegation. The act of conferring authority upon another; the body of delegates or representatives from a particular state or political subdivision, e. g. the delegation from New York in Congress or in the National Convention of the Democratic Party. A novation; a substitution of debtors. Adams v Power, 48 Miss 450, 454.
See **imperfect delegation**.

delegation of authority. See **delegation of power**.

delegation of legislative power. An attempt by a legislature to amplicate its legislative power by delegating to another the power to enact a law, whether in form or effect, or to bestow upon another the power to determine the effectiveness of a specific act. 16 Am J2d Const L § 240. There is, of course, a sense of the term "delegation of legislative power," as to which there is no impropriety, that is, the delegation of power made to a legislature by a constitution. 16 Am J2d Const L § 211. It is also well settled that it is within the power of the legislature to delegate to a municipal corporation for municipal purposes, to be exercised within the municipal limits, the three most essential powers of the state, namely, the police power, the power of taxation, and the power of eminent domain. 37 Am J1st Mun Corp § 111.

delegation of powers. An essential in the creation of an agency. 3 Am J2d Agency § 2; the appointment of a subagent by an agent. 3 Am J2d Agency § 152; a vesting of authority in an administrative agency, as to which meticulous precision of language is neither expected nor required. Russell Motorcar Co. v United States, 261 US 514, 67 L Ed 778, 43 S Ct 428.
See **delegation of legislative power**.

Delegatus debitor est odiosus in lege (de-le-gā'tus de'bi-tor est ō-di-ō'sus in lē'je). A substituted debtor is obnoxious to the law.

Delegatus non potest delegare (de-le-gā'tus non po'-test de-le-gā're). A representative cannot delegate his authority. Jamesville & Washington R. Co. v Fisher, 109 NC 1, 13 SE 698. The principle is that where personal trust or confidence is reposed in an agency of the government and especially where the exercise and application of the power is made subject to the judgment or discretion of the agency, the authority is purely personal and cannot be delegated to another unless there is a special power of substitution either expressly or necessarily implied. 2 Am J2d Admin L § 222. The maxim is not applicable to a general agent of an insurance company, since the business of such an agent, either in issuing policies or in soliciting insurance, is not of such a discretionary or personal nature that it cannot be delegated. 29 Am J Rev ed Ins § 148.

de leproso amovendo (dē le-prō'sō ā-mō-ven'dō). A writ for the removal of a leper.

delete (dẹ-lēt'). To expunge; to erase; to blot out.

deletion. The obliteration, expunging, or crossing out of words or letters of an instrument, such as a will. 57 Am J1st Wills § 508.

Deliberandum est diu quod statuendum est semel (dē-li-be-ran'dum est dī'ū quod sta-tū-en'dum est se'-mel). That which is to be settled once and for all should be deliberated at length.

de libera piscaria (dē li'be-ra pis-kā'ri-a). A writ of free fishery to enforce a person's exclusive right to fish.

deliberate. Verb: To consider with care; to plan beforehand; to premeditate. Adjective: By plan or design; considered action; avoiding hasty or ill-conceived acts.
By the use of the word "deliberate" in describing a crime, the idea is conveyed that the perpetrator weighs the motives for the act and its consequences, the nature of the crime, or other things connected with his intentions, with a view to a decision thereon; that he carefully considers all these, and that the act is not suddenly committed. State v Boyle, 28 Iowa 522, 524.

deliberate and premeditated. Connoting careful consideration and examination of the reasons for and against a choice or measure; some plan thought out before the commission of the act and a decision to act according to a plan. People v Bender, 27 Cal 2d 164, 163 P2d 8; People v Gonzales, 87 Cal App 2d 867, 198 P2d 81.

deliberately. Carefully, designedly, unhurriedly.
As used in defining murder, the word means in a cool state of the blood. It does not mean brooded over, considered, reflected upon for a week, a day, or an hour, but it means an intent to kill, executed by a party not under the influence of a violent passion suddenly aroused by some just or lawful cause of provocation to passion, but in the furtherance of a formed design to gratify a feeling of revenge or to accomplish some other unlawful act. State v Forsha, 190 Mo 296, 88 SW 505. See also Commonwealth v Tucker, 189 Mass 457, 76 NE 127.

deliberate speed in desegregation of schools. A concept enunciated by the United States Supreme Court several years ago after having declared that state laws requiring or permitting segregation of pupils in public schools, that is, denying Negro children admission to public schools attended by white children, were unconstitutional. Brown v Board of Education, 349 US 294, 99 L Ed 1083, 75 S Ct 753. The concept has never countenanced indefinite delay, although it was once recognized that a court properly might conclude that the relevant facts in a particular case justified school authorities in not attempting immediate nonsegrated admission of all qualified Negro children. Cooper v Aaron, 358 US 1, 20, 3 L Ed 2d 5, 19, 78 S Ct 1401. But much time has passed since the issue first arose, and it is to be said now that delays in the segregation of public school systems are no longer tolerable. Bradley v School Board of Education, 382 US 103, 15 L Ed 2d 187, 86 S Ct 224.

deliberate violation. An unexcused or wilful violation. 8 Am J2d Auto § 705.

deliberation. A careful and thoughtful consideration; slowness in action; thinking and reflecting, having volition to make a choice and refrain from doing the homicidal act. No particular period of time is essential to "deliberation" as an element of murder in the first degree. A very brief period will suffice, provided the formed intent to kill was consciously conceived in the mind of the slayer before the homicidal act was committed. 26 Am J1st Homi § 42.
See **premeditation.**

de libero passagio (dē lī'be-rō pas-sā'ji-ō). A writ of free passage, which lay to enforce a right to pass over private water.

de libertate probanda (dē li-ber-tā'te prō-ban'da). For proving freedom,—a writ whereby a villein might establish his status as a freeman.

de libertatibus allocandis (dē li-ber-tā'ti-bus al"lō-kan'dis). A writ to enforce certain liberties of burgesses and citizens.

Delicatus debitor est odiosus in lege (de-li-kā'tus de'bi-tor est ō-di-ō'sus in lē'je). A luxurious debtor is detestable to the law.

de licentia transfretandi (dē lī-sen'she-a trans"fre-tan'dī). A writ for leave to cross the sea.

delict (dē-likt'). A tort; a wrong; a criminal offense; a misdemeanor.

delicti (dē-lik'tī). See **corpus delicti.**

delicto (de-lik'to). See **ex delicto; flagrante delicto; in delicto.**

delictum (dē-lik'tum). A wrongful act; a tortious act; a criminal act; a misdemeanor. See 3 Bl Comm 117.
See **actions ex delicto; ex delicto.**

delictus (de-lik'tus). See **delictum; locus delicti.**

delimit. To limit; to mark with a boundary line.

delineate. To picture or describe by drawn lines, as by lines made on a map.

delinquency. A failure or omission of duty, a fault, a misdeed, an offense, a misdemeanor, a crime. People's Sav. Bank v Retail Merchants Mut. Fire Ins. Co. 146 Iowa 536, 123 NW 198.
See **delinquent children.**

delinquency proceeding. A proceeding in juvenile court, usually civil in nature for the purpose of placing a delinquent child under the control of the court; a proceeding in juvenile court for an adjudication of the status of a child in the nature of a guardianship imposed by the state as parents patriae to provide the care and guidance that under normal circumstances would be furnished by the child's parents. 31 Am J Rev ed Juv Ct § 53; within the meaning of the Uniform Insurers Liquidation Act, a proceeding for the rehabilitation of an insurance company in financial difficulties. Anno: 46 ALR2d 1186.

Delinquens per iram provocatus puniri debet mitius (de-lin'quenz per ī'ram prō-vō-kā'tus pu-nī'rī de'bet mi'she-us). A wrongdoer who has been provoked to anger ought to be punished less severely.

delinquent. Noun: A person failing in duty; a person offending by neglect of duty. Peoples Sav. Bank v Retail Merchants' Mut. Fire Ins. Co. 146 Iowa 536, 123 NW 198; a person whose acts do not measure up to the proper standard of conduct expected of civilized people. Adjective: Guilty of improper conduct; behind in payment of an obligation.
See **delinquent children.**

delinquent children. A generic term. Children who have committed offenses against the law, or who are found to be falling into bad habits, or who knowingly associate with vicious or immoral persons, or who are growing up in idleness and crime. 31 Am J Rev ed Juv Ct § 36; children who have committed acts which but for the ages of the perpetrators would be criminal offenses punishable as such. State v Dubray, 121 Kan 886, 250 P 316.
As used in juvenile laws the terms "incorrigibility" and "delinquency" are two different offenses. The former has in it the element of continuous disobedience of parental commands, viciousness, and general bad conduct. The latter may be, and often is, a single offense—violation of any law of the state or any city or borough ordinance. Anno: 45 ALR 1533, s. 85 ALR 1099.

delirious. See **delirium.**

delirium. A state of mind in which a person is wholly unconscious of surrounding objects or conceives them to be different from what they really are; a state of mind in which the mind acts without being directed by the power of volition which is partially or entirely suspended. 29 Am J Rev ed Ins Per § 3.

delirium febrile (de-li'ri-um fe'bri-le). A fever accompanied with delirium.

delirium tremens. A mental disease brought on by the use of intoxicants, 21 Am J2d Crim L § 44; a

DELITO [329] DELIVERY

form of insanity resulting from the collapse of the human system as a result of habitual drunkenness, immediately produced by sudden abstinence from liquor. 29 Am J Rev ed Ins Per § 3; known as "mania a potu" in the extreme stage where the victim is virtually a madman, deprived of all reason for intermittent periods during which he sustains attacks or so-called fits. State v Reidell, 14 Del (9 Houst) 470, 473, 14 A 550.

delito (day-lee′to). (Spanish.) A crime.

deliver. To hand over; to surrender possession to another. Marcus v Pennsylvania Trust Co. (CA3 Pa) 23 F2d 303; to give forth, as a speech; to assist in the birth of a child.

deliverance (dē-liv′ẽr-ans). A delivery; the verdict of a jury.

delivered. Delivery completed.
A child is delivered only when it is born alive. State v Joiner, 11 NC (4 Hawks) 350, 353. The fact that a bastard child was born dead before institution of a proceeding to recover the expenses incident to its mother's confinement precludes the maintenance of the proceeding where the statute which authorizes it contemplates that the child be born alive in providing for the making of a provision for the child's support, and that it may be instituted by a woman if "pregnant with child which, if born alive, may be a bastard child" and that "before proceeding to trial the complainant must file a declaration stating that she has been delivered of a bastard child begotten by the accused." Inman v Willinski, 144 Me 116, 65 A2d 1, 7 ALR2d 1390.

delivering carrier. The carrier performing the linehaul service nearest to a point of destination, not a carrier performing merely a switching service at the point of destination. 49 USC § 20 (11).

delivery. A handing over; the surrender of possession to another; a release from imprisonment.
As used in a statute against fraudulent conveyances, the word implies the surrender of the control of the property by the vendor and the assumption of possession by the vendee, and mere words will not constitute such a delivery. O. W. Perry Co. v Mullen, 81 Mont 482, 263 P 976, 56 ALR 514.
For some purposes, a delivery is accomplished by nothing more than making a thing available to another, placing it within his reach, notwithstanding there is no actual handing of the thing from one person to another. Ross v Pan American Airways, 299 NY 88, 85 NE2d 880, 13 ALR2d 319 (airline ticket).
See **claim and delivery; conditional delivery; constructive delivery; jail delivery; writ of delivery;** also terms and expressions beginning **delivery** which follow.

delivery as an escrow. A delivery on some collateral condition, which must be consistent with the contract, on the happening of which condition alone the contract is to take effect. 28 Am J2d Escr § 1.

delivery bond. A bond, otherwise known as a forthcoming bond or a redelivery bond, given by the defendant in an action aided by attachment, in obtaining the release of the attached property from the custody of the officer who seized it under the writ of attachment, although not from the lien of the attachment, the condition of the bond being that if judgment in the action is rendered against the defendant, the property shall be forthcoming to satisfy the execution on such judgment, otherwise that the sureties will be bound to the extent of the value of the property, in some instances, and to the amount of the indebtedness in other instances. 6 Am J2d Attach § 523; a bond containing comparable conditions given in obtaining the release of property seized under a writ of execution. 30 Am J2d Exec § 277; a bond furnished by the defendant in a replevin action in having the property replevied returned to him. 46 Am J1st Replev § 86.

delivery by carrier. The surrender of the goods by the carrier to the right person, in a proper manner, and at a proper place and time. 13 Am J2d Car § 406.

delivery of bastard child. The birth of a child to parents not husband and wife; for some purposes the birth of a live child. Inman v Willinski, 144 Me 116, 65 A2d 1, 7 ALR2d 1390.

delivery of bill or note. A voluntary transfer of possession of the instrument. 15 Am J2d Com C § 7.

delivery of deed. A condition of the operative effect of the instrument. A transfer of the instrument from the grantor to the grantee or his agent or to a third person for the grantee's use, in such manner as to deprive the grantor of the right to recall it at his option, and with intent to convey title. Marshall v Marshall, 140 Cal App 2d 475, 259 P2d 131. A transfer of possession, either actual or constructive, from one person to another. Uniform Negotiable Instruments Act § 191.

delivery of gift. An actual, symbolical, or constructive transfer of possession of the subject matter to the donee personally or to some person acting as his agent, trustee, guardian, or bailee, the operation of physically handing over giving way at times, as where the subject matter is bulky, to such acts and declarations as the situation reasonably permits, it being essential, however, whatever the act employed may be, that it manifest the donor's intention to divest himself of title and possession. 24 Am J1st Gifts §§ 24 et seq.
To make a valid gift of corporate stock by assignment on a separate document, the Uniform Stock Transfer Act requires delivery of both the separate document and the stock certificate. Lyons v Freshman, 124 Mont 485, 226 P2d 775, 23 ALR2d 1165.

delivery of insurance policy. An insurance policy becomes effective as by the delivery of the instrument where it appears that there is an intention to part with the control of the instrument and to place it in the possession or control of the insured, or some person acting for him, and an act evincing such a purpose. 29 Am J Rev ed Ins § 216. Mailing or otherwise delivering a policy to the agent of the insurer with unconditional instructions to deliver the instrument to the insured is generally deemed sufficient to constitute a delivery of the policy. Mutual Life Ins. Co. v Otto, 153 Md 179, 138 A 16, 53 ALR 487.

delivery of ship. As with other unwieldy property, the delivery may be purely constructive, and may be effected by delivery of the vessel's documents of title, which supplies not merely a symbol, but the mode of enabling the buyer to take actual possession as soon as circumstances permit. 48 Am J1st Ship § 67. The transfer of a ship at sea by the delivery of a bona fide bill of sale, mortgage, or assignment in trust is valid, even as against the vendor's creditors, although possession is not given at once, provided the vendee takes prompt possession when the property comes within his reach. 48 Am J1st Ship § 69.

delivery of warehouse receipt. The voluntary transfer of possession from one person to another. Uniform Warehouse Receipts Act § 58.

delivery order. An order drawn by the owner of goods on the bailee of them, directing their delivery to a third party.

delivery service. The delivery of small packages by messenger or delivery boy, which, under some circumstances, puts the proprietor in a classification of a common carrier. Portland v Western Union Tel. Co. 75 Or 37, 146 P 148.

delivery table. The table upon which a woman is placed for delivery in giving birth. Anno: 37 ALR2d 1291.

delivery to carrier. The placing of a shipment in the exclusive possession, custody, and control of the carrier for the purpose of immediate transportation, and an acceptance by the carrier. 13 Am J2d Car § 256. It is a well-established general rule that when goods are to be shipped to the buyer, a delivery by the seller to a carrier designated by the buyer is a delivery to the buyer, on the theory that the carrier is made the agent of the buyer to accept the delivery. 46 Am J1st Sales § 172.

de lucro captando (dē lū′krō kap-tan′dō). For the sake of taking a profit. The position of a plaintiff in an action who seeks to gain a profit by maintaining his suit. Jones v Sevier, 11 Ky (1 Litt) 50.

de lunatico inquirendo (dē lū-nat′i-kō in-kwi-ren′dō). A writ for an inquisition of lunacy. Hart v Deamer (NY) 6 Wend 497, 498.
See **commission of lunacy.**

delusion. A belief based upon a concept for which there is no reasonable foundation and which is ordinarily incredible to a sane person. Kimberly's Appeal, 68 Conn 428, 36 A 847. An extreme misconception; partial insanity, sometimes called delusional insanity. 21 Am J2d Crim L § 41.
See **insane delusion.**

delusional insanity. See **delusion; insane delusion; paranoia.**

dem. An abbreviation of **demise.**
See **ex dem.**

Dem. Abbreviation of Democrat, also of Democratic.

de magna assisa eligenda (dē mag′na as-sī′sa ē-li-jen′da). Of choosing the grand assize; a writ for choosing the grand assize. See 3 Bl Comm 351.

demain (dẹ-mān′). To-morrow. Also, same as **demesne.**

De majori et minori non variant jura (dē mā-jō′rī et mi-nō′rī′′ non va′ri-ant jū′ra). Whether the matter is great or small, the laws do not vary.

de mal de lit. See **essoin de mal de lit.**

de mal de venue. See **essoin de mal de venue.**

De Malefactoribus in Parcis (dē ma-le-fak-tō′ri-bus in par′sis). Of wrongdoers in the forests,—the title of the statute of 21 Edward I, st. 2 (1293). Under this statute if trespassers in forests, parks, or warrens refused to surrender themselves to the keepers, the keepers might kill them. See 4 Bl Comm 180.

de malo (dē ma′lō). Of sickness.

de malo lecti (dē ma′lō lek-tī). See **essoin de malo lecti.**

de malo veniendi. See **essoin de malo veniendi.**

demand. A claim; a legal obligation; a request to perform an alleged obligation; a written statement of a claim, Brennan v Swasey, 16 Cal 141; a requisition or request under a claim of right, Brackenridge v Texas, 27 Tex App 513, 11 SW 630; the assertion of a right to recover a sum of money from the person upon whom the demand is made. Mack v Hugger Bros. Constr. Co. 153 Tenn 260, 283 SW 448, 46 ALR 389, 392.
See **claim; cross demand; payable on demand; reciprocal demands; statement of demand.**

demanda (de-man′da). A demand.

demand against a decedent. Any debt or claim enforceable in law or equity against a person since deceased which must be presented to his executor or administrator in order to obtain allowance and payment. 31 Am J2d Ex & Ad § 276.

demandant (dẹ-mȧn′dạnt). A person who makes a demand; a plaintiff.

demand certificate of deposit. See **certificate of deposit.**

demand deposit. A bank deposit payable on demand or within a specified number of days after demand. 10 Am J2d Banks § 356.

demand for change of venue. A formal application for change of venue, presenting the ground upon which a change is demanded, and supported by affidavit. 56 Am J1st Ven § 60.

demand for exemption. See **notice of exemption.**

demand for jury trial. A prerequisite in many jurisdictions to a right to a jury trial. The demand is made by filing a formal demand or notice that a jury trial is desired, even by merely placing the case upon the list or calendar of jury cases. 31 Am J Rev ed Jur § 40.

demand for rent on the due date. The ancient common-law rule, as reported by Coke, was "that the landlord must ask for the precise sum due, at a convenient time before sunset upon the day when the rent is due, upon the land, at the most notorious place of it, though there be no person on the land to pay." The details must be strictly observed by the landlord; thus, Coke says "he cannot demand it at the back door of the house but at the fore door." In rejecting the rule as absurdly impractical in modern times, Circuit Judge Frank has delved deeply into a well of medieval lore, concluding convincingly that our ancestors were the slaves of form and that judicial discretion is a product of a later and better world. United States v Forness (CA2 NY) 125 F2d 928.

demand for struck jury. A demand for a jury from a panel that is struck or chosen for a particular case, not from the regular panel for the term of court. 31 Am J Rev ed Jur § 90.

demand in attachment. The debt or obligation upon which the remedy of attachment is available. 6 Am J2d Attach §§ 40 et seq. The statutory liability of a stockholder of a corporation arising out of the obligation of the corporation to pay an assessment, is contractual and constitutes a "demand" or "debt" which will support an attachment. Caldwell v Morfa (DC Tex) 24 F2d 106.

demand in embezzlement. A demand as a prerequisite to a prosecution for embezzlement must be an actual demand. In civil actions constructive demands may be and are recognized, but not so in the criminal prosecution of a defendant for an offense having as one of its statutory ingredients a refusal to pay on demand. Shoener v Pennsylvania, 207 US 188, 191, 52 L Ed 163, 165, 28 S Ct 110.

demand in reconvention. The civil-law equivalent of counterclaim. 20 Am J2d Countcl § 5.

demand note. A promissory note payable on demand. 11 Am J2d B & N § 167.

demand oyer. See **oyer.**

demand paper. Commercial paper payable upon demand. 11 Am J2d B & N § 167.
  The term "payable on demand" imports that the debt evidenced by the note is already due. The obligation is absolute and present; the only element not fixed with certainty is the time of payment; and as that is at the option of the creditor, and the debtor must be prepared eo instante, the time of payment, and with it the statute of limitations, begins to run at once. Cook v Carpenter, 212 Pa 165, 61 A 799.

demandress (dẹ-màn'dres). A female plaintiff.

demands. See **demand,** also terms and expressions following that word, which begin **demand.**

de manucaptione (dē ma-nū-kap-she-ō'ne). A writ to compel the sheriff to release a prisoner and take mainpernors or sureties as bail. See 3 Bl Comm 128.

de manutenendo (dē ma-nū"te-nen'dō). A writ of maintenance which lay against a person who had committed maintenance.

de me (dē mē). From me.

demease. Death; demise.

de medietate linguae (dē me-di-e-tā'te lin'gwē). Of divided tongue or language. The characterization of a jury composed one-half of English speaking persons and one-half of persons speaking the language of the accused. Respublica v Mesta (Pa) 1 Dow 73, 1 L Ed 42.

de medio (dē mē'di-ō). Of mesne,—an ancient writ which lay for the tenant against the mesne lord, when the lord paramount had distrained the tenant for the rent due to him—the lord paramount—from the mesne lord. See 3 Bl Comm 234.

de melioribus damnis (dē mē-li-ō'ri-bus dam'nis). For better damages; the plaintiff's election to proceed against one defendant after having dismissed the action as to the others.

demembration (dẹ-mem-brā'shọn). The criminal offense of severing a limb from a person's body.

demens (dē'menz). A person who is demented; a person who has lost his mind.

dementenant en avant (de'mon-te-nän on avän). From the present time henceforth.

dementia (dẹ-men'shi-ạ). An impaired state of the mental powers, feebleness of mind. Dennett v Dennett, 44 NH 531.

dementia precox paranoid (dē-men'she-a prē'kox pa'-ra-noid). That form of dementia in which the patient exhibits ideas of persecution and has delusions; mental disorder occurring in early life; sometimes called schizophrenia. Rasmussen v George Benz & Sons, 168 Minn 319, 321, 210 NW 75, 76.

De Mercatoribus (dē mer-ka-tō'ri-bus). The statute 13 Edward I (1285) allowing the charging of lands of a merchant with debts contracted in trade. The statute was also called Acton Burnel. See 2 Bl Comm 160; 4 Bl Comm 426.

demesne (de-mēn'). Own; his own; lands of the lord himself which were not held by him of a superior. A manor was a district of land which was held by a lord or great personage, who kept in his own hands as much land as he required for his household. Such lands were called demesne lands. See 2 Bl Comm 90.

demesne, as of fee. There is a distinction between a corporeal inheritance, of which a man is said to be seised in his demesne as of fee, and an incorporeal inheritance, of which he is said merely to be seised as of fee, and not in his demesne, because incorporeal hereditaments are by nature merely collateral to lands and houses, as a rent issuing out of those lands or houses, and the owner has no property, dominicum, or demesne in the thing itself. See 2 Bl Comm 106.

demesne lands. See **demesne.**

demesne lands of the crown. The share of land which was reserved to the crown at the original distribution of landed property, or such as came to it afterwards by forfeitures or other means. These lands were anciently very large and extensive, comprising many manors, honors and lordships, the tenants of which had very peculiar privileges. See 1 Bl Comm 286.

demesnial (de-mē'ni-ạl). Pertaining to a demesne.

demeure. See **en demeure.**

demeyne. See **en demeyne.**

demeyne come de fee. See **en son demeyne come de fee.**

demi (dẹ-mī'). One-half.

demidietas (de-mĭ-di-ē'tas). One-half.

De Militibus (dē mī-li'ti-bus). The statute of 1 Edward II (1307) whereby vassals of the king were compelled to be knighted, or to pay a fine. This practice "was exerted as an expedient for raising money by many of our best princes, particularly by Edward the Sixth and Queen Elizabeth." See 2 Bl Comm 69.

demi-mark. A sum of money tendered and paid into court in certain cases in the trial of a writ of right by the grand assize. The amount tendered was six shillings and eightpence. See 3 Bl Comm appendix V.

de minimis (dē mi'ni-mis). Concerning trifles. NLRB v Suburban Lumber Co. (CA3) 121 F2d 829.

de minimis non curat lex. The law is not concerned with trifles. Loeffler v Roe (Fla) 69 So 2d 331, 47 ALR2d 319. A maxim leading to the rule that accepts substantial performance as a sufficient performance of a contract, 17 Am J2d Contr § 370; sometimes applied to exclude the recovery of nominal damages, where no unlawful intent or disturbance of a right or possession is shown and where all possible damage is expressly disproved, 22 Am J2d Damg § 2; and applied at other times to preclude reversal on appeal, 5 Am J2d A & E § 790. The maxim has no application to money demands. Kennedy v Gramling, 33 SC 367. It will not prevent the recovery of nominal damages for an invasion of one's rights, as by a trespass upon his lands, especially where the invasion, if not penalized, may result in obtaining a prescriptive right. 22 Am J2d Damg § 5.

De minimis non curat praetor (dē mi'ni-mis non kū'rat prē'tor). (Roman law.) The praetor does not concern himself with trifles.

de minis (dē mi'nis). A writ against threats; that is, a writ to keep the peace.

De minoribus rebus principes consultant, de majoribus omnes (dē mi-nō'ri-bus rē'bus prin'si-pēz konsul'tant, dē mā-jō'ri-bus om'nēz). In matters of less importance, rulers take counsel, in those of greater import, the people. See 1 Bl Comm 147, footnote.

deminutio (dē-mi-nu'she-ō). Diminution; subtraction; deprivation.

demisable (dẹ-mī'zạ-bl). Capable of being demised.

demi-sangue (dem'i-sang). Half blood.

demise (dē-mīz'). Noun: A deed, lease, conveyance of the fee or of a life estate; a grant of land. Chandler v Hart, 161 Cal 405, 119 P 516; Atlantic & North Carolina Railroad Co. v Atlantic & North Carolina Co. 147 NC 368, 61 SE 185. The transfer of property by will. The word, appearing in a lease, implies a covenant on the part of the lessor of good right and title to make the lease. 32 Am J1st L & T § 268. The word also means death, this meaning having originated in the reluctance of people in an earlier time to speak of the possibility of the king's death, perferring to cloak the disaster of his dissolution by referring to it in the less harsh term "demise," the passing of the crown to his heir. Verb: To grant; to lease; to bequeath; to pass on the death of the owner by bequest or inheritance.

demise and re-demise. A kind of agreement which in effect is a mutual leasing of the same land, under which the owner pays only a nominal rental.

demise charter. See **charter of demise**.

demise of the crown. The transfer of the kingdom to a dead king's successor. When we say the demise of the crown, we mean only that, in consequence of the disunion of the king's natural body from his body politic, the kingdom is transferred or demised to his successor; and so the royal dignity remains perpetual. See 1 Bl Comm 249.

demisi (de-mī'sī). I have demised; I have let.

demissione. See **ex demissione**.

demissio regis, vel coronae (dē-mi'she-ō rē'jis, vel ko-rō'ne). The demise of the king or the crown. See 1 Bl Comm 249.

de mittendo tenorem recordi (dē mit-ten'dō te-nō'rem re-kor'dī). A writ to send the tenor of a record, or to exemplify the record.

demi-vill (dem'i-vil). One-half of a vill or tithing. A tithing comprised ten freemen and their families.

demo. See **damage**.

democracy. Popular government; rule by the people. Not to be confused with the Democratic Party or the policies of such party.

See **pure democracy; representative democracy**.

de moderata misericordia capienda (dē mo-de-rā'ta mi-se-ri-kor'di-a kā-pi-en'da). A writ for taking a moderate amercement, which lay to reduce an excessive amercement.

de modo decimandi (dē mō'dō de-si-man'dī). Of the manner of tithing. A discharge by custom or prescription is where, time out of mind, certain persons or lands have been discharged from the payment of tithes. This immemorial usage is either de modo decimandi or de non decimando. A modus decimandi, often called a "modus," is any means whereby the general law of tithing is altered, and a new method of taking them is introduced. A prescription de non decimando is a claim to be entirely discharged of tithes, and pay no compensation in lieu of them. See 2 Bl Comm 29, 31.

De molendino de novo erecto non jacet prohibitio (dē mo-len'dī-nō dē nō'vō ē-rek'tō non jā'set pro-hi-bi'she-ō). Prohibition does not lie against a newly erected mill.

demolition loss. A deduction in an income tax return for loss suffered by the taxpayer on the demolition of a building. Commissioner v Estate of Appleby (CA1) 23 F2d 700.

de moneta (dē mō-nē'ta). Concerning the currency.

demonstrate To prove indubitably, as, to demonstrate a proposition of geometry; to teach by exhibition of examples, as, anatomy is demonstrated by exhibition of the dissected parts of the body. Espenhain v Barker, 121 Or 621, 625, 256 P 766.

demonstratio (de-mon-strā'she-ō). A description; a designation; a denomination.

demonstration. A designation; a manifestation; a showing.

None but mathematical truth is susceptible of that high degree of evidence, called demonstration, which excludes all possibility of error, and which, therefore, may reasonably be required in support of every mathematical deduction. People v Risley, 214 NY 75, 108 NE 200.

See **false demonstration**.

demonstrative evidence. Usually the equivalent of real evidence. 29 Am J2d Ev § 769. Narrowly, evidence which has no probative value in itself, serving merely as a visual aid to jury or trier of the fact in comprehending the verbal testimony. Smith v Ohio Oil Co. 10 Ill App 2d 67, 134 NE2d 526, 58 ALR2d 680.

See **real evidence**.

demonstrative legacy. A legacy which differs from a general legacy in that it refers to a particular fund or particular property as a primary source of payment, the two essentials of such a legacy being an unconditional gift in the nature of a general legacy and a designation of a particular fund or particular property as a primary source of payment but not such a designation as evinces an intent to relieve the general estate from liability if the particular fund or particular property fails as a source of payment. Nusly v Curtis, 36 Colo 464, 85 P 846; Rogers v Rogers, 67 SC 168, 45 SE 176.

demonstrator. An automobile used by an automobile salesman to demonstrate the particular model and type and the operation of the vehicle to a prospective buyer. Anything used to show the operation of a thing of its kind, particularly for the purpose of making a sale. A person who demonstrates things or processes, e.g. a person who makes coffee in a grocery store for the purpose of advertising the brand of coffee used.

De Monticolis Walliae (dē mon-ti-kō'lis wal'li-ē). Of the Welsh mountaineers,—the name given to an ancient statute of the time of King Ethelred, whereby Welshmen, who at that time were aliens, might demand a trial by a jury composed of six Welshmen and six Englishmen. See 3 Bl Comm 360.

demorage. Same as **demurrage**.

demorari (de-mo-rā'rī). To demur.

De morte hominis nulla est cunctatio longa (dē mor'te ho'mi-nis nul'la est kunk-tā'she-ō lon'ga). With respect to a man's death no delay is regarded as long.

de mot en mot (dē mo ān mo). From word to word; word for word.

demotion. The lowering of the grade of a civil service officer or employee. 15 Am J2d Civ S § 33.

dempster. Same as **deemster**.

demur. To interpose a demurrer; to hesitate; to object.

demurrable. Subject to attack by demurrer.
See **demurrer**.

demurrage. A sum of money due by way of compensation for the loss of earnings of a vessel by an improper delay or detention of the vessel. 48 Am J1st Ship § 606. A word derived from the maritime law but applied to railroad cars, meaning, in this respect, the charges imposed by a carrier by rail for the detention of the cars beyond the time reasonably required for the loading or unloading thereof. 13 Am J2d Car § 480.

demurrage lien. The lien of a carrier by rail upon a shipment for unpaid demurrage charges. 13 Am J2d Carriers § 501. The lien of a shipowner upon cargo for demurrage charges unpaid, enforceable in admiralty by an action in rem. 48 Am J1st Ship § 615.

demurrant. A party to an action who interposes a demurrer to a pleading of an adverse party.

demurrer. A method of raising an objection to the sufficiency in law of a pleading. 27 Am J2d Eq § 299; 41 Am J1st Pl § 204.
While demurrers are abolished in many jurisdictions by statute, the abolition is superficial, being essentially one of terminology, the office of the demurrer being performed under the new and simplified systems of pleading by motion or answer. 41 Am J1st Pl § 204.

demurrer book. A transcript of the pleadings in an action leading up to an issue of law.

demurrer ore tenus (dē-mur'ėr o're te'nus). A demurrer made orally at the time of argument in support of a demurrer of record, pointing out the defect in the pleading to which it is addressed. Wetherell v Eberle, 123 Ill 666, 14 NE 675. A demurrer in the form of an objection to evidence on the ground that the complaint, declaration, or petition fails to state a cause of action. Cleveland v Bateman, 21 NM 675, 158 P 648.

demurrer to evidence. A method of taking a case from the jury, being an objection made by the defendant to the plaintiff's evidence as a whole, which concedes the truth of all that the evidence tends to establish in favor of the plaintiff, but that the facts thus conceded do not establish in law a right to recover. The use of a demurrer to evidence is rare in modern practice; it has been supplanted by a motion for a directed verdict or the equivalent of such motion. 53 Am J1st Trial §§ 427, 428.

demurrer to form. A special objection to a pleading on grounds of form rather than substance. 41 Am J1st Pl § 206.
See **demurrer**.

demurrer to indictment. A pleading attacking the sufficiency of an indictment for a defect which appears on the face of the indictment, the failure to state an offense, or the failure to state an offense with the clearness and precision required in an indictment. 27 Am J1st Indict § 144.

demurrer to interrogatory. A reason offered by a witness for refusing to answer a question.

demurrer to plea. A method by which the plaintiff tests the sufficiency of the answer or plea of the defendant; such a demurrer calls into question the sufficiency in law of the plaintiff's own pleadings, and all the facts and attendant circumstances revealed in all the pleadings must be taken into consideration in determining the demurrer. 41 Am J1st Pl § 234. A method of objecting to the sufficiency in law of a special plea by the defendant in a criminal case. 21 Am J2d Crim L § 465.

demurrer to plea in abatement. A method by which the plaintiff tests the legal sufficiency of the defendant's plea in abatement. 41 Am J1st Pl § 211.

demurrer to substance. A demurrer testing the sufficiency of a pleading in respect of a matter of substance. 41 Am J1st Pl § 211.

demurrer to the jurisdiction. A demurrer to plaintiff's pleading which raises the objection of a want of jurisdiction over the person of the defendant or the subject matter of the suit apparent on the face of the pleading. 41 Am J1st Pl § 213.

demurrer to the person. A demurrer raising the question of the competency of the plaintiff to maintain the suit. 39 Am J1st Parties § 105.

demy sangue (dĕ-mi sang). Same as **demi sangue**.

demy sanke. Same as **demi sangue**.

denarii (de-nā'ri-ī). Plural of **denarius**.

denarius (de-nā'ri-us). A Roman silver coin equivalent to about fourteen cents. Also, the English pence.

denarius Dei (dē-nā'ri-us dē'ī). God's penny,—earnest money given to bind a bargain.

denarius Petrii (dē-nā'ri-us pē'tri-ī). Peter's penny or Peter's pence,—an annual general contribution to the Pope.

de nativo habendo (dē nā'ti-vō ha-ben'dō). A writ which lay for the lord of the manor to secure the return of a fugitive villein.

denaturalize (dē-nat'ụ-ral-īz). To deprive a person of his citizenship, whether acquired by naturalization or not.

denatured. Deprived of natural qualities; changed in nature.
See **denatured alcohol**.

denatured alcohol. Alcohol which has been so adulterated with poisonous or other chemicals as to render it fatally dangerous or otherwise unfit for use as a beverage.

denaturized. Same as **denatured**.

denial. A contradiction; a traverse; a withholding; a refusal to grant; a refusal. In pleading, a controverting of affirmative allegations in the pleading of an adversary.
Under the Federal Rules of Civil Procedure, a denial of statements made in a plaintiff's demand for admissions is not made by a denial of "the accuracy" of statements made in the demand, or by a refusal "to admit the truth" of such statements. Southern R. Co. v Crosby (CA4 SC) 201 F2d 878, 36 ALR2d 1186.
See **general denial**; **negative pregnant**; **specific denial**.

denier (dẹ-nī'ėr). A penny.

denier a Dieu. Same as **denarius Dei**.

De nihilo, nil (dē ni'hi-lo, nil). Nothing out of nothing. A void contract can no more give rise to a right

denization. [334]

of action than a void deed can create title in the grantee. West Maryland R. R. Co. v Blue Ridge Hotel Co. 102 Md 307, 62 A 351.

denization. A proceeding known to the English by which an alien acquires the status of a denizen. McClenaghan v McClenaghan, 32 SCL (1 Strobh) 295.
See **denizen.**

denize (de-nīz'). To effect a denization.
See **denization.**

denizen. One in a middle state between an alien and a natural born citizen, and who, though subject to some of the disabilities of the former, is entitled to many of the privileges of the latter. 3 Am J2d Aliens § 1.

Denman's Act. See **Lord Denman's Act.**

denominatio (de-no-mi-nā'she-ō). A denomination.
See **denomination.**

Denominatio est a digniore (dē-no-mi-nā'she-ō est ā dig-ni-ō're). Denomination is from the more worthy.

Denominatio fieri debet a dignioribus (de-no-mi-nā'she-ō fī'e-rī de'bet ā dig-ni-ō'rī-bus). Denomination should be made from the more worthy.

denomination. Name; the act of naming. A coin of a stated value. A religious society of a particular faith, the name usually being carried in some form by members in professing the faith, e. g. "Methodists," "Presbyterians," "Baptists," etc.

De nomine proprio non est curandum cum in substantia non erretur; quia nomina mutabilia sunt, res autem immobiles (dē nō'mi-ne prō'pri-ō non est kū-ran'dum kum in sub-stan'she-a non er-rē'ter; qui'a nō'mi-na mū-tà-bi'li-a sunt, rēz â'tem īm-mō'bi-lēz). As to the proper name, it is not to be regarded when there is no substantial error, because names are changeable; but things, that is, facts, are not.

De non apparentibus et de non existentibus eadem est ratio (dē non ap-pa-ren'ti-bus et dē non eg-zis-ten'ti-bus e-ā'dem est rā'she-ō). The same reasoning applies to those things which are not proved as to those which have no existence. United States v Wilkinson (US) 12 How 246, 253, 13 L Ed 974, 977.

De non apparentibus, et non existentibus, eadem est lex (dē non ap-pa-ren'ti-bus, et non eg-zis-ten'ti-bus, e-ā'dem est lex). As to matters which are not proved and as to those which do not exist, the law is the same. State ex rel. Lasserre v Michel, 105 La 741, 30 So 122.

de non decimando (dē non de-si-man'dō). See **de modo decimando.**

de non desidentia clerici regis (dē non dē"si-den'she-a kle'ri-sī rē'jis). A writ to exonerate a clergyman abroad in the service of the king for his non-residence.

de non procedendo ad assisam (dē non prō-sē-den'dō ad as-sī'sam). A writ to prohibit the judges of the assize from proceeding with the cause.

de non sane memorie (dē non sa'ne me'mo-ri). Of unsound memory,—of unsound mind.

denouncement (dē-nouns'ment). Same as **denuncia.** A denunciation. The reporting of a mine to the authorities as unoccupied or abandoned; the claiming of the right to work a mine; the reporting of the discovery and pre-emption of a mine; the claiming of a mine as a new one. Stewart v King, 85 Or 14, 166 P 55.

See **denunciation.**

de novo (dē nō'vō). Anew; over again; a second time. See 1 Bl Comm 186.
See **trial de novo.**

de novo trial. See **trial de novo.**

dense smoke. Dark smoke as it comes from the smokestack or where common chimney soft or bituminous coal is used for fuel in any considerable quantities. St. Paul v Haugbro, 93 Minn 59, 100 NW 470. Also the smoke created by the burning of certain types of heating oil.

dentist. One whose profession is to clean and extract teeth, repair them when diseased, and replace them, when necessary by artificial ones; one sometimes said to be a surgeon practicing upon teeth. 41 Am J1st Phys & S § 2.

dentistry. The profession of the dentist; a medical science concerned with the teeth and the care of teeth.
See **dentist.**

dentists' liability insurance. A form of liability insurance which protects a dentist against loss resulting from his liability for acts or omissions in the treatment of a patient. 29A Am J Rev ed Ins § 1358.

Dent operam consules ne quid respublica detrimenti capiat (dent o'pe-ram kon'su-lēz nē quid res-pub'li-ka de-tri-men'tī kā'pi-at). Let the consuls take heed lest the state suffer harm. See 1 Bl Comm 136.

Dentur omnes decimae primariae ecclesiae ad quam parochia pertinet (den'ter om'nēz de'si-mē prī-mā'ri-ē e-klē'si-ē ad quam pa-rō'ki-a per'ti-net). Let all tithes be given to the head church to which the parish belongs. See 1 Bl Comm 112.

De nullo, quod est sua natura indivisibile, et divisionem non patitur nullam partem labebit vidua, sed satisfaciat ei ad valentiam (dē nul'lō, quod est su'a nā-tū'ra in-di-vi-si'bi-le, et di-vi-zhe-ō'nem non pa'-ti-ter nul'lam par'tem la-bē'bit vi'du-a, sed sa-tis-fā'she-at e'i ad val-len'she-am). A widow shall have no part of that which is in its own nature indivisible, and will not suffer division, but she shall be satisfied with its value.

De nullo tenemento, quod tenetur ad terminum, fit homagii, fit tamen inde fidelitatis sacramentum (dē nul'lō te-ne-men'tō, quod te-nē'ter ad ter'mi-num, fit ho-mā'ji-ī, fit ta'men in'de fī-de-li-tā'tis sa-kra-men'tum). There is no homage in a tenement for a term of years, but in such case there is the oath of fealty (to the lord).

denumeration (dē-nū-me-rā'shon). A payment down at the present time.

denuncia (dā-nön'thi-ä). A judicial proceeding under Spanish-American law to establish a claim to real property which had been acquired by another without observing the requirements of the law. In its substantive characteristics, the denouncement or denuncia was equivalent to the inquest of office found of the common law. De Merle v Mathews, 26 Cal 455, 477.

denunciation. The condemning of a person, a practice, or an idea as evil; the reporting of a person to the authorities as one to be prosecuted.
See **denouncement; denuncia.**

denuntiatio (de-nun-she-ā'she-ō). A public notice; a bulletin.

deny (dẹ-nī'). To deny means to withhold, to refuse

to grant. To contradict. Beck v Allen, 58 Miss 143, 162.
See **denial**.

deodand (dē'ō-dand). Any chattel which caused a person's death, and which was in consequence, under the old common law, forfeited to the crown. Goldsmith-Grant Co. v United States, 254 US 505, 65 L Ed 376, 41 S Ct 189. See also Fields v Metropolitan Life Ins. Co. 147 Tenn 464, 249 SW 798, 36 ALR 1250, 1251.

deodand for pious uses (dē'ō-dand). See **pious uses**.

de odio et atia (dē ō'di-ō et ā'she-a). For hatred and ill will,—an ancient writ which was directed to the sheriff, commanding him to inquire whether a prisoner charged with murder was committed upon just cause of suspicion, or merely propter odium et atiam, for hatred and ill will. If the inquisition showed the latter cause, another writ issued for the sheriff to admit the prisoner to bail. See 3 Bl Comm 128.

de office (dē o-fi-s). Of office; officially.

De Officio Coronatoris (dē of-fi'she-ō ko-rō-nā-tō'ris). Of the office of coroner,—the statute of 4 Edward the First (1276) prescribing the principal functions and duties of the coroner, and specifically his duties in holding inquests. See 1 Bl Comm 348.

de onerando pro rata portione (dē ō-ne-ran'dō pro rā'ta por-she-ō'ne). A writ which lay for a tenant in common or a joint tenant to compel his cotenant to contribute rent.

de outre mere. See **essoin de outre mere**.

de pace et imprisonamento (dē pa'se et im-pri-so-na-men'tō). A writ in the nature of an appeal of crime for breach of the peace and imprisonment.

de pace et legalitate tuenda (dē pā'se et le-ga-li-tā'te tu-en'da). A writ for keeping the peace and good conduct.

de pace et plagis (dē pā'se et plā'jis). A writ for breach of the peace and wounding.

de pace et roberia (dē pā'se et ro-be'ri-a). A writ for breach of the peace and robbery.

de pace infracta (dē pā'se in-frak'ta). A writ for breach of the peace.

de palabra (dē pa-la'bra). By parol; oral.

de parco fracto (dē par'kō frak'tō). For breaking into a pound. When goods had been distrained and had been actually impounded, and had been taken out of the pound by force, the distrainor had his remedy by the writ of pound-breach, or de parco fracto. See 3 Bl Comm 146.

depart (dē-pärt'). To go away; to part; to partition; to divide; to separate; to change the cause of action or defense in amending a pleading or in pleading further by way of reply or other subsequent pleading. 41 Am J1st Pl §§ 184, 185.
See **departure**.

de partitione facienda (dē par-ti-she-ō'ne fā-she-en'da). For making partition,—a writ for the partition of lands of coparceners.

department. A division of the executive department of the national or state government.

departmental doctrine. A limitation of the fellow servant rule to employees engaged in the same department of the employer's business or establishment. 35 Am J1st M & S § 382.

department head. See **head of a department**.

department of government. One of the three great divisions of government between which the powers of the United States Government are separated, namely the legislative, executive, and judicial departments. A comparable division in a state. A part or division of the executive branch of the government of the United States, such as the **Justice Department, State Department,** etc. 54 Am J1st US § 39. A division of the executive branch of a state government, even of a municipal government.
See **cabinet; head of a department**.

department rule. An administrative regulation or order. 2 Am J2d Admin L §§ 277 et seq.
See **departmental doctrine**.

department store. A big merchandising establishment, divided into departments according to the kind of merchandise handled, such as men's wear, ladies' wear, groceries, shoes, hardware, etc., often having branches established and operating in suburban locations.

department store index. An index of department store prices, grouped according to the various categories of goods, such as infant's wear, women's underwear, men's furnishings, notions, etc., prepared by the Bureau of Labor Statistics.

departure. A leaving, such as the departure of a bus from the station; a turning aside from a usual route. A changing of the cause of action or defense alleged in a pleading, either in substance or the law upon which it is founded, in an amendment to the pleading, a reply, rejoinder, or other subsequent pleading. 41 Am J1st Pl §§ 184, 185.

The test whether new matter introduced by the way of an amendment is a departure is whether a different character of evidence is required for its support than would be required for proof of the antecedent pleading and whether proof of additional facts will be required to sustain the later pleading. Gerstel v William Curry's Sons Co. 155 Fla 471, 20 So 2d 802.
See **deviation**.

departure in amended pleading. A change in the cause of action or defense pleaded in the original complaint or answer by an amendment thereto. 41 Am J1st Pl § 306.

departure in despite of court. The failure of a tenant to appear in court in a real action against him on being summoned, although he had appeared previously.

depasture (dē-pàs'tūr). To pasture; to graze; to denude of grass or feed; to strip.

depeculation (dē-pek'ū-lā'shon). The embezzlement of public moneys.

depend. To be subject to a contingency; to hang upon a condition. To look to another for support.

dependency. A colony of a country; a territory which is subordinated to the authority and laws of a mother country. 29 Am J Rev ed States § 7. The status of a dependent person.
See **dependent**.

dependent. The status of one in need of aid or support because he entirely or partially lacks the means of supporting himself, Utah Fuel Co. v Industrial Com. 80 Utah 105, 15 P2d 297, 86 ALR 858; one who looks to another for support and maintenance.

58 Am J1st Workm Comp § 162. One who is sustained by, or who relies for support upon, the aid of another. Royal League v Shields, 251 Ill 250, 96 NE 45. One entitled to support as a wife or child, even an illegitimate child entitled to support. 30 Am J Rev ed Intox L § 534. One in such relationship to the taxpayer that the latter is granted an exemption for him in making return for income tax. IRC § 151(e).

See dependent child; partial dependent; support; total dependent.

dependent bill. A bill in equity, otherwise known as a "bill not original," being a pleading relating to some matter already litigated in the court by the same parties and depending on the prior suit; that is, it supplements or continues the former suit or seeks relief in respect of some matter growing out of that suit and connected with it. 27 Am J2d Eq § 179.

dependent child. A term applied to a normal child without means for self-support who must be supported by someone other than the person to whom he naturally could look for support, that is, a parent or guardian. Re Souers, 135 Misc 521, 238 NYS 738. Dependency on the part of a child is something different from the right of the child to have support, or the duty of a parent to support his children. The mere fact that the father is legally and morally bound to support his children does not necessarily establish that they are either partly or wholly dependent upon him. Dependency connotes the need of aid or support by one who entirely or partially lacks the means of supporting himself. 39 Am J1st P & C § 2.

As used in statutes providing for the care of dependent, neglected and delinquent children, the term means dependent upon the public for support. State ex rel. Stearns County v Klasen, 123 Minn 382, 143 NW 984; any child under the age of 18 who is destitute, or whose home by reason of neglect by the parents or either of them is an unfit place for such child, or whose father, mother, guardian, or custodian, does not properly provide for such child. Re Hudson, 13 Wash 2d 673, 126 P2d 765. The statutes on dependent children usually define what is meant by the expression "dependent child." It is said that a legislative classification of dependent children as distinguished from delinquent children is not unreasonable. Under some statutes, however, the terms "dependent child" and "delinquent child" are largely synonymous. 31 Am J Rev ed Juv Ct § 38.

See delinquent children; neglected children.

dependent contract. A contract the performance of which depends upon the performance of another contract.

See dependent covenants.

dependent covenants. Covenants made by the parties to a deed or agreement which are of such character that the act covenanted to be performed enters into the whole consideration for the covenant or promise on the other part, or where the acts or covenants of the parties are concurrent and are to be performed at the same time, so that neither party can maintain an action against the other without first proving full performance on his part. 20 Am J2d Cov § 8. A "dependent covenant" in a contract for the sale of land is one which depends upon the prior performance of some act or condition or, as otherwise defined, an agreement to do or omit to do something with reference to a thing on which it depends and to which it relates. 55 Am J1st V & P § 102.

dependent jurisdiction. Another term for ancillary jurisdiction.

See ancillary jurisdiction.

dependent person. See dependent; dependent child.

dependent proceeding. An action or proceeding in which the court exercises dependent or ancillary jurisdiction.

See ancillary jurisdiction; ancillary proceeding.

dependent promises. Promises in a bilateral contract which are mutually dependent, that is, the one promise is the condition of the enforcement of the other. 17 Am J2d Contr § 322; 55 Am J1st V & P § 102.

See dependent covenants.

dependent relative revocation. The doctrine that if a testator revoke a will with a present intention to make a new will as a substitute for the old, and the new will is not made, or if made fails of effect for some reason, it will be presumed that the testator preferred the old will to intestacy, and this testament will be given effect. 57 J1st Wills § 514. The doctrine is also known as that of "conditional" or "provisional" revocation.

dependents. See dependent.

dependent stipulations. Mutual agreements which go to the whole of the consideration on both sides of a contract. 55 Am J1st V & P § 102.

See dependent covenants; dependent promises.

depending. Relying on; being conditional or contingent on something. Ancient usage seems to have included the meaning of "pending," so that a "depending action" was a "pending action." 3 Bl Comm 450.

See words and phrases beginning dependent.

de perambulatione facienda (dē per-am-bu-lā-she-ō'ne fā-she-en'da). A writ for the establishment of a boundary line.

de persona. See constat de persona.

depesas (de-pā'sas). A word found in Spanish-American grants signifying spaces of ground reserved in the vicinity of a town, when it was being laid out, for commons or public pasturage. Strother v Lucas (US) 12 Pet 410, 442, footnote, 9 L Ed 1137, 1150, footnote.

de pignore surrepto furti, actio (dē pig-nō're sur-rep'tō fur'tī, ak'she-ō). (Roman law.) An action to recover a stolen pledge.

de placito (dē pla'si-tō). Of a plea.

de plagis et mahemio (dē plā'jis et ma-he'mi-ō). A criminal appeal for wounding and mayhem.

de plano (dē plā'nō). Clearly; immediately.

de plegiis acquietandis (dē ple'ji-is ak-qui-e-tan'dis). A writ under which a surety could compel his principal to reimburse him for loss.

de pleine age (dē plī-è-n â-j). Of full age.

depletion deduction. A deduction allowed in an income tax return to the owner of an economic interest in mineral deposits or standing timber. IRC § 613(a).

de pone (dē pōn'). A writ to remove a cause to a superior court.

depone (dē-pōn). To depose; to give a deposition.

de ponendo sigillum ad exceptionem (dē pō-nen'dō si-jil'lum ad ek-sep-she-ō'nem). A writ to place the court seal on an exception taken to a ruling of the court.

deponent. One whose deposition is given. 23 Am J2d Dep § 1; a witness; an affiant; a person who gives testimony under oath or affirmation, whether by deposition, affidavit, or otherwise. Bliss v Shuman, 47 Me 248, 252.

deponer (day-po'ner). A deponent.

depopulatio agrorum (de-po-pū-lā'she-ō a-grō'rum). Laying waste the fields,—the crime of destroying or ravaging a country, bordering upon treason. See 4 Bl Comm 373.

deportation. The expulsion of an alien from the country. 3 Am J2d Aliens § 71; a maritime tort, if illegal. 2 Am J2d Adm § 78.

Under the Federal statute providing that an alien's deportation must take place within three years after his entry, the time is not determined by the date of his actual deportation but by the date of his arrest for that purpose. United States ex rel. Filippini v Day (DC NY) 18 F2d 781.

See **to the country whence they came.**

deportation proceeding. An administrative proceeding conducted by immigration officers to determine by hearing whether or not an alien should be deported, and, if the finding is in the affirmative, to issue an order and warrant for deportation. 3 Am J2d Aliens §§ 82 et seq.

depose. To state or affirm a fact by affidavit or deposition; in a broader sense, to testify as a witness; to remove from an office, or position of authority, particularly a king.

deposit. Verb: To put down, as a deposit of earnest money; to put money or things in a place for storage or safekeeping; to put money in a bank at interest or on checking account. Noun: An accumulation; money or an article deposited.

See **bank deposit; certificate of deposit; depositary; deposit for collection; deposit in court; depositor; depositors' guaranty fund; general deposit; joint deposit; special deposit.**

depositary. A person, firm or corporation receiving a deposit for safekeeping; a depository.
See **depository.**

deposit box. See **safe deposit box**

deposit company. See **safe deposit company.**

deposited for record. See **filed for record.**

deposit for collection. A transaction wherein a customer delivers commercial paper to a bank and the bank undertakes as agent for the customer the duty of making the collection. 10 Am J2d Banks § 403.

deposit in court. A payment or delivery into court, pursuant to court order, of money or anything capable of delivery. 24 Am J1st Funds & D §§ 1-3.
See **payment into court.**

Deposit Insurance Corporation. An agency of the United States established for the purpose of insuring bank deposits by setting up a permanent insurance fund for that purpose and the payment of deposits upon the closing of any insured bank, to preserve the solvency of insured banks, and to keep open the channels of trade and commercial exchange. 10 Am J2d Banks § 427.

deposit in trust. See **trust deposit.**

deposition. The written testimony of a witness given under oath in the course of a judicial proceeding, either at law or in equity, in advance of the trial or hearing, upon oral examination or in response to written interrogatories and where an opportunity is given for cross-examination; in a less refined sense, an affidavit, an oath; a statement under oath. 23 Am J2d Dep § 1.

See **deposition de bene esse; in perpetuam rei memoriam; letter rogatory.**

deposition de bene esse (dep-ō-zish'on dē be'ne es'se). A deposition taken during the pendency of an action for use as evidence therein, provided the personal attendance of the witness for oral examination cannot be secured. 23 Am J2d Dep § 2.

deposito (day-po'se-to). (Spanish.) A bailment of goods which is determinable at the will of the bailor.

deposit of earnest money. See **earnest money.**

depositor. One who makes a deposit, particularly one who makes a deposit in a bank whether on open account, special account, or at interest, the term including the holder of a certificate of deposit, but according to some definitions, not the holder of a cashier's check or certified check. Re Citizen's State Bank, 44 Idaho 33, 255 P 300 (statutory definition).

A depositor is not the owner of any specific money in the bank. He is simply the owner of a right and credit against the bank. Wright v Holmes, 100 Me 508, 62 A 507. But as used in bank guaranty laws, the word depositor should be taken in its commonly understood sense, and not so as to include creditors generally, who would not in common parlance, be regarded as depositors in a bank. Anno: 111 ALR 229.

depositors' guaranty fund. A fund to which the banks of a state contribute according to the amount of their deposits, established for the protection of depositors, that is, to make the currency of checks secure and also to protect the depositors in respect of their deposits. 10 Am J2d Banks § 424.

See **permanent insurance fund.**

depository. A storehouse; a place where money or valuable articles are put for safekeeping; a depositary; an official custodian of monies or other property paid into court under order of court. 23 Am J2d Deposit In Ct § 4; a banking institution designated by the judge of a bankruptcy court as the place of deposit of the funds of estates in bankruptcy. 9 Am J2d Bankr § 1240.

As used in a criminal statute forbidding the possession of tools and implements adapted and designed for forcing or breaking open a building, room, vault, safe, or other depository, the term is not confined to depositories substantially similar to vaults or safes, but extends to whatever is commonly used for the safekeeping of money or other personal property. Commonwealth v Tilley, 306 Mass 412, 28 NE2d 245, 129 ALR 381.

deposit slip. A slip of paper containing entries made by the person making a bank deposit, showing his name, the amount of cash deposited, and a listing of the checks deposited by the name of the bank upon which drawn or the use of numbers representing the drawee bank, the amount of each character of items deposited, and the total deposit. The rules of the bank in respect of deposits are often printed on the slip. 11 Am J2d B & N § 341.

deposits tax. See **bank deposits tax.**

deposit subject to final payment. See **subject to final payment.**

depositum. (Civil law.) A naked bailment, without reward, of goods to be kept for the bailor, by one who is usually called a depositary. Anno: 4 ALR 1196.

de post disseisina (dē post dis-sē'si-na). A writ of post disseisin.

depot. A stopping place for trains or motorbuses where there is a building more or less permanent for the accommodation of passengers and freight. A railroad depot includes not only a stopping place for railroad trains, but also a building for the accommodation of passengers and freight, together with all passageways, or platforms prepared for passengers in boarding and leaving trains. 44 Am J1st RR § 254.
A place where military stores or supplies are kept or troops assembled. United States v Caldwell (US) 19 Wall 264, 22 L Ed 114. A storehouse.
See **railroad station; union station.**

depot grounds. The grounds or land upon which a railroad station or depot stands, together with such surrounding territory as may be required to satisfy the reasonable convenience and necessity of the public while engaged in transacting business with the railroad company, and which is actually used for such purpose. 44 Am J1st RR § 169.

De Praerogativa Regis (dē pre-rō-ga-tī'va rē'jis). Of the king's prerogative,—the title of the statute 17 Edw. II, c. 11, by which many of the prerogatives of the king were confirmed by parliament. See 2 Stephen's Commentaries 509. This statute affirmed the king's ancient right of committing waste and taking the profits of an attainted felon's land for a year and a day. See 4 Bl Comm 386.

de praesenti (dē pre-zen'tī). For the present.

depreciated book value—As used in a statute requiring "depreciated book value" of personal property to be considered for purposes of taxation, the term means the cost price of the personal property, including the cost of installation, entered on the books of the company in ordinary course of business, less the depreciation set up on the books in a regular and consistent manner for reflecting such depreciation, including reasonable allowance for obsolescence. Wheeling Steel Corp. v Evatt, 143 Ohio St 71, 54 Ne 132.

depreciated value. Cost less depreciation. Brennan v Brennan, 164 Ohio St 29, 57 Ohio Ops 71, 128 NE2d 89, 50 ALR2d 1259.

depreciation. The lessening in worth of any property caused by weather, time, and use, including obsolescence and inadequacy. 43 Am J1st Pub Util § 145. A deduction allowed in an income tax return for the gradual loss of usefulness of tangible property used in business or in the production of income. IRC § 167(a).
"Dépréciation" for which allowance is to be made in fixing the rate base for a public utility is the loss, not restored by current maintenance, which is due to all the factors causing the ultimate retirement of the property, embracing wear and tear, decay, inadequacy, and obsolescence. Lindheimer v Illinois Bell Tel. Co. 292 US 151, 78 L Ed 1182, 54 S Ct 658.

depreciation recapture. An income tax rule whereby a gain on the sale of property is treated as ordinary income, or partly as ordinary income, to the extent of depreciation taken on the property. Internal Revenue Code §§ 1245, 1250.

depredation (dep-rẹ-dā'shọn). The act of plundering; a robbing; a pillaging. Deal v United States, 274 US 277, 71 L Ed 1045, 47 S Ct 613. An informal, illegitimate war. 56 Am J1st War § 5.

depressing bids. Stifling or chilling bids at a judicial sale. 30A Am J Rev ed Jud S § 98.

depression. A natural way or means for the drainage of surface water. 56 Am J1st Wat § 76. A disastrous condition of the economy, characterized by unemployment, forced sales of property, and falling prices.
See **Great Depression.**

deprivation. A taking of property, rights, or privileges from a person. An ecclesiastical term applied to one of the several ways in which a parson or vicar may cease to be so. Deprivation may be effected by the sentence of the ecclesiastical court or pursuant to certain penal statutes which declare the benefice void either by reason of the incumbent's omission of duty or his active commission of some forbidden act or crime. See 1 Bl Comm 393.

deprivation without due process. Wherever the operation and effect of any general regulation is to extinguish or destroy that which by the law of the land is the property of any person, so far as it has that effect, it is unconstitutional and void as being a deprivation of property without due process of law. Brown v Grant, 116 US 207, 29 L Ed 598, 6 S Ct 357.

deprive. To take from one some property, right, or privilege which he enjoys and which he is entitled to enjoy; to cause a deprivation.
See **deprivation.**

de proavo (dē pro'ā-vō). Of the great grandfather,—a writ whereby an heir secured land entered upon by a stranger upon the death of the heir's great grandfather who had died seised. See 3 Bl Comm 186.

de probioribus et potentioribus comitatus sui in custodes pacis (dē pro-bi-ō'ri-bus et po-ten-she-ō'ri-bus ko-mi-tā'tus su'ī in kus-tō'dēz pa'sis). From the most excellent and powerful of their county as keepers of the peace. See 1 Bl Comm 350.

de proprietate probanda (dē prō-prī-e-tā'te prō-ban'da). For proving ownership,—a writ which lay for a plaintiff who had replevined goods from the possession of a distrainor who thereupon claimed the goods, to try by an inquest before the sheriff and determine in whom the property subsisted prior to the distress. See 3 Bl Comm 148.

depuis (dē-puî). Since.

deputy. One appointed to act for another, a substitute, a delegate, an agent. 37 Am J1st Mun Corp § 273; 43 Am J1st Pub Of § 218. A person who is a subordinate of a public officer, performing the duties of the office under powers conferred for that purpose, but only in the name of the officer, except in jurisdictions where he is recognized as an independent public officer. 43 Am J1st Pub Of §§ 460 et seq.

deputy clerk of court. In some jurisdictions, a mere agent of the principal clerk performing as of right only ministerial acts, but in other jurisdictions, an independent public officer vested with authority to discharge any of the official duties of his principal save that of appointing a deputy. 15 Am J2d Clk Ct §§ 38, 41.

deputy judge. A paradox; there can be no delegation of judicial authority, hence no deputy judge. State ex rel. Hovey v Noble, 118 Ind 350, 21 NE 244.

deputy sheriff. An officer who acts for the sheriff, in some jurisdictions his powers being limited to the performance of ministerial acts, but in other jurisdictions, being given authority equivalent to that of the sheriff, even authority for the execution of conveyances of lands sold under execution. 47 Am J1st Sher § 154.

de quarentina habenda (dē qua-ren-tī'na hā-ben'da). For securing her quarantine,—a common law writ whereby a widow might secure her right of quarantine, that is, to continue to occupy the mansion house or other dowable residence of her husband for forty days after his death. Aikin v Aikin, 12 Or 203, 6 P 682.

de ques en ça (dē kuès ān sä). From which time until the present.

de quibus (dē qui'bus). Of which things or persons.

de quibus sur disseisin (dē qui'bus ser dis-sē'sin). A kind of writ of entry.

de quo (dē quō). Of which; of whom.

de quodam ignoto (dē quō'dam ig-nō'tō). From a certain person unknown.

de quota litis (dē quō'ta lī'tis). (Civil law.) An agreement for a contingent fee.

de quoy (dē koa). Of which.

deraign (dẹ-rān'). To prove; to prove in detail; to vindicate; to prove by disproving the allegations of an adversary.

deraignment of title. A statute requiring the complainant to set forth the "deraignment of his title" means that he must show (a) title in himself from the government, (b) title in himself by adverse possession, (c) title in himself from the defendant, or a better title than that of the defendant, tracing both his title and that of the defendant to a common source. Smith v Overstreet, 205 Miss 488, 38 So 2d 923.

deranged (dẹ-rānjd'). Disordered in mind; insane. Hiett v Shull, 36 W Va 563, 565.
See **insane.**

de raptu haeredis (dē rap'tū hē-rē'dis). A writ whereby a guardian might secure the custody of his ward after she had been abducted.

de raptu virginum (dē rap'tū vir'ji-num). An appeal of felony for the rape of a maiden.

de rationabili parte (dē ra-she-ō-nā'bi-lī par'te). A writ of right which lay for a person against his cotenant who had assumed exclusive possession.

de rationabili parte bonorum (dē ra-she-ō-nā'bi-lī par'te bō-nō'rum). Of a reasonable share of the goods,—a writ for the recovery of that part of a decedent's personal property which he had, in his lifetime, alienated against the rights of the wife and children. The shares of the wife and children were called their reasonable parts. See 2 Bl Comm 492.

de rationalibus divisis (dē ra-she-ō-nā'li-bus di-vī'sis). A writ for the establishment of boundaries.

de rebus (dē rē'bus). Concerning things,—the title of the third part of the Digests or Pandects.

de rebus dubiis (dē rē'bus du'bi-is). In doubtful matters.

derecho (dā-rā'chō). (Spanish.) A right; a lawful claim.

de recordo et processu mittendis (dē re-kor'dō et prō-ses'sū mit-ten'dīs). A writ in the nature of a writ of error to send the record and process of an action to a higher court.

de recto (dē rek'tō). A writ of right, which lay to recover a person's full rights to property.

de recto clause. See **briefe de recto claus.**

de recto de advocatione (dē rek'tō dē ad-vo-kā-she-ō'ne). A writ of right of advowson.

de recto de dote (dē rek'tō dē dō'te). A writ of right of dower.

de recto deficere (dē rek'tō dē-fi'se-re). To fail of right; to fall short of justice.

de recto patens (dē rek'tō pā'tenz). A writ of right patent.

de redisseisina (dē re-dis-sē'si-na). A writ of redisseisin,—a writ which lay for one who had been disseised and who was disseised again by the same disseisor after he had recovered possession.

dereine. Same as **deraign.**

derelict. A vagrant; a person who is without substance, means, or an apparent purpose in life. A vessel abandoned without hope of recovery and without intention of returning to it, whether the abandonment arises from accident, necessity, or a purely voluntary measure. Mengel Box Co. v Joest, 127 Miss 461, 90 So 161. In the maritime sense, a vessel, cargo, or other property is derelict when it is abandoned without hope of recovery or without intention of returning thereto. 48 Am J1st Ship § 647.

dereliction. Failure in performance of duty; neglect of duty. Abandonment of property; abandoned property. A reliction, that is land made by the withdrawal of the waters by which it was previously covered. 56 Am J1st Wat § 476.
See **reliction; renunciation.**

de religiosis (dē re-li-ji-ō'sis). Concerning religious persons.

de reparatione (dē re-pa-rā-she-ō'ne). Of repair,—an ancient writ now practically obsolete, which was brought by one tenant in common to recover of his cotenant a due proportion of the expense of making necessary repairs. Ballou v Ballou, 94 Va 350, 26 SE 840.

de reparatione facienda (dē re-pa-rā-she-ō'ne fā-she-en'da). Of making repairs,—an old writ seldom used whereby one joint tenant or tenant in common could compel the others to unite in the expenses of the necessary reparation of a house or mill owned by them, but which did not apply to fences enclosing wood or arable land.

de replegiare (dē re-ple-ji-ā're). A writ of replevin.

de rescussu (de res-kus'sū). A writ of rescue, which lay to recover a person who had been rescued from an arrest or cattle which had been rescued from a distress.

de retorno habendo (dē re-tor'nō hā-ben'dō). A writ whereby a defendant who has prevailed in an action of replevin might have goods which were distrained and then replevied returned again into his custody, to be sold or disposed of as if no replevin had been made. See 3 Bl Comm 149.

dereyn. Same as **deraign.**

de rien culpable (dē ri-īn kul-pa-bl). Guilty of nothing,—not guilty.

de rigore juris (dē ri'go-re jū'ris). According to strict law.

de rigueur (dė rē-gųr'). (French.) By indispensable rule.

Derivativa postestas non potest esse major primitiva (de-ri-va-tī'va po-tes'tās non po'-test es'se mā'jor pri-mi-tī'va). Delegated authority cannot be greater than that which was originally given.

derivative. Something not original; something derived from another thing.

derivative action. An action brought by one or more stockholders of a corporation to enforce a corporate right or to prevent or remedy a wrong to the corporation in cases where the corporation, because it is controlled by the wrongdoers or for other reasons, fails and refuses to take appropriate action for its own protection. Price v Gurney, 324 US 100, 89 L Ed 776, 65 S Ct 513.

derivative conveyances. Conveyances of a secondary sort, which presuppose some other conveyance precedent, and only serve to enlarge, confirm, alter, restrain, restore, or transfer the interest granted by an original conveyance. See 2 Bl Comm 324. Derivative conveyances are releases, confirmations, surrenders, assignments, and defeasances. See 2 Bl Comm 310.

derivative fee. See **feudum improprium.**

derivative feud. Same as **feudum improprium.**

derivative jurisdiction. The jurisdiction of a certain court derived from another court, the term being best illustrated by jurisdiction on appeal, where the appellate court has jurisdiction of the cause on appeal only as the lower court had jurisdiction. 20 Am J2d Cts § 99.

derivative liability. See **vicarious liability.**

derivative suit. Same as **derivative action.**

derive. To receive as from a source or origin; to originate or acquire characteristics from a source which is traceable.

dernier (dėr'ni-ėr). See **au dernier.**

dernier resort (dėr'ni-ėr or der-nyā). The last resort.

derogation (der-ǫ-gā'shǫn). Nullification, avoidance or abrogation, in whole or in part, as a statute nullifying common-law rights. 1 Am J2d Adm L § 43.

derogatory clause (dę̄-rog'ą-tō-ri). A clause which a testator has secretly inserted in his will, the will containing a provision that any will thereafter made by him without the precise clause is to be void. The provision is anomalous to the same extent that an irrevocable will is anomalous. 57 Am J1st Wills § 15.

Derogatur legi, cum pars detrahitur; abrogatur legi, cum prorsus tollitur (de-ro-gā'ter lē'jī, kum parz de-tra'hi-ter; ab-ro-gā'ter lē'jī, kum pror'sus tol'li-ter). A law is derogated when part of it is taken away; a law is abrogated when it is wholly abolished.

derrick barges. Vessels carrying derricks. 2 Am J2d Adm § 33.

de salva guardia (dē sal'va gar'di-a). A writ of safeguard for the license and protection of strangers.

de salvo conductu (dē sal'vō con-duk'tū). A writ of safe conduct.

de sa vie (dē sa vî). For his own life; for his own lifetime.

De Scaccario (dē ska-kā'ri-ō). Of or concerning the exchequer,—the title of a statute enacted in the reign of Henry the Third.

descend. To come down; to pass by inheritance; to vest in a descendant or heir by operation of law on the death of the ancestor. 23 Am J2d Desc & D § 2.

descendant. A descendant is an individual proceeding from an ancestor in any degree; a child, a grandchild, a great grandchild, anyone, near or remote, in the line from the ancestor. Turner v Monteiro, 127 Va 537, 103 SE 572, 13 ALR 383, 387. Issue of any degree. Soper v Brown, 136 NY 244, 32 NE 768.

See **lineal descendant; posterity.**

descender (dę-sen'dėr). To descend.

descending from airplane. The phrase "descending from", in a life insurance policy excluding accidental death benefit for death resulting from "operating, riding in, or descending from" an airplane, includes things different from those included in the phrase "riding in," such as a voluntary descent by parachute, or leaving the plane after it has landed. Willingham v Life & Casualty Ins. Co. (CA5 Ga) 216 F2d 226, 47 ALR2d 1017.

descending line of descent. See **direct descending line.**

Descensus tollit intrationem (de-sen'sus tol'lit in-trā-she-ō'nem). A descent tolls or removes the right of entry.

descent. Hereditary succession. Freeman v Allen, 17 Ohio St 527. Technically, the transmission of real estate, or some interest in real estate, on the death of its owner intestate; to be distinguished from the transmission of personal property, the title to which, on the death of the owner intestate, passes to the personal representative and, after the payment of all debts and claims against the estate, is governed by the rules of distribution. But often used loosely to refer to succession to either real or personal property. 23 Am J2d Desc & D § 1.

As the term is used in the Federal estate tax law, the time of the acquisition of the property of a decedent is the date of his death and not the date of distribution. See Hopkins v Commissioner (CA7) 69 F2d 11, 96 ALR 1358.

See **canons of descent; collateral descent; establishment of heirship; heirs; immediate descent; inherit; inheritance; intestate; issue; next of kin; per capita; per stirpes; presumptive heir; primogeniture; prospective heir; shifting descents doctrine; statute of distribution; stirps; stock of descent; succession; title by descent; vacant succession.**

descent cast. Literally, the devolving of title to real estate upon the heir upon the death of his ancestor intestate. A term used for the most part in designation of the acquisition of color of title by heirs where the ancestor, although possibly a trespasser originally, died in possession under claim of right. 3 Am J2d Adv P § 122.

describe. To define by properties or characteristics; to represent by words or other signs; to give an account; to relate; to give the boundaries of real estate.

description. A portrayal of a subject by reference to its features and incidents; a representation in words. As it applies to property, a delineation in a mortgage, deed, contract, or other instrument affecting the title to property, by means of which

the property involved in the transaction may be identified. Ehret v Price, 122 Okla 277, 254 P 748.
See **description of real estate; sufficient description.**

description of real estate. A statement of the boundaries by monuments, courses, distances and quantity or by reference to maps, plats, or surveys. 12 Am J2d Bound §§ 3 et seq.

description of timber. See **now standing; when cut.**

descriptio personae (de-skrip′she-ō per-sō′nē). Description of the person; a word or phrase used for the purpose of identifying or pointing out a person. Milam v Settle, 127 W Va 271, 32 SE2d 269. Words descriptive of the person, such as "president," "manager," "agent," etc.

descriptive calls. Courses and distances referred to in describing a surveyed boundary of land, as distinguished from landmarks, monuments, and other physical objects which are known as locative calls. Holmes v Trout (US) 7 Pet 171, 8 L Ed 646.

de scutagio habendo (dē sku-tā′ji-o hā-ben′dō). A writ to recover escuage.

de se bene gerendo (dē sē be′ne je-ren′dō). For or during his good behavior.

desecration of burial place. An unnecessary disturbance or wanton violation of a burial place. 14 Am J2d Cem § 39.

de secta ad molendinum (dē sek′tā ad mo-len′di-num). Of suit at the mill,—a writ to compel a person to grind his corn at the plaintiff's mill. See 3 Bl Comm 235.

desegregation. The elimination of the color of a person as a test or qualification of his or her right to be present at a school, a place of employment, a place of entertainment or refreshment, a place of commerce, or the depots and conveyances of a common carrier. See 15 Am J2d Civ R §§ 18 et seq.

desert (dē-zėrt′). Verb: To abandon or forsake, although not beyond the possibility of returning. People v Board of Police (NY) 26 Barb 481, 501.
See **desertion.**

desert (dez′ėrt). Noun: Arid land.

desertion. The act of forsaking or abandoning a person, a cause or a post of duty. A continued abandonment of a ship by a seaman, during the term of service provided by his contract, with intention not to return, and without sufficient cause. 48 Am J1st Ship § 190. The criminal offense under the Uniform Code of Military Justice committed by any member of the armed forces where (1) without authority he goes or remains absent from his unit, organization, or place of duty with intent to remain away therefrom permanently; (2) quits his unit, organization, or place of duty to avoid hazardous duty or to shirk important service; or (3) without being permanently separated from one of the armed forces, enlists or accepts an appointment in the same or another one of the armed forces without fully disclosing the fact that he has not been regularly separated, or enters any foreign armed service except when authorized by the United States; also committed by any commissioned officer of the armed forces where, after tender of his resignation and before notice of its acceptance, quits his post or proper duties without leave and with intent to remain away therefrom permanently. 10 USC § 885.
The abandonment of a child in neglect of the duty of support. 39 Am J1st P & C § 104. The abandonment of wife or child penalized by the statutes of most of the states, including the Uniform Desertion and Nonsupport Act. 23 Am J2d Desert § 1. Quitting the society of wife and children and renouncing the duties owed them as a husband and father. Kelley v State, 218 Miss 459, 67 So 2d 459, 44 ALR2d 881.
As a ground for divorce, "desertion" is a voluntary separation of one of the parties to a marriage from the other or the voluntary refusal to renew a suspended cohabitation, without justification either in the consent or the wrongful conduct of the second party; a wilful absence by one spouse from the society of the other with the intention to live apart in spite of the wishes of the other and without any intention to return to cohabitation. 24 Am J2d Div & S § 96.
See **constructive desertion; wilful desertion.**

Desertion and Nonsupport Act. One of the uniform laws. 23 Am J2d Desert § 125.

desertion by seaman. See **desertion.**

desertion by soldier or other person in armed services. See **desertion.**

Desert Lands Act. A federal statute, commonly called the Carey Act, which sets forth a scheme for aiding the reclamation of arid lands in the public land states. 30 Am J1st Irrig § 101.

deserving. Worthy of assistance or of reward. Nichols v Allen, 130 Mass 211, 218.

de servitio regis. See **essoin de servitio regis.**

des gens. See **droit des gens.**

desideratum (dē-sid-e-rā′tum). That which is desired or called for.

design. A purpose, usually combined with a plan, of action; an intent or aim. State v Grant, 86 Iowa 216, 222. A sketch, plan, or pattern. To form a plan. To make a sketch or plan.
See **architectural design; formed design.**

designate. To mark out and make known; to point out; to name; to indicate. State v Madison State Bank, 77 Mont 498, 251 P 548. To locate definitely, as on a map. Southern Pacific Railroad Co. v United States, 168 US 1, 54, 42 L Ed 355, 378, 18 S Ct 18. To appoint a person to a position to be filled. County of Santa Barbara v Janssens, 177 Cal 114, 169 P 1025.

designation. A marking out; a pointing out; a selection; a naming, e. g. a naming of candidates by a county committee of a political party.
As used in an election law providing that the ballots shall be of plain, white paper, without ornaments, "designation," symbol, or mark, unless there is something in the statute to prevent it, the word must be construed as meaning only such a designation as is in the nature of a mark. State v Saxon, 30 Fla 668, 12 So 218.

designation of beneficiary. The naming by the insured under a life insurance policy of a third person as the one to receive the proceeds of the insurance upon the death of the insured. The clause in a life insurance policy wherein the person to receive the proceeds upon insured's death is named.

designation of homestead. The selection by formal declaration of the land which one desires to stand as his homestead, exempt from a forced sale, required under some statutes as a condition of a homestead right. 26 Am J1st Home § 88.

DESIGNATIO

designatio personae (de-sig-nā'she-o per-sō'nē). A description of the person.
See **descriptio personae**.

Designatio unius est exclusio alterius, et expressum facit cessare tacitum (de-sig-nā'she-ō ū'ni-us est ex-klu'she-ō al-te'ri-us, et ex-pres'sum fā'sit ses-sā're ta'si-tum). The designation of one is the exclusion of the other, and that which is expressed chokes that which is silent.

designed. Planned. Jacobs v Danziger, 328 Mo 458, 41 SW2d 389, 77 ALR 1237, cert den 284 US 675, 76 L Ed 571, 52 S Ct 130.
See **design**.

design patent. A patent of a design giving a new and pleasing appearance to an article of manufacture, whereby its sale is enhanced. Smith v Whitman Saddle Co. 148 US 674, 37 L Ed 606, 13 S Ct 768; Viehmann v D. F. H. Novelty Furniture Co. (DC NY) 27 F Supp 566.

design to kill. An intent to kill held for an appreciable, even if very brief, period of time. 26 Am J1st Homi § 42.

De similibus ad similia eadem ratione procedendum est (dē si-mi'li-bus ad si-mi'li-a e-a'dem rā-she-ō'ne prō-se-den'dum est). Proceeding in similar matters is by the same rule.

De similibus idem est judicium (dē si-mi'li-bus ī'dem est jū-di'she-um). The same judgment is rendered in similar cases.

desire. To wish; to express a wish. A precatory term, but in the proper context, a word of disposition or gift in a will. 57 Am J1st Wills § 1328. A mandatory direction as it appears in a will providing for the payment of inheritance taxes from the residue of the estate. 28 Am J1st Inher T § 488.

desire to improve the premises. A clause in a cancelation provision of a lease, the connotation of which is a desire accompanied by a definite intention of execution and attainment. Woods v Posto Telegraph-Cable Co. 205 Ala 236, 87 So 681, 27 ALR 834.

desmaintenant (de-mant'naw). From the present time; henceforth.

desmemoriados (des-may-mo-re'ah-dos). (Spanish.) A person who is bereft of memory.

de son done (dē sōn dōn). By his own gift.

de son fee. See **hors de son fee**.

de son gree (de sōn gre'). Of his own accord.

de son tort (dē sōn tor). By his own tort or wrong.
See **executor de son tort; guardian de son tort; trustee de son tort**.

de son tort demesne sans tiel cause (dē sōn tŏr de-mēn' sān ti-īl kâ-z). By his own wrong without such cause.

desormes (de'zor-me'). From the present time, henceforth.

desoubs (de'zoob). Same as **dessous**.

despatch (des-pach'). Same as **dispatch**.

desperate chose in action. See **desperate debt**.

desperate debt. An obligation as to which there is no hope of collection. Schultz v Pulver (NY) 11 Wend 363, 365.

despitus (des'pi-tus). A despised person.

despoil. To deprive a person of property of which he

DESTROYED

is in possession by violence or by some clandestine means. Sunol v Hepburn, 1 Cal 255, 268.

desponsation (des-pon-sā'shǫn). A betrothal.

desponsorio (des-pon-sō'ri-ō). (Spanish.) Mutual promises to marry.

despot. An absolute ruler; a tyrant.

despotism. (des'pǫt-izm). The rule of a tyrant.

desrenable. Unreasonable.

dessication. See **de debitore in partes secando**.

dessous (dĕ-soû). Under; underneath; below.

dessus (de-sü'). Above.

de statuto mercatori (dē sta-tū'tō mer-ka-tō'rī). A writ of statute merchant.

de statuto stapulae (dē sta-tū'tō stā'pu-lē). A writ of statute staple.

destination. The place to which something is sent. The place at which the trip of a passenger, or a shipment of goods, by carrier is to end, which, in the case of a through shipment over two or more lines, is the final or last termination. Home Furniture Co. v United States, 271 US 456, 460, 70 L Ed 1033, 1035, 46 S Ct 545.

The term is not limited to the premises of the carrier where the shipment is unloaded, but means the town or city to which the shipment is sent. Anno: 1 ALR 912.

A succession of beneficiaries provided for in a will.
See **port of destination**.

destine. To set, ordain, or appoint to a use, purpose, estate or place; to appoint unalterably. United States v Philadelphia & New Orleans (US) 11 How 609, 659, 13 L Ed 834, 855.

destitute. Poor, indigent. 41 Am J1st Poor L § 4. Without means of support either in property or in a person legally bound to furnish support. Supreme Council Catholic Benev. Legion v Grove, 176 Ind 356, 96 NE 159.
See **destitute circumstances**.

destitute child. See **destitute circumstances; destitute person**.

destitute circumstances. A relative term. A wife or child is in "destitute circumstances" when in need of the necessities of life, meaning not only primitive physical needs, things absolutely indispensable to human existence and decency, but also things which are in fact necessary to him or her as an individual. State v Waller, 90 Kan 829, 136 P 215.

destitute person. A poor or indigent person. 41 Am J1st Poor L § 4.
See **destitute circumstances**.

destitute wife. See **destitute circumstances; destitute person**.

destroy. To tear down; to cause to perish; to break into pieces; to burn up; to make useless for service, beyond hope of recovery of value, as by wrecking a ship through casting her upon rocks or shoals. United States v Johns (US) 4 Dall 412, 417, 1 L Ed 888, 890. But a thing may lose its value without being destroyed, as where a hotel or inn in the country is taken out of the main stream of traffic by a relocation of highway. Jones v Erie & Wyoming Valley Railroad Co. 151 Pa 30, 25 A 134.

destroyed by fire. Total destruction or such damage as renders the property unfit or incapable of being used without rebuilding, not simply repairing. 32 Am J1st L & T § 506.

See **total destruction; total loss; wholly destroyed.**

destruction. A wrecking, tearing down, breaking up, or burning up. Sometimes synonymous with "loss." Electric Reduction Co. v Lewellyn (CA3 Pa) 11 F 493. Sometimes accomplished indirectly, without touching the property physically, as where the property is rendered useless. Jones v Erie & Wyoming Valley Railroad Co. 151 Pa 30, 46. But a thing can lose its value without being destroyed. Jones v Erie & Wyoming Railroad Co. 151 Pa 30.

See **destroyed by fire; total destruction; wholly destroyed.**

destruction of subject matter. The destruction of a thing, the continued existence of which is essential to the performance of a contract. 17 Am J2d Contr § 411.

De sturgione observetur, quod rex illum habebit integrum; de balena vero sufficit, si rex habeat caput, et regina caudam (dē ster-ji-ō'ne ob-zer-vē'ter, quod rex il'lum hā-bē'bit in'te-grum; dē ba-lē'na vē'rō suf'fi-sit, sī rex hā'be-at ka'put, et rė-jī'na kâ'dam). As to the sturgeon, it is to be noted, that the king shall have the whole of it, but as to the whale, it sufficeth if the king have the head, and the queen the tail. See 1 Bl Comm 222.

desuetude (des'wẹ-tūd). Disuse.

de suit. See **droit de suit.**

de superoneratione pasturae (dē su-per-ō-ne-rā-she-ō'ne pas-tū'rē). A writ of surcharge of the common of pasture. See 3 Bl Comm 238.

de supersedendo (dē su-per-se-den'dō). A writ of supersedeas, which, directed to an officer, commands him to desist from the execution of another writ which he is about to execute, or which may come into his hands.

desus. Same as **dessus.**

detached dwelling. A term familiar in restrictive covenants limiting construction to "detached dwellings," the courts disagreeing as to whether a covenant in such terms precludes the construction of apartment houses. Anno: 14 ALR2d 1403, § 8.

detachiare (dē-ta-she-ar'ē). To seize.

detail. A small part or item; an account of a happening which deals minutely with it. A term of the military for a small detachment put to special duty or special tasks, but subject to recall to the ordinary line of duty. State ex rel. Dawson, 39 Ala 367, 379.

detailmen. Employees of an industry whose duties are to travel and discuss and explain the products of the industry, not to wholesalers, but to persons interested as prospective purchasers and users. Eli Lilly & Co. v Sav On Drugs Inc. 366 US 276, 6 L Ed 2d 288, 81 S Ct 1316.

detain. To hold; to keep in custody; to keep. To detain goods as amounting to a conversion of them means wrongfully to hold them and keep them in one's custody. Wails v Farrington, 27 Okla 754, 116 P 428.

detainer (dẹ-tā'nėr). The act of withholding land from the rightful owner; the restraint of a person without his consent.

See **forcible detainer; unlawful detainer.**

detainment of kings. See **restraints of kings.**

detainment of princes. See **restraints of princes.**

detainment of vessel. Holding in possession or custody, something more than a blockade, since the master is in control of a blockaded vessel. Olivera v Union Ins. Co. (US) 3 Wheat 183, 189, 4 L Ed 365, 366.

de tarris. See **judgment de tarris.**

detection. Bringing to light; finding out, particularly the person who committed a crime.

detective. One engaged in the detection of crime as a member of a police force or privately.

de tempore cujus contrarium memoria hominum non existat (dē tem'po-re kū'jus kon-trā'ri-um me-mō'ri-a ho'mi-num non eg-zis'tat). From the time when the memory of man runneth not to the contrary.

de tempore in tempus, et ad omnia tempora (dē tem'-po-re in tem'pus, et ad om'ni-a tem'po-ra). From time to time, and at all times.

de temps dont memorie ne court (dē tān dōn me'mo-rē nē kour). From the time when memory runneth not to the contrary.

detention. Holding one arrested on a charge of crime. Wong Wing v United States, 163 US 228, 235, 41 L Ed 140, 142, 16 S Ct 977.

See **commitment; detainment of vessel; restraints of kings; restraints of princes.**

deter. To stop one from acting by frightening him; to discourage the performance of an act. Printup v Alexander & Wright, 69 Ga 553, 556.

detergent. A cleansing substance, other than soap, used in washing clothes, dishes, etc., and sometimes added to lubricating oil.

determinable. That which may be determined, found out, definitely decided upon, or settled; as the date of an instrument which, to be negotiable, must, under the Negotiable Instruments Law, be payable at a "determinable" future time. McCornick & Co. v Gem State Oil & Products Co. 38 Idaho 470, 222 P 286, 34 ALR 867, 872.

determinable fee. An estate limited to a person and his heirs, with a qualification annexed by which it is provided that the estate must determine whenever that qualification is at an end; otherwise known as a base fee, qualified fee, or a defeasible fee. Staack v Detterding, 182 Iowa 582, 161 NW 44; King County v Henson Invest. Co. 34 Wash 2d 112, 208 P2d 113.

Upon the grant of a determinable fee there remains in the grantor a possibility of reverter. Donehue v Nilges (Mo) 266 SW2d 553, 45 ALR2d 1150.

determinable future time. A fixed period after the occurrence of a specified event, which is certain to happen, though the time of happening is uncertain. Uniform Negotiable Instruments Law § 4(3); 11 Am J2d B & N § 171.

determinate (dẹ-ter'mi-nāt). Ascertained; made certain; definite; having fixed limits.

determination. Firm intention; a conclusion; a cessation; an ending; a termination. A technical term applied to an allowance or disallowance in correcting an error in taxation. See 34 Am J2d Fed Tax ¶ 9172.

determination letter. A written statement issued by the district director of internal revenue in response to a taxpayer's inquiry as to the tax treatment of a particular transaction, primarily with respect to a completed transaction.

determination of adverse claims. A statutory remedy for the determination of adverse claims to real property which is an enlargement upon the equitable remedies of quieting title and removing a cloud on title; designed to afford an easy and expeditious mode of quieting title to real estate. 44 Am J1st Quiet T § 5.

determination of will. Firm intention. The manifestation of the termination of that intention or state of mind which keeps alive an estate at will, by some appropriate act or omission on the part of the lessor or lessee. See 2 Bl Comm 146.

determinative powers. A term more useful than exact, the aim of which is to describe powers and functions involving the decision or determination by an administrative agency of the rights, duties, and obligations of specific individuals and persons, as contrasted with powers of administrative agencies which, while they may involve decisions or determinations in the broadest sense, involve persons generally rather than specially and usually operate only prospectively. 1 Am J2d Admin L § 138.

determine. To terminate; to cease; to end. To put an end to controversy by deciding the issue or issues, by making a settlement, or by adjustment. Field v Auditor, 83 Va 882, 887. Same as "hear and determine" when used by statute with reference to court action, but meaning merely "ascertain," where used in matters not pertaining to judicial process. Ex parte Anderson, 191 Or 409, 229 P2d 633, 230 P2d 770, 29 ALR2d 1051.
See **hear and determine.**

de terra sancta (dē ter'ra sank'ta). Of the holy land.
See **essoin de terra sancta.**

de terre seynte. See **essoin de terre seynte.**

de testamentis (dē tes-tā-men'tis). Of testaments or wills,—the title of the fifth part of the Digests or Pandects.

de theolonio (dē the-ō-lō'ni-ō). A writ for the recovery of tolls.

detinet (det-i'net). He detains.
See **debet et detinet.**

detinue (det-i-nū). A common-law remedy for the recovery in specie of chattels wrongfully withheld from the plaintiff.
See **non detinet; writ of detinue.**

detinuit (de-ti'nu-it). A plaintiff is said to be "in the detinuit" when he is in possession of the goods under a writ of replevin.

detractare (de-trak-tā're). To draw; to drag along.

detraction. Disparagement. A taking away.
See **duties of detraction.**

de transgressione (dē trans-gre-she-ō'ne). A writ of trespass.

detriment. As consideration for a contract, some forbearance, loss, or responsibility, given, suffered, or undertaken by the party; any prejudice suffered or agreed to be suffered by a contracting party other than such as he is at the time of contracting lawfully bound to suffer. 17 Am J2d Contr § 96. Loss or harm suffered in person or in property. Moberg v Scott, 38 SD 422, 161 NW 998; Brown v Brown, 42 Okla 124, 140 P 1022.

detunicari (de-tu-ni-kā'rī). To discover; to uncover.

Detur digniori (de'ter dig-ni-ō'rī). Let it be given to the more deserving one.

de ultra mare (dē ul'tra ma're). Of beyond the sea, —a kind of essoin.
See **essoin de ultra mare.**

de una parte (dē ū'na par'tē). Of one side; unilateral; binding upon but one of the parties.

Deus solus haeredem facere potest, non homo (dē'us sō'lus hē'rē'dem fā'se-re po'test, non hō'mō). God alone can make an heir, man cannot.

deuterogamy (dū-tę-rog'a-mi). The marriage of a person after the death of that person's former spouse. Some authorities confine the definition to the remarriage of a widower.

de uxore abducto. See **trespass de uxore abducto.**

de uxore rapta et abducta (dē ux-ō're rap'ta et ab-duk'ta). Of the rape and abduction of a wife,—a writ which lay for a husband to recover damages for the abduction of his wife, whether the act was by force, fraud or persuasion. See 3 Bl Comm 139.

devadiatus (de-va-di-ā'tus). A person charged with crime who was at large without bail or sureties.

devant (dē-văn). Before.

devant le roy (dē-văn lē roa). Before the king.

devastation. A state of destruction. Waste. See 2 Bl Comm 508.

devastaverunt (de-vas-tā-vē'runt). They have committed waste.

devastavit (dev-as-tā'vit) Mismanagement of the estate and effects of a decedent, or a misapplication or waste of the assets, in violation of the duty imposed upon an executor or administrator. 31 Am J2d Ex & Ad § 265.

de vasto (dē vas'tō). A writ of waste.

developed water. Such subterranean or underground water as is discovered and brought to the surface by the exploitation of man, and which otherwise would run to waste. Rock Creek Ditch & Flume Co. v Miller, 93 Mont 248, 17 P2d 1074, 89 ALR 200.

developing land. See **land development.**

development of mine. See **mine development.**

devenerunt (de-ve-nē'runt). A writ directing the escheator to ascertain what lands which were held by a tenant in capite should, upon his death, escheat to the king.

Devenio vester homo (de-ve'ni-ō ves'ter hō'mō). I become your man,—formal words which were used by the vassal in the ceremony of homagium, or manhood, whereby the tenant or vassal, after having made oath of fealty, became bound to the lord, under the feudal system. See 2 Bl Comm 54.

devenit (de-vē'nit). He comes; he comes into.

de ventre inspiciendo (dē vontr in-spi-she-en'do). A writ to ascertain whether a woman convicted of a capital crime was quick with child, which was allowed by the common law, in order to guard against the taking of the life of an unborn child for the crime of the mother. The writ was also used in civil cases to protect the rightful succession to the property of a decedent against fraudulent claims of bastards, when a widow was suspected of feigning pregnancy in order to produce a supposititious heir to the estate, in which case the heir or devisee might have this writ to examine whether the woman was pregnant or not, and if she was, to keep her under proper restraint until she was delivered. Union Pacific Ry. Co. v Botsford, 141 US 250, 253, 35 L Ed 734, 738, 11 S Ct 1000.

de verbo in verbum (dē ver′bō in ver′bum). From word to word,—word for word.

de verborum significatione (dē ver-bō′rum sig-ni-fi-kā-she-ō′ne). Of or concerning the meaning of words,—the title of that part of the Digests or Pandects which defined words and phrases of the Roman law.

devest (dẹ-vest′). To deprive.

deviation. A departure by the owner of an easement of way from the path or road over the servient tenement which he is entitled to use. 25 Am J2d Ease § 70.
See **deviation from route.**

deviation by carrier. See **deviation from route.**

deviation by ship. See **deviation from route.**

deviation doctrine. A doctrine involving the liability of the master for the negligence of his servant in driving the master's car, that if the use to which the automobile is being put is only a slight deviation from the use for which permission was originally granted, the permission is not vitiated. Johnson v Maryland Casualty Co. (CA 7 Wis) 125 F2d 337.

deviation from route. A change from the usual or customary route, a term usually employed in the law in reference to a carrier or other bailee entrusted with property for transportation. 4 Am J2d Ani § 7. A technical term in the law of carriers, of maritime origin but extended to include land transportation, meaning a change of route from the customary route, such being actionable only where it was voluntary and without necessity or reasonable cause. 13 Am J2d Car § 324. A voluntary variation constituting an abandonment of the voyage insured by a marine policy. Wilkins v Tobacco Ins. Co. 30 Ohio St 317.

Deviation by a ship is a voluntary departure, without necessity or reasonable cause, from the regular and usual or agreed course of a voyage. It may consist also in other departures from the agreed or customary route or method of transportation, such as taking another vessel in tow, shipping by a vessel other than the one specified in the contract of affreightment, shipping part of the way by rail when all water carriage was stipulated, or carrying the goods beyond the delivery point. Whether there has been a deviation or not, upon given facts, is a question of law for the court to determine. 48 Am J1st Ship § 393. The term "deviation" in a marine insurance policy means a voluntary departure without necessity or justifiable cause, from the regular and usual course of the voyage. 29A Am J Rev ed Ins § 1000.
See **involuntary deviation.**

device. Something ingeniously conceived and skilfully made, especially something whereby to work a trick or perpetrate a fraud. Armour Packing Co. v United States, 209 US 56, 71, 52 L Ed 681, 690, 28 S Ct 428. A distinguishing mark, as upon an election ballot; an emblem, a symbol, such as "O.-K." State ex rel. Baxter v Ellis, 111 NC 124, 15 SE 938. A placard, a banner, or a sign, displayed and maintained by strikers near the employer's place of business for the purpose of deterring workmen from entering the place or remaining at work. Arthur v Oakes (CA7 Wis) 63 F 310. As the term is used in connection with patents it means a thing devised or formed by design,—a contrivance, an invention. Bliss Co. v United States, 248 US 37, 43, 63 L Ed 112, 116, 39 S Ct 42.
See **gambling device; safety device.**

de vicineto (dē vi-sī′ne-tō). From the particular neighborhood, as distinguished from the county at large. See 3 Bl Comm 360.
See also **de corpore comitatus.**

devier (dè vi-e′). To swerve; to deviate.

devil. A term of the printing trade of an older day for boy in the shop who ran errands and did odd jobs.

"It sometimes happens that a junior barrister will be given work which a brother barrister, through press of business, is unable to do. Where a barrister obliges a friend in this way he is said to "devil" for him. Formerly the "devil" got no fee, but at the present day it is usual for him to receive [in the Chancery Division, but not seemingly in the King's Bench Division] half the fee marked on his friend's brief." Marston Garcia, A New Guide to the Bar (6th Ed. 1928) p. 124.

de vi laica amovenda (dē vī la′i-ka ā-mō-ven′da). For removing the force of the laity,—a writ which lay to prevent laymen from giving aid by force to a clergyman in his strife with another one for possession of a church.

devilish character. An eccentric, roguish, quarrelsome, or even a mean person, but not an insane person. 29 Am J Rev ed Ins Per § 35.

de viridi et venatione (dē vi′ri-dī et ve-nā-she-ō′ne). Of vert and venison. The court of attachments, a forest court, was held before the verderers of the forest once in every forty days to inquire into all offenses against vert (the greensward where the deer fed) and venison (the killing of deer). See 3 Bl Comm 71.

devisa (dē-vī′sa). A boundary.

devisavit vel non (de-vis-ā′vit vel non). The issue which arises upon the contest of a will. 57 Am J1st Wills § 774. An issue of fact as to whether a will in question was made by the testator as his own responsible act. Asay v Hooper, 5 Pa 21, 25.

devise (dē-vīz′). A testamentary gift of real estate. 57 Am J1st Wills § 1399. Sometimes used loosely to include a testamentary gift of either personalty or real estate, but by the weight of authority, when used in a statute, the word is to be given its technical meaning and is held to apply only to real property, unless it clearly appears that the intention of the legislature was otherwise. 57 Am J1st Wills § 1400. The meaning restricted to real estate, however, will not prevail against language in the will which indicates the testator's intention to include personal property despite his use of the term "devise." 57 Am J1st Wills § 1400. Although in their technical sense the words "devise" and "bequest" are generally applied to the testamentary disposition of real and personal property respectively, a nonlapse statute providing that the lineal descendants of a "devisee" shall take the estates given by the will "in the same manner as the devisee would have done had he survived the testor" will be interpreted as including bequests of personalty as well as devises of realty where the legislature has in other statutes used the terms in a nontechnical sense, where the evident legislative intent is to carry out the will of the testator, and where an intent to dispose of realty and personalty on the same basis appears in the will. Hoellinger v Molzhon, 77 ND 108, 41 NW2d 217, 19 ALR2d 1147.

devise and bequeath. Words which in their ordinary legal meaning, also in common usage, refer to real as well as personal property. Caracci v Lillard, 7 Ill 2d 382, 130 NE2d 514, 53 ALR2d 1053.

devise and grant. Apt words of conveyance in creating a covenant to stand seised. 28 Am J2d Est § 347.

devisee. The beneficiary named in a devise which in the best legal sense is a testamentary gift of real estate.
See **devise; residuary devisee.**

devisor (dē-vi'zor). A testator who makes a devise by his will.

devoir (dev-wor'). Duties; customs.

devolution (dev-ō-lū'shon). The transfer of property from one person to another by operation of law.
See **clause of devolution.**

devolve. To roll or tumble down or descend; to be transmitted by a course of events, or by operation of law; to transfer from one person to another; to pass by transmission to another; to pass by operation of law upon the death of the owner. Fitzpatrick v McAlister, 121 Okla 83, 248 P 569.
An estate "devolves" upon another when by operation of law, and without any act of the previous owner, it passes from one person to another; but it does not devolve from one person to another as the result of some positive act or agreement between them. Francisco v Aguirre, 94 Cal 180, 185, 29 P 495.

devyer. Same as **devier.**

de warrantia chartae (dē war-ran'she-a kar'tē). A writ of warranty of charter.

de warrantia diei (dē war-ran'she-a dī'ē-ī). A writ of warranty of day, under which a man might save himself from suffering a default by reason of his absence in the service of the king.

d'execution. See **droit d'execution.**

d. h. An abbreviation of the word "deadhead."
See **deadhead; deadhead message.**

diabetes (dī-a-bē'tēz). A disease having various types but in its most common form characterized by excessive sugar in the blood and urine. Duggan v McBreen, 78 Iowa 591, 593. Usually responding favorably to treatment with insulin.

diagnosis (dī-ag-nō'sis). Etymologically and in its general interpretation, the word signifies a discrimination, a passing of judgment as to physical conditions. Baker v State, 91 Tex Crim 521, 240 SW 924, 22 ALR 1163, 1166. It is an analysis by a physician of the trouble of his patient. 41 Am J1st Phys & S § 92. The professional opinion of a physician based on his examination.

diagram. An illustrative outline of a tract of land, or something else capable of linear projection, which is not necessarily intended to be perfectly correct and accurate. At best, it is but an approximation. It is a common and usual method of pointing out localities and lines. Shook v Pate, 50 Ala 91, 92.

diarium (di-ā'ri-um). Sufficient food for one day.

diatim (dī'a-tim). From day to day; daily.

dicasts (dī'kasts). Athenian judges who were chosen by lot and who passed upon questions of both law and fact.

dice. Small cubes of bone or plastic, convenient for tossing, marked in the sides by spots in varying numbers running from one to six, used in games of chance by gamblers. Loaded dice.
See **cogging.**

Dicebatur fregisse juramentum regis juratum (dī-se-bā'ter fre-jis'se ju-ra-men'tum rē'jis ju-rā'tum). He was said to have broken the sworn oath of a king. See 1 Bl Comm 268.

dicere et non dare legem (di'se-re et non da're lē'jem). To expound, but not to make the law. The Curtis, The Camden & The Welcome, 37 F 705.

dicing (dī'sing). The gambling game of throwing dice.

di colonna (dī kō'lon-na). A contract under which the owner of a ship and everyone connected with the ship are entitled to share in the profits of the voyage.

dict. (dikt). An abbreviated form of **dictum.** An abbreviation of "dictionary."

dicta (dik'ta). Plural of **dictum.** Often referred to as obiter dicta or obiter, being expressions in an opinion of the court which are not necessary to support the decision. Lawson v United States, 85 App DC 167, 176 F2d 49, cert den 339 US 934, 94 L Ed 1352, 70 S Ct 663, reh den 339 US 972, 94 L Ed 1379, 70 S Ct 994. Language unnecessary to a decision; ruling on an issue not raised, or the opinion of a judge which does not embody the resolution or determination of the court, and made without argument or full consideration of the point. Lawson v United States, 85 App DC 167, 176 F2d 49; 20 Am J2d Cts § 74.
Stare decisis does not attach to such parts of the opinion of a court as are mere dicta. Of course, if nothing can be found in point except dicta, counsel does not hesitate to cite the case which contains it. There is, moreover, a distinction between mere obiter and judicial dicta. The latter term applies to expressions of opinion on a point deliberately passed upon by the court. 20 Am J2d Cts § 74. Judicial dicta, as such, is sometimes given effect as holdings. 20 Am J2d Cts § 190.
While mere obiter is not law of the case, judicial dicta are not excluding from the applicability of the doctrine of the law of the case. 5 Am J2d A & E § 753.

dictate. To pronounce, word by word, what is designed to be written by another. Hamilton v Hamilton (La) 6 Mart NS 143, 146. To give orders with authority.

dictator. An absolute ruler, answerable to no other power or authority.

dictionary. Dictionaries do not give to words their meaning; they only chronicle that which has been done, and the use must precede the chronicling. State v Olson, 26 ND 304, 144 NW 661.

dicto majoris partis. See **ex dicto majoris partis.**

dictores (dik-tō'rēz). Arbitrators.

dictum (dik'tum). An expression in an opinion which is not necessary to support the decision reached by the court. Parker v Stonehouse Drainage Dist. 152 Kan 188, 102 P 1017. A statement in an opinion with respect to a matter which is not an issue necessary for decision. Tillinghast v Maggs, 82 RI 478, 111 A2d 713, 52 ALR2d 1004. A writ employed to obtain the correction of a record on appeal. 4 Am J2d A & E § 478.

The plural of dictum is **dicta**. For effect of dictum as precedent or law of the case. See **dicta**.

dictum of Kenilworth (dik'tum of Kenilworth). A compromise of their differences between Henry the Third and Parliament in 1266.

dictus. See **alias dictus**.

did then and there. Familiar words in alleging time and place of the commission of an offense. 26 Am J1st Homi §§ 267 et seq.; 27 Am J1st Indict § 70.

die. To lose one's life. This does not necessarily import that death must result from an accident or that it must occur in some unforeseen manner. Hershey v Agnew, 83 Colo 89, 262 P 526.

Diebus Dominicis mercari, judicari vel jurari non debet (dī-ē'bus do-mi'ni-sis mer-kā'rī, jū-di-kā'rī vel jū-rā'rī non de'bet). On the Sabbath there ought not to be any trading, any giving judgment, nor any holding of court. A maxim of the civil law. Richardson v Goddard (US) 23 How 28, 16 L Ed 412, 417.

die by his own hand. Die by suicide. Unless the words are qualified by some other expression, they import a criminal act of self destruction. Hence they do not include a case of suicide while insane. Breasted v Farmers' Loan & Trust Co. 8 NY 299.

die by suicide. Die by his own hand. A self-killing by an insane person, understanding the physical nature and consequences of his act, but not its moral aspect, is not a death by suicide within the meaning of the phrase. Manhattan Life Ins. Co. v Broughton, 109 US 121, 131, 27 L Ed 878, 882, 3 S Ct 99.

died by his own hand. See **die by his own hand; death by his own hand**.

diei dictio (dī'e-ī dik'she-ō). A notice given by a Roman magistrate of his intention to impeach a citizen upon a certain day.

Diem clausit extremum (dī'em klâ'sit ex-trē'mum). He closed his last day; that is, he died,—a writ by which the heir of a deceased tenant in capite compelled the escheator to ascertain what land should escheat to the king.

dies (dī'ēz). A day.

dies ad quem (dī'ēz ad quem). The day to which.

dies amoris (dī'ēz a-mō'ris). A day of grace, favor, or indulgence.

dies a quo (dī'ēz ā quō). The day from which; the day from which or upon which a period of time begins to run. 52 Am J1st Time § 17.

dies communes in banco (dī'ēz kom-mū'nēz in ban'kō). Common days in banc,—fixed days for appearance in court.

dies consilii (dī'ēz kon-si'li-ī). A day set for an argument or hearing.

dies datus (dī'ēz dā'tus). A given day; a day given or set.

Dies Dominicus non est juridicus (dī'ēz do-mi'ni-kus non est jū-ri'di-kus). The Lord's day is not a juridical day. That is, it is not a day upon which legal proceedings may be conducted. Moss v State, 131 Tenn 94, 173 SW 859.

Diesel engine. An internal combustion engine without sparkplugs, ignition being accomplished by heat.

Diesel-powered single-car unit. Not a train with the meaning of a full-crew statute. Western Pac. R. R. Co. v State, 69 Nev 66, 241 P2d 846, 45 ALR2d 429.

dies excrescens (dī'ēz ex-kre'senz). The extra day—the twenty-ninth day of February—which is added in leap-years.

dies fasti (dī'ēz fas'tī). (Civil law.) Those days on which the business of the courts could be transacted. In the Roman calendar there were in the whole year but twenty-eight judicial or triverbial days allowed to the praetor for deciding causes. 3 Bl Comm 424.

dies feriati (dī'ēz fe-ri-ā'tī). Days of rest or idleness; holidays.

dies gratiae (dī'ēz grā'she-ē). A day of grace, favor, or indulgence.

Dies inceptus pro completo habetur (dī'ēz in-sep'tus prō kom-plē'tō hā-bē'ter). A day begun is regarded as completed. The law does not recognize fractions of a day.

Dies incertus pro conditione habetur (dī'ēz in-ser'tus prō kon-di-she-ō'ne hā-bē'ter). An uncertain day is regarded as a condition.

dies intercisi (dī'ēz in-ter-si'sī). Days upon which the court was in session during only a part of each day.

Dies interpellat pro homine (dī'ēz in-ter-pel'lat prō ho'mi-ne). The due date makes the demand for the man (the creditor).

dies juridici (dī'ēz jū-ri'di-sī). Plural of **dies juridicus**.

dies juridicus (dī'ēz jū-ri'di-kus). A juridical day,—a day upon which court can lawfully be held; a court day. 50 Am J1st Sun & H § 73.

dies legitimus (dī'ēz lē-ji'ti-mus). A lawful day; a term day of court; a law day; an appearance day.

dies lunaris (dī'ēz lu-nā'ris). A lunar day.

dies nefasti (dī'ēz ne̢-fas'tī). (Civil law.) Those days of the year in which the business of the courts could not be lawfully transacted. See 3 Bl Comm 276.

dies non (dī'ēz non). An abbreviation of **dies non juridicus**. Havens v Stiles, 8 Idaho 250, 67 P 919.

dies non juridicus (dī'ēz non jū-ri'di-kus). A day not for litigation. Vidal v Backs, 218 Cal 99, 21 P2d 952, 86 ALR 1134.
See **nonjuridical day**.

dies solaris (dī'ēz sō-lā'ris). A solar day.

dies solis (dī'ēz sō'lis). The day of the sun,—Sunday.

dies utiles (dī'ēz u'ti-lēz). Available days,—days upon which a proposed or agreed act could be lawfully done.

diet (dī'et). A legislative assembly; a meeting of delegates. One's daily food; a selection of food made for reasons of health or for reducing weight.

dieta (dī-ē'ta). A day's work; a day's expenses; a reasonable day's journey. See 3 Bl Comm 218.

diet of compearance. A day set for a party's appearance in court.

Dieu et mon droit (diė ā mȯn drwo). God and my right,—the battle slogan of Richard the First which subsequently became the motto of the royal arms of England.

Dieu son acte (diė sōn akt). God's own act,—an act of God; vis major.

die without issue. A phrase common in testamentary gifts, appearing in the form of "to A, but if he dies without issue, then to B," and presenting the ques-

DIFFACERE [348] DIMES

tion of construction as between a definite and an indefinite failure of issue, the interpretation whereby the testator is taken to have meant the death of A without surviving issue being termed the "definite failure" construction and the interpretation whereby the testator is taken to have meant the death without surviving issue of A's last descendant, whenever that might be, being called the "indefinite failure" construction.

While at common law, the "indefinite failure" construction was preferred, the "definite failure" construction was made mandatory in England by statute in 1837, in the absence of a clear testatorial intention to the contrary. In the United States, in the absence of statute, there are two lines of authority, one upholding and one rejecting the common-law rule. In many states, statutes have been enacted requiring the adoption of the "definite failure" construction in the absence of any clear expression of a contrary intention. 57 Am J1st Wills § 1238.

The words "die without issue," and other expressions of the same import, mean an indefinite failure of issue. At common law, in the absence of words making a different intent apparent, the established interpretation of such expressions in a will is that they import a general indefinite failure of issue, and not a failure at the death of the first taker. Parkhurst v Harrower, 142 Pa 432, 21 A 826.

diffacere (dif-fa'se-re). To mutilate; to destroy.

differences. See **compounding for differences; controversy; issue.**

differentiated tax (dif-ẹ-ren'shi-āt'ed). See **graduated tax.**

differentiation of taxes (dif-ẹ-ren-shi-ā'shọn). See **graduated tax.**

Difficile est ut unus homo vicem duorum sustineat (dif-fi'si-le est ut ū'nus hō'mō vi'sem du-ō'rum susti'ne-at). It is distressing that one man should suffer for the vice of two.

difforciare (dif-for-si-ā're). To deny or keep from a person.

dig. To excavate. To mine. An abbreviation of **digests.**

digama (dī-gam'ạ). Same as **deuterogamy.**

digamy (dig'ạ-mi). Same as **deuterogamy.**

digests (di-jests'). The Pandects or body of Roman laws compiled under the Emperor Justinian. Law books arranged in an alphabetical order of titles and presenting in analytical distribution summaries and syllabi of cases.

digging. A mine. A slang term for one's living quarters.

dignitary. A person of importance. In an older day, the term was applied to any ecclesiastical officer of a rank or station higher than that of a priest or canon.

dignities (dig'nị-tēz). A species of incorporeal hereditaments bearing a near relation to offices. They were originally annexed to the possession of certain estates in land. See 2 Bl Comm 37.

dike. An embankment employed to prevent the inundation of land; a structure of earth or other material usually placed upon the bank of a stream or near the shore of a lake, bay, etc., the ends of which extend across low land to higher ground, forming a continuous bulwark or obstruction to water, and designed to keep it without the inclosure thus formed. Morton v Oregon Short Line Railway Co. 48 Or 444, 87 P 151.

See **flee to the wall.**

dilacion (de-lah-the-on'). A postponement or extension of time granted to a litigant.

dilapidations (di- or dī-lap-i-dā'shọns). Ruins. A kind of ecclesiastical waste, either voluntary, by pulling down; or permissive, by suffering the chancel, parsonage-house and other buildings thereunto belonging to decay. For such wrong an action lay, either in the spiritual court by the canon law, or in the courts of common law. See 3 Bl Comm 91.

dilation (dil-ạ or di-lạ'shọn). A delay; a continuance; a postponement.

Dilationes in lege sunt odiosae (dī-lā-she-ō'nēz in lē'je sunt ō-di-ō'sē). Delays are obnoxious to the law.

dilatoria. See **exceptio dilatoria.**

dilatory defenses. Defenses which delay the action without destroying the cause or right of action; defenses pleaded in abatement. 41 Am J1st Pl § 115.

dilatory motion. A motion made for delay. 37 Am J1st Motions § 3.

dilatory plea. Any plea belonging to a class which tends to delay a trial of the case on the merits; such as a plea in abatement or a plea in bar. Parks v McClellan, 44 NJL 552, 557.

See **dilatory defenses.**

diligence (dil'i-jẹns). Active attention to some matter in hand. Heintz v Cooper, 104 Cal 670, 38 P 512. The opposite of laches. 27 Am J2d Eq § 152. A relative term incapable of precise definition, its meaning being dependent upon the particular circumstances of the case.

Under Scotch law, the word is applied to an execution proceeding for the collection of a debt.

See **diligent inquiry; due diligence; extraordinary diligence; ordinary diligence; prudence; reasonable diligence; slight diligence.**

diligence of bailee. See **high diligence.**

diligentia (di-li-jen'she-a). In the civil law, there are three degrees of diligence; *diligentia* or ordinary diligence; *exactissima diligentia* or extraordinary diligence; and *levissima diligentia* or slight diligence. Likewise, there are three degrees of fault or neglect; *lata culpa* or gross fault or neglect; *levis culpa* or ordinary fault or neglect; and *levissima culpa* or slight fault or neglect. Brand v Troy & Schenectady Railroad Co. (NY) 8 Barb 368, 378.

Diligentia quam suis rebus adhibere solet (di-li-jen'-she-a quam su'is rē'bus ad-hi'be-re so'let). The diligence which it is customary to exercise in the management of one's own affairs.

diligent inquiry. Such inquiry as a diligent man, intent upon ascertaining a fact, would usually and ordinarily make,—inquiry, with diligence, and in good faith, to ascertain the truth. Van Matre v Sankey, 148 Ill 536, 36 NE 628.

diligiatus (di-li-ji-ā'tus). A person who was outlawed; an outlaw.

dillonques (dī-lōngk). Thenceforth; afterward.

diluvion (di- or dī-lū'vi-un). The gradual washing away and consequent loss of soil along the banks of a river. Hagen v Campbell (Ala) 8 Port 9. Opposite of **alluvion.**

dimes (dīms). Tenths; tithes. United States coins of the value of ten cents.

dimidietas (di-mi-di-ē′tas). One half of anything.

dimidium (di-mi′di-um). An undivided one-half interest in anything.

diminished liability clause. A provision in an accident insurance policy for a decrease of benefits upon the insured engaging in an occupation more hazardous than the one under which he was insured. 29 Am J Rev ed Ins § 768.

diminutio (di-mi-nu′she-ō). Diminution.

diminution. A taking away or lessening.

diminution of damages. See **mitigation of damages**.

diminution of salary. The lowering of a salary. Not comprehending the placing of a burden upon a salary in the form of an income tax.

diminution of the record. A term applied to a record on appeal which is in some respect inaccurate or incomplete. State v Reid, 18 NC 382.

dimisi (di-mī′sī). I have demised.

Dimisi, concessi, et ad firman tradidi (di-mī′sī, kon-ses′sī, et ad fir′mam tra′di-dī). I have demised, granted and leased to farm.

dimisit (di-mī′sit). He has demised.

dimittere (di-mit′te-re). To dismiss; to release.

dimming headlights. A requirement in driving a motor vehicle imposed in many jurisdictions as a safety measure, preventing a glare interfering with approaching drivers. 7 Am J2d Auto § 226.

dinarchy. A government with two rulers.

Dingley Act. The protective tariff act passed by Congress in 1884.

diocesan courts (dī′ō-sē-san or dī-os′e-san). Ecclesiastical courts held by the bishop or his chancellor in each diocese.

diocese (dī′ō-sēs). The see or jurisdiction of a bishop. See 1 Bl Comm 111.

diode (dī′ōd). A vacuum tube for radio or television. Lewis v Avco Mfg. Corp. (CA7 Ill) 228 F2d 919, 926.

dip. In mining,—the downward course of the vein. "Dip" and "depth" are of the same origin—"dip" is the direction or inclination toward the "depth"—and it is throughout their depth that veins may be followed, and that is surely their downward course. Duggan v Davey, 4 Dak 110, 141, 26 NW 887.

diploma. An instrument conferring some privilege, honor, or authority; now almost wholly restricted to certificates of degrees conferred by schools, universities and colleges. Halliday v Butt, 40 Ala 178, 183.

diplomatic officers. Ambassadors, envoys extraordinary, ministers plenipotentiary, ministers resident, commissioners, chargés d'affaires, agents and secretaries of legation. Ex parte Baiz, 135 US 403, 419, 34 L Ed 222, 227, 10 S Ct 854. Officers however denominated who possess the functions, rights, and privileges as agents of their respective governments for the transaction of diplomatic business abroad. 4 Am J2d Ambss § 1.

diplomatics (dip-lō-mat′iks). The science of deciphering ancient documents or that of passing upon their genuineness.

dippers (dip′ērs). Certain officers of a court baron who received and depended upon gratuities for their compensation. Weller v Baker (Eng) 2 Wilson 422.

dipping. The placing of animals in a chemical bath for disinfection and removal of parasites such as ticks. Anno: 65 ALR 543.

dipsomania (dip-sō-mā′ni-ạ). An irresistible craving for alcoholic beverages; an irresistible impulse to indulge in intoxication, either through the medium of alcohol or other drugs, such as opium. This mania or disease is classed as one of the minor forms of insanity. Ballard v State, 19 Neb 609, 614, 28 NW 271.

direct. Verb: To guide; to regulate; to control. Sometimes creative of a trust as a precatory term. Collister v Fassitt, 163 NY 281, 57 NE 490. Adjective: Immediate or proximate as distinguished from remote. Ermentrout v Girard Fire & Marine Ins. Co. 63 Minn 305, 65 NW 635; Mork v Eureka-Security F. & M. Ins. Co. 230 Minn 382, 42 NW2d 33, 28 ALR2d 987.

direct ascending line. The line of descent traced upward from intestate son, grandson, daughter, granddaughter, great grandson, great granddaughter, etc., to the ancestor. 23 Am J2d Desc & D § 36.

direct attack. A challenge of the integrity of a judgment, in the action wherein the judgment was rendered, by a proceeding maintained for the express purpose of vacating, suspending, annulling, reversing, or modifying the judgment. Mitchell v Village Creek Drainage Dist. (CA8 Ark) 158 F2d 475; Hall v Huse, 122 Ark 67, 182 SW 535; Mastin v Gray, 19 Kan 458, 466. Some authorities regard a suit to obtain equitable relief by way of an injunction against the enforcement of a judgment or by the annulment or setting aside of a judgment as a direct attack upon the judgment. Other authorities say that such a suit is an indirect attack upon the judgment, although not to be regarded as a collateral attack. 30A Am J Rev ed Judgm § 856.

direct bounty. A certain amount paid upon the production or exportation of particular articles. The act of Congress of 1895, allowing a bounty upon the production of sugar, and Rev. Stat. §§ 3015-3027 (U. S. Comp. Stat. 1901, pp. 1989-1994), allowing a drawback on certain articles exported, are examples of direct bounties. Downs v United States, 187 US 496, 502, 47 L Ed 275, 277, 23 S Ct 222.

direct cause. An active and efficient cause, that is, a proximate cause.
See **proximate cause**.

direct competition. See **competition**.

direct contempt. Words spoken or acts done in the presence of the court, or during its intermissions, which tend to subvert, embarrass or prevent justice, such as telling the judge that he is ignorant and unfair. State v Goff, 28 SC 17, 88 SE2d 788, 52 ALR2d 1292.

direct corporate purpose. A characterization of a purpose of the exercise of power by a municipal corporation which operates with direct and immediate consequences upon the interests of the corporation, such as the suppression of vice and the promotion of good order. State ex rel. Thompson v Memphis, 147 Tenn 658, 251 SW 46, 27 ALR 1257, 1264.

direct criminal contempt. Conduct directed against the power and dignity of the court during a session of court and in the immediate view and presence

of the court. Lynn v State, 38 Okla Crim 313, 260 P 1069.
See **criminal contempt**.

direct damages. In one sense, damages which result from a wrongful act without the intervention of any other efficient cause. Loiseau v Arp, 21 SD 566, 114 NW 701. In another sense, the direct or proximate, as distinguished from the remote, consequences of a wrongful act. 22 Am J2d Damg § 20.

direct descending line. The line of descent from intestate to his children, grandchildren, great grandchildren, etc. 23 Am J2d Desc & D § 54.

directed. Guided, regulated, controlled.
As used in a statute by which someone is "directed" to perform an act, the word, if standing alone, may well be construed as implying something mandatory, but other words in the context may so control it as to give it the effect of importing discretionary action on the part of the person "directed." Binney v Chesapeake & Ohio Canal Co. (US) 8 Pet 201, 212, 8 L Ed 917, 921.

directed verdict. A verdict which a jury returns as directed by the court. 53 Am J1st Trial §§ 332 et seq.
See **motion for directed verdict**.

direct evidence. Proof which speaks directly to the issue, requiring no support by other evidence; proof in testimony out of the witness' own knowledge, as distinguished from evidence of circumstances from which inferences must be drawn if it is to have probative effect. 29 Am J2d Ev § 264.

direct examination. The examination in chief of a witness by the party who called him to the stand.
See **examination in chief; question in chief; redirect examination**.

direct infringement. An infringement of a patent by one's own act, as distinguished from a contributory infringement. See **contributory infringement; infringement of patent**.

directing powers. See **determinative powers**.

direct injury. The direct result of the violation of a legal right. Alabama Power Co. v Ickes, 302 US 464, 82 L Ed 374, 58 S Ct 300.
See **direct damages; proximate cause**.

direction. A command; an order; an instruction to an agent or servant; a court's instruction to a jury; the complainant's address to the court in a bill in equity; control; management; superintendence.
See **direct; directed; directed verdict**.

direction against apportionment. A special type of tax clause in a will aimed at avoiding or overcoming a statute providing for proration of the estate tax. 28 Am J Rev ed Inher T § 489.

directional signals. Equipment upon a motor vehicle for use in warning other drivers before making a turn. 7 Am J2d Auto § 157.

directional survey. A survey had by way of discovery to ascertain whether an oil well is draining oil from adjoining premises. 23 Am J2d Dep § 184.

direct line. See **direct ascending line; direct descending line**.

direct loss or damage by fire. Loss or damage occurring with fire as the destroying agency, as distinguished from fire as a remote agency of loss. 29A Am J Rev ed Ins § 1288. A loss which is immediate or proximate, as distinguished from remote or incidental. Clouse v St. Paul F. & M. Ins. Co. 152 Neb 230, 40 NW2d 820, 15 ALR2d 1008. But proximate results may include other things than combustion, such as the resulting fall of a building. O'Connor v Queen Ins. Co. 140 Wis 388, 122 NW 1038.

directly. In a direct manner; in a straight line or course; without curving, swerving, or deviation. State ex rel. Norton v Van Camp, 36 Neb 9, 13.

directly affected. See **involved**.

directly essential to production. Under the Fair Labor Standards Act covering an employee in an occupation "closely related" and "directly essential" to the production of goods for commerce, the employee's work need not be indispensable to production. General Electric Co. v Porter, 208 F2d 805, 44 ALR2d 854.

directly interested in labor dispute. Interested as the employer; interested as an employee in hours, wages, or working conditions involved. Anno: 28 ALR2d 338, 339.

directo. See **ex directo**.

Director of the Census. The head of the Federal Bureau of the Census, appointed by the President with the advice and consent of the Senate, and directed by law to perform such duties as may be imposed upon him by statute, regulations, or orders of the Secretary of Commerce. 14 Am J2d Census § 3.

directors. Agents and executive representatives of a corporation, who, acting as a board or unit, manage the business of the corporation, constituting, as it has been said, the mind and soul of the corporation, acting according to their best judgment, and beyond control by the stockholders in respect of any particular action taken. 19 Am J2d Corp §§ 1079 et seq.
Corporate directors act as a board, this is, as a unit, in representing the corporation, and transacting its business, but as individuals in the performance of some of their duties, such as inspection of corporate records. State ex rel. Keller v Grymes, 65 W Va 451, 64 SE 728.
See **dummy director**.

directors' meeting. The coming together of the directors of a corporation to determine their course of action in corporate affairs as an official body. 19 Am J2d Corp §§ 1118 et seq.

directors of bank. Executive representatives of a banking corporation elected by the stockholders, who, acting as a board, manage and control the affairs and business of the corporation. 10 Am J2d Banks §§ 77, 176.

directory. Noun: A listing of the names and addresses of the persons in a particular city, of the members of a fraternal order, club, or profession, or of the subscribers to telephone service in a city or area. Adjective: That which is merely advisory or instructive, as opposed to that which is mandatory.

directory part of a statute. The part which directs that which is to be done or not to be done, the other parts being the declaratory and vindicatory portions. 50 Am J1st Stat § 151. The provision of a statute which is directory or permissive, as distinguished from mandatory provisions of the same statute. 50 Am J1st Stat § 18.
See **directory statute**.

directory statute. A statute whose provisions are a matter of form only, are not material, do not affect any substantial right, and do not relate to the es-

directory trust. A trust in which, by the terms of the trust, the trust funds are to be invested in a particular manner until the time arrives at which they are to be appropriated. Deaderick v Cantrell, 18 Tenn 263.

direct payment. A payment which is absolute and unconditional as to time, amount, and the persons by whom and to whom it is to be made. Ancient Order of Hibernians v Sparrow, 29 Mont 132, 74 P 197. A payment made directly to the obligee, not to an intermediary.

direct proceedings. A direct attack upon a judgment.
See **direct attack.**

direct property tax. The primary form of taxation in most states. 51 Am J1st Tax § 408.
See **direct taxes.**

direct settlement. A term common in board of trade transactions, signifying the method of settlement consisting simply in setting off contracts to buy a certain amount of a given commodity at a certain time, against contracts to sell a like amount of it at the same time, and paying the difference of price in cash, at the end of the business day. Chicago Board of Trade v Christie Grain & Stock Co. 198 US 236, 247, 49 L Ed 1031, 1037, 25 S Ct 637.

direct taxes. Capitation or poll taxes levied without regard to property, profession or other circumstances; taxes on land. Springer v United States, 102 US 586, 26 L Ed 253. Also, taxes levied directly on personal property because of ownership. Pollock v Farmers' Loan & T. Co. 157 US 429, 39 L Ed 759, 15 S Ct 673. Such taxes may be distinguished from taxes on importations, consumption, manufacture and sale of commodities, and taxes on business and occupation privileges and the like which Congress may impose without apportionment. The Federal income tax is a direct tax but the requirement of the Constitution that it be apportioned among the states according to population was removed by the Sixteenth Amendment.

direct trust. Same as **express trust.**

diribitores (di-ri-bi-tō'rēz). Persons who distributed the ballots to the voters at a Roman election.

dirimant impediments (di'ri-mant im-pe'di-ments). Those bars to lawful matrimony which are not removed by a consummation.

dirk. A deadly weapon. 56 Am J1st Weap § 3.
See **dagger.**

dirt. Loose earth as distinguished from firm rock. Highley v Phillips, 176 Md 463, 5 A2d 824. Anything unclean. Gossip.
See **visible dirt.**

disability. A deprivation of ability; a state of being disabled. Miller v American Mut. Acci. Ins. Co. 92 Tenn 167, 21 SW 39. Want of competent power, strength, or physical ability; weakness; incapacity; impotence. Hill v Travelers' Ins. Co. 146 Iowa 133, 124 NW 898. Loss of earning power; loss of a limb or member. 58 Am J1st Workm Comp § 282. Under some workmen's compensation statutes, impairment of physical efficiency, even though earning power has not been lost. 58 Am J1st Workm Comp § 282. As used in a policy of accident insurance, the bare term "disability" means disability from performing the occupation which the insured was following at the time of the accident, and not some vocation which he might be able to follow after the accident. Ozark Mut. Life Asso. v Winchester, 116 Okla 116, 243 P 735; 29A Am J Rev ed Ins § 1518. For the purposes of the Social Security Act, inability by reason of a medically determinable physical or mental impairment, to engage in substantial and gainful activity, commensurate with his age, educational attainments, training, experience, and mental and physical capacities. Teeter v Fleming (CA7 Ind) 270 F2d 871, 77 ALR2d 636.

Want of legal capacity, such as infancy, insanity, and loss of rights consequent to the conviction of a crime. Berkin v Marsh, 15 Mont 152, 44 P 528; 23 Am J2d Crim L § 616.

See **legal disability; total disability; total mental disability; total physical disability.**

disability clause. A clause in a policy of life insurance providing for a waiver of premiums in the event of the disability of the insured occurring while the policy is in effect, sometimes for monthly or other periodical payments to be made to the insured during the continuance of the disability so incurred.

disability provisions. The terms of health and accident insurance policies, and life insurance policies with disability features, which define and describe the risk covered by the policy. 29A Am J Rev ed Ins § 1504.

disable. To make unfit physically or to incapacitate one to transact business. As used in a statute defining mayhem, the word is held to import a permanent disability, and not a mere temporary one. Vawter v Commonwealth, 87 Va 245, 12 SE 339; Anno: 58 ALR 1320.

disabled from earning a livelihood. Physically incapacitated. Also where a man is so inattentive or forgetful as a result of mental disorder that he cannot be trusted to carry on even simple forms of work, he is as truly disabled from earning a livelihood as one who must refrain from work on account of the condition of his vital organs. United States v Taylor (CA4 NC) 110 F2d 132.

disabling statutes. The statutes, also called the "restraining statutes," passed in the reign of Elizabeth, which curbed the leasing of lands by the church and by eleemosynary corporations, and resulted in the turning over to Elizabeth of much valuable land by the prelates, for which she paid nothing. See 2 Bl Comm 320.

disadvantage to promisee. See **detriment.**

disadvocare (dis-ad-vo-kā're). To disavow; to deny.

disaffirm. To repudiate a voidable obligation or deed.

disaffirmance. The repudiation of a voidable obligation or deed, sometimes by the subsequent conveyance of the same premises to a third person. Searcy v Hunter, 81 Tex 644.

disafforest (dis-a-for'est). To release a forest from the operation of the forest laws. Many forests were thus stripped of their oppressive privileges and regulations by the Charta de Foresta, 9 Henry III. See 2 Bl Comm 416.

disaffranchise. Same as **disfranchise.**

disagreement. A jurisdictional term in the federal statute in reference to veterans' insurance, meaning a denial of a claim for insurance benefits, after consideration of its merits, by the Administrator of Veterans' Affairs or any employee or organizational unit of the Veterans Administration designated therefor by the Administrator of Veterans' Affairs. 29A Am J Rev ed Ins § 1988.

disagreement of jury. See **hung jury.**

disallow. To overrule; to reject; to deny.

disalt. To disable.

disappropriation (dis-a-prō-pri-ā'shon). The severing of an appropriation from the benefice to which it was annexed, either by presentation of a clerk by the appropriator or patron and his induction to the parsonage, or by the dissolution of the corporation which had the appropriation. See 1 Bl Comm 385.

disapprove. To refuse to approve, confirm, ratify, sanction, or consent to some act or thing done by another. Stewart v Yellowtail (DC Mont) 35 F Supp 799.

disaster relief. Aid to farmers suffering financially from drought, crop failure, calamity, or disaster. 3 Am J2d Agri § 32. Also aid to the inhabitants of a particular city or political subdivision who have suffered losses of property from fire, hurricane, flood, or extremely cold and bitter weather. Emergency relief in furnishing food, clothing, medical and nursing services.

disavow. To repudiate; to disclaim.

disband. To cease to exist as a body. To dissolve a body, such as a school district. Briggs v Borden, 71 Mich 87, 38 NW 712.

disbar. To pronounce a judgment or make an order of disbarment of an attorney; to revoke an attorney's license to practice law. 7 Am J2d Attys § 12.

disbarment. The revocation by judgment or order of court of the right of an attorney at law to practice. 7 Am J2d Attys § 12.
See **grounds for disbarment.**

disbarment proceeding. A proceeding instituted by an aggrieved client, the state's attorney, a bar association, a committee of a bar association, an individual attorney at law, or a group of attorneys at law not constituting a committee of a bar association, or instituted by the court on its own motion, seeking the disbarment of an attorney at law for cause or causes stated. 7 Am J2d Attys §§ 60 et seq.

disbocation (dis-bo-kā'shon). The clearing of wooded land; the changing of wooded or forest land into pasture.

discarcare (dis-kar-kā're). To discharge or unload a cargo.

discargare (dis-kar-gā're). Same as **discarcare.**

disceptatio causae (dis-sep-tā'she-ō kâ'zē). Same as **disceptio causae.**

disceptio causae (dis-sep'she-ō kâ'zē). The argument of a cause by counsel.

discharge. Noun: The performance of an obligation or duty. A release because of performance or as a matter of grace. Union Bank v Powell's Heirs, 3 Fla 175. A release of a debtor in insolvency proceedings by operation of law. 29 Am J Rev ed Insolv § 88. A release from custody, as the discharge of an accused, or release from the performance of a duty, as the discharge of a juror. The separation of a civil service officer or employee from the service. 15 Am J2d Civ S § 33. The release of a member of one of the armed services from such service. 36 Am J1st Mil § 36. The dismissal of an employee. Verb: To perform obligations; to release from a prison or from duty. To release a member of one of the armed services from the service. To dismiss an employee. To unload or deliver cargo from a vessel or freight from a railroad car.
See **honorable discharge.** See also terms and expressions following which commence **discharge.**

discharged. The termination of a contract by performance in accordance with its terms. 17 Am J2d Contr § 482. Released from performance of duty; dismissed from employment; released from one of the armed services. 36 Am J1st Mil § 36.
A convict is "discharged" from prison when he is restored to freedom. It may not mean that he has been given the right of suffrage, or the right to hold office, if he lost those rights by conviction, but it does mean that in all other respects he is a citizen, and fully protected in his rights under the organic law. Ex parte Schatz, 307 Mo 67, 269 SW 383, 38 ALR 1032, 1035. As the word is used in a statute exempting a person from jury service who has been "discharged" as a juror within a year, it means one who is discharged from the panel, or for the term, and not one who has been discharged from a case at the close of a trial. White v United States (CA9 Cal) 16 F2d 870.

discharge for money. A receipt for money; a receipted bill; a voucher for money spent. Commonwealth v Brown 147 Mass 585, 18 NE 587.

discharge from draft. A certificate given one who has reported to his draft board for immediate military service but is permitted to return home, without entering the service, because of the termination of hostilities. Patterson v Lamb, 329 US 539, 91 L Ed 485, 67 S Ct 448.

discharge from military service. See **discharge.**

discharge from payment of tithes. See **de modo decimandi.**

discharge in bankruptcy. The release of a bankrupt from all of his debts which are provable in bankruptcy, except such as are excepted from discharge by the Bankruptcy Act. Bankruptcy Act § 1(15); 11 USC § 1(15).

discharge of attachment. The dissolution of an attachment (1) upon the occurrence of certain events after the levy, e. g. the loss of legal possession of the goods attached, (2) upon the entry or receipt of security, or (3) as the result of some proceeding taken for the express purpose of defeating or nullifying the attachment. 6 Am J2d Attach § 408.

discharge of bill or note. An expression with a dual aspect, meaning the discharge of the instrument itself and the discharge of the persons primarily and secondarily liable thereon. The NIL provides for discharge of the instrument by specified methods and for discharge of persons secondarily liable by specified methods. The Commercial Code takes a new approach to the concept of discharge. The Code generally does not speak of discharge of the instrument but of discharge of all parties and the discharge of any single party. The methods of discharge are collected and referred to in a single section. 11 Am J2d B & N § 901.

discharge of guardian. The release of a guardian from his trust, either by order of court or by a settlement with his ward when the ward becomes of age or ceases to be incompetent. Berkin v Marsh, 18 Mont 152, 44 P 528.

discharge of jury. The remedy of the prejudiced party upon a mistrial. 53 Am J1st Trial § 965. The release of a jury from further service in a case or a release of all jurors upon the list upon completion of their work at the term.

discharge of officer in armed forces. A separation from the service at the request of the officer. In any other connection, the term implies some measure of discredit. United States v Sweet, 189 US 471, 473, 47 L Ed 907, 908, 23 S Ct 638.

discharge of prisoner. A remedy sought by motion on presenting exceptions to the return to a writ of habeas corpus. Ex parte Mooney, 26 W Va 36.

discharge of surety. The release of a surety upon performance of the obligation or by operation of law. 50 Am J1st Suret § 40.

discharge of watercourse. The place where a stream or watercourse empties or discharges itself into some other watercourse or body of water. See 56 Am J1st Wat § 10.

discipline. Good conduct; training in good conduct. The maintenance of good order in a voluntary association or club, in a last resort by suspension or even expulsion of a member. 6 Am J2d Asso & C § 32. As applied to a soldier or militiaman, the word means system of drill; systematic training; training to act in accordance with established rules; accustoming to systematic and regular action. State ex rel. Poole v Peake, 22 ND 457, 135 NW 197.
See **corporal punishment.**

disclaimer. A renunciation or refusal to accept. A refusal to recognize the existence of an obligation. A refusal to retain title obtained as the grantee of a deed not accepted by the grantee. 23 Am J2d Deeds § 127. The object of a deed is to transfer property, but the object of a disclaimer is to prevent a transfer. Watson v Watson, 13 Conn 83, 85.
In patent law procedure, a statement filed by the patentee for the surrender of a separate claim in the patent, or some other distinct and separable matter, which can be exscinded without mutilating or changing what is left standing. 40 Am J1st Pat § 105.
A pleading filed by a defendant in a suit in equity, setting forth that he has no interest in the subject matter of the suit. 27 Am J2d Eq § 196.

disclaimer of paternity. A refusal to acknowledge a child as one's own. 10 Am J2d Bast § 29.

disclaimer of tenure. The disclaimer of a tenant in an action against him for rent.

disclamation (dis-klā-mā'shon). Same as **disclaimer.**

disclose. To make known that which before was unknown.

disclosed principal. A situation where the other party to a transaction conducted on the one side by an agent knows that the agent is acting for a principal and has notice of the principal's identity. 3 Am J2d Agency § 307.

discommission. To deprive a person of his office or commission.

discommon. To deprive of a right of common; to change common property into private property.

discontinuance. In the modern sense of the term, a voluntary dismissal or the taking of a nonsuit; at early common law, the failure of a litigant to continue his suit regularly from day to day or from term to term between the commencement of the action and final judgment. 24 Am J2d Dism § 2. The abandonment of work on a project. The abandonment of a use which is nonconforming under a zoning ordinance. Anno: 18 ALR2d 729.

discontinuance of estate. The termination or interruption of an estate tail by a grant by the tenant in tail of a larger estate than he had, thereby either defeating the estate of the tenant in tail or that of the remainderman or reversioner. See 3 Bl Comm 171.

discontinuance of highway. The abolition or vacation of a highway. 25 Am J1st High § 127.

discontinuance of service. The conduct of a public service corporation in refusing to continue operations to supply existing needs. 43 Am J1st Pub Util § 78. Shutting off service to customer for nonpayment of bill for service furnished. 43 Am J1st Pub Util § 64.

discontinued. Abandoned. The term as used in a zoning ordinance provision that if a nonconforming use is discontinued, any new use of the premises shall be in conformity with the provisions of the ordinance, connotes a voluntary act and is synonymous with abandon. Anno: 18 ALR2d 729.

discontinous easement. An easement characterized by a use not so continuous as to be compsicuous. 25 Am J2d Ease § 32. An easement which can only be enjoyed by the intervention of a human agency, such as a right of way. In some states continuous easements will pass by implication in a grant and discontinuous easements will not. Anno: 34 ALR 234.

disconvenable. Improper; inappropriate.

discooperta. Same as **discovert.**

discount. In the broad sense, a deduction from a sum in gross; a reduction from a regular price of an article offered for sale. In a technical sense, interest reserved from the amount lent at the time of making the loan. 30 Am J Rev ed Int § 12. In the banking business, a charge for a loan in advance, whether called interest, compensation, or premium, the amount of the discount being deducted from the principal and retained by the bank at the time of making the loan. 10 Am J2d Banks § 689. A rate applied in the commutation of periodical payments to a payment in a lump sum. Anno: 105 ALR 242.

discounting commercial paper. The lending of money upon commercial paper and the deducting of the interest or premium in advance. 10 Am J2d Banks § 689.

discover. Ascertain by sight, hearing, or smell, and by information obtained from others. Carroll v United States, 267 US 132, 69 L Ed 543, 45 S Ct 280, 39 ALR 790.

discovered. Having acquired actual knowledge of something, such as defalcation by an employee within the coverage of a fidelity bond. Anno: 23 ALR2d 1076.
See **after-discovered; discover.**

discovered peril. For all practical purposes the doctrine of discovered peril is the same in scope and effect as the last clear chance doctrine. Soards v Shreveport Rys. Co. (La App) 8 So 2d 343, 344.
See **last clear chance.**

discovert (dis-kuv'ért). The condition or status of a woman who is at present without a husband, whether she be unmarried, widowed or divorced.

discoverture (dis-kuv'ẻr-tụr). The changing of the

discovery. The finding of something, perchance a cure for a disease, a new land, a new planet, or a mechanical principle which may be adapted to produce an article which has the requisite of patentability. 40 Am J1st Pat § 39. A finding of mineral, the primary factor in the perfection of a mining claim. 36 Am J1st Min & M § 83. The showing of mineral must be of such character that a person of ordinary prudence, whether he is a miner or not, would feel justified in expending further time and money in development of the property in view of prospects of profit. 36 Am J1st Min & M § 87. A remedy for the sole purpose of compelling the adverse party to answer its allegations and interrogatories, and thereby to disclose facts within his own knowledge, information, or belief, or to disclose and produce documents, books and other things within his possession, custody or control, being usually employed to enable a party to prosecute or defend an action. 23 Am J2d Depos § 141.

status of a married woman by the death of her husband or the obtaining of a divorce from him.

See **bill of discovery; discovery and occupation; pure bill of discovery; statutory discovery.**

discovery and occupation. A method of acquiring territory on behalf of a nation. 30 Am J Rev ed Internat L § 42; 54 Am J1st US § 77.

By the law of nations, dominion of new territory may be acquired by discovery and occupation, as well as by cession or by conquest; and when citizens or subjects of one nation, in its name and by its authority or with its assent, take and hold actual, continuous, and useful possession (although only for the purpose of carrying on a particular business, such as catching and curing fish or working mines) of territory unoccupied by any other government or its citizens, the nation to which they belong may exercise such jurisdiction and for such period as it sees fit over territory so acquired. Downes v Bidwell, 182 US 244, 45 L Ed 1088, 21 S Ct 770.

discovery shaft. A shaft which the mining laws of some states require to be sunk within a prescribed number of days after discovery. 36 Am J1st Min & M § 88.

discredit. To injure a person's credit or reputation; to refuse credence; to distrust; to discredit the testimony of a witness is to distrust it, to disbelieve it, to regard it as false. People v Clark, 84 Cal 573, 24 P 313.

discrepancy (dis-krep'an-si or dis'kre-pan-si). Difference appearing upon comparison; inconsistency. A variance between a party's pleading and his proof.

Discretio est discernere per legem quid sit justum (dis-krē'she-ō est dis-ser'ne-re per lē'jem quid sit jŭs'tum). Discretion is the discernment, through the law, of that which is just. "That is, to discern by the right line of law, and not by the crooked cord of public opinion." Commonwealth v Anthes, 71 Mass (5 Gray) 185, 204.

Discretio est scire per legem quid sit justum (dis-kre'she-ō est si're per lē'jem quid sit jus'tum). Discretion is the knowledge of that which is just through the law. Le Roy v Corporation of New York (NY) 4 Johns Ch 352, 356.

discretion. The equitable decision of what is just and proper under the circumstances; the liberty or power of acting without other control than one's own judgment. The S.S. Styria v Morgan, 186 US 1, 9, 46 L Ed 1027, 1033, 22 S Ct 731. The power or right conferred upon an officer of acting officially under certain circumstances according to the dictates of his own judgment and conscience, uncontrolled by the judgment or conscience of others. United States ex rel. Accardi v Shaughnessy, 347 US 260, 98 L Ed 681, 74 S Ct 499; Farrelly v Cole, 60 Kan 356, 56 P 492; 2 Am J2d Admin L § 191.

See **abuse of discretion; age of discretion; judicial discretion; legal capacity.**

discretionary divorce. A divorce granted by a court under a statute permitting the granting of a divorce for such cause or causes as the court may find sufficient.

discretionary duty. A duty imposed upon an officer for the performance of an act which involves the exercise of discretion by the officer, the duty not being defined with such precision and certainty as to leave nothing to the exercise of discretion. State ex rel. Linden v Bunge, 192 Wash 245, 73 P2d 516.

discretionary interest. Interest which is awarded by way of damages in any case where it is a matter within the discretion of the court to award interest or to refuse to do so. Redfield v Ystalyfera Iron Co. 110 US 174, 28 L Ed 109, 3 S Ct 208. A discretionary rate of interest allowed as damages. 22 Am J2d Damg § 182.

discretionary trust. An anomalous term from the standpoint of absolute discretion in the trustee, since unbridled discretion in a trustee negatives the necessary separation of legal and equitable ownership. Best defined as a trust in which a broad discretion is vested in the trustee to be exercised in carrying out purposes and objectives for the benefit of another, which are required by the terms of the trust. 54 Am J1st Trusts § 36. A trust which exists when, by the terms of the trust, no direction is given to the trustee as to the manner in which the trust funds are to be invested, until the time arrives at which they are to be appropriated in satisfaction of the trust. Deaderick v Cantrell, 18 Tenn 263. A trust designed to prevent alienation by lodging discretion in the trustee as to the payment of income and withholding from the beneficiary a vesting of the equitable right to compel the distribution. Re Bucklin's Estate, 243 Iowa 312, 51 NW2d 412, 34 ALR2d 1327.

discretion of administrative agency. A power or right, conferred upon an agency by law, of acting officially in certain circumstances according to the dictates of their own judgment and conscience as to what is just and proper under the circumstances, uncontrolled by the judgment or conscience of others. 2 Am J2d Admin L § 191.

discretion of court. A scope of authority of determination granted to a trial court which, in the absence of abuse of discretion, accords finality to a determination made, so that it is not reviewable by a higher court. 4 Am J2d A & E § 80. Necessarily a sound discretion, or as it is sometimes stated, a legal discretion. 20 Am J2d Cts § 69. Exercising the best of judgment upon the occasion that calls for it. Tompkins v Sands (NY) 8 Wend 462. Nothing more nor less than a discretion to do in any particular case what the ends of justice demand. Sioux Falls v Marshall, 48 SD 378, 204 NW 999, 45 ALR 447, 451. The sound choosing by the court, subject to the guidance of the law, between doing or not doing a thing, the doing of which cannot be demanded as an absolute right. Chapman v Dorsey, 230 Minn 279, 41 NW2d 438, 16 ALR2d 1015.

A court without discretion would be a hobby horse. Watts v State, 22 Tex App 572, 577.

DISCRIMINATING [355] DISFIGUREMENT

discriminating duty. An additional customs duty imposed on an imported article of a kind for the manufacture, production, and export of which in and from this country a bounty is paid. 21 Am J2d Cust D § 14.

discrimination. Failure to treat everyone alike according to the standards and rule of action prescribed, that is, unreasonable and arbitrary action. 2 Am J2d Admin L § 193. Class legislation and the denial of equal protection of the laws. Arbitrary inclusions or exclusions of persons from the list for jury duty. 31 Am J Rev ed Jur § 93. A purposeful and systematic exclusion of persons from the jury list on the basis of race or color. 31 Am J Rev ed Jur § 12. The denial of suffrage on the basis of a classification according to race. 25 Am J2d Elect § 55.

See **advantage, concession, and discrimination; class legislation; equal protection; price discrimination.**

discrimination by common carrier. Any act, device, or arrangement by a common carrier which operates to give to one or more patrons rates, services, or privileges not accorded to all under similar conditions or circumstances, or, vice versa, which operates to render unavailable to some patrons rates, services, or privileges which are available to others similarly situated. 13 Am J2d Car § 197.

As applied to freight rates, the term implies a charge to shippers of freight, as compensation for railroad transportation, of unequal sums of money for the same quantity of freight, for equal distances, more for a shorter than a longer distance, more in proportion of distance for a shorter than a longer distance; more for "local freights," than for "through freights;" more for the former, in proportion of the distance such freights may be carried, than the latter, the railroads being prompted to make such charges by unreasonable competition between two or more of them at competing points. Freight Discrimination Cases, 95 NC 434, 446.

To constitute an "unjust discrimination" in passenger rates, the carrier must charge or receive directly from one person a greater or lesser compensation than from another, or must accomplish the same thing indirectly by means of a special rate, rebate or other device; but, in either case, it must be for a like and contemporaneous service in the transportation of a like kind of traffic, under substantially similar circumstances and conditions. Interstate Commerce Com. v Baltimore & Ohio Railroad Co. 145 US 263, 281, 36 L Ed 699, 705, 12 S Ct 844.

discumberment (dis-kum'bẽr-mẽnt). A release of property from an encumbrance or lien.

discussion. A civil law term meaning the seizure and sale of the property of the principal to satisfy the demand against him before proceeding against that of the surety. Schmidt v New Orleans, 33 La Ann 17, 18.

See **benefit of discussion.**

disease. In a strict or literal sense, any departure from a perfect norm of health, even including some ailments which are more or less trivial. Mutual Life Ins. Co. v Simpson, 88 Tex 333. Better understood in a legal sense as an ailment or disorder of an established or settled character to which the insured is subject, having no reference to a temporary disorder which is new and unusual, and arises from some sudden and unexpected derangement of the system, although it may produce or cause unconsciousness. 29A Am J Rev ed Ins § 1211. As the term "disease" appears in a health insurance policy it is not the equivalent of sickness; sickness is a condition interfering with one's usual activities, whereas disease may exist without such result. 29A Am J Rev ed Ins § 1154. A "disease in any organ of the body" is not every disorder or ailment affecting an organ, lasting for a brief period only and unattended by substantial injury or inconvenience, or prolonged suffering, but is an affection so well defined and marked as materially to derange for a time the functions of that organ. Connecticut Mut. Life Ins. Co. v Union Trust Co. 112 US 250, 258, 28 L Ed 708, 711, 5 S Ct 119.

In an accident policy the words "bodily infirmity or disease" have a well understood meaning. They are practically synonymous and refer to an ailment or disease of a settled character and all the definitions given by the courts negative the idea that they could possibly include a personal peculiarity not in any way impairing bodily health or strength and not in any way interfering with the functioning of the organs of the body. Mutual Life Ins. Co. v Dodge (CA4 Md) 11 F2d 486.

In a strict or literal sense, any departure from an ideal or perfect norm of health is a disease or an infirmity, but when considered with relation to a policy insuring against death caused by "accidental means alone" something more must be shown. If there is no active disease, but merely a frail general condition, so that powers of resistance are easily overcome, or merely a tendency to disease, which is started up and made operative, whereby death results, then there may be recovery even though the accident would not have caused that effect upon a healthy person in a normal state. Bush v Order of United Commercial Travellers (CA2 Vt) 124 F2d 528.

See **chronic; contagious disease; exposed to disease; idiopathic disease; illness; incurable disease; industrial disease; infectious disease; occupational disease; serious ailment; serious illness; sickness; sound health; sound physical condition; traumatic disease.**

disembargo. To release from the restrictions of an embargo.

disencumber. To remove an encumbrance, as, to pay off a mortgage debt; to relieve of a burden.

disencumbrance. The removal of an encumbrance, such as a mortgage; the removal of a burden.

disentail (dis-en-tāl'). To break the entail of an entailed estate. This was effected by a disentailing deed whereby the tenant in tail conveyed an absolute title to his grantee, which was authorized by statute in the reign of William the Fourth.

disentailing deed. See **disentail.**

disestablish. A labor law expression which means the divesting of an agent for collective bargaining of his authority as such. 31 Am J Rev ed Lab § 281.

disfigure. To cause a disfigurement.
See **disfigurement.**

disfigurement. "That which impairs or injures the beauty, symmetry, or appearance of a person or thing; that which renders unsightly, misshapen, or imperfect, or deforms in some manner." Superior Mining Co. v Industrial Com. 309 Ill 339, 141 NE 165. A change of external form for the worse. Dickson v United States Sheet & Window Glass Co. 3 La App 83.

As used in a statute defining mayhem, the word

disforest means a permanent and not a mere temporary disfigurement. State v Taylor, 105 W Va 298, 142 SE 254. The offense of disfiguring a domestic animal may be complete with no injury of a permanent character. Thus, to shave a horse's mane or tail is a disfiguring of the horse. State v Harris, 11 Iowa 414, 415.

disforest. To clear wooded land of trees.

disfranchise. To effect a disfranchisement.
See **disfranchisement**.

disfranchisement. The taking away of a franchise, a person's citizenship, or his right of suffrage. The absolute expulsion of a member from a corporation, and the taking away of his franchise of being a member. White v Brownell (NY) 2 Daly 329, 357.
See **amotion**.

disgavel (dis-gav'el). To remove from land the incidents of gavelkind tenure, under which the lands descended equally to all of the sons of the tenant.

disgrace. A cause of shame or reproach; that which dishonors; a state of ignominy, dishonor, or shame. Slawson v State, 39 Tex Crim 176, 178. Loss or respect; disrepute; an element of actionable defamation. 33 Am J1st L & S § 45.

disgrade. To deprive a person of a title or dignity.

disguise. Verb: To conceal identity by assuming or giving a false appearance or guise, as by wearing an unusual clothing or dress. Noun: Clothing, dress, wigs, goggles, or other device put on to conceal identity. Artifice in speech or manner employed to conceal identity. Darneal v State, 14 Okla Crim 540, 174 P 290, 1 ALR 638, 641.

dishabilitation (dis-ha-bil-i-tā'shǫn). Corruption of blood. A sentence of dishabilitation was imposed as a punishment for treason.

disherison (dis-her'i-zǫn). Same as **disinheritance**.

disheritor (dis-her'i-tǫr). A testator who disinherits his heir.

dishes. Containers for serving food and holding food; in one sense, household furniture. 29 Am J Rev ed Ins § 298.

dishonesty. Want of honesty; lying; stealing; defrauding. Something more than mere negligence, mistake, error in judgment, or incompetence. Irvin Jacobs & Co. v Fidelity & Deposit Co. (CA7 Ill) 202 F2d 794, 37 ALR2d 889. But not necessarily such conduct as imports a criminal offense. Citizens' Trust & Guaranty Co. v Globe & Rutgers Fire Ins. Co. (CA4 NC) 229 F 326.

dishonor. Loss of respect; shame and disgrace. Nonpayment of a bill or note. Nonacceptance of a bill or draft.
See **fraud or dishonesty**.

dishonor by nonacceptance. A term of the commercial law.
A bill is dishonored by nonacceptance when it is duly presented for acceptance and the prescribed acceptance is refused or cannot be obtained, or when presentment for acceptance is excused and the bill is not accepted. 11 Am J2d B & N § 736.

dishonor by nonpayment. A negotiable instrument is dishonored by nonpayment when it is duly presented for payment and payment is refused or cannot be obtained, or when presentment is excused and the instrument is overdue and unpaid. 11 Am J2d B & N § 739.

disincarcerate (dis-in-kär'se-rāt). To release a prisoner from imprisonment.

disincorporate. To relinquish a corporate charter; to cause a corporation to cease to exist as a corporation.

disinherison. Same as **disinheritance**.

disinheritance. Disinheriting an heir; depriving an heir of his inheritance of right to succeed to the estate of his ancestor.

disinter. To exhume or remove a body that has been buried in the earth; to take out of the grave. People v Baumgartner, 135 Cal 72, 74, 66 P 974.
See **body snatching; disturbing dead body**.

disinterested. Having no interest in a matter or cause. Jones v Larrabee, 47 Me 474, 476.
See **interested**.

disinterested appraiser. An appraiser who not only is without any pecuniary interest in the property appraised, but one who is not biased or prejudiced in reference to the parties or the property. L. D. Hickerson & Co. v German-American Ins. Co. 96 Tenn 193, 33 SW 1041. The mere fact of other employment by insurance companies does not, as a matter of law, disqualify one from selection as a "disinterested appraiser." Schreiber v Pacific Coast Fire Ins. Co. 195 Md 639, 75 A2d 108, 20 ALR2d 951.

disinterested juror. A juror without a disqualifying interest such as relationship to a party within a degree prohibited as to jurors. Jewell v Jewell, 84 Me 304, 24 A 858.

disinterested malevolence (dis-in'tėr-es-ted mạ-lev'ō-lęns). An epigrammatic phrase coined by Mr. Justice Holmes, which is supposed to mean that the genesis which will make a lawful act unlawful must be a malicious one unmixed with any other and exclusively directed to injury and damage of another. Beardsley v Kilmer, 236 NY 80, 140 NE 203.

disinterested witness. A witness who is not biased by reason of any interest in the action.

disinterment. The removal of a body from a grave.
See **disinter**.

disjunctim (dis-jungk'tim). Separately; severally; disjunctively.

disjunctive allegations (dis-jungk'tiv al-ẹ-gā'shǫnz). Allegations in a pleading in the disjunctive form, that is, an alternative form, and the clauses of which are usually separated by the word "or." The general principle is that allegations in such form vitiate a pleading. 41 Am J1st Pl § 41. An indictment, information, or affidavit is rendered bad by allegations in the disjunctive, unless such form is authorized by statute. 27 Am J1st Indict § 127.

disjunctive condition. A condition which depends upon the happening of but one of several events.

disjunctive denial. The form of denial required in responding to conjunctive allegations in an adversary's pleading. 41 Am J1st Pl § 193.

disjunctive term. A term or expression in an alternative form. Deihl v Perie (Pa) 2 Miles 47, 49.

dislawyer (dis-lâ'yėr). An ancient word meaning to disbar a lawyer.

dislocation. A condition of disarrangement. A bone out of joint.

dismes. Tenths; tithes.

dismiss. To discontinue; to order a cause, motion, or prosecution to be discontinued, quashed, or dismissed as finally adjudicated against the plaintiff. The term was not originally applied to common-law proceedings, but seems to have been borrowed by the law courts from proceedings in the court of chancery, where in practice it is applied to the removal of a cause out of court, without any further hearing. It is applied to the removal or disposal of the cause itself, and not to the mere annulment of the writ. Bosley v Bruner, 24 Miss 457, 462.
See **dismissal**.

dismissal. An order for the termination of a case without a trial of any of its issues; a voluntary discontinuance by the plaintiff. 24 Am J2d Dism § 1. A judgment dismissing a cause as finally adjudicated against the plaintiff. The termination of a criminal case by the prosecuting attorney, the result of which is to free the defendant. Brackenridge v State of Texas, 27 Tex Crim 513, 11 SW 630. The discharge of an employee; a termination of employment in public or private capacity at the instance of the employer. The Fort Gaines (DC Md) 18 F2d 413.
See **discontinuance; nolle prosequi; voluntary dismissal; want of prosecution**.

dismissal compensation. A payment made by an employer to an employee, in addition to wages or salary then owing by the employer to such employer, upon the termination of the employment, particularly where the employment is under a contract which entitles the employer to terminate the employment and discharge the employee at will. Anno: 147 ALR 151; 40 ALR2d 1044. Sometimes called separation wage; sometimes severance pay.

dismissal of action. See **dismissal**.

dismissal of appeal. The refusal by the appellate court to examine the merits of the cause—that is, a dismissal on a ground not involving the merits of the cause. 5 Am J2d A & E § 905.

dismissal without prejudice. A voluntary dismissal of an action or proceeding without an adjudication of the cause that would prevent the bringing of a new action upon the same cause. 24 Am J2d Dism §§ 6 et seq. An order of dismissal of an action reciting that it is without prejudice, the effect of which is to prevent the dismissal from operating as a bar to any new suit which the plaintiff might thereafter desire to bring on the same cause of action. W. T. Raleigh Co. v Barnes, 143 Miss 597, 600, 109 So 8.
See **two-dismissal rule**.

dismissal with prejudice. An order of dismissal granted on motion of the defendant made without reservation as to prejudice. 24 Am J2d Dism §§ 53 et seq. An adjudication on the merits of the case, a final disposition of the controversy which bars the right to bring or maintain an action on the same claim or cause of action. Roden v Roden, 29 Ariz 549, 243 P 413; Pulley v Chicago, R. I. & P. Ry. Co. 122 Kan 269, 251 P 1100.

dismissed. As the word is used in an appeal bond, the removal or disposal of the cause itself. 5 Am J2d A & E § 1031.
Where the entry "dismissed" is made as a minute order on motion of a plaintiff who wishes to abandon his action, such an entry is undistinguishable from an entry "dismissed" made by the court's order after a full examination of the evidence, and is a decision on the merits, while the other is a mere non pros. To avoid the bar presumptively arising from such a decree the entry of the motion to dismiss should be made on the record, or the entry should be made "without prejudice." Brown v Brown, 37 NH 536.
See **dismissed**.

dismissed agreed. An order "dismissed agreed" not only puts an end to the pending suit but is a bar to any subsequent suit on the same cause of action by the same parties. Virginia Concrete Co. v Board of Supervisors, 197 Va 821, 91 SE2d 415, 56 ALR 1283, except as the plaintiff obtain relief against such order on the theory that the dismissal is entirely the act of the parties and does not involve the exercise of judgment by the court. McDonnell v Wasenmiller (CA8 Neb) 74 F2d 320.

dismortgage. To free or redeem property from a mortgage.

disobedience. See **wilful disobedience**.

disorderly. Against or in violation of the peace, good order, morals, decency or safety of the public.

disorderly conduct. An act which tends to breach the peace or to disturb those people who hear or see it, or to endanger the morals, safety, or health of the community or of a class of persons or a family. 12 Am J2d Breach P § 30.

disorderly house. Any place where unlawful and illegal practices are habitually carried on. Marvel v State, 127 Ark 595, 193 SW 259, 5 ALR 1458. A place where acts are performed that tend to corrupt the morals of the community or to promote breaches of the peace, or a place kept for the purpose of public resort for thieves, drunkards, prostitutes or other idle and vicious people, without regard to whether there is any actual disturbance of the public peace and quiet. 24 Am J2d Disord H § 1.
See **house of ill fame; whorehouse**.

disorderly persons. Persons guilty of disorderly conduct.
See **disorderly conduct**.

disparagation. Same as **disparagement**.

disparage (dis-par'āj). To suffer or permit a disparagement. To discredit.

disparagement. Discredit; detraction. The wrong suffered by an infant ward at the hands of the guardian in providing an unequal or unsuitable marriage. As a survival of many of the abuses of feudal tenure, the guardian had and exercised the right of selling the ward in marriage for his own profit. See 2 Bl Comm 70, 71.

disparagement of property. Criticism which discredits the quality of merchandise or other property offered for sale. Anno: 57 ALR2d 848; 33 Am J1st L & S § 344.

disparagement of title. Words or conduct which bring or tend to bring in question the right or title of another to particular property. 33 Am J1st L & S § 344.

disparagium (dis-pa-rā'ji-um). Inequality in blood or station.

Disparata non debent jungi (dis-pa-rā'ta non de'bent jun'jī). Dissimilar matters ought not to be connected together.

dispark (dis-pärk'). To change the use or character of land from that of a park or game preserve.

dispatch. Verb: To send; to act promptly; to put an end to something; to kill. Noun: A message; speed; an article transmitted to a news agency.
See **customary despatch.**

dispatch company. A company engaged in the business of transporting goods through the agency and over the lines of other carriers selected by them, the company not owning or controlling any means of conveyance. 13 Am J2d Car § 50.

dispauper (dis-pâ′pėr). To declare officially that a person who has been a pauper, is no longer a pauper; to deprive or deny a person the right of suing in forma pauperis.

dispensaries. State or municipal places where intoxicating liquors are sold at retail. 30 Am J Rev ed Intox L § 204. Places where medicines are prepared or dispensed.

dispensary act. A statute which forbids the manufacture or sale of intoxicating liquors as a beverage, within the limits of the state, by any private individual, and vests the right to manufacture and sell such liquor in the state exclusively, through certain designated officers and agents. McCullough v Brown, 41 SC 220, 19 SE 458.

Dispensatio est vulnus, quod vulnerat jus commune (dis-pen-sā′she-ō est vul′nus, quod vul′ne-rat jūs kom-mū′ne). A dispensation is a wound, because it wounds common right.

dispensation. Distribution; delivery. An exemption from certain duties or penalties imposed or prescribed by law.

dispensing of drug by physician. The actual delivery of a drug by the physician to the patient, from the physician's office supply, generally, though not always, excluding other actual delivery. Anno: 13 ALR 871.

dispensing power. The authority of an administrative agency to exempt from or relax a general prohibition or to relieve from an affirmative duty. 1 Am J2d Admin L § 141.

dispersonare (dis-per-so-nā′re). To scandalize.

displace. To take the place of; to remove; to remove a person from an office or position and put another person in his place. As applied to the act of a master of a ship in "displacing" an officer or seaman, to displace means to degrade or reduce to a lower station on the ship. Potter v Smith, 103 Mass 68, 69.

displaced person. A product of the ravages of war; a person left in a foreign country without a home because of a war.

displacement waves. Waves produced by a larger vessel proceeding at a high rate of speed, often causing injury to smaller craft. 48 Am J1st Ship § 280.

disposal. Arrangement; the transfer or alienation of property, even by gift, trade, or barter.
See **disposition.**

disposal plants. Places where the carcasses of animals are rendered into usable products; places where sewage is treated and reduced to the point where it is not harmful or annoying to the senses. A place provided by a municipality for receiving and disposing of garbage, such disposal being by incineration or other method of treatment. A municipal use within the meaning of a zoning ordinance. Lees v Sampson Land Co. 372 Pa 126, 92 A2d 692, 40 ALR2d 1171.

dispose. To arrange; to put in place. To alienate, sell, or transfer. United States v Hacker (DC Cal) 73 F 292, 294; Hubbell v Hubbell, 135 Iowa 637, 113 NW 512. To grant; to convey, even by way of barter or exchange. Phelps v Harris (US) 11 Otto 370, 380, 25 L Ed 855, 859. As the word appears in a statute providing a ground for attachment, it has a broader significance than "transfer," but does not include the mere secretion of property. 6 Am J2d Attach § 237.

disposing mind. A test of testamentary capacity, being a mind capable of knowing and understanding the disposition to be made of one's property by will and the persons upon whom bounty is to be bestowed, notwithstanding some element of mental unsoundness. Freeman v Easly, 117 Ill 317, 321. The mind of a testator who is fully capable of comprehending the testamentary disposition which his will has made of his property. Yardley v Cuthbertson, 108 Pa 395.
See **sound and disposing mind and memory.**

disposition. Frame of mind; nature or temperament. An arrangement. A transfer of property. The power of disposal.
See **fraudulent disposition of property; testamentary disposition.**

dispositive mind. Same as **disposing mind.**

dispossess. To oust; to put out of possession.

dispossession. Changing from the possession of one person to that of another; ouster; a wrong or injury that carries with it the amotion of possession thereby getting the wrongdoer into the actual occupation of the land or hereditament, and obliging him who has a right to seek his legal remedy in order to gain possession, and damages for the injuries he has sustained. See 3 Bl Comm 167.

dispossess proceeding. A summary proceeding brought to oust from possession a tenant who is in default.
See **ejectment; forcible entry and detainer.**

dispossess warrant. A warrant issued by the court in dispossess proceedings for the ouster of the tenant.
See **writ of possession.**

disprison (dis-priz′n). To liberate from prison.

disproof. Proof which tends to rebut or negative other evidence.

disproportionate. Out of proportion, as an award of damages bearing no reasonable proportion to the injury sustained. 22 Am J2d Damg § 366.

disprove. To refute; to negate.

disputable. Rebuttable; capable of being rebutted or refuted.

disputable presumption. A rebuttable presumption. A presumption which can be removed in no other way than by evidence sufficiently strong to rebut it. Joyner v South Carolina Railway Co. 26 SC 49, 55, 1 SE 52.

disputatio fori (dis-pu-tā′she-ō fō′rī). (Civil law.) An argument before the court.

dispute. A controversy. An allegation of fact by one person denied by another person, each acting with some show of reason. Knight's Appeal, 19 Pa 493, 494.
See **labor dispute; matter in dispute.**

disputed claim. As the subject of an accord and satisfaction, a dispute as to the amount of the sum

DISPUTES [359] DISSIPATION

actually due, as to whether anything is due, or as to the construction of the terms of the contract between the parties, which is bona fide, honest, and based upon a reasonably tenable or plausible ground. 1 Am J2d Accord § 27.

disputes clause. The provision in a contract for the construction of a public improvement that a dispute concerning a question of fact shall be conclusively settled by an administrative decision. Anno: 94 L Ed 263; 96 L Ed 119.

disqualification. Want of qualification, especially for a public office or for jury duty. It may be from want of an abstract qualification, such as a requirement for education, or from an element such as interest in the matter to be handled.
See **ineligible.**

disqualified judge. A judge disqualified to act in a particular case because of personal interest in the subject matter of the suit or because he is within a certain degree of relationship to one of the parties. 30A Am J Rev ed Judges § 89.

disqualified juror. A juror subject to challenge for want of a requisite qualification such as literacy, character, mental disability, prejudice, bias, relationship to a party, or interest in the suit. 31 Am J Rev ed Jur §§ 157 et seq.

disqualified witness. A witness incompetent to testify because of his mental condition, want of sensibility to the obligation of an oath, the privileged nature of the communication or other source of his knowledge of the facts, or interest in the result of the suit in a case where he is called to testify on his own behalf, in an action in which the adverse party is a personal representative of a decedent or the guardian or committee of an incompetent, concerning a transaction with the person since deceased or become incompetent. 58 Am J1st Witn §§ 102 et seq.

disqualify. To incapacitate; to disable; to divest or deprive of qualifications. Matter of Maguire, 57 Cal 604.
See **disqualification.**

disrationare (dis-ra-she-ō-nā're). To exonerate one's self; to establish innocence.

disregard. To take no notice of; to give no credence to, as in following an instruction by the court to the jury to disregard certain testimony stricken from the record. Anno: 4 ALR2d 1088.

disregarding corporate entity. Treating a corporation and the individual or individuals owning all its stock as identical; graphically stated, piercing the veil of the corporate entity. Anno: 1 ALR 610; 34 ALR 597.

disruptive discharge. See **brush discharge.**

dissasina (dis-sa'si-na). Same as **disseisin.**

dissection. The severance of a dead body into parts, sometimes very minute parts, for study of the anatomical structure, or the detection of infection or disease.

disseisee (dis-sē-zē'). A person who has been disseised or ousted.

disseisin (dis-sēz'zin). An ouster or wrongful dispossession of one in possession of real property who is seised of a freehold therein. 3 Am J2d Adv P § 52. More broadly defined as the wrongful dispossession or exclusion of a person entitled to possession. 25 Am J2d Eject § 47.

Disseisinam satisfacit, qui uti non permittit possessorem, vel minus commode, licet omnino non expellat (dis-sē'sin-am sa-tis-fā'sit, qui u'ti non per-mit'tit po-zes-sō'rem, vel mī'nus kom'mo-de, li'set om-nī'nō non ex-pel'lat). A person who commits a disseisin is one who does not permit the possessor to enjoy his property or who renders his enjoyment less comfortable, although he does not expel him altogether.

disseisin by construction of law. Acts committed without force, in themselves equivocal, and not necessarily amounting to an entire and immediate ouster of the freehold, but which the owner may, if he pleases, treat as usurpations of his freehold for the purpose of vindicating his title by an action at law. 25 Am J2d Eject § 47.

disseisin by election. A legal fiction under which an owner might elect to admit disseisin and consider himself disseised for the purpose of securing or availing himself of the remedy by action of novel disseisin against an adverse claimant; but if he did not elect to consider himself disseised, the freehold was not divested, but still continued in him. Varick v Jackson (NY) 2 Wend 166.
See **disseisin by construction of law.**

disseisin in fact. An actual ouster or dispossession of the owner of the freehold which deprives him even of constructive possession, leaving him a mere right of entry or of property. Varick v Jackson (NY) 2 Wend 166.

disseisor (dis-sē'zor). A person who effects or commits a disseisin.

disseisoress (dis-sē'zor-es). A female who effects or commits a disseisin.

disseminate. To spread information. The word creates the same picture as broadcast by radio. Norman v Century Athletic Club, 193 Md 584, 69 A2d 466, 15 ALR2d 777.

dissension. A disagreement, particularly in religious societies, leading to heated debate, even angry words, strife, discord, quarrels, and sometimes a disunion or breaking apart. McKinney v Griggs, 68 Ky (5 Bush) 401, 417.

dissent. To disagree with another or with others; to render a minority opinion in the decision of a case. Disagreement of an individual juror with the verdict, announced on the polling of the jury. 21 Am J2d Crim L § 371.

dissenting stockholders. A minority who oppose the action taken by the majority.

dissignare (dis-sig-nā're). To break a seal.

Dissimilium dissimilis est ratio (dis-si-mi'li-um dis-si'mi-lēz est rā'she-ō). The rule as to matters which are dissimilar; dissimilar.

Dissimulatione tollitur injuria (Dis-si-mu-lā-she-ō'-ne tol'li-ter in-jū'ri-a). An injury is extinguished by the condonation of the person injured.

dissipate. To squander; to waste; to scatter completely; to disperse and cause to disappear—used especially of the dispersion of things that can never again be collected or restored. Hughes v Carr, 101 Wash 109, 172 P 224. To over-indulge in pleasure.

dissipation of funds. The free spending by a debtor in failing circumstances without regard for his obligations to creditors; for all practical purposes, a destruction of property within the meaning of opposition to discharge in bankruptcy. 9 Am J2d Bankr § 711.

dissolution. The separation of a thing into its component parts; a breaking up.

dissolution bond. A bond given by the defendant in an action in which property has been attached, for the purpose of obtaining an entire dissolution of the attachment, the condition of the bond being that the defendant will perform or satisfy whatever judgment is obtained against him in the action. 6 Am J2d Attach § 523.

dissolution of association. The winding up of the affairs of a voluntary association, including the payment of claims against the organization and the distribution of remaining assets, if there be such assets, among the members. 6 Am J2d Asso & C §§ 59 et seq.

dissolution of attachment or garnishment. The termination of an attachment or garnishment upon the happening of certain events or contingencies after the levy, upon the entry or receipt of security, or as the result of some act or proceeding taken for the express purpose of defeating or nullifying the attachment or garnishment. There is a distinction between the "dissolution" of an attachment and the quashing of a levy; in a proper case a levy may be set aside and the writ of attachment stand. 6 Am J2d Attach § 408.

dissolution of corporation. The termination of the existence of the corporation and its utter extinction and obliteration as an entity or body. 19 Am J2d Corp § 1586.
See **de facto dissolution; winding up.**

dissolution of injunction. The termination or vacation of an injunction upon cause shown for such relief. 28 Am J Rev ed Inj § 306.

dissolution of marriage. See **annulment of marriage; divorce a vinculo matrimonii.**

dissolution of partnership. That change in the partnership relation which ultimately culminates in its termination. The change of the relation of partners caused by any partner's ceasing to be associated in the carrying on of the business. 48 Am J1st Partn § 233. Dissolution is not in itself a termination of the partnership or of all the rights and powers of partners, for many of these persist during the winding-up process which follows dissolution. Under statutory provision distinguishing between dissolution of a partnership and winding-up the business, the conduct of a partner inconsistent with the continuance of a partnership results in the dissolution of the partnership in spite of the fact that liquidation is not completed or some appearances of the partnership continue. Fooshe v Sunshine, 96 Cal App 2d 336, 215 P2d 66, 16 ALR2d 1142.

dissolve. To effect a dissolution; as to dissolve a partnership or a corporation.

dissuade (di-swād'). To persuade one not to follow a certain course or perform a certain act.

distances. Indications in describing the boundaries of a tract of real estate.
See **assured clear distance; courses; striking distance.**

distemper. A contagious disease affecting animals; an emotional state.

distillation. See **distilling.**

distiller. A person whose occupation is to extract spirits by distillation. Johnson v State, 44 Ala 414, 416.

distillery. A place or building where alcoholic liquors are distilled or manufactured. The term does not, as ordinarily used, apply to every building where the process of distillation is used, such as a paraffin oil factory. Atlantic Dock Co. v Libby, 45 NY 499, 502.

distilling. A refinement of a liquid by the process of heating it to the boiling point, collecting the vapor, and cooling the vapor, thereby reducing it to a liquid of greater strength and purity than the original; a process in the manufacture of alcoholic beverages. The application of heat to liquid by which means it is converted into steam and afterward converted into liquid, the steam being run through a coil which is kept cool, either by water or other process, cool enough so as to condense the steam into liquid. Whisnant v State, 39 Okla Crim 214, 264 P 837, 839; State v Scott, 119 Or 446, 249 P 817.

distinct. Clear to the senses or mind; easily perceived or understood; plain; unmistakable. Hill v Norton, 74 W Va 428, 438, 82 SE 363.

distincte et aperte (dis-tink'te et a-per'te). Distinctly and openly.

distinctively. Characteristically, or peculiarly; not necessarily exclusively. Western Union Tel. Co. v Green, 153 Tenn 59, 281 SW 778, 48 ALR 301, 314.

distinctive name. As defined in the departmental regulations for the enforcement of the provisions of the Food and Drugs Act of 1906, the term means a trade, arbitrary, or fancy name which clearly distinguishes a food product, mixture, or compound from any other food product, mixture, or compound. United States v Forty Barrels & Twenty Kegs of Coca Cola, 241 US 265, 286, 60 L Ed 995, 1005, 36 S Ct 573. The later statutes in this field do not contain the "distinctive name" provisions of the former act. 35 Am J2d Food § 45.

distinct offenses. Distinct violations of law, even though they may grow out of the same transaction. The test of identity of offenses is whether the same evidence is required to sustain them; if not, then the fact that both charges relate to and grow out of one transaction does not make a single offense where two are defined by the statutes. Morgan v Devine, 237 US 632, 59 L Ed 1153, 35 S Ct 712.

Distinguenda sunt tempora; aliud est facere, aliud perficere (dis-tin-gwen'da sunt tem'po-ra; a'li-ud est fā'se-re, a'li-ud per-fi'se-re). Times must be distinguished; it is one thing to act and another to finish. The maxim has been applied as asserting the doctrine that the law should be construed in a manner to some extent affected by public sentiment. Bloss v Tobey, 19 Mass 320, 327.

Distinguenda sunt tempora; distingue tempora, et concordabis leges (dis-tin-gwen'da sunt tem'po-ra; dis-tin'gwe tem'po-ra, et kon-kor-dā'bis lē'jēz). Times must be distinguished; distinguish times and you will reconcile laws.

Distingue tempora, et concordabis leges (dis-tin'gwe tem'po-ra, et kon-kor-dā'bis lē'jīs). Distinguish times and you will reconcile laws.

distinguishing mark. Birthmark, scar, or other mark of identification; such a mark on a ballot, whether letter, figure, character, cut corner, or mere crease, as shows an intention on the part of the voter to distinguish his particular ballot from others of its class.

A distinguishing mark invalidates a ballot, since

DISTRACTED [361] DISTRIBUTIVE

it furnishes a means of evading the law as to the secrecy of the ballot. 26 Am J2d Elect § 265.

distracted. Diverted; worried, sometimes to the point of derangement.

distractio (dis-trak'she-ō). (Civil law.) A creditor's sale of hypothecated property; a pledgee's sale of a pledge.

distrahere (dis-trā'he-re). To withdraw; to sell at public auction; to put up for sale.

distrain. To seize the animals or goods of another, as to take up or withhold the cattle or goods of a tenant for the non-payment of rent, or other duties due the landlord. 32 Am J1st L & T § 613. To seize and impound a trespassing animal. 4 Am J2d Ani § 55. A "distraint" involves the actual seizure of the property distrained. No distraint is shown by a mere sale of a tax lien on property without disturbance of the debtor's property ownership. Kroell v New York Ambassador (CA2 NY) 108 F2d 294.
See **distress.**

distress. The act of distraining the goods or cattle of another; the taking of possession of a personal chattel out of the possession of a wrongdoer into that of the party injured, to procure satisfaction for the wrong done. 3 Bl Comm 6. The common-law writ under which a distress was effected. Barnet v Ihrie (Pa) 1 Rawle 44.
See **distress damage feasant; distress for rent.**

distress damage feasant (dis-tres' dam'āj fe'sant). A landowner's seizure and impounding of animals found trespassing and doing damage on his land, and holding them until compensation for the damage sustained is made. 4 Am J2d Ani § 55.

distress for rent. A common-law remedy for the collection of rent in arrears which permits the landlord to go upon the demised premises and seize anything he may find there as security for rent in arrears, and hold it without sale until the rental is paid. In a number of jurisdictions, distress for rent either has been expressly abolished by statute or impliedly abolished by statutes providing other remedies for the recovery of rent. In most if not all of the states in which the remedy still exists, its exercise is regulated by statute. 32 Am J1st L & T § 613.

distress infinite (in'fi-nit). A series of distresses made one after another until satisfaction for the wrong done has been made by the owner of the distrained property. A distress of this nature has no bounds with regard to its quantity and may be repeated from time to time until the stubbornness of the party is conquered. It is used sometimes for extraordinary purposes such as summoning jurors. See 3 Bl Comm 231.

distress warrant. A term of variable meaning. In some jurisdictions, a judicial writ in the nature of an execution. Inhabitants of Baileyville v Lowell, 20 Me 178, 182. In other jurisdictions, a writ within a requirement that all writs run in the name of the state, but not judicial process within the requirement of having such process returnable before a court or justice of the peace. State ex rel. Myers v Hodge, 129 W Va 820, 42 SE2d 23. In another jurisdiction, a mere power of attorney by which a landlord delegates the exercise of his right of distraint to an agent. Re Koizim, (DC NJ) 52 F Supp 357. In some jurisdictions, a remedy for the collection of taxes. 28 Am J Rev ed Inher T § 455.

distributable. Divisible.
See **allocable.**

distribute. To divide; to apportion; to make distribution of the property of a decedent's estate to the persons entitled thereto.
See **pro-rate.**

distributees. Persons who are entitled, under the statute of distributions, to the personal estate of one who has died intestate. Henry v Henry, 31 NC (9 Ired L) 278, 279. In the nontechnical sense, all persons in whom the law may vest any part of the property of a decedent. Terral v Terral, 212 Ark 221, 205 SW2d 198, 1 ALR2d 1092.
See **heirs; next of kin.**

distributing literature. A means of advertising and promoting a cause. Pierce v United States, 252 US 239, 253, 64 L Ed 542, 549, 40 S Ct 205.

distribution. Division. The transmission of personal property of a decedent by the passing of title to the personal representative for the payment of decedent's debts and claims against the estate, and finally to distribute the remainder to the persons entitled by the law of intestate succession. 23 Am J2d Desc & D § 1. Swift & Co. v Johnson (CA8 Minn) 138 F 867. Sometimes having reference to real as well as personal property. Foster v Clifford, 87 Ohio St 294, 101 NE 269. Sometimes applied to the disposal of the estate of a testate decedent by the executor. Johnson v Knights of Honor, 53 Ark 255, 13 SW 794.
See **decree of final distribution; descent; distributees; distributive share; establishment of heirship; final distribution; hotchpot; statute of distribution.**

distribution of capital. The distribution of capital assets of a corporation to the stockholders, thereby depriving creditors of property which is primarily liable to the payment of their claims. Davis v Hemming, 101 Conn 713, 127 A 514, 39 ALR 133. The term does not include an issue of new stock. Trefry v Putnam, 227 Mass 522, 116 NE 904.

distribution of powers. See **division of powers.**

distribution policy. See **deferred dividend policy.**

distributive finding of the issue. A finding of facts for both parties, partly for the plaintiff and partly for the defendant.

distributive justice. A concept exemplified by the maxim:—"Unto each shall be rendered that which is his." A guaranty of the due process clause.
Due process of law, in spite of the absolutism of continental governments, is not alien to that Code which survived the Roman Empire as the foundation of modern civilization in Europe, and which has given us that fundamental maxim of distributive justice. Hurtado v California, 110 US 516, 531, 28 L Ed 232, 237, 4 S Ct 111, 292.

distributive share. The share in the personal estate of an intestate, after the payment of his debts and claims against the estate, to which a distributee or heir is entitled. 22 Am J2d Desc & D § 22.
The term has also been applied with less precision to the share of a legatee, sometimes to a share in the real estate left by an intestate, even to the share of a devisee. 31 Am J2d Ex & Ad § 550. Strictly speaking, a distributee is not entitled to a share of the specific rights and credits, goods, and chattels of the decedent in the hands of his personal representative, but only to a share in the fund produced by administering them. Wright v Holmes, 100 Me 508, 62 A 507.

district. A word of variable meaning in the law. A portion of the state with limits set by law for governmental purposes. Chicago & Northwestern Railway Co. v Oconto, 50 Wis 189, 6 NW 607. A judicial district. State ex rel. Brockmeier v Ely, 16 ND 569, 113 NW 711. The area or vicinity of an event. State ex rel. Funck v McCarty, 52 Ohio St 363, 39 NE 1041.

district attorneys. Public officers elected or appointed, as provided in the several state constitutions or by statute, to conduct suits, generally criminal, on behalf of the state in their respective districts. They are sworn ministers of justice, quasi judicial officers representing the commonwealth. 42 Am J1st Pub Of § 2.
See **United States District Attorney.**

district courts. Usually, courts of record having general jurisdiction. In some jurisdictions, constitutional courts. 20 Am J2d Cts § 17. Courts of limited jurisdiction in some states.

district courts of the United States. See **United States District Courts.**

district director of internal revenue. An officer in the field organization of the Internal Revenue Service. 34 Am J2d Fed Tax ¶ 9261.

districtio (dis-trik'she-ō). A distress. See 3 Bl Comm 6.

District of Columbia. The seat of government of the United States, having an area of 69 square miles, situated on the Potomac River, on the border of Maryland opposite Virginia, and subject to the power of Congress to exercise exclusive legislation in reference thereto. 49 Am J1st States § 122. It occupies a unique position, being neither state nor organized territory in the usual sense of such terms. Hepburn v Ellzey (US) 2 Cranch 445, 2 L Ed 332. But it is a state as the word is used in reference to the making of treaties with foreign powers. Geofroy v Riggs, 133 US 258, 33 L Ed 642, 10 S Ct 295.

districts. See **district.**

district school. A public school open to all children of school age. In some cities such schools are denominated "ward schools." Maxcy v Oshkosh, 144 Wis 238, 128 NW 899. Many district schools have been eliminated of recent years by the creation and operation of centralized or consolidated schools.

districtus (dis-trik'tus). A district; a distress.

distringas (dis-tring'gas). A writ of distress; a writ to enforce the attendance of jurors by distress of their goods or seizure of their persons; a proceeding in equity to enforce the obedience of a corporation to a summons; a form of execution. "Whether the writ of execution is called a *distringas* or an *habere facias seisinam*, is of little consequence, provided it is calculated to carry the judgment into effect." Barnet v Ihrie (Pa) 1 Rawle 44, 51.

distringas juratores (dis-trin'gas jū-rā-tō'rēz). A writ to enforce the attendance of jurors at court by the distress of their goods or by the seizure of their persons. See 3 Bl Comm 355.

distringas nuper vice comitem (dis-trin'gas nū'per vī'se ko'mi-tem). A writ of distress which lay against a man who had been sheriff for nonfeasance while in office.

distringas vice comitem (dis-trin'gas vī'se ko'mi-tem). A writ of distress which lay against a sheriff who neglected to execute a writ.

distringere (dis-trin'je-re). To distrain.

disturb. To throw into disorder or confusion; to derange; to interrupt the settled state of; to excite from a state of rest. Watkins v Kaolin Mfg. Co. 131 NC 536, 42 SE 983.

disturbance (dis-tėr'bans). A wrong done to some incorporeal hereditament, by hindering or disquieting the owners in their regular and lawful enjoyment of it. See 3 Bl Comm 236.

disturbance of common. The incommoding or diminishing of a right of common. See 3 Bl Comm 237.

disturbance of franchises. Such a disturbance as happens when a man has the franchise of holding a court-leet, of keeping a fair or market, of free-warren, of taking toll, of seising waifs or estrays, or any other species of franchise, and he is disturbed or incommoded in its lawful exercise. See 3 Bl Comm 236.

disturbance of patronage (pat'ron-āj or pā'tron-āj). A hindrance or obstruction of a patron to present his clerk to a benefice. This disturbance differed from usurpation which was an absolute dispossession of the patron and happened when a stranger without right presented a clerk who was forthwith admitted and instituted. See 3 Bl Comm 242.

disturbance of public worship. See **disturbance of worship.**

disturbance of repose. A violation of sepulture in unauthorized exhumation and removal of remains or the desecration of a grave, such being an actionable wrong and a criminal act as well. 22 Am J2d Dead B § 18.

disturbance of tenure. The breaking of the relation which subsisted between a lord and his tenant. To have an estate well tenanted was an advantage to every landlord and the driving away of a tenant from his estate was a considerable injury for the redress of which an action on the case lay at common law. See 3 Bl Comm 242.

disturbance of the peace. A breach of peace. 12 Am J2d Breach P § 4.
See **breach of peace; riot.**

disturbance of ways. A species of disturbance which happened chiefly when a person who had a right of way over the land of another, by grant or prescription, was obstructed by enclosures or other obstacles, or by ploughing across it, whereby he could not use the way at all, or at least in a less convenient manner than he might have done. See 3 Bl Comm 241.

disturbance of worship. The common-law offense of disturbance of persons gathered for the purpose of religious worship, extended by statute to the protection of all lawful meetings against the wilful and tumultuous conduct of persons attempting to make a disturbance. 24 Am J2d Disturb M § 1. Any act which is disorderly and subversive of the solemnity and decorum due to the occasion and the place, which is committed while a congregation is assembled for public worship; as where a member of the congregation arose from his seat and interrogated the minister, while the latter was taking up the collection, as to remarks made in his sermon. Wall v Lee, 34 NY 141, 149.

disturber. A person who commits a disturbance.

disturbing. See **disturbing meeting;** and see also terms and expressions beginning **disturbance.**

disturbing meeting. Wilful and tulmultuous conduct of persons making, or attempting to make, a disturbance at a religious meeting or other lawful assembly. People v Malone, 156 App Div 10, 141 NYS 149. Any conduct which is contrary to the usages of the particular sort of meeting and class of persons assembled and interferes with its due progress or annoys the assembly in whole or in part is a disturbance. It may consist of a physical act, a verbal expression, an indecent gesture, or generally anything violative of the character and purpose of the particular meeting. 24 Am J2d Disturb M § 5.

disuse. See **nonuser.**

diswarren (dis-wor'en). To change the use or character of land from that of a warren.

ditch. A hollow space in the ground, either natural or artificial, where water is collected or drained away. Barton v Drainage Dist. 174 Ark 173, 294 SW 418. A way or course of drainage of surface water. Anno: 81 ALR 263.

ditch company. See **irrigation companies.**

dites ouster (dēt ūs-ter'). You say over again,—a formal expression used in a judgment of respondeat ouster. See 3 Bl Comm 303.

dittay (dit'ā). The charge of crime contained in an indictment.

ditto mark. The mark ", used to indicate that the word in a line, under which the mark appears, is to be considered duplicated in the line below.

divers (dī'vėrz). Different, various, sundry, several.

diverse (di-vėrs' or dī'vėrs). Different; varied.

diverse citizenship. See **diversity of citizenship.**

diverse considerations. Not sufficient, at common law, as an allegation of a money consideration. Hartley v McAnulty (Pa) 4 Yeates 95.

diversion of goods. The right and act of a shipper by common carrier in changing the destination of the shipment at any intermediate point through which the goods pass before reaching their original destination. 13 Am J2d Car § 393.

diversion of stream. Changing the course or channel of a natural stream. 56 Am J1st Wat § 14.
See **diversion of water.**

diversion of water. The extraction of water from a stream or other body of water for the purpose of making use of it, such constituting an actionable wrong to a lower riparian owner where it is not limited to a taking for a reasonable use, causes a material diminution of the stream, and materially interferes with the rights of the lower riparian owner. Parker v Griswold, 17 Conn 288, 299.
See **diversion of stream.**

diversis diebus et vicibus (di-ver'sis dī-ē'bus et vī'si-bus). At divers days and times.

diversity cases. Actions properly before federal courts because of diversity of citizenship of the parties. 20 Am J2d Cts § 13.
See **diversity of citizenship.**

diversity jurisdiction. The jurisdiction of a federal court arising from diversity of citizenship of the parties. 20 Am J2d Cts § 13.
See **diversity of citizenship.**

diversity of citizenship. A ground for invoking the original jurisdiction of a Federal District Court, the basis of jurisdiction on such ground being the existence of an actual and substantial controversy between citizens of different states. There is a diversity of citizenship, in a case involving a plurality of parties, where all the parties on one side of a controversy are citizens of different states from all those on the other side. Indianapolis v Chase Nat. Bank, 314 US 63, 86 L Ed 569, 62 S Ct 355. The same principle applies in determining diversity of citizenship for the purpose of removing a case from a state court to a federal court. Gainesville v Brown-Crummer Invest. Co. 277 US 54, 72 L Ed 781, 48 S Ct 454.

diversity of person. A plea interposed after a judgment of conviction denying the identity of the prisoner with that of the convicted defendant.

diverso intuitu (di-vėr'sō in-tū'i-tū). With a different purpose or motive. Where the original consideration flows from A, not solely upon the promise of B or C, but upon the promise of both, diverso intuitu, each becomes liable to A, not upon a joint, but a several original undertaking. D'Wolf v Rabaud (US) 1 Pet 476, 500, 7 L Ed 227, 237.

diversorium (di-ver-sō'ri-um). A place of entertainment; an inn.

divers persons. At least three or more persons. State v Lustig, 13 NJ Super 149, 80 A2d 309.

dives costs (dī'vēz kosts). A rich man's costs,—ordinary costs, as opposed to costs taxed to a defendant who appears in forma pauperis.

divest. To deprive or cause the loss of a right or title.

divestiture (di-ves'ti-tụ̄r). A being divested, as by a surrender of a right or title.

divestive fact (di-ves'tiv fakt). A fact, the existence of which divests or modifies a right.

divide. The severance or partition into two equal parts, except as the word may be qualified by other terms. Groves v Jones, 252 Mich 446, 233 NW 375. In common usage, to sever into two parts; to cut or part into several or many pieces. Graves v White, 43 Colo 131, 134.

divide and pay over rule. The rule that where the only words of gift in a testamentary disposition of property are found in the direction to divide or pay at a time subsequent to the death of the testator, time is to be taken as of the essence of the gift and the interest is future and contingent, rather than immediate and vested. See Lytle v Guilliams, 241 Iowa 523, 41 NW2d 668, 16 ALR2d 1377.

divided court. A division of the judges or justices on the decision to be rendered. Division does not affect the character of the case as a precedent, unless the court is equally divided, in which case, the doctrine of stare decisis has no application. 20 Am J2d Cts § 195.

divided custody. An alternating custody of a child between divorced parents. 24 Am J2d Div & S § 799.

divided damages rule. The rule in admiralty that where two parties are jointly responsible for a tort to a third, each is primarily liable only for half of the damages. 2 Am J2d Adm § 212.

divided fractional part. Used in the granting clause of a deed, the term indicates an intention to convey in severalty. 23 Am J2d Deeds § 196.

divided highway. A highway in which traffic moving in one direction is separated from traffic moving in the other direction by a raised portion of the way, a low wall, or an open space.

divided reputation. A paradoxical expression for diversity of evidence as to general reputation. Jackson v Jackson, 82 Md 17, 33 A 317.

Divide et impera, cum radix et vertex imperii in obedientium consensu rata sunt (di-vī'de et im'pe-ra, kum rā'dix et ver'tex im-pe'ri-ī in ō-bē-di-en'shē-um kon-sen'sū rā'ta sunt). Divide and rule, for the root and pinnacle of empire are rated in the consent of the obedient.

dividend. A gain or profit. Hellmich v Hellman (CA8 Mo) 18 F2d 239. A division into shares; one of such shares. A payment made by a corporation to its stockholders out of surplus earnings and under authority of a resolution by the board of directors which declares the policy of a paying a portion or all of such surplus to the stockholders. Lamb v Lehmann, 110 Ohio St 59, 143 NE 276, 42 ALR 437. A disbursement by a business trust to its members. A payment made to general creditors in a proceeding in bankruptcy; sometimes used in a broader significance as including a payment made in satisfaction of priority debts. 9 Am J2d Bankr § 1262. A payment made to creditors in insolvency proceedings.

Used in the limitation of a life estate and a remainder in connection with a provision for the disposition of extraordinary dividends and distributions as between life tenant and remainder, the term "dividend" is equivalent to "income." 33 Am J1st Life Est § 378.

See **cash dividend; cumulative dividends; dividend additions; dividend in scrip; dividend on insurance policy; dividend warrant; guaranteed dividends; non-cumulative dividends; stock dividend.**

dividenda (di-vi-den'da). An indenture; one of the two parts of an indenture.

dividend addition. A term usually applied to paid-up insurance purchased by a dividend, but at other times understood to mean dividends. 29 Am J1st Ins § 648.
See **paid-up addition.**

dividend declared. See **declaration of dividend.**

dividend in kind. A corporate dividend in any medium other than money. Commissioner v First State Bank (CA5) 168 F2d 1004, 7 ALR2d 738.

dividend in liquidation. A payment made to creditors in a bankruptcy proceeding. 9 Am J2d Bankr § 1262. A payment made to creditors in insolvency proceedings. A distribution to stockholders in a corporation or members of a firm or business enterprise of the fund remaining after the liquidation of the business and the payment of creditors. Hellman v Helvering, 63 App DC 18, 68 F2d 763.

dividend in scrip. A certificate issued by a corporation to its stockholder evidencing the holder's title to the same extent of interest in the property and franchise as a stock dividend, except that the corporation has the right to pay the dividend out of future earnings, and except also that the scrip dividend confers no right to vote. Bailey v New York Cent. & Hudson River Railroad Co. (US) 22 Wall 604, 22 L Ed 840.

dividend off. A sale of a corporate stock not carrying to the purchaser a dividend previously declared; same as **ex dividend.** 19 Am J2d Corp § 892.

dividend on. A characterization of a sale of corporate stock carrying a dividend previously declared. 19 Am J2d Corp § 892.

dividend on insurance policy. A payment made by an insurance company to policyholders from the surplus of the company, either in cash, by way of credit on the premium, or by applying it to the purchase of paid-up insurance called a dividend addition. 29 Am J Rev ed Ins § 110.
See **dividend addition.**

dividend policy. A most common form of life insurance policy issued under a plan whereby each policyholder pays annually in advance a fixed sum which, when added to like payments by others, probably will create a fund larger than necessary to meet all maturing policies and estimated expenses. At the end of each year the actual insurance costs and expenses incurred are ascertained. The difference between their sums and the total of advance payments and other income, then becomes the "overpayment" or surplus fund for immediate pro rata distribution among policyholders as dividends or for such future disposition as the contracts provide. An "annual dividend" policyholder receives his proportionate part of this fund each year in cash, as a credit upon or abatement of his next premium, or in the form of paid-up insurance purchased by the dividend. New York Life Ins. Co. v Edwards, 271 US 109, 115, 70 L Ed 859, 861, 46 S Ct 436.

dividend warrant. A warrant or order on a corporation treasury for the amount of a stockholder's dividend.

divinare (di-vi-nā're). To divine; to guess; to prophesy.

Divinatio non interpretatio est, quae omnino recedit a litera (di-vi-nā'she-ō non in-ter-pre-tā'she-ō est, kwē om-nī'nō re-sē'dit ā li'te-ra). It is guesswork and not interpretation which wholly departs from the literal.

divine. Pertaining to God.

divine law (di-vīn' lâ). A law which has God for its author, as distinguished from man-made law. The definition is sometimes refined by recognizing two types, natural law and positive or revealed law. Borden v State, 11 Ark 519.

divine right of kings. The old theory that the king derived his power from God.
There has never been any sensible reason for asserting that the title to the throne of England was by divine right. 1 Bl Comm 191.

divine service. Religious worship.
See **tenure by divine service.**

divining-rod (di-vī'ning-rod). A rod or twig held in the hand and supposed to indicate the location of subterranean water by being pulled down by a mysterious force at the farther end.

divisa (di-vī'sa). A boundary.

Divisibilis est semper divisibilis (dī-vī-si'bi-lis est sem'per dī-vī-si'bi-lis). That which is divisible is always divisible.

divisibility of statute. See **severability of statute.**

divisible. Susceptible of being divided or separated into component parts.

divisible contract. A contract of which a part is susceptible of separate or independent treatment with respect to some particular right or remedy. 46 Am

DIVISIBLE [365] DIVORCED

J1st Sales § 140. A contract, the performance of which is divided into different groups, each set embracing performances which are the agreed exchange for each other; in other words, on performance by one side of one of the successive divisions, the other party becomes liable for his performance of that division. 17 Am J2d Contr § 324; 46 Am J1st Sales § 140. A contract enforceable as to a part which is valid, although another part is invalid and unenforceable. 17 Am J2d Contr § 230. An insurance policy under which there may be recovery for the loss of one of several items covered by the policy, notwithstanding a breach of warranty or condition precludes recovery as to another item or items. 29 Am J Rev ed Ins § 283.
See **severability of contract.**

divisible divorce. The phrase used in reference to a decree of divorce which is valid insofar as it grants a divorce, but may be invalid insofar as it purports to adjudicate separable personal rights, because of want of personal service of process within the state. Estin v Estin, 334 US 541, 92 L Ed 1561, 68 S Ct 1213, 1 ALR2d 1412. The "divisible divorce" doctrine is a recognition of the fact that dissolution of the marital status by a divorce may or may not extinguish all the obligations of a husband originally created as incidents thereof, including the duty to support the former wife. Pawley v Pawley (Fla) 46 So 2d 464, 28 ALR2d 1358. Under the "divisible divorce" concept, a divorce decree may be completely effective to dissolve a marriage and yet be completely ineffective to alter certain legal and economic incidents of that marriage. Lynn v Lynn, 302 NY 193, 97 NE2d 748, 28 ALR2d 1335.

divisible judgment. See **severable judgment.**

divisible statute. See **severability of statute.**

divisim (di-vī'sim). Severally; separately.

divisim et conjunctim (di-vī'sim et kon-junk'tim). Severally and jointly.

division. Separation. The ascertainment of a legislative vote by separating the members. A dissension or schism between groups of members of the congregation of a church, causing it to split into factions, each faction claiming to be the true body or congregation of the church. Poynter v Phelps, 129 Ky 381, 111 SW 699.
See **benefit of division; political division.**

divisional court. An English court composed of two or more judges of the high court of justice and sitting only in special cases.

division fence. See **partition fence.**

division of administrative body. Organization of a board or commission by panels or divisions, each of which shall have and exercise all the jurisdiction and powers of the board or commission. 2 Am J2d Admin L § 196.

division of commission. See **splitting commission.**

division of fees. A permissible practice as between attorneys at law representing a client jointly, the division being equal in the absence of a contract to the contrary. 7 Am J2d Attys § 260. A reprehensible practice, which is a ground for disbarment or suspension of license, where performed in consideration of the solicitation of business by the person with whom the fee is split. Utz v State Bar of California, 21 Cal 2d 100, 150, 130 P2d 377; Re Tuthill, 256 App Div 539, 10 NYS2d 643, app den 256 App Div 1059, 11 NYS2d 842. Also a reprehensible practice, known as fee-splitting, where it consists in the conduct of an employment agency in charging a fee to the worker and paying a part of it to the employer; a practice akin to job-selling by foremen and superintendents. Ribnik v McBride, 277 US 350, 72 L Ed 913.

division of opinion. The disagreement in opinion of the judges of a court when they do not concur in rendering their decisions.
See **divided court.**

division of powers. The system under the constitution of the United States wherein the powers of government are divided between the federal and the state governments. 16 Am J2d Const L § 198.
See **separation of powers.**

division wall. A wall on the line or abutting the line between the property of adjoining landowners. Such may become a party wall by agreement or prescription.
See **party wall.**

divisum imperium (dī-vī'sum im-pe'ri-um). A divided authority; the concurrent jurisdiction of different tribunals over the same subject matter. See 1 Bl Comm 110.

divorce. A dissolution of the marriage relation between husband and wife, the term, standing alone, importing a complete severance of the tie by which the parties were united. Miller v Miller, 33 Cal 353.
A divorce decree is a judgment. Jelm v Jelm, 155 Ohio St 226, 98 NE2d 401, 22 ALR2d 1300.
See **absolute divorce; alimony; collusive divorce; discretionary divorce; divorce a mensa et thoro; divorce a vinculo matrimonii; divorced; divorceé; foreign divorce; Indian divorce; interlocutory decree; judicial divorce; judicial separation; legislative divorce; limited divorce; separate maintenance; separation; separation agreement.**

divorceé (dē-vor'sā). A divorced man.

divorce a mensa et thoro (di-vōrs ā men'sa et thō'rō). A judicial decree which terminates the obligation and right of cohabitation but does not affect the status of the parties as married persons or dissolve the marriage. 24 Am J2d Div & S § 1. A limited, partial or qualified divorce which suspends the marriage relation and modifies the duties and obligations but leaves the marriage bond in full force,— a judicial separation. Givens v Givens, 121 Fla 271, 63 So 574; People v John, 181 Misc 921, 44 NYS2d 806.
A final judgment for divorce, if the divorce granted is an absolute divorce, dissolves the marriage bond and changes the status of the parties; if the divorce is limited, or, as sometimes called, a decree of separation from bed and board, it merely relieves the parties from their obligations and rights as to cohabitation, support, and property interests. 24 Am J2d Div & S § 1.

divorce a vinculo matrimonii (di-vōrs a vin-ku-lō matri-mō'ni-ī). A judicial dissolution or termination of the bonds of matrimony, because of matrimonial misconduct or other statutory cause arising after the marriage ceremony, with the result that the status of the parties is changed from coverture to that of single persons. 24 Am J2d Div & S § 1.

divorced. Marriage dissolved absolutely. Miller v Miller, 33 Cal 353.
A husband against whom an interlocutory decree only has been entered is not divorced within the definition. Re Newman, 88 Cal App 186, 262 P 1112.

divorcée (di-vōr'sā). A divorced woman.

divorce from bed and board. Same as **divorce a mensa et thoro.**

divorcement. Divorce; divorcing.
See **bill of divorcement.**

divorce proctor. A public official upon whom the process in a suit for divorce must be served. Smythe v Smythe, 80 Or 150, 149 P 516, 156 P 785.

Divorce Recognition Act. One of the uniform laws. 24 Am J2d Div & S § 494.

divortium (di-vor'she-um). Divorce.

Divortium dicitur a divertendo, quia vir divertitur ab uxore (di-vor'she-um di'si-ter ā di-ver-ten'do, quī'a vir di-ver'ti-ter ab ux-ō're). Divorce is said to be from "divertendo," because a man is diverted or turned away from his wife.

divot. See **feal and divot.**

divulge. To reveal.
Under a statute forbidding the interception or divulging of a telephone communication without the authority of the sender, to shunt a conversation so that a third person may and does hear it is to "divulge" a communication even though the person doing the shunting does not hear the conversation. United States v Gruber (CA2 NY) 123 F2d 307.

dixième (di-ziè-m). One-tenth.

dixit. See **ipse dixit.**

do (dō). I give; I grant.
See **dedi.**

Dobson Rule. A decision of the United States Supreme Court that a Tax Court decision must stand if the appellate court cannot separate the elements of the decision so as to identify a clear cut mistake of law and the decision of such court has warrant in the record and a reasonable basis in the law. Dobson v Commissioner, 320 US 489, 88 L Ed 248, 64 S Ct 239, reh den 321 US 231, 88 L Ed 691, 64 S Ct 494.

dock. Noun: In common parlance, a wharf or pier. Technically, the space between wharves; a slip. Boston v Lecraw (US) 17 How 426, 15 L Ed 118. An artificial basin in connection with a harbor, used for the reception of vessels in the taking on or discharging of their cargoes, sometimes provided with gates for preventing the rise and fall of the waters occasioned by the tides. The Robert W. Parsons, 191 US 17, 48 L Ed 73, 24 S Ct 8. The word is also used to designate the place reserved in the courtroom for a prisoner on trial. Verb: To bring a vessel into dock. To clip or bob, as to "dock" a horse's tail. Bland v People, 32 Colo 319, 324, 76 P 359.
See **dry dock; graving dock.**

dockage. Compensation for use of a wharf; the charge made against a vessel for the privilege of mooring to a wharf or in a slip; also called wharfage. 56 Am J1st Whar § 30.
See **double wharfage.**

dockage lien. See **wharfage lien.**

docket. Noun: A term somewhat confusing because of variation in meaning between jurisdictions. Literally, a list or register of cases, whether for trial in the nisi prius court (53 Am J1st Trial §§ 5-7) or for hearing on appeal. 5 Am J2d A & E § 678. A record of cases and of the proceedings had in a case, although not a record in the extended form of a journal of the proceedings of a court. Verb: To enter upon the docket. An appeal is docketed when the appropriate papers are received by the clerk of the appellate court and the case has been entered by him on the docket, whether or not the clerk has received the docket fees. Drennen v Johnson, 65 Colo 381, 176 P 479.
See **calendar; docketing judgment; striking a docket.**

docketed. See **docket; docketing judgment.**

docket fees. Sums collected for placing the case on the docket or calendar; fees allowable to attorneys under a federal statute. Anno: 22 ALR 1208.

docketing judgment. Noting a judgment, which has been entered of record, upon the judgment docket, so that notice may be taken readily by anyone concerned, and that execution may be issued. 30A Am J Rev ed Judgm § 93. The entry of a judgment is a proceeding distinct from that of docketing. Rockwood v Davenport, 37 Minn 533, 35 NW 377.
See **entry of judgment.**

docking. See **dock.**

dock line. Same as **harbor line.**

dock warrant. A warehouse receipt.

doctor. A term most commonly applied to a physician. Witty v State, 173 Ind 404, 90 NE 627. Equally applicable to a dentist, even to a veterinarian. Applicable in fact to a person who has attained a doctorate conferred by a university in any branch of learning—medicine, law, divinity, philosophy, etc. State v MacKnight, 131 NC 717, 42 SE 580.
The degree of M. D. is something more than a mere honorary title. It is a certificate attesting the fact that the person upon whom it has been conferred has successfully mastered the curriculum of study prescribed by the authorities of an institution created by law, and by law authorized to issue such certificate. It thus has a legal sanction and authority. But it has more. In practical affairs, it introduces its possessor to the confidence and patronage of the general public. Its legal character gives it a moral and material credit in the estimation of the world, and makes it thereby a valuable property right of great pecuniary value. Townshend v Gray, 62 Vt 378, 19 A 635.
The term is applied with a degree of levity to drug clerks, male nurses, hospital attendants, etc. Of course, calling a person "doctor" or "doc" does not qualify him as a professional. A person licensed to practice drugless healing is not a "doctor" and rules of law pertaining distinctively to the latter are not applicable to the former. Kelly v Carroll, 36 Wash 2d 482, 219 P2d 79, 19 ALR2d 1174.
See **physician.**

doctor and patient. See **physician and patient.**

Doctor and Student. An ancient treatise on the common law which is written in the form of a dialogue between a teacher and his pupil.

doctor of medicine. See **M.D.; physician.**

Doctors' Commons. An institution near St. Paul's Cathedral, where the ecclesiastical and admiralty courts are held. In 1768, a royal charter was obtained, by virtue of which the members of the society and their successors were incorporated under the name and title of "The College of Doctors of Laws exercent in the ecclesiastical and admiralty courts."—Wharton's Law Dict.

Doctor's Draft Act. A federal statute providing for the induction of members of the medical profession into military service for assignment to the Medical Corps as commissioned officers of rank or grade commensurate with education, experience, and ability. Nelson v Peckham (CA4 Va) 210 F2d 574.

doctrine. A rule or principle of law which has been developed by the decisions of the courts.

For definition of a particular doctrine, see the concrete term, such as **anticipatory breach; earmark; inverse order of alienation; laches; pin money; res ipsa loquitur; shifting descents; tacking, virtual representation;** etc.

document. Any matter expressed or described upon any substance by means of letters, figures or marks, or by more than one of these means, intended to be used, or which may be used, for the purpose of recording that matter. 29 Am J2d Ev § 834. The term is broadly applied to writings, to words printed, lithographed or photographed, to seals, plates, or stones on which inscriptions are cut or engraved, to photographs and pictures, to maps and plans. Arnold v Pawtucket Valley Water Co. 18 RI 189, 26 A 55. The term is applicable as an instrument having operative effect in itself, such as a document of title, as well as to writings of evidentiary effect.

documentary evidence. Tangible objects capable of expressing a fact or tending to establish the truth or untruth of a matter at issue, including all kinds of documents, records, and writings. 29 Am J2d Ev § 834. In oral evidence, the witness is the person who speaks; in documentary evidence, the witness is the thing that speaks. Curtis v Bradley, 65 Conn 99, 31 A 591.

documentary bill. Same as **document bill.**

documentary exchange. Same as **document bill.**

documentary stamp tax. See **stamp taxes.**

document bill. A bill of exchange drawn by a consignor on a consignee of the goods with negotiable bill of lading attached to the bill of exchange evidencing collateral security, whereby the consignor is enabled to get immediate payment on account of the price of his goods.

document of title. A bill of lading, dock warrant, dock receipt, warehouse receipt, or order for the delivery of goods, and also any other document which in the regular course of business or financing is treated as adequately evidencing that the person in possession of it is entitled to receive, hold, and dispose of the document and the goods it covers. 15 Am J2d Com C § 7.

do, dico, addico (dō, di′kō, ad-di′kō). I give judgment, I expound the law, I execute the law. These were the words which the Roman law permitted the praetor to use on triverbial days upon which he was allowed to decide cases. See 3 Bl Comm 424.

Doe. See **John Doe.**

doer. A person who does an act; an actor; an agent; an attorney.

dog. A canine animal useful in hunting, driving livestock, preventing intrusions upon property, and a source of pleasure as a pet. A thing of value within the meaning of a statute on burglary. 13 Am J2d Burgl § 24.

The old rule of the common law that a dog was not property and accordingly could not be the subject of larceny is preserved in a very few states, but dogs are now generally regarded as chattels and as subjects of larceny. 32 Am J1st Larc § 79.

Stealing a dog was not larceny at common law, because it was deemed not fit that a person should die for a dog. State v Soward, 83 Ark 264, 103 SW 741.

According to some authorities, dogs are livestock within the meaning of statutes relating to the duty of a railroad company toward livestock upon its track, but other authorities are to the contrary. 44 Am J1st R R § 591.

dogdraw (dog′drâ). An arrest for killing deer made while the person arrested was on the scent with a dog.

dog hole (dog hōl). A nickname which was given to the Court of the Second Vice-Chancellor of England.

dogma (dog′mä). An order of the Roman senate. A belief, especially in the field of religion; an opinion asserted with arrogance.

dog racing. An amusement. A game within the meaning of some statutes penalizing the placing of bets upon a game. 24 Am J1st Gaming § 22. In some jurisdictions, conducted on a pari-mutuel basis for legalized betting.

dog tag. A metal tag with identification number obtained upon the registration of a dog. 4 Am J2d Ani § 23. Jargon of the military for the identification tag worn by a man in the armed service.

doing business. Carrying on business; engaging in business. In the case of a corporation, the exercise of some of the functions and the carrying on of the ordinary business for which the corporation was organized. Home Lumber Co. v Hopkins, 107 Kan 153, 190 P 601, 10 ALR 879, 886.

doing business in state. A foreign corporation is doing, transacting, engaging in, or carrying on, business in the state when, and ordinarily only when, it has entered the state through its agents and is there engaged in transacting through them some substantial part of its ordinary or customary business, usually continuous in the sense that it may be distinguished from merely casual, sporadic, or occasional transactions and isolated acts. 36 Am J2d For Corp § 317. A combination of acts or transactions may constitute doing business, where neither of the acts or transactions taken separately amounts to doing business. 29 Am J Rev ed Ins § 68. A foreign corporation may safely be said to be doing business wherever an important combination of functions is being performed, such as the ownership, possession, or control of property, dealing with others in reference to the property, the exercise of discretion, the making of business decisions, the execution of contracts, the marketing of a product by advertising and solicitation, and collecting for the sold product. 36 Am J2d For Corp § 319.

doing equity. See **he who seeks equity must do equity.**

doit (doit). Same as **doitkin.**

doitkin (doit′kin). A small base coin the use of which was forbidden by statute under Henry the Fifth.

dole (dōl). A division of ore among miners; a payment to the unemployed; a gift by way of charity.

do, lego (dō, le′gō). I give and bequeath.

dolg bote (dŏlg′ bōt). A compensation paid for inflicting a wound.

doli capax (dō′lī kā′paks). (Civil law.) Capable of mischief. Between the ages of ten and a half to fourteen children were punishable for crime if they were proved capable of committing it. See 1 Bl

Comm 464. (Common law.) Between the ages of seven and fourteen children were punishable for crime if they could discern good from evil. See 4 Bl Comm 23.
See **doli incapax.**

doli incapax (dō'lī in-kā'paks). Incapable of mischief. At common law a child under seven was doli incapax; that is, he could not be guilty of felony, but between the ages of seven and fourteen he was only prima facie doli incapax; that is, if it appeared to the court and the jury that he was doli capax and could discern between good and evil, he could be convicted and punished capitally. See 4 Bl Comm 23.
See **doli capax.**

doli mali. See **exceptio doli mali.**

dollar. The legal currency of the United States; State v Downs, 148 Ind 324, 327; the unit of money consisting of one hundred cents. The aggregate of specific coins which add up to one dollar. 36 Am J1st Money § 8. In the absence of qualifying words, it cannot mean promissory notes, bonds, or other evidences of debt. 36 Am J1st Money § 8.

dollar sign. An abbreviation ($) for a dollar or dollars. 1 Am J2d Abbr § 9.

dolo (dō'lo). (Spanish.) Malice; fraud.

dolo malo. See **de dolo malo; ex dolo malo.**

Dolosus versatur in generalibus (do-lō'sus ver-sā'ter in je-ne-rā'li-bus). A deceiver deals in generalities.

dolphin (dol'fin). A cetacean. A mammal of the sea, being a kind of whale. A porpoise. A buoy or float used as a mooring for a boat and also as a means of boarding a boat.

Dolum ex indiciis perspicuis probari convenit (dō'lum ex in-di'she-is per-spi'ku-is pro-bā'rī kon-vē'nit). Fraud should be established by clear proofs.

dolus (dō'lus). Malice; fraud; deceit.

Dolus auctoris non nocet successori, nisi in causa lucrativa (dō'lus âk-tō'ris non no'set suk-ses-sō'rī, nī'sī in kâ'za lu-kra-tī'va). The fraud of one prejudices not his successor, unless a valuable consideration is wanting.

dolus circuitu non purgator (dō'lus ser-kū'i-tū non per-gā'tor). Fraud is not purged by circuity.

dolus dans locum contractui (dō'lus danz lō'kum kon-trak'tu-ī). Fraud giving occasion for the contract; false representation, inducing a contract.

Dolus est machinatio, cum aliud dissimulat aliud agit (dō'lus est ma-shi-nā'she-ō, kum a'li-ud dis-si'mu-lat a'li-ud ā'jit). Deceit is an artifice, because it pretends one thing and does another.

Dolus et fraus nemini patrocinentur; patrocinari debent (dō'lus et frâs nē'mi-nī pa-trō-si-nen'ter, pa-trō-si-nā'rī de'bent). Deceit and fraud will protect no one; they require protection.

Dolus latet in generalibus (dō'lus la'tet in je-ne-rā'li-bus). Fraud lies hidden in generalities.

dolus malus (dō'lus ma'lus). Actual fraud arising from facts and circumstances of imposition.

Dolus versatur in generalibus (dō'lus ver-sā'ter in je-ne-rā'li-bus). Fraud deals in generalities.

domain. The land of one who has paramount title and absolute ownership. People v Shearer, 30 Cal 645, 658.
See **demesne; public domain.**

Dombec. Same as **Dome Book.**

Domboc (dom'bōk). Same as **Dome Book.**

dome (dōm). A judgment.

Dome Book. Also called "Liber Judicialis,"—a compilation made in the time of Alfred, about 887, which was said to contain the principal maxims of the common law, the penalties for misdemeanors, and the forms of judicial proceedings. See 1 Bl Comm 64.

Domesday Book. A famous book in two volumes published during the reign of William the Conqueror and finished a short time before his death in 1087. The book contained the great survey of all England, except the counties of Cumberland, Northumberland, Durham, and part of Lancashire, and of all the manors held in ancient demesne, and it came to be of great value and assistance in the establishment of land titles. The book is said to have received its name because it was as general and conclusive as the last judgment will be. See 1 Bl Comm 49, 99; 3 Bl Comm 331.

domesmen. The judges of certain inferior courts in England.

domestic. Adjective: Belonging to the household or home; inhabiting the house. Thurston v Carter, 112 Me 361, 92 A 295. Local as distinguished from foreign. Noun: One employed as a servant in the home.
See **domestic servant.**

domestic animal. A tame animal, associated with family life, or accustomed to live in or near the habitation of men. Thurston v Carter, 112 Me 361, 92 A 295; Commonwealth v Flynn, 285 Mass 136, 188 NE 627, 92 ALR 206.

domestic association. An association existing in and sanctioned by the laws of a state. United States v Cambridge Loan & Bldg. Co. 278 US 55, 73 L Ed 180.

domesticated animal. An animal wild by nature which has been so reclaimed as to become tame and under the dominion and control of its master. Hurley v State, 30 Tex App 333.

domestication. Taming an animal wild by nature so as to bring it under the dominion and control of its master. 4 Am J2d Ani § 17. The procedure by which a foreign corporation is given the status of the domestic corporation. 36 Am J2d For Corp § 374. The term is used at times in reference to procedure in licensing a foreign corporation or granting it a franchise to operate as a public utility and also to the actual reincorporation of a foreign corporation. 36 Am J2d For Corp § 376.

domestic attachment. An attachment which is levied on the property of a debtor who resides in the state where the levy is made. The term is significant in contrast to foreign attachment.
See **foreign attachment.**

domestic bill of exchange. A bill of exchange which is drawn on a drawee who resides in the same state as the drawer of the bill.

domestic citizenship. Citizenship of a state as distinguished from citizenship of the United States. Dred Scott v Sanford (US) 19 How 393, 15 L Ed 691. This case was decided in 1857. The Fourteenth Amendment declaring citizens of the United States to be "citizens of the State wherein they reside," was adopted in 1868.

domestic commerce. See **intrastate commerce.**

domestic corporation. A term contrasting with "foreign corporation," meaning a corporation of the state, that is, a corporation organized and created under the laws of the state. Sometimes, more elaborately defined by statute as a corporation created by or under the laws of the state, or located in the state and created by or under the laws of the United States. First Nat. Bank v Doying (NY) 13 Daly 509, 510. As the term is used in Federal statutes in connection with corporations or partnerships, its usual meaning is created or organized in the United States, and the word "foreign" in the same connection usually means created or organized outside the United States. Hecht v Malley, 265 US 144, 154, 68 L Ed 949, 956, 44 S Ct 46.
See **foreign corporation.**

domestic fixtures. Such chattels as have been affixed to a dwelling house for the comfort or convenience of the tenant. Such fixtures include stoves and ranges fixed in brickwork, furnaces, gas fixtures, pumps, clocks, window blinds, bath tubs. The tenant may lawfully remove domestic fixtures which have been annexed to the premises by himself for the more advantageous use thereof, provided no material injury results to the realty or to the substantial characteristics of the articles. Raymond v Strickland, 124 Ga 504, 52 SE 619.

domestic judgment. A judgment rendered by a court in the sovereignty or jurisdiction wherein rights or liabilities under the judgment are involved in an action. The term is significant only by way of contrasting such a judgment with a "foreign judgment." 30A Am J Rev ed Judgm § 232.
See **foreign judgment.**

domestic medicine. See **domestic remedy.**

domestic purposes. Uses of the services of a public utility which contribute to health, comfort, and convenience of a family in the enjoyment of their dwelling as a home. 43 Am J1st Pub Util § 182; 56 Am J1st Wat Wk § 57. Sometimes more elaborately defined by statute in reference to water rights and irrigation to include water for the household and an additional amount for domestic animals. Anno: Ann Cas 1912, 612.
As the term "domestic use" is used in an ordinance fixing water rates, it means the use to which water is applied by the family, or for family use, and includes all uses to which water is applied around the home; but it does not include the use of water in public parks or public pleasure resorts maintained by the city. Water Supply Co. v Albuquerque, 17 NM 326, 128 P 77.
See **family use.**

domestic remedy. An herb or other plant having, or believed to have medicinal value. The expression frequently occurs in statutes regulating the practice of medicine, and as there used the words refer to the administration of medicine in the family or in the household, without the aid of a physician. State v Huff, 75 Kan 585, 90 P 279.

domestics. Same as **domestic servants.**

domestic servants. Household employees rather than farm laborers or chauffeurs working outside. 57 Am J1st Wills § 1395. Servants who receive wages and stay in the house of the person paying and employing them for service to him or his family, such as valets, footmen, cooks, butlers and others who reside in the house. Cook v Dodge, 6 La Ann 275, 277.

domestics infra moenia (in'fra moi'ni-a). Domestics within the walls,—menial servants employed in and about a dwelling house. 35 Am J1st M & S § 530.

domesticum. See **forum domesticum.**

domesticus (do-mes'ti-kus). A steward.

domestic use. See **domestic purposes.**

domicil. The relationship which the law creates between an individual and a particular locality or country. The place where a person has his true fixed permanent home and principal establishment, and to which place he has, whenever he is absent, the intention of returning, and from which he has no present intention of moving. 25 Am J2d Dom § 1.
In a particular context, it may be the same as residence. Anno: 12 ALR2d 759; 57 Am J1st Wills § 766. It is not exactly synonomous with residence. It is (1) the fact of residence and (2) the intention to remain. Ex parte Weissinger, 247 Ala 113, 22 So 2d 510; McIntosh v Maricopa County, 73 Ariz 366, 241 P2d 801, 31 ALR2d 770. A person may have his residence in one place and his domicil in another. Missouri Pacific R. Co. v Lawrence, 215 Ark 718, 223 SW2d 823, 12 ALR2d 748. He can have only one domicil at the same time, though he may have more than one residence. State v Allen, 48 W Va 154, 160, 35 SE 990.
He who stops even for a long time in a place for the management of his affairs, has a simple habitation there, but has no domicil. Re Thompson (NY) 1 Wend 45.
See **change of domicil; commercial domicil; corporate domicil; domicil by operation of law; domicil of origin; floating intention; habitancy; habitation; home; loss of domicil; matrimonial domicil; national domicil; permanent abode; place of abode; place of usual abode; residence; settlement of a pauper; voluntary domicil.**

domicil by operation of law. That domicil which the law attributes to a person independent of his own intention or selection. This results generally from the domestic relations of husband and wife, or parent and child, the domicil of the wife or the child following that of the husband or father as a legal consequence. Re Estate of Jones, 192 Iowa 78, 182 NW 227, 16 ALR 1286, 1289; Re Weber, 187 Misc 674, 64 NYS2d 281.
The words "resides" as used in a statute providing that proceedings to remove disabilities of a minor shall be instituted in the county where he resides, does not mean his bodily presence, but his legal domicil, which is that of his father. Gulf, C. & S. F. R. Co. v Lemons, 109 Tex 244, 206 SW 75, 5 ALR 943.

domicile (dom'i-sil). Same as **domicil.**

domiciled note. A promissory note payable at a designated bank. 11 Am J2d B & N § 22.

domiciliary administrator (dom-i-sil'i-ạ-ri). An administrator of a decedent's estate appointed and acting at the place of the decedent's domicil. 31 Am J2d Ex & Ad § 681.

domiciliary executor. An executor appointed and acting at the place of the testator's domicil. See 31 Am J2d Ex & Ad § 688.

domiciliate (dom-i-sil'i-āt). To establish one's domicil in a place.

domicilii. See **forum domicilii.**

domicilii actoris. See **forum domicilii actoris.**

domicilii rei. See **forum domicilii rei.**

domicilium ex proprio motu. (Latin.) Domicil of one's own choice.
See **domicil of choice.**

domicilium originis. (Latin.) Domicil of origin; the domicil assigned to a child at his birth. 25 Am J2d Dom § 13.
See **domicil of origin.**

domicil of child. See **domicil by operation of law.**

domicil of choice. The true domicil; the place which a person has voluntarily chosen for himself to displace his previous one. Ex parte Weissinger, 247 Ala 113, 22 So 2d 510; Re Estate of Jones, 192 Iowa 78, 182 NW 227, 16 ALR 1286, 1289.
See **domicil of prisoner.**

domicil of corporation. See **corporate domicil.**

domicil of matrimony. See **matrimonial domicil.**

domicil of nativity. The place of a person's birth.
See **domicil of origin.**

domicil of origin. The domicil assigned to a child at its birth. 25 Am J2d Dom § 13; Kowalski v Wojtkowski, 19 NJ 247, 116 A2d 6, 53 ALR2d 556. The domicil which a person acquires at birth, it being the domicil of his parents or of the person upon whom he is legally dependent. Ex parte Weissinger, 247 Ala 113, 22 So 2d 510; Re Estate of Jones, 192 Iowa 78, 182 NW 227; 16 ALR 1286, 1289; Re Weber, 187 Misc 674, 64 NYS 281.

domicil of a prisoner. A paradoxial expression. A prisoner, being under legal restraint, cannot acquire a domicil in his prison; his former domicil continues during his imprisonment. Likewise, where a prisoner is compelled to live within the liberties of the prison, he acquires no domicil there; his residence there is merely a continuation of his imprisonment. Nor would his desire to live within the prison make it his domicil. Wendel v Hoffman (DC NJ) 24 F Supp 63.

domicil of wife. See **domicil by operation of law; matrimonial domicil.**

domigerium (do-mi-je'ri-um). The power or dominion which one person has over another.

domina (dom'i-nạ). A dame; a woman who held a barony in her own right.

dominant (dom'i-nạnt). Controlling; principal; ruling.

dominant estate. Same as **dominant tenement.**

dominant part (dom'i-nạnt pärt). If the purchaser of trade-marked goods would be more likely to remember one part of a mark than another part as indicating origin of the goods, such word is the dominant part of the mark. As, the dominant part of the mark "Wheato-Nuts" is "nuts," and considered in its entirety this mark is confusingly similar to "Grape-Nuts," a mark whose dominant part is the same. Langendorf United Bakeries v General Foods Corp. 29 Cust & Pat App (Pat) 831, 125 F2d 159.

dominant tenement. A tenement for the benefit of which an easement in the form of a charge or burden is imposed upon a servient tenement. 25 Am J2d Ease § 8.

domination. Rule or control.
See **interference and domination.**

dominical (dọ-min'i-kạl). Pertaining to the Lord or to Sunday.

dominicide (dō-min'i-sīd). The killing of his master by a servant, slave or vassal.

dominicum (do-mi'ni-kum). A demesne; a church.
See **demesne.**

dominicum antiquum (do-mi'ni-kum an-tī'kwu-um). Same as **ancient demesne.**

dominio (dō-mē'ne-ō). A term used in Spanish-American grants, meaning the right of power to dispose freely of a thing, if the law, the will of the testator, or some agreement does not prevent. Castillero v United States (US) 2 Black 1, 17 L Ed 360, 400.

dominio directo (do-mē'ne-o de-rek'to). The term used in Spanish-American grants, meaning the right a person has to control the disposition of a thing, the use (utilidad) of which he has ceded. Castillero v United States (US) 2 Black 1, 17 L Ed 360, 400.

dominion (dō-min'yọn). Control; ownership. The rights of dominion or property are those rights which a man may acquire in and to such external things as are unconnected with his person. See 2 Bl Comm 1.

dominion over premises. A present ability to control plus an intent to exclude others from control. 3 Am J2d Adv P § 13.

dominio pleno y absoluto (do-mē'ne-o play'no ee ab-so-loo'to). A term used in Spanish-American grants, meaning, the power one has over anything to alienate independently of another—to receive its fruits—to exclude all others from its use. Castillero v United States (US) 2 Black 1, 17 L Ed 360, 400.

dominio util (do-mē'ne-o oo'tėel). A term used in Spanish-American grants, meaning the right to receive all the fruits of a thing subject to some contribution or tribute, which is paid to him who reserves in it the dominium directum. Castillero v United States (US) 2 Black 1, 17 L Ed 360, 400.

dominium (dō-min'i-um). Dominion; control; ownership.

dominium directum (do-mi'ni-um di-rek'tum). Direct ownership, i. e. allodial or legal tenure.

dominium directum et utile (do-mi'ni-um di-rek'tum et u'ti-le). The complete and absolute dominion in property; the union of the title and the exclusive use. See Fairfax's Devisee v Hunter's Lessee (US) 7 Cranch 603, 618, 3 L Ed 453, 458.

dominium eminens (do-mi'ni-um ē'mi-nenz). (Civil law.) The right of eminent domain. Gilmer v Lime Point, 18 Cal 229, 251.

Dominium non potest esse in pendenti (do-mi'ni-um non po'test es'se in pen-den'tī). Ownership cannot be held in suspense.

dominium plenum (do-mi'ni-um plē'num). Full or complete ownership of property.

dominium utile (do-mi'ni-um u'ti-le). Equitable or beneficial ownership of property.

domino volente (do'mi-nō vo-len'te). With the consent of the owner.

dominus (do'mi-nus). Lord; master; principal.

Dominus capitalis feodi loco haeredis habetur, quoties per defectum vel delictum extinguitur sanguis tenentis (do'mi-nus ka-pi-tā'lēz fē'o-dō lō'kō hē-rē'-dis hā-bē'ter, quō'she-ēz per dē-fek'tum vel de-lik'-tum ex-tin'gwi-ter san'gwis te-nen'tis). The chief lord of the fee is regarded as heir whenever the blood of the tenant becomes extinct either through failure of heirs or attainder. See 2 Bl Comm 247.

dominus ligius (do'mi-nus li'ji-us). Liege lord, the king. See 1 Bl Comm 367.

dominus litis (do'mi-nus li'tis). A person who controls a litigation.

dominus manerii (do'mi-nus ma-ne'ri-i). The lord of the manor.

dominus navis (do'mi-nus nā'vis). The master of a ship.

Dominus non maritabit pupillum nisi semel (do'mi-nus non ma-ri-tā'bit pu-pil'lum ni'si se'mel). A lord cannot give his ward in marriage more than once.

dominus pro tempore (do'mi-nus prō tem'pō-rē). The temporary master of a ship. The charterer of a vessel may be to some purposes such a master. Laugher v Pointer, 5 Barn & C 547, 108 Eng Rep 204.

Dominus rex nullum habere potest parem, multo minus superiorem (do'mi-nus rex nul'lum hā-bē're po'test pa'rem, mul'tō mī'nus su-pe-ri-ō'rem). The king cannot have an equal, much less a superior.

domitae (do'mi-tē). Reclaimed; domesticated; domestic.

domitae naturae (do'mi-tē nā-tū'rē). Animals which are naturally tame and gentle or which, by long continued association with man, have become thoroughly domesticated and reduced to such a state of subjection that they no longer possess the inclination or disposition to escape. 4 Am J2d Ani § 2.

domo reparanda (do'mō re-pa-ran'da). A writ to compel a person to repair his house and thus prevent its falling upon his neighbor's property.

dom. proc. An abbreviation of **domus procerum**,— the house of lords.

domus (dō'mus). A house; a dwelling house; a home; a domicil; a residence.

domus capitularis (dō'mus ka-pi-tu-lā'ris). A chapter house.

domus Dei (dō'mus dē'i). The house of God,—a church; a hospital.

domus mansionalis (dō'mus man-she-ō-nā'lis). Mansion house.
See **mansion house**.

domus mansionalis Dei (dō'mus man-she-ō-nā'lis dē'i). The mansion house of God. Lord Coke said that burglary could be committed in a church because it was the mansion house of God. See 4 Bl Comm 224.

domus procerum (dō'mus prō'se-rum). The English house of lords.

Domus sua cuique est tutissimum refugium (dō'mus su'a ki'kwe est tu-tis'si-mum re-fu'ji-um). A man's home is his safest refuge. Davison v People, 90 Ill 221, 229.

Domus tutissimum cuique refugium atque receptaculum (dō'mus tu-tis'si-mum ki'kwe re-fu'ji-um at'kwe re-sep-ta'ku-lum). The home of each person is his safest refuge and asylum.

dona (dō'nạ). Gifts.

Dona clandestina sunt semper suspiciosa (dō'na klandes-ti'na sunt sem'per sus-pi-she-ō'sa). Secret gifts are always open to suspicion.

donare (dō-nā're). To give.

Donari videtur quod nulli jure cogente conceditur (dō-nā'ri vi-dē'ter quod nul'li jū're ko-jen'te kon-sē'di-ter). That is considered as given which is transferred under no legal compulsion.

donatarius (dō-na-tā'ri-us). A person who receives a gift; a donee.

donate. To give, generally for a specific object; to bestow freely. State v Sioux City & Pacific Railroad Co. 7 Neb 357, 373.

donatio (dō-nā'she-ō). That which is given; gift.

donatio causa mortis. See **gift causa mortis**.

donatio feudi (dō-nā'she-ō fū'di). The gift of a fee.

donatio inter vivos (dō-nā'she-ō in'ter vi'vos). Same as **gift inter vivos**.

donatio mortis causa. See **gift causa mortis**.

donation. The act by which the owner of a thing voluntarily transfers the title and possession of the same without any consideration. Georgia Penitentiary Co. v Nelms, 65 Ga 499.
The word is synonymous with gift. Mills v Stewart, 76 Mont 429, 247 P 332, 47 ALR 424.
See **gift**.

Donationes sint stricti juris, ne quis plus donasse praesumatur quam in donatione expresserit (dō-nā-she-ō'nēz sint strik'ti jū'ris, nē quis plus dō-nās'se prē-zu-mā'ter quam in dō-nā-she-ō'ne expres'se-rit). Gifts should be of strict construction, lest anyone may be presumed to have given more than is described in the gift. See 2 Bl Comm 108.

donation inter vivos. Same as **gift inter vivos**.

donation lands. Lands reserved by the state of Pennsylvania and allotted to citizens of that state who fought in the Revolutionary War.

Donatio non praesumitur (dō-nā'she-ō non prē-zu'-mi-ter). A gift is not presumed to have been made.

Donationum alia perfecta, alia incepta, et non perfecta; ut si donatio lecta fuit et concessa, ac traditio nondum fuerit subsecuta (dō-nā-she-ō'num a'li-a per-fek'ta, a'li-a in-sep'ta, et non per-fek'ta; ut si dō-nā'she-ō lek'ta fu'it et kon-ses'sa, ak trā-di'she-ō non'dum fu'e-rit sub-se-kū'ta). Some gifts are complete, others are either incipient or not complete, as if a gift were considered and agreed upon, but delivery had not yet followed.

Donatio perficitur possessione accipientis (dō-nā'she-ō per-fi'si-ter po-zes-she-ō'ne ak-si-pi-en'tis). A gift is perfected by the possession of the donee. A maxim of the ancient English law. Hatch v Atkinson, 56 Me 324.

donatio propter nuptias (dō-nā'she-ō prō'ter nup'she-as). A gift in consideration of marriage.

donatio regis. See **ex donatio regis**.

donatio velata (dō-nā'she-ō ve-lā'ta). A veiled or hidden gift; a gift for a pretended consideration.

donative advowson (don'ạ-tiv). Same as **advowson donative**.

donative intent. The intent to make a gift. Commissioner v Duberstein, 363 US 278, 4 L Ed 2d 1218, 80 S Ct 1190.

donator (dō-nā'tọr). A person who makes a gift; a donor.

donatorius (dō-nā-tō'ri-us). A person who receives a gift; a donee.

Donator nunquam desinit possidere antequam donatarius incipiat possidere (dō-nā'tor nun'quam dē'si-nit pos-si-dē're an'te-quam dō-nā-tā'ri-us in-si'pi-at pos-si-dē're). A donor never ceases to possess until the possession of the donee begins.

donatory (don'a-tō-ri). A person who receives a gift from the crown.

donc (dōn). Then.

done. Completed.
See **de son done.**

donec (dō'nek). Until; while; as long as.

donee (dō-nē'). A person to whom a gift is made; a grantee.

donee-beneficiary. A third person designated to receive the benefit of performance by one of two contracting parties under the terms of the agreement with the other, who is a stranger to the consideration and is to receive the benefit of performance as a pure donation by the promisee. Breaux v Banker (Tex Civ App) 107 SW2d 382.

Dongan charter. A charter granted for the city of New York under James the Second in 1686, by Thomas Dongan as lieutenant-governor.

donkey. A domestic animal, often known as a jackass. 4 Am J2d Ani § 22.

Donkey Case. See **Davies v Mann.**

donor (dō'nor). A person who makes a gift.

donque (dōnk). Same as **donc.**

donum (dō'num). A gift.

doom (döm). A judgment. A tragic fate.

dooming. The practice of county assessors in "estimating" the value of property belonging to persons liable to taxation, in cases where such persons have failed or neglected to make returns thereof. Thurston v Little, 3 Mass (3 Tyng) 429, 433.

Doomsday Book (dömz'dā buk). Same as **Domesday Book.**

door. A movable panel for closing the entrance to a building or room.
See **open doors; outer door.**

dormant (dôr'mant). Sleeping; silent; inactive for the time being; in abeyance.

dormant claim. A claim held in abeyance; a claim barred by the statute of limitations.

dormant execution. An execution which has lost its priority from delay in making any levy under it. A writ of execution duly made out and signed by the clerk of court, and otherwise ready for levy, but marked "to lie," and not issued to an officer for levy. Davis v Roller, 106 Va 46, 55 SE 4.

dormant judgment. A judgment no longer active, its active period having been terminated by the death of a party or the lapse of time and the failure to take any steps to continue or enforce it. 30A Am J Rev ed Judgm § 568. A judgment which must be revived before execution will be issued thereon and before other steps in enforcement may be taken. 30A Am J Rev ed Judgm § 570.

dormant lien of judgment. The lien of a judgment which is in abeyance while the land is exempt from execution, but which becomes active or potential when the exemption ceases to exist. 26 Am J1st Home § 94. The lien of a dormant judgment during the period of dormancy in jurisdictions which adhere to the view that upon the revival of a dormant judgment, the lien of the judgment is considered to have been a continuous lien from the date of entry of the judgment. 30A Am J Rev ed Judgm § 579.

dormant partner. A silent partner, one whose connection with the firm is concealed from the public and who takes no part in the conduct of the business or affairs of the firm. 40 Am J1st Partn § 15.
See **silent partner.**

dormant titles. A title to real estate held in abeyance, unasserted.
See **buying and selling dormant titles; trading in dormant titles.**

dormitory. A room or building with sleeping accommodations for a number of people. United Cerebral Palsy Asso. v Zoning Board, 282 Pa 67, 114 A2d 331, 52 ALR2d 1093.

Dormiunt aliquando leges, nunquam moriuntur (dor'mi-unt a-li-quan'dō lē'jēz, nun'quam mo-ri-un'ter). Although the laws sometimes sleep, they never die.

Dorr's Rebellion. A rebellion against the state government of Rhode Island in 1842, led by Thomas W. Dorr. Luther v Borden (US) 7 How 1, 12 L Ed 581.

dorso recordi. See **in dorso recordi.**

dorsum (dôr'sum). The back of anything.

dorture. A lodging place; a dormitory.

dos (dō'). A dowry; dower. Roman law dower. 25 Am J2d Dow § 12.

Dos de dote peti non debet (dōs dē dō'te pe'tī non de'bet). Dower ought not to be sought from dower. Brooks v Everett, 95 Mass (13 Allen) 457, 459.

dos rationabilis (dōs ra-she-ō-nā'bi-lis). Reasonable or legitimate dower. If no specific dotation was made at the church porch, at the time of the marriage, the common law endowed the wife of a third part of such lands and tenements as the husband was seised at the time of the marriage, and no other. This third part was her dos rationabilis. See 2 Bl Comm 133.

Dos rationabilis vel legitima est cujuslibet mulieris de quocunque tenemento tertia pars omnium terrarum et tenementorum, quae vir suus tenuit in dominio suo ut de feodo (dōs ra-she-ō-nā'bi-lis vel lē-ji'ti-ma est kū-jus'li-bet mu-lī'e-ris dē quō-kun'kwe te-ne-men'tō ter'she-a parz om'ni-um ter-rā'rum et te-ne-men-tō'rum, kwē vir su'us te'nu-it in do-mi'ni-o sū'o ut dē fe'o-do). Reasonable or legitimate dower is for every woman a third part of all the lands and tenements which her husband held in his demesne as of fee.

dot. See **dotal property; dowry.**

dotage. Feebleness of the mental faculties which proceeds from old age. 29 Am J Rev ed Ins Per § 3.

dotalitium (dō-ta-li'she-um). Dower.

dotal property. That property which a wife brings to the husband to assist him in bearing the expenses of the marriage establishment. 15 Am J2d Community Prop § 3.
Dotal property as here defined was not known to the common law, but appears to be peculiar to the state of Louisiana. Hayes v Pratt, 147 US 550, 37 L Ed 276, 13 S Ct 495.

dotation (dō-tā'shon). The endowment of a woman with a dowry or marriage portion; any other endowment, as that of a public charity.

dote (dōt). To be delirious, silly, or insane. Gates v Meredith, 7 Ind 440, 441.

dote assignanda (dō'te as-sig-nan'da). A writ that lay for a widow, where it was found by office that the king's tenant was seised of tenements in fee or fee tail at the day of his death, and that he held of the king in chief. In such case, the widow came into chancery, and there made oath that she would not marry without the king's leave, and she had this writ to the escheators. These widows were called "king's widows."—Holthouse's Law Dict.

Dote lex favet; praemium pudoris est, ideo parcatur (do'tī lex fa'vet; prē'mi-um pu-dō'ris est, i'de-ō par-kā'ter). The law favors dower; it is the reward of virtue, therefore it should be spared or kept alive.

dote unde nihil habet (dō'te un'de ni'hil hā'bet). Dower from whence she has nothing,—a writ of dower which lay for a widow against a tenant of lands to whom her husband had conveyed them and of which her husband was solely seised in fee simple, or fee tail, and of which she was dowable. See 1 Bl Comm 182.

dotis administratio (dō'tis ad-mi-nis-tra'she-ō). The admeasurement of dower; that is, the assignment or adjustment of a widow's dower.

dotissa (do-tis'sa). A dowager; an endowed widow.

Douay Bible (Doo'ay Bī'ble). The translation or version of the Bible used by the Roman Catholic Church, the name coming from Douay, a municipality of France, where the Old Testament of such translation or version was published early in the 17th century.

double adultery. Adultery committed where both parties to the offense are married persons. Hunter v United States (Wis) 1 Pinney 91.

double agency. An agency on the part of one agent acting for two principals. 11 Am J2d B & N § 479.

double allegiance. See **dual nationality.**

double avail of marriage. Two times the ordinary or single value of a marriage.
See **value of the marriage.**

double bond. A bond providing a penalty for its nonfulfillment, as distinguished from a single bond which carries no penalty.

double comma. Same as **ditto mark.**

double complaint. A complaint made before an ecclesiastical court against both the judge who delayed or refused justice and the defendant in the cause in which the grievance arose.
See **double pleading; joinder of causes of action.**

double contingency. See **remainders on a contingency with a double aspect.**

double conversion. That which takes place when land is directed to be sold and converted into money, and these proceeds are directed to be laid out again in land, the whole forming one continuous obligation. The property, in such case, is considered to be in that state in which it is ultimately to be converted; that is, to be land. Double conversion does not differ from single conversion, but the property is treated as if already converted into that species of property into which it is directed to be changed, no matter whether the steps are more or less numerous. Ford v Ford, 80 Mich 42, 53.
See **reconversion.**

double costs. Additional allowances imposed against a party because of the nature of the action or delaying tactics. Where a statute gives double costs, they are to be calculated thus: the common costs; and then half the common costs. Van Auken v Decker, 2 NJL 108, 111.

double cousin. The relationship of cousin traceable through both the paternal and maternal lines; the same degree of relationship as an ordinary cousin. 23 Am J2d Desc & D § 61.

double creditor. A term connected with marshaling assets, meaning a creditor who holds a lien upon two separate and distinct funds or securities. Newby v Norton, 90 Kan 317, 133 P 890.

double damages. Multiple damages awarded under statutory authority for certain classes of wrongs, some courts regarding the excess of the award over the amount of injury actually sustained as an extraordinary liability imposed by way of penalty, others regarding it as an extraordinary liability imposed under a statute which is remedial and nonpunitive. 22 Am J2d Damg §§ 267, 268. The damages awarded for waste in some jurisdictions. 56 Am J1st Waste § 36. A term for an allowance on inconsistent theories. Anno: 17 ALR2d 1323.
See **exemplary damages.**

double deadwoods. See **buffers.**

double-decker. A bus with two levels for passengers. 7 Am J2d Auto § 163. Also, a large sandwich.

double derivative suit. An action, brought by a stockholder in a corporation which holds stock in a second corporation for wrongs to the second corporation, where it appears that neither corporation is willing to enforce the right of action. Anno: 154 ALR 1296.

double fine. Same as **fine sur done grant et render.**

double gibbet. A gibbet with arms projecting in opposite directions for double executions.

double indemnity. A double recovery under an insurance policy for loss occurring under certain conditions, for example, an accidental death of one insured under a life insurance policy.

double insurance. Coverage of the same risk and same interest by different insurers. Western Union Tel. Co. v Houghton, 146 Pa 561, 23 A 248.
See **contribution between insurers; excess insurance; other insurance clause.**

double jeopardy. See **prior jeopardy.**

double letter. A term of significance in communications of an older period, meaning a letter consisting of two sheets. Williams v Wells, Fargo & Co. Express (CA8 Ark) 177 F 352.

double liability. Double recovery for a single liability. St. Louis S.W.R.Co. v Meyer (Mo) 272 SW2d 249, 46 ALR2d 964.
See **double damages.**

double liability of stockholder. See **superadded liability.**

double meaning. See **ambiguity.**

double parking. The parking of a vehicle on the roadway side of any vehicle parked or standing at the edge or curb of a street. 7 Am J2d Auto § 236.

double patenting. The obtaining of a second patent by the same applicant on the same invention. McIlvaine Patent Corp. v Walgren Co. (DC Ill) 44 F Supp 530.

double plea. A plea setting up two or more several

and distinct defenses. Handy v Waldron, 18 RI 567, 29 A 143.

double pleading. A pleading which in one count or paragraph sets out two or more several and distinct causes of action or two or more several and distinct defenses. Handy v Waldron, 18 RI 567, 29 A 143.
See **duplicity.**

double possibility. See **possibility on a possibility.**

double punishment. The punishment of a person two or more times for the same offense, such being within the prohibition of provisions against double jeopardy.
See **former jeopardy.**

double quarrel. Same as **double complaint.**

double rent. A common statutory penalty of double the amount of the agreed rental for a holding over by the tenant after the time specified in the landlord's notice to quit.

double taxation. In a very broad sense, any situation in which it can be contended with some show of reason that the same person or property has been subjected to more than one tax burden. 51 Am J1st Tax § 284. More precisely, for the purposes of a constitutional prohibition, taxing twice, for the same purpose, by a tax of the same kind, in the same year, some of the property in the taxing district, without imposing the same levies upon all the property of the same kind in the district. 51 Am J1st Tax § 284.

double voucher. A form of common recovery wherein the praecipe or writ was brought against an indifferent person to whom a conveyance of an estate of freehold had been made as a matter of form, and who then vouched the tenant in tail, the latter thereupon vouching the common vouchee. See 2 Bl Comm 359. See also 2 Bl Comm Appx V.

double waste. Cutting timber to obtain material for making repairs to buildings, without making the repairs.

double wharfage. Double the amount of the usual charge for the use of a wharf, recoverable by statute when a vessel leaves a wharf without paying wharfage. 56 Am J1st Whar § 30.

double wills. Another term for reciprocal wills in which the testators name each other as beneficiaries under similar testamentary plans. 57 Am J1st Wills § 681. See mutual wills; reciprocal wills.

doubt. Uncertainty. That state of a person's mind which exists where evidence in reference to the fact to be proved fails to generate a rational belief of the existence of the fact. Rowe v Baber, 93 Ala 422, 425.
See **reasonable doubt.**

doubtful title. A title which is open to reasonable doubt; one for which a purchaser who takes it probably will be subjected to contest and litigation; one which can be established only by parol testimony difficult to procure; one that an ordinarily prudent man would not accept if he were buying the property or taking it as security for a loan. Wanser v De Nyse, 188 NY 378, 80 NE 1088.

dough. The mixture of flour and other ingredients from which bread and pastries are baked. A slang term for money or wealth.
See **dot.**

Do ut des (dō ut dēz). I give that you may give. This was the first species of consideration under the civil law, and applied to a giving of money or goods under a promise of repayment in money or goods, and to loans of money, and contracts of sale. See 2 Bl Comm 444.

Do ut facias (dō ut fā'she-as). I pay in order that you may perform. This was the fourth species of consideration under the civil law and was the counterpart of the third (facio ut des); as when I agree with the servant to give him such wages upon his performance. See 2 Bl Comm 445.

doves. Birds of intrinsic value because the carcass is food, but which constitute a subject of property only when in the care and custody of the owner. 4 Am J2d Ani § 19. A term recently applied to members of Congress and other public figures opposed to the escalation of the Vietnam War.

dowable (dou'ạ-bl). The state or condition of a widow who is entitled to dower out of the real property of her deceased husband. The term is also applied to lands or other property of the husband which are subject to, or chargeable with, dower.

dowager (dou'ạ-jėr). A widow to whom her dower has been assigned. See 2 Bl Comm 136.

dowager queen. The widow of the king of England, at present the gracious and well-beloved Elizabeth, widow of George VI.

dower (dou'ėr). The legal right or interest which the wife acquires by marriage in the real estate of her husband. At common law it consists in the use, during her natural life after the death of her husband, of one-third of all the real estate of which her husband was beneficially seised, at any time during the marriage, by a title such as might pass by inheritance to the children of the marriage. The same term is often used to describe the rights given to widows in the real estate of their husbands by statute, even where the statutory rights differ from the common-law estate of dower. Sometimes the term is used to describe a widow's statutory rights in her husband's real and personal estate, even personal estate alone, and the rights of a husband in the real estate of his deceased wife. 25 Am J2d Dow § 1.
See **admeasurement of dower; assignment of dower; dowable; dower consummate; inchoate right of dower; jointure; quarantine; release of dower; tenant in dower; widow's third.**

dower ad ostium ecclesiae (dower ad os'ti-um e-klē'-si-ē). Dower at the door of the church,—a form of dower given openly at the time of a marriage ceremony, at the very door of the church wherein the marriage was celebrated by a tenant in fee simple of full age, who after "affiance made and troth plighted," endowed his wife with the whole or a part of his lands, publicly specifying her portion in such manner that after his death she might enter upon the same without further ceremony.

dower by particular custom. That species of dower to which a widow is entitled because of a particular custom, such as that she should have half of her husband's lands, or in some places the whole, and in some others only a quarter. See 1 Bl Comm 132.

dower consummate. The right of a widow to her dower in her husband's real property which accrues to her immediately upon his death. Upon the husband's death, the widow's right of dower becomes consummate. It has ceased to be a contingency. But still it remains a mere right in the nature of a chose in action. She has the right to have the estate assigned to her, but she has no estate until it has been assigned. Underground Electric Railways Co. v

Owsley (CA2 NY) 196 F 278. Once assigned, the consummate dower is a vested right in the property assigned and the widow's rights in other lands of the decedent cease altogether. 25 Am J2d Dow § 8.

dower de la plus belle (dŏw-er de la plū bel). Dower of the fairest part,—a species of dower which was assigned to the widow from the fairest part of her husband's lands and which was abolished with the military tenures, of which it was a consequence. See 2 Bl Comm 132.

dower ex assensu patris (dower ex as-sen'su pa'tris). Dower by the consent of the father,—a form of dower wherein the husband endowed his wife openly at the time of the marriage and at the door of the church, with lands upon which she might enter upon his death without further ceremony, but in this case it was the father of the bridegroom who was seised in fee of the lands in question, and the father's consent, expressly given, was a necessary part of the son's right to designate such lands as the dower of his wife. By this form of dower, a wife might enter upon her dower after the death of her husband although the father still lived.

dower unde nihil habet (dower un'de ni'hil hā'bet). Same as **de dote unde nihil habet.**

dowle stones. Stones employed to mark a boundary.

dowment. Same as **endowment.** Also, same as **dower.**

dowment ad ostium ecclesiae (dow'ment ad os'ti-um e-klē'si-ē). Same as **dower ad ostium ecclesiae.**

down draft. A term familiar in aviation, signifying a turbulent atmospheric condition. 8 Am J2d Avi § 96.

Downes v Bidwell. See **Foraker Act.**

dowress (dou'res). A woman who is entitled to dower.

dowry (dou'ri). A term of several meanings, dependent upon the historical source, but not the same as the **dower** of the common law.

The "dowry" of biblical times bore no resemblance to common-law "dower," but was a gift made by the suitor to the father or other near relatives of the intended bride. A similar custom prevailed among the Greeks, but Aristotle states that it had come to be looked upon as a relic of barbarism in their ancestors, as it was virtually a purchase of their wives. Neither is it like the dower, called "dot" of the Roman law (or the "dot" still in France), which was the marriage portion which the wife brought to her husband, in land or money. The French "dot" (pronounced "doe"), with its attraction to foreign suitors of American heiresses, is the origin of the slang word "dough" for property. State ex rel. Corporation Com. v Dunn, 174 NC 679, 94 SE 481.

See **dotal property.**

doz. Abbreviation for dozen.

dozein. An ancient municipal district which was composed of twelve families.

dozer (dō'zėr). Same as **bulldozer.**

D. P. An abbreviation of domus procerum, the English house of lords. Also an abbreviation for displaced person.

dr. Common abbreviation for debtor.

Dr. An abbreviation for Doctor.

Draconian laws (drā-kọ'ni-ạn lâs). A code of laws compiled by Draco the "lawgiver" of Athens; the term is applied to laws which are unreasonably harsh or severe.

draff (dràf). Dirt dregs, impurities. Sometimes confused with "draft," the arbitrary deduction from gross weight of an imported article, formerly employed in customs offices to assure the importer that he was not prejudiced by the scales used.

draft. An order in writing by one person on another to pay a sum of money therein specified to a third person on demand or at a future time therein stated. 11 Am J2d B & N § 14. A term completely synonymous with "bill of exchange." See State v Di Nocla, 163 Ohio St 140, 56 Ohio Ops 185, 126 NE2d 62. A term preferable to bill of exchange in the connotation of commercial paper. UCC § 3–104(2)(a). In military parlance, the enforcement of the duty of a citizen to perform military service. Lanahan v Birge, 30 Conn 438, 443. An arbitrary deduction from the gross weight of an imported article, formerly employed in customs offices to assure the importer that he was not prejudiced by the scales used. 21 Am J2d Cust D § 87; sometimes spelled "draught." A copy of an instrument, such as a will, otherwise known as a first draft, from which the executed instrument was drawn. A rough copy of a plan for the construction of a building or other structure.

A bank draft is a bill of exchange drawn by a bank; where drawn upon another bank, it has the same general effect as a check drawn by an ordinary person. 11 Am J2d B & N § 14.

See **military draft; overdraft; selective draft.**

draft dodger. One who evades a draft for service in the armed forces of the country.

See **Selective Draft Law.**

draftsman. A scrivener; the person who prepares a deed, will or other instrument. A person skilled in drawing designs or plans for buildings, other works of construction, and machines.

dragnet clause. A provision of a mortgage which broadens the security clause to cover all indebtedness of the mortgagor to the mortgagee of past or future origin, existing indebtedness, advances to be made by the mortgagee to the mortgagor, and indebtedness of the mortgagor to the mortgagee created subsequent to the execution of the mortgage. Anno: 172 ALR2d 1082.

dragnet of conspiracy. A phrase applied to the tendency of prosecutors, in prosecuting for the crime of conspiracy, to charge as defendants all persons who have been associated in any degree whatsoever with the main offenders. United States v Falcon (CA2 NY) 109 F2d 579.

dragoman (drag'ō-mạn). A Turkish court interpreter.

drain. A hollow space in the ground, either natural or artificial, where water is collected or drained away. Barton v Drainage Dist. 174 Ark 173, 294 SW 418. The word has been construed as being broad enough to include a sewer. Barton v Drainage Dist. 174 Ark 173, 294 SW 418.

See **drainway; natural drainway.**

drainage. The conveying from land, by natural or artificial means, of water not absorbed by the soil. "This word is not inept to express the concept of water which has escaped from a reservoir by percolation and is drawn off when it appears again on the surface." United States v Warmsprings Irrig. Dist. (DC Or) 38 F 239.

See **cutoff drainage; right of drainage.**

drainage district. A governmental corporation of limited powers, in the nature of a public or quasi-public corporation, similar to a municipal corporation, although not created for political purposes or for the administration of civil government, but for the purpose of creating and maintaining a project for the drainage of lands within the district. 25 Am J2d Drains § 6.

drainage ditch. A ditch dug for the purpose of drainage of land; not a "water course" in the true sense of the term. 56 Am J1st Water § 151.

drainway. A way for the drainage of surface water. 56 Am J1st Water § 76.

See **drain; drainage; natural drainway.**

dram. An alcoholic beverage in a small portion. Lacy v State, 32 Tex 227, 228.

drama. A story represented by action, the representation being as if the real persons were introduced and employed in the action itself. 4 Am J2d Amuse § 3.

It is ordinarily designed to be spoken, but may be represented in pantomime, when the actors use gesticulations, but do not speak; in the form of ballet where the portrayal is by dance; or in opera where music takes the place of poetry and of ordinary speech, and the dramatic treatment is essentially different from the other methods of representation. Bell v Mahn, 121 Pa 225, 15 A 523.

dram shop. A place where intoxicating liquor is sold at a public bar. 30 Am J Rev ed Intox L § 20.

draw. Noun: A small stream; a creek, Aldritt v Fleischauer, 74 Neb 66, 103 NW 1084; a way for the drainage of surface water. 56 Am J1st Water § 76. The movable section of a drawbridge. Savannah, Florida & Western R. Co. v Daniels, 90 Ga 608, 17 SE 647. Verb: To write in due form; to prepare a draft of, as to draw a memorial, a deed, or a bill of exchange. Hawkins v State, 28 Fla 363, 367. To obtain as a prize.

draw a prize. To ascertain, by chance or otherwise, who is entitled to a particular result, or a particular thing, by means of some pre-arranged mode of ascertaining the result.

As soon as the number, which entitles the ticket holder to the money or article, is drawn from the wheel, or otherwise ascertained, the prize is said to be drawn. The receiving of the prize is a separate act. People v Kent, 6 Cal 89.

drawback. The refund of duties paid upon the importation of materials used in the manufacture or production of articles in the United States, when such articles are exported. 21 Am J2d Cust D § 16.

Dram Shop Acts. Same as **Civil Damage Acts.**

draught. See **draft.**

drawbridge. A bridge, one or more sections of which can be lifted or moved aside to permit the passage of boats. Savannah, Florida & Western R. Co. v Daniels, 90 Ga 608, 17 SE 647.

drawee. The person upon whom a draft or bill of exchange is drawn; the person to whom the paper is presented for acceptance and payment.

drawer. The maker of a draft or bill of exchange.

drawing. To pull. To drag a person along the ground or pavement to the place of execution, as a part of his punishment, particularly for the crime of treason. State v Woodward, 68 W Va 66, 69 SE 385. See 4 Bl Comm 92.

See **draw.**

drawing account. The account of an employee, usually a salesman working on a commission or part-commission basis, with the employer, upon which advances are made to the employee at intervals fixed by the contract of employment or upon request by the employee. Anno: 95 ALR2d 505. The privilege of having a drawing account as defined above.

drawing jurors. See **selection of grand jurors; selection of jurors.**

drawlatches. Thieves; robbers.

drawn. See **draw.**

drawn in blank. See **in blank.**

draw on. To prepare, sign, and deliver a draft for acceptance by another.

draw poker. The conventional form of the game of poker, the play being upon a hand of five cards obtained upon one deal or by way of replacement of discards. 24 Am J1st Gaming § 20.

dray (drā). A wagon with detachable sides, horse-drawn, and used for the transportation for hire of goods, wares, merchandise, and other property.

A dray has been held to be exempt from execution, under a statute exempting a wagon. Cone v Lewis, 64 Tex 331.

drayage. The transportation of commodities by drays. Soule v San Francisco Gas-light Co. 54 Cal 241.

See **drayman.**

drayman. A wagoner or cartman, the forerunner of the modern trucker, his vehicle being pulled by horses. 13 Am J2d Car § 17.

Dr. Bonham's Case. A famous English case which held that a statute impossible of performance or against common right and reason was void at common law.

dredge. A vessel equipped for the removal of accumulated dirt, stone, and refuse in a harbor or waterway; a vessel within admiralty jurisdiction. 2 Am J2d Adm § 33. But not a watercraft for all purposes. Bartlett v Steam Dredge, 107 Mich 74.

dredging. Scooping dirt, rocks, or debris from the bottom of a harbor or river to deepen the harbor or channel, thereby improving navigation; opening a ditch through a swamp or other area to give better drainage.

Dred Scott Case. The famous case of Scott v Sanford (US) 19 How 393, 15 L Ed 691, holding that the United States courts had no jurisdiction over the question as to whether slaves who had been permitted to pass from the state of their domicil into a free state acquired thereby a right to freedom after their return to the state of their domicil, but that the courts of the latter state alone could decide as to their status or condition as free or slave.

dreit dreit (drea drea). Same as **droit droit.**

dreng. A tenant in capite; that is, a tenant who held his land immediately of the king.

drengage (dreng'āj). The land tenure of a dreng.

dressing. The clothing of a person. An application of drugs or materials to a wound for the purpose of hastening healing and preventing infection. The preparation of a carcass to make it edible and tasty. The process is concluded when the meat is placed in the cooler; it does not include packing, loading, grading, or shipping. Fleming v Swift & Co. (DC Ill) 41 F Supp 825, affd (CA7) 131 F2d 249.

DRIFTING [377] DROIT

drifting. Moving with the wind. The movement of cattle undirected by man, often prompted by weather conditions. In mining parlance, taking earth, gravel, or ore from a position made accessible by means of a tunnel. It is not the same as running a tunnel, which is construction work. Jurgenson v Diller, 114 Cal 491, 493, 46 P 610.

driftland (drift'land). An annual tribute paid by certain tenants for the privilege of driving their cattle through a manor.

drift of the forest. A driving together of all the cattle in a forest at certain stated periods for much the same purposes as those of a modern "round-up" in the western parts of the United States.

driftway. A common way for driving cattle. Swenson v Marino, 306 Mass 582, 29 NE2d 15, 130 ALR 763.

driller's lien. A special lien to a person contributing labor or materials toward the drilling of a gas and oil well. 24 Am J1st Gas & O § 114.

drilling. Making a hole in wood, metal, or other substance; penetrating the earth for oil or gas; preparing a cavity in a tooth for a filling.
See **turn key job.**

drilling fluid. See **rotary drilling.**

drill stem. See **rotary drilling.**

drink. A liquid beverage of any kind, except as the context in which the word appears indicates an alcoholic beverage. 30 Am J Rev ed Intox L § 8. The portion of an alcoholic beverage consumed at one time. A court will take judicial notice that a "drink" of intoxicating liquor is less than one quart in volume. Sappington v Carter, 67 Ill 482, 485.

As used in a town ordinance prohibiting the sale of "drinks" on Sunday, the word was held to include any soft drink usually sold as a beverage, but not to include water, coffee, tea, milk or anything not classed as a beverage. Coca-cola was held to be among the prohibited potations. State v Weddington, 188 NC 643, 125 SE 257, 37 ALR 573.

drinkable. Literally, capable of being drunk, but more practicably, suitable for drinking, that is, potable. Anno: 11 ALR 1237.

drinks. See **drink.**

drip. The falling of rain-water from the eaves of a house.
See **eaves-drip.**

drive. To compel, urge, or control movement in some manner or direction, for example, a team of horses or a herd of cattle. Howell v J. Mandelbaum & Sons, 160 Iowa 119, 122, 140 NW 397.
See **driving a motor vehicle.**

drive-in. A development of the automobile age, wherein a business, such as a bank, a lunch room, a confectionery, or an ice cream vendor, serves its customers in their automobiles driven upon the premises.

drive-in theater. A place of entertainment, peculiar in the fact that the patrons drive their automobiles into an enclosure within good view of the screen or stage and view the picture or performance from their seats in the vehicle.

drive-it-yourself system. The business of renting out motor vehicles without drivers. 13 Am J2d Car § 18.
See **renting automobiles.**

drive other cars clause. A clause in an automobile liability policy which protects the named assured in using an automobile other than the one described in the policy. 7 Am J2d Auto Ins § 105.

driver's license. See **operator's license.**

driver's training. Instruction in driving an automobile, obtained as a preliminary to the test for a license or required under a judgment rendered in a prosecution for violation of the Motor Vehicle Law.

driving a motor vehicle. Controlling the motive power. Commonwealth v Crowninshield, 187 Mass 221, 72 NE 963. More precisely, controlling the motive power or movement of a motor vehicle in motion, albeit the movement be only a few feet. 7 Am J2d Auto § 256.
See **driving while intoxicated; operating motor vehicle; reckless driving.**

driving range. An area, usually a part of a regular golf course, wherein golfers may practice driving the ball.

driving while intoxicated. A criminal offense, known in some jurisdictions as drunken driving, or driving while under the influence of intoxicating liquor or of drugs, the elements of which are the control of a motor vehicle by the accused while it is in movement under power within his control, and while the accused is intoxicated, in an intoxicated condition, under the influence of intoxicating liquor, intoxicated or in any degree under the influence of intoxicating liquor, the statutes varying in the terms which describe the condition of the driver contemplated by the legislature in determining the nature of the conduct to be proscribed. 7 Am J2d Auto §§ 253 et seq.
See **operation of motor vehicle while intoxicated.**

drofland. Same as **driftland.**

droit (drwo). (French.) A right. Opel v Shoup, 100 Iowa 407, 69 NW 560.

droit administratif (drwo ad-mĕ-nĕs-trä-tēf'). The French system of administrative law based upon the principle of freedom of administrative action in the determination of causes growing out of the relationship of government to individuals. 1 Am J2d Admin L § 9.

droit commun (drwo ko-mūn). The common law.

droit d'accroissement (drwo d'a-kroa-s-mān). The right of survivorship.

droit d'ainesse (drwo d'ê-nè-s). A birthright.

droit d'aubaine (drwo d'o-bān). The right of a stranger,—the right assumed and exercised by the French government of seizing and confiscating all of the real and personal property situate in France and belonging to an alien who dies in that country. Opel v Shoup, 100 Iowa 407, 69 NW 560.
See **jus albinatus.**

droit de corvees (drwo dĕ kŏr-ve'). A right to feudal service.

droit de déshérence (drwo dĕ de'ze'ran-s). The right of escheat.

droit de detraction. (French.) A tax levied upon the removal from one country to another of property acquired by succession or testamentary disposition. 28 Am J Rev ed Inher T § 36. A survival from medieval European law. Melson v Johnson, 279 US 47, 73 L Ed 607.

droit d'eignesse (drwo dān-yes). The right of the eldest.

droit des gens (drwo dā zhǫn). (French.) The law of nations; international law.

droit de suit (drwo dē sui). A person's right to pursue the property of his debtor in the hands of a third party; stoppage in transitu.
See **stoppage in transitu**.

droit d'execution (drwo d'eks-e-kū'sion). The right of a broker to sell what he has bought for his principal for the account of his principal after the latter has refused to accept delivery.

droit droit (drwo drwo). A double right consisting of the right of possession joined with the right of property. It is an ancient maxim of the law that no title is completely good without this double right. See 2 Bl Comm 199.

droit écrit (drwo ê-cri). The written law,—statute law.

droit international (drwo in-ter-năc-ion-al). International law.

droit ne done pluis que soit demaunde (drwo né dōn pluî kĕ soa dē-män-de'). The law gives no more than is demanded.

droit ne poet pas morier (drwo né poa' pa mō-ri-e'). Right cannot die.

droits civils (drwot si-vil). Civil or private rights.

droits of admiralty (drwot of admiralty). The rights of the admiralty,—goods which have been abandoned found at sea; goods captured in time of war by a non-commissioned ship.

droitural (droi'tū-ral). Concerning or pertaining to a person's right or title to property, as distinguished from his right to the possession of it.

droitural action (droi'tū-ral ak'shǫn). An action to recover land of which the plaintiff had lost both the possession and the right thereto.

drop letter (drop'let"ĕr). A letter posted for delivery by the local post office.

drover (drō'vĕr). A buyer of cattle for a distant market. A person taking cattle to market or in charge of cattle being taken to market.

drove road. A road where cattle may be driven.

drover's pass. A pass for free transportation on a railroad train of a person in charge of a shipment of livestock. The status of the person carried is that of a passenger for hire. 14 Am J2d Car § 756.

drug. Broadly defined, any substance used as a medicine or in the composition of medicine for internal or external use, including patent and proprietary remedies that possess or are reputed to possess curative or remedial properties. Kelly v Carroll, 36 Wash 2d 482, 219 P2d 79. Technically, articles recognized in the official United States Pharmacopoeia, official Homeopathic Pharmacopoeia of the United States, or official National Formulary, or any supplement to any of them; articles intended for use in the diagnosis, cure, mitigation, treatment or prevention of disease in man or other animals; articles, other than food, intended to affect the structure or any function of the body of man or other animals; and articles intended for use as a component of any articles specified in the foregoing clauses. 21 USC § 321(G), a part of the Federal Food, Drug and Cosmetic Act.
See **Food, Drug, and Cosmetic Act; medicine; narcotics**.

druggist. Essentially a dealer in drugs, who acquires a professional standing by being licensed as a pharmacist, pharmaceutical chemist, a druggist, or an apothecary; one qualified by education and training to compound drugs and fill prescriptions. 25 Am J2d Drugs § 4. Narrowly defined, one who deals in uncompounded medicinal substances, vegetable, animal or mineral. State v Holmes, 28 La Ann 765.

druggists' liability insurance. A policy protecting a druggist against liability for injury or sickness resulting from malpractice, error, or mistake. 29A Am J Rev ed Ins § 1358.

drugless therapeutics (drugless ther-a-pū'tiks). Hydrotherapy, dietetics, electrotherapy, radiography, sanitation, suggestion, or mechanical and manual manipulation for the stimulation of physiological and psychological action to establish a normal condition of mind and body, but in no way including the giving, prescribing or recommending of pharmaceutic drugs and poisons for internal use. Kelly v Carroll, 36 Wash 2d 482, 219 P2d 79, 19 ALR2d 1174.

drum. An instrument played as one of the instruments of a band or orchestra, being so constructed as to present a taut membrane to be beaten by a small stick, known as a drumstick. A container in the shape of a keg or barrel, usually made of steel, and used for holding explosive or inflammable liquids.

drumhead court-martial. A summary military trial.

drummer. A musician whose instrument is a drum. A traveling salesman in the sense of one who solicits order but carries no stock, except samples, and makes no deliveries. Re Wilson (Dist Col) 8 Mackey 341; Thomas v Hot Springs, 34 Ark 553.

drunk. One in a state of drunkenness; a drunkard; an habitual drunkard.
See **drunkard; habitual drunkard; drunkenness**.

drunkard. A person given to inebriety and the excessive use of intoxicating liquor, who has lost the power or will, by frequent indulgence, to control his appetite for it. 29A Am J Rev ed Ins § 1230. The definition is sometimes extended to include excessive use of either intoxicating liquor or narcotics. Re House, 23 Colo 87, 46 P 117.
See **habitual drunkard**.

drunken driving. See **driving while intoxicated**.

drunkenness. That state or condition of a person which inevitably follows from taking excessive quantities of an intoxicant, meaning to some men the condition of being under the influence of an intoxicant to such an extent as to render one helpless, to others a lesser degree of effect, even a slight influence. 30 Am J Rev ed Intox L § 21.
See **habitual drunkenness; intoxication**.

drunk-o-meter. An instrument to determine the intoxication or extent of intoxication by exposing the breath to chemicals, thereby determining the amount of alcohol in the system. Hill v State, 158 Tex Crim 313, 256 SW2d 93.

dry. Want of moisture. A term applied to one who is opposed to traffic in alcoholic beverages and advocates legislation and strict law enforcement to put an end to it. State v Shumaker, 200 Ind 623, 157 NE 769, 58 ALR 954.

dry-craeft. Witchcraft.

dry dock. A watertight dock provided with machinery for pumping out the water in order that a

docked vessel may be repaired. Maryland Casualty Co. v Lawson (CA5 Fla) 101 F2d 732. All injuries suffered by the hulls of vessels below the water line by collision or stranding must necessarily be repaired in a dry dock, to prevent the inflow of water. While the vessel is in such a dock, she is not on land and is within the jurisdiction of the admiralty court. Perry v Haines, 191 US 17, 33, 48 L Ed 73, 80, 24 S Ct 8.
See **graving dock**.

dry exchange. A pretended exchange of property employed to conceal a transaction which was in fact usurious.

dry gas. Gas produced by an oil well, from which the gasoline has been removed, thereby rendering it fit for use for the purposes of heat and power. Standard Oil Co. v United States (CA9 Cal) 107 F2d 402.

dry goods. Textiles; cloth. Levy v Friedlander, 24 La Ann 439, 441.
Sometimes considered broadly as including everything in a stock of general merchandise, except groceries.

dry law. A statute prohibiting the manufacture, sale or other disposition of intoxicating liquors.

dry mortgage. A mortgage containing a provision that there shall be no personal liability on the part of the mortgagor for the payment of the obligation secured by the mortgage, beyond the value of the mortgaged property. Frowenfeld v Hastings, 134 Cal 128, 66 P 178.

dry rent. Rent seck,—a rent reserved by deed, without the covenant or clause of distress. 32 Am J1st L & T § 1040.

dry territory. A term peculiar to liquor law, having reference to a county or lesser political subdivision in which, by virtue of local option, the traffic in intoxicating beverages is prohibited.

dry trust. A trust in which the trustee has no duties to perform, and in which the cestui que trust has the entire management of the estate. 54 Am J1st Trusts § 13. A voting trust of corporate stock in which the trustees have no beneficial interest and concerning which they have no duties other than to vote the stock. Anno: 98 ALR2d 387 § 9.
See **passive trust**.

d/s. An abbreviation of day's sight, as used in negotiable instruments. Thus, 30 d/s would mean 30 days after sight.

d. s. b. Abbreviation of **debitum sine breve**.

d. s. b. judgment. An abbreviation of judgment debitum sine brevi.

D. Sc. Abbreviation of Doctor of Science.

D. S. T. Abbreviation of daylight saving time.

dual agency. A situation where an agent is acting for both parties to a transaction. 29 Am J Rev ed Ins § 140. A reprehensible practice in acting for both parties to a transaction, without disclosing the dual representation to both parties. 3 Am J2d Agency § 233.

dual citizenship. A status long recognized in law as existing where a person is claimed as a subject or citizen or two states. The concept recognizes that a person may have and exercise rights of nationality in two countries and be subject to the responsibilities of both. 3 Am J2d Aliens § 118. One nation may claim his allegiance because of his birth within its territory, and the other demand it because at the time of his birth in foreign territory his parents were its nationals. Perkins v Elg, 307 US 325, 83 L Ed 1320, 59 S Ct 884.

dual nationality. See **dual citizenship**.

duarchy (dū'är-ki). A government with two rulers.

Duas uxores eodem tempore habere non licet (du'ās ux-ōr'ēz e-ō'dem tem'po-re hā-bē're non lī'set). It is unlawful to have two wives at the same time. See 1 Bl Comm 436.

Duas uxores eodem tempore habere non potest (du'ās ux-ōr'ēz e-ō'dem tem'po-re hā'bē-re non po'test). A man cannot have two wives at the same time.

dub. An abbreviation of **dubitatur**,—it is doubted. To confer a title, a name, or a nickname.

dubii juris (dūb'ī-ī jū'ris). Of doubtful right or law.

dubitans (dū'bi-tạns). Doubting.

dubitante (du-bi-tan'te). Doubting.

dubitatur (du-bi-tā'ter). It is doubted; it is doubtful.

dubitavit (du-bi-tā'vit). He has doubted; he doubted.

duces tecum (dū'sēz tē'kum). Bring with you.
See **subpoena duces tecum**.

duces tecum licet languidus (du'sēz tē'kum lī'set lan'-gwi-dus). A writ which lay to bring a person into court notwithstanding his illness.

duchy court of Lancaster (duch'i kōrt). A court of equity of special jurisdiction in cases relating to lands held of the king in right of the Duchy of Lancaster.

Ducitur in absurdum (dū'si-ter in ab-ser'dum). It is led into absurdity. Nichols v Fearson (US) 7 Pet 103, 110, 8 L Ed 623, 626.

ducking stool. Also called a cucking stool. A stool or chair upon which a defendant was placed to be plunged three times in the water as a punishment under the early common law for the offense of being a common scold. 15 Am J2d Comm S § 3.

due. Owing; payable. The United States v State Bank of North Carolina (US) 6 Pet 29, 36, 8 L Ed 308, 311; Allen v Patterson, 7 NY 476; currently payable. 6 Am J2d Attach § 264. Fitting; suitable.

due bill. An acknowledgment of a debt in writing. Erickson v Sophy, 10 SD 71, 74, 71 NW 758.

due care. Care according to the circumstances of the case. 38 Am J1st Negl § 29. That degree of care which a man of ordinary prudence would exercise in similar circumstances. Gahagan v Boston & Maine Railroad, 70 NH 441, 50 A 146. As the term appears in an exception from the risk in an accident insurance policy, it means the measure of caution and care that would be required of a reasonably prudent man in like circumstances. 29A Am J Rev ed Ins § 1160.
See **due diligence; ordinary care; reasonable care**.

due compensation. Just compensation; the compensation to which a person is entitled. As the term is used in the law of eminent domain, it means the compensation which ought to be made; that is, compensation which will make the owner whole pecuniarily for the appropriation or injury of his property by an invasion of it cognizable by the senses, or by interference with some right in relation to property whereby its market value is lessened as the direct result of the public use. King v

Vicksburg Railway & Light Co. 88 Miss 456, 42 So 204.

due consideration. Giving such thought or weight to a fact as it merits under all the circumstances of the case. New York Tel. Co. v James, 309 NY 569, 132 NE2d 850.

due course. The ordinary course of events; not highlighted by unusual or extraordinary events.
See **holder in due course.**

due course holder. Same as **holder in due course.**

due course of justice. The due course of proceedings in the administration of justice, whether leading to a judgment for the plaintiff or a judgment for the defendant, whether to an acquittal or conviction. 39 Am J1st Obst J § 1.

due course of law. According to the law of the land; due process of law. Hanson v Krehbiel, 68 Kan 670, 75 P 1041.
See **due process of law; remedy by due course of law.**

due course of trade. In the ordinary course of business. The circumstances attendant upon a transaction in the ordinary course of business, such as a sale and payment of the price comtemporaneously.

due course of transit. Property being carried with the intent to deliver it at a specific destination. Anno: 80 ALR2d 447.
See **deviation from route.**

due course payment. See **payment in due course.**

due date (dū dāt). The date on which a promissory note or other obligation, by its terms, falls due.

due-days (dū′dāz). Same as **boom-days.**

due diligence. Constancy or steadiness of purpose or labor by men who desire a speedy accomplishment of their purposes and such assiduity in the prosecution of the enterprize as manifest to the world a bona fide intention to complete the task within a reasonable time. Ophir Silver Mining Co. v Carpenter, 4 Nev 534. In reference to conduct negativing negligence or contributory negligence, that amount of diligence which a reasonable and prudent man would exercise under the circumstances. Perry v Cedar Falls, 87 Iowa 315, 316. As a prerequisite to a continuance on the ground of the absence of a witness, due diligence in attempting to procure the attendance of the witness means that a party avail himself of the means provided by law, when practicable, to force the attendance of the witness. Fritsch v J. M. English Truck Line, Inc. 151 Tex 168, 246 SW2d 856.
See **due care.**

due east. A compass point, directly east. 23 Am J2d Deeds § 248.

due in advance. A clause used in loan contracts, requiring payment of interest in advance. 30 Am J Rev ed Int § 12.

duel. A combat with deadly weapons between two persons, according to the terms of a precedent agreement and under certain agreed and prescribed rules. Ward v Commonwealth, 132 Ky 636, 116 SW 786; Griffin v State, 100 Tex Crim 641, 274 SW 11. A criminal offense under modern law. 25 Am J2d Duel § 1.

duelling (dū′el-ing). Fighting a duel.
See **duel.**

duello (dū-el′ō). A duel.

duellum (dū-el′lum). A duel.

due north. A compass point, directly north. 23 Am J2d Deeds § 248.

due notice. Sufficient notice. The notice prescribed by law in the case of where notice is prescribed. Where a statute requires notice to be given, it is the general rule of law that actual personal notice is required, and the notice must be personally served on the person to be notified. 39 Am J1st Notice § 9. Due notice of a trial upon charges made against a person, means that he is to be put upon trial at a specified time upon specified charges; and the notice must be given in season to afford him a reasonable opportunity to make preparation to meet the charges by summoning witnesses in his behalf. Brennan v United Hatters of North America, 73 NJL 729, 65 A 165.
See **due process of law; due publication.**

due process. See **due process of law.**

due process of law. A phrase impossible of precise definition; one which asserts a fundamental principle of justice rather than a specific rule of law. 16 Am J2d Const L § 545. Law in the regular course of administration through courts of justice according to those rules and forms which have been established for the protection of private rights. Endicott-Johnson Corp. v Smith, 266 US 291, 69 L Ed 293, 45 S Ct 63.

"Due process of law" implies and comprehends the administration of laws equally applicable to all under established rules which do not violate fundamental principles of private rights, and in a competent tribunal possessing jurisdiction of the cause and proceeding by hearing upon notice. State ex rel. Sweezer v Green, 360 Mo 1249, 232 SW2d 897, 24 ALR2d 340. "Due process of law" requires in each case an evaluation based on a disinterested inquiry pursued in the spirit of science, on a balanced order of facts exactly and fairly stated, on the detached consideration of conflicting claims, and on a judgment not ad hoc and episodic but duly mindful of reconciling the needs both of continuity and of change in any progressive society. Rochin v California, 342 US 165, 96 L Ed 183, 72 S Ct 205, 25 ALR2d 1396.

One of the most famous and perhaps the most often quoted definition of "due process of law" is that given by Daniel Webster in his argument in the Dartmouth College case (Dartmouth College v Woodward (US) 4 Wheat 518, 4 L Ed 629), wherein he declared that by due process of law was meant "the law which hears before it condemns; which proceeds upon inquiry, and renders judgment only after trial.
See **day in court; deprivation without due process; hearing; law of the land; life, liberty and property; life, liberty and the pursuit of happiness.**

due proof. Sufficient proof.
See **due proof of loss; sufficient evidence.**

due proof of loss. As required by an insurance policy, reasonable and satisfactory proof; a proof which makes out a prima facie case against the insurer by furnishing information which is substantial and trustworthy enough to enable the insurer to form an intelligent estimate. 29A Am J Rev ed Ins § 1403. Evidence proper in form and sufficient in character to indicate the truth of the facts stated and to show the happening of the event upon which the insurer agreed to pay the loss or claim. Howe v National Life Ins. Co. 321 Mass 283, 72 NE2d 425, 170 ALR 1254.

due publication. A publication in the manner and form and for the time required by law. Laugel v Bushnell, 197 Ill 20, 63 NE 1086.

due regard. See **due consideration**.

due regard for the safety of others. See **due care**.

dues. Annual or other regular payments made by a member of an association, club, society, or fraternal order. The sums of money which a member of a mutual benefit society or benevolent association must pay toward the support of the society in order to retain his membership therein. 36 Am J2d Frat O § 80. The term has been used in the unusual sense of contract obligations, even liability for torts. Whitman v National Bank of Oxford, 176 US 559, 44 L Ed 587, 590, 20 S Ct 477.

due south. A compass point, directly south. 23 Am J2d Deeds § 248.

due to conditions of employment. A phrase in a workmen's compensation statute which serves to emphasize the necessity for a causal relationship between the employment and the injury. 58 Am J1st Workm Comp § 209.

due west. A compass point, directly west. 23 Am J2d Deeds § 248.

duke. A leader; an English hereditary title which is next in rank below that of a prince.

dulocracy (dū-lok′ra̧-si). A government by slaves.

duly. The word has acquired a fixed legal meaning, and when used before any word implying action, it means that the act was done properly, regularly, and according to law. It is often used before such words as "convened," "arrested," "qualified," "served," "presented," "discharged," and many others, and in such cases it has the meaning of the word "legally" or "properly," "according to law." O'Donnell v People, 224 Ill 218, 79 NE 639. Citing Am & Eng Encyc of Law.

duly adjudged. Adjudged according to law,—that is, according to the statute governing the subject, and implying the existence of every fact essential to perfect regularity of procedure, and to confer jurisdiction both of the subject matter and of the parties affected by the judgment. Any step in the cause before the court is necessarily the exercise of jurisdiction, and that step cannot be "duly" taken unless jurisdiction exists. The final step—in particular, the making of the judgment—cannot be "duly" taken unless all of the preliminary steps upon which it is based have likewise been "duly" taken. Brownell v Greenwich, 114 NY 518, 22 NE 24.

duly authorized agent. An agent with authority either express or implied to act in a particular situation, for example, the receiving of notice or proof of loss. 29A Am J Rev ed Ins § 1398.

duly negotiated. Commercial paper transferred from one person to another in such manner and form that the transferee becomes the holder thereof. Uniform Negotiable Instruments Act § 30. The negotiation of a negotiable document of title in the manner stated in the Uniform Commercial Code to a holder who purchases it in good faith without notice of any defense against or claim to it on the part of any person and for value, unless it is established that the negotiation is not in the regular course of business or financing, or that it involves receiving the document in settlement or payment of a money obligation. UCC § 7-501(4).

duly performed. Fully performed.

In some jurisdictions, where the statute permits a party in a contract action to allege generally that he has "duly performed" all of the conditions on his part, if he would avail himself of this provision, he must comply strictly with the statute, and the omission of the word "duly" would seem fatal. Accordingly, a substitution of the word "substantially" for the word "duly" was held to be an insufficient allegation of performance. Lusk Lumber Co. v Independent Producers Consol. 35 Wyo 381, 249 P 790.

duly recorded. The term not only imports that the instrument has been filed for record and copied in the proper record book of the registrar, but also that it was in form and substance an instrument which was by law entitled to be recorded. See Marden v Dorthy, 160 NY 39, 54 NE 726.

duly sworn. Having been put under oath, before an officer authorized to administer oaths, in the manner and form required by law. Garner v State, 28 Fla 113. An allegation that one did depose and swear is not the equivalent of alleging that being "duly sworn," he did depose and say. A man may depose as well before an oath has been administered to him as afterwards. Likewise a person may "swear" who is not duly sworn. United States v M'Conaughy (DC Or) 33 F 168, 169.

See **swear**.

dum. While; as long as; in so far as.

dumb. Lacking the power of speech. Mute. Such disability is not one of mental incapacity. A colloquial expression for stupid.

dumb-bidding. Bidding at an auction sale where all bids below a previously arranged secret figure are to be rejected by the auctioneer.

dum bene se gesserit (dum be′ne sē jes′se-rit). As long as he should well behave himself,—during good behavior. 43 Am J1st Pub Of § 156.

dumboc. Same as **Dome Book**. See 1 Bl Comm 46.

dumb person. See **deaf mute**; **dumb**.

dumb waiter. A small elevator or lift in a house for sending food, laundry, trash, etc. from one floor to another. A serving table.

dum fervet opus (dum fer′vet ō′pus). While the work is going on; during the transaction.

dum fuit infra aetatem (dum fu′it in′fra ē-tā′tem). While he was under age.

dum fuit in prisona (dum fu′it in pri′zō-na). While he was in prison,—a writ to recover land conveyed under duress of imprisonment.

dum fuit non compos mentis suae, ut dicit (dum fu′it non kom′pos men′tis su′ē, ut dī′sit). While he was of unsound mind, as he says. See 2 Bl Comm 291.

dummodo (dum-mō′dō). Provided; provided that.

dummodo constat de persona (dum-mō′dō kon′stat dē per-sō′na). Provided that it is clear as to the person.

dummy. One posing or represented as acting for himself, but in reality acting for another; a tool or straw man for the real parties in interest.

dummy corporation. A corporation organized and acting ostensibly as a corporation, but in reality having no real corporate purpose, having been organized with the motive of avoiding personal liability on the part of the incorporator and sole stockholder. Chesapeake Stone Co. v Holbrook, 168 Ky 128, 181 SW 953.

dummy director. A person who, although nominally a director of a corporation is a mere figurehead and discharges no duties. Goldenrod Mining Co. v Bukvich, 108 Mont 569, 92 P2d 316. A person to whom a share of stock in a corporation is transferred in order to qualify him as a director. Hoopes v Basic Co. 69 NJ Eq 679, 61 A 979.

dummy engine. A small railroad locomotive used only in the yards of a railroad or on the tracks of an industrial plant, sometimes having a muffled exhaust. Birmingham Mineral Railroad Co. v Jacobs, 92 Ala 187, 9 So 320.

dum non fuit compos mentis (dum non fu'it kom'pōs men'tis). While he was of unsound mind.

dump. Noun: The place where the accumulated refuse of a city or center of population is dumped. Bruce v Kansas City, 128 Kan 13, 276 P 284, 63 ALR 325. Verb: To throw away; to unload in a heap, as rubbish.
See **dumping; mine dump.**

dumping. The sale in the United States of foreign merchandise at less than its fair value. 21 Am J2d Cust D § 15. Cutting the price of merchandise for a quick sale. Unloading a truck filled with heavy material such as coal or ore; unloading refuse at a dump.
See **dump.**

Dumpor's Case. An old English case from which there was developed the rule that once the condition upon which an estate was granted is waived and therefore gone, it is gone forever. 28 Am J2d Est § 169.

dump truck. A truck equipped so that the power of the motor can be applied to unloading the vehicle by raising the front end of the body, thereby permitting the contents of the load to slide out. A motor vehicle. Anno: 77 ALR2d 948.

dum recens fuit maleficium (dum re'senz fu'it ma-lefi'she-um). While the offense was fresh or recent.

dum sola (dum sō'la). While unmarried.

dum sola et casta vixerit (dum sō'la et kas'ta vix'erit). While she shall live unmarried and chaste.

dun. A statement of account with request for payment.
See **bum-bailiff.**

dunces. See **parliament of dunces.**

dungeon (dun'jun). An underground prison or cell of a prison.

dunnage. Material for the packing or shoring of a ship's cargo. 21 Am J2d Cust D § 49. Chips, planks, boughs, and other pieces of wood placed in the bottom of the hold of a vessel to keep the cargo above the water which collects in the hold. Materials used to steady the cargo and prevent one part from rubbing against another. Great Western Insurance Co. v Thwing (US) 13 Wall 672, 20 L Ed 607.

duodecemvirale judicium (du-ō-de-sem-vi-rā'le jū-di'she-um). A trial by twelve men, a trial by jury.

duodecima manus (du-ō-de'si-ma man'us). The twelfth hand; twelve hands. The term was used to refer to the twelve right hands of the eleven compurgators and the defendant himself which were raised when the twelve were sworn in a trial by wager of law. See 3 Bl Comm 343.

duodena (du-ō-dē'na). A jury composed of twelve men.

duodenitis (dū"ō-dẹ-nī'tis). A bodily ailment consisting of the stricture or obstruction of the duodenum, sometimes caused by an external physical injury, such as a fall or a twisting of the body, and often causing death. See United States Mutual Accident Association v Barry, 131 US 100, 109, 33 L Ed 60, 64, 9 S Ct 755.

duo non possunt in solido unam rem possidere (du'ō non pos'sunt in so'li-dō ū'nam rem pos-si-dē're). Two persons cannot each possess one thing exclusively.

duorum in solidum dominium vel possessio esse non potest (du-ō'rum in so'li-dum do-mi'ni-um vel po-ze'she-ō es'se non po'test). Sole ownership or possession cannot be in two persons.

duo sunt instrumenta ad omnes res aut confirmandas aut impugnandas,—ratio et auctoritas (du'ō sunt in-stru-men'ta ad om'nēz rēz ât kon-fir-man'das ât im-pug-nan'das,—rā'she-ō et âk-tō'ri-tas). There are two instrumentalities for the confirmation or repudiation of all things,—reason and authority.

duplex (dū'pleks). A dwelling or apartment house consisting of two family units. One of the units of a two-family house or apartment.

duplex querela (dū'pleks kwe-rē'la). A double complaint; an appeal from an ordinary to his next superior, as from the decision of a bishop to an archbishop. See 3 Bl Comm 247.

duplex valor maritagii (du'pleks va'lor ma-ri-tā'ji-ī). Double the value of the maritagium. The amount of the penalty which a ward had to pay if he married without his guardian's consent and thus cut off the guardian's maritagium. See 2 Bl Comm 70.

duplicate (dū'pli-kāt). Verb: To make an exact copy or double of something. Noun: The double of anything. Lorch v Page, 97 Conn 66, 115 A 681, 24 ALR 1204, 1206. An instrument, sometimes called a duplicate original, of exact identity with another instrument, executed as an original the same as the other instrument, and having all the legal effect of an original. Anno: 24 ALR 1209; 17 Am J2d Contr § 284; 50 Am J1st Stat § 289. The most significant distinction between a mere copy and a duplicate or duplicate original is that the best evidence rule, which applies to a copy does not apply to a duplicate. 29 Am J2d Ev § 487. The better view is that the different numbers or impressions of a writing produced by placing carbon paper between sheets of paper and writing upon the exposed surface are duplicate originals, of which any may be introduced in evidence without accounting for the nonproduction of the others. Maston v Glen Lumber Co. 65 Okla 80, 163 P 128; 29 Am J2d Ev § 488.

duplicate bill. See **bills in a set; duplicate bill of lading; duplicate paper.**

duplicate bill of lading. An extra copy of a bill of lading made for the convenience and information of consignor or consignee, which, under statute, must bear the word "duplicate" or some other word or words appropriate to show that the document is not an original bill. 13 Am J2d Car § 268.

duplicate paper. A substitute for a negotiable instrument which has been lost, destroyed, or mutilated. 11 Am J2d B & N § 59.
See **bills in a set.**

duplicate taxation. Same as **double taxation.**

duplicate will. A will which has been executed in duplicate so that the two copies can be placed in the hands of different persons. 57 Am J1st Wills § 495.
See **double wills; reciprocal wills.**

duplicatio (du-pli-kā'she-ō). A Roman law pleading corresponding to the common-law rejoinder, being the defendant's reply to the actor's replicatio. See 3 Bl Comm 310.
See **rejoinder.**

duplication. The making of a duplicate. In admiralty, a pleading replying to the replication of the defendant.

duplicationem possibilitatis lex non patitur (du-pli-kā-she-ō'nem pos-si-bi''li-tā'tis lex non pā'ti-ter). The law does not permit the doubling of a possibility.

duplicatum jus (du-pli-kā'tum jūs). A double right.

duplicem valorem maritagii (du'pli-sem va-lō'rem ma-ri-tā'ji-ī). See **duplex valor maritagii.**

duplicitous (dū-plis'i-tus). See **duplicity; duplicity in indictment or information; duplicity in pleading.**

duplicity. Deception, particularly in double dealing.
See **duplicity in indictment or information; duplicity in pleading.**

duplicity in indictment or information. Charging two different and distinct offenses in one count. Frohwerk v United States, 249 US 204, 63 L Ed 561, 39 S Ct 249; 27 Am J1st Indict § 124.

duplicity in pleading. A defect in pleading as in violation of the rules which tend to produce singleness or unity in the issue. A declaration, complaint, or petition is duplicitous where it joins in one and the same count different grounds of action of different natures, or of the same nature, to enforce a single right of recovery; or where it is based on different theories of the defendant's liability. A plea or answer is bad for duplicity if it contains more than one independent fact, or set of facts, any of which alone is a sufficient answer to the declaration, complaint, or petition, and this, whether the defense is in abatement, in bar, or both. 41 Am J1st Pl §§ 44, 45.
See **duplicity in indictment or information.**

duplo. See **in duplo.**

duply (dū-plī'). A Scotch pleading corresponding to the rejoinder of the common law, being the same as the Roman law **duplicatio.**

dura lex scripta tamen (dū'ra lex skrip'ta ta'men). Harsh though it be, the law is thus written. Landry v American Creosote Works, 119 La 231, 43 So 1016.

durante (du-ran'te). During; pending.

durante absentia (du-ran'te ab-sen'she-a). See **administration durante absentia; administrator of absentee.**

durante animo vitio administrator. See **administrator animo vitio.**

durante bene placito (dū-ran'tē bē'nę plas'i-tō). During the pleasure. Before the statute 13 William III, c. 2, the judges of the superior courts held their offices at the pleasure of the king. See 1 Bl Comm 267. It seems also that a sheriff might be appointed during the pleasure of the king. See 1 Bl Comm 342.

durante furore (du-ran'te fu-rō're). During the period of a person's insanity.

durante itinere (du-ran'te ī-ti'ne-re). During the time when a person is on a journey.

durante minore aetate (du-ran'te mī-nō're ē-tā'te). During the age of minority.

durante minoritate administrator (du-ran'te mi-nō-ri-tā'te ad-min-is-trā-tōr). See **administrator durante minoritate administratoris.**

durante minoritate administratoris. See **administrator durante minoritate administratoris.**

durante viduitate (du-ran'te vi-du-i-tā'te). During widowhood, while she was a widow. See 2 Bl Comm 124.

durante virginitate (dū-ran'te vir-ji-ni-tā'te). During virginity,—during the time a woman remains unmarried.

durante vita (dū-ran'tē vī'tą). During a person's lifetime.

duration. The period of existence, People v Hill, 7 Cal 97; continuance in time; the portion of time during which anything exists. Hence, a statute providing that a session should be "limited to sixty days' duration" means sixty days counting one after another, including Sundays, holidays, and any days of temporary adjournment. Cheyney v Smith, 3 Ariz 143, 23 P 680.

duration of risk. The extent of time within which the losses covered by a policy of insurance must occur in order for the insurer to be liable. 29 Am J Rev ed Ins § 317. The period of time between the effective date of the policy and the termination of the risk by expiration of the period of coverage, cancellation of the policy, or breach of condition.

duration of war. In a legal sense the period continuing to and terminating at the time of a formal proclamation of peace by competent authorities; in common usage by laymen, the period of time terminating on the cessation of actual hostilities. When such term is used in a contract the meaning to be attributed is one of intent of the parties to be determined upon the consideration of the instrument itself and evidence produced as to the circumstances surrounding its execution and the purposes which the party sought to accomplish. Malbone Garage v Minkin, 272 App Div 109, 72 NYS2d 327, affd 297 NY 677, 76 NE2d 331.

duress. Any wrongful act of one person that compels a manifestation of apparent assent by another to a transaction without his volition. Compulsion or restraint by which a person is illegally forced to do, or forbear from doing, some act. 25 Am J2d Dur § 1. A species of fraud in which compulsion in some form takes the place of deception. 25 Am J2d Dur § 1. As a defense in a criminal prosecution, a present, imminent, and impending coercion of such a nature as to induce a well-grounded apprehension of death or serious bodily injury if the act is not done. 21 Am J2d Crim L § 100.
The existence of duress is to be determined by the subjective standard of whether the free will of the victim was, rather than whether that of a person of ordinary courage and firmness would be, overcome thereby. Wise v Midtown Motors, 231 Minn 46, 42 NW2d 404, 20 ALR2d 735.
See **business compulsion; coercion; undue influence.**

duress by imprisonment. See **duress of imprisonment.**

duress by public utility. The exaction of a payment demanded for services under threat of terminating service, thereby causing great injury to the property or business of the customer. 25 Am J2d Dur § 8.

duress by threat. See **duress per minas.**

duress of family. See **duress per minas.**

duress of goods. See **duress of property.**

duress of imprisonment. An arrest for improper purposes without just cause; an arrest for a just cause but without lawful authority; an arrest for a just cause and under lawful authority for an improper purpose; or ill treatment of a prisoner under imprisonment originally lawful. 25 Am J2d Dur § 4.

duress of property. The refusal of one in possession or control of property of another to surrender the possession or control of it to the owner except upon compliance with an unlawful demand. A contract made by the owner under such circumstances to emancipate the property is to be regarded as made under compulsion and duress and is voidable by the owner. 25 Am J2d Dur § 5. A contract procured by threats inducing fear of the destruction of one's property, and compelling him to act against his will may be avoided on the ground of duress, there being in such a case only the bare form of a contract, wholly lacking the voluntary assent necessary for a binding contract. Cleaveland v Richardson, 132 US 318, 33 L Ed 384, 10 S Ct 108.

duressor (dū-res'ọr). A person who employs duress in his dealing with another.

duress per minas (dū-res' per mī'nas). Compulsion exercised by threat of imprisonment, mayhem, or taking of life or limb. 25 Am J2d Dur § 11. As defined at common law, such duress existed only where the party entered into a contract or performed an act for fear of imprisonment, mayhem, or loss of life or limb; threats or menace of mere battery to the person, or of trespass to lands or loss of goods were not sufficient to constitute such duress as to void obligations entered into because of such threats. 25 Am J2d Dur § 11. By many, if not most, of the modern authorities, however, the true doctrine of duress is held to be that a contract, deed, or any obligation obtained by so oppressing a person by threats regarding the safety or liberty of himself, or of his property, or of a member of his family, as to deprive him of the free exercise of his will and prevent the meeting of minds necessary to a valid contract, may be avoided on the ground of duress, whether the oppression was formerly deemed duress, and relievable at law as such, or was deemed wrongful compulsion remediable only in equity. 25 Am J2d Dur § 12.

Durham Test. A test of insanity constituting a defense in a criminal case, otherwise known as the "product test," which determines criminal responsibility on whether the unlawful act was the product of "mental disease or mental defect." 21 Am J2d Crim L § 39.

See **mental disease or mental defect.**

during. Throughout a period of time. A point of time within a period, as during the month of January, or during the widowhood of the grantee of a deed. Glendale Mfg. Co. v Protection Ins. Co. 21 Conn 19, 38.

during coverture. While marriage lasts. State ex rel. Hamilton v Guinotte, 156 Mo 513, 57 SW 281.

during good behavior. See **good behavior.**

during natural life. During the lifetime of a person. See **Shelley's Case.**

during the hours of service. A period which includes the hours of active labor on the premises of the employer and the time necessary for going to and from the place of employment where the latter is expressly or impliedly included in the terms of the employment. Any period during which the employee was on the premises of the employer due to his employment. 58 Am J1st Workm Comp § 214.

during the term. During the time or period for which the officer is elected or appointed. State ex rel. Hamilton v Guinotte, 156 Mo 513, 57 SW 281. Within the period during which a tenant is entitled to possession under his lease.

during trial. See **trial.**

dusting. Spreading poisonous dust upon crops or land to control or eradicate pests. The operation is normally performed with the aid of an airplane. 3 Am J2d Agri § 47.

dustyfoot (dus'ti-fut). See **courts of piepoudre.**

Dutch auction. An auction where the property is put up at a price usually greater than its value and the price is then gradually lowered until someone closes the sale by accepting the offer and thus becoming the purchaser. Anderson v Wisconsin C. R. Co. 107 Minn 296, 120 NW 39.

Dutch net. Also called a "pod net" or "pound net," —a kind of fisherman's net so set with stakes as to form a large trap or weir for fish and from the pod or inner compartment of which they cannot escape. Rea v Hampton & Nichols, 101 NC 51.

dutiable (dū'ti-ạ-bl). Subject to import duty.

duties. Obligations, whether imposed by the common law, statute, or contract; when a right is invaded, a duty is violated. Lake Shore & Michigan Southern Railway Co. v Kurtz, 10 Ind App 60, 67, 37 NE 303. A particular kind of levy or tax made by a government on the importation of commodities into the country. 21 Am J2d Cust D § 1. Not merely duties on the act of importation, but duties on the thing imported. Brown v Maryland (US) 12 Wheat 419, 6 L Ed 678.

See **customs duties.**

duties and imposts. As used in Clause 1, Section 8, Article I of the United States Constitution, a particular kind of tax commonly applied to levies on imports, but probably comprehending every species of tax or contribution not included under the ordinary terms "taxes" and "excises." Steward Mach. Co. v Davis, 301 US 548, 81 L Ed 481, 24 S Ct 305.

See **duties, imposts and excises.**

duties, imposts and excises. Words which are often used comprehensively and cover customs and excise duties imposed on importation, consumption, manufacture, and sale of certain commodities, privileges, particular business transactions, vocations, occupations, and the like, being, when so used, subject to construction under the rules that apply to license taxes. Thomas v United States, 192 US 363, 48 L Ed 481. One of the two great classes of taxes, the other being direct taxes, and the two, taken together, including every kind of tax appropriate to sovereignty.

See **customs duties; duties and imposts; excises; imposts.**

duties of detraction. Duties imposed on legacies payable to aliens and residents of other states. Mager v Grima (US) 8 How 490, 493, 12 L Ed 1168, 1170.

duties on imports. See **customs duties; duties.**

duties required of him by law. A common phrase appearing as a condition of the bond required of an executor or administrator, the effect of which is to extend the obligation to all duties in reference to the administration of the estate, including the payment of debts and the distribution of the remainder of the estate among those entitled to receive it. Williams v State, 68 Miss 680, 10 So 52.

duty. See **duties.**

duty of disclosure. See **duty to communicate.**

duty of support. A duty of supporting wife or child imposed or imposable by law, or by any court order, decree, or judgment, whether interlocutory or final, and whether incidental to a proceeding for divorce, judicial separation, separate maintenance, or otherwise. Uniform Reciprocal Enforcement of Support Act § 2(f); 23 Am J2d Desert § 131. The obligation to support a parent or other relative imposed by statute. 39 Am J1st P & C § 122. The obligation to support a person under an agreement for support. 50 Am J1st Sup Per § 2.

duty of tonnage. See **tonnage duty.**

duty to communicate. An agent's duty to make a full disclosure to his principal of all material facts relevant to the agency; to make a prompt, full, and frank disclosure and account to the principal of all matters concerning the agency; to give the principal any information that the latter would desire to have and which can be communicated to him without violating a superior duty to a third person. 3 Am J2d Agency § 200. The duty to communicate criminatory matter to a person having a corresponding interest or duty, not confined to legal duties which may be enforced by indictment, action, or mandamus, but including moral and social duties of imperfect obligation as well. Harrison v Bush, 5 Ellis & Blackburn (Eng) 344.

duty to lessen damages. See **mitigation of damages.**

duty to retreat. See **retreat.**

duumviri (dū-um'vī-rī). Two Roman magistrates possessing the same powers and functions who were elected or appointed as a pair.

dux (duks). A chief; a leader.

D. V. M. Abbreviation of Doctor of Veterinary Medicine.

D. V. S. Abbreviation of Doctor of Veterinary Science.

dwell. To inhabit; to reside; to have a fixed place of residence. Eatontown v Shrewsbury, 49 NJL 188, 190.
See **dwelling; residence.**

dwelling. A place of abode for people. 43 Am J1st Pub Util § 183. A dwelling house. The act of inhabiting or residing in a place.
See **dwell; dwelling house.**

dwelling house. A building used as a place of abode for people. 43 Am J1st Pub Util § 183. A building suitable as a dwelling house, whether or not it is occupied at the time. 29A Am J Rev ed Ins § 904. For the purpose of the offense of arson, any house intended to be occupied as a residence, or a house in which human beings usually stay, lodge, or reside. 5 Am J2d Arson § 19. For the purpose of the crime of burglary, the apartment, room in a hotel, building, or cluster of buildings in which a man resides with his family, or any permanent building in which a person may dwell and sleep. 13 Am J2d Burgl § 3.
See **house; mansion house; residence.**

dwelling house of another. As the term is used in the law of arson, a dwelling house of which a person other than the accused is in possession; the person in possession may or may not be the owner. 5 Am J2d Arson § 39.

dwelling-place (dwel'ing-plās). See **dwell; dwelling house.**

DWI. Abbreviation for driving while intoxicated.

Dyer Act. The National Motor Vehicle Theft Act of 1919, making it an offense to transport a motor vehicle in interstate or foreign commerce with knowledge that the same has been stolen or to receive, conceal, barter or sell a motor vehicle in interstate or foreign commerce, knowing the same to have been stolen. 7 Am J2d Auto § 305.

dying declaration. A declaration by the victim of a homicide or of an abortion resulting in the death of the woman, made while in extremis. 1 Am J2d Abort § 23. More precisely, a statement made by the victim of a homicide while about to die, and without any hope of recovery, concerning the facts and circumstances under which the fatal injury was inflicted, and offered in evidence on the trial of the person charged with having caused the death of the declarant. 26 Am J1st Homi § 385.

dying intestate. Dying without leaving a valid will. Also death without making an effective testamentary disposition. Bradford v Leake, 124 Tenn 312, 137 SW 96.

dying without issue. Dying without a child born either before or after the decedent's death. A term often appearing in devises of real estate, sometimes construed as meaning a definite failure of issue, that is no issue living at the time of the first taker's death, while other authorities construe the phrase as providing for an indefinite failure of issue, thereby invalidating the limitation on the ground of remoteness. 28 Am J2d Est § 272. Of course, the limitation is not evaluated according to its bare bones, the context of the entire instrument must be considered in determining whether the expression is one of a definite failure of issue or an indefinite failure of issue. 28 Am J2d Est § 272. Although it has been held that in executory bequests of personal estates any words in the will may be laid hold of to restrain the generality of the words "dying without issue" and confine them to a dying without issue living at the time of the person's decease, in order to support the intention of the testator, yet even in the limitation of personal estates, the words "dying without issue," standing alone, without the concurrence of any other circumstances indicating an intention of restricting them, will not signify a dying without issue living at the death of the first taker. 28 Am J2d Est § 273.

dying without leaving issue. See **dying without issue.**

dyke. Another spelling of **dike.**

dynamo (dī'na-mō). A device for converting mechanical energy into electricity by magnetic induction. Thomson-Houston Electric Co. v Western Electric Co. (CC Ill) 65 F 615, 616.

dynasty (dī'nas-ti). A royal family succession to a throne or sovereignty.

dysnomy (dis'nō-mi). Bad legislation; the enactment of unwarrantable laws.

dyvour (dī'vör). An insolvent person who had made an assignment of his property for the benefit of his creditors; a bankrupt.

dyvour's habit The costume which the law prescribed to be worn by a dyvour.

E

e. An abbreviation of "east" in descriptions of land, whether in stating the course of a boundary, e. g. "running e. 80 rods," or designating the fractional part of a section under the Congressional Survey, e. g. "the e. 1/2 of the NW quarter of Section 6."
In Latin, a preposition, the equivalent of "ex," meaning from, out of.

E [2]. An abbreviation of a fractional part of a section of land of 640 acres under the Congressional Survey, the figure whether 2, 4, 16, or whatever, indicating the fraction of the section designated, as 1/2, 1/4, 1/16, etc. of a numbered section. For example, E[2] NW[4] Sec 10 means 80 acres comprising the east half of the northwest quarter of section 10. Power v Bowdle, 3 ND 107, 54 NW 404.

each. Every one of the two or more comprising the whole. Adams Express Co. v Lexington, 83 Ky 657, 660. Indicating generally, as it appears in a designation of beneficiaries in a will, a gift to individuals rather than to a class. 57 Am J1st Wills § 1265. Significant in the same connection as tending to show intent for distribution per capita. 57 Am J1st Wills § 1296.

each accident. See **per accident clause.**

each party. Every one of two or more parties. Appearing in a statute giving "each party" a designated number of peremptory challenges to a juror, the term, in a case involving plural parties, means each side, notwithstanding the parties on one side plead separately, at least where their interests are common and their pleadings are substantially identical. 31 Am J Rev ed Jury § 238.

eadem causa. See **in eadem causa.**

Eadem causa diversis rationibus coram judicibus ecclesiasticis et secularibus ventilatur (ē'a-dem kâ'za dī-ver'sis ra-she-ō'ni-bus kō'ram jū-di'si-bus e-klē-si-as'ti-sis et se-kū-lā'ir-bus ven-ti-lā'ter). The same cause is argued with different reasons before both the ecclesiastical and the secular judges.

Eadem est ratio, eadem est lex (ē'a-dem est rā'she-o, ē'a-dem est lex). The reason being the same, the law is the same. Follett v United States Mut. Acci. Asso. 110 NC 377, 14 SE 923.

Eadem mens praesumitur regis quae est juris et quae esse debet, praesertim in dubiis (ē-ā'dem menz prē-zū'mi-ter rē'jis kwē est jū'ris et kwē es'se de'bet, prē-ser'tim in du'bi-is). The king's mind is presumed to be in accord with law and as it should be, especially in doubtful matters.

eadling (ed'ling). Same as **atheling.**

Ea est accipienda interpretatio, quae vitio caret (ē'ā est ak-si-pi-en'da in-ter-pre-tā'she-ō, kwē vi'she-ō ka'ret). That interpretation is to be accepted which is without fault.

eagle (ē'gl). A United States gold coin of the value of ten dollars. Withdrawn from circulation, along with other gold coin, in 1933.

ea intentione (ē'ā in-ten-she-ō'ne). With that intention.

ealdor biscop. A chief bishop, an archbishop.

ealehus (ăl-hŭs). An alehouse.

e. and o.e. An abbreviation of "errors and omissions excepted," often noted upon financial statements and accounts.

Ea quae commendandi causa in venditionibus dicuntur si palam appareant venditorem non obligant (e'ā kwē kom-men-dan'dī kâ'za in ven-di-she-ō'ni-bus di-kun'ter sī pa'lam ap-pa're-ant ven-di-tō'rem non ob'li-gant). Those statements which are made in commendation at sales, if they appear openly, do not bind the seller.

Ea quae dari impossibilia sunt, vel quae in rerum natura non sunt, pro non adjectis habentur (e'ā kwē da'rī im-pos-si-bi'li-a sunt, vel kwē in rē'rum nā-tū'ra non sunt, prō non ad-jek'tis hā-ben'ter). Those things which it is not possible to give, or which in the nature of things have no existence, are not regarded as included (in the contract).

Ea quae in curia nostra rite acta sunt debitae executioni demandari debent (e'a kwē in kū'ri-a nos'tra rī'te ak'ta sunt de'bi-tē ex-e-kū-she-ō'nī de-man-dā'rī de'bent). Those things which are regularly done in our court should be committed to a due execution.

Ea quae raro accidunt, non temere in agendis negotiis computantur (e'a kwē ra'rō ak'si-dunt, non te'me-rē in ā-jen'dis ne-gō'she-is kom-pu-tan'ter). Those things which rarely happen are not to be taken into account in business transactions without sufficient reason.

ear. The organ of hearing. Grains of corn and the cob to which they are affixed by nature. In a mechanical sense, a part projecting from the side of anything. Consolidated Vapor-Stove Co. v Elwood Gas-Stove & Stamping Co. (CC Pa) 63 F 698.

earl (ĕrl). An English title of nobility below that of a marquis and above that of a viscount in rank. The custody of the shire is said to have been committed to an earl at the first division of the kingdom into counties, but later, by reason of their attendance on the king and other duties, the labor of the office was transferred to the vice-comes or sheriff, the earl, however, retaining the honor. See 1 Bl Comm 339.

earldom (ĕrl-dum'). The jurisdiction, seigniory, or dignity of an earl.

earles-penny (ĕrlz'pen''i). A piece of money given as an earnest to bind a bargain.

earliest possible convenience. As a limitation upon a promise to pay, "earliest possible convenience" means payment when the promisor is able to pay, that is, has the means to pay. Halladay v Weeks, 127 Mich 363, 86 NW 799.

earl marshal (ĕrl' mär'shạl). The eighth great officer of state in England. At one time the earl marshal presided over the court of chivalry when it was held as a military court, or court of honor and when this court was held as a criminal court, it was presided over by the lord high constable jointly with the earl marshal. See 4 Bl Comm 268.

earl palatine (ĕrl pal'ạ-tin). Same as **count palatine.**

earmark. Any mark or means by which a thing can be identified or distinguished from other things of the same sort. A slit made in one or both ears of cattle, sheep, or hogs, for their identification.

earmark doctrine. The doctrine, now obsolete, that where a trustee or other fiduciary dies, the owner

EARN [387] EASEMENT

of money which has been entrusted to the decedent shares as a general creditor in the assets of the decedent's estate, unless the money so held had an "earmark" and was thus distinguishable from the mass of the decedent's own property. Such doctrine appears to have given way to the modern principle that the owner can recover the money or its equivalent whenever it can be traced to the estate, no matter what form it may take. First Nat. Bank v Hummell, 14 Colo 259, 23 P 986.

earn. To gain, obtain, or acquire as the reward of labor or performance of some service. Lewis' Estate, 156 Pa St 337, 340.

earned premium. See **premium earned.**

earned surplus. The surplus of a corporation derived from undistributed profits, not from a reduction of capital stock. Willcutts v Milton Dairy Co. 275 US 215, 72 L Ed 247.

earnest. Another term for **earnest money.**

earnest money. A downpayment of part of the purchase price made to bind the bargain. A part payment of the purchase price, within the meaning of the statute of frauds. Goddard v Monitor Mut. Fire Ins. Co. 108 Mass 54; 49 Am J1st Stat of F § 265. A downpayment or deposit required at an auction sale. 7 Am J2d Auct § 45.

earning capacity. The power of a person or a business enterprise to earn money or show a profit; to earn money or show a profit in a particular sum. The power to create property from earnings. Local Loan Co. v Hunt, 292 US 234, 78 L Ed 1230, 54 S Ct 695. An element considered in measuring damages recoverable for a personal injury. 22 Am J2d Damg § 92. The best test of the value of a going commercial enterprise; a test to be employed in the valuation of a corporation for the purpose of reorganization under the Chapter X of the Bankruptcy Act. For such purpose, "earning capacity" means normal capacity rather than an abnormal capacity consequent upon business conditions which cannot reasonably be expected to continue. 9 Am J2d Bankr § 1591.

A person may have an earning capacity, even though not employed at any labor or occupation at the particular time in question. 22 Am J2d Damg § 89.

earning power. Same as **earning capacity.**

earnings. In a pristine sense, the gains of a person from his services or labor, without the aid of capital. 22 Am J2d Damg § 89; 31 Am J2d Exemp § 39. In the modern sense and development of the term, it includes profits from the employment of capital, as illustrated by the earnings of a corporation. 19 Am J2d Corp § 823. The term is equivalent to "income" where used in the limitation of a life estate and a remainder in connection with a provision for the disposition of extraordinary dividends and distributions as between life tenant and remainderman. 33 Am J1st Life Est § 378.

See **future earnings; net earnings; personal earnings; surplus earnings.**

earnings and profits. Wages of labor and income from business. 27 Am J1st H & W § 466.
See **earnings; profits.**

earth. The planet on which we live; the world. Soil of all kinds, including gravel, clay, loam, and the like, in distinction from the firm rock. Dickinson v Poughkeepsie, 75 NY 65, 76.

earthquake. A movement of the crust of the earth due to faults in the structure or rock or pressure originating in the interior of the earth; an act of God. 1 Am J2d Act of God § 6; a casualty for the purpose of deducting losses for income tax purposes. Anno: 41 ALR2d 711-713.

ear-witness. A witness who gives hearsay testimony.

ease. Comfort, contentment, enjoyment, happiness, pleasure and satisfaction. National Surety Co. v Jarett, 95 W Va 420, 121 SE 291

easement. A servitude imposed as a burden on land. The right which one person has to use the land of another for a specific purpose not inconsistent with a general property in the owner and not including the right to participate in the profits of the soil charged with it. Precisely, a liberty, privilege, or advantage in land without profit, existing distinct from the ownership of the soil. 25 Am J2d Ease § 1.

easement appendant. Same as **easement appurtenant.**
See **affirmative easement; apparent easement; continuous easement; discontinuous easement; dominant tenement; license; lost grant; necessary easement; negative easement; praedial servitude; praedium dominans; praedium serviens; prescriptive easement; public easement; quasi easement; secondary easement; servient tenement; urban easements; way of necessity.**

easement appurtenant. An easement of the conventional type, one that is appurtenant to a dominant tenement. An incorporeal right, a servitude, attached to, and belonging with, some greater or superior right—something annexed to another more worthy thing with which it passes as an incident, being incapable of existence separate and apart from the particular land to which it is annexed and to which it bears a relationship connected with the use of the dominant estate. 25 Am J2d Ease § 11.

easement by custom. A right acquired by custom, in the nature of an easement but lacking a dominant tenement, for example, a right of way by custom in favor of the inhabitants of a particular locality. Such easements have received little, if any, recognition in this country. 25 Am J2d Ease § 19.

easement by implication. See **implied easement.**

easement by implied grant. Same as **implied easement.**

easement by natural right. See **easement ex jure naturale.**

easement by prescription. See **prescriptive easement.**

easement ex jure naturale (ex jū're na-tū-rā'le). Not a true easement, since not created by the act of man. A right, such as subjacent and lateral support or the right of an owner of land to have surface water flow freely from his land to that of his neighbor, arising by law and existing as a so-called natural right. 25 Am J2d Ease § 6.

easement for years. An easement created to endure for a specified period of time. 25 Am J2d Ease § 99.

easement in gross. An easement not supported by a dominant estate, consisting of a mere personal interest in or right to use the land of another. 25 Am J2d Ease § 12. A right, usufructuary in its nature and character, which entitles the owner to the use of the land for the profits which may be derived from its rents, or from quarrying and digging it for ores, or from harvesting its fruits, crops, and vintages, etc. Smith v Cooley, 65 Cal 46, 48, 2 P 880. A right of way which is personal to the grantee and

easement of highway. See **highway easement.**

easement of drip. The servitude of the dripping of water from the eaves of a building on to the land of the adjoining owner. 1 Am J2d Adj L § 31.

easement of natural support. The easement or right which a landowner has to the lateral and subjacent support of his land in its natural condition. Booth v Rome, Watertown & Ogdensburg Terminal R. Co. 140 NY 267, 35 NE 592. An easement ex jure naturale rather than a true easement.
See **easement ex jure naturale; lateral support; subjacent support.**

easements of light, air, and view. Express or implied easements for the enjoyment of light, air, and view without obstruction by structures on the adjoining premises. 1 Am J2d Adj L §§ 89 et seq.
See **ancient lights.**

east. A direction; the direction of sunrise; a compass point, the point at which the sun rises at the equinox. A compass point which, appearing in a deed, means due east, in the absence of qualifying words in the instrument. 23 Am J2d Deeds § 248.

Easter (ēs'tẽr). An annual Christian festival in commemoration of the resurrection of Christ. The date of the festival, as fixed by the first Council of Christian Churches in Nicaea in 325 A. D., is the first Sunday after the first full moon that occurs on or after March 21. For table of Easter dates for the 20th century, see **The World Almanac,** index reference "Easter Sunday."

Easter dues. Same as **Easter offerings.**

easterly. Due east, in the absence of qualifying words. 23 Am J2d Deeds § 248. When other words are used for the purpose of qualifying its meaning, it means precisely what the qualifying words make it mean. Fratt v Woodward, 32 Cal 213, 227.
See **east.**

eastern time (ēs'tẽrn tīm). See **standard time.**

Easter offerings (ēs'tẽr of'ẽr-ings). Dues which were paid to the clergy at Easter.

Easter term (ēs'tẽr tẽrm). An English term of court which begins on April fifteenth and ends on the eighth day of May.

East Greenwich (ēst gren'ich). A royal manor in Kent.

Eastman formula. A formula, said to have been suggested to Congress by Commissioner Eastman of the Interstate Commerce Commission, that fixed charges, under a plan for the reorganization of a railroad, should not exceed eighty per cent of the net available for interest in the three worst years of the last ten. Denver & R. G. W. R. Co. (DC Colo) 38 F Supp 106.

east one-half. See **fraction of section.**

Ea sunt animadvertenda peccata maxime, quae difficillime praecaventur (ē'a sunt a-ni-mad-ver-ten'da pe-kā'ta ma'xi-mē, kwē dif-fi-sil'li-mē prē-kā-ven'tẽr). Those offenses should be most severely punished which are most difficult to prevent. See 3 Bl Comm 16.

easy coal. A technical term in coal-mining, designating coal which is to be handled with care, since its value is greatly impaired by breakage. Chesapeake & O. Ry. Co. v Kaltenbach (CA4 Va) 124 F2d 375.

easy-divorce state. A state having a number of grounds of divorce, a short residence requirement, and judges who are not inclined to doubt the plaintiff's testimony. Elwert v Elwert, 196 Or 256, 248 P2d 847, 36 ALR2d 741.

easy girl. Slang for a female who is easily seduced.

easy virtue. Willingness to engage in immoral practices, particularly on the part of a girl.

Eat inde sine die (e'at in'de sī'ne dī'e). Let him go hence without day,—formal words used in a judgment of acquittal on a charge of crime.

eau (ō). (French.) Water.

eaves. The edges of the roof of a building, projecting beyond the face of the walls. Proprietors of Center St. Church v Machias Hotel Co. 51 Me 413.

eaves-drip. Water which drips from the eaves of a house.
See **easement of drip.**

eavesdropper. A person who listens under the windows or eaves of a house to hear the discourse therein and thereupon proclaim slanderous and mischievous tales. Such persons were regarded as nuisances at common law, and were required, in the discretion of the court, to find sureties for their good behavior. Pavesich v New England Life Ins. Co. 122 Ga 190, 50 SE 624. It is the habitual commission of the acts stated above which seems to constitute the gist of the common-law offense of eavesdropping, and the proof necessary for conviction must be such as will permit the jury to infer the habit of eavesdropping. State v Davis, 139 NC 547, 51 SE 897.

eavesdropping. See **eavesdropper.**

ebb. The falling or going out of the tides; the receding of the tide, moving back to the sea.

ebba (eb'ba). Same as **ebb.**

ebb and flow. The coming in and the falling back of the tide. A rejected test of navigability of water. 56 Am J1st Wat § 178.

ebermord (ē-ber-mŏrd). Same as **aberemurder.**

E bonds. A convenient term for referring to series E of United States Savings Bonds, the distinguishing characteristic of which is an increasing redemption value in lieu of an expressly stated rate of interest.

Ebor. Latin for **York.**

E.b S. Abbreviation for east by south.

eccentricity. Deviation from the ordinary. Oddity in a person's conduct or manners, often so pronounced as to attract attention.
Even glaring eccentricity is not the equivalent of insanity. 29 Am J Rev ed Ins Per § 7.

eccl. An abbreviation of ecclesiastical.

eccles. An abbreviation of ecclesiastical.

ecclesia (e-klē'zi-ą). A church; a place of divine worship; a parsonage.

ecclesia commendata (e-klē'si-a kom-men-dā'ta). Also called "commenda,"—a church living commended by the crown to the care of a clerk, to hold until a proper pastor is provided for it. This might be temporary for from one to three years; or perpetual: being a kind of dispensation to avoid the vacancy of the living, and is called a commenda retinere. There was also a "commenda recipere," which was to take a benefice de novo, in the bishop's own gift, or the gift of some other patron consenting to it. See 1 Bl Comm 393.

Ecclesia decimas non solvit ecclesiae (e-klē'si-a de'si-mas non sol'vit e-klē'si-ē). The church pays no tithes to the church. See 2 Bl Comm 31.

Ecclesia ecclesiae decimas solvere non debet (e-klē'si-a e-klē'si-ē de'si-mas sol've-re non de'bet). A church ought not to pay tithes to a church.

Ecclesiae de feudo domini regis non possunt in perpetuum dari, absque assensu et consensione ipsius (e-klē'si-ē dē fū'dō do'mi-nī rē'jis non pos'sunt in per-pe'tū-um da'rī, abs'kwe as-sen'sū et kon-sen-she-ō'ne īp-sī'us). Parsonages partaking of the king's fee cannot be given in perpetuity without his approval and consent. See 2 Bl Comm 269, note.

Ecclesia est domus mansionalis omnipotentis Dei (e-klē'si-a est dō'mus man-she-ō-nā'lis om-ni-pō-ten'tis dē'ī). The church is the mansion house of God Almighty.

Ecclesia est infra aetatem et in custodia domini regis, qui tenetur jura et haereditates ejusdem manu tenere et defendere (e-klē'si-a est in'fra ē-tā'tem et in kus-tō'di-a do'mi-nī rē'jis, quī te-nē'ter jū'ra et hē-rē-di-tā'tēz ē-jus'dem ma'nū te-nē're et de-fen'de-re). The church is under age and in the custody of the king, who is bound to support and defend her rights and inheritances.

Ecclesia fungitur vice minoris; meliorem conditionem suam facere potest, deteriorem nequaquam (e-klē'si-a fun'ji-ter vī'se mī-nō'ris; me-li-ō'rem kon-di-she-ō'nem su'am fā'se-re po'test, de-te-ri-ō'rem ne-quä'quam). The church occupies the position of a minor; she can make her own condition better, but never worse.

Ecclesia magis favendum est quam personae (e-klē'si-a mā'jis fa-ven'dum est quam per-sō'nē). The church is more to be favored than the individual.

Ecclesia non moritur (e-klē'si-a non mo'ri-ter). The church does not die.

ecclesiastic (e-klē-zi-as'tik). Ecclesiastical; a churchman.

ecclesiastical (e-klē-zi-as'ti-kạl). Religious; pertaining to the church.

ecclesiastical commission (e-klē-zi-as'ti-kạl kọ-mish'ọn). A court which was instituted by Queen Elizabeth and which was clothed with great powers in religious matters.

ecclesiastical corporations (kôr-pọ-rā'shọnz). Corporations, either sole or aggregate, the members composing which are all spiritual persons, such as bishops, certain deans, and prebendaries, all archdeacons, parsons, and vicars, all of which are corporations sole, and such corporations aggregate as deans and chapters, prior and convent (formerly), abbots and monks, and the like. See 1 Bl Comm 470; 18 Am J2d Corp § 7.

See **religious corporations; religious societies.**

ecclesiastical council. Another name for a church court or tribunal taking cognizance of spiritual matters and internal controversies.

See **ecclesiastical courts.**

ecclesiastical courts. In Amercian usage, church tribunals taking cognizance of spiritual matters and internal controversies. English courts presided over by members of the clergy, which, in the course of time, have exercised jurisdiction over spiritual matters and some matters deemed temporal today. The ecclesiastical court was not made a part of the judicial system of the United States or of the several states. Edgerton v Edgerton, 12 Mont 122, 29 P 966.

ecclesiastical law. That system of jurisprudence which prevails in the ecclesiastical courts of England. There is a conflict of opinion as to whether the ecclesiastical law of England has been adopted as part of the common law of American states. 15 Am J2d Comm L § 10.

ecclesiastical notary. A secretary or clerk employed in the ecclesiastical courts and councils.

ecclesiastical offense (ọ-fens'). See **heresy.**

ecclesiastical officer (of'i-sėr). A person in the hierarchy of control in the Church. Known as a "dignitary" if of a rank superior to that of a priest or canon.

ecclesiastical tribunal. See **church tribunal.**

ecclesiastical waste. Waste occuring to church property—chancel, parsonage, or other buildings thereunto belonging—of a voluntary or permissive character. 3 Bl Comm 91.

eccliasticum. See **forum ecclesiasticum.**

eclampsia (ek-lamp'si-ạ). A toxic condition of the body, particularly a toxic condition during pregnancy. Walker v Distler, 78 Idaho 38, 296 P2d 452, 454.

eclectic. Gathered from various sources by choosing; not bound to a conventional system.

eclectic practice of medicine. An unusual and perhaps eccentric system of treating human maladies; selecting methods of treatment from various sources of learning rather than following one school. Bradbury v Bardin, 34 Conn 453.

economic adulteration. The substitution of less expensive ingredients, or the diminution of the proportion of more expensive ingredients, so as to make the product, although not in itself deleterious, inferior to that which the consumer expects to receive when purchasing the product. Anno: 56 ALR2d 1132. The use of foreign and artificial ingredients as coloring matter in food to deceive or defraud the consuming public. 22 Am J1st Food § 3.

economic burden. Literally, any expense, e. g. supporting a mother-in-law. A speculative abstraction in taxation, signifying the intangible, unascertainable result borne by everybody when a tax is imposed on anybody, the theory being that tax burdens are passed on to be borne by the ultimate consumer. Cudahy Packing Co. v United States (DC Ill) 37 F Supp 563.

economic compulsion. See **business compulsion.**

economic depression. An unhappy state in commerce and industry, carried over to the entire populace, resulting from decreasing business, falling prices, the closing down of factories, wide-spread unemployment, and increasing numbers of people subsisting on public welfare.

See **Great Depression.**

economic pressure. The force of circumstances in the field of economics that controls the course taken in a business or industry. The condition which forces one to sell on a low market or purchase on a high market.

See **business compulsion; economic depression.**

economics. A study in the abstract of the production and distribution of wealth and the problems related thereto, such as those of taxation, finance, labor, etc.

economic waste. An overproduction of oil and gas, relief against which is obtained by proration of production. 24 Am J1st Gas & O § 150.

economizer. Something working in the interest of economy. An attachment to a steam boiler. 29A Am J Rev ed Ins § 1365.

e contra (ē kon'trā). On the contrary; on the other hand.

e converso (ē kon-ver'sō). Conversely; turned around.

écrit. See **droit écrit.**

ecumenical (ek-ū-men'i-kạl). Universal; pertaining to the Christian church in its entirety; disregarding denominations in order to view the Church as a whole. Belonging to the whole of the Christian church.

ed. Abbreviation of edition.

edge lease. An oil and gas lease located on the edge of an oil bearing structure. Carter Oil Co. v Mitchell (CA10) Okla 100 F2d 945.

edict (ē'dikt). A command or prohibition promulgated by a sovereign and having the effect of law.

Edict of Theodoric. See **Edictum Theodorici.**

edictum (ē-dik'tum). Same as **edict.**

edictum perpetuum (ē-dik'tum per-pe'tū-um). A perpetual edict.

Edictum Theodorici (ē-dik'tum the-o-dō'ri-sī). The Edict of Theodoric,—a code of laws compiled in the sixth century, A. D., under the Roman Emperor Theodoric.

edile (ē'dīl). Same as **aedile.**

edition. The total of copies of a book, magazine, or newspaper printed and published at one time or during a period of time, e. g. the second edition of American Jurisprudence, cited Am J2d.

editus (e'di-tus). Issued; promulgated.

Edmunds Anti-polygamy Law. A federal statute of 1892 which punished bigamy and also the act of cohabitation with more than one woman at the same time. 10 Am J2d Big § 5.

Edmundus autem latusferreum, rex naturalis de stirpe regum, genuit Edwardum et Edwardus genuit Edgarum, cui de jure debebatur regnum Anglorum (Ed-mun'dus â'tem lā-tus-fer're-um rex na-tū-rā'lis dē ster'pe rē'gum, je'nu-it Ed-war'dum et Ed-war'dus je'nū-it Ed'ga-rum, ki dē jū're de-bē-bā'ter reg'num Ang-lō'rum). But Edmund Ironside, natural king from the race of kings, begat Edward and Edward begat Edgar, to whom the kingdom of England belonged of right. See 1 Bl Comm 199.

educate. To lead forth, to train, to develop physically and mentally. McNair v School Dist. 87 Mont 423, 288 P 188, 69 ALR 866.
See **education.**

education. The cultivation of the mind, the improvement of moral and religious natures, and the development of physical faculties. German Gymnastic Asso. v Louisville, 117 Ky 958, 80 SW 287.

Herbert Spencer said, "to prepare us for complete living is the function which education has to discharge." McNair v School Dist. 87 Mont 423, 288 P 188, 69 ALR 866.

educational appliance. Something necessary or useful to enable the teacher to teach the school children, such as a blackboard, map, or dictionary, but not an ordinary school book. Honaker v Board of Education, 42 W Va 170, 24 SE 544.

educational corporation. A corporation not for profit but for an educational purpose, particularly the establishment and maintenance of a school, college, or university. Public or private according to its foundation; founded by private individuals or supported by private funds or privately endowed, it is a private corporation. Founded and supported by the state or a municipal subdivision thereof, it is a public corporation. See 15 Am J2d Colleges § 3.

educational institution. An institution for the teaching and improvement of its students or pupils; a school, seminary, college, or university. Anno: 95 ALR 63. An institution giving a course of instruction for the cultivation of the mind, the inculcation of a clearer sense of moral and spiritual values, or the obtaining of a better physical development. German Gymnastic Asso. v Louisville, 117 Ky 958, 80 SW 201. Art galleries, museums, public libraries, even labor union buildings have at times been held to be educational institutions. 51 Am J1st Tax § 620.
See **general educational institution.**

educational purpose. Broadly, the establishment and maintenance of any kind of educational institution, but sometimes acquiring a more restricted meaning from the context in which it appears. In the ordinary and commonly accepted sense, the term does not include a general hospital which has, as an incident to its main purpose and usefulness an educational feature. Cedars of Lebanon Hospital v Los Angeles County, 35 Cal 2d 729, 221 P2d 31, 15 ALR2d 1045. While a public library is in one sense an educational agency, it is not an educational purpose within the meaning of a constitutional provision that no sum shall be raised by taxation for education other than in common schools, etc. Ramsey v Shelbyville, 119 Ky 180, 83 SW 116.
See **educational institution.**

education expense. A deduction in an income tax return where required to retain salary, status or employment.

Edward I. (Ed'wärd). Edward the First, king of England from November 20th, 1272, to July 7th, 1307.

Edward II. Edward the Second, king of England from July 8th, 1307, to January 25th, 1327.

Edward III. Edward the Third, king of England from January 25th, 1327, to June 21st, 1377.

Edward IV. Edward the Fourth, king of England from May 4th, 1461, to April 9th, 1483.

Edward V. Edward the Fifth, king of England from April 9th, 1483, to June 26th, 1483.

Edward VI. Edward the Sixth, king of England from January 28th, 1547, to July 6th, 1553.

Edward VII. Edward the Seventh, king of England from January 22nd, 1901, to May 7th, 1910.

Edward VIII. Edward the Eighth, king of England from Jan. 20, 1936, to Dec. 11 of the same year, when he abdicated, giving up the throne, as he said, because, as king, he could not marry "the woman I love," the divorced Mrs. Wallis Warfield of Baltimore, Maryland, better known in the press of the United States as Mrs. Simpson.

EDWARD [391] EGALITY

Edward the Confessor (kon-fes′or). King of England from 1043 to 1066. He was so called because of his reputation for piety.

eé (ē). To be.

e. e. An abbreviation of the words "errors excepted," frequently used in accounts.
See **e. and o.e.**

eeg. Abbreviation for electroencephalogram.

effect. Verb: To accomplish. Noun: An impression. A belonging, especially one of a personal nature.
See **effects**; **in effect.**

effecting a loan. Arrangement of terms and completion of a loan of money; to be distinguished from the renewal of a loan. State v Love, 170 Miss 666, 150 So 196, 90 ALR 506.

effective (e-fek′tiv). In force; in effect.

effective absence. The absence of an officer upon an occasion which demands the immediate exercise of his powers. State v Lahiff, 146 Wis 490, 131 NW 824; Anno: 98 ALR 1149.

effective blockade. A blockade so effective as to make it dangerous in fact for vessels to attempt to enter the blockaded port; the question of effectiveness is not controlled by the number of the blockading force. One modern cruiser may suffice. 56 Am J1st War § 173.

effective date. The date when a code of laws, a constitution, or single statute or constitutional amendment becomes binding as law. Anno: 132 ALR 1060.
A bill introduced in the legislature is ordinarily regarded as becoming a law upon its enactment, but the time as of which its provisions become operative may be earlier by application of a legal fiction, or later by the application of an express statutory or constitutional provision. 56 Am J1st Stat § 502.

effective height. The height of a mill dam at which, the dam, being in good condition, will flow land, unaffected by changes in seasons or occasional leakage. Carr v Piscataquis Woolen Co. 110 Me 184, 85 A 497.

effective money (mun′i). Coin.

effective possession. Otherwise known as virtual possession, being an actual occupancy of part of a tract under color of title, sufficient where continued for the statutory period to support a claim of title to the whole tract as acquired by adverse possession. Sometimes called "constructive possession," but to be distinguished from the conventional constructive possession which follows the title where the owner of the title is not in actual possession and there is no adverse possession. Wheeler v Clark, 114 Tenn 117.

effects. One's belongings, especially things of a personal nature. Personal property. 57 Am J1st Wills § 1344.
In the context of a statute such as one defining the offense of false pretenses, the term may include real as well as personal property. State v Newell, 1 Mo 248. As the word appears in a treaty respecting inheritance rights of aliens, the term may be sufficiently broad, in the light of the context, to include real estate. 3 Am J2d Aliens § 33. Construed in the light of the entire context of a testamentary gift, the term may include both real and personal property. 57 Am J1st Wills § 1346.
See **goods and effects.**

Effectus punitur licet non sequatur effectus (ef-fek′-tus pu′ni-ter lī′set non se-quā′ter ef-fek′tus). The act may be punished that the consequence may not follow.

Effectus sequitur causam (ef-fek′tus se′qui-ter kâ′zam). The effect follows the cause.

effets. (French.) Effects.
The word "effets" when used in a will, has the same meaning as the English word "effects," and this depends largely upon the context. In some cases the word has been properly held to cover the whole personal estate of the testator. In other cases it has been limited by the accompanying words. Ennis v Smith (US) 14 How 400, 421, 14 L Ed 472, 482.

efficient. Producing outward effects; of a nature to produce a result; active; causative; acting or able to act with due effect; adequate in performance; bringing to bear the requisite knowledge, skill, and industry; capable; competent. Thayer v Denver & R. G. R. Co. 25 NM 559, 185 P 542.

efficient cause. The primary responsible cause of a legal liability, even though, being first of a chain of events leading to the infliction of injury, it is most remote in point of time of any event preceding the injury and connected therewith. Stacy v Williams, 253 Ky 353, 60 SW2d 697. The proximate cause. 38 Am J1st Negl § 50. The cause that necessarily sets the other causes in operation; the act or omission which directly brings about the happening complained of, and in the absence of which the happening complained of would not have occurred. White v Ellison Realty Corp. 5 NJ 228, 74 A2d 401, 19 ALR2d 264.

efficient intervening cause. A cause intervening the negligence of the defendant and the occurrence of injury to the plaintiff, without which the injury would not have occurred. 38 Am J1st Negl § 68. A new and independent force, which breaks the causal connection between the original wrong and the injury, and itself becomes the direct and immediate—that is, the proximate—cause of an injury. Pullman's Palace Car Co. v Laack, 143 Ill 242, 32 NE 285; Ney v Yellow Cab Co. 2 Ill 2d 74, 117 NE2d 74, 51 ALR2d 624; Hall v Coble Dairies, 234 NC 206, 67 SE2d 63, 29 ALR2d 682.

effigy. A stuffed figure made to represent some person. A form of libel where exposing the subject to ridicule. 33 Am J1st L & S § 55.

efflux (ef′luks). A flowing.

efflux of time. The lapse of time.

efforce (e-fōrs′). To force; to effect an entry by force.

efforcialiter (ef-for-she-ā′li-ter). Forcibly.

effraction (e-frak′shon). A breaking effected by force.

effractor (ef-frak′tōr). A housebreaker; a burglar.

effractores (ef-frak-tō′rēz). Plural of **effractor**.

effranchise (e-fran′chiz). Same as **enfranchise**.

effray (e-frā′). Same as **affray**.

effusio sanguinis (ef-fu′she-ō san′gui-nis). The shedding of blood; bloodshed.

e. g. An abreviation of "exempli gratia," meaning for or by way of example.

egalitarian. A person who advocates equality of political and social rights between all men.

egality (ẹ-gal′i̧-ti). Equality.

egetter. To eject.

egglise. Same as **eglise.**

egidos (ay-hē′dos). Same as **exidos.**

eglise (ê-glî-z). A church.

ego (ē′gō). The self. Colloquial term for conceit. (Latin.) The pronoun I.
See **alter ego.**

ego, talis (ē′go, tā′lis). I, such a one.

egrediens et exeuns (ē-grē′di-enz et ex′e-unz). Going forth and issuing.

egreditur personam (ē-grē′di-tur per-sō′nam). It issues out of his person; that is, he is the author of it. Scott v Shepherd, 2 William Blackstone (Eng) 892.

egress. A means of exit.

egressus. See **ingressus et egressus.**

eia. An island.

Eighteenth Amendment. The Eighteenth Amendment to the Constitution of the United States, since repealed by the Twenty-First Amendment, established national prohibition of the traffic in intoxicating liquors.

eight-hour law. A term of dual meaning. A statute which restricts absolutely the length of a day's labor to eight hours; a statute which provides that eight hours shall be a lawful day's work. 31 Am J Rev ed Lab § 780. The federal statute fixing an eight hour day for the purposes of compensation of railroad employees, with certain exceptions. 31 Am J Rev ed Lab § 799.

eighty per cent credit. A credit provided against federal estate tax for estate, inheritance, or succession taxes paid a state. 28 Am J Rev ed Inher T § 426.

eigne (ān or ā′ne). The eldest.

eignesse. The share of the eldest son. Same as **esnecy.**

Ei incumbit probatio qui dicit, non qui negat (e′ī in-kum′bit pro-bā′she-ō quī di′sit, non quī ne′gat). The burden of proof is upon him who alleges, not upon him who denies. Patterson v Gaines (US) 6 How 550, 596, 12 L Ed 553, 572.

Ei incumbit probatio, qui dicit, non qui negat; cum per rerum naturam factum, negantis probatio nulla sit (e′ī in-kum′bit prō-bā′she-ō, quī di′sit, non quī ne′gat; kum per rē′rum na-tū′ram fak′tum, ne-gan′-tis pro-bā′she-ō nul′la sit). The proof is incumbent upon him who asserts, not on him who denies; since in the nature of things there can be no proof of a negative. See 3 Bl Comm 366.

eik (ēk). An addition.

ei legitur in haec verba. See **et ei legitur in haec verba.**

einecia (ē-nē′she-a). Same as **einetia.**

einetia (ē-nē′she-a). The share of the eldest son. Same as **esnecy.**

Ei nihil turpe, cui nihil satis (e′ī ni′hil ter′pe, ki ni′hil sa′tis). Nothing is base to a person to whom nothing is sufficient.

eins ceo que. Inasmuch as.

eirant. Errant; wandering.

eire. Same as **eyre.**

Eire (ār). The Republic of Ireland.

Eisdem modis dissolvitur obligatio quae nascitur ex contractu, vel quasi, quibus contrahitur (e-is′dem mō′dis dis-sol′vi-ter ob-li-gā′she-ō kwē na′si-ter ex kon-trak′tū, vel quā′sī, quī′bus kon-trā′hi-ter). An obligation which arises in contract or quasi contract is dissolved in the same manner in which it is contracted.

eisna. The eldest.

eisnetia (ēz-nē′she-a). The share of the eldest son. Same as **einetia.**

either. Preferably, one or the other of two. Permissibly, one or another of several. Never, one of many. Messer v Jones, 88 Me 349, 356.

either extremity. Any one of the four extremities of the body, that is, of the hands and feet. Brotherhood of Locomotive Firemen & Engineers v Aday, 97 Ark 425, 134 SW 928.

either or survivor. A term used in leasing a safe deposit box; a joint tenancy with right of survivorship is not necessarily created by the use of such term. 10 Am J2d Banks § 474.

eject. To turn out; to expel.

ejecta (ē-jek′tạ). Refuse matter; offal.

ejection. Compelling a person to leave a place, whether by force administered to his person or by order or command to leave, as where the conductor of a passenger train explicitly orders a passenger to leave the train. 14 Am J2d Car § 1092. An ouster or turning out of a person in possession of land. See 3 Bl Comm 198.

ejection and intrusion (ē-jek′shọn and intrö′zhọn). An action to recover real property and also for damages sustained, by a plaintiff who was forcibly dispossessed.

ejectione custodiae (ē-jek′she-ō′ne kus-tō′di-ē). See **de ejectione custodiae.**

ejectione firmae (ē-jek-she-ō′ne fir′mē). A writ or action of trespass in ejectment which lay when lands or tenements had been let for a term of years, and afterwards the lessor, reversioner, remainderman, or a stranger, ejected or ousted the lessee of his term. See 3 Bl Comm 199.

ejectment. An action which is purely possessory; a form of action in which the right of possession to corporeal hereditaments may be tried and possession obtained. Kingsnorth v Baker, 213 Mich 294, 182 NW 108. At common law a purely possessory action; even as modified by statute, and though based upon title, it is essentially of that nature. 25 Am J2d Eject § 1.
See **equitable ejectment; writ of ejectment.**

ejector. The person or thing by which a person or thing is ejected.
See **casual ejector.**

ejectum (ē-jek′tum). Wreckage which has been cast upon the shore by the sea.

ejercitoria (ay-her-the-to′ri-a). (Spanish.) An action against the owner of a ship for an indebtedness incurred by the master of the ship.

ejettement. Same as ejectment.

ejettement de garde. Ejectment of ward.

ejidos (ā-hē′dōs). (Spanish.) Commons. Lands used in common by the inhabitants of a place for pasture, wood, threshing-ground, etc.; particular

EJURARE [393] **ELECTION**

names are assigned to each, according to its particular use. Hart v Burnett, 15 Cal 530, 554.

ejurare (ē-jū-rā're). To abjure; to renounce by oath; to resign.

ejusdem generis (ē-jus'dem je'ne-ris). Of the same kind or class. The rule of construction that where general words are used in a contract after specific terms, they are to be confined to things of the same kind or class as the things previously specified. 17 Am J2d Contr § 270. The principle applicable in the construction of wills that where certain things are enumerated and a more general description is coupled with the enumeration, the general expressions are understood to cover only things of a like kind with those enumerated. 57 Am J1st Wills § 1130. The rule of statutory construction that where general words follow a designation of particular subjects or classes or persons, the meaning of the general words will ordinarily be presumed to be restricted by the particular designation, and to include only things or persons of the same kind, class or nature as those specifically enumerated, unless there is a clear manifestation of a contrary purpose. 50 Am J1st Stat § 249.

The rules as stated above are not to be applied by rote against the obvious intent of the contracting parties, the testator, or, in the case of a statute, the legislature. If upon consideration of the whole subject matter of the contract or the law upon the subject in the case of a statute and the purposes sought to be effected, it is apparent that the intention was that the general words should go beyond the class specifically designated, the rule does not apply. Moreover, if the particular words exhaust the class, then the general words must have a meaning beyond the class, or be discarded altogether. Kansas City Southern Railway Co. v Wallace, 38 Okla 233, 132 P 908.

ejusdem negotii (ē-jus'dem ne-gō'she-ī). Of the same transaction.

Ejus est interpretari cujus est condere (ē'jus est inter-pre-tā'rī kū'jus est kon'de-re). It is for him who writes or composes anything to give it interpretation.

Ejus est nolle, qui potest velle (ē'jus est nol'le, quī po'test vel'le). He who can consent can refuse.

Ejus est non nolle qui potest velle (ē'jus est non nol'le quī po'test vel'le). He who can consent should not be noncommittal.

Ejus est periculum cujus est dominium aut commodum (ē'jus est pe-ri'ku-lum kū'jus est do-mi'nium ât kom'mo-dum). He should have the hazard who has the ownership or profit of a thing.

Ejus nulla culpa est cui parere necesse sit (ē'jus nul'la kul'pa est ki pa-rē're ne-ses'se sit). No blame attaches to a person who is compelled to obey.

ekg. Abbreviation for **electrocardiogram.**

elaborare (e-la-bo-rā're). To acquire by labor or effort.

elapse. To pass or slip by; to expire as a period of time; to intervene points of time. Logsdon v Logsdon, 109 Ill App 194.

elder brethren (el'dėr). A name which is applied to the masters of Trinity House, an official board having charge of English buoys and lighthouses.

eldest (el'dest). Oldest; firstborn.

elect. Verb: To make a choice. To select a person for office by a majority or a plurality of votes. State ex rel. Cook v Doss, 102 W Va 162, 134 SE 749. Noun: A person elected to public office but awaiting inauguration or installation.
See **appoint**; **election.**

Electa una via, non datur recursus ad alteram (ē-lek'ta ū'na vī'a, non dā'ter re-ker'sus ad al'te-ram). Having chosen one course, he is not allowed to have recourse to another.

elected. Chosen. In the most ordinary significance, chosen by vote, usually by popular vote, but applicable also to a choice by a restricted vote. Clarke v Irwin, 5 Nev 111, 121.

elected domicil. The domicil of a party or parties to a contract as fixed by the contract for the purposes of the contract. Woodworth v Bank of America (NY) 19 Johns 391.

Electio est creditoris (ē-lek'she-o est kre-di-tō'ris). The creditor has his election.

Electio est debitoris (ē-lek'she-ō est de-bi-tō'ris). The debtor has his election.

Electio est intima (interna), libera, et spontanea separatio unius rei ab alia, sine compulsione, consistens in animo et voluntate (ē-lek'she-ō est in'ti-ma (in-ter'na), li'be-ra, et spon-ta-nē'a se-pa-rā'she-ō ū'ni-us rē'ī ab a'li-a, sī'ne kom-pul-she-ō'ne, konsis'tenz in a'ni-mō et vo-lun-tā'te). Election is the internal, free, and spontaneous separation of one thing from another, without compulsion, and consists of intention and will.

election. In the most common usage, the expression of a choice by the voters of a body politic, or the means by which a choice is made by the electors. State ex rel. La Follette v Kohler, 200 Wis 518, 228 NW 895, 69 ALR 348. Precisely, a choosing or selection, by those having a right to participate, of persons to fill public offices or of public measures which shall be adopted or rejected. 25 Am J2d Elect § 1. The choosing of a public officer by an organized body, such as the legislature of a state. Speed & Worthington v Crawford, 60 Ky (3 Met) 207, 211. The designation of corporate directors by the vote of the stockholders and the designation of corporate officers by the vote of the directors. 19 Am J2d Corp §§ 1081, 1082. In an abstract sense, a choice between two or more substantive rights, either one or any one of which may be asserted at the will of the person making the choice, which are so inconsistent that a choice once made is binding upon beyond recall. Wilhorn Builders v Cortaro Management Co. 81 Ariz 381, 307 P2d 94, supp op 82 Ariz 48, 308 P2d 251. The choice which a person must make between the acceptance of a benefit under an instrument, and the retention of some property already his own, which the same instrument purports to dispose of to another. McDermid v Bourhill, 101 Or 305, 199 P 610, 22 ALR 428, 433. The right or privilege, accorded by statute in some states to the eldest heir, if of age, of taking the whole estate of the deceased ancestor, upon paying to the others their just proportions of the value in money.

If the eldest refuse, the next eldest succeeds to the right of election until all the adults have enjoyed the opportunity of election. If all refuse, the property is sold and the proceeds divided. Catlin v Catlin, 60 Md 573, 575.

The doctrine of election is applicable to a taxpayer having a choice of two legal methods of computing his tax, and having chosen one he is not permitted to change his mind to the detriment of

ELECTION [394] ELECTIO

the revenue. Ross v Commissioner (CA1) 169 F2d 483, 7 ALR2d 719.

See **corrupt practices acts; cumulative voting; general election; primary election; referendum; registration; special election; suffrage.**

election auditor. An officer who audits and publishes an account of election expenses.

election bet. The subject of a criminal offense as prescribed by statute in most jurisdictions. A transaction, whatever the name given it, the real effect of which, as intended, is that one party may lose, and the other may gain, money or property, or the representative of either may so gain or lose, according to whether the election terminates for or against a particular person, or may result in one way or another. 26 Am J2d Elect § 378. To bet that one of the candidates will or will not obtain a stated number of votes is an election bet. Commonwealth v Brandon, 43 Ky (4 B Mon) 1, 2.

election between causes of action. See **election of counts.**

election between defenses. See **election of defenses.**

election between dower and will. The doctrine that puts the surviving spouse to an election between her right to dower and the benefits provided for her by the will. 57 Am J1st Wills § 1560.

election between offenses. See **election of counts.**

election by ballot. Nothing less than an election by secret ballot. Ex parte Arnold, 128 Mo 256, 30 SW 768.

See **Australian Ballot System; ballot; distinguishing mark; marked ballot.**

election contest. See **contest of election.**

election district. A territorial unit of a state or of a county or municipality established with reference to various offices to be filled by election, such as legislative, congressional, or councilmanic districts, and often with reference to apportionment according to population. 25 Am J2d Elect §§ 12 et seq. A small territorial unit, otherwise known as an election precinct, established for administrative purposes and laid out with the view of accommodating the voters of the district at a single voting place. Kerlin v Devils Lake, 25 ND 207, 141 NW 756.

election dower. The estate which a widow may elect to take in lieu of dower. Chrisman v Linderman, 202 Mo 605, 100 SW 1090.

See **election between dower and will.**

electioneering. The solicitation of votes. A criminal offense where conducted at certain times and places on election day. 26 Am J2d Elect § 374.

Electiones fiant rite et libere sine interruptione aliqua (ē-lek-she-ō'nēz fī'ant rī'te et lī'be-re sī'ne in-ter-rup-she-ō'ne a'li-qua). Elections should be made regularly and freely and without any interruption.

election of counts. The doctrine under which the prosecution may be required to elect on which charge it will proceed to the trial under an indictment which is in two or more counts for separate and distinct offenses. 27 Am J1st Indict § 133. The doctrine that a plaintiff, who has misjoined causes of action in his declaration, complaint, or petition will be required upon motion of the adverse party to elect upon which cause of action or count he will proceed in the action. 41 Am J1st Pl § 357.

election of defenses. The doctrine that a defendant who has joined defenses improperly may be required to elect upon which defense he shall rely. 41 Am J1st Pl § 358.

election officers. Wardens, clerks, tellers, inspectors, etc. and sometimes town or township officers, such as selectmen, trustees, and town clerks, whose official duties include taking part in the conduct of a general or special election. 25 Am J2d Elect § 39.

election of place of payment. The right of the holder of a note, payable, by its terms, at any one of several places, to choose the particular place at which payment shall be made. Also, the right of the maker of such note to choose the place of payment, once he has called upon the holder to elect and the holder has failed to elect. 11 Am J2d B & N § 972.

election of remedies. The choosing between two or more different and co-existing modes of procedure and relief allowed by law on the same state of facts. Mansfield v Pickwick Stages, 191 Cal 129, 215 P 389. The doctrine, not a rule of substantive law but a technical rule of procedure, that the adoption, by an unequivocal act, of one of two or more inconsistent remedial rights has the effect of precluding a resort to the others. Arzuaga v Gonzalez (CA1 Puerto Rico) 239 F 60.

election precinct. See **election district.**

election returns. The report made by the polling officials to the higher authority as to the number of votes cast for each candidate, or the number of votes cast for or against the propositions or questions submitted to the voters at the election. Bond v Rogers, 219 Ark 319, 241 SW2d 371. An official statement of the votes cast at an election, transmitted to some authorized custodian, for the purpose of being canvassed by some proper authority. State v Common Council of St. Paul, 25 Minn 106, 108.

See **canvass.**

elections. See **election.**

election to fill vacancy in office. The next election at which a successor to the incumbent of the office would have been elected if there had been no vacancy, or the election next in point of time after the vacancy occurs, the divergence of view arising in the construction of statutes containing such varied phrases as "first annual election," "next election," "regular election," and "proper election." Anno: 132 ALR 574.

election to hold agent. The doctrine applicable in a case of undisclosed principal that since the liability of an undisclosed principal and his agent is an alternative liability, rather than a joint liability or a joint and several liability, the third party, after he becomes aware of the agency and the identity of the principal, is put to an election to hold either the agent or the principal; he cannot hold both. 3 Am J2d Agency § 308.

election under will. The doctrine that one who is given a benefit under a will must choose between such benefit and an estate or interest in the testator's property which he claims but which is taken from him by the terms of the will. 57 Am J1st Wills § 1526. The making of an election to take under or against a will. 57 Am J1st Wills § 1534.

Electio semel facta, et placitum testatum, non patitur regressum (ē-lek'she-o se'mel fak'ta, et pla'si-tum tes-tā'tum, non pā'ti-ter re-gres'sum). An election once made, and the plea witnessed, is not permitted to be revoked.

Electio semel facta non patitur regressum (ē-lek'she-o se'mel fak'ta non pā'ti-ter re-gres'sum). An elec-

tion which has once been made is not permitted to be revoked.

elective. Contingent upon a selection or choice; subject to choice; dependent upon the votes to be cast at an election by voters.

elective franchise. The right, rather the privilege, of voting at an election; not a natural right or a civil right, but a political right or privilege conferred and existing only by law, that is, by constitution or statute. Chamberlin v Wood, 15 SD 216, 88 NW 109.
See **suffrage**.

elector. A person having constitutional and statutory qualifications which entitle him to vote, including not only one who votes, but one who is qualified, yet fails to exercise the right of suffrage. 25 Am J2d Elect § 52.
See **elective franchise; presidential electors; suffrage**.

electoral college. The presidential electors considered as a body.
See **presidential electors**.

electors of president. See **presidential electors**.

electric company. A public utility engaged in the production, transmission, or furnishing of electricity to customers for heating, lighting, or other domestic, mechanical or scientific purposes.

electric eye. A device whereby a ray is controlled to open a door, turn on a lamp, etc.; a game played on a machine called the "electric eye," whereby a ray or beam of light is shot at a target. Anno: 135 ALR 158.

electricity. A subtle agency that pervades all space and evades successful definition. A dangerous, invisible, subtle, silent, deadly, and instantaneous force. Austin v Public Service Co. 299 Ill 112, 132 NE 458, 17 ALR 795.

electric line. A line of insulated wire for conducting electricity.
See **power line**.

electric meter. See **meter**.

electric plant. See **plant; public utility**.

electric power line. See **power line**.

Electric Safety Code. A code of regulations with respect to the installation and maintenance of electrical equipment and wires, issued by the Bureau of Standards of the United States Department of Commerce. 26 Am J2d Electr § 44.

electric telegraph. An apparatus or instrument used to transmit intelligence to a distant point with the aid of electricity. Western Union Tel Co. v Hill, 163 Ala 18, 50 So 248.

electric wire. See **electric line**.

electric work. Construction, installation, operation, alteration, removal or repair of electrical apparatus. Hollingsworth v Berry, 107 Kan 544, 192 P 763, 11 ALR 151.

electrocardiogram. The record of the test made of a heart by an electrocardiograph.

electrocardiograph. An instrument by which the contractions of the heart are measured.

electrocution. Death caused by electricity. A method of executing the death penalty; passing through the body of the convict a current of electricity of sufficient intensity to cause his death. People ex rel. Kemmler v Durston, 119 NY 569, 579.

electrodes. The poles or terminals of an electric circuit or source, such as a battery. California Electrical Works v Henzel (CC Cal) 48 F 375, 378.

electroencephalogram. A record of a medical study of the brain with the aid of apparatus whereby waves of the brain are recorded.

electrolysis (ē-lek'trō-sis). The action of an electric current passing through a chemical compound in a fluid condition or solution; a source of destruction of water mains and steel reinforcements in buildings where a current escapes from a wire to the ground. Lowrey v Cowles Electric Smelting & Aluminum Co. (CC Ohio) 68 F 354, 366.

electrolyte (ē-lek'trō-līt). A chemical substance which, when dissolved in a liquid, will be dissociated and render the liquid conductive of an electric current. Ruben v Ariston Laboratories (DC Ill) 40 F Supp 551.
See **electrolysis**.

electronic eavesdropping. A recording of speech or conversation by an electronic apparatus operating without the knowledge of the speaker. Anno: 97 ALR2d 1288.

electrotherapy. The use of different forms of electric machines for therapeutic purposes. Joyner v State, 181 Miss 245, 179 So 573, 115 ALR 954.

eleemosyna (el-ē-mos'i-na). Alms.

eleemosynarius (ĕl-lē-e-mos-in-ā'ri-us). A person who dispenses or bestows alms.

eleemosynary (el-ē-mos'i-nā-ri). Charitable. People ex rel. Ellert v Cogswell, 113 Cal 129, 45 P 270.

eleemosynary corporation. A corporation created for or devoted to charitable purposes or one supported by charity. 15 Am J2d Char § 145. A corporation created, not for private gain or profit, but for the administration of a charitable trust or for a charitable purpose, such as the maintenance of a hospital. Gilbert v McLeod Infirmary, 219 SC 174, 64 SE2d 524, 24 ALR2d 60.

eleemosynary purpose (el-ē-mos'i-nā-ri pėr'pọs). A charitable purpose. A "charitable purpose" as such term is used and understood in treatises and decisions upon the subject of trusts. Estate of Wirt (Cal App) 263 P 271, 272.

eleganter (e-le-gan'ter). Accurately; with due regard to form.

elegit (ē-lē'jit). A writ, provided by the Statute of Westminster 2, ch. 18, Edw. 1, for the enforcement of a judgment, by virtue of which the sheriff seized and delivered a moiety of the defendant's lands until the debt was levied out of the rents and profits. 30 Am J2d Exec § 29.
See **estate by elegit; tenant by elegit**.

element. Any one of the four substances or elements, earth, air, fire, and water. A component or essential part, such as proximate cause in liability for negligence.

elementary (el-ē-men'tạ-ri). Pertinent to the elements, rudiments, or first principles of anything; initial; rudimental. Livingston v Davis, 243 Iowa 21, 50 NW2d 592, 27 ALR2d 1237.

elementary school. A school for the elementary education of children. Livingston v Davis, 243 Iowa 21, 50 NW2d 592, 27 ALR2d 1237.

elements. The four substances believed by former generations to constitute all matter of a physical nature: earth, air, fire and water. Sudden, unusual or unexpected manifestations of the forces of na-

ture, such as floods, tornadoes, etc. 32 Am J1st L & T § 505. Sometimes considered the equivalent of act of God. 32 Am J1st L & T § 811.
See **damage by the elements**.

elevated railway. A railway elevated above the streets upon an overhead roadbed. 55 Am J1st Urb Trans § 12.

elevator. A car, platform, or cage, known in England as a "lift," used for the vertical conveyance of persons or property between the floors of a building. More broadly defined as the car, platform, or cage and the power machinery propelling such device, the cables or connections by means of which the power is supplied, and the shaft in which the carriage moves. 26 Am J2d Elev § 1. Cases construing the term as it appears in the double indemnity clause of an accident insurance policy are divided in opinion, some holding that the term is confined to the car, platform, or cage, while others hold that it includes, not only the car, platform, or cage, but the shaft as well. 29A Am J Rev ed Ins § 1235.
A lifter or conveyer, in the form of an endless belt or chain bearing cups or scoops for picking up threshed grain, or other material which handles easily, and carrying it above to another floor or a higher point for processing, is called an "elevator." Also called an "elevator" is a structure used for the storage of grain, usually referred to as a "grain elevator."
See **escalator; freight elevator; grain elevator; passenger elevator**.

elevator attendant. The person or individual who is engaged in the actual operating, running, or handling of the elevator car, platform, or cage. 26 Am J2d Elev § 1.

elevator operator. An elevator attendant. A person other than the owner of the building who may nevertheless be under duties with regard to an elevator, such as a managing agent in control, or any other person who has general charge of the elevator. 26 Am J2d Elev § 1.

elevator insurance. Insurance against liability arising from the death of or injury to a person or persons caused by the operation of an elevator.

eligibility. Fitness for selection. Fitness for election or appointment to a public office. 42 Am J1st Pub Of § 37.
See **eligible to an office; qualification**.

eligible alien. An alien who may become a citizen of the United States, having the qualifications and meeting the requirements imposed by Congress in granting the privilege of naturalization. Terrace v Thompson, 263 US 197, 68 L Ed 255, 44 S Ct 15.

eligible list. A list of applicants for a Civil Service position found upon a test to possess the qualifications requisite for the position. State v Frear, 146 Wis 302, 131 NW 834.

eligible to an office. A person legally qualified and capable of holding the office at the commencement of the term for which he may be elected or appointed. Demaree v Scates, 50 Kan 275, 32 P 1123.

elimination. The act of removing, getting rid of, or leaving out of consideration.

elinguation (ē-ling-gwā'shǫn). An ancient punishment for crime by cutting out the tongue of the offender.

elisor (ē-lī'zǫr). A person appointed to perform certain duties pertaining to certain officers, when the latter are disqualified. More specifically, a person who is appointed to perform functions of a sheriff or coroner in cases where they are disqualified or unable to act. Bruner v Superior Court, 92 Cal 239, 245, 28 P 341.

Elizabeth I. Queen of England from November 17th, 1558, to March 24th, 1603.

Elizabeth II. The present Queen of the United Kingdom and Northern Ireland, and Head of the Commonwealth, having reigned since Feb. 6, 1952, and having been crowned on June 2, 1953.

Elkins Act. A federal statute making it a criminal offense for one knowingly to accept a rebate from a railroad common carrier subject to the provisions of the Interstate Commerce Act. Lehigh Coal & Navigation Co. v United States, 250 US 556, 63 L Ed 1138, 40 S Ct 24.

ell (el). A lineal cloth measure equal to about one yard.

elogium (ē-lō'ji-um). A will, a testament.

eloign (ē-loin'). To take beyond the jurisdiction of the court, particularly to avoid seizure. To take personal property subject to a lien out of the county. Garneau v Port Blakeley Mill Co. 8 Wash 467, 36 P 463. A return to a writ of replevin where the property has been put out of reach.

eloigner (ē-loin'er). One who eloigns.
See **eloign**.

eloignment (ē-loin'męnt). See **eloign**.

eloin (ē-loin'). Same as **eloign**.

eloinate (ē-loi'nāt). To eloign.
See **eloign**.

eloinment (ē-loin'męnt). Same as **eloignment**.

elongare (ē-lon-gā're). To eloign.

elongata (ē-lon-gā'ta). Eloigned,—a sheriff's return on a writ of replevin if the goods are carried out of the county, or concealed; that is, eloigned. See 3 Bl Comm 148.

elongatus (ē-lon-gā'tus). Eloigned.
See **eloign**.

elongavit (e-long-gā'vit). He has eloigned.

elope. To engage in an elopement.
See **elopement**.

elopement. The abandonment of a husband by a wife who leaves his home and goes to live with an adulterer. Cogswell v Tibbets, 3 NH 41, 42. The innocent act of lovers, both unwed, in going away secretly to be married.

elsewhere. In any other place. In another place suggested by the context. Commonwealth v Bowser, 61 Pa Super 107.

eluviones (e-lu-vi-ō'nēz). Spring tides.

emanare (e-ma-nā're). To spring from; to issue.

emanavit (e-ma-nā'vit). It issued.

emancipate. To release; to set free, as to release a minor from parental control.
See **emancipation; emancipation of minor**.

emancipation. Liberation from slavery or bondage; release of a minor from parental control.
See **emancipation of minor**.

emancipation by marriage. That emancipation from a parent's control of the time and earnings of his minor child, which necessarily results from the marriage of the child, whether with or without the parent's consent. See 39 Am J1st P & C § 65.

emancipation of minor. The relinquishment by a parent of control and authority over his minor child, conferring on him the right to his earnings, and terminating the parent's legal duty to support the child. Swenson v Swenson (Mo App) 227 SW2d 103, 20 ALR2d 1409.
See **express emancipation; implied emancipation; partial emancipation; statutory emancipation.**

emasculate. To castrate; to remove the testicles. To deprive of virility or strength.
See **eunuch.**

embalmer. A person trained and skilled in the process of treating and preserving a dead body against decay. State ex rel. Kempinger v White, 177 Wis 541, 188 NW 607, 23 ALR 67, 70.
See **undertaker.**

embalmer's license. A license required of an embalmer by the state under its police power. 54 Am J1st Und & E § 5.

embankment. A bank of earth, usually produced artificially for flood control.
See **dike; levee.**

embargo. The exclusion of an article from interstate or foreign commerce. 15 Am J2d Com §§ 73-75. An edict or order of a government forbidding the entry or departure of ships at ports within the dominions of the government, sometimes imposed in carrying on war, at other times imposed merely in the control of trade and the advancement of commerce, in which case it may be total or partial, as when imposed on domestic ships to prevent trade with a particular country. Gibbons v Ogden (US) 9 Wheat 1, 6 L Ed 23. The refusal of a common carrier to accept certain kinds of freight on its line, or freight to be carried between certain points, for a limited or indefinite period of time. Froehling Supply Co. v United States (CA7 Ill) 194 F2d 637.
See **disembargo; hostile embargo.**

embarrassed. Ill at ease. Impeded.
See **financially embarrassed.**

embassy. The trust, charge, or mission of the ambassador of a foreign nation; the residence of the ambassador of a foreign nation.
See **diplomatic officers; legation.**

embedded property. See **imbedded property.**

embezzlement. A statutory offense, not a common law crime; the fraudulent appropriation or conversion by an agent, an employee, a corporate officer, a trustee, a public officer, or other person acting in a fiduciary capacity or character, of money or property, the possession of which has been entrusted to him by another. 18 Am J1st Embez § 2. The word includes misappropriation of trifling sums, made with intent to restore in due time, and with ample present and prospective ability to restore. United States v Summers (DC Va) 19 F 627. In statutes imposing a double liability in damages for the "embezzlement" of property of a decedent prior to the granting of letters testamentary or letters of administration, the term means the fraudulent appropriation or concealment to one's own use of estate property in one's possession. Anno: 29 ALR2d 256.

embezzlement by agent. The crime of embezzlement committed by one in possession of the converted or misappropriated property by virtue of his employment by a principal and the delegation of authority to do something in the name and stead of such principal. 26 Am J2d Embez § 26.

embezzlement by bailee. The offense of embezzlement committed by one in possession of the converted or misappropriated property as bailee. Although the hirer of property has been held not to be within a statute of embezzlement which includes "any bailee or other agent," it has also been held that a statute making it a crime for any carrier, bailee, or other person to embezzle or convert to his own use property delivered to him, is not confined to bailments for the sole benefit of the bailor, but extends to the bailee of an automobile under a hiring agreement, who fails to return the automobile. 26 Am J2d Embez § 24.

embezzlement by employee. The criminal offense of embezzlement committed by a person who is in the employ of another and who, in the discharge of his duties, is subject to the immediate control and direction of his employer. 26 Am J2d Embez § 25.

embezzlement by fiduciary. The crime of embezzlement committed by an executor, administrator, guardian, or broker. 26 Am J2d Embez § 31. A statute defining embezzlement by a "trustee or factor, carrier or bailee," applies to trustees, factors, carriers, or bailees for artificial persons as well as private persons. Anno: 41 ALR 474.

emblavence de bled (em'bla-vens de blèd). Profits of the crop, that is, emblements.

emblements. Corn, wheat, rye, potatoes, garden vegetables, and other crops, which are produced annually, not spontaneously, but by labor and industry; a classification which is important in reference to the doctrine of a tenant's rights in crops after the termination of the tenancy, which has come to be known as the doctrine of emblements. 21 Am J2d Crops § 2.

embler. To sow; to steal.

embody. To include or incorporate as a part of something; to include in a written instrument or statute.

embolism (em'bō-lizm). The plugging of a blood vessel by a blood clot. Anno: 20 ALR 81.
See **cerebral embolism; pulmonary embolism.**

embowel. A rare, if not obsolete, word meaning disembowel.

embrace. To hug a person in demonstrating or expressing affection; to encircle; to encompass, to surround or inclose; to include as parts of a whole, or as subordinate divisions of a part; to accept; to use to advantage.

embraceor (em-brā'sọr). Same as **embracer.**

embracer. A person who has committed the crime of embracery.
See **embracery.**

embracery. The criminal offense of attempting to corrupt, influence, instruct, or induce a jury in any way, except by the strength of evidence and the arguments of counsel in open court, to be more favorable to one side of the case than the other. 26 Am J2d Embr § 1.

embrothel. To place or harbor a person in a brothel.
See **brothel.**

emenda (e-men'da). Amends; that which is given to mend or satisfy an injured party.

emendare (ē-men-dā're). To make amends; to compensate for an injury.

emendatio (ē-men-dā'she-ō). An amendment; a rectification; a correction; amends; compensation for injury.

e mera gratia (ē me'ra grā'she-a). Of mere grace, favor, or indulgence.

emergency. Confrontation by sudden peril. 38 Am J1st Negl § 41. A pressing necessity; an exigency; an event or occasional combination of circumstances calling for immediate action or remedy. 38 Am J1st Mun Corp § 450. An unforeseen occurrence or condition calling for immediate action to avert imminent danger to life, health, or property. 43 Am J1st Pub Wks § 136.

The term in the Hours of Service Act is used in its ordinary or popular sense, not synonymous with accident, casualty, or act of God. While unexpected sickness of an employee or the delay of a train caused by a wreck is an emergency, such is not true of an ordinary accident incidental to the operation of a railroad. 31 Am J Rev ed Lab § 803.

See **financial emergency; sudden emergency.**

emergency appointment. A temporary or provisional appointment to a civil service position. 15 Am J2d Civ S § 25.

emergency brakes. Hand brakes on a motor vehicle, required and regulated by statute in many jurisdictions. 7 Am J2d Auto § 151.

emergency call. A call by telephone for a physician, police, firemen, ambulance, etc. A call of nature requiring immediate attention.

emergency employment doctrine. The rule that an employee under regular employment possesses implied authority to employ an assistant to aid him in performing a task or tasks within the scope of his employment in case of emergency which renders the engaging of such assistance absolutely necessary, it being impossible for the employee working by himself or with the aid of other employees in regular service to overcome the emergency conditions. Standard Oil Co. v Adams, 271 Ky 221, 111 SW2d 668.

emergency fund. A fund of an insurance company or mutual benefit society provided for use in the event of the occurrence of losses in excess of common experience.

emergency landing. The landing of an aircraft in a place or at a time not within the flight plan.

emergency measures. Acts performed in an emergency. 38 Am J1st Negl § 41. Legislation enacted in an emergency; laws necessary for the immediate preservation of the public peace, health, or safety. 28 Am J Rev ed Init & R § 10. Statutes which, because of the existence of an emergency as declared in the legislation, do by their terms take effect immediately, or from or after their passage, or from or after their approval by the governor. 50 Am J1st Stat §§ 491-493. A municipal ordinance relating to the preservation of public peace, property, health, safety, or morals, taking effect, according to its terms, immediately upon passage. 37 Am J1st Mun Corp § 152.

emergency operation. Surgery required immediately. An abortion necessary for saving the life of the woman. State v Unosawa, 48 Wash 2d 616, 296 P2d 315.

emergency ordinance. See **emergency measures.**

emergency price control. The regulation of prices in an emergency, such as the country being at war, which otherwise might result in the inflation of prices of goods most in demand, especially food and clothing, to the disadvantage, discomfort, and suffering of many people. 56 Am J1st War § 39.

emergency relief. Appropriations for relief of distress after a disaster caused by a tornado, hurricane, flood, earthquake, drought, pestilence, unemployment resulting from a sudden shut-down of industries, etc. 41 Am J1st Poor L § 22.

emergency rent laws. Statutes, the primary purpose of which is to limit rents for a period when an unexpected demand for, or a shortage in, housing inflates rentals to an unrealistic amount.

emergency statutes. See **emergency measures.**

emergency vehicles. Fire trucks, police cars, ambulances, utility repair cars, etc. 7 Am J2d Auto § 206.

emeritus (ē-mer'i-tus). Retired from service but retaining the title of office.

e.m.f. Abbreviation of electromotive force.

emigrant. A native or national of a country who is leaving the country to take up permanent residence elsewhere. 3 Am J2d Aliens § 48.

emigrant agent. A person engaged in employing laborers for work outside the state. 31 Am J Rev ed Lab § 762.

emigration. The act of foreigners in leaving their former country for purposes of permanent residence in another country. The term is the correlative of immigration, denoting their coming into a country. That is, a person is an emigrant as to the country which he leaves, and he is an immigrant as to the country to which he comes. 3 Am J2d Aliens § 48.

eminent domain. The power of the nation or a sovereign state to take, or to authorize the taking of, private property for a public use without the owner's consent, conditioned upon the payment of a just compensation. 26 Am J2d Em D § 1. The theory of such power, otherwise known as compulsory purchase or expropriation, is that all lands are held mediately or immediately from the state, upon the implied condition that the eminent domain, the superior dominion, remains in the state, authorizing it to take the same for public uses, when necessity requires it, by paying therefor an equivalent in money. It resembles the ancient prerogative of purveyance whereby the crown enjoyed the right of buying up provisions and other necessaries for the use of the royal household at an appraised valuation, and in preference to all others, even without the consent of the owner. Re Barre Water Co. 62 Vt 27, 30 A 109.

See **condemnation; just compensation; public use.**

emisset (e-mis'et). He bought.

emission. The act of sending forth or issuing, such as issuing bills of credit to circulate as currency. 36 Am J1st Money § 17. The discharge of seminal fluid from the male organ. 2 Am J2d Adult § 1; 44 Am J1st Rape § 4.

emit. To send forth; to issue.
See **emission.**

emmenagogue (e-men'a̱-gog). Medicine or drugs administered to a woman to produce menstruation, or to cause an abortion.

emoluments. The profit arising from office or employment; that which is received as compensation for services, or which is annexed to the possession of office as salary, fees, and perquisites; advantage; gain, public or private. State ex rel. Todd v Reeves, 196 Wash 145, 82 P2d 173, 118 ALR 177. Indirect or contingent remunerations which may or may not

EMOTIONAL [399] EMPLOYERS'

be earned; remunerations in the nature of compensation or in the nature of reimbursement. Waller v United States, 86 App DC 93, 180 F2d 194, 16 ALR2d 1328.

emotional insanity. Passion or frenzy produced by anger, jealously, or other emotion, sometimes of overwhelming force. 21 Am J2d Crim L § 37. The state of mind of one who, while in possession of his ordinary faculties and unaffected by any mental disease, gives way to his passions to such an extent as to become a temporary maniac. 29 Am J Rev ed Ins Per § 3.

empalement. Same as **impalement**.

empannel (em-pan'el). Same as **impanel**.

emparlance. Same as **imparlance**.

emparler (äm-par-lay). Same as **imparl**.

emphyteusis (em-fi-tū'sis). (Roman law.) A kind of lease of real property, the term of which was usually forever or for a very long period, and which provided for the improvement of the property, reserving an annual rent.

emphyteuta (em-fi-tū'tạ). (Roman law.) A tenant who held land by emphyteusis.

empire. See **American Empire**.

empiricism (em-pir'i-sizm). Searching for knowledge by experiment. A practice of medicine founded on mere experience without the aid of science or the knowledge of scientific principles. Nelson v State Board of Health, 22 Ky LR 438, 57 SW 501.

emplazamiento (em-plah-thah-me-en'to). (Spanish.) A summons or citation to appear before a court.

emplead. Same as **implead**.

employ. To engage the services of another, usually by contract or agreement for the performance of the services and the payment of a compensation therefor. Pinkerton Nat. Detective Agency v Walker, 157 Ga 548, 122 SE 202, 35 ALR 557, 560. One may employ a person without paying him compensation, for example, making use of a minor in a place of entertainment (31 Am J Rev ed Lab § 768) or in a place where intoxicating liquors are dispensed. Lutkevicz v Brennan, 128 Conn 651, 25 A2d 66.

employed. Being engaged in rendering services or being under contract for the rendition of services. United States v Morris (US) 14 Pet 464, 475, 10 L Ed 543, 548. The services may be intellectual or physical. 31 Am J Rev ed Lab § 783.

employed in agriculture. See **farm laborer**.

employed in manufacture. Made use of in manufacture. Hamilton Mfg. Co. v Lowell, 274 Mass 477, 175 NE 73, 74 ALR 1213.

employed in trade. Made use of in business or commerce. Working in a commercial enterprise.

employee. An expression more euphonious than "servant" but ordinarily meaning the same. 35 Am J1st M & S § 2. One who is in such a relation to another person that the latter may control the work of the former and direct the manner in which it shall be done. 35 Am J1st M & S § 2.

One is an "employee" for the purposes of Social Security and Unemployment Compensation where in rendering services for another he acts under the control and direction of the latter, not only as to the result to be accomplished, but as to the means and details by which the result is accomplished.

United States v Silk, 331 US 704, 91 L Ed 1757, 67 S Ct 1463; Schwing v United States (CA3 Pa) 165 F2d 518, 1 ALR2d 548. Only persons who perform menial services, manual labor, or work which is subordinate in its nature, and immediately subject to the directions and orders of the superior, are within the contemplation of statutes imposing liability upon corporate stockholders for debts of the corporation owing to laborers, servants, "employees", etc. Anno: 104 ALR 765. In other contexts, the term has a broader meaning, for example, in exemption statutes, where, under the rule of liberal construction, persons engaged in positions requiring services far above those of a menial character, such as sales manager, auditor, comptroller, etc., are deemed "employees." 31 Am J2d Exemp § 20. An officer of a corporation may be an "employee" for the purposes of Social Security. 48 Am J1st Soc Sec § 16.

See **public employee; servant**.

employee of the United States. Broadly, any person in the employ of the government. For the purposes of the Federal Tort Claims Act, one acting under the control of the government, unaffected from the standpoint of control by any intervening sovereignty, independent agency, or independent contractor. Anno: 57 ALR2d 1449-1453.

Employees' Pay Act. A federal statute providing a method for the division of time and computation of pay for services rendered by persons employed by the United States. 5 USC § 84.

employee stock option. A plan whereby a corporation gives to its employees, or employees who qualify under conditions imposed by the plan, an option to purchase stock of the corporation at a certain price, often the market price on a certain day, sometimes somewhat less than the market price on a certain day, to run for a period prescribed by the plan, irrespective of the market price during the period.

employer. One, formerly known as "master," who is in such relation to another person that he may control the work of that other person and direct the manner in which it is to be done. 35 Am J1st M & S § 2. The person by and for whom an independent contractor is engaged. 27 Am J1st Ind Contr § 27.

The concept of the term in labor legislation is broader than the common law or usual statutory concept. Anno: 1 L Ed 2d 2078. As defined by the National Labor Relations Act, an employer includes any person acting as an agent of an employer, directly or indirectly. 29 USC § 152(2). Expressly excluded from the definition of "employer" in the National Labor Relations Act are the United States, any wholly owned government corporation, any federal reserve bank, or any state or political subdivision of a state; national banks are not excluded. 31 Am J Rev ed Lab § 185.

employers' association. An association of employers, normally of employers engaged in the same industry.

employers' liability acts. Statutes in reference to an employer's liability for negligence resulting in injury to an employee, the most of which abrogate the fellow servant doctrine and limit the defenses of contributory negligence and the doctrine of assumption of risk (35 Am J1st M & S §§ 395 et seq.), including the Federal Employers' Liability Act relative to common carriers by railroad engaged in

interstate commerce and their employees. 35 Am J1st M & S §§ 398 et seq.
See **workmen's compensation acts**.

employers' liability insurance. Insurance which protects an employer against liability for the death or injury of an employee occurring within the scope of the employment. 29A Am J Rev ed Ins § 1351.
See **workmen's compensation insurance**.

employing unit. An employer.
For the purpose of determining the right to a reduced compensation contribution rating as a "qualified employer" under the unemployment compensation act, an "employer" and "employing unit" are synonymous, and are not intended to include a part or department of a going business or to embrace a unit which has no legal entity even though isolated from other units owned, managed, and controlled by the employer. Canada Dry Bottling Co. v Board of Review, 118 Utah 619, 223 P2d 586, 22 ALR2d 664.

employment. The act of employing or being employed. The occupation, business, or profession to which one devotes his services, time, and attention, and which he depends upon for livelihood or profit. Lyons-Thomas Hardware Co. v Perry Stove Mfg. Co. 86 Tex 143, 24 SW 16. The scope of an employee's duties and authority. 26 Am J2d Embez § 15. For the purposes of Social Security, any service, of whatever nature, performed within the United States by an employee for the person employing him, irrespective of the citizenship or residence of either. 48 Am J1st Soc Sec § 15. This comprehends, not only work actually done, but the entire employer-employee relationship for which compensation is paid to the employee by the employer. Social Secur. Board v Nierotko, 327 US 359, 90 L Ed 718, 66 S Ct 637, 162 ALR 1445. In some jurisdictions, for the purposes of workmen's compensation statutes, the term "employment" includes only occupations carried on by the employer for pecuniary gain, excluding employment in public or governmental service and service for charitable institutions. 58 Am J1st Workm Comp § 80.
See **casual employment; permanent employment; scope of employment**.

employment agency. A business having the purpose of obtaining employment for persons who make application to it for employment, the agency being compensated by the applicants, usually in the form of a percentage of wages or salaries obtained in the employments in which the applicants are placed by the agency. Adams v Tanner, 244 US 590, 61 L Ed 1336, 37 S Ct 662.

employment at will. A hiring for an indefinite period of time. 35 Am J1st M & S § 19.

employment contract. A contract between employer and employee; a collective labor agreement.
See **collective labor agreement; contract of hire**.

employment security. The protection given by labor laws. Another term for **unemployment insurance**.

empower (em-pou'ėr). To authorize; to commission; to delegate; to depute.

emprestido (em-prays'te-do). (Spanish.) A loan.

emptio (emp'she-ō). A buying; a purchase.

emptio bonorum (emp'she-ō bo-nō'rum). The purchase of goods.

emptio et venditio (emp'she-ō et ven-di'she-ō). Purchase and sale.

emptionis venditionis contractae argumentum (emp-she-ō'nis ven-di-she-ō'nis kon-trak'tē ar-gu-men'-tum). An earnest or token of a buying and selling contract; an arra. See 2 Bl Comm 447.

empto. See **ex empto**.

emptor (emp'tor). A buyer; a purchaser.
See **bona fidei emptor; caveat emptor**.

Emptor emit quam minimo potest, venditor vendit quam maximo potest (emp'tor e'mit quam mi'ni-mō po'test, ven'di-tor ven'dit quam ma'xi-mō po'test). The purchaser buys for the least he can, the vendor sells for the most he can. Michoud v Girod (US) 4 How 503, 554, 11 L Ed 1076, 1099.

emtio. Same as **emptio**.

emtor. Same as **emptor**.

emtrix. A female purchaser or buyer.

en (en). In; into; on.

enabling act. An act of emancipation. A statute which removes a disability, for example, the disability of a married woman at common law. 26 Am J1st H & W § 20. A statute which grants new powers or authority to a person or a corporation; the statute 32 Henry VIII, c. 28 (1540) which enabled three classes of persons to make leases which would last for three lives or twenty-one years. See 2 Bl Comm 319. A statute authorizing a particular act, such as the sale of land of a person under disability. 16 Am J2d Const L § 236.
See **curative act**.

enabling power. The power of approving or licensing something which the law undertakes to regulate. 1 Am J2d Admin L § 140.

enabling statute. See **enabling act**.

enact. To establish by law; to perform or effect; to decree. Re Senate File 31, 25 Neb 864, 876.

enacting clause. An orderly, and in some jurisdictions a mandatory, part of a statute, proclaiming the authority by which the statute was enacted, usually in some such form as "Be it enacted by the legislature [general assembly] of the State of [name of state], as follows." 50 Am J1st Stat §§ 153-155.

enactment. The process by which a legislative bill becomes law. Creating a law, that is, giving it an existence, or, as in some jurisdictions, giving it effectiveness. Anno: 132 ALR 1060.

enagenacion (ay-nah-hay-nā'ci-on). A word encountered in Spanish-American grants, which in its ordinary sense means a transfer of the title, the fee, but in a more enlarged sense it may include the transfer of every estate known to the law, from a fee simple to an estate at will or sufferance; and in this enlarged sense it is equivalent to the English word "alienation." Mulford v Le Franc, 26 Cal 88, 103, 104.

enajenacion. Same as **enagenacion**.

en aprés (on a-prê). In the future; hereafter; henceforth.

en ariere (on a-rėr). In the past.

en autre droit (on ô-tr drwo). In the right of another person.

en autre soile (on ô-tr soil). On the land of another person.

en avant (oṅ a-vȯn'). In the future; for the future.

en banc (oṅ bangk). (French.) On the bench.
See **full bench**.

en barre (on bär). In bar.

en bloc (oṅ blok). In a mass; as a whole; as a unit.

en bonne foy (on bōn foa). In good faith.

en ce (oṅ sė). In this.

enceinte (ȯn-saṅt'). Pregnant; with child.

encephalogram (en-sef'a̱-lō-gram). See **electroencephalogram.**

en chemin (on shė-man'). On the way.

encheson. A cause or reason for anything.

en chiefe (on chief). In chief.

enclave. A territory or area foreign to, or apart from, that by which it is surrounded completely. See **federal enclave.**

enclose. Same as **inclose.**

enclosure. See **inclosure.**

en coste (on kost). On the side; collateral.

encourage. To give hope and impart courage. To incite; to induce; to abet.

en court (on kōrt). In court.

encroach. To effect an encroachment. See **encroachment.**

encroachment. A movement upon the property, authority, or rights of another; a gradual movement upon and occupancy of the land of another. In the broad sense, a trespass upon real estate, but in the legal sense, usually confined to an intrusion upon a highway by occupying it, fencing or walling in a portion of it, or erecting a structure which protrudes into it. State v Pomeroy, 73 Wis 664, 665; Chase v Oshkosh, 81 Wis 313, 51 NW 560. See **trespass.**

encumber. To effect or suffer an encumbrance. See **encumbrance.**

encumbrance. Literally a hindrance, impediment, or obstruction, such as an object in a highway. 25 Am J1st High § 272. The significance in the law is that of any right to, or interest in land conveyed, which may subsist in a third party, to the diminution of the value of the land, but at the same time consistent with the passage of the fee thereto. 20 Am J2d Cov § 81; 55 Am J1st V & P § 225. Including whatever charges, burdens, obstructs, or impairs the use of the land, depreciates it in value, or impedes its transfer, such as a lien, a mortgage, deed of trust, or an easement. Anno: 57 ALR 1376; 55 Am J1st V & P § 225. "Encumbrances" fall into two general classes: (1) Those which affect or relate to the title or the record thereof, and (2) those which affect or relate to the actual physical conditions upon the realty such as a path or roadway indicating a servitude. Anno: 64 ALR 1480.

The application of the term "encumbrance" is almost invariably made to real estate, although it would seem entirely proper to speak of a chattel mortgage or lien upon personal property as an "encumbrance."
See **covenant against encumbrances.**

encumbrancer. The holder of an incumbrance; as a person who holds a mortgage. A person who has a legal claim upon an estate. Warden v Sabins, 36 Kan 165, 169.

end. Finish; terminus; termination. An objective or purpose.
See **duration; end of will; end on.**

endangering life. Acting so as to imperil the life of a human. Not necessarily by acts of physical violence. Anno: 5 ALR 712.

endeavor. To attempt; to try; to experiment. Success is not an attribute of endeavor. Experimental approach toward the commission of a crime is an endeavor. Guilt is incurred by the trial,—success may aggravate, it is not a condition of it. United States v Russell, 255 US 138, 143, 65 L Ed 553, 555, 41 S Ct 260.

en declaration de simulation (on de-kla-rä'ti-on de si-mu-lä'ti-on). A form of action in France and Louisiana, the object of which is to have an unbelievable act declared to have been feigned. Erwin v Bank of Kentucky, 5 La Ann 1, 4.

en demeure (on dė-meu-r). In default.

en demeyne (on dė-main). In demesne.
See **demesne; demesne, as of fee.**

endenizen (en-den'i-zn). Same as **denize.**

endless chain contract. A contract, ostensibly for the sale of the right to vend an article in a designated territory, but in reality cloaking an undertaking by the purchaser to enter into similar contracts with others. 46 Am J1st Sales § 122.

end lines. The boundary lines of a mining claim which cross the lode or vein. 36 Am J1st Min & M § 111.

The legal end lines of the original or discovery vein of a mining claim are the end lines of all veins within the surface boundary with respect to extralateral rights. Jefferson Mining Co. v Anchoria-Leland Min. & Mill. Co. 32 Colo 176, 75 P 1070.

end of war. See **duration of the war.**

end of will. An expression clothed with pertinency by statutory requirements that a will be signed at the foot or end. Two variant definitions have evolved from the application of such statutes: (1) the physical end of the writing, the point spatially the farthest removed from the beginning; (2) the logical end, the end of the disposition of property wherever that end may appear in the paper, the sequential end, the end as determined by the unmistakable sequence which the testator intended to give to the writing as revealed upon the face of the instrument. 57 Am J1st Wills § 268.

end on. Ships approaching each other from opposite directions, or on such parallel lines as to involve risk of collision on account of their proximity. Brown v Slanson (US) 7 Wall 656, 19 L Ed 157.
See **head on.**

endorse. Same as **indorse.**

endorsement. Same as **indorsement.**

endow. In a narrow sense, to give one's wife an estate of dower upon taking the marital vows or entering into the marriage with her. In a broader sense, to bestow property upon a person or an institution, such as a college. Gupton v Gupton, 40 Tenn (3 Head) 487, 489.

endowment. The assignment to a widow of her dower upon the death of her husband. The provision made for the maintenance of officiating ministers by setting apart a glebe or land and by appointing tithes. Such endowments were established when lords of manors first built churches on their own demesnes. See 2 Bl Comm 21. The endowment of an institution, such as a college, is commonly understood as including all property, both real and personal, given to the institution for

its permanent support. Millsaps College v Jackson, 275 US 129, 72 L Ed 196, 48 S Ct 94, 95.
See **assignment of dower; fine for endowment.**

endowment insurance. In modern terminology, a life insurance policy which provides for the payment of the proceeds of the policy at a stated time after the date of the instrument, sometimes 20, sometimes 30 or more years, but upon the death of the insured if it occurs prior to the expiration of the stated period. 29 Am J1st Ins § 6. In former times, endowment policies appear to have had features of the tontine policy, one of which was that the insurer came under no liability to an insured who did not survive the endowment or tontine period. Such policies have been referred to at times as "pure endowment insurance."
See **tontine policy.**

en droit (on drwo). In right; in point of law.
See **defense en droit.**

ends of justice. In furtherance of justice.

end-use factor. A test of practicability employed before issuance of a certificate of public convenience and necessity. Anno: 5 L Ed 2d 1004. The ultimate use of the product to be supplied by a utility seeking a certificate of public convenience and necessity required as a condition of lawful operation. Anno: 5 L Ed 2d 1004.

enecius (e-nē'she-us). Same as **anecius.**

enemy. Another nation with which the country is in a state of war; more broadly defined for the purposes of some statutes, as including the individuals and corporations of a nation with which the country is at war. 56 Am J1st War § 83. Narrowly interpreted, an "enemy" is always the subject of a foreign power, who owes no allegiance to our government or country. United States v Greathouse (CC Cal) 4 Sawy 457, 466, F Cas No 15254. Reasonably, a person engaged against the United States in a rebellion or civil war is an "enemy." 56 Am J1st War § 62. The status of a person as an "enemy" for the purposes of the application of the Trading with the Enemy Act is determined with reference to domicil or residence in the territory of the nation which is a belligerent against the United States rather than according to nationality. 56 Am J1st War § 83. For the purposes of such statute, an "enemy" may be a partnership, corporation, or other body of individuals. 56 Am J1st War § 83.
See **alien enemy; public enemy.**

enemy alien. See **alien enemy.**

enemy property. All property within enemy territory. If suffered to remain in the hostile country after the war breaks out, it becomes impressed with the national character of the belligerent where it is situated without regard to the owner's sentiments or political opinions, or whether he is an enemy or a friend. The Peterhoff (US) 5 Wall 28, 18 L Ed 564. Under the Trading with the Enemy Act, money and all kinds of property of enemies, both tangible and intangible, including patents, copyrights, applications therefor, trademarks, choses in action, and claims of every character and description, owing to, belonging to, or held for, by, or on account of, or for the benefit of, the enemy may be sequestered. 56 Am J1st War § 85.

enemy waters. Storm, freshet and flood waters of a river, as distinguished from its ordinary and usual flow. Herminghaus v Southern California Edison Co. 200 Cal 81, 252 P 607. Surface waters referred to as the common enemy in supporting the common-law rule that the owner of the lower tenement or estate may at his option lawfully obstruct or hinder the flow of surface water thereon, and in so doing may turn it back or away from his own lands, and onto and over the lands of other proprietors without liability for such obstruction or diversion. 56 Am J1st Wat § 69.

En eschange il covient que les estates soient egales (on ā'shänj eel ko-vya' ker lays es-tāts' swat ā-gal'). In an exchange it is proper that the estates should be equal.

enetius (e-nē'she-us). Same as **anecius.**

en fait (on fay). In fact.

enfeoff (en-fef'). To vest a person, the feoffee, with a fee.
See **feoffee; feoffment; feoffor.**

enfeoffment (en-fef'ment). Same as **feoffment.**

enforceable legal right. A right recognized by law and executed by the law, executed by force within the law where force is necessary. Shaw v Proffitt, 57 Or 192, 109 P 584.

enforceable trust. A trust in which some person or class of persons have a right to all or a part of a designated fund, and can demand its transfer to them, and in case such demand is refused, may sue the trustee in a court of equity, and compel compliance with the demand. Tilden v Green, 130 NY 29, 28 NE 880. In a broader sense, a trust recognized in equity as valid and subsisting. 54 Am J1st Trusts §§ 570 et seq.

Enforcement of Foreign Judgments Act. One of the uniform laws. Anno: 72 ALR2d 1259, § 3. A uniform law, the purpose of which is to give to holders of foreign judgments, with respect to claims on the judgment debtor's property and the remedies of levy and garnishment thereon, the same rights and remedies as the holder of a domestic judgment. Sullivan v Sullivan, 168 Neb 850, 97 NW2d 348, 72 ALR2d 1251.

enfranchise (en-fran'chiz). To confer a franchise upon; to free; to permit a person to vote.
See **franchise.**

enfranchisement (en-fran'chiz-ment). The act of enfranchising.
See **enfranchise; franchise.**

enfranchisement of copyhold. The act of the lord of the manor in conveying a fee simple title to a copyholder, thus changing the tenure of the land from copyhold to freehold.

engage. In the oldest sense of the term, to give as a gage or pledge; to pledge property as security. To take part in; to be employed in, however the employment may arise. Anno: 15 ALR 1283. To cooperate actively or take part in an enterprise. Benefit Asso. of R. Employees v Hayden, 175 Ark 565, 299 SW 995, 57 ALR 622. To embark; to bind by appointment or by contract; to bind by promise of marriage. To enter into conflict with an enemy or test of strength and athletic ability with an opponent.

engaged. Taking an active part.
See **engage.**

engaged in aviation operations. Taking part in the operation of an airplane in some direct way other than merely being a passenger in an airplane. Price v Prudential Ins. Co. 98 Fla 1044, 124 So 817.
See **participating in aeronautics.**

engaged in business. Occupied or employed in business as a sustained, progressive, and continuous activity. Lewellyn v Pittsburg, B. & L. E. R. Co. (CA3 Pa) 222 F 177.

See **carrying on business; doing business; doing business in state; engaging in or transacting business.**

engaged in interstate commerce. In the meaning of the term as it appears in the Fair Labor Standards Act, engaged in activities so closely related to interstate commerce as to be for all practical purposes and in legal contemplation a part of it. Mitchell v C. Vollmer & Co. 349 US 427, 99 L Ed 1196, 75 S Ct 860. Similarly defined for the purposes of the Federal Employers' Liability Act. Southern Pacific Co. v Industrial Com. of Utah, 71 Utah, 248, 264 P 965, 968.

See **commerce; interstate commerce.**

engaged in manufacturing. Working with machinery to produce a finished product from raw materials or to convert manufactured articles into a different product. Hotchkiss v District of Columbia, 44 App DC 73.

engaged in military service. Being in the military service. Bradshaw v Farmers' & Bankers' Life Ins. Co. 107 Kan 681, 193 P 332, 11 ALR 1091, 1096. Having passed the examination or examinations, having taken the oath, having been enrolled, and having become subject to the orders of the military authorities. 29A Am J Rev ed Ins § 1204.

engaged in or about. A phrase used in workmen's compensation statutes to emphasize the necessity for a causal relationship between the employment and a compensable injury. 58 Am J1st Workm Comp § 209.

engage in practice. To pursue a profession such as law, medicine, architecture, etc. or a skilled occupation by a course of professional or business activities, not by single isolated acts. Dane v Brown (CA1 Mass) 70 F2d 164.

engagement. An agreement; a contract; an agreement consisting of mutual promises to marry.

engagements of bank. All pecuniary liabilities and obligations of a bank. Oppenheimer v Harriman Nat. Bank & Trust Co. 300 US 206, 81 L Ed 142, 57 S Ct 719.

engagement to marry. An agreement or contract to marry arising out of the mutual promises of the parties. 12 Am J2d Breach P §§ 2, 3.

engaging in business. See **engaged in business.**

engaging in or transacting business. To constitute "engaging in or transacting business" in a state, so as to be found or be present there for purposes of personal service of process, a nonresident corporation's activities must be substantial, continuous, and regular, as distinguished from casual, single, or isolated acts. Steinway v Majestic Amusement Co. (CA10 Okla) 179 F2d 681, 18 ALR2d 179.

engine. A skilfully contrived mechanism or machine, the parts of which concur in producing an intended effect; a machine for applying any of the mechanical or physical powers to effect a particular purpose; especially a self-contained mechanism for the conversion of energy into useful work; as a hydraulic engine for utilizing the pressure of water; a steam, gas, or air engine, in which the elastic force of steam, gas, or air is utilized. Haddad v Commercial Motor Truck Co., 146 La 897, 84 So 197, 9 ALR 1380.

See **road engine; switch engine; wild-cat engine.**

engineer. A graduate of an engineering college. One in charge of the running of an engine, especially a locomotive. One certified as an engineer in charge of the engines of a ship, but not one engaged to perform purely mechanical work on the engines of a ship. Baggaley v Aetna Ins. Co. (CA7 Ill) 111 F2d 134. As the term appears in a clause of an automobile liability insurance policy permitting use of the car in certain occupations, including that of engineers, a person who is not a graduate of an engineering school and has never been licensed as an engineer, but being a general superintendent of a steel company has practical knowledge of the processes involved in the manufacture of steel, and, at the time of the accident in question, is travelling to inspect mechanical equipment for possible use in the steel industry, is an engineer. Employers Liability Assur. Corp. v Accident & C. Ins. Co. (CA6 Ohio) 134 F2d 566, 146 ALR 1186.

engineering work. Any work of construction, alteration, or repair. 58 Am J1st Workm Comp § 108.

engineer's certificate. See **certificate of architect or engineer.**

England. The mother country and the source of our common law. 15 Am J2d Comm L § 5.

englecery. Same as **engleshire.**

englescherie. Same as **engleshire.**

engleshire (onglushayree). A word originating in the time of King Canute, meaning proof, in an action to amerce the inhabitants of a town or hundred for the death of a man occurring by homicide committed in the town or hundred, that the victim was an Englishman.

English. Our language. The people of England.

English church. The established Church of England.
See **Church of England.**

English consols. See **consols.**

English institutions. See the particular institution under concrete title or popular name, such as **Church of England; Parliament,** etc.

Englishman. A native of England; a citizen of England. One of English ancestry.
See **Once an Englishman always an Englishman.**

English mile. See **mile.**

English rule or doctrine. See the specific rule or doctrine under concrete title or popular name, such as **fifty per cent rule; market overt,** etc.

English rulers (rö'lėrs). The kings and queens of England.
See **regnal years.**

English Ruling Cases. A publication in the form of a set of books of leading cases decided by the courts of England.

englishry (ing'glish-ri). Same as **engleshire.**
See **presentment of englishry.**

English statutes. Acts of Parliament.
For particular statute, see the concrete title or popular name, such as **corn laws; mortmain statutes,** etc.

English tables. Mortality tables accepted by the courts of England. The Carlisle and Northampton tables.
See **mortality tables.**

en gross (on grōs'). In gross.

engross. To prepare a document; to express in legal form; to prepare a legislative bill for enrollment; to demand close attention. To gain a monopoly.

engrossed bill. A legislative bill which has been engrossed or copied for enrollment and is ready to be passed or enacted into a statute.

engrossing. The common-law and sometimes statutory offense of buying up large quantities of a commodity, such as grain, in order to control the market. 36 Am J1st Monop Etc. § 20. Demanding close attention. Making a clear copy of a rough draft of an instrument or writing.

Eng. Rul. Cas. An abbreviation of **English Ruling Cases.**

enhanced. Increased, especially in value. Thornburn v Doscher, (CC Or) 32 F 810, 812.

enhancement of damages. See **aggravation of damages; exemplary damages.**

enitia pars (e-ni'she-a parz). The part or share of the eldest.

enjoin. To forbid; to restrain by injunction; to command; to order. Ordinarily an imperative, but may be given less than mandatory force in the light of the entire context in which it appears. Good v Fichthorn, 144 Pa 287, 22 A 1032. Imperative in legal parlance, except as the mandatory character gives way to the entire context in which the word appears or to common parlance. Clifford v Stewart, 95 Me 38, 49 A 52; Good v Fichthorn, 144 Pa 287, 22 A 1032.
See **injunction.**

enjoy. See **enjoyment.**

enjoyment. Receiving the benefit of something; receiving substantial economic benefit rather than a technical vesting of title or estate. 28 Am J Rev ed Inher T § 193. Something less than consumption. 33 Am J1st Life Est § 241. That which gives value to property, including the beneficial use, interest, and purpose to which the property may be put. Pollock v Farmers' Loan Trust Co. 157 US 581, 39 L Ed 759, 15 S Ct 673.
See **beneficial enjoyment; covenant of quiet enjoyment; occupation; possession.**

enlarge. To free or set at large, as cattle within an enclosure. To increase in size; to expand. To grant to a party to an action an extension of time within which he may comply with a requirement of law or an order of court, as to enlarge his time to plead.

Enlarged Homesteads Act. A federal statute providing for entry of 320 acres or less of public lands in certain states, of a character which is nonmineral, nonirrigable, unreserved, and unappropriated, and for additional entries under certain circumstances. 43 USC § 218.

enlarged liability. An increased liability; a liability to which an obligation has been added or annexed. Buck v Davenport Sav. Bank, 29 Neb 407.
See **indorsement with enlarged liability.**

enlargement of estate. Adding to an estate in property, thereby increasing the estate in importance and in value, as where the remainderman conveys or releases his interest to the life tenant or tenant for years.

enlarger l'estate (on-larg-e' l'es-tāt). Enlargement of estate.

enlarging statute. A statute is a remedial statute, according to Blackstone (1 Bl Comm 86), which supplies defects, and abridges superfluities, in the former law. This is done by enlarging or restraining the former law, and these remedial statutes are therefore called enlarging or restraining statutes, depending on whether they supply or abridge. 50 Am J1st Stat § 15.

en le mercie (on lē mèr-si). In mercy, liable to amercement.

enlist. To enter one of the armed services other than as a commissioned officer. In the popular sense, to enter the service voluntarily.

enlistment. Entry into one of the armed services other than as a commissioned officer. In the popular sense, entering the service voluntarily. The contract of service which one other than a commissioned officer enters into with the government. 36 Am J1st Mil § 26. Constituting either an original undertaking or a renewal of an original undertaking known as a reenlistment. 10 USC § 3251.

enlistment service. See **recruiting and enlistment service.**

en masse (on mas). In one piece.
See **execution sale en masse.**

en mort meyne (on mor mīn). In mortmain.
See **mortmain.**

ennoyer (an-no-iā'). Same as **anoyer.**

Enoch Arden Statutes. Legislation which facilitates proof of death from absence, particularly for the benefit of the spouse of the absentee.

enormia (e-nor'mi-a). Wrongs; crimes; any acts of an unlawful character.

enormis (e-nor'mis). Excessive; enormous; wicked.

en oultre (on ôl-tr). Furthermore; besides.

en owel main. In equal hand.

en pais (on pè). Same as **in pais.**

enparler (on-par-le'). Same as **imparl.**

en passant (on pas-soń'). In passing; incidentally.

enpleet. Same as **implead.**

en plein vie (on plīn vî). In full life; that is in life in fact as well as in law.

en poigne. Same as **en poin.**

en poin (on poa). In the hand.

en primes (on pri-m). In the first place.

enquest. Same as **inquest.**

enquet. Same as **inquest.**

enrichment. Receiving something of value; being enriched. A thing that enriches.
See **unjust enrichment.**

enroll. To enter upon a roll or record; to record.

enrolled bill. A legislative bill in its final form as enacted and deposited with the official custodian of the statutory laws. 50 Am J1st Stat § 148.

enrolled bill rule. The rule that an enrolled bill imports absolute verity, so that the courts will not look beyond it to ascertain whether it has been regularly enacted or whether it expresses the terms of the statute as enacted. 50 Am J1st Stat § 149.

enrolled order. An order prepared for the signature of the judge and to be entered as the judgment of the court, once his signature has been appended.

enrolled ship. See **enrollment of vessel.**

enrollment. The act of entering something upon a roll or record. The recording of a deed.
See **clerk of enrollments; Statute of Enrolments.**

enrollment for military service. The listing in a register of the names of persons subject to military service; not a draft or an actual calling of the men. 36 Am J1st Mil § 7. Sometimes used as the equivalent of enlistment.

enrollment of judgment. The ministerial act in entering a judgment upon the record of the court to stand as a perpetual memorial of the court's action and to afford a means of proving the judgment. 30A Am J Rev ed Judgm § 92. The act of making up the judgment roll.
See **judgment roll.**

enrollment of vessel. The listing of a vessel of 20 tons or over in the office of the collector of the revenue of that district which includes the port to which she belongs at the time, the purpose being to evidence the national character of the vessel and enable her to obtain a coasting license. 48 Am J1st Ship § 48.
See **registration of vessel.**

enrollment of voters. The registration of voters. The listing of voters by party affiliation, by which eligibility to vote in a primary election is determined.

enrolment. Same as **enrollment.**

en route (oṅ röt). On the journey; during the journey.

ens (enz). Existence; a being; a creature.

enschedule (en-skedʹụl). To place or incorporate in a schedule.

enseal (en-sēlʹ). To seal; to affix a seal.

enseint (on-sańtʹ). Same as **enceinte.**

ensemble (oṅ-somʹbl). All together.

ensement. Also; likewise; similarly.

enserver. To subject to a service; to subject to servitude.

ensi (on-zi). Thus; so; likewise.

ensign (en-sīnʹ or enʹsīn). A flag. A commissioned officer of the United States Navy, being the lowest in rank of the commissioned officers.

ensilage. Corn in the stalk, clover, alfalfa, or other feed and roughage for livestock, stored while green or partly green in a silo, and allowed to cure therein.

ens legis (ānz lēʹjis). A creature or being of the law.

en son damage (on sōn da-mäzh). In his damage; while doing damage; damage feasant.

en son demeyne come de fee (on sōn dē-main kōm dē fē). In his demesne as of fee.

ensue. To follow or come after, sometimes importing a connection with that which precedes, as where a statute provides that one who administers a drug to a woman pregnant with a quick child, with intent to destroy the child, is guilty of manslaughter if the death of such woman "ensues." 26 Am J1st Homi § 196.

ensure (en-shörʹ). Same as **insure.**

en suspence (on sus-pān-s). In suspense; in abeyance; in statu quo.

ensy. Same as **ensi.**

entail (en-tālʹ). To settle property upon a person with limitations in respect of the succession. Precisely, to create an estate in tail, that is, a fee tail, in conveying or devising real property. To involve, e. g., the trial of a law suit "involves" much preparation.
See **fee tail.**

entailed-money. Money to be applied on account of the purchase of an estate-tail.

entencion. (Old French.) A plaintiff's declaration or first pleading in an action; a count or cause of action set forth in a declaration.

entendment. Understanding.

entente (oṅ-toṅtʹ). An understanding or agreement, especially an agreement between nations.

enter. To go into; to pass in or upon; as to enter a house or a close, sometimes for the purpose of taking possession. To list by name in a competition, as to "enter" a horse for a race. To make note of a fact by way of making a record thereof to be preserved. To make an entry of any kind.
See **entry.**

entering. See **enter; entry.**

entering the common rule (enʹtėr-ing). In the old common-law action of ejectment, the entry by the clerk of an order of court requiring the casual ejector, if he was a stranger, to give notice to the tenant in possession that he had been sued and would make no defense, and that unless the tenant in possession should defend, he would be turned out. 25 Am J2d Eject § 2.

enter into. To join with another or with others; as, to enter into a contract, to enter into a conspiracy.

enterlesse. Omitted; left out.

enterprise. An undertaking, a project, especially an undertaking or project involving hazard. United States v Ybanez (CC Tex) 53 F 536, 538. Initiative; readiness to engage.
See **business enterprise; gift enterprise; joint enterprise; military enterprise.**

entertainer. One who entertains, particularly one in the profession of entertainment, such as a comedian, an acrobat, a clown, etc.

entertainment. Diversion; amusement; something of interest. Hospitality.
See **house of entertainment.**

entertainment expense. A deduction in an income tax return where an ordinary and necessary business expense by way of entertainment, amusement, or recreation furnished a customer, client, or prospective customer or client. IRC § 274(a).

entertainment of suit. Taking jurisdiction, especially for the purpose of a trial or hearing on the merits. Denholm & McKay Co. v Commissioner (CA1) 132 F2d 243; Fernandez v Carrasquillo (CA1 Puerto Rico) 146 F2d 204.

entertainment tax. See **admissions tax.**

en tesmoignance (on toymwanyonce). In testimony; in witness.

entice. To allure or tempt by artifice, the word importing an initial, active and wrongful effort. State v Norris, 82 Or 680, 162 P 859. To lure animals onto one's premises by putting out food by way of bait. 4 Am J2d Ani § 139.
It is true that the word "entice" may be used in a good sense, but that is not its natural meaning, and when so used it is but figurative. Mooney v State, 8 Ala 328, 331.
See **induce; inveigle; procure; solicitation.**

enticement of child. The abduction or wrongful taking of a minor child from the custody of the parents for which the parent may have an action for damages based upon loss of the child's services. 39 Am J1st P & C § 72. A possible method of kidnapping. 1 Am J2d Abduct § 13.

enticement of servant. A form of tortious interference, consisting in maliciously inducing an employee in the actual service of his employer to desert and leave his service, to the injury of the employer. 30 Am J Rev ed Interf § 6.

entire. Whole; undivided; not participated in with others. Heathman v Hall, 38 NC (3 Ired Eq) 414, 421. Indivisible. 46 Am J1st Sales § 140.

entire compensation. As used in a statute providing for the recovery of "entire compensation" for the unlicensed use by the government of a patented invention, the term includes interest upon the damages found to have been suffered. Waite v United States, 282 US 508, 75 L Ed 494, 51 S Ct 227.

entire contract. The whole of the contract to be considered in construction. 17 Am J2d Contr § 258.
See **entirety of contract.**

entire day. A day of twenty-four hours, beginning and ending at midnight. To assure the intervention of a certain number of "entire days" between two specified days, both the first and last days are excluded. 52 Am J1st Time § 17.

entire interest. See **all title and interest.**

entire loss of hands or feet. Amputation, severance, or complete destruction of use of a member, as by paralysis. Fuller v Locomotive Engineers' Mut. Life & Acci. Ins. Asso. 122 Mich 548, 81 NW 326.

entire loss of sight. The loss of ability to see or perceive objects with the eye or the loss which leaves no sight left for practical use, notwithstanding the ability to distinguish between light and dark, but not a condition where there is limited or partial vision, although not sufficient for the pursuit of the victim's occupation or profession. 29A Am J Rev ed Ins § 1513.

entire output. A term designating the subject matter of a sale of manufactured goods, binding the seller, if he makes any of the product, to sell it to the buyer at the agreed price, and binding the buyer, to take all the product made by the seller at the time the buyer may choose to terminate the agreement. 46 Am J1st Sales § 65.

entire property and assets. Necessarily including cash, notes, accounts, and leases of personal property. Krell v Krell Piano Co. 23 Ohio NP NS 193.

entire tenancy. Sole ownership; ownership which is neither joint nor in common.

entirety. A whole of anything, as distinguished from a part of it; an undivided whole. The joint estate of husband and wife. 26 Am J1st H & W § 66.
See **estate by entireties.**

entirety of cause of action. A quality to be tested according to the identity of the essential facts; if the same evidence will support both actions, there is deemed to be but one cause of action, although the mere fact that the same evidence may be admissible under the pleadings in each action is not necessarily controlling. 1 Am J2d Actions § 128.

entirety of contract. A confusing term, sometimes meaning that there is but one, rather than several, contracts; at other times meaning that a contract is not divisible or severable. 17 Am J2d Contr § 324.
See **divisible contract; severability of contract.**

entirety of statute. The quality of a statute which renders it impossible to give effect to one part where another part is invalid. 16 Am J2d Const L §§ 181 et seq.

entitle. To vest the title to anything in a person; to furnish a right or claim to a thing. Barron Estate Co. v Waterman, 32 Cal App 171, 162 P 410. To give a name; to give a title; to supply a heading for a document or pleading.
See **beneficially entitled.**

entitled. See **entitle; vested interest; vested estate.**

entity. An existence; a being, actual or artificial.

entity of corporation. See **corporate entity.**

entity of partnership. See **partnership.**

entrance. The means or place of entering, as a door or gate. Renfo Drug Co. v Lewis, 149 Tex 507, 235 SW2d 609, 23 ALR2d 1114.

entrance fee. A payment made for admission to a place of entertainment; the charge made for obtaining membership in a labor union.

entrap. To catch; to ensnare; hence to catch by artifice; to involve in difficulties or distresses; to catch or involve in contradistinctions. Roane v State, 55 Okla Crim 332, 29 P2d 990.
See **entrapment.**

entrapment. The inducement of one to commit a crime not contemplated by him, for the mere purpose of instituting a criminal prosecution against him. People v Makovsky, 3 Cal 2d 366, 44 P2d 536; State v Marquardt, 139 Conn 1, 89 A2d 219, 31 ALR2d 1206. Measures used to entrap a person into crime in order, by making him a criminal, to aid the instigator in the accomplishment of some corrupt private purpose of his own. Woo Wai v United States (CA9 Cal) 223 F 412.

entre. In; within; between; entry.

entrebat. An intruder; a stranger; an interloper.

entrega (en-tray'ga). (Spanish.) A delivery.

entrepot (oñ'tr-pō). A warehouse; a storehouse; a freight depot; a place where goods are temporarily stored awaiting shipment. Coe v Errol, 116 US 517, 525, 29 L Ed 715, 718, 6 S Ct 475.

entruster. Same as **truster.**

entry. The act of one who enters. In burglary, the act of going into a place; it may consist of the insertion, for the purpose of committing a felony, of any part of the body or of any instrument connected with the body, such as a hook or a gun. 13 Am J2d Burgl § 10. Going upon land. The act of making something of record by noting it in a book or upon a paper.
See **book of original entry; breaking and entering; right of entry; writ of entry.**

entry ad communem legem (en'tri ad kom-mū'nem lē'jem). Entry at common law,—a writ under which the holder of a reversion could secure the possession of the land, upon the death of the particular tenant.

entry ad terminum qui praeteriit (en-tri ad ter'mi-num kwī prē-ter'i-it). An entry at the end of a term which has expired,—a writ of entry for the landlord at the expiration of the tenant's lease.

entry at customhouse. The exhibition or depositing by a ship's officer of the papers required by law, at the customhouse, or the giving of information to customs authorities with respect to the ship's cargo, for the purpose of securing permission to land or to discharge such cargo. 48 Am J1st Ship § 19. A written statement by the consignee of imported merchandise or his agent which gives such facts in regard to the importation as is required for the purpose of assessing duties and of securing a proper examination, inspection, appraisement, and liquidation. 21 Am J2d Cust D § 75. The listing by a person entering the United States of merchandise or other articles brought into the country by him. 21 Am J2d Cust D § 74.

For the purposes of tariff schedules, the term "entered" means entered, or withdrawn from warehouse, for consumption in the customs territory of the United States; the term "entered for consumption" does not include withdrawals from warehouse for consumption. 21 Am J2d Cust D § 33.

entry book. The record in the office of a recorder or register of titles where the filing or recording of an instrument is noted, usually under the names of both grantor and grantee, mortgagor or mortgagee. 15 Am J2d Chat Mtg § 92.

See **book of original entry.**

entry cui ante divortium (en′tri ki an′te di-vor′she-um). A writ which lay for a woman who had secured a divorce from her husband to secure lands which had been alienated by him. See 3 Bl Comm 183.

entry in casu consimili (en′tri in ka′sū kon-si′mi-lī). Entry in a similar case,—a writ of entry which lay to recover a reversion in land which had been alienated by a tenant.

entry into automobile. Stepping into the vehicle or at least making some move in reference to the vehicle other than merely approaching it for the purpose of entering it. New Amsterdam Casualty Co. v Fromer (Mun Ct App Dist Col) 75 A2d 645, 19 ALR2d 509.

entryman. A person who makes an entry of public lands under the homestead laws.

entry of alien. The physical act of coming into the geographical territory of the United States, a coming from outside, from some foreign port or place. 3 Am J2d Aliens § 54.

entry of amendment to state constitution. Entry of the full text of a proposed amendment to the constitution on the journal of each house of the legislature; an entry on the journal of each house sufficient to identify the resolution proposing the amendment, the resolution itself being in the possession of each house when it is passed by the house. 16 Am J2d Const L § 33.

entry of appearance. Indicating the appearance of the defendant in an action by the filing or service of a formal appearance or the announcement in open court that the defendant appears, in both of which methods the name of the attorney appearing for the defendant is given, unless the appearance is pro se.

entry of court order. The placing of an order of court of record by the clerk, after the court has made the order by announcing it or signing it. 37 Am J1st Motions § 29.

See **entry of judgment.**

entry of decree. Same as **entry of judgment.**

entry of homestead. See **entry on public land.**

entry of imports. See **entry at customhouse.**

entry of judgment. Recording a judgment in judgment book. 30A Am J Rev ed Judgm § 93. Spreading the judgment in full length upon the records of the trial court. 30A Am J Rev ed Judgm § 104. The enrolling of a judgment on the records of the court; a ministerial rather than a judicial act. 30A Am J Rev ed Judgm § 94.

See **docketing judgment.**

entry on public land. See **entry under homestead law.**

entry-taker. A state officer whose functions correspond closely with those of registers of United States land offices under Federal statutes. Chotard v Pope (US) 12 Wheat 587, 6 L Ed 737.

entry under homestead law. The act by which an individual acquires an inceptive right to a portion of the unappropriated soil of the public domain, consisting in the filing of a claim in the proper land office of the United States or, in case of the public domain of a state, in the office of an entry-taker or other officer with similar authority. 42 Am J1st Pub L §§ 19 et seq.

See **contest of land entry; original entry; preemption entry.**

enumerate. To count; to specify; to mention in detail; to enumerate property is to specify with precision its amount, quality or number. San Francisco v Pennie, 93 Cal 465, 29 P 66.

To place articles among those designated as "enumerated" in the Tariff Act, it is not necessary that they should be specifically mentioned. It is sufficient that they are designated in any way to distinguish them from other articles. Junge v Hedden, 146 US 233, 36 L Ed 953, 13 S Ct 88.

Enumeratio infirmat regulam in casibus non enumeratis (ē-nu-me-rā′she-ō in-fir′mat rē′gu-lam in kā′si-bus non ē-nu-me-rā′tis). Enumeration or specification disaffirms the rule in cases which are not specified or enumerated.

Enumeratio unius est exclusio alterius (ē-nu-me-rā′she-ō ū′ni-us est ex-klū′she-ō al-te′ri-us). The enumeration or inclusion of one is in effect the exclusion of another. Re Washburn (NY) 4 Johns Ch 106.

enure. Same as **inure.**

en ventre sa mere (on văn-tr sa mè-r). (French.) In the womb of the mother. Same as the Latin **in utero matris.**

envers (on-vêr). Against.

en vie (on vî). In life; while alive.

envoy (en′voi). A messenger sent by one government to another for the purpose of transacting some business of an international character.

See **diplomatic officers.**

eoath. An oath.

eodem delicto (ē-ō′dem de-lik′tō). In the same wrong; equally guilty of the offense. Conant v Conant, 10 Cal 239, 245.

eodem flatu (e-ō′dem flā′tū). In the same breath. Green v Biddle (US) 8 Wheat 1, 103, 5 L Ed 547, 572.

Eodem ligamine quo ligatum est dissolvitur (ē-ō′dem li-gā′mi-ne quō li-gā′tum est dis-sol′vi-ter). A bond is released by the same means by which it was made binding.

Eodem modo quo oritur, eodem modo dissolvitur (ē-ō'dem mō'dō quō ō'ri-ter, ē-ō'dem mō'dō dis-sol'vi-ter). Anything is dissolved or discharged in the same manner in which it was created.

Eodem modo quo quid constituitur, eodem modo destruitur (e-ō'dem mō'dō quō quid kon-sti-tu'i-ter, e-ō'dem mō'dō de-stru'i-ter). Anything is released in the same manner in which it is made binding.

eo instante or eo instanti (ē'ō in-stan'te or ē'ō in-stan'tī). At that moment; instantly; immediately. 1 Bl Comm 196.

eo intuitu (ē'ō in-tu'i-tū). With that intention; with that intent.

eo ipso (ē'ō ip'sō). By the thing itself; by the very thing.

eo loci (ē'ō lō'sī). In that place; in that state, condition, or situation.

eo nomine (ē'ō no'mi-ne). By or in that name or designation.

eo quod plerumque fit. See **ex eo quod plerumque fit.**

eorl (ėrl). Same as **earl.**

epidemic disease. A disease prevalent and spreading in the community.
See **contagious disease; infectious disease.**

epilepsy. A chronic disease of the nervous system characterized by paroxysms or convulsions, such seizures at times resulting in unconsciousness. Gould v Gould, 78 Conn 242, 61 A 604. Corbit v Smith, 7 Iowa 60. The older view that the inevitable course of epilepsy was to insanity has vanished in the light of better medical knowledge of the subject and improvement in medical treatment. It is also negatived by the fact that some great figures in history were afflicted with epilepsy.

epiqueya (ay-pe-kay'yah). (Spanish.) The word is practically the equivalent of our word "equity."

episcopacy (ē-pis'kō-pạ-si). The rule or government of the church by bishops.

episcopal. Administered and governed by bishops.
See **archiepiscopal.**

Episcopal Church. The Protestant Episcopal Church of the United States; the Church of England.

episcopalia (ē-pis-ko-pā'li-a). Certain dues which were paid by the clergy to the bishops.

episcopus (ē-pis'kō-pus). A Roman overseer or manager; a bishop of the church of England.
See **archiepiscopus.**

Episcopus alterius mandato quam regis non tenetur obtemperare (e-pis'ko-pus al-ter'i-us man-dā'tō quam rē'jis non te-nē'ter ob-tem-pe-rā're). A bishop is not bound to obey any other command than that of the king.

epistola (e-pis'to-la). A written communication; a letter.

epistolae (e-pis'to-lē). Opinions of the Roman emperors on matters and questions which were propounded to them.

e pluribus unum (ē plö'ri-bus ū'num). One out of many; one composed of many,—the motto of the United States government.

equal (ē'kwạl). Adjective: Impartial; not discriminating; unbiased; uniform. Verb: To make equivalent to, to recompense fully, to answer in full proportion. Fry v Hawley, 4 Fla 258, 279.

equal election. An election in which every elector has the right to have his vote counted for all it is worth in proportion to the whole number of qualified electors desiring to exercise their privilege. McKinney v Barker, 180 Ky 526, 203 SW 303. An election where the vote of every elector is equal in its influence upon the result to the vote of every other elector; where each ballot is as effective as every other ballot. Blue v State, 206 Ind 98, 188 NE 583, 91 ALR 334.

equal equities. The equity of one party shown to be equal to the equity of the other; one party as well situated as the other to foresee and prevent the prejudicial consequence. 27 Am J2d Eq § 145.

equal guilt. See **recrimination.**

equality. The state or condition of being equal; uniformity. A state not exclusive of distinctions, provided the distinctions are based upon reason. State v Finch, 78 Minn 118, 80 NW 856. The absence of arbitrary distinctions.

equality clause. A clause which anciently was commonly inserted in charters of common carriers, requiring the carrier to furnish transportation to its patrons on equal terms. Hilton Lumber Co. v Atlantic Coast Line Railroad Co. 141 NC 171, 53 SE 823.

equality is equity. A maxim of equity. 27 Am J2d Eq § 125. The basis of the doctrine of advancements. 3 Am J2d Advancem § 3.

equalization. The act or process of making things equal, of producing uniformity.

equalization board. See **board of equalization.**

equalization of assessments. A proceeding the general purpose of which is to bring the assessments of different parts of a taxing district to the same relative standard so that no one of the parts may be compelled to pay a disproportionate part of the tax. Huidekoper v Hadley (CA8 Mo) 177 F 1. Used with less precision to designate the process of raising or lowering the amount of a tax assessment upon an individual piece of property to render it equal to the assessments on other individual pieces of property of the same class in the taxing district. 51 Am J1st Tax § 741.

equalization of taxes. A process necessary properly to fulfil constitutional requirements of equality and uniformity in taxation. The process of adjusting the aggregate values of property as between different taxing districts, so that the value of the whole tax imposed on each taxing district shall be justly proportioned to the value of the taxable property within its limits, in order that one county or taxing district shall not pay a higher tax in proportion to the value of its taxable property than another. People ex rel. Bracher v Orvis, 301 Ill 350, 133 NE 787, 24 ALR 325. The process of raising or lowering the total assessments on all the property in a taxing district to equalize them with the total assessments in other taxing districts of the same kind in the state, or of raising or lowering the entire assessment on a given class of property, such, for example, as mining rights, in order to equalize it with the total assessment made with respect to other classes of property in the taxing district in question, or other taxing districts, or with the total assessment on the same class of property in other taxing districts. 51 Am J1st Tax § 741.

EQUALIZE [409] EQUITABLE

equalize. To make equal; to produce uniformity.
See **equalization**.

equally. In an equal degree or quantity. Gulf, Colorado & Santa Fe Railroad Co. v Warlick, 1 Indian Terr 10, 16, 35 SW 235. Importing a division per capita when used to indicate an equal division among a class, but not necessarily requiring a per capita equality of division, being satisfied at times by an equality between a class and a legatee named, and always subject to control by a context which calls for a per stirpes distribution. 57 Am J1st Wills § 1297.
See **share and share alike**.

equally between. Appearing in a legacy or devise, usually, but not necessarily, indicating a bequest to individuals rather than to a class. 57 Am J1st Wills § 1265.

equally divided court. The number of justices holding for affirmance equalling the number holding for reversal, so that the judgment of the lower court must stand. 5 Am J2d A & E § 902.

equal protection of the laws. A phrase not susceptible of exact definition; generally, a guaranty under the Fourteenth Amendment to the United States Constitution that no person or class of persons shall be denied the same protection of the law which is enjoyed by the other persons or other classes under like circumstances, in their lives, liberty, property, and in pursuit of happiness. Truax v Corrigan, 257 US 312, 66 L Ed 254, 42 S Ct 124, 27 ALR 375. Concisely stated, the guaranty of equal protection means that the rights of all persons must rest upon the same rule under the same circumstances, both in privileges conferred and in liabilities imposed. Hartford Steam Boiler Inspection & Ins. Co. v Harrison, 301 US 459, 81 L Ed 1223, 57 S Ct 838.

equal rights statutes. The designation sometimes given to those statutes enacted since the civil war and the abolition of slavery which exemplify the changed feeling of the people towards the African race and are intended to place the colored man upon a perfect equality with all others before the law. Ferguson v Geis, 82 Mich 358. The modern terminology is "civil rights acts." But statutes removing the disabilities of married women and forbidding discrimination against women are sometimes referred to as "equal rights laws" or "equal rights statutes."
See **civil rights acts**.

equal watches. Successive and continuous watches of sailors on a vessel at sea. To be constituted in numbers as nearly equal as the sum of the whole number will permit. New York & Cuba Mail S. S. Co. v Continental Ins. Co. (CA2 NY) 117 F2d 404.

eques (ē′kwēz). A knight.

equip. To furnish for service, or against a need or exigency; to fit out; to supply with whatever is necessary to efficient action in any way; to furnish with means for the prosecution of a purpose. Anno: 24 ALR 743.

equipage (ek′wi-pāj). An outfit or equipment for a particular purpose, such as a trip or expedition. Anno: 24 ALR 743.
See **equipment**.

equipment. The means with which a task can be accomplished; an outfit. The personal luggage of a traveler or passenger. Metz v California Southern Railroad Co. 85 Cal 329, 24 P 610. As the word is used in construction contracts, it means the outfit necessary to enable the contractor to perform the agreed service, the tools, implements, and appliances which might have been previously used, or might be subsequently used by the contractor in carrying on other work of like character. United States Rubber Co. v Washington Engineering Co. 86 Wash 180, 149 P 706. As used in the Federal Employers' Liability Act, the term "equipment" has reference more to personal and movable property than to fixed real property. 35 Am J1st M & S § 426.
See **railroad equipment**.

equitable. Just. 27 Am J2d Eq § 23. The characterization of a right which should be recognized, even though it is not a legal right or title. 27 Am J2d Eq § 63.

equitable action. An expression that has lost much of its significance because of the enactment of statutes and the promulgation of rules of procedure abolishing the distinction between an action in equity and an action at law. Where the distinction still prevails, an "equitable action" is one to be prosecuted and tried in accordance with the modes of procedure known to courts of equity. 27 Am J2d Eq § 177. Although the distinction between an action in equity and an action at law may have been abolished in a particular jurisdiction, an action in equity in such jurisdiction still has a distinctive character in respect of the relief sought, relief which historically has been obtainable only in equity, relief demanded, not only on account of the substantive character of the right sought to be enforced, but also on account of the inadequacy of the legal remedy. 27 Am J2d Eq § 5. An "equitable action" is an action which is not only remedial in its nature, but which may be brought for the purpose of restraining the infliction of contemplated wrongs or injuries, and the prevention of threatened illegal action, which may be the occasion of serious injury to others. Thomas v Musical Mut. Protective Union, 121 NY 45, 24 NE 24.

equitable adoption. The principle that a contract or agreement to adopt a child, clear and complete in its terms, and entered into by persons capable of contacting, which has been fully and faithfully performed on the part of the child so that relief for him is required as a matter of justice and equity, will be enforced in equity to the extent of decreeing that the child occupy in equity the status of an adopted child, and be entitled to the same rights of inheritance in intestate property of the promisor to which he would have otherwise been entitled had the intended adoption proceedings been legally consummated. 2 Am J2d Adopt § 16.

equitable approximation doctrine. The principle applied in a few cases whereby a testamentary gift is saved from defeat by the rule against perpetuities by the contrived reasoning that the intent of the testator was that the donee should have the property and that the time of vesting of the property in the donee was a matter of subordinate consequence. Anno: 95 ALR2d 808.
See **cy pres**.

equitable assets. Rights or interests, which may be either real or personal, but require the aid of the court of equity for their subjection. Agee v Saunders, 127 Tenn 680, 157 SW 64. Lands or personalty in which a debtor has an equitable estate or interest, so that they may be reached by a creditor's bill, notwithstanding the legal title is in another. 21 Am J2d Cred B § 33.

equitable assignment. An order, writing, or act by the assignor which makes an absolute appropriation of a chose in action or fund to the use of the assignee with the intent of transferring a present interest, but not amounting to a legal assignment. An executory agreement or declaration of trust, not enforceable as an assignment by a court of law, which a court of equity, exercising a sound discretion will enforce. 6 Am J2d Assign § 1.

equitable chattel mortgage. Any contract so convincingly established as to show that there was a clear intention to give a lien on specified chattels of, and in the possession of, the lienee, and that the contract ought, in good conscience and equity, to be enforced according to that intention. An agreement founded on a valuable consideration to give a mortgage on a chattel, an instrument inartificially drawn, a mortgage defectively executed, or an imperfect attempt to create a mortgage, or to appropriate specific property to the discharge of a debt. 15 Am J2d Chat Mtg § 3.

equitable chose in action. A personal right of which equity will take cognizance for the purpose of granting relief, such, for example, as a right against a trustee to enforce the execution of a trust. McIlvaine v Smith, 42 Mo 45.

equitable claim. A claim of which equity will take cognizance for the purpose of granting relief, especially a claim for breach of duty by a fiduciary. Seminole Nation v United States, 316 US 286, 86 L Ed 1480, 62 S Ct 1049.

equitable construction. The construction of a statute by either restraining or enlarging the letter of the statute. Riggs v Palmer, 115 NY 506, 22 NE 188. The interpretation of instruments agreeably to and in conformity with the principles and rules of equity. By and large, the rules for the construction of a contract are the same in equity as in law. Neither a court of law nor a court of equity can interpolate in a contract what the contract does not contain either in words or by necessary implication. 17 Am J2d Contr §§ 241, 242.

equitable conversion. That constructive alteration in the nature or character of property whereby, in equity, real is for certain purposes considered as personalty, or whereby personalty for similar considerations, is regarded as real estate, and in either instance, it is deemed to be transmissible and descendible in its converted form. 27 Am J2d Eq Conv § 1.

equitable defense. A defense which recognized by courts of equity acting solely upon the inherent rules and principles of equity, altogether outside and independent of those rules and defenses which obtain in a court of law. Kelly v Hurt, 74 Mo 561, 565, 569. A concept of little significance in most jurisdictions, modern rules of practice permitting the pleading in an action of defenses either legal or equitable. 27 Am J2d Eq § 19.

equitable easements. A term frequently applied to covenants running with the land. Werner v Graham, 181 Cal 174, 183 P 945. Restrictive covenants as to the use of land or the location or character of buildings or other structures thereon are primary examples. 20 Am J2d Cov § 166.

equitable ejectment. A paradoxical expression, since ejectment is a legal, not an equitable remedy, but nevertheless applied to an equitable remedy employed in obtaining the specific performance of contracts for the sale of real estate and in some other instances. McKendry v McKendry, 131 Pa 24, 18 A 1078.

equitable election. Essentially, the principle of election.
See **election.**

equitable estate. An equity; an estate or interest in property recognized only in equity, especially a trust. McIlvaine v Smith, 42 Mo 45.
See **equitable title.**

equitable estate of wife. See **separate estate of wife.**

equitable estoppel. A term which, for all practicable purposes, is the same as estoppel in pais; an estoppel of a party to plead or prove an otherwise important fact, because of something which he has done or omitted to do. 28 Am J2d Estop § 27.
See **estoppel in pais.**

equitable execution. Any one of the procedures whereby equity enforces its decrees; writ of assistance; sequestration; distringas, receivership, etc. 27 Am J2d Eq § 252.

equitable foreclosure. See **foreclosure.**

equitable garnishment. A form of judgment creditor's action, statutory proceeding under which, when an execution has been returned wholly or partly unsatisfied, the judgment creditor may maintain an action against the judgment debtor and any other person to compel the discovery of any property belonging to the judgment debtor, and of any money, thing in action, or other property due him, or held in trust for him, and to procure satisfaction of the judgment out of such property. Giest v St. Louis, 156 Mo 643, 57 SW 766.

equitable interest. See **equitable right; equitable title.**

equitable jointure. The satisfaction of a wife's right to dower made by a settlement before marriage, enforceable in equity where it consists of a competent livelihood to take effect upon the husband's death and to continue at least for the life of the wife, and was accepted by her in lieu of, or as the equivalent of, dower. 25 Am J2d Dow § 114.

equitable lien. A right, not recognized at law, to have a fund or specific property, or its proceeds, applied in whole or in part to the payment of a particular debt or class of debts. 33 Am J1st Liens § 18.

equitable maxim. See **maxim.**

equitable mortgage. An instrument not effective as a mortgage at law but regarded as a mortgage and given the effect of a mortgage in equity, the same as if a mortgage in due form had been executed, under various circumstances, such as the reservation of a lien on property which is conveyed, an appropriation of specific property to secure the performance of an obligation, an attempt to create a mortgage, and an agreement to give a mortgage, provided the instrument does not merely assume that a lien has been or will be created, but purports through its own terms and efficacy to create the lien. 36 Am J1st Mtg § 13. Another term for vendor's lien. Gessner v Palmater, 89 Cal 89, 26 P 789.
See **equitable chattel mortgage; imperfect mortgage.**

equitable owner. See **equitable title.**

equitable partition. See **partition.**

equitable plaintiff. Broadly, the plaintiff in an action or suit in equity. Precisely, the holder of the beneficial interest where a suit has been instituted by or

EQUITABLE [411] EQUITY

in the name of the holder of the legal title as nominal plaintiff for the benefit of the owner of the beneficial interest. 39 Am J1st Parties § 15.

equitable plea. A plea in an action at law which presents an equitable defense.
See **equitable defense.**

equitable rate of interest. A rate of interest chargeable against a fiduciary, as fixed by a court of equity, usually lower than the statutory rate. 30 Am J Rev ed Int § 35.

equitable recoupment. A reduction of the claim affirmatively urged in an action so far as in reason and action it ought to be reduced. Gooch Mill & Elevator Co. v Commissioner (CA8) 133 F2d 131, revd on other grounds 320 US 418, 88 L Ed 139, 64 S Ct 184. The doctrine of recoupment exists in equity as well as at law, and has been said to be equitable in nature. 20 Am J2d Count § 6.
See **recoupment.**

equitable rescission. Relief by way of rescission had in a court of equity without restoration by the plaintiff, prior to the commencement of the action, of that which he received from the defendant under the contract which he seeks to have rescinded. Morgan Munitions Supply Co. v Studebaker Corp. 226 NY 94, 123 NE 146.

equitable right. A right which equity will protect, even though it is not a legal right or title. 27 Am J2d Eq § 63. A right recognized by a court of equity and enforceable only by a court of equity, except as statutes or modern rules of practice have wiped out the distinction between an action at law and a suit in equity. Brown v Circuit Judge of Kalamazoo County, 75 Mich 274, 42 NW 831; Estate of Folwell, 68 NJ Eq 728, 62 A 414.
See **equitable title.**

equitable rule. Literally, the rule followed by equity courts. A rule which is just.

equitable seisin (sē'zin). By analogy to legal seisin, the possession of land coupled with the right to possess it by virtue of a freehold estate therein which equity will recognize and protect.

equitable servitude. See **equitable easements.**

equitable setoff. A remedy open to the defendant where, from the nature of the claim or the situation of the parties, it is impossible to obtain justice by plea or cross action—in other words, in those cases where, through no fault of the defendant, he has no adequate remedy at law. 20 Am J2d Countcl § 24.

equitable title. A title which is recognized as ownership in equity, whatever cognizance may be taken of it at law, for example, the title of the vendee under a contract for the sale of real estate. 56 Am J1st V & P § 356. A title which is not a legal title and is enforceable only in a court of equity, except as statutes or modern rules of practice have wiped out the distinction between an action at law or a suit in equity. A title derived through a valid contract or relation, and based on recognized equitable principles; the right in the party, to whom it belongs, to have the legal title transferred to him. Harris v Mason, 120 Tenn 668, 115 SW 1146; Estate of Folwell, 68 NJ Eq 728, 62 A 414.

equitable trust fund doctrine. See **trust fund doctrine.**

equitable waste. Acts which at law would not be deemed waste under the circumstances of the case, but which, in the view of a court of equity are regarded as waste from their manifest injury to the inheritance, although such acts are not inconsistent with the legal rights of the party who commits them. 56 Am J1st Waste § 5.

equitas. A corruption of **aequitas.**

equitatura (e-qui-tā-tū'ra). The equipment of a traveler.

equites aurati (e'qui-tēz â-rā'tī). Knights were called "aurati" from the gilt spurs which they wore, and "equites" because they always served on horseback. See 1 Bl Comm 404.

equities being equal, the law prevails. A maxim of equity, meaning that where two persons have equal equitable claims upon, or interests in, the same subject matter, or, in other words, if each is equally entitled to the protection and aid of a court of equity with respect to his equitable interest, and one of them in addition to his equity has obtained also the legal estate in the subject matter, he who thus has the legal estate will prevail. 27 Am J2d Eq § 150.

equity. A term having a variety of meanings. The mitigating principles, by the application of which substantial justice may be attained in particular cases wherein the prescribed or customary forms of ordinary law seem to be inadequate. A complex system of established law and jurisprudence. The standing of a party to claim relief. An interest in property which a court of equity will protect. 27 Am J2d Eq § 1.
See **at law and in equity; bill in equity; court of equity; decree; equity term; in equity; strong arm of equity.**

equity acts in personam. A maxim in equity. The Latin form, **aequitas agit in personam** (ē'qui-tas ā'jit in pėr-sō'nam). Schmaltz v York Mfg. Co. 204 Pa 1, 53 A 522.
Equity deals primarily with the person, and usually only through him with the res. Atlantic Seaboard Natural Gas Co. v Whitten, 315 Pa 529, 173 A 305, 93 ALR 615. The operation of the maxim has been greatly modified by statute. Although an equity court still has the power to act in personam, by force of statute, its judgment or decree also operates in rem to establish a title or right. 27 Am J2d Eq § 122.

equity aids no man to the injury of another. A maxim of equity. The Latin form is **aequitas neminem juvat cum injuria alterius** (ē'qui-tas nē'mi-nem ju'vat kum in-jū'ri-a al-te'ri-us).

equity aids the vigilant and diligent. A maxim of equity, sometimes stated as "equity aids the vigilant, not the sluggards." The Latin form is **aequitas subvenit vigilantibus non dormientibus** (ē'qui-tas sub-vē'nit vi-ji-lan'ti-bus non dor-mi-en'ti-bus). In application, the maxim is essentially the equivalent of the doctrine of estoppel. Equity will not take rights acquired by one who has been vigilant and give their benefit to one who has lost them through inaction. 27 Am J2d Eq § 130.

equity assists ignorance, but not carelessness. A maxim of equity. The Latin form is **aequitas ignorantia opitulantur, oscitantiae non item** (ē'qui-tas ig-nō-ran'she-a ō-pi-tu-lan'ter, o-si-tan'she-ē non ī'tem). The meaning is that equity should deny relief to those who do not take care of themselves, and who thereby suffer losses which ordinary care would have prevented. Tackett v Bolling, 172 Va 326, 1 SE2d 285.

equity corrects a law which is too broad in that particular in which it is defective. A principle or maxim of equity. The Latin form is **aequitas est correctio legis generaliter latae, qua parte deficit** (ē'qui-tas est kor-rek'she-ō lē'jis je-ne-rā'li-ter lā'te, quā par'te dē'fi-sit). Riggs v Palmer, 115 NY 506, 22 NE 188.
See **equitable construction.**

equity corrects errors. A familiar function of equity. 27 Am J2d Eq § 28. The Latin form is **aequitas erroribus medetur** (ē'qui-tas er-rō'ri-bus mē-dē'ter).

equity court. See **court of equity.**

equity credits. The credits to which a member of a co-operative association is entitled in the revolving capital fund accumulated by the association from operating profits or a portion of the operating profits. 18 Am J2d Co-op Asso § 15.

equity delights in amicable adjustments. A maxim of equity; a maxim addressed to the judicial conscience and intended to govern the court in the determination of disputes between litigants. Troll v Spencer, 238 Mo 81, 141 SW 855.

equity dislikes superfluity. The Latin form is **aequitas supervacua odit** (ē'qui-tas su-per-va'ku-a ō'dit).
See **equity regards substance and intent rather than form.**

equity does justice completely, not by halves. A maxim of equity. 27 Am J2d Eq § 119.

equity does not change the nature of a thing. The Latin form is **aequitas naturam rei non mutat** (ē'qui-tas nā-tū'ram rē'ī non mū'tat).

equity does not confuse jurisdiction. The Latin form is **aequitas jurisdictiones non confundit** (ē'qui-tas ju-ris-dik"she-ō'nēz non kon-fun'dit).

equity does not cure defects in positive requirements of the law. The Latin form is **aequitas non medetur defectu eorum quae jure positivo requisita alium** (ē'qui-tas non mē-dē'ter dē-fek'tu e-ō'rum kwē jū're po-si-tī'vō re-qui-sī'ta a'li-um). 27 Am J2d Eq § 124.

equity does not make the law, but assists the law. A maxim of equity. The Latin form is **aequitas non facit jus, sed juri auxiliatur** (ē'qui-tas non fa'sit jūs, sed jū'rī â-xi-li-ā'ter).

equity does not permit a person to get double satisfaction for the same grievance. The Latin form of the principle is **aequitas non sinit ut eandem rem duplici via simul quis persequatur** (ē'qui-tas non si'nit ut e-an'dem rem du'pli-sī' vī'a si'mūl quis per-se-quā'ter).

equity does not suffer him who holds a true right to prosecute it to extremes. The Latin form of the principle is **aequitas non sinit eum qui jus verum tenuit, extremum jus persequi** (ē'qui-tas non si'nit e'um quī jūs ve'rum te'nu-it, ex-trē'mum jūs per'se-quī).

equity does not supply those things which may be in the hands of the complainant. The Latin form of the principle is **aequitas non supplet ea quae in manu orantis esse possunt** (ē'qui-tas non sup'plet e'a kwē in mā'nū ō-ran'tis es'se pos'sunt).

equity favors the redemption of a pledge. An undoubted principle of equity. 41 Am J1st Pldg & Col § 105. The Latin form is **aequitas rei oppignoratae redemptionibus favet** (ē'qui-tas rē'ī op-pig-no-rā'tē re-demp-she-ō'ni-bus fa'vet).

equity follows the law. The Latin form is **aequitas sequitur legem** (e'qui-tās se'qui-tēr lē'jem). A maxim of equity which is subject to various interpretations, but the main purpose seems to be to keep judicial action within the boundaries which have been established by the prior course of adjudication, in line with the precepts that equity will follow established rules and precedents and will not change or unsettle rights which are defined and established by existing legal principles. 27 Am J2d Eq § 123. Assuredly, equity is bound by statutes. 49 Am J1st Stat of F § 535.

equity for a settlement. A married woman's right, recognized and enforced by courts of equity, for a suitable allowance or a settlement out of her choses in action, interest in a decedent's estate, and other personalty which at common law became the property of her husband when he reduced them into his possession. 26 Am J1st H & W § 48.

equity for marshaling. See **equity to marshal assets.**

equity gives the power of the law to him who wishes to observe it. The Latin form of the principle is **aequitas in eum qui vult summo jure agere summum jus intendit** (ē'qui-tas in e'um quī vult sum'mō jū're ā'je-re sum'mum jūs in-ten'dit).

equity imputes an intention to fulfil an obligation. The maxim embodies a statement of a general presumption upon which a court of equity acts. It is commonly applied in cases involving the performance and satisfaction of covenants, the rule being that wherever a deceased person has covenanted to do an act and has done that which may pro tanto be considered as a performance of his covenant, he will be presumed to have done the act with that intention and his estate will be treated as if he had been a trustee to complete the performance. 27 Am J2d Eq § 128.

equity is a certain perfect reasoning which interprets and amends the written law; not embraced in any writing, but consisting simply in true reason. The Latin form is **aequitas est perfecta quaedam ratio quae jus scriptum interpretatur et emendat; nulla scriptura comprehensa, sed solum in vera ratione consistens** (ē'qui-tas est per-fek'ta kwē'dam rā'she-ō kwē jūs skrīp'tum in-ter-pre-tā'ter et ē-men'dat; nul'la skrip-tū'ra kom-pre-hen'sa, sed sō'lum in ve'ra rā-she-ō'ne kon-sis'tēnz).

equity is a relaxing or alleviation of the law. It is a mitigating principle by the application of which substantial justice may be attained in particular cases wherein the prescribed or customary forms of law seem to be inadequate. 27 Am J2d Eq § 1. The Latin form of the principle is **aequitas est laximentum juris** (ē'qui-tas est lak-si-men'tum jöris). Pomeroy's Equity Jurisprudence, § 46.

equity is equality, and equality is equity. A maxim of equity. The Latin forms are **aequitas est aequalitas** (ē'qui-tas est ē-quā'li-tas) and **aequitas est quasi aequalitas** (ē'qui-tas est quā'sī ē-quā'li-tas). As sometimes stated, equity delights in equality. Equity treats all members of a class on an equal footing, and imposes burdens and distributes rights without preference, either equally or in proportion to the several interests. 27 Am J2d Eq § 125.

equity is not vague and uncertain but has fixed boundaries and limits. The Latin form of the statement is **aequitas non vaga atque incerta est, sed terminos habet atque limites praefinitas** (ē'qui-tas non va'ga at'kwē in-ser'ta est, sed ter'mi-nos hā'bet at'kwē li'mi-tēz prē-fī-nī'tas). But a want of equity jurisdiction is not inferred from the novelty of the question. The fact that there is no precedent for the precise relief sought is not fatal to equity jurisdiction. 27 Am J2d Eq § 13.

equity jurisdiction. A broad and flexible jurisdiction to grant remedial relief where justice and good conscience demands it, but without purporting to create rights, being limited to determining what rights the parties have and whether or in what manner it is just and proper to enforce them. A jurisdiction in two categories, the one dependent upon the substantive character of the right sought to be enforced, the other dependent upon the inadequacy of the legal remedy. 27 Am J2d Eq § 5.

equity jurisprudence. That portion of our system of jurisprudence traditionally expounded and administered by courts of equity. 27 Am J2d Eq § 1. It remains a distinct part of the system, notwithstanding in many jurisdictions legal and equitable remedies have been commingled in one form of civil action and a court of general jurisdiction may hear both law and equity cases. 27 Am J2d Eq § 4.

equity never aids contention where it can give a remedy. The Latin form of the principle is **aequitas nunquam liti ancillatur ubi remedium potest dare** (ē'qui-tas nun'quom lī'tī an-sil-lā'ter ū'bi re-mē'di-um po'test da're).

equity never contravenes the law. The Latin form of the principle is **aequitas nunquam contravenit legis** (ē'qui-tas nun'quom kon-tra-vē'nit lē'jis). The principle is a corollary of the principle that **equity follows the law.**

equity of partner. The right to have the partnership assets applied in liquidation of the partnership debts before any one of the partners or his creditors can claim any right or title to them, and to have the surplus assets divided among the members of the firm. 40 Am J1st Partn § 404.

equity of redemption. The right, recognized by courts of equity from early times, of a mortgagor, following a breach of the condition of the mortgage, to redeem property from the forfeiture by discharging the obligation secured within a reasonable period; such right is a real and beneficial estate in the land under the concept of a court of equity that despite its terms, a mortgage is a transaction of security, not of purchase. 36 Am J1st Mtg § 180. See **foreclosure.**

equity of statute. The reason and spirit underlying a statute as aids to its interpretation. 50 Am J1st Stat § 304.

equity pleading. A pleading in a suit in equity, whether bill, complaint, petition, answer, plea, or cross bill, etc., governed by traditional equity practice. In most jurisdictions today, distinctive rules of equity pleading have been largely, if not entirely, supplanted by statutory provisions or rules of court which prescribe rules of pleading, especially in those jurisdictions where law and equity courts have been combined or in which there is but one form or kind of action in a civil case, known as a "civil action." 27 Am J2d Eq § 179.

equity prevents mischief. A maxim of equity, a maxim addressed to the judicial conscience. Funk v Voneida (Pa) 11 Serg & R 109.

equity receiver. A receiver appointed by a court by virtue of its equity jurisdiction and without reference to statutory authority. 45 Am J1st Rec § 3.

equity receivership. A remedy for the dissolution or reorganization of a corporation in financial distress.

equity regards as done that which ought to be done. A maxim of equity which means that a court of equity, in determining a dispute between litigants, regards and treats as done that which, in fairness and good conscience ought to be or should have been done. 27 Am J2d Eq § 126.

equity regards substance and intent, rather than form. A maxim of equity sometimes stated as "equity regards form and circumstance as of less consequence than the subject matter itself." The Latin form is **aequitas rem ipsam intuetur de forma et circumstantiis minus anxia** (ē'qui-tas rem ip'sam in-tu-ē'ter dē for'ma et sėr-kum-stan'she-is mī'nus an'xi-a). The meaning of the maxim is that the rights of the parties are not to be sacrificed to the mere letter, but that the intent or spirit of a contract, agreement, or transaction will in equity at least be the paramount consideration. 27 Am J2d Eq § 127.

equity relieves against accidents. An undoubted principle of equity. 27 Am J2d Eq § 44. The Latin form of the principle is **aequitas casibus medetur** (ē'qui-tas kā'si-bus mē-dē'ter).

equity rules of practice. A set of rules supplanted by the Federal Rules of Civil Procedure, effective September 16, 1938. Schlaefer v Schlaefer, 71 App DC 350, 112 F2d 177.

equity seeks to do justice. A maxim of equity reflecting the principle that the first principle of equity is justice. Tompers v Bank of America, 217 App Div 691, 217 NYS 67.

equity side. The sitting of a court having jurisdiction in both law and equity but sitting for the time as a court of equity.

equity supplies defects. A maxim or principle of equity. 27 Am J2d Eq § 2. The Latin form is **aequitas defectus supplet** (ē'qui-tas dē-fek'tus sup'plet).

equity term (tėrm). A term or session of court without a jury, such being the term at which equity cases are tried.

equity to a settlement. See **equity for a settlement.**

equity to marshal assets (mär'shal as'ėts). The equity to marshal the assets, securities and funds of a debtor is the right of a creditor who has a junior lien on or interest in only a part of the assets, securities, or funds of the debtor to have a creditor who has a prior lien on or interest in the same assets, securities or funds, before resorting to the assets, securities and funds thus charged, to exhaust other assets, securities or funds of the debtor on which the prior creditor has a lien or in which he has an interest, but on which or in which the junior creditor has no lien or interest. 35 Am J1st Marsh A § 2.

equity which is prior in time is better in right. A principle or maxim of equity. The Latin form is **qui prior est tempore potior est jure** (quī prī'or est tem'po-re, pō'she-or est jū're). The meaning is that where opposing equities are otherwise equal, the one which is prior in time is entitled to precedence or preference. 27 Am J2d Eq § 149.

equity will not do or require the doing of a vain or useless thing. A maxim of equity, meaning that a court of equity must look to the practicalities of the situation and the relief sought to be had. 27 Am J2d Eq § 119.

EQUITY [414] ERROR

equity will not suffer a wrong to be without a remedy. A maxim of equity. The legal maxim is: Where there is a right, there is a remedy. [ubi jus, ibi remedium (u'bi jūs i'bi re-mē'di-um).] 27 Am J2d Eq § 120.

equivalent. Adjective: Of equal value, weight, force, etc. Noun: A thing of equal value, weight, force, etc. In patent law, a device which accomplishes the same result as that achieved by a patent alleged to have been infringed. 40 Am J1st Pat § 156.
See **seller's option.**

equivocal (ē-kwiv'ọ-kạl). Possessing a double or doubtful meaning.

equivocum (ē-qui'vo-kum). A double meaning.

equuleus (e-kwö'lę-us). A kind of rack which was employed by the Romans for the purpose of extorting the confessions of persons accused of crime.

era. A period of time characterized by outstanding events, such as Christian era, machine era, and atomic era.

eradication. The annihilation of something, for example, the suppression and prevention of animal diseases. 4 Am J2d Ani § 34.

Erant in Anglia quodammodo tot reges vel potius tyranni quot domini castellorum (e'rant in Ang'li-a quō-dam-mō'dō tot rē'jēz vel pō'she-us ti-ran'nī quot do'mi-nī kas-tel-lō'rum). There were in England as many kings or rather tyrants as there were lords of castles. See 1 Bl Comm 263.

Erant omnia communia et indivisa omnibus, veluti unum cunctis patrimonium esset (e'rant om'ni-a kom-mū'ni-a et in-di-vī'sa om'ni-bus, ve'lu-tī ū'num kunk'tis pa-tri-mō'ni-um es'set). All things were common and undivided, as if there were a single patrimony for all. See 2 Bl Comm 3.

erase. To rub, scrape, or wipe out.

erasure. A rubbing, scraping, or wiping out; a method of alteration of an instrument. 4 Am J2d Alt Inst § 36. Sometimes an effective revocation of a will or a portion of a will. 57 Am J1st Wills §§ 502 et seq.
See **obliteration.**

erection. The construction of a building or structure complete from the ground up or of some part of the building or structure, such as the foundation, a pillar, or support, even a driveway serving the building or structure. Red Lake Falls Milling Co. v Thief River Falls, 109 Minn 52, 122 NW 872. A building or structure. Strauss v Ginzberg, 218 Minn 57, 15 NW2d 130, 155 ALR 1000.

erer. To plough.

ergo (ĕr'gō). Therefore; consequently; accordingly.

ergo hic (er'gō hik). Therefore here.

ergot (ĕr'gọt). A drug sometimes used in abortions, the tendency of which is to contract the uterus and throw out the foetus. State v Alcorn, 7 Idaho 599, 64 P 1014.

Erie R. Co. v Tompkins. A landmark case, overruling a doctrine theretofore followed for many years, and establishing the doctrine that, under the Federal Judiciary Act, except as to matters governed by the United States Constitution, Acts of Congress, or treaties, the law to be applied in any case in the federal court is the law of the state, and that the phrase "the laws of the several states" refers, not only to state law as enacted by the state legislature, but to the law of a state as declared by its highest court, whether the law thus declared is local in nature or is general, common, or commercial. The case is reported in 304 US 64, 82 L Ed 1188, 58 S Ct 817, 114 ALR 1487, and the case long cited as authority for the principle which was overruled is Swift v Tyson (US) 16 Pet 1, 10 L Ed 865.

erigimus (e-ri'ji-mus). We establish; we erect.

erosion. The gradual eating away of the soil by the operation of currents or tides, so that the portion of land which is eaten away is lost to the riparian or littoral owner, except and until it be restored to him by accretion. Mulry v Norton, 100 NY 426, 3 NE 581. A gradual wearing away or disintegration from any cause.

erotic mania (e-rot'ik mā'ni-ạ). A form of mental disease better known in modern times as nymphomania.
See **nymphomania.**

errant (er-ạnt). Wandering; itinerant; traveling from place to place.
See **bailiff errant.**

erraticum (er-rā'ti-kum). Same as **estray.**

erroneous. Wrong, mistaken. Particularly, in reference to a determination made by a court. Deviating from, or contrary to, the law, as an erroneous ruling. It means or imports the power to act, but error in its exercise. The word does not appear to be used either by courts or text writers as applying to a corrupt or evil act. Mitchell v Bowers (CA9 Cal) 15 F2d 285.

erroneous judgment. A judgment rendered according to the course and practice of the courts, but contrary to law; that is, based upon an erroneous application of legal principles. Stafford v Gallops, 123 NC 19, 21.

erroneously or illegally charged. As used in a statute providing for a refund of taxes so exacted, the phrase is held to refer to a jurisdictional defect as distinguished from a mere error of judgment, and it is generally held that no recovery of taxes paid under protest can be had under such statutes on the theory that there has been a mistake in the valuation of the property, which resulted in an excessive assessment. Anno: 110 ALR 670.

erronice (er-ron'is-e). Erroneously; through error or mistake.

error (er'ọr). A mistake of law or fact; a mistake of the court in the trial of an action; a writ to review a judgment of an inferior court in a higher court for errors appearing on the face of the record. A proceeding under a writ of error, distinct, under the older practice, from an appeal, in respect primarily of the scope of review, the typical error proceeding calling for a trial de novo. 4 Am J2d A & E § 2.
See **appeal and error; assignable error; assignment of errors; clerical error; common error; confession of error; cross errors; favorable error; fundamental error; harmless error; invited error; judicial error; palpable; prejudicial error; proceeding in error; reversible error; substantial error; technical error; writ of error.**

error apparent. A manifest, plain, or obvious error. An error on the face of a proceeding, in the pleadings, judgment, or decree, as distinguished from an error in the evidence discoverable only upon the examination of the record. Milliken v McKenzie (Tex Civ App) 285 SW 1110, 1111.

error coram nobis (er'ror kō'ram nō'bis). See **coram nobis.**

error coram vobis (er'ror kō'ram vō'bis). See **coram vobis**.

Errores ad sua principia referre, est refellere (er-rō'rēz ad su'a prin-si'pi-a re-fer're, est re-fel'le-re). To refer errors to their source is to refute them.

Error fucatus nuda veritate in multis est probabilior, et saepenumero rationibus vincit veritatem error (er'ror fu-kā'tus nū'da ve-ri-tā'te in mul'tis est pro-bā-bi'li-or, et sē-pe-nū'me-rō rā-she-ō'ni-bus vin'sit ve-ri-tā'tem er'ror). Error disguised is in many instances more probable than naked truth, and error very often overcomes truth in argument.

error in extremis. A mistake committed in good faith while in great danger, so that it must be weighed according to a standard different from that applied to an error committed under less distressing and distracting circumstances. 48 Am J1st Ship § 233.

error juris (er'ror jū'ris). An error or mistake of law; ignorance of law.

Error juris nocet (er'ror jū'ris no'set). An error of law works an injury.

error lapsus (er'ror lap'sus). An error by mistake or slip, as distinguished from an error through ignorance, as by ignorance of law.

Error nominis nunquam nocet, si de identitate rei constat (er'ror nō'mi-nis nun'quam no'set, sī dē ī-den-ti-tā'te rē'ī kon'stat). A mistake or error in a name is never prejudicial, if the identity of the thing is clear.

error of fact. A mistake of fact as distinguished from a mistake of law. A finding of fact by the trial court contrary to the weight of the evidence. Southern Surety Co. v United States (CA8 NM) 23 F2d 55, 59.

See **ignorance of fact**; **mistake of fact**.

error of judgment. A mistaken conclusion. Not negligence if committed in good faith in the observance of the standard or ordinary or reasonable care. 38 Am J2d Negl § 33.

If one, assuming to act as an expert, has knowledge of the facts and circumstances connected with the duty he is about to perform, and, bringing to bear all his experience and skill, weighs those facts and circumstances, and decides upon a course of action which he faithfully attempts to carry out, his want of success would be due to error of judgment, and not to negligence. Luka v Lowrie, 171 Mich 122, 136 NW 1106.

Although a druggist is not necessarily responsible for the results of an error of judgment which is reconcilable and consistent with the exercise of ordinary skill and care, a presumption or an inference sufficient to require the druggist to disprove negligence arises upon proof of mistake or inadvertence on his part. 25 Am J2d Drugs § 56.

error proceeding. See **proceeding in error**.

Error qui non resistitur approbatur (er'ror quī non re-sis'ti-ter ap-prō-bā'ter). An error which is not objected to is waived.

Error scribentis nocere non debit (er'ror skri-ben'tis no-sē're non de'bit). An error or mistake of a scrivener ought not to prejudice.

Erubescit lex filios castigare parentes (ē-ru-bē'sit lex fi'li-os kas-ti-gā're pa-ren'tēz). The law blushes at reproofs which children administer to their parents.

erysipelas (er-i-sip'e-las). A painful affection of the skin, or mucous membrane, characterized by local inflammation and fever. Owing's Case (Md) 1 Bland Ch 370. An affliction of the body, but not a mental or bodily infirmity within the meaning of a warranty in an insurance policy. 29 Am J Rev ed Ins § 749.

esartum (e-sar'tum). Same as **assart**.

escaeta. Same as **escheat**.

escaetor. Same as **escheator**.

escalator (es'ka-lā-tor). A power-driven moving stairway, used in department stores, airports, underground parking places, banks, office buildings, etc., made up of interconnected platforms and risers, usually of grooved metal, normally inclined at an angle of about 45 degrees, so constructed that it can be moved either up or down, at speeds which may be varied within limits, and having the distinguishing characteristics of being in constant motion, operating under the control of neither attendant nor passenger, and available to passengers so that they enter and leave the conveyance at any floor by merely stepping on and off. 26 Am J2d Elev § 78. An elevator within the meaning of the double indemnity provision of an accident insurance policy. 29A Am J Rev ed Ins § 1235.

escalator clause. A clause in a contract of sale or lease, made during a period when prices and rentals are limited in amount by law, which gives the vendor or landlord the benefit of such increases in the price or rent as may be made by law during the life of the contract or lease.

escaldare (es-kal-dā're). To scald.

escambio (es-kam'bī-ō). Exchange; a writ to authorize the drawing of bills of exchange on persons who are in a foreign country.

escambio monetae. See **de escambio monetae**.

escambium (es-kam'bi-um). Exchange.

escape. A criminal offense at common law, and by statute in most jurisdictions, consisting in the unlawful departure of a legally confined prisoner from custody or the act of a prisoner in regaining his liberty before being released in due course of law. The criminal offense committed by a jailer, warden, or other custodian of a prisoner in permitting him to depart from custody unlawfully. 27 Am J2d Escape § 1. In common usage, the flight of a person seeking to avoid arrest, also any act or movement by a person to avoid a peril. An animal's departing the custody of its owner, the effects of which, in the case of an animal ferae naturae, is to deprive the owner of his rights as such. 4 Am J2d Ani § 19.

See **prison breaking**; **rescue**.

escape clause. A clause in the lease of a tenant-stockholder in a cooperative apartment which permits him to assign his stock and lease to the cooperative association without receiving compensation therefor but enabling him to escape continuing liability to the association for payments otherwise coming due under the lease. 15 Am J2d Con Apt § 27. A clause in a contract relieving a promisor of liability for nonperformance in the event of contingent developments rendering performance impossible. 17 Am J2d Contr § 404.

escape warrant. A warrant which directed any sheriff in England to arrest a person who had escaped from an imprisonment on civil process.

escaping fire. A fire which has spread out of the place where it is ordinarily maintained, thereby becoming a "hostile fire." 29A Am J Rev ed Ins § 1287.

escaping substances. The doctrine, often called the doctrine of Rylands v Fletcher, or Fletcher v Rylands (LR 1 Exch 265, LR 3 HL 330, 4 Hurlst & C 263, 1 Eng Rul Cas 236), that a person who, for his own purposes, brings on his lands and collects and keeps there anything likely to do mischief if it escapes must keep it in at his peril; and if he does not do so, he is prima facie liable for all the damage which is the natural consequence of its escape. 38 Am J1st Negl § 139.

escapium (es-kā'pi-um). An escape; an accident; that which happened by chance.

eschaeta. See **de eschaeta.**

Eschaetae vulgo discuntur quae decidentibus iis quae de rege tenent, cum non existit ratione sanguinis haeres, ad fiscum relabuntur (es-kē'tē vul'gō diskun'ter kwe dē-si-den'ti-bus ī'is kwē dē rē'je te'nent, kum non eg-zis'tit rā-she-ō'ne san'gwi-nis hē'rēz, ad fis'kum re-lā-bun'ter). They are commonly called escheats which, upon the dying out of those who hold of the king when there is no heir by consanguinity, revert to the treasury.

Esch Car Service Act. See **car service.**

escheat (es-chēt'). An obstruction of the course of descent by chance or accident. 27 Am J2d Esch § 1. The preferable right of the state to an estate left vacant because of the absence of persons legally entitled to make claim thereto. University of North Carolina v High Point, 203 NC 558, 166 SE 511. The reversion of property to the state when the title fails. Delaney v State, 42 ND 630, 174 NW 290. The state does not take as an heir; escheat is not succession. 27 Am J2d Esch § 1.

A word deriving from the French or Norman French which, in its most comprehensive scope, means the reversion or forfeiture of property to the government upon the happening of some chance event or default. 27 Am J2d Esch § 1. In England, real estate escheats, but the Crown takes personal property, where there is no owner, that is bona vacantia. 27 Am J2d Esch § 1.

escheat grant. See **escheat patent.**

escheator (es-chē'tor). An English county officer who looked into and made report of escheats reverting to the king. A public officer or public body upon whom rests the duty of bringing actions for escheat or for a sale or conveyance of escheated lands. 27 Am J2d Esch § 32.

escheat patent. The formal deed or conveyance by which escheated lands are regranted by the state. 27 Am J2d Esch § 43.

escheat propter defectum sanguinis (es-chēt prop'ter dē-fek'tum san'gwi-nis). Escheat for failure of blood relations.

escheat propter delictum tenentis (es-chēt prop'ter de-lik'tum te-nen'tis). Escheat for the fault of the tenant; as through the attainder of the tenant.

escheat warrant. Same as **escheat patent.**

escheceum (es-chek'um). A jury; an inquisition.

eschoir (ays-chwär'). To escheat.

escippare (es-sip-pā're). To ship. Same as **eskipper.**

escribano (es-kre-bah'no). A term encountered in Spanish-American grants, being the name of an officer whose functions are quite similar to those of a notary public under our law. Panaud v Jones, 1 Cal 488, 502.

escrier. To proclaim.

escript (es-kript'). A writing; a written instrument.

escrit (e'krî). Same as **escript.**

escritura (es-kre-too'rah). (Spanish.) A deed; a writing; a written instrument.

escrow. A written instrument which by its terms imports a legal obligation and which is deposited by the grantor, promisor, or obligor, or his agent, with a stranger or third party to be kept by the depository until the performance of a condition or the happening of a certain event, and to be delivered over to the grantee, promisee, or obligee. 28 Am J2d Escr § 1.

In its origin, the doctrine of escrow applied only to deeds of grant or conveyances of land, but it was soon extended to other sealed instruments and has come to apply to a variety of instruments, including bonds, contracts for the sale of land, contracts for the purchase of personal property, corporate stocks, deeds, discontinuances and releases of cause of action, contracts for the settlement of will contests, commercial paper, applications for insurance, and subscription papers. 28 Am J2d Escr § 2.

See **delivery as an escrow.**

escrow account. A bank account created by a special deposit to be held in escrow and returned to the depositor upon the occurrence of a specified contingency. 10 Am J2d Banks § 366.

escrow holder. The third party to an escrow. See **escrow.**

escrowl. Same as **escrow.**

escuage (es'kū-āj). Also called "scutagium," or "servitium scuti," derived from "scutum," which was at one time a common word for money, and meaning the pecuniary satisfaction which a tenant paid to his lord for a release from the the troublesome and inconvenient personal attendance of knight-service. At first the tenant was permitted to send a substitute and later escuage developed. See 2 Bl Comm 74.

See **king-geld.**

esketores (es-ke-tō'rēz). Robbers; pillagers.

Eskimos. Native inhabitants of Alaska, so similar in features to Orientals, especially Orientals in Siberia across the Bering Sea from Alaska, as to suggest what many anthropologists state after scientific observations, that they emigrated from Siberia some thousands of years ago. Classified as Indians by statute. United States v First Nat. Bank, 234 US 245, 58 L Ed 1298, 34 S Ct 846.

eskippamentum (es-kip-pa-men'tum). The tackle of a ship; skippage.

eskippare (es-kip-pā're). To ship.

eslier (ay-lee-ay'). To choose; to select.

eslisor (ay lee zor). Same as **elisor,** a person who chose or selected a jury.

esloigner (e'loa-gne'). Same as **eloign.**

esne (en). A person in a condition of servitude.

esnecy (es'ne-si). The right or privilege of seniority. The privilege or prerogative given to the eldest among coparceners, to have the first choice after the inheritance is divided.

espera (es'pe-ra). The time which a court has fixed for the performance of an act.

esperons. Spurs.

espionage. Spying, especially for military purposes; a criminal offense where the activity is employed against the United States. 47 Am J1st Sedit Etc. § 5. The obtaining of national defense information and communicating it to a foreign nation in time of war. Rosenberg v United States, 346 US 273, 97 L Ed 1607, 73 S Ct 1152.

Espionage Act. The federal statute which denounces and provides for the punishment of actual espionage and deals in addition with a wide variety of matters relating to and connected with the national defense and war activities of the United States. 50 USC §§ 31 et seq.

esplees (es-plēz'). The products and profits of land which it yields, such as the hay of the meadows, the herbage of the pasture land, the corn of the arable land, rents, services, etc. Fosgate v Herkimer Mfg. & Hydraulic Co. (NY) 9 Barb 287, 293.

espousals (es-pou'zạls). The mutual promises of a man and a woman to marry each other.

espouse (es-pouz'). To engage to marry; to give or bestow in marriage; to engage in the defense of another; as, to espouse his cause.

espurio (es-pu'ri-ō). (Spanish.) A spurious offspring; a bastard.

esq. An abbreviation of **esquire.**

esquire (es-kwīr'). The term is applied to barristers-at-law, and in the United States it is customary to append the title to attorneys at law in addressing them by letter.
   Blackstone has said it is a matter somewhat unsettled what constitutes the distinction between a gentleman and an esquire, or who is a *real* esquire. See 1 Bl Comm 406.

essart. Wooded land which has been cleared and cultivated.

essartum (es-sar'tum). Same as **essart.**

esse (es'se). To be; being; to appear.
   See **in esse.**

essence (es'ẹns). The gist or substance of anything; the vital constituent of a thing.
   See **time is of the essence.**

essence of the contract. The gist or substance or vital constituent of the contract; an important part of a contract.

essendi quietam de theolonia (es-sen'dī qui-ē'tam dē the-ō-lō'ni-a). An exemption from the payment of tolls.

essendo quietum de theolonio. See **de essendo, etc.**

essentialia negotii (es-sen-she-ā'li-a ne-gō'she-ī). The essentials of the transaction or business.

Esse optime constitutam republicam quae ex tribus generibus illis, regali, optimo, et populari, sit modice confusa (es'se op'ti-mé kon-sti-tū'tam re-pub'li-kam kwē ex tri'bus je-ne'ri-bus il'lis, rē-gā'lī, op'ti-mō, et po-pu-lā'rī, sit mo'di-se kon-fū'sa). That the best constituted republic is that which is moderately composed of three elements, royalty, aristocracy and democracy. 1 Bl Comm 50.

essoign (e-soin'). An excuse made to the court by a defendant who failed to appear according to the summons of a writ. See 3 Bl Comm 278.

essoign day. That day of a term of court, which was called the essoign day of the term, upon which the court sat to take or hear essoigns. See 3 Bl Comm 278.

essoign roll. The record of essoigns.

essoin (e-soin'). Same as **essoign.**

essoin day. Same as **essoign day.**

essoin de infirmitate (e-soin' dē in-fir'mi-tā-te). An essoign of illness or infirmity.

essoin de mal de lit (e-soin' dē mal dē li). Same as **essoin de malo lecti.**

essoin de mal de venue (e-soin' dē mal dē vẹ-nû). Same as **essoin de malo veniendi.**

essoin de malo lecti (e-soin' dē mā'lō lek'tī). An essoign that the defendant was sick in his bed.

essoin de malo veniendi (e-soin' dē mā'lō ve-ni-en'dī). An essoign that the defendant met with an accident on his journey to court.

essoin de outre mer (e-soin' dē ô-tr mēr). Same as **essoin de ultra mer.**

essoin de servitio regis (e-soin' dē ser-vi'she-ō rē'jis). An essoign that the defendant was away in the service of the king.

essoin de terra sancta (e-soin' dē ter'ra sank'ta). An essoign that the defendant was absent in the holy land.

essoin de terre seynte (e-soin' dē têr sīnt). Same as **essoin de terra sancta.**

essoin de ultra mer (e-soin' dē ul'tra ma're). An essoign that the defendant was beyond seas.

essoineour. Same as **essoiniator.**

essoiniator (e-soin'i-ā-tor). The person who presented an essoign to the court in behalf of the defendant who failed to appear.

essoin service del roy (e-soin' sèr'vi-s del roa). Same as **essoin de servitio regis.**

est. It is; he is; there is.

establish. To originate, to create; to found and set up; to put or fix on a firm basis; to put in a settled or efficient state or condition. State, ex rel. Bragg v Rogers, 107 Ala 444, 19 So 909.
   As used in an instruction requiring a party to clearly "establish" a fact by evidence, it means to settle certainly or fix permanently what was before uncertain, doubtful, or disputed, and is therefore improper as applied to the party having the burden of proof in a civil case, in that it requires too high a degree of proof, that is, it requires a higher degree than is reached by a mere preponderance, which is sufficient. Fisher v Travelers' Ins. Co. 124 Tenn 450, 138 SW 316.
   To establish may mean to settle or fix unalterably, but that is not its necessary meaning. As used in a statute authorizing the establishment of water rates, the word does not convey the idea of permanency and it has no such meaning. The power of the board is not exhausted by one exercise nor has its result unalterable fixity. Knowlton v Moore, 178 US 22, 38, 44 L Ed 961, 969, 20 S Ct 860.

established business. A business which has an element of fixity and permanence. A doctor's office or a farm of a farmer, which is the locally established center from which he distributes what he has to sell may be said to be a place where he has an established business. Allen v Commonwealth, 188 Mass 59, 74 NE 287.

established highway. A highway which has been located, created by dedication, prescription, or by the direct action of the public authorities, and opened for use by the people of the state at their pleasure for the purpose of travel. Palatka & Indian River Railroad Co. v State, 23 Fla 546.

establishing a market. Nothing more than designating a space within a city or town where goods of a certain character may be bought and sold. 35 Am J1st Mark & M § 4.

establishing credit. See **opening a credit.**

establishment. The fixing of something on a firm basis; making certain that which before was uncertain. The place in which one is permanently fixed for residence or business; residence with grounds, furniture, equipage, etc., with which one is fitted out; also, any office or place of business, with its fixtures. Trustees of Academy v Bohler, 80 Ga 159, 162. An industrial plant or other place of employment. Matson Terminals v California Employment Com. 24 Cal 2d 695, 151 P2d 202.

establishment clause. The provision of the First Amendment to the Constitution of the United States concerning establishment of religion, the meaning of which is that neither a state nor the federal government can set up a church; neither can pass laws which aid one religion, aid all religions, or prefer one religion over another; neither can force nor influence a person to go to or remain away from church against his will or force him to profess a belief or disbelief in any religion. Illinois ex rel. McCollum v Board of Education, 33 US 203, 92 L Ed 649, 68 S Ct 461, 2 ALR2d 1338; Everson v Board of Education, 330 US 1, 91 L Ed 711, 67 S Ct 504, 168 ALR 392, reh den 330 US 855, 91 L Ed 1297, 67 S Ct 962.

establishment of dower. Same as **assignment of dower.**

establishment of grade. The fixing of the grade of a street or highway at an official grade, either by a direct act of the legislature or under authority delegated by the legislature to municipalities, or to private corporations or individuals. Nicholsen v New York, N. H. R. Co. 22 Conn 74. Required in some jurisdictions as a condition precedent to improvement. 25 Am J1st High § 59.

establishment of heirship. A part of the ordinary administration of an estate, either by one claiming the right under the statute to administer, or by one claiming a distributive share. An incident of some action in which the court has general jurisdiction. 23 Am J2d Desc & D § 104.
See **heirship proceeding.**

establishment of religion. See **establishment clause.**

estadal (es-tä-däl). A Spanish lineal measure equivalent to about eleven English feet.

estadia (es-tah-dee'ah). (Spanish.) The time for which demurrage is chargeable for the delay of the charterer or the consignee in unlading the cargo of a vessel.

Est aliquid quod non oportet, etiam si licet; quicquid vero non licet certe non oportet (est a'li-quid quod non o-por'tet, ē'she-am sī lī'set; quik'quid vē'rō non lī'set ser'te non o-por'tet). A thing may not be proper, although it is lawful, but certainly anything which is not lawful is not proper.

est ascavoir (ā a-sah-vwar). It is understood; that is to say; to wit; viz. For practical purposes, synonymous with **scilicet.**

estate. In the pristine technical sense, the degree, quantity, nature, and extent of interest which a person has in real property. 28 Am J2d Est § 1. Otherwise, a word of several meanings, neither of which imports a legal entity: the property left by a decedent, the property of a ward, a mentally incompetent person, or a bankrupt; in its most popular sense including both real and personal property. Re Glassford's Estate, 114 Cal App 2d 908, 34 ALR2d 1259. Including every vested right and interest attached to and growing out of property. Lee v Hill, 87 Va 497, 12 SE 1052. Including tangible and intangible property. Anno: 34 ALR2d 1271. Including even a contract of employment for personal services. Lee v Hill, 87 Va 497, 12 SE 1052. When used in a will, usually, but not necessarily, comprehending all property of the testator whether real or personal in character. 57 Am J1st Wills § 1337. It includes both real and personal property, and is sufficient to pass a fee in land, unless restricted by words expressing a different intention. It has long been held that the devise of all a man's "estate," where there are no words to restrain or control its operation, should be construed not merely to mean his lands, but the quantity of interest which he has in them. The word may likewise include an equitable interest. However, the word "estate" in a will is not to be understood as a word of art, but of interpretation, and its meaning may be affected by other clauses and disposition in the will. 57 Am J1st Wills § 1337.

A person's degree or rank in life.

estate at sufferance. Same as **estate by sufferance.**

estate at will. A lease of lands or tenements to be held at the will of the lessor but actually determinable at the will of either party. 28 Am J2d Est §§ 130, 131. The estate of a tenant who has entered upon the premises under a lease to hold during the joint wills of the parties. Public Service Co. v Voudomas, 84 NH 387, 151 A 81, 70 ALR 480.

estate by elegit (ē-lē'jit). The interest of a creditor in land of which he is in possession by virtue of a writ of elegit. 2 Bl Comm 160.

estate by entireties. An estate predicated on the legal unity of husband and wife, being taken, upon a conveyance or devise to them, to hold as a single person with the right of survivorship as an incident, so that when one dies, the entire estate belongs to the other by virtue of the title originally vested. 26 Am J1st H & W § 66.

estate by new acquisition. Same as **estate by purchase.**

estate by purchase. An estate acquired by sale or gift, or by any other method, except only that of descent, there being no distinction known to the law between a gift or devise by a stranger, and a gift or devise by an ancestor. See Hall v Jacobs (Md) 4 Harr & J 245, 254, wherein the question was as to whether an estate became vested in the deceased by descent or by purchase so as to admit the half blood.

estate by statute merchant. The interest or estate of the creditor in land conveyed to him under the statute 13 Edward I, De Mercatoribus, and therefore called a statute merchant. This conveyance was by way of security to be held by the creditor as "tenant by statute merchant" until the income and profits from the land conveyed should discharge the debt, which was an ascertained and definite sum. This transaction was entered into between the parties before the chief magistrate of some trading town. See 2 Bl Comm 160.

estate by statute staple. The interest or estate of the creditor in land conveyed to him under the statute 27 Edward III. c. 9, before the mayor of the staple, that is the grand mart for the principal commodities or manufactures of the kingdom in certain trading towns, and therefore called a statute staple. This conveyance was by way of security to be held by the creditor as "tenant by statute staple" until the income and profits from the land thus held by him should discharge the debt which was an ascertained and definite sum. See 2 Bl Comm 160.

estate by sufferance. A holding by one who came into possession rightfully, after the termination of the interest under which he came into possession, for example, the continuance in possession after the termination of a life estate by a person who had entered under a lease from the life tenant. 28 Am J2d Est §§ 130, 131.
See **tenancy at sufferance.**

estate by the curtesy. See **curtesy.**

estate duty. See **estate tax.**

estate for years. An estate which must expire at a period certain, fixed in advance. United States v First Nat. Bank (CA5 Ala) 74 F2d 360. An interest arising from an agreement or contract for the possession of lands or tenements for some definite period, such estate being regarded at common law as a chattel. 28 Am J2d Est § 136. A chattel real rather than real estate, except as a contrary definition is provided by statute or a reasonable construction of a will in which the term appears demands that it be deemed inclusive of a leasehold. Anno: 103 ALR 826; 57 Am J1st Wills § 1337.

estate from year to year. An estate for an uncertain term for which an annual rent is reserved. See 2 Bl Comm 147.
See **tenancy from year to year.**

estate in bankruptcy. Assets which vest in the trustee in bankruptcy. 9 Am J2d Bankr § 847.

estate in common. The common estate of persons holding as tenants in common. 20 Am J2d Coten § 2.

estate in coparcenary (es-tāt' in kō-pär'se-nā-ri). An estate known to the common law but virtually obsolete under modern statutes, whereby joint heirs hold as tenants in common. 20 Am J2d Coten § 1.

estate in dead pledge. See **dead pledge.**

estate in expectancy. See **expectant estate.**

estate in fee. See **fee simple.**

estate in fee conditional. See **fee conditional.**

estate in fee simple. See **fee simple.**

estate in fee tail. See **fee tail.**

estate in gage. See **dead pledge; living pledge; mortgage; pledge.**

estate in joint tenancy. An estate held by two or more persons jointly, with equal rights to share in its enjoyment during their lives, and having as its distinguishing feature the right of survivorship, by virtue of which the entire estate goes to the survivor (or in case of more than two joint tenants, to the survivors, and so on to the last survivor), free and exempt from all charges made by his deceased cotenant or cotenants. 20 Am J2d Coten § 3.

estate in land. The degree, quantity, nature, or extent of interest which a person has in land. Robertson v Vancleave, 129 Ind 217, 29 NE 781.
See **estate; landed estate.**

estate in mortuo vadio (mor'tu-o va'di-o). Estate in dead pledge.
See **dead pledge; mortgage.**

estate in pledge. See **dead pledge; living pledge; mortgage; pledge.**

estate in plurality. An estate in which there is always a plurality of tenants, that is, more than one. Such estates are of three varieties, estates in joint tenancy, estates in coparcenary and estates in common. See 2 Bl Comm 179.

estate in possession. An estate under which the owner has an immediate right to the possession of the land. Sage v Wheeler, 3 AD 38, 37 NYS 1107.
See **vested estate.**

estate in remainder. See **remainder.**

estate in reversion. See **reversion.**

estate in severalty. An estate held by a person as the sole tenant thereof in his own right only, without any other person being joined or connected with him in point of interest, during his estate therein. This is the most common and usual way of holding an estate, and all estates are supposed to be of this sort unless expressly declared to be otherwise. See 2 Bl Comm 179.

estate in vadio (es-tāt' in va'di-o). Estate in pledge.
See **dead pledge; living pledge; mortgage; pledge.**

estate in vivo vadio (es-tāt' in vī'vō va'di-o). Estate in living pledge.
See **living pledge.**

estate jure uxoris (es-tāt' jū're u-xō'ris). See **jure uxoris estate.**

estate less than freehold. Any estate the duration of which is regarded in law as being less than that of a life estate, in real property either corporeal or incorporeal. An estate for years, an estate at will, or an estate at sufferance. Decatur Coal Co. v Clokey, 332 Ill 253, 163 NE 702.

estate not of inheritance. A freehold estate for life. See 2 Bl Comm 104. Broadly, any interest, whether in real or personal property, which passes to the executor or administrator rather than directly to the heir or heirs. 23 Am J2d Desc & D § 18.

estate of cestui que trust. See **trust estate.**

estate of deceased person. Broadly speaking, such an estate may be deemed to exist only from the death of the decedent until it is finally wound up by an order of the court having jurisdiction of it. After the property of the decedent's estate has been paid out or otherwise distributed to those entitled thereto in accordance with the court's orders, and thereupon the estate has been declared closed, it can no longer be said to exist. State ex rel. Petters & Co. v District Court, 76 Mont 143, 245 P 529.
See **administration; administrator; descent; executor; heirs, probate; residuary estate.**

estate of freehold. See **freehold.**

estate of freehold not of inheritance. A freehold estate which does not pass to the heirs of the holder but is only for his lifetime or that of another person. Such estates are conventional, that is, expressly created by the acts of the parties; or they are legal, that is, they are created by construction and operation of law. See 2 Bl Comm 119.

estate of inheritance. A freehold interest in land, otherwise called a fee, where the tenant is not only entitled to enjoy the land for his own life, but where, after his death, it is passed by the law upon the person or persons who successfully represent him in perpetuum in right of blood, according to a certain established order of descent. 28 Am J2d Est § 8.

estate of tenant by the curtesy initiate. See **tenant by the curtesy initiate.**

estate of trustee. See **trust estate.**

estate on condition. An estate in real property with a qualification annexed by which it may, on the happening of a particular event, be created, enlarged, or destroyed. Munro v Syracuse L. S. & N. R. R. Co. 200 NY 224, 93 NE 516. The conditions annexed to estates are those implied by law and those expressed in the grant or devise which creates the estate. Express conditions are those declared or set forth in the instrument creating an estate or superimposed by a collateral agreement. Conditions implied in law are those which the law itself annexes to either certain estates or estates held under certain circumstances. 28 Am J2d Est § 132.
See **fee conditional.**

estate on condition precedent. See **condition precedent.**

estate on condition subsequent. See **condition subsequent.**

estate pur autre vie (es-tāt'pur ô-tr vî). An estate which is to endure for the life of a person other than the grantee or devisee. 33 Am J1st Life Est § 3.

estates of the realm. One of the two constituent parts of parliament, consisting of the lords spiritual, the lords temporal and the commons, the other part being the king. The king and these three estates form the great corporation or body politic of the kingdom, of which the king is the head. See 1 Bl Comm 153.

estate tail. See **fee tail.**

estate tail after possibility of issue extinct. See **fee tail after possibility of issue extinct.**

estate tail female. See **fee tail female.**

estate tail general. See **fee tail general.**

estate tail male. See **fee tail male.**

estate tail special. See **fee tail special.**

estate tax. A tax upon the transmission of property by a deceased person, that is, upon the privilege of transmitting property. 28 Am J Rev ed Inher T § 5. A tax imposed upon the net or taxable estate of a decedent without reference to the relationship of the recipients to the decedent or to the amount which a recipient takes. 28 Am J Rev ed Inher T § 5. A tax upon the transfer of property at death by a decedent, as distinguished from a succession tax, which, in its essence, is a tax upon the right to receive property from the estate of a decedent. McLaughlin v Grenn, 136 Conn 138, 69 A2d 289, 15 ALR2d 1210.
See **Federal estate tax.**

estate upon condition. Same as **estate on condition.**

estate upon condition expressed in grant or devise. See **estate on condition.**

estate upon condition implied in law. See **estate on condition.**

estate upon limitation. See **estate on condition; words of limitation.**

estate vested in interest. See **vested estate.**

estate vested in possession. An estate whereof there is a right of present enjoyment. 28 Am J2d Est § 2. See **vested estate.**

estate vested subject to defeasance. An estate subject to a condition subsequent. Anno: 131 ALR 712.
See **condition subsequent.**

Est autem jus publicum et privatum, quod ex naturalibus praeceptis aut gentium, aut civilibus est collectum; et quod in jure scripto jus appellatur id in lege Angliae rectum esse dicitur (est â'tem jūs pub'li-kum et prī-vā'tum, quod ex na-tū-rā'li-bus pre-sep'tis ât jen'she-um, ât si-vi'li-bus est kol-lek'-tum; et quod in jū're skrip'tō jūs ap-pel-ā'ter id in le'je an'gli-ē rek'tum es'se di'si-ter). Public and private law is that which is collected from natural precepts or from nations or from citizens; and that which in the written law is called "jus," in the law of England is called "right."

Est autem vis legem simulans (est â'tem vīs lē'jem si'mu-lanz). Violence may also be masquerading as law.

Est boni judicis ampliare jurisdictionem (est bo'nī jū'di-sis am-pli-ā're jū-ris-dik-she-ō'nem). It is the duty of a good judge to interpret his jurisdiction liberally.

este (es'te). Been.

ester in judgment (es'ter in juj'ment). To enter an appearance as a party to a pending action.

esthetic. See **aesthetic.**

estimate. Verb: (es'ti-māt). To form an opinion from data as to the weight, value, etc. of something. Duncan v National Mut. Fire Ins. Co. 44 Colo 472, 98 P 634. Noun: (es'ti-mat). An approximation or rough calculation of the size, weight, etc. of something.

estimated. The equivalent of more or less. Jeffreys v Weekly, 81 Or 140, 158 P 522. Appearing in a written contract, an indication that the quantity or amount of the subject matter is not attempted to be stated with mathematical exactness, and that the instrument must not be interpreted as if it contained an exact statement of the quantity or amount. 17 Am J2d Contr § 282. In connection with the designation of the amount of goods to be delivered under a contract of sale, it is an indefinite term comparable to the terms "about" or "more or less," and does not require or constitute a guaranty that the amount so estimated will be delivered. 46 Am J1st Sales § 156. A word of precaution in describing an area of land, intended to cover slight and unimportant inaccuracies. 55 Am J1st V & P § 131.

estimated cost. The reasonable cost of a building erected in accordance with certain plans and specifications, not necessarily the amount of some actual estimate made by a builder, an estimate agreed upon by the parties, or an estimate or bid duly accepted. Lambert v Sanford, 55 Conn 437, 12 A 519.

estimated tax. An income tax estimated as to amount, prior to the actual accrual of the entire income, as a basis for payment in instalments during the year and, if the taxpayer is employed, for withholding of a certain amount by the employer from each salary or wage payment, to be turned over to the government and credited to the employee in his income tax return for the year in which withheld.

estimation. See **by estimation; estimate; estimated.**

Est ipsorum legislatorum tanquam viva vox; rebus et non verbis legem imponimus (est ip-sō'rum le-jis-lā-tō'rum tan'quam vī'va vŏx; rē'bus et non ver'bis lē'jem im-pō'ni-mus). The voice of the lawmakers is like the living voice; we impose law upon things and not upon words. The meaning of the maxim is that legislative acts should be interpreted as ordinary language is understood.

esto (es'tō). Be it; let it be.

estop (es-top'). To bar; to stop; to prevent; to operate as an estoppel.
See **estoppel.**

esto perpetua (es'tō per-pe'tu-a). Be it perpetual or everlasting.

estopped. See **estoppel.**

estoppel. A bar which stoppeth a person or closes up his mouth to allege or plead what actually may be the truth. 2 Coke, Littleton 352a. A bar which precludes a person from denying or asserting anything to the contrary of that which has, in contemplation of law, been established as the truth, either by the acts of judicial or legislative officers or by his own deed or representations, express or implied. 28 Am J2d Estop § 1.

A waiver, being the intentional relinquishment of a known right, is consensual in nature and is distinguished from an estoppel which is not consensual, but is given effect to defeat the inequitable intent of the party estopped. Seavey v Erickson, 244 Minn 232, 69 NW2d 889, 52 ALR2d 1144.

The elements of estoppel by acts or representations are reliance by a person entitled to rely on the acts and representations, the misleading of such person, and, in consequence, a change of position to his detriment, so that the person responsible for the misleading will not be permitted to deny the truth of his own statements, express or implied. 29A Am J Rev ed Ins § 1009. Although the terms "waiver" and "estoppel" are not convertible, the distinction between the two terms is not entirely clear in insurance cases. Grantham v State Farm Mut. Auto. Ins. Co. 126 Cal App 2d Supp 855, 272 P2d 959, 48 ALR2d 1088.

See **judicial estoppel; promissory estoppel; waiver.**

estoppel by bond. The preclusion of a party to a bond to deny the truth of the recitals in the instrument, the estoppel operating similarly to estoppel by deed. 28 Am J2d Estop § 25.

estoppel by conduct. An equitable estoppel or estoppel in pais. 28 Am J2d Estop § 27.
See **estoppel in pais.**

estoppel by contract. A bar against denying the truth of facts agreed upon and settled by force of entering into a contract. Gress v Gress (Tex Civ App) 209 SW2d 1003, 15 ALR2d 700; a bar arising from acts done under or in performance of the contract. Re Schofield's Estate, 101 Colo 443, 73 P2d 1381.

estoppel by deed. A bar which precludes one party to a deed and his privies from asserting as against the other party and his privies any right or title in derogation of the deed or from denying the truth of any material facts asserted in it. 28 Am J2d Estop §§ 4, 5, 8.

estoppel by inaction. See **estoppel by silence; estoppel by standing.**

estoppel by judgment. Technically, the bar of a judgment against the relitigation of particular facts and issues, but used sometimes to indicate a bar against the relitigation of particular causes of action. 30A Am J Rev ed Judgm § 328.
See **res judicata.**

estoppel by mortgage. An estoppel operating from the recitals in the bond or the mortgage, similar to estoppel by deed.
See **estoppel by bond; estoppel by deed.**

estoppel by oath. The bar of a party to deny in subsequent litigation that which he has previously stated on oath in a former litigation, in a pleading, deposition, or oral testimony. Such bar is limited in most jurisdictions to persons who were parties to the former suit. 28 Am J2d Estop § 71.

estoppel by record. The preclusion to deny the truth set forth in a record, whether legislative or judicial, and also to deny the facts adjudicated by a court of competent jurisdiction. 28 Am J2d Estop § 2.

estoppel by silence. An estoppel in pais. An estoppel which arises where a person who by force of circumstances is under a duty to another to speak, refrains from doing so and thereby leads the other to believe in the existence of a state of facts in reliance upon which he acts to his prejudice. Engelhardt v Gravens (Mo) 281 SW 715, 719. An estoppel by standing by. 28 Am J2d Estop §§ 43, 53.

estoppel by standing by. See **estoppel by silence.**

estoppel by verdict. A bar to the relitigation of particular facts and issues. 30A Am J Rev ed Judgm § 328.

estoppel in pais. Otherwise known as equitable estoppel. 28 Am J2d Estop § 33. A term applied to a situation where, because of something which he has done or omitted to do, a party is denied the right to plead or prove an otherwise important fact. 28 Am J2d Estop § 27. It arises out of the acts and conduct of the party estopped, such being the characteristic which distinguishes it from a technical estoppel by deed, record, or judgment. Sequin v Maloney, 198 Or 272, 253 P2d 252, 256 P2d 514, 35 ALR2d 1412.

Estoveria sunt ardendi, arundi, construendi, et claudendi (es-to-ve'ri-a sunt ar-den'dī, a-run'dī, kon-stru-en'dī, et klâ-den'dī). Estovers are of burning, ploughing, building, and fencing.

estoveriis habendis (es-to-ve'ri-is hā-ben'dis). See **de estoveriis habendis.**

estoverium (es-tō-ve'ri-um). Same as **estovers.**

estovers (es-tō'vèrz). The right of a tenant of farm land, whether for life or for years, to take from the leased premises such amount of wood or timber as is sufficient or necessary for fuel, the repair of buildings, the repair of implements of husbandry, the repair of fences, and other agricultural needs. 32 Am J1st L & T § 219. Another sense of the term is that of support.

Est quiddam perfectius in rebus licitis (est quĭd'dam per-fek'she-us in re'bus lĭ-sī'tis). There is something more perfect in things which are permitted.

Est quidem alia praestatio quae nominatur heriettum; ubi tenens, liber vel servus, in morte sua, dominum suum, de quo tenuerit, respicit de meliori averio suo, vel de secundo meliori, secundum diversam locorum consuetudinem (est quĭ'dem a'li-a pre-stā'she-ō kwē no-mi-nā'ter he-ri-et'tum; ŭ'bi te'-nenz, lī'ber vel ser'vus, in mor'te su'a, do'mi-num su'um, dē quō te-nu'e-rit, re'spi-sit dē me-li-ō'rī a-ve'ri-ō su'ō, vel dē se-kun'dō me-li-ō'rī, se-kun'dum dī-ver′sam lō-kō′rum kon-su-e-tū′di-nem). There is a certain other sort of prestation which is called a heriot; where a tenant, whether a freeman or a slave, at his death provides the lord of whom he held with his best beast or with the second best, according to the custom of the place. See 2 Bl Comm 424.

estrapamento. See **de estrapamento**.

estray. A beast, by nature tame or reclaimable, in which there is a valuable property, such as a cow, pig, or horse, found wandering at large or lost, its owner being unknown. 4 Am J2d Ani § 46.

estreat (es-trēt′). To extract; to take out. Where a bond or recognizance to keep the peace was broken, the bond became forfeited and was "estreated," that is, it was taken out from among the other records, and it was sent up to the exchequer, whereupon the sureties on the bond became the absolute debtors of the king. See 4 Bl Comm 253.

estrepamentum (es-tre-pa-men′tum). Same as **estrepement**.

estrepe (es-trēp′). To strip, to lay bare, to lay waste; to commit waste.

estrepement (es-trēp′ment). Waste; extirpation; a common-law writ which lay after judgment in any real action, and before the sheriff delivered possession, to stop any waste which the losing party might be tempted to commit in lands which were determined to be no longer his. See 3 Bl Comm 225.

estrepement pendente placito (es-trēp′ment pen-den′te pla′si-tō). Estrepement pending suit; a writ given by the statute of Gloucester to prevent waste pending the outcome of any real action. See 3 Bl Comm 226.

estrepment. Same as **estrepement**.

estuary. The wide mouth of a tidal stream; a bay or inlet.

et. And; also.

et ad huc detinet (et ad hūk de-ti′net). And he still detains.

et adjournatur (et ad-jur-nā′ter). And it is adjourned.

et al. An abbreviation of the Latin "et alius," meaning and another, and also of "et alii," meaning and others. Re McGovern's Estate, 77 Mont 182, 250 P 812.

et alii (et a′li-ī). And others.

et alii e contra (et a′li-ī ē kon′trā). And others to the contrary.

et alios (et a′li-ōs). And others.

et alius (et a′li-us). And another.

et allocatur (et al-lō-kā′ter). And it is allowed.

et als. An abbreviation of "et alios,"—and others.

etc. Abbreviation of et cetera, and so forth, sometimes written "&c." 1 Am J2d Abbr § 8. And others; other things of a like kind. 57 Am J1st Wills § 1335.

et cetera (et set′er-ạ). And so forth, and others, and other things, and the rest, and so on. 1 Am J2d Abbr § 8.
 The meaning of the term depends so much upon the context of the instrument, the description and enumeration of matters and things preceding it and the subject matter to which it is applied that in one instance it may mean one thing and a different thing in another. Muir v Kay, 66 Utah 550, 244 P 901. See **etc.**

et curia consentiente (et kū′ri-a kon-sen-she-en′te). And the court consenting.

Et de ceo se mettent en le pays (é dē say suh metahn ōn lu payes). And as to this matter, they put themselves on the country; that is, they leave it to the jury to decide.

Et de hoc ponit se super patriam (et dē hōk pō′nit sē sū′per pa′tri-am). And of this he puts himself on the country. That is, he leaves it for the jury to decide.

et ei legitur in haec verba (et ē′ī le′ji-ter in hec ver′ba). And it is read to him in these words.

eternal law. The moral law; the law of nature. The law which God in the creation of man infused into him for his direction and preservation. Calvin's Case (Eng) 7 Co Rep la.

et habeas ibi tunc hoc breve (et hā′be-as i′bi tunk hōk brē′ve). And have you then there this writ.

et habuit (et hā′bu-it). And he had it.

ethical. In accord with ethics.
 See **ethics**.

ethics. A code, system, or body of moral principles or good conduct, particularly a system for a group of people or a profession, such as law or medicine. In a profession, the sum of professional experience as to standards of professional behavior. Abelson's, Inc. v New Jersey State Board of Optometry, 5 NJ 412, 75 A2d 867, 22 ALR2d 929.
 See **judicial ethics; legal ethics**.

Ethiopian. A native of Ethiopia. Used loosely, any African of the black race.

ethling (ēth′ling). Same as **atheling**.

et hoc paratus est verificare (et hōk pa-rā′tus est ve-ri-fi-kā′re). And this he is ready to verify; that is, to prove.

et hoc petit quod inquiratur per patriam (et hōk pē′tit quod in′′qui-rā′ter per pa′tri-am). And this he prays may be inquired of by the country; that is, by the jury.

et hoc ponit se super patriam (et hōk po′nit sē sū′per pa′tri-am). And of this he puts himself upon the country. This was the formal conclusion of a defendant's traverse or denial of the plaintiff's allegations, whereby he—the defendant—tendered the issue and thus submitted himself to the judgment of his peers, that is, to the verdict of the jury. See 3 Bl Comm 313.

ethyl alcohol. Ordinary or common alcohol.

et inde petit judicium (et in′de pe′tit jū-di′she-um). And thereof he prays judgment.

et inde producit sectam (et in′de prō-du′sit sek′tam). And thereupon he brings suit. The formal conclusion of a common-law declaration was always in these words. Originally, they meant that the plaintiff came with his witnesses or followers. He was then required to use them to make out at least a prima facie case by their testimony before the defendant was put to the trouble of answering the charge. This latter practice was discontinued in the reign of Edward the Third, but the form of it survived. See 3 Bl Comm 295.

et issint (et is′sint). And so.

et modo ad hunc diem (et mō′dō ad hunk dī′em). And now, at this day.

et non. And not.

et non allocatur (et non al-lo-kā'ter). And it is not allowed.

et petit auxilium (et pe'tit âk-zi'li-um). And he prays aid.

et praedictus X similiter (et pre-dik'tus X si-mi'li-ter). And the said X likewise.

Et quod non habet principium, non habet finem (et quod non hā'bet prin-si'pi-um, non hā'bet fī'nem). And that which has no beginning, has no end.

et semble (e' sān-bl). And it seems.

et seq. An abbreviation of **et sequitur.**

et sequitur (et se'qui-ter). And as follows.

et sic (et sīk). And so.

et sic ad judicium (et sīk ad jū-di'she-um). And so to judgment.

et sic ad patriam (et sīk ad pa'tri-am). And so to the country; that is, to the jury.

et sic fecit (et sīk fē'sit). And he did so.

et sic pendet (et sīk pen'det). And so the matter hangs or rests.

et sic ulterius (et sīk ul-te'ri-us). And so further; and so forth.

et sim. An abbreviation of et similis, meaning and the like. Penas v Chicago, Milwaukee & St. Paul Ry. Co. 112 Minn 203, 127 NW 926.

et similis (et si'mi-lis). And the like. See **et sim.**

Et stet nomen universitatis (et stet nō'men ū-ni-ver-si-tā'tis). And the name of the corporation may remain. See 1 Bl Comm 469.

et ux. An abbreviation of **et uxor.**

et uxor (et u'xor). And his wife.

eugenics. The improvement of the race by scientific controls, based on study of hereditary factors.

eugenics laws. Statutes having a background in eugenics, for example, a statute which requires a medical examination and certificate of freedom from venereal disease before issuance of a marriage license. Peterson v Widule, 157 Wis 641, 647.

Eum qui nocentem infamat, non est aequum et bonum ob eam rem condemnari; delicta enim nocentium nota esse oportet et expedit (ē'um quī no-sen'tem in'fā-mat, non est e'kwu'um et bō'num ob ē'am rem kon-dem-nā'rī; dē-lik'ta e'nim no-sen'-she-um nō'ta es'se o-por'tet et ex-pē'dit). If anyone defames a bad man, it is not just and right that he should on that account be condemned, for it is proper and expedient that the crimes of wicked men should be made known.

eundo, redeundo et morando (e-un'dō, re-de-un'dō et mo-ran'dō). In going, in returning and in remaining.

eunuch (ū'nuk). A castrated male of the human species. Eckert v Van Pelt, 69 Kan 357, 76 P 909.

EURATOM. Abbreviation for European Atomic Energy Community. This community is composed of the governments of France, West Germany, Italy, Belgium, Holland and Luxemburg. 6 Am J2d Atomic E § 41.

EURATOM Co-operation Act. A federal statute providing for a joint nuclear power program between the United States and the European Atomic Energy Community. 42 USC § 2291 (c); 6 Am J2d Atomic E § 41.

European plan. A system of hotel operation under which a guest engages a room for a charge which does not include meals, although a dining room is operated by the hotel, such being available to the guest if he desires, he to pay for such meals as he may order there. New Galt House v Louisville, 129 Ky 341, 111 SW 351; Wellsboro Hotel Co's Appeal, 336 Pa 171, 7 A2d 334, 122 ALR 1396.

evade. To escape; to slip away; to take refuge in flight or artifice. Keegan v United States, 325 US 478, 89 L Ed 1745, 65 S Ct 1203.

evangelist. A minister of the gospel who, traveling from church to church or city to city, preaches sermons intended and usually effective to obtain conversions to the religion espoused.

Evangelists. The four writers of the gospels, the first four books of the New Testament.

evaporation. Changing into vapor; a problem in conducting water through irrigation ditches. 30 Am J Rev ed Irrig § 24.

evasio (ē-vā'she-ō). An escape.

evasion. Avoiding something by flight or artifice, especially a penalty or obligation. Keegan v United States, 325 US 478, 89 L Ed 1745, 65 S Ct 1203.

evasion marriage. A marriage entered into for the purpose of avoiding military service under the Selective Training and Service Act. United States v Baird (DC NY) 39 F Supp 388.

evasion of tax. See **tax evasion.**

event. The consequence of anything; the issue, end, conclusion; that in which an action, operation, or series of operations, terminates. Fitch v Bates (NY) 11 Barb 471, 473. The culmination or end that the means may have produced or brought about. Continental Casualty Co. v Willis, 28 F2d 707, 61 ALR 1069.

event causing injury. As the expression is used in an accident insurance policy covering disability immediately following the event causing the injury, the "event" is not the injury itself but it is the accidental means by which the effect on the body —the injury—is caused. Hatch v United States Casualty Co. 197 Mass 101, 83 NE 398.

eventual waste. Waste done by an admitted particular tenant after the institution of a suit involving the title or a partition suit. 56 Am J1st Waste § 6.

Eventus est qui ex causa sequitur; et dicitur eventus quia ex causis evenit (ē-ven'tus est quī ex kâ'za se'qui-ter; et di'si-ter ē-ven'tus qui'a ex kâ'zis ē-vē'nit). An event is that which follows from the cause; and it is called an event because it comes out of the causes.

Eventus varios res nova semper habet (ē-ven'tus va'ri-ōs rēz nō'va sem'per hā'bet). A new circumstance always holds possibility of a different result.

everlasting. See **perpetual.**

every. All of a whole collection or aggregate number, considered separately, one by one; each, considered as a unitary part of an aggregate number. Salo v Pacific Coast Casualty Co. 95 Wash 109, 163 P 384. Appearing in a statute, generally regarded as a word of inclusion. 50 Am J1st Stat § 286.

every corporation. A term broad enough to include foreign, as well as domestic, corporations. 36 Am

J2d For Corp § 152. Not including municipal corporations, where it appears in a statute, the obvious intent of which is against the inclusion of such corporations. Phillips v Baltimore, 110 Md 431, 72 A 902.

everyone. All of a group or body, considered separately, one by one. For some purposes, as in a statutory definition of a crime, including a corporation. 19 Am J2d Corp § 1436.

every other reasonable hypothesis. A conventional term in an instruction to the jury in a criminal case on circumstantial evidence, the admonition being to "exclude every other reasonable hypothesis." Jones v State, 34 Tex Crim 490, 30 SW 1059, 31 SW 664.

everything. All of a group or collection of things, considered separately, one by one. A term subject to limitation in scope by the application of the rule of ejusdem generis. 57 Am J1st Wills § 1362.

evesche. The diocese of a bishop.

evesque. A bishop.

eviction. Dispossession, actual or constructive. A term with peculiar reference to a tenant, being the disturbance of his possession, his expulsion or amotion, depriving him of the enjoyment of the demised premises, or any portion thereof, by title paramount or by entry and act of the landlord. 32 Am J1st L & T § 245. A breach of covenant of quiet enjoyment. 20 Am J2d Cov § 101. A breach of a covenant of warranty. 20 Am J2d Cov § 54.
See **constructive eviction; eviction by title paramount.**

eviction by title paramount. The eviction of a tenant by one whose title is superior to that of the landlord. 32 Am J1st L & T § 245. A breach of a title covenant of quiet enjoyment. 20 Am J2d Cov § 101; a breach of a title covenant of warranty. 20 Am J2d Cov § 54.
Within the meaning of a covenant in a deed against eviction by "paramount right," the term includes any right which commencing before the deed is not passed by it, but exists independently of it, and can be asserted with the effect of rightfully evicting the tenant under the deed. Davis v Logan's Heirs, 44 Ky (5 B Mon) 341, 342.

evidence. The means by which any matter of fact, the truth of which is submitted to investigation, may be established or disproved. That which demonstrates, makes clear, or ascertains the truth of the very fact or point in issue, either on the one side or the other. Lynch v Rosenberger, 121 Kan 601, 249 P 682, 60 ALR 376.
The law of evidence embraces those rules which determine what testimony is to be admitted or rejected in the trial of a civil action or a criminal prosecution and what weight is to be given to evidence which is admitted. 29 Am J2d Ev § 1.

evidence aliunde (al-i-un'de). Same as **extrinsic evidence.**

evidence by comparison. Evidence admitted to prove the quality of a thing by comparing one thing with another under such circumstances that the similarity of the subjects of comparison is reasonably sufficient to give the result of the comparison sound probative force. 46 Am J1st Sales § 310.
See **comparison of handwriting.**

evidence in mitigation. Proof of facts tending to show that the conceded or assumed cause of action does not entitle the plaintiff to as large an amount of damages as might otherwise be recoverable. 22 Am J2d Damg § 291.

evidence introduced. See **introduced evidence.**

evidence of debt. Any written instrument for the payment of money.

evidence offered. See **offered evidence.**

evidence of title. A deed or other instrument establishing title to property, particularly real estate.

evident. Plainly seen or understood; manifest; obvious.
Under a constitutional provision guaranteeing the right to bail except in capital cases when the proof is "evident," the word has been viewed as meaning manifest, plain, clear, obvious, apparent, and notorious. 8 Am J2d Bail § 50. In a more technical and precise sense, such probative facts as are requisite to prove ultimate facts. Ultimate facts are the facts which are pleaded and probative and evidentiary facts are those which supply the proof of the ultimate facts. 41 Am J1st Pl § 8.

evidentiary facts. The facts admissible in evidence.

evidently. In an evident manner.
See **evident.**

evil. That which is wicked, morally bad.

evil spirits. See **conjuration; witchcraft.**

ew. Marriage.

ewage. A toll paid for passage over water.

ewbrice. Breach of marriage; adultery.

ewe (ū). A female sheep.

ex (eks). From; out of; in; of; in accord with; because of; by reason of.

ex. Sometimes used as an abbreviation of "exhibit." (Latin.) Out of, from.

ex abundanti cautela (ex a-bun-dan'tī kâ-tē'la). From or out of abundance of caution.

Ex abuso non arguitur ad usum (ex ab-u'sō non argu'i-ter ad ū'sum). The utility of anything cannot be argued from the abuse of it.

exaction. The excessive or unauthorized taking or collecting of moneys as fees or dues by an officer or by a person pretending to be an officer. An excessive demand. An amount demanded and taken without right.
See **extortion.**

exactissima diligentia (eg-zak-tis'si-ma di-li-jen'she-a). Extraordinary diligence.

exactor (eg-zak'tor). One who makes an exaction. (Latin.) Collector, especially of taxes and duties.

exactor regis (eg-zak'tor rē'jis). An officer who collected taxes and other moneys for the royal treasury. A sheriff.

exact science. Mathematics.
See **books of exact science.**

ex adverso (ex ad-ver'sō). On the other side.

ex aequitate (ex e-qui-tā'te). According to equity.

ex aequo et bono (ex e'quō et bō'nō). In equity and good conscience. Scott v Ford, 45 Or 531, 80 P 899.

exaltare (eg-zal-tā're). To raise; to lift; to elevate.

exaltare stagnum (eg-zal-tā're stag'num). To raise the water in a pond or pool.

ex altera parte (ex al'te-ra par'te). Of the other part.

EXAMEN [425] EXCEPTANT

examen (eg-zā'men). A trial.

examination. Inspection, close observation; investigation, usually by questioning a person or persons. In connection with legal proceedings, commonly understood to mean an examination under oath or affirmation. Edelstein v United States (CA8 Minn) 149 F 636.

The right of the insurer to "examine" the body of the insured, conferred by a clause in an accident policy, does not include the right to make an autopsy, dissection, or exhumation. Suddath v Travelers' Ins. Co. (CC Ky) 106 F 822.

See **investigation**.

examination before trial. See **deposition; discovery.**

examination in chief. The first or direct examination of a witness by the party who has called him to testify. Webber v Barry, 66 Mich 127, 33 NW 289.

examination of bankrupt. An examination provided by the Bankruptcy Act at which the bankrupt is required to submit, under oath, to questioning concerning the conduct of his business, the cause of his bankruptcy, his dealings with his creditors and other persons, the amount, kind, and whereabouts of his property, and, in addition, all matters which may effect the administration and settlement of his estate or the granting of his discharge. Bankruptcy Act § 7(a)(10); 11 USC § 25(a)(10); 9 Am J2d Bankr §§ 606, 611.

examination of juror. An examination of a juror called for a particular case to ascertain by questioning him whether or not he is subject to a challenge for cause, and, if not, whether he should be kept off the jury by a peremptory challenge. 31 Am J Rev ed Jur § 136. The court is not bound by the answers of the juror, but may take such other means as may be necessary to determine his competency. 31 Am J Rev ed Jur § 145.

examination of witness. The obtaining of the testimony of a witness by oral questions and answers made under oath in open court. 58 Am J1st Witn § 553.

See **cross examination; depositions; direct examination; leading questions.**

examined copy. A copy proved by oral evidence to have been examined with the original document and to correspond therewith. 29 Am J2d Ev § 910.

examiner. An officer or other person who is authorized to conduct an examination. A person appointed in a corporate reorganization proceeding, where the debtor is continued in possession, to prepare and file a plan of reorganization and to perform other duties prescribed for trustees in corporate reorganization proceedings. 9 Am J2d Bankr § 1540.

See **bank examiner; bar examiner; medical examiner; trial examiner.**

examiners in chancery. Officers appointed by the English court of chancery to take the testimony of witnesses and to return the same to the court.

examining court. A committing magistrate; a magistrate authorized to act, and presiding as, a magistrate inquiring into an accusation of the commission of a crime, preferred against a person by complaint, information, or affidavit, for the purpose of binding the accused over to await the action of the grand jury upon finding that there is probable cause to believe that an offense has been committed and that the accused committed it. State v Rogers, 31 NM 485, 247 P 828; Childers v State, 30 Tex App 160.

examining trial. A trial or hearing held before a magistrate while presiding as such in an examining court for the purpose of inquiring into a criminal accusation which has been preferred against a person. Childers v State, 30 Tex App 160.

ex animo (eks an'i-mō). From the mind; arising from one's conscience.

ex antecedentibus et consequentibus (eks an-ti-si-den'ti-bus et kon-se-kwen'ti-bus). From those matters which precede and those which follow that is, from the whole instrument. Brannan v Mesick, 10 Cal 95, 101.

Ex antecedentibus et consequentibus fit optima interpretatio (ex an-te-sē-den'ti-bus et kon-se-quen'ti-bus fit op'ti-ma in-ter-pre-tā'she-ō). The best interpretation is made from those matters which precede and those which follow. State ex rel. Patton v Marron, 22 NM 632, 167 P 9.

ex arbitrio judicis (ex ar-bi'tri-ō jū'di-sis). At the will or discretion of the judge. See 4 Bl Comm 394.

ex assensu curiae (ex as-sen'su kū'ri-ē). With the consent of the court.

ex assensu patris (ex as-sen'su pa'tris). With the consent of the father.

ex assensu suo (ex as-sen'su su'ō). With his own consent.

ex audito (ex â'di-tō). From what has been heard; from hearsay.

ex bonis (ex bō'nis). From or of the goods.

ex bonis maternis (ex bō'nis ma-ter'nis). From maternal goods; from the goods inherited from the mother.

ex bonis paternis (ex bō'nis pa-ter'nis). From paternal goods,—from the goods inherited from the father.

excambia (ex-kam'bi-ä). See **excambium.**

excambiator (eks-kam'bi-ā-tor). One who exchanges; a broker; an agent employed to effect an exchange of real property.

excambion (eks-kam'bi-on). Same as **excambium.**

excambium (eks-kam'bi-um). Exchange; an exchange of property; a place where merchants met; a contract for an exchange of lands.

See **billa excambia.**

ex capite doli (ex ka'pi-te dō'lī). On the ground of deceit.

ex capite fraudis (ex ka'pi-te frâ'dis). On the ground of fraud.

ex cathedra (eks kath'ē-drą or ka-thē' drą). From the chair; from authority.

ex causa (ex kâ'za). From or with cause; by title.

ex causa lucrativa (ex kâ'sa lu-krā-tī'va). From voluntary consideration; by gratuity; gratuitously.

except. Verb: To object; to take or reserve an exception to a ruling or order of the court in a judicial proceeding. Preposition: Other than.

excepta dignitate regali (ex-sep'ta dig-ni-tā'te rē-gā'lī). With the exception of royal dignity. See 1 Bl Comm 205.

exceptant (ek-sep'tant). A party to an action who causes an exception to be entered.

except by accident. An occurrence which is unexpected, not according to the usual course of events. Hutcherson v Sovereign Camp, W. W. 112 Tex 551, 251 SW 491, 28 ALR 832.

excepted. Excluded; taken out. Occasionally confused with "accepted."
Where the word has been written across the face of a draft with the signature of the party, courts have admitted parol evidence to show that the word "accepted" was intended. "The law is not a system of quirks and quibbles upon which courts may seize to defeat rights, but a system of rules and principles, and it is the duty of a court to disregard mere pretexts." Cortelyou v Maben, 22 Neb 697.

excepted risk. See **exception in insurance policy**.

excepting. Leaving out. Making an exception. See **exception**.

exceptio (ek-sep'she-ō). An exception; a plea; a defense; an objection. A Roman law pleading corresponding to the "plea" of the common law. See 3 Bl Comm 310.

exceptio ad breve prosternendum (ek-sep'she-o ad brē've prō-ster-nen'dum). A plea in abatement.

exceptio dilatoria (ek-sep'she-ō di-la-tō'ri-a). (Roman law.) A plea which was interposed for delay.

exceptio doli mali (ek-sep'she-o do'lī ma'lī). (Roman law.) A plea of fraud.

Exceptio ejus rei cujus petitur dissolutio nulla est (ek-sep'she-ō ē'jus rē'ī kū'jus pē'ti-ter dis-so-lu'she-ō nul'la est). A plea of the same transaction of which a dissolution or discharge is sought, is a nullity.

Exceptio falsi omnium ultima (ek-sep'she-ō fal'sī om'ni-um ul'ti-ma). A false plea is the worst of all.

Exceptio firmat regulam in casibus non exceptis (ek-sep'she-ō fir'mat rē'gu-lam in kā'si-bus non ek-sep'tis). An exception confirms the rule in cases not excepted.

Exceptio firmat regulam in contrarium (ek-sep'she-o fir'mat rē'gu-lam in kon-trā'ri-um). The exception affirms the rule to be the contrary.

exceptio juris jurandi (ek-sep'she-o jū'ris jū-ran'dī). (Roman law.) A plea of an oath,—a plea that the defendant had, at the instance of the plaintiff, sworn that he owed the plaintiff nothing.

exceptio metus (ek-sep'she-o me'tus). (Roman law.) A plea of fear, compulsion or duress.

exception. Someone or something excluded. A protest against the ruling of the trial court upon a question of law, designed for the protection of the court so that it may reconsider its action and of the opposing counsel so that he may consent to a change by the court in its ruling, but primarily designed to bring upon the record on appeal, by a bill of exceptions, the ruling objected to, which otherwise would not constitute a part of the record. 5 Am J2d A & E § 558; 53 Am J1st Trial § 132.
In Louisiana the word is a comprehensive term referring to defenses. Buty v Goldfinch, 74 Wash 532, 133 P 1057.
See **bill of exceptions; objection; peremptory exception; reservation**.

exceptional. The rare—the unusual or extraordinary case or circumstance. Re Irving-Austin Bldg. Corp. (CA7 Ill) 100 F2d 574.

exceptional and extremely unusual hardship. A matter of suspension of the deportation of an alien, for determination by the Attorney General acting with a sound discretion, according to whether deportation will result in exceptional and extremely unusual hardship to the alien or to his spouse, parent or child, who is a citizen or an alien lawfully admitted for permanent residence. 8 USC § 1254 (a); Jay v Boyd, 351 US 345, 100 L Ed 1242, 76 S Ct 919.

exceptional bailment. A bailment which affects the public interest in such a way that the law imposes on the bailee a somewhat different liability from that of the ordinary bailee for hire, for example, a bailment to a carrier or innkeeper. 8 Am J2d Bailm § 6.

exception in admiralty. A plea filed in a suit in admiralty corresponding to a plea in abatement or a special plea in bar in an ordinary civil action. United States Shipping Board Emergency Fleet Corp. v Rosenberg Bros. & Co. 276 US 202, 72 L Ed 531, 48 S Ct 256. An objection to the sufficiency, fullness, distinctness, relevancy, or competency of any pleading or interrogatory. Rules of Practice in Admiralty and Maritime Cases, Rule 27.

exception in an equity suit. Written objections to a pleading, filed in the suit.

exception in contract. Something omitted from the operation of the contract in reference to the subject matter.
As the word is frequently used in contracts, it usually indicates that something is taken out from the principal matter provided for in the clause or paragraph in which the word is found, and not that something is taken out of or changed from other provisions in other clauses of the entire contract. Anvil Mining Co. v Humble, 153 US 540, 548, 38 L Ed 814, 817, 14 S Ct 876.

exception in deed. A withdrawal of some part of the thing granted by the general description which otherwise would pass to the grantee, which was in esse at the time of the conveyance, and which until such conveyance and the severance thereby was comprised in the thing granted. 23 Am J2d Deeds § 262. Although distinguishable, the terms "exception" and "reservation" are quite commonly used as interchangeable. 23 Am J2d Deeds § 262.
See **reservation**.

exception in insurance policy. A provision of a contract of insurance which withdraws a certain risk or risks from the coverage of the contract. 29A Am J Rev ed Ins §§ 1132 et seq.

exception in lease. The exclusion of some part of the demised premises from the operation of the lease by the terms thereof. 32 Am J1st L & T § 185.

exception in statute. A clause in a statute which takes away from the operation of the measure that which, but for it, would be included. State ex rel. Crow v St. Louis, 174 Mo 125, 73 SW 623.
An "exception" is similar to a "proviso," although undoubtedly there is a technical distinction between them.
See **proviso in statute**.

exception taken on trial. See **exception**.

exception to bail. A formal objection to the sureties on a bail bond, or to the amount of the bond.

exception to hearsay rule. Hearsay evidence taken out of the general rule against the admissibility of hearsay in the interest of justice, and in accord with sound policy, so as to be admissible notwithstanding the rule, for example, a dying declaration, a declaration against interest, etc. 29 Am J2d Ev §§ 495, 496.

Exceptio nulla est versus actionem quae exceptionem perimit (ek-sep'she-o nul'la est ver'sus ak-she-ō'nem kwē ek-sep-she-ō'nem per'i-mit). There is no plea against an action which destroys the plea.

exceptio pacti conventi (ek-sep'she-ō pak'tī kon-ven'tī). (Roman law.) A plea that the plaintiff had agreed with the defendant that he would not sue.

exceptio pecuniae non numeratae (ek-sep'she-o pe-kū'ni-ē non nū-me-rā'tē). (Roman law.) A plea that the money had not been paid to the defendant.

exceptio peremptoria (ek-sep'she-o per-emp-tō'ri-a). (Roman law.) A peremptory plea,—a plea which denied the right of the plaintiff to sue.

Exceptio probat regulam (ek-sep'she-o prō'bat rē'gu-lam). The exception proves the rule. Where the rule is stated and the exceptions are stated and the matter is not within the exceptions, the rule governs. Lamkin & Foster v Ledoux, 101 Me 581, 64 A 1048.

Exceptio probat regulam de rebus non exceptis (ek-sep'she-ō prō'bat rē'gu-lam dē rē'bus non ek-sep'-tis). The exception proves the rule in matters not excepted. He who asserts the right to an exclusive privilege in any department of business must bring himself under the protection of some recognized exception to the rule of unrestricted liberty in the practice of all arts and trades. P. C. Wiest Co. v Weeks, 177 Pa 412, 35 A 693.

Exceptio quae firmat legem, exponit legem (ek-sep'-she-o kwē fir'mat lē'jem, ex-pō'nit lē'jem). An exception which confirms the law, expounds it. Neary v Philadelphia, Wilmington & Baltimore Railroad Co. 12 Del (7 Houst) 419, 438.

Exceptio quoque regulam declarat (ek-sep'she-o quō'kwe rē'gu-lam dē-klā'rat). An exception also declares or affirms the rule.

exceptio rei adjudicatae (ek-sep'she-o rē'ī ad-jū-di-kā'tē). (Roman law.) A plea of res adjudicata,— that the same matter had been previously determined by a judgment in an action between the same parties.

exceptio rei venditae et traditae (ek-sep'she-o rē'ī ven'di-tē et trā'di-tē). (Roman law.) A plea that the thing was sold and delivered.

Exceptio semper ultima ponenda est (ek-sep'she-o sem'per ul'ti-ma pō-nen'da est). An exception should always be placed last.

exceptio temporis (ek-sep'she-ō tem'po-ris). (Roman law.) A plea that the plaintiff's cause of action has expired by lapse of time.

exceptor (ek-sep'tor). A party to an action who makes or reserves an exception to a ruling of the court.

excerpta (ek-sėrp'tạ). Extracts; excerpts.

excerpts. Extracts.

ex certa scientia (ex ser'ta sī-en'she-a). Of or from certain knowledge.

excess. Surplus; indulgence to an extreme.
See **corporate excess; overtime; surplus.**

excess baggage. The weight of baggage in excess of the maximum weight of baggage of a passenger which will be carried free of charge. 14 Am J2d Car § 1221.

excess insurance. Insurance which, by a provision in the policy, is relieved from contributing to other insurers of the same risk; such a policy renders the insurer liable only for the amount of loss or damage in excess of the coverage provided by another policy or policies covering the same risk. 29A Am J Rev ed Ins § 1715.

A liability insurance policy issued to a lessor of automobiles and covering liability of the lessee, which expressly provides for its inapplicability to liability "for such loss as is covered on a primary, contributory, excess, or any other basis by insurance in another insurance company," does not constitute "other valid and collectible insurance" within the meaning of a liability insurance policy issued with respect to the lessee's own automobile, but covering the insured while driving another car, subject to the proviso that such insurance "shall be excess insurance over any other valid and collectible insurance available to the insurance . . .". Continental Casualty Co. v Weeks (Fla) 74 So 2d 367, 46 ALR2d 1159.

excessive. Running or operating to excess; extreme.

excessive award. An award by arbitrators which embraces matters not contained in the submission. 5 Am J2d Arb & A § 150.
See **excessive damages.**

excessive bail. An imposition prohibited by both the United States Constitution and state constitutions, being bail set at an amount higher than reasonably calculated to insure that the accused will appear to stand trial, considering the factors of the ability of the accused to give bail, the nature of the offense charged, the penalty for the offense charged, the character and reputation of the accused, the health of the accused, the kind and strength of the evidence, the probability of the accused appearing at trial, the forfeiture of other bonds, and whether the accused was a fugitive from justice when arrested. 8 Am J2d Bail § 71.

excessive damages. An award of damages by verdict which appears to have been given under the influence of passion or prejudice; an award so large as to shock the judicial conscience; an award so out of proportion to the damages proved as to indicate an abuse of the jury's discretion. 22 Am J2d Damg § 366. See also 5 Am J2d A & E § 896.

excessive deposit. A deposit or account in excess of the amount which a savings bank is authorized to receive or carry. 10 Am J2d Banks § 275.

excessive fine. An imposition prohibited by the Constitution of the United States and many of the state constitutions; a relative matter, dependent upon many factors, including the financial status of the person penalized. An imposition so disproportionate to the offense as to present a plain conflict between the constitutional prohibition and those of the statute prescribing the punishment. 21 Am J2d Crim L § 601.

A fine imposed in a criminal case is excessive, even though within the maximum provided by statute, if it is apparently beyond the power of the defendant to pay it forthwith, or even during a lifetime of effort. State v Ross, 55 Or 450, 104 P 596.

excessive force. Force which is unnecessary and unreasonable in the performance of an act otherwise lawful, such as the use of force in self-defense so far beyond a necessity of the case as to appear vindictive. 6 Am J2d Asslt & B § 162. Force used

in making an arrest in excess of the force reasonably necessary to apprehend the offender or effect the arrest. 5 Am J2d Arr § 80. Ham v Santa Rosa Bank, 62 Cal 125.

excessive homestead. A selected homestead exemption which exceeds in value the amount fixed by the statute which creates the exemption. 26 Am J1st Home § 43. Not a selection which creditors can attack successfully as illegal, their remedy being to reach the excess in value.

excessive levy. A levy upon more property of the defendant than in the opinion of a reasonably prudent man is necessary to satisfy the debt, interest, and costs, considering various factors, such as incumbrances upon the property, the fact that a forced sale usually results in a sacrifice, and the convenience of division or separation of the property for purposes of levy and sale. 6 Am J2d Attach § 294; 30 Am J2d Exec §§ 96, 97. A form of abuse of process. 1 Am J2d Abuse P § 10.

excessive loan. A loan in an amount in excess of the amount which the lender, a bank, is authorized by statutory or charter provision to make. 10 Am J2d Banks § 684.

excessive or unusual noise. Appearing in a statute which requires a muffler as equipment on a motor vehicle to prevent "excessive or unusual noise," the expression means any noise from the operation of a motor vehicle in excess of what is usual when a muffler in sound condition is used. Smith v Peterson, 131 Cal App 2d 241, 280 P2d 522, 49 ALR2d 1194.

excessive sentence. A sentence for a term in excess of what the law permits as punishment for the particular offense. 21 Am J2d Crim L § 536. A sentence which should be reduced in the exercise of a sound discretion by the court, notwithstanding it is not in excess of the maximum penalty prescribed for the offense of which the defendant was convicted. State v Ross, 55 Or 450, 104 P 596.

excessive speed. Motor vehicle: Speed in excess of the limit fixed by law or the rate which is reasonable and prudent under the circumstances. 8 Am J2d Auto §§ 717, 718. Vessel: A speed such as will not permit the vessel seasonably and effectually to avoid collision by slackening speed, or by stopping and reversing, within the distance at which an approaching vessel can be seen. Macham v New York (CC NY) 35 F 604, 609.

excessive use of intoxicating liquors. Such an indulgence in intoxicants as tends to impair the health or mental faculties of the insured, or to render the insurance risk more hazardous. 29 Am J Rev ed Ins § 775.

excessive verdict. See **excessive damages.**

Excessivum in jure reprobatur; excessus in re qualibet jure reprobatur communi (ek-ses'si-vum in jū're re-prō-bā'ter; ek-ses'sus in rē quā'li-bet jū're re-prō-bā'ter kom-mū'nī). Excess is reprehended in the law; any kind of excess is reprehended in the common law.

excess of jurisdiction. An act which, although within the general power of the judge, is not authorized and therefore void with respect to the particular case, because the conditions which alone authorize the exercise of his general power in that particular case are wanting, and hence the judicial power is not lawfully invoked. 30A Am J Rev ed Judges § 78.

excess of privilege. A basis of liability for defamation, notwithstanding the subject matter of the communication lies within the field of privilege, where the statement goes beyond the duty or interest of the publisher or utterer, is irrelevant or extraneous to the field of privilege, is defamatory to a person outside the privilege, is violent or intemperate, or goes beyond the duty to publish or communicate which supports the privilege. 33 Am J1st L & S §§ 183 et seq.

excess profits tax. A type of income tax based on net income in excess of a certain percentage of the taxpayer's invested capital and imposed at progressive rates. Greenport Basin & Constr. Co. v United States, 260 US 512, 67 L Ed 370, 43 S Ct 183.
See **invested capital.**

excess waters. The waters of a stream subject to appropriation for beneficial use over and above what may reasonably be subjected to a beneficial use on the lands bordering the stream. Rindge v Crags Land Co. 56 Cal App 247, 205 P 36.

exch. An abbreviation of "exchange," "exchequer."

exchange. A voluntary association or corporation organized for the purpose of furnishing its members a convenient and suitable place to transact their business, of promoting uniformity in the customs and usages of merchants, of inculcating principles of justice and equity in trade, of facilitating the speedy adjustment of business disputes, of acquiring and disseminating valuable commercial and economic information, and generally of securing to its members the benefits of co-operation in the furtherance of their legitimate pursuits. 50 Am J1st Stock Ex § 2. An organized and established place of business wherein the marketing of securities is conducted and accomplished. Fratt v Robinson (CA9 Wash) 203 F2d 627, 37 ALR2d 636. A stock exchange, a place where securities are bought and sold; a commodity exchange, a place where grain, cotton, wool, etc. is bought and sold. 50 Am J1st Stock Ex § 2. An association acting in the mutual exchange of insurance contracts by the subscribers thereto under a system of reciprocal or interinsurance. 29 Am J Rev ed Ins § 102. An exchange of the money of one country for the money of another at a rate which depends upon the respective values of the two currencies in the money markets of the world. 36 Am J1st Money § 26. A transfer of money from one person to another at a distant place at an agreed or customary rate of exchange. A word indicating negotiability where it appears on the face of an instrument calling for the payment of money to a named payee. UCC § 3–110(1).

A reciprocal transfer of property for property, in other words a trade, barter, or swap. 30 Am J2d Ex P § 1. An executed contract which operates per se as a reciprocal conveyance of the thing given and of the thing received in exchange, each of the parties being individually considered in the double light of vendor and vendee. Preston v Keene (US) 14 Pet 133, 10 L Ed 387. For tax purposes, a bona fide transfer of property for property other than money or a cash equivalent.

See **arbitration of exchange; barter; bill of exchange; dry exchange; first of exchange; loan for exchange; par of exchange; rate of exchange; sale and exchange; second of exchange; set of exchange; stipulation for exchange; trade.**

Exchange Act. See **Securities Exchange Act.**

exchange broker. A broker who makes and concludes bargains for others in matters of money or

EXCHANGE [429] EXCLUSIVE

merchandise; learns the rate of exchange, and notifies his employers. Portland v O'Neill, 1 Or 218, 219. A broker who negotiates bills of exchange drawn on foreign countries or on other places in the United States. Little Rock v Barton, 33 Ark 436, 446. A broker who transacts business on a stock or commodity exchange. 50 Am J1st Stock Ex § 20.

exchange certificate. A certificate of membership in a stock or commodity exchange. Anno: 44 ALR2d 947, § 16.

Exchange Commission. See **Securities and Exchange Commission.**

exchange of goods. See **barter; exchange; trade.**

exchange of judges. A practice expedient in relieving a crowded trial calendar in a court circuit or district, whereby a judge of another circuit or district is brought in temporarily to assist the regular judges. York v State, 91 Ark 582, 121 SW 1070.

exchange of policy. The substitution of one policy for another accomplished by the agreement of the insurer and insured or pursuant to a policy provision. Baine v Continental Assur. Co. 21 Cal 2d 1, 129 P2d 396, 142 ALR 1253.
See **conversion of insurance policy.**

exchanges. See **exchange.**

exchanging work. Practice of farmers in helping one another, in which case, they do not work as employees. 7 Am J2d Auto Ins § 132.

exchequer (eks-chek'ẽr). The English department of revenue. A very ancient court of record, set up by William the Conqueror, as a part of the aula regia, and intended principally to order the revenues of the crown, and to recover the king's debts and duties. It was called exchequer, "scaccharium," from the checked cloth, resembling a chessboard, which covers the table.
See **barons of the exchequer; Black Book of the Exchequer; chancellor of the exchequer; court of exchequer; exchequer bills; information in the exchequer; receipt of the exchequer.**

exchequer bills. English bills of credit issued by the government under the authority of parliament.

exchequer chamber. See **court of exchequer chamber.**

excisable. Subject to or liable for excise taxes.

excise (ek-sīz'). Same as **excise tax.**

excise tax. A tax which does not fall within the classification of a poll tax or a property tax, and embraces every form of tax burdens not laid directly upon persons or property. Idaho Gold Dredging Co. v Balderston, 58 Idaho 692, 78 P2d 105. A tax imposed on the sale, even the use, of a certain article and on certain transactions and occupations.
Sums assessed as meals taxes and paid, on the claim of the commissioner of taxation, under protest and duress to avoid imposition of penalties, are received "as excise on account of the Commonwealth" within the meaning of constitutional and statutory provisions requiring the tax collector to pay money so collected into the treasury of the commonwealth, even though they were illegally exacted. Oakley Country Club v Long, 325 Mass 109, 89 NE2d 260, 14 ALR 377.
See **corporation excise tax; duties; income excise tax; license tax; privilege tax.**

excitement. Impulsion; agitation. The act of exciting, or the state of having increased action. That which excites or rouses; that which moves, stirs or induces action; a motive. Morris v Territory, 1 Okla Crim 617, 99 P 760.

excluding. Taking out; keeping out; excepting. Often used as synonymous with "reserving." 23 Am J2d Deeds § 262.
See **excepting; reserving.**

exclusive. Pertaining to the subject alone; not including, admitting, or pertaining to any other or others; undivided; sole; as, an exclusive right or privilege; exclusive jurisdiction. Vicksburg v Vicksburg Waterworks Co. 202 US 453, 471, 50 L Ed 1102, 1112, 26 S Ct 660. Restrictive, as in the case of a club with membership restricted to a distinct class.
A computation of time by including one terminal day and excluding the other has been applied in a case where a statute required the performance of acts a certain number of days, "exclusive," before a known future date. Anno: 98 ALR 1372.

exclusive agency. A term embracing three classes of situations: (1) where the contract does not prevent the principal from making direct sales but deprives him of the right to appoint other agents; (2) where the agent is the only one with any right to sell; and (3) where the exclusive agency is accompanied with a stipulated right to commissions on all sales whether made through the agent or not. 3 Am J2d Ag § 259.
The use of the terms "exclusive agency," or "exclusive sale" in a contract giving one the right to sell for another is not conclusive that the right given is an exclusive one, but all the circumstances must be considered. Navy Gas & Supply Co. v Schoech, 105 Colo 374, 98 P2d 860, 126 ALR 1225.
An exclusive agency to sell having been granted, the owner may still sell the property without incurring liability to the broker for commission, unless the broker has procured a purchaser able and willing to buy prior to the time that the owner makes the sale. Anno: 64 ALR 395; 12 Am J2d Brok § 226.
See **exclusive right of sale.**

exclusive agency to sell. See **exclusive agency.**

exclusive control. A control which is limited in respect of the person by whom exercised, but not necessarily limited to one person. Mack v Reading Co. 377 Pa 135, 103 A2d 749, 41 ALR2d 927.
The word "exclusive" when used to define the nature of the control necessary to invoke the doctrine of res ipsa loquitur does not connote that such control must be in a single person, and the fact that a collapsing scaffold causing the injury was in control of both defendants, a general contractor and his subcontractor, does not preclude operation of the doctrine. Meny v Carlson, 6 NJ 82, 77 A2d 245, 22 ALR2d 1160.

exclusive fishery. An exclusive right to fish in a given place, either with or without the property in the soil at such place, no person other than the owner of the fishery being lawfully entitled to take fish at such place. 35 Am J2d Fish § 6.

exclusive lease. In loose usage, an exclusive license.
See **exclusive license.**

exclusive license. A license to pursue a calling or occupation which in effect creates a monopoly in the licensee. 33 Am J1st Lic § 23. A grant by the proprietor of a patent to another person of the right to make, use, or sell the patented article, including the condition that the grantor will grant no further license of the kind in respect of such article to any other person. 40 Am J1st Pat § 146.

The mere grant by a state of an "exclusive ferry lease" for a specified distance along a river does not prevent the state from erecting a bridge within the prescribed limits. Larson v South Dakota, 278 US 429, 73 L Ed 441, 49 S Ct 196.

exclusively. With the exclusion of all others; without admission of others to participation.

Under a statute exempting from taxation property used "exclusively" for a public purpose, the word has been held to mean "substantially all" or "for the greater part." Anoka County v St. Paul, 194 Minn 554, 99 ALR 1137, 261 NW 588.

exclusive possession. An exclusive dominion over land and an appropriation of it to one's own use and benefit. 3 Am J2d Adv P § 50. Possession of land by a claimant for himself, as his own, and not for another. 3 Am J2d Adv P § 50.

exclusive power of appointment. A power of appointment under which there is granted to the donee the right to exclude from the distribution any of the designated objects of the power. Anno: 100 ALR 343.

exclusive representative. An exclusive agent. For the purpose of collective bargaining under the National Labor Relations Act, the sole and exclusive bargaining agency of all the employees it represents for the purpose of bargaining as to rates of pay, wages, hours of employment or other conditions of employment. International Union, U. A. A.A.I.W. v J. I. Case Co. 250 Wis 63, 26 NW2d 305, 170 ALR 933.

See **exclusive agency.**

exclusive right. A sole and undivided right or privilege. Vicksburg v Vicksburg Waterworks Co. 202 US 453, 471, 50 L Ed 1102, 1112, 26 S Ct 660.

See **exclusive right of sale.**

exclusive right of sale. The right of an agent to be the sole sale's agent appointed by his principal and to be free from competition by the principal personally. 3 Am J2d Ag § 259. Not the same exactly as an exclusive agency.

An exclusive agency to sell having been granted to a broker, the owner may still sell the property without incurring liability to the broker for a commission, unless the broker has procured a purchaser able and willing to pay prior to the time that the owner makes the sale. But where a broker is given an exclusive right to sell property, as distinguished from an exclusive agency, he is held entitled to the agreed commission, or at least damages, where a sale is made by the owner, and it is immaterial that he was not the procuring cause thereof, provided, however, that the employment contract is supported by consideration and is not a mere unilateral offer, and provided also, according to some cases, that the broker has produced a ready, able, and willing purchaser or can show damage. 12 Am J2d Brok § 226.

exclusive sale. See **exclusive agency; exclusive right of sale.**

exclusive sales contract. A contract by which a manufacturer or wholesale dealer agrees to sell his commodities exclusively to a dealer in a particular locality, or the dealer agrees to purchase exclusively from the manufacturer or wholesaler. Such a contract is valid where not monopolistic in tendency, and where there is no combination to control prices or to stifle competition. 36 Am J1st Monop etc. § 32.

See **exclusive agency; exclusive right of sale.**

exclusive use. A use which gives rise to a prescriptive right, not because it excludes the holder of the legal title or other persons from the premises, but because it is not dependent upon a similar right in another person. Marta v Trincia, 26 Del Ch 94, 22 A2d 519; Jurgensen v Ainscow, 155 Neb 701, 53 NW2d 196.

ex colore (ex ko-lō're). Under color of; by the pretence of.

ex comitate (ex ko-mi-tā'te). By comity; by courtesy; by public policy.

excommengement (ā-kō-monj-mon'). Same as **excommunication.**

ex commodato (ex kom-mo-dā'tō). From a loan.

ex commodo (eks kom'ō-dō). At one's convenience; leisurely.

excommunicate. To impose a sentence or order of excommunication.

See **excommunication.**

excommunication (eks-ko-mū-ni-kā'shon). Expulsion from membership in a church. Nance v Busby, 91 Tenn 303, 333. A sentence of excommunication, by an ecclesiastical court. This sentence was of two grades. The lesser excluded the person from partaking of the sacraments; the greater excluded him from the company of all Christians. See 3 Bl Comm 101.

excommunicato capiendo (ex-kom-mū-ni-kā'tō kā-pi-en'dō). See **de excommunicato capiendo.**

excommunicato deliberando. See **de excommunicato deliberando.**

Excommunicato interdicitur omnis actus legitimus, ita quod agere non potest, nec aliquem convenire, licet ipse ab aliis possit conveniri (ex-kom-mū-ni-kā'tō in-ter-di'si-ter om'nis ak'tus lē-ji'ti-mus, i'ta quod ā'je-re non pō'test, nek a'li-quem kon-ve-nī're, li'set ip'se ab a'li-is pos'sit kon-ve-nī'rī). Every legal act is forbidden a person who has been excommunicated, so that he cannot act, nor can he sue anyone, but he himself can be sued by others.

excommunicato recapiendo. See **de excommunicato recapiendo.**

ex comparatione scriptorum (ex kom-pa-rā-she-ō'ne skrip-tō'rum). By comparison of handwritings.

ex concessione (ex kon-se-she-ō'ne). By or out of grant.

ex concessis (ex kon-ses'sis). From or out of the things which have been granted.

ex concesso (eks kon-ses'ō). From what has been conceded or granted.

See **argumentum ex concesso.**

ex concessu (ex kon-ses'su). Same as **ex consesso.**

ex consulto (ex kon-sul'tō). With or from consultation or deliberation.

ex continenti (ex kon-ti-nen'tī). At once; forthwith; immediately.

ex contractu (ex kon-trak'tu). Arising out of a contract; founded upon contract, as an obligation ex contractu, or an action ex contractu. See 3 Bl Comm 117.

See **action ex contractu; quasi ex-contractu.**

ex culpa levissima (ex kul'pa le-vis'si-ma). From the least fault or negligence.

exculpatory clause. A clause in a trust instrument relieving the trustee from liability for any act performed by him under the trust instrument in good faith. Anno: 78 ALR2d 36.

ex curia (eks kū'ri-ą). Out of court; elsewhere than in court.

excursion. A round trip taken for pleasure or health, usually at a reduced rate. 14 Am J2d Car § 845.

excursion permit. A permit issued to authorize a vessel certified for the carriage of passengers to carry additional passengers or to go out of the waters over which it is authorized by its certificate to ply. 48 Am J1st Ship § 360.

excursion rate. A round trip and reduced rate for passengers on an excursion. 14 Am J2d Car § 845.

excursion river boat. A place of amusement and entertainment. Shannon v Streckfus Steamers, Inc. 279 Ky 649, 131 SW2d 833.

excursus (eks-kėr'sus). A running out; a departure; a deviation; a frolic of one's own. Bugge v Brown (Austr) 26 CLR 110.

excusable (eks-kū'zą-bl). Deserving excuse or pardon; that which is forgiven or condoned; that which is not wholly free from fault, but for which there is no liability.

excusable homicide. A homicide committed in doing a lawful act, without any intention to hurt, as by accident or misadventure, or a homicide committed in self-defense. 26 Am J1st Homi § 102.

excusable neglect. See excusable negligence.

excusable negligence. A paradoxical phrase, since if the failure to exercise reasonable care under the circumstances is excusable, there is no negligence. 38 Am J1st Negl § 12.

As the term is used in statutes authorizing the opening of a default and allowing a party to defend on the merits, the courts appear to be in irreconcilable conflict as to what constitutes "excusable neglect," but well considered cases have seemed to agree that a reasonable excuse is sufficient, where it appears that the defense is meritorious and no substantial prejudice will result from setting aside the default. Citizens' Nat. Bank v Branden, 19 ND 489, 126 NW 102.

excusable trespass. A trespass for which no action will lie because the law forgives or pardons it. A trespass for which there is justification.

Generally speaking, justification as a defense to an action of trespass must be specially pleaded. 52 Am J1st Tresp § 68.

Excusat aut extenuat delictum in capitalibus, quod non operatur idem in civilibus (ex-kū'zat ât ex-te'nu-at de-lik'tum in ka-pi-tā'li-bus, quod non ō-pe-rā'ter ī'dem in si-vi'li-bus). That excuses or extenuates fault in capital cases which would not operate similarly in civil cases.

excusatio (ex-kū-zā'she-ō). An excuse.

Excusatur quis quod clameum non opposuerit, ut si toto tempore litigii fuit ultra mare quacunque occasione (ex-kū-zā'ter quis quod klā'me-um non oppō-zu'e-rit, ut sī tō'tō tem'po-re li-ti'ji-ī fu'it ul'tra ma're quā-kun'kwe o-kā-zhe-ō'ne). A person is excused for not resisting a claim if during the whole period of the litigation, he is for some reason, beyond seas.

excuse (eks-kūz). Verb: To relieve from liability; to relieve from a duty or obligation. (eks-kūs). Noun: A grant of relief from duty or obligation. A reason for being relieved from duty or obligation. A reason for relieving a person from jury duty. 31 Am J Rev ed Jur § 70.
See **justification**.

excused. Relieved from duty or liability.
See **excuse**.

excuss (eks-kus'). To seize goods under process of a court.

excussio (ex-ku'she-ō). (Civil law.) The exhaustion by a creditor of his remedies against the principal debtor before resorting to the surety.

ex damno absque injuria non oritur actio (ex dam'nō abs'kwe in-jū'ri-a non ō'ri-ter ak'she-ō). From loss or damage, without the violation of a legal right, no action arises.
See **damnum absque injuria**.

ex debito justitiae (ex de'bi-tō jūs-ti'she-ē). From a debt of justice; from that which is owing; from one's right; as of right. Thompson v Jackson, 24 Va (3 Rand) 504.

ex debito naturali (ex de'bi-tō nā-tū-rā'lē). From natural obligation.

ex defectu juris (ex dē-fek' jū'ris). From or because of a defect or failure of right.

ex defectu natalium (ex de-fek'tū nā-tā'lī-um). From failure of lawful birth; because of being born out of wedlock. A phrase that loses meaning with the mitigation by statute of the rigors of the common law concerning the status and rights of an illegitimate child. 10 Am J2d Bast § 8.

ex defectu sanguinis (ex dē-fek'tu san'gwi-nis). From or because of failure of blood; for want of issue.

ex delicto (ex de-lik'tō). From or out of a wrongful act; tortious; tortiously.
See **action ex delicto; chose ex delicto**.

ex delicto quasi ex contractu (ex de-lik'tō quā'sī ex kon-trak'tu). An action wherein there is combined a cause or ground of action for breach of a special contract with a cause or ground of action for a tort in violation of a common-law duty. Nelson v Great Northern Railroad Co. 28 Mont 297, 72 P 642.

ex dem. An abbreviation of **ex demissione**.

ex demissione (ex de-mi-she-ō'ne). From or on the demise of.

ex dicto majoris partis (ex dik'tō mā-jō'ris par'tis). By the order or command of the larger side; by the voice of the majority.

ex directo (ex dī-rek'tō). Directly; forthwith; immediately.

Ex diuturnitate temporis, omnia praesumuntur solemniter esse acta (ex dī-u-ter-ni-tā'te tem'po-ris, om'ni-a prē-su-mun'ter so-lem'ni-ter es'se ak'ta). From length or lapse of time, all things are presumed to have been duly performed.

ex dividend. An expression familiar to corporate officers and directors, stockbrokers, and persons who deal in stocks, meaning that a quotation of a price for a stock is for a sale not including a dividend previously declared by the corporation. This is in accord with the modern corporate practice according to which corporations declare dividends payable to stockholders of record on a specified date, after which date the stock is said to be "ex dividend." 19 Am J2d Corp § 891.

ex dolo malo (ex dō'lō ma'lō). From or out of fraud.

Ex dolo malo non oritur actio (ex dō'lō ma'lō non ō'ri-ter ak'she-ō). No action can arise out of fraud; no court will lend its aid to a man who founds his cause of action upon an immoral or an illegal act. Hill v Walker, 41 Ga 449.

Ex donationibus autem feoda militaria vel magnum serjeantium non continentibus oriter nobis quoddam nomen generale, quod est socagium (ex dō-nā-she-ō'ni-bus â'tem fe-ō'da mi-li-tā'ri-a vel mag'num ser-je-an'sheum non kon-ti-nen'ti-bus ō'ri-ter nō'bis quod'dam nō'men je-ne-rā'le, quod est so-kā'ji-um). From grants containing neither military fees nor grand serjeanty, a certain general name has sprung up among us which is "socage." See 2 Bl Comm 79.

ex donatio regis (ex dō-nā'she-ō rē'jis). By the gift of the king.

exeat. See **ne exeat**.

exec. An abbreviation of **executor**.

execration (ek'sē-krā'shǫn). A form of trial by purgation, consisting in feeding the accused a small bit of consecrated cheese or bread, and at the same time praying for his ability to swallow it if innocent and to choke to death on it if guilty; the morsel given the accused in the purgation. 4 Bl Comm 345.

execute. To complete; to sign; to sign, seal, and deliver. Perko v Rock Springs Commercial Co. 37 Wyo 98, 259 P 520. To perform or carry out a mission, a command, a duty, or obligation. To put a man to death pursuant to a sentence of death.

executed. Signed. Signed, sealed, and delivered, that is, the completion of the transaction. Bensimer v Fell, 35 W Va 15, 12 SE 1078. See also Worthley v Worthley, 33 Cal App 473, 165 P 714. Equivalent of "signed, sealed, and delivered," for the purpose of a certificate of acknowledgment. 1 Am J2d Ack § 75.

Put to death pursuant to a sentence of death.

executed agreement. See **executed contract**.

executed and recorded. As an allegation in a pleading, the equivalent of executed and delivered. McReynolds v Grubb, 150 Mo 352, 51 SW 822.

executed compromise. The full and complete performance of a compromise agreement, whether the agreement is an executory accord or a substituted contract, such performance often involving a surrender and release of rights. 15 Am J2d Compr § 24.

executed consideration. A past consideration; something given and received before the making of a promise. 17 Am J2d Contr § 125.

See **past consideration**.

executed contract. A contract, the terms of which have been fully performed. Henehan v Hart, 127 Cal 656, 60 P 426. A contract performed in fulfillment of the object of the contract and the accomplishment of everything required to be done under it. 17 Am J2d Contr § 6.

executed contract of sale. A present conveyance, that is a contract sufficient in itself to convey title to real estate. 55 Am J1st V & P § 100. A land contract which has been performed by both vendor and purchaser, the purchase price having been paid and the deed executed and delivered. Miller v Kemp, 157 Va 178, 160 SE 203, 84 ALR 980. A contract of sale of personal property so fully performed that nothing remains to be done under it, title having passed to the buyer and the risk of loss or destruction of the chattel having been shifted from the seller to him. 46 Am J1st Sales § 412.

executed deed. A deed completely prepared for delivery; more appropriately, a deed which has been signed, also sealed, acknowledged, and attested, as may be required by statute, and delivered to the grantee or someone in his behalf. Turlington v Neighbors, 222 NC 694, 24 SE2d 648.

executed estate. Same as **estate in possession**.

executed insurance policy. A policy of insurance that has been signed by or on behalf of the insurer and, if the instrument so provides as conditions of effectiveness, countersigned and delivered. 29 Am J Rev ed Ins §§ 214, 215.

executed gift. A gift which has been delivered by the donor with the intent to transfer title and accepted by the donee. 24 Am J1st Gifts § 22.

executed license. An irrevocable license in real property. 33 Am J1st Lic § 99. A license in return for which the licensee has paid a consideration to the licensor, or upon the faith and in consequence of which the licensee has made valuable improvements or expended money or invested capital. Flickinger v Shaw, 87 Cal 126, 25 P 268.

executed remainder. An old term for vested remainder. See 2 Bl Comm 168.

executed trust. In one sense, an intention to create a trust, executed by a definite and unequivocal disposition of property in accordance with the intention; in another, and more familiar sense, a trust that is final and definite in respect of the limitations of the equitable interest, so that no aid by an equity court is required to settle and model the limitations in accordance with the intention of the creator of the trust. 54 Am J1st Trusts § 7.

executed unilateral contract. An offer fully performed in accordance with the conditions of the offer, including a limitation of time. Bethlehem Silk Co. v Commissioner (CA3) 124 F2d 649. An offer accepted by part performance to the extent that the offer can not be revoked or withdrawn. 17 Am J2d Contr § 37.

executed use. A use which has become a legal interest under the Statute of Uses or its equivalent in American jurisdictions. 28 Am J2d Est § 344.

executed will. Broadly, a will which has been signed by the testator and attested in accord with statutory requirements. More narrowly defined in the terms of what the testator must do, that is, a will signed by the testator. Re Johnson (ND) 75 NW2d 313, 55 ALR2d 1049.

executed writ. A writ, the command of which has been fully executed or complied with by the officer to whom the writ was directed.

executio (ex-e-kū'she-ō). Execution; administration; management; full performance; full compliance; fulfillment.

executio bonorum (ex-e-kū'she-ō bo-nō'rum). The administration or management of goods.

Executio est executio juris secundum judicium (ex-e-kū'she-ō est ex-e-kū'she-ō jū'ris se-kun'dum jū-di'-she-um). Execution is the fulfillment of the law in accordance with the judgment.

Executio est finis et fructus legis (ex-e-kū'she-ō est fī'nis et frūk'tus lē'jis). Execution is the end and the fruit of the law.

Executio juris non habet injuriam (ex-e-kū'she-ō jū'-ris non hā'bet in-jū'ri-am). The fulfillment or carrying out of the law cannot operate as an injury.

execution. A writ or process for the enforcement of a judgment. A remedy afforded by law for the enforcement of a judgment, which is not an action but is included in the phrase "process in an action." 30 Am J2d Exec § 1.

The signing of an instrument; signing, coupled with sealing, acknowledgment, and attestation, as such may be required by statute, and the delivery of the instrument. 23 Am J2d Deeds § 18. The signing and delivery of a negotiable instrument. Re Tynans Estate, 142 Neb 671, 7 NW2d 628.

The performance of a duty, assignment, or obligation. The acts of a sheriff in serving the writ or process of execution. 30 Am J2d Exec § 207. The performance of a promisor's obligation under a contract. 17 Am J2d Contr § 355. The imprisonment of a person pursuant to a sentence; putting a man to death by hanging, electrocution, or gas pursuant to a death sentence. 21 Am J2d Crim L §§ 590 et seq.

See **fieri facias**; **ground writ**; **levy of execution**; **pluries writs**; **supplementary proceedings**.

execution against the person. A writ or process for the enforcement of a judgment, usually a judgment of a particular nature in reference to the obligation adjudicated, by arresting and detaining the judgment debtor until he be legally discharged. 30 Am J2d Exec § 865. A form of execution well known at common law and effected by the writ of capias ad satisfaciendum, which was directed to the sheriff or coroner, and commanded him to take the person therein named and him safely keep so that he might have the body in court on the return day of the writ, to satisfy the party who had recovered judgment against him. 30 Am J2d Exec § 873.

execution creditor. A person who, having recovered a judgment against one obligated to him, has caused an execution to be issued on such judgment. Anno: 61 ALR 984.

executione judicii. See **de executione judicii**.

executioner (ek-sẹ-kū'shọn-ėr). A person who executes a death sentence; a headsman; a gangman.

execution in duplicate. The signing and putting into effect of two or more instruments identical in content, each instrument being made thereby an original. 17 Am J2d Contr § 284.

execution lien. A lien created by or as an inseparable incident of the levy of an execution. 30A Am J Rev ed Judgm § 479. A constructive lien insofar as the levy is upon real estate without a manual seizure or taking possession. 30A Am J Rev ed Judgm § 480.

execution of instrument. See **executed**; **executed deed**; **executed insurance policy**; **executed will**.

execution paree (èg-ze'kû-si-ōn paray). A proceeding under the law of France under which a creditor can seize and sell the property of his debtor to satisfy a judgment by confession.

execution sale. A sale, usually at public auction, by a sheriff or other ministerial officer of property seized by him in levying an execution, pursuant to and under the authority of the writ or process of execution, for the purpose of obtaining from the proceeds of the sale an amount sufficient to satisfy the execution and the judgment whereunder it was issued. Sometimes the term "judicial sale" is used in the reported cases to include a sale under execution, and sometimes, judicial sales are referred to as "special execution sales." 30 Am J2d Exec § 304.

See **certificate of sale**; **redemption**; **sale en masse**; **sheriff's deed**.

execution sale en masse. See **sale en masse**.

executive. Noun: One who manages or administers. One who enforces the law as distinguished from one who makes the law or one who interprets the law. Adjective: Pertaining to the administration or enforcement of the law. State ex rel. Jameson v Denny, 118 Ind 382, 21 NE 252.

executive agencies. See **administrative agencies**.

executive agreement. An agreement made by the President of the United States, acting within his exclusive powers as the executive, with the authorized representative of a foreign government. Russia v National City Bank (CA2) 69 F2d 44.

executive capacity. An administrative capacity. The status of one in business or industry who manages the business or a department thereof or directs operations of the industry. Anno: 40 ALR2d 332.

See **executive employee**.

executive committee. A committee of a voluntary association or club, the authority of which is determined by the constitution or bylaws. 6 Am J2d Asso & C § 44. A committee chosen from among the directors of a corporation, authorized to act for the board, during intervals between meetings of the board, in respect of the ordinary business of the corporation. 19 Am J2d Corp § 1160.

executive department. The department of government, headed by the President in the case of the United States Government and by the governor in the case of a state government, in whom the executive, as distinguished from the legislative or judicial, power is vested. 16 Am J2d Const L § 216. One of the major administrative or executive agencies of the federal or a state government, such as the State Department, War Department, Department of Justice, etc.

executive employee. An employee who may have administrative duties but has at least some managerial authority. 31 Am J Rev ed Lab § 668.

executive officer. Any officer in whom executive power of a state or other government is vested. The President is the chief executive officer of the United States. The respective governors are the chief executive officers in the several states. 42 Am J1st Pub Of § 25.

An officer of a corporation having at least some degree of managerial responsibility for the affairs of the corporation generally, and having a close connection with the board of directors and high officers of the company. Bruce v Travelers Ins. Co. (CA5 La) 266 F2d 781; Flight Equipment & Engineering Corp. v Shelton (Fla) 103 So 2d 615.

The cashier of a bank is an executive officer. First Nat. Bank v Mee, 126 Okla 265, 259 P 523.

See **cashier**.

executive order. An order promulgated by the President of the United States or the governor of a state.

executive ordinance. A municipal ordinance passed in the exercise of administrative or executive, rather than legislative power, and accordingly not subject to referendum. 37 Am J1st Mun Corp § 209.

executive power. The power vested in the executive department of the United States Government or the government of a state; the power vested in executive officers of a county, town, municipality, or other political subdivision; the power to administer and enforce the laws. State ex rel. Jameson v Denny, 118 Ind 382, 21 NE 252.

See **executive department**; **executive officer**; **supreme executive power**.

executive proceeding. Action taken by an executive officer or executive department without invoking the jurisdiction or aid of a court, for example, the summary collection of taxes by distraint and seizure of property of a person liable for payment of the taxes. 34 Am J2d Fed Tax ¶ 9403.

executive warrant. See **extradition warrant**.

executor. The person nominated by a testator to carry out the directions and requests in his will and to dispose of the property according to his testamentary provisions after his decease. One to whom a testator has given his goods, chattels, and personal estate for the purpose of paying all his debts. 21 Am J2d Ex & Ad § 3.

It is not to be implied that in order to name an executor by will, the will must dispose of property. There is an abundance of authority for the proposition that an instrument properly executed as a will may be probated as a will if it names or nominates an executor, notwithstanding it does not purport to dispose of any property further than to provide for the payment of debts which the law would require the personal representative to pay if the estate was intestate. Reeves v Duke, 192 Okla 519, 137 P2d 897, 147 ALR 634.

See **domiciliary executor**; **foreign executor**; **independent executor**; **instituted executor**; **joint executor**; **renunciation of executorship**; **substituted executor**; **substitutionary executor**.

executor de son tort (eg-zek'ū-tor dē sōn tor). Literally, executor of his own wrong. A person who, without authority granted by the decedent or a court of probate, assumes, by interference with the estate of a decedent, to act as executor or administrator and performs such acts with respect to the personal property of that estate as can legally be done only by a properly appointed executor or administrator; one who intrudes himself into the office of personal representative of a decedent without legal authority, and of his own authority enters into the possession or assumes the management of, or intermeddles with, the property of the decedent. 31 Am J2d Ex & Ad § 661. A quasi executor for the purpose only of being sued or made liable for the assets with which he has intermeddled. Grace v Seibert, 235 Ill 190, 85 NE 308.

executorial trustee. A person who is executor of a decedent's estate but is given powers and duties as a trustee, in reference to a testamentary trust created by the will, beyond the powers and duties of an executor. 31 Am J2d Ex & Ad § 163.

executor's bond. The bond required of an executor as a condition of his right to act as personal representative of the decedent, the amount, form, and conditions of which are usually prescribed by statute. 31 Am J2d Ex & Ad § 126.

executorship. The office of executor in relation to a particular estate of a decedent.
See **executor**.

executor's right of retainer. See **retainer**.

executor to the tenor. A person who, without any appointment as executor, performs certain of the functions of an executor.
See **executor de son tort**.

executory. Not yet executed; not yet fully performed, completed, fulfilled or carried out; to be performed either wholly or in part.

executory accord. An accord which has not been fully performed. 1 Am J2d Accord § 52. A compromise agreement which provides for the acceptance in the future of a stated performance in satisfaction of the antecedent claim. 15 Am J2d Compr § 24.

executory bequest. A testamentary gift of personal property on a contingency after an absolute gift to another. Robinson v Harris, 73 SC 469, 53 SE 755.

executory consideration. A consideration for a promise or an act, which consideration has not yet been performed and which the party who is to perform is either bound by contract to perform or not.

If a promissory note is given for future services of the payee, his rendition of the services furnishes a consideration to uphold the note which is equally valid whether or not he made a binding promise to render them. Miller v McKenzie, 95 NY 575.

executory contract. A contract to be performed, each party having bound himself to do or not to do a particular thing. 17 Am J2d Contr § 6.

executory contract of sale. A contract, the terms and conditions of which must be performed before title passes. 46 Am J1st Sales § 412. A land contract under which the execution and delivery of a further instrument is necessary for the passing of title to the purchaser. 55 Am J1st V & P § 100. A contract which gives the purchaser an interest in the land involved as the subject matter of the contract. 29A Am J Rev ed Ins § 832.

executory devises. Estates in futuro consisting of executory interests created by devises, recognized in equity and validated by the Statute of Uses and the Statute of Wills, but invalid under the early common law as in contravention of the rigid rules against a limitation of a fee on a fee or the taking effect of a future estate by the cutting short of a prior estate. 28 Am J2d Est §§ 333, 334.

executory estate. An estate which is to vest in possession at a future time.
See **executory interests**.

executory instrument. A written instrument which has not been fully executed or made effective by the parties; as a written contract which has been signed by the parties but has not yet been delivered. Stiebel v Grosberg, 202 NY 266, 95 NE 692.

executory interests. Estates in futuro created by executory devises or by conveyances to uses, recognized in equity and validated by the Statute of Uses, but invalid under the early common law as in contravention of the rigid rules against a limitation of a fee on a fee or the taking effect of a future estate by the cutting short of a prior estate. 28 Am J2d Est 333.

executory judgment. A judgment which remains unpaid; a judgment which has not been satisfied by voluntary payment, by an execution, or other method of enforcement. 30A Am J Rev ed Judgm § 119.

executory limitation. Same as **executory interest**.

executory process. A proceeding under the civil law to enforce a judgment by confession by the seizure and sale of the property of the debtor. The term in French is "execution paree."

executory trust. In one sense, a trust not completely achieved in legal effect. In another sense, a trust

executory indefinite in limitations of the equitable interest, so that it may be necessary to invoke the jurisdiction of equity to settle the limitations and model the trust in accordance with the intention of the creator of the trust. 54 Am J1st Trusts § 7.

executory use. A use which is to come into existence at a future time; a springing use, which arises from the seisin of the grantor with no estate preceding it.
See **executory interest; shifting use; springing use; Statute of Uses.**

executory warranty. A promissory warranty.
See **promissory warranty.**

executress (eg-zek′ū-tres). Same as **executrix.**

executrix (eg-zek′ū-triks). Feminine of **executor.**

executry (eg-zek′ū-tri). That portion of the personal property of a decedent which passes to his executor, as distinguished from that portion which goes to his heirs.

exegence. Same as **exigent.**

Exempla illustrant non restringunt legem (eg-zem′pla il-lus′trant non res-trin′gunt lē′jem). Examples illustrate the law; they do not restrict it.

exemplary damages. Damages given as an enhancement of compensatory damages because of the wanton, reckless, malicious, or oppressive character of the acts complained of, and by way of punishment of the defendant and a deterrent to others. 22 Am J2d Damg § 236. Damages awarded to punish the defendant for a wilful act and to vindicate the rights of a party in substitution for personal revenge, thus safeguarding the public peace. Winkler v Hartford Acci. & Indem. Co. 66 NJ Super 22, 168 A2d 418.

exempli causa (eg-zem′plī kâ′za). For or by way of example.

exemplification. A portrayal by example. The authentication of a copy by attestation or certification under seal.
See **exemplified copy.**

exemplified copy. An authenticated copy; a copy of a public document or record verified by the great seal or the seal of the court. 29 Am J2d Ev § 910.

exempli gratia (eg-zem′plī grā′she-a). For or by way of example. The expression is commonly abbreviated, "e. g." or "ex. gr."

exemplum (eg-zem′plum). An example; a copy; a transcript; a model.

exempt. Noun: A person who is free from any charge, burden, or duty. Re Strawbridge & Mays, 39 Ala 367, 379. Adjective: Free of an obligation which is binding on others.

exempt income. Income exempt from payment of income tax. Income not subject to levy or garnishment.

exemption. A privilege, sometimes referred to as a right, granted to a debtor by the grace and favor of the state on the grounds of public policy for a humane and generous purpose, which permits him to retain a portion of his property or earnings free from seizure or sale by his creditors under judicial process. 31 Am J2d Exemp §§ 1, 2. Freedom or release from duty or obligation, such as military service or service on a jury, not granted to others indiscriminately. Maine Water Co. v Waterville, 93 Me 586, 45 A 830; Green v State, 59 Md 123. An allowance of a deduction in computing net income for tax purposes by way of a personal exemption, an old-age exemption, or a blindness exemption. IRC § 151. The person for whom an exemption may be claimed in an income tax return. IRC § 151.
See **limitation of liability.**

exemption from arrest. The privilege, granted by constitutional provision or statute, of being free from arrest in a criminal case or a criminal case of a certain character. The privilege granted by constitutional provision, statute, or the common law of being free from arrest in a civil case. 5 Am J2d Arr § 95.

exemption from income tax. A fixed amount allowed by statute to the taxpayer for himself, spouse, and dependents against net income in determining taxable income; income of a certain nature, such as interest on certain bonds, rendered not subject to income tax by statute or common-law principle.

exemption from jury duty. The release of a class of persons by force of statute from the general duty of serving as a juror.
Such exemption is to be distinguished from an excuse granted a juror from service in a particular case or at a particular term of court. 31 Am J Rev ed Jur § 70.

exemption from military service. A release of a class of persons from compulsory military service or from certain phases of such service. 36 Am J1st Mil § 23.

exemption from self-incrimination. See **self-incrimination.**

exemption from service of process. A privilege, granted by constitutional provision or statute, or given by the courts upon grounds of public policy, to be free at certain times from the service of process in a civil action or proceeding, examples of which are attorneys at law while in attendance at court, persons in the active military service, members of Congress or of a state legislature while in attendance upon their legislative duties, etc. 42 Am J1st Proc § 135.

exemption from taxation. In the broad sense, all property not taxed; in a narrower sense, the grant of immunity, express or implied, to particular persons or corporations, or to persons or corporations of a particular class, from a tax upon property or an excise which persons and corporations generally within the same taxing district are obliged to pay. 51 Am J1st Tax § 495.
See **tax exempt income; tax exemption; tax exempt organization.**

exemptions. See **exemption.**

ex empto (ex emp′tō). From purchase; arising from or out of purchase.

exempt offices. Offices and employments excluded from the operation of civil service law. 15 Am J2d Civ S § 14.

ex eo quod plerumque fit (ex ē′ō quod plē-rum′kwe fit). From that which frequently happens.

exequatur (ek-sē-kwā′tėr). (Latin.) Let it be executed. The formal grant of authority to a foreign consul by the country to which he is sent and by virtue of which he is able to exercise his official functions within its territorial limits. 4 Am J2d Ambss § 12.

exercise. To avail or make use of, as to use a peremptory challenge to a juror or to take up an option.

exercise of judgment. Acting advisedly; using sound judgment; acting with due care.

exercise of judicial discretion. See **judicial discretion.**

exercise of power of appointment. A disposition of property. 28 Am J Rev ed Inher T § 216. A disposition of property made in accord with the mode or manner of execution provided for or designated in the power. 41 Am J1st Pow § 35.

exercitorial action. (eg-zėr-si-tō′ri-ạl ak′shọn). An action against the owner for breach of a contract made by the master of a ship.

exercitor maris (eg-zer′si-tor ma′ris). (Civil law.) A person who outfits a ship for a voyage; a "ship's husband."

exercitor navis (egs-zer′si-tor nā′vis). The charterer of a ship.

ex facie (eks fā′shi-ē). On the face; as, on the face of an instrument.

ex facto (ex fak′tō). From the act; from the fact; by reason or in consequence of an act or fact.

Ex facto jus oritur (ex fak′tō jūs ō′ri-ter). The law springs from the fact; law is born of fact.

ex fictione juris (ex fik-she-ō′ne jū′ris). By fiction of law; by legal fiction.

exfrediare (ex-fre-di-ā′re). To commit a breach of the peace.

Ex frequenti delicto augetur poena (ex fre-quen′tī de-lik′tō â-jē′ter pē′na). Punishment is increased by the frequency of crime.

ex. gr. Abbreviation of exempli gratia; abbreviation of ex gratia.

ex gratia (ex grā′she-a). Not a matter of right, but resting in the exercise of a sound discretion to determine the demands of justice. 5 Am J2d A & E § 998.

ex gravi querela (ex gra′vī kwe-rē′la). From or on the grievous complaint,—an ancient writ for the recovery of land by a devisee from whom it was wrongfully withheld by the heir of the testator.

exhaeres (ex-hē′rēz). A person who has been disinherited by his ancestor.

exhaeridatio (ex-hē-rē-dā′she-ō). A disinheritance.

exhausted. Tired out; drained; used up. The application of all the assets of a debtor to the claims of his creditors, so that further executions on judgments against him will be returned unsatisfied. Globe Publishing Co. v State Bank of Nebraska, 41 Neb 175, 59 NW 683.

exhausting security. The necessity of a creditor to look to a lien which secures him alone before seeking satisfaction from a lien which secures other creditors as well as him. 35 Am J1st Marsh A § 2.

exhaustion of remedy. The doctrine that where an administrative remedy is provided, relief must be sought exhausting such remedy before the courts will act. 2 Am J2d Admin L § 595.

exheredate (eks-her′ẹ-dāt). To disinherit.

exhibere (eg-zi-bē′re). To produce; to produce in a court of justice; to offer as an exhibit.

exhibit. A copy of a written instrument on which a pleading is founded, annexed to the pleading and by reference made a part of it. 41 Am J1st Pl § 55. Any paper or thing offered in evidence and marked for identification. Item of real or demonstrative evidence offered in evidence for observation by court or jury. 29 Am J2d Ev § 771. Something on exhibition.

See **exhibition.**

exhibitant (eg-zib′i-tạnt). A party to an action who offers an exhibit.

exhibitio billae (eg-zi-bi′she-ō bil′lē). The exhibition of a bill,—the filing of a suit.

exhibition. A fair; a show; a presentation of works of art or of trade and commerce for viewing by the public or a class of persons. A suit to compel a person to produce writings.

exhumation. The removal of a body from the grave.

ex hypothesi (ex hī-po′the-sī). Upon the hypothesis or supposition.

exidos (ek-se-dos′). Vacant spaces for exercise, and for threshing corn, or other general uses, which were reserved or set apart for such purposes in the laying out of Spanish-American towns. Strother v Lucas (US) 12 Pet 410, 444, note, 9 L Ed 1137, 1150, note.

exigence (ek′si-jẹns). Same as **exigency.**

exigency (ek′si-jẹn-si). An urgency; a demand; a need; a requirement; a condition.
See **public exigency.**

exigency of a bond. The condition upon which the enforcement of the bond depends.

exigendary (ek-si-jen′dạ-ri). Same as **exigenter.**

exigent (ek′si-jẹnt). A writ which was used in outlawry proceedings when the defendant could not be found. The writ required the sheriff to cause the defendant to be proclaimed, required or exacted in five county courts successively, to render himself, and if he did, to take him. If he did not appear, he was outlawed by the coroners of the county. See 3 Bl Comm 283.

exigenter (ek′si-jen-tėr). An officer of the English court of common pleas who issued writs of exigent.

exigible (ek′si-ji-bl). Capable of being demanded or required; as the payment of a debt.

exigi facias (ex′i-jī fā′she-as). Same as **exigent.**

exile (ek′sīl, formerly eg-zīl). To banish, to send a person out of the country as a punishment for crime; banishment; a person who has been banished. See 1 Bl Comm 137.

Exilium est patriae privatio, natalis soli mutatio, legum nativarum amissio (eg-zi′li-um est pa′tri-ē prī-vā′she-ō, nā-tā′lis sō′lī mu-tā′she-o, lē′gum nā-ti-vā′rum ā-mi′she-ō). Exile or banishment is a deprivation of country, a change of natal soil, a loss of native laws.

ex improviso (ex im-prō-vī′zō). Without any preparation.

ex incontinenti (ex īn-kon-ti-nen′tī). With incontinence; incontinently; immediately; summarily.

ex industria (ex in-dus′tri-a). On purpose; purposely; intentionally. Martin v Hunter's Lessee (US) 1 Wheat 304, 334, 4 L Ed 97, 104.

ex insinuatione (ex in-si-nū-ā-she-ō′ne). Upon the information of; upon the suggestion of.

ex integro (ex in′te-grō). Anew; over again; afresh.

ex intervallo (ex in-ter-val′lō). After an interval.

exire (ex-ī′re). To go out; to come out; to issue forth; to issue.

exist (eg-zist′). To be; to have being; to come into existence; to have existence.

existence. Life; a state of being; a corporation endowed with the capacity to transact the legal business for which it was created. 18 Am J2d Corp § 43.
See **entity; potential existence.**

existimatio (eg-zis-ti-mā'she-ō). An opinion which one man has of another; estimation; reputation; the award of an arbitrator.

existing. Existent; in existence; having being.

existing creditors. As the term appears in a statute which provides for the avoidance of a fraudulent transfer or conveyance as to "existing creditors," persons having subsisting obligations against the grantor or donor at the time of the transfer or conveyance, whether or not the obligations had been reduced to judgment at that time, even immature or contingent obligations. Carr v Davis, 64 W Va 522, 63 SE 326; Sallaske v Fletcher, 73 Wash 593, 132 P 648; Uniform Fraudulent Conveyance Act § 1. For some purposes, an "existing indebtedness" is a liquidated demand or a sum of money due by certain and express agreement.
See **existing indebtedness.**

existing debt. See **existing indebtedness.**

existing equity. An existing right enforceable in equity, if not at law.
The right of a carrier to deny as to the shipper receipt of the goods for which its agent has issued a bill of lading is an "existing equity" within the provision of the Federal Bill of Lading Act that a straight bill cannot be negotiated free from existing equities. Chesapeake & O. R. Co. v State Nat. Bank, 280 Ky 444, 133 SW2d 511, 130 ALR 1306.
See **equitable right.**

existing indebtedness. For some purposes, a liquidated demand or a sum of money due by certain and express agreement. Craig v Gaddis, 171 Miss 379, 157 So 684, 95 ALR 1494 (availability of remedy of attachment); Wing v Slater, 19 RI 597, 35 A 302 (personal liability of stockholders for existing debts of corporation). In other connections, one may have the status of an "existing creditor," even though the obligation owing to him is immature or contingent.
See **existing creditors.**

existing insurance. Other insurance on the same risk in existence at the time of application for insurance. 29 Am J Rev ed Ins § 778.
Benefit certificates in mutual aid societies have been held not to constitute "existing insurance" as the term is employed in applications for life insurance, but there is respectable authority to the contrary. Penn Mut. Life Ins. Co. v Mechanics' Sav. Bank & Trust Co. (CA6 Tenn) 72 F 413, reh den 73 F 653.

existing law. A broad term but, in the particular context in which it appears, it may be limited to statutory law, as distinguished from common law, or to Federal law, as distinguished from state law. Chicago, St. Paul etc. R Co. v Latta, 226 US 519, 57 L Ed 328, 33 S Ct 155; Adams Express Co. v Croninger, 226 US 491, 57 L Ed 314; 33 S Ct 148 (application of provision of Carmack Amendment).

existing use. A familiar term in zoning ordinances and regulations, usually employed in characterizing a nonconforming use excepted from the application of the ordinance or regulation, and meaning an actual, as distinguished from a mere contemplated, use, existing at the time of the enactment of the ordinance or the passage of the regulation, but not necessarily a use in actual operation at that time or a use which utilizes the entire tract involved. De Felice v Zoning Board of Appeals, 130 Conn 156, 32 A2d 635, 147 ALR 161.

exit. Verb: To go out. (Latin.) To issue something, for example, a writ or process. Noun: A way out, particularly a way out of a building or off a stage in a theater.

exitu. See **in exitu.**

exitus (ek'si-tus). An issue. An issue, "exitus," being the end of all the pleadings, is the fourth part or stage of an action, and is either upon matter of law, or matter of fact. See 3 Bl Comm 314.

exit wound. A wound made by a sword or other weapon or instrument at the point where it comes out of the body after having passed through it.

ex jure naturale (ex jū're na-tū-rā'le). From the law of nature.
See **natural law; natural rights.**

ex justa causa (ex jus'ta kâ'za). From or with a just or lawful cause; by a just or legal title.

ex latere (ex la'te-re). From the side or flank; collaterally.

exlegalitas (ex-lē-gā'li-tās). Outlawry.

exlegare (ex-lē-gā're). To cause a felon to be outlawed.

exlegatus (ex-lē-gā'tus). Outlawed; an outlaw.

ex lege (eks lē'jē). According to law; by law; as a matter of law.

ex legibus (ex lē'ji-bus). According to the laws; by the laws.

exlex (eks'leks). An outlaw, a felon who has been outlawed.

ex licentia regis (ex lī-sen'she-a rē'jis). By leave or license of the king.

ex locato (ex lō-kā'tō). From a lease; from a letting.

ex majore cautela (eks mā-jō're kâ'te-la). For greater caution.

Ex mala causa non oritur actio (ex ma'la kâ'za non ō'ri-ter ak'she-ō). From an unlawful transaction, no cause of action arises. Commercial Nat. Bank v First Nat. Bank, 118 NC 783, 24 SE 524.

ex maleficio (ex ma-le-fi'she-ō). From or out of wrongdoing; tortious; tortiously.
See **trustee ex maleficio.**

Ex maleficio non oritur contractus (ex ma-le-fi'she-ō non ō'ri-ter kon-trak'tus). A contract cannot be born of wrongdoing.

Ex malis moribus bonae leges natae sunt (ex ma'lis mō'ri-bus bō'nē lē'jēz nā'tē sunt). Good laws are born of bad morals.

ex malitia (ex ma-li'she-a). From or out of malice; maliciously.
See **malice.**

ex malitia sua praecogitata (ex ma-li'she-a su'a prē-ko-ji-ta'ta). With his malice aforethought; with malice aforethought.

ex merito justitiae (ex me'ri-tō jūs-ti'she-ē). For the benefit of or in the interest of justice.

ex mero motu (ex me'rō mō'tu). On the court's own motion, without application made by either party.

ex mora (ex mo'ra). From or by reason of delay.

ex mora debitoris (ex mo′ra de-bi-tō′ris). From or by reason of the delay of the debtor.

ex more (ex mō′re). By or according to the custom or usage.

Ex multitudine signorum, colligitur identitas vera (ex mul-ti-tū′di-ne sig-nō′rum, kol-li′ji-ter ī-den′ti-tas vē′ra). From a large number of signs or marks the true identity of anything is gathered or established.

ex mutuo (ex mu′tu-ō). From or out of the loan of a thing.

ex natura rei (ex nā-tū′ra rē′ī). From the nature of the thing.

ex necessitate (eks nę-ses-i-tā′tē). From or by reason of necessity.

ex necessitate legis (ex ne-ses-si-tā′te lē′jis). By necessity of law; by legal necessity; as where a woman is capitally convicted and pleads her pregnancy, it is cause to stay execution until her delivery. See 4 Bl Comm 394.

ex necessitate rei (ex ne-ses-si-tā′te rē′ī). From the necessity of the thing; from the exigency or urgency of the matter.

Ex nihilo nihil fit (ex ni′hi-lō ni′hil fit). Nothing comes from nothing.

Ex nudo pacto non oritur actio (ex nu′dō pak′tō non ō′ri-ter ak′she-ō). No action can accrue out of a mere naked promise, that is, a promise for which there is no consideration. Cook v Bradley, 7 Conn 57.

ex officio (ex of-fi′she-ō). From or by virtue of the office. A right or privilege in an office arising from one's status as the holder of another office, for example, the right of a justice of the peace to membership on a town board.

ex officio informations (ex of-fi′she-ō in-for-ma′tions). Informations charging crime filed by the attorney general of England.

ex officio justice of the peace. An officer having all the powers of a justice of the peace, without being actually elected or appointed to that office, the powers and duties being attached to some other office, such as that of mayor or magistrate of a municipality. 31 Am J Rev ed J P § 5.

exonerare (eg-zo-ne-rā′re). To exonerate; to discharge; to release from liability; to free.

exoneration. Absolving of a charge or imputation of guilt; the lifting of a burden; a discharge; a release from liability; the application of the personal property of an intestate to the payment of his debts and the relief of his real property therefrom. 21 Am J2d Ex & Ad § 391.
See **contribution; indemnity**.

exonerationae sectae. See **de exoneratione sectae**.

exoneration of bail. The release from liability of the sureties on a bail bond either by their surrender of their principal to the proper authorities; by his surrender of himself before the day stipulated in the bond; by the acquittal of the principal or the termination of the prosecution by any other means before the forfeiture of the bond or undertaking. 8 Am J2d Bail § 120.

exoneration of surety. The discharge of a surety. 50 Am J1st Suret § 40.
See **exoneration of bail**.

exoneretur (eg-zo-ne-rē′ter). Let him be discharged, —a notation made on a bail-piece discharging the sureties from liability.

exor. An abbreviation of executor.

ex ordine (ex or′di-ne). From or according to the order.

Ex pacto illicito non oritur actio (ex pak′tō il-li′si-to non ō′ri-ter ak′she-ō). From an unlawful agreement, no action can arise.

ex parte (ex par′te). Of or from one side or party. Application made to the court without notice to the adverse party.

ex parte deposition. A deposition taken without notice in cases of necessity and in cases where all that is sought in the way of testimony is mere formal proof or proof of an isolated fact. Walsh v Rogers (US) 13 How 283, 14 L Ed 147.

ex parte injunction. An injunction issued without prior notice to the adverse party. 28 Am J Rev ed Inj § 248.

ex parte materna (ex par′te ma-ter′na). On the maternal or mother's side.

ex parte motion. A motion made to the court without notice to the adverse party. 37 Am J1st Motions § 26.

ex parte order (ex par′te or-der). An order made by the court upon the application of one of the parties to an action without notice to the other. 37 Am J1st Motions § 26.

ex parte paterna (ex par′te pa-ter′na). On the paternal or father's side.

expatriate (eks-pā′tri-āt). Verb: To quit one's country, renouncing citizenship in and allegiance to that country and taking residence in and becoming a citizen of another country. 3 Am J2d Aliens § 120. Noun: One who has expatriated himself.

expatriation. A voluntary change of allegiance from one country to another, effecting an absolute termination of all civil and political rights as of the date of such act. 3 Am J2d Aliens § 120.
The concept of expatriation has no application to the removal from this country of a native citizen during minority. In such case the voluntary action which is the essence of the right of expatriation is lacking. That right is fittingly recognized where a child born here, who may be, or may become, subject to a dual nationality, elects on attaining majority citizenship in the country to which he has removed. Perkins v Elg, 307 US 325, 83 L Ed 1320, 59 S Ct 884.
See **expatriate**.

Ex paucis dictis intendere plurima possis (ex pâ′sis dik′tis in-ten′de-re plū′ri-ma pos′sis). It is possible to express very much in a few words.

expect. To anticipate. A secondary meaning of "to demand". Sillman v Spokane Sav. & Loan Soc. 103 Wash 619, 175 P2d 296.

expectancies. Estates in anticipation, not in present possession or enjoyment. 28 Am J2d Est § 2. Reversions, remainders, and estates in the nature of remainders known as executory interests. A mere naked possibility not coupled with an interest. Hart v Gregg, 32 Ohio St 502. The bare hope of succession to the property of another, something so inchoate as to have no attribute of property. Johnson v Breeding, 136 Tenn 528, 190 SW 545.
See **possibility**.

expectancy of life. See **expectation of life.**

expectancy tables. See **mortality tables.**

expectant estates. Future interests, whether vested or contingent or of an executory nature. 23 Am J2d Desc & D § 30. Reversions, remainders, vested or contingent, and executory interests. But not including the mere possibility of a reverter, which the grantor has after he has conveyed in fee on condition subsequent. Upington v Corrigan, 151 NY 143, 45 NE 359.

expectant fee. See **expectant estates; fee-expectant.**

expectant heir. See **heir apparent.**

expectant right. See **expectancies; expectant estates.**

expectation. See **anticipation; expectancies; in expectation.**

expectation of life. The presumption of the continuance of life. 22 Am J2d Dth § 294. The expected duration of the life of a man or woman of a particular age, as calculated according to the statistics of mortality and listed in mortality tables.
See **mortality tables.**

expected return. The total amount or the estimated amount to be received under an annuity contract. IRC § 72(c) (2).

expect to pay. Words importing a desire, a willingness, or an intention to pay, but not a promise. Coe v Rosene, 66 Wash 73, 118 P 881.

expediency of measure. The wisdom or propriety of a measure adopted by an administrative agency to which the formulation and execution of policy has been entrusted. 2 Am J2d Admin L § 677.

expedient. Advantageous; suitable for the particular purpose.

expediente (ex-pay-de-en'tay). A complete statement of every step taken in the proceedings to acquire a Mexican grant. Ainsa v United States, 161 US 208, 40 L Ed 673, 16 S Ct 544.

expeditate (eks-ped'i-tāt). To cut off the feet.

expeditation of dogs (eks-ped-i-tā'shon). Also called the "lawing" of dogs,—the practice of cutting off the claws and ball or pelote of the forefeet of mastiffs, to prevent them from running after deer in the king's forests. See 3 Bl Comm 72.

expeditio (ex-pe-di'she-ō). Service; execution.

expeditio brevis (ex-pe-di'she-ō brē'vis). The execution or service of a writ.

expeditio contra hostem (ex-pe-di'she-ō kon'tra hos'tem). Military service against an enemy, a part of the "tri-noda necessitas" or three-fold burden to which every man's estate was subject under the ancient laws of England. Butler v Perry, 240 US 328, 60 L Ed 672, 36 S Ct 258.

expedition. A journey by several persons or a body of persons; ordinarily not inclusive of a journey by one person, notwithstanding hazard to the person in making the trip. King v Equitable Life Assur. Soc. 232 Iowa 541, 5 NW2d 845, 155 ALR 1022.
See **aeronautic expedition; military expedition.**

Expedit reipublicae ut sit finis litium (ex'pe-dit rē-ī-pub'li-sē ut sit fī'nis lī'she-um). It is of advantage to the state that litigation should come to an end. Eastman v Cooper, 32 Mass (15 Pick) 276.

Expedit republicae ne sua re quis male utatur (ex'pe-dit rē-pub'li-sē nē su'a rē quis ma'le ū-tā'ter). It is for the welfare of the state that no one should make an ill use of his property.

expel. To drive out or put out. To terminate the membership of a person in a club, lodge, or association. Macauley v Tierney, 19 RI 255, 33 A 1.
See **expulsion.**

expended. Actually paid out or disbursed. School Dist. v Smith, 82 Or 443, 161 P 706.

expenditors (eks-pen'di-tors). Paymasters.

expenditure. A word impossible of precise definition, the meaning of which must be determined from the circumstances under which it is used. United States v CIO, 335 US 106, 92 L Ed 1849, 68 S Ct 1349. For some purposes, a necessary outlay of money, that is, an expense. Natural Gas Pipe Line Co. v State Commission of Revenue, 155 Kan 416, 125 P2d 397, 140 ALR 1341. For other purposes, a contribution, for example, an expenditure in aid of a candidate for political office. 31 Am J Rev ed Lab § 175.
See **capital expenditures.**

expensae (expen'sē). Expenses; charges; costs.

expensae circa funus (ex-pen'sē ser'ka fu'nus). Expenses at the time of a funeral; funeral expenses.

expensae litis (ex-pen'sē lī'tis). Costs of suit.

expense. The cost of a thing or of services; the charge made for something; a paying out for something.
See **expenditure; family expenses; funeral expenses; operating expenses; ordinary and necessary expense; overhead expenses.**

expense incurred. An expense for which one has become liable, even though not defrayed. Brown v Helvering, 291 US 193, 78 L Ed 724, 54 S Ct 356.

expense of litigation. Court costs and attorneys' fees. As the expression is used in an indemnity insurance policy giving the insurer the right to control the litigation, it embraces all the expenses the assured was put to by the litigation, including costs, damages and interest, although there are decisions which do not include these items in ruling on such policies. Aetna Life Ins. Co. v Bowling Green Gaslight Co. 150 Ky 732, 150 SW 994.

expense ration. Terminology of insurers; an amount arrived at by measuring expenses incurred, including all expenses incurred in acquiring, writing and servicing business, but excluding loss adjustment expenses, against premiums written.

expenses of administration. See **administration expenses.**

expenses of family. See **family expenses.**

expenses of last illness. See **death-bed expenses; funeral expenses.**

expensis civium et burgensium. See **de expensis,** etc.

experience. Work, pleasure, any facet of life gone by, as distinguished from that which is only imagined or anticipated. That from which a degree of proficiency in a profession or occupation is expected to result. The proficiency of an employee at his work, including his knowledge of the work, particularly dangers inherent therein. 35 Am J1st M & S § 290. An insurer's record of losses in respect of a particular class of risks carried, such as automobile liability, inland marine, and plate glass. The result of the operation of an unemployment compensation law in the state in reference to all employers and employees engaged under the act. Broadway v Alabama Dry Dock & Shipbuilding Co. 246 Ala 201, 20 So 2d 41.

Under a credit insurance policy which permits

credit to be extended according to the previous "experience" of the insured with the customer, the word thus used denotes closed transactions, that is, indebtedness which has been paid. Philadelphia Casualty Co. v Cannon & Buyers Millinery Co. 133 Ky 745, 118 SW 1004.

experience tables. See **mortality tables.**

Experientia per varios actus legem facit. Magistra rerum experientia (ex-pe-ri-en'she-a per vā'ri-ōs ak'tus lē'jem fā'sit. Ma-jis'tra rē'rum ex-pe-ri-en'she-a). Experience by various acts makes law. Experience is the mistress of things.

experimental evidence. Proof of a fact by way of an experiment performed in court, at any rate in the presence of judge and jury, or evidence of experiments performed out of court under similar conditions and like circumstances to those existing in the case at issue. People v Levine, 85 Cal 39, 22 P 969, 24 P 631.

expert. One who is so qualified, either by actual experience or by careful study, as to enable him to form a definite opinion of his own respecting a division of science, branch of art, or department of trade about which persons having no particular training or special study are incapable of forming accurate opinions or of deducing correct conclusions. Scott v Astoria & C. River R. Co. 43 Or 26, 72 P 594.

Accountants, engineers, clerks, and stenographers are properly to be considered experts within the meaning of a statutory provision which authorizes a public service commission to employ experts to assist the members of the commission in obtaining extensive information regarding public utilities. Anno: 10 ALR 1453, s. 18 ALR 946.

See **expert witness.**

expert opinion. See **expert testimony; expert witness.**

expert testimony. The opinion of an expert witness; the testimony of persons who are particularly skilled, learned, or experienced in a particular art, science, trade, business, profession, or vocation a thorough knowledge of which is not possessed by men in general, in regard to matters connected therewith. 31 Am J2d Exp & Op § 1.

See **expert witness; medical evidence.**

expert witness. A person who is so qualified, either by actual experience or by careful study, as to enable him to form a definite opinion of his own respecting a division of science, branch of art, or department of trade about which persons having no particular training or special study are incapable of forming accurate opinions or of deducing correct conclusions. 31 Am J2d Exp & Op § 1. A witness qualified by scientific or specialized knowledge or experience so as to be permitted to testify not only to the facts, but to his opinion respecting the facts, so far as necessary to inform the jury and enable them to understand the issues of fact and arrive at a proper conclusion. 26 Am J1st Homi § 432.

expilare (ex-pi-lā're). To despoil; to pillage; to plunder; to rob.

expiration. Coming to an end; termination by lapse of time.

expiration of policy. The termination of an insurance policy by expiration of the period of coverage stated in the instrument.

See **expirations.**

expiration of term. An ending of the term of a lease by the lapse of the time provided by the lease for its duration. 32 Am J1st L & T § 138. Any termination of a lease, whether by expiration of the period of the lease or by the occurrence of a condition which calls for a termination. Pringle v Wilson, 156 Cal 313, 104 P 316.

See **option to terminate.**

expirations. A technical term in the insurance business; a record kept by an insurance agent of policies issued which contains the dates of issuance, names of the insureds, expiration dates, the amounts of the policies issued, the amounts of the premiums, the properties covered, and particular terms of the insurance. Anno: 124 ALR 1356.

expire. To exhale. To emit the last breath; to perish; to cease; to come to an end; to conclude; to terminate.

See **expiration.**

expired. Having come to an end. Having died.

See **expiration; expire.**

expiry of the legal (eks'pi-ri). The expiration of the period of time within which property subjected to a judgment might be redeemed.

explees. Same as **esplees.**

explicatio (ex-pli-kā'she-ō). A pleading under the civil law which corresponded to the surrejoinder of the common law.

exploration expenditure. The cost of geological or geophysical work in prospecting for oil and gas or other minerals.

See **mine exploration costs.**

exploratory drilling test. A test had by way of discovery to ascertain the extent of mineral deposits. 23 Am J2d Dep § 184.

explosion. A bursting with violence and loud noise caused by internal pressure; a sudden bursting or breaking up or in pieces from an internal or other force. 31 Am J2d Explos § 1. A violent bursting or expansion, following the production of great pressure, or a certain release of pressure. 29A Am J Rev ed Ins § 1296.

explosive. Any substance the decomposition or combustion of which generates gas with such rapidity that it can be used for blasting, in firearms, or for the generation of power. 31 Am J2d Explos § 1. Material from which through nuclear transformation tremendous forms of energy are released. 6 Am J2d Atomic E § 2.

exportation. The sending of goods from one country to another country.

export certificate. A certificate issued by the keeper of the English Stud Book when a horse entered in the book is exported, by means of which the foreign purchaser is enabled to register the horse in his own country. Halbronn v International Horse Agency & Exchange [1903] 1 King's Bench 270.

exports. Articles shipped from a port of the United States to a foreign country. 21 Am J2d Cust D § 5. Goods and merchandise exported to foreign countries. 51 Am J1st Tax § 104.

export value. The value of imported goods in the country of export. 21 Am J2d Cust D § 83.

expose. To disclose; to make known; to exhibit; to leave unprotected.

exposed to disease. Subjected to existing conditions under which a disease may be communicated. Re Smith, 146 NY 68, 40 NE 497.

expose for sale. To exhibit goods to persons solicited to purchase, or to have them in hand in the presence of such persons and to offer to exhibit them without actually doing so. Commonwealth v Hana, 195 Mass 262, 81 NE 149.

exposing buildings. A term familiar in insurance; such buildings as tend to increase the risk of loss by fire and naturally may be considered in fixing the rate of premium. Macatawa Transp. Co. v Fireman's Fund Ins. Co. 168 Mich 365, 134 NW 193.

exposing for sale. See **expose for sale.**

expositio (ex-pō-zi'she-ō). Exposition; interpretation; explanation.

Expositio, quae ex visceribus causae nascitur, est aptissima et fortissima in lege (ex-pō-zi'she-ō, kwē ex vis-se'ri-bus kā'zē na'si-ter, est ap-tis'si-ma et for-tis'si-ma in lē'je). That interpretation which springs from the essence of a cause is the most apt and the most powerful in law.

expository statute. A statute which does not purport or attempt to amend an existing statute, but which provides a rule or manner for its construction or interpretation. Lindsay v United States Sav. & Loan Co. 120 Ala 156, 24 So 171.

ex post facto (eks pōst fak'to). After the thing is done; after the act is committed. Calder v Bull (US) 3 Dall 386, 1 L Ed 648. Signifying something done after, or arising from or to affect, another thing committed before. State v Masino, 216 La 352, 43 So 2d 685, 14 ALR2d 720.

ex post facto law(eks pōst fak'to lâ). A law which, in its operation, makes that criminal which was not so at the time of the act, or which increases the punishment, or, in short, which, in relation to the offense or its consequences, alters the situation of a party to his disadvantage. Lindsey v Washington, 301 US 397, 81 L Ed 1182, 57 S Ct 797. A law that deprives a person accused of crime of a substantial right in which he was protected and granted immunity by the law in force at the time of the commission of the offense. Murphy v Commonwealth, 172 Mass 264, 52 NE 505. A law which operates upon a subject not liable to it at the time the law was made. State v Masino, 216 La 352, 43 So 2d 685, 14 ALR2d 720.

exposure. The state of being exposed; openness to danger; accessibility to anything that may affect, especially detrimentally. In the business of fire insurance, a source of danger external to the insured property itself. Davis v Western Home Ins. Co. 81 Iowa 496, 46 NW 1073.

See **indecent exposure; involuntary exposure; unnecessary exposure.**

exposure of person. See **indecent exposure.**

ex praecogitata malicia (ex prē-ko-ji-tā'ta ma-li'she-a). With malice aforethought.

ex praemissis (ex prē-mis'sis). From the premises.

express. Adjective: Stated, explicit, clear; declared; not left to implication. State ex rel. Holt v Denny, 118 Ind 447, 21 NE 274. Noun: A method of transportation of property or remittance of money.

express acceptance. An acceptance of an offer expressed in words of acceptance, leaving nothing to inference or implication. 17 Am J2d Contr § 44. The acceptance of a dedication by formal ratification by the proper official board of the municipality or other public body concerned, the adoption of a municipal ordinance, the vote of a town council, the signing of a written instrument by the proper authorities, the execution of an official map by a city showing the street offered to be dedicated, or the act of the legislature incorporating a town, or adopting a map showing its limits. 23 Am J2d Ded § 50.

express agency. An actual agency created as a result of the oral or written agreement of the parties. 3 Am J2d Ag § 18.

express aider. The doctrine that a defect in pleading is aided if the adverse party pleads over to or answers the defective pleading in such a manner that an omission or informality therein is supplied or rendered formal or intelligible. Cross v Chicago, 198 Ill App 177.

Expressa nocent; non expressa non nocent (ex-pres'sa no'sent; non ex-pres'sa non no'sent). That which is expressed may injure; that which is not expressed will not.

Expressa non prosunt quae non expressa proderunt (ex-pres'sa non prō'sunt kwē non ex-pres'sa prō-dē'runt). Things which are expressed may be detrimental which if not expressed would be beneficial.

express assumpsit (express as-sump'sit). An undertaking supported by an express promise.

express authority. Such authority as is directly granted to or conferred upon an agent or employee in express terms. 3 Am J2d Ag § 69.

express business. See **express company.**

express cars. The cars of an express company carried on railroad trains.

express color. A characterization of an evasive plea setting up feigned matter.

express company. A common carrier, its business being that of transporting over a regular route and at regular times money, goods in packages of limited size, and other small but valuable parcels for the public generally. 13 Am J2d Car § 15. At one time the most outstanding example of a joint stock company. 30 Am J Rev ed Jnt Stk Co § 8.

A person who carries goods from one city to another, and from one place to another in either city, solely on call and at special request without making regular trips or going over regular routes, is merely a truckman and is not in the express business. Retzer v Wood, 109 US 185, 27 L Ed 900.

express condition. Literally, a condition stated rather than implied. A qualification annexed to an estate in real property by the terms of the instrument which creates the estate. Raley v County of Umatilla, 15 Or 172, 13 P 890.

express consideration. A consideration which is expressed in the contract.

express contract. A contract, the terms of which are stated by the parties. 17 Am J2d Contr § 3. A contract which expresses the intentions of the parties in words. 58 Am J1st Wk & L § 2.

Where there is an actual promise, a contract is said to be express; where there is no actual promise, a contract is said to be implied. Damron v Stewart & Weir, 253 Ky 394, 69 SW2d 683.

express covenant. A covenant stated in words more or less distinctly exposing the intent to covenant. 20 Am J2d Cov § 11.

express dedication. A dedication made explicitly by

deed, note, memorandum, or oral declaration. 23 Am J2d Ded § 1.

express direction. As the term appears in a statute of frauds which requires a writing signed by the party to the contract sought to be charged or by another at his "express direction":—any word or act intended as a direction to sign, the term not being limited to a direction in words. Ex parte Leonard, 39 SC 302, 18 SE 216.

express easement. An easement created by grant, reservation, exception, agreement or covenant. See 25 Am J2d Ease §§ 20–22.

express emancipation. That emancipation which takes place when the parent freely and voluntarily agrees with his child, who is able to take care of and provide for himself, that he may leave home, earn his own living, and do as he pleases with his earnings. 39 Am J1st P & C § 64.

express invitation. An invitation extended by an owner of property in terms to a person or persons to come upon the premises, to make use of them, or to do something thereon. Robinson v Leighton, 122 Me 309, 119 A 809, 30 ALR 1386, 1389.

Expressio eorum quae tacite insunt nihil operatur (ex-pre'she-ō ē-ō'rum kwē ta'si-te in'sunt ni'hil ō-pe-rā'ter). The statement of those things which are tacitly understood can avail nothing. Stuart v Easton, 170 US 383, 395, 42 L Ed 1078, 1082, 18 S Ct 650.

expressio falsi (ex-pre'she-ō fal'sī). A falsehood; an untrue statement.

expression of opinion. See **expert testimony; opinion; opinion evidence.**

Expressio non prosunt quae non expressa proderunt (ex-pre'she-o non prō'sunt kwē non ex-pres'sa prō-de'runt). Things which are expressed may be disadvantageous which not expressed would benefit.

expressio unius est exclusio alterius (ex-pre'she-ō ū'-ni-us est ex-klū'she-ō al-te'ri-us). The expression of one thing implies the exclusion of another thing. A maxim applied in a construction of contracts to the effect that the expression in a contract of one or more things of a class implies the exclusion of all not expressed. 17 Am J2d Contr § 255. A principle of statutory construction, but as an aid to construction, not a rule of law, the principle being of limited use and application. 50 Am J1st Stat §§ 244, 245.

express lien. A charge upon property for the payment or discharge of a debt or duty created in stated and explicit terms.

expressly. Clearly, directly, plainly, distinctly. State ex rel. Holt v Denny, 118 Ind 447, 21 NE 274.

express malice. A deliberate or premeditated design to inflict injury or take life. 26 Am J1st Homi § 38. For the purposes of the law of defamation, malice in fact as distinguished from implied malice. 33 Am J1st L & S § 111.

See **malice in fact.**

express messenger. An employee of an express company in charge of the express car on a railroad train. Louisville N. O. & T. R. Co. v Douglass, 69 Miss 723, 11 So 933.

express notice. Actual notice by direct information. 39 Am J1st Notice § 6.

express permission. As the term appears in a statute rendering an automobile owner liable for injury caused by the car in operation by another with "express permission"—prior knowledge of the intended use and an affirmative and active consent to it. 8 Am J2d Auto § 605.

express ratification. The ratification of an unauthorized act by spoken or written words. 3 Am J2d Agency § 162.

express trust. A trust which arises out of a direct or positive declaration of trust. A trust that comes into existence by the execution of an intention to create it by the person having legal and equitable dominion over the property made subject to it. 54 Am J1st Trusts § 30.

Expressum facit cessare tacitum (ex-pres'sum fā'sit ses-sā're ta'si-tum). The express declaration puts to an end anything which silence might signify. Slegel v Herbine, 148 Pa 236, 23 A 996.

express warranty. A part of a contract of sale of personalty:—being a statement in so many words that the subject of the sale has a certain quality or condition. 46 Am J1st Sales § 299. In a contract of insurance:—an agreement contained in the policy whereby the insured stipulates that certain facts relating to the risk are or shall be true, or that certain acts relating to the subject of the insurance have been or shall be done. 29 Am J Rev ed Ins § 709.

expressway. A superior highway.

See **limited-access highway.**

Ex procedentibus et consequentibus optima fit interpretatio (ex prō-sē-den'ti-bus et kon-se-quen'ti-bus op'ti-ma fit in-ter-pre-tā'she-ō). The best interpretation or explanation is made from the matter which precedes and follows.

ex professo (eks prō-fes'ō). By profession; professedly.

Expromissio (ex-pro-mī'she-ō). A kind of novation in the civil law, whereby the creditor accepted a new debtor in the place of the original one and released the latter.

expromissor (eks-prō-mis'ọr). (Civil law.) A person who assumed the payment of a debtor's obligation, thus releasing the original debtor upon the creditor's acceptance of the new debtor.

expromittere (ex-prō-mit'te-re). To become bound as an expromissor.

See **expromissor.**

expropriate (eks-prō'pri-āt). In modern usage, to condemn for public use; in older usage, a surrender or renunciation of a claim to property.

expropriation. The English and Canadian term for eminent domain.

See **eminent domain.**

ex proprio motu (ex prō'pri-ō mō'tu). Of his own motion; of his own accord.

ex proprio vigore (ex prō'pri-ō vi-gō're). Of its own force; by its own force; automatically.

ex provisione hominis (ex prō-vi-zhi-ō'ne ho'mi-nis). By provision of man; that is, by a man's own act, not by operation of law.

ex provisione mariti (ex prō-vi-zhi-ō'ne ma'ri-tī). By or from the provision of the husband.

ex provisione viri (ex prō-vi-zhi-ō'ne vi'rī). By or from the provision of the husband.

expulsion. A driving out with force. An enforced withdrawal from or termination of membership in a lodge or mutual benefit society. 36 Am J2d Frat

EXPURGATION [443] EXTENSION

O § 64. The removal of a member of a nonprofit corporation from the list of members and the elimination of his rights as a member. 18 Am J2d Corp § 473. The dismissal of a student from a university or college. 15 Am J2d Colleges § 25. The dismissal of a public school pupil for breach of a rule, regulation or requirement of the school authorities. 47 Am J1st Sch § 177.

See **deportation; excommunication.**

expurgation (eks-pėr-gā'shọn). A purging; a cleansing; a purification.

ex quasi contractu (ex quā'sī kon-trak'tu). As if from a contract; as if arising out of a contract.

ex rel. An abbreviation of **ex relatione.**

ex rel. action. An action in which a relator appears as one beneficially interested, the action being maintained on his behalf.

See **relator.**

ex relatione (ex rē-lā-she-ō'ne). On the relation of; on the information of.

See **relator.**

ex rigore juris (ex ri-gō're jū'ris). From or according to the rigor or harshness of the law.

exrogare (ex-rō-gā're). (Roman law.) To adopt a part of an old law in the enactment of a new one.

exscript (eks-kript'). A copy; a transcript.

ex scriptis olim visis (ex skrip'tis ō'lim vī'sis). From writings formerly seen.

ex ship. In connection with the stipulated price in a contract for the sale of merchandise: all expenses incurred to the time the goods leave the ship's tackle are to be borne by the seller; all expenses incurred after that time are to be borne by the buyer. Harrison v Fortlage, 161 US 57, 40 L Ed 616, 16 S Ct 488.

A bill of sale of goods in bulk at the time of the sale in a foreign country, to be delivered "ex vessel" in New York Harbor, means that the merchandise should be delivered at New York, and not at the place where it was when sold. Tinsley v Weidinger, 15 Daly 534, 8 NYS 476.

ex speciali gratia (ex spe-she-ā'lī grā'she-a). From special grace, favor, or indulgence.

ex speciali gratia, certa scientia, et mero motu regis (ex spe-she-ā'lī grā'she-a, ser'ta sī-en'she-a, et me'rō mō'tū rē'jis). By special favor, certain knowledge, and mere motion of the king: a usual clause in a king's grant. See 2 Bl Comm 347.

ex statuto (ex sta-tū'tō). According to the statute.

ex tempore (ex tem'po-re). For the time being; for the occasion; temporarily; from lapse of time.

extend. To stretch; to lengthen; to prolong. Quinn v Valiquet, 80 Vt 434, 68 A 515. To levy a writ of extent. Den ex dem. Murray v Hoboken Land & Improv. Co. (US) 18 How 272, 15 L Ed 372. To make a complete record of a judicial proceeding.

extended insurance. Life insurance for the full amount of the policy, less contractual deductions, for the period contemplated by the nonforfeiture table. 29 Am J Rev ed Ins § 619.

extendi facias (ex-ten'dī fā'she-as). A form of writ of execution, also known as a writ of extent, against the body, goods, and lands of the judgment debtor. 30 Am J2d Exec § 29. In some jurisdictions, a writ under which lands are seized by the sheriff and delivered to the plaintiff for the purpose of the recovery of the debt out of the rents and profits, but appraised at their full extended value before delivery to the plaintiff. 30 Am J2d Exec § 29.

Extenditur haec pax et securitas ad quatuordecim dies, convocato regni senatu (ex-ten'di-ter hēk pax et se-kū'ri-tas ad qua-tu-or'de-sim dī'ēz, kon-vo-kā'tō reg'nī se-nā'tū). This tranquillity and protection is extended to fourteen days from the assembling of the senate of the kingdom. See 1 Bl Comm 165.

extension (eks-ten'shọn). A stretching; a lengthening; a prolongation; a continuance; a grant of further time. An addition to the system of lines of a public utility for the purpose of serving new territory. State ex rel. Mason v Consumers' Power Co. 119 Minn 225, 137 NW 1104. A railroad running off a main line like a spur but constituting a part of the railroad system to be operated as a common carrier. 44 Am J1st RR § 231.

extension of building. An enlargement of a building. An addition to a building. 29 Am J Rev ed Ins § 294.

extension of charter. A prolongation of the existence of a corporation by statute or pursuant to statute. 18 Am J2d Corp § 69.

While the term "extension" has frequently been used synonymously with "renewal", it has been held that to "extend" a charter is to give one which now exists greater or longer time to operate in than that to which it was originally limited, while "renewal" of a charter is to give a new existence to one which has been forfeited, or which has lost its vitality by lapse of time. Moers v Reading, 21 Pa 188.

extension of debt. See **extension of time.**

extension of lease. The lengthening of the term of a lease by mutual agreement or by the exercise by the lessee of an option contained in the lease. 32 Am J1st L & T §§ 953 et seq.

In some of the cases, the courts seem to disregard any distinction in meaning between a renewal and an extension. However, generally a distinction is drawn between a provision in a lease for a renewal and a provision for the extension of the term at the option of the lessee, the courts treating the latter, upon the exercise of the privilege, as a present demise for the full term to which it may be extended and not a demise for the shorter period with a privilege for a new lease for the extended term. 32 Am J1st L & T § 956.

There is a distinction between a stipulation in a lease to renew it for an additional term and one to extend it, in that a stipulation to renew requires the making of a new lease, while a stipulation to extend does not. Grant v Collins, 157 Ky 36, 41, 162 SW 539.

extension of mortgage. The extension of the maturity of the obligation secured. 36 Am J1st Mtg § 381. The extension of the security of the mortgage to cover an additional indebtedness or future advances. 36 Am J1st Mtg §§ 67, 68.

extension of note. See **extension of time.**

extension of record. The preparation of the complete record of an action or proceeding in court from the processes and pleadings on file. 15 Am J2d Clk Ct § 23.

extension of term. See **extension of lease.**

extension of time. The prolongation of a period previously fixed. Modification of an obligation by giving additional time for performance. 11 Am J2d B & N § 297. Prolonging the time for payment of

extenso a note to a date beyond the due date stated in the note. Rossville State Bank v Heslet, 84 Kan 315, 113 P 1052. Relief granted to a debtor by a court of bankruptcy in respect of unsecured indebtedness in an arrangement proceeding under the Bankruptcy Act. 9 Am J2d Bankr § 1317.
See **extension of lease**.

extenso. See **in extenso**.

extensores (ex-ten-sō'rēz). Officers appointed to extend or appraise lands.

extent (eks-tent'). A writ or process usually called an "extent" or "extendi facias," because the sheriff is to cause the property seized to be appraised at its full extended value, before he delivers it to the plaintiff, that it may be known how soon the debt will be satisfied. This writ or process was commonly used upon forfeitures of recognizances on statutes merchant or statutes staple when body, lands and goods of the debtor might all be taken on execution. See 21 Am J2d Exec § 29.
Size, amount, coverage, applicable to time, space, proportion, etc., in fact a word which varies in meaning according to the subject to which it is applied. Wilson v Rousseau (US) 4 How 646, 698, 11 L Ed 1141, 1164. A writ of execution, otherwise known as extendi facias.
See **extendi facias**.

extent in chief. A writ of extent sued out at the instance of the king.

extenuate. To lessen; to weaken; to palliate; to excuse to some extent.

extenuating circumstances. Facts which reduce the damages in a civil case or the penalty in a criminal case.

extenuation. The mitigation of damages or of punishment for crime; a fact warranting mitigation.

extermination. The abatement of an agricultural nuisance by preventing the spread of insect pests or diseases detrimental to agriculture. 3 Am J2d Agri § 43.

exterminator. A substance in powder, liquid, or fumes for use in eliminating insect pests from house or lands. A person whose occupation is that of eliminating pests.

external administration. That part of the law which is concerned with the legal relations between administrative authorities and private interests. 1 Am J2d Admin L § 5.

external and visible signs of injury. A condition of recovery under many accident insurance policies, the purpose being to protect the insurer against sham claims. 29A Am J Rev ed Ins §§ 1169, 1170.

external means. A term limiting the coverage of an accident policy for the purpose of protecting the insurer against hidden or secret diseases where there is no manifestation of harm to the external body. American Acci. Co. v Reigart, 94 Ky 547, 23 SW 191. Not limiting recovery to a case where the external means should itself cause injury or death, the limitation being only that the cause be external to the person, although it may act on the insured internally. 29A Am J Rev ed Ins § 1165.

external or visible evidence. A familiar term in accident insurance policies covering injury sustained while riding in a motor vehicle, requiring as a condition of the insurer's liability that there be external or visible evidence of a collision or accident on the motor vehicle in which the insured alleges that he was riding when injured. 29A Am J Rev ed Ins § 1246.

external, violent, and accidental means. A clause limiting the risk of loss in an accident insurance policy, meaning that in order to support a recovery, it must be shown, not only that the means were external and violent, but also that they were accidental; in other words, all three tests must be met before coverage is afforded. Schonberg v New York Life Ins. Co. 235 La 461, 104 So 2d 171.
See **accidental means; violent means**.

external, violent, or accidental means. A disjunctive statement of coverage in an accident insurance policy, so that if an injury is external and violent, it need not be accidental in order to be covered. 29A Am J Rev ed Ins § 1165.
See **accidental means; violent means**.

exterritoriality. See **extraterritoriality**.

Exterus non habet terras (ex-te'rus non hā'bet ter'-res). An alien cannot hold land.

ex testamento (ex tes-ta-men'tō). By the will or testament.

extinct. Extinguished; having come to an end; discharged; released.

Extincto subjecto, tollitur adjunctum (ex-tink'tō sub-jek'to, tol'li-ter ad-junk'tum). The subject having become extinct, the adjunct or incident of it disappears.

extinguish. To terminate; to put an end to; to cancel; to discharge.

extinguishment. Discharge; destruction; termination; cancellation.

extinguishment of common. The termination of a right of common from any cause, for example, the acquisition of title by the person holding the right.

extinguishment of copyhold. The conversion of the tenure of a copyhold tenant to a freehold.

extinguishment of debt. The extinction or cancellation of a debt; as, by payment, by merging of the debtor and the creditor, by novation, or by the merger of a debt in a judgment. 30A Am J Rev ed Judgm § 321.

extinguishment of easement. The termination of an easement, as by abandonment of use, merger of dominant and servient estates, release, etc. 25 Am J2d Ease §§ 101 et seq.

extinguishment of rent. The termination of a tenant's liability for rent, as, by his acquisition of title to the land or by a release granted by the landlord.

extorsively (eks-tôr'siv-li). With intent to commit the crime of extortion. Leeman v State, 35 Ark 438.

extort. To commit the offense of extortion.
See **extortion**.

Extortio est crimen quando quis colore officii extorquet quod non est debitum, vel supra debitum, vel ante tempus quod est debitum (ex-tor'she-ō est kri'-men quan'dō quis ko-lō're of-fi'she-ī ex-tor'quet quod non est de'bi-tum, vel sū'pra de'bi-tum, vel an'te tem'pus quod est de'bi-tum). Extortion is a crime when anyone under color of office extorts that which is not due, or more than is due, or before the time when it is due.

extortion. Oppression under color or right; the criminal offense of obtaining money or other valuable thing by compulsion, actual force, or force of motives applied to the will; more technically defined as the unlawful taking by an officer of the law, by color of his office, of any money or thing of value that is not due to him, or the taking of more than is due, or the taking of money before it is due. Bush v State, 19 Ariz 195, 168 P 508; 31 Am J2d Extort § 1. A method of abuse of process. 1 Am J2d Abuse P § 12.

Ex tota materia emergat resolutio (ex tō′ta ma-te′ri-a ē-mer′gat re-so-lū′she-ō). The explanation or solution should arise out of the whole subject matter.

extra. Outside of; out of; beyond; better than expected; additional.

extra allowances. See **additional allowances**.

extra baggage. See **excess baggage**.

extra compensation. Compensation over and above that fixed by contract for the work agreed to be done. Weston v State, 262 NY 46, 186 NE 197, 88 ALR 1219. Money paid out of public funds to a public officer or servant in excess of his regular salary for the performance of services that are within the scope of his official duties. Mullane v McKenzie, 269 NY 369, 199 NE 624.

extract. Noun: That which is extracted or taken from something else; a copy of a portion of a record or document; a selection, as from a treatise or a book. Verb: To take something out of something else.

extraction. The removal of a tooth. The descent of a person in reference to the nationality of his ancestors.

extradition. The surrender by one nation or state to another of an individual accused or convicted of an offense outside of the former's territory and within the territorial jurisdiction of the latter, which, being competent to try and punish him, demands the surrender. State ex rel. Treseder v Remann, 165 Wash 92, 4 P2d 866, 78 ALR 412.

Extradition Act. One of the uniform laws.

extradition treaty. A treaty between two or more nations which provides for the extradition from each of the countries to any of the others of persons charged with specified offenses.

extradition warrant. The formal warrant of arrest issued by the governor or executive of the state or country for the apprehension and detention of the person whose surrender has been demanded of that state or country by another state or country. 31 Am J2d Extrad §§ 61, 62.

extra dividend. Sometimes called an "extraordinary dividend;" a dividend, whether cash or stock, paid by a corporation and representing an accumulated excess of earnings over normal return on capital invested and constituting a distribution or a capitalization of surplus profits remaining after distribution of ordinary dividends. 19 Am J2d Corp § 810.

extradotal property (eks-trạ-dō′tạl). Same as **paraphernal property**.

extra feodum (ex′tra fe′o-dum). Out of the fee; out of the seigniory.

extrahazardous. A descriptive term applicable to articles insured or articles permitted to be kept on insured premises; something beyond hazardous; extra dangerous. 29A Am J Rev ed Ins § 927.

extra-hazardous employment. A relative term. An occupation attended by a risk of danger to the person employed greater than in an ordinary employment. 58 Am J1st Workm Comp § 90.

extrahura (ex-tra-hu′ra). An estray.

extrajudicial (eks″trạ-jö-dish′ạl). Aside from or without the intervention of a court; outside of the court's jurisdiction.

extrajudicial confession. A confession made elsewhere than before a magistrate or in court. Stewart v State, 41 Okla Crim 117, 271 P 959.

extrajudicial identification. A former identification made out of court; sometimes imbued with such trustworthiness because of the circumstances under which it was made as to be competent evidence. 29 Am J2d Ev §§ 372, 373.

extrajudicially. In a manner other than judicial; by means outside of court.

extrajudicial oath. An oath which is not administered in the due and regular course of judicial proceedings which is not authorized by law, and which, accordingly, is not binding upon the person making it. State v Bowman, 90 Me 363.

extrajudicial opinion. An opinion on a question not presented or necessary to a decision in the case; obiter. Warner v Steamer Uncle Sam, 9 Cal 697, 732.

See **obiter**; **obiter dictum**.

extra judicium (ex′tra jū-di′she-um). Outside of court; extrajudicial.

extra jus (ex′tra jūs). Beyond the law; beyond the requirements of the law.

extralateral rights. A doctrine of mining law which refers to that part of a vein which, on the dip, lies outside of the side lines of the location within whose surface lines the apex of the vein appears, and not to any part of such vein, either the outcrop or the segments on the dip thereof, which lie wholly within planes drawn downwards coincident with the surface boundaries of the location.

The extralateral rights of the locator of a lode mining claim do not attach until after, in pursuit of his vein on its dip, he crosses the side lines of his location. Jefferson Mining Co. v Anchoria-Leland Mining & Milling Co. 32 Colo 176, 75 P 1070.

extra legem (ex′tra lē′jem). Outside of the law; beyond the protection of the law.

extra legem positus (ex′tra lē′jem po′zi-tus). Placed outside the law; subjected to civil death, an accompaniment of attainder of treason or felony whereby the attainted person was disqualified as a witness, as a plaintiff or as having capacity to perform any legal function; legally dead. 21 Am J2d Crim L §§ 626 et seq.

Extra legem positus est civiliter mortuus (ex′tra lē′jem pō′zi-tus est si-vi′li-ter mor′tu-us). A person who is placed outside the law (that is, outlawed) is civilly dead.

extraliminal rights (ex-tra-lim′i-nal rītz). Same as **extralateral rights.**

extraneous. Not pertinent. Something coming from outside.

extraneus (eks-trā′nẹ-us). An alien; a foreigner; a stranger.

Extraneus est subditus qui extra terram, i. e., potestatem regis natus est (ex-trā′ne-us est sub′di-tus quī ex′tra ter′ram, i. e., po-tes-tā′tem rē′jis nā′tus est). An alien or foreigner is a subject born outside the land; that is, outside the power of the king.

extraordinary. Beyond or out of the common order

EXTRAORDINARY [446] EXTRA

or rule; not usual, regular or of a customary kind; not ordinary; remarkable; uncommon; rare. Ten Eyck v Rector, etc. of Albany (NY) 65 Hun 194, 197, 20 NYS 157.

extraordinary care. A very high degree of care. 14 Am J2d Car § 916. More than ordinary care; great care. 8 Am J2d Bailm § 202.

Even the standard of "due care" varies with the danger involved and is proportionate thereto. 38 Am J1st Negl § 31. What a prudent man will do, and what a very prudent and thoughtful man will do under special circumstances, are questions for the jury. Wallace v Clayton, 42 Ga 443, 448.

extraordinary costs. See **additional allowances**.

extraordinary diligence. See **extraordinary care**.

extraordinary dividend. See **extra dividend**.

extraordinary flood. A flood of unprecedented magnitude; a flood frequently regarded as an act of God. 56 Am J1st Wat § 91. A flood, the magnitude and destructiveness of which could not have been anticipated or provided against by the exercise of ordinary foresight. Schweiger v Solbeck, 191 Or 454, 230 P2d 195, 29 ALR2d 435.

extraordinary physical effort. As the term applies in a statute prescribing a maximum and minimum age limit for certain positions in the civil service requiring "extraordinary physical effort," a physical effort of long duration or an effort involving extraordinary exertion at times, but not necessarily an effort beyond the ordinary, in respect of exertion of strength, which is continuous. Deodati v Kern, 280 NY 366, 21 NE 355, 122 ALR 1446.

extraordinary proceedings. See **extraordinary remedies**.

extraordinary remedies. Remedies, developed by the application of common-law or prerogative writs and confirmed with modifications by statute, intended to make available types of relief not obtainable in an ordinary action in law or equity, most notable of which are those employed in reference to the acts and determinations of administrative agencies:—certiorari, mandamus, and prohibition. 2 Am J2d Admin L § 708. Other administrative remedies:—assistance under writ, 6 Am J2d Assist § 1; quo warranto or proceeding in the nature of quo warranto, Casey v McElrath, 177 Ga 35, 169 SE 342; and receivership. Prudential Securities Co. v Three Forks, H.& N.V.R. Co. 49 Mont 567, 144 P 158.

extraordinary repairs. Such repairs as are made necessary by some unusual or unforeseen occurrence which does not destroy the building but merely renders it less suited to the use for which it was intended. Courtney v Ocean Acci. & G. Corp. 346 Mo 703, 142 SW2d 858, 130 ALR 234.

extraordinary risk. A term of application in reference to the safety of the working place; not a risk which is uncommon or unusual in the sense that it is rare, but one which arises out of unusual conditions resulting from the employer's negligence. Van Kirk v Butler, 19 NM 597, 145 P 129.

extraordinary session. See **special session**.

extraparochial (eks″trä-pạ-rō′ki-ạl). Some lands, either because they were in the hands of irreligious and careless owners, or were situated in forests and desert places, or for other reasons, were never united to any parish. See 1 Bl Comm 113.

extra praesentiam mariti (ex′tra prē-zen′she-am ma′-ri-tī). Outside the presence of the husband.

extra provincial company. A Canadian term for foreign corporation.
See **foreign corporation**.

extra quatuor maria (ex′tra qua′tu-or ma′ri-a). Beyond the four seas; that is, outside the kingdom of England. See 1 Bl Comm 457.

extra regnum (ex′tra reg′num). Outside the kingdom.

extra services. Services performed by an agent additional to or beyond the scope of the contract made by him with the principal, 3 Am J2d Agency § 248; services not covered by the contract but performed by a building contractor at the request or without objection on the part of the owner, the other contracting party, 13 Am J2d Bldg Contr § 19; services, by one hired to perform work and labor, beyond the stipulations of the contract, 58 Am J1st Wk & L § 34; services of a public officer incident to his office but for which no compensation is provided by law. Board of Comrs. v Blake, 21 Ind 32, 34.

extra session. See **special session**.

extraterritorial. Outside of the boundaries of the state or country.

extraterritoriality. The operation of the laws of a state or country beyond or outside of its physical boundaries. The fiction that a diplomatic officer, although actually in a foreign country, remains in the territory of his sovereign, applied in support of the immunities and privileges of ambassadors and other public ministers serving in a foreign country. 4 Am J2d Ambss § 4.

extraterritorial wrong. A wrong according to the law of the place where it occurred rather than the law of the jurisdiction wherein the action is brought. 1 Am J2d Actions § 6.

extra territorium (ex′tra ter-ri-tō′ri-um). Beyond or outside the territorial boundaries.

Extra territorium jus dicenti non paretur impune (ex′-tra ter-ri-tō′ri-um jūs di-sen′tī non pa-rē′ter im-pū′nē). A person may not with impunity obey the law laid down by a body exercising jurisdiction outside of its territorial limits.

extravagance. Excess, especially in dress, manner of living, or expenditures of public funds.
See **sumptuary laws**.

Extravagantes Communes (ex-tra-va-gan′tēz kom-mū′nēz). Common extravagants, the decrees of the popes who followed Pope John XXII. See 1 Bl Comm 82.

Extravagantes Joannis (ex-tra-va-gan′tēz Jo-an′nis). The twenty constitutions of Pope John XXII. See 1 Bl Comm 82.

extra viam (ex′tra vī′am). Outside the way; off the highway.

extra viam rights. The right of a traveler upon the highway to travel over the abutting property where the highway is out of repair and impassable for practical purposes. 25 Am J1st High § 615. The right of one having an easement of way to depart from the regularly traveled way or path and pass over the abutting land of the servient owner where the latter has obstructed the private way or made it impassable. 25 Am J2d Ease § 70.

extra vires (ex′tra vī′rēz). Same as **ultra vires**.

extra work. Services additional to that undertaken by a contractor. 58 Am J1st Wk & L § 34.

extreme. Outermost; utmost. Sometimes employed as the opposite of moderate, but more often as meaning far advanced or excessive, e. g. "extreme cruelty." Estate of Nelson, 132 Cal 182, 191.

extreme care. Such care as a prudent man would exercise in a place of danger. Schlosstein v Bernstein, 293 Pa 245, 142 A 324.

extreme cruelty. As a ground of divorce, the same in meaning as "cruel and inhuman treatment" and "intolerable severity." 24 Am J2d Divorce § 32. Not confined to physical violence, but including conduct that wounds the feelings and sensibilities so grievously as to impair physical or mental health. 24 Am J2d Div & S § 35.

extreme tide. The tide which occurs when the difference between high tide and low tide is the greatest.

extremis (ex-trē'mis). See **in extremis**.

Extremis probatis, praesumuntur media (ex-trē'mis prō'bā-tis, prē-su-mun'ter mē'di-a). When the extremes have been proved, those things which are between them are presumed.

extremity. The outermost; the hands and feet. Danger. The end of life.
See **either extremity**.

extrinsic (eks-trin'sik). Outside; from outside; foreign; derived from outside.

extrinsic evidence. See **parol evidence**.

extrinsic fraud. The character of fraud which will afford a ground for setting aside a judgment, that is, fraud which is collateral to the issues tried in the case wherein the judgment was rendered. 30A Am J Rev ed Judgm § 657. For the purpose of a ground of equitable relief against a judgment, fraud which has prevented a party from having a trial, from presenting all his case to the court, or has so affected the manner in which the judgment was taken that there has not been a fair submission of the controversy to the court. Farley v Davis, 10 Wash 2d 62, 116 P2d 263, 155 ALR 1302. For the purpose of serving as a defense to an action on a foreign judgment, any fraudulent conduct of the successful party in the foreign action, practiced directly and affirmatively on the defeated party outside the actual trial of the case, whereby he was prevented from presenting his side of the cause fully and fairly. Britton v Gannon (Okla) 285 P2d 407, 55 ALR2d 667. Actual fraud characterized by an evil intent to take undue advantage of another person for the purpose of actually and knowingly defrauding him. Flood v Templeton, 152 Cal 148, 92 P 78.

extum (ex'tum). Thence.

ex turpi causa (ex ter'pī kâ'za). A claim, asserted as a cause of action, which arises from the transgression of a positive law. 11 Am J2d B & N § 1001.

Ex turpi causa non oritur actio (ex ter'pī kâ'za non ō'ri-ter ak'she-ō). No cause of action can arise out of an immoral (or illegal) inducement (or consideration). 1 Am J2d Actions § 51.

Ex turpi contractu actio non oritur (ex ter'pī kontrak'tu ak'she-ō non ō'ri-ter). From an immoral (or illegal) contract no action can arise. Anheuser-Busch Brewing Asso. v Mason, 44 Minn 318, 46 NW 558.

exuere patriam (ex-u'e-re pa'tri-am). To renounce allegiance to the government of one's country; to expatriate one's self.

exulare (ex-u-lā're). To exile; to banish.

ex una parte (ex ū'na par'te). Of or from one part or side.

Ex uno disces omnes (ex ū'nō dis'sēz om'nēz). From one thing you can find out all.

ex usu (eks ū'sū). From the use; by using.

ex utraque parte (ex ut-rā'kwe par'te). From both sides.

ex utrisque parentibus conjuncti (ex ūt-ris'kwe paren'ti-bus kon-junk'tī). Connected with both parents; related by ties of full blood.

ex vessel. See **ex ship**.

ex vi aut metu (ex vī ât me'tu). By or from force or fear.

ex visceribus (ex vis-se'ri-bus). From the bowels; from the vitals.

ex visceribus testamenti (ex vis-se'ri-bus tes'tamentī). From the vitals of the will, that is, from the whole will; a rule of construction. Homer v Shelton, 48 Mass (2 Met) 194, 213.

ex visitatione Dei (ex vi-si-tā-she-ō'ne Dē'ī). By the visitation of God; by divine dispensation.

ex visu scriptionis (ex vī'sū skrip-she-ō'nis). From the sight of the writing; from seeing the person write.

ex vi termini (ex vi ter'mi-nī). By the force of the term; by the intrinsic import of the term or expression.
See **right of way ex vi termini**.

ex vi terminorum (eks vī tėr-mi-nor'um). By the force of the terms or words used: that is, by their intrinsic import.

ex voluntate (ex vo-lun-tā'te). Emanating from the will; voluntary; voluntarily; of one's own volition.

ey. Water; a place surrounded by water; an island.

eye. See **sight**.

eyesight. See **sight**.

eyewitness. A person who testifies to what he has seen. Ellis v Interstate Business Men's Acci. Asso. 183 Iowa 1279, 168 NW 212.
A person may be an eyewitness to his own injury. Lewis v Brotherhood Acci. Co. 194 Mass 1, 79 NE 802.

eyewitness provision. A clause in an accident insurance policy which requires proof of the accidental character of an injury by eyewitnesses other than the insured or claimant. 29A Am J Rev ed Ins § 1933.

eyewitness testimony. Testimony by a witness to what he has seen.
See **eyewitness**.

eygne (ī-gn). The eldest.

eyott (āt). A small island; an islet.

eyre (ār). A journey; the journey of a judge from place to place upon his circuit.
See **justices in eyre**.

eyrer. To journey; to travel.

F

f. Abbreviation for Fahrenheit, also for fathom. The brand by which the hand of a convicted felon was marked in olden times in England.

F. A. A. Abbreviation of free from all average.
See **free from all average**.

fabricare (fa-bri-kā're). To fabricate; to falsify; to forge; to make false coins; to counterfeit.

fabricate (fab'ri-kāt). To construct, especially by assembling parts. To falsify; to forge; to make false coins; to counterfeit. 20 Am J2d Counterf § 1.

fabrication. Making or preparing; deception by making up a story or tale. 20 Am J2d Counterf § 1.

fabric lands. Lands which were given for the erection and upkeep of churches and cathedrals.

fabrika (fa'bri-ka). The coinage of money.

fabula (fā'bu-la). An agreement; a covenant; a contract.

face (fās). The matter which appears on document, pleading, statute, writ or other written or printed instrument, without explanation or addition.

face amount certificate company. An investment company. 15 USC § 80a-4.

face amount of policy. The amount of straight life insurance provided by a life insurance policy, without giving effect to additional indemnity provisions. Pierce v Businessmen's Assur. Co. (Mo) 333 SW2d 97.

face of instrument. The side of an instrument upon which the terms and conditions appear.

face of insurance policy. The entire insurance contract contained in the policy. Julius v Metropolitan Life Ins. Co. 299 Ill 343, 132 NE 435, 17 ALR 956.

face of judgment. The sum or amount for which the judgment was rendered, without interest. Osgood v Bringolf, 32 Iowa 265, 270.

face of mine. See **working face**.

face of the record. The entire record of a case in court up to the point at which reference is made to it. State v Haines, 51 La Ann 731, 25 So 372.

facere (fā'se-re). To do; to make; to act; to cause.

face to face. The confrontation of a witness in court with the opportunity to cross-examine him. State v Heffernan, 24 SD 1, 118 NW 1027.

face value. The full amount to be paid, principal and interest, according to the terms of the instrument. Anno: 91 ALR 30, 31. The par value of corporate stock which has a par value. Goodyear Tire & Rubber Co. v United States, 273 US 100, 71 L Ed 558, 47 S Ct 263.
For the purpose of computing a stock transfer tax, the "face value" of the shares transferred is to be determined from the provisions of the corporate charter, not from the face of the certificate. Goodyear Tire & Rubber Co. v United States, 273 US 100, 71 L Ed 558, 47 S Ct 263.

facias (fā'she-as). You do it; you cause.
See **exigi facias**; **extendi facias**; **fieri facias**; **levari facias**; **replegiari facias**; **scire facias**; **venire facias**.

facie. See **ex facie**.

facie curiae. See **in facie curiae**.

faciendo (fā-she-en'dō). In doing; in making; in causing.

facies (fā'shi-ēz). Same as **face**.

facilitate (fạ-sil'i-tāt). To make easy or less difficult; to free from difficulty or impediment; as to facilitate the execution of a task or the completion of a trip. Pon Wing Quong v United States (CA9 Cal) 111 F2d 751.

facilitation. Assistance rendering a task easier of accomplishment.
See **facilitate**.

facilities. Appliances and services necessary or convenient in keeping house or operating a business or industry. Utilities; conveniences; restrooms. Equipment of a carrier.
As the word was at one time used in promissory notes which provided that they were payable in "facilities," the word was understood to mean certain notes of some of the banks in the state of Connecticut, which were made payable in two years after the close of the war of 1812. Springfield Bank v Merrick, 14 Mass (14 Tyng) 322.

facilities tax. A tax upon the amount paid or collected for the use and enjoyment of certain facilities and services. 26 USC §§ 4231 et seq.

facility. Singular of **facilities**. A state of mental unsoundness warranting the appointment of a guardian or other legal intervention.

facility of payment clause. An appointment by the parties to an insurance contract of persons or classes of persons who may receive payment of the benefits or proceeds accruing under the contract, give receipt therefor to the insurer so as to discharge it from liability, and thereafter hold the amount received for the benefit of the person ultimately entitled thereto. Anno: 166 ALR 12. Better known is the clause in industrial life insurance policies whereby the insurer is permitted to discharge its liability for the proceeds by payment to the beneficiary named or to any other person appearing to the insurer to be equitably entitled to the proceeds. Annos: 28 ALR 1350; 49 ALR 939.

facility of transportation. A means of transportation, an automobile, a motorcycle, even a riding horse. Bernardine v New York, 249 NY 361, 62 NE2d 604, 161 ALR 364.

Facinus quos inquinat aequat (fa'si-nus quōs in-qui'-nat ē'quat). An evil deed or a crime levels those whom it contaminates.

Facio ut des (fā'she-ō ut dēz). (Civil law.) I perform so that you are to pay. This was the third species of consideration under the civil law and signified an agreement to perform anything for a price, either specifically mentic.ned, or left to the determination of the law to set a value on it. See 2 Bl Comm 445.

Facio, ut facias (fā'she-ō, ut fā'she-as). (Civil law.) I perform so that you are to perform. This was the second species of consideration under the civil law and signified a man's agreement to do work for another if the other will do work for him; or to do any other positive acts on both sides. Or, it may be to forbear on one side on consideration of something done on the other. See 2 Bl Comm 444.

facit (fā'sit). He or it does or acts.

Facit ex curvo rectum, ex nigro album (fa'sit ex kur'vō rek'tum, ex ni'gro al'bum). It renders straight that which is crooked and white that which is black. Jeter v Hewitt (US) 22 How 352, 364, 16 L Ed 345, 348.

facsimile (fak-sim'i-lē). An exact and precise copy of anything. An exact reproduction, for example, the signature reproduced by rubber stamp. 11 Am J2d B & N § 210.

fact. A deed; an act; that which exists; that which is real; that which is true, an actuality; that which took place, not that which might or might not have occurred. Churchill v Meade, 92 Or 626, 182 P 368.

facta (fak'ta). Facts; deeds; acts.

Facta sunt potentiora verbis (fak'ta sunt po-ten-she-ō'ra ver'bis). Acts or deeds are more powerful than words.

Facta tenent multa quae fieri prohibentur (fak'ta te'-nent mul'ta kwē fī'e-rī prō-hi-ben'ter). Deeds contain many things, the doing of which is prohibited.

fact-finding body. The board or body of an administrative agency in which is vested the power of decision. Wilson & Co. v NLRB (CA7 Ill) 126 F2d 114.

fact findings. See findings.

fact in issue. The fact upon which the plaintiff proceeds by his action, and which the defendant controverts in his pleadings. Garwood v Garwood, 29 Cal 514.

factions. Groups within a body which are united in opinion and endeavor, such as factions in a church. 45 Am J1st Reli Soc § 44.

factio testamenti (fak'she-ō tes-ta-men'tī). (Roman law.) The making of a will,—the ability to make a will.

facto (fak'tō). In fact; in deed.
See **ex facto; ex post facto; ipso facto.**

fact of general notoriety. A fact of a public, as distinguished from a private, nature; historical facts, not within the memory of living men, but provable by historical works of deceased authors of established reputation. Bixby v Omaha & Council Bluffs Ry. & Bridge Co. 105 Iowa 293, 75 NW 182.

factor. A person employed specially to receive and take possession of goods from a principal and to sell them for a compensation called "factorage" or "commission." Sometimes called a consignee or commission merchant. Under some definitions, the term includes an agent empowered to purchase, as well as to sell. 22 Am J2d Fact § 1.
See **del credere factor; interim factor; supercargo.**

factorage. Commissions paid to a factor for his services as such. 22 Am J2d Fact § 1.

factorage financing. A method of financing wherein the security arrangement leaves the security more or less in possession of, and subject to sale or handling by, the debtor, as part of a going business; usually substitutions of security from time to time are required to keep the collateral adequate in amount. 9 Am J2d Bankr § 965.

factoring process. A synonym of garnishment process. 6 Am J2d Attach § 2.
See **garnishment.**

factorizing. A proceeding more commonly known as garnisheeing. Cross v Brown, Steese & Clarke, 19 RI 220, 248, 33 A 147.

See **garnishment.**

factorizing process. See **factorizing.**

Factors' Acts. An English statute and its counterpart in many American states, the object of which is to make a factor's possession of goods and merchandise such evidence of ownership as to enable him to do all acts which the true owner might, thus making the owner responsible for the factor's acts and protecting bona fide purchasers in any transaction fairly effected with the apparent owner. 22 Am J2d Fact § 53.

factor's lien. The general lien which a factor has on goods of his principal in his possession, their proceeds and securities taken for the price, for advances, expenses, and commissions, and extending to the general balance of his accounts, to debts connected with the agency, which the factor has undertaken as surety or for the accommodation of the principal, and to interest on subsequent advances, but not to debts outside the agency. 22 Am J2d Fact §§ 20, 21.

factory. A place where an industrial operation is conducted; a place where mechanical power is used. 58 Am J1st Workm Comp § 117; a place where natural substances are converted to articles of value and use. 51 Am J1st Tax § 592. A mill, workshop, or other manufacturing establishment. Anno: 16 ALR 539. Any place where goods or products are manufactured or repaired, cleaned or sorted. Ritchie v People, 155 Ill 98, 40 NE 454. A settlement maintained by factors for trading.
See **manufacturing establishment.**

factory weight. The weight of a motor vehicle as it is driven or hauled from the factory, often taken as the weight for the purpose of fixing the amount of a license or registration fee; sometimes the measure of fees charged motor vehicles used in the business of transportation. Dixie Ohio Exp. Co. v State Revenue Com. 306 US 72, 83 L Ed 495, 59 S Ct 435.

fact questions. See **questions of fact.**

facts. See **fact.**

factum (fak'tum). The fact; the existence; the doing; the making.
See **ante-factum; factum of will.**

Factum a judice quod ad ejus officium non spectat non ratum est (fak'tum a jū'di-se quod ad ē'jus of-fi'she-um non spek'tat non rā'tum est). The act of a judge which does not belong to his office is void.

Factum a judice quod ad officium ejus non pertinet ratum non est (fak'tum a jū'di-se quod ad of-fi'she-um ē'jus non per'ti-net rā'tum non est). The act of a judge which does not pertain to his office is void.

Factum cuique suum, non adversario, nocere debet (fak'tum kī'kwe su'um, non ad-ver-sā'ri-ō, no-sē're de'bet). A person's act ought to prejudice himself and not his adversary.

Factum infectum fieri nequit (fak'tum in-fek'tum fī'e-rī ne'quit). A thing which has been done cannot be undone.

Factum negantis nulla probatio (fak'tum ne-gan'tis nul'la pro-bā'she-o). The denial of a fact requires no proof; he who denies a fact need not prove his denial.

Factum non dicitur quod non perseverat (fak'tum non di'si-ter quod non per-se-vē'rat). A thing is not spoken of as done which is not finished.

factum of will (fak'tum ov wil). The making of a will, not the mere signing and publication, but acting with knowledge of the contents of the instrument and its effect as a disposition of property. Dorsey v Sheppard (Md) 12 Gill & J 192.

factum probandum (fak'tum pro-ban'dum). A fact to be proved.

factum probans (fak'tum prō'banz). A proving fact; a fact of probative value; a fact tending to establish the existence of another fact.

Factum reputabitur pro voluntate (fak'tum re-pu-tā'bi-ter prō vo-lun-tā'te). The act will be considered according to the intent.

Factum unius alteri nocere non debet (fak'tum ū'ni-us al'te-rī no-sē're non de'bet). The act of one person should not prejudice another.

Facultas probationum non est angustanda (fa-kul'tās prō-bā-she-ō'num non est an-gus-tan'da). The right of offering proof is not to be curtailed.

faculty. The ability to perform a particular act. The operation of one of the senses, as the faculty of speech or hearing. The authority vested in an agent, or other representative, by his principal or other constituent. The teaching staff, professors, associate professors, assistant professors, and instructors of a university, college, or school. 15 Am J2d Colleges § 15.
See **allegation of faculties; court of faculties; husband's faculties.**

faculty of advocates. An association of lawyers practicing in the highest courts of Scotland.

faggot (fag'ǫt). The ancient form of punishment of a person by burning him alive.

faggot votes (fag'ǫt vōts). Votes cast by persons who were merely nominal owners of the amount of land necessary to qualify them as electors; sham or illegal votes.

faida. A spirit of revenge; malice.

fail (fāl). To refuse; to neglect; to become insolvent.
Although the word has in law the same general meaning as "refuse," as where the condition to be performed depends on the will of the party who fails or refuses, yet where the condition does not depend upon the party's will, but upon the will of those whom he cannot control, there is a manifest distinction. One is an act of the will, the other may be an act of inevitable necessity. Taylor v Mason (US) 9 Wheat 325, 344, 6 L Ed 101, 106.
The word sometimes has the meaning of to become worthless, but it may also mean to become worthless in part or to a certain extent, as where consideration "fails." Shirk v Neible, 156 Ind 66, 59 NE 281.

failed bank. A bank which is insolvent, or has failed to meet its obligations to depositors and other creditors, and has been taken over by the banking department for liquidation and closing of its affairs. Godfrey v Terry (US) 7 Otto 171, 24 L Ed 944; 10 Am J2d Banks §§ 754 et seq.
See **insolvency of bank.**

failing circumstances. The circumstances of an individual or a business wherein the debts become increasingly difficult of payment; the approach of insolvency. Utley v Smith, 24 Conn 290.

failing of record. The failure of a party to produce a record after pleading it.

faillite (fī-yĕt'). (French.) Failure; bankruptcy; insolvency.

failure. Inability to meet obligations as they become due; insolvency. Boyce & Henry v Ewart, 14 SC Eq (Rice) 126, 140.
See **failing circumstances.**

failure of bank. See **failed bank.**

failure of consideration. The circumstance or combination of circumstances under which the consideration for a contract, which was sufficient at the inception of the contract, has become worthless, has ceased to exist, or has been extinguished, whether by nonperformance or an innate defect in the thing to be given. 11 Am J2d B & N § 237; 17 Am J2d Contr § 397.

failure of evidence. See **total failure of evidence.**

failure of issue. See **definite failure of issue; indefinite failure of issue.**

failure of proof. Want of proof of a fact alleged or proof which departs so far from the cause of action or defense pleaded that it may fairly be said that the facts alleged remain unproved. E. B. Ryan Co. v Russel, 52 Mont 596, 161 P 307.

failure to file a tax return. Want of a properly executed income tax return within the time prescribed by law for filing; not the filing of a return which is incorrect in reference to the amount of the tax. Plunkett v Commissioner (CA1) 118 F2d 644.

failure to make delivery. Failure to make any delivery or, for some purposes, a misdelivery. 14 Am J2d Car § 582. The failure of the seller of personal property to deliver the goods to the purchaser in accord with the terms of the contract, fairly construed. 46 Am J1st Sales §§ 161 et seq.

failure to prosecute. See **want of prosecution.**

failure to provide. See **nonsupport.**

faint action (fānt ak'shǫn). Same as **feigned action.**

fainting spell. Temporary loss of consciousness caused by want of sufficient blood supply for the brain; not a disease or bodily infirmity. 29 Am J Rev ed Ins § 749.

faint pleading (fānt plē'ding). A false or collusive manner of pleading, with the purpose of deceiving persons who are not parties to the action.

fair. An exhibition of industrial or agricultural products, sometimes of the artistic and mechanical products of a school, a state hospital, or orphans' home, coupled with various amusements and entertainments. In an old and primary sense of the term, a market for the buying and selling of exhibited goods, livestock, and other articles. State v Long, 48 Ohio St 509, 510.
See **agricultural fair.**

fair and equitable. A term of art, developed in corporate reorganizations in equity receiverships and applied as well in reorganizations under the Bankruptcy Act and other statutes, to characterize the necessity, in formulating and adopting plans of reorganization, of according to creditors and classes of creditors the priorities to which they are entitled by contract and to stockholders of one class the superior position to which they are entitled by the charter of the corporation over stockholders of another class. Securities & Exchange Com. v United States Realty & Improv. Co. 310 US 434, 84 L Ed 1293, 60 S Ct 1044; Otis & Co. v Securities

& Exch. Com. 323 US 624, 89 L Ed 511, 65 S Ct 483.

fair and impartial trial. A guaranty of due process, requiring a competent and impartial tribunal, the right to be represented by counsel, the right to cross-examine adverse witnesses, the right to offer testimony on one's own behalf, and the right to have such advance notice of trial as will permit preparation for trial. 21 Am J2d Crim L §§ 221, 222. A jury trial in an action of such nature that a party is entitled to a jury trial, as in a prosecution for desertion and nonsupport, unless he has voluntarily and knowingly waived such right. 23 Am J2d Desert § 43.

See **fair trial.**

fair and legal. A redundant expression, since the word "fair" can add no force to the word "legal." Wood v Strother, 76 Cal 545.

fair and true value. Market value, and in the absence of a standard market for the particular kind of property involved, a fair value as determined by reference to all relevant facts in evidence. State v Wagner, 233 Mich 241, 46 NW2d 676, 23 ALR2d 762.

fair à scavoir (fare a savwar). To make to know. Ray Consol. Copper Co. v United States, 268 US 373, 69 L Ed 1003, 45 S Ct 526.

fair average value. For the purpose of assessing capital stock of a corporation for excise tax, a value determined in part according to the fair net value of the assets of the corporation, not entirely by the value of the aggregate shares of the stock.

fair book value. A contract price for corporate stock to be determined by ascertaining the net worth of all the assets and deducting therefrom the liabilities, without allowance of more than a nominal amount for good will. Early v Moore, 249 Mass 223, 144 NE 108, 33 ALR 362.

fair cash value. Actual cash value. The price which the property in question will bring in a fair market, after fair and reasonable efforts have been made to find the purchaser who will give the highest price; the fair or reasonable cash price for which the property can be sold in the market. Birmingham Fire Ins. Co. v Pulver, 126 Ill 329, 18 NE 804.

The term as used in a statute providing that, upon a merger or consolidation of corporations, a dissenting stockholder shall be entitled to receive a "fair cash value" of his shares, means the intrinsic worth of his stock, which is to be arrived at after an appraisal of all the elements of value. Adams v United States Distributing Corp. 184 Va 134, 34 SE2d 244, 162 ALR 1227.

fair comment. Comment on a matter of public interest which is confined to comment on things and the acts of persons and does not extend to attacks upon personal character or to imputing immoral or corrupt motives. 33 Am J1st L & S § 162. Any criticism of a book or other literary production which does not go beyond the critic's honest opinion, does not misstate any material fact contained in the work, and does not attack the character of the author. 33 Am J1st L & S § 164. Criticism of dramatic productions and public entertainers based upon facts and not actuated by malice or evil purpose, however hostile and pointed it may be in holding the subject up to ridicule. 33 Am J1st L & S § 165.

fair competition. A phrase of the National Industrial Recovery Act enacted during the first administration of President Franklin D. Roosevelt but held unconstitutional by the United States Supreme Court, meaning open, equitable, and just competition, fair to competitors and to customers. United States v National Garment Co. (DC Mo) 10 F Supp 104.

fair consideration. An adequate, just, or proper consideration; something more than a nominal consideration. Rude v Levy, 43 Colo 482, 96 P 560. A consideration fairly proportioned to the money, property, or services furnished by the contracting party. Manello v Bornstine, 44 Wash 769, 270 P2d 494, 45 ALR2d 494. The discharge of an antecedent debt, provided it is the obligation of the contracting party. Hansen v Cramer, 39 Cal 2d 321, 245 P2d 1059, 30 ALR2d 1204.

As defined by the Bankruptcy Act for the purpose only of that portion of the statute dealing with the avoidance of fraudulent transfers, a consideration given for the property or obligation of a debtor is "fair" (1) when, in good faith, in exchange and as a fair equivalent therefor, property is transferred or an antecedent debt is satisfied, or (2) when such property or obligation is received in good faith to secure a present advance or antecedent debt in an amount not disproportionately small as compared with the value of the property or obligation obtained. 9 Am J2d Bankr § 1113.

fair, concise summary. A condensation which is accurate and does not destroy the substance. Sears v Treasurer & Receiver General, 327 Mass 310, 98 NE2d 621.

fair construction. A reasonable, rational, and just construction of a contract. 17 Am J2d Contr § 252.

fair criticism. See **fair comment.**

fair dealing. Good faith (this index).

faire. To do; to make; to act.

fair employment practices legislation. Statutes intended to prohibit employers from discriminating in the hiring of employees on the ground of race, color, creed, or national origin. 31 Am J Rev ed Lab § 12.

fair enjoyment. The measure of the right of the dominant owner in the use of an easement; a right of use consistent with the purpose and character of the easement and also with the correlative right of the servient owner to use the premises for any purpose which does not interfere with the lawful use of the easement. Unversagt v Miller, 306 Mich 260, 10 NW2d 849; Malher v Brumder, 92 Wis 477, 66 NW 502.

fair knowledge. Ordinary knowledge; reasonable knowledge. Jones v Angell, 95 Ind 376, 382.

Fair Labor Standards Act. A federal statute, commonly known as the Wage and Hour Law, regulating the hours and wages of employees engaged in interstate commerce or in the production of goods for interstate commerce. 29 USC §§ 201 et seq.

fairly. Impartially; in a manner free from prejudice, bias or improper influence.

The word is not synonymous with "truly." Language may be truly, yet most unfairly repeated. The answer of a witness may be truly written down, yet it may convey a meaning quite different from that which the witness intended to convey, and did convey. Moreover, language may be fairly reported, yet not in accordance with strict truth. Lawrence v Finch, 17 NJ Eq 234, 239.

fairly and legally. In good faith. People v Mancuso, 255 NY 463, 175 NE 177, 76 ALR 514 (construing term respecting fraudulent insolvency of corporation).

fair market price. Market value; clear market value. 28 Am J Rev ed Inher T § 359. The result of the opposing views of the willing seller not compelled to sell and a willing purchaser not required to buy. Vale v Du Pont, 37 Del 254, 182 A 668, 103 ALR 946.

See **clear market value**; **fair market value**.

fair market value. Actual value or value in money. Re Patton, 227 Wis 407, 278 NW 866, 117 ALR 140. That which property will sell for as between one who wants to purchase and one who wants to sell; in the absence of a ready market and a market price, a constructive value determined upon an appropriate basis selected by the court. 28 Am J Rev ed Inher T § 609.

See **clear market value**.

fairness of plan. See **fair and equitable**.

fair-play men. A court which was held in Pennsylvania before the Revolutionary War.

fair pleader (făr plē'dĕr). A prohibition addressed to the sheriff directing him not to take a fine for a bad pleading.

fair pleading (făr plē'ding). Pleading fairly or aptly, or to the purpose.

fair preponderance of evidence. A characterization of the degree of proof required in some civil cases, particularly in reference to proof of fraud. 37 Am J2d Fraud §§ 468, 470. Not the larger number of witnesses, but the probability of truth. Schargel v United Electric Light & Power Co. 127 Misc 24, 25, 215 NYS 217, 218.

See **preponderance of evidence**.

fair return. An expression much employed in the fixing of public utility rates, meaning a reasonable return on the value of the property used in rendering the services. 52 Am J1st Teleg & T § 57. A reasonable return on the investment of a public utility, determinable only by the exercise of sound judgment and common sense, being a matter of fair approximation, not capable of exact mathematical demonstration. 43 Am J1st Pub Util § 156.

The term has a double aspect, one legislative and the other judicial. In the judicial aspect it is the equivalent of nonconfiscatory. Judicially, a rate is unreasonable only when it yields a return less than the minimum which the capital invested may of right demand. In the legislative aspect, the return may exceed such amount; for the legislature or the commission may add to it to carry out some public policy rates which are substantially higher than the line between validity and unconstitutionality properly may be deemed to be just and reasonable, and not excessive or extortionate. Idaho Power Co. v Thompson (DC Idaho) 19 F2d 547.

fair sale. A sale conducted with fairness as respects the rights and interests of the parties affected by it. Lalor v M'Carthy, 24 Minn 417, 419. A judicial sale conducted according to law at auction at which all persons have the right to appear and bid. 30A Am J Rev ed Jud S § 67.

Fair Sales Act. A statute prohibiting sales of commodities below cost, except under particular circumstances. Anno: 118 ALR 506, supplemented 128 ALR 1126.

Fair Trade Acts. Statutes which remove or except price-maintenance agreements of the vertical type, that is, agreements between the producer and distributors of trademarked, tradenamed, or branded articles, from the operation of the rules and provisions relating to monopolies and restraints of trade, thereby authorizing and protecting such agreements. 52 Am J1st Tradem § 173.

fair trial. A legal trial; a trial conducted in all material things in substantial conformity to law. People v Wolf, 183 NY 464, 472, 76 NE 592, 594. In a criminal case, a trial before an impartial judge, an honest jury, and in an atmosphere of judicial calm. 21 Am J2d Crim L § 235. A trial, not only with observance of the naked forms of law, but in a recognition and just appreciation of its principles. Sunderland v United States (CA8 Neb) 19 F2d 202. A trial according to law, not necessarily free from all error, but from substantial error. State v Schimsky, 243 Minn 533, 69 NW2d 89; People v Becker, 210 NY 274, 311, 104 NE 396, 409.

The right of one charged with the commission of a crime to a fair trial does not embrace the right to be tried by any particular judge or jury, but is enough if the jury is impartial and the judge one whose neutrality is indifferent to every factor in the trial but that of administering justice. State ex rel. Brown v Dewell, 131 Fla 566, 179 So 695, 115 ALR 857.

See **fair and impartial trial**.

fair use doctrine. The principle which entitles a person to use copyrighted material in a reasonable manner, including the use of the mere theme or idea, without the consent of the copyright owner. 18 Am J2d Copyr § 109.

fair valuation. For the purpose of determining "insolvency" within the definition provided by the Bankruptcy Act (Bankr Act § (19); 11 USC § 1 (19)), the fair market value of the property as between one who wants to buy and one who wants to sell, or the value that can be made promptly effective by the owner of the property for payment of debts. Nicolai-Neppach Co. v Smith, 154 Or 450, 58 P2d 1016, 60 P2d 979, 107 ALR 1124.

See **fair value**.

fair value. For the purpose of, and as a base for, fixing the rates of a public utility: —the present value of the property of the utility as determined, not by formula, such as original cost, prudent investment, or cost of reproduction, but by consideration of all relevant factors entering into the worth of the property at the time of the inquiry made for rate-fixing. 43 Am J1st Pub Util § 105. As used in a statute permitting dissenting stockholders to obtain the "fair value" of their stock: —the intrinsic worth of the stock, which is to be arrived at after an appraisal of all the elements of value. Lucas v Pembroke Water Co. 205 Va 84, 135 SE2d 147.

See **fair and true value**; **fair average value**; **fair book value**; **fair cash value**; **fair market value**; **fair valuation**.

fairway. The navigable channel of a river, gulf, or other body of water, variously called "thalweg," "main channel," "midway." Louisiana v Mississippi, 202 US 1, 49, 50 L Ed 913, 930. Any one of the parts of a golf course, lying between a tee and a putting green, where the grass is cut fairly short.

faisant (fĕ-zōn). Same as **feasant**.

fait (făt). A fact; a deed; an act; an act done. See **en fait**.

fait enrolle (fāt ān-rōl). A deed which has been enrolled.

faith. The assent of the mind to what is stated or put forward by another; trust or confidence in the veracity of another. Patzwald v United States, 7 Okla 232, 54 P 458.
See **abiding faith**; **articles of faith**; **bad faith**; **good faith**; **religion**.

faithful. Noun: Those who believe in and sincerely practice the principles of a religious faith. Adjective: In temporal affairs, diligent, without unnecessary delay; as a faithful officer, a faithful servant, in applying to their duties. Den ex dem. Perry v Thompson, 16 NJ L 72, 73.
The guaranty of the "faithful" discharge of the duties of a county treasurer, contained in the bond required of, and furnished by, him is a guaranty, not only of personal honesty, but also of competency, skill and diligence in the discharge of the treasurer's duties. The word is held to imply that the bonded person has assumed that measure of responsibility laid on him by law, had no bond been given; and everything is unfaithfulness which the law does not excuse. Thurston County use of Vesely v Chmelka, 138 Neb 696, 294 NW 857, 132 ALR 1077.

faith healing. The restoration, or attempted restoration, of health by prayer and religious faith. 41 Am J1st Phys & S § 30.
See **Christian Science**.

faitours (fā'tọrs). Vagrants; vagabonds; idle persons.

fake. Noun: A swindler; an imposter. A trick employed to obtain money. Midland Publishing Co. v Implement Trade Journal Co. 108 Mo App 223, 83 SW 298. A false pretense. Adjective: Spurious, counterfeit.

falcare (fal-kā're). To cut; to mow.

falcidia (fal-si'di-a). The falcidian part or portion of an ancestor's estate; that is, the one fourth part of it, of which he could not, under the Falcidian Law of Rome, deprive his heir by his will.

falcidia lex. Same as **Falcidian Law**.

Falcidian Law. A Roman statute, enacted in 714 A. D., which restricted the disposition of property by will to the extent that one fourth of the property of a testator, who was the father of a family, was reserved from the exercise of testamentary power in such manner as to deprive the heir or heirs thereof. United States v Perkins, 163 US 625, 41 L Ed 287, 16 S Ct 1073.

Falcidian portion. The one-fourth part of a father's property which, under the Falcidian Law of Rome, he could not dispose of by will. United States v Perkins, 163 US 625, 41 L Ed 287, 16 S Ct 1073.
See **Falcidian Law**.

faldae cursus (fal'dē ker'sus). A sheep trail.

faldage (fāl'dāj). The right of the lord of the manor to have the sheep of his tenant manure his land; the term was also applied to the fee paid by the tenant to the lord for exemption from the service of thus manuring.

faldata (fāl-dā'ta). A flock of sheep.

fald-fee (fāld'-fē). Same as **faldage**.

faldsoca (fald-sō'ka). Same as **faldage**.

faldworth. A person who had attained an age which qualified him to be one of the ten of a decennary.

falk-land (fâk-land). Same as **folk-land**.

fall. Noun: The autumn season. A sudden dropping from a higher to a lower position. Verb: To come down, to move down involuntarily. To descend, as in the devolution of property from ancestor to heir. M'Cullough's Heirs v Gilmore, 11 Pa 370, 373.

fall due. To become due. White v Leyden, 112 Neb 774, 201 NW 637.

falling of the womb. See **prolapsus uteri**.

fallo (fahl'yo). (Spanish.) A final judgment or decree.

fall of hammer. The completion of the sale of an article at an auction; the signal that the bidding is closed. 7 Am J2d Auct §§ 20, 21.

fall of land. A parcel of land equivalent to the one hundred and sixtieth part of an acre.

fall of soil. Caving or washing. 1 Am J2d Adj L § 43.

fallout. The dropping of radioactive particles following an atomic explosion.

fall out. The words of command given by the officer or noncommissioned officer in charge of a military formation to release the men from the formation.

fallow land (fal'ō land). Land which has been ploughed up but which has been left unseeded in order to allow it to recuperate its fertility.

falsa demonstratio (fal'sa de-mon-strā'she-ō). False or erroneous description.

Falsa demonstratione legatum non perimi (fal'sa de-mon-strā-she-ō'ne lē-gā'tum non per'i-mī). An erroneous description will not nullify a legacy.
It was a rule of the civil law, that a legacy should not perish by reason of a false description, but the statute of wills modifies the maxim to some extent. Roman Catholic Orphan Asylum v Emmons (NY) 3 Bradf 144, 149.

Falsa demonstratio non nocet, cum de corpore constat (fal'sa de-mon-strā'she-ō non no'set, kum dē kor'po-re kon'stat). An erroneous description is harmless, when it is clear as to the person intended. 57 Am J1st Wills §§ 1048, 1199.

Falsa grammatica non vitiat chartum (fal'sa gramma'ti-ka non vi'she-at kar'tum). Faulty grammar will not vitiate an instrument.

falsa moneta (fal'sa mo-nē'ta). False money; counterfeit money.

Falsa orthographia, sive falsa grammatica, non vitiat concessionem (fal'sa or-thō-gra'fi-a, si've fal'sa gram-ma'ti-ka, non vi'she-at kon-se-she-ō'nem). Neither faulty spelling nor faulty grammar will vitiate a grant.

falsare (fal-sā're). To falsify; to forge; to make false coins.
See **counterfeiting**; **forgery**.

falsarius (fal-sā'ri-us). A counterfeiter; a forger.
See **counterfeiting**; **forgery**.

false. Sometimes meaning untrue, at other times, designedly untrue, implying an intention to deceive, as where it is an element of actionable fraud. 37 Am J2d Fraud § 2. Unlawful. Mahan v Adam, 144 Md 355, 124 A 901.

false account. An account which is morally false,—known to be untrue. Putnam v Osgood, 51 NH 192, 207.
See **false oath or account**.

false action (fâls ak'shọn). Same as **feigned action**.

false advertising. Untrue and fraudulent statements and representations made by way of advertising a product or a service. 3 Am J2d Advertg § 2.

false affidavit. The statutory offense of perjury in an affidavit authorized by law. 41 Am J1st Perj § 26. A false claim against the government, such having reference to the form of the paper rather than its legal character, so that an affidavit may be "false," irrespective of the absence of an oath administered by an officer qualified to administer oaths. Williams v Territory, 13 Ariz 27, 108 P 243.

false and fraudulent. Having the dual quality of falsity and intent to deceive. 37 Am J2d Fraud § 2.

false appeal. An older English term for unsuccessful appeal of felony. See 4 Bl Comm 316.

false answer. A criminal offense in wilfully giving a false answer to a question propounded by a taker of the federal census. 14 Am J2d Census § 9. Perjury by a witness. 41 Am J1st Perj § 2.

false arrest. The unlawful restraint by one person of the physical liberty of another under an asserted legal authority to enforce the processes of the law. 22 Am J2d False Imp §§ 1, 2.

false bank note. A forged paper in the similitude of a bank note, or which on its face appears to be such a note. Williams v Territory, 13 Ariz 27, 108 P 243.

false brand. See misbranding.

false branding. See **misbranding**.

false certificate of acknowledgment. A misstatement of a material fact, especially a misstatement respecting the identity of the person acknowledging. 1 Am J2d Ack §§ 117, 118. Additional elements of negligence and wilful misconduct imposed by statutes rendering the officer taking the acknowledgment liable in civil or criminal aspect. 1 Am J2d Ack §§ 118, 119.

false certificate of citizenship. A certificate of citizenship which is false in its recital of facts. Dolan v United States (CA8 Mo) 133 F 440.

false certification of check. The statutory offense committed by an officer of a national bank in wilfully certifying a check the drawer of which has not on deposit at the time an equal amount of money. Potter v United States, 155 US 438, 39 L Ed 214, 15 S Ct 144.

Although the certification of checks by a national bank without an equivalent amount of money on deposit is in violation of the National Bank Act, a valid debt of the bank is created thereby. Thompson v St. Nicholas Nat. Bank, 146 US 240, 36 L Ed 966, 13 S Ct 66.

false character. A fraudulent letter of recommendation concocted to aid a person who is seeking employment as a servant.

See **false personation**.

false check. A check drawn upon a bank in which the drawer has no funds or which he has no reason to believe will honor it. Williams v Territory, 13 Ariz 27, 108 P 243.

false claims against the government. Claims presented against the government and also allegations, as in income tax returns, which cause pecuniary or property loss to the government. Capone v United States (CA7 Ill) 51 F2d 609, 76 ALR 1534, cert den 284 US 669, 76 L Ed 566, 52 S Ct 44.

See **false affidavit**.

false colors. Colors carried on a vessel different from those of the nation of registration. 56 Am J1st War § 200. An impersonation.

See **impersonation**.

false demonstration. The doctrine that where the description of a person or a thing in a will is made up of more than one part, and one part is true while the other is inexact or false, then, if the part which is true describes the subject or object of the gift with sufficient certainty, the untrue part may be rejected and the gift sustained. 57 Am J1st Wills § 1199.

falsedad (fal-say-dahd'). (Spanish.) Falsity; deception; fraud.

false document. A document purporting to be made by a person who did not make the same, or a document purporting to be made by some person who did not in fact exist. Williams v Territory, 13 Ariz 27, 108 P 243.

See **forgery**.

false entry. Literally, an entry in a book or record which does not speak the truth. A criminal offense by a bank officer or employee in making false entries in reports or statements of the bank with the intent to injure or defraud. 10 Am J2d Banks § 234.

false financial statement. An inaccurate statement by a public accountant, through the medium of the balance sheet, of the financial condition of the client. 1 Am J2d Accts § 16. A ground of opposition to a discharge in bankruptcy where consisting of a materially false statement in writing respecting the financial condition of the bankrupt made or published by the bankrupt in obtaining money or property on credit or in obtaining an extension or renewal of credit. 9 Am J2d Bankr § 701.

falsehood. A lie; a wilful act or declaration contrary to truth, as the more common meaning. Putnam v Osgood, 51 NH 192, 207.

false imprisonment. The unlawful restraint by one person of the physical liberty of another. 22 Am J False Imp § 1. An unlawful violation of the personal liberty of another, whether considered as a tort or a crime. Parrot v Bank of America Nat. Trust & Sav. Asso. 97 Cal App 2d 14, 217 P2d 89, 35 ALR2d 263.

To constitute an unlawful arrest or a false imprisonment, it is not necessary that force be used. The wrong done is one which may be committed by acts or by words, or by both. An unlawful restraint of the person, or an interference with his personal liberty, is essential, but he is deemed to have been put under restraint if words or acts induced a reasonable apprehension that force would be used, if he did not submit. In short, any unlawful exercise or show of force, by which a person is compelled to remain where he does not wish to remain or to go where he does not wish to go is an unlawful arrest. Durgin v Cohen, 168 Minn 77, 209 NW 532.

false instrument. A forged instrument; a counterfeit instrument; an instrument which carries on its face the semblance of that for which it is counterfeited. People v Bendit, 111 Cal 274, 43 P 901.

false judgment. An English writ for the correction or reversal of a judgment of an inferior court not a court of record.

false Latin. A term used in the earlier English cases for the erroneous use of Latin in a court record or a writ.

See **vicious for false Latin**.

falsely. Implying, as the word is used in a statute prescribing the offense of forgery, that the paper or writing in question is not genuine but false or counterfeit. 36 Am J2d Forg § 6. Implying, in reference to the obtaining of money or property by false pretenses, fraud rather than mistake or mere untruth. 32 Am J2d False Pret § 72.

false making. As applied to the crime of forgery, the making of a writing which falsely purports to be the writing of a person other than the writer. People v Bendit, 111 Cal 274, 43 P 901. Not to change or form an instrument to resemble an existing genuine instrument or to represent that it is the act of a genuine and existing obligor, but rather to make an instrument which has no original as such and no genuine maker whose work is copied, although in form it may resemble a type of recognized security. Pines v United States (CA8 Iowa) 123 F2d 825.

false measures. Fraudulently constructed measures or containers for measuring size or capacity, employed to defraud.

false oath. In reference to a bankruptcy proceeding, an intentional untruth stated under oath respecting a matter material to an issue which is itself material. 9 Am J2d Bankr § 694.
See **false swearing; perjury.**

false packed. Goods or commodities, which are sound and merchantable, so packed or loaded, with intent to defraud a purchaser, as to conceal defective or unmerchantable goods or commodities underneath in the same box, basket, barrel, crate, or other container. Garretson v Ferrall, 83 Ga 684, 10 SE 360.

false personation. See **impersonation.**

false pleading. A pleading good in form but sham for want of good faith in making the allegations. 41 Am J1st Pl § 50.
See **sham pleading.**

false pretense. Literally, a false representation of a fact or circumstance calculated to mislead. 32 Am J2d False Pret § 2. Any trick or device whereby the property of another is obtained. 37 Am J2d Fraud § 2. As an essential element of the offense of obtaining property or money by false pretenses, an intentional false statement concerning a material matter of fact, in reliance on which the title or possession of property is relinquished. 32 Am J2d False Pret § 3. As the basis of the exception from discharge in bankruptcy of a liability for obtaining money or property by false pretenses, a false and intentional pretense or representation which induced the creditor to part with money or property to be repaid or paid for later. 9 Am J2d Bankr § 782.
See **false advertising.**

false registry. The term usually applied to the registration of a vessel in violation of the Federal registry statutes which provide that if any certificate of registry or record is fraudulently, or knowingly used for any ship or vessel not then actually entitled to the benefit thereof, according to the true intent of the act, such ship or vessel shall be forfeited to the United States, with her tackle, apparel, and furniture. See 48 Am J1st Ship § 23.

false report. A criminal offense by a corporate officer or director. 19 Am J2d Corp § 1354.
See **false entry.**

false representation. A misrepresentation. 22 Am J2d False Pret § 72.
See **false pretense; representation.**

false return. A criminal offense by a census officer or employee, consisting in wilfully and knowingly making a false certificate or fictitious return. 14 Am J2d Census § 8. A return of process by a sheriff or other officer to whom the writ was issued for service which is false in reference to the acts performed by him in respect of the writ or other facts regarding the service or attempted service which it is his duty to report on the return. 47 Am J1st Sher § 78. An income tax return falsified for the purpose of evading the tax owing by the taxpayer. Capone v United States (CA7 Ill) 51 F2d 609, 76 ALR 1534, cert den 284 US 669, 76 L Ed 566, 52 S Ct 44. The wilful making, subscribing, and verifying of a return which he does not believe to be true and correct by one liable for an internal revenue tax 34 Am J2d Fed Tax ¶ 9386. A return of taxable property falsified with intent to deceive or mislead or with culpable negligence. Ratterman v Ingalls, 48 Ohio St 468, 28 NE 168, 171.

false statement. A statement which is false. For most purposes of the law, a statement which is wilfully false. Fougera & Co. v New York, 224 NY 269, 120 NE 642, 1 ALR 1467, 1473.
See **false representation.**

false suit. Same as **feigned action.**

false swearing. Knowingly and intentionally stating upon oath that which is not true; swearing corruptly, or wilfully and knowingly deposing falsely in a sworn statement before some officer authorized to administer an oath, concerning some fact. Schoenfeld v State, 56 Tex Crim 103, 119 SW 101. Distinguished from perjury under the common law in the respect that false oath in perjury must be made in a judicial proceeding, whereas in false swearing it need not be made in such a proceeding. 41 Am J1st Perj § 3.
As a matter of defense to an insurer, "false swearing" means false statements wilfully made with respect to a material matter and with the intention of deceiving the insurer thereby. 29A Am J Rev ed Ins § 1419.

false teeth. A denture, often referred to as a plate where complete in reference to the number of teeth contained, the preparation and fitting of which, is distinctly a part of the practice of dentistry. Anno: 83 ALR2d 114, 151, 284 et seq.

false testimony. See **false oath; false swearing; perjury.**

false token. A devise for the effecting of a cheat or the obtaining of money by false pretenses; a device having the semblance of authenticity to the public but spurious; a false weight or measure; impersonation of another person. 22 Am J2d False Pret § 20.
See **counterfeit.**

false verdict. A verdict not reached by due deliberation upon the evidence and under the instructions given by the court; a verdict arrived at by chance rather than by understanding, such as a verdict arrived at by drawing lots or casting dice, or a quotient verdict. 53 Am J1st Trial §§ 1029, 1030.

false weights. Weighing devices so constructed as to enable a tradesman to cheat and defraud his customers; a kind of false token. 22 Am J2d False Pret § 22. A crime at common law and under statute in most jurisdictions. 56 Am J1st Wts & L § 46.

falsi crimen (fal′sī kri′men). An offense characterized by fraud through concealment, untruthfulness, false weights, forgery, etc. An offense involving un-

falsifier. A liar. One who wilfully makes untruthful statements. Tawney v Simonson, Whitcomb, & Hurley Co. 109 Minn 341, 124 NW 229.

falsify. To misrepresent the facts. To tell a falsehood. Fraudulently to alter a record or document. To disprove. To disprove the correctness of an account which is prima facie presumed to be correct. Rehill v McTague, 114 Pa 82, 7 A 224.

falsify a judgment. Formally to declare against the court for having rendered a false or erroneous judgment. This liberty was allowed by the Assizes of Jerusalem, but the person availing himself of it was obliged to fight all the members of the court including both judges and suitors, one after another. The privilege was seldom claimed.

falsifying evidence. The offense, distinct from that of perjury or subornation of perjury, of giving, offering, or promising to give, something to a witness or prospective witness in order to induce him to give false testimony. People v Teal, 196 NY 372, 89 NE 1086.

falsing. The crime of falsifying; the crime of forgery.

falsing of dooms. Objecting to, protesting against, or pointing out errors in a sentence or judgment of a court.

falso clamore. See **in misericordia.**

falsonarius (fal-so-nā′ri-us). A forger.

falso retorno brevium (fal′sō re-tor′nō brē′vi-um). A writ against a sheriff who made a false return of his disposition of process.

falsum (fal′sum). Something falsified, counterfeit, or forged.

falsus in uno, falsus in omnibus. False in one thing, false in everything.

The maxim expresses the general principle of law that where a witness has testified falsely to some material matter in a cause, the jury are at liberty to disregard his testimony in other respects, unless it is corroborated by other proof. 58 Am J1st Witn § 872.

fama (fā′mä). A person's good name or reputation; report; rumor.

famacide (fā′ma-sīd). A reputation killer; a defamer; a slanderer.

Fama, fides, et oculus non patiuntur ludum (fā′ma, fī′dēz, et ō′ku-lus non pa-ti-un′ter lū′dum). Good name, faith and eyesight cannot endure deceit.

Fama, quae suspicionem inducit, oriri debet apud bonos et graves, non quidem malevolos et maledicos, sed providas et fide dignas personas, non semel sed saepius, quia clamor minuit et defamatio manifestat (fa′ma, kwē sus-pi-she-ō′nem in-dū′sit, ō-rī′rī de′bet a′pud bo′nōs et gra′vēz, non qui′dem ma-le′vo-los et ma-le-dī′kos, sed prō-vī′das et fī′dē dig′nas per-sō′nas, non se′mel sed sē′pi-us, qui′a klā′mor mi′nu-it et dē-fa-mā′she-ō ma-ni-fes′tat). Rumor, which induces suspicion, ought to have its origin among good and serious minded persons, not indeed from the malevolent and evil-tongued, but from cautious and worthy persons, not once, but often, because praise dies out and evil gossip spreads.

familia (fa-mi′li-a). The family.

familiares regis (fa-mi-li-ā′rēz rē′jis). Familiars of the king,—certain clerks of the English chancery courts were so referred to.

familiarities. Undue liberties taken with a person, whether in speech, by touching him or her with the hands, or by otherwise coming in contact with him or her physically. 6 Am J2d Asslt & B §§ 98, 106.

family. A word of great flexibility, its meaning varying according to the connection in which it appears. Tomlyanovich v Tomlyanovich, 239 Minn 250, 58 NW2d 855, 50 ALR2d 108. Primarily, the collective body of persons who live in one house and under one head or management; secondarily, those persons who are of the same lineage, or have descended from one common progenitor. Dodge v Boston & P. R. Co. 154 Mass 299, 28 NE 243. Within the meaning of welfare statutes:—those, and only those, persons for whose support and maintenance the law requires the person who seeks relief to provide. Newbury v Brunswick, 2 Vt 151. For some purposes, synonymous with household, as in the clause of an automobile theft insurance policy excluding theft by a member of the household. 7 Am J2d Auto Ins § 56. As the word appears in the rule that services rendered for a member of the "family" are presumed to have been rendered gratuitously:—persons living together in a state of mutual dependence irrespective of how close the tie of blood between them may be. Robinson v Johnson, 119 Kan 639, 240 P 962. As used in an exemption statute:—those who reside with, or compose the household of, the debtor. 22 Am J2d Exemp § 27. For the purposes of a statutory exemption of the homestead:—two or more persons who reside in a common household under the direction of one of them who is designated expressly or impliedly the head of the family. 26 Am J1st Home § 68. As used in the charter of, or certificate issued by, a mutual benefit association:—parents, wife, children, brothers, sisters, or other relatives, even stepchildren, so long as they comprise a part of the household of the member. 38 Am J2d Frat O § 143. As used in those provisions of workmen's compensation acts which specify persons entitled to compensation as dependents of a deceased employee:—persons having an abode in common with the employee as the single head or in single management of the group. 58 Am J1st Workm Comp § 172. Within the meaning of a statute providing for substituted service of process by leaving a copy with one of defendant's family:—persons living together permanently and continuously within the same domestic establishment, irrespective of what the blood relationship, if any, between them may be. 42 Am J1st Proc § 63. Expressly defined in some zoning laws:—any number of persons living or cooking together as a single housekeeping unit; a number of individuals living together on the premises as a single nonprofit housekeeping unit, including domestic servants. Carroll v Arlington County, 186 Va 575, 44 SE2d 6, 172 ALR 1169. In reference to free transportation of the employee of a carrier or the members of his "family":—wife, parents or children of the employee living in the same household with him in a state of mutual dependence or reciprocal duties beyond those arising from the ties of consanguinity. Wentz v Chicago, B. & Q. R. Co. 259 Mo 450, 168 SW 1166. But not all members of the household for the purposes of a clause in a fire insurance policy covering wearing apparel of the insured and his "family." 29 Am J Rev ed Ins § 303.

As used in a statute providing for an allowance

out of the estate of a decedent for his "family":—the widow and minor children of the decedent; the widow alone, if she has no children or no children who are minors; broadly defined by some authorities as including all persons who constituted the family of the decedent at the time of his death. 21 Am J2d Ex & Ad §§ 329–331.

Appearing in a will, the term "family" has such a variety of meanings that little of a general nature can be said as to its proper interpretation. 57 Am J1st Wills § 1392. Much depends upon the context of the entire will or of the pertinent portion. Anno: 154 ALR 1414. Sometimes, it means children or wife and children; at other times, a group of persons related to each other by marriage or blood living together under a single roof and comprising a household the head of which is usually the father or husband. 57 Am J1st Wills § 1392.

See **branch; consanguinity; member of household; members of a family; relative.**

family agreement. Same as **family settlement.**

family allowance. An allowance in a judgment for divorce or separation for the support of the child or children of the parties, often granted in a unitary award for wife and child or children. 24 Am J2d Div & S § 664. An award to be paid by the personal representative of a decedent's estate out of the assets of the estate to provide for daily necessities of the surviving family during the period of readjustment following the death of the breadwinner, until such time as a final settlement or award can be determined and effectuated. 31 Am J2d Exec & Ad § 24.

family arrangement. An expression characterizing the method of operation of a private boarding school; a family association for pupils and headmasters under a common roof, by a common fireside, in a common lodging, and at a common table. State ex rel. Spillers v Johnson, 214 Mo 656, 113 SW 1083.

family Bible. A Bible which has been used in a family for years, sometimes passed down from one generation to another in the family; often the place of recording events of important, even sacred, significance, such as births, deaths, marriages, baptisms, etc.

family burial ground. See **family cemetery.**

family car doctrine. See **family purpose doctrine.**

family cemetery. A family burial ground in which no lots are sold to the public and in which burials are restricted to a group of persons related to each other by blood or marriage. Union Cemetery Asso. v Cooper, 414 Ill 23, 110 NE2d 239.

family corporation. A corporation, the stock of which is held for the most part by the members of one family. 18 Am J2d Corp § 13.

family expense. An expenditure for an article or service which contributes to the comfort or enjoyment of the family as a unit, at least where reasonable and necessary. 26 Am J1st H & W § 387.

family history. The family record, often found in a family Bible, of births, deaths, marriages, baptisms, confirmations, etc. A medical term for the prevalence among members of a family of a particular disease, physical disability or bodily weakness.

family immunity. The absence of liability for an act, otherwise a tort, because of a family relationship between the person who performed the act and the injured person.

family meeting. An advisory jury, differing radically from an ordinary jury in that it is constituted with direct reference to its members having a bias, a partiality, an affection for those whose affairs it is called to deliberate. It is called to aid the court in determining affairs in which the members of the family are interested, such as the appointment of the curator of an interdict, a lunatic or an infant. Interdiction of Bothick, 44 La Ann 1037, 1041, 11 So 712. See also Lemoine v Ducote, 45 La Ann 857, 12 So 939.

family member. See **members of a family.**

family name. See **surname.**

family of a pauper. Those, and those only, for whom the law requires a pauper to provide. Newbury v Brunswick, 2 Vt 151.

family physician. The physician who usually attends and is consulted by the members of a family in the capacity of physician. 29 Am J Rev ed Ins § 759.

One may stand in the relationship of family physician to another, notwithstanding the latter has not consulted him or been attended by him. 29 Am J Rev ed Ins § 759.

family purpose doctrine. The rule that the owner of a motor vehicle purchased or maintained for the pleasure of his family is liable for injuries inflicted by the negligent operation of the vehicle while it is being used by members of the family for their own pleasure, on the theory that the vehicle is being used for the purpose or business for which it was kept, and that the person operating it is therefore acting as the owner's agent or servant in using it. 8 Am J2d Auto § 588. A doctrine which has been considered in reference to the operation of motorboats. 12 Am J2d Boats § 39.

family settlement. An agreement between the members of a family settling the distribution of family property among them.

family use. The use of a public service, such as that of a municipal waterworks, appropriate to the needs of the individual members of the household and of the household in a collective capacity for drinking, bathing, laundering, etc. Spring Valley Water Works v San Francisco, 52 Cal 111, 120.

See **domestic purposes.**

famosi libelli (fa-mō'sī lī-bel'lī). Plural of **famosus libellus.**

famosus libellus (fa-mō'sus li-bel'lus). A libelous book or publication; a libel.

fanatica mania (fa-na'ti-ka mā'ni-a). A form of insanity produced by a morbid state of religious feeling. Ekin v McCracken (Pa) 11 Phila 534, 540.

fanega (fah-nay'gah). A Spanish land measure equal to about sixty-four hundred square yards.

fan-tan. A card game, usually played by gamblers; a Chinese gambling game involving the guessing of the number of counters.

farce. A short dramatic entertainment in which ludicrous qualities are greatly exaggerated for humor. Society for the Reformation of Juvenile Delinquents (NY) 60 Barb 152, 156.

farcy (fär'si). Same as **glanders.**

fardage (fär'dăj). Same as **dunnage.**

fardel (fär'del, -dl). A fourth part.

farding deal (fär'ding dēl). A one-fourth of an acre of land.

fare. The price for the transportation of a passenger by a carrier. 14 Am J2d Car § 781. A passenger in a taxicab or other vehicle of a carrier.

According to one view, a fare is a payment made when the right of carriage is claimed, so that the purchase of a ticket is not the payment of a fare, the ticket becoming a fare only when accepted by the conductor and not before. Shelton v Erie R. Co. 73 NJL 558, 66 A 403.

fare-paying passenger. Ordinarily but not universally a person who has paid his fare in money of his own or in money supplied by a third person. 29A Am J Rev ed Ins § 1271.

farinagium (fa-ri-nā′ji-um). A mill where grain was ground into meal.

farleu (fär′lö). Money paid by the tenant to the lord of the manor in lieu of a heriot.

farlingarii (far-lin-gā′ri-ī). Panderers; procurers.

farm. A tract of land, consisting of one or any number of acres, having one or many fields, located in one or more than one township or county, devoted to agriculture, either to the raising of crops or pasturage, or both. People ex rel. Rodgers v Caldwell, 142 Ill 434, 32 NE 691, 693; Dorsett v Watkins, 59 Okla 198, 158 P 608, 9 ALR 278, 281.

Appearing in a will as the subject of a devise, the term will include lands accessory to a cultivated farm, notwithstanding they are not actually cultivated, for example, woodland. 57 Am J1st Wills § 14. Even noncontiguous lands may be included in a devise of a farm, if such tracts were used by the testator for farming purposes or for purposes incidental to the operation of his farm. 57 Am J1st Wills § 1342.

See **county farm**; **penal farm.**

farm aid. Aid extended by the government, directly or indirectly, to persons engaged in agriculture. 3 Am J2d Agri §§ 16 et seq.

farm commodities. The products of the farm, such as grain, meat, milk, etc.

Farm Credit Administration. A federal agency in the Department of Agriculture with facilities to be expanded in time of economic depression in agriculture and utilized for the refinancing of farm indebtedness. 12 USC §§ 636-1148d.

farm credit institutions. Federal land banks, joint stock land banks, national farm loan associations, federal intermediate credit banks, Central Bank for Cooperatives, regional banks for cooperatives, federal credit unions, regional and local agricultural credit corporations, and other institutions of a similar nature. 51 Am J1st Tax § 251.

farm crossing. A passage across, under, or over a railroad track running across a farm, for the use and convenience of the proprietor or tenant of the farm. Wheeler v Rochester & Syracuse Railroad Co. (NY) 12 Barb 227, 230.

farmer. In an older meaning, the lessor or lessee of a farm; the eldest son of such tenant or lessee; a yeoman. In the modern sense of the term, a person who earns his living by, or follows the occupation or profession of farming or agriculture, whether he be the owner or tenant of the land in his use. Hickman v Cruise, 72 Iowa 528. As defined in the Bankruptcy Act:—an individual personally engaged in farming or tillage of the soil, including an individual personally engaged in dairy farming or in the production of poultry, livestock, or poultry or livestock products in their unmanufactured state, if the principal part of his income is derived from any one or more of such operations. Bankr § 1(17); 11 USC § 1(17).

A debtor's act in growing garden products for the use of his table, upon premises adjacent to his residence, does not make him a farmer for the purpose of the exception of farmers from involuntary bankruptcy. Nicholson v Williams & S. Co. (CA4 SC) 121 F2d 740.

If a debtor's vocation or business is that of a farmer, he will be entitled to the exemptions from execution granted by statute to a "farmer," although he is not at the time of the levy engaged in farming, or doing any specific thing as a farmer, and may not own a farm or have one leased at the time. 22 Am J2d Exemp § 23.

Farmer Cooperative Service. A federal agency in the Department of Agriculture.

farmers' cooperative. A cooperative association of farmer-producers. 18 Am J2d Co-op Asso § 1.

farm implements. Machines, tools, and utensils commonly used in farming; the implements of husbandry. 22 Am J2d Exemp § 60.

See **implements of husbandry.**

farming. The ancient and honorable occupation, business, or profession of cultivating land, including horticulture, viticulture, and gardening. Estate of Slade, 122 Cal 434, 55 P 158.

See **agriculture.**

farming on shares. See **croppers**; **share rent.**

farming out convicts. See **hiring out convicts.**

farming utensils. See **farm implements.**

farm laborer. One employed upon a farm in raising and harvesting crops, doing general farm work, or employed in a special line of farm work, such as production of milk for distribution over a retail milk route. 3 Am J2d Agri § 3. One employed in the cultivation of the soil and its fruits or in such processes or steps as are necessary and incident to the raising, harvesting, and processing of the harvested products for consumption or marketing. Anno: 53 ALR2d 406; 48 Am J1st Soc Sec § 30. One employed by a farmer to perform work which ordinarily is incidental to farming. 58 Am J1st Workm Comp § 97. For the purposes of the National Labor Relations Act, one employed in any one of the following enterprises: farming in all its branches, including, among other things, the cultivation and tillage of the soil; dairying; the production, cultivation, growing, and harvesting of agricultural or horticultural commodities; the raising of livestock or poultry, etc. 31 Am J Rev ed Lab § 685.

A man is not a farm laborer when in the employ of a man who travels about from farm to farm with a corn-husking machine, engaged in the business of husking corn for a stated compensation. Roush v Heffelbower, 225 Mich 664, 196 NW 185, 35 ALR 196, 198, 199.

farm let. Formal words in a lease, expressed in the Latin form, "ad firmam tradidi," signifying a letting on a certain rent payable in produce. See 2 Bl Comm 317.

Farm Loan Act. A federal statute enacted to provide loans on farm lands or assistance in obtaining such loans. 3 Am J2d Agri § 25. An act of Congress providing for the creation of federal land banks and joint stock land banks to facilitate the making of loans upon farm security at low rates of interest.

FARM [459] FATTY

12 USC §§ 641 et seq., 810 et seq.; 10 Am J2d Bks § 21.

The beneficent purpose of loans under this statute is to enable farmers who are in debt, and without ability to make payment, to constitute the federal agency the sole creditor and thereby eliminate, by way of compromise, all other creditors. International Harvester Co. v Young, 288 Mich 436, 285 NW 12.

farm manager. An agent intrusted with the management of a farm, but ordinarily not authorized to borrow money on the credit of his principal only as borrowing is indispensable to the operation of the farm. 3 Am J2d Ag § 89.

farm produce. See **farm products.**

farm products. Products of the pursuit of farming or agriculture, including swine, horses, cattle, and sheep, as well as grain, vegetables, fruit, eggs, milk, butter, lard, and other provisions consumed as food. 3 Am J2d Agri § 2. Including for the purpose of tax or licensing statutes products of the field and garden, fruit trees, livestock, poultry, eggs, dairy products, meats, nuts, and honey. 3 Am J2d Agri § 2. Crops, livestock, or supplies used or produced in farming operations. UCC § 9-109(3).
See **crops.**

farm relief. The relief of burdensome indebtedness of farmers by means of refinancing farm mortgages at low rates of interest through governmental agencies. 3 Am J2d Agri § 30. A form of relief under the Bankruptcy Act, known as agricultural compositions and extensions, provided as a temporary measure in 1933 but continuing until March 1, 1949, and even beyond that date as to proceedings then pending, the primary objective of which was to enable the farm debtor to hold onto his property and keep operating under extensions of time for payment or redemption. 9 Am J2d Bankr § 162.

farm tractor. See **tractor.**

farm use. As the term appears in an automobile insurance policy, use in pursuance of the profession of farming. Anno: 10 ALR2d 674.

farm vehicles. Motor vehicles employed in transporting or delivering dairy or other farm products or livestock. 7 Am J2d Auto § 78.

faro (fā'rō). A card game played by gamblers. 24 Am J1st Gaming § 37.

farrago libelli (far-rā'gō lī-bel'lī). Books compiled or written in a confused or disorderly manner.

farrier. One who shoes horses; a person who takes care of sick horses.

farsightedness. Better vision for distant than near-by objects.

farthing. A British coin of very small value practically out of circulation. Anything of extremely small value.
See **smoke farthings.**

farthing damages. Nominal damages; that is, such damages as are awarded when judgment is for the plaintiff and no actual damages have been or can be shown.

Faryndon Inn. One of the ancient inns of court in London.

f.a.s. Abbreviation of free alongside steamer.
See **free alongside steamer.**

fas (fās). That which is right or just in the sight of God, as distinguished from "jus," which more frequently refers to that which is right in the aspect of man-made law. See 3 Bl Comm 2.

Fascist. One who advocates, or is a member of an organization which advocates, the establishment of a totalitarian dictatorship.

fast. Speedy. Living in a state of dissipation. Tied.
In railroading, a train is going fast within the meaning of yard rules when traveling at the full authorized rate of fifteen miles an hour. Missouri Pacific R. R. Co. v Baldwin (CA8 Ark) 117 F2d 510.

fast bill of exceptions. A bill of exceptions which is entitled to review by the higher court without the usual delay. Sewell v Edmonston, 66 Ga 353.

fastening seat belt. A precaution to be taken by one riding in an airplane at time of takeoff or landing or during a turbulence. 8 Am J2d Avi § 96.

fast estate. An unusual term for real property. Jackson ex dem. Decker v Merrill (NY) 6 Johns 185, 191.

fasti (fas'tī). Those days on which the praetor could administer justice under the Roman law.

fast writ. Any matter or proceeding which is entitled to precedence on the calendar of the court. Young v Hamilton, 135 Ga 339, 69 SE 593.

fast writ of error. A proceeding by writ of error entitled to precedence on the court docket. Gordon v Gordon, 109 Ga 262, 34 SE 324.

fatal. Causing death; deadly or mortal. Boyer v State, 84 Neb 407, 121 NW 445.

fatale. See **damnum fatale.**

fatal error. See **prejudicial error.**

fatal injury. A personal injury resulting in death. Provident Life & Acci. Ins. Co. v Johnson (Tex Civ App) 235 SW 650.
See **personal injury.**

fatal variance. A material variance between the pleading and the proof, a variance which actually misleads the opposing party to his prejudice in maintaining his cause of action or defense. 41 Am J1st Pl § 371.

fate. Inevitability; destiny.

Fatetur facinus qui judicium fugit (fa-tē'ter fa'si-nus qui jū-di'she-um fu'jit). A person who flees from judgment admits his guilt.

father. A person's male parent; a male who has begotten a child. An adoptive male parent. Lind v Burke, 56 Neb 785, 790, 77 NW 444, 445. A priest; a person honored or respected because of age or position.

father's natural guardianship. The modern status of the father as the natural guardian of the person of all his children until they have attained the age of twenty-one. 25 Am J1st 10 G & W § 6.

fatigue life. The useful life of a metal, it being recognized as a scientific fact that even hard metal may in time, by the action of the elements, stress, and strain, cease to have the resistance which makes it useful. Northwest Airlines Inc. v Glenn L. Martin Co. (CA6 Ohio) 224 F2d 120, 50 ALR2d 882, reh den 229 F2d 434, 50 ALR2d 897.

fatty degeneration. Abnormality in the appearance of particles of fat in tissues; not a bodily infirmity as a matter of law. Modern Woodmen Acci. Asso. v Shryock, 54 Neb 250, 74 NW 607.

fatua mulier (fa′tu-a mu′li-er). A ruined woman; a whore.

fatuitas (fa-tu′i-tās). Fatuity; idiocy.

fatuity. Stupidity. Folly.

fatum (fā′tum). Fate; vis major.

fatuous person (fat′ū-us). A silly person. In rare usage, an idiot.

fatuum judicium (fa′tu-um jū-di′she-um). A fatuous, foolish, or idiotic judgment.

fatuus (fa′tu-us). Fatuous; foolish; idiotic; an idiot.

Fatuus, apud jurisconsultos nostros, accipitur pro non compos mentis; et fatuus dicitur, qui omnino desipit (fa′tu-us, a′pud jū-ris-kon-sul′tos nos′tros, ak-si′pi-ter prō non kom′pos men′tis; et fa′tu-us di′si-ter, quī om-nī′nō de′si-pit). "Fatuus," among our men learned in the law, is treated as meaning not in one's right mind, and he is called "fatuus" who is altogether foolish.

Fatuus praesumitur qui in proprio nomine errat (fa′-tu-us prē-zu′mi-ter quī in pro′pri-ō no′mi-ne er′rat). He is presumed incompetent who mistakes his own name. Van Alst v Hunter (NY) 5 Johns Ch 148, 161.

faubourg (fō′börg). In Louisiana,—a suburban town or community.

fauces terrae (fâ′sēz ter′rē). Headlands inclosing a bay.

fault. A wrongful act, omission, or breach. UCC § 1-201(16). An error or defect of judgment or conduct; any deviation from prudence, rectitude, or duty; any shortcoming or neglect of care or performance, resulting from inattention, incapacity, or perversity; a wrong tendency, course, or act; including but not limited to negligence; not necessarily imputing moral delinquency. Louisville, Evansville & St. Louis Railroad Co. v Berry, 2 Ind App 427, 431.

fausse (fōs). False.

fautor (fâ′tor). A patron; a supporter; an abettor.

faux (fō). False.

fauxer. To falsify; to forge.

favor. Grace; indulgence; prejudice; bias.
See **challenge to the favor.**

favorabilia in lege sunt fiscus, dos, vita, libertas (fa-vō-rā-bi′li-a in lē′je sunt fis′kus, dōs, vī′ta, li-ber′-tas). Favorites of the law are the revenue, dower, life, and liberty.

Favorabilia in lege sunt vita, fiscus, dos, libertas (fa-vō-rā-bi′li-a in lē′je sunt, vī′ta, fis′kus, dōs, li-ber′tas). Life, the revenue, dower and liberty are favorites of the law. State ex rel. Corporation Com. v Dunn, 174 NC 679, 94 SE 481.

Favorabiliores rei potius quam actores habentur (fa-vō-rā-bi-li-ō′rez rē′ī po′she-us quam ak-tō′rēz hā-ben′ter). Defendants are favored rather than plaintiffs.
 Both parties are the objects of the law's equal protection, but to make the protection equal, a certain position is assigned to the defendant; he is so placed that he may not be overcome by surprise. Hunt v Rousmanier's Administrators (US) 8 Wheat 174, 195, 5 L Ed 589, 594.

Favorabiliores sunt executiones aliis processibus quibuscunque (fa-vō-rā-bi-li-ō′rēz sunt ex-e-ku-she-ō′nēz a′li-is prō-ses′si-bus qui-bus-kun′kwe). Executions are more favored than all other processes.

favorable construction. See **liberal construction.**

favorable error. An error of the trial court which is favorable to a party and is therefore one which he cannot assign as error either on a motion for a new trial or on appeal. 5 Am J2d A & E § 784.

favored vessel. A vessel to be favored by other craft in navigation. Connolly v The Ace (CA2 NY) 164 F2d 86. The ship, boat, or other watercraft to which other vessels must give way in order to avoid collision and injury. 12 Am J2d Boats § 80; 48 Am J1st Ship §§ 250 et seq. The one of two vessels approaching each other which is required by the rules of navigation to keep her course and speed. The Knoxville City (CA9 Cal) 112 F2d 223.

Favores ampliandi sunt; odia restringenda (fa-vō′rēz am-pli-an′dī sunt; ō′di-a rēs-trin-jen′da). Favorable comments should be encouraged, expressions of hatred should be restrained.

favoritism. See **bias; discrimination; favor; prejudice.**

favor of. On the side of, as in announcing the score of a game or contest. An informal term for the creation of a fiduciary relationship.
 A check made payable to the order of one person "favor of" another person makes the payee upon accepting the check a fiduciary for the other person and the words "favor of" are equivalent to "collect for" or "for account of." White v National Bank, 102 US 658, 26 L Ed 250.

f. b. Abbreviation of freight bill.

FBI. Abbreviation of **Federal Bureau of Investigation.**
See **Bureau of Investigation.**

FCC. Abbreviation of **Federal Communications Commission.**

fcp. Abbreviation of foolscap.

FDA. Abbreviation of **Food and Drug Administration.**

feal (fēl). Faithful; loyal.

feal and divot. A servitude of taking sod, corresponding closely to the English common of turbary.

fealte. Same as **fealty.**

fealty. An incident of feudal tenure, being the obligation of fidelity which a tenant owed to his lord. 19 Am J2d Est § 3.

fear. A state of agitation and anxiety prompted by the nearness or imagined nearness of danger or evil. A basic element of the instinct of self-preservation.
 Fear consists in capitulating to the human instinct of self-preservation. The bravest of men know what it is. It is not a ridiculous malady, nor one that a person need be ashamed of under ordinary circumstances. Everett v Paschall, 61 Wash 47, 111 P 879.
 In robbery, the fear which moves the victim to part with his goods may be the apprehension of injury to his person, property or reputation. No matter how slight the cause creating the fear may be, nor by what other circumstances the taking may be accomplished, if the transaction be attended with such circumstances of terror, such threatening by word or gesture, as in common experience are likely to create an apprehension of danger, and to induce a man to part with his property for the safety of his person, he is put in fear. See 46 Am J1st Rob § 16.

The fear of disease, which is sometimes an element in depriving a person of the comfortable enjoyment of his property, is real in that it affects the movements and conduct of men. Such fears are actual and must be recognized by the courts as other emotions of the human mind. Everett v Paschall, 61 Wash 47, 111 P 879.
See **fright**.

fearm (fērm). Same as **farm**.

fear of death. See **fear**; **gift causa mortis**.

feasance (fē'sans). A doing; a making; putting into effect.
See **malfeasance**; **misfeasance**; **nonfeasance**.

feasant (fē'sant). The process of acting or putting into effect.
See **damage feasant**.

feasibility. Capability of accomplishment. Gilmartin v D. & N. Transp. Co. 123 Conn 127, 193 A 726, 113 ALR 1322.

feasor (fē'sor). One who performs or commits.

feasts (fēsts). Ecclesiastical festivals or holidays. Rent days and days for holding court were often fixed by reference to these feasts.

febrile (fē'bril). Feverish.
See **delirium febrile**.

featherbedding. The exaction of pay for services not to be performed. 31 Am J Rev ed Lab § 261.

feciales (fē-she-ā'lēz). Ancient Roman officers upon whom devolved the functions of declaring war and peace.

fecial law. The ancient Roman law governing declarations of war and peace.

federal. Joined in a union having central and predominate authority. Appertaining to the community of sovereign states, the United States of America. Piqua Bank v Knoup, 6 Ohio St 342.
See terms and expressions beginning **federal**; **national**; **United States**.

federal act. See **federal statute**.

federal agencies and instrumentalities. Agencies, boards, bureaus, commissions, institutions, and services of the United States Government.
For particular agency, bureau, commission, service, or instrumentality, see the pertinent title or popular name, such as **Bureau of Investigation; Civil Service Commission; Deposit Insurance Corporation; Housing and Home Finance Agency; Mediation and Conciliation Service; Power Commission**, etc.

federal agency. A federal administrative board or commission. A means or agency used by the Federal government. Capitol Bldg. & Loan Asso. v Kansas Com. 148 Kan 446, 83 P2d 106, 118 ALR 1212.
See **federal agencies and instrumentalities**.

federal aid. The use of federal funds in giving financial aid to states or state agencies, for particular purposes, such as the construction of highways, the elimination of slums, the control of disease, etc.
See **foreign aid**.

federal airports. Airports in the continental United States in, or in close proximity to, national parks, national monuments, and national recreation areas. 16 USC §§ 7a–7e.

federal airway. A portion of the navigable air space of the United States designated by the Administrator of the federal aviation agency as a federal airway. 49 USC § 1301(18).

federal bureaus. See **federal agencies and instrumentalities**.

federal census. The census taken every 10 years by the Federal Government. 14 Am J2d Census §§ 1–4.

Federal Code. See **United States Code**.

federal commissioner. See **United States Commissioner**.

federal commissions. See **federal agencies and instrumentalities**.

federal common law. A concept intriguing to legal theorists. Strictly speaking, a nonentity. 15 Am J2d Com L § 4. In a less than strict usage, the common law enforced generally throughout the United States. Western Union Tel. Co. v Call Pub. Co. 181 US 92, 45 L Ed 765, 21 S Ct 561.
While there is no common law of the United States in the sense of a national customary law, the courts of the United States enforce the law as they find it in the several states and apply the common law, as a national institution, in the interpretation of the constitution. State ex rel. Powell v State Bank, 90 Mont 539, 4 P2d 717, 80 ALR 1494.
Although there is no national common law in the United States distinct from the common law which each state has adopted for itself and applies as its local law subject to alteration by statute, there is a federal common law in the sense that the United States Constitution, treaties, and statutes are construed in the light of common law principles and in the further sense that the federal courts also apply common law principles in cases involving substantive matters in transactions substantially involving the interests or obligations of the federal government or its instrumentalities. 15 Am J2d Com L § 4.
"Notwithstanding Erie Railroad v Tompkins, 304 US 64, 82 L Ed 1188, 58 S Ct 817, 114 ALR 1487, there still exist certain fields where legal relations are governed by a Federal common law, a body of decisional law developed by the Federal courts untrammeled by state court decisions." O'Brien v Western Union Telegraph Co. (CA1 Mass) 113 F2d 539.

Federal Control Act. The statute which provided for the operation of the railroads by the federal government during World War I. 31 USC § 191.

federal corporation. A corporation chartered by act of Congress or organized under federal laws. 23 Am J2d For Corp §§ 112, 113.

federal courts. See **United States Courts**.

federal district. An area for the seat of government in a country under the federal system; the District of Columbia in the United States. A judicial district in the federal system of courts.

federal enclave. A federal institution, such as a military base, within a state. A place falling within the special maritime and territorial jurisdiction of the United States. 21 Am J2d Crim L § 395.

Federal Government. The government of the United States; the government of a community of independent and sovereign states, united by compact. Piqua Bank v Knoup, 6 Ohio St 342, 394.
See **United States**.

federal grant. A transfer of title to public lands of the United States by act of Congress, through treaty provisions, or by patent under general laws. 42 Am J1st Pub L § 30.

federal instrumentality. A means or agency used by the Federal government. Capitol Bldg. & Loan Asso. v Kansas Com. 148 Kan 446, 83 P2d 106, 118 ALR 1212.

See **federal agencies and instrumentalities.**

Federalist. A series of political essays on the United States Constitution, written by Alexander Hamilton, James Madison, and John Jay in advocating the adoption of the great document, to which recourse has often been had in the interpretation of the constitution. 16 Am J2d Const L § 89.

federal judge. A judge of a court of the United States. Fong Yue Ting v United States, 149 US 698, 37 L Ed 905, 13 S Ct 1016.

federal lands. See **public lands.**

federal legislation. See **federal statute.**

federal offenses. Offenses defined by Congress and for which Congress prescribes punishment. 21 Am J2d Crim L § 15.

An offense created by a statute which is operative only within the District of Columbia is an offense against the United States. Beard v Bennett, 72 App DC 269, 114 F2d 578.

federal police power. A power analagous to the police power of the states; the police power appropriate to the exercise of any attribute of sovereignty specifically granted the federal government by the Constitution of the United States. 16 Am J2d Const L § 276.

federal powers. The powers granted the federal government by the Constitution of the United States.
See **resulting powers.**

federal prison. A prison erected under authority of Congress at any place within the jurisdiction of the United States for the confinement of persons sentenced to imprisonment under the laws of the United States or a state prison designated by Congress under arrangement with a state for the reception of Federal prisoners. 41 Am J1st Pris & P § 7.

federal question. A genuine and substantial controversy, arising under the Constitution, a law, or treaty of the United States, presented in such form that the judicial power is capable of acting upon it, and so directly involved in a case that a determination thereof is necessary to a decision. Kansas v Colorado, 206 US 46, 51 L Ed 956, 27 S Ct 655; Smith v Kansas City Title & Trust Co. 255 US 180, 65 L Ed 577, 41 S Ct 243.

Federal Register. An official publication in daily issues of executive orders and proclamations of the President, rules, regulations, etc. of the federal departments, commissions, and agencies. A publication prescribed by law wherein every federal agency shall publish: (1) descriptions of its central and field organization, including delegations by the agency of final authority and the established places at which, and methods whereby, the public may secure information or make submittals or requests; (2) statements of the general course and method by which its functions are channeled and determined, including the nature and requirements of all formal or informal procedures available as well as forms and instructions as to the scope and contents of all papers, reports, or examinations; and substantive rules and statements of general policy. 5 USC 1002.
See **Code of Federal Regulations.**

federal reserve. See **reserve system.**

federal reserve bank. See **reserve bank.**

Federal Rules of Civil Procedure. A comprehensive set of rules governing procedure in the United States District Courts, promulgated by the United States Supreme Court under power delegated to the court by Congress, replacing the Conformity Act and the Federal Rules of Equity Practice.

Federal Rules of Criminal Procedure. A comprehensive set of rules governing the procedure in criminal cases in the United States District Courts, promulgated by the United States Supreme Court.

Federal Rules of Equity Practice. A set of rules, adopted by the United States Supreme Court, governing the practice and procedure in equity suits in the United States District Courts, since supplanted by the Federal Rules of Civil Procedure which govern in all suits in such courts of a civil nature whether cognizable as cases at law or in equity.

federal statute. The written will of Congress as expressed formally by an Act of Congress. 50 Am J1st Stat § 2.

For particular statute, see the pertinent title or popular name, such as **Alcohol Administration Act; Bank Conservation Act; Farm Loan Act; Interpleader Act; Miller Act; Ship Mortgage Act,** etc.

federal taxes. See **internal revenue.**

federation. A combination of states or bodies to which the components surrender at least some measure of their powers. A combination of labor unions.

fee. The royalty paid for the use of a patent or copyright under license. The charge made for services of a professional man, such as a lawyer, physician, or abstracter. 1 Am J2d Abstr T § 3, the charges for the services of a public officer in his official capacity (Rose v Superior Court, 80 Cal App 739, 252 P 765), especially the services of the clerk of court. 15 Am J2d Cl C § 14. A charge imposed upon students for an incidental, such as a fee for use of library or laboratory, a student-union fee, an athletic fee, or a matriculation fee. 15 Am J2d Colleges § 19. A perpetual annuity. 4 Am J2d, Annui § 7.

An estate in real property, which, unless qualified by additional terminology, is an estate in inheritance where the tenant is not only entitled to enjoy the land for his own life, but where, after his death, it is cast by law upon the persons who successfully represent him in perpetuum in right of blood, according to a certain established order of descent. 19 Am J2d Est § 8. Often used as a synonym of fee simple.

The word was originally used in contradistinction to the word "allodium," and signifies that which was held of another, on condition of rendering him a service. And although the word is now generally used to express the quantum of the estate, it is also used to designate a fee simple. Hay's Estate v Commissioner (CA5) 181 F2d 169, 39 ALR2d 453; Wendell v Crandall, 1 NY 491, 495.

See **conditional fee; determinable fee; fee tail.**

feeble-minded. A condition of incomplete development of mind of such a degree or kind as to render the individual incapable of adjusting himself to his social environment in a reasonably efficient and harmonious manner and to necessitate external care, supervision, or control. Re Masters, 216 Minn 553, 13 NW2d 487, 158 ALR 1210. Having a subnormal mentality. 21 Am J2d Crim L § 28.

fee conditional. See **conditional fee.**

feed. Noun: Provender for cattle and other animals. Verb: To supply food, as to "feed" the starving of the world out of our abundance.

feeder. A canal which intersects another and larger canal to which it brings traffic; a railroad line which intersects a trunk line with which it exchanges traffic; a steer or heifer of such size and condition as to be ready for feeding preparatory to marketing the animal.

Feed Grain Program. Various activities of the Federal Government carried on to reduce the acreage of land planted to feed grains, conducted for the purpose of stabilization of prices.

feed loans. Government loans for livestock feed made when, by reason of drought, destruction or failure of crops, farmers are unable otherwise to procure them. 3 Am J2d Agri § 33.

fee-expectant. A fee which is limited to a man and his wife and the heirs of their bodies.
See **expectant estates.**

fee farm (fē färm). A letting of lands to farm in fee-simple, instead of the usual methods for life or years. See 2 Bl Comm 43.
See **rent charge.**

fee farm rent. The rent reserved in letting a fee farm.
See **rent charge.**

fee in abeyance. See **in abeyance.**

feelings. Emotions.
Injury to feelings is often used as synonymous with the term mental suffering. Bovee v Danville, 53 Vt 183, 191.

fees. See **fee.**

fee schedule. See **minimum fee schedule.**

fee simple. The largest estate in land known to the law and implying absolute dominion over the land; an estate of inheritance clear of any condition, limitation, or restriction, to particular heirs. 28 Am J2d Est § 10. An estate of lawful inheritance or pure inheritance, "fee" standing for inheritance and "simple" for pure or lawful. A legal or equitable estate in land constituting the largest estate and implying absolute dominion, although possibly subject to executory limitations or conditions subsequent. Hay's Estate v Commissioner (CA5) 181 F2d 169, 39 ALR2d 453; Ford v Unity Church Society, 120 Mo 498, 25 SW 394.
See **fee simple.**

fee simple absolute. A fee simple.

fee simple conditional. Same as **conditional fee.**

fee splitting. See **division of fees.**

feet. See **foot.**

fee tail. A legal or equitable estate in which lands and tenements are given to one and the heirs of his body begotten, in other words, an estate of inheritance which is to pass by lineal descent only. 19 Am J2d Est § 45. An estate resulting from the application of the Statute de Donis to the conditional fee. 19 Am J2d Est § 45.
The name was borrowed from the feudists, among whom it signified any mutilated or truncated inheritance from which the heirs general were cut off, or, as some say, because ownership of the subject was cut in two parts, one going to the donee and the heirs of his body, and the other remaining as a reversion in the donor. Gannon v Albright, 183 Mo 498, 81 SW 1162.

See **barring the entail; common recovery; fine to bar entail; Statute de Donis.**

fee tail after possibility of issue extinct. An estate which is not a conventional one, but is of the legal kind and arises when a tenant is tenant in special tail and a person from whose body the issue was to spring, dies without issue; or, having left issue, that issue becomes extinct. In either of these cases the surviving tenant in special tail becomes tenant in tail after possibility of issue extinct. 2 Bl Comm 124.

fee tail female. An estate tail in which the distinctive limitation is to female heirs of the donee's body. 28 Am J2d Est § 45.

fee tail general. An estate tail where the limitation is to the heirs of a man's body generally. 28 Am J2d Est § 45.

fee tail male. An estate tail in which the distinctive limitation is to male heirs of the donee's body. Restatement, Property § 78, Comments b, c, d; 28 Am J2d Est § 45.

fee tail special. See **special estate tail.**

fegangi (fe-gan'jī). A fleeing thief who was captured with the stolen goods in his possession.

feigned accomplice. One who participates in an act, otherwise criminal, with the intent, not to accomplish that which constitutes a crime, but to secure the apprehension of the other participant or participants. 13 Am J2d Burgl § 26.

feigned action. A fictitious suit; a suit instituted to obtain a judicial opinion, without an actual or existing controversy between the parties. 1 Am J2d Actions § 56.

feigned appearance. Disguise. A false registration of emotions.

feigned conduct. Disguising one's feelings, emotions, intent, or purpose by assuming a posture.

feigned injury. A pretended personal injury asserted by way of exaggerating a claim for damages.

feigned issue. An issue in a suit in equity presented for trial at law before a jury under the guise of a fictitious wager. 27 Am J2d Equity § 240.
Feigned issues were also frequently used in courts of law, by consent of the parties, to determine some disputed right without the formality of pleading, thus saving time and expense. See 3 Bl Comm 452.

FELA. Abbreviation of Federal Employers' Liability Act.

feldspar. A mineral. Anno: 86 ALR 984.

fele. Same as **feal.**

Felix qui potuit rerum cognoscere causas (fē'lix quī po'tu-it rē'rum kog-nō'se-re kä'zas). He is fortunate who is able to understand the causes of things.

fellow-heir (fel'ō). A joint heir; a co-heir; a person sharing an inheritance with another or with others.

fellow servant doctrine. The common-law rule which absolves an employer from liability to one engaged in his employment for injuries incurred or suffered solely as the result of the negligence, carelessness, or misconduct of others who are in the service of the employer and who are engaged in the same common or general employment as the injured employee. 35 Am J1st M & S § 334.

fellow servants. Literally, co-workers in the same employment. For the purposes of the fellow servant doctrine:—the injured person and the person who caused the injury engaged in the service of the same employer and acting at the time the injury was sustained within the scope of their employment. 35 Am J1st M & S § 377. With refinements:—servants of a common master, who are engaged in and about a common work under one common master workman or superintendent, and who in doing their work can observe and influence each other's conduct and suggest delinquencies to a correcting power. Relyea v Kansas City, Fort Scott & Gulf Railroad Co. 112 Mo 86, 93, 20 SW 480.

All the members of the crew on the same vessel, with the exception, according to some authorities, of the master or other commanding officer, are fellow servants of each other, though their duties and functions differ; and the same is true of workmen engaged in building, repairing, loading or unloading a ship. 48 Am J1st Ship § 127.

felo (fē'lō). A felon.

felo de se (fē'lō dē sē). A self-destroyer; a suicide.

felon. One who has been convicted of a felony and whose disabilities arising from such conviction have not been removed. An infection of finger or toe extruding pus and very painful. 29A Am J Rev ed Ins § 1173.

felonia (fe-lō'ni-a). A felony.

feloniae, per quas vasallas amitteret feudum (fe-lō'ni-ē, per quas vas-sal'las a-mit'te-ret fū'dum). Felonies through which a vassal would lose his fee. See 2 Bl Comm 284.

Felonia, ex vi termini, significat quodlibet capitale crimen felleo animo perpetratum (fe-lō'ni-a, ex vī ter'mi-nī, sig-ni'fi-kat quod'li-bet ka-pi-tā'le kri'-men fel'le-ō a'ni-mō per-pe-trā'tum). Felony, by the force of the term, signifies any capital crime perpetrated with felonious intent.

Felonia implicatur in qualibet proditione (fe-lō'ni-a im-pli-kā'ter in quā'li-bet pro-di-she-ō'ne). Felony is implied in every treason.

felonice (fe-lo'ni-sē). Feloniously. An allegation that the criminal act was committed "feloniously" or "felonice," was a vital formality in every indictment charging the commission of a felony. See 4 Bl Comm 307.

Felonice abduxit unum equum (fe-lō'ni-se ab-duks'it ū'num e'kwu-um). He feloniously led away one horse.

felonice cepit (fe-lō'ni-se sē'pit). He feloniously took.

felonious. Having the quality of a felony; malignant; malicious; villainous; perfidious; in a legal sense, done with intent to commit a crime. State v Bush, 47 Kan 201, 207.

See **felonious intent.**

felonious homicide. Murder, in some one of the degrees of the offense, or manslaughter, depending upon the presence or absence of malice, express or implied, or upon the fact that the homicide was committed by the slayer while in the perpetration of another felony. 26 Am J1st Homi § 2.

The killing of a human creature of any age or sex, without justification or excuse. This may be done either by killing one's self, or another man. The term therefore includes self-murder, murder and manslaughter. See 4 Bl Comm 188–190.

felonious intent. The intent to commit a felony. As an element of the crime of larceny:—an absence of color, of right or excuse for the act, combined with an intent to deprive the owner permanently of his property, sometimes including an element of concealment. 32 Am J1st Larc § 36.

It is not sufficient in an indictment for burglary, to charge simply intent to commit a felony; the particular felony intended must be specified. 13 Am J2d Burgl § 36.

feloniously. Acting with intent to commit a felony or to do that which constitutes a felony under the law even perhaps without knowledge of the legal effect. Acting with an evil heart or purpose. State v Clark, 83 Vt 305, 75 A 534. A technical, but in many jurisdictions an essential, word in an indictment charging a felony, at least where the offense is a felony at common law. 27 Am J1st Indict § 67.

feloniously and burglariously. A conventional expression in an indictment for burglary employed in charging an intent to commit a felony. State v Wiley, 173 Md 119, 194 A 629, 113 ALR 1267.

felony. A generic term for certain high crimes, such as murder, treason, robbery, and larceny, for the purpose of distinguishing them from minor offenses known as misdemeanors. 13 Am J2d Burgl § 36. An offense punishable by death, or by the imprisonment in a state prison or penitentiary. Briggs v Board of County Comrs. 202 Okla 684, 217 P2d 827, 20 ALR2d 727. Such a serious offense as was formerly punishable by death or by forfeiture of lands or goods. Bannon v United States, 156 US 464, 39 L Ed 494, 15 S Ct 467.

Within the meaning of a statute which provides that a homicide committed in the perpetration of a felony is murder, a "felony" is an act punishable either capitally or by imprisonment in state prison, whether the act is one proscribed by the common law or by statute. 26 Am J1st Homi § 39.

female. One of the sex that bears offspring. State v Hemm, 82 Iowa 609, 48 NW 971.

See **chaste female; fee tail female; virtuous female.**

female disease. A disease not common to both sexes, peculiar to females. 29A Am J Rev ed Ins § 1158.

female estate tail. An estate tail in which the distinctive limitation is to female heirs of the donee's body. 28 Am J2d Est § 45.

feme (fem). A woman.

feme covert (fem co'vert). A married woman.

feme sole (fem sōl). An unmarried woman.

feme sole trader. A married woman who engages in business on her own account. M'Daniel v Cornwell 10 SC Eq (1 Hill) 428, 429.

femicide (fem'i-sīd). The killing of a woman.

femme (fem). A woman.

fen. A marsh or swamp.

See **submerged fen.**

fenatio (fe-nā-she-ō). The breeding season of deer.

fence. An inclosure about a field or other space, or about any object, especially an inclosing structure of wood, iron, or other material, intended to prevent intrusion from without or straying from within; a visible or tangible obstruction which may be a hedge, ditch, wall, trestle, frame of wood, wire, rails, or any line of obstacle interposed between two portions of land so as to part off and shut in the land and set it off as private property or for the purpose of using it separately from adjacent land of the same owner. 35 Am J2d Fen § 1. A place where thieves, robbers, and burglars may dispose of their plunder. State v Rosenbaum, 80 Conn 327, 68 A 250.

See **lawful fence**; **partition fence**; **spite fence**.

fence district. Same as **fencing district**.

fence-mouth (fens'munth). The closed or fawning season for deer.

fence operation. Receiving stolen property; receiving stolen vehicles. 7 Am J2d Auto § 307.

fence viewer. An officer, usually a township officer, having the duty of ascertaining the true boundary between adjoining landowners in case of dispute, and, in some jurisdictions, authorized to determine the sufficiency of a fence on a boundary line.

fencing district. A district established under statute for the purpose of requiring the owners of livestock within such district to keep their animals restrained against trespassing upon the premises of other persons, in order that crops may be cultivated on unfenced premises. 4 Am J2d Ani § 51.

fender. A guard and protection against danger. State, Cape May, etc. Railway Co. v Cape May, 59 NJL 396, 403, 36 A 696. A metal pattern placed over the wheels of a motor vehicle to prevent the splashing of mud and the throwing of particles from the highway. The cowcatcher of a locomotive.

feneration (fen-e-rā'shon). The lending of money at interest; interest; usury.

fengeld (fen'geld). A tax imposed for warding off or repelling enemies.

feod (fe'od). A fee, a fief.

feodal. Same as **feudal**.

feoda; actions. Same as **feudal actions**.

feodality (fū-dal'i-ti). Same as **fealty**.

feodal law. Same as **feudal law**.

feoda propria et impropria (fe'o-da prō'pri-a et im-prō'pri-a). Proper (military) and improper (nonmilitary) feuds. See 2 Bl Comm 58.

feodary. Same as **feudary**.

feodatory. Same as **feudatory**.

feodi firma. Same as **fee-farm**.

feodo. See **de feodo**.

feodum. Same as **feudum**.

feoffment. A common law method of conveying the title to real estate, accompanied by traditional and conventional livery of seisin. 23 Am J2d Deeds § 11.

feodum antiquum (fe'o-dum an-tē'kwu-um). An ancient fee. Same as **feudum antiquum**.

Feodum est quod quis tenet ex quacunque causa, sive sit tenementum sive redditus (fe'o-dum est quod quis te'net ex quā-kun'kwe kâ'za, sī've sit te-ne-men'tum sīve red'di-tus). A fee is something that a person holds from whatever cause, whether it be tenement or rent.

Feodum est guod quis tenet sibi et haeredibus suis, sive sit tenementum, sive reditus, etc. (fe'o-dum est quod quis te'net si'bi et he-red'i-bus su'is, si've sit te-ne-men'tum, si've re'di-tus). A fee is that which one holds for himself and his heirs, whether it be a tenement or a rent.

feodum nobile. Same as **feudum nobile**.

feodum novum. Same as **feudum novum**.

Feodum simplex quia feodum idem est quod haereditas, et simplex idem est quod legitimum vel purum; et sic feodum simplex idem est quod haereditas legitima vel haereditas pura (fe'o-dum sim'-plex qui'a fe'o-dum ī'dem est quod hē-rē'di-tas, et sim'plex ī'dem est quod le-ji'ti-mum vel pū'rum; et sik fe'o-dum sim'plex ī'dem est quod hē-rē'di-tas le-ji'ti-ma vel hē-rē'di-tās pū'ra). It is called a "fee simple," because "fee" is the same as inheritance and "simple" is the same as lawful or pure; and so "fee simple" is the same as lawful inheritance or pure inheritance.

feodum talliatum, i. e., haereditas in quandam certitudinem limitata (fe'o-dum tal-li-ā'tum, i. e., he-rē'di-tas in quan'dam ser-ti-tū'di-nem li-mi-tā'ta). A fee tail, that is, an inheritance limited in a certain descent.

feoffamentum (fē-of-fa-men'tum). A feoffment,— derived from feoffare or infeudare, to give one a feud. See 2 Bl Comm 310.

feoffare (fē-of-fā're). To enfeoff; to grant a fee.

feoffator. Same as **feoffor**.

feoffatus (fē-of-fā'tus). Same as **feoffee**.

feoffavit (fē-of-fā'vit). He has enfeoffed.

feoffee (fe-fē'). A person to whom a fee is conveyed; a person to whom a feoffment is made; the donee of any corporeal hereditament; one who is enfeoffed. See 2 Bl Comm 310.

feoffee to uses. A person to whom a fee is conveyed to the use of another person, who is called the cestui que use.

feoffment (fef'ment). The act of enfeoffing or investing a person with a fee. The transfer of a fee, a freehold or a corporeal hereditament by livery of seisin.

See **livery of seisin**.

feoffor (fef-or'). A person who conveys a fee; a person who makes a feoffment; one who gives any corporeal hereditament to another; one who enfeoffs another. See 2 Bl Comm 310.

feoh. A fee; a reward.

feorme. Same as **farm**.

ferae bestiae (fē'rē best'she-ē). Wild beasts; wild animals.

ferae igitur bestiae, et volucres, et omnia animalia quae mari, coelo et terra nascuntur, simul atque ab aliquo capta fuerint, jure gentium statim illius esse incipiunt. Quod enim nullius est, id naturali ratione occupanti concediture (fē'rē i'ji-ter best'she-ē, et vo-lū'krez, et om'ni-a a-ni-ma'li-a kwē ma'rī, sē'lō et ter'ra nas-kun'ter, sī'mul at'kwē ab a'li-quo kap'ta fu'e-rint, jū're jen'she-um sta'tim il-lī'us es'se in-si'pi-unt. Quod e'nim nul-lī'us est, id na-tu-rā'lī ra-she-ō'ne o-ku-pan'tī kon-sē'di-ter). (Roman law). Hence, wild animals and birds, and all animals which spring from the sea, the air and the earth as soon as they have been taken by anyone by the law of nations forthwith become his. For what belongs to no one by natural reason is given to the one taking it. See 2 Bl Comm 411.

ferae neturae (fē'rē na-tū're). Wild animals. 4 Am J2d Ani §§ 2, 4.

ferdwit (fėrd'wit). (Saxon.) A fine for not joining a military expedition.

ferens ligna in sylva (fe'renz lig'na in sil'va). Carrying wood to the forest; superfluous.

The expression is applied to the tautologous use of adjectives, as a "round" ball, an "open" assumption of marital rights, duties, and obligations. Sharon v Sharon, 75 Cal 1, 75, 16 P 345, 379.

feria (fē′ri-ą). A fair; a ferry; a holiday.

feriae (fē′ri-ē). Plural of **feria**.

ferial days (fē′ri-al dāz). Holidays; also, working-days other than Sundays.

ferita (fe′ri-ta). A wound.

ferme. Same as **farm**.

fermented liquor. Alcoholic beverages prepared in part by utilizing the natural process of fermentation.

fermer. Same as **farmer**.

ferret. See **tax ferret**.

ferriage (fer′i-ąj). Transportation by ferry. The price or fare fixed by law for the transporation of the traveling public, with such goods and chattels as they may have with them, across a river, bay, or lake. People v San Francisco & Alameda Railroad Co. 35 Cal 606, 619.

ferry. Verb: To transport persons and their belongings across a river or other body of water. 35 Am J2d Ferr § 1. Noun: A place where persons are taken across a river or other body of water in boats or other vessels for hire. A boat, barge, or raft, which, plying back and forth across a stream or other body of water for the conveyance of passengers and their belongings, thereby serves as a connection of the highways located on the opposite banks or shores. 35 Am J2d Ferr § 1. A merchant vessel. Re Ellingson (DC Cal) 300 F 225. The right or franchise granted by the state or an authorized political subdivision to continue, by means of watercraft, an interrupted land highway over interrupting waters and to charge a fee for the use thereof by the public. See 35 Am J2d Ferr § 2.

ferry boat. See **ferry**.

ferry bridge. A structure floating on water, which is hinged or chained to a wharf. 47 Am J1st Salv § 4.

ferry customers. Persons transported by ferry. Persons wishing to go along the highway, of which the ferry constitutes a part, and whom the proprietor of the ferry would be bound to transport on being called by them, and not such as wish to travel from one of the ferry landings to a point out of the highway. Taylor v Wilmington & Manchester Railroad Co. 49 NC (4 Jones L) 277, 282.

ferry franchise. The right or privilege, usually exclusive, granted by or under the authority of the legislature, to operate a ferry at a certain designated place. A public right obtained under a grant by the state or an authorized political subdivision to a designated person vesting in him the authority to continue an interrupted land highway over interrupting waters. 35 Am J2d Ferr § 6.

ferryman. A person operating a ferry.
In the understanding of the common law, a ferryman was a person who had the exclusive right of transporting passengers over rivers and other watercourses, for hire, at an established rate; and no other person could keep or employ a boat to his prejudice, either at the same place, or within a limited distance above or below him; and he was bound at all times to be ready with good boats and craft to convey passengers backwards and forwards, otherwise an action would lie against him. Clarke v State, 7 SC Eq 2 M'Cord 47.

ferry ramp. The sloping way leading from the land portion of a highway down to a ferry landing or up from a ferry landing to the land portion of a highway; a part of the highway generally but not necessarily a "highway" for all applications of a traffic regulation. Dilich v Templemen Bros. (La App) 164 So 261.

fertilizer. A substance, natural, as in the case of manure, or artificial, as in the case of bone meal, applied to the soil to increase fertility.

fesaunt. Same as **feasant**.

Festinatio justitiae est noverca infortunii (fes-ti-nā′-she-o jūs-ti′she-ē est no-ver′ka in-for-tun′ni-ī). The hastening of justice is the stepmother of misfortune.

festingman (fes′ting-man). A surety.

festing penny (fes′ting pen′′i). Money paid over as an earnest to bind a contract of hiring.

festinum remedium (fes′ti-num re-mē′di-um). A speedy remedy.

festival. A celebration, especially an annual celebration of a religious event. A merrymaking with music and other entertainment.
See **feasts**.

festuca (fes-tū′ką). Same as **fistuca**.

festum (fes′tum). A feast; a festival.

fet (fet). Done; made; a fact; a deed.

fete. An entertainment held outdoors; a festival.

fetiales (fe-she-ā′lēz). Same as **feciales**.

fetial law (fē′shial lâ). Same as **fecial law**.

feticide (fē′ti-sīd). The killing of the foetus in the uterus; a criminal abortion.

fetters (fet′ers). Manacles; shackles; irons and chains used to secure prisoners.

fetus (fē′tus). Same as **foetus**.

feu (fū). Fire; a hearth; a fee; a Scotch land tenure under which the holding was by the payment of rent either in produce or in money.

feu annuals. (Scotch.) The annual rent paid by the holder of a feu.

feuar (fū′är). (Scotch.) The holder or tenant of a feu.

feud. A long continued enmity, especially a quarrel between families lasting for generations. Another term for fee or fief.
See **fee**; **fief**; **vendetta**.

feuda antiqua (fū′da an-tī′qua). Plural of **feudum antiquum**.

feuda individua (fū′da in-di-vi′du-a). Impartible feuds or fees; that is, feuds or fees which were so made that they could descend only to the eldest son. See 2 Bl Comm 215.

feudal (fū′dal). Pertaining to that kind of land tenure under which the land was held of a superior, as opposed to allodial, where it was not. Pertaining to the feudal system of the medieval period.

feudal actions. Real actions,—actions which concerned real property only. Formerly, these actions were employed to settle all disputes concerning real property, but owing to their complicated nature they were superseded by more expeditious proceedings for trying titles. See 3 Bl Comm 117.

feudal canons of descent. The five canons of the English law of descent during the feudal period, their primary purpose being to support military power by preventing diffusion of the ownership of real property and promoting the accumulation of such property in the hands of a few. 23 Am J2d Desc & D § 7.

feudalism (fū'dạl-izm). Same as **feudal system**.

feudalize (fū'dạl-īz). To invest lands with the feudal system of tenure.

feudal law (fū'dạl lâ). The law pertaining to the feudal system of land tenure.

feudal system. The economic and social control of the medieval period, characterized by a stratification of the populace into classes of lords, men of arms, and serfs, its most important feature from the standpoint of the law being the system of land tenure.
See **feudal tenure**.

feudal tenure. That system of land tenure which had as its foundation the principle or fiction that the king is the universal lord and original proprietor of all the lands in his kingdom and that no man possesses or can possess any part of such lands which has not mediately or immediately been derived as a gift from the king, to be held upon feudal services. See 2 Bl Comm 51. The system which gave birth to the feud or fief.
See **bordage**; **fealty**; **fief**; **free services**; **homage, et seq.**; **honorary services**; **investiture**; **knight-service**; **primer seisin**; **relief**; **services**; **subinfeudation**.

feuda nova (fū'da nō'va). Plural of **feudum novum**.

feudary (fū'dạ-ri). Pertaining to the feudal system of land tenure; a tenant who held his land by feudal tenure, a feudatory.

feudatory (fū'dạ-tọ-ri). A person to whom a feud had been granted by his superior. See 2 Bl Comm 46.

feudbote (fūd'bōt). A fine imposed for engaging in a feud or quarrel.

feude. Deadly hatred; vengeance.
See **feud**.

feudist (fū'dist). A writer or commentator on the law connected with the feudal system of land tenure. One having a long-continued enmity toward another or one participating in a family feud.
See **feud**.

feudo (fay'oo-do). (Spanish.) A feud; a fee.

feudum (fū'dum). A feud; a fee; a fief.

feudum antiquum (fū'dum an-tī'kwu-um). An ancient feud; a feud which a person inherited by descent from his ancestors. See 2 Bl Comm 212.
According to the doctrine of the feudists, interests in land were divided into but two kinds, feuda antiqua and feuda nova, which are defined to be those to which the possessor succeeds as heir to his ancestor, and those which he has acquired in some other way. Priest v Cummings (NY) 20 Wend 338, 349.

feudum apertum (fū'dum a-per'tum). A free or open feud or fee,—a feud or fee which, by reason of the lack of an heir, on the death of the person last seized, reverted to the lord of the fee, by whom, or by those whose estate he had, it was given. See 2 Bl Comm 245.

feudum francum (fū'dum fran'kum). A free feud; a frank fee.

feudum hauberticum (fū'dum hâ-ber'ti-kum). A feud or fee held by the service of being present in full armor at the call of the lord.

feudum improprium (fū'dum im-prō'pri-um). An improper or derivative feud; that is, a feud having extraordinary incidents in its creation, such, for instance, as were originally bartered and sold to the feudatory for a price. See 2 Bl Comm 58.

feudum individuum (fū'dum in-di-vi'dū-um). An impartible feud or fee; that is, a feud or fee so made that it could descend only to the eldest son. See 2 Bl Comm 215.

feudum laicum (fū'dum lā'i-kum). A lay fee.

feudum ligium (fū'dum li'ji-um). A liege fee,—a fee or feud held directly of the king, with no intermediate lord.
"Allegiance is the tie, or ligamen, which binds the subject to the king, in return for that protection which the king affords the subject." See 1 Bl Comm 366.

feudum maternum (fū'dum ma-ter'num). A maternal fee; that is, a feud or fee which could only descend to heirs on the mother's side of the family. See 2 Bl Comm 212.

feudum militare (fū'dum mi-li-tā're). A knight's fee, —a determinate quantity of land held under tenure by knight-service, the measure of which was about twelve ploughlands and its value was about twenty pounds a year. See 2 Bl Comm 62.

feudum militus (fū'dum mi'li-tus). A knight's fee.
See **feudum militare**.

feudum nobile (fū'dum nō'bi-le). A feud or fee which was held by guard service, fealty, and homage.

feudum novum (fū'dum nō'vum). A new fee; a fee acquired in a manner other than succession or inheritance.

feudum novum ut antiquum (fū'dum nō'vum ut an-tī'kwu-um). A new fee held as an ancient one; that is, a new fee with all the qualities annexed to a fee descended from ancestors. See 2 Bl Comm 212.

feudum paternum (fū'dum pa-ter'num). A paternal fee; that is, a feud or fee which could only descend to heirs on the father's side of the family. See 2 Bl Comm 222.

feudum proprium (fū'dum prō'pri-um). A proper feud or fee; that is a feud or fee held by services which were strictly military. See 2 Bl Comm 58.

feudum simplex (fū'dum sim'plex). Same as **fee simple**.

Feudum sine investitura nullo modo constitui potest (fū'dum sī'ne in-ves-ti-tū'ra nul'ō mō'dō kon-sti'-shu-ī po'test). A fee cannot be created in any manner without an investiture.

feudum talliatum (fū'dum tal-li-ā'tum). Fee-tail. See 2 Bl Comm 112, note.

feu holding. The tenancy of lands under a feu right.

few (fū). Noun: A fee. Adjective: Small in number.

f. f. An abbreviation of **fieri facias**.

f.f.a. Abbreviation of "free from alongside."
See **free alongside steamer**.

f.g.a. Abbreviation of free of general average.
See **free from general average**.

FHA. Abbreviation for Federal Housing Administration.

fiance' (fi-än'sā). The male party to an engagement to wed.

fiancée (fi-än-sā). The female party to an engagement to wed.

fiancer (fī-ān-se'). To promise; to engage; to pledge.

fiar (fē'ạr). The holder of a fee or feu.

fiar prices. Prices at which grain could be sold, as fixed by the sheriffs of the several counties.

fiat (fī'at). An order emanating from an authoritative source and in the positive terms of "let it be done."

fiat in bankruptcy. An English term; an order signed by the lord chancellor authorizing the issuance of a commission in bankruptcy and the prosecution by the creditors of their complaint.

Fiat justitia (fī'at jūs-ti'she-a). Let justice be done.

Fiat justitia ruat coelum (fī'at jūs-ti'she-a ru'at sē'-lum). Let justice be done though the heavens fall asunder. Missouri, Kansas & Texas Railroad Co. v Merrill, 65 Kan 436, 70 P 358.

Fiat prout fieri consuevit; nil temere novandum (fī'at prō'ut fī'e-rī kon-su-ē'vit; nil te'me-rē no-van'dum). Let it be done in the customary manner; nothing should be adopted rashly.

Fiat ut petitur (fī'at ut pē'ti-ter). Let it be done as he asks or demands.

fictio (fik'she-o). A fiction.

Fictio cedit veritati (fik'she-ō sē'dit ve-ri-tā'tī). Fiction gives way to truth. Louisville v Portsmouth Sav. Bank (US) 14 Otto 469, 478, 26 L Ed 775, 778.

Fictio cedit veritati. Fictio juris non est, ubi veritas (fik'she-o se'dit ve-ri-tā'tī. fik'she-ō jū'ris non est, u'bi ve'ri-tās). Fiction gives way to truth. A fiction of law will not prevail where the fact appears.

Fictio est contra veritatem, sed pro veritate habetur (fik'she-o est kon'tra ve-ri-tā'tem, sed prō ve-ri-tā'te hā-bē'ter). Fiction is opposed to truth, but a fiction is taken for the truth.

Fictio juris non est ubi veritas (fik'she-ō jū'ris non est u'bi ve'ri-tās). A fiction of law will not prevail where the fact appears. Louisville v Portsmouth Sav. Bank (US) 14 Otto 469, 478, 26 L Ed 775, 778.

Fictio legis inique operatur alieni damnum vel injuriam (fik'she-ō lē'jis in'ik-wē o-pe-rā'ter ā-li-ē'nī dam'num vel in-jū'ri-am). A legal fiction should not be employed to work loss or injury to another.

Fictio legis neminem laedit (fik'she-o lē'jis ne'mi-nem lē'dit). A legal fiction injures no one.

fiction. In the sense of a fiction of law, a contrived condition or situation; the simulation of a status or condition with the purpose of accomplishing justice, albeit justice reached by devious means, as the fiction of casual ejector whereby the action of ejectment was converted into an action for the determination of title to real estate. 25 Am J2d Eject § 2. As a literary work, a novel, a portrayal with imaginary characters. In pleading, a false averment on the part of the plaintiff which the defendant is not allowed to traverse, the object being to give the court jurisdiction. Snider v Newell, 132 NC 614, 625, 44 SE 354.

For particular fictions of the law, see the specific term, such as **lost grant**.

fictione juris. Fiction of law. See **fiction**.

fiction of law. See **fiction**.

fictitious. Imaginary; not real; counterfeit; false; not genuine. State v Tinnin, 64 Utah 587, 232 P 543, 43 ALR 46, 48.

fictitious action. A feigned action. See **feigned action**.

fictitious bidding. Bidding at an auction without purpose of purchasing, merely to augment the final bid. 7 Am J2d Auct §§ 26, 27. See **puffing**.

fictitious credit. An indorsement on a promissory note, made without the authority of the maker or any indorser, of credit for a payment not made. 4 Am J2d Alt Inst § 62.

Such an indorsement is sometimes made by payee or indorsee for the purpose of tolling the statute of limitations. 34 Am J1st Lim Ac § 347.

fictitious debt. A feigned debt; one not real or genuine; a debt arbitrarily invented and set up, to accomplish an ulterior object; such as to defraud the revenue laws and the state. West Virginia Mortgage & Discount Corp. v Newcomer, 101 W Va 292, 296, 132 SE 748.

fictitious increase in capital stock. The issuance of stock in a corporation otherwise than for money paid, labor done, or property actually received. Stein v Howard, 65 Cal 616, 4 P 662.

fictitious name. Any name which a person adopts or assumes either for business purposes or in his social relations, other than the name of his parents. 38 Am J1st Name § 11. A name artificially contrived or adopted. General American Oil Co. v Wagoner Oil & Gas Co. 118 Okla 183, 247 P 99. A purely artificial name or a name that is or may be applied to a natural person. Pease v Pease, 35 Conn 131. A name other than the true name of a corporation, used by the corporation in transacting business or conducting its affairs. 18 Am J2d Corp § 143.

A feigned or pretended name employed by one relating it to another, not to himself. Soekland v Torch, 123 Ark 253, 185 SW 262. A name selected by a person perpetrating a fraud involving the employment of commercial paper, without intent that it represent any person, notwithstanding there is a person in the community who bears that name. Jordan-Marsh Co. v National Shawmut Bank, 201 Mass 397, 87 NE 740.

fictitious party. A party in whose name an action has been brought without any authority from him.

If committed in any of the king's superior courts, it was punishable as a high contempt to bring an action in the name of a person who did not exist, or of one who was ignorant of the suit. See 4 Bl Comm 134.

See **fictitious payee; John Doe**.

fictitious payee. A fictitious person, as where the name is feigned or pretended or where a name is inserted as payee without any intention that payment shall be made only in conformity therewith. 11 Am J2d B & N § 128.

It is well settled that an existing person may be a fictitious person within the meaning of the Negotiable Instruments Law. The rule is that when an instrument is made payable to an existing person, but with no intention that he shall have any interest in it, the name being used entirely as a matter of form, it is considered to be payable to a fictitious payee and so payable to bearer. Pennsylvania Co. v Federal Reserve Bank (DC Pa) 30 F Supp 982.

fictitious person. An imaginary person. See **fictitious payee**.

fictitious plaintiff. See **fictitious party**.

fictitious proceeding. See **feigned action**.

fictitious purchase. A purchase reported by a broker to a customer, although not actually made. 12 Am J2d Brok § 126.

fictitious receipt. A warehouse receipt issued for goods not actually in storage. Sykes v People, 127 Ill 117, 19 NE 705. A receipt issued by a seller of goods under a pretense of warehousing. Anno: 133 ALR 250.

fictitious return. A criminal offense by an officer or employee of the federal census, consisting in wilfully and knowingly making a feigned or pretended return. 14 Am J2d Census § 8.

fictitious sale. A sale reported by a broker to a customer, although not actually made. 12 Am J2d Brok § 126. A sale by a broker to a dummy for the purpose of securing the securities for himself. 12 Am J2d Brok § 153.

fictitious stock. Watered stock. Corporate stock not actually paid up but issued as fully paid up. 19 Am J2d Corp § 764.

fictitious suit. See feigned action.

fictitious warrants. Warrants purporting to have been issued by a public body, which are in fact fictitious and therefore void, even in the hands of innocent purchasers. People v Hayes, 365 Ill 318, 6 NE2d 645.

fide. See bona fide.

fide commissary (fī'de kom'i-sā-ri). A euphonious term suggested as a euphonious substitute for the awkward tongue-crippling "cestui que trust." Brown v Brown (NY) 83 Hun 160, 164, 31 NYS 650.

fidei commissa (fī'dē-ī kom-mis'sa). Plural of fidei commissium.

fidei-commissarius (fī'dē-ī). Same as fide commissary.

fidei commissum (fī'dē-ī kom-mis'sum). A trust arising upon a bequest with directions to deliver the subject matter or some portion of it to another person; in equity, an estate in possession, encumbered with the charge to surrender it to another. McDonough's Executors v Murdoch (US) 15 How 367, 407, 14 L Ed 732, 750; Succession of Meunier, 52 La Ann 79, 26 So 776.

See precatory trust; precatory words.

fidei laesione. See de fidei laesione.

fide-jubere (fī'de-ju-bē're). (Civil law.) To become surety for the obligation of another person.

fide-jussio (fī'de-ju'she-ō). (Civil law.) The transaction or agreement whereby one person becomes surety for the performance of the obligation of another person.

fide-jussor (fī-dẹ-jus'or). (Civil law.) A surety; a guarantor; a person who undertakes to answer for the debt or obligation of another.

fidelis (fī-dē'lis). Faithful; loyal.

fidelitas (fī-de'li-tās). Fidelity; fealty.

fidelitate. See de fidelitate.

fidelity. See good faith.

fidelity bond. A bond conditioned upon payment of loss resulting from embezzlement by an officer or employee, usually construed as an insurance contract, notwithstanding it is nominally in the form of a contract of suretyship.

See fidelity guaranty insurance.

fidelity guaranty insurance. A contract whereby one, for a consideration, agrees to indemnify another against loss arising from the want of integrity or fidelity of employees or persons holding positions of trust. People ex rel. Kasson v Rose, 174 Ill 310, 51 NE 246. In substance and effect a contract to be construed as a policy of insurance notwithstanding it may be nominally in the form of a contract of suretyship, having a principal, surety, and obligee. Anno: 7 ALR2d 946; 50 Am J1st Suret § 324.

fidem. Trust, confidence.

fidem mentiri (fī'dem men-tī'rī). To break the oath of fealty; that is, the oath of fealty which a tenant had made to his lord.

fide-promissor (fī'de-prō-mis'sor). Same as fide-jussor.

fides (fī'dēz). Faith; trust; confidence; a trust.
See bona fides.

Fides est obligatio conscientiae alicujus ad intentionem alterius (fī'dēz est ob-li-gā'she-ō kon-shen'she-ē a-li-kū'jus ad in-ten-she-ō'nem al-te'ri-us). A trust is an obligation of conscience of one person to the wishes of another.

fides facta (fī'dez fak'ta). Formal acts symbolizing the contracting of an obligation.

fides servanda (fī'dēz ser-van'da). Good faith is to be observed or kept.

"Fides servanda is indeed a rule of law, as well as of morality, and will be vigorously enforced in favor of one who is chargeable with no culpable negligence or inattention to his own interest. But to one so chargeable the law will not afford relief." Bostwick v Mutual Life Insurance Co. 116 Wis 392, 89 NW 538, 92 NW 246.

Fides servanda est (fī'dēz ser-van'da est). Good faith is to be observed. Smith v Richards (US) 13 Pet 26, 43, 10 L Ed 42, 50.

Fides servanda est; simplicitas juris gentium praevaleat (fī'dēz ser-van'da est; sim-pli'si-tās jū'ris jen'-she-um prē-va'le-at). Good faith is to be observed; the simplicity of the law of nations should prevail.

fiducia (fi-du'she-a). (Roman law.) A kind of pledge in which a transfer of the goods was made on condition that after satisfaction of the transferee's claim, he would retransfer them. See Mackeldey's Roman L § 334.

fiducial relation. Same as fiduciary relation.

Fiduciaries Act. One of the uniform statutes. 54 Am J1st Trusts § 271.

fiduciary (fi-dū'shi-ā-ri). Adjective: Held or founded in trust or confidence. Noun: A trustee, at least where the trust is an express trust. Svanoe v Jurgens, 144 Ill 507, 513, 33 NE 955.

The word embraces those and only those who are bound for the discharge of express trusts—technical trusts, where bond is required to be given by law—and it does not include those engaged in the execution of trusts springing from contract. Barnard & Co. v Sykes, 72 Miss 297, 302.

fiduciary capacity. The position of one in whom special confidence is reposed, and who is bound in equity and good conscience to act in good faith with due regard to the interest of the person reposing the confidence. Illinois v Riggins, 8 Ill 2d 78, 132 NE2d 519, 56 ALR2d 1149. For practical purposes, the capacity in which a trustee acts. Svanoe v Jurgens, 144 Ill 507, 513, 33 NE 955.

fiduciary. As the term is used in reference to exception from discharge in bankruptcy of debts created in a fiduciary capacity, it has reference to technical or express trust, not to those trusts which the law implies from a contract or from the position of parties to a transaction. Anno: 16 ALR2d 1152 § 2; 9 Am J2d Bankr § 802.

fiduciary contract. A contract which embraces trust and confidence reposed by one party in the other, refers to the integrity and fidelity of the party trusted rather than his credit or ability, and contemplates good faith rather than legal obligation. Smith v Vogilvie, 127 NY 143, 27 NE 807.

fiduciary fund. A fund entrusted to a fiduciary. See **trust fund**.

fiduciary relation. Often, but perhaps somewhat loosely, considered as the equivalent of confidential relation.
There is a technical distinction between a fiduciary relation and a confidential relation, the former being more correctly applicable to legal relationships between parties, such as guardian and ward, administrator and heirs, trustee and cestui que trust, principal and agent, etc., while the latter includes such relationships and also every other relationship wherein confidence is rightfully reposed and is exercised. Roberts v Parsons, 195 Ky 274, 242 SW 594.
See **confidential relation**.

fief (fēf). An estate in fee in real property, otherwise known as a feud; an inheritable estate. Dowdel v Hamm (Pa) 2 Watts 61, 65. Under the feudal system, an estate held by the performance of services for the grantor; a tenure by service rendered a superior lord.
Feuds originated in the military policy of the northern or Celtic nations who swarmed all over Europe on the decline of the Roman Empire. The conquering general allotted large districts of land to the superior officers of the army, and they, in turn made allotments to the soldiers. These allotments were the feuds which were given out as rewards or stipends for faithful services to be rendered by the donees in peace and in war; and in the event of a failure to render such services, the land reverted to him who granted it. See 2 Bl Comm 45.
See **derivative feud; Book of Fiefs; honorary feud; impartible feud; improper feud; military feuds; proper feud.**

fief d'haubert (fēf d'ô-ber). The Norman designation of a knight's fee. See 2 Bl Comm 62.

fief tenant (fēf ten'ant). The holder of a fief or fee.

field. A cultivated tract of land. State v McMinn, 81 NC 585, 587. A tract of land cultivated or pastured. An area where athletic games are played, for example, Soldiers' Field, in Chicago. An area of special knowledge or scientific endeavor, as the field of geology.
See **common field**.

field audit. An examination of the books and records of the taxpayer to determine the accuracy of his income tax return.

field book. A book containing the notes made by a surveyor in the field while making a survey, which describe by course and distance, and by natural or artificial marks found or made by him, the running of the lines, and the establishment of the corners. 12 Am J2d Bound § 1.

field manager. An employee or agent of a corporation rather than an officer of the company. Badger Oil & Gas Co. v Preston, 49 Okla 270, 152 P 383.

field notes. The notes in a surveyor's field book. See **field book**.

field warehousing. A device whereby manufacturers, jobbers, wholesalers, and others borrow money on the security of goods remaining stored in warehouses, or on storage ground, on their own premises, the procedure being to give as security warehouse receipts issued by a warehouseman placed in possession of the goods. Anno: 133 ALR 234. A method of business financing wherein the security is left more or less in possession of, and subject to handling and sale by, the debtor, as part of a going business, and often involving the substitutions of security from time to time as required to keep the collateral adequate in amount. 9 Am J2d Bankr § 965.

field work. Farm work. Scientific work close to nature, e. g. the observation by a biologist of ground squirrels in a meadow.

fierding courts. Ancient Gothic courts of very inferior jurisdiction which were so named because there were four of them in every superior district or hundred. See 3 Bl Comm 34.

fieri. See **in fieri**.

fieri facias (fī'e-rī fā'shi-as). A writ of execution; the ordinary writ for the seizure and sale of property of a judgment debtor. 30 Am J2d Exec § 28.
See **testatum writ**.

fieri facias de bonis testatoris (fī'e-rī fā'-she-as dē bō'nis tes-tā-tō'ris). A writ of execution against an executor as such, on account of a debt due from his testator and which can only be levied on property which belonged to the testator.

fieri feci (fī'e-rī fē'sī). I have caused it to be done or made,—formal words used in the sheriff's return on a fieri facias after he has made a levy under the writ.

Fieri non debet, sed factum valet (fī'e-rī non de'bet, sed fak'tum vā'let). Although it ought not to have been done, having been done, it is valid. Nichols v Ketcham (NY) 19 Johns 84, 92.

fi. fa. An abbreviation of **fieri facias**.

fifteenths (fif-tēnths'). Temporary aids issuing out of personal property, and granted to the king by parliament. These aids which were said to have been first granted under Henry the Second for the crusades, were first levied in tenths and later in fifteenths were a form of tax representing that fraction of the valuation of all personal property. See 2 Bl Comm 309.

FIFO. Abbreviation of **first in, first out**.

Fifth Amendment. An amendment to the Constitution of the United States, contained in the Bill of Rights, which, in popular parlance and legal literature, is synonymous with the privilege against self-incrimination. Quinn v United States, 349 US 155, 99 L Ed 964, 75 S Ct 668, 51 ALR2d 1157.

fifth degree of kinship. A second cousin under the civil law method of computing degrees of kinship which has been adopted in most American jurisdictions. 23 Am J2d Desc & D § 48.

fifty-fifty. Division into halves. Chafin v Main Island Creek Coal Co. 85 W Va 459, 102 SE 291, 11 ALR 657.

fifty per cent rule. The rule of marine insurance that where the loss or cost of repair equals or exceeds 50 per cent of the value of the vessel, there may be an abandonment and recovery as for a total loss. 29A Am J Rev ed Ins § 1577.

fight. Verb: To strive for victory in battle or over an opponent in single combat; an attempt to defeat an opponent or the enemy by blows or weapons. Sullivan v State, 67 Miss 346, 351. To work hard for a cause against opposition; to strive for success in an endeavor. Noun: An altercation accompanied by blows. The meeting of opponents or opposing forces in battle or contest. The striving for a cause or for success in an endeavor.
See **challenge to fight; combat; fighting; prize fight.**

fighting. Engaging in a fight, irrespective of which participant is the aggressor. United States Mut. Acci. Asso. v Millard, 43 Ill App 148.

fightnite. Same as **fightwite.**

fightwite (fīt'wīt). A fine for the offense of disturbing the peace by fighting.

filacer (fĭl'ạ-sėr). One of the clerks in the English superior court at Westminster who filed writs and issued process.

filare (fī-lā're). To file.

filch. To steal, particularly something of petty value. Peck v Bez, 129 W Va 247, 50 SE2d 1.

file. Verb: To deposit an instrument or document with a public officer at his office with the purpose of having him preserve the instrument or document as one of the records of his office. 45 Am J1st Recds § 67. To place an instrument, document, even an exhibit or small object, in a place of deposit, usually indexed or marked in a manner making location of the subject convenient. To receive an instrument or document officially, as where a clerk of court receives a pleading and notes the fact of the filing and the date thereof by way of an indorsement on the pleading. Meridian Nat. Bank v Hoyt & Bros. Co. 74 Miss 221, 21 So 12. Noun: A place where instruments, documents, exhibits, etc. are deposited and kept, preferably in covers so marked and tabbed that the subjects may be readily located.

file clerk. An employee, sometimes a public employee, whose duty it is to file instruments under a system of separate categories and keep the files in a usable condition.

filed for record. Deposited with a proper officer at his office with direction, express or implied, for recording. 45 Am J1st Recds § 67.
Indorsing the fact and time of its deposit is not an essential part of the filing. Neither does it appear to be an essential that the deposit be made within the hours fixed by law for keeping the office open. Edwards v Grand, 121 Cal 254, 53 P 796.

filiate. See **affiliate.**

filiatio (fī-li-ā'she-ō). Filiation; paternity.

filiation. See **affiliation.**

Filiatio non potest probari (fī-li-ā'she-ō non pō'test prō-bā'rī). Paternity cannot be proved. Powell v State ex rel. Fowler, 84 Ohio St 165, 95 NE 560.

filiation proceeding. See **affiliation proceeding.**

filing. See **file; filed for record.**

filing articles of incorporation. The depositing of articles of incorporation in the public office specified by statute as the place of filing with the intent that the document is to remain on file in the office. 18 Am J2d Corp § 39.

filing bill in equity or other pleading. See **file.**

filing claim in bankruptcy. The delivery of a proof of claim against a bankrupt to the clerk of the district court, the referee, if the case has been referred, or to the trustee in bankruptcy. 9 Am J2d Bankr § 449.

filing date. The time as of which a claim or demand must be filed. The date of filing as indorsed upon an instrument or pleading by the officer who receives it.
The filing date of an application for a patent is the date upon which the application was filed in the patent office, and not the date on which the filing fee was paid. Hazeltine Corp. v Electric Service Engineering Corp. (DC NY) 18 F2d 662.

filing fee. The fee charged by a public officer for the filing of a pleading, an instrument, or document in his office. The amount to be paid to the clerk of court upon filing a petition in bankruptcy or a petition for relief in the bankruptcy court by way of reorganization or plan for rehabilitation of a debtor. 9 Am J2d Bankr § 1627.

filing laws. Statutes which require the filing of an instrument as a condition of complete effectiveness.

filing libel. Commencement of action in admiralty. 2 Am J2d Adm § 153.

filiolus (fi-li-ō'lus). A godson.

filius (fī'li-us). A son.

Filius est nomen naturae, sed haeres nomen juris (fī'li-us est nō'men nā-tū'rē, sed hē'rēz nō'men jū'ris). "Son" is the natural name, but "heir" is the legal name.

filius familias (fī'li-us fa-mi'li-ās). A son of the family,—a son who is under the control of his parents.

Filius in utero matris est pars viscerum matris (fī'li-us in u'te-rō mā'tris est parz vi'ser-um mā'tris). A son in his mother's womb is part of his mother's vitals.

filius mulieratus (fī'li-us mu-li-e-rā'tus). A mulier; a mulier puisne; that is, the legitimate son of a woman who, before her marriage to his father, gave birth to a bastard by the same father. See 2 Bl Comm 248.

filius nullius (fī'li-us nul-lī'us). The child of nobody; the common law status of an illegitimate child. 10 Am J2d Bast § 8.

filius populi (fī'li-us pop'ū-lī). The child of the people; the common law status of an illegitimate child.

filizer. Same as **filacer.**

fill. A roadbed, whether for railroad or highway, which is raised by an embankment above the natural level of the land. O. & R. V. R. Co. v Severin, 30 Neb 318, 322; 25 Am J1st High § 67. A method of reclamation. 56 Am J1st Water § 501.

fill an office. To accept and discharge the duties of an office. Johnston v Wilson, 2 NH 202, 203.

fille (fē). A girl; a daughter.

filled cheese. A cheese enriched by adding food elements in manufacture.

filled cheese tax. A federal tax upon the manufacture, importation, or dealing in the product known as filled cheese. 30 Am J1st Int Rev § 113.

filled land. Land which has been artificially raised in elevation by depositing or dumping dirt, refuse, or rubble thereon. An area where the grade has been raised. 1 Am J2d Adj L § 27.

filling. Bringing a highway or a railroad to a proper grade by raising an embankment. Dumping dirt, refuse, or rubble on a tract of low land.
See **fill; filled land.**

filling blanks. The completion of an operative deed by filling in blanks above the grantor's signature, with the authority of the grantor. 23 Am J2d Deeds § 138. An alteration of an instrument delivered as a complete instrument, notwithstanding it contains some blank spaces. 4 Am J2d Alt Inst § 39. An act which may be authorized by a grantor, maker, or obligor, either expressly or impliedly. 50 Am J1st Suret § 26.

filling in instrument. See **filling blanks.**

filling prescription. Furnishing, preparing, and combining the requisite materials in due proportion as prescribed. 25 Am J2d Drugs § 5.

filling station. See **gasoline filling station.**

fill out. To complete a document by writing in the blank spaces left for that purpose.
See **filling blanks.**

filly. A young mare. An obsolete expression for a lively, roistering, or wanton girl. Lunsford v State, 1 Tex App 448, 450.

fils (fil). A son.

filtering. Removing foreign matter from water intended for domestic use. 56 Am J1st Watwk § 76.

filthy. Dirty, foul, corrupt. In application to food; containing dirt, refuse, offal, or impurities, or adulterations, so as to be unfit for consumption. Anno: 45 ALR2d 861. As used in federal statutes respecting the use of the mails: nasty, dirty, vulgar, indecent, offensive in the moral sense, morally depraving. Anno: 76 L Ed 850.

filum (fī'lum). A thread; an edge.

filum aquae (fī'lum a'kwē). The thread of the water, —the middle or center line of a river or stream. Ingraham v Wilkinson, 21 Mass (4 Pick) 268.

filum forestae (fī'lum fo-res'tē). The edge or boundary of a forest.

filum viae (fī'lum vī'ē). The thread or center line of a way, street, or road.

fin (fin). The end.

final. Conclusive; terminating all controversy, doubt or dispute; the end, ultimate, or last. Saylor v Duel, 236 Ill 429, 86 NE 119.
See **finality.**

final account. See **final report.**

final and appealable order. See **final order.**

final appealable order. See **final order.**

final appeal court. The court of delegates,—which was at one time a court of final appeal in English admiralty and ecclesiastical cases.

final assessment. A special assessment from the confirmation of which no appeal is taken within the time for appeal. 25 Am J2d Drains § 52.

final concord (kon'kord). The final agreement of the parties in levying a fine.

final costs. The costs of suit as allowed and awarded upon entry of final judgment or the termination of the litigation; the costs awarded to the party ultimately prevailing. 20 Am J2d Costs § 9.

final decision. For the purpose of appellate review: a decision which disposes of the whole case, adjudicates all rights including questions of liability and compensation, ends litigation on the merits, and leaves nothing for the court to do but execute the judgment, Lewis v E. I. Du Pont De Nemours & Co. (CA5 Ga) 183 F2d 29, 21 ALR2d 757; a decision which terminates the suit and puts the case out of court, although it does not adjudicate the merits of the litigated controversy, 4 Am J2d A & E § 55; a decision which terminates an action or proceeding, although it does not dispose of the whole subject matter in litigation. 4 Am J2d A & E § 53.

A "final decision" rendered appealable by 28 USC 1291 involves the idea of a definitive judgment, order, or decree determining something more than a mere procedural incident in a lawsuit, and a judgment definitively adjudicating a claim for relief in a civil action clearly comes within the term. Bendix Aviation Corp. v Glass, 195 F2d 267, 38 ALR2d 356.

final decision on the merits. A determination of the merits of a cause which will, in due time, by operation of law, lead to a final judgment in the cause. Fisher v Sun Underwriters Ins. Co. 55 RI 175, 179 A 702, 103 ALR 1097.

final decree. The decree rendered by a court of bankruptcy whereby the estate of a debtor undergoing readjustment or reorganization in bankruptcy is closed, the receiver or trustee, if any discharged, and such other relief by way of injunction or otherwise, as may be equitable is granted. A decree in equity which disposes of the cause or a part thereof, reserving no question or direction for future determination in reference to the cause or the part of the cause adjudicated, 27 Am J2d Eq § 245; the practical equivalent of final judgment in modern practice.

According to some authorities, a decree may be partly final and partly interlocutory—final as to its determination of all issues of fact and law, and interlocutory as to its mode of execution. 27 Am J2d Eq § 245.
See **final judgment.**

final distribution. The final allocation of the property in the estate of a decedent under order of court to the person or persons entitled thereto. Kemster v Evans, 81 Wis 247, 51 NW 327.

final estimate. For the purpose of a limitation of time for suit upon a contractor's bond:—the conclusion and determination of a person having final authority to make the estimate. Consolidated Indem. & Ins. Co. v Fischer Lime & Cement Co. 187 Ark 131, 58 SW2d 928.

final hearing. The hearing which results in a final decision or adjudication. 27 Am J2d Eq § 235.

final injunction. A final decree of injunction which adjudicates the merits of the cause. 28 Am J Rev ed Inj § 319.
See **permanent injunction.**

finalis concordia (fī-nā'lis kon-kor'di-a). Same as **final concord.**

finality. Conclusiveness; completeness. 2 Am J2d Admin L § 483. The quality in a judgment or decision of being a full and unconditional determination. 4 Am J2d A & E § 51. The quality of conclusiveness, which may be the result of statute or, as in the case of an agreement for arbitration, of contract. 5 Am J2d Arb & A § 29.

See **final**.

final judgment. A judgment which determines and disposes of the whole merits of the cause before the court by declaring that the plaintiff is or is not entitled to recovery by the remedy chosen, or completely and finally disposes of a branch of the cause which is separate and distinct from other parts thereof. 30A Am J Rev ed Judgm § 121. A judgment which determines a question in such a manner as to terminate or end the matter so completely as to preclude all future inquiry concerning the truth itself. Re Enger, 225 Minn 229, 30 NW2d 694, 18 ALR2d 1048. A judgment which puts at an end the judicial labor in a cause. Ruth v United States Fidelity & Guaranty Co. (Fla) 83 So 2d 769, 55 ALR2d 541. For any purpose of the application of the doctrine of res judicata:—any judicial decision upon a question of law or fact which is not provisional and subject to change in the future by the same tribunal. Bannon v Bannon, 270 NY 484, 1 NE2d 975, 105 ALR 1401. For the purposes of appeal:—a judgment which terminates the litigation between the parties on the merits and leaves nothing to be done but to enforce by execution what has been determined. St. Louis, Iron Mountain & S. R. R. Co. v Southern Express Co. 27 L Ed 638, 108 US 24, 2 S Ct 6.

The sentence in a criminal case. Miller v Aderhold, 288 US 206, 77 L Ed 702, 53 S Ct 325.

As used in the federal statute conferring jurisdiction on the Supreme Court to review the "final judgment" of a state court, the expression is defined as applying to all judgments and decrees which determine the particular case, that is, such as terminate the litigation between the parties on the merits of the case, so that, in case of affirmance in the federal court, the court below would have nothing to do but to execute the judgment or decree it had already rendered. Georgia R. & Power Co. v Decatur, 262 US 432, 67 L Ed 1065, 43 S Ct 613.

final judgment or decree. See **final decree; final judgment**.

final jurisdiction. A jurisdiction which, once exercised, is exclusive of the exercise of jurisdiction over the same matter by any other court. Saylor v Duel, 236 Ill 429, 86 NE 119. A term of particular reference to criminal cases, being jurisdiction to convict and sentence or acquit and discharge, as distinguished from jurisdiction over a preliminary hearing wherein the accused may be released from custody or bound over to the grand jury. State v Fox, 83 Conn 286, 76 A 302.

finally compelled. In reference to a public utility "finally compelled" to put lower rates in effect:— the entry by a court of a final order making effective a challenged rate structure. Texarkana v Arkansas, Louisiana Gas Co. 306 US 188, 83 L Ed 598, 59 S Ct 448.

final meeting. The meeting of creditors in a bankruptcy proceeding, to be held, as ordered by the court, whenever the affairs of the estate are ready to be closed, wherein there shall be considered the trustee's statement of his administration of the estate, his accounts, the discharge of the trustee, and the closing of the estate, and such other matters as may be required for determination. 9 Am J2d Bankr § 584.

final order. A final decision or judgment for purposes of an appeal. An administrative order which is conclusive; an administrative order which has reached such stage of completeness that it can be subjected to judicial review. 2 Am J2d Admin L § 483.

An order affecting a substantial right in an action, when such order, in effect, determines the action and prevents a judgment, and an order affecting a substantial right, made in a special proceeding or upon a summary application in an action after judgment. Exchange Trust Co. v Oklahoma State Bank, 126 Okla 193, 259 P 589.

In habeas corpus proceedings, an order which either discharges the writ or discharges the relator is a final order and appealable, but an order which sustains the writ and remands the relator to custody that a rehearing may be had, is not final. United States v Curran (CA2 NY) 18 F2d 958.

See **final decision; final judgment**.

final passage. The completion of legislative action in the adoption of a bill or other legislative measure as one to become law. Norman v Kentucky Board of Managers, 93 Ky 537, 20 SW 901. The passage of a bill over a veto. 50 Am J1st Stat § 504.

final process. Process issued in an action or proceeding after judgment has been entered; as a writ of execution. Amis v Smith (US) 16 Pet 303, 313, 10 L Ed 973, 976.

final proof. The showing made by a homesteader which will entitle him to a patent. 42 Am J1st Pub L §§ 23, 73.

final report. The report required of a trustee in bankruptcy, wherein he is required to set forth a detailed statement of his administration of the estate. 9 Am J2d Bankr § 1260. The final account and report by an executor or administrator, a guardian, a receiver, or other fiduciary, of his acts in the administration, his receipts and disbursements, and the money and property in his hands for disposition.

Regardless of how designated, any report as to the last or final acts of a guardian, on which a hearing is had and on which the court fixes and determines the amount due the ward's estate from a guardian then or theretofore removed from office, is the final account of such guardian, in so far as the guardian is concerned. Re Kostohris' Estate, 96 Mont 226, 29 P2d 829.

final settlement. An agreement fully settling the rights of partners after a dissolution of the partnership. 40 Am J1st Partn § 489. The winding up of the affairs in the estate of a decedent, a receivership, a guardianship, or other fiduciary engagement, preliminary to the closing of the estate and the discharge of the fiduciary.

When used in connection with a public transaction and account, the term connotes an administrative determination of the amount due, that is, an appropriate administrative determination of the amount which the government is finally bound to pay, or entitled to receive, as indicated by some public or official act; it does not depend upon the existence of a dispute with the other party. Antrim Lumber Co. v Hannan (CA10 Okla) 18 F2d 548; Anno: 119 ALR 280.

final submission. As the ending of the period within which a case may be dismissed, or otherwise voluntarily terminated, without prejudice:—in a jury case, the moment when the court directs the jury to retire in charge of an officer for their consideration of the case, or to enter upon consideration of the case without retiring, 24 Am J2d Dism § 33; in a trial before the court without a jury, the moment when the court takes the case under advisement, the evidence having been presented, the

FINANCE [474] FINE

arguments made, and the briefs filed. 24 Am J2d Dism § 34.

finance (fi-nans' or fī'nans). The public revenue; public or government funds; the management of money.

finance charges. See **carrying charges**.

finance company. A company engaged in making loans, usually on the security of additional sale contracts, instalment sale contracts, chattel mortgages, or trust receipts.

financial circumstances. See **financial condition**.

financial condition. The wealth of a person and his income, whether from property or his earnings.

financial corporation. A familiar term in taxation statutes, the meaning of which varies according to the nature of the activities of the particular entity involved and the context of the entire statute, one of the broader interpretations including all classes of corporations organized and created for business purposes, as distinguished from public, charitable or other corporations. 51 Am J1st Tax § 930.

financial depression. An economic depression.

financial emergency. In reference to the condition frequently appearing in trusts for the benefit of the widow of a testator whereunder the trustee is authorized to withdraw funds from principal for payment to the widow in event of a "financial emergency":—not a temporary unavailability of resources to meet a need, but a situation where the widow's financial resources, including her income from the trust estate are, in the best informed judgment of the trustee in considering an urgent need of the widow, in such a state of insufficiency or unavailability that the encroachment upon principal will be immediately necessary for the widow's maintenance, comfort, and general welfare. Lyter v Vestal, 355 Mo 457, 196 SW2d 769, 2 ALR2d 1375.

Widespread unemployment is an "emergency," especially during severe winter weather. 38 Am J1st Mun Corp § 450.

financially embarrassed. Incumbered with debt; beset with urgent claims and demands; unable to meet pecuniary engagements. Hayes v Press Co. 127 Pa 642, 18 A 331.

financial rating. See **credit standing**.

financial reports. The reports periodically issued by a corporation to stockholders, showing the financial condition of the corporation. 18 Am J2d Corp § 174.

financial responsibility laws. Statutes requiring proof of financial responsibility as a condition of the granting of a driver's license or certificate of registration; statutes providing for the suspension or revocation of a driver's license or certificate of registration for failure to satisfy a final judgment or furnish proof of responsibility after an accident or a violation of a motor vehicle statute. 7 Am J2d Auto § 135. Statutes requiring insurance as a condition of the operation of a motor vehicle.
See **compulsory insurance**.

financial standing. See **credit report**; **credit standing**.

financial statement. A statement in writing often required of a borrower of money from a bank stating fully all of his assets and liabilities. Re Sine (DC W Va) 25 F Supp 800.
See **credit statement**.

financial worth. The value of a person's property less what he owes, or the value of his resources less his liabilities. Boney v Central Mut. Ins. Co. 213 NC 470, 196 SE 837.

find. To discover a lost chattel. To discover a person with whom one has been out of touch. To learn or become apprised of something. To arrive at a decision or, if a jury is involved, at a verdict. State ex rel. Higgins v Beloit, 74 Wis 267, 42 NW 110. To ascertain by judicial inquiry. State ex rel. Morris v Bulkeley, 61 Conn 287, 23 A 186.

find and establish. To ascertain and confirm that which was previously doubtful; as, for example, the pre-existing line, on the respective sides of which the parties had held the title ever since they became the proprietors of the adjoining lots. Weeks v Trask, 81 Me 127, 16 A 413.

find bail. To furnish or provide bail; to secure bail or to secure persons to act as sureties on a bail bond.

finder. A person who discovers personal property lost by him or by another. For the purpose of the crime of larceny by finder, one who discovers lost property with knowledge that it is lost property. Weeks v Hackett, 104 Me 264, 71 A 858.
See **lost property**; **treasure-trove**.

finder's lien. The lien of a finder of lost property upon the property for his expenses in caring for the property, 1 Am J2d Aband § 31, also for the reward offered for the restoration of the property. 1 Am J2d Aband § 25.

finding. Discovering property which has been lost. Becoming apprised of something. The ascertainment of a fact by the judge or chancellor in an equity suit. 27 Am J2d Equity § 238. A judicial statement of a conclusion of law or fact. State ex rel. Higgins v Beloit, 74 Wis 267, 42 NW 110. A determination made by an administrative agency. 2 Am J2d Admin L § 434.
See **finding of fact**.

finding of fact. The result of reasoning from the evidentiary facts. Greenberg v Lee, 196 Or 157, 248 P2d 324, 35 ALR2d 567. A conclusion drawn by the trial court from the facts without the exercise of legal judgment. 53 Am J1st Trial § 1132. A written statement of an ultimate fact as found by the court, signed by the court, and filed in court, often required by statute as support for the decision and judgment in a trial to the court. 53 Am J1st Trial § 1131. A finding made by arbitrators. 5 Am J2d, Arb & A § 127. Finding of referee or master. The finding of a coroner or medical examiner at an inquest conducted to ascertain the cause of death of a person. 18 Am J2d Corn § 16.

In a trial to the court, the court makes findings. A jury, on the other hand, ordinarily makes no findings of fact. It arrives at a verdict, making findings of fact only as special findings or a special verdict is required in a particular case. State ex rel. Higgins v Beloit, 74 Wis 267, 42 NW 110.
See **special finding**; **special verdict**.

fine. A sum of money exacted of a person guilty of an offense as a pecuniary punishment, the amount of which may be fixed by law or left to the discretion of the court. 21 Am J2d Crim L § 599. A payment required of a member of a club, society, or fraternal order for misconduct or delinquency in attendance or payment of dues. 6 Am J2d Asso & C § 32.

See **excessive fine**; **fine to bar entail**; **joint fine**.

Fine and Recoveries Act. A statute enacted in England in 1833, abolishing fines and common recoveries and providing for conveyances by deed instead.

fine capiendo pro terris. See **de fine capiendo pro terris.**

fine for alienation (fīn fôr āl-yen-ā'shọn). A sum of money which was exacted by the lord from his tenant in chivalry whenever the tenant had occasion to make over his land to another person. See 2 Bl Comm 71.

fine force (fīn fors). Absolute necessity; actual compulsion.

fine for endowment (fīn fôr en-dou'mẹnt). A sum of money exacted from a widow by the feudal lord upon the assignment of her dower. This was one of the oppressions which was remedied first by the charter of Henry the First, and afterwards by Magna Charta. See 2 Bl Comm 135.

finem facere (fī'nem fā'se-re). To impose a fine; to pay a fine.

fine non capiendo pro pulchre placitando. See **de fine non capiendo pro pulchre placitando.**

fine pro redisseisina capiendo. See **de fine pro redisseisina capiendo.**

fine sur cognizance de droit come ceo que il ad de son done (fi-n ser kon'i-zạns dē droa kom kē il ad dē sōn dōn). A fine of land upon the acknowledgment of the right (of the cognizee) as that which he has by the gift (of his cognizor); wherein the cognizor acknowledges his gift of the land to the plaintiff, the cognizee.

This was the best and surest kind of a fine; for thereby the deforciant, in order to keep his covenant with the plaintiff, of conveying to him the lands in question, and at the same time to avoid the formality of an actual feoffment and livery, acknowledged in court a former feoffment, or gift in possession, to have been made by him to the plaintiff. See 2 Bl Comm 352.

fine sur cognizance de droit tantum (fi-n ser kon'i-zạns dē droa tan'tum). A fine upon acknowledgment of the right merely; not with the circumstance of a preceding gift from the cognizor. This fine was commonly used to pass a reversionary interest, which was in the cognizor. See 2 Bl Comm 353.

fine sur concessit (fīn ser kon-ses'sit). A fine of land wherein the cognizor, in order to make an end of disputes, though he acknowledges no precedent right, yet grants to the cognizee an estate de novo, usually for life or years, by way of supposed composition. And this may be done reserving a rent, or the like; for it operates as a new grant. See 2 Bl Comm 353.

fine sur done, grant et render (fīn ser dōn, grān e render). A double fine, comprehending both the "fine sur cognizance de droit cum ceo," etc., and the fine "sur concessit." This fine might be used to create particular limitations of estate, whereas the fine sur cognizance de droit cum ceo, etc., conveyed nothing but an absolute estate, either of inheritance or at least of freehold. See 2 Bl Comm 353.

fine to bar entail. A method, long since obsolete, if not entirely illegal, of defeating a fee tail, being a fictitious proceeding under which the entail could be barred, consisting of the acknowledgement in a feigned suit in open court of a previous conveyance by the tenant in tail. 28 Am J2d Est § 47.

See **common recovery.**

fine to convey. A collusive proceeding at common law whereby a married woman by uniting with her husband in a suit upon a purported agreement was enabled to effect a conveyance of her real estate.

fingerprinting. Taking and preserving the fingerprints of a person for purposes of identification and of connecting him or exculpating him from participation in a criminal offense. 21 Am J2d Crim L § 369.

fingerprints. Marks left by a person's fingers on objects, the most singular characteristic of which is the dissimilarity between the fingerprints of any two persons, which has rendered fingerprints most desirable evidence for purposes of identification. Impressions of the fingers taken and preserved on cards so as to be readily available for purposes of identification of the person as such may ultimately be required.

The fact that every fingertip has a series of convolutions in the skin surface, no two of which are alike, and which students of the subject can classify and describe so as to facilitate search, has made identification of a criminal almost certain whenever a clear impression of bloody or dirty fingers has been left on the scene of the crime. See 29 Am J2d Ev § 770.

finibus levatis. See **de finibus levatis.**

finire (fī-nī're). To finish; to end; to fine; to impose a fine; to pay a fine.

finis (fī'nis). A finish; a fine; the end; the limit; a boundary.

Finis est amicabilis compositio et finalis concordia ex consensu et concordia domini regis vel justiciarum (fī'nis est a-mi-kā'bi-lis kom-po-zi'she-ō et fi-nā'lis kon-kor'di-a ex kon-sen'sū et kon-kor'di-a do'mi-nī rē'jis vel jūs-ti-she-ā-rum). A fine is a friendly settlement and final concord by the consent of our lord the king or the justices.

Finis finem litibus imponit (fī'nis fī'nem lī'ti-bus im-pō'nit). The termination of a suit puts an end to litigation. State v Lee, 65 Conn 265, 30 A 1110.

finished article. A completed article for the purposes of a tariff act. 21 Am J2d Cust D § 44.

Finis rei attendendus est (fī'nis rē'ī at-ten-den'dus est). The completion of anything ought to be attended to.

Finis unius diei est principium alterius (fī'nis ū'ni-us dī'ē-ī est prin-si'pi-um al-te'ri-us). The end of one day is the beginning of another.

finitio (fi-ni'she-ō). The finish; the end; the completion.

finium regundorum actio (fī'ni-um re-gun-dō'rum ak'she-ō). (Civil law.) An action to establish a boundary line.

firdnite. Same as **ferdwit.**

fire. Verb: To discharge an employee; to make or keep something burning; to supply fuel, as to a furnace. Noun: A burning; a conflagration. As used in a fire insurance policy: a hostile, rather than a friendly fire. 29A Am J Rev Ins § 1287.

See **destroyed by fire; friendly fire; hostile fire; loss by fire.**

fire and sword. See **letters of fire and sword.**

firearms. Rifles, shotguns, revolvers, any weapon by which a shot is discharged by an explosive force. Weapons which act by the force of gunpowder. Harris v Cameron, 81 Wis 239, 243.

As used in a statute prohibiting parades of unauthorized bodies with firearms, any gun which to the ordinary observer appears to be an efficient weapon capable of being discharged is held to be a firearm whether it has in fact been rendered harmless or not. Commonwealth v Murphy, 166 Mass 171, 44 NE 138.

Firearms Act. A federal statute having for its purpose the regulation and taxation of the transfer of certain firearms. 26 USC §§ 2700 et seq.

fire bell. A fire alarm.

firebote (fīr'bōt). The right of estovers. See **estovers**.

fire clause. A clause common in bills of lading exempting the carrier from loss or damage to the freight caused by fire. 14 Am J2d Car § 570.

fire department. An agency of a municipality or town created, organized, and equipped to extinguish fires.

fire door. A door of fireproof material, to be kept closed as a precaution against the spread of fire in a building. 29A Am J Rev ed Ins § 930.

fire extinguisher. A portable device containing a chemical element which can be sprayed upon a fire for the purpose of controlling or extinguishing it; required equipment upon a motorboat under some statutes. 12 Am J2d Boats § 12.

fireguard. A person employed to maintain a watch against the breaking out of fire. Anno: 12 ALR2d 1142. A fire door; a screen to prevent the spread of an open fire.

fire hazard. A building of such structure and in such condition as to be in danger of catching on fire. Any collection of combustible material, but particularly material easily ignited. An industrial operation which emits sparks.

fire insurance. A contract to indemnify the insured against loss by fire to the property insured. 29 Am J Rev ed Ins § 4. A personal contract between the insurer and the insured. 29 Am J Rev ed Ins § 183. A form of automobile insurance. 7 Am J2d Auto Ins § 43.

fire insurance policy. A personal contract to indemnify the insured against loss by fire to the property insured; a contract of indemnity to reimburse the insured for his actual loss not exceeding an agreed sum. 29 Am J Rev ed Ins § 4. A contract of indemnity by which the insurer agrees to indemnify the insured against loss or damage to the insured property by fire, not exceeding the amount of the insurance. Citizens Ins. Co. v Foxbilt, Inc. 226 F2d 641, 53 ALR2d 1376.

fire limits. An area wherein the erection of buildings is regulated in reference to the kinds of building materials used, the purpose of regulation being to avoid or lessen the risk of fire. 13 Am J2d Bldgs § 19.

fire loss. The risk covered by a fire insurance policy. Inclusive of the destruction of property directly or indirectly pursuant to the orders of civil authorities. Anno: 76 ALR2d 1140, 1146, 1147. Loss from a hostile fire, not loss from a friendly fire. 29A Am J Rev ed Ins § 1287. Including a loss caused by an explosion resulting from a fire. German American Ins Co. v Hyman, 42 Colo 156, 94 P 27.
Loss or damage by fire, as the terms are used in fire insurance policies, means loss or damage of which fire was the immediate or proximate cause. The damage need not be caused by direct contact with the fire and it is not necessary that any part of the insured property actually ignite or be consumed by fire; as where it was held that the fall of the insured building was within the policy, although no part of it ignited or was consumed by fire. Russell v German fire Ins. Co. 100 Minn 528, 111 NW 400.
See **fire**.
See **destroyed by fire**.

fireman. A man on the force of a fire department. A man who feeds and maintains the fire in an engine or furnace.

firemen's pensions. Pensions paid to superannuated or disabled firemen. 40 Am J1st Pens § 18.

fire ordeal. See **trial by fire**.

fire policy. See **fire insurance policy**.

fireproof. Literally, incombustible or proof against fire, but, in the ordinary legal sense, indestructible by an ordinary fire. Diebold Safe & Lock Co. v. Huston, 55 Kan 104, 39 P 1035.
See **incombustible**.

fireproof safe clause. Same as **iron-safe clause**.

fire regulations. Regulations relating to the materials used, location, and method of construction of buildings, having the purpose of reducing the fire hazard, particularly in business sections and thickly populated areas. 13 Am J2d Bldgs §§ 12 et seq. Statutes or ordinances requiring fire drills and periodic inspections for fire hazards.

fire underwriters. See **underwriters**.

firkin (fėr'kin). A liquid measure equivalent to eight and four-fifths American gallons or nine imperial or English gallons.

firm. Noun: An unincorporated business, particularly a partnership; the members of a partnership, collectively. Ryder v Wilcox, 103 Mass 24, 28. Adjective: Binding.

firma (fir'ma). Same as **farm**.

firma alba (fir'ma al'ba). White rents,—rents payable in silver money.

firma feodi (fir'ma fū'dī). Same as **fee-farm**.

firman (fėr'mạn or fėr-män'). A passport; a license; a permit.

firmaratio (fir-ma-rā'she-ō). The right of a tenant to his lands.

firmarius (fir-mā'ri-us). A tenant who held his land for life or for a term of years.

firme. Same as **farm**.

Firmior et potentior est operatio legis quam dispositio hominis (fir'mi-or et po-ten'she-or est o-pe-rā'she-ō lē'jis quam dis-pō-zi'she-ō ho'mi-nis). The operation of the law is more firm and more powerful than the disposition of man.

firm name. See **partnership name**.

firm name and style. See **partnership name**.

first aid clause. Another term for the medical expense provision of an automobile liability policy whereunder the insurer contracts to pay for medical expenses, within specified limits, incurred by persons injured as a result of the condition or use of the automobile. 7 Am J2d Auto Ins § 154.

first annual election. See **election to fill vacancy in office**.

first bite. The old doctrine that every dog is entitled to one bite, enunciated in relieving an owner from liability for the first bite; a doctrine long since disavowed as out of keeping with a modern humanitarian society. Perkins v Drury, 57 NM 269, 258 P2d 379.

first board. The board of directors of a corporation as it appears in the articles of incorporation, the names of the directors being noted. 18 Am J2d Corp § 36.

first class. A word descriptive of chattels offered for sale, implying the best of their kind in general use, not the best of a single manufacturer, unless the situation is one in which the two superlatives coincide. 46 Am J1st Sales § 150.

first class dwelling. A superior dwelling place, but not necessarily excluding quarters in a multiple dwelling. Bowers v Fifth Ave. & Seventy-seventh Street Corp. (Sup) 209 NYS 743.

first-class funeral. A funeral in keeping with the previous social status and financial condition of the person to be interred. Mackovsky v Manhattan Railway Co. 11 NY 649, 650.

first-class investments. Investments permissible for the employment of trust funds. Investments producing income consistent with safety of the principal. 54 Am J1st Trusts § 371. Investments which require little or no personal care or supervision in order to avoid loss. Sparks Mfg. Co. v Newton, 57 NJ Eq 367, 41 A 385.

first-class mail (fėrst'klás māl). Written matter, comprising letters and postal cards; matter sealed or closed against inspection. 41 Am J1st P O § 56.

first-class misdemeanant. A person who has been found guilty of a misdemeanor but who has been adjudged to be deserving of leniency.

first-class passage. Transportation by a carrier at a fare higher than for ordinary passage, usually with accommodations superior to those of ordinary passage.

first-class state of repair. As a term descriptive of the tenant's obligation under a covenant to repair:—a variable term, the meaning in a particular case to be ascertained from the entire context of the lease and the surrounding circumstances. Puget Invest. Co. v Wenck, 36 Wash 2d 817, 221 P2d 459, 20 ALR2d 1320.

first-class theater. A term descriptive of the character of the performance within the building, rather than of the building itself. Asa G. Chandler, Inc. v Georgia Theater Co. 148 Ga 188, 96 SE 226.

first-class title. A marketable title; a good and valid title, at least a title free from reasonable doubt. Vought v Williams, 120 NY 253, 24 NE 195.

first class turn-key job. An expression of the construction industry, meaning the building of a complete house, one ready for occupancy as a dwelling. 13 Am J2d Bldg Contr § 10.

first conviction. As the term appears in an habitual criminal statute which makes provision for determining the length of a sentence for a subsequent conviction by multiplying the time imposed for the first conviction:—the first conviction for the subsequent offense for which the defendant has presently been convicted. Anno: 82 ALR 380, s. 116 ALR 236.

first cousin. The child of an uncle or an aunt. Anno: 54 ALR2d 1011. A relationship in the fourth degree according to the civil-law method of computing degrees of kinship which prevails in most American jurisdictions. 23 Am J2d Desc & D § 48.

first cousin once removed. A child of a first cousin. 54 ALR2d Anno: 54 ALR2d 1012. A relationship in the fifth degree. 23 Am J2d Desc & D § 48. Often called a second cousin.

first degree manslaughter. See **manslaughter**.

first-degree murder. See **murder in the first degree**.

first-degree principal. See **principal in first degree**.

first domestic processing. An internal revenue term; the first use in the United States, in the manufacture or production of an article intended for sale, of the article with respect to which the tax is imposed. 26 USC § 4512.

first-fruits (fėrst'fröts'). The annates or profits of the first year of a church preferment or living. See 1 Bl Comm 284.

first impression. An action without precedent to govern it. 1 Am J2d Actions § 49.

first in, first out. A method of recording inventory for the purpose of taxation of a stock of merchandise. Anno: 66 ALR2d 834. A rule applied in the valuation of inventory for purposes of federal taxation, that where goods are so intermingled that they cannot be identified with specific invoices, the goods in the inventory will be considered to be the goods most recently purchased or produced. The rule that, for income tax purposes, securities sold are charged off against the earliest purchase, in order to compute gain or loss, where the identity of the securities sold cannot be determined.
See **first money in, first money out**.

first in payment of taxes. The rule which determines rights by adverse possession where taxes paid by both adverse claimant and owner. 3 Am J2d Adv P § 127.

first in possession is first in right. The rule as between persons who are both intruders upon real estate. 3 Am J2d Adv P § 237.

first in time. The principle that, as between courts of concurrent jurisdiction, the first to exercise jurisdiction has exclusive jurisdiction to proceed further in the case. 20 Am J2d Cts § 128.
See **priority**.

first in time, first in right. A maxim applicable where the equities otherwise are equal. Walton v Hargroves, 42 Miss 18.

first inventor. He who first reduces an invention to practice. 40 Am J1st Pat § 70.

first meeting. The first meeting of creditors of a bankrupt, to be held not less than 10 nor more than 30 days after the adjudication, for the allowance of claims of creditors, the examination of the bankrupt, the election of a trustee in bankruptcy, and such other matters as may be pertinent and necessary for the promotion of the best interests of the estate. Bankruptcy Act § 55(c); 11 USC § 91(c); 9 Am J2d, Bankr §§ 581, 582.

first money in, first money out. A rule applied in determining the existence of a lien upon a fund, such as a bank deposit, where during a period, there are various deposits and withdrawals. Mississippi Cottonseed Products Co. v Canal Bank & Trust Co. 172 Miss 105, 159 So 404. The rule under which a particular credit in a bank is not regarded as having been drawn on until there is drawn an amount of money greater than the amount in the account at the moment prior to such credit and the credit is completely withdrawn when the depositor has drawn a sum equal to the amount in the account when the credit was entered plus the amount of the credit. 11 Am J2d B & N § 342.

first mortgage (fėrst môr'gāj). A mortgage having priority as a lien over the lien of any other mortgage of the same property. A mortgage having priority over any other lien on the same property.

first name. See **Christian name.**

first occupant. The rule that by the law of nature unclaimed goods belonged to the first finder. See 1 Bl Comm 298.
See **first in possession is first in right.**

first of exchange (fėrst' of eks'chānj). The first of a set of bills of exchange, drawn in duplicate or triplicate, the honoring of any one of which avoids the others. Bank of Pittsburgh v Neal (US) 22 How 96, 16 L Ed 323.
See **bills in a set.**

first option. The preferential right of a lessee to a new lease to run after the expiration of the existing lease under which he holds. Landowners Co. v Pendry, 151 Kan 674, 100 P2d 632, 127 ALR 890.

first papers. Declaration by an alien of his intention to become a citizen of the United States. 3 Am J2d, Aliens § 147.

first privilege. See **first option.**

first processing. The operations in the canning and packing of fruits and vegetables which precede the point where the fresh fruit or vegetables are converted to a nonperishable form. McComb v Hunt Foods, Inc. (CA9 Cal) 167 F2d 905, cert den 335 US 845, 93 L Ed 395, 69 S Ct 69.

first publication. The common law right of an author, sometimes spoken of as "copyright before publication." 18 Am J2d Copyr § 1. The earliest date when copies of the first authorized edition were placed on sale, sold, or publicly distributed by the proprietor of a copyright or under his authority. 17 USC § 26.

first purchaser. He who first acquired the estate to his family, whether the same was transferred to him by sale or by gift, or by any other method, except only that of descent. Blair v Adams (CC Tex) 59 F 243, 247.

first resolution in Wild's Case. A famous and much controverted rule that an estate tail is created by a devise to a person and his children or issue if such person then has no issue, but if such person has issue at the specified time, the words are words of purchase and no estate tail is created. 28 Am J2d Est § 52.

first return. A term of application in matters of internal revenue, meaning a tax return for the first year of tax, including a timely amended return for that year. Haggar Co. v Helvering, 308 US 389, 84 L Ed 340, 60 S Ct 337.

firsts. In mercantile usage, articles of best quality. Iselin v United States, 271 US 136, 138, 70 L Ed 872, 873, 46 S Ct 458.

fisc (fisk). The treasury of a state, a government, or a prince.

fiscal affairs. The financial affairs of a public body; business transactions, the raising of revenue, the issuance of securities to obtain funds for public improvements, appropriations, and the disposition of public funds. 49 Am J1st States § 64. In the case of a county, the performance of such duties as are placed upon the county board or such as uniformly pertain to the office of its members. Martin v Tyler, 4 ND 278, 60 NW 392.

fiscal agent. An agent acting for a public body in reference to its financial affairs. An agent invested with the funds and the conduct of the financial affairs of another person, business, association, society, or club.

fiscal court. See **county court.**

fiscal year. An accounting period of twelve months, such as that of the United States Government which ends on June 30th of each year. The annual period on the basis of which the taxpayer regularly computes his income in keeping his books. IRC § 441(c).

fiscus (fis'kus). A fisc.
See **fisc.**

fish. Cold-blooded animals, with backbones, living in water, and having gills for breathing. Animals ferae naturae where wild, unconfined, and in a state of nature. 35 Am J2d Fish § 2.
The term is sufficiently comprehensive to include shellfish, such as oysters, clams, lobsters, and crabs. State v Savage, 96 Or 53, 184 P 567, 189 P 427.

fish and game laws. Statutes, enacted in the interest of conservation of natural resources in fish and game in the wild state, which limit the taking of fish and game by establishing open and closed seasons and in some instances absolutely prohibiting the taking at any time of certain species.

fishery. In common usage, a place for fishing. In a legal sense, a right, other than one arising from ownership of a particular shore or beach, to employ within a particular stretch of water, lawful means for the taking of fish which may be found there. 35 Am J2d Fish § 6.
See **common fishery; common of fishery; exclusive fishery; fishing right; free fishery; royal fishery; several fishery; shellfishery.**

fish for evidence. See **fishing expedition.**

fishgarth (fish'gärth). A fish-trap or fish-weir.

fishing bill. A derogatory term for a bill in equity in which the plaintiff shows no cause of action, and endeavors to compel the defendant to disclose one in the plaintiff's favor. Carroll v Carroll (NY) 11 Barb 293, 298.

fishing expedition. A discovery, not so much in aid of a cause of action, as to determine whether there is a cause of action. 23 Am J2d Dep § 150. Using a subpoena duces tecum for the purpose of discovering evidence. 58 Am J1st Witn § 25. Seeking an order against an adverse party to compel the production of books, paper, and writings, for the purpose only of searching for evidence and witnesses. 29 Am J2d Ev § 843.

fishing place. See **fishery; fishing right.**

fishing preserve. See **private preserve.**

fishing right. The right to fish on the premises of another. The right to fish in all the arms of the sea and other public waters of the state; a right to fish granted by the United States or a state. 35 Am J2d Fish § 6. A profit a prendre. 25 Am J2d Ease § 4.
See **fishery.**

FISHING [479] FIXED

fishing tool. A term used by oil well drillers for an instrument employed to grapple with or otherwise engage an object in a drill pipe for the purpose of removing such object. Raymond v Wickersham, 27 Cust & Pat App (Pat) 1079, 110 F2d 863.

fish net. See **net**.

fish royal (fish roi'al). Fish which when brought ashore were the property of the king; such fish were confined to sturgeons, whales, and porpoises.
The whale was called a royal fish because by an ancient perquisite of the crown, when taken on the coast of England, the head was the property of the king and the tail went to the queen to furnish her wardrobe with whalebone. See 1 Bl Comm 222.
Actually, neither whale nor porpoise is a real fish. See **porpoise; whale**.

fishtail. The lateral movement of the rear of a motor vehicle in a skid. A controlled movement of an airplane to reduce speed for landing.

fishway. A way, provided in the construction of a dam, whereby fish may journey from below to above the dam or vice versa. 55 Am J1st Supp Water § 23.

fisk (fisk). Same as **fisc**.

fissionable material. Substances of such atomic structure that the atom may be split, thereby releasing energy.

fisticuffs. A fight in which the blows are delivered only by the fists. A boxing match arranged by agreement. Champer v State, 14 Ohio St 437.

fist-law (fist-lâ). The law of the fist; that is, the law of force.

fistuca (fis-tū'kạ). A rod or staff used as a symbol in making livery of seisin.

fistula (fis'tū-lạ). An abscess, particularly a large abscess on a horse, characterized by a hollow passage. (Civil law.) A water conduit or pipe.

fit (fit). Adjective: Proper; suitable; befitting; adapted to. Noun: A medical term for a convulsion in which the victim usually becomes unconscious.

fit for cultivation. Such a condition of the soil, in its natural condition, as will enable a farmer bringing to business a reasonable amount of skill, to raise regularly and annually by tillage, grain or other staple crops. Keeran v Griffith, 34 Cal 580, 581.

Fit juris et seisinae conjunctio (fit jū'ris et sē'si-ne kon-junk'she-ō). A joining is made of right and seisin.

fitness. The condition of being fit.
See **warranty of fitness**.

fitness of parent. An issue raised in awarding custody of a child or children in a suit for divorce, to be determined not alone from financial condition or even specific instances of moral weakness, but upon the primary consideration of the welfare of the child, coupled with recognition of the fact that misconduct toward a spouse is not necessarily moral unfitness for taking custody of a child. 24 Am J2d Div & S § 788.

fitting or suited to the public need. Public convenience. Milwaukee Co. of Jehovah's Witnesses v Mullen, 214 Or 281, 330 P2d 5, 74 ALR2d 347, app dismd and cert den 359 US 436, 3 L Ed 2d 932, 79 S Ct 940.

fittings. The furniture, appliances, or other equipment in a building or vessel.

fitz (fits). A son. A prefix to surnames, such as Fitzgerald and Fitzpatrick.

five civilized tribes (fīv siv'i-līzd trībs). The Creeks, Cherokees, Chickasaws, Choctaws, and Seminoles. Keokuk v Ulam, 4 Okla 5, 10.

Five Mile Act (fīv mīl akt). A statute enacted in England in 1665, which restricted the right of certain non-conformists to preach. The statute was repealed in 1689.

Five Ports. The ports of Hastings, Romney, Hythe, Dover, and Sandwich, all on the southern coast of England.

fix. Verb: To fasten securely; to mend or repair. To arrange, establish, or prescribe. Colloquially, to bribe a juror or a judge. Noun: A determined position in navigation. Colloquially, a predicament or awkward situation. Also colloquially, a portion of narcotic drugs taken by one other than for medicinal purposes.
See **increase and fix**.

fix by law. To arrange, establish, or prescribe by statute, for example, the qualifications for a public office. Anno: 34 ALR2d 178.

fixed by law. Allowed or prescribed by law. Daggs v Phoenix Nat. Bank, 177 US 549, 44 L Ed 882, 20 S Ct 732.

fixed charges. The expenses to be defrayed by a business or industry whether or not the place of business or plant is in operation for the time, being for charges which spread over the entire establishment, such as taxes, mortgage interest, insurance, depreciation, or rent, according to whether the plant is owned or leased. Standard Printing & Publishing Co. v Bothwell, 143 Md 303, 122 A 195, 31 ALR 1269, 1275.

fixed liability. Literally, an absolute or certain liability. A liability "evidenced by a judgment or an instrument in writing, absolutely owing at the time of the filing of a petition in bankruptcy by or against the debtor, whether then payable or not, with any interest thereon which would have been recoverable at that date or with a rebate of interest upon such liability as was not then payable and did not bear interest. Bankr Act § 63 (a) (1); 11 USC § 103 (a) (1).

fixed premium. A premium is a definite fixed sum, for example the premium paid annually upon an old-line life insurance policy or the premium paid upon obtaining a loan from a building and loan association. 13 Am J2d B & L Assoc § 54. A noncompetitive premium charged a borrower by a building and loan association, that is, a premium not determined by competitive bidding, 13 Am J2d B & L Assoc § 55.

fixed prices. Agreed-upon prices, not necessarily uniform prices. United States v Food & Grocery Bureau (DC Cal) 43 F. Supp 966.
See **price-fixing**.

fixed route. A definite route followed by a carrier.

fixed schedule. The schedule by which the vehicles or trains of a common carrier are operated, the periods of their arrival and departure being fixed, not beyond all possibility of change in the future, but subject only to such changes as may be approved by the regulatory authority.

fixed standard. A standard so capable of ascertainment that it can be stated in definite terms of

money, for the purposes of a testator in giving a third person a power to determine the amount of a bequest within limits of a "fixed standard." 28 Am J Rev ed Inher T § 332.

fixed tenure. The term of a public officer, the length of which is definitely prescribed by constitution or statute. 43 Am J1st Pub Of §§ 156, 158. A term sometimes applied to the protection against termination of employment given by civil-service laws to an employee after a certain number of years of satisfactory service.

fixed termini. The starting and ending points in the route of a common carrier, such places being fixed, not beyond the possibility of change in the future, but subject to only such changes as may be approved by the regulatory authority.

fixing bail. The determination by the court or judge of the amount of bail or a bond which a prisoner must furnish to effect his release from custody.

fixture. An article, once a chattel, but which, by being physically annexed or constructively affixed to the realty, has become accessory to it and part and parcel of it. 35 Am J2d Fixt § 1. Something so annexed to the freehold for use in connection therewith that it cannot be removed without injury to the freehold and accordingly has become a part of the freehold, losing its original identity as personal property. 35 Am J2d Fixt § 2.

See **constructive annexation; trade fixtures.**

flag. Verb: To droop; to lose speed. To signal with a flag. To signal a bus or train to stop for a passenger. Noun: Flat stones used in making a sidewalk or the portion of a street set apart for use by pedestrians, occasionally used in paving ways for vehicles. Re Phillips, 60 NY 16, 21. An emblem of cloth, usually in colors and usually on a staff, particularly the emblem of the nation or state.

"The flag is the emblem of national authority. To the citizen it is an object of patriotic adoration, emblematic of all for which his country stands,— her institutions, her achievements, her long roster of heroic dead, the story of her past, the promise of her future; and it is not fitting that it should become associated in his mind with anything less exalted, nor that it should be put to any mean or ignoble use." Halter v State, 74 Neb 757, 105 NW 298.

A public flag cannot always be considered as a true indication of the arms of the country to which it belongs; for most countries have two banners— the one borne by vessels of war, and the other by those engaged in commerce. Kirksey v Bates (Ala) 7 Port 529.

See **fly the flag; law of the flag; red flag.**

flagellat (fla-jel'lat). Whipped with a scourge.

flagellis et fustibus acriter verberare uxorem (fla-jel'-lis et fus'ti-bus a'kri-ter ver-be-rā're u-xō'rem). To beat his wife violently with scourges and sticks. See 1 Bl Comm 445.

flagging. See **flag.**

flagman. A trainman, also a watchman at a railroad crossing.

flagrans (flā'granz). Burning; raging; in course of perpetration, as a crime.

flagrans crimen (flā'granz kri'men). While the crime was being perpetrated or committed.

flagrant. Outrageous; notoriously bad.

flagrante bello (flạ-gran'tē bel'ō). During the time the war is raging.

flagrante delicto (flā-gran'tē dẹ-lik'tō). In the perpetration of the crime; in the very act of committing the offense. See 4 Bl Comm 307.

flagrantly against the weight of the evidence. A verdict not supported by substantial evidence. 5 Am J2d, A & E § 835.

flagrant necessity. Burning need; such necessity as will excuse an act which otherwise would be unlawful.

flag salute. A ceremony in opening school and at the beginning of a meeting of a youth organization, consisting in saluting the national flag by raising the right hand to the head, or in other chosen and appropriate form, and in reciting the pledge of allegiance. 47 Am J1st Sch § 170.

flag station. A railroad station at which the trains or some of the trains stop only on signal.

See **flag.**

flare. A light, usually produced by the burning of an inflammable liquid in a container closed except for a small orifice from which flame appears, used as a warning signal, particularly on vehicles left standing on a street or highway during hours of darkness. 7 Am J2d Auto § 157.

flash boards. Boards fastened to the top of the permanent structure of a dam, by the use of which, it is possible to raise the water above the ordinary height of the dam. Lammot v Ewers, 106 Ind 310.

flashing light. Equipment on a police car, ambulance, or other emergency vehicle. 8 Am J2d Auto §§ 756, 757. A signal light on the highway which flashes on and off or changes from red to green. 8 Am J2d Auto § 745. Signal at railroad crossing warning of the approach of a train.

flashover. A technical term in electricity, meaning an electrical discharge through the air to the ground from a high potential source or between two conducting portions of a machine or structure.

flash signal. See **flashing light.**

flat. An apartment or suite of rooms for housekeeping purposes on one story of a building; an edifice which contains suites of rooms for housekeeping purposes; a multiple dwelling or multiple family house. Elterich v Leicht Real Estate Co. 130 Va 224, 107 SE 735, 18 ALR 441.

See **flats.**

flat house (flat' hous). See **flat.**

flat marker. The marker of a grave, flush with the ground, required in cemeteries of the memorial park type. 14 Am J2d Cem § 35.

flat race. A horse race wherein the horses are ridden by jockeys. A race by thoroughbreds.

flats. Flat lands, especially tidelands and lands along a river.

Mr. Justice Story defined shores or flats to be the space between the margin of the water at low stage and the banks which contain it in its greatest flow; Lord Hale defined the term "shore" to be synonymous with flat, and substituted "flat" for "shore." Mr. Justice Parker did the same. Alabama v Georgia (US) 23 How 505, 514, 16 L Ed 556, 560.

A mussel bed over which the water flows at every tide is not an island but is flats. Fowler v Wood, 73 Kan 511, 85 P 763.

See **flat.**

flattery. An effort to influence another by the use of false or excessive praise; insincere complimentary language or conduct. Hall v State, 134 Ala 90, 32 So 750.

flatu. See **eodem flatu.**

flax. The plant which produces the fiber from which linen is made and the seeds from which linseed oil is produced; sometimes deemed a grain. State v Cowdery, 79 Minn 94, 81 NW 750.

flection (flek'shon). See **flexion.**

fledwit (fled'wit). The pardon of a person who had been outlawed; the price which such a person paid for his pardon.

flee. See **fleeing from justice; flight.**

fleece (flēs). To cheat; to defraud; to rob.

fleeing from justice. Departing a place with the intention of avoiding prosecution for a crime, whether or not a prosecution has been commenced or is pending. Streep v. United States, 160 US 128, 40 L Ed 365, 16 S Ct 244.
See **flight; fugitive from justice.**

Fleet. An ancient London prison, famous as a place where persons were imprisoned for debt. The naval force of the country.

fleet coverage. The inclusion within the risk covered by an automobile liability policy of the entire number of cars operated by the insured, coverage being extended automatically when newly acquired vehicles are added to those already insured. Anno: 34 ALR2d 946, 947 §§ 13, 14.

flee to the wall. See **retreat to the wall.**

flem (flem). An outlaw; a fugitive from justice.

flemens-firth (flē'menz-fèrth). The offense of harboring a fugitive from justice, or giving him aid.

flet (flet). A house; a home.

fleta (flē'ta). An ancient treatise on the English law which is believed to have been written about 1300 by a judge while he was imprisoned in the Fleet prison in London.

Fletcher v. Rylands. See **Rylands v. Fletcher.**

fleth. Same as **flet.**

flexion (flek'shon). Sometimes referred to as "flection." A bending, especially the bending of a limb.

flichwite. Same as **fightwite.**

flight. The act of flying. The scheduled trip of an airplane over a prescribed route at a prescribed time. 8 Am J2d Avi § 38. The common-law offense of running away upon an accusation of crime. See 4 Bl Comm 387.
See **escape; fleeing from justice.**

flight risk. A term used in the law of aircraft insurance:—coverage, or the exclusion of coverage, while the insured craft is in flight, as distinguished from coverage, or the exclusion of coverage, of ground risk, that is, the risk of loss sustained while the craft is on the ground. 29A Am J Rev ed Ins § 1363.

flight to avoid killing. See **retreat to the wall.**

flightwite. Same as **fledwit.**

float. As certificate issuing out of the United States land office authorizing the person to whom it was issued to enter a specified amount—such as a quarter section—of the public lands. Marks v Dickson (US) 20 How 501, 15 L Ed 1002.

floatability. See **floatable waters.**

floatable waters. Streams which, while not navigable by vessels, are usable for the transportation of certain kinds of property, such as logs and timber, by floating, or which are navigable only downstream. 56 Am J1st Wat § 188. Any stream which is capable in its natural condition of being commonly and generally used for floating saw logs, posts, ties, etc. cut from the timber along its banks. Anno: 47 ALR2d 386; 34 Am J1st Logs § 57.

floatage (flō'tāj). Same as **flotsam.**

floater. A voter whose vote is for sale; one who makes a practice of voting in places where he is not qualified by residence for voting. One who puts down no roots in a locality but changes residence frequently. A blanket policy of insurance.
See **blanket policy.**

floating bethel. A church for sailors which is moored to a wharf and kept in place by piles. 47 Am J1st Salv § 3.

floating capital. Funds of a corporation or other business institution which have been set apart for the payment of general expenses.

floating charge. The term used in England for floating security.
See **floating security.**

floating debt. Same as **floating indebtedness.**

floating drydock. A drydock moored or attached to a wharf but floating. 48 Am J1st Ship § 36.

floating indebtedness. Indebtedness of a municipality for the payment of which there is no fund in the treasury specifically designated or particular means of providing funds by taxation or other method. Huron v Second Ward Sav. Bank (CA8 SD) 86 F 272.

floating intention. An expression frequently applied in the law of domicil to the intention of a person, upon departing one place to live at another, to return at some indefinite future time to the former place of abode. 25 Am J2d Dom § 27.

floating pier. A pier built to float on the surface of the water. The Haxby (DC Pa) 94 F 1016.

floating policy. Another term for blanket policy.
See **blanket policy.**

floating security. A form of security by equitable charge wherein the property standing as security is left with the debtor to be handled and even sold in the due course of a business, with provisions for replenishing the security whenever it becomes depleted. Pennsylvania Co., etc. v United Railways, etc. (DC Me) 26 F Supp 379.
It is what might be called an equitable lien, a continuing charge on the assets of the company creating it, but permitting the company to deal freely with the property in the usual course of business until the security holder shall intervene to enforce his claim, whereupon the lien or charge becomes fixed or crystallized and the company which gave it has no further authority to deal with the property. Nor can the general creditors take the property charged with the lien after the secured creditor has intervened to enforce the lien. Pennsylvania Co., etc. v United Railways, etc. (DC Me) 26 F Supp 379.

float policy. Another term for blanket policy.
See **blanket policy.**

flodemark (flud′màrk). The highest mark left by the sea on the shore at high tide.

flogging. Inflicting punishment by whipping. State v Cannon, 55 Del 587, 190 A2d 514; Commonwealth v Wyatt, 27 Va (6 Rand) 694.

flood. An overflow of water, classified as an ordinary or extraordinary flood. 56 Am J1st Wat § 91. An overflow of a natural watercourse. 29A Am J Rev ed Ins § 1332. An Act of God, particularly if unprecedented. 1 Am J2d Act of God § 5. A relative term which may refer to mere surface water causing temporary inconvenience or which may refer to a collection of water so great as to amount to an inundation. Tulsa v Grier, 114 Okla 93, 243 P 753.
See **extraordinary flood**; **ordinary flood**.

flood channel. The channel of a river when swollen by rains and melting snows, extending over the bottom lands along the regular channel. Cole v Missouri, Kansas & Oklahoma Railroad Co. 20 Okla 227, 94 P 540.

flood control. An enterprise, sometimes private, but usually public, in character, whereby artificial channels are dug, dams constructed, storage basins created, and dikes built, for the purpose of preventing floods, or if they do occur, preventing great damage therefrom. 56 Am J1st Wat §§ 95 et seq.
See **conservancy districts**.

Flood Control Act. A federal statute providing Flood Control Act. A federal statute providing for the control of floods along the Mississippi River. 56 Am J1st Wat § 97.

Flood Control Acts. Federal and state statutes, including the Mississippi Flood Control Act, providing for the control of floods by various means and methods. 56 Am J1st Wat § 97.

flood insurance. A policy of insurance protecting the insured against loss of or damage to property caused by flood. 29A Am J Rev ed Ins § 1332.

floodlight. An intense artificial light, covering an area of considerable dimension, usually with the aid of a reflector; blinding to motorists within the beam. Anno: 22 ALR2d 413 § 26.

flood-tide. The rising or in-coming tide of the sea. A river out of its banks, inundating land not normally covered by its flow. Perkins v Byrnes, 364 Mo 849, 269 SW2d 52, 48 ALR2d 97.

flood waters. Waters above the highest line of the ordinary flow of the stream. Texas Co. v Burkett, 117 Tex 16, 296 SW 273, 54 ALR 1397. Forming a continuous body with the water flowing in the ordinary channel, or, if temporarily overflowing presently to return to such channel, to be regarded as still a part of the stream. 56 Am J1st Wat § 92; Anno: 20 ALR2d 656.

floor. The surface of a room, house, or other building at the bottom; the surface that an occupant uses. A single story of a building two or more stories in height, including the walls. 32 Am J1st L & T § 166.
See **story**.

floor area restrictions. Zoning laws prescribing minimum floor areas for dwellings to be erected in a certain district. 58 Am J1st Zon § 53.

floor tax. A tax levied under act of Congress upon liquor and tobacco produced in or imported into the United States upon which the internal revenue tax previously imposed had been paid, and which thereafter are held for sale or for use in the manufacture of an article intended for sale. Leeb v United States (DC NY) 16 F2d 937.

Florentine Pandects (flor′ęn-tin or tīn pan′dekts). A copy of the Pandects or Digests of Justinian which was found at Amalphi in Italy in 1137.

florin (flor′in). An English coin which at one time was the equivalent of six shillings, but later, since 1849, two shillings. A coin of medieval Florence.

flotage. Same as **flotsam**.

flotation of securities. Issuing securities and selling the issue for the purpose of beginning or financing a business.

floterial district. A multimember legislative district. 25 Am J2d Elect § 25.

flotsam (flot′sam). Goods cast into the sea in order to save a ship, or by shipwreck, and floating. 48 Am J1st Ship § 647. Odds and ends of little value.

flotsan. Same as **flotsam**.

flow. See **flowage**; **return flow**.

flowage. A right to overflow the land of another in the accumulation and maintenance of an artificial body of water, acquired by grant or prescription, or reserved in conveyance. Union Falls Power Co. v Marionette County, 238 Wis 134, 298 NW 598, 134 ALR 958.

flowage right. See **flowage**.

floud-marke. Same as **flode-mark**.

fluctus (fluk′tus). Same as **flood-tide**.

flues. Chimneys; tubes in a steam boiler for the passage of hot air and smoke.

flume. An artificial waterway in the nature of an inclined chute or narrow channel for transporting logs or other materials down a mountainside or conducting water for power purposes.

flumen (flū′men). An old term for eavesdrip.
See **easement of drip**.

Flumina et portus publica sunt; ideoque jus piscandi omnibus commune est (flū′mi-na et por′tus pub′li-ka sunt; i-de-ō′kwe jūs pis-kan′dī om′ni-bus kom-mū′ne est). Rivers and ports are public and the right to fish is therefore common to all.

Fluminis naturalem cursum non avertere (flū′min-is nat-ū̇-rā′lem kėr′sum non ạ-vėrt′ę-rę). A stream should flow unimpeded in its natural course. Cubbins v Mississippi River Com. 241 US 351, 60 L Ed 1041, 36 S Ct 671.

fluorspar. A mineral. Anno: 86 ALR 984.

flushing streets. A governmental function. Hale v Knoxville, 189 Tenn 491, 226 SW2d 265, 15 ALR2d 1283.

fluvius (flu′vi-us). A river; a stream.

fluxus (flu′xus). The flow of the tides.

flying machine. An obsolete term for airplane.

flying nondescript. A facetious characterization of a sleeping car company.

flying school. A school for instruction in the science and art of flying and in the repair, alteration, maintenance, and overhauling of aircraft. 8 Am J2d Avi § 36.

flying switch. A method of switching railroad cars wherein at one point in the operation a car or cars run free, having been "kicked", that is shoved violently by a locomotive. Chicago & Northwestern R. Co. v Calumet Stock Farm, 194 Ill 9, 61 NE 1095.

flyma (flī'ma). A fugitive from justice; a fugitive.

flyman-frymth (flī'man). Same as **flemens-firth**.

fly the flag. Acts of possession which put the true owner of real estate upon notice that his land is held under an adverse claim of ownership. 3 Am J2d Adv P § 23.

flywheel insurance. Casualty insurance covering injuries from a flywheel.

FM. Abbreviation of frequency modulation.
See **frequency modulation**.

f.o.b. Abbreviation of free on board.
See **free on board**.

f.o.b. acceptance final. See **free on board acceptance final**.

f.o.b. cars. See **free on board cars**.

focage (fō'kāj). A right of estovers.
See **firebote**.

focale (fō'kal). Same as **focage**.

fodder. Roughage for animals, usually the stalk and leaves of the corn plant.

fodder shed. A building for the storage of fodder or other roughage for animals; a structure to be distinguished from a barn. 5 Am J2d Arson § 21.

foderum (fo'de-rum). Fodder.

foedus (fē'dus). (Latin.) A compact or agreement between individuals or between nations; a league; a treaty between nations.

Foeminae ab omnibus officiis civilibus vel publicis remotae sunt (fe'mi-nē ab om'ni-bus of-fi'she-is si-vil'li-bus vel pub'li-sis re-mō'tē sunt). Women are excluded from all offices whether private or public.

Foeminae non sunt capaces de publicis officiis (fe'mi-nē non sunt ka-pā'sēz de pub'li-sis of-fi'she-is). Women are not qualified for public office.

foemina viro co-operta (fe'mi-na vī'rō ko-o-per'ta). A feme covert,—a married woman.

foeneration. Same as **feneration**.

foenus (fē'nus). That which is produced; the interest of money.

foenus nauticum (fē'nus nâ'ti-kum). An agreement for the repayment of a marine loan, with extraordinary interest. See 2 Bl Comm 458.

foeticide (fē'ti-sīd). The killing of a foetus or unborn child; a criminal abortion.

foetura (fe-tū'ra). The increase of animals; fruit.

foetus (fē'tus). An unborn child.

foetus in utero. See **pregnant woman**.

fog. Technically, water vapor in fine particles lying close to the surface of the earth or sea. In the law of navigation, a generic term, descriptive of all conditions of the atmosphere increasing the perils of navigation by obscuration. Flint & Pere Marquette R. Co. v Marine Ins. Co. (CC Mich) 71 F 210, 215. In common usage, something that prevents clear thought.

fogagium (fo-gā'ji-um). A kind of rank grass available for feed only at certain times of the year.

foghorn. A horn or other device for giving sound signals in time of fog; required equipment under rules of navigation. 48 Am J1st Ship § 271.

fogy pay (fō'gi pā). Same as **longevity pay**.

foi (fwa). Fealty; loyalty.

foil. To prevent the accomplishment of the purpose of another.
See **counterfoil**.

foinesun. Same as **fenatio**.

foirfault. Same as **forfeit**.

foirthocht. Aforethought; premeditated.

fois (fwa). Time.

foiterers (foi'ter-erz). Vagrants; vagabonds.

folc-gemote. Same as **folcmote**.

folc-land (folk'länt). Same as **folk-land**.

folcmote (folk'mōt). An ancient Saxon assembly of the people.

folc-right (folk'rīt). A jus commune,—a law to all the people of the kingdom; the common law. See 1 Bl Comm 67.

foldage (fōl'dāj). Same as **faldage**.

folgarii (fol-ga'ri-ī). Followers; menial servants.

folgere (fol'je-re). A follower; a retainer; a menial servant.

folgers. Same as **folgarii**.

folio. A large sheet of paper folded so as to form two leaves, making available four pages for a manuscript or book numbered on both sides of the leaves. A unit for the measurement of the length of a legal document; in the United States, a page of one hundred words; in England, as used in conveyancing, seventy-two words; in English parliamentary, chancery and probate matters, ninety words.

In this country, in counting, each figure in a folio is counted as a word, and when there are over fifty and under a hundred words, they are counted as one folio, but a less number than fifty words is not counted, unless the whole document contains less than fifty words. Erwin v United States (DC Ga) 37 F 470.

Folio Edition. An edition of the Year books, otherwise known as the Vulgate Edition or the Edition of 1679.
See **Year Books**.

folk. The people, particularly the common people.
See **borel folk**.

folk-land (folk-länd). Land which was held by no assurance in writing, but distributed among the common folk or people at the pleasure of the lord, and resumed at his discretion. See 2 Bl Comm 90.

folkmote (fōk'mōt). Same as **folcmote**.

follow. To come after; to result from; to pursue. To adhere to a decision as a precedent.
See **ensue**.

following federal rule. The binding effect of federal court decisions in state court.

following fund. See **following trust fund or property**.

following proceeds of sale. The right of a mortgagee under a chattel mortgage to the proceeds of a sale of the property by the mortgagor. 15 Am J2d Chat Mtg § 161.

following state court decisions. The duty of a federal court, not only as to questions of the statutory law of the state, but also as to questions of general common law or commercial law. Erie Railroad Co. v Tompkins, 304 US 64, 82 L Ed 1188, 58 S Ct 817, 114 ALR 1487; Fashion Originators' Guild v Federal Trade Com. 312 US 457, 85 L Ed 949, 61 S Ct 703.

following too closely. Negligence or even negligence per se on the part of a motorist. 8 Am J2d Auto § 773.

following trust fund or property. Pursuing property wrongfully converted by a fiduciary for the purpose of compelling restitution to the beneficiary, such pursuit encompassing a following through all changes in state and form, so long as such property, its product, or its proceeds are capable of identification and so long as the property has not passed into the hands of a bona fide purchaser for value. 54 Am J1st Trusts § 248. A practice in favor of a surety on the bond of a trustee who has diverted funds. 50 Am J1st Subro § 132. Tracing specific funds in the hands of a trustee in insolvency or assignee for the benefit of creditors and enforcing the trust therein. 6 Am J2d Assign for Crs § 116. Identifying or tracing trust funds for the purpose of reclaiming them from an insolvent trust company or bank. 10 Am J2d Bks § 805.

foment (fō-mĕnt'). To encourage; to incite; to abet.

fond. See **au fond; au fond en droit; au fond en fait.**

fonsadera (fŏn-sä-da'y-rä). (Spanish.) A loan or tribute paid to the king for the purpose of carrying on war.

fontana (fon-ta'na). A fountain; a spring.

food. Anything eaten for the nourishment of the body. 35 Am J2d Food § 1. Articles used for food or drink for man or animals and the components of any such article. 21 USC § 321. All articles used for food, drink, confectionery, or condiment by man or other animals, whether simple, mixed, or compound. 35 Am J2d Food § 2.

Food and Drug Administration. A federal agency of the Department of Health, Education, and Welfare.

food coloring. See **coal tar colors.**

Food, Drug and Cosmetic Act. A statute regulating interstate traffic in food, drugs and cosmetics, covering such matters as adulteration, misbranding, false guaranties against adulteration or misbranding, the alteration, obliteration, removal, or destruction of labels, and having the purpose in general of keeping dangerous products out of interstate commerce, preventing fraud, and protecting the public health. 21 USC § 331(a)-(k).

food premium. Something of value given a purchaser of food in addition to the commodity purchased. 52 Am J1st Trad St § 11.

food preservative. See **preservative.**

fool natural. An idiot.

foot. A lineal measure, consisting of 12 inches. The segment of the limb of a vertebrate upon which the body rests in standing.

The human foot consists of three parts: the ankle or torsus, the instep or metatarsus, and the toes or phalanges. Jones v Continental Casualty Co. 189 Iowa 678, 179 NW 203, 18 ALR 1329.
See **loss of feet.**

foot acre. A method of determining the value of coal land for tax purposes, applying the measure of one acre of coal one foot thick, but excluding exhausted areas, barrier pillars, areas entirely unminable because of physical conditions, or areas of unproved minability, unless development and exploration discloses minable coal therein. Re Hudson Coal Co. 327 Pa 247, 193 A 8.

footage drilling. The drilling of an oil well under a contract whereby the contracting driller is paid at an agreed rate per foot of well drilled, plus the cost of equipment. Walker v Chitty (CA6 Ohio) 112 F2d 79.

foot frontage. A basis of apportionment of a special or local assessment. 48 Am J1st Spec A § 67.

footgeld (fut'geld). An amercement which was imposed under the forest laws for failure to expeditate a dog.
See **expeditation of dogs.**

footing. A base or support. A place to stand.

footman. A male servant in the household. A person on foot; a pedestrian.

A person riding on a bicycle is not a footman or pedestrian, whether he is riding on the sidewalk or elsewhere. Mercer v Corbin, 117 Ind 450, 20 NE 132.

foot of the fine (fŭt of the fīn). The fifth or concluding part of a fine. This part included the whole proceeding, reciting the parties, day, year, and place, and before whom the fine was acknowledged or levied. Indentures of this were made, or engrossed at the chirographer's office, and delivered to the cognizor and the cognizee; usually beginning, "haec est finalis concordia," this is the final agreement, and then reciting the whole proceeding at length. See 2 Bl Comm 351.

footpath. See **path.**

footpound. A unit of energy; the energy required to raise a weight of one pound one foot.

footstool. A stool placed below the lower step of a railroad passenger car for the use of passengers in boarding or leaving the car. 14 Am J2d Car § 1010.

footway. A sidewalk; a path.
See **iter; public footway.**

for. Because of, on account of, by reason of. Glassell Development Co. v Citizens' Nat Bank, 191 Cal 375, 216 P 1012, 28 ALR 1427, 1434. In consideration of Brooks v Coppedge, 71 Idaho 156, 228 P2d 248, 27 ALR2d 645. Throughout or during the continuance of a period of time. Finlayson v Peterson, 5 ND 587.

A designation of agency in the execution of a contract by an agent on behalf of his principal, that is, purporting to sign "for" for the principal, e.g. Robert Roy, Agent "for" John Smith, by which liability is imposed upon the principal and not the agent. 3 Am J2d Ag § 190.

for account of. A form of indorsement of commercial paper for collection. 10 Am J2d Bks § 407; 12 Am J2d B & N § 1277.

for account of whom it may concern. See **on account of whom it may concern.**

forage. Verb: To search for food or other need. Noun: Rough feed for domestic animals; fodder; hay.

Foraker Act. An act of Congress approved April 12, 1900, entitled "An Act Temporarily to Provide Revenues and a Civil Government for Porto Rico, and for Other Purposes." Downes v Bidwell, 182 US 247, 45 L Ed 1088, 21 S Ct 770.

foraneus (fo-rā'ne-us). A foreigner; an alien.

forathe. A term used in the forest laws meaning a witness who would testify in one's behalf.

forbalca (for-bal'ka). Same as **forebalk.**

forbannitus (for-ban'ni-tus). A person who had been banished or exiled.

forbarrer (for-bar'rer). To bar out; to exclude; to estop.

forbatudus (for-bā'tu-dus). An aggressor who was killed in an encounter.

forbearance. Submitting without complaint. Giving a debtor additional time for payment. Withholding of action constituting a sufficient consideration for a guaranty. Anno: 78 ALR2d 1418.
It has long been settled that the term, as applied to usury laws, cannot be predicated of any other transaction than a loan of money. Title Guaranty & Surety Co. v Klein (CA3 Pa) 178 F 689.

forbearance to sue. Refraining from the commencement of an action. Abandonment of the right to institute or assert a claim in legal proceedings. 15 Am J2d Compr § 17.
See **covenant not to sue.**

for cause. For legal cause, e.g. the challenge of a juror on voir dire for want of the qualifications prescribed by law, 31 Am J Rev ed Jur § 147, or the removal of a public officer upon a ground of removal provided by constitution or statute. State ex rel. Nagle v Sullivan, 98 Mont 425, 40 P2d 995, 99 ALR 321.

force. The impetus of power; physical power or strength exerted against a person or thing. 5 Am J2d Arr § 80; 6 Am J2d Asslt & B §§ 5, 39. Not necessarily confined to a physical manifestation; there may be an exertion of force through the practice of a deceit. Commonwealth v Stratton, 114 Mass 303.
As an essential ingredient of rape, "force" does not necessarily imply the positive exertion of actual physical force in the act of compelling submission; but force or violence threatened as the result of noncompliance, and for the purpose of preventing resistance, or extorting consent, is equivalent to force actually exerted. 44 Am J1st Rape § 5.
See **actual force; armed force; constructive force; duress; excessive force; force and violence; forcible entry and detainer; fresh force; irresistible force; superior force.**

force account. A contract between a contractor and his employer under which the workmen are paid by the foot or yard, the contractor hiring the labor and supervising the job and receiving from the employer an agreed percentage above the total cost. Anno: 55 ALR 292.

force and arms. Actual violence. Taylor v State, 25 Tenn (6 Humph) 284, 286.

force and violence. As used in a statutory definition of riot:—something more than the force necessary to do an unlawful act; a defiance of constituted authority or of the rights of a person injured, or of his effort to protect such rights. Walter v Northern Ins. Co. 370 Ill 283, 18 NE2d 906, 121 ALR 244. As an element of the crime of robbery:—actual force, which implies personal violence, and constructive force which includes all demonstrations of force, menaces, and other means by which the person robbed is put in fear sufficient to suspend the free exercise of his will or prevent resistance to the taking. State v Snyder, 41 Nev 453, 172 P 364.

forced heir. A person who, in reference to a certain portion of his ancestor's property, can not be disinherited by the will of the ancestor, except where there is a just and legal cause to disinherit him.
The doctrine of forced heir is one of the Roman law and the civil law of the Continent of Europe, and is preserved in Louisiana by a provision of the state constitution. 23 Am J2d Desc & D § 90.

forced landing. An aircraft landing in an emergency, caused by lack of fuel, weather turbulence, or mechanical mishap.

forced sale. A sale other than at the will and pleasure of the owner. An execution sale; a sale on foreclosure; a sale made under the authority of any judicial proceeding at law or in equity which seeks to appropriate the property to the payment of debts, whether or not denominated a sale. 26 Am J1st Home § 99.

force majeure (fôrs' mä-zur'). (French.) The equivalent of **vis major.**

force with force. Repelling an unlawful use of force with force. State v Durham, 141 NC 741, 53 SE 720.

forcheapum (for-che-a'pum). Same as **forestalling.**

forcible detainer. The unlawful holding or detention of real property by force, threats, or menaces after the making of a peaceable, though unlawful, entry thereon. 35 Am J2d Forc E & D § 1.
See **forcible entry and detainer.**

forcible entry. An entry by breaking doors to make an arrest or a search of premises. 5 Am J2d Arr §§ 86, 87. An entry, with at least some degree of actual force, for the purpose of committing a felony. 13 Am J2d Burgl §§ 11, 12. An entry on real property peaceably in the possession of another, against his will, without authority of law, by actual force, or with such an array of force and apparent intent to employ it for the purpose of overcoming resistance, that the occupant, in yielding and permitting possession to be taken from him, must be regarded as acting from a well-founded apprehension that resistance by him would be perilous or unavailing. 35 Am J2d Forc E & D § 1.
See **forcible entry and detainer.**

forcible entry and detainer. A common-law offense against the public peace committed by violently taking or keeping possession of lands and tenements, with menaces, force and arms, and without the authority of law. 4 Bl Comm 148. A remedy to obtain restitution to possession of one turned or kept out of possession of real property by strong hand, violence, or terror. 35 Am J2d Forc E & D § 5.

forcible trespass. A trespass amounting to a breach of the peace. Carroll v State, 23 Ala 28.

forcibly. With force, as in a breaking and entry for the purpose of committing a felony. 13 Am J2d Burgl §§ 11, 12.

forcibly to defile. To commit rape. State v Montgomery, 79 Iowa 737, 45 NW 292.

for clearing house purposes only. An ordinary form of indorsement of a check by a bank holding it for collection; an indorsement which does not constitute a representation that the bank is the owner. 10 Am J2d Bks § 840.

for collection. A form of restrictive indorsement. 12 Am J2d B & N § 1278. A form of restrictive indorsement of commercial paper left with a bank for collection, whereunder the bank becomes a mere agent of the depositor for the purpose of obtaining funds upon the paper. 10 Am J2d Bks § 402. An indorsement which warns the drawee bank that the responsibility of determining the genuineness of the paper is placed upon it. 10 Am J2d Bks § 615.

for commerce. See production of goods for commerce.

for compensation. For a consideration. A test of the character of a company as a public utility; not the equivalent of "for profit." Mountain States Tel. Co. v Project Mut. Tel. & Electric Co. PUR 1916F 370.
See **for hire; for hire or compensation.**

ford. A place for crossing a stream where there is no bridge.

forda (for'da). A ford.

fordanno. The aggressor in an encounter.

for deposit. A form of restrictive indorsement. 11 Am J2d B & N § 362. A restrictive indorsement which indicates that the indorsee bank is an agent for collection, not the owner. 10 Am J2d Bks § 403.

for deposit only. A form of restrictive indorsement. 11 Am J2d B & N § 362.
See **for deposit.**

fordyka. Grass growing on the bank of a dyke or ditch.

fore (fôr). Before.

forebalk. A strip of land left unploughed on lands adjoining a highway.

foreclose. To obtain an order for foreclosure or otherwise to proceed with a foreclosure.
See **foreclosure.**

foreclosure. In the original inception of the term, a suit to extinguish the equity of redemption. A proceeding in a court of justice, conducted according to legal forms, in and by which a mortgagee, or assigns, or successor, or anyone who has by law succeeded to the rights and liabilities of a mortgagee, undertakes to dispose of, or bar, or cut off the legal or equitable claims of lien-holders, or of the mortgagor, or those who have succeeded to the rights and liabilities of the mortgagor. Arrington v Liscom, 34 Cal 365. In the ordinary present-day sense of the term, the enforcement of a lien, deed of trust, or mortgage in any method provided or sanctioned by law. Arrington v Liscom, 34 Cal 365.

foreclosure by action and sale. A suit to obtain a decree of foreclosure and a sale of the mortgaged premises in accordance with that decree, the proceeds to be applied, first to the payment of the costs of suit, the mortgage debt, and interest thereon, second to junior encumbrancers, and third to the owner of the premises. McMillan v Richards, 9 Cal 365, 411.

foreclosure by entry and writ of entry. The remedy in some jurisdictions for enforcing a mortgage by entry and possession by the mortgagee. 37 Am J1st Mtg § 531.
Upon a foreclosure by entry and possession after a breach of the condition of the mortgage, and by holding such possession for the period allowed for redemption, the mortgage debt will be deemed paid to the extent of the value of the land. 37 Am J1st Mtg § 531.

foreclosure by sale. A summary method of foreclosure of a mortgage or deed of trust by sale of the mortgaged premises under a power of sale contained in the mortgage or deed of trust, or even in a separate instrument. 37 Am J1st Mtg § 647.
See **foreclosure of chattel mortgage.**

foreclosure of chattel mortgage. An action to declare judicially the forfeiture for condition broken and to obtain a sale and transfer of title to the subject of the mortgage. 15 Am J2d Chat Mtg § 208. A sale of the property covered by the mortgage, upon a default by the mortgagor, under a power of sale contained in the instrument. 15 Am J2d Chat Mtg § 211.

foreclosure receivership. See **receivership in foreclosure.**

foreclosure sale. A sale, judicial or otherwise, made in the enforcement of a lien, mortgage, or deed of trust.

foreclosure suit. See **foreclosure by action and sale.**

forefault. Same as **forfeit.**

foregift. A premium or bonus paid for a leasehold in addition to rent.

foregoer. A progenitor; an ancestor.

foregoing instrument. An identifying term commonly used in acknowledgments. 1 Am J2d Ack § 59.

forehand rent. Rent paid in advance. Also the bonus or foregift paid by the tenant upon the making of the lease.
See **foregift.**

foreign. Belonging to another nation or country.
In a political sense, we call every country foreign which is not within the jurisdiction of the same government. In this sense, Canada, Mexico, and all transatlantic countries are foreign to the United States. Cherokee Nation v Georgia (US) 5 Pet 1, 56, 8 L Ed 25, 45.

foreign acknowledgment. An acknowledgment taken outside the state wherein the efficacy of the instrument authenticated is to be determined. 1 Am J2d Ack § 26.

foreign administration. The administration of property belonging to the estate of a decedent situated in a jurisdiction other than that of his residence; otherwise known as ancillary administration. 31 Am J2d Ex & Ad § 680.

foreign administrator. See **foreign representative.**

foreign adoption. An adoption under a decree granted by a court in state or country other than that wherein effect is sought to be given to it. 2 Am J2d Adopt §§ 12, 115.

foreign affidavit. An affidavit involving a matter of concern in one state but taken in another state or country before an officer of that state or country. 3 Am J2d Affi § 19.
Statutes relating to the authentication of affidavits taken in a foreign state may require, in addition to the ordinary attestation with the seal of the notary or other officer, that the affidavit be accompanied by a certificate of the county clerk or other proper officer of the foreign state, under his hand and official seal, stating that the officer before whom the affidavit was taken is duly commissioned and authorized by the statutes of his state to administer oaths. Turtle v Turtle, 31 AD 49, 52 NYS 857.

Foreign Agents Registration Act. A federal statute enacted for the purpose of protecting the national defense, internal security, and foreign relations of the United States, by requiring public disclosure by persons engaged in propaganda and other activities for or on behalf of foreign governments, foreign political parties, and other foreign principals, so that the government and people of the United States may be informed of the identity of such persons and may appraise their statements and actions in the light of their associations and activities. 47 Am J1st Sedit etc. § 10.

foreign aid. The making of loans and of grants of money and property, particularly grain, by the United States for the benefit of foreign nations, intended for the rehabilitation of countries in distress economically, thereby assisting them to establish and maintain stable government of the democratic form.

foreign attachment. The attachment of property within the jurisdiction but owned by a nonresident defendant. Greene v Johnston, 34 Del Ch 115, 99 A2d 627, 42 ALR2d 906.

foreign award. An award made in arbitration in another state or country. 5 Am J2d Arb & A § 153.
See **foreign judgment.**

foreign bank. A bank in a foreign country; a bank incorporated under the laws of another state.

foreign bill. A bill of exchange which is not, or does not purport to be, both drawn and payable within the state. Uniform Negotiable Instruments L § 129.
The primary importance of the distinction between an inland and a foreign bill of exchange lies in the necessity of protest of a foreign bill upon nonacceptance or nonpayment. 11 Am J2d B & N § 790.

foreign broker. A broker from without the state. 12 Am J2d Brok § 17.

foreign building and loan association. A building and loan association operating outside the jurisdiction of its origin or domicil. 13 Am J2d B & L Assoc § 122.

foreign cause. A cause of action arising under the laws of another jurisdiction.

foreign charity. A charity which by the terms of the instrument creating it is to be administered in a state or country other than the one in which it is created. Taylor v Trustees of Bryn Mawr College, 34 NJ Eq 101, 104. A charitable institution or operation outside the jurisdiction of the domicil of the donor. 15 Am J2d Char § 109.

foreign commerce. Commerce between citizens of the United States and citizens or subjects of foreign nations; every species of commercial intercourse between the United States and foreign nations, including the entrance of ships, the importation of goods and property, and the bringing of persons into the ports of the United States. 15 Am J2d Com § 4.

foreign consul. See **consul; exequatur.**

foreign corporation. In respect of a particular state or country:—a corporation created by, or organized under, the laws of another state, government, or country. 36 Am J2d For Corp § 1. As the term is used in federal statutes:—a corporation created or organized outside the United States. Hecht v Malley, 265 US 144, 154, 68 L Ed 949, 956, 44 S Ct 46. For income tax purposes, a corporation which is organized outside the United States or under any law other than that of the United States, a state or the District of Columbia. IRC § 7701(a)(3), (4), (9).
See **residence of corporation.**

foreign country. A country exclusively within the sovereignty of a foreign nation, and without the sovereignty of the United States. De Lima v Bidwell, 182 US 1, 45 L Ed 1041, 21 S Ct 743.

foreign court. A court of a foreign state or nation. See **foreign judgment.**

foreign credit. Credit provided by a bank to a customer in a foreign country or another state by the transmission of funds. 10 Am J2d Banks § 308.

foreign currency. The coin or bills constituting money in a foreign country.

Foreign Depositions Act. One of the uniform laws, adopted in a number of states, with modifications in some instances, concerned with the taking of depositions within the enacting state to be used in a foreign jurisdiction. 23 Am J2d Dep § 12.

foreign divorce. A divorce granted in another state or country.

foreigner. A citizen of a foreign country; an alien who has not been naturalized. Lessee of Spratt et al. v Spratt (US) 1 Pet 343, 7 L Ed 171.
See **transient foreigner.**

foreign exchange. Foreign money; commercial paper payable in foreign money; the rate at which money of one country is converted to the money of another by exchange; the transfer of credits from one country to another in settlement of debts of residents of the former owing to residents of the latter.

foreign executor. See **foreign representative.**

foreign extradition. International extradition, that is, extradition to the United States from a foreign country or from the United States to a foreign country. See 31 Am J2d Extrad § 7.

foreign government. The government of a foreign country. The recognized government of a foreign country. Zaph v Ridenour, 198 Iowa 1006, 200 NW 618.

foreign guardian. A guardian appointed in a jurisdiction other than that of the ward's residence. 25 Am J1st G & W § 215.

foreign investment. The investment of trust funds in property, securities, and obligations, where the property or obligor is outside the state. Merchants Loan & Trust Co. v Northern Trust Co. 250 Ill 86, 95 NE 59.

foreign investment company. A foreign corporation which is either (a) registered as a management company, or a unit investment trust under the 1940 Investment Company Act, or (b) engaged in the investment business at a time when a majority interest is held by United States investors—United States citizens or residents, domestic partnerships or corporations, and "domestic" (nonforeign) trusts. IRC § 1246(b); IRC § 7701(a)(30).

foreign judgment. A judgment rendered by a foreign court or a court of an independent unconnected jurisdiction. 30A Am J Rev ed Judgm § 232. Narrowly defined, a judgment rendered by a court of a foreign country. 30A Am J Rev ed Judgm § 232. Precisely, any judgment, decree or order of a court of the United States or of any state or territory which is entitled to full faith and credit. Anno: 72 ALR2d 1256, quoting provisions of Uniform Enforcement of Foreign Judgments Act.

foreign jurisdiction. A jurisdiction other than that of the forum.

foreign law. The law of a state or country other than the forum. The law of a state or jurisdiction other than the state or jurisdiction in which it is sought to enforce such law. Marshall v Sherman, 148 NY 9, 42 NE 419.
See **conflict of laws**.

foreign minister. In the diplomatic use of the term, any minister who comes as the representative of another jurisdiction or government. Cherokee Nation v Georgia, (US) 5 Pet 1, 56, 8 L Ed 25, 45.
See **diplomatic officers**.

foreign nation. A political union or community of people under a sovereignty other than that of the United States.
 A nation is foreign to another nation, that is, it is a foreign nation with reference to that nation, unless the two nations owe a common allegiance; so that the term is applicable by either nation to the other. Cherokee Nation v Georgia (US) 5 Pet 1, 8 L Ed 25.

foreign office. That department of a government which carries on the communications of its government with those of foreign countries.

foreign pauper. An indigent person who has no legal settlement in the city, town, district, or county in which aid is sought to be obtained for him from the department of public welfare. Opinion of the Justices, 42 Mass (1 Met) 572, 578.

foreign personal holding company. A foreign corporation, the primary part of the income of which is personal holding company income and the stock of which is owned to the extent of 50 percent in value by less than six individual United States citizens or residents. IRC § 554.

foreign port. Precisely, a port in a foreign country. Sometimes applied more broadly to a port of a foreign country or of another state of the Union. Cohen v Charleston Fire & Marine Ins. Co. 23 SCL (Dud) 147.

foreign representative. An ambassador or other diplomatic officer. A consul. An agent representing his principal in a foreign country. The status of an executor or administrator in a state other than that of the domicil of the decedent in which he was appointed. An ancillary executor or administrator. Hopper v Hopper, 125 NY 400.

foreign state. Another state; another country.
 For all national purposes embraced by the Federal Constitution, the states and the citizens thereof are one; united under the same sovereign authority, and governed by the same laws. But in other respects the states are necessarily foreign to and independent of each other. See Cherokee Nation v Georgia (US) 5 Pet 1, 57, 8 L Ed 25, 45.

foreign surety company. A corporation organized in one state for the purpose of transacting business as surety on the obligations of persons or corporations, authorized by statute of another state to transact business therein, upon compliance with certain specified conditions, the most common of which is assuring its financial responsibility by the deposit of securities with a specified officer of the authorizing state. 50 Am J1st Suret § 315.

foreign tax credit. A credit against income tax designed to ease the burden of double taxation by permitting a dollar-for-dollar credit against the United States tax for the tax paid to a foreign country. IRC § 901(a).

foreign trademark. A trademark registered or used in a foreign country and not registered in this country or established in this country by actual use. 52 Am J1st Tradem § 27.

foreign-trade zone. An isolated policed area adjacent to a port of entry where foreign goods may be unloaded for immediate transhipment or stored, repacked, sorted, mixed, or otherwise manipulated without being subject to import duties. 21 Am J2d Cust D § 17.

foreign will. A will made and executed in, and in conformity with, the laws of a state of the Union other than the state in which it is offered for probate, or made and executed in, and in conformity with, the laws of a foreign country. Estate of Clark, 148 Cal 108, 82 P 760.

forein. Same as **foreign**.

forejudge (fōr-juj'). To expel from the court; to take away by a judgment; to banish.

forejudger (for-juj'er). A judgment by which a person is forejudged.

foreman. A man in charge of a group of employees in an industrial plant or in construction work. Moore v Dublin Cotton Mills, 127 Ga 609, 56 SE 839. One of the jury appointed by it, or, in some jurisdictions, by the court, as the spokesman of the jury. Burk v Hodge, 211 Mass 156, 97 NE 920.
 The foreman of the jury is not an officer of the court; he can neither exercise authority over the jury nor control their deliberations. 53 Am J1st Trials § 849.
See **foreman of grand jury**.

foreman of grand jury. A member of the grand jury appointed by the court to act as such, thus constituting him the organ through which their inquisitions and proceedings are reported to the court, and upon whom particular duties are devolved which are distinct from the duties of the other members of the jury. Cody v State, 4 Miss (3 How) 27, 29.

forensic. Pertaining to or belonging to the courts. In the field of public discussion or debate.

forensic medicine. Medical jurisprudence, that is, the science of medicine as connected with law.

forensis (fo-ren'sis). Same as **forensic**.

fore-rent (fōr'rent). Same as **forehand rent**.

foreright. The first or preferred right to inherit; the right of primogeniture.

foresaid. Aforesaid; previously mentioned in the same instrument.

foreseeable. The characteristic of an event making it one to be anticipated. 14 Am J2d Car § 914; 38 Am J1st Negl § 24.

foresight. Prudence in anticipation of an event, particularly one fraught with danger. 14 Am J2d Car § 914; 38 Am J1st Negl § 24.

foreshore. The territory lying between the lines of high water and low water, over which the tide ebbs and flows. 12 Am J2d Bound § 13.

forest. See **forests**.

forestage (for'es-tąj). Duties which were exacted by the royal foresters.

forestagium (fo-res-tā'ji-um). Same as **forestage**.

forestal (for'es-tal). Pertaining or relating to the royal forests.

FORESTALL [489] FORFENG

forestall. To prevent something by anticipating it and taking obstructive tactics against it. To forestall the market.
See **forestalling the market**.

forestaller. A person who committed the ancient offense of forestalling the market. 36 Am J1st Monop etc. § 20. A tenant who by an ancient method of forestalling worked a disseisin of freehold rent either by besetting the way with force and arms or by threats of bodily violence so frightening the landlord as to keep him off the premises. See 3 Bl Comm 170.

forestalling the market. Buying victuals on their way to market before they reach it, with intent to sell them again at a higher price, or in dissuading persons from buying merchandise there; every practice or device by act, word, or news to enhance the price of victuals or other merchandise. 36 Am J1st Monop etc. § 20.

forestarius (fo-res-tā'ri-us). Same as **forester**.

forest courts. Courts which were instituted for the government of the king's forests in different parts of England, and for the punishment of all injuries done to the king's deer or venison, to the vert or greensward, and to the covert in which the deer were lodged. These were the courts of attachments, of regard, of sweinmote, and of justice-seat. See 3 Bl Comm 71.

forester (for'es-tėr). One of the officers of the king who had charge of the royal forests and of the wild game therein.

forest law. The laws pertaining to the royal forests.
See **Charta de Foresta**; **disafforest**.

forest liberties (lib'ėr-tēz). The royal grant of the right or privilege of hunting in royal forests.

forest products. Logs, timber, lumber, turpentine, tar, etc.

forest reserves. National Forest Areas of the United States, under supervision and control of the Forest Service of the Department of Agriculture; state forests in areas reserved from private acquisition, developed and maintained in the interests of conservation and recreation.

forests. Woodlands. In an earlier time in England, waste grounds belonging to the king, replenished with all manner of beasts of chase or venery and under the king's protection, for the sake of his royal recreation and delight. For the preservation of the king's game, there are particular laws, privileges, courts and offices belonging to the king's forests. See 2 Bl Comm 38, 289.
See **beasts of the forest**; **drift of the forest**; **logs**; **timber**.

Forest Service. A federal agency under the Department of Agriculture, exercising authority over National Forest Areas, National Grasslands, land utilization projects, and other special areas, and engaging in the acquisition of land for National Forests.

forethought. See **aforethought**; **malice aforethought**.

forethought felony. Premeditated felony; felony previously planned.

forever. A word not necessarily inconsistent with the grant of a life estate, where it appears in the granting clause of a deed. Johnson v Barden, 86 Vt 19, 83 A 721. A word ineffective in the grant of an estate to vest more than a life estate, in the absence of a limitation to "heirs." 28 Am J2d Est § 14.

forfang (for'fang). The recaption of goods which have been stolen; a reward paid for the return of stolen goods.

forfault. Same as **forfeit**.

forfaulture. Same as **forfeiture**.

forfeit. Verb: To lose, particularly in consequence of a default or an offense. 36 Am J2d Forf & P § 3. Noun: That which is forfeited or lost by neglect of duty, or, in other words a fine, a mulct, a penalty, a forfeiture. State v Baltimore & Ohio Railroad Co. (Md) 12 Gill & J 399.
See **forfeiture**.

forfeitment. Same as **forfeiture**.

forfeiture. A word often used as a synonym of "penalty" but which is, precisely, a divestiture of property without compensation, in consequence of a default or an offense, 36 Am J2d Forf & P § 1; an enforced and involuntary loss of a right. Storm v Barbara Oil Co. 177 Kan 589, 282 P2d 417.
A judicial act, such as the forfeiture of a bail bond or recognizance. Re Wright, 228 NC 584, 46 SE2d 696. An incident of the old attainder whereby, as a form of punishment for crime, the estate of a convicted felon was extinguished, the property going to the king. 21 Am J2d Crim L § 616. An incident of attainder consequent upon the flight of a felon. 23 Am J2d Desc & D § 91.

forfeiture by alienation (for'fi-tūr by āl-yen-ā'shọn). The forfeiture of land to the crown by the alienation of it to a stranger. See 2 Bl Comm 274.

forfeiture of bail. The consequence of a breach of the condition of a bail bond, particularly, the failure of the surety to deliver the principal into the custody of the proper officer of the law, or to procure his attendance in court, as required by the bond. 8 Am J2d Bail § 139.

forfeiture of bond. A breach of condition in consequence of which the obligee is entitled to declare a forfeiture.
See **forfeiture of bail**.

forfeiture of insurance. See **nonforfeiture provisions**.

forfeiture of lease. The forfeiture of a leasehold at common law, as in the case of a disclaimer of title, by virtue of a statutory provision, or under a clause in the lease providing for a forfeiture upon breach of covenant or condition. 32 Am J1st L & T § 847.

forfeiture of marriage (of mar'āj). A forfeiture or penalty exacted of a ward in chivalry for marrying without the consent of his guardian.

forfeiture of mining claim. The loss of the right to a mining claim consequent to the failure to perform conditions imposed by law, particularly the condition requiring the performance of annual development work. 36 Am J1st Min & M § 115.

forfeiture of mining lease. The forfeiture of a mining lease for nonpayment of rent or the breach of other conditions of the lease. 36 Am J1st Min & M §§ 58 et seq. The forfeiture of a mining lease of property constituting public lands of the United States for default in nonpayment of royalty or the violation of other provisions of the lease. 36 Am J1st Min & M § 141.

Forfeitures Abolition Act (ab-ọ-lish'ọn akt). An English statute enacted in 1870 which abolished the forfeiture of property as a punishment for felony.

forfeng. Same as **forfang**.

forgavel (for-ga'vel). A small rent which was payable in money.

forge. To shape by beating, particularly metal. In law, to fabricate an instrument by imitation with intent to defraud. People v Mitchell, 92 Cal 590, 28 P 597; State v Sotak, 100 W Va 652, 131 SE 706, 46 ALR 1523, 1526. To commit a forgery.
See **forgery**.

forged check. In common parlance, a check upon which the maker's name is forged. Kleinman v Chase Nat. Bank, 124 Misc 173, 207 NYS 191.

forged deed. A deed of conveyance to which the grantor's name has been forged, such instrument being absolutely void and wholly ineffectual to pass title, even to a subsequent innocent purchaser. 23 Am J2d Deeds § 139.

forgery. A criminal offense at common law and under statutes defining the term variously. 36 Am J2d Forg § 1. Essentially, the false making or material alteration, with intent to defraud, or, under some statutes, intent to injure. (Green v State (Fla) 76 So 2d 645, 49 ALR2d 847), of any writing which, if genuine, might apparently be of legal efficacy or the foundation of a legal liability. 36 Am J2d Forg § 1.

For the purposes of a policy of forgery insurance: an act which, under applicable principles of criminal law, will amount to the crime of forgery. 29A Am J Rev ed Ins § 1339. Of course, where a policy insuring against "forgery" contains its own definition of the term, such definition rather than a technical definition of the crime of forgery will prevail. Anno: 52 ALR2d 209.

Falsification of a paper or the making of a false paper of legal efficacy apparently capable of effecting a fraud and a fraudulent intent are essentials of the offense of forgery; and the falsity of the writing relates to the want of genuineness in its making and not to the truth or falsity of the statements contained therein. To constitute forgery, the name signed on writings designed and used as instruments of fraud need not be identical with that of the person whose signature it purports to be, but merely idem sonans; and the use of a recurrent middle initial not in the simulated signature is not a fatal variance. Peoples Bank & T. Co. v Fidelity & Casualty Co. 231 NC 510, 57 SE2d 809, 15 ALR2d 996.

forgiveness. See **condonation**; **reconciliation**.

for good cause. See **good cause**.

forgotten invention. An art or device which has been forgotten, thereby becoming unknown and of no use to society. 40 Am J1st Pat § 38.

forgotten notice doctrine. A rule applicable where one taking a negotiable instrument contends that he did not have notice of an infirmity in the instrument at that time, although he had such notice at a prior time, the principle being that a lapse of memory or inadvertent omission to look for the notice is mere negligence, not bad faith destroying the taker's status as a holder in due course. 11 Am J2d B & N § 429.

forgotten property. Property of which the owner has no recollection.
See **mislaid property**.

for hire. A test applied in determining the character of a company as a public utility; a test by which a mutual company furnishing telephone service without profit held not to be a public utility. State ex rel. Buffum Tel. Co. v Public Service Com. 272 Mo 627, 199 SW 962, PUR1918C 158.
See **for compensation**; **for hire or compensation**.

for hire or compensation. In reference to a motor vehicle:—a vehicle operated to carry passengers or freight of other persons for a direct charge, not a vehicle used for the delivery of one's own property or products. 7 Am J2d Auto § 74.

Transactions in which a company delivering goods to customers outside the city makes a direct charge to them for the cost of transportation are within the contemplation of a statute requiring the licensing or registration of motor vehicles for hire or compensation. Collins-Dietz-Morris Co. v State Corp. Com. 154 Okla 121, 7 P2d 123, l0 ALR 561.

forinsecus (fo-rin'se-kus). Same as **forinsic**.

forinsic (for-in'sik). Foreign; outside; extrinsic; external.

foris (fō'ris). Outside; without; abroad; foreign.

forisbanitus (fō-ris-ba'ni-tus). Banished; exiled.

forisfacere (fō-ris-fa'se-re). To forfeit.

Forisfacit omnia quae juris sunt (fō-ris-fā'-sit om'ni-a kwē jū'ris sunt). He has forfeited all of his legal rights.

Forisfacit patriam et regnum, et exul efficitur (fō-ris-fā'sit pa'tri-am et reg'num, et ex'ul ef-fi'si-ter). He has forfeited his country and his kingdom and has been made an exile.

Forisfacit utlagatus omnia quae pacis sunt (fō-ris-fā'sit ut-la-gā'tus om'ni-a kwē pa'sis sunt). An outlaw forfeits all things which pertain to peace.

forisfacta (fō-ris-fak'ta). Lands and goods whereof the property is gone away or departed from the owner; that is, which have been forfeited to the king for offenses. The underlying reason for such forfeitures appears to be that since the individual has derived his property from society, as a right conferred upon him in exchange for the natural freedom which he relinquishes as a member of society, it is just that for good cause the state should resume the property which the laws had assigned to him. See 1 Bl Comm 299.

forisfactum (fō-ris-fak'tum). Singular of **forisfacta**.

forisfactura (fō-ris-fak-tū'ra). Same as **forfeiture**.

forisfactura maritagii. See **de forisfactura maritagii**.

forisfactus (fō-ris-fak'tus). A person who has forfeited his life; a felon.

forisfamiliated (fō"ris-fạ-mil'i-ā-ted). A son provided for by his father in the latter's lifetime instead of inheriting after his father's death. See 2 Bl Comm 220.

forisfamiliatus (fō-ris-fa-mi-li-ā'tūs). Same as **forisfamiliated**.

forisjudicatio (fō-ris-jū-di-kā'she-ō). Same as **forejudger**.

forisjudicatus (fō-ris-jū-di-kā'tus). Forejudged.
See **forejudge**.

forisjurare (fō-ris-jū-rā're). To forswear; to abjúre, to renounce by oath.

forjudge (fôr-juj'). Same as **forejudge**.

forjurer. Same as **forisjurare**.

fork. A term unfamiliar in present usage for the practice of delaying the progress of litigation against joint defendants by entering appearances at intervals instead of all at once.

form. The antithesis of substance; the appearance or superficial aspect rather than the substance or the essence. State v Japone, 202 Iowa 450, 455, 209 N W 468, 471. Shape or configuration of a body; the figure as defined by lines and surfaces. See Sherill v O'Brien, 188 NY 185, 81 NE 124. A printed or typed formulatory contract or other instrument with blank spaces for the insertion of the names of the parties and such other particulars as may be required to make it a complete instrument. Mutual Ben. Life Ins. Co. v Welch, 71 Okla 59, 175 P 45, 48. A printed or typed composition of allegations typical of a particular kind of a pleading, motion, court order, or judgment, containing blanks for the insertion of the names of parties and allegations required to adapt the composition to use in a particular case.
See **common form; matter of form.**

forma (for'ma). Form.
See **modo et forma; pro forma.**

Forma dat esse (for'ma dat es'se). Form imparts existence.

Forma dat esse rei (for'ma dat es'se rē'ī). The form of the thing imparts to it its existence. District of Columbia v Bailey, 171 US 161, 178, 43 L Ed 118, 126, 118 S Ct 868.

forma et figura judicii (for'ma et fi-gū'ra jū-di'she-ī). The forms and shapes of judgment or judicial action. See 3 Bl Comm 271.

formal conclusion. A conclusion drawn by the court in the exercise of its legal judgment as a basis of the decision in the case. 53 Am J1st Trial § 1132. The concluding statement in a special verdict that "if on the facts found, the law is with the plaintiff, then we find for the plaintiff; if the law is with the defendant, then we find for the defendant." 53 Am J1st Trial § 1092.

formal contract. A written contract duly executed, also under seal where a seal is required by law.

formaldehyde. An organic compound oxidation product of alcohol. St. Louis v Schuler, 190 Mo 524, 89 SW 621. In solution, a disinfectant and preservative.

Forma legalis forma essentialis (for'ma lē-gā'lis for'ma es-sen-she-ā'lis). Legal form is essential form.

formal error. Harmless error. 5 Am J2d A & E § 776.

formalities. The prescribed robes of office.

formality (for-mal'i-ti). Adherence to forms and customs.

formal party. A classification of parties to an action. A nominal party rather than a necessary or indispensable party. Minnis v Southern Pacific Co. (CA9 Cal) 98 F2d 913. A person having no interest in the subject matter of the action but whose joinder as a party is required by statute. Tregear v Etiwanda Water Co. 76 Cal 537, 18 P 658.

Forma non observata, infertur adnullatio actus (for'ma non ob-zer-vā'ta, in-fer'ter ad-nul-lā'she-ō ak'tus). If form is not observed, it is inferred that the act is a nullity.

forma pauperis (for'ma pâ'pe-ris). See **in forma pauperis.**

form a quorum. See **quorum.**

formata brevia (for-mā'ta brē'vi-a). Same as **brevia formata.**

formed action (fôrmd ak'shon). An action in which a set form of words has been established or prescribed.

formed design. A plan or course of conduct deliberately conceived with premeditation. Lang v State, 84 Ala 1.

formedon (fôr'mẹ-don). An ancient writ of right which lay to recover lands according to the form of a gift or grant in tail.

formedon in the descender (fôr'mē-don in the dē-sen'dėr). A writ which lay where a gift in tail was made, and the tenant in tail aliened the lands entailed, or was disseised of them and then died. In such a case the heir in tail had his writ of formedon in the descender to recover these lands so given in tail against him who was then the actual tenant of the freehold. See 3 Bl Comm 192.

formedon in the remainder (in the rē-mān'dėr). A writ which a remainderman had against a stranger who intruded and kept him out of possession of land upon the death of the tenant for life or in tail without issue inheritable. See 3 Bl Comm 192.

formedon in the reverter (in the rē-vėr'tėr). A writ which a reversioner had where there was a gift in tail, and then by the death of the donee or his heirs without issue of his body the reversion fell in upon the donor, his heirs or assigns. See 3 Bl Comm 192.

former. Prior in point of time.
See terms and expressions beginning "prior", such as **prior adjudication; prior jeopardy; prior testimony.**

formerly. See **heretofore.**

formido periculi (for'mi-dō pe-ri'ku-lī). The fear of danger.

form of action. The designation by which an action is known in the law, as trover, trespass, assumpsit, an action ex delicto or an action ex contractu.
While technical forms of action have been abolished in most jurisdictions, leaving only one form of action in civil suits, known as the "civil action," in all jurisdictions, the fundamental and substantial distinctions upon which the old common-law forms of actions were based, remain. 1 Am J2d Actions § 5.

formula. A set or prescribed form of words which remains in use but has lost its original meaning, having become a merely conventional expression. A list of ingredients and directions for preparing or compounding a food or medicine. 25 Am J2d Drugs § 3.

formulae (for'mū-lē). Plural of **formula.**

Formulary. An official list of medicines with description of method of compounding. 25 Am J2d Drugs § 1.

fornagium (for-nā'ji-um). Same as **furnage.**

fornication. At common law, the act of illicit intercourse by a man, married or single, with an unmarried woman; more broadly defined by modern authorities as illicit sexual intercourse, whether between married or unmarried persons. 2 Am J2d Adult § 1. Particularly defined by some authority as the living together and having intercourse with each other, or habitual intercourse without living together, of a man and a woman, neither of whom is married. 2 Am J2d Adult § 1.
The word is derived from the Latin word "fornix," which originally meant the forceps of a beetle, then an arch, then an underground vault or cavern,

FORNICATION / FORTUNETELLING

then a brothel, because in Roman cities brothels were kept in underground vaults or caverns. A "fornicator," then, was one who carried on illicit sexual intercourse in a brothel or for hire; that is, what we now term a "prostitute." State v Phillips, 26 ND 206, 144 NW 94.

fornication statutes. Modern statutes which place fornication in the catalogue of crimes. 2 Am J2d Adult § 8.

fornicator. See **fornication.**

fornix (fôr'niks). A brothel; a house of prostitution.

forno (for'nō). An oven; a bakehouse.

foro (fō'rō). In the forum; within the jurisdiction; in the court.

foro seculari (fō'rō se-ku-lā'rī). In the secular court.

for other purposes. A phrase in the title of a statute which calls attention to provisions in the body of the statute germane to the general subject, although not referred to expressly in the title. 50 Am J1st Stat § 175.

for own use. A limitation or restriction.
For meaning of term as it pertains to the rights and duties of a life tenant with power to anticipate or enjoy the principal, see Anno: 2 ALR 1266.

for plaintiff. See **verdict for plaintiff.**

forprise (for'prīz). Something withheld; an exception or reservation in a grant or conveyance.

for public use. As a test of the character of a company as a public utility:—of or belonging to the people; open to all the people to the extent of the capacity of the plant. State Public Utilities Com. v Monarch Refrigerator Co. 267 Ill 528, 108 NE 716.

for purpose of argument. A phrase often used in qualifying a concession. 5 Am J2d A & E § 712.

Forrester intoximeter test. An alcohol breath test used to determine intoxication. 7 Am J2d Auto § 332.

for so long as he shall occupy. A phrase which gives a life estate. 28 Am J2d Est § 63.

forsque (fŏr-kē). Only; but.

forstal. Same as **forestall.**

forstellarius (for-stel-lā'ri-us). A forestaller.

Forstellarius est pauperum depressor, et totius communitatis et patriae publicus inimicus (for-stel-lā'ri-us est pâ'pe-rŭm de-pres'sor, et tō'she-us kom-mū-ni-tā'tis et pa'tri-ē pub'li-kus in-i-mī'kus). A forestaller is an oppressor of the poor and is a public enemy of the whole community and the country.

forswear (fôr-swār'). To abjure; to swear falsely; to commit perjury.

forsworn. Having made a false statement under oath; sometimes, but not necessarily, the committing of perjury. Sheely v Biggs (Md) 2 Harr & J 363.

fort. A place, usually a location having some natural advantages pertinent to the purpose, equipped for defense against an attacking force and protected by heavy walls or embankments of earth. United States v Tichenor (CC Or) 12 F 415, 424.

fortax (fōr-taks'). To tax heavily or immoderately.

forthcoming (fōrth'kum-ing). An action to carry out an arrestment.

forthcoming bond. Same as **delivery bond.**

for the purpose and consideration stated. A formal clause in an acknowledgment. 1 Am J2d Ack § 77.

for the uses and purposes herein set forth. A formal clause in an acknowledgment. 1 Am J2d Ack § 77.

forthwith. With all reasonable diligence and dispatch. Within a reasonable time. As a limitation of time in a covenant for repairs contained in a lease: —with all reasonable celerity, not immediately. 32 Am J1st L & T § 800. As a limitation of time for the giving of a notice:—with reasonable promptness, 8 Am J2d Auto § 869; 32 Am J1st L & T § 800; with promptness according to the exigency of the occasion, such as the necessity of locating the person to receive notice. Northwestern Nat. Ins. Co. v Cohen, 138 Va 177, 121 SE 507.

fortia (for'she-a). Force; violence.

fortia frisca (for'she-a fris'ka). Same as **fresh force.**

fortility (for-til'i-ti). A fort; a stronghold; a castle.

fortior (for'she-or). Stronger; more forcible; greater; more powerful; more effective.

Fortior est custodia legis quam hominis (for'she-or est kus-tō'di-a lē'jis quam ho'mi-nis). The custody of the law is stronger than that of man.

Fortior et equior est dispositio legis quam hominis (for'she-or et e'qui-or est dis-po-zi' she-ō lē'jis quam ho'mi-nis). The disposition of the law is stronger and fairer than that of man. See Jackson v Gardner (NY) 8 Johns 393, 401.

Fortior et potentior est dispositio legis quam hominis (for'she-or et po-ten'she-or est dis-pō-zi'she-ō lē'jis quam ho'mi-nis). The disposition of the law is stronger and more powerful than that of man.

fortiori (for-she-ō'rī). See **a fortiori; multo fortiori.**

fortis (fôr'tis). Strong; forcible; effective; powerful.

fortius contra proferentem (for'she-us kon'tra prō-fe-ren'tem). More strictly against the party offering. Dodge v Walley, 22 Cal 224, 228.

fortuit (for'tu-it). Fortuitous; accidental; occurring by the arbitrament of chance.
See **cas fortuit.**

fortuitment (fŏr-tu-it-mān). Same as **fortuit.**

fortuitous. Accidental. Zappala v Industrial Acci. Com. 82 Wash 314, 144 P 54. Occurring by the arbitrament of chance.

fortuitous collision. An accidental collision of vessels without fault on either side. Peters v Warren Ins. Com. (US) 14 Pet 99, 112, 10 L Ed 371, 378.

fortuitous event. An accident; something happening by chance. Stertz v Industrial Ins. Com. 91 Wash 588, 158 P 256.
No sound distinction can be made between those injuries to employees resulting from accident and those resulting from some fortuitous event. See Zappala v Industrial Acci. Com. 82 Wash 314, 144 P 54.

fortuitum. See **forum fortuitum.**

fortunam faciunt judicem (for-tū'nam fā'she-unt jū'-di-sem). They make fortune or chance the judge.

forty (fôr'ti). A word in common use, especially in the middle west and west, to designate a quarter of the quarter section of land, that is, a forty acre tract.

forty-days court. One of the ancient English forest courts.

fortunetelling. The craft of looking into the future and foretelling or predicting events to occur, particularly those which bear upon the life of a particular person. 36 Am J2d Fortunetelling § 1.

forum (fō'rum). A court; a tribunal; a jurisdiction; a place where justice is administered; the place of jurisdiction.
See **law of the forum.**

forum actus (fō'rum ak'tus). The place of jurisdiction over the act.

forum conscientiae (fō'rum kon-she-en'she-ē). The court or forum of conscience; a term sometimes used to characterize a court of equity.

forum contractus (fō'rum kon-trak'tus). The forum of the contract, the place where the contract is entered into.

forum domesticum (fō'rum do-mes'ti-kum). A domestic forum or jurisdiction.

forum domicilii (fō'rum dō-mi-si'li-ī). The forum of domicile; the place or jurisdiction where a man resides and has the right to be sued.

forum domicilii actoris (fō'rum dō-mi-si'li-ī ak-tō'ris). The forum or jurisdiction of the plaintiff's domicile.

forum domicilii rei (fō'rum dō-mi-si'li-ī rē'ī). The forum or jurisdiction of the domicile of the defendant.

forum ecclesiasticum (fō'rum e-klē-si-as'ti-kum). An ecclesiastical court or forum.

forum fortuitum (fō'rum for-tū'i-tum). The forum of chance; that is, the jurisdiction in which the action happens to be filed.

forum ligeantiae actoris (fō'rum li-je-an'she-e ak-tō'ris). The forum of the plaintiff's allegiance; that is the court or forum of the country to which the plaintiff owes allegiance.

forum ligeantiae rei (fō'rum li-je-an'she-ē rē'ī). The forum of the defendant's allegiance; that is, the court or forum of the country to which he owes allegiance.

forum litis motae (fō'rum lī'tis mō'tē). The forum or jurisdiction in which the action is brought.

forum non conveniens. (Latin.) The doctrine or principle that where, in a broad sense, the ends of justice strongly indicate that the controversy may be more suitably tried elsewhere, jurisdiction should be declined and the parties relegated to relief to be sought in another forum. Universal Adjustment Corp. v Midland Bank, 281 Mass 303, 184 NE 152, 87 ALR 1407. The doctrine that an American court has power to decline to assume jurisdiction where the litigation is between aliens or nonresidents, or can more appropriately be conducted in a foreign tribunal. Canada Malting Co. v Paterson Steamships, 258 US 413, 76 L Ed 837, 52 S Ct 413.

forum originis (fō'rum ō-ri'ji-nis). The forum or jurisdiction in which the person was born.

forum regis (fō'rum rē'jis). The king's court.

forum rei (fō'rum rē'ī). The forum of the defendant; that is, the forum or jurisdiction of the residence of the defendant; also the forum or jurisdiction of the subject matter of the action.

forum rei gestae (fō'rum rē'ī jes'tē). The forum or jurisdiction where the act was done or committed.

forum rei sitae (fō'rum rē'ī sī'tē). The forum or jurisdiction where the subject matter of the action is situated.

forum saeculare (fō'rum se-ku-lā're). A secular court, as distinguished from an ecclesiastical court.

for value. For consideration.
See **purchaser for value; trust for value.**

for value received. An admission of the receiving of value by way of consideration. 29 Am J Rev ed Ins § 659. Importing, where used in a contract, that the promisor did receive something of some value. Sullivan v Lear, 23 Fla 463. Importing, where used in a deed, a consideration sufficient to raise a use in the bargainee. Jackson ex dem. Hudson v Alexander (NY) 3 Johns 484.
See **having received full value; value received.**

forward. Adverb: Onward; toward the front. Adjective: Advanced; precocious. Verb: To dispatch; to transmit; in one sense, to put something on its way to an ultimate destination, not including the idea of completing a delivery. Nicoletti v Bank of Los Banos, 190 Cal 637, 214 P 51, 27 ALR 1479, 1483. In reference to the obligation of a receiving carrier:
—To undertake under the terms of the contract with the shipper for through transportation to a point beyond the carrier's own line. 14 Am J2d Car § 691.
See **forwarder.**

forwarder. A lawyer who sends an item of business accepted from a client to another lawyer, usually a lawyer at a distance, who, by reason of jurisdictional considerations or of proximity to a party or the subject matter of the business, can handle it more expeditiously. 7 Am J2d Attys § 259. One who, without owning or controlling the actual means of carriage, such as ships, railroad cars, etc., arranges for the transportation of the goods of a consignor in the ships or vehicles of an actual carrier. Anno: 141 ALR 919; 93 L Ed 831.

With the appearance of the practice by railroad companies of offering shippers greatly reduced freight rates for shipments in carload quantities, a modern concept of the term "forwarder" arose, as one who picked up the less-than-a-carload shipment at the shipper's place of business and engaged to deliver it safely at its ultimate destination, charging a rate covering the entire transportation and making its profit by consolidating the shipment with others in carload quantities to take advantage of the spread between the carload rates paid by him to the railroad company and the higher rates, approximating less-than-carload rates, which he charged the various shippers. United States v Chicago Heights Trucking Co. 310 US 344, 84 L Ed 1243, 60 S Ct 931.

Forwarder Act. A federal statute which subjects freight forwarders and their operations to the jurisdiction of the Interstate Commerce Commission. 49 USC §§ 1001 et seq.; Anno: 93 L Ed 831.

forwarder's receipt. The receipt for goods given by a forwarder. Another term for bill of lading.

forwarding. See **forwarder.**

forwarding bank. A bank which transmits an item for collection to another bank.

forwarding fee. The part of the fee for handling a matter of legal business forwarded by one attorney to another attorney to which the forwarder is entitled. 7 Am J2d Attys § 259.

forwarding suit papers. The obligation of one insured under an automobile liability policy, arising under a co-operation clause or an express provision of the policy, which requires the insured to forward immediately to the insurer every demand, notice, summons, other process, or pleadings received by him or his representative in connection with a claim made or suit brought against him based upon a liability alleged to arise out of the use and operation of the vehicle covered by the policy. 7 Am J2d Auto Ins § 185.

forwards and backwards at sea. From port to port in the course of the voyage.

for whom it may concern. A phrase which, appearing in an insurance policy, may extend the protection to any person having an insurable interest and within the contemplation of the parties at the time of the execution and delivery of the policy. 29 Am J Rev ed Ins § 241.

fossa (fos'ä). A ditch; a grave; a water hole where female felons were drowned; a castle moat.

fossage (fos'äj). A tax or duty paid by the inhabitants of a town for the upkeep of a moat surrounding the town.

fossagium (fos-sā'ji-um). Same as **fossage**.

fossatorium operatio (fos-sā-tō'ri-um o-per-ā'she-ō). Work or service performed on moats or ditches.

fossatum (fos-sā'tum). A ditch; a dyke; a moat.

fossway (fos'wā). One of the ancient roads constructed by the Romans in England.

fosterage (fos'tėr-āj). The rearing of the child of another as one's own.

foster-child (fos'tėr-chīld). The child of another who is being reared by a person as his or her own.

fosterland (fos'tėr-land). Land which has been assigned or set apart for the support of a person or an institution.

fosterlean (fos'ter-lēn). Remuneration given to a foster-parent for the rearing of a foster-child.

foster-parent (fos'tėr-pār'ent). One who is rearing the child of another as his or her own.
See **adoptive parent**.

foto-patrol. A device, similar to the photo-traffic camera, for measuring the speed of an automobile, operating on an electronic impulse which activates a light and a camera. People v Pett, 13 Misc 2d 975, 178 NYS2d 550.
See **photo-traffic camera**.

fouage (fū'āj). Same as **fuage**.

fouling waters. Corrupting waters. 56 Am J1st Wat §§ 405 et seq.

found. Room and board. Past tense of verb "find": Determined as a fact or facts; a finding made. Discovered or ascertained, as where, for jurisdictional purposes, a corporation is "found" to be doing business in a given judicial district. Haskell v Aluminum Co. of America (DC Mass) 14 F2d 864.
See **finding of fact**; **office found**.

foundation. A support, as of a building. The preliminary basis required for the admission of certain evidence.
A term often applied in modern times to a charitable organization, especially where a large fund of money is involved in the dispensing of charity. The endowment of a charitable or educational institution.

founded on statute. A proposition of law for which a statute is cited or which involves the application of statute. Compagnie Transatlantique v United States (DC NY) 21 F2d 465.

founded upon contract. Any action based on a contract which requires the support of the contract to sustain it. Republic Iron Mining Co. v Jones (CC Ga) 37 F 721.

founder (foun'dėr). The person who makes the first gift for the foundation of a college, a hospital or other eleemosynary institution. In the sense that the king alone could incorporate a society, he was called the founder of all corporations. See 1 Bl Comm 481.

founderosa (foun-de-rō'sa). Founderous; out of repair; in need of repair.

foundling. A child of very tender years abandoned by unknown parents. Anno: 16 ALR 1027.

foundling home. A charitable institution for the care of abandoned children.

fountain-pen gun. A weapon for the discharge of tear gas, of such size as to be carried easily and secretly. Bates v Taylor, 115 W Va 4, 174 SE 485, 92 ALR 1093.

fourcher (four-she'). To fork,—a practice of delaying the progress of a litigation against two or more defendants by entering their appearances at intervals instead of all at once.

fourching. Delaying a litigation.

four corners. A figurative expression signifying the whole face of an instrument, omitting nothing in arriving at its meaning and intent.

four seas. The four seas surrounding the British Isles.
See **beyond the four seas**.

Fourteenth Amendment. The amendment to the Constitution of the United States which extends citizenship to all persons born or naturalized in the United States and subject to the jurisdiction thereof, and contains the due process and equal protection clauses.

fourteen-year-old child. See **child of fourteen**.

fourth branch of government. The administrative agencies. 1 Am J2d Admin L § 11.

fourth class mail. See **parcel post**.

fourth-degree manslaughter. See **manslaughter**.

Fourth of July. See **Independence Day**.

four unities. Essentials in the creation and existence of an estate by the entireties; interest; title, time, and possession. Anno: 44 ALR2d 603.

fowl. Domesticated birds, especially large birds used for food; poultry. In one sense, any bird. Domestic fowl and wild fowl, the distinction being whether the fowl has been tamed and subjected so as to constitute property. 4 Am J2d Ani § 12.

fowls of warren (fouls of wor'en). Wild fowl which were protected from promiscuous killing by the English forest laws. These fowls were of three classes, campestres, as partridges, rails and quails; sylvestres, as woodcocks and pheasants; and aquatiles, as mallards and herons. See 2 Bl Comm 38, note.

fox hunt. Literally, a hunt for a fox. In popular usage, an elaborate enterprise with social significance, referring to a group of riders from a hunt club or assembled by invitation, mounted on wellbred horses known as "hunters," and following hounds directed by a master of the hunt in pursuit of a fox raised from cover or one turned loose for the purpose of chasing him.

fox raising and pelting. Agricultural labor. Fromm Bros. v United States (DC Wis) 35 F Supp 145.

foy (foi). Fealty; fidelity; allegiance.
See **en bonne foy.**

f.p. Abbreviation of fire policy, also of floating policy.

FPC. Abbreviation of Federal Power Commission.
See **Power Commission.**

fr. Abbreviation of fractional, often used in descriptions of real estate.

fractio (frak′she-ō). A fraction; a fragment; a fractional part; a division.

fraction. A quantity less than the whole of something, expressed as a decimal or by numerator and denominator. A fragment; a fragmentary part of a whole, disconnected and distinct within itself, rather than an undivided interest; a several, not a joint, interest. Jory v Palace Dry-goods & Shoe Co. 30 Or 196, 46 P 786.

fractional. Small, comprising no more than a fraction of the whole.

fractional lot. A city or village lot containing an area less than that of the normal lot laid out by a survey.

fractional part. A fraction of an entire unit.
A conveyance of a fractional part of a designated tract of land, without specifying the location within the tract, is construed as conveying an undivided interest to the extent of the fraction. 23 Am J2d Deeds § 246.

fractional section. A section of land laid off in the governmental survey with less than the normal 640 acres, by way of allowance for the convergence of the meridians in running toward the pole.
See **fraction of section.**

fractional share. A fractional part of a share of corporate stock, such being nonvoting, except as voting has been authorized by statute. Commonwealth ex rel. Cartwright v Cartwright, 350 Pa 638, 40 A2d 30, 155 ALR 1088.

fractionem diei non recipet lex (frak-she-ō′nem dī′ē-ī non rē′si-pit lex). The law does not recognize fractions of a day.

fraction of a day. A fractional part of a day. A division of a day; a half-day; an hour or a minute.
At common law, fractions of a day are generally rejected in computing the time for the performance of an act. 52 Am J1st Time § 15.
The maxim that there are no fractions of a day is a fiction of law, and when it is material to distinguish, the truth may be shown; for a fiction of law, introduced for the sake of convenience and justice, ought never to be allowed to work a wrong; thus, when it is necessary to determine the priority of two attachments, the precise time of each attachment may be shown; and so in many other cases. Westbrook Manufacturing Co. v Grant, 60 Me 88.

fraction of section. A section of a section of land as laid out by the government survey, designated in words or figures, for example, "northeast quarter" or "NE4".
Throughout those portions of the United States in which the government system of land surveys is used, initials of the points of the compass, followed by the figure "2" or the figure "4," are employed to describe fractional portions of a 640-acre section of land, the figure "4," written as above, meaning one quarter, and the figure "2," thus written, meaning one half; thus E2 NE4 sec. 10 means eighty acres comprising the east half of the northeast quarter of section 10. Power v Bowdle, 3 ND 107, 54 NW 404.
See **fractional section.**

fractura navium (frak-tū′ra nā′vi-um). The breaking up of ships; shipwrecks.

fracture. A break, crack, or split in a bone. A crack or break in a steam boiler. 29A Am J Rev ed Ins § 1365.
See **Pott's fracture.**

fragentibus prisonam. See **de fragentibus prisonam.**

fragmentary appeals. Successive appeals from the same decision. 4 Am J2d A & E § 49.

frais (frè). Costs; expenses; charges.

frais de justice (frè dē jus-tis). Costs incurred in an action; costs of suit.

frame. Verb: To give a shape to something. To put a border around something, e.g. a picture. To draft the outline of a constitution or a form of government. Frieszleben v Shallcross 14 Del (9 Houst) 1, 19 A 576. A term on the border between slang and accepted usage for producing a case to convict an accused, without scruples as to the propriety or the trustworthiness of the evidence offered.

franc (frangk). Free. The standard unit of the currency of France, also of Switzerland and Belgium.

franc aleu (frangk a-leu). Free land; allodial land; land held free from any service to a superior.

franchilanus (fran-ki-lā′nus). A freeman; a free tenant.

franchise. In the most general sense of the term, a right or privilege conferred by law, e.g. the right to vote. 23 Am J2d Franch § 2. A privilege conferred by law upon a corporation or an individual which permits the recipient to make use of a street or public place in an activity or operation which, except for the grant of the franchise, would constitute a wrong or trespass. People ex rel. New York C. & H. R. Co. v Gourley, 198 NY 486, 92 NE 398. In a narrower sense, the privilege of doing something which does not belong to all citizens as a matter of common right. 23 Am J2d Franch § 2; a privilege or immunity of a public nature which cannot be legally exercised without a legislative grant. 23 Am J2d Franch § 2. A special privilege, conferred by the state on an individual, which did not theretofore exist and which does not belong to the individual as a matter of right. Madden v Queens County Jockey Club, 296 NY 249, 72 NE2d 697, 1 ALR2d 1160. A grant to a public service corporation or public utility conferring the right to carry on business, which, when accepted by the grantee, constitutes a contract between the parties by which their rights and obligations are to be determined in accordance with its terms and conditions. 43 Am J1st Pub Util § 16.
A primary corporate franchise, the result of a grant of special privileges to incorporators which enables them to act for certain designated purposes as a single individual and exempts them, unless otherwise specially provided, from individual liability; a secondary corporate franchise in the powers granted to a corporation by the sovereign and specified in its charter. 18 Am J2d Corp § 66.
See **special franchise.**

franchise taxes. Taxes in five classes:—(1) organization taxes, or fees exacted of domestic corporations for the grant of corporate powers; (2) excises levied periodically, usually annually, upon the franchise of domestic corporations; (3) excises charged foreign corporations for the privilege of entering and doing business within the state; (4) excises upon special privileges enjoyed by particular corporations; (5) ad valorem taxes on franchises as property. 51 Am J1st Tax § 809.

Francigena (fran-si-je'na). A native of France; hence, an alien in the United States until naturalized.

franclaine (fron-clen). A freeholder; a freeman.

franc tenancier (frank ten-an-ci-e). A freeholder.

francum. See **feudum francum.**

francus (fran'kus). Free; a freeman.

francus bancus (fran'kus ban'kus). Same as **free bench.**

francus homo (fran'kus hō'mō). A freeman.

francus plegius (fran'kus ple'ji-us). Same as **frank-pledge.**
See **frank-pledges.**

francus tenens (fran'kus te'nēnz). A freeholder.

frank. Free. The privilege of sending mail matter without postage. The mark or indorsement used in exercising such privilege.
See **franking privilege.**

frankalmoign tenure. A form of land tenure whereby a religious corporation held lands of the donor to them and their successors forever. Tenure in free alms,—a Saxon tenure which survived the Norman revolution, and under which tenure an ecclesiastical corporation held land without fealty and merely by prayer service for the soul of the donor. See 2 Bl Comm 101.

frank bank (frangk' bangk). Same as **free bench.**

frank chase (frangk' chās). Free chase,—the exclusive liberty or privilege of hunting within a prescribed area. The granting of such a liberty was a prohibition against the cutting of any wood on the land, even by the owner, without the consent of the king's forester. See 2 Bl Comm 39.

frank fee (frangk' fē). A species of freehold tenure which was exempt from all services, but not from homage. Copyhold lands could be altered into frank fee by means of a fine levied in the king's court, but a writ of deceit lay to change it back to copyhold. See 2 Bl Comm 368, footnote.

frank ferme (frangk' fėrm). A species of socage tenure which was exempt from homage, ward, marriage and relief, and with respect to which the nature of the fee was changed by feoffment out of chivalry or knight service for certain yearly services. See 2 Bl Comm 80.

frank fold (frangk' fōld). Same as **faldage.**

franking privilege. A privilege conferred by statute upon certain persons and certain classes of mail matter by virtue of which certain matters may be transmitted by mail without postage, subject to conditions prescribed in the statute. 39 USC §§ 321 et seq.

frank law (frangk' lâ). The aggregate rights of a freeman or a citizen.

franklyn (frangk'lin). A freeholder; a freeman.

frank marriage (frangk' mar'āj). A species of entailed estate which was created when an estate-tail special was given to a man and his wife, the near relative of the donor, and to the heirs of their bodies to the fourth generation, free of all service but fealty. See 2 Bl Comm 115.

frank-pledges (frangk' plej'es). Free pledges. The tithings or decennaries of the Saxons were so called because each of the members of a tithing was a surety or free pledge to the king for the good behavior of the other members, and if any offense was committed in the district, they were bound to produce the offender. See 1 Bl Comm 114.

frank tenant (frangk' ten'ạnt). A freeholder.

frank tenement (frangk' ten'ẹ-ment). A free tenement; a freehold.

frank tenure. Same as **free tenure.**

frassetum (fras-sē'tum). A tract of wooded land.

frater (frā'tėr). A brother.

frater consanguineus (frā'ter kon-san-gwi'ne-us). A brother born of the same father, but a different mother.

frater fratri uterino non succedet in haereditate paterna (frā'ter frā'trī ū-te-rī'nō non suk-sē'det in hē-rē-di-tā'te pa-ter'na). A brother shall not succeed his uterine brother in the paternal inheritance. See 2 Bl Comm 233.

fraternal beneficial society. A mutual benefit society. As defined by statute in one jurisdiction, a corporation, society, or voluntary association, organized and carried on for the sole benefit of its members, and their beneficiaries, and not for profit, and in which the payment of death benefits shall be for families, heirs, blood relatives, affianced husband or wife, or dependents. Lafferty v Supreme Council Catholic Mut. Ben. Asso. 259 Pa 452, 103 A 280.
See **mutual benefit society.**

fraternal benefit society. See **mutual benefit society.**

fraternal insurance (frạ-tėr'nạl in-shör'ạns). Mutual life, accident, and health insurance which is issued to their members by fraternal orders or societies.

fraternal order or society. An organization of men created and maintained for the improvement of its members by instruction through rituals and lectures in the principles of true brotherhood, real charity, and loyalty to country, for fellowship, and for aiding the widows and orphans of members, often by providing mutual benefit or fraternal insurance. Re Mason Tire & Rubber Co. 56 App DC 170, 11 F2d 556.

fraternia (fra-ter'ni-a). A fraternity; a brotherhood.

fraternity. A fraternal order or society; an organization of college students, usually providing living quarters for the members. An organization of high-school students.
See **fraternal order or society.**

frater nutricius (frā'ter nu-tri'she-us). A bastard brother.

frater uterinus (frā'ter u-te-rī'nus). A uterine brother,—a brother by the mother's side; that is one who had the same mother but a different father. See 2 Bl Comm 232.

fratriage. Inheritance by a younger brother.

fratricide (frat'ri-sīd). The killing of a brother or a sister; a person who kills a brother or a sister.

fraud. Deceit, deception, artifice, or trickery operating prejudicially on the rights of another, and so intended, by inducing him to part with property or surrender some legal right. 23 Am J2d Fraud § 2. Anything calculated to deceive another to his prejudice and accomplishing the purpose, whether it be an act, a word, silence, the suppression of the truth, or other device contrary to the plain rules of common honesty. 23 Am J2d Fraud § 2. An affirmation of a fact rather than a promise or statement of intent to do something in the future. Miller v Sutliff, 241 Ill 521, 89 NE 651.

For the purpose of the exception to discharge in bankruptcy of debts incurred by officers and fiduciaries through "fraud":—positive fraud, fraud in fact, involving moral turpitude or intentional wrong. 9 Am J2d Bankr § 801. As a ground for annulment of a marriage:—concealment or deception affecting the free consent of the injured party, involving such matters as identity, birth, rank, family, fortune, health, character, morality, habits, temper, reputation, etc. 35 Am J1st Mar § 90.

See **badge of fraud; constructive fraud; deceit; extrinsic fraud; fraudulent conveyance; legal fraud; misrepresentation; positive fraud.**

fraud in equity. A conception of fraud which includes whatever amounts to actionable fraud in law and other acts, transactions, and circumstances, wherein it appears that one person has obtained an unconscionable advantage over another, from which equity conceives the existence of a constructive fraud. Gierth v Fidelity Trust Co. 93 NJ Equity 163, 115 A 397, 18 ALR 976.

fraud in the factum. Fraud exercised in reference to the manual acts of signing and delivering an instrument, sometimes by a substitution of documents accomplished by deception. Blackburn v Morrison, 29 Okla 510, 118 P 402. Gomillion v Forsythe, 218 SC 211, 62 SE2d 297, 53 ALR2d 169.

fraud in the inducement. Fraud exercised in inducing the signing of an instrument. Gomillion v Forsythe, 218 SC 211, 62 SE2d 297, 53 ALR2d 169.

fraud of creditors. See **fraudulent conveyance.**

fraud order. An order by the Postmaster General directing the return of mail to the sender upon finding that the addressee is engaged in conducting prohibited schemes, enterprises, or devices. 41 Am J1st P O § 97.

fraud or dishonesty. As a phrase expressive of the undertaking of the surety in a fidelity bond:—acts extending beyond those which are criminal; a phrase inclusive under a broad construction against a paid surety of acts and circumstances whereby loss is caused the obligee, even though not such as would support a criminal prosecution. Prior Lake State Bank v National Surety Corp. 248 Minn 383, 80 NW2d 612, 57 ALR2d 1306.

frauds, statute of. See **Statute of Frauds.**

fraudulent. That which is done with intent to defraud. Luttrell v State, 85 Tenn 232.
See **fraud.**

fraudulent assignment. An assignment for the benefit of creditors made with intent to prevent the immediate application of the property to the payment of assignor's debts. 6 Am J2d Assign for Crs § 63.

fraudulent concealment. The suppression of, or silence concerning, a fact material to be known and which the party is under a duty to communicate because of a confidential relationship between the parties or the particular circumstances of the case. American Nat. Bank v Fidelity & Deposit Co. 131 Ga 854, 63 SE 622. As a bar to discharge in bankruptcy:—the failure of the bankrupt to disclose his property to his trustee in bankruptcy after having had reasonable opportunity so to do. 9 Am J2d Bankr § 695. As a criminal offense against the Bankruptcy Act:—knowingly to conceal from the receiver, custodian, trustee, marshal, or other officer of the court charged with the custody or control of property, or from creditors in any proceeding under the Bankruptcy Act, any property belonging to the estate of a bankrupt; to conceal property knowingly, in contemplation of a bankruptcy proceeding, with intent to defeat the bankruptcy law. 18 USC § 152, paragraphs (1),(6).

fraudulent contract of marriage. A ground of absolute divorce consisting of fraud perpetrated upon the plaintiff in inducing him or her to enter into a marriage which is void because of consanguinity, imbecility, or other circumstance rendering the marriage void from the beginning. Gould v Gould, 74 Conn 242, 61 A 604.

fraudulent conversion. An essential element of the crime of embezzlement, which may consist either of an appropriation of the money or other personal property to the personal use of the accused, that is, of his disposition of it for his own personal benefit and his own private business, or in putting it to some other use than a proper discharge of the trust imposed, or after obtaining lawful possession, in failing to account for or pay over on proper or lawful demand. Blake v State, 12 Okla Crim 549, 160 P 30. A conversion by a fiduciary made with intent to deprive the beneficiary of the money permanently, or at least until restoration should be compelled. United States v Summers (DC Va) 19 F2d 627.

fraudulent conveyance. A conveyance in fraud of creditors. A transaction by means of which the owner of real or personal property has sought to place the land or goods beyond the reach of his creditors, or which operates to the prejudice of their legal or equitable rights, or a conveyance which operates to the prejudice of the legal or equitable rights of other persons, including subsequent purchasers. 37 Am J2d Frd Conv § 1.
See **Bulk Sales Acts; fraudulent transfer.**

Fraudulent Conveyance Act. One of the uniform laws. 37 Am J2d Frd Conv § 3.

fraudulent disposition of property. A disposition of property with respect to which three things must concur:—first, the thing disposed of must be of value, out of which the creditor could have realized all, or a portion of his claim; second, it must be transferred or disposed or by the debtor, and, third, it must be done with intent to defraud. Hoyt v Godfrey, 88 NY 669, 670.

fraudulent enlistment or appointment. The procuring of one's own enlistment or appointment in the armed forces by false representations or deliberate concealment as to his qualifications for the enlistment of appointment and receiving pay or allowances thereunder. 10 USC § 883. The effecting by one person of an enlistment or appointment in the armed forces of one known by him to be ineligible for such enlistment or appointment. 10 USC § 884.

fraudulent exchange. An exchange of property fraudulent as to the creditors of one of the parties. 37 Am J2d Frd Conv § 59.

fraudulent joinder. A plaintiff's joinder of a resident of the state as a party defendant without the right to do so and in bad faith, but in order to prevent a removal of the cause to the federal court. Good v Hartford Acci. & Indem. Co. (DC SC) 39 F Supp 475.

fraudulently. Acting with a deliberately-planned purpose and intent to deceive and thereby to gain an unlawful advantage. Bank of Montreal v Thayer (CC Iowa) 7 F 622, 625. A word insufficient in itself as an allegation of fraud, a sufficient allegation being nothing less than a statement of the fraudulent conduct. Garst v Hall & Lyon Co. 179 Mass 588, 61 NE 219.

fraudulent mortgage. A mortgage fraudulent as to the creditors of the mortgagor. 37 Am J2d Frd Conv § 58.

fraudulent practice. Literally, the practice of fraud— that is, fraudulent conduct. In reference to conduct proscribed by a Blue Sky Law, all acts which have a tendency to deceive or mislead the purchasing public, whether or not they originate in an actual evil design or contrivance to perpetrate fraud or do injury to the rights of another person. People v Federated Radio Corp. 244 NY 33, 154 NE 65.

fraudulent preference. Giving a creditor an undue advantage over other creditors in securing his agreement to a composition. 15 Am J2d Comp Cred § 8. The act of a debtor in preferring one of his creditors by making payment to him with intent thereby to hinder, delay, or defraud other creditors. 37 Am J2d Frd Conv §§ 87 et seq.
 A preferential transfer voidable under the Bankruptcy Act is not necessarily fraudulent. In the actual cases, however, a purpose to prefer, which is usually aimed at benefiting relatives or business associates, is important for consideration in determining whether there was also a purpose to defraud. Van Iderstine v National Discount Co. 227 US 575, 57 L Ed 652, 33 S Ct 343.

fraudulent representation. A representation proceeding from, or characterized by, fraud, and the purpose of which is to deceive. 37 Am J2d Fraud § 2. A representation that is knowingly untrue, or made without belief in its truth, or made recklessly, and, in any event, for the purpose of inducing action upon it. Clark v Haggard, 141 Conn 668, 109 A2d 358, 54 ALR2d 655.

fraudulent separation. The procuring of one's own separation from the armed forces by false representations or deliberate concealment as to his eligibility for separation. 10 USC § 883. The effecting by one person of the separation of another from the armed forces, knowing the latter to be ineligible for separation. 10 USC § 884.

fraudulent transfer. A transfer voidable in bankruptcy because made with actual intent to hinder, delay, or defraud existing or future creditors, or a transfer fraudulent in law, without reference to an actual fraudulent intent on the part of the bankrupt, because of the insolvency of the bankrupt at the time of the transfer and the absence of a fair consideration. 9 Am J2d Bankr § 1115.
 See **fraudulent conveyance.**

fraudulent use of process. A form of abuse of process; the use of legal process for a fraudulent purpose, as by attempting to enforce a judgment on a fictitious claim or the use of legal process as a mere cover for the creditors in obtaining property of the defendant in order to put it to their own use. 1 Am J2d Abuse P §§ 9-12.

fraudum legis. See **in fraudum legis.**

fraunche (frän-sh). Free. Same as **frank.**

fraunchise. Same as **franchise.**

fraunke. Free. Same as **frank.**

fraunke ferme. Same as **frank ferme.**

fraunk homo (fraunk hō'mō). A freeman.

fraus (frâs). Fraud.

fraus dans locum contractui (frâs danz lo'kum kontrak'shu-ī). Fraud inducing the making of the contract.

fraus est celare fraudem (frâs est se-lā're frâ'dem). It is fraud to conceal a fraud. Anno: 50 ALR 807.

fraus est odiosa, et non praesumenda (frâs est ō-di-ō'sa, et non prē-zu-men'da). Fraud is odious and will not be presumed.

fraus et dolus nemini patrocinari debent (frâs et do'- lus ne'mi-nī pat-rō-si-nā'rī dē'bent). Fraud and deceit ought not to excuse anyone.

fraus et jus nunquam cohabitant (frâs et jūs nun'- quam ko-ha'bi-tant). Fraud and justice never live together.

fraus latet in generalibus (frâs la'tet in je-ne-rā'li- bus). Fraud lurks or lies hidden in generalities.

fraus legis (frâs lē'jis). Fraud of the law; fraud upon the law.

fraus meretur fraudem (frâs me-rē'ter frâ'dem). Fraud merits or begets fraud.

fray (frā). An affray.

frectare (frek-tā're). To freight; to load.

frectum (frek'tum). Freight.

frednite. Immunity or exemption from fine or amercement.

fredum (fre'dum). A payment made to obtain a pardon where the offense was breach of peace. A sum paid to a magistrate for protection against vengeance.

free. Without restraint or coercion; not enslaved; not bound; exonerated. Thrown open, or made accessible to all; to be enjoyed without limitations; unrestricted; not obstructed, engrossed, or appropriated; open for use or enjoyment without charge. Flaherty v Fleming, 58 W Va 669, 52 SE 857. Not subject to customs duty. 21 Am J2d Cust D § 36.

free alms. See **frankalmoign; in libera eleemosyna.**

free alongside steamer. Free alongside ship; a term in commercial usage which binds a seller to delivery of the goods to the buyer at the dock. Iwai & Co. v Hercules Powder Co. 162 Ga 795, 802, 134 SE 763.

Free Baptists. A religious body of the Baptist persuasion generally, characterized in particular by adherence to the doctrine of conditional election and reprobation as opposed to absolute predestination. Park v Champlin, 96 Iowa 55, 64 NW 674.

free bed. An endowed bed in a hospital or sanitorium. Kapiolani Maternity & G. Hospital v Wodehouse (CA9 Hawaii) 70 F2d 793.

free bench (frē' bench). A widow's dower in copyhold lands, which she usually held subject to the condition that she should remain chaste and unmarried. See 2 Bl Comm 129.

free-borough men (frē'-bur"ō men). The inhabitants of a free burgh.

free burgh. A borough which had its charter rights from the crown.

free competition. A free and open market among

both buyers and sellers for sale and distribution of commodities. Maple Flooring Mfrs. Asso. v United States, 268 US 563, 69 L Ed 1093, 45 S Ct 578. The requisite of the bidding at a judicial sale. 30A Am J Rev ed Jud S § 98.

free course (kōrs). A vessel sailing with a favorable wind.

free delivery. A service rendered by some retail establishments.
See **rural free delivery.**

free delivery limits. The boundaries of the area within which a telegraph company will deliver messages without charge.

freedman. A person who has been freed from bondage, involuntary servitude or slavery. Slaughter House Cases (US) 16 Wall 36, 21 L Ed 395.

freedom. Liberty; absence of restraint.
See also **liberty** and phrases beginning **"liberty."**

freedom of contract. Same as **liberty of contract.**

freedom of movement. The right to travel—to go where and when one pleases—only so far restrained as the rights of others may make restraint necessary for the welfare of all other citizens. 16 Am J2d Const L § 359. The right of removal from one state to another. 16 Am J2d Const L § 478.

freedom of religion. A constitutional guaranty under the First Amendment, and the due process clause of the Fourteenth Amendment, to the Constitution of the United States and the provisions of some state constitutions, embracing the two concepts of freedom to believe and freedom to act, the first being absolute and beyond interference by legislation, the second being subject to regulation to prevent acts subversive of the civil government or otherwise criminal. Oney v Oklahoma City (CA10 Okla) 126 F2d 861; 16 Am J2d Const L §§ 336 et seq. One of the liberties included within and protected by the due process clause of the Fourteenth Amendment. Hamilton v Regents of the University of California, 293 US 245, 79 L Ed 343, 55 S Ct 197.

freedom of speech and of the press. A constitutional guaranty under the First Amendment, and the due process clause of the Fourteenth Amendment, to the Constitution of the United States and provisions in many state constitutions, embracing the concept that free discussion is essential to the growth, development, and well being of our free society under a democratic form of government and should be limited by regulation only to prevent abuse of the right. 16 Am J2d Const L §§ 341 et seq.
Liberty and freedom of speech under the Constitution do not mean the unrestrained right to do and say what one pleases at all times and under all circumstances, and certainly they do not mean that, contrary to the will of Congress, one may make of the post office establishment an agency for the publication of his views of the character and conduct of others, as distinguished from the carriage of the mails. Warren v United States (CA8 Kan) 183 F 718.

freedom of the press. See **freedom of speech and of the press.**

free election. An election at which the voter is left in the untrammeled exercise, whether by civil or military authority, of his right or privilege,—that is, where no impediment or restraint of any character is imposed upon him either directly or indirectly whereby he is hindered or prevented from participation at the polls. 25 Am J2d Elect § 7. An election where the voters are subject to no intimidation or improper influence, and where every voter is allowed to cast his ballot as his own judgment and conscience dictate. Blue v State, 206 Ind 98, 188 NE 583, 91 ALR 334.

free employment agency. A state employment agency. 31 Am J Rev ed Lab § 761.

free fee. See **feudum apertum.**

free feud. See **feudum francum.**

free fishery. The exclusive liberty of taking and killing fish in a public stream or river. By an express provision of Magna Charta no new franchise of this liberty could be granted by the crown. See 2 Bl Comm 417.

free flow of labor. The right of a prospective employer to be free from unlawful interference with the employment of workmen who wish to enter his employment, not a right to employ workmen who for any reason do not wish to enter such employment. Boylston Housing Corp. v O'Toole, 321 Mass 538, 74 NE2d 288, 172 ALR 1251.

freefold. Same as **faldage.**

free from average unless general. A limitation of liability in a marine insurance policy, having the same effect as the clause **free from particular average.** 29A Am J Rev ed Ins § 1585.

free from particular average. A clause in a marine insurance policy used in a limitation of liability, generally defeating liability of the insurer for a partial loss. 29A Am J Rev ed Ins § 1585.

free government. A government of the republican form, the powers of which are divided between departments, preferably, legislative, executive, and judicial, each of which is separate from the others, neither being subordinated to nor encroaching upon the functions of the others, and each operating as a check upon the activities of the others, thereby preventing the usurpation of absolute power by any one of the separate departments. Re Davies, 168 NY 89, 61 NE 118; State ex rel. Zillmer v Kreutzberg, 114 Wis 530, 90 NW 1098.

free handicap. A horse race as to which no liability for entrance fee or stake is incurred until acceptance of the weight allotted to the entry, either by direct acceptance or omission to declare the horse out of the race. Stone v Clay (CA7 Ill) 61 F 889.

freehold. Any estate of inheritance or for life, in either a corporeal or incorporeal hereditament, existing in, or arising from, real property of free tenure. 28 Am J2d Est § 8.
See **freehold estate not of inheritance; freehold estate of inheritance.**

freeholder. The owner of a freehold. One who owns lands, having an estate of inheritance or an estate for life, not merely a contingent or an expectant estate. State ex rel. Cain v Toomey, 27 SD 37, 129 NW 563. For the purpose of qualification as a voter in certain elections:—one having legal title to real estate or one in the possession and control of real estate as the apparent owner thereof. 25 Am J2d Elect § 80.
See **chosen freeholders; freehold; freeholder voter of such city; resident freeholder.**

freeholder voter of such city. As a qualification of the signer of a petition for a local option election: —a voter as well as a freeholder of the city, not including a voter of the city whose only land is located outside the city or a man who lives in the city but has no interest in real estate in the city other than the contingent or expectant interest of a husband in real estate owned by his wife. State ex rel. Cain v Toomey, 27 SD 37, 129 NW 563.

freehold estate. Same as **freehold**.

freehold estate not of inheritance (es-tāt' not of in-her'i-tans). A freehold estate for the life of the grantee or some other person. 28 Am J2d Est § 8.

freehold estate of inheritance. A freehold estate in fee simple absolute, fee simple conditional, fee simple determinable or defeasible, and estates in fee tail. 28 Am J2d Est § 8.

freehold in law (in lâ). A freehold to which a person is lawfully entitled, but upon which he has not entered.

freehold land societies. Societies formed for the assistance of workingmen in acquiring freeholds.

freehold tenure. Same as **free tenure**.

free justice. A constitutional guaranty against the sale of justice under the guise of exorbitant fees imposed on litigants or demands by judges for gratuities for giving or withholding decisions. 16 Am J2d Const L § 382.

free labor market. The right of one conducting a business or industry to have a free flow of labor for the purpose of carrying on the business or industry, such being not merely an abstract right, but one recognized as the basis of a cause of action where there is an unlawful interference therewith. L. D. Willcutt & Sons Co. v Driscoll, 200 Mass 110, 85 NE 897. A right to a market in which no compulsion is put upon the will of others; a right to a market in which transactions proceed according to the ordinary laws of trade, without interference other than may be occasioned by the bona fide exercise of rights by others. Anno: 6 ALR 913, 16 ALR 230, 27 ALR 652, 32 ALR 779, 116 ALR 485.

free legal advice. A ground for disciplinary proceedings against an attorney at law when offered in an advertisement. Re Cohen, 261 Mass 484, 159 NE 495, 55 ALR 1309.

free list. A list of articles on the importation of which no duties are charged, contained in the former § 1201 of Title 19 of the United States Code.

In the present tariff schedules, the dutiable list and the free list are combined in 19 USC § 1202 by specifying, in the "rates of duty" columns, either the particular duty payable or the word "free."

freeman. One born free; one who has been freed from the bonds of slavery. A person in possession in all the civil rights to which a person may be entitled. McCafferty v Guyer, 59 Pa 109, 116. In the feudal period, a freeholder, as distinguished from a villein.

freeman's roll (frē'mans rol). A list of those persons who are entitled to participate in the government of a village.

Freemasons. See **Masons**.

free negro. See **freedman; freeman; free woman of color**.

free of average. See **free from all average; free from average unless general**.

free of duty. The characterization of an article which may be imported without payment of customs duty. 21 Am J2d Cust D § 36.

free on board. A commercial term, familiar in sales contracts under the abbreviation "f.o.b." which, where no place is designated, binds the seller to deliver the goods upon car, truck, or vessel at the usual place of shipping goods of the kind sold, without expense to the buyer for such delivery, but leaving to the buyer the responsibility for the payment of charges for the transportation from such point of delivery; and which means, where it appears as "f.o.b." point of destination, that the charges for delivery and transportation to the point of destination are to be paid by the seller. 46 Am J1st Sales § 188.

No agreement by the consignee of goods to pay the freight charges thereon will be implied from his acceptance of the goods from the carrier, where the goods have been purchased by the consignee under an agreement providing for their delivery "free on board" at the place of destination. 13 Am J2d Car § 475.

free on board acceptance final. A regulation adopted under the authority of the Secretary of Agriculture, whereunder a buyer accepting produce f.o.b. cars at shipping point is without recourse against a seller because of change in condition of the produce while in transit. Anno: 21 ALR2d 845.

free on board cars. A sale upon the terms that the subject of the sale is to be placed on the cars for shipment without any expense or act on the part of the buyer, and that as soon as so placed the title is to pass absolutely to the buyer, and the property be wholly at his risk, in the absence of any circumstances indicating a retention of such control by the seller as security for purchase money, by preserving the right of stoppage in transitu. Geogehan Sons & Co. v Arbuckle Bros. 139 Va 92, 123 SE 387, 36 ALR 399.

Sometimes construed as meaning merely that the seller is required to load the property for shipment without expense to the purchaser, not involving the matter of time of passing of title. Sadler Machinery Co. v Ohio Nat. Inc. (CA6 Ohio) 202 F2d 887, 38 ALR2d 649.

free pass. See **pass**.

free passage. The passage of vehicles in the ordinary course of traffic on the improved portion of the highway; a sufficient width of the improved portion of the highway left unobstructed to permit the passage of vehicles in separate adjacent lanes of traffic. Pugh v Akron-Chicago Transp. Co. 64 Ohio App 479, 18 Ohio Ops 211, 32 Ohio L Abs 159, 28 NE2d 1015, aff'd 137 Ohio St 164, 17 Ohio Ops 511, 28 NE2d 501.

free right of way. A right of way unobstructed by any act of the servient owner. Flaherty v Fleming, 58 W Va 669, 52 SE 857.

free services. See **gratuitous services**.

free ships. Ships of nations which are neutral during a war.

free socage (frē sok'āj). Tenure of land by services which were certain, free and honorable. See 2 Bl Comm 62.

free socmen (frē sok'men). Tenants in free socage. See 2 Bl Comm 79.

freestone. A mineral. 36 Am J1st Min & M § 35. A stone fit for the facade or any exterior wall of a

FREE [501] FREIGHT

building because it is easily shaped or cut without splitting.

free tenure (frē ten'ūr). Freehold tenure; tenure by free services; that is, by services which were becoming a freeman or a soldier. See 2 Bl Comm 62, 89, 90.

free textbooks. A means of aid to poor persons. 41 Am J1st Poor L § 32. A service in education in the public schools and high schools in many states, being applied without reference to financial circumstances of the parents of the recipients. 47 Am J1st Sch § 204.

free time. Hours or days not counted in determining liability for demurrage. 13 Am J2d Car § 482.

free transportation. The transportation of pupils to and from school at public expense. 47 Am J1st Sch § 160. Discrimination by a common carrier. 13 Am J2d Car § 204.
See **pass.**

free warren. The liberty, franchise or royalty, derived from the crown, of taking or killing all inferior species of game, called beasts and fowls of warren. See 2 Bl Comm 417.

freeway. A public highway, particularly, a superior or divided highway for fast movement of traffic, for the use of which there is no toll.

freewheeling. Coasting in an automobile, unimpeded by the motor. Anno: 78 ALR2d 231, § 6. A slang term for unrestrained action.

free white. See **white person.**

Free Will Baptists. See **Free Baptists.**

free woman of color. A female of African descent freed from slavery. Hearn v Bridault, 37 Miss 209.

freeze. An Act of God where unprecedented as to time or violence. 1 Am J2d Act of God § 5.

freezer. A device for freezing anything. A place for the preservation of meat or poultry where the temperature is kept below the freezing point,—from zero up to thirty-two degrees. Allen v Somers, 73 Conn 355, 47 A 653.

freezing. Subjecting something to freezing temperature, causing it to harden or solidify. Preserving the status quo—for example, prohibiting withdrawals from, or additions to, a fund in litigation.

fregit. See **clausum fregit.**

freight. A freight train. The load or cargo carried by a carrier by land or water. The charge or hire for a carrier's services in the transportation and delivery of property, 48 Am J1st Ship § 424; it is in such sense that the term appears in a marine insurance policy on "freight." 29A Am J Rev ed Ins § 1308.
See **dead freight; lien for freight; local freight.**

freight agent. An agent of a carrier authorized to receive freight and make contracts for transportation thereof at least over the line of the carrier and, under certain circumstances, over connecting lines in order to accomplish through transportation. 14 Am J2d Car § 690.

freight booking. The making, in advance, of specific arrangements for the transportation of goods by a particular vessel. Ocean S.S. Co. v Savannah Locomotive Works. 131 Ga 831, 837, 63 SE 577.

freight car. A railroad car for the transporation of goods, merchandise, and other property, not of passengers.

freight charges. The charges made by a carrier for the transportation of property. 13 Am J2d Car §§ 461 et seq.

freight collected from consignee. A stipulation in a contract of sale of personalty or a bill of lading, indicating that the charges for transportation are to be collected from the consignee. 13 Am J2d Car § 477.

freight depot. A place provided by a carrier for the receiving and delivery of freight.

freight elevator. A classification sometimes made on the basis of the regular and primary use of the instrumentality in carrying goods, merchandise, and other property, irrespective of its form or size; at other times made according to the construction of the instrumentality. 26 Am J2d Elev § 2.

freighter. A ship used for carrying cargo primarily; also the owner of the vessel hired under a contract of affreightment. The latter definition derives from the French and is not accepted in common-law jurisdictions without some disagreement. At times, the person to whom the vessel is let is called the "freighter."

freight forwarder. See **forwarder.**

Freight Forwarder Act. See **Forwarder Act.**

freight lien. See **carrier's lien.**

freight line company. A company furnishing or leasing cars to railroads for freight transportation. Cudahy Packing Co. v Minnesota, 246 US 450, 452, 62 L Ed 827, 829, 38 S Ct 373.

freight prepaid. A term familiar in sales contracts, imposing upon the seller the obligation of payment of freight charges. A term, which, when marked or stamped on a bill of lading, does not necessarily, but may, under the circumstances of a particular case, estop the carrier to deny the prepayment of freight charges. 13 Am J2d Car § 479.

freight pro rata (frāt prō rā'ta). Or **freight pro rata itineris peracti,**—freight for the completed portion of the voyage; freight in the proportion that the part of the voyage performed bears to the entire length of it, the right to which is exclusively a matter of contract, express or implied. 48 Am J1st Ship § 432.

freight pro rata itineris (frāt prō rā'ta i-ti'ne-ris). Freight charges proportioned to the voyage.
See **freight pro rata.**

freight pro rata itineris peracti (frāt prō rā'ta i-ti'ne-ris per-ak'tī). See **freight pro rata.**

freight rate. The rate according to which a carrier is compensated for the transportation of goods, merchandise, and other property. 13 Am J2d Car §§ 105 et seq. Not necessarily the rate for transportation by railroad, the term being applicable as well to the rate for transportation by truck. Lyman-Richey Sand & Gravel Co. v State, 123 Neb 674, 243 NW 891, 83 ALR 1301.
See **class rate.**

freight shipment. See **shipment by freight.**

freight train. A railroad train which carries freight alone, and which has a caboose attached to it for the use of the train crew. Arizona Eastern Railroad Co. v State, 29 Ariz 446, 242 P 870. A railroad train provided by a carrier primarily for the carriage of freight, but used incidentally for the carriage of passengers. 14 Am J2d Car § 860.

French. The people of France. The language of France.
See **Law French.**

French pool. The pari-mutuel system in betting, particularly on horse races.
See **pari-mutuel.**

French Spoliation Claims. Claims of two classes:— (1) claims of American citizens arising out of depredations by French naval forces against American ships between 1793 and 1798, used by the United States government as an offset against claims of France against the United States in effecting a treaty with France, thereby becoming claims against the United States, some of which remain unpaid to this day, particularly claims held by insurance companies under the right of subrogation; (2) claims growing out of French seizure and confiscation of American ships and cargoes under a series of decrees issued by Napoleon, finally settled for about sixty cents on the dollar of the total award of damages made by a special commission.

frendlesman. Same as **friendlesman.**

frendwit (frend'wit). A fine imposed upon a person for the offense of harboring a friend who had been outlawed.

freneticus (frẹ-net'i-kus). A madman; a lunatic.

frentike. Same as **freneticus.**

frenzy. A state of delirium of short duration, approaching madness or insanity. Lowe v State, 118 Wis 641, 96 NW 417.
See **blood-frenzy.**

freoborgh. Same as **frank pledge.**

frequency. The number of times something occurs within a stated period. A term pertaining particularly to electricity, signifying the number of cycles per second of an alternating electric current.

frequency modulation. Abbreviated FM; reproduction of sound over the radio in which exactness is maintained by changing the frequency of the wave in accord with the sound intended to be transmitted.

frequent. Adjective: Occurring at short intervals. Verb: To visit or resort to a place often.
To frequent a gaming house is to make a habit of going there. A person may be guilty of frequenting a gaming house for the purpose of gaming without actually engaging in any game. Green v State, 109 Ind 175, 176.

frequenter. One who comes to a place often. A person, other than an employee, in a place of employment who, by reason of the circumstances, particularly the acquiesence of the employer in many past visits by such person, is not to be regarded as a trespasser. Sullivan v School Dist. 179 Wis 502, 191 NW 1020, 22 NCCA 863 (statutory definition).

Frequentia actus multum operatur (fre-quen'she-a ak'tus mul'tum o-pe-rā'ter). The frequency of an act effects much.

fresh (fresh). New; recent; recently produced; uncured; not salty.

fresh disseisin. Recent disseisin, such disseisin as the person disseised might resist with force.

freshet. The sudden overflow of a stream from a heavy rain or an accumulation of water from melting snow or other source.

freshet waters. See **enemy waters; storm waters.**

fresh fine (fresh fīn). A fine of land which had been levied within the year next preceding.

fresh force. Recent force, that is force used to effect a disseisin within the next preceding forty days.
See **assize of fresh force.**

fresh pursuit. The pursuit of a person for the purpose of arresting him, which has been continued without substantial interruption from the time of the issuance of the warrant for his arrest or from the time of the commission of the offense, or the discovery of the offense, where the arrest is to be made without a warrant. An "immediate pursuit" in a reasonable sense of the term. People v Pool, 27 Cal 573. A pursuit maintained purposefully, albeit with some interruptions, such as a delay for the purpose of seeking assistance. 5 Am J2d Arr § 33. A pursuit of a thief immediately after the theft to apprehend him and recover the property. 1 Bl Comm 297.

fresh suit. An Old English term for **fresh pursuit.**

fresh water. See **inland waters.**

fresh-water river. A river which has banks, not shores such as are characteristic of a tidal river. State v Faudre, 54 W Va 122, 46 SE 269.

fret (fret). Verb: To worry; to be irritated. Noun: An irritation. (French.) Freight.

freter (frutay). (French.) To freight.

freteur (fruturr). (French.) See **freighter.**

frettum (fret'tum). Freight. The charge for carrying a shipment.

fretum (frē'tum). An arm of the sea; a strait.

friars (frī'ạrs). The members of certain religious orders who lived in monasteries.

friborg. Same as **frank pledge.**

friction-hoist elevator. An elevator in which the lifting power is transmitted by friction gears instead of the conventional gears with teeth.

fridborg (frĭd'bŏrg). Same as **frank pledge.**

friend. An acquaintance for whom one has at least some degree of fondness. An alien enemy residing in this country but not adhering to the enemy. 3 Am J2d Aliens § 173. Insufficient as a designation of beneficiary of a trust. 54 Am J1st Trusts § 140.
See **next friend.**

friendlesman (frend'les-mạn). One who could not, by law, have a friend; an outlaw. Drew v Drew, 37 Me 389, 381.

friendly fire. A fire lighted and contained in a usual place for fire, such as furnace, stove, incinerator, and the like, and used for the purposes of heating, cooking, manufacturing, or other common and usual every day purposes. Youse v Employers Fire Ins. Co. 172 Kan 111, 238 P2d 473.

friendly receivership. A receivership constituted where contending parties have agreed to the appointment of a receiver of certain property for a certain purpose in a bona fide case by a court with jurisdiction. 45 Am J1st Rec § 3. A receivership which is obtained indirectly by the debtor himself or with his connivance, wherein through his attorney or otherwise he contrives to cause his creditor to institute proceedings for the appointment of the receiver. Harkin v Brundage, 276 US 36, 72 L Ed 457, 48 S Ct 268.

friendly society (frend'li sọ-sī'e-ti). A mutual aid or benefit society.

friendly suit. Same as **amicable action.**

friend of the court. Same as **amicus curiae.**

fright. Sudden fear; apprehension of immediate injury to the person. 6 Am J2d Asslt & B § 4.
 The fright of one who is robbed must be under the law an objective fright, as contradistinguished from subjective fright; it must have been due to some act on the part of the accused, and not arise from the mere temperamental timidity of the person whose property happens to be stolen from his person or presence. State v Parker, 262 Mo 169, 170 SW 1121.
 See **fear.**

frigidity. Want of normal sexual desires, but not equivalent to impotency. S. v S. 211 Ga 365, 86 SE2d 103.

frilingi (fri-lin'jī). Freemen.

fringe benefits. Benefits received by any employee in addition to wages or salary, such as group insurance, pension rights, etc.

friscus (fris'kus). Fresh; recent; new; not salty.

friscus fortia (fris'kus for'she-a). Same as **fresh force.**

frisk. To filch; to steal; to search a person, particularly by running the hands over his clothing. Mason v Wrightson, 205 Md 481, 109 A2d 128.

frithbote (frith'bōt). A fine imposed for a breach of the peace.

frithbreach (frith'brēch). A breach of the peace.

frithman (frith'man). A member of a company or fraternity.

frithsocne. Same as **frithsoken.**

frithsoken (frith'sō"ken). Power to preserve the peace.

frithsplot (frith'splot). Sacred ground, where fugitives from justice might safely hide; a sanctuary; an asylum.

frivolous. So clearly and palpably bad and insufficient as to require no argument or illustration to show the character as indicative of bad faith upon a bare inspection; as a pleading, argument, motion, or objection. Strong v Sproul, 53 NY 497, 499.

frivolous answer. An answer which does not, in any view of the facts pleaded, present a defense to the action; an answer which forms or tenders no material issue; a false answer; a sham answer. 41 Am J1st Pl § 50.

frivolous appeal. An appeal where the exceptions are so obviously frivolous on their face as to require no argument. Dachrach v Manhattan R. Co. 154 NY 178, 47 NE 1087.

frivolous claim. A claim asserted where there is no bona fide dispute between the parties. Excercycle Corp. v Maratta, 9 NY2d 329, 214 NYS2d 353, 174 NE2d 463.

frivolous demurrer. A demurrer which is so clearly untenable, the insufficiency of which is so manifest upon a bare inspection of the pleadings, that the court or judge is able to determine its character without argument or research. Farmers & Millers' Bank v Sawyer, 7 Wis 379, 383.

frivolous plea. A plea which does not in any view of the facts pleaded present a defense to the action; a plea which tenders no material issue; a false or sham plea. 41 Am J1st Pl § 50.

frivolous pleading. A pleading good in form but false in fact and not pleaded in good faith. 41 Am J1st Pl § 50. A pleading palpably and manifestly false on its face. Commonwealth ex rel. Meredith v Murphy, 295 Ky 466, 174 SW2d 681.
 See **frivolous answer.**

frivolous question. A question presented to the court which is devoid of substance or so clearly determined by previous decisions as to foreclose the subject. California Water Service Co. v Redding, 304 US 252, 82 L Ed 1323, 58 S Ct 865.

frivolous suit. A suit without purpose to determine an actual controversy, as where the parties control by interest both sides of the litigation. 1 Am J2d Actions § 56.

frl. An abbreviation of fractional, often used in descriptions of real estate.

frodmortel. An exemption or immunity from punishment for manslaughter.

frog. In common parlance, a small four-legged creature developing from a tadpole and living in water or on land, characterized by ability to leap. In the parlance of a railroad man, a section of a rail, or of several rails combined, at a point where two railways cross or at the point of a switch from a line to a siding or to another line, its function being to enable a car or train to be turned from one track to another track. 35 Am J1st M & S § 221.
 See **blocked frog; unblocked frog.**

frolic of his own. The activity of an agent or an employee who has departed from the scope of the agency or the employment and is not while thus engaged a representative of his principal or employer or one whose acts are binding upon, or productive of liability of, the principal or employer.

from. As the word appears in a statement of the voyage covered by a marine insurance policy, e.g. "from" New York to Port au Prince:—the risk attaches at the time of weighing anchor and breaking ground for the voyage, but is not exclusive of intermediate ports stated in the policy. Bradley v Nashville Ins. Co. 3 La Ann 708. As the word appears in the designation of a boundary of real estate, e.g. "from" the [a designated monument or object]:—the designation is exclusive of the monument or object specified, except as the entire context requires its inclusion. Bonney v Morrill, 52 Me 252.
 A word productive of some confusion in determining whether it denotes inclusion or exclusion of the day from which a reckoning is to be made, the courts, however, ordinarily proceeding on the theory that the word is not per se a word either of inclusion or exclusion, but is to be construed as one or the other according to the tenor of the instrument or the intent of the parties and the equities of the particular case. 52 Am J1st Times § 23.
 When the words "from" a day named, are used in connection with the creation of an estate or interest, and it is not contrary to the express intention of the parties, the date named from which the estate or interest is to exist is to be included, and the estate vests on that day. Budds v Frey, 104 Minn 481, 117 NW 158.

from and after. A term ordinarily signifying the exclusion of the day from which the reckoning is to be made, but not so considered where such construction will defeat the purpose of the contract or statute in which the term appears. 52 Am J1st Time § 27. An expression of futurity but, as it appears in a testamentary gift of a remainder, following a

life estate, it does not make the remainder contingent, in the absence of anything else on the face of the will to show that vesting was postponed or intended to be postponed beyond the death of the testator. 33 Am J1st Life Est § 111.

from and after passage. A provision in a statute specifying the effective date, sometimes interpreted as meaning that the statute takes effect on the day of its passage, but in other cases interpreted as rendering the statute effective the day following passage. 50 Am J1st Stat § 506.

from the making. A common term in a provision of the statute of frauds respecting agreements not to be performed within one year "from the making" thereof; the words excluding the day on which the agreement was made. Nickerson v Harvard College, 298 Mass 484, 11 NE2d 444, 114 ALR 414.

from the person. See **taking from the person.**

from time to time. At intervals. First Nat. Bank v Stover, 21 NM 453, 155 P 905.

from whatever cause arising. An expression in a bill of lading or other contract of carriage in reference to relief of the carrier from liability for damage to the shipment. 14 Am J2d Car § 566.

front. Noun: That which faces forward. Appearance. A union which has complied with the National Labor Relations Act acting on behalf of a union which has not complied with such statute. 31 Am J Rev ed Lab § 222. Verb: To stand opposite something. A store operating in a basement which extends under the sidewalk and out to the curb of a street, from which an entrance was made to the store, "fronts" on that street within the meaning of a provision in a lease giving the lessee the exclusive right to sell cigars and tobacco in that part of the building "fronting" on such street. Anno: 90 ALR 1461.

The narrow end of a lot "fronts" on the street upon which it abuts; it does not front on another street although it is a corner lot which abuts on both streets. The end of an unimproved lot fronts on the street upon which it abuts, toward which the house, when constructed, is intended to face according to the plan or usage in the particular block or district. Rhinehart v Leitch, 107 Conn 400, 140 A 763. But some authority holds that a corner lot "fronts" on both streets. Des Moines v Dorr, 31 Iowa 89, 93.

frontage. The measure in feet or other linear unit of measurement of the boundary between a street or highway and an abutting property. The measure of the line between a river or other body of water and land abutting thereon. The buildings fronting upon a street, whether business or residential. 7 Am J2d Auto § 191.

In determining "frontage" occupied by business buildings, for the purpose of applicability of a speed limit prescribed by statute for business districts, an intersecting street or highway is not included. Hinson v Dawson, 241 NC 714, 86 SE2d 585, 50 ALR2d 333.

frontage cost. The entire cost of a local improvement in front of the property assessed. 48 Am J1st, Spec A § 66.

front door of the courthouse. A good and sufficient designation of the place where a judicial sale of real estate shall be made at auction.

front foot plan. A plan or method of levying local assessments for street work upon the property abutting on the portion of the street to be improved, in proportion to the length of the frontage of each lot along the improvement. Crummey v Popp, 79 Cal App 230, 249 P 29.

fronting. See **front.**

fronting and abutting property. A term, frequently used in statutes providing for street improvement by special assessment, for property between which and the improvement there is no intervening land. Wilburton v McConnell, 119 Okla 242, 249 P 708.

front tooth. A part or member of the body within the meaning of the offense of mayhem. High v State, 26 Tex App 545.

Whether a corner tooth is a front tooth is a question of fact for the jury. High v State, 26 Tex App 545.

frost damage. Injury by freezing.

frozen navigable river. A public highway, a way on which a traveler has the paramount right of passage. 56 Am J1st Wat § 208.

fructuarius (fruk-tu-ā′ri-us). A person entitled to the fruits and profits of property; a lessee.

fructus (fruk′tus). Fruit; fruits; increase; usufruct.

Fructus augent haereditatem (fruk′tus â-jent hē-rĕ-di-ta′tem). The fruits go to increase the inheritance.

fructus civiles (fruk′tus si′vi-lēz). Civil fruits; revenues; recompenses; compensations.

fructus industriae. Same as **fructus industriales.**

fructus industriales (fruk′tus in-dus-tri-ā′lez). Crops that must be planted or sown each year and which require the attention of man to produce them. 21 Am J2d Crops § 2.

See **emblements.**

fructus legis (fruk′tus lē′jis). The fruit or product of the law,—execution.

fructus naturales (fruk′tus na-tu-rā′lez). Crops produced by the powers of nature alone. 21 Am J2d Crops § 2. The fruits and produce of perennial trees, bushes, and grasses.

fructus pecudum (fruk′tus pe′ku-dum). The produce of the flocks; such as the wool and milk of sheep and goats.

fructus pendentes (fruk′tus pen-den′tēz). Hanging fruits; unplucked fruits.

Fructus pendentes pars fundi videntur (fruk′tus pen-den′tēz parz fun′dī vi-den′ter). Unplucked fruits are regarded as part of the soil.

Fructus perceptos villae non esse constat (fruk′tus per-sep′tos vil′le non es′se kon′stat). Gathered fruits are not a part of the farm.

fructus rei alienae (fruk′tus rē′ī ā-li-ē′nē). The fruit or product of the property of another.

fructus separati (fruk′tus se-pa-rā′tī). Severed fruit; plucked fruit.

fruges (fru′jēz). Fruits; produce.

fruit. The seed of plants, or that part of plants which contains the seed, and especially the juicy, pulpy products of certain plants, covering and containing the seed. Nix v Hedden, 149 US 304, 37 L Ed 745, 13 S Ct 881.

See **first-fruits; natural fruits.**

fruitless. Unproductive; unavailing.

As applied to a congressional investigation, the word means that it could result in no valid legislation on the subject to which the inquiry refers. Sinclair v United States, 279 US 263, 73 L Ed 692, 49 S Ct 257.

fruits of crime. Loot; booty; anything acquired in or by the commission of a criminal offense.

fruits of property. Gains and profits from property.

Frumenta quae sata sunt solo cedere intelliguntur (fru-men'ta kwē sā'ta sunt sō'lō sē'de-re in-tel-li-gun'ter). Grain which has been sowed is understood to go with the soil.

frumentum (frö-men'tum). (Civil law.) Grain; anything which grows on an ear.

frumgild (frum'gild). The initial recompense paid to the relatives of a person who has been murdered.

frusca terra (frus'ka ter'ra). Barren, waste, or desert land; uncultivated land.

frussura (frus-sū'ra). A breaking up or ploughing.

frustra (frus'tra). In vain; vainly; unsuccessfully; to no purpose.

Frustra agit qui judicium prosequi nequit cum effectu (frus'tra ā'jit quī jū-di'she-um pro'se-quī ne'quit kum ef-fek'tū). He sues vainly who is unable to prosecute his judgment with effect.

Frustra est potentia quae nunquam venit in actum (frus'tra est pō-ten'she-a kwē nun'quam vē'nit in ak'tum). A power or authority is a vain one if it is never exercised.

Frustra expectatur eventus cujus effectus nullus sequitur (frus'tra ex-pek-tā'ter ē-ven'tus kū'jus ef-fek'tus nul'lus se'qui-ter). It is vain to look forward to an event which is not to be followed by any result.

Frustra feruntur leges nisi subditis et obedientibus (frus'tra fe-run'ter lē'jēz nī'sī sub-di'tis et ō-be-di-en'ti-bus). Laws are made to no purpose unless for those who are subject and obedient.

Frustra fit per plura, quod fieri potest per pauciora (frus'tra fit per plū'ra, quod fī'e-rī po'test per pâ-si-ō'ra). That is done or executed vainly through many means or agencies, if it could be done through few.

Frustra legis auxilium quaerit qui in legem committit (frus'tra lē'jis âk-zi'li-um kwē'rit quī in lē'jem kom-mit'tit). A person who has transgressed the law vainly seeks the law's aid.

Frustra petis, quod mox es restiturus (frus'tra pe'tis, quod mox es re-sti-tū'rus). You vainly seek to get what you must immediately restore. Jarvis v Rogers, 15 Mass (15 Tyng) 389, 407.

Frustra petis quod statim alteri reddere cogeris (frus'tra pe'tis quod sta'tim al'te-rī red'de-re ko-jē'ris). You vainly seek that which you will be compelled to restore to another immediately.

Frustra probatur quod probatum non relevat (frus'tra pro-bā'ter quod prō-bā'tum non re'le-vat). It is idle to prove that which when proved is irrelevant. Farnum v Farnum, 79 Mass (13 Gray) 508, 511.

frustrated expectations. Developments or absence of developments contrary to expectations; not the equivalent of failure of consideration. 11 Am J2d B & N § 245.

frustrum terrae (frus'trum ter'rē). A piece or parcel of land lying segregated from other land.

frustration. The prevention of accomplishment of purpose.

See **commercial frustration; frustrated expectations.**

frustration of ancestral or testamentary intention. The violation by heir, devisee, or legatee of a promise to the testator to hold an inheritance, device, or legacy, for another or to give it to another, upon which the testator relied in the making or changing of his will in order to favor such other person. 54 Am J1st Trusts § 242.

frustration of contract. See **commercial frustration.**

frustration of conversion. See **reconversion.**

frutex (frö'teks). Singular of **frutices.**

frutices (fru'ti-sēz). Bushes; shrubs.

frutos (froo'tos). (Spanish.) Fruits; profits; products.

frythe. Clear land between woods; a strait; an arm of the sea.

FSLIC. Abbreviation for Federal Savings and Loan Insurance Corporation.

ft. An abbreviation of "feet" or "foot."

FTC. Abbreviation of Federal Trade Commission.

ft-lb. Abbreviation of foot pound.

fuage (few'āj). An old tax of England. A duty or tax paid by custom to the king for every chimney in the house; hearth-money, a tax upon every hearth or fireplace.

fuel oil. Oil used for fuel in industrial plants, also in dwelling houses.

fuer (foo-ayr'). To fly; to flee; flight.

fuer en fait (fua an fā). Flight in fact; actual flight; the physical act of fleeing.

fuer en ley (fua in lā). Flight in law, a failure to appear in court when summoned.

fuero (fwā'rō). (Spanish.) A use and custom combined, having the force of law. See Strother v Lucas (US) 9 Pet 410, 446, 9 L Ed 1137, 1151.

fuero de Castilla (fwā'rō day cas-teel'yah). The ancient law of the Castillians.

fuero de correos y caminas (fwā'rō da kor-ray'os y kah-mee'nas). A Spanish tribunal which had jurisdiction over post offices and roads.

fuero de guerra (fwā'rō day gayr'rah). A Spanish tribunal which had jurisdiction over military matters.

fuero de marina (fwā'rō day mah-ree'nah). A Spanish tribunal which had jurisdiction over naval affairs.

fuero juzgo (fwā'rō hooth'go). The ancient Visigothic law of Spain.

fuero municipal (fwā'rō moo-ne-the-pahl'). The charter of a Spanish town or city.

fuga catallorum (fö'gä ka-tal-lō'rum). A drove of cattle.

fugacia (fö-gä'she-a). A chase; a hunt.

fugam fecit (fū'gam fē'sit). He has fled.

fugatio (fö-gä'she-ō). A privilege of hunting.

fugator (fö-gä'tor). A driver.

fugatores carucarum (fö-gä-tō'rēz ka-ru-kā'rum). Wagon drivers.

fugie (fū'ji). A fugitive.

fugie-warrant (fū'ji-wor'ant). A warrant for the arrest of a debtor who has fled.

fugitate (fū'ji-tāt). To outlaw a person accused of crime.

fugitation (fū-ji-tā'shọn). Outlawry; the flight of a criminal from justice.

fugitive. A person fleeing from danger or from justice. People ex rel. Merklen v Enright, 217 App Div 514, 517, 217 NYS 288.
See **fugitive from justice.**

fugitive from justice. A person who commits a crime and then withdraws himself from the jurisdiction, whether or not such jurisdiction is his home state. 31 Am J2d Extrad § 15. A person who, having committed a crime, is absent from the state when he is sought to answer therefor and is found within the jurisdiction of another state. 31 Am J2d Extrad § 15. One who, with knowledge that he is being sought pursuant to court process, absents himself or flees, even though he believes himself innocent. Tobin v Casaus, 128 Cal App 2d 588, 275 P2d 792, 49 ALR2d 1419. Under federal law:— a person who, having committed a crime in violation of the laws of the United States, flees from the jurisdiction of the court where the crime was committed, or departs from his usual place of abode and conceals himself within the district. United States v Farrell (CA8 Minn) 87 F2d 957. See, also, Greene v United States (CA5 Ga) 154 F 401.

fugitive oil and gas. A redundant expression, since oil and gas in their natural state in the earth are always fugitive in nature, possessing no fixed situs in any particular portion of the area where they may be, having the power, as it were, of self-transmission. 24 Am J1st Gas & O § 2. Oil and gas drained from premises by operations on adjoining property. 24 Am J1st Gas & O § 43.
See **hot oil.**

fugitive slave. (slāv). A slave who had fled from his master.

Fugitive Slave Acts. The Act of Congress of February 12, 1793, and that of September 18, 1850, recognizing the existence of slavery, the object and purposes of the acts being to authorize and enable the owners to recover their fugitive slaves who should escape from their service and flee into a state where slavery did not exist. McElvain v Mudd, 44 Ala 48.

fugitive witness. A person wanted as a witness who has left the jurisdiction in order to avoid service of a subpoena upon him. A person wanted as a witness who is a fugitive from justice. 17 Am J2d Contin § 31.

fugitivus (fū-ji-tī'vus). A fugitive; a fugitive from justice.

fuit coactus (fū'it ko-ak'tus). He was compelled.

full. Ample; complete; perfect; not wanting in any essential quality. Mobile School Com. v Putnam, 44 Ala 506, 537.

full actual loss. The entire loss, which, in the case of goods damaged in transit, is ordinarily established by the difference between the fair market value of the goods undamaged and their fair market value as delivered in damaged condition. Meltzer v Baltimore & Ohio R. Co. (DC Pa) 38 F Supp 391.

full admiral. An admiral, as distinguished from a vice admiral or rear admiral.
See **admiral.**

full age. The status of a person who has reached the age of majority, usually, as at common law, the completion of the twenty-first year, but in some jurisdictions, in respect of females, the end of the eighteenth year. 27 Am J1st Inf § 5. The status of a person who has become an adult in the eyes of the law by a proceeding removing the disability of infancy or, as provided by statute in some jurisdictions, by marriage. 27 Am J1st Inf § 5.

full and fair statement of all the facts. As an element of a defense to an action for malicious prosecution: —all the facts within the knowledge of the person making the statement, not all facts discoverable. 34 Am J1st Mal Pros § 7.

full and satisfactory evidence. A refinement of the law which imposes a requirement in reference to the degree of proof in a civil case beyond that of a preponderance of the evidence. 30 Am J2d Evi §§ 1167.

A statute which provides that a divorce may be granted only upon "full and satisfactory evidence" does not mean that plaintiff's testimony must be corroborated in all cases. Anno: 15 ALR2d 186, § 5.

full and true value. A value determined by reference to all relevant facts in evidence; not a fictional value in cases where there is no standardized market for the subject of valuation. State v Wagner, 233 Minn 241, 46 NW2d 676, 23 ALR2d 762. The amount the owner would be entitled to receive as just compensation upon a taking of the property by a state or the United States in the exertion of the power of eminent domain. Great Northern R. Co. v Weeks, 297 US 135, 80 L Ed 532, 56 S Ct 426.

So far as respects the rule by which the duties on imported goods are to be ascertained, the true value shall be deemed to be the actual cost of the goods to the importer at the place from which they were imported, and not the current market value of the goods at that place. United States v Tappan (US) 11 Wheat 419, 424, 6 L Ed 509, 510.

full answer. An answer to a bill in equity which is full and complete; that is an answer which is ample and sufficient. See Bentley v Cleaveland, 22 Ala 814, 817.

full bench. The court with all the qualified judges sitting in a case, particularly an appellate court.
See **in bank.**

full blood. The relationship between children of the same father and mother.

full cash value. As the criterion for the assessment of property for taxation:— the amount at which the property would be appraised if taken in payment of a just debt due from a solvent debtor. State v Virginia & Truckee Railroad Co. 23 Nev 283, 46 P 723 (statutory definition.)

full court. Same as **full bench.**

full cousin. A first cousin. Anno: 54 ALR2d 1011.

full crew law. A statute requiring crews of a certain minimum in number of employees on a railroad locomotive or train. 44 Am J1st RR § 405.

full faith and credit. The measure of the recognition required by Article IV, section 1, of the Constitution of the United States to be accorded by a court to the public acts, records, and judicial proceedings of a state other than that in which the court is sitting. 16 Am J2d Const L § 585. The requirement that the public acts of every state shall be given the same effect by the courts of another state that they have by law and usage at home. Chicago & Alton Railroad Co. v Wiggins Ferry Co. 119 US 615, 30 L Ed 519, 7 S Ct 398. A provision of the United States Constitution, one essential purpose of which is that litigation once pursued to judgment shall be

FULL [507] FUNCTIONAL

as conclusive of the rights of the parties in every other court as in that in which the judgment was rendered, so that a cause of action merged in a judgment in one state is likewise merged in every other. Magnolia Petroleum Co. v Hunt, 320 US 430, 321 US 801, 88 L Ed 149, 64 S Ct 208, 150 ALR 413.

full hearing. A hearing in which ample oportunity is afforded to all parties to make, by evidence and argument, a showing fairly adequate to establish the propriety or impropriety, from the standpoint of justice and law, of the steps asked to be taken. 2 Am J2d Admin L § 415.

The right to a full hearing in a quasi-judicial proceeding conducted by an administrative agency embraces not only the right to present evidence, but also a reasonable opportunity to know the claims of the opposing party and to meet them. The full hearing upon which the Packers and Stockyards Act conditions the power of the Secretary of Agriculture to fix maximum rates to be charged by market agencies at stockyards requires that the agencies under investigation be fairly advised of what the government proposes and be heard upon its proposals before it issues its final command, even where the proceeding is not of an adversary character but is initiated as a general inquiry. Morgan v United States, 304 US 1, 82 L Ed 1129, 58 S Ct 773, 999.

full income. As the term appears in a bequest of the income from designated securities purchased at a premium:—the annual interest paid in on the securities, without deducting therefrom a progressively increasing sum in each year to meet the wearing away of the premiums as the times of the maturity of the securities approach. McLouth v Hunt, 154 NY 179, 48 NE 548.

full indorsement. An indorsement of a bill or note which is not a mere signature; an indorsement with words added, such words varying from those of special indorsement adding the name of the indorsee, to words of assignment and transfer, waiver, or other agreements. 11 Am J2d B & N § 359.

full life. Life or existence both in law and in fact, de jure and de facto.

full name. In a literal sense, first name, middle name, if any, and surname, or, with almost equal formality, first name, initial of middle name, and surname. In a practical sense, the name which provides the most certainty of identification, the whole of such name as is used by a person and his associates to identify him. Laflin & Rand Powder Co. v Steytler, 146 Pa 434, 23 A 215.

The early rule that both first and middle names of a person were essential to a proper designation of a person no longer prevails. 38 Am J1st Name § 6.

full officer. An officer of the military holding a regular commission, as distinguished from an officer holding a rank by brevet. United States v Hunt (US) 14 Wall 550, 20 L Ed 739.

full pardon. A pardon which remits the punishment and blots out the existence of guilt, so that in the eyes of the law the offender is as innocent as if he had never committed the offense. Ex parte Garland (US) 3 Wall 333, 380, 18 L Ed 366, 371.

full priority. See **strict priority.**

full proof. A degree of proof higher than the degree of preponderance of evidence usually prevailing in civil cases; evidence which satisfies the minds of the jury of the truth of the fact in dispute, to the entire exclusion of every reasonable doubt. Kane v Hibernia Mut. Ins. Co. 38 NJL 441.

full prosecution. The prosecution of an action or proceeding to a final judgment. Bensley v Mountain Lake Water Co. 13 Cal 307.

full settlement. See **in full settlement.**

full stop. A complete stop by a vehicle, a stop to the extent that no wheel turns. 7 Am J2d Auto § 228.

full time. The characterization of an employee in regular rather than casual, seasonal, or temporary employment. 58 Am J1st Workm Comp § 92. As used in a provision of a workmen's compensation act making the basis of compensation the average weekly earnings of the workman when at work on full time during the preceding year; the normal labor period for the kind of work which the workman is hired to perform, and not to such time during the preceding year as the employer had work for him. Cote v Bachelder-Worcester Co. 85 NH 444, 160 A 101.

Compensation for a week or other period without deduction for absence or hours of work missed.

full-time child. Under an older view, a child whose birth is forty weeks after conception. Young v Makepeace, 103 Mass 50, 51. In the modern view, a child born within or after the thirty-sixth week of gestation, especially if he has a birth weight over 5-1/2 pounds.

fullum aquae (ful'lum a'kwē). An aqueduct or flume; a stream of water.

full value. See **full cash value.**

fully. Amply; sufficiently; clearly; distinctly. Riley v State (Miss) 18 So 117, 118.

fully accounted. A full account rendered, not necessarily a proper expenditure of all money received. Kane v Kane, 120 Conn 184, 180 A 308.

full year. As an element of a legal settlement of a pauper, the full space of one year continuously and without interruption. Eaton Town v Shrewsbury, 49 NJL 188, 6 A 319.

fully equipped. Literally, completely equipped, but subject to explanation by parol evidence of usage. Halifax Auto Co. v Redden, 48 NS 20, 12 BRC 307, 15 DLR 34.

fully paid stock. Corporate stock for which the full par value has been paid to the corporation. 18 Am J2d Corp § 494.

fulmen. See **brutum fulmen.**

fumage. Same as **fuage.**

fumes. Gases which may be inhaled. 29A Am JRev ed Ins § 1277.

function. Whatever a person is employed or appointed to do; the duty of an office or officer. The operation of a mechanism. 40 Am J1st Pat § 15.

See **judicial function; ministerial functions; quasi-judicial functions.**

functional. Having or performing a function. Affecting the purpose, action, or performance of goods, or the facility or economy of processing, handling, or using them. J. C. Penney Co. v H. D. Lee Mercantile Co. (CA8 Mo) 120 F2d 949.

Where used in patent law with reference to the exact point of novelty in an invention, "means" or "mechanism" may expose the inventor's claim of

FUNCTIONAL [508] FUNERAL

patentability to attack on the ground that it is functional, but where used with reference to the makeup of the field in which the real invention finds its usefulness or with reference to the connecting parts which permit the salient novelty of the invention to accomplish its function, these words are only a convenient formula of the broadest equivalency of which the real invention permits. Goodwin v Carloss Co. (CA6 Tenn) 116 F2d 644.

functional depreciation. As considered in the valuation of property for taxation:—the result of lack of adaptation to function; the result of change of conditions and surroundings which renders the structure ill adapted to the work, especially a growth of business which calls for the substitution of other equipment and structures. Central Railroad Co. v Martin (DC NJ) 30 F Supp 41.

functionary (fungk'shọn-ạ-ri). A public officer.

functus (fungk'tus). Dead; expired; void; of no effect. Manning v Louisville & Nashville Railroad Co. 95 Ala 392, 11 So 8.

functus officio (fungk'tus o-fish'i-ō). Having performed its office; legally defunct.
The term is applied to a process which has been returned; to an agent or officer whose authority has expired; to an association which has ceased to function. Allen v Long, 80 Tex 261.

fund. Noun: A sum of money, either in hand or on deposit in a bank or other institution. A deposit or accumulation of resources, such as the assets of a decedent's estate, from which supplies are drawn, out of which expenses are provided, or which may be available for the payment of debts or the discharge of liabilities. Jewett v State, 94 Ind 549, 552. As used in a disposing clause in a will:—an accumulation of money, a security, an evidence of indebtedness, etc., but ordinarily not any kind of property. Anno: 67 ALR2d 1445. A designation of one of the accounts of a state or public body to be applied to a particular purpose, e.g. a school fund. People v New York Cent. Railroad Co. (NY) 34 Barb 123, 135. Verb: To convert an indebtedness, such as a warrant, into a more permanent form with an extended time of payment. 43 Am J1st Pub Sec § 155.
See **blended fund; current funds; funded debt; funding system; guaranty fund; public funds; school fund; sinking fund; slush funds; surplus funds.**

fundamental. At the foundation; basic.

fundamental error. An error of such character as to render a judgment void, as where the lower court proceeded without jurisdiction of the subject matter of the action. State v Cruikshank, 138 W Va 332, 76 SE2d 744. An error of the court which goes to the foundation of the case, or which takes from a defendant a right essential to his defense on appeal. Morrison v State, 37 Okla Crim 359, 258 P 1050. An error of the court which, in some jurisdictions, will be considered on appeal, notwithstanding the absence of an exception in the lower court or of an assignment of the error on appeal. Hollywood v Wellhausen, 28 Tex Civ App 541, 544, 68 SW 329.

fundamental law. Those principles, some in the form of declaration, others by way of implied or express provision, and some in the form of grant, deemed supposed to be limitations essential to conserve human liberty, security, equality and happiness, and not to be subject to change except in a way calculated to arouse the highest judgment and the most efficient, deliberate, and considered choice. State ex rel. Mueller v Thompson, 149 Wis 488, 137 NW 20.

fundamental rights and privileges. Life, liberty and property, except as such may be declared to be forfeited by the judgment of one's peers of the law of the land; the inherent rights common to all citizens. 16 Am J2d Const L § 328. Freedom of religion, freedom of speech and press, due process, etc. Individual rights immutable against all hostile legislation not required by considerations of public health or safety. National Mut. Ins. Co. v Tidewater Transfer Co. 337 US 582, 93 L Ed 1556, 69 S Ct 1173.
See **bill of rights.**
The preservation of fundamental rights by principle is primarily an Anglo-American concept. Conger v Pierce County, 116 Wash 27, 198 P 377, 18 ALR 393.

fundamus (fun-dā'mus). We found:—a formal word used in the king's letters patent or charter upon his creation of a corporation. Other similar words thus used were "creamus," we create; "erigimus," we erect; "incorporamus," we incorporate. See 1 Bl Comm 473.

fundatio (fun-dā'she-ō). A foundling.

fundator (fun-dā'tor). A founder; a person who makes an endowment to an institution.

funded debt. A debt for which revenues have been provided to pay the interest and to make payments upon the principal so that the debt will be gradually reduced. Ketchum v Buffalo, 14 NY 356, 367.

fundi (fun'di). Lands.

funding. See **fund.**

funding system. A plan whereby on the creation of a debt for money borrowed provision is made for the revenues whereby the interest can be paid and the principal gradually reduced. Merrill v Monticello (CC Ind) 22 F 589, 596.

fund in hand. Cash on hand or money due. Parsons v Armor (US) 3 Pet 413, 70 L Ed 724; Marrow v Marrow, 45 NC 148.
See **fund.**

fundi patrimoniales (fun'dī pa-tri-mō-ni-a'lēz). Lands of inheritance.

fundi publici (fun'dī pub'li-sī). Public lands; lands belonging to the state.

funditores (fun-di-tō'rēz). Pioneers.

fundus (fun'dus). Land; soil; a farm; an estate. See 3 Bl Comm 209.

funds. See **fund; fund in hand.**

funeral. A ceremony or service conducted upon the burial or cremation of a dead person.
See **first-class funeral; funeral director; funeral expenses; monument; undertaker.**

funeral director. A person who follows the profession or business of arranging and conducting funerals.
See **undertaker.**

funeral expenses. Those necessary and, in fact, compulsory expenditures, the necessity for which arises immediately upon and after the death of a person and which embrace the embalming, arraying, coffining, and sepulture or cremation of his body, together with those accustomed forms and ceremonies which attend upon the present disposition of his remains. 31 Am J2d Ex & Ad § 322. Allowable as a debt of a decedent's estate or an expense of administration where reasonable in amount in the light of the station in life, pecuniary circumstances, and social condition of the decedent. 31 Am J2d Ex & Ad § 321.

funeral expenses clause. A clause usually contained in standard automobile liability policies which provide, by way of extra coverage, for the payment of funeral expenses of a person killed as a result of the condition or use of the automobile covered by the policy. 7 Am J2d Auto Ins § 154.

funeral procession. See **procession.**

funeral vehicles. The hearse and other vehicles in a funeral procession.

fungible (fun'ji-bl). Consumable by use, and returnable in kind.

fungible goods. Goods of such nature that one unit is identical with another unit and is a replacement for another unit, the primary example being grain, such as wheat, oats, or corn. 1 Am J2d Access § 15.

fungible goods or securities. Goods or securities of which any unit is, by nature or usage of trade, the equivalent of any other like unit. UCC § 1–201(17).

F. U. R. See **homo trium litterarum.**

fur. The hair on the bodies of certain animals. A processed skin of a fur-bearing animal with the fur on it; merchandise within the meaning of an insurance policy covering loss by robbery. Kaplan v United States Fidelity & Guaranty Co. 343 Ill 44, 174 NE 834. (Latin.) A thief; a person who has committed larceny.

furandi animo (fū'ran'dī a'ni-mō). With intent to steal.

furandi animus (fū-ran'dī a'ni-mus). Intent to steal.

fur-bearing animals. Animals whose skins are well covered with fur, especially such animals as the mink, beaver, etc., which bear fur that thickens and becomes more valuable with the onset of winter.

furca (fėr'ką). A fork; a gallows; a gibbet.

furca et flagellum (fer'ka et fla-jel'lum). Gallows and whip,—the name of the lowest form of servile tenure, wherein the body and the life itself of the tenant were in the hands of the lord.

furca et fossa (fer'ka et fos'sa). Gallows and pit,—signifying the punishment of men by hanging and that of women by drowning.

furcare (fer-kā're). To fork. Same as **fourcher.**

fur diurnus (fer dī-er'nus). A daytime thief.

furem, si aliter capi non posset, occidere permittunt (fu'rem, sī a'li-ter kā'pī non pos'set, ok-si'de-re permit'tunt). They allow one to kill a thief if he cannot otherwise be taken. See 4 Bl Comm 179.

furent criblés (für krĕ-blā'). They were debated.

furigeldum (fū-ri-jel'dum). The payment of a fine for stealing.

Furiosi nulla voluntas est (fū-ri-ō'sī nul'la vo-lun'tās est). A madman has no will.

furiosity (fū-ri-os'į-ti). Raving madness.

furiosus (fū-ri-ō'sus). Mad; insane; a madman; a lunatic who is violent.

Furiosus absentis loco est (fu-ri-ō'sus ab-sen'tis lō'kō est). A madman is in the same position as a person who is absent.

Furiosus furore solo punitur (fu-ri-ō'sus fu-rō're sō'lō pu'ni-ter). A lunatic is punished by his madness alone. State v Strasburg, 60 Wash 106, 110 P 1020.

If a man becomes non compos after he commits a crime, he shall not be indicted; if after conviction, he shall not receive judgment; if after judgment, he shall not be ordered for execution. Nobles v Georgia, 168 US 398, 407, 42 L Ed 515, 518, 18 S Ct 87.

Furiosus furore solum punitur (fu-ri-ō'sus fu-rō're so'lum pu'ni-ter). Only because of his insanity, a lunatic is not punished. See 4 Bl Comm 24.

Furiosus nullum negotium contrahere (gerere) potest (quia non intelligit quod agit) (fu-ri-ō'sus nul'lum ne-gō'she-um kon-trā'he-re (je're-re) po'test (qui'a non in-tel'li-jit quod ā'jit). An insane person cannot make a contract (because he cannot understand what he is doing.)

Furiosus nullum negotium gerere potest, quia non intelligit quod agit (fu-ri-ō'sus nul'lum ne-gō'she-um je're-re po'test, qui'a non in-tel'li-jit quod ā'jit). A lunatic cannot transact any business, because he does not understand what he is doing.

It is a rule, not merely of municipal law, but of universal law, that contracts of all such persons are utterly void. The Roman law adopted this doctrine as expressed in the maxim. See American Trust & Banking Co. v Boone, 102 Ga 202, 29 SE 182.

Furiosus stipulari non potest nec aliquod negotium agere, qui non intelligit quid agit (fu-ri-ō'sus sti-pu-lā'rī non po'test nek a'li-quod nē-gō'she-um ā'je-re, quī non in-tel'li-jit quid ā'jit). An insane person who does not understand what he is doing, cannot contract nor transact any business.

furlong (fėr'lông). An eighth of a mile.

furlough (fėr'lō). Leave of absence for more than three days granted to an enlisted member of the armed forces. Williams v Brents, 171 Ark 367, 372, 284 SW 56.

fur manifestus (fer ma-ni-fes'tus). A person who is manifestly or palpably a thief,—a thief who is caught in the act of stealing.

furnage (fer'nāj). Fees exacted from tenants for the use of the oven or bakehouse of the lord of the manor.

furnish. To supply, provide, equip, or fit out. Tibbets v Moore, 23 Cal 208; Dickinson v Gray, 10 Ky LR 292, 8 SW 876, 9 SW 291.

Although it has been said that "furnish" is synonymous with "deliver," the terms are usually not synonymous. 17 Am J2d Contr § 281. But a person indicted for "furnishing" opium may be convicted upon evidence of a sale and delivery of the narcotic. Territory v Hu Seong, 20 Hawaii 669.

furnishing. The furniture and fixtures in a room or house. Attaway v Hoskinson, 37 Mo App 132. See **furnish.**

furnishing instrumentality for commission of crime. The handing or delivery of an instrumentality ordinarily used for lawful purposes to one who uses it in the commission of a crime. 21 Am J2d Crim L § 116.

furnishing liquor. Selling, disposing, or making a gift of liquor. 30 Am J Rev ed Intox L § 219.

furniture of a store. Implements and instruments used in carrying on the business. 15 Am J2d Chat Mtg § 77. The equipment or outfit of a trade or business; whatever may be supplied to a stock of goods or to a business, to make it convenient, useful, or gainful. Brody v Chittenden, 106 Iowa 524, 526.

furniture. Articles of common household use or ornament, excluding articles which have a personal history or peculiar relation as keepsakes to the proprietor or his family or which are kept for some special purpose which is independent of housekeeping. 15 Am J2d Chat Mtg § 77. As the word is used in an exemption statute:—about everything of the nature of personalty with which a house or any other building or place may be equipped. 31 Am J2d Exemp § 73.
See **household furniture.**

furniture of a ship. Everything required to be furnished a ship in order to make her seaworthy.

fur nocturnus (fer nok-ter'nus). A nighttime thief.

furor brevis (fū'rôr brē'vis). Sudden anger.

furor contrahi matrimonium non sinit, quia consensu opus est (fu'ror kon-trā'hī ma-tri-mō'ni-um non si'-nit, qui'a kon-sen'su ō'pus est). Insanity prevents a marriage from being contracted, because consent is essential.

furrow. A groove or rut 12 to 14 inches in width from which the earth has been turned by a plow.

further. Adjective: Farther out; at a greater distance. Adverb: A word of comparison; additional; moreover; furthermore; something beyond what has been said; likewise; also. Jones v Executors of Creveling, 19 NJL 127, 133.

further advance An additional loan made to a mortgagor, often secured in anticipation by the original mortgage.
See **future advances.**

further assurance. See **covenant for further assurance.**

further assessment. See **additional assessment.**

further disability. See **new and further disability.**

further proceedings. Additional proceedings, usually in the same case. Schlaefer v Schlaefer, 71 App DC 350, 112 F2d 177, 130 ALR 1014.

furtively (fėr'tiv-li). Stealthily; by stealth.

furto (fer'tō). A theft, a taking by stealth.

furtum (fėr'tum). Theft; larceny; anything which has been stolen.

furtum conceptum (fer'tum kon-sep'tum). Discovered or detected larceny or theft.

furtum est contrectatio fraudulosa, lucri faciendi gratia, vel ipsius rei, vel etiam usus, possessionisve (fer'tum est kon-trek-tā'she-ō frâ-du-lō'sa, lū'krī fa-she-en'dī grā'she-a, vel ip-sī'us rē'ī, vel e'she-am ū'sus, po-ze-she-ō-nis've). Larceny is the fraudulent taking or making use of a thing, or of the possession of it, for the sake of making gain.

furtum est contrectatio rei alienae fraudulenta, cum animo furandi, invito illo domino cujus res illa fuerat (fer'tum est kon-trek-tā'she-ō rē'ī ā-li-ē'nē frâ-du-len'ta, kum a'ni-mō fū-ran'dī, in-vī'to il'lō do'-mi-no kū'jus rēz il'la fu'e-rat). Larceny is the fraudulent taking of the goods of another with intent to steal and against the will of the person in whose control they were.

furtum grave (fer'tum gra've). Aggravated larceny.

furtum manifestum (fer'tum ma-ni-fes'tum). Manifest, open, palpable theft; as, where the thief is caught in the act of stealing.

furtum non est ubi initium habet detentionis per dominum rei (fer'tum non est u'bi in-i'she-um hā'-bet dē-ten-she-ō'nis per do'mi-num rē'ī). It is no larceny where the detention of the thing has its beginning through the owner of it.

furtum oblatum (fer'tum ob-lā'tum). The offering of stolen property; the offense of receiving stolen goods.

fuse. A device for setting off an explosion without injury to the person. An explosive cap, sometimes employed by railroad trainmen to signal a stop by placing it on the rail ahead of an approaching train. An electrical term; a wire of low melting point inserted in an electric circuit as a safety measure taken against the possibility of a current exceeding the safety level, the fuse wire melting and breaking upon an unwanted increase in the current, thereby breaking the circuit and cutting off the current.

Fusian Caninian Law. See **Lex Furia Caninia.**

fustigatio (fus-ti-gā'she-ō). An old form of punishment for certain offenses by beating the culprit with a club or cudgel.

fustis (fus'tis). A staff. Same as **fistuca.**

futile act. See **vain act.**

future acquired property. See **after acquired property.**

future advances. Loans made by a mortgagee to a mortgagor after the initial loan for which the mortgage was given, usually secured by the mortgage under an express affirmative provision therein. 36 Am J1st Mtg § 64.

future damages. The consequences of the defendant's wrongful act to occur in the future, that is, after the commencement of action. 22 Am J2d Damg § 26.

future debt. An existing debt which is not yet due.
See **future advances.**

future earnings. Wages, salaries, or the net income from an occupation, profession, or business to be earned or accrue later.

future estates. Estates to vest, either in title or in enjoyment, at a future time, whether or not under a limitation that creates an intervening estate. Moore v Little, 41 NY 66, 75.
See **expectancies; future interests.**

future fund. A fund to accrue and be developed in the future.

future interests. Remainders, reversions, executory interests, and other interests to come into possession or enjoyment in the future, whether vested or contingent, and whether or not supported by a particular estate. The title of an advanced course on the law of property in law schools.
See **expectancies.**

future premiums. As the term appears in a waiver of premiums clause in an accident insurance policy: —all premiums which the insurer would otherwise be entitled to demand after the commencement of the disability of the insured. 29 Am J Rev ed Ins § 581.

future rent. Rent to accrue in the future.

future right. A right, expected to mature in the future under a contract already in existence, but conditional rather than absolute. Re New York, N. H. & H. R. Co. (DC Conn) 25 F Supp 874.
See **future interests.**

futures. Contracts for the sale of securities, such as bonds and stocks, or of certain commodities, such as grain and cotton, which call for delivery at a future time, the value of such a contract fluctuating with changes in the market value of the security or commodity. Lemonius v Mayer, 71 Miss 514, 521, 14 So 33. Transactions upon stock and commodity exchanges calling for future delivery and payment, wherein it is understood that the vendor is not at the time of the transaction the owner of the property which is the subject matter of the transaction but that he intends to purchase it on or before the date of delivery. 50 Am J1st Stock Ex § 24. Transactions in stocks or commodities ostensibly calling for future delivery and payment but which actually do not contemplate delivery under any circumstances, the arrangement, as understood by the parties, being for a settlement between the parties to be made according to the rise and fall of the market. 24 Am J1st Gaming § 66.

Those who deal in "futures" are divided into three classes: First, those who use them to hedge, i.e. to insure themselves against loss by unfavorable changes in price at the time of actual delivery of what they have to sell or buy in their business; second, legitimate capitalists, who, exercising their judgment as to the conditions, purchase or sell for future delivery with a view to profit based on the law of supply and demand; and, third, gamblers, or irresponsible speculators, who buy or sell as upon the turn of a card. United States v New York Coffee & Sugar Exchange, 263 US 611, 619, 68 L Ed 475, 477, 44 S Ct 225.

See **margin; matching; option.**

future sales. In a sense developed in some commercial activities, a sale under terms calling for delivery later in the current month, or in some future month. Board of Trade v United States, 246 US 231, 62 L Ed 683, 38 S Ct 242.

futuri (fu-tū'rī). Persons of the future; persons who have not yet come into existence.

futuro. See **de futuro; in futuro.**

fyhtwite. Same as **fightwite.**

fyrdwite. Same as **ferdwit.**

G

G. A slang term for one thousand dollars. Standing for four hundred, as a Roman numeral.

g. a. Abbreviation of general average, also of general agent.

G. A. Abbreviation of General Assembly.

gabel (gā'bel). Same as **gavel**.
See **land-gabel**.

gabella (gă-bel'ă). Same as **gavel**.

gablum (gā'blum). Same as **gavel**.

gabulus denariorum (gā'bu-lus de-nā-ri-ō'rum). Rent paid in money.

Gadsden Purchase. See **Gadsden Treaty**.

Gadsden Treaty. A treaty made December 30, 1853, between the United States and Mexico, whereby, under the so-called "Gadsden Purchase," the United States added a strip along the southern boundary of the Territory of New Mexico. Ainsa v United States, 161 US 208, 220, 40 L Ed 673, 677, 16 S Ct 544.

gafol. Same as **gavel**.

gafolgild. The payment of taxes, tribute or rent.

gafol-land. Land which was liable to the payment of gafolgild.

gag. Something forced into a person's mouth to prevent outcry.

gage (gāj). Noun: A pledge; a challenge; a wager. Verb: To pledge; to wage; to challenge.

gager (gā'jėr). Verb: To pledge; to wage; to challenge. Noun: A government revenue officer charged with the duty of measuring the contents of liquor casks.

gager de deliverance (gā'jer de de-li'ver-anz). To give security; to give pledge for the delivery of goods by the person who had distrained them, after an action had been brought against him for their recovery.

gager del ley (gā'jer dĕl lā). Wager of law.

gain. That which is acquired or comes as a benefit; profit. Thorn v de Breteuil, 86 App Div 405, 416, 83 NYS 849.

gainage (gā'nāj). The gain or profit accruing to a farmer from his crops; animals and implements employed in the raising of crops.

gain derived from capital. Not a growth or increment of value in the investment; but a gain, a profit, something of exchangeable value proceeding from the property, severed from the capital, however invested or employed, and coming in, being derived, that is, received or drawn in by the recipient for his separate use, benefit, and disposal. Eisner v Macomber, 252 US 189, 64 L Ed 521, 40 S Ct 189, 9 ALR 1570, 1577.
See **capital gain**.

gainery (gā'nėr-i). Same as **gainage**.

Gaius. See **Institutes of Gaius**.

gale. A strong or violent wind; technically, a wind of the velocity of from 35 or 40 to 75 or 80 miles per hour. Missouri Pacific Railroad Co. v Columbia, 65 Kan 390, 69 P 338. An older term for a license in real estate and the rent paid for such license.

Gales (gāls). Wales, now a part of Great Britain, but at one time a separate kingdom.

gallery. The section of a theater in which the least expensive seats are located. A walk having a roof supported by pillars. A collection of works of art. The place of business of a professional photographer.
See **rogues' gallery**.

gallows (gal'ōz or gal'us). A framework made of two upright posts and a bar across on which criminals convicted of capital offenses are put to death by hanging. Anciently it was sometimes made with but one upright post or by a bar across the fork of a tree.

gallows-tree (gal'ōz-trē). Same as **gallows**.

galravage (gal-rav'āj). Same as **gilravage**.

gamacta (gā-mak'ta). An assault; a battery; a stroke; a blow.

gamalis (ga-ma'lis). A legitimate child; a child born of parents who are married to each other; a child born of parents who are engaged to marry each other, but who are not yet married.

gamble. To play at any game for any sum of money or other property of any value. State v Book, 41 Iowa 550. To take a monetary risk on the chance of receiving a monetary gain, 24 Am J1st Gaming § 2; in short, to stake money or property on a chance. 24 Am J1st Gaming § 2.
To play any game for cigars or drinks, or under an agreement that the loser shall treat to cigars, drinks or other refreshments, is a form of gambling. Zotalis v Cannellos, 138 Minn 179, 164 NW 807.

gambler. One who gambles; a person who follows or practices games of chance or skill, with the expectation and purpose of thereby winning money or other property. See Buckley v O'Niel, 113 Mass 193.
See **common gambler**; **gamble**; **professional gambler**.

gambling. See **gamble**.

gambling contract. A contract in which the parties, in effect, stipulate that they shall gain or lose on the happening of an event which is uncertain of occurrence and in which they have no interest except that arising from the possibility of such gain or loss. 24 Am J1st Gaming § 62. A contract wherein the parties stake their property or money on an event which in its nature may or may not happen, and whereby one of them is to lose and the other is to win. State v Stripling, 113 Ala 120, 21 So 409.

gambling den. Another term for "gambling house." Buckley v O'Niel, 113 Mass 193.

gambling device. The tangible means, instrument, contrivance or thing with or by which money may be lost or won, as distinguished from the game itself. 24 Am J1st Gaming § 31. Gilley v Commonwealth, 312 Ky 584, 229 SW2d 60, 19 ALR2d 1224. An instrument or device used for the purpose of gambling, although capable of use for another purpose. 24 Am J1st Gaming § 31. Any machine which is so contrived that the player is attracted by the chance that he will either immediately or ultimately receive something for nothing. Marvin v Sloan, 77 Mont 174, 250 P 443.

GAMBLING [513] GARAGE

gambling house. A house kept for the purpose of permitting persons to resort to it for gambling. 24 Am J2d Disord H § 3. A place to which persons are permitted to resort for gambling. Buckley v O'Niel, 113 Mass 193. A place whose use is intended to facilitate gambling and where sporting characters are invited to congregate for purposes of illegal amusement and gain, and to stake money or other thing of value upon trials of chance, skill, or endurance. St. Louis Fair Asso. v Carmody, 151 Mo 566, 52 SW 365.
See **common gaming house; house money; keeper of common gaming house.**

gambling machine. See **gambling device.**

gambling partnership. A partnership organized for the purpose of gambling. 40 Am J1st Partn § 29.

gambling policy. A wager policy; that is, a policy of life insurance wherein the person for whose use it was issued has no pecuniary interest in the life of the insured. Gambs v Covenant Mut. Life Ins. Co. 50 Mo 44, 47. An insurance policy in which the insured has no insurable interest in the subject of the insurance. 29 Am J Rev ed Ins §§ 432 et seq.

gambling room. A room to which persons are permitted to resort for gambling. Any room with books, apparatus, or paraphernalia for the purpose of recording or registering bets or wagers or of selling pools. People v Weithoff, 93 Mich 631.
See **gambling house.**

gambling table. A table adapted, devised, and designed for the playing of a game or games of chance for money or property. Any table kept and used for gambling, being characterized, not by structure or appliances attached, but by the use to which it is put. 24 Am J1st Gaming § 32.

gambling verdict. A verdict reached by chance, for example, by tossing a coin or drawing lots. Anno: 73 ALR 94; 53 Am J1st Trials § 1029.

game. A contest for success or superiority in a trial of chance, skill or endurance; in its connection with gambling, a means of playing for money or other things of value, so that the result depends more on chance than skill. James v State, 4 Okla Crim 587, 112 P 944.
Birds and beasts of a wild nature obtained by hunting and trapping. 35 Am J2d Fish §§ 1, 2. All animals of both land and sea which are hunted for sport:—fish, deer, pheasants, partridges, and even wild bees. State v Higgins, 51 SC 51, 28 SE 15. Sometimes construed to include animals and birds which are by nature wild although bred in captivity and confined, being thereby to a certain extent domesticated. 35 Am J2d Fish §§ 1, 2.
A contest for success or superiority in a trial of chance, skill or endurance; a sporting event, such as a game of football or baseball. 24 Am J1st Gaming § 13. In the narrower sense of a connection with gambling, an activity employed as a means of playing for money or other thing of value; as a means of determining who wins a bet. 24 Am J1st Gaming § 13.

gamecock. See **cock fight.**

gamekeeper (gām'kē″pėr). A person employed to guard wild game in a park or game preserve and to prevent poaching.

game laws. See **fish and game laws.**

game of chance. Such a game as is determined entirely or in part by lot or mere luck, and in which judgment, practice, skill, and adroitness play no part at all or are thwarted by chance. 24 Am J1st Gaming § 18.

game preserve (gām' prḗ-zėrv″). A private park or tract, stocked with wild game for hunting.
A tract of publicly owned land closed to hunting or in which hunting is limited according to season or kind of game, the tract being maintained in the interest of conservation.

game warden. Same as **gamekeeper.**

gaming. To play at any game for money or property; in short to stake money or property on a chance. 24 Am J1st Gaming § 2. Essentially the same as gambling.
See **gamble.**

gaming contract. Same as **gambling contract.**

gaming device. See **gambling device.**

gaming house. See **gambling house.**

gaming table. See **gambling table.**

ganancial property (ga-nan'she-al pro'per-ti). (Spanish.) That property which husband and wife, living together, acquire during matrimony, by a common title, lucrative or onerous; or that which husband and wife, or either, acquire by purchase, or by their labor and industry, as also the fruits of the separate property which each brings to the matrimony or acquires by lucrative title during the continuance of the partnership. Cartwright v Cartwright, 18 Tex 626, 634.

ganancias (gah-nahn'the-ah). (Spanish.) The income derived from the community property of a husband and his wife.

gang. A number of persons associated together for work or sport. A group of employees directed by a foreman. A body of persons organized and directed for criminal purposes. An old term for currency or current money.

gang-days (gang-dās). Same as **gang-week.**

gangiatori (gan-ji-a-tō'rī). Ancient officers whose duty it was to inspect weights and measures.

gangplank. A movable platform or stairway for boarding or leaving a ship.

gangster. One of a gang organized for and directed in the commission of crime; one of a gang of roughs or hirelings. State v Gaynor, 119 NJL 582, 197 A 360.

gangway. Passageway.

gang-week (gang'wĕk). Rogation week; that is, the week in each year when the boundaries of parishes and manors were surveyed.

gantlet (gȧnt'let). Same as **gauntlet.**

gantlope (gant'lōp). Same as **gauntlet.**

gaol (jāl). Same as **jail.**

gaol delivery. Same as **jail delivery.**

gaoler (jā'lėr). Same as **jailer.**

gaol liberties. See **liberties of the jail.**

gaol limits. See **liberties of the jail.**

garage. A word appropriated from the French, meaning a place where a motor vehicle is housed or housed and kept in condition. 24 Am J1st Garag § 2. A "workshop" within the meaning of a workmen's compensation statute, as a place where repairs are made on the vehicles of customers. 58 Am J1st Workm Comp § 110.
See **private garage; public garage.**

garage liability insurance. A liability insurance policy specifically designed to protect garage-keepers, operators of service and repair stations, rental agencies, or automobile dealers, against loss by reason of the inflicting of injury to the person or property of others in the pursuit of business operations. 7 Am J2d Auto Ins § 96.

garageman's lien. The lien of the keeper of a garage for service upon, or storage of, a motor vehicle. 24 Am J1st Garag § 48.

garandia (ga-ran'di-a). A warranty.

garathinx (ga'ra-thinx). A gift.

garaunt. A warranty.

garaunter (gah'rôn-tā'). To warrant.

garauntor. A warrantor.

garba (gar'ba). A bundle or sheaf of unthreshed grain.

garbage. The accumulation as refuse of animal, fruit, or vegetable matter, liquid or otherwise, that attends the preparation, use, cooking, dealing in, or storing of meat, fish, fowl, fruit, or vegetables; any worthless or offensive matter. 37 Am J1st Mun Corp § 298.

garbage disposal plant. See **disposal plants.**

garbales decimae (gar-bā'lēz de'si-mē). Tithes of grain.

garble. To mix up a story; to distort the facts in relating an occurrence or event. In very rare usage, to sort the good from the bad in a quantity of a commodity.

garbling coins. In rare usage, the practice of dealers in money of taking the good coins out of circulation for melting and keeping the worn ones in circulation.

gard (gärd). A guard; a guardianship; care; custody; wardship.

garde (gärd). Same as **gard.**

gardein. A guardian; a keeper; a warden.

garden. A tract, usually of a limited area, for the growing of vegetables or flowers. A part of the curtilage of the dwelling house. 5 Am J2d Arson § 1.

garden apartment. An apartment in an apartment house, the occupants of which are entitled to join with the occupants of other apartments in the use and enjoyment of open areas around the apartment building. Shapiro v Baltimore, 230 Md 199, 186 A2d 605, 99 ALR2d 861.

gardianus (gar-di-ā'nus). A guardian; a keeper; a warden.

gardinum (gar'di-num). A garden.

garene. A warren or private game preserve where wild game and wild fowl were kept for hunting.

garner (gär'nėr). To warn, being the word from which the term "garnishment" derives. Lynch v Johnson, 196 Va 516, 84 SE2d 419. To garnish; to garnishee.
See **garnishment.**

garnetted wool (gär'nett-ed wůl). Wool shorn from the animal which bore it, cleaned, and partially processed. Interstate Commerce Com. v Wagner (DC Tenn) 112 F Supp 109.

garnir. Another spelling of **garner.** Lynch v Johnson, 196 Va 516, 84 SE2d 419.

garnish. To warn; to notify; to cause a garnishment to be levied on a garnishee; to garnishee.

garnishee (gär-ni-shē'). Noun: The person upon whom a garnishment is served, usually a person indebted to, or in possession of property of, the defendant in the main action. Verb: To commence a garnishment proceeding; to serve a notice of garnishment; to effect a garnishment of a debtor of the defendant in the main action. Burlington & Missouri River Railroad Co. v Thompson, 31 Kan 180, 1 P 622.
See **garnishment.**

garnishee execution. The employment of the remedy of garnishment under an execution issued upon a judgment. Sarver v Towne, 285 NY 264, 34 NE2d 313, 138 ALR 1344.

garnishee process (gär-ni-shē' pros'es). Same as **garnishment.**

garnishing process. Same as **garnishment.**

garnishment. A proceeding by a creditor to obtain satisfaction of the indebtedness out of property or credits of the debtor in the possession of, or owing by, a third person; the person instituting the proceeding being generally referred to as the creditor or plaintiff, the person indebted to the creditor being called the debtor or defendant, and the person holding the property of, or who is indebted to, the defendant being called the garnishee. In effect, an action by the defendant against the garnishee for the use of the plaintiff, or a suit by the defendant in which the plaintiff is subrogated to the rights of the defendant; sometimes called a compulsory novation. 6 Am J2d Attach § 2. Known in some states as factoring process or trustee process. 6 Am J2d Attach § 2. Distinguished from attachment in the respect that it reaches funds, effects, or credits belonging to the defendant which are in the hands of third persons and that property reached by the proceeding is left in the hands of the garnishee pending the outcome of the principal action. 6 Am J2d Attach § 3.

garnishment bonds. A bond required in obtaining a garnishment as a provisional remedy, the condition of which is that the plaintiff shall pay the costs and damages which the defendant may sustain if the writ has been sued out wrongfully. 6 Am J2d Attach § 518. A bond, otherwise known as a "forthcoming" or "delivery" bond, given by the defendant to obtain a release of property reached by a garnishment, the condition of which is that the property will be forthcoming in the event judgment is rendered against the defendant in the main action. 6 Am J2d Attach § 523. A bond furnished in obtaining a dissolution of the garnishment, the condition of which is that the defendant will perform and satisfy whatever judgment is obtained against him in the main action. 6 Am J2d Attach § 523.

garote (ga-rot'). Same as **garrote.**

garrant. A warrant; authority.

garrantie. A warranty.

garrena (gar-rē'na). A warren; a game preserve.

garrote (ga-rot'). A form of capital punishment, adopted by some countries; strangulation or the severance of the spinal cord by an iron collar tightened by a screw.

garsumne (gar-sum'ne). A fine; an amercement.

garter (gär'tėr). The badge of the order of the garter, which was also called the order of St. George, and was the highest order of British knighthood. The members of this order ranked next after the nobility. See 1 Bl Comm 403.

garth (gärth). A yard; a small enclosure; a fish-weir.

gas. A substance of such nature that it can expand indefinitely, thereby completely filling its container; a form neither liquid nor solid, in other words, a vapor. An inflammable used for lighting and heating. A colloquial term for gasoline. As the word appears in an insurance policy provision excluding the risk of death or injury from "gas:" —any substance in an aeriform state, having noxious or poisonous qualities. Anno: 92 ALR 167.
See **carbon monoxide; casing head gas; natural gas; wet gas.**

gas company. A company engaged in the business of supplying artificial or natural gas to ultimate consumers for lighting, power, or heating purposes. See 26 Am J2d Electr §§ 6-9. A public utility rendering service to industrial plants, business buildings, mercantile establishments, residences, etc.
See **natural gas company.**

gas franchise. The right to use the streets of a city or village or public highways outside a city or village for laying pipes, mains, etc. through which gas may be conveyed and furnished for public or private use. See 26 Am J2d Electr § 18.

gas jet. A flame of burning gas. The burner on a gas fixture.

gas lease. See **oil and gas lease.**

gas meter. See **meter.**

gasoline. A volatile and inflammable liquid produced from crude oil by successive distillations; used as fuel in engines, particularly the engines in motor vehicles, and for other domestic and industrial purposes. United States v Gulf Refining Co. 268 US 542, 69 L Ed 1082, 45 S Ct 597.

gasoline clause. A clause in a fire insurance policy whereby the policy is rendered void if gasoline is kept or used on the insured premises without the written consent of the insurer. German American Ins. Co. v Hyman, 42 Colo 156, 94 P 27.

gasoline filling station. A place of business, located on premises abutting on a street or highway, supplying motorists with gasoline, lubricating oil, and some automobile accessories, and furnishing services connected with motor vehicles, such as tire repair, lubrication, washing, and even repairs upon the vehicle itself.

gasoline license. A municipal license required for the storage or keeping of gasoline. 24 Am J1st Gas & O § 154.

gasoline permit. See **gasoline license.**

gasoline premium. Something given a purchaser of gasoline in addition to the product itself, usually trading stamps. 52 Am J1st Trad St § 11.

gas station. See **gasoline filling station.**

gast (gȧst). Waste; whatever is done to land to impair the value of the inheritance.

gastaldus (gas-tal'dus). A bailiff; a steward.

gaster (gas'tẻr). To commit waste.

gastine. Waste land; uncultivated land.

gastric analysis. The removal of food contents from the stomach by pump, followed by an analysis of such contents to determine the chemicals present, the chemical action, even the presence of radioactive material. Cardinal v University of Rochester, 188 Misc 823, 71 NYS2d 614, affd 271 App Div 1048, 69 NYS2d 352.

gastric lavage (gas'trik lav'āj). The withdrawal of the contents of the stomach to prevent disastrous effects of poison therein or for the purpose of making an analysis of the contents.

gastritis. A disease of the stomach, particularly an inflammation of the lining, but not necessarily a serious disease within the meaning of a life insurance policy. Anno: 153 ALR 723 et seq.

gas well. A well which produces gas in such quantities and under such pressure that it can be operated commercially or at least that the gas produced can be used profitably on the premises. Prichard v Freeland Oil Co. 75 W Va 450, 84 SE 945. Not a mine. 36 Am J1st Min & M § 2.

gas works. A plant for the manufacture of artificial gas.

gate. A barrier which can be swung or raised to permit passage; an opening in a fence or wall, sometimes with, sometimes without, a movable barrier. Bars at a railroad crossing which may be raised or lowered to permit or restrain traffic on the highway. In a peculiar sense of the term, a servitude or easement for the pasturage or passage of cattle.
See **toll gate.**

gatemen. Railroad employees at railroad crossings, whose primary duty is to raise and lower the gates according to the movement of trains and traffic upon the highway.

gathered crop. A mature and harvested crop. 21 Am J2d Crops § 1.

gauge. A measure; an instrument for taking a measure. The width of a railroad track, meaning the distance between the rails.

gauging. An operation for determining the physical, chemical, or other properties or characteristics of an article for the purpose of the application of customs duties. 21 Am J2d Cust D § 62.

gaugeator (ga-je-ā'tor). Same as **gager.**

gauger (gā'jer). Same as **gager.**

gaugetum (gā-jē'tum). The measure of the capacity of a barrel, cask or other like container.

gauntlet (gänt'let). A former type of military punishment in which the offender was required to pass between two files of soldiers who struck him with sticks or whips as he passed. A punishment sometimes imposed by a "kangaroo court."

gavel. A tax; an excise; a duty; rent. A mallet used by a presiding officer or judge holding court to obtain order and decorum by rapping it on the table or bench.

gavelbred (gav'el-bred). Rent paid in bread or provisions.

gaveled (gav'eld). Held by gavelkind tenure.

gavelet and cessavit (gav'el-et and ses-sā'vit). A common-law process, long since in disuse, by which a landlord could seize the land itself for rent in arrear and hold it until payment was made. 32 Am J1st L & T § 613.

gavelgeld (gav-el'geld). Yearly profit, toll, or tribute; the subject of such profit, toll, or tribute.

gavelherte. A service of ploughing rendered by customary tenants.

gaveling men. Tenants who paid rent and who rendered customary services.

gavelkind (gav'el-kīnd). A form of socage tenure which originated in Kent and of which the principal characteristics were: (1) That the tenant could dispose of his estate by feoffment at the age of fifteen. (2) That the estate did not escheat in case of attainder and execution of the tenant for felony, under the maxim "The father to the bough, the son to the plough." (3) In most places, the tenant could pass his lands by devise, even before statute permitted it. (4) The lands descended to all the sons together, and not to any one of them. See 2 Bl Comm 84.
See **Irish gavelkind; tenure in gavelkind.**

gaveller (gav-el'lėr). An officer appointed by the king, who had charge of coal mining in certain districts of England.

gavelman (gav'el-man). A tenant who held his land under gavelkind tenure.

gavelmed (gav'el-med). The customary service, rendered by tenants, of mowing meadows.

gavelrep (gav'el-rep). The service of reaping at the command of the lord of the manor.

gavelwerk (gav'el-werk). Customary services of tenants rendered by manual labor or with carts.

gazette. Noun: A magazine or other periodical. Verb: To publish in an official publication, especially in the British Gazette.
See **Gazette.**

Gazette (ga-zet'). A British official newspaper announcing declarations of bankruptcy, official promotions and public events.

gebocced (gĕ-bōk'ed). Conveyed, the term being derived by a flagrant corruption of Latin.

gebocian. To convey; to convey by a writing.
See **gebocced.**

gebur (ge-bör'). A person who owned an allotment of land.

geburscript. A neighborhood; a village.

Geiger counter. An instrument which detects radiation, one of the important uses of which is the discovery of radioactive minerals. Anno: 66 ALR2d 560.

geld. Noun: A sum of money; a fine; a tribute; a tax. A castrated horse. Verb: To castrate a horse.

geldabilis (gel-dā'bi-lis). Same as **geldable.**

geldable (gel'da-bl). Taxable; liable to pay a tax or tribute.

gelded (gel'ded). See **gelt.**

gelding (gel'ding). See **gelt.**

gelt. See **geld.**

gem. A precious stone fit for cutting and polishing as a jewel.
A singular distinction appears in old authority—a jewel is a stone which is valuable but kept as a curiosity; a gem is a valuable stone prepared and mounted for wear. Cavendish v Cavendish (Eng) 1 Bro Ch 409.

gemma (jem'ä). A gem; a jewel; a precious stone.

gemot (ge-mōt'). A meeting; an assembly.

gemote. Same as **gemot.**

genealogy. Family history. The tracing of a person's descent from his ancestors. The science of tracing the history of a family in respect of lineage.

genearch (jen'ē-ärk). The head or chief of a family or tribe.

geneath. A villein; a vassal.

gener (je'ner). A son-in-law.

general. Common to many, or the greatest number; widely spread; prevalent; extensive though not universal; having a relation to all; common to the whole. Koen v State, 35 Neb 676, 53 NW 595, quoting Webster.

general acceptance. An acceptance of a bill of exchange by the drawee whereby he engages to pay according to the tenor of the bill, without qualification. Uniform Negotiable Instruments L § 139. Cox v National Bank, 100 US 704, 25 L Ed 739.

general accident policy. A contract insuring against accidents happening to the person of the insured, without limitation as to the means of or the occasion, that is, not limited to accidents involving motor vehicles, airplanes, etc. Employers' Liability Assur. Corp. v Merrill, 155 Mass 404, 29 NE 529, 530.

general act. Same as **general statute.**

General Accounting Office. The accounting and auditing office of the United States, headed by the Comptroller General, and the Assistant Comptroller General, of the United States, having a European Branch and a Far East Branch, and various Divisions for distinct parts of the work, such as Defense Accounting and Auditing Division, Civil Accounting and Auditing Division, and Field Operations Division.

general administrative law. Administrative law which is common to all or to many different types of administrative agencies. 1 Am J2d Admin L § 7.

general administrator. An administrator who administers the whole of the estate of a decedent. Clemens v Walker & Brickell, 40 Ala 189, 198.

General Advisory Committee. A committee established by the Atomic Energy Act to advise the Atomic Energy Commission on scientific and technical matters. 42 USC § 2036.

general agent. An agent authorized to perform all acts connected with the business or employment in which he is engaged; one authorized to conduct on behalf of a principal a series of transactions involving a continuity of service; one authorized to bind his principal by an act within the scope of his authority, notwithstanding it may be contrary to his special instructions. 3 Am J2d Agency § 6. An agent of a corporation with responsibility, but not necessarily an officer. 19 Am J2d Corp § 1080.
See **general agent of foreign corporation; general agent of insurance company.**

general agent of foreign corporation. One who is authorized to transact all the business of the principal at a particular place or of a particular kind generally. Anno: 113 ALR 83.

general agent of insurance company. An agent authorized to transact all the business of the company of a particular kind or in a particular place, and whose powers are prima facie coextensive with the business entrusted to his care. Southern States Fire Ins. Co. v Kronenberg, 199 Ala 164, 74 So 63.

general and notorious recognition. As a means of legitimation of a child born out of wedlock: —open and extensive recognition; not necessarily universal recognition; such conduct and bearing of the father toward the child that a substantial portion of the community believes that the child is his. 10 Am J2d Bast § 52.

general appearance. An appearance whereby the person appearing submits himself to the jurisdiction of the court, regardless of whether process has been served upon him, and renders himself before the court for all further proceedings in the cause or incidental to the original suit. 5 Am J2d Appear § 1. An appearance by invoking the judgment of the court in any manner on any question other than that of the jurisdiction of the court over his person, thereby waiving any defects in the jurisdiction of the court for want of valid summons or a proper service thereof. Re Blalock, 233 NC 493, 64 SE2d 848, 25 ALR2d 818.

General Assembly. The official title of the legislature in nineteen of the states. The body highest in the government of the United Presbyterian Church in the United States of America.

general assignment. As an act of bankruptcy:—any conveyance at common law or by statute by which one intends to make an absolute and unconditional appropriation of all his property to pay his creditors, share and share alike. Anno: 57 ALR 859.

See **general assignment for benefit of creditors**; **general assignment of error**.

general assignment for benefit of creditors. A conveyance by a debtor without consideration from the grantee of substantially all his property to a party in trust to collect the amount owing to him, to sell and convey the property, to distribute the proceeds of all the property among his creditors, and to return the surplus, if any, to the debtor. 6 Am J2d Assign for Crs § 1.

general assignment of error. An assignment of error on appeal which does not clearly indicate the particular rulings of which complaint is made by appellant. 5 Am J2d A & E § 670.

general assize (a̱-sīz'). An old name for the British parliament.

general assumpsit. Assumpsit in the common courts: indebitatus assumpsit, quantum meruit, quantum valebant, money had and received, money lent, money paid, and insimul computassent or count on account stated. 1 Am J2d Actions § 13.

general average. A contribution by all the parties in a sea adventure to make good the loss sustained by one of their number on account of sacrifices voluntary made of part of the ship or cargo to save the residue and the lives of those on board from an impending peril, or for extraordinary expenses necessarily incurred by one or more of the parties for the general benefit of all the interests embarked in the enterprise. An obligation resting upon the vessel, the cargo, and the freight, in proportion to their respective values, and upon the owners of each, in proportion to the value of their property at risk, and enforceable by resorting to a lien upon the property saved from the common peril, or by actions against the persons bound to contribute. 48 Am J1st Ship § 621.

While general average is not, eo nomine, insured against in marine policies, where it is payable in consequence of a peril insured against, the insurer is liable therefor. Peters v Warren Ins. Co. (US) 14 Pet 99, 10 L Ed 371.

In case of a general average loss, the insurer is directly liable for the whole of the insured value of the property sacrificed for the general benefit, and upon payment is subrogated to the rights of the insured for contribution. Dickenson v Jardine (Eng) LR 3 CP 639, 14 ERC 431.

See **free from average unless general**.

general average bond. A kind of bond, also called an "average bond," which it is customary and lawful for the master of a ship to exact as a condition precedent to the delivery of the cargo in case a dispute has arisen as to liability for general average, or where investigation is necessary before claims can be adjusted; which bond is conditioned upon the payment of such average, if any, as may be found due upon proper adjustment conformably to law and the usage of the port.

The legal operation and effect of such a bond is to fix the measure of the obligor's liability, and to secure the payment of the amount, unless it shall afterward appear that it was not a case of general average. 48 Am J1st Ship § 645.

general average contribution. See **general average**.

general average lien. See **general average**.

general average loss. See **general average**.

general ballot. A ballot which contains the names of all candidates for both local and state offices to be voted upon at an election. Re Ballot Act, 16 RI 766, 19 A 656.

general benefits. For the purposes of the rule that "general benefits" are not to be deducted from compensation or damages in eminent domain:—those benefits from the improvement which are enjoyed, not only by the property of the condemnee concerned in the litigation, but also by other property. 27 Am J2d Em D § 367.

general bequest. See **general legacy**.

general building scheme. A scheme or plan under which the owner of a large tract of land divides it into building lots, to be sold to different persons for separate occupancy, and to be conveyed to them by deeds which contain uniform covenants restricting the use which the several grantees may make of their premises. Besch v Hyman, 221 App Div 445, 223 NYS 231.

general cancellation. A sweeping and general termination by one act and at one time of all the outstanding policies issued by an insurance company. State Mut. Fire Underwriters v Glen Cove Mut. Ins. Co. (CA8 SD) 124 F2d 681.

general character. The estimation of a person by the members of the community in which he resides. Douglas v Tousey (NY) 2 Wend 352, 354. The reputation of a person.

See **reputation**.

general charge. See **general instruction**.

general circulation. See **newspaper of general circulation**.

general claim. See **general creditor**.

general construction business. The business of constructing houses, buildings in industrial plants, office buildings, and other structures. A term broad enough to include the making of boxes, crates, and parts for prefabricated houses. Gilman Paint & Varnish Co. v Legum, 197 Md 665, 80 A2d 906, 29 ALR2d 286.

general constructive possession. That possession which the law attaches to the title to real property where there is no actual possession in the owner of the title, and no one in adverse possession of the property; to be distinguished from that constructive possession known as "effective possession" or "virtual possession." Wheeler v Clark, 114 Tenn 117, 85 SW 258.

General Court. The official title of the legislature in Massachusetts and New Hampshire.

general court-martial. The highest in rank of the three kinds of courts-martial, conducted before a body of at least five persons who shall be commissioned officers, except as one of them must be an enlisted man where the accused, an enlisted man, so demands, and usually convened for the trial of capital cases.

general covenant of warranty. A warranty of title to real estate unrestricted as to claims or claimants, that is, a warranty against the lawful claims of all persons whomsoever. Burton v Price, 105 Fla 544, 141 So 728.

general credit. The general reputation of a witness for veracity.

general creditor. A creditor whose claim is unsecured by mortgage, judgment lien, or other lien, and is not entitled to priority. Stepp v McAdams (CA9 Cal) 97 F2d 874; Dempsey v Pforzheimer, 86 Mich 652, 49 NW 465; Wolcott v Ashenfelter, 5 NM 442, 23 P 780.

general criminal intent. A matter of conscious wrongdoing from which a prohibited result follows, without a subjective desire for the accomplishment of that result. State v Daniels, 236 La 998, 109 So 2d 896.

general custom. A custom which prevails throughout a country or a large portion of a country and becomes its law, its existence being determined by the court. 21 Am J2d Cust & U § 6.

A custom observed generally in a particular trade or locality. United States v Stanolind Crude Oil Purchasing Co. (CA10 Okla). 113 F2d 194.

general damages. Those damages which are the natural and necessary result of the wrongful act or omission asserted as the foundation of liability. Parker v Harris Pine Mills, 206 Or 187, 291 P2d 709, 56 ALR2d 382. Those damages which are traceable to, and are the probable and necessary result of, the injury complained of, or which are presumed by, or implied in, law to have resulted therefrom. 22 Am J2d Damg § 15.

general damages in defamation. Such damages as will compensate for the natural and probable consequences of the publication. Turner v Hearst, 115 Cal 394, 47 P 129.

general damages in eminent domain. Properly, those damages which result from the taking of the property, including compensation for the property taken and injury to adjacent land of the condemnee. 26 Am J2d Em D § 159. In a very special sense of the term, damages common to the entire community through which or in which the project of condemnation is established. Lewisburg & Northern Railroad Co. v Hinds, 134 Tenn 293, 183 SW 985.

general damages in sales. For breach by seller:—the difference between what the buyer agreed to pay, and the sum for which he could have supplied himself with goods of the same character at the place of delivery, or if not obtainable there, then at the nearest available market, plus any additional freight resulting from the breach. Lawrence v Porter (CA6 Mich) 63 F 62. For breach by buyer: —the difference between the contract price and the market or current price at the time or times when the goods ought to have been accepted, or, if no time was fixed for acceptance, then at the time of the refusal to accept. 46 Am J1st Sales § 616.

general demurrer. A demurrer directed to a matter of substance and attacking a pleading on the ground that the averments are insufficient in substance to state a cause of action or defense. 41 Am J1st Pl § 204.

In equity, where the practice is not controlled by rules of practice, a general demurrer challenges, in general terms, the right of the plaintiff to have any relief, or discovery and relief, on the facts stated in the bill. Its usual form is that of the general demurrer for want of equity on the face of the bill. Marsh v Marsh, 16 NJ Eq 391.

general denial. A pleading in modern practice which bears a close analogy to the general issue in common law pleading; a pleading, in response to what purports to be an affirmative allegation of a cause of action, which operates as a denial of every material allegation of such complaint or other pleading as fully as if it had been specifically and separately denied. 41 Am J1st Pl §§ 148, 149. A pleading by a defendant which goes to destroy the plaintiff's clause of action but presents no defense grounded on new matter or matter in avoidance. 41 Am J1st Pl § 149.

general deposit. A delivery of money or funds into the possession of a bank, whose property the deposit becomes, in return for which the depositor receives a credit of the amount represented by the deposit, against which credit the depositor may draw in the usual course of the bank's business. 10 Am J2d Banks § 360.

general deputy sheriff. An under sheriff,—a deputy sheriff who, by virtue of his appointment, has authority to execute all the ordinary duties of the office of sheriff. Allen v Smith, 12 NJL 159, 162.

general devise. A devise which does not refer to real estate by a specific designation or description of the property but instead is inclusive of perhaps several distinct properties, as where the devise is of "all" or the "remainder" of the testator's real property. 57 Am J1st Wills § 1404. In much less common usage, a devise without words of limitation, that is, without any words which limit the quantity of the estate devised. Doe, d. Hitch v Patten, 13 Del (8 Houst) 334, 16 A 558.

Generale dictum generaliter est interpretandum (je-ne-rā'le dik'tum je-ne-rā'li-ter est in-ter-pre-tan'-dum). A general statement should be interpreted generally.

general disability clause. A disability provision of a health or accident insurance policy, which provides for benefits for total disability preventing the insured from performing any work or following any occupation for compensation or profit, or which indicates in some other way that the insured's disability, in order to be total, is not limited merely to inability to perform the duties of his own particular occupation or profession. 29A Am J Rev ed Ins § 1516.

general educational institution. A common school; a public school. So defined by some authority as to be more mythical than real:—a school with kindergarten, primary, preparatory, and collegiate departments, with courses of instruction in all the elementary and advanced sciences, and ancient and modern languages, and with courses of instruction, in the advanced departments, usual in the colleges of the state. Parsons Business College v Kalamazoo, 166 Mich 305, 131 NW 553.

general election. An election recurring at stated intervals as fixed by law, without any superinducing cause other than the passage of time. 25 Am J2d Elect § 3. An election held for the purpose of selecting an officer to succeed to the office on the expiration of the full term of the incumbent. People ex rel. Elder v Quilici, 309 Ill App 466, 33 NE2d 492; Grant v Payne, 60 Nev 250, 107 P2d 307, 132 ALR 568.

general emancipation. The release of a child from custody and control by the parent upon the child's reaching the age of majority. A complete severance by the parent of the filial tie in releasing his minor child permanently from custody and control and authorizing the child to make its own contract of service and to collect and spend its wages and other earnings. 39 Am J1st P & C § 64.

Generale nihil certum implicat (je-ne-rā'le ni'hil ser'-tum im'pli-kat). A general expression implies nothing certain.

general estate. The entire estate both real and personal of a person, but particularly the entire property left by a decedent. In a more narrow sense, that part of the estate of a decedent, a bankrupt, a debtor in receivership, or an assignor under an assignment for the benefit of creditors, which is available for the payment of claims of general creditors. In a more technical sense, the residuary estate, the property of the decedent not specifically devised or bequeathed. 28 Am J Rev ed Inher T § 515.

Generale tantum valet in generalibus, quantum singulare in singulis (je-ne-rā'le tan'tum va'let in je-ne-rā'li-bus, quan'tum sin-gu-lā're in sin'gu-lis). That which is general prevails in general matters, as that which is particular prevails in particular matters.

general execution. The ordinary execution issued upon a judgment; a writ which directs the sheriff to levy upon property of the defendant which is not exempt in such amount as to satisfy the judgment, as distinguished from a special execution, as in a mortgage foreclosure, where the writ directs levy upon the property covered by the mortgage.

general executor. An executor who has been appointed to administer the whole of the estate of a decedent.

general exemption from taxation. An exemption applicable to all persons of a certain class or of all property of a certain kind; a prerogative of the legislature except as controlled by constitutional provision. Eyers Woolen Co. v Gilsum, 84 NH 1, 146 A 511, 64 ALR 1196.

general finding. A finding of fact by the trial court, in a trial to the court, in terms such as "all the issues of fact presented under the pleadings are determined in favor of the plaintiff," such finding usually being sufficient to support a judgment in the absence of a statute or rule of practice to the contrary, since it imports a finding of every subsidiary fact. 53 Am J1st Trial § 1141. A finding of the ultimate facts and all the special facts necessary to sustain the finding. 2 Am J2d Admin L § 456.

general franchises. The primary corporate franchise which grants special privileges to incorporators, enabling them to act for certain designated purposes as a single individual and usually exempts them from individual liability; and the secondary corporate franchise consisting in the powers granted to a corporation and specified in its charter. 18 Am J2d Corp § 66.

The right to be a corporation, or the corporate right of life, is inseparable from the corporation itself. It is a part of it, and cannot be sold or assigned. That franchise is general and dies with the corporation, for it cannot survive dissolution or repeal. Lord v Equitable Life Assur. Soc. 194 NY 212, 87 NE 443.

general freight agent. A carrier's agent authorized to make contracts for transportation, even for through transportation to a point beyond the line of the carrier. 14 Am J2d Car § 690.

general guaranty. A guaranty which is addressed to persons generally and may be acted upon and enforced by anyone to whom it is presented, the requisite meeting of minds occurring when advantage is taken of the general guaranty by the creation of a debt thereunder. Burckhardt v Bank of America Nat. Trust & Sav. Asso. 127 Colo 251, 256 P2d 234, 41 ALR2d 1207.

general guardian. A guardian of the person of the ward, or of all of the property of the ward situated within the jurisdiction of the court which appointed him, or of both the person and of such property. To be distinguished from a guardian ad litem or special guardian.

general heir. See **heir general.**

general hypothecation. The hypothecation by a debtor of all of his property for the benefit of his creditors.

Generalia praecedunt; specialia sequuntur (je-ne-rā'li-a prē-sē'dunt; spe-she-ā'li-a se-kwu-un'ter). General matters precede; special matters follow.

Generalia specialibus non derogant (je-ne-rā'li-a spe-she-ā'li-bus non dē'ro-gant). General terms do not control special ones. Burnett v Maloney, 97 Tenn 697, 37 SW 689.

Generalia sunt praeponenda singularibus (je-ne-rā'li-a sunt prē-pō-nen'da sin-gu-lā'ri-bus). General matters should be placed before particular matters.

Generalia verba sunt generaliter intelligenda (je-ne-rā'li-a ver'ba sunt je-ne-rā'li-ter in-tel-li-jen'da). General words are to be understood generally.

Generalibus specialia derogant (je-ne-rā'li-bus spe-she-ā'li-a dē'ro-gant). Special words derogate or take away from the meaning of general ones.

general income tax. An income tax, which taxes income from all sources, with certain definite exceptions. United States v Safety Car Heating & Lighting Co. 297 US 88, 80 L Ed 500, 56 S Ct 353, reh den 297 US 727, 80 L Ed 1010, 56 S Ct 495.

general indefinite failure of issue. See **indefinite failure of issue.**

general indorsement. An indorsement of a bill or note made without qualification. Uniform Negotiable Instruments L § 66; 11 Am J2d B & N § 359. An indorsement in which no indorsee is named. Santa Marina Co. v Canadian Bank of Commerce (CA9 Cal) 254 F 391.

general insanity. An expression sometimes used in distinguishing partial insanity and illusion from insanity generally. Reeves v State, 196 Ga 604, 27 SE2d 375. Madness on all subjects. National Life & Acci. Ins. Co. v Hannon, 214 Ala 663, 666, 108 So 575.

general instruction. An instruction by the court to the jury of such a nature that it is required, or at least proper, in all cases, for example, the charge that the jury shall consider only the evidence and the instructions given them by the court in arriving at a verdict. A charge to the jury in the form of an affirmative statement with a hypothesis, such being proper in some jurisdictions where there is no conflict in the evidence and where the facts testified to, if proved, entitle one party, plaintiff or defendant, to a verdict, the charge, in effect, stating that the jury shall find for such party if they believe the evidence or if they are satisfied that the facts are as testified. 53 Am J1st Trial § 550.

A general charge in a criminal case is an instruction that the jury shall find the defendant guilty if they believe the evidence produced by the state, or, more properly, if they are satisfied beyond a reasonable doubt that the facts are as testified; such a verdict is never proper unless the evidence justifies a conviction and any other verdict would be inconsistent with the evidence as a whole. 53 Am J1st Trial § 551.

general intent. See **general criminal intent.**

general interrogatories. Interrogatories contained or referred to in a bill in equity, constituting a definite part of such a bill under traditional equity practice. 27 Am J2d Equity § 181.

generalis clausula non porrigitur ad ea quae antea specialiter sunt comprehensa (je-ne-rā'lis klâ'zu-la non por-ri'ji-ter ad e'a kwē an'te-a spe-she-ā'li-ter sunt kom-pre-hen'sa). A general clause is not extended to include those things which have been previously specially included.

generalis regula generaliter est intelligenda (je-ne-rā'lis re-gū'la je-ne-rā'li-ter est in-tel-li-jen'da). A general rule should be generally understood.

general issue. A common law pleading, abolished as such in most states using a reformed system of pleading, consisting of a denial in short form of all that is material in the complaint or declaration. Somewhat analogous to the general denial of modern code and rules procedure. 41 Am J1st Pl § 140.
See **general denial.**

generality of custom. A requisite of a binding custom; the element of universality from which knowledge of the custom may well be presumed; in the case of a custom becoming a part of a contract, such general practice that it is a fair inference that both parties had knowledge of the custom and contracted with reference thereto. 21 Am J2d Cust & U § 5.

general judgment. A judgment in personam. Smith v Colloty, 69 NJL 365, 55 A 805.
See **judgment in personam.**

general jurisdiction. The jurisdiction of a trial court which is generally, although not absolutely, without limitation. 20 Am J2d Cts § 103.
See **court of general jurisdiction.**

general jurisdiction clause. A clause of a bill in equity consisting of an allegation in general terms to the effect that the acts complained of are contrary to equity and tend to the injury of the plaintiff, and that the plaintiff has no remedy, or no adequate remedy, without assistance from the court of equity.

The clause will not confer jurisdiction where the case otherwise made in the bill is not one of equitable cognizance. 27 Am J2d Equity § 181.

General Land Office. That agency of the government which was established to supervise the various proceedings whereby a conveyance of the title from the United States to portions of the public domain is obtained, and to see that the requirements of different acts of Congress are fully complied with. Steel v St. Louis Smelting & Refining Co. 106 US 447, 450, 27 L Ed 226, 228. An agency of the past, its functions having been transferred to the Bureau of Land Management in the Department of the Interior. 43 USC § 1, note.

general law. A statute having a uniform operation, that is a statute operating equally or alike upon all persons, entities, or subjects within the relations, conditions, and circumstances prescribed by the law, or affected by the conditions to be remedied. 50 Am J1st Stat § 6.
See **general public law.**

general legacy. A legacy designated primarily by quantity or amount, such as a gift of a stated amount of money, and which may be satisfied out of the general assets of the testator, without the necessity of delivering any particular chattel or fund to the legatee. Spinney v Eaton, 111 Me 1, 87 A 378; Re Goggin's Estate, 43 Misc 233, 88 NYS 557; Crabtree v Kelly, 65 ND 501, 260 NW 262.

general legislation. See **general law.**

general letter of credit. A letter of credit addressed to any and every person, and therefore giving to any person to whom it may be shown authority to make loans and advances upon it, the effect of the letter and the making of a loan or advance in response thereto being to bind as guarantor the person who issued the letter. 24 Am J1st Guar § 22.

general lien. The right to retain particular chattels as a security, not merely for the sum due in respect of those chattels, but for the entire amount owing on a general balance of account in respect of business done, but not in respect of loans or other transactions outside the regular course of trade. 33 Am J1st Liens § 5. The retaining lien of an attorney at law.
See **retaining lien.**

generally appear. Entering a general appearance or taking or agreeing to take some step or proceeding in the cause other than one to contest jurisdiction. 5 Am J2d Appear § 14.

general malice. Malice toward a group of persons rather than specifically toward one's victim in a homicide. 26 Am J1st Homi § 40. Wickedness; a disposition to do wrong; a black and diabolical heart, regardless of social duty and fatally bent on mischief. State v Long, 117 NC 791, 799, 23 SE 431.

general manager. A formal term for an executive in charge of a business; the status of a business officer under another title who is actually in the general management of the business. The person to whom the general business of a corporation is entrusted; the principal officer of a corporation, having general charge of the business matters for the carrying on of which the company was incorporated, and having the implied or ostensible authority for the performance of any act which is usual or necessary in the ordinary transaction of the company's business. 19 Am J2d Corp § 1174. One of the trustees of the business trust designated by the trustees to manage the operations of the trust, with power and authority to execute notes. Martin v Security Nat. Bank (Tex Civ App) 257 SW 645.

general notoriety. See **fact of general notoriety.**

general objection. An objection which does not point out the specific ground; an objection to evidence as incompetent, irrelevant, and immaterial, not coupled with any statement of the specific grounds or reasons why the evidence is not admissible. Hicks v Demer, 187 Ill 164, 58 NE 252.

general obligation bond. A bond issued by a public body as the obligation of the body payable from its general resources raised by taxation, as distinguished from a bond issued by such a body but payable from a special fund only. 43 Am J1st Publ Sec § 282.

general occupant. A person who took and retained possession of land, as anyone might do, after the death of a tenant for the life of another, and while the person for whose life the estate had been granted still lived. See 2 Bl Comm 258. He was also called "common occupant."

general orders. Standing orders of the court, issued, not in a particular suit or proceeding, but for application in any action or proceeding to which the substance is pertinent, the best illustration of which is found in the General Orders in Bankruptcy. 37 Am J1st Motions § 25.

General Orders in Bankruptcy. Orders formulated and prescribed by the Supreme Court of the United States for the purpose of carrying the Bankruptcy Act into force and effect. 9 Am J2d Bankr § 108.

general or retaining lien. See **retaining lien.**

general owner. One having unqualified dominion over a thing. Farmers' & Merchants' Nat. Bank v Logan, 74 NY 568, 581. The person in ultimate ownership, as distinguished from a person interested as a bailee, lessee, mortgagee, or lienor.
See **larceny by general.**

general ownership. See **general owner.**

general partner. A partner in an ordinary partnership, as distinguished from the special or limited partner in a limited partnership. 40 Am J1st Partn § 510. The member of a limited partnership who has rights and powers analogous to those possessed by the members of an ordinary general partnership. Uniform Limited Partnership Act § 9.

general partnership. The ordinary partnership, as distinguished from a limited partnership or partnership association.
See **partnership.**

general power of appointment. A power of appointment exercisable without limitation as to the person appointed, except as to the rule of some jurisdictions which limit exercise to exercise by will, in which event the donee cannot appoint himself, although he can appoint his estate. Lyon v Alexander, 304 Pa 288, 156 A 84, 76 ALR 1427. For the purpose of the federal estate tax:—a power which is exercisable in favor of the decedent, his creditors, or the creditors of his estate except certain powers limited by an ascertainable standard and certain powers exercisable by the decedent only in conjunction with another person. 26 USC § 2041(b)(1).

general power of attorney. See **power of attorney.**

general prayer. A prayer of a bill in equity whereby the plaintiff seeks generally such relief as he is entitled to under the allegations of the bill. Usually, a prayer, joined with a prayer for special relief, for such other and further relief as plaintiff may be entitled to in the premises. 27 Am J2d Equity § 182.

general proxy. A proxy for representation of a corporate stockholder at a corporate meeting which empowers the proxy to do all that the principal might do if present at the meeting. 19 Am J2d Corp § 673.

general publication. An expression familiar in the law of copyright and literary property; such a disclosure, communication, circulation, exhibition, or distribution of the subject matter of a literary work, tendered or given to one or more members of the general public, as implies dedication to the public. 18 Am J2d Copyr § 79.
See **newspaper of general circulation.**

general public law. That body of law under which due process of law is accorded; the law which is binding upon all members of the community under all circumstances, including no private or special acts affecting only the rights of certain individuals or certain classes of individuals especially favored. Eden v People, 161 Ill 296, 43 NE 1108.

general receivership. A receivership under which the receiver takes custody of all the property of a corporation or of an individual for some general purpose, such as the administration of such property for the benefit of creditors. 45 Am J1st Rec § 3.

general recognition. As a means of legitimation of a child born out of wedlock:—extensive recognition; not necessarily universal recognition. Van Horn v Van Horn, 107 Iowa 247, 77 NW 846; Record v Ellis, 97 Kan 754, 156 P 712.
See **general and notorious recognition.**

general relief. Relief sought by a bill, complaint, or petition in equity in terms of a prayer for such relief as is equitable in the premises. 27 Am J2d Equity § 182.

general replication. A pleading which raises an issue on affirmative matter pleaded in the answer by controverting it in general terms, such pleading being unnecessary under reformed practice in some jurisdictions, such practice dispensing with a replication by deeming affirmative matter in the answer denied as a matter of course. 41 Am J1st Pl § 175.

general reply. See **general replication.**

general reputation. The evidence to which proof of the good or bad character of a party to a civil action or the defendant in a criminal prosecution is confined. 29 Am J2d Ev §§ 339, 344-346.
The determining factor in measuring the worth and weight of evidence of a man's good character is whether the community in which he has lived his life is sufficiently large for the persons to become acquainted with his character and to form a general opinion of it. This we call general reputation. People v Colantone, 243 NY 134, 139, 152 NE 700.

general reputation in the family. Evidence of kinship, pedigree, births, deaths, and other matters of family history; tradition handed down by the declarations of deceased members of the family made ante lite motam. Re Estate of Hurlburt, 68 Vt 366, 35 A 77.

general repute. See **general reputation; general reputation in the family.**

general restraint of marriage. See **restraint of marriage.**

general restraint of trade. A restraint which constitutes a monopoly or unlawful restraint of trade. Not necessarily a complete monopoly. Any contract or combination to the end of a complete monopoly and to the deprivation of the public of the advantages which flow from free competition. 36 Am J1st Monop etc § 13.

A contract is said to be in general restraint of trade when it contains an agreement not to carry on a certain business or occupation anywhere. Kellogg v Larkin (Wis) 3 Pinney 123, 3 Chandler 133.

general retainer. The engaging of the professional services of an attorney at law by a client for a specified period of time, often a year, such services to be rendered only upon the request of the client, but the attorney being bound not to accept any retainer in opposition to the client for the period and accordingly entitled to be paid for the retainer in any event. Rhode Island Exchange Bank v Hawkins, 6 RI 198, 206.

See **retaining fee.**

general revival acts and rules. Statutes and rules of practice which make the common-law rule that all pending personal actions abate on the death of a sole plaintiff or defendant of historical interest only by setting up a procedure to prevent such an arbitrary cessation of an action, in cases where the cause of action survives, and providing for the substitution of the personal representative or other proper party and the continuation of the matter in his name. 1 Am J2d Abat & R § 47.

general sales tax. A tax applicable to goods or commodities in general. 47 Am J1st Sales T § 1.

general sessions. See **clerks of the general sessions of the peace; Court of General Sessions.**

general saving provision. A provision of constitution or statute intended to prevent the retrospective operation of the repeal of a statute by providing that the repeal of a statute shall not affect any right, liability, or penalty accrued or arising prior to the effective date of the repealing statute. 50 Am J1st Stat §§ 573, 574.

general ship. A vessel in which the master or the owners engage separately with a number of persons unconnected with each other, to convey their respective goods to the place of the vessel's destination.

While a general ship is abroad, the master has power to make contracts in relation to freight which will be binding upon the owners. Ward v Green (NY) 6 Cow 173.

general statute. See **general law.**

general strike. A strike against all the employers in an industry or a territory. 31 Am J Rev ed Lab § 369.

general superintendency. The scope of supervisory jurisdiction exercised by some appellate courts over the lower courts. 20 Am J2d Cts § 115.

general survival acts. Numerous statutes in the various states providing for survivorship of many causes of action that did not survive at common law, some of them providing in sweeping terms that all causes of action survive the death of either the person in whom the cause is vested or the person liable thereon, while others provide for general survival of personal tort actions, except for those matters that are secondary to the principal cause of action and are purely personal to the person injured. 1 Am J2d Abat & R § 52.

general tax. The customary annual tax imposed upon all taxable property within the taxing district to provide revenue for the usual and ordinary day-to-day expenses of the government, being imposed without reference to return by the government of special benefit to any property, only securing to the taxpayer the general benefit which results from protection to his person and property and the promotion of various enterprises and schemes which have for their object the welfare of all residents of the district. 51 Am J1st Tax § 27.

general tenancy. Such a tenancy as was not fixed and made certain in point of duration by the agreement of the parties. Brown's Admrs. v Bragg, 22 Ind 122, 123.

See **tenancy at will.**

general ticket. See **general ballot.**

general usage. See **general custom.**

general verdict. The final declaration by the jury as to the truth of the matter submitted to their determination and at issue between the parties. 53 Am J1st Trial § 1005. The response to and decision upon the issues between the parties upon the evidence adduced, rendered with such certainty and in such form that judgment can be entered thereon. Stafford v King, 30 Tex 257.

A general verdict for the plaintiff imports a finding of all issues in the plaintiff's favor and, in a case where the evidence was susceptible to different inferences, that the jury drew inferences favorable to the plaintiff. Railway Express Agency v Little (CA3 Pa) 50 F2d 59, 75 ALR 963.

general welfare. A generic term often employed in connection with protection of the peace, safety, health, and good morals of the people. Allinder v Homewood, 254 Ala 525, 49 So 2d 108, 22 ALR2d 763. The safety, prosperity, health and happiness of the people. 16 Am J2d Const L § 6.

See **public welfare.**

generation. Production, particularly electricity. Bringing into being, particularly by birth, as the increase of animals. 15 Am J2d Chat Mtg § 28.

One level in the succession of living beings. In this connection, the word has no technical meaning and hence it must be considered as used in the sense of succession, its ordinary import, rather than as meaning a degree of removal, in computing descents. McMillan v School Committee of Croatan Dist. 107 NC 609, 12 SE 330.

generator. Electrical term meaning a machine for converting mechanical into electrical energy by moving a coil in a magnetic field, so as to embrace a varying flux, thereby inducing an electromotive force.

generic. Applicable or referring to a kind, class, or group; inclusive.

generis (je'ne-ris). Kind.

See **ejusdem generis.**

generosi filius (je-ne-rō'sī fi'li-us). The son of a gentleman.

generosus (je-ne-rō'sus). A gentleman.

Geneva Award. See **Alabama Claims.**

Geneva Copyright Convention. See **Universal Copyright Convention.**

genitals. The reproductive or sex organs.

genito-urinary ailment. Affliction centering in the genitals or the urinary tract. Anno: 53 ALR2d 702.

gens (jenz). A Roman tribe composed of families of the same name, all of whom were descended from a common ancestor. In French, people, folk, men, servants, attendants.

gentes (jen'tēz). Plural of **gens.**

gentile (jen'til). One who is not a Jew. Among Mormons, one not a Morman.

gentiles (jen'tils or -tīls). Members of the same gens. See **gens.**

gentleman. In a former period, any man who ranked above a yeoman; a man who had the right to use a crest or coat-of-arms. In the modern sense, a courteous man, a well-behaved man.

gentlewoman. A woman of the same rank or status as that of a gentleman. In a more modern sense, a refined woman.

gents (jents). People; persons.

genuine. Real or original, as opposed to adulterated, false, fictitious, simulated, spurious, or counterfeit. Baldwin v Van Deusen, 37 NY 487, 492. Free of forgery or counterfeiting. UCC § 1–201(18).

genuineness of the instrument. The validity of an instrument in respect of it being what it purports to be. Warranted by an indorsement of a negotiable instrument. 11 Am J2d B & N § 611.

genus. A class embracing two or more species. Smythe v State, 17 Tex App 244, 251.
See **species.**

geodectic survey. See **coast and geodetic survey.**

geographical mile. See **mile.**

geology. The science and course of study which deals with the structure of the earth, particularly the crust.
See **aereal geology.**

George the First. The king of England from August 1st, 1714, to June 11th, 1727.

George the Second. The king of England from June 11th, 1727, to October 25th, 1760.

George the Third. The king of England from October 25th, 1760, to January 29th, 1820. To Americans, the despicable character who ruled England during the Revolution.

George the Fourth. The king of England from January 29th, 1820, to June 26th, 1830.

George the Fifth. King of the United Kingdom of Great Britain and Northern Ireland from May 7th, 1910 to Jan. 20th, 1936.

George the Sixth. King of the United Kingdom of Great Britain and Northern Ireland from Dec. 11th, 1936 to March 24th, 1953. Honored in England and respected in the United States as a courageous ruler during the perilous period of the Second World War.

gerefa (gĕ-rā'fah). A reeve; a shire-reeve; a sheriff.

gerens (je'renz). Bearing; carrying on; engaging in.

gerens datum (je'renz da'tum). Bearing date.

gerere (je're-re). To act; to behave; to carry on; to engage in.

gerere pro haerede (je're-re prō hē-rē'de). To act as heir.

germain. Same as **germane.**

german (jėr'mąn). Germane; fully related, as brothers of the same parents.

german cousin. A first cousin.

germane (jėr-mān'). Closely allied; relevant. Roark v People, 79 Colo 181, 244 P 909.

germane to the title. An essential of a statute; a statute, the subject matter of which is fairly and reasonably expressed, embraced, or indicated by the title. Roark v People, 79 Colo 181, 244 P 909.

germanus (ger-mā'nus). Of the same parents; of the same stock.

gerrymandering. A word derived from the name of Hon. Elbridge Gerry, a former governor of Massachusetts. So contriving in fixing the boundary lines of legislative districts as to give an unfair advantage to one political party. Anno: 2 ALR 1337; 25 Am J2d Elect § 18. An unfair method adopted by a political party in control of the legislature, whereby the boundaries of election districts are altered and arranged as to prevent a majority vote in such districts in favor of the opposing political party, which, under a fair and normal apportionment, would represent a majority vote in those districts. State ex rel. Morris v Wrightson, 56 NJL 126, 28 A 56. Fixing school attendance zones in such manner as to segregate the races in the schools. 15 Am J2d Civ R § 39.

gersome. Same as **gersume.**

gersume (gėr'som). A reward; a recompense; a fine imposed for an offense; an exaction from a tenant for permitting him to transfer his tenancy to another; a bonus paid for a rebate in rent on a lease.

gest (jest). (Saxon.) A guest; a stranger who stayed at a house a second night.

gesta (jes'ta). Plural of **gestum.**

gestation. The development of the foetus in the body of the mother from conception to birth.

gestation period. See **period of gestation.**

geste (jest). Same as **gest.**

gestio (jes'she-ō). An act; behavior; conduct; a performance; a transaction.

gestio pro haerede (jes'she-ō pro hē-rē'de). Behavior or conduct as an heir; such conduct as renders the heir liable for the debts of his ancestor.

gestor (jes'tor). (Civil law.) A person who transacts business for another; an agent.

gest-taker. Same as **agister.**

gestu et fama. See **de gestu et fama.**

gestum (jes'tum). (Roman law.) Something done; a deed; an act; a transaction; business.

gestura (jest-ur'a). Behavior.

gewitnessa (ge-wit'nes-sa). (Saxon.) Testifying as a witness.

gewrite. (Saxon.) Written instruments, such as deeds and charters.

gibbet (jib'et). An upright post with a projecting arm from which capital offenders were hanged.
See **double gibbet.**

gift. A voluntary transfer of property by one to another without any consideration or compensation therefor; anything given or bestowed, or any piece of property voluntarily transferred by one person to another. 24 Am J1st Gifts § 2. As the word is used in liquor legislation:—a transfer without price or reward; a gratuitous transfer without any equivalent. Parkinson v State, 14 Md 184.
See **sham gift; substitutional gift.**

gift causa mortis (gift kâ′za mor′tis). A gift of personal property made in expectation of the donor's death and upon condition that the property shall belong fully to the donee in case the donor dies as anticipated, leaving the donee surviving him, and the gift is not in the meantime revoked. 24 Am J1st Gifts § 4.

All gifts are necessarily inter vivos, for a living donor and donee are indispensable to a valid donation; but when the gift is prompted by the belief of the donor that his death is impending, and is made as a provision for the donee, if death ensues, it is distinguished from the ordinary gift inter vivos, and is called donatio causa mortis. But by whatever name called, the elements necessary to a complete gift are not changed. Walsh's Appeal, 122 Pa 177, 15 A 470.

gift enterprise. A scheme for the division or distribution of certain articles of property, to be determined by chance, among those who have taken shares in the scheme. A sporting artifice by which a merchant or tradesman sells his wares for their market value, but by way of inducement gives to each purchaser a ticket which entitles him to a chance to win certain prizes, to be determined after the manner of a lottery. 34 Am J1st Lot § 10.

gift exhibition. See **lottery**.

gift in contemplation of death. A gift impelled by the thought of death, as distinguished from a purpose associated with life. United States v Wells, 283 US 102, 75 L Ed 867, 51 S Ct 446.
See **in contemplation of death**.

gift of contemplation of marriage. A transaction which is something less than a real gift, since in such case the donor may recover back the property if the "donee" breaks the engagement to marry. Williamson v Johnson, 62 Vt 378.

gift inter vivos (gift in′ter vī′vōs). A real gift. A gift between living persons; a voluntary transfer of property by one living person to another living person, without any valuable consideration, which becomes absolute and irrevocable during the lifetime of the parties. 24 Am J1st Gifts § 4.

gift in trust. A gift which withholds the legal title from the donee.

Legal title may be transmitted to a third person, or it may be retained by the donor, but in either case the equitable title has gone from him, and unless the declaration of trust contains the power of revocation, or the wide discretion of chancery attaches, it leaves him powerless to extinguish the trust. Bath Sav. Institution v Hathorn, 88 Me 122, 33 A 836.

gift nominatim. A gift to individuals described by name. 57 Am J1st Wills § 1261.

gift note. A donor's promissory note payable to the donee. 24 Am J1st Gifts § 93.

gift of bastardy. The gift by the crown of the property of a bastard who died intestate and without heirs.

gift of public money. Any appropriation of public money for the benefit of one who has no claim to be compensated which is enforceable at law or in equity, irrespective of what the moral obligation may be under the circumstances. Conlin v San Francisco Board of Supervisors, 99 Cal 17, 33 P 753.

gift over. A limitation of an estate to follow the termination of a prior estate.

gift tax. An excise tax on the transfer by a living person of money or other property by gift. A tax imposed on the transfer of property by gift inter vivos without relation to the death of the donor, being distinguished from succession or estate taxes imposed on certain inter vivos transfers, such as gifts made in contemplation of death or intended to take effect in possession or enjoyment at or after death.

The tax is imposed on the transfer, not on the property transferred, since it applies even though the property transferred may be exempt from income or other taxes. IRC § 2501(a).

gift to a class. A gift of an aggregate sum to a body of persons uncertain in number at the time of the gift, to be ascertained at a future time, who are all to take in equal or some other definite proportions, the share of each being dependent for its amount upon the ultimate number. 57 Am J1st Wills § 1256.

gild. Verb: To apply a substance to metal or stone so as to give luster such as that of gold. Noun: A guild; an English mutual benefit society. A term sometimes used for "geld" in the sense of a sum of money, tribute, or tax. A surface or covering which makes a substance appear more valuable than it really is. In one sense, same as **guild**.
See **ceapgild; cenegild**.

gildable (gil′dạ-bl). Same as **geldable**.

gilda mercatoria (gil′da mer-ka-tō′ri-a). A mercantile company or corporation; a mercantile meeting or assembly. See 1 Bl Comm 473.

gildam mercatorium (gil′dam mer-ka-tō′ri-um). A grant by the king to a body of men establishing them as a mercantile corporation. See 1 Bl Comm 473.

gild hall (gild′hâl). The meeting place of a gild.

gildo (gil′do). A member of a gild.

gill net. A fish net so constructed that the fish is caught by its gills when it attempts to escape from the meshes of the net.

Such nets are regulated as to their use in some jurisdictions and forbidden in others. State v Lewis, 134 Ind 250, 33 NE 1024; Barker v State Fish Com. 88 Wash 73, 152 P 73.

gillravage. Same as **gilravage**.

gilour. A beguiler; a betrayer; a cheat; a deceiver.

gilravage (gil-rav′ạj). To ravage; to plunder; to pillage.

gilt-edged bonds. Securities reputed to be most safe for investment.

gin. An intoxicating alcoholic liquor. Skaggs v State (Okla Crim) 276 P2d 267, 49 ALR2d 760. A liquor distilled from grain and flavored with the juice of juniper berries. A machine used to remove the seed from the fiber of the cotton plant.

gin men. Laborers in a mine without special employment but performing tasks of a general nature as ordered and directed. Smith v North Jellico Coal Co. 131 Ky 196, 114 SW 785.

ginning. The process of separating the fiber of cotton from the seeds.

Girl Scouts. A world-wide organization for training girls in citizenship and leadership and promoting patriotism, which qualifies as having a charitable purpose. 15 Am J2d Char § 68.

girth (gėrth). A linear measure equivalent to a yard or thirty-six inches. The circumference of an object or of the waist of a person. A band placed around the body of a horse to hold a saddle or pack upon the back of the animal.

gisant (ji'zant). Resting; lying; reclining.

gisel (giz'el). A pledge.

gisement. Same as **agistment.**

giser. To lie; to rest; to recline.

gisetaker. Same as **agister.**

gist. The main point of a question or of a discussion. The pith of a matter. Hoffman v Knight, 127 Ala 149, 156, 28 So 593.
See **gravamen.**

gist of an action. The cause for which an action will lie; the ground or foundation of a suit, without which it would not be maintainable; the essential ground or object of a suit, and without which there is not a cause of action. First Nat. Bank v Burkett, 101 Ill 391, 394.

give. To make a gift; to convey; to transfer; to grant. A word of grant in a conveyance. 23 Am J2d Deeds § 35.

give and grant. Apt words in creating a covenant to stand seized. 28 Am J2d Est § 348. Words of conveyance sufficient in themselves in a deed to indicate the intent to effect an immediate transfer of title. Smith v Furbish, 68 NH 123, 44 A 398.
See **devise and grant; give, grant, sell, and convey.**

giveaway program. A radio or television program calling for the distribution of prizes to listeners, selected wholly or in part on the basis of chance, as an award for correctly solving a given problem or answering a question.
Such a program is not a lottery or gift enterprise. Federal Communications Com. v American Broadcasting Co. 347 US 284, 98 L Ed 699, 74 S Ct 593.

give, grant, bargain, etc. Words in a deed appropriate to indicate an intent to effect an immediate transfer of title. 23 Am J2d Deeds § 35.
See **give, grant, sell, and convey.**

give, grant, sell, and convey. Words in a deed appropriate to indicate an intent to effect an immediate transfer of title. 23 Am J2d Deeds § 35. Words of transfer or conveyance usually considered appropriate to convey an estate in fee. 28 Am J2d Est § 17. Not in themselves implying a covenant of warranty. 20 Am J2d Cov § 13.

given as collateral security with agreement. A means of referring in a bill of exchange or promissory note to an extrinsic contract, thereby depriving the bill or note of negotiability. Toledo Scale Co. v Gogo, 186 Mich 442, 152 NW 1046.

given for a patent right. A required recital in a promissory note, under statutes of some jurisdictions, where the consideration is a patent right. 11 Am J2d B & N § 189.

given for life insurance. A required recital in a promissory note, under the statutes of some jurisdictions, where the consideration is the initial premium for a policy of life insurance.

given name. See **Christian name.**

give precedence. To accord a priority. To recognize superior importance. Kansas City Terminal Railway Co. v Central Union Trust Co. 271 US 445, 455, 70 L Ed 1028, 1033, 46 S Ct 549.

giver. One who gives. The maker of a gift.

giving aid and comfort to enemy. As an element of the offense of treason:—overt acts committed which, in their natural consequence, if successful, would encourage and advance the interests of the enemy. Young v United States, 97 US 39, 24 L Ed 992.

glanders. A dangerous and highly contagious and infectious disease of horses and mules affecting the glands beneath the lower jaw. Pearson v Zehr, 138 Ill 48, 29 NE 854.

glare. See **blinding lights.**

gleaning. The gathering together of crops which have been reaped. Going over a harvested field and collecting grain not taken by the harvesters. Obtaining information in bits.

gleba (glē'bạ). Same as **glebe.**

glebae. See **adscriptus glebae.**

glebae ascriptitii (glē'bē a-skrip-ti'she-ī). Villeins in socage tenure who were regarded as fixtures while they performed services due.

glebe (glēb). A parcel of tillable land attached to a parish church. Pawlet v Clark (US) 9 Cranch 292, 326, 3 L Ed 735, 747.

glebe-land. Same as **glebe.**

glider. An aircraft without motive power. Anno: 54 ALR2d 413.

gloss. A translation; an explanation; an interpretation. Superficiality. Luster.

glossa (glos'ạ). Same as **gloss.**

glossary. An alphabetical list of terms taken from a book, appearing in the back of the volume, with explanations intended to be of assistance to the reader.

glossator (glo-sā'tor). A translator; a commentator; an annotator.

‘Glossa viperina est quae corrodit viscera textus (glos'sa vī-pe-rī'na est kwē kor-rō'dit vī'se-ra tex'- tus). It is a viperous gloss or interpretation which eats out the vitals of the text.

Gloucester. See **Statute of Gloucester.**

glove contest. A boxing match, a mere exhibition of skill in sparring with gloves, not calculated to do great bodily injury. See State v Olympic Club, 46 La Ann 935, 15 So 190.

glove-money (gluv'mun"ī). Money to buy gloves,— money given by the sheriff to certain officers of the court when there were no offenders left for execution.

glove-silver (gluv'sil"vėr). Same as **glove-money.**

glyn (glin). A glen; a ravine.

go. To move along, physically as in walking or running or figuratively as in the transmission or devolution of a title from one person to another.
See **shall go.**

goat. A cud-chewing domestic animal. 4 Am J2d Ani § 2. A slang expression for scapegoat.

gobernaciones (go-ber-nah-the-on'es). A Spanish term applied to the former provinces of Spain in the New World and the governments of such provinces. Footnote in Strother v Lucas (US) 12 Pet 410, 441, 9 L Ed 1137, 1149.

go-between. An intermediary. An agent who acts for both of the parties in a transaction.

God and my country. See **by God and my country.**

godbote (god'bōt). A fine imposed for an ecclesiastical offense.

go-devil. A crude conveyance consisting of two poles attached one to each side of a horse with the ends dragging behind, somewhat like a sled, on which goods are carried. Hamp v Pend Oreille County, 102 Wash 184, 172 P 869.

God's acre. A cemetery. A place for the burial and repose of the dead. Hertle v Riddell, 127 Ky 623, 106 SW 282.

God's penny. Earnest money paid to bind a bargain.

goggles. A disease of sheep, constituting a breach of warranty of soundness. 46 Am J1st Sales § 399. Large eyeglasses worn to protect the eyes against dust and small particles carried by the wind or blown in the air by industrial processes.

goging stole. Same as **cucking-stool.**

go hence acquitted. Formal words in a judgment of acquittal. State v Buchanan (Md) 5 Harr & J 317.

go hence without day. To leave the court without the necessity of returning; to be discharged or exonerated. Hiatt v Kinkaid, 40 Neb 178, 185, 58 NW 700.

go in evidence. To be considered as in evidence.
A stipulation that documents are "to go in evidence" means that the documents are to be considered in evidence; that is, as having been received and admitted as a part of the evidence before the court, and the expression does not mean that they may be read or offered and received as evidence. Protection Life Ins. Co. v Palmer, 81 Ill 88, 91.

going and coming rule. The rule which determines the right of an employee to workmen's compensation benefits for injuries sustained by him while going to or returning from work. 58 Am J1st Workm Comp § 217.

going business. See **going concern.**

going concern. A business in operation for the purpose for which it is organized, unhampered by insolvency or legal prohibitions.
A corporation is a going business or establishment when it is still in good faith prosecuting its line of business, with the prospect and expectation of continuing to do so, even though its assets are insufficient to discharge its liabilities in full. Corey v Wadsworth, 99 Ala 68, 11 So 350.

going-concern value. The amount by which the assets of a business as a whole, assembled for the conduct of the business, exceeds the aggregate of the value of the separate items of property in the business. Pacific State Sav. & Loan Co. v Hise, 25 Cal 2d 822, 155 P2d 809, 158 ALR 955. The aggregate value of items of property in a place of business, not as isolated articles separated from the whole, but as parts of the whole business and as useful in the business. Re Nathanson Bros. Co. (CA6 Ohio) 64 F2d 912. The value of the plant of an established business as distinguished from the plant of a concern whose business is not yet established. 43 Am J1st Pub Util § 139. A term in common use in the fixing of rates for the service of public utility companies, meaning the value of the plant as a whole upon which the company is entitled to a fair return, as distinguished from its bare physical value. Pioneer Tel. & Tel. Co. v State, 64 Okla 304, 167 P 995.
Used as a test of determining solvency or insolvency, the term may have two distinct meanings: it may denote (1) the value which could be realized by a sale of an enterprise as an operating unit as opposed to piecemeal liquidation; or (2) the value of the enterprise to its owners. Anno: 158 ALR 968.

going forward with the evidence. The burden of proof in the sense of the duty of producing evidence to meet the evidence produced or the prima facie case made by one's adversary. 29 Am J2d Ev § 124.

going, going, gone. The chant of an auctioneer, given immediately before the closing of the bidding. 7 Am J2d Auct § 31.

going to the country. Arriving at an issue of fact by the pleadings in an action preparatory to the submission of such an issue to the jury. The submission of a case to a jury.

going value. Same as **going concern value.**

going witness. A person whose testimony is sought in an action and who is about to depart from the jurisdiction of the court.

gold. A mineral. 36 Am J1st Min & M § 5. A precious metal so highly regarded as to have served for a period reaching into the remote past as a medium of exchange and the substance of coinage.
The act of Congress of 1792 established a mint for the purpose of a national coinage. It was the result of very careful and thorough investigation of the whole subject, in which Jefferson and Hamilton took the greatest parts. It provided that the gold of coinage should consist of eleven parts fine and one part alloy, which alloy was to be of silver and copper in convenient proportions, not exceeding one half silver; and that the silver of coinage should consist of fourteen hundred and eighty-five parts fine, and one hundred and seventy-nine parts of an alloy wholly of copper. Bronson v Rodes (US) 7 Wall 229, 247, 19 L Ed 141, 145.
The coinage of gold has been discontinued and gold coins withdrawn from circulation. 36 Am J1st Money § 16.
See **bullion; queen-gold.**

gold certificates. A form of currency circulating in the United States prior to the withdrawal thereof from circulation by act of Congress in 1933, such certificates being backed by, and redeemable in, gold. 36 Am J1st Money § 16.

gold clause. The provision of a contract, bond, or mortgage requiring payment in gold, all such clauses having been nullified by an Act of Congress in 1933. Norman v Baltimore & Ohio R. Co. 294 US 240, 79 L Ed 885, 55 S Ct 407, 95 ALR 1352.

gold coinage. See **gold.**

golden rule. A guide for jurors in their deliberations, sometimes suggested in arguments of counsel, that the jurors place themselves in the position of a litigant. Norton Bros. v Nadebok, 92 Ill App 541, affd 190 Ill 695, 60 NE2d 843. An erroneous principle that in assessing damages the jurors should put themselves in the injured person's place and render such a verdict as they would wish to receive were they in his position. 22 Am J2d Damg §§ 342, 346.

gold or its equivalent. A clause which purports to establish the medium of payment of an obligation, meaning payment in gold or any kind of money which is legal tender. 40 Am J1st Paym § 58.

gold reserve. The gold of the United States set aside as a backing for the currency.

gold scales. See **weigh with gold scales.**

goldsmiths' notes. Notes issued by English banks or bankers, called goldsmiths' notes because all of the bankers were at one time goldsmiths.

gold standard. A monetary system in which the basic unit of currency is redeemable in a specified quantity of gold, the United States having withdrawn from such standard in 1933 by legislation calling in all gold coin from circulation. 36 Am J1st Money § 16.

Gold Star Mothers. A membership corporation composed of numerous chapters throughout the United States, organized for patriotic and charitable purposes, every member being a mother of one killed in the service of his country in the armed forces in wartime. American Gold Star Mothers, Inc. v National Gold Star Mothers, Inc. 89 App DC 269, 191 F2d 488, 27 ALR2d 948.

golf course. An area for the playing of the game of golf, consisting of either 9 or 18 holes, each of which is surrounded by a putting green of close cropped grass; fairways, such being open spaces between the greens, kept mowed fairly short; and spaces adjacent to the fairways known as "the rough" wherein the grass is usually long and the surface somewhat rough.

gong. A bell used as a warning, particularly at railroad crossings.

gonorrhea. A venereal disease, not so serious as syphilis. 29 Am J Rev ed Ins § 745.
See **gram stain test.**

good. Beneficial rather than harmful; effective rather than ineffective; genuine rather than forged or counterfeited. As applied to commercial paper, genuine rather than certain of collection. Commonwealth v Stone, 45 Mass (4 Met) 43, 48. As applied to articles offered for sale, of a merchantable quality. Northern Supply Co. v Wangard, 123 Wis 1, 100 NW 1066.

As used in a representation by a restaurant owner that he would serve a customer a "good" sandwich, the term signifies no more than agreeable to the taste, and is too indefinite to be the basis of an express warranty of the quality of the food. Albrecht v Rubinstein, 135 Conn 243, 63 A2d 158, 7 ALR2d 1022.
See **certified check.**

good abearing (a-bãr'ing). Good behavior, lawful conduct. See 4 Bl Comm 256.

good accounts. Accounts of a merchant which are worth their face value, and which are collectable in the ordinary course of business and by usual business methods, resort to suit or execution not being necessary. Stillman v Lynch, 56 Utah 540, 192 P 272, 12 ALR 552, 559.

good and indefeasible title. A title which enables the owner to exercise absolute and exclusive control as against all others. Adams v Henderson, 168 US 573, 42 L Ed 584, 18 S Ct 179.

good and lawful men. As the expression appears in the caption of an indictment:—freeholders. 27 Am J1st Indict § 36. As applied to the members of a grand jury:—including every statutory, as well as every common-law, qualification required of them. Jerry v State (Ind) 1 Blackf 395, 396.

good and sufficient deed. A condition to be performed by the vendor in a land contract by the delivery of a deed sufficient in form and conveying a good and sufficient title in compliance with the terms of the contract. 55 Am J1st V & P § 162.

good behavior. Conduct of a prisoner warranting a deduction in time to be served. 41 Am J1st Pris & P §§ 41 et seq. The condition of a bond given as security to keep the peace. 12 Am J2d Breach P § 44. For the purpose of an order suspending sentence during good behavior:—no higher standard than conduct conformable to law. Ex parte Hamm, 24 NM 33, 172 P 190. In reference to the removal of the incumbent of a public office for breach of "good behavior":—behavior from the standpoint of official action, without regard to conduct outside the office, however immoral it may be. Commonwealth v Williams, 79 Ky 42.

good cause. Substantial reason, a legal excuse. Pines v District Court in Woodbury County, 233 Iowa 1284, 10 NW2d 574. Legal cause, in reference to the right of the state to dissolve a corporation and recall the franchise granted to it. Wheeler v Pullman Iron & Steel Co. 143 Ill 197, 820, 32 NE 420. As a ground for the revocation of a certificate of convenience and necessity, the failure to comply with a condition precedent to the issuance of the certificate. Midwestern Motor Transit, Inc. v Public Utilities Com. 126 Ohio St 317, 185 NE 194. As ground for a continuance, something which deprives the applicant of a fair trial if forced to proceed at the appointed time. Ex Parte Venable, 86 Cal App 585, 261 P 731; People v O'Connor, 88 Cal App 568, 263 P 866; People v Clayton, 89 Cal App 405, 264 P 1105. As an excuse for failure to file a claim for workmen's compensation within the period provided by statute:—a mistake on the part of claimant or other reasonable cause. 58 Am J1st Workm Comp § 414. A vague and unintelligible term, as it appears in a clause of a contract providing for termination of the contract by either party for "good cause." Cummer v Butts, 40 Mich 322.

As used in unemployment compensation statutes that an employee shall be ineligible for compensation if he has voluntarily left work without "good cause", it has been held that removal from the area of employment because of marital obligation is such cause as to entitle the claimant to the statutory benefits. Such holdings have, however, been criticized as opening the door to fraud. Anno: 13 ALR2d 875, 876.

good character. See **good moral character.**

good commercial title. Such a title as an attorney for a purchaser should advise his client to accept. Ward v James, 83 Or 695, 164 P 370.

good condition. A relative term; an expression to be construed according to the context in which it appears.

As used in a lessee's covenant to keep and yield up the leased premises in good condition, the words do not have a fixed or technical meaning which is always the same regardless of the character and use of the building to which they refer. A building adapted for use as a tannery might be in good condition for that purpose and absolutely untenantable as a watch factory. Codman v Hygrade Food Products Corp. 295 Mass 195, 3 NE2d 759, 106 ALR 1354.

good condition and repair. As a phrase stating the obligation of a tenant in reference to the state of the premises upon his surrender thereof:—a reasonable state of repair, allowing for the age and condition of the premises at the inception of the tenancy. 32 Am J1st L & T §§ 803 et seq.

GOOD [528] GOOD

good conduct. See **good behavior**.

good consideration. A consideration founded either on love and affection toward one to whom a natural duty exists, such as a near relative by either consanguinity or affinity, or on a strong moral obligation supported either by some antecedent legal obligation, although unenforceable at the time, or by some present equitable duty. 23 Am J2d Deeds § 64. The consideration, sometimes called a meritorious consideration, of blood, of natural love and affection, or of love and affection based on kindred by blood or marriage. Williston on Contracts (3d ed) § 110.

good custom. See **custom**.

good faith. Fairness and equity. The antithesis of fraud and deceit. Acting in the absence of circumstances placing a man of ordinary prudence on inquiry. Pennington County Bank v First State Bank, 110 Minn 263, 125 NW 119 (accepting a forged check.) Acting with a sincere belief that the accomplishment intended is not unlawful or harmful to another. Smith v State, 214 Ind 169, 13 NE2d 562 (a physician prescribing a narcotic drug.) Acting in the belief that a prudent and sensible man would hold in the ordinary conduct of his own business affairs. Kelly v Fourth of July Mining Co. 21 Mont 291, 53 P 959 (issuance of stock.) Absence of improper motive and of a negligent disregard of the rights of others. Allen v Pioneer Press Co. 40 Minn 117, 41 NW 936 (rebutting malice in utterance or publication alleged to be defamatory.) Acting without culpable negligence or a wilful disregard of the rights of others and in the honest and reasonable belief that the act is rightful. Anno: 21 ALR2d 393 (a trespasser upon land taking property therefrom.)

good faith declarant. An alien who may, and who intends to, become a citizen of the United States, and who in good faith has made the declaration required by the naturalization laws.

good faith holder. See **holder in due course**.

good faith in adverse possession. For practical purposes in most jurisdictions, actual, open, notorious, exclusive and hostile possession; in other jurisdictions, by force of statute, occupancy under a bona fide belief in one's title as a valid title. 3 Am J2d Adv P § 98.

good faith in collective bargaining. An honest and sincere intent and purpose to explore all possibilities of settlement of the matters in dispute, until the exhaustion of all reasonable efforts and the arrival at a point where a definite decision is reached, presupposing freedom from any fixed purpose to employ the machinery of negotiation as a cloak for other designs, or to disregard either the objects or methods of negotiation prescribed by the statute. 31 Am J Rev ed Lab § 268.

good faith in filing petition for reorganization. Something more than honesty of purpose and good intention; a filing with reasonable belief that reorganization is attainable. 9 Am J2d Bankr § 1527.

good faith in possession. See **possession in good faith**.

good faith of occupant making improvement. A reasonable and honest belief of the occupant in his right or title, such state of mind not being negatived by any showing that diligence would have revealed the absence of any title held by him. 27 Am J1st Improv § 14.

good faith operation. See **bona fide operation**.

good faith purchaser. See **bona fide purchaser**.

good faith residence. See **bona fide residence**.

good firms. See **terms good firms**.

good for this day only. A provision in a passenger's ticket, usually held ineffective to preclude a stopover privilege as against a ticket agent's representation of the existence of such privilege. 14 Am J2d Car § 840.

Good Friday. A day observed in remembrance of the crucifixion of Christ; a legal holiday in some states. 50 Am J1st Sun & H § 77.

good health. Sound health; the absence of any grave, important, or serious disease, or ailment seriously affecting the general soundness or healthfulness of the system. 29 Am J Rev ed Ins § 746.

good moral character. A quality which varies according to the particular circumstances, and from one generation to another; conduct which comports with a good character; a character which measures up as good among the people of the community, that is, up to the standard of the average citizen. Anno: 22 ALR2d 250, § 3. Character evidenced by conduct which conforms to the generally accepted moral conventions current at the time. Anno: 22 ALR2d 250, § 3.

An habitual violator of the law, "especially the laws regulating the conduct of the liquor traffic," is not a person of good moral character, no matter how honest he may be in business or clean in his private life. Whissen v Furth, 73 Ark 366, 84 SW 500.

Even a single lapse from marital fidelity by an applicant for naturalization is not, in the absence of extenuating circumstances, consistent with the requirement of five years of unbroken "good moral character," and the burden of proof of the extenuating circumstance rests upon the applicant. Johnson v United States (CA2 NY) 186 F2d 588, 22 ALR2d 240.

good mortgage. A mortgage which is legal and constitutes sufficient security for the obligation. DuFlon v Powers (NY) 14 Abb Pr NS 391.

good note. A collectible note. Hammond v Chamberlin, 26 Vt 406, 413.

good order. A term often used in describing goods in a contract of sale which is somewhat flexible in meaning and varies according to the understanding of the particular trade or business, but not necessarily requiring absolute soundness or perfection. 46 Am J1st Sales § 150.

As applied to streets, the term is not synonymous with "good repair." A portion of a street might be in good repair as a dirt road, or as cobblestone pavement, and yet might be in bad order, plight, or condition to bear the increased burdens and accommodate the travel of a modern city. Danville v Danville Railway & Electric Co. 114 Va 382, 76 SE 913.

The term as it appears in a naturalization statute which provides that no person shall be naturalized unless he is well disposed to the "good order" of the United States, is a term of vague content, which of necessity must be construed with the purpose of the statute in mind, that is to admit to citizenship only persons who are in accord generally with the basic principles of the community. 3 Am J2d Aliens § 138.

good order and condition. A recital in a bill of lading respecting the condition of the subject of the bill. 13 Am J2d Car § 285.

Good Parliament. The reform parliament of 1376 in England.

good potatoes. Merchantable potatoes. Northern Supply Co. v Wangard, 123 Wis 1, 100 NW 1066.

good repair. Reasonable or proper repair. 32 Am J1st L & T § 789 (condition in lease respecting obligation of tenant.)
See **good order**; **habitable repair**.

good repute. Good reputation. State v Wheeler, 108 Mo 658, 665, 18 SW 924. Good character. Commonwealth v Davis, 3 Pa Dist 271 (pertaining to prosecutrix in prosecution for rape.)

good right to convey. See **covenant of good right to convey**.

goods. A term of variable meaning, sometimes having the significance of personal property. Tisdale v Harris, 37 Mass (20 Pick) 9. Sometimes inclusive of corporate stock. Spencer v McGuffin, 190 Ind 308, 130 NE 407, 14 ALR 385.
In other connections, limited to merchandise kept for sale. McPartin v Clarkson, 240 Mich 390, 215 NW 338, 54 ALR 1535. Sometimes having reference to chattels or merchandise in storage or about to be placed in storage. 56 Am J1st Wareh § 3 (Uniform Warehouse Receipts Act.) Constituting articles, wares, or merchandise for the purpose of a revenue law imposing customs duties. 21 Am J2d Cust D § 1.
See **confusion of goods**; **dry goods**; **fungible goods**; **green goods**; **lawful goods**; **mislaid goods**; **shipwrecked goods**; **worldly goods**.

goods administered. Goods, chattels, or credits of the decedent which have been changed, altered, or converted by the executor or administrator before the appointment of an administrator de bonis non. Chamberlin's Appeal, 70 Conn 363, 39 A 734.

good safety. See **in good safety**; **mooring in good safety**.

goods and chattels. Subjects of personal property which are perceptible to the senses and deliverable in specie. 42 Am J1st Prop § 24. Sometimes exclusive of commercial paper and money. 57 Am J1st Wills § 1343.

goods and effects. In common parlance, chattels or movables, but in some connections including real as well as personal property. 52 Am J1st Treat § 41; 57 Am J1st Wills § 1343.

goods and merchandise. Usually having reference to goods kept for sale or purchased with the intent of placing them in a stock of merchandise.

goods and movables. See **goods**.

goods bargained and sold. The subject of an action; an action of general assumpsit. 1 Am J2d Actions § 15.

goods, effects, and credits. A very comprehensive term, covering tangibles and intangibles, but not inclusive of a claim for unliquidated damages not in judgment. Wilde v Mahaney, 183 Mass 455, 67 NE 337.

goods not administered. Goods, chattels, and credits which had been the property of the decedent and remained in specie, unchanged and unconverted, when an administrator de bonis non was appointed. Chamberlin's Appeal, 70 Conn 363, 39 A 734.

goods of another. For the purpose of a definition of larceny:—property owned by another or in the possession of another so as to be presumptively his property. People v Davis, 97 Cal 194, 31 P 1109.

goods sold and delivered. The subject of an action; an action of general assumpsit. 1 Am J2d Actions § 15.

good standing. The status of a member of a fraternal order or mutual benefit association or society whose dues and obligations to the order or society have been paid or are not delinquent and whose conduct has not been such as to bring him in bad repute as a member and to subject him to expulsion or suspension. Overton v Woodmen of the World, 206 Ala 584, 91 So 485, 23 ALR 337, 340.

goods to arrive. A term in a contract for the sale of personal property which ordinarily renders the obligation of the seller to perform the contract by an actual transfer of the property contingent upon the arrival of the goods. 46 Am J1st Sales § 201.

goods, wares, and merchandise. Goods or things which are kept for sale and which are constantly sold or replaced by other merchandise. 37 Am J2d Frd Conv § 252. Imported articles within the meaning of the revenue laws imposing customs duties. 21 Am J2d Cust & D § 1.

good time. That length of time, fixed by statute, by which the prison term of a convict is shortened by reason of his good behavior while in prison. Re Canfield, 98 Mich 644, 645, 57 NW 808.

good title. A valid title and a marketable title. 55 Am J1st V & P § 166. Not merely a title which is valid in fact, but a marketable title which can again be sold to a reasonable purchaser, or mortagaged to a person of reasonable prudence as security for the loan of money. Moore v Williams, 115 NY 586, 22 NE 233. A title free from litigation, palpable defects, and grave doubts, and fairly deducible of record. Reynolds v Borel, 86 Cal 538, 25 P 67.

good watch. See **constant watch**.

good will. The expectation of continued public patronage. Stott v Johnston, 36 Cal 2d 864, 229 P2d 348, 28 ALR2d 580. The probability that old customers will resort to the old place. Every positive advantage acquired, arising out of the business of the old firm, whether connected with the premises where it was carried on, with the name of the old firm, or with any other matter carrying with it the benefit of the business of the old firm. The advantage or benefit which is acquired by an establishment beyond the mere value of the capital stock, funds, or property employed therein, in consequence of the general public patronage and encouragement which it receives from constant or habitual customers on account of its local position, or common celebrity, or reputation for skill, or affluence, or punctuality, or from other accidental circumstances or necessities, or even from ancient partialities or prejudices. 24 Am J1st Good W § 2. A species of property of an intangible nature so connected with a going concern or business as to be disposable only in connection with a disposition of such concern or business. 24 Am J1st Good W § 4.

go quit (gō kwit). To be dismissed by the court's order; to be exonerated.

gorge. A defile between hills or mountains; that is, a narrow throat or outlet. Gibbs v Williams, 25 Kan 214, 217. A natural drainway of surface water in a hilly or mountainous area. Anno: 81 ALR 271.

goring. A specific kind of India rubber fabric. Robertson v Salomon, 144 US 603, 36 L Ed 560, 12 S Ct 752.

goshawk (gos'hâk). A hawk used by falconers in hunting; the modern chicken hawk.

gossip. Veritable hearsay, inadmissible in any court. Re Mantell, 157 Neb 900, 62 NW2d 308, 43 ALR2d 1122.

gote (gōt). A gutter; a drain.

go to protest. A negotiable instrument being protested for nonacceptance or nonpayment.
See **protest**.

gouge. Noun: A blade for making groves or holes. Verb: To make a hole or a groove with a gouge. Also, to cheat in a bold or brutal manner; to overreach in a bargain; to deceive and defraud; to impose upon; to trick; to mislead. Shubert v Variety, Inc. 128 Misc 428, 429, 219 NYS 233.

govern. To direct and control; to regulate; to influence; to restrain; to manage. State v Ream, 16 Neb 681, 683.

governing law. See **conflict of laws**.

government. Management; administration; control; power or authority to check or restrain. See St. Louis v Howard, 119 Mo 41, 24 SW 770.
The ligament that holds the political society together; the public political authority which guides and directs the body politic, or society of men called the "state," united together to promote their safety and advantage by means of their union. Thomas v Taylor, 42 Miss 651. The political agency through which the state acts. Texas v White (US) 7 Wall 700, 19 L Ed 227. A term usually applied to the government of the Unites States, but equally applicable to the government of any of the states.

governmental act. An act done in pursuance of some duty imposed by the state on a person, individual or corporate, which duty is one pertaining to the administration of government, and is imposed as an absolute obligation on a person who receives no profit or advantage peculiar to himself from its execution. Markwardt v Guthrie, 18 Okla 32, 90 P 26. More broadly, an act of the government.
See **governmental functions**.

governmental agencies. See **administrative agencies**.

governmental duties. See **governmental functions**.

governmental functions. The performance of duties imposed upon a municipal corporation by the state as a part of the sovereignty of the state to be exercised by the municipality for the benefit of the whole public living both within and without the corporate limits. Pass Christian v Fernandez, 100 Miss 76, 56 So 329. The functions of a municipal corporation which are to be exercised, not only in the interest of the inhabitants, but also in advancing the public good or welfare as affecting the public generally, including the promotion of public peace, health, safety, and morals. 37 Am J1st Mun Corp § 114. Acts performed by a municipality for the common good of all, not for the special benefit or profit of the corporate entity. 38 Am J1st Mun Corp § 574.

governmental immunity. See **immunity**.

governmental lien. A lien to repayment of public money expended for the benefit of individuals engaged in agriculture. 3 Am J2d Agri § 15.
See **tax lien**.

governmental power. The power exercised by the government as a sovereign, being distinguished from power exercised by the government in a proprietary or business capacity. Omaha Water Co. v Omaha, 147 F 1.
See **governmental functions**.

governmental purposes. Imposing punishment for crime, prevention of wrong, the enforcement of a private right, or in some manner preventing wrong from being inflicted upon the public, or upon an individual, or redressing some grievance, or in some way enforcing a legal right, or redressing or preventing a public or individual injury. Owensboro v Commonwealth ex rel. Stone, 105 Ky 344, 49 SW 320.
See **governmental functions; municipal purpose**.

governmental subdivision. A public body, such as a county, town, township, city, village, or other municipal corporation, even a public corporation such as an irrigation district, created and vested with powers by the state. Platt Valley P. P. & I. Dist. v Lincoln County, 144 Neb 584, 14 NW2d 202, 155 ALR 412.

governmental survey. The survey of the public domain, sometimes known as the Congressional Survey, by which the land is laid out in townships, sections, quarter sections, and quarters of quarter sections, the section being one mile square and containing 640 acres.

government bond. A United States bond. A contract which imports a loan of money by an individual to the government at a stipulated rate of interest, payable at a designated time and place. New York Life Ins. & Trust Co. v Baker, 165 NY 484, 59 NE 257.

government contracts. Contracts with the United States; public contracts.

government corporation. A corporation created by statute through which a function or functions of the government are exercised. Federal Housing Administration v Burr, 309 US 242, 84 L Ed 724, 60 S Ct 488.
See **Home Owners' Loan Corporation; public corporation**.

government de facto. See **de facto government**.

government grant. A deed of public lands by the federal or state government.

government lands. See **public lands**.

government of paramount force. A de facto government. 30 Am J1st Internat L § 12.

government survey. See **governmental survey**.

government traffic. Vehicular traffic of the army and navy and of governmental agencies. Golden Gate & Highway District v United States (CA9 Cal) 125 F2d 872 (involving free use of Golden Gate bridge at San Francisco, Cal.)

governor. The chief executive of a state in the restricted or local meaning of the word "state"—that is, one of the United States. Texas v White (US) 7 Wall 700, 19 L Ed 227, ovrld on other grounds Morgan v United States 113 US 476, 28 L Ed 1044, 5 S Ct 588. The chief executive officer of a state or territory of the United States. Whitsett v Forehand, 79 NC 230, 233.

governors of the Federal Reserve System, see **Reserve Board**.

go without day. To go out of the court without any

day appointed for returning; hence, to be dismissed by order of the court.
See **go hence without day**.

grab. A seizure or acquisition by violent or unscrupulous means. Smith v Pure Oil Co. 278 Ky 430, 128 SW2d 931.

grab irons. Handholds on railroad cars, required by law for the safety of employees. 45 USC §§ 4, 11.

grace. Indulgence, favor, mercy, and clemency.
See **act of grace; days of grace**.

grace period. See **days of grace**.

gracias. (Spanish.) Thanks. Thank you.
See **gratia**.

gradatim (grā-dā'tim). Step by step; by degrees; gradually.

grade. Noun: An inclination, as in a highway. The lay of the land in reference to the elevation of adjoining lands. The amount of difference between the "grade line" and a level or horizontal line. Davies v East Saginaw, 66 Mich 37, 39. A degree or rank, in order or dignity. People v Rawson (NY) 61 Barb 619, 631. The rank of a class in school. The rank of a thing or product in order of merit or excellence, as grade A eggs. Verb: To bring the surface of a street to the grade line, whether by excavation or fill. Davies v East Saginaw, 66 Mich 37. To determine an order of excellence or merit, for example, rating the quality of grain in a granary. To classify positions in the civil service. 15 Am J2d Civ S § 16.

grade crossing. The intersection formed by a railroad and a highway at a common grade. Cowles v New York, New Haven & Hartford Railroad Co. 80 Conn 48, 66 A 1020.

grade crossing elimination. The elimination of a grade crossing by relocation of the railroad line or the highway or by the construction of an underpass or overpass. 44 Am J1st RR §§ 300 et seq.

graded income tax. See **progressive tax**.

graded probate fee. See **progressive tax**.

graded tax. See **graded income tax; progressive tax**.

grade line. The line which determines the grade of a highway or street where such highway or street is constructed otherwise than as a level or horizontal way.
The grade of a street is the amount of difference between the "grade line" and a level or horizontal line. To grade a street means to bring the surface of the street to the grade line. The term includes excavation and filling, so as to make the surface conform to the grade line. See Davies v East Saginaw, 66 Mich 37, 39.

grade of street. See **street grade; grade line**.

grader. See **road grader**.

grade school. See **elementary school**.

grades of crime. Classification according to felony, misdemeanor, or a mere offense or violation. Classification according to the measure of punishment meted out on conviction and the consequences to the person convicted, the severity of the punishment varying according to the heinousness of the crime and the injury inflicted thereby upon society. People ex rel. Stezer v Rawson (NY) 61 Barb 619, 631.

grading. See **grade; street grade**.

gradual decrease. Not necessarily an equal or uniform reduction per year. Moss v Aetna L. Ins. Co. (CA6 Tenn) 73 F2d 339.
The term, appearing in a clause of a life insurance policy relative to surrender charges, does not require equal or uniform reductions, particularly not, if the policy shows the net sums available at the close of each year of the policy. Anno: 111 ALR 974.

graduate. Noun: A person who has honorably passed through that prescribed course of study and received a certificate or diploma to that effect. Sweitzer v Fisher, 172 Iowa 266, 154 NW 465. Of a college:—one who has received a degree upon the completion of a prescribed course or curriculum. People ex rel. Johnson v Eichelroth, 78 Cal 141, 20 P 364; People ex rel. Johnson v Eichelroth, 78 Cal 141, 20 P 364. Verb: To receive a degree, diploma, or certificate, upon the completion of a prescribed course of study in a school, college, or university.

graduated license fee. A fee varying according to the weight, power, or value, of the instrumentality licensed, especially a motor vehicle. 7 Am J2d Auto § 63.

graduated tax. A term sometimes applied to a progressive tax. Precisely, an inheritance or succession tax under rates which change according to the degree of relationship between the decedent and the heir or successor. State ex rel. Foot v Bazille, 97 Minn 11, 106 NW 93.
See **progressive tax**.

graduate nurse. A person who has graduated from an accredited training school for nurses. Moore v Fidelity & C. Co. 203 Cal 465, 265 P 207, 56 ALR 860.

graduate work. Postgraduate study, usually for a higher degree in a college or university.

graduation. The act of graduating from a school, college, or university. The satisfactory completion of the courses of study required for a degree or diploma, as determined by the faculty. 15 Am J2d Colleges § 28. A successive raising or lowering of a figure in proportion to some external control, for example, changes in freight rates corresponding to differences in value of the goods shipped. 13 Am J2d Car § 107.

gradus (grā'dus). A step; a grade; a degree; a status; a degree of relationship.

gradus parentelae (grā'dus pa-ren-te'le). A genealogy; a family tree.

graf (gräf). A magistrate; a chief.

graffarius (graf-fā'ri-us). Same as **graffer**.

graffer (graf'er). A notary; a scrivener; a copyist.

graft. Gain by taking advantage of one's position, particularly a position in public office. A dishonest transaction in relation to public or official acts. Quinn v Review Publishing Co. 55 Wash 69, 104 P 181. The fraudulent obtaining of public money unlawfully by the corruption of public officers. 33 Am J1st Lib & Sl § 27.

grafter. One who grafts; a swindler or dishonest person. One who takes or makes graft, or dishonest private gain, especially in positions of trust, and in ways peculiarly corrupt. State v Sheridan, 14 Idaho 222, 93 P 656.

grain. Wheat, corn, oats, barley, rye, flax, and sorghum. Trusler v Crooks, 269 US 475, 479, 70 L Ed 365, 366, 46 S Ct 165. (Federal Futures Trading Act.) More broadly, the seed of any cereal plant.

grainage (grā'nāj). A duty of the twentieth part collected by the mayor of London on all salt imported by aliens.

grain broker. A person who, for commission or other compensation, is engaged in selling or negotiating the sale of grain belonging to others. Braun v Chicago, 110 Ill 188, 191.

grain company. A corporation, sometimes a co-operative association, which handles grain by buying from producers and shipping it to mills or other markets, and often deals in grain futures.

grain doors. Inside doors for freight cars, required in shipping loose products, such as grain. 13 Am J2d Car § 470.

grain elevator. A building for the storage of grain. A warehouse for grain, equipped with elevators, hoppers, spouts, motors, etc. to facilitate the rapid handling of the product in receiving and storing it, and in moving it to railroad cars and trucks for transfer to mill or market.

grain in stacks. Unthreshed grain in bundles erected into stacks, but not unthreshed grain in mow in a barn. 29 Am J Rev ed Ins § 299.

grain rent. See **crop rent**.

grain rust. A plant disease caused by fungi, especially prevalent in growing crops of grain, indicated by red or dark brown spots on stalks and leaves. 29A Am J Rev ed Ins § 1330.

Grammatica falsa non vitiat chartam (gram-ma'ti-ka fal'sa non vi'she-at kar'tam). Faulty grammar does not vitiate a deed.

grammatical construction. The construction of a contract, deed, or other instrument according to the rules of grammar, such construction giving way to a contrary intent apparent from the context. 17 Am J2d Contr § 278; 23 Am J2d Deeds § 210.

gram stain test. A laboratory test for symptoms of gonorrhea, universally used, and considered to be practically conclusive, certainly so when the objective symptoms are present. Peterson v Widule, 157 Wis 641, 147 NW 966.

granage (gran'āj). Same as **grainage**.

granary. A structure or room or bin within a structure devoted particularly to the storage of grain. Anno: 10 ALR2d 226; 29 Am J Rev ed Ins § 299. See **grain elevator**.

granatarius (grā-na-tā'ri-us). The manager of a granary.

grand assize (grand a-sīz'). The great jury, instituted by Henry II,—a jury composed of sixteen knights, before whom a tenant or defendant in a writ of right might have a trial, if he chose this course in preference to a trial by battle. See 3 Bl Comm 351.

grand bill of sale. An English term for a bill of sale conveying the title to a vessel. Thuret v Jenkins (La) 7 Mart 318, 355.

grand cape (grand căp). Same as **cape magnum**.

grandchild. A child of one's child. A child of one's legally adopted child. Batchelder v Walworth, 85 Vt 322, 82 A 7. Including an illegitimate child of one's own child only where the context in which it appears indicates a clear intent to include an illegitimate child. 10 Am J2d Bast §§ 138, 142. Included in a designation of "child" or "children" only where the context of the instrument or the surrounding facts and circumstances clearly indicate that such construction is required to accord with the intent of the grantor or maker. Bennett v Humphreys, 159 Kan 416, 155 P2d 413. A "child" for the purpose of the doctrine of advancements. 3 Am J2d Advancem § 25. A "child" within the meaning of the designation of dependents in a workmen's compensation statute. 58 Am J1st Workm Comp § 174. Ordinarily not a "child" within the meaning of such term appearing in a deed or will. 23 Am J2d Deeds § 216; Anno: 14 ALR2d 1242; 23 Am J2d Deeds § 216; 53 Am J1st Wills §§ 1364, 1366. Not a "child" within the meaning of a designation of beneficiaries of a life insurance policy. 29A Am J Rev ed Ins § 1658.

The word "children" in a statute relating to descent and distribution to brothers and sisters of the decedent and to "children" of any deceased brother and sister by right of representation does not include grandchildren. Dennis v Omaha Nat. Bank, 153 Neb 865, 46 NW2d 606, 27 ALR2d 674.

grand days (dās). English court holidays which are celebrated by elaborate banquets at the inns of court.

grand distress (dis-tres'). A writ issued in an action of quare impedit, after the defendant has defaulted, to distrain all of his property situated in the county for the purpose of forcing him to appear.

grandfather. See **grandparent**.

grandfather clause. A clause in a licensing statute which exempts persons already engaged in the regulated business or occupation. Application of Richardson, 199 Okla 406, 24 P2d 642. A provision in a statute requiring a certificate of public convenience and necessity which excepts carriers currently operating. 13 Am J2d Car §§ 85, 86. The popular designation of a provision found in the constitutions of southern states exempting from property and literacy restrictions on suffrage descendants of persons voting before 1867, or descendants of persons who were in military service of the United States or the Confederate states in time of war. Anno: 4 ALR2d 670.

grand juror. A person serving upon a grand jury.

grand jury. A body composed of a number, which varies from state to state, sometimes six, sometimes twelve, and occasionally more than twelve, to which is committed the duty of inquiring into crimes committed in the county from which the members are drawn, the determination of the probability of guilt, and the finding of indictments against supposed offenders. 24 Am J1st Grand J § 2.

See **foreman of grand jury; indictment; minutes; presentment; special grand jury; true bill**.

grand jury report. See **report by grand jury**.

grand larceny. At common law, larceny wherein the value of the property stolen exceeded twelve pence. Under modern statutes, the offense of the larcenous taking of property above a specified value, also such a taking of property of a specified kind, from a specified place, or from the person of another, irrespective of the value of the property taken. 32 Am J1st Larc § 3.

grand list. A schedule of the polls and ratable estate of the inhabitants upon which taxes are to be assessed. Wilson v Wheeler, 55 Vt 446, 452.

grandmother. See **grandparent**.

grandnephew. The son of one's nephew or niece. Ordinarily not a "nephew" within the meaning of such term as it appears in a will. 57 Am J1st Wills § 1390. Ordinarily not inclusive of a male child adopted by a nephew or niece. 57 Am J1st Wills § 1390.

grandniece. The daughter of a nephew or niece. Ordinarily not included in a bequest to a "niece." 57 Am J1st Wills § 1390. Ordinarily not inclusive of a female child adopted by a nephew or niece. 57 Am J1st Wills § 1390.

grandparent. The parent of one's father or mother. A relative in the second degree according to the civil-law method of computing degrees of kinship which prevails in most American jurisdictions. 23 Am J2d Desc & D § 48.

grand serjeanty (sär' or sėr'jęn-ti). A tenure in capite like knight service, but which did not include either personal attendance on the king or escuage. See 2 Bl Comm 73.

grand serjeanty, per magnum servitium (grand sär'jen-ti, per mag'num ser-vi'she-um). Grand serjeanty by distinguished service,—whereby the tenant was bound, instead of serving the king generally in his wars, to do some special honorary service to the king in person; as to carry his banner, his sword, or the like; or to be his butler, champion, or other officer, at his coronation. See 2 Bl Comm 73.

grand stand. Adjective: A colloquial term characterizing an act or performance intended primarily to win applause. Noun: The covered structure occupied by the spectators at a sporting event, such as a baseball game.

grand theft. Another term for **grand larceny.**

grange (grānj). A farm, with all of its barns, sheds, stables, and other buildings. An organization of farmers intended for the promotion of their welfare and service in the national interest.

grangiarius (grān-ji-ā'ri-us). The steward or keeper of a grange.

grant. Noun: A conveyance or transfer of real property, especially of public lands. The conferring of something by one person upon another. Nicholas & Co. v United States, 249 US 34, 39, 63 L Ed 461, 465, 39 S Ct 218. As the term appears in a treaty: —any concession, warrant, order, or permission to survey, possess, or settle, whether evidenced by writing or parol, or presumed from possession. Strother v Lucas (US) 12 Pet 410, 9 L Ed 1137. Verb: A word of conveyance or transfer. An apt word of conveyance, effective to create a covenant to stand seised. 28 Am J2d Est §§ 255-257.

The word is not a technical word like the word "enfeoff," and although, if used broadly, without limitation or restriction, it would carry an estate or interest in the thing granted, still it may be used in a more restricted sense, and be so limited that the grantee will take but a mere naked trust or power to dispose of the thing granted, and to apply the proceeds arising out of it to the use and benefit of the grantor. Rice v Minnesota & Northwestern Railroad Co. (US) 1 Black 358, 17 L Ed 147, 153.

See **capitation grant; congressional grant; devise and grant; give; give, grant, bargain, etc.; grant, bargain and sell; grantor; grant to uses; hereby granted; inclusive grant; lie in grant; lost grant; office grant; presumed grant; railroad grant; recession; regrant; reservation; right of way by grant; royal grant.**

grant and demise. A term in a lease for years creating an implied warranty of title and a covenant for quiet enjoyment. Stott v Rutherford (US) 2 Otto 107, 23 L Ed 486.

grant, bargain, and sell. Words of conveyance with contractual significance, operating under statute in some jurisdictions as a warranty against incumbrances made or suffered by the grantor. Mullanphy Sav. Bank v Schott, 135 Ill 655.

grantee. A person to whom a grant is made. The party in a deed to whom the conveyance is made. 23 Am J2d Deeds § 41.

granting clause. Apt words of grant which manifest the grantor's intent to make a present conveyance of the land by his deed, as distinguished from an intention to convey it at some future time. De Bergere v Chaves, 14 NM 352, 93 P 762, Affd 231 US 482, 58 L Ed 325, 34 S Ct 144; New Home Bldg. Supply Co. v Nations, 259 NC 681, 131 SE2d 425.

grant of patent. A transfer in writing of an entire patent for an invention, of an undivided part thereof, or of an exclusive right for a limited or unlimited territory to make and use or vend the thing patented. Moore v Marsh (US) 7 Wall 515, 19 L Ed 37, 39.

grantor. A person who makes a grant. The party to a deed who makes the conveyance. 23 Am J2d Deeds § 41.

grant to uses. A grant of land made to one person for the use or benefit of another person called the cestui que use.

grantz. Grandees; noblemen.

granum crescens (grā'num kres'enz). Growing grain.

graph. A writing. A representation by means of a line imposed upon a series of bars of changes appearing in a variable quantity or amount, such as stock market quotations, populations, temperatures, etc.

grass. A perennial plant for pasturage or the beautification of a lawn or public grounds. Superior Oil Co. v Griffin (Okla) 357 P2d 987, 87 ALR2d 224.

grass colt. A colt having an unknown sire. A slang expression for an illegitimate child.

grasshearth (gràs'härth). A customary service of a single day's work for the lord of the manor.

grassum (gras'sum). Same as **gersome.**

grass widow. A term of little, if any, legal significance, for a woman who has been divorced from or is living separate and apart from her husband.

gratia (grā'she-a). (Latin.) Favor; indulgence. Thanks.

See **a gratia; bona gratia; de gratia; Dei gratia; exempli gratia; ex gratia; ex speciali gratia; lucri gratia.**

Gratian (grā'she-an). See **Decretum Gratiani.**

gratification. Pleasure or satisfaction. A gratuity bestowed voluntarily upon a person for services rendered or benefits received.

gratis (grā'tis). As a favor; for nothing; gratuitously; without consideration.

gratis appearance (grā'tis a-pėr'ans). An appearance in an action by a defendant without waiting for or requiring service of process.

gratis dictum (grā'tis dik'tum). A gratuitous statement; a statement made for no particular purpose; a statement made without any intention that it should be relied or acted upon. Medbury v Watson, 47 Mass (6 Met) 246, 260.

gratuities received in the usual course of business. Tips received by an employee in work, such as that of a waiter in a restaurant, a bell hop, or porter, at a place where it is customary for customers or guests to give gratuities and for the employee to keep them as part of his compensation. 58 Am J1st Workm Comp § 314.

gratuitous. By way of gift; without consideration.

gratuitous agent. An agent acting as such without compensation.

gratuitous bailee. See **gratuitous bailment.**

gratuitous bailment. A bailment without compensation; according to some authority a bailment intended for the sole benefit of the bailor or a bailment intended for the sole benefit of the bailee. 8 Am J2d Bailm § 7.

In view of the fact that some courts regard a gratuitous bailment as on only for the sole benefit of the bailor, it is perhaps better to avoid altogether a classification of bailments as "gratuitous", and to adopt instead the three-fold general classification of (1) those for the sole benefit of the bailor; (2) those for the sole benefit of the bailee; and (3) those for the mutual benefit of both parties. 8 Am J2d Bailm § 7.

gratuitous contract. An anomaly in the field of contracts; a contract the purpose of which is to benefit the promisee, but without any consideration given or promised from the promisee. Georgia Penitentiary Co. v Nelms, 65 Ga 499.

gratuitous conveyance. A conveyance made without consideration.

gratuitous pension. See **pension.**

gratuitous guest. A person served or entertained without charge, particularly a person transported in an automobile without charge.

gratuitous licensee. A person using a common passageway in a building occupied by several tenants, at the invitation of an employee of a tenant; such guest is a gratuitous licensee of the employer and accordingly an invitee of the landlord. Snyder v Jay Realty Co. 30 NJ 303, 153 A2d 1, 78 ALR2d 95.

gratuitous rider. See **guest.**

gratuitous services. Work or labor rendered without charge. A matter for disciplinary proceedings against an attorney at law where offered by advertisement. 7 Am J2d Attys § 43. Services rendered by a public utility for a municipality, without charge, under contract with the municipality. 56 Am J1st Watwk § 54. The carrying of a passenger on a pass. 14 Am J2d Car § 946.

Such services attached to feudal tenure as were becoming a freeman or a soldier, such as were not base. The service was free, but uncertain under tenure by knight-service, and it was free and certain under free socage tenure. See 2 Bl Comm 62.

See **liberum servitium.**

gratuity. A present; a recompense; a gift; a reward; a tip. Georgia Penitentiary Co. v Nelms, 65 Ga 499.

gratulance (grat'ū-lans). A bribe.

gravamen (gra-vā'men). Gist; essence; substance; sting.

gravatio (gra-vā'she-o). A charge; an accusation.

grave. A place of burial.

gravel. A mixture of sand and small rocks. A species of stone which is a mineral. Wright v Carrollton Gravel & Sand Co. (Ky) 242 SW2d 751, 26 ALR2d 1449. Disintegrated rock.

gravel pit. A digging upon land where gravel in saleable quantities is obtainable. Williamson v Jones, 43 W Va 562, 27 SE 411.

gravel road. A road, the surface of which is gravel applied, by a spreader, for the purpose of making the way passable in wet weather.

graveyard. See **cemetery.**

graving dock. A dock which is put to use somewhat as a floating dock but is permanently attached to the land. 2 Am J2d Adm § 35. Except for details of construction, the same as a dry dock. Maryland Casualty Co. v Lawson (CA5 Fla) 101 F2d 732.

gravi querela. See **ex gravi querela.**

gravis (gra'vis). Grave; grievous; important; serious.

gravity. A term familiar in oil price quotations, referring to what is called "Baume" gravity, under which the lighter the oil the higher the gravity. Ohio Oil Co. v Conway, 281 US 146, 74 L Ed 775, 50 S Ct 310.

gravity switch. A switching of railroad cars from one track to another by allowing them to run detached from a locomotive down grade over the switch. 44 Am J1st RR § 454.

gravius (gra'vi-us). Same as **graf.**

Gravius est divinam quam temporalem laedere majestatem (gra'vi-us est di-vi'nam quam tem-po-re'lem lē'de-re ma-jes-tā'tem). It is more serious to offend divine majesty than temporal.

Gray's Inn (grās in). One of the inns of court at London.

grazing right. The right to graze animals on the land of another; a profit a prendre. 25 Am J2d Ease § 4.

great. Important; extraordinary; paramount; grave; serious.

great aunt. The aunt of one's father or mother. A relative in the fourth degree of kinship according to the civil law method of computing kinship which prevails in most American jurisdictions. 23 Am J2d Desc & D § 48.

great bodily harm. See **great bodily injury.**

great bodily injury. A phrase so self-expressive as to be difficult of definition. An injury great in degree as contrasted with a trifling hurt. Lawlor v People, 74 Ill 228, 231.

What constitutes such an injury, and whether the circumstances were such as to justify one in believing that such an injury is about to be committed upon him, is a matter which, to a great extent, must be left to the jury. Rogers v State, 60 Ark 76, 29 SW 894.

Great Body of Laws (bod'i of lâs). A code of statutes adopted in the Province of Pennsylvania in 1682. James v Commonwealth (Pa) 12 Serg & R 220, 232.

Great Britain. England, Scotland, and Wales; a division of the United Kingdom and the Commonwealth.

great calamity. See **calamity.**

great cape. See **cape magnum.**

great care. Extraordinary diligence; that degree of care or diligence which a very prudent person takes of his own concerns, or which a person of ordinary prudence usually exercises about his own affairs of great importance. 8 Am J2d Bailm § 206.

great cattle (grāt kat′l). Cattle which have reached their full growth.

Great Charter. See **Magna Charta**.

great emergency. See **great necessity or emergency**.

Great Depression. The extremely unfavorable economic condition of the United States which began in 1929 and continued in various degrees of intensity for ten years, the period being marked by business failures, much unemployment, and low prices for agricultural products. 3 Am J2d Agri § 26.

great diligence. See **great care**.

greater rate. As the term appears in the provision of a statute on taxation that national bank shares shall not be taxed at a "greater rate" than the tax on other moneyed capital, it means that neither the rate of assessment nor the valuation shall be higher than on other moneyed capital. New York v Weaver, 100 US 539, 25 L Ed 705.

greatest convenience to the parties in interest. A phrase relative to the venue of a bankruptcy proceeding, without absolute meaning, to be applied according to the circumstances of each case—proximity to the court of bankrupt, creditors, and witnesses, the location of assets, and the economic and efficient administration of the estate. 9 Am J2d Bankr § 35.

great fee (grat fē). A fee held directly of the king.

great-grandchild. The son or daughter of one's grandchild. Ordinarily not a "grandchild" within the meaning of such term as it appears in a will by way of designation of a beneficiary, although such construction will be adopted where necessary to carry out the intention of the testator as such appears from the entire context. Anno: 104 ALR 309. A relative in the third degree of kinship according to the civil law method of computing degrees of kinship which prevails in most American jurisdictions. 23 Am J2d Desc & D § 48.

great grandparent. The father or mother of one's grandmother or grandfather. A relative in the third degree of kinship according to the civil law method of computing degrees of kinship which prevails in most American jurisdictions. 48 Am J2d Desc & D § 48.

great-great-grandparent. The father or mother of one's great-grandparent. A relative in the fourth degree of kinship according to the civil law method of computing degrees of kinship which prevails in most American jurisdictions. 23 Am J2d Desc & D § 48.

great jury. Same as **grand assize**.
See **grand jury**.

Great Lakes. Inland seas; open seas except for the characteristic freshness of water and the absence of observable tides. Illinois C. R. Co. v Illinois, 146 US 387, 36 L Ed 1018, 13 S Ct 110. Sometimes included within the classification of high seas. United States v Rodgers, 150 US 249, 37 L Ed 1071, 14 S Ct 109.

Great Law. Same as **Great Body of Laws**.

great necessity or emergency (nẹ-ses′i̧-ti or ẹ-mẽr′jẹn-si). As the word is applied to a necessity or emergency authorizing an extra tax levy:—of grave character and serious moment. San Christina Investment Co. v San Francisco, 167 Cal 762, 141 P 384.

great ponds. A term familiar in the New England states; ponds covering over 10 acres. 56 Am J1st Wat § 53.

great prejudice. Material pecuniary loss, not mere temporary inconvenience, or temporary impairment of income, slight in comparison with the value of the property for the uses for which it is suitable. Williamson Invest. Co. v Williamson, 96 Wash 529, 165 P 385 (the term appearing in a statute authorizing a sale of the property in an action for partition where an actual partition cannot be made "without great prejudice" to the owners.)

great seal. A seal of state; the seal of the United States; the seal of a state; the seal of Great Britain, of which the lord high chancellor is the custodian.
See **seal of the United States**.

great tithes. Tithes of corn, hay, wood or grain.

great uncle. The uncle of one's father or mother. A relative in the fourth degree of relationship according to the civil law method of determining kinship which prevails in most American jurisdiction. 23 Am J2d Desc & D § 48.

great writ of liberty. The writ of habeas corpus.

greave. An old and obsolete form of "grove."

greaves. A substance which remains in solid form when fat is melted; a crackling.

gree (grē). An agreement; a satisfaction for an injury; a consent; to effect a compromise.
See **de son gree**.

Greek bearing a gift. See **onerous gift**.

Greek letter fraternities. College fraternities, sometimes high school fraternities, having names composed of Greek letters.
See **fraternities**.

green. See **Gretna Green**.

greenback. Paper money, the term deriving from the green color of the back of the bill or note. Levy v State, 79 Ala 259, 261. A derogatory term applied to paper money not supported by a deposit or reserve of gold or silver.

green cloth. An English court which was held in the royal household.

green goods (grēn gůdz). An American slang expression signifying counterfeit paper money.

greengrocer. A retail dealer in fresh fruits and vegetables.

greenhouse. A building constructed principally of glass, usually provided with artificial heat for protection against the ravages of the weather, wherein plants, flowers, and sometimes vegetables are raised for purposes of sale. Hultin v Klein, 301 Ill 94, 133 NE 660, 20 ALR 230; Needham v Winslow Nurseries, Inc. 330 Mass 95, 111 NE2d 453, 40 ALR2d 1450.

greenhouse business. The cultivation of plants, flowers and vegetables in a greenhouse for disposal to purchasers. Needham v Winslow Nurseries, Inc. 330 Mass 95, 111 NE2d 453, 40 ALR2d 1450.

Green River ordinance. A type of ordinance forbidding uninvited entry by peddlers, solicitors, and the like. Anno: 77 ALR2d 1225.

green silver (grēn sil′vẽr). A feudal customary annual rent.

greeve (grēv). Same as **gerefa**.

Gregorian Calendar (grẹ-gō'ri-ạn kal'en-dạr). The calendar so named after Pope Gregory who corrected the errors of several centuries in the calculation of time and put in force a new style by which the error is reduced to one day in thirty centuries.

Christian nations have generally adopted the Gregorian Calendar, authorized by Pope Gregory in 1582, numbering the years from the birth of Christ, and when a year is mentioned in legislative or judicial proceedings, and no mention is made of any other system of reckoning, the Gregorian or Christian Calendar is understood. 52 Am J1st Time § 9.

Gregorian Code. A compilation of Roman laws made by the jurist Gregorianus in the fourth century.

Gregorian epoch. The period of time beginning in 1582, when the Gregorian Calendar was adopted, and continuing to the present.

Gregorianus. See **Gregorian Code**.

Gregory, Pope. See **Gregorian Calendar**.

gremio legis. See **in gremio legis**.

gremium (gre'mi-um). Lap; bosom; breast.

gressame. Same as **gersome**.

gressum (gres'sum). Same as **gersome**.

gressume. Same as **gersome**.

Gretna Green (gret'na grēn). A place in Scotland very near the Scotch border where English runaway couples went to marry and thus escape publication of the banns and other formalities required by English law. A term applied in the United States to any city or village, to which many couples resort for marriage, for the purpose of escaping requirements imposed in other locations, of preserving secrecy respecting the marriage, or of having the ceremony performed in pleasant surroundings.

Gretna Green marriage (mar'ạj). A marriage which was valid in Scotland and required only the mutual declarations of the parties made in the presence of witnesses. A marriage performed in a literal or figurative Gretna Green.
See **Gretna Green**.

grievance. A cause for complaint or protest. The crux of an industrial or labor dispute. Anno: 158 ALR 1176; 31 Am J Rev ed Lab § 369.

grievance day. The day on which the complaint of a taxpayer concerning the assessment of his property is to be made. 51 Am J1st Tax §§ 728 et seq.

grieved. Aggrieved.

griff (grif). A term familiar in Louisiana; the child of a Negro and a mulatto; a person too black to be a mulatto and too light in color to be a Negro. State v Treadway, 126 La 300, 52 So 500.

grippe. A disease caused by a virus, similar to a severe cold. 29 Am J Rev ed Ins § 745.

gripping efficiency. The efficiency of brakes on a motor vehicle.
See **braking distance**.

grist (grist). A quantity of grain, particularly an amount taken by a farmer to a mill to be ground into flour and collateral products for the farmer. A term sometimes applied to the amount of flour retained by the miller for his services in grinding the grain.

grith (grith). (Saxon.) Peace; the public peace.

grithbrech. (Saxon.) A breach of the peace.

grithstole. (Saxon.) A seat or place of peace; a sanctuary.

grocer. A dealer in groceries. An engrosser.

grocery store. A building or structure in which groceries are kept for sale. Goldstine v State, 230 Ind 343, 103 NE2d 438.

gros (grō). Large; great.

gross. Noun: Twelve dozen. Adjective: Without deduction. As a whole or in an entirety; total. Large; lacking refinement. Braun's Appeal, 105 Pa 414, 415.
See **in gross**.

gross abuse of discretion. An arbitrary, unreasonable, individualistic, unjust, and unconscionable act or decision. 5 Am J2d A & E § 774.

gross adventure. Bottomry; a maritime loan.
See **bill of gross adventure**.

gross allowance. A lump-sum award of alimony. 24 Am J2d Div & S § 614.

gross average. Same as **general average**.

Grosscup Rule. A rule applied in determining the rights and liabilities of a borrowing member of a building and loan association in the event of the insolvency or dissolution of the association. 13 Am J2d B & L Assoc § 121.

grosse avanture. Same as **gross adventure**.

grosse bois (grōs bwä). Great wood; timber.

grossement (grōs'mânt). Greatly.

gross estate of decedent. The value of all property left by a decedent, determined as of the date of death. For federal tax: the value of all property to the extent of the decedent's interest therein at the time of his death; virtually all property transferred either by the will of the decedent or under the local intestacy laws. Estate of Kinney v Commissioner (CA9) 80 F2d 568. For the purposes of the statute which provides for an estate tax lien:—the estate or property on which the tax chargeable to the decedent's estate is computed, including property which does not pass as part of the estate but by right of survivorship. Detroit Bank v United States, 317 US 329, 87 L Ed 304, 63 S Ct 297.

gross immorality. Wilful, flagrant, or shameful immorality, showing a moral indifference to the opinions of the good and respectable members of the community and to the just obligations of the position held by the delinquent. Moore v Strickling, 46 W Va 515, 33 SE 274 (involving ground for removal from public office.)

gross inadequacy of consideration. Inadequacy of consideration which is shocking to the conscience; which implies fraud, oppression, or the taking of advantage of a relationship of trust or dependence. 17 Am J2d Contr § 102. Inadequacy of value received so great as to evidence fraud or imposition. 11 Am J2d B & N § 217.

gross income. The whole or entire profit arising from a business or pursuit. Braun's Appeal, 105 Pa 414, 415. For income tax purposes: the total income of the taxpayer; the income from all sources without deductions or allowance for exemptions; the total of gains and profits of the taxpayer, irrespective of immorality or viciousness in the method of acquisition. Steinberg v United States (CC NY) 14 F2d 564.

That portion of the gross profits arising out of the sale of capital assets which represents gain or increase acquired must be regarded as "gross income" within the meaning of the Federal Corporation Excise Tax Act. Doyle v Mitchell Bros. Co. 247 US 179, 62 L Ed 1054, 38 S Ct 467.

gross income from the property. For the purpose of a percentage depletion for income tax computation involving income from oil or gas well: the amount for which the taxpayer sells oil or gas in the immediate vicinity of the well. If the oil or gas is not sold on the premises but is, before sale, manufactured or converted into a refined product or transported from the premises: the equivalent of the representative market or field price, at the well head on the date of sale, before conversion or transportation. If sold in place and extracted by the buyer: it does not include the buyer's cost of extraction. 34 Am J2d Fed Tax ¶ 7684.

gross incompetency or recklessness. Act or conduct which is grossly incompetent or reckless according to the common judgment, that is, in the judgment of the people. Klafter v State Board of Examiners, 259 Ill 15, 102 NE 193 (ground for revocation of a professional license).
See **gross negligence.**

gross lewdness in an open place. Not to be confounded with "open and gross lewdness." The former has reference to the place where the act is committed, while the latter has not, but simply means lewdness which is not secret. Burroughs v Eastman, 88 Wis 180, 59 NW 580.
See **open and gross lewdness.**

gross misdemeanor. A misdemeanor of a more serious nature than the ordinary misdemeanor. 21 Am J2d Crim L § 21. A term invented to permit a distinction between petty offenses and those of a more serious nature. State v Kelly, 218 Minn 247, 15 NW2d 554, 162 ALR 477.

gross misdemeanor of public school pupil. Gross misbehavior but not necessarily criminal conduct; persistent disobedience of the proper and reasonable rules and regulations of the school. Holman v Trustees of School Dist. 77 Mich 605, 43 NW 996.

gross national product. The market value of all the goods and services our economy produces in a given period.

gross neglect of duty. As a ground for divorce:—neglect attended with circumstances of indignity or aggravation; such a glaring, shameful neglect of marital duties as to be obvious from common understanding and inexcusable under all the relevant facts of the case. Morris v Morris, 132 Okla 291, 270 P 833. By a public officer:—a dereliction which, from the gravity of the situation or the frequency of instances, becomes so serious as to endanger or threaten the public welfare; not necessarily inclusive of every instance of wilful neglect or intentional official wrongdoing. Attorney-General, ex rel. Rich v Jochim, 99 Mich 358, 58 NW 611. Clearly beyond mere inadvertence. Clemens v State, 176 Wis 289, 185 NW 209, 21 ALR 1490. Acting with such an utter disregard of consequences as to suggest something of an intent to cause injury. Astin v Chicago, M. & St. P. R. Co. 143 Wis 477, 128 NW 265.

gross negligence. A classification as difficult as any classification according to degrees of negligence. 38 Am J1st Negl § 43. Negligence characterized by the want of even slight care. Acting, or omitting to act in a situation where there is a duty to act, not inadvertently but wilfully and intentionally with a conscious indifference to consequences so far as other persons may be affected. 38 Am J1st Negl § 47.

gross negligence in homicide. Aggravated or culpable negligence; conduct constituting such a departure from the conduct of an ordinarily prudent or careful man under the same circumstances as to be incompatible with a proper regard for human life; conduct amounting to a disregard of human life or an indifference to consequences to human life. 26 Am J1st Homi § 210.

gross negligence of bailee. An expression without a precise or definite meaning; a concept to be considered in the light of all the circumstances surrounding the bailment. Broadly, the failure to exercise reasonable care, skill and diligence, or the failure to exercise that care which the property in its particular situation demands. 8 Am J2d Bailm § 212.

gross negligence of carrier. In respect of limitation of liability to passenger riding on a pass:—a term not susceptible of precise definition; a question to be resolved ultimately in the factual situation of the case. 14 Am J2d Car § 951.

gross negligence toward guest in automobile. A term not susceptible of precise definition; a question to be resolved according to the circumstances of the particular case, Broadly, an entire failure to exercise care, or the exercise of so slight a degree of care as to justify the belief that there was an indifference to the things and welfare of others; that want of care which raises a presumption of conscious indifference to consequences; indifference to present legal duty and utter forgetfulness of legal obligations. 8 Am J2d Auto § 487.

gross proceeds. The entire proceeds. The proceeds of a sale or of a collection without deduction for cost, commissions, or any other expenses whatsoever. Ross Jewelers, Inc. v State, 260 Ala 682, 72 So 2d 402, 43 ALR2d 851; Duhame v State Tax Commission, 65 Ariz 268, 179 P2d 252, 171 ALR 684.

gross receipts. The entire earnings of a business without deduction; the total as opposed to the net. Greene County Bldg. & Loan Asso. v Milner Hotels, Inc. 240 Mo App 1048, 227 SW2d 111. For the purpose of a sales tax:—the proceeds of sales of personal property without deduction on account of cost of the property or any other expense whatsoever. Ross Jewelers, Inc. v State, 260 Ala 682, 72 So 2d 402, 43 ALR2d 851.

Receipts from employees' purchases at wholesale cost, voluntarily allowed, constitute "gross receipts" derived from trades, businesses or commerce, taxable under a gross income tax law. Walgreen Co. v Gross Income Tax Div. 225 Ind 418, 75 NE2d 784, 1 ALR2d 1014.

gross sales. The entire amount of the entire sales of a business for a specific period of time.

As used in a tax statute imposing a privilege tax on the "gross sales" of wholesale dealers, the term means the gross prices paid for the products named. Pure Oil Co. v State, 244 Ala 258, 12 So 2d 861, 148 ALR 260.

grossome. Same as **gersome.**

gross premium. The net premium, which is the cost of the insurance, that is, the amount required on an actuarial basis to carry the risk, plus loading for expenses and contingencies. Fox v Mutual Ben. Life Ins. Co. (CA8 Mo) 107 F2d 715.

gross production tax. A state tax upon the gross production of certain industries which is substituted for and takes the place of an ad valorem tax imposed under general tax laws; a tax in lieu of all other taxes on the leases and minerals or the equipment used in producing or in the operation of oil wells or mines. New England Oil & Pipe Line Co. v State Board of Equalization, 121 Okla 277, 249 P 914.

gross ton. A measure of avoirdupois weight. The equivalent of 2,240 pounds.

gross weight (wāt). The weight of a thing or commodity without any allowance or deduction.

Grotius. One of the earlier outstanding authorities on international law.

ground. The earth or soil. An electrical term, meaning an object of metal buried in the earth whereby an electrical connection is made with the earth. A point; a reason; support for a cause of action. The basis for taking a step in an action, for example, a ground of attachment. 6 Am J2d Attach § 218.

groundage (groun'dạj). A fee charged by port authorities for allowing a ship to remain in a port.

ground annual (ground' an"ū-ạl). An annual rent.

ground collision. A collision between aircraft on take-off or landing.

ground crew. A detail of men necessary for the landing and handling of an airship on the ground. Preferred Acci. Ins. Co. v Rhodenbaugh (CA6 Ohio) 160 F2d 832, 834; Miner v Western Casualty & Surety Co. 241 Iowa 530, 41 NW2d 557, 14 ALR2d 1358.

ground vessel. A stranded vessel.

ground for disbarment or discipline. Misconduct of an attorney at law, either within or outside his professional activities, which shows that he is unfit to discharge the duties of his profession or unworthy of confidence. 7 Am J2d Attys § 25.

ground for divorce. A legal cause for divorce. 24 Am J2d Div & S § 20. Misconduct of a spouse which, as provided by statute, entitles the other spouse to a divorce. 24 Am J2d Div & S § 20.

ground landlord. A landlord to whom a tenant pays ground rent.
See **ground rent.**

ground of action. Essentially, the cause of action. Johnston v Sikes, 56 Conn 589, 594. The basis of an action as determined under the law and upon the facts pleaded.

ground rent. A rent reserved to himself and his heirs by a grantor of land, out of the land itself, constituting real estate and having the usual characteristics of an estate in fee simple. 32 Am J1st L & T § 1039.

ground rent lease. An expression familiar in Maryland but anomalous in some other jurisdictions.
The chief characteristics of the Maryland ground rent leases are (1) the owner of the land in fee leases it to the named lessee for the period of ninety-nine years, (2) with covenant for renewal from time to time forever, upon payment of a small renewal fine (3) upon the condition, however, of the payment of a certain sum of money (usually payable semi-annually) and (4) upon the further condition that if the payment of the rent is in default for a stipulated time the lessor may reenter and avoid the lease. The grantee also covenants to pay all taxes upon the whole property; and under the present (1941) taxing system the taxes are assessed to the lessee. Jones v Magruder (DC Md) 42 F Supp 193.
The typical Pennsylvania ground rent is not created by a lease but results from a conveyance by the absolute owner of the land to the grantee in fee, subject to the payment of rent. The difference between the Maryland and Pennsylvania ground rent systems is said to be attributable to the somewhat different provisions of the respective royal charters to Cecelius Calvert and William Penn for the proprietary provinces of Maryland and Pennsylvania, with respect to the application of the Statute of Quia Emptores. Jones v Magruder (DC Md) 42 F Supp 193.

ground risk. The risk of any direct loss or damage to an aircraft while not in flight. Acme Flying Service v Royal Ins. Co. (Sup) 83 NYS2d 740, affd without op 275 App Div 766, 88 NYS2d 904.

ground writ. An English writ running to a county outside of the county in which it was issued and upon the authority of which a writ of execution is issued in the outside county.

group. A number of persons or things existing or brought together with or without interrelation, orderly form, or arrangement. Hope v Flentage, 140 Mo 390, 41 SW 1002.

group annuity. A contract providing annuities for the members of a defined group of persons, usually the employees of a business or industry, or of such part of them as desire to participate and are eligible under the arrangement or plan provided, the conditions of the contract being stated in a master policy and the participation by an individual being noted in a certificate of insurance issued to him.

grouping of contracts. A theory of conflict of laws otherwise known as the "center of gravity theory." 16 Am J2d Confl L § 42.
See **center of gravity theory.**

group insurance. A contract providing life, accident, or health insurance for the members of a defined group of persons, usually the employees of a business or industry, or of such part of them as desire to participate and are eligible under the arrangement or plan provided, the conditions of the contract being stated in a master policy and the participation by an individual being noted in a certificate issued to him.

group medicine. Arrangement by contract, certificate, or policy, having the purpose of providing medical treatment for special groups or classes of people, especially those of limited means. 41 Am J1st Phys & S § 25.

growing concern value. The value which inheres in a public utility plant having an established business, as distinguished from a plant which has yet to establish its business; a property right which should be considered in determining the value of the property upon which a public utility company has a right to a fair return. 43 Am J1st Pub Util § 139.

growing crop. Literally, a crop in the process of growth, an unmatured crop. But a disputed term in legal parlance.
Some authorities hold that a growing crop may be either above or below the surface of the soil, while other authorities hold that a crop is not a growing crop unless it shows above ground, and that underground sprouts do not constitute such a

crop. Again, some authorities hold that a crop is growing from the time the seed is planted until the harvest, while other authorities hold that a matured, ungathered crop is not growing. 21 Am J2d Crops § 2. Whether grass in a pasture is a growing crop is also a controverted question. Anno: 87 ALR2d 238.

growing timber. Trees in the process of growth; live trees. Exclusive of felled or dead trees. Anno: 72 ALR2d 740.
See **growth of timber.**

growing value. The value which inheres in a public utility plant having an established business, as distinguished from a plant which has yet to establish its business; a property right which should be considered in determining the value of the property upon which a public utility company has a right to a fair return. 43 Am J1st Pub Util § 139.

growth corporation. A corporation characterized, not by growth in earnings but by growth in plant, capabilities for the future, and in expansion of sales outlets.

growth half-penny (grōth häf'pen''i). A tax which was imposed on oxen and other non-producing cattle.

growth of timber. Literally, timber growing on premises, but sometimes meaning future growth. Baker v Kenney, 145 Iowa 638, 124 NW 901.

growth theory. The rule that rights in respect of pure or technical trademarks are the result of growth, that is, of increasing amount of use over a period of time. 52 Am J1st Tradem § 22.

gruarii (gru-ā'ri-ī). The chief officers of a forest.

grubbing contract. A contract to take out the roots, stumps, and obstacles imbedded in the surface of the ground along the right of way of a railroad, except where not required on account of cuts or fills. Cervien v Erickson Constr. Co. 94 Wash 500, 162 P 567.

grubstake. An advance made to a person about to engage in a venture for living expenses. A vernacular term coined by miners, used loosely in legal opinions for various kinds of joint ventures in prospecting. Anno: 70 ALR2d 907.

grubstake contract. A contract between one person known as an outfitter and another person known as the miner, wherein the former agrees to supply the latter in a mining adventure which the latter agrees to follow for a prescribed period. 36 Am J1st Min & M §§ 171, 172. An arrangement by which one of the parties undertakes to supply finances, supplies, or equipment which the other party is to use in discovering and locating mineral claims on the public domain, the parties to share in any claims located. Anno: 70 ALR2d 907. Sometimes spoken of as a prospecting partnership, but to be distinguished from a mining partnership. Anno: 70 ALR2d 907.

Guadalupe Hidalgo Treaty. The treaty, perhaps better called the Treaty of Queretaro, of Feb. 2, 1848, which ended the War between the United States and the Republic of Mexico. 9 Stat 923.

guadia (gwa'di-a). A pledge.

guarantee. The creditor under a contract of guaranty, being the person to whom the principal debtor is primarily liable and to whom the guarantor is secondarily liable. 24 Am J1st Guar § 2. In another sense, a guaranty.

See **guaranty.**

guaranteed annual wage. An undertaking by an employer that he will pay a specified total amount in wages during the year to an employee employed by the hour or the day.

guaranteed dividends. An expression which is somewhat anomolous so far as it relates to corporate dividends, since dividends are payable only from net profits or surplus earnings, and is ordinarily construed to mean only that dividends are guaranteed in the event there are net profits from which they may properly be dispersed. 19 Am J2d Corp § 872. A "guaranty of dividend" by a corporation is nothing more than a pledge of the funds, legally applicable to the purposes of a dividend. Taft v Hartford P. & F. R. Co. 8 RI 310.

guaranteed insurability rider. A rider attached to a life insurance policy at time of issuance, permitting the insured to obtain, without medical examination, policies of life insurance, subject to limitation upon amount contained in the rider. Otherwise known as purchase option rider.

guaranteed sales. See **sales guaranteed.**

guaranteed stock. See **preferred stock.**

guaranteed title. A title to real estate such as designated title insurance company will approve and insure.
See **title insurance.**

guarantor. The person bound, by a contract of guaranty. 24 Am J1st Guar § 2. One who undertakes to answer for the debt, default, or miscarriage of another.

guaranty. An undertaking or promise, on the part of one person called the guarantor, which is collateral to a primary or principal obligation on the part of another, and which binds the guarantor to performance in the event of nonperformance by such other person, the latter being primarily bound to perform. 24 Am J1st Guar § 3. Concisely, a promise to answer for the debt, default, or miscarriage of another person, provided such person does not respond by payment or performance. Hickory Novelty Co. v Andrews, 188 NC 59, 123 SE 314.

The fundamental difference between a contract of guaranty and one of suretyship is that the guarantor's contract is collateral to and independent of the contract the performance of which he guarantees, while that of a surety is an original obligation. 24 Am J1st Guar § 11.

See **absolute guaranty; collateral guaranty; conditional guaranty; continuing guaranty; general guaranty; guaranty insurance; letter of credit; limited guaranty; merger of guaranty; offer to guarantee; prior indorsements guaranteed; special guaranty; suretyship; warranty.**

guaranty fund. See **depositors' guaranty fund; reserve.**

guaranty insurance. A guaranty or insurance against loss in case a person named shall make a designated default, or be guilty of specified conduct. People ex rel. Kasson v Rose, 174 Ill 310, 51 NE 246.

See **credit insurance; fidelity guaranty insurance; title insurance.**

guaranty of collection. A guaranty which is not absolute but implies that the creditor will make diligent effort to enforce the collection of the obligation from the principal debtor. To be distinguished from a guaranty of payment. 24 Am J1st Guar § 17.

guaranty of dividend. See guaranteed dividend.

guaranty of liberty. The guaranty under the Fourteenth Amendment to the United States Constitution that no state shall deprive any person of life, liberty, or property without due process of law.

guaranty of payment. A guaranty which binds the guarantor to pay the debt of another, known as the principal debtor, at maturity, in the event the money has not been paid by the principal debtor, the obligation of the guarantor becoming fixed upon the default of the latter. 24 Am J1st Guar § 17.

guaranty of prior indorsements. See prior indorsements guaranteed.

guaranty policy. An insurance policy whereby the insurer undertakes to pay the insured creditor in the event of nonpayment by his debtor.

See credit insurance; guaranty insurance; solvency policy.

guard. Noun: A person whose duty it is to protect the person or property of another. A watchman. A railing around a shaft in a building, open hole in a highway or street, or other place of danger to pedestrians or drivers. Verb: To keep watch against danger; to protect the person or property of another. To control or restrain.

See castleguard; cattleguard; custodia; safeguards.

guardage (gär'dāj). Wardship.

guardia (gar'di-a). The ward of a guardian.

guardian. A person to whom the law has intrusted the custody and control of the person, or estate, or both, of an infant, lunatic or incompetent person. A person in a trust relation of the most sacred character, known as a guardianship, in which he acts for another person called the "ward," whom the law regards as incapable of managing his own affairs. Harrison v Harrison, 21 NM 372, 155 P 356. Sometimes in the relationship of in loco parentis with the ward. 25 Am J1st G & W § 62.

The guardian, at common law, performs the office of tutor or curator of the Roman civil law, the former of whom had charge of the maintenance and education of the minor, the latter the care of his fortune. Mercer v Watson (Pa) 1 Watts 330, 348.

See committee; conservator; general guardian; joint guardian; protutor; special guardian; testamentary guardian.

guardian ad litem. A person appointed by the court during the course of litigation, in which an infant or a person mentally incompetent is a party, to represent and protect the interests of the infant or incompetent.

guardian by custom. A person who, by the custom of the place, had the right to act as guardian.

guardian by election. A person selected by an infant as his guardian and appointed by the court to act in such capacity. 25 Am J1st G & W § 5.

guardian by infant's election. See guardian by election.

guardian by judicial appointment. The most common kind of guardian, being a person appointed by the court as the guardian of the person, of the property, or of both person and property, of an infant or mental incompetent.

guardian by nature. The father of an infant, 25 Am J1st G & W § 6; the mother of an infant upon the death of the father, upon his removal as guardian, or upon his abandonment of wife and children. 25 Am J1st G & W § 7. In some jurisdictions, although not in others, the next of kin of an infant where the parents are both deceased. 25 Am J1st G & W § 7. One having a right to the custody of the person of the ward, but no right of custody or control over his estate, except as such right is conferred by statute or other law. 25 Am J1st G & W § 10.

At common law guardianship by nature was a guardianship of the person only, was limited to the eldest son, and continued until the ward became twenty-one. 25 Am J1st G & W § 5.

guardian by nurture. A common-law guardian of the person only, the guardianship being that of the father and extending to all his children, and continuing until the ward reached the age of fourteen if a boy, or sixteen if a girl. A type of guardianship long since succeeded by that of guardianship by nature. 25 Am J1st G & W §§ 5, 6.

See guardian by nature.

guardian by statute. An expression which, in England, designates a guardian appointed by the father's will. Huson v Green, 88 Ga 722, 725, 16 SE 255.

guardian de son tort (gär'diạn dē sōn tor). A person who, without legal appointment or qualification, assumes the functions of a guardian by exercising control over the person, or estate, or both, of a minor or insane person. Maish v Valenzuela, 71 Ariz 426, 229 P2d 248, 25 ALR2d 747.

guardian for nurture. See guardian by nurture.

guardian in chivalry. A status acquired by a lord of the manor, upon the death of a tenant holding by knight service, in reference to children of the tenant, such guardian having the right to the custody of the ward's person, and to take the profits of his land, as recompense for the loss of knight service, the guardianship terminating when the ward, if a male, reached the age of 21, or, if a female, the age of 14. 25 Am J1st G & W § 5.

guardian in socage. A guardian of an infant under 14 years inheriting lands held in socage, the guardian being the next of blood to the heir and one who could by no possibility inherit the socage estate in guardianship. 25 Am J1st G & W § 5.

guardian of spendthrift. A guardian appointed by a court, on the institution of appropriate proceedings for that purpose, to take charge of the estate of an improvident person, profligate, spendthrift, or drunkard, the appointment of such a guardian being authorized by statute in some states. 25 Am J1st G & W § 20.

guardian of the spiritualities. See custos spiritualium.

guardian of the temporalities. See custos temporalium.

guardian's bond. The bond required of guardian by judicial appointment. 25 Am J1st G & W § 47. The bond sometimes required of a natural guardian. 25 Am J1st G & W § 47.

guardian's commission. The fees of a guardian for performance of the duties of his office; the compensation to which a guardian is entitled. 25 Am J1st G & W § 182.

guardianship. The office of a guardian; the functions and duties pertaining to the office of a guardian. A trust relation of the most sacred character, in which one person, called a "guardian," acts for another, called the "ward," whom the law regards as incapa-

ble of managing his own affairs. Harrison v Harrison, 21 NM 372, 155 P 356.
See **guardian**.

guardians of the peace. Same as **conservators of the peace**.

guardians of the poor. The board or body having charge of the care and support of the persons of a county who are dependent upon the county for their support.

guardianus (gar-di-ā'nus). Same as **gardianus**.

guardrail. A protection around a stairway, open shaft, or other place of danger; an additional rail at an intersection of railroads, intended to prevent cars from jumping the track.
See **handrails**.

guarra (gar'ra). War.

guastald. Same as **gastaldus**.

gubernator (gū''bėr-nạ̄'tȯr). A helmsman; a pilot; a governor.

gubernatorial (gū''bėr-nạ-tō'ri-ạl). Pertaining to or connected with the office of a governor.

gue (gū). A vagrant; a vagabond.

guerpi. Abandoned; deserted.

guerra (gayr'rah). War.

guerre. Same as **guerra**.

guess. A conjecture; an estimate made without knowledge of the facts.

guessing contest. A contest at prophesying or predicting, for a prize, the best answer to the question or the nearest approximation to a figure, the correctness of which answer or prediction will determine the winner of the prize; not a lottery where skill or judgment is the dominant element in determining the winner. 34 Am J1st Lot § 12.

guest. One invited or received at the home, table, or other place of another, for food, lodging, entertainment, or sociability. A person stopping at an inn, hotel, motel, or other place of public accommodation, for food or lodging, without becoming a permanent resident or tenant. 29 Am J1st Innk § 12.
See **business visitor; visitor**.

guest in aircraft. A person who is not a passenger for hire or an employee but is carried in an aircraft with the knowledge and consent of the owner or operator. Anno: 12 ALR2d 657; 8 Am J2d Avi § 81.

guest in motor vehicle. One who is invited, either directly or by implication, to enjoy the hospitality of the owner or operator of a motor vehicle, and who accepts such hospitality and takes a ride either for his own pleasure or on his own business, without making any return to or conferring any benefit upon the owner or operator of the motor vehicle other than the mere pleasure of his company. 8 Am J2d Auto § 475.
This term does not include one becoming a passenger for the substantial benefit of the owner or operator. Antonen v Swanson, 74 SD 1, 48 NW2d 161, 28 ALR2d 1.

guest statutes. Statutes relative to the liability of the owner or operator of a motor vehicle, aircraft, or pleasure boat, for injury to a guest. 8 Am J2d Auto § 471; Avi § 81; 12 Am J2d Boats § 37.

guest-taker. Same as **agister**.

guia (gwī'ạ). (Spanish.) A way; a right of way.

guidage (gī'dāj). A reward or compensation paid by a traveler to a guide for his safe conduct in a strange country.

guide. A person whom others follow for the purpose of arriving at a specific destination. A person who conducts tourists or strangers in a region through the region and buildings and other points of interest therein. Something to follow, be it a book, a design, or a plan.

guide book. A compilation depicting, describing, and furnishing information as to points of interest, historical and natural attractions in a city or region, prepared for tourists and also with the idea of advertising the city or region so as to attract tourists. A writing of an author within the meaning of the copyright law. 18 Am J2d Copyr § 38.

Guidon De La Mer (gē-dön dē lah mare). The title of an authoritative treatise on maritime law, written about 1670.

guild. A term, more familiar in England than in the United States, for a union of men in the same craft, trade, or occupation, or for an association for mutual aid and improvement of the members.

guild-hall. The meeting place of a guild.

guilt. Criminality; culpability; guiltiness; the antithesis of innocence.

guilty (gil'ti). The plea of a defendant in a criminal prosecution who admits having committed the crime with which he is charged. Having guilt; justly chargeable with a crime; not innocent; criminal. The state of a person who has committed an offense. Commonwealth v Walter, 83 Pa 105, 108.
See **plea of guilty**.

guilty knowledge. An element of offenses, such as receiving stolen property or accepting bank deposits with knowledge of insolvency of the bank, consisting of actual knowledge of the relevant fact or of notice of facts and circumstances from which knowledge of the relevant fact may be implied, but not merely of an innocent bona fide ignorance arising from neglect to keep posted or to inquire. Utley v Hill, 155 Mo 232, 55 SW 1091.

guilty mind. General criminal intent. 21 Am J2d Crim L §§ 81, 82.
See **mens rea**.

guilty plea. See **plea of guilty**.

gulch. A natural waterway for the drainage of surface water, characterized by precipitous banks. 56 Am J1st Wat § 76. A deep or precipitous cleft, especially the sharply hollowed-out bed of a torrential intermittent stream; a ravine; a deep gully. Popham v Holloron, 84 Mont 442, 275 P 1099.

gule of August (gūl). The first day of the month of August.

gulf. An arm of the ocean or of an inland sea extending into the land.

gullible. Easily imposed upon or cheated.

gully. A ravine or gulch; a natural watercourse for the drainage of surface waters. Not necessarily a watercourse, although sometimes considered to be such. Anno: 40 ALR 852.

gun. In military parlance, a heavy weapon with a long barrel, such as a cannon. In common parlance, a rifle, pistol, revolver, machine gun, or other instrumentality having a barrel or tube from which a bullet or other projectile is discharged by force, usually the force generated by the explosion of gunpowder. Harris v Cameron, 81 Wis 239.

See **firearm; spring gun.**

Gunpowder Plot. The name given to a conspiracy to kill James I of England, and blow up the House of Parliament, by an explosion, in retaliation for anti-Catholic legislation, most of which had been enacted in the reign of Elizabeth I.

gunwale. The upper edge of the side of a watercraft.

gurgites. Gullies or pools of water on a man's land, isolated from other water, in which he has the exclusive right of taking fish. Arnold v Mundy, 6 NJL 1.

gust (gust). A burst of wind or rain. A Saxon term for a guest, especially a guest for two nights running.

gutter. A long receptacle and conduit hung on a building to catch the eavesdrip. A narrow ditch along the side of a street or highway for drainage.

Guy Fawkes. The chief of the conspirators in the Gunpowder Plot.

See **Gunpowder Plot.**

guy wire. A wire which holds a pole, building, or other structure to the ground, being attached to an upper portion and running downward but laterally to the ground, wherein it is anchored, its purpose being to support the pole or other structure against stress, especially that produced by high wind.

gwabr merched. A fee paid to the lord of the manor upon the loss of her maidenhood, by marriage or otherwise, of the daughter of a tenant.

gwalstow. A place where capital offenders were put to death.

gwayf. Stolen property which was dropped in the highway to avoid discovery.

gylwite. Amends or compensation paid to settle a fraud or a trespass.

gymnasium. A building or room for the practice of gymnastic exercises, as distinguished from field athletics, but often including a rowing tank, a cage for winter practice of baseball, etc.; a place or building where athletic exercises are performed; a school of gymnastics. McNair v School Dist. 87 Mont 423, 288 P 188, 69 ALR 866. An adjunct of schools in modern times. 47 Am J1st Schools § 75.

gymnasium fee. An incidental charge imposed upon a student in college or university. 15 Am J2d Colleges § 19.

gynarchy (jin'ạr-ki). A government ruled by a woman; as, by a queen.

gypsum. A mineral. 36 Am J1st Min & M § 5.

gyro compass. A form of compass used for steering a ship consisting of a rapidly spinning rotor so swung as to maintain its axis in the geographical meridian in pointing to the true north, often equipped with a course recorder so that the course of the vessel is recorded automatically on a graph which shows the heading of the vessel, in degrees on the compass, at any and all times. The Sakito Maru (DC Cal) 41 F Supp 769.

gyrotiller (jī'rō-til-ėr). A self-propelled plowing device, used by sugar planters throughout the West Indies, so constructed and equipped as to turn the soil, pulverize it, and prepare the ground for planting, all in one operation. Central Aguirre Sugar Co. v Domenech (CA1 Puerto Rico) 115 F2d 502.

gyves (jīvz). Handcuffs; shackles.

H

H. A. Abbreviation of "in this year," being derived from "hoc anno."

hab. corp. An abbreviation of **habeas corpus.**

habeas corpora (hā'be-as kor'po-ra). Same as **habeas corpora juratorum.**

habeas corpora juratorum (hā'be-as kor'po-ra jū-rā-tō'rum). That you have the bodies of the jurors,— a writ of the court of common pleas commanding the sheriff to have the bodies of jurors named in the panel, or else to distrain them by their lands and goods, to compel their appearance in court upon the day appointed. See 3 Bl Comm 354.

habeas corpus (hā'bē-as kôr'pus). A high prerogative writ of ancient origin, the vital purposes of which are to obtain immediate relief from illegal confinement; to liberate those who may be imprisoned without sufficient cause, and to deliver them from unlawful custody; or to obtain a proper custody of persons illegally detained from the control of those who are entitled to the custody of them. 25 Am J1st Hab C § 2. A generic term in one sense, being applicable to each of several different writs, but as used generally, referring to the writ of habeas corpus ad subjiciendum. 25 Am J1st Hab C § 2.

Habeas Corpus Act (hā'be-as kor'pus act). An English statute (31 Car. II) passed to remedy a condition of indifference or disregard of the rights of the people which had through royal influence and other causes reached the point where the common law writ became so little respected that it no longer afforded real or substantial benefits to English subjects.

The act had the desired effect, although it introduced no new principle, conferred no right upon the subject and made no change in the practice of the courts in granting the writ, but it did correct certain imperfections of the common law writ and tended to make the prisoner's remedy a speedy one. 25 Am J1st Hab C § 6.

habeas corpus ad deliberandum et recipiendum (hā'be-as kor'pus ad dē-li-be-ran'dum et re-si-pi-en'dum). A writ of habeas corpus which issues where it is necessary to remove a prisoner in order that he may be tried in the proper jurisdiction— namely, that wherein the act was committed. 25 Am J1st Hab C § 4.

habeas corpus ad faciendum et recipiendum (hā'be-as kor'pus ad fā-she-en'dum et re-si-pi-en'dum). A common writ of habeas corpus which issues where a person is sued and arrested in some inferior jurisdiction and is desirous of removing the action into a superior court, commanding the inferior judges to produce the body of the defendant and to state the day and cause of his caption and detainer. 25 Am J1st Hab C § 4.

habeas corpus ad prosequendum (hā-be-as kor'pus ad prō-se-quen'dum). A writ of habeas corpus which issues for the purpose of removing a prisoner in order to prosecute him in the proper jurisdiction, namely, that wherein the act was committed, or to enable him to become the prosecuting witness in a criminal case. 25 Am J1st Hab C § 4.

habeas corpus ad respondendum (hā-be-as kor'pus ad res-pon-den'dum). A writ of habeas corpus which issues where one has a claim against another, who is in custody under process of an inferior court, in order to remove the prisoner and prefer the claim against him in the higher court. 25 Am J1st Hab C § 4.

habeas corpus ad satisfaciendum (hā'be-as kor'pus ad sa-tis-fa-she-en'dum). A writ of habeas corpus which issues where a prisoner has had judgment against him in an action, and the plaintiff is desirous of bringing him up to some superior court to charge him with process of execution. 25 Am J1st Hab C § 4.

This writ is not available in the United States, because here one court never awards execution on the judgment of another. 25 Am J1st Hab C § 4.

habeas corpus ad subjiciendum (hā'be-as kor'pus ad sub-ji-she-en'dum). The ordinary writ of habeas corpus.

See **habeas corpus.**

habeas corpus ad testificandum (hā'be-as kor'pus ad tes-ti-fi-kan'dum). A writ of habeas corpus, although not a high prerogative writ, its issuance lying in the sound discretion of the court, which issues to remove a prisoner in order for him to bear testimony. 25 Am J1st Hab C § 4.

habeas corpus cum causa (hā'be-as kor'pus kum kâ'za). The same as **habeas corpus ad faciendum et recipiendum.**

habeas ibi tunc hoc breve. See **et habeas ibi tunc hoc breve.**

Habemus optimum testem, confitentem reum (hā-bē'mus op'ti-mum tes'tem, kon-fi-ten'tem rē'um). We have the best witness, a defendant who is confessing.

habendum clause. That part of a deed, usually following the premises, which sets forth the estate to be held and enjoyed by the grantee.

Words of inheritance are commonly used, but contrary to the rule at common law, under the statutes now in force in most states, such are not necessary to pass a title in fee simple. 23 Am J2d Deeds § 38.

habendum et tenendum (hā-ben'dum et te-nen'dum). To have and to hold.

habentes homines (hā-ben'tēz ho'mi-nēz). Men who have things; wealthy men.

habentia (hā-ben'she-a). Riches.

habere (hạ-bē're). To have.

habere facias possessionem (hā-bē're fā'she-as po-ze-she-ō'nem). The technical term applied to a writ of possession for the execution of a judgment in favor of a plaintiff in ejectment. 25 Am J2d Eject § 133. A writ of possession directed to the sheriff of the county commanding him to give actual possession to the plaintiff who had established his right to recover a chattel interest in land in a real or mixed action. See 3 Bl Comm 412.

Habere facias seisinam (hā-bē're fa'she-as sē'si-nam). That you give him seisin,—a writ of seisin of a freehold,—a writ directed to the sheriff of the county commanding him to give actual possession to the plaintiff, who had established his right to recover land in a real action. See 3 Bl Comm 412.

habere facias visum (hā-bē're fā'she-as vī'sum). A writ which directs the sheriff to view the premises in controversy.

habere licere (hā-be′re lī′se-re). To allow to hold, to allow a person to take possession.

Habeto tibi res tuas (hā-bē′tō ti′bi rēz tu′as). Take your effects or belongings to yourself—a Roman formula for divorcing a wife.

hab. fa. An abbreviation of **habere facias possessionem.**

habiles ad matrimonium (ha′bi-lēz ad ma-tri-mō′ni-um). Fit for marriage.

habilis (ha′bi-lis). Suitable; proper; fit; capable.

habit. A customary method of doing a thing. See 29 Am J2d Ev § 303. Customary conduct, deriving as a tendency arising from frequent repetition. Knickerbocker Life Ins. Co. v Foley, 105 US 350, 26 L Ed 1055.

When a person has repeatedly acted in a particular way at intervals, whether regular or irregular, for such length of time as that we can predicate with reasonable assurance that he will continue so to act, we may affirm that this is his habit. State ex rel. Atty. Gen. v Savage, 89 Ala 1, 7 So 183.

It would be incorrect to say that a man has a habit of anything from a single act. A habit of early rising, for instance, could not be affirmed of one because he was once seen abroad before sunrise; nor could intemperate habits be imputed to him because his appearance and actions might indicate a night of excessive indulgence. Knickerbocker Life Ins. Co. v Foley (US) 15 Otto 350, 26 L Ed 1055.

habitable. Fit for habitation; tenantable; reasonably fit for occupation by a tenant of the class which occupies it. Miller v McCardell, 19 RI 304, 33 A 445.

habitable repair. Good repair; such state of repair as renders a building fit for occupancy by an inhabitant.

habitancy. Residence or domicil; a residence at a place with the intent to make and regard it as a home. Lyman v Fiske, 34 Mass (17 Pick) 231.
See **domicil; residence.**

habit and repute. Habits and reputation.

habitatio (ha-bi-tā′she-ō). Same as **habitation.**

habitation. A component part of the concept of domicil, as an abiding in a place. Re Lester, 377 Pa 411, 105 A2d 376. A place of abode, either permanent or temporary. Union Hotel Co. v Hersee, 79 NY 454.

habit-forming drugs. Narcotic drugs.

habitual. By habit; constant; customary, accustomed, usual; common; ordinary; regular; familiar. Peltz v Printz, 186 Pa 347, 349.

habitual carnal intercourse. Sexual intercourse, had at least more than one time, between persons not husband and wife. 2 Am J2d Adult § 3.

habitual criminal. A second or subsequent offender; a convicted person with a prior criminal record. A term usually defined with precision by statute in a jurisdiction where the status permits or requires an increase in term of imprisonment imposed for a crime.
See **sterilization.**

habitual criminal statute. A statute which imposes a greater punishment for a second or subsequent offense than for the first. Tucker v State, 14 Okla Crim 54, 167 P 637.

Such statutes have been enacted in order that one who persists in the commission of crime may be put away permanently and the state may rid itself of the depravity when its efforts to reform have failed. Coleman v Commonwealth, 276 Ky 802, 125 SW2d 728.

habitual drunkard. One who drinks intoxicating liquors to excess and with habitual frequency, as the opportunity permits. One who has lost the power or will to control his appetite for intoxicating liquors or narcotics, and has the fixed habit of drunkenness. 29 Am J Rev ed Ins Per § 8.

habitual drunkenness. A very frequent condition of intoxication. The result of indulging a natural or acquired appetite for intoxicating liquors, by continued use, until it becomes a customary practice. 29 Am J Rev ed Ins Per § 8. A disease of mind and body, analogous to insanity. Leavitt v Morris, 105 Minn 170, 117 NW 393. As ground for divorce:— habitually drinking intoxicating drinks immoderately and a habit of getting drunk. Anno: 120 ALR 1177.

habitual intemperance. A very frequent condition of intoxication.
See **habitual drunkenness.**

habitual intoxication. Same as **habitual drunkenness.**

habitually. By habit, customarily. By frequent practice.

The word does not appear to mean "exclusively" or "entirely." Stanton v French, 91 Cal 274, 27 P 657.

habitual user. A drug addict.
See **habitual drunkenness.**

habitum et tonsuram clericalem (ha′bi-tum et ton-shu′ri-am kle-ri-kā′lem). The clerical garb and tonsure. See 4 Bl Comm 367.

habitus (hab′i-tus). Habit; garb; appearance; apparel.

habitus et tonsura clericalis (ha′bi-tus et ton-shū′ra kle-ri-kā′lis). The dress and tonsure of a priest or clergyman.

hacienda (as-i-en′dä). (Spanish). An estate; the public domain.

hack. A vehicle for hire in the transportation of persons. A term inclusive of automobiles in so far as a regulation of the transportation of passengers for hire is concerned. Fletcher v Bordelon (Tex Civ App) 56 SW2d 313, error ref.
See **taxicab.**

hadbote (had′bōt). A fine or mulct imposed for the offense of committing an assault on a clergyman.

Haddock Case. A decision of the United States Supreme Court in a divorce case (Haddock v Haddock, 201 US 562, 50 L Ed 867, 26 S Ct 525) involving the application of the full faith and credit clause of the United States Constitution to a divorce decree obtained against a nonresident defendant upon constructive service of process, once regarded as a leading authority upon the question determined, but now to be considered in the light of more recent decisions of the same court. 24 Am J2d Div & S § 951.

hade (hād). A grassy slope.

haderunga (ha-de-run′ga). Hatred; ill will; malevolence.

hadgonel. A tax.

Hadley v Baxendale. An English case notable for the principle that the damages recoverable for breach of contract are such as may fairly and reasonably be considered as arising naturally—that is, according to the usual course of things—from the breach of the contract itself, or such as may reasonably be supposed to have been in the contemplation of both parties at the time they made the contract, as the probable result of its breach. 9 Exch 341, 156 Eng Reprint 145.

Haec est conventio (hēk est kon-ven'she-ō). This is the agreement.

Haec est finalis concordia (hēk est fī-nā'lis kon-kor'-di-a). This is the final agreement,—the formal words which usually formed the beginning or introductory part of the indentures which after being engrossed were delivered to the cognizor and cognizee, and which recited at length all of the steps in the levying of a fine at common law. See 2 Bl Comm 351.

Haec quae nullius in bonis sunt, et olim fuerunt inventoris de jure naturali, jam efficiuntur principis de jure gentium (hēk kwē nul-lī'us in bō'nis sunt, et o'lim fu'e-runt in-ven-to'ris dē jū're na-tū-rā'lī, jam ef-fi-she-un'ter prin'si-pis dē jū're jen'she-um). These things which are the goods of no one and which were formerly the property of the finder by natural right, now are made those of the king by the law of nations. See 1 Bl Comm 299.

Haec sunt institutiones, quas Rex Edmundus et episcopi sui cum sapientibus suis instituerunt (hēk sunt in-sti-tū-she-ō'nēz, quas Rex Ed-mun'dus et e-pis'-ko-pī su'ī kum sa-pi-en'ti-bus su'is in-sti-shu-ē'runt). These are the institutions which King Edmund and his bishops and his wise men have established. See 1 Bl Comm 148.

Haec sunt judicia quae sapientes consilio regis Ethelstani instituerunt (hēk sunt jū-di'she-a kwē sa-pi-en'tēz kon-si'li-ō rē'jis E-thel-stā'nī in-sti-shu-ē'runt). These are the decrees which the wise men with the advice of King Ethelstane have ordained. See 1 Bl Comm 148.

haec verba (hēk ver'ba). See **in haec verba; pleading in haec verba.**

haereda (hē-rē'da). The name given to the hundred-court in the Gothic constitution. See 3 Bl Comm 35.
 See **hundred-court.**

haerede deliberando. See **de haerede deliberando, etc.**

Haeredem Deus facit, non homo (hē-rē'dem Dē'us fā'sit, non hō'mō). God makes an heir, not man.

haerede rapto et abducto. See **de haerede et abducto.**

haeredes (hē-rē'dēz). Heirs, plural of **haeres.**

Haeredes est nomen collectivum (hē-rē'dēz est nō'men kol-lek-tī'vum). Heirs is a collective name.

haeredes extranei (hē-rē'dēz ex-trā'nē-ī). (Civil law.) Foreign heirs; that is, heirs who were neither the children nor the slaves of the decedent.

haeredes facti (hē-rē'dēz fak'tī). (Civil law.) Made heirs; that is, beneficiaries under the will of the decedent.

haeredes necessarii (hē-rē'dēz ne-ses-sā'ri-ī). (Civil law.) Heirs of necessity; that is, heirs who were so without their election to become heirs.

haeredes proximi (hē-rē'dēz prok'si-mī). Nearest heirs, next heirs, children or descendants of the decedent.

haeredes recti (hē-rē'dēz rek'tī). Right heirs.
 See **right heirs.**

haeredes remotiores (hē-rē'dēz re-mō-she-ō'rēz). More remote heirs; that is heirs of more remote relationship than haeredes proximi.

haeredes sui et necessarii (hē-rē'dēs su'ī et ne-ses-sā'ri-ī). (Civil law.) Descendants of the deceased and haeredes necessarii.

Haeredi magis parcendum est (hē-rē'dī mā'jis par-sen'dum est). An heir should be dealt with more leniently.

haeredipeta (hē-rē-di'pe-ta). A person seeking an inheritance; that is, the next heir.

Haeredipetae suo propinquo vel extraneo periculoso sane custodi nullus committatur (hē-rē-di'pe-tē su'ō pro-pin'quō vel ex-trā'ne-ō pe-ri-ku-lō'sō sā'ne kus-tō'dī nul'lus kom-mit-tā'ter). No one should be committed to his next heir or to a stranger, certainly a dangerous guardian.

haereditas (hē-rē'di-tās). An inheritance.

Haereditas, alia corporalis, alia incorporalis; corporalis est, quae tangi potest et videri; incorporalis quae tangi non potest nec videri (hē-rē'di-tās, a'li-a kor-po-rā'lis, a'li-a in-kor-po-rā'lis; kor-po-rā'lis est, kwē tan'jī po'test et vi-dē'rī; in-kor-po-rā'lis kwē tan'jī non po'test nek vi-dē'rī). An inheritance is either corporeal or incorporeal; corporeal is that which can be touched or seen; incorporeal is that which can neither be touched nor seen.

haereditas damnosa (hē-rē'di-tās dam-nō'sa). A detrimental or burdensome inheritance; that is, an inheritance which would render the heir liable for debts of the deceased ancestor.

Haereditas est successio in universum jus quod defunctus habuerat (hē-rē'di-tās est suk-se'she-ō in ū-ni-ver'sum jūs quod de-funk'tus hā-bu'e-rat). Inheritance is the succession to every right which the deceased had.

haereditas jacens (hē-rē'di-tās jā'senz). (Roman law.) A fallen or prostrate inheritance; an inheritance which the heir has not yet received or accepted; an inheritance with no owner. See 2 Bl Comm 259.

haereditas luctuosa (hē-rē'di-tās luk-tu-ō'sa). (Civil law.) A sorrowful or mournful inheritance,—an inheritance in the ascending line, as by parents from children was considered as disturbing the natural order of inheritance. See 4 Kent Comm 397.

Haereditas nihil aliud est, quam successio in universum jus, quod defunctus habuerit (hē-rē'di-tās ni'hil a'li-ud est, quam suk-se'she-ō in ū-ni-ver'sum jūs, quod de-funk'tus hā-bu'e-rit). An inheritance is nothing but the succession to all the rights which the deceased had.

Haereditas nunquam ascendit (hē-rē'di-tās nun'-quam a-sen'dit). An inheritance never ascends. This very ancient maxim was recorded in writings in the time of Henry the Second and was probably of feudal origin and formed the basis of the first canon of descent that inheritances should lineally descend to the issue of the person who last died actually seised in infinitum; but should never lineally ascend. See 2 Bl Comm 208, 211.
 See **haereditas luctuosa.**

haereditas paterna (hē-rē'di-tās pa-ter'na). A paternal inheritance, an inheritance from the heir's father.

Haeredum appellatione veniunt haeredes haeredum in infinitum (hē-rē′dum ap-pel-lā-she-ō′ne ve′ni-unt he-rē′dēz he-rē′dum in in-fī-nī′tum). Under the name "heirs" come the heirs of heirs without limit.

haeres (hē′rēz). (Roman law.) A person who succeeds to the rights of a decedent in real or personal property, whether by the law of descent or under a will. Adams v Akerlund, 168 Ill 632, 639, 48 NE 454.

haeres actu (hē′rēz ak′tū). (Roman law.) A person who became such by the act or appointment of the deceased in his lifetime.

haeres astrarius (hē′rēz as-trā′ri-us). An heir in the actual possession of his inheritance.

haeres de facto (hē′rēz dē fak′tō). Same as **haeres factus**.

Haeres est alter ipse, et filius est pars patris (hē′rēz est al′ter ip′se, et fi′li-us est parz pa′tris). An heir is a man's other self, and the son is a part of his father.

Haeres est aut jure proprietatis aut jure representationis (hē′rēz est ât jū′re pro-prī-e-tā′tis ât jū′re re-pre-sen-tā-she-ō′nis). A person is an heir either by right of property or by right of representation.

Haeres est eadem persona cum antecessore (hē′rēz est e-ā′dem per-sō′na kum an-te-ses′sō-re). An heir is the same person as his ancestor.

Haeres est nomen collectivum (hē′rēz est nō′men kol-lek′tī-vum). Heir is a collective name.

Haeres est nomen juris; filius est nomen naturae (hē′rēz est nō′men jū′ris; fi′li-us est nō′men nā-tū′rē). Heir is the legal name, son is the natural name.

Haeres est pars antecessoris (hē′rēz est parz an-te-ses′sō-ris). The heir is a part of his ancestor. Schoonmaker v Sheely (NY) 3 Hill 165, 167.

Haeres est quem nuptiae demonstrant (hē′rēz est quem nup′she-ē de-mon′strant). The heir is the person whom the marriage shows to be the heir.

haeres ex asse (hē′rēz ex as′se). (Civil law.) An heir to the whole estate of the deceased; a sole heir.

haeres extraneus (hē′rēz ex-trā′ne-us). (Civil law.) A foreign heir,—an heir who was neither a slave nor a child of the deceased.

haeres factus (hē′rēz fak′tus). (Civil law.) A made heir,—an heir appointed by will or by settlement, as distinguished from an heir born; a devisee. See 1 Bl Comm 196.

haeres fideicommissarius (hē′rēz fī-dē-ī-kom-mis-sa′ri-us). (Civil law.) A beneficiary heir,—a testamentary cestui que trust.

haeres fiduciarius (hē′rēz fi-du-she-ā′ri-us). (Roman law.) A fiduciary heir, a fiduciarius or trustee who was made haeres by will for the benefit of the fideicommissarius. Mackeldey's Roman Law § 783.

Haeres haeredis mei est meus haeres (hē′rēz hē-rē′dis mē′ī est mē′us hē′rēz). The heir of my heir is my heir.

haeres legitimus (hē′rēz le-ji′ti-mus). A lawful heir,—an heir born out of lawful wedlock.

Haeres legitimus est quem nuptiae demonstrant (hē′rēz le-ji′ti-mus est quem nup′she-ē de-mon′-strant). He is the lawful heir whom the marriage points out to be such. Jackson v Jackson, 82 Md 17, 33 A 317.

Haeres minor uno et vigenti annis non respondebit, nisi in casu dotis (hē′rēz mī′nor ū′nō et vi-jen′tī an′nis non re-spon-dē′bit, nī′sī in kā′sū dō′tis). An heir who is under twenty-one years of age is not answerable, except in the matter of dower.

haeres natus (hē′rēz nā′tus). A born heir; an heir who is entitled to inherit by descent. See 1 Bl Comm 196.

haeres necessarius (hē′rēz ne-ses-sā′ri-us). Singular of **haeredes necessarii**.

Haeres non tenetur in Anglia ad debita antecessoris reddenda, nisi per antecessorem ad hoc fuerit obligatus, praeterquam debita regis tantum (hē′rēz non te-nē′ter in An′gli-a ad de′bi-ta an-te-ses-sō′ris red-den′da, ni′sī per an-te-ses-so′rem ad hōc fu′er-it ob-li-gā′tus, prē-ter′quam de′bi-ta rē′jis tan′tum). The heir is not bound in England to pay his ancestor's debts unless he was bound to this by the ancestor, excepting whatever is owed to the king.

haeres rectus (hē′rēz rek′tus). A right heir. See **right heir**.

haeres suus (hē′rēz su′us). (Civil law.) His own heir, —a proper heir; an heir by descent.

haeretare (hē-re-tā′re). To attach an hereditary character to a gift.

haeretico comburendo (hē-re′ti-kō kom-bū-ren′dō). See **de haeretico comburendo**.

haesitabant (hez-i-ta′bànt). They were in doubt.

hafne courts (haf′ne korts). Haven courts,—courts anciently held in ports of England.

haga (ha′ga). A house; a house in a city or borough.

Hague Tribunal. A name applied first to an international court of arbitration established by the International Peace Conference of 1889, later to the Permanent Court of International Justice established under the auspices of the League of Nations in 1920, but now to the International Court of Justice established as the judicial branch of the United Nations. 30 Am J Rev ed Internat L § 54.

haie. (French.) A hedge; an enclosure.

haiebote. Same as **haybote**.

haill. Whole; the whole.

hailworkfolk. Same as **halywercfolk**.

haimsucken. Same as **hamesecken**.

hair stylist. A hairdresser. 10 Am J2d Barbers § 2.

hale. Healthy.

halegemot. Same as **halmote**.

half. A fraction. The part obtainable in an equal division. As descriptive of the premises in a deed: —an undivided interest of one half. 23 Am J2d Deeds § 246. A half section of land.

half blood. Broadly defined, relatives by blood but having only one common ancestor. The relationship between children who have but one of their parents in common. Butler v King, 10 Tenn (2 Yerg) 115, 118.

In a number of cases wherein the language of the will was unambiguous or there was no expression of an intent to the contrary, it has been held that half bloods share equally with whole bloods in a testamentary gift to "heirs," "heirs at law," "legal heirs," etc. Anno: 49 ALR2d 1369. In other cases, however, it has been held that half bloods do not share equally in such gifts. Anno: 49 ALR2d 1372.

half brother. A man or boy related to one through a common parentage limited to one parent. Wood v Mitcham, 92 NY 375, 379.
See **half blood.**

half-endeal (haf-en'dĕl). One-half.

half fare. A reduced charge made by a carrier of passengers for certain persons, especially children and students. 14 Am J2d Car § 847.

half gelt. A horse castrated to the extent only of removing one of his testicles. Douglas v Moses, 89 Iowa 40.

half-notes. Notes which were given as payment and torn in half; half of each note was given to the seller when the buyer ordered the goods and the other half upon delivery of them.

half pilotage. The fee to which a pilot is entitled under compulsory pilotage laws where his services are offered but declined. 48 Am J1st Ship § 204.

half-proof. An obsolete term for proof by a single witness or by a single document. 3 Bl Comm 370.

half-section. Three hundred twenty acres of land according to the government survey.

half sister. A woman or girl related to one through a common parentage limited to one parent. Wood v Mitcham, 92 NY 375, 379.
See **half blood.**

half-tongue. A term applied to a jury, part of whom speak one language and part another.

half-truth. Deceit consisting in only a partial disclosure of the facts. 37 Am J2d Fraud § 151. A fraud where spoken with a design of influencing the opposite party who does not have equal means of knowledge. Addison v Wilson, 238 Ky 143, 37 SW2d 7.

half-year (häf'yĕr). One hundred and eighty-two days, odd hours being rejected in the computation. 52 Am J1st Time § 15.

hali-gemote. Same as **halle-gemote.**

Halimass. Same as **Hallowmass.**

hallage (hâ'lāj). A toll charged for the privilege of selling goods in a hall or fair.

hallazco (al-lyath-ko). (Spanish.) The acquisition of title to goods which have been abandoned by finding them.

hall day. A court day.

halle-gemote. A manor court; a court baron.

Halloween. The evening of Oct. 31; the evening preceding All Saints Day, generally celebrated by masquerading, especially by children who go from house to house seeking treats under threat of "tricks."

Hallowmass (hal'ō-mąs). All Saints' Day, the first day of november.

hallucination. A morbid error in one or more of the senses; a perception of objects which do not, in fact, make any impression on the external senses.
The basic distinction between an hallucination and a delusion is that the former is a matter of false perception, the latter a matter of false idea or belief. 29 Am J Rev ed Ins Per § 3.

halmote. Same as **court-baron.**

halt. Infirm. A stop. To stop, especially on command.

halywercfolk. Tenants who held their land by the service of repairing or defending a church.

ham. A home; a house; a dwelling house. In the more modern sense, meat of the hog taken from the quarters, usually marketed after curing; the thigh and buttock. A slang term for an incompetent actor or an actor who overplays.

hamble (ham'bl). To hamstring an animal; to expeditate a dog, that is, to remove the balls of his feet to prevent the chasing of game.

hamel (ham'el). A village.

hamesecken (hām'sek-en). Home-sacking,—the ancient word for burglary, or nocturnal housebreaking. See 4 Bl Comm 223.

hamesucken (hām'suk-n). Same as **hamesecken.**

hamfare (ham'far). An assault upon a person committed within a house or dwelling.

hamlet (ham'let). A small village; a vill.

hamma (ham'ma). Same as **curtilage.**

hamsocne. Same as **hamesecken.**

hamsoken. Same as **hamesecken.**

hamstring. To disable an animal by severing the hamstring, the tendon in the hock. To place such restraint upon a person that he is unable to act.

hanaper (han'ą-pėr). A hamper; a receptacle where writs and their returns were kept. See 3 Bl Comm 49.

hanaper office (han'ą-pėr). An old term for an office in the English court of chancery where original writs pertaining to subjects, as distinguished from writs relating to the crown, were issued. Yates v People (NY) 6 Johns 337, 363.

Hanc Tuemur, Hac Nitimur (hank tu-ē'mer, hāk ni'-ti-mer). This we defend, this we lean upon.
The words are those of a motto which appears on the face of a medallion on the title page of the journal of the proceedings of the Colonial Congress of 1774, representing Magna Charta as the pedestal on which was raised the column and cap of liberty, supported by twelve hands; one for each of the twelve colonies. Hurtado v California, 110 US 516, 554, 28 L Ed 232, 245, 4 S Ct 111, 292.

hand. The terminal of the arm; a member of man and apes adapted for grasping things. Champlin Refining Co. v State Industrial Com. 153 Okla 45, 4 P2d 1. A lineal measure of four inches. A word often used to indicate handwriting.
See **beat hand; bloody hand; clean hands; entire loss of hands or feet; note of hand; strong hand; unclean hands; witness my hand; witness my hand and seal.**

hand baggage. See **baggage.**

handbill. A printed sheet of advertising, of a convenient size for passing out along the street or from house to house. A circular. People v McLaughlin, 33 Misc 691, 693, 68 NYS 1108.

handborow (hand'bor''ō). A hand pledge; a pledge; a frank pledge.

handcar. A small car upon which railroad trackmen ride to and from work, the term continuing in use notwithstanding handpower has been replaced by diesel or electric power. Any small cart or vehicle pushed by hand.

handcuffing. Putting handcuffs on a person.

handcuffs. Manacles; shackles. Metal rings or chains placed around the wrists and locked to prevent the use of the hands and incidentally the escape of a prisoner. 5 Am J2d Arr § 75.

handfasting. A kind of trial marriage which prevailed anciently in parts of Scotland, referred to in The Monastery by Sir Walter Scott, Chapter XXV.
See **trial marriage**.

hand grith (hand grith). Protection at the hands of the king himself.

handhabend. Same as **bacberend**.

handholds. See **grab irons; handrail**.

handicap. Something that hampers a person in an endeavor or activity. A game, especially golf or bowling, in which the competition is equalized by artificially burdening the better players and favoring the players with an inferior record by adding to or subtracting points from the actual score as the plan or scheme of the game play requires. The number of points imposed to the disadvantage of a particular player. A horse race in which the horses are weighted according to the estimate of the handicapper for the purpose of equalizing their chances of winning. Stone v Clay (CA7 Ill) 61 F 889.

handicapper. One who fixes the handicaps of horses in a race or of players in a game such as bowling or golf.
See **handicap**.

handled. Moved or manipulated by the hand. Bought or sold in commerce. For the purposes of the Fair Labor Standards Act:—every kind of incidental operation preparatory to putting goods in the stream of commerce. Western Union Tel. Co. v Lenroot, 323 US 490, 89 L Ed 414, 65 S Ct 335.

handling (hand'ling). As used in the Federal Fair Labor Standards Act of 1918, the word has been defined as those physical operations customarily performed in obtaining agricultural or horticultural commodities from producers' farms, transporting them to and receiving them at the establishment, weighing them or otherwise determining on what basis the producer is to be paid, placing them in the establishment where further operations are to be performed, and delivering the commodities to warehouses. Gordon v Paducah Ice Mfg. Co. (DC Ky) 41 F Supp 980.

handling charges. Charges covering a variety of small services by brokers, banks, even cooperative associations, in completing transactions on behalf of customers or clients.

handling firearms. Using firearms or merely carrying firearms. 29A Am J Rev ed Ins § 1284.

handling, slaughtering or dressing. An expression pertaining to labor relations, meaning work in reference to the processing of meat and poultry concluded when the product is placed in the cooler, thus not including packing, loading, grading, or shipping. Shain v Armour & Co. (DC Ky) 50 F Supp 907.

handrail. A metal or wooden handhold securely fastened along a stairway to give support to users. A handhold of metal affixed to passenger cars for the convenience and protection of passengers boarding or leaving; also a metal handhold at points inside a passenger car for the protection of passengers standing or walking when the car sways on curves or is stopped abruptly.

handsale. A sale made under the ancient custom of the northern countries by shaking hands to bind the bargain; later the same word came to be used to signify the price or earnest which was given immediately after the shaking of hands, or instead of shaking hands. See 2 Bl Comm 448.

handsel (hand'sel). Same as **handsale**.

hand signals. Signals made by movement of the arm and hand, especially those made by a brakeman on a railroad train or a motorist.

hand sled. See **sled**.

hands of justice. A familiar term in exceptions from the risk found in life insurance policies, meaning an act performed under public authority, as by a police officer in the discharge of his duty. Not including the killing by a husband of the paramour of his wife, although under the circumstances and the law, such killing is a justifiable homicide. Supreme Lodge, K. T. v Crenshaw, 129 Ga 195, 58 SE 628.

handsworn. See **mainsworn**.

handwriting. Chirography; penmanship. In the broad sense, anything written by the hand. Commonwealth v Webster, 59 Mass (5 Cush) 295.
See **comparison of handwriting; court hand**.

handwriting expert. A person qualified by study and practice to identify handwriting as that of a particular person by comparison with a sample of handwriting known to be that of such person, irrespective of whether or not he makes a business of identification of handwriting. Christman v Pearson, 100 Iowa 634, 635.

hangar. The structure in which aircraft are sheltered, repaired, or serviced.

hanging. A method of execution of the death penalty. 21 Am J2d Crim L § 613. Suspending a person convicted of a capital offense by the neck until he is dead, as the penalty for such an offense.

hanging-gale (hang'ing-gāl). An old term for overdue rent.

hanging in chains. The practice, at one time common in England, of suspending the body of a murderer, who had been executed, by chains in a public place.

hangman. An executioner; a person employed to execute a capital sentence by hanging the convict.

hangwite (hang'wīt). The ancient practice of hanging a thief without bringing him to trial; a fine for permitting a thief to escape.

hanse (hans). An association formed by the merchants of different towns and cities for their mutual protection, welfare, and advantage.

hanseatic (han-sē-at'ik). Relating to a hanse or to the Hanse towns.

Hanseatic League (han-sē-at'ik lēg). A politico-commercial association or league of cities in the north of Germany and adjoining states during the middle ages.

Hanse towns (hans touns). Those towns which were associated together as members of the Hanseatic League.
See **Hanseatic League**.

hantelode. An arrest.

happiness. Contentment, consisting in many things or depending upon many circumstances, such as the right of an individual to follow his preference in selecting an occupation. Ruhstrat v People, 185 Ill 133, 57 NE 41.
See **life, liberty and the pursuit of happiness**.

harangue (ha-rang'). A noisy, bombastic, ranting speech. Commonwealth v Brown, 309 Pa 515, 164 A 726, 86 ALR 892.

harassing litigation. Vexatious or oppressive litigation. 28 Am J Rev ed Inj § 210.

HARASSMENT [549] HARTER

harassment. Torment. A form of abuse of process. 1 Am J2d Abuse P § 10.
See **harassing litigation.**

harbor. Noun: A haven for a vessel. A place on navigable waters, either landlocked or artificially protected, where vessels may resort for safety. 48 Am J1st Ship § 223. A word sometimes used as synonymous with "port", which is in fact a broader term. 48 Am J1st Ship § 223. Verb: To secrete or conceal a person. Jones v Van Zandt (US) 5 How 215, 12 L Ed 122. To keep, shelter, or protect.

harbor dues. Fixed charges for a ship's use of a harbor.

harboring a criminal. Almost indistinguishable from being an accessory after the fact; secreting a criminal or acting as a go-between to enable him to escape arrest and punishment. 39 Am J1st Obst J § 17.

harboring an alien. Keeping, maintaining, or aiding an alien to reside in the United States contrary to law. 3 Am J2d Aliens § 104.
Within the meaning of the Federal statutes dealing with the importation and harboring of alien girls not lawfully entitled to enter or to reside within the United States, to harbor means only that the girls shall be sheltered from the immigration authorities and shielded from observation to prevent their discovery as aliens. United States v Smith (CA2 NY) 112 F2d 83.

harboring an animal. Giving shelter and protection to an animal, as by keeping it in one's house or place of business. McClain v Lewiston Interstate Fair & Racing Asso. 17 Idaho 6, 104 P 1015.

harbor lines. Limits established in a navigable body of water by the federal government, a state, or a municipality for the erection of wharves, piers, or other structures to be available for convenient use in the loading or unloading of vessels. 56 Am J1st Wat § 201.

harbor master. The officer who enforces the public regulations pertaining to a harbor. 56 Am J1st Whar § 27.

harbor watch. One or a small number of men detailed to keep a lookout for the safety of a vessel while it is in harbor. O'Hara v Luchenbach Steamship Co. 269 US 364, 70 L Ed 313, 46 S Ct 157.

Harbor Worker's Compensation Act. See **Longshoremen's and Harbor Workers' Compensation Act.**

hard action. A tort action or an action to recover a penalty. Cronemillar v Duluth-Superior Milling Co. 134 Wis 248, 114 NW 432.

hard cider. Cider which has fermented. 30 Am J Rev ed Intox L § 17.

hard labor. A special condition of imprisonment for crime. 21 Am J2d Crim L § 615.
Describing the labor as hard, in a sentence imposing imprisonment at hard labor, does not signify that it shall be of unusual severity. It means no more than that it is compulsory, and continuous during the term of imprisonment. Brown v State, 74 Ala 478, 483.

hard money. Specie; a coin of the precious metals, of a certain weight and fineness, with the government stamp thereon, denoting its value as a medium of exchange, or currency. Henry v Bank of Salina (NY) 5 Hill 523, 536.

hardpan. A hard stratum of earth. Dickinson v Poughkeepsie, 75 NY 65, 76. Earth difficult to dig because of its hardness:—(1) semi-indurated clay, with or without admixture of stony matter; (2) cemented gravel; or (3) clay, with or without admixture of stony matter, which is very tough because of its strong cohesion. Newport v Temescal Water Co. 149 Cal 531, 87 P 372; Baker v Multnomah County, 118 Or 143, 246 P 352.

hardship. Suffering privations; financial loss suffered in the performance of a contract. 17 Am J2d Contr § 402. Conditions making life miserable and productive activities difficult. 49 Am J1st Spec Per § 59.

Hare System. A form of proportional representation, whereby candidates for public office are not elected by their obtaining a majority or plurality of the votes cast, but by their obtaining a quota of a designated number of votes or a certain proportion of the entire vote, the electors being permitted to express second, third, or additional choices. Johnson v New York, 274 NY 411, 9 NE2d 30, 110 ALR 1502.

Harger drunkometer. A device used in taking a breath test for the purpose of determining intoxication according to the amount of alcohol in the breath. 7 Am J2d Auto § 332.

hariot. Same as **heriot.**

harlot. A whore; a prostitute.

harm. Hurt; injury.
See **bodily harm; great bodily harm; serious bodily harm.**

harmless. Not causing or productive of harm. In a more rare sense, unharmed.

harmless error. Trivial, formal, or merely academic error; a determination which although erroneous, is not prejudicial to the substantial rights of the party who assigns it and in no way affects the final outcome of the case. State v Britton, 27 Wash 2d, 336, 178 P2d 341.

harmonizing. Preserving a statute or part of a statute against repeal by another statute or part of a statute by construction which reconciles the statutes and parts with one another so that effect may be given to all provisions. 50 Am J1st Stat § 363. Reconciling clauses or provisions of a contract in construction, so as to ascertain the meaning of the contract by reasoning which dispels apparent repugnancy between the clauses or provisions. 17 Am J2d Contr § 267. Giving effect to an entire will by reconciling apparent inconsistencies, on the theory that the testator intended all parts of the will to operate. 57 Am J1st Wills § 1129. Reconciling apparent conflicts in testimony for the purpose of giving effect to all testimony, if possible. State v Pettit, 33 Idaho 326, 193 P 1015.

harnasca (har-nas'ka). Harness; armor.

haro. Hue and cry.

Harrison Narcotic Act. See **Narcotic Act.**

harrou. Hue and cry.

harsh contract. A hard bargain, even a foolish contract, from the standpoint of a party, but not necessarily the result of undue advantage having been taken of his trust and confidence. 17 Am J2d Contr § 192.

Harter Act. An act of Congress approved February 13th, 1893, which was designed to fix the relations between the cargo and the vessel and to prohibit contracts restricting the liability of the vessel and owners in certain particulars connected with the construction, repair and outfit of the vessel and the care and delivery of the cargo. 48 Am J1st Ship § 447.

harth-penny. Same as **chimney-money.**

harvest. Noun: A crop produced and taken from the ground. The time when crops of small grain, such as wheat, oats, and rye, are gathered; not applicable to the cutting of a second crop grown on a field from which one crop was taken during the same season. Wendall v Osborne & Co. 63 Iowa 99, 103. Verb: To sever a crop from the soil and take it in hand for giving it such care at the time as is necessary to conserve it for ultimate use or processing as food or clothing.

As used in a statute providing that crops raised and harvested pass with a judicial sale of the land, raised is used in the sense of "matured" and harvested in the sense of "severed." The words are not thus used synonymously, for it is well known that there are a variety of crops that are harvested before their maturity, grain especially. McNulty v Dean, 154 Wash 110, 281 P 9, 66 ALR 1417.

harvesting ice. The cutting and taking of ice from the water upon which it has formed. 52 Am J1st Tresp § 17.

has been. A term which, as it appears in a statute, may be construed to permit retrospective operation, provided such construction is not in violation of constitutional provisions. Nervo v Mealy, 175 Misc 952, 25 NYS2d 632.

haspa (has'pa). The hasp of a door, which was often used in making livery of seisin of the land on which the building stood.

hasp and staple. See **seizin by hasp and staple.**

hasten death. In legal effect, to cause death. Avignone Freres, Inc. v Cardillo, 73 App DC 149, 117 F2d 385.

Hastings. A city of England, the name of which has been given to the battle of Oct. 14, 1066, near the English Channel, in which the Normans, invading from across the channel, defeated the Anglo Saxons, thereby winning a victory which lead ultimately to Norman control of all England.

hasty legislation. Statutes enacted without time for due consideration by the legislative body. 50 Am J1st Stat § 71.

hatch. An opening in the deck of a vessel; an opening in the roof or the floor of a building permitting access below.
See **hatchway.**

Hatch Act. A federal statute making it unlawful for any person employed in the executive branch of the Federal Government, or any agency or department thereof, to use his official authority or influence for the purpose of interfering with an election or affecting the result thereof, or for any such officer or employee to take any active part in political management or in political campaigns, although such person maintains the right to vote as he may choose and to express his opinions on all political subjects and candidates. 5 USC § 118i(a).

hatchway. An opening through the deck of a vessel to a lower deck or the hold. An opening through a sidewalk over an areaway. 25 Am J1st High § 263. Not a stairway or basement-way. State v Armstrong, 97 Neb 343, 350, 149 NW 786.

See **hatch.**

hat-money. Primage,—compensation paid to the master of a ship for his care of goods entrusted to him.

hauberk (hâ'bėrk). A coat of mail.

haubert. Same as **hauberk.**

hauberticum. See **feudum hauberticum.**

haugh (hâ). Low lands which were sometimes overflowed by a river.

haul. A pull. The movement of railroad cars whether on the main line or in switching operations. United States v Erie R. Co. 237 US 402, 59 L Ed 1019, 35 S Ct 621.
See **line haul; long-and-short haul.**

haula (hâ'la). A hall; a court.

hauled or used. A term employed in safety appliance acts in reference to railroad cars. Hauled in a train or otherwise used. United States v St. Louis S. W. R. Co. (CA5 Tex) 184 F 28.

hauler. One who hauls goods, merchandise, or other things for compensation.
See **contract hauler.**

hauling crosscut. A way in the underground workings of a mine. Anno: 15 ALR 1504.

haul-out. The removal of a yacht or other watercraft from the water for storage, repairs, and care. 12 Am J2d Boats § 30.

haur (hawr). Hate; malevolence.

haustus (hâs'tus). A drawing, as of water from a well.

haut (hât). High.

haut bois (ōt bwä). High wood.

haut chemin (ōt she-mâ'). A highway.

haut en bas. See **de haut en bas.**

haut estret (ōt es-trā'). A high street.

Havana. The capital of Cuba. A cigar made in Cuba or of Cuban tobacco. El Moro Cigar Co. v Federal Trade Com. (CA4) 107 F2d 429.

have. To possess, either temporarily or permanently. State v Lowry, 166 Ind 372, 77 NE 728.

have and hold. See **to have and to hold.**

haven. A shelter or place of safety. A bay, recess, or inlet of the sea, or the mouth of a river, which affords a good anchorage and a safe station for ships. Lowndes v Huntington, 153 US 1, 23, 38 L Ed 615, 621, 14 S Ct 758.

having a car under control. See **control of vehicle.**

having an interest. See **interest.**

having due regard. A directory phrase, as it appears in a statute, not of mandatory or all-controlling influence. Lape v Lape, 99 Ohio St 143, 124 NE 51, 6 ALR 187.

having lottery tickets in possession. An offense by ordinance or statute passed to suppress lotteries, some of which make it an offense to have the tickets in one's possession, unless it is shown that the possession is innocent or for a lawful purpose. See 34 Am J1st Lot § 26.

having received full value. A recital in a deed, insufficient in itself to establish a good or valuable consideration. 23 Am J2d Deeds § 65.
See **for value received.**

Hawaii. The fiftieth state of the Union, admitted in 1959.

Hawaiian Islands. A group of islands in the Pacific Ocean, formerly incorporated as a territory of the United States, now contained in the fiftieth state of the Union, the State of Hawaii.

hawker. A peddler who makes noise in advertising his product, either by crying or shouting, or by ringing of bells, or by other means. 40 Am J1st Ped § 3. One who not only carries goods for sale, but seeks for purchasers, either by outcry, by actual exhibition or exposure of the goods, by placards or labels, or by a conventional signal, such as the sounding of a horn for the sale of fish. South Bend v Martin, 142 Ind 31, 41 NE 315.

Hawkeye. An Indian chief, whose name has been given to residents of Iowa and the athletic teams of the University of Iowa at Iowa City, Iowa.

hawser. A tow line. 48 Am J1st Ship § 503.

hay. A harvested crop growing annually from grasses, such as clover, alfalfa, or timothy. Baumgartner v Sturgeon River Boom Co. 120 Mich 321, 323, 79 NW 566, 567.

haybote (hā′bōt). One of the three estovers implied in England from the mere leasing of land, whereby a tenant for life or years may take from the land a sufficient amount of timber for repairing hedges and fences. 32 Am J1st L & T § 219.

hay grinder. A machine on wheels, used in the grinding or shredding of hay into small particles for blowing into a silo or for commercial use; a vehicle within the exception of the use of an insured automobile for towing any vehicle. Moffitt v State Auto. Ins. Asso. 140 Neb 578, 300 NW 837.

Haymarket Riot. The violent result in deaths and serious injuries, sometimes attributed to anarchists, of a demonstration by the forces of labor at Haymarket Square in Chicago, Illinois, March 4, 1886.

hay press. A machine for bailing hay. Phoenix Ins. Co. v Stewart, 53 Ill App 273.

haywards (hā′wârds). Officers regularly appointed whose duty it is to impound estrays. Adams v Nichols (Vt) 1 Aik 316, 319.

hazard. Danger; peril. In the parlance of insurance, risk, the likelihood or probability of loss. State Ins. Co. v Taylor, 14 Colo 499, 24 P 333.
See **increase of hazard**; **moral hazard**.

hazardous. Subject to hazard, that is to possibility of danger or of loss.

hazardous contract. A contract, the performance of which depends on an uncertain event.

hazardous employment or occupation. A relative term in the absence of qualifying terms, meaning an employment or occupation attended with greater risk of injury or death than is true of other employments or occupations under consideration. 58 Am J1st Workm Comp § 90.

hazardous goods. Articles or substances which are explosive or highly inflammable. A classification of goods made for the purpose of prohibited-article clauses of fire insurance policies; a classification not inclusive of articles or substances which are specially hazardous or extra-hazardous. Pindar v Continental Ins. Co. 38 NY 364.

hazing. Horseplay and practical jokes perpetrated on a freshman student, or neophyte in an organization, by way of initiation or discipline. 15 Am J2d Colleges § 27.

H. B. M. An abbreviation of His or Her Britannic Majesty.

H-bomb. A hydrogen bomb.

H. C. An abbreviation of House of Commons. Also an abbreviation of habeas corpus.

h.c. of l. Abbreviation of high cost of living.

head. A leader or commander. Nautical slang for a toilet.

headborough (hed′bur″ō). Same as **headborow**.

headborow (hed′bur″ō). The head or chief man of a borough; a frank pledge or tithing.

head gate. A gate controlling the flow of water in an irrigation canal or other canal as at a lock. 30 Am J Rev ed Irrig § 14.

heading. See **caption**.

headings. Words and phrases placed at the head of main subdivisions of codes and other law books to indicate the character of matter contained therein. 50 Am J1st Stat § 157.
See **caption**.

headland (hed′land). A strip of unploughed land left at the end of a ploughed field.

headlights. The lights on a motor vehicle which illuminate the way in front of the vehicle as it advances. The front lights carried by locomotives.

head money. A gratuity distributed among the officers and crew of a ship in the same manner as prize money is distributed. A reward for the taking of a person wanted for prosecution, or an escaped convict, dead or alive. An admission tax.

Head Money Cases. Certain famous cases in which the United States Supreme Court sustained the validity of the Act of August 3, 1882, imposing upon the owners of steam or sailing vessels bringing passengers from a foreign port a duty of fifty cents for each such passenger not a United States citizen. Cunard S.S. Co. v Robertson, 112 US 580, 28 L Ed 798, 5 S Ct 247.

headnote lawyer. A term applied to a lawyer who relies on the headnotes of decisions and omits the reading of the decisions.

headnotes. Statements in summary and concise form, otherwise known as syllabi, which appear in law reports at the head of the reported cases, to indicate the propositions decided by a case and, in general, the order in which various propositions declared in a case appear in the opinion. 18 Am J2d Copyr § 44. Usually the work of the court reporter, but sometimes of the court itself, in which event they may constitute the official opinion of the court under a rule of court to such effect. 20 Am J2d Cts § 77. Often prepared by members of the editorial staff of the publisher of court reports.

head of a department. A person in charge of a department, whether it be in a business or industry or in the municipal, state, or national government.
As the term is used in connection with the Federal Government, it means the secretary in charge of a great division of the executive branch of the government, such as the state, treasury, and war, who is a member of the cabinet. The term does not include the heads of bureaus or lesser divisions. Burnap v United States, 252 US 512, 515, 64 L Ed 692, 694, 40 S Ct 374; Brooks v United States (DC NY) 33 F Supp 68.

head of a family. A phrase familiar in statutes pro-

viding exemption from execution, especially the exemption of the homestead The person who is under a legal or moral obligation for the support of a family, consisting of two or more persons, living in one household. Moyer v Drummond, 32 SC 165, 10 SE 952. The person who has assumed the burden of supporting such a family although under no duty to do so. Holloway v Holloway, 86 Ga 576, 12 SE 943; Sternberg v Levy, 159 Mo 617, 60 SW 1114.
See **householder**.

head of stream. In common parlance, the source of a stream, whether it be a spring, a lake, or a swamp. Technically, the highest point on a stream which furnishes a continuous stream, not necessarily the longest fork or sprong. Uhl v Reynolds, 23 Ky LR 759, 64 SW 498.

head of water. That quantity of water which will flow each second through an opening one foot square. Watkins Land Co. v Clements, 98 Tex 578, 86 SW 733. More precisely, the quantity of water which will flow in a given time, through an opening of a specified size, from a source defined in terms of a measurement taken with the water at rest. 56 Am J1st Wat § 263.

head-on. A term descriptive of a collision of motor vehicles in which the impact of each vehicle is against the front of the other vehicle.
See **end on**.

head pistareen (hed pĭs″tȧ-rēn′). A Spanish silver coin which in 1835 passed current in the United States for twenty cents, or one fifth of a dollar; not a coin made current by the laws of the United States. United States v Gardner (US) 10 Pet 618, 9 L Ed 556.

headquarters of state officer. A room for the discharge of duties; something more than mere space in the capitol. People v Peck, 138 NY 386, 34 NE 347.

headright certificate. A certificate issued by the United States Land Office representing a conditional grant of 640 acres of land. Cannon v Vaughan, 12 Tex 399, 400.

headspring. A spring which is the original surface source of the water which flows away from it.
"Toyah creek is a stream with well-defined channels and banks, its source being what is called a 'headspring,' which flows twelve heads of water." See Watkins Land Co. v Clements, 98 Tex 578, 86 SW 733.

headstone. A cornerstone; a stone marker placed at the head of a grave.

head tax. See **poll tax**.

headwater. See **head of stream; head of water**.

healer. A person or thing that heals.
See **Christian Science healer**.

healgemote. Same as **halmote**.

healing. Making better; making well.

healsfang. A pillory, a means of punishment for certain offenses, consisting of a wooden bar, through which the head and hands of the culprit protruded, affixed across the top of an upright post.

health. The condition of a living being in reference to well-being and the presence or absence of sickness or disease afflicting him. Absence of disease; soundness of body; freedom from pain, sickness or disease.
The word is said to be derived from an Anglo-Saxon word which is to be traced through the word "hale," and which may be rendered "whole" or "sound." State, etc., v Paterson, 45 NJL 310.
See **bill of health; good health; sound health**.

health board. See **board of health**.

health insurance. A contract wherein one known as the insurer agrees, in consideration of the premium paid and to be paid by the other party known as the insured, to indemnify the latter for losses caused by illness, providing indemnification for both expenses and loss of time resulting from sickness and disease. 29A Am J Rev ed Ins § 1154.
For the purpose of the exemption from taxable income under the Internal Revenue Code, the term "health insurance" is not limited to the particular forms of conventional insurance made available by commercial companies, but includes sickness benefits payable under an employer's plan. Haynes v United States, 353 US 81, 1 L Ed 2d 671, 77 S Ct 649.

health laws. Statutes and bylaws or ordinances pertaining to sanitation and the preservation of the health of the public.
See **health regulations**.

health officers. Members of a board of health and administrative officers empowered to enforce ordinances, rules, bylaws, and regulations, as well as statutes, enacted and promulgated for the purpose of preserving public health.

health plan. An arrangement or contract for medical services or medical supplies. 29 Am J Rev ed Ins § 12.
See **health insurance**.

health regulations. Statutes, ordinances, and administrative regulations in the interest of promoting or preserving health, for example regulations respecting the installation in buildings of water closets, flush bowls, etc. 13 Am J2d Bldgs § 29.

health resort. A place to which people resort for improvement of health, often having hot or mineral springs for bathing or even imbibing. A boarding house rather than an inn or hotel. 29 Am J Rev ed Innk § 10.

healthy. In good health. Free from disease or bodily ailment, or a state of the system peculiarly susceptible or liable to disease or bodily ailment. Bell v Jeffreys, 35 NC (13 Ired L) 356, 357.
See **health**.

healthy condition. In the condition of good health. In reference to a sale of animals, a healthy as opposed to a diseased condition. 46 Am J1st Sales § 150.

hear. To exercise the sense of hearing. To try a case; to consider a motion upon presentation thereof by counsel.
As the verb "to hear" is used in an artistic sense, it requires certain procedural minima to insure an informed judgment by the one who has the responsibility of making the final decision and order. Southern Garment Mfrs. Asso. v Fleming, 74 App DC 228, 122 F2d 622.

hear and determine. To try and decide all the questions involved in a controversy presented to court. Quarl v Abbett, 102 Ind 233, 1 NE 476. The disposal of a case by a referee by proceeding to trial and decision of the matter as distinguished from the function of a referee under a reference to hear and report. 45 Am J1st Ref § 22.

hear and report. The function of a referee under a reference to take testimony and report it to the court for decision by the court. 45 Am J1st Ref § 22.

hear and see. Literally, the exercise of the senses of sight and hearing. A metaphor in expressing apprehension or conscious knowledge.

A person may hear or see and yet not observe; that is, he may not have a conscious knowledge of the object or noise he actually sees or hears, and, ordinarily, when questioned as to the fact, he will say that he did not see or hear. Seaboard Air Line Railway Co. v Myrick, 91 Fla 918, 109 So 193, 195.

Heard Act. A federal statute of 1894 requiring a contractor's bond, containing conditions prescribed by the statute, in any case of a contract for the construction, alteration, or repair of any public building or other public improvement of the United States. 17 Am J2d Cont Bond § 43. The statute has been succeeded by the Miller Act of 1955. 40 USC §§ 270a–270d.

hearing. The physical sense through which sound becomes audible, thereby constituting a means of communication. A term originating in equity but almost as familiar in present-day law actions. A prerequisite to a finding of facts. Re Anderson, 191 Or 49, 229 P2d 633, 230 P2d 770, 29 ALR2d 1051, 1073. A constitutional right of one accused of crime. 21 Am J2d Crim L § 309. An essential of due process of law. Denver v State Invest. Co. 49 Colo 244, 112 P 789.

The presentation and consideration of proofs and arguments, and determinative action with respect to the issue. Re Enger, 225 Minn 229, 30 NW2d 694, 1 ALR2d 1048; Handlon v Belleville, 4 NJ 99, 71 A2d 624, 16 ALR2d 1118. Either an interlocutory hearing, the purpose of which is to get the case into such shape that it may, in the end, be properly heard and finally adjudicated on the merits, or the final hearing in which the case is absolutely determined. 27 Am J2d Equity § 235. The presentation of a case or defense before an administrative agency, with opportunity to introduce evidence in chief and on rebuttal, and to cross-examine witnesses, as may be required for a full and true disclosure of the facts. 2 Am J2d Admin L § 397. An arbitration at which the arbitrators are present to hear the persons whose rights are affected, such persons having been given notice and opportunity to be heard. 5 Am J2d Arb & A § 122.

Where statute provides for a "hearing," the term necessarily implies the power to administer some adequate remedy. See Adams v Shelbyville, 154 Ind 467, 57 NE 114.

See **final hearing; interlocutory hearing; rehearing; rehearing on appeal; trial.**

hearing officer. An examiner in an administrative proceeding, similar to an auditor or special master in a plenary action. 2 Am J2d Admin L § 407.

hearsay. Evidence, whether oral or written, which derives its value, not solely from the credit to be given to the witness upon the stand, but in part from the veracity and competency of some other person. 29 Am J2d Ev § 493. Evidence which is inadmissible because the statements thus made are not subjected to the ordinary tests required by law for ascertaining their truth, the author not being exposed to cross-examination in the presence of a court of justice and not speaking under the sanction of an oath, no opportunity being afforded to investigate his character and motives, and his deportment not being subject to observation. 29 Am J2d Ev § 493.

hearsay evidence. See **hearsay.**

heart attack. A sudden impairment of the heart. See **coronary occlusion.**

heart balm statutes. Legislation abolishing the right of action for breach of promise to marry. 12 Am J2d Breach P § 18.

hearth money. A duty or tax laid by the king upon the hearth of every dwelling; abolished in 1688 by the statute 1 W. & M., st. 1, c. 10. See 1 Bl Comm 324.

hear ye, hear ye, the polls are now closed. The formal statement made by an election officer at the closing of the polls.

hear ye, hear ye, the polls are now open. The formal statement made by an election officer at the opening of an election, the polls.

hear ye, hear ye, this honorable court is now in session. The formal statement made by the bailiff at the opening of court.

heating service. The furnishing of steam by a public utility to heat business places and dwellings. Milligan v Miles City, 51 Mont 374, 153 P 276.

heat of passion. The expression for a mental state on the part of the accused reducing the offense of the killing of a person from murder to manslaughter; heat in the sense of an emotional state, produced by an adequate or reasonable provocation and before a reasonable time has elapsed for the blood to cool and reason to assume its habitual control. State v Forsha, 190 Mo 296, 88 SW 746; State v Seaton, 106 Mo 198, 204; Johnson v State, 129 Wis 146, 108 NW 55.

heat prostration. Same as **heat stroke.**

heatstroke. A morbid condition of the person resulting from exposure to excessive heat. Continental Casualty Co. v Johnson, 74 Kan 129, 85 P 545.

hebberman. A person who fished in the Thames below London bridge, which was against the law.

he be out of the state. An expression common in statutes of limitation, meaning the personal absence of the debtor from the state. 34 Am J1st Lim Ac § 219.

hectare (hek′tăr). A land measure under the metric system; the equivalent of 2,471 acres. Ainsa v United States, 161 US 208, 219, 40 L Ed 673, 677, 16 S Ct 544.

hedagium (he-dā′ji-um). A toll charged for landing goods at a wharf.

hedge-bote (hej′bōt). Same as **hay-bote.**

hedgerow. A row of shrubs, usually shrubs with prickles or needles, and usually kept trimmed to a height between 5 and 6 feet, maintained as a fence.

hedging. A transaction by which one who has made a contract for the sale or purchase of a commodity protects himself against loss through a fluctuation in the market by making a countercontract for purchase or sale of an equal quantity of the commodity; a practice generally recognized as a legitimate and useful method of insuring against losses on contracts for future delivery. 24 Am J1st Gaming § 94.

See **sales against the box.**

hedging bets. The placing of a bet or bets upon a team or contestant in a sporting event after having made a bet or bets upon the opposing team or contestant, the purpose being to minimize losses.

hedging sales. See **hedging; sales against the box.**

heed. To pay attention, especially to an instruction or direction as to conduct in a situation fraught with some danger.

heedlessness. Carelessness or negligence. Silver v Silver, 108 Conn 371, 143 A 240, 65 ALR 943.

Hegira (he-jī'ra). The escape of Mohammed from the Meccans on Friday, July sixteenth, 622 A. D., which date marks the beginning of the calendar used by the Arabians and the Turks.

heifer (hef'ėr). A female calf of the bovine species, from the end of the first year, until she has had a calf; a young cow. Freeman v Carpenter, 10 Vt 433, 435.

height regulations. Statutes or municipal ordinances which limit the height of buildings in the promotion of public health, safety, and welfare. 13 Am J2d Bldgs § 16. Zoning ordinances establishing a maximum or minimum height for buildings in certain districts. 58 Am J1st Zon § 49.

heir. Broadly, one who succeeds to either real or personal property of a decedent who dies intestate. Re Rawnsley's Estate, 94 Cal App 2d 384, 210 P2d 888. At common law and by modern technical usage in some jurisdictions, one who succeeds to the real property of one dying intestate. 23 Am J2d Desc & D § 43.
See **heirs.**

heir apparent. A person who stands in such relationship to another that he is sure to inherit the estate of the latter if he outlives the latter and the latter dies intestate.
See **heir presumptive.**

heir beneficiary. An heir who has accepted his inheritance under an inventory regularly made.

heir by adoption. One who inherits by force of a legal adoption of him as the child of another or by or through a relationship created by the legal adoption of a child. 2 Am J2d Adopt § 100.

heir by custom. A term used in England for one who inherits in accordance with a local custom.

heir by devise. An anamolous expression applied to a person to whom land is devised by will.

heir collateral. See **collateral descent; collateral heir.**

heir conventional. A person who succeeds to an estate under a contract or agreement, usually between him and the decedent.
See **heir of provision.**

heiress. A female who is an heir.
See **heir.**

heir expectant. See **heir apparent.**

heir general. An heir who inherits an estate by the ordinary rules of descent.

heir hunter. One who makes a business of ascertaining and contacting potential distributees of estates. 7 Am J2d Attys § 87.

heir institute. A term of the Scotch law for an heir conventional.
See **heir conventional.**

heir-land (ār'land). Land which descended to an heir upon the death of his ancestor.

heir legal. (Civil law.) An heir who succeeded to the estate of his ancestor by descent under the law of succession, as distinguished from an heir who took under a will or a contract.

heirloom. A piece of property that goes to an heir along with an estate, being defined in this respect as property which is not altogether real or altogether personal, but a compound of both. 42 Am J1st Prop § 28.

Such goods and personal chattels, as, contrary to the nature of chattels, go by special custom to the heir along with the inheritance, and not to the executor, of the last proprietor. Loom is from the Saxon, meaning a limb or member. Hence, an heirloom is a limb or member of the inheritance. See 2 Bl Comm 427.

heir of conquest. An heir who succeeded to property which his ancestor acquired by conquest.

heir of line. An heir who succeeded to an estate as a lineal descendant of his ancestor.

heir of provision. A person who succeeded to property of a decedent under the provision of some instrument.
See **heir conventional.**

heir of tailzie (ār'of tāl'zē). Same as **heir special.**

heir presumptive. One who would be the heir if the ancestor were to die at the contemplated time, but whose possibility of inheritance may be destroyed by the birth of some one more nearly related, as well as by his death before that of the ancestor.
See **heir apparent.**

heirs. The plural of **heir**; persons taking by descent. Designation of grantees in a deed:—the persons who are entitled under the law of intestate succession. 23 Am J2d Deeds § 215. Sometimes construed as meaning children, as where otherwise the deed will be void for uncertainty. 23 Am J2d Deeds § 215.

Designation of beneficiaries under a wrongful death statute:—kin of the decedent who would inherit from him under the governing statute of descent and distribution. 22 Am J2d Dth § 47. Designation of beneficiaries of a life insurance policy:—those persons entitled under the statutes of descent to the personal estate of the insured in the event of his intestacy. 29A Am J Rev ed Ins § 1659. Designation of beneficiaries of a certificate or policy issued by a mutual benefit society:—those persons entitled under the statutes of descent to the personal estate of the member or insured in the event of his intestacy. 36 Am J2d Frat O § 154.

A word of art in a grant or devise, constituting a word of limitation rather than of purchase. 33 Am J1st Life Est § 147; 28 Am J2d Est § 119. Essential at common law to the passing of a fee by deed, such requirement having been eliminated by statute in many jurisdictions. 28 Am J2d Est §§ 14-16.

Used as a designation of beneficiaries in a will, the primary significance of the word "heirs" is, in the absence of context to the contrary, the persons who would take the property of the person designated as ancestor in case of his death intestate. Generally speaking, the term, as used in a will, will apply to a gift of personal property notwithstanding the applicable statute of the jurisdiction designates different persons for taking an intestate's personalty from those indicated to take his real property. 57 Am J1st Wills § 1369. The term may be interpreted as the equivalent of "children" or

HEIRS [555] HELMET

"next of kin," where the context so requires. 33 Am J1st Life Est § 140; 57 Am J1st Wills § 1369.
Sufficient as a designation of the beneficiaries of a trust. 54 Am J1st Trusts § 140.
See behavior as heir; bodily heirs; co-heir; defect of heirs; fellow-heir; forced heir; heir; illegitimate child; irregular heirs; joint heir; last heir; lawful heirs; lineal heirs; natural heirs; nearest heir; nearest male heir; present heirs; presumptive heir; pretermitted heir; right heirs; unconditional heirs.

heirs and assigns. Words which are used in the habendum clause of a deed and which have a well defined and settled meaning in the law as words apt and appropriate to pass a fee simple absolute, if not followed or accompanied by other modifying words. Jamaica Pond Aqueduct Corp. v Chandler, 91 Mass (9 Allen) 159, 168. Words of inheritance or limitation in the grant of an easement. Riley v Pearson, 120 Minn 210, 139 NW 361.
The words of the statute, "the patentee, his heirs and assigns," whether construed according to the rules of grammar or to the intent of Congress mean "the patentee, or his heirs or assigns." They comprehend the legal representatives, assignees in law, and assignees in fact, and the phraseology raises no limitation in the sense of the strict common law rule applied to realty. De La Vergne Refrigerating Machine Co. v Featherstone, 147 US 209, 37 L Ed 138, 13 S Ct 283.

heirs at law. Essentially the same as the more simple term "heirs." Mullen v Reed, 64 Conn 240, 29 A 478. Sometimes construed as words of purchase. 28 Am J2d Est § 118. Designation of beneficiaries of contract or certificate issued by a mutual benefit society:—those persons who under the statutes of distribution would be entitled to the personal estate in the event of the member's intestacy. 36 Am J2d Frat O § 154. Sufficient designation of beneficiaries of a trust. 54 Am J1st Trusts § 140.
Used in a will, the term "heirs at law" indicates those persons on whom the law casts the descent of real estate or admits to participation in the distribution of personal property, except as a contrary intention may be exhibited in the context of the instrument considered in its entirety. 57 Am J1st Wills § 1371.

heirs by blood. Words of limitation sufficient to confer a fee simple title when used in a deed. 23 Am J2d Deeds § 215. As words of purchase, persons whose relationship is by consanguinity.

heirship. The status of an heir; the right of an heir to inherit.

heirship movables. Certain personal property of a decedent which under the law went to the heir and not to the executor. In a will, sometimes equivalent to "issue," "heirs," or "natural heirs." 57 Am J1st Wills § 1371.
See bodily heirs.

heirship proceeding. A special proceeding, authorized only by statute, to determine the heirs and distributees of the property of a decedent. 23 Am J2d Desc & D § 104.

heirs of her body begotten. A technical term but sometimes construed as words of purchase. 28 Am J2d Est § 118. Technical words used in creating an estate in fee tail, being construed as words of limitation except as the entire context discloses an intention of the testator to use them as words of purchase. 28 Am J2d Est § 49.

heirs of the body. Ordinarily considered to be a technical legal term, or word of art, constituting words of limitation, not of purchase. 28 Am J2d Est § 119.

heir special. An heir in respect of an entailed estate.

heir substitute, in a bond. The obligee of a bond payable on the death of a creditor.

heir testamentary. A person to whom property is left by will.

Hejira (he-jī'ra). Same as **Hegira.**

held. Having grasped or clutched. In reference to property, a word of variable meaning; actual possession; the right to possession; invested with title. Federal National Bank v Miller, 128 Okla 82, 261 P 206, 208.
See hold.

held for sale. Property in the possession of an agent authorized to sell it. Merchandise or stock of goods in place of business. A clause describing the subject matter of a dealers' collision insurance policy, so that the protection of the dealer's automobile continues until the sale thereof, whether absolute or conditional, has been completed, by transfer of title if absolute, or of possession if conditional. 7 Am J2d Auto Ins § 73.

held in trust. Property in the possession of a trustee; property in the possession of one other than the owner, such as an agent, bailee, factor, etc., who must account to the owner for the property or the proceeds thereof.
As used in fire insurance policies, phrases describing property as held in trust, or on commission, and kindred terms in a policy to an agent, factor, or the like, have been held to give to the owner a right to take the place of the insured, to adopt the contract, and enforce it in his own name or that of his agent. Waring v Indemnity Fire Ins Co. 45 NY 610.

helicopter. An aircraft the propeller of which is placed on top the fuselage, thereby enabling a craft to rise without the take-off required for an ordinary aircraft; an aircraft becoming increasingly useful in the transportation of passengers in populated areas and also as a military plane.

hell. A place under the English exchequer chamber where debtors of the king were confined. A profane word for a very disagreeable experience. The place to which, according to the Christian faith as expressed by fundamentalists, sinners and unbelievers are sent at death.
"There are those who, for reasons satisfactory to themselves, contend that there is no such place; but even this class will admit that, if there is such a place, there is nothing there which is consistent with honesty, decency, or the right conception of things. Both the popular and the theological idea of hell has nothing in it to make any connection with the place either desirable or comfortable from a physical or spiritual point of view. The word is a synonym for all that is evil and corrupt in the grossest and basest sense of those terms." Atlanta News Publishing Co. v Medlock, 123 Ga 714, 51 SE 756.

hell and high-water rule. A term for the liberal rule in the construction of the omnibus clause of an automobile liability insurance policy. United States Fidelity & Guaranty Co. v Smith (CA9 Ariz) 279 F2d 678.

helmet. A head covering worn for protection of members of the armed services in combat, of par-

ticipants in violent sports, and persons exposed to the sun.
See **branding-helmet**.

hemiplegy (hem′i-plē-ji). A brain disease, usually caused by a tumor pressing on the brain or by a blow, resulting in a paralysis of one-half of the body.
The disease may be either complete or incomplete. When it is complete, one-half of the body is paralyzed; when incomplete, one-half of the body is only partially paralyzed. If the disease comes on quickly, it is called quick hemiplegy; if it comes on gradually, it is called chronic. Quick hemiplegy is more apt to affect the mental faculties than chronic. Baughman v Baughman, 32 Kan·538, 542.

he must protect himself if he can do so at trifling expense. A principle of the law of damages; the obligation of an injured person to take steps of alleviation, even by incurring expense, where such is small in relation to the consequential damages. 22 Am J2d Damg § 32.

henceforward. Henceforth; hereafter.
The word does not necessarily convey the idea of perpetuity; it means no more than the word "hereafter," which may import a temporary or a permanent arrangement, according to the general tenor of the instrument, and the nature of the subject matter about which it is used. Adams v Bucklin, 24 Mass (7 Pick) 121, 128, footnote.

hence without day. See **go hence without day**.

henfare (hen′fār). A fine which was imposed upon a person for having fled from a charge of murder.

henghen. A prison; a house of correction.

hengwyte. Same as **hangwite**.

Henricus vetus (hen-rī′kus ve′tus). Henry the Elder, —a name which was applied to Henry the First to distinguish him from the subsequent kings of that name.

Henry I. (hen′ri fėrst). Henry the First, the king of England from August 5th, 1100, to December 1st, 1135.

Henry II. Henry the Second, the king of England from December 19th, 1154, to July 6th, 1189.

Henry III. Henry the Third, the king of England from October 28th, 1216, to November 16th, 1272.

Henry IV. Henry the Fourth, the king of England from September 30th, 1399, to March 20th, 1413.

Henry V. Henry the Fifth, the king of England from March 21st, 1413, to August 31st, 1422.

Henry VI. Henry the Sixth, the king of England from September 1st, 1422, to March 4th, 1461.

Henry VII. Henry the Seventh, the king of England from August 22nd, 1485, to April 21st, 1509.

Henry VIII. Henry the Eighth, the king of England from April 22nd, 1509, to January 28th, 1547.

heordwerch. Same as **herdwerck**.

he or they paying freight. A term in a bill of lading indicating the consignee's obligation for payment of freight charges. 13 Am J2d Car § 477.

Hepburn Act. An act of Congress amendatory of the Interstate Commerce Act, June 29, 1906, 34 Stat 589.

heptarchy (hep′tạr-ki). A government by seven rulers; that period of English history beginning with the coming of the Saxons in 449 and the uniting of the seven kingdoms of Northumbria, Mercia, East Anglia, Essex, Kent, Sussex and Wessex, in 828.

herald. A messenger; an English officer in charge of matters pertaining to heraldry.

heraldry (her′ạld-ri). The office of a herald in England; the art of tracing genealogy and inheritable titles and decorations.

Heralds' College. A corporation chartered by the king (Richard the Third) in 1483, for the purpose of tracing and preserving the records of heraldry.

herbage (ėr′ or hėr′bȧj). The right or easement of pasturing one's cattle on the land of another.

herbagium (her-bā′ji-um). Same as **herbage**.

herbagium anterius (her-bā′ji-um an-tē′ri-us). A first crop of grass or hay.

herb doctor. One who treats sick persons by herbs, sometimes combining such treatment with massage. 41 Am J1st Phys & S § 31.

herbergare (her-ber-gā′re). To entertain at an inn; to harbor; to accommodate with lodgings.

herbery (hėr′bėr-i). An inn.

herd. Noun: A collection of many beasts assembled together. Brimm v Jones, 13 Utah 440, 448. Verb: To form beasts into a large body for care or for moving the animals. A colloquial term for attending animals to keep them from straying or from encroaching upon growing or matured crops in field.

herdbook. A record kept of the breeding of animals, particularly cattle, which show the date of breeding of a female, the sire, and the date, also facts respecting the date of birth of the progeny.

herdwerck. Herd work,—the work of a herdsman or shepherd.

hereafter. A word of futurity. Keller v Ashford, 133 US 610, 33 L Ed 667, 10 S Ct 494. Sometimes, but not necessarily, conveying the idea of perpetuity; importing a temporary or permanent arrangement according to the tenor of the context in which it appears. Adams v Bucklin, 24 Mass (7 Pick) 121, 128, footnote.

hereby granted. See **there is hereby granted**.

heredad (ay-ray-dahd′). (Spanish.) Farmed land.

heredad yacente (ay-ray-dahd′ yah-then′tay). (Spanish.) Same as **haereditas jacens**.

heredero (ay-ray-day′ro). A term frequently encountered in Spanish-American title records, which means the person who by a testamentary disposition or by law succeeds to the rights which a deceased person held at the time of his death. Emeric v Alvarado, 64 Cal 529, 2 P 418.

hereditaments. A comprehensive term, including anything capable of being inherited, be it corporeal, incorporeal, real, personal or mixed. 42 Am J1st Prop § 17.
See **corporeal hereditament; incorporeal hereditament**.

hereditary. Something inherited. Passed along by inheritance. Douglas v Lewis, 131 US 75, 33 L Ed 53, 9 S Ct 634.

hereditary disease. A disease arising in a physical or mental weakness inherited from an ancestor.
See **hereditary insanity**.

hereditary insanity. Mental illness of a character to

hereditary be transmitted from parent to child or later descendant.
"There is nothing unreasonable in referring wild, furious and unnatural actions, not otherwise accounted for, to the aberrations of a mind the reflux of that of a crazy parent." People v Smith, 31 Cal 467; Prewitt v State, 106 Miss 82, 6 ALR 1476, 1478, 63 So 330.

hereditary real estate. Real estate of inheritance. Douglas v Lewis, 131 US 75, 33 L Ed 53, 9 S Ct 634.

hereditary succession. The passing of title under the laws of descent.

hereditary successor. A successor by hereditary succession.

hereditas (he-rē'di-tās). Same as **haereditas**.

heredity. The universal law of organic life, the biological law by which all things living tend to repeat themselves in their descendants; the natural tendency to reproduce in offspring the characteristics of the parent organ or body. Prewitt v State, 106 Miss 82, 63 So 330, 6 ALR 1476.

heredium (hẹ-rē'di-um). (Roman Law.) The homestead or hereditary domain allotted as the private property of a citizen, and which was inheritable and alienable; comprising space for house, yard, and garden,—usually about one and a quarter acres.

heregeat. Same as **heriot**.

heregeld. A tax or tribute levied for the support of an army.

heregild. Same as **heregeld**.

herein. A locative adverb, the meaning of which varies according to the context, referring to a certain part, page, or paragraph of a writing, or, in other connections, to the entire writing, such being true whether the word be used in a statute or a private writing or document. Re Pearsons, 98 Cal 603, 33 P 451.

hereinafter. Relating to a thing or matter mentioned in a later part of a private writing or statute.

hereinbefore. Relating to a thing or matter mentioned in a preceding part of a private writing or statute.

heres (he'rēz). (Civil law.) Same as **haeres**.

heresy. The ecclesiastical offense of entertaining religious views or beliefs which are not in harmony with those of the established church; the entertainment of an erroneous religious belief. Any political or philosophical view contrary to established view.

heretofore. At a time before the present; formerly. Andrews v Thayer, 40 Conn 156.
As used in the constitutional phrase "the right of trial by jury as heretofore enjoyed," the word relates to the past and to determine the true meaning of the phrase, it is necessary to go back to the common law of England. See State v Hamey, 168 Mo 167, 67 SW 620.

hereunder. A word of location in a private writing or a statute, the meaning varying according to the context, sometimes referring to the entire instrument, and, at other times, to only a clause, paragraph, section or other division or subdivision of the writing or statute. Pringle v Wilson, 156 Cal 313, 104 P 316.

hereyeld. Same as **heregeld**.

heriot (her'i-ọt). A fruit or appendage of copyhold tenure consisting of a render of the best beast or other thing (as the custom may be) to the lord of the manor on the death of the tenant. See 2 Bl Comm 97.

heriot custom (her'i-ọt kus'tum). A heriot due under custom or usage.

heriot service (sẽr'vis). A heriot which was due the lord of the manor under a special reservation in his grant.

herischild. A species of military service under feudal tenure.

heritable (her'i-tạ-bl). Inheritable; capable of being inherited; subject to inheritance.

heritable bond (bond). A bond secured by inheritable property; that is, by land.

heritable jurisdiction (jö-ris-dik'shọn). A royal grant of criminal jurisdiction to a family.

heritable rights. Rights in real property. Rights capable of being inherited.

heritable security (sẹ-kū'rị-ti). The pledge of an inheritance as security for the fulfillment of an obligation.

heritage. An inheritance; an inheritable estate. Dowdel v Hamm (Pa) 2 Watts 61, 65. A culture handed down from one generation to another.

heritor (her'i-tor). The proprietor of an inheritance.

hermandad (er-màn-dàd'). A Spanish society organized for the preservation of public peace and order.

hermaphrodite (her-maf'rō-dīt). A human being with sexual organs, more or less perfect, of both sexes.
In some of the states, to say of a woman that she is a hermaphrodite is actionable as defamation without alleging special damages. Eckert v Van Pelt, 69 Kan 357, 76 P 909.

Hermaphroditus tam masculo quam foeminae comparatur, secundum prevalentiam sexus incalescentis (her-mā-frō-dī'tus tam mas'kū-lō quam fē'mi-nē kom-pa-rā'ter, se-kun'dum pre-va-len'she-am se'xus in-kā-lē-sen'tis). A hermaphrodite is regarded as male or female according to the predominance of the attributes of sex.

hermer (hẽr'mer). A great lord.

hernia. As commonly understood by laymen,—a rupture or noticeable protrusion from some part of the abdominal cavity. 29A Am J Rev ed Ins § 1217.
What constitutes "hernia" within exclusionary clause of health or accident insurance policy. Anno: 55 ALR2d 1020.

heroin (her'oin). A habit forming narcotic; a derivative of opium. Chadwick v United States (CA5 Tex) 117 F2d 902; Baker v State, 123 Tex Crim 209, 58 SW2d 534. An item of the illegal traffic in narcotic drugs. 25 Am J2d Drugs § 2.

herring silver (her'ing sil'vẽr). Customary money payments made for the purpose of supplying a religious house with herring.

herus (he'rus). Master; owner; lord; head of a household.

Herus dat, ut servus faciat (he'rus dat, ut ser'vus fā'she-at). The master gives or pays that the servant may work. See 2 Bl Comm 445.

hesia (hē'zhe-a). An easement.

hetaeria (he-tē'ri-ạ). (Roman law.) An association; a society.

heterogeneous goods (het-ę-ro-ge′ne-us gủdz). Articles or substances dissimilar in kind. Goods of different structure. The antithesis of homogeneous goods.

he that hath committed inequity shall not have equity. A maxim of equity. 27 Am J2d Equity § 136.

heuvelborh. (Saxon). A guarantor; a surety.

he who comes into equity must come with clean hands. A maxim of equity. 27 Am J2d Eq § 136.
See **clean hands doctrine.**

he who made the loss possible must suffer. A maxim applicable especially in the law of bailments. 8 Am J2d Bailm §§ 198 et seq.

he who owns land owns to the sky above it. A maxim which is qualified as between adjoining owners, giving way to a rule of convenience more just, equitable, and beneficial to both parties. 1 Am J2d Adj L § 22. A maxim considerably modified in adjudicating rights in air space for the operation of aircraft. 8 Am J2d Avi § 3.

he who owns the soil, owns to the heavens. Same as **he who owns land owns to the sky above it.**

he who seeks equity must do equity. A maxim of equity. 27 Am J2d Eq §§ 131 et seq. A condition of injunctive relief. 28 Am J Rev ed Inj § 34. A maxim which requires one who seeks the cancellation of an instrument to restore to the defendant the position occupied by the latter before the transaction sought to be nullified. 13 Am J2d Canc Inst § 2.

heybote (hā′bōt). Same as **hay-bote.**

HHFA. Abbreviation for **Housing and Home Finance Agency.**

hidage (hī′dạj). A tax which was levied by the king on each hide of land.

hidalgo (hi-dal′gō). A Spanish nobleman of lower rank.

hidden defects. Those imperfections which cannot be discovered by simple inspection. Bulkley v Honold (US) 19 How 390, 15 L Ed 663.
The term is a relative one and what may be apparent in the daytime may become a pitfall in darkness or in dim light, and conditions obvious to one with opportunity to investigate may be a trap to one precluded by nature of his work from making careful examination. Franklin v Maine Amusement Co. 133 Me 203, 175 A 305.

hidden meaning. A refined or subtle meaning. 50 Am J1st Stat § 238.

hidden property. See **conceal; treasure trove.**

hide. A raw or tanned skin of an animal. An ancient measure of land, a quantity of land which could be worked by one team of oxen.
The number of acres contained in a hide varies in the works of different writers and has been variously estimated at from thirty to one hundred and twenty.
See **conceal; secrete; treasure trove.**

hide and gain (hīd ạnd gān). Ploughable land; arable land.

hidegild (hīd′gild). A tax levied on each hide of land.

hidel. A hiding place; a sanctuary; an asylum.

hide lands. Lands allotted in hides.
See **hide.**

hierarchy (hī′ę-rär-ki). The government of a church, such as the Roman Catholic Church, by ecclesiastics in an ascending scale of authority.

higgling. A stock-exchange term for negotiations by offers to sell and offers to purchase through which a price is agreed upon and a sale accomplished. Nicol v Ames, 173 US 509, 518, 43 L Ed 786, 792, 19 S Ct 522.

high. As stated of things, not of persons, tall and lofty; elevated in reference to some other level. That which is common, open, and public, such as a road, way, or navigable river which used freely by the public. United States v Rodgers, 150 US 249, 258, 37 L Ed 1071, 1074, 14 S Ct 109. Slang for intoxicated.

high bailiff (hī bā′lif). In England, an officer of the county court who performs certain services which are not within the duties of a sheriff; in Vermont, an officer with functions similar to those of an elisor.

highbinder (hī′bīn″dėr). An old term for a member of a Chinese tong or society organized for blackmailing or murder, or both.

High Commission Court (hī ko-mish′ọn kōrt). An English ecclesiastical court which was "justly abolished by statute" in 1641, because of its having arbitrarily usurped powers which were almost despotic. See 3 Bl Comm 67.

high constable (hī kon′stạ-bl). The constable or peace officer of a hundred. They were appointed by the court leets of the franchise or hundred over which they presided. See 1 Bl Comm 355.

High Court of Admiralty. An English court of admiralty which was presided over by the lord high admiral until its jurisdiction and functions were taken over by the high court of justice.

High Court of Chancery. An English court which appears to have attained its full development in the reign of Edward II, 1307-1327, and which by reason of the royal prerogative could afford relief above and beyond that available in the common-law courts.

High Court of Delegates. An English court, no longer existing, which formerly had jurisdiction of appeals from the ecclesiastical and admiralty courts.

High Court of Justice. A division of the English supreme court of judicature, established in the reign of Victoria.

High Court of Parliament. The English parliament comprising the house of lords and the house of commons; the house of lords in the exercise of its judicial functions.

high crimes and misdemeanors. Such immoral and unlawful acts as are nearly allied and equal in guilt to felony, yet, owing to some technical circumstance, do not fall within the definition of felony. State v Knapp, 6 Conn 415.
The term "high misdemeanor" is of statutory origin, invented to permit a distinction between petty offenses and those of a more serious nature. State v Kelly, 218 Minn 247, 15 NW2d 554, 162 ALR 477.
See **gross misdemeanor.**

high degree of care. Great care; more than ordinary care. 8 Am J2d Bailm § 205.

high diligence. Great care; more than ordinary care. 8 Am J2d Bailm § 205.

higher and lower scales. The two scales or schedules regulating the fees to be paid to counsel in England.

Higher Education Facilities Act. A federal statute of 1963 enacted to authorize assistance to public and other nonprofit institutions of higher education in financing the construction, rehabilitation, or improvement of needed academic and related facilities in undergraduate and graduate institutions. 20 USC §§ 701 et seq.

higher schools. Public schools which includes grades above the eighth grade.

highest and best. A term in reference to price; the best price obtainable under the circumstances, even the price offered by one bidder, where he is the only bidder present. Lathrop v Tracy, 24 Colo 382, 51 P 486.

highest bidder. The successful bidder at an auction, but the unsuccessful bidder at the letting of a contract.

highest court. See **court of last resort; highest court of a state.**

highest court of a state. A state court, the decision of which is not subject to review by a higher state court by appeal or otherwise. Southern Electric Co. v Stoddard, 269 US 186, 70 L Ed 227, 46 S Ct 71.
 A judgment rendered by a division of the state supreme court, consisting of four of the seven judges of that court, is not reviewable in the United States Supreme Court, as one of the highest courts of a state, where the state constitution, although providing that the state court shall consist of two divisions, and that the judgments of either division shall have the force and effect of a judgment of the court, also authorizes the transfer of a cause from a division to the court en banc, and requires such a transfer, on the application of the losing party, "when a federal question is involved," and the rules of the state supreme court authorize a transfer from either division to the court en banc after final disposition of the cause by a division. Gorman v Washington University, 316 US 98, 86 L Ed 938, 5 S Ct 369.

highest degree of care. Care in an extraordinary degree. The standard of care required of a common carrier of passengers. 14 Am J2d Car § 916.

highest legal interest. Any rate of interest up to that fixed by statute as the maximum rate. Daniel v Gibson, 72 Ga 367.

highest point. The apex of a vein of mineral.

high justice. The right or jurisdiction of a feudal lord to try all crimes.
 See **high Court of Justice.**

high justicier (jus-ti′si-er). A feudal lord who asserted the right or jurisdiction of high justice.

high line. A line carrying an electric current of high voltage.

high misdemeanor. A misdemeanor of a more serious nature than the ordinary misdemeanor. 21 Am J2d Crim L § 21.
 See **gross misdemeanor; high crimes and misdemeanors.**

high power accelerator. An organic accelerator used in the vulcanization of crude rubber, the outstanding feature of which is efficiency in permitting vulcanization, without pressure, at a relatively low degree of heat. Vultex Corp. v Heveatex Corp. (CA1 Mass) 100 F2d 838.

high prerogative writ. A writ issued not as an ordinary writ, of strict right, but at the discretion of the sovereign acting through that court in which the sovereign is supposed to be personally present. Ex parte Thompson, 85 NJ Eq 221, 96 A 102.

high-pressure gas line. A line of pipe through which gas is conveyed at a high pressure, as contrasted with a line which conveys gas for household use at a pressure which is safe for use in household appliances. McKenna v Bridgewater Gas Co. 193 Pa 633, 45 A 52.

high school. A school where the higher branches of a common school education are taught. Whitlock v State ex rel. School Dist. 30 Neb 815, 822. One of the common or public schools, usually including grades 9 to 12, inclusive, but sometimes divided so as to have a junior high and a senior high school. McLeod v State, 154 Miss 468, 122 So 737, 63 ALR 1161.

high seas. Rough water. The waters of the oceans and the arms thereof beyond the territorial jurisdiction of any nation. Including waters on the sea coast without the boundaries of low-water mark, such as the waters of the port of Yokohama. Ross v McIntyre, 140 US 453, 471, 35 L Ed 581, 588, 11 S Ct 897. Also including any large body of navigable water other than a river, which is of an extent beyond the measurement of one's unaided vision, and is open and unconfined, and not under the exclusive control of any one nation or people, but is the free highway of adjoining nations or people. United States v Rodgers, 150 US 249, 259, 37 L Ed 1071, 1075, 14 S Ct 109.

high-tension wire. A wire carrying electric current of high voltage.

high tide. The highest line to which the tide rises. The time of day at which the tide reaches such line.
 See **mean high tide; neap tide; spring tide.**

high treason. Treason against the king or the government.
 See **treason.**

high water. See **flood; high tide; high-watermark.**

high-watermark. As applied to tidal waters:—the line marked by the periodical flow of the tide, excluding the advance of the water above the line, occasioned by wind, storm, or other unusual condition; usually construed to indicate the "ordinary" high water—that is, the line of the medium high tide between the spring and the neap tide. 12 Am J2d Bound § 13. As applied to fresh water lakes and streams:—the mark where the presence and action of the water are so common and usual as to mark upon the soil of the bed a character distinct from that of the banks in respect to vegetation as well as to the nature of the soil itself. Re Minnetonka Lake Improv. 56 Minn 513, 58 NW 295. The line to which the water rises in the seasons of ordinary high water; the line at which the presence of water is continued for such length of time as to mark upon the soil and vegetation a distinct character. 56 Am J1st Wat § 448.
 Bounding a grant on a pond does not per se extend title to the center if the boundary of the tract is indicated by an old and definite line following the high watermark. Jennings v Marston, 121 Va 79, 92 SE 821, 7 ALR 855.
 See **ordinary high-watermark.**

highway. A generic term including all public roads and ways. Carlin v Chicago, 262 Ill 564, 104 NE

905. A way open to the public at large, for travel or transportation, without distinction, discrimination, or restriction, except such as is incident to regulations calculated to secure to the general public the largest practical benefit therefrom and enjoyment thereof. 25 Am J1st High § 2. In a broad or general sense, every common way for travel in any ordinary mode or by any ordinary means, which the public has the right to use either conditionally or unconditionally, including turnpikes and toll roads, bridges, canals, ferries, navigable waters, lanes, pent roads, and crossroads. 25 Am J1st High § 5.

See **by-road; cartway; common highway; country road; established highway; intersection; lane; neighborhood road; park strips; pavement; pent road; right of way; road; rules of the road; shun pike; thoroughfare; town way; turnpike.**

highway by prescription. A highway the right to maintain which has been obtained by prescription. Brown v Peck, 125 Iowa 624, 625, 101 NW 443.

highway by user. A highway established by long continued use, that is, a prescriptive way. 25 Am J1st High § 11.

See **highway by prescription.**

highway commission. An agency of the state, a subdivision of the state, or a municipal corporation, exercising governmental functions pertaining to highways. 25 Am J1st High § 600.

highway district. An improvement district established for the construction and maintenance of highways. 25 Am J1st High § 601.

highway easement. An easement belonging to the public embracing all public travel not prohibited by law, on foot, in carriages, omnibuses, stages, sleighs, or other vehicles, as the wants and habits of the public demand. Carli v Stillwater Street Railway and Transfer Co. 28 Minn 373.

"Whether it be travel, the transportation of persons and property, or the transmission of intelligence, and whether accomplished by old methods or new ones, they are all included within the public highway easement, and impose no additional servitude upon the land, provided they are not inconsistent with the reasonably safe and practical use of the highway in other and usual necessary modes, and provided they do not unreasonably impair the special easements of abutting owners in the street for purposes of access, light and air." Cater v Northwestern Tel. Exchange Co. 60 Minn 539, 63 NW 111.

highway intersection. See **intersection.**

highwayman. A person who commits the crime of highway robbery. Anderson v Hartford Acci. & Indem. Co. 77 Cal App 641, 247 P 507. A robber who finds his prey on highways.

highway patrol. Police or other law enforcement officers assigned to the highways; an independent department of law enforcement officers organized for service upon highways.

highway robbery. The common-law crime of robbery committed on the highway. Anderson v Hartford Acci. & Indem. Co. 77 Cal App 641, 247 P 507.

high wind. See **gale; storm.**

higler. Same as **huckster.**

higuela. (Spanish.) A receipt for his inheritance, signed by the heir.

H. I. H. An abbreviation of His or Her Imperial Highness.

hiis testibus (hī'is tes'ti-bus). With these witnesses.

hiis testibus clause (hī'is tes'ti-bus klâz). An attestation clause.

hiis testibus Johanne Moore, Jacobo Smith, et aliis, ad hanc rem convocatis (hī'is tes'ti-bus Jo-han'ne Moore, Ja-kō'bō Smith, et a'li-is, ad hank rem kon-vo-kā'tis). By these witnesses, John Moore, Jacob Smith and others gathered together for that purpose, i. e. as witnesses to attest the deed. See 2 Bl Comm 307.

hijacker. A robber. Franklin v State (Tex Crim) 283 SW 802, 803. More precisely, one who robs by taking property in transit, especially property such as intoxicating liquors or narcotic drugs illegally possessed or transported.

hijodalgo. Same as **hidalgo.**

Hikenild Street. One of the four great ancient Roman roads in England, also known as Ikenild street.

Hilary rules (hil'a-ri rūls). A set of English rules and forms of pleading and practice which were adopted by the superior courts in 1834.

Hilary term (hil'a-ri tėrm). An English term of court which began with the eleventh of January and ended on the thirty-first.

himself order. Words of negotiability, the same as "himself or order." Day & Night Bank v Coffee (CA6 Ky) 25 F2d 403, 58 ALR 1002.

himself or order. A phrase appended to the payee of an instrument, making the instrument negotiable. Day & Night Bank v Coffee, (CA6 Ky) 25 F2d 403, 58 ALR 1002.

hinc inde (hink in'de). On each side; mutually; reciprocally.

hind (hīnd). An agricultural servant; a field hand; a rustic.

Hinde Palmer's Act. An English statute of 1869, placing specialty debts and simple contract debts in the same rank in the settlement of decedents' estates.

hindering and delaying creditors. Acts which impede or retard creditors in their lawful efforts to subject the property of their debtor to their lawful claims, performed with the fraudulent intent to defraud. Clayton v Clark, 76 Kan 832, 92 P 1117. An act impeding or retarding creditors, whether done innocently or with intent to hinder and delay them; a sale of property by a debtor at less than the fair value. Mente & Co. v Old River Co. (CA5 Tex) 17 F2d 350.

Hindu. A name applied to one of the peoples of India. One who is a believer in the religion of Hinduism.

hine. Same as **hind.**

hinny (hin'i). The hybrid offspring of a horse and a jennet or female donkey.

hipoteca (e-po-tay'cah). (Spanish.) A real property mortgage.

hire. Verb: To employ a person. To rent or engage the use of an article, receiving it as a bailee under obligation to return the article at the end of the term of the hiring. Farquhar v McAlevy, 142 Pa, 233. Noun: The amount paid or to be paid for the services of a person. The amount paid or to be paid for the use of a chattel. Bledsoe v Nixon, 69 NC 89.

See **bailee for hire; carrier for hire; contract of hire; operator for hire.**

hired automobile clause. The clause of an automobile liability insurance policy which provides coverage for the insured while operating a rented automobile, but usually excluding from coverage the owner of such vehicle or his employee. 7 Am J2d Auto Ins § 108.

hired driver. One employed for the specific purpose of driving, not including one whose duties under employment by another include driving, for example one employed to sell soft drinks and proceeding from house to house to make sales from the vehicle. Anno: 138 ALR 425.

hire or retain. To engage the services of another, especially professional services.
The phrase as used in a statute making it a criminal offense to "hire or retain" any person to go beyond the limits of the United States with intent to be enlisted in a foreign military or naval service means to pay for services, or to engage services, and the consideration need not be pecuniary or be paid at once. United States v Blair-Murdock Co. (DC Cal) 228 F 77.

hirer. A person who by contract acquires the right to use a thing belonging to another. Turner v Cross, 83 Tex 218, 18 SW 578. One who employs a person to render service for him.
See **hire.**

hiring. See **hire; hiring at will; hiring out convicts.**

hiring at will. A hiring which can be terminated by either of the parties at any time, subject to such notice of intent to terminate as may be required by the contract of hire. Warden v Hinds (CA4 Va) 163 F 201.

hiring automobile. See **drive-it-yourself system; renting automobiles; taxicab.**

hiring hall. A place where prospective employers may engage the services of persons available for employment, maintained by a labor union. 31 Am J Rev ed Lab § 250.

hiring-hall agreement. A provision in a collective labor agreement respecting the maintenance of a hiring hall by the union, the characteristic feature of which is the clause respecting discrimination against prospective employees because of the presence or absence of union membership. International Brotherhood of T. C. W. & H. v NLRB, 365 US 667, 6 L Ed 2d 11, 81 S Ct 835.

hiring out prisoners. See **convict labor; convict labor contract.**

hirst (hèrst). Same as **hurst.**

his heirs. See **heirs; heirs and assigns.**

his mark. Words frequently employed in identifying a signature by mark, in a form such as: "his x mark," but not essential to the validity of the signature, authenticity being sufficiently assured by the attestation required by law. 23 Am J2d Deeds § 25.

His saltem accumulem donis, et fungar inani munere (his sal'tem a-kū'mu-lem dō'nis, et fun'gar in-ā'nī mu-ne're). At least I have added to what he has given and I have served to defend one who is dead. Briscoe v Bank of Kentucky (US) 11 Pet 257, 350, 9 L Ed 709, 746.

historical society. A society the purpose of which is to preserve historical records and mementos and to arouse an interest in history and the realization of its significance. Mitchell v Reeves, 123 Conn 549, 196 A 785, 115 ALR 1114.

his verbis. See **in his verbis.**

hit-and-run. See **leaving scene of accident.**

hit-and-run driver. See **leaving scene of accident.**

hitch. A fastener or coupler by means of which one object is attached to another, as a trailer to a motor vehicle. Slang for a period of enlistment in the armed services.

hitchhiker. A person who stands in the highway close to the paved or traveled portion for the purpose of obtaining a ride, usually indicating such purpose by gestures.

hitching. Tying an animal to a post, tree, or other object, so as to prevent him from running at large. Tying an object to an engine or vehicle under power for the purpose of towing the object.

hithe. A harbor; a port.

hit the jackpot. To win the stake in a game of chance. To have a great success.

H. L. An abbreviation of **house of lords.**

hlaford. A lord.

hlafordswice. Betraying a lord; treason.

hlothbote. (Saxon.) A fine for attending a hlothe or unlawful assembly.

hlothe. An unlawful assembly.

H. M. Abbreviation of His Majesty or Her Majesty.

H$_2$O. The symbol representing the chemical compound of water; two parts of hydrogen and one part of oxygen.

hoard. Noun: An accumulation of savings. A supply held in reserve. Verb: To accumulate by way of having a reserve.
As defined by the Lever Act which was a war measure of Congress passed in 1917 and amended in 1919, "necessaries shall be deemed to be hoarded when withheld, whether by possession or under any contract or arrangement, from the market by any person for the purpose of unreasonably increasing or diminishing the price." United States v Cohen Grocery Co. 255 US 81, 65 L Ed 516, 41 S Ct 298, 14 ALR 1045, 1052.

hoarding. Noun: A protective board fence; a palisade; a billboard. Verb: See **hoard.**

Hobbs Act. A federal Anti-racketeering Act. 18 USC § 1951. A statute manifesting a purpose to use all the constitutional power of Congress to punish interference with interstate commerce by extortion, robbery, or physical violence. Stirone v United States, 361 US 212, 4 L Ed 2d 252, 80 S Ct 270.

Hobson's choice. An election by compulsion or without freedom of choice; a choice without an alternative. Pictorial Review Co. v Helvering, 68 F2d 766.

hoc (hōk). This; with, by, or in, this. See **absque hoc; ad hoc.**

hoccus saltis (ho'kus sal'tis). A salt-pit.

hochepot. Same as **hotchpot.**

hock (hok). Noun: The joint between the upper and lower bones of the hind leg of an animal or the leg of a fowl. Verb: To hamstring an animal. Slang for pawning.

hock-day (hok-dā). An ancient English festival, the second or third Tuesday after Easter.

hockey. A game, usually played on ice by teams on skates, the players using sticks curved at the end, the object being to make goals constituting scores by driving a disc, known as a puck, into the goal of the opposing team. A popular spectator sport where played by professionals in indoor arenas. 4 Am J2d Amuse § 79.

hockle (hok'l). Same as **hamstring.**

hock-money (hok'mun''i). Contributions for the celebration of hock-day.

Hoc paratus est verificare (hōk pa-rā'tus est ve-ri-fi-kā're). This he is ready to verify.

Hoc paratus est verificare per recordum (hōk pa-rā'tus est ve-ri-fi-kā're per re-kor'dum). This he is ready to verify by the record.

hoc paratus verificare. See **et hoc paratus verificare.**

hoc petit quod inquiratur per patriam. See **et hoc petit quod inquiratur pro patriam.**

hoc ponit se super patriam. See **et hoc ponit se super patriam.**

Hoc quidem perquam durum est, sed ita lex scripta est (hōk qui'dem per'quam dū'rum est, sed i'ta lex skrip'ta est). This indeed is very hard, but such is the written law. See 3 Bl Comm 430.

Hoc servabitur quod initio convenit (hōk ser-vā'bi-ter quod in-i'she-ō kon-vē'nit). That shall be preserved which is useful in the beginning.

hoc titulo (hōk ti'tu-lō). Under this title.

Hoc vobis ostendit (hōk vō'bis os-ten'dit). This makes clear to you; this shows you.

hoc voce (hōk vō'se). By or under this word.

hodge-podge (hoj'poj). Same as **hotchpot.**

hog. A domestic animal which provides ham, bacon, and lard upon butchering. 4 Am J2d Ani §§ 2, 21, 22. Slang for a greedy person.

hoghenhyne. (Saxon.) A domestic servant; a house servant.

hogshead. A big barrel. A measure of volume or capacity equivalent to sixty-three gallons.

hoist. Noun: A device for lifting materials or articles. Verb: To lift or raise.

H.O.L.C. An abbreviation of Home Owner's Loan Corporation.

hold. Verb: To stand fast. To maintain a grip on something. To own or have title to something. To retain in one's keeping; to possess, occupy, and maintain authority over real property, whatever the source of title or authority may be. Miller v Oliver, 54 Cal App 495, 202 P 168; Ure v Ure, 185 Ill 216, 217; Cooke v Doron, 215 Pa 393, 64 A 595. Noun: The space in a ship below deck for cargo.
See **held.**

holder. A person who holds; a person who is in the actual or constructive possession of land. State v Wheeler, 23 Nev 143, 44 P 430. A technical term of the law merchant, the Negotiable Instruments Law, and the Uniform Commercial Code. The person in possession of a bill or note which is payable to bearer. Capitol Hill State Bank v Rawlins Nat. Bank, 24 Wyo 423, 160 P 1171, 11 ALR 937, 950. A person in legal possession of a negotiable instrument and entitled to demand payment in accordance with its terms, whether in his own right or as an agent. Bowling v Harrison (US) 6 How 248, 258, 12 L Ed 425, 429. The payee or indorsee of a bill or note, who is in the possession of it, or the bearer thereof. Uniform Negotiable Instruments L § 191. A person who is in possession of a document of title or an instrument or an investment security drawn, issued, or indorsed to him or his order or to bearer or in blank. UCC § 1–201 (20). One in possession of a negotiable instrument and entitled to maintain an action at law on it or anyone in actual or constructive possession of such an instrument and entitled to recover or receive its contents from the parties to it. Buckman v Hill Military Academy, 182 Or 621, 189 P2d 575.

holder for value. One who has given a legal consideration for a negotiable instrument. Birket v Elward, 68 Kan 295, 74 P 1100.
See **holder in due course.**

holder in due course. Broadly, a bona fide holder for value without notice. 11 Am J2d B & N § 397. A holder of a negotiable instrument or document of title who has taken the instrument under the following conditions: that it is complete and regular upon its face; that he became the holder of it before it was overdue, and without notice that it had previously been dishonored, if such was the fact; that he took it in good faith and for value; that at the time it was negotiated to him he had no notice of any infirmity in the instrument or defect in the title of the person negotiating it. Uniform Negotiable Instruments L § 52. A holder who takes a negotiable instrument, document of title, or an investment security, for value, in good faith, and without notice that it is overdue or has been dishonored or of any defense against or claim to it on the part of any person. UCC § 3–305; 11 Am J2d B & N § 397.

holder in good faith. One who has accepted a bill or note without notice that it is overdue or has been dishonored or of any defense to it or claim thereto on the part of any person.
See **bona fide holder**; **holder in due course.**

holder of life insurance policy. The named insured or an assignee, for the purpose of obtaining the cash surrender value under a nonforfeiture provision of the policy. 29 Am J Rev ed Ins § 686.

holder of warehouse receipt. A person who has both actual possession of, and a right of property in, a warehouse receipt. Uniform Warehouse Receipts Act § 58. The person in possession of a document of title which is a warehouse receipt. UCC § 1–201(5).

holding. The land which is held by a person; a tenure. Possessing; occupying.
See **hold.**

holding company. A supercorporation which owns or at least controls such a dominant interest in one or more other corporations that it is enabled to dictate their policies through voting power, or which is in position to control or materially to influence the management of one or more companies by virtue, in part at least, of its ownership of securities in the other company or companies. 18 Am J2d Corp § 12. A term often applied to a corporation which owns banks. 10 Am J2d Bks § 60. A device sometimes employed to obtain a monopoly or suppress competition between the constituent companies. 36 Am J1st Monop etc § 94.

holding corporation. See **holding company.**

holding court. The act of a judge in presiding over a term or session of a court. Keeping a court open, the judge and all officers of the court being present.

holding for ransom or reward. An element of the offense of kidnapping. Gooch v United States, 297 US 124, 80 L Ed 522, 56 S Ct 395.

holding out. Assuming a status, for example holding out to be a carrier. 13 Am J2d Car §§ 2, 5. Refusing to join in an agreement or course of action entered into or upon by others.

holding over. Any actual retention of possession by a tenant under a lease, without the consent of the landlord, after the expiration of the term of the lease. 32 Am J1st L & T § 920. The acts of a public officer, elected or appointed for a fixed term, in continuing to exercise the functions and duties of the office after the expiration of such term. State v Simon, 20 Or 365, 26 P 170. The act of a bailee under a bailment for a definite term of holding the property after the expiration of the term. 8 Am J2d Bailm § 277. A method of adverse possession. 3 Am J2d Adv P § 229.
See **hold over.**

holding period. The period of time that the taxpayer holds property before disposing of it, such being determinative of whether a gain is short term or long term. IRC § 1222.

holding track. See **hold track.**

holdman. One who works, within the hold of a ship. Union Stevedoring Corp. v Norton (CA3 Pa) 98 F2d 1012.

hold over. A public officer who continues in office after the expiration of the term for which appointed or elected, sometimes by re-election or re-appointment, sometimes for want of a successor, sometimes under color of right or title but without legal authority. 43 Am J1st Pub Of § 484. A tenant under a lease who continues in possession without the consent of the landlord after the expiration of the term of the lease.
See **holding over.**

hold pleas. To take jurisdiction as a court or judicial tribunal. Thus, the county court might hold pleas of debt or damages under the value of forty shillings. See 3 Bl Comm 35.

hold to bail. See **affidavit to hold to bail; binding over.**

hold track. A railroad track used by a railroad company for cars awaiting movement to the place where the freight carried shall be delivered ultimately to the consignee. State ex rel. Crow v Atchison, T. & S. F. R. Co. 176 Mo 687, 75 SW 776.

holdup. A robbery committed by threats and the use of deadly weapons. Leo v State, 63 Neb 723, 724, 89 NW 303.

holiday. A day set aside for worship, or reverence to the memory of a great leader and benefactor of humanity, to rejoice over some great national or historical event, or to rekindle the flame of an ideal. Gidal v Backs, 218 Cal 99, 21 P2d 952. A day declared a holiday by statute.
See **feasts; grand days; legal holiday; nonjuridical day.**

holimote. Same as **halmote.**

Hollywood muffler. A muffler on a motor vehicle so constructed that the noise from the exhaust is much louder than that permitted by a standard type muffler. 7 Am J2d Auto § 158.

holm (hōlm or hōm). A small island.

holografo (o-lo'grah-fo). (Spanish.) A holographic will.

holograph (hol'ō-gráf). A writing which is wholly in the handwriting of the ostensible author. A holographic will.

holographic will. A will that is entirely written and signed by the testator in his own handwriting. 57 Am J1st Wills § 632.
The requirement of attestation is not imposed in the case of a holographic will, since a successful counterfeit of another's handwriting is exceedingly difficult and the requirement that the instrument be in the testator's own handwriting is a sufficient protection against forgery. If a date is required, as it is in some jurisdictions by statute, the date must also be in the handwriting of the testator. 57 Am J1st Wills § 632.

holt (hōlt). A grove; a piece of wooded land.

holymote (hō'li-mōt). Same as **halmote.**

holy orders (hō'li or'dėrs). The rank or station of ecclesiastical officers.

homage (hom' or om'ąj). A formal acknowledgment or profession of fealty by a feudal vassal or tenant to his lord upon investiture.
The vassal or tenant knelt openly and humbly, ungirt and uncovered, and holding up his hands together between those of the lord, who sat before him, he there professed that "he did become his man, from that day forth of life and limb and earthly honor," and then the lord kissed him. The feudists called the ceremony "homagium" or "manhood." See 2 Bl Comm 53.

homage ancestral (ąn-ses'tral). A feudal tenure wherein a man and his ancestors had immemorially held land of another by the service of homage. This also bound the lord to warranty, the homage being an evidence of such a feudal grant. See 2 Bl Comm 300.

homage jury (hom'ąj jö''ri). The jury of a court-baron drawn from tenants. See 2 Bl Comm 54.

homager (hom' or om'ąj-ėr). A tenant or vassal by homage.

homagio respectuando. See **de homagio respectuando.**

homagium (ho-mā'ji-um). Same as **homage.**

homagium ligium (ho-mā'ji-um lī'ji-um). Liege homage; that is, such homage as is due the king irrespective of land tenure.

Homagium, non per procuratores nec per literas fieri potuit, sed in propria persona tam domini quam tenentis capi debet et fieri (ho-mā'ji-um, non per prō-ku-rā-tō'rēz nek per li'te-räs fī'e-rī po'tu-it, sed in prō'pri-a per-sō'na tam do'mi-nī quam te-nen'tis kā'pī de'bet et fī'e-rī). Homage cannot be done by proxy nor by letter, but ought to be received and made in the proper person of the lord as well as that of the tenant.

homagium planum (ho-mā'ji-um plā'num). Plain homage; that is, homage made by the service of fidelity alone.

homagium reddere (hō-mā'ji-um red'de-re). To renounce homage.

hombre bueno (om'br bwä'nō). (Spanish.) A good or worthy man; a district judge.

home. A word so suggestive of love, affection, and security as to be one of the most pleasantly sounding words in the English language. A place where a husband and wife may live in the enjoyment of each other's society and rear their offspring. Anno: 38 ALR 340. The place to which, when weary, one can go and sit, with shoes unlaced, and rest. Johnson v Harvey, 261 Ky 522, 88 SW2d 42. The place where a family lives in the close relation of people who enjoy the company of each other and the comfort and security of abiding together or where some are dependent upon others for care and protection.

A word of variable meaning in legal significance. A house in one respect, but in a proper sense including not only the house, but the entire surroundings and appurtenances enjoyed with the house. 57 Am J1st Wills § 1356. Sometimes, but not necessarily, the equivalent of domicil, since one may abandon his home without losing his domicil at the place (25 Am J2d Dom § 7) and incidental references to a place as "my home" are not conclusive against the existence of the domicil of the declarant in another place. Dodd v Lorenz, 210 Iowa 513, 231 NW 422. Sometimes including not only a place of abode, but also support and maintenance. Anno: 101 ALR 1487.

In ancient law French, the word also signified a man.

As to what passes under a devise of my "home." Anno: 38 ALR2d 840.

home consumption. The consumption of merchandise either by use or by its being manufactured into another product. J. H. Cottman & Co. v United States, 20 Cust & Pat App 344, cert den 289 US 750, 77 L Ed 1495, 53 S Ct 695.

home factor. A factor who resides in the same state or country as his principal. Ruffner v Hewitt, 7 W Va 585.

home farm. The farm upon which a family, some of whom, at least, are farmers, make their home. Doolittle v Blakesley (Conn) 4 Day 265.

home loan bank. A financial institution organized and operating under Title 12 of the United States Code, making loans to its members consisting of building and loan associations, savings and loan associations, and homestead associations, and also to certain non-member borrowers.

Home Loan Bank Board. A federal agency directing the operations of the federal home loan bank system and the federal savings and loan insurance corporation. 12 USC § 1464(a).

Home Loan Bank System. A creation of the federal government for providing a reserve credit pool for member home-finance institutions.

Home ne sera puny pur suer des briefes en court le roy, soit il a droit ou a tort (ôm nē se-rah pu-nē pūr soo-ay day brief ôn kūr lē rwah, swat ēl ah drwah oo ah tor). A man shall not be punished for suing out writs in the king's court, whether he is right or wrong.

home occupation. An occupation, customarily incidental to the use of a building as a residence, carried on in a home or a building accessory thereto, by an occupant of the dwelling, usually the owner or some member of his immediate family, without employees or assistants other than resident members of the family or other occupants of the dwelling. Anno: 73 ALR2d 442.

home office (hōm of'is). The office or department of the British government which supervises the internal affairs of the empire.

homeopath. A physician of the school which teaches that a disease is cured by the administration in small amounts of a drug which will produce the disease if administered in large amounts to a person theretofore healthy. Anno: 78 ALR 699.

Homeopathic Pharmacopoeia. See **United States Homeopathic Pharmacopoeia.**

Home Owners Loan Act. A chapter of the United States Code which provides for the organization, incorporation, examination, operation, and regulation of associations to be known as Federal Savings and Loan Associations, delegating authority to the Federal Home Loan Bank Board to give charters to and regulate such associations. 13 Am J2d B & L Assoc § 10.

Home Owners' Loan Corporation. A corporation established by Act of Congress in 1933 to refinance the indebtedness of homeowners threatened by foreclosure; liquidated in 1951.

home place. The dwelling house and the entire estate and appurtenances which surround it. 57 Am J1st Wills § 1356. In the usage of the Middle West, a farm which is held and occupied by the owner as his place of residence.

As to what passes under a device of "my home place." Anno: 38 ALR2d 840.

home port. The port where a documented vessel of the United States is registered or enrolled, or the place in the same district where the vessel was built, or where one or more of the owners resides. 46 USC § 47.

home rule. The powers of local self-government conferred upon municipalities by constitutional provision. 37 Am J1st Mun Corp § 102.

home rule charter. A charter of a municipal corporation which is framed by the municipality itself and is adopted by popular vote of its own people.

The constitutions of many states authorize such charters. In some of them the state legislature must confirm the charter before it can become effective, and the legislature is permitted to alter and amend the submitted charter both before and after confirmation. In other states, the legislature is given no power of confirmation, alteration, or amendment, the charter becomes final upon its adoption by vote of the people of the municipality and it may be amended by them at future elections. 37 Am J1st Mun Corp § 103.

homesoken. Same as **hamesecken.**

homestall (hōm'stâl). A word used in the ancient law to designate the mansion house. Dickinson v Mayer, 58 Tenn (11 Heisk) 515, 521.

homestead. In a popular sense, the place of the home —the residence of the family; it represents the dwelling house in which the family resides, with the usual and customary appurtenances, including the outbuildings of every kind necessary or convenient for family use, and the lands used for the purposes thereof. In a legal sense, a term strictly American, but susceptible to a variety of conceptions, one being immunity from the claims of creditors, another the restriction of the conveyance or incumbering of such property, still another a provision for surviving spouse and minor children to be made out of the lands of a decedent, which may or may not be property to which a homestead exemption has attached, and, in still other senses, the right, based on residence and cultivation, to acquire a tract of land out of the public lands of the United States, and the subject of such a right. 26 Am J1st Home § 1.

Used in a will by way of describing the subject matter of a devise, it is uniformly held that the term "homestead" is not limited to the quantity or value of land denominated in applicable statutes as constituting an exemption from execution. 57 Am J1st Wills § 1356.

See **abandonment of homestead; admeasurement of homestead; declaration of homestead; entry under homestead law; excessive homestead; head of family; homestall; homestead entry; homesteader; homestead ex vi terminis; homestead right; householder; probate homestead; reassignment of homestead; right of homestead; rural homestead; urban homestead.**

homestead association. An association comparable to a savings and loan association.

homestead entry. See **entry under homestead law.**

homesteader. The claimant of a homestead; one who has made a homestead entry on public lands and is residing, upon the lands entered, for the purpose of perfecting his entry and ultimately acquiring title. 42 Am J1st Home §§ 19 et seq.

homestead exemption. The exemption created by act of Congress declaring that no lands acquired under federal homestead and timber culture laws shall be liable for the satisfaction of any debt contracted prior to their acquisition from the government. 42 Am J1st Pub L § 27. The exemption from execution, provided by constitution or statute, of a prescribed amount or tract of land occupied by the debtor as the head of the family residing thereon. 26 Am J1st Home §§ 2 et seq.

homestead ex vi termini (homestead ex vī ter′mi-nī). A homestead by the force of the term or expression; that is, in its ordinary meaning, the family seat or mansion. Turner v Turner, 107 Ala 465, 18 So 310.

homestead laws. The statutes relative to the acquisition of a homestead out of the public domain. 42 Am J2d Pub L § 20.

See **homestead exemption; pre-emption laws.**

homestead right. A quality annexed to land whereby an estate is exempted from sale under execution for debt. Littlejohn v Egerton, 77 NC 379, 384. A statutory privilege which may be asserted where the homestead property of the family is sought to be subjected to the payment of a debt not a lien, whereunder either or both spouses may claim the homestead as exempt from seizure. Thompson v Marlin, 116 Okla 159, 243 P 950. The right to enter upon unappropriated public land for the purpose of occupying a tract and ultimately acquiring title to it under the homestead laws. 42 Am J1st Pub L §§ 19 et seq.

homestead servants. Domestic servants. 57 Am J1st Wills § 1395.

homework. Industrial work performed at home according to instructions and directions given by the employer, a good example of which is needlework on clothing. Anno: 143 ALR 420.

homeworker. One who performs industrial work in his or her own home for others. Anno: 143 ALR 419.

homicidal insanity. See **homicidal mania.**

homicidal mania. A morbid and uncontrollable appetite for man-killing. 29 Am J1st Homi § 3. A heart totally depraved and fatally bent on mischief. Leache v State, 22 Tex Crim 279.

homicide. The killing of a human being under any circumstances, by the act, agency, or omission of another. 26 Am J1st Homi § 2.

The word is generic and embraces every mode by which the life of one man is taken by the act of another man. It may be lawful, as where a man is killed in war or put to death under the valid sentence of a court, or it may be unlawful. It may also be justifiable or excusable, as in the prevention of a violent felony or in self-defense. The word includes both murder and manslaughter. Commonwealth v Webster, 59 Mass (5 Cush) 295.

See **criminal homicide; felonious homicide; femicide; fratricide; infanticide; manslaughter; matricide; murder; parricide; patricide; prolicide; regicide; retreat to the wall; self-defense; suicide; uxoricide.**

homicide by misadventure. An accidental killing of a human being. 26 Am J1st Homi § 220. A killing by pure accident, that is, where a man, doing a lawful act, without any intention of hurt, unfortunately kills another; as where a man is at work with a hatchet, and the head of it flies off and kills a by-stander. See 4 Bl Comm 182.

homicide per infortunium (hom′i-sīd per in-for-tū′ni-um). Same as **homicide by misadventure.**

homicide se defendendo (homicide sē dē-fen-den′dō). The killing of a human being in self-defense.
See **self-defense.**

homicidium (ho-mi-sī′di-um). Same as **homicide.**

homicidium in rixo (ho-mi-sī′di-um in rik′sō). The killing of a human being while engaged in a quarrel.

homicidium per infortunium (ho-mi-sī′di-um per in-for-tū′ni-um). Same as **homicide by misadventure.**

homicidium per misadventure (ho-mi-sī′di-um per misadventure). Same as **homicide by misadventure.**

homicidium se defendendo (ho-mi-sī′di-um sē dē-fen′den-dō). Same as **homicide se defendendo.**

hominatio (ho-mi-nā′she-ō). Same as **homage.**

homine capto in withernam (ho′mi-ne kap′tō in withernam). See **de homine capto in withernam.**

homine eligendo (ho′mi-ne ē-li-jen′dō). A writ which directed the members of a corporation to select a successor to a dead man who had held one part of an indenture under a statute merchant.

homine replegiando (ho′mi-ne rē-ple-ji-an′dō). See **de homine replegiando.**

homines (ho′mi-nēz). Plural of homo; men.

homines ligii (ho′mi-nēz li′ji-ī). Liege Men,—the vassals of their sovereign or liege lord under that exalted species of fealty called feudum ligium, a liege fee. See 1 Bl Comm 367.

hominium (ho-mi′ni-um). Same as **homage.**

Hominum causa jus constitutum est (hō′mi-num kâ′za jūs kon-sti-tū′tum est). Law is constituted for the benefit of mankind.

homiplagium (ho-mi-plā′ji-um). Mayhem.

homme (ôm). A man.

hommes de fief (ôm dē fēf). Men of the fief or feud,
—feudal tenants or vassals.

hommes feodaux (ôm fē′ō-dō′). Same as **hommes de fief.**

homo (hō′mō). A man; a feudal tenant or vassal.

homo astrer (hō′mō as′trer). A householder.

homo chartularis (hō'mō kar-tu-lā'ris). A freeman by deed or charter.

homo commendatus (hō'mō kom-men-dā'tus). A freeman who voluntarily placed himself under the subjection of a lord in order to secure his protection.

homo ecclesiasticus (hō'mō e-klē-si-as'ti-kus). A vassal or bond slave of the church.

homo exercitalis (hō'mō ex-er-si-tā'lis). A man of the army; a soldier.

homo feodalis (hō'mō fū-dā'lis). A man of the feud; a feudal tenant; a vassal.

homo francus (hō'mō fran'kus). A freeman.

homogenous goods (hō-moj'e-nus güdz). Uniform in structure; composed of the same elements. Substances, such as seeds of grass, which are indistinguishable when intermingled. The antithesis of heterogenous goods.

homo ingenuus (hō'mō in-je'nū-us). A freeman.

homo liber (hō'mō li'ber). A freeman.

homo ligius (hō'mō li'ji-us). Singular of **homines ligii**.

homologacion (o-mo-lo-gah-the-on'). (Spanish.) Same as **homologation**.

homologare (ho-mo-lo-gā're). Same as **homologate**.

homologate (hō-mol'ō̬-gāt). (Civil law.) To say the like, homos logos similiter dicere. Viales' Syndics v Gardenier (La) 9 Mart 324, 325.

homologation (hō-mol-ō̬-gā'shọn). A confirmation; an approval; saying the same. Hecker v Brown, 104 La 524, 527, 29 So 232.

homo novus (hō'mō nō'vus). A new man; that is, a feudal tenant who took a new fee.

homonymiae (ho-mo-ni'mi-ē). (Civil law.) Cases containing repetitions of the same principles and rules of law which had been set down in previous cases.

homo pertinens (hō'mō per'ti-nenz). A feudal vassal who went with the soil.

Homo potest esse habilis et inhabilis diversis temporibus (hō'mō po'test es'se ha'bi-lis et in-ha'bi-lis dī-ver'sis tem-po'ri-bus). A man can be capable and incapable at different times.

homo regius (hō'mō rē'ji-us). A man of the king, a king's vassal.

homo Romanus (hō'mō rō-mā'nus). A Roman.

homosexual. One, especially a male, whose desire for sexual relations is directed to a person of the same sex.

homosexuality. Sexual relations between persons of the same sex, males especially.
    See **sodomy**.

homos logos similiter dicere (hō'mos lō'gos si-mi'li-ter dī'se-re). See **homologate**.

homo sui juris (hō'mō su'ī jū'ris). See **datio in adoptionem**.

homo trium litterarum (hō'mō tri'um lit-te-rā'rum). A man of three letters; that is "f" "u" "r," meaning a thief.

Homo vocabulum est naturae; persona juris civilis (hō'mō vo-kā'bu-lum est nā-tū'rē; per-sō'na jū'ris si'vi-lis). Man is a natural word; person is a term of the civil law.

homsoken. Same as **hamesecken**.

homstd. An abbreviation of "homestead," sometimes employed in descriptions of real estate, but the use of which is not recommended, since it is only a little shorter than the whole word.

Hon. An abbreviation of **Honorable**.

honest. Descriptive of one who does not lie or cheat. See **true**.

honeste vivere (ho-nes'tē vī've-re). To live honorably or respectably.

Honeste vivere, alteri non laedere suum cuique tribuere (ho-nes'tē vī've-re, al'te-rī non lē'de-re su'um kī'kwē tri-bu'e-re). Live honorably, injure no one else, render to each man that which is his.

honesty. The quality of being honest, neither cheating nor lying.
    The word is derived from the Latin "honestus," and is essentially one which takes its meaning from its context. Primarily, it means suitable, becoming, or decent. In money transactions, it means financial integrity. In affairs of state, it means loyalty. In matters of friendship, it means steadfast. In sexual relations, it imports fidelity. State v Snover, 63 NJL 382, 384, 43 A 1059.

honey. A product of bees, whether produced in a hive or in the hollow of a tree by wild bees. 4 Am J2d Ani § 18. A term of endearment.

honor. Verb: To pay or to accept and pay. UCC § 1–201(21). Noun: Adherence to right principles of conduct; integrity. Respect accorded another. A seigniory consisting of an aggregation of manors held under one lord paramount was so called, especially if it had belonged to an ancient feudal baron, or had been at any time in the hands of the crown. See 2 Bl Comm 91.
    See **acceptance for honor**; **payment for honor**.

honorable. An English title bestowed upon younger sons of earls and upon the children of viscounts and barons; in the United States, a title of courtesy applied to judges, members of Congress and state legislatures, and other federal and state officers of rank.

honorable discharge. A formal final judgment passed by the government upon the entire military record of a soldier, and an authoritative declaration by the government that the soldier has left the service in a status of honor. United States v Kelly (US) 15 Wall 34, 21 L Ed 106.

honorarium (on-ō-rā'ri-um). A fee paid for professional services rendered gratuitously or under such conditions that there is no legal obligation for payment.

honorary. As an honor; without profit, fee or reward, and in consideration of the honor conferred by holding a position of responsibility and trust. Haswell v New York, 81 NY 255, 258.

honorary feud. A feudal honorary rank or title of nobility, which was not of a divisible nature and which could only be inherited by the eldest son. See 2 Bl Comm 56.

honorary office. A public office to which no fees or salary are annexed; an office accepted from desire to be of service to the public. State v Stanley, 66 NC 59. An office in an association, society, or corporation created to honor an incumbent, not to impose duties upon him.

honorary rank. See **brevet**; **emeritus**; **honorary office**.

honorary services. Feudal services of a special nature rendered to the king in person, such as carrying his banner or his sword. See 2 Bl Comm 73.
See **honorary office.**

honorary trust. An alleged trust predicated upon nothing more than a moral, ethical, or honorary obligation. 54 Am J1st Trusts § 15.

honor-court. A court held within an honor or seigniory.

honoring paper. See **honor.**

honoris causa (ho-nō'ris kâ'za). As a mark of honor.

honour (on'ǫr). Same as **honor.**

hood. Slang for hoodlum or gangster.

hoodlum. A rowdy. A gangster.
See **gangster.**

Hooper ratings. A system used to ascertain the number of listeners tuned in to a particular radio program. Stanley v Columbia Broadcasting System, 35 Cal 2d 653, 221 P2d 73, 23 ALR2d 216.

hootch (höch). Slang for an alcoholic beverage. State v Vesper (Mo) 289 SW 862, 863.
"We should take judicial notice that the words hootch, moonshine, white mule, etc., are generally used in connection with the unlawful manufacture of whisky." State v Wright, 312 Mo 626, 632.

hop ale. A drink akin to hop beer.
See **hop beer.**

hop beer. A nonintoxicating malt liquor, otherwise known as near beer, widely marketed during the period of National Prohibition. 30 Am J Rev ed Intox L § 11.
A court will not recognize, by way of taking judicial notice, that hop beer or hop jack is an intoxicating liquor. Jacob Ruppert, Inc. v Caffey, 251 US 264, 64 L Ed 260, 40 S Ct 141.

hope. A desire; an expectation. A precatory word; the equivalent of a command or direction in a will where coming from a testator who has the power to command. Pembroke Academy v Epsom School Dist. 75 NH 408, 75 A 100. A term of the old English for valley.

hopelessly insolvent. Irretrievably insolvent; such state of insolvency that it is manifestly impossible to continue in business and meet obligations. Forsythe v First State Bank, 185 Minn 255, 241 NW 66, 81 ALR 1074.
Where, at the time in question, there is a reasonable hope and expectation on the part of the officers of a bank that a consolidation plan may be consummated and that the business of the bank may be continued and its fortunes retrieved, the bank is not hopelessly and irretrievably insolvent. Washington Shoe Mfg. Co. v Duke, 126 Wash 510, 218 P 232, 37 ALR 611.

hope of benefit. As an inducement to a confession: —a temporal or worldly benefit, the hope of escaping punishment in whole or in part, not hope of a moral or spiritual benefit. 29 Am J2d Ev § 560.

hop jack. Same as **hop beer.**

hopping car. Boarding a vehicle while it is in motion, especially the car of a carrier.

hops. A crop mainly dependent on annual cultivation, used in the making of beer. 21 Am J2d Crops § 4.

horae judiciae (hō'rē jū-di'she-ē). The hours of the sessions of a court.

Hora non est multum de substantia negotii, licet in appello de ea aliquando fiat mentio (hō'ra non est mul'tum de sub-stan'she-a ne-gō'she-ī, li'set in appel'lō dē e'a a-li-quan'do fī'at men'she-ō). The hour (of the day) is not of much consequence in business affairs, but mention of it is sometimes made in appeals.

hord. See **bock hord.**

hordera (hor'de-ra). A treasurer.

horizontal. Toward the horizon; lateral rather than vertical; across the board; uniform.
"It was not the intention to prohibit carriers from making reductions in tariffs at will, provided such reductions were uniform,—what are frequently called 'horizontal reductions.'" Steenerson v Great Northern Railway Co. 60 Minn 461, 472, 62 NW 826.

horizontal agreement. An agreement entered into between competing producers or dealers whereby they seek to control the market price of a commodity. 52 Am J1st Tradem § 173.

horizontal measurement. The use of the chain in measuring land which is mountainous or hilly in such manner that it is kept level rather than following the acclivities or depressions. The antithesis of the surface measurement wherein the chain is run along the surface, following the acclivities and depressions. 12 Am J2d Bound § 58.

Horizontal Property Acts. Statutes relative to condominiums or similar structures under other names. 15 Am J2d Con Apt § 1.

horizontal union. Same as **trade union.**

horn. A musical instrument used in an orchestra or band, occasionally in a solo; a device on a motor vehicle to signal its approach by sound.

hornage. Same as **cornage.**

horngeld (hôrn'geld). A tax which was levied on horned animals in a forest.

horning. An ancient practice under the Scotch law whereby a debtor was summoned by the sounding of a horn to satisfy his obligation under pain of imprisonment for default. Borden v State, 11 Ark 519; Fisher, Brown & Co. v Fielding, 67 Conn 91, 34 A 714.

hornswoggle (hôrn-swog'l). Slang for cheat or swindle. United States Fidelity & Guaranty Co. v Rochester (Tex Civ App) 281 SW 306, 314.

horn tenure. Same as **cornage.**

horoscope reading. A purported demonstration of the determination of the destiny of a person by examing the position of the planets and other heavenly bodies at the time of his birth. State v Neitzel, 69 Wash 567, 125 P 939.

hors (ôr). Out; outside; out of; without.

hors de combat (ôr dė koṅ-bä'). Out of the combat or struggle; worsted.

hors de court (ôr de kor). Out of or away from court.

hors de son fee (ôr dē sôn fay). Out of his fee.
In England at common law, the property of the tenant could never be taken after the disruption of the relation of landlord and tenant and a removal from the demised premises. In such cases the tenant pleaded "Hors de son fee." That was to say, "I am no longer your tenant and am with my goods out of your land." In other words, "I am out of your seigniory." Mather v Wood, 12 Pa Co 3, 4.

horse. A domestic animal. 4 Am J2d Ani § 2. A large four-footed animal, characterized by flowing mane and tail and solid hoofs. In one sense limited to a gelding or stallion; in another sense, inclusive of a female or mare as well as a male. McCarver v Griffin, 194 Ala 634, 69 So 920; State v Dunnavant, 5 SCL (3 Brev) 9.

See **colt; filly; gelding; mare; ridgling; work horse.**

horse game. See **horseplay.**

horseless carriage. An obsolete term for motor vehicle.

horseplay. Having fun in a rough and boisterous manner, often at hazard of personal injury to participant or spectator. The "good, clean, fun" of assaulting a victim from behind, when his attention is directed elsewhere, by rushing at him and violently pushing him forward. Markley v Whitman, 95 Mich 236, 54 MW 763.

See **rush.**

horsepower. A unit of measure first used in reference to steam engines but now employed for other engines and motors. The unit in estimating the power required to drive machinery. Eastern Pennsylvania Power Co. v Lehigh Coal & Navigation Co. 246 Pa 72, 77, 92 A 47. The power required to lift a weight of 550 pounds 1 foot in 1 second.

horsepower rating. The rating of a watercraft or vehicle according to the horsepower of its motor or engine, sometimes noted for purposes of identification in licensing.

horse race. A contest by way of sport wherein horses are pitted against each other, either a flat race wherein the horses are ridden by jockeys, or a harness race wherein they are driven by drivers riding in light carts known as sulkies. A game or gaming within the meaning of some statutes prohibiting gambling or gaming. 24 Am J1st Gaming § 22.

As defined by the American racing rules, a race is any contest for purse, stake, premium, or wager for money, or involving admission fees, on any course, and in the presence of a judge or judges. Stone v Clay (CA7 Ill) 61 F 889, 890.

See **bookmaking; French pool; handicap; pool; pool selling; parimutuel; purse; race meeting; sweepstakes.**

horse show. An exhibition of horses, often including a demonstration of the gaits of the animals.

horse trailer. A trailer towed by a motor vehicle and used for the transportation of a horse or horses.

horseway. A private way usable for a rider on horseback. Jones v Venable, 120 Ga 1, 47 NE 549

horsing around. A slang expression for activities directed toward no serious purpose and often of a mischievous nature.

hors pris (or prē). Taken out; except.

horticulture. A branch of agriculture; the science or art of cultivating the soil and its fruits. 3 Am J2d Agri § 1.

hortus (hôr′tus). A garden.

hospes (hos′pēz). See **hospitium.**

hospital. A place for the reception of persons sick or infirm in body or in mind; a building founded through charity, where the sick and disabled may be treated solely at their own expense, or at the expense of the institution. An institution for receiving, maintaining and, as far as possible, ameliorating the condition of persons suffering from bodily defects, mental maladies, or other misfortunes affecting health and physical condition adversely. 26 Am J1st Hospit § 2.

A hospital is primarily a service organization. It serves three groups: the patients, its doctors, and the public. It furnishes the place where the patient, whether poor or rich, can be treated under ideal conditions. It makes available room, special diet, X-ray, laboratory, surgery, and a multitude of other services and equipment now available through the advances of medical science. Cedars of Lebanon Hospital v Los Angeles County, 35 Cal 2d 729, 221 P2d 31, 15 ALR2d 1045.

As the term appears in a policy of hospital insurance, it does not include a nursing home, a convalescent home, or a private dwelling. 29A Am J Rev ed Ins § 1532.

See **public hospital.**

hospitaler. Another spelling for **hospitaller.**

hospital fee. An incidental charge imposed upon a student in a university or college. 15 Am J2d Colleges § 19. Broadly, a fee charged by a hospital for a service rendered a patient.

hospital insurance. A policy or contract whereby the one party, known as the insurer, in consideration of the payment of premiums by the other party, known as the insured, agrees to pay the hospital expenses of the insured or members of his family for care required because of sickness, disease, or disability suffered or incurred during the term of the policy.

hospitalization contract. See **Blue Cross; hospital insurance; hospital service contract.**

hospitaller (hos′pi-tal-ėr). A member of an order of knighthood which cared for the sick and the poor.

hospital liability insurance. A contract of insurance insuring a hospital against liability in damages for the death of or injury to a patient. 29A Am J Rev ed Ins § 1355.

hospital service contract. A contract issued by a corporation, ordinarily one organized as a nonprofit body, whereby the corporation agrees to provide the members with hospitalization as such may be required by a member or the members of his family. 29 Am J Rev ed Ins § 12.

See **Blue Cross; blue cross contract.**

hospital service corporation. See **hospital service contract.**

hospital staff. The officers and employees of a hospital, especially professional people such as physicians, surgeons, and nurses. 26 Am J1st Hospit § 8.

hospital zone. An area surrounding a hospital wherein motor vehicle traffic is regulated as to the speed of the vehicles and sometimes the sounding of horns.

hospitator (hos′pi-tā-tor). A host; an innkeeper.

hospitelarius (hos-pi-tel-lā′ri-us). A host; an innkeeper.

hospites (hos′pi-tēz). The proprietors or hosts in mansions of ancient Rome.

See **hospitium.**

hospitia (hos-pi′she-a). Plural of **hospitium.**

hospitia curiae (hos-pi′she-a kū′ri-ē). The inns of court.

hospiticide (hos-pit′i-sīd). The killing of a host or the guest at an inn; the person who did the killing.

hospitium (hos-pish'i-um). An inn; a hostel; a household.
 Among the ancient Romans, on either side of the spacious mansions of the wealthy patricians were smaller apartments, known as the "hospitium," or place for the entertainment of strangers, and the word "hospes" was a term to designate the proprietor of such a mansion, as well as the guest whom he received. Cromwell v Stephens (NY) 2 Daly 15, 17.
 See **intra hospitium**.

host. Noun: An innkeeper. One who receives another for refreshment, lodging, or entertainment. Verb: To be a host on a particular occasion. In a usage now obsolete, to put up at an inn. Cromwell v Stephens (NY) 2 Daly 15, 20.

hostage (hos'tăj). An inn; a lodging; a person held in unlawful custody for the purpose of obtaining the performance of demands made by the person holding him.

hosteler (hos'tel-ėr). A host; an innkeeper.

hostelier (ōs-tĕ'lē-ay). Same as **hosteler**.

hostellagium (hos-tel-lā'ji-um). A lord's right of lodging on the premises of his tenant.

hostelry (hos'tel-ri). An inn; a lodginghouse; a hotel.

hostes (hos'tēz). Enemies.

Hostes hi sunt qui nobis, aut quibus nos, publice bellum decrevimus; caeteri latrones aut praedones sunt (hos'tēz hī sunt quī nō'bis, ât qui'bus nos, pub'li-sē bel'lum de-krē'vi-mus; sē'te-rī la-trō'nēz ât prē-dō'nēz sunt). Those are enemies who have publicly declared war against us, or against whom we have done so; the others are thieves or robbers. See 1 Bl Comm 257.

hostes humani generis (hos'tēz hu-mā'nī je'ne-ris). Enemies of the human race.

Hostes sunt qui nobis vel quibus nos bellum decernimus; caeteri traditores vel praedones sunt (hos'tēz sunt quī nō'bis vel qui'bus nos bel'lum de-ser'nimus; sē'te-rī trā-di-tō'rēz vel prē-dō'nēz sunt). Enemies are those against whom we declare war or who declare it against us; others are either traitors or pirates.

host-guest relationship. See **guest**.

hosticide (hos'ti-sīd). The killing of an enemy; a person who kills an enemy.

hostile (hos'til or tīl). Belonging to an enemy; appropriate to an enemy; showing ill-will and malevolence, or a desire to thwart and injure; occupied by an enemy or a hostile people; inimical; a hostile country; hostile to a sudden change. Ballard v Hansen, 33 Neb 861, 865, 50 NW 295; Brewer v Brewer, 238 NC 607, 78 SE2d 719, 40 ALR2d 763.

hostile act. An act of war; that is, an act which tends to involve one nation in war with another nation; an act committed with intent to injure another.

hostile embargo. An embargo directed against the ships of a present or prospective enemy nation. See **embargo**.

hostile fire. A term familiar in the law of fire insurance as signifying the opposite of friendly fire. A fire unexpected, unintended, not anticipated, in a place not intended for it to be and where fire is not ordinarily maintained, or a fire which has "escaped" in the usual and ordinary sense of the word. 29A Am J Rev ed Ins § 1287.
 See **escaping fire**.

hostile in its inception. Referring to an adverse claim by a disseisor; relating, not to the orginal entry of the disseisor, but to the act by which the possession became adverse. 3 Am J2d Adv P § 33.

hostile paramount title. An element of constructive eviction of tenant; an assertion of title which justifies the bona fide belief that the threat of dispossession will be carried out in the foreseeable future. Anno: 172 ALR 37.

hostile possession. Possession of land under a claim of an exclusive right thereto, thereby denying the right of any other person. An open and notorious possession of such a character that a claim of ownership inconsistent with the existence of a right on the part of any other person is unquestionably to be inferred. 3 Am J2d Adv P § 34.
 Ill will, malevolence or a desire to thwart and injure are not essential characteristics of hostile possession. Brewer v Brewer, 238 NC 607, 78 SE2d 719, 40 ALR2d 763.

hostile witness. A witness who is subject to cross-examination by the party who called him, because of his evident antagonism toward that party as exhibited in his direct examination.

hostilian law. See **lex hostilia**.

hostilities. Actual operations, offensive or defensive, in the conduct of war. Anno: 95 L Ed 80.

hostility. See **bias**; **hostile**; **hostilities**; **prejudice**.

hot. Stolen or otherwise involved in illegal operations. People v Carrow, 207 Cal 366, 278 P 857.

hot cargo clause. A provision in a collective labor agreement under which union members have the right to refuse to handle unfair or struck goods. 31 Am J Rev ed Lab § 255.

hotchpot. The blending and mixing of property belonging to different persons in order to divide it equally. Pitts v Metzger, 195 Mo App 677, 187 SW 610. The grouping with the assets of a decedent's estate of the value of property given by him by way of advancement to heirs or distributees during his lifetime, so that the whole may be divided so far as possible in accordance with the statutes of descent and distribution, each share being charged with what has already been received. 3 Am J2d Advancem § 54. In admiralty practice, the adding of all the items of damage to both ships injured in a collision, once it has been determined that both contributed to the collision, for the purpose of dividing the loss between the two ships. Cayzer, Irvine Co. v Carron Co. (Eng) LR 1883–1884, 9 App Cas 873.

hot dog. See **wiener**.

hotel. A word usually considered synonymous with "inn." A house which is held out to the public by the proprietor as a place where transient persons who come in a fit condition will be received and entertained as guests for compensation. 29 Am J Rev ed Innk § 2. Sometimes considered an inn of the better class. Dixon v Robbins, 246 NY 169, 158 NE 63, 53 ALR 986.

hotel keeper. See **innkeeper**.
 See **American plan**; **apartment hotel**; **European plan**; **tavern**.

hot-foot. An ill-conceived practical joke in secretly placing a match between the sole and vamp of a person's shoe and then igniting the match.

hot gasoline. Gasoline manufactured from hot oil.

United States v Socony-Vacuum Oil Co. (CA7 Wis) 105 F2d 809.
See **hot oil**.

hot iron ordeal. An ancient form of trial for crime.

hot oil. Crude oil produced in violation of state prorating statutes limiting oil production. United States v Socony-Vacuum Oil Co. (CA7 Wis) 105 F2d 809.
See **Connally Act**.

hot pursuit. See **fresh pursuit**.

hot rod. A slang term for an automobile, usually an older vehicle, which has been equipped by some form of supercharger for high speed.

hot vulcanization. The process of incorporating vulcanizing ingredients, such as sulphur, and accelerators, into a mass of crude dry rubber by milling, and subjecting the mass to heat and pressure. Vultex Corp v Heveatex Corp. (CA1 Mass) 100 F2d 838.

hot-water ordeal. An ancient form of trial for crime in which the defendant's arms were plunged into scalding hot water.

hound-bailiff. Same as **bound-bailiff**.

hours for presentment. The hours for presenting a bill of exchange or draft for acceptance. 11 Am J2d B & N § 732. The hours for presenting a bill or note for payment, for the purpose of charging a person secondarily liable. 11 Am J2d B & N §§ 755, 756.

hours of banking. See **banking hours**.

hours of business. See **business hours**.

hours of labor. The time in hours per day or per week spent by an employee in the service of his employer. Statutes enacted under the police power, in consideration of the health of laborers and the safety of the public, applicable in certain occupations which are particularly fatiguing, such statutes being distinguishable from those which prescribe what shall constitute a day's work in the absence of an agreement by the parties on the point. 31 Am J Rev ed Lab § 780.

As used in the Federal Fair Labor Standards Act, the term includes not only the hours that employees were actually engaged in manual labor, but also such hours during which they were charged with the operation of the plant. Fleming v Rex Oil & Gas Co. (DC Mich) 43 F Supp 951.

Whether sleeping time allowed an employee at his station is work time within the meaning of the Fair Labor Standards Act depends upon the express or implied agreement of the parties and, in the absence of an agreement, upon the nature of the service. General Electric Co. v Porter (CA9 Wash) 208 F2d 805, 44 ALR2d 854.
See **day's work**; **Hours of Service Act**.

hours of service. See **day's work**; **hours of labor**; **Hours of Service Act**.

Hours of Service Act. A federal statute intended to promote the safety of employees and travelers upon railroad by regulating and limiting the hours of labor of railroad employees who are engaged in or connected with the movement of train in interstate or foreign commerce. 31 Am J Rev ed Lab § 799.

hours of voting. See **voting hours**.

hours worked. See **day's work**; **hours of labor**; **Hours of Service Act**.

housage (hou'zăj). A fee or charge paid for the storage of goods.

house. A building, Simmons v State, 234 Ind 489, 129 NE2d 121. Any building, edifice, or structure enclosed with walls and covered. State v Beckwith, 135 Me 423, 198 A 739; Mulligan v State, 25 Tex App 199, 7 SW 664. A building, whether for private or public use. State v Beckwith, 135 Me 423, 198 A 739. A structure intended or used for human habitation; especially a human habitation which is fixed in place and is intended for the private occupation of a family or families. Bolin v Tyrol Invest Co. 273 Mo 257, 200 SW 1059. For some purposes, a dwelling house. 5 Am J2d Arson § 19; 13 Am J2d Burgl § 6. Sometimes confined to a single-family residence. 20 Am J2d Cov § 196. For other purposes a single room. Wolcott v Ashenfelter, 5 NM 442, 23 P 780, landlord's lien statute. Including for some purposes, outhouses, party walls, and subsidiaries necessary to convenient occupancy. 5 Am J2d Arson § 20; 29 Am J Rev ed Ins § 293. Including, where it is the subject of a grant, an interest in land upon which the structure is located, except as the contrary appears by other terms of the instrument. 23 Am J2d Deeds § 244. Including, where it indicates the subject of a devise, not only the land physically covered, but an additional amount, necessary or convenient to the enjoyment of the structure itself. 57 Am J1st Wills § 1356.

house boat. A vessel within admiralty jurisdiction. 2 Am J2d Adm § 33.

housebote (hous'bōt). A right of estover; the right of a tenant to cut and take timber and wood for the repair of buildings and fences and for fuel. 32 Am J1st L & T § 219.

housebreaking. The breaking and entering into the dwelling house of another; an element of the crime of burglary. Sometimes a statutory offense similar to burglary.

house-burning. See **arson**; **pyromania**.

house confinement clause. A clause of a health and accident policy, generally understood to be intended to show the extent of disability rather than to impose a strict condition of absolute confinement to a house. A clause which calls for substantial confinement by reason of illness or accident, not confinement so close as to exclude a period of disability during which the insured went out for exercise or visits to his physician. 29A Am J Rev ed Ins § 1530. A clause which is satisfied by confinement in a hospital or sanitarium, as well as at home. Anno: 29 ALR2d 1427.

household. Noun: Persons who dwell together as a family. Arthur v Morgan, 112 US 495, 499, 28 L Ed 825, 5 S Ct 241. A family residing together in one dwelling, using common living quarters and facilities under such domestic arrangements and circumstances as create a single family unit or establishment. Anno: 88 ALR2d 923. A family relation of a character both permanent and domestic, not that of persons abiding together as strangers or mere boarders. Robbins v Bangor Railway & Electric Co. 100 Me 496, 62 A 136. Quite the same as "family" for the purpose of the exclusion, in a policy of automobile theft insurance, of "theft" by a member of insured's "household." Anno: 48 ALR2d 93. Adjective: Pertaining to or belonging to the house or family. Rydstrom v Queen Ins. Co. 137 Md 349, 112 A 586, 14 ALR 212, 214.

household effects. Articles having some connection with the management of a household. 57 Am J1st Wills § 1347.

See **household furniture.**

householder. For some purposes, the head of a family, not necessarily an owner of property. The head, master, or person who has charge of and provides for a family. Nelson v State, 57 Miss 286. (Qualification as a juror). For the purpose of a homestead exemption:—the head or master of a family who provides for it. 26 Am J1st Home § 17. For the purpose of exemption statutes generally, a person owning or holding and occupying a house. 31 Am J2d Exemp § 26.

Under some statutes, a person may qualify, as a "householder," for a homestead exemption notwithstanding he or she is not the head of a family. 26 Am J1st Home § 17.

household furnishings and effects. An expression which, appearing in a will, may include all of the testator's personal property. 57 Am J1st Wills § 1347.

See **household effects; household furniture.**

household furniture. Not necessarily synonymous with "household goods". As the term appears in a statement of the subject matter of a fire insurance policy:—a variety of articles chiefly associated with the household in their general nature and use. Anno: 41 ALR2d 720; 29 Am J Rev ed Ins § 298. As the term appears in a statute exempting certain property from execution:—those articles which, not becoming fixtures, are designed in their manufacture originally as instruments of the household, essential or useful for comfortable living persons. 31 Am J Rev ed Exemp § 73.

See **necessary household furniture.**

household goods. Not necessarily synonymous with "household furniture." 57 Am J1st Wills § 1347. As the term appears in the statement of the subject matter of a fire insurance policy:—articles in great variety, associated with the household in their general nature and use. 29 Am J Rev ed Ins § 298.

household servant. Domestic servant. 57 Am J1st Wills § 1395.

See **menial servant.**

household stuff. See **household effects; household furnishings and effects; household furniture.**

housekeeper. A woman who takes care of a house or supervises servants of the household.

Generally speaking, the term has reference to services performed in the taking care of a house in connection with the inmates residing therein, but exactly what special and particular duties are to be regarded as embodied within the term must always be decided by the duties which are actually performed under the agreement as made. Edgecomb v Buckhout, 146 NY 332, 40 NE 991.

housekeeping unit. A family under certain zoning laws. 58 Am J1st Zon § 56.

house money. The sum put up for play by the proprietor of a gambling house. Anno: 1 ALR 1403. The percentage of the pool claimed by the proprietor of a gambling house.

house number. The number of a house on a designated street. Sufficient as a description of property conveyed by deed where the municipality, having a known system of numbering, is designated. 23 Am J1st Deeds § 229.

house of assignation. A bawdyhouse or house of ill fame; a house resorted to for purposes of prostitution. McAlister v Clark, 33 Conn 91, 92.

House of Commons. The lower house of the English parliament.

house of correction. An institution for the reception and care of orphans, indigent, wayward, incorrigible, or vicious youths, children whose parents are incapable or unworthy, and, in some instances, adults, such as unfortunate or abandoned women, first offenders, and other particular classes, where they may be taught habits of industry, morality, and religion, and be freed from the corrupting influence of improper associates. 26 Am J1st House of C § 2.

house of entertainment. A tavern; an inn. Bonner v Welborn, 7 Ga 296, 304.

house of his usual abode. The house where a person resides which, in the case of a married man, is prima facie or presumptively the house wherein his wife and family reside. Berryhill v Sepp, 106 Minn 458, 119 NW 404.

house of ill fame. A disorderly house. A house resorted to for the purpose of prostitution. Anno: 74 ALR 314, 320 et seq. A place kept for the convenience of people of both sexes in resorting to lewdness; a place many people may frequent for immoral purposes; a house where one may go for immoral purposes without an invitation. 24 Am J2d Disord H § 2.

House of Keys. The lower house of the legislature of the Isle of Man.

house of legislature. One of the bodies of a bicameral legislature. The membership of a house of the legislature or a majority of the members of such a house. According to some usage, the number of members constituting a quorum. State v McBride, 4 Mo 303.

House of Lords. The upper house of the English parliament; the supreme court of England which is composed of those members of the house of lords who have performed judicial functions.

house of prostitution. A house of ill fame. A house resorted to for the purpose of prostitution. 42 Am J1st Prost § 3.

See **house of ill fame.**

house of public worship. Any building which is primarily devoted to the worship of God and to such incidental exercises and functions as are usually connected with such worship. St. Paul's Church v Concord, 75 NH 420, 75 A 531.

A schoolhouse does not become a house of religious worship merely because the Bible is read to the classes without note or comment thereon by the teachers. Hackett v Brooksville School Dist. 120 Ky 608, 87 SW 792.

See **church.**

house of reformation. Same as **house of correction.**

house of refuge. Essentially the same as **house of correction.**

house of religious worship. See **church; house of public worship.**

House of Representatives. The lower house of the Congress of the United States. One of the houses of a bicameral state legislature.

house of usual abode. See **house of his usual abode.**

house physician. A resident physician in a hospital; a physician available in a hotel for the treatment of guests.

house rules. The regulations provided by a hotel, apartment house, co-operative apartment, or lodg-

HOUSE [572] HUNDREDORS

ing house, respecting the conduct of the guests and occupants and their visitors with reference to the safety of the premises and the comfort and convenience of all concerned.

house to house. Advertising by distribution of circulars and bills. 3 Am J2d Advertg § 11.

house trailer. See **trailer.**

Housing Administration. An agency of the United States within the Housing and Home Finance Agency, operating programs for the improvement of housing conditions and the creation of a sound mortgage market.

Housing and Home Finance Agency. A federal agency created for the purpose of co-ordinating federal functions in reference to housing projects.
See **Housing Administration.**

Housing laws. See **public housing.**

housing projects. Arrangements for the construction of a number of houses in a particular locality, often for the construction of public housing.

hovel. A hut; a shed.

hovering vessel. Any vessel found or kept off the coast of the United States, if from its history, conduct, character, or location, it is reasonable to believe that such vessel is being used or may be used to introduce or promote or facilitate the introduction or attempted introduction of merchandise into the United States in violation of the revenue laws. 19 USC §§ 1401(n), 1709(d).

howe. A word of the Old English for hill.

hoy (hoi). A small sailboat usually employed in and about a harbor for lightering larger craft.

hoyman (hoi'man). A man in charge of a hoy.

H. R. H. An abbreviation of his or her royal highness.

hstd. An unrecommended abbreviation of homestead.

huckster. A dealer in smaller items of merchandise; a peddler rather than a merchant. One who carries his stock with him, going house to house to make sales. Mays v Cincinnati, 1 Ohio St 268, 272.

huckstering. The business or trade carried on by a huckster.

hue and cry (hū and crī). "The old common-law process of pursuing with horn and with voice, all felons, and such as have dangerously wounded another." 4 Bl Comm 293.
See **Statute of Hue and Cry; vociferatio.**

huebra (oo-ay'brah). A land measure used in Spanish-American grants, signifying as much land as two oxen can plough up in a day.

huis (wee). Same as **huy.**

huisher (wee'shay). Same as **huissier.**

huissier (wee'she-ay). (French.) A court usher; a process server.

hull. An outer covering. As a marine term, the body of a ship; the container of the cargo. 29 Am J Rev ed Ins § 304.

hullus (hul'lus). A hill.

humagium (hu-mā'ji-um). A humid or moist place.

human. Of the form and characteristics of man.

human being. A person, male or female.

human body. See **body.**

humane. Kind, tender, compassionate. Disposed to eliminate the cause of suffering of man or beast.
Humane differs from the ordinary use of "merciful," in that it expresses active endeavors to find and relieve suffering, and especially to prevent it, while "merciful" expresses the disposition to spare one the suffering which might be inflicted. Willett v Willett, 197 Ky 663, 247 SW 739, 31 ALR 426, 428.

Humane Society. An organization for the prevention of cruelty to animals. 4 Am J2d Ani § 30

humanitarian considerations. Feelings of kindliness and sympathy as illustrated by the motivation of the good Samaritan to minister to the sick and wounded at the roadside. 38 Am J1st Negl § 16.

humanitarian doctrine. A doctrine, unsupported in law, which would render one liable for the injurious consequences of an accident which was within his power to avert, because of the existence of a moral duty, where he was under no legal duty to act. Oklahoma Natural Gas Co. v Young (CA10 Okla) 116 F2d 720. Another term for the doctrine of "last clear chance." 38 Am J1st Negl § 215

human laws. Laws made by man; not divine law. Borden v State, 11 Ark 519.

humbug. An impostor; a deceiver; a cheat.

humdinger. A slang expression for a case decided in another jurisdiction, but well-considered and clearly in point.

humiliating insults. Personal indignities, sometimes constituting a ground for divorce. 24 Am J2d Div & S § 150.

humiliation. The feeling that one is disgraced or made to seem weak, unimportant, foolish, or contemptible. An element of damages for tort, but measured by no precise rules of damages. 22 Am J2d Damg § 86.

hunc modum. See **in hunc modum.**

hundred (hun'dred). The round number of ten times ten. A superior division made up of ten towns or tithings, which, in turn, were each composed of ten families of freeholders. In some of the more northern counties these hundreds were called "wapentakes." See 1 Bl Comm 115.
See **bailiffs of hundreds; century; Chiltern hundreds; wapentakes.**

hundredarius (hun-dre-dā'ri-us). Same as **hundredary.**

hundredary (hun'dred-ari). The chief officer of a hundred.

hundred court (hun'dred kōrt). A larger court-baron which was held for all the inhabitants of a particular hundred, instead of a manor. Not a court of record. See 3 Bl Comm 34.

hundreders (hun'dred-èrz). Those members of a hundred who were liable to jury service.

hundredfeh. Same as **hundred-penny.**

hundred gemote (hun'dred gē-mōt'). An assembly of the freeholders of a hundred.

hundred lagh. The law of the hundred; liability of members of a hundred to attend the hundred court.

hundredman. Same as **hundreders.**

hundredors (hun'dred-orz). Same as **hundreders.**

hundred-penny (hun'dred-pen"i). A tax levied on a hundred and collected by the sheriff or by the lord of the hundred.

hung jury. A trial or petit jury which cannot reach a unanimous verdict or a verdict supported by the requisite number of jurors.

hunting. Looking for that which is lost. Looking for a person whose whereabouts for the time are unknown. The pursuit and taking of wild game.
See **season; closed season.**

hunting heirs. See **heir hunter.**

hunting license. A license required in most, if not all of the states, under statutes which usually prescribe the fee to be paid therefor and make the procuring of such a license a prerequisite to hunting wild game in the state. 24 Am J1st Game § 45.

hunting preserve. See **game-preserve.**

hunting privilege. See **hunting license; hunting right.**

hunting right. The right to hunt on the land of another; a profit a prendre. 25 Am J2d Ease § 4.

hurdle (hėr'dl). A sledge on which a person convicted of high treason was dragged or drawn to the gallows. See 4 Bl Comm 92.

hurricane. A violent storm characterized by the vehemence of the wind and its sudden changes. Queen Ins. Co. v Hudnut Co. 8 Ind App 22, 26, 35 NE 397. Known in recent years as a storm originating in tropical seas, often moving to land in the temperate zone, causing terrific losses in life and property by the violence of the wind and the heavy rains which accompany it. Not to be confused with the cyclone or tornado.
See **cyclone; tornado.**
It appears that for the purposes of insurance, the terms "hurricane," "tornado," and "windstorm" are often treated as synonymous. See **windstorm insurance.**

hurricane insurance. See **windstorm insurance.**

hurst (hėrst). A grove; a wooded place.

hurt. Noun: A very general term for an injury to the body or even the feelings. Montgomery v Lansing City Electric Railway Co. 103 Mich 46, 61 NW 543. In an application for life insurance:—an injury to the body causing an impairment of health or strength, or rendering the person more liable to contract disease or less able to resist its effects. Bancroft v Home Benefit Asso. 120 NY 14, 23 NE 997. Verb: To injure; to cause pain.

husband. Noun: The male of the two parties to a marital relationship. A farmer; a manager. Verb: To farm; to till the soil; to engage in husbandry. To conserve, for example, a supply of food in the wilderness.
See **husbandry; ship's husband.**

husband and wife. A natural and legal relation. The relation between a man and a woman created by their valid marriage to each other giving rise to the mutual rights, duties and liabilities arising out of that relation. 26 Am J1st H & W § 2.
See **marriage; married woman; unity of husband and wife; wife.**

husband de facto (huz'band dē fak'tō). A husband in conjugal relation, not living apart.

husband de jure (huz'band dē jọ'rē). A husband by a legal marriage.

husband infra brachia (huz'band in'fra brā'ki-a). A husband both de jure and de facto.

husbandry. Care and management, especially of a farm. The business of a farmer, comprehending the various branches of agriculture. Estate of Slade, 122 Cal 434, 55 P 158. The business of a farmer, comprehending agriculture or tillage of the ground, the raising, managing, and fattening of cattle and other domestic animals, the management of the dairy and whatever the land produces. Slycord v Horn, 179 Iowa 936, 162 NW 249, 7 ALR 1285, 1290.
See **animal husbandry; implements of husbandry.**

husband's faculties. The financial condition and the ability and power of a husband to earn money, whether or not he exerts such power, considered with reference to the determination of the amount of an award of alimony. Fowler v Fowler, 61 Okla 280, 161 P 227.

husbrece. Same as **housebreaking.**

huscarle. A household or domestic servant.

husgablum (hus-gä'blum). House rent; a tax levied on houses.

hustings (hus'tings). Same as **hustings court.**

hustings court (hus'tings kōrt). A city police court with jurisdiction in criminal cases similar to that of a justice of the peace. Smith v Commonwealth, 47 Va (6 Gratt) 696, 697. Formerly, the county court of the city of London.
There where also hustings courts at York, Winchester and Lincoln. See 3 Bl Comm 80.

hustler. An employee of a house of prostitution. 24 Am J2d Disord H § 35.

hutesium et clamor (hu-tē'she-um et klā'-mor). Same as **hue and cry.**

hybrid class action. An action maintained by one on behalf of others, not as a typical class suit, since the requisite community of interest is absent, the interests of the members of the class being several, not joint or common, support for the action in such form existing in the presence of property in which all members of the class have an interest and a mutuality of interest in the question involved. Deckert v Independent Shares Corp. (DC Pa) 39 F Supp 592.

hydraulic mining. A method of mining free gold wherein a large volume of water is thrown with great force through a pipe or hose upon the sides of a hill, the gold-bearing earth and gravel thereby being washed down so that the gold can readily be separated. Jennison v Kirk, 98 US 453, 25 L Ed 240.

hydraulic power. Power developed by the movement and force of a liquid, such as the power applied to the brakes on a motor vehicle or to a lifting jack. 58 Am J1st Workm Comp § 108.

hydrophobia. See **rabies.**

hydroplane. An airplane equipped to land on water; a light motor boat with a flat bottom, such structure rendering it possible to skim at the surface of a water at high speed.

hydrostatic pressure. The pressure of water coming from a higher to a lower level. 1 Am J2d Adj L § 22. A phenomenon of Alaska due to the fact that the source of many of the streams is in the mountains at a high altitude.

hymen. The membrane that covers part of the opening of the vagina in a virgin. 44 Am J1st Rape § 3.

hypermetropia (hī"pėr-me-trō'pi-ą). An affection of the eye commonly described as farsightedness.

Baker v State, 91 Tex Crim 521, 240 SW 924, 22 ALR 1163, 1165.

hypersensitiveness. Undue sensitivity to some unpleasant thing, such as a surgical operation. Cody v John Hancock Mut. Life Ins. Co. 111 W Va 518, 163 So 4, 86 ALR 354.

hypersusceptibility. A peculiarity which renders a person subject to painful consequences of the administration of a certain drug, such as penicillin or novocain. 29A Am J Rev ed Ins § 1211.

hypnotism. A state of artificial catalepsy or induced somnambulism. 29 Am J Rev ed Ins Per § 3.

hypobolum (hī-pob'ọ-lum). A testamentary gift of a husband to his wife in addition to her dowry.

hypothec (hī-poth'ek). Same as **hypothecation**.

hypotheca (hī-po-the'ka). (Roman law.) A mortgage of real property; a mortgage or pledge of personal property.

hypothecaria actio (hī-po-the-kā'ri-a ak'shè-ō). Same as **hypothecary action**.

hypothecary action (hī-poth'ẹ-kạ-ri ak'-shọn). A term known in Louisiana, being an action brought by a creditor against the property which has been hypothecated to him by his debtor, in order to have it seized and sold for the payment of the debt. Lovell v Cragin, 136 US 130, 142, 34 L Ed 372, 376, 10 S Ct 1024.

hypothecate (hī-poth'ẹ-kāt). To enter into a contract whereby certain specified real or personal property is designated as security for the performance of an act, without any transfer of the possession of the property. Spect v Spect, 88 Cal 437, 26 P 203.

hypothecation (hī-poth-ē-kā'shọn). A Roman-law name for a pawn or pledge wherein the feigned pledge remained in the possession of the pledgor. 41 Am J1st Pldg & Col § 2. A contract whereby, without change of possession, specific property is designated as security for the payment of a debt or the performance of an obligation.

The contract does not include a transfer of possession as one of its essentials and, therefore, when, in addition to the contract of hypothecation, the debtor gives to his creditor the possession of the premises, he thereby pledges to him the land also as security for the debt, and confers upon him such rights as are incident to a pledge. Spect v Spect, 88 Cal 437, 26 P 203.

See **general hypothecation**; **maritime hypothecation**; **tacit hypothecation**.

hypothecation bond. The bond given under a contract of bottomry or respondentia.

See **bottomry**; **respondentia**.

hypotheque (hī'pô-thêk'). Same as **hypothecation**.

hypothesi. See **ex hypothesi**.

hypothesis (hī-poth'e-sis). A supposition, a proposition, or principle which is assumed or taken for granted, in order to draw a conclusion or inference for proof of the point in question; something not proved, but assumed for the purpose of argument, or to account for a fact or an occurrence. People v Ward, 105 Cal 335, 38 P 945, quoting Webster's Dictionary.

hypothetical case. A case, the facts of which are assumed for the purpose of explaining and discussing the law applicable.

hypothetical instruction. An instruction to the jury as to the law on a hypothetical statement of facts, submitting to the jury the question whether such facts are proved. 53 Am J1st Trial § 547.

hypothetical question. A question addressed to an expert witness, based upon assumed facts stated. 23 Am J2d Dep § 103. A question addressed to an expert witness which assumes or hypothesizes the existence of a certain state of facts and asks for the opinion of the expert witness based upon such facts. 31 Am J2d Expert § 53; 53 Am J1st Trial § 605. A question designed to elicit the opinion of an expert witness on a given condition or state of facts in evidence in the case, the things which counsel claims or assumes to have been proved being stated as an hypothesis and the opinion of the expert asked thereon. Shaughnessy v Holt, 236 Ill 485, 86 NE 256.

hysterical diathesis (his-ter'i-cal di-ath'ẹ-sis). A highly emotional state of congenital origin which may aggravate an injury. 22 Am J2d Damg § 123.

hysterotomy (his-tẹ-rot'ọ-mi). Same as **caesarean operation**.

hythe. Same as **hithe**.

I

I. Roman numeral for 1.

The personal pronoun in the singular of the nominative case. Sufficiently connected with the person executing the instrument where it appears in the body of a deed, that he is bound, although his name does not appear above his signature. 23 Am J2d Deeds § 49.

I am satisfied. A phrase which, appearing in an acknowledgment, is insufficient as a statement of the officer's knowledge of identity of the person acknowledging. Newton Finance Corp. v Conner, 161 Tenn 441, 33 SW2d 95, 72 ALR 1286.

I believe. Not necessarily indicative of a conclusion; a phrase which, appearing in the testimony of a witness, indicates that the witness is speaking from observation and recollection or from what he remembers. See 31 Am J2d Ex & Op § 35.

ibi (i'bi). There; at that place; then; thereupon.

ibid (ī'bid). Same as **ibidem.**

ibidem (i-bī'dem). In the same place; in that very place. In the same book.

Ibi esse poenam, ubi et nox est (i'bi es'se pē'nam, u'bi et nox est). Where the crime is, there the punishment should be also. A principle of the Roman law which precluded forfeiture as a punishment of posterity. See 4 Bl Comm 383.

Ibi jus, ibi remedium (i'bi jūs i'bi rē-mēd'i-um). A maxim of the common law. See **equity will not suffer a wrong, etc.**

Ibi semper debet fieri triatio ubi juratores meliorem possunt habere notitiam (i'bi sem'per de'bet fī'e-rī tri-ā'she-o u'bi jū-rā-tō'rēz me-li-ō'rem pos'sunt hā-bē're no-ti'she-am). The trial of an action ought always to be held in that place where the jurors can have the better information.

I.C. Abbreviation of inspected and condemned. Bergen v Riggs, 34 Ill 170.

I.C.C. Abbreviation of Interstate Commerce Commission.

ice. Frozen water; in its uncut state, partaking of the nature of real estate as an accession or increment to the land. 27 Am J1st Ice § 2. But capable of being transferred as personalty, either in a cut or uncut state. 27 Am J1st Ice § 11. A profit a prendre in taking from the premises of another by right. 25 Am J2d Ease § 4. Underworld slang for diamonds.

icebox. A refrigerator in which ice is the cooling element.

ice cream. A frozen food consisting of cream or milk to which eggs and other food elements and flavorings are added. 35 Am J2d Food § 61.

ice hockey. See **hockey.**

ice house. A building or cave in which ice is stored for purpose of later use.

ice plant. A building in which artificial ice is frozen. Also, a place where ice is stored.

ice rack. A rack of wood construction, carried upon an ice wagon, and loaded with ice. Anno: 2 ALR 828.

ice skating. See **skates; skating rink.**

ice wagon. A truck carrying ice for delivery from door to door; familiar to all in an older day but fast disappearing with the extension of electric lines furnishing current for refrigerators.

icing cars. The supplying of old style refrigerator cars on railroads with ice.

ictus (ik'tus). A bruise; a blow; a stab; a thrust; a stroke.

ictus orbis (ik'tus or'bis). A blow or stroke making a bruise without breaking the skin.

id. It; that.

id certum est quod certum reddi potest (id ser'tum est quod ser'tum red'dī po'test). That is certain which can be made certain. 11 Am J2d B & N § 113; 17 Am J2d Contr § 77; 55 Am J1st V & P § 6; 57 Am J1st Wills § 35.

An agreement need not contain definitely and specifically every fact in detail to which the parties may be agreeing; it is sufficient if the phrases can be made certain by proof. 17 Am J2d Contr § 77.

Id certum est quod certum reddi potest, sed id magis certum est quod de semetipso est certum (id ser'tum est quod ser'tum red'dī po'test, sed id mā'jis ser'tum est quod dē sē-met-ip'sō est ser'tum). That is certain which can be rendered certain, but that is more certain which is certain in itself.

idea. A concept; a product of the mind.

See **copyright; literary property; patent.**

ideal lien creditor. A term of the law of bankruptcy relative to the preferred status of a trustee in bankruptcy in asserting priorities; a hypothetical creditor holding a lien by legal or equitable proceedings at the date of bankruptcy, whereby the trustee in bankruptcy, being armed with such a lien by virtue of a provision of the Bankruptcy Act, is enabled to assert priorities as against secret liens, unfiled or unrecorded mortgages, and the like. 9 Am J2d Bankr § 857.

idem (ī'dem). The same; the same thing.

Idem agens et patiens esse non potest (ī'dem ā'jenz et pa'she-enz es'se non po'test). A person cannot at the same time be the person acting and the person acted upon. Brotherhood of Railroad Trainmen v Barnhill, 214 Ala 565, 108 So 456, 47 ALR 270, 281.

Idem est facere, et nolle prohibere cum possis (ī'dem est fā'se-re, et nol'le prō-hi-bē're kum pos'sis). It is the same thing to do a thing as not to prohibit it when you can.

Idem est nihil dicere et insufficienter dicere (ī'dem est ni'hil dī'se-re et in-suf-fi-she-en'ter dī'se-re). It is the same thing to say nothing as not to say enough.

Idem est non probari et non esse; non deficit jus sed probatio (ī'dem est non prō-bā'rī et non es'se; non dē'fi-sit jūs sed prō-bā'she-ō). A thing is the same when not proved as when non-existent; the law is not lacking, but the proof is.

Idem est scire aut scire debet aut potuisse (ī'dem est sī're ât sī're de'bet ât po-tu-is'se). To know, to be bound to know and to be able to know, are all the same thing.

Idem non esse est non apparere (ī'dem non es'se est non ap-pā-rē're). Not to exist is the same thing as not to appear.

The maxim applies to a purchaser, without notice

of an unrecorded deed. Neslin v Wells Fargo & Co. (US) 14 Otto 428, 439, 26 L Ed 802, 806.

idem per idem (ī'dem per ī'dem). The same for the same; like for like.

idem quod (ī'dem quod). The same as.

Idem semper antecedenti proximo refertur (ī'dem sem'per an-te-sē-den'tī prox'i-mō re-fer'ter). "Idem" (the same) always refers to the immediate antecedent. Stewart v Stewart (NY) 7 Johns Ch 229, 248.

idem sonans (ī'dem sō'nanz). The same sound. The doctrine, applicable in all legal proceedings, that the use of a name being merely to designate the person intended, such object is fully accomplished where the name given to him has the same sound as his true name. State v Wahl, 118 Kan 771, 236 P 652. The doctrine that in all proceedings, whether civil or criminal, a mistake in spelling the name of a party is immaterial if both the correct and the incorrect mode of spelling has the same sound. Bennett v Winegar, 103 Neb 843, 174 NW 512. A doctrine applied in determining the effect of mistakes as to the names of parties in entering, docketing, and indexing of judgments, with the result that if two names may be sounded alike without doing violence to the power of the letters formed in the variant orthography, the variance is immaterial. 30A Am J Rev ed Judgm § 111.

Names are idem sonans if the attentive ear find difficulty is distinguishing them when pronounced, or if common and long-continued usage has by corruption or abbreviation made them identical in pronunciation. 38 Am J1st Name § 36.

identical. The same exactly. A word sometimes construed according to the context in which it appears. 23 Am J2d Desc & D § 86.

Under a statute which provides that the rights of inheritance of the heirs of the deceased spouse of an intestate shall accrue only where the intestate dies possessed of the "identical" property which came from such deceased spouse, the word "identical" will not be given such a strict and literal construction as to deprive the statute of meaning; a mere change in the evidence of ownership does not require the conclusion that the property owned by an intestate at death is not the "identical" property acquired from a deceased spouse. Millar v Mount Castle, 161 Ohio St 409, 119 NE2d 626, 49 ALR2d 381.

identical causes of action. See **identity of causes of action.**

identical crimes. See **identity of offenses.**

identical goods. See **fungible goods.**

identical offenses. See **identity of offenses.**

identical parties. See **identity of parties.**

identical property. See **fungible goods; identical.**

identifiable event. Within the rule that a deductible loss for income tax purposes based on the worthlessness of a stock must be one fixed by an "identifiable event":—an incident or an occurrence that points to or indicates a loss. Industrial Rayon Corp. v Commissioner (CA6) 94 F2d 383; Bartlett v Commissioner of Internal Revenue (CA4) 114 F2d 634.

identification. The means or act of identifying a person, an instrument, or property. Proof that a person or thing is the person or thing it is supposed or represented to be. A Roman law term for imputable negligence. Duval v Atlantic Coast Line Railroad Co. 134 NC 331, 46 SE 750.

identification of instrument. See **identification.**

identifying number. See **account number.**

identifying trust fund. See **following trust fund or property.**

Identitas vera colligitur ex multitudine signorum (ī-den'ti-tās vē'ra kol-li'ji-ter ex mul-ti-tū'di-ne sig-nō'rum). True identity is gathered from a multitude of signs.

identitate nominis (ī-den-ti-tā'te nō'mi-nis). A writ which lay for the release of a prisoner who had been committed under the same name as that of the real offender.

identity. Sameness; the state of being the same as someone or something assumed, described, or represented. For some purposes, the means of identification. State v Evjue, 253 Wis 146, 33 NW2d 305, 13 ALR2d 1201.

identity certificate. See **certificate of identity.**

identity of causes of action. The same cause of action in two cases, an essential element of res judicata. 30A Am J Rev ed Judgm § 363. Two actions asserting the same rights, demanding the same relief, and founded on the same facts. Anno: 31 ALR2d 446 § 3. Not necessarily a matter of identity of subject matter. Creek v Laski, 248 Mich 425, 227 NW 817, 65 ALR 1113. Tested generally according to whether or not the same evidence would sustain both causes of action. 30A Am J Rev ed Judgm § 365.

A prerequisite to a plea of abatement on the ground of prior action pending; a term characterizing two actions of the same character, for the same cause and relief, and in all respects identical. McAllister v McAllister, 147 Fla 647, 3 So 2d 351. Actions of the same character, for the same cause and relief, and in all respects identical, or actions having the same subject matter, although not demanding exactly the same specific relief. 1 Am J2d Abat & R § 26.

Identity exists irrespective of whether the same specific relief be demanded, if the subject matter of both actions is the same, the ultimate inquiry being whether a judgment in the one action being first rendered first, will be conclusive on the parties with respect to the matters involved in the second. 1 Am J2d Abat & R § 26.

identity of interests. See **identity of parties.**

identity of issues. See **identical causes of action.**

identity of legal personalities. The unity of husband and wife under the common law. 26 Am J1st H & W § 3.

identity of offenses. A matter of prior jeopardy, the common law rule and the constitutional provisions against second jeopardy applying only to a second prosecution for the same act and crime, both in law and in fact, on which the first prosecution was based; the test being whether the two offenses are essentially independent and distinct or not—whether one offense can be committed without necessarily committing the other. State v Westbrook, 79 Ariz 116, 285 P2d 161. Another test being whether the same evidence is required to prove the offenses. 21 Am J2d Crim L § 182.

As the term "same offense" is used in the constitutional provision that no person shall be twice put in jeopardy for the same offense, or another offense of which the first is a necessary element and constitutes an essential part. People v Stephens, 79 Cal 428, 21 P 856.

If a man simultaneously commits two offenses, either of which may be committed without the other and is then prosecuted for each of the offenses, even if the two prosecutions are based on the same acts, he is not twice put in jeopardy for the same offense; a fortiori, if the two prosecutions are based on different acts though committed simultaneously. Berry v United States, 72 App DC 229, 113 F2d 183. A matter of res judicata.

The plea of res judicata may be available in cases where there is no such identity of offenses in the two prosecutions that a plea of former jeopardy could be sustained. Anno: 147 ALR 992.

identity of parties. The prerequisite to joinder of causes of action that all causes should affect all parties to the action, both parties defendant and parties plaintiff. State ex rel. Alderson v Halbert, 133 W Va 337, 56 SE2d 114. Not a mere matter of form, but of substance, since parties nominally the same may be, in legal effect different; and parties nominally different may be, in legal effect, the same. Chicago Rock Island & Pacific R. Co. v Schendel, 270 US 611, 70 L Ed 757, 46 S Ct 420, 53 ALR 1265. A prerequisite to a plea of abatement on the ground of prior action pending; the same parties on both sides in two or more actions, appearing in the same capacity in each action, and representing the same interest. 1 Am J2d Abat & R § 26.

identity of the person (of the pèr'son). A collateral issue which may be pleaded in bar of execution after a judgment of attainder against the defendant, whereby the question is raised as to whether he is the same person who was thus attained. See 4 Bl Comm 396.

See **identity of parties.**

ideo (ī'de-ō). Therefore; on that account.

ideo consideratum est (i'de-ō kon-si-de-rā'tum est). Therefore it is considered.

Ideo consideratum est per curiam (i'de-ō kon-si-de-rā'tum est per kū'ri-am). Therefore, it is considered by the court. Prohibitions Del Roy (Eng) 12 Coke's Rep 63.

ides (īdz). The name given under the ancient Roman calendar to the 15th day of the months of March, May, July, and October and to the 13th day of all the other months. Rives v Guthrie, 46 NC 84.

"Beware the ides of March." The warning to Caesar·in Act I, Scene II, of Shakespeare's "Julius Caesar."

id est (id est). That is; it is; that is to say.

idiochira (ī-dī-ō-kī'rah). A privately executed instrument.

idiocy. A total absence of mind or reason; a condition of hopeless mental incapacity existing from birth. Slaughter v Heath, 127 Ga 787, 57 SE 69; Owing's Case (Md) 1 Bland Ch 370.

idiopathic disease (id''i-ọ-path'ik di-zēz'). A disease which develops gradually, or at least imperceptibly, and, while it may be attributable to external conditions, is also dependent in part on conditions inherent in the individual; a disease which cannot be regarded as an injury by accident. Iwanicki v State Industrial Acci. Com. 104 Or 650, 205 P 990, 29 ALR 682, 688.

idiosyncracy (id''ī-ọ-sin'krạsi). A peculiarity in the temperament of a person; an element of individuality.

See **hypersusceptibility.**

idiot. One in the state of idiocy.

See **idiocy.**

idiota a casu et infirmitate (i-di-ō'ta ā kā'sū et in-fir-mi-tā'te). An idiot by accident and infirmity.

idiota a nativitate (i-di-ō'ta ā nā-ti-vi-tā'te). An idiot from birth, a natural fool,—a person who was without understanding from the time of his birth, and therefore is presumed by law never likely to attain any. See 1 Bl Comm 302.

idiota inquirendo (i-di-ō'ta in-qui-ren'dō). See **de idiota inquirendo.**

idle. Not employed. In the case of an industrial plant, not operating in production. Anno: 87 ALR 1144.

idle funds. Unappropriated public funds. Uninvested funds in a trust.

idoneare (i-dō-ne-ā're). To prove one's own innocence; to disprove one's own guilt.

idoneus (ī-dō'nẹ-us). Appropriate; fit; capable; adequate; suitable; qualified.

idonietas (i-dō-ni-ē'tās). Fitness; adequacy; capability.

Id perfectum est quod ex omnibus suis partibus constat (id per-fek'tum est quod ex om'ni-bus su'is par'ti-bus kon'stat). That is perfect which is correct in all of its parts.

Id possumus quod de jure possumus (id pos'su-mus quod dē jū're pos'su-mus). We may do that which we are able to do lawfully.

Id quod est magis remotum, non trahit ad se quod est magis junctum, sed e contrario in omni casu (id quod est mā'jis rē-mō'tum, nōn tra'hit ad sē quod est mā'jis junk'tum, sed ē kon-tra'ri-ō in om'nī kā'sū). That which is more remote does not draw to itself that which is more proximate, but the contrary, in every case.

Id quod nostrum est, sine facto nostro, ad alium transferri non potest (id quod nos'trum est, sī'ne fak'tō nos'trō, ad a'li-um trans-fer'rī non po'test). That which is ours cannot be transferred to another without our act.

Id solum nostrum quod debitis deductis nostrum est (id so'lum nos'trum quod de'bi-tis de-duk'tis nos'-trum est). That only is ours which is ours after the deduction of our debts.

Id tantum possumus quod de jure possumus (id tan'-tum pos'su-mus quod dē jū're pos'su-mus). We may do only so much as we are able to do lawfully.

Id tenementum dici potest socagium (id te-ne-men'-tem dī'sī po'test so-kā'ji-um). That tenure may be called socage. See 2 Bl Comm 79.

idus (i'dus). Same as **ides.**

i. e. An abbreviation of id est, meaning that is; that is to say.

if. A word implying a condition; showing that the expectation of a fulfilment is uncertain, and presupposing that it may not occur. Doe v Wilson, 20 Miss 12 Smedes & M 498, 504. Ordinarily, a term of contingency in a will. 57 Am J1st Wills §§ 1222, 1333. An apt term in a contract to indicate a condition. 17 Am J2d Contr § 320.

if affirmed. A stipulation in an appeal bond, meaning finally affirmed, so that the bond guarantees the

payment of the judgment if affirmed finally, even though it may have been first reversed and then affirmed on rehearing or, in the case of an appeal to an intermediate court, it may have been reversed there but subsequently affirmed on a final appeal to the highest court. 5 Am J2d A & E § 1031.

if any. In reference to children of a life tenant:— having the effect of making a remainder contingent. Anno: 57 ALR2d 128.

The charter of a bridge company requiring the payment of damages "if any," by reason of the erection of the bridge, means all damages including consequential damages. Buckwalter v Black Rock Bridge Co. 38 Pa 281.

if any remains. A clause which, appearing in a will following a gift of personal property, shows the testator's intention to give the legatee the specific property, with the right to use it for his or her benefit and to consume it in such use if his or her judgment should dictate or his or her necessities compel that course. Anno: 108 ALR 551, 558, 564.

if appeal is dismissed. A stipulation in an appeal bond, the effect of which may be to render the sureties liable upon dismissal of the appeal, even though the dismissal be erroneous, but not to render them liable where the writ of error is merely quashed for formal defect in the writ itself, since such would not be a disposal of the cause itself. 5 Am J2d A & E § 1031.

"if" condition. A condition which goes to the existence of an obligation. 11 Am J2d B & N § 141.

if living at his death. A reference to children of a life tenant to whom the remainder is bequeathed which has the effect of making the remainder contingent. Collins v Crawford (Mo) 103 SW 537, affd on reh 214 Mo 167, 112 SW 538.

I. F. L. W. U. Abbreviation of International Fur and Leatherworkers Union.

if no agreement is reached. A clause having reference to condemnation of property under the power of eminent domain; the condition of absence of agreement, not imposing upon the public body or condemner the duty of attempting to acquire the property by purchase. Re New York, 45 Misc 184, 91 NYS 987.

Other authority adheres to a general principle that a bona fide effort to purchase the property by agreement is a condition precedent to the initiation of condemnation proceedings. 27 Am J2d Em D § 387.

if practicable. A condition which looks to the aspects of time, space, and physical effort.

As used in a traffic regulation providing it to be the duty of motorists passing in opposite directions to reasonably turn to the right so as to give half the traveled portion of the highway "if practicable" and a fair and equal opportunity to the person so met to pass, the term is not restricted in operation to the physical condition of the highway, but may properly be regarded as applying also to situations created by the person met, as by invasion by the latter of the operator's right side of the road, of itself or in conjunction with other circumstances rendering compliance with the statutory direction impracticable. Gilmartin v D. & N. Transp. Co. 123 Conn 127, 193 A 726, 113 ALR 1322.

if you believe. A phrase used in formulating a hypothetical instruction to jury. 53 Am J1st Trial § 549.

iglise. Same as **eglise.**

ignis judicium (ig'nis jū-di'she-um). Trial by fire.

ignitegium (ig-ni-tē'ji-um). Same as **curfew.**

ignition. Catching on fire; setting on fire; the means by which a fire is set. The device in an internal combustion engine which ignites the explosive mixture in the cylinder. The instrument on the instrument panel of a motor vehicle whereby the device for igniting is actuated, such instrument usually being provided with a lock, so that the motor can be started only by the use of a key. 7 Am J2d Auto Ins § 29.

ignition lock. A lock placed in the instrumentality of a motor vehicle known as the ignition, which, when used, as usually required by statute, is a deterrent to theft and also a safety device in the respect that it prevents interference with the vehicle's stationary condition and mechanical immobility. Kass v Schneiderman, 21 Misc 2d 518, 197 NYS2d 979.

ignominy (ig'nō-min-i). Infamy, reproach, dishonor, public disgrace; public hatred or detestation. Mahanke v Cleland, 76 Iowa 401.

See **public ignominy.**

ignoramus (ig-nō-rā'mus). Noun: An ignorant person; a vain pretender to knowledge; a dunce. See Pentuff v Park, 194 NC 146, 138 SE 616, 53 ALR 626. Verb: Not to know; to take no notice. A word indorsed by the grand jury on the back of the bill when they thought the charge it made was groundless, the intimation being that it might be true but that they did not know. Commonwealth v Miller (Pa) 2 Ashm 61.

ignorance. A passive state, a want of knowledge. Not a matter of being mistaken. Lawrence v Beaubien, 18 SCL (2 Bail) 623, 649.

ignorance of fact. Literally, want of knowledge. Equivalent in legal terminology to "error of fact," occurring either when some fact, which really exists, is unknown, or when some fact, which is supposed to exist, really does not exist.

ignorance of the law. An expression having reference, for the purpose of the presumption that every one knows the law and the corollary that ignorance of the law is no defense, to knowledge of the law of one's own state or country, not the laws of other states or other countries. Haven v Foster, 26 Mass 112.

ignorance of the law is no excuse. A maxim applicable in criminal cases. 21 Am J2d Crim L § 94. A maxim applicable in both civil and criminal cases. 29 Am J2d Ev § 222. A maxim of equity. 27 Am J2d Equity § 37.

"Law" for the purposes of the maxim is general law, the ordinary law of the country. The maxim has no application to a private law in support of a private right. Freichnecht v Meyer, 39 NJ Eq 551, 560.

ignorantia (ig-nō-ran'she-a). Ignorance.

Ignorantia eorum quae scire tenetur non excusat (ig-nō-ran'she-a e-ō'rum kwē sī're te-nē'ter non ex-kū'zat). Ignorance of those things which a person is deemed to know is no excuse.

Ignorantia excusatur, non juris sed facti (ig-nō-ran'-she-a ex-kū-zā'ter, non jū'ris sed fak'tī). Ignorance excuses, that is, ignorance of fact, but not ignorance of law.

Ignorantia facti excusat (ig-nō-ran'she-a fak'tī ex-kū'zat). Ignorance of fact is an excuse.

Ignorantia facti excusat, ignorantia juris non excusat (ig-nō-ran'she-a fak'tī ex-kū'zat, ig-nō-ran'she-a jū'ris non ex-kū'zat). Ignorance of fact excuses, ignorance of the law does not excuse. Scott v Ford, 45 Or 531, 78 P 742.

Ignorantia judicis est calamitas innocentis (ig-nō-ran'she-a jū'di-sis est ka-la'mi-tās in-no-sen'tis). The ignorance of a judge is the misfortune of an innocent person.

Ignorantia juris haud excusat (ig-nō-ran'she-a jū'ris hâd ex-kū'zat). Ignorance of the law is by no means an excuse. 21 Am J2d Crim L § 94.

Ignorantia juris neminem excusat (ig-nō-ran'she-a jū'ris ne'mi-nem ex-kū'zat). Ignorance of the law excuses no one. 21 Am J2d Crim L § 94.

Ignorantia juris non excusat (ig-nō-ran'she-a jū'ris non ex-kū'zat). Ignorance of the law does not excuse. Freichnecht v Meyer, 39 NJ Eq 551, 560; Scott v Ford, 45 Or 531, 80 P 899.

Ignorantia juris quod quisque tenetur scire, neminem excusat (ig-nō-ran'she-a jū'ris quod quis'kwe te-nē'ter sī're, nē'mi-nem ex-kū'zat). Ignorance of the law, which everyone is presumed to know, does not excuse. Haven v Foster, 26 Mass (9 Pick) 112. Rankin v Mortimere (Pa) 7 Watts 372, 374.

Ignorantia juris sui non praejudicat juri (ig-nō-ran'-she-a jū'ris su'ī non prē-jū'di-kat jū'rī). Ignorance of one's own right does not prejudice the right.

Ignorantia legis neminem excusat (ig-nō-ran'she-a lē'jis ne'mi-nem ex-kū'zat). Ignorance of the law excuses no one. 29 Am J2d Ev § 222.

Ignorantia legis non excusat (ig-nō-ran'she-a lē'jis non ex-kū'zat). Ignorance of the law does not excuse. 29 Am J2d Ev § 222.

Ignorantia praesumitur ubi scientia non probatur (ig-nō-ran'she-a prē-zu'mi-ter u'bi sī-en'she-a non prō-bā'ter). Ignorance is presumed when knowledge is not proved. Ignorance of the law is no defense. 2 Am J2d Adult § 15.

ignorare (ig-nō-rā're). To be ignorant of; to ignore.

Ignorare legis est culpa (ig-nō-rō-rā're lē'jis est kul'pa). To be ignorant of the law is negligence.

Ignorare legis est lata culpa (ig-nō-rā're lē'jis est lā'ta kul'pa). To be ignorant of the law is gross negligence.

ignoratio elenchi (ig-nō-rā'she-o e-len'chī). In argument, a mistake or misapprehension of the question under discussion. Statute for Distribution (Va) Wythe 302, 309.

Ignoratis terminis artis, ignoratur et ars (ig-nō-rā'tis ter'mi-nis ar'tis, ig-nō-rā'ter et arz). The terms employed in an art being unknown, the art is also unknown.

ignore. In common parlance, to refuse to take notice, to refuse to consider. To reject or throw out as false or unfounded, as where a grand jury refuses to indict, thereby rejecting the bill. See Ex parte Morton, 69 Ark 48, 51, 60 SW 307.

Ignoscitur ei qui sanguinem suum qualiter redemptum voluit (ig-nōs'si-ter ē'ī qui san'gwi-nem su'um quā'li-ter re-demp'tum vo'lu-it). He is excused who chooses to defend his own life. See 1 Bl Comm 131.

ignotum per ignotius (ig-nō'tum per ig-nō'she-us). That which is unknown by one who is still more unknown.

iisdem terminis. See in iisdem terminis.

Ikenild Street. One of the four great ancient Roman roads in England.

il (eel). He; it.

il covient (ēl kō-vē-en'). It is fitting.

Il est communement dit (eel ay côm-moon'ē-môn dee). It is commonly said.

ilet (ī'let). A small island.

illegal. Unlawful; contrary to law; illicit. State v Haynorth, 35 Tenn 64, 65.
See **illicit; unlawful.**

illegal acts. A very general and all inclusive term, ineffective, in an injunction, to describe the acts to be restrained. Anno: 120 ALR 349, 124 ALR 776, 127 ALR 888.

illegal agreement. See **illegal contract.**

illegal ballot. A ballot which because of the method of preparation, the method of marking, or the want of qualification of the voter, should not be counted in determining the result of an election. 26 Am J2d Elect §§ 291 et seq. A ballot which is not to be counted, because not received according to law. 26 Am J2d Elect § 292.

illegal branding. The statutory offense of branding or marking cattle without the consent of the owner, and with intent to defraud. State v Hall, 27 Tex 333. The misbranding of a product for the purpose of deceiving the public. 56 Am J1st Wts & L § 64.

illegal conditions. See **illegal contract.**

illegal consideration. An act or forbearance, or a promise to act or forbear, which is contrary to law or public policy. 17 Am J2d Contr § 157.
An illegal consideration is insufficient to support a contract, and an agreement founded upon it is illegal. Smith v Southwestern Bell Tel. Co. (Okla) 349 P2d 646, 83 ALR2d 454.

illegal contract. An agreement contrary to law, morality, or public policy. 17 Am J2d Contr § 156. A contract founded upon a consideration contrary to good morals, against the principles of sound public policy, in fraud, or in contravention of the provisions of some statute. Goodrich v Tenney, 144 Ill 422, 33 NE 44; Ovitt v Smith, 68 Vt 35, 33 A 769. Precisely, an agreement, the intent of which conflicts with a statute, a well-clarified rule of the law set forth by judicial decision, or the recognized rights of others so as to threaten the life, disturb the peace, or endanger the safety or morals of other citizens. Wm. Lindeke Land Co. v Kalman, 190 Minn 601, 252 NW 650, 93 ALR 1393.

illegal entry. A federal offense by an alien entering the United States at an unauthorized time or place, or to elude examination or inspection, or to obtain entry fraudulently. 8 USC § 1325.

illegal fee. A fee collected by a public officer for private gain, whether collected from a private individual or from the state, a county, or a municipality. Skeen v Craig, 31 Utah 20, 86 P 487.

illegal gaming. The making of a wager, the placing of bets, in violation of law.
The term implies gain and loss between the parties by betting such as would excite a spirit of cupidity. Hankins v Ottinger 115 Cal 454, 47 P 254.

illegal interest. Usury; interest in excess of the rate allowed by law. 30 Am J Rev ed Int § 2.

illegality. Unlawfulness; the state of being illegal. The word is not synonymous with irregularity. Illegality denotes a radical defect, while irregularity is a want of adherence to some prescribed rule or mode of proceeding. United States v Salomon (DC La) 231 F 461, aff (Ca5) 231 F 928.

illegality of contract. See **illegal contract.**

illegally procured. Procured in violation of law.
As used in the naturalization law providing for the cancellation of a certificate "unlawfully procured," the term means procured by subornation or some other illegal means used to impose upon the court; it does not mean that the certificate was issued through error of law. See United States v Luria (DC NY) 184 F 643.

illegal operation. A surgical operation in violation of law, such as an abortion.

illegal transaction. Something beyond a mere intent to violate the law. An illegal intention, accompanied by an act which is criminal or prohibited by law. Smith v Blachley, 188 Pa 550, 41 A 619.
See **illegal contract.**

illegal vote. See **illegal ballot; illegal voting.**

illegal voting. A criminal offense consisting, not merely in voting when not possessed of the proper qualifications, but in doing so wilfully, that is, designedly or purposely, involving either knowledge of disqualification or a reckless disregard of the question of qualification. 26 Am J2d Elect § 375.

illegitimate. Broadly, contrary to law. Usually understood in the narrower sense of being born out of wedlock.
See **illegitimate child.**

illegitimate child. A natural child, a child born out of wedlock, or born to a married woman under conditions where the presumption of legitimacy is not conclusive and has been rebutted. 10 Am J2d Bast § 1. Not an "heir" within the meaning of a devise or bequest to "heirs," unless the context indicates an intent to consider such child as included or a statute gives an illegitimate child the status of an heir. 10 Am J2d Bast § 135. Not an "heir" of either parent, for the purposes of descent, unless a right of inheritance has been conferred upon such child by statute. 10 Am J2d Bast § 146. Not "issue" within the meaning of such term in the designation of the beneficiary of a gift, unless the intention to include an illegitimate child is clearly deducible from the entire context. 10 Am J2d Bast § 136. Not included in a legacy or devise to "children," unless it appears clearly and unmistakably in other parts of the instrument that the intention of the testators was to include an illegitimate child or children. 57 Am J1st Wills § 1074.
Statutes which provide generally for the distribution of intestate property of a deceased person among certain classes of persons without mentioning illegitimates, are construed to refer to legitimates only, unless there is something in the language of the particular statute which indicates a different intention on the part of the legislature. Anno: 48 ALR2d 764,§ [3c]; 10 Am J2d Bast §149. But the term "issue" appearing in a statute of descent may include children born out of wedlock, where they are capable of inheriting. 10 Am J2d Bast § 149.
The term "illegitimate child" shall not be used in any local law, ordinance, or resolution, or in any public or judicial proceeding, or in any process, notice, order, judgment, record, or other public document or paper, but there shall be used in place of such term the expression "child born out of wedlock." New York General Construction L § 59.

illegitimate war. An unlawful war under the law of nations; conquest and depredation. 56 Am J1st War § 5.

Ille non habet, non dat (il'le non hā'bet, non dat). A person cannot grant a thing which he has not. Pennock v Coe (US) 23 How 117, 16 L Ed 436, 441.

illeviable (i-lev'i-ạ-bl). Not leviable; exempt from levy.

ill fame. Bad; repute.
See **house of ill fame.**

illicenciatus (il-lī-sen-she-ā'tus). Unlicensed; not licensed or permitted.

illicit. Unlawful; illegal; prohibited or forbidden by law. State v Miller, 60 Vt 90, 92, 12 A 526.

illicit cohabitation. A term more narrow than illicit intercourse; living together as man and wife, though not married. Thomas v United States (DC Mass) 14 F2d 229.

illicite. Unlawfully; illegally.

illicit intercourse. See **adultery; fornication; illicit cohabitation.**

illicit relation. Literally, an illegal relation; usually having reference to an illegal sexual relation, such as **adultery** or **illicit cohabitation.**

illicitum collegium (il-li'si-tum kol-lē'ji-um). (Civil law.) An unlawful corporation,—a voluntary association of persons attempting to form a corporation contrary to law. See 1 Bl Comm 472.

Illinois Rule of Liquidation. Same as **Grosscup Rule.**

illiteracy. Inability to read or write; want of education. The state of one who is illiterate.
See **illiterate.**

illiterate. Unlettered; ignorant of letters or books; untaught, unlearned; uninstructed in science.
A person who can sign his name, may still be illiterate. Hence it is improper to describe a person who cannot sign his name by the word "illiterate." Re Succession of Carroll, 28 La Ann 388, 389.

illiterate person. See **illiteracy; illiterate.**

illness. Sickness; disease. For some purposes inclusive of both severe and slight attacks, even attacks of a less grave and serious character than a disease. Connecticut Mut. Life Ins. Co. v Union Trust Co. 112 US 250, 259, 28 L Ed 708, 712, 5 S Ct 119. For the purposes of an application for life insurance, a disease or ailment of such a character as to affect the general soundness and health of the system seriously, and not a mere temporary indisposition, which does not tend to undermine or weaken the constitution of the applicant. Metropolitan Life Ins. Co. v Brubaker, 78 Kan 146, 96 P 62.
See **confined; disease; last illness; serious ailment; serious illness; severe illness; sickness.**

illocable (i-lō'kạ-bl). Not capable of being hired or let out to hire.

ill treatment. Cruelty; abuse. Unfairness.

illud (il'lud). That; that thing.

Illud dici poterit foedum militare (il'lud dī'sī po'te-rit fū'dum mi-li-tā're). That shall be called military tenure. See 2 Bl Comm 79.

Illud, quod alias licitum non est necessitas facit licitum; et necessitas inducit privilegium quod jure

ILLUD [581] IMMEDIATE

privatur (il'lud, quod a'li-as li'si-tum non est neses'si-tās fā'sit li'si-tum; et ne-ses'si-tās in-dū'sit pri-vi-lē'ji-um quod jū're pri-vā'ter). That which is otherwise not lawful, necessity makes lawful; for necessity produces a privilege which dispenses with law.

Illud, quod alteri unitur extinguitur neque amplius per se vacare licet (il'lud, quod al'te-rī ū'ni-ter extin'gwi-ter ne'kwe am'pli-us per sē va-kā're li'set). That which is united to another thing is extinguished, nor can it again be detached.

illuminated signs. Advertising signs characterized by flashing, intermittent, or steady lights. Anno: 72 ALR 374.

illuminating oil. See **kerosene**.

illumination of way. See **lighting way**.

illusion. That which a person believes that he sees, but which he does not really see. A false conception. See **hallucination**.

illusory. Permeated with illusion; deceiving.

illusory appointment. An insubstantial or merely nominal disposition of property made under a power of appointment. 41 Am J1st Pow § 64.

illusory promise. A promise so conditioned that the performance thereof is a matter of promisor's option, such promise not being sufficient as consideration for another promise. 17 Am J2d Contr § 105.

illustrious. An honorary designation applied to a person who has been born to rank or has attained rank. A term of infrequent use in the United States, except in fraternal orders.

ill will. See **malice**.

imaginary damages. A paradoxical term sometimes applied to punitive or exemplary damages. 22 Am J2d Damg § 236.

imagine. To conceive in the mind.

iman (i'män). A Mohammedan chief.

imbargo. Same as **embargo**.

imbasing of money. Same as **debasing coin**.

imbecile. A person weak or decrepit in mind. Campbell v Campbell, 130 Ill 466, 22 NE 620. A person with a pronounced mental deficiency. In loose usage, a stupid or very foolish person.
See **imbecility**.

imbecility. A term inclusive of many conditions and forms of mental weakness, which may or may not amount to incompetency. 29 Am J Rev ed Ins Per § 3.
See **imbecile**.

imbedded property. Property embedded in the earth. 1 Am J2d Aband § 4. Precisely, property other than gold or silver, found imbedded in the soil under circumstances indicating that some person had placed it where found. Ferguson v Ray, 44 Or 557, 77 P 600.

imbezzle. Same as **embezzle**.

imbladare (im-bla-dā're). To sow grain.

imbracery. Same as **embracery**.

imitation. Sometime contrived with the purpose of having it appear to be the same as another product. 35 Am J2d Foods § 19.
See **colorable imitation**.

immaterial. Not material; not pertinent; of no consequence.

immaterial allegation. An unessential allegation in a pleading; an allegation which can be stricken from the pleading without leaving it insufficient; an allegation which need not be proved or disproved. Green v Palmer, 15 Cal 411, 416.

immaterial alteration. An alteration of an instrument which does not change its legal effect. An alteration of an instrument which does not vary, or have any tendency to vary, the meaning in any essential particular, does not change in any manner the rights or interests, duties or obligations, of either of the parties, and does not mislead any person. 4 Am J2d Alt Inst § 5.

immaterial averment. Same as **immaterial allegation**.

immaterial evidence. Evidence which is offered to prove or disprove a fact or proposition which is not at issue. 29 Am J2d Ev § 252.
See **material evidence**.

immaterial issue. An issue which occurs where a material allegation in the pleadings is not answered, but an issue is taken on some point which will not determine the merits of the case, so that the court must be at a loss to determine for which of the parties to give judgment. Garland v Davis (US) 4 How 131, 146, 11 L Ed 907, 914.

immaterial representation. A representation in an application for insurance, particularly life or accident insurance, concerning a matter which, if truly stated by the applicant, would not prompt further inquiry by the insurer, does not increase the chance of loss so substantially as to bring about the rejection of the risk or the charging of an increased premium, and is not expressly made material by the terms of the contract of insurance. 29 Am J Rev ed Ins § 701.

immaterial variance. A variance between pleading and proof which is not so substantial as to mislead the adverse party to his prejudice in maintaining his cause of action or defense. 41 Am J1st Pl § 371.

immature claim. A claim upon an obligation which is not due.

immature crop. See **growing crop**.

immaturity. Lacking discretion or judgment because of youth. Lacking full growth. The quality of an obligation arising from the fact that it is not yet due or payable.

immediate. A word of qualification of both time and distance but having no one precise signification in either respect, being relative to the event. People v Pool, 27 Cal 573. As the word appears in a provision for forwarding papers, contained in a liability insurance policy:—with reasonable dispatch. Harmon v Farm Bureau Mut. Auto. Ins. Co. 172 Va 61, 200 SE 616.

With reference to locality the word imports not far apart or distant, but like the word presence, it is elastic and is used relatively. In robbery, it is dependent on circumstances or conditions; the distance which property might intervene between the victim and the property taken might vary considerably and still be in the "immediate" presence of the victim. People v Lavender, 137 Cal App 582, 31 P2d 439.

immediate cause of injury. A phrase often used in defining proximate cause but which itself is incapable of precise definition. Rodgers v Missouri Pacific Railway Co. 75 Kan 222, 88 P 885.

immediate death. Death resulting within a short time

after an injury, not necessarily instantaneously. 22 Am J2d Dth § 26.

As an example of an "immediate" rather than an "instantaneous" death, one court has suggested the situation in which a blow on the head produces unconsciousness and renders the victim incapable of intelligent thought, speech, or action for several minutes until he dies. Sawyer v Perry, 88 Me 42, 33 A 660. A death resulting about five and one half days after injury, during which time the victim never regained consciousness, has been held to come within a statute authorizing an action for injuries causing "immediate" death. Farrington v Stoddard (CA1 Me) 115 F2d 96, 131 ALR 1344.

immediate delivery. A delivery with expedition, with reasonable haste consistent with fair business activity. 46 Am J1st Sales § 163.

The term does not mean a delivery instanter; the character of the property, its situation, and all the circumstances must be taken into consideration in determining whether there was a delivery within a reasonable time so as to meet the requirement of the statute, and this will often be a question of fact for the jury. Feeley v Boyd, 143 Cal 282, 76 P 1029.

immediate descent. In one sense of the term, a descent cast directly upon the heir, as where the descent is to a grandson of the intestate, the father or intermediate person being dead. In another and distinct sense, a descent directly from the intestate without intervening link or degree of consanguinity, as from father to son, but not from grandfather to grandson, the latter descent being mediate from this standpoint. Lessee of Levy v M'Cartee (US) 6 Pet 102, 8 L Ed 334.

immediate disability. A disability which follows directly from an accidental hurt, within such time as the processes of nature consume in bringing the person affected to a state of incapacity. Rathbun v Globe Indem. Co. 107 Neb 18, 184 NW 903, 24 ALR 191, 201 (term as used in an accident insurance policy).

See **immediate injury.**

immediate family. As the word appears in a mutual benefit certificate or in the rules and regulations of a mutual benefit society:—those members of the same household to which the insured belongs who are bound together by ties of relationship, such as one's parents, wife, children, brothers and sisters, excluding no one within the household for the reason only that he or she is not one whom the head of the family is legally bound to support. 36 Am J2d Frat O § 144.

immediate hazard. As a situation for the application of a rule of the road for yielding the right of way, the imminence of collision when the relative speeds and distances of the two vehicles are considered; circumstances from which it must appear to a person of ordinary prudence in the position of a driver that if the two vehicles continue on their respective courses at the same rate of speed, a collision is probable. 7 Am J2d Auto § 202.

immediate injury. An injury resulting directly from an act rather than an injury ensuing the act. Mulchanock v Whitehall Cement Manufacturing Co. 253 Pa 262, 98 A 554.

See **immediately disability.**

immediately. Promptly, with expedition, with reasonable haste consistent with fair business activity. 46 Am J1st Sales § 163. As used in a request made to a carrier for freight cars:—at once. 13 Am J2d Car § 153. As an adverb of time in the clause of an accident policy providing for certain indemnity in case of injury causing total disability "immediately":—proximity of time with the injury, as presently, or without any substantial interval between the accident and the disability. 29A Am J Rev ed Ins § 1526. As a limitation of time for the commencement of an action:—within a reasonable time and without unnecessary delay. Putnam v Putnam, 86 Mont 135, 282 P 855.

Courts, looking at the substance of contracts and statutes, have, during the last two centuries, repeatedly declared that the word "immediately," although in strictness it excludes all meantimes, yet to make good the deeds and intents of the parties, it shall be construed "such convenient time as is reasonably requisite for doing the thing." Anno: 16 ALR 609.

immediately adjacent. Adjoining or abutting, rather than in the vicinity. Parsons v Wethersfield, 135 Conn 24, 60 A2d 771, 4 ALR2d 330 (term in a statutory provision requiring a unanimous vote of the commission on a question of rezoning property over the protest of 20 per cent of the owners of lots "immediately adjacent").

immediately due at the option of the holder. Immediately due upon or after the holder's election to exercise the option. Damet v Aetna Life Ins. Co. 71 Okla 122, 179 P 760, 5 ALR 434.

immediately on demand. Payment after a reasonable opportunity for complying with the demand. 40 Am J1st Paym § 15.

immediate medical assistance. As the word appears in a "first-aid" clause in a liability insurance policy: —within a reasonable time after the accident, considering the facts and circumstances of the particular case. United States Casualty Co. v Johnston Drilling Co. 161 Ark 158, 255 SW 890, 34 ALR 727.

immediate notice of defects. Notice within a reasonable time. Anno: 41 ALR2d 853 (notice of defects constituting breach of warranty).

immediate notice of dishonor. A broad characterization of the requirements of the Negotiable Instruments Law, which provides that unless delay is excused, notice of dishonor must be given within the time fixed by the statute. Legal Discount Corp. v Martin Hardware Co. 199 Wash 476, 91 P2d 1010, 129 ALR 420 (having reference to Uniform Negotiable Instruments L § 102).

immediate notice of loss. Notice to insurer:—notice given with reasonable dispatch, and within a reasonable time, in view of all the facts and circumstances of the case, 29A Am J Rev ed Ins § 1379; notice within such convenient time as is reasonably requisite for communication, after knowledge of the fact comes to the person charged with the duty of giving the notice. Anno: 16 ALR 609. Automobile theft insurance: notice given with due diligence and reasonable promptness under the circumstances of the case. Friedman v Orient Ins. Co. 278 Mass 596, 180 NE 617. Fidelity bond or policy of fidelity insurance. Notice within such time after the discovery of the loss as is reasonable under all the circumstances of the case. Anno: 23 ALR2d 1083.

immediate payment. See **immediately on demand.**

immediate surgical relief. As the expression appears in a "first-aid" clause of a liability insurance policy:

—emergency or firsthand relief, as distinguished from relief in the usual and ordinary course of treatment of the victim of an accident continued for some time in order to restore him, if possible, to his normal condition. 29A Am J Rev ed Ins § 1443.

immediately upon arrival. Phrase appearing in direction to factor to sell:—as soon after arrival as a sale can be made, irrespective of loss, the factor being precluded from exercising his discretion. Courcier v Ritter (CC Pa) F Cas No 3282.

immediate vicinity. A place adjoining or abutting. 23 Am J2d Deeds § 243. An expression not capable of precise definition, its meaning depending upon the context in which it appears, sometimes indicating actual contact, while at other times and in other connections applicable even where there is an intervening space between the objects or tracts of real estate under consideration. Smith v Furbish, 68 NH 123, 44 A 398.

immemorial. Before the time of legal memory; time out of mind. Kripp v Curtis, 71 Cal 62, 11 P 879.
See **legal memory**.

immeubles (i-mė'bls). Same as **immovables**.

immigrant. Every alien in the country except an alien within one of the classes of non-immigrant aliens specified in the Immigration and Nationality Act. 8 USC § 1101(a)(15).

immigrant alien. An alien entering the United States for permanent residence with the view of becoming a citizen of the United States. 8 USC §§ 1101(a)(15), 1181, 1184.

immigrant visa (im'i-grant vē'zạ). A visa required by law of an alien entering the country as an immigrant, issued by a consular officer of the United States. 8 USC § 1101 (16); 3 Am J2d Aliens § 55.

immigration. The coming of foreigners into the country for purposes of permanent residence. 3 Am J2d Aliens § 48.

Immigration and Nationality Act. A comprehensive federal statute controlling the immigration, admission, entry, and exclusion of aliens, also the naturalization and admission of aliens to citizenship. 8 USC §§ 1101 et seq.

Immigration and Naturalization Service. A federal agency in the Department of Justice, for the administration of immigration laws, particularly the Immigration and Nationality Act. 5 USC §§ 342b; 8 USC § 1101(34); 3 Am J2d Aliens § 52.

immigration officer. Any employee of the Immigration and Naturalization Service designated to perform functions in reference to the admission, naturalization, etc. of aliens. 8 USC § 1101 (18).

immigration quota. See **quota**.

Immigration Service. See **Immigration and Naturalization Service**.

imminence of danger. The presence of danger of death or great bodily harm, as will justify a killing in self-defense. 26 Am J1st Homi § 137.
See **imminent peril**.

imminence of death. The approach of death, not merely the expectation of death which all mortals must entertain. 28 Am J Rev ed Inher T § 128.

imminent. Overhanging, about to materialize, especially something of a dangerous nature. Threatening; full of danger. Collins v Liddle, 67 Utah 242, 247 P 476.

imminent insolvency. Insolvency likely to occur at any moment. Arnold v Globe Exchange Bank, 40 F2d 555.

imminently dangerous article. An article, such as poison or an explosive, which contains within itself the elements which render it dangerous to life and limb at all times and under all conditions. An article of a kind in common use without disastrous results, but dangerous to life and limb unless safely and properly constructed, such as a machine operated by power. Olds Motor Works v Shaffer, 145 Ky 616, 140 SW 1047.

imminently dangerous motor vehicle. A motor vehicle which because of defective construction is reasonably certain to place life and limb in peril when put to use. 8 Am J2d Auto § 658.

imminent peril. Threatened peril; danger immediately at hand.
See **imminence of danger**.

immiscere (im-mi'se-re). To mingle; to mix.

immittere (im-mit'te-re). To put into possession; to admit.

immobilia (im-mō-bi'li-a). Immovables.
See **bona immobilia**.

Immobilia situm sequuntur (im-mō-bi'li-a si'tum sequ-un'ter). Immovable things follow their location (as to the law which governs them).

immobilis (im-mō'bi-lis). Immovable.

immoderate. Beyond reasonable limits.

immoral. Wicked. Hostile to the welfare of the general public; having a tendency to mischievous or pernicious consequences. Jones v Dannenberg Co. 112 Ga 426, 37 SE 729. Unrestrained by law or principles of good conduct in sexual relations; licentious.

immoral consideration. A consideration, the furnishing of which is against public morals and public decency, a stock example of which is the commencement or continuance of meretricious sexual intercourse. 17 Am J2d Contr §§ 183, 184.

immoral contract. An agreement clearly repugnant to sound morality. Veazey v Allen, 173 NY 359, 66 NE 103.
See **immoral consideration**.

immorality. Conduct, behaviour, or practices which are immoral, that is, in violation of principles of decency and good conduct, especially meretricious sexual relations; licentiousness. 17 Am J2d Contr §§ 183, 184. Something more than the mere refusal of a minority to obey the wishes of the majority, or to subscribe to every view the majority may express as to their religious convictions. Poynter v Phelps, 129 Ky 381, 111 SW 699.
See **gross immorality**; **poverty and immorality**.

immoral purpose. Literally, a purpose to commit an act which is immoral. A term to be construed according to the context in which it appears.

As used in a provision of the Immigration Act excluding aliens who are prostitutes or persons coming into the United States for the purpose of prostitution or for any other "immoral purpose," the term is limited to purposes of like character with prostitution, and does not include extramarital relations, short of concubinage. Hansen v Haff, 291 US 559, 78 L Ed 968, 54 S Ct 494.

The interstate transportation, by a member of a religious sect, one of whose tenants is polygamy, of a plural wife either for the purpose of cohabiting with her or for the purpose of aiding another member of the cult in such a project, is for an "immoral purpose" within the meaning of the term as it is used in the Mann Act making an offense the transportation in interstate commerce of any woman or girl for the purpose of prostitution or debauchery, or for any other "immoral purpose." Cleveland v United States, 329 US 14, 91 L Ed 12, 67 S Ct 13.

See **debauchery** and **immoral purpose.**

immortality of corporation. One of the most important attributes of a corporation, as spoken of in the Dartmouth College Case. Dartmouth College v Woodward (US) 4 Wheat 518, 4 L Ed 629. Meaning only the capacity of continuous succession during the time of the existence of the corporation, whether that is definite or indefinite. 18 Am J2d Corp § 94.

immovable property. Real property and some things attached to realty but not in the nature of freehold and constituting personalty rather than realty. 42 Am J1st Prop § 24. Land and chattels real. Sneed v Ewing, 28 Ky (5 JJ Marsh) 460.

immovables. Immovable property.

immunity. A personal favor granted by law, contrary to the general rule. Ex parte Levy, 43 Ark 42. A privilege or special privilege; a favor granted; an affirmative act of selection of special subjects of favors not enjoyed in general by citizens under constitution, statute, or laws. Hammer v State, 173 Ind 199, 89 NE 850. A right in the negative form of freedom from action or restraint which otherwise might be taken against or imposed upon a person, such as the right of a witness to be free from arrest while attending court.

See **exemption; privilege; privileges and immunities; waiver of immunity.**

immunity bath. A person availing himself of the opportunity to give testimony which incriminates him in order to take advantage of statutory immunity granted a witness. 58 Am J1st Witn § 86.

immunity clause. A provision in a deed of trust securing corporate bonds which limits the trustee's liability, usually in providing that the trustee shall not be answerable for anything except his own gross negligence or wilful misconduct in the discharge of his duties. Anno: 57 ALR 470, s. 71 ALR 1414.

immunity from arrest. A privilege of narrow scope whereunder a few persons are rendered not subject to arrest on a criminal charge. 5 Am J2d Arr § 95. A privilege of broader scope whereunder a person of a certain class or performing a particular function at the time is rendered not subject to civil arrest, such privilege usually being applicable to mesne process as well as body executions. 5 Am J2d Arr § 95.

See **sanctuary.**

immunity from liability. An exemption from liability based on the nature of the defendant, such as a charitable corporate body; not nonliability under the application of tort law. Anno: 25 ALR2d 36. The rule that a judge is not civilly liable for acts done in the exercise of his judicial functions. 30A Am J Rev ed Judges § 73. The immunity of a public officer or administrative agency for discretionary, judicial, or quasi-judicial acts. 2 Am J2d Admin L § 799; 43 Am J1st Pub Of § 274.

See **limitation of liability.**

immunity from process. The privilege of exemption from service of civil process of persons acting in certain capacities, or occupying a certain status, at the time, such as Congressmen, members of a legislature, and parties or witnesses in attendance at court. 42 Am J1st Proc §§ 135 et seq.

immunity from suit. The removal of certain persons or things from the exercise of jurisdiction for reasons of public policy. The established principle of jurisprudence, applicable in favor of the United States and a state, that the sovereign cannot be sued in its own courts, or in any other court, without its consent and permission. 49 Am J1st States § 91; 54 Am J1st US § 127.

There can be no legal right as against the authority that makes the law on which the right depends. A sovereign is exempt from suit, not because of any formal conception of obsolete theory, but on this logical and practical ground. Holmes, J., in Kawananakoa v Polybank, 205 US 349, 51 L Ed 834, 27 S Ct 526.

Such immunity is a high attribute of sovereignty —a prerogative of the state itself—which cannot be availed of by public agents when sued for their own torts. The Eleventh Amendment to the Federal Constitution was not intended to afford them freedom from liability in any case where, under color of their office, they have injured one of the state's citizens. To grant them such an immunity would be to create a privileged class free from liability for wrongs inflicted or injuries threatened. Public agents must be liable to the law, unless they are to be put above the law. Old Colony Trust Co. v Seattle, 271 US 426, 431, 70 L Ed 1019, 1022, 46 S Ct 552.

immunity of witness. See **immunity from process; immunity provisions; judicial immunity of witness; self-incrimination.**

immunity provisions. Constitutional and statutory provisions intended to render available testimony from a witness, who otherwise would remain silent under the privilege against self-incrimination, by granting him immunity from prosecution. 21 Am J2d Crim L § 148.

See **immunity bath.**

immurement (i-mūr'ment). Imprisonment; incarceration.

impair. To make worse; to diminish in quality, value, excellence, or strength; to deteriorate. Swinburne v Mills, 17 Wash 611, 50 P 489.

impairment of capital. A deficiency in the capital of a bank, but not necessarily a condition of insolvency. 10 Am J2d Bks § 41. Distribution reducing capital of corporation. 19 Am J2d Corp § 819.

impairment of earning ability. Decrease in earning capacity. 22 Am J2d Damg § 89.

impairment of justice. See **obstruction of justice.**

impairment of memory. Forgetfulness. A condition of the mind in which recollection of past events becomes difficult, if not impossible. 27 Am J2d Eq § 170.

impairment of mind. Mental weakness or incompetency.

impairment of obligation of contract. Within the meaning of the constitutional provision, known as the contract clause appearing in Article I, Section 10, of the United States Constitution:—the effect of a statute enacted subsequently to the making of a contract which annuls it or changes its terms by adding or releasing material conditions, provisions,

or stipulations or which changes the remedy for a breach, so that the new remedy is not substantially the equivalent of the old one, thereby lessening the value of the agreement. 16 Am J2d Const L §§ 444 et seq.
In determining whether state legislation unconstitutionally impairs contract obligations, no unchanging yardstick can be fashioned, applicable at all times and under all circumstances, by which the validity of every statute may be measured; each case must be determined upon its own circumstances. Re People (Title and Mortgage Guaranty Co.) 264 NY 69, 190 NE 153, 96 ALR 297.

impairment of vested rights. See **retrospective legislation.**

impalare. To impound.

impalement (im-pāl'ment). An inclosure. The execution of the death penalty, as in ancient times, by thrusting a stake through the body.

impanel (im-pan'el). To place the names of the jurors on a panel; to make a list of the names of those persons who have been selected for jury duty; to go through the process of selecting a jury which is to try the cause. 31 Am J Rev ed Jur § 129.

impanelment of jury. See **impanel; panel.**

imparcare (im-par-kā're). To impound; to imprison.

impargamentum (im-par-ga-men'tum). An impounding; the right to impound.

imparl (im-pärl'). To discuss a controversy in an effort to effect an amicable settlement after action pending. See 3 Bl Comm 299.

imparlance (im-pär'lans). A discussion between the parties to a pending action in an effort to effect an amicable settlement of the controversy. See 3 Bl Comm 299.

imparsonee (im-pär-sǫ-nē'). Inducted into and placed in possession of a benefice; the clergyman who has been thus inducted and placed.

impartial. Being indifferent as between parties. Sunderland v United States (CA8 Neb) 19 F2d 202.

impartial hearing. A fair and open hearing, without bias or prejudice; indifferent as between the parties. 2 Am J2d Admin L § 412.

impartiality. Absence of bias or prejudice. Indifference as between the parties.

impartial juror (jö'ror). A juror who will render an impartial verdict on the evidence. International News Service v News Publishing Co. 118 Okla 113, 247 P 87.

impartial trial. See **fair and impartial trial.**

impartible fee. Same as **impartible feud.**

impartible feud (im-pär'ti-bl fūd). A feud or fee which was so conditioned in its creation that it could only descend to the eldest son. See 2 Bl Comm 215.

impatronization (im-pā''trǫn-i-zā'shǫn). The induction of a parson or clergyman into a benefice and vesting him with the possession of it.

mpeach. To effect an impeachment.
See **impeachment.**

impeachable for waste. A phrase indicating the liability of the life tenant for waste as to conduct in encroaching upon the corpus of the estate. 33 Am J1st Life Est §§ 313 et seq. Also indicating the liability of a tenant under a lease for years for waste. 32 Am J1st L & T §§ 779 et seq.

See **without impeachment of waste.**

impeachment. The act of discrediting a person or a thing. Calling the integrity or ability of a person into question. The imputation of fault or of defective performance, particularly that of a public officer. Shanks v Julian, 213 Ky 291, 303, 280 SW 1081, 1085. Showing imperfection or error, for example, attacking the certified record on appeal by comparing it with the transcript. 4 Am J2d A & E § 503. Questioning the authenticity of a document or the veracity of a witness.
To impeach, as applied to a person, is to accuse, to blame, to censure him. It includes the imputation of wrongdoing. To impeach his official report or conduct is to show that it was occasioned by some partiality, bias, prejudice, inattention to, or unfaithfulness in, the discharge of that duty; or, that it was based upon such error that the existence of such influences may be justly inferred from the extraordinary character or grossness of that error. Bryant v Glidden, 36 Me 36, 47.

impeachment court. A court for the trial of an impeached officer. 20 Am J2d Cts § 34. The upper house of a legislative body. 20 Am J2d Cts § 34.
In the impeachment of an officer of the United States, the accusation is made by the House of Representatives, and tried by the Senate, under section 3 of article I of the United States Constitution. In some of the states the same procedure is followed. In other states, the legislature has relegated impeachment cases to the courts. Re John J. Marks, 45 Cal 199.

impeachment of account. Questioning correctness of an account. 1 Am J2d Accts § 35.

impeachment of acknowledgment. Disproving the facts stated in the certificate. 1 Am J2d Ack § 98.

impeachment of award. A proceeding at law or in equity for the setting aside of an arbitration award which is void or where cause for setting it aside may be shown. 5 Am J2d Arb & A § 167.

impeachment of public officer. Seeking the removal of a public officer upon charges, formally made, of the commission of a crime or of official misconduct or neglect. Technically, the adoption of articles of impeachment upon inquiry by the lower house of Congress or the legislature, the filing of such articles with, and their acceptance by, the United States Senate in the case of a federal officer, or the upper house of the legislature or court of impeachment in the case of a state officer. 43 Am J1st Pub Of §§ 175, 178.

impeachment of title or right to office. An action to determine the title or right of a judge to the office. 30A Am J Rev ed Judges § 235.

impeachment of verdict. An attack against a verdict based upon grounds concerning the deliberations of the jury and the manner of arriving at a verdict. 53 Am J1st Trial §§ 1105 et seq.

impeachment of waste. See **impeachable for waste.**

impeachment of witness. An attack on the credibility of a witness by the testimony of other witnesses that the facts about which he has testified are other than as he has stated; by proof that his general reputation is bad; by proof that he has previously made contradictory or inconsistent statements, or by proof of his bias, interest, or hostility. Harris v Tippett, 11 Eng Rul Cas 144. Any means through proof of impairing the credit of the witness, involving matters affecting the general credit of a witness as well as those affecting his credit in the particular case. 58 Am J1st Witn §§ 674 et seq.

impechiare (im-pē-chi-ā're). To impeach.

impediens (im-pē'di-enz). A person who impedes or hinders; a person who withholds land from the true owner; a defendant.

impediment. An obstruction, for example, an obstruction in a highway. 25 Am J1st High § 272. A bar; a disqualification, for example, insanity barring marriage. 35 Am J1st Mar § 17.
See **canonical impediments; dirimant impediments; impediments to marriage; legal impediment; manifest impediment.**

impedimento (im-pay-de-men'to). (Spanish.) An impediment or bar to matrimony.

impediments to marriage. Disqualifications, such as nonage, mental incapacity, etc.
See **prohibitive impediments; relative impediment.**

impeditor (im-ped'i-tor). A person who interferes with the right of a patron to make presentation to a benefice.

impensae (im-pen'sē). (Civil law.) Expenses; moneys spent or laid out for expenses.

imperative. Mandatory; commanding.

imperative direction. An essential of equitable conversion; an expression in some form of an absolute intention that a conversion shall be effected, that is, that land shall be sold and turned into money, or that money shall be expended in the purchase of land. 27 Am J2d Eq Conv § 4.

imperative power. A power in trust. The essential distinction between a power of appointment and a trust, the former being discretionary, the latter imperative. 41 Am J1st Pow § 3.

imperative statute. A mandatory statute; that is, one which plainly commands something to be done or refrained from, as distinguished from a statute which is merely directory and hence leaves a choice between doing or not.

imperative words. Words of command rather than precatory words.
When in a will words of recommendation, request, and the like are used in direct reference to the testator's estate, they are prima facie testamentary and imperative and not precatory. While the desire of a testator for the disposal of his estate is a mere request when addressed to his devisee, it is to be construed as a command when addressed to his executor. All expressions indicative of his wish or will are commands. Estate of Tooley, 170 Cal 164, 149 P 574.

imperator (im-pē-rā'tor). Emperor,—a title frequently appended to the name of the king of England in charters which were granted before the time of the Norman Conquest. See 1 Bl Comm 242.

Imperator solus et conditor et interpres legis existimatur (im-pe-rā'tor sō'lus et kon'di-tor et in-ter'-prēz lē'jis eg-zis-ti-mā'ter). The emperor alone is deemed to be both the founder and the interpreter of the law. 1 Bl Comm 74.

imperceptible process. In reference to the rule of accretion:—imperceptibility in progress, notwithstanding perceptibility after a long lapse of time. 56 Am J1st Wat § 484.

imperfect. Incomplete; lacking in some essential; defective.

imperfect delegation. A substitution of a new debtor for an old one without releasing the old one.

imperfect gift. A gift incomplete because of the omission of act or circumstance which the law requires as necessary to pass title. 24 Am J1st Gifts § 43.

imperfect mortgage. A mortgage good in equity, although not at law. Another term for vendor's lien. Gessner v Palmater, 89 Cal 89, 26 P 789.

imperfect obligation. An obligation not enforceable by suit, depending for fulfillment upon the will and conscience of the obligor. Edwards v Kearzey, 96 US 595, 24 L Ed 793.

imperfect right. A right which is not a full or perfect right because he who would enjoy it has been guilty of some wrong, fault, or blame in the matter out of which the right accrued; as where a man sets up the plea of self-defense when he was the original aggressor. Wallace v United States, 162 US 466, 40 L Ed 1039, 16 S Ct 859.

imperfect sexual intercourse. See **sexual intercourse.**

imperfect trust. A trust, the legal effect of which has not been achieved or, if achieved, is not complete and final in its limitations. 54 Am J1st Trusts § 7.

imperfect war. A war not formally declared and limited as to places, persons, and things, but nevertheless an external contention by force between members of the two nations, authorized by the legitimate powers. 56 Am J1st War § 4.

imperial parliament. A name once used for the parliament of England.

Imperii majestas est tutelae salus (im-pe'ri-ī ma-jes'-tās est tū-tē'le sa'lus). The majesty of the empire is the safety of its protection.

imperite (im-pe-rī'tē). Unskillfully; without skill.

imperitia (im-pe-rī'she-a). Unskillfulness; lack of skill.

Imperitia culpae adnumeratur (im-pe-rī'she-a kul'pe ad-nu-me-rā'ter). Unskillfulness is rated as negligence.

Imperitia est maxima mechanicorum poena (im-pe-rī'she-a est mak'si-ma me-ka-ni-kō'rum pē'na). Lack of skill is the greatest sin of mechanics.

imperium (im-pē'ri-um). Rule; power; authority. The power vested in a Roman magistrate to command the citizen to the end of preserving order in time of peace and discipline in time of war.

imperium in imperio (im-pe'ri-um in im-pe'ri-ō). A government within a government.

impersonal. Without reference to any person.

impersonalitas (im-per-so-na'li-tās). Impersonality; the quality of referring to no person.

Impersonalitas non concludit nec ligat (im-per-so-nā'li-tās non kon-klū'dit nek li'gat). Impersonality neither concludes nor binds.

impersonal payee. A payee of a bill or note designated as "cash," "bills payable or order," or otherwise than in the name of a person, association, partnership, or corporation, the consequence being that the instrument is payable to bearer. 11 Am J2d B & N § 124.

impersonal trademark or trade name. A trademark or trade name not of a character representing in itself a personal element in the production of the article but which may be associated with kind and quality so as to identify the article. 52 Am J1st Tradem §§ 47 et seq.

impersonation. Assuming the name and identity of another person. 11 Am J2d B & N § 132. A means of committing a fraud. 27 Am J2d Fraud § 28. Representing oneself as another person, such constituting the offense of false pretenses, when done for the purpose of defrauding another. 32 Am J2d False Pret § 18. Assuming the character or personality of another, for example assuming the personality of another for the purpose of voting in his name at election. 26 Am J2d Elect § 375.

impertinence. Rudeness; insolence. Matter in a complaint, bill, answer or other pleading not properly before the court for decision at any stage of the suit (27 Am J2d Eq §§ 187, 198, 201) particularly, scandalous allegations. 27 Am J2d Eq 187; 41 Am J1st Plead § 351.

impertinent matter. See **impertinence**.

impescare (im-pes-kā′re). Same as **impeach**.

impetere (im-pe′te-re). To impeach.

impetitio vasti (im-pe-ti′she-ō vas′tī). Same as **impeachment of waste.**

impetrare (im-pe-trā′re). To obtain by asking.

impetration (im-pe-trā′shon). The obtaining of a thing by request or petition.

impie. (French.) Reprobate. Infidel.

impier (am′pī-ay′). An arbiter; an umpire.

impierment (im-pi′er-ment). Impairment.

impignorata (im-pig-nō-rā′ta). Pledged; mortgaged.

impignoration (im-pig-nọ-rā′shọn). A pledge; a mortgage; pledging or mortgaging property.

Impius et crudelis judicandus est qui libertati non favet (im′pi-us et kru-dē′lis jū-di-kan′dus est quī li-ber-tā′tī non fa′vet). He should be adjudged impious and cruel who does not favor liberty.

implacitare (im-plā-si-tā′re). Same as **implead**.

implead (im-plēd′). To sue; to make a person a party to an action or suit. To bring into an action as a party a person not named as a party in the action as originally instituted.

impleader. Broadly, the joining of a person as a party to an action. As known under modern code or rules practice, the bringing into an action as a party of a person liable over to or liable with the defendant. 39 Am J1st Parties § 90. The bringing into an action of either a person or a thing, whether wholly or in part liable or liable only by way of remedy over or contribution. 2 Am J2d Adm § 151.
See **third-party practice**.

implement. Noun: A tool, instrument, utensil, or machine for carrying on work, particularly a machine for agricultural work. A thing necessary to a trade and without which the work cannot be performed. Anno: 2 ALR 818. As used in an exemption statute:—a usable article, an instrument employed as a means to effect an end in debtor's trade or occupation. 31 Am J2d Exemp § 51. Verb: To put into effect; to provide with means for accomplishing a purpose.

As used in a statute with reference to the power of the board of county supervisors to purchase or hire "implements" and material and employ labor in connection with the reconstruction or repair of highways, the term embraces such road machines as tractors, graders, etc., especially where the statute expressly provides that the board may do any and all things necessary to be done to construct, reconstruct, and maintain the public roads. Mississippi Road Supply Co. v Hester, 185 Miss 839, 188 So 281, 124 ALR 574.

implements of husbandry. Farm implements. As something exempt from a statutory requirement of registration of motor vehicles, a vehicle designed and used primarily as a farm vehicle but which may be operated or moved temporarily upon the highway. Allred v J. C. Engelman, 123 Tex 205, 61 SW2d 75, 91 ALR 417.

A statutory definition of an "implement of husbandry" as a "vehicle which is designed for agricultural purposes and exclusively used by the owner thereof in the conduct of his agricultural operations" includes a grain combine being hauled on the highway by a tractor, so as to bring such combine within the statutory exception of "implements of husbandry temporarily moved upon a highway" from restrictions as to width of vehicles on the highway, although at the time of the accident the combine was being hauled by its owner, a farmer, to the farm of another, some eighteen miles away, to be used by the owner in combining soybeans for a fixed fee. Worthington v McDonald, 246 Iowa 466, 68 NW2d 89, 47 ALR2d 135.

Any instrument used directly in the business of farming, and for no other purpose is an implement of husbandry. Horse rakes, gang plows, headers, threshing machines, and combined harvesters are as clearly implements of husbandry as are hand rakes, single plows, sickles, cradles, flails, or an old fashioned machine for winnowing. There is no ground for excluding an implement from the operation of the exemption statute because it is an improvement, and supplants a former implement used with less effectiveness for the same purpose. Estate of Klemp, 119 Cal 41, 50 P 1062.

implication. Something implied. The evident consequence, or some necessary consequence resulting from the law, or the words of an instrument, in the construction of which the words, the subject, the context, the intention of the person using them, are all to be taken into view. Rhode Island v Massachusetts (US) 12 Pet 657, 723, 9 L Ed 1233, 1260. The matter of being involved, as in a crime.
See **implied**.

implied. Accepted as that which was intended although not stated expressly. Understood. Suggested.

implied abandonment. In some jurisdictions, the nonuser of a highway. 25 Am J1st High § 112.

implied abrogation. See **implied repeal**.

implied acceptance. An acceptance understood from acts and circumstances where not expressly stated. The acceptance of an offer implied from acts or conduct, including performance by the offeree of his undertaking. Cole-McIntyre-Norfleet Co. v Holloway, 141 Tenn 679, 214 SW 817, 7 ALR 1683. Duquesne Lumber Co. v Keystone Mfg. Co. 90 W Va 673, 112 SE 219. An acceptance of an offer of dedication through positive conduct on the part of the authorized public officers evincing their consent on behalf of the public. Blowing Rock v Gregorie, 243 NC 364, 90 SE2d 898; Henry v Ionic Petroleum Co. (Okla) 391 P2d 792. An acceptance of a deed implied where the intention to accept is manifested by conduct such as that of retaining possession of the deed, conveying the property, or otherwise exercising the rights of an owner, provided the grantee had, at the time he acted, knowledge of the conveyance. 23 Am J2d Deeds § 128. The acceptance of a gift operating entirely to the

IMPLIED [588] IMPLIED

benefit of the donee. 24 Am J1st Gifts § 117. Of a draft or bill of exchange:—an acceptance by the drawee implied from circumstances such as his retention or destruction of the instrument, 11 Am J2d B & N § 509; a concept at variance with the provision of the Uniform Commercial Code that the signed engagement of the acceptor must be written on the bill or draft. 11 Am J2d B & N § 510.

implied accord. The usual situation of accord in which a sum less than the whole claim is remitted or tendered on condition that it be accepted as full satisfaction, and accord and satisfaction resulting from its acceptance. Shinn v Kitchens, 208 Ark 321, 186 SW2d 168; Virginia-Carolina Electrical Works, Inc. v Cooper, 192 Va 78, 63 SE2d 717.

implied actual notice. See **implied notice.**

implied admission. An admission by act, conduct, or silence. 29 Am J2d Ev § 623.

implied agency. An actual agency, the existence of which as a fact is proved by deductions or inferences from the other facts and circumstances of the particular case, including the words and conduct of the parties. Turnbull v Shelton, 47 Wash 2d 70, 286 P2d 676.

implied assignment. An assignment by operation of law, for example, the passing of a decedent's personal assets to the executor or administrator of his estate. 6 Am J2d Assign § 2.

implied assumpsit (im-plīd' a-sump'sit). General assumpsit or indebitatus assumpsit. 1 Am J2d Actions § 11.

implied authority. The actual authority of an agent, circumstantially proved, which the principal is deemed to have actually intended the agent to possess; authority of an agent arising independently of any express grant of authority, as from some manifestation by the principal that the particular authority in question shall exist in the agent, or arising as a necessary or reasonable implication in order to effectuate other authority expressly conferred, embracing authority to do whatever acts are incidental to, or are necessary, usual, and proper to accomplish or perform the main authority expressly delegated to the agent. Annotation: 55 ALR2d 27, § 4[a]; 3 Am J2d Agency § 71.
See **implied powers.**

implied banker's lien. A lien of a bank for the balance owing upon a general account upon the securities of the customer or depositor in the possession of the bank, implied from the usages of the banking business or the law merchant. 10 Am J2d Banks § 660.

implied bequest or devise. A bequest or devise inferred from expressions in a will raised for the purpose of carrying out what the testator appears on the whole to have really meant, but failed to express as distinctly as he should have done. O'Hearn v O'Hearn, 114 Wis 428, 90 NW 450.

implied bias. Presumed bias; bias which is supposed to exist on account of the relation which the juror bears either to the cause or to some of the parties thereto. 31 Am J Rev ed Jury § 171.

implied coercion. Existing where a person is induced to do an act contrary to his will in consequence of his legal subjection to another. Fluharty v Fluharty, 38 Del 487, 193 A 838.

implied condition. A condition which is not expressed but which is either implied by the law or by the common intention of the parties. As applied to estates in real property, a condition otherwise known as a condition in law, a condition which the law implies either from its being always understood to be annexed to certain estates, or as annexed to estates held under certain circumstances. Raley & Johns v Umatilla County, 15 Or 172, 13 P 890.
See **estate upon condition.**

implied confession. Admissions by the accused from which guilt may be inferred, whether by words, acts, or, in some instances silence. See 29 Am J2d Ev § 523. A confession which is implied by law where a defendant, in a criminal case not capital, does not directly own himself guilty, but in a manner admits it by yielding to the state's mercy, and desiring to submit to a small fine. Commonwealth v Shrope, 264 Pa 246, 107 A 729, 6 ALR 690, 692.

implied consent. Acquiescence. By the prosecutrix in a prosecution for rape:—conduct of such nature as to create in the mind of the accused an honest and reasonable belief of free submission to the carnal act, 44 Am J1st Rape § 12; failure to oppose the carnal act when one is awake, of mature years, of sound mind, and not in fear. 44 Am J1st Rape § 12.

implied consideration. The consideration for an act performed or forborne at the request of another without an express stipulation as to compensation or other consideration. Bixler v Ream (Pa) 3 Penr & W 282, 284.

implied constitutional provision. A condition implied in a constitution, whether the Constitution of the United States or a state constitution, because deemed within the meaning and intention of the constitution on judicial inspection thereof. 16 Am J2d Const L § 72.

implied contract. A contract inferred from the conduct of the parties, although not expressed in words. Corriveau v Jenkins Bros. 144 Conn 383, 132 A2d 67. Implied in fact:—a real contract but one inferred from the circumstances, the conduct, acts, or relation of the parties, rather than from their spoken words, Gleason v Salt Lake City, 94 Utah 1, 74 P2d 1225. A contract to pay the reasonable value of services performed by one person for another, where there is no express agreement as to the compensation, but the circumstances, particularly the conduct of the person for whom the work was done, is such as to justify an understanding by the person performing the work that the former intended to pay for it. Anno: 54 ALR 549; 58 Am J1st Wk & L § 3. Implied in law:—a quasi or constructive contract implied by law on the grounds of justice and equity, usually to prevent unjust enrichment. 58 Am J1st Wk & L § 2.

implied contract of sale. A contract for the sale of goods implied from the facts and circumstances of the case creating an obligation on the part of the buyer to pay for goods received from another. Ordinarily when one person receives goods or merchandise from another, the law implies a contract on his part to pay therefor, which will support an action for goods sold and delivered. 46 Am J1st Sales § 37.

implied covenant. A covenant in law; a covenant which may reasonably be inferred from the whole agreement and the circumstances attending its execution. 20 Am J2d Cov § 12. Such a covenant as the law will imply from the making of a lease or from the use of certain words in the lease; a covenant of quiet enjoyment free from any interference with the lessee's occupation of the premises by the lessor and a covenant of good title and right to make the lease on the part of the lessor. 32 Am J1st L & T § 143.

The theory of estoppel by deed under which an after-acquired title passes to the grantee. 23 Am J2d Deeds § 294. The theory upon which a dedication occurs from the sale of land with reference to a map or plat. 23 Am J2d Ded § 25.

implied dedication. An acquiescence by the owner of land in a public use thereof; acts or conduct of the owner of land manifesting an intent to devote the property to public use. 23 Am J2d Ded § 1.

implied delivery. A constructive delivery to bailee, meaning all those acts which, although not truly comprising real possession of the goods transferred, have been held, by legal construction, equivalent to actual delivery, including, in this sense, symbolical or substituted delivery. 8 Am J2d Bailm § 55.

implied devise. See **implied bequest or devise**.

implied easement. An easement by implication in favor of a grantor or grantee, being a creature of the common law, existing only in connection with a conveyance, and based on the theory that whenever one conveys land adjacent to land owned and retained by him, he includes or intends to include in the conveyance whatever is necessary for its beneficial use and enjoyment and to retain whatever is necessary for the use and enjoyment of the land retained. Trattar v Rausch, 154 Ohio St 286, 43 Ohio Ops 186, 95 NE2d 685.

To create an easement by implication there must be (1) a separation of title; (2) a use, before the separation, so long continued, obvious, and manifest as to show the use was meant to be permanent; and (3) a use essential to the beneficial enjoyment of the land granted or retained. Kling v Ghilarducci, 3 Ill 2d 454, 121 NE2d 752, 46 ALR2d 1189.

implied election. An election to take under or against a will implied from the acts or conduct of the beneficiary on whom the election evolves, or, as it is occasionally stated, evidenced by matters in pais. 57 Am J1st Wills § 1534.

implied emancipation. That emancipation of a child which results when the parent without any express agreement, impliedly consents by his acts and conduct that the child may have his own time and the control of his earnings, or such consent is inferred from or shown by circumstances. 39 Am J1st P & C § 64.

implied exception. An exception of a right or easement from the grant made by an absolute conveyance in fee where such right or easement is essential to the enjoyment of land remaining in the grantor's ownership. 23 Am J2d Deeds § 270.

implied finding. A negative finding implied where the findings by the trial court leave some issue or material fact undetermined, the implication being that such issue or fact was not proved by the party having the burden of proof thereon. 53 Am J1st Trial § 1143. An anomaly in an administrative proceeding where express findings are required as a matter of procedural law. 2 Am J2d Admin L § 449.

implied force. The employment of words or conduct to put another in fear of bodily harm if he does not give way or submit. See 35 Am J2d Forc E & D § 58.

implied franchise. A franchise to use the streets, for the purpose of rendering service as a public utility, conferred by necessary implication from the negotiations between the city and the company claiming the franchise. Eichels v Evansville St. R. Co. 78 Ind 261.

implied illegality. That which, although neither expressly forbidden nor authorized, is contrary to the plain implication of a statute. Luria v United States, 231 US 9, 58 L Ed 101, 34 S Ct 10.

implied in fact. See **implied contract**.

implied in law. See **implied contract**.

implied intent. A guilty intention inferable from the act relied upon by the prosecution as constituting the offense. 21 Am J2d Crim L § 81.

implied invitation. An act of the owner or occupant of premises, or of someone else with his permission, which he knows, or reasonably should know, may give rise to the belief, in a mind of a person ordinarily discerning, that the owner or occupant intended such person to come upon the premises. Black v Central R. Co. 85 NJL 197, 89 A 24.

In its real value and significance, as derived from its application in the adjudged cases, the term imports knowledge by the defendant of the probable use by the plaintiff of the defendant's property so situated and conditioned as to be open to, and likely to be subjected to such use. Lepnick v Gaddis, 72 Miss 200, 16 So 213.

See **implied license**.

implied lease. The relation of landlord and tenant existing under an implied contract, that is, a relation from the acts and conduct of the parties consistent only with the existence of a lease and the creation of the relation of landlord and tenant thereunder. 32 Am J1st L & T § 24.

implied license. A license to perform an act or acts upon the land of another existing by virtue of acquiescence of the owner or inferred from the acts of the parties, their relations with each other, from custom, or from the habits of the country, but giving the licensee no interest in the land. McKee v Gratz, 200 US 127, 67 L Ed 167, 43 S Ct 16 (license to go upon land for purpose of hunting or fishing).

The principle on which an implied license may be distinguished from an implied invitation is that where the privilege of user exists for the common interest or mutual advantage of both parties, it will be held to be an invitation; but if it exists for the mere pleasure and benefit of the party exercising the privilege, it will be held to be a license. Douglas v Bergland, 216 Mich 380, 185 NW 819, 20 ALR 197.

implied lien. A lien which may be created in the absence of an express contract, based upon the fundamental maxims of equity and which may be implied and declared by a court of equity out of general considerations of right and justice as applied to the relations of the parties and the circumstances of their dealings. 33 Am J1st Liens § 21. The lien in favor of a vendor who has conveyed the legal title to real estate to a purchaser, as security for the unpaid purchase money. 55 Am J1st V & P § 462.

implied malice. An expresssion of dual meaning, sometimes being used in the sense of constructive malice and at other times indicating presumed malice. The mental state of ill will, spite, wicked intention, or enmity which the law infers from or imputes to certain acts. Griswold v Horne, 19 Ariz 56, 165 P 318. The inference or implication from a wilful and intentional act performed for the accomplishment of a wrongful object or ulterior purpose. 1 Am J2d Abuse P § 6. An application of the presumption that one intends the natural and probable consequences of his voluntary and deliberate acts. Taylor v State, 201 Ind 241, 167 NE 133. As an element of the crime of murder:—the absence of a deliberate mind and formed design to take life, but where the killing, nevertheless, is done without justification or excuse, and without provocation, or without sufficient provocation to reduce the offense to manslaughter. State v Trott, 190 NC 674, 130 SE 627, 42 ALR 1214. The showing of an abandoned or malignant heart by all the circumstances. People v Crenshaw, 298 Ill 412, 131 NE 576, 15 ALR 671.

It is a matter of the greatest difficulty to distinguish between express malice and implied malice so as to render those terms intelligible to a jury. Turner v Commonwealth, 167 Ky 365, 180 SW 768.

implied notice. A kind of actual notice rather than constructive notice; sometimes referred to as implied actual notice. 39 Am J1st Notice § 6. Notice inferred from the means of knowledge open to a person, without proof that he used them. Texas Co. v Aycock, 190 Tenn 16, 227 SW2d 41, 17 ALR2d 322. Sometimes confused with "constructive notice" which is a matter of legal inference rather than actual notice. 39 Am J1st Notice § 6. Hunt v Ellis, 27 NM 397, 201 P 1064.

implied obligation. See **implied contract.**

implied permission. See **implied license; implied permission to use motor vehicle.**

implied permission to use motor vehicle. A sufferance of use or passive permission deduced from a failure to object to a known past, present or intended future use under circumstances where the use should be anticipated. Bradford v Sargent, 135 Cal App 324, 27 P2d 93.

implied powers. The powers necessary to effectuate the powers expressly conferred. Re Munger, 168 Iowa 372, 150 NW 447 (powers of executor or administrator). Sometimes in loose usage referred to as inherent powers. Re Berman, 245 NC 612, 97 SE2d 232. The powers of a public officer which, although incidental and collateral, are germane to, or serve to promote or benefit, the accomplishment of the principal purposes of the office. Moore v Nation, 80 Kan 672, 103 P 107. Federal powers under an implied grant in the United States Constitution. 16 Am J2d Const L § 199. The powers of a corporation to effectuate the powers expressly granted and to accomplish the purposes for which the corporation was formed, except as the particular act is prohibited by law or by the charter. 19 Am J2d Corp § 953.

The implied powers which a corporation has in order to carry into effect those expressly granted and to accomplish the purposes of the creation of the corporation are not limited to such as are indispensable for these purposes, but comprise all that are necessary, in the sense of appropriate and suitable, including the right of reasonable choice of means to be employed. 19 Am J2d Corp § 953.

See **implied authority.**

implied publication. The communication by the testator to the attesting witnesses by word, sign, motion, or conduct, his intent that the instrument take effect as his will. 57 Am J1st Wills § 283.

implied ratification. An inference from a course of conduct, lapse of time, or acquiescence, indicating an intention to approve, confirm, and adopt something which in the first instance he might have successfully avoided. Peter v Irwin, 69 W Va 200, 71 SE 115. Recognizing the validity of a transaction, or remaining silent when called upon to speak, whereby others have been injured. Anno: 48 ALR 425, 54 ALR 1246. Of contract:—accepting the benefits growing out of it or remaining silent or acquiescing in a contract for any considerable length of time after opportunity is afforded to avoid it or have it annulled, or recognizing the validity of the contract by acting upon it. 25 Am J2d Dur § 28. An election, definitely manifested, by one, after reaching majority, to let a contract made by him while an infant stand in force. Hermenu v Zazzarino, 108 NJ Eq 451, 155 A 459. Of act or transaction by agent:—any act, words, or course of conduct on the part of the principal which reasonably tends to show an intention on his part to ratify the unauthorized acts or transactions of the alleged agent. 3 Am J2d Agency § 162. The ratification of an agent's acts by accepting the benefits thereof or failing to repudiate the acts after notice that the agent has exceeded his authority. Howell v Grocers Inc. (CA6 Mich) 2 F2d 499.

An alteration of an instrument is ratified where the obligor under the instrument, with knowledge of the alteration, agrees to pay the amount of the instrument as altered, renews the instrument, or accepts and retains benefits under the instrument with knowledge that it has been altered. 4 Am J2d Alt Inst § 67.

implied rejection. A rejection of an offer of dedication by acts of the authorized public officers indicating an intention to reject. Ramstad v Carr, 31 ND 504, 154 NW 195.

implied remainder. A remainder created by implication according to the intention of the testator or grantor, as where a remainder is deemed to have been devised by words of gift directing a payment or distribution in the future. 33 Am J1st Life Est § 62.

implied repeal. The superseding of a rule of the common law, without an express directive to that effect, as by adoption of a statute dealing comprehensively with the subject to which the common law rule relates. Banko v Weber, 9 App Div 2d 720, 192 NYS2d 260, affd 7 NY2d 758, 193 NYS2d 670, 162 NE2d 750. The repeal of a statute by a later statute, in the absence of an express repeal by the later statute, where there is such a positive repugnancy between the provisions of the old and the new statutes that they cannot stand together or be harmonized. Pacific Milling Elevator Co. v Portland, 65 Or 349, 133 P 72. The repeal of a statute by the adoption of an amendment to the constitution which is inconsistent with and repugnant to the provisions of the statute. 16 Am J2d Const L § 49. The repeal of a provision of a constitution by the adoption of an amendment to the constitution which is inconsistent with such provision. 16 Am J2d Const L § 27.

A portion of a statute may also be repealed by implication, as where it is in conflict with a provision of a later statute. State v Atlantic Coast Line R. Co. 56 Fla 617, 47 So 969.

implied representation. A representation made, not directly by words, but indirectly by words, acts, or conduct from which the representation of a fact may be implied. See 32 Am J2d False Pret § 17, A conclusion which, while not expressed directly in a statement, is one clearly to be drawn from the statement. 29 Am J Rev ed Ins § 698.

implied rescission. A rescission of a contract which the law implies when the parties make a new contract concerning the same matter with terms so inconsistent with the terms of the former contract that they cannot stand together. 17 Am J2d Contr § 493. A rescission of a contract by acts or conduct of the parties inconsistent with the continued existence of the contract. 17 Am J2d Contr § 494.

implied reservation. A reservation of a right or easement from the grant made by an absolute conveyance in fee where such right or easement is essential to the enjoyment of land remaining in the grantor's ownership. 23 Am J2d Deeds § 270.

implied review. A constitutional right of review of an administrative determination. State ex rel. Watson v Lee, 157 Fla 62, 24 So 2d 798, 163 ALR 862.

implied revocation of will. A revocation by operation of law consequent to certain important changes in the family or domestic relations of the testator, such as marriage or the birth of a child after the making of the will, or changes involving the property of the testator or the beneficiaries of the will. 57 Am J1st Wills §§ 521 et seq. The revocation of a will by a later will or codicil which is inconsistent with the prior will, 57 Am J1st Wills § 474; a question of the intention of the testator as such appears from the general tenor and structure of the later will and the nature and character of the provisions contained therein. Kearns v Roush, 106 W Va 663, 146 SE 729.

implied tenancy. See **implied lease; implied tenancy at will.**

implied tenancy at will. The tenancy of one who enters on land by permission of the owner for an indefinite period without the reservation of any rent. 32 Am J1st L & T § 66.

implied trust. A trust which comes into existence through the application of intention to create a trust as a matter of law. A term also used for what is really a constructive trust, a trust by operation of law irrespective of and even contrary to the intention of him who is charged as trustee. 54 Am J1st Trusts § 5.
See **constructive trust.**

implied use. An implied trust.
See **implied license.**

implied waiver. A waiver shown by the acts and conduct of the parties from which an intention to waive reasonably may be inferred. 56 Am J1st Waiver § 17. A waiver implied as a reasonable inference from the act or silence of the party who has the power to waive. Roumage v Mechanics' Fire Ins. Co. 13 NJL 110. The waiver of notice of the taking of a deposition or of defects in such a notice by failure to object in writing. 23 Am J2d Dep § 37.

implied warranty. A statement, description, or undertaking by the insured under a marine policy which binds the insured as though expressed in the contract. Procacci v United States Fidelity Ins. Co. 118 NJL 423, 193 A 180. In sale of personal property:—a warranty by the seller of the quality or condition of the goods sold, imposed by operation of law, that is, a warranty inferred by law irrespective of any intention of the seller to create it, 46 Am J1st Sales § 332; a warranty of quality or condition implied from affirmations of the seller made without using technical words of warranty but with apparent intention to warrant, such being a warranty implied in fact rather than a warranty implied in law. 46 Am J1st Sales § 332. The obligation of an indorser of a negotiable instrument, apart from statute. 11 Am J2d B & N § 610.

import. Verb: To bring or carry a substance or article into the country from outside. Cunard S.S. Co. v Mellon, 262 US 100, 67 L Ed 894, 43 S Ct 504, 27 ALR 1306 (intoxicating liquor.) Within the meaning of the law of customs duties, to bring an article into the country from the outside, usually but not necessarily through a custom house. Pomplaim v United States (CA5 La) 42 F2d 203, cert den 282 US 886, 75 L Ed 881, 51 S Ct 89, following Cunard S.S. Co. v Mellon, 262 US 100, 67 L Ed 894, 45 S Ct 504, 27 ALR 1306. For some purposes, to bring articles into a state from another state. 24 Am J1st Game § 18. Noun: A substance or article carried into the country from abroad; a shipment from a foreign country to the United States. Faber v United States, 221 US 649, 55 L Ed 897, 31 S Ct 659.

An "imported" article is an article brought or carried into this country from abroad. A steam yacht coming into a port of the United States under her own steam is not an imported article. The Conqueror (DC NY) 49 F 99, 102.

As the term is used in the tenth section of the first article of the Federal Constitution, declaring that "no state shall without the consent of Congress lay any imposts or duties on imports or exports," it refers to articles imported from foreign countries into the United States, and it does not refer to those articles which are carried from one state of the Union into a sister state. Brown v Houston, 114 US 622, 29 L Ed 257, 5 S Ct 1091.

Within the meaning of section 9 of article I of the United States Constitution providing that the migration or importation of such persons as any of the states now existing shall think proper to admit, shall not be prohibited by the Congress prior to the year one thousand eight hundred and eight, the word "migration" had exclusive reference to persons of the African race. The two words "migration" and "importation" refer to the different conditions of this race as regards freedom from slavery. When the free black man came here, he "migrated;" when the slave came, he was imported. The latter was property and could be taxed as an import. People v Compagnie Générale Transatlantique (US) 17 Otto 59, 27 L Ed 383, 2 S Ct 87.

importation. An import. The act of importing.
See **import.**

import cost. The price at which an article is freely offered for sale in the ordinary course of trade in the usual wholesale quantities for exportation to the United States, plus all necessary expenses of bringing it to the United States when these are not included in such price. 19 USC § 1332(e)(2).

import duties. See **customs duties.**

imported. See **import.**

importer. A person who brings goods and merchandise into the United States from a foreign country; the consignee of a shipment to the United States from a foreign country. Meredith & Ellicott v United States (US) 13 Pet 486, 493, 10 L Ed 258, 262. One bringing articles, particularly intoxicating liquors, into a state from another state. 30 Am J Rev ed Intox L § 129.

import-export clause. Clause 2 of Section 10 of Article I of the Constitution of the United States which provides that no state shall, without the consent of Congress, lay any impost or duties on imports or exports, except what may be absolutely necessary for executing its inspection laws.

imports. See **import.**

import taxes. Taxes imposed on certain articles imported into the United States. 26 USC §§ 4521 et seq; 21 Am J2d Cust D § 1.
See **customs duties.**

importunity. Persistent solicitation; continued begging. Persistent request or entreaty. 47 Am J1st Seduc § 67. A form of undue influence. 25 Am J2d Dur § 36.

impose. To place a burden upon a person, for example, a tax. Hertz v Woodman, 218 US 205, 54 L Ed 1001, 30 S Ct 621.
See **imposition; impost.**

imposed duties. Literally, duties, the burden of which is imposed upon a person. In a technical sense, those duties of a municipal corporation which are superadded to merely governmental functions, like the special private corporate duty to maintain streets in a safe condition for public travel, or the special, private corporate duty to maintain and manage corporate property so that city employees shall have safe places in which to work. Edson v Olathe, 81 Kan 328, 105 P 521.

impositio (im-pō-zi'she-ō). Same as **imposition.**

imposition. Fraud, deception. Taking advantage of good nature to impose a burden. Any form of tax or enforced contribution to the public treasury. State v Heppenheimer, 58 NJL 633, 34 A 1061.

impossibilis (im-pos-si'bi-lis). Same as **impossible.**

impossibilitas facti (im-pos-si-bi'li-tas fak'-tī). The impossibility of doing a thing; that is, the inability of a person to perform an act, as distinguished from an act which in the nature of the thing is impossible. Klauber v San Diego Street Car Co. 95 Cal 353, 30 P 555.

impossibilitas rei (im-pos-si-bi'li-tas rē'ī). An impossibility in the nature of the thing, as distinguished from an inability of the person to do it. Klauber v San Diego Street Car Co. 95 Cal 353, 30 P 555.

impossibility. That which is impossible.
See **impossibility of performance; impossible; physical impossibility.**

impossibility of performance. Impossibility of accomplishment. Something beyond mere difficulty in performance. Impossibility having reference to the nature of the thing to be accomplished, not to the inability of the person. Mineral Park Land Co. v Howard, 172 Cal 289, 156 P 458. Original impossibility, an impossibility of performance existing when the contract was entered into, so that the contract was to do something which was from the outset impossible; supervening impossibility, that is impossibility from something developing after the inception of the contract. 17 Am J2d Contr § 404. No excuse for nonperformance of condition precedent to the vesting of an estate. 28 Am J2d Est § 158. A reason for extinguishment of condition subsequent whereby the estate vests free from the condition. 28 Am J2d Est § 158.

impossibility of proof. A fact, such as damages in certain peculiar cases, not susceptible of proof. 27 Am J2d Eq § 98. The impossibility of determination after the facts are in.
Whether or not any such impossibility of determination will exist is a question which properly should await the ascertainment of the facts. Anniston Manufacturing Co. v Davis, 301 US 337, 81 L Ed 1143, 57 S Ct 816.

impossibility of relief. A ground of jurisdiction in equity; the impossibility of evaluating damages in dollars and cents; damages not susceptible of proof. 27 Am J2d Eq § 98.

Impossibilium nulla obligatio est (im-pos-si-bi'li-um nul'la ob-li-gā'she-ō est). There is no obligation to do the impossible.
The law never requires the doing of an impossible thing, though it often awards damages for a failure to perform express contract stipulations where performance was rendered impossible by reason of intervening overpowering causes other than act of God. First Nat. Bank v McConnell, 103 Minn 340, 114 NW 1129.

impossible. Not capable of accomplishment. For some purposes, not reasonably practical, as where a statute prohibits under penalty the parking of a motor vehicle upon the traveled portion of a highway, unless it is "impossible to avoid stopping and temporarily leaving the vehicle" in such position. 7 Am J2d Auto § 235.
See **impossibility of performance.**

impossible condition. A condition precedent or subsequent in a contract which, at the time when the contract is entered into, purports to bind a party to do that which is absolutely impossible in itself. Jones v United States (US) 6 Otto 24, 24 L Ed 644.

impossible contract. A contract to do a thing which is in the nature of things impossible.
Such a contract is to be distinguished from one which could be performed by anyone possessing the means, skill and knowledge requisite for performance, but which the party is unable to perform; as a contract binding a party to pay money who is without funds to pay. Klauber v San Diego Street Car Co. 95 Cal 353, 30 P 555.

impossible statement. A representation so extravagant that only a credulous person will believe it. 23 Am J2d Fraud § 156.

impost. Any tax or imposition, but particularly a duty on imports. 21 Am J2d Cust D § 1.
The word "impost" is derived from the Latin word "impono," which was generally used among the Romans as meaning to lay or levy a tax, and in our language has scarcely had any other meaning than a tax, however assessed, levied or collected by a government, although by usage "impost" has acquired the more restricted meaning of taxes or duties imposed by government on imports. Neary v Philadelphia, Wilmington & Baltimore Railroad Co.12 Del (7 Houst) 419, 440.

impostor. One who poses as another. In a restricted sense, a person who misrepresents himself as another person, or as agent for another person. Anno: 54 ALR 1330. One who perpetrates a fraud by impersonation. Comment to UCC § 3-405.
See **impersonation.**

impotence (im'pō-tens). Same as **impotency.**

impotency (im'pō-tent-si). A term applying to both male and female. 4 Am J2d Annul § 32. Incapacity, whether from malformation or organic defect, to have natural and complete sexual intercourse. 4 Am J2d Annul § 32. Incapacity for ordinary and complete sexual intercourse, whether arising from malformation or absence of the sexual parts or organs or genital weakness. 35 Am J1st Mar § 121. Inability to engage in, or lack of capacity for, normal sexual intercourse. Anno: 65 ALR2d 778 § 2.

Excessive sensibility rendering sexual intercourse practically impossible on account of the pain it would inflict is within the meaning of impotency which renders a marriage voidable. S. v S. 192 Mass 194, 77 NE 1025.

See **triennial test; viripotens.**

impotency quoad hoc (im'pō-tent-si kwō'ad hok). Incapacity for sexual intercourse with this person.

impotent. In a state of impotency.
See **impotency.**

Impotentia excusat legem (im-po-ten'she-a ex-kū'zat lē'jem). Impossibility cuts out or dispenses with law. See 2 Bl Comm 127.

impotentiam (im-po-ten'she-am). See **property propter impotentiam.**

impound. To place animals taken up or distrained in a building or enclosure known as a pound. 4 Am J2d Ani § 40. To hold animals, goods, or funds in legal custody.
See **pound.**

impounded animal. Any animal in the custody of an animal pound. 4 Am J2d Ani § 48.

impounded funds. Funds held in legal custody.

impounded property. Movable property held in legal custody.

impoverishment. See **pauper.**

impracticable. Not feasible. Not capable of successful or worthwhile accomplishment.

In matters of business, a thing is commonly treated as "impracticable" when it cannot be done without laying out more money than the thing is worth. Devitt v Providence Washington Ins. Co. 61 App Div 390, 70 NYS 654.

imprescriptibility (im-prę-skrip-ti-bil'i-ti). Incapability of being acquired by prescription.

imprescriptible right (im-prę-skrip'ti-bl rīt). A right which a person cannot secure by prescription; such as a right to maintain a nuisance.

impression. An image fixed in the mind; a belief. Riggs v Tayloe (US) 9 Wheat 483, 6 L Ed 140. An indentation, fissure, or other mark made by the weight of one object applied to another or by the hammering of an object.

impressment. Forcing into service, particularly public service or military service. The seizure of seafaring men for compulsory service in the navy.

The power to impress seamen appears to have had a common-law origin, but even the early English statutes greatly curtailed it. See 1 Bl Comm 419. The impressment of American citizens into service in the English navy, however, was one of the causes of the War of 1812.

imprest. See **auditors of the imprest.**

imprest money (im'prest mun"i). Money paid for the impressment of seamen.

impretiabilis (im-pre-she-ā'bi-lis). Without price; invaluable.

imprimatur (im-pri-mā'tėr). Let it be printed,—a license from the government which was formerly required in England for the publication of a book.

imprimere (im-pri'me-re). To impress; to print.

imprimis (im-prī'mis). Especially; first of all; principally.

imprison. To deprive a person of his liberty without his consent. Efroymson v Smith, 29 Ind App 451, 453, 63 NE 328.

imprisoned on a criminal charge. The state or condition of a person who is imprisoned, but not yet convicted. Mitchell v Greenough (CA9 Wash) 100 F2d 184.

imprisonment. The holding of a person from the time of his commitment to the time of his discharge. 41 Am J1st Pris & P § 2. The holding of a person as a prisoner under a commitment ordered pursuant to a sentence for a crime or a commitment for temporary detention pending the disposition of a criminal charge. Any restraint placed upon a person contrary to his wishes and amounting to a physical detention of his person. United States ex rel. Carapa v Curran (CA2 NY) 297 F 946, 36 ALR 877. Any exercise of force, or express or implied threat of force, by which in fact a person is deprived of his liberty, compelled to remain where he does not wish to remain, or to go where he does not wish to go. 32 Am J2d False Imp § 11.

See **close confinement; commitment; false imprisonment; hard labor; prison; prisoner; solitary confinement.**

imprisonment at hard labor. See **hard labor.**

imprisonment for debt. Imprisonment under an execution against the person of the judgment debtor. 30 Am J2d Exec § 865. Taking and holding a person in custody under mesne process to secure his presence until final judgment. 5 Am J2d Arr § 52.

Most of the state constitutions contain provisions which, although varying considerably in terminology and application, prohibit imprisonment for debt. In some jurisdictions, imprisonment for debt is prohibited by statute. 5 Am J2d Arr § 54.

The effect of a commitment for contempt for failure to comply with an order of court requiring a trustee to turn over assets is not an imprisonment for debt. Watkins v Rives, 75 App DC 109, 125 F2d 33.

imprisonment on civil process. Imprisonment for debt, whether under execution against the person or under mesne process; imprisonment for contempt in failing to comply with an order of court. 17 Am J2d Contpt §§ 104 et seq.

See **imprisonment for debt.**

impristi (im-pris'tī). Sympathizers; partisans; allies; backers.

improbare (im-prō-bā're). To disallow; to disapprove; to reject; to overrule.

improbation (im-prǫ-bā'shǫn). An action to have an instrument declared void on the ground of forgery.

improbatory. See **articles improbatory.**

improper. That which is not suitable; unfit; not suited to the character, time and place. Chadbourne v Newcastle, 48 NH 196, 199. Not fitted to the circumstances. Pennsylvania Co. v Sloan, 125 Ill 72, 80.

improper conduct. Such conduct as a man of ordinary and reasonable care and prudence, would not have been guilty of, under the circumstances, par-

ticularly, conduct which is immoral. Palmer v Concord, 48 NH 211, 214.
See **immorality**.

improper fee. Same as **improper feud**.

improper feud (fūd). A fee or feud such as was originally sold to the feudatory for a price; such as was held upon base or less honorable services, or upon a rent, in lieu of military service; such as was in itself alienable, without mutual license; and such as might descend indifferently either to males or females. See 2 Bl Comm 58.

improperly. Acting in a manner which is unsuitable, unfitting, or wrong, especially in reference to the time, place, and circumstances. In connection with the conduct of a person, acting in a manner much different from that which a man of ordinary and reasonable care and prudence would have followed under the circumstances of the case. Cairnes v Hillman Drug Co. 214 Ala 545, 547, 108 So 362.

improper navigation. Navigation of a vessel in a manner contrary to the rules of navigation; navigation of a vessel not in a fit condition for navigation with safety to the vessel or cargo. The Manitoba (DC NY) 104 F 145, 155.

improper use doctrine. The doctrine of patent law, also known as the unclean hands doctrine, which denies the owner of a patent relief against one who supplies unpatented material to a licensee of the patent, although there is an agreement between the patent owner and the licensee that all unpatented materials used in connection with the patent shall be purchased from the patent owner, the latter having no right to exact such an agreement of the licensee. Carbice Corporation of America v American Patents Development Corp. 283 US 27, 75 L Ed 819, 51 S Ct 334.

impropriate rector (im-prō'pri-āt rek'tor). A layman who had been invested with a benefice and thus made a rector.

impropriation (im-prō-pri-ā'shọn). The investiture of a benefice in a layman or in a lay corporation.

impropriator (im-prō'pri-ā-tor). A layman or lay corporation holding the appropriation of a benefice. An impropriate rector.

improprium (im-pro'pri-um). See **feudum hauberticum**.

improve. To become better. To use to good purpose. To make better; to increase the value of something by alteration or addition. To construct buildings, put up fences, and provide drainage ditches on land. The performance of any act, whether on or off a lot or tract of land, the direct and proximate tendency of which is to enhance its value in the market. Vandall v South San Francisco Dock Co. 40 Cal 83, 90. In a meaning peculiar to Scotch law, to disprove; to impeach; to annul.

improved land. Land used or employed to good purpose, or turned to profitable account. Johnson v Frederick, 163 Ala 455, 50 So 910. Land upon which buildings have been erected to render the use of the land more profitable and more convenient. Vandall v South San Francisco Dock Co. 40 Cal 83.

improvement. A change for the better. Anything that enhances the value of real property permanently for general uses, including buildings, fixtures, fences, wells, orchards, etc., including additions to existing buildings. 27 Am J1st Improv § 2; 36 Am J1st Mech L § 43. Original construction or substantial reconstruction as distinguished from repair. Hazard v Main Street Realty Co. (Ky) 262 SW2d 87, 41 ALR2d 609 (statutory definition for purposes of special assessment.)

Although there is some authority to the contrary, it has been held in a few instances that labor performed in clearing, grading, landscaping, and the like, did not come within the meaning of the words "improvement" under mechanic's lien statutes covering erection, construction, alteration, repair, or other improvements with regard to buildings, structures, and appurtenances. Anno: 39 ALR2d 870.

An "improvement" contemplated by a provision in a lease for its cancellation in case the lessor "desires" to improve the premises has been held to be something substantial in character, as distinguished from that which is petty or minute; and it must be permanent in its use and value, as distinguished from that which is ephemeral or subject to easy and frequent change. 32 Am J1st L & T § 835.

See **improvement on invention**; **public improvement**.

improvement bond. A bond issued by a municipality or other public body to be paid from no source other than an improvement fund. Manker v American Sav. Bank & Trust Co. 131 Wash 430, 230 P 406, 42 ALR 1021. An obligation of an improvement district payable only from the fund provided by special assessment. Northern Trust Co. v Wilmette, 220 Ill 417, 77 NE 169.

improvement district. A drainage district, sewer district, or other area organized for the construction and maintenance of a public improvement. An area or district within which property is specially benefited by a local public improvement with the consequence that a special or local assessment is made against such property to finance the improvement. 48 Am J1st Spec A § 114. A public debtor within the provisions of the Bankruptcy Act for relief to public debtors. 9 Am J2d Bankr § 1416.

improvement lien. A lien recognized in equity in a proper case for the benefit of one who claims compensation for an improvement made on the land of another. 27 Am J1st Improv § 30.

See **mechanic's lien**; **special assessment lien**.

improvement on invention. That which improves on a patentable or patented invention. 40 Am J1st Pat § 18. A change in a machine by introducing some mechanical principle or mode of operation not previously existing in the machine. 40 Am J1st Pat § 52. An achievement which marks a distinct advance in an art. 40 Am J1st Pat § 54. The selection and adaptation of an existing form beyond the mere exercise of the imitative faculty, the result of which is in effect a new creation. Smith v Whitman Saddle Co. 148 US 674, 37 L Ed 606, 13 S Ct 768.

improvement patent. A term applied to the vast majority of patents and covering discoveries made in the fields where others have already labored but have failed to obtain that state of perfection which frequently follows experience, further study, and experimentation. Northwest Engineering Corp. v Keystone Driller Co. (CA7 Wis) 70 F2d 13.

improvement petition. A petition for a public improvement, the expense of which is to be defrayed by special assessments.

improvements. See **improvement**; **public improvement**.

improvidence. Want of thrift. Amado v Aguirre, 63 Ariz 213, 161 P2d 117, 160 ALR 1126. Carelessness, indifference, prodigality, wastefulness, or negligence in reference to the care, management, and preservation of property. Re Davis' Estate, 10 Mont 228, 25 P 105.

improvident contract. A contract which is unwise, unprofitable or oppressive, resulting from bad calculation or the want of vigilance on the part of the party who seeks relief therefrom. 27 Am J2d Eq § 25. A contract disadvantageous to one of the parties; a contract financially improvident or a contract so unreasonable and such an abnegation of legal rights that, for protection of the public, it should not be enforced; a contract, the enforcement of which will bring about an unreasonable restriction of the liberty of a person to exercise his profession or occupation or earn his living. 17 Am J2d Contr § 192.

improvident person. A spendthrift. One given to improvidence.
See **improvidence.**

improviso. See **ex improviso.**

impruiamentum (im-pru-i-ā-men'tum). Same as **improvement.**

impruiare (im-pru-i-ā're). To improve; to erect improvements on land.

impubes (im-pu'bēz). (Civil law.) A child over seven years of age who has not yet reached the age of puberty.

impulse. Sudden force. A spontaneous inclination of the mind prompting an immediate involvement in something not theretofore in contemplation. Curry v Federal Life Ins. Co. (Mo) 287 SW 1053, 1056.
See **irresistible impulse; uncontrollable impulse.**

impulsive insanity. That form of insanity by which a person is irresistibly impelled to the commission of an act, sometimes accompanied by delusions and sometimes not, sometimes apparent and sometimes concealed. Mutual Life Ins. Co. v Terry (US) 15 Wall 580, 21 L Ed 236. Otherwise known as **irresistible impulse.**

impunitas (im-pū'ni-tas). Same as **impunity.**

Impunitas continuum affectum tribuit delinquendi (im-pū'ni-tas kon-ti'ny-um af-fek'tum tri'bu-it dē-lin-quen'dī). Impunity offers a constant opening to the delinquent.

Impunitas semper ad deteriora invitat (im-pū'ni-tās sem'per ad de-te-ri-ō'ra in-vī'tat). Impunity always invites greater offenses.

impunity. Freedom or exemption from punishment.
See **immunity.**

impure. Adulterated; containing foreign matter, especially deleterious substances. Immoral.

impure water. Water injurious to health or unreasonably muddy so as to be unfit for use in a laundry. 56 Am J1st Watwk § 75.

Impuris manibus nemo accedat curiam (im-pū'ris ma'ni-bus nē'mō ak-sē'dat kū'ri-am). Let no one approach the court with unclean hands.

imputable negligence. See **indentification; imputed negligence.**

imputatio (im-pū-tā'she-ō). (Civil law.) Legal responsibility.

imputation of payments (im-pū-tā'shọn of pā'ments). A term of the civil law for application of payments.

imputed. Attributed or charged to a person, not as the one who personally perpetrated the wrong or created the situation from which injury has resulted, but as one who, because of his relationship to another person, is responsible for the acts or omissions of that person. Anno: 42 ALR 719.

imputed intent. See **implied intent.**

imputed knowledge. An agent's knowledge which is binding upon his principal because of the agency relationship between them. 3 Am J2d Agency § 273; 29A Am J Rev ed Ins § 1019. Knowledge of a fact or facts charged to a person because the circumstances are such that a person of ordinary common sense would know them. 29 Am J2d Ev § 27. That which it is one's duty to know and concerning which he has the means of knowing. Darling & Co. v Petri, 138 Kan 666, 27 P2d 255.

imputed negligence. The negligence of one person which, by reason of his relation to another person, is chargeable to that person. 38 Am J1st Negl § 234. A ground for defeating liability for negligence by charging the plaintiff with the concurrent negligence of a third person, thereby rendering the defense of contributory negligence available. 38 Am J1st Negl §§ 235 et seq. Also a basis for charging the negligence of one person to another in establishing the liability of the latter to a third person. 38 Am J1st Negl § 253.

in. Within, as "in an hour." Indicating a location, as "in Boston." Rogers v Galloway Female College, 64 Ark 627, 44 SW 454. Abbreviation of inch, also of inches.
With Latin words and phrases the word, as a preposition, has many meanings; in; on; to; into; within; according to; in the course of; at; among.

in abeyance (ạ-bā'yạns). Said of a fee when there is no person in being in whom it can vest and abide, although the law considers it as always potentially existing, and ready to vest whenever a proper owner appears. See 2 Bl Comm 107.

inability. Want of ability or capacity to act or perform. Want of physical capacity or of capacity in an abstract sense, as inability of a trust company to act as trustee under a deed of trust, arising from its insolvency. State ex rel. Bannister v Gantley, 330 Mo 943, 62 SW2d 397.

inability to bear. Inability to become a mother, which may or may not arise from impotency. 4 Am J2d Annul § 30.

inability to beget. Inability to be a father or sire, which may or may not arise from impotency. 4 Am J2d Annul § 30.

inability to pay. Not insolvency in itself. 9 Am J2d Bankr § 160.

inability to testify. Mental or physical inability to testify. Hansen-Rynning v Oregon-Washington R. & Nav. Co. 105 Or 67, 209 P 462.

inability to work. For the purposes of allowing workmen's compensation, inability to carry on one's usual employment. Clini v New Haven Brewing Co. 119 Conn 556, 177 A 745.
See **physical inability to work.**

in absentia (in ab-sen'she-à). In the absence.

in absurdum. See **ducitur in absurdum.**

inaccessible. In a place which cannot be reached.
Whether or not a witness beyond the jurisdiction of the state is inaccessible, in the sense in which the word is used in a statute making his inaccessibility

an excuse for failure to produce him, is a question for the trial judge to determine. In the absence of such a statute, a witness so situated would doubtless be deemed inaccessible. Atlanta & Charlotte Air-Line Railway Co. v Gravitt, 93 Ga 369, 371, 20 SE 550.

inaction. A condition or state of no action or motion. A matter of not speaking or acting.
See **estoppel by inaction.**

in action. A right asserted in, and awaiting determination by, an action.
Property is "in action," where one is not in the occupation of it, but has a bare right to occupy or possess it, which he may enforce in an action or suit. See 2 Bl Comm 396.
See **chose in action.**

inaction by Congress. The absence of congressional legislation, particularly in the field of interstate commerce. 15 Am J2d Com § 20.

inactive account. A savings bank account which has stood for years without a deposit or withdrawal. 10 Am J2d Banks § 416.

inactive concert or participation. A nonparty who, while engaging in the prohibited act, aids and abets, or is legally identified in interest with, an enjoined defendant, who likewise engages in the enjoined act. Rule 65(d) Fed Rules of Civ Proc; Anno: 97 ALR2d 491.

in actual use. As the term appears in a statute exempting wearing apparel from import duties:—apparel being worn at the time and also apparel in a passenger's trunks or luggage intended for and awaiting use in wearing it. Astor v Merritt, 111 US 202, 28 L Ed 401, 4 S Ct 413.

inadequacy of plant. The condition of a public utility plant where an increase in business requires the replacement of equipment by new equipment fitted more adequately to the demands of the service. 43 Am J1st Pub Util § 145.

inadequacy of price. The price obtained at a judicial sale:—inadequacy so gross as to shock the conscience and raise a presumption of fraud, unfairness, or mistake. 30A Am J Rev ed Jud S § 135.

inadequate damages. An award so small as to indicate passion, prejudice, partiality, or corruption on the part of the jury, or to make it appear that the jury disregarded the instructions of the court or labored under a vital mistake or misapprehension of the principles by which they should have been governed in making the award. 22 Am J2d Damg § 398. An award in an amount so small as to bear no reasonable relation to the loss suffered by the plaintiff or to indicate an evident failure of justice. 22 Am J2d Damg § 398.

inadequate remedy at law. A remedy which, although available at law, is not plain, clear and certain, prompt or speedy, sufficient, full and complete, practical, efficient to the attainment of the ends of justice, and final. 27 Am J2d Equity § 94. A remedy which is circuitous or doubtful, or is not as plain, complete, and efficient as an equitable remedy. 49 Am J1st Spec Per § 11. Specifically, a remedy limited to compensatory damages which under the circumstances of the case does not do complete justice between the parties. 49 Am J1st Spec Per § 10.

inadmissible (in-ad-mis′i-bl). Not receivable as evidence.

in adversum (in ad-ver′sum). Against an adverse party; against the will or without the consent.

inadvertence. The state of one acting in an inadvertent manner. Absence of intention. Harris v Piggly Wiggly Stores, 236 Ill App 392. Acting without thought or premeditation. 38 Am J1st Negl § 5. A mistake; oversight. Tremont Trust Co. v Burack, 235 Mass 398, 126 NE 782, 9 ALR 1067, 1069. An unplanned occurrence.

inadvertent. See **inadvertence.**

inaedificatio (in-ē-di-fi-kā′she-ō). (Civil law.) A building; so constructing a building as to encroach upon the land of another; constructing a building on one's own land with materials belonging to another.

In aedificiis lapis male positus non est removendus (in ē-di-fi′she-is la′pis ma′le pō′zi-tus non est rē-mō-ven′dus). In buildings, a stone badly placed cannot be removed.

in aequali jure (in ē-kwā′lī ju′rē). In equal right. An essential element in the application of the principle of contribution. 18 Am J2d Contrib § 1.

In aequali jure melior est conditio possidentis (in ē-quā′lī ju′re me′li-or est kon-di′she-ō pos-si-den′tis). In a case of equal right the situation of the party in possession is the better.

In aequali jure potior est conditio possidentis (in ē-quā′lī ju′re po′she-or est kon-di′she-ō pos-si-den′-tis). In a case of equal right, the situation of the party in possession is the stronger.

in aequali manu (in ē-quā′lī mā′nū). Same as **in aequa manu.**

in aequa manu (in ē′qua ma′nū). In equal hand; that is, in the hands of an indifferent person.

in aid of its jurisdiction. A phrase permissive of the power of a federal court to stay by injunction a proceeding in a state court. 28 USC § 2283.

inalienability. The quality of being nontransferable.
By giving to certain lands allotted to Indian tribes the character of inalienability, it is held that Congress has thereby made the lands nontaxable, because in order to make the restriction against alienation properly effective, nontaxability follows as an implied concomitant. Colonial Trust Co. v Lewellyn (DC Penn) 12 F2d 481.

inalienable. Incapable of being aliened, transferred, or conveyed; non-transferable.

inalienable rights. The fundamental rights and privileges; the right to personal liberty and individual ownership of property, freedom of religion, freedom of speech and press; due process of law, etc. 16 Am J2d Const L § 328.

in alieno solo (in ā-li-ē′nō sō′lō). On the land of another.

in alio loco (in a′li-ō lō′kō). In another place.

in all likelihood. With reasonable certainty. Coppinger v Broderick, 37 Ariz 473, 295 P 780, 81 ALR 419.

in all probability. The highest degree of probability; with reasonable certainty. Coppinger v Broderick, 37 Ariz 473, 295 P 780, 81 ALR 419.

In alta proditione nullus potest esse accessorius sed principalis solummodo (in al′ta pro-di-she-ō′ne nul′-lus po′test es′se ak-ses-sō′ri-us sed prin-si-pā′lis sō-lum-mō′dō). In high treason no one can be an accessory but each one is a principal. Ex parte Bollman and Ex parte Swartout (US) 4 Cranch 75, 126, 2 L Ed 554, 571.

In alternativis electio est debitoris (in al-ter-nā-tī′vis ē-lek′she-ō est de-bi-tō′ris). In alternatives, the debitor has his election.

In ambigua voce legis ea potius accipienda est significatio quae vitio caret, praesertim cum etiam voluntas legis ex hoc colligi possit (in am-bi′gu-a vō′se lē′jis e′a pō′she-us ak-si-pi-en′da est sig-ni-fi-kā′she-ō kwē vi′she-o ka′ret, prē-ser′tim kum e′she-am vo-lun′tās lē′jis ex hōk kol′li-jī pos′sit). In an ambiguous expression of law, that construction ought rather to be adopted which renders it free from fault, especially when the intent of the law can thus be gathered.

In ambiguis casibus semper praesumitur pro rege (in am-bi′gu-is kā′si-bus sem′per prē-zu′mi-ter prō rē′je). In doubtful cases, the presumption is always on the side of the crown.

In ambiguis orationibus maxime sententia spectanda est ejus qui eas protulisset (in am-bi′gu-is ō-rā-she-ō′ni-bus mak′ si-mē sen-ten′she-a spek-tan′da est ē′-jus quī e′as prō-tu-lis′set). In ambiguous expressions, the intent of him who made them ought to be regarded as most important.

In ambiguo sermone non utrumque dicimus sed id duntaxat quod volumus (in am-bi′gu-ō ser-mō′ne non u-trum′kwē dī′si-mus sed id dun-ta′xat quod vo′lu-mus). In ambiguous discourse or conversation, we do not say either one thing or the other, but neither more nor less than we wish.

in amity (in am′i-ti). In peace.
In amity with the United States is an expression commonly used in acts of Congress dealing with the Indian tribes and means at peace, or more specifically, carrying on no hostilities toward the United States, its citizens or its property. Leighton v United States, 161 US 291, 40 L Ed 703, 16 S Ct 495.

in a motor vehicle. A phrase indicating a relationship between a person and a vehicle, such as riding in the vehicle or being in the process of entering or leaving the vehicle, but not limited to one sitting in the vehicle in the place provided for the accommodation of driver or passenger. 29A Am J Rev ed Ins § 1241.

in and on the body. A phrase used in an indictment charging the use of an instrument in an abortion or attempted abortion. State v Longstreth, 19 ND 268, 121 NW 1114.

in an elevator. A clause in an accident insurance policy or double indemnity provision of a life insurance policy; comprehending an injury, the moving or primary cause of which originates in an elevator, for example, a fall down the shaft subsequent to an accident involving the elevator car, or an injury consequent to a fall by one intending to be a passenger into the pit of the shaft. 29A Am J Rev ed Ins § 1235.

In Anglia non est interregnum (in An′gli-a non est in-ter-reg′num). In England there is no interregnum. The king never dies, for immediately upon his decease, his kingship is vested in his heir. See 1 Bl Comm 249.

in an intoxicated condition. Under the influence of intoxicating liquor. 7 Am J2d Auto § 257.
There is, however, authority to the effect that while all persons intoxicated by the use of alcoholic liquors are "under the influence of intoxicating liquor," the reverse is not true. 7 Am J2d Auto § 257.

in another state. See **arising in another state.**

in any degree under the influence of intoxicating liquor. Intoxicated. Anno: 13 ALR2d 1003.

in aperta luce (in a-per′ta lū′se). In open daylight.

in apicibus juris (in ā-pi′si-bus jū′ris). In the extremes of the law.

inapplicable. No applicable. In one sense, not suitable. Freedman v Petty, 93 Ga App 590, 92 SE2d 588, 589.

in a public conveyance. See **in or on a public or passenger conveyance.**

in arbitrio judicis (in ar-bi′tri-ō jū′di-sis). In the discretion of the court; for the decision of the court. Rhodes v Whitehead, 27 Tex 304.

in arbitrium alieno (in ar-bi′tri-um ā-li-ē′nō). In the discretion of another person.

in arbitrium judicis (in ar-bi′tri-um jū′di-sis). In the decision or discretion of the court.

in arcta et salva custodia (in ark′ta et sal′va kus-tō′di-a). In close and safe custody.

in articulo (in är-tik′ụ-lō). At the point; at the moment.

in articulo mortis (in är-tik′ụ-lō môr′tis). At the point of death.
See **in extremis.**

In atrocioribus delictis punitur affectus licet non sequatur effectus (in a-trō-si-ō′ri-bus dē-lik′ tis pu′-ni-ter af-fek′tus li′set non se-quā′ter ef-fek′tus). In the more atrocious crimes, the attempt is punished although the result does not follow.

in auditu (in â-dī′tū). Within the hearing. Brown v Brashier (Pa) 2 Penr & W 114.

inauguration. The installation into office of a person elected or appointed to a high office of state. Making a beginning; putting into effect.

Inauguration Day. The day, January 20, following their election, for the inauguration of the President and Vice President of the United States. The day fixed by law of a state for the inauguration of the Governor.

in auter droit (ēn ō′trŭh drwo). In the right of another person. 2 Bl Comm 177.

in bad faith. With actual intent to deceive or mislead. Penn Mut. Life Ins. Co. v Mechanics' Sav. Bank & Trust Co. (CA6 Tenn) 73 F 653.
See **bad faith.**

in banco (in bang′kō). On the bench; in bank, that is, when all of the judges of the court are sitting.

in bank (in bangk). With all of the judges of the court sitting.

in bar. See **plea in bar.**

in being. In existence; alive.

An unborn child, after conception, if it is subsequently born alive and so far advanced to maturity as to be capable of living, is considered as "in esse" from the time of its conception where it is for the benefit of the child that it should be so considered. Hone v Van Schaick (NY) 3 Barb Ch 488, 509.

For the purpose of taking any estate which is for his benefit, whether by descent, devise, or under the statute of distributions, a person is held both in England and in the United States to be "in being" from the time of his conception, the commencement of foetal existence being placed at a time nine months before birth. 23 Am J2d Desc & D § 88; 57 Am J1st Wills § 154. If the child is born dead or in such an early stage of gestation as to be incapable of living, the situation is as though he had never been conceived or born. 23 Am J2d Desc & D § 88; 57 Am J1st Wills § 154.

See **in.**

in blank. An instrument drawn and executed with blank spaces left to be filled later.

See **indorsement in blank.**

inblaura (in-blâ′ra). Produce of the soil; the profit of such produce.

inboard. Stowage of cargo under deck or, at least, with no part projecting over the rail of the vessel.

inboard motorboat. A motorboat, the engine of which is mounted within the hull.

in body. See **in person.**

in bona fide operation. An expression in the "grandfather clause" of the Federal Motor Carrier Act indicating prior service that was actual rather than simulated and legal rather than in defiance of the laws of the state. McDonald v Thompson, 305 US 263, 83 L Ed 164, 59 S Ct 176, reh den 305 US 676, 83 L Ed 437, 59 S Ct 356.

See **grandfather clause.**

in bonis (in bō′nis). Among the goods; in the property.

in bonis defuncti (in bō′nis dē-funk′tī). Among the goods or in the property of the deceased.

in bonis, in terris, vel persona (in bō′nis, in ter′ris, vel per-sō′na). In either his goods, his lands or his person. See 1 Bl Comm 141.

inborow. A gatehouse between principalities.

inbound common. A common with definite boundaries but not fenced.

In Britannia tertia pars bonorum decedentium ab intestato in opus ecclesiae et pauperum dispensanda est (in Bri-tan′ni-a ter′she-a parz bō-nō′rum de-sē-den′she-um ab in-tes-tā′tō in o′pus e-klē′si-ē et pâ′pe-rum dis-pen-san′da est). In Britain a third part of the goods left by an intestate is to be distributed for the needs of the church and the poor. See 2 Bl Comm 495.

in camera (in kam′ę-ra). In chambers; in private. A trial in which the court excludes the public from the courtroom. 24 Am J2d Div & S § 334.

incapable. Unfit for work, or for the performance of a particular task, for want of physical strength, education, or mentality. Having physical or mental disability. Ineligible; disqualified.

A statute which provided for certain action to be had upon the death or disability of the judge would ordinarily be construed to refer to the physical or mental disability of the judge. Used in this connection, it would not in the customary use of language be construed to mean if the judge was incapable to act because of disqualification. Todd v Bradley, 97 Conn 563, 117 A 808, 25 ALR 22, 25.

incapable of being ascertained. The absence of any rule for the guidance of the jury or the trier of the facts for the determination of the amount of actual damages from breach of contract, wherefrom a stipulation in the contract may be deemed a provision for liquidated damages, not a penalty. 22 Am J2d Damg § 218.

incapacitated. See **incapacity; physically incapacitated.**

incapacity. In the broader meaning, physical or mental inability to act. In some contexts, confined to mental disability or incapability. Ellicott v Ellicott, 90 Md 321, 45 A 183 (incapacity to pursue a college education.) For the purposes of workmen's compensation:—inability to procure employment or incapacity to perform the service. 58 Am J1st Workm C § 282.

See **mental incapacity; physical incapacity.**

incapacity for work. A familiar phrase in workmen's compensation statutes; including not merely want of physical ability to work, but lack of opportunity for work; loss of earning power as a workman in consequence of the injury, whether the loss manifests itself in inability to perform such work as may be obtainable, or inability to secure work to do. Ray v Frenchmen's Bay Packing Co. 122 Me 108, 119 A 191, 33 ALR 112, 114.

incapacity of physician. See **manifest incapacity.**

incapacity to defend. Infancy. 27 Am J1st Inf § 116. Insanity. 29 Am J Rev ed Ins Per § 123.

incapacity to sue. Want of capacity arising from infancy, incompetency, lack of authority, etc., as a result of which the plaintiff lacks standing to maintain the action. 39 Am J1st Parties §§ 105 et seq.

incapax. See **doli incapax.**

in capita (in kap′i-tą). To the polls.

A challenge in capita, or to the polls, is a challenge to a particular juror. See 3 Bl Comm 361.

in capite (in kap′i-tē). In chief.

See **tenure in capite.**

incarcerate (in-kär′sę-rāt). To imprison; to confine in a prison or jail.

in case of need. See **referee in case of need.**

in cash. A requirement imposed upon the insured under some insurance policies as a condition in reference to the payment of premium. 29 Am J Rev ed Ins § 542.

See **cash.**

in casu consimili (in kā′sū kon-si′mi-lī). In a similar case.

In casu extremae necessitatis omnia sunt communia (in kā′sū ex-trē′mē ne-ses-si-tā′tis om′ni-a sunt kom-mū′ni-a). In a case of extreme necessity, all things are common property.

in casu proviso (in ka′sū prō-vī′sō). In the case provided.

incaustum (in-kâs′tum). Ink.

incautacion. (Spanish.) A taking of property without thought of restitution, somewhat by way of punishment, as in the expropriation of property of a deposed king. The Navemar (DC NY) 24 F Supp 495.

Incaute factum pro non facto habetur (in-kâ′te fak′-tum prō non fak′tō hā-bē′ter). An act which is done carelessly is regarded as not having been done.

incautious. Careless; negligent; lacking in circumspection.

incendiarism (in-sen′di-a̱-rism). A wilful, as distinguished from an accidental, starting of a fire. Williamsburgh City Fire Ins. Co. v Willard (CA9 Cal) 164 F 404.

incendiary. Adjective: Kindled. Wilfully set on fire. Noun: A person guilty of arson or an attempt to commit arson.

incendi crimen. (Latin.) Arson.

Incendit et combussit (in-sen′dit et kom-bus′sit). He set on fire and burned.

Incendium aere alieno non exuit debitorem (in-sen′-di-um ē′re ā-li-ē′nō non ex′u-it de-bi-tō′rem). A fire does not discharge a debtor of his debt.

incentive compensation. Bonus and profit-sharing plans for corporate officers and employees. 19 Am J2d Corp § 1413. Stock options for executives.

incentive plan. See **bonus plan.**

incentive wages. Bonuses or other payments made to employees in addition to guaranteed hourly wages. 31 Am J Rev ed Labor § 615.
See **incentive compensation.**

inception. An initial stage. The beginning.
The word does not refer to a state of actual existence, but to a condition of things or circumstances from which the thing may develop, as the beginning of work on a building. Oriental Hotel Co. v Griffiths, 88 Tex 574, 33 SW 652.

inception of lien. The commencement or attachment of a lien, particularly a lien predicated upon judgment or execution. 30A Am J Rev ed Judgm §§ 520 et seq.

inception of risk. Assuming the consummation of a contract of insurance, the attachment of the risk covered by the policy. 29 Am J Rev ed Ins § 309.

inception of title doctrine. The doctrine of community-property law that property is acquired, for the purpose of classification as separate or community, at inception of spouse's title. Hollingsworth v Hicks, 57 NM 336, 258 P2d 724.

Incertam et caducam hereditatem relevabat (in-ser′-tam et ka-dū′kam hē-rē-di-tā′tem re-le-vā′bat). It freed the uncertain and fallen inheritance. See 2 Bl Comm 56.

Incerta pro nullis habentur (in-ser′ta prō nul′lis hā-ben′ter). Uncertain things are regarded as nullities.

Incerta quantitas vitiat actum (in-ser′ta quan′ti-tas vi′she-at ak′tum). An uncertain quantity vitiates the act.

incest. Sexual intercourse, either habitual or in a single instance, and either under form of marriage or without it, between persons too closely related in consanguinity or affinity to be entitled to intermarry; sexual intercourse between persons so closely related that marriage between them would be unlawful. 27 Am J1st Incest § 1.

incestuous adultery. Incest committed by a person who is married.

incestuous bastard. A person whose conception was in the perpetration of the crime of incest by his parents; a bastard born of the incestuous relations of his parents with one another.

incestuous marriage. A marriage between persons forbidden by law to intermarry, because they are related to one another in a certain degree. 35 Am J1st Marr § 140.

inch. A unit of linear measurement, one-twelfth of a foot or 254.00 centimeters. Am J2d Desk Book Document 156. Also a measure of surface area and of volume, respectively a square inch and a cubic inch.
See **inch of water; miner's inch.**

in charge of motor vehicle. Being in control of the movement of a motor vehicle, whether by application of the power of the motor or steering the vehicle while it is being towed or pushed by another vehicle. Anno: 47 ALR2d 585, § 5[c].

in chief. See **examination in chief; question in chief.**

Inchmaree Clause. A clause of a marine insurance policy, covering loss of, or damage to, the hull or machinery, through the negligence of master, mariners, engineers or pilots, or through explosions, bursting of boilers, or breaking of shafts, or through any latent defect in the machinery or hull, provided such loss or damage has not resulted from want of due diligence by the owners of the vessel or any of them or by the manager. Anno: 91 ALR2d 1296; 98 ALR2d 953.

inchoate (in-kō′āt). Imperfect; incipient; not completely formed.

inchoate battery. An assault. Johnson v Sampson, 167 Minn 203, 208 NW 814, 46 ALR 772.

inchoate curtesy. A term variously defined as the right of the husband akin to the inchoate right of dower of the wife; the right of the husband in a jurisdiction in which the husband's right of curtesy is by statute the same as the right of dower, such right attaching the moment the wife becomes seized in fee simple during coverture; the doctrine that on the birth of issue, even though the husband has no greater interest in the wife's property during her life because of the Married Woman's Act, he nevertheless has a potential life estate in his wife's real property conditional on his surviving her. 25 Am J2d Dow § 2.

inchoate dower. See **inchoate right of dower.**

inchoate lien. A lien that has not actually attached to the property, as in the case of a tax lien prior to the assessment of the tax. 51 Am J1st Tax § 1020. The state of a mechanic's lien before filing or giving of notice. 36 Am J1st Mech L § 167.

inchoate right. A rudimentary interest.

inchoate right of dower. The right, or expectation of a future right, that a wife has in real estate, of which her husband has become seized, while he is still living, such right becoming consummate as her dower if he dies leaving her surviving and she has not previously released her interest. American Blower Co. v MacKenzie, 197 NC 152, 147 SE 829, 64 ALR 1047.

inch of candle. See **auction by inch of candle.**

inch of water. A measurement of rainfall. Flowing water:—an indefinite term, without meaning in and of itself in the absence of extrinsic evidence indicating the kind of inch or the method of measurement. 56 Am J1st Wat § 4. In some jurisdictions, the amount of water that flows through an orifice one inch square in a vertical position and under a standard head prescribed by custom or by statute. New Brantner Extension Ditch Co. v Kramer, 57 Colo 218, 141 P 498.

incidence of tax. The burden of a tax, that is, where the burden of payment is ultimately imposed, as where a person obligated to pay a stamp tax shifts the burden to another by charging him directly or indirectly the amount of the tax paid. 49 Am J1st Stamp T § 20.

incident. An event, happening, or thing, of moment because of its connection with a main or principal event, happening, or thing. Commonwealth use of Vicars v Wampler, 104 Va 337, 51 SE 737.

incidental authority. See **implied authority.**

incidental beneficiary. A person to whom the benefits of a contract accrue merely as an incident to the performance of the contract.

A person for whose benefit a contract is made may maintain an action thereon. It must definitely appear, however, that the contract was made for his benefit; it is not sufficient that he is merely an incidental beneficiary. Shapiro Bros. Factors Corp. v Automobile Ins. Co. (DC NJ) 40 F Supp 1.

incidental fees. Student union fee, matriculation fee, hospital fee, laboratory fee, athletic fee, etc., collected by a state university or college, admission to which is generally free by constitutional or statutory provision. 15 Am J2d Univ & C § 19.

incidental jurisdiction. See **ancillary jurisdiction.**

incidental power. A power that is directly and immediately appropriate to the execution of the specific power granted. Nicollet National Bank v Frisk-Turner Co. 71 Minn 413, 74 NW 160; People ex rel. Peabody v Chicago Gas Trust Co. 130 Ill 268, 22 NE 798.

See **implied authority.**

incidental proceeding. An ancillary proceeding, that is a proceeding which stems from a main or principal action or proceeding.

See **ancillary proceeding.**

incidental relief. Relief granted by a court of equity beyond that specifically requested in the bill or complaint. 27 Am J2d Equity § 108.

incidental rights. See **appurtenant rights.**

incidental third-party beneficiary. Same as **incidental beneficiary.**

incidental use. The use of a highway for a purpose other than travel or transportation, which is conducive to public convenience or tends to make the highway of greater utility, or for the purpose of travel or transportation by a special instrumentality or mode of conveyance not inconsistent or incompatible with the primary purpose of a highway or its use in the customary manner. 25 Am J1st High § 168. A familiar term in zoning laws; a use of premises dependent on or pertaining to the principal or main use. Needham v Winslow Nurseries, Inc. 330 Mass 95, 111 NE2d 453, 40 ALR2d 1450. A use accessory to a permitted use, sometimes limited to a use on the same premises or a use other than for business or industrial purposes. 58 Am J1st Zoning § 46.

incident and appurtenant. A characterization of those things which pass by a conveyance of lands, though not designated in the conveyance. 23 Am J2d Deeds § 256.

incidents of ownership. A test of taxability of the proceeds of life insurance under an estate tax law. 28 Am J Rev ed Inher T § 254.

incident to employment. A characterization of those dangers in the work and injuries compensable under a workmen's compensation statute, although not located or occurring directly on the premises of the employer. Kozdeba v Peoples Gas Light & Coke Co. 232 Ill App 495. A characterization of a basis for recognizing the authority of an agent or the duties and scope of employment of a servant.

incidere (in-si′de-re). To happen; to occur; to attack.

Incidit in Scyllam evitare Charybdin (in′ci-dit in sil′-lam ē-vi-tā′re ka-rib′din). He falls upon Scylla in avoiding Charybdis.

As where counsel, in his effort to prove his client innocent of one offense, shows him to be guilty of another. Commonwealth v Eagan, 190 Pa 10, 42 A 374.

incinerator. A large receptacle of metal for receiving and burning rubbish and other trash. 39 Am J1st Nuis § 94. A structure equipped for the burning of the rubbish and waste of the inhabitants of a city.

incipitur (in-si′pi-ter). It is begun.

incite. To arouse to action, sometimes to violence, mob action or riot, even to revolution. State v Diamond, 27 NM 477, 202 P 988, 20 ALR 1527, 1532. To solicit the commission of a crime, such as larceny. 32 Am J1st Larc § 91.

incitement. An arousing to action.

See **incite.**

inciting fraudulent litigation. A form of obstruction of justice. 39 Am J1st Obst J § 4.

incivile (in-si′vi-le). Unjustly; tyrannically; improperly; unfairly.

Incivile est, nisi tota lege prospecta, una aliqua particula ejus proposita, judicare vel respondere (in-si′vi-le est, nī′sī tō′ta lē′je prō-spek′ta, ū′na a′li-qua par-ti′ku-la ē′jus prō-pō′zi-ta, ju-di-kā′re vel res-pon-dē′re). It is unfair, unless the whole of the law has been examined to adjudge or to advise respecting some particular provision of it.

The word "prospecta" in the maxim is sometimes written as "perspecta."

Incivile est, nisi tota sententia inspecta, de aliqua parta judicare (in-si′vi-le est, nī′sī to′ta sen-ten′she-a in-spek′ta, dē a′li-qua par′te jū-di-kā′re). Unless the whole of a sentence has been examined, it is unfair to pass judgment upon any certain portion of it.

In civilibus ministerium excusat, in criminalibus non item (in si-vi′li-bus mi-nis-te′ri-um ex-kū′zat, in kri-mi-nā′li-bus non i′tem). In civil cases agency is an excuse, but it is not so in criminal cases.

incivility. Rudeness; conduct which may constitute a ground for divorce as an indignity. 24 Am J2d Div & S § 159.

incivism (in′si-vizm). The failure of a person to perform his duty as a citizen.

In claris non est locus conjecturis (in klā′ris non est lō′kus kon-jek-tū′ris). In matters which are clear there is no room for conjecture.

inclausa (in-klâ′sa). An inclosure; an enclosed space.

inclement weather. Bad weather.

in clientelam recipere (in kli-en-tē′lam re-si′pe-re). To take into protection or patronage. See 2 Bl Comm 21.

inclination. An encroachment, as where the wall tips or leans over adjoining premises. 3 Am J2d Adv P § 44.

incline. A hill or grade.

inclose. To encompass, bound, fence, or otherwise part off or hem in a tract of land on all sides. White Chapel Memorial Asso. v Wilson, 260 Mich 238, 244 NW 460; Kimball v Carter, 95 Va 77, 27 SE 823. To place in an envelope, particularly with a letter; the same as "enclose."

inclosed land. Fenced land. Land surrounded by a fence, hedge, ditch, wall, or any line of obstacles interposed so as to part off and shut in the land and set it off as private property, but not necessarily so securely as to prevent the passing of cattle to and from the premises. Kimball v Carter, 95 Va 77.

inclosure. A fence, wall, hedge, rail, or other tangible obstruction protecting premises against encroachment. The area protected by such visible or tangible obstruction.

As used in a statute relating to damage done by cattle, it was held to mean a tract of land surrounded by an actual fence together with such fence, and not to include that part of a public highway of which the fee belonged to the owner of an adjoining inclosure. Peck v Williams, 24 RI 583, 54 A 381.

See **ancient inclosure; fence; possession by inclosure.**

include. To comprise, embrace, contain, or comprehend as a component part or member. Montello Salt Co. v Utah, 221 US 452, 55 L Ed 810, 31 S Ct 706; Red Wing Malting Co. v Willcuts (CA8 Minn) 15 F2d 626, 49 ALR 459, 464.

included offense. A criminal offense included, within an indictment for a more serious offense, as a lesser offense, or one of a lower degree of the same general class as the more serious offense, for which the accused may be convicted under the indictment, provided he is not convicted of the more serious offense. 27 Am J1st Indict § 105.

including. The present participle of "include," used in the sense of "inclusive of." A term of enlargement rather than limitation. Montello Salt Co. v Utah, 221 US 452, 464, 55 L Ed 810, 814, 31 S Ct 706.

See **include.**

Inclusio unius est exclusio alterius (in-klu'she-ō ū'ni-us est ex-klū'she-ō al-te'ri-us). The inclusion of one is the exclusion of the other. Ex parte Cox, 44 Fla 537, 33 So 509.

inclusive. Embracing; comprehensive; forming a part of.

See **include; including.**

inclusive deed (dēd). See **inclusive grant.**

inclusive grant. A term applied to a deed without exception of acreage excepted in the conveyance under which the grantor holds. Logan v Ward, 58 W Va 366, 52 SE 398.

inclusive survey. See **cadastral survey.**

incola (in'ko-la). An inhabitant; a person who dwells in a place.

incolae territorii (in'ko-lē ter-ri-tō'ri-ī). The inhabitants of the territory.

incolas domicilium facit (in'ko-lās do-mi-si'li-um fā'-sit). Residence makes the domicil. Arnold v United Ins. Co. (NY) 1 Johns Cas 363, 366.

incombustible. Incapable of being burned or consumed by fire, at least an ordinary fire. Sylvania v Hylton, 123 Ga 754, 51 SE 744.

income. A word having different meanings, dependent upon the connection in which it is used and the result intended to be accomplished. Equitable Trust Co. v Prentice, 250 NY 1, 164 NE 723, 63 ALR 263. For tax purposes, the gain derived from capital, from labor, or from both combined (Eisner v Macomber, 252 US 189, 64 L Ed 521, 40 S Ct 189, 9 ALR 1570), including profit gained through a sale or conversion of capital assets. Doyle Case, 247 US 183, 62 L Ed 1054, 38 S Ct 467. In reference to a life tenant, something produced by capital and severed from capital, leaving the property or principal intact. Rhode Island Hospital Trust Co. v Tucker, 51 RI 507, 155 A 661, 83 ALR 1253, mod on reh 52 RI 277, 160 A 465, 83 ALR 1259. Ordinarily, but not necessarily, cash or money; sometimes taking the form of property. United States v Siegel (CA8 Mo) 52 F2d 63, 78 ALR 672, cert den 284 US 679, 76 L Ed 574, 52 S Ct 140. In the usual signification, net, rather than gross, income. 33 Am J1st Life Est § 284. Profits earned rather than a fixed annuity. 4 Am J2d Annui § 3.

See **gross income; net income; ordinary income.**

income and revenues. That which will accrue to a municipality from all sources of its operations and employment of its taxing power, including delinquent taxes which are collectible. 38 Am J1st Mun Corp § 479.

income averaging. An elective method of computing income tax by an individual, not a corporation or trust, who has unusually large income in the current taxable year as compared with the four preceding years, whereby the taxpayer may elect to have the excess taxed, in effect, as if he had received it over five years instead of all in a single year. IRC §§ 1301, 1302, 1305.

income bearing. Productive of income. Re Briggs' Estate, 139 Cal App 2d 802, 294 P2d 478, 481.

income excise tax. See **income tax.**

income execution. Garnishment for the purpose of collecting a judgment out of income of the judgment debtor. 30 Am J2d Exec § 774.

income, rents, and profits. As the term appears in a will, deed, or trust instrument:—net income. 33 Am J1st Life Est § 285.

income tax. A tax based on income, gross or net. Powell v Gleason, 50 Ariz 542, 74 P2d 47, 114 ALR 838. Usually regarded as an excise rather than a property tax. Sims v Ahrens, 167 Ark 557, 271 SW 720; Miles v Department of Treasury, 209 Ind 172, 199 NE 372, 97 ALR 1474, 101 ALR 1359, app dismd 298 US 640, 80 L Ed 1372, 56 S Ct 750.

Income tax laws do not profess to embody perfect economic theory. They ignore some things that either a theorist or a businessman would take into account in determining the pecuniary condition of the taxpayer. Weiss v Wiener, 279 US 333, 73 L Ed 720, 49 S Ct 337.

income tax return. See **tax return.**

in commendam (in kom-men'dam). In trust.

In commodato haec pactio, ne dolus praestetur, rata non est (in kom-mo-dā'tō hēc pak'she-ō, nē do'lus prē-stē'ter, rā'ta non est). (Civil law.) In a commodatum, an agreement that fraud is not to be answered for is not valid.

Incommodum non solvit argumentum (in-kom'modum non sol'vit ar-gu-men'tum). An inconvenience does not settle an argument.

in common. Participating or sharing in ownership, use or enjoyment of anything. Land open to public use. 35 Am J2d Fen § 19.
See **estate in common.**

in communi (in kom-mū'nī). In common.

incommunication (in-kọ-mū-ni-kā'shọn). The confinement of a prisoner in such a manner as to prevent his seeing or conversing with other persons.

incompatibility. Conflicts in personalities and dispositions. As a ground for divorce:—conflicts in personalities and dispositions which are so deep as to be irreconcilable and irremediable, and which render it impossible for the parties to continue to live together in a normal marital relationship. Burch v Burch (CA3 Virgin Islands) 195 F2d 799. Such conflict of personalities as to destroy the legitimate ends of matrimony and the possibility of reconciliation. Wegener v Wegener (Okla) 365 P2d 728.
See **incompatible offices; incompatible things.**

incompatible. See **incompatibility; incompatible offices; incompatible things.**

incompatible offices. Public offices which cannot be held by one person at the same time. 42 Am J1st Pub Of § 70. Two public offices having respectively such duties and functions that the performance of the duties of the one will so interfere with the performance of the duties of the other that it will be impossible for the same incumbent to discharge the duties of both offices faithfully, impartially, and efficiently. Haymaker v State ex rel. McCain, 22 NM 400, 163 P 248; State ex rel. Metcalf v Goff, 15 RI 505, 9 A 226.

incompatible things. Things which cannot coexist without disturbance at the same time and place. Commonwealth v Staunton Mut. Tel. Co. 134 Va 291, 114 SE 600.

incompetence. See **incompetency.**

incompetency. Inefficiency; a lack of some requisite ability. Anno: 4 ALR3d 1095. Inadequacy or insufficiency, either physical or mental, as the incompetency of a child for hard labor or of an idiot for intellectual labor. Brandt v Godwin, 24 NYSE 305, 3 NYS 807, 811. Want of qualification or eligibility. Of public officer:—the absence of a physical, moral, or intellectual quality, incapacitating one to perform the duties of his office, characterized by gross neglect of duty or gross carelessness in the performance of duty, lack of judgment, and want of sound discretion. State ex rel.Hardie v Coleman, 115 Fla 119, 155 So 129, 92 ALR 988. Of a schoolteacher:—want of knowledge of the subject matter to be taught; inability to maintain discipline; physical mistreatment of pupils; even improper conduct outside of school. Anno: 4 ALR3d 1102, 1109, 1117. Of an employee:—want of ability suitable to the task, as regards natural qualities or experience, or deficiency of disposition to use one's ability and experience properly. 35 Am J1st M & S § 197. Of fellow servant:—want of ability suitable to the task with which the fellow employee is charged, either as regards natural ability or experience, or deficiency of disposition to use one's ability and experience properly; qualities and characteristics calculated to cause reasonable apprehension that the admission to the service or the retention therein of the incompetent will or may imperil the safety of other employees. Still v San Francisco & Northwestern Railway Co. 154 Cal 559, 98 P 672; 35 Am J1st M & S § 350.
See **mental incapacity; physically incapacitated.**

incompetency proceeding. A proceeding for the determination of the competency or incompetency of a person for the purpose of determining whether the state may or should assume jurisdiction over his person or property, or for the purpose merely of giving public notice of the existence of such status. 29 Am J Rev ed Ins Per §§ 9 et seq. A special action within the meaning of a statute providing for appeal from a final order made in a special action. State ex rel. McPherson v Rakey, 236 Iowa 876, 20 NW2d 43.

incompetent. See **incompetency; incompetent person.**

incompetent, irrelevant, and immaterial. A very general objection to the admissibility of evidence, usually held insufficient, when standing alone, for want of a statement of specific ground or reason. 53 Am J1st Trial § 138.

incompetent person. Literally and broadly, one lacking competency, physical or mental. Usually having reference in the law to an insane or feeble-minded person; a person lacking the mental capacity to make a contract or engage in business transactions. Sometimes inclusive of any one incapacitated for the making of a contract or the transaction of business, whether his incapacity arises from mental unsoundness or infancy. Walgreen Co. v Industrial Com. 323 Ill 194, 153 NE 831, 48 ALR 1199, 1202.
See **incompetency; spendthrift.**

incomplete dedication. A defective statutory dedication or an ineffectual attempt to make a statutory dedication, operating by way of estoppel when accepted by the public or when rights are acquired under it by third persons. Hooper v Haas, 332 Ill 561, 164 NE 23, 63 ALR 658.

incomplete gift. See **imperfect gift.**

incomplete possession. Literally, a possession of less than the whole or which lacks the quality of complete dominion. Technically, a possession of land involving a struggle with another claimant to maintain it or under such circumstances that such struggle appears imminent. 35 Am J2d Forc E & D § 18.

incomplete trust. See **executory trust.**

inconclusive. Not conclusive; subject to disproof; subject to rebuttal.

in confidence. In a confidential relationship; in secret and to be kept a secret.

in confinio comitatus (in kon-fi'ni-ō ko-mi-tā'tus). Within the boundary of the county.
It is said in Co. Litt. 154a that "for a common of pasture, of turbary, of pischary, of estovers and the like in one county, appendant or appurtenant to land in another county, in assize in confinio comitatus did lye at common law, and so it is of a nusans done in one county to lands lying in another county, the like assize did lye at common law." Worster v Winnipiseogee Lake Co. 25 NH 525, 532.

in confusum. See **mittere in confusum.**

In conjunctivis oportet utramque partem esse veram (in kon-junk-tī'vis o-por'tet u-tram'kwe par'tem es'se vē'ram). In conjunctives it is necessary that each part should be true.

in consequence of. As the result of; because of. Tierney v Occidental L. Ins. Co. 89 Cal App 779, 265 P 400.

in consequence of intoxication. A clause found in dram-shop or civil damage acts, meaning that intoxication was the proximate cause, or at least a contributory cause, of the injury for which recovery may be had under such statute. 30 Am J Rev ed Intox L § 541.

inconsequential error. An error occurring on trial which perpetrates no injustice and denies no substantial right. 39 Am J1st New Tr § 28.

in consideratione inde (in kon-si-de-rā-she-ō'ne in'de). In consideration thereof.

in consideratione legis (in kon-si-de-rā-she-ō'ne lē'jis). In consideration of law; in contemplation of law.

in consideratione praemissorum (in kon-si-de-rā-she-ō'ne prē-mis-sō'rum). In consideration of the premises.

In consimili casu, consimile debet esse remedium (in kon-si'mi-lī kā'sū, kon-si'mi-le de'bet es'se rē-mē'di-um). In a similar case, there ought to be a similar remedy.

inconsistency. Want of harmony or accord. The quality of being inconsistent. Want of harmony between two clauses of an instrument, as where there are conflicting descriptions in a deed of the property conveyed. 23 Am J2d Deeds § 237. Repugnancy in a pleading; an inconsistency between allegations such that one destroys the effect of the other. 41 Am J1st Pl § 47.

See **inconsistent counts**; **inconsistent defenses**; **repugnancy**.

inconsistent. Repugnant; not in harmony or accord. Contradictory of one another.

inconsistent counts. Causes of action pleaded which are repugnant to each other. 41 Am J1st Pl § 48.

inconsistent defenses. Defenses pleaded in an answer which disagree with one another. 41 Am J1st Pl § 48. Defenses which contradict each other or disprove each other, thus being mutually destructive. 41 Am J1st Pl § 163. Defenses which raise issues triable by different methods or by different courts. 41 Am J1st Pl § 163.

inconsistent offices. See **incompatible offices**.

inconsistent pleading. See **inconsistency**; **inconsistent counts**; **inconsistent defenses**.

inconsistent position. A position assumed in litigation directly contrary to one previously assumed by the party, constituting an estoppel in pais where he had, or was chargeable with, full knowledge of the facts and another will be prejudiced by his action. 28 Am J2d Estop § 68.

inconsistent remedies. For the purposes of the doctrine of election of remedies:—two or more co-existing remedies available to the litigant at the time of the election which are repugnant and inconsistent, 25 Am J2d Elect R § 10; not, in reality, an inconsistency between the remedies themselves, but an inconsistency between a certain state of facts relied on as the basis of a certain remedy and another certain state of facts relied on as the basis of another remedy. Brady v State Ins. Co. 100 Neb 497, 160 NW 882.

Remedies are inconsistent when the right to any of them necessarily yields or concedes the right to another. Crane v Atlanta & Lowry Nat. Bank, 40 Ga App 83, 49 SE 58.

inconsistent things. Things which are opposed to each other. Commonwealth v Staunton Mutual Tel. Co. 134 Va 291, 114 SE 600.

inconsistent verdict. A verdict which is self-contradictory, as where, on a charge of conspiracy, one of the two defendants is convicted and the other is acquitted. Sasser v United States (CA5 Ga) 29 F2d 76.

in conspectu ejus (in kon-spek'tū ē'jus). Within his view; in his sight.

In consuetudinibus, non diuturnitas temporis sed soliditas rationis est consideranda (in kon-sū-ē-tu-di'ni-bus, non dī-u-ter'ni-tās tem'po-ris sed so-li'di-tas rā-she-ō'nis est kon-si-de-ran'da). In customs or usages, not lapse of time, but the soundness of the reason for their existence should be considered.

inconsulto (in-kon-sul'tō). (Civil law.) Without being advised; inadvisedly; unintentionally.

in contemplation of bankruptcy. See **contemplation of bankruptcy**.

in contemplation of death. See **contemplation of death**.

in contemplation of insolvency. See **contemplation of insolvency**.

in contempt. The status of a person who has committed a contempt of court and who has not expiated his offense.

incontestability provision. A provision in a life insurance policy to the effect that the policy shall be incontestable from date or incontestable after a specified period, sometimes subject to express reservation of enumerated specific circumstances under which the provision shall not be operative, the effect of such a provision being to preclude the insurer from contesting the validity of the contract as such, the truthfulness of the answers to questions propounded to the applicant, and other matters ordinarily constituting defenses, such preclusion, of course, being subject to the terms of the provision and the reservations contained therein. 29A Am J Rev ed Ins §§ 1107 et seq.

incontestable clause. See **incontestability provision**.

incontinent. Want of restraint, especially in sexual activity. 33 Am J1st L & S §§ 35 et seq.

incontinenti (in-kon-ti-nen'tī). Immediately; at once.

In contractibus, benigna, in testamentis, benignior, in restitutionibus, benignissima interpretatio facienda est (in kon-trak'ti-bus, be-nig'na, in tes-ta-men'tis, be-nig'ni-or, in res-ti-tu-she-ō'ni-bus, be-nig-nis'si-ma in-ter-pre-tā'she-ō fā-she-en'da est). In contracts, a liberal, in wills, a more liberal, and in restitutions, a most liberal construction should be adopted.

In contractibus, rei veritas potius quam scriptura perspici debet (in kon-trak'ti-bus, rē'ī vē'ri-tās po'she-us quam skrip-tū'ra per'spi-sī de'bet). In contracts, the truth of the matter ought to be regarded as of more consequence than the writing.

In contractibus, tacite insunt quae sunt moris et consuetudinis (in kon-trak'ti-bus, ta'si-tē in'sunt kwē sunt mō'ris et kon-su-ē-tū'di-nis). In contracts, matters of custom and usage are tacitly implied.

In contrahenda venditione, ambiguum pactum contra venditorem interpretandum est (in kon-tra-hen'da ven-di-she-ō'ne, am-bi'gu-um pak'tum kon'tra ven-di-tō'rem in-ter-pre-tan'dum est). In the negotiation of a sale, an ambiguous clause is to be interpreted or construed against the vendor.

in control of a motor vehicle. In control of the movement of a motor vehicle, whether by application of the power of the motor or by steering the vehicle while it is being towed or pushed by another vehicle. Anno: 47 ALR2d 585, § 5 [c].

incontrovertible. So clear and certain as not to admit of dispute. McCreary v Skinner, 75 Iowa 412, 413.

inconvenience. Disquiet; uneasiness; annoyance; trouble. Jenson v Chicago, St. Paul, Minneapolis & Omaha R. Co. 86 Wis 589, 57 NW 359.

inconvenience of legal remedy. Vexatious irritation, annoyance, or embarrassment consequent on a recourse to a court of law. Cook v Carpenter, 212 Pa 165, 61 A 799.

inconveniences of trial. Difficulties and burdens in transporting witnesses, taking depositions, transporting books and documents, employing local counsel, expenditures of time by the parties and the loss of time of their employees, the necessity of proving foreign law, and the possibility of the necessity of trial in another jurisdiction. 28 Am J Rev ed Inj § 224.

inconvenient forum. The doctrine that where the plaintiff could have brought the action in a court other than that in which he instituted the suit, in other words had a choice of forum, the court may, in the exercise of sound discretion, decline to assume or exercise jurisdiction of the case brought before it by the plaintiff, if it believes that the case may more conveniently, yet justly, proceed in another court before which the plaintiff may bring it after refusal of the exercise of jurisdiction by the court in which the action was first brought. 20 Am J2d Cts § 173.

inconvenienti. See **ab inconvenienti.**

In conventionibus contrahentium voluntas potius quam verba spectari placuit (in kon-ven-she-ō'ni-bus kon-tra-hen'she-um vo-lun'tās po'she-us quam ver'ba spek-tā'rī pla'ku-it). In contracts, it is well to regard the intention of the parties rather than their mere words. Jackson ex dem. Craigie v Wilkinson (NY) 17 Johns 146, 150.

Incorporalia bello non adquiruntur (in-kor-po-rā'li-a bel'lō non ad-qui-run'ter). Incorporeal things are not acquired in war.

incorporalis (in-kor-po-rā'lis). Same as **incorporeal.**

incorporamus (in-kor-po-rā'mus). We incorporate. A formal word employed in the king's grant of a corporation charter. See 1 Bl Comm 473.

incorporate. To combine in one unit. To form a corporation.
See **incorporation.**

incorporated. Combined with something else. Made or formed as a corporation.
While the usual meaning of the term, as applied to an association of persons, imports that they have formed a corporation, as the word is used in a statute providing that every corporation, joint-stock company or association "incorporated" under the laws of the state shall pay a specified tax, "incorporated" is not to be taken in a technical or restricted meaning and confined to an association brought into being according to the formality of a statute, but as including any combination of individuals upon terms which embody or adopt as rules or regulations of business the enabling provisions of the statutes. People, ex rel Platt v Wemple, 117 NY 136, 22 NE 1046.

incorporated company. A business or stock corporation, as distinguished from a charitable, religious, literary, or membership corporation. Catlin v Trinity College, 113 NY 133, 20 NE 864.

incorporated territory. A territory incorporated into the United States so as to be a part thereof. 49 Am J1st States § 4. Territory included in the incorporation of a municipality or added later to the municipality.

incorporating state. The state wherein a corporation was created by law and became an entity. 36 Am J2d For Corp § 85.

incorporation. The creation of a corporation whether directly by special legislative act, or by compliance with general laws. 18 Am J2d Corp §§ 24 et seq. An incorporated company; a corporation. The combining of one thing with another. The addition of a material to a building or other structure. 36 Am J1st Mech L § 72.

incorporation by reference. The doctrine that a will, duly executed and witnessed according to statutory requirements, may incorporate into itself by an appropriate reference a written paper or document which is in existence at the time of the execution of the will, irrespective of whether such document is one executed by the testator or a third person, whether it is executed and attested as a will, or whether it is in and of itself a valid instrument, provided the document referred to is identified by clear and satisfactory proof. 57 Am J1st Wills § 233. The permissible practice of referring to, and thereby making a part of one count or defense, the whole or a part of the allegations of another count or defense in the same pleading. 41 Am J1st Pl § 58. Making a map, plat, or writing a part of a deed by reference thereto in the deed, particularly for the purpose of furnishing a description of the property conveyed. 23 Am J2d Deeds § 232. Making prior certificates in an abstract of title a part of the last certificate by a reference in the latter. 1 Am J2d Abstr T § 20. Making a separation agreement a part of decree of divorce by reference thereto in the decree. 24 Am J2d Div & S § 907. Making an extraneous writing a part of a written contract by reference thereto in the contract in terms of making it a part of the contract. 17 Am J2d Contr § 263.

incorporation fees. Fees the payment of which is required by the constitutions and statutes of many states as a prerequisite to the exercise of corporate powers. 18 Am J2d Corp § 41.

incorporation under general laws. The usual method of incorporation, calling for compliance with statutes imposing requirements generally relative to the formation of a corporation and the exercise of powers thereby. 18 Am J2d Corp §§ 23 et seq.

incorporation under special laws. Acquiring corporate status under a special act conferring upon designated persons and their associates the right to be a corporation and exercise corporate powers. 18 Am J2d Corp § 26.

incorporator. Same as **corporator.**

in corpore (in kor'po-re). In body; in substance.

incorporeal. Having no body or substance; intangible; without physical existence.

incorporeal chattel. Same as **chose in action.**

incorporeal hereditament. A right without the substance of a body but issuing out of a substance of real or personal property, such as rent issuing out of land, and capable of being inherited. 42 Am J1st Prop § 17.

incorporeal property. Property that has no corporeal tangible substance. Transcontinental Oil Co. v Emmerson, 298 Ill 394, 131 NE 645, 16 ALR 507. Intangibles without the substance of a body, but sometimes issuing out of corporeal property, which the law gives effect to as property by attaching to them certain sanctions enforceable in the courts. Curry v McCanless, 307 US 357, 83 L Ed 1339, 59 S Ct 900, 123 ALR 162.
See **chose in action; intangible; intangible property.**

incorrigibility. See **incorrigible child.**

incorrigible child. A child unmanageable by parents or guardians. Annos: 45 ALR 1533, 85 ALR 1099. A child incapable of being corrected or reformed in his present situation and under his present control. Re Hook, 95 Vt 497, 115 A 730, 19 ALR 610, 615.
See **delinquent children.**

in course of employment. See **in the course of employment.**

in court. Literally, one's presence during a session of court. Having appeared in an action in which named as a party. Having been subjected to service of legal process, so as to be bound by the proceedings in court.
See **day in court.**

in crastino (in krăs'ti-nō). On the morrow; tomorrow.

in crastino animarum (in kras'ti-nō a-ni-mā'rum). On the morrow of all souls; a return day for writs in Michaelmas term at Westminster. See 1 Bl Comm 342.

increase. Verb: Deriving from the Latin "crescere"; to grow. To augment in size or in value. Anno: 32 ALR 854. Noun: Growth or augmentation; amount of growth.
See **accession; accretion; increase of livestock.**

increase and fix. A term found in statutes involving the salary of a public officer or employee; importing stability, not the power to decrease compensation. Cochnower v United States, 248 US 405, 63 L Ed 328, 39 S Ct 137.

increase of capital. An increase in the stated capital of a corporation the same involving a fundamental change in the corporation, and authorized only where the power to increase is expressly conferred by law. 18 Am J2d Corp § 226.

increase of hazard. Same as **increase of risk.**

increase of livestock. A term familiar in chattel mortgages covering livestock, particularly cattle. That which is added to the original stock by augmentation, or growth; produce; profit; interest; progeny; issue; offspring. Stockyards Loan Co. v Nichols (CA8 Okla) 243 F 511, 1 ALR 547, 551. Ordinarily, not inclusive of the wool grown on sheep. 15 Am J2d Chat Mtg § 68.

increase of risk. Something which increases the probability of the occurrence of the loss insured against under the terms of an insurance policy. Some alteration in or change in the situation or condition of the property insured which tends to increase the risk—something of duration, and not a casual change of a temporary character. Angier v Western Assur. Co. 10 SD 82, 71 NW 761.

increase of shares. See **increase of capital; natural increase of shares.**

increment. Increase; gain. The amount of increase or growth.

incrementa (in-kre-men'ta). Increments; increases.

incrementum (in-kre-men'tum). Increment; increase.

increscitur. (Latin.) The act of the appellate court in increasing the amount of damages awarded by the verdict, the defendant being put to the choice of accepting the increased verdict or having a new trial. 5 Am J2d A & E § 946.

In criminalibus, probationes debent esse luce clariores (in kri-mi-na'li-bus, pro-bā-she-ō'nēz de'bent es'se lū'se kla-ri-ō'rēz). In criminal cases, the proofs ought to be clearer than light.

In criminalibus, sufficit generalis malitia intentionis, cum facto paris gradus (in kri-mi-na'li-bus, suf'fi-sit ge-ne-rā'lis ma-li'she-a in-ten-she-ō'nis, kum fak'tō pa'ris grā'dus). In crimes, general malicious intent accompanied by an act of equal degree is sufficient. Isham v State, 38 Ala 213, 220.

In criminalibus, voluntas reputabitur pro facto (in kri-mi-nā'li-bus, vo-lun'tās rē-pu-tā'bi-ter prō fak'-tō). In criminal cases, the will will be taken for the deed.

incriminate. To charge with a crime. Davis v State, 51 Neb 301, 323, 70 NW 984. To make it appear that one is guilty of a crime.

incriminating circumstance. A circumstance which tends to show that a crime has been committed, or that some particular person committed it. Davis v State, 51 Neb 301, 323, 70 NW 984.

incriminating statement. An accusation in the presence of the accused. A statement by the accused which involves him in the crime charged.
See **self-incrimination.**

incrimination. The act of accusing or charging with the commission of a crime or of making it appear that one is guilty of a crime. Rendering a person liable to a criminal prosecution, as by giving or furnishing evidence against him. Counselman v Hitchcock, 142 US 547, 35 L Ed 1110, 12 S Ct 195.

incrimination of self. See **self-incrimination.**

incroachment. Same as **encroachment.**

In cujus rei testimonium (in kū'jus rē'ī tes-ti-mō'nium). In witness of which transaction; in witness whereof.

In cujus rei testimonium huic chartae (vel scripto) nostra sigilla apposuimus (in kū'jus rē'ī tes-ti-mō'nium hu'ik kar'te (vel skrip'tō) nos'tra si-jil'la ap-po-su'i-mus). In witness whereof we have set our seals to this charter (or writing).

inculpate. To incriminate; to accuse a person of crime or fault.

inculpatory. Incriminatory; accusing.

incumbent. One who holds an office, particularly one who holds it under legal authority to discharge the duties of the office. State v McCollister, 11 Ohio St 46, 50.

incumber. Same as **encumber.**

incumbrance. Same as **encumbrance.**

incumbrancer. Same as **encumbrancer.**

incur. To bring upon one's self. To become subject to liability by act or by operation of law. Maryland Casualty Co. v Martin (Tex Civ App) 289 SW2d 655.

incurable. Not curable; beyond the power and skill of medicine. Not susceptible of cure; applied to both patients and disease. Freeman v State Board of Medical Examiners, 54 Okla 531, 154 P 56.

incurable disease. A disease which is incurable according to the general state of knowledge of the medical profession at the time in question. Freeman v State Board of Medical Examiners, 54 Okla 531, 154 P 56.

in curia (in kū'ri-a). In court.

incuria (in-kū'ri-a). Negligence; carelessness; absence of care.

incuria dans locum injuriae (in-kū'ri-a dān lō'kum in-jū'ri-i). Negligence at the place or locality of the injury. Thomas v Quartermaine, L. R. (Eng) 18 QBD 685.

In curia domini regis, ipse in propria persona jura decernit (in kū'ri-a do'mi-nī rē'jis, ip'se in prō'pri-a per-sō'na jū'ra dē-ser'nit). In the king's court, the king himself in person, decides the cases.

incurramentum (in-ker-ra-men'tum). Liability to fine or amercement.

incurred. See **incur.**

in currency. In any kind of money in circulation and constituting legal tender. 40 Am J1st Paym § 58.

in current funds. In funds equal in value to the current coin of the country, such as is received and paid on debts, in the purchase of property, and in ordinary business transactions, at par, and without discount. 40 Am J1st Paym § 58.

in custodia legis (in kus-tō'di-ạ lē'jis). See **custodia legis; custody of the law.**

in custody. In jail or prison. Under the direct or indirect restraint of an officer of the law armed with authority to restrain.
A prisoner who is at large on bail is not in custody, but, although a prisoner to whom a parole has been granted is permitted to go and remain at large under the supervision of the court, he is held to be in custody. Carpenter v Lord, 88 Or 128, 171 P 577.

in damno (in dam'nō). In damage; doing damage.

inde (in'dē). Thence; from there; from that place; from thence; then; thereupon; from that time.

indebitatus (in-de-bi-tā'tus). Indebted.

indebitatus assumpsit (in-de-bi-tā'tus as-sump'sit). Being indebted, he undertook. A common-law form of action. In its specific sense, that form of assumpsit which is available for the recovery of any simple common-law debt without regard to any express promise to pay the debt; in its enlarged sense, a remedy embracing all cases in which the plaintiff has equity and conscience on his side and the defendant is bound by ties of natural justice and equity to pay the money, even being applied to all the common counts, namely the quantum counts, the money counts, and the count upon an account stated. 1 Am J2d Actions § 13.

indebitatus nunquam (in-de-bi-tā'tus nun'quam). Never indebted.

indebiti solutio (in-de'bi-tī so-lu'she-ō). An undue payment, that is, the payment of that which is not due or owing.

indebitum (in-de'bi-tum). Not due; not owing.

indebitus (in-de'bi-tus). Not owed; not due.

indebted. Obligated to make a payment for money, property, or services. Obligated upon a debt, although not necessarily a debt due.
As the word appears in a statute prescribing the contents of an affidavit for attachment, to say that a "debt" is due means that it is presently owing and due; to state that a defendant "is indebted" is not the equivalent of saying that he owes a debt which is due. 6 Am J2d Attach § 264.
See **debt; deeply indebted; mutually indebted.**

indebtedness. The aggregate of a person's debts. A single debt. The state of being obligated upon a debt or debts. For the purpose of deducting interest in computing net income for tax purposes:—an unconditional obligation. Gilman v Commissioner (CA8) 53 F2d 47, 80 ALR 209; Johnson v Commissioner (CA8) 108 F2d 104.
The term in former constitutional or statutory provisions imposing personal or superadded liability upon stockholders of a corporation was said not to include a claim for unliquidated damages. 19 Am J2d Corp § 779. As the word appears in a constitutional provision limiting the amount of indebtedness of a municipal corporation:—every obligation contracted for which there is no present means of payment. 38 Am J1st Mun Corp § 410.
Tax liabilities have frequently been held included in agreement for assumption or payment of another's indebtedness. Anno: 4 ALR2d 1315.
See **bonded indebtedness; debt; involuntary indebtedness.**

indebtedness of decedent. For the purpose of a deduction from the estate in determining an estate or inheritance tax; debts of the decedent allowed in the administration proceeding, not including expenses of administration. 28 Am J Rev ed Inher T § 387.
See **claim against decedent's estate.**

indecency. A state of being indecent, some forms being punishable as criminal offenses. 33 Am J1st Lewd etc. § 3.
See **indecent.**

indecent. Lewd, lascivious, obscene, grossly vulgar, unbecoming, unseemly, unfit to be seen or heard, or violating the proprieties of language or behavior. 33 Am J1st Lewd etc § 3. Not decent; unfit to be seen or heard. United States v Bebout (DC Ohio) 28 F 522, 524. The characterization of an act which is a violation of modesty or an offense to delicacy, such as an exhibition of obscene pictures or the exhibition of one's naked body in public. Timmons v United States (CA6 Ohio) 85 F 204, 205; McJunkins v State, 10 Ind 140, 144.
See **indecency.**

indecent assault. The act of a man in taking indecent liberties with the person of a female, such as fondling her in a lewd and lascivious manner. 6 Am J2d Asslt & B § 41. An indecent proposal followed by actual or attempted physical contact. Lynch v Commonwealth, 131 Va 762, 109 SE 427. The act of a man in taking indecent liberties with another man. 6 Am J2d Asslt & B § 42. Taking indecent liberties with the person of a child. Tidd v Skinner, 225 NY 422, 122 NE 247, 3 ALR 1145.
See **indecent proposal.**

indecent exposure. An exposure of the person in such manner and at such time and place as to offend against public decency, occurring by intent or by recklessness from which an intent may be inferred.

Anno: 93 ALR 998. Exposing another person in an indecent or compromising attitude. 33 Am J1st Lewd etc § 6.

An indecent exposure of the person committed once does not constitute the common-law offense of committing or maintaining a public nuisance, but the latter offense is committed by continuous and repeated exposures on the public streets thereby creating a more or less existing condition prejudicial to the sense of decency. Nuchols v Commonwealth, 312 Ky 171, 226 SW2d 796, 13 ALR2d 1478.

indecent gesture. A movement of the body or some portion of the body in a manner which is obscene or suggestive of obscenity. A method of interrupting and disturbing a public meeting or assembly. 24 Am J2d Disturb M § 5.

indecent language. Language which is obscene, profane, or shocking to the moral sense.

indecent proposal. A proposal made directly or indirectly for unlawful or improper sexual relations. Barbknecht v Great Northern R. Co. 55 ND 104, 212 NW 776.

indecimable (in-des′i-mạ-bl). Non-titheable; not liable to the payment of tithes.

Inde datae leges ne fortior omnia posset (in′de dā′tē lē′jēz nē for′she-or om′ni-a pos′set). Laws were made lest the stronger might become all powerful.

in deed. In fact.
See **possession in deed.**

indefeasible. Not to be defeated or avoided.

indefeasibly vested. Vested and not subject to divestiture. Keepers v Fidelity Title & D. Co. 56 NJL 302, 28 A 585.

indefensus (in-dē-fen′sus). Not defended; not denied; a defendant who does not plead.

indefinite award. An award of arbitrators which leaves open the possibility or probability of future disputes and litigation. 5 Am J2d Arb & A § 151.

indefinite contract. A term appearing in some teachers' tenure statutes; the right of a permanent teacher upon the expiration of his or her contract, such being a protected contractual right entitling the teacher to a succession of definite contracts having terms in accord with and meeting the requirements of other statutes governing teachers' contracts. Lost Creek School Twp. v York, 215 Ind 636, 21 NE2d 58.

indefinite failure of issue. A failure of issue whenever it shall happen, sooner or later, without any definite period within which it must happen. Downing v Wherrin, 19 NH 9. A period when the issue or descendants of the first taker become extinct and when there is no longer any issue of the issue of the grantee, without reference to any particular time or any particular event. 28 Am J2d Est § 363. Death without issue of the last descendant of the devisee. 57 Am J1st Wills § 1238.
See **die without issue.**

indefinite imprisonment. The punishment of imprisonment prescribed by a sentence for crime, the term of which is fixed or rendered calculable by neither the sentence nor statute. 21 Am J2d Crim L § 534.

A sentence prescribing imprisonment until a fine, the amount of which is specified, is paid, does not prescribe an indefinite imprisonment, because, under it, there need be no imprisonment at all. Ex Parte Bryant, 24 Fla 278, 4 S 854.
See **indeterminate sentence.**

indefiniteness. The quality of not being sufficiently specific.

indefiniteness of pleading. Want of certainty of allegation, a defect constituting a ground of attack upon the pleading by motion or demurrer in accordance with the practice of the jurisdiction. 41 Am J1st Pl §§ 30 et seq.

indefinite sentence. See **indefinite imprisonment; indeterminate sentence.**

Indefinitum aequipollet universali (in-dē-fī-nī′tum ē-qui-pol′let ū-ni-ver-sā′lī). That which is unlimited is equivalent to the whole.

Indefinitum supplet locum universalis (in-dē-fī-nī′tum sup′plet lō′kum ū-ni-ver-sā′lis). The undefined supplies the place of the whole.

indelicacy. Want of tact, good taste, or good manners, but not necessarily immorality. 33 Am J1st L & S § 46.

in delicto (in dē-lik′tō). In fault; in the wrong. In the wrong, although not in equal wrong with the other party. 37 Am J2d Fraud § 304.
See **in pari delicto.**

indemnatus (in-dem-nā′tus). Uncondemned.

indemnification. The act of indemnifying; being indemnified. Payment made by way of compensation for a loss suffered.
See **indemnify; indemnity.**

indemnificatus (in-dem-ni-fi-kā′tus). Indemnified.

indemnify. To save harmless; to secure against future loss or damage; to give indemnity. To recompense for a past loss. 27 Am J1st Indem § 2.
See **indemnity.**

indemnify and save harmless. See **to indemnify and save harmless.**

indemnifying bond. See **indemnity bond.**

indemnis (in-dem′nis). Undamaged; unharmed; harmless.

indemnitee. One for whose benefit a contract of indemnity is made; one whom another is under obligation to indemnify.

indemnities. In common usage, the plural of **indemnity.** A technical term of the grain market or board of trade.

For many years prior to August 24, 1921, members of grain exchanges bought and sold in large quantities agreements for contracts for purchase or sale of grain subject to acceptance within a definite time thereafter, commonly known as "indemnities." When the holder of one of these elected to exercise his rights, the specified amount of grain was bought and sold on the exchange indicated for future delivery, and the agreement was thus finally consummated. By far the larger percentage of such agreements were subject to acceptance during the following day at a price ordinarily within one fourth of a cent of the price prevailing when the market closed on the day of the agreement. During many years the uniform consideration paid was one dollar per thousand bushels. Trusler v Crooks, 269 US 475, 481, 70 L Ed 365, 367, 46 S Ct 165.

indemnitor. One who indemnifies another; one upon whom there rests an obligation to indemnify or save another from a legal consequence of the conduct of one of the parties to the obligation or of some other person. 27 Am J1st Indem § 2.

indemnity. A term inclusive of two primary concepts: (1) compensation in money or property for a loss suffered; (2) a contract to save another from the legal consequences of the conduct of one of the parties or of a third person. Also inclusive in a proper sense of the security by way of deposit or bond furnished for the performance of an undertaking to save another harmless. Builders Supply Co. v McCabe, 366 Pa 322, 77 A2d 368, 24 ALR2d 319; 27 Am J1st Indem § 2. An obligation or duty resting on one person to make good any loss or damage another has incurred while acting at the request of the former or for his benefit. 27 Am J1st Indem § 2. The right of one who has been compelled to pay that which another person should have paid. Security to protect against loss in assuming a status such as that of a guarantor or surety. From the standpoint of an insurance contract:—the stipulated desideratum to be paid to the insured in case he suffers loss or damage through the risk specified and covered by the contract. Physicians' Defense Co. v Cooper (CA9 Cal) 199 F 576.

indemnity and guaranty. Two distinct undertakings, in that a guaranty is a collateral undertaking, and presupposes some contract or transaction to which it is collateral, while an indemnity is essentially an original contract. Anderson v Spence, 72 Ind 315.

indemnity belt. The designated strip or belt of land from which indemnity lands may be selected. Elling v Thexton, 7 Mont 330, 338, 16 P 931, 933.
See **indemnity lands.**

indemnity bond. A bond to indemnify the obligee or indemnitee against loss from the conduct of the obligor or indemnitor or from the conduct of a third person. 12 Am J2d Bonds § 1. A bond, the condition of which is the indemnification of the obligee against loss from the incurrence of liability from an act, for example a bond indemnifying a sheriff in seizing and holding property claimed by a person other than the defendant under the process with which the sheriff is armed. 30 Am J2d Exec § 752.

Where the legislature in licensing occupational groups, requires a bond as a part of the general scheme of protection of the public, the bond is an indemnity rather than a penal bond. Anchor Casualty Co. v Commissioner of Securities, 259 Minn 277, 107 NW2d 234.

indemnity contract. A contract whereby one agrees to save another from the legal consequence of the conduct of one of the parties or of some other person. 27 Am J1st Indem § 2.
See **indemnity; indemnity bond.**

indemnity for damage to the person. Compensation for everything then on, about, or belonging to the person, as well as for all bodily injuries which are proved to be the result of the accident. Woodman v Nottingham, 49 NH 387.

indemnity insurance. Insurance under a policy providing indemnification for actual loss or damage suffered by the insured (Shealey v American Health Ins. Corp. 220 SC 79, 66 SE2d 461, 27 ALR2d 942) as distinguished from insurance, particularly insurance under a policy covering a life, which provides for the payment of a specified sum upon the occurrence of the event insured against without reference to what the actual loss or damage arising from the event may be. 29 Am J Rev ed Ins § 4. A policy of insurance protecting the insured against loss due to injuring the property or person of a third person, under which the insurer does not become liable to the insured until the latter has sustained an actual loss in the discharge of liability to the third person, being distinguished in this respect from a liability policy under which the liability of the insurer attaches when the liability of the insured attaches, notwithstanding the insured has not sustained a loss in payment, voluntary or involuntary, made to the third person. 7 Am J2d Auto Ins § 81; 29A Am J Rev ed Ins § 1343.

indemnity lands. Lands which, by statute, are allowed to be selected by the grantee under a grant in aid of railroad construction, in lieu of parcels lost from the designated or granted lands by previous disposition or reservation. 42 Am J1st Pub L § 49.
See **indemnity belt.**

indemnity mortgage. A mortgage executed to indemnify the mortgagee against future loss.
A mortgage given to secure future advances which may be made by the mortgagee to the mortgagor is such a mortgage. Lawrence v Tucker (US) 23 How 14, 16 L Ed 474.

indemnity policy. See **indemnity insurance.**

indemnity provision. A provision in a building or construction contract or subcontract whereby the contractor or subcontractor, as indemnitor, agrees to indemnify or hold harmless the owner or principal contractor, as the case may be, for injuries resulting from the indemnitor's own negligence. 13 Am J2d Bldg Contr § 141.

indempnis (in-demp'nis). Same as **indemnis.**

indenization (in-den-i-zā'shọn). Same as **denization.**

indent (in-dent'). To prepare a deed or an agreement in the form of an indenture. To enter into articles of apprenticeship.
See **indenture.**

indented deed. See **indenture.**

indenture. In modern sense, a deed executed by both grantor and grantee or all parties to the instrument. The term derives from an old practice of actually "indenting" the deed executed by both grantor and grantee or all parties to the instrument. Sterling v Park, 129 Ga 309, 58 SE 828. Anciently, deeds of indenture were deeds which were made in two parts formed by cutting or tearing a single sheet across the middle in a jagged or indented line, so that the two parts might be subsequently matched, and they were executed by both grantor and grantee. Later the indenting was discontinued, yet the term came to be applied to all deeds which were executed by both parties. See 2 Bl Comm 295.

indenture of apprenticeship. A contract executed in duplicate by which an apprentice becomes bound to the service of a master.
See **apprentice; articles of apprenticeship.**

indenture of fine. The indenture of the foot of a fine.
The fifth step, or concluding part, of a fine for the alienation of land included the whole proceeding, reciting the parties, day, year, and place, and before whom the fine was levied or acknowledged. Indentures of this were made, or engrossed at the chirographer's office, and delivered to the cognizor or cognizee; usually beginning, "haec est finalis concordia," this is the final agreement, and then reciting the whole proceeding at length. See 2 Bl Comm 351.

indenture of trust. See **trust indenture.**

indenture trustee. The trustee named in an indenture which creates a trust.

independence. The state of being free from the control of another. The state of a country free from and unfettered by control exercised by another nation.
See **Declaration of Independence.**

Independence Day. July Fourth, a national holiday of the United States in celebration of the adoption of the Declaration of Independence on July Fourth, 1776.

independent advice. As a statutory condition precedent to the validity of a legacy or devise to a person in a fiduciary or confidential relationship toward the testator:—advice given to the testator by one with whom the testator had a full and private conference respecting such legacy or devise before the preparation and execution of the will, who was not only competent to inform him correctly as to its legal effect, but who was, furthermore, so disassociated with the interests of the legatee or devisee as to be in a position to advise with the testator impartially and confidentially as to the consequences to himself of his proposed benefaction. Post v Hagan, 71 NJ Eq 234, 65 A 1026.

independent adjuster. An adjuster of claims against insurance companies, who usually represents the company, although, at times, the insured, occupying in neither instance the status of a regular employee of his principal.

independent candidate. A candidate for public office, entitled by virtue of having been legally nominated to have his name on the ballot, but who is not the nominee of any existing political party. Stanfield v Kozer, 119 Or 324, 249 P 631.

independent condition. A condition in a contract which can be enforced without showing the performance of any other condition. 17 Am J2d Contr § 322.

independent consideration. A consideration furnished a guarantor other than that furnished the principal debtor. 24 Am J1st Guar § 49.

independent contract. A contract, the enforcement of which does not depend upon the performance of any other contract. The engagement made by an independent contractor for the performance of services.
See **independent contractor.**

independent contractor. One who, exercising independence in respect of his choice of work to be performed by him, contracts to do or perform certain work for another person according to his own means and methods, without being subject to the control of such other person except as to the product or result of the work. NLRB v Steinberg (CA5) 182 F2d 850; United States Fidelity & G. Co. v Spring Brook, 135 Conn 294, 64 A2d 39, 13 ALR2d 769; Hammond v El Dorado Springs, 362 Mo 530, 242 SW2d 479, 31 ALR2d 1367; Gomillion v Forsythe, 218 SC 211, 62 SE2d 297, 53 ALR2d 169; Hanks v Landert, 37 Wash 2d 293, 223 P2d 443, 30 ALR2d 1012. Not a "laborer" for the purposes of a statutory exemption. 31 Am J2d Exemp § 20.

The principal test in determining whether one rendering services for another is an independent contractor is whether the employer has the right to control the details of the work, although the place of the work, the time of the employment, the method of payment, and the right of summary discharge, are also to be considered. Huebner v Industrial Com. 234 Wis 239, 290 NW 145, 126 ALR 1113.

independent covenant. A covenant which relates to only a part of the consideration upon both sides of a contract or deed, is of such nature that a breach may be compensated in damages, and for the breach of which an action may be maintained without an averment by the plaintiff of performance or an offer to perform on his part. 20 Am J2d Cov § 8; 55 Am J1st V & P § 102.
See **independent promises.**

Independenter se habet assecuratio a viaggio navis (in-de-pen-den′ter sē hā′bet as-sē-kū-rā′she-ō ā vi-ā′ji-ō nā′vis). Insurance of the voyage is independent of the voyage of the ship.
"If a ship sails on a voyage from Saint Malo to Toulon, and is insured from Saint Malo to Cadiz, the latter is the voyage insured, but the former is the voyage of the ship." See 3 Kent Comm 318, footnote.

independent executor. The executor named to execute a will without administration in the probate court, thus avoiding the usual costs of regular administration. 21 Am J2d Ex & Ad § 824.

independent fires. Fires started by different causes, as where one is traceable to a person and the other attributable to some unknown or irresponsible origin. 35 Am J2d Fires § 40.

independent intervening cause. A cause which operates in succession to and independent of a prior wrong as a proximate cause of an injury. Ft. Worth & D. C. R. Co. v Smithers (Tex Civ App) 228 SW 637.

independently engaged. For the purposes of an exception to a provision for unemployment compensation, a business or trade established and conducted independently of an employer. Fuller Brush Co. v Industrial Com. 99 Utah 97, 104 P2d 201, 129 ALR 511.

independent promises. The mutual promises of the parties to a contract so plainly independent of each other that the one can never by fair construction be a condition of the performance of the other. 17 Am J2d Contr § 322.

Courts will not and ought not to construe promises as independent unless no other construction is possible and such construction appears to have been the deliberate intention of the parties at the time the instrument was executed. Palmer v Fox, 274 Mich 252, 264 NW 361, 104 ALR 1057; Summer v Fabregas, 52 NJ Super 399, 145 A2d 659.
See **independent covenant.**

independent school district. A school district which has not been consolidated with any other school district. See Harp v Consolidated School Dist. 115 Okla 48, 241 P 787. A school district whose affairs are administered independently of a school township, ordinarily conterminous with, or located in, a city or village.

independent stipulation. See **independent covenant; independent promises.**

independent tortfeasors. Tortfeasors who injured the same person or the same property but who acted without common design or concert of action and in the absence of any circumstance, such as common duty, joint enterprise, or relationship, which would make them joint tortfeasors. Husky Refining Co. v Barnes (CA9 Idaho) 119 F2d 715.

inde petit judicium. See **et inde petit judicium.**

inde producit sectam. See **et inde producit sectam.**

in descendu (in de-sen′dū). By descent.

indeterminate. Uncertain; not ascertained; not fixed; not made certain.

indeterminate damages. A little-used and unsatisfactory term for punitive or exemplary damages.

indeterminate permit. A kind of franchise granted public service corporations, provided for by statute in some jurisdictions, to continue in force until such time as the municipality shall exercise its option to purchase as provided by the statute. Superior Water, Light & Power Co. v Superior, 263 US 125, 132, 68 L Ed 204, 209, 44 S Ct 82.

indeterminate sentence. A sentence imposed for a crime, not for a precise period of time, but in terms of a minimum period and a maximum period of imprisonment as provided by statute for the particular offense. 21 Am J2d Crim L § 540.

index. Titles or subjects with lines thereunder in brief form suggestive of subject matter, all in alphabetical order, and so prepared and arranged as to point out the page, or volume and page in case of a multi-volume work, where the discussion of a particular point or bit of subject matter may be found.

Index animi sermo (in′dex a′ni-mī ser′mō). Speech is the index of the mind.

Where a law is plain and unambiguous whether it is expressed in general or limited terms, the legislature should be understood to mean what they have plainly expressed, and consequently no room is left for construction. Where the intention is clearly ascertained, the courts have no other duty to perform than to execute the legislative will, without any regard to their own views as to the wisdom or justice of the particular enactment. Shellenberger v Ransom, 41 Neb 631, 59 NW 935.

index on appeal. See **index to transcript of record.**

index to judgments. See **judgment index.**

index to records of title. An index of instruments of title recorded or filed in the office of clerk of court, registrar of titles, or county recorder, usually under the names of both grantor and grantee, mortgagor and mortgagee, lienor and lienee, pointing out the book and page of the records of title upon which a particular instrument is recorded or the file in which a particular instrument is filed. 45 Am J1st Recds § 72.

An index to the record of an instrument is the means provided for pointing out or indicating where the record may be found. It may in many cases be indispensable in order to secure the full benefit of the record to the public. But its office is to facilitate the researches of those having occasion to examine the records; and strictly, in the absence of statute, it cannot be said to form part of the record. Green v Garrington, 16 Ohio St 548.

Where the statute makes the indexing part of the record, the record is not complete as to notice if the index is not properly made. Re Labb (DC NY) 42 F Supp 542.

index to transcript of record. A convenience for the appellate court required by rule of court in some jurisdictions. 4 Am J2d A & E § 406.

Indian. A member of the aboriginal race which inhabited the continents of North America and South America at the time of the discovery by Columbus. 27 Am J1st Indians § 2. A word descriptive of race, that is, the red race, so that a white man or negro does not become an "Indian" by adoption into an Indian tribe. 27 Am J1st Indians § 2. In a meaning secondary in the United States, a person of India. If born or naturalized in the United States, a citizen of the United States and of the state wherein he resides. 3 Am J2d Aliens § 116.

See **mestizo; mixed blood; pueblo dwellers; reservation Indians.**

Indian adoption. An adoption of a child in pursuance of a tribal custom. Non-She-Po v Wa-Win-Ta, 37 Or 213, 62 P 15. Adoption of a person by a tribe of Indians, having the effect of bestowing on the person adopted the privileges and immunities of the other members and subjecting him to the laws and usages of the tribe. 27 Am J1st Indians § 2.

Indian Affairs Bureau. A federal agency in the Department of the Interior, headed by the Commissioner of Indian Affairs who is appointed by the President by and with the advice and consent of the Senate, the purpose of the agency being to facilitate and simplify the administration of the laws governing Indian Affairs. 25 USC §§ 1, 1a.

Indian agent. A United States government officer who lives on or near an Indian reservation as the representative of the government in its relations with the tribe and whose duty it is to serve the interests of the Indians of the tribe.

Indian allotment. A conveyance of land by the United States to an individual Indian, usually the head of a family, made in pursuance of a policy adopted in reference to the Indians. 27 Am J1st Indians § 27. A term also applied to any allotment of land to Indians, the title of which is held in trust by the United States or which remains inalienable without the consent of the United States. 27 Am J1st Indians § 45.

Indian band. A company of Indians, not necessarily, though often, of the same race or tribe, united under the same leadership in a common design. Connors v United States, 180 US 271, 45 L Ed 525, 21 S Ct 362.

Indian chief. The leader of a tribe. That officer of an Indian nation, such as the Cherokee Nation, who discharges the duties which usually pertain to the office of governor. Whitsett v Forehand, 79 NC 230, 233.

Indian country. The territory formerly held by Indians and to which their title remains unextinguished, also any tract of land, which, being a part of the public domain, is lawfully set apart as an Indian reservation, and also any Indian allotment, the title of which is held in trust by the government or which remains inalienable by the allottee without the consent of the United States. 27 Am J1st Indians § 45.

Indian divorce. A divorce of husband and wife married and continuing to live in Indian territory, in accordance with established custom among the Indian tribe, effected completely by separation of mutual consent. 24 Am J2d Div & S § 8. A divorce in accordance with tribal custom, effected by mutual consent or the abandonment of one spouse by the other. Cyr v Walker, 29 Okla 289, 116 P 934.

Indian lands. Lands allotted to and in the possession

of an Indian tribe. Lands reserved under acts of Congress for occupancy by Indian tribes. United States v Powers, 305 US 527, 83 L Ed 330, 59 S Ct 344. Lands held in trust for Indians by the United States. McCurdy v United States, 264 US 484, 68 L Ed 801, 44 S Ct 345. Lands owned by the United States and subject to sale by it, but in the manner and for the purposes provided for in the special agreements of the government with the Indians. Ash Sheep Co. v United States, 252 US 159, 166, 64 L Ed 507, 511, 40 S Ct 241. Lands to which Indians have a right of perpetual occupancy with the privilege of using them in such manner as they see fit until such right of occupation has been surrendered to the United States, the fee of such land being vested in the United States. 27 Am J1st Indians § 24.

See **Indian title.**

Indian maize (māze). See **corn.**

Indian marriage. A marriage contracted by members of an Indian tribe, who are living with the tribe in tribal relation and subject to the tribal government, in accordance with the laws and customs of the tribe. 35 Am J1st Mar § 40.

Indian nation. A large tribe of Indians, or a group of affiliated tribes, as, bear witness, the Iroquois. 27 Am J1st Indians § 6.

Indian reservation. Land set apart from the public domain by treaty or executive order for perpetual occupancy by Indians or until the right of occupation has been surrendered to the United States. 27 Am J1st Indians § 24.

See **reservation Indians.**

Indian territory. A former territory, now a part of the state of Oklahoma.

See **Indian country.**

Indian title. By virtue of prior occupancy of the continent of North America, at best, nothing more than a right of occupancy. Northwestern Bands of Shoshone Indians v United States, 324 US 335, 89 L Ed 985, 65 S Ct 690; nothing more than permissive occupancy; not a title which could be conveyed so as to transfer to the grantee a title which the United States was bound to recognize. Johnson and Graham's Lessee v M'Intosh (US) 8 Wheat 543, 574, 5 L Ed 681, 688. A right not beyond that of permissive occupancy, except as Congress might recognize a right of permanent occupancy not to be disturbed. Tee-Hit-Ton Indians v United States, 348 US 272, 99 L Ed 314, 75 S Ct 313.

The right of Indians to occupy lands in the United States over which they had sovereignty prior to conquest by the white man is not a property right but amounts to a right of occupancy which the sovereign grants and, although protecting against intrusion by third parties, may terminate; such lands may be fully disposed of by the sovereign itself without any legally enforceable obligation to compensate the Indians. Tee-Hit-Ton Indians v United States, 348 US 272, 99 L Ed 314, 75 S Ct 313.

Exclusive title to American lands passed to the white discoverers subject to the Indian title, with power in the white sovereign alone to extinguish that right by purchase or conquest. Northwestern Bands of Shoshone Indians v United States, 324 US 335, 89 L Ed 985, 65 S Ct 690.

Indian treaties. Treaties made and entered into between the various American Indian tribes and the United States. Worcester v The State of Georgia (US) 6 Pet 515, 8 L Ed 483.

Indian tribe. A body of Indians, united in a community under one leadership or government, and inhabiting a particular territory. 27 Am J1st Indians § 4.

See **commerce with the Indian tribes; Indian adoption.**

Indian tribe member of adoption. See **Indian adoption.**

Indian war. A war in which American Indians engaged the whites. 27 Am J1st Indians § 12.

indicare (in-di-kā′re). To indicate; to designate; to show; to declare; to make known; to reveal.

indication. Something which points to, or gives direction to the mind. Coyle v Commonwealth, 104 Pa 117, 133.

indicavit (in-di-kā′vit). A writ of prohibition which a person who was sued in the ecclesiastical court might obtain. State v Commissioners of Roads, 8 SCL (1 Mill Const) 55.

indicia (in-dish′iạ). Plural of **indicium.**

indicia of ownership (in-dish′i-a of ō′ner-ship). Evidence of title; as, a deed to land, or a bill of sale of personal property.

indicium (in-di′she-um). A mark; a sign; a token; a symbol; a disclosure; a thing furnishing information.

indicia of fraud. Badges of fraud; circumstances such as insolvency, or heavy indebtedness on the part of a grantor, and lack of consideration which indicate, in the absence of explanation to the contrary, that a conveyance was made in fraud of creditors. 24 Am J1st Frd Conv § 14.

indict. To charge one with the commission of a crime by an indictment.

See **indictment.**

indictable. Subject to indictment; as, a person who has committed a felony. The proper subject of an indictment; as, an offense amounting to felony.

indictable attempt. A direct ineffectual act performed intentionally toward the commission of an indictable offense. Commonwealth v Crow, 303 Pa 91, 154 A 283. Broadly, any attempted offense subject to prosecution by indictment under the law of the jurisdiction.

indictable nuisance. A common law offense against the public peace, the public health, or the public morals. State v Waymire, 52 Or 281, 97 P 16. A public, as distinguished from, a private nuisance. 39 Am J1st Nuis § 178.

indictable offense. A crime to be prosecuted under an indictment; in some jurisdictions, any felony. In some jurisdictions, any felony and any misdemeanor of a certain class, particularly a misdemeanor of a serious nature. State v Berlin, 42 Mo 572, 576. At common law, treason, a capital offense, or a felony. 27 Am J1st Indict § 5.

indictare (in-dik′-tā′re). To indict.

indicted. Charged with the commission of a crime by the filing of an indictment or an information of weight equal to an indictment under the law of the jurisdiction. United States v Borger (CC NY) 7 F 193, 196.

indictee. A person against whom a grand jury has returned an indictment.

indictio (in-dik'she-ō). An indictment; a proclamation; a declaration.

indictment. An accusation or charge of the commission of an indictable offense, made in writing by a grand jury against one or more persons upon evidence heard by the grand jury and presented by them under oath at the instance, and by the authority, of the state or the government. State v Hamilton, 133 W Va 394, 56 SE2d 544, 12 ALR2d 573.

See **indictable offense; information.**

Indictment de felony est contra pacem domini regis, coronam et dignitatem suam, in genere et non in individuo; quia in Anglia non est interregnum (in-dict'ment dē fe-lo'ni est kon'trā pa'sem do'mi-nī rē'jis, ko-rō'nam et dig-ni-tā'tem su'am, in je'ne-re et non in in-dī-vi'du-ō; qui'a in Ang'li-a non est in-ter-reg'num). An indictment for felony reads "against the peace of our lord the king, his crown and dignity," in general, and not against the king individually, because in England there is no interregnum.

indictment for wrongful death. A form of proceeding formerly authorized by statute in some states for the recovery of damages for death by wrongful act.
These statutes have been everywhere superseded by laws modeled on Lord Campbell's Act allowing a civil action. 22 Am J2d Dth § 2.

indictor (in-dī'tor). A person who causes another to be indicted.

in diem (in dī'em). For a day; on a day; at a day.
See **de die in diem.**

indifferent. Neutral as to the parties or subject-matter involved in a dispute, controversy, or litigation; impartial; unbiased.

indifferent person. One without interest in favoring either party to an action or in doing anything to the prejudice of either party. 45 Am J1st Rec § 131. A person so situated with reference to certain other persons that there is not such a relation between him and them as could bias his mind and induce him to act with partiality. Mitchell v Kirtland, 7 Conn 228, 231.

indigena (in-di'je-na). A native subject or a subject who has been naturalized.

indigent. In need; in want of a comfortable subsistence; poor.

indigent person. One destitute of property or means of comfortable subsistence. Juneau County v Wood County, 109 Wis 330, 333, 85 NW 387. A poor person. A pauper. Risner v State, 55 Ohio App 151, 9 NE2d 151; Lynchburg v Slaughter, 75 Va 57, 62. A person who has no money or property, or insufficient money or property available for his immediate relief from want, is without credit, and is unable to maintain himself because of inability to work or to obtain employment. 41 Am J1st Poor L § 17. A person who has neither money nor estate, is without credit, and is unable to maintain himself because of inability to work or to obtain employment. 41 Am J1st Poor L § 17.

indigent relief. See **poor relief.**

indigestion. A physical condition of the body resulting from the inability of the stomach to change its content of food to a form capable of assimilation. Not a serious disease within the meaning of an application for life or accident insurance. 29 Am J Rev ed Ins § 745.

indignity. Insult; an affront to one's sensibilities. An affront to self respect. Conduct humiliating to another. A matter of compensatory, rather than punitive or exemplary, damages. 22 Am J2d Damg § 197. Unmerited contemptuous conduct; any act towards another which manifests contempt for him; contumely, incivility or injury accompanied with insult and amounting to a species of cruelty to the mind. Lynch v Lynch, 87 Mo App 32, 37. As a ground for divorce under some statutes: humiliating and degrading conduct of such a character and continuity as to manifest a settled hate and estrangement, or to render the plaintiff's condition intolerable and life burdensome. Kranch v Kranch, 17 Pa Super 169, 84 A2d 230.

See **dutrage and indignity; personal indignity.**

indirect. Not direct, circuitous, as an indirect road. Not leading to the fulfillment of a purpose by the plain and obvious course, but obliquely or by remote means; roundabout; not resulting directly from an act or cause, but more or less remotely connected with or growing out of it. Maryland Casualty Co. v Scharlack (DC Tex) 31 F Supp 931.

indirect bounty. A bounty indirectly paid by the government by the remission of taxes upon the exportation of articles which are subjected to a tax when sold or consumed in the country of their production, of which the laws permitting distillers of spirits to export the same without payment of internal revenue tax or other burden, is an example. Downs v United States, 187 US 496, 502, 47 L Ed 275, 277, 23 S Ct 222.

indirect contempt. An act committed elsewhere than in the presence of the court or judge, which tends to obstruct the administration of justice, or to bring the court, or judge, or the administration of justice into disrespect. Re Dill, 32 Kan 668, 5 P 39; Osborne v Purdome (Mo) 244 SW2d 1005, 29 ALR2d 1141. An act committed, not in the presence of the court, but at a distance from it, generally characterized by disobeying or resisting process, intimidating a witness out of the presence of the court, making a false report of a proceeding pending before the court, etc. La Grange v State, 238 Ind 689, 153 NE2d 593, 69 ALR2d 668. Sometimes referred to as constructive contempt.

indirect corporate purpose. A purpose which does not in its direct and immediate consequences operate upon the corporators, but the beneficial effects of which are to be experienced in a remoter degree, and which have to be traced to their source before they can be duly comprehended and appreciated. State, ex rel. Thompson, v Memphis, 147 Tenn 658, 251 SW 46, 27 ALR 1257, 1265.

indirect evidence. Evidence of value and weight because of the presumptions and inferences arising therefrom.
See **circumstantial evidence.**

indirect review. A collateral attack on a judgment. 2 Am J2d Adm L § 494.

indirect solicitation. A term found in statutes prohibiting and penalizing ambulance chasing by attorneys; any circuitous means of reaching the injured person and obtaining control of the claim. Hightower v Detroit Edison Co. 262 Mich 1, 247 NW 97, 86 ALR 509.

indirect tax. Categorically, a tax other than one imposed directly upon property according to its value, for example, an occupation tax. Foster & Creighton Co. v Graham, 154 Tenn 412, 285 SW 570, 47 ALR

971, 975. Loosely, a tax paid by a person who can shift the burden to another person or who is not under legal compulsion to pay. 51 Am J1st Tax § 25.

In disjunctivis sufficit alteram partem esse veram (in dis-junk-tī′vis suf′fi-si• al′te-ram par′tem es′se vē′-ram). In disjunctives it is sufficient if either part be true.

indispensable. That which cannot be dispensed with; vital; essential.

indispensable evidence. Evidence the absence of which renders the proof of a given fact impossible.

indispensable party. A person materially interested either legally or beneficially in the subject matter of the suit. Green v Brophy, 71 App DC 299, 110 F2d 539, 9 ALR2d 1. A person who must be joined as a party if the action is to succeed. McAndrews v Krause, 245 Minn 85, 71 NW2d 153, 53 ALR2d 312. A person who has an interest in the subject matter of the controversy in litigation of such nature that the final judgment cannot be rendered between the other parties to the suit without radically and injuriously affecting that interest, or without leaving the controversy in such a situation that its final determination may be inconsistent with equity and good conscience. 39 Am J1st Parties § 5.

The true rule as to indispensability of parties calls for a reconciliation of the desirability, on the one hand, of preventing multiplicity of suits and obtaining a complete and final decree between all interested parties, and, on the other hand, of having some adjudication if at all possible rather than none. Gauss v Kirk, 91 App DC 80, 198 F2d 83, 33 ALR2d 1085.

indispensable repairs. See **necessary repairs.**

indisputable. Not subject to dispute; undeniable; irrebuttable; conclusive.

indisputable presumption. Same as **irrebuttable presumption.**

in dispute (in dis-pūt′). See **dispute.**

indissolvable union. The Union of the States in the United States. 49 Am J1st States § 11.

indistributable. Incapable of being distributed.

inditee (in-dī′tē″). Same as **indictee.**

individual. Adjective: Single. Pertaining to one person alone. Noun: A person. A natural person, as distinguished from a corporation. Commonwealth ex rel. Reinboth, v Councils of Pittsburgh, 41 Pa 278.

The purchaser may recover for injuries resulting from drinking liquor where the remedy is given by dramshop or civil damage act to "individuals" who sustain damage. 30 Am J Rev ed Intox L § 539.

See **quasi individual.**

individual banker. Same as **private banker.**

individual enterprise. See **private enterprise.**

individual estate. See **separate estate of wife.**

individual liability. See **personal liability; superadded liability of stockholders.**

individually. As an individual or person; personally. State v Robinson, 71 ND 463, 2 NW2d 183, 148 ALR 332.

Where lands were conveyed to husband and wife to be held by them "individually," they were held to take the lands by moieties, as tenants in common, and not by the entirety. Distributing Co. v Carraway, 189 NC 420, 127 SE 427.

individual operator's license. See **operator's license.**

individual rights. See **fundamental rights and privileges.**

individuo. See **in individuo.**

individuum (in-dĭ-vi′dū-um). Incapable of division; indivisible; inseparable.

indivisible. Incapable of division; inseparable.

indivisible contract. A contract impossible of division so as to render a valid part enforceable pro tanto where another part is invalid. 17 Am J2d Contr § 230. A contract impossible of division so as to render a party liable upon performance by the other party of one of successive divisions. 17 Am J2d Contr § 324.

See **divisible contract; entirety of contract; severability of contract.**

indivisible statute. A statute of such nature that a part of it will not be enforced where another part is invalid. 16 Am J2d Const L §§ 181 et seq.

indivisibility. The quality of something that cannot be divided.

See **entirety.**

indoctrination of prospective jurors. The instruction of prospective jurors upon court procedure and general principles of law, a practice which, while perhaps salutary in theory, is deemed dangerous in practice and is generally condemned by the courts. Anno: 2 ALR2d 1104.

in dominico (in do-mi′ni-kō). In demesne.

See **demesne.**

indorsat (in-dor′sat). Indorsed.

indorse. A verb derived from the Latin words "in," meaning "on" and "dorsum" meaning "the back." To write one's own name on the back of an instrument. Commonwealth v Spilman, 124 Mass 327. Implying delivery. Babbitt Bros. Trading Co. v First Nat. Bank, 32 Ariz 588, 261 P 45; Cady v Bay City Land Co. 102 Or 5, 201 P 179, 21 ALR 1367. To approve as worthy of support, as to indorse a candidate for election.

indorsed note. A promissory note indorsed by the payee or by payee and prior indorsee.

See **approved indorsed note.**

indorsed over. Indorsed and delivered. Babbitt Bros. Trading Co. v First Nat. Bank, 32 Ariz 588, 261 P 45.

indorsee. The person named in a special indorsement of a bill or note.

The holder of an instrument on which the only or last indorsement is a blank indorsement is a "bearer," rather than an "indorsee." 11 Am J2d B & N § 371.

indorsee in due course. A person who in good faith, in the ordinary course of business, for value, before its apparent maturity or presumptive dishonor, and without knowledge of its actual dishonor, acquires a negotiable instrument duly indorsed to him, or indorsed generally, or payable to bearer. Reese v Bell (Cal) 71 P 87.

See **holder in due course.**

indorsement. Literally, as derived from the Latin "indorsa," a writing on the back; employed in common as well as legal usage to designate the transaction whereby the holder of a bill or note transfers his right to such instrument to another person and incurs the liabilities incident to the transfer under the law. 11 Am J2d B & N § 349. The writing of one's own name on the back of a negotiable instrument, whereby one not only transfers one's full legal title to the paper but likewise enters into a contract, implied or express, dependent upon whether or not the signing of the name is accompanied by other words, and the particular words used, such as an implied guaranty that the instrument will be paid. Glaser v Connell, 47 Wash 2d 622, 289 P2d 364. An additional contract on the instrument; a new, independent, and substantive contract. 11 Am J2d B & N § 349. (For liability of indorser, see 11 Am J2d B & N §§ 598 et seq.) Signing one's name on the face of a bill or note with words indicating the character of the signature as an indorsement or the character of the signer as an indorser. Peoples Nat. Bank v Dicks, 258 Mich 441, 242 NW 825. A signature on a security in registered form or on a separate document assigning or transferring the security or granting a power to assign or transfer it, or the mere signature on the back of a security of a person having the right or authority to assign or transfer the instrument or empower another person to assign or transfer it. UCC § 8–308(1).

Broadly, a writing on the back of an instrument for any purpose, not necessarily the purpose of transfer or assumption of liability. 11 Am J2d B & N § 349. Technically confined to the theory of negotiability, but commonly used in application to the writing of a name on the back of a nonnegotiable instrument. Bank of America v Butterfield, 77 SD 170, 88 NW2d 909.

A signature upon the back of a will. 57 Am J1st Wills § 263. Most broadly, a writing upon either the back or margin of an instrument, for example, a writing indicating part payment. 34 Am J1st Lim Ac § 347. The marking of an envelope which contains a deposition to indicate such content and the title of the cause. 23 Am J2d Dep § 82.

See **backing; blank indorsement; for account of; for clearing house purposes only; for collection; for deposit; full indorsement; general indorsement; guaranty of previous indorsements; irregular indorsement; previous indorsements guaranteed; proper indorsement; qualified indorsement; regular indorsement; restrictive indorsement; special indorsement; transfer by indorsement; usual course of business; waiver of presentment; waiver of protest; without recourse.**

indorsement after maturity. An indorsement of a bill or note, the legal effect of which is, in general, that the holder takes the instrument subject to all the equities which existed between the original parties. 11 Am J2d B & N § 481.

indorsement before due. An indorsement of a bill or note the legal effect of which is that the holder takes the instrument discharged of all defenses which could arise out of equities which existed between the original parties. 11 Am J2d B & N § 398.

indorsement for account of. See **for account of.**

indorsement for clearing house purposes only. See **for clearing house purposes only.**

indorsement for collection. See **for collection.**

indorsement for deposit. See **for deposit.**

indorsement in blank. See **blank indorsement.**

indorsement in full. See **full indorsement.**

indorsement of ballot. A statutory requirement in reference to ballots delivered to voters at an election; the initialing of a ballot upon the back thereof by an election official. 26 Am J2d Elect § 255.

indorsement of deed. Words of conveyance indorsed on an instrument to give it operation as a conveyance of property. 23 Am J2d Deeds § 37.

See **in the within deed.**

indorsement on indictment. Words written upon an indictment denoting its character as a "true bill." 27 Am J1st Indict § 42.

indorsement on information. Giving the names of witnesses for the state. 27 Am J1st Indict § 46; 6 Am J2d Attach §§ 312, 316; 30 Am J2d Exec § 552.

See **return of process.**

indorsement on instruction. The noting by the judge at the trial on each written instruction presented to him by counsel, the fact of giving or refusing it, by writing thereon either "given" or "refused" as the case may be. The court's error in omitting this practice is generally regarded as harmless. 53 Am J1st Trial § 534.

indorsement on policy. A physical addition to an insurance policy by written, typed or printed matter appearing on the margin of the instrument, on the back of the instrument, or on a separate sheet or sheets attached to the instrument, or in any manner other than in the body of the instrument. 29 Am J Rev ed Ins § 267.

indorsement on writ. In effect a return of the process by the officer to whom it was issued, noting the acts performed by him under the writ or the absence of service of the process.

indorsement sans recours. Indorsement without recourse.

See **without recourse.**

indorsement with enlarged liability. An indorsement of a bill or negotiable instrument with the written words "demand, notice, and protest waived, and payment guaranteed," appearing above the signature of the indorser. Buck v Davenport Sav. Bank, 29 Neb 407.

indorsement without recourse. See **without recourse.**

indorser. One who indorses; one who signs as an indorser; even one who signs on the face of the instrument, provided he indicates his character as an indorser in writing appearing with the signature. Peoples Nat. Bank v Dicks, 258 Mich 441, 242 NW 825. One who indorses a registered security by way of transferring or assigning the instrument or granting another the authority to assign or transfer it. 15 Am J2d Com C § 32.

See **accommodation indorser; indorsement; satisfactory indorser.**

indorser duly notified in writing. A phrase used in the entry of the protest of a negotiable instrument. Bell v Perkins, 7 Tenn (Peck) 261.

indorser not holden. See **without recourse.**

indorser's liability. The liability incurred by the indorsement of a negotiable instrument. 11 Am J2d B & N §§ 598 et seq.

in dorso (in dor'sō). On the back.

in dorso recordi (in dor'sō rē-kor'dī). On the back of the record.

In dubiis, benigniora praeferenda sunt (in du'bi-is, bē-nig-ni-ō'ra prē-fe-ren'da sunt). In doubtful cases, the more liberal constructions are to be preferred.

In dubiis, magis dignum est accipiendum (in du'bi-is, mā'jis dig'num est ak-si-pi-en'dum). In doubtful cases, the more worthy is to be adopted or accepted.

In dubiis, non praesumitur pro testamento (in du'bi-is, non prē-zu'mi-ter prō tes-ta-men'tō). In doubtful cases, there is no presumption in favor of a will.

in dubio (in du'bi-ō). In doubt; in case of doubt; in a doubtful case.

In dubio, haec legis constructio quam verba ostendunt (in du'bi-ō, hĕk lē'jis kon-struk'she-ō quam ver'ba os-ten'dunt). In a doubtful case, that construction which the words indicate should be adopted.

In dubio, pars mitior est sequenda (in du'bi-ō, pärz mī'she-or est se-quen'da). In a doubtful case, the milder course should be pursued.

In dubio pro dote, libertate, innocentia, possessore, debitore, reo, respondendum est (in du'bi-ō prō dō'te, li-ber-tā'te, in-no-sen'she-a, po-ze-sō're, de-bi-tō're, re'ō, re-spon-den'dum est). In case of doubt the response is in favor of dower, liberty, innocence, of the possessor, of the debtor, and of the defendant. Chrisman v Linderman, 202 Mo 605, 100 SW 1090.

In dubio, pro lege fori (in du'bi-ō, prō lē'je fō'rī). In case of doubt, the law of the forum governs.

In dubio, sequendum quod tutius est (in du'bi-ō, se-quen'dum quod tu'she-us est). In a doubtful case, that course should be followed which is the safer one.

indubitable proof. Evidence that is not only credible, but is of such weight and directness as to make out the facts alleged beyond a doubt. Hart v Carroll, 85 Pa 508.

induce. To lead on, to influence, to prevail on, or move by persuasion or influence. Bradbury v Brooks, 82 Colo 133, 257 P 359.

induce and encourage. A term broad enough to include every form of influence and persuasion. International Brotherhood, E. W. v NLRB, 341 US 694, 95 L Ed 1299, 71 S Ct 954.

induced error. See **invited error**.

inducing cause. See **procuring cause**.

inducement. That which prevails on a person to promote an act or acts by him, for example, fraud inducing the making of a contract. 23 Am J1st Fraud § 111. That part of a declaration or complaint in an action for libel or slander the office of which is to narrate the extrinsic circumstances which, coupled with the language published or uttered by the defendant affect its construction, and render it actionable, where, standing alone and not thus explained, the language would appear either not to concern the plaintiff, or, if concerning him, not to affect him injuriously. 33 Am J1st L & S § 239.

See **entrapment**.

induciae (in-dū'she-ē). An armistice; a truce; a suspension of hostilities; an indulgence.

induct. To lead or conduct. To place a person formally in the possession of an office or a benefice. To place or install a person in an office. To bring into one of the armed forces a person called for service under a compulsory service act. 36 Am J1st Mil § 24.

inducted. Led or conducted. Placed in an office or a benefice. Made a member of one of the armed forces after having been called under a compulsory service act. 36 Am J1st Mil § 24.

A registrant has been "inducted" when he has appeared before his local board, has been passed by its medical examiners on the preliminary or screen examination, has passed his blood test at the local hospital or state board of health, has passed his medical examination at the hands of the army doctors at the induction center, and has taken the oath as a member of the armed forces of the United States. Hoellman v Abel, 293 Ky 776, 170 SW2d 26.

inductio (in-duk'she-ō). (Civil law.) A cancellation; an obliteration.

induction. Being made a member of one of the armed forces after having been called under a compulsory service act. 36 Am J1st Mil § 24. The flow of electricity, through the medium of the atmosphere, from one wire to another without actual contact. 26 Am J2d Electr § 2. Producing an effect in a conductor of electricity.

Being formally placed in office. The investing of a clergyman with the actual possession of the temporalities of a benefice by means of some symbolic act. Godwin v Lunan (Va) Jeff 96, 99

in due course. See **holder in due course**.

in due course of transportation. Between delivery of the shipment to the carrier and delivery to the consignee or one acting for the consignee. Anno: 80 ALR2d 447, 452. For the purposes of stating the risk of protection by an insurance policy, prior periods of actual movement or periods of rest while property is being carried from one place to another with the intention to take it to a destination conceived in the mind, not the mere possession of something in the course of a casual wandering. Anno: 80 ALR2d 447.

indulgence. The granting of a favor, such as an extension of time to a creditor. 34 Am J1st Lim Ac § 367. In the Roman Catholic Church, a remission of punishment for sin. In other connections, a grant of religious liberties to persons not members of the established church.

indulto (in-dul'to). (Spanish.) A pardon by the king for the commission of an offense.

indument. Same as **endowment**.

in duplo (in du'plō). In double the amount.

in duplum (in du'plum). In double the amount.

industria. See **ex industria**.

industrial. Pertaining to industry.

industrial accident commission. A special agency or board administering the workmen's compensation act of the jurisdiction. 58 Am J1st Workm Comp § 371. An agency known in other states as the **workmen's compensation commission**.

industrial accident fund. See **state insurance fund**.

industrial arts. Mechanical arts.

industrial bank. A bank of a particular type, operating with the primary purpose of giving credit to wage earners of good character on an instalment-payment basis.

industrial blindness. Impairment of vision to the extent of preventing one from engaging in an industrial pursuit. Powers v Motor Wheel Corp. 252 Mich 639, 234 NW 122, 73 ALR 702.

industrial bounties. Bounties to industry provided by Act of Congress in promotion of national defense. 12 Am J2d Bount § 2.

industrial commission. Same as **industrial accident commission.**

industrial development. An area devoted to industries, that is, a section in which industrial plants have been built and are operating. The process of creating an area for industries, the obtaining of industries for the section, and the construction of industrial plants.

industrial disease. A disease peculiar to a certain employment because of the place of employment and conditions affecting the health in such place. A sudden and unexpected development of a traumatic origin in an employment. 58 Am J1st Workm Comp § 246. An infirmity which does not arise by "accident" and, in the absence of an express provision in the act, is not an injury or personal injury within the meaning of a compensation statute. 58 Am J1st Workm Comp § 246.

industrial dispute. See **labor dispute; strike.**

industrial district. See **industrial zone.**

industriales. See **fructus industriales.**

industrial establishment. A place for engaging in an industry, particularly manufacturing, requiring both capital and labor. State ex rel. Kansas City Power & Light Co. v Smith, 342 Mo 75, 111 SW2d 513.

industrial exhibition. An exhibition in which industries of the state or locality, depending upon the sponsor, exhibit their products and demonstrate some of their manufacturing operations. 37 Am J1st Mun Corp § 128.

industrial homework. See **homework; homeworker.**

industrial hospital. A hospital maintained by a railroad or industrial corporation for the benefit of the employees, supported usually by the employer or partly by the employer and partly by the employee. 26 Am J1st Hospit § 15.

industrial insurance. A form of life insurance, the primary purpose of which is to provide for the expenses of the last illness and burial of the insured, characterized by the relatively small amounts in which the policies are written, the circumstance that the premiums are payable monthly, and the additional circumstance that ordinarily the premiums are collected by collectors employed by the insurer who make house to house calls.

industrial life insurance. See **industrial insurance.**

industrial railroad. A railroad within the limits of an industrial plant operated for the benefit or convenience of the industry. 13 Am J2d Car § 12.

industrial relations. The relations between the employing industry and the workers, often referred to today as capital and labor.

As the words are used in the title of an act relating to an administrative body for the regulation of industrial relations, the word industrial means relating to industry, and industry embraces those departments devoted to public service. The word relations has the meaning of "affairs." Fifty years ago the words would have conveyed little or no information, but in the light of common knowledge of the science of government, and particularly the regulation of industry by administrative tribunals as they now exist, anyone whose interests might be affected by the legislation would be directed to details by the title. State ex rel. Hopkins v Howat, 109 Kan 376, 198 P 686, 25 ALR 1210, 1228.

industrial relations court. An administrative board established for the regulation of industrial relations. State ex rel. Hopkins v Howat, 109 Kan 376, 198 P 686, 25 ALR 1210, writ of error dismd 258 US 181, 66 L Ed 550, 42 S Ct 277.

industrial relations department. A department of a state government administering the workmen's compensation act; otherwise known in some jurisdictions as the **workmen's compensation commission.**

industrial school. An institution for the reception, education, and training of wayward, incorrigible, or vicious youths or youths from broken homes or whose parents are incapable or unworthy of caring for children, where they may be inculcated with habits of industry and morality and be free from the corrupting influence of bad associates. 26 Am J1st House of C § 2.

industrial solids. Refuse and waste from an industrial plant.

industrial union. A labor union organized on an industrial basis without regard to the particular occupations or skills of the members, taking in as members all employees of a particular industrial unit. 31 Am J Rev ed Lab § 13.

industrial zone. An area where the construction and operation of industrial plants is permitted under zoning ordinances. 58 Am J1st Zon § 33.

industry. Diligence in employment or self-employment, exercised bodily or mentally. Carver Mercantile Co. v Hulme, 7 Mont 566, 571. A business, plant, or enterprise for the production of goods, merchandise, machines, motor vehicles, etc. for sale, particularly a manufacturing plant employing many people and requiring the support of large capital. A distinct branch of trade or business, such as the sugar industry, the printing industry, or the clothing industry. State ex rel. Kansas City Power & Light Co. v Smith, 342 Mo 75, 111 SW2d 513. A thing involving capital and labor but distinct from both.

industry affecting commerce. As defined by the Taft-Hartley Act, any industry or activity in commerce or in which a labor dispute would burden or obstruct commerce or intend to burden or obstruct commerce or the free flow of commerce. Shirley-Herman Co. v International Hod Carriers, Bldg. & C. L. Union (CA2 NY) 182 F2d 806, 17 ALR2d 609.

indutiae (in-dū'she-ē). Same as **induciae.**

in eadem causa (in e-ā'dem kâ'za). In the same cause; in the same case; in the same suit or action; in the same condition or state. A person in a condition of chronic inebriety, whether caused by the excessive use of intoxicating liquors, morphine, or other narcotics. Leavitt v Morris, 105 Minn 170, 117 NW 393 (statutory definition.)

inebriate. Noun: An habitual drunkard. 29 Am J Rev ed Ins Per § 8. A drunken person. Verb: To intoxicate or make drunk.

inebriated. Intoxicated.

inebriation. Same as **intoxication.**

inebriety. Same as **intoxication.**

in effect. In force; in operation; effective. In fact.

ineffectual judgment. A judgment which grants full relief to the successful party but is unenforceable

inefficiency. Incompetency; a lack of some requisite ability. Anno: 4 ALR3d 1095. Incapability, as for a public office. State ex rel. Rockwell v State Board of Education, 213 Minn 184, 6 NW2d 251, 143 ALR 503.
See **efficient**.

In ejus unius persona veteris reipublicae vis atque majestas per cumulatas magistratuum potestates exprimebatur (in e'jus ū-nī'us per-sō'na ve'te-ris rē-ī-pub'li-sē vis at'kwe ma-jes'tās per ku-mu-lā'tās ma-jis-trā'tu-um po-tes-tā'tēz ex-pri-mē-bā'ter). The power and majesty of the old commonwealth were represented in that one man through the combined powers of the magistrates. 1 Bl Comm 251.

ineligibility. The state of being ineligible.
See **ineligible**.

ineligible. Want of eligibility. The lack of the legal qualifications essential for an office or trust. Barnum v Gilpin, 27 Minn 466, 8 NW 375.
See **eligibility**.

in emulationem vicini (in e-mu-lā-she-ō'nem vi-sī'nī). In envy or hatred of a neighbor.

In eo quod plus sit, semper inest et minus (in ē'ō quod plus sit, sem'per in'est et mī'nus). The less is always included in the greater.

in equal shares. Sometimes, although not always, indicating a gift to individuals rather than to a class. 57 Am J1st Wills § 1265.

in equal wrong. See **in pari delicto**.

inequitable. Unjust; not according to the principles of equity.

inequitable conduct. A course of conduct contrary to the principles of equity. Unconscionable conduct; unfairness; conduct prompted by bad motive. 27 Am J2d Eq § 138.

in equity. In a court of equity; through or by means of proceedings in equity.

in esse (in es'ē). Alive; living; in being.
See **in being**.

in essentialibus (in es-sen-she-ā'li-bús). In the essentials.

Inesse potest donationi, modus, conditio sive causa; ut modus est; si conditio; quia causa (in-es'se po'test do-nā-she-ō'nī, mō'dus, kon-di'she-ō sī've kâ'za; ut mō'dus est; sī kon-di'she-ō; qui'a kâ'za). There can be manner, condition, or cause in a gift; "ut" is for the manner; "si" is for the condition; and "quia" for the cause.

Inest de jure (in'est dē jū're). It is implied in law.

in evidence. Before the court, after having been offered or introduced, and received, as evidence.

inevitable. Not to be avoided; unavoidable.

inevitable accident. A purely accidental occurrence, the origin of which is either in the agency of men or in a natural force. King v Richards-Cunningham Co. 46 Wyo 355, 28 P2d 492. An unusual, unexpected, or extraordinary occurrence. French v Pirnie, 240 Mass 489, 134 NE 353, 20 ALR 1098. A collision of ships which occurs, even though both parties have endeavored, by every means in their power, with due care and caution and a proper display of nautical skill, to prevent it, and in spite of everything that nautical skill, care, and precaution can do to keep the vessels from coming together. 48 Am J1st Ship § 232.

An Act of God is an inevitable accident because no human agency can resist it, but the expression "inevitable accident" is broader and more comprehensive than "Act of God." 38 Am J1st Negl § 6. But as the term is employed in the law of common carriers, it is a technical expression and "a loss by inevitable accident" is held to be synonymous with "a loss by act of God." Neal v Saunderson, 10 Miss 2 Smedes & M 572.
See **inevitable casualty; unavoidable accident**.

inevitable casualty. A term, apparently favored in the drafting of leases, meaning inevitable accident. An occurrence of an unusual, unexpected, or extraordinary character, without the direct participation of either landlord or tenant. Anno: 20 ALR 1101; 32 Am J1st L & T § 505.
See **inevitable accident**.

inewardus (in-e-war'dus). A warden; a guard; a watchman.

in excambio (in ex-kam'bi-ō). In exchange.

in execution under sentence of the court. The state or condition of a person who is imprisoned in execution of a sentence. Mitchell v Greenough (CA 9 Wash) F2d 184.

in exitu (in ex'i-tū). Same as **in issue**.

in expectancy. See **estate in expectancy; expectancy**.

in expectation. In anticipation rather than in present enjoyment or endurance.

As used with reference to estates, the term is used in contradistinction to the term "in possession." Both terms contemplate a title vested and indefeasible, but in one instance the right of enjoyment is immediate, "in possession;" in the other it is postponed, "in expectation." People v McCormick, 208 Ill 437, 70 NE 350.

inexperience. Want of experience. Want of judgment in matters of business arising from lack of participation in such matters; not the incompetency which justifies the appointment of a guardian. 29 Am J Rev ed Ins Per § 6.
See **experience**.

In expositione instrumentorum, mala grammatica, quod fieri potest, vitanda est (in ex-po-zi-she-ō'ne in-stru-men-tō'rum, ma'la gram-ma'ti-ka, quod fī'e-rī po'test, vi-tan'da est). In the drawing of instruments, bad grammar is to be avoided as much as possible.

in extenso (in eks-ten'sō). At length; in full; verbatim.

in extremis. In the last stage and extremity of the last illness. As a characterization of the circumstance under which a declaration becomes admissible in a prosecution for homicide as a dying declaration, the victim being the declarant:—at the point of death from the wound to which the declaration refers, although not necessarily taking the last breath. 26 Am J1st Homi § 405.

in eyre. (in ār). See **adjournment in eyre**.

in facie curiae (in fā-she-ē kū'ri-ē). In the face or presence of the court. Cooke v United States, 267 US 517, 536, 69 L Ed 767, 773, 45 S Ct 390.

in facie ecclesiae (in fā'shi-ē e-klē'si-ē). In the face of the church, that is, in a church.
See **marriage in facie ecclesiae**.

in faciendo (in fā-she-en′dō). In doing; in making; in performing. In fact. In truth. In reality. In existence rather than in theory. In circumstances rather than in law.

See **assignee in fact**; **attorney in fact**; **possession in fact**.

in facto (in fak′tō). In fact; in deed.

In facto quod se habet ad bonum et malum, magis de bono quam de malo lex intendit (in fak′tō quod sē hā′bet ad bō′num et ma′lum, mā′jis dē bō′nō quam dē ma′lō lex in-ten′dit). In a deed which may be held to be either good or bad, the law directs its attention more to the good than to the bad.

infamia (in-fā′mi-a). Infamy; disgrace; dishonor; ignominy; ill repute.

infamia facti (in-fā′mi-a fak′tī). Infamy in fact; the infamy which in fact exists where a person is supposed to be guilty of a crime, but it has not been judicially proved.

He who has been declared infamous in one country is infamous in a foreign country in fact, but not in law. Commonwealth v Green, 17 Mass (17 Tyng) 515, 541.

infamia juris (in-fā′mi-a jū′ris). Infamy in law; that is, infamy established by law as a consequence of crime. Commonwealth v Green, 17 Mass (17 Tyng) 515, 541.

infamis (in-fā′mis). Of ill repute; infamous; disreputable.

infamous. See **infamia facti**; **infamous crime**.

infamous crime. A term of more than one connotation; sometimes referring to the manner of punishment, at other times to the effect of a conviction upon the credibility of the delinquent. 21 Am J2d Crim L § 23. Determined by the nature of the punishment rather than the circumstances of the commission of the particular offense for which punishment imposed. Briggs v Board of Comrs. 202 Okla 684, 217 P2d 827, 20 ALR2d 727. At common law, a crime infamous in the opinion of the people respecting the mode of punishment or infamous in respect of the future credibility of the delinquent. 21 Am J2d Crim L § 23. An offense punishable by death or by imprisonment in a prison or penitentiary, particularly if the period of imprisonment is more than one year. Anno: 24 ALR 1004; 27 Am J1st Indict § 10. Within the meaning of the Fifth Amendment of the Federal Constitution, an offense punishable by imprisonment in a state prison or penitentiary with or without hard labor. Ex parte Mills, 135 US 263, 267, 34 L Ed 107, 109, 10 S Ct 762. Treason, felony, and those crimes of dishonesty included within the term "crimen falsi." 21 Am J2d Crim L § 23. In one sense of the term, any felony. State ex rel. Anderson v Fousek, 91 Mont 448, 8 P2d 312, 84 ALR 303.

An offense which is typified by collateral results such as disqualification for voting or holding office. 21 Am J2d Crim L § 23. An offense which can be prosecuted only by indictment by a grand jury or the equivalent in an information. 21 Am J2d Crim L § 23. An offense expressly declared "infamous" by statute. People ex rel. Latimer v Randolph, 13 Ill 2d 552, 150 NE2d 603, cert den 358 US 852, 856, 3 L Ed 2d 85, 90, 79 S Ct 80, 89.

In determining whether a crime is infamous, the punishment which the statute authorizes is regarded, and not the punishment which is actually awarded. 27 Am J1st Indict § 9.

infamous crime against nature. See **pederasty**; **penetration per anum**; **sodomy**.

infamous offense. Same as **infamous crime**.

infamous punishment. Punishment characterized by infamy; punishment for a felony rather than punishment for a misdemeanor. 27 Am J1st Indict § 9.

Two hundred years ago, punishments clearly infamous were death, gallows, pillory, branding, whipping, confinement at hard labor, and cropping. Whipping and being put in the stocks were not so regarded in colonial times, but would probably be considered infamous today. Punishment by confinement in a state prison or penitentiary, or other similar institution is held to be infamous punishment. Ex parte Wilson, 114 US 417, 428, 29 L Ed 89, 93, 5 S Ct 935.

infamy. Disgrace; loss of reputation. The stigma which attaches to a person who has been convicted of an infamous crime. Schuylkill County v Copley, 67 Pa 386, 390. Disgrace resulting from the conviction of a crime whereby the privileges attendant upon citizenship are lost or one's competency or credibility as a witness adversely affected. Ex parte Wilson, 114 US 417, 422, 29 L Ed 89, 91, 5 S Ct 935.

infancy. A status created by law; the status of nonage; in other words, the status of an infant.

See **infant**.

infangenthef. The right or privilege of the lord of the manor to pass judgment on a thief taken within the manor.

infangthefe. Same as **infangenthef**.

infans (in′fānz). (Civil law.) A child under the age of seven years.

Infans non multum a furioso distat (in′fānz non mul′-tum ā fu-ri-ō′sō dis′tat). An infant does not differ much from a lunatic.

infant. In ordinary usage, a child of a tender and helpless age. In law, a person who has not reached the age of majority, usually 21 years, at which the law recognizes a general contractual capacity. 27 Am J1st Inf § 2.

In some states females become of age at the end of the eighteenth year and the statutes of some states make all persons adults upon their marriage. See 27 Am J1st Inf § 5.

See **emancipation of minor**; **legal capacity**; **majority**; **natural infancy**.

infantia (in-fan′she-a). (Civil law.) Childhood from birth to the age of seven years.

infanticide (in-fan′ti-sīd). The killing of a young child shortly after its birth.

infantile paralysis. See **poliomyelitis**.

Infants' Marriage Act. An English statute which enabled an infant to enter with court sanction into a valid marriage settlement. 18 & 19 Vict c 43.

infanzon (in-fan-thone′). (Spanish.) A person of noble birth.

infatuation. An attraction without reason.

In favorabilibus magis attenditur quod prodest quam quod nocet (in fa-vō-rā-bi′li-bus mā′jis at-ten′di-ter quod prō′dest quam quod no′set.) In matters which are favored, more attention is paid to that which is beneficial than to that which is harmful.

in favorem libertatis (in fa-vō′rem li-ber-tā′tis). In favor of liberty. Re Justus, 3 Okla Crim 111, 104 P 933.

in favorem prolis (in fa-vō'rem prō'lis). In favor of the offspring or descendants.

in favorem vitae (in fa-vō'rem vī'tē). In favor of life.

in favorem vitae, libertatis, et innocentiae, omnia praesumuntur (in fa-vō'rem vī'tē, li-ber-tā'tis, et in-no-sen'she-ē, om'ni-a prē-zu-mun'ter). All things are presumed in favor of life, liberty, and innocence.

infected. Having an infection or having caused an infection.
See **infection**.

infection. The state or condition of a person or animal whose body is affected with a disease, or in or on whose body the germs of a disease are present. Summers v Houston, 62 Okla 280, 162 P 474. The transmitting of a disease from one person to another. An absorption of germs at a definite external point of contact on the human body, such as a scratch, abrasion, or vulnerable tissue, or through the nose, mouth, or other normal channel of entry. 58 Am J1st Workm Comp § 251. The transmitting of a feeling, perchance gaiety, from one person to others.

infectious. Capable of transmitting a feeling, particularly a feeling of gaiety. In a somber sense, capable of causing an infection leading to a disease. Having a contaminating character in the literal sense or in a figurative sense, as where it is said contraband articles are "infectious" in a cargo, subjecting the whole to condemnation. 56 Am J1st War § 157.

infectious disease. A disease caused by bacteria, virus, or other parasite in the body. A disease likely to be spread to other persons by infection.
A disease which presupposes a cause acting by hidden influences, like the miasma of prison ships or marshes, or through the pollution of water or the atmosphere, or from the various dejections from animals. As applied to Texas fever, if it were infectious, it would be communicated by cattle carrying the germs of the disease from the infected district, and depositing them upon the range and waters occupied by other cattle susceptible to the infection, so that they would become infected therefrom. Grayson v Lynch, 163 US 468, 477, 41 L Ed 230, 233, 16 S Ct 1064.
An infectious disease may or may not be contagious, that is, communicable by contact or body exhalation. Grayson v Lynch, 163 US 468, 41 L Ed 230, 16 S Ct 1064.

in fee. A term descriptive of the highest and most enlarged estate in real property, meaning "in fee simple." 28 Am J2d Est § 9.
"When it is said that a man is seised in fee, without more saying, it shall be intended in fee simple; for it shall not be intended by this word 'in fee,' that a man is seised in fee tayle, unless there be added to it this addition, fee tayle." "When the terms in fee, without adjunct, are used as applied to estates, they are to be taken as descriptive of the highest and most enlarged estate, as contradistinguished from a fee conditional at the common law, or a fee tail by the Statute De Donis." Pennington v Pennington, 70 Md 418, 17 A 329.
See **fee simple**.

in fee simple. See **fee simple**.

in fee tail. See **fee tail**.

infeft (in-feft). Same as **enfeoff**.

infeftment (in-feft'ment). Same as **enfeoffment**.

infeodare (in-fū-dā're). To enfeoff; to invest with a fee.

infeodatio (in-fū-dā'she-ō). Same as **enfeoffment**.

infeodation (in-fū-dā'shon). Same as **enfeoffment**.

infeodo (in-fū'do). In fee.

infeoffment (in-fef'ment). Same as **enfeoffment**.

infer. To reason and conclude from a known fact. Derived from the Latin word "inferre," compounded of "in," meaning from, and "ferre," to carry or bring; so, its strict meaning is to bring a result or conclusion from something back of it; that is, from some evidence or data from which it may be logically deduced. Morford v Peck, 46 Conn 380, 385.

inference. In common usage, that which is inferred. In legal usage, a permissible deduction from the evidence before the court which the jury may accept, reject, or accord such probative value as they desire. 29 Am J2d Ev § 161. A permissible deduction which the trier of the facts may adopt, without an express deduction of law to that effect. Rose v Missouri Dist. Tel Co. 328 Mo 1009, 43 SW2d 562, 81 ALR 400. In a proper sense, the thing proved. Not guesswork. Whitehouse v Bolster, 95 Me 458, 50 A 240. A presumption of fact, but not a presumption of law.
See **presumption; presumption of fact**.

inferential. Inferable or deducible from facts which have been proved.

inferior. Less or lower in power, authority, rank, or station; subordinate.

inferior agent. An ordinary agent or employee of a corporation, who acts in an inferior capacity, and under the direction of superior authority, both in regard to the extent of the work and the manner of its execution.
Such an agent is to be distinguished from a managing agent who is invested with general power, involving the exercise of judgment and discretion. The distinction is made in reference to the statutes which have usually provided that service of process may be made on a foreign corporation by service upon its managing agent. Foster v Charles Betcher Lumber Co. 5 SD 57, 58 NW 9.

inferior court. A classification of somewhat flexible character, but usually meaning that the court is one whose proceedings are not endowed with the presumption of jurisdiction. 20 Am J2d Cts § 28. A court of limited jurisdiction. 20 Am J2d Cts § 28. A court of original jurisdiction as distinguished from a court having appellate jurisdiction; a court of original jurisdiction as distinguished from a court exercising supervisory control over it. 20 Am J2d Cts § 28. A court subject to control under a writ of mandamus directed to it by another court. 35 Am J1st Mand § 250.

inferior equity. A right subordinate to another or other rights from the standpoint of the relative standing of the parties in equity. The degree of right of the party who is shown to have been in the better position to avert the loss, injury, or prejudice now to be borne by the one or the other. Champa v Consolidated Finance Corp. 231 Ind 580, 110 NE2d 289, 36 ALR2d 185.
See **junior equity**.

inferior use. A public use of land of lesser rank in respect of public necessity than another public use for which it is sought to condemn the property. 26 Am J2d Em D § 90.

inferred. Concluded from a known fact.
See **infer; inference**.

infeudation (in-fū-dā'shǫn). Same as **enfeoffment**.

infeudation of tithes (of tīthz). The investing of a layman with the right to receive tithes.

in feudis stricte novis (in fū'dis strik'te nō'vis). In feuds strictly new. See 2 Bl Comm 229.

in feudis vere antiquis (in fū'dis vē'rē an-ti'quis). In feuds really ancient.

inficiari (in-fi-she-ā'rī). (Civil law.) To deny; to repudiate an obligation; to deny liability.

inficiatio (in-fi-she-ā'she-ō). (Civil law.) A denial; a denial or repudiation of liability; a denial or repudiation of an obligation.

In fictione juris consistit aequitas (in fik-she-ō'ne jū'ris kon-sis'tit ē'qui-tās). In the fictions of law, equity supports it.

In fictione juris semper aequitas existit (in fik-she-ō'ne jū'ris sem'per ē'qui-tas eg-zis'tit). In a fiction of law, an equity always survives; that is, a fiction of law is always consistent with equity.

"All fictions of law, we have been taught, were created to enable the court to do justice, and where to indulge a fiction is to cause injustice, its just limit has been found." Estate of Walker, 125 Cal 242, 57 P 991.

In fictione juris semper est aequitas (in fik-she-ō'ne jū'ris sem'per est ē'qui-tās). In fiction of law, equity always exists. To apply a legal fiction to work a wrong is a violation of the maxim. Emerson v Thompson, 19 Mass (2 Pick) 473, 495.

In fictione juris subsistit aequitas (in fik-she-ō'ne jū'ris sub-sis'tit ē'qui-tās). In the application of a fiction of the law, equity will prevail. State ex rel. Watson v Standard Oil Co. 49 Ohio St 137, 30 NE 279.

A fiction is maintained where it may contribute to the advancement of justice; it will not be allowed to work an injury or prejudice to any party. Low v Little (NY) 17 Johns 346, 348.

infidel. One without trust in God or belief in immortality. State v Rozell (Mo) 225 SW 931, 16 ALR 400, later app (Mo) 279 SW 705. In a parochial view, one who does not believe in the Bible or believe that Jesus Christ was the true Messiah, the Son of God; one who necessarily must be both anti-Catholic and anit-Protestant. Hale v Everett, 53 NH 9.

infidelis (in-fi-dē'lis). An infidel; an unbeliever; a person who violated his oath of fealty.

infidelitas (in-fi-dē'li-tas). Infidelity; unfaithfulness; disloyal to one's oath of fealty.

infidelity. In one sense, the state of being an infidel. In modern usage and generally the usage in the law, unfaithfulness in marriage; practically synonymous with adultery; a stated ground of divorce under the statutes of some jurisdictions. Bradshaw v Tinker, 129 Okla 244, 264 P 162.

See **adultery**; **infidel**.

in fieri (in fī'ę-rī). In the making; unfinished; incomplete.

At common law, misspellings and other clerical errors could be amended while all the proceedings were "in paper," and therefore subject to the control of the courts, but when the record was made up, no amendment could be made unless within the term of court in which the record was made. Later, however, the law relaxed and permitted such an amendment to be made at any time before judgment was given, because until then, the proceedings were considered as being "in fieri." See 3 Bl Comm 406.

infiht. (Saxon.) An assault upon a person who lived in the same house as the assailant.

in fine (in fī'ne). At the end; as, at the end of a page; at the end of a book.

infinite. Without limit.

See **distress infinite**.

infinitum. Endlessly.

Infinitum in jure reprobatur (in-fī-nī'tum in jū're re-prō-bā'ter). Endlessness is disapproved in the law.

infirm. Weak; sickly; feeble in mind or body, particularly from old age. Lacking purpose.

infirmary. A building or part of a building devoted to the care of sick and disabled persons.

infirmative (in-fėr'mạ-tiv). Tending to weaken or lessen.

infirmitate. See **de infirmitate**; **essoin de infirmitate**.

infirmity. Disease; physical or mental weakness. Including abnormal weaknesses, such as impaired heart functions, as well as acute diseases. 29A Am J Rev ed Ins § 1211. Something beyond a temporary disorder; an ailment of a somewhat established or settled character which, at least, has a tendency to impair a person's health and physical vigor. Anno: 26 ALR 1515. As the word appears in an application for life, health, or accident insurance or in any representation, warranty or condition contained in such a policy:—a defective condition of a substantial character which in some material degree impairs the physical condition and health of the applicant, and increases the chance of death, sickness, or accident against which the insurance company is asked to issue insurance. 29 Am J Rev ed Ins § 749.

infirmity exemption. A homestead exemption granted an infirm person, although he is not the head of a family. 26 Am J1st Home § 15.

in flagrante delicto (in flā-gran'te dē-lik'tō). In the act of committing the offense; "red-handed." State v Smith, 156 NC 628, 72 SE 321.

inflammable. A substance easily ignited.

inflammable substance. See **inflammable**.

inflation. An economic condition characterized by rising prices and a decrease in the purchasing power of money. 22 Am J2d Damg § 87; 27 Am J2d Em D § 274.

inflict. To impose as a burden. To cause, as to produce injury by striking. To impose as punishment pursuant to sentence.

The word does not necessarily imply direct violence. There is no more appropriate use of the word than in connection with punishment and to inflict punishment clearly includes imprisonment and involuntary restraint, as well as hanging, beheading, or whipping. Commonwealth v Macloon, 101 Mass 1.

inflicted injury. Any bodily harm which is caused to be suffered by the act of one person upon another. Commonwealth v Macloon, 101 Mass 1. For some purposes, confined to an injury intentionally produced, not including an injury caused by an insane person. Great Southern Life Ins. Co. v Campbell, 148 Miss 173, 114 So 262, 56 ALR 681 (phrase appearing in exception stated in double indemnity provision of life insurance policy.) Noun: The quality possessed by a person through ability, educa-

INFLUENCE [621] INFORMER

tion, social standing, or wealth to affect the course of conduct or of the acts of another.

influence. Verb: To alter, move, sway, or affect. State v Ventola 122 Conn 635, 191 A 726, 110 ALR 578. In some connotations, as in labor relations, pressure applied to corrupt or over-ride the will, at least something beyond innocent communications and friendly intercourse between employer and employee. Texas & N.O. R. Co. v Brotherhood of R. & S.S. Clerks, 281 US 548, 74 L Ed 1034, 50 S Ct 427.

See **undue influence.**

influence of liquor. See **under the influence of liquor.**

influencing election. Restricting the liberty of an elector to vote according to his best judgment and conscience or bringing to bear any influence calculated to affect adversely the purity of an election. 26 Am J2d Elect § 385.

influencing jurors. Bringing a bad influence to bear upon jurors for the purpose of obtaining a desired verdict. 31 Am J Rev ed Jury § 66.

influenza. An inflammation of the respiratory tract. A common disease. 58 Am J1st Workm Comp § 244. But a disease which spreads rapidly by infection and may be deadly, especially in its aftereffects, unless medical treatment is obtained.

in force. In effect; operative, as in the case of a contract which is in force until it is abrogated or rescinded voluntarily or in judicial proceedings, or it terminates in accordance with a provision for termination contained in the contract. Malanti v Metropolitan Life Ins. Co. 127 Misc 674, 675, 216 NYS 643, 644.

informal. Lacking in form; not according to formal rules or requirements.

informality. The quality of being informal. In pleading, a deviation, in alleging necessary facts and circumstances, from the well approved forms of expression, and a substitution in lieu thereof of other terms, which nevertheless constitute plain, intelligible and explicit language. State v Gallimore, 24 NC (2 Ired L) 372, 377.

in forma pauperis (in fôr'mạ pâ'pẹ-ris). In the status of a poor person. The characterization of an action or proceeding authorized by statute by a person who by reason of poverty is unable to give security for the payment of costs, where the statute requires security to be given. Anno: 6 ALR 1285. The characterization of an appeal by a poor person, especially in a criminal case. 4 Am J2d A & E § 345.

See **dispauper; dives costs; poverty affidavit.**

information. In common parlance, acquired knowledge or knowleding of facts which advise and lead to the acquisition of knowledge. In the technical legal sense, an accusation of the commission of a crime, otherwise known as a complaint or affidavit, upon which an accused is brought to trial and prosecuted for a misdemeanor or trivial offense or, if a felony is charged, whether there is probable cause for the accusation so that the accused should be held for, or bound over to await the action of, the grand jury. 21 Am J2d Crim L § 441. In another sense of the term, a written accusation of crime preferred by a public prosecuting officer without the intervention of a grand jury. 27 Am J1st Indict § 27.

See **libel of information.**

informational agencies. Administrative agencies with investigatory or inquisitorial powers. 1 Am J2d Admin L § 85.

information and belief. See **upon information and belief.**

information for an intrusion. A prosecution against intruders upon the public domain; a method of redress for a trespass committed on the lands of the commonwealth in the nature of an action of trespass quare clausum fregit. Commonwealth v Hite, 33 Va (6 Leigh) 588.

information in chancery. A bill in chancery filed in behalf of the crown. For all practical purposes in modern times, the same as a bill in equity, although at one time distinguishable from an ordinary bill in equity in the regard that, since filed on behalf of the crown, all that was required was a statement of facts, it not being necessary for the crown to assume the position of a suitor or orator and pray for relief.

information in equity. See **information in chancery.**

information in rem. A proceeding instituted by the government for the forfeiture of goods imported from a foreign country, for failure to pay import duties thereon. Boyd v United States, 116 US 616, 29 L Ed 746, 6 S Ct 524.

information in the exchequer (in the eks-chek'ẽr). The institution of a suit in the English court of exchequer on behalf of the king for money, or an action in the king's behalf for damages for trespass.

information in the nature of quo warranto (in the nā'tūr of kwŏ wôr'an-to). A remedy often considered to be the same as quo warranto, although actually a remedy substituted for the latter, an older remedy under writ of quo warranto. 44 Am J1st Quo W § 2. A common law proceeding more modern than the writ of quo warranto, and properly a criminal prosecution, instituted not only to fine a usurper, but to oust him from an office, franchise, or liberty. 44 Am J1st Quo W § 3.

See **quo warranto.**

information of intrusion (in-trū'zhọn). See **information for an intrusion.**

information of title. A common-law proceeding for the confirmation of title by escheat. 27 Am J2d Esch § 29.

information return. A return required by tax law of an employer, bank, corporation, etc. of the amounts paid by way of wages, salaries, interst, dividends, etc. to employees, customers, stockholders, etc.

informatus non sum (in-for-mā'tus non sum). I am not informed,—a species of judgment by default which is given against a defendant when his attorney declares that he has no instruction to say anything in answer to the plaintiff, or in defense of his client. See 3 Bl Comm 397.

informer. One giving notice to the authorities of a violation of law; one who swears to an information for prosecution. In a more technical sense, one who prosecutes an action on behalf of the state for the recovery of a penalty, usually for the purpose of sharing in the penalty. 36 Am J2d Forf & P § 79. One who communicates to the revenue authorities information which he has of the violation of revenue laws; 34 Am J2d Fed Tax ¶ 9381. A person not an officer of the United States who detects and seizes any vessel, vehicle, merchandise, or baggage, subject to seizure and forfeiture under the customs laws and who reports the same to an officer of the customs, or who furnishes to a United States attorney, to the Secretary of the Treasury, or to any customs officer original information concerning any fraud upon the customs revenue, or a violation of the customs laws, perpetrated or contemplated. 21 Am J2d Cust D § 110.

informer's action. Broadly, any action brought by an informer. Technically, a qui tam action.
See **informer; qui tam action.**

in foro (in fō'rō). In the forum; in the court; in the jurisdiction.

in foro conscientiae (in fō'rō kon-she-en'she-ē). In the forum of conscience, in good faith. See footnote in Laidlaw v Organ (US) 2 Wheat 178, 185, 4 L Ed 214, 215.

in foro contentioso (in fō'rō kon-ten-she-ō'sō). In the forum of contention; in a court of litigation.

in foro domestico (in fō'rō dǫ-mes'ti-kō). In the domestic forum; in the home.

in foro ecclesiastico (in fō'rō e-klē-si-as'ti-kō). In the ecclesiastical court.

in foro legis (in fō'rō lē'jis). In a court of law.

in foro saeculari (in fō'rō sē-ku-lā'rī). In a secular court.

infortunium (in-for-tu'ni-um). Misfortune; misadventure; accident; ill luck.

infra (in'fra). Below; beneath; under; within; during.

infra aetatem (in'fra ē-tā'tem). Under age.

infra annos nubiles (in'fra an'nōs nū'bi-lēz). (Civil law.) Below marriageable age; that is, the condition of a woman under the age of twelve years.

infra annum (in'fra an'num). Within a year.

infra annum clause (in'fra an'num klâz). The within a year clause,—that clause of the Statute of Frauds which relates to "any agreement that is not to be performed within the space of one year from the making thereof. 49 Am J1st Stat F § 23.

infra annum luctus (in'fra an'num luk'tus). (Civil law.) Within the year of mourning. See 1 Bl Comm 457.

infra brachia (in'fra brā'ki-a). Within her arms.

infra civitatem (in'fra si-vi-tā'tem). Within the state.

infra comitatum vel extra (in'fra ko-mi-tā'tum vel ex'tra). Within the county or without.

infra corpus comitatus (in'fra kor'pus ko-mi-tā'tus). Within the body of the county; within the physical boundaries of the county. Waring v Clarke (US) 5 How 441, 464, 12 L Ed 226, 237; Commonwealth v Macloon, 101 Mass 1.

infraction. A violation of law, particularly a traffic rule or regulation. Ando v Woodberry, 8 NY2d 165, 203 NYS2d 74, 168 NE2d 520. A breach or violation of a duty, or obligation.

infra dig. (in'fra dig). An abbreviation of **infra dignitatem.**

infra dignitatem (in'fra dig-ni-tā'tem). Beneath the dignity.

infra dignitatem curiae (in'fra dig-ni-tā'tem kū'ri-ē). Below the dignity of the court. Moore v Little (NY) 4 Johns Ch 183, 184.

infra furorem (in'fra fu-rō'rem). During insanity; while insane.

infra hospitium (in'fra hos-pi'she-um). Within the inn. 29 Am J Rev ed Innk § 107.

infra jurisdictionem (in'fra jū-ris-dik-she-ō'nem). Within the jurisdiction.

infra ligeantiam domini regis (in'fra li-je-an'she-am dǫ'mi-nī rē'jis). Within the territory of our lord the king. Commonwealth v Macloon, 101 Mass 1.

infra ligeantiam regis (in'fra li-je-an'she-am re'jis). Within the allegiance of the king.

infra maneria (in'fra ma-ne'ri-a). Within the manors.

infra metas (in'fra me'tas). Within the metes or boundaries.

infra moenia (in'fra mē'ni-a). Within the walls; about the house.

infra praesidia (in'fra prē-si'di-a). Within the walls; under the protection; within complete subjection.

infra quatuor maria (in'fra qua'tu-or ma'ri-a). Within the four seas; that is, in England.

infra quatuor parietes (in'fra qua'tu-or pa-ri-ē'tēz). Within the four walls; in prison.

infra regnum (in'fra reg'num). Within the kingdom.

infra sex annos (in'fra sex an'nos). Within six years.

infra tempus semestre (in'fra tem'pus se-mes'tre). Within six months.

infra triduum (in'fra trī'du-um). Within three days.

in fraudem creditorum (in frâ'dem kre-di-tō'rum). In fraud of creditors.

in fraudem legis (in frâ'dem lē'jis). In fraud of the law.

In fraudem legis facit, qui salvis verbis legis, sententiam ejus circumvenit (in frâ'dem lē'jis fā'sit, quī sal'vis ver'bis lē'jis, sen-ten'she-am e'jus ser-kum-vē'nit). He works a fraud upon the law, who, observing the letter of the law, circumvents its spirit. State ex rel. Matthews v Forsyth, 147 Ind 466, 44 NE 593.

infringement. A violation of a right or privilege; an encroachment.

infringement of copyright. Copying, in whole or in part, in haec verba or by colorable variation, that which is protected under the Federal Copyright law; doing anything that the owner of a copyright alone has the right to do, without the consent of such owner. 18 Am J2d Copyr § 104.

infringement of name. The adoption by a corporation of a name so similar to that of another corporation, association, or firm as will result in confusion or deception. 18 Am J2d Corp § 156.
See **infringement of tradename.**

infringement of patent. A tort. Carbice Corp. v American Patents Development Corp. 283 US 27, 75 L Ed 819, 51 S Ct 334. The violation of a right secured to the inventor by the Patent Law. The manufacture, use, or sale of the patented process or instrumentality without authorization on the part of the patentee. Goodyear Shoe Machinery Co. v Jackson (CA 1 Mass) 112 F 146. The use of a patented invention beyond the valid terms of a license. General Talking Pictures Corp. v Western Electric Co. 305 US 124, 83 L Ed 81, 59 S Ct 116, reh den 305 US 675, 83 L Ed 437, 59 S Ct 355.

infringement of trademark. A use or imitation of one's trademark by another on the latter's goods in such manner that the purchasers of such goods are deceived, or likely to be deceived, and induced to believe that they were manufactured or sold by the owner of the trademark. 52 Am J1st Tradem § 84.

infringement of tradename. Such a colorable imitation of a tradename that the general public, in the exercise of reasonable care, might think that it is the name of the one first appropriating it. 52 Am J1st Tradem §§ 127 et seq.

infugare (in-fu-gā're). To chase; to compel to flee; to put to flight.

infula (in'fu-lạ). A band or fillet; a coif; a head dress.

in full. In complete performance, especially in reference to an obligation for money. A phrase written upon a check or appearing in a letter accompanying a check, employed for the purpose that the acceptance of the check may operate as an accord and satisfaction. 1 Am J2d Accord § 18.
See **full indorsement**; **receipt in full**.

in full life. Alive both civilly and physically.

in full settlement. A phrase indicating receipt of payment in full or acknowledging payment or performance accepted as the equivalent of complete performance or satisfaction.
Under a contract executed "in full settlement of all claims and demands," the phrase covers all rights, demands, claims or disputes as to property existing at the time of execution of the contract. Golden v Golden, 155 Okla 10, 8 P2d 42.

in futuro (in fū-tū'rō). In the future; at a future time.

In generalibus versatur error (in je-ne-rā'li-bus ver-sā'ter er'ror). Error thrives on general terms. Underwood v Carney (1 Cush) 55 Mass 285, 292.

in generali passagio (in je-ne-rā'lī pas-sā'ji-ō). In the general passage; that is, in the journey with the Crusaders to the Holy Land.

in genere (in jen'ẹ-rē). In kind.

In genere quicunque aliquid dicit sive actor sive reus, necesse est ut probat (in je'ne-re quī-kun'kwe a'li-quid dī'sit, sī've ak'tor sī've rē'us, ne-ses'se est ut prō'bat). In general, whoever alleges anything, whether plaintiff or defendant, is under the necessity of proving it.

ingenium (in-jē'ni-um). A trick; a fraudulent scheme or device.

ingenui (in-je'nū-ī). Plural of **ingenuus**.

ingenuitas (in-je-nu'i-tās). The condition of a freeman or that of a manumitted slave.

ingenuitas regni (in-je-nu'i-tās reg'nī). The freemen or yeomanry of the kingdom.

ingenuus (in-jen'ū-us). A native who was born a freeman.

in gold or the equivalent thereof in United States legal tender notes. A provision under which an obligation is completely discharged by a payment in legal tender notes, dollar per dollar. Killough v Alford, 32 Tex 457.

in good faith. With honesty, whether done negligently or not. Uniform Warehouse Receipts Act § 58.

in good order. See **good order**.

in good safety. A warranty phrase in marine insurance, amounting to a stipulation by the insured that the insurance shall not attach in case the vessel or cargo shall have been lost or damaged at the time appointed for the attachment of the risk. Alexander, Ramsay & Kerr v National Union Fire Ins. Co. (CA2 NY) 104 F2d 1006.

in good standing. See **good standing**.

ingredients. The two or more substances which are the components of a thing. The two or more substances from which a drug is fabricated. 25 Am J2d Drugs § 31.

in gremio legis (in grē'mi-ō lē'jis). In the bosom of the law,—that is, in abeyance. A term expressive of the status of the fee during the period intervening between the creation and the termination of a contingent remainder. 28 Am J2d Est § 223.

ingress. Access; entrance; means of entry. A going in; entry; a right to enter.

ingressu (in-gres'ū). A writ of entry.

ingressus (in-gres'sus). Same as **ingress**.

ingress and egress. The right or privilege of entering upon land and departing therefrom.

ingressus et egressus (in-gres'sus et ē-gres'sus). Ingress and egress; the right or liberty of entering upon land and departing therefrom.

in gross. Without deduction; considered as a whole. Braun's Appeal, 105 Pa 414. In one sum. At large; attached to a person rather than appurtenant to land.
See **alimony in gross**; **common in gross**; **easement in gross**.

ingrossator (in-gros-sā'tor). Same as **engrosser**.

ingrossing. An obsolete form of **engrossing**.

inhabitability. The condition of premises such as to permit occupancy as living quarters.

inhabitancy. A term, the meaning of which may vary according to the context in which it appears. Literally, the state or condition of an inhabitant. For some purposes, a dwelling house. For other purposes, domicil or legal residence. Thayer v Boston, 124 Mass 132.
The word will not be construed as involving the idea of domicil where it reasonably appears that such meaning is not consistent with the legislative intent. 25 Am J2d Dom § 10.
See **inhabitant**.

inhabitant. A word impossible of precise and inclusive definition, since the meaning varies according to the context in which it appears, particularly where the matter is one of determining the legislative intent in a statute. 25 Am J2d Dom § 10. Narrowly, a dweller or householder, whether he be a tenant in fee simple, a life tenant, a tenant for years, a tenant at will, or one who has no interest in the premises other than that it is his habitation and dwelling. One having a domicil in a particular place. 25 Am J2d Dom § 10. One domiciled in or having a fixed residence in a given locality. Anno: 53 ALR 1394. One, who, although he may not be a citizen, dwells or resides in a place permanently, or has a fixed residence therein, as distinguished from an occasional lodger or visitor. Re Wrigley (NY) 4 Wend 602, 603. Synonymous with the term "resident" where used in a general sense in a statute respecting requisites to jurisdiction of an action for divorce. 24 Am J2d Div & S § 247. For income tax purposes:—sometimes regarded as the equivalent of a domiciled person; at other times regarded as a resident. Anno: 82 ALR 982. A corporation in the state of incorporation. 36 Am J2d For Corp § 34.
See **inhabitancy**; **inhabitants**.

inhabitants. The plural of **inhabitant**; synonymous with population for the purpose of a statute respecting the census. Ludwig v Board of County Comrs. 170 Neb 600, 103 NW2d 838.

inhabited house duty. An English tax or duty which was imposed upon each inhabited dwelling-house.

in hac parte (in hak pär'tē). On this side; in this behalf.

in haec verba (in hēc ver'ba). In these words.

In haeredes non solent transire actiones quae poenales ex maleficio sunt (in hē-rē'dēz non sō'lent trans-ī're ak-she-ō'nēz kwē pē-nā'lēz ex ma-le-fi'she-ō sunt). Actions which are penal and which arise out of the commission of crime do not pass to the heirs.

inhalation. The breathing in of air and sometimes, in unfortunate situations, of fumes, gases, dust, or other harmful elements. 58 Am J1st Workm Comp § 252. For some purposes, a voluntary act, as in an exception in a life or accident policy of death or injury from "inhalation" of gas. Travelers' Ins. Co. v Ayers, 217 Ill 391, 75 NE 506 (noting a division of authority.)

inherent. An inseparable quality or part of a thing or a person; intrinsic to a thing or a person. Anno: 23 ALR 1095.

inherent condition. A condition not added by a separate clause but contained in the agreement as an intrinsic part of the substantial provisions. A condition which is not newly imposed but previously existing.

inherent covenant. A covenant in a deed which relates directly to the grant.

inherent danger in work. A danger incidental to, and characteristic of, certain work, not one arising solely from the method of performance of the details of the work. Anno: 23 ALR 1095.

inherent jurisdiction. The jurisdiction of a court existing under a grant of general jurisdiction to the court, not by a grant of jurisdiction for a specific purpose. Kelly v Conner, 122 Tenn 339, 123 SW 622.

See **inherent power of court.**

inherently dangerous article. An article fraught with danger lying in the character and content of the article, albeit the disastrous consequences are caused immediately by an external force. 46 Am J1st Sales § 814. An article, the use of which is dangerous because of the nature or character of the article, for example, gun powder. 46 Am J1st Sales § 815.

inherent power. The doctrine that the federal government has sovereign and inherent powers in addition to the powers given to it expressly or impliedly by the United States Constitution; a doctrine refused recognition as law by the United States Supreme Court. Kansas v Colorado, 206 US 46, 51 L Ed 956, 27 S Ct 655.

inherent power of court. A power essential to the very existence of the court or its ability to function in dispensing justice; the power to punish contempt, 17 Am J2d Contpt § 62; the power to grant a continuance in the interest of justice. State ex rel. Buck v McCabe, 140 Ohio St 535, 24 Ohio Ops 552, 45 NE2d 763. A power included within the scope of a court's jurisdiction which a court possesses irrespective of specific grant by constitution or legislation; a power which can neither be taken away nor abridged by the legislature. State ex rel. Ricco v Biggs, 198 Or 413, 255 P2d 1055, 38 ALR2d 720.

inherent power of officer or agent. A power native to the position, although it may not be sanctioned by an express grant of authority. 10 Am J2d Banks § 99.

inherent right. A term denoting the functional character of rights of members of a community in an unorganized state. State ex rel. McGrael v Phelps, 144 Wis 1, 128 NW 1041.

See **fundamental rights and privileges.**

inheretrix (in-he're-trix). An heiress; a woman who inherits property.

inherit. To take as an heir at law by descent. 23 Am J2d Desc & D § 1. The succession to the property of a decedent by those entitled to it. Glascott v Bragg, 111 Wis 605, 87 NW 853. Technically, to take by descent or succession rather than by will. Warren v Prescott, 84 Me 483, 24 A 948. But, appearing in a will, sometimes construed to include a taking by devise. 57 Am J1st Wills § 1329.

inheritable blood. Hereditary blood; relationship by blood through which an inheritance may be transmitted. See 2 Bl Comm 254.

inheritance. In strict usage, the taking of property by descent or intestate succession. In common parlance, the taking of real or personal property by either will or intestate succession. 28 Am J Rev ed Inher T § 8; 57 Am J1st Wills § 1329. An estate which has descended to the heir and has been cast upon him by the single operation of law. Estate of Donahue, 36 Cal 329. Property inherited; in common usage, property acquired by descent or through a will.

As used in a provision of the Bankruptcy Act that all property which vests in the bankrupt within six months after bankruptcy by bequest, devise, or "inheritance" shall vest in the trustee, the word is confined to property, both real and personal, coming to the bankrupt by intestate succession and is not to be distorted by making it apply to something that accrues as a result of a death but is not acquired through intestate succession. Thus, the word, could not include a recovery under the Federal Employers' Liability Act. Friedman v McHugh, 168 F2d 350, 11 ALR2d 733.

See **descent; words of inheritance.**

Inheritance Act (akt). The statute of 3 and 4 Wm. IV., c. 106, which amended the English law of descents.

For an outline of this statute see footnote in 2 Cooley's Blackstone, Commentaries 201.

inheritance tax. A succession tax; a tax on the privilege of taking property of a decedent in accordance with law or on the right to receive property of a decedent. Not a tax on decedent's privilege of disposition of his property. 28 Am J Rev ed Inher T § 8. A tax on the right to succession to property, and not on the property itself, and collectible out of each specific share or interest, and not out of the general property of the estate. Re Estate of Kennedy, 157 Cal 517, 108 P 280. Not a debt. Anno: 150 ALR 1287; 47 ALR2d 1015.

Although the term "inheritance tax" has been sometimes so employed as to include taxes of the nature of estate duties, proper regard for the etymology of the term is sufficient to restrain extension of its meaning beyond succession duties. The term as used in a private document, however, may well be deemed to have been intended to cover taxes

which are technically estate taxes as well as those which are strictly inheritance taxes. 28 Am J Rev ed Inher T § 8.
See **collateral inheritance tax; estate tax; lineal inheritance tax; net estate; net succession; progressive tax.**

inherited and equally divided. A phrase in a will suggestive of an immediate taking of the interest devised. 57 Am J1st Wills § 1329.

inhibition. A prohibition; a writ to prohibit a judge from proceeding further in a matter.

inhibition against a wife. A writ to prohibit business transactions with a married woman.

in his demesne (in his dē-mēn'). See **demesne, as of fee.**

in his demesne as of fee. See **demesne, as of fee.**

In his enim quae sunt favorabilia animae, quamvis sunt damnosa rebus, fiat aliquando extentio statuti (in his e'min kwē sunt fa-vo-ra-bi'li-a a'ni-mē, quam'vis sunt dam-nō'sa rē'bus, fī'at a-li-quan'dō ex-ten'she-ō sta-tū'tī). In matters which are good for the soul, though they may be injurious to material things, some elasticity should be given to the statute.

in his own favor. As a phrase of a statute rendering incompetent the testimony of the surviving party to a contract in an action between him and the personal representative of the deceased party:—testimony which will tend to establish a present legal interest in the contract of cause of action to which it has reference. Proulx v Parrow, 115 Vt 232, 56 A2d 623.

in his own right. A phrase which excludes acquisition in a clearly representative capacity. Sigler v Sigler, 98 Kan 524, 158 P 864.

in his presence. See **presence.**

In his quae de jure communi omnibus conceduntur, consuetudo alicujus patriae vel loci non est allegenda (in his kwē dē jū're kom-mū'nī om'ni-bus kon-sē-dun'ter, kon-su-e-tū'dō a-li-kū'jus pa'tri-ē vel lō'sī non est al-le-jen'da). In those matters which in law are conceded to be common to all, a custom of a particular county or place should not be alleged.

in his verbis (in his ver'bis). In these words.

in hoc (in hok). In this.

inhonestus (in-ho-nes'tus). Dishonorable; shameful; disgraceful.

inhumanity. See **inhuman treatment.**

inhuman treatment. Cruelty; want of mercy.
See **cruel and unusual punishment; cruelty to animals; inhuman treatment which endangers life.**

inhuman treatment which endangers life. A ground of divorce under some statutes; not confined to physical or violent acts; may consist wholly of abusive and insulting words, much depending upon the moral, mental, and spiritual qualities of the victim. Thompson v Thompson, 186 Iowa 1066, 173 NW 55, 5 ALR 710; Ekerson v Ekerson, 121 Or 405, 255 P 480.

in hunc modum (in hunk mō'dum). In this manner.

in iisdem terminis (in i-is'dem ter'mi-nis). In the same terms.

in individuo (in in-dī-vi'du-ō). In its individual character; that is intact; in specie. Wright v Payne, 62 Ala 340.

in infinitum (in in-fi-nī'tum). To infinity; without end or limit.

in initialibus (in in-i-she-ā'li-bus). In the beginnings.

in initio (in in-i'she-o). In the beginning; at the commencement.

in initio litis (in in-i'she-ō lī'tis). At the beginning of the action or litigation.

in integrum (in in'tē-grum). Anew; over again.

in interest. Interested; having an interest.
See **real party in interest.**

in interstate commerce. See **engaged in interstate commerce; interstate commerce.**

in invidiam (in in-vi'di-am). In prejudice of; to the prejudice.

in invitum (in in-vī'tum). Against the will; without consent.

in ipsis faucibus (in ip'sis fâ'si-bus). In the very entrance.

in ipso articulo temporis (in ip'sō ar-ti'ku-lō tem'po-ris). At the very moment of time; on the very instant.

Iniquissima pax est anteponenda justissimo bello (in-i-quis'si-ma pax est an-te-pō-nen'da jus-tis'si-mō bel'lō). A most unfavorable peace is to be preferred to a war which is most just. Root v Stuyvesant (NY) 18 Wend 257, 305.

iniquity (i-nik'wi-ti). Want of justice. A judicial error; an error of the court or judge.

Iniquum est alios permittere, alios inhibere mercaturam (in-ī'qu-um est a'li-ōs per-mit'te-re, a'li-ōs in-hi'be-re mer-ka-tū'ram). It is unfair to permit some to carry on trade and to prohibit others.

Iniquum est aliquem rei sui esse judicem (in-ī'qu-um est a'li-quem rē'ī su'ī es'se jū'di-sem). It is improper for a person to be a judge in his own cause.

Iniquum est ingenuis hominibus non esse liberam rerum suarum alienationem (in-ī'qu-um est in-ge'-nu-is ho-mi'ni-bus non es'se li'be-ram rē'rum su-ā'rum ā-li-ē-nā-she-ō'nem). It is unjust for freemen not to be at liberty to alienate their own property.

in issue. Regularly and properly in controversy before the court. Timken Roller Bearing Co. v Pennsylvania Railroad Co. 273 US 665, 71 L Ed 829, 47 S Ct 550.

initial. Adjective: The first. Noun: The first letter of a name, often used in place of the name in a signature, especially in place of the middle name. Verb: To sign with an initial or initials.
See **initials.**

initial carrier. The first carrier in a pair or series of connecting carriers, the carrier who received the goods from the shipper. 14 Am J2d Car § 700.
It has also been held that the term refers to the carrier contracting with the shipper, and is not necessarily the one whose line constitutes the first link in transportation. Knapp v Minneapolis, St. P & S. S. M. Ry. Co. 33 ND 291, 156 NW 1019.

initial court. See **nisi prius.**

initialia testimonii (in-i-she-ā'li-a tes-ti-mō'ni-ī). The preliminary examination of a witness.

initialibus. See **in initialibus.**

initial notice of loss. A summary or abbreviated form of notice of loss of, or damage to, goods in the possession of a carrier, sometimes required by

INITIALING [626] IN

stipulation in the contract of carriage. 14 Am J2d Car § 584.

initialing protest (i-nish'al prō'test). Same as **noting protest**.

initials. The first letters of a person's christian name or names and the first letter of his surname or family name, e.g. J. F. K. for John F. Kennedy. 38 Am J1st Name § 7. Sufficient as a designation of the creditors of a bankrupt in the schedule of creditors. 9 Am J2d Bankr § 373. Sufficient as a signature of a negotiable instrument. Merchants Bank v Spicer (NY) 6 Wend 443. Insufficient as a signature binding a person as bail. 8 Am J2d Bail § 64. Not a proper signature to a bill of exceptions. 4 Am J2d A & E § 466.

initiate. Verb: To start a movement. To commence something, for example a proceeding. To propose for approval. Idaho Power Co. v Thompson (DC Idaho) 19 F2d 547. To bring a person into an activity, a fraternal order, association, or social club. Noun: One newly brought into a fraternal order, association, or club.

initiate curtesy. See **curtesy initiate**.

initiate tenant by curtesy. See **curtesy initiate**.

initiated law. A statute enacted by the people as an initiative measure.
See **initiative**.

initiation. A ceremony, formal or informal, by which one is received into a fraternal order, social group, or membership corporation.

initiation fee. A sum paid by a member to a club or other association for the privilege of joining the club. Masonic Country Club v Holden (CA 6 Mich) 18 F2d 553. The charge imposed by a labor union upon one joining the union.

initiative. The power reserved to the people to propose laws and amendments to the constitution and to enact or reject the same at the polls, generally independent of the legislature. 28 Am J Rev Init & R § 2. The name which has been given to a proceeding which has been authorized in a number of states by constitutional amendments of comparatively recent adoption, whereby the people reserve to themselves the right to propose laws to be enacted by the legislature and submitted to the vote of the electors of the state. 28 Am J Rev ed Init & R §§ 3 et seq. As applied to municipalities:—the power reserved to the people of a municipality residing therein to propose laws or ordinances and amendments to the charter. 37 Am J1st Mun Corp § 204.

in itinere (in ī-ti'ne-re). On the journey, particularly a journey made with the purpose of acquiring a new domicile. 25 Am J2d Dom § 35. On the voyage; on the circuit; in transit.

initio (i-nish'i-ō). A beginning; a commencement.
See **ab initio**.

initio litis. See **in initio litis**.

initium (in-i'she-um). A beginning; a commencement.

injection. See **hypodermic injection**.

in jeopardy. A technical expression used in stating the rule of former jeopardy or double jeopardy; on trial before a court of competent jurisdiction, on an indictment sufficient in form and substance to sustain a conviction, the jury having been charged with deliverance, that is, having been impaneled and sworn. 21 Am J2d Crim L §§ 175, 176.

in judgment. In a court. Merged in judgment.
See **ester in judgment**.

In judiciis, minori aetati succurritur (in jū-di'she-is, mī-nō'rī ē-tā'tī su-kur'ri-ter). Persons of minor age are assisted in judicial proceedings.

in judicio (in jū-dish'i-ō). In the presence of a judge; before a judge; in court.

In judicio non creditur nisi juratis (in jū-di'she-ō non kre'di-ter nī'sī jū-rā'tis). In a court of justice no one is believed who is not sworn.

injunction. A term of dual meaning, having reference to a suit to enjoin or to the writ, process, or restraining order issued pursuant to an order or decree obtained in the suit. 28 Am J Rev ed Inj § 2. In the former aspect, a form of action in equity which is designed to protect a plaintiff from irreparable injury to his property or other rights of which a court of equity will take cognizance, by prohibiting or commanding the doing of certain acts. Ladner v Siegel, 298 Pa 487, 148 A 699, 68 ALR 1172. In the latter aspect, a formal command of the court couched in the form of an order, writ, or process, as the local practice may require, directing the persons named therein to refrain from doing certain specified acts which appear to be against equity or conscience, or, where the relief is mandatory in form, commanding them to take certain steps to undo the wrong or injury with which they are charged—a command to refrain from, or to do a particular act. 28 Am J Rev ed Inj § 2.

In the legal usage of the term in some jurisdictions, reference to an "injunction" is to what is known in other jurisdictions as a temporary injunction. In such jurisdictions, an injunction in the sense of a final order which determines a controversy is deemed essentially the same as any other judgment or decree in equity, notwithstanding the order may include the enjoining of the performance of an act or an order requiring the performance of an act.

See **common injunction**; **irreparable injury**; **mandatory injunction**; **preliminary injunction**; **prohibitory injunction**; **restraining order**; **special injunction**; **temporary injunction**.

injunction against suit. See **stay**.

injunction bond. A bond required of the plaintiff as a condition of obtaining relief by a preliminary or interlocutory injunction. 28 Am J Rev ed Inj § 301.

injunction in labor dispute. A pertinent classification because of the prevailing pendency to regulate such relief closely by statute. 31 Am J Rev ed Lab §§ 490 et seq.

injunction pendente lite (injunction pen-den'te lī'te). A temporary injunction which is to operate pending a hearing of the suit on its merits, or until the final decree of the court is rendered. 28 Am J Rev ed Inj § 12.

in jure (in jū'rē). In law; in right.

injure. To harm; to hurt; to wound, but short of causing death at the time. Interstate Business Men's Acci. Asso. v Dunn, 178 Ky 193, 198 SW 727, 6 ALR 1333, 1336. To harm, damage, or reduce the value of property directly, or indirectly, as by obstructing access. Jones v Erie & Wyoming Valley Railroad Co. 151 Pa 30, 46.

in jure alterius (in jū're al-te'ri-us). In the right of another.

In jure causa proxima non remota spectatur (in jū're kâ'za pro'xi-ma non re-mō'ta spek-tā'ter). In law,

INJURED [627] IN

the proximate, and not the remote, cause is regarded.

injured. Hurt, damaged, wounded.
See **injure**.

injured party. A person wronged by the action of the other. Lee v Lee, 182 NC 61, 108 SE 352. The plaintiff; a person having a right of action, particularly a person having a ground of divorce.

A statute specifying incurable insanity as a permissible cause for divorce does not, in providing that divorces may be decreed upon the application of the "injured party," make the divorce unattainable because there is no injury to the other party to the marriage, the term referring only to a husband or wife who, by the plain terms of the act, is intended to have a right of action for divorce on the grounds of incurable insanity. State v Brown, 213 Ind 118, 11 NE2d 679, 113 ALR 1243.

See **innocent or injured person**.

In jure non remota causa sed proxima spectatur (in jū´re non rē-mō´ta kâ´za sed pro´xi-ma spek-tā´ter). In law, not the remote cause, but the proximate cause is regarded. Maryland Steel Co. v Marney, 88 Md 482, 42 A 60.

in jure proprio (in jū´re pro´pri-ō). In a person's own right.

injuria (in-jū´ri-a). A wrong; the violation of a legal right. See 3 Bl Comm 2. In the Roman law, a legal wrong for which redress would be granted, whether against the person or against property. Pavesich v New England Life Ins. Co. 122 Ga 190, 50 SE 68. A tortious act, whether intentional or accidental. Wright v Chicago & Northwestern Railway, 7 Ill App 438, 446.

injuria absque damno (in-jū´ri-a abs´kwe dam´nō). Wrong without damage. 1 Am J2d Act § 69.

But a direct invasion of a legal right imports damage. 52 Am J1st Torts § 6.

injuria atque damnum (in-jū´ri-a at´kwē dam´num). The violation of a legal right coupled with actual loss.

Injuria fit ei cui convicium dictum est, vel de eo factum carmen famosum (in-jū´ri-a fit ē´ī kī kon-vi´she-um dik´tum est, vel dē ē´ō fak´tum kar´men fa-mō´sum). An injury is done to him of whom reviling things are said, or concerning whom a defamatory poem is composed.

Injuria illata judici, seu locum tenenti regis, videtur ipsi regi illata maxime si fiat in exercentem officium (in-jū´ri-a il-lā´ta jū´di-sī, sū lō´kum te-nen´tī rē´jis, vi-dē´ter ip´sī rē´jī il-lā´ta mak´si-mē sī fī´at in ex-er-sen´tem of-fi´she-um). An injury offered to a judge or to a person holding the place of the king, seems to be as if it were offered to the king himself, if done while the person is in the exercise of his office.

Injuria non excusat injuriam (in-jū´ri-a non ex-kū´zat in-jū´ri-am). An injury does not excuse an injury.

Injuria non praesumitur (in-jū´ri-a non prē-zu´mi-ter). Injury is not presumed.

Injuria propria non cadet beneficium facientis (in-jū´ri-a prō´pri-a non kă´det be-ne-fi´she-um fā-she-en´tis). No benefit shall accrue to a person from his own wrongdoing.

Injuria servi dominum pertingit (in-jū´ri-a ser´vī do´-mi-num per-tin´jit). The wrongdoing of the servant attaches to the master.

injuria sine damno (in-jū´ri-a sī´ne dam´nō). The violation of a legal right without damage,—an obvious impossibility as pointed out by Lord Holt, for the reason that every injury imports damage in the nature of it. See 52 Am J1st Torts § 6.

injuriously affected. As a condition of the right to damages in eminent domain, the consequences of an act which would have given a right of action if the act had not been authorized by the statute. Memphis & Charleston Railroad Co. v Birmingham, Sheffield & Tennessee River Railroad Co. 96 Ala 571, 11 So 642.

injury. The invasion of a legal right. Bowman v Davenport, 243 Iowa 1135, 53 NW2d 249, 63 ALR2d 853. To be distinguished from "damage," which is the loss, hurt, or harm resulting from the "injury." 22 Am J2d Damg § 1.

As the word appears in an application for life, health or accident insurance:—a substantial injury affecting the general health. 29 Am J Rev ed Ins § 750. As the term is used in a workmen's compensation statute:—any lesion or change in the structure of the body, causing harm thereto and a lessened facility of its natural and normal use. Sullivan's Case, 265 Mass 497, 164 NE 457, 62 ALR 1458. Damage or harm to the physical structure of the body, although not necessarily presenting external or visible signs of its existence, 58 Am J1st Workm Comp § 194; sometimes construed to include simple and common diseases, 58 Am J1st Workm Comp § 244; including also nonoccupational diseases and disorders of an idiopathic nature, as well as those having a definitely traumatic origin. 58 Am J1st Workm Comp § 244.

injury arising by accident. See **accident**.

injury arising out of employment. The existence of a direct cause and effect relationship between the injury and the employment. Gage v Connecticut General Life Ins. Co. (Mo App) 273 SW2d 761, 47 ALR2d 1234.

injury by the elements. Such an injury as results from the operation of the most common destructive forces of nature against which buildings need to be protected. Hanchett v O'Reilly, 76 NJL 212, 68 A 1066.

injury in his property. An injury to his property; also the diminishing of his property by a transfer of property, or a payment of money, induced by fraud. Wheeler-Stenzel Co. v National Window Glass Jobbers Asso. (CA3 NJ) 152 F 864. Harm or damage resulting to his property directly or indirectly. Jones v Erie & Wyoming Valley Railroad Co. 151 Pa 30, 46.

injury in person or property. An expression in the disjunctive, often used in statutes for comprehensive effect in providing for recovery of damages caused by a violation of the statute, e.g., in a civil damage or dramshop act. Anno: 6 ALR2d 798.

injury to life or limb. A personal or bodily injury. Bailey v Bailey, 97 Mass 373. Not limited to such an injury as results in death or the actual loss of a limb. Iola v Birmbuam, 71 Kan 600, 81 P 198.

See **bodily injuries; personal injury**.

injury to property. Something materially affecting the capacity of particular property for ordinary use and enjoyment. Evans v Reading Chemical Fertilizing Co. 160 Pa 209, 219, 28 A 702.

injury to the person. See **personal injury**.

In justitia recipienda, minimo de regno suo comparetur (in jūs-ti´she-a re-si-pi-en´da, mi´ni-mō dē reg´nō su´ō kom-pa-rē´ter). In receiving justice, he should be placed on a level with the meanest person in the kingdom. Chisholm v Georgia (US) 2 Dal 419, 460, 1 L Ed 440, 458.

Injustum est, nisi tota lege inspecta, de una aliqua ejus particula proposita judicare vel respondere (in-jus'tum est, nī'sī tō'ta lē'je in-spek'ta, dē ū'na a'li-qua ē'jus par-ti'ku-la prō-pō'zi-ta jū-di-kā're vel respon-dē're). Without having examined the whole of a law, it is unfair to judge or to give an opinion concerning some particular provision of it.

in jus vocando (in jūs vo-kan'dō). By calling or summoning into court. See 3 Bl Comm 279.

in jus vocare (in jūs vō-kā're). To call or summon to court.

ink. See **recording; writing.**

in kind. In produce or goods in place of money. 32 Am J1st L & T § 61. In the same or a similar commodity or kind of goods.
As the expression is used in a statute providing that the commissions of a tax collector shall be paid "in kind," it is held to mean that the commission shall be paid in the same kind of funds that the collector has legally received in payment of the tax. Wilson v State, 51 Ark 212, 213.
See **in specie.**

inlagare (in-la-gā're). To restore an outlaw to the protection of the law.

inlagation (in-lạ-gā'shọn). Restoration of an outlaw to the protection of the law.

inlagh. A person who is under the protection of the law.

inland bill. A bill of exchange which is, or on its face purports to be, both drawn and payable within the state. 11 Am J2d B & N § 20.

inland bill of exchange. Same as **inland bill.**

inland marine insurance. A term suggestive of risks carried upon ships or cargoes to be found on inland waters of the United States but employed by insurers in an indiscriminate manner for a much broader category of insurance, including various risks having no relation to transportation by water, even some, such as floating policies on jewels, clothing, etc., which have only a tenuous connection with transportation of any kind.

inland navigation. Navigation upon waters lying wholly within the boundaries of a state, and hence not including any of the great lakes. Moore v American Transportation Co. (US) 24 How 1, 16 L Ed 674. Navigation upon inland waters.
See **inland rules of navigation; inland waters.**

inland rules of navigation. Special navigation rules made by local authority relative to river, lake, or other inland water. 33 USC § 1092.

inland waters. Rivers, lakes, great ponds, and other bodies of water within, or partly within, the boundaries of the United States, which are not tidal waters. Chamberlain v Hemingway, 63 Conn 1, 27 A 239.
"All the gulfs, all the inland seas, form only portions detached, but not entirely separated from that universal sea denominated the ocean." The Orient (CC La) 16 F 916, 920.
As the expression "inland waters of the United States" was used in the act of Congress regulating prize proceedings and the distribution of prize money, it referred to all waters of the United States upon which a naval force could go, other than bays and harbors on the sea coast. In most instances, property of the enemy on them could be taken, if at all, by an armed force, without the aid of vessels of war. United States v Vessels of War (US) 16 Otto 607, 27 L Ed 286, 1 S Ct 539.
See **Great Lakes.**

inland waters of the United States. See **inland waters.**

inlantal. Same as **demesne land.**

inlaughe. (Saxon.) Under the protection of the law.

inlaw (in-lâ'). To restore from a condition of outlawry back to the protection of the law; to pardon a person of attainder.

in-law. A blood relative of one's spouse. A relative by marriage.
See **brother-in-law; sister-in-law.**

in law. As it is according to law. Existing under the law. Implied by law; presumed by law. In law, as distinguished from equity.

inleased (in-lēsd'). Trapped; ensnared.

in lecto (in lek'to). In bed.

in lecto mortali (in lek'tō mor-ta'lī). On one's deathbed.

in libera eleemosyna (in li'be-ra ē-le-em-os'in-a). In free alms. See 2 Bl Comm 101. Same as **frankalmoign tenure.**

in libero soccagio (in li'be-rō so-kā'ji-ō). In free socage.
See **free socage.**

in lieu of. In substitution for or in place of. Ordinarily implying the existence of something to be replaced. Lamb v Milliken, 78 Colo 564, 243 P 624.
But a mere statement in a lease that a certain paragraph is "in lieu of" prior paragraphs does not necessarily eliminate such prior paragraphs. Milan Bldg. Co. v Dannelley (Tex Civ App) 57 SW2d 345.

in limine (in lim'i-nē). On the threshold; at the outset.

in linea recta (in li'ne-a rek'ta). In the direct line.

in litem (in li'tem). In or during the suit or litigation.

in loco (in lō'kō). In the place.

in loco parentis (in lō'kō pạ-ren'tis). See **person in loco parentis.**

in majorem cautelam (in ma-jō'rem kâ-tē'lam). By way of greater caution; for greater security.

in majorem cautelam, si qua forte sit irregularitas (in mā-jō'rem kâ-tē'lam, sī quā for'te sit ir-re-gū-la'ri-tās). For greater caution, if perchance there might be irregularity.

In majore summa continetur minor (in mā-jō're sum'ma kon-ti-nē'ter mī'nor). The lesser sum is contained or included in the greater.

in malam partem (in ma'lam par'tem). In an evil sense.

In maleficiis voluntas spectatur, non exitus (in ma-le-fi'she-is vo-lun'tas spek-tā'ter, non ex'i-tūs). In criminal offenses, the intent and not the outcome is regarded.

In maleficio, ratihabitio mandato comparatur (in ma-le-fi'she-ō, rā-tī-ha-bi'she-ō man-dā'to kom-pa-rā'ter). In tort, a ratification is regarded as a command.

in manu (in ma'nū). In his hand.
See **with the mainour.**

inmate. A co-lodger; a person who lives in the same abode with another or others. A person confined with others in a state prison, penitentiary, jail, state hospital, etc.

In maxima potentia minima licentia (in ma'xi-ma po-ten'she-a mi'ni-ma li-sen'she-a). Where power is greatest freedom is least.

In mediam viam tutissimus ibis (in me'di-am vī'am tu-tis'si-mus ī'bis). In the middle of the road you will journey most safely. Bledsoe v Nixon, 69 NC 89.

in medias res (in mē'di-as rēz). Into the midst of the thing; into the meat of the matter.

In mercibus illicitis non sit commercium (in mer'si-bus il-li'si-tis non sit kom-mer'she-um). There should be no commerce in illicit merchandise.

in mercy. Liable to amercement.
At the early common law, if a plaintiff failed in his suit, he was at the mercy of the king with regard to the fine which was to be imposed upon him for his false claim. Day v Woodworth (US) 13 How 362, 14 L Ed 181.

in mero jure (in me'rō jū're). Of mere right; on the mere right.

in misericordia (in mi-se-ri-kor'di-a). Liable to amercement for unjust detention from the plaintiff.
At one time, by the common law, if the plaintiff failed to recover, he was amerced pro falso clamore (sentenced to pay a fine for bringing a false claim), but if he recovered judgment, the defendant was in misericordia for his unjust detention of the plaintiff's debt. Day v Woodworth (US) 13 How 362, 14 L Ed 181.

in misericordia domini regis pro falso clamore suo (in mi-se-ri-kor'di-a do'mi-nī rē'jis prō fal'sō kla-mō're su'ō). At the mercy of the king for his false claim. See 3 Bl Comm 376.

in mitiori sensu (in mi-she-ō'rī sen'sū). In the milder or less harmful sense.
It was a doctrine of the early common law, since departed from, that when words charged as defamatory were capable of two constructions, the court would presume that they were intended to be used in the less harmful sense. Bash v Sommer, 20 Pa 159, 162.

in modum assisae (in mō'dum as-sī'sē). In the manner of an assize.

in mora (in mo'ra). In delay; in default.

in mortmain (in mort'mān). See **mortmain**.

in mortu manu (in môr'tū mā'nū). In mortmain. See **mortmain**.

inn. A public house of entertainment for all who choose to visit it. 29 Am J Rev ed Innk § 2. Elaborately defined, a house held out to the public by the proprietor thereof as a place where transient persons who come in a fit condition will be received and entertained as guests for compensation. 29 Am J Rev ed Innk § 2.

innamium (in-na'mi-um). A pledge.

in naturali laxitate (in na-tū-rā'lī la-xi-tā'te). In a natural state of freedom; the unconfined and unrestrained state of wild animals. Geer v Connecticut, 161 US 519, 524, 40 L Ed 793, 795, 16 S Ct 600.

in naufragorum miseria et calamitate tanquam vultures ad praedam currere (in nâ-fra-gō'rum mi-se'ri-a et ka-la-mi-tā'te tan'quam vul'tu-rēz ad prē'dam ker're-re). To run like vultures to their prey amidst the misery and misfortune of those suffering shipwreck. See 1 Bl Comm 293.

innavigability. The state of a ship which is unseaworthy; the state of a waterway which is impassable for ships.

innavigable. Descriptive of the condition of innavigability.
See **innavigability**.

inner barrister. An English barrister who is privileged to plead within the bar.

inner house (in'ẽr hous). The superior department of the high court of sessions in Scotland.

inner temple (in'ẽr tem'pl). See **inns of court**.

innings (in'ings). Tide lands which have been reclaimed by man. The successive periods in a baseball game in which both teams come to bat. Figuratively, opportunity.

innkeeper. The proprietor of an inn. 29 Am J Rev ed Innk § 2.
See **inn**.

innkeeper's lien. The lien of the proprietor of an inn or hotel upon the effects of a guest in the inn or hotel for the amount of unpaid reasonable charges for the keeping and entertainment of the guest. 29 Am J Rev ed Innk § 145.

innocence. Freedom from guilt.
See **presumption of innocence**.

innocent. Free from wrongdoing or from guilty participation therein. Not guilty.

innocent agent. A person who acts in violation of law, being moved to the act by another, but incurs no guilt, because either he lacks the capacity to commit a crime or was entirely unaware of the circumstances which made his act a violation. Smith v State, 21 Tex App 107, 132, 17 SW 552.

innocent conversion. See **technical conversion**.

innocent conveyance. A conveyance which transfers only the title of the grantor, as opposed to a tortious conveyance which purports to convey a larger estate than the grantor has.

innocent holder for value. One who has acquired property from another for value without notice of a third person's equities in or claims to the property.
In order that a payee of trust funds may prevail as an innocent holder for value, in addition to being innocent of its trust character at the time of its receipt, he must have parted with some value, suffered some detriment, or forborne the exercise of some right which he might otherwise have asserted. Aetna Casualty & Surety Co. v Local Building & Loan Asso. 162 Okla 141, 19 P2d 612, 86 ALR 526.
See **holder in due course**; **innocent indorsee**.

innocent indorsee. One who has acquired the instrument by indorsement without notice of defects in the instrument, prior dishonor, or of a third person's equities in or claims to the instrument. Christensen v Farmers' Warehouse Asso. 5 ND 438, 67 NW 300.
See **holder in due course**.

innocent or injured person. The status of a party to an action for annulment of a marriage on the ground of a prior undissolved marriage, which is negatived by knowledge of the existence of the prior marriage at the time of entering into the marriage sought to be dissolved. 4 Am J2d Annul § 56.
See **innocent party**.

innocent party. One who did not participate in the disputed transaction understandingly, intention-

INNOCENT

ally, or of his own free will, and could not have ascertained the facts by the exercise of due diligence. 27 Am J2d Eq § 22.

See **innocent or injured person.**

innocent purchaser. See **bona fide purchaser.**

innocent trespasser. One who trespasses under color of right, or in good faith by mistake. Hughett v Caldwell County, 313 Ky 85, 230 SW2d 92, 21 ALR2d 373.

innocent woman. A woman who has never had illicit sexual intercourse with a man. State v Shoemaker, 101 NC 690, 693.

innominate (i-nom′i-nāt). (Civil law.) Unclassified; not assigned to any particular class.

In nomine Dei, Amen (in nō′mi-ne Dē′ī, ā′men). In the name of God, Amen.
  Formerly, a will was ordinarily thus begun. Today it is common practice to begin a will with the same words in English.

innonia (in-no′ni-a). An inclosure; a close.

In nostra lege unum comma evertit totum placitum (in nos′tra lē′je ū′num kom′ma ē-ver′tit tō′tum pla′-si-tum). In our law one comma overturns a whole plea. See 3 Bl Comm 410, note.

innotescimus (in-no-tes′si-mus). We make known.

in notis (in nō′tis). In the notes.

innovation (in-ō-vā′shọn). A change in method. A novation; a mode of extinguishing one obligation by another.

In novo casu novum remedium apponendum est (in nō′vō ka′sū nō′vum re-mē′di-um ap-pō-nen′dum est). In a novel case, a new remedy must be applied.

innoxiare (in-no-xi-ā′re). To exculpate; to purge an accused person of guilt.

inns. See **inns; inns of chancery; inns of court.**

inns of chancery. Associations of solicitors in London, existing originally for the purpose of instruction in chancery law and practice, later as preparatory schools for students intending to enter one of the inns of court, both of which functions have long been in disuse.
  See **Barnard's Inn; Clifford's Inn.**

inns of court. Associations of lawyers at London existing for the purpose of the instruction of students in the law and the practice of law and of calling men to the bar, the four principal inns being The Inner Temple, The Middle Temple, Lincoln's Inn, and Gray's Inn.
  See **Gray's Inn; Farydon Inn; inns of chancery.**

in nubibus (in nū′bi-bus). Among the clouds, that is, in abeyance. A term expressive of the status of the inheritance or fee during the period intervening between the creation and the termination of a contingent remainder, meaning in abeyance. 28 Am J2d Est § 223.

in nuce (in nū′sē). In a nutshell; concisely.

innuendo. A meaning conveyed by indirection. An allegation in the complaint, declaration, or petition, in an action for defamation, the purpose of which is to show the meaning of the publication or utterance and bring out its defamatory character and effect by reference to the antecedent matters contained in the inducement and the colloquium. 33 Am J1st L & S § 241.

in nullius bonis (in nul′li-us bō′nis). In the goods of no one.

in nullo est erratum (in nul′lō est er-rā′tum). No error has been committed. A form of pleading filed by the defendant in error in proceedings for review by writ of error. Edwards v Elliott (US) 21 Wall 532, 549, 22 L Ed 487, 489.

In obscura voluntate manumittentis, favendum est libertati (in ob-skū′ra vo-lun-tā′te ma-nu-mit-ten′-tis, fa-ven′dum est li-ber-tā′tī). In the case of a doubtful wish for the manumission of a slave, liberty is to be favored.

In obscuris, inspici solere quod verisimilius est, aut quod plerumque fieri solet (in ob-skū′ris, in′spi-sī so-lē′re quod ve-ri-si-mi′li-us est, ât quod plē-rum′kwe fī′e-rī so′let). In obscure or doubtful matters, it is customary to inquire into what is probable or what is ordinarily done.

In obscuris, quod minimum est sequimur (in ob-skū′-ris, quod mi′ni-mum est se′qui-mer). In obscure or doubtful matters, we follow that which is the least so.

in octavis (in ok-tā′vis). In eight (days).

inoculation. The injection of a virus into the body for the purpose of causing a disease in a mild form, thereby building up an immunity. 25 Am J1st Hlth § 35.

in odium spoliatoris (in ō′di-um spo-li-ā-tō′ris). To the prejudice of the pirate; a presumption applied in infringement of patent cases. Coffin v Ogden (US) 18 Wall 120, 21 L Ed 821, 823.

In odium spoliatoris omnia praesumuntur (in ō′di-um spo-li-ā-tō′ris om′ni-a prē-zu-mun′ter). All things are presumed to the prejudice of the pirate or the despoiler.

inofficiosum (in-of-fi-she-ō′sum). Neglectful of natural duty, or contrary thereto; unkind; unnatural.

inofficiosum testamentum (in-of-fi-she-ō′sum test-ta-men′tum). An undutiful or unkind will. See 2 Bl Comm 503.

inofficious testament (in-ọ-fish′us). Same as **inofficious will.**

inofficious will. A will omitting the testator's nearest relatives; a will deficient in natural duty. See 2 Bl Comm 503.

In omni actione ubi duae concurrunt districtiones, videlicet, in rem et in personam, illa districtio tenenda est quae magis timetur et magis ligat (in om′nī ak-she-ō′ne u′bi du′ē kon-ker′runt dis-trik-she-ō′nez, vi-de-lī′set, in rem et in per-sō′nam, il′la dis-trik′she-ō te-nen′da est kwē mā′jis ti-mē′ter et mā′jis li′gat). In every action where two distresses concur, that is to say, in rem and in personam, that distress will hold which is the more dreaded, and which binds the more firmly.

in omnibus (in om′ni-bus). In all things, in everything.

in omnibus causis motis et movendis (in om′ni-bus kâ′zis mō′tis et mo-ven′dis). In all cases pending and in all cases which may be instituted. Per Holt, C. J., in Parker v Kett (Eng) 1 Salk 95, 96.

In omnibus contractibus, sive nominatis sive innominatis, permutatio continetur (in om′ni-bus kon-trak′ti-bus, sī′ve no-mi-nā′tis sī′ve in-nō-mi-nā′tis, per-mu-tā′she-ō kon-ti-nē′ter). In all contracts, whether nominate or innominate, a consideration is contained.

In omnibus imperatoris excipitur fortuna; cui ipsas leges Deus subjecit (in om′ni-bus im-pe-rā-tō′ris ex-si'pi-ter for-tū'na; kī ip'sās lē'jēz Dē'us sub-jē'sit). The property of the emperor should in all matters be excepted; with respect to him, God has subjected the laws themselves. 1 Bl Comm 239.

In omnibus obligationibus in quibus dies non ponitur, praesenti die debetur (in om'ni-bus ob-li-gā-she-ō'ni-bus in qui'bus dī'ēz non pō'ni-ter, prē-zen'tī dī'ē de-bē'ter). (Civil law.) In all obligations in which no time is designated for their fulfillment, the obligation is presently due.

In omnibus poenalis judiciis, et aetati et imprudentiae succurritur (in om'ni-bus pe-nāl'is jū-di'she-is, et ē-tā'tī et im-prū-den'she-ē su-ker'ri-ter). In all penal judgments, both youth and lack of prudence are favored.

In omnibus quidem, maxime tamen in jure, aequitas spectanda sit (in om'ni-bus qui'dem, mak'si-mē ta'-men in jū're, ē'qui-tas spek-tan'da sit). In all matters indeed, but especially in matters of right, equity should be regarded.

In omni re nascitur res quae ipsam rem exterminat (in om'nī rē na'si-ter rēz kwē ip'sam rem ex-ter'mi-nat). In all things, something arises which exterminates the thing itself.

in open court. Before the court while it is in public session, as distinguished from a judge or judges of the court in chambers. Conover v Bird, 56 NJL 228, 230, 28 A 428.
See **open court.**

inoperative deed. A deed ineffectual to convey legal title, although possibly operating contractually. 23 Am J2d Deeds § 137.

inoperative patent. A patent for an invention which fails to secure to the inventor a monopoly of his actual invention. National Nut Co. v Sontag Chain Stores Co. (CA9 Cal) 107 F2d 318.

inoperative will. A will which is ineffective because of statutory restrictions upon the disposition attempted by the will. Re Houston, 383 Pa 466, 119 A2d 304.

inopportune. Unseasonable in time; at the wrong time. Pennsylvania Co. v Sloan, 125 Ill 72, 80.

inops consilii (in'ops kon-si'li-ī). Without the aid of counsel. Den ex dem. Davenport v Wynne, 28 NC (6 Ired L) 128.

in or about. A phrase having reference to an area and expressing the idea of physical proximity. 58 Am J1st Workm Comp § 86.

inordinatus (in-or-di-nā'tus). An intestate; a person who dies without leaving a valid will.

in ore (in ō're). In the mouth.

in or on a motor vehicle. A clause depicting the risk of loss under a policy of accident insurance which, as such, is to be construed in favor of the insured. 29 Am J Rev ed Ins § 262. Having the body in some sort of physical contact with the automobile, not necessarily sitting in the place provided for the seating of passengers. 29A Am J Rev ed Ins § 1241.
The insured does not have to be actually or wholly on the car in the sense of being entirely off the ground. In some instances, the coverage has been held to extend to situations in which there was actually no physical contact, before injury, between the person injured and the automobile, it appearing, however, that such person was either preparing to enter the automobile or in close proximity thereto after alighting. 29A Am J Rev ed Ins § 1241.

in or on a public or passenger conveyance. Within the meaning of a provision of an accident policy which depicts the coverage or a double indemnity provision of a life insurance policy:—riding inside the conveyance and, as well, riding on the platform or even while being in the act of boarding or alighting from a bus or car. 29A Am J Rev ed Ins § 1254.

in or upon. See phrases beginning **in or on.**

in ovo (in ō'vō). In the egg; in the first stage; at the beginning.

in pacato solo (in pa-kā'tō sō'lō). On peaceful soil.

in pace Dei et regis (in pa'se Dē'ī et rē'jis). In the peace of God and the king.

in pais (in pā). In the country; outside of the court; away from court; out of court. In free translation:—in an informal manner rather than in a formal attempt to comply with the law.
See **estoppel in pais; notice in pais.**

in paper. The state of the proceedings in a case, in reference to a memorandum or record thereof, before the complete record is extended. 3 Bl Comm 406.

in pari causa (in pa'rī kâ'za). In a similar or like case; under similar or like conditions.

In pari causa possessor potior haberi debet (in pa'rī kâ'za po-ze'sor po'she-or hā-bē'rī de'bet). Under like conditions, the party who is in possession ought to be deemed the stronger.

In pari causa potior est conditio possidentis (in pa'rī kâ'za po'she-or est kon-di'she-ō pos-si-den'tis). Under similar conditions, the situation of the party who is in possession is the stronger.

in pari delicto (in pa'rī de-lik'tō). In equal wrong; equally at fault. 27 Am J2d Eq § 72. The status of both parties to an illegal agreement or transaction where they are equally at fault. 1 Am J2d Acctg § 56; 17 Am J2d Contr § 221.
It is a trite and commonplace maxim that where parties are equally in wrong, the court will not give one legal redress against the other but will leave them where it finds them. Anno: 116 ALR 1018. So, where the parties are equally at fault the defendant and the party in possession hold the strong position. 17 Am J2d Contr § 221.

In pari delicto melior est conditio defendentis (in pa'rī de-lik'tō me'li-or est kon-di'she-ō dē-fen-den'tis). Where the parties are equally at fault, the situation of the defendant is the more favorable.
If a person suffers injury while violating a public law, the other party being also a transgressor, he cannot recover for the injury, if his unlawful act was the cause of the injury. Gilmore v Fuller, 198 Ill 130, 65 NE 84.

In pari delicto melior est conditio possidentis (in pa'rī de-lik'tō me'li-or est kon-di'she-ō pos-si-den'tis). Where the parties are equally at fault, the situation of the party in possession is the preferable one. Fawcett v Supreme Sitting of Order of Iron Hall, 64 Conn 170, 29 A 614.

In pari delicto potior est conditio defendentis (in pa'rī de-lik'tō po'she-or est kon-di'she-ō de-fen-den'tis). Where the parties are equally at fault, the defendant holds the stronger position.
The general rule of the maxim applies not only to the original parties to an illegal, immoral or fraudulent transaction, but to their heirs, and to all parties claiming under them or by title derived from them, where no equitable rights intervene to protect

such parties. Dennehy v McNulta (CA7 Ill) 86 F 825.

In pari delicto, potior est conditio defendentis et possidentis (in pa′rī de-lik′tō, po′she-or est kon-di′she-ō de-fen-den′tis et pos-si-den′tis). Where the parties are equally at fault, the defendant and the party in possession hold the stronger position.

In pari delicto potior est conditio possidentis (in pa′rī de-lik′tō po′she-or est kon-di′she-o pos-si-den′tis). Where the parties are equally at fault, the situation of the party in possession is the stronger one. Morrison v Bennett, 20 Mont 560, 52 P 553.

in pari jure (in pa′rī jū′rē). In equal right. 27 Am J2d Eq § 148.

in pari materia (in pa′rī ma-te′ri-a). In relation to the same matter, subject, or object. Winston v State, 186 Ga 573, 198 SE 667, 118 ALR 719.

Statutes which relate to the same thing or to the same subject or object are in pari materia, although they were enacted at different times and it is a fundamental rule of statutory construction that such statutes should be construed together for the purpose of learning and giving effect to the legislative intention. 1 Am J2d Admin L § 40; 50 Am J1st Stat § 348.

in pari passu (in pa′rī pas′sū). On equal footing.

in part. Less than the whole, as a stock of goods consisting "in part" of inflammables.

in part of. A characteristic description of an article for the purpose of customs duties, meaning that the article contains a significant quantity of the named material. 19 USC, Headnote 9(f).

in patiendo (in pa-she-en′dō). In suffering; in allowing; in permitting.

in paying quantities. A clause familiar in oil and gas leases. A yield of oil or gas in excess of operating costs. Barnard v Gibson, 100 Cal App 2d 527, 224 P2d 90. Characterizing the production of a gas well in excess of the producing and marketing cost. Benedum-Trees Oil Co. v Davis (CA6 Tenn) 107 F2d 981; Barbour, Stedman & Herod v Tompkins, 81 W Va 116, 93 SE 1038.

Under the usual habendum clause, which fixes the duration of the lease at a designated number of years and so long thereafter as gas or oil shall be produced in "paying quantities," the right to an extension accrues only in the event of attainment of profitable production within the fixed term. Anno: 67 ALR 526.

in payment. See **in full; in full settlement; note in payment of an account.**

in pectore judicis (in pek′to-re jū′di-sis). In the breast of the court.

in pejorem partem (in pe-jō′rem par′tem). In the worse part; on the worse side.

in pendente (in pen-den′te). In suspense.
See **pendente lite.**

inpeny (in′pen-i). The customary payment which a tenant made to his landlord upon entering upon his tenancy.

in performance of duty. See **in the course of the employment.**

in perpetuam (in per-pe′tu-am). In perpetuity; forever.

Where land was conveyed in fee, and, as a part of the consideration, the grantor imposed a condition as to maintaining fences which was to be "perpetually" binding on the owners of the land, it was held that the condition did not impose an obligation on the grantee in perpetuam, but only upon the owners of the land, whoever they might be. Hickey v Lake Shore & Michigan Southern Railway Co. 51 Ohio St 40, 36 NE 672.
See **perpetual.**

in perpetuam rei memoriam (in per-pe′tu-am rē′ī me-mō′ri-am). For the perpetuation of the memory of the matter. The characterization of a deposition taken in advance of trial, for use in the event the attendance of the witness at the trial cannot be secured. Richter v Jerome, 115 US 55, 29 L Ed 345, 5 S Ct 1162.

in perpetuity. Of endless duration. Central R. Co. v New York Tel. Co. 101 NJL 353, 128 A 160.
See **perpetuity.**

in perpetuum (in pėr-pet′ū-um). In perpetuity; forever.

in perpetuum rei testimonium (in per-pe′tu-um rē′ī tes-ti-mō′ni-um). In perpetual memory of the matter; establishing a matter forever.

in person (in pėr′son). Appearing without counsel in the conduct of one's action or defense. For some purposes, in body, as where a civil damage or dramshop act provides for the recovery of damages for an injury "in person."

in persona (in pėr-sō′nạ). In person; appearing in an action without the aid of counsel.

in personam (in pėr-sō′nam). Against the person; involving the person.
See **judgment in personam; right in personam.**

In personam actio est, qua cum eo agimus qui obligatus est nobis ad faciendum aliquid vel dandum (in per-sō′nam ak′she-ō est, qua kum ė′ō ā′ji-mus qui ob-li-gā′tus est nō′bis ad fā-she-en′dum a′li-quid vel dan′dum). An action in personam is one in which we sue a person who is obligated to us to do something or to give something.

in personam action (in pėr-sō′nam ak′shọn). An action having the objective of a judgment against the person, as distinguished from a judgment against property, being an action to enforce personal rights and obligations, brought against the person and based on jurisdiction of the person, notwithstanding it may involve his right to, or the exercise of ownership of, specific property, or seek to compel him to control or dispose of it in accordance with the mandate of the court. Atlantic Seaboard Natural Gas Co. v Whitten, 315 Pa 529, 173 A 305, 93 ALR 615. A proceeding against a person involving his personal rights and based on jurisdiction of his person. McCormick v Blaine, 345 Ill 461, 178 NE 195, 77 ALR 1215.

in personam judgment. See **judgment in personam.**

in personam jurisdiction. See **jurisdiction in personam.**

in personam, not in rem. A maxim characterizing equity jurisdiction, indicating that remedies administered in equity are made effectual by decrees operating in personam. 27 Am J2d Eq § 122.

in pios usus (in pī′os ū′sus). For religious uses or purposes. See 2 Bl Comm 505.

in place. Descriptive of minerals unsevered from the soil, constituting a part of the freehold. Williams v Gibson, 84 Ala 228.

in plena vita (in plē'na vī'ta). In full life; that is, both civilly and physically alive.

in pleno comitatu (in plē'nō ko-mi-tā'tu). In the full county court. See 3 Bl Comm 36.

in pleno lumine (in plē'nō lū'mi-ne). In full light; in the daytime.

in plurality (in plọ̈-ral'ị̈-ti). See **estate in plurality**.

In poenalibus causis benignius interpretandum est (in pē-nā'li-bus kâ'zis be-nig'ni-us in-ter-pre-tan'dum est). In penal cases, the more liberal interpretation is to be adopted.

in poenam (in pē'nam). In punishment; by way of punishment or penalty.

in posse (in pos'ē). In possibility; in potentiality, as opposed to "in esse."

in possession. Holding possession.
See **chose in possession; estate in possession; estate vested in possession.**

in posterum (in pos'te-rum). In the future.

in potentia (in pō-ten'shi-ą). In possibility.

In potestate parentis (in pō-tes-tā'tē pā-ren'tis). Under the control of a parent.

in praemissorum fidem (in prē-mis-sō'rum fī'dem). In the attestation of the premises. A phrase used in technical language of a notary.

In praeparatoriis ad judicium favetur actori (in prē-pa-rā-tō'ri-is ad jū-di'she-um fa-vē'ter ak-tō'rī). (Civil law.) In those matters which precede the judgment, the plaintiff is favored.

in praesenti (in prẹ-zen'tī). At the present time; at once; immediately effective. Van Wyck v Knevals (US) 16 Otto 360, 27 L Ed 201, 1 S Ct 336.

in praesentia (in prē-zen'she-a). In the presence.

in praesentia diversorum (in prē-zen'she-a dī-ver-sō'rum). In the presence of divers persons.

in praesentia et auditu aliorum (in prē-zen'she-a et â-dī'tu al-i-o'rum). In the presence and hearing of others. Broderick v James (NY) 3 Daly 481.

In praesentia majoris potestatis, minor potestas cessat (in prē-zen'she-a ma-jō'ris po-tes-tā'tis, mī'nor po-tes'tās ses'sat). In the presence of the superior power, the inferior power ceases. In presence of the major the power of the minor ceases. See Broom's Maxims 111.

in prender (in pren'der). Characterization of incorporeal hereditaments which the landlord had the right to take. See 3 Bl Comm 15.

in presence. See **in the presence of the testator; presence; presence of the court.**

In pretio emptionis et venditionis, naturaliter licet contrahentibus se circumvenire (in pre'she-ō emp-she-ō'nis et ven-di-she-ō'nis, nā-tū-rā'li-ter lī'set kon-tra-hen'ti-bus sē ser-kum-ve-nī're). In respect to the price, in buying and selling, it is naturally permitted to the contracting parties to cheat one another.

in primis (in prī'mis). In the first place; at first; at the outset.

in principio (in prin-si'pi-ō). In the beginning. In principle.

in privity. See **privity**.

in promptu (in promp'tu). Impromptu; in readiness.

In propria causa nemo judex (in prō'pri-a kâ'za nē'mō jū'dex). No one can be a judge in his own cause.

in propria persona (in prō'pri-ą pėr-sō'ną). In one's own person or behalf. Appearing in an action without counsel.

in proximo gradu (in pro'xi-mō grā'dū). In the next or nearest degree.

in puris naturalibus (in pū'ris na-tur-al'i-bus). In a quite natural state; naked; unclothed.

in quantum lucratus est (in quan'tum lu-krā'tus est). To the extent to which he has profited.

inquest. An investigation conducted by a coroner or medical examiner, sometimes with the aid of a jury, to determine the cause of death of a person in a case where death is due, or is supposed to be due, to violence or other unlawful means. 18 Am J2d Corn § 7.
See **post mortem inquisitio.**

inquest in lunacy. A hearing to determine the sanity of a person. 26 Am J1st Homi §§ 82, 83.

inquest jury. A jury summoned by a coroner, medical examiner, or comparable officer to determine the cause of death of a person in a case in which death is due, or is supposed to be due, to violence or other unlawful means. 18 Am J2d Corn § 12.

inquest of drunkard. A statutory proceeding, similar to that provided for the determination of sanity, to ascertain whether a person is incapable of conducting his own affairs in consequence of habitual drunkenness. 29 Am J Rev ed Ins Per § 11.

inquest of office. An inquiry made by a jury before a sheriff, coroner, escheator, or other government officer, or by commissioners specially appointed, concerning any matter that entitled the sovereign to the possession of lands or tenements, goods or chattels, by reason of an escheat, forfeiture, idiocy, and the like. Hughes v Jones, 116 NY 67, 22 NE 446. Anno: 23 ALR 1233. An inquest conducted by a sheriff to determine the title to goods levied upon by him. 47 Am J1st Sher § 153.

inquest of title. A trial of the title to goods levied upon by a sheriff; not a judicial proceeding or part of a judicial proceeding—merely an inquest of office to indemnify the sheriff in making his return to the writ. 47 Am J1st Sher § 153.

inquilinus (in-kwi-lī'nus). (Roman law.) A person who dwells in a place not his own; a tenant; a lodger.

in quindena (in quin-dē'na). In fifteen days.

inquirendo (in-kwi-ren'dō). An authorization to institute an inquiry on behalf of the government.

inquiry. A seeking for information. An examination or investigation.
See **court of inquiry; diligent inquiry; judicial inquiry; writ of inquiry.**

inquisitio (in-qui-zi'she-ō). An inquisition; an inquest; an investigation; an inquiry.

inquisition. A church tribunal for the discovery and suppression of heresy. In law, an inquest.
See **inquest; inquest in lunacy; inquest of office; inquest of title.**

inquisitio post mortem (in-qui-zi'she-ō post mor'-tem). An inquisition or inquest after death.
See **post mortem.**

inquisitor (in-kwiz'i-tọr). An official investigator.

inquisitorial power. Investigating authority. 24 Am J1st Grand J § 33. The power of an administrative agency to inspect accounts, records, etc. or to require the disclosure of information through the testimony of witnesses or the production of documents. 1 Am J2d Admin L § 85.

in quo (in quō). In what; in which.
See **locus in quo.**

In quo quis delinquit, in eo de jure est puniendus (in quō quis de-lin'quit, in e'ō dē jū're est pu-ni-en'dus). In that wherein a person has committed an offense, he is to be punished by the law.

in re (in rē). In the matter; in the transaction.

in re aliena (in rē ā-li-ē'na). In the affair or business of another; in the property of another.

in rebus (in rē'bus). In matters; in transactions.

In rebus manifestis, errat qui auctoritates legum allegat; quia perspicua vera non sunt probanda (in rē'bus ma-ni-fes'tis, er'rat quī âk-tō-ri-tā'tēz lē'jum al'le-gat; quī'a per-spi'ku-a vē'ra non sunt prō-ban'da). He errs who cites authority of law in respect to things which are manifest, because plain truths do not have to be proved.

In rebus quae sunt favorabilia animae, quamvis sunt damnosa rebus, fiat aliquando extensio statuti (in rē'bus kwē sunt fa-vō-rā-bi'li-a a'ni-mē, quam'vis sunt dam-nō'sa rē'bus, fī'at a-li-quan'dō ex-ten'she-ō sta-tū'tī). In matters where the intent is good, although there is damage to property, there should be given some elasticity to the statute.

In re communi neminem dominorum jure facere quicquam, invito altero, posse (in rē kom-mū'nī nē'mi-nem do-mi-nō'rum jū're fā'se-re quik'quam, in-vī'tō al'te-rō, pos'se). No one of the owners of common property may exercise any dominion over it against the will of another of them.

In re communi potior est conditio prohibentis (in rē kom-mū'nī po'she-or est kon-di'she-ō prō-hi-ben'tis). In relation to property held in common, the position of the one who holds back (the conservative partner) is the more favorable.

In re dubia, benigniorem interpretationem sequi, non minis justius est quam tutius (in rē du'bi-a, be-nig-ni-ō'rem in-ter-pre-tā-she-ō'nem se'quī, non mī'nis jus'she-us est quam tu'she-us). In a doubtful matter, to follow a more liberal construction is no less the more just than it is the more safe.

In re dubia magis infitiatio quam affirmatio intelligenda (in rē dū'bi-a mā'jis in-fi-she-ā'she-o quam af-fir-mā'she-ō in-tel-li-jen'da). In a doubtful matter, the negative rather than the affirmative is to be understood.

In re lupanari, testes lupanares admittentur (in rē lu-pa-nā'rī, tes'tēz lu-pa-nā'rēz ad-mit-ten'ter). In a matter involving a brothel, the inmates are admitted as witnesses. Van Epps v Van Epps (NY) 6 Barb 320, 324.

in rem (in rem). Against a thing and not against a person; concerning the condition or status of a thing. Re Will of W. F. Storey, 20 Ill App 183, 190.

In rem actio est per quam rem nostram quae ab alio possidetur petimus, et semper adversus eum est qui rem possidet (in rem ak'she-ō est per quam rem nos'tram kwē ab a'li-ō pos-si-dē'ter pe'ti-mus, et sem'per ad-ver'sus e'um est quī rem pos'si-det). An action in rem is one by means of which we seek our property in the hands of another, and is always against him who holds possession of the property.

in rem action. In the more strict sense of the term, a proceeding to determine the right in specific property, against all the world, equally binding on everyone, but taking no cognizance of the owner or person with a beneficial interest, being against the thing or property itself directly, and having for its object the disposition of the property without reference to the title of individual claimants. 1 Am J2d Actions § 40. Most clearly illustrated by the proceeding against a vessel in a court of admiralty. 2 Am J2d Adm §§ 93, 94. Inclusive in the broad sense of actions quasi in rem.
See **quasi in rem action.**

in remainder. See **estate in remainder; remainder.**

in rem judgment. See **judgment in rem.**

in rem jurisdiction. See **jurisdiction in rem.**

in rem proceeding (in rem prō-sē'ding). See **in rem action.**

in rem process. See **process in rem.**

in rem suam (in rem su'am). In his own business; in his own affair.

in rem versum (in rem ver'sum). Used in one's business; used to one's advantage.

in render (in ren'der). Characterization of incorporeal hereditaments which the tenant was required to render to the landlord. See 3 Bl Comm 15.

In re pari potiorem causam esse prohibentis constat (in rē pa'rī po-she-ō'rem kâ'zam es'se prō-hi-ben'tis kon'stat). In a matter of equal rights the cause of the party who is seeking to prohibit is deemed the stronger. Griswold v Waddington (NY) 16 Johns 438, 491.

in re propria (in rē prō'pri-a). In one's own business; in one's own affair.

In re propria iniquum admodum est alicui licentiam tribuere sententiae (in rē prō'pri-a in-ī'qu-um ad'-mo-dum est a'li-kī lī-sen'she-am tri-bu'e-re sen-ten'-she-ē). It is most unfair for anyone to assign to himself the privilege of deciding his own case.

In republica maxime conservanda sunt jura belli (in rē-pūb'li-ka ma'xi-mē kon-ser-van'da sunt jū'ra bel'lī). It is of the highest importance that the laws of war be observed in the state. Tyler v Pomeroy, 90 Mass (8 Allen) 480, 484.

in rerum natura (in rē'rum nạ-tū'rạ). In the nature of things.

In restitutionem, non in poenam haeres succedit (in re-sti-tū-she-ō'nem, non in pē'nam hē'rēz suk-sē'-dit). An heir succeeds to a restitution, but not to a penalty.

In restitutionibus benignissima interpretatio facienda est (in res-ti-tu-she-ō'ni-bus be-nig-nis'si-ma in-ter-pre-tā'she-ō fā-she-en'da est). In restitutions, the most liberal construction is adopted.

in reversion. See **estate in reversion; reversion.**

in rixa (in ri'xa). In a quarrel.

inroll (in'rōl). Same as **enroll.**

inrollment (in'rōl-mẹnt). Same as **enrollment.**

insane. Of unsound mind; afflicted with insanity.
See **insanity.**

insane delusion. The product of a diseased mind or brain. 26 Am J1st Homi § 81. A belief which cannot be dispelled by reason and can be accounted for only as the product of mental disorder. A belief in things which do not exist and which no rational mind would believe to exist. 57 Am J1st Wills § 80. A belief in something impossible in the nature of things or under the special circumstances; a belief in a state or condition of things which no rational person would believe and which refuses to yield either to evidence or reason. Jackman v North, 398 Ill 90, 75 NE2d 324, 175 ALR 868. Such an aberration as indicates an unsound and deranged condition of the mental faculties. Brown v Ward, 53 Md 376. Insanity, in effect, as to an act, such as to render one incapable of entertaining criminal intent. 26 Am J1st Homi § 81.

insane person. A person afflicted with insanity.

The term is a generic one and includes idiots, lunatics, persons who are non compos mentis, and persons who are deranged. Hiett v Shull, 36 W Va 563, 565.

See **insanity**.

insanity. An unsound, deranged, delirious, or distracted condition of mind. Manley v Staples, 62 Vt 153, 19 A 983. A condition of mind so impaired in function, or so deranged, as to induce a deviation from normal conduct in the person so afflicted. 29 Am J Rev ed Ins Per § 2. Such a degree of mental incapacity as renders one unable to understand and deal with the common affairs of life. Lewis v Lewis, 199 SC 490, 20 SE2d 107. Such impairment of the mind as renders it impossible for one to understand the nature and consequences of his acts, or the character of a transaction in question. 29 Am J Rev ed Ins Per § 2. A sickness. Robillard v Société St. Jean Baptiste De Centreville, 21 RI 348, 43 A 635. A physical disease, consisting of a diseased or disordered condition or malformation of the organs or tissues, through which the mind receives impressions, and operates, and by which the will and judgment are impaired, and conduct rendered irrational. Blackstone v Standard Life & Acci. Ins. Co. 74 Mich 592, 42 NW 156.

Defense in criminal case. Incapacity to form a guilty intention. People v Schmidt, 216 NY 324, 110 NE 945. Mental disease or mental defect producing the unlawful act. 21 Am J2d Crim L § 39. Such a condition of mind and want of reason as to act from irresistible impulse. 21 Am J2d Crim L § 36. Want of substantial capacity, as a result of mental disease or defect, to appreciate the criminality or wrongfulness of conduct or to conform conduct to the requirements of law. American Law Institute Model Penal Code, proposed official draft § 4.01(1). Such defect of reason, from disease of the mind, as not to know the nature and quality of the act, or if the accused did know it, that he did not know that what he was doing was wrong; such being the definition of the celebrated M'Naghten Case, 10 Clark & F 200, 8 Eng Reprint 718. Sometimes tested, in homicide cases, according to the ability to distinguish between right and wrong. 26 Am J1st Homi §§ 78, 79. Inability to understand the nature and quality of the act or inability to distinguish right from wrong in respect to the act. 21 Am J2d Crim L § 34.

At time of trial for crime. The want of capacity to comprehend one's position, to understand the nature and object of the proceedings, to conduct his defense in a rational manner, and to co-operate with his counsel to the end that any available defense may be interposed. People v Burson, 11 Ill 2d 360, 143 NE2d 939.

At the time punishment for crime to be imposed, particularly the execution of the death penalty. The want of sufficient intelligence to understand the nature of the proceedings, what the trial was for, the purpose of punishment, the impending fate, or of sufficient understanding to know any fact which might exist making punishment unjust or unlawful, or of intelligence requisite to convey such information to attorneys or the court. 21 Am J2d Crim L § 76.

As a condition which operates to prevent or suspend the running of a statute of limitations. Such a mental impairment as renders one incompetent to manage his own affairs and endangers his person or property. Brown v Smith, 119 Colo 469, 205 P2d 239, 9 ALR2d 961.

As a matter of avoidance of the effect of an exception in a life insurance policy of death by suicide. An impairment of the reasoning faculties so far that one is not able to understand the moral character, the general nature, the consequences and effect of an act he is about to commit, or is impelled to the act by an impulse which he is not able to resist. 29A Am J Rev ed Ins § 1144.

See **idiocy; imbecility; inquest in lunacy; non compos mentis; right and wrong test; total mental disability; wild beast test.**

Insanus est qui, abjecta ratione, omnia cum impetu et furore facit (in-sā'nus est quī, ab-jek'tā rā-she-ō'ne, om'ni-a kum im'pe-tū et fu-rō're fā'sit). A person is insane who, deprived of reason, does everything in violence and fury.

In satisfactionibus non permittitur amplius fieri quam semel factum est (in sa-tis-fak-she-ō'ni-bus non per-mit'ti-ter am'pli-us fī'e-rī quam se'mel fak'tum est). In settlements more should not be paid than was paid once for all.

in scaccario (in ska-kā'ri-o). In the exchequer.

inscribe. To mark or engrave words, letters, or signs in such manner and upon such substance that they will have some degree, at least, of permanency.

inscribere (in-skri'be-re). To inscribe; to write in or on; to charge with the commission of a crime.

in scrinio judicis (in skri'ni-ō jū'di-sis). Among the notes or papers of the judge; that is, not contained in the record.

inscriptio (in-skrip'she-ō). (Civil law.) A written accusation of crime; the consent of an accuser to suffer the penalty prescribed for the offense with which he charges the accused, in the event of the acquittal of the accused.

inscription. Words, letters, or signs marked or engraved upon stone, metal, or other enduring substance so that they will stand in some degree of permanancy, at least. Another term for the registration or recording of a deed, mortgage, or other instrument entitled to be inscribed or recorded in the public records. Bondurant v Watson (US) 13 Otto 281, 26 L Ed 447.

See **reinscription.**

in se (in sē). In itself; in themselves.

See **mala in se.**

insecticide. A substance sprayed or dusted upon the soil or vegetation to kill or prevent the propagation of insect pests. 1 Am J2d Adj L § 35.

insect infestation. The overrunning of plants and growing things, particularly crops, by insect pests. A risk of loss under crop insurance pursuant to the Federal Crop Insurance Act. 21 Am J2d Crops § 6.

insecure clause. Same as **insecurity clause.**

insecurity clause. A provision in a chattel mortgage which gives the mortgagee a right to take possession of the mortgaged chattels whenever he deems himself insecure. 15 Am J2d Chat Mtg § 202. A clause in an instrument for the payment of money which authorizes acceleration of maturity if and when the holder deems his claim insecure. 11 Am J2d B & N § 185.

insensible. Unconscious; unintelligible; meaningless.

in sensu et re ipsa (in sen'sū et rē ip'sa). In the meaning or intention and regarding the very thing itself. Culpeper Agricultural & Mfg. Soc. v Digges, 27 Va (6 Rand) 165.

inseparable error. An error by the trial court affecting all coparties of such nature that a reversal must apply to all such parties notwithstanding less than all of them appealed. 5 Am J2d A & E §§ 951, 952.

in separali (in se-pa-rā'lī). In severalty.

insert. Verb: To add a line or lines between lines or even a page between pages. Noun: A line or lines or even a page added to a writing.
See **write-in candidates.**

in session. A court engaged in the administration of justice and the business of the court, with the judge on the bench and discharging his official function. The status of a court between the time that it has convened for the term and the time that it adjourns sine die. State v Root, 5 ND 487, 67 NW 590.

in severalty. The character of a holding of land by one person in his own right only, without any other person being joined or connected with him in point of interest during the continuance of his estate in the land. State ex rel. Anderton v Somers, 242 Wis 484, 8 NW2d 263, 145 ALR 1324.

inside a motor vehicle. Inside the vehicle in the place ordinarily occupied by one driving or riding. Anno: 39 ALR2d 961 (construing phrase as it appears in an accident insurance policy or the accident feature of a life insurance policy).

inside information. The information acquired by a director or officer of a corporation by reason of his position. 19 Am J2d Corp § 1326.

inside lane. The lane nearest the center line of the highway on a highway containing more than one lane of traffic proceeding in the same direction. Richards v Warner Co. 311 Pa 50, 166 A 496, 87 ALR 1159.

insiders. Officers and directors of a corporation who acquire knowledge of the business and condition of the corporation by their official position. 19 Am J2d Corp § 1326.

insider short-swing transaction. A term of the Securities Exchange Act, typifying a transaction in the stock of a corporation by a director, officer, or principal stockholder, buying and selling on the basis of information obtained by him through his position in the company. Anno: 40 ALR2d 1349.

insidiatio viarum (in-si-di-ā'she-ō vī-ā'rum). Lying in wait for one on the highway,—a common-law felony for which benefit of clergy was not allowed, because it was said to be one of those offenses which bordered on treason. See 4 Bl Comm 373.

insidiator (in-sid'i-ā-tǫr). A spy; a waylayer; a traitor; a lurker.

insidiatores viarum (in-si-di-a-tō'rēz vī-ā'rum). Highwaymen; highway robbers; persons lurking in the highways to commit crime.

insidious machination. A deceitful scheme or plot with evil design, or, in other words, with a fraudulent purpose. Strong v Repide, 213 US 419, 53 L Ed 853, 29 S Ct 521.

insignia. Coats of arms; armorial bearings; emblems of rank. Pins, badges or ribbons worn by members of a club. 6 Am J2d Asso & C § 17.

In the days of chivalry and knight errantry, and at the present time, where distinctions are recognized by law, between wealth and other adventitious influences, and poverty or weakness, the adventurous and the great have adopted their insignia, suggested by valorous achievement, or other causes. These are called their arms or family escutcheon, and are usually engraved on their seals. Kirksey v Bates (Ala) 7 Port 529.

As the term is used with reference to notarial seals, it means the armorial ensign of a state or political community, intended to distinguish it from others, and which is usually transferred to its national flag or banner. Yet, perhaps a public flag cannot always be considered as a true indication of the arms of the country to which it belongs; for most countries have two banners—one borne by vessels of war, and the other by those engaged in commerce. Kirksey v Bates (Ala) 7 Port 529.

insilium (in-si'li-um). Rash advice; bad counsel.

in simile materia (in si'mi-lī ma-te'ri-a). In a like or similar matter.

in simplici peregrinatione (in sim'pli-sī pe-re-grinā-she-ō'ne). In simple pilgrimage.

insimul (in'si-mul). At the same time; together; jointly.

insimul computassent (in'si-mul kom-pu-tas'sent). Literally, they accounted together. A common count in assumpsit pleaded in an action upon an account. 1 Am J2d Acctg § 37.

insinuacion (in-sin-ū-ā'shǫn). (Spanish.) The submission of a public document to a judge for his approval.

insinuare (in-si-nu-ā're). To deposit in the records of the court; to declare or acknowledge before a judge.

insinuatio (in-si-nu-ā'she-ō). Suggestion; information.

insinuation. A suggestion of something, particularly bad or criminal conduct. 33 Am J1st L & S § 9. (Civil law.) Copying anything into a public record.

insinuatione (in-sin-ū-ā'shǫn). Insinuation.
See **ex insinuatione.**

insinuation of a will. (Civil law.) The production of a will of a decedent for probate.

in situ (in sī'tū). As located; in its place.

insolence. The conduct of one who is insolent.
See **insolent.**

insolent. Rude; insulting; abusive; offensive. State v Bill, 35 NC (13 Ired L) 373, 377.

in solido (in sol'i-dō). In a lump; in a lump sum; in one payment; as a whole; for the whole sum.

As used in the Louisiana code, the term appears to have the meaning of jointly and severally, so that debtors bound "in solido" must be all obliged to do the same thing, so that each may be compelled for the whole. Henderson v Wadsworth, 115 US 264, 29 L Ed 377, 6 S Ct 40.
See **creditors in solido; debitors in solido.**

in solidum (in sō'li-dum). As a whole; for the whole.

in solo (in sō'lō). In the soil; on the land; on the ground. By one's self alone.

in solo proprio (in sō'lō prō'pri-ō). On one's own land.

in solutum (in so-lū'tum). In payment.

insolvency. The insufficiency of the entire property and assets of an individual to pay his debts. 29 Am J Rev ed Insolv § 2. In a practical commercial sense, the inability of a person to pay his debts as they become due in the ordinary course of his business, such being the sense of the term as applied to traders and merchants, permitting a determination of insolvency, although the debts of the person actually may be paid at some future time on a settlement and winding up of his affairs (29 Am J Rev ed Insolv § 2) but apparently giving to a debtor the advantage of the use of his credit to raise money for the payment of his debts. United States v Anderson Co. (CA7 Ind) 119 F2d 343.

By definition in the Bankruptcy Act, controlling for the purpose of determining the commission of an act of bankruptcy:—the status of a person whenever the aggregate of his property exclusive of any property which he may have conveyed, transferred, concealed, removed, or permitted to be concealed or removed, with intent to defraud, hinder, or delay his creditors, shall not at the fair valuation be sufficient in amount to pay his debts. Bankr Act § 1(19); 11 USC § 1(19); 9 Am J2d Bankr § 160. For the purpose of determining whether a transfer is fraudulent under the Bankruptcy Act:—the status of a person when the present fair salable value of his property is less than the amount required to pay his debts. Bankruptcy Act § 67 (d) (1) (d); 11 USC § 107 (d) (1) (d). (This definition is controlling as against the preceding definition, also from the Bankruptcy Act, inasmuch as Congress intended less stringent requirement in proof of insolvency in fraudulent transfer cases than in other phases of bankruptcy. Holohan v Lewis (DC Fla) 182 F Supp 473.)

In reference to the qualification of a person to administer the estate of a decedent, not the mere not owning of property, but the owing of debts in excess of the value of property. 31 Am J2d Ex & Ad § 68.

A debtor is "insolvent" within the meaning of a statute giving priority to debts due the United States from an insolvent debtor, if, not having sufficient property to pay all his debts, he either makes a voluntary assignment of his property for the benefit of his creditors or commits an act of bankruptcy. United States v Gotwals (CA10 Okla) 156 F2d 692, 169 ALR 619. No lien is created by the statute; the priority established can never attach while the debtor continues the owner and in the possession of the property, although he may be unable to pay all his debts; no evidence can be received of the insolvency of the debtor until he has been divested of his property in one of the modes stated in the statute. 29 Am J Rev ed Insolv § 68.

See **acts of insolvency**; **assignee in insolvency**; **hopelessly insolvent**; **open insolvency**.

insolvency laws. See **insolvency statutes**.

insolvency of bank. An expression of dual meaning: —(1) the insufficiency of assets to pay liabilities within a reasonable time; (2) an insufficiency of assets to pay liabilities as they become due in the ordinary course of business. Anno: 85 ALR 812.

See **hopelessly insolvent**; **receiving deposits while insolvent**.

insolvency of building and loan association. Inability to satisfy the demands of members. Anno: 98 ALR 111; 13 Am J2d B & L Assoc § 101. Inability to pay back to members the amount of their contributions dollar for dollar. Rummens v Home Sav. & L. Asso. 182 Wash 539, 47 P2d 845, 100 ALR 570.

insolvency of corporation. An insufficiency of assets to pay debts. In a more commercial sense, an inability to pay debts as they become due in the ordinary course of business. 19 Am J2d Corp § 1569.

See also **insolvency**.

insolvency of insurance company. A depletion of assets to the extent that they are insufficient for the payment of the just debts and obligations of the company. 29 Am J Rev ed Ins § 116.

An insurance company is not insolvent when the value of its property is greater than the amount of its liabilities and it is able to pay its debts when they mature, although the excess of the value of its property above its liabilities may be less than the par value of its stock. Shearer v Farmers' L. Ins. Co. (CA8 Mo) 262 F 861.

Actuarial solvency of a mutual benefit company requires that the funds of the company on hand and the present value of future payments to be made by the members shall be equal to the accrued obligations and the present value of the insurance in force. Jenkins v Talbot, 338 Ill 441, 170 NE 735, 80 ALR 638, app dismd 283 US 782, 75 L Ed 1412, 51 S Ct 342.

insolvency of lessee. In reference to re-entry by the lessor:—the failure of a lessee to meet obligations as they mature, or such financial condition as throws the lessee's relations into confusion, delays payment of the rent, impounds his property for an indefinite time, and in general makes it important for the lessor to be free to re-enter. Re Wil-Low Cafeterias Inc. (CA2 NY) 95 F2d 306, 115 ALR 1184, cert den 304 US 567, 82 L Ed 1533, 58 S Ct 950.

insolvency of partnership. Insufficiency of the aggregate joint property to pay the firm liabilities, without reference to the solvency or insolvency of the individual partners. 40 Am J1st Partn § 256.

In determining insolvency of a partnership for the purposes of ascertaining whether a transfer is fraudulent under the Bankruptcy Act, there shall be added to the partnership property the present fair salable value of the separate property of each general partner in excess of the amount required to pay his separate debts, and also the amount realizable on any unpaid subscription to the partnership of each limited partner. Bankr Act § 67 (d) (1) (d); 11 USC § 107 (d) (1) (d).

insolvency of savings and loan association. See **insolvency of building and loan association**.

insolvency proceedings. See **proceedings in insolvency**.

insolvency statutes. State statutes, comparable to the National Bankruptcy Act, which provide a proceeding by or against a debtor to have him declared insolvent and his property brought into court for disposition among his creditors in accordance with law. Vanuxem v Hazelhursts, 4 NJL 192.

insolvent. Characterizing a person who either has ceased to pay his debts in the ordinary course of business, cannot pay his debts as they become due, or is insolvent within the meaning of the Federal Bankruptcy Act. UCC § 1—201(24). One in a condition of insolvency.

See **insolvency**.

INSOLVENT [638] INSTALMENT

insolvent bank. See **insolvency of bank.**

insolvent building and loan association. See **insolvency of building and loan association.**

insolvent corporation. See **insolvency of corporation.**

insolvent estate. The estate of a decedent which is to be administered according to a special statutory method because of the fact of insolvency. 31 Am J2d Ex & Ad § 312.

insolvent law. See **insolvency statutes.**

insolvent partnership. See **insolvency of partnership.**

insomnia. Inability to sleep; prolonged sleeplessness. United States v Ridgeway (CC Ga) 31 F 144, 147.

in spe (in spē). In hope; in expectation.

in specie. Payment in the designated number of gold or silver dollars of the coinage of the United States; in gold or silver coin of the United States. 40 Am J1st Paym § 58.

inspect. To look upon; to examine for the purpose of determining quality, detecting what is wrong, and the like; to view narrowly and critically; as to inspect conduct. Fairchild v Ada County, 6 Idaho 340, 55 P 654.

inspectator (in-spek′tā-tor). An adversary.

inspected and condemned. See **US brand.**

inspection. The act of inspecting, whether it be articles offered for sale, real estate, or the conduct of a person. The right by which, as a general rule, the buyer of goods is entitled to a fair opportunity to inspect or examine the article or commodity tendered by the seller to see if it conforms to the contract, and if it does not do so, to reject it. 46 Am J1st Sales § 247. Under an inspection law:—an examination to determine whether the article inspected is fit for use or commerce; something which can be accomplished by looking at or by weighing or measuring the thing to be inspected or applying to it some crucial test, without resort to other evidence. 29 Am J Rev ed Insp L § 2.

"Inspection" of the home by a health officer is a "search" thereof within the meaning of the Fourth Amendment to the Constitution of the United States prohibiting unreasonable searches. District of Columbia v Little, 85 App DC 242, 178 F2d 13, 13 ALR2d 954.

See **inspect; physical examination; right of visitation; trial by inspection.**

inspection by customs. An examination by customs officers of goods, merchandise, and baggage brought into the United States from a foreign country. 21 Am J2d Cust D §§ 73, 74.

inspection charges. Duties laid by the states on goods imported to, and exported from them, under the authority of section ten, article one, of the United States Constitution, for services rendered in executing their inspection laws. Turner v Maryland (US) 17 Otto 38, 27 L Ed 370, 2 S Ct 44. An exception to the prohibition on the states to lay duties on imports or exports. Brown v Maryland (US) 12 Wheat 419, 6 L Ed 678.

Inspection Division. An agency established within the Atomic Energy Commission for gathering information as to whether or not contractors, licensees, officers, and employees of the commission are complying with the statutes and the rules and regulations of the commission. 42 USC § 2035.

inspection duties. Same as **inspection charges.**

inspection laws. Police regulations, designed to safeguard the public against fraud, imposition, or injury and to promote the public health, safety, and welfare, by providing for the examination or inspection of property by an authorized public official in order to determine whether prescribed standards are met by compliance therewith. Anno: 51 L Ed 78, s. 63 L Ed 180, 83 L Ed 776. Characterized by concern with the quality of the article, the form, capacity, dimensions, and weight of a package, the manner of putting up, and the markings and brandings of various kinds, all these matters being supervised by a public officer having authority to pass or not to pass the article as lawful merchandise, according to the prescribed requirements. Turner v Maryland, 107 US 38, 27 L Ed 370, 2 S Ct 44.

inspection of corporate records. See **inspection of records.**

inspection of documents. The preliminary examination of documents by the party who is opposing the party who offers the documents in evidence.

inspection officer. See **inspector.**

inspection of records. A right which entails access to, free examination of, and the taking of copies from, public records. 1 Am J2d Abstr T § 8; 45 Am J1st Recds §§ 14 et seq. The right of a stockholder to examine the books of the corporation by virtue of the fact of ownership of stock. 18 Am J2d Corp §§ 178 et seq.

See **interested person.**

inspection of vessels. Inspection under federal statutes for the purpose of ascertaining whether there has been compliance with requirements respecting construction and equipment. 48 Am J1st Ship § 58.

inspector. A common term for a person of rank in a detective or police force. Often a public officer, for example, a building inspector, customs inspector, grain inspector, or health inspector. 42 Am J1st Pub Of § 16. A public officer, quasi-public officer, or merely a public employee, engaged in the administration of inspection laws, particularly by conducting inspections in accord with such laws. 29 Am J Rev ed Insp L § 7.

inspectors of election. The persons conducting an election of directors of a corporation at a corporate meeting. 19 Am J2d Corp § 629. The title of officers of election who administer election laws in the conduct of the voting in precincts and districts.

Inst. See **Institutes of Coke.**

install. To induct or place in office. To place a pastor elect formally in the pastoral relation to the congregation. 45 Am J1st Reli Soc § 29. To place and establish a machine or other instrumentality in position and use, as to "install" a furnace.

Unless modified by other terms, a contract to "install" certain equipment, binds the promisor, not only to set up and connect the parts, but also to furnish suitable and adequate material. Bernstein v Alcorn, 194 Iowa 1109, 190 NW 975.

installation. The act of installing.

See **install.**

installation services. The assembling and setting up of machinery, household appliances, and other apparatus as an incident of the sale of such things. 15 Am J2d Com § 43. More broadly, any act of installing.

See **install.**

instalment. One of successive parts of a performance, such as delivery of goods or the payment of money.

INSTALMENT [639] INSTIGATION

instalment contract. A contract the consideration in which is expressed in separate and distinct items. A contract calling for payment or performance in instalments; not necessarily a divisible contract. 17 Am J2d Contr § 328. A contract for the purchase of real estate which provides for payment of the purchase price to be made in instalments, and for the conveyance of the title to be made on the completion of the payments. 55 Am J1st V & P § 106.

A provision in a contract for payment in instalments, which instalments are not referable to severable items or portions of the performance but are referable to the performance of the whole, does not render or characterize such contract as severable. Condon v H. C. Hazen Contracting Co. 122 Ohio St 100, 170 NE 870.

instalment judgment. A judgment for a sum to be paid in instalments; a judgment calling for instalment payments, such as a judgment for the payment of alimony at stated periods. United States v Ewing (DC Miss) 19 F2d 378.

instalment legacy. A bequest of a certain amount payable in stated instalments at definite periods in the future. A legacy in the form of an annuity created by the will. 4 Am J2d Annui § 4.

instalment note. A promissory note the principal of which is payable in two or more certain amounts at different stated times.

instalment payments. Partial payments on account of a larger sum. Payments at fixed intervals until the entire principal and interest on an obligation is satisfied, according to a provision contained in a contract, note, conditional sale contract, chattel mortgage, or trust receipt. Partial payments to be made to a building contractor as the work progresses. Anno: 22 ALR2d 1343.

instalment sale. A sale of personal property in which the purchase price is payable in instalments. 47 Am J1st Sales § 830. Usually, although not necessarily, a conditional sale in reference to the security provided by the contract for the payment of the purchase price. 47 Am J1st Sales § 830.
See **conditional sale.**

instalments of insurance. Payments of a stated amount at recurring intervals, such as disability benefits payable under a policy of life or accident insurance. 29A Am J Rev ed Ins § 1508. Fixed instalments of the proceeds of a life insurance policy paid at regular intervals; not constituting an annuity, unless the person entitled to the proceeds has himself made a contract with the insurer, separate and distinct from the insurance policy, for the payment of the proceeds in instalments, can properly be regarded as an annuity. Commonwealth v Beisel, 338 Pa 519, 13 A2d 419, 128 ALR 978.

instance. A request; a precedent; instigation; solicitation. An occasion.

instance court. One of the two branches of the admiralty court; the branch which exercises jurisdiction in reference to maritime contracts and maritime torts. Percival v Hickey (NY) 18 Johns 257. The other branch is the **prize court.**

instancia (ins-tahn'the-àh). (Spanish.) The filing of an action and the prosecution of it to judgment.

Instans est finis unius temporis et principium alterius (in'stanz est fī'nis ū'ni-us tem'po-ris et prin-si'pi-um al-ter'ri-us). An instant is the end or termination of one time and the beginning of another.

instantaneous. Done or occurring in an instant, or without any perceptible duration of time; as the passage of electricity appears to be instantaneous. Not synonymous with "immediate." Sawyers v Perry, 88 Me 42, 48.

instantaneous death. A death occurring in an instant or without any appreciable duration of time after an injury or seizure. 22 Am J2d Dth § 26.

Although the possibility of a death that is truly simultaneous with the injury that caused it has been denied, it has been pointed out that death may be so contemporaneous with the fatal injury as to be instantaneous in the sense that there can be no recovery for the victim's pain and suffering. Moffett v Baltimore & O. R. Co. (CA4 W Va) 220 F 39.

instantaneous seisin. The doctrine that a transitory seisin for an instant, when the same act which conveys an estate to a person conveys it away from him, is not a seisin to "abide" in him, that is, to be in him "beneficially for his own use," which will permit such a right as dower, homestead, mechanic's lien or vendor's lien, to attach to the land. Lassen v Vance, 8 Cal 271; Libbey v Tidden, 192 Mass 175, 183.

instante. See **eo instante.**

instanter (in-stan'tėr). Instantly; on the instant; at once; immediately.

instantly. Without delay; immediately. Not the equivalent of "then and there" in an indictment. Lester v State, 9 Mo 666, 667.

instar (in'stär). An image; a likeness; like; equal.

instar dentium (in'star den'she-um). Like teeth; indented, as in an indenture. See 2 Bl Comm 295.

instar omnium (in'star om'ni-um). Equal to all.

in statu quo (in sta'tū quō). In the situation in which he was. As that situation which is preserved by restraining order or preliminary injunction:—the last actual, peaceable, noncontested status preceding the pending controversy, as distinguished from a status effected by a wrongdoer before institution of the suit. Steggles v National Discount Corp. 326 Mich 44, 39 NW2d 237, 15 ALR2d 208; State ex rel. Pay Less Drug Stores v Sutton, 2 Wash 2d 523, 98 P2d 680.

Within the meaning of the rule which requires that a party to an executory contract, who for proper cause would rescind the contract, must as a condition precedent to such rescission place the other party to the contract "in statu quo," the expression means that he shall place him "in the same position" in which he was at the time of the inception of the contract which is sought to be rescinded. Daly v Bernstein, 6 NM 380, 28 P 764.

in statu quo ante bellum (in sta'tū quō an'te bel'-lum). In the state in which it was before the war.

in statu quo ante fuit (in sta'tū quō an'te fu'it). In the state in which it was before.

instaurum (in-stâ'rum). Farming equipment.

instigate. To stimulate or goad to an action, especially a bad act. State v Fraker, 148 Mo 143, 165. To incite, to foment, especially the commission of a crime. 36 Am J2d Forf & P § 69; 32 Am J1st Larc § 27.
See **entrapment.**

instigation. The act of instigating.
See **instigate.**

instinct of self-preservation. See **self-preservation.**

instinctive statements. See **res gestae.**

In stipulationibus cum quaeritur quid actum sit verba contra stipulatorem interpretanda sunt (in sti-pu-lā-she-ō'ni-bus kum kwē'ri-ter quid ak'tum sit ver'ba kon'trā sti-pu-lā-tō'rem in-ter-pre-tan'da sunt). In agreements, when it is questioned as to what was done, the words are to be construed against the stipulator.

In stipulationibus, id tempus spectatur quo contrahimus (in sti-pu-lā-she-ō'ni-bus, id tem'pus spektā'ter quō kon-tra'hi-mus). In agreements, the time at which we contract is regarded.

In stipulationibus quum queritur quid actum sit verba contra stipulatorem interpretanda sunt (in sti-pu-lā-she-ō'ni-bus qu'um kwē'ri-ter quid ak'tum sit ver'ba kon'trā sti-pu-lā-tō'rem in-ter-pre-tan'da sunt). In agreements, when it is questioned as to what was done, the words are to be construed against the stipulator.

instirpare (in-ster-pā're). To establish.

in stirpes (in ster'pēz). According to the roots.
See **taking per stirpes.**

institor (in'sti-tôr). (Civil law.) A factor; a broker; an agent; a huckster; a peddler.

institorial action (in-sti-tō'ri-al ak'shon). (Civil law.) An action against a principal on a contract made for him by his "institor" or agent. See Mackeldey's Roman L § 513.

institorial power (pou'ėr). The power or authority of an agent.

institute. Verb: To start; to establish. Noun: An educational institution, especially a school or college providing training for particular work. An established principle of law. A treatise on law. A person appointed by will and by the will directed to transfer property by the will devised to him, to a person called the "substitute."
See **institution; teachers' institute.**

institute an action. To begin an action.
The word differs from the word "maintain." An action must be instituted before it can be maintained. National Fertilizer Co. v Fall River Five Cents Sav. Bank, 196 Mass 458, 82 NE 671.

instituted. Commenced; established.

instituted executor. An executor who is appointed by the testator without any condition.

institute heir. See **heir institute.**

institutes. Plural of **institute.**

Institutes of Caius (of kā'us). Same as **Institutes of Gaius.**

Institutes of Coke. A treatise on the common law which was written in four volumes by Sir Edward Coke.
The first volume is an extensive comment on the treatise on tenures which was compiled by Judge Littleton in the reign of Edward the Fourth, and is cited as Coke's Littleton, abbreviated "Co. Litt." or "1 Inst." The second volume is a comment on many old acts of parliament. The third is a treatise of the pleas of the crown; and the fourth is an account of the several species of courts.
The three volumes following the first are cited respectively as "2 Inst.," "3 Inst.," and "4 Inst."

Institutes of Gaius (gā'us). An elementary treatise on the Roman law written by Gaius, a Roman jurist who preceded Justinian and whose work is said to have formed the basis for the Institutes of Justinian.

Institutes of Justinian. An elementary treatise on the Roman law written in the sixth century A. D.

institutio haeredis (in-sti-tū'she-ō hē-rē'dis). (Roman law.) The appointment of an heir by will.

institution. The act of instituting or establishing something. Something that has been established, particularly a place where an educational or charitable enterprise is conducted. Trustees of Kentucky Female Orphan School v Louisville, 100 Ky 470, 36 SW 921. A school, library, hospital, or auditorium, provided by a municipal corporation. 38 Am J1st Mun Corp §§ 559 et seq.
A charitable institution for the reformation of girls and women does not become a "state institution" or a governmental agency, so as to become immune from liability for the torts of its employees, simply because the state law authorizes a magistrate to commit a girl to its custody. Gallon v House of Good Shepherd, 158 Mich 361, 122 NW 631.
See **institute.**

institutional decision. A decision made by an organization, not by an individual or agency head. 2 Am J2d Admin L § 435, 2 Davis, Admin L p 36.

institution and prosecution of action. The filing or service of a proper complaint, declaration, or petition, the service of process, or obtaining the waiver of process, to bring the parties into court, and judicial inquiry according to the rules and practice of the court. Zanesville v Zanesville Tel & Tel Co. 64 Ohio St 67, 59 NE 781.

institutiones (in-sti-tū-she-ō'nēz). Same as **institutes.**

institution of a clergyman. The formal act of the bishop of the diocese of investing a clergyman or clerk with the actual possession of the temporalities of a parsonage or vicarage. The clergyman was thus "instituted" by some symbolic act of the bishop after he had been presented to the bishop by his patron. See 1 Bl Comm 389.

institution of action. The commencement of an action at law or in equity.
See **institution and prosecution of action.**

institution of learning. Broadly, an educational institution, any school. In a narrower sense of the term, as it appears in a tax exemption statute, an enterprise conducted for educational purposes which includes a grade or grades higher than are included in the public schools, not limited to incorporated or public enterprises. Montgomery v Wyman, 130 Ill 17, 22 NE 845.

in stricto jure (in strik'tō jū're). In strict law; in strict right.

instruct. To direct; to advise; to impart knowledge; to order; to give instructions.
See **instructions.**

instructed verdict. See **directed verdict.**

instruction. The imparting of knowledge. The directing of an employee or subordinate.
See **instructions to jury; sectarian instruction; shipping instruction.**

instructions to jury. To final charges given by the court to the jury upon the submission of the case to the jury, explaining the law of the case and pointing out the essentials to be proved on the one side or the other, the purpose being to furnish guidance to the jury in their deliberations, and to aid them in arriving at a proper verdict, so far as it is competent for the court to assist them. 53 Am J1st Trial § 509.

As usually understood, the term does not include anything which the court might say during the progress of the trial as to the purpose for which certain evidence is admitted or as to what facts have been admitted by one side or the other; oral directions to the jury to reject evidence, made when it is given; directions during the trial to disregard improper or incompetent evidence given in the examination of the witness, or to disregard prejudicial remarks of counsel; oral directions as to the form of the verdict, or other comment and statements of the trial judge as to collateral matters made during trial. 53 Am J1st Trial § 508.

See **abstract instruction; additional instructions; advisory instruction; argumentative instruction; conditional instruction; contradictory instruction; general instruction; indorsement of instructions; peremptory instruction.**

instructor. A teacher, whether in a university or college, a public or private school, an art school, a dancing school, or a factory the processes of which are such that new employees must be instructed therein.

instrument. A negotiable instrument. Uniform Negotiable Instruments L § 2; UCC § 3–102(1)(e). A negotiable instrument or a security or any other writing evidencing a right to the payment of money, and of a type transferred in the ordinary course of business by delivery with any necessary indorsement or assignment. UCC § 9-105(1)(g). A writing or document, such as a contract deed or mortgage. Cardenas v Miller, 108 Cal 250, 39 P 783, 41 P 472. Compare Nash v Rehmann Bros. (CA8 Iowa) 53 F2d 624 (holding that the bilateral nature of a contract may preclude it from falling within the meaning of the term "instrument").

A tool; a device for performing work or accomplishing a purpose, sometimes the performance of highly skilled services, such as those of a physician, surgeon, or dentist. An inclusive term where it appears in a statute respecting the mode of committing an offense. Lee v State, 66 Tex Crim 567, 148 SW 567. Inclusive of a substance, such as carbolic acid. Lee v State, 66 Tex Crim 567, 148 SW 567. In a very broad sense, things animate and inanimate, even witnesses presented to the court in the process of producing evidence upon a trial. Cardenas v Miller, 108 Cal 250, 39 P 783, 41 P 472. As used in an exemption statute:—a usable article employed as a means to effect an end. 31 Am J2d Exemp § 53.

See **implement; tool.**

instrumenta (in-stru-men'ta). Unsealed writings admitted as evidence in a trial.

instrumentality. An agency, a means of accomplishment.

See **dangerous instrumentality; federal instrumentality.**

instrument flying. Flying an aircraft, the course of which is kept by instruments, the pilot being free for the performance of other duties. 14 CFR §§ 600.1 et seq.

instrument for the payment of money. An instrument which acknowledges an absolute obligation to pay, not conditional or contingent; one, the execution of which being admitted, it would be incumbent on the plaintiff, in an action to enforce it, only to offer the instrument in evidence to entitle him to a recovery,—that is, an instrument that admits an existing debt. Ancient Order of Hibernians v Sparrow, 29 Mont 132, 74 P 197. A promissory note.

instrument inter partes (in'strö-ment in'ter par'tēz). An instrument which records in writing a transaction between two or more persons; an instrument between the persons named therein as executing it. Smith v Emery, 12 NJL 53, 60.

See **deed inter partes.**

instrument of appeal. A petition on appeal in a divorce suit in England.

instrument of evidence. A document, witness or thing which may be presented in evidence for inspection. Cardenas v Miller, 108 Cal 250, 39 P 783, 41 P 472. In a more common sense, a document or writing presented and admitted in evidence.

instrument of war. An instrument subject to embargo as a military instrument. Gibbons v Ogden (US) 9 Wheat 1, 6 L Ed 23.

instrumentum patrisfamilias domesticum et quotidianum (in-stru-men'tum pa-tris-fa-mi'li-ās do-mes'ti-kum et quō-ti-di-ā'num). The domestic and everyday conveniences of the family; that is, household stuff, such as tables, chairs, beds, pots, pans, kettles and the like. Hoope's Appeal, 60 Pa 220.

instrument under seal. See **sealed instrument; specialty.**

insubordination. Refusal to obey directions.

in subsidium (in sub-si'di-um). By way of subsidy; in aid of.

in substantialibus (in sub-stan-she-ā'li-bus). In substance; substantially.

insufficiency of repair. A state of neglect or disrepair. In reference to a highway:—inadequacy of original construction, subsequent deterioration, and such obstacles or defects as render the use of the highway dangerous to one exercising ordinary care. 25 Am J1st High § 476.

See **defective highway.**

insufficient consideration. See **sufficient consideration.**

insufficient funds. The want of sufficient funds in a bank account for the payment of a check drawn by the depositor. 11 Am J2d B & N § 763.

See **overdraft.**

insufficient pleading. A pleading which will not stand against a demurrer or motion which is the equivalent of a demurrer. State v Burgdoerfer, 107 Mo 1, 17 SW 646.

insufficient record. See **defective record.**

insula (in'sū-lä). An island; a detached building; a building let out to several poor families.

insular courts. Courts established by Congress and invested with jurisdiction to be exercised in insular possessions of the United States.

insulated car. A freight car insulated to exclude the cold and prevent the freezing of perishable goods. 13 Am J2d Car § 170. Also, insulated to exclude heat where the car is cooled artificially.

insulation. Material used to prevent the passage or leakage of electricity, heat, or sound. A wrapping of nonconductive material around a wire intended to carry an electric current, for the purpose of preventing the discharge of electricity from the wire and of preventing disastrous consequences if the wire should happen to come in contact with a heavily and dangerously charged wire. Western Union Tel. Co. v State, 82 Md 293, 33 A 763; Lynch v Carolina Tel. & Tel. Co. 204 NC 252, 167 SE 847. The process of insulating structures or wires.

insulator. A material or device which serves as insulation, particularly a glass or porcelain device affixed to pole or cross bar of pole, whereto telephone, telegraph, or electric lines are attached. Owen v Appalachian Power Co. 78 W Va 596, 89 SE 262.

See **insulation.**

insulin. A drug taken for diabetes, capable of inducing intoxication within the meaning of statutes prohibiting driving a motor vehicle while intoxicated. 7 Am J2d Auto § 258.

insult. An indignity; a humiliation by word or gesture. An affront to self respect; in some jurisdictions an item of compensatory damages, in other jurisdictions an item of punitive damages. 22 Am J2d Damg § 197.

insultus (in-sul'tus). An assault.

in summa (in sum'ma). On the whole.

in summo jure (in sum'mō jū're). In strictest law; in strictest right.

in suo genere (in su'ō je'ne-re). Of its own kind.

In suo quisque negotio hebetior est quam in alieno (in su'ō quis kwe ne-go'she-ō he-be'she-or est quam in ā-li-ē'nō). Everyone is more stupid in his own business than in that of another.

insuper (in-sū'pėr). Above; over; over and above; moreover; besides.

in superficie (in su-per-fi'she-ē). On the surface; superficially.

insurability. The quality or condition of being insurable. Kahn v Continental Casualty Co. 391 Ill 445, 63 NE2d 468, In reference to life insurance:—all those physical and moral factors reasonably taken into consideration by life insurance companies in determining coverage or matters affecting the risk. Rosenbloom v New York Life Ins. Co. (DC Mo) 65 F Supp 692, remanded (CA8) 163 F2d 1. As a condition of the reinstatement of a life insurance policy:—good health; good health plus circumstances rendering the risk desirable from the standpoint of the insurance company. 29 Am J Rev ed Ins § 371.

insurable interest. An essential of a valid contract of insurance, being, in general, that which takes a contract out of the class of wagering policies; best defined in reference to the particular risk or thing insured. 29 Am J Rev ed Ins § 432.

See **interest or no interest clause; wager policy.**

insurable interest in liability. The interest that the insured has in the possibility of death of or injury to third persons, or of the destruction of or injury to the property of third persons, which may be the basis of a liability established against him or, at least, of suits brought against him. Anno: 77 ALR 1256.

insurable interest in life. One's interest in his own life. Any reasonable expectation of benefit or advantage from the continued life of another person, which advantage or benefit need not be capable of pecuniary estimation, but may be predicated upon any relation which is such as warrants the conclusion that the person claiming an insurable interest has an interest, whether pecuniary or arising from dependence or natural affection, in the life of the person insured. 29 Am J Rev ed Ins § 474.

Any pecuniary interest in the continued life of another is an insurable interest. Butterworth v Mississippi Valley Trust Co. 362 Mo 133, 240 SW2d 676, 30 ALR2d 1298.

insurable interest in property. An interest in property to the extent that the owner of the interest derives a benefit from the existence of the property and will suffer a loss from its destruction. 29 Am J Rev ed Ins § 438. Any interest in property or any relation thereto or liability in respect thereof which is of such a nature that a contemplated peril might directly cause the insured a loss. Farmer's Union Mut. Protective Asso. v San Luis State Bank, 86 Colo 293, 281 P 366, 66 ALR 1166.

It is not necessary, to constitute an insurable interest, that the interest be such that the event insured against would necessarily subject the insured to loss; it is sufficient that it might do so and that pecuniary injury would be the natural consequence. Rogers v Lumbermen's Mut. Casualty Co. 271 Ala 348, 124 So 2d 70; United States Fidelity & Guaranty Co. v Reagan, 256 NC 1, 122 SE2d 774.

A property or estate, legal or equitable, in the thing insured is not essential to an "insurable interest," which term is more extensive than property or estate and includes a qualified or limited interest in, or a reasonable expectation of legitimate profit or pecuniary benefit from the continued existence of, the subject of insurance. North British & M. Ins. Co. v Sciandra, 256 Ala 409, 54 So 2d 764, 27 ALR2d 1047; American Indem. Co. v Southern Missionary College, 195 Tenn 513, 260 SW2d 269, 39 ALR2d 714.

insurable risk. Any foreseeable risk of loss, except one caused by the insured's own misconduct or one of such nature that to insure it is prohibited by law or sound public policy. 29A Am J Rev ed Ins § 1133.

insurance. A contract whereby one undertakes to indemnify another against loss, damage, or liability arising from an unknown or contingent event. Meyer v Building & Realty Service Co. 209 Ind 125, 196 NE 250, 100 ALR 1442. An agreement by which one person for a consideration promises to pay money or its equivalent, or to perform some act of value, to another on the destruction, death, loss, or injury of someone or something by specified perils. 29 Am J Rev ed Ins § 3. A contract of indemnity where it affords protection against actual loss or damage; not where, as, in the case of life insurance, payment is to be made by the insurer upon the occurrence of the event insured against, without reference to the actual loss in dollars and cents. 29 Am J Rev ed Ins § 4.

The nature of a contract as one of insurance depends upon its contents and the true character of the contract actually entered into or issued—that is, whether a contract is one of insurance is to be determined by a consideration of the real character of the promise or of the act to be performed, and by a consideration of the exact nature of the agreement in the light of the occurrence, contingency, or circumstances under which the performance becomes requisite. 29 Am J Rev ed Ins § 5.

insurance adjuster. See **adjuster.**

insurance agent. A person expressly or impliedly authorized by an insurance company to represent it in dealing with third persons in matters relating to insurance. 29 Am J Rev ed Ins § 135. One who represents an insurance company as a solicitor of

INSURANCE

business or as a collector of premiums. Home Beneficial L. Ins. Co. v Unemployment Compensation Com. 181 Va 811, 27 SE2d 159. One who represents another in making application for insurance or otherwise in dealing with an insurance company in reference to insurance, called agent of insured. A person within an exemption from execution in favor of any mechanic, miner, or other person. Wilhite v Williams, 41 Kan 288, 21 P 256.

An insurance agent over whom the company retains no control in regard to the physical acts incidental to the performance of his general duties is not an agent of the company, but an independent contractor, in relation to the operation of his automobile while making collections and calling on clients. American National Ins. Co. v Denke, 128 Tex 229, 95 SW2d 370, 107 ALR 409.

See **insurance broker; soliciting agent.**

insurance agent's lien. See **insurance broker's lien.**

insurance broker. One who acts as a middleman between the insured and the insurer, and who solicits insurance from the public under no employment from any special company, but having secured an order, either places the insurance with a company selected by the insured, or in the absence of any selection by the latter, then with a company selected by himself. 29 Am J Rev ed Ins § 135.

Whether an insurance broker represents the insurer or the insured is a question which cannot be answered categorically but which depends upon the circumstances of the particular case. Under certain circumstances and for certain purposes, an insurance broker may represent either the insured or the insurer or both. 29 Am J Rev ed Ins § 139.

insurance broker's lien. A lien of an insurance broker or agent of the insured upon all policies in his hands procured by him for his principal, and also upon all moneys received by him upon such policies, for the payment of the amount due him for commissions, disbursements, advances, and services in and about the negotiation of that particular insurance and all past insurance, but not for the balance of a general account embracing items wholly disconnected with the business of placing insurance. 29 Am J Rev ed Ins § 175.

insurance business. The business of writing and issuing contracts of insurance, that is, insurance policies. 29 Am J Rev ed Ins § 5.

The business of insurance consists in accepting a number of risks, some of which will involve losses, and of spreading such losses over all risks so as to enable the insurer to accept each risk at the slightest fraction of possible liability upon it. Home Title Ins. Co. v United States (CA2 NY) 50 F 107.

insurance carrier. A familiar term in workmen's compensation cases, referring to the state fund, corporation, or association with which the employer has insured. Sheehan Co. v Shuler, 265 US 371, 373 (footnote), 68 L Ed 1061 (footnote), 44 S Ct 546. In the broad sense of the term, a company engaged in the business of insurance.

insurance collector. A person authorized by an insurance company to collect premiums becoming due under policies issued by it, particularly insurance companies engaged in the business of industrial insurance.

insurance commissioner. The head of a state department regulating insurance companies.

insurance company. A company engaged in the business of making contracts by which it agrees to indemnify the other parties thereto from a loss or damage which they may suffer from a specified peril. Strictly construed, an insurance company regularly incorporated and doing business as an old-line company, not a benevolent society or fraternal order providing insurance benefits for its members. 29 Am J Rev ed Ins § 781. An investment company within the meaning of § 3(a) of the Federal Investment Company Act. 15 USC § 80a-3(a).

As the term appears in a tax statute:—an incorporated organization, as contrasted with an unincorporated company or association; including a mutual company, a guaranty or surety company, a hospital service association, and an insurance association created by the legislature as an integral part of a workmen's compensation act. On the other hand, it has been held, under the statutory phraseology and facts and circumstances of a particular case, that for the purposes of such statute, the term may not be applied to a reciprocal insurance exchange, to a company dealing in industrial group insurance, to a mutual company, or to a corporation engaged in the business of servicing mortgages, investing in, and buying and selling bonds and mortgages, and originating and selling mortgage loans. Anno: 146 ALR 464 et seq.

See **benevolent insurance company; mutual benefit society; mutual insurance company; old line company; stock insurance company.**

insurance contract. A contract whereby one person undertakes to indemnify another against loss, damage or liability arising from an unknown or contingent event. An agreement by which one party for a consideration promises to pay money, or its equivalent, or do some act of value, to the assured, upon the destruction or injury of something in which the other party has an interest. State v Willett, 171 Ind 296, 86 NE 68. A contract whereby the insurer in return for a stated consideration agrees on the happening of a specified event to pay the insured a fixed or ascertainable sum of money. Re Barry's Estate, 208 Okla 8, 252 P2d 437, 35 ALR2d 1052.

See **binder; blanket policy; cash-surrender value; floating policy; insurance; oral insurance contract; rider; slip.**

insurance cost. A term significance primarily in life insurance.

Cost is established by mortality tables and invariably increases with age. It is the sum necessary to be paid in during the period of expectancy to amount with interest accretions to the face of the policy. It has nothing to do with rates. It is the toll annually taken from the insurer's assets. Jenkins v Talbot, 338 Ill 441, 170 NE 735, 80 ALR 638.

insurance department. A state agency for the supervision or regulation of insurance companies.

insurance exchange. An association of insurance companies or insurance agents for the purpose of promoting the business, welfare, and convenience of the members, and to secure uniformity in the insurance business. 29 Am J Rev ed Ins § 109. In another and distinct sense, the operation of the system known as reciprocal insurance, interinsurance, or interindemnity, whereby individuals, partnerships, or corporations, engaged in a similar line of business, undertake to indemnify each other against a certain kind or kinds of losses by means of a mutual exchange of insurance contracts, usually through the medium of a common attorney in fact appointed for that purpose by each of the underwriters, under agreements whereby, as between

INSURANCE

themselves, each member separately becomes both an insured and an insurer with several liability only. 29 Am J Rev ed Ins § 102.

insurance fund. See **state insurance fund.**

insurance money. Money recoverable on a policy of insurance by the insured against the insurance company which issued the policy. Stacey v Fidelity & Casualty Co. 21 Ohio App 70, 73, 152 NE 794, 795.

insurance patrol. A salvage corps operated by an insurance company, or insurance companies in combination, for the purpose of attending at fires and salvaging or protecting the imperiled property. Coleman v Fire Ins. Patrol, 122 La 626, 48 So 130.

insurance policy. The name by which the formal written instrument in which a contract of insurance is embodied is known. 29 Am J Rev ed Ins § 186.
See **insurance contract.**

insurance premium. The agreed price for assuming and carrying the risk—that is, the consideration paid an insurer for undertaking to indemnify the insured against a specified peril. State ex rel. Sheets v Pittsburgh, Cincinnati, Chicago & St. Louis Railroad Co. 68 Ohio St 9, 67 NE 93.

insurance rate. The premium rate. 29 Am J Rev ed Ins § 503.
See **manual rates.**

insurance reserve. See **reserve.**

insurance solicitor. An insurance agent who solicits business for his company in the form of insurance policies or contracts. 29 Am J Rev ed Ins § 135.
See **insurance agent.**

insurance trust. See **life insurance trust.**

insure. To contract to indemnify a person against loss from stated perils; to enter into a contract of insurance as insurer.

insured. Ordinarily, synonymous with "assured." 29 Am J Rev ed Ins § 239. The person in whose favor a contract of insurance is operative and who is indemnified against, or is to receive a certain sum upon, the happening of a specified contingency or event. 29 Am J Rev ed Ins § 239. Protected by insurance. The person protected by an automobile liability policy, although not the insured named in the policy, by virtue of the standard provision of the policy extending the protection to any person using the vehicle covered by the policy with the permission of the named insured. Libero v Lumbermen's Mut. Casualty Co. 141 Conn 574, 108 A2d 533, 47 ALR2d 550.

The circumstance that one who takes out a policy of insurance on his own life may never obtain the benefits of the insurance directly is of no weight against considering him as the "insured," such a contract being his, at least in part. Heffelfinger v Commissioner (CA8) 87 F2d 991, 109 ALR 1045, cert den 302 US 690, 82 L Ed 533, 58 S Ct 10.

When used as a noun in fire insurance policies, the word should be construed to include the person whose property is insured and his legal representatives, but, in the absence of clauses protecting other persons, it should not be extended to include any other persons, such as a mortgagee of the property. Collinsville Sav. Soc. v Boston Ins. Co. 17 Conn 676, 60 A 647.

See **loss payable clause; mortgagee clause; standard mortgagee clause.**

insured bank. A bank, the deposits of which are insured by the Federal Deposit Insurance Corporation. Anno: 59 ALR2d 972.

insured deposit. A bank deposit insured by the Federal Deposit Insurance Corporation. The net amount due to any depositor for a deposit in an insured bank (after deducting offsets), less any part thereof which is in excess of $10,000. 12 USC § 1813(m).

insured premises. The real property covered by a policy of insurance protecting against loss or damage or against liability for an injury to a third person occurring on the premises.

insured's permission. See **permission of insured.**

insured title. A title to real estate insured by a policy of title insurance. A title to real estate such as a designated title insurance company will approve and insure. 55 Am J1st V & P § 165.
See **title insurance.**

insurer. The party to a contract of insurance who assumes the risk and undertakes to indemnify the second party known as the insured or to pay a certain sum on the happening of a specified contingency. 29 Am J Rev ed Ins § 238.

insurer's liability. Literally, the liability of an insurer. In common usage, a term of art importing absolute liability. A liability which is absolute except as the injury is caused by the public enemy or an act of God or is self-inflicted. Anderson Hotels of Oklahoma, Inc. v Baker (CA10 Okla) 190 F2d 741, cert den 342 US 869, 96 L Ed 654, 72 S Ct 111.

Insurers' Liquidation Act. One of the uniform laws. 29 Am J Rev ed Ins § 118.

insurgent. A person who engages with others in an insurrection; partaking of or relating to an insurrection. A term of politics for a member of a party who goes against the leadership either in advocacy of principle or in an attempt to overthrow the leadership.

insurrection. A rising against civil or political authority, more than a mob or riot, sometimes amounting to a rebellion, at least, an incipient or limited rebellion. Gitlow v Kiely (DC NY) 44 F2d 227, affd (CA2) 49 F2d 1077, cert den 284 US 648, 76 L Ed 550, 52 S Ct 29; County of Allegheny v Gibson, 90 Pa 397.

In a marine insurance policy on a cargo of slaves, the words "insurrection" and "mutiny" were held to be substantially identical in meaning. McCargo v New Orleans Ins. Co. (La) 10 Rob 202.
See **rebellion.**

insurrectionaries. The individual participants in an insurrection or rebellion.

insurrectionists. Same as **insurrectionaries.**

in suspenso (in sus-pen'sō). In suspense; in abeyance.

in syllabis et verbis (in sil'la-bis et ver'bis). In syllables and words.

intact value. The real value of a share of corporate stock as distinguished from its book value. 18 Am J2d Corp § 219.

intake. The opening in a pipe in lake, pond, or river through which water is taken for a public water supply. 56 Am J1st Watwk § 51.

intaker (in'tā-kėr). A receiver of stolen goods.

in tali casu editum et provisum (in tā'lī kā'sū e'di-tum et prō-vī'sum). In such case made and provided.

In tali conflictu magis est, ut jus nostrum, quam jus aliorum servemus (in tā'lī kon-flik'tū mā'jis est, ut jūs nos'trum, quam jūs a-li-ō'rum ser-vē'mus). In such conflict it is better that we obey our own law than the laws of other nations. That is, in the conflict between the lex fori and the lex loci contractus, the comity of nations should not prevail over our law. McMahan v Green, 12 Ala 71.

intangible. Adjective: Incorporeal; without physical substance; difficult to appraise. Noun: A chose in action; a thing, perhaps of value, but without physical substance in itself.

See **chose in action; intangible property.**

intangible property. Rights not related to physical things, being merely relationships between persons, natural or corporate, which the law recognizes by attaching to them certain sanctions enforceable in the courts. Curry v McCanless, 307 US 357, 83 L Ed 1339, 59 S Ct 900, 123 ALR 162. Property rights protected by the due process clause equally with ordinary real and personal property. 16 Am J2d Const L § 365. For purpose of taxation:—enforceable claims and solvent credits such as bills, notes, and other obligations to pay money, and shares of corporate stock. 51 Am J1st Tax § 420.

An unallowed claim for a refund of Federal income taxes is taxable as "other taxable intangibles" rather than as "credits," under statutes taxing money, credits, investments, deposits, and other intangible property, defining "credits" as the excess of current accounts receivable over current accounts payable, defining "current accounts" as items receivable or payable on demand or within one year of the date of inception, and defining "other taxable intangibles" as including every valuable right, title, or interest not comprised within or excluded from the preceding statutory sections of a specific nature. Glidden Co. v Glander, 151 Ohio St 344, 86 NE2d 1, 9 ALR2d 515.

See **chose in action; incorporeal property; situs; situs for taxation.**

intangible res. An intangible, such as a claim for freight, made the defendant in a proceeding in rem. United States v The Mt. Shasta, 274 US 466, 71 L Ed 1156, 47 S Ct 666.

intangible value. A right or value in a public utility plant evidenced by no physical object but for the development of which the owner has incurred expense and which is properly considered in evaluating the plant for rate-making purposes. 43 Am J1st Pub Util § 132. Going-concern value.

in tantum (in tan'tum). In so much.

integer (in'tē-jėr). Whole; entire; undiminished; unharmed; blameless.

integral. Lacking nothing of completeness. Tebeau v Ridge, 261 Mo 547, 170 SW 871. In mechanics, all of one piece, as of metal or wood. Heuberger v Becker, 27 Cust & Pat App 746, 107 F2d 601.

integral part. A part essential to completeness. A test employed in determining whether an employer whose business is restricted to selling merchandise in a local market at retail is within the jurisdiction of the National Labor Relations Board, the doctrine being that if the retailer is an "integral part" of an interstate system of distribution, as where he operates under a franchise from, and is subject to the control of, a national manufacturer, his business affects interstate commerce and he is subject to the jurisdiction of the board. Anno: 98 L Ed 221.

integrated bar. A governmental body created by statute or rules of court, composed of all the practicing attorneys in the state, their membership in the body being compulsory, operating to control the practices of attorneys by requiring adherence to a code of ethics and instituting disciplinary proceedings for infractions of the code. 7 Am J2d Attys § 7.

integrated bar association. In effect, a bar association to which all practicing attorneys must belong.

See **integrated bar.**

integrated contract. A written contract which contains all the terms and conditions of the agreement. 17 Am J2d Contr § 260.

integration. In the most modern sense of the term, the bringing together of people of all races, but particularly of the black and white races, in all the common concerns of men—educational, political, industrial, religious, and social—by removing all bars of discrimination based on race or color. As a term of economics, the status of an industry operating in continuity from the extraction of the raw materials to the last process in the completion of the product. United States v United States Steel Corp. 251 US 417, 438, 64 L Ed 343, 348, 40 S Ct 293.

integration of the bar. See **integrated bar.**

integration theory. The theory that the business situs of intangible property, for the purposes of property taxation in a state other than the domicile of the owner, is determined according to whether or not the intangibles have become an integral part of some business activity, and their possession and control localized in an independent business or investment away from the owner's domicile, so that their substantial use and value primarily attach to and become an asset of the outside business, or, in other words, that the local independent business controls and utilizes the intangible property in its own operations. Anno: 143 ALR 367; 51 Am J1st Tax § 470.

integrity. Uprightness of character and soundness of moral principle; honesty; probity. Crocheron v Babington, 16 Idaho 441, 101 P 741.

A married woman's unfaithfulness to her husband and her violation of marital obligations, does not tend to show her lack of integrity to qualify as administratrix of his estate, under a statute making "lack of integrity" a disqualification. Estate of Newman, 124 Cal 688, 57 P 686.

integro. See **de integro; ex integro.**

integrum. See **in integrum.**

intellectual insanity. Mental unsoundness to the extent of being unable to distinguish between right and wrong, or, as sometimes stated, incapacity to understand the nature and quality of the act or, if aware of such, inability to know that it is wrong to commit such act. 26 Am J1st Homi §§ 78, 79.

intellectual property. Those property rights which result from the physical manifestation of original thought. Weil, Copyright L 1917 § 6.

intelligence office. An unusual term for an office kept for the purpose of obtaining places of employment for female domestic servants or other laborers. Keim v Chicago, 46 Ill App 445, 446.

intelligence quotient. A rating by number of the level of intelligence of a particular person.

intemperance. Want of restraint in habits and conduct. The intemperate use of intoxicating liquor. Anno: 26 ALR 1291. The habitual and excessive use of intoxicating liquor. Deadwyler v Grand Lodge, K. P. 131 SC 335, 126 SE 437. Indulging in intoxicants excessively whenever the occasion offers. Tatum v State, 63 Ala 147, 152. Overindulgence in the use of intoxicating liquors so frequently as to constitute a habit. 29 Am J Rev ed Ins § 774.

See **habitual intemperance; intoxication.**

intemperant use of intoxicating liquor. An expression found in the form of a question propounded by the insurer in an application for life insurance, meaning indulgence to the point of impairment of mental or physical health, thereby rendering the risk more hazardous. Anno: 26 ALR 1291.

See **intemperance.**

intemperate habits. See **intemperance; habitual intemperance.**

intend. To intend is to fix the mind upon; to have a design; to purpose. People v Vanderpool, 1 Mich NP 264, 267.

intendant (in-ten'dạnt). A superintendent; a manager; an important officer.

intended. Fixed in the mind; designed; purposed.
As used in a statute barring a right to recover the purchase price of preparations intended or designed for illegal use, the words are held to include a design and intention on the part of the vendor that the preparation sold by him will be used in an unlawful manufacture. The word intended is held to mean more than mere knowledge and to import knowledge of the seller accompanied by some act on his part indicating consent to or encouragement in the unlawful use. Jacobs v Danciger, 328 Mo 458, 77 ALR 1237, 41 SW2d 389.

intending passenger. A person who enters upon the premises of a carrier of passengers with the bona fide intention of becoming a passenger, and awaits the arrival of his train or other conveyance at a proper place, in a proper manner, and within a reasonable time before the arrival of such train or other conveyance. Palmer v Willamette Valley Southern Railway Co. 88 Or 322, 171 P 1169.

intendment. The meaning of a word. Legal meaning. 27 Am J1st Indict § 55.

See **common intendment; rule of intendment.**

intendment of law. A presumption of law; legal meaning; meaning peculiar to the law.

intent. Adjective: With fixed purpose; earnest; determined; engrossed. Noun: Purpose. The purpose to use a particular means to effect a certain result. Baker v State, 120 Wis 135, 97 NW 566. A constituent element of all criminal acts, but not necessarily conscious wrongdoing. 21 Am J2d Crim L § 81. An inference of law from facts proved. State v La Page, 57 NH 245.

See **common intent; criminal intent; design; felonious intent; general criminal intent; legal intent; rational intent; specific intent.**

intentio (in-ten'she-ō). (Civil law.) Intent; intention; meaning; the formal complaint of the actor or plaintiff in an action.

Intentio caeca mala (in-ten'she-ō sē'ka ma'la). A concealed intention or meaning is bad.

ntentio inservire debet legibus, non leges intentioni (in-ten'she-ō in-ser-vī're de'bet lē'ji-bus, non lē'jĕz in-ten-she-ō'nī). Intention should be subservient to the laws, not the laws to intention.

Intentio mea imponit nomen operi meo (in-ten'she-ō me'a im-pō'nit nō'men o'pe-rī mē'ō). My intent stamps or impresses a name upon my act.

intention. Purpose. That which is intended.
See **declaration of intention; floating intention; intend; intent.**

intentional. Performed or done with intent.
In the law of private nuisance an invasion of another's interest in the use and enjoyment of land is intentional when the person whose conduct is in question as a basis for liability acts for the purpose of causing it, or knows that it is resulting from his conduct, or knows that it is substantially certain to result from his conduct. Anno: 54 ALR2d 769.

intentional injury. An injury inflicted by positive, willful, and aggressive conduct; an injury inflicted with design and foresight, as distinguished from an injury caused by negligence or sustained by mishap. Cleveland, Cincinnati, Chicago & St. Louis. Railway Co. v Tartt (CA7 Ill) 99 F 369; American Acci. Co. v Carson, 99 Ky 441, 36 SW 169.

intentionally. In an intentional manner, with design, of purpose. McNamara v St. Louis Transit Co. 182 Mo 676, 81 SW 880.

intention of parties. The primary consideration in determining the making, as well as in the interpretation of a contract.

intention of testator. The intention manifested in the terms of the will, not necessarily the intention existing in the mind of the testator. Yeates v Yeates, 179 Ark 543, 16 SW2d 996, 65 ALR 466.

intent to commit a felony. See **burglary; felonious intent.**

intent to defraud. An intent to commit a fraud.
The words as used in a statute making it an offense to pretend to be an officer or employee acting under the authority of the United States, do not require more than that the person charged has, by artifice and deceit, sought to cause the deceived person to follow some course he would not have pursued but for the deceitful conduct. United States v Lepowitch, 318 US 702, 87 L Ed 1091, 63 S Ct 914.

See **fraud.**

intent to kill. See **assault with intent to kill; intent to take life; murder.**

intent to nuncupate (in'tent to nung'kụ-pāt). The intention of one who is in extremis to make a nuncupative will. 57 Am J1st Wills 656.

intent to rape. See **assault with intent to rape.**

intent to steal. The intent or purpose which a thief has to deprive another of his goods. The intent of one taking personal property without the consent of the owner to deprive the owner permanently of his property or its value. 32 Am J1st Larc § 36.

intent to take life. The willingness to take, or unwillingness to respect, human life. 26 Am J1st Homi § 34.

inter (in-tėr'). Between; among; amid; in; during.

inter absentes (in'ter ab-sen'tēz). Among or between persons who are absent.

inter alia (in-tėr ā'li-ạ). Among other things or matters. See 4 Bl Comm 129.

Inter alias causas acquisitionis, magna, celebris, et famosa est causa donationis (in'ter a'li-as kâ'zas akqui-zi-she-ō'nis, mag'na, se'le-bris, et fa-mō'sa est kâ'za dō-nā-she-ō'nis). Among other means of acquisition, there is a great, frequently used and famous means, that of gift.

inter alios (in'ter a'li-ōs). Among others; between other persons.

inter alios acta (in'ter a'li-os ak'ta). Acts or transactions between other persons; acts or transactions between persons other than those before the court.

Inter alios res gestas aliis non posse praejudicium facere saepe constitutum est (in'ter a'li-os rēz jes'tas a'li-is non pos'se prē-jū-di'she-um fā'se-re sē'pe kon-sti-tū'tum est). It has often been decided that matters which were transacted between some persons cannot operate as a prejudice to other persons.

Inter-American Coffee Agreement. An agreement made by the President of the United States with the representatives of coffee producing countries of the Western Hemisphere, providing quotas for the importation of coffee into the United States from such countries. 19 USC § 1356.

inter amicos (in'ter a-mī'kos). Among or between friends.

inter apices juris (in'ter ā'pi-sez jū'ris). Among the extremities or subtleties of the law. Hinsdale v Miles, 5 Conn 331, 334.

Inter arma silent leges (in'ter ar'ma sī'lent lē'jēz). Amidst arms the laws are silent; that is, in time of war.

inter brachia (in-tėr brā'ki-a). Between arms.

inter caeteros (in'ter sē'te-ros). Among or between other persons.

intercalare (in-tėr-ka-lā'rē). To insert; to insert or intercalate a month or a day in the calendar.

intercalary month (in-tėr'ka-la-ri munth). An extra month in the calendar inserted at intervals by the Jews, Arabs and Turks, who still use the lunar month, as did the ancient Greeks, for the purpose of reconciling solar time with lunar time.

inter canem et lupum. (Latin.) Literally, between the dog and the wolf. Figuratively, the twilight, the time when the dog goes to rest and the wolf to hunt.

intercedere (in-ter-sē'de-re). (Civil law.) To stand between; to intervene; to interpose as a mediator; to stand surety.

intercepted shipment. A shipment of goods by the seller which the buyer intercepts before it reaches its original destination, thereby actually and lawfully obtaining possession. Anno: 7 ALR 1385; Uniform Sales Act § 58(2)(a).

intercepting merchandise on way to market. See **forestalling the market.**

intercepting telephone conversation. A breach of privacy in listening without the consent of the communicants, whatever the method used to hear or record the conversation may be. United States v Polakoff (CA2 NY) 112 F2d 888, 134 ALR 607. Obtaining a telephone communication or message by wiretapping device. Benanti v United States, 355 US 96, 2 L Ed 2d 126, 78 S Ct 155.

interchangeably. In the way, mode or form of exchange.
"A term constantly used in the concluding clause of indentures (in witness whereof the said parties have hereunto interchangeably set their hands and seals) and properly imputing not only an execution by all the parties, but an actual interchange of signatures and seals and such as takes place in the case of instruments executed in duplicate, or in part and counterpart, where the signature and seal of each party are affixed to the part given to the other." Roosevelt v Smith, 17 Misc 323, 325, 40 NYS 381.

interchange of cars. The practice in railroading whereby the cars of one company are transported over the lines and in the trains of other companies. Jacobson v Wisconsin M. & K. R. Co. 71 Minn 519, 74 NW 893, aff'd 179 US 287, 45 L Ed 194, 21 S Ct 115.

interchange of traffic. The movement of freight, also of passengers, from a carrier to a connecting carrier. 14 Am J2d Car § 662.

intercommon. To enjoy mutual rights of common in adjoining lands; as where the beasts of each of two adjoining owners stray mutually into the field of the other, without any molestation from either. See 2 Bl Comm 33.

intercommoning (in-tėr-kom'on-ing). Enjoying the rights of intercommon in adjoining lands.
See **intercommon.**

inter conjuges (in'ter kon'ju-jēz). Between a husband and his wife.

inter conjunctas personas (in'tėr kon-junk'tas per-so'nas). Between conjunct persons.
See **conjunct persons.**

intercourse. A commingling; intimate connections between persons or nations, as in common affairs and civilities, in correspondence or trade; communication; commerce, especially interchange of thought and feeling; association; communion. Not necessarily sexual intercourse. People v Howard, 143 Cal 316, 320, 76 P 1116.
See **commerce; sexual intercourse.**

interdict. Verb: To prohibit. Noun: An interdiction.
See **interdiction.**

interdiction. An authoritative prohibition. An order of a high ecclesiastical officer prohibiting divine services in certain specified places or under the direction of certain specified persons.

interdiction of commerce. A reprisal by one nation against another whereunder, by order promulgated by the authorities of the former, all trade between it and the other must cease for the time. The Edward Scott (US) 1 Wheaton 261, 272, 4 L Ed 86, 88. The closing of a port to commerce. Craig v United Ins. Co. (NY) 6 Johns 226.

interdiction of fire and water (of fīr and wâ'tėr). An interdict ordering a person to be banished from the kingdom and prohibiting any person from furnishing him with either fire or water.

interdictum salvianum (in'ter-dik'tum sal-vi-ā'num). (Roman law.) The foreclosure of a pledge of the goods of a tenant given by him as security for the payment of rent.

Interdum evenit ut exceptio quae prima facie justa videtur, tamen unique noceat (in-ter'dum ē-ve'nit ut ex-sep'she-ō kwē prī'ma fā'shē jus'ta vi-de'ter, ta'men ū'ni-kwe no'se-at). It sometimes happens that a plea which on its face seems just, is nevertheless unfair and inequitable.

interesse (in-tėr-es'ē). Interest; an interest.

interesse termini (in-ter-es'ē tėr'mi-nī). The interest of a lessee acquired upon the execution of the lease and before taking possession of the premises. 32 Am J1st L & T § 27.

interest. A right in, or share of, something. Concern. The compensation allowed by law, or fixed by the parties, for the use, detention, or forbearance of money or its equivalent. 30 Am J Rev ed Int § 2. Compensation payable on a contractual basis or allowed by way of damages. 22 Am J2d Damg § 179. A means of compensation, as distinguished from a penalty which is a means of punishment. United States v Childs, 266 US 304, 69 L Ed 299, 45 S Ct 110. As taxable income:—the compensation paid for the use of money. Sayles v Commissioner of Corp. & Taxation, 286 Mass 102, 189 NE 579, 91 ALR 1267.

The word as used in a codicil may, depending upon the context and the presence or absence of qualifying words, have the meaning of "income" in one part of the instrument and "share" in another. Hilton v Kinsey, 88 App DC 14, 185 F2d 885, 23 ALR2d 830.

See **absolute interest; adverse interest; affected with a public interest; appealable interest; beneficial interest; declaration against interest; interest in property; party in interest; power coupled with an interest.**

interest annually. See **annual interest; at interest; compound interest; conventional interest; customary interest; discount; discretionary interest; Jewish interest; legal interest; legal rate of interest; marine interest; maritime interest; mercantile rule; moratory interest; per annum; rests; simple interest; United States rule; with interest; with interest annually.**

interest-bearing stock. Another term for preferred stock. 19 Am J2d Corp § 872.
See **preferred stock.**

interest by way of damages. Sometimes called moratory interest,—interest allowed in actions for breach of contract or tort as damages for the unlawful detention of the money found to be due, not by way of contract or arbitrary rule, but by way of reparation as justice demands. 22 Am J2d Damg § 179.

interest coupons. Instruments attached to a note or bond to evidence the interest maturing at stated intervals over the term of the principal debt, usually executed in a form which constitutes them separate promissory notes distinct from the obligation to which attached. 11 Am J2d B & N § 21.
See **interest from bond.**

interest, dividends, rents and profits. As the term appears in stating the subject of a gift or grant by will, deed, or trust instrument:—net income. Re Heaton, 89 Vt 550, 96 A 21.

interested. Having an interest.
See **interested person.**

interested in estate. One having some pecuniary interest in the estate of a decedent, so as to be entitled to notice of hearing upon the final report and prayer for discharge of the personal representative. Re Holman, 216 Iowa 1186, 250 NW 498, 98 ALR 1363.

interested in patent. Owning the exclusive right at the time an infringement was committed. Moore v Marsh (US) 7 Wall 515, 19 L Ed 37, 39 (construing statute authorizing action for infringement by person interested.)

interested person. A person concerned or having an interest. Within the meaning of a statute designating persons eligible to contest a will:—one who has such an interest as may be impaired or defeated by the probate of the will or benefitted by setting it aside. Re Plaut, 27 Cal 2d 424, 164 P2d 765, 162 ALR 837. In reference to the right to appeal from a judgment, one who has some immediate legal right, or is under some legal liability, that may be enlarged or diminished by the judgment. 4 Am J2d A & E §§ 182 et seq. As a person incompetent to testify against the personal representative of a deceased person, a person having a direct legal interest, a pecuniary interest, in the result of the suit. 58 Am J1st Witn § 287. In reference to the right to intervene in an action, an interest in the matter in litigation of such direct and immediate character that the intervener will either gain or lose by the direct legal operation and effect of the judgment. 39 Am J1st Parties § 61.

A statute disqualifying a judge for relationship to "any person" interested in the proceedings has been held to disqualify a judge on the basis of his relationship to an attorney in the cause before him, where the attorney's fee was dependent upon his success. Vine v Jones, 13 SD 54, 82 NW 82.

As to who is a "person interested" in the estate of a decedent under statutes apportioning the estate tax among persons interested, see Anno: 37 ALR2d 215.

interest eo nomine (in′tĕr-est ē′ō no′mi-ne). Interest on money specially provided for by statute. Oppenheim v Hood, 33 SW2d 265.

interest equalization tax. A tax on the acquisition of foreign securities, being an economic device imposed to increase the cost to foreigners of borrowing United States capital, for the purpose of cutting down the flow of United States capital abroad, thereby improving the position of the United States respecting the balance of international payments. IRC § 4911(a).

interest from bond. Interest payable in the usual sense, that is, as compensation for the use of money, notwithstanding the obligation is encompassed in a coupon. Sayles v Commissioner of Corps. & Taxation, 286 Mass 102, 189 NE 579, 91 ALR 1267; Commissioner of Corps. & Taxation v Williston, 315 Mass 648, 54 NE2d 43, 151 ALR 1395.

interest in case. A pecuniary or property interest in the event or subject matter of the action or in the judgment to be rendered. Anno: 10 ALR2d 1320.
See **interest in subject matter.**

interest in contract. A term familiar in statutes respecting the private concern of a public officer in a public contract negotiated by him, meaning any interest which prevents him from exercising absolute loyalty and undivided allegiance to the best interests of the public body which he serves, not necessarily an interest involving direct financial gain upon his part. Miller v Martinez, 28 Cal App 2d 364, 82 P2d 519.

interest in land. See **interest in property.**

interest in litigation. See **interest in subject matter.**

interest in property. In the broader sense of the term, ownership of a particular property, whether of the full or a lesser interest. More precisely, a right in or to property which is less than ownership or title, 29A Am J Rev ed Ins § 825. A right less than an estate. Garner v Milwaukee Mechanics' Ins. Co. 73 Kan 127, 84 P 717. In free usage, an estate. Embracing both legal and equitable rights. Gibb v

Philadelphia Fire Ins. Co. 59 Minn 267, 61 NW 137.

Under a statute requiring a license to engage in the business of buying and selling interests in real estate, there is strong support for the view that a person engaged in buying or selling businesses as going concerns, including real estate as a part of the subject matter of the transfer, is not within the statute. But there is authority to the contrary. 12 Am J2d Brok § 15.

The term "interest in land," as used in the statute of frauds, means some portion of the title or right of possession, and does not include agreements which may affect land but which do not complete the transfer of any title, ownership, or possession. 49 Am J1st Stat of F § 154.

See **change of interest; chattel interest; estate; executory interests; insurable interest; landed interest; license coupled with an interest; life interest; limited interest; possessory interest; power coupled with an interest; public interest; qualified interest; royalty interest; unity of interest; vested in interest; vested interest.**

interest in real property. See **interest in property.**

interest in subject matter. For the purpose of intervention, some legal or equitable interest in the subject of the action which a judgment or decree will or may affect. Universal Oil Products Co. v Standard Oil Co. 6 F Supp 37. For the purpose of a statute rendering one interested in the subject matter incompetent as a witness in an action by or against a legal representative of a decedent, one having a direct pecuniary interest in the subject matter of the litigation before the court so as to constitute him at the time an "opposite party" to the estate of deceased. Beaupre v Holzbaugh, 327 Mich 101, 41 NW2d 338, 27 ALR2d 532. In reference to parties on appeal, one whose interest may be adversely affected by the decision on appeal. 4 Am J2d A & E § 276.

interest in the event. One's position in reference to an action being such that he will either gain or lose by the direct legal operation and effect of the judgment of the court disposing of the facts in dispute, or such that the record of a judgment will be legal evidence for or against him in some other action. 58 Am J1st Witn § 288.

interest may appear. See **as interest may appear.**

interest on indebtedness. Compensation for the use or forbearance of money. Deputy v DuPont, 308 US 488, 84 L Ed 416, 60 S Ct 363.
See **interest.**

interest on interest. A middle course between simple interest and compound interest. 30 Am J Rev ed Int § 61.
See **compound interest.**

interest on money. See **interest.**

interest or no interest clause. A clause or provision in an insurance policy whereby the insurer waives the right to question the interest or ownership of the insured in the property insured. 29A Am J Rev ed Ins §§ 1013, 1015.

interest policy. A true rather than a wager policy; a policy protecting a real and substantial interest of the insured. Sawyer v Dodge County Mut. Ins. Co. 37 Wis 503, 539.

interest upon condition precedent. A contingent interest. Anno: 71 ALR 1053, 1054.

interest upon condition subsequent. A vested interest subject to be divested. Anno: 71 ALR 1053, 1054.

Interest reipublicae ne maleficia remaneant impunita (in'ter-est rē-ī-pub'li-sē ne ma-le-fi'she-a rē-mā'ne-ant im-pū-nī'ta). It is to the interest of the commonwealth that malefactors do not go unpunished. Abbott v Territory, 20 Okla Crim 1, 94 P 179.

Interest reipublicae ne sua quis male utatur (in'ter-est rē-ī-pub'li-sē nē su'a quis ma'le u-tā'ter). It is in the interest of the state that no one make a bad use of his own property.

Interest reipublicae quod homines conserventur (in'ter-est rē-ī-pub'li-sē quod ho'mi-nēz kon-serven'ter). It is in the interest of the state that men should be protected.

Interest reipublicae res judicatas non rescindi (in'ter-est rē-ī-pub'li-sē rēz jū-di-kā'tas non re-sin'dī). It is of interest to the state that judgments should not be reversed or set aside.

Interest reipublicae suprema hominum testamenta rata haberi (in'ter-est rē-ī-pub'li-sē su-prē'ma ho'mi-num tes-ta-men'ta rā'ta hā-bē'rī). It is of interest to the state that the last wills of men should be held valid.

Interest reipublicae ut carceres sint in tuto (in'ter-est rē-ī-pub'li-sē ut kar'se-rēz sint in tū'tō). It is of interest to the state that the prisons should be safe.

Interest reipublicae ut pax in regno conservetur, et quaecunque paci adversentur provide declinentur (in'ter-est rē-ī-pub'li-sē ut pax in reg'no kon-servē'ter, et kwē-kun'kwe pa'sī ad-ver-sen'ter prō-vī'de dē-klī-nen'ter). It is of interest to the state that peace should be preserved within the kingdom, and whatever things are opposed to peace should be prudently avoided.

Interest reipublicae ut quilibet re sua bene utatur (in'ter-est rē-ī-pub'li-sē ut quī'li-bet rē su'a be'ne u-tā'tėr). It is in the interest of the state that each person should make a good use of his own property.

Interest reipublicae ut sit finis litium (in'ter-est rē-ī-pub'li-sē ut sit fī'nis lī'she-um). It is in the interest of the state that there should be an end of a lawsuit.

interests. See **interest.**

interest suit (sūt). A contest between parties interested in the estate of a deceased person for the right to administer it.

interest upon interest. See **interest on interest.**

interference. A tort in violating the right of another to be secure in his business and contract relationships and in his relationship with another as an employer or employee. A tort actionable as malicious in the legal sense where not justified or constituting an exercise of an absolute right. 30 Am J Rev ed Interf § 2. An employer's restraint or coercion of employees in respect of their exercise of rights guaranteed by the Labor Management Relations Act, particularly the right of collective bargaining. 31 Am J Rev ed Lab § 226. The acts of a labor union in impeding the exercise of the right of a worker to dispose of his services in a free labor market. 31 Am J Rev ed Lab § 144. The acts of a labor union, performed maliciously and without justifiable cause, to induce third persons to leave an employment, to induce others not to enter into the service, or to combine to injure an employer by inducing workmen not to enter into employment with him. 31 Am J Rev ed Lab § 140. Another term for **interference proceeding.** 40 Am J1st Pat § 73.

An obstruction or hindrance to use, such as the placing of railings or barriers in a highway. 25 Am J1st High § 532.

interference and domination. The participation of a corporation employer in revamping or recasting the organization of an independent labor union. Continental Oil Co. v NLRB (CA 10) 113 F2d 473.

interference proceeding. A proceeding before officers of the Patent Office for the purpose of determining the relative priority of two inventions which conflict with each other. 40 Am J1st Pat § 73.

interference with burial. A tort consisting in interfering with the right to the solace of burying the body of one's spouse or kin, whether by mutilation of the body after death, disturbing it otherwise, withholding it, or preventing entrance to the cemetery. 22 Am J2d Dead B § 17. An unconstitutional interference with private rights in refusal, on the part of a public officer, to permit one to bury the body of his friend or relative except under unreasonable restrictions. 22 Am J2d Dead B § 2.

interference with mail. Any obstruction to or hindering of the transportation and delivery of the mail. 41 Am J1st P O § 72.

interference with military activities. A criminal offense in obstructing or interfering with the recruiting or enlistment services of the United States, or other military, naval, or war activities or efforts. 47 Am J1st Sedit etc. § 12.

interference with trade or calling. A term applied to the tort of intermeddling in certain relations affecting a man's trade, occupation, profession, or means of gaining a livelihood. 30 Am J Rev ed Interf § 44.

interfere with. Affirmative conduct essentially; not including a refusal to deal with employees collectively. Anno: 123 ALR 622; 83 L Ed 691.

interim (in'tėr-im). Meanwhile; in the meantime. Hence, temporary, as interim receipt.

interim allowance. See **temporary allowance.**

interim certificate. A receipt issued on a subscription for corporate stock or a purchase of bonds or other securities, to be held by the subscriber or purchaser until the securities purchased are ready for delivery, being in effect the promise or obligation of the issuer to deliver the securities when issued. 11 Am J2d B & N § 28.

interim committitur (in'te-rim kom-mit'ti-ter). An order of commitment directing temporary custody of a person.

interim curator (kụ-rā'tọr). A temporary guardian or custodian of property.

interim dividend. A corporate dividend payable on a date between regular dividend paying dates; a dividend which may be rescinded or revoked where such action is made advisable by an adverse change in the circumstances of the corporation. Lagunas Nitrate Co. v Schroeder & Co. (Eng) 85 LT NS 22, 17 Times L 625.

interim factor (fak'tor). A temporary trustee appointed to take charge of the property of a bankrupt.

interim officer (of'i-sėr). An officer appointed to take charge and to perform the duties of an office temporarily; an officer pro tempore.

interim order. A provisional order of court, such as a temporary injunction. A provisional or temporary order by an administrative agency. 2 Am J2d Admin L § 466. An interlocutory order.

See **interlocutory order; provisional order.**

interim ordinance. A zoning ordinance intended to preserve the status quo of a particular section or sections of the municipality pending the adoption of permanent zoning regulations, the purpose of the ordinance being to prevent the evasion of a comprehensive zoning plan in prospect by entering upon a course of construction during the time that it takes to work out the details of and enact a complete zoning plan. 58 Am J1st Zon § 137.

interim receipt. In insurance parlance, a binder or contract of temporary insurance. 29 Am J Rev ed Ins § 205.

See **interim certificate.**

interim receiver. Same as **temporary receiver.**

interim report. A report by a fiduciary of the condition of the estate and his administration thereof, furnished between the filing of the inventory of the estate and the final report, either as required by law or by order of the court. A report required of a trustee in bankruptcy concerning the condition of the estate in bankruptcy, the amount of money on hand, and such other details as may be required by the court, one to be furnished within the first month after the appointment of the trustee, and one every two months thereafter, unless otherwise ordered by the court. 9 Am J2d Bankr § 1259.

interindemnity. Same as **reciprocal insurance.**

interinsurance. Same as **reciprocal insurance.**

interinsurance association. An association engaged in providing reciprocal insurance for its members. 29 Am J Rev ed Ins § 102.

See **reciprocal insurance.**

Interior Department. An executive department of the United States Government, headed by a Secretary of the Interior, who is charged with supervision of public business relating to public lands, Indians, mines, reclamation, fish and wildlife service, geological survey, and other subjects and agencies. 54 Am J1st US § 52.

interline. To write between lines already written, for the purpose of adding to, or correcting what is written. Russell v Eubanks, 84 Mo 82, 88.

interlineation. The act of interlining. That which is interlined. An alteration of an instrument. 4 Am J2d Alt Inst § 36.

See **interline.**

interlocking device. A device at a railroad crossing installed to control the signals and gates so that one will not be working independently of the other. Anno: 40 ALR 758.

interlocking directorate. The relationship between two or more corporations who have directors or officers in common. 19 Am J2d Corp § 1307.

interlocking directors. Directors common to the boards of two or more corporations. 19 Am J2d Corp § 1307.

interlocutio (in-ter-lo-kū'she-ō). Same as **imparlance.**

interlocution. The making of an interlocutory application or the rendition of an interlocutory decree or judgment during the pendency of an action or suit.

interlocutor (in-tėr-lok'ụ-tọr). A judgment, order, or decree of a court.

interlocutory. Not decisive of the cause but determining an intervening matter relating to the cause. Mora v Sun Mut. Ins. Co. (NY) 13 Abb Pr 304, 307. Intermediate.

interlocutory accounting. See **intermediate accounting.**

interlocutory application. A motion made during the progress of a case invoking provisional or interlocutory relief rather than a final judgment or decree. An application for an order by way of getting the case in such shape that in the end it may be properly heard and finally adjudicated. 27 Am J2d Eq § 235.

interlocutory award. An award made by arbitrators, not final in character because of incompleteness or other cause. Jones v Jones, 229 Ky 71, 16 SW2d 503.

interlocutory costs. Costs or disbursements on an intermediate motion or proceeding. Cardoff v Cardoff, 152 Minn 399, 189 NW 124. Costs allowable, taxable, and payable during the progress of a case. Goodyear v Sawyer (CC Tenn) 17 F 2, 6.

interlocutory decision. See **interlocutory; interlocutory judgment.**

interlocutory decree. A decree intended, not as a final adjudication, but as a determination made for the purpose of presenting the case in such form that it may, in the end, be heard on the merits and finally adjudicated. 27 Am J2d Eq § 235. The determination of a matter preliminary to trial or hearing for the rendition of a final decree. Comans v Tapley, 101 Miss 203, 57 So 567. A decree of divorce, that is, a decree which determines that a party is entitled to a divorce, such decree not to be final until after the expiration of the period of time prescribed by the statute. 24 Am J2d Div & S § 427.
See **interlocutory judgment.**

interlocutory divorce. See **interlocutory decree.**

interlocutory hearing. Any hearing for the purpose, not of an ultimate determination and final adjudication, but to obtain a presentation of the case in such form that it may, in the end, be properly heard and adjudicated finally on the merits. 27 Am J2d Eq § 235.

interlocutory injunction. A provisional or temporary injunction. 28 Am J Rev ed Inj § 12.
See **temporary injunction.**

interlocutory judgment. An intermediate judgment, a judgment which lacks finality. United States v Howe (CA2 Vt) 280 F 815, 23 ALR 531, cert den 259 US 587, 66 L Ed 1077, 42 S Ct 590. A judgment which "speaks between", that is does not speak the last word which the court may be required to speak in the case. Keffer v Keffer, 307 Ky 831, 212 SW2d 314. A judgment rendered in the middle of a cause upon some plea, proceeding, or default, which is only intermediate and does not finally determine or complete the suit. Jacoby v Carrollton Federal Sav. & Loan Asso. (Ky) 246 SW2d 1000. A judgment which is made before a final decision, for the purpose of ascertaining a matter of law or fact preparatory to a final judgment, or which determines some preliminary or subordinate point or plea, or settles some step, question, or default arising in the progress of the case, but does not adjudicate the ultimate rights of the parties or finally put the case out of court. 30A Am J Rev ed Judgm § 121.

A judgment on the merits defining and settling the rights of the parties is not rendered interlocutory by the fact that further orders may be necessary to carry into effect the rights settled by the judgment. 30A Am J Rev ed Judgm § 122.
See **interlocutory decree.**

interlocutory judgment or decree of divorce. A judgment or decree which determines that a party is entitled to an absolute divorce, such decree not to be final until after the expiration of the period of time prescribed by the statute. 24 Am J2d Div & S § 427.

interlocutory motion. See **interlocutory application.**

interlocutory order. An order rendered in an action or proceeding by way of provisional relief or upon a motion or application made during the course of the action or proceeding by way of determining the manner or form in which the case shall be presented for a final trial or hearing and an adjudication on the merits; not in itself an adjudication on the merits. Re Blalock, 233 NC 493, 64 SE2d 848, 25 ALR2d 818; People v Priori, 163 NY 99, 57 NE 85, 87; Mackowain v Gulf Oil Corp. 369 Pa 581, 87 A2d 314, 37 ALR2d 584.
See **interlocutory decree; interlocutory judgment.**

interloper. A trader operating without the license required by law. A party who takes an appeal or participates in an appeal taken by others who has no financial interest or other right which could be affected either adversely or favorably by the outcome of the litigation. Re Bush's Trust, 249 Minn 51, 82 NW2d 221.

interlude. An intervening event. A short dramatic piece, generally accompanied with music, usually represented or performed between the acts of longer performances. Society for Reformation of Juvenile Delinquents v Diers (NY) 60 Barb 152, 156.

intermarriage. The act of marrying. People v Bord, 243 NY 595, 596, 154 NE 620.

intermarry. To enter into a marriage.

intermeddler. One who stirs up litigation.
A person who officiously intrudes into a business to which he has no right.
The distinction between an intermeddler and a trespasser is not in any case very great. Vassor v Atlantic Coast Line Railroad Co. 142 NC 68, 950, 954, 54 SE 849.

intermeddling. A form of maintenance. Anno: 139 ALR 650.
See **intermeddler.**

intermediary. A go-between. One through whom a transaction is performed for another, for example, a person paying the rent of another with funds provided by the latter. 3 Am J2d Agency § 22.

intermediary bank. A bank which receives a collection from another bank and forwards it to a third bank for collection. Any bank to which an item is transferred in course of collection except the depositary or payor bank. UCC § 4—105(c).

intermediate. Occurring between two events. Interlocutory; intervening.
See **interlocutory.**

intermediate accounting. An accounting by a fiduciary at intervals between the filing of the inventory of the estate and the final accounting. 54 Am J1st Trusts § 511.

intermediate administrative appeal. An appeal from an administrative order to an officer on an inter-

INTERMEDIATE [652] INTERNAL

mediate level, a subsequent appeal to the head of the department or agency being available. 2 Am J2d Admin L § 540.

intermediate appellate court. Same as **intermediate court of appeal**.

intermediate carrier. One of three or more connecting carriers, who is neither the initial nor the terminal carrier. 14 Am J2d Car § 662.

intermediate costs. Same as **interlocutory costs**.

intermediate court of appeal. The lower court of a two-level appellate system; a court whose decision is subject to review by a higher appellate court. 4 Am J2d A & E § 11.

intermediate estate. An estate intervening the interest giving a right of present possession and the remote future interest, the effect of which is to prevent a merger of such present and future interests to create a fee simple. 28 Am J2d Est § 374.

intermediate hearing. See **interlocutory hearing**.

intermediate injunction. See **interlocutory injunction**.

intermediate interest. An interest in real estate so limited as to be between a life estate and an ultimate interest by way of remainder. McCreary v Coggeshall, 74 SC 42, 53 SE 978.
See **intermediate estate**.

intermediate judgment. See **interlocutory judgment**.

intermediate landing field. See **landing area**.

intermediate lien. See **intervening lien**.

intermediate order. See **interlocutory order**.

intermediate point. A place along the route of a shipment of goods between the place of shipment and the place where the shipment is to be delivered according to the terms of the contract of carriage. 13 Am J2d Car § 393.

intermediate port. A port between the sailing port and the port of termination of a voyage. 29 Am J Rev ed Ins § 332.

intermediate rate. A freight rate established expressly for a shipment between designated places, such as Chicago and Omaha. 13 Am J2d Car § 119.

intermediate witness. A witness who testifies to a fact on the strength of other testimony, and not of his own knowledge.

intermediator. One who settles or attempts to settle a dispute or controversy between others.
See **arbitrator**.

interment. See **burial**.

intermingling. For the purpose of the application of the doctrine of confusion of goods, a wilful and tortious mixture and confusion of goods by the owner with the goods of another so that they are indistinguishable and not susceptible of division according to the rights of each owner. 1 Am J2d Access § 15.
See **commingling of funds; commingling of goods**.

inter minora crimina (in'ter mi-nō'ra kri'mi-na). Among the minor crimes.

in terminis terminantibus (in ter'mi-nis ter-mi-nan'-ti-bus). In determinate or determinating terms; in express terms.

intermittent easement. An easement which is only used occasionally, or that is used or usable only at times; such as a right of occasionally flooding the lands of one's neighbor. Eaton v Boston, Concord & Montreal Railroad, 51 NH 504.

intermittent injury. The opposite of constant and continuous injury; temporary, depending on future conditions which may or may not arise. Harvey v Mason City & Fort Dodge R. Co. 129 Iowa 465, 105 NW 958.

intermittent stream. Same as **intermittent watercourse**.

intermittent watercourse. A watercourse, which although dry at times, has a well-defined and substantial existence; a watercourse with a usual or frequent flow which occurs regularly at certain seasons, and upon which dependence may be placed. 56 Am J1st Wat § 9. A stream in which the flow of water is discontinuous. 56 Am J1st Wat § 9.

intern. Verb: (in-tèrn'). To apprehend, restrain, and detain an enemy alien. To confine prisoners of war in the interior of the country. To hold a person as a political prisoner. On the part of a neutral, to detain ships, sailors, soldiers, or property of a belligerent. Noun: (in'tèrn). A physician, usually one in the first year after graduation from medical college, who serves in a hospital in a professional capacity, assisting the physicians on the staff and attending upon patients in the hospital under the direction of their physicians or members of the hospital staff.
See **interned alien; internment**.

internal administration. Public administration on the institutional side, that is, as a going concern, including the legal structure or organization of administration, the legal aspects of its institutional activities, and the legal questions involved in overall management of such activities. 1 Am J2d Admin L § 5.

internal affairs of corporation. Of private corporation: —transactions and relations which affect only the corporation and the stockholders as between themselves. Edwards v Schillinger, 245 Ill 231, 91 NE 1048. Something which concerns one solely in his capacity as a member of a corporation, whether as corporator, stockholder, director, president, or other officer, and is the act of the corporation, whether acting in stockholders' meeting or through its agents, the board of directors. 23 Am J2d For Corp § 410. Of municipal corporation:—such business as a municipal corporation of like character is normally required to transact in order to effectuate the purpose of its charter, such as providing a police force, a jail, buildings for offices, etc. Lewis v Pima County, 155 US 54, 39 L Ed 67, 15 S Ct 22.

internal commerce. Commerce which is completely internal within a state of the Union, which is carried on between man and man in a state, or between different parts of the same state, and which does not extend to, or affect other states. North River Steamboat Co. v Livingston (NY) 3 Cow 713, 731.

internal improvement. A highway, toll road, canal, or other public improvement. 38 Am J1st Mun Corp § 559.
See **works of internal improvement**.

internal medicine. A branch of the practice of medicine. Treatment of diseases of the internal organs.

internal revenue. Revenues of the federal government. California ex rel. McColgan v Bruce (CA9 Nev) 129 F2d 421, 147 ALR 782.

Internal Revenue Bureau. An older terminology for

what is now known as the "Internal Revenue Service."

Internal Revenue Code. Title 26 of the United States Code, inclusive of sections on income taxes, estate taxes, gift taxes, excises on alcohol and tobacco, and various other excises, together with provisions on the administration of such tax laws and the procedure to be followed.

internal revenue law. See **Internal Revenue Code; revenue law.**

internal revenue officers. See **Internal Revenue Service; revenue officers.**

Internal Revenue Service. The organization which administers the Internal Revenue Code, headed by the Commissioner of Internal Revenue and embracing a national office in Washington, D. C. and a field organization of revenue regions, each headed by a regional commissioner, and internal revenue districts, each headed by a district director. 34 Am J2d Fed Tax ¶ 9260.

internal revenue stamps. See **revenue stamps.**

internal revenue tax. An exaction for the support of the federal government; a contribution imposed on individuals by the government for its services. Bailey v Drexel Furniture Co. 259 US 20, 66 L Ed 817, 42 S Ct 449, 21 ALR 1432. More narrowly defined as federal taxes with the exception of customs duties. Leeb v United States (DC NY) 16 F2d 937.

Internal Security Act. Legislation intended to protect the government and the people against subversive activities tending to the overthrow of the government.

international. A characterization in a general manner of business or transactions between nations or between persons of different nations. Koehler v Sanders, 122 NY 65, 25 NE 235.
See **public.**

international agreement. A treaty between nations. A contract in which nations are the contracting parties.

international airport of entry. An airport designated as an international airport of entry for purpose of collecting customs duties. 21 Am J2d Cust D § 60.

international bank. A bank which engages in business transactions in foreign countries. 10 Am J2d Banks § 835.

International Bank for Reconstruction and Development. See **World Bank.**

international commerce. See **foreign commerce.**

International Co-operation Administration. A federal agency in the Department of State.

international copyright. A copyright which by force of international agreement is extended, in reference to the protection granted an author, beyond the territorial limits of the jurisdiction in which it was obtained. 18 Am J2d Copyr § 76.

International Copyright Act. An English statute growing out of the Berne Convention of 1887.

International Court of Justice. The principal judicial organ of the United Nations, established by Ch. XIV of the United Nations Charter. Am J2d Desk Book Document 16.

international courts. The international court of arbitration, known as the Hague Tribunal, established by the International Peace Conference in 1899; the Permanent Court of International Justice, established under the auspices of the League of Nations in 1920, which was the successor of the Hague Tribunal; and the International Court of Justice established as the judicial branch of the United Nations Organization, which is the successor to the Permanent Court of International Justice. 30 Am J Rev ed Internat L § 54.

international extradition. The surrender by one nation of an individual accused or convicted of an offense outside of the territory of the former and within the territorial jurisdiction of the latter, which, being competent to try and to punish him, demands the surrender. 31 Am J2d Extrad § 1.

international labor union. See **international union.**

international law. The rules and principles which govern the relations and dealings of nations with each other. New Jersey v Delaware, 291 US 361, 78 L Ed 847, 54 S Ct 407. The usage of all civilized nations. United States v Arre Don Do (US) 6 Pet 691, 8 L Ed 547.
International law in its widest and most comprehensive sense includes not only questions of right between nations, governed by what has been appropriately called the law of nations, but also questions arising under what is generally called private international law, or the conflict of laws, and concerning the rights of persons within the territory and dominion of one nation, by reason of acts, private or public, done within the dominion of another nation. Such was the force accorded the term "jus gentium" by the Roman juris-consults, but today private international law is deemed quite separate and distinct from the law of nations. 30 Am J Rev ed Internat L § 1.
See **private international law; public international law.**

International Monetary Fund. A fund established by Articles of Agreement adopted by a large number of nations at the Bretton Woods Conference in 1944, constituting in gold and national currencies the largest source of quickly available international credit.

International Nautical Mile. See **nautical mile.**

International Organization Immunities Act. A federal statute pertaining to the status of international organizations in reference to their capacity as parties. 22 USC § 288a.

International Peace Conference. A conference held in 1899, to which the leading nations of the world sent representatives, best remembered for its establishment of the international court of arbitration, known as the Hague Tribunal. 30 Am J Rev ed Internat L § 54.

international public law. The law which governs nations in their dealings and relations with one another. 30 Am J Rev ed Internat L § 1.

International Refugee Organization. An organization functioning under the United Nations Charter. International Refugee Organization v Republic S.S. Corp. (CA4) 189 F2d 858.

International Rules for Navigation at Sea. Federal statutes applying generally to all public and private vessels of the United States, also referred to as Regulations for Preventing Collisions at Sea. 33 USC §§ 143–147(d). Substantially, a code of navigation law, similar to that adopted by the leading maritime nations. 48 Am J1st Ship § 245.

International Rules to Prevent Collisions. Same as **International Rules for Navigation at Sea.**

international sight draft. A sight draft drawn in a foreign country against a drawee bank of this country. 10 Am J2d Banks § 494.

international union. A labor union whose organization and activities transcend the territorial limits of the country. A union of nations; the United Nations.

interne. Same as **intern.**

interned alien. An enemy alien confined pursuant to an order issued by the President; for the purposes of a writ of habeas corpus, confined as a prisoner of war. 56 Am J1st War § 68. A status which does not prevent the enforcement of contract rights or the right of the alien to sue in the courts of the country in which he is interned. 56 Am J1st War § 141.

internist. One qualified as a physician who specializes in internal medicine.

internment. The detention of a resident enemy alien during the existence of a declared war between his country and the United States. Johnson v Eisentrager, 339 US 763, 94 L Ed 1255, 70 S Ct 936. The apprehension, restraint, and removal of an enemy alien to a designated place pursuant to an order by the President. 56 Am J1st War §§ 67, 68. The confinement of prisoners of war in the interior of a country. The act of a neutral nation in detaining ships, sailors, soldiers or property of a belligerent.

inter nos (in'tèr nōs). Between ourselves.

internuncio (in-tèr-nun'shi-ō). A representative of the pope of Rome at a minor court.

internuncius (in-tèr-nun'shi-us). A messenger; a joint agent acting between two parties.

inter partes (in'ter par'tēz). Between the parties.
See **deed inter partes; instrument inter partes.**

interpellation (in"tèr-pe-lā'shọn). A citation to appear before a court; a summons.

interplea. A proceeding by an adverse claimant, somewhat in the nature of an action in replevin, wherein all of his rights in property attached may be determined. Farmers State Bank v Hess, 138 Okla 190, 280 P 305, 66 ALR 894.
See **interpleader.**

interplead. To interpose or file an interpleader in a pending suit.

interpleader. A remedy, equitable in origin, devised and exercised on behalf of one in possession of property as a disinterested stakeholder, or obligated for the payment of a debt or the performance of a legal duty, to prevent loss or embarrassment to him from separate suits by rival claimants seeking to cover the same property from him or to enforce against him the same debt or obligation, the efficacy of the remedy lying in its function of requiring the rival claimants to litigate their demands without embroiling the stakeholder or debtor in the controversy. 30 Am J Rev ed Interpl § 3.
See **bill in the nature of interpleader.**

Interpleader Act. A statute which, as adopted in 1917 and subsequently amended, gives to the federal courts original jurisdiction of bills of interpleader and of bills in the nature of interpleader. 30 Am J Rev ed Interpl § 19.

interpolation. Adding words to an instrument or manuscript; a method of altering an instrument. 4 Am J2d Alt Inst § 36. Reading words and clauses into a contract in the construction of the contract. 29 Am J Rev ed Ins § 253.
See **interlineation.**

interposing a defense. To plead a defense in an answer or to insist upon it at any stage of the action. Rosa v Butterfield, 33 NY 665, 667.

interposition. Intervention. In a distinct sense, a fully discredited and disavowed concept that the United States is a compact of states, any one of which may interpose its sovereignty against the enforcement within its orders of any decision of the Supreme Court or Act of Congress, irrespective of the fact that the constitutionality of the act has been established by a decision of the Supreme Court, and that, a state having so acted, the law or decision is not enforceable in the interposing state until approved by an amendment to the Constitution of the United States. Bush v Orleans Parish School Board (DC La) 188 F Supp 916, affd per curiam op 365 US 569, 5 L Ed 2d 806, 81 S Ct 754.
See **intervening cause; intervention.**

inter praesentes (in'ter prē-zen'tēz). Among or between persons present.

interpret (in-tèr'pret). To construe; to explain; to expound; to translate from a foreign language.

Interpretare et concordare leges legibus est optimus interpretandi modus (in-ter-pre-tā're et kon-kor-dā're lē'jēs lē'ji-bus est op'ti-mus in-ter-pre-tan'dī mō'dus). To interpret and reconcile laws with laws is the best manner of explaining them or construing them.

Interpretatio chartarum benigne facienda est, ut res magis valeat quam pereat (in-ter-pre-tā'she-ō kar-tā'rum be-nig'ne fā-she-en'da est, ut rēz mā'jis va'le-at quam per'e-at). The construction of deeds or charters should be liberal in order that the transaction may be effective rather than impotent.

Interpretatio chartarum benigne facienda est, ut res magis valeat quam pereatquando res non valet ut ago valeat quantum valere potest (in-ter-pre-tā'she-ō kar-ta'rum be-nig'ne fā-she-en'da est, ut rēz mā'jis va'le-at quam per'e-at-quan'dō rēz non va'let ut ā'gō va'le-at quan'tum va-lē're po'test). The construction of instruments should be liberal, that the transaction may be effective rather than impotent—when the transaction is not valid as I do it, let it have as much validity as it can have. Bond v Bunting, 78 Pa St 210, 219.

Interpretatio fienda est ut res magis valeat quam pereat (in-ter-pre-tā'she-ō fī-en'da est ut rēz mā'jis va'le-at quam per'e-at). Construction should be such that the transaction may be effective rather than perish.

interpretation. A translation. The art of finding the true sense of any form of words or symbols. Bloomer v Todd, 3 Wash Terr 599, 19 P 135.
The term is not synonymous with "construction," the latter meaning the determination, not of the sense of the words or symbols, but of the legal meaning of the entire contract. 17 Am J2d Contr § 240.
See **rational interpretation; restrictive interpretation.**

interpretation clause. A clause contained in many statutes which governs the construction of the statute, or which defines one or more terms of the statute.

interpretation test. A test given to prospective voters, involving the interpretation of any section of the federal or state constitution. 25 Am J2d Elect § 89.

Interpretatio talis in ambiguis semper fienda est ut evitetur inconveniens et absurdum (in-ter-pre-tā'-she-ō ta'lis in am-bi'gu-is sem'per fī-en'da est ut e-vi-tē'ter in-kon-vē'ni-enz et ab-ser'dum). Such construction of ambiguous expressions should be made that inconvenience and absurdity shall be avoided.

interpretative regulation. A regulation by an administrative body purporting to interpret a statute of doubtful meaning. A regulation issued as a Treasury Decision, designed to interpret the doubtful meaning of a tax statute. Anno: 153 ALR 1191.

interpreter. One who interprets, particularly one who interprets words written or spoken in a foreign language. A person appointed by the court to interpret the testimony of a witness who speaks a foreign tongue because he does not understand and speak the English language. 53 Am J1st Trial § 29. A person employed in the taking of a deposition to translate into English for the benefit of the reporter questions and answers given in a foreign language. 23 Am J2d Dep § 51.

interpretive regulation. Same as **interpretative regulation.**

inter quatuor parietes (in'ter qua'tu-or pa-ri-ē'tēz). Within the four walls.

interracial marriage. A marriage between persons of different races.
See **miscegenation.**

interregnum (in-tėr-reg'num). The interval of time between the death of an hereditary sovereign and the beginning of the reign of his successor.
Theoretically, there can be no interregnum in England because upon the death of the king, the right of the crown vests instantly in his heir, whence the saying, "The king is dead. Long live the king." See 1 Bl Comm 196.
The eleven-year period from 1649 to 1660, between the execution of Charles I and the reign of his son, Charles II; that is, the period of the commonwealth under Cromwell, is often referred to as "The Interregnum," but Blackstone refers to that unpleasantness as "the rebellion" which "broke out" in the reign of Charles I, and, following "the trial and murder of their sovereign" (Charles I), continued into the reign of Charles II until his "restoration." That is, Blackstone does not admit any break in the royal succession. See 4 Bl Comm 437.

interrogating. Propounding questions; questioning, especially, a witness, a prospective witness, or one suspected of the commission of a crime.

interrogating part of bill in equity. A term familiar in discussions of pristine equity pleading. The part of a bill in equity following the general jurisdiction clause and generally comprising two features:—the general interrogatory and the special interrogatories.
The general interrogatory calls on the defendant to make full, true and perfect answer to each and every allegation of the bill, or, what is the same in effect, it prays the court to require the defendant to appear in court and answer those allegations. The special interrogatories constitute the interrogating part of the bill as more generally understood and are properly put in series very much as the interrogatories for the taking of a deposition, being consecutively numbered for reference. 27 Am J2d Eq § 181.

interrogatories. Questions addressed to a person, especially a witness. Questions propounded in writing or orally in obtaining a deposition. 23 Am J2d Dep § 1. Questions propounded in obtaining a discovery. Questions submitted in writing by the plaintiff for answer by a garnishee, constituting, in effect, a form of discovery of assets of the defendant in the hands of the garnishee. 6 Am J2d Attach § 346. Questions submitted by one party to another in a case in admiralty by way of obtaining a discovery. 2 Am J2d Adm § 140. Questions submitted to the jury upon request for special verdict or special findings. 53 Am J1st Trial §§ 1063 et seq. Preliminary questions, propounded to a person called as a witness, for the purpose of determining his capacity, particularly in reference to a witness who is obviously a minor or mentally deficient. Den v Vancleve, 5 NJL 695, 765.
See **cross interrogatories; special interrogatories.**

in terrorem (in tė-rō'rem). By way of warning or intimidation. Tending to inspire fear or dread, for example, the punishment for crime or contempt. State v Shepherd, 177 Mo 205, 228, 76 SW 79. A condition subsequent in a gift or devise, void as in terrorem, in itself or for want of a limitation over, the absence of a limitation over indicating that the primary purpose was to intimidate. 28 Am J2d Est § 145. A condition in restraint of marriage, appearing in a deed or gift of property, imposed with the view of preventing marriage rather than in furtherance of a legitimate purpose, especially where there is no gift over. 35 Am J1st Mar §§ 247, 266.

in terrorem populi (in ter-rō'rem po'pu-lī). To the terror of the populace. Commonwealth v Runnels, (10 Tyng) 10 Mass 518, 520.

interruptio (in-ter-rup'she-ō). (Civil law.) Same as **interruption.**

Interruptio multiplex non tollit praescriptionem semel obtentam (in-ter-rup'she-o mul'ti-plex non tol'lit prē-skrip-she-ō'nem se'mel ob-ten'tam). Repeated interruption will not defeat a prescription after it has been acquired.

interruption-of-business insurance. See **business interruption insurance.**

interruption of possession. An interruption of the continuity of the possession of an adverse claimant; any substantial interruption in the possession of an adverse claimant. 3 Am J2d Adv P § 68.
The effect is to restore constructive possession to the owner. 3 Am J2d Adv P § 54.

interruption of prescription. Any unambiguous act of the owner of land evincing his intention to exclude others from the interrupted use of the right claimed, thereby preventing the acquisition of an easement in the land by prescription. Red Star Yeast & Products Co. v Merchandising Corp. 4 Wis 2d 327, 90 NW2d 777. Under the civil law, an entry by the owner into and upon immovables or his taking away movables. Innerarity v Heirs of Mims, 1 Ala 660, 674.

interruption of statute. The suspension of the running of a statute of limitations. 34 Am J1st Lim Ac §§ 186 et seq.
See **suspension of statute of limitations.**

inter rusticos (in'ter rus'ti-kos). Among or between rustics; among or between persons who are illiterate.

inter se (in'tėr sē). Among or between themselves.

intersecting lines. One railroad line connecting with or crossing over another railroad line. 44 Am J1st RR § 283.

intersecting streets or highways. Streets or highways meeting with one another. 7 Am J2d Auto § 203.

Some authorities include the meeting of one way with another even though one of the streets stops at and does not cross the other; but in a few cases it has been held, in view of the language of the particular statute or ordinance, that the two ways must actually cross each other in order to be intersecting. 7 Am J2d Auto § 203.

The intersection of a public thoroughfare with a private way does not come within the terms of a statute which, by language or definition, relates to the intersection of "highways," or which defines the intersecting way as any "public highway, street, avenue, road, alley, park, or parkway. Anno: 50 ALR 204; 7 Am J2d Auto § 204.

intersecting veins. Veins of minerals which cross one another. 36 Am J1st Min & M § 112.

intersecting way. See **intersecting streets or highways.**

intersection. The space of intersecting streets or roadways common to both the ways as determined by a continuation of the curb or similar lines. Neuman v Apter, 95 Conn 695, 112 A 350, 21 ALR 970; Stewart v Olson, 188 Wis 487, 206 NW 909, 44 ALR 1292. The point at which railroad lines intersect; the city or village in which railroad lines intersect.

See **intersecting lines; intersecting streets or highways.**

inter se liability. (in'tėr sē li-a-bil'i-ti). Liability as between themselves, such as liability as between the shareholders of a business trust. 13 Am J2d Bus Tr § 41.

inter se rights. (in'tėr sē rīts). Rights as between themselves, such as rights as between the shareholders in a business trust. 13 Am J2d Bus Tr § 41.

inter sese (in'ter sē'sē). Same as **inter se.**

interspousal transfers. Transfers of property between husband and wife.

interstate commerce. Literally, commerce between states. A practical rather than a technical legal conception, impossible of comprehensive definition, but having the distinguishing feature and indispensible element of importation into one state from another state. 15 Am J2d Com § 3. A term comprehending all commercial intercourse between different states and all the component parts of that intercourse. 15 Am J2d Com § 3. As defined in the Federal Employers' Liability Act:—acts which shall in any way directly or closely and substantially affect commerce between the states. 45 USC § 51. Interstate transportation or work so closely related thereto as to be practically a part of it. 35 Am J1st M & S § 442.

There is no single concept of interstate commerce which can be applied to every federal statute regulating commerce. McLeod v Threlkeld, 319 US 491, 87 L Ed 1538, 63 S Ct 1248.

See **commerce clause; engaged in interstate commerce.**

Interstate Commerce Act. A federal statute creating the Interstate Commerce Commission and providing for the regulation, supervision, and investigation of interstate carriers by the commission. 49 USC § 11.

interstate commerce clause. See **commerce clause.**

Interstate Commerce Commission. A body corporate, essentially an administrative board invested with administrative powers of supervision and investigation, although exercising quasi-judicial powers. 13 Am J2d Car § 33. A federal agency created in 1887 by the Interstate Commerce Act in order to bring into existence a body which, from its special character, would be best fitted to deal with interstate carriers and, among other things, to determine whether, upon the facts in a given case, there was an unjust discrimination against interstate commerce. Florida v United States, 292 US 1, 78 L Ed 1077, 54 S Ct 603.

interstate extradition. See **extradition.**

interstate ferry. A ferry operating between landing places in different states.

interstate free pass. A pass for free transportation of a passenger on a trip between states, forbidden by law, subject to certain exceptions, particularly drovers or caretakers of livestock in charge of a shipment. 14 Am J2d Car § 756.

interstate highway. A highway of a superior nature constructed with federal aid, intended to facilitate the movement of traffic between states.

interstate surface water. Water flowing over the surface of lands located in two states. Caldwell v Gore, 175 La 501, 143 So 387.

interstate traffic. Traffic that is moving from one state or territory into or through some other state or territory. United States v Chicago Great Western Co. (DC Iowa) 162 F 775.

See **interstate commerce.**

interstate watercourse. A watercourse which borders upon or passes through two or more states. 56 Am J1st Wat §§ 373 et seq.

interterritorial. Between one territory and another.

interurban. See **interurban railroad.**

interurban bus. A bus running between cities or other centers of population.

interurban railroad. Literally a railroad running between cities, but known more particularly as a railroad line of limited extent in length, making use of electric passenger cars quite similar to streetcars. 44 Am J1st RR § 7. A means of transportation which became widely established with the advent and extended use of electric passenger cars, but has since been almost completely replaced in the United States by busses. Partaking somewhat of the nature of an ordinary railroad and of a street railway, resembling the former when operated on its private right of way, outside the traveled portion of a public highway, and the latter when operating over a public street. 44 Am J1st RR § 7. More in the nature of a railroad than a street railway. Louisville & N. R. Co. v Anchors, 114 Ala 492, 227 So 279.

See **commercial railroad.**

interurban railway passenger traffic. The transportation of passengers between cities without rendering streetcar service in any city. Milwaukee v Milwaukee Electric R. & Light Co. 173 Wis 400, 180 NW 339, 181 NW 821, 13 ALR 802.

interval. A space of time or distance.
See **lucid interval.**

intervallo (in-ter-val'lō). See **ex intervallo**.

intervene. To come between. To become a party to an action by way of intervention. See **intervention**.

intervener. One who intervenes. One who becomes a party to a suit by the proceeding of intervention. 39 Am J1st Parties § 55. See **intervention**.

intervening. As a matter of designation of time:— intermediate; implying an exclusion of both first and last terminal days. Anno: 98 ALR2d 1369. Acquiring the status of a party to an action by way of intervention. See **intervention**.

intervening agency. An act or omission which comes between cause and effect. Ahern v Oregon Tel. & Tel. Co. 24 Or 276, 33 P 403, 35 P 549. See **intervening cause**.

intervening cause. A cause which supersedes a prior wrong as the proximate cause of an injury by breaking the sequence between the prior wrong and the injury. Mahoney v Beatman, 110 Conn 184, 146 A 762, 66 ALR 1121.
The test of the sufficiency of an intervening cause to defeat recovery for negligence is not to be found in the mere fact of its existence, but rather in its nature and the manner in which it affects the continuity of operation of the primary cause, or the connection between it and the injury. Sandel v State, 115 SC 168, 104 SE 567, 13 ALR 1268, ovrld on other grounds Sirrine v State, 132 SC 241, 253, 128 SE 172.
See **efficient intervening cause**.

intervening damages. Damages resulting to an appellee from the delay caused by the appeal. Peasely v Buckminster (Vt) 2 Tyler 264, 267.

intervening efficient cause. See **efficient intervening cause**.

intervening force. See **intervening cause**.

intervening human agency. The instrumentality of man. The antithesis of act of God. Cachick v United States (DC Ill) 161 F Supp 15.

intervening lien. A lien which, in point of time or of record comes between other liens or other conveyances or transfers of the same property.

intervention. The act or fact of intervening—any interference that may affect the interest of others. In legal terminology, the proceeding by which one not originally a party to an action is permitted, on his own application, to appear therein and join one of the original parties in maintaining the action or defense, or to assert a claim or defense against some or all of the parties to the action as originally instituted. 39 Am J1st Parties § 55. A proceeding within an attachment or garnishment proceeding wherein third party claimants assert their rights. 6 Am J2d Attach § 577. An appearance by a consul on behalf of his nation interested in the estate of a decedent. Anno: 157 ALR 108. A proceeding in admiralty by a third person to establish a claim to property or the proceeds of property brought into court in a suit in admiralty, where the suit is in rem, or to establish the right or rights of the third person in a proceeding for limitation of a shipowner's liability. 2 Am J2d Adm § 184.

intervention on appeal. A practice generally refused after the case has reached the appellate court, or after the time for appeal has expired, parties being brought in to an appeal by order of the appellate court only where the effective administration of justice demands it. Mullaney v Anderson, 342 US 415, 96 L Ed 458, 72 S Ct 428.

intervertebral discs. The structure of the spine. 22 Am J2d Damag § 374.

interview. The method of obtaining information by conversation. An informal method of obtaining answers to interrogatories propounded in obtaining a discovery. 23 Am J2d Dep § 289.

inter virum et uxorem (in'ter vi'rum et u-xō'rem). Between husband and wife.

inter vivos (in'ter vī'vos). Between living persons. See **gift inter vivos**.

inter vivos gift. See **gift inter vivos**.

inter vivos instrument. An instrument taking effect during the life of the grantor, mortgagor, or lienee.

inter vivos transfer (in'ter vī'vos tràns'fèr). A transfer effective during the life of the transferor.

inter vivos trust (in'ter vī'vos trust). Same as **trust inter vivos**.

intestabilis (in-tes-tā'bi-lis). Disqualified from being a witness; disqualified to make a will; dishonored; infamous.

intestable (in-tes'tạ-bl). A person who is not qualified to make a will; as, a lunatic.

intestacy. The status or condition of a person who dies without leaving a valid and operative will. Re Noble, 194 Iowa 733, 190 NW 511, 26 ALR 86. More precisely, the status of the estate or property of a decedent who dies without leaving a valid or operative will. Murdoch v Murdoch, 81 Conn 681, 72 A 290.
See **dying intestate**; **partial intestacy**.

In testamentis et ultimis voluntatibus tractatur de probanda voluntate defuncti post ejus mortem (in tes-ta-men'tis et ul'ti-mis vol-un-tat'i-bus trak-ta'tur dē prō-ban'da vol-un-tā'tē dē-funkt'ī post ē'jus mor'tem). In the case of testaments and last wills matters shall be administered according to the proven wishes of the deceased, after his death. Panaud v Jones, 1 Cal 488, 505.

In testamentis plenius testatoris intentionem scrutamur (in tes-ta-men'tis plē'ni-us tes-tā-tō'ris in ten-she-ō'nem skru-tā'mer). In wills, we should search thoroughly for the intention of the testator.

In testamentis plenius voluntates testantium interpretantur (in tes-ta-men'tis plē'ni-us vo-lun-tā'tēz tes-tan'she-um in-ter-pre-tan'ter). In wills, the intentions of the testators should be fully determined.

In testamentis ratio tacita non debet considerari, sed verba solum spectari debent; adeo per divinationem mentis a verbis recedere durum est (in tes-ta-men'tis rā'she-ō ta'si-ta non de'bet kon-si-de-rā'rī, sed ver'ba sō'lum spek-tā'rī de'bent; a'de-ō per di-vi-nā-she-ō'nem men'tis ā ver'bis rē-sē'de re du'rum est). In wills a secret intention ought not to be considered, but only the words ought to be regarded; it is so difficult to recede from the words by guessing at the intention.

intestate. The characterization of a person, or of the estate or property of a person, who dies in the status or condition of intestacy, that is, without leaving a valid and operative will. Re Noble, 194 Iowa 733, 190 NW 511, 26 ALR 86. One who dies without leaving a valid and operative will. Kohny v Dunbar, 21 Idaho 258, 121 P 544.
See **dying intestate**; **intestacy**; **partial intestacy**.

intestate estate. The estate of a person who dies without leaving a valid and operative will.
See **partial intestacy.**

intestate laws. The body of statutes which provide and prescribe the devolution of estates of persons who die without disposing of their estates by last will or testament. Guiness v State, 40 Wash 2d 677, 246 P2d 433.

intestate property. See **intestate estate; partial intestacy.**

intestate succession. Succession or inheritance from a person who dies without leaving a valid or operative will. Not a natural or inherent right. 23 Am J2d Desc & D § 11.

intestato (in-tes-tā′tō). See **ab intestato.**

intestatus (in-tes-tā′tus). (Civil law.) Intestate; without leaving a will; an intestate.

Intestatus decedit qui aut omnino testamentum non fecit; aut non jure fecit; aut id quod fecerat ruptum irritumve factum est; aut nemo ex eo haeres exstitit (in-tes-tā′tus de-sē′dit qui ât om-nī′nō tes-ta-men′-tum non fē′sit; ât non jū′re fē′sit ât id quod fē′se-rat rup′tum ir-ri-tum′ve fak′tum est; ât nē′mō ex ē′ō hē′rēz ex-sti′tit). A person dies intestate who either made no will, or made one not according to law, or the one which he made has been broken or rendered ineffectual, or who is one whom no devisee survives.

in testimonium (in tes-ti-mō′ni-um). In testimony; in witness whereof.

in the air. Literally, an operation off the ground, such as flying an aircraft. Figuratively, without basis or foundation.
Proof of negligence in the air, so to speak, will not do. Martin v Herzog, 228 NY 164, 126 NE 814.

in the alternative. One in the place of another, not the two taken together. Montgomery Ward & Co. v Duncan, 311 US 243, 85 L Ed 147, 61 S Ct 189.
See **alternative.**

in the bosom of the country. An expression used in relation to the situs of articles of commerce.
Such articles are in the "bosom of the country" before they become articles of foreign commerce or commerce between the states of the Union. Turner v Maryland (US) 17 Otto 38, 27 L Ed 370, 2 S Ct 44.

in the bosom of the court. See **breast of the court.**

in the cepit (in the sē′pit). See **replevin in the cepit.**

in the course of the employment. A phrase sometimes understood to mean the same as within the scope of the employment, at other times construed to mean during the period of employment, such variation, of course, being most confusing where it is sought to impose liability on the employer for an injury occurring to a third person by the act of an employee. Penas v Chicago, Milwaukee & St. Paul Railway Co. 112 Minn 203, 127 NW 926. While engaged in the service of the employer; not synonymous with the phrase "during the period covered by his employment." Hickson v W. W. Walker Co. 110 Conn 604, 149 A 400, 68 ALR 1044; Slater v Advance Thresher Co. 97 Minn 305, 107 NW 133. Engaged in that activity which he was employed to pursue; not engaged in a pursuit of his own. White v Eastern Mfg. Co. 120 Me 62, 112 A 841, 16 ALR 1165, 1168; Jackson v American Tel. & Tel.Co. 139 NC 347, 51 SE 1015. Performing the work of the employer pursuant to the employer's directions. Braen v Pefeifer Oil Transp. Co. 361 US 129, 4 L Ed 2d 191, 80 S Ct 247. At work in the employer's service. Cox v Kansas City Refining Co. 108 Kan 320, 195 P 863, 19 ALR 90. Engaged in matters fairly incidental to the employment relationship. Gage v Connecticut General Life Ins. Co. (Mo App) 273 SW2d 761, 47 ALR2d 1234 (provision of group accident policy.) For the purposes of workmen's compensation:—within the period of employment, at a place where the employee reasonably may be in the performance of his duties, and while he is fulfilling those duties or engaged in doing something incidental thereto, or, as otherwise stated, engaged in the furtherance of the employer's business. 58 Am J1st Workm Comp § 212.
See **scope of employment.**

in the custody of the law. See **custody of the law.**

in the debet and detinet (in the deb′et and det′i-net). See **debet et detinet.**

in the detinuit (in the de-ti′nu-it). In possession by virtue of a writ of replevin.

in the employ. Working for another whether as a menial, a mechanic, or a manager of the business. Kay v General Cable Corp. (CA3 NJ) 144 F2d 653.

in the event. A phrase setting up a condition. 11 Am J2d B & N § 141.

in the nature of quo warranto. See **information in the nature of quo warranto.**

in the opinion of the agency. A clause in a statute delegating powers to an administrative agency, the effect of which is to confer unwarranted policy-making power upon the agency. State v Marana Plantations, Inc. 75 Ariz 111, 252 P2d 87.

in the ordinary course of business. In the course of business of mercantile men generally, not those engaged in a particular trade. Romeo v Martucci 72 Conn 504, 45 A 1. A sale such as made in the regular course of business, not one such as will be made only a few times in the life of a merchant. Sternberg v Rubenstein, 305 NY 235, 112 NE2d 210, 36 ALR2d 1136. According to the usages and customs of commercial transactions. Christensen v Farmers' Warehouse Asso. 5 ND 438, 67 NW 300.
As to whether sales are made in "ordinary course of trade or business" within the meaning of the Federal income tax rules as to property deemed held primarily for sale to customers in ordinary course of trade or business, see Anno: 46 ALR2d 649.

in the premises. A familiar phrase used in a prayer for relief in equity, meaning on the case as made by the plaintiff, for example:—wherefore plaintiff demands [specific relief requested, such as foreclosure, injunction, etc.] and such other and further relief as he may be entitled to in the premises.

in the presence. See **in the presence of the testator; presence.**

in the presence of the court. See **presence of the court.**

in the presence of the testator. A signing of the will within the view of the testator, such view being uninterrupted and the testator conscious. A signing within the actual range of vision of the testator. 57 Am J1st Wills § 338.
It has been held that the words "in the presence of the testator," in a statute relating to the execution and attestation of wills, do not necessarily mean that the testator and the witnesses must be in the same room, or that he must have actual sight

or inspection of the process of signing by the witnesses, but there is respectable authority to the contrary. Cook v Winchester, 81 Mich 581, 46 NW 106.

Due regard must be had to the circumstances of each particular case, as it is well settled by all the authorities that the statute does not require absolutely that the witnessing of the signing by the testator must be done in the actual sight of the testator, nor yet within the same room with him. If the witnesses sign within his hearing, knowledge, and understanding, and so near as not to be substantially away from him, they are considered to be in his presence. Re Will of Cunningham, 80 Minn 180, 83 NW 58.

in the public domain. See **public domain**.

in the residence. As the term appears in a statute giving a landlord a lien upon all property of the tenant situated "in the residence":—all property on the premises. 32 Am J1st L & T § 586.

in the service of the ship. See **service of the ship**.

in the trial. At the trial; during the trial; while the case is actually being tried. Carpenter v Winn, 221 US 533, 539, 55 L Ed 842, 845, 31 S Ct 683.

in the vicinity. See **vicinity**.

in the within deed. An indorsement of a deed which may have the effect of conveying the property described by the instrument. 23 Am J2d Deeds § 37.

in this state. A phrase embracing all territory within the geographical limits of the state. Collins v Yosemite Park & C. Co. 304 US 518, 82 L Ed 1502, 58 S Ct 1009.

intimacy. A friendly relationship. In another sense, an illicit, improper, and degrading relationship; an illicit sexual relationship. Collins v Dispatch Publishing Co. 152 Pa 187, 191.

intimate. Closely acquainted. In one sense, having illicit sexual relations. 33 Am J1st L & S § 39.

A man and woman not married to each other are said to have been intimate when it is intended to convey the meaning that they have indulged in sexual intercourse together. Crosslands v Hamilton, 128 Okla 213, 262 P 196, 198.

As applied to the relations between a man and a woman, the adjective does not necessarily import misconduct. To charge a woman with being intimate with a man does not of itself amount to a charge of unchastity, although the word "intimate" is capable of use in a defamatory sense, and if it is so used it is actionable per se in many jurisdictions. 33 Am J1st L & S § 39.

intimation. A hint or suggestion. A mere conclusion from something said—that something should have been stated. Miller v Miller (Pa) 2 Serg & R 266.

intimidate. To put one in fear. To cause a state of intimidation.
See **intimidation**.

intimidation. The act of putting another in fear or a state of timidity by means of a threat or declaration of an intention or determination to injure such person by the commission of an unlawful act. Payne v Western & Atlantic Railroad Co. 81 Tenn (13 Lea) 507. Not necessarily implying an overt act of violence, or even a direct threat of violence. United Constr. Workers v New Burnside Veneer Co. (Ky) 274 SW2d 787.
See **business compulsion; duress**.

intimidation of voter. Producing fear sufficient to deter a voter from the exercise of his free will, thereby affecting the integrity of an election, irrespective of the degree in which force is displayed. 26 Am J2d Elect § 286.

intitle. Same as **entitle**.

into. Toward and within.

There is no difference, so far as a lessor's covenant to repair is concerned, between entrances leading "to" the premises and entrances leading "into" it. Renfro Drug Co. v Lewis (Tex) 235 SW2d 609, 23 ALR2d 1114.

The prohibition of a federal statute against transporting intoxicating liquor in interstate commerce "into" any state or territory the law of which prohibits the manufacture and sale of intoxicating liquors for beverage purposes does not include the movement through a dry state as a mere incident of the transportation to another state, whether such transportation is by personal carriage or by common carrier, the word "into" referring to the state of destination, and not to the means by which that end is reached. United States v Gudger, 249 US 373, 63 L Ed 653, 39 S Ct 323.

intol and uttol. Tolls or duties which were levied on imports and exports.

intolerable indignity. An indignity amounting to a species of mental cruelty, thereby constituting a ground of divorce under some statutes. Wirthman v Wirthman, 225 Mo App 692, 39 SW2d 404.

intolerable severity. As a characterization of cruelty constituting a ground for divorce:—extreme cruelty. Mathewson v Mathewson, 81 Vt 173, 69 A 646.

intolerance. Bigotry; narrow-mindedness. An intrusion upon our traditional concept of religious liberty. United States Nat. Bank v Snodgrass, 202 Or 530, 275 P2d 860, 50 ALR2d 725.

in totidem verbis (in tō-tī′dem vėr′bis). In so many words; in just as many words.

in toto (in tō′tō). In the whole; altogether; wholly.

In toto et pars continetur (in tō′tō et parz kon-ti-nē′ter). In the whole a part is also contained, or embraced, or included.

intoxicants. Any substance which intoxicates.
See **intoxicating liquors**.

intoxicated. In common parlance, in which sense it is used in an application for life insurance, drunk or inebriated. Mutual Life Ins. Co. v Johnson, 64 Okla 222, 166 P 1074. In a state of intoxication. Within the meaning of a limitation of risk in a life or accident insurance policy:—a disturbance of mental or physical faculties substantially or materially impairing a sense of responsibility, arising from the use of an alcoholic beverage or a drug or drugs. Anno: 13 ALR2d 987, 999.
See **intoxicated condition; intoxication**.

intoxicated condition. Under the influence of intoxicating liquor. 7 Am J2d Auto § 257.
See **intoxication**.

intoxicating bitters. An alcoholic beverage. 30 Am J Rev ed Intox L § 16.
See **bitters**.

intoxicating liquor. A liquor intended for use as a beverage, or capable of being so used, which contains alcohol in such percent that it will produce intoxication when imbibed in quantities that practically may be drunk. 30 Am J Rev ed Intox L § 4.

A liquor which contains alcohol capable of producing intoxication when taken into the stomach in such quantities as the stomach may reasonably contain. 30 Am J Rev ed Intox L § 4. Liquors defined by statute as "intoxicating," regardless of their alcoholic content or intoxicating quality. 30 Am J Rev ed Intox L § 6.

See **alcoholic beverage; alcoholic liquor; sale of intoxicating liquor.**

intoxicating quality. The distinctive characteristic of an intoxicating liquor, being that quality which renders a beverage such that when used it will produce intoxication to some extent. 30 Am J Rev ed Intox L § 5.

intoxication. An undue abnormal excitation of the passions or feelings, or the impairment of the capacity to think and act correctly and efficiently. 30 Am J Rev ed Intox L § 21. As a ground for cancellation of a contract, such an impairment of capacity as deprives a person of reason and renders him bereft of the power to understand the nature and effect of his act in the transaction. 29 Am J Rev ed Ins Per § 83. A state of inebriation or drunkenness. That state or condition of a person which inevitably follows from taking excessive quantities of an intoxicant. 30 Am J Rev ed Intox L § 21. To some persons, being under the influence of an intoxicant to such an extent as to render one helpless; to other persons, a person even only slightly under such influence. 30 Am J Rev ed Intox L § 21.

See **habitual drunkenness; involuntary intoxication.**

intra (in'trạ). Within; in the space of; within the bounds of.

intra anni spatium (in'tra an'nī spā'she-um). Within the space of a year.

in trade. In commerce; in business.

As used in the Federal Income Tax Act that losses actually sustained during the year, incurred "in trade," shall be allowed as a deduction, the term means the trade or trades in which the person making the return is engaged; that is, in which he has invested money otherwise than for the purpose of being employed in isolated transactions, and to which he devotes at least a part of his time and attention. Mente v Eisner (CA2 NY) 266 F 161, 11 ALR 496.

See **payable in trade.**

In traditionibus scriptorum, non quod dictum est, sed quod gestum est, inspicitur (in tra-di-she-ō'ni-bus skrip-tō'rum, non quod dik'tum est, sed quod jes'tum est, in-spi'si-ter). In the delivery of written instruments, not what was said, but what was done, is regarded.

intra family. Within the family, between the members of a family.

intra fidem (in'tra fī'dem). Within belief; credible.

intra hospitium (in'tra hos-pi'she-um). Within the precincts of the inn.

in trajectu (in tra-jek'tū). In passing over.

intra luctus tempus (in'tra luk'tus tem'pus). Within the time of mourning.

intra moenia (in'tra mē'ni-a). Within the walls; pertaining to the household. See 1 Bl Comm 425.

in transit. Literally, in the course of passing from point to point. Technically, between delivery to the carrier and delivery to the consignee or one acting for the consignee. Anno: 80 ALR2d 448, 452. For the purpose of an insurance risk, periods of actual movement or periods of rest while property is being carried from one place to another with the intention to take it to a destination conceived in the mind, not the mere possession of something in the course of a casual wandering. Anno: 80 ALR2d 447.

The term includes not only the carriage of goods to their destination, but also their delivery there in accordance with the terms of the contract with the carrier. Anno: 7 ALR 1389.

See **in transitu.**

in transitu (in tran'si-tū). In transit. A phrase familiar in the law of sales, meaning the period while the goods are in the possession of a carrier, whether by land, water, or air, until they are delivered into the possession of the consignee, whether or not the carrier has been designated by the buyer. 46 Am J1st Sales § 530.

See **in transit; stoppage in transitu.**

intra parietes (in'tra pa-ri-ē'tēz). Inside the walls of the house; among friends.

intra praesidia (in'tra prē-si'di-a). Same as **infra praesidia.**

intra quatuor maria (in'tra qua'tu-or ma'ri-a). Inside or within the four seas; that is, in England.

intrastate (in'trạ-stāt). Wholly within the external boundaries of a single one of the United States.

intrastate commerce. Commerce within the limits of one state.

Substance, not form, controls in the determination of the character of the transaction; the courts look to practical considerations and the established course of business. NLRB v Jones & L. Steel Corp. 301 US 1, 81 L Ed 893, 57 S Ct 615, 108 ALR 1352.

intra-urban (in-trạ-ėr'bạn). Within the limits of a city.

intra vires (in'tra vī'rēz). Within the powers; within the authority given by law.

See **ultra vires.**

intrinsic danger. See **inherent danger in work.**

intrinsic fraud. Fraud practiced in procuring a transaction. Toledo Scale Co. v Computing Scale Co. 261 US 399, 67 L Ed 719, 43 S Ct 458. In the trial of an action:—perjury, forgery, bribery of a witness, and other frauds which could have been relieved by the court in the action itself. Caldwell v Taylor, 218 Cal 471, 23 P2d 758, 88 ALR 1194. In reference to relief from a judgment:—fraudulent acts pertaining to an issue involved in the original action, or fraudulent acts which were or could have been litigated in the original action. 30A Am J Rev ed Judgm §§ 657, 784.

intrinsic value (in-trin'sik val'ụ). The true, inherent, and essential value of a thing, not depending upon accident, place, or person, but the same everywhere and to everyone. Bank of North Carolina v Ford, 27 NC (5 Ired L) 692, 698. Of corporate stock:—the amount which the assets behind the stock will bring at a sale fairly conducted. Jackson Co. v Gardiner Invest. Co. (CA1 NH) 217 F 350, affd on reh 220 F 297, app dismd 239 US 628, 60 L Ed 475, 36 S Ct 164.

introduced evidence. Evidence offered by a party on the trial of a case and admitted or received by the court. Tuttle v Story County, 56 Iowa 316, 9 NW 292.

introduction. A bringing in. A preliminary by way of explanation of what follows. In pristine equity

practice, a distinct part of a bill in equity indicating the names of the parties and the capacity in which the plaintiff brings the suit if it is brought in the right of another. 27 Am J2d Eq § 180.
See **clandestine introduction.**

intruder. A person who commits an intrusion. A person entering upon premises without invitation, especially a person expressly prohibited from entering. One who usurps a public office, having neither title nor color of right. Hamlin v Kassafer, 178 SC 351, 183 SE 145, 114 ALR 1130. An entry by a stranger on lands after a particular estate of freehold in them is determined and before entry by the remainderman or reversioner. See 3 Bl Comm 169.
See **information for an intrusion; monstrans de droit; purpresture.**

intrusion. The act of an intruder.
See **intruder.**

intrusione. See **de intrusione.**

intrust (in-trust'). To transfer or deliver property to another to hold as trustee.

in trust. The status of property held by a trustee. A phrase in an instrument strongly indicative of the intent to create a trust rather than convey an absolute estate. Anno: 147 ALR 609, 611. A phrase generally inconsistent with the idea that the grant of an absolute estate was intended, but not conclusive in such respect. Flynn v Palmer, 270 Wis 43, 70 NW2d 231, 51 ALR2d 1000. A clause which, appearing in a will, strongly but not conclusively indicates the creation of a trust. 57 Am J1st Wills § 1323.

in trust for any purpose. Limited to technical or special trusts; not inclusive of a trust implied from the situation of the parties or the nature of the transaction. Schaack v Reiter, 372 Ill 328, 23 NE2d 714, 125 ALR 1482.

intuitu. See **eo intuitu.**

intuitu matrimonii (in-tū'i-tu ma-tri-mō'ni-ī). In comtemplation of marriage.

intuitu mortis (in-tū'i-tū mor'tis). In contemplation of death.

intuitus (in-tū'i-tus). View; contemplation; consideration.

in tuto (in tu'tō). In safety; safe; secure.

inundation. A flood.

inure (in-ūr'). To accrue to the benefit of a person; to devolve upon a person. Malachowski v Varro, 76 Cal App 207, 244 P 936.

inurement of title. The benefit of the title of one for another, for example, the title of one cotenant benefitting another cotenant. 20 Am J2d Coten § 69. The passing of title to property from one person to another, without any writing or other formality than some act which thereafter estops the grantor from asserting title to the property as against his grantee. Dickerson v Colgrove (US) 10 Otto 578, 583, 25 L Ed 618, 620. The transfer of an after-acquired title of the grantor to the grantee of a deed by operation of law. 23 Am J2d Deeds § 308.

in utero matris (in u'te-rō mā'tris). In the womb of the mother.
See **unborn child.**

Inutilis labor et sine fructu non est effectus legis (in-u'ti-lis lā'bor et sī'ne fruk'tū non est ef-fek'tus lē'jis). Useless and fruitless labor is not the end of the law.

in utroque jure (in u-trō'kwe jū're). In both laws.

in vacation. See **vacation of court.**

in vacuo (in vak'ụ-ō). In space.

invade (in-vād'). To make an invasion; to assault.

invadiare (in-vā-di-ā're). To pledge; to mortgage.

invadiatio (in-vā-di-ā'she-ō). A pledge; a mortgage.

invadiatus (in-vā-di-ā'tus). The principal debtor in a contract of pledge or suretyship; a person who has had pledges given for him.

in vadio (in vā'di-ō). In gage; in pledge; by way of security.
See **estate in vadio.**

invalid (in-val'id). Adjective: Illegal, having no force or effect or efficacy; void; null. State ex rel. MacKenzie v Casteel, 110 Ind 174, 182. Noun: (in'val-id) A sick person, especially one without hope of restoration to health.

invalidated. Rendered illegal or deprived of legal effect.
A provision in a fire insurance policy that a mortgagee's interest in the policy shall not be invalidated by any act of the owner, means that the interest of the mortgagee in the policy shall not be injuriously affected thereby. Tarleton v De Veuve (CA9 Cal) 11" F2d 290, 132 ALR 343.

invalid chair. A wheelchair.

invalidism. A condition of chronic ill health, sometimes coinciding with mental incompetency, but by no means the equivalent of mental incompetency. Groff v Stitzer, 77 NJ Eq 260, 77 A 46.

invalidity. See **illegality.**

invalid pension (pen'shọn). See **pension.**

invasion. An intrusion upon the property or rights of another. The entry of a hostile military force. The hostile entry of a public enemy. Aetna Ins. Co. v Boon (US) 5 Otto 117, 24 L Ed 395.

invasion of corpus. Taking from the principal of a trust estate when the income is insufficient for the payment of annuities to, or the defrayment of expenses of, the beneficiaries as provided by the indenture of trust. 4 Am J2d Annui § 18.

invasion of privacy. A violation of the right of privacy.
See **privacy.**

invasion of province of jury. The decision by the court of a question of fact within the province of the jury or interference by the court with the jury in attempting to control or determine the verdict to be rendered by them. 39 Am J1st Tr § 48.

invecta et illata (in-vek'tā et il-lā'ta). (Civil law.) Things which were carried and brought,—the goods of a tenant which he brought on the land and pledged to the landlord to secure his rent.

inveigle. To deceive for the purpose of accomplishing an evil purpose. State v Lacoshus, 96 NH 76, 70 A2d 203. To allure, incite, instigate, seduce, or entice into the doing of an improper act. Mooney v State, 8 Ala 328, 331.

inveniendo (in-ve-ni-en'dō). Finding.

Inveniens libellum famosum et non corrumpens punitur (in-ve'ni-enz lī-bel'lum fa-mō'sum et non korrum'penz pu'ni-ter). A person who finds a defamatory libel and does not destroy it, is punished.

invent. To create. Bliss Co. v United States, 248 US 37, 63 L Ed 112, 39 S Ct 42. To think of somthing, especially a new device, and of a method of creating it, and to follow through with the creation of the thing.

inventio (in-ven'she-ō). (Civil law.) A finding of goods.

invention. A creation of something new. Within the meaning of the patent laws:—an operation of the intellect, a product of intuition, of something akin to genius, as distinguished from mere mechanical skill. 40 Am J1st Pat § 40. A word impossible of definition affording any substantial aid in determining whether a particular device involves an exercise of the inventive faculty or not. 40 Am J1st Pat § 40.
See **caveat; caveator; improvement; patent; patentable invention.**

inventor. The orginator of an invention.
See **patent; patentable invention.**

inventory. An itemized list or schedule of articles in a stock of goods or merchandise, usually including notations of values. 29A Am J Rev ed Ins § 946. The foundation of the bookkeeping required by the bookkeeping clause of a fire insurance policy covering a stock of merchandise. Hartford Fire Ins. Co. v Farris, 116 Va 880, 83 SE 377. A list of the goods and merchandise to be offered at an auction sale, sometimes setting forth the cost of the several items; an inventory of all goods and merchandise sold at an auction sale, giving the prices received for the items listed. Steinberg-Baum & Co. v Countryman, 247 Iowa 923, 77 NW2d 15. A list made by an officer serving a writ of execution of the items of personal property subjected to the levy. 30 Am J2d Exec § 298. A list made by the sheriff or other officer to whom a writ of attachment was issued, of the property seized by him in serving the writ. 6 Am J2d Attach § 310. A list made by an executor or administrator of the personal assets of the decedent. 31 Am J2d Ex & Ad §§ 209 et seq. A complete list, to be prepared and filed by a trustee in bankruptcy or a trustee in an arrangement or reorganization proceeding in the bankruptcy court, of all the property of the bankrupt or debtor that comes into his possession, except where a receiver or other officer of the court has previously prepared and filed such an inventory. 9 Am J2d Bankr § 1259. A schedule to be made and filed by a bankrupt showing the amount and kind of property owned by him, the location thereof, and its money value, in detail. 9 Am J2d Bankr § 378. A detailed list of property to be prepared, verified, and filed by a bankrupt, when required by the court, showing the cost to him of his merchandise or of such other property as may be designated, as of the date of his bankruptcy. 9 Am J2d Bankr § 381.

inventory goods. Goods held by a person for sale, lease, or furnishing under a contract of service, raw materials, work in process, or materials used or consumed in a business. UCC § 9-109(4).

in ventre sa mere (in ven'trĕ sa mār). In the womb of the mother.

inventus (in-ven'tus). Found.

In veram quantitatem fidejussor teneatur, nisi pro certa quantitate accessit (in vē'ram quan-ti-tā'tem fĭ-de-jus'sor te-ne-ā'ter, nī'sĭ prō ser'ta quan-ti-tā'te ak-ses'sit). A surety should be held for the true quantity, unless he agreed for a certain quantity. Bean v Parker, 17 Mass (17 Tyng) 591, 597.

In verbis, non verba, sed res et ratio, quaerenda est (in ver'bis, non ver'ba, sed rēz et rā'she-o, kwē-ren'da est). In expressions, not the words, but the thing itself and the meaning, are to be inquired into.

inveritare (in-ve-ri-tā're). To verify; to prove.

inverse condemnation. The taking of property by an actual interference with or disturbance of property rights, without an actual entry upon the property. 26 Am J2d Em D §§ 157 et seq.

inverse order of alienation. The doctrine that where land subject to a paramount encumbrance is subsequently sold or encumbered in parts or parcels at different times, no intention being disclosed in the instrument that the purchaser or the encumbrancer of the part should pay the whole or his proportion of the paramount encumbrance, the parcel retained by the grantor should be first subjected to the discharge or payment of the paramount encumbrance, and the parcels alienated or encumbered should be reached only in the event the parcel retained by the grantor is not sufficient to pay the paramount encumbrance in full, and then only to the extent of the deficiency and in the inverse order of alienation; and that if all of the land covered by the paramount encumbrance has been successively alienated or encumbered in parcels, the parcel last alienated or encumbered must be first exhausted for the payment or discharge of the paramount encumbrance, before the parcel alienated or encumbered next preceding to the last may be reached, and so on in that order until the parcel first alienated or encumbered is reached, if need there be, provided the alienee or the junior encumbrancer of the party against whose parcel recourse must be had had notice of the prior alienation or encumbrance of another part. 35 Am J1st Marsh A § 32. A doctrine analogous to but at the same time in contrast with the doctrine of marshaling assets. 35 Am J1st Marsh A § 33.

invest. To vest; to clothe with authority; to confer upon. To make an investment of money or other property; that is, to place it where it will yield an income or revenue. Savings Bank of San Diego County v Barrett, 126 Cal 413, 58 P 914; Drake v Crane, 127 Mo 85, 29 SW 990.

invested. See **invest; invested capital; investment.**

invested capital. Literally, the money or property put into an enterprise. For the purpose of the wartime federal revenue acts, actual cash paid in, or the actual cash value of tangible property paid in, other than cash, for stock or shares in the corporation, or paid-in or earned surplus and undivided profits. Duffy v Mutual Ben. Life Ins. Co. 272 US 613, 71 L Ed 439, 47 S Ct 205.

investigate. To inquire; to make an investigation. See **investigation.**

investigation. An administrative function, the exercise of which ordinarily does not require a hearing. 2 Am J2d Adm L § 257. In a more complete sense, an inquiry, judicial or otherwise, for the discovery and collection of facts concerning a certain matter or matters.
Authority to a legislative committee to make an investigation includes the power to call witnesses and to compel them to testify under oath. People v Sharp, 107 NY 427.

Investigation Bureau. See **Bureau of Investigation.**

investigatory powers. Powers conferred on administrative agencies to inspect, secure or require the

disclosure of information. 1 Am J2d Admin L § 85. Judicial powers or other powers to inquire and collect facts concerning a certain matter or matters.
See **investigation**.

investitive fact (in-ves'ti-tiv fakt). A fact the existence of which gives rise to a right.

investiture. The act of making livery of seisin; the act of investing or clothing a person with actual possession.
The ancient custom of feudal tenure whereby, while feuds were precarious, the vassal on descent of lands was admitted in the lord's court and there received his seisin. This was in the nature of a renewal of his ancestor's grant in the presence of the feudal peers. At a later period, when the right of succession became indefeasible, an entry on any of the lands within the county was considered as equivalent to the formal grant of seisin and made the tenant capable of transmitting his estate by descent. See 2 Bl Comm 209.

investment. The act of placing money where it will yield an income or revenue. Savings Bank of San Diego County v Barrett, 126 Cal 413, 58 P 914; Drake v Crane, 127 Mo 85, 29 SW 990. The laying out of money in such a manner that it may produce a revenue, whether the particular method be a loan, or the purchase of stocks, securities or other property. Putting money on interest, either by way of loan, or the purchase of income-producing property. Drake v Crane, 127 Mo 85, 29 SW 990. A note, bond, or share of stock purchased for income.
This word, within the meaning of a clause authorizing executors and trustees to retain investments or any property in which the estate may be "invested" at the time of the testator's death, means property from which an income or profit is expected to be derived in the ordinary course of events. Anno: 47 ALR2d 196.
See **investiture**.

investment adviser. Any person who, for compensation, engages in the business of advising others, either directly or through publications or writings, as to the advisability of purchasing or selling securities, or who, for compensation and as a regular business, issues analyses or reports concerning securities, excluding certain persons, such as lawyers, accountants, teachers, and engineers, who may incidentally engage in such activities. 15 USC § 80b-1.

Investment Advisers Act. A federal statute having the general objective of protecting the public and investors against malpractices by persons paid for advising others about securities. 15 USC § 80b-6.

investment bonds. The obligations of private and public bodies taken by the holders as investments. 12 Am J2d Bonds § 49.

investment brokers. A person or corporation licensed to deal, and actually dealing with the general public in the purchase and sale of securities. Trading Associates Corp. v Magruder (CA4 Md) 112 F2d 779.

investment company. A company which either itself or through others engages in business within the state of selling or offering for sale securities issued by itself, including a foreign corporation. 47 Am J1st Secur A § 32. Any issuer of securities which is engaged primarily in the business of investing, reinvesting, or trading in securities or in the business of issuing face-amount certificates of the instalment type. 15 USC § 80a-3(3).

Investment Company Act. A comprehensive federal statute regulating investment companies as defined in the act. 15 USC §§ 80a-1 et seq.

investment contract. A contract providing for the investment of capital in a way intended to secure income or profit from its employment. State v Evans, 154 Minn 95, 191 NW 425, 27 ALR 1165. An investment, as well as a contract, since the purchasers rely upon the efforts of other persons to make the investment a profitable one. 47 Am J1st Supp Secur A § 16.
If a corporation issues its securities to purchasers who pay their money justly expecting to receive an income or profit from their investment, there results an investment contract such as is referred to in blue sky laws. State v Heath, 199 NC 135, 153 SE 855, 87 ALR 37.

investment credit. A direct credit against the federal income tax applied where certain depreciable property having a useful life of at least four years is placed in service during the taxable year, the amount of the credit being seven per cent of the qualified investment which in turn depends upon the useful life of the property. IRC §§ 46(c)(1), 48(a)(1).

investment scheme. A plan for the making of an investment or investments. Sometimes a lottery, as where a fund is created by the payment of designated sums at stated intervals by the holders of certificates, which shall be matured and paid to the investor in an amount dependent upon chance. 34 Am J1st Lot § 14.

investment security. A security dealt in upon securities exchanges or markets or commonly recognized in any area in which it is issued or dealt in as a medium for investment, evidencing a share, participation, or other interest in property, or in an enterprise, or evidencing an obligation of the issuer. UCC § 8-102(1)(a).
A security normally traded on securities markets, as distinguished from ordinary commercial paper. This distinction is of importance in the case of bonds of private or public bodies, since, prior to the enactment of the Uniform Commercial Code in a particular jurisdiction, such bonds were subject to the requirements of the Negotiable Instruments Act, while, under the code, such bonds are subject to the code article dealing with "investment securities." 12 Am J2d Bonds § 49.

investment trust. A corporation which keeps its assets invested in stocks or bonds and distributes the returns by way of dividends and profits to the shareholders of the trust.

investment value. The real value of a share of corporate stock as an investment, as distinguished from book value. 19 Am J2d Corp § 520. The value calculated by the capitalization of income from the property. 27 Am J2d Em D § 286.

invidiam. See **in invidiam**.

in vinculis (in vĭn'ku-lis). In chains; in bondage; under duress. Under undue influence. 25 Am J2d Dur § 36.

inviolable. Not to be violated; immunity from being violated; immunity or exemption from violence.

inviolate. Unhurt, uninjured, unpolluted, unbroken. Flint River Steam Boat Co. v Roberts, Allen & Co. 2 Fla 102, 114. Freedom from substantial impairment. Commonwealth v Almeida, 362 Pa 596, 68 A2d 595, 12 ALR2d 183, cert den 339 US 924, 94

L Ed 1346, 70 S Ct 614, and cert den 340 US 867, 95 L Ed 633, 71 S Ct 83.

in viridi observantia (in vi'ri-dī ob-zer-van'she-a). In fresh attention; present in one's mind.

in vita (in vī'tạ). In life; living; alive.

invitation. A direct or implied inducement by the owner or occupier of premises to another person to enter or pass over such premises. Sweeny v Old Colony & Newport R. R. Co. 92 Mass (10 Allen) 368.

See **express invitation; implied invitation; invitee.**

invited error. An error induced or provoked by the party who complains thereof on appeal. Pettingill v Perkins, 2 Utah 2d 266, 272 P2d 185.

invited visitor. See **invitee.**

invitee. A person on the premises of another at the express or implied invitation of the latter for business purposes, for mutual advantage, or for purely social purposes. Smith v Kroger Grocery & Baking Co. 339 Ill App 501, 90 NE2d 500, 20 ALR2d 1; Strand Enterprises v Turner, 223 Miss 588, 78 So 2d 769, 47 ALR2d 1431; English v Thomas, 48 Okla 247, 149 P 906; Southcote v Stanley (Eng) 1 H & N 247.

A guest of an employee of a tenant is an invitee of the landlord in the use of a common passageway. Snyder v L. Jay Realty Co. 30 NJ 303, 153 A2d 1, 78 ALR2d 95.

See **business visitor; guest.**

invito (in-vī'tō). See **ab invito.**

Invito beneficium non datur (in-vī'tō be-ne-fi'she-um non dā'ter). A benefit is not conferred upon a person against his will.

invito debitore (in-vī'to de-bi-tō're). Against the will or without the consent of the debtor.

invito domino (in-vī'tō do'mi-nō). The lord or master being unwilling,—against the will of the owner.

invitum. See **in invitum.**

invitus (in-vī'tus). Against the wish; against the will; unwilling; without consent.

in vivo vadium. See **estate in vivo vadium.**

In vocibus videndum non a quo sed ad quid sumatur (in vō'si-bus vi-den'dum non ā quō sed ad quid su-mā'ter). In discourse it should be observed not from what but to what end it is leading.

invoice. A list of all the goods in a mercantile establishment, or in a department of a mercantile establishment, sometimes with the values of the items listed, such being prepared at regular times for the purpose of ascertaining the net worth of the store. A mere list of the items of personalty included in a sale—not in itself, a bill of sale. 46 Am J1st Sales § 452. A list of items included in a shipment, usually forwarded by mail to the purchaser or consignee.

See **inventory.**

invoice price. Literally, the amount of value placed upon an item of goods or merchandise in the invoice in which the item appears.

Appearing in a stipulation in a contract of carriage that the liability in case of loss of the goods shall be limited to the invoice price at the point of shipment, the term "invoice price" is not rendered meaningless by the fact that no invoice was actually made out or agreed upon; by application of the rule of reasonable construction, it should be considered to mean the actual value of the goods where loaded and ready for transportation. Pierce v Southern Pacific R. Co. 120 Cal 156, 47 P 874, 52 P 302.

See **invoice purchase price.**

invoice purchase price. A familiar term in contracts for the sale of a stock of goods; a price to be determined on appraisement according to what the seller paid for the articles when he bought them, not at what it would cost to buy them at the time of appraisement. 46 Am J1st Sales § 179.

invoice value. The invoice price. The cost price rather than the actual value. Knopfler v Flynn, 135 Minn 333, 160 NW 860.

See **invoice price.**

involuntary. Not voluntary; unintentional; without willing; independent of volition or consent; accidental. Riley v Interstate Business Men's Acci. Asso. (Iowa) 169 NW 488, 2 ALR 57, 62.

involuntary adjudication. An adjudication in bankruptcy on an involuntary petition. Bankruptcy Act § 1(2); 11 USC § 1(2). A determination, whether by decree or by operation of law, that a person is a bankrupt. 29 Am J2d Bankr § 264. A determination, whether by decree not sought by him or by operation of law, that a person is a bankrupt. 29 Am J2d Bankr § 264. In a broader sense, any judgment other than a consent judgment.

involuntary admission. A self-incriminating statement by one accused of crime influenced by hope, fear, or the calamity of a situation. 29 Am J2d Ev § 612.

involuntary alienation. A parting with the title to property resulting from its attachment, levy and sale for taxes or debts due from the owner, or from proceedings in insolvency, bankruptcy, or otherwise, whereby the owner is deprived of his interest in the property. Manierre v Welling, 32 RI 104, 78 A 507.

involuntary assent. An anomaly; a consent obtained by force, duress, or undue influence.

involuntary assignment. An assignment by operation of law, for example, the passing of a decedent's choses in action to the executor or administrator of his estate. 6 Am J2d Assign § 2. The transfer of the choses in action of a bankrupt to the trustee in bankruptcy. An assignment for the benefit of creditors by operation of law where a preferential or fraudulent transfer or conveyance has been made by the debtor. 6 Am J2d Assign for Cr § 3.

involuntary assignment for benefit of creditors. See **involuntary assignment.**

involuntary association. An association, such as a professional society, membership in which constitutes a valuable right, not merely a social privilege. 6 Am J2d Asso & C § 18.

involuntary bailee. A bailee under an involuntary bailment.

See **involuntary bailment.**

involuntary bailment. A bailment arising by the accidental leaving of personal property in the possession of any person, without negligence on the part of its owner. Grossman Co. v White, 52 Okla 117, 152 P 816. The deposit or placing of goods in a person's possession without his consent, as where a departing lodger leaves goods behind; or lost goods are found on land. Preston v Neale, 78 Mass (12 Gray) 222, 223. A bailment resulting from the action of the elements in moving property onto the premises of one other than the owner of the property, for example, the stranding of goods or merchandise carried by a flood onto another's land. Mitchell v Oklahoma Cotton Growers Asso. 108 Okla 200, 235 P 587, 41 ALR 1011.

involuntary bankruptcy proceeding. A proceeding in a court of bankruptcy instituted by the creditors of a person, firm, or corporation, without his or its consent, to have him or it adjudicated and declared to be a bankrupt. Re Murray (DC Iowa) 96 F 600, 602.

See **involuntary adjudication.**

involuntary confession. A confession obtained under the influence of fear, especially fear induced by threats of bodily harm, torture, personal violence, or abuse, by methods known as "sweating" or "third degree" or by holding out a promise or hope of a reward or immunity—in short, a confession which is forced or extorted in any manner by over persuasion, promise, or threats. 29 Am J2d Ev § 543.

involuntary consent. See **involuntary assent.**

involuntary conveyance. See **involuntary alienation.**

involuntary deposit. An involuntary bailment.
See **involuntary bailment.**

involuntary deviation. A deviation by a ship from the voyage, neither planned nor necessarily anticipated upon leaving port.

If the circumstances under which a ship leaves port are such that it must be known that she will be compelled to deviate from her voyage, as, for example, with a shortage of fuel, the deviation is voluntary. But if the ship leaves port unseaworthy, which includes a ship badly stowed, even if it was known, she does not voluntarily deviate if she seeks a port of refuge. The Malcolm Baxter, Jr. (CA2 NY) 20 F2d 304.

Literally, there is no such thing as an "involuntary deviation," since one of the elements of a deviation is voluntariness of the departure. See 29A Am J Rev ed Ins § 1000.

involuntary discontinuance. The forcing of a case out of court for some error in pleading, technical omission, etc., better called an involuntary dismissal. Hunt v Griffin, 49 Miss 742.

involuntary dismissal. The dismissal of an action on motion by the defendant. 24 Am J2d Dism § 53. The ultimate dismissal by a judgment against the plaintiff upon the verdict of the jury or the decision of the court in a case tried to the court.

involuntary exposure. A merely inadvertent and unintentional exposure to a known danger, under peculiar circumstances not affording opportunity for deliberate action, or an exposure to an unknown danger, through a voluntary act. Diddle v Continental Casualty Co. 65 W Va 170, 63 SE 962.

involuntary indebtedness. An indebtedness incurred in the performance of a duty and obligation imposed by the law of the state;—a debt incurred by a county in holding a special election as directed by statute. State v Stannard, 84 Or 450, 165 P 571.

involuntary insolvency. A proceeding under a state insolvency statute brought against an alleged insolvent. 29 Am J Rev ed Insolv § 14.
See **involuntary bankruptcy.**

involuntary intoxication. Drunkenness characterized by an absence of exercise of independent judgment and volition in taking the intoxicant, as where intoxication results from taking drugs prescribed for medical treatment or from deception respecting the character of the substance taken. Johnson v Commonwealth, 135 Va 524, 115 SE 673, 30 ALR 755; 21 Am J2d Crim L § 108.

involuntary losses. Losses of capital not intentionally or voluntarily incurred. New England Trust Co. v Paine, 317 Mass 542, 59 NE2d 263, 148 ALR 262.

involuntary manslaughter. The unintentional killing of another occasioned by a person engaged at the time in doing some unlawful act not amounting to a felony and not likely or naturally tending to endanger life, or engaged in the doing of a lawful act in an unlawful manner. 26 Am J1st Homi § 18. The killing of another without malice and unintentionally, (1) in doing some unlawful act not amounting to a felony or naturally tending to cause death or great bodily harm, or (2) in negligently doing some act lawful in itself, or (3) by the negligent omission to perform a legal duty. Commonwealth v Comber, 374 Pa 570, 97 A2d 343, 37 ALR2d 1058.

involuntary nonsuit. See **nonsuit.**

involuntary payment. A payment forced or compelled. A payment made against the will of the person who pays, that is, a payment made under some fact or circumstance which overcomes the will and imposes a necessity of payment in order to escape further ills. 40 Am J1st Paym § 162. A payment, as of taxes, made under an immediate and urgent necessity. 51 Am J1st Tax § 1185. A payment made because of some actual or threatened exercise of power possessed, or believed to be possessed, by the party exacting or receiving the payment over the person or property of another, for which the latter has no other means of immediate relief than by making the payment. 40 Am J1st Paym § 162; 51 Am J1st Tax § 1185.

involuntary peonage. A redundancy, since peonage, however arising or created, is involuntary servitude. Ex parte Hollman, 79 SC 9, 60 SE 19.
See **peonage.**

involuntary petition. A petition filed in a court of bankruptcy which seeks an adjudication of bankruptcy against the defendant. 9 Am J2d Bankr § 207.

involuntary plea of guilty. A plea of guilty made under such inducements as would cause an innocent person to confess guilt. Pennington v Smith, 35 Wash 2d 267, 212 P2d 811.

involuntary self-destruction. Death at one's own hand but unintended.

The expression includes all cases where a person, without intending to accomplish his own death, carelessly and negligently does acts which may naturally and probably result, and do in fact result, in death. It would thus include all cases where there exists on the part of such person any direct and immediate legal or moral responsibility for his own death. But as the term is used in a life insurance policy it would not include cases where the act of the insured contributed to shorten or terminate his life, without design or negligence on his part. Courtemanche v Independent Order of Foresters, 136 Mich 30, 98 NW 749.

involuntary separation of jury. The separation of the jurors after the submission of the cause to them, from overwhelming necessity, such as tempest, fire, or the like. Armleder v Lieberman, 33 Ohio St 77.

involuntary servitude. Compulsory labor under bondage. Slavery or peonage, except as imposed by way of punishment for a crime whereof the party shall have been duly convicted.

involuntary trust. A trust founded on a contract supported by a consideration; a trust arising by operation of law. 54 Am J1st Trusts § 5. Another term for constructive trust. Newman v Newman, 60 W Va 371, 55 SE 377.
See **constructive trust.**

involved. Implicated; affected or concerned in some degree.
A subject matter, a question, or specific property is said to be "involved" in an action when it is "affected" or "directly affected" by such action. Williams v Western Union Tel. Co. 1 NY Civ Proc 194, 199.

in withernam (in with'er-nam). In retaliation; by way of reprisal or requital.

in witness whereof. A formal expression commonly used at the beginning of the attestation clause of any signed document, making it clear that the persons signing are witnesses.

in writing. See **writing.**

iodine (ī'ō-dīn). An antiseptic. A drug or medicine within the meaning of various statutory provisions. State Board of Pharmacy v Matthews, 197 NY 355, 90 NE 966.

iota. A Greek letter. A most minute quantity.

I.O.U. A memorandum of debt, consisting of the three letters, "I.O.U.," a statement of the amount, and debtor's signature, constituting an instrument for the unconditional payment of money only, and, according to some but not all the authorities, a promissory note. 11 Am J2d B & N § 140.

I promise to pay. The obligating phrase in a promissory note. 11 Am J2d B & N § 570.
See **I, we, or either of us.**

Ipsae leges cupiunt ut jure regantur (ip'sē lē'jēz ku'pi-unt ut jū're re-gan'ter). The very laws themselves are desirous of being ruled by what is right.

Ipsa utilitas justi prope mater et aequi (ip'sa u-ti'li-tăs jūs'tī prō'pe mā'ter et ē'qui). Utility itself is very nearly the mother of that which is just and equitable.

ipse (ip'sē). He, himself; himself.

Ipse dixit (ip'sē dik'sit). He himself spoke. That is, it was his own statement not made on the authority of any precedent.

ipsis faucibus. See **in ipsis faucibus.**

ipsissimis verbis (ip-sis'si-mis ver'bis). By the very words themselves. Gardiner v New York Central & Hudson River R. Co. 201 NY 387, 94 NE 876.

ipsius patris bene placito (ip-sī'us pā'tris be'ne pla'si-tō). By the kindly grace of his father. See 1 Bl Comm 351.

ipso. Itself; by itself.

ipso articulo temporis. See **in ipso articulo temporis.**

ipso facto (ip'sō fak'tō). By the fact itself; by the very fact; by the act itself. State v Lansing, 46 Neb 514, 64 NW 1104.

ipso facto et ipso jure (ip'sō fak'tō et ip'sō jū're). By the very act and by the law itself.

ipso jure (ip'sō jū're). By the law itself.

ipsum matrimonium (ip-sum' ma-tri-mō'ni-um). Marriage itself. Holt v Clarencieux (Eng) 2 Strange 937.

i. q. An abbreviation of idem quod, meaning "the same as."

I.Q. Abbreviation of intelligence quotient.

Ira furor brevis est (ī'ra fu'ror brē'vis est). Anger is brief insanity.
"Short, however, as it is, the policy of the law is to restrain its natural operation. A few moments is all the toleration that can be given to it." Beardsley v Maynard (NY) 4 Wend 336, 355.

ira motus (ī'ra mō'tus). Excited or enraged by anger or passion.

irato. See **ab irato.**

IRC. Abbreviation of Internal Revenue Code.

ire ad largum (ī're ad lar'gum). To go at large; to go free of restraint.

Ireland. See **Eire.**

Irish corporation. A corporation incorporated in Ireland, such being a foreign corporation in England. 36 Am J2d For Corp § 1.

Irish gavelkind (ī'rish gav'el-kīnd). A kind of land tenure under which upon the death of the proprietor there was a fresh division of all the lands in this district, including his own.

iron. A mineral. 36 Am J1st Min & M § 5. A metal. A tool made of iron. A term for a shackle.
See **carry the iron; pig iron; trial by the iron.**

Iron Age. One of the ages of man, characterized by the introduction of tools, weapons, and other instruments made of iron into the life of man.

iron ordeal. An ancient form of trial for crime wherein the prisoner was handed a hot iron which he carried in his hand for nine feet, whereupon his hand was bandaged and sealed to the iron and kept so for three nights. Then the bandages were removed. If the iron was clean, he was pronounced innocent, but if unhealthy matter was found upon it, he was adjudged guilty. Sayre's Cases on Criminal Law 30.

iron ore. A substance containing iron which can be extracted by a process.

iron puddler. A person performing the process of making wrought iron from pig iron by heating and stirring it. Adcock v Smith, 97 Tenn 373, 37 SW 91.

iron safe clause. A provision, in a policy of insurance covering a stock of goods or merchandise, that the insured shall make and keep inventories and books of account which shall be kept in an iron or other fire proof safe, or other secure place, and that the insured shall, upon demand, produce such books and inventories for the inspection of the insurer, in default of which the policy shall be void. Diebold Safe & Lock Co. v Huston, 55 Kan 104, 39 P 1035; Westchester Fire Ins. Co. v Gray (Ky) 240 SW2d 825, 33 ALR2d 608.

irrebuttable presumption. Same as **conclusive presumption.**

irrecusable (ir-ē-kū'za-bl). Not to be avoided, although made an obligation without one's consent. See 8 Harvard L Rev 200.

irredeemable. Not subject to redemption.
See **redemption.**

irredeemable ground rent. A rent reserved to himself and his heirs by the grantor of land, out of the land itself. It is not granted like an annuity or rent charge, but is reserved out of a conveyance of the land in fee. It is a separate estate from the ownership of the ground, and is held to be real estate, with the usual characteristics of an estate in fee simple, descendible, devisable, alienable. Wilson v Iseminger, 185 US 55, 59, 46 L Ed 804, 806, 22 S Ct 573.

irregular (i-reg'ū-lạr). Lacking adherence to some prescribed rule or mode of proceeding, either in omitting to do something that is necessary for the due and orderly conduct of a suit, or in doing it in an unreasonable time or improper manner. Ex parte Gibson, 31 Cal 620, 625.
See **irregularity**.

irregular deposit. A deposit of money for safe-keeping whereunder the depositee is not to return the specific money deposited, but he is to return an equal sum to the depositor. Rozelle v Rhodes, 116 Pa 129.

irregular heirs (ārs). (Civil law.) Those persons who took the land of a deceased person by statute in case there were neither testamentary heirs nor legal heirs.

irregular indorsement. Sometimes referred to as an "anomalous indorsement," meaning an indorsement for the purpose other than to transfer the instrument, an indorsement by a stranger to the instrument or a person not in an actual or apparent chain of title, or an indorsement made prior to delivery of the instrument to the payee, the purpose of such an indorsement usually being that of adding the indorser's credit to the instrument. 11 Am J2d B & N § 364.

irregular indorser. One who makes an irregular indorsement of a negotiable instrument.
See **irregular indorsement**.

irregularity. A failure to follow appropriate and necessary rules of practice or procedure, omitting some act essential to the due and orderly conduct of the action or proceeding, or doing it in an improper manner. Sache v Gillette, 101 Minn 169, 112 NW 386. A violation or nonobservance of established rules and practices. State ex rel. West v Des Moines, 96 Iowa 521, 65 NW 818. The failure to observe that particular course of proceeding which, conformably with the practice of the court, ought to have been observed in the case. Griggs v Hanson, 86 Kan 632, 121 P 1094. Such a defect as consists either in omitting to do something that is necessary to the due and orderly conduct of a suit, or doing it in an unseasonable time or improper manner. Salter v Hilgen, 40 Wis 363, 365.

The word must be given a broad enough meaning to cover a case where the court has acted upon an erroneous understanding of the facts. Such has been the practical construction placed upon it. Cooper v Rhea, 82 Kan 109, 107 P 799.

A direct violation of an ordinance in regard to the manner in which a municipal corporation shall enter into a contract is not a mere irregularity, but is a substantial defect rendering such a contract unenforceable. Holbrook v Girand, 52 Ariz 291, 80 P2d 695.

irregular judgment. A judgment rendered or entered with a want of adherence to some prescribed rule or mode of procedure, consisting either in omitting to do something that is necessary, or in doing it at an unreasonable time or in an improper manner. Murray v United Zinc Smelting Corp. (Mo) 263 SW2d 351. A judgment which, for want of conformity to the course and practice of the courts, is subject to vacation or reversal, but which may stand until vacated or reversed. Stafford v Gallops, 123 NC 19, 31 SE 265.

irregular process. Process not conforming to law. Defective process.

Sometimes the term has been defined to mear process absolutely void, and not merely erroneous and voidable, but, usually, the term has been applied to all process not issued in strict conformity with the law, whether the defects appear upon the face of the process, or by reference to extrinsic facts, and whether such defects render the process absolutely void or only voidable. Doe v Harter, 2 Ind 252, 253.

irregular water course. See intermittent water course.

irrelevancy. Want of pertinency, whether in a pleading or in evidence. Not pertinent; not forming or tendering any material issue in the case; redundant. People v McCumber, 18 NY 315. A term descriptive of the quality facts and circumstances which throw no light and have no logical relation the facts in issue which must be established by one party or disproved by the other; facts and circumstances which are remote and collateral. 29 Am J2d Ev §§ 251, 252.

irrelevant. Having the quality of irrelevancy.
See **irrelevancy**.

irreparable damage. See **irreparable injury**.

irreparable injury. As the term applies in the law of injunctions: —an injury of such a character that a fair and reasonable redress may not be had in a court of law, so that to refuse the injunction would be a denial of justice—in other words, where, from the nature of the act, or from the circumstances surrounding the person injured, or from the financial condition of the person committing it, the injury cannot be readily, adequately, and completely compensated for with money. Miller v Lawlor, 245 Iowa 1144, 66 NW2d 267, 48 ALR2d 1058.

To be irreparable, the injury need not be beyond the possibility of repair or beyond possible compensation in damages, nor need it be very great. The term "irreparable damage" does not have reference to the amount of damage caused, but rather to the difficulty of means measuring the amount of damages inflicted. 28 Am J Rev ed Inj § 48.

irrepleviable (ir-ȩ̄-plev'i-ạ-bl). Incapable of being recovered in an action of replevin.

irresistible force. A force incapable of being resisted, repelled or overcome; an overwhelming force, such as that of a mob.

irresistible impulse. A form of insanity, frequently termed "impulsive insanity," by which a person is irresistibly impelled to the commission of an act, for example, the killing of a person. 29 Am J Rev ed Ins Per § 3. A product of mental insanity, as distinguished from moral insanity. 21 Am J2d Crim L § 36. An impulse to commit an act, otherwise criminal, which one is powerless to control in consequence of a disease of the mind or brain, although he may be able to comprehend the nature and consequences of his act and know that it is wrong. 21 Am J2d Crim L § 36. An impulse produced by and growing out of some mental disease affecting the volitive as distinguished from the perceptive powers, so that the person afflicted, while able to understand the nature of the consequences and to perceive that the act is wrong, is unable because of such mental disease to resist the insane impulse to do it. Durham v United States, 94 App DC 228, 214 F2d 862, 45 ALR2d 1430

Insanity constituting a ground for divorce, where generated by a diseased mind. Willis v Willis (Mo App) 274 SW2d 621.

It is essential carefully to distinguish between instances of irresistible impulse and those situations where persons in the possession of their reasoning faculties are impelled by passion to the commission of acts which in their calmer moments would prove repulsive. Mutual Life Ins. Co. v Terry (US) 15 Wall 580, 21 L Ed 236.

irresistible superhuman cause. An act of God. A natural cause, the effect of which cannot be prevented by the exercise of prudence, diligence, and care, and the use of those appliances which the situation of the party renders it reasonable that he should employ. Fay v Pacific Improv. Co. 93 Cal 253, 261, 26 P 1099.

irretrievably insolvent. See **hopelessly insolvent.**

irreversible (ir-ẹ-vėr'si-bl). Not capable of being reversed or annulled.

irrevocability. The want of power to recall or nullify a grant. 23 Am J2d Deeds § 6. The characteristic of a deed which distinguishes it from a will. 23 Am J2d Deeds § 6.

See **irrevocable.**

irrevocable. Not revocable at the will of one party. Re Zimmerman, 236 NY 15, 139 NE 764.

The usual meaning of the word is never to be revoked; never to be abrogated, annulled, or withdrawn. But a court will not so interpret the word when such a construction would be unreasonably harsh. Mutual Reserve Fund Life Asso. v Boyer, 62 Kan 31, 61 P 387.

Even an agreement made irrevocable by statute is revocable by the mutual consent of the parties. 5 Am J2d Arb & A § 41.

Irrevocable election. An election between inconsistent remedies made by a party, with knowledge of the facts, and in the absence of fraud or imposition. 25 Am J2d Elect R § 32. Flickinger v Shaw, 87 Cal 126, 25 P 268. Also, in some jurisdictions, a license in connection with which the licensee has made expenditures in maintenance and improvement. 33 Am J1st Lic § 103.

It is a general rule that a license in the nature of a special privilege conferred by a public body may be withdrawn at the discretion of the body or sovereignty which granted it. 33 Am J1st Lic § 65.

irrigate (ir'i-gāt). To convey water to or upon anything; to wet or moisten. Charnock v Higuerra, 111 Cal 473, 44 P 171.

irrigating plant. A mechanical device installed upon land for the purpose of irrigation. Gracy v Gracy, 74 Fla 63, 76 So 530.

irrigation. The artificial watering of agricultural land in regions where the rainfall is insufficient for crops; application of water to land for the production of crops, whether by channels, by flooding, or merely by sprinkling. 30 Am J Rev ed Irrig § 2.

See **return flow.**

Irrigation Act. See **Reclamation Act.**

irrigation company. A private company organized for the purpose of constructing and operating irrigation works as an independent business enterprise. A mutual company of individual landowners in association for the purpose of obtaining water and using it for the irrigation of their own lands. A company organized for the purpose of the purchase and development of tracts of arid land and the construction of irrigation works in connection with the enterprise, with the view of the subsequent sale of smaller tracts with appurtenant irrigation rights. 30 Am J Rev ed Irrig § 46. A public utility subject to regulation and control as such where it holds itself out generally to serve for compensation all who may apply for water within the area served by its irrigation system. 30 Am J Rev ed Irrig § 47.

irrigation district. An improvement district established under government authority to accomplish the purpose of irrigation by the united efforts of landowners. 30 Am J Rev ed Irrig § 60. A public debtor within the meaning of the provisions of the Bankruptcy Act for the composition of the indebtedness of certain public agencies or instrumentalities. 9 Am J2d Bankr § 1416. Sometimes regarded as a governmental subdivision. Platt Valley & I. Dist. v Lincoln County, 144 Neb 584, 14 NW2d 202, 155 ALR 412. Not a public service corporation in the sense of being a common carrier, since its operations are confined to the business of carrying and supplying water for the irrigation of lands within its area. Stephenson v Pioneer Irrigation Dist. 49 Idaho 189, 69 ALR 1225, 288 P 421.

irritancy (ir'i-tạn-si). Becoming void; making void; avoiding.

irritant (ir'i-tạnt). Rendering void or null.

irritant clause (klâz). A clause in a deed or other instrument containing a condition the happening of which will render the instrument void.

irritant poison. A poison such as arsenic which, when administered internally, causes severe irritation of some or all parts of the alimentary canal.

The most general effect of irritant poisoning is acute inflammation of the stomach. Joe v State, 6 Fla 591, 605.

irritus (ir'ri-tus). Ineffectual; void.

irrogare (ir-ro-gā're). (Civil law.) To inflict; to impose; to levy; as, a tax.

irrotulatio (ir-rō-tu-lā'she-ō). An enrollment; a record; a roll.

is cui cognoscitur (is kī kog-nō'si-ter). He to whom it is acknowledged; a cognizee.

Islam. The Mohammedan religion and its followers. See **Mohammedanism.**

island. A body of land surrounded by water. 56 Am J1st Wat § 504.

To constitute an island in a river, the formation or body must be of a permanent character, not merely surrounded by water when the river is high, but permanently surrounded by a channel of the river, and not a sand bar subject to overflow by the rise of the river and connected with the main land when the river is low, but it is not necessary that the formation on the bed of the river and extending above its surface be suitable for agricultural purposes in order to constitute it an island. Howler v Wood, 73 Kan 511, 85 P 763.

isolated transaction. A transaction which stands alone, not one of repeated or successive transactions. Brannan, Beckham & Co. v Ramsaur, 41 Ga App 166, 152 SE 282.

isolation hospital. A hospital wherein persons having contagious or infectious diseases are confined.

isotope (ī-sọ-tọp). See **radioiostope.**

is qui cognoscit (is quī kog-nō'sit). He who acknowledges; a cognizor.

issint (is'sint). Thus.

issuable. Prepared and ready for issue, as bonds. Capable of being raised as an issue.

issuable facts. Ultimate facts, as distinguished from matters of evidence. Heyward v Long, 178 SC 351, 183 SE 145, 114 ALR 1130.

issuable plea. A plea which goes to the merits of the case. Welsh v Blackwell, 14 NJL 344, 346.

issuable terms (tèrms). The terms of court at which the issues were made up for the assizes. See 3 Bl Comm 353.

issuance. The act of issuing.
See **issue**.

issue. Verb: To come forth; to come out. To put forth, as to issue corporate securities. Noun: That which is issued at a particular time, as a bond issue. An increment, product, profit, or crop arising from real estate. 33 Am J1st Life Est § 313. All the copies of a newspaper or magazine issued at one time. An essential of the proper disposition of a case in court; a single, certain, and material point or question arising out of the pleadings of the parties, being either of law or of fact. 41 Am J1st Pl § 362.

All the persons who may occupy the position of a descendant of one ancestor, Re Farmers' Loan & Trust Co. 213 NY 168, 107 NE 340, 2 ALR 910; embracing all future descendants. 57 Am J1st Wills §§ 1377-1384. Including, when used in a deed, descendants of every degree in the absence of an explanatory context to the contrary. 23 Am J2d Deeds § 216. Under a power to appoint to "issue:" —not limited to children but including descendants in any degree, unless an intent to limit to children is apparent. 41 Am J1st Pow § 58. But sometimes construed, when it appears in a will, as meaning "children" and not including grandchildren. Watterson v Thompson, 404 Ill 515, 89 NE2d 381, 14 ALR2d 1239.

Prima facie a word of limitation equivalent to "heirs of the body." 57 Am J1st Wills §§ 1377–1384.

A word of limitation creating an estate tail. 28 Am J2d Est § 51. But not a technical word either of limitation or of purchase, readily yielding to construction in this respect in accordance with the intention of the testator or grantor. 28 Am J2d Est § 120. Construed as a word of purchase in a will where the context of the instrument demands such construction. 28 Am J2d Est § 43. A word of limitation or of purchase in a will depending upon a sound construction of the instrument. 57 Am J1st Wills §§ 1377 et seq. Appearing in a deed ordinarily as a word of limitation, but as a word of purchase if the grantee has issue living at the time of the deed or if the context of the deed shows that the word is not used in a technical sense but refers specifically to children. Anno: 114 ALR 619.

issue at law. A question or point of law arising in a case upon demurrer or motion.

Under the equity practice of submitting an issue at law to be tried by a jury, the words "issue at law" mean such an issue as has always been known and employed in the administration of equity jurisprudence. Brady v Carteret Co. 70 NJ Eq 748, 64 A 1078.

issue begotten of her body. As the phrase appears in a will, sometimes but not necessarily indicating "children." 57 Am J1st Wills § 1380.

issue by marriage. Children, except as the entire context indicates to the contrary. Anno: 2 ALR 937.

issue devisavit vel non (ish'ō de-vī-sā'vit vel non). See **devisavit vel non**.

issue extinct. See **possibility of issue extinct**.

issue in law. See **issue at law**.

issue joined. See **joinder of issue**.

issue legally begotten. Sometimes, but not necessarily, importing inheritance and procreation, thereby, as a limitation, creating a fee simple conditional. 28 Am J2d Est § 41.

issue of fact. A single, certain, and material part of dispute arising upon a denial of a material allegation in the adversary's pleading, or where by force of statute a material allegation is to be considered controverted without further pleading. 41 Am J1st Pl § 362. Such an issue as is made by the pleadings in a civil action, where the facts alleged, constituting the cause of action, are denied. Dean v Willamette Bridge R. Co. 22 Or 167, 29 P 440.

Arising when a fact or conclusion of fact is maintained by one party, and is controverted by the other in the pleadings. Harris v San Francisco Sugar Refining Co. 41 Cal 393, 404.

In a criminal prosecution an issue of fact may arise upon a plea of not guilty, or upon a plea of former conviction, or acquittal of the same crime. State v Walton, 50 Or 142, 91 P 490.

issue of his body. Words of limitation converting a fee simple into a fee tail, being words of inheritance as well as words of procreation. 28 Am J2d Est § 51.

issue of patent. The grant of letters patent for an invention upon application made therefor, together with a description and a drawing, specimen, or model of the device. 40 Am J1st Pat §§ 40 et seq.

issue of riens per descent (ish'ō of ri-en' per des-sôn'). See **riens per descent**.

issuer. In general one who issues something. A person who places or authorizes the placing of his name on a security (otherwise than as authenticating trustee, registrar transfer agent, or the like) to evidence that it represents a share, participation, or other interest in his property or in an enterprise or to evidence his duty to perform an obligation evidenced by the security; directly or indirectly creates fractional interests in his rights or property which fractional interests are evidenced by securities; or becomes responsible for or in place of any other person described as an issuer. UCC § 8—201(1).

issue roll. A record upon which the issues in an action were entered as soon as they were reached by the pleadings filed.

issues. See **issue**.

issuing bonds. See **bond issue**.

issuing execution. See **issuing writ of process**.

issuing insurance policy. A phrase variously construed:—(1) the signing and execution of the policy by the officers of the insurance company; (2) act of delivery of the policy fully executed; (3) the certain date indicated by the policy as the effective date. 29 Am J Rev ed Ins § 312.

issuing money. The act of the government in putting coins and bills into circulation, the purpose being to have them circulate as money. 36 Am J1st Money §§ 11 et seq.

issuing negotiable instrument. The first delivery of a negotiable instrument complete in form to a person taking it as a holder. Uniform Negotiable Instruments L § 191.

An instrument is "issued" rather than negotiated to the original payee. Firestone Tire & Rubber Co. v Central Nat. Bank, 159 Ohio St 423, 50 Ohio Ops 364, 112 NE2d 636; Texas Gulf Trust Co. v Notias (Tex Civ App) 352 SW2d 925 error ref n r e.

issuing stock. All the process of authorizing, executing, and delivering the certificates of stock to the subscribers, thereby conferring upon and vesting in them the rights and privileges of stockholders. Majestic Household Utilities Corp. v Stratton, 353 Ill 86, 186 NE 522, 89 ALR 852; Don Johnston Drilling Co. v Howard (Okla) 347 P2d 640, 78 ALR2d 824.

Something more than merely procuring contracts of subscription to the stock of the corporation not in being, but which may be organized in the future. Felton v Highlands Hotel Co. 165 Ga 598, 141 SE 793, 57 ALR 987.

The issuance of new stock certificates to replace lost certificates or to evidence a stock transfer, or upon a split up of outstanding existing shares of stock, does not involve "issuance of new or additional stock," within a statute subjecting a public service corporation to the payment of a fee for each authorized "issue of securities." Lake Superior Dist. Power Co. v Public Service Com. 250 Wis 39, 26 NW2d 278, 170 ALR 680.

When certificates of stock are officially executed and delivered by a corporation to its stockholders they are "issued" in the ordinary sense, but when such stock is called in and canceled as of record the original shares can no longer be said to be "issued." Majestic Household Utilities Corp. v Stratton, 353 Ill 86, 186 NE 522, 89 ALR 852.

issuing writ or process. The preparing, signing, sealing, and delivering of the writ or process to the sheriff or other proper officer for service or levy. Ball v Jones (Fla) 65 So 2d 3, 37 ALR2d 922; Pease v Ritchie, 132 Ill 638, 24 NE 433.

ita (i'ta). Thus; so.

Ita est (i'ta est). It is thus; it is so.

Ita lex scripta est (i'ta lex skrip'ta est). The law is thus written; such is the written law. Hawaii v Mankichi, 190 US 197, 248, 47 L Ed 1016, 1034, 23 S Ct 787.

ita quod (i'ta quod). So that.

Ita semper fiat relatio ut valeat dispositio (i'ta sem'per fī'at re-lā'she-ō ut va'le-at dis-pō-zi'she-ō). Let the reference always be so made that the disposition may prevail.

Ita te Deus adjuvet (i'ta tē Dē'us ad-ju'vet). So help you God.

Ita utere tuo ut alienum non laedas (i'ta ū'te-re tu'ō ut ā-li-ē'num non lē'das). So use your own property that you do not injure that of another.

it being understood. Words of qualification; the equivalent of:—if such and such is true, then it is agreed. Phoenix Iron & Steel Co. v Wilkoff Co. (CA6 Ohio) 253 F 165, 1 ALR 1497. A phrase which, appearing in a grant, imports a covenant rather than a condition. 28 Am J2d Est § 146.

item. A particular, a detail; a distinct and severable part.

itemize. To state in items or by particulars. Lovell v Sny Island Levee Drainage Dist. 159 Ill 188, 42 NE 600.

item of gross income. Any item or amount which affects gross income as such exists for the purpose of an income tax. Anno: 54 ALR2d 573.

items of appropriation. The distinct subjects of appropriation in an appropriation bill. Anno: 35 ALR 602.

iter (ī'tėr). A footway. Jones v Venable, 120 Ga 1, 47 NE 549.

iteratio (i-te-rā'she-ō). An iteration; a repetition.

Iter est jus eundi, ambulandi hominis, non etiam jumentum agendi vel vehiculum (i'ter est jūs e-un'dī, am-bu-lan'dī ho'mi-nis, non e'she-am jū'men'tum ā-jen'dī vel ve-hi'ku-lum). A way is a right of going or walking by man, and not of driving a beast of burden or a vehicle.

I think. Not necessarily indicating a conclusion; consistent with considering the testimony of a witness, who uses the expression as a preface, as a matter of his own observation and recollection. Losey v Atchison, Topeka & Santa Fe Railway Co. 84 Kan 224, 114 P 198. An expression capable of construction as an allegation of fact. 41 Am J1st Perj § 9.

itinera (ī-ti'ne-ra). Plural of **iter**.

itinerant (ī-tin'e-rant). Traveling from place to place; wandering; a person who roams or travels from place to place.

itinerant dealer. One who establishes himself in business in a locality with the intention and determination to remain there for a short period of time only, whether such period is a definite or indefinite one, such as a period of one or more weeks or months, or until a particular stock of merchandise is disposed of, or until the local market for the commodity handled by the dealer has been exhausted, and who for such limited period engages or occupies a building or other place for the exhibition and sale of his goods or wares. Anno: 94 ALR 1084, 1088. Sometimes called an "itinerant merchant." Carrolton v Bazzette, 159 Ill 284, 42 NE 837. Distinguished from a peddler in the respect that he has a definite place for the exhibition and sale of his goods, however temporary his stay at such place may be. Anno: 94 ALR 1083.

itinerant domicil. The domicil of a person in the course of a trip from an old to a new home, such being the old domicil until the new is reached. 25 Am J2d Dom § 35.

itinerant merchant. Same as **itinerant dealer.**

itinerant photographer. A photographer without any fixed place of business who obtains his orders by soliciting them from house to house or place of business to place of business. Anno: 116 ALR 1377, s. 134 ALR 1382.

itinerant physician. A physician not entitled to a license to practice, because of the want of a fixed place for the practice of his profession and further because of the solicitation of patients. Anno: 61 ALR 346.

itinerant vender. A hawker, peddler, or itinerant merchant.

A statutory definition of the term includes all persons, both principals and agents, who engage in a temporary or transient business in this state, either in one locality or in traveling from place to place selling goods, wares, and merchandise, and who, for the purposes of carrying on such business,

ITINERE

hire, lease, or occupy any building or structure for the exhibition and sale of such goods, wares, and merchandise. A person having a permanent place of business may still be an itinerant vender elsewhere within the state. State v Foster, 22 RI 163, 46 A 833.

See **hawker**; **itinerant merchant**; **peddler**.

itinere. See **durante itinere**; **in itinere**.

it is lawful. A permissive term in a statute, especially where the act involved does not affect third persons, and is not clearly beneficial to them, or to the public generally. 50 Am J Stat § 28.

it is understood. Same as **it being understood**.

I, we, or either of us. A series of pronouns referring to the makers of a promissory note, the effect of which is to render the promise to pay joint and several. 11 Am J2d B & N § 587.

J

J. An abbreviation of **judge**, also of **justice**.

J. A. An abbreviation of **judge advocate**.

ja. Now; yet. Yes, in German.

Jac. I. An abbreviation of Jacobus I, meaning **James I**.

Jac. II. An abbreviation of Jacobus II, meaning **James II**.

jacens (ja'senz). Lying down; in abeyance.

jacens haereditas (ja'senz hē-rē'di-tas). An estate which is lying in abeyance.

jacet in ore (ja'set in ō're). It lies in the mouth.

jack. A male, especially a male jackass.
See **lifting jack; standing jacks**.

jackass. A male donkey, one of the characteristics of which is the making of a loud noise called braying. 4 Am J2d Ani § 22. A silly or stupid person; a person whose purposes of accomplishment are ill-conceived and unfortunate in result.

jacket. A cover, especially the cover on a book to protect it while on shelf for sale. A coat.
See **straightjacket**.

Jack Ketch (jȧk kech). A name sometimes given to an English hangman or executioner.

jacknifing. A familiar cause of highway accidents, being a movement of a trailer contrary to the movement of the tractor, so that, joined together, they bend in the middle. 8 Am J2d Auto § 715.
The movement known as jacknifing will result from the application of brakes to the tractor without putting on the brakes of the trailer. Fruehauf Trailer Co. v Gusewelle (CA8 Mo) 190 F2d 248, cert den 342 US 866, 96 L Ed 651, 72 S Ct 105.

Jack of lent (jȧk' of lent'). An effigy personifying the lenten season.

jackpot. A game of chance. Anno: 135 ALR 129. The stake in a game of chance, particularly a game of cards in which the stake is cumulative with the progression in the betting. The amount in a slot machine which may be released to a winner.

jactitation. A false boast. In medical terminology, any involuntary convulsive muscular movement. Leman v Manhattan Life Ins. Co. 46 La Ann 1189, 15 So 388.

jactitation of marriage. The wrongful boasting or giving out by a person that he or she is married to a certain person, contrary to the fact, whereby a common rumor of their marriage may ensue. See 3 Bl Comm 93.

jactitation of tithes (of tīthz). A person's false boasting of his right to take tithes.

jactitation of title. An action, the object of which is to force a party who is not in possession, but who asserts a right to the property out of court, to come into court and disclaim or assert the right judicially. The procedure used in some jurisdictions to recover damages for slander of title. 33 Am J1st L & S § 354.

jactivus (jak-tī'vus). Thrown away; cast away; lost.

jactura (jak-tū'ra). A word used in the civil law with the same meaning as the English word **jettison**.

jactura evitanda. See **de jactura evitanda**.

jactus (jak'tus). A throwing; a cast; a throw. Jettison. Barnard v Adams (US) 10 How 270, 303, 13 L Ed 417, 431.

jactus lapilli (jak'tus la-pil'lī). Throwing down a stone.
Under the civil law this was an act which was symbolic of an assertion of right or title in land and was employed to bar the acquisition of a prescriptive right or title by adverse possession.

jail. A prison pertaining to a county or municipality in which are confined for punishment persons convicted of misdemeanors committed in the county or municipality; also a place in which persons accused of crime, who are not able to furnish bail, or are not entitled to furnish bail, pending action by the grand jury, or the filing of an information, are confined, prior to being brought on for trial. 41 Am J1st Pris & P § 2.
See **common jail; lockup; state jail**.

jail breaking. The offense of breaking out of a jail through any confining wall by force or violence.
A mere constructive breaking, as by walking out through an open door, or an escape accomplished by stratagem is not a jail breaking, unless accompanied by force, but force used to overcome a jailer or turnkey is sufficient. State v Clark, 121 Kan 816, 250 P 300.

jail delivery. The clearing out or ridding a jail of the persons committed there to await their trials, by disposing of their cases. See 4 Bl Comm 270.

jail delivery judges. See **judges of gaol delivery**.

jailer. The custodian or keeper of a jail. 41 Am J1st Pris & P § 5. A public officer subject to the commands of courts to receive and retain prisoners committed to their custody by legal process. 41 Am J1st Pris & P § 10.

jail liberties. See **liberties of the jail**.

jail limits. See **liberties of the jail**.

jake. A slang term for Jamaica ginger. 30 Am J Rev ed Intox L § 19.

Jamaica ginger. An extract of ginger with an alcoholic content. State v Intoxicating Liquors & Vessels, 118 Me 98, 106 A 711, 4 ALR 1128. Generally regarded as an intoxicating liquor because of its use as an intoxicant. 30 Am J Rev ed Intox L § 19.

James I. James the First, the king of England from March 24th, 1603, to March 27th, 1625.

James II. James the Second, the king of England from February 6th, 1685, to 1689.

jamundilingi. Same as **jamunlingi**.

jamunlingi. Freemen who voluntarily placed themselves and their property under the duties of subjection and service of a man of wealth in order to secure his protection.

janitor. A person who cares for a building, such as an apartment house, in respect of keeping it clean and orderly. A doorkeeper.

Japanese curfew. A restriction in the form of a curfew established by executive order against all persons of Japanese ancestry residing in the West Coast Military Area during the war between the

United States and Japan. Yasui v United States, 320 US 115, 87 L Ed 1793, 63 S Ct 1392.

Japanese evacuation. The evacuation of Japanese from certain areas on the West Coast and their relocation elsewhere at the beginning of the war with Japan, as authorized by Act of March 21, 1942 and Executive Orders 9066, 9102.

Japanese exclusion. A policy, since abrogated, of excluding Japanese, along with other members of the yellow race, from immigation. Japanese Immigrant Case (Yamataya v Fisher) 189 US 86, 47 L Ed 721, 23 S Ct 611. The former policy, since abrogated, of excluding Japanese, along with other members of the yellow race, from naturalization. Re Yamashita, 30 Wash 234, 70 P 482. The exclusion of Japanese from certain areas on the West Coast at the beginning of the war with Japan, as authorized by Act of March 21, 1942 and Executive Order 9066.

jar. A container, usually earthenware. A shock. The technical name for a tool used by oil well drillers to dislodge objects which have become fastened in a well. Raymond v Wickersham, 27 Cust & Pat App 1079, 110 F2d 863.

Jason Clause. A clause in a maritime bill of lading, the effect of which is to invest the master of the carrying vessel with authority and responsibility to act directly for cargo in relation to contribution in general average. Aktieselskabet Cuzco v The Sucarseco, 294 US 394, 79 L Ed 942, 55 S Ct 467.

jaundice. A disease characterized by the presence of bile in the blood; sometimes resulting from transfusions of blood following an injury. Duvall v T. W. A. 98 Cal App 2d 106, 219 P2d 463. Often developing as a direct result of injuries. Helms v Leonard (DC Va) 170 F Supp 143.

javelour (zhah″vĕ-loor′). A jailer.

jaw-strap. An iron bar on a railroad car used for hauling coal, running below and between the ends of the axles under the body of the car. Coates v Boston & Maine Railroad, 153 Mass 297, 26 NE 864.

jaywalking. A pedestrian crossing a street diagonally, or at other than right angles, or crossing at a place other than an intersection or designated crossing. 7 Am J2d Auto § 243.

J. C. D. Abbreviation of Doctor of Civil Law.

J. D. Abbreviation of Doctor or Laws.

Jedburgh justice. An ancient name for modern lynch law, under which a prisoner is put to death without a trial.
 Sir Walter Scott refers to a species of lynching when he refers to what was called "Jedwood" justice, "hang in haste and try at leisure." State v Lewis, 142 NC 626, 55 SE 600.

Jeddart justice. Same as **Jedburgh justice.**

Jedwood justice. Apparently the same as **Jedburgh justice.**

jeep. A small but sturdy motor vehicle adaptable to the purposes of a small truck as well as to the carrying of passengers, but not a passenger automobile of the pleasure-car type. Pennell v United Ins. Co. 150 Tex 541, 243 SW2d 572.

Jehovah's Witnesses. A religious sect, the practices of which in living up to the precepts of their belief have brought them into litigation repeatedly, particularly criminal prosecutions.

 The Witnesses claim and are entitled to the constitutional guaranties of freedom of speech and of religion within the conditions of the application of such guaranties. 12 Am J2d Breach P § 14.

Jencks Act. A federal statute the major concern of which is with limiting and regulating defense access to government papers, the provision being that in any criminal prosecution brought by the United States, no statement or report in the possession of the United States which was made by a government witness or prospective government witness (other than the defendant) to an agent of the government shall be the subject of subpoena, discovery, or inspection until said witness has testified on direct examination in the trial of the case. 18 USC § 3500; Palermo v United States, 360 US 343, 3 L Ed 2d 1287, 79 S Ct 1217.

jennet. A female donkey.

jeofail (jef′āl). A mistake or error in a pleading.

jeofaile. Same as **jeofail.**

jeofail statute (jef′āl stat̲′ūt). A statute curing imperfections in pleading, civil or criminal. Witte Iron Works v Holmes, 62 Mo App 372.

jeopardy. Danger. In a criminal case, the danger of punishment which the defendant incurs when brought to trial before a court of competent jurisdiction, on an indictment, presentment, or information which is sufficient in form and substance to sustain a conviction, and a jury has been charged with his deliverance. 21 Am J2d Crim L §§ 169 et seq.
 See **prior jeopardy.**

jepardy. Same as **jeopardy.**

jerguer. An English customs officer.

jerk. A sudden movement of a railroad car occurring as a result of the stress produced by a sudden start or stop of the train. Foley v Boston & Maine R. Co. 193 Mass 339, 79 NE 765. A sudden moving of the body or a part of the body by an abrupt application of force, as where a motor vehicle in which a person is riding suddenly stops. A slang term for a silly person.
 See **lurch.**

Jerusalem assizes. See **assizes of Jerusalem.**

jest. A joke. A remark made in a taunting manner.

jet. An airplane propelled by jets of gas and developing great speed as compared with an airplane powered by the conventional piston engine.

jet routes. The routes prescribed by the Federal Aviation Agency for jet planes. 14 CFR §§ 600.1 et seq.

jetsam (jet′sạm). Goods cast into the sea in order to save a ship, or by shipwreck, which sink and remain under water. 48 Am J1st Ship § 647. A subject of salvage. 47 Am J1st Salv § 3.

jetsom. Same as **jetsam.**

jetsome. Same as **jetsam.**

jettage (jet′ạj). A tax laid on incoming ships.

jetting. A technical term of the construction industry for the process of filling an excavation with the same material as that removed in excavating and soaking the fill with water. Leo F. Piazza Paving Co. v Bebek & Brkich, 141 Cal App 2d 226, 296 P2d 368, 369, footnote.

jettison (jet′i-sọn). The voluntary casting overboard of part of the cargo in order to relieve the ship in

distress. 48 Am J1st Ship § 633. A peril of the sea within the meaning of a marine insurance policy. 29A Am J Rev ed Ins § 1314.

jetty. A structure, usually in the form of a wall, sometimes a dam built and extending into a river or other body of water for the purpose of deflecting the current, thereby protecting a harbor by deepening the channel and strengthening the banks of the stream. Morton v Oregon Short Line Railroad Co. 48 Or 444, 87 P 151.

jeux de bourse (zhĕr dĕ boorse). (French.) Speculations in stocks or futures.

jewelry. Ornaments used for personal adornment. Anno: 40 ALR2d 871. Inclusive also of useful articles such as a watch, tie-clasp, etc. Rains v Maxwell House Co. 112 Tenn 219, 79 SW 114. Including gems, whether mounted or unmounted. Automobile Ins. Co. v Denny (CA8 Mo) 206 F2d 401, 40 ALR2d 865.

Jewish interest. An expression, common in England in an older day, for usury.

Jews. The chosen people of the Old Testament. Persons whose ancestors were the ancient Hebrews.
See **Judaism.**

jigsaw puzzle. A puzzle in the assembling of the severed parts of a picture, presenting a problem requiring ingenuity in solution; not a game within the meaning of a tax on games. White v Aronson, 303 US 16, 82 L Ed 20, 58 S Ct 95.

Jim Crow car. A car provided by a carrier for the carriage of colored passengers only, such passengers not being permitted to ride in coaches with whites; an instrumentality of unlawful segregation. 15 Am J2d Civ R § 35.

jim-jams. A slang term for delirium tremens, also slang for a nervousness, even for a belly-ache.

jimmy (jim'i). A prying-bar used by burglars for opening doors and windows. United States ex rel. Guarino v Uhl (CA2 NY) 107 F2d 401.

jitney. An automobile which carries passengers on a regular route for a relatively small fare. Memphis v State, 133 Tenn 83, 179 SW 631. A competitor of the streetcar in an older day. Columbia v Alexander, 125 SC 530, 119 SE 241, 32 ALR 746. A slang expression for a nickle.

jitney bus. Same as **jitney.**

jitters. A slang term for nervousness.

JJ. An abbreviation of "judges."

J. K. B. An abbreviation of "justice of the king's bench."

jobber. A middleman, a dealer in merchandise who buys from the manufacturer, wholesaler, or importer and sells to retailers. Steward v Winters (NY) 4 Sandf Ch 587, 590. One who does piece work.
See **piece work.**

jobbers' association. An association by the jobbers of a locality for the purpose of obtaining cooperation in purchasing and distribution of commodities. Arkansas Brokerage Co. v Dunn (CA8) 173 F 899.

jobbery. A form of extortion; the misuse of a public office for private gain.

job differential. A circumstance such as undesirable hours, disagreeable work, or danger in the work, for which wages are paid at premium rates. Bay Ridge Operating Co. v Aaron, 334 US 446, 92 L Ed 1502, 68 S Ct 1186.

job lot. A commercial term for goods of various kinds or of various makes brought together for sale in one lot. 46 Am J1st Sales § 361.

job printing. The business or occupation of furnishing special printed matter upon orders from customers, such as letterheads, calling cards, circulars, mail-order catalogues, printed briefs of attorneys, etc.

job selling. A term of the profession for fee-splitting.
See **division of fees.**

jocalia (jō-kā'li-a). Jewels.

jocelet. A small farm.

jockey. Verb: To maneuver for position or advantage. Noun: A person employed by the owner to ride a horse in a race. Moore v Clarke, 171 Md 39, 187 A 887, 107 ALR 924.

jocus (jō'kus). A game of chance.

jocus partitus (jō'kus par-tī'tus). An ancient means of deciding a case by chance.

John (jon). The king of England from May 27th, 1199, to October 19th, 1216.

John XXIII. His Holiness, The Pope, 1958-1963, revered by Roman-Catholic, Protestant, and Jew alike, as an enlightened, progressive, and gracious spiritual leader.

John Doe. A fictitious name of a person which is often substituted in an action or proceeding for a party's real name until the latter can be ascertained.

John Doe action. An action brought against "John Doe" as an unknown uninsured motorist. 7 Am J2d Auto Ins § 137. Any action in which the defendant is designated as "John Doe," his real name being unknown to the plaintiff.

John Doe summons. A summons in which the name of the defendant being unknown to the plaintiff at time of issuance, the defendant is designated as John Doe, his true name to be added after service. 42 Am J1st Proc § 16.

John Doe warrant. A warrant for the arrest of a person designated as John Doe or by some other fictitious name because his real name is unknown. 5 Am J2d Arr § 9.

Johnson Act. A federal statute which limits the jurisdiction of the federal courts in state tax cases to cases where the state courts do not give a plain, speedy and efficient remedy. 28 USC § 1341.

join. To unite; to act jointly with another person or with other persons; to act together; as where a husband and wife join or act together in the execution of a deed. Nolan v Moore, 96 Tex 341, 72 SW 583.

joinder. Acting jointly with one or more other persons; joining.

joinder in demurrer. The formal acceptance by the adverse party to an action of the issue of law which is tendered by a party's demurrer to such adverse party's pleading.

joinder in issue. A party's formal acceptance of the tender of an issue of fact which is made by the pleadings on file in the action.
See **joinder of issue.**

joinder of actions. See **consolidation of actions; joinder of causes of action.**

joinder of causes of action. Union of two or more causes of action, each of which could be made the basis of a separate suit, in the same complaint, declaration, bill, or petition. Linscott v Linscott, 243 Iowa 335, 51 NW2d 428, 30 ALR2d 789. An impropriety in joining in one and the same count different causes of action of the same nature or of different natures in support of a single right of recovery. 41 Am J1st Pl § 44.
See **joinder of counts.**

joinder of counts. The inclusion in a complaint, declaration, or petition, of two or more counts intended to present separate causes of action or to plead the same count in different ways in order to meet any possible phase of the evidence. 41 Am J1st Pl § 106. The joinder of distinct offenses by including separate counts in an indictment or information, each count being in legal effect a separate indictment or information. 27 Am J1st Indict § 129.

joinder of defenses. Different and distinct defenses set up in the same plea or answer. 41 Am J1st Pl § 161.

joinder of issue. The raising and presentation for trial of an issue of fact. 41 Am J1st Pl § 362. In a criminal case, a plea of not guilty in response to an indictment information or complaint. 21 Am J2d Crim L § 458.

joinder of motions. Presenting two or more motions as one, sometimes resulting in a combination of demands for relief of a different nature, depending on different facts and circumstances wholly unrelated. 37 Am J1st Motions § 68.

joinder of offenses. The charging of two or more offenses in separate counts in a single indictment, information or presentment. 27 Am J1st Indict § 129. Duplicity in the joinder of two or more distinct and separate offenses in the same count of an indictment or information. 27 Am J1st Indict § 124.

joinder of parties. The uniting of two or more parties as plaintiffs or as defendants in an action or suit. See 39 Am J1st Parties §§ 24 et seq.
See **fraudulent joinder.**

joined. United.

joint. Adjective: Operating or acting in unity. Merrill v Pepperdine, 9 Ind App 416, 36 NE 921. Noun: Slang for a restaurant, cigar store, pool hall, or similar place, of an inferior quality, especially one frequented by criminals, narcotic addicts, pimps, or prostitutes. State v Shoaf, 179 NC 744, 102 SE 705, 9 ALR 426, 428.

joint action. An action which is prosecuted or defended by two or more persons acting for their common interest.

joint administrators. Two or more persons duly appointed, qualified, and acting in the administration of a decedent's estate. 31 Am J2d Ex & Ad §§ 624 et seq.

joint adventure. The relationship created when two or more persons combine in a joint business enterprise for their mutual benefit with the understanding that they are to share in the profits or losses and that each is to have voice in its management. Chisholm v Gilmer (CA4 Va) 81 F2d 120, affd 299 US 99, 81 L Ed 63, 57 S Ct 65, reh den 299 US 623, 81 L Ed 458, 57 S Ct 229. An association of persons in a single business enterprise for profit, for which purpose they combine their property, money, effects, skill, and knowledge, without forming a partnership or corporation. Summers v Hoffman, 341 Mich 686, 69 NW2d 198, 48 ALR2d 1033; Brooks v Brooks, 357 Mo 343, 208 SW2d 279, 4 ALR2d 826. More precisely, an association of persons with intent, by way of contract, express or implied, to engage in and carry out a single business adventure for joint profit, for which purpose they combine their efforts, property, money, skill, and knowledge, but without creating a partnership in the legal or technical sense of the term, or a corporation, and they agree that there shall be a community of interest among them as to the purpose of the undertaking, and that each coadventurer shall stand in the relation of principal, as well as agent, as to each of the other coadventurers, with an equal right of control of the means employed to carry out the common purpose of the adventure. 30 Am J Rev ed Jnt Adv § 2.
See **joint enterprise.**

joint agency. An agency conferred on two or more persons which is to be exercised jointly by the designated agents, the principal having bargained for and obtained the combined personal ability, experience, judgment, integrity, and other personal qualities of the agents. Egner v States Realty Co. 223 Minn 305, 26 NW2d 464, 170 ALR 500.

joint and mutual will. A will executed jointly by two persons, the provisions of which are reciprocal, and which shows on its face that the devises are made one in consideration of the other. 57 Am J1st Wills §§ 680 et seq.

joint and several. A term importing unity, as distinguishing from separate or several which implies division or distribution. Merrill v Pepperdine, 9 Ind App 416, 36 NE 921.

joint and several bond. A bond in which the obligors are, by its terms, bound both jointly and individually to pay the full amount of the bond.
The rule is that where an instrument worded in the singular is executed by several, the obligation is a joint and several one, and those who so execute it may be sued either separately or together. It is not necessary to use the technical words "joint and several" in the bond in order to make the obligation thereunder a joint and several one; it is sufficient for this purpose if any of the terms import the meaning of a joint and several obligation. 12 Am J2d Bonds § 29.

joint and several contract. A contract with two or more contracting parties on one side, presenting distinct engagements and rights, each contractor being liable and entitled individually and the two or more of them being liable and entitled jointly. 17 Am J2d Contr § 298.
The use of the pronoun "we" usually creates a joint obligation, although despite the use of that word, the language of some contracts permits of a construction that the parties were intended to be bound severally as well as jointly. If an instrument worded in the singular is executed by several parties, the obligation is a joint and several one. 17 Am J2d Contr § 298.

joint and several covenant. A covenant under which the two or more covenantees on one side bear the burden or receive the benefit not only jointly, but severally. 20 Am J2d Cov § 10.

joint and several demurrer (and sev′ėr-ạl dẹ-mėr′ėr). A demurrer in which the parties demurring to a pleading assail it both collectively and individually.

A demurrer may be joint, several, or both joint and several as to the parties demurring; for the defendants may assail the complaint collectively or individually, or collectively and individually. Merrill v Pepperdine, 9 Ind App 416, 36 NE 921.

joint and several judgment. A judgment against two or more parties and each of them. Tucker v Gautier, 196 Okla 267, 164 P2d 613. A judgment in the ordinary form as taken against two or more defendants.

joint and several liability. The liability of joint tortfeasors. 52 Am J1st Torts § 110. The liability of the two or more contracting parties on one side under an agreement in such terms as to engage the two or more jointly and each one individually.
See **joint and several bond; joint and several contract; joint tortfeasors.**

joint and several note. A promissory note which is the note of all and of each of the makers as to its legal obligation between the parties to it.
A promissory note in the form, "I promise to pay," etc., and signed by two persons is as much a joint and several note as one which reads, "We jointly and severally promise to pay," similarly signed. Ladd v Baker, 26 NH 76; UCC § 118(e) and Comment 6; Uniform Negotiable Instruments L § 17(7).

joint and survivorship annuity. An annuity contract providing for payments to be made during the lives of two annuitants and to continue, after the death of one, for the life of the surviving annuitant. 4 Am J2d Annui § 6.

joint and survivorship estate. A joint tenancy; an estate held by two or more jointly to continue during their joint lives and to vest upon the death of one in the remaining joint tenant or joint tenants, and so on, in a case of more than two joint tenants, until the survivor of all of them takes the entire estate.

joint appeal. A proceeding on appeal or in error in which two or more parties join. 4 Am J2d A & E § 276.

joint authorship. Joint participation in the production of a literary work giving rise to joint ownership. Silverman v Sunrise Pictures Corp. (CA2 NY) 273 F 909, 19 ALR 289.

joint bank account. A bank account in the names of two or more persons which may or may not embrace a survivorship feature. A bank account so created that two persons shall be joint owners during their mutual lives, and the survivor take the whole on the death of the other. 10 Am J2d Bks § 369.

joint bill of exceptions. A bill of exceptions filed by appellant in which the respondent has incorporated his exceptions. 4 Am J2d A & E § 440.

joint bond. A bond on which the obligors are only liable in combination, that is, jointly, and not severally. Municipal Court v Whaley, 25 RI 289, 55 A 750.
See **joint and several bond.**

joint cause of action. A cause of action pleaded by the obligees under a joint contract, also a cause pleaded by two or more persons upon claims presenting a single question of law or fact common to all the plaintiffs. Commodores Point Terminal Co. v Hudnall (DC Fla) 283 F 150.

Joint Chiefs of Staff. A body in the Department of Defense headed by a chairman and made up as follows:—Chief of Staff of the Army, Chief of Naval Operations, Chief of Staff of the Air Force, and the Commandant of the Marine Corps.

Joint Committee on Atomic Energy. A committee of Congress established by the Atomic Energy Act, with the authority and duty to make continuing studies of activities of the Atomic Energy Commission and of problems relating to the development, use, and control of atomic energy, and to conduct hearings on the state of the atomic energy industry. 42 USC § 2252.

joint contract. A contract under which an obligation is incurred by or a right given to two or more persons, there being absent any distinct word of severance indicating or producing a several responsibility or right. Dean v Dean, 229 SC 430, 93 SE2d 206.
See **joint and several contract.**

joint covenant. A covenant made with two or more covenantees who carry the burden or receive the benefit as one person. 20 Am J2d Cov § 10.
See **joint and several covenant.**

joint creditors. Creditors who can only enforce their claims by acting together; the obligees under a contract giving them joint rights.
See **joint contract.**

joint debtors. Persons who are jointly indebted. Walsh v Miller, 51 Ohio St 462, 487, 38 NE 381. The obligors under a contract joint as to them.
See **joint contract.**

joint debtors' acts. Statutes found in most jurisdictions which permit the rendition of judgment against one or more of joint obligors. 30 A Am J Rev ed Judgm § 78.

joint defense. A defense in which two or more defendants in an action join. 41 Am J1st Pl § 119.

joint demurrer. A demurrer in which two or more parties unite to raise an objection to the sufficiency in law of a pleading. 41 Am J1st Pl § 230.

joint deposit. See **joint bank account.**

joint donees. Two or more persons holding a single power of appointment. 41 Am J1st Pow § 29. Two or more persons designated to receive together the whole of a specific item of property.

joint donors. Two or more persons who unite in making a gift.

joint drawees. Two or more persons upon whom a bill of exchange is drawn. 11 Am J2d B & N § 502.

joint enterprise. A term pertinent in the law of imputed negligence. The pursuit of an undertaking by two or more persons having a community of interests in the objects and purposes of the undertaking, and an equal right to direct and govern the movements and conduct of each other. St. Louis & San Francisco Railroad Co. v Bell, 58 Okla 84, 159 P 336; Fox v Lavender, 89 Utah 115, 56 P2d 1049, 109 ALR 105.
Persons riding in an automobile are not, within the law of negligence, engaged in a joint enterprise unless there is a community of interest in the object and purposes of the undertaking and an equal right to direct and govern the driving of the car, and to determine the point of destination. Sizemore v Hall, 148 Kan 233, 80 P2d 1092; Gardner v Hobbs, 69 Idaho 288, 206 P2d 539, 14 ALR2d 478.

joint execution. An execution against all defendants against whom the judgment rendered. 30 Am J2d Exec § 66.

joint executors. Two or more persons acting jointly as executors in the administration of a decedent's estate. 31 Am J2d Ex & Ad §§ 624 et seq.

joint feasors in pari delicto. See **in pari delicto**; **joint tortfeasors.**

joint fiat. See **joint order.**

joint fine. An anomaly, since two or more defendants, although jointly charged, are sentenced separately upon both or all having been found guilty. 21 Am J2d Crim L § 533.

joint gift. See **joint donees**; **joint donors.**

joint grantees. Two or more persons named in a deed as the persons to receive the grant.

joint grantors. The two or more persons named in a deed as the persons conveying.

joint guarantors. Two or more guarantors of the same obligation by the same contract of guaranty.

joint guardians. Two or more persons appointed, qualified, and acting with joint and several authority as guardians over the same fund, property, or person. 25 Am J1st G & W § 214.

joint heir. A co-heir; a person who inherits jointly with another heir or other heirs.

joint indictment. An indictment charging two or more persons as defendants, such being a permissible finding and return where the offenses arise wholly out of the same joint act or where the same evidence as to the act constituting the crime applies to all the persons indicted. 27 Am J1st Indict § 123.

jointist. A person who runs a joint. A Kansas concept of a bootlegger, not an ordinary bootlegger, but one who has risen above his class by maintaining a place of business wherein he may obtain support for the little woman and wee bairns at home by selling intoxicating liquors, albeit unlawfully. Scriven v Lebanon, 99 Kan 602, 162 P 307, 309.
See **joint.**

joint letters of administration. Letters of administration granted and issued to two or more persons jointly. 31 Am J2d Ex & Ad § 45.

joint liability. The liability of two or more persons as one, so that, in the absence of statute, where one of them is sued, the other or others liable with him must be joined as defendants if living and within the jurisdiction. 39 Am J1st Parties § 37.
See **joint and several liability.**

joint lives. A period of time which will terminate upon the death of any one of two or more specified persons.

jointly. Unitedly; sharing together; in unity of interest or liability. Soderberg v Atlantic Lighterage Corp. (DC NY) 15 F2d 209. Appearing in the habendum of a deed, not necessarily indicative of a joint tenancy. 20 Am J2d Coten § 13. As a matter of ownership of property within the meaning of the ownership clause of an insurance policy:—an affirmance that the insureds together own the property and that no other person is interested in it, not a representation that the insureds are tenants in common. Webster v Dwelling House Ins. Co. 53 Ohio St 558, 42 NE 546.

jointly and severally. See **in solido**; **joint and several liability.**

joint maker. A person who with another, or with others, signs a negotiable instrument on the face thereof and thereby becomes primarily liable for its payment. First Nat. Bank v Guardian Trust Co. 187 Mo 494, 86 SW 109. As to the status of an irregular indorser as a comaker, see 11 Am J2d B & N § 522.

joint mine. A term of uncertain origin that has not been widely accepted.
For convenience, a mine served by one carrier is called a "local mine," and a mine served by two or more carriers is called a "joint mine." United States v New River Co. 265 US 533, 68 L Ed 1165, 44 S Ct 610.

joint negligence. See **joint tortfeasors.**

joint obligor. One of two or more persons bound by a joint obligation or a joint and several obligation. One of two or more persons jointly liable upon a negotiable instrument as makers, indorsers, accommodation indorsers, etc.

joint offenders. Participants in the same criminal offense. 21 Am J2d Crim L § 115.

joint offense. A criminal offense committed by two or more persons participating as joint offenders. State ex rel. Flaherty v Ermston, 209 Ind 117, 197 NE 908.
See **joint offenders.**

joint order. An order directed against two or more persons.

joint owners. Co-owners.
See **cotenancy.**

joint parties. Parties to an action on the same side, as either plaintiffs or defendants.

joint patent. A patent issued to two or more persons jointly where both have participated in the process of discovery and invention. 40 Am J1st Pat § 66.

joint payees. The persons to whom a negotiable instrument drawn payable to the order of two or more persons jointly is payable. Uniform Negotiable Instruments L § 8(4); 11 Am J2d B & N § 117.
The Commercial Code declares that an instrument payable to order may be payable to the order of two or more payees together or in the alternative, eliminating the word "jointly" as used by the NIL in order to avoid any implication of survivorship. Comment 1 to UCC § 3–110.

joint policy. An adaption of the tontine plan, being a policy on the lives of two or more persons, the proceeds payable to the survivor.
See **tontine policy.**

joint possession. A possession of premises held by two or more persons jointly, as by tenants in common, coparceners, partners, and the like.
Such persons are seized for themselves and for each other. All are equally entitled to possession, and the possession of any one of them is the possession of all. Knapp v Reed, 88 Neb 754, 130 NW 430.

joint rate. The freight rate for a through shipment by connecting carriers, often called a through rate. 13 Am J2d Car § 206.
Such charge is so apportioned to the separate carriers that each shall receive a just and reasonable part of the joint charge. Burlington, Cedar Rapids & Northern Railroad Co. v Dey, 82 Iowa 312, 48 NW 98.
A through rate is not necessarily a joint rate. It may be an aggregation of separate rates fixed independently by the carriers involved in the through transportation. St. Louis Southwestern Railway Co. v United States, 245 US 136, 139, note, 62 L Ed 199, 205, note, 38 S Ct 49.

joint resolution. A resolution concurred in by both houses of a legislative body, but which, in most jurisdictions, does not have the effect of a statute, at least not without the approval of the executive. 50 Am J1st Stat § 4.

joint return. A single return for income tax made by husband and wife, reporting their combined incomes, deductions, and exemptions.

joint sentence. A sentence of two or more defendants under a joint indictment, which imposes the punishment jointly against them. Ex parte Gafford, 25 Nev 101, 57 P 484. An anomaly, since two or more defendants, although jointly charged, are sentenced separately upon both or all having been found guilty. 21 Am J2d Crim L § 533.

joint session. A meeting of the upper and lower houses of a legislative body in combination, usually for ceremonial purposes or the reception of the executive and the reading of his message or other communication to the legislature. Snow v Hudson, 56 Kan 378, 43 P 260.

joint-stock association. Same as **joint-stock company.**

joint stock bank. See **joint-stock land bank.**

joint-stock company. An unincorporated association of individuals for the purpose of carrying on business and making profits, having a capital stock contributed by the members, which is commonly divided into shares of which each member possesses one or more and which are transferrable by the owner; governed by articles of association which, subject to statutory and other limitations, prescribe its objects, organization, and the rights and liabilities of its members, and usually provide that its business shall be under the control of selected individuals called "managers" or "directors." Earlsboro Gas Co. v Vern H. Brown Drilling Co. 175 Okla 320, 52 P 730.

A joint-stock company created solely by agreement of its members and in which their individual rights and liabilities are not merged as in the case of a corporation is not a stock corporation. People, ex rel.Winchester v Coleman, 133 NY 279, 31 NE 96.

joint-stock land bank. A federal bank authorized by and created under the Federal Farm Loan Act. 10 Am J2d Bks § 21.

joint tenancy. An estate held by two or more persons jointly, with equal rights to share in its enjoyment during their lives, and having as its distinguishing feature the right of survivorship, or jus accrescendi, by virtue of which the entire estate, upon the death of a joint tenant, goes to the survivor (or, in the case of more than two joint tenants, to the survivors, and so on to the last survivor), free and exempt from all charges made by his deceased cotenant or cotenants in which he did not concur. 20 Am J2d Coten § 3.

See **joint bank account.**

joint tenant. Precisely, one of two or more tenants under a joint tenancy. In loose usage, a cotenant. See **joint tenancy.**

joint through rate. See **joint rate.**

joint tort. See **joint tortfeasors.**

joint tortfeasors. Two or more persons who unite in committing a tort, or whose acts concur in contributing to and producing a single indivisible injury upon a third person. 52 Am J1st Torts §§ 110 et seq. Two or more persons jointly or severally liable in tort for the same injury to person or property, whether or not judgment has been recovered against all or some of them. Anno: 34 ALR2d 1108 (referring to Joint Tortfeasor Act of the Uniform Laws.)

To make tortfeasors liable jointly, there must be some sort of community in the wrongdoing, and the injury must be in some way due to their joint work, but it is not necessary that they be acting together or in concert if their concurring negligence occasions the injury. Brose v Twin Falls Land & Water Co. 24 Idaho 266, 133 P 673.

All the tortfeasors are jointly and severally liable for all the damages done the injured party where the tort is committed by two or more persons jointly by force applied directly, or in the pursuit of a common purpose or design, or by concert, or in the advancement of a common interest, or as the result of joint concurrent negligence, although the wrongful conduct or negligence of some may have contributed less than that of others to the injury. Hale v Knoxville, 189 Tenn 491, 226 SW2d 265, 15 ALR2d 1283.

A tort jointly committed by several may be treated as joint or several at the election of the aggrieved party. 52 Am J1st Torts § 110.

jointress (join'tres). A married woman upon whom a jointure has been settled.

See **jointure.**

joint trespass. A trespass committed by the united action of two or more persons, or by the action of one or more of them with the authority or assent of the others. Bonte v Postell, 109 Ky 64, 58 SW 536.

See **joint trespassers.**

joint trespassers. Two or more persons who unite in the act of committing a trespass; two or more persons, one or more of whom commit a trespass with the authority, encouragement, advice, countenance, cooperation, or aid of the others. 52 Am J1st Tresp § 31.

joint trial. See **consolidation of actions.**

joint trustees. See **cotrustees.**

jointure. A provision made for a wife by way of a marriage settlement. 26 Am J1st H & W § 308. Precisely, the settlement on the wife before marriage, in satisfaction of dower, of a competent livelihood by way of a freehold in the husband's property, to take effect in possession immediately after his death and to continue at least for the life of the wife. 25 Am J2d Dow § 114.

jointuress (join'tūr-es). Same as **jointress.**

joint venture. See **joint adventure; joint enterprise.**

joint will. A single testamentary instrument which contains the wills of two or more persons, is executed jointly by them, and disposes of property owned jointly, in common, or in severalty by them. Anno: 169 ALR 12.

See **joint and mutual will; mutual wills; reciprocal wills.**

joists. Heavy bases that hold up the floor of a building, being tied into the frame in such manner as to take up the stress. 13 Am J2d Bldgs § 13.

joke. See **jest; practical joke.**

joker. One who jests. A slang term for an inefficient person.

See **practical joke.**

jolt. See **jerk.**

Jones Act. A federal statute which enlarges the rule of liability under the maritime law by providing that any seaman who shall suffer personal injury in the course of his employment may, at his election, maintain an action for damages at law, and that in such action, all statutes of the United States modifying or extending the common-law right or remedy in cases of personal injury to railway employees shall apply. 46 USC § 688; 48 Am J1st Ship § 179.

jostling. Crowding a person. 4 Am J2d Amuse § 60.

jour (jėr). A day.

jour en banc (jer on bângk). A day in bank. See **in bank.**

journal. A publication, such as a magazine. A formal record of court proceedings. A court record in which judgments are entered. 30A Am J Rev ed Judgm § 91. The book in which the proceedings of a house of a state legislature are recorded, particularly the proceedings in the enactment of a law. 49 Am J1st States § 37; 50 Am J1st Stat § 137. The record in which the minutes of a city council meeting are recorded. 37 Am J1st Mun Corp §§ 64, 65. In bookkeeping, a daybook, but, more precisely, the record to which original entries are transferred.

journal entry. An entry on a journal. See entry of judgment; journal.

journal entry rule. The rule that courts have recourse to journals of either house of the state legislature for ascertaining whether a law has in fact been passed in accordance with constitutional requirements. 49 Am J1st States § 37.

Journal of Congress. See **Congressional Record.**

journée (jėr'nā). A court day; a day for holding court.

journey. A trip. Traveling from place to place.

The original meaning of the word was a day's travel. It is now applied to travel from place to place without restriction to time, but when thus applied, it is employed to designate a traveling which is outside the ordinary habits, business, or duties of the person, to a distance from his home, and beyond the circle of his friends and acquaintances. This is held to be the meaning of the word as it is used in a statute prohibiting the carrying of concealed weapons, except when traveling or setting out on a "journey." Gholson v State, 53 Ala 519.

journeyman. A worker who has learned the trade, having progressed beyond the status of an apprentice. One who has become qualified at his trade or occupation, for example, a journeyman plumber. Re Means, 14 Cal 2d 254, 93 P2d 105, 123 ALR 1378.

journeys account. A common-law rule often said to have been the origin of statutes which operate to prevent the bar by statute of limitations of a new action commenced after the expiration of the limitation period, following the failure of an action commenced within such period. 34 Am J1st Lim Ac § 279.

An ancient common-law practice or doctrine under which the plaintiff might in certain cases cause a suit which had abated to be revived by the issuance of a new writ. At one time the plaintiff had as many days within which to apply to the court of chancery for the new writ as he was days' journeys from the court, allowing twenty miles for each day, but this time was later arbitrarily fixed at thirty days. The practice was referred to as being "antiquated" in 1814. Richards v Maryland Ins. Co. (US) 8 Cranch 84, 3 L Ed 496.

journey-work. The work of a journeyman.

joyride. A ride taken in an automobile purely for pleasure, often in the vehicle of another person taken without his consent. Fredericksen v Employers Liability Assur. Corp. (CA9 Cal) 26 F2d 76; United States Fidelity & Guaranty Co. v Brann, 297 Ky 381, 180 SW2d 102. A ride in a motor vehicle at a dangerously high rate of speed, for the purpose merely of enjoying the exhilarating and pleasurable sensations incident to the swirl and dash of rapid transit. Farmers' Bank & Trust Co. v Henderson, 179 Ky 220, 200 SW 330.

JP. Abbreviation for Justice of the Peace. 1 Am J2d Abbr § 5.

J. Q. B. An abbreviation of "justice of the queen's bench."

Jr. Abbreviation of Junior. No part of a man's name. Foshier v Narver, 24 Or 441, 34 P 21.

jubere (ju-bē're). (Civil law.) To order; to command.

jubilacion (hoo-be-lah-the-on'). (Spanish.) The retirement of a government officer without depriving him of either his title of office or his salary.

J. U. D. An abbreviation of **juris utrius doctor.**

Judaism (jō'dā-izm). The religion of the Jews. Hale v Everett, 53 NH 9.

Judaismo. See **de Judaismo.**

Judaismus. Same as **Judaism.**

judex (jū'dex). A judge.

judex ad quem (jū'dex ad quem). A judge to whom; that is, a judge to whose court a cause has been removed by appeal.

Judex aequitatem semper spectare debet (jū'dex ē-qui-tā'tem sem'per spek-tā're de'bet). A judge ought always to regard equity.

Judex ante oculos aequitatem semper habere debet (jū'dex an'te ō'ku-los ē-qui-tā'tem sem'per hā-bē're de'bet). A judge ought always to have equity before his eyes.

judex a quo (jū'dex ā quō). A judge from whom; that is, a judge from whose court a cause has been removed by an appeal.

Judex bonus nihil ex arbitrio suo faciat, nec propositione domesticae voluntatis, sed juxta leges et jura pronunciet (jū'dex bō'nus ni'hil ex ar-bi'tri-ō su'ō fa'she-at, nek prō-pō-zi-she-ō'ne do-mes'ti-sē volun-tā'tis, sed jux'ta lē'jēz et jū'ra pro-nun'she-et). A good judge should do nothing of his own choice, nor from the prompting of his private wish, but he should pronounce judgment according to laws and justice.

Judex damnatur cum nocens absolvitur (jū'dex damnā'ter kum no'senz ab-sol'vi-ter). A judge is condemned when a guilty man is acquitted.

judex datus (jū'dex dā'tus). (Roman law.) An appointed judge; that is, a judge appointed by the praetor to try a case.

Judex debet judicare secundum allegata et probata (jū'dex de'bet jū-di-kā're se-kun'dum al-le-gā'ta et prō-bā'ta). A judge ought to decide according to the pleadings and the proofs.

judex delegatus (jū'dex de-le-gā'tus). A delegated judge, a judge specially appointed.

Judex est lex loquens (jū'dex est lex lō'quenz). The judge is the law speaking; that is, he is the mouthpiece of the law.

judex fiscalis (jū'dex fis-kā'lis). A judge with jurisdiction in matters pertaining to the fiscus or public treasury.

Judex habere debet duos sales, salem sapientiae ne sit insipidus, et salem conscientiae, ne sit diabolus (jū'dex hā-bē're de'bet du'ōs sā'lēz, sā'lem sa-pi-en'she-ē, nē sit in-si'pi-dus, et sā'lem kon-si-en'she-ē, nē sit di-a'bo-lus). A judge ought to have two salts, the salt of wisdom, that he be not foolish, and the salt of conscience, that he be not diabolical.

Judex non potest esse testis in propria causa (jū'dex non po'test es'se tes'tis in prō'pri-a kâ'za). A judge cannot be a witness in his own case.

Judex non potest injuriam sibi datam punire (jū'dex non po'test in-jū'ri-am si'bi dā'tam pu-nī're). A judge cannot punish a wrong which has been inflicted upon himself.

Judex non reddit plus quam quod petens ipse requirit (jū'dex non red'dit plus quam quod pe'tenz ip'se re-quī'rit). A judge should not render judgement for a larger sum than the plaintiff himself demands.

judex ordinarius (jū'dex or-di-nā'ri-us). (Civil law.) An ordinary judge; that is, a judge having jurisdiction in his own right as judge, as distinguished from a judge appointed or delegated for the trial of a particular case.

judex pedaneus (jū'dex pe-dā'ne-us). (Roman law.) A judge appointed by the praetor to try a case of lesser importance.

judex selectus (jū'dex se-lek'tus). Singular of **judices selecti.**

judge. A public officer who, by virtue of his office, is clothed with judicial powers. Better understood as one who conducts or presides over a court of justice. 30A Am J Rev ed Judges § 2. Clearly to be distinguished from "court" but often used interchangeably and indiscriminately with the latter term, even in some statutes. Broadfoot v Florence, 253 Ala 455, 45 So 2d 311. A title applied in some states to members of a so-called "county court" or board of supervisors or county commissioners who are in no proper sense judicial officers or charged with judicial duties.

Within the meaning of the rule that words spoken by a judge in the course of a judicial proceeding over which he is presiding, and in relation to the subject of the proceeding are absolutely privileged, the following officers have been held to be included within the term "judge," for the purpose of enjoying this protection from suits for libel or slander, when in the discharge of judicial duties; magistrates, justices of the peace, judges in other courts of inferior and superior jurisdiction, equity judges, coroners, members of courts-martial, and receivers in making reports to the courts appointing them. 33 Am J1st L & S § 177.

See **justice; justice of the peace.**

judge ad quem (juj ad quem). The judge to which,—the judge of the court to which a case comes on appeal from a lower court,—from a judge a quo.

Judge Advocate. See **Judge Advocate General; staff judge advocate.**

Judge Advocate General. Severally, the Judge Advocates General of the Army, Navy, and Air Force, and except when the Coast Guard is operating as a service in the Navy, the General Counsel of the Department of the Treasury. 10 USC § 801(1).

Judge Advocate General's Department. A department of the Army, Navy, and Air Force, headed by a **Judge Advocate General.**

judge a quo (juj a quō). The judge from which,—the judge of the court from which the case is appealed to the judge ad quem,—of the higher court.

judge de facto (juj dē fak'to). See **de facto judge.**

judge in chambers. A judge of a court of record acting out of court. Frawley v Cosgrove, 83 Wis 441, 53 NW 689.

See **chambers decision; chambers judgment; chambers order.**

judge-made law. See **judicial legislation.**

judgement. Another spelling for **judgment.**

judge ordinary (juj ôr'di-nạ-ri). A judge of the English court of probate for divorce and matrimonial causes.

judge pro tem (juj prō tem). A temporary judge; a substitute judge.

judge's calendar. A calendar of cases prepared for the use of a judge, often with room on the separate sheets for the individual cases for the writing of his minutes.

See **judge's minutes.**

judge's certificate. A statement signed by the judge before whom a case was tried awarding a party his costs in the action. Any certificate given by a judge in his official capacity.

judge's chambers. See **chambers.**

judge's minutes. The entries made by a judge upon his calendar or other book or sheet in reference to the proceedings taken in the cases brought before him as the court or in chambers, particularly the granting of orders for judgments. 30A Am J Rev ed Judgm § 93.

judge's notes. Same as **judge's minutes.**

judges of elections. Officers conducting elections and assisting in the canvassing of returns. 25 Am J2d Elect § 39.

judges of gaol delivery (of jāl dẹ-liv'ėr-i). Judges who were specially commissioned to hear and determine the cases of persons imprisoned in a jail.

judgment (juj'mẹnt). The final consideration and determination by the court of the rights of the parties, as those rights presently exist, upon matters submitted to it in an action or proceeding. The judicial determination or sentence of the court upon a matter within its jurisdiction. 30A Am J Rev ed Judgm § 2. More precisely, the conclusion of the law upon the matters contained in the record, or the application of the law to the pleadings and to the facts as they appear from the evidence in the case, and as found by the court or jury, admitted by the parties, or as deemed to exist upon their default in the course of judicial proceedings. State ex rel. McDonald v Lollis, 326 Mo 644, 33 SW2d 98. In a criminal case, the action of a court of criminal jurisdiction formally declaring to the accused the legal consequences of the guilt which he has confessed or of which he has been convicted. 21 Am J2d Crim L § 525. Sometimes synonymous with decision, as where both words are used in a statute requiring a liberal construction. 30A Am J Rev ed Judgm § 14. In theory, a determination sought by a motion.

In common parlance, the formation of an opinion or notion concerning something by exercising the mind upon it.

The word is distinguished from desire which imports a wish of more or less intensity. Cleveland Clinic Foundation v Humphreys (CA6 Ohio) 97 F2d 849.

See **decree**.

judgment book. A court record in which judgments are entered. 30A Am J Rev ed Judgm § 91.

judgment by cognovit actionem (juj'mẹnt bī kog-nō'vit ak-she-ō'nem). A judgment rendered, after service of process upon the defendant, upon his acknowledgment and confession that the plaintiff's cause of action is just and rightful. 30A Am J Rev ed Judgm § 156.

judgment by confession. A judgment entered by confession of the defendant. 30A Am J Rev ed Judgm § 156.

judgment by confession relicta verificatione (juj'mẹnt bī kon-fesh'ọn re-lik'ta ve-ri-fi-kā-she-ō'ne). A judgment rendered against the defendant where, after pleading and before trial, he has both confessed the plaintiff's cause of action and withdrawn or abandoned his plea or other allegations, the judgment being entered upon such confession. 30A Am J Rev ed Judgm § 156.

judgment by consent. See **consent judgment**.

judgment by default. See **default judgment**.

judgment by default and inquiry. A judgment which establishes a right of action in the plaintiff as declared in the complaint, the precise character, extent, and amount of which remains to be determined by a hearing in damages and a final judgment thereon. De Hoff v Black, 206 NC 687, 175 SE 179.

judgment by default final. A default judgment in final form, effective by way of estoppel and res judicata, upon the allegations of the complaint. De Hoff v Black, 206 NE 687, 175 NE 179.

judgment by nil dicit. Same as **judgment nihil dicit**.

judgment by non sum informatus (juj'mẹnt bī non sum in-for-mā'tus). A judgment rendered when, instead of entering a plea or answer, the defendant's attorney says he is not informed of any answer to be given to the action. 30A Am J Rev ed Judgm § 119.

judgment by one's peers. See **judgment of his peers**.

judgment creditor. A creditor who has secured a judgment against his debtor for the amount of his debt; a person in whose favor a judgment has been entered, which has not been satisfied.

judgment creditor's action. As usually understood, an action in equity or of an equitable nature to enforce the payment of the judgment out of property or interests of the debtor which cannot be reached by ordinary legal process. 21 Am J2d Cred B § 1.

judgment debitum sine brevi (juj'mẹnt de'bi-tum sī'ne brē'vi). He owes without declaration filed; debt evidenced by confession of judgment without suit. 30A Am J Rev ed Judgm § 156.

judgment de bonis intestati (dē bō'nis in-tes-tā'tī). A judgment affecting the property of the intestate,— a proper form of judgment in all cases where an administrator is a party defendant and the estate of his deceased intestate is liable for the debt. 31 Am J2d Ex & Ad § 759.

judgment de bonis testatoris (dē bō'nis tes-tā-tō'ris). A judgment affecting the property of the testator, —a proper form of judgment in all cases where an executor is a party defendant and the estate of his decedent is liable for the debt. 31 Am J2d Ex & Ad § 759.

judgment debt. An indebtedness evidenced by a judgment; a debt owing on a judgment.

judgment debtor. A person against whom a judgment has been entered and which has not been satisfied.

judgment debtor summons. A summons issued against a debtor under the English Bankruptcy Act.

judgment de melioribus damnis (juj'mẹnt dē me-li-ō'ri-bus dam'nis). A judgment for the highest amount found by the jury, where its verdict differs in amounts as to the different defendants who are liable as cotortfeasors.

judgment de tarris. A judgment obtained on a dower charge on land. Byers v Byers, 339 Pa 146, 14 A2d 93.

judgment docket. A book kept and prepared in the office of the clerk of court wherein there is noted the facts respecting judgments entered and recorded, such as the date of entry, the parties, satisfaction, execution taken and returned, the page of the complete record of the court upon which a particular judgment appears, etc. 30A Am J Rev ed Judgm § 91.

judgment d. s. b. Same as **judgment debitum sine brevi**.

judgment for want of prosecution. See **judgment of nolle prosequi; judgment of non pros**.

judgment fund statute. A statute which provides an indemnity fund for losses caused by uninsured or unknown motorists. 7 Am J2d Auto § 301.

judgment index. An index of the judgments entered in a court, alphabetically arranged, usually under the names of both plaintiff and defendant.

judgment in error. The judgment of the higher court rendered on a writ of error.

judgment in personam. A judgment, necessarily on a personal obligation, which follows the person wherever he may be, and which may be enforced by action or levy, wherever he may be found, binding the person of the defendant. A money judgment which is rendered in an action in personam, which proceeds, not against the property, but against the person; and binds only those who are parties to the action, and those in privity with them. Bardwell v Anderson, 44 Minn 97, 46 NW 315.

judgment in rem. A judgment pronounced upon the status of some particular subject matter, or rendered in a proceeding instituted against property, or brought to enforce a jus in re, with no cognizance taken of the owner or persons having a beneficial interest in the property. Combs v Combs, 240 Ky 155, 60 SW2d 368, 89 ALR 1095.

judgment lien. Security for the judgment debt. 30A Am J Rev ed Judgm § 480. A lien predicated upon the rendition or entry of judgment, the same being the right given the judgment creditor to subject by levy or seizure the property of the judgment debtor to the satisfaction of the judgment. Jones v Hall, 177 Va 658, 15 SE2d 108.

judgment nihil (or nil) dicit (juj'ment nil di'sit). A judgment against a party taken upon his failure to plead. Graves v Cameron, Castles & Storey, 77 Tex 273, 275, 14 SW 59. Substantially the same as a judgment by default. Wilbur v Maynard, 6 Colo 483, 485; Stevens v State, 100 Vt 214, 136 A 387.

judgment nisi (judgment nī'sī). A rule to show cause why judgment should not be rendered. Young v M'Pherson, 3 NJL 895, 897.
See **decree nisi**.

judgment non obstante veredicto (juj'ment non obstan'te vē-re-dik'tō). See **judgment notwithstanding the verdict**.

judgment non sum informatus (juj'ment non sum in-for-mā'tus). Same as **judgment by non sum informatus**.

judgment note. Same as **cognovit note**.

judgment notwithstanding the verdict. A judgment rendered upon a motion made after verdict but before rendition of judgment on the verdict, in which the applicant prevails in showing that he is entitled to judgment under the law notwithstanding the verdict returned against him by the jury. 30A Am J Rev ed Judgm § 292.

Although the motion for judgment notwithstanding the verdict was available only to the plaintiff at common law, it is now generally available to both parties, either as a result of judicial relaxation of the common-law rule confining the remedy to the plaintiff, or as a result of express statutory provisions granting the remedy to defendants. 30A Am J Rev ed Judgm § 292.

judgment nunc pro tunc (nunk prō tunk). See **nunc pro tunk judgment**.

judgment of affirmance. See **affirmance**.

judgment of assets in futuro (juj'ment of assets in fu-tū'rō). A judgment which is enforceable against a future interest of the defendant in real property.

judgment of cassetur billa (juj'ment of kas-ē'ter bil'-la). A decree of a court of equity ordering a dismissal of the bill.

judgment of cassetur breve (juj'ment of kas-ē'ter brē've). Same as **judgment of cassetur billa**.

judgment of conviction. A judgment against the defendant in a criminal case; a judgment denoting the action of a court of criminal jurisdiction formally declaring to the accused the legal consequences of the guilt which he has confessed or of which he has been convicted. Ellis v State, 100 Fla 27, 129 So 106, 69 ALR 783.

judgment of dismissal. See **dismissal; dismissal without prejudice; dismissal with prejudice**.

judgment of God. See **judicium Dei**.

judgment of his peers. A trial by a jury who are the peers of the party accused, being of like condition and equality in the state. 31 Am J Rev ed Jur § 7.

judgment of interpleader. Same as **decree of interpleader**.

judgment of nil capiat (nil ka'pi-at). A judgment that he (the plaintiff) take nothing.

A judgment which is entered when the defendant has pleaded in bar and the plaintiff's demurrer to the plea is overruled. Such a judgment should be entered, although there may be also one or more issues of fact; because, upon the whole, it appears that the plaintiff had no cause of action. La Tourette v Burton (US) 1 Wall 25, 53, 17 L Ed 604, 609.

judgment of nil capiat per billam (juj'ment of nil kā'pi-at per bil'lam). Same as **judgment of nil capiat per breve**.

judgment of nil capiat per breve (juj'ment of nil kā'pi-at per brē've). A judgment rendered in favor of the defendant on an issue raised by a plea in bar or by a plea in abatement.

judgment of nolle prosequi (juj'ment of nol'le prō'se-quī). A judgment rendered in favor of the defendant upon the formal refusal of the plaintiff to proceed with the action; sometimes styled nol. pros. Commonwealth v Casey, 94 Mass (12 Allen) 214, 218. A type of judgment superseded in many jurisdictions by judgment of nonsuit. Steele v Beaty, 215 NC 680, 2 SE2d 854.

judgment of nol. pros. (juj'ment of nol pros). Same as **judgment of nolle prosequi**.

judgment of non pros. (juj'ment of non pros). Abbreviation of **judgment of non prosequitur**.

judgment of non prosequitur (juj'ment of non pro-se'qui-ter). A judgment entered when the plaintiff at any stage of the proceedings fails to prosecute his action, or any part of it, in due time. 24 Am J2d Dism § 4. An old form of judgment displaced by the more modern form of involuntary nonsuit. Steele v Beaty, 215 NC 680, 2 SE2d 854.

judgment of nonsuit. See **nonsuit**.

judgment of ouster. See **ouster judgment**.

judgment of repleader. See **repleader**.

judgment of respondeat ouster (juj'ment of res-pon'de-at ous'ter). A judgment rendered against a defendant upon an issue of law raised by his dilatory plea, the effect of which is to overrule the plea and require the defendant to answer to the merits of the action.

A judgment on demurrer against the defendant should be respondeat ouster. Cooke v Crawford, 1 Tex 9.

judgment of restitution. See **restitution**.

judgment of retraxit (rē-trak'sit). A judgment rendered against a plaintiff who has withdrawn his action.
See **retraxit**.

judgment of the iron (of the ī'ern). See **judicium ferri**.

judgment of water. See **judicium aquae**.

As used in a statute giving a right to a new trial in ejectment when the judgment is rendered on either default or verdict, it has been held that the term "judgment on a verdict" was intended to embrace all cases where the decision upon which the judgment was rendered had been given on contestation, as distinguished from a "judgment on default," and that such statute applies in cases where judgment is entered on the mandate of an appellate court. Smalles v Mitchell, 143 US 99, 36 L Ed 90, 12 S Ct 353.

judgment on demurrer. The judgment rendered upon the determination made by the court after hearing a demurrer.

For conclusiveness of judgment rendered upon sustaining or overruling a demurrer, see 41 Am J1st Pl §§ 251 et seq.

judgment on the merits. A judgment based on legal rights as distinguished from mere matters of practice, procedure, jurisdiction, or from—in other words, a judgment that determines, on an issue either of law or fact, which party is right. Rosenthal v McMann, 93 Cal 505, 29 P 121.

judgment on the pleadings. A judgment rendered on motion:—in favor of the defendant for failure of the plaintiff to state a good cause of action in his complaint, declaration, or petition; in favor of the plaintiff where the defendant fails to state in his answer a defense sufficient in law to the cause of action alleged by the plaintiff or fails to tender any real issue of facts in the case. 41 Am J1st Pl § 335.

judgment on the verdict. A judgment rendered on a verdict of a jury as distinguished from a judgment rendered on a decision by the court in a trial to the court without a jury.

judgment paper. The paper on which the final judgment of the court in an action is written and signed.
See **judgment roll.**

judgment par contumace (pär kon-tu-mä'sē). In French law, a judgment condemning a person to death. President of United States v Kelly (CA2 NY) 96 F2d 787.

judgment pro confesso (juj'ment prō kon-fes'o). A **judgment by confession.**

judgment pro retorno habendo (juj'ment prō retor'nō ha-ben'dō). A judgment ordering a restoration of goods.

judgment quando acciderint (juj'ment quan'dō aksi'de-rint). A judgment rendered against an heir or an executor which can only be enforced against assets which may afterwards come into his hands.

judgment quasi in rem (juj'ment quā'sī in rem). A judgment, the object of which is to determine as between particular persons, the title to particular property or the right to possession of particular property, or to subject certain property of a particular person to the payment of a particular obligation of such person, either because such personal obligation is secured by a lien on the property, or because jurisdiction over the person of the obligor cannot be acquired. Sometimes regarded as a qualified judgment in personam rather than a qualified judgment in rem. 30A Am J Rev ed Judgm § 126.

judgment quod computet (juj'ment quod kompū'tet). A judgment ordering the defendant to render an account.

judgment quod eat inde quietus (juj'ment quod e'at in'de quī-ē'tūs). Judgment that he go hence acquitted,—a judgment of acquittal on a criminal charge. State v Buchanan (Md) 5 Harr & J 317.

judgment quod partes replacitent (juj'ment quod par'tēz re-pla'si-tent). A judgment that the parties replead.
See **repleader.**

judgment quod partitio fiat (juj'ment quod par-ti'sheō fī'at). A judgment that a partition be made, a judgment ordering a partition of property.

judgment quod recuperet (juj'ment quod rē-ku'peret). A judgment that he should recover, that is, a judgment rendered in favor of the plaintiff otherwise than on a dilatory plea.

judgment record. The record of a judgment.

judgment rendered. A judgment by judicial action. Dieffenbach v Roch, 112 NY 621, 20 NE 560.
See **rendition of judgment.**

judgment rendered and satisfied. Indicating for the purpose of a limitation provision in a liability insurance policy, the time when a final judgment is paid and satisfied. Anno: 83 ALR 759; 29A Am J Rev ed Ins § 1798.

judgment roll. A collection of papers including every part of the action or proceeding, or such parts as the statute may specify, to be preserved where the action or proceeding is in a court of record, usually the summons, affidavit of service, pleadings, instructions to the jury, minutes of the verdict or findings, the decision, if the trial was to the court, and judgment, the common practice being to include all the papers that would be printed upon an appeal. Peerson v Mitchell, 205 Okla 530, 239 P2d 1028, 26 ALR2d 1362, cert den 342 US 866, 96 L Ed 652, 72 S Ct 106.

judgment satisfied. An entry on the record indicating payment and satisfaction of a judgment.
The entry of "judgment satisfied" is not a part of the judgment of the court. It is an entry of record to be used as evidence in case there is a question about the plaintiff's right afterwards to collect the judgment. The entry has no effect on the plaintiff's right to appeal from the judgment itself. Preston v Henshaw, 192 Mass 34, 77 NE 1153.

judgment setoff. See **setoff of judgments.**

judgment vacated, verdict set aside, and new trial granted. The formal order for a new trial to be entered in the court record. Fisher v Hestonville, Mantua & Fairmount Passenger Railway Co. 185 Pa 602, 40 A 97.

Judicandum est legibus, non exemplis (jū-di-kan'dum est lē'ji-bus, non ex-em'plis). We must judge by the laws, not by examples. See 4 Bl Comm 405.

judicare (jū-di-kā're). To judge; to decide; to determine.

judicata. See **doctrine of res judicata.**

judicatio (jū-di-kā'she-ō). (Civil law.) The announcement or rendition of a judgment; the passing of a sentence.

judicatores terrarum (jū-di-kā-tō'rēz ter-rā'rum). Tenants in certain parts of England who, under their tenure, performed judicial functions.

judicatories (jö'di-kā-tō-rēz). See **church judicatory; judicatory.**

judicatory (jö'di-kạ-tō-ri). A court of justice. Macon v Shaw, 16 Ga 172, 185.
See **church judicatory.**

judicato solvendo. See **de judicato solvendo.**

judicature (jö'di-kạ-tūr). Judicial power; jurisdiction; a judicatory; a court of justice.

judicature acts (akts). Statutes which were enacted in the reign of Victoria providing for the reorganization of the courts of England.

Judicature Commission. An instrumentality of judicial reform created to make recommendations for improvement in judicial procedure and the administration of the business of the courts.

judices delegati (jū'di-sēz de-le-gā'tī). Plural of **judex delegatus.**

Judices non tenentur exprimere causam sententiae suae (jū'di-sēz non te-nen'ter ex-pri'me-re kâ'zam sen-ten'she-ē su'ē). Judges are not bound to give the reasons for their decisions.

judices ordinarii (ju'di-sēz or-di-nā'ri-ī). Plural of **judex ordinarius.**

judices pedanei (jū'di-sēz pe-da'ne-ī). Plural of **judex pedaneus.**

judices selecti (jū'di-sēz se-lek'tī). (Civil law.) Selected or chosen judges; judges chosen by the praetor to try and decide questions of fact in criminal cases, bearing remarkable resemblances to the jury of the common law. See 3 Bl Comm 366.

judicia (jū-di'she-a). (Roman law.) Trials; lawsuits; judgments; decisions.

Judicia in curia regis non adnihilentur, sed stent in robore suo quosque per errorem aut attinctum adnullentur (jū-di'she-a in kū'ri-a rē'jis non ad-ni-hi-len'ter, sed stent in ro-bō're su'ō quōs'kwe per er-rō'rem ât at-tink'tum ad-nul-len'ter). Judgments in the king's court are not to be ignored, but they stand in force until they are annulled by error or attaint.

Judicia in deliberationibus crebro maturescunt, in accelerato processu nunquam (jū-di'she-a in dē-li-be-rā-she-ō'ni-bus krē'brō ma-tū-rēs'kunt, in ak-se-le-rā'tō pro-se'su nun'quam). Judgments often mature through deliberations, never through hurried proceedings.

judicial. Characterizing whatever emanates from a judge as such, or whatever proceeds from courts of justice. State of Indiana ex rel. Hovey v Noble, 118 Ind 350, 21 NE 244; Merchants' Nat. Bank v Jaffray, 36 Neb 218, 54 NW 258. Pertaining to courts and their functions. Well-considered; decided or determined upon facts and the law.

judicial act. The act of a judge in applying the law to the situation presented, as distinguished from a legislative act which predetermines what the law shall be for future cases. Wulzen v Board of Supervisors, 101 Cal 15, 35 P 353. The act of a judge, or an officer other than a judge, performing a duty which is judicial or quasi judicial in nature. Motor Credit Co. v Tremper, 121 NJL 91, 1 A2d 301. An act performed in the exercise of judicial power. People ex rel. Riordan v Hersey, 69 Colo 492, 196 P 180, 14 ALR 631, 635.

judicial action. An adjudication upon the rights of parties who, in general, appear or are brought before the court by notice or process, and upon whose claims some decision or judgment is rendered.
See **judicial act.**

judicial admission. An admission made by a party in the course of judicial proceedings. 29 Am J2d Ev § 615.

judicial branch. See **judiciary.**

judicial business. The business transacted by courts. See **judicial act.**

judicial circuit. See **circuit.**

Judicial Code. Title 28 of the United States Code, covering the Federal Courts and Judicial Procedure.

judicial comity. See **comity.**

judicial committee of the privy council (kǫ-mit'ē of the priv'i koun'sil). An English tribunal which had jurisdiction of appeals in admiralty and lunacy cases until 1873.

Judicial Conference of the United States. A conference of judges of the United States courts on a representative basis, held pursuant to statute, the primary functions of which are to consider measures for expediting the business of the federal courts and to maintain a continuous study of the general rules of practice and procedure now or hereafter in use in such courts. 28 USC § 331.

judicial confession. A confession made before a committing magistrate or in a court in the due course of legal proceedings. 29 Am J2d Ev § 524. Narrowly defined as a plea of guilty made by the accused in a fit state of mind to plead, before a court which is competent to try him for the offense charged and which, upon the entry of the plea, is competent to enter judgment and fix the penalty. 29 Am J2d Ev § 524.

judicial contempt. Same as **contempt of court.**

judicial control. The control by a court of its own officers, such as receivers, referees, masters, etc., in the exercise of their duties. The exercise of jurisdiction to declare legislative or executive acts void as unconstitutional.

judicial convention. An agreement entered into between the parties to an action pursuant to an order of the court. A convention of delegates meeting for the nomination of candidates for judicial offices.

Judicial Council. A permanent instrumentality of judicial reform, created to study the organization and operation of the judicial system and to suggest improvements in procedure and administration.

Judicial Council of the Circuit. A council of the circuit judges for the circuit, held pursuant to statute in each federal circuit to consider the necessity of and to make orders in the interest of the effective and expeditious administration of the business of the federal courts in the circuit. 28 USC § 332.

judicial cy pres (jǫ-dish'ạl sē prā'). See **cy pres.**

judicial day. A day upon which court is in session. State v C.C.A. Judges, 48 La Ann 1079, 20 So 282. (Civil law.) One of the twenty-eight days which were allowed in each year to the praetor for deciding cases.

These days were called triverbial days, because on these days the praetor announced his jurisdiction in the words: do, dico, addico,—I give, I say, I adjudge. See 3 Bl Comm 424.

judicial decision. A decision by the court. See **decision.**

judicial decree. See **decree.**

judicial definition. The definition of a term as made by a court. Robinson v Rogers, 237 NY 467, 143 NE 647, 33 ALR 1291.

judicial department. One of the three independent departments of government which derives none of its power from either the legislative or executive departments but directly from the Constitution.

This is true of both the National Government of the United States and also of the state governments.

judicial department of the United States. The department created by article III of the Federal Constitution, consisting of one Supreme Court and of such inferior courts as Congress shall, from time to time, ordain and establish.

In these courts is vested the judicial power of the United States. This power of Congress to create inferior courts does not make it a matter of discretion to create them or not at its pleasure, but is rather a duty to vest the whole judicial power. Martin v Hunter (US) 1 Wheat 304, 4 L Ed 97.

judicial dicta. An expression of opinion by a court on a point not necessary to a decision but deliberately passed upon by the court. Scovill Mfg. Co. v Cassidy, 275 Ill 462, 114 NE 181. Sometimes given effect as a holding of the court. 20 Am J2d Cts § 190.

judicial discretion. A discretion to be exercised judicially rather than arbitrarily. A discretion founded upon the facts and circumstances presented to the court, from which it must draw a conclusion governed by the law. People v Rosner, 78 Cal App 497, 248 P 683.

The discretion conferred by statute upon courts with respect to the vacation of judgments is a legal discretion to be exercised in conformity with the spirit of the law and in a manner to subserve and not defeat the ends of justice. King v Mitchell, 188 Or 434, 214 P2d 993, 216 P2d 269, 16 ALR2d 1128.

A statutory provision authorizing a public functionary to act in his "discretion" may be construed to mean judicial discretion or not, according to the subject matter involved. Re Anderson, 191 Or 409, 229 P2d 633, 230 P2d 770, 29 ALR2d 1051, 1073.

judicial district. A division of a state for judicial purposes, sometimes as a matter of jurisdiction, at other times as a matter of venue. State ex rel. Brockmeier v Ely, 16 ND 569, 113 NW 711. The territorial unit of a federal district court.

judicial divorce. A dissolution of the marriage contract by decree of court after a judicial inquiry to ascertain the breach of the contract. Starr v Pease, 8 Conn 540, 546. A divorce granted by the court as distinguished from a legislative divorce.

judicial documents. Documents in the files of a court, constituting proof of its proceedings in particular cases. Hammatt v Emerson, 27 Me 308, 337.

judicial duty. Such a duty as legitimately pertains to an officer in the department of the government designated by the Constitution as "judicial," that is, an officer of the judiciary. State ex rel. Hovey, v Noble, 118 Ind 350, 21 NE 244.

See **judicial act.**

Judicial equity. Equity administered by a court of justice, decreeing the aequum et bonum of the case, let who or what be the parties before them. Rhode Island v Massachusetts (US) 12 Pet 657, 738, 9 L Ed 1233, 1266.

judicial error. An error into which the court itself falls. State v District Court, 55 Mont 324, 176 P 608. An error in the decision as distinguished from an error in entering the decision or making it of record. Anno: 14 ALR2d 233.

judicial estoppel. An estoppel arising from sworn statements made in the course of judicial proceedings. Helfer v Mutual Ben Health & Acci. Asso. 170 Tenn 630, 96 SW2d 1103, 113 ALR 921. Otherwise known as "estoppel by oath."

judicial ethics. Canons adopted by the American Bar Association, published in Am J2d Desk Book, Document 67.

judicial foreclosure. Foreclosure of a mortgage or lien by an action, as distinguished from foreclosure by seizure and sale.

The function of a judicial foreclosure is to declare judicially the forfeiture for condition broken, to obtain an order for sale, and to perfect a transfer of title to the purchaser. Larson v Anderson, 97 Wash 484, 166 P 774.

judicial function. A function exercised by the employment of judicial powers. People ex rel. Riordan v Hersey, 69 Colo 492, 196 P 180, 14 ALR 631, 635.

Counting, weighing, and measuring are not judicial functions, they are ministerial functions. Pickering v Moore, 67 NH 533, 32 A 828.

See **judicial power; quasi-judicial function.**

judicial immunity. The freedom of a judicial officer from personal liability for his decisions or acts.

judicial immunity of witness. An exemption from criminal prosecution promised a witness by the court in consideration of his giving testimony that may tend to incriminate him. 58 Am J1st Witn § 93.

judicial inquiry. An inquiry which investigates, declares, and enforces liabilities as they stand on present or past facts and under laws supposed already to exist. Keller v Potomac Electric Power Co. 261 US 428, 67 L Ed 731, 43 S Ct 445.

judicial intervention. A court review of an administrative determination or a restraint by the court of an administrative act.

judicial knowledge. See **judicial notice.**

judicial legislation. An uncomplimentary term applied to certain decisions. Encroachment by the court upon the function of the legislature; making law rather than declaring, construing, or enforcing the law. 16 Am J2d Const L § 225.

judicial location. The determination of the location of an easement by a court of equity. 25 Am J2d Ease § 68.

judicially. Belonging to, or emanating from, a judge. Commonwealth ex rel. Bressler v Gane (Pa) 3 Grant Cas 447, 459.

judicial mortgage. Same as **judgment lien.**

judicial notice. The cognizance of certain facts which a judge under rules of legal procedure or otherwise may properly take or act upon without proof because they are already known to him or because of that knowledge which a judge has, or is assumed to have by virtue of his office. Riley v Wallace, 188 Ky 471, 222 SW 1085, 11 ALR 337.

Judicial notice takes the place of proof and is of equal force. It displaces evidence, since it stands for the same thing. 29 Am J2d Ev § 14.

Judicial Notice of Foreign Law Act. One of the uniform laws.

judicial oath. An oath authorized by law and administered in the due and regular course of judicial proceedings. State v Bowman, 90 Me 363. The qualifying oath of a judge.

judicial office. An office constituting a part of the judicial department of government. People v Ransom, 58 Cal 558. An office, the duties and functions of which are principally judicial. People v Jackson, 191 NY 293, 84 NE 65. An office for the administration of justice by the person appointed or elected to the office, not by one acting under delegated authority. Twenty Per Cent Cases (United States v Fitzpatrick) (US) 13 Wall 568, 20 L Ed 707.

judicial officer. A judge; an incumbent of a judicial office.

See **judge; judicial office.**

judicial opinion. See **opinion of court.**

judicial partition. A compulsory partition in action by which co-owners of property cause it to be divided into as many shares as there are owners, according to their interests therein, or, if that cannot be done equitably, to be sold for the best obtainable price and the proceeds distributed. Michael v Sphier, 129 Or 413, 272 P 902, 73 ALR 1.

judicial power. That power which is granted to a court or judicial tribunal. Rhode Island v Massachusetts (US) 12 Pet 657, 738, 9 L Ed 1233, 1266. That part of the sovereign power which belongs to the courts or, at least, does not belong to the legislative or executive department. 16 Am J2d Const L § 222. A power which a regularly constituted court exercises in matters which are brought before it in the manner prescribed by statute or established rules of practice, and which do not come within the powers granted to the executive or vested in the legislative department of the government. 16 Am J2d Const L § 220. The power of a court to decide and pronounce a judgment and carry it into effect between persons who bring a case before it for decision. Muskrat v United States, 219 US 346, 55 L Ed 246, 31 S Ct 250; People ex rel. Riordan v Hersey, 69 Colo 492, 196 P 180, 14 ALR 631, 635.

The term is not capable of more precise definition but it is to be said that the common source of the power and authority of every court, and all questions concerning jurisdiction of a court must be determined according to the constitution, with the exception of certain inherent powers belonging to all courts. Re Buckles, 331 Mo 405, 53 SW2d 1055.

See **quasi judicial power.**

judicial power of the United States. The power vested in the United States Supreme Court, and such inferior courts as Congress shall from time to time ordain and establish, under and in accordance with Article III of the United States Constitution. Martin v Hunter (US) 1 Wheat 304, 4 L Ed 97.

judicial precedent. See **precedent.**

judicial proceedings. Proceedings before a court of justice or before a judge acting in a judicial capacity.

As to what constitutes a judicial proceeding within the rule of privilege as to defamatory matter published in the course of such proceedings, see 33 Am J1st L & S § 147.

judicial process. A part of the legal system, contrasting with the administrative process. 1 Am J2d Adm Law § 16. Broadly, all the acts of the court from the beginning of an action or proceeding to the end. Blair v Maxbass Secur. Bank, 44 ND 12, 176. In a more narrow sense, the means of acquiring jurisdiction over person or thing or the means of enforcing and carrying out the judgment of the court, in other words the ordinary concept of process.

See **process.**

judicial proof. A clear and evident declaration and demonstration of a matter which was before doubtful, conveyed in a judicial manner. Powell v State, 101 Ga 9, 29 SE 309. Broadly, evidence admissible under the rules of evidence. In another sense of the term, sufficient proof under the rules which determine the weight of evidence.

See **juridical proof.**

judicial question. A question within the province of the court to decide.

See **question of law.**

judicial record. See **court record.**

judicial remedy. A remedy to be pursued in a court rather than before an administrative body.

judicial review. The review of administrative action by an action or proceeding in court.

See **appeal.**

judicial sale. A sale made under the judgment or order of a court of competent authority by the sheriff or other legally appointed and commissioned to sell, the court being the vendor, while the officer appointed to sell is a mere ministerial agent. Hayes v Betts, 227 Ala 630, 151 So 692, 95 ALR 1484.

See **bid; execution sale; redemption; reserved price; stifling bids; upset price.**

judicial separation. An establishment by a decree or judgment of a competent court of the right of one spouse to live apart from the other and of the rights of property and the custody of their children, without divorce. In effect, a divorce a mensa et thoro.

judicial visit. See **visitation.**

judicial writs. Writs which were issued in an action subsequently to the issuance of the original writ or summons, and which issued under the private seal of the court and not under the great seal of England.

They were not tested in the king's name, but in the name of the chief justice if there was one, and in the name of the senior justice if there was not. See 3 Bl Comm 282.

Judicia posteriora sunt in lege fortiora (jū-di'she-a pos-te-ri-ō'ra sunt in lē'je for-she-ō'ra). The more recent decisions are the stronger in law.

judiciary. A judge; a justice. A court; the system of courts in a state or nation. A department of justice. Re Davies, 168 NY 89, 61 NE 118.

Judiciary Act (akt). An act of Congress passed in 1789, which under the Federal Constitution created the courts which were to exercise the judicial functions of the government. United States v Holliday (US) 3 Wall 407, 18 L Ed 182.

judiciary court (kōrt). The principal criminal court of Scotland.

judiciary police. Members of the police department, especially magistrates, whose function it is to prevent crimes by punishing criminals. State ex rel. Walsh v Hine, 59 Conn 50, 21 A 1024.

Judicia sunt tanquam juris dicta, et pro veritate accipiuntur (jū-di'she-a sunt tan'quam jū'ris dik'ta, et prō ve-ri-tā'te ak-si-pi-un'ter). Judgments are, as it were, the sayings of the law, and are received as truth. Laun v Kipp, 155 Wis 347, 145 NW 183, 5 ALR 655, 668.

Judiciis posterioribus fides est adhibenda (jū-di'she-is pos-te-ri-ō'ri-bus fī'dēz est ad-hi-ben'da). Confidence should be reposed in the more recent decisions.

Judici officium suum excedenti non paretur (jū'di-sī of-fi'she-um sū'um ex-sē-den'tī non pa-rē'ter). A judge need not be obeyed when he exceeds his jurisdiction.

judiciously. With the exercise of good judgment. Cotes & Patchin v Davenport, 9 Iowa 227, 236.

Judici satis poena est quod Deum habet ultorem (jū'di-sī sa'tis pē'na est quod Dē'um hā'bet ul-tō'rem). It is a sufficient punishment for a judge that he has God as his avenger.

Judicis est in pronuntiando sequi regulam, exceptione non probata (jū'di-sis est in prō-nun-she-an'dō se'quī re-gū'lam, ex-sep-she-ō'ne non prō-bā'ta). The exception not having been proved, it is the duty of the judge to follow the rule.

Judicis est judicare secundum allegata et probata (jū'di-sis est jū-di-kā're se-kun'dum al-le-gā'ta et prō-bā'ta). It is the duty of the judge to decide in conformity with the pleadings and the proofs.

Judicis est jus dicere non dare (jū'di-sis est jūs dī'ke-re non da're). It is the duty of the judge to administer justice and not to make law.

Judicis officium est opus diei in die suo perficere (jū'di-sis of-fi'she-um est o'pus dī'ē-ī in dī'ē su'ō per-fi'se-re). It is the duty of the judge to complete the day's work within the day.

Judicis officium est ut res ita tempora rerum quarere; quaesito tempore tutus eris (ju'di-sis of-fi'she-um est ut rēz i'ta tem'po-ra rē'rum kwē're-re; kwē-si'tō tem'po-re tū'tus e'ris). It is as much the duty of the judge to inquire into the times of things as into the things themselves; by inquiring into the time you will be safe.

judicium (jū-di'she-um). A trial; an action; a decision; an opinion; a judgment; a proceeding before a "judex" or judge. State ex rel. Moreland v Whitford, 54 Wis 150, 157.

Judicium a non suo judice datum nullius est momenti (jū-di'she-um ā non su'ō jū'di-se dā'tum nul-lī'us est mo-men'tī). A judgment rendered by a person who is not a judge is of no avail.

judicium aquae (jū-di'she-um ā'kwē). The judgment of water.

This judgment represented the outcome of a trial by water-ordeal, which was performed either by plunging the defendant's bare arm up to the elbow in boiling water, or by casting him into a pool of water. If he escaped harm from the boiling water, or sank in the plunge, he was deemed innocent and acquitted, but if he was scalded by the hot water, or if he floated when thrown into the pool, he was adjudged guilty. See 4 Bl Comm 343.

judicium capitale (jū-di'she-um ka-pi-tā'le). A judgment or sentence of death.

judicium Dei (jū-di'she-um Dē'ī). The judgment of God,—the judgment which was the culmination of a trial by ordeal of fire or water, and was sometimes called vulgaris purgatio—common purgation—to distinguish it from the canonical purgation which was by the oath of the party. See 4 Bl Comm 342.

Judicium est quasi juris dictum (ju-di'she-um est quā'sī jū'ris dik'tum). A judgment is, as it were, a command of the law.

judicium ferri (jū-di'she-um fer'rī). The judgment of the iron.

This judgment was the culmination of a trial by fire-ordeal, which was performed either by taking up in the hand a piece of red-hot iron of from one to three pounds weight, or else by walking barefoot and blindfold over nine red-hot ploughshares, laid lengthwise at equal distances. If the accused escaped unhurt, he was acquitted, but if otherwise, as was usually the case, he was adjudged guilty. See 4 Bl Comm 342.

judicium ignis (jū-di'she-um ig'nis). The judgment of fire.

See **judicium ferri**.

Judicium non debet esse illusorium; suum effectum habere debet (jū-di'she-um non de'bet es'se il-lū-sō'ri-um; su'um ef-fek'tum hā-bē're de'bet). A judgment ought not to be illusory; it ought to have its effect.

judicium parium (jū-di'she-um pa'ri-um). The judgment of his peers.

judicium pro rege (jū-di'she-um prō rē'je). A judgment in favor of the king.

Judicium redditur in invitum (jū-di-she-um red'di-ter in in-vī'tum). A judgment is rendered against one's will. It is not a contract and is not to be so considered. O'Brien v Young, 95 NY 428.

Judicium redditur in invitum in praesumptione legis (jū-di'she-um red'di-ter in in-vī'tum in prē-zump-she-ō'ne lē'jis). In presumption of law, a judgment is rendered against one's will.

Judicium semper pro veritate accipitur (ju-di'she-um sem'per prō ve-ri-tā'te ak-si'pi-ter). A judgment is always accepted as true.

jug. An earthenware, plastic, or glass container of liquids, having a small mouth. Slang for jail or prison.

jugerum (jö'je-rum). A Roman land measure which was equivalent to a little more than half a modern acre, and specifically, measured 240 by 120 feet.

jugulator (jö'gū-lā-tor). A cutthroat; an assassin; a murderer.

jugum (jö'gum). (Civil law.) An ox-yoke; a yoke of land, being a quantity which was ploughable by one ox-team in a day.

jugum terrae (jö'gum ter'rē). A yoke of land.
See **yoke**.

juicio (hoo-ee'the-o). (Spanish.) An action; a suit; a trial; a judgment.

juicio de apeo (hoo-ee'the-o day ah-pay'o). (Spanish.) A decree establishing a boundary.

juicio de concurso de acreedores (hoo-ee'the-o day con-coor'so day ay-cray-ay-dor'es). (Spanish.) A judgment against an insolvent debtor directing a pro rata payment to his creditors out of the assets of his estate.

juke box. A record player, found in restaurants and saloons, which operates upon the dropping of a coin in a slot; expressly declared an amusement by statute in some jurisdictions. Fierri v Williamsport, 384 Pa 568, 120 A2d 889.

Julian calendar (jö'lyan kal'en-dar). The calendar instituted by Julius Caesar in 46 B. C., dividing the year into twelve months to consist alternately of thirty and thirty-one days, with the exception of February, which was to have twenty-nine days in ordinary years and thirty in leap years, and every third year was a leap year.

The Julian Calendar assumed the length of the year to be 365-1/4 days, whereas it is eleven minutes and some seconds shorter, making an error of three fourths of a day in a century. The Gregorian Calendar reduced this error to one day in thirty centuries.

See **Gregorian Calendar**.

Julian law of treason. See **lex Julia majestatis**.

jument (jö'ment). A plough ox.

jumenta (jö-men'tạ). (Civil law.) Beasts of burden; animals used for carrying or draughting.

jump bail (jump bāl). To flee while released on bail.

jumper. A technical term for a wire used to intercept or cut out a part of an electric circuit. Ballard v State, 68 Okla Crim 39, 95 P2d 239. A wire used in starting the motor of an automobile without a key to the ignition. Edwards v Hartford, 145 Conn 141, 139 A2d 599.

jumper wire. See **jumper**.

Jun. An abbreviation of junior, infrequently used.

Juncta juvant (junk'ta ju'vant). United, they flourish. Things which are void severally may be valid jointly.

junction. In its ordinary acceptation as applied to railroads, the point or locality where two or more lines of railway meet.

Two lines of distinct companies, or separate roads of the same company, or a main line and a branch road of the same company, may have points of union or meeting, styled junctions, but this can hardly be predicated of a single continuous road from one point to another. United States v Oregon & California Railroad Co. 164 US 526, 41 L Ed 541, 17 S Ct 165.

See **intersection**.

junior. Adjective: Younger; of secondary consequence, standing, or rank; that is junior over which something else stands prior in right. Noun: A suffix appended to a name to indicate a person as the son of a person of the same name; no part of the legal name, being nothing more than a mere title. Huff v State Election Board, 168 Okla 277, 32 P2d 920, 93 ALR 906. Abbreviated "Jr." and "Jun." Carleton v Townsend, 28 Cal 219. No part of a man's name; not essential to the docketing of the judgment against a son, although his father has the same name and resides in the same county. Foshier v Narver, 24 Or 441, 34 P 21.

junior college. A school offering courses of instruction on the level of difficulty for the first two years above high school level, irrespective of the breadth or variety of the field of education covered. Nixon-Clay Commercial College v Woods (Tex Civ App) 176 SW2d 1015, error ref. Best understood as a college providing instruction equivalent to the first two years of an ordinary college, intended to provide a general education so far as the period of study and instruction permits, also to qualify graduates to transfer to other colleges and universities for further work. Pollitt v Lewis, 269 Ky 680, 108 SW2d 671, 113 ALR 691. Not a common school or a public school. Anno: 113 ALR 711.

junior creditor. A creditor whose claim is subject to the claim or claims of another creditor or creditors which have priority by force of law.

junior encumbrance. A mortgage or other lien which is inferior in point of priority in law to another mortgage or lien.

junior encumbrancer. A person holding a lien or encumbrance which is in point of priority in law to another lien or encumbrance.

junior equities. Equitable interests in real estate which are junior in point of priority in law to other equities. 55 Am J1st V & P §§ 678 et seq.

See **inferior equity**.

junior execution. An execution levied after a levy on the same property under another execution issued upon a different judgment. 30 Am J2d Exec § 515. A writ of execution bearing a date subsequent to that of an execution against the same defendant issued upon a different judgment. Continental Distributing Co. v Hays, 86 Wash 300, 150 P 416.

junior high. See **high school**.

junior incumbrance. See **junior encumbrance**.

junior incumbrancer. See **junior encumbrancer**.

junior judgment. A judgment which is inferior in point of priority in law to another judgment entered against the same defendant.

junior mortgage. A mortgage over which another mortgage has priority in law.

junior operator's license. A license for the operation of a motor vehicle, with restrictions in reference to the hours of driving, the presence of an adult licensed driver in the vehicle, etc., imposed due to the youth of the licensee. 7 Am J2d Auto § 97.

junior-right (jō-nyọr-rīt). Also called borough-English,—the right of the youngest son to inherit the estate of his deceased father.

junior widow. The surviving spouse of a decedent, claiming dower in lands to which the surviving spouse of an ancestor of the decedent is entitled to dower. 25 Am J2d Dow § 87.

juniperus sabina (jō-ni′pe-rus sā-bī′na). A plant sometimes called "savin," the product of which is employed in producing abortions.

junk. A word of nautical origin, meaning old or condemned cable and cordage cut into small pieces, which, when untwisted, were used for various purposes on the ship. 47 Am J1st Sec H D § 2. Articles of no value except for the reclaimable material in them. Worn-out or discarded material that still may be turned to some use, especially old metals, ropes, rags, glass, paper, or clothing. State v Shapiro, 131 Md 168, 101 A 703.

Secondhand furniture is not junk. Duluth v Bloom, 55 Minn 97, 56 NW 580.

junk dealer. A person who makes it his business to buy or sell junk as a trader. State v Rosenbaum, 80 Conn 327, 68 A 250; State v Shapiro, 131 Md 168, 101 A 703.

junking motor vehicles. The business of buying up used cars and placing them in a junk yard where they will be available for the removal and sale of their parts or for sale as mere junk. 47 Am J1st Sec H D § 11.

junk shop. A building or room in which junk is sold. Duluth v Bloom, 55 Minn 97, 56 NW 580.

junk yard. A place where junk is stored or stored and sold.

junta (jun′tạ). Same as **junto**.

junto (jun′tō). A secret political council; a political faction.

jura (jū′ra). Rights. Laws.

jura ad personam (jū′ra ad per-sō′nam). Rights in personam, rights against the person.

jura ad rem (jū′ra ad rem). Rights in rem; rights against the thing.

jura coronae (jū′ra ko-rō′nē). Private rights of the crown. Geiger v Filor, 8 Fla 325, 337.

Jura ecclesiastica limitata sunt infra limites separatos (jū′ra e-klē-si-as′ti-ka li-mi-tā′ta sunt in′fra lī′-mi-tēz se-pa-rā′tōs). Ecclesiastical laws are limited within distinct confines.

Jura eodem modo destituuntur quo constituuntur (jū′ra ē-ō′dem mō′dō des-ti-tu-un′ter quō kon-sti-tu-un′ter). Laws are repealed in the same manner in which they are enacted.

jura fiscalia (jū′ra fis-kā′li-a). Fiscal rights,—rights in the royal revenue. See 3 Bl Comm 45.

jura in re (jū′ra in rē). Rights in a thing.

jura in re aliena (jū′ra in rē ā-li-ē′na). (Civil law.) Rights in property belonging to another person. See Mackeldey's Roman Law § 237.

jural (jö′rạl). Pertaining or relating to law or to legal matters.

jura majestatis (jū'ra ma-jes-tā'tis). (Civil law.) The rights of sovereignty.
    Among these rights is the jus eminens, or the supreme power of the state over its members and whatever belongs to them. When applied to property alone, it is called dominium eminens, or the right of eminent domain; that is, the right of the sovereignty to use the property of its members for the public good or public necessity. Gilmer v Lime Point, 18 Cal 229, 251.

juramenta (jū-ra-men'ta). Plural of **juramentum**.

juramentum (ju-ra-men'tum). (Civil law.) An oath.

juramentum calumniae (jū'ra-men'tum ka-lum'ni-ē). (Civil law.) The oath of calumny,—an oath disclaiming malice, which was required of each of the parties to an action before trial.

Juramentum corporalis (jū-ra-men'tum kor-po-rā'lis). A corporal oath, an oath taken by swearing on the Bible.

Juramentum est affirmatio vel negatio de aliquo, attestatione sacrae rei firmata (jū-ra-men'tum est af-fir-mā'she-ō vel ne-gā'she-ō dē a'li-quō, at-tes-tā-she-ō'ne sak're rē'ī fir-mā'ta). An oath is an affirmation or a denial concerning any matter, confirmed by the attestation of a sacred thing.

Juramentum est indivisibile; et non est admittendum in parte verum et in parte falsam (jū-ra-men'tum est in-dī-vī-si'bi-le; et non est ad-mit-ten'dum in par'te vē'rum et in par'te fal'sam). An oath is indivisible; and it is not to be accepted as partly true and partly false.

juramentum fidelitatis (jū-ra-men'tum fī-de-li-tā'tis). The oath of fealty, which was the oath which bound the tenant to his lord's service under feudal tenure. See 2 Bl Comm 45.

juramentum necessarium (jū-ra-men'tum ne-ses-sā'ri-um). (Civil law.) A necessary oath,—an oath as to the truth of any matter which a party was required to make on the demand of the other party, and which when so made was binding on such other party.

juramentum voluntarium (jū-ra-men'tum vo-lun-tā'ri-um). (Civil law.) The voluntary oath,—an oath which a party to an action was not required to make, but when made, the other party was required to answer it under oath.

Jura naturae sunt immutabilia (jū'ra nā-tū'rē sunt im-mu-ta-bi'li-a). The laws of nature are unchangeable. Anderson v Wilkins, 142 NC 154, 55 SE 272.

jura personarum (jū'ra per-so-nā'rum). The rights of persons,—such rights as belong to every person. See 1 Bl Comm 122.

jura praediorum (jū'ra prē-di-ō'rum). (Civil law.) The rights of landed estates.

jura publica (jū'ra pub'li-ka). Public rights, also called "jura communia," among which are the rights of navigation and fishery; so called in contradistinction to jura coronae, the private rights of the crown. Geiger v Filor, 8 Fla 325, 337.

Jura publica anteferenda privatis (jū'ra pub'li-ka an-te-fe-ren'da prī-vā-tis). Public rights are to be preferred to private rights.

Jura publica ex privato promiscue decidi non debent (jū'ra pub'li-ka ex prī-vā'tō prō-mis'ku-e dē'si-dī non de'bent). Public rights ought not to be decided promiscuously with private right.

jurare (jū-rā're). To swear; to make oath; to affirm on oath.

Jurare est Deum in testum vocare, et est actus divini cultus (jū-rā're est Dē'um in tes'tum vō-kā're, est est ak'tus di-vī'nī kul'tus). To swear is to call upon God to witness, and it is an act of divine reverence.

jura regalia (jū'ra rē-gā'li-a). Royal rights,—a term comprehending not only those rights which pertain to the political character and authority of the king, but also those rights which are incidental to his regal dignity, and may be severed at his pleasure from the crown and vested in his subjects.

jura regia (jū'ra rē'ji-a). Same as **jura regalia**.

Jura regis specialia non conceduntur per generalia verba (jū'ra rē'jis spe-she-ā'li-a non kon-sē-dun'ter per je-ne-rā'li-a ver'ba). Special rights are not granted by the crown in general terms.

jura rerum (jū'ra rē'rum). The rights of things,—such rights as a man may acquire over external objects, or things unconnected with his person. See 1 Bl Comm 122.

Jura sanguinis nullo jure civili dirimi possunt (jū'ra san'gwi-nis nul'lō jū're si-vi-lī di'ri-mī pos'sunt). The rights of blood cannot be destroyed by any provisions of the civil law. Jackson v Phillips, 96 Mass (14 Allen) 539, 562.

jura summi imperii (jū'ra sum'mī im-pe'ri-ī). The rights of sovereignty.

jurat (jū'rat). The evidence that an affidavit has been duly sworn by the affiant; a certificate evidencing the fact that the affidavit was properly made before a duly authorized officer, the usual and proper form being "Subscribed and sworn to before me," followed by the date, signature, and title of the officer. 3 Am J2d Affi § 16.
    Although it has been said that, strictly speaking, the jurat is not a part of the affidavit, common prudence dictates that a properly executed jurat be attached to every affidavit. Cox v Stern, 170 Ill 442, 48 NE 906.
    See **jurats**.

jurata (jū-rā'ta). A jury; a trial jury.

juration (jū-rā'shọn). The taking of an oath; the administration of an oath by one authorized.

Jurato creditur in judicio (jū-rā'tō kre'di-ter in jū-di'she-ō). A person who is sworn is to be believed in a judicial proceeding.

jurator (jū-rā'tor). A juror or member of a jury; a compurgator.
    See **distringas juratores**.

juratores (jū-rā-tō'rēz). Plural of jurator.

Juratores debent esse vicini, sufficientes et minus suspecti (jū-rā-tō'rez de'bent es'se vi-sī'nī, suf-fi-she-en'tez et mī'nus sus-pek'tī). Jurors ought to be of the vicinage, sufficiently well off, and free from suspicion.

Juratores sunt judices facti (ju-rā-tō'rēz sunt jū'di-sēz fak'tī). The jurors are the judges of fact.

juratory (jō'rạ-tọ-ri). Relating or pertaining to an oath.
    See **caution juratory**.

jurats (jū'rats). Sworn officers who formed the governing body in certain communities in England.
    Plural of **jurat**.

jure (ju're). In right; in law; by right; by law.

jure alluvionis (jū're al-lu-vi-ō'nis). By the right of alluvion,—by the right to land formed by the gradual washing up of sand and earth on the shore of a river.

jure alterius. See **in jure alterius.**

jure belli (jū're bel'lī). By the law of war. See **prize goods.**

jure civile (jū're si'vi-le). By the civil law of the Romans.

jure coronae (jū're ko-ro'nē). By right of the crown; by royal right. Arnold v Mundy, 6 NJL 1.

jure divino (jū're di-vī'nō). By divine right.

jure ecclesiae (jū're e-kle'si-ē). By right of the church; by the ecclesiastical law.

jure emphyteutico (jū're em-fi-tu'ti-kō). (Roman law.) By right of emphyteusis. See **emphyteusis.**

jure gentium (jū're jen'she-um). By the law of nations.

jure mariti (jū're ma'rī-tī). By the right of a husband.

jure naturae (jū're na-tū'rē). By the law of nature.

Jure naturae aequum est neminem cum alterius detrimento et injuria fieri locupletiorem (jū're nā-tū'rē ē'qu-um est nē'mi-nem kum al-te'ri-us de-tri-men'tō et in-jū'ri-a fī'e-rī lo-ku-ple-she-ō'rem). By natural law it is just that no one be enriched through the loss or injury of another. Berry v Stigall, 253 Mo 690, 162 SW 126.

jure propinquitatis (jū're pro-pin-qui-tā'tis). By right of relationship.

jure proprio. See **in jure proprio.**

jure representationis (jū're re-pre-zen-tā-she-ō'nis). By right of representation.

"There is no difference between the descent to George and the descent to John his son, who, jure representationis, is the same with the father." Lessee of Levy v M'Cartee, (US) 6 Pet 102, 115, 8 L Ed 334, 339.

jure uxoris (jū're u-xō'ris). In the right of the wife.

jure uxoris estate (jū're u-xō'ris es-tāt'). The common-law freehold estate of a husband in real property of which his wife is, at the time of the marriage, seised in fee or in which she has a life estate; also extending to real estate of which the wife becomes seised after the marriage. An estate in the right of the wife, entitling the husband to the possession, use, income, and usufruct of the property, but not continuing beyond the death of either of the spouses. Hopper v Gurtman, 126 NJL 263, 18 A2d 245, 133 ALR 624.

juridical (jū-rid'i-kal). Pertaining to the law; pertaining to the administration of justice.

juridical days. Days which are legal for the holding of court.

juridical proof. A clear and evident declaration or demonstration of a matter which before was doubtful, conveyed in a judicial manner. Powell v State, 101 Ga 9, 21. See **judicial proof.**

juridicus (jū-ri'di-kus). Same as **juridical.**

Juri non est consonum quod aliquis accessorius in curia regis convincatur antequam aliquis de facto fuerit attinctus (jū'rī non est kon-sō'num quod a'li-quis ak-ses-sō'ri-us in kū'ri-a rē'jis kon-vin-kā'ter an'te-quam a'li-quis dē fak'tō fu'e-rit at-tink'tus). It is not consonant with the law that any accessory should be convicted in the king's court before anyone has been attainted of the fact.

juris consultus (jū'ris kon-sul'tus). Learned in the law.

jurisdictio (jū-ris-dik'she-ō). Same as **jurisdiction.**

Jurisdictio est potestas de publico introducta, cum necessitate juris dicendi (jū-ris-dik'she-ō est potes'tās dē pub'li-kō in-trō-duk'ta, kum ne-ses-si-tā'te jū'ris dī-sen'dī). Jurisdiction is a power introduced for the public welfare, through the necessity of administering the law.

jurisdiction. A term used in two senses as it applies to a court: (1) In a general sense, the abstract right of a court to exercise its powers in causes of a certain class; (2) in a particular sense, the right of a tribunal to exercise its power with respect to a particular matter. In other words, the power of the court over the subject matter, over the res or property in contest, and for the rendition of the judgment or decree the court assumes to make. 20 Am J2d Cts §§ 87, 88. Summarily stated, the power to act judicially. Industrial Addition Asso. v Commissioner, 323 US 310, 89 L Ed 260, 65 S Ct 289; Monarch Anthracite Mining Co. (CA3 Pa) 102 F2d 337. The power to hear, determine, and adjudicate. Mellette County v Arnold, 76 SD 210, 75 NW2d 641, 644. In criminal case, the jurisdiction which exists for the punishment of crimes; the power of a court to inquire into the fact, to apply the law, and to declare the punishment, in a regular course of judicial proceeding, embracing every kind of judicial action on the subject matter, from finding the indictment to pronouncing the sentence. State v Smith, 29 RI 513, 72 A 710.

Sometimes referring to the power or authority of administrative or executive agencies, even to the power of the state. 20 Am J2d Cts § 87. Sometimes referring to the territorial area, national or state, by way of indicating the law applicable to a case or the place where a cause was tried.

jurisdictional. Vital or essential to the jurisdiction of the court or other tribunal before which a matter is pending.

jurisdictional amount. See **amount in controversy.**

jurisdictional defect. A defect, whether of omission or commission, in process, pleading, parties, or procedure which deprives the court of jurisdiction.

Neither the fact that an action is brought in the wrong county, nor that other persons should have been joined as parties is necessarily a jurisdictional defect. Stratton v Beaver Farmers' Canal & Ditch Co. 82 Colo 118, 257 P 1077.

jurisdictional dispute. Conflicting claims by labor unions over representation of employees or over the right to do certain types of work. 31 Am J Rev ed Labor § 391.

jurisdictional fact doctrine. The principle that even though supported by evidence, an administrative determination of certain fundamental facts bearing upon a constitutional or jurisdictional issue is not conclusive upon the courts, and that, with respect to such a determination, the courts have the power and duty to exercise their own independent judgment. 2 Am J2d Admin L § 692.

jurisdictional plea. A plea in contest of the jurisdiction of the court; either a plea in abatement or a plea in bar, according to whether the objection is to a particular court or to the subject matter in

JURISDICTION [691] JUROR

controversy whatever the particular court may be. United States v J. L. Hopkins & Co. (DC NY) 288 F 173.

jurisdiction clause. That essential clause in a bill in equity upon which the complainant bases his claim of the jurisdiction of the court in which the suit is brought.

jurisdiction in equity. See **equity jurisdiction.**

jurisdiction in personam. Jurisdiction over the person of the defendant which can be acquired only by service of process upon the defendant in the state to which the court belongs or by his voluntary submission to jurisdiction. Pennoier v Neff, 95 US 714, 24 L Ed 565.

jurisdiction in rem. Jurisdiction over a res or thing situated in the state, which may be property or a status or relation. Hamm v Hamm, 30 Tenn App 122, 204 SW2d 113, 175 ALR 523. That jurisdiction of the property in contest in an action which is obtained by a seizure under process of the court, whereby it is held to abide such order as the court may make concerning it. Cooper v Reynolds' Lessee (US) 10 Wall 308, 19 L Ed 931, 932.

jurisdiction of federal courts. The power of the court to hear and determine the subject matter in controversy between parties to a suit—the power to decide a justiciable controversy. Binderup v Pathe Exchange, 263 US 291, 68 L Ed 308, 44 S Ct 96. Jurisdiction as conferred by the United States Constitution and acts of Congress enacted under the authority of the Constitution and in conformity therewith. Lockerty v Phillips, 319 US 182, 87 L Ed 1339, 63 S Ct 1019.

jurisdiction of the cause. In the broader sense, the power of the court to proceed to the administration of justice in a particular case, considered from any angle affecting such power, be it want of service of process, the absence of the requisite amount in controversy, etc. In a more precise sense, the power over the subject matter, given by the law of the sovereignty in which the tribunal exists. Re Taylor, 7 SD 382, 64 NW 253.

jurisdiction of the person. See **jurisdiction in personam.**

jurisdiction of the res. See **jurisdiction in rem.**

jurisdiction of the subject matter. The power of a court to hear and determine cases of the general class to which the action in question belongs. Schillerstrom v Schillerstrom, 75 ND 667, 32 NW2d 106, 2 ALR2d 271. A jurisdiction not dependent upon the state of facts which may appear in a particular case, or the ultimate existence of a good cause of action in the plaintiff therein. Parker Bros. v Fagan (CA5 Fla) 68 F2d 616.

jurisdiction quasi in rem. Jurisdiction neither strictly in personam nor strictly in rem; an action in personam where a thing or res is indirectly affected by the decision. Hanson v Denekla, 357 US 235, 2 L Ed 1283, 78 S Ct 1228, reh den 358 US 858, 3 L Ed 2d 92, 79 S Ct 10. Jurisdiction in a proceeding affecting a status or relation, for example, a marital status. Hamm v Hamm, 30 Tenn App 122, 204 SW2d 113, 175 ALR 523.

Juris effectus in executione consistit (jū′ris ef-fek′tus in ex-e-ku-she-ō′ne kon-sis′tit). The effectiveness of the law lies in its execution. An execution is the end of the law. Central Nat Bank v Stevens, 169 US 432, 465, 42 L Ed 807, 819, 18 S Ct 403.

juris et de jure (jū′ris et dē jū′re). Of law and by or from law.
The expression is one which is applied to conclusive presumptions; that is presumptions of law which the law does not permit to be disputed or disproved.

juris et seisinae conjunctio (jū′ris et sē′zi-nē konjunk′she-ō). The union of right and seisin, that is the double right, of possession joined with the right of property, which is essential to every good and complete title to real property. See 2 Bl Comm 199.

juris gentium (jū′ris jen′she-um). Of the law of nations.

Juris ignorantia est, cum jus nostram ignoramus (jū′ris ig-nō-ran′she-a est, kum jūs nos′tram ig-nō-rā′mus). It is ignorance of the law when we are ignorant of our own rights. Haven v Foster, 26 Mass (9 Pick) 112.

juris jurando. See **exceptio juris jurando.**

jurisperitus (jū-ris-per-ī′tus). Skilled or learned in the law.

juris positivi (jū′ris po-si-tī′vī). Of positive law.

Juris praecepta sunt haec, honeste vivere, alterum non laedere, suum cuique tribuere (jū′ris prē-sep′ta sunt hēk, ho-nes′te vi′ve-re, al′te-rum non lē′de-re, su′um kī′kwe tri-bu′e-re). The precepts of the law are these, to live honestly, not to injure another, and to give to each one his due.

juris privati (jū′ris prī-vā′tī). Of private right; not clothed with a public interest. Munn v Illinois, 94 US 113, 24 L Ed 77.

jurisprudence. The science of law. A division of law, such as admiralty. A treatise on the law or particular subjects of the law, such as American Jurisprudence or Ohio Jurisprudence.

jurisprudentia (jū-ris-pru-den′she-a). Same as **jurisprudence.**

Jurisprudentia est divinarum atque humanarum rerum notitia; justi atque injusti scientia (jū-ris-pruden′she-a est di-vi-nā′rum at′kwe hu-man-ā′rum rē′rum no-ti′she-a; jus′tī at′kwe in-jus′tī sī-en′she-a). Jurisprudence is the knowledge of things divine and human; it is the science of justice and injustice.

Jurisprudentia legis communis Angliae est scientia, socialis et copiosa (jū-ris-pru-den′she-a lē′jis kommū′nis An′gli-ē est si-en′she-a, so-she-ā′lis et kō-pi-ō′sa). The jurisprudence of the common law of England is a science, social and rich.

juris publici (jū′ris pub′li-sī). Of public or common right.

jurist (jū′rist). A person who is learned in the law.

juristic act (jū-ris′tik akt). An act which is calculated to have legal effect.

juris utrius doctor (jū′ris u-trī′us dok′tor). Doctor of both laws; that is, doctor of civil and canon law, a university degree, abbreviated J. U. D.

juris utrum (jū′ris ut′rum). A writ sometimes called the parson's writ of right, which lay for an incumbent parson or prebendary at common law and for a vicar by statute, to recover land alienated by his predecessor. See 3 Bl Comm 252.

juro (hoo′ro). A kind of pension which is granted by the king of Spain in recognition of public service.

juror. A person on the jury list or roll—any person in a county, city, district, or other venue listed for jury service for a definite period, such as a year, or for an indefinite period. A person whose name has been drawn from the jury list or roll and placed in the jury wheel or box. In common usage, a venireman—a person whose name has been drawn from the wheel for a venire or special venire and who has been summoned by a writ of venire and is thereby upon the jury panel for a term of court, or part of a term, or a panel from which jurors are to be selected for a particular case. 31 Am J Rev ed Jur § 3. Most narrowly defined, a member of a jury which has been sworn to try a case. Anno: 34 ALR 1119.

jury. A body of laymen selected by lot, or by some other fair and impartial means, to ascertain, under the guidance of a judge, the truth in questions of fact arising in either a civil or criminal proceeding. 31 Am J Rev ed Jur § 2. A body of 12 jurors at common law. 31 Am J Rev ed Jur § 121.
See **challenge for cause; demand for a jury; grand jury; hung jury; instructions to jury; packing a jury; peremptory challenge; separation of jury; special jury; struck jury; talesmen; traverse jury; venire; voir dire examination.**

jury box. That portion of the court room in which the jury are seated during the trial of a case.
See **jury wheel.**

jury commissioner. An officer having administrative duties in reference to the compiling of a jury list, the drawing of jurors for a panel, and the summoning of jurors on the panel for duty.

jury de medietate linguae (ju'ri de me-di-e-tā'te lin'gwē). A jury seldom, if ever, known to American Jurisprudence, but existing in England from 1353 until abolished by the statute, 33 Victoria, Chapter 14, composed one-half each of English speaking persons and of persons speaking the language of the accused, a foreigner, on trial. Respublica v Mesca (Pa) 1 Dall 73, 1 L Ed 42.

jury list. A list of names of all persons in a county, city, district, or other venue subject to call for jury service. 31 Am J Rev ed Jur § 3.

juryman. See **juror.**

jury of annoyance. A special jury which was summoned to investigate and return a report upon public nuisances alleged to exist within the county.

jury of coroner. See **inquest jury.**

jury of inquest. See **inquest jury.**

jury of jealous women. A jocose expression for a jury composed of women, or of women for the most part, in a case where a beautiful girl or young woman is a party, especially where the reputation of such party is drawn in issue.

jury of matrons. A jury employed in England until well into the 19th century, and on rare occasions in the United States, to determine the pregnancy of a woman condemned to death, also to determine the fact of pregnancy where a woman was under suspicion of feigning pregnancy by her deceased husband as a reason for withholding land from the next heir. Union Pacific R. Co. v Botsford, 141 US 250, 35 L Ed 734, 11 S Ct 1000.

jury of peers. See **peer.**

jury of physicians. A jury to inquire into the pregnancy of a woman sentenced to punishment by death. New York Criminal Code § 500.

jury of sheriff. See **sheriff's jury.**

jury of the country. A jury of peers of the accused, being persons of like condition and quality. 31 Am J Rev ed Jur § 7.

jury of the county. A jury drawn from the entire area of venue, as distinguished from an ancient jury drawn from the immediate vicinity of the event giving rise to the action or criminal prosecution. State v Brown, 103 Vt 312, 154 A 579, 76 ALR 1029.

jury of view. A jury in condemnation proceedings and proceedings to vacate certain ways as nuisances. 31 Am J Rev ed Jur § 2.
See **view by jury.**

jury panel. The jury list. The jury empaneled for the trial of a particular case.
See **jury list.**

jury process. The process of a court employed to summon jurors to attend court and to compel their attendance.
See **venire.**

jury roll. Same as **jury list.**

jury room. The room in a courthouse wherein the jury conduct their deliberations.

jury tampering. See **tampering with jury.**

jury trial. See **trial by jury.**

jury view. See **view by jury.**

jury wheel. A receptacle from which the names of persons on the jury list are drawn for summoning as jurors for a term of court, or a part of a term, or for service in a particular case. 31 Am J Rev ed Jur § 3.

jurywoman. A woman serving as a juror.
See **jury of matrons.**

jus (jus). Right; justice; law. Freichnecht v Meyer, 39 NJ Eq 551, 560.

jus abstinendi (jūs ab-sti-nen'dī). (Civil law.) The right of renouncing, also called potestas abstinendi (the power of renouncing),—that is, the right which an heir had to renounce his paternal inheritance. See Mackeldey's Roman Law § 733.

jus abutendi (jūs ab-u-ten'dī). The right of abusing; that is the right of doing what one pleases with his own; hence, full ownership.

jus accrescendi (jūs a-kre-sen'dī). The right of survivorship, which vests in the remaining joint-tenants upon the death of one of their number. See 2 Bl Comm 184.

Jus accrescendi inter mercatores locum non habet, pro beneficio commercii (jūs a-kre-sen'dī in'ter mer-ka-tō'rēz lō'kum non hā'bet, prō be-ne-fi'she-ō kom-mer'she-ī). The right of survivorship has no place among merchants, which is for the benefit of commerce.

Jus accrescendi praefertur oneribus (jūs a-kre-sen'dī prē-fer'ter ō-ne'ri-bus). The right of survivorship is preferred to incumbrances.

Jus accrescendi praefertur ultimae voluntati (jūs a-kre-sen'dī prē-fer'ter ul'ti-mē vol-un-ta'tī). The right of survivorship is given preference over the last will. See 2 Bl Comm 186 and note.

jus ad rem (jūs ad rem). See **jus in rem.**

jus aesneciae (jūs es-ne'she-e). The right of esnecy, the right of the first-born to have the first choice on a division of an inheritance between coparceners.

jus albinatus (jūs al-bi-nā'tus). Also called the "droit d'aubaine,"—the right of the king, under the law of France, to all the property of a deceased alien, unless he had a peculiar exemption. See 1 Bl Comm 372.

jus alluvionis (jus a-lū'vi-ō-nis). The right to an increase of land by the natural process of alluvion. Fowler v Wood, 73 Kan 511, 85 P 763.

jus angariae (jūs an-ga'ri-ē). The right of the lord of the manor to exact service of a vassal.

jus Anglorum (jūs Ang-lō'rum). The law of the Anglo-Saxons.

jus aquam ducendi (jūs a'quam dū-sen'dī). Same as **jus aqueductus**.

jus aqueductus (jūs a-kwē-duk'tus). The right of drainage which existed under the civil law, and which is an easement giving the owner of land the right to bring down water through or from the land of another, either from its source or from any other place. Nellis v Munson, 108 NY 453, 459, 15 NE 739.

jus banci (jūs ban'sī). The right of bench,—the right of particular judges to have an elevated seat.

jus belli (jūs bel'lī). The law of war; the right of war.

jus bellum dicendi (jūs bel'lum di-sen'dī). The right to declare war, or to proclaim war.

jus canonicum (jūs ka-nō'ni-kum). The canon law. The term is applied to both the canon or ecclesiastical law of England and to the ancient law of the church of Rome.

jus civile (jūs si'vi-le). The civil law.

Jus civile est quod quisque sibi populus constituit (jūs si'vi-le est quod quis'kwe si'bi po'pu-lus kon-sti'tu-it). Municipal or civil law is that which a people establishes for itself.
This was Justinian's definition of municipal law, and although strictly municipal law refers to the particular customs of one single free town, or "municipium," yet it may properly be applied to any one state or nation, which is governed by the same laws and customs. See 1 Bl Comm 44.

Jus civile est quod sibi populus constituit (jūs si'vi-le est quod si'bi po'pu-lus kon-sti'tu-it). The civil law is that law which the people establish for themselves. Jackson v Jackson (NY) 1 Johns 424, 426.

jus civitatis (jūs si-vi-tā'tis). (Roman law.) The right of citizenship.

jus cloacae (jūs klō'a-sē). The right of sewage or drainage.

jus commune (jūs kom-mū'ne). The common or public law. The common law of England, of the United States, and other countries who have derived it from England.

jus commune, et quasi gentium (jūs kom-mū'ne, et quā'sī jen'she-um). The common law, and as it were the law of nations.

Jus constitui oportet in his quae ut plurimum accidunt, non quae ex inopinato (jūs kon-sti'tu-ī ō-por'tet in his kwē ut plu'ri-mum ak'si-dunt, non kwē ex in-op-in-ā'tō). Law ought to be established in respect to those matters which occur most frequently, and not in respect to those which are not to be expected.

jus coronae (jūs ko-rō'nē). The right of succession to the throne. See 1 Bl Comm 191.

jus cudendae monetae (jūs kū-den'dē mo-nē'tē). The right of coining money.

jus curialitatis (jūs kū-ri-ā-li-tā'tis). The right of curtesy.

jus dare (jūs da're). To make or enact the law. The Pedro, 175 US 354, 44 L Ed 195, 175 S Ct 138.

jus deliberandi (jūs dē-li-be-ran'dī). (Civil law.) The right of deliberating,—the right of an heir to take sufficient time for determining whether he will take or reject the estate of the deceased person.

Jus descendit, et non terra (jūs de-sen'dit, et non ter'ra). The right descends, and not the land.

jus dicere (jūs dī'se-re). The right to speak. To declare or state the law; to expound the law. The Pedro, 175 US 354, 44 L Ed 195, 195 S Ct 138.

Jus dicere, et non jus dare (jūs dī'se-re, et non jūs da're). To declare the law, and not to make the law. State ex rel. Barker v Chicago & Alton Railroad Co. 265 Mo 646, 178 SW 129.

Jus dicere, non jus dare (jūs dī'se-re, non jūs da're). To declare the law, not to make the law. Barry v Mandell (NY) 10 Johns 563, 566.

jus disponendi (jūs dis-pō-nen'dī). The right of disposing; that is, the right which a man has to dispose of his property as he pleases. Vanderbilt v Mitchell, 72 NJ Eq 910, 67 A 97.

jus dividendi (jūs dī-vi-den'dī). The right to devise one's real property by will.

jus duplicatum (jūs du-pli-kā'tum). A double right, particularly the right of possession joined with the right of property or title.

jus eminens (jūs ē'mi-nenz). (Civil law.) The supreme power of the state over its members and whatever belongs to them; the basis of the right of eminent domain. Gilmer v Lime Point, 18 Cal 229, 251.

jus est ars boni et aequi (jūs est arz bō'nī et ē'quī). Law is the science of that which is good and just.

Jus est norma recti; et quicquid est contra normam recti est injuria (jūs est nor'ma rek'tī; et quik'quid est kon'trā nor'mam rek'tī est in-jū'ri-a). Law is the rule of right; and whatever is contrary to the rule of right is an injury.

Jus et fraus nunquam cohabitant (jūs et frâs nun'-quam ko-ha'bi-tant). Right and fraud never live together.

jus et seisinam (jūs et sē'zi-nam). The right and the seisin.

Jus ex injuria non oritur (jūs ex in-jū'ri-a non ō'ri-ter). A right cannot spring from a wrong.

jus feciale (jūs fe-she-ā'le). Fecial law,—the ancient Roman law governing relations with other nations and declarations of war.

jus fiduciarum (jūs fī-du-she-ā'rum). (Roman law.) A right in trust, for which there was a remedy in conscience. See 2 Bl Comm 328.

jus fluminum (jūs flū'mi-num). (Civil law.) The right of using rivers.

jus fodiendi (jūs fo-di-en'dī). The right to dig in the land of another.

jus futurum (jūs-fu-tū'rum). (Civil law.) A right expected to be acquired.

jus gentium (jūs jen'she-um). The law of nations. See **international law; private international law**.

jus gladii (jūs gla'di-ī). The right of the sword,—the executory power of the law, to prosecute criminal offenses, which resides in the sovereign power. See 4 Bl Comm 177.

jus habendi (jūs hā-ben'dī). The right of having possession of property.

jus habendi et retinendi (jūs hā-ben'dī et re-ti-nen'dī). The right of having and retaining,—the right of having and keeping the rewards and fruits of a rectory or parsonage.

jus haereditatis (jūs hē-rē-di-tā'tis). The right of inheritance; the right to succeed as heir.

jus hauriendi (jūs hâ-ri-en'dē). (Civil law.) The right or servitude of drawing water.

jus honorarium (jūs ho-no-rā'ri-um). (Roman law.) The law which was instituted by the edicts of the magistrates. See Mackeldey's Roman Law § 37.

jus immunitatis (jūs im-mū-ni-tā'tis). (Civil law.) The right of immunity from service in public office.

jus incognitum (jūs in-kōg'ni-tum). An unknown law.

jus individuum (jūs in-dī-vi'du-um). An indivisible right; a right which cannot be separated into parts; an individual right.

jus in personam (jūs in per-sō'nam). A right against a person, such as a right arising out of a personal obligation.

jus in re (jūs in rē). A right in a thing; a right of property; a property right.
See **jus in rem.**

jus in re aliena (jūs in rē ā-li-ē'na). A right in the property of another person.

Jus in re inhaerit ossibus usufructuarii (jūs in rē in-hē'rit os'si-bus ū-su-fruk-tu-ā'ri-ī). The right in anything clings to the (bones) person of him who has the right to use it, the usufructuary.

jus in rem (jūs in rem). A right in rem or in re, which implies the absolute dominion over property, the ownership of it independently of any particular relation with another person.
    The jus ad rem, the right to a thing, is a right which has its foundation in an obligation incurred by another person. The assignment of a bill of lading transfers the jus ad rem, but not necessarily the jus in rem. The Carlos F. Roses, 177 US 655, 666, 44 L Ed 929, 933, 20 S Ct 803.

jus in re propria (jūs in rē prō'pri-a). A right in the thing itself; complete ownership.

jus Italicum (jūs ī-tạ'li-kum). (Roman law.) The common right or rights of the people of Italy outside of Rome; the common right or rights of Roman colonists.

Jusjurandi forma verbis differt, re convenit; hunc enim sensum habere debet, ut Deus invocetur (jus-jū-ran'dī for'ma ver'bis dif'fert, rē kon-vē'nit; hunk e'nim sen'sum hā-bē're de'bet, ut Dē'us in-vō-sē'ter). The form of an oath differs in wording, but agrees in the substance; for it ought to have this meaning,—that God is invoked.

jus jurandum (jus jū-ran'dum). Same as **jusjurandum.**

jusjurandum (jūs-jū-ran'dum). An oath.

Jusjurandum inter alios factum nec nocere nec prodesse debet (jūs-jū-ran'dum in'ter a'li-ōs fak'tum nek nō-sē're nek prō-des'se de'bet). An oath made between other parties ought neither to harm nor profit.

jus Latii (jūs la'she-ī). (Roman law.) The law of Latium (the district of Italy in which Rome was situated), exclusive of the law which governed the city of Rome.

jus legitimum (jūs lē-ji'ti-mum). (Roman law.) A legal right, a violation of which was remedied by the ordinary course of law. See 2 Bl Comm 328.

jus mariti (jus ma'ri-ti). The right of a husband.

jus merum (jūs mē'rum). A mere right. A mere right of property, the jus proprietas, without either possession or even the right of possession. See 2 Bl Comm 197.

jus naturae (jūs nā-tū'rē). The law of nature.

jus naturale (jūs nā-tū-rā'le). Natural law; law the principles of which accord with natural reason.

Jus naturale est quod apud homines eandem habet potentiam (jūs nā-tū-rā'le est quod a'pud ho'mi-nēz e-an'dem hā'bet po-ten'she-am). Natural law is the law which has the same power among all mankind.

jus naturalis aut divini (jūs na-tū-rā'lis ât di-vī'nī). Natural or divine law.

jus navigandi (jūs na-vi-gan'dī). The right of navigation.

jus necis (jūs nē'sis). The right of death,—the right which a Roman father had of putting his children to death.

Jus non habenti, tute non paretur (jūs non hā-ben'tī, tū'tē non pa-rē'ter). He who has no right is safely disobeyed.

Jus non patitur ut idem bis solvatur (jūs non pa'ti-ter ut ī'dem bis sol-vā'ter). The law does not suffer the same thing to be paid twice.

jus non scriptum (jūs non skrip'tum). The unwritten law,—the law which is expressed or sanctioned by the tacit and unwritten customs and consent of men; the common law. See 1 Bl Comm 64.

jus pascendi (jūs pa-sen'dī). The right to pasture cattle.

jus patronatus (jūs pa-tro-nā'tus). (Ecclesiastical law.) A commission from the bishop, directed usually to his chancellor and others of competent learning, who were to summon a jury of six clergymen and six laymen, to inquire into and examine as to who was the rightful patron of a living. See 3 Bl Comm 246.

jus personarum (jūs per-sō-nā'rum). Singular of **jura personarum.**

jus possessionis (jūs po-ze-she-ō'nis). The right of possession. See 3 Bl Comm 177.

jus postliminii (jūs post-li-mi'ni-ī). The right under which persons and things taken by an enemy in war are restored to their former state on coming again into the power of the nation to which they belonged. Leitensdorfer v Webb, 1 NM 34, 44.

jus praesens (jūs prē'senz). (Civil law.) A present or existing right; a right which has been completely acquired, as distinguished from jus futurum, which is a right expected to be acquired, but which has not been completely acquired. See Mackeldey's Roman Law § 191.

jus praetorium (jūs prē-tō'ri-um). (Civil law.) The discretion of the praetor,—the power to pronounce the rule of law, and to apply it to particular cases by the principles of equity. See 3 Bl Comm 49.

jus precarium (jūs pre-kā′ri-um). (Roman law.) A right obtained by begging or asking for it; that is, a right in courtesy, for which the remedy was only by entreaty or request. See 2 Bl Comm 328.

jus presentationis (jūs pre-zen-tā′she-ō-nis). (Ecclesiastical law.) The right of a patron to present a clergyman to a benefice. See 3 Bl Comm 246.

jus privatum (jūs prī-vā′tum). A private right.
Any right held by the king of England in his individual capacity was known as jus privatum. Any right which he held in a representative capacity was known as jus publicum, a public right. Lewis Blue Point Oyster Cultivation Co. v Briggs, 198 NY 287, 91 NE 846.

jus projiciendi (jūs prō-ji-she-en′dī). (Civil law.) The servitude or right to build a projection, such as a balcony or gallery, from one's house over the land of his neighbor. See Mackeldey's Roman Law § 317.

jus proprietas (jūs prō-pri′e-tās). See **jus merum.**

Jus prosequendi in judicio, quod alicui debetur (jūs prō-se-quen′dī in jū-di′she-ō, quod a′li-kī de-bē′ter). The right of prosecuting to judgment, which is due to everyone. See 3 Bl Comm 116.

jus protegendi (jūs prō-te-jen′dī). (Civil law.) The right to construct a shed on one's house in such manner that it projected over his neighbor's land. See Mackeldey's Roman Law § 317.

jus publicum (jūs pub′li-kum). A public right; a right held by the king in a representative capacity. Lewis Blue Point Oyster Cultivation Co. v Briggs, 198 NY 287, 91 NE 846.

Jus publicum et privatum quod ex naturalibus praeceptis aut gentium aut civilibus est collectum; et quod in jure scripto jus appellatur, id in lege Angliae rectum esse dicitur (jūs pub′li-kum et prī-vā′tum quod ex nā-tū-rā′li-bus prē-sep′tis ât jen′she-um ât si-vi′li-bus est kol-lek′tum; et quod in jū′re skrip′to jūs ap-pel-lā′ter, id in lē′je Ang′li-ē rek′tum es′se di′si-ter). Law, both public and private, is that which is collected from natural precepts either of nations or states; and that which in the written law is called "jus," in the law of England is called "right."

Jus publicum privatorum pactis mutari non potest (jūs pub′li-kum prī-vā-tō′rum pak′tis mū-tā′rī non pō′test). A public law or right cannot be altered by the agreements of individuals. Mitchell v First National Bank, 180 US 471, 476, 45 L Ed 627, 630, 21 S Ct 418.

jus quaesitum (jūs kwē-sī′tum). The right of demanding or recovering a thing.

jus quiritium (jūs qui-rī′she-um). (Roman law.) The law of Rome, which at first extended only to the patricians, but later to the whole of the Roman people.

Jus quo universitates utuntur est idem quod habent privati (jūs quō ū-ni-ver-si-tā′tēz ū-tun′ter est ī′dem quod hā′bent prī-vā′tī). The law which governs corporations is the same as that which governs private persons.

jus regium (jūs rē′ji-um). Royal right.
That right of the people of a state, as the sovereign of the state, to regulate, improve, and secure for the common benefit of every individual citizen, is nothing more than what is called the jus regium. Arnold v Mundy, 6 NJL 1.

jus relictae (jūs re-lik′tē). The right of a widow in the personal property which belonged to her deceased husband.

Jus respicit aequitatem (rē-spī′sit ē-qui-tā′tem). Law regards equity.

jus sacrum (jūs sa′krūm). (Roman law.) The law relating to public worship.

jus sanguinis (jūs san′gwi-nis). The law of the place of one's descent or parentage. The rule of descent or blood. United States v Wong Kim Ark, 169 US 649, 42 L Ed 890, 18 S Ct 456.

jus scriptum (jūs skrip′tum). The written law,—the statutes, acts, or edicts, made by the king's majesty, by and with the consent of parliament, the oldest of which, extant and printed in the English statute-books, is the famous Magna Charta. See 1 Bl Comm 85.

jus singulare (jūs sin-gu-la′rē). A peculiar rule of law established for a special occasion or special reason.

jus soli (jus sol′ī). The right of the soil or the land. The law of the place of one's birth.

jus stapulae (jūs stā′pu-lē). The right of staple,—an ancient right of some English towns to force the sale of imports to their own people, exclusively.

jus strictum (jūs strik′tum). Strict law; the law enforced with precision and severity.

Jus superveniens auctori accrescit successori (jūs super-ve′ni-enz âk-tō′rī a-kre′sit suk-ses-sō′rī). A right coming to the holder of an estate accrues to his successor.

just. Right or fair according to law. Legally right, lawful.
All human actions are either just or unjust as they are in conformity to or in opposition to law. Borden v State, 11 Ark 519.

justa causa (jus′ta kâ′za). (Civil law.) A just cause; a lawful or proper motive; a lawful claim. See Mackeldey's Roman Law § 283.

just and unextinguished title. A title to land good upon its face, not manifestly frivolous, but not necessarily one which shall be determined to be valid in the ultimate test. United States v Conway, 175 US 60, 44 L Ed 72, 20 S Ct 13 (phrase appearing in a private land claim act).

just beyond. Barely beyond; a very little space beyond. Carroll v Cave Hill Cemetery Co. 172 Ky 204, 189 SW 186.

just cause. A legal cause; a fair cause relied upon in good faith. For the removal, discharge or demotion of an officer or employee in the classified civil service:—legal cause or a cause based upon acts or omissions detrimental to the public service. People ex rel. Polen v Hoehler, 405 Ill 322, 90 NE2d 729. See justification.

just cause of provocation. See provocation.

just claim. A claim or demand enforceable in a court of justice. Bostwick v Mutual Life Ins. Co. 116 Wis 392, 92 NW 246.

just compensation. A familiar term in constitutional provisions and statutes granting or regulating the exercise of the power of eminent domain in the condemnation and taking of private property. Reasonable compensation. A compensation which is just, not merely to the individual whose property is taken, but to the public which is to pay for it. 27 Am J2d Em D § 266. The full and perfect equivalent of the property taken and the damages inflicted by the taking. 27 Am J2d Em D § 266.

It is not the investment, but the "value of the interest" in land taken by eminent domain that is guaranteed to the owner; the government may neither confiscate the owner's bargain, nor be required to assume his loss. Kinter v United States (CA3 Pa) 156 F2d 5, 172 ALR 232.

just consideration. A consideration legally sufficient. Moruzzi v Federal Life & Casualty Co. 42 NM 35, 75 P2d 320, 115 ALR 407.

Under a statute requiring a chattel mortgage when filed to be accompanied by an affidavit stating inter alia that the mortgage is "just," a statement that the mortgage is given "for value received" and "in good faith" is not sufficient. A consideration may well be for value and yet not "just," and that the mortgage is given in good faith merely indicates that it is not collusive or fraudulent and a denial of collusion or fraud is not an affirmation that the claim due the creditor is just. Schuster v Wendling (CA6 Ohio) 116 F2d 596.

just debts of decedent. All claims which could have been enforced by action against the decedent in his lifetime. 31 Am J2d Ex & Ad § 276. Not estate or inheritance taxes or claims upon indebtedness incurred by personal representative of the decedent. Anno: 37 ALR2d 136.

jus tertii (jūs ter'she-ī). The right of a third person. 11 Am J2d B & N § 655.

Jus testamentorum pertinet ordinario (jūs tes-tā-men-tō'rum per'ti-net or-di-nā'ri-ō). The right of testaments belongs to the ordinary.

justice. That end which ought to be reached in a case by the regular administration of the principles of law involved as applied to the facts. Sioux Falls v Marshall, 48 SD 378, 204 NW 999, 45 ALR 447, 451. Nothing more nor less than exact conformity to some obligatory law. Borden v State, 11 Ark 519.

The title of a judge, especially the judge of a high court, such as the United States Supreme Court or the highest court of a state.

See **justice of the peace.**

justice ayres (ārs). The circuits of Scotch judges.

justice court. A term erroneously applied at times to a justice's court, the court of a justice of the peace.

justice de facto. See **de facto justice of the peace.**

justice de jure (jus'tis de jū're). An officer who has the lawful right or title to the office of justice of the peace, with or without the possession of the office. 31 Am J Rev ed J P § 6.

Justice Department. One of the executive departments of the United States, headed by the Attorney General, whose primary duty is to supervise the conduct of all suits brought by or against the United States, and to give advice to the President and the heads of the other departments of the government. 54 Am J1st US § 54. A comparable department of a state government.

justice of the peace. An office of ancient origin, established in the United States as part of the English judicial system under the common law. Brown v Knox County, 187 Tenn 8, 212 SW2d 673, 5 ALR2d 1264. A magistrate; often a township officer, although exercising county-wide jurisdiction, and sometimes regarded as a county officer. 31 Am J Rev ed J P § 3. Essentially a magistrate, a judicial officer, although vested with some administrative or ministerial powers. 31 Am J Rev ed J P § 2. A judicial office of limited jurisdiction, the jurisdiction usually being limited to actions, other than those involving title to real property, wherein the amount in controversy is relatively small, and in criminal cases, to prosecutions for minor offenses and misdemeanors, and preliminary hearings upon charges of felony or serious misdemeanor. The incumbent of the office of justice of the peace. Not a judge for all purposes, for example, not within the meaning of a statute fixing an age limit for "judges." People v Mann, 97 NY 530. But a judge within the meaning of the rule that words spoken by a "judge" in the course of a judicial proceeding over which he is presiding, and in relation to the subject of the proceeding, are absolutely privileged. 33 Am J1st L & S § 177.

justice's court. The title of the court of a justice of the peace.

See **justice of the peace.**

justice's docket. The book required to be kept by a justice of the peace wherein he shall enter a record of each step taken in an action, suit, or proceeding before him, from the issuance of process to the rendition and entry of judgment, and the issuance of an execution as such may be required for the enforcement of the judgment. 31 Am J Rev ed J P § 59. A docket wherein a justice of the peace shall show the institution and disposition of criminal causes brought before him for prosecution or by way of a preliminary hearing.

justices in eyre. Justices on circuit,—judges who were regularly established under Henry the Second in 1176, with a delegated power from the king's great court, or aula regia, being regarded as members of it and who afterwards made their circuit around the kingdom once in seven years to try causes.

Later, by Magna Charta, they were directed to be sent into every county once a year, to take recognitions or assizes. See 3 Bl Comm 57.

justices itinerant. Justices on circuit.

See **justices in eyre.**

justice's judgment. A judgment rendered by a justice of the peace.

Such a judgment is the judgment of a court not of record, and therefore cannot be established as a record, but is to be established as a public writing, not of record, by evidence. Hamilton v Wright, 11 NC (4 Hawks) 283, 286.

As to filing a transcript of a justice's judgment in a court of record so as to give effect to the judgment as one of a court of record, see 31 Am J Rev ed J P § 94.

justices of assize (a-sīz'). Justices of the superior courts of England, who tried causes on their circuits.

justices of gaol delivery (of jāl dẹ-liv'ėr-i). Judges who were commissioned to hear the cases of persons who were in jail.

justices of laborers (lā'bọr-ėrs). Justices specially appointed to hear and determine controversies between workingmen and their employers.

justices of nisi prius (jus'ti-ses of nī'sī prī'us). See **nisi prius.**

justices of oyer and terminer (jus'ti-ses of oy'er and ter'mi-ner). The judges of the courts of assize and nisi prius.

justices of the Jews (of the jöz). Judges who were appointed by Richard the First to enforce the usury laws against the Jews.

justices of the peace. See **justice of the peace.**

justices of the sessions (of the sesh'ọnz). Two or more justices of the peace who preside at the English sessions of the peace, for the execution of the authority given them by their commission and certain acts of Parliament. People v Powell (NY) 14 Abb Pr 91, 93.

justiciable case. A case which presents a justiciable controversy.
See **justiciable controversy.**

justiciable controversy. A controversy appropriate for judicial inquiry or adjudgment. 20 Am J2d Cts § 80. A controversy not so exclusively or predominantly involved with political questions as to come within the prerogative of the legislative or administrative branch of the government. Chicago & Southern Airlines v Waterman SS Corp. 333 US 103, 92 L Ed 568, 68 S Ct 431. For the purposes of declaratory relief:—a controversy involving something more than a mere difference of opinion; a controversy involving persons adversely interested in matters in respect of which a declaration is sought. 22 Am J2d Dec J § 11.

justiciar (jus-tish'i-ạr). A justice; a judge. See 3 Bl Comm 38.

justiciarii ad omnia placita (jūs-ti-she-ā'ri-ī ad om'ni-a pla'si-ta). Justices for all pleas.

justiciarii in itinere (jūs-ti-she-ā'ri-ī in i-ti'ne-re). Justices on circuit. Same as **justices in eyre.**

justiciarii itinerantes (jus-ti-she-ā'ri-ī ī-ti-ne-ran'tēz). Same as **justices in eyre.**

justiciarii residentes (jus-ti-she-ā'ri-ī re-si-den'tēz). The English judges who resided at Westminster.

justiciary. A judge or justice.
See **court of justiciary.**

justicier. (French.) A judge. A lover of justice.

justicies (jus-tish'i-ēz). A special writ by which the sheriff of the county was empowered for the sake of dispatch, to sit in the county court of his county and try causes.
Under this writ, the sheriff could take cognizance of many real actions and all personal actions, to any amount, which without the writ would be tried at Westminster. See 3 Bl Comm 36.

justifiable. By legal sanction. Defensible.

justifiable cause for nonsupport. A cause legally relieving the husband of the duty of support. 23 Am J2d Desert § 15. A cause which he has not helped to create, a result which has not been in any measure caused by his own misconduct,—such as her adultery without guilt or connivance on his part. White v White, 87 NJ Eq 354, 100 A 235.

justifiable homicide. An excusable homicide. State v Trent, 122 Or 463, 259 P 893. A homicide committed: (1) by unavoidable necessity without any will, intention, desire, inadvertence, or negligence on the part of the person killing, (2) for the advancement of public justice, or (3) for the prevention of any atrocious crime attempted to be committed by force. Erwin v State, 29 Ohio St 186.

justifiable trespass. An intentional trespass which the law has authorized; as, an entry into a house through an open door to serve a civil process. In reality, not a trespass, justification being a defense, albeit one to be pleaded specially. 52 Am J1st Tresp § 68.

justification. A showing by sureties of their qualifications as householders or freeholders and of their ability to respond in the amount of the suretyship obligation. Wilson v Eagleson, 9 Idaho 17, 71 P 613. A reason for committing an act which otherwise would constitute an actionable wrong or tort. 52 Am J1st Torts § 85. Just cause or excuse for the commission of an act otherwise criminal. State v Williams, 166 SC 63, 164 SE 415. Good cause for abandoning, deserting, or failing to support wife. 23 Am J2d Desert § 15. The defense of truth in an action for libel or slander. 33 Am J1st L & S § 117. In reference to the rule imposing liability for procuring breach of contract:—the presence of exceptional circumstances showing that no tort has been in fact committed, the term connoting lawful excuse which excludes malice, actual or legal, for example, procuring the breach of a contract without knowledge of the contract, or acting in the exercise of an equal or superior right. Childress v Abeles, 240 NC 667, 84 SE2d 176, reh dismd 242 NC 123, 86 SE2d 916.
See **justifiable homicide.**

justificators (jus'ti-fi-kạ-tọrs). Compurgators,—persons who, in a trial by wager of law, swore to the innocence of the defendant.

justifying bail. The justification of the sureties on a bail bond.
See **justification.**

Justinian (jus-tin'i-ạn). Emperor of the Byzantine Empire from 527 to 565, renowned for codification of the Roman law.
See **Florentine Pandects; Institutes of Justinian; Novels; Pandects.**

Justinian Code. Same as **Corpus Juris Civilis.**

justinianist. A student of Roman law.

justitia (jūs-ti'she-a). Justice.

Justitia debet esse libera, quia nihil iniquius venali justitia; plena, quia justitia non debet claudicare; et celeris, quia dilatio est quaedam negatio (jūs-ti'she-a de'bet es'se li'be-ra, qui'a ni'hil in-ī'qui-us vē-nā'lī jūs-ti'she-a; plē'na, qui'a jūs-ti'she-a non de'bet klâ-di-ka're; et se'le-ris, qui'a dī-lā'she-ō est kwē'dam ne-gā'she-ō). Justice ought to be free, because nothing is more iniquitous than venal justice; full, because justice ought not to halt; and speedy, because delay is a sort of denial.

Justitia est constans et perpetua voluntas jus suum cuique tribuendi (jūs-ti'she-a est kon'stanz et per-pe'tu-a vo-lun'tās jūs su'um kī'kwe tri-bu-en'dī). Justice is the constant and perpetual wish to render to each one his rights.

Justitia est duplex, viz., severe puniens et vere praeveniens (jūs-ti'she-a est du'plex, viz., se-vē'rē pu'ni-enz et vē'rē prē-ve'ni-enz). Justice is double, that is to say, severely punishing and truly preventing.

Justitia est virtus excellens, et Altissimo complacens (jūs-ti'she-a est vir'tus ex-sel'lenz, et Al-tis'si-mō kom-plā'senz). Justice is excellent goodness, and is pleasing to the Most High.

Justitia firmatur solium (jūs-ti'she-a fir-mā'ter sō'li-um). Justice confirms sovereign power.

Justitia nec differenda nec neganda est (jus-ti'she-a nek dif-fe-ren'da nek ne-gan'da est). Justice is neither to be delayed nor denied.

Justitia nemini neganda est (jŭs-tĭ′she-a nĕ′mĭ-nī ne-gan′da est). Justice is to be denied to no one.

Justitia non est neganda, non differenda (jŭs-tĭ′she-a non est ne-gan′da, non dĭf-fe-ren′da). Justice is neither to be denied nor delayed.

Justitia non novit patrem nec matrem; solum veritatem spectat justitia (jŭs-tĭ′she-a non no′vit pa′trem nek mā′trem; sō′lum ve-ri-tā′tem spek′tat jŭs-tĭ′she-a). Justice knows neither father nor mother; justice looks only at the truth.

justitia piepoudrous (jŭs-tĭ′she-a pyā′poo-droo). Speedy justice.
See **court of piepoudre.**

justitium (jŭs-tĭ′she-um). (Civil law.) A suspension of the business of the courts.

jus tripertitum (jŭs tri-per-tī′tum). The law of wills.

Jus triplex est,—proprietatis, possessionis, et possibilitatis (jŭs trī′plex est,—prō-pri-e-tā̆′tis, po-ze-she-ō′nis, et pos-si-bi-li-tā̆′tis). A right is threefold, —proprietary, possessory, and in possibility.

jus trium liberorum (jŭs trī′um lĭ-be-rō′rum). (Roman law.) The right of three children; that is, the extraordinary rights, privileges and immunities which the Roman law accorded to a father of three or more children. See 2 Bl Comm 247.

just title. The equivalent of color of title. A title that is imperfect, but not so obviously that the imperfection is apparent to one not skilled in the law. Fernandes & Bros. v Ayllon y Ojeda, 266 US 144, 146, 69 L Ed 209, 211, 45 S Ct 52 (applying law of Porto Rico); 3 Am J2d Adv P § 96.

Justum non est aliquem antenatum mortuum facere bastardum, qui pro tota vita sua pro legitimo habetur (jus′tum non est a′li-quem an-te-nā′tum mor′tu-um fā̆′se-re bas-tar′dum, quī prō tō′ta vī′ta su′a prō lē-jĭ′ti-mō hă-bē′ter). It is not just to make a dead man a bastard, who throughout his whole life was regarded as legitimate.

justness. The quality or state of being just, equitable or right; conformity to truth or justice, lawfulness; rightfulness; honorableness. Correctness; exactness; accuracy. Fuchs v Lehman, 47 ND 58, 188 NW 85.
See **just.**

jus utendi (jŭs ū-ten′dī). The right to make use of a thing.

jus vagum et incertum (jus vā′gum et in-sėr′tum). Vague and uncertain law. See 1 Pomeroy's Equity Jurisprudence § 60.

jus venandi et piscandi (jŭs vē-nan′dī et pis-kan′dī). The right to hunt and fish on the land of another.

Jus vendit quod usus approbavit (jŭs ven′dit quod ū′sus ap-prō-bā̆′vit). The law recommends that which use or custom has approved.

jus vocando. See **in jus vocando.**

juvenile court. A court having special jurisdiction, of a paternal nature, over delinquent and neglected children. 31 Am J Rev ed Juv Ct § 3.

juvenile delinquent. A generic term, embracing every lapse into wrongdoing from murder to habitual truancy, even certain acts of incorrigibility rather than crime. 31 Am J Rev ed Juv Ct § 36.
See **delinquent children.**

juxta (juks′tă). Near; according to.

juxta formam statuti (jux′ta for′mam sta-tu′tī). According to the form of the statute.

juxta tenorem sequentem (jux′ta te-nō′rem se-quen′-tem). According to the following tenor.

juzgado (hooth-gah′do). (Spanish.) The judiciary; that faction of a court which concurs in a decree or judgment.

K

k. Abbreviation of **kilogram,** of the nautical term **knot,** and of the electrical term **kilowatt.**

K. Roman numeral for 250.

kadi (kä'di or kā'di). A Turkish civil magistrate.

kaia (kai'a). A quay.

kaiagium (kai-ā'jī-um). Same as **quayage.**

kain (kān). A tax; rent paid in produce.

kaiser (kī'zėr). An emperor.

kalendae (ka-len'dē). The first day of the month of the Roman calendar.

kalendar (kal'en-dạr). Same as **calendar.**

kalends (ka'lendz). Same as **kalendae.**

kangaroo court. A mock court, especially one held by the inmates of a jail. 41 Am J1st Pris & P § 20. A court set up without warrant or authority of law on the frontier for quick trial of an alleged criminal, especially a horse thief or a murderer, usually in anticipation and by way of justification of a lynching.

karat (kar'ạt). A weight of four grains, used in weighing gems, usually written "carat."

karl (kârl). A churl, a person belonging to one of the lowest classes of freemen.

kavil (ka'vil). A staff or stick used in choosing by lot; a choosing by lot.

K. B. An abbreviation of **king's bench;** also, an abbreviation of **knight of the bath.**

K. C. An abbreviation of **King's Counsel.**

keelage (kē'lāj). A duty or toll charged for permitting a ship to enter and anchor in a port or harbor.

keelhaul (kēl'hâl). To punish a sailor for disobedience or misconduct by dragging him under the ship's keel with a rope.

keels (kēls). Coal barges; ships carrying coal.

keep. Verb: To maintain; to carry on; to conduct; to manage; to hold in custody. State v Irvin, 117 Iowa 469, 470, 91 NW 760. Noun: The central structure of a feudal castle.

keep arms. See **bear arms.**

keeper. One who has the care, custody, or superintendence of anything; as the keeper of a park, a pound, a gate, and (in the English law) keeper of a forest, great seal, and privy seal. One in charge of a jail. A person in charge of animals. Fishell v Morris, 57 Conn 547, 18 A 717. One in possession of a thing, place, or business, whether or not the owner or proprietor. Schultz v State, 32 Ohio St 276, 281.

keeper of dog. A person who keeps, or permits a dog to be kept and maintained on his premises, provided he has at least some possession and control of the animal. Anno: 17 ALR2d 469.

keeper of gambling house. One in charge of a gambling house, irrespective of interest or ownership in or of the property or instrumentalities involved. State v Rand, 238 Iowa 250, 25 NW2d 800, 170 ALR 289.

See **keeping common gaming house.**

keeper of the forest (of the for'est). The chief officer of a forest; a forest warden.

keeper of the great seal (of the grāt sēl). The chancellor or lord keeper, who was the custodian of the king's great seal, and an officer of great importance and power in the kingdom. In rank he was superior to every temporal lord and held a large number of offices and honors, ex officio. See 3 Bl Comm 47.

keeper of the king's conscience (of the king's kon'shens). The lord chancellor of England. See 3 Bl Comm 47.

keeper of the privy seal (of the priv'i sēl). An English officer who was the custodian of the privy seal and as such inspected all documents requiring the great seal.

The sign manual was the warrant to the privy seal, and the privy seal was the warrant to the great seal. See 2 Bl Comm 347.

keeper of the rolls. The incumbent of an old office in England. The keeper of the rolls or records of the county, who was the principal justice of the peace. 1 Bl Comm 349.

keep-friend (kēp'frend). An iron ring fastened to a chain, used for holding prisoners.

keeping books. See **bookkeeping.**

keeping common gaming house. A common-law offense, indictable as a criminal nuisance on account of its tendency to bring together disorderly persons, promote immorality, and lead to breaches of the peace.

By judicial evolution and legislative enactment the common-law offense has been so broadened in its scope as to include any place wherein persons are allowed to assemble for the purpose of betting, wagering, gaming, or gambling, and especially where such practices are encouraged by the proprietor. 24 Am J1st Gaming §§ 38 et seq.

See **keeper of gambling house; keeping gambling resort.**

keeping disorderly house. A common-law offense; a statutory offense in most American jurisdictions. 24 Am J2d Disord H § 14. Keeping a lewd house, a house of ill fame, a house of prostitution, or a house to which people resort for a commission of acts contrary to law and subversive of public morals. 24 Am J2d Disord H § 14.

keeping explosives. The common-law offense of keeping large quantities of gunpowder and other explosives in, or dangerously near to, public places, such as villages and highways. 31 Am J2d Explos § 121.

keeping gambling device. A statutory offense committed by setting up, keeping, or exhibiting gaming or gambling devises, such being the tables and any other apparatus, device, or machine of any kind or description constituting the tangible means, instrument, or thing with or by which money may be won or lost by the arbitrament of chance, as distinguished from the game itself. 24 Am J1st Gaming § 31.

Neither a single act of play at a gaming table, nor even a single day's use of it on the race field, is keeping a common gaming table. United States v Smith, 27 F Cas No 1155.

keeping gambling resort. The maintenance of a place to which persons resort for gambling; a common-law offense irrespective of whether the gambling is lawful or unlawful, since it tends to bring together

keeping [700] **KICKBACK**

disorderly persons, promote immorality, and lead to breaches of the peace. 24 Am J1st Gaming § 38.

keeping good a tender. See **keeping tender good.**

keeping house of ill fame. See **keeping disorderly house.**

keeping intoxicating liquor. Within the meaning of liquor laws, keeping for sale or barter, except in the most sumptuary legislation forbidding possession for private or family use. Street v Lincoln Safe Deposit Co. 254 US 88, 65 L Ed 151, 41 S Ct 31, 10 ALR 1548, 1551.

keeping or storing. For the purposes of the prohibitory clause of an insurance policy:—warehousing or safekeeping of deposited goods, not the possessing of a small quantity of the designated articles or substances customarily found on premises such as those insured. 29A Am J Rev ed Ins § 921.

keeping place for disorderly conduct. See **keeping disorderly house.**

keeping place for gambling. See **keeping gambling resort.**

keeping place for unlawful sale of liquor. A criminal offense in some jurisdictions distinct from that of making unlawful sales of liquor. 30 Am J Rev ed Intox L § 263. An offense embracing the possession, management, and control of the liquor and the place. Schultz v State, 32 Ohio St 276.

keeping tender good. Maintaining a readiness and ability to make payment after a tender has been refused. Depositing the sum tendered in court. 52 Am J1st Ten § 28.

keeping to the right. An elementary rule of the road, formally adopted by statute in some jurisdictions. Cupples Mercantile Co. v Bow, 32 Idaho 774, 189 P 48, 24 ALR 1296, ovrld on another point Hamilton v Carpenter, 49 Idaho 629, 290 P 724; O'Mally v Eagan, 43 Wyo 233, 350 P2d 1063, 5 P2d 276, 77 ALR 582.

keeping, using or allowing. For the purposes of a prohibitory clause in an insurance policy:—the permanent or habitual keeping or using of the designated articles in considerable quantities, not the temporary or occasional use of a small quantity of the articles. 29A Am J Rev ed Ins § 922.

keep in repair. In reference to a highway:—maintaining the highway in such physical condition as will make it reasonably safe for travel. 25 Am J1st High § 476. As an undertaking by a lessee under a covenant in the lease:—to keep the premises in as good repair as they were when the lease was made. St. Joseph & St. Louis R. Co. v St. Louis I. M. & S. R. Co. 135 Mo 173, 36 SW 602.

keep school. To teach school. To maintain school in session. Borchers v Taylor, 83 NH 564, 145 A 666, 63 ALR 874.

keep the peace. To maintain public order and decorum; to prevent breach of the peace; to refrain from violence
See **bond to keep the peace.**

Kelly Girl. A female employee obtained for temporary work through a service organization.
See **service organization.**

kelp (kelp). A kind of seaweed, sometimes taken for the extraction of iodine therefrom.

kelp-shore. Same as **seashore.**

Kenilworth Edict (ken'il-wėrth ē'dikt). An award for the pacification of the kingdom made by Henry the Third and the English parliament in 1266.

kenning to a terce (ken'ing to a tėrs). A reckoning of the third,—a computation or assignment by the sheriff of a widow's third or dower.

keno. A game of chance played by gamblers. 24 Am J1st Gaming § 28. A gambling game in which there is a "banker" and which is operated with ninety numbered ivory balls placed inside of a rotating oblong wheel. Miller v State, 48 Ala 122, 125. A name applied without circumspection to the game **bingo.**

kentledge (kent'lej). The pig iron ballast of a ship.

Keogh plan. A relatively new pension plan which offers self-employed business and professional people the chance to obtain for themselves advantages long enjoyed by employees of many businesses.

kept. Maintained; supported. Possessed or held in custody. Even possessing a thing for a short period of time, as in the case of intoxicating liquor in a restaurant brought there by a patron for immediate consumption. Fritzel v United States (CA7 Ill) 17 F2d 965. As the word appears in a statute declaring that a place where intoxicating liquor is manufactured, sold, kept, or bartered in violation of the act, shall constitute a common nuisance:—kept for sale, barter, or other commercial purpose. Street v Lincoln Safe Deposit Co. 254 US 88, 65 L Ed 151, 41 S Ct 31, 10 ALR 1548.
See **stored or kept.**

kept woman. A paramour or mistress. 33 Am J1st L & S § 39.

kern (kėrn). A vagrant; a vagabond.

kerosene. A thin oil derived by process of distillation from crude oil or coal, formerly much used in lamps for the purpose of illumination, particularly in dwellinghouses; sometimes called coal oil.

key. A metal instrument for moving the bolt of a lock, thereby locking or unlocking. A wharf. An island, for example, Key Largo off the southern tip of Florida. The means of solving a difficult problem.
See **cone and key; keys.**

keyage. The money or toll taken for lading or unlading wares at a key or wharf. Rowan's Executors v Portland, 47 Ky (8 B Mon) 232, 253.

keys (kēz). The house of keys,—the lower house of the Manx legislature.
See **key.**

kg. Abbreviation of keg.

K. G. An abbreviation of **knights of the garter.**

Khedive (ke-dēv'). The viceroy or governor of Egypt.

kick. To strike with the foot. A colloquial term for an objection or complaint.

kickback. The forced return of a part of one's wages. Boehm v United States (CA8 Mo) 123 F2d 791. The payment of money or property to an individual for causing his employer, client, patient, customer, or principal to buy from, to use the services of, or to deal otherwise with, the person making the payment.

Kickback Act. A federal statute which provides that whoever induces any person employed in the construction or repair of any public building or work, or building or work financed by loans or grants from the United States, to give up any part of the compensation to which he is entitled under his contract of employment, is subject to fine or imprisonment, or both. 18 USC § 874.

kickback agreement. An agreement between an employer and an employee under which the latter agrees to surrender to the former part of the compensation to which the latter is entitled under the contract of employment. 31 Am J Rev ed Lab § 173.

kicked car. See **kicking cars**.

kicking cars. A railroad operation in switching wherein the locomotive having given impetus to a car or cars, the locomotive is quickly stopped and disengaged, permitting the car or cars to roll under their own momentum. Chicago, St. Louis & Pittsburg Railroad Co. v Champion, 9 Ind App 510; Promer v Milwaukee, L. S. & W. R. Co. 90 Wis 215, 63 NW 90.

kidder. An engrosser; a forestaller. Slang for one who seeks to impose upon the credulity of another.

kidnaping. Same as **kidnapping**.

kidnapping. At early common law:—the forcible abduction or stealing of a man, woman, or child from his own country and sending him into another; an aggravated species of false imprisonment. 1 Am J2d Abduct § 1. The offense under statutes generally: the taking or detaining of a person against his will and without lawful authority. Anno: 114 ALR 870. A wilful and intentional detention for an unlawful purpose against one's will and without authority of law. People v Florio, 301 NY 46, 92 NE2d 881, 17 ALR2d 993.

kidnapping for extortion. An aggravated offense of kidnapping. Kidnapping for the purpose of holding the victim for a ransom. 1 Am J2d Abduct § 3.

Kidnapping Law. A federal statute, commonly known as the Lindbergh Law, which prescribes the crime of kidnapping for ransom, reward, or otherwise, where the victim is transported from one state to another or to a foreign country. 18 USC § 1201 (a); 1 Am J2d Abduct §§ 5, 18.

Kiel beer. Near beer; a beer of low alcoholic content.

kilderkin (kil'dėr-kin). A cask or keg holding about half a barrel or eighteen imperial gallons.

kill. Verb: To cause death. To put an end to something, as to "kill" a bill in the legislature. Noun: A stream or creek, the word in this sense being derived from the Holland Dutch.

killed instantly. See **instantaneous death**.

killing by accident. See **accidental death**.

killyth-stallion. The customary duty of the lord of the manor to provide a stallion for the breeding of his tenants' mares.

kiln. See **brick kiln**.

kilogram (kil'ọ-gram). A unit of weight in the metric system, equivalent to 2.2046 pounds.

kilometer (kil'ọ-mē-tėr). A unit of linear measure in the metric system, equivalent to 0.62137 miles.

kilowatt (kil'ọ-wot). A unit of electrical power, equivalent to 1000 watts. See **watt**.

kilter (kil'tėr). A colloquial expression for good order or working condition of an instrumentality. See **out of kilter**.

Kimbell-Diamond doctrine. The doctrine of income tax law, otherwise known as the unitary transaction rule, that where a taxpayer, who is interested primarily in obtaining a corporation's assets, first purchases the stock of the corporation and then liquidates the corporation in order to acquire the desired assets, the separate steps taken to accomplish the primary objective are treated as a single transaction, and even though the objective is accomplished in form by a purchase of stock, the substance of the transaction is regarded as a purchase of property. United States v Mattison (CA9 Idaho) 273 F2d 13, 83 ALR2d 706.

kin. Relatives. Primarily, relatives by the tie of consanguinity or blood. State v Tucker, 174 Ind 715, 93 NE 3; Re Stoler, 293 Pa 433, 143 A 121, 59 ALR 1402. But including for the purposes of a statute respecting competency to testify as to a transaction with one since deceased, otherwise known as a dead man's statute, relatives by marriage as well as by blood. French v French, 84 Iowa 655, 51 NW 145.

See **collateral kinsmen; kindred; nearest blood kin; nearest kin; next of kin**.

kinbote (kin'bōt). An ancient pecuniary compensation among the Saxons for the killing of a relative. The portion of a regicide's fine which was paid to the community.

kind. Adjective: Gentle, friendly, and considerate. Noun: A class; a variety.
See **in kind**.

kindergarten. Literally in the translation of the German from which it derives, a children's garden. Actually, a class in school which precedes the first grade; the class which, except for a child which has attended nursery school, is the place in which a child's education by schooling begins, albeit the purpose is to have him become accustomed to school and pleased with it rather than to present a formal course of study. Sinnott v Colombet, 107 Cal 187, 40 P 329.

kindlie (kīnd'lė). The right of a tenant to have his lease renewed.

kindling. A substance easily ignited, used in starting a fire. The act of starting a fire.

kindred. Relatives. Kin. Usually relatives by blood, but for some purposes only relatives born in lawful wedlock, as where the word appears in a statute of descent. Anno: 48 ALR2d 764, § 3 (c); 10 Am J2d Bast § 149. For some purposes, including relatives by marriage. French v French, 84 Iowa 655, 51 NW 145 (statute relative to competency as a witness to testify concerning a transaction with a person since deceased).

Aliens incapable of inheriting are not such "kindred" as can defeat the right of a surviving spouse to take the whole of the estate of the deceased spouse if there are no kindred. Wunderle v Wunderle, 144 Ill 40, 33 NE 195, error dismd 154 US 524, 38 L Ed 1078, 14 S Ct 1156.

kindred rule. A rule related to another rule, such as the doctrine of the law of the case to the doctrine of res judicata. United States v United States Smelting Refining & Mining Co. 339 US 186, 94 L Ed 750, 70 S Ct 537, reh den 339 US 972, 94 L Ed 1379, 70 S Ct 994.

king. The ruler or sovereign of a kingdom. The lord paramount under the early feudal system of holding real property in England. 28 Am J2d Est § 3.

king de facto (king dē fak'to). See **de facto king**.

king de jure (king dē jū're). See **de jure king**.

kingdom. The dominion of a king or queen; a country whose sovereign is a king or a queen.

king-geld (king'gĕld). Escuage,—money paid by the tenant in lieu of knight-service.

King James Bible. A leading Protestant version of the Bible, taking its name from King James I of Great Britain, its publication date, 1611, being within his reign, the preparation of the Bible having been ordered by him in 1604.

king's advocate. The legal advisor of the king of England.
See **King's Counsel.**

kings and queens of England. See **regnal years.**

king's bench. See **court of king's bench.**

king's bench division. A department of the English high court of justice.

king's chambers. The harbors of England; probably so called because they were a part of the territorial waters of the crown.

king's council. A court which, during the Norman period, followed the person of the king.

King's Counsel. See **Queen's Counsel.**

king's court. A court which was the successor of the very ancient witenagemote of the Saxons.

king's evidence. Same as **state's evidence.**

king's highways. The federal highways in Canada. See **royal streams.**

king's justiciars (jus-tish'i-ạrs). Certain persons learned in the law who acted as assistants to the high officers of state who composed the aula regia. See 3 Bl Comm 38.

king's keys. Such axes, bars, and other implements as were used to force an entry to serve a warrant of the king.

kings of England. See **regnal years.**

king's peace. See **peace of the king.**

king's premier serjeant. The first in rank of the king's serjeants, so constituted by letters patent and having the first right of pre-audience. See 3 Bl Comm 28, note.

king's silver (sil'vėr). Sometimes called the post fine, —an ancient revenue of the king which was due him by royal prerogative and which was required to be paid into the royal treasury at the second stage of a proceeding of levying a fine for alienation of land. See 2 Bl Comm 350.

king's widow (wid'ọ). The widow of a tenant of the king, who could not marry again without the consent of the king.

king's year, day and waste. See **year, day and waste.**

kinless. Without kindred; without relatives.

kinsbote. Same as **kinbote.**

kinship. The matter of being kin.
See **kin.**

kinsmen. People who are one's kin.
See **kin; kindred.**

kintledge (kint'lej). Same as **kentledge.**

kip (kip). A brothel; a bawdyhouse.

Kirby's quest (ker'bēs kwest). John de Kirby's inquest,—a record of ancient English surveys made by de Kirby in the reign of Edward the First.

kissing the Book. The act of kissing the Bible or Testament, often performed in taking an oath, especially an oath of office administered to one qualifying for high office, but not essential to the validity of any oath. 39 Am J1st Oath § 13.

kitchen range. See **range.**

kitchen sink. See **sink.**

kith (kith). A person's home or birthplace.

kiting checks. A practice, not to be recommended, indulged by a person short in both cash and credit, in taking care of an overdraft in one bank by depositing therein a check drawn on a bank at some distance, that is, in another city or village, which will result in an overdraft in the second bank until another worthless check is presented in that bank, and so on until the denouement which inevitably occurs except as a windfall takes care of the last check written.

KKK. Abbreviation of **Ku Klux Klan.**

kleptomania. A morbid propensity to steal, whether consciously or unconsciously. The disease of stealing; an irresistible impulse to steal. 29 Am J Rev ed Ins Per § 3. A species of insanity; a weakening of the will power to such an extent as to leave one powerless to control his impulse to appropriate the personal property of others, without regard to whether such impulse is inspired by avarice, greed, or idle fancy. State v McCullough, 114 Iowa 532, 87 NW 503. In some, although not all, jurisdictions, a complete defense in a prosecution for larceny. 32 Am J1st Larc § 42.

Kluxer. Slang for a member of the **Ku Klux Klan.**

knave. A swindler; a cheat; a servant; a rogue; one who has been guilty of dishonest acts. Harding v Brooks, 22 Mass (5 Pick) 244.

knife. An instrument for cutting. In some categories, a deadly weapon. 26 Am J1st Homi § 7; 56 Am J1st Weap § 3.

knight. A man who had attained the dignity of knighthood, which was the first personal dignity, after the nobility.

A knight, therefore, in order of rank or precedence, followed a baronet. See 1 Bl Comm 403.

knighthood. The rank, dignity, or station of a knight.

knight marshal. A keeper of decorum within the royal household of the king of England.

knights bachelors (nīts bach'e-lọrs). The most ancient, though the lowest, order of knighthood. See 1 Bl Comm 404.

knights banneret (ban'ėr-et). Knights of the order which after certain other dignities ranked below the knights of the order of St. George, or of the garter. See 1 Bl Comm 403.

knight-service. A species of tenure under the feudal system under which each knight or soldier held a knight's fee and was bound to attend the king in his wars forty days in each year.

This service in time degenerated into pecuniary commutations or aids until the military part of the feudal system was abolished in the reign of Charles the Second. See 1 Bl Comm 410.

knight's fee. An estate sufficiently large to maintain a knight.

knights of St. George. Same as **knights of the garter.**

knights of the bath (of the bạth). An order of knighthood which ranked next after the knights bannerets; so called from the ceremony of bathing the knights before their creation. See 1 Bl Comm 403.

knights of the chamber. Knights bachelors who attained knighthood in times of peace.

knights of the garter (of the gär'tėr). The highest order of knighthood, ranking next after the nobility.

The order was first instituted by Edward the Third in 1344, and was also called the order of St. George. See 1 Bl Comm 403.

knights of the shire. Members of Parliament representing counties rather than municipal corporations or boroughs.

Knight Templars. See **Templars.**

knocked down. Struck down; knocked off one's feet by a violent blow. An expression used in auction sales, meaning "sold." 7 Am J2d Auct § 31.

In the language of the auction room, and in common parlance, property is said to be "struck off" or "knocked down" when the auctioneer, by the fall of his hammer, or by any other audible or visible announcement, signifies to the bidder that he is entitled to the property on paying the amount of his bid, according to the terms of the sale. Sherwood v Reade (NY) 7 Hill 431, 439.

As to the meaning of the term "knocked down" as it appears in an accident insurance policy, See Anno: 138 ALR 411.

knot. A nautical mile. Something that binds, such as a marriage, the bonds of matrimony.
See **nautical mile.**

know. To be aware or informed of something. To have reason to believe. Shaw v Merchants' Nat. Bank (US) 11 Otto 557, 25 L Ed 892.

knowingly. With knowledge; having knowledge. As part of the statutory definition of a criminal offense: —a term without a single fixed and uniform meaning, the meaning in the particular case to be determined according to the character of the offense charged. Riss & Co. v United States (CA8 Mo) 262 F2d 245; sometimes construed as intentionally, in which case it must appear that the person charged was aware of the illegality of his conduct. 21 Am J2d Crim L § 88; more often construed as having knowledge, not of the act's unlawfulness, but merely knowledge of those facts which are essential to make it unlawful. People v Shapiro, 4 NY2d 597, 176 NYS2d 632, 152 NE2d 65, 69 ALR2d 973. As the word is used in federal statutes relating to the use of the mails:—not necessarily a matter of having actual knowledge or intent, the knowledge of circumstances from which the indecent character of matter and the likelihood that the disposition made of it will probably result in the use of the mails, being sufficient. 41 Am J1st P O § 99.

As used in a statute giving a lien to any person doing work under a contract with the owner or with one whom the owner has authorized or "knowingly permitted" to improve the property, the phrase is satisfied if the owner, knowing that the work is being done, fails to object. However, it has also been held, that mere knowledge and a failure to object by the owner, is not sufficient. Anno: 4 ALR 694.

knowingly and wilfully. A purposeful failure to obey the law, with knowledge of the facts. Missouri K. & T. R. Co. v United States (CA8 Kan) 178 F 15; St. Louis & S. F. R. Co. v United States (CA8 Mo) 169 F 69. An essential term in an indictment where it constitutes a part of the statutory definition of the offense. 27 Am J1st Indict § 67.

knowingly misrepresent. See **to knowingly misrepresent.**

knowingly permitted. See **knowingly.**

knowledge. The perception of the mind as to facts; information and intelligence. Utley v Hill, 155 Mo 232, 55 SW 1091, 1102. As an element of a criminal offense, awareness of those facts which are essential to the unlawfulness of the act alleged as criminal. 21 Am J2d Crim L § 88. Within the meaning of a clause of an insurance policy for voiding the contract upon the commencement of foreclosure proceedings "with the knowledge of the insured": actual knowledge or actual notice. 29A Am J Rev ed Ins § 860.

It has been generally held that under a fidelity bond or policy providing for notice of loss within a specified time after the insured has "knowledge of," "learned of," "discovered," or "become aware of" a loss or a dishonest act, the insured is not required to act respecting the notice provision until he has actual knowledge of the loss or dishonest act. Anno: 23 ALR2d 1076.

See **actual knowledge; actual notice; guilty knowledge; notice.**

knowledge of custom. Actual or constructive knowledge of a custom consistent with the contract of which it is alleged to be a part. 21 Am J2d Cust & U § 17.

known. A conventional term in a certificate of acknowledgment, indicating the officer's knowledge of the identity of the person acknowledging. 1 Am J2d Ack § 70.

known equivalent. A patent law term; a known device used as a substitute which effects the same result. 40 Am J1st Pat § 160.

known mine. An actual and opened mine which has been worked or is capable of being worked. Colorado Coal & I. Co. v United States, 123 US 307, 31 L Ed 182, 8 S Ct 131.

known personally. A conventional term in a certificate of acknowledgment, indicating the officer's knowledge of the identity of the person acknowledging. 1 Am J2d Ack § 70.

known vein. A mining law term referring to a vein or lode whose existence is known, as contradistinguished from one which has been appropriated by location.

It must either have been known to the applicant for the patent or known to the community generally, or else disclosed by workings and obvious to anyone making a reasonable and fair inspection of the premises for the purpose of obtaining title from the government. Iron Silver Mining Co. v Mike & Starr Gold & Silver Mining Co. 143 US 394, 36 L Ed 201, 12 S Ct 543.

knuckles. See **brass knuckles.**

koshuba (ko-shū-vä'). A Jewish marriage contract or marriage settlement. Hurwitz v Hurwitz, 216 App Div 362, 363, 215 NYS 184, 185.

Ku Klux Act. A federal statute which creates a civil liability for conspiracy interfering with civil rights. 42 USC § 1985(3); 15 Am J2d Civ R § 16.

Ku Klux Klan. A secret society, the membership of which is limited to white men, against which legislation has been directed on account of alleged anti-Negro and anti-Semitic practices.

kyn (kin). Same as **kin.**

kyth. Same as **kith.**

L

la (lä). (French.) The, for the feminine.

là (lą̈). (French.) There.

label. A small card or piece of paper attached to an article of goods or merchandise and indicating the manufacturer, brand, weight, size, dimension, etc. 56 Am J1st W & L §§ 54 et seq. A slip or tag of paper, or other material, bearing the description in the form of a word or words, name, monogram, letter, scroll, or trademark indicating the character, origin, or destination of the article to which it is attached. National Battery Co. v Western Molded Products Co. (DC Cal) 39 F Supp 954. A small card or piece of paper attached to a can or package of food, showing the contents, the nature and ingredients of the food. 35 Am J2d Food § 25. A strip of paper upon which a seal is affixed and which is attached to a written instrument.

See **misbranding; union label.**

labeling of narcotic. Written, printed, or graphic matter upon any wrapper or container of a narcotic, or accompanying such substance. 21 USC § 321m.

The term applies to circulars shipped simultaneously with the articles to which they relate and kept in the same room of a warehouse for distribution to retail stores. United States v Research Laboratories (CA9 Wash) 126 F2d 42, cert den 317 US 656, 87 L Ed 528, 63 S Ct 54.

labor. Narrowly defined as purely physical toil. 31 Am J2d Exemp § 19; 31 Am J Rev ed Lab § 1. Services in a manual occupation; work requiring little skill or special training. 36 Am J1st Mech L § 53; 58 Am J1st Workm Comp § 91. Services in following a manual occupation rather than an intellectual pursuit. Michigan Trust Co. v Grand Rapids Democrat, 113 Mich 615, 71 NW 1102. Better defined as work with the hands or with the mind including the application of professional and trade skills. 31 Am J2d Exemp § 19; 31 Am J Rev ed Lab § 1. Toil with the brains as well as toil with the hands. Commonwealth v John T. Connor Co. 222 Mass 299, 110 NE 301. In a broad but none the less accurate sense, services of a person whether they be rendered by his hands or by the application of learning and professional skill, including the work of high-salaried corporate officers, engineers, architects, actors, painters, builders, etc. 31 Am J Rev ed Lab § 1. In political economy, the position held by workers collectively. 31 Am J Rev ed Lab § 1.

An effort is no less labor because it is carried on with the use of machinery instead of hand tools. Timber Structures v C. W. S. Grinding & Machine Works, 191 Or 231, 229 P2d 623, 25 ALR2d 1358 (within the meaning of a statute granting a mechanic's lien for labor performed.)

labor agitator. One actively engaged in promoting the interests of labor.

The term does not imply the use of unlawful or improper means. Wabash Railroad Co. v Young, 162 Ind 102, 69 NE 1003.

labor a jury. To tamper with a jury or a juror in order to influence the jury's verdict.

labor and material payment bond. A contractor's bond which guarantees the owner that all bills for labor and materials contracted for and used by the contractor will be paid by the surety if the contractor defaults. Standard Acci. Ins. Co. v Rose, 314 Ky 233, 234 SW2d 728.

laborariis (la-bo-rā'ri-is). An old English writ to compel a pauper to work.

laboratory fee. A student's fee for the use of laboratories in the institution. 15 Am J2d Colleges § 19.

laboratory report. A scientific report respecting a matter in issue, made by qualified technicians. 23 Am J2d Dep § 322.

laboratory test. A test conducted by a scientist in the field, in a laboratory, by means of instruments adapted to the problem at hand and the use of such chemicals or other materials as are required to reach a conclusion on a scientific basis. Petersen v Widule, 157 Wis 641, 147 NW 966.

labor combination. See **labor union.**

Labor Day. The first Monday in September, observed as a legal holiday in all the states in honor of labor. State v Thomas, 61 Ohio St 444, 56 NE 276.

Labor Department. An administrative department of the United States Government, headed by the Secretary of Labor. A comparable department of a state government.

labor dispute. A controversy between an employer and his employees as to terms and conditions of the employment. 31 Am J Rev ed Lab § 369. Any controversy over wages, hours, working conditions, or terms of employment. Anno: 28 ALR2d 297 (involving right to unemployment compensation). For the purposes of the application of the Norris-LaGuardia Act and state anti-injunction laws of a similar nature, any controversy concerning terms or conditions of employment, or concerning the association or representation of persons in negotiating, fixing, maintaining, changing, or seeking to arrange terms or conditions of employment, regardless of whether or not the disputants stand in the proximate relation of employer and employee. 31 Am J Rev ed Lab § 546.

A labor dispute exists, within the meaning of the Pennsylvania Labor Anti-Injunction Act, where the employees of one plant of the employer, who are on strike following the expiration of a collective bargaining agreement, are picketing another plant of the employer where no labor dispute exists. American Brake Shoe Co. v District Lodge of International Asso. of Machinists, 373 Pa 164, 94 A2d 884, 37 ALR2d 675.

See **jurisdictional dispute; strike.**

labor dispute insurance. Insurance against loss resulting from strikes or labor disputes. 29A Am J Rev ed Ins § 1371. Insurance of employers of labor in the manufacturing business against loss or damage resulting directly or indirectly from any interference with or interruption or suspension of business or use or operation of plant by reason of employees' strikes. Buffalo Forge Co. v Mutual Secur. Co. 83 Conn 393, 396.

labor done. A type of consideration frequently authorized by statute as acceptable in payment of a subscription to corporate stock. 18 Am J2d Corp § 261.

See **service; work.**

laborer. One who performs labor.
See **labor**.

laborer's lien. A lien upon a chattel for work performed thereon.
See **mechanic's lien**.

labor laws. Those constitutional provisions, statutes, ordinances, and administrative regulations which regulate labor relations in such matters as hours of labor, wages, unemployment insurance, Sunday observance, preference of wage claims in bankruptcy and insolvency proceedings, minimum wages, collective bargaining, etc.
See **contract labor law; labor relations acts**.

Labor-Management Panel. A federal agency composed of six representatives of management and six of labor, to advise upon request in the avoidance of industrial controversies and the manner in which mediation and voluntary adjustment shall be administered. 29 USC § 175.

labor market. See **free labor market**.

labor organization. In the usual sense of the term a labor union. In a less precise sense, an organization in which employees participate. Di Georgio Fruit Corp. v NLRB, 89 App DC 155, 191 F2d 642, 28 ALR2d 377. An organization of any kind, or any agency or employee representation committee or plan, in which employees participate and which exists for the purpose, in whole or in part, of dealing with employers concerning grievances, labor disputes, wages, rates of pay, hours of employment, or conditions of work. 29 USC § 152(5).
Spontaneous or informal activity of employees as that of "labor organization" within protection of National Labor Relations Act. Anno: 19 ALR2d 566.

labor relations acts. The statutes, state and federal, which purport to regulate the relation between capital and labor for the purpose of avoiding industrial disputes and strikes. The National Labor Relations Act, known as the Wagner Act, of 1935 and the Labor-Management Relations Act of 1947, known as the Taft-Hartley Act, amending the Act of 1935, such statutes being codified as Chapter 7, Labor Management Relations, of Title 29 of the United States Code.

Labor Relations Board. A national public agency created by statute to enforce the provisions of the Federal Labor Relations Act; not a tribunal for the enforcement of private rights through administrative remedies. An agency of the United States, an entity apart from its members, having legal capacity to sue in the federal courts to carry out its statutory functions; located in the District of Columbia. 31 Am J Rev ed Lab § 210.

labor representative. Any representative of a labor organization, whether an officer or lessee agent, and whether elected or appointed. State v Provenzano, 34 NJ 318, 169 A2d 135 (term appearing in statute penalizing bribery).

Labor Standards. A bureau in the Department of Labor of the federal government.

Labor Standards Act. See **Fair Labor Standards Act**.

Labor Statistics. A bureau of the United States Department of Labor.

labor ticket. A certificate or memorandum given to an employee, showing him entitled to a certain amount of pay for a certain amount of work. Anno: 76 ALR 1305. In practical politics, the group of candidates at a general election supported by organized labor.

labor union. An association of workers existing for the purpose, in whole or in part, of bargaining on behalf of workers with employers about the terms or conditions of employment. A combination of workmen organized for the ultimate purpose of securing through united action the most favorable conditions, as regards wages, hours of labor, conditions of employment, etc., for its members. 31 Am J Rev ed Lab § 13.
See **industrial union; trade union**.

laceration. A tear or wound, on face or body, characterized by jagged or irregular edges. Moriarty v New York Cent. R. Co. (Sup) 124 NYS2d 284.

laches. A doctrine, otherwise known as the doctrine of stale demand, by which equitable relief is denied to one who has been guilty of unconscionable delay, as shown by surrounding facts and circumstances, in seeking that relief. Anno: 34 ALR2d 1314 § 1. More precisely, such neglect or omission to assert a right, taken in conjunction with lapse of time and other circumstances causing prejudice to an adverse party, as will operate as a bar to relief in equity. Re O'Donnell's Estate, 8 Ill App 2d 348, 132 NE2d 74; Boehnke v Roenfanz, 246 Iowa 240, 67 NW2d 585, 54 ALR2d 1; Simmerman v Ft. Hartford Coal Co. 310 Ky 572, 221 SW2d 442, 11 ALR2d 381; Aronovitch v Levy, 238 Minn 237, 56 NW2d 570, 34 ALR2d 1306.

lack-learning parliament. Same as **parliament of dunces**.

lack of. See words and phrases beginning "want of."

La conscience est la plus changeante des règles (lah con-shi-ôns ay lah ploo shan-zhan day re-glē). Conscience is the most changeable of rules.

La court se voet aviser de cest issue (lä cūr sē vō-et ä-vē-zā dē cest is'sū). The court will take this issue under advisement or consideration.

lacta (lak'ta). Lack of weight; short weight.

lacus (lā'kus). (Civil law.) A large body of water; a lake. In older English law, an alloy of silver used in coinage.

lada (la'da). (Saxon.) A trial by purgation.

ladder. A means of climbing in the realistic or figurative sense. A series of handholds vertically arranged on the corner of a railroad car, affording a means for the climbing of the car by an employee. 45 USC § 11.

laden in bulk (lā'den in bulk). A shipping term signifying loaded with a loose, unboxed cargo.

lading. See **bill of lading**.

lading and unlading. Same as **loading and unloading**.

Lady Day. The twenty-fifth day of March. Doe D. Hall v Benson (Eng) 4 Barn & Ald 588.

lady's friend (lā'diz frend). The title of an officer in the English house of commons who looked to the enforcement of orders for the support and maintenance of women who had been divorced from their husbands by acts of parliament.

laesa majestas (lē'sa ma-jes'tās). Injured majesty; high treason. 4 Bl Comm 75.

laga (lā'ga). Law; a law.

lagan (lā'gan). Same as **ligan**.

lage. Same as **laga**.

lage day. Same as **law day.**

lage man. A lawful man; a man qualified for jury duty; a juror.

lager beer. Beer aged by storing. 30 Am J Rev ed Intox L § 10. A malt beverage; neither a spiritous liquor or a vinous liquor. Sarlls v United States, 152 US 570, 38 L Ed 556, 14 S Ct 720.

laghslite. (Saxon.) An unlawful act; a fine or punishment for breaking the law.

la grippe (lä grip). A disease, quite similar to a severe cold, otherwise known as "grippe." 29 Am J Rev ed Ins § 745.

lagu (lah-goo). Law.

lahman. (Saxon.) A law man; a lawyer.

laicum. See **feudum laicum.**

laicus (lā'i-kus). A layman, as distinguished from a person connected with the church.

lairesite. A fine imposed by the lord of the manor for committing adultery or fornication.

lais gents (lay zhôn). Men of the laity; laymen.

laity (lā'i-ti). Same as **laymen.**

lake. A body of water in its natural state, substantially at rest, usually of fresh water. Trustees of Schools v Schroll, 120 Ill 509, 12 NE 248.

lake peril. See **perils of the river, lake, or canal.**

lake navigation. See **navigation.**

La ley favour la vie d'un homme (lah lay fah-voor lah vee d'ùn ôm). The law favors human life.

La ley favour l'inheritance d'un homme (lah lay fah-voor l'in-ĕr-i-täns d'ŭn ôm). The law favors the inheritance of a man.

La ley voit plus tost suffer un mischiefe que un inconvenience (lah lay vwah ploo tōst soof-fay ŭn mischief kĕ ŭn ăn-côn-vay-ni-ôns). The law will rather suffer a mischief than an inconvenience.

Lambeth degree (Lam'beth dē'grē). A degree of Oxford or Cambridge conferred by the archbishop of Canterbury. See 1 Bl Comm 381.

lammas land (lam'as land). Land which was thrown open after harvest as a common pasture for the cattle of the landowner and others.

lanceti (lan'se-tī). Feudal vassals who labored one day in each week for the lord of the manor, at certain seasons of the year.

land. A general term including not only the soil, but everything attached to it, whether attached by the course of nature, as trees, herbage, and water, or by the hand of man, as buildings, fixtures, and fences. 42 Am J1st Prop § 14. A corporeal thing, but exclusive of a franchise connected with land. Southern Pacific Co. v Riverside County, 35 Cal App 2d 380, 95 P2d 688. A word of art; extending from the surface downward to the center of the earth and upwards indefinitely to the skies. 42 Am J1st Prop § 14. The solid material of the earth; real property, tenements, and hereditaments, and all rights thereto and interests therein, equitable as well as legal. 42 Am J1st Prop § 50. Broadly, town and city lots as well as rural property. 1 Am J2d Adj L § 1. The character of an interest in real estate. 42 Am J1st Prop § 14.

See **estate in land; real estate; real property.**

land agent. Historically, an agent for the sale of vast tracts of unimproved lands. An agent for sale of large acreages of land in the western states or Canada. In modern parlance, a real estate broker.

land bank. A bank organized under an Act of Congress known as the Federal Farm Loan Act for the purpose in general of making loans upon farm security at low rates of interest. 10 Am J2d Bks § 21.

landboc (land'bok). (Saxon.) A deed or charter evidencing title to land.

land carrier. See **carrier.**

landceap. A customary fine paid to the lord of the manor on a transfer of land, in certain manors and boroughs.

land certificate. The obligation of the government entitling the owner to secure the designated quantity of land by following the requirements of the law. Waterman v Charlton, 102 Tex 510, 120 SW 171.

See **certificate of entry.**

landcheap. Same as **landceap.**

Land claim. See **claim.**

land contract. A contract whereby one party agrees to sell and the other to purchase real estate. Pike Rapids Power Co. v Minneapolis, St. P. & S. S. M. R. Co. (CA8 Minn) 99 F2d 902. A contract for the transfer of the title to real estate in consideration of a money price or its equivalent passing from the purchaser to the vendor. Recognized in equity as a transfer of ownership to the purchaser. 55 Am J1st V & P § 356.

land-cop (land'kop). A sale of land.

"The lord will take a small fine for this land-cop, this sale of land, and soon it may seem that the purchaser acquires his title to the land rather from the lord than from the vendor." Maitland's Doomsday Book and Beyond 323.

Land Department. A federal authority consisting of the General Land Office with the Secretary of the Interior at its head, vested by statute with substantially exclusive jurisdiction to determine, in the first instance, all questions of fact respecting the acquisition, disposition, and control of the public lands, so long as the title thereto remains in the United States. 42 Am J1st Pub L § 57. A comparable agency of state government.

land development. Improving and subdividing a tract of land preparatory to the erection of residential, commercial, or industrial buildings; the improvement of land for agricultural purposes. A planned scheme for the construction of houses, street improvements, utility structures, etc. in a particular area, usually with covenants restricting the use of the lots in the area by business or industry.

landed. Owning land. In another sense, having come or been brought ashore.

Persons aboard a ship are landed when they are brought ashore, but sailors on a ship have not landed unless they permanently leave the ship, since it is necessary for commerce that sailors should go ashore temporarily and return to the ship. Taylor v United States, 207 US 120, 52 L Ed 130, 28 S Ct 53.

landed estate. An interest in, and pertaining to, land. Police Jury v Harris, 10 La Ann 676, 677.

See **estate in land.**

landed interest. The interest or estate which a person holds or owns in land or in the possession of land.

See **estate in land; landed estate.**

landed property. Real estate. While the term would ordinarily include a railway company's right of way, such a right of way will not be held to be included in a statutory exemption of landed property from taxation, where the spirit of the exemption statute is against such inclusion. United Railways & Electric Co. v Baltimore, 93 Md 630, 49 A 655.

landed proprietor. See **landed estate; landed property.**

landefricus (lan-de-frī′kus). A landlord.

landegandman. A tenant of a manor of an inferior class.

land entry. See **entry under homestead law; original entry.**

land-gabel (ga′bel). A tax or rent paid for the use of land.

land grant. Broadly, a transfer of title to real estate. In the accepted sense of the term, a grant of public lands by the United States or a state. A grant of land in the public domain made by Congress from time to time for the support of education in the various states. 15 Am J2d Colleges § 30. A grant of land by the government to a railroad company by way of aid in the construction of a railroad. 13 Am J2d Car § 118.

land grant institutions. Educational institutions which have received a land grant made by Congress for the support of education. 15 Am J2d Colleges § 30.

land-grant rates. Favorable rates for railroad transportation of government property or armed forces, obtained because of the fact that the railroad company had obtained a land grant to assist in construction of the line. 13 Am J2d Car § 118.

landing. A pier, other structure, or unimproved area at which the cargo of a vessel can be unloaded or passengers disembark. A place on a river, or other navigable water, for loading and unloading goods, or for the reception and delivery of passengers; either the bank or the wharf, to or from which persons or things may go or be carried to or from some vessel in the contiguous waters. 56 Am J1st Whar § 2. A place for loading or unloading vessels, but not a harbor. 48 Am J1st Ship § 223. A platform maintained by a carrier for receiving or delivering freight or for the use of passengers in boarding and leaving trains. 14 Am J2d Car § 871. The act of a pilot of an aircraft in bringing it to the ground. 8 Am J2d Avi § 102.

landing area. A locality, either of land or water, including an airport or intermediate landing field, which is used, or intended to be used, for the landing and takeoff of aircraft, whether or not facilities are provided for the shelter, servicing, or repairs of aircraft, or for receiving or discharging passengers or cargo. 49 USC § 1301 (22).

landing card. A card handed an alien upon approval of his entry into the country, for presentation to an immigration officer upon the pier.

landing cargo. See **loading and unloading.**

landing certificate. A requirement by regulation of the Secretary of the Treasury in reference to merchandise landed for exportation or to residue cargo. 19 USC § 1622.

landing field. See **landing area.**

landing in safety. The responsibility of a carrier in reference to the condition in which a passenger finds himself immediately after he has alighted from the carrier's conveyance. Harries v Atlantic Greyhound Corp. 243 NC 346, 90 SE2d 710, 58 ALR2d 939.

land jobber. A person who makes a particular business of buying and selling land to obtain profit. Vanderbilt University v Cheney, 116 Tenn 259, 94 SW 90.

landing lights. Artificial lights placed close to the ground on a landing field for illumination to permit safe landing of aircraft during hours of darkness. Lights on an aircraft located in such position as to illuminate the landing area for safe landing during hours of darkness. Plewes v Lancaster, 171 Pa Super 312, 90 A2d 279.

landing net. A net used to land a fish after it is hooked. Commonwealth v Wetherill, 8 Pa Dist 653, 655.

landing place. See **landing; landing area.**

landlord. A lessor. One under whom another holds premises as a tenant or lessee. 32 Am J1st L & T § 2.

landlord's attachment. A remedy provided a landlord by statute for the enforcement or protection of his landlord's lien. 32 Am J1st L & T § 583.

landlord's lien. At common law, a lien for rent in arrears acquired by an actual seizure of property upon the leased premises by the levy of a distress for rent in arrears. 32 Am J1st L & T § 564. A lien in favor of the landlord for the rent, reserved in a lease, on the crops raised or personal property of the tenant brought upon the leased premises. 32 Am J1st L & T § 566. A statutory lien for rent upon property of the tenant brought upon the leased premises and, in the case of farm land, crops raised upon the leased premises. 32 Am J1st L & T § 575.

land lottery. A scheme for the division of land by chance, which is to cut a plot of land into several parcels of uniform size, but of unequal value, and to have each purchaser of a parcel pay a uniform price and select his parcel by lot. 34 Am J1st Lot § 11. Any lottery wherein land in the form of farm or building lot is the prize. Branham v Stallings, 21 Colo 211, 40 P 396.

landman. A tenant of land; a holder of land; a person in the occupation of land.

Land Management Bureau. A federal agency in the Department of the Interior, exercising functions formerly within the province of the General Land Office. 43 USC § 1, note.

landmark. A natural or artificial object having sufficient permanency to serve as a monument or marker of a land boundary. 12 AM J2d Bound § 4. A structure of historical significance. An event illuminative of an historical period, such as the Boston Tea Party. A reported case of great importance in establishing a legal proposition of law.

land measure. Area measure. Measuring by units of acres, square rods, square feet, etc.

land mile. See **mile.**

Land Office. See **General Land Office.**

land office records. Records of the General Land Office, kept under official sanction of the government. 30 Am J2d Ev § 999.

landowner. An owner of real property. Sometimes inclusive of a tenant for years. 32 Am J1st L & T

§ 4. As a person entitled to redeem from an execution sale:—any owner of real estate whose interest was subject to the payment of the judgment upon which it was sold, without regard to whether he is the judgment debtor or claims under him. Anno: 2 ALR 794, s. 95 ALR 1095. As one qualified to object to the issuance of a liquor license:—a holder of the legal title, exclusive of lessee, life tenant, or person vested with title for the sole purpose of qualifying as a signer. 30 Am J Rev ed Intox L § 147. As one to be named in a petition for the establishment of a highway:—any person who has an interest of record in the land over which the highway is to be located. Anno: 2 ALR 788, s. 95 ALR 1091. As the word is used in a mechanic's lien statute:—the owner of the fee or of any interest in lands, legal or equitable, fee simple, or leasehold, including life estates, estates for years, interest as cotenant, lessee, trustee, or vendee in possession under an executory contract of sale. Anno: 2 ALR 795, s. 95 ALR 1095; 36 Am J1st Mech L § 84. Within the meaning of statutes penalizing hunting over property without the consent of the owner:— a natural person, a corporation, or a quasi-person or entity such as a partnership, including one who owns an undivided fractional interest, one in possession under a parol contract of purchase, and, under some statutes, one who owns the hunting rights over lands. Anno: 2 ALR 799, s. 95 ALR 1099.

land patent. A conveyance to an individual of that which is the absolute property of the government and to which, but for the conveyance, the individual would have no right or title.
A transfer by the government to the entryman of land covered by a homestead entry, upon payment for the land and proof of settlement, residence, and cultivation. 42 Am J1st Pub L § 31.

land-poor. The condition of one whose ownership of land imposes a financial burden, being unproductive of net revenue. Matteson v Blackmer, 46 Mich 393, 397.

land-reeve (land'rēv). An overseer or superintendent of a portion of a farm or estate.

land regulations. Laws relating to the mode and requisites of a conveyance of title or any interest in real property. Laws relating to the use of premises, such as those relating to restrictive covenants, nuisances, and zoning.

lands available for mining. See **valuable for mining.**

lands beneath navigable waters. The beds of navigable rivers.
For detailed statement made for the purposes of the Submerged Lands Act, see 43 USC § 1301.

Lands' Clauses Act. An English statute passed in 1845, governing proceedings for the condemnation of private property for public use.

land scrip. See **scrip.**

land settlement. The settlement of public lands by homesteaders. A settlement upon public lands under a project primarily for the benefit of veterans. 56 Am J1st Vet & V A § 14. The closing of the transaction comprehended by a land contract by payment of consideration, transfer of title to purchaser, etc. A settlement of a controversy respecting the title to or the location of boundaries of real estate.

land's lagh. The title of a universal body of the common law of Sweden compiled out of the particular customs established by the laghman of every province, about 1250, and analogous to the common law of England.

lands let to lease. Lands conveyed only for life, years, or at will. Wright v Hardy, 76 Miss 524, 24 SW 697.

landslide. A falling or slipping of a large amount of earth or rock from a cliff, mountain, or hill onto lower ground, becoming a destructive manifestation of nature in wrecking buildings and obstructing highways. 25 Am J1st High § 111. A heavy vote in favor of a candidate at an election.

Landsteiner test. A blood test, otherwise known as the Bernstein blood test, devised to assist in the determination of parentage, postulated upon the inheritability of a blood type. 29 Am J2d Ev § 370.

lands, tenements, and hereditaments. Inheritable lands or interests therein amounting to freehold estates. Hutchinson v Bramhall, 42 NJ Eq 372, 383, 7 A 873.
See **freehold.**

land-tax. A tax imposed upon the beneficial owner of land.
See **real estate tax.**

land-tenant. A holder of land; a person in the actual possession or occupation of land. A lessee in possession.

land tenure. See **estate; tenure.**

land-waiter (land'wā"tėr). An English customs officer who measured and weighed and classified imported goods on their arrival at a port.

lane. A narrow way or passage, as distinguished from a public road or highway. Wiggins v Tallmadge (NY) 11 Barb 457, 465.

lanes of traffic. See **traffic lanes.**

Langdeau Case. A comparatively recent decision of the United States Supreme Court respecting the venue of actions against national banks. Mercantile Nat. Bank v Langdeau, 371 US 555, 9 L Ed 2d 523, 83 S Ct 520.

language. The spoken or written word as a means of communication. The words, sounds, and the forms thereof in grammatical composition, as used in a particular country, or by a particular group of people, as a means of communication.
While it is true that the word is broad enough to include words which are written as well as words which are spoken, it is generally held that statutes regulating the use of objectionable language refer to oral speech only unless written language is specifically mentioned in the statute. Stevenson v State, 90 Ga 456, 458.
See **ordinary and concise language.**

languidus (lan'gwi-dus). Sick; ill.

languidus in prisona (lan'gwi-dus in pri'so-na). Sick or ill in prison.

lanzas (lan'thas). (Spanish.) An annual money service paid by nobles and grandees to the government, as a substitute for military aid.

lapidation (lap-i-dā'shọn). Stoning to death; the execution of the death penalty by stoning the defendant.

lappage. The area as to which title deeds of rival claimants tend to lap upon each other. Vance v Guy, 224 NC 607, 31 SE2d 766.

lapse. A termination, particularly of a right or privilege. A forfeiture caused by one's failure to perform some necessary act. Winsor v Brown, 48 RI 200, 204, 136 A 434, 435. A policy of insurance becoming ineffective, according to the provisions of the policy, for failure to pay the premium. 29 Am J Rev ed Ins § 587.

lapsed benefice (lapst ben'ē-fis). The loss or forfeiture by a patron of his right to present a clergyman to a benefice, by not doing so in season.

lapsed land. Land entered by a homesteader upon the public domain under an entry which he did not perfect so as to be entitled to a patent or other conveyance of title by the government. 42 Am J1st Pub L §§ 19 et seq. Land covered by a patent which the patentee has lost by his failure to make payments or to comply with other conditions of the patent; such as the failure to pay quitrents or to cultivate the land. Wilcox v Calloway, 1 Va (1 Wash) 38, 39.

In the early settlement of the country, the man who received a grant of land and failed, at first in three, and afterwards in five years, to seat and improve it, was held to have abandoned it; it received the denomination of "lapsed land," and was declared to be forfeited. Hawkins v Barney's Lessee (US) 5 Pet 457, 468, 8 L Ed 190, 194.

lapsed patent. See **lapsed land.**

lapsed policy. See **lapse.**

lapse of legacy or devise. The falling back of the subject matter of a legacy or devise into the testator's estate. Anno: 3 ALR 1689. A legacy or devise which was good when the will was made, but has failed since then by some event which occurred before the testator's death. Occurring under a variety of circumstances, the most frequent of which is the death of the legatee or devisee before the death of the testator. 57 Am J1st Wills §§ 1424 et seq.

lapse of term of court. The ending of a term of court because of the judge's failure to appear on the day fixed by law for the opening of the term. 20 Am J2d Cts § 45.

lapsus. See **error lapsus.**

lapsus linguae (lap'sus ling'gwē). A slip of the tongue, language differing from that which the speaker intended to say. Chattanooga, Rome, & Columbus Railroad Co. v Liddell, 85 Ga 482, 11 SE 853; State v Owens, 243 NC 673, 91 SE2d 900, 902 (in charge to jury).

larboard watch (lär'bōrd wach). See **watch.**

larcenous. In a thievish manner; connected with the commission of larceny.

larceny. Stealing or theft. People v Campbell, 89 Cal App 646, 265 P 364. At common law:—the felony of taking by trespass and carrying away the goods or things personal of another, without the latter's consent and with the felonious intent permanently to deprive the owner of his property and to convert it to the taker's own use or the use of some person other than the owner. 32 Am J1st Larc § 2. As a statutory offense:—the taking of personal property accomplished by fraud or stealth, with intent to deprive another thereof. State v Ugland, 48 ND 841, 187 NW 237; the felonious stealing, taking, and carrying, leading, riding, or driving away the personal property of another. People v Lardner, 300 Ill 264, 133 NE 375, 19 ALR 721.

See **grand larceny; petit larceny.**

larceny after a trust. Embezzlement by bailee. Almand v State, 110 Ga 883, 36 SE 215.

larceny by bailee. An offense as defined by statute. An offense at common law only as it appears that possession was obtained by the bailee from the bailor with the felonius intent of appropriating the thing bailed to his own use and depriving the bailor thereof. 32 Am J1st Larc § 57.

larceny by finder. The taking and carrying away of the lost personal property of another with a felonious intent permanently to deprive the owner of his property and to convert it to his own, the finder's, use. 32 Am J1st Larc § 64.

larceny by fraud. The offense of taking personal property, accomplished by fraud or stealth and with intent to deprive the owner of his property permanently. Bivens v State, 6 Okla Crim 521, 120 P 1033.

larceny by general owner. The taking and carrying away of personal property by the general owner from the possession of a person holding possession under some special right or title, with the felonious intent of depriving such person of his rights, or of charging him with the value of the property. 32 Am J1st Larc § 53.

larceny by trick. The offense of taking personal property, accomplished by trick and with intent to deprive the owner of his property permanently. Commonwealth v Eichelberger, 119 Pa 254, 13 A 422.

larceny from the person. The statutory felony of stealing any article attached to the person of the owner or under his immediate personal protection.

Of course, larceny is "from the person," in any case, in the sense that the taking is with the intent to deprive another of his property.

larceny of mislaid goods. The felonious taking and carrying away of the mislaid goods of another, without his consent, and with the felonious intent permanently to deprive the owner of his property, and to convert it to his own, the finder's, use, which felonious intent may exist at the time of the finding, or subsequently to the finder's taking possession. 32 Am J1st Larc § 72.

larcyn (lär'sn). Larceny.

laron (la'ron). A thief.

lascivious. Loose; wanton; lewd; lustful; tending to produce voluptuous or lewd emotions. United States v Britton (Comrs Ct Ohio) 17 F 731; United States v Bebout (DC Ohio) 28 F 522, 524. As used in the laws relating to the use of the mails, immorality in the sense of sexual impurity. 41 Am J1st P O § 116.

See **lewd and lascivious conduct.**

lascivious carriage and behavior. Wanton acts between persons of different sexes, flowing from the exercise of lustful passions, which are grossly indecent and unchaste, and which are not otherwise punished as crimes against chastity and public decency. Fowler v State (Conn) 5 Day 81, 84.

lashlit (lash'lit). Same as **lagslite.**

last. Adjective: Coming after all others. Noun: A measure of carrying capacity, particularly of a ship, for which purpose it is equivalent to six thousand pounds in some places, but a lesser amount in others. A form over which shoes are built or repaired.

lastage. The load or ballast of a ship; a duty or custom charged at certain fairs or markets to permit a purchaser to go where he pleased with his purchase.

last and usual place of abode. As the place for substituted service of process by leaving a copy with a member of the family or household, the place of residence or domicil in the state at which the defendant last abided. Tilden v Johnson, 60 Mass (6 Cush) 354.

last antecedent. For the purposes of the rule of construction of a statute that qualifying words, phrases and clauses are ordinarily confined to the last antecedent:—the last words which can be made an antecedent without impairing the meaning of the sentence. Travers City v Blair Township, 190 Mich 313, 157 NW 81.

last antecedent clause. The principle that relative and qualifying words, phrases, or clauses are to be applied to the words, phrases, or clauses immediately precedent, and not extended to other words, phrases or clauses more remote. Montgomery Light & Traction Co. v Avant, 202 Ala 404, 80 So 497, 3 ALR 384.

last clear chance. The doctrine that the negligence of the plaintiff does not preclude a recovery for the negligence of the defendant where it appears that the defendant by exercising reasonable care and prudence might have avoided injurious consequences to the plaintiff notwithstanding the plaintiff's negligence. 38 Am J1st Negl § 215. The principle that a collision of vessels is attributed to the fault of the vessel which had the last clear chance to avoid the collision. 48 Am J1st Ship § 230.

The practical import of the doctrine is that a negligent defendant is held liable to a negligent plaintiff, or even to a plaintiff who has been grossly negligent in placing himself in peril, if the defendant, aware of the plaintiff's peril, or, according to some but not all authorities, although unaware of the plaintiff's peril, reasonably in the exercise of due care should have been aware of it, had in fact a later opportunity than the plaintiff to avoid an accident. Anno: 92 ALR 50, s. 119 ALR 1044; 7 Am J2d Auto § 376.

last commanded. The settled law. Flaherty v Thomas, 94 Mass (12 Allen) 428.

last court. See **last resort.**

last-court (làst′kōrt). An ancient English court which was held in the marshes of Kent.

last day. The final day for payment or performance without penalty for delay.
See **default day.**

last heir. The lord of the manor, or the king, as the case might be, to whom the land of the tenant, upon his death, escheated for want of lawful heirs.

last illness. The illness or sickness which was the cause of the decedent's death, covering the period during which it was continuously operative after it became serious or pronounced. Long v Northrup, 225 Iowa 132, 279 NW 104, 116 ALR 1475. In some connections, a sickness from which a person believed he would not recover, and from which he did not recover, but died. Harrington v Stees, 82 Ill 50.

last in, first out. A method of recording inventory in assessing a stock of merchandise. Anno: 66 ALR2d 834-836. A method of inventory valuation for income tax purposes which assumes that the most recently purchased merchandise is the first sold.

By treating current purchases as being sold first, the method seeks to eliminate from income profits which arose solely from an advance in the price level, thus more accurately matching costs against revenues.

last known address. The place to which the mail is to be directed for service of process by mail where actual personal service cannot be obtained. 42 Am J1st Proc § 60.

As used in a statute authorizing the service of summons on a non-resident defendant by mailing a copy of the summons and complaint to his last known address, the term means not his last address known to the plaintiff, but the plaintiff is required to ascertain at his peril, the last known address of the defendant as a matter of fact, and his failure to do so will amount to a failure to comply with the statute and render the service invalid. State v Belden, 193 Wis 145, 211 NW 916, 214 NW 460, 57 ALR 1218.

last resort. Characterizing a court from the judgments or decisions of which no appeal can be taken.

last sickness. See **last illness.**

last will. The effective will. Occidental Life Ins. Co. v Powers, 192 Wash 475, 74 P2d 27, 114 ALR 531.

As used in a will which the testator designated as his "last will," the term is not equivalent to "sole," and does not necessarily revoke all former wills. Freeman v Freeman, 27 Eng L & Eq 351.
See **will.**

last will and testament. See **last will; will.**

lata culpa (lā′ta kul′pa). Gross fault or neglect.

Lata culpa dolo aequiparatur (lā′ta kul′pa do′lō ē-qui-pa-rā′ter). An expression of the principle that gross fault—or gross negligence—is equivalent to fraud.

late. Out of time. Tardy.

late a resident. Last a resident. Beckett v Selover, 7 Cal 215.

latens (lā′tenz). Same as **latent.**

latent. Hidden from view; concealed; not discoverable by ordinary inspection. Miller v Moore, 83 Ga 684, 10 SE 360.

latent alteration. An alteration of an instrument not manifest or visible upon the face of the instrument. Miles City Bank v Askin, 119 Mont 581, 179 P2d 750, 171 ALR 790.

latent ambiguity. An ambiguity in a writing which does not appear until the writing is applied to the circumstances. Putnam v Bond, 100 Mass 58, 60. An uncertainty in an instrument which does not appear on the face, but which is shown to exist for the first time by matter outside the writing. Equivocality of expression, or obscurity of intention, arising not from the words of the instrument themselves, but from the ambiguous or obscure state of extrinsic circumstances to which the words of the instrument pertain, and which is susceptible of explanation by a mere development of extraneous facts without altering or adding to the written language or requiring more to be understood thereby than will fairly comport with the ordinary or legal sense of the words used in the instrument. 30 Am J2d Ev § 1073.

In a will:—an ambiguity which is not discoverable from reading the will, but which appears upon consideration of the extrinsic circumstances, for example, a bequest to "my cousin John," it appearing that the testator has two or more cousins "John." 57 Am J1st Wills § 1042.

latent danger. A hidden danger.

latent deed. A deed kept hidden in a secret place for twenty years or more. Den ex dem. Wright v Wright, 7 NJL 175.

latent defect. A defect not observable on casual inspection. A hidden defect in a structure, machine, or article of merchandise. A defect in an article constituting the subject matter of a sale, not discoverable on a reasonable examination of the property. 46 Am J1st Sales § 94. A secret defect arising out of the manner in which the article was manufactured. Hoe v Sanborn, 21 NY 552, 555.
A defect in the title to real estate not readily observable even though a matter of public record. Anno: 33 ALR 994.

latent injury. An injury not apparent at the time but capable of producing pain and suffering at a later time. 6 Am J2d Atomic E § 51.

lateral. From or toward the side.

lateral branch. See **lateral railroad.**

lateral railroad. A railroad line constituting an offshoot from the main line or stem; a feeder of the main line. Blanton v Richmond, Fredericksburg & Potomac Railroad Co. 86 Va 618, 620. A railroad connected, indeed, with the main line, but not a mere incident of it; not constructed simply to facilitate the chief railway, but designed to have a business of its own, for the transportation of persons or property. Baltimore & Ohio Railroad Co. v Waters, 105 Md 396, 66 A 685.

lateral support. The right to support of soil in its natural state from land adjoining it. 1 Am J2d Adj L § 37. Precisely, the right of an adjoining property owner to support for his land in its natural state from his neighbor's land in its natural state. Carrig v Andrews, 127 Conn 403, 17 A2d 520, 132 ALR 993.

latere. See **ex latere.**

lath (làth). A thin strip of wood, formerly used extensively on walls to form a base for plaster.

lathe. A machine for cutting and shaping wood or metal.
In some counties in England, an intermediate division between a shire or county and a hundred, containing about three or four hundreds, as the lathes in Kent. In Sussex, these divisions were called rapes. Each lathe had its lathe-reeve, and each rape had its rape-reeve, corresponding to the shire-reeve or sheriff of the shire or county. See 1 Bl Comm 116.

lathe-reeve. See **lathe.**

latifundium (lat-i-fun'di-um). (Civil law.) A large landed estate.

latifundus (la-ti-fun'dus). (Civil law.) The owner or holder of a large landed estate.

Latin. A designation applicable to ancient Rome and the people and things of ancient Rome, particularly the language.

Latins (lat'ins). The inhabitants of Latium, the district of Italy in which Rome was situated.

latitare (la-ti-tā're). To lie hidden; to be concealed.

latitat (la'ti-tat). He lies hidden; a writ running outside the county to summon one who lay concealed there to the king's bench. See 3 Bl Comm 286.

Latitat et discurrit (la'ti-tat et dis-ker'rit). He lies hidden, or lurks, and wanders about,—formal words used in a writ of latitat. See 3 Bl Comm 286.

latitatio (la-ti-tā'she-ō). (Civil law.) A concealment of one's person; a lying hidden.

Latium (lā'she-um). The district of Italy in which the city of Rome was situated.

lator (lā'tor). (Roman law.) A messenger; the bearer of a message; the proposer of a law.

latori praesentium (la-tō'rī prē-sen'she-um). To the bearer of these presents.

lato sensu (lā'tō sen'sū). In a broad sense; broadly speaking.

latro (la'trō). A thief; a robber; a brigand; a freebooter; a bandit.

latrocination (lat″rō-si-nā'shọn). Pillage; robbery committed by force or violence. American Ins. Co. v Bryan & Maitland (NY) 26 Wend 563, 573.

latrocinium (lat-rọ-sin'i-um). Same as **latrocination.**

latrociny (lat'rọ-si-ni). Larceny.

latter. Comparative in reference to point of time or of place. The word may mean later in point of time, but as applied to two conflicting provisions in the same code it has reference to place or arrangement in the code. Armstrong v Phillips, 76 Okla 192, 184 P 109.

laudamentum parium suorum (lâ-da-men'tum pā'rium su-ō'rum). The finding of his peers; that is, the verdict of a jury. See 2 Bl Comm 285.

laudanum. (lâ'da-num). A narcotic drug, a solution of opium in alcohol. Michigan Mut. Life Ins. Co. v Naugle, 130 Ind 79, 29 NE 393.

laudare (lâ-dā're). (Civil law.) To name; to cite; to quote; to show one's title or authority; to testify favorably as to a person's character. To advise; to arbitrate.

laudatio (lâ-dā'she-ō). (Roman law.) Testimony favorable to a person's character.

laudator (lâ-dā'tọr). A witness who testifies favorably as to a person's character; an arbitrator; an adviser.

laudemium (lâ-de'mi-um). (Civil law.) A fiftieth part of the purchase price, or if there was no sale, a fiftieth part of the true value of the estate, paid to the owner for his acceptance of a new tenant or emphyteuta upon the latter's acquisition of the estate by gift, devise, exchange, or sale. See Mackeldey's Roman Law § 328.

laudum (lâ'dum). An award of arbitrators. A sentence or judgment; a doom.

laughe. A frank-pledge,—an old English pledge or bond given to secure the good behavior of members of a tithing by the other members.

laughlesman (law'les-man). A lawless man; a man who had lost his law; an outlaw.

launch. Noun: A relatively small watercraft with motive power. Verb: To start an enterprise. To let a newly-constructed vessel slide from the way to the water.

laundry. A place wherein the trade of washing and ironing clothing and linen is pursued. 33 Am J1st

LAUNDRY [712] LAWFUL

Laundries § 1. Not a manufacturing establishment. Anno: 31 ALR 535.

laundry route. A list of the customers of a laundry by name and street address. Adkins v Model Laundry Co. 92 Cal App 575, 268 P 939.

laundry-supply service. Same as **linen-supply service.**

laus Deo (lâs Dē'ō). Praise be to God. Bills of exchange at one time were written with this sanctimonious beginning.

lavatory. A toilet; a men's room; a powder room for women.

law. The whole body of rules of conduct applied and enforced under the authority of established government in determining that which is proper and should be permitted and that which should be denied, or even penalized, in respect of the relation between a person and the state, between him and society, or between him and another individual, including a provision of a constitution, a legislative enactment or statute, a municipal ordinance, a principle declared in an authoritative decision of a court, a rule of practice prescribed by a legislature or promulgated by a court acting with authority, even, to some extent, a usage or custom. Strother v Lucas (US) 12 Pet 410, 9 L Ed 1137.

There is no word in the language which, in its popular and technical application, takes a wider or more diversified signification. In its popular sense, and in common acceptation, by those for whom laws are made, the word includes the whole body or system of rules of conduct, but it does not include that refined, technical and astute idea which recognizes nothing within the meaning of the term which is not constitutionally and technically perfect. Miller v Dunn, 72 Cal 462, 14 P 27. See also 1 Bl Comm 44.

The constitution of the state is "a law of the state" within the meaning of the Constitution of the United States, prohibiting states from passing laws impairing the obligation of contract. Bier v McGehee, 148 US 137, 37 L Ed 397, 13 S Ct 580.

law action. See **action at law.**

law and motion day. A court day, in some jurisdictions, upon which issues of law and motions are heard by the court.

lawbook. A book primarily for use by lawyers, such as a digest, law report, text, or a volume of an encyclopedic work such as American Jurisprudence or Corpus Juris.

law borgh. A pledge or security for a person's appearance in court.

law-burrows (lâ'bur''ōz). Security to keep the peace.

law charges. Costs,—the court and official charges in an action or proceeding.

law clerk. A person employed in a law office, usually for the performance of duties for which admission to the bar is not required. A person following the employment for the purpose of obtaining instruction in the law and the practice of law preliminary to his admission to the bar.

law conclusion. See **conclusion of law.**

law court. A court having jurisdiction of cases at law as distinguished from cases in equity; a classification no longer of moment in most jurisdictions. 20 Am J2d Cts § 25.

law-day. The exact day specified in a contract upon which money was to be paid. Moore v Norman, 43 Minn 428, 45 NW 857. The day named for the performance of the obligation of a mortgagor. 36 Am J1st Mtg § 380.

The adoption of the lien theory has been regarded as abolishing the significance of a law day, or at least as extending the term to include any day prior to foreclosure. Murray v O'Brien, 56 Wash 361, 105 P 840.

See **law and motion day.**

law digest. See **digest.**

law enforcement officer. A policeman, sheriff, deputy sheriff, constable, or other officer whose duty it is to be vigilant in discovering violations of the criminal laws and ordinances and to arrest offenders.

law French. The Norman French which was brought into use in all court proceedings at the time of the Norman Conquest.

Many of its terms survive in modern law.

lawful. According to law. In accord with the spirit of the law, not merely the forms of law. State ex rel. Van Nice v Whealey, 5 SD 427, 431, 59 NW 211.

See **legal,** also words and phrases following beginning "lawful" and words and phrases beginning "legal".

lawful business. A business lawful as to all who wish to engage in it. Re Co-operative Law Co. 198 NY 479, 92 NE 15.

lawful charges. Impositions lawfully imposed. Charges made in accord with rates prescribed by law.

As the term is used in a statute requiring a party who redeems from a mortgage foreclosure sale to pay all "lawful charges," it is one of very large signification and includes every lien or incumbrance or claim the purchaser may have upon the premises, and for which, at law or in equity, he would be entitled to hold the lands as security, and for the satisfaction of which a court of equity would condemn them. First National Bank v Elliott, 125 Ala 646, 27 So 7.

lawful day. A day which is lawful for the transaction of business or the making of a particular contract.

See **legal holiday; nonjuridical day; Sunday.**

lawful fence. A good and sufficient fence within the statutory requirement for a fence, frequently prescribed as one such as good husbandmen generally keep. 35 Am J2d Fen § 1.

lawful force. The extent of the force permitted to be used in self-defense, that is, the degree of violence permitted in resisting an attack upon one's person; such degree of violence as is necessary, or is honestly and reasonably believed by the person attacked to be necessary, for his defense. 6 Am J2d Asslt & B §§ 72, 162. That degree of force which a peace officer is permitted to employ in making an arrest; such force as is reasonably necessary to apprehend the offender or effect the arrest. 5 Am J2d Arr § 80.

lawful goods. Articles or substances which are not contraband and may be held, sold, or exported without violating the law. Seton & Co. v Low (NY) 1 Johns Cas 1, 5.

lawful heirs. Those persons upon whom the descent of real property is cast upon the death of the owner intestate. 23 Am J2d Desc & D § 43. As the term appears in a will, those persons on whom the law passes the descent of real estate or admits to participate in the distribution of personalty, except as a contrary intention appears in the context of the will in which the clause appears. White v Inman, 212 Miss 237, 54 So 2d 375, 30 ALR2d 380. Ordinarily a term of art, constituting words of limitation. 28 Am J2d Est § 118. But sometimes constituting words of purchase. Conger v Lowe, 124 Ind 368, 24 NE 889; 28 Am J2d Est § 118 (construed as meaning "children"). According to some, although not all, authority, inclusive of half bloods as well as whole bloods. Anno: 49 ALR2d 1369-1372.

lawful holder. One entitled to possession and in possession.
For definition of term as it appears in a provision of the Carmack Amendment to the Interstate Commerce Act (49 USC § 20(11)), see Pennsylvania R. Co. v Carr, 243 US 587, 61 L Ed 914, 37 S Ct 472; Pennsylvania R. Co. v Olivit Bros. 243 US 574, 61 L Ed 908, 37 S Ct 468.
See **holder in due course.**

lawful interest. Any rate of interest up to that fixed by statute as the maximum rate at which interest can be charged by contract. Re Hoerman's Estate (Mo) 247 SW2d 762.
See **legal interest.**

lawful issue. In the broader sense, all the descendants of a person; the technical equivalent of heirs of the body. 57 Am J1st Wills § 1379. Primarily words of limitation, but words of purchase where it appears on the face of a will that the clause should be construed as a word of purchase, as where a devise is to "lawful issue as tenants in common." 57 Am J1st Wills § 1377. A term exclusive of a child born out of wedlock. Olmsted v Olmsted, 190 NY 458, 83 NE 569.

lawful man. A freeman; a man who could make oath and testify as a witness; a man who had not been outlawed or attainted.

lawful money. Gold and silver coin of the United States, or paper money which by act of Congress has been made the equivalent of such coin. Bronson v Rodes (US) 7 Wall 229, 19 L Ed 141.
See **legal tender.**

lawful order. Any order of court which is not erroneous; any order which may not be reversed on appeal for error. Ex parte Cohen, 5 Cal 494, 495.

lawful rate. The rate for transportation which a carrier must exact and which the shipper must pay. Duholm v Chicago, N. & St. P. Ry. Co. 146 Minn 1, 177 NW 772.
See **lawful interest; legal interest.**

lawful representative. Same as **legal representative.**

lawful structure. A structure which conforms to law and is permitted and authorized by law. Pike Rapids Power Co. v Minneapolis, St. P. & S. S. M. R. Co. (CA8 Minn) 99 F2d 902.

lawful war. A war which is lawful by the law of nations. A thing which can never exist without the express concurrence of the war-making power. 56 Am J1st War § 5.

lawful wedlock. Matrimony; the ceremony or state of marriage. State v Coliton, 73 ND 582, 17 NW2d 546, 156 ALR 1403.

lawing a mastiff (lâ'ing a màs'tif). The practice of cutting off the claws and ball or pelote of the forefeet, to prevent the dogs from running after deer in the king's forest. See 3 Bl Comm 72.

law Latin. The Latin language, considerably mutilated, as used in the old forms and proceedings in England for four centuries, "until the subversion of our ancient constitution under Cromwell." See 3 Bl Comm 319, 322.

lawless. The characterization of a person who does not submit to be governed by the law. Arkansas v Kansas & T. Coal Co. (CC Ark) 96 F 353, 362.

lawless court. A curious ancient court held at Essex in England at cock-crowing, without lights, ink, or pen, whereat all speech was in whispers.

lawless man. A man who had lost his law; an outlaw.

law list. An annual compilation of statistics and important and interesting matters concerning the profession of the law in England. A published list of attorneys at law used in law offices in referring matters and cases to attorneys at a distance.

law lords. Those members of the upper house of the English parliament, the house of lords, who have held high judicial offices.

law martial. See **military law.**

law merchant. A body of commercial law embracing the usages of merchants in different commercial countries, but not resting exclusively on the institutions and local customs of any particular country, consisting of certain principles of equity and usages of trade which general convenience and a common sense of justice have established to regulate the dealings of merchants and mariners in all the commercial countries of the civilized world. Bank of Conway v Stary, 51 ND 399, 200 NW 505, 37 ALR 1186. Long recognized as a part of the common law. 15 Am J2d Com L § 8. The basis of the jurisprudence regulating bills of exchange and promissory notes, particularly the negotiability of such instruments and the rights and liabilities of persons becoming parties to the instrument. 11 Am J2d B & N § 36.
The law merchant or lex mercatoria was originally a separate body of law, and, like equity and admiralty law, was administered in separate or special courts. It bore some analogy to the Roman system known as "jus gentium." The lex mercatoria was not, like the common law, the custom of a place or territory; it was the recognized custom of merchants and traders who had business relations in all the countries of Europe, including England. The merchant class and the controversies of its members arising out of commercial transactions, were not subject to the common law. During the sixteenth century the admiralty court declared the principles of the law merchant. Later, the common law judges encroached upon the field of admiralty over commercial transactions. Thus, the law merchant gradually became a part of the legal system of England. Bank of Conway v Stary, 51 ND 399, 200 NW 505, 37 ALR 1186, 1193.

Law of Alaric. A statute book or code of laws which was published in 506 A. D., by Alaric II, often referred to as Lex Romana Visigothorum.
It borrowed much from the code of Theodosius, some from the Gregorian code and some from the Hermogenian code.

law of citations. In the broad sense, the effect of precedent. In a technical sense, a law of ancient Rome prescribing the relative authority of the works of Roman law writers.

law of damages. A term of art applied to the body

of principles which determines the size of a verdict. 22 Am J2d Damg § 22.

law office clerk. See **law clerk**.

law officer. A public officer having powers and duties in the enforcement of the penal laws. A commissioned officer who presides at a general court-martial.

See **peace officer**.

law of marque. The law of nations governing the seizure of property of a hostile nation on the high seas.

See **letters of marque and reprisal**.

law of nations. Same as **international law**.

law of nature. See **natural law**.

law of payment. The law relating to performance of the contract.

law of retaliation. The principle that one should be punished for a crime by inflicting upon him the same injury that he inflicted upon the victim of the offense.

law of ship's flag. See **law of the flag**.

law of the case. The principle that instructions given by the court to the jury during the trial of a case, become, for the time being, the law of the case, binding upon the jury, court and counsel. 53 Am J1st Trial § 492. A rule kindred to the doctrine of res judicata. United States v United States Smelting, Refining & Mining Co. 339 US 186, 94 L Ed 750, 70 S Ct 537, reh den 339 US 972, 94 L Ed 1379, 70 S Ct 994. The principle that a decision of the appellate court, unless properly set aside is controlling at all subsequent stages of the litigation, including the rule that on remand the trial court must strictly follow the mandate of the appellate court. 5 Am J2d A & E § 744. Also inclusive of the principle that if an appellate court has passed on a legal question and has remanded the cause to the court below for further proceedings, the legal questions thus determined by the appellate court will not be differently determined on a subsequent appeal in the same case. Todd v State, 229 Ind 664, 101 NE2d 45 (concurring opinion). The rule that the final judgment of a court on an appeal from the action taken by an administrative agency governs the agency in all further proceedings in the case. Federal Power Com. v Pacific Power & Light Co. 307 US 156, 83 L Ed 1180, 59 S Ct 766; State ex rel. Spurck v Civil Service Board, 226 Minn 240, 32 NW2d 574.

law of the flag. The law of the state or nation whose flag is flown by the vessel involved. 2 Am J2d Adm § 90. The law of the sovereignty to which the ship belongs. 48 Am J1st Ship § 545. A doctrine, perhaps the most venerable and universal rule of maritime law bearing on conflict of laws, that certain maritime matters are determined pursuant to the law of the state or nation whose flag the vessel flies. 2 Am J2d Adm § 90.

law of the forum. The law of the jurisdiction in which the cause is litigated. 16 Am J2d Confl L § 11.

law of the land. The law of the state in which the proceeding is brought, whether common law or statutory law. 16 Am J2d Const L § 547. An implement of the guaranty of due process of law, having reference to the common law as modified by statute and as suited to the wants and conditions of the people. 16 Am J2d Const L § 543.

The term in a constitutional provision that "no person ought to be taken, imprisoned, or divested of his freehold, liberty, or privileges, or outlawed or exiled, or in any manner deprived of his life, liberty, or property but by the law of the land," is synonymous with due process of law. State v Ballance, 229 NC 764, 51 SE2d 731, 7 ALR2d 407.

law of the place. The law of the place in which the circumstances arose on which the litigation is based. 16 Am J2d Confl L § 11.

law of the road. See **rules of the road**.

law of the staple. The law administered in the enforcement of a statute staple; the law merchant.

See **law merchant; statute staple**.

law of war. That part of the law of nations which prescribes for, and regulates the conduct of, war and the status, rights and duties of enemy nations and of enemy individuals. Ex parte Quirin, 317 US 1, 87 L Ed 3, 63 S Ct 2.

law question. See **question of law**.

law report. A publication containing the opinions of a court or courts in actual cases, sometimes, as in the case of the American Law Reports, containing annotations showing additional cases upon or cognate to the point or points decided in the reported case.

law review. A publication of special interest to lawyers and professors in law schools, usually emanating from a law school as the work of professors of law and law students of the more capable and scholarly type, and containing articles on points of law of the most current interest.

law side. The sitting of a court having jurisdiction in both law and equity but for the time sitting as a court of law.

Laws of Oleron. A code of maritime laws which are received by all nations in Europe as the ground and foundation of all their maritime constitutions.

This code was compiled by Richard the First at the Isle of Oleron on the coast of France which was then a possession of the English crown. See 1 Bl Comm 418. The Laws of Oleron have been held in peculiar respect by England, and have been incorporated into her maritime jurisprudence. Per Story, J., in (US CC A) 2 Mason 548.

Laws of the Bretts and Scotts. An ancient Scotch code which was abolished under Edward the First.

laws of the country. In the broader sense of the term, the laws of the United States and the state and local laws.

As the expression is used in a treaty providing that if any citizen of either country shall die in the territory of the other, the consul of the nation to which he belonged shall have the right to administer the decedent's estate, conformably with the "laws of the country," so far as the United States is concerned, the phrase means the local laws of administration and procedure of the respective states of the Union. If the right asserted is necessarily contrary to those laws, it cannot be said to conform to them. Estate of Ghio, 157 Cal 552, 108 P 516.

laws of the several states. As laws to be applied by the federal courts:—statutes and the rules of law as declared by the highest court of the state in the field of the common or decisional law, including matters of general or commercial law. Erie Railroad Co. v Tompkins, 304 US 64, 82 L Ed 1188, 58 S Ct 817, 114 ALR 1487.

As to what actions arise under the laws and treaties of the United States so as to vest jurisdiction in federal courts, see Anno: 14 ALR2d 992.

law spiritual. The ecclesiastical law.

law student. A person engaged in the study of law with the purpose of obtaining admission to the bar or of engaging in a business in which knowledge of the law is helpful, usually in a college of law but sometimes as a law clerk.
See **inns of chancery; law clerk.**

lawsuit. An action or proceeding in a civil court in law or in equity, but not a criminal prosecution. Patterson v Standard Acci. Ins. Co. 178 Mich 288, 144 NW 491.

law worthy. Worthy of the protection of the law; entitled to such protection.

lawyer. An attorney or counsellor at law; a barrister; a solicitor; a person licensed by law to practice the profession of the law who thus practices.
A lawyer need not appear in any court, advertise himself as a lawyer, or earn his living by the services he performs as a lawyer, if he occupies some of his time in doing the proper work of a lawyer which contributes to his support, to fall within the term as it is used in a statute exempting the library of a "lawyer" from execution. Equitable Life Assur. Soc. v Goode, 101 Iowa 160, 70 NW 113.
See **attorney; common lawyer; crown lawyer; practicing lawyer.**

Lawyers' Edition. The United States Supreme Court Reports as published by the Lawyers Co-operative Publishing Company of Rochester, New York.

lawyer's liability policy. See **lawyer's protective policy.**

lawyer's protective policy. A policy insuring an attorney at law against any claim against him arising out of the performance of professional services as a lawyer and caused by any negligent act, error, or omission for which he would be legally liable, excluding claims arising out of fraudulent or criminal misconduct. Anno: 72 ALR2d 1249.

Lawyers' Reports Annotated. A predecessor of the American Law Reports.
See **American Law Reports.**

Lawyers' Reports Annotated (New Series). A successor to Lawyers' Reports Annotated and a predecessor of American Law Reports.
See **American Law Reports.**

laxative. A drug or medicine, the effect of which is to induce a bowel movement. Kelly v Carroll, 36 Wash 2d 482, 219 P2d 79, 19 ALR2d 1174.

lay. Adjective: Pertaining to laymen or the laity, as opposed to the clergy. Verb: To place or put in position. A slang expression meaning to engage with in sexual intercourse.

lay a bet. To place a wager.

lay corporation. A corporation the purposes of which are secular, as opposed to religious; a corporation composed of laymen.

lay damages. To allege damages, particularly in a pleading, such as a complaint.

lay days. The days specified in a contract of affreightment during which the charterer of a vessel is permitted to detain her for loading or unloading without incurring liability for demurrage. 48 Am J1st Ship § 608.

lay fee. A feud or fee held by services which were not religious.

lay gents. Same as **laymen.**

lay impropriator (im-prō'pri-ā-tor). (Ecclesiastical law.) A layman who held the appropriation of a benefice; an impropriate rector; a lay rector.

laying basis. See **laying foundation.**

laying foundation. Introducing evidence for the purpose of showing the relevancy and materiality of other evidence sought to be introduced. 53 Am J1st Trial § 117.

laying off. The election and designation of a homestead. 26 Am J1st Home §§ 87 et seq. An employer's act in terminating the employment temporarily. A slang term for desisting from critical comments. A gambler's term for not placing a wager on a particular event.
See **laying out; layoff.**

laying on of hands. The striking or touching of one person by another. 6 Am J2d Asslt & B § 5.

laying out. Locating and establishing a new highway. Borrowdale v Board of County Comrs. 23 NM 1, 163 P 721.
See **laying off.**

laying the venue. Stating in the caption of a declaration, complaint, or petition the court and jurisdiction in which the action or proceeding is brought.

lay judge. A person sitting as a judge, usually, if not always, as an assistant, who is not versed or learned in the law.

layman. Singular of **laymen.**

laymen. Persons not of the profession, whether it be that of the clergy, of lawyers, of actors, or of physicians, but particularly that of the clergy.

layoff. A temporary suspension of employment of a person at the instance of his employer. The act of an employer in suspending the employment of one or more employees during an exigency, such as lack of materials, an oversupply of manufactured articles, etc. Prudential Ins. Co. v Bridgman, 256 Ky 575, 76 SW2d 639.
The courts are divided in view as to whether or not a layoff constitutes a termination of employment within the meaning of a group insurance policy. 29A Am J Rev ed Ins § 1772.
See **laying off.**

layoff status. The status of an employee receiving no pay during a shutdown. Golubski Unemployment Compensation Case, 171 Pa Super 634, 91 A2d 315, 30 ALR2d 362.

layout. A sketch of a building to be constructed. Walter M. Ballard Corp. v Dougherty, 106 Cal App 2d 35, 234 P2d 745. The plan or scheme determining the style and arrangement of a printed page, a newspaper, or an advertisement.
See **mine layout.**

layover ticket. A ticket issued by a carrier which permits the passenger to break the journey at various points, resuming travel at his convenience and pleasure, subject to certain overall limitations of time. Chicago Rock Island & P. R. Co. v Boyce, 73 Ill 510.

lay people. Laymen, particularly jurors.

lay taxes. To levy taxes.

lay tenure. Any tenure which was not of a spiritual nature; that is, a tenure under which lands were held by services which were not religious. See 2 Bl Comm 101.

lay witness. A witness, other than an expert in the field, whose opinion is sought to be introduced in evidence.

lazaret (laz-a-ret'). A place of quarantine, particularly on a ship, where persons having contagious diseases may be isolated, thus preventing the spreading of the disease.

lazaretto (laz-a-ret'ō). Same as **lazaret.**

le (le). (French.) The, for the masculine.

Le action bien gist (le ak'sion bē'en jist). The action well lies.

leading astray. The seduction of a female by persuasion or inducements. 47 Am J1st Seduc § 2.

leading a use. Making a deed to show the object or use previously to a fine or recovery.

If fines or recoveries were levied or suffered without any good consideration, and without any uses declared, they inured only to the use of him who levied or suffered them, unless their force and effect were directed by other deeds expressing particular uses. If such deeds were made before the fine or recovery, they were called deeds to lead the uses. If they were made subsequently, they were called deeds to declare the uses. See 2 Bl Comm 363.

leading case. A case often referred to by the courts and by counsel as having finally settled and determined a point of law.

leading counsel. The counsel or attorney who has charge of his side of a case with other counsel assisting him.

leading devise. A devise which operates to control or vary other distinct provisions of the will which by themselves would have tended toward the creation of an interest or estate other than indicated by the leading devise. Lewis v Payne, 113 Md 127, 77 A 321.

leading question. A question put to a witness which suggests the answer desired, or which assumes to be proved a fact which is not proved, or which, embodying a material fact, admits of an answer by a simple negative or affirmative. Deans v Deans, 171 Ga 664, 156 SE 691, 74 ALR 222; Turney v State, 16 Miss (8 Smedes & M) 104.

lead pencil. See **pencil.**

lead poisoning. An occupational disability of painters, of idiopathic as distinguished from traumatic origin. Adams v Acme White Lead & Color Works, 182 Mich 157, 148 NW 485.

leaflet. A brochure, often used in advertising, especially in political campaigns, being distributed from house to house.

league. An association or society. 6 Am J2d Asso & C § 1. A unit of linear measure, equivalent to 3 miles. A mexican unit of area measure.

The Mexican league as used in Texas and applicable to Spanish grants in the Neutral Ground has always been estimated at 4,428.4 acres, being a square of 5,000 varas on each side, the vara being considered 33-1/3 American inches, and grants of leagues in the Neutral Ground should be estimated at that rate. The true vara is slightly less than 33-1/3 inches, but it is by usage estimated at 33-1/3 in Texas, and in California at 33 inches. United States v Perot (US) 8 Otto 428, 25 L Ed 251.

See **business league; marine league.**

League of Nations. A governmental and juridical agency of international status organized to deal with questions of an international character, being in existence from January 10, 1920 until its dissolution on January 10, 1946, its successor being the United Nations. 30 Am J Rev ed Internat L § 9.

leak. A divulging of information intended to be kept secret.

See **leakage.**

leakage. The escape of a liquid or a vapor. Loss in a ship's cargo by leaking or breaking in transit.

As used in bills of lading, the term appears to be applied not only to the leaking of liquids from their casks or other containers, but also to the loss attendant upon breaking alone, such as the breakage of glass show cases stowed in a cargo. Thomas v Ship Morning Glory, 13 La Ann 269.

leal (lēl). Loyal; lawful; liege.

lealte (lēl-te). Legality; loyalty.

lean-to. A shed, or other dependent structure, the supports of which rest upon or lean against another building.

leap year. A year of 366 days, occurring after a sequence of three common years, that is, years of 365 days, the extra day of the leap year being the 29th day of February.

By the statute 21 Henry III, it was provided that in certain cases of pleading, where February 29th of a leap year intervened, the 28th and 29th were to be counted as one day and statutes in this country have provided that whenever "year" or "years" is used, the year shall be taken to consist of 365 days; and the added day of a leap year, and the day immediately preceding, if they shall occur in any period so to be computed, shall be reckoned together as one day. But each of the 28th and 29th days of February, in the leap year, is a day of twenty-four hours' duration, and where these two days occur in any period of days less than one year, they ought to be and must be regarded as two days, and not as one day, for any purpose. See 52 Am J1st Time § 10.

learned in the law. Having much learning in the law. More precisely admitted to the practice of law or entitled to be admitted to practice without examination. Jamieson v Wiggin, 12 SD 16, 80 NW 137; Danforth v Egan, 23 SD 43, 119 NW 1021.

learned of. Having acquired actual knowledge of. Anno: 23 ALR2d 1076.

lease. Noun: A contract for the possession and profits of lands and tenements on the one side, and a recompense of rent or other income on the other. A conveyance by one to be known as the "landlord" to another to be known as the "tenant," ordinarily for a term of years, but sometimes at will or for the life of the tenant, in consideration of payment of rent or other recompense. 32 Am J1st L & T § 2. Undoubtedly a "conveyance," although it conveys a lesser interest than does a deed. 32 Am J1st L & T § 3. Inclusive in modern times, of the bailment of a chattel, such as an automobile or a computer. Verb: To create a tenancy. Mallory Associates, Inc. v Barving Realty Co. 300 NY 297, 90 NE2d 468, 15 ALR2d 1193. To make a bailment of a chattel.

See **leasehold.**

lease and release. A form of conveyance, in general use at one time in England, but rarely used in the United States. 23 Am J2d Deeds §§ 14, 15.

A highly artificial method once in use in England for conveying real property, consisting, first, of a

LEASED [717] LEDGER

lease (or bargain and sale for a year) which by force of the Statute of Uses put the lessee or bargainee in possession, and while he was thus in possession, although by a mere fiction, the lessor or bargainor executed to him a deed of release, which operated by way of enlargement of the estate, and was effectual to transfer the entire title to the lessee or bargainee. Hall's Lessee v Ashby, 9 Ohio 96.

leased aircraft. An aircraft held under a lease. 8 Am J2d Avi § 24.

leased automobile. A rented automobile.
See **renting automobiles.**

lease for years. A contract between lessor and lessee by which the lessor contracts to grant the possession and enjoyment of land, or hereditaments of a demisable nature, for a period of years certain, and the lessee usually agrees to render to the lessor a rent in money, or any other kind of payment, at the end of stated periods during the term. 32 Am J1st L & T § 61.
See **estate for years.**

leasehold. The interest of a lessee. An interest in real estate. 26 Am J1st H & W § 233. An estate in real property which is conveyed to a tenant by his landlord when the landlord makes a lease of the property to the tenant; an estate entirely separate and distinct from the estate which the landlord retains. Stubbings v Evanston, 136 Ill 37, 26 NE 577. Included in a devise of "land" where the testator has no lands which he owns in fee. 57 Am J1st Wills § 1337.
See **estate for years.**

leasehold estate. Same as **leasehold.**

leasehold interest. Same as **leasehold.**

lease in reversion. A lease that becomes effective only at the expiration of the term of the prior lease.
That the lease is to have this effect may be expressed in two ways, i. e., the time set for the beginning of the term in the second lease may be made to correspond with the time set for the expiration of the term of the prior lease, or the second lease may contain a reference to the first, and be so worded as to become effective at the expiration of the term thereof. 32 Am J1st L & T § 94.

lease of personalty. See **bailment.**

lease on shares. A lease providing for the payment of grain or crop rent.

lease renewable forever. A lease for a term of years, often for ninety-nine years, with unlimited option for renewal. 32 Am J1st L & T § 1039.

lease with option to purchase. A lease in the ordinary form with the usual provisions, and in addition thereto, providing that in consideration of the payment of a specified sum and the stipulated rent and a full compliance with all the terms of the lease, the lessee is to have the option at the end of the term to purchase the property for a specified sum. Cawthorn v McAlister, 217 Ky 551, 552, 290 SW 316.

Leasing Act. A federal statute enacted in 1920, which, as amended, regulates the exploration and development of gas, oil, and mineral lands included within the public domain. 24 Am J1st Gas & O § 46; 36 Am J1st Min & M § 65.

leaute (lay′ō-tay′). Legal sufficiency.

leave. Verb: To deposit or put a thing in place. To make a disposition of something, particularly by a will. Williams v Kidd, 170 Cal 631, 151 P 1. To refrain from assuming possession of property in the hands of another, thereby committing it to his custody and management. Allen v McFarland, 150 Ill 455, 461. Noun: Permission.

leave and license. The permission of the plaintiff, set up by the defendant as a defense in an action of trespass.

leave of absence. Absence from work with the permission of the employer, Anno: 174 ALR 576, sometimes with pay. Nolan v State (Ct Cl) 44 NYS2d 328. The absence of one in the Civil Service, from work, with the permission of his superior. 15 Am J2d Civ S § 31.

leave of court. Permission of court; an order of court granting permission to take a certain step in an action, usually, where it is discretionary with the court to give or refuse the permission. Copperthwait v Dummer, 18 NJL 258, 260.

leave standing. An expression familiar in reference to statutes and ordinances prohibiting or regulating the parking of vehicles on the streets and other public highways.
As used in a statute making it unlawful to leave standing on a highway any vehicle, whether attended or not, without leaving fifteen feet of the traveled portion of the highway clear for traffic on the left, the words "leave standing" are held to mean "stopping at all without leaving the required clearance." The word "leave" means to put, place, deposit, deliver, or the like. Stand means to cease from movement or progress; to pause; to stop; to remain stationary or inactive. Jaggers v Southeastern Greyhound Lines (DC Tenn) 34 F Supp 667.

leaving process at place of abode. A method of substituted service of process. 42 Am J1st Proc § 60.

leaving scene of accident. The act of one of a callous class known as "hit-and-run" drivers, the purpose being to evade civil or criminal consequences by escape before identity can be established. 7 Am J2d Auto § 246.

leaving vehicle. See **alighting from vehicle.**

Le batel est oblige a la marchandise et la marchandise au batel (lē bä-tĕl ät ō-blē-jä ä lä mar-shän-dēs ä lä mar-shän-dēs ō bä-tel). The ship is liable to the cargo and the cargo to the ship.
The owner of the cargo has a lien, by the maritime law, upon the ship for the safe custody, due transport, and right delivery of the same, as much as the ship-owner has upon the cargo for the freight, as expressed in the maxim. The Maggie Hammond v Morland (US) 9 Wall 435, 19 L Ed 772, 777.

leccator (le-kā′tor). A lecherous person.

lecherous. Lustful; characterized by lechery. Jones v State, 38 Tex Crim 87, 40 SW 807, 41 SW 638.

lechery. Excessive indulgence in sex.

lecherwite. Same as **lairesite.**

le contrat fait la loi (le kon′trạ fā lä lwa). The contract makes the law.

lecto mortali. See **in lecto mortali.**

L Ed. Abbreviation of **Lawyers' Edition.**

ledge. A lode or vein of mineral in its natural state.
See **lode; vein.**

ledger. A book of account, the entries of which are taken from books of original entry or journals.
See **post.**

ledgrevius (led-gre'vi-us). Same as **lathe-reeve**.

lees (lēz). The dregs of the barrel or vat used in wine-making.

leet (lēt'). An ancient English criminal court.

leftovers. Merchandise which remains unsold after it has been offered and displayed for sale for some time.

left turn. The movement of a motor vehicle across traffic at an intersection for the purpose of proceeding to the left on the intersecting street or highway. 8 Am J2d Auto § 799.

leg. A limb; the lower limb of the human body. A support, as of a table. A partial accomplishment of an undertaking or task.
According to its common definition, the word leg does not include the foot or any of the bones in the foot. Butler v Eminent Household, 116 Miss 85, 1137, 1139, 76 So 830.

lega (le'ga). An alloy used in making coins.

legabilis (le-gā'bi-lis). Chattels which were subject to bequest; whatever could be bequeathed by will.

legacy. A testamentary gift of personal property; a bequest. 57 Am J1st Wills § 1400. In loose usage, inclusive of testamentary gifts of real estate as well as of personal property. 57 Am J1st Wills § 1400.

legacy duty. See **legacy tax**.

legacy tax. A succession tax or duty on the passing of personal property by will. Knowlton v Moore, 178 US 41, 44 L Ed 969, 20 S Ct 747. An inheritance tax, rather than estate tax. Re Inman, 101 Or 182, 199 P 615, 16 ALR 675.

legal. According to the principles of law; according to the method required by statute; by means of judicial proceedings. Estate of Folwell, 68 NJ Eq 728, 62 A 414. According to law rather than equity.
See **lawful**, also words and phrases following, beginning "legal," and words and phrases beginning "lawful."

legal accumulation. The withholding by a trustee of the income of a minor for the purpose of creating an increased fund. Anno: 61 ALR 679.
See **unlawful accumulations**.

legal action. An action at law.

legal age. The age of majority, that is, the age, usually fixed by law at 21 years, at 18 years for females in some jurisdictions, at which an infant acquires the capacity to bind himself by contract, make conveyances and transfers of property, and conduct business as an adult. 27 Am J1st Inf § 5. The age at which a person acquires the capacity to act in reference to certain things, which may be prior to the age of majority. Montoya De Antonio v Miller, 7 NM 289, 34 P 40. The age fixed by the common law, 14 years for males, 12 years for females, or the more common increased age prescribed by statute, at which a person can enter into a marriage. 35 Am J1st Mar § 16.
Although the term in strictness means the age at which a person reaches his majority, which is usually twenty-one years, yet in construing a will, where it appeared to be the testator's intention, it was held that the term applied to the age at which a female beneficiary would be entitled by law to receive her estate from her guardian, although that age was eighteen. See McKim v Hardy, 4 Md Ch 228, 236.

legal assets. Assets left by a decedent available for administration without the aid of a court of equity. Agee v Saunders, 127 Tenn 680, 157 SW 64. Moneys in the hands of an executor as administrator arising from the sale of personal property, as distinguished from moneys in his hands arising from the sale of real estate. 31 Am J2d Ex & Ad § 193.

legal assignment. An assignment enforceable without the aid of equity.
A "legal assignment" is a transfer of property or an interest therein from one person to another; and unless in some way qualified, it is properly a transfer of the entire interest. Purman's Estate, 358 Pa 187, 56 A2d 86, 175 ALR 1129.

legal authority. See **lawbook; precedent**.

legal capacity. The ability to make contracts, conveyances, mortgages, etc. which are binding and beyond nullification for disability of the person arising from infancy, mental incompetency, etc. Pratt v Northern Pacific Express Co. 13 Idaho 373, 90 P 341.

legal cause. The proximate cause of damage. 22 Am J2d Damg § 20. The proximate cause of an injury. 38 Am J1st Negl §§ 49 et seq.
See **proximate cause**.

legal compulsion. That compulsion which is presumed in law, as distinguished from actual compulsion or compulsion in fact; as, where the law presumes the compulsion of the husband if the wife commits a crime in his presence. 21 Am J2d Crim L § 102.

legal conclusion. A conclusion of law.

legal consideration. A consideration legally sufficient in support of a contract, although not in the nature of pecuniary gain or benefit to the person assuming the obligation. Albert Lee College v Brown, 88 Minn 524, 93 NW 672.

legal constraint. The holding of a person or property under legal process; not duress. State ex rel. Cabel v Sewerage & Water Board (La App) 138 So 2d 856.

legal custody. Custody in accordance with law, for example, the custody of a child by a person appointed guardian of his person. The restraint of a person or of property pursuant to writ or process or otherwise in accordance with law.

legal damages. Such losses or detriments as the law compensates in consequence of a wrong committed. 22 Am J2d Damg § 1.
See **legal injury**.

legal day. A day in which legal and judicial business can be transacted, as distinguished from dies non.
It is distinguished also from a judicial day, which is a day in which the court is in session. State v Judges of the Court of Appeals, 48 La Ann 1079, 1080, 20 So 282.

legal dependent. A person whom one is legally bound to support. Caldwell v Little, 158 NC 351, 74 SE 10. One who has the right to invoke the aid of the law to require another to support him. National Council J. O. U. A. M. v Tate, 212 NC 305, 193 SE 397, 113 ALR 1514.

legal disability. Incapacity to contract; infancy; unsoundness of mind. Re Price's Estate, 87 Ohio App 23, 93 NE2d 769. Any condition which renders a person unable to act for himself or bind himself so that the law will not regard his acts as void or voidable.

A disability which may relate to the power to contract or to bring suits, and which may arise out of want of sufficient understanding, as idiocy, lunacy, or want of freedom of will, as in the case of married women and persons under duress; or out of the policy of the law, as alienage when the alien is an enemy, outlawry, attainder, praemunire, and the like. The disability is something pertaining to the person of the party—a personal incapacity— and not to the cause of action, or his relation to it. For the existence of legal disability, there must be a present right of action in the person, but some want of capacity to sue. Berkin v Marsh, 18 Mont 152, 44 P 528.

legal discretion. See **legal capacity**; **judicial discretion**.

legal duty. That which the law requires to be done or forborne to a determinable person, or to the public at large, being correlative to a right vested in such determinate person, or the public at large. Bragdon v Perkins-Campbell Co. (CA3 Pa) 87 F 109.

legal easement. A liberty, privilege, or advantage without profit, which the owner, as such, of one parcel of land, may have in the lands of another. Weletoff v Kohl, 105 NJ 181, 147 A 390, 66 ALR 1317.
See **easement**.

legal entity. An organization or association recognized in law as an entity apart from the individual members.

legal estate. An estate in property recognized at law, not merely in equity. At common law, strictly speaking, the only estate. Sayre v Mohney, 30 Or 238, 47 P 197.

legal estoppel. An estoppel recognized in law, as distinguished from equitable estoppel or estoppel in pais.

legal ethics. Canons of Professional Ethics adopted by the American Bar Association, published in Am J2d Desk Book Document 91. The usages and customs among members of the legal profession involving their moral and professional duties toward one another, toward their clients and toward the courts.

The principles which guide an attorney at law in his professional conduct are not enforced by the court as legal principles, but an attorney may be disciplined for not observing them. Re Heirich, 10 Ill 2d 357, 140 NE2d 825, 67 ALR2d 827, cert den 355 US 805, 2 L Ed 2d 49, 78 S Ct 22.

legal evidence. Evidence which is legally admissible.
Legal evidence is not confined to the human voice or oral testimony; it includes every tangible object capable of making a truthful statement, such evidence being roughly classified as documentary evidence. In oral evidence the witness is the man who speaks; in documentary evidence the witness is the thing that speaks. In either case the witness must be competent,—that is, must be deemed competent to make a truthful statement. See Curtis v Bradley, 65 Conn 99, 31 A 591.

legal examiners. Members of a state board conducting the examination of applicants for admission to the bar. State ex rel. Clyatt v Hocker, 39 Fla 477, 22 So 721.

legal expenses. See **attorney's fee**; **costs**.

legal fiction. See **fiction**.

legal fraud. Often regarded as synonymous with constructive fraud. Precisely, actual fraud, that is, fraud of which the law will take cognizance as a cause of action or foundation of a defense.

Fraud without damage, or damage without fraud gives no cause of action, but when these two concur, an action lies. This has long been recognized as the governing rule. But the rule has been obscured by the judges in their use of the phrase "legal fraud," which has sometimes been interpreted as meaning fraud by construction, and as indicating that something less than actual fraud may sustain an action for deceit. The gravamen of the action, however, is actual fraud, and nothing less will sustain it. Kountze v Kennedy, 147 NY 124, 41 NE 414.
See **constructive fraud**.

legal heirs. Essentially the same as heirs, but sometimes subject to construction, as where the term appears in a will. Those persons on whom the law passes the descent of real estate or admits to participate in the distribution of personalty, except as a contrary intention appears in the context of the will in which the clause appears. 57 Am J1st Wills § 1371. Ordinarily a term of art, constituting words of limitation. 28 Am J2d Est § 15. Sometimes construed as words of purchase, 28 Am J2d Est § 118, as where deemed synonymous with "children." 28 Am J2d Est § 118. In one sense, legal representatives.

Where a testator directed a sum of money to be "equally divided among all my children, or their legal heirs," the words "or their legal heirs" were held to be used, not to individuate grandchildren, but to supply a legal succession in the event of the death of anyone, and to mean simply legal representatives; that is, in case of the death of one of the children, his share would not go to the survivors, but would be considered as vested in the deceased child. Reed's Appeal, 118 Pa 215, 11 A 787.

legal holiday. A day declared a holiday by statute, the terms of which, such as provisions respecting the closing of banks, exchanges, public offices, etc., determine the nature of the business which can be legally transacted upon the day.

A statutory declaration that a certain day shall be a "legal holiday" does not indicate an attempt to elevate its status to that of Sunday. 50 Am J1st Sun & H § 2.

The courts do not regard "legal holidays" as nonjuridical days unless constrained to do so by the terms or the necessary effect of statutes. 50 Am J1st Sun & H § 77. Compare State v Duncan, 118 La 702, 43 So 283.

legal impediment. The lack of a quality or qualification provided for by law as a condition precedent.
Residence for a period less than required by statute, or being below the minimum age, may be a legal impediment to marriage. State v Randall, 166 Minn 381, 382, 208 NW 14, 15.

legal incapacity. See **disability**; **legal capacity**.

legal injury. An invasion of a legal right; a wrong from which the law imports damage. Allen v Stowell, 145 Cal 666, 79 P 371. An injury for the redress whereof an action will lie.

"The much-argued and interesting case of Allen v Flood (1898) A. C. 1, illustrates the general doctrine that, however harmful to others individual or combined action may be, if it is not unlawful, the damage or harm so inflicted does not constitute legal injury at common law." Wheeler-Stenzel Co.

v National Window Glass Jobbers' Asso. (CA3 NJ) 152 F 864.

legal insanity. Insanity of which the law takes cognizance in recognizing it as a defense in a criminal case, as a ground for committing the person to an asylum or state hospital, or as a ground for the appointment of a committee or guardian.

legal intent. A presumed intent, for example, the intent to accomplish the natural and probable consequences of one's acts. 29 Am J2d Ev § 204. A term applied without circumspection to the intent of a testator.

In strict reasoning, a testator can have but one intent,—his own actual intent. To speak of a testator's legal intent is strictly a solecism; there is no such thing. So that, when it is said that a testator's legal intent is to be gathered from the decisions of the court of his domicil, nothing more is meant than that whatever his actual intent may have been, if he has used in his will certain technical terms to which the courts of his domicil have attached a crystallized and settled judicial meaning which has become a rule of property in that state, then such will, wherever it comes under construction in other states, will have the same meaning given to those technical words which the courts of his domicil gave them. That is what the phrase "legal intent" means, and this rule about the legal intent being governed by the courts of his domicil means. In truth, we should only speak of a testator's actual intent, for that is all the testator ever had. If it violates no law, it stands. If it violates the law, the will fails, unless either statute or the settled decisions of the courts have given the terms which he has used a meaning which will save the will. Ball v Phelan, 94 Miss 293, 49 So 956.

legal interest. That rate of interest prescribed by the law which will prevail in absence of any contract between the parties fixing the rate. 30 Am J Rev ed Int § 2.

As to what constitutes the "legal interest" which one seeking equitable relief from a usurious transaction must offer to pay as the condition of obtaining such relief, the courts are not in entire agreement. While there is authority for the view that "legal interest" is to be computed at the rate prevailing in the absence of an agreement, it has also been held that it should be computed at the maximum legal rate, and not at the lesser rate prevailing in the absence of an agreement between the parties regarding interest. 55 Am J1st Usury § 108.

See **lawful interest.**

legal investment. One of a list of permissible trust investments presented by statute as authorized trust investments. 54 Am J1st Trusts § 381.

legalis homo (le-gā′lis hō′mō). Same as **lawful man.**

legalis moneta Angliae (lē-gā′lis mo-nē′ta Ang′li-ē). Lawful money of England.

legality. The matter or question of being in accord, or in conflict, with the law.

legalization. Legalizing; the making lawful of something otherwise unlawful.

See **legitimation; validation.**

legalize. To make legal that which otherwise is illegal. To confirm something already done; not to authorize something in the future. Barker v Chesterfield, 102 Mass 127.

legalized nuisance. A concept of the legalization by legislative act of that which otherwise would be a nuisance. 38 Am J1st Mun Corp § 650.

legal jeopardy. See **prior jeopardy.**

legal liability. Liability at law.

legal life estate. A life estate coming into existence by operation of law, such as dower and curtesy, as distinguished from a life estate created by will or grant. 28 Am J2d Est § 56.

legal limit. A limit fixed by law such as a speed limit, a limit upon the amount of municipal indebtedness, or a limit upon the rate of interest which may be charged by contract.

legal lottery. A lottery authorized by law. Clark v Washington (US) 12 Wheat 40, 6 L Ed 544.

legally. According to law; properly.

As the word is used in a statute referring to the legally administered affairs of a bank, it is held to import a compliance with the statutes of the state, and particularly a compliance with the statutes regulating the management of banks. People v Mancuso, 255 NY 463, 175 NE 177, 76 ALR 514.

legally adopted. Adopted according to law, that is, according to the statutes relating to adoption of children. Anno: 141 ALR 1303.

legally constituted court. A court existing under the authority of the law, so that its judgments and decrees are not open to collateral attack. State ex rel. Bales v Bailey, 106 Minn 138, 118 NW 676.

legally dead. See **presumption of death.**

legally insufficient title. A title which, not being free from reasonable doubt, is not a marketable title. 55 Am J1st V & P §§ 157, 158.

legally interested. Having a legal interest, in property, in a specific fund, or in the subject matter of litigation. Ward v San Diego School Dist. (Cal App) 259 P 349.

legally proved. Established by evidence legally admissible. Paiva v California Door Co. 75 Cal App 323, 242 P 887.

legally sufficient title. A marketable title. Cowdery v Greenlee, 126 Ga 786, 55 SE 91.

legally sworn. Put under oath. Being bound by an oath.

A person can only be "legally sworn" in a matter "judicially pending" before the court in which he makes oath to give true testimony. If the court is wholly without jurisdiction, the matter is not "judicially pending," and a witness therein cannot be "legally sworn." Smiddy v Commonwealth, 214 Ky 100, 102, 282 SW 774.

legal malice. See **malice in law.**

legal maxim. See **maxim.**

legal memory. See **time of legal memory.**

legal name. The given or Christian name in combination with the surname or family name. Butler v Smith, 84 Neb 78, 120 NW 1106; 38 Am J1st Name § 1.

But for all practical and legal purposes, a man's name is the designation by which he is known and called in the community in which he lives and is known. 38 Am J1st Name § 2.

legal notice. Notice complying with the requirements of the law; notice which the law implies either from knowledge of actual facts or from failure to make inquiry where a duty arises to make such inquiry. Jennings v Lentz, 50 Or 483, 93 P 327, 329.

Legal or implied notice is the same as constructive notice and is notice which cannot be controverted by proof. It is a legal inference from established facts, and, like other legal presumptions, does not admit of dispute. A recorded deed is an instance of such notice. It is of no consequence whether the second purchaser has actual notice of the prior deed or not. He is bound to take, and is presumed to have, the requisite notice. Notice to an agent also is constructive notice to the principal. The law imputes such notice to the party whether he has it or not. See Cooper v Flesner, 24 Okla 47, 103 P 1016.

legal obligation. A debt; an obligation enforcible in an action at law. An obligation to do and perform what the law of the land, as it exists at the time, requires a person to do.

legal officer. A de jure officer. Also inclusive, for some purposes, of a de facto officer.

A person who actually obtains an office, with the legal indicia of title to that office is a legal officer until ousted. Hallgren v Campbell, 82 Mich 255, 46 NW 381.

legal possession. Same as **possession in law.**

legal presumption. A presumption of law rather than a presumption founded on the basic fact of the experience of men. Gulick v Loder, 13 NJL 68.
See **presumption of law.**

legal proceeding. In the broad sense, any action or special proceeding in court. In a narrower sense, an action or special proceeding at law rather than in equity.

As used in the Bankruptcy Act nullifying liens obtained by legal proceedings within four months prior to the filing of a petition in bankruptcy, the term contemplates proceedings against the insolvent debtor, and not voluntary proceedings by him. 9 Am J2d Bankr § 1025.

legal process. Process which is fair on its face, lawfully issued for a lawful purpose. State v Knopf, 50 Wash 229, 96 P 1076.

legal provocation. See **considerable provocation; reasonable provocation.**

legal rate. See **lawful rate.**

legal representative. In primary meaning, an executor or administrator; in secondary meaning, one who succeeds to the rights of another, such as an heir, next of kin, devisee or legatee, assignee, trustee, receiver, etc. 12 Am J2d Bonds § 24; 23 Am J2d Desc & D § 44; 31 Am J2d Ex & Ad § 4. As a designation of beneficiary of a life insurance policy:—the executor or administrator of the insured, unless a contrary intention in such respect is manifested by the context of the policy or the surrounding circumstances. 29A Am J Rev ed Ins § 1656.

legal research. A study of the authorities, whether case or text, for the purpose of supporting a proposition or the development of an article for publication.

legal reserve. See **reserve.**

legal reserve insurance. A policy of life insurance issued and maintained on the level-premium basis and supported by a reserve set aside, as required by law, with which to mature or liquidate a claim accrued under the policy. 29 Am J Rev ed Ins § 56.

legal residence. The place which the law accepts as the residence of a person, notwithstanding it is not the place where he is presently to be found. The equivalent of domicil. Phillips v South Carolina Tax Com. 195 SC 472, 12 SE2d 13; Restatement, Conflict of Laws § 9.
See **domicil; residence.**

legal settlement. Same as **legal residence.** Louriston v Swift County Comrs. 89 Minn 91, 93 NW 1052.
See **settlement of pauper.**

legal residuum rule (lē′gal rę̄-zid′ū-um röl). The rule that, even though an administrative agency is not bound by the rules and evidence applicable in court and may accept, in its discretion, any evidence that is offered, still in the end there must be a residuum of legal evidence to support the finding of the administrative agency. Carroll v Knickerbocker Ice Co. 218 NY 435, 113 NE 507.

legal reversion. The time within which property sold for debt could be redeemed.

legal right. A claim recognizable and enforceable at law. See Estate of Folwell, 68 NJ Eq. 728, 62 A 414.

legal right of redemption. The right of a mortgagor, in a jurisdiction where a mortgage has the effect of vesting title in the mortgagee, to pay the mortgage debt and thus avoid the effect of the mortgage as a transfer of title. Stevens v Turlington, 186 NC 191, 119 SE 210, 32 ALR 870, 873.

legal sanity. A mental condition whereunder a person is held responsible for his acts, contracts, and other transactions. Not necessarily a mental condition of perfection, devoid of the least aspect of mental weakness. People v Baker, 42 Cal 2d 550, 268 P2d 705.
See **legal insanity.**

legal situs. See **situs.**

legal standing. See **capacity; standing to sue.**

legal strike. A simultaneous cessation or quitting of work by a body of workmen acting in combination for the coercion of their employer in a lawful economic struggle or competition between employer and employee as to the share or division between them of the joint product of labor and capital, hours of work, or working conditions. 31 Am J Rev ed Lab § 383. As between employees and their union, a strike authorized by the union or its officers empowered to call a strike. Toledo, Ann Arbor & North Michigan Railway Co. v Pennsylvania Co. (CC Ohio) 54 F 730 (involving right to strike benefits.)

legal subrogation. A right of subrogation existing independently of custom or statute and not dependent upon contract, assignment, privity, or strict suretyship, occurring as the legal consequence of the acts and relationship of the parties. 50 Am J1st Subro § 5.
See **subrogation.**

legal system. The historic and traditional system, including the legislative and judicial process, as contrasted with the emergent or lately adopted system which includes the legislative, administrative, and judicial process. 1 Am J2d Admin L § 16.

legal tender. That sort of money in which a debt, or other obligation calling for money, may be lawfully paid, if a specific medium of payment is not required by statute or the terms of the contract or obligation. 36 Am J1st Money § 22.

Legal Tender Acts. Acts of Congress, particularly the act of February 25, 1862, making treasury notes of the United States a legal tender for the payment of all debts. Legal Tender Cases (US) 12 Wall 457, 20 L Ed 287.

Legal Tender Cases. Two cases decided together upholding the constitutionality of the Acts of Congress of 1862 and 1863 providing for the issue of paper money by the United States and making such money legal tender for the payment of private debts. (US) 12 Wall 457, 20 L Ed 287.

legal-tender notes. Notes declared legal tender by Act of Congress. State v Beebe, 17 Minn 241.

legal title. A title under rules of law as distinguished from a title recognized in equity according to equitable principles.
See **legally sufficient title.**

legal visitors. Official visitors.
See **visitors.**

legal voter. A person authorized by law to cast his ballot at an election. A person who possesses the qualifications for voting prescribed by law and who also has registered as a voter in accordance with the statute. Re Opinion of Justices, 247 Mass 583, 143 NE 142.

legal waste. Voluntary waste in acts done and permissive waste in acts suffered by neglect. 56 Am J1st Waste § 4.

legare (le-gā're). (Civil law.) To bequeath; to leave as a legacy.

legatary (leg'a-tā-ri). Same as **legatee.**

legatee. One who takes personal property as beneficiary under a will. A word sometimes inclusive, as a generic term, of a person taking either real or personal property as beneficiary under a will. 57 Am J1st Wills § 1400.

legates (leg'āts). Representatives or ambassadors of the pope of Rome; nuncios.

Legatine Constitutions (leg'ā-tin kon-sti-tu'shons). Ecclesiastical laws enacted in national synods, held under the cardinals Otho and Othobon, legates from Pope Gregory IX and Pope Clement IV, in the reign of Henry the Third, about 1220 and 1268. See 1 Bl Comm 83.

legation. An embassy; a diplomatic minister of a foreign country, and his assistants; the place of business or residence of a foreign embassy.

legatory (le'ga-tō-ri). That part of a man's personal property which he can dispose of by will. See 2 Bl Comm 492.

Legatos violare contra jus gentium est (lē-gā'tōs vi-ō-lā're kon'trā jūs jen'she-um est). To offer violence to ambassadors is against the law of nations.

legatum (lē-gā'tum). (Civil law.) A legacy; a bequest.

Legatum morte testatoris tantum confirmatur, sicut donatio inter vivos traditione sola (lē-gā'tum mor'te tes-tā-tō'ris tan'tum kon-fir-mā'ter, si'kut dō-nā'-she-ō in'ter vī'vos tra-di-she-ō'ne sō'la). A legacy is confirmed by the death of the testator, just as a gift between living persons is confirmed by delivery alone.

Legatus regis vice fungitur a quo destinatur, et honorandus ets sicut ille cujus vicem gerit (lē-gā'tus rē'jis vī'se fun'ji-ter ā quō des-ti-nā'ter, et ho-no-ran'dus est sik'ut il'le kū'jus vī'sem je'rit). An ambassador functions in the place of the king by whom he is sent, and he should be honored as much as that king whose place he holds.

lege. See **ex lege.**

legem. See **extra legem.**

legem amittere (lē'jem a-mit'te-re). To lose one's law. When a man was condemned as a recreant, amittere liberem legem—to lose his free law—that is, to become infamous, and not to be accounted liber et legalis homo—a free and lawful man—he was supposed thereby to be forsworn, and therefore never to be put upon a jury or allowed to testify as a witness in any cause. This was one of the disgraceful consequences attending a champion's defeat in trial by battle. See 3 Bl Comm 340.

Legem enim contractus dat (le'jem e'nim kon-trak'-tus dat). The contract makes the law.

legem facere (lē'jem fā'se-re). To make an oath; to wager one's law.

legem ferre (lē'jem fer're). (Roman law.) To submit a proposed law to the people.

legem habere (lē'jem hā-bē're). To have one's law; to have the right to give testimony under oath.

legem jubere (lē'jem ju-bē're). (Roman law.) To ratify a proposed law which had been submitted to the people.

legem positus. See **extra legem positus.**

Legem terrae amittentes perpetuam infamiae notam inde merito incurrunt (lē'jem ter'rē a-mit-ten'tēz per-pe'tu-am in-fā'mi-ē nō'tam in'de me'ri-tō in-ker'runt). Persons who lose the law of the land thereby justly incur the everlasting mark of disgrace.

legem vadiare (lē'jem va-di-ā're). To wage law.
See **wager of law.**

legend. A notation, mark, or character upon a map or plat, explanatory of the representation made. Anno: 108 ALR 1424.

legerwite. Same as **lairesite.**

leges (lē'jēz). Laws, plural of **lex.**

Leges Angliae sunt tripartitae; jus commune, consuetudines, ac decreta comitiorum (lē'jēz Ang'li-ē sunt tri-par-tī'tē; jūs kom-mū'ne, kon-su-ē-tū'di-nēz, ak dē-krē'ta ko-mi-she-ō'rum). The laws of England are threefold, the common law, the customs or usages, and the resolutions of parliament.

Leges figendi et refigendi consuetudo est periculosissima (lē'jēz fi-jen'dī et re-fi-jen'dī kon-su-ē-tū'dō est pe-ri-ku-lō-sis'si-ma). The custom of making and remaking laws is most dangerous.

Leges humanae nascuntur, vivunt, et moriuntur (lē'-jēz hu-ma'nē nas-kun'ter, vī'vunt, et mo-ri-un'ter). Human laws are born, live, and die.

leges legum (lē'jēz lē'gum). The law of laws; the characterization of the laws of nature. Anderson v Wilkins, 142 NC 154, 55 SE 272.

Leges naturae perfectissimae sunt et immutabiles; humani vero juris conditio semper in infinitum decurrit, et nihil est in eo quod perpetuo stare possit (lē'jēz nā-tū'rē per-fek-tis'si-mē sunt et im-mū-tā'bi-lēz; hu-ma'nī ve'rō jū'ris kon-di'she-ō sem'per in in-fi-nī'tum de-ker'rit, et ni'hil est in ē'ō quod per-pe'tu-ō stā're pos'sit). The laws of nature are the most perfect and immutable, but the condition of human law always runs into infinity, and there is nothing in it which can stand permanently.

leges non scriptae (lē'jēz non skrip'tē). The unwritten or common law, as distinguished from the leges scriptae, the written or statute law. See 1 Bl Comm 63.

Leges non verbis sed rebus sunt impositae (le'jēz non ver'bis sed rē'bus sunt im-pō'zi-tē). Laws are imposed not upon words but upon things.

Leges posteriores, priores contrarias abrogant (lē'jēz pos-te-ri-ō'rēz, pri-ō'rēz kon-trā'ri-as ab'rō-gant). New statutes repeal old ones which are repugnant to them. See 1 Bl Comm 89.

Leges quae retrospiciunt raro, et magna cum cautione sunt adhibendae neque enim Janus locatur in legibus (lē'jēz kwē re-tro-spi'she-unt ra'rō, et mag'na kum kâ-she-ō'ne sunt ad-hi-ben'dē ne'kwe e-nim Jā'nus lō-kā'ter in lē'ji-bus). Laws which are retrospective are rarely and cautiously received, for Janus has really no place in the laws.

The maxim expresses the well-recognized doctrine that retrospective laws are not favored, and although they are not prohibited by the Federal Constitution, nor by the constitutions of many of the states, courts will always, where possible, give a construction which avoids a retrospective meaning. 50 Am J1st Stat § 477.

leges scriptae (le'jēz skrip'tē). The written or statute laws. See 1 Bl Comm 63.

Leges sola memoria et usu retinebant (lē'jēz sō'la me-mō'ri-a et ū'sū re-ti-nē'bant). They retained laws solely by memory and usage. See 1 Bl Comm 63.

leges sub graviori lege (lē'jēz sub gra-vi-ō'rī lē'je). Laws subservient to higher laws. See 1 Bl Comm 84.

Leges suum ligent latorem (lē'jēz su'um li'jent la-tō'rem). Laws should bind their own sponsor or proposer.

leges tabellariae (lē'jēz ta-bel-lar'i-ē). The laws of the ballot; that is, the laws governing elections.

Leges vigilantibus non dormientibus factae sunt (lē'jēz vi-ji-lan'ti-bus non dor-mi-en'ti-bus fak'tē sunt). The laws aid the vigilant and not those who slumber on their rights. 27 Am J2d Eq § 130.

Leges vigilantibus, non dormientibus subveniunt (lē'jēz vi-ji-lan'ti-bus, non dor-mi-en'ti-bus sub-ve'ni-unt). The laws aid the vigilant, not those who slumber. 27 Am J2d Eq § 130.

legibus. See ex legibus.

legibus patriae obtime instituti (le'ji-bus pā'tri-ē op'-ti-mē in-sti-tū'tī). Those best instructed in the laws of their country. See 1 Bl Comm 69.

legibus solutus (lē'ji-bus so-lū'tus). (Civil law.) Immune or exempt from the operation of the laws,— the condition of the emperor.

Legibus sumptis desinentibus, lege naturae utendum est (lē'ji-bus sump'tis de-si-nen'ti-bus, lē'je nā-tū'rē ū-ten'dum est). When artificial laws fail, the law of nature must be invoked.

legis (lē'jis). Of the law.

Legis constructio non facit injuriam (lē'jis kon-struk'-she-ō non fā'sit in-jū'ri-am). The construction of the law does not work injury.

Legis figendi et refigendi consuetudo periculosissima est (lē'jis fi-jen'dī et re-fi-jen'dī kon-su-ē-tū'dō pe-ri-ku-lō-sis'si-ma est). The custom of making and remaking the law is a very dangerous one.

Legis interpretatio legis vim obtinet (lē'jis in-ter-pre-tā'she-ō lē'jis vim ob'ti-net). The interpretation of the law obtains the force of law.

legislation. The product of a legislative body in laws made. The process of making laws.

Legislation looks to the future and changes existing conditions by making a new rule to be applied thereafter to all or some part of those subject to its power. 1 Am J2d Admin L § 163.

legislative act. A law or statute enacted by the legislature. An act which predetermines what the law shall be for the regulation of future cases falling under its provisions.

It is to be distinguished from a judicial act, which is a determination of what the law is in relation to some existing thing done or happened. Wulzen v Board of Supervisors, 101 Cal 15, 35 P 353.

Legislative Assembly. A legislative body provided by Congress for the District of Columbia which ceased to exist on the adoption of the Temporary Organic Act of June 20, 1874, followed by the Organic Act of June 11, 1878. 24 Am J2d DC § 3. The lower house of the legislature in some states.

legislative control. A term applied in the law of corporations to control by the legislature of the affairs of a private corporation. 19 Am J2d Corp § 1447.

legislative court. A court created by legislative action, that is, by statute, rather than by constitutional provisions. 20 Am J2d Cts § 18. A federal court created by Congress under authority derived from provisions of the Constitution of the United States other than Article 3, section 1. 20 Am J2d Cts § 8.

legislative days. Days during which the legislature is in session.

legislative definition. A statement in a statute defining the sense in which words are employed in the statute. 50 Am J1st Stat § 261.

legislative department. One of the three main departments of government, the other two being the executive and judicial departments.

Under the principle of the separation of governmental powers, the legislative power of the state is vested in the state legislature and that of the Federal Government is vested in Congress.

legislative divorce. A divorce granted, without judicial inquiry, by an act of the legislature directed particularly to a specific union of husband and wife and declaring it to be dissolved. Starr v Pease, 8 Conn 540, 541.

legislative intent. The vital part, heart, soul and essence of statutory law; the guiding star in the interpretation of a statute. 50 Am J1st Stat § 223.

legislative journal. See journal.

legislative measure. A statute; an act or joint resolution of the legislature. A measure passed by a municipal council in the exercise of its legislative, rather than administrative or executive, powers. 37 Am J1st Mun Corp § 209.

legislative power. The power to make, alter, and repeal laws. 16 Am J2d Const L § 227. The determination of legislative policy and its formulation and promulgation as a defined and binding rule of conduct. Yakus v United States, 321 US 414, 88 L Ed 834, 64 S Ct 660. That power which in the Federal Government is vested in Congress, and, in the several states, in their state legislatures. 49 Am J1st States § 28.

legislative record. The record of the proceedings of the legislature. The daily journals, wherein the proceedings of the bodies are recorded, and copies thereof, such copies being bound and distributed under the direction of a state officer, usually the secretary of state. 49 Am J1st States § 37.
See **Congressional Record**.

legislative regulation. A term familiar in the field of administrative law; a regulation having the force and effect of law, intended to supplement a statute in accord with the terms of the statute by filling in the details of the rule of conduct sought to be prescribed. Anno: 153 ALR 1191.
See **interpretative regulation**.

legislator. A lawmaker; a member of a legislative body; a member of the legislature.

Legislatorum est viva vox, rebus et non verbis, legem imponere (le-jis-la-tō'rum est vī'va vŏx, rē'bus et non ver'bis, lē'jem im-pŏ'ne-re). The voice of the legislators is the living voice, to impose law upon things, and not upon words.

legislature. Broadly, any body having legislative power. One of the three branches of state government, the law-making branch, usually consisting of two bodies, a senate and a house of representatives made up of members representing districts and elected respectively by the voters of the districts. 49 Am J1st States § 28.
See **contempt of legislature**.

Legis minister non tenetur, in executione officii sui, fugere aut retrocedere (lē'jis mi-nis'ter non te-nē'ter, in ex-e-kū-she-ŏ'ne of-fi'she-ī su'ī, fu'je-re ât re-trō-sē'de-re). A servant of the law is not bound in the execution of his office, either to flee or to retreat.

legisperitus (lē-jis-pe'rī-tus). A person who is skilled or learned in the law; skilled or learned in the law.

legitim (lē'ji-tim). The share of a father's movable property to which his children became entitled upon his death.

legitimacy. In the broad sense, the matter of lawfulness. In the usual sense, the matter of having a lawful parentage, that is, of having been born in lawful wedlock. Pratt v Pratt, 5 Mo App 539, 542.
See **illegitimate child; legitimate child**.

legitima potestas (lē-ji'ti-ma pō-tes'tās). Lawful power.

legitimate (lę-jit'i-māt). Adjective: Lawful; of lawful parentage. Verb: To make lawful; to make legitimate. To effect a legitimation of an illegitimate child. McKamie v Baskerville, 86 Tenn 459, 461.
See **legitimation**.

legitimate child. A child born or begotten in lawful wedlock or a child born out of wedlock who has acquired the status of legitimacy by legitimation.
At common law, a legitimate child is one either born or begotten in wedlock, and where conception takes place during lawful wedlock, the subsequent dissolution of the marriage by death or divorce before birth of the child does not affect its legitimacy. Kowalski v Wojtkowski, 19 NJ 247, 116 A2d 6, 53 ALR2d 556.
See **legitimation**.

legitimate inferences. Those inferences that necessarily follow from certain evidence; legal inferences reasonably and legally to be drawn from the evidence. Re Little's Estate, 46 Cal App 776, 189 P 818.

legitimacy test. A blood-grouping test helpful in the determination of parentage. 23 Am J2d Dep § 211.

legitimated child. A child born out of wedlock who has acquired the status of legitimacy by the subsequent marriage of its parents or other method of legitimation. Hunter v Whitworth, 9 Ala 965.
See **legitimation**.

legitimation. In the broad sense, the act of giving the character of lawfulness to that which was unlawful. In the accepted sense, the act of giving the status of a legitimate child to one born out of wedlock, such being done sometimes by statute, at other times by a proceeding provided by statute, but most frequently by the subsequent marriage of the parents. 10 Am J2d Bast §§ 45 et seq.

legitimatio per subsequens matrimonium (le-ji-ti-mā'-she-ō per sub'se-quenz ma-tri-mō'ni-um). Legitimation through subsequent marriage, that is, the legitimation of a bastard child by the subsequent marriage of the child's parents. Blythe v Ayres, 96 Cal 532, 31 P 915.

legitimo modo acquietatus (lę-jit'i-mŏ mō'dō ak-qui"-ē-tā'tus). Acquitted in a lawful manner. Poulterer's Case, 9 Coke 55b, 77 Eng Rep 813.

legitime (lej'i-tim). In Louisiana,—that portion of a father's estate reserved by law for those of his legitimate children who are living at the time of his death. Bauman v Pennywell, 160 La 555, 562, 107 So 425. That portion of a decedent's estate of which a forced heir is not to be deprived. Cox v Von Ahlefeldt, 50 La Ann 1266, 23 So 959.
See **forced heir**.

Legitime imperanti parere necesse est (lē-ji'ti-mē im-pe-ran'tī pa-rē're ne-ses'se est). It is necessary to obey a person who gives a lawful command.

legitimize (lę-jit'i-mīz). To legitimate; to make lawful.
See **legitimation**.

legitimus (lē-ji'ti-mus). Lawful; legitimate.

Legitimus haeres et filius est quem nuptiae demonstrant (lē-ji'ti-mus hē'rēz et fi'li-us est quem nup'-she-ē de-mon'strant). The lawful son and heir is he whom the marriage shows to be such.

Legit ut clericus (lē'jit ut kle'ri-kus). He reads as a clerk.

Legit vel non? (lē'jit vel non). Does he read or not? This was the question put by the bishop to the ordinary upon presenting a convict who claimed benefit of clergy. The usual answer was, "Legit ut clericus," "He reads as a clerk."

Lego (lē'gō). (Latin.) I bequeath. I appoint.

leguleius (le-gu-lē'us). A person learned or versed in the law.

legum Anglicanarum conditor (lē'gum Ang-li-ka-nā'rum kon'di-tor). The founder of the English laws, i. e., Alfred the Great.

le haut meer (lē ŏt mēr). (French.) The high sea.

leidgreve. Same as **lath-reeve**.

leipa (le'pa). A fugitive; a fugitive from justice.

Le ley de Dieu et le ley de terre sont tout un, et l'un et l'autre preferre et favour le common et publique bien del terre (luh lay duh Dyû ay luh lay duh tare sôn toot ŭn, ay l'ŭn ay l'ō-tre prē-fare ay fah-voor luh côm-môn ay poo-bleek bī-ĕn del tare). The law of God and the law of the land are all one, and both the one and the other preserve and favor the common and public good of the land.

Le ley est le plus haut enheritance que le roy ad, car par le ley, il mesne et touts ses sujets sont rules, et si le ley ne fuit, nul roy ne nul enheritance serra (luh lay ay luh ploo ōte ôn-ēr-ī-tôns kuh luh rwah äd, kar par luh lay, eel mēs-nĕ ay too say soo-zhay sôn rool, ảy see luh lay nuh fwee, nool rwah nuh nool ôn-ēr-ī-tôns sēr-rah). The law is the highest inheritance which the king has, for by the law he himself and all his subjects are ruled, and if there were no law, there would be neither king nor inheritance.

Le mort saisit le vif (lĕ mor sä-zē′ lĕ vēf). The death invests the living. Succession of Meunier, 52 La Ann 79, 26 So 776.

lend. To make a loan. Subject to construction, in a proper case where it appears in a will, as a word of gift, conveyance, or bequest. 57 Am J1st Wills § 1334.

lending agency. A loan company, a bank, or building and loan association.

lending credit. Standing as surety or guarantor of a person for the purpose of enabling him to obtain funds on credit or to obtain an extension of credit.

Lent. A period of forty weekdays preceding Easter Sunday, observed by Christians, as a period of great religious significance, in attendance at daily religious services and sometimes in fasting.
  See **Jack of Lent.**

leod. The people; the country; the nation.

leodes (le-ō′dēz). A vassal; a liege man.

leonina societas (le-o′ni-na so-si′e-tās). A Roman-law term for a partnership deemed unlawful because one partner was wholly excluded from a share in the profits.

leper. A person afflicted with the disease of leprosy. Baltimore v Fairfield Improv. Co. 87 Md 352, 39 A 1081.

leper hospital. An institution for the confinement and care of lepers. 26 Am J1st Hospit § 19.

leproso amovendo (le-prō′sō ā-mō-ven′dō). See **de leproso amovendo.**

leprosy (lep′rọ-si). An infectious disease communicated by close contact characterized by scabs on the skin and in its extremity the wasting away of parts of the body, especially the fingers and toes.

Le roi veut en deliberer (luh rwah vur ôn day-lee′be-ray). The king wishes to deliberate upon it.

Le roy le veut (luh rwah luh vur). The king so wills it. See 1 Bl Comm 184.

Le roy remercie ses loyal subjects, accept leur benevolence, et ausi le veut (luh rwah rĕ-mer-see say lwah-yal soo-zhay, äc-cept lur bay-nay-vō-lôns, ay ō-see luh vur). The king thanks his loyal subjects, accepts their benevolence, and wills it to be so.— The formal expression of the king's assent to a bill of supply after it had passed both houses of parliament and had been presented to him for his approval. See 1 Bl Comm 184.

Le roy s'avisera (luh rwah s′ah-vee-sēr-ah). The king will advise upon it.—The formal expression of the king's refusal to assent to a bill which had passed both houses of parliament. See 1 Bl Comm 184.

les (lä). (French.) The article "the" in the plural.

Le salut du peuple est la supreme loi (luh sah-loo doo pur-plĕ ay la soo-prĕm lwah). The welfare of the people is the supreme law.

lesbian. A female who is a homosexual. In the vernacular, a lady lover.

lese majeste (lēz′ maj′es-ti). High treason.

Les fictions naissent de la loi, et non la loi des fictions (lay feek-si-ôn ness duh lah lwah, ay nôn la lwah dā feek-si-ôn). Fictions arise from law, and not law from fictions.

lesion (lē′zhọn). A hurt, loss, or injury to the body, or any morbid change in structure of organs or parts of the body. Warbende v Prudential Ins. Co. of America (CA7 Ill) 97 F2d 749. (French.) Loss. The injury suffered by one who does not receive a full equivalent for what he gives in a commutative contract.
  The remedy given for this injury is founded on its being the effect of implied error or imposition. See Linkswiler v Hoffman, 109 La 948, 34 So 34.

Les lois ne se chargent de punir que les actions exterieures (lay lwah nuh suh sharzh duh poo-neer kuh lās äk-si-ôns ĕx-tĕr′i-er′). The laws do not assume to punish other than overt acts.

lespedeza (les-pe-dē′zä). An annual reseeding plant; a clover. Superior Oil Co. v Griffin (Okla) 357 P2d 987, 87 ALR2d 224.

lespegend. A subordinate forest officer.

Les prelats, seigneurs, et commons, en ce present parliament assemblees, au nom de touts vous autres subjects, remercient tres humblement votre majeste, et prient a Dieu vous donner en sante bone vie et longue (lä prä′lä, sä-nyür′, ā com-môn, ôn sē prä′sôn pär-liä-mônt äs-sôm-blä, ō nôm dē too voos ō′trē sū-jä, rĕ-mer-cē trä hum-blĕ-môn vō-trē mä-jes-tä, ā prēt ä Dyuh voo don′nä ôn sän′tä bo-ne vĕ ä long). The prelates, lords, and commons, in this present parliament assembled, in the name of all your other subjects, most humbly thank your majesty, and pray to God to grant you in health and wealth long to live. See 1 Bl Comm 84.

less or more. See **more or less.**

lessa (les′sa). A legacy.

lessee. The party to a lease known as the tenant. The bailee under a lease of personalty.
  There is authority to the effect that the presence or absence of possession of the premises is a distinguishing factor between the relationship of landlord and tenant and that of lessor and lessee—that is, the one relation is referable only to the contract, and the other to both the contract and the change in the possession of the premises. Thus, it has been said that the lessee is not a tenant until he enters into possession. Usually, however, the word "lessee" means the same as "tenant." 32 Am J1st L & T § 2.

lesser offense. See **included offense.**

lessor. One who has leased property to another. The party to a lease known as the landlord, at least where possession of the premises has been delivered under the lease. 32 Am J1st L & T § 2. The bailor under a lease of personalty.
  See **lease; lessee.**

lessor of the plaintiff. The real party in interest who institutes the action in an action of ejectment.

less than freehold. A characterization of estates for

years, estates at will, and estates at sufferance. 28 Am J2d Est § 130.

lestage. Same as **lastage.**

leswes. Pasture land.

let. To select a contractor from two or more bidders for the job. To lease or demise property.

The verbs "to let" and "to demise" are usually applied to real estate, and mean to lease or to convey, but both words contain the idea of a grant, and where they could only have been intended to convey the meaning of "assign," they will be given that meaning; as where the parties have used them as operative words applied to a transfer of timber rights and contracts passing such interest for ninety-one years. Atlantic & North Carolina Railroad Co. v Atlantic & North Carolina Co. 147 NC 368, 61 SE 185.

let contract. See **letting.**

lethal (lē'thạl). Capable of producing death or great bodily harm. State v Godfrey, 17 Or 300, 20 P 625.

lethal weapon. A deadly weapon. 56 Am J1st Weap § 3. A weapon capable of producing great bodily harm.

A gun, sword, knife, pistol, or the like, is a lethal weapon, as a matter of law, when used within striking distance from the person assaulted; and all other weapons are lethal or not, according to their capacity to produce death or great bodily harm in the manner in which they are used. State v Godfrey, 17 Or 300, 20 P 625.

letter. A symbol of the alphabet, representing a sound, at least in theory. A communication, usually through the mail, by one person to another in the form of writing or typewriting. A classification of mailable matter; the first class of mailable matter. 41 Am J1st P O § 56.

As used in the statutes concerning thefts by postoffice employees, a letter is a writing or document, which bears the outward semblance of a genuine communication, and comes into the possession of the employee in the regular course of his official business, regardless of what he may know of its contents or genuineness. Hence, a decoy letter is as much a letter as any other, if it is regularly transmitted through the mails. See Goode v United States, 159 US 663, 671, 40 L Ed 297, 301, 16 S Ct 136. See **letters.**

letter box. See **mailbox.**

letter carrier. A government employee as a carrier in the delivery of mail. 41 Am J1st P O § 32.

letterhead. The name, address, and usually the telephone number of the person, operation, partnership, or other business enterprise appearing at the top of the paper used in correspondence, together with short pertinent statements respecting the nature of the business.

letter missive (mis'iv). A summons issued by the chancellor directing a peer to defend a suit in equity; a royal letter nominating a bishop.

letter of advice. A written notice of an act which has been done by the writer. A drawer's communication to the drawee that a described draft has been drawn. UCC § 3–701(1). An instrument employed to decrease the risk of forgery of an international sight draft, notifying the drawee that a draft has been drawn and will be forthcoming. 11 Am J2d B & N § 60.

letter of attorney. See **power of attorney.**

letter of credence. A letter furnished to a diplomatic agent by the sovereign or other chief magistrate of his own state, which, being addressed to the sovereign or state to which such agent is delegated, states the general object of his mission and requests that full faith and credit be given to what he may say in behalf of his government. 4 Am J2d Ambss § 2.

letter of credit. Succinctly, a letter authorizing the addressee to pay money or supply a commodity to a third person on the credit of the writer. 24 Am J1st Guar § 20.

Wilbert Ward, in his "American Commercial Credits" at page 9, says: "A buyer who can place in the hands of a seller a written instrument by the buyer's bank, authorizing the seller to draw in accordance with certain terms, and stipulating in legal form that such bills will be honored, has at his command an instrument which will make his business more attractive to the seller than would otherwise be the case. An instrument by which a bank gives formal evidence of its willingness to undertake this class of operation for one of its customers is what has come to be known as a commercial letter of credit." Ernesto Foglino & Co. v Webster, 217 App Div 282, 293, 216 NYS 225, 234.

letter of introduction. A letter introducing a person to the addressee, sometimes mailed to the addressee but often carried and presented to him in person by the person to be introduced.

letter of license. An agreement entered into between an insolvent person and his creditors extending his time for payment.

letter of recall. A notice sent to a foreign government by another government of the recall of its ambassador or diplomatic representative.

letter of recommendation. A letter commending the services of a former employee and speaking of him in such terms as will tend to bring him to the favorable notice of one to whom he may apply for employment; sometimes being directed to whom it may concern and handed to the former employee to be carried by him, and sometimes directed specially to one to whom he proposes to make application for employment. 35 Am J1st M & S § 39.

letter of recredentials (rek"rē-den'shals). The reply of a foreign government to a letter of recall. See **letter of recall.**

letter of service. A letter of recommendation; a character reference. 35 Am J1st M & S § 39. A clearance card.

See **clearance card; letter of recommendation.**

letter press. An instrumentality formerly in general use in offices but rarely in use at present, for the making of copies of documents and letters.

letter press copy. A copy made by the use of a letter press.

letter requisitory (let'ėr rē-kwiz'i-tọ-ri). Same as **letter rogatory.**

letter rogatory (let'ėr rog'a-tọ-ri). A request by a court made of a foreign court in writing to secure the aid of the foreign court, backed by its power, in obtaining desired information in the form of a deposition by a person within the jurisdiction of the foreign court or to obtain the production of a record within the jurisdiction of such court. 23 Am J2d Dep § 23.

While it is usual for a letter rogatory to be accompanied by written interrogatories, this is not essential, unless required by statute; in the absence of any such statutory provision, the testimony may be taken upon oral examination. The absence of written interrogatories may, however, affect the question whether the court in its discretion will honor the letters. Anno: 9 ALR 967, s. 108 ALR 384; 23 Am J2d Dep § 23.

letters. A public or private document granting or delegating some power or authority.
See **letter**.

letters ad colligendum bona defuncti (ad kol-li-jen'-dum bō'na dē-funk'tī). Letters to collect the goods of the deceased.
Letters were thus designated which were issued to a person authorizing him to gather and keep in his safe custody the goods of a deceased person. Such letters neither made the person so appointed the executor nor the administrator of the estate of the decedent. See 2 Bl Comm 505.

letters avocatory (a-vok'a-tō-ri). Letters officially summoning a citizen to return to his own country from a country with which it is at war, or warning him against the commission of unlawful acts.

letters close. Same as **close writs.**

letters of abolition (of ab-ō-lish'ǫn). (Civil law.) Letters whereby a punishment for crime was remitted; but the infamy remained unless the letters had been issued before sentence.

letters of administration. The official exemplification of the record of the appointment of an administrator of a decedent's estate by the court. 31 Am J Ex & Ad § 89. Letters granted to a person by a probate court evidencing such person's authority to act as administrator of the estate of a person who has died without leaving a valid will. Mutual Ben. Life Ins. Co. v Tisdale, 91 US (1 Otto) 238, 23 L Ed 314.

letters of administration with the will annexed. Letters of administration issued in case no executor is appointed in the will or in case the person appointed in the will cannot qualify or refuses to do so.

letters of collection. Letters authorizing a person to gather and keep in his safe custody the goods of a deceased person; not the equivalent of letters testamentary or letters of administration. See 2 Bl Comm 505.

letters of fire and sword. Letters which were anciently directed to the sheriff of the county requesting him to gather all the force necessary to dispossess a tenant who remained in possession of land unlawfully.

letters of marque and reprisal (of märk and rē-prī'-zal). A commission issued during a state of war by one of the belligerent governments authorizing a privateer to attack the ships and seize the property of a hostile nation on the high seas. See 41 Am J1st Pir § 2.

letters of request. A written waiver of its jurisdiction by a lower ecclesiastical court to a higher one, requesting the higher court to take jurisdiction of a matter.

letters of safe conduct. Passports issued by a government in time of war.

letters of special administration. Letters issued to a special administrator upon his qualifying for the office.
See **special administrator.**

letters overt (ō'vėrt). Same as **letters patent.**

letters patent. The instrument evidencing the grant of a patent for an invention. 40 Am J1st Pat § 2. A royal or governmental grant of property, status, title, authority, or privilege.

letters rogatory. See **letter rogatory.**

letters testamentary. An official exemplification of the record of the appointment of an executor by the court. 31 Am J Ex & Ad § 91. Letters issued by a court of probate to a person as evidence of his authority and office as the executor of a deceased person's estate.

letting. An Americanism for the act of a public body or private owner for engaging a contractor for the construction of a building or other improvement, normally after bids for the work have been received, thus entailing the selection of a contractor from a number of bidders. Eppes v Mississippi, Gainesville & Tuskaloosa Railroad Co. 35 Ala 33, 55.
See **letting contract.**

letting contract. The steps in the formation and execution of a contract, particularly a public contract, including an advertising for bids, the reception of bids, and the award of the contract to the lowest bidder, provided he appears to be a responsible bidder.

letting of ship "on a lay." See **letting of ship on shares.**

letting of ship on shares. The transaction whereby the owner of a vessel lets her to the master who operates on shares or, as sometimes stated "on a lay."
The master is intrusted with entire possession and control, with the right to employ and navigate the vessel as he sees fit, and is required to victual and man her at his own expense. He collects the freights, and after deducting the expenses, divides the net earnings between himself and the owner in the agreed proportions. At a time when vessels were small, this practice was much in vogue. 48 Am J1st Ship § 335.

letting on shares. The making of a lease for crop rent.
See **crop rent; letting of ship on shares.**

letting out work. See **letting contract.**

letting premises. The making of a lease.

lettre de change (de shänj). (French.) A bill of exchange.

leucite. An ore from which aluminum can be made. United States v Aluminum Co. of America (DC NY) 44 F Supp 97.

leukemia (lū-kē'mi-ạ). A disease of the blood, the effects of which appear in the bone marrow, generally considered fatal. Kundiger v Prudential Ins. Co. 219 Minn 25, 17 NW2d 49.

levandae navis causa (le-van'dē na'vis kâ'za). For the purpose of lightening the ship.

levant (lev'ant'). (French.) Rising up.

levantes et cubantes (le-van'tēz et ku-ban'tēz). Same as **levant et couchant.**

levant et couchant (lev'ant ā kö'shänt). Rising up and lying down.
Cattle could not be distrained by a landlord if the lands were not sufficiently fenced to keep them out, until they had been levant et couchant; that is, until they had been there at least one night. See 3 Bl Comm 9.

levari facias (lẹ-vā'rī fā'shi-as). A common law writ similar to the writ of equitable origin known as sequestration. 47 Am J1st Seques § 2. A writ of execution commanding the sheriff to levy the plaintiff's debt on the lands and goods of the defendant and authorizing the sheriff to seize all the defendant's goods and receive the rents and profits of the land until satisfaction is made to the plaintiff. 30 Am J2d Exec § 29.

levee. An artificial embankment constructed to contain the flood waters of a river. Anno: 70 ALR 1275, 1278; 26 Am J2d Em D § 65. A landing place for vessels, and for the delivery of merchandise to and from such vessels, and, as incident to that, for the temporary storage of the merchandise. St. Paul v Chicago, Milwaukee & St. Paul Railway Co. 63 Minn 330, 63 NW 267, 65 NW 649, 68 NW 458.

levee commissioner. A public officer having duties in reference to the construction and maintenance of levees. Shelby v Alcorn, 36 Miss 273.

levee district. An improvement district created for the construction and maintenance of a levee. A quasi-public corporation like a railroad, not a political or civil division of the state and not created for political purposes nor for the administration of civil government, but created by statute with only such powers as are expressly or impliedly conferred. Board of Directors of St. Francis Levee District v Kurn (CA5 Mo) 98 F2d 394.

level premium. A life insurance premium in the same amount from year to year, such amount being computed on the basis that mortality cost is less during the early years of the insurance and greater in later years. 29 Am J Rev ed Ins § 56.

The level rate method is a recognized method of fixing rates of life insurance whereby the insured begins at once to pay an amount each year which will in the period of his expectancy be sufficient, with interest accretions to pay the face of his policy. Whether the step rate or level rate plan is used, the total amount paid is the same. Jenkins v Talbot, 338 Ill 441, 170 NE 735, 80 ALR 638.

level rate. See **level premium.**

level road. For the purposes of a statute requiring the headlights of motor vehicles to be such that under normal atmospheric conditions and on a "level road" they will produce a driving light sufficient to render clearly discernible all vehicles, persons, or substantial objects a specified distance ahead: —a road with a uniform grade, the provision applying irrespective of whether a car is traveling on a straight level stretch of road which is horizontal, or on an up grade or down grade. O'Rourke v Washington, 304 Pa 78, 155 A 100, 78 ALR 811.

Lever Act. A federal statute of August 10, 1917, re-enacted in the act of October 22, 1919, § 2 (41 Stat 297, c 80), penalizing the exaction of excessive prices upon the sale of necessaries in wartime. United States v L. Cohen Grocery Co. 255 US 81, 65 L Ed 516, 41 S Ct 298.

levir (le'vir). (Roman law.) The brother of a wife's husband; a wife's brother-in-law.

levis culpa (le'vis kul'pa). Ordinary fault or neglect.

levissima culpa (le-vis'si-ma kul'pa). Slight fault or neglect.

levissima diligentia (le-vis'si-ma di-li-jen'she-a). Slight diligence. Brand v Troy & Schenectady Railroad Co. (NY) 8 Barb 368, 378.

Levitical degrees (lẹ-vit'i-kạl dē-grēz'). The degrees of relationship between a man and a woman which bar their marriage to each other, as stated in the eighteenth chapter of Leviticus.

levy. An imposition whether of a tax, a burden upon property as authorized by a writ, or compulsory military service. Of tax: The acts of imposing and collecting a tax under authority of law. State v Camp Sing, 18 Mont 128, 44 P 516. The establishment or fixing of a rate of taxation by a duly authorized board or body. More narrowly defined as the imposition of the burden of the tax in the abstract, as distinguished from the ministerial duties in listing and assessment of property and the apportionment of the tax. Borrowdale v Socorro County, 23 NM 1, 163 P 721. Of attachment:—the seizure or taking of possession or custody of property under a writ of attachment by sheriff or other authorized officer. 6 Am J2d Attach § 288. An act symbolizing that land has become bound by the lien of an attachment, and indorsement on the writ of attachment that such has been levied upon property of the defendant, describing the same and noting the date and time of day of the levy, and some form of actual or constructive notice to the defendant of the levy. 6 Am J2d Attach § 311. Of execution:— an absolute appropriation of property of a judgment debtor to the payment of the judgment debt; a ministerial act. 30 Am J2d Exec § 95.

At common law a levy on goods consisted of an officer's entering the premises where they were and either leaving an assistant in charge of them or removing them after taking an inventory. Today courts differ as to what is a valid levy, but by the weight of authority there must be an actual or constructive seizure of the goods. 30 Am J2d Exec § 238. In most states, a levy on land must be made by some unequivocal act of the officer indicating his intention of singling out certain real estate for the satisfaction of the debt. The cases are not agreed on what this act must be, but the better considered ones hold that, in the absence of statute, a valid levy may be made by the sheriff by an indorsement thereof upon the records without even seeing the land, if he is sufficiently informed to describe it properly. 30 Am J2d Exec §§ 245 et seq.

levy at the risk of the plaintiff. An indorsement upon the writ of execution by the execution officer meaning, not only that the execution creditor has agreed to indemnify the execution officer for a wrongful levy, but also that the property may be left with the execution debtor until the sale at the risk of the execution creditor, so that the officer is relieved from responsibility to the execution creditor if the property is not produced at the date of the sale. Keyser's Appeal, 13 Pa 409.

levy court. The body which was at one time charged with the administration of the ministerial and financial duties of Washington county in the District of Columbia; a board which corresponded to the county commissioners and county supervisors of various states of the Union. Levy Court v Woodward (US) 2 Wall 501, 17 L Ed 851.

levying fine. A fictitious proceeding at common law to effect an alienation of land.

See **fine to bar entail; fine to convey.**

levying war. A term including, not only the act of making war for the purpose of overturning the government, but also any combination forcibly to oppose the execution of any public law of the United States, if accompanied or followed by an act of forcible opposition to such law in pursuance of such combination. Druecker v Salomon, 21 Wis 621.

War is actually levied when a body of men are actually assembled for the purpose of effecting by force a treasonable object. See Burr's Case (US) 4 Cranch 473, 2 L Ed 686.

levy of attachment. See levy.

levy of execution. See levy.

lewd. A characterization of an act of lewdness. See lewdness.

lewd and lascivious association. An offense dependent upon repetition of the acts proscribed, single or occasional acts of sexual intercourse unaccompanied by any pretense of living together being insufficient to constitute the offense. Boswell v State, 48 Tex Crim 47, 85 SW 1076.

See lewd and lascivious conduct.

lewd and lascivious behaviour. See lewd and lascivious conduct.

lewd and lascivious conduct. An offense distinct from adultery. 2 Am J2d Adult § 16. Including in some instances acts of illicit intercourse but not the exact equivalent of illicit intercourse; continuing conduct in defiance of the standards of decency and constituting an affront to society. State v Brooks, 215 Wis 134, 254 NW 374, 94 ALR 401.

lewd house. A house to which people resort for lewd acts.

See house of ill fame.

lewdness. The unlawful indulgence of lust; sexual impurity; gross indecency with respect to the sexual relation. State v Rayburn, 170 Iowa 514, 153 NW 59.

The common-law offense of "lewdness" means open and public indecency, and in order to amount to an indictable crime it must always amount to a common nuisance, committed in a public place, and seen by persons lawfully in that place. 33 Am J1st Lewd etc § 2.

If a man and woman resort to a house of ill fame for the purpose of having sexual relations, her purpose is prostitution, and his, lewdness. State v Gardner, 174 Iowa 748, 156 NW 747, ovrld on other grounds State v Frey, 206 Iowa 981, 988, 221 NW 445.

lewdly (lūd′li). Lustfully. With unlawful indulgence in lust. State v Lawrence, 19 Neb 307, 313.

lex (leks). Law; a law; the law.
See the singular lex.

Lex aequitate gaudet; appetit perfectum; est norma recti (lex ē-qui-tā′te gâ′det; ap-pe′tit per-fek′tum; est nor′ma rek′tī). The law delights in equity; it grasps at perfection; it is the rule of right.

lex aeterna (leks ē-ter′na). The eternal law; the moral law; the law of nature; the law which God at the time of the creation of the nature of man infused into his heart, for his preservation and direction. Calvin's Case (Eng) 7 Co Rep la.

lex agraria (lex a-grā′ri-a). The agrarian law of the Romans, which limited the amount of land which could be held by a Roman citizen, and provided for the allotment of public lands among the people.

lex alimentaria (lex a-li-men-tā′ri-a). The Roman law which provided for the distribution of bread among the poor.

Lex aliquando sequitur aequitatem (lex a-li-quan′dō se′qui-ter ē-qui-tā′tem). The law sometimes follows equity.

lex amissa (lex a-mis′sa). A person who has lost his law; a person outlawed; one civilly dead.

Lex Angliae (lex Ang′li-ē). The law of England.

Lex Angliae est lex misericordiae (lex Ang′li-ē est lex mi-se-ri-kor′di-ē). The law of England is the law of mercy.

Lex Angliae non patitur absurdum (lex Ang′li-ē non pa′ti-ter ab-ser′dum). The law of England does not suffer an absurdity.

Lex Angliae nunquam matris, sed semper patris conditionem imitari partum judicat (lex Ang′li-ē nun′quam mā′tris, sed sem′per pa′tris kon-di-she-ō′nem i-mi-tā′rī par′tum jū′di-kat). The law of England never adjudges that their issue shall partake of the condition of the mother, but always of that of the father.

Lex Angliae nunquam sine parliamento mutari potest (lex Ang′li-ē nun′quam sī′ne par-li-a-men′tō mū-tā′rī po′test). The law of England never can be changed without parliament.

lex annale (lex an-nā′le). The Roman law governing minimum ages for high officials.

lex apparens (lex ap-pa′renz). Apparent law; manifest law; that is, the law which is apparent or made manifest in a trial by battel or trial by ordeal.

lex atilia (lex a-ti′li-a). The atilian law,—the Roman law governing the appointment of guardians.

lex atinia (lex a-ti′ni-a). The atinian law,—the Roman law which prohibited the acquisition of title to stolen goods by long-continued possession.

Lex beneficialis rei consimili remedium praestat (lex be-ne-fi-she-ā′lis rē′ī kon-si′mi-lī rē-mē′di-um prē′-stat). A beneficial law furnishes a remedy in a similar case or matter.

lex brehonia (lex bre-hō′ni-a). Brehon law,—an ancient system of Irish law.

Lex citius tolerare vult privatum damnum quam publicum malum (lex si′she-us to-le-rā′re vult prī-vā′-tum dam′num quam pub′li-kum ma′lum). The law would rather tolerate a private loss than a public evil.

lex commissoria (lex kom-mis-sō′ri-a). A Roman law under which a pledge securing the payment of money was ipso facto forfeited upon the failure to make payment on the due date.

lex communis (lex kom-mū′nis). The common law.

lex contractus (lex kon-trak′tus). The law of the contract.

Lex contra id quod praesumit probationem non recipit (lex kon′trā id quod prē′zu-mit prō-bā-she-ō′nem non re′si-pit). The law receives no proof which is contrary to that which it presumes.

lex Cornelia de falsis (lex kor-nē′li-a dē fal′sis). The Cornelian law of falsifying,—a Roman law for the punishment of the forgery of the will of a person dying in captivity.

lex Cornelia de injuriis (lex kor-nē′li-a dē in-jū′ri-is). A Roman law providing a civil action for injury suffered by a beating, or in the forcing into a strange dwelling. See Mackeldey's Roman Law § 489.

lex Cornelia de sicariis et veneficis (lex kor-nē′li-a dē si-kā′ri-is et ve-nē′fi-sis). (Roman law.) The Cornelian law for the punishment of assassins and poisoners.

Lex deficere non potest in justitia exhibenda (lex dē-fi'se-re non po'test in jŭs-ti'she-a ex-hi-ben'da). The law cannot be deficient in allowing justice.

Lex de futuro; judex de praeterito (lex dē fu-tū'rō; jŭ'dex dē prē-te'ri-tō). The law provides for the future; the judge for the past.

lex dilationes semper exhorret (lex di-lā-she-ō'nēz sem'per ex-hor'ret). The law always abhors delays.

lex domicilii (lex dō-mi-si'li-ī). The law of the domicil.

Lex est ab aeterno (lex est ab ē-ter'nō). Law is from eternity, that is, its origin is in eternity.

Lex est dictamen rationis (lex est dik'ta-men rā-she-ō'nis). Law is the dictate of reason.

Lex est norma recti (lex est nor'ma rek'tī). Law is the rule of right.

Lex est ratio summa quae jubet quae sunt utilia et necessaria, et contraria prohibet (lex est rā'she-ō sum'ma kwē jū'bet kwē sunt ū-ti'li-a et ne-ses-sā'ri-a, et kon-trā'ri-a pro'hi-bet). Law is the consummation of reason, which commands those things which are useful and necessary, and prohibits the contrary.

Lex est sanctio sancta, jubens honesta, et prohibens contraria (lex est sank'she-ō sank'ta, ju'benz hones'ta, et prō'hi-benz kon-trā'ri-a). Law is a sacred sanction, commanding that which is right and prohibiting the contrary.

Lex est summa ratio insita a natura quae jubet ea, quae facienda sunt prohibetque contraria (lex est sum'ma rā'she-ō in'si-ta ā na-tū'ra kwē ju'bet ē'a, kwē fa-she-en'da sunt pro-hi-bet'kwe kon-trā'ri-a). Law is the highest reason implanted in us by nature, which commands what should be done and prohibits the contrary.

Lex est tutissima cassis; sub clypeo legis nemo decipitur (lex est tū-tis'si-ma kas'sis; sub klip'e-ō lē'jis ne'mō de-si'pi-ter). Law is the safest helmet; under the shield of the law no one is deceived.

lex et consuetudo parliamenti (lex et kon-suē-tū'dō par-lī-a-ment'ī). The law and the custom of parliament. See 1 Bl Comm 163.

Lex et consuetudo regni nostri (lex et kon-suē-tū-dō reg'nī nos'trī). The law and the custom or usage of our kingdom; that is, the common law of England.

lex Falcidia (lex Fal-si'di-a). The Falcidian law,—a Roman statute of 714 A. D., which restricted the disposition of one's property by will or testament.

Lex favet doti (lex fa'vet dō'tī). The law favors dower.

lex feudi (lex fū'dī). The law of the fee or feud.

Lex fingit ubi subsistit aequitas (lex fin'jit u'bi sub-sis'tit ē'qui-tās). The law fabricates where equity subsists.

lex fori (lex fō'rī). The law of the jurisdiction in which the litigation occurs, controlling all that part of the litigation which is concerned merely with remedy. 16 Am J2d Confl L § 11.

lex Furia Caninia (lex fu'ri-a ka-ni'ni-a). The Fusian Caninian law,—a Roman law which limited the manumission of slaves by will or testament.

lex Hostilia de furtis (lex hos-ti'li-a dē fer'tis). (Roman law.) The Hostilian law concerning theft or larceny. See 4 Bl Comm 236.

lexicographical definition. A definition as given in a dictionary.

A correct construction of legislative language may not always be reached by a dogmatic adherence to the lexicographical definition. Anno: 101 ALR 566.

Lex intendit vicinum vicini facta scire (lex in-ten'dit vi-sī'num vi-sī'nī fak'ta sī're). The law presumes that a neighbor is cognizant of the acts of his neighbor.

Lex judicat de rebus necessario faciendis quasi de re ipsa factis (lex jū'di-kat de rē'bus ne-ses-sa'ri-ō fā-she-en'dis quā'sī dē rē ip'sa fak'tis). The law judges of things which must necessarily be done as if they were really done.

lex Julia majestatis (lex jū'li-a ma-jes-tā'tis). (Roman law.) The Julian law concerning treason. See 4 Bl Comm 76.

lex ligeantiae (lex li-je-an'she-ē). The law of the country of a person's allegiance.

lex loci (lex lō'sī). The law of the place in which the circumstances on which the action is based arose or occurred, controlling that part of the litigation concerned with the substantive right or basis of the cause of action. 16 Am J2d Confl L § 11.

lex loci actus (lex lō'sī ak'tus). The law of the place of the act.

lex loci celebrationis (lex lō'sī se-le-brā-she-ō'nis). The law of the place where the contract or other obligation is solemnized, controlling on questions of form or of formal validity of a contract. Pritchard v Norton (US) 16 Otto 124, 27 L Ed 104, 1 S Ct 102.

lex loci commissi (lex lō'sī kom-mis'sī). the law of the place where the act was committed, controlling in reference to matters of substantive right or basis of a cause of action. 16 Am J2d Confl L § 11.

lex loci contractus (lex lō'sī kon-trak'tus). The law of the place of the contract,—that is, the law of the place where the contract is made.

As to the law governing the validity and construction of contracts see 16 Am J2d Confl L §§ 38 et seq.

lex loci delictis (lex lō'sī de-lik'tis). The law of the place of the crime, the wrong, the tort.

lex loci rei sitae (lex lō'sī rē'ī si'tē). The law of the place where the subject matter is situated.

lex loci sitae rei (lex lō'sī si'tē rē'ī). The law of the place where the property lies. Crapo v Kelly (US) 16 Wall 610, 21 L Ed 430, 438.

lex loci solutionis (lex lō'sī so-lū-she-ō'nis). The law of the place of payment or performance. Pritchard v Norton (US) 16 Otto 124, 27 L Ed 104, 1 S Ct 102.

lex manifesta (lex ma-ni-fes'ta). Same as **lex apparens**.

lex mercatoria (lex mer-ka-tō'ri-a). The law merchant. 11 Am J2d B & N § 36.
See **law merchant**.

Lex necessitatis est lex temporis, i. e., instantis (lex ne-ses-si-tā'tis est lex tem'po-ris, i. e., in-stan'tis). The law of necessity is the law of the time; that is, of the present time.

Lex neminem cogit ad impossibilia (lex nē'mi-nem kō'jit ad im-pos-si-bi'li-a). The law compels no one to perform that which is impossible.

This maxim is the foundation of the rule that an act of God excuses the failure to discharge a duty. Southern Pacific Co. v Schoer (CA8 Utah) 114 F 466.

Lex neminem cogit ad vana seu inutilia peragenda (lex nē'mi-nem kō'jit ad vā'na su in-ū-ti'li-a per-ā-jen'da). The law does not compel anyone to perform vain or useless acts. Gordon v Massachusetts Fire & Marine Ins. Co. 19 Mass (2 Pick) 249, 259.

Lex neminem cogit ostendere quod nescire praesumitur (lex nē'mi-nem kō'jit os-ten'de-re quod ne-sī're prē-zu'mi-ter). The law does not compel anyone to divulge that of which he is presumed to be ignorant.

Lex nemini facit injuriam (lex nē'mi-nī fā'sit in-jū'ri-am). The law works injury to no one.

Lex nemini operatur iniquum, nemini facit injuriam (lex nē'mi-nī ō-pe-rā'ter in-ī'qu-um, ne'mi-nī fā'sit in-jū'ri-am). The law works injustice to no one, does injury to no one.

Lex nil facit frustra, nil jubet frustra (lex nil fā'sit frus'tra, nil ju'bet frus'tra). The law does nothing in vain, commands nothing in vain.

Lex nil frustra facit (lex nil frus'tra fā'sit). The law does nothing in vain.

Lex non cogit ad impossibilia (lex non kō'jit ad im-pos-si-bi'li-a). The law does not compel that which is impossible.

Lex non cogit ad vana seu inutilia (leks non koj'it ad van'a sū in-ū-til'i-a). The law does not compel vain or useless things.

Lex non cogit seu ad vana aut impossibilia (lex non kō'jit su ad vā'na ât im-pos-si-bi'li-a). The law does not compel either useless or impossible things. Green v Liter (US) 8 Cranch 229, 246, 3 L Ed 545, 551.

Lex non curat de minimis (lex non kū'rat de mi'ni-mis). The law does not pay attention to trifles.

Lex non deficit in justitia exhibenda (lex non de'fi-sit in jus-ti'she-a ex-hi-ben'da). The law is not deficient in dispensing justice.

Lex non exacte definit, sed arbitrio boni viri permittit (lex non eg-zak'te dē-fī'nit, sed ar-bi'tri-ō bō'nī vi'rī per-mit'tit). The law does not define exactly, but allows for the judgment of a fair man. See 1 Bl Comm 61.

Lex non favet votis delicatorum (lex non fa'vet vō'tis de-li-kā-tō'rum). The law does not favor the wishes of the fastidious.

"Trifling results are disregarded, for the courts proceed with great caution, and will not interfere with the use of property by the owner thereof, unless such use is unreasonable, the injury material and actual, not fanciful or sentimental." McCarty v Natural Carbonic Gas Co. 189 NY 40, 81 NE 549.

Lex non intendit aliquid impossibile (lex non in-ten'-dit a'li-quid im-pos-si'bi-le). The law does not require anything which is impossible. Chew Heong v United States, 112 US 536, 554, 28 L Ed 770, 776, 5 S Ct 255.

Lex non patitur fractiones et divisiones statuum (lex non pa'ti-ter frak-she-ō'nēz et di-vī-zhe-ō'nēz sta-tu'um). The law does not intend fractions and divisions of estates.

Lex non praecipit inutilia (lex non prē'si-pit in-u-ti'-li-a). The law does not require vain or useless things.

The maxim expresses rather an ideal than an accomplished fact. Rock Island, Arkansas & Louisiana Railroad Co. v United States, 254 US 141, 65 L Ed 188, 41 S Ct 55.

Lex non praecipit inutilia, quia inutilis labor stultus (lex non prē'si-pit in-ū-ti'- li-a, qui'a in-u'ti-lis la'-bor stul'tus). The law does not command useless acts, because useless labor is silly.

Lex non requirit frustra (lex non re-quī'rit frus'tra). The law does not require a vain or useless thing.

Lex non requirit verificari quod apparet curiae (lex non re-quī'rit ve-ri-fi-kā'rī quod ap'pa-ret kū'ri-ē). The law does not require that which is apparent to the court to be proved.

lex non scripta (lex non skrip'ta). The unwritten law.

lex parliamenti (lex par-li-ā-men'tī). The laws of parliament. Kilbourn v Thompson (US) 13 Otto 168, 186, 26 L Ed 377, 385.

lex patriae (lex pa'tri-ē). The law of one's country.

Lex plus laudatur quando ratione probatur (lex plus lâ-dā'ter quan'dō rā-she-ō'ne prō-bā'ter). The law is more to be praised when it is approved by reason.

Lex posterior derogat prior (lex pos-te'ri-or de'ro-gat pri-ō'rī). A later law repeals an earlier one.

Lex prospicit, non respicit (lex prō'spi-sit, non re'spi-sit). The law looks forward, it is not retrospective.

Lex punit mendacium (lex pu'nit men-dā'she-um). The law punishes falsehood or mendacity.

Lex pure poenalis obligat tantum ad poenam, non item ad culpam; lex poenalis mixta et ad culpam obligat et ad poenam (lex pū'rē pē-nā'lis ob'li-gat tan'tum ad pē'nam, non ī'tem ad kul'pam; lex pē-nā'lis mix'ta et ad kul'pam ob'li-gat et ad pē'nam). A law purely penal looks most at the punishment, not at the crime; a mixed penal law looks at both the crime and the punishment.

lex regia (lex rē'ji-a). The law which was ordained by the Roman emperor.

lex rei sitae (lex rē'ī si'tē). The law of the locality of the thing,—that is, the law in force at the place where the subject matter is situated, controlling all matters concerning the title and disposition of real property. 16 Am J2d Confl L § 14.

Lex rejicit superflua, pugnantia, incongrua (lex rē'ji-sit su-per'flu-a, pug-nan'she-a, in-kon'gru-a). The law rejects those matters which are superfluous, repugnant, or incongruous.

Lex reprobat moram (lex re-prō'bat mo'ram). The law disapproves of delay.

Lex respicit aequitatem (lex re'spi-sit ē-qui-tā'tem). The law regards equity.

Lex Rhodia de jactu (lex rō'di-a dē jak'tū). The Rhodian law concerning jettison.

Historically, this law contributed to form the modern law of general average in marine insurance. Barnard v Adams, (US) 10 How 270, 303, 13 L Ed 417, 431.

lex Romana Visigothorum (lex rō-mā'na vi-sī-go-thō'rum). See **law of Alaric**.

lex Salica (lex sa'li-ka). Same as **Salic law**.

lex scripta (lex skrip'ta). Singular of **leges scriptae**.

Lex semper dabit remedium (lex sem'per da'bit rē-mē'di-um). The law always gives a remedy; a common-law maxim. Smith v Bonsall (Pa) 5 Rawle 80, 89.

Lex semper intendit quod convenit rationi (lex sem'per in-ten'dit quod kon-vē'nit rā-she-ō'nī). The law always intends what is agreeable to reason. Williams v Hays, 157 NY 541, 52 NE 589.

lex situs (lex si'tus). Same as **lex rei sitae.**

lex solutionis (lex so-lū-she-ō'nis). The law of payment,—that is, the law relating to the performance of the contract.
See **lex loci solutionis.**

Lex spectat naturae ordinem (lex spek'tat nā-tū'rē or'di-nem). The law regards the order of nature.

lex sub graviore lege (lex sub gra-vi-ō're lē'je). A law subordinate to higher law.
"A state which has not the exclusive dominion over its territory, is more or less dependent and weak; and its 'eminent domain,' modified by the will of others, is lex sub graviore lege." Sneed v Ewing, 28 Ky 460.

Lex succurrit ignoranti (lex su-ker'rit ig-nō-ran'tī). The law succors ignorance.

Lex succurrit minoribus (lex su-ker'rit mī-nō'ri-bus). The law aids minors.

lex talionis (lex ta-li-ō'nis). The law of retaliation.
See **retaliation.**

lex terrae (lex ter'rē). The law of the land.

Lex uno ore omnes alloquitur (lex ū'nō o're om'nēz al-lō'qui-ter). The law speaks to all with one mouth.

Lex vigilantibus favet (lex vi-ji-lan'ti-bus fa'vet). The law favors those who are vigilant.

Lex vigilantibus, non dormientibus (lex vi-ji-lan'ti-bus, non dor-mi-en'ti-bus). The law is for the vigilant, not for those who slumber. Toole v Cook (NY) 16 How Pr 142, 144.

Lex vigilantibus, non dormientibus subvenit (lex vi-ji-lan'ti-bus, non dor-mi-en'ti-bus sub-vē'nit). The law aids the vigilant, not those who slumber.

ley (lā). Law; the law; an oath.

ley civile (lā si-vēl'). The civil law; the civil law of the Romans.

ley gager (lay gah'zhay). To wage one's law.
See **wager of law.**

leze majesty (lays mah'zhēs-ty). Same as **lèse majesté.**

liability. Legal responsibility, either civil or criminal. The condition of being bound in law and justice to pay an indebtedness or discharge some obligation. Feil v Coeur D'Alene, 23 Idaho 32, 129 P 643. The state or condition of a person after he has breached his contract or violated any obligation resting upon him. Lattin v Gillette, 95 Cal 317, 30 P 545. A word of different meanings, the pertinent one to be gathered from the context in which it appears, construed in the light of surrounding circumstances. Evans v Kroh (Ky) 284 SW2d 329, 58 ALR2d 1446. Sometimes synonymous with "debt." Anno: 58 ALR2d 1453. Within the meaning of a statute of limitations:—under one view, a contract obligation; under another view, responsibility, embracing tort liability as well as contract liability. 34 Am J1st Lim Ac § 94. As the word appears in a limitation on the creation of debt or liability of a state in excess of a prescribed amount:—a term having special reference to the warrant and legislative authority on which a state contract must rest, and on which alone a public debt must find its sanction in order to obligate the state. 49 Am J1st States § 66.

liability created by statute. A liability created by a statute which discloses an intention, express or implied, that from disregard of the statutory command, a liability for damages will arise which would not exist but for the statute. Schmidt v Merchants Despatch Transp. Co. 270 NY 287, 200 NE 824, 104 ALR 450, reh den 271 NY 531, 2 NE2d 680. A liability which would not exist but for the statute. See Fidelity & Deposit Co. v Lindholm (CA9 Cal) 66 F2d 56, 89 ALR 279. A liability that comes into being solely by statute and has no existence prior to the enactment creating it. Steel v National Surety Corp. 74 Ariz 193, 245 P2d 960, 32 ALR2d 1236.
A cause of action recognized for centuries by the common law cannot be regarded as a "liability created by statute" within the meaning of a statute of limitations. Fratt v Robinson (CA9 Wash) 203 F2d 627, 37 ALR2d 636.
When the statute merely defines, in the interest of the general public, the degree of care which shall be exercised under certain specified circumstances, it does not "create" a new liability, but merely changes the standard which must be applied in an action to recover damages caused by lack of care. 35 Am J1st M & S § 467.

liability insurance. A policy or contract of insurance whereby the insurer agrees to protect the insured against liability arising from an act or omission of the insured which causes injury to the person or the property of a third person, the liability of the insurer attaching upon the determination that the insured is liable for such act or omission, notwithstanding the insured has not sustained a loss in payment, voluntary or involuntary, made to the third person. 7 Am J2d Auto Ins § 81; 29A Am J Rev ed Ins § 1343.
Such insurance is of recent origin when compared with fire insurance, and was unknown in this country prior to 1887, when it was introduced from England. Employers' Liability Assur. Corp. v C. E. Carnes & Co. (DC La) 24 F 128.

liability reserve. See **reserve.**

liability without fault. See **absolute liability.**

liable. Under liability or legal responsibility.
See **liability.**

libel. An initial pleading in a suit in admiralty; the pleading whereby litigation is brought into an Admiralty Court. 2 Am J2d Adm § 175. A malicious publication, expressed either in printing, writing, typewriting, or by signs and pictures, tending either to blacken the memory of one who is dead, or the reputation of one who is alive, and expose him to public hatred, contempt, or ridicule. 33 Am J1st L & S § 3.
See **innuendo; privileged communication; privileged occasion; publication.**

libelant. Same as **libellant.**

libelee. Same as **libellee.**

libel in admiralty. The initial pleading in a suit in admiralty, corresponding to the declaration, complaint, or petition in an action or proceeding at law. 2 Am J2d Adm § 175.
See **libel of information**

libellant (lī'bel-ạnt). The complaining party in an admiralty or ecclesiastical suit.

libellee (lī'bel-ē). The defendant in an admiralty or ecclesiastical suit.

libellous (lī'bel-us). Same as **libelous**.

libellus famosus (lī'bel-us fam-o'sus). (Civil law.) a defamatory publication.

libel of accusation (of ak-ū-zā'shon). A formal accusation charging a person with the commission of a criminal offense; an indictment.

libel of information. A pleading in a proceeding brought to obtain a forfeiture containing a substantial statement of the offense upon which the forfeiture is predicated. 23 Am J1st Forf & P § 15. A pleading in admiralty demanding a forfeiture because of breach of revenue, navigation, or other laws of the United States. 2 Am J2d Adm § 176. A pleading asking for the seizure and condemnation of property, such as adulterated or misbranded drugs. 21 USC § 334(a), (b).

libel of information for a forfeiture. See **libel of information**.

libel of review. A procedure provided for by the rules of some Admiralty Courts for demanding that the court correct or change its decree after the rendition thereof, and after expiration of the term in which it was rendered. 2 Am J2d Adm § 221.

libelous (lī'bel-us). Containing or constituting a libel; defamatory.

libelous per quod (li'bel-us per quod). Words which are not defamatory in themselves but may be shown, under proper allegation in the pleading and the proof, to constitute a libel. McDonald v Lee, 246 Pa 253, 92 A 135.

libelous per se. Written or printed words of such kind that when applied to a person they will necessarily cause injury to him in his personal, social, official, or business relations of life, so that legal injury may be presumed or implied from the bare fact of publication. 33 Am J1st L & S § 5. Written or printed words so obviously hurtful to the person aggrieved by them that no explanation of their meaning and no proof of their injurious character is required in order to make them actionable. Jerald v Huston, 120 Kan 3, 242 P 472.

liber (lī'bėr). Noun: A book; a volume; one of the units of a published work, either literary or professional; a book in which public records are made. Adjective: Free; freed.

libera chasea (li'be-ra cha'se-a). Free chase,—the exclusive right to hunt in a chase or park.

libera eleemosyna (li'be-ra ē-le-e-mo'si-na). Frankalmoign or free alms,—a Saxon land tenure, which survived the Norman revolution, under which tenure an ecclesiastical corporation held land without fealty and merely by prayer service for the soul of the donor. See 2 Bl Comm 101.

libera falda (li'be-ra fal'da). Frank-fold or faldage,—the right of the lord of the manor to have the sheep of his tenant manure his land; a term also applied to the fee paid by the tenant to the lord for exemption from the service of thus manuring.

liberal construction. A broad construction. A construction of the words of a contract, either singly or in connection with the subject matter, giving the words full effect so as to carry out the intention of the parties. 17 Am J2d Contr § 253. An interpretation of a statute which is within the reason and spirit of the statute or public policy which animates it, rather than the strict letter thereof; a fair or favorable construction so as to give the statute, if possible, a beneficial operation, one which will tend to promote and effectuate justice, in the interest of the public good, and avoid harsh or incongruous results. International Mercantile Marine Co. v Lowe (CA2 NY) 93 F2d 663, 115 ALR 896, cert den 304 US 565, 82 L Ed 1532, 58 S Ct 948; Fox Park Timber Co. v Baker, 53 Wyo 467, 784 P2d 736, 120 ALR 1020. An interpretation of an administrative rule in a manner similar to that applied in giving a statute a broad and liberal construction. Anno: 40 ALR2d 337, § 2[a].

libera lex (li'be-ra lex). Frank law,—the aggregate rights of a freeman or a citizen.

liberam legem amittere (li'be-ram lē'jem ā-mit'te-re). Same as **legem amittere**.

libera piscaria (li'be-ra pis-kā'ri-a). Free fishery,—the exclusive right of fishing in a public river. Arnold v Mundy, 1 NJL 1.

liberare (li-be-rā're). To liberate; to deliver; to set free; to manumit; to discharge from a debt or other obligation; to release; to restore.

liberari facias (li-be-rā'rī fā'she-as). A writ of execution which commands the sheriff to set off real estate taken by him under the writ to the judgment creditor instead of selling it and appropriating the proceeds to the payment of the debt, the lands being appraised at the instance of the sheriff, so that the amount of the credit upon the judgment may be ascertained and made of record. See 7 Stand Pa Proc §§ 140 et seq.

liber assisarum (lī'ber as-si-sā'rum). The book of the assizes,—the fourth volume of decisions reported in the reign of Edward the Third.

Liberata pecunia non liberat offerentem (li-be-rā'ta pe-kū'ni-a non li'be-rat of-fe-ren'tem). A restoration of money does not free the offeror. That is, from a criminal charge.

liberate. Verb: To set free; to release from custody. Noun: A conditional writ, ordering the sheriff to cause goods, which have been taken on an extent sued out upon a statute staple, to be appraised, and to deliver them to the creditor, if he will accept them on the valuation thus set, by the appraisement, which he may do, or not, at his election. Re Reed, 21 Vt 635, 640.

liberatio (li-be-rā'she-ō). Livery; delivery; a payment for the delivery of a thing.

liberation. The act of setting free, discharging or releasing from custody. (Civil law.) A payment made for the discharge of, or release from, a contract.

See **emancipation; independence**.

libera warrena (li'be-ra war're-na). Free warren,—the liberty, franchise, or royalty, derived from the crown, of taking or killing all inferior species of game, called beasts and fowls of warren. See 2 Bl Comm 417.

liber bancus (li'ber ban'kus). Free bench,—a widow's dower in copyhold lands, which she usually held subject to the condition that she should remain chaste and unmarried. See 2 Bl Comm 129.

liber et legalis homo (li'ber et lē-gā'lis hō'mō). A free and lawful man; a juryman.

Liber Feudorum (li'ber fū-dō'rum). The book of fiefs or feuds,—a code of feudal law which was compiled and published in the twelfth century.

liber homo (lī'ber hō'mō). A freeman; one who owns a freehold and has freedom of mind; that is, a man who, as a member of a jury, can render an unbiased verdict. Turner v State, 128 Tenn 27, 157 SW 67.

liberi (lī'be-rī). (Saxon.) Freemen; landholders whose tenure was allodial,—who did not hold under a superior. (Latin.) Children. The young.

liberi et legales homines (lī'be-rī et lē-gā'lēz ho'mi-nēz). Freeholders and lawful men. Turner v State, 128 Tenn 27, 157 SW 67. Qualified for duty as jurors as having, not only a freehold, but freedom of mind to stand indifferent as between the persons involved in the litigation, no more inclining to the one than to the other. Turner v State, 128 Tenn 27, 157 SW 67.

liberi et legales homines de vicineto (lī'be-rī et lē-gā'lēz ho'mi-nēz dē vī-sī'nē-tō). Free and lawful men of the vicinage, that is, freeholders, without just exception, and of the visne or neighborhood; which is interpreted to be of the county where the fact is committed. People of California v Powell, 87 Cal 348, 25 P 481.

liberis. See **liberi.**

liberi sokemanni (lī'be-rī so-ke-man'nī). Tenants in free socage; tenants who held their lands by services which were not only certain, but honorable. See 2 Bl Comm 79.

Liber Judicialis (lī'ber jū-di-she-ā'lis). The Dome Book of King Alfred which probably contained the principal maxims of the common law, the penalties for misdemeanors, and the forms of judicial proceedings. 1 Bl Comm 65.

Liber Judiciarum (lī'ber jū-di-she-ā'rum). Same as **Liber Judicialis.**

libero maritagio (lī'ber-ō ma-ri-tā'ji-ō). Same as **liberum maritagium.**

libero passagio. See **de libero passagio.**

libertas (li-ber'tās). Liberty; freedom; a license; a privilege; an immunity; a franchise.

libertas ecclesiastica (li-ber'tās ē-klē-si-as'ti-ka). Ecclesiastical liberty or immunity.

Libertas est naturalis facultas ejus, quod cuique facere libet, nisi quod de jure aut vi prohibetur (li-ber'tās est nā-tu-rā'lis fa-kul'tas ē'jus, quod ki'kwe fā'se-re lī'bet, nī'sī quod dē jū're ât vi prō-hi-bē'ter). Liberty is a person's natural power of doing as it may please him, unless that is prohibited by law or by force.

Libertas inaestimabilis res est (li-ber'tās in-ēs-ti-mā'-bi-lis rēz est). Liberty is a thing of inestimable value.

Libertas non recipit aestimationem (li-ber'tās non re'si-pit ēs-ti-ma-she-ō'nem). Liberty does not admit of valuation.

Libertas omnibus rebus favorabilior est (li-ber'tās om'ni-bus rē'bus fa-vō-rā-bi'li-or est). Liberty is more favored than all other things.

libertate probanda. See **de libertate probanda.**

Libertates regales ad coronam spectantes ex concessione regum a corona exierunt (li-ber-tā'tēs rē-gā'lēz ad ko-rō'nam spek-tan'tēz ex kon-se-she-ō'ne re'-jum ā ko-rō'na ex-i-ē'runt). Royal privileges relating to the crown have issued from the crown by royal grant.

libertatibus allocandis. See **de libertatibus allocandis.**

liberti (li-ber'tī). (Roman law.) Persons who were freed from slavery; freedmen.

liberticide (lib'ėr-ti-sīd or li-bėr'ti-sīd). A destroyer of liberty or freedom.

liberties. Privileged communities or districts. The fundamental rights and privileges of the people guaranteed by the Constitution of the United States and the state constitutions.
See **liberty.**

liberties of the jail. Graphically, an extension of the walls of a jail. Peters v Henry (NY) 6 Johns 121. The area, within limits prescribed by statute, wherein a prisoner for debt may live or sojourn upon giving bond or other security for such accommodation. Dole v Moulton (NY) 2 Johns Cas 205, 206.
See **liberty of the rules.**

libertine (lib'ėr-tin). One who lacks moral restraint. A licentious person.

libertini (li-ber-tī'nī). Same as **liberti.**

Libertinum ingratum leges civiles in pristinam servitutem redigunt; sed leges Angliae semel manumissum semper liberum judicant (li-ber-tī'num in-grā'tum lē'jēz si'vi-lēz in pris-ti-nam ser-vi-tū'-tem re'di-gunt; sed lē'jēz Ang'li-ē se'mel ma-nū-mis'sum sem'per lī'be-rum jū'di-kant). The civil laws reduce an ungrateful freedman to his former servitude, but the laws of England adjudge a person who has been once manumitted or freed to be always free.

libertinus (li-ber-tī'nus). Same as **libertus,** the singular of **liberti.**

libertus (li-ber'tus). Singular of **liberti.**

liberty. Absence of servitude and restraint. A most broad and extensive concept, embracing every form and phase of individual right that is not necessarily taken away by some valid law for the common good. Wright v Hart, 12 NY 330, 75 NE 404. The right to do such acts as one may judge best for his interest, not inconsistent with the rights of others. Ex parte Drexel, 147 Cal 763, 82 P 429. The right to protection from violation of any of the fundamental conceptions of justice which lie at the base of our civil and political institutions. 16 Am J2d Const L § 358.

As the word is used in the United States Constitution, it means not only freedom of the citizen from servitude and restraint, but is deemed to embrace the right of every man to be free in the use of his powers and faculties, and to adopt and pursue such avocation or calling as he may choose, subject only to the restraints necessary to secure the common welfare. There can be no liberty, protected by government, that is not regulated by such laws as will preserve the right of each citizen to pursue his own advancement and happiness in his own way, subject only to the restraints necessary to secure the same right to others. The fundamental principle upon which liberty is based, in free and enlightened government, is equality under the law of the land. Braceville Coal Co. v People, 147 Ill 66, 35 NE 62.

See **life, liberty, and property; life, liberty, and pursuit of happiness.** See also "freedom" and phrases beginning "freedom."

liberty guaranty. See **guaranty of liberty.**

liberty of contract. The right to make a contract and the right to terminate a contract subject only to civil liability for unwarranted termination, both of which rights are protected by the United States Constitution. 16 Am J2d Const L § 373. The right to acquire and possess property and to contract concerning it. Lawrence v Rutland Railroad Co. 80 Vt 370, 67 A 1091. Not an absolute guaranty of freedom to contract without reference to the nature of the contract as perversive, contrary to good morals, or in contravention of sound public policy, but a guaranty against arbitrary or unreasonable restraint upon the right to contract. Lochner v State, 198 US 45, 49 L Ed 937, 25 S Ct 539; Moore v Grillis, 205 Miss 865, 39 So 2d 505, 10 ALR2d 1425; State ex rel. Davis-Smith Co. v Clausen, 65 Wash 156, 117 P 1101. The right granted by a statute to vary the operation of the statute in particular respects by agreement. UCC § 1–102(3)(4).

liberty of port. A phrase in a marine insurance policy which permits use to be made by the insured vessel of a specified port.

The words, "with liberty" of a certain port, do not necessarily give notice to the insurer that the object of the privilege is to trade at that port, and procuring such words to be inserted is not an unequivocal intimation of the nature of the cargo insured; nor is it an intimation to the underwriters that the insured looks to such port, under any circumstances in the contemplation of the parties, as that at which the voyage is designed to terminate. 29A Am J Rev ed Ins § 992.

liberty of speech. See **freedom of speech and of the press.**

liberty of the globe (of the glōb). As used in a policy of marine insurance, an expression employed to signify that the vessel shall have the liberty to go to any part of the world. Eyre v Marine Insurance Co. (Pa) 6 Whart 247, 254.

liberty of the press. See **freedom of speech and of the press.**

liberty of the rules. A privilege, which was sometimes allowed an imprisoned debtor, of living outside the prison, but within prescribed limits.

The territory or district, which is also called "bounds," surrounding the walls of a jail or prison, where a prisoner who has been accorded the "liberty of the prison rules" may go. Ever since the establishment of the prison rules in England, the courts there have held the rules as being in effect an extension of the walls of the jail. The jailer is not bound to allow a prisoner the liberty of the prison rules, unless he shall give bond and security not to depart therefrom. Steinman v Tabb, 6 Ky (3 Bibb) 202.

liberty pole. A flagpole, usually one erected in exhibiting a patriotic spirit during wartime. A pole raised by rioters as a symbol of dissatisfaction with the government. Commonwealth v Morrison (Pa) 1 Addison 274, 275.

See **pole-raising.**

liberty to contract. See **liberty of contract.**

liberty to hold pleas (to hōld plēz). The privilege of holding a court, which was allowed certain manors.

Liberum corpus aestimationem non recipit (li'be-rum kor'pus ēs-ti-ma-she-ō'nem non re'si-pit). The body of a freeman does not admit of valuation.

Liberum est cuique apud se explorare an expediat sibi consilium (li'be-rum est kī'kwe a'pud sē ex-plō-rā're an ex-pē'di-at si'bi kon-si'li-um). Each one is free to determine for himself whether he requires counsel or advice.

liberum et commune socagium (li'be-rum et kommū'ne so-kā'ji-um). Free and common socage. See 2 Bl Comm 82.

liberum maritagium (li'be-rum ma-ri-tā'ji-um). Frankmarriage.

An estate in liberum maritagium or frankmarriage was a kind of entailed estate where a tenement was given by one man to another, together with a wife, who was the daughter or cousin of the donor, to hold in frankmarriage; that is, the donees were to have the tenement to them, and the heirs of their two bodies begotten and they were tenants in special tail. See 2 Bl Comm 115.

liberum servitium (li'be-rum ser-vi'she-um). Free service.

Free services, under the feudal system, were such as were not unbecoming the character of a soldier or a freeman to perform; as to serve under the lord in his wars, to pay a sum of money, and the like. See 2 Bl Comm 60.

liberum socagium (li'be-rum so-kā'ji-um). Free socage.

liberum tenementum (li'be-rum te-ne-men'tum). A freehold estate. A plea in an action of trespass quare clausum brought by a person in actual possession of the land, asserting title to the property in the defendant, and the right to immediate possession, but admitting possession in the plaintiff and a color of right thereto. 52 Am J1st Tresp § 69.

liblac (lib'lak). (Saxon.) Witchcraft.

liblacum (lib-lā'kum). Same as **liblac.**

libra (lī'brạ). A pound; a pound in English money.

libra arsa (li'bra ar'sa). A burned pound; that is, a pound tested by melting and assaying.

libra numerata (li'bra nu-me-rā'ta). A numbered or counted pound, a pound in English money, ascertained by counting the coins.

libra pensa (li'bra pen'sa). A weighed pound, a pound in English money, ascertained by weighing the coins.

librarian. A person in charge of a library, often with special training in library work, having the status of a public officer where the library is a public library maintained by state, county, or city. Anno: 140 ALR 1085.

Librarian of Congress. A federal officer in general charge of the Congressional Library.

librarius (lī-brā'ri-us). (Roman law.) A transcriber of books; a copyist; an amanuensis.

library. A public or private place wherein books are kept for reference and use, often for lending to patrons of the city, village, or vicinity.

See **public library.**

library fee. The fee paid by a college student for use of the library. 15 Am J2d Colleges § 19.

Admission into the Kansas State University is made free by statute, and the Board of Regents has no power to collect a fee for the use of the library or to exclude students from the use of the library for the nonpayment of such fee. State ex rel. Little v University of Kansas, 55 Kan 389, 40 P 656.

Library of Congress. A library established by Congress in 1800 for its use, the services of which have been extended for benefit of governmental agencies, other libraries, students, and the public, such institution occupying buildings opposite the Capitol at Washington D.C.

librata (li-brā'ta). A pound-land; a piece of land yielding an annual rent of one pound.

libripens (li'bri-penz). (Roman law.) A scale holder; a weigher.

Librorum appellatione continentur omnia volumina, sive in charta, sive in membrana sint, sive in quavis alia materia (li-brō'rum ap-pel-lā-she-ō'ne kon-ti-nen'ter om'ni-a vo-lū'mi-na, sī've in kar'ta, sī've in mem-brā'na sint, sī've in quā'vis a'li-a ma-te'ri-a). Within the meaning of the term "books" is included all volumes, whether of paper, of parchment, or of some other material.

Libson Shops. A leading case wherein the United States Supreme Court ruled that a net operating loss carry over could be used in reduction of taxable income only against income from the very same business which incurred the loss. Libson Shops, Inc. v Koehler, 353 US 382, 1 L Ed 2d 924.

licenciado (le-then-the-ah'do). (Spanish.) An attorney; a lawyer.

license. Unrestrained conduct. A special privilege, not a right common to all. The privilege conferred by a public body on a person for the doing of something which otherwise he would not have the right to do. 33 Am J1st Lic § 2. Permission to exercise a right or privilege which has been subjected to regulation. Madden v Queens County Jockey Club, 296 NY 249, 72 NE2d 697, 1 ALR2d 1160. A requirement imposed by way of regulation of an occupation or business such as the business of selling intoxicating liquors. 30 Am J Rev ed Intox L § 116.

A transfer by the owner of a patent right of an interest therein less than that passing by an assignment, being the granting to the licensee of the right to make, use, or vend the patented article. 40 Am J1st Pat § 146. Permission to make use of a copyrighted work exclusive of others or to use the work in a particular manner or for particular purposes. Black v Henry G. Allen Co. (CC NY) 42 F 618.

See **certificate; implied license; irrevocable license; leave and license; parol license.**

license coupled with an interest. A license in real property which confers the right, not the mere permission, to perform an act or acts upon the property, thereby being irrevocable and constituting an interest in the land itself. 33 Am J1st Lic § 101.

licensed material. Source material, special nuclear material, or by-product material received, possessed, used, or transferred under a general or specific license issued by the Atomic Energy Commission pursuant to the regulations of such Commission. 10 CFR Cum Supp § 20.3(a) (8).

licensed vessel. A vessel licensed by the United States for use in the coasting trade and fisheries. 48 Am J1st Ship § 48.
See **registry of vessel.**

licensee. A person who enters upon the property of another for his own convenience, pleasure, or benefit, his presence being tolerated, not invited, by the person in possession. Greenfield v Miller, 173 Wis 184, 180 NW 834, 12 ALR 982. A person possessing a license, such as a license to practice a particular profession.

license fee. The charge made for the issuance of a license, such being a tax where imposed for revenue, not merely to defray the expense of issuing the license. An imposition or exaction on the right to use or dispose of property, to pursue a business, occupation, or calling, or to exercise a privilege. 33 Am J1st Lic § 2.

license in real property. A personal, unassignable, and ordinarily revocable, privilege conferred either by writing or parol for the doing of one or more acts on land without possessing any estate therein, thereby rendering legal an act or acts which otherwise would be trespasses. 33 Am J1st Lic § 91.
See **license coupled with an interest.**

license plate. A metal or plastic plate upon which the license or registration number of an automobile or motor truck appears, the requirement being that such plate shall be attached to the automobile in such manner and at such a place that the number be clearly visible.

license tax. Same as **license fee.**

license to mine. See **mining license.**

licensing driver. See **operator's license.**

licensing motor vehicle. A statutory requirement, the purpose of which is to facilitate the supervision of such vehicles, their movement and control, and to establish their identity in relation to the public and to any resultant damage or injury they may cause. 7 Am J2d Auto § 50.

licensor (lī-sen-sor'). The grantor of a license.

licentia concordandi (lī-sen'she-a kon-kor-dan'dī). Leave to agree the suit.

In levying a fine to effect a conveyance of land, as soon as the action was brought, the defendant, knowing himself to be in the wrong, was supposed to make overtures of peace to the plaintiff, whereupon the plaintiff asked the court's leave to agree to a settlement or concord. See 2 Bl Comm 350.

licentia loquendi (lī-sen'she-a lō-quen'dī). The liberty of speaking; that is, time for the defendant to talk to the plaintiff for the purpose of ending the controversy without further litigation. See 3 Bl Comm 299.

licentia regis. See **ex licentia regis.**

licentia surgendi (lī-sen'she-a ser-jen'dī). The privilege of rising,—the duration of the time allowed upon an essoin de malo lecti, that is, upon an excuse for nonappearance at court by reason of illness in bed.

licentiate (lī-sen'shi-āt). The holder of a license permitting him to practice a profession or calling.

licentia transfretandi (lī-sen'she-a trans-fre-tan'dī). A writ to cause a port warden to honor a royal license permitting the holder to pass out of the port.

licentiously (lī-sen'shus-li). In a licentious manner; freely; loosely; dissolutely. State v Lawrence, 19 Neb 307, 314.

licentiousness (lī-sen'shus-nes). Lack of moral restraint. The acts of a libertine. In an older sense, ruthless disregard of the rights of others.

licere (lī'sē-re). To be allowed or permitted by law; to be lawful.

licet (lī'set). It is allowed or permitted by law; it is lawful. Adverb: Although; notwithstanding.

Licet cepit non asportavit (lī'set sē'pit non as-por-tā'vit). Although he took, he did not carry away.

Licet dispositio de interesse futuro sit inutilis, tamen potest fieri declaratio praecedens quae sortiatur effectum interveniente novo actu (lī'set dis-pō-zi'-she-ō dē in-ter-es'se fu-tū'rō sit in-ū'ti-lis, ta'men po'test fī'e-rī de-kla-rā'she-ō prē-sē'denz kwē sor-ti-ā'tēr ef-fek'tum in-ter-ve-ni-en'te nō'vō ak'tū). Although the disposition of a future interest is ineffectual, yet a declaration precedent can be made which will take effect upon the intervention of a new act.

licet saepe requisitus (lī'set sē'pe re-qui-zī'tus). Although often requested or demanded.

licet saepius requisitus (lī'set sē'pi-us re-qui-zī'tus). Although he was often requested,—a general averment in formal words, which strictest rules of pleading required the plaintiff to insert in a common law declaration for breach of contract. Lent v Padelford, 10 Mass (10 Tyng) 230, 239.

Licita bene miscentur, formula nisi juris obstet (lī'si-ta bē'nē mis-sen'ter, for'mula nī'sī jū'ris ob'stet). Things which are allowed by law may well be mingled, unless a form of law forbid.

licitare (lī-si-tā're). (Roman law.) To bid; to bid at a public sale or auction; to outbid at an auction sale.

licitation (lis-i-tā'shon). (Civil law.) Also called "cant,"—a mode of dividing property held in common by two or more persons. Hayes v Cuny (La) 9 Mart 87, 89. (Roman law.) The bidding at an auction sale.

licitator (lī-si-tā'tor). (Roman law.) A bidder at an auction or sale.

Lidford law (lid'ford lâ). Same as **Jedwood justice**.

lie (lī). Verb: To be appropriate as a remedy. To tell a falsehood knowingly. Noun: A prevarication; an untruth told knowingly.

lie detector. An instrument, sometimes called a pathometer, whose advocates claim for it that when attached to a witness, it will indicate whether he is testifying truthfully or not. People v Forte, 279 NY 204, 18 NE2d 31, 119 ALR 1198. An instrumentality used with some success to determine whether a person is telling the truth, being adapted to the registering of the blood pressure of a person being interrogated as he responds with answers to the questions propounded to him, the principle being that the blood pressure of a person changes upon the exertion of a conscious effort to tell an untruth. Anno: 34 ALR 147, s. 86 ALR 616. An instrumentality comparable to the blood pressure test but applied to the respiration, its operation being based upon the hypothesis that a person's breathing varies according to whether or not he is telling the truth. 29 Am J2d Ev § 831.
See **truth serum**.

lie detector test. A test made by lie detector.
See **lie detector**.

liege (lēj). The state of a person who is bound in fealty to a superior.

liege fee (fē). See **feudum ligium**.

liege homage (hom'- or om'āj). Such homage or allegiance as was due the king alone, irrespective of tenure. See 1 Bl Comm 367.

liege lord (lôrd). A superior lord; a sovereign lord; the king.

liegeman (lēj'man). A person from whom allegiance was due to a superior.

liege poustie (lēj pous'ti). The condition of a person's health prerequisite to his freedom in alienating his property either by deed or by will.

lie in franchise. Descriptive of the status of property open to be taken without resort to an action.

lie in grant. Descriptive of a status of property.
Property lies in grant when it can be transferred from one person to another by grant alone; as in the case of incorporeal hereditaments such as advowsons, commons, rents, and reversions, which pass by deed alone, since delivery of them cannot be made. See 2 Bl Comm 317.

lie in livery. Descriptive of a status of property.
Property lies in livery when livery of seisin is essential to its transfer from one person to another; as in the case of all corporeal hereditaments, such as lands and houses. See 2 Bl Comm 317.

lie in prender. See **in prender**.

lie in render. See **in prender**.

lie in wait. See **lying in wait**.

lien. A charge upon property for the payment or discharge of a debt or duty. The right which the law gives to have a debt satisfied out of a particular thing; a proprietary interest which, in a given case, may be exercised over the property of another. 33 Am J1st Liens § 2. In the aspect of a common-law lien, the mere right in one person to retain that which is in his possession belonging to another until certain demands of the person in possession are satisfied. Agnew v American Ice Co. 2 NJ 291, 66 A2d 330, 10 ALR2d 232.

The word "lien" is of the same origin as the word "liable," and the right of lien expresses the liability of certain property for a certain legal duty, or a right to resort to it in order to enforce that duty. Wood's Appeal, 30 Pa 274, 277.

There are a great variety of liens, such as **banker's lien**; **factor's lien**; **mechanic's lien**, etc.

lien by judicial proceeding. An expression, of particular significance in the law of bankruptcy, for a lien obtained by attachment, judgment, levy, or other legal or equitable process or proceeding. 9 Am J2d Bankr § 1022.
See **attachment lien**; **judgment lien**.

lien by legal proceeding. See **lien by judicial proceeding**.

lien creditor. A creditor who holds a lien for the debt owed to him.

lienee. The owner of property subject to a lien.

lienholder. The holder or owner of a lien.

lienor. The holder or owner of a lien upon the real or personal property of another.

lieu. See **in lieu of**.

lieu conus (lū kon'ū). A well-known place.

lieu lands. Lands of the public domain open to settlement by persons holding unperfected but bona fide claims to public lands, in lieu of the lands covered by such claims. 42 Am J1st Pub L § 15.

lieu taxes. Taxes on transportation or communication companies measured by the amount of their gross receipts, imposed in lieu of all other taxes upon the property of such concern or in lieu of taxes on certain classes of their property, such as that necessary to the carrying on of the business for which they were organized. Anno: 80 ALR 261, 277-279.

lieutenant. A deputy; a substitute; an agent. An officer of the United States Army, either a first lieutenant or a second lieutenant, the latter being the lowest in rank of the commissioned officers, the former being intermediate in rank between second lieutenant and captain. An officer of the United

States Navy, ranking immediately below lieutenant commander and immediately above lieutenant junior grade.

lieutenant colonel. An officer of the United States Army, also of the Air Force, in rank immediately above major and immediately below colonel.

lieutenant commander. An officer of the United States Navy, in rank immediately below commander and immediately above lieutenant.

lieutenant general. A high ranking officer of the United States Army, ranking immediately below a general and immediately above a major general.

lieutenant governor. A state officer, usually the presiding officer of the senate or higher body of the state legislature, and usually the officer succeeding to the duties of the governor in the event of the latter's death, resignation, removal, incapacity, or other event rendering him incapable of performing the duties of the office. 24 Am J1st Gov § 8.

lieutenant junior grade. An officer of the United States Navy, ranking immediately above an ensign and immediately below a lieutenant.

life. Existence as an animate being.
See **beginning of life; expectation of life; full life; lives in being; natural life.**

life annuity. An obligation to pay to a specified person a specified sum each year during the remainder of lifetime.
See **annuity.**

life assurance (a-shör'ans). Same as **life insurance.**

lifeboat. A boat carried by a ship for use in event of a forced abandonment of the ship. 48 Am J1st Ship § 361. A boat used by the Coast Guard in rescuing shipwrecked crew or passengers of vessels or other persons in danger of perishing in the sea.

life estate. An estate to be held by grantee or devisee for the term of his own life, or for that of another person, or for more lives than one. 28 Am J2d Est § 56; 33 Am J1st Life Est § 2. An estate of freehold, not of inheritance. 28 Am J2d Est § 56.
A life estate in land is real estate. Croasdale v Butell, 177 Kan 487, 280 P2d 593, 49 ALR2d 1112.
Under the modern law, a life estate and future interest, usually by way of remainder, may be created in personal property. 33 Am J1st Life Est § 5.

life estate by operation of law. A life estate which comes into existence without any act of the parties, such as that which springs from curtesy or dower. 33 Am J1st Life Est § 2.

life expectancy. See **expectation of life.**

life expectancy table. See **mortality table.**

lifeguard. A person employed at a beach, swimming pool, or on a ship or boat to effect a rescue of persons in danger of drowning or to prevent swimmers from getting into dangerous waters.

life imprisonment. Imprisonment as punishment for a criminal offense for the lifetime of the offender. State v Evans, 73 Idaho 50, 245 P2d 788.

life insurance. A contract, known as a policy, by which the insurer in consideration of the payment to it by the insured of a certain sum, or certain sums, of money known as a premium or premiums, measured and proportioned in amount according to factors affecting the risk of death, such as the age, health, and occupation of the insured, assumes the risk of insured's death by agreeing to pay a fixed amount to the estate of the insured or a beneficiary designated by the insured; or, in the case of an endowment policy, agrees to pay the insured the amount of the policy in one sum, or in an annuity, upon the expiration of the endowment period during the life of the insured. Tyler v Treasurer, 226 Mass 306, 115 NE 300; Fox v Swartz, 235 Minn 337, 51 NW2d 80, 30 ALR2d 739; St. John v American Mut. Life Ins. Co. 13 NY 31. Not a contract of indemnity. 29 Am J Rev ed Ins § 4.

life insurance company. A corporation engaged in the business of issuing policies or contracts of life insurance.
See **mutual insurance company; reserve; stock company.**

life insurance contract. See **life insurance.**

life insurance policy. See **life insurance.**

life interest. An interest in property which is to terminate upon the death of the holder of the interest, or upon the death of some other designated person.
See **life estate.**

life, liberty, and property. A phrase encompassing every right to which a member of the body politic is entitled under the law. Gillespie v People, 188 Ill 176, 58 NE 1007. The rights of self-defense, freedom of speech, religious and political freedom, exemption from arbitrary arrest, the right freely to buy and sell as others may, the right to labor, to follow an occupation, to contract, to terminate contracts, to acquire property, and the right to all liberties, personal, civil, and political—in short, all that makes life worth living. 16 Am J2d Const L § 357.
The term within the meaning of constitutional guaranties of life, liberty, and property does not consist simply of the right to freedom from arbitrary physical restraints or servitude, but includes the right to be free in the use of one's faculties in all lawful ways, to earn one's livelihood where and how he will, subject to such restraints as are necessary for the common welfare. State v Ballance, 229 NC 764, 51 SE2d 731, 7 ALR2d 407.

life, liberty, and pursuit of happiness. Inalienable, fundamental and inherent rights. 16 Am J2d Const L § 346. Substantially the same rights comprehended by the phrase **life, liberty, and property.** Ruhstrat v People, 185 Ill 133, 57 NE 41; Wyeth v State, 200 Mass 474, 86 NE 925. Inclusive of the enjoyment of all the comforts and pleasures which man's physical, intellectual, and moral nature is capable of acquiring and enjoying by the application and exercise of the various faculties with which he is endowed, and of all that the world can afford him. Lawrence E. Tierney Coal Co. v Smith, 180 Ky 815, 203 SW 731, 4 ALR 1540.

life or limb. See **injury to life or limb.**

life peerage. The dignity or rank of a baron conferred upon a man by letters patent of the king, to endure for the lifetime of the man and no longer. That is, the dignity of a life peerage does not descend to the heir. See 1 Bl Comm 401.

life policy. A written contract of life insurance. See **life insurance.**

life preserver. A garment or other device worn in water for the purpose of keeping the body afloat, thereby saving the person from drowning. A weapon carried for self-defense.

life-rent (lif'rent). Same as **life estate.**

life-renter (līf'ren"tėr). The holder of a life-rent.

lifesaving station. A building at the seashore for the housing of men and boats to be used as necessary for the saving of the lives of persons imperiled by shipwreck or other marine disaster, or otherwise placed in peril of drowning.

life sentence. See **sentence.**

life tables. See **mortality tables.**

life tenancy. See **life estate**; **life tenant.**

life tenant. A person who has a life estate, such interest giving him the status of a freeholder. 28 Am J2d Est § 56.
See **life estate.**

lifetime transfer. Same as **inter vivos transfer.**

life trustee. A trustee of a business trust holding the office for life. Anno: 156 ALR 138.

LIFO. Abbreviation of last in, first out.

lift. A lifting jack. An elevator in England.
See **lifting jack.**

lifting corporate veil. Disregarding the corporate entity where to recognize it as something distinct from the incorporators or stockholders results in a violation of public policy. 18 Am J2d Corp § 14.

lifting hand. A formality in the taking of an oath. 39 Am J1st Oath § 13.

lifting jack. A device for raising heavy objects, particularly motor vehicles, for convenience in accomplishing repair work or servicing upon the vehicle. 24 Am J1st Gas Sta § 23. An elevator in England.

liga (lī'ga). A league; an association.

ligan (lī'gan). Goods cast into the sea by shipwreck or in order to save a ship, tied to a buoy. 48 Am J1st Ship § 647. A subject of salvage. 47 Am J1st Salv § 3.

ligare (li-gā're). To bind together; to unite; to join a league.

ligealty (lī'je-al-ti). Allegiance.
The fundamental principle of the common law with regard to English nationality was birth within the allegiance, also called "ligealty," "obedience," "faith," or "power," of the king. The principle embraced all persons born within the king's allegiance, and subject to his protection. United States v Wong Kim Ark, 169 US 649, 655, 42 L Ed 890, 893, 18 S Ct 456.

ligeance (lē'jans). Allegiance.
See **ligealty.**

ligeantia (li-jē-an'she-a). Ligeance; allegiance.
See **ligealty.**

ligeantia actoris. See **forum ligeantiae actoris.**

ligentiae rei. See **forum ligeantiae rei.**

Ligeantia est quasi legis essentia; est vinculum fidei (li-je-an'she-a est quä'sī lē'jis es-sen'she-a; est vin'-ku-lum fī-dē'ī). Allegiance is, as it were, the essence of the law; it is the bond of faith.

Ligeantia naturalis nullis claustris coercetur, nullis metis refraenatur, nullis finibus premitur (li-je-an'she-a nā-tū-rā'lis nul'lis klâs'tris ko-er'sē-ter, nul'lis me'tis rē-frē-en-nā'ter nul'lis fī'ni-bus pre'mi-ter). Natural allegiance is restrained by no bars, held by no boundaries, compressed by no limits.

light. See **ancient lights**; **easements of light, air, and view.**

light, air, and view. Neither appurtenances nor hereditaments in the absence of an easement. 1 Am J2d Adj L § 89.
See **easements of light, air, and view.**

light and air. See **easements of light, air, and view.**

light company. See **electric company**; **gas company.**

light easement. See **easements of light, air, and view.**

lighter. A vessel of shallow draft used in transporting cargo to and from a ship anchored in deep water, shallow water preventing the docking of the ship at the wharf. The Mamie (DC Mich) 5 F 813, 820. A vessel for the purpose of admiralty jurisdiction. The Mackinaw (DC Or) 165 F 351.

lighterage. The transportation of goods by lighter or barge; the charge for transportation by lighter. Western Transportation Co. v Hawley (NY) 1 Daly 327, 332.

lighterman (lī'tėr-man). The proprietor of a lighter.

light fixture. An instrumentality affixed to the ceiling or wall of a building, through which insulated wires carrying electricity are run and to which bulbs for illumination are fastened.
The authorities are conflicting as to whether gas and electric light fixtures retain their quality of personal property when put into place in buildings. Some of the authorities consider that such attachments are fixtures in the true sense of the term, but the greater number of authorities hold that they should not so be considered. 35 Am J2d Fixt § 127.

lighthouse. A comparatively tall structure erected at or near the shore of the ocean or body of water, wherein a light is displayed for the purpose of warning ships during hours of darkness of dangers in shoals or rock.

lighting regulations. Building regulations promulgated primarily for purposes of health. Daniels v Portland, 124 Or 677, 265 P 790, 59 ALR 512.

lighting way. Illuminating a highway or street by artificial lights. 25 Am J1st High § 70.

light manufacturing district. A zoning law classification intended to keep out heavy industries such as cement works, steel mills, paper mills, etc. 58 Am J1st Zon § 33.

light money. A duty, additional to tonnage duties, paid upon all vessels not of United States registry which enter the ports of this country. 48 Am J1st Ship § 650.

lightning. A sudden discharge of electricity from a cloud to the earth, or from the earth to a cloud, or from one cloud to another, that is, from a body positively charged to one negatively charged, producing a vivid flash of light, and usually a loud report called thunder. Spensley v Lancashire Ins. Co. 54 Wis 433, 441. One of the elements of nature. 32 Am J1st L & T § 811. An act of God in its origin, but not necessarily in its consequences. Short v Kerr, 104 Ind App 118, 9 NE2d 114.

lightning clause. A clause in, or attached as a rider to, a fire insurance policy, relative to the risk of loss by lightning. Russell v German Fire Ins. Co. 100 Minn 528, 111 NW 400.

lightning insurance. Insurance against loss or damage by lightning, provided by an independent policy or by a clause in an ordinary fire insurance policy. Anno: 15 ALR2d 1017.

lights. See **ancient lights**; **headlights**; **load lights**;

side lights; tail light; also words and phrases beginning "light."

ligium. See **feudum ligium.**

ligius (li'ji-us). Same as **liege.**

Ligna et lapides sub "armorum" appellatione non continentur (lig'na et la'pi-dēz sub ar-mō'rum appel-lā-she-ō'ne non kon-ti-nen'ter). Sticks and stones are not included in the term "arms."

lignagium (lig-nā'ji-um). The right to gather fuel in a wood.

lignum (lig'num). Wood; firewood; cut wood as distinguished from that which is growing.

like effect. Like result. Fine v Soifer, 288 Pa 164, 135 A 742.

likelihood. See **in all likelihood.**

likely. Adjective: Credible, although often employed in sarcasm, as a "likely" story. Adverb: Probable, but not more than "probable" and sometimes less than "probable" depending upon the context. Not the equivalent of reasonably certain. 22 Am J2d Damg § 352.

In the law of proximate cause, when it is said that an injury is the "likely," and not the improbable result of the wrongful act, the word "likely" is used in the sense of something more than possible, and less than probable. Conchin v El Paso & Southwestern Railroad Co. 13 Ariz 259, 108 P 260.

likeness. A picture; a resemblance.

like result. Like effect. Fine v Soifer, 288 Pa 164, 135 A 742.

limb for a limb. A sentence of one convicted of mayhem, on the principle of retaliation, that he should lose the member of his own body corresponding to the member of which he had deprived the victim of the offense.

By the ancient law of England a person convicted of mayhem was sentenced to lose that member of his own body corresponding to the member of which he had deprived his victim. This method of punishment became obsolete partly because of its inadequacy and partly because it could not be repeated in the case of a repetition of precisely the same act. See 4 Bl Comm 206.

lime kiln. An oven wherein limestone is heated for the purpose of obtaining lime. 32 Am J1st L & T § 493.

limestone. A mineral. Anno: 86 ALR 985; 36 Am J1st Min & M § 5. The raw material from which lime is obtained by the application of heat. Also a building stone.

limine. See **in limine.**

limit. A boundary, a border, the outer line of a thing. A restraining line, often figurative, as "debt limit." Casler v Connecticut Mut. Life Ins. Co. 22 NY 429, 431.

limitatio (li-mi-tā'she-ō). A limitation.

limitation. In the broad sense a limit. In a technical sense, a clause or provision in deed, grant, or will which states a condition of the grant or devise, especially a condition which terminates an estate without act performed by the taker of the next estate or interest or a condition which determines the quality of the estate granted or devised. A provision in a lease whereby the lease terminates upon the happening or not happening of a certain event or upon the performance or nonperformance of a condition. 32 Am J1st L & T § 825. The period of time subsequent to the event giving rise to a cause of action or cause for criminal prosecution during which the action or prosecution must be commenced. 34 Am J1st Lim Ac § 3. The period of time during which adverse possession of property must be maintained in order to ripen into title. 3 Am J2d Adv P §§ 9 et seq.

See **conditional limitation; estate upon condition; executory limitation; words of limitation.**

limitation of action. The policy of the state as expressed in a statute of limitations prescribing the period of time within which an action or proceeding in law or in equity must be brought. 34 Am J1st Lim Ac § 3. The policy of the state as expressed in a statute of limitations prescribing the period of time within which a criminal prosecution must be commenced. 21 Am J2d Crim L § 154. The policy of the parties to a contract as expressed by a provision of the contract limiting the period of time within which an action or proceeding may be brought upon the contract. 34 Am J1st Lim Ac § 67.

limitation of estate. See **limitation.**

limitation of indebtedness. A provision in a state constitution, as found in a number of states, that the state will not, through its legislature, create any debt or liability, except for certain purposes, in excess of a prescribed amount, or a provision that the legislature shall not create an indebtedness to exceed a certain per cent on the assessed value of the taxable value property of the state. 49 Am J1st States § 66. A provision of the state constitution, statute, or charter which places a limit upon the amount of indebtedness which a municipal corporation can lawfully incur. 38 Am J1st Mun Corp § 408. The limit on the amount of indebtedness of the United States as fixed and modified from time to time by Congress.

limitation of liability. A limitation upon a liability otherwise contracted or assumed by entering into a particular relationship, the most common of which is found in contracts of bailment, limiting the liability of the bailee, 8 Am J2d Bailm § 132, such as a carrier, 14 Am J2d Car § 537, the keeper of a hotel or inn, 29 Am J Rev ed Innk § 86, or a warehouseman, Lancaster Mills v Merchants' Cotton-Press & Storage Co. 89 Tenn 1, 14 SW 317, especially in reference to those bailments in which, in the absence of a limitation, the bailee is under an absolute or insurer's liability.

A contractual, statutory, or customary limitation of a shipowner's liability for loss of or injury to goods or merchandise carried on board the vessel. 48 Am J1st Ship §§ 445 et seq. A limitation appearing in a policy of insurance upon the amount of loss for which the insurer is liable. 7 Am J2d Auto Ins § 189; 29 Am J Rev ed Ins § 227. A contractual limitation of a telegraph company's liability for negligence in the transmission of a message. 52 Am J1st Teleg & T § 143. A stipulation in a contract between a credit-reporting agency and a customer which provides that the agency shall not be liable for the negligence of its agents, and that it does not guarantee the verity or accuracy of the information given. Corrigan v Dun & Bradstreet, Inc. (DC RI) 91 F Supp 424. A provision in the indenture of a business trust which states expressly that the shareholders shall not be individually liable for debts or liabilities incurred by the trustees on behalf of the trust, or that persons dealing with the trustees shall look for satisfaction of their demands only to the property and assets of the trust. 13 Am J2d Bus Tr § 37. A clause in the indenture of a business trust which provides that the trustees shall not be personally liable on contracts made by them on behalf of the trust. Anno: 156 ALR 165. The condition of a sale at auction that all complaints must be made at a specified time after the sale. 7 Am J2d Auct § 54.

A contract against liability for negligence is in contravention of public policy. Anno: 175 ALR 39.

See **limited liability acts.**

limitation of time. A rule prescribed by statute, order of court, or the common law, whereby a certain action must be taken within a specified time under pain of inability to take such action at a later time.

See **limitation of action.**

limitation on jurisdiction. See **limited jurisdiction.**

limitation over. The disposition made by deed or will of an estate or interest following the termination of a prior estate, the stock example of which is a remainder limited after a life estate. Ewing v Shropshire, 80 Ga 374, 377, 7 SE 554.

limitation period. See **limitation; limitation of action.**

limited. Narrow, restricted, circumscribed, inclosed within a certain limit; hemmed in; confined; bounded. Cheney v Smith, 3 Ariz 143, 23 P 680, 685. Abbreviated **ltd.** A word used to indicate the corporate status, especially in England and Canada, the connotation being that the liability of a shareholder is limited to his investment in shares. A word used to signify a partnership other than a general partnership.

See **limited partnership.**

limited-access highway. A superior highway so constructed with feeder lines as to eliminate the intersection of traffic at right angles, the construction permitting an entering vehicle to approach the lane desired in the same general direction as the movement of traffic in the lane and to come into such lane with the least disturbance of the movement of traffic.

limited adoption. The selective adoption of principles of the common law, that is, the adoption by the state of only such common-law principles as are deemed salutary in the light of the conditions existing in the state. Cahoon v Pelton, 9 Utah 2d 224, 342 P2d 94.

limited company. See **limited; limited partnership.**

limited constitution. A constitution which contains certain specified exceptions to the legislative authority; such, for instance, as that it shall pass no bills of attainder, no ex post facto laws, and the like.

Limitations of this kind can be preserved in practice no other way than through the medium of the courts of justice. Per Alexander Hamilton in The Federalist, No. 78.

limited covenant of warranty. See **special warranty.**

limited divorce. Otherwise known as a divorce from bed and board or divorce a mensa et thoro. Kelley v Kelley, 183 Or 169, 191 P2d 656. A divorce which varies in its consequences from state to state, but may be defined generally as a judicial decree which terminates the obligation and right of cohabitation but does not affect the status of the parties as married persons or dissolve the marriage. 24 Am J2d Div & S § 1.

limited emancipation. The act of a parent in releasing his child from care, custody, or control for only a part of the period of minority or from only a part of the rights of the parent. Porter v Powell, 79 Iowa 151, 44 NW 295.

limited estate. Any estate less than a fee.

limited fee. See **conditional fee; determinable fee; qualified fee.**

limited guaranty. A contract of guaranty which is restricted in its operation with respect to obligee, transactions covered, locality, items for which credit may be extended, amount of credit, etc. 24 Am J1st Guar § 72.

limited indorsement. See **conditional indorsement; qualified indorsement.**

limited interest. An interest which is qualified or which falls short of being an absolute interest. Griffith v Charlotte, Columbia & Augusta Railroad Co. 23 SC 25.

See **limited estate.**

limited jurisdiction. A phrase having reference to inferior courts. Jurisdiction which does not extend to the general administration of justice. Den ex dem. Obert v Hammel, 18 NJL 73, 79

See **court of limited jurisdiction.**

limited legal investments. A term of significance to trustees.

This term as used in the New Jersey Prudent Man Investment Statute, does not make such investments any less legal than the fiduciary investments authorized by other statutes and labeled "legal investments"; the limitation relates solely to the percentage of the trust which the trustee may invest therein. Fidelity Union Trust Co. v Price, 11 NJ 90, 93 A2d 321, 35 ALR2d 980.

limited legitimation. The legitimation of a child born out of wedlock for some purposes but not to the extent of equalizing its status with that of a legitimate child. 10 Am J2d Bast § 57.

limited liability acts. Statutes which restrict liability to a less amount than the common law would allow. Federal statutes limiting the liability of a shipowner for loss, damage, or injury, enacted for the purpose of encouraging the investment of capital in the building and navigation of ships, by enabling the owners of American ships to compete upon equal terms of liability with foreign shipowners. 48 Am J1st Ship § 567.

limited liability of shipowner. See **limited liability acts.**

limited owner. An owner whose interest in the property is not absolute, but qualified. Griffith v Charlotte, Columbia & Augusta Railroad Co. 23 SC 25.

See **limited estate.**

limited partnership. A partnership in which the liability of some, but not all, members is limited, being formed under laws permitting an individual to contribute a specified sum to the capital of the firm and then limit his liability for losses to that amount, provided compliance is had with certain established requirements. 40 Am J1st Partn §§ 504 et seq.

As to the effect of writing "limited" or "ltd" after the signatures of the members of a limited partnership appended to a contract, see Bernard & Less Mfg. Co. v Packard & Calvin (CA3 Pa) 64 F 309, 310.

See **partnership association.**

limited power of appointment. A power of appointment which is exercisable only in favor of persons or a class of persons designated or described in the instrument creating the power. Marx v Rice, 1 NJ 574, 65 A2d 48, 9 ALR2d 584.

In Pennsylvania, a general power of appointment is not converted into a special power by reason of spendthrift provisions protecting the income during the lifetime of the donee. Legg's Estate v Commissioner (CA4) 114 F2d 760.

limited power of disposal. A qualified power of disposition, a power dependent on a contingency or definitely qualified. 33 Am J1st Life Est § 25.

limited predestination. A doctrine of the Primitive Baptist Church that God predestinated things which may come to pass with reference to the salvation of souls only, repudiating the idea that God predestinated the happening of things in this material world. Bennett v Morgan, 112 Kan 512, 520, 66 SW 289.

limited publication. A publication which communicates the contents of a manuscript or other intellectual production to a definitely selected group and for a limited purpose, and without the right of diffusion, reproduction, distribution, or sale, or under conditions which expressly or impliedly preclude its dedication to the public. 18 Am J2d Copyr § 79.

Prior to publication an author may, without forfeiture of the right of a general publication, make copies of his production and enjoy the benefit of limited or restricted publication, such as performance of a dramatic or musical composition before a select audience, or private circulation of a manuscript. Stanley v Columbia Broadcasting System, 35 Cal 2d 653, 221 P2d 73, 23 ALR2d 216.

limited ticket. A railroad ticket which entitles the holder to ride only certain trains. 14 Am J2d Car § 754.

limited train. A through train, that is, one stopping at only a few stations; a train carrying only first class or extra-fare passengers.

limited voting. Same as **restrictive voting.**

limits of the jail. See **liberties of the jail.**

limits on speed. See **speed limits.**

limousine service. A service, sometimes operating under an exclusive franchise, for the transportation of people to and from a public airport, passengers boarding and leaving the limousines at hotels and other places in the downtown area. 8 Am J2d Avi § 56.

Lindbergh Law. See **Kidnapping Act.**

line. A wire for the transmission of telegraph messages or the transmission of sound by telephone. A wire through which electricity is conducted for the use of customers. The pipes of a gas company. A course of descent or succession. McIntyre v Ramsey, 23 Pa 317, 320.

See **boundary; route.**

linea (lin'ē-ạ). Same as **line.**

lineage. Race; progeny; descendants in a line from a common progenitor. Lockett v Lockett, 94 Ky 289, 291.

lineal (lin'ē-ạl). In a direct line.

lineal ascendants. The parents, grandparents, great-grandparents, etc. of a person. 23 Am J2d Desc & D § 42.

lineal consanguinity. The blood relationship which subsists between persons of whom one is descended in a direct line from the other; as between the son, the father and the grandfather, in the ascending line, and between the father, son, and grandson, and so on downward, in the descending line.

lineal descendants. Blood relatives in the direct line of descent. Re Smith's Estate, 343 Mich 291, 72 NW2d 287, 51 ALR2d 287. The children, grandchildren, great-grandchildren, etc. of a person. 23 Am J2d Desc & D § 42.

lineal descent. A descent in the direct line of an intestate, as, for example, from father or grandfather to son or grandson, or from son or grandson to father or grandfather. 23 Am J2d Desc & D § 42.

lineal heirs. Persons entitled to the property of an intestate as heirs by lineal descent.

See **lineal descent.**

lineal inheritance tax. A succession tax imposed upon the passing of property of a decedent to persons connected with him by lineal descent. Estate of Macky, 46 Colo 79, 102 P 1075.

See **lineal descent.**

lineal measure. The measurement of distance, employing units such as the foot, yard, rod, etc.

lineal warranty. A warranty which existed where the heir derived, or might by possibility have derived, his title to the land warranted, either from or through the ancestor who made the warranty; where a father, or an elder son in the lifetime of the father, released to the disseisor of either themselves or the grandfather, with warranty, this was lineal to the younger son. See 1 Bl Comm 301.

linea recta (lī'ne-a rek'ta). A straight line; a line of direct descent.

Linea recta est index sui et obliqui; lex est linea recti (lī'ne-a rek'ta est in'dex su'ī et ob'li-quī; lex est lī'ne-a rek'tī). A straight line is its own index or criterion and is also that of an oblique or indirect line; law is the line of rectitude.

Linea recta semper praefertur transversali (lī'ne-a rek'ta sem'per prē-fer'ter trans-ver-sā'lī). A direct line of descent is always preferred to a collateral line.

linea transversalis (lī'ne-a trans-ver-sā'lis). A collateral line.

line haul. The transportation of goods by railroad from an initial point to a terminal point on the same road or on a connecting road.

Switching service is not a line haul but is an incident to a line haul. Cummings Sand & Gravel Co. v Minneapolis & St. Louis Railroad Co. 182 Iowa 955, 166 NW 354.

line-haul charge. A charge made by a carrier for transportation, inclusive of accessorial or incidental service in receiving or delivering freight in carload lots on private or industrial sidings or spur tracks. 13 Am J2d Car § 467.

lineman. An employee of an electric company, telephone company or telegraph company whose duties are concerned with the erection and maintenance of the power or communication lines. A railroad worker, sometimes known as a section hand, employed in the maintenance of roadbed and track.

linen-supply service. A service for supplying tablecloths, bedsheets, pillow cases, towels, etc., week by week, in cleaned and laundried form, for rent, the customers being hotels, restaurants, industrial, and business concerns. Lonas v National Linen Service Corp. (CA6 Tenn) 136 F2d 433, 150 ALR 697, cert den 320 US 785, 88 L Ed 472, 64 S Ct

157; Harper v Alderson, 126 W Va 707, 30 SE2d 521, 153 ALR 819.

line of causation. The test of proximate cause. 38 Am J1st Negl § 56.

line of credit. A margin of credit maintained by a customer with a firm through keeping the amount of his account within a certain amount by payments on account from time to time. Schneider-Davis Co. v Hart, 23 Tex Civ App 529, 57 SW 903.

line of descent. See **collateral descent; lineal descent.**

line of duty. The course of duty whether in the military or in civilian employment.

line of high water. See **ordinary high-water mark.**

line tree. A tree marking a boundary line or corner.

lineup. A practice by the police in which prisoners held pending preliminary hearing are brought into view for inspection and identification. Owens v Commonwealth, 186 Va 689, 43 SE2d 895.

link-in-chain. The rule which applies the privilege against self-incrimination to protect an individual not only against requiring answers by him that are in themselves directly incriminating, but also against requiring answers that may provide a link in the chain of evidence against him. Estes v Potter (CA5 Tex) 183 F2d 865, cert den 340 US 920, 95 L Ed 664, 71 S Ct 356.

lion's share. The whole of the profits going to one partner.

liquere (li-kwē're). To be fluid; to be clear; to be evident; to be apparent.

liquet (li'quet). It appears; it is evident; it is clear.

liquet satis (li'quet sa'tis). It is clear enough; it is sufficiently evident; it appears clearly enough.

liqueur (li-kėr'). An aromatic, alcoholic cordial, including creme de menthe and absinthe. Erhardt v Steinhardt, 153 US 177, 38 L Ed 678, 14 S Ct 775.

liquidate. To pay a debt. Flecker v Bank of United States (US) 8 Wheat 338, 5 L Ed 631; Austin v Tecumseh Nat. Bank, 49 Neb 412, 68 NW 628. To obtain by agreement or by action the ascertainment of the amount of a debt. To settle the affairs of a business by selling assets, making collections of accounts receivable, applying the proceeds thus obtained to the payment of the debts of the business, and, if there be a surplus after such debts are paid, dividing it among the owners of the business.

liquidated. Paid. Wound up, as in reference to the affairs of a business. Determined as to amount, as in reference to a debt.

liquidated account. An account the amount of which is agreed upon by the parties, or is fixed by operation of law. State v Staub, 61 Conn 553, 568.

liquidated damages. A sum stipulated and agreed upon by the parties, at the time of entering into a contract, as being payable as compensation for loss suffered in the event of a breach. 22 Am J2d Damg § 212.

As to the distinction between penalties and liquidated damages, see 22 Am J2d Damg § 213.

liquidated debt. A debt which has been paid. A debt, the amount of which has been determined by agreement between the parties or by legal proceedings.

A debt is liquidated when it is certain what is due and how much is due; cum certum est an et quantum debeatur. For although it may appear that something is due, if it does not also appear how much is due, the debt is not liquidated. Roberts v Prior, 20 Ga 561, 562.

liquidated demand. A demand ascertained in reference to the amount. A demand which is undisputed as to amount.
See **liquidated debt.**

liquidating partner. A partner who accomplishes or participates in the liquidation of the firm. Garretson v Brown, 185 Pa 447, 452, 40 A 293.

Under the provisions of the Uniform Partnership Act, unless otherwise agreed, the partners who have not wrongfully dissolved the partnership or the legal representative of the last surviving partner, not bankrupt, has the right to wind up the partnership affairs, provided, however, that any partner, his legal representative or his assigneee, upon cause shown may obtain winding up by the court. Uniform Partnership Act § 37.

liquidating trust. A trust, the purpose of which is liquidation as soon as the circumstances will permit, albeit it may be carrying on a business, where the engagement in business is incidental and necessary to the preservation of assets. Helvering v Washburn (CA Minn) 99 F2d 478.

An incidental intention to liquidate in case of unsuccessful business operations is not sufficient to make a liquidating trust out of what would otherwise be a taxable association under the income tax statute. Jackson v United States (CA9 Cal) 110 F2d 574.

liquidation. The extinguishment of a debt by payment. Flecker v Bank of United States (US) 8 Wheat 338, 5 L Ed 631. The ascertainment of the amount of a debt or demand by agreement or by legal proceedings. In a more common sense of the term, the winding up of a corporation, partnership, or other business enterprise upon dissolution by converting the assets to money, collecting accounts receivable, paying debts, and distributing the net proceeds, if any, among the shareholders, partners, or owners of the business. Garrett Co. v Morton, 35 Misc 10, 71 NYS 17. The winding up of the affairs of a corporation by reducing its assets, paying its debts, and apportioning the surplus, if there be a surplus. Young v Blandin, 215 Minn 111, 9 NW2d 313.
See **partial liquidation.**

liquidation dividend. Same as **dividend in liquidation.**

liquidation of corporation. See **liquidation.**

liquidation of duties. The ascertainment and settlement of the amount of custom duties to be paid upon imported merchandise. 21 Am J2d Cust D § 80.

liquidation of partnership. See **liquidation.**

liquidator. In the broad sense, one who liquidates. In a technical sense, especially in England and Canada, one who liquidates a corporation in receivership for dissolution; in other words, a receiver. 45 Am J1st Rec § 3.

liquid gas. A product captured and compressed at oil and gas wells, for shipment in containers to individual customers. 26 Am J2d Electr § 5.

liquid measure. The measurement of liquids, the units being pint, quart, gallon, etc.

liquor. Any sort of liquid or fluid substance, but in common parlance a beverage with an intoxicating quality. 30 Am J Rev ed Intox L § 8. A beverage of high potency produced by distillation. 30 Am J Rev ed Intox L § 8. Broadly, an alcoholic or spiritu-

ous liquor, either distilled or fermented. Luther v State, 83 Neb 455, 120 NW 125.
See **intoxicating liquor.**

Liquor Control Act. The title given in several jurisdictions to the statute regulating the traffic in alcoholic beverages.

liquor dealer. See **dealer in liquor.**

liquor dispensary. See **dispensaries.**

Liquor Enforcement Act. A federal statute enacted following the termination of National Prohibition which is concerned with the interstate transportation of liquor, defining several offenses in connection therewith. 18 USC §§ 1262-1265.

liquor license. A license to manufacture, sell, serve, store, or traffic in any respect in intoxicating beverages.

liquor nuisance. A place of business selling intoxicating liquors as declared a nuisance by statute or ordinance or so conducted as to constitute a material annoyance, inconvenience, discomfort, or hurt to an individual or the public. The selling and delivering of intoxicating liquor on the streets of a municipality in violation of law, repeatedly and persistently. 30 Am J Rev ed Intox L § 415.

liquor traffic. Trade or commerce in intoxicating liquors.
A foreign corporation is a "trafficker" in intoxicating liquors, within the meaning of a statute imposing a tax on the business, where it maintains a storehouse in the state, at which it sells and delivers beer and collects payment. Reyman Brewing Co. v Brister, 179 US 445, 45 L Ed 269, 21 S Ct 201.

lis (lis). (Latin.) A suit; action; controversy, or dispute. State ex rel. Hamilton v Guinotte, 156 Mo 513, 57 SW 281.

lis alibi pendens (lis a'li-bī pen'denz). An action pending in another place; a plea of an action pending elsewhere.

lis mota (lis mō'ta). The commencement of a controversy; the commencement of a suit or action.

lis pendens. (lis pen'denz). Literally, a pending suit; in law, the jurisdiction, power, or control that a court has, during the pendency of an action, over the property involved therein. 34 Am J1st Lis P § 1.
See **notice of lis pendens.**

list. Verb: To make an orderly memorandum of things, persons, or events. To register or enroll real property with a real estate broker or agent, authorizing him to conduct negotiations with prospective purchasers for the sale of the property. E. A. Strout Co. v Gay, 105 Me 108, 72 A 881. To enroll the stock or other security issued by a corporation or a commodity, such as wheat, soybeans, etc. on a stock of commodity exchange for the purpose of the handling of purchases and sales by the exchange. Noun: An orderly memorandum of things, persons, or events, such as a list of customers of a business, 19 Am J2d Corp § 1282, or of the stockholders of a corporation. 18 Am J2d Corp § 188.
See **blacklist; cause list; civil list; eligible list; grand list; inventory; jury list; Lloyd's Lists; tax list; unfair list.**

listed price. The price at which a landowner lists his property for sale with a real estate broker. 12 Am J2d Brok § 111.

listen. See **look and listen.**

lister (lis'tėr). A person who lists persons and property and who values the latter for purposes of assessment or taxation; an appraiser; an assessor.

listing. See **list.**

listing contract. A so-called contract whereby an owner of real property employs a broker to procure a purchaser without giving the broker an exclusive right to sell. Under such an agreement, it is generally held that the employment may be terminated by the owner at will, and that a sale of the property by the owner terminates the employment. Such an agreement is not in fact a contract, but is a mere offer, which, if not sooner revoked, ripens into a contract if the broker produces a purchaser while the owner still holds the property. Harris v McPherson, 97 Conn 164, 115 A 723, 24 ALR 1530, 1534.
See **list.**

list of creditors. A list of the creditors of the seller of a stock of merchandise, required by bulk sales statutes. 24 Am J1st Frd Conv § 237. A schedule of the debts of a bankrupt, including the names and addresses of creditors and a description of the debts with details respecting amount, consideration, and security, to be provided by a bankrupt. 9 Am J2d Bankr §§ 367 et seq.

list of property. A schedule of property required of a bankrupt. 9 Am J2d Bankr § 378.
See **inventory.**

list of proved claims. A requirement made by a General Order in Bankruptcy of the person with whom proofs of claim or of interest are filed. 9 Am J2d Bankr § 497.

list of referred cases. A statement required of a referee in bankruptcy, showing a list of the proceedings referred to him which have remained open for more than 18 months, giving the reasons in each instance why they have not been closed, the same to be in duplicate and verified, and filed in the office of the clerk of court.
One copy shall be transmitted by the clerk, forthwith upon its receipt, to the Administrative Office of the United States Courts. Order 26, General Orders in Bankruptcy.

list system. A system of voting for public officers. 26 Am J2d Elect § 273.
Under this system, the names of candidates are put on the ballot in lists or blocks, so that those of similar views are grouped together. The elector has but one vote to cast and he casts it for one candidate on one of the lists. This vote counts one in determining how many candidates the adherents of that list are to elect and it also counts one toward the election of a single candidate on that list. The proportion of the total vote which is cast for a single list determines the number of representatives which are chosen from that list; and when that number has been determined, the highest candidates on the list are chosen. Thus an elector may vote for a candidate who is defeated, yet at the same time further the election of another candidate from the same list of the party. 26 Am J2d Elect § 273.

litem (lī'tem). Of or pertaining to litigation.
See **in litem; litis.**

litem motam. See **ante litem motem.**

litem suam facere (lī'tem su'am fā'se-re). (Roman law.) To make the action his own. A judge who exhibited partiality was said to do this.

lite pendente (lī'te pen-den'te). See **pendente lite.**

liter. A unit of measure, equivalent to 1.057 liquid quarts and 0.908 dry quart.

litera (li'ter-ra). A letter. Singular of **literae.**

litera acquietantiae (li'te-ra ak-qui-e-tan'she-ē). A letter of discharge or acquittance.

literacy. Ability to read and write.

literacy qualification. A qualification for jury duty, sometimes imposed directly as a certain minimum or fair education, sometimes imposed indirectly by requiring literacy as a prerequisite to registering as a voter, and then requiring jurors to be selected from the list of registered voters. 31 Am J Rev ed Jury § 168.

literacy test. A test to determine the qualification of a voter according to his ability to read and write or ability to read and understand any section of the State or Federal Constitution. 25 Am J2d Elect § 89.

literae (li'te-rē). Letters; written instruments; words; the words.

literae clausae (li'te-rē klâ'sē). Close letters,—letters or grants from the king, sealed with his great seal, but directed to particular persons, and for particular purposes, and which, not being proper for public inspection, were closed up and sealed on the outside. See 2 Bl Comm 346.

literae mortuae (li'te-rē mor'tu-ē). Dead letters,—superfluous words.

literae patentes (li'te-rē pa-ten'tēz). Open letters; letters patent.

Literae patentes regis non erunt vacuae (li'te-rē pa-ten'tēz rē'jis non ē'runt va'ku-ē). The letters patent of the king shall not be void.

literae procuratoriae (li'te-rē pro-kū-rā-tō'ri-ē). Letters procuratory; letters of procuration; letters of attorney; a power of attorney.

literae recognitionis (li'te-re re-kog-ni-she-ō'nis). A bill of lading.

Literae scriptae manent (li'te-rē skrip'tē ma'nent). Written words endure.

literae sigillatae (li'te-rē si-ji-lā'tē). Sealed letters.

litera excambii (li'te-ra ex-kam'bi-ī). A bill of exchange.

literal (lit'ẹ-rạl). Adhering strictly to the letter; closely following the precise words.

literal construction. A construction, usually narrow, according to the letter or the word rather than according to the intention of the parties as gathered from the entire context. Bear v Millikin Trust Co. 336 Ill 366, 168 NE 349, 73 ALR 173; 16 Am J2d Const L § 71. A construction of a statute which adheres to the mere letter, the literal or strict meaning of the words of the statute. 50 Am J1st Stat § 240. A technical construction of a word or term of a contract which may or may not convey the real meaning of the parties. Lemons v Knox, 72 Ariz 177, 232 P2d 383.

literal contract. (Roman law.) A contract which was wholly in writing, and which was binding on him who signed it, although without consideration.

literal proof (pröf). (Civil law.) Proof made by writings received in evidence.

literary journal. A publication devoted to the special interests of literature; a publication of articles selected because of literary merit. 39 Am J1st Newsp § 9.

literary property. An intellectual conception embodied in a form whereby it may be disseminated by the production of multiple copies. 18 Am J2d Copyr § 2. The interest of an author, or of those who claim under him, in his works, whether before or after publication or before or after a copyright has been secured, being in essence, a right to exclude others, to a greater or lesser extent, from making some or all use of the express thoughts of the author. Records Inc. v Mercury Records Corp. (CA2 NY) 221 F2d 657.

literary proprietor. One who owns literary property. An author or his assigns. Keene v Wheatley (CC Pa) F Cas No 7644.
See **literary property.**

Litera scripta manet (li'te-ra skrip'ta ma'net). The written word or letter endures.

literatura (li-te-ra-tū'ra). Education.

literature. See **literary property.**

literis obligation. (li'te-ris ob-li-gā'she-ō). (Roman law.) An obligation arising out of entries made in certain books of account.

lithograph. The reproduction of a picture or of printed matter by the process known as lithography. Arthur v Moller, 97 US 365, 24 L Ed 1046.

litigant. A person engaged in a litigation; a party to a suit or action.

litigare (li-ti-gā're). To litigate; to go to law; to maintain or defend an action as a party thereto.

litigate. To go to law; to maintain or defend an action as a party thereto; to sue or to be sued.

litigated. Subjected to litigation.
Facts, matters, or questions are said to have been litigated when they have formed the subject matter of litigation. Only those facts are said to have been "litigated" in an action which were necessarily within the issue presented and without proof of which the judgment rendered in the action could not have been rendered. Eastman v Symonds, 108 Mass 567, 569.

litigation. An action or suit; a series or group of related suits or actions.

litigation expenses. A reasonable attorney's fee incurred in any necessary litigation and all other necessary expenses incurred by the personal representative of a decedent or other fiduciary in litigation for the benefit of the estate. 21 Am J2d Ex & Ad § 545.
See **allowance; attorney's fee; costs; suit money.**

litigiosity. The pendency of a suit or action.

litigious (li-tij'us). Contested in a suit or action; eager to enter into a litigation, suit or action.

litigious right. A right contested in a suit. The right ceases to be litigious when judgment has been rendered. See Cucullu v Hernandez (US) 13 Otto 105, 26 L Ed 322.

litis (lī'tis). (Civil law.) Of a litigation suit, or action.

litis aestimatio (lī'tis ēs-ti-mā'she-ō). (Civil Law.) The measure of damages.

litis contestatio (lī'tis kon-tes-tā'she-ō). (Civil and canon law.) The contest of an action or suit; an issue; joinder of issue; a general denial in an ecclesiastical suit.

litis dominium (lī′tis do-mi′ni-um). (Civil law.) The control or direction of an action or litigation.

litis dominus (lī′tis do′mi-nus). (Roman law.) A person who controls or directs an action or litigation.

litis magister (lī′tis ma-jis′ter). (Roman law.) Same as **litis dominus.**

litis motae. See **forum litis motae.**

Litis nomen actionem significat, sive in rem, sive in personam sit (lī′tis nō′men ak-she-ō′nem sig-ni′fi-kat, si′ve in rem, sī′ve in per-sō′nam sit). The word "lis" signifies an action, whether an action in rem or an action in personam.

litispendence (lī-tis-pen′dens). The pendency of a suit or action.

litre (lē′tẻr). Same as **liter.**

little cape. A writ of old vintage, summoning a tenant to answer for default in payment of rent.

little more than. A comparative. About the same. Pierce v Lefort, 197 La 1, 200 So 801.

Littleton. Sir Thomas Littleton, a famous English jurist; the author of a treatise on land tenures which he wrote about 1470, and which formed the basis of Lord Coke's Commentaries.

littoral (lit′ọ-ral). Bordering on the shore; pertaining to the shore of the sea.

littoral owner. Same as **littoral proprietor.**

littoral proprietor (lit′ọ-ral prọ-prī′e-tọr). The owner of premises on the shores of the sea or a lake. 56 Am J1st Wat § 273.

If an owner's lands abut upon a river he is deemed a riparian owner. Peck v Alfred Olsen Constr. Co. 216 Iowa 519, 238 NW 416, 89 ALR 1132.

littoral rights (lit′ọ-ral rīts). The rights of a littoral owner.

littoral waters. Coastal waters, whether of the sea or a lake.

litura (li-tū′rạ). (Civil law.) An erasure, correction, or blot on a written instrument.

Litus est quousque maximus fluctus a mari pervenit (lī′tus est quo-us′kwe ma′xi-mus fluk′tus ā ma′rī per-vē′nit). (Civil law.) The shore is as far as the greatest wave has come up from the sea.

litus maris (lī′tus mar′is). The shore of the sea.

live (līv) See **alive.**

live (liv). To be animate. To reside or abide in a place. For some purposes merely to sojourn in a place.

For the purpose of taking a deposition, a witness "lives" where he can be found, and is sojourning, residing, or abiding for any lawful purpose. Mut. Ben. Life Ins. Co. v Robison (CA8 Iowa) 58 F 723.

See **living.**

live birth. The birth of a child which breathes after delivery from the womb.

live issue. Issue by a live birth. For the purposes of an estate by curtesy, one delivered or expelled from the body of the mother and living by respiration independent of the mother. 25 Am J2d Dower § 34.

live rail. Same as **third rail.**

livery. The keeping of horses and vehicles ready for hire. Keen v Ross, 186 Ky 256, 216 SW 605. A private carrier, not a common carrier. Stanley v Steele, 77 Conn 688, 60 A 640.

Delivery. When a male heir arrived at the age of twenty-one, or a female heir at sixteen, they could "sue out their livery" or ousterlemain; that is the delivery of their lands out of their guardian's hands; and for this they paid a fine equal to half a year's profits of the land. See 2 Bl Comm 68.

See **livery of seisin.**

livery conveyance. A motor vehicle or, as in the old days, a horse-drawn vehicle used to convey passengers for hire.

See **public conveyance.**

livery in law. The transfer of the possession of land while the parties are in sight of it, but without making an actual physical entry upon it.

liveryman. A person who keeps a livery stable. Elliott v Hodgson, 133 Ga 209, 65 SE 405.

livery of seisin. A ceremonial delivery of possession of real estate, long since obsolete, made in the presence of witnesses in the transfer of title to lands by feoffment. 23 Am J2d Deeds § 11.

livery stable. A building in which either horses or vehicles are kept or let for hire. Elliott v Hodgson, 133 Ga 209, 65 SE 405. A place where horses are kept or boarded for compensation.

See **livery.**

livery stable lien. Similar to an **agister's lien.**

lives (livs). Being in a state of animation.

lives (līvs). The plural of life.

See **joint lives; lives in being.**

lives in being. Within the meaning of the rule against perpetuities, any lives in being at the time the interest is created, selected expressly or by plain implication for a limitation of the estate. 41 Am J1st Perp § 14.

"Lives in being" within the meaning of the rule against perpetuities, has reference to those in being at the date of the testator's death, not at the time of the execution of the will. Story v First Nat. Bank & Trust Co. 115 Fla 436, 156 So 101.

Within the meaning of the rule against perpetuities which allows the postponement of the vesting of an estate or interest for the period of lives in being and twenty-one years and the period of gestation, there is generally no restriction on the number of lives in being which may be selected as the measure of the period of time permitted by the rule; the only limitation being that the lives in being must not be so numerous that there is not some reasonable way of proving the decease of the survivor of them. 41 Am J1st Perp § 14.

livestock. Domestic animals, particularly cattle, hogs, sheep, and horses.

Livestock includes fur bearing animals domesticated, and raised in captivity. The breeding, raising, and pelting of foxes is agricultural labor as that term is used in the Federal Social Security Act. Fromm Bros. v United States (DC Wis) 35 F 145.

livestock car. A railroad car constructed especially for the transportation of livestock.

livestock feed. See **feed.**

livestock insurance. A contract of insurance by which the insurer agrees to indemnify the insured against such loss as he may sustain by reason of injury to or death of livestock by the happening of specified risks or causes. Abraham v Ins. Co. of North America, 117 Vt 75, 84 A2d 670, 29 ALR2d 783.

livestock market. A place where livestock is taken for sale and at which prospective purchasers assemble for the purpose of buying livestock, often operating as an auction sale.

livestock producer. A person who produces livestock by feeding and caring for cattle, hogs, sheep, etc.; a "farmer" as such term is defined in the Bankruptcy Act. 11 USC 1(17).

livestock register. A record of purebred livestock showing the sire and dam of an animal entitled to registration as purebred.
See **purebred livestock.**

live storage. The safe-keeping of goods in a warehouse or other depository, to be moved or replaced with other goods at the will of the patron. Tipp v District of Columbia, 69 App DC 400, 102 F2d 264. The storage of a motor vehicle in running condition and equipped for operation, the battery being in operating position and connected with the ignition system.

live together. See **living together.**

live trust. An **active trust.** Also, a **trust inter vivos.**

live wire. A wire charged with an electric current, especially where the current is deadly or potent with danger to the person. Phelan v Louisville Electrical Co. 122 Ky 476, 91 SW 703. A colloquial term for an active and energetic person.

living. Being in a state of animation. The state of a person from birth to death and, for some purposes in civil cases, the existence of the animate foetus in the womb. Hall v Hancock, 32 Mass (15 Pick) 255.
See **born alive; church living.**

living apart. Separation of husband and wife, ignoring the marital relationship and with design or agreement to be separated. 26 Am J1st Husband and Wife § 7. Living in the same house or place of residence but not in an actual marital relationship. 26 Am J1st H & W § 7.

living in adultery. Living together openly as if married and indulging in acts of intercourse. 2 Am J2d Adult §§ 10-12.

living in disorderly house. Being an inmate or resident of a house of ill fame.

living in fornication. Openly living together as if the legal relationship of husband and wife existed and indulging in acts of sexual intercourse. 2 Am J2d Adult §§ 10 et seq.

living persons. See **live; living.**

living pledge. An estate which arises when a person borrows a specific sum and grants property to the lender to hold until the rents and profits shall repay the sum so borrowed, whereupon the property reverts to the borrower. Spect v Spect, 88 Cal 437, 26 F 203.

living proof. Proof by living witness or witnesses.

Livingston v Jefferson. The litigation between Edward Livingston and Thomas Jefferson wherein it was decided that a suit for wrongful entry on land in Louisiana could not be maintained in a court in Virginia. (CC Va) 1 Brock 203, 4 Hughes 606, F Cas No 8411.

living then. See **then living.**

living together. See **cohabit; family, household; living together as husband and wife.**

living together as husband and wife. Living as husband and wife, with voluntary recognition of the relationship and in the absence of design or agreement to live apart free from reciprocal marital rights and duties, irrespective of whether or not there is a common place of living. 26 Am J1st H & W § 7.
See **cohabit; living in adultery.**

living trust. An **active trust.** Also, a **trust inter vivos.**

livre (lē'vėr). A book; a pound weight.

L. J. An abbreviation of "law judge."

LL.B. An abbreviation of Legum Baccalaureus, Bachelor of Laws.

LL.D. An abbreviation of Legum Doctor, Doctor of Laws.

Lloyd's. Often referred to as Lloyd's of London, an association of individual insurers or underwriters, which takes its name from the coffee house in London at which insurers, then engaged in marine insurance only, formerly met for the transaction of business. Not an insurance company in the American sense of the term.
   Although the Lloyd's insurers originally engaged in marine insurance only, so-called Lloyd's policies are now issued upon risks of almost every conceivable nature.

Lloyd's association. Sometimes known as an American Lloyd's. An unincorporated association engaged in the insurance business. 29 Am J Rev ed Ins § 51.

Lloyd's bond. An instrument in writing under seal issued by a corporation, acknowledging value received, and promising to pay a certain sum of money.

Lloyd's lists. Published statements of the arrival and departure of vessels and of marine losses and accidents.

Lloyd's of London. See **Lloyd's.**

loaded cane. A walking stick or cane in which metal has been inserted to make it a deadly weapon. Anno: 30 ALR 816.

loaded dice. Dice which are weighted or carved so that, when thrown, one side will come up much more frequently than would be the case without such tampering therewith.
See **cogging.**

loaded gun. A firearm charged with powder and ball, that is, with a bullet.

loading. The placing of goods on a ship, railroad car, or truck. Adding to the weight of something. The addition by an insurer, in calculating a premium rate, of a charge for operating expenses or for the contingency of increases in the risk or in the expense of doing business which cannot be foreseen in advance. Fox v Mutual Ben. Life Ins. Co. (CA8 Mo) 107 F2d 715; United States Life Ins. Co. v Spinks, 126 Ky 405, 96 SW 889. The inclusion in calculating a rate or charge for any service of items which have no material bearing upon what is a reasonable and proper charge.
See **loading and unloading.**

loading and unloading. The transfer of cargo from wharf or landing to ship and from ship to wharf or landing. 48 Am J1st Ship § 381. A comparable operation in the transportation of goods, merchandise, or other articles by land carrier. 13 Am J2d Car § 319. The business of a wharfinger. 56 Am J1st Whar § 19.
   As a general rule, the carrier has the primary

duty to load and unload goods or inanimate freight shipped in less than carload lots, and is liable for damages resulting from its failure to perform that duty in a proper manner. The shipper or consignee, however, has the duty to load and unload freight shipped in carload lots, or where for the shipper's convenience the cars to be loaded or unloaded are placed at his warehouse or on public tracks. 13 Am J2d Car § 319.

See **complete operation doctrine; loading and unloading clause.**

loading and unloading clause. A familiar clause in liability insurance policies covering trucks and commercial vehicles, providing in substance that the use of the insured vehicle for the purposes stated in the policy includes the loading and unloading of the vehicle, or, to the contrary, that such operation is excluded from the risk insured. 7 Am J2d Auto Ins § 87.

As a general principle, in construing a policy insuring a truck owner against liability for damage arising out of the use of his trucks, including loading and unloading, the mission or transaction being performed by the insured's employees at the time of the accident is the controlling element in determining whether the situation from which the accident occurred is included in loading and unloading. Pacific Auto Ins. Co. v Commercial Casualty Ins. Co. 108 Utah 500, 161 P2d 423, 160 ALR 1251.

loading charge. See **loading.**

loading tipple. See **tipple.**

load lights. Lights displayed at the end of load which projects from the side or rear of a vehicle. Anno: 21 ALR2d 85, § 27; 8 Am J2d Auto § 713.

load line. See **Plimsoll Line.**

loadman (lōd′man). One who directs the course of a ship, not from the vessel itself, but from a small boat propelled in advance of the vessel.

loadmanage. The piloting of a vessel by a loadman. See **loadman.**

loafing. Idling; avoiding work; loitering. See **vagrancy.**

loan. Verb: To deliver or transfer personal property or money to a borrower, that is, one who receives it and promises to return it or its equivalent, often with compensation for the use thereof by him, as where he promises to pay interest upon a loan of money. Nichols v Fearson (US) 7 Pet 103, 109, 8 L Ed 623, 625; Kent v Quicksilver Mining Co. 78 NY 159, 177; First Nat. Bank v Tjosevig (Wash) 254 P 951. Sometimes, as where it appears in a will, a word of grant. 57 Am J1st Wills § 1334. Noun: The act of making a loan. An asset of the lender, upon completion and before payment.

loan association. See **building and loan association; savings and loan association.**

loan broker. See **personal-property loan broker.**

loan company. A company engaged in the making of loans, usually secured loans.

loaned employee. Same as **loaned servant.**

loaned servant. A general employee of one person performing service for another. 58 Am J1st Workm Comp § 343. One having the status of an employee who is lent or hired out by his employer to another person for some special service so as to become, as to that service, the employee of such third person, the test being whether, in the particular service which he is engaged to perform, he continues to be under the direction and control of his regular employer or becomes subject to that of the person to whom he has been lent or hired. 35 Am J1st M & S § 18.

loaned servant doctrine. The test by which the status of a person as a loaned servant is determined. See **loaned servant.**

loan for consumption. A lending of goods to be consumed and to be returned in kind.

loan for exchange. A contract by which one delivers personal property to another, and the latter agrees to return to the lender a similar thing at a future time, without reward for its use. Section 1902, California Civil Code.

loan for use. A contract by which one gives to another the temporary possession and use of personal property, and the latter agrees to return the same thing to him at a future time, without reward for its use. Section 1884, California Civil Code.

loan of money. See **loan.**

loan of shares. See **loan ticket.**

loan on life insurance policy. By insurer: not a "loan" in the ordinary sense of the term, being merely an advance by the insurer of a sum which the insurer ultimately must pay the borrower, that is, the insured. 29 Am J Rev ed Ins § 615. A loan by a bank or other financial institution in which the policy is assigned to the bank or other institution by way of security.

loan society. An association of individuals formed for the purpose of lending money to its members or to others.

See **building and loan association.**

loan ticket. A ticket or instrument evidencing a transaction commonly known in the stock-brokerage business as a "loan" of shares of stock.

The loan of stock is usually, though not necessarily, incidental to a "short sale," that is, a contract for the sale of shares which the seller does not own, or the certificates for which are not within his control to be available for delivery at the time when delivery must be made. Provost v United States, 269 US 443, 449, 450, 46 S Ct 152.

loathsome disease. A disease shocking to the senses of other persons. Anno: 5 ALR 1022, s. 8 ALR 1540.

lobby. See **lobbying.**

lobbying. Services in attempting to obtain the passage of favored legislation. The practice of addressing or soliciting members of a legislative body, in the lobby off the chamber or elsewhere, for the purpose of influencing their votes. Chippewa Valley & Superior Railway Co. v Chicago, St. Paul, Minneapolis & Omaha Railway Co. 75 Wis 224, 44 NW 17.

Lobbying Act. A federal statute regulating lobbying in reference to the Congress of the United States. Anno: 98 L Ed 1006-1007.

lobbying contract. Any agreement which tends to introduce personal influence and solicitation as elements in procuring and influencing legislative action. Houlton v Nichol, 93 Wis 393, 67 NW 715. A contract in which one of the parties undertakes to perform lobbying services.

See **lobbying.**

lobby member. A person who frequents the lobby of a house of legislation for the purpose of influencing measures therein pending. Chippewa Valley & Superior Ry. Co. v Chicago, St. Paul, Minneapolis & Omaha Ry. Co. 75 Wis 224, 44 NW 17.

lobbying services. See **lobbying**.

L'obligation sans cause, ou sur une fausse cause, ou sur cause illicite, ne peut avoir aucun effet (l'ŏ-blī-gah-sī-ôn sôn cōz, oo soor ūne fōs cōz, oo soor cōz il-li-seet, nuh pert ah-vwor ō-kŭn ay-fay). An obligation without any consideration, or with a false one, or with an unlawful one, cannot have any effect.

local. Pertaining to a particular place, or to a fixed or limited portion of space, as local circumstances; limited or confined to a spot, place, or definite district, as a local custom. Graves v Alsap, 1 Ariz 274, 293.

local acceptance. An acceptance of a bill of exchange or draft whereby the drawee agrees to pay only at a particular place. Uniform Negotiable Instruments Law § 141; 11 Am J2d B & N § 517.

local action. At common law, an action which can be brought only where the cause of action arose, since the cause is one that in its nature can arise in one place only. 56 Am J1st Ven § 3. The antithesis of a transitory action.

In most jurisdictions, the venue of actions is now wholly regulated by statute, and frequently the character of an action as local or transitory is important in reference to venue only when a foreign cause of action is involved. 56 Am J1st Ven § 3.

local affection. See **local disease**.

local agent. An agent of a corporation representing it at a given place or within a definite district. Anno: 113 ALR 84, 85. In the insurance business, a term characterizing an agent of an insurance company in reference to the territory in which his services are to be employed on behalf of the company, not in reference to his authority respecting a particular transaction. 29 Am J Rev ed Ins § 152.

As used in statutes authorizing the service of process on the local agent of a foreign corporation, a local agent who represents the corporation in the promotion of the business for which it was incorporated has been held to be an agent at a given place or within a definite district, but every person who may be employed in any capacity by it is not a local agent. An agent with authority to borrow money and execute notes and deeds of trust in the name of the corporation, a resident sales agent, and a bookkeeper having charge of the finances of the corporation have each been held to be a local agent under such statutes. 36 Am J2d For Corp § 563.

local allegiance. The allegiance which a foreigner owes to the king during his residence in England. See 1 Bl Comm 370.

local assessment. Same as **special assessment**.

local assessment lien. See **special assessment lien**.

local benefit. The benefit of a public improvement limited to the inhabitants of a small locality. 26 Am J2d Em D § 31.

local board. The administrative board of the selective draft for the armed forces.

local bounty. A bounty provided by a municipality or other political subdivision of the state. 12 Am J2d Bount § 6.

local cause of action. An action which could have arisen in only one place. 56 Am J1st Ven § 3.

local chattel. A fixture,—something so attached to the realty as to become, for the time being, a part of the freehold.

local civil service. Municipal civil service. 15 Am J2d Civ S § 7.

local court. A court the jurisdiction and process of which are confined to a certain locality. Geraty v Reid, 78 NY 64, 67. A city court, municipal court, police court, or court of a justice of the peace. 20 Am J2d Cts § 30.

local custom. A custom which prevails in some county, city, town, parish, district, or place, the existence of which is to be determined as a matter of fact upon proof. 21 Am J2d Cust & U § 6.

local disease. An affection sufficiently developed to have some bearing on the general health. Cady v Fidelity & Casualty Co. 134 Wis 322, 113 NW 967.

locale. The neighborhood.

local election. An election of local officers. See **municipal election**.

local freight. Freight shipped from either terminus of a railroad to a way station, or vice versa, or from one way station to another, that is, over a part of the one railroad only. Mobile & Montgomery Railway Co. v Steiner, McGehee & Co. 61 Ala 559, 579.

local freight train. See **local train**.

local government. Municipal as distinguished from the state or national government. The government of a county, city, town, or district.

local history. The history of a municipality, a county, a township, or other political subdivision or definite area.

local improvement. A building or other work of construction, the cost and expense of which is chargeable upon private property by way of a special assessment.

An improvement chargeable upon private property and possessing at least two essential elements: (1) It must be of a public nature, that is, it must be such an improvement as the muncipality would be justified in constructing and maintaining by general taxation; and (2) it must confer a special benefit on the property sought to be specially charged with its creation and maintenance, over and above that conferred generally upon property within the municipality. Some courts have added a third element, that of permanency, denying the power of local assessment for an improvement of an evanescent type or nature. 48 Am J1st Spec A §§ 21 et seq.

local improvement bond. See **improvement bond**.

local improvement district. See **improvement district**.

local improvement lien. See **special assessment lien**.

local improvement tax. Same as **special assessment**.

local influence. That influence which might operate in the minds of the people to prevent a citizen of one state sued in the state court of another state from obtaining justice in such state. Gaines v Fuentes, 92 US 10, 23 L Ed 524. A ground at one time for removal of a cause from a state to a federal court, no longer of moment. 28 USC § 1441, reviser's notes.

See **local prejudice**.

locality. A place. The vicinity or neighborhood. An area relative in size to the circumstances involved, sometimes measurable in rods, at other times, in miles. Connally v General Constr. Co. 269 US 385, 394, 70 L Ed 322, 330, 46 S Ct 126.

localization doctrine. The doctrine that a foreign loan association voluntarily subjects itself to the local laws by doing business for a length of time in a state and cannot thereafter abrogate those laws by contractual stipulations to the effect that its local contract shall be governed by the usury laws of the state of its domicil. National Mut. Building & Loan Asso. v Brahan, 193 US 635, 48 L Ed 823, 24 S Ct 532.

local law. The law of the jurisdiction in which the action or proceeding is pending. The state, as distinguished from the federal, law. A law enacted by a municipal council or other law-making body of a political subdivision. A statute which in fact, if not in form, is directed only to a specific part of the state, being confined in its operation to the property or persons of a limited portion of the state, touching only a portion of the territory and people of the state. 50 Am J1st Stat §§ 8-10.

As applied to statutes, the term is of modern origin, and is used to designate an act which operates only within a single city, county, or other particular division or place, and not throughout the entire legislative jurisdiction. in this sense, the term "local" is the antithesis of the word "general." State ex rel. Anderson v Tillamook, 62 Or 332, 124 P 637.

See **ordinance**.

local legislation. The enactment of local laws.
See **local law**.

local mine. A term of uncertain origin that has not been widely accepted.

For convenience, a mine served by one carrier is called a "local mine," and a mine served by two or more carriers is called a "joint mine." United States v New River Co. 265 US 533, 534, 68 L Ed 1165, 1169, 44 S Ct 610.

local mining rules. See **miners' rules and customs**.

local nature. See **action of a local nature**.

local necessity. Geographic and local considerations determining the validity of a statute made applicable only to a segregated area or district. Des Moines v Manhattan Oil Co. 193 Iowa 1096, 184 NW 823, 188 NW 921, 23 ALR 1322.

local officers. Public officers of a county, township, or municipality, sometimes charged with duties to be performed on behalf of the state government as well as duties on behalf of their own bailiwick. 42 Am J1st Pub Of § 21.

local operation. A maritime operation which is so local in nature as to permit the application of state workmen's compensation laws. Southern Pacific Co. v Jensen, 244 US 205, 61 L Ed 1086, 37 S Ct 524.

local option. The right given a township, county, or other political subdivision to determine for itself by an election whether or not a certain law shall take effect in such area or district. People v Stimer, 248 Mich 272, 226 NW 899, 67 ALR 552. Laws which provide for leaving to the decision of the electors of a county, municipality, or other prescribed territory the matter of the expediency of permitting or forbidding the sale of intoxicating liquors, or the issuance of licenses for such sale, in any part of the territory in which the vote is had. 30 Am J Rev ed Intox L § 81. Primarily concerned with laws respecting the traffic in intoxicating liquors.

local option election. An election in a county, township, or other political subdivision through which the right of local option is exercised. 30 Am J Rev ed Intox L § 89.
See **local option**.

local passenger train. See **local train**.

local prejudice. Prejudice arising out of peculiar local conditions, such as social or economic conditions, racial constituencies, and religious beliefs. 39 Am J1st New Tr § 57. Feeling or excitement in the county rendering it impossible for an accused or a party to a civil action to obtain a fair trial in the county. 56 Am J1st Ven § 56. A strong current of public opinion as to the guilt of an accused such as to render an impartial trial in the locality impossible. Oborn v State, 143 Wis 259, 125 NW 737. A ground at one time for removal of a cause from a state to a federal court, no longer of moment. 28 USC § 1441, reviser's notes.
See **local influence**.

local rules. Court rules applicable in a single district.

local self-government. The right of self-government as to local affairs; the right of a city, borough, or town to elect local officers from their own citizens and to manage purely local affairs. 37 Am J1st Mun Corp § 77.
See **home rule**.

local statute. See **local law**.

local sun time. The time of day in a given place as shown by a sun dial at that place. Anno: 35 LRA NS 611.

local tax. A tax imposed in and for the benefit of a municipality, county, town, or district as distinguished from a state tax or tax of general application throughout the state. People ex rel. Pratt Institute v Assessors of Brooklyn, 141 NY 476, 477, 36 NE 508.
See **special assessment**.

local train. A freight train which stops at any siding or station along the line where there is freight to load and unload, be the quantity what it may, as distinguished from a freight train which takes and leaves freight only at certain definite stops, and which is generally called a through train.

Passenger trains are similarly classified. Arizona Eastern Railroad Co. v State, 29 Ariz 446, 242 P 870.

local venue. Venue or jurisdiction which is confined to a single county.

local union. A voluntary association of laborers in a particular locality, subordinate to its national union, but a separate and distinct body, owing its creation and continued existence to the will of its own members. 31 Am J Rev ed Lab § 42.

local usage. See **local custom**.

local words. Words having a meaning determined by a peculiar local usage. Collender v Dinsmore, 55 NY 200.

locare (lō-kā're). To let out to hire; to bestow in marriage.

locarium (lō-kā'ri-um). Compensation for hire; rent.

locataire (lō-cah-tär'). (French.) A lessee; a tenant.

locatarius (lō-kā-tā'ri-us). A despositary,—a person who receives a deposit; a depositee.

locate. To place; to set in a particular spot or position; to select, survey, and settle the boundaries of a particular tract of land; or to designate a particular portion of land by limits; to designate and determine a place for something. Murdock v Memphis, 47 Tenn (7 Coldw) 483, 501. To discover where something is by a search therefor.

locatio (lō-kā'she-ō). (Civil law.) A letting out to hire; a leasing; a contract of letting and hiring; a lease.

locatio conductio (lō-kā'she-ō kon-duk'she-ō). (Civil law.) A bailment of goods for reward or hire.

locatio custodiae (lō-kā'she-ō kus-tō'di-ē). The hiring of care or services to be performed or bestowed on the thing delivered under a bailment. 8 Am J2d Bailm § 5.

locatio et conductio (lō-kā'she-ō et kon-duk'she-ō). A bailment where goods are left with a bailee for some use or service by him, such bailment always being for some reward. 8 Am J2d Bailm § 5.

location. The act of locating, that is, designating a place for something or, in the case of land, designating the boundaries or otherwise describing it so that another may know where it lies and its extent. A statement in a description to real estate of the town, county, or state in which the land is situated; a description of real property by house number in a city. 23 Am J2d Deeds § 223. The selection of a homestead upon the public domain for entry. 42 Am J1st Pub L §§ 19 et seq. A series of acts by which the locator appropriates a portion of the public mineral lands and establishes his right to exploit it to the exclusion of all others. Creede & C. C. Mining & Milling Co. v Uinta Tunnel Mining & Transp. Co. 196 US 337, 49 L Ed 501, 25 S Ct 266. Another word for mining claim. 36 Am J1st Min & M § 69.

location of claim. See **location**.

location of railroad. The designation and adoption of a route, at least where such is followed by construction of the line. 44 Am J1st RR § 204.

The location of the route is, in its nature, a proceeding preliminary to the acquisition of land therefor by appraisal and condemnation; and the statute regulation must be complied with before the route can be located. The filing of the profile and map required by that section is not the location of the route, but the proposal of one, which may or may not become the actual route, as shall be determined by the subsequent proceedings. Re Niagara Falls Railway Co. (NY) 46 Hun 94, 97.

location of way. The determination of the course of a highway, made as a part of the establishment of the highway. 25 Am J1st High §§ 9 et seq.

location restrictions. Regulations and restrictions respecting the part of a lot or tract upon which buildings and other structures may be erected. 58 Am J1st Zon § 50.

locatio operis (lō-kā'she-ō o'pe-ris). A contract to repair a thing and to supply the materials.

The obligations imposed by the locatio operis and capable of enforcement by an action on the contract are: (a) To do the work which is the subject of the undertaking; (b) to do it within the time agreed on, or within what may be, in view of all the circumstances, a proper time; (c) to do it in a proper manner; (d) to surrender the property on which the labor has been expended on payment for the work done. Zell v Dunkle, 156 Pa 353, 357, 27 A 38.

locatio operis faciendi (lō-kā'she-ō o'pe-ris fa-she-en'dī). The hiring of work or labor to be performed upon a thing. 8 Am J2d Bailm § 5.

locatio operis mercium vehendarum (lō-kā'she-ō o'pe-ris mer'she-um ve-hen-dar'um). The hiring of the carriage of goods, when they are bailed, either to a public carrier, or to a private person, for the purpose of being carried from place to place. 8 Am J2d Bailm § 5.

locatio rei (lō-kā'she-ō rē'ī). The hire of a thing, whereby the hirer gains the temporary use thereof. 8 Am J2d Bailm § 5.

locative calls. Landmarks, monuments, and other physical objects marking the surveyed line of a boundary, as distinguished from courses and distances which are descriptive calls. Holmes v Trout (US) 7 Pet 171, 194, 8 L Ed 646, 655.

locato. See **ex locato**.

locator. The bailor in a "locatio" or bailment for hire. One who locates a claim, such as a mining claim, or a homestead claim, to public lands.
See **location**.

locatum (lo-kā'tum). The same as **locatio et conductio**.

loc. cit. Abbreviation of **loco citato**,—in the place cited.

loci (lō'sī). Plural of **locus**.

lock. A basin in a canal, of sufficient size to hold vessels of the size using the waterway, having gates which may be opened or closed to permit the entry or discharge of water, thereby changing the level of the water as required to permit vessels to advance from a lower to a higher level of the canal, or vice versa. Dawson v Western M. R. Co. 107 Md 70, 68 A 301. A mechanical device for holding fast the door of a building, room, chest, box, or vehicle against opening except by key or known combination.
See **ignition**.

locked car. A private car on a railroad. 14 Am J2d Car § 860.

locked ignition. The effect of removing the key from the instrumentality of ignition on a motor vehicle. 7 Am J2d Auto § 234.

locked wheel. A disablement of a motor vehicle. Anno: 15 ALR2d 917, § 7.

locker plant. A place where individual lockers for cold storage of food are furnished to customers at a monthly or weekly rental, sometimes furnishing services in cutting meat and otherwise preparing meat and other food for storage.

locker system. An arrangement in a social club whereby a member purchases his own liquor and places it in his own locker, in the club building, to which only he has a key. 30 Am J Rev ed Intox L § 229.

lockjaw. See **tetanus**.

lockout. An employer's discharge of his employees because of a labor dispute or because of his dislike of his employees' activities as a union. Anno: 173 ALR 675. The temporary closing of the place of employment by the employer without formally discharging the employees, the object being to discourage union activities or to gain acceptance of his views or a compromise which is more favorable to him than the demands made by the employees. 31 Am J Rev ed Lab § 487.

lockup. A place for the temporary and compulsory confinement and detention of persons under arrest. 41 Am J1st Pris & P § 2.

locmen (lok'men). (French.) Local mariners engaged as pilots of vessels coming in or departing from a harbor or traversing a river. Martin v Farnsworth 33 NY Super Ct (1 Jones 48) 246, 261.

loco citato (lō'kō si-tā'tō). In the place cited; abbreviated, "loc. cit."

locomotive. The instrumentality which supplies the motive power for the movement of a train, usually placed at the head of the train. A railroad car for the purposes of the application of Safety Appliance Acts. Baltimore & Ohio R. Co. v Jackson, 353 US 325, 1 L Ed 2d 862, 77 S Ct 842.

locomotive engineer. The person in charge of the operation of a railroad locomotive.

loco parentis (lō'kō pā-ren'tis). See **person in loco parentis**.

locum (lō'kum). See **locus**.

locum tenens (lō'kum tē'nenz). Holding the place.
A person whose term of office was expired, is said to be merely locum tenens until he shall be superseded by some person authorized by law to be inducted into the office. State ex rel. Everding v Simon, 20 Or 365, 26 P 170, 174.

locuples (lo'ku-plēs). (Civil law.) Wealthy; financially responsible; able to respond to a judgment.

locus (lō-kus). A place; a location; a piece of ground; a neighborhood.
See **eo loci**.

locus contractus (lō'kus kon-trak'tus). The place of the contract,—the place where the contract is entered into.

Locus contractus regit actum (lō'kus kon-trak'tus rē'jit ak'tum). The place of the contract governs the act. A principle having reference to the act of solemnization. Scudder v Union Nat. Bank, 91 US 406, 410, 23 L Ed 245, 248.

Locus criminis (lō'kus kri'mi-nis). The place of the crime,—the place where the crime was committed.

locus delicti (lō'kus de-lik'tī). The place of wrongdoing,—the place where the crime or the tort was committed.

locus in quo (lō'kus in quō). The place in which; the premises described in the writ. Moor v Campbell, 15 NH 208, 211.

locus paenitentia (lō'kus pe-ni-ten'she-ä). A place for repentance. The opportunity which a man engaged in the commission of a crime may have to withdraw before its consummation, without incurring criminality. Hyde v United States, 225 US 347, 356, 56 L Ed 1114, 1122, 32 S Ct 793.

Locus pro solutione reditus aut pecuniae secundum conditionem dimissionis aut obligationis est stricte observandus (lō'kus prō so-lū-she-ō'ne re'di-tus ât pe-kū'ni-ē se-kun'dum kon-di-she-ō'nem di-mi-she-ō'nis ât ob-li-gā-she-ō'nis est strik'te ob-ser-van'-dus). The place for the payment of rent or money is to be strictly adhered to according to the provision of the demise or obligation.

locus publicus (lō'kus pub'li-kus). A public place.

Locus regit actum (lō'kus rē'jit ak'tum). The place governs the act.
The meaning of the maxim is that the place where a contract is entered into governs the manner in which it shall be formally solemnized. Pritchard v Norton, 106 US 124, 27 L Ed 106, 1 S Ct 102.

locus rei sitae (lō'kus rē'ī si'tē). The place where the thing or the property is situated.

locus sigilli (lō'kus si-jil'lī). The place of the seal. Abbreviated "L. S."
As to the effect of the letters "L. S." appearing on an instrument, as a seal, see 47 Am J1st Seals § 4.

locus standi (lō'kus stan'dī). A place to stand; a standing.
"He was in the position of an alien enemy, and hence could have no locus standi in that forum." Daniels v Homer, 139 NC 219, 51 SE 992.

lode. A term of mining law, brought to this country by miners from Cornwall as an alteration of the word "lead." A vein or two or more veins constituting a seam or fissure in the crust of the earth filled with quartz or other rock containing gold, silver, or other valuable mineral. 36 Am J1st Min & M § 69.

lode claim. A mining claim that embraces one or more continuous veins, lodes, or ledges of mineral lying within well-defined seams or fissures in the surrounding rock, often deep within the bowels of the earth. 36 Am J1st Min & M § 70.

lode location. A mining claim where the appropriation purports to be a claim to a lode.
In the location of mining claims there are two kinds of locations, lode and placer, which differ somewhat. A discovery within the limits of the claim is equally essential to both. But to sustain a lode location the discovery must be of a vein or lode of rock in place, bearing valuable mineral; and to sustain a placer location it must be of some other form of valuable mineral deposit, one such being scattered particles of gold found in the softer covering of the earth. A placer discovery will not sustain a lode location, nor a lode discovery a placer location. Cole v Ralph, 252 US 286, 295, 64 L Ed 567, 577, 40 S Ct 321.

lodeman (lōd-man). Same as **loadman**.

lodemanage (lōd'man-āj). Same as **loadmanage**.

lodge. A small house. A fraternal order; a secret society. State ex rel. Bradford v National Asso. of Farmers' etc. 35 Kan 51, 57.
See **fraternal order or society**.

lodger. One who resides in a lodging house or rooming house. 29 Am J Rev ed Innk § 6. A person who, for the time being, has his home at his lodging place. 29 Am J Rev ed Innk § 12.

lodging house. A house where bedrooms as such are supplied to guests for compensation usually known as room rent. 29 Am J Rev ed Innk § 6. Characterized by at least some degree of permanency of residence by the guests. Anno: 64 ALR2d 1167.

lodging house keeper. The proprietor or keeper of a lodging house.

lodging house keeper's lien. The statutory lien of the keeper of a lodging house upon goods of a lodger brought upon the premises for the former's charges against the latter for the lodging and services appertaining to the lodging, the lien sometimes being extended by statute to goods of a third person brought upon the premises by the lodger. 29 Am J Rev ed Innk §§ 145 et seq.

lods et ventes (lō ay vän). A fine which was formerly imposed for the alienation of land.

log. The section of a tree which has been cut or sawed from the trunk after the latter has been severed from the stump. Craddock Mfg. Co. v Faison, 138 Va 665, 123 SE 535, 39 ALR 1309. The record of an airplane flight kept by the pilot. Ogden v Transcontinental Airport of Toledo, 390 Ohio App 301, 177 NE 536; Liberty Mut. Ins. Co. v Boggs (Tex Civ App) 66 SW2d 787. The rather minute record of the voyage of a ship kept by the master or other officer, containing entries respecting the course and nature of the voyage, the weather encountered, and daily events, especially those pertaining to the operation of the vessel and the administration of discipline upon the vessel. A record required of certain vessels by federal statute. 48 Am J1st Ship § 220.

logbook. The book or journal in which a log is kept. See **log**.

log boom. See **boom**.

log brand. See **log mark**.

log-driving company. A corporation supplying facilities to the general public for floating logs and carrying on a large-scale business of driving and rafting logs for other persons. 34 Am J1st Logs § 85.

logger's lien. A lien upon the product of the work for work performed in connection with the cutting of timber, the hauling and rafting of logs, and the sawing of timber into marketable lumber products. 34 Am J1st Logs § 101.

logging. The operation of cutting and taking logs out of standing timber. 34 Am J1st Logs §§ 52 et seq. Felling trees, cutting them into logs, and transporting them to mill or market. Fox Park Timber Co. v Baker, 53 Wyo 467, 84 P2d 736, 120 ALR 1020 (involving workmen's compensation.)

logging license. A license to enter upon land and to cut and remove timber. 34 Am J1st Logs §§ 43 et seq.

logging railroad. A railroad operated by a logging company for the purpose of transporting its own products or materials to be used in logging operations. 13 Am J2d Car § 12.

logia (loj´ạ). A lodge.

logical end of instrument. The place where the draftsman stopped writing in the consecutive order of composition, as revealed by a reading of the instrument naturally and consecutively without deviating from the order of the instrument to have the sense continuous. The end of the disposition of property, wherever that may appear in the instrument. 57 Am J1st Wills § 268. The termination of the sequence which the testator intended to give to the writing as revealed upon the face of the instrument. Stinson's Estate, 228 Pa 475, 77 A 807.

logical relevancy. See **relevancy**.

log jam. A pile of logs lodged in a river or other stream of water so firmly and extensively as to block the use of the river or stream for the purpose of transportation. Elder v Delcour, 364 Mo 835, 269 SW2d 17, 47 ALR2d 370.

log laborer. One who labors on timber or logs in respect of the production and transportation of logs or timber, with his physical powers, in the service and under the direction of another, for fixed wages. Rogers v Dexter & P. R. Co. 85 Me 372, 27 A 257.

log mark. A mark or brand upon logs transported by floatage. 34 Am J1st Logs § 112.

log measure. The measurement of a log for the purpose of ascertaining the number of feet of lumber which may be obtained from the log. Craddock Mfg. Co. v Faison, 138 Va 665, 123 SE 535, 39 ALR 1309.

See **board foot; wood measure**.

logrolling. A term applied to the submission of a constitutional amendment to the voters in such form that a voter is required to vote for something which he disapproves in order to register approval of other propositions. Fugina v Donovan, 259 Minn 35, 104 NW2d 911. A term applied to a similar practice in drafting and submitting a bill to the legislature for adoption and enactment into law, especially as an expedient in obtaining the passage of special and local legislation. 50 Am J1st Stat § 49. A political term applied to the practice in legislative bodies whereby one member votes for the bill of another member in order to obtain the latter's support and vote for a measure of the former or in which the former is interested.

log timber. Trees such as can be cut into logs convenient in size for sawing into lumber. Ladnier v Ingram Day Lumber Co. 135 Miss 632, 100 So 369.

log wagon. A horse-drawn vehicle, sturdy in construction, formerly in use for the hauling of logs and other heavy material.

loiter. See **loitering**.

loitering. Being dilatory; standing around or spending one's time idly. State v Badda, 97 W Va 417, 125 SE 159. Idling or lounging upon a street or other public way, especially in such manner or to such an extent as to interfere with or annoy travelers. 25 Am J1st High § 189. Wandering on the streets or in public places. 55 Am J1st Vag § 7.

In reference to a statute rendering it a criminal offense on the part of the proprietor of a place for the sale of intoxicating liquors in permitting a minor to "loiter" in a saloon, some authorities take the position that a minor is "loitering" in such a place if he stays for an appreciable period of time, say 10 or 15 minutes. 30 Am J Rev ed Intox L § 260.

See **vagrancy**.

lollardy (lol´ạr-di). The offense of being a member of a religious sect known as the Lollards which sprang up in the reign of Henry IV, made indictable by 2 Hen. V, c. 7.

lond. land.

London custom. See **custom of London**.

London Prize Ring Rules. Rules applied in prize fights. States v Olympic Club, 46 La Ann 935, 15 So 190.

Londres (Lôn-druh). (French.) The city of London.

long. Extended; not short.

In the language of stockholders, a transaction is "long" where an order is given to a broker to buy, or where the broker receives an order to credit the account with certain stocks. Baldwin v Flagg, 36 NJ Eq 48, 56. A trader is said to be long on the market when he takes the full price risk, whereby he gains if the market price goes up and loses in the event of a decline in the market. Valley Waste Mills v Page (CA5 Ga) 115 F2d 466.

long-and-short haul. See **long haul rate**.

Longa patientia trahitur ad consensum (lon´ga pa-she-en´she-a tra´hi-ter ad kon-sen´sum). Long sufferance is interpreted as consent.

Longa possessio est pacis jus (lon´ga po-ze´she-o est pa´sis jus). Long-continued possession is the law of peace.

Longa possessio jus parit (lon'ga po-ze'she-o jūs pa'rit). Long-continued possession ripens into right.

Longa possessio parit jus possidendi, et tollit actionem vero domino (lon'ga pō-ze'she-o pa'rit jūs pos-si-den'dī, et tol'lit ak-she-ō'nem ve'rō do'minō). Long possession ripens into the right to possession, and deprives the true owner of his right of action. Campbell v Holt, 115 US 620, 623, 29 L Ed 483, 484, 6 S Ct 209.

long arm statute. A statute providing for constructive or substituted service of process on a nonresident motorist in case such motorist becomes involved in an accident while using the highways in the jurisdiction in which such statute has been enacted, and leaves the jurisdiction before any legal action against him growing out of the accident can be commenced. 8 Am J2d Auto § 849.

longevity pay. An allowance and payment made to certain officers of the armed forces, in addition to regular pay, of a specified per cent of their current yearly pay for each period of a specified number of years of service. 36 Am J1st Mil § 64.

long haul rate. The rate of a carrier which, considered in proportion to the charge made for a shorter distance, is more favorable to the shipper than the ordinary rate. 13 Am J2d Car § 205.

Long Island Sound. The body of water between Long Island and the mainland to the north, not inclusive of the independent bays connected therewith. Tiffany v Oyster Bay, 209 NY 1, 102 NE 585 (Colonial Long Island Charters, bounding grants by the Sound); Re Site for Hunts Point Sewage Treatment Works, 281 App Div 315, 119 NYS2d 391.

long on the market. See **long**.

long parliament. The English parliament under Charles the First in 1640, reduced in numbers in 1648, dissolved by Cromwell in 1653, and restored in 1659, and finally dissolved in 1660.

long quinto. Literally, long fifth. A name given to the Year Book containing a long and separate set of reports for the 5th year of the reign of Edward IV. This set of reports is distinct from the reports of the same year which are found in their proper chronological order in the Year Books 1-22 Edward IV. The fact that the separate reports were so great in number as to make an entire volume achieved for them the name "Long Quinto."
See **Year Books**.

longshoremen. See **stevedores**.

Longshoremen and Harbor Workers Compensation Act. A federal statute which provides, with certain exceptions, for compensation, for injuries occurring in maritime employment, in cases where recovery for the resulting disability or death through workmen's compensation proceedings may not validly be provided by state law. 33 USC §§ 901 et seq; 58 Am J1st Workm Comp § 124.

long-staple wool. See **worsted**.

long ton. A measure of avoirdupois weight; the equivalent of 2,240 pounds.

Longum tempus, et longus usus, qui excedit memoria hominum, sufficit pro jure (lon'gum tem'pus, et lon'gus ū'sus, quī ex-sē'dit me-mō'ri-a ho'mi-num, suf'fi-sit prō jū're). Long time and long use, which go beyond the memory of man, take the place of right.

long vacation (lông vā-kā'shọn). The vacation of the English courts which was from August tenth to October twenty-fourth in the law courts, and to October twenty-eighth in chancery, but is now from August thirteenth to October twenty-third for both.

looking and listening. The duty of a person upon approaching a railroad track with the purpose of crossing it. The duty of using the senses in a way that an ordinarily prudent person would do under similar circumstances in order to determine whether it is safe to cross at that time and place. 44 Am J1st RR § 546.

lookout. Exercising the sense of sight with concentration, particularly for the purpose of avoiding injury to one's self or another. Constant vigilance on the part of a locomotive engineer to discover persons and things upon the track. 44 Am J1st RR § 386. Vigilance on the part of a motorist in anticipating and discovering the presence of other persons upon the highway. 7 Am J2d Auto § 355. A vigilant watch ahead required of the operator of a bus in order to prevent injury to other users of the street, whether such users are in vehicles or on foot. Alabama Power Co. v Bass, 218 Ala 586, 119 So 625, 63 ALR 1. A person other than the master, pilot, helmsman, or other officer or member of the crew of a vessel, whose sole business when on duty shall be to look for and report vessels and dangers ahead. 48 Am J1st Ship § 268. One who participates in the execution of a criminal offense by watching at the proper distance to prevent surprise of confederates at the scene of the crime. 26 Am J1st Homi § 65.

This word, as used in connection with the operation of a motor vehicle, has no technical legal significance; its meaning depends on the context. Devore v Schaffer, 245 Iowa 1017, 65 NW2d 553, 51 ALR2d 1041.

loom. A machine for weaving cloth. Hopewell Mills v Taunton Sav. Bank, 150 Mass 519, 23 NE 327.

loom beam. A fixture as an essential part of the loom in a cotton mill. Hopewell Mills v Taunton Sav. Bank, 150 Mass 519, 23 NE 327.

loose character. See **loose woman**.

loose-leaf account book. An account book in a form other than a bound volume, the book being so devised that sheets containing the accounts of individuals may be inserted or withdrawn at will.

loose wire. A wire, particularly a wire carrying an electric current, which has become detached from the pole or other device to which it is normally secured.

loose woman. A woman of loose character. An unchaste woman; a woman who is sexually impure. Foster v Hanchett, 68 Vt 319, 35 A 316.

loquela (lō-kwē'lạ). A discourse; a conversation; a talk; a speech; language.

Loquendum ut vulgus; sentiendum ut docti (lo-quen'dum ut vul'gus; sen-ti-en'dum ut dok'tī). A person should speak as the masses speak, and think as the learned think.

lord. A member of the British peerage; a feudal proprietor; an official title.

lord advocate (ad'vọ-kāt). The principal crown counsel in civil causes and the chief public prosecutor in criminal prosecutions.

Lord Brougham's Act. An English statute removing the disqualification of a party as a witness. 14 & 15 Vict c 99.

Lord Cairn's Act. An English statute conferring jurisdiction upon the court of chancery which permits it to award damages in lieu of an injunction. 28 Am J Rev ed Inj § 292.

Lord Campbell's Act. An English statute passed in 1846, allowing an action for death caused by the wrongful act, neglect, or default of another. 9 & 10 Vict c 93; 22 Am J2d Dth § 2.

lord chancellor. See **Lord High Chancellor.**

Lord Chesterfield's Act. An English Statute passed in 1751, adopting the Gregorian calendar.

lord chief baron (chēf bar'ọn). An English judicial officer who was formerly the chief judge of the court of exchequer.

lord chief justice (jus'tis). The chief judge of the English court of king's (or queen's) bench.

Lord Coke. See **Coke.**

Lord Cranworth's Act. An English statute passed in 1860 facilitating the functions of trustees and mortgagees by giving them the powers which they usually have by contract or appointment.

Lord Denman's Act. An English statute removing the disqualification of interest in reference to the competency of a witness. 6 & 7 Vict c 85.

Lord Eldon. One of the greatest and most conservative English chancellors. Edgerton v Edgerton, 12 Mont 122, 29 P 966.

lord high admiral (hī ad'mi-rạl). The highest officer of the British navy, and formerly the chief officer of the British courts of admiralty.

Lord High Chancellor. The presiding officer of the House of Lords in Great Britain.

Historically, the highest judicial officer in the kingdom, in rank superior to every temporal lord, created by the mere delivery to his custody of the king's great seal, a privy counsellor and prolocutor of the house of lords by prescription. He had the appointment of all justices of the peace, was keeper of the king's conscience, visitor in the king's right of all hospitals and colleges, the general guardian of all infants, idiots, and lunatics, and supreme judge of the court of chancery. See 3 Bl Comm 47.

lord high constable. See **constable of England.**

lord high steward. A member of the English house of lords appointed to preside therein in cases of felony and impeachment.

lord high treasurer. An officer who was formerly the chief treasurer of England.

lord in gross (in grōs). A feudal lord whose lordship was not attached to any manor.

lord justice clerk (jus'tis klėrk). The second highest judicial officer in Scotland.

lord keeper. An English officer who was the keeper of the great seal of the kingdom.

Lord Lyndhurst's Act. An English statute rendering void marriages of persons within certain degrees of relationship.

lord mayor's court (mā'ọrz kort). An English court of limited jurisdiction in both law and equity cases, held in London.

lord of a manor (of a man'ọr). The proprietor or owner of a manor.

lord paramount. The king of England.

Lord's day (lôrdz' dā). The Sabbath day; Sunday.

lordship. The jurisdiction of the lord of a manor; a manor. The title by which a lord is addressed, usually preceded by "your" or "his."

lords marchers (mär'chėrs). The lords of the marches of Wales and Scotland.

lords of articles (of är'ti-kls). A parliamentary committee which prepared bills for enactment and which was designed to increase the power of the crown, long since abolished by statute.

lords of parliament. The members of the English house of lords, the upper house of parliament.

lords spiritual (spir'i-tụ-ạl). Those bishops and archbishops who are members of the English house of lords.

lords temporal (tem'pọ-rạl). The lay lords,—those members of the English house of lords who are not lords spiritual,—who were neither bishops nor archbishops.

Lord Tenterden's Act. An English statute (9 Geo. IV, ch. 14) providing that no new promise should take a case out of the statute of limitations unless in writing, and signed by the party to be charged. 34 Am J1st Lim Ac § 289. Also extending the statute of frauds to cover a representation or assurance made or given, concerning or relating to the conduct, credit, ability, trade or dealings, of any other person, to the intent or purpose that such other person may obtain credit, money or goods thereon. 49 Am J1st Stat of F § 8.

lose. To fail of winning or of accomplishing a tie. To drop or otherwise handle something inadvertently so that one is unable to find it later.

To lose is not to place or put anything carefully and voluntarily in the place one intends and then to forget it; it is casually and involuntarily to part from the possession; and the thing is then usually found in a place or under circumstances to prove to the finder that the owner's will was not employed in placing it there. To place a pocketbook, therefore, upon a table, and to omit or forget to take it away, is not to lose it in the sense in which it is referred to as lost property. Foulke v New York Consol. Railroad Co. 228 NY 269, 127 NE 237, 9 ALR 1384, 1387.

loser. One who has lost something. One who has failed of winning or of accomplishing a tie.

As the word is used in a statute authorizing the "loser" in any game of chance to sue for and recover the amount he has lost, the term refers only to the person in whose name the bet or wager has been made, whether he be a principal or only an agent. Haywood v Sheldon (NY) 13 Johns 88, 90.

loss. A deprivation. Damage; also the act of losing and the thing lost. 22 Am J2d Damg § 1.

The word is not one of limited, hard and fast meaning. There are many kinds of loss, besides money out of pocket. No man would doubt that he might rightly call a "loss" that event which changed his status from solvency to insolvency. In the strictest sense of the word a man against whom a tort judgment has become final has suffered a loss. Schambs v Fidelity & Casualty Co. (CA5 La) 250 F 6, 6 ALR 1231, 1233.

Even though a showing of losses may be necessary to constitute the particular transaction a joint adventure, the term "loss" does not necessarily mean actual monetary loss. There is a loss if one's

LOSS [756] LOST

time has been for nought. Summers v Hoffman, 341 Mich 686, 69 NW2d 198, 48 ALR2d 1033.
See **actual total loss; constructive total loss; direct loss; fire loss; indemnity insurance; liability insurance; proof of loss; risk and causes of loss; total loss.**

loss and loss expense reserve. Terminology of insurers; the estimated amount payable for losses reported but not yet settled, plus a reserve for losses incurred but not yet recorded, including the estimated expenses of adjustment.

loss by breaking. See **breaking.**

loss by fire. See **fire loss.**

loss by theft. As a deduction in computing income tax:—a loss in the sense that the taxpayer is worse off financially as a result of the crime. Anno: 62 ALR2d 590.
See **theft insurance.**

loss claims reserve. See **loss and loss expense reserve; reserve.**

losses and loss expenses incurred. A phrase common to insurers; representing the total claims and losses paid during the year for which the insurer is reporting, plus the outstanding reserves for unpaid losses and claims at the end of the year, less the reserves for outstanding losses and claims as of the end of the previous year; also including the expense of adjusting and processing all losses and claims paid during the year plus the outstanding reserves for loss and claim expense at the end of the current year, less the reserve for loss and claim expense at the end of the previous year.

loss from liability. The loss which arises immediately upon one becoming liable to another and not the loss which arises upon the payment or extinguishment thereof. Anno: 37 ALR 646.
See **liability insurance.**

loss of arm. See **loss of member.**

loss of business time. An insurance term, meaning disability from working at one's specific occupation, irrespective of ability to perform other work. Anno: 31 ALR2d 1222.

loss of capital. See **capital loss.**

loss of consortium. The loss of a wife's society, companionship, and services. 27 Am J1st H & W § 505. The loss of society and sexual intercourse. 27 Am J1st H & W § 525.

loss of domicil. A matter of change of domicil, involving an abandonment of one domicil with an intent not to return to it as a domicil, and the acquisition of a new domicil by actual residence in such place with an intention of making it a permanent home. 25 Am J2d Dom § 16.

loss of earning capacity. An element of future damages resulting from a personal injury where the effect of the injury extends beyond the time of trial of the action for the injury in a decrease in earning capacity. 22 Am J2d Damg § 89.

loss of earnings. See **loss of earning capacity; loss of time.**

loss of eye. The actual deprivation of an eye or the deprivation of use of an eye for any practical purpose. Order of United Commercial Travelers v Knorr (CA10 Kan) 112 F2d 679.

loss of foot. A complete loss of the member by severance or an entire destruction of use of the member, as by paralysis. Fuller v Locomotive Engineers' Mut. Life & Acci. Ins. Asso. 122 Mich 548, 81 NW 326; Sheanon v Pacific Mut. Life Ins. Co. 77 Wis 618, 46 NW 799.

loss of jurisdiction. The cessation of the right to adjudicate concerning the subject matter in a given case, either by the termination of the power of the court or the destruction or removal of the subject matter. 20 Am J2d Cts §§ 149, 150.

loss of leg. See **loss of member.**

loss of limb. See **loss of member.**

loss of member. Loss of arm or leg. 29A Am J Rev ed Ins § 1510. Sometimes meaning an actual severance, at other times including loss of use. 58 Am J1st Workm Comp § 287.
See **loss of foot.**

loss of profits. See **lost profit.**

loss of sight. The deprivation of the use of one's eyes for any practical purpose.
It has been held that an accident resulting in a ninety per cent loss of sight of both eyes was not a loss of sight where the loss could be reduced to fifty per cent by the use of proper glasses. Cline v Studebaker Corp. 189 Mich 514, 155 NW 519.
See **loss of eye; total loss of sight.**

loss of time. An element of damages for personal injury confined to time prior to trial of the action therefor, being inability of the plaintiff to follow his ordinary pursuits regardless of whether he was being compensated therefor at the time of the accident. 22 Am J2d Damg § 89. Loss of working time. 29A Am J Rev ed Ins § 1514.
See **loss of business time.**

loss of use. An element of damages as an interference with the plaintiff's right to use the property involved, usually measured by rental value or the reasonable cost of hiring a replacement. 22 Am J2d Damg § 152.
See **loss of member.**

loss of wife's society. See **loss of consortium.**

loss payable clause. A provision in a policy of insurance on property taken out by the owner that the loss, if any, shall be paid to a mortgagee, or other person having an' interest in the property, as his interest may appear. 29 Am J Rev ed Ins §§ 728 et seq.

loss ratio. Terminology of insurers; a ratio arrived at by measuring losses incurred, plus loss adjustment expenses, incurred against premiums earned.
See **premium earned.**

lost corner. A point of a survey of land, the position of which cannot be determined beyond reasonable doubt, either from traces of the original marks or from acceptable evidence or testimony bearing on the original position, and the location of which can be restored only by reference to one or more independent corners. Reid v Dunn, 201 Cal App 2d 612, 20 Cal Rptr 273.

lost deed. See **lost instrument.**

lost grant. The fiction whereunder it is presumed from long possession and exercise of a right in real estate with acquiescence of the owner that there must have been originally a grant by the owner which has become lost. 25 Am J2d Ease § 39. The presumption that one, who has for a long time been in interrupted possession of real property and committing acts thereon ostensibly of a proprietary nature, maintained such possession and committed such acts under an ancient or lost grant of title. 3 Am J2d Adv P § 3.

lost instrument. A written instrument, such as contract, deed, mortgage, etc., which cannot be found after careful and thorough search, sometimes including an instrument which has been stolen, burned, or otherwise destroyed. 34 Am J1st Lost Papers § 2.

lost log. A log which in the course of floating upon a stream by way of transportation to a sawmill, has been washed ashore and stranded. 34 Am J1st Logs § 76.

lost monument. A monument mentioned in a description of real estate as marking a boundary, which has been destroyed or misplaced. 12 Am J2d Bound §§ 70, 71.

lost or not lost. A clause in a marine insurance policy whereby the coverage extends to a loss occurring prior to the date of the policy. 29 Am J Rev ed Ins § 327. A stipulation against past as well as future losses, and the law upholds it. Hooper v Robinson (US) 8 Otto 528, 25 L Ed 219.

lost profits. In contract actions, the profit which the nondefaulting promisee expected to make from the breached contract, or the profit which he expected to make from the collateral transactions based upon the promised performance. In tort actions, the expected gains from transactions which the injured party expected to complete had it not been for the tort. 22 Am J2d Damg § 171.

lost property. Personal property from which the owner has involuntarily parted through neglect, carelessness, or inadvertence. Danielson v Roberts, 44 Or 108, 74 P 913. Property casually and unknowingly dropped by the owner. Flood v City Nat. Bank, 218 Iowa 898, 253 NW 509, 95 ALR 1168.

lost record. A public record which cannot be found after careful and thorough search. 34 Am J1st Lost Papers § 3.

lost time. See **loss of time.**

lot. A small area of land; a building lot. as in a municipality. A wood lot, house lot, or store lot. A tract of land smaller than a field. Kaufman v Stein, 138 Ind 49, 37 NE 333. In a technical sense, a tract in a township duly laid out as a lot by the original proprietors. White v Gay, 9 NH 126. A tract of land indicated as a lot in the plan or map of a land development. As the word is used in a mechanic's lien statute:—the entire separate tract upon which the improvement or building, for which the lien is claimed, is asserted. Anno: 84 ALR 124.

In a distinct sense, a determination by chance; an object for determining by chance, be it nothing more than a bundle of long straws and short straws. Lynch v Rosenthal, 144 Ind 86, 42 NE 1103. That which one receives in a determination by chance.

See **cemetery lot; street water lots.**

lot and scot. See **scot and lot.**

lot book. A plat book.

lotion. A soothing or healing liquid applied to the skin, much used by barbers. 10 Am J2d Barbers § 19.

lot number. A designation referring to a number ascribed to a lot in the original plat, or an addition thereto, of a city or town. White v Gay, 9 NH 126. The number given a lot laid out by a survey, its purpose being to afford a means of description of the premises. 12 Am J2d Bound § 7.

lottery. A scheme for the distribution of a prize by lot or by chance. A scheme for the distribution of a prize or prizes by chance through selling tickets with numbers corresponding to numbers on tickets in a wheel or box from which the lucky number or numbers are drawn at a time previously announced. 34 Am J1st Lot § 2. A generic term, including any device whereby anything of value is, for a consideration, allotted by chance, State ex rel. Home Planners Depository v Hughes, 299 Mo 529, 253 SW 229, 28 ALR 1305, including policy playing, gift exhibition, prize contest, raffle, and other forms of gambling. 34 Am J1st Lot § 2.

lottery ticket. See **having lottery tickets in possession; lottery.**

lotto. A game of chance, a gambling device where played for money. 24 Am J1st Gaming § 36.

See **bingo.**

loud and raucous. The characterization of a sound interfering with the peace and quiet of a person. Haggerty v Associated Farmers of California, Inc. 44 Cal 2d 60, 279 P2d 734.

Louisiana law. The law of the State of Louisiana which has its background in the civil or continental law rather than the common law.

L'ou le ley done chose, la ceo done remedie a vener a ceo (loo luh lay dōn shōz, la sō dōn rē-mē-dee ah vĕ-nay ah sō). Wherever the law gives a right, it gives a remedy to recover.

lounging. See **loitering.**

love and affection. A good but not a valuable consideration necessary to support a bill or note. 11 Am J2d B & N § 222. A good consideration for a deed where extended toward one to whom a natural duty exists, such as near relatives by either consanguinity or affinity, or based upon a strong moral obligation supported either by some antecedent legal obligation, unenforceable at the time, or by some present equitable duty. 23 Am J2d Deeds § 64.

lovely claim. A donation made by the general government, of two quarter sections of the public lands, according to the legal subdivisions of the public surveys, to a particular class of persons, who are embraced by the act of Congress of the twenty-fourth of May, 1828, and who have complied with the conditions therein imposed, and also with the stipulations of the treaty ratified between the United States and the Cherokee nation of Indians on the twenty-eighth of May, 1828. Logan v Moulder, 1 Ark 313.

love-making. One of the arts of seduction. 47 Am J2d Seduc § 68.

low. Lacking in dignity, refinement, or principle; vulgar; groveling; abject; mean, base; in a mean condition, as a low-born fellow. Arkansas v Kansas & T. Coal Co. (CC Ark) 96 F 353, 362.

low bote (lō bōt). Compensation for the killing of a person in a riot or tumult.

lowboy. A chest of drawers standing on short legs. A trailer used in the trucking and draying business to transport heavy objects. Utica Carting, Storage & Contracting Co. v World Fire & Marine Ins. Co. 277 App Div 483, 100 NYS2d 941, 36 ALR2d 500, reh and leave to app den 278 App Div 629, 102 NYS2d 637.

low-cost housing. Housing for people of small means or persons on welfare.

lower court. An expression of dual meaning: (1) a trial court as distinguished from the court to which an appeal from its judgment is taken; (2) an inferior court.

lower house. The less important of the two houses of a legislative body; as the house of representatives of the Congress of the United States.

lowering grade. An alteration of a highway by cutting away a hill or incline.

lower offense. See **included offense.**

lower owner. A riparian owner whose land is downstream in reference to the land of another such owner.

lowers (lō'ers). Derived from the French "louer;" a seaman's wages.

lowest balance doctrine. The modern rule that in order to trace a trust fund, deposited as such in a bank, into the hands of a receiver of the bank, it is only necessary to show that the lowest level of cash in the vaults of the bank never fell below the amount of the fund. Ferguson v Reed (DC Pa) 44 F 387.

lowest reasonable rate. A rate which is not confiscatory in the constitutional sense. Federal Power Com. v Natural Gas Pipeline Co. 315 US 575, 86 L Ed 1037, 62 S Ct 736.

lowest responsible bidder. A bidder on a public contract to be selected by the officers with the exercise of sound discretion, not necessarily the lowest bidder in dollars, but just as clearly not the highest bidder. McIntosh Road Materials Co. v Woolworth, 365 Pa 190, 74 A2d 384.

A municipality may exercise a reasonable discretion in determining the lowest responsible bidder on items of equipment not capable of precise specifications and, in so doing, may consider, in addition to the bid price, substantial differences in quality, suitability, and adaptability of the equipment for the intended use. Otter Tail Power Co. v Elbow Lake, 234 Minn 419, 49 NW2d 197, 27 ALR2d 906.

See **responsible bidder.**

low flying. An unwarranted interference with a surface proprietor's rights. 8 Am J2d Avi § 4.

low-pressure gas line. A line of pipe through which gas for household use is conveyed at a pressure which renders it safe for household appliances. McKenna v Bridgewater Gas Co. 193 Pa 633, 45 A 52.

low temperature accelerators. See **cold vulcanization.**

low tide. The lowest point reached by the ebbing tide.

See **mean low tide.**

low-water channel. The channel of a river when, because of dry weather a minimum of water is in the channel. Cole v Missouri, Kansas & Oklahoma Railroad Co. 20 Okla 227, 94 P 540.

low water line. The line in the bed of a stream to which the water falls in the season of ordinary low water.

low-watermark. The lowest line made by the receding tide, not the lowest line which a stream of fresh water emptying into the sea, or a cove, or tidal river makes with the land. 12 Am J2d Bound § 13.

See **ordinary low-watermark.**

loyal. Faithful; lawful or legal in the sense of following constituted authority.

loyalty. Adherence to the government, a person, or a principle. Faithfulness or devotion to the government or to law, or to an employer, master, or superior.

loyalty check. A test of one's attitude toward the government and the possibility of his being involved in subversive activities by a course of detection respecting the character of meeting which he attends, the persons with whom he associates, and his past political record, also any criminal record which he may have.

loyalty oath. An oath, required of a public officer or employee, as a condition of employment or continued employment, by which the affiant not only pledges himself in the customary form to support the Constitution of the United States and of his particular state, but also affirms that he is not a member of certain designated organizations, such as the Communist Party, or of any organization believing in or advocating the doctrine of the overthrow of the Government of the United States by force or any unlawful means, and that he does not believe in or advocate such doctrine. 15 Am J2d Colleges § 12. An oath once required as a prerequisite, in certain instances, to maintaining or defending a civil action, the statute so requiring later being held unconstitutional. Pierce v Carskadon (US) 16 Wall 234, 24 L Ed 676.

L. R. Abbreviation of Lloyd's Register.

L.R.A. An abbreviation of **Lawyers' Reports Annotated.**

L.R.A. (N.S.) An abbreviation of **Lawyers' Reports Annotated (New Series).**

l.s. Abbreviation of **locus sigilli,** the place of the seal.

As to the effect of the letters "L.S." appearing on an instrument, as a seal, see 47 Am J1st Seals § 4.

l.t. Abbreviation of **long ton.**

ltd. Abbreviation of **limited.**

Lubricum linguae non facile trahendum est in poenam (lu'bri-kum lin'gwē non fa'si-le tra-hen'dum est in pē-nam). A slip of the tongue ought not to be readily subjected to punishment.

lucid interval. A period of sanity intervening periods of insanity.

The term means more than a mere remission of the manifestations of a person's insanity. It must be such a full return of his mind to sanity as places him in possession of the powers of his mind, enabling him to understand and transact his affairs as usual. Ekin v McCracken (Pa) 11 Phila, 534, 539.

lucrative bailee. The bailee of a lucrative bailment; a bailee for hire.

lucrative bailment. A bailment for hire. A bailment in which the parties contemplate some price or compensation in return for benefits flowing from the fact of bailment. 8 Am J2d Bailm § 9.

lucrative office. Same as **office of profit.**

lucrative succession. The gift by an ancestor to his heir of all or a portion of the property which the heir would inherit, rendering him liable for the debts of his ancestor.

lucrative title. A term having an origin in the Spanish law. A title derived by donation, inheritance, or

LUCRI [759] LUST

devise without onerous conditions attached. Fuller v Ferguson, 26 Cal 546.

lucri causa (lū′krī kâ′za). For the sake of gain. Anno: 12 ALR 804.

lucri gratia (lū′krī grā′she-a). For the sake of gain. Mann v State, 47 Ohio St 556, 26 NE 226.

lucro captando. See **de lucro captando.**

Lucrum facere ex pupilli tutela tutor non debet (lū′krum fā′se-re ex pu-pil′lī tū-tē′la tū′tor non de′bet). (Roman law.) A guardian ought not to make gain out of the guardianship of his ward. Manning v Manning (NY) 1 Johns Ch 527, 535.

luctuosa haereditas (luk-tu-ō′sa hē-rē′di-tās). (Civil law.) A sorrowful or mournful inheritance,—an inheritance in the ascending line, as by parents from children. 4 Kent Comm 397.

luctus. See **annus luctus.**

luctus tempus. See **intra luctus tempus.**

luggage. See **baggage.**

lumber. The product manufactured from logs. Building material. Craddock Mfg. Co. v Faison, 138 Va 665, 123 SE 535, 39 ALR 1309.

lumbering. The operation of taking logs from timber and sawing them into lumber. 34 Am J1st Logs §§ 52 et seq.

lumber measure. The actual number of board feet which have been obtained from the sawing of a log. Craddock Mfg. Co. v Faison, 138 Va 665, 123 SE 535, 39 ALR 1309.
See **board foot; log measure.**

lumberyard. A place where lumber is kept in large quantities for sale at retail.

lumen (lū′men). (Civil law.) Light; light in a house; a window; the right to receive light.

luminal. Another term for **phenobarbital.**

Lumley v Gye. An historical and famous case which enunciated the doctrine of liability for interference with a contract relationship. 2 El & Bl 216, 118 Eng Reprint 749, 1 ERC 706.

lumber. See **lumping.**

lumping. Making a sale for one sum in the aggregate without pricing by unit of measure, such as so much per pound, per bushel, per yard, etc. Vernacular in the field of labor law:—employing a so-called "contractor," who actually is a mere figurehead or "lumper" from the contractual standpoint, furnishing the labor and acting as superintendent of construction, the owner purchasing the material and assuming the responsibility in connection with the contract. People v Weinseimer, 117 App Div 603, 102 NYS 579.

lump-sale. See **sale en masse.**

lump sum. One sum covering all amounts to be paid.

lump-sum alimony. An award of alimony in gross, that is, an award of one definite sum in the aggregate, whether or not it is to be paid in instalments or in one sum. 24 Am J2d Div & S § 614.

lump-sum payment. A payment in one sum, as distinguished from payment in instalments or at intervals.

lump-sum price. See **lumping.**

lump-sum settlement. The commutation of periodical payments into one lump sum to be accepted as in full payment and satisfaction. 58 Am J1st Workm Comp § 548.

lump-sum verdict. A verdict in one sum without specification of the amounts allowed for separate items of damages or as interest. 53 Am J1st Trial §§ 1053, 1054.

lunacy. A misguided or erroneously directed condition of the mind. An impairment of one or more of the mental faculties sufficient to cause instability of mental powers and want of full capacity to reason. 29 Am J Rev ed Ins Per § 3.
See **lunatic.**

lunacy proceeding. A proceeding to determine the mental competency of a person, the purpose being to commit the person to an institution if found to be mentally deranged so that he should be confined, or to obtain the appointment of a guardian or committee for him if found mentally incompetent to manage his own affairs.

lunar month. A month of 28 days. 52 Am J1st Time § 11.

lunatic. An insane person. People v Wells, 33 Cal 2d 330, 202 P2d 53, cert den 338 US 836, 94 L Ed 510, 70 S Ct 43. One incapable from unsoundness of mind to control himself or his affairs. 29 Am J Rev ed Ins Per § 3.

lunatico inquirendo. See **de lunatico inquirendo.**

Lunaticus, qui guadet in lucidis intervallis (lu-nā′tikus, quī gâ′det in lū′si-dis in-ter-val′lis). He is a lunatic who enjoys lucid intervals.

lunation (lū-nā′shǫn). Same as **lunar month.**

lunch hour. The time taken off from employment or occupation for eating lunch; a variable time but normally one hour.

lunch vendor. A person who goes through a train selling lunches and sometimes other small articles of merchandise to passengers. 14 Am J2d Car § 913.

lung disease. A phrase usually associated with tuberculosis, although inclusive of any affliction of the lungs.

lung examination. An examination of the lungs for the detection of any diseased condition. A physical examination made by way of discovery. 23 Am J2d Dep § 220.

lupanatrix (lu-pā-nā′trix). A she-wolf; a prostitute.

lupinum caput (lu-pī′num ka′put). A wolf head, a person whom anyone might kill and receive a reward for his head,—an outlaw.

lupinum caput gerere (lu-pī′num ka′put je′re-re). To have one's head regarded as a wolf's, with a bounty for its capture,—to be outlawed.

lupus (lū′pus). A wolf.

lurch. A sudden and unexpected movement of an aircraft due to turbulent atmospheric conditions or other manifestation of nature. 8 Am J2d Avi § 96. A roll, pitch, or sway of a vehicle, in rounding a corner or otherwise changing direction abruptly.

lure to improvidence. The giving of a premium by a dealer to a purchaser of goods or a particular article. 52 Am J1st Trad St § 11.

luring. See **entice.**

lust. A strong desire for sexual relations. Anno: 19 ALR 1526.

lustful. Having lust.
See **lust.**

Lydford law. An allusion to violent acts in the nature of lynching, recorded in literature by Sir Walter Scott in the introduction to his Border Minstrelsy. Daniels v Homer, 139 NC 239, 51 SE 992.
"I oft have heard of Lydford law, How in the morn they hang and draw And sit in judgment after." State v Lewis, 142 NC 626, 55 SE 600.

lyef geld. (Saxon.) A fine which was exacted for leave to till the soil and raise crops.

lying. See **lie.**

lying at anchor. A vessel floating on the water, but held by her cable and anchor. Reid v Lancaster Fire Ins. Co. 19 Hun 284, 285.

lying-in expenses. Medical, nursing, and hospital expenses in childbirth.

lying in grant. See **lie in grant.**

lying in livery. See **lie in livery.**

lying in wait. Ambushing or concealing oneself for the purpose of taking a victim unawares. 26 Am J1st Homi § 16. Concealing oneself in a position to wait and watch for a victim with the intention of inflicting bodily injury upon such person or of killing him. People v Thomas, 41 Cal 2d 470, 261 P2d 1.

lying on. Bounding.
As the words are used in any instrument in the description of metes and bounds and location of land, as in the expression "lying on the north side of the mill road," they import in law, as well as in fact, that it extends to and borders upon the boundary designated in the description. Carson v Doe d. Hickman, 9 Del (4 Houst) 328, 337.

lying up. A vessel at berth. Dows v Howard Ins. Co. 28 NY Super Ct (5 Robt) 473, 475.

lynching. Putting a person to death, usually by hanging, ostensibly for the commission of a crime, but without authority of law.

lynch law. Something done without the warrant or sanction of law. State v Aler, 39 W Va 549, 559.
For discussion of derivation of the term, see State v Aler, 39 W Va 549, 558, 20 SE 585.
See also dissenting opinion of Brown, J., in State v Lewis, 142 NC 626, 55 SE 600.

M

M. A numerical symbol for one thousand, being the first letter of the word "mill," the one thousandth part of a dollar. The Roman numeral for one thousand. An abbreviation also of "meridian," signifying noon.
See **em**.

M. A. Abbreviation of Master of Arts.

macadam (mak-ad'am). A kind of surface of a highway.
See **macadamize**.

macadamize (mak-ad'am-īz). The making of a road surface by spreading successive layers of broken rock and binding such together by the application of tar or asphalt, the term deriving from the name of a Scottish engineer. 25 Am J1st High § 67.

Macedonian decree (mas-ē-dō'ni-an dē-krē'). A Roman law for the protection of young men against usury and denying an action to recover money from them if lent at a usurious rate.

mace proof (mās pröf). Immune from arrest.

macgrief (mak'grēf). A buyer of stolen meat or provisions.

machination (mak-i-nā'shon). A scheme, plot, or conspiracy to defraud.

machine. Something which utilizes, applies, or modifies force or translates motion. Rosenblad Corp. v United States, 49 Cust & Pat App 81. A device, either simple or complex, whose function is to increase the intensity of an applied force, or to change its direction, or to change one form of motion or energy into another form. Durst Mfg. Co. v United States, 50 Cust & Pat App 56. With less precision, a mechanical device or combination of devices to perform some function and produce a certain effect. Central Trust Co. v Sheffield & B. Coal, Iron & R. Co. (CC Ala) 42 F 106.

machine for voting. See **voting machine**.

machine gun. An automatic firearm firing a continuous stream of bullets. Commonwealth v Colton, 333 Mass 607, 132 NE2d 398, 399.

Machine Gun Act. One of the uniform statutes. 56 Am J1st Weap § 5.

machinery. A machine plus appurtenances necessary to the working of the machine. Anno: 91 ALR 541; 32 Am J1st L & T § 843. A machine or the constituent parts of a machine taken collectively; any combination of mechanical means designed to work together in accomplishing a given result. Murphy v O'Neil, 204 Mass 42, 90 NE 406. A machine or engine and its working parts, also the means, appliances, and attachments by which the machine or engine becomes effectively operative for its purpose. 29 Am J Rev ed Ins § 302.

mactator (mak-tā'tor). A murderer.

mad. Madness.

mad dog. A dog afflicted with rabies.
See **rabies**.

made. Signed and delivered as a negotiable instrument. 12 Am J2d B & N § 1103.
See **case made**.

made and executed. In reference to a deed, usually the equivalent of signed, sealed, and delivered. 23 Am J2d Deeds § 20.

made known to me by introduction. A clause in a certificate of acknowledgment showing the source of the officer's knowledge of the identity of the person acknowledging the instrument. 1 Am J2d Ack § 71.

made land. Land which has been reclaimed from the waters by filling out into a lake or other body of water from the shore. Carli v Stillwater Street Railway & Transfer Co. 28 Minn 373, 10 NW 205.

madman. See **madness**.

madness. Insanity or mental derangement, especially in a form resulting in violent acts or other manifestation of acute derangement of the mind. A word which was apparently employed by the earlier writers on the subject of insanity to include almost every form of mental derangement. Owing's Case (Md) 1 Bland Ch 370.

mad parliament (mad pär'li-ment). A council held in 1258 to adjust the differences existing between King Henry the Third and the barons, which provided for the king's closer observance of Magna Charta and other reforms.

mad point. The idea or object upon which a monomania, in any given case, is centered. Owing's Case (Md) 1 Bland Ch 370.
See **monomania**.

maeg. (Saxon.) A kinsman.

maegbot. Same as **maegbote**.

maegbote (Saxon.) Compensation for the killing of a kinsman.

maelstrom (māl'strom). A violent whirlpool. A state of agitation, literal or figurative. Any destructive or wide-reaching noxious influence. Wisner v Nichols, 165 Iowa 15, 143 NW 1020.

maeremium (mē-re'mi-um). Lumber for building.

magazine. A receptacle in which anything is stored; a storehouse; a warehouse. State v Sprague, 149 Mo 409, 419, 50 SW 901. Particularly a place for the storage of explosives. A periodical publication.

magis (ma'jis). More; the more; in a higher degree.

Magis de bono quam de malo lex intendit (mā'jis dē bō'nō quam dē mā'lō lex in-ten'dit). The law inclines rather toward that which is good than toward that which is bad.

Magis dignum trahit ad se minus dignum (mā'jis dig'-num trā'hit ad sē mī'nus dig'num). The more worthy appropriates to itself the less worthy.

Magis fit de gratia quam de jure (mā'jis fit dē grā'shē-a quam dē jū're). It was done more as a matter of favor than of right.

magister (ma-jis'tėr). A master; a chief; a head; a ruler; an instigator; a manager.

magister ad facultates (ma-jis'ter ad fa-kul-tā'tēz). An ecclesiastical officer who granted dispensations.

magister cancellariae (ma-jis'ter kan-sel-lā'ri-ē). A master in chancery.

magisterial (maj-is-tē'ri-al). Relating or pertaining to a magistrate or his functions.

magisterial precinct. The area or district which constitutes the territorial jurisdiction of a justice of the peace and sometimes serves as an election district or precinct. Breckinridge County v M'Cracken

(CA6 Ky) 61 F 191, 194 (referring to the term as known to the bar in Kentucky.)

magister litis (ma-jis'ter li'tis). The master or person in control of the suit or litigation.

magister navis (ma-jis'ter nā'vis). The master of a ship.

Magister rerum usus (ma-jis'ter rē'rum ū'sus). Use is the master of things.

Magister rerum usus; magistra rerum experientia (ma-jis'ter rē'rum ū'sus; ma-jis'tra rē'rum ex-pe-ri-en'she-a). Use is the master of things; experience is the mistress of things.

magister societatis (ma-jis'ter so-si-e-tā'tis). (Civil law.) The manager of an association or partnership.

magistra (ma-jis'tra). A mistress; female manager.

magistralia brevia (ma-jis-trā'li-a brē'vi-a). Magisterial writs,—writs which were drawn by masters in chancery.

magistrate. A judge or justice of an inferior court; a mayor; a justice of the peace. A judge of court, such as a police court, mayor's court, or justice's court, the jurisdiction of which is restricted to the trial of misdemeanors and the conducting of preliminary hearings upon charges of more serious offenses.

In a broader sense, a magistrate is a public civil officer invested with some part of the legislative, executive, or judicial power given by the Constitution. The President of the United States is the chief magistrate of the nation; the governors are the chief magistrates in their respective states. Childers v State, 30 Tex App 160, 195, 16 SW 903. For the purposes of extradition, any person regarded as a magistrate under the law of the state where the alleged crime was committed. 31 Am J2d Extrad § 39.

See **committing magistrate; preliminary hearing.**

magistrate's certificate. A certificate required by the terms of some fire insurance policies to accompany proofs of loss, to be procured by the insured from the nearest magistrate, notary public, or other officer, stating that the loss was sustained without fraud. Kelly v Sun Fire Office, 141 Pa 10.

magistratus (ma-jis-trā'tus). (Civil law.) A magistrate; a high Roman official.

magna assisa (mag'na as-sī'sa). The grand assize,—an optional substitute for a trial by battel, which was a trial before a jury of sixteen men. See 3 Bl Comm 341.

magna assisa eligenda (mag'na as-sī'sa e-li-jen'da). A writ for the choosing of the grand assize.

magna avena (mag'na a-vē'na). Great cattle,—animals of the bovine species.

Magna Carta (mag'nạ kär'tạ). Same as **Magna Charta.**

Magna Charta. A charter of liberties, now found to be embodied in some form in every one of the American Constitutions; guaranteeing that every person shall be protected in the enjoyment of his life, liberty, and property, except as they may be declared to be forfeited by the judgment of his peers or the law of the land; issued by King John, at the demand of the barons, June 15, 1215, confirmed, with some changes, 9 Hen. III and 25 Edw. I.

For the full text of Magna Charta, see Am J2d Desk Book Document 4.

Magna Charta et Charta de Foresta sont appele les deux grand charters (mag'na kar'ta et kar'ta de fo-res'ta sôn a-pel'lā duh grän chär'ters). Magna Charta and Charta de Foresta—the Charter of the Forest—are called the two great charters.

magna componere parvis (mag'na kom-pō'ne-re par'vis). To compare great things with little things.

magna culpa (mag'na kul'pa). Gross negligence; great fault.

Magna culpa dolus est (mag'na kul'pa do'lus est). Gross neglect or fault is the equivalent of fraud.

magna curia. See **curia magna.**

Magna negligentia culpa est; magna culpa dolus est (mag'na neg-li-jen'she-a kul'pa est; mag'na kul'pa do'lus est). Gross negligence is fault; gross fault is equivalent to fraud. Beers v Boston & Albany Railroad Co. 67 Conn 417, 34 A 541.

magna precaria. See **precariae.**

magna serjeantia (mag'na ser-je-an'she-a). Grand serjeanty,—a tenure in capite like knight service, but which did not include either personal attendance on the king or escuage. See 2 Bl Comm 73.

magnesia. See **milk of magnesia.**

magnetic healer. One who practices a special or limited system of healing the sick. 41 Am J1st Phys & S § 31.

magnetic meridian. A great circle of the earth which passes through the magnetic, rather than the geographical, poles of the earth. 12 Am J2d Bound § 59. A meridian established by the employment of a magnetic compass without allowing for deviations in direction from the true meridian on account of magnetic variations in the needle of the compass.

In the earlier private surveys made in the United States, it seems to have been the practice to run lines on the ground according to the magnetic meridian, and not according to the true meridian. 12 Am J2d Bound § 59. The Congressional survey of public lands is according to the true meridian. 43 USC § 751.

magnetic variation. The variation from a geographical or true line caused by the influence of terrestrial magnetism upon the needle of the compass. 12 Am J2d Bound § 59.

magnum cape (mag'num kā'pe). Grand cape,—a judicial writ which lay to recover the possession of land when the tenant defaulted in a real action.

magnum concilium (mag'num kon-si'li-um). The great council,—the English parliament.

magnum concilium regis, curia magna, conventus magnatum vel procerum, assisa generalis (mag'num kon-si'li-um rē'jis, kū'ri-a mag'na, kon-ven'tus mag-nā'tum, vel prō-sē'rum as-sī'sa je-ne-rā'lis). The great council of the king, the high court, the assembly of the nobles, and the general assize. See 1 Bl Comm 148.

magnus rotulus statutorum (mag'nus rō'tu-lus sta-tū-tō'rum). The great roll of statutes, the great statute roll, beginning with Magna Charta and including the statutes following through the reign of Edward the Third.

maiden. An instrument anciently used in England for beheading capital offenders. A virgin but not in the absolute sense in all contexts. A young, unmarried woman, or female, but not necessarily a virgin and not necessarily one who has preserved her chastity. State v Shedrick, 69 Vt 428, 431.

maiden assize (a̱-sīz'). An assize which did not convict any person of a capital offense.

maidenhead. Same as **hymen**.

maiden name. The surname of a female before her marriage.

maiden rents. A fine paid by the tenant to the lord of the manor for license to marry off his (the tenant's) daughter.

maihem. Same as **mayhem**.

maihematus (mā-he-mā'tus). Maimed; wounded.

maihemium (mā-he'mi-um). Same as **mayhem**.

Maihemium est homicidium inchoatum (mā-he'mium est ho-mi-sī'di-um in-ko-ā'tum). Mayhem is inchoate or unfinished homicide.

Maihemium est inter crimina majora minimum, et inter minora maximum (mā-he'mi-um est in'tēr kri'-mi-na ma-jō'ra mi'ni-mum, et in'ter mī-nō'ra ma'ximum). Mayhem is the least among the greater crimes, and the grossest among the lesser ones.

Maihemium est membri mutilatio, et dici poterit ubi aliquis in aliqua parte sui corporis effectus sit inutilis ad pugnandum (mā-he'mi-um est mem'brī mu-ti-lā'she-ō, et dī'sī po'te-rit u'bi a'li-quis in a'li-qua par'te su'ī kor'po-ris ef-fek'tūs sit in-u'ti-lis ad pugnan'dum). Mayhem is the mutilation of a member of the body, and may be said to take place when anyone is so injured in any part of his body as to be rendered useless for fighting.

mail. Verb: To place a letter or other mail matter, properly enveloped or packaged, addressed and stamped, in a mail slot, mail chute, or mail box, provided by the post office department for the reception of mail, or to deliver a letter or other mail matter so prepared to a postman or letter carrier employed by the department. Anno: 63 ALR 932; 29 Am J2d Ev §§ 195, 196. Within the meaning of a cancellation clause in an insurance policy:—to deposit a letter containing a notice of cancellation in the mail, irrespective of its actual receipt by the insured. 29 Am J Rev ed Ins § 386. Noun: Letters, packets, etc. deposited or received for transmission by post to the person or persons to whom they are addressed, in accordance with the postal regulations. 41 Am J1st P O § 48.

The original meaning of the word was a covering, and the word thus came to be applied to the bag or packet in which letters and messages were placed, and later to the contents of the bag or packet.

See **acceptance by mail**; **competition with the mails**; **first-class mail**; **fourth-class mail**; **franking**; **letter**; **mailable matter**; **packet**; **parcel post**; **post-office**; **registered letter**; **second-class mail**; **third-class mail**; **using mails to defraud**.

mailability. The quality or condition of a matter which renders it mailable, that is, acceptable for transportation as mail. 41 Am J1st P O § 49.

mailable matter. Matter which may be lawfully conveyed in the United States mails, or be delivered by a postmaster or letter carrier. United States ex rel. Milwaukee Social Democratic Publishing Co. v Burleson, 255 US 407, 410, 65 L Ed 704, 708, 41 S Ct 352.

mailbag. The container in which mail is transported.

mail box. A receptacle for the deposit of mail, whether outgoing mail to be picked up by a carrier or mail arriving for a particular person.

mail car. The car on a train in which United States mail is transported. Cincinnati, Lebanon & Springfield Turnpike Co. v Neil, 9 Ohio 11, 12.

mail carrier. An employee of the government, through the post office department, for the free delivery of mail. 41 Am J1st P O § 32.

mail catcher (māl kach'ẽr). See **mail crane**.

mail clerk. A clerk engaged in the distribution of mail in a mail car on a train.
See **post-office clerk**.

mail coach. See **mail car**.

mail contract. A contract entered into between the government and a carrier for carrying mail matter over a fixed route for a definite period of time, at a specified rate of compensation. 41 Am J1st P O § 73.

mail correspondence course. See **correspondence course**.

mail crane. An upright post planted close to a railroad track with an arm which, when not in use, hangs by the side of the post, but when in use is extended horizontally toward the track, and from which a suspended mail sack may be taken while the train is in motion by means of an iron hook or "mail catcher" attached to the door of the mail car and operated by the mail clerk. International & Great Northern Railway Co. v Stephenson, 22 Tex Civ App 220, 222.

maile (mal). Rent-money.

mailed. See **mail**.

mail fraud. See **using mails to defraud**.

mailing. See **mail**.

mailing process. See **substituted service**.

mail matter. Letters, packets, etc. deposited or received for transmission by government post to the person or persons to whom they are addressed, in accordance with the postal regulations. 41 Am J1st P O § 48.
See **mailability**; **mailable matter**.

mail offense. An offense directed against the United States mail or an instrumentality of the mail service, such as a post office. A violation of postal laws. 41 Am J1st P O § 98.

mail-order divorce. Otherwise known as a Mexican divorce; a divorce in which the plaintiff, without ever becoming a resident of Mexico, corresponds with an attorney of that country who prepares the necessary papers, plaintiff signing and returning them to him, whereupon a divorce is granted in Mexico, without the presence of either party to the marital relation severed by the divorce.

Such a divorce is generally regarded as absolutely void. 24 Am J2d Div & S § 965.

mail stage. A stage coach used in carrying mail in an earlier day.

mail train. Any railroad train carrying United States mail; a railroad train carrying only United States mail.

mail zones. See **parcel post zones**.

maim. To mutilate a limb, member, or any essential part of the body of another. To commit the crime of mayhem.

The word is also used as a noun, and as thus used it has the same meaning as the word mayhem. See State v Johnson, 58 Ohio St 417, 51 NE 40.
See **mayhem**.

main. Adjective: Principal; leading; chief in importance, strength, extent, or length. Oregon, C. & E. Ry. Co. v Blackmer, 154 Or 388, 59 P2d 694. Noun: A pipe or conduit for the conveyance of water or gas, particularly along a street or highway. A mainsail or mainmast. The sea. In a sense now obsolete, a hand.

See **en owel main.**

main action. Same as **principal action.**

mainad. False swearing; perjury.

main a main (măn ah măn). At once; immediately.

main channel. The channel through which the current courses to best advantage, usually the deeper and more navigable channel of a river of two or more channels at a particular point of the stream.

The description of a boundary line as formed by the center of the "main channel" of a designated river is too indefinite, in many instances, to constitute a description which can be traced. Michigan v Wisconsin, 270 US 295, 311, 70 L Ed 595, 602, 46 S Ct 290.

See **main river.**

main employment. See **principal employment or business.**

mainoevre. Same as **mainovre.**

mainour (mā′nọr). See **in manu; with the mainour.**

mainovre (ma-noo′vre). Handwork; manual labor.

mainpernable (măn′pẽr-nạ-bl). Bailable; that is, admitting of bail, as, a bailable offense; entitled to bail, as, a bailable prisoner.

mainpernors (măn′pẽr-nọrs). Sureties on a bond or undertaking for the appearance of a defendant.

See **mainprise.**

mainprise (măn′prīz). A writ directed to the sheriff, either generally, when a man was imprisoned for a bailable offense, and bail had been refused, or specially, when the offense or cause of commitment was not properly bailable below, commanding him to take mainpernors, or sureties, for the prisoner's appearance. See 3 Bl Comm 128.

The word is often used in the old books as synonymous with the word "bail," and both are obligations for the appearance of a party and to save him from imprisonment, and the chief difference is said to be that a man's mainpernors are barely his sureties, and cannot imprison him themselves to secure his appearance, as his bail may. Toles v Adee, 84 NY 222, 240.

main river. The principal stream of a river system, as distinguished from the branches or tributaries.

See **main channel.**

main seas. The high seas. United States v Bevans (US) 3 Wheat 336, 4 L Ed 403.

main stem. A slang expression for main line of a railroad. Anno: 80 ALR 279. Also slang for the principal street of a municipality.

main stream. See **main river.**

mainstream. A new word coined in political circles for the current general course of social, economic, and political events.

main street. See **main stem; main thoroughfare.**

mainsworn (măn′sworn). Handsworn,—the condition of a person who has committed perjury after having made oath with his hand on the Book.

maintain. To support; to keep in condition; to sustain.

When the word is used with the word construct, it must be held to relate more closely to the structure itself of a building than to such an operation as keeping the floors of the building clean. Juul v School Dist. 168 Wis 111, 169 NW 309, 9 ALR 904, 907.

"We cannot yield our assent to the contention that the word 'maintain' ordinarily means to maintain indefinitely or forever. Its meaning in that respect depends upon the context in which it appears and the subject matter to which it relates." Hasman v Elk Grove Union High School, 76 Cal App 629, 245 P 464.

maintainable action. An action capable of being maintained; capable of being sustained or entertained by a court. McLaughlin v Upton, 2 Wyo 32, 45.

maintain an action. To uphold, continue on foot, and keep from collapse a suit already begun. Smallgood v Gallardo, 275 US 56, 72 L Ed 152, 48 S Ct 23; National Fertilizer Co. v Fall River Five Cents Savings Bank, 196 Mass 458, 82 NE 671.

As used in § 16(b) of the Fair Labor Standards Act providing that an action to recover unpaid overtime and liquidated damages "may be maintained in any court of competent jurisdiction," it has been held that the phrase was merely used to confer jurisdiction on the state courts and not to restrict the operation of the removal statute. But a majority of the cases hold that the phrase in effect amends, or creates an exception to the operation of, the removal statute, giving the employee the right to select the forum in which to prosecute the action to a conclusion, and deprives the defendant of the right to remove the action. The disagreement is due almost entirely to the uncertainty as to the true meaning of the word "maintained." The courts following the first view hold that it means merely that the action may be "commenced" in any court of competent jurisdiction, and that if it is brought in a state court it may be prosecuted to a conclusion there if the defendant does not remove it; but the majority interpret the word "maintained" to mean "prosecute to judgment," so that the statute in effect provides that if the plaintiff brings the action in a state court of competent jurisdiction he may prosecute it there to judgment notwithstanding the desire of the defendant to remove the case to the Federal court. Anno: 172 ALR 1163.

maintain and provide for. In reference to the duty of a husband, the furnishing of support which is reasonable under the circumstances, particularly the husband's financial condition. State v Fredercici, 269 Mo 689, 192 SW 464.

maintain in any court of competent jurisdiction. See **maintain an action.**

maintainor (măn-tā′nọr). A person guilty of the offense of maintenance.

maintenance. Making repairs and otherwise keeping premises or instrumentalities in good condition. Support of a person. Wall v Williams, 93 NC 327. The act of improperly, for the purpose of stirring up litigation and strife, encouraging others either to bring actions or to make defenses that they have no right to make. Schaferman v O'Brien, 28 Md 565. An unlawful taking in hand or upholding of quarrels or sides, to the disturbance or hindrance of common right. Anno: 139 ALR 648. An officious intermeddling in a suit which in no way belongs to the intermeddler by maintaining or assisting either party to the action with money or otherwise, to prosecute or defend it; the intermeddling in a suit by a stranger, one having no privity or concern in the subject matter and standing in no relation of duty to the suitor. Gruber v Baker, 20 Nev 453, 23 P 858.

See **champerty; separate maintenance; support; trading in dormant titles.**

maintenance and cure. A term of the maritime law the real meaning of which is maintenance and care.

The duty to make provision for maintenance and cure is annexed as an inseparable incident to the relation of a seaman and his employers. The right of such maintenance is not restricted to those cases where the seaman's employment is the cause of his illness. Moreover, the obligation may continue after the termination of the voyage in which an injury is sustained or an illness begins. Calmar S.S. Corp. v Taylor, 82 L Ed 993, 303 US 525, 58 S Ct 651.

maintenance curialis (măn′te-nąns kū-ri-ā′lis). Maintenance in a court of justice,—as where one officiously intermeddles in a suit which is not his by assisting either party with money, or otherwise, in the prosecution or defense.

maintenance employee. An employee engaged in the repairing and upkeep of the premises of a business or industry, rather than in production or sales work.

maintenance of action. See **maintain an action.**

maintenance of highway. Keeping a highway in a state of repair. 25 Am J1st High §§ 52 et seq.

maintenance ruralis (măn′ten-ąns ru-rā′lis). Maintenance committed in the country, as where one assists another in his pretensions to certain lands, or stirs up quarrels and suits in the country, in relation to matters wherein he is no way concerned.

maintenant (măn′te-nąnt). Now.

maintes fois (mănt fwah). Many times; often.

main thoroughfare. A main street, particularly a street upon which a transit line operates. An interstate, intercounty, or farm to market highway. Heidle v Baldwin, 118 Ohio St 375, 161 NE 44, 58 ALR 1186.

mainzie. Same as **mayhem.**

maire (măr). (French.) A mayor.

mais (mă). (French.) But; but yet; however.

maison de Dieu (mă-zôn′ dŭh Dyŭh). (French.) A house of God; a hospital.

majestas. (ma-jes′tăs). (Roman law.) Majesty; royal power; sovereignty.

major. Adjective: Greater; more powerful; more important; more eminent. Noun: A military officer, ranking immediately below a lieutenant colonel and immediately above a captain.

majora et minora regalia (mă-jō′ra et mī-nō′ra rē-gā′li-a). The greater and lesser royal prerogatives. See 1 Bl Comm 241.

major and minor fault rule. The rule in admiralty, relative to collisions between vessels that were not equally at fault, that there is a rebuttable presumption, in favor of the vessel with the minor fault, that the major fault of the other vessel was the exclusive contributing cause of the collision. 2 Am J2d Adm § 206; 12 Am J2d Boats § 73.

major annus (mă′jor an′nus). A greater year,—a leap year with its three hundred and sixty-six days.

majora regalia (mă-jō′ra rē-gā′li-a). The greater royal prerogatives, including the royal dignity, the high political character of the king, his perfection, his sovereignty or pre-eminence, the sacred quality of his person and indeed all of the royal prerogatives excepting the rights of revenue. See 1 Bl Comm 241.

Majora regalia imperii praeeminentiam spectant; minora vero ab commodum pecuniarium immediate attinent; et haec proprie fiscalia sunt, et ad just fisci pertinent (mă-jō′ra rē-gā′li-a im-pe′ri-ī prē-ē-mi-nen′she-am spek′tant; mī-nō′ra vē′rō ab kom′modum pe-kū-ni-ā′ri-um im-me-di-ā′te at′ti-nent; et hĕk prō′pri-e fis-kā′li-a sunt, et ad jūs fi′sī per′tinent). The greater royal prerogatives appertain to the dignity of royal power; but the lesser have to do immediately with the acquisition of money; and these are properly fiscal and pertain to the right of revenue. See 1 Bl Comm 241.

Major continet in se minus (mă′jor kon′ti-net in sē mī′nus). The greater includes the lesser within itself.

Majore poena affectus quam legibus statuta est, non est infamis (mă-jō′re pē′na af-fek′tus quam lē′ji-bus stă-tū′ta est, non est in-fā′mis). A person who undergoes a greater punishment than that fixed or established by law is not infamous.

majores (mă-jō′rēz). (Roman law.) Persons of consequence.

major general. A high ranking officer of the United States Army, ranking immediately below a lieutenant general and immediately above a brigadier general.

Major haereditas venit unicuique nostrum a jure et legibus quam a parentibus (mă′jor hē-rē′di-tăs vē′nit ū-nī-ki′kwe nos′trum ā jū′re et lē′ji-bus quam a paren′ti-bus). A greater heritage comes to each one of us from justice and the laws than from our parents.

Majori summae minor inest (mă-jō′rī sum′mē mī′nor in′est). The lesser sum or amount is included in the greater.

majority. The age at which infancy terminates and the person acquires contractual capacity. 27 Am J1st Inf § 5. More than half of anything. Re Denny, 156 Ind 104, 59 NE 359.

See **age of majority.**

majority award. An award in arbitration in which the majority of, but not all, arbitrators concur. 5 Am J2d Arb & A § 131.

majority decision. A decision of the court concurred in by a majority but not all the judges sitting in the case, such decision generally being determinative of the case. 20 Am J2d Cts § 67.

majority interest. See **controlling interest.**

majority of electors. See **majority vote.**

majority of members. See **majority vote.**

majority of qualified electors. See **majority vote.**

majority opinion. In effect the opinion of the court; an opinion prepared or approved by a majority of the judges sitting in the case. 20 Am J2d Cts § 71.

majority stockholders. Stockholders of a corporation sufficient in respect of the number of shares held in the aggregate to elect directors and ultimately to control and direct the action of the corporation. 18 Am J2d Corp § 496.

See **majority vote.**

majority rule. The foundation of the republican system of government. Maynard v Board of Canvassers, 84 Mich 228, 47 NW 756.

majority verdict. A verdict having the assent of a majority of the jury. 53 Am J1st Trial § 1032.

majority vote. A vote of more than half for a candidate for office or a proposition submitted to the voters at an election. Necessarily the vote received by the winning candidate where there are only two candidates. 26 Am J2d Elect § 309. Of electors:—the choice of the majority of the persons voting, except as constitutional or statutory requirements call for a choice by the majority of all the eligible or qualified voters. 26 Am J2d Elect §§ 309 et seq. Of board of directors:—a majority of the directors present and constituting a quorum, unless there are specific provisions in statute, charter, or bylaws of the corporation requiring a larger number of directors to act. As to the Uniform Business Corporation Act, see 19 Am J2d Corp § 112. Of stockholders of a corporation:—a vote of a majority of the stock represented at a legally constituted meeting of the shareholders of a corporation, such being sufficient to decide any question properly presented, in the absence of statute, charter provision, or bylaw requiring more. 19 Am J2d Corp § 627. A majority in interest rather than in number of stockholders. Weinburgh v Union Street Railway Advertising Co. 55 NJ Eq 640, 646.
As to what constitutes a majority of members of a municipal council voting on an issue, see Anno: 43 ALR2d 698.
The "majority" contemplated by the provision of the Railway Labor Act that "the majority" of any craft or class of employees shall have the right to determine who shall be the representative of the craft or class, is a majority of those voting, although such majority may be less in number than a majority of the entire eligible membership. Virginian Ry. Co. v System Federation, 300 US 515, 81 L Ed 789, 57 S Ct 592.

Major numerus in se continet minorem (mā′jor nu′me-rus in sē kon′ti-net mī-nō′rem). The greater number includes in itself the lesser.

Majus dignum trahit ad se minus dignum (mā′jus dig′num tra′hit ad sē mī′nus dig′num). The more worthy appropriates or draws to itself the less worthy.

Majus est delictum seipsum occidere quam alium (mā′jus est de-lik′tum sē-ip′sum ok-si′de-re quam a′li-um). It is a greater wrong to kill one's self than to kill another.

majus jus (mā′jus jūs). A greater right; a better right.

Majus jus nostrum quam jus alienum servemus (mā′jus jūs nos′trum quam jūs ā-li-ē′num ser-vē′mus). We obey our own laws rather than those of another country. Smith v Union Bank of Georgetown (US) 5 Pet 518, 526, 8 L Ed 212, 215.

make. Verb: To build or construct. To accomplish. To execute an instrument, as, to make a promissory note; to sign; to collect money on an execution. Noun: A style or type.
See **made; made and executed.**

make a contract. To arrive at an agreement and to put it into effect as a binding obligation, including, in the case of a written contract, reduction of the terms of the agreement to writing and the execution of the instrument thus prepared.

make an assignment. To assign a chose in action, but in the most common sense of the term to assign property for the benefit of creditors. 6 Am J2d Assign § 1.

make an examination. To inspect public records. 45 Am J1st Recds § 14. To inspect corporate records. 18 Am J2d Corp § 178.
See **physical examination.**

make default. To come into default.
See **default.**

make few laws. A maxim of questionable propriety which is extended with less propriety:—make few laws, make them easy to obey and hard to break, and hang the man who breaks one.

make one's faith. Scottish for **to make one's law.**

make one's law. See **to make one's law.**

maker. One who obligates himself by entering into a contract, executing a promissory note, or drawing a bill of exchange.

makeweight. Something added to fill up space.
An argument was thus characterized in Pennsylvania v West Virginia, 262 US 553, 67 L Ed 1117, 43 S Ct 658.

making an order. The act of the court in announcing or otherwise rendering its order.
See **entry of court order.**

making false entry. See **false entry.**

making his law. See **to make one's law.**

making love. One of the arts of seduction. 47 Am J1st Seduc § 68.

making record. The mechanical act of preparing a record in writing, typewriting, or printing. The presentation of evidence for the record, usually with an appeal in mind.
See **offer of proof.**

making up train. The work in gathering the cars from sidings and placing them in a train for a trip. 35 Am J1st M & S § 446.

mala (ma′la). Bad; evil. Bad things; evil things; wicked things.

maladministration. Inefficient administration; bad but not necessarily corrupt administration. Minkler v State, 14 Neb 181, 183.

mala fide (mā′lạ fī′dē). In bad faith.

mala fides (mā′lạ fī′dez). Bad faith.

Mala grammatica non vitiat chartam (ma′la gram-ma′ti-ka non vi′she-at kar′tam). Bad grammar does not vitiate a deed.

Mala grammatica non vitiat chartam; sed in expositione instrumentorum mala grammatica quoad fieri possit evitanda est (ma′la gram-ma′ti-ka non vi′she-at kar′tam; sed in ex-pō-zi-she-ō′ne in-stru-men-tō′rum ma′la gram-ma′ti-ka quō′ad fī′e-rī pos′sit e-vi-tan′da est). Bad grammar does not vitiate a deed; nevertheless, in the drawing of instruments, bad grammar should, as far as possible, be avoided.

mala in se (ma′la in sē). Inherently wicked, naturally evil, as adjudged by the sense of a civilized community; illegal from the very nature of the transaction, upon principles of natural, moral, and public law; immoral in its nature and injurious in its consequences, without regard to the fact of its being noticed or punished by the law of the state. 21 Am J2d Crim L § 25. A wrong involving moral turpitude or delinquency. Horrabin v Des Moines, 198 Iowa 549, 199 NW 988, 38 ALR 544. Offenses

involving moral turpitude. Du Vall v Board of Medical Examiners, 49 Ariz 329, 66 P2d 1026.
See **contracts mala in se.**

Malam cerevisiam faciens, in cathedra ponebatur stercoris (ma'lam se-re-vi'she-am fā'she-enz, in ka-thē'dra po-nē-bā'ter ster-kō'rēz). The maker of bad beer was placed in a dung cart,—the punishment for knavish brewers during the reign of Edward the Confessor. See 4 Bl Comm 157.

mala mens (ma'la menz). Evil mind; bad intention. Flood v Templeton, 152 Cal 148, 92 P 78.

malam partem. See **in malam partem.**

malandrinus (ma-lan-drī'nus). A robber; a thief; a pirate.

mala praxis (ma'la pra'xis). Same as **malpractice.**

mala prohibita (ma'la prō-hi'bi-ta). Wrong only as forbidden by positive law. 21 Am J2d Crim L § 25. A crime not involving moral turpitude. Du Vall v Board of Medical Examiners, 49 Ariz 329, 66 P2d 1026. Evil because prohibited by law. 17 Am J2d Contr § 167. Wrong because prohibited by law but not immoral. Horrabin v Des Moines, 198 Iowa 549, 199 NW 988, 38 ALR 544.
See **contracts mala prohibita.**

malaria (mạ-lā'ri-ạ). A morbid condition of the body, formerly believed to be caused by inhalation of bad air coming off decaying vegetation in swamps and marshes, St. Louis v Galt, 179 Mo 8, 77 SW 876; now known as an infectious disease transmitted through the bite of a mosquito. Sometimes a chronic disease. American Life & Acci. Ins. Co. v Nirdlinger, 113 Miss 74, 73 So 875, 4 ALR 871.

mala soi qui mala pens (ma'la swä kē ma'la pens). Evil to him who evil thinks.

mala tolta (ma'la tol'ta). A heavy tax or toll; a burdensome or oppressive tax.

malconduct. A term sometimes applied to the unprofessional conduct of a lawyer. People v McCabe, 18 Colo 186, 32 P 280.
See **misconduct; misconduct in office.**

mal de lit. See **essoin de mal de lit.**

mal de venue. See **essoin de mal de venue.**

male (māl). A person or animal of the masculine sex; of the sex that begets offspring; of masculine gender.

male citizen. A citizen of the male sex.
The rule of construction under which females are included in words importing the masculine gender has been held not to apply in the interpretation of a code section prescribing rules for the admission of "male citizens" to the bar. Re Maddox, 93 Md 727, 50 A 487.

male creditus (ma'le kre'di-tus). Of bad credit; of bad or unfavorable reputation.

Maledicta est expositio quae corrumpit textum (ma-le-dik'ta est ex-pō-zi'she-ō kwē kor-rum'pit tex'-tum). That is a very bad interpretation which corrupts the text. State v Norfolk Southern Railroad Co. 168 NC 103, 82 SE 963.

malediction. A curse. Evil speaking. An ecclesiastical curse or anathema which was incorporated into grants to the church and which was directed at anyone who should thereafter interfere with their enjoyment or question their validity.

male estate tail. An estate tail in which the distinctive limitation is to male heirs of the donee's body. Restatement, Property § 78, comments B, C, D; 29 Am J2d Est § 45.

malefactor (mal'ẹ-fak-tọr). A person convicted of crime; a criminal.

malefactoribus in parcis. See **de malefactoribus in parcis.**

malefactors in parcis. See **Statute of Malefactors in Parcis.**

Maleficia non debent remanere impunita, et impunitas continuum affectum tribuit delinquenti (ma-le-fi'she-a non de'bent re-ma-nē're im-pū'nī-ta, et im-pū'ni-tās kon-ti-nu-um af-fek'tum tri'bu-it dē-lin-quen'tī). Evil deeds ought not to remain unpunished, for impunity offers constant encouragement to the wrongdoer.

Maleficia propositis distinguuntur (ma-le-fi'she-a prō-pō'zi-tis dis-tin-gu-un'ter). Evil deeds are distinguishable from plots; evil deeds are distinguishable by their purposes.

maleficio. See **ex maleficio.**

maleficium (ma-le-fi'she-um). An evil deed; a wrongful act; a tort; a crime.

male heir. An heir of the male sex.
See **nearest male heir.**

maleson (ma'le-son). A curse; a malediction.

malevolence. Ill will.
See **disinterested malevolence.**

malfeasance. The doing of an act which is positively unlawful or wrong. Allas v Rumson, 115 NJL 593, 181 A 175, 102 ALR 648. An act forbidden by law, or illegal, causing injury to the person or property of another. 35 Am J1st M & S § 588. Of public officer:—the performance of an act in an official capacity that is wholly illegal and wrongful. People ex rel. Johnson v Coffey, 237 Mich 591, 213 NW 460, 52 ALR 1.

malformation. An abnormal condition in the structure of the body or an organ thereof.

malgre' (mal-grā'). (French.) Against the will.

malice. A state of mind, being ill will, hatred, or hostility entertained by one person toward another. 34 Am J1st Mal § 2. More precisely, that state of mind which prompts the intentional doing of a wrongful act without legal justification or excuse. State v Heinz, 223 Iowa 1241, 275 NW 10, 114 ALR 959; Sall v State, 157 Neb 688, 61 NW2d 256. As a mental element in crime:—sometimes a connotation of ill will, but frequently merely the state of mind prompting a wrongful act without legal justification or excuse. 21 Am J2d Crim L § 86. As an element of murder:—a condition of mind prompting one to commit or direct an act wilfully; a wicked and corrupt disregard of the lives and safety of others; including all those states and conditions of mind accompanying a homicide committed without legal excuse or extenuation. 26 Am J1st Homi § 40. An intent to do the deceased great bodily harm. Commonwealth v Buzard, 365 Pa 511, 76 A2d 394, 22 ALR2d 846. As an element of malicious prosecution:—either personal malice or the malice indicated by an improper motive. 34 Am J1st Mal Pros § 45. Not necessarily ill will, hatred, or express malice, but a want of probable cause. Schnathorst v Williams, 240 Iowa 561, 36 NW2d 739, 10 ALR2d 1199. As an ingredient of libel or slander:—malice in law; malice in fact or express malice. 33 Am J1st L & S § 111. Importing a publication that is false and without legal excuse. Dixon v Allen, 69 Cal 527, 529. As an element of alienation of affections:—any wrongful or improper motive or intent to do a wrongful or improper act; not limited to a malignant and revengeful disposition and intent. 27 Am J1st H & W § 530. As an element of wrongful and malicious attachment:—either actual malice or legal malice. Brown v Guaranty Estates Corp. 239 NC 595, 80 SE2d 645, 40 ALR2d 1094. An improper motive, not necessarily positive malignity; a wilful disregard of the rights of another, whether in accomplishing an unlawful purpose or a lawful purpose by an unlawful means. 6 Am J2d Attach § 598.

See **actual malice; express malice; general malice; implied malice; particular malice; wilful and malicious act.**

malice aforethought. See **with malice aforethought.**

malice in fact. Actual malice; a positive desire and intention to annoy or injure another person. Gamble v Keyes, 43 SD 245, 178 NW 870. In overcoming privilege, a motive which induces the defendant to defame the plaintiff. Hemmers v Nelson, 138 NY 517, 34 NE 342.

malice in law. The intentional performance of an act harmful to another without just or lawful cause or excuse. Brown v Guaranty Estates Corp. 239 NC 595, 80 SE2d 645, 40 ALR2d 1094. The intent unlawfully to take human life in cases where the law neither mitigates nor justifies the killing. Mann v State, 124 Ga 760, 53 SE 324. The wilful violation of a known contract right. 30 Am J Rev ed Interf § 27. A wicked or mischievous intention; a wanton inclination to mischief; an intention to do wrong or injury to another; a depraved inclination to disregard the rights of others. Morasca v Item Co. 126 La 426, 52 So 565. As an ingredient of libel or slander:—a presumption of malice arising from the use of certain words, not necessarily inconsistent with an honest or even laudable purpose, implying neither ill will, personal malice, hatred, nor a purpose to injure. 33 Am J1st L & S § 111.

malice prepense. Same as **malice aforethought.** See **with malice aforethought.**

malicious. Actuated by malice. Wicked and perverse. Commonwealth v York, 50 Mass 93. Intentional in reference to the commission of a wrongful act by one person toward another, without legal justification or excuse. 34 Am J1st Mal § 2.

malicious abuse of process. A wilful and intentional abuse or misuse of process to attain an objective which is unlawful in itself or beyond the purposes for which the process may be legally employed. Anno: 14 ALR2d 322; 1 Am J2d Abuse P § 6.

malicious act. A wrongful act intentionally done without legal justification or excuse. High v State, 26 Tex App 545, 10 SW 238; 9 Am J2d Bankr § 786 (relating to liability excepted from discharge in bankruptcy). An act committed in a state of mind which shows a heart regardless of social duty and fatally bent on mischief. Bowers v State, 24 Tex App 542, 7 SW 249.

malicious arrest. The term applied where the arrest on which an action for malicious prosecution is based was under civil, not criminal, process; an action not essentially different from an action for malicious prosecution. Waters v Winn, 142 Ga 138, 82 SE 537. Causing an arrest by maliciously bringing a suit upon false charges, or maliciously making a false affidavit. Everett v Henderson, 146 Mass 89, 14 NE 932.

malicious attachment. See **malice; probable cause.**

malicious burning. An essential element of common-law arson. 5 Am J2d Arson § 11. An act of setting fire performed with a condition of mind that shows a heart regardless of social duty and bent on mischief, evidencing a design to do an intentional wrongful act toward another, or toward the public, without legal justification or excuse. Love v State, 107 Fla 376, 144 So 843.

malicious injury. A wrongful injury intentionally inflicted by one person upon another. State ex rel. Durner v Huegin, 110 Wis 189.

See **wilful and malicious injury.**

malicious interference with contract. See **interference.**

maliciously. With harmful motive and in wilful disregard of the rights of others. 34 Am J1st Mal § 2. For some purposes the equivalent of "wilfully and unlawfully." Chapman v Commonwealth, (Pa) 5 Wharton 427; 27 Am J1st Indict § 67.

malicious mischief. The wilful and unlawful injury to or destruction of the property of another with the malicious intent to injure the owner; a malicious physical injury to the rights of another, which impairs utility or materially diminishes value; a malicious or mischievous physical injury, either to the rights of another or to those of the public in general. 34 Am J1st Mal Mis § 2. As used in an insurance policy:—wilful or malicious physical injury to or destruction of the insured property; a reckless disregard of the owner's rights in deliberately injuring his property. General Acci. Fire & Life Assur. Corp. v Azar, 103 Ga App 215, 119 SE2d 82.

As to what constitutes "malicious mischief" within the meaning of an automobile comprehensive policy, see Anno: 43 ALR2d 604.

malicious misconduct. The wrong of an election officer for which he may be held liable to electors or to a candidate for public office. 25 Am J2d Elect §§ 47 et seq.

See **malicious mischief.**

malicious prosecution. A criminal prosecution begun in malice, without probable cause to believe it can succeed, and finally ending in failure. 34 Am J1st Mal Pros § 2. An action for damages brought by one against whom a criminal prosecution, civil suit, or other legal proceeding has been instituted maliciously and without probable cause, after the termination of such prosecution, suit, or other proceeding in favor of the defendant therein. Shedd v Patterson, 302 Ill 355, 134 NE 705, 26 ALR 1004; 34 Am J1st Mal Pros § 2. An action for the wrong of instituting a civil action without probable cause, especially where there is in such action a seizure of property or of the person of the defendant or other circumstances giving rise to special damages. 34 Am J1st Mal Pros § 10.

malicious prosecution of civil action. See **malicious prosecution.**

malicious use of process. In essence a form of malicious prosecution. The use of civil process without probable cause. Nix v Goodhil, 95 Iowa 282, 63 NW 701.

malign. To defame.

malignancy. A dangerous condition of the body, especially a cancerous condition. A condition of ill will or malevolence.

MALIGNANT [769] MANAGEMENT

malignant pustule (mạ-lig'nạnt pus'tųl). See **woolsorter's disease.**

malignare (ma-lig-nā're). To malign; to defame; to maim.

malinger (mạ-ling'gėr). To pretend or feign illness or sickness, usually to avoid labor, but sometimes with the idea of enhancing damages or collecting insurance.

malison (mal'i-zọn). Same as **maleson.**

malitia (ma-li'she-a). Malice.
See **ex malitia.**

Malitia est acida; est mali animi affectus (ma-li'she-a est a'si-da; est ma'lī a'ni-mī af-fek'tus). Malice is sour; it is an affection of an evil heart.

malitia implicita (ma-li'she-a im-pli'si-ta). Implied malice.

malitia praecogitata (ma-li'she-a prē-kō-ji-tā'ta). Malice aforethought; malice prepense; evil intended beforehand. See 4 Bl Comm 198-200.
See **with malice aforethought.**

Malitia supplet aetatem (ma-li'she-a sup'plet ē-tā'tem). Malice supplies age, a maxim is applied to offenses committed by children between the ages of seven and fourteen years. See 4 Bl Comm 23.

malo animo (ma'lō ā'ni-mō). With bad intent; with a wicked or evil heart.

malo lecti. See **essoin de malo lecti.**

malo sensu (ma'lō sen'sū). In a bad sense; with an evil or wicked meaning.

malo veniendi. See **essoin de malo veniendi.**

malpractice. The violation of a professional duty to act with reasonable care and in good faith without fraud or collusion, as in the case of a public accountant, 1 Am J2d Accts § 15, or a beautician. Ocean Acci. & Guarantee Corp. v Herzberg's Inc. (CA8 Neb) 100 F2d 171. By an attorney at law:—the failure to exercise on behalf of his client the knowledge, skill, and ability ordinarily possessed and exercised by members of the legal profession, whereby an actual loss is caused the client. 7 Am J2d Attys §§ 167 et seq. By physician or surgeon: —the wrong, for which a physician or surgeon is answerable to his patient where it results in injury to the patient, consisting in the want of that reasonable degree of learning, skill, and experience which ordinarily is possessed by others of his profession, the omission to exercise reasonable care and diligence in the exertion of his skill and the application of his knowledge, or his failure to exert his best judgment in the case entrusted to him. 41 Am J1st Phys & S §§ 79, 82. A cause of action predicated by law on the relation which exists between physician and patient, although supported by some cases on the theory of liability under a contract implied by law. 41 Am J1st Phys & S § 79.

malpractice insurance. See **physician's liability insurance.**

malt. Barley or other grain processed for brewing. Grain within the meaning of a statute imposing, in lieu of other taxes, a tax of a stated amount per bushel upon all "grain" received in or handled by an elevator or warehouse. Joseph Schlitz Brewing Co. v Milwaukee, 232 Wis 118, 286 NW 602, 122 ALR 1432.

malt beverage. See **malt liquor; near beer; small brew.**

malt extract (mâlt' eks"trakt). See **malt liquor; near beer; small brew.**

malt liquor. An alcoholic beverage produced by the fermentation of malt. 30 Am J Rev ed Intox L § 9.
See **small brew.**

malt mead. Same as **near beer.**

malt-tax (mâlt'taks). A tax of six pence a bushel on malt and a proportionate sum on certain liquors, such as cider and perry, first levied by parliament in 1697, the whole yielding an annual sum of seven hundred and fifty thousand pounds a year. See 1 Bl Comm 313.

Malum hominum est obviandum (ma'lum ho'mi-num est ob-vi-an'dum). The wickedness of men is to be opposed.

malum in se (ma'lum in sē). See **mala in se.**

Malum non habet efficientem, sed deficientem causam (ma'lum non hā'bet ef-fi'she-en-tem, sed dē-fi-she-en'tem kâ'zam). Evil has not an efficient cause, but a deficient one.

Malum non praesumitur (ma'lum non prē-zu'mi-ter). Evil is not presumed.

malum prohibitum (ma'lum prō-hi'bi-tum). See **mala prohibita.**

Malum quo communius eo pejus (ma'lum quō kom-mū'ni-us ē'ō pe'jus). The more common an evil, the worse it is.

malus animus (ma'lus a'ni-mus). Evil or bad intent. Flood v Templeton, 152 Cal 148, 92 P 78.

Malus usus est abolendus (mā'lus ū'sus est ab-ō-len'-dus). A bad custom should be abolished. Evans v Waln, 71 Pa 69, 75.

malveilles (măl-vā'yuh). Malevolence; ill will.

malveis procurors (mal'vay pro-kū'rorz). Persons who packed jurors, who used improper or corrupt means in their selection.

malversation (mal-vėr-sā'shọn). Official misconduct; corruption in office.

man. In the generic sense, a human being, whether male or female; all human beings; mankind. In the narrow sense, a male human being who has reached the age of majority, at least an age above puberty. State v Seiler, 106 Wis 343, 82 NW 167.

manacles. Handcuffs.

manage. To direct; to control; to govern; to administer; to oversee. Ure v Ure, 185 Ill 216, 218.
It has been held in a majority of the cases that a testamentary authorization for an executor or trustee to "manage" property includes the power of sale. Anno: 134 ALR 405; 23 ALR2d 1011.

management. Government; control; superintendence; physical or manual handling or guidance; the act of managing by direction or regulation; administration,—as the management of a family or of a household, or of servants, or of great enterprises, or of great affairs. Re Sanders, 53 Kan 191, 36 P 348. The executives in charge of a business, considered collectively.

management contract. A contract for the management, agency, or representation of an actor, musician, dancer, or other professional artist or entertainer. Anno: 175 ALR 621.

management functions clause. A clause in a collective labor agreement under which the right to select, hire, promote, discharge, and discipline employees and to determine work schedules is the sole prerogative of the employer, and his decision with respect to such matters is not subject to arbitration. NLRB v American Nat. Ins. Co. 343 US 395, 96 L Ed 1027, 72 S Ct 824.

Management Relations Acts. See **Labor Relations Acts.**

manager. One who has the conduct or direction of anything, as the manager of a theater. Commonwealth v Johnson, 144 Pa 377, 381. One in charge of the business or operations of another. The officer of a private corporation to which the general business of the corporation is entrusted; in some corporations, the head of one of several departments. 19 Am J2d Corp § 1174. The title of an officer of a business trust who is in charge of the business and managing its affairs. 13 Am J2d Bus Tr § 44. Descriptio personae as appended to the name of a payee of a bill or note and not destroying negotiability of the instrument. 11 Am J2d B & N § 115.

manager form of government. See **city manager.**

managing agent. A person invested by a corporation with general powers involving the exercise of judgment and discretion. Anno: 113 ALR 70 et seq. An executive of a co-operative apartment association. 15 Am J2d Con Apt § 21. As one upon whom service of process binding a foreign corporation can be made:—an officer or agent whose position, right, and duties make it reasonably certain that the corporation will be apprised of service made upon him. 36 Am J2d For Corp § 558. An agent whose contract of agency demands of him the exercise of judgment in the business affairs of his principal, and who has charge of all of the business of his principal in the territory covered by his contract. Ord Hardware Co. v J. I. Case Threshing Machine Co. 77 Neb 847, 110 NW 551. As one through whom a corporation may be examined by way of discovery or deposition:—one authorized to exercise judgment and discretion in dealing with corporate matters and expected to identify himself with the interest of the corporation. Anno: 98 ALR2d 626, 627, § 3[a, b].

managing employee. A term in an automobile liability insurance policy extending the coverage to one other than the named insured; an employee of the named insured who, at the time of an accident giving rise to liability, had the named insured's car under his control and direction and was acting within the scope of his duties. Continental Casualty Co. v Phoenix Constr. Co. 46 Cal 2d 423, 296 P2d 801, 57 ALR2d 914.

managing owner of ship (ō'nėr of ship). One of the several owners of a ship who acts as manager for them all.

managium (ma-nā'ji-um). A mansion,—a dwellinghouse and all within the curtilage thereof.

manas mediae (ma'nas mē'di-ē). Inferior persons.

man-bote (man'bōt). (Saxon.) A recompense paid to the lord of a manor for the killing of one of his tenants.

manche present (môn-sh pray-sôn). A present from the hand of the owner; a bribe.

mancipare (man-si-pā're). (Roman law.) To sell; to sell in a formal manner; to transfer; to give up.

mancipation (man-si-pā'shọn). (Roman law.) A sale of property attended with certain essential formalities.

mancipia quasi manu capti (man-si'pi-a quā'sī ma'nū kap'tī). Sold, as if taken by the hand. See 1 Bl Comm 423.

mancipium (man-si'pi-um). (Roman law.) An old form of purchase in which the thing sold was taken by the hand in the presence of five witnesses; a slave purchased in the manner above stated; a formal purchase or transfer.

mancomunal (man-co-moo-na'hl). (Spanish.) An undertaking to answer for the debt or obligation of another person.

mandamiento (man-dah-me-en'to). (Spanish.) A power of attorney.

mandamus. A command by order or writ issuing from a court of law of competent jurisdiction, in the name of the state or sovereign, directed to some inferior court, tribunal, or board, or to some corporation or person, requiring the performance of a particular duty therein specified, which duty results from the official station of the party to whom the writ is directed, or from operation of law. A coercive writ, one that commands performance, not desistance. 34 Am J1st Mand § 2. An extraordinary remedy. State ex rel. Ricco v Biggs, 198 Or 413, 255 P2d 1055, 38 ALR2d 720.

A writ of mandamus was originally a prerogative writ, but in this country, in modern practice, it is nothing more than an action at law between the parties and is not now regarded as a prerogative writ. 34 Am J1st Mand § 5.

Since mandamus was originally a prerogative writ, issuing in the king's name, it was not a civil action, but the character of the proceeding and the nature of the writ have been so changed by statute that in most of the states of the Union it is now regarded as a civil proceeding. Nevertheless the supreme court has repeatedly held that it is not a suit of a civil nature at common law or in equity within the meaning of the acts of Congress defining the jurisdiction of the federal courts. Western Union Tel. Co. v State ex rel. Hammond Elevator Co. 165 Ind 492, 76 NE 100.

See **alternative mandamus; peremptory mandamus; writ of mandamus.**

mandans (man'dans). Commanding; committing; entrusting.

mandant (man'dạnt). Same as **mandans.**

Mandata licita strictam recipiunt interpretationem, sed illicita latam et extensam (man-dā'ta lī'si-ta strik'tam re-si'pi-unt in-ter-pre-tā-she-ō'nem, sed il-lī'si-ta lā'tam et ex-ten'sam). Lawful commands receive a strict interpretation, but unlawful ones receive a broad and elastic one.

mandatarius (man-da-tā'ri-us). Same as **mandatary.**

Mandatarius terminos sibi positos transgredi non potest (man-da-tā'ri-us ter'mi-nos sī'bi pō'si-tōs trans'gre-dī non po'test). A mandatory cannot transgress the limits of his powers.

mandatary (man'dạ-tā-ri). The person to whom a mandate has been given. A bailee under a bailment of the class known as mandatum.

See **mandatum.**

mandate. An order; an authoritative command by the court. In technical significance, the official communication made of the judgment of a reviewing court to the court below and the direction given by the reviewing court as to the enforcement, reversal, or vacation, as the case may be, of the judgment below. 5 Am J2d A & E § 989.

mandator (man-dā'tor). (Civil law.) The person who makes a bailment of **mandatum;** one who gives a mandate.

mandatory. Imperative. Required to be done or performed. Compulsory, not a matter of discretion.
See **mandatary.**

mandatory clause. The part of an alternative writ of mandamus in the form of a command. 35 Am J1st Mand § 351.

mandatory constitutional provision. A provision of a constitution which leaves no discretion to the legislature in respect of obedience to, or disregard of, it, the use of the word "shall" sometimes being emphasized in construction as indicative of mandatory character. 16 Am J2d Const L §§ 90-92.

mandatory continuance. A continuance resulting by operation of law, as where a case is not reached for trial by the end of a term. 17 Am J2d Contin § 1. A continuance to which a party is entitled as a matter of right, for example, in some jurisdictions, a continuance because of the absence of counsel in attendance upon the legislature. Anno: 49 ALR2d 1074 § 1.

mandatory counterclaim. Same as **compulsory counterclaim.**

mandatory franchise. A franchise, performance of which by conducting the operation licensed is obligatory upon the grantee. Murray v Roberts (CA2 NY) 103 F2d 889.

mandatory injunction. An injunction which compels some positive action involving a change of existing conditions—some affirmative act or acts essential to restore the status quo. 28 Am J Rev ed Inj § 17.

mandatory order. An order which requires affirmative action to be taken. 2 Am J2d Admin L § 468.

mandatory provision. See **mandatory clause; mandatory constitutional provision; mandatory statute.**

Mandatory Securities Valuation Reserve. A reserve fund required to be maintained by insurance companies in some states for the purpose of absorbing fluctuations in prices of securities.

mandatory statute. A statute which leaves nothing to the discretion of the court in respect of compliance with its terms; a statute which relates to matters of substance, affects substantial rights, and is of the very essence of the thing required to be done. 1 Am J2d Admin L § 45; 50 Am J1st Stat §§ 180 et seq.
A "mandatory provision" in a statute is one which if not followed renders the proceeding to which it relates illegal and void. State v Parnell, 109 Ohio St 246, 142 NE 611.

mandatum (man-dā'tum). A bailment of goods without recompense, where the mandatary or person to whom the property is delivered, undertakes to do some act with respect to the thing bailed, as simply to carry it; a bailment of something for some gratuitous service upon it by the bailee. Briggs v Spaulding, 141 US 132, 148, 35 L Ed 662, 669, 11 S Ct 924; Maddock v Riggs, 106 Kan 808, 190 P 12, 11 ALR 216.

Mandatum nisi gratuitum nullum est (man-dā'tum nī'sī gra-tū'i-tum nul'lum est). A mandatum (bailment), unless gratuitous, is not one.

Mandavi ballivo (man-dā'vī bal'li-vō). I have commanded the bailiff,—a form of sheriff's return on a writ executed by his bailiff.

manens (ma'nenz). Remaining.

manerium a manendo (ma-ne'ri-um ā man-en'dō). "Manor," from "manendo," a place to remain or reside.
See **manor.**

Manerium dicitur a manendo, secundum excellentiam, sedes magna, fixa et stabilis (ma-ne'ri-um di'si-ter ā ma-nen'dō, se-kun'dum ex-sel-len'she-am, se'dēz mag'na, fi'xa et stā'bi-lis). Manor is derived from "manendo, par excellence," a great, fixed, and stable abode.

mangle. A machine constituting part of laundry equipment, being used for ironing. Quinn v Electric Laundry Co. 155 Cal 500, 101 P 794.
See **maim.**

manhandle. To handle a person roughly; to maul him.

Manhattan. A borough of New York City, consisting of the island of the same name. A cocktail, strong and stimulating, made of whisky, vermouth, and sometimes a dash of bitters, served cold after shaking in cracked ice.

manhole. An opening in a street or highway, permitting a man to go below for the purpose of inspection or work upon subsurface instrumentalities such as telephone wires, sewers, and pipe lines.

manhood. Resolute strength of character. The state of being a man. A feudal ceremony by which the vassal or tenant became the lord's man "from that day forth, of life and limb and earthly honor." See 2 Bl Comm 54.

mania (mān'i̯a). Violent insanity; an obsession or craze.
See **moral mania.**

mania a potu (mān'i̯a ā pō'tū). The same as **delirium tremens.**

maniac (mā'ni-ak). A madman; an insane person; a lunatic.

mania transitoria (man'i̯a trans-i-tō'ri-a). Emotional insanity; that is, the case of one in the possession of his ordinary reasoning faculties, who allows his passions to convert him into a temporary maniac. Mutual Life Ins. Co. v Terry (US) 15 Wall 580, 21 L Ed 236, 239.

manifest. Adjective: Evident to the senses; evident to the mind; obvious to the mind. Love v Mt. Oddie United Mines Co. 43 Nev 61, 184 P 921. Noun: In maritime law, a record or statement in writing, carried by a vessel, containing information with respect to the vessel's cargo, passengers, and other matters required by statute or regulation. 19 USC §§ 1431 et seq.; 46 USC §§ 91 et seq. A summary of all the bills of lading for the cargo of a vessel. The Newton Bay (CA2 NY) 36 F2d 729. One of a ship's papers; one to be presented to the customs officers upon the entry of any vessel into the United States. New York & Cuba Mail S.S. Co. v United States (DC NY) 125 F 320, 321.

Manifesta non indigent probatione (ma-ni-fes'ta non in'di-jent pro-bā-she-ō'ne). Those facts which are manifest do not require proof. Riley v Wallace, 188 Ky 471, 222 SW 1085, 11 ALR 337, 340.

Manifesta probatione non indigent (ma-ni-fes'ta prō-bā-she-ō'ne non in'di-jent). Manifest facts do not require proof.

manifest impediment. An impediment which operates to prevent a military court from exercising its

jurisdiction over a soldier charged with a military offense.
Such an impediment may consist of his being continuously a prisoner in the hands of the enemy, or of his being imprisoned under sentence of a civil court for crime, and the like. Re Davison (DC NY) 4 F 507, 510.

manifest incapacity. Obvious incapacity. In reference to a physician, a want of power to comprehend or to act, so obvious that no proof is necessary to establish it other than proof of the act or omission itself. Yoshizawa v Hewitt (CA9 Hawaii) 52 F2d 411, 79 ALR 317.

manifest injustice. As a ground for withdrawing a plea of guilty:—something more than the expectation of a sentence less severe than that actually imposed. Injustice from conduct improperly inducing accused to expect lenient punishment or from the accused's misunderstanding, reasonably entertained, of the trial judge's remarks, regarding the severity of the sentence that might be imposed. 21 Am J2d Crim L § 511.

manifest intent. The meeting of the minds of the parties to a contract as manifested by conduct, act, or sign. The intent of an instrument as it appears from the face thereof.

manifestly. Obviously.
Language which "manifestly" tends to the corruption of the youth must be such language as obviously and incontrovertibly has that tendency. It is not sufficient that it might tend to corrupt. Commonwealth v Buckley, 200 Mass 346, 86 NE 910.

manifesto (man-i-fes'tō). A public statement issued under the governmental authority of one nation, describing its reasons for its acts or attitude toward another nation. A statement to the public by an organization or group of people, social, economic, or scientific, of its policy or position with supporting reasons.

manifest theft. Same as **open theft.**

manifestus. See **fur manifestus.**

manipulation of prices. The artificial control or stabilization of security prices by a pooling arrangement or other joint adventure. 47 Am J1st Secur A § 12; 50 Am J1st Stock Ex § 26.

Mann Act. Same as **White Slave Traffic Act.**

manner. Way of performing or executing; method; custom; habitual practice. People ex rel. Ahrens v English, 139 Ill 622, 629.

mannire (man-nī're). To cite an adverse party to appear in court; a citation issued at the instance of one of the parties to an action requiring his adversary to appear in court.

mannopus (man-nō'pus). Stolen goods which have been taken from the hands of a thief.

man of straw. See **straw man.**

manor (man'or). The feudal estate of a lord; a barony; a lordship.

manorial court (ma-nō'ri-al kôrt). A court-baron,— a court held within certain manors in which the tenants litigated and were tried.

manor lease. An estate, formerly legal in New York, now expressly forbidden in that state by constitutional provision, similar to ground rent. 32 Am J1st L & T § 1039.

manqueller (man'kwel"ėr). (Saxon.) A man-killer; a murderer.

manred (man'red). Same as **manrent.**

manrent (man'rent). A vassal's bond or promise of fidelity and service in return for the protection he is to receive from his lord.

manse (mans). A dwelling house, particularly one in which a Protestant clergyman resides.

manser (man'sėr). An illegitimate child; a bastard.

mansion. See **mansion house.**

mansion house. Deriving from the Latin "mansio," a place where one remains or sojourns. Including, not only the dwelling house, but also the outhouses, such as barns, stables, cow houses, dairy houses and the like, if they be parcel of the messuage, though they be not under the same roof, or joining contiguous to it. State v Brooks, 4 Conn 446, 448.
See **quarantine.**

manslaughter (man'slâ"tėr). The unlawful killing of another, without malice, and either voluntary, as when the act is committed with a real design and purpose to kill, but through the violence of sudden passion, occasioned by some great provocation, which in tenderness for the frailty of human nature, the law considers sufficient to palliate the offense, or involuntary, when the death of another is caused by some unlawful act, not accompanied with any intention to take life. 26 Am J1st Homi § 17. A crime in various degrees under the statutes, there being inconsistency between jurisdictions as to particulars. First degree:—involuntary manslaughter; a killing by negligence. 26 Am J1st Homi § 219. Second degree:—the killing of one human being by another when committed without a design to effect death. People v Rochester Railway & Light Co. 195 NY 102, 88 NE 22. Third degree:—the killing of a human being in the heat of passion, without a design to effect death. Clemens v State, 176 Wis 289, 185 NW 209, 21 ALR 1490. Fourth degree:— an involuntary killing of a human being in the heat of passion. Clemens v State, 176 Wis 289, 185 NW 209, 21 ALR 1490. A killing by inadvertence amounting to culpable negligence. 26 Am J1st Homi § 219.

manstealing. The offense of kidnapping, or the forcible abduction or stealing away of a man, woman or child from his own country and sending him to another. See 4 Bl Comm 219.

mansuetae naturae (man-su-ē'tē nā-tū'rē). Gentle or tame by nature. 4 Am J2d Ani § 2.

mansueta, quasi, manui assueta (man-su-ē'ta, quā'sī, ma'nu-ī as-su-ē'ta). Domesticated, made accustomed to the hand, as it were. See 2 Bl Comm 391.

mansuetus (man-su-ē'tus). Tamed; gentle; domesticated.

mansum capitale (man'sum ka-pi-tā'le). A manor house.

man trap. A dangerous instrumentality maintained upon one's premises as a protection against trespassers or burglars. 38 Am J1st Negl § 114. A device, such as a spring gun or spring trap, set for the protection of property, but which is a lethal instrument. 26 Am J1st Homi § 200.

manu. See **in manu.**

manual. Directions for the manner of performance of certain work, particularly the assembly of machines and appliances and the operation of machines. Meccano Ltd. v Wagner (DC Ohio) 234 F 912, affd (CA6) 246 F 603.
See **sign manual.**

manual delivery. A hand to hand or physical delivery of an instrument or article by one person to another. 23 Am J2d Deeds § 91.

manual gift. A gift by the donor's own hand. Succession of Gomez, 223 La 859, 67 So 2d 156.

manual labor. Labor under physical power of the laborer, in the service and under the direction of another, for fixed wages. Rogers v Dexter & P. R. Co. 85 Me 372, 27 A 257. Within the meaning of the immigration laws, including both skilled and unskilled work, even work in the mechanical trades, although not professional services. 3 Am J2d Aliens § 62.

manual laborer. See **manual labor**.

manual rates. The premium rates to be charged for insurance covering risks on property as fixed by a rating bureau or underwriters' association after inspection of the properties. Commercial Standard Ins. Co. v Remer (CA10 Okla) 119 F2d 66; 29 Am J Rev ed Ins § 109.

manual seizure. An actual seizure, particularly under a writ of execution. 30 Am J2d Exec § 238.

manual test. A physical test such as that given to determine the degree of intoxication of a person by requiring him to walk along a straight marked line. Alexander v State (Okla Crim) 305 P2d 572.

manual training. Training in work in wood and metals and in other arts and crafts, particularly as given in the public schools. Maxcy v Oshkosh, 144 Wis 238, 128 NW 899.

manu brevi (ma'nū brē'vī). With short hand; briefly; directly.

manucapere (ma-nū-kā'pe-re). To become surety of mainprise.
See **mainprise**.

manucaptio (ma-nū-kap'she-ō). Same as **mainprise**.

manucaptione. See **de manucaptione**.

manucaptors (man-ụ-kap'tọrs). Same as **mainpernors**.

manufactory. A house or place where anything is manufactured. Halpin v Insurance Co. of North America, 120 NY 73, 23 NE 989.
See **factory**.

manufacture. Verb: To make and fabricate from raw materials or processed materials by the hand, by art, or by machinery, into a form fit and convenient for use. Attorney General v Lorman, 59 Mich 157, 26 NW 311; Bell v Lamborn, 18 Colo 346, 32 P 989; 51 Am J1st Tax § 592. Noun: The process of converting a raw material into a form fit and convenient for use, that is, into finished parts or products. Anno: 10 ALR 1276; 34 ALR 544. An article upon the material of which labor has been expended to make the finished product. Comptroller of Treasury v Crofton Co. 198 Md 398, 84 A2d 86, 30 ALR2d 1434.

manufactured article. An article made either by hand or by machinery into a new form, capable of being used, and designed to be used, in ordinary life. Lawrence v Allen (US) 7 How 785, 793, 12 L Ed 914, 917.

manufacturer. One engaged in manufacturing.
See **manufacture**.

manufacturers' bounties. Payments of public funds to manufacturers for the purpose of stimulating production. 12 Am J2d Bount § 3.

manufacturer's liability. See **products liability**.

manufacturing corporation. A private corporation organized and operating in reducing raw or processed materials by hand or by machinery into a form fit for use or consumption. 18 Am J2d Corp § 32. A corporation engaged in manufacturing, as its principal business, and not as a mere minor incident to some larger work. Friday v Hall & Kaul Co. 216 US 449, 54 L Ed 562, 30 S Ct 261.

manufacturing establishment. A factory or industrial plant. A place where machinery or mechanical power is utilized in connection with the employment of the individual. 58 Am J1st Workm Comp § 117. A place where there is an organized force of laborers working with machinery to produce the finished product from raw materials, or converting manufactured articles into a different product. Hotchkiss v District of Columbia, 4 App DC 73 (involving statutes fixing hours of labor or prescribing provisions as to child labor.) For practical purposes, any plant or factory where raw material is converted into a finished product, complete and ready for the final use for which it is intended, or so completed as that in the ordinary course of business of the concern it is ready to be put upon the open market for sale to any person wishing to buy it. Louisville v Zinmeister & Sons, 188 Ky 570, 222 SW 958, 10 ALR 1269, 1273.

manufacturing explosives. The common-law offense of manufacturing explosives near a public place, such as a city or highway. 31 Am J2d Explos § 127.

manu forti (ma'nū for'tī). With strong hand; an expression used to characterize an entry upon real estate as partaking of criminality due to its forcible or violent nature. 35 Am J2d Forc E & D § 4.

manu forti et cum multitudine gentium (ma'nū for'tī et kum mul-ti-tū'di-ne jen'she-um). With strong hand and a multitude of people.

manu longa (ma'nū lon'ga). With long hand,—indirectly; in a roundabout manner.

manumission. Liberation from a condition of servitude by the voluntary act of the master. Fenwick v Chapman (US) 9 Pet 461, 472, 9 L Ed 193, 197. The emancipation of a child by his parent, terminating the parent's right to the services of the child. 39 Am J1st P & C § 82.

Manumittere idem est quod extra manum vel potestatem ponere (ma-nū-mit'te-re ī'dem est quod ex'-tra ma'num vel po-tes-tā'tem po'ne-re). To manumit is the same thing as to put out of the hand or power.

manurable (mạ-nūr'ạ-bl). Capable of being manured or cultivated; tillable; capable of being handled; corporeal; tangible.

manure (mạ-nūr'). Verb: To work on by hand; to cultivate; to spread with manure. Noun: Animal excrement applied to the soil to increase fertility. Snow v Perkins, 60 NH 493. Droppings of cattle composted with earth and vegetable matter taken from the land and used to supply the drain made on the soil in the production of crops, which would otherwise become impoverished and barren; sometimes regarded as appurtenant to the real estate. 42 Am J1st Prop § 31.

manure clause. A covenant by a tenant to leave the manure on the land. 32 Am J1st L & T § 814.

manus (mā'nus). A hand; an oath made with the hand on the Book; an oath; a compurgator.

manuscript. Written or typewritten matter, particularly of a book or article proposed for publication. Becoming property when placed on the market for use or profit. Leon Loan & Abstract Co. v Equalization Board of Leon, 86 Iowa 127, 53 NW 94.

manus mortua (ma'nus mor'tu-a). Same as **mortmain.**

Manus mortua, quia possessio est immortalis, manus pro possessione et mortua pro immortali (ma'nus mor'tu-a, qui'a po'ze-she-ō est im-mor-tā'lis, ma'-nus prō po-ze-she-ō'ne et mor'tu-a prō im-mor-tā'lī). "Manus mortua," dead hand or mortmain, because it is an immortal possession; "manus" stands for possession, and "mortua" for immortal.

manutendo. See **de manutendo.**

manutenentia (ma-nū-te-nen'she-a). Same as **maintenance.**

manworth (man'wėrth). The value of a man's life or that of a man's head.

many. A multitude. A number relatively large as compared with the whole or possible number of persons or things. Louisville & Nashville R. Co. v Hall, 87 Ala 708, 6 So 277.

map. A condensed representation, usually according to a scale noted, of an area of the earth's surface, large or small, of a nation, a state, a county, a municipality, etc., showing on a flat surface by lines and characters boundaries and peculiarities of the earth's surface, such as watercourses, other bodies of water, mountains, swamps, etc., and man's accomplishments in cities, towns, and villages established by him, even particular structures erected by him, such as bridges. Banker v Caldwell, 3 Minn 94, 103.
See **plat.**

marathon. An athletic event consisting in a long race; any endurance contest, sometimes one in dancing. State ex rel. Bluemound Amusement Park v Milwaukee, 207 Wis 199, 240 NW 847, 79 ALR 281.

marauder (ma-râ'dėr). A soldier or deserter who robs or steals. Curry v Collins, 37 Mo 324, 328. Broadly, one who roves for pillage and plunder.

marble. A mineral. A stone valuable for use in building and sculpture, resulting in nature from the subjecting of limestone to metamorphism. 36 Am J1st Min & M § 5.

marca (mar'ka). Same as **march.**

march. Verb: To walk in an orderly manner, as in a military formation. Noun: A mark; a boundary; a limit; a frontier.

marchers (mär'chėrs). Noblemen of the marches or frontiers between England and Scotland who exercised a petty sovereignty and made and enforced their own laws. Persons marching.

marcheta (mär'kȧ-ta). The lord's customary right of spending the first night with the bride of a tenant following the marriage. (English.) Same as **maiden rents.**

marchioness (mär'shon-es). An English noblewoman with a rank corresponding to that of a marquis.

mare (mār). A female of the horse family. Precisely, a female horse, donkey, mule, or zebra.

mare (mā're). The sea.

mare altum (mā're al'tum). The high sea.
Lord Hale says: "The sea is either that which lies within the body of a county or without. The part of the sea which lies not within the body of a county is called the main sea or ocean." By the main sea, Lord Hale undoubtedly means the same as is expressed by "high sea," "mare altum," or "le haut meer." United States v Bevans (US) 3 Wheat 336, 340, 4 L Ed 404, 405, argument of Honorable Daniel Webster.

mare apertum (mā're a-per'tum). The open sea.

maretum (ma're-tum). Overflowed marshes.

margarine. See **oleomargarine.**

margin. A sum of money, or its value in securities, deposited with a broker to protect him against loss in buying or selling for his principal. Assigned Estate of Taylor, 192 Pa 304, 43 A 793.

marginal hazard. A source of peril to a traveler on the highway, although located along the margin or outside of the highway, not on the traveled portion. 25 Am J1st High § 528.

marginal notations. Notes appearing in the margin of a document offered in evidence. 53 Am J1st Tr § 111. Words and figures written on an instrument outside the body of the instrument. 11 Am J2d B & N § 66. A part of a bill or note where placed thereon at the time of the execution of the instrument with the intention of making them a part of the contract. 11 Am J2d B & N § 66. Notes appended to the sections of a code of statutes by way of explanation of the codification and for convenience in search and examination. 50 Am J1st Stat § 157.

marginal notes. Same as **marginal notations.**

marginal purchase. A purchase wherein the full price or cost of the stock or commodity purchased is not given to the broker at the time of the execution of the order of the customer, without regard to whether the purchase was made as an investment with the expectation on the part of the customer of later making full payment and acquiring the ultimate possession, or as a speculation with the intention of reselling upon a rise in the market and without any intention of making full payment therefor or acquiring possession thereof. Austin v Hayden, 71 Mich 38, 137 NE 317.

marginal sale. See **short sale.**

marginal signature. The signature of a testator appearing in the margin of the instrument. 57 Am J1st Wills § 274.

marginal well. A term of the oil industry.
The term is defined by a Texas statute regulating the production of oil wells as any pumping well having a daily output of production of twenty barrels or less. The statute prohibits restriction of the production of any marginal well as thus defined. Railroad Com. v Rowan & Nichols Oil Co. (CA5 Tex) 107 F2d 70.

margin of credit. The amount of credit which a merchant will extend to a customer over and above a fixed limit in the latter's indebtedness to the merchant upon account, it being understood that the indebtedness will be kept within such limit by payments upon the account from time to time. Schaffran v Mount Vernon-Woodbury Mills (CA3 NJ) 70 F2d 963, 94 ALR 543; Schneider-Davis Co. v Hart, 23 Tex Civ App 529, 530, 57 SW 903.

margin of safety. The margin, to be noted by a trustee in making an investment of funds of the trust, between the value of the security and the amount of the investment. 54 Am J1st Trusts § 426.

margin on sale. The sum of money or its value in securities required by a broker of his customer in making a short sale, such being for the protection of the broker. 12 Am J2d Brok § 114.
See **short sale.**

margin transaction. A transaction in stocks or commodities made through a broker, usually as a speculation, wherein no more than an advance is made by way of payment to the broker. 24 Am J1st Gaming § 72.
See **margin; marginal purchase; margin on sale.**

marijuana (mä-rẹ-hwä′nạ). A substance derived from a hemp plant, generally classified as a narcotic. 25 Am J2d Drugs §§ 2, 16.

marinarius (ma-ri-nā′ri-us). A mariner.

marine (mạ-rēn′). Pertaining or relating to the sea; pertaining or relating to navigation.
A person serving in the Marine Corps.
See **Marine Corps.**

marine contract. Same as **maritime contract.**

Marine Corps. A military body in the regular service of the United States, but identified with the Navy. Wilkes v Dinsman (US) 7 How 89, 124, 12 L Ed 618, 634.
While the Marine Corps partakes more of a military body than a naval one and is sometimes loosely referred to as the third branch or element of the military establishment, it is a branch of the navy designed to perform military services. United States v Dunn, 120 US 249, 30 L Ed 667, 7 S Ct 507.

marine hospital. A hospital for sick and disabled seamen. 48 Am J1st Ship § 175.

marine insurance. A policy or contract of insurance covering the risk of loss to ship, cargo, or freight from a peril or perils of the sea. 29A Am J Rev ed Ins §§ 1308 et seq. A maritime contract or guaranty, on the part of the insurer, that the ship or goods shall pass safely over the sea, and through its storms and its many casualties, to the port of its destination; and that if they do not pass safely, but meet with disaster, from any of the misadventures insured against, the insurer will pay the loss sustained. New England Marine Ins. Co. v Dunham (US) 11 Wall 1, 20 L Ed 90. Probably the oldest form of insurance.

marine interest. The interest allowable on bottomry and respondentia bonds, such being at an exceptionally high rate on account of the hazard of loss of both principal and interest. 48 Am J1st Ship § 601.
Although bottomry and respondentia bonds usually make provision for the payment of maritime interest, an agreement for such interest is not a necessary element of a bottomry contract. Force v The Ship Pride of the Ocean (DC NY) 3 F 162, 164.

marine league. The equivalent of three geographical miles. Manchester v Massachusetts, 139 US 240, 257, 35 L Ed 159, 164, 11 S Ct 559.

marine lien. See **mariner's lien; maritime lien.**

marine mile. Same as **nautical mile.**

marine protest. A written statement under oath, made by the master of a vessel after the occurrence of an accident or disaster in which the vessel or cargo is lost or injured, with respect to the attending circumstances, being intended to show that the loss or damage resulted from a peril of the sea or other cause for which neither the master nor the owner was responsible, concluding with protestation against any liability of the owner for such loss or damage. 48 Am J1st Ship § 221.

mariner. Every person whose employment is on the sea and who is attached to a ship. Spinetti v Atlas S.S. Co. 80 NY 71, 81.
See **seaman.**

marine railway. A railway so constructed as to permit a ship to be rather conveniently loaded on a conveyor and pulled from the water. An inclined structure at the water's edge which extends below the water. It carries a cradle which moves on rollers or wheels. The cradle runs below the water and receives the vessel which is then hauled out. Maryland Casualty Co. v Lawson (CA5 Fla) 101 F2d 732, citing Bradford, Glossary of Sea Terms.

mariner's lien. The lien of a mariner for his wages. It is one of the oldest and best recognized of maritime liens. It exists as a rule in favor of every one who, in justice, can be regarded as a seaman. It follows the ship and its proceeds into whatever hands they go. Sheppard v Taylor (US) 5 Pet 675, 8 L Ed 269.

marine tort. Same as **maritime tort.**

maris. See **exercitor maris**

Maris et foeminae conjunctio est de jure naturae (ma′ ris et fē′mi-nē kon-junk′she-ō est dē jū′re nā-tū′rē). The union of the male and the female is according to the law of nature.

maritagio amisso per defaltam (ma-ri-tā′ji-ō a-mis′sō per dē-fal′tam). An old writ for the recovery of lands of which a tenant in frankmarriage had been disseised.

maritagium (ma-ri-tā′ji-um). The right of marriage, which is to be distinguished from matrimonium, and in its feudal sense signifies the power the lord or guardian in chivalry had of disposing of his infant ward in matrimony. See 2 Bl Comm 70.

Maritagium est aut liberum aut servitio obligatum; liberum maritagium dicitur ubi donator vult quod terra sic data quieta sit et libera ab omni seculari servitio (ma-ri-tā′ji-um est ât li′be-rum ât ser-vi′she-o ob-li-gā′tum; li′be-rum ma-ri-tā′ji-um di′si-ter u′bi do-nā′tor vult quod ter′ra sik dā′ta qui-ē′ta sit et li′be-ra ab om′nī se-ku-lā′rī ser-vi′she-o). Marriage is either frankmarriage or obligated with service; it is called frankmarriage when the giver wills it that land so given be secure and free from all secular service.

marital (mar′i-tạl). Pertaining or relating to the marriage relation.

marital deduction. A deduction in computing the taxable estate for federal estate tax purposes, limited to one-half of the decedent's adjusted gross estate, of property passing to the surviving spouse. IRC § 2056(a).

marital discord. Unhappy relations between husband and wife.

marital duties. The personal consequences and incidents of the marital relationship, duties reciprocal to the rights of consortium. 26 Am J1st H & W § 5.
See **consortium.**

marital infidelity. See **infidelity.**

marital portion (pōr′shọn). (Louisiana terminology.)

The rightful share or portion of a widow in the estate of her deceased husband.

marital relationship. The natural and legal relationship of husband and wife; the peculiar relationship growing out of marriage, based upon the reciprocal rights and duties of the spouses. 26 Am J1st H & W § 2.

marital rights. The rights of spouses as such. The personal consequences and incidents of the marital relationship; the rights of consortium. 26 Am J1st H & W § 5.
See **consortium.**

marital rights, duties and obligations. Such rights, duties, and obligations as arise from the contract of marriage, and constitute its object, and therefore embracing what the parties to such a contract mutually agree to perform toward each other and toward society. Kilburn v Kilburn, 89 Cal 46, 26 P 636.
See **marital duties; marital rights.**

marital settlement. See **marriage settlement.**

marital status. The status of one as a single or married person.

maritima incrementa (ma-ri'ti-ma in-kre-men'ta). Marine increment or increase,—lands reclaimed from the sea.

maritime. Of the sea. Pertaining to the sea; pertaining to navigable waters. Eclipse Mill Co. v Department of Labor & Industries, 141 Wash 172, 251 P 130.

maritime assizes of Jerusalem (a-sī'zes of je-rūs'a-lĕm). That part of the assizes of Jerusalem dealing with maritime law.

maritime belt. That part of the sea which, in contradistinction to the open sea, is under the sway of the littoral or bordering states, which can exclusively reserve the fishery within their respective maritime belts for their own citizens, whether fish, or pearls, or amber, or other products of the sea. Louisiana v Mississippi, 202 US 1, 52, 50 L Ed 913, 932, 26 S Ct 408, 571.

maritime blockade. See **blockade.**

Maritime Code. A code of laws pertaining to the navigation of the Mediterranean Sea formerly in effect, having been compiled about 1000 A. D.

Maritime Commission. An administrative agency of the United States, dealing with maritime things and activities, many of its duties being those of the former United States Shipping Board. Isbrandtsen-Moller Co. v United States, 300 US 139, 81 L Ed 562, 57 S Ct 407.

Maritime Commission Liens. The title of Chapter XIV of the Bankruptcy Act relating to the rights of the United States as a mortgage or lien creditor in the receivership or trusteeship of a shipping corporation. Bankruptcy Act §§ 701-703; 11 USC §§ 1101-1103.

maritime contract. A contract relative to a matter, transaction, or service that depends on, assists, or furthers transportation on navigable waters. Basically, a contract the whole substance of which has a connection with navigation of a ship, with her equipment or preservation, or with the maintenance or preservation of her crew. 2 Am J2d Adm § 61.

maritime courts. Courts established in England during the middle ages with jurisdiction over maritime matters.

See **admiralty court.**

maritime employment. Employment on a vessel, in the operation and repair of vessels, in loading and unloading vessels, and other longshore work. Anno: 83 ALR 1039; 58 Am J1st Workm Comp § 124.
A service is not necessarily a maritime service because it is rendered upon the high seas or a navigable river. To be a maritime service it must have some relation to commerce or navigation; some connection with a vessel employed in trade,—with her equipment, her preservation or the preservation of her crew. Cope v Vallette Dry-Dock Co. (CC La) 16 F 924.

maritime hypothecation. See **bottomry; respondentia.**

maritime insurance. See **marine insurance.**

maritime interest. Same as **marine interest.**

maritime law. The law which deals with rights, duties, and liabilities with respect to, or arising out of, the use of navigable waters for the transportation of persons or property by means of ships or vessels, either commercially or noncommercially. 48 Am J1st Ship § 3.
The United States has its own system of maritime law, coextensive with and operating uniformly throughout its boundaries. The basis of this system is the general maritime law but the latter has no inherent force of its own and is operative in this, as in any country, only so far as it has been adopted by the laws and usages thereof. 48 Am J1st Ship § 3.
See **admiralty.**

maritime lien. A lien on a vessel, enforceable by suit in rem, in favor of any person furnishing repairs, supplies, towage, use of drydock or marine railway or other necessaries, to any vessel, foreign or domestic. 46 USC § 971. To be distinguished from a common-law lien on a vessel which depends upon possession. 48 Am J1st Ship § 551. A lien on a vessel by contract, even by tort. 48 Am J1st Ship §§ 553 et seq.
See **mariner's lien.**

Maritime Lien Act. A comprehensive federal statute on the subject of maritime liens. 46 USC §§ 971 et seq.

maritime loan. A loan wherein the lender loses all the money lent in the event of the total loss of the security, or pro rata in the event of a partial loss.
See **bottomry; respondentia**

maritime service. See **maritime employment.**

maritime state. A collective name sometimes applied to the officers and men of the English navy.

maritime supplies. Articles and substances used in the operation of vessels on navigable waters.

maritime tort. An injury to person or property of which admiralty will take jurisdiction because of its origin on navigable waters in a maritime matter, including torts resulting from malfeasance or negligence, as well as those committed by direct force. 2 Am J2d Adm §§ 77 et seq.; 48 Am J1st Ship § 531.
So long as a tort is committed on navigable waters, it is not essential to its classification as a maritime tort that it be committed on board a vessel. Newport News Shipbuilding & Dry Dock Co. v O'Hearne (CA4 Va) 192 F2d 968.

maritime transaction. See **maritime contract**; **maritime lien**; **maritime tort**.

maritus (ma'ri-tus). A married man; a husband.

Maritus potest perdere, dissipare, abuti (ma'rī-tus po'test per'de-re, dis-si-pā're, ab-ū'tī). The husband can lose, squander and waste. Garrozi v Dastas, 204 US 64, 81, 51 L Ed 369, 379, 27 S Ct 224.

mark. See **signature by mark**; **trademark**; **visible mark or injury**.

marked ballot. A ballot marked by the voter to indicate his choice of a candidate or candidates, normally, in accord with statute, by making a cross in the square appearing opposite the name of the candidate. 26 Am J2d Elect § 258. A ballot having distinguishing marks, permitting it to be identified among all the ballots cast. 26 Am J2d Elect § 263.

marked card. A playing card secretly marked by minute mark, so that a player can identify the card in play.

marked crosswalk. A way for pedestrians across a street marked by lines, usually in white. 7 Am J2d Auto § 421.

marked line. A boundary line based upon monuments, such prevailing, in the construction of a description of real estate, over calls for courses and distances. 12 Am J2d Bound § 72.

marked tree. A tree marked by slash or cut of an axe for identification, particularly for use as a monument of a land boundary.

marker. A stone or metal piece placed at a grave, lettered for the purpose of identifying a body at rest in a grave. 14 Am J2d Cem §§ 33-35.
See **monument**.

market. At common law, a franchise conferring a right to hold a concourse of buyers and sellers. 35 Am J1st Mark & M § 3. In the modern sense, a place designated by municipal or town authority for the sale of articles necessary or convenient for the subsistence of men and domestic animals. 35 Am J1st Mark & M § 2. Within the meaning of occupation or privilege tax statutes:—a designated place to which all persons can go who wish to buy things necessary for subsistence or for the convenience of life which are there exposed for sale. Jacksonville v Ledwith, 26 Fla 163, 7 So 885. The state of business and prices upon a stock or commodity exchange as active, slow, rising or falling.
The word is derived from the Latin word "mercatus," which signifies trade or traffic, or buying and selling. Re New York, 127 Misc 710, 723, 217 NYS 544.
See **corner**; **forestalling the market**.

marketable title. A title good as a matter of law, its validity not being dependent upon the determination of any question of fact. Wurzweiler v Cox, 138 Or 110, 5 P2d 699; First Nat. Bank of St. Johnsbury v Laperle 117 Vt 144, 86 A2d 635, 30 ALR2d 958. A title that a person of reasonable prudence and intelligence, guided by competent legal advice, will be willing to take and pay for according to the fair value of the land. Campbell v Doherty, 53 NM 280, 206 P2d 1145, 9 ALR2d 699. A title not subject to such reasonable doubt as will create a just apprehension of its validity in the mind of a reasonable, prudent and intelligent person. Campbell v Doherty, 53 NM 280, 206 P2d 1145, 9 ALR2d 699. A title free from reasonable doubt both as to matters of law and fact, at law and in equity; a title which a reasonable purchaser, well informed as to the facts and their legal bearings, willing and ready to perform his contract, would, in the exercise of that prudence which businessmen ordinarily bring to bear upon such transactions, be willing to accept and ought to accept. Robinson v Bressler, 122 Neb 461, 240 NW 564, 90 ALR 600. Such ownership as enables and insures to the owner the peaceable enjoyment and control of the land as against all others. Barnard v Brown, 112 Mich 452, 70 NW 1038. A title free from liens or encumbrances, and dependent for its validity on no doubtful questions of law or fact—a title either of record, or, if dependent upon facts extrinsic to the record, dependent only upon facts sure to be easily accessible at all times in the future to a vendee, should his title at any time be attacked. Anno: 57 ALR 1284. A title which the purchaser of real estate under a contract is impliedly bound to accept in the absence of a provision requiring a particular kind of title. Anno: 46 ALR2d 547.

market agency. A person engaged in the business of buying and selling for others on a commission basis livestock in interstate commerce at a stockyard. Tagg Bros. & Moorhead v United States, 280 US 420, 74 L Ed 524, 50 S Ct 22.

market corner. See **corner**.

market house. The building in which a market is housed.

marketing agreement. See **marketing contract**.

marketing association. An organization having the purpose of promoting the marketing of agricultural products, sometimes of a particular product.
See **co-operative marketing association**.

marketing contract. The most vital instrumentality of a co-operative association. Hiroshi Kaneko v Jones, 192 Or 523, 235 P2d 768. A contract between a co-operative association and its members whereby the latter undertake to market their products exclusively through the association for a stated period, and the association undertakes to obtain the best price possible for the products. 18 Am J2d Coop Asso § 21. An agreement between administrative authorities of the federal or state government with a producer, processor, or other person engaged in the handling of agricultural commodities, entered into under the authority conferred by an agricultural adjustment and marketing act and as a means of effectuating the purposes of such statute. Yarnell v Hillsborough Packing Co. (CA5 Fla) 70 F2d 435, 92 ALR 1475.

marketing quota. See **quota**.

market license. A license to occupy a stall in a public market. Re Emrich (DC Pa) 101 F 231.

market of competition. A market in which two litigants involving trademark or trade-name protection compete in business, irrespective of geographical remoteness from one another. 52 Am J1st Tradem § 107.

market overt (ō'vert). An open, public, and legally constituted market.
In England, sales in market overt are an exception to the rule that no one can transfer even to a bona fide purchaser any greater or better title than he himself has. The established American doctrine is that a purchaser in a public, open market acquires no better title to goods than if he had bought them elsewhere. 46 Am J1st Sales § 462.

market price. A price determined by the demand for

the commodity in relation to the supply; the price in an open market. 46 Am J1st Sales § 180.

If the market is not open but subject to control by all who offer a commodity of like kind, by fixing a price, either by a common, although unexpressed, understanding, the term "market price" means merely quoted price. 46 Am J1st Sales § 180.

market quotations. A list of current or latest prices for commodities or securities bought and sold on a board of trade, stock exchange, or other market. Board of Trade v L. A. Kinsey Co. (CA7) 130 F 507, affd 198 US 236, 49 L Ed 1031, 25 S Ct 637.

market rate. The rate at which a commodity is commonly sold. Gold Brand Confectionery Co. v Dimmick, 276 Mass 386, 177 NE 547.
See **market price.**

market report. The report of the prices paid for particular commodities or securities upon a particular day or during a certain period of time.
See **market quotations.**

market value. The price for which an article is bought and sold in the ordinary course of business. 22 Am J2d Damg § 146. The price which would be agreed upon at a voluntary sale between an owner willing to sell and a purchaser willing to buy. 27 Am J2d Em D § 267. Of real estate:—the highest price obtainable in the open market for cash. Anno: 48 ALR 71, s. 68 ALR 152. The resultant of the prediction of many minds as to the usability of real property and probably financial returns from that use, projected into the future as far as reasonable, intelligent men can foresee the future. Palmer v Connecticut R. & Lighting Co. 311 US 544, 85 L Ed 336, 61 S Ct 379, reh den 312 US 713, 85 L Ed 1143, 61 S Ct 609. In condemnation proceedings, the fair market value. 27 Am J2d Em D § 267. As a standard of valuation for inheritance tax:—fair market price; cash value; actual value. Anno: 57 ALR 1158, s. 83 ALR 939 and 117 ALR 143.

In order for it to be said that a thing has a market value, it is necessary that there shall be a market for such commodity—that is, a demand therefor and an ability from such demand to sell the same when a sale thereof is desired. 22 Am J2d Damg § 146.

The courts have recognized the lack of correlation between "market value" and "book value" of corporate stock. Anno: 51 ALR2d 612.
See **clear market value; market price.**

market wagon. A vehicle, formerly in frequent use on the streets of cities and villages, wherefrom the proprietor dispensed groceries, vegetables, and other articles of merchandise from door to door and house to house. Re Flaherty, 105 Cal 558, 38 P 981.

marking ballot. A part of the process of voting.
See **marked ballot.**

marking document. Identifying a document by a mark placed upon it upon introducing or offering it in evidence. State v Rhoads, 81 Ohio St 397, 91 NE 186.

mark it off. An expression in the nature of a request accompanying the return of a binder to an insurance company, but insufficient as a request for the cancellation of the policy, the theory being that in insurance parlance a request for cancellation is not unconditional but carries with it the understanding that the policy shall be considered as having never been in force and that the insurer abandons any claim for premiums under such policy. Boutwell v Globe & Rutgers Fire Ins. Co. 193 NY 323, 85 NE 1087.

marksman. A person who, being unable to write his name, signs an instrument by making his mark, either as a witness or a principal. 57 Am J1st Wills § 250.

Marlborough. See **Statute of Marlborough.**

marque. See **law of marque; letters of marque and reprisal.**

marque and reprisal. See **letters of marque and reprisal.**

marquee. An awning or roof projecting from a building, especially a theater, over the sidewalk at the main entrance, sometimes supported by columns. Gilbert v Repertory, Inc. 302 Mass 105, 18 NE2d 437.

marquis. An English nobleman ranking next below a duke. See 1 Bl Comm 405, note.

Marquis of Queensbury Rules. Rules governing boxing and sparring exhibitions. State v Olympic Club, 46 La Ann 935, 15 So 190.

marriage. An institution; the foundation of the family and of society. 35 Am J1st Mar § 8. The status or relation of a man and a woman legally united as husband and wife. Baker v State, 86 Neb 775, 126 NW 300. A personal relation arising out of a civil contract to which the consent of the parties is essential. The voluntary union for life of one man and one woman as husband and wife, to the exclusion of all others, for the discharge to each other and to the community, of the duties legally incumbent on those whose association is founded on the distinction of sex. The act of becoming married. 35 Am J1st Mar § 4.
See **clandestine marriage; common-law marriage; companionate marriage; coverture; morganatic marriage; putative marriage.**

marriageable age. The age of consent, upon arriving at which one becomes capable of entering into a marriage. 35 Am J1st Mar § 16.
See **age of consent.**

marriage articles. The articles of an agreement made by parties in contemplation of marriage, usually in anticipation of the drafting of a formal marriage settlement. 26 Am J1st H & W § 278.
See **marriage settlement.**

marriage banns. See **publication of marriage banns.**

marriage benefit insurance. A contract by which the insurer becomes bound to pay either a stated sum of money to the beneficiary or his wife on his marriage, if the beneficiary will remain unmarried for a certain time, or a sum of money the amount of which is proportioned to the length of time during which the beneficiary remains single.

Such a contract is held void, both as being a wagering contract and as holding out an inducement for the postponement of marriage. White v Equitable Mut. Ben. Union, 76 Ala 251.

marriage broker. See **marriage brokerage.**

marriage brokerage. The business of a "marriage broker," who undertakes for compensation to procure spouses for those who seek them.

At one time the courts differed as to whether such contracts could be set aside without fraud, deceit, coercion, or a total failure of consideration, but since the House of Lords declared them to be against public policy this view has been quite generally followed in the United States as well as in England. 35 Am J1st Mar § 283.

marriage ceremony. The giving utterance to and public evidence of the contract of marriage. 35 Am J1st Mar § 25.

marriage certificate. A certificate of the solemnization of a marriage, prepared by the person officiating. 35 Am J1st Mar § 27.

marriage in facie ecclesiae (mar'āj in fā'she-e e-klē'-she-ē). A marriage in the face of the church. A marriage solemnized by a clergyman of the church. 35 Am J1st Mar §§ 25, 26.

marriage license. A license to marry; a condition precedent to the solemnization of a marriage. 35 Am J1st Lic § 23.

marriage per verba de futuro cum copula (mar'āj per ver'ba de fu-tu'rō kum ko'pu-la). A common-law marriage through carnal intercourse after an agreement to be married in the future, the law presuming a present consent from such agreement and intercourse. 35 Am J1st Mar § 42.

marriage per verba de praesenti (mar'āj per ver'ba dē prē-zen'tī). Marriage by means of words of present assent. That is, a common-law marriage entered into by the parties simply by their joint consent, without the interposition of any person authorized to solemnize the marriage and without formal solemnization of any sort. 35 Am J1st Mar § 28.

marriage portion. The same as the "dot" of the French. The property which a woman brings to her husband upon her marriage. Croft, Petitioner, 162 Mass 22, 27, 37 NE 784.

marriage register. A public record of marriages. A church record of marriages.

marriage settlement. A settlement of property by one spouse on the other or an agreement with respect to the rights of one spouse in the property of the other, as surviving spouse or otherwise, or with respect to the disposition of property, or with respect to support and maintenance. 26 Am J1st H & W § 274.
See **antenuptial settlement; property settlement.**

marriage speculation contract. A contract whereby an unmarried man in consideration of payments to be made by him receives the promise and engagement of the other contracting party to pay a stated sum to his wife, upon his marriage, provided such marriage does not occur until after a specified time running from the date of the contract. Anno: 63 ALR 733, s. 100 ALR 1457, 119 ALR 1246.
See **marriage benefit insurance.**

married woman. A status no longer of much more legal significance than the comparable status of married man.
Blackstone said: "By marriage, the husband and wife are one person in law,—that is, the very being or legal existence of the woman is suspended during the marriage, or at least is incorporated and consolidated into that of the husband, under whose wing, protection, and cover, she performs everything." 1 Bl Comm 442. But modern legislation has made one change after another until "what there is left of subjugation by her husband or subjection to him to incapacitate her to make any kind of contract she pleased is difficult to perceive." Harrington v Lowe, 73 Kan 1, 84 P 570.
See **Married Women's Acts.**

married woman's acknowledgment. An acknowledgment by a married woman of an instrument in the execution of which she joins with her husband, the examination and the act of acknowledgment being separate from the acknowledgment by the husband. 26 Am J1st H & W § 154. A distinctive form of acknowledgment, characterized by a privy examination of a married woman making an acknowledgment before the officer taking the acknowledgment, formerly required generally but now required in only a few states. 1 Am J2d Ack § 2.

married woman's equity for a settlement. See **equity for a settlement.**

married woman's separate estate. See **separate estate of wife.**

Married Women's Acts. Statutes or constitutional provisions, now found in most, if not all, American jurisdictions, enacted for the benefit of married women, abolishing common-law restrictions upon their right to contract, sue and be sued, acquire, hold, and convey property in their own right free from interference by their husbands. 26 Am J1st H & W § 20.

Married Women's Property Acts. Essentially the same as Married Women's Acts. 26 Am J1st H & W § 20.
See **Married Women's Acts.**

marsh. A wet tract of land.

marshal. A court officer. An officer vested with power and authority for the execution of process. A town or village police officer in some jurisdictions.
See **earl marshal; knight marshal; provost marshal; United States Marshal.**

marshal court. Same as **court of chivalry.**

marshaling assets. The principle that where two or more creditors seek satisfaction out of the assets of their debtor, the creditor who has a lien on only a part of the assets shall be protected so far as possible without doing violence to the rights of the other creditor or creditors. 35 Am J1st Marsh A § 2. The principle that where two or more creditors seek satisfaction out of the assets of their debtor and one of them can resort to two sources whereas another creditor has recourse to only one of the sources—for example, where a senior or prior mortgagee has a lien on two parcels of land, and a junior mortgagee has a lien on only one of the parcels—the former may be required to seek satisfaction out of the fund which the latter creditor cannot touch, in order that the latter may, if possible, have his claim satisfied out of the fund which is subject to the claims of both creditors. Showmaker v White-Dulaney Co. 131 Wash 347, 230 P 162, 232 P 695.
See **inverse order of alienation.**

marshaling liens. Determining the priority as between two or more liens. An expression sometimes loosely used for marshaling assets.
See **marshaling assets.**

marshaling securities. Same as **marshaling assets.**

marshal of the king's household. Same as **knight marshal.**

Marshalsea (mär'shạl-sē). An old prison in London which formerly belonged to the court of king's bench.
See **court of the Marshalsea.**

mart (märt). A market; a public market.

martial law. Law as applied by military authorities for the government of the civilian population in portions of the country in a state of war, operative only until pacification. 16 Am J1st Const L § 52. That law which is promulgated and administered by and through military authorities and agencies for the maintenance of public order and the protection of persons and property in territory wherein the agencies of the civil law have been paralyzed, overthrown, or overpowered, and are unable, for the time being, fully to operate and function. 36 Am J1st Mil § 84. The law of military necessity in the actual presence of war. United States v Diekelman, 92 US 520, 23 L Ed 742. The will of the military commander in the field. Re McDonald, 49 Mont 454, 143 P 947.

It is to be distinguished from military law which applies to those rules enacted by the legislative power for the government and regulation of the army and navy, and the militia when called into the active service of the United States. Johnson v Jones, 44 Ill 142.

See **military law.**

martini. A cocktail made of gin, a dash of bitters, and vermouth, cooled by shaking it in cracked ice.

martyrs. See **acta martyrum.**

Mary (mā′ri). The queen of England from July 6th, 1553, to November 17th, 1558, known to some as Bloody Mary.

mask. A covering over the face or part of the face, worn as a disguise in committing or attempting to commit a crime or in fun, as at a costume ball or party.

mason. A layer of stone or brick. One who builds of brick or stone.

Mason. A member of the secret fraternal order of Masonry, otherwise called Freemasonry, through a masonic lodge.

Masonic lodge. A lodge of Masons or Freemasons, organized and operating in the exemplification of the principles of Masonry. A charitable organization in some jurisdictions, but not in others. 15 Am J2d Char § 149.

masonry. Stone or brick construction.

Masonry. A fraternal and secret order, often called Freemasonry, existing throughout the civilized world in grand lodges and local lodges. The principles taught by Masons in Masonic lodges.

mass. Bulk. A quantity of articles, goods, or substances, usually large in size.

Mass. The service in the Roman Catholic Church.

Mass is an act of public worship, in celebration of the Eucharist as observed in the Roman Catholic Church, and formerly observed in the Church of England, and still observed in some Anglican churches. It is common, and public to all as a religious ceremony, and is therefore a religious or pious use, and is a public charity, as distinguished from a private charity, which it might be if restricted to masses for the souls of designated persons. Ackerman v Fichter, 179 Ind 392, 101 NE 493.

massa (mas′a). (Civil law.) A mass; a lump; raw material before it has been fabricated.

Massachusetts Colony Ordinance. An important statutory provision pertaining to the boundaries of lands bordering water courses, and the right of a town to grant away a great pond, such provision having been extended by judicial construction to cover the entire state of Massachusetts and apparently having become a part of the common law of Maine. 12 Am J2d Bound § 36.

Massachusetts trust. Same as **business trust.**

massage. A method of treating the superficial soft parts of the body for remedial or hygienic purposes, consisting in rubbing, stroking and kneading, tapping, etc. with the hands or an instrument. Rubin v United States, 59 App DC 195, 37 F2d 991; Florida Board of Massage v Underwood (Fla) 45 So 2d 184, 17 ALR2d 1181.

See **masseur.**

mass convention. A political convention of electors as distinguished from a convention of delegates chosen by the electors. 25 Am J2d Elect § 120. A political convention of voters held for the purpose of nominating candidates for office to be voted for at an ensuing election, at which convention every voter represents himself and himself only, as distinguished from a delegate convention at which the delegates vote as representatives. Manston v McIntosh, 58 Minn 525, 60 NW 672.

Masses. See **Mass.**

masseur (må-sėr). One accomplished in massage, that is in rubbing or kneading muscles or joints so as to relieve pain or stiffness by stimulating the circulation. Anno: 17 ALR2d 1190. A person who practices, administers or teaches the art of body massage. Florida Board of Massage v Underwood (Fla) 45 So 2d 184, 17 ALR2d 1181.

mass picketing. The use of pickets in great numbers in a labor dispute. 31 Am J Rev ed Lab § 365.

mass sale. See **sale en masse.**

mast. A pole raised vertically from the deck of a vessel to support the sails and yards. 48 Am J1st Ship § 641.

master. The person in command of a vessel. 48 Am J1st Ship § 113. An official of court assisting in the administration of the functions of the court. An officer similar to commissioner or referee. 20 Am J2d Cts § 4. An outdated term for "employer." 35 Am J1st M & S § 2.

The words "employer" and "employee" are the outgrowth of the old terms "master" and "servant"; they have been adopted by reason of the shift of the relation in general from a personal to an impersonal one, and are the terms now commonly used to describe the relationship. 35 Am J1st M & S § 2.

See **master in chancery.**

master and servant. The relationship which exists when one person who employs another to do certain work exercises the right of control over the performance of the work to the extent of prescribing the manner in which it is to be executed. 35 Am J1st M & S § 2. The equivalent of the more modern term "employer and employee."

master at common law. A ministerial officer of an English superior court with functions and duties corresponding to those of a master in chancery.

master builder. A contractor who employs men to build. Little Rock, Hot Springs & Texas Railway Co. v Spencer, 65 Ark 183, 198. A person skilled in building, in making plans for building, or in supervision of construction.

master chief petty officer. A noncommissioned

officer of the Navy, of a rank comparable to that of sergeant major of the Army.

master in chancery. An officer of the court. A referee in a suit in equity. An assistant of the chancellor having the function of performing acts, either judicial or ministerial in nature, which the chancellor may see fit, in accordance with equity practice, to require of him. 27 Am J2d Eq § 225.

Master of Arts. A postgraduate degree in the liberal arts, humanities, or social sciences.

Master of Science. A postgraduate degree in science.

master of ship. The person, usually called "captain," in command of the vessel, including control of the crew, chief charge of the government and navigation of the vessel, and supervision over the care of the vessel and cargo. 48 Am J1st Ship § 113.

master of the crown office (of the kroun of'is). An important English officer performing the functions of public prosecutor in the court of king's bench, and also acting as coroner to the king.

master of the rolls (of the rōls). An assistant judge of the English chancery court, holding a court of his own ranking next below that of the lord chancellor.

master of vessel. See **master of ship**.

master plumber. A skilled plumber. A plumber qualified to work without supervision.

master pro hac vice (măs-tèr prō hăk vī'se). A master appointed to act in a particular case and for such case only. 27 Am J2d Eq § 225.

master's mate. See **mate**.

master sergeant. The highest in rank of noncommissioned officers of the United States Army.

masthead. A term of the printing and publishing business for the part of a page of a publication upon which there is noted the name of the publication, the names of the owner, publisher, and editor, the place of publication, business-office address, the address of the editorial office, and the titles of any prior publications which have been merged or consolidated with the reporting publication. American Photographic Publishing Co. v Ziff-Davis Publishing Co. 27 Cust & Pat App 1014, 127 F2d 308.

mastiff. A large dog formerly in common use for hunting, also as a watchdog.
See **lawing**.

masturbation. Self-abuse; onanism; the self-excitement of the genitals, usually by manipulation. Sometimes a serious disease within the meaning of an application for life insurance. 29 Am J Rev ed Ins § 745.

mat. A removable covering for the floor or part of the floor, often placed in vestibules and aisles of the cars of a carrier to prevent passengers from falling on a slippery floor.

match. See **boxing match**; **matched orders**; **matching**.

matched orders. Orders to sell or purchase the same securities in substantially the same amounts, at substantially the same prices, and at substantially the same times at which sales or purchases are made; a means of illegal manipulation of prices on an exchange. 50 Am J1st Stock Ex § 26.

matching. A stock exchange term designating the practice, when dealing in futures, of settling contracts by offsetting purchases against sales. United States v New York Coffee & Sugar Exchange, 263 US 611, 616, 68 L Ed 475, 476, 44 S Ct 225.

mate. A ship's officer, subordinate to the captain. Sometimes regarded as a seaman, although clearly of a rank above an ordinary seaman. 48 Am J1st Ship § 144.
The officers of a ship are the master and the mate. The mate is the first officer under the master. He is sometimes called the "master's mate," and is neither a seaman nor a mariner. Ely v Peck, 7 Conn 239, 242.
Two masters of whaling vessels are said to mate when they enter into a contract of mateship. Baxter v Rodman, 20 Mass (3 Pick) 435.
See **contract of mateship**.

materfamilias (mā″ter-fa-mi′li-as). (Civil law.) The mother of a family; a woman in the position of head of the household.

materia (ma-tē′ri-a). Materials; matter; subject matter.
See **in pari materia**.

material. Adjective: Important; relating to the substance rather than form; going to the merits and essence. Noun: Metal, wood, or any substances used in the fabrication of a product. Wood, brick, stone, steel, etc. used in the construction of a building or other improvement. 36 Am J1st Mech L § 69. Collected facts or ideas used by a writer in the preparation of an essay or thesis.
See **immaterial**. See also terms and expressions beginning **immaterial**.

material allegation. A statement in a pleading upon which an issue in the action can be made. Miller v Brumbaugh, 7 Kan 343, 353. A statement in a pleading essential to the claim or defense, and which cannot be stricken from the pleading without leaving it insufficient. Tucker v Parks, 7 Colo 62, 67.

material alteration. A change in the terms of a written instrument which gives it a legal effect different from that which it originally had. Barton Sav. Bank & Trust Co. v Stephenson, 87 Vt 433, 89 A 639. An intentional act performed upon an instrument after it has been fully executed, by one of the parties thereto, without the consent of the other, which changes the legal effect of the instrument in any respect. O. N. Bull Remedy Co. v Clark, 109 Minn 396, 124 NW 20. An alteration of an instrument which destroys the identity of the instrument or of the contract evidenced thereby, or which so changes its terms as to give it different legal effect from that which it originally had, and thus works some change in the rights, obligations, interest, or relations of the party. 4 Am J2d Alt Inst § 5. The completion of an executed but incomplete instrument, in a manner other than that is authorized, so as to change the contract. UCC § 3-115(a).
Elimination of words which had no legal effect at the time the contract was signed and delivered is not a material alteration. Cities Service Oil Co. v Viering, 404 Ill 538, 89 NE2d 392, 13 ALR2d 1448.
An instrument is "materially altered" if the change increases the liability of, or injuriously affects, a party or parties. Newman v Cover, 300 Pa 267, 150 A 595.

material breach. A breach of contract which goes to the whole consideration; a breach which gives to the injured party the right to rescind the contract or to maintain an action for damages for a total breach. 17 Am J2d Contr § 446.

material change. An expression which, in reference to a building or construction contract, is so well understood that to attempt to define it in instructing the jury is more likely to confuse than to aid the jury. Nance v Patterson Bldg. Co. 140 Ky 564, 131 SW 494.
See **material alteration.**

material concealment. A concealment upon which fraud may be predicated where the fact concealed is such that had it been known to the other party he would not have entered into the contract or engaged in the transaction. 37 Am J2d Fraud § 178. In an application for insurance, the concealment of a fact material to the risk. 29 Am J Rev ed Ins § 689.
In contracts of life insurance, a concealment is material when the knowledge or ignorance of the fact involved will influence the judgment of the insurer as to whether or not it will enter into the contract. Travelers Ins. Co. v Wilkins (DC Fla) 33 F 117.

material error. See **prejudicial error.**

material evidence. Evidence which bears so closely upon the issues of the case as to warrant its being considered by jury or court as the trier of the facts. 20 Am J Rev ed Ev §§ 253 et seq. Evidence which goes to the substantial matters in dispute or has a legitimate and effective influence or bearing on the decision of the case. Lynch v Rosenberger, 121 Kan 601, 249 P 682. Evidence which has a substantial, as distinguished from a formal, bearing upon the merits of the controversy. David Bradley Mfg. Co. v Eagle Mfg. Co. (CA7 Ill) 57 F 980, 986.
Testimony is deemed "material testimony," the falsity of which warrants a conviction of perjury, if it might have substantially influenced the jury's consideration of the merits or the credibility of other testimony going to the merits. People v Kresel, 147 Misc 241, 264 NYS 464.

material facilities. Instrumentalities for the production of special nuclear material. 6 Am J2d Atomic E § 12.

material fact. See **material.**

material fraud. A fraud which so influenced the conduct of the injured party in leading him to enter into the transaction that without it he would not have done so. Boulden v Stilwell, 100 Md 543, 60 A 609.
See **material concealment; material representation.**

material injury. An injury resulting in damages of a substantial nature as distinguished from merely nominal damages. Anno: 16 ALR 633. To the freehold:—the term as used in the provisions of a conditional sales act making severability without "material injury to the freehold" a factor in determining the rights, as against third persons, of the seller of the goods which are affixed by the purchaser to realty, does not have reference to the diminution of value or usefulness of the freehold resulting from a removal, but to cases in which the articles sold have been so closely attached to or incorporated into the realty as to lose its identity as personal property. People's Sav. & Trust Co. v Munsert, 212 Wis 449, 249 NW 527, 88 ALR 1306.

materiality. The state of a thing in reference to whether or not it is material or the degree in which it is material.

See **material.** See also terms and expressions beginning **material.**

materially altered. See **material alteration.**

materialman. A person who supplies materials for use in the construction of a building or other structure. A person to whom the protection of a mechanic's lien statute is now generally extended.
See **mechanic's lien.**

materialman's lien. A lien now generally provided under mechanic's lien statutes for the protection of one who supplies materials for use in the construction of a building or other improvement.
See **mechanic's lien.**

materialman's maritime lien. The lien upon a ship under federal or state statute for necessary materials or supplies furnished the vessel in port, especially her home port. 48 Am J1st Ship §§ 552 et seq.

material misrepresentation. See **material representation.**

material mistake. A mistake substantially affecting the rights and obligations of the parties to an instrument. 45 Am J1st Reform Inst § 48. A mistake so great that the parties obviously did not act with knowledge of the true facts, since such would have defeated the very object of the transaction. Anno: 1 ALR2d 79.

material payment bond. See **labor and material payment bond.**

material representation. As an element of fraud:—a representation of fact which influences a person to act, as to enter into a contract or transaction which, in the absence of the representation, would not have been a subject of engagement by him. 37 Am J2d Fraud § 178; 55 Am J1st V & P § 64. An element of estoppel in pais. Douglass v Belknap Springs Land Co. 76 NH 254, 81 A 1086. In application for insurance:—a representation of a fact which reasonably careful and intelligent underwriters would regard as substantially involved in the risk of loss and rate of premium to be charged. 29 Am J Rev ed Ins § 701.

material testimony. See **material evidence.**

material variance. See **variance.**

materia prima (ma-te′ri-a ri′ma). The primary matter,—the groundwork of all natural knowledge. See 3 Bl Comm 322.

maternal. Pertaining to or emanating from the mother.

maternal fee. See **feudum maternum.**

maternal property. Property which has come from the maternal or mother's side of the family.

maternal welfare. Relief by welfare payments to mother.
See **mother's pension.**

materna maternis (ma-ter′na ma-ter′nis). Maternal things to maternal.
The expression is an abbreviated form of the common-law rule that property which has come through the mother descends to maternal relatives. See 2 Bl Comm 236.

maternity. Motherhood; the state or condition of being a mother.

maternum. See **feudum maternum.**

mateship. See **contract of mateship.**

mathematical evidence. Evidence established by

computation or demonstration; evidence of a very certain and reliable character.

mathematical symbols. Arabic numerals and Roman letters for numbers. 1 Am J2d Abbr § 9.

matima (ma'ti-ma). A godmother.

mating. Taking a spouse; being married. The act of the masters of two whaling ships whereby they enter into a contract of mateship. Baxter v Rodman, 20 Mass (3 Pick) 435.
See **contract of mateship.**

matricide (mat'ri-sīd). The murder of one's own mother; a person who murders his own mother.

matricula (mạ-trik'ụ-lạ). A register containing the names of the members of an institution, association, or society.

matriculation. Enrollment as a student in an educational institution, particularly a college or university. A contract, complete upon payment of the required tuition fee, containing two implied conditions: (1) that no student shall be arbitrarily expelled; and (2) that the student will submit himself to reasonable rules and regulations for the breach of which, in a proper case, he may be expelled. 15 Am J2d Colleges § 25.

matriculation fee. The fee paid by a student upon matriculation at a college or university. 15 Am J2d Colleges § 19.

Matrimonia debent esse libera (ma-tri-mō'ni-a de'-bent es'se li'be-ra). Marriages ought to be free.
It was a loose application of this maxim of the old Roman law under which the Romans permitted voluntary divorces. Knost v Knost, 229 Mo 170, 129 SW 665.

matrimonial acquets (mat-ri-mō'ni-al ạ'kwets). (Civil law.) Property acquired otherwise than by descent by a husband or wife during the marriage.

matrimonial action. An action predicated upon the marital relation, such as an action for divorce, for separate maintenance, or for an annulment of a marriage.
Causes involving the marriage relation; causes involving injuries respecting the rights of marriage, including jactitation of marriage (formerly), specific performance of marriage contracts, restoration of conjugal rights, separate maintenance and alimony. See 3 Bl Comm 92 et seq.

matrimonial causes. See **matrimonial action.**

matrimonial cohabitation. The living together by a man and a woman, ostensibly as husband and wife, either with or without sexual intercourse between them. It is stated, however, that from such cohabitation the carnal act is presumed. Cox v State, 117 Ala 103, 23 So 806; Stevens v Allen, 139 La 658, 71 So 936.

matrimonial domicil. The domicil of the husband which is that of the wife by virtue of the marital relation, her domicil merging into that of her husband.
The unity of the domicil of husband and wife is in reality no more than a fiction of the law. It should not prevail in divorce cases where the purpose is to sever the marital relation and the incidents thereof. 24 Am J2d Div & S § 257.

matrimonial offense. An offense against the vows of marriage. Richardson v Richardson [1950] Prob 16, [1949] 2 All Eng 330, 16 ALR2d 579.

matrimonium (ma-tri-mō'ni-um). (Roman law.) Matrimony; marriage.

Matrimonium subsequens tollit peccatum praecedens (ma-tri-mō'ni-um sub'se-quenz tol'lit pe-kā'tum prē-sē'denz). Subsequent marriage obliterates precedent sin or offense.

matrimony. The state or status of being married. Married life.

matrix (mā'triks or mat'riks). (Civil law.) An original document, as distinguished from copies.

matron. A married woman or widow. A woman serving as an attendant or guard in an institution for females, such as a hospital or prison, or in a similar capacity in a department for females in an institution.
See **jury of matrons.**

matter. Substance or material. A fact or facts constituting the whole or a part of a ground of action or defense, not to be confused with "evidence," which is that which tends to prove the existence of a fact or facts. Nelson v Johnson, 18 Ind 329, 332. In one sense of the term, a fact or facts material to the issue which is being tried. Bishop v Shurly, 237 Mich 76, 84, 211 NW 75, 78.
The word is often used as synonymous with the word "subject," and sometimes simply to avoid repetition, as in the constitutional clause, "every act shall embrace but one subject, and matters properly connected therewith, which subject shall be expressed in the title." The word "subject" is here used to indicate the chief thing about which legislation is had, and "matters," the things which are secondary, subordinate, or incidental. State ex rel. Duensing v Roby, 142 Ind 168, 41 NE 145.

Matter en ley ne serra mise en bouche del jurors (ôn lay nuh ser-rah mēz ôn boosh del zhoo-ror). A matter of law shall not be placed in the mouth of the jurors.

matter in controversy. The subject of the litigation; the matter for which suit is brought and upon which the trial of the action proceeds. Lee v Watson (US) 1 Wall 337, 17 L Ed 557. The claim presented on the record of a case in court to the legal consideration of the court, ordinarily the amount demanded by the plaintiff's pleading. St. Paul Mercury Indem. Co. v Red Cab Co. 303 US 283, 82 L Ed 845, 58 S Ct 586 (relative to removal of case to federal court from a state court).
See **amount in controversy; matter in issue.**

matter in deed. A matter contained in an instrument under seal.

matter in dispute. Same as **matter in controversy.**

matter in issue. In the usual sense, the question or questions of fact presented by the pleadings.
Within the meaning of the rule that a judgment is only conclusive upon the matter which was directly in issue upon the former trial, the "matter in issue" is that matter upon which the plaintiff proceeds by his action, and which the defendant controverts by his pleadings. The declaration and other pleadings may show specifically what this is, or they may not. If they do not, the party may introduce other evidence to show what was in issue. But facts offered in evidence to establish the matters in issue are not themselves in issue within the meaning of the rule, although they may be controverted on the trial. King v Chase, 15 NH 9.
See **matter in controversy.**

matter in pais (in pā). A matter of fact, as opposed to a matter of law. A matter not of record. A matter not in writing, so susceptible of proof only by oral testimony.

matter of defense. An affirmative defense.

matter of fact. See **question of fact**.

matter of form. A formality involving in the law a technical aspect, particularly in reference to a fixed procedure, the form of an action, or manner of pleading, as distinguished from a matter of substance going to the existence of a cause of action. Meath v Board of Mississippi Levee Comrs. 109 US 268, 27 L Ed 930, 3 S Ct 284; Lake Shore & Michigan Southern Railway Co. v Kurtz, 10 Ind App 60, 75, 37 NE 303.

matter of law. See **question of law**.

matter of probate. Such a matter as the probate of a will or the administration of a decedent's estate which is within the jurisdiction of a probate court.

There is a "matter of probate," within the term as used in a state constitution, if the status of heirship or nonheirship, whether dependent on matters of legal or equitable cognizance, becomes material in the probate of a will or in any proceedings incident thereto. Re Stoiber, 101 Colo 192, 72 P2d 276, 112 ALR 1416.

matter of record. A matter entered on the records of a court of record; a matter recorded in the place and manner required by law. Croswell v Byrnes (NY) 9 Johns 287, 290.

matter of substance. A matter going to the existence of a cause of action or defense as distinguished from a matter of formal pleading or procedure. Meath v Board of Mississippi Levee Comrs. 109 US 268, 277 L Ed 930, 3 S Ct 284.

If the right of the party pleading sufficiently appears to the court, the pleading, if defective at all, is defective in a matter of form. If such right does not sufficiently appear to the court from the pleading, the pleading is defective in a matter of substance. Lake Shore & Michigan Southern Railway Co. v Kurtz, 10 Ind App 60, 37 NE 303.

mature. Adjective: Full-grown. Ripe. Fully developed. Due and payable. Verb: To ripen; to develop. To reach maturity; to become due and payable, as in the case of a promissory note. To accelerate the maturity of an instrument, as to exercise an option to declare it payable at a time before the due date prescribed in the instrument. Vestal v Texas Employers' Ins. Asso. (Tex Com App) 285 SW 1041, 1045.

matured crop. A crop that has come to maturity. Anno: 103 ALR 469. A crop that has stopped growing and is ready for harvesting. 21 Am J2d Crops § 2. A crop which has ceased to draw sustenance from the soil, notwithstanding it may require seasoning before it is ready to be stored or marketed, and therefore may be left standing for a time. Myers v Steele, 98 Kan 577, 158 P 660.

Maturiora sunt vota mulierum quam virorum (ma-tu-ri-ō'ra sunt vō'ta mu-li'e-rum quam vi-rō'rum). The desires of women are earlier than those of men.

maturity. The state of full growth and development. The time specified in a negotiable instrument for the payment thereof. 11 Am J2d B & N § 285.

See **acceleration of maturity**.

maxim. A precise expression developed over the years in elucidating a principle of law by reasoning. A time-tried rule of thumb, not a law in itself. Ackroyd v Winston Bros. Co. (CA9 Mont) 113 F2d 657. Maxim of equity:—a rule or principle formulated by equity courts for the government and regulation of judicial action. 27 Am J2d Eq § 119. Divisible, with respect to the mode of their operation, into four groups, as follows: (1) maxims governing the action of the chancellor or court; (2) maxims connoting the right or standing of the party to claim a remedy or relief; (3) maxims describing the relative standing of litigants where the question is whether one party or another has the prior or superior right or "equity"; and (4) maxims prescribing the mode of disposition of the case where the "equities" of the parties are shown to be of equal dignity. 27 Am J2d Eq § 119.

Maxime ita dicta quia maxima est ejus dignitas et certissima auctoritas, atque quod maxime omnibus probetur (ma'xi-mē i'ta dik'ta qui'a ma'xi-ma est ē'jus dig'ni-tās et ser-tis'si-ma âk-tō'ri-tās, at'kwe quod ma'xi-me om'ni-bus prō-bē'ter). A maxim is so called because its dignity is greatest and its authority is the most certain, and because it is approved most by all.

Maxime paci sunt contraria, vis et injuria (ma'xi-mē pa'sī sunt kon-trā'ri-a, vīs et in-jū'ri-a). Those elements which are most opposed to peace are violence and wrong.

maxims of equity. See **maxim**.

maximum amount. A constitutional or statutory provision which deprives a court of jurisdiction where the amount or value in controversy exceeds a stated amount. 20 Am J2d Cts § 154. A statutory limitation of a penalty. 36 Am J2d Forf & P § 64. A limit on the amount to be allowed by way of workmen's compensation. 58 Am J1st Workm Comp § 320. A prescribed limit on the amount of damages recoverable under a wrongful death statute. 22 Am J2d Dth § 117. A stipulation in an airplane ticket limiting the amount of the recovery for the passenger's death to a specified amount. Conklin v Canadian-Colonial Airways, 266 NY 244, 194 NE 692. A limitation placed by statute upon the amount of damages recoverable for infringement of a copyright. 18 Am J2d Copyr § 137.

maximum height restriction. A limitation in linear measurement or by a stated number of stories, placed upon the height of buildings within a definite area by restrictive covenant. 20 Am J2d Cov § 263. A limitation placed upon the height of buildings by a restrictive covenant in terms of comparison with other described structures. 20 Am J2d Cov § 263.

maximum hours. A limitation placed upon hours of labor in certain occupations.

See **hours of labor; Hours of Service Act**.

maximum number. A limitation placed by statute upon the number of signatures to be affixed to a nominating petition. 25 Am J2d Elect § 171.

maximum rate. The highest rate of interest warranted by law. 55 Am J1st Usury §§ 36 et seq.

maximum sentence. The longest sentence provided by statute for a particular criminal offense. A limit placed by statute upon the length of the sentence of an habitual criminal. State v Malusky, 59 ND 501, 230 NW 735, 71 ALR 190.

See **indeterminate sentence**.

Maximus erroris populus magister (ma'xi-mus er-rō'ris po'pu-lus ma-jis'ter). The greatest master of error is the people; the people may be the greatest master or error.

may. An auxiliary verb qualifying the meaning of another verb by expressing ability, contingency, liability, possibility or probability. United States v Lexington Mill & Elevator Co. 232 US 399, 58 L Ed 658, 34 S Ct 337. Ordinarily a permissive, rather than a mandatory, term in a statute. Burnett v Graves, 230 F2d 49, 56 ALR2d 1; 50 Am J1st Stat § 28. Permissive rather than mandatory and, appearing in a constitutional provision, not to be construed as "shall," unless from the whole context, it plainly appears to be mandatory. State ex rel. Greaves v Henry, 87 Miss 125, 40 So 152. Discretionary in its grammatical sense, but subject to construction as mandatory where the sense of the entire context impels such construction, 1 Am J2d Admin L § 46, as where used in a statute providing that when the bank commissioner has reasonable cause to consider a bank insolvent, he "may" immediately apply for a receiver. State use of Mills v American Surety Co. 26 Idaho 652, 145 P 1097. Frequently construed as mandatory where relating to the duty of a public officer. 34 Am J1st Mand § 72.

A provision in a trust agreement that the trustee "may" use the principal for the beneficiary, has been regarded as mandatory. Re Ward, 186 App Div 261, 174 NYS 182.

may declare due. Terms of an optional provision for acceleration of maturity. 11 Am J2d B & N § 294.

may elect to declare due. Terms of an optional provision for acceleration of maturity. 11 Am J2d B & N § 294.

Mayflower Compact. A compact made and signed by 41 adult male members of the Pilgrims aboard the Mayflower, off the coast of what later became the state of Massachusetts, in 1620, binding the signers under solemn covenant to form a civil body politic to operate under just and equal laws, acts, ordinances, and constitutions to be enacted from time to time for the good of the Colony.

mayhem. At early common law, the deprivation of the use of a limb or member of the body by which one was rendered unable to defend himself or annoy his adversary. Anno: 16 ALR 955, s. 58 ALR 1320. Under modern statutes, a malicious injury which disables or disfigures the person of another. An offense which is ordinarily a felony. 36 Am J1st May § 2.

mayhemavit (may-he-mā′vit). He has maimed.

maynover. The product of hand labor.
See **manure.**

mayor. A municipal officer, usually the highest, charged with administrative duties to be performed on behalf of the municipality. Sometimes having judicial duties as the magistrate of a mayor's court. Waldo v Wallace, 12 Ind 569, 577.

mayor of the staple (of the stā′pl). The chief officer of the staple or great market at Westminster who acted as one of the substitutes for the chief justices, out of term, in taking acknowledgments of recognizances similar in their nature to statutes staple as security for debts acknowledged to be due. See 2 Bl Comm 160.

mayor's court. A municipal or city court presided over by the mayor.

mazuma (ma-zoo-mah). Slang for money, especially money taken illegally or employed for an ulterior purpose.

McCarran Act. A federal statute supporting the power of a state to tax and regulate foreign insurance companies doing business in the state. 15 USC §§ 1011 et seq.

McCarren-Walter Act. See **Immigration and Nationality Act.**

McGuire Act. A federal statute, the primary significance of which is in allowing states to permit enforcement of fair trade laws against nonsigners of fair trade agreements. Anno: 12 L Ed 2d 1210, 1215.

M.D. Abbreviation of **Doctor of Medicine.**
See **doctor; physician.**

mead. A mild fermented beverage made of honey, malt, and spices, with yeast added; sometimes akin to near beer. 30 Am J1st Intox L § 11. Under poetic license, a meadow.

meadow. Grassland, especially grassland kept for the hay crop to be grown thereon.

The term is also applied to the tracts which lie above the sea shore, and are overflowed by spring and extraordinary tides only, and yield grasses which are good for hay. Church v Meeker, 34 Conn 421, 429.

meadow grass. Hay. 21 Am J2d Crops § 23.

meal rent. Rent paid by a tenant in meal.

mean. Adjective: Vicious; bad-tempered. Of little importance; inferior. In a distinct sense, intermediate or in the middle. Noun: An average; a state between extremes.

meander. Verb: To follow a winding or flexuous course. Turner v Parker, 14 Or 340, 12 P 495. Noun: Same as **meander line.**

meander line. A line established by a survey, defining the sinuosities of a stream which constitutes a land boundary. A line established in surveying land adjacent to a river or stream, whether navigable or not, running from one point to another along or near the bank or margin of the stream in such a manner as to leave a quantity of land lying between the line and the thread or bank of the stream. 12 Am J2d Bound § 29.

A meander line, although not in itself a boundary, affords a means of ascertaining the quantity of land to be paid for by a purchaser of a tract bounded in part by a river. Anno: 71 ALR 1256; 12 Am J2d Bound § 29.

mean high tide. The average height of all the high waters at a place over a considerable period of time. A line, to be determined by taking an average of the rise of the water above sea level for a period of 18.6 years, that fixes the boundary between tideland and upland. Borax Consolidated v Los Angeles, 296 US 10, 80 L Ed 9, 56 S Ct 23.

mean low tide. The line of the average low tide. The average taken at a specific point on a shore of the extreme low tide and the highest line of an ebbing tide.

mean person. A cruel, vicious, or corrupt person. A person without compassion or charity. In an older sense, a person of low degree.

mean reserve. A well-recognized term in the insurance business which, as applied to individual insurance policies may be defined as the mean of the reserve at the beginning of the policy year after the premium for such year is paid and the terminal at the end of such policy year. When applied to the whole business of a life insurance company, the

term "mean" as ordinarily understood is that reserve which is in the middle or that which is intermediate, or a condition that is equally removed from two opposite extremes. Western & Southern Life Ins. Co. v Huwe (CA6 Ohio) 116 F2d 1008.
See **reserve**.

means. Financial resources. An instrumentality for the accomplishment of a purpose. 16 Am J2d Consp § 7.
See **accidental means; available means**.

means of support. In a general sense, all those resources from which the necessaries and comforts of life are or may be supplied, such as lands, goods, salaries, wages or other sources of income. In a limited sense, any resource from which the wants of life may be supplied. Meidel v Anthis, 71 Ill 241, 246.
See **visible means of support**.

mean solar time. A measure of time calculated upon the motion of a fictitious sun called "the mean sun," which is imagined to move with perfect uniformity, being sometimes behind the true sun, and sometimes in advance of it. Anno: 143 ALR 1238.

mean sun. See **mean solar time**.

mean sun time. See **mean solar time**.

mease (mēs or mēz). A house.

meason (mē'zôn). Same as **mease**.

measure. Verb: To determine the size, weight, or value of something by the use of a recognized standard. Noun: A standard or unit of measure, such as a bushel or a gallon. The size or weight of anything as ascertained by applying a standard. A statute or resolution enacted by a legislative body. McBride v Kirby, 32 Okla 515, 260 P 435.

measured in wall. A term of measurement of mason work, subject to explanation by custom or usage. Miller v Wiggins, 227 Pa 564, 76 A 711.

measure of care. See **standard of care**.

measure of damages. The rule of law established by statute or decision for arriving at the amount of the plaintiff's damages which he is entitled to recover in a given case. 22 Am J2d Damg § 45.

measure with gold scales. See **gold scales**.

Meat Inspection Act. A federal statute providing for an elaborate system of inspection of animals before slaughter, of carcasses after slaughter, and of meat food products, with the view of preventing the shipment of impure, unwholesome, and unfit meat and meat food products in interstate and foreign commerce. 34 Stat at L 674, ch 3913; 22 Am J1st Food § 46.

meat processing. Slaughtering and butchering livestock in the preparing of the various parts of the carcass for distribution and sale, the process ending when the meat is placed in the cooler. Shain v Armour & Co. (DC Ky) 50 F Supp 907.

mechanic. For the purposes of laws granting an exemption against claims for indebtedness:—narrowly, a skilled workman employed in shaping materials, such as wood, metal, or stone, into a structure, machine or other object requiring the use of tools in its construction; more commonly and more broadly, any person who works with machines or instruments, including a baker, barber, tailor, even a dentist. 31 Am J2d Exemp § 21. As the term is used in a mechanic's lien statute:—a skilled workman. 36 Am J1st Mech L § 53. For the purposes of a workmen's compensation act:—a person in a manual occupation. 58 Am J1st Workm Comp § 91.

mechanical. Of or pertaining to, or concerned with manual labor, especially as performed by an artisan. Of, pertaining to, or concerned with machinery or mechanism; made or performed by machinery or with tools. Arizona Eastern Railroad Co. v Matthews, 20 Ariz 282, 180 P 159, 7 ALR 1149, 1155. By rote or settled rule rather than by use of the intellect.

mechanical device for aerial navigation. An aircraft, including a glider and a seaplane. 29A Am J Rev ed Ins § 1263.

mechanical equivalent. A term of art in patent law. A device which accomplishes the same result as that achieved by the patent alleged to be infringed. 40 Am J1st Pat § 156.

The term, when applied to the interpretation of a pioneer patent, has a broad and generous signification, but when applied to a patent for a slight improvement, its meaning is narrow and limited. The range of equivalents depends upon the degree of invention. If the patent is primary in character, the patentee is entitled to a broad range of equivalents. But if the patent is for a slight improvement on an old device or combination which performs the same function before as after the improvement, the range of equivalent is narrow. Mason Corp. v Halliburton (CA10 Okla) 118 F2d 729.

mechanical establishment. In the broad sense, any place or plant where machinery is used in production or other work. Within the meaning of a statute regulating hours of labor, a place where the mechanical element predominates in the activity, thereby excluding a newspaper plant. 31 Am J Rev ed Lab § 784.

mechanical failure. An accident occurring from a defect inherent in an instrumentality rather than from the act or omission of the operator.

mechanical labor. Work performed by a mechanic or one practicing a mechanical art; the shaping or uniting of materials into any structure, machine, or object, the construction of which requires the use of tools. Arizona Eastern Railroad Co. v Matthews, 20 Ariz 282, 180 P 159, 7 ALR 1149, 1155. Broadly, the work of a mechanic. Labor performed according to rule or rote rather than by use of the intellect.
See **mechanic; mechanical pursuit**.

mechanical musical device. See **jukebox**.

mechanical pursuit. An occupation or trade in which the object realized is not dependent for its perfection on the exertion of a controlling intellect, but rather on the adaption of some helpful mechanism, or use of some auxiliary tool or instrument. 33 Am J1st Lic § 39.
See **mechanical labor**.

mechanical skill. A term contrasted in patent law with inventive faculty.

As distinguished from invention, the term imports simply the display of the expected skill of the calling; it involves the exercise of the ordinary faculties of reasoning, aided by the special knowledge and the facility of manipulation which is acquired through habitual and intelligent practice of the art; and it is in no sense the creative work of that inventive faculty which it is the purpose of the Constitution and the patent laws to encourage and reward. Callison v Dean, 70 F2d 55.

mechanic's lien. A claim created by law for the purpose of securing a priority of payment of the price or value of work performed and materials furnished in erecting or repairing a building or other structure, usually attaching to the land as well as to the buildings erected thereon. Schwartz v Whelan, 295 Pa 425, 145 A 525, 65 ALR 277. A lien upon moneys withheld by a public body from a contractor in favor of a laborer or materialman for the amount of his claim for labor or materials furnished the contractor upon the improvement under construction by him pursuant to a contract with the public body. Anno: 112 ALR 816.

mechanic's maritime lien. A lien for repairs made upon a vessel provided by the Federal Maritime Lien Act of 1910, re-enacted in 1920, which superseded state legislation upon the same subject. 46 USC §§ 971 et seq.; 48 Am J1st Ship § 555.

See **materialman's maritime lien.**

mechanism. Working parts of a machine, a watch, or other instrumentality or device.

meddler. See **intermeddler.**

medfee (med'fē). A bribe; a reward; the return given in an unequal exchange.

media annata (mē'di-a an-nā'ta). (Civil law.) Half-yearly profits. McMullen v Hodge, 5 Tex 34, 79.

media concludendi (me'di-a kon-klu-den'dī). Plural of **medium concludendi.**

mediae et infimae manus homines (me'di-ē et in'fi-mē ma'nus ho'mi-nēz). Men of mean and lowly condition.

mediam viam. See **in mediam viam.**

media nox (mē'di-a nox). Midnight.

mediante altero (mē-di-an'te al'te-rō). Mediate through another. Intermediate.

See **mediate descent.**

mediante patre (mē-di-an'te pa'tre). Mediate through the father. Lessee of Levy v M'Cartee (US) 6 Pet 102, 114, 8 L Ed 334, 339.

medias res. See **in medias res.**

mediate descent. In one sense of the term, a descent not cast immediately, as where a grandson takes by descent land once owned by his intestate grandfather, but not directly from his grandfather, the descent having first been cast upon his father and then from his father upon him. In a more practical and different sense, a descent cast directly upon the heir but through an intermediate link or degree of consanguinity, as from grandfather to grandson, the father being dead, but nevertheless constituting an intermediate link or degree of consanguinity. Lessee of Levy v M'Cartee (US) 6 Pet 102, 112, 8 L Ed 334, 338. Comparably, a descent to a cousin, the latter not inheriting immediately from the intestate but only mediately through the parents of each of them. Cramer v McCann, 83 Kan 719, 112 P 832.

mediate powers. Those powers which are incidental to authority which has been granted or delegated.

mediate testimony. Same as **secondary evidence.**

mediation. The settlement of disputes between sovereign nations by the arbitration thereof. 30 Am J Rev ed Internat L § 52. The settlement of labor disputes.

See **mediation of labor disputes.**

Mediation and Conciliation Service. An independent federal agency, operating under a Director and having regional offices throughout the country, the duties of which are to assist parties to labor disputes to settle such disputes through conciliation and mediation. 29 USC §§ 172-174; 31 Am J Rev ed Lab § 371.

mediation of labor disputes. The settlement of labor disputes by conciliation or by arbitration of the matters in dispute. 31 Am J Rev ed Lab § 371.

mediators of questions. Persons who were appointed under the authority of a statute passed in the reign of Edward the Third to settle disputes arising among merchants.

medical. Pertaining or relating to the science of medicine or to the practice or study of medicine. Lowman v Kuecker, 246 Iowa 1227, 71 NW2d 586, 52 ALR2d 1380.

medical aid. Relief pertaining to the science of medicine for one injured, sick, disabled, or distressed. Olmstead v Lamphier, 93 Conn 20, 104 A 488, 7 ALR 542, 544.

medical attendance. Attendance by a physician for the purpose of medical treatment or medical advice. 29 Am J Rev ed Ins § 756.

As the term is used in a penal statute requiring a parent to furnish food, clothing, shelter, and "medical attendance" to his minor child, it means attendance by a regularly licensed physician. People v Pierson, 176 NY 201, 68 NE 243.

medical benefits. Aid furnished by a corporation for employees injured in the performance of their duties. 19 Am J2d Corp § 1054. In the broad sense of the term, payments under Social Security, workmen's compensation, or any contract of insurance, to cover medical expenses.

medical boards. Boards established under legislative authority in most, if not all, of the states of the Union, whose chief functions are to supervise the practice of medicine and surgery in their states, to examine applicants for licenses to practice, and to issue and revoke such licenses. 41 Am J1st Phys & S § 19.

medical clinic. See **clinic.**

medical college. An institution, usually one of the colleges of a university, for the education and training of men and women for the medical profession, teaching the nature, source, and causes of disease, the nature and effect of the various drugs, surgery, and whatever is necessary to adequate education in the constantly expanding field of medicine and surgery. Nelson v State Board of Health, 108 Ky 769, 57 SW 501.

medical college hospital. A hospital maintained in connection with a medical school, normally for the purpose of giving students opportunity for clinical observation and instruction.

medical consultation. Consultation with a physician for the purpose of obtaining medical treatment or medical advice. 29 Am J Rev ed Ins § 756.

medical evidence. Expert testimony of physicians and surgeons. 31 Am J2d Ex & Op §§ 1 et seq.

The opinions of medical men are constantly admitted as to the cause of disease, or of death, or the consequences of wounds, and as to the sane or insane state of a person's mind, as collected from a number of circumstances, and as to other subjects of professional skill. Estate of Toomes, 54 Cal 509.

medical examination. An examination of a person by a physician for the purpose of giving medical treatment or medical advice. 29 Am J Rev ed Ins § 756. An examination by a physician to determine the state of health of the person examined, apropos the need for medical or surgical treatment or his acceptability as a life insurance risk. An examination by a physician to determine whether or not a person has a communicable disease. 25 Am J1st Hlth § 32. An examination to determine the existence of venereal disease. 25 Am J1st Hlth § 34. An examination of a litigant for the purpose of determining his physical condition, involving, not only observation of the body, but also an inquiry by questions and answers as to the cause and character of a disability. 23 Am J2d Dep §§ 210 et seq.

See **mental examination; physical examination.**

medical examiner. A physician engaged by an insurance company to examine applicants for life insurance. In some jurisdictions, an officer who has succeeded to the authority of the coroner to make inquests and reports. 18 Am J2d Corn § 1. In the broadest sense of the term, a physician making a medical examination.

medical insanity. Some unsoundness of mind but not necessarily such as relieves from legal responsibility for crime. 21 Am J2d Crim L § 32.

medical insurance. Insurance providing for the payment of medical expenses in the event of sickness or disability.

See **blue shield; physicians' liability insurance.**

medical journal. A publication devoted to the special interests of physicians and surgeons. 39 Am J1st Newsp § 9.

medical jurisprudence (jö-ris-prü′dens). That part or branch of the science of medicine which has to do with questions of law.

medical or surgical treatment. All things performed by a physician or surgeon on the body of a patient in the diagnosis of the ailment or in treatment or operation to effect a cure. Provident Life & Acci. Ins. Co. v Hutson (Tex Civ App) 305 SW2d 837, 65 ALR2d 1443, error ref n r e.

medical practice. The professional practice of a physician.

medical preparations. Substances treated or compounded for administration or use to obtain cure or relief from sickness or pain. Grace v Collector of Customs (CA9 Cal) 79 F 313, 314.

See **medicine; patent medicine.**

medical record. A record kept in the office of a physician or surgeon or in a hospital of observations made in the course of a medical examination of a patient, of treatment administered to him, and of surgery performed upon him.

medical science. The science in which physicians and surgeons are trained. The branch of science dealing with the human body, disease, the treatment of sickness, and the alleviation of pain and suffering.

medical school. See **medical college.**

medical service corporation. See **blue cross; blue shield.**

medical testimony. See **medical evidence.**

medical therapy. Curative treatment by physician.

medical treatment. The administration of treatment by a physician. 29 Am J Rev ed Ins § 756.

See **medical or surgical treatment; regular care of physician.**

medicine. Any substance administered in the treatment of disease; a remedial agent; a remedy. State v Stoddard, 215 Iowa 534, 245 NW 273, 86 ALR 616; Kelly v Carroll, 36 Wash 2d 482, 219 P2d 79, 19 ALR2d 1174; Waldo v Poe (DC Wash) 14 F2d 749. Anything, however simple, administered in the treatment of disease or disorder of the human system. Kelly v Carroll, 36 Wash 2d 482, 219 P2d 79, 19 ALR2d 1174. The science and art of preserving health and preventing and curing disease. Lowman v Kuecker, 246 Iowa 1227, 71 NW2d 586, 52 ALR2d 1380. A technical word, denoting a science or art comprehending, not only therapeutics, but the art of understanding the nature of diseases, the causes that produce them, as well as knowing how to prevent them,—hygiene, sanitation, and the like. Bragg v State, 134 Ala 165, 32 So 767. The practice of medicine.

See **curative medicine: medicinal preparations; patent medicine.**

medicine chest. A wooden or metal box with cover and lock, having compartments or slots in which drugs and medicines may be safely carried for use as needed by any member of an expedition going abroad or afield. Required equipment of a ship under certain statutes. 48 Am J1st Ship § 176.

medietas advocationis (me̞-dī′e-tas ad-vo-kā-she-ō′nis). The moiety of an advowson; a half right of presentation which existed when two patrons shared the right to present one clerk or parson.

medietas linguae (me̞-dī′e-tas ling′gwē). See **jury de medietate linguae.**

medietate linguae. See **de medietate linguae.**

medio. See **de medio.**

medio tempore (mē′di-ō tem′po-re). In the meantime.

meditatio fugae (med-i-tā′shi-ō fū′jē). The intention of fleeing or running away.

medium. A person who professes ability to communicate with departed spirits. McMasters v State, 21 Okla Crim 318, 207 P 566, 29 ALR 292. One in a confidential relationship to the person advised professionally by him in the realm of spiritualism. Lyon v Home (Eng) LR 6 Eq 655. One who purports to heal disease by the application of forces beyond the physical world. 41 Am J1st Phys & S § 31.

medium concludendi (mē′di-um kon-klu-den′dī). A means of reaching a conclusion; a course of reasoning, as to reach the same result by a different medium concludendi. United States v California & Oregon Land Co. 192 US 355, 358, 48 L Ed 476, 479.

medium deferens (me′di-um de′fe-renz). The medium or means of descending; that is the intervening ancestor through whom property descends to the heir from a more remote ancestor; as where a grandson inherits from his grandfather, the grandson's father being dead, the dead father is the medium deferens of the descent or consanguinity. Lessee of Levy v M'Cartee (US) 6 Pet 102, 113, 8 L Ed 334, 338.

medium filum (me′di-um fī′lum). The middle thread.

medium filum aquae (me′di-um fī′lum a′kwē). The middle thread of the water or river.

medium of payment. Money, currency, current funds. 11 Am J2d B & N § 153. Money or, by agreement of the parties, anything of value which the debtor is to give and the creditor to receive as a satisfaction of a debt. 11 Am J2d B & N § 155; 40 Am J1st Paym § 40.

medius ancestor (me'di-us an'ses-tor). Same as **medium deferens**.

medletum (měd-lē'tum). Same as **medley**.

medley (med'li). A mixture of a heterogeneous character. In an old sense, a sudden fight; a melée; an affray.

medscheat. A bribe. Same as **medseat**.

medseat. A bribe.

meet. See **meeting**.

meeting. Coming together by approaches from opposite directions; coming face to face; joining. An assembly or convening of persons in large or small numbers.
See **directors' meeting; family meeting; race meeting; regular meeting; religious meeting; stockholders' meeting; town meeting**.

meeting each other. A phrase not meaning merely persons passing each other while going in opposite directions, but implying a coming together in such manner that there would be an actual collision or an apparent danger of one, if they should pursue their course without change of direction. Riepe v Elting, 89 Iowa 82, 56 NW 285.

meeting of creditors. See **creditors' meeting**.

meeting of directors. See **directors' meeting**.

meeting of minds. See **meeting of the minds**.

meeting of stockholders. See **stockholders' meeting**.

meeting of the minds. A concurrence of intention between a promisor and a promisee. The mutual assent of the parties on all the essential elements or terms of a contract. 17 Am J2d Contr § 18.

meeting of vehicles. An exigency for which rules of the road are provided, particularly where physical features of the way obscure the approach of the one vehicle to the driver of the other. 8 Am J2d Auto §§ 687 et seq.

meeting of vessels. An exigency for which steering, sailing, and other pertinent rules of navigation are provided. 48 Am J1st Ship §§ 250 et seq.

meeting place. See **place of meeting**.

megbote (meg'bōt). Same as **maegbote**.

meindre age (měn'druh äzh). Under age,—under the age of majority.

melancholia (mel-ạn-kō'li-ạ). A disease of the brain which, in its simple form, is characterized by deep depression, by inconsolable sorrow, by weary grief, and yet withal by no impairment of the intellectual powers. See Browne, Med. Jurisprudence of Insanity, section 266.
That form of melancholia which creates a prevailing propensity to suicide, consists in the unfounded and morbid fancies of the sufferer regarding his means of subsistence or his position in life, or in distorted conceptions of his relations to society or his family, of his rights or duties, or of dangers threatening his person, property or reputation. When fully developed, the hallucination becomes the sole object of attention; the evil seems overwhelming and hopeless. See Connecticut Mutual Life Ins. Co. v Green, 86 Pa 92.

meldfeoh. (Saxon.) A reward paid to an informer.

melior (me'li-or). Better; more advantageous; preferable.

meliorating waste. An act which, although technically waste, results in improving instead of injuring the inheritance. J. H. Bellows Co. v Covell, 28 Ohio App 277, 162 NE 621.

melioration. The equitable doctrine which recognizes the right of compensation for improvements made by an occupying claimant. 27 Am J1st Improv § 26. A betterment; a permanent improvement made upon land.
"It is a maxim suggested by nature, that reparations and meliorations bestowed upon a house, or on land, ought to be defrayed out of the rents." Green v Biddle (US) 8 Wheat 82, 5 L Ed 547, 567.

Meliorem conditionem ecclesiae suae facere potest praelatus, deteriorem nequaquam (me-li-ō'rem kon-di-she-ō'nem e-klē'si-ē su'ē fā'se-re po'test prē-lā'tus, de-te-ri-ō'rem ne-quā'quam). A prelate can make the condition of his own church better, but in no wise, or by no means, worse.

Meliorem conditionem suam facere potest minor, deteriorem nequaquam (me-li-ō'rem kon-di'she-ō'nem su'am fā'se-re po'test mī'nor, de-te-ri-ō'rem ne-quā'quam). A minor can make his own condition better, but in no wise, or by no means, worse.

Melior est causa possidentis (me'li-or est kâ'za pos-si-den'tis). The cause of the party who is in possession is the more advantageous.

Melior est conditio defendentis (me'li-or est kon-di'-she-ō de-fen-den-'tis). The position of the defendant is superior. Osborn v Baxter (4 Cush) 58 Mass 406, 408.

Melior est conditio possidentis et rei quam actoris (me'li-or est kon-di'she-ō pos-si-den'tis et rē'ī quam ak-tō'ris). The position of the party in possession and that of the defendant is more advantageous than that of the plaintiff.

Melior est conditio possidentis, et rei quam actoris, ubi neuter jus habet (me'li-or est kon-di'she-ō pos-si-den'tis, et rē'ī quam ak-tō'ris, u'bi nū'ter jūs hā'-bet). The position of the party in possession and that of the defendant is more advantageous than that of the plaintiff, where neither has the right.

Melior est conditio possidentis, ubi neuter jus habet (me'li-or est kon-di'she-ō pos-si-den'tis, u'bi nū'ter jūs hā'bet). The position of the party in possession is the more advantageous, where neither party has the right.

Melior est justitia vere praeveniens quam severe puniens (me'li-or est jūs-ti'she-a vē'rē prē-ve'ni-enz quam se-vē'rē pū'ni-enz). Truly preventive justice is better than severe punishment.

melioribus damnis. See **de melioribus damnis**.

Melius est in tempore occurrere, quam post causam vulneratum remedium quaerere (me'li-us est in tem'po-re o-ker're-re, quam post kâ'zam vul-ne-rā'tum re-mē'di-um kwē're-re). It is better to hasten to meet a thing in time than to seek a remedy after his situation has been injured.

Melius est jus deficiens quam jus incertum (me'li-us est jūs dē-fī'she-enz quam jūs in-ser'tum). A deficient law is better than an uncertain one.

Melius est omnia mala pati quam malo consentire (me'li-us est om'ni-a ma'la pa'tī quam ma'lo kon-sen-tī're). It is better to suffer every ill than to consent to evil.

Melius est petere fontes quam sectari rivulos (me'li-us est pe'te-re fon'tēz quam sek-tā'rī ri'vu-lōs). It is better to seek out the springs or sources than to follow the little streams.

Melius est recurrere quam malo currere (me'li-us est re-ker're-re quam ma'lō ker're-re). It is better to recede than to rush into error.

melius inquirendum (me'li-us in-quī-ren'dum). To be better inquired into,—an ancient writ ordering a further inquiry into a matter.

melting. Dissolving under heat.

member. One who belongs to an organization, such as cooperative association, fraternal order, or membership corporation. Smith v Iron M.T. Terminal Co. 46 Mont 13, 125 P 649. An incorporator or the successor of an incorporator of a corporation which has no capital stock. 18 Am J2d Corp § 460. A hand, foot, arm, leg, finger, toe, testicle, or other organ of the body. See 4 Bl Comm 205.

member of Congress. A member of the lower house, the House of Representatives, of the Congress of the United States. In a broader sense, a member of either the House of Representatives or the Senate.

member of crew. One of a crew of a vessel or of a work force.

As to the meaning of "member of a crew" within Social Security and Unemployment Compensation Acts see Anno: 161 ALR 842.

member of family. Narrowly, one of a group related by blood or marriage. Sometimes limited to a close relative, such as widow, child, or parent. Fennimore v Pittsburg-Scammon Coal Co. 100 Kan 372, 164 P 265 (workmen's compensation statute). Broadly, one of a group living in the same household. Within the meaning of a statute permitting substituted service of process upon the defendant in an action by leaving a copy with a "member of his family": —any person living permanently and continuously with the defendant in the same domestic establishment. Anno: 136 ALR 1505.

The purpose of a clause of an automobile liability insurance policy excluding from coverage an injury to "any member of the family of the insured residing in the same household as the insured" is to exempt the insurer from liability to those persons to whom the insured, on account of close family ties, would be apt to be partial in case of injury, and cases defining the word "family", but involving an entirely different situation, are not authoritative. Tomlyanovich v Tomlyanovich, 239 Minn 250, 58 NW2d 855, 50 ALR2d 108.

The question as to who is a member of the insured's "family" within the coverage clause of a property insurance policy depends upon the precise terminology of the particular policy involved and the particular circumstances present. Anno: 1 ALR2d 561.

member of household. An inmate or resident of a house in which two or more persons reside. A member of the insured's family for the purpose of a clause of an automobile theft insurance policy excepting from coverage a theft by a "member of the household" of the insured. Anno: 48 ALR2d 93, § 32. Within the meaning of a clause of an automobile liability insurance policy excluding from coverage "members of the insured's household":—a person living in the same household as the insured, whether or not the insured is the head of the household. Anno: 50 ALR2d 122, § 3.

The question as to who is a member of the insured's household within the coverage clause of a property insurance policy depends upon the precise terminology of the particular policy involved and the particular circumstances present. Anno: 1 ALR2d 561.

member of the human body. See **member.**

membership. A condition or status of being a member. In reference to a building and loan association, a matter of contract and ordinarily acquired by taking and holding stock, such being evidenced by the issuance and delivery of a certificate or certificates of stock to the member and the inscription of his name on the books of the association. 13 Am J2d B & L Assoc § 16.

membership certificate. See **certificate of membership.**

membership corporation. A distinct kind of corporation authorized under the statutes of most jurisdictions, existing for purposes other than profit, often for charitable, fraternal, social, or religious purposes, in which the participants acquire the status of members rather than stockholders. 18 Am J2d Corp § 460.

membership in exchange. See **seat on exchange.**

membership list. A list of the members of a building and loan association, constituting one of the records of the association. 13 Am J2d B & L Assoc § 18.

membership organization. A voluntary organization which is a charity only as its stated purposes, and the nature and extent of its operations make it so, considering the objective of applicable statutes. 15 Am J2d Char § 149.

See **membership corporation.**

members of a family. See **member of family.**

membrana (mem-brā'na). Membrane; parchment.

membrum pro membro (mem'brum prō mem'brō). A limb for a limb.

memoranda. Plural of **memorandum.**

memorandum. An informal writing. A brief writing to preserve a thing or an event against loss of memory in respect thereof. A writing used by a witness to assist and refresh his memory while on the witness stand. 29 Am J2d Ev § 876. A writing which records the terms of an agreement preliminary to the drafting and execution of a more formal instrument. A writing evidencing a transaction, for example, a sale by auction. 7 Am J2d Auct § 34. As a requirement of the statute of frauds:—a writing which contains the names of the parties to the contract, the terms and conditions of the contract, and a description of the subject matter sufficient to render it capable of identification. 49 Am J1st Stat § 32. A writing submitted by the attorney of the losing party to the attorney of the successful party embodying his objections to the decree as drafted by the latter. 27 Am J2d Eq § 250. A draft of a decree in equity, filed with the clerk of court, not as a record, but merely as a memorandum of the decree to be entered. 27 Am J2d Eq § 250. A written opinion of an equity court. 27 Am J2d Eq § 235.

memorandum articles. See **memorandum clause.**

memorandum clause. A limitation of liability of a marine insurer for partial loss of articles perishable in their nature or peculiarly susceptible to damage. 29A Am J Rev ed Ins § 1584. Not a finding of fact. Gould v McCormick, 75 Wash 61, 134 P 676. To be regarded as an order of court where its substance is clearly that of an order. Feenaughty Machinery Co. v Turner, 44 Idaho 363, 257 P 38.

memorandum check. An instrument in the ordinary form of a bank check, with the word "memorandum" written across its face, not intended for immediate presentation, but simply as evidence of an indebtedness of the drawer to the holder. United States v Isham (US) 17 Wall 496, 21 L Ed 728.

memorandum decision. The decision of an appellate court usually contained in a single very brief paragraph, announcing the bare result of the court's decision, without an opinion.

memorandum of alteration. A disclaimer filed by a patentee under the patent laws of England whereby he denied making any claim to certain rights to which he was not entitled in order to prevent the total loss of his patent.

memorandum of association. Same as **articles of incorporation.**

memorandum of costs. A bill of costs; an itemization of the costs or disbursements to be filed by the party entitled to costs, a copy of which is served upon the adverse party. 20 Am J2d Costs § 91.

memorandum of levy. An entry made by the sheriff upon a writ of attachment of the levy made by him under the writ. 6 Am J2d Attach § 312. A comparable entry made by a sheriff on a writ of execution delivered to him for service. 30 Am J2d Exec § 563.

memorandum of protest. Same as certificate of protest.
See **protest.**

memorandum sale. Same as **sale on approval.**

memorial. A manifestation of recognition of a person or an event to stand as a reminder in the future of services or sacrifices made by the person or of the importance of the event. A memorandum; a means of reminding of something to be done. A short note, abstract, memorandum, or rough draft of the orders of court from which the records thereof may at any time be fully made. State v Shaw, 73 Vt 149, 165, 50 A 863.

memorial building. A building erected as a memorial to deceased and living veterans of the armed forces but usually available for public meetings and entertainments of various kinds under conditions prescribed by the management.

Memorial Day. A national holiday, also a legal holiday in most of the states, observed on May 30, in memory of the deceased members of the armed forces, with special recognition to those who made the supreme sacrifice while in service. A legal holiday in some of the southern states in memory of deceased members of the armed forces, including the armed forces of the Confederate States.

memoriter (mẹ-mor'i-tėr). From memory; that is with nothing to refresh the mind with respect to past events or circumstances.

memory. The power of retaining knowledge in the mind; the mental power of recognizing past knowledge. State v Coyne, 214 Mo 344, 114 SW 8.
See **impairment of memory; refreshing memory; time of legal memory.**

men. See **man.**

menace. A threat of harm, of confinement, of personal injury. Morrill v Nightingale, 93 Cal 452, 28 P 1068.

menagerie. A collection of wild or strange animals in an enclosure for exhibition and sometimes for performances. 4 Am J2d Amuse § 3.

menial. Low; servile. A menial servant.

menial servant. A servant whose duties involve the most simple of domestic tasks, requiring little, if any, exercise of discretion, and often consisting in tasks of a degrading nature.
Menials or menial servants were originally so called because they were employed to serve their masters intra moenia, within the walls; that is, in the house. They were domestic or household servants. See 1 Bl Comm 425.

meningitis (men-in-jī'tis). A bodily infirmity. First Nat. Bank v Equitable Life Assur. Soc. 225 Ala 586, 144 So 451. A disease of the brain and the spinal cord often resulting in mental derangement and insanity. Tiffany v Tiffany, 84 Iowa 122, 126.

men of straw. See **straw man.**

mens (menz). (Latin.) Mind; intention; reason; judgment; understanding; conscience.

mensa (men'sạ). A table; a dining table; board; sustenance; support.

mensa et thoro (men'sa et tho'rō). Bed and board.
See **divorce a mensa et thoro.**

menses (men'sēz). The periodic flow experienced by a woman from puberty to menopause.
See **suppression of menses.**

mensis (men'sis). A month.

mensis vetitus (men'sis ve'ti-tus). The prohibited month,—the summer closed season for deer hunting, also called "fence month."

mens legislatories (mēnz le-jis-la-tō'ris). The intention of the legislature; the legislative intent.

mensor (men'sor). (Civil law.) A measurer; a surveyor.

mens rea (mēnz re'a). An evil intent; a guilty mind. Durham v United States, 94 App DC 228, 214 F2d 862, 45 ALR2d 1430; Brown v State 23 Del (7 Penn) 159, 74 A 836. Referring not to one state of mind, but to many different ones for many different offenses. Brown v State, 23 Del (7 Penn) 159, 74 A 836.

Mens testatoris in testamentis spectanda est (mēnz tes-tā-tō'ris in tes-ta-men'tis spek-tan'da est). In wills, the intention of the testator should be regarded.

mensularius (men-su-lā'ri-us). (Civil law.) A moneychanger; a money dealer.

mensura (men-sū'ra). A measure.

mensura domini regis (men-sū'ra do'mi-nī rē'jis). The measure of our lord, the king.
The original standard of measure was so called, and that of weight was called pondus regis, weight of the king. These standards were established by parliament and subsequent statutes directed them to be kept in the exchequer and required that all weights and measures should conform to them, but the requirement was most difficult to enforce. See 1 Bl Comm 276.

mental abstraction. Want of awareness of one's surroundings, even of circumstances fraught with peril. 38 Am J1st Negl § 187.

mental anguish. Grief. Mental suffering as distinguished from physical pain, but inclusive of the mental reaction to physical pain and suffering caused by a personal injury. 22 Am J2d Damg § 195.

mental capacity. The condition or quality of the mind which renders one criminally responsible for his acts; an essential of criminal responsibility. State v Pinski (Mo) 163 SW2d 785. Sufficient capacity to know and understand in a reasonable manner the nature and character of the transaction engaged in. Shelton v Shelton, (Tex Civ App) 281 SW 331, 334.
See **capacity**; **mental incapacity**.

mental condition. The state of mind of a person in reference to his consciousness, senses, and perceptions. Mutual Life Ins. Co. v Terry (US) 15 Wall 580, 588, 21 L Ed 236, 241.
See **insanity**; **mental capacity**; **mental incapacity**.

mental cruelty. As ground for divorce, misconduct which impairs or threatens to impair physical or mental health of the complainant in the action, 24 Am J2d Div & S § 35; conduct on the part of the defendant which renders it impracticable for the complainant to perform the marital duties. 24 Am J2d Div & S § 37.

mental defect. A defect in the mind of a person. For the purposes of the Durham or product test of criminal responsibility, a condition which is not considered capable of either improving or deteriorating, and which may be either congenital, the result of injury, or the residual effect of a physical or mental disease. Durham v United States, 94 App DC 228, 214 F2d 862, 45 ALR2d 1430.
See **mental disability**.

mental disability. Any abnormal condition of the mind, regardless of its medical label, which substantially affects mental or emotional processes and substantially impairs behavior controls. Blocker v United States, 116 App DC 78, 320 F2d 800, cert den 375 US 923, 11 L Ed 2d 167, 84 S Ct 269.
A witness who has a "mental disqualification" is one who has not the capacity to receive, to record, and to recall impressions and to testify intelligently concerning them. Batterson v State, 52 Tex Crim 381, 107 SW 826.
See **insanity**; **mental incapacity**; **total mental disability**.

mental disease. A disease affecting the mind. For the purposes of a Durham or product test in determining criminal responsibility, a condition which is considered capable of either improving or deteriorating. Durham v United States, 94 App DC 228, 214 F2d 862, 45 ALR2d 1430.
See **insanity**.

mental disorder. An affliction of the mind.
See **insanity**.

mental disqualification. See **mental disability**.

mental endurance contest. A form of public competition for prizes conducted in a place of amusement. 4 Am J2d Amuse § 28.

mental examination. An examination by a psychiatrist to determine the condition of the mind, sometimes conducted as part of a proceeding for the commitment of a person as insane or for the appointment of a committee or guardian of his person or property. An examination by a psychiatrist conducted by way of perpetuating testimony through taking a deposition. 23 Am J2d Dep § 46. An examination of the defendant in a criminal prosecution to determine his criminal responsibility, his ability to stand trial, or his condition while awaiting execution in the event the death penalty has been imposed.

mental healer. One engaged in a peculiar system of practicing medicine. 41 Am J1st Phys & S § 31.

mental illness. See **insanity**.

mental inbecility. See **imbecility**.

mental incapacity. A condition of outright insanity or other weakness or deficiency of mind which renders the person afflicted incapable of understanding the nature and effect of a business transaction. 13 Am J2d Canc Inst § 13.
Old age, weakening of the memory and understanding, and occasional strange and eccentric acts are not of themselves mental incapacity. Beckley National Bank v Boone (CA4 W Va) 115 F2d 513.
See **incompetent person**.

mental incompetent. See **incompetent person**; **insane person**; **mental incapacity**.

mental institution. See **asylum**; **state hospital**.

mental reservation. The secret understanding of a party to a contract concerning the meaning of the agreement. 17 Am J2d Contr § 248.

mental shock. See **nervous shock**; **shock**.

mental suffering. See **mental anguish**.

mentiri (men-tī′rī). To lie; to falsify; to deceive; to counterfeit; to misrepresent; to break one's word or promise.

Mentiri est contra mentem ire (men-tī′rī est kon′trā men′tem ī′re). To lie is to go contrary to the mind, to do a foolish thing.

mentis (men′tis). See **compos mentis**; **non compos mentis**.

mention (men-tish′ọn). A lie; a deceit; a falsification.

mephitic (mẹ-fit′ik). Neither more nor less than what common folks refer to as "stinking."

mer. Abbreviation of meridian.

mera gratia. See **e mera gratia**.

mera noctis (me′ra nok′tis). Midnight.

mercable. Merchantable.

mercantile. Commercial. Pertaining to trade and commerce in merchandise.
Although the word includes trade, it is of a larger significance, being extended to all commercial operations, so that we speak of shipping merchants, commission merchants, and forwarding merchants. But the dishes of a restaurant could not with propriety be described as merchandise, or the proprietor as a merchant, or as engaged in mercantile pursuits. Swift & Co. v Tempelos, 178 NC 276, 101 SE 8, 7 ALR 1581, 1583.

mercantile agency. A person, firm, or corporation, engaged in the business of collecting information relating to the financial standing, credit, character, responsibility, and general reputation of persons, firms, and corporations engaged in business, and furnishing this information to subscribers for a consideration. Annotation: 54 ALR2d 889, § 5; 15 Am J2d Collect § 3. A term sometimes applied to a collection agency.
See **collection agency**; **commercial agency**.

mercantile business. The business of buying and selling articles of merchandise. State v Winneshiek Co-op. Burial Asso. 237 Iowa 556, 22 NW2d 800, 165 ALR 1092.

mercantile contract. A contract for the purchase or

sale of goods, wares, and merchandise. A contract between merchants or persons in trade.

mercantile custom. A custom of merchants.
See **custom; trade usage.**

mercantile establishment. Any place where goods, wares, and merchandise are offered for sale. Anno: 16 ALR 542. Within the meaning of statutes regulating or limiting hours of labor or otherwise restricting the employment of women and children: —a place where the buying and selling of articles of merchandise are conducted as an employment. 31 Am J Rev ed Lab § 784.

mercantile law. Same as **law merchant.**

Mercantile National Bank Case. A recent decision by the United States Supreme Court in respect of the venue of actions against national banks. Mercantile Nat. Bank v Langdeau, 371 US 555, 9 L Ed 2d 523, 83 S Ct 520.

mercantile paper. Same as **commercial paper.**

mercantile partnership. A trading firm engaged in buying and selling goods.

mercantile restrictions. Limitations placed by covenant upon the location of places of business within a designated and described locality.

mercantile rule. A rule for the application of partial payments as between interest and principal, by which interest is charged on each item of principal on the debit side and credited on each item on the credit side of the account, and a balance of such interest is struck and added to the balance of the principal. In other words, the rule is to compute the interest on the principal debt until maturity or any given time, and the interest on payments made, for the time when made, until such time, and then deduct the one sum from the other. 30 Am J Rev ed Int § 49.

mercat (mer'kat). A market.

mercative (mėr'ka̧-tiv). Pertaining to trade.

mercatoribus. See **De Mercatoribus.**

mercatum (mer-kā'tum). Same as **mercatus.**

mercatus (mer-kā'tus). A market; a fair; a public place for the transaction of business.

mercenarius (mer-se-nā'ri-us). A mercenary; a hired soldier; a hired servant.

Mercen-Lage. The Mercian laws, which were observed in many of the midland counties of England, and those bordering on the principality of Wales, the retreat of the ancient Britons.
These laws were very probably intermixed with the British or Druidical customs. See 1 Bl Comm 65.

merces (mer'sēz). (Civil law.) Wages for labor.

merchandise. Noun: Goods, wares, and commodities commonly bought and sold in trade or market by merchants. All kinds of personal property ordinarily bought and sold in the market. Blackwood v Cutting Packing Co. 76 Cal 212, 18 P 248. Goods or things kept for sale, constantly sold and replaced by another supply. Root Refineries v Gay Oil Co. 171 Ark 129, 284 SW 26, 46 ALR 979; McPartin v Clarkson, 240 Mich 390, 215 NW 338, 54 ALR 1535. For the purposes of customs duties, articles, goods, and wares. 21 Am J2d Cust D § 1. As an entry on a ship's manifest, wares, and chattels of every description, even contraband articles the importation of which is forbidden by law. United States v Sischo, 262 US 165, 67 L Ed 925, 43 S Ct 511. Verb: To trade or traffic in goods and wares ordinarily bought and sold by merchants. Ellis v Commonwealth, 186 Ky 494, 217 SW 368, 11 ALR 1030, 1031.
See **stock of merchandise.**

merchandise broker. A person who negotiates the sale of merchandise for others without having it in his possession or control. See Robinson, Norton & Co. v Corsicana Cotton Factory, 124 Ky 435, 99 SW 305; Jones v Pittsburg, 176 Pa Super 154, 106 A2d 892.

Merchandise Marks Act. An English statute passed in 1862, to protect trademarks from infringement.

merchant. In most common usage, a retailer of merchandise. In a more accurate sense, one who buys and sells merchandise as an entrepreneur.
See **commission merchant.**

merchantability. See **merchantable.**

merchantable. Of good quality and salable, but not necessarily the best. Anno: 21 ALR 368; 46 Am J1st Sales § 149. Being at least of medium quality, of such quality as to bring the average price for goods of a similar kind. 46 Am J1st Sales § 149.
The term includes what the law requires. "The Uniform Sales Act carries an implied warranty of merchantable quality. Therefore the defendant's sale to the plaintiff warranted that the kerosene was of the statutory proof." Manning Manufacturing Co. v Hartol Products Corporation (CA2 Vt) 99 F2d 813.
One meaning of the term, as applied to the sale of goods, is that the article sold shall be reasonably suitable for the ordinary uses it was manufactured to meet. Giant Mfg. Co. v Yates-American Machine Co. (CA8 Iowa) 111 F2d 360.

merchantable coal. Coal which is not only salable but salable at a profit. Anno: 28 ALR2d 1031.

merchantable quality. See **merchantable.**

merchantable timber. Trees suitable for the production of lumber. Anno: 72 ALR2d 734. Trees which will produce any salable product. Anno: 72 ALR2d 735. Timber of a grade or quality to be profitably used, a matter determinable by experts with approximate certainty. Lee Lumber Co. v Hotard, 122 La 850, 48 So 286.

merchantable title. A marketable title. A title which a reasonably prudent man would accept in the ordinary course of business after being fully apprised of the facts and the law applicable thereto. Holliday v Arthur, 241 Iowa 1193, 44 NW2d 717, 24 ALR2d 1302; Campbell v Doherty, 53 NM 280, 206 P2d 1145, 9 ALR2d 699.
See **marketable title.**

merchantable title, abstract, and deed. A phrase expressive of a vendor's obligation, meaning that he must furnish an abstract of title showing in itself a marketable title of record in the vendor and execute a deed conveying a marketable title of record to the purchaser. Campbell v Doherty, 53 NM 280, 206 P2d 1145, 9 ALR2d 699.

merchantman. Same as **merchant vessel.**

merchant marine. The entire body of ships and their personnel used in commerce of the nation.

Merchant Marine Act. See **Jones Act; Merchant Seamen's Act.**

merchants' accounts. Such accounts as concern the trade of merchandise between merchant and mer-

MERCHANT [794] MERGER

chant, their factors or servants. 34 Am J1st Lim Ac § 98.

merchant seamen. Men employed on private vessels of any nation, as distinguished from men employed on public vessels or in naval forces. United States v Sullivan (CC Ore) 43 F 602, 604.

Merchant Seamen's Act. A federal statute which provides that any seaman who has signed an agreement and is discharged before commencement of the voyage or before one month's wages are earned, without fault on his part and without his consent, is entitled to receive from the master or owner, in addition to any wages he may have earned, a sum equal to one month's wages, on adducing evidence satisfactory to the court hearing the case. 46 USC § 594.
See **Jones Act.**

merchant vessel. A vessel which carries cargo. A vessel which is wholly engaged in commercial service. Petition of United States, 250 US 246, 256, 63 L Ed 962, 968, 39 S Ct 460.

merchet (mûr'chêt). Same as **marcheta.**

merciament (mėr'si-ạ-mẹnt). Amercement.

Mercian laws (mėr'sian lâs). See **Mercen-Lage.**

merciful. Disposed to spare another the suffering which might be inflicted upon him. Willett v Willett, 197 Ky 663, 247 SW 739, 31 ALR 426.
See **humane.**

Mercis appellatio ad res mobiles tantum pertinet (mer'sis ap-pel-lā'she-ō ad rēz mō'bi-lēz tan'tum per'ti-net). The term "merx" (merchandise) pertains only to movable things.

Mercis appellatione homines non continere (mer'sis ap-pel-lā-she-ō'ne ho'mi-nēz non kon-ti-nē're). The term "merx" (merchandise) does not apply to men.

mercy. See **in mercy; merciful; recommendation of mercy.**

mere (mēr). Adjective: Nothing more. Noun: The sea. A term of old English for boundary.
See **mere-stone.**

mere (măr). (French.) Mother

mere droit (măr drwah). Same as **mere jus.**

mere irregularity. See **irregularity.**

mere jus (mēr jūs). A bare right.
See **mere right.**

mere motion (mēr mō'shọn). Of a person's own free will; a voluntary act.

mere possibility. See **possibility.**

mere right. The jus mereum, or mere right of property, without either possession or even the right of possession. See 2 Bl Comm 197.

mere-stone. A stone marking a boundary line or corner.

meretricious (mer-ẹ-trish'us). Lewd; sexually immoral.

meretricious relation. A sexual relation which is immoral, if not illicit.

meretricious union. A marriage in which either or both of the parties is legally incapable; hence, one which is not a matrimonial union.
Such incapacity or disability may result from having another husband or wife still living; from want of age; from want of consent of parents or guardians; or from want of sufficient mental capacity. See 1 Bl Comm 436.

mere volunteer. See **volunteer.**

merge. To sink or disappear in something else; to be swallowed up; to lose identity or individuality, Marfield v Cincinnati, Dayton & Toledo Traction Co. 111 Ohio St 139, 144 NE 689, 40 ALR 357, 369, as the negotiations for a contract unite and lose identity in the written contract as finally executed, Price v Block (CA7 Ill) 124 F2d 738, as one agreement is lost in a later agreement substituted for it by the parties, 17 Am J2d Contr § 459, as prior negotiations between vendor and purchaser are swallowed up by the deed, 23 Am J2d Deeds § 161, and as a claim by the state disappears in state ownership as acquired by escheat. 27 Am J2d Esch § 39.

merger in judgment. The extinguishment of claim pleaded as a cause of action in the judgment rendered for the plaintiff. Anno: 32 ALR2d 1147. The extinguishment of an obligation for the payment of money existing under a separation agreement in a judgment for alimony. 24 Am J2d Div & S § 908.

merger of action in criminal prosecution. The ancient doctrine of the common law that all civil remedies in favor of one injured by a felony are merged in the felony. 1 Am J2d Actions § 45.

merger of corporations. A combination whereby one of the constituent companies remains in being, absorbing the other or all the other constituent corporations. 19 Am J2d Corp § 1492. A union or combination of pre-existing corporations wherein all but one go out of existence leaving a designated survivor. Anno: 27 ALR2d 777. A union, or amalgamation by which the stock of two corporations is made one, their property and franchises combined into one, their powers become the powers of one, and the identity of the two practically, if not actually, runs into one. State, ex rel. Nolan, v Montana Railway Co. 21 Mont 221, 53 P 623.

A distinction exists between a merger and a consolidation of corporations: in a merger, one of the combining corporations continues in existence and absorbs the others; in a consolidation, all the combining corporations are deemed dissolved and lose their identity in a new corporate entity which takes over the properties, powers, and privileges, as well as the liabilities, of the constituent companies. Dodier Realty & Invest. Co. v St. Louis Nat. Baseball Club, 361 Mo 981, 238 SW2d 321, 24 ALR2d 683; Marfield v Cincinnati, Dayton & Toledo Traction Co. 111 Ohio St 139, 144 NE 689, 40 ALR 357, 369. But the terms "consolidation" and "merger" have been used rather indiscriminately, and some of the courts and text writers have used the terms interchangeably, and, in cases of doubt, conjunctively, to express the idea of complete corporate union, whether a new corporation, normally results or whether a constituent corporation is normally preserved. Alabama Power Co. v McNinch, 68 App DC 132, 94 F2d 601.

merger of crimes. See **merger of offenses.**

merger of custom. The extinguishment of a custom by a statute which deals with the subject matter. Creekmore v F. T. Justice & Co. 152 Ky 514, 153 SW 738.

merger of estates. The absorption of one estate in another, where a greater estate and a lesser coincide and meet in one and the same person without any intermediate estate. 28 Am J2d Est § 374. The uniting of the legal and equitable interests in the same person. 54 Am J1st Trusts § 88.

merger of offenses. The common law doctrine that if a misdemeanor is an ingredient of a felony, the misdemeanor is an integral part of the felony and prosecution can only be for the felony. 21 Am J2d Crim L § 9. The embracing of one offense necessarily involved in another in the latter offense, for the purposes of determining the penalty upon conviction on a plea of guilty, for example, rape involving fornication, and robbery involving both assault and larceny. 21 Am J2d Crim L § 9. The doctrine that where an indictment charges more than one offense and the jury returns a general verdict of guilty, such verdict is understood to find the higher offense if there is testimony to support it. State v Nelson, 48 SCL (14 Rich) 169. The encompassing of an attempt to commit a crime in the crime itself when the latter is consummated. Anno: 59 ALR2d 998, § 42.

merger of personalities. The unity of husband and wife.

merger of school districts. Two or more school districts joining in a new or enlarged district. 47 Am J1st Sch § 22.

meridian. Adjective: At noon. Noun: A line of longitude, running north and south from pole to pole.
See **magnetic meridian; principal meridian; true meridian.**

meridies (mę-rid'i-ēz). Noon; midday.

Merito beneficium legis amittit, qui legem ipsam subvertere intendit (me'ri-tō be-ne-fi'she-um lē'jis a-mit'tit, quī lē'jem ip'sam sub-ver'te-re in-ten'dit). He justly loses the protection of the law who attempts to subvert it.

merito justitiae. See **ex merito justitiae.**

meritorious condition. See **condition meritorious.**

meritorious consideration. A consideration for a promise confined to three duties, that of charity, that of paying one's creditors, and that of maintaining a wife and children. Fischer v Union Trust Co. 138 Mich 612, 101 NW 852. A good consideration of natural love and affection, of love and affection based on kindred by blood and marriage. Williston, Contracts 3d ed § 110.

meritorious defense. A defense worthy of a hearing or judicial inquiry, because raising a question of law deserving some investigation and discussion or a real controversy as to essential facts arising from conflicting or doubtful evidence, albeit not a perfect defense or defense assured of prevailing at a trial. 30A Am J Rev ed Judgm § 682.

merits of case. The essential issues. The substantive rights presented by an action. The strict legal rights of the parties to an action, as contradistinguished from those mere questions of practice which every court regulates for itself, and from all matters which depend upon the discretion or favor of the court. Chouteau v Parker, 2 Minn 118, 121.
See **affidavit of merits; judgment on the merits; meritorious defense; pleading to the merits.**

merit system. The system in the Civil Service whereby appointments and promotions are made according to the merit and fitness rather than by way of political favor. 15 Am J2d Civ S § 20.

merit wage increase. A raise in pay ostensibly in recognition of individual aptitude and industry.
Where a union has been recognized as a bargaining agent of the employees, merit increases in wages cannot be made by the unilateral action of the employer, without being guilty of an unfair labor practice within the meaning of the statute requiring collective bargaining. 31 Am J Rev ed Lab § 243.

mero jure. See **in mero jure.**

mero motu (me'rō mō'tū). See **ex mero motu.**

Merton. See **Statute of Merton.**

merum (me'rum). Mere; bare; naked.

merry-go-round. An amusement device having carriages or wooden horses upon a revolving platform, particularly appealing to children. Condon v Forest Park, 278 Ill 218, 115 NE 825. A figure of speech for a continual round of work or pleasure.

merx (merks). Merchandise.

Merx est quicquid vendi potest (merx est quik'quid ven'dī po'test). Merchandise is whatever can be sold. Baldwin v Williams, 44 Mass (3 Met) 365, 367.

merx peculiaris (merx pe-kū-li-ā'ris). (Civil law.) The property of a slave invested in his own business.

mesaventure. Same as **misadventure.**

mescroyant (may"crwah-yant'). An unbeliever; an infidel; an agnostic.

mese (mēs). A house.

mesmerism (mez'mėr-izm). Same as **hypnotism.**

mesnality (mē'nal-i-ti). The manor or estate of a mesne lord.

mesne (mēn). Intermediate; intervening; the middle between two extremes. Davis v Dantzler Lumber Co. 261 US 280, 67 L Ed 387, 43 S Ct 349, 28 ALR 834, 836.

mesne conveyance (mēn kon-vā'ans). A conveyance prior to one, but subsequent to another, conveyance of the same property.

mesne damage (mēn dam'āj). The damage allowed in ejectment based upon the profits of the land during the time it was held tortiously by the defendant. 25 Am J2d Eject § 148.

mesne encumbrance (mēn en-kum'brans). An encumbrance which is prior in right to one encumbrance and subsequent in right to another one.

mesne lord (mēn lôrd). A lord in the middle, standing between those tenants holding of him and the king of England or lord paramount under whom he holds. De Peyster v Michael, 6 NY 467.

mesne process (mēn prō'ses). Process issued between the beginning of a suit and final judgment, especially process in invoking a provisional remedy, such as attachment or civil arrest.

mesne profits (mēn prof'its). Intermediate profits; profits accruing between two points of time. Profits accruing from land during an intermediate period, such as a period of tortious holding by the defendant in an action in ejectment. 25 Am J2d Eject § 148.

mesprision (mes-pri'zhun). Same as **misprision.**

mesque (mėsk). Unless; except.

message. A communication from one person to another. A communication received for transmission for telegraph. 52 Am J1st Teleg & T § 103.
See **dead-head message.**

messenger. One who delivers written telegrams. One

MESSENGER [796] MEZZANINE

employed for the delivery of messages, running errands, or services of a comparable character.

The term, by its fair import and significance, does not apply to a public officer acting in an original capacity in the discharge of duties imposed upon him by law, but presupposes a superior in authority whose servant the messenger is and whose mandate he executes, not as a deputy, with power to discriminate and judge, or to bind his superior, but as a mere bearer and communicator of the will of his superior. Pfister v Central Pacific Railroad Co. 70 Cal 169, 11 P 686.

See **express messenger**.

messenger service. A service, sometimes conducted by a telegraph company in addition to its usual business of transmitting messages by telegram, consisting in furnishing persons for delivering messages or performing other errands. 52 Am J1st Teleg & T § 102.

Messis sementem sequitur (mes'sis se-men'tem se'-qui-ter). The crop follows the sower.

messuage (mes'wąj). A house. In some contexts, a dwelling house, with its adjacent buildings, orchard, garden, and curtilage. Gibson v Brockway, 8 NH 465.

mestizo (mes-tē'zō). The offspring of parents of different races, particularly the offspring of a Spaniard and an American Indian.

See **mustizo**.

meta (mēt'ą). An object marking a boundary; a monument; a boundary.

metabolism (me-tab'ǫ-lizm). The processes in the human body by which food is converted for assimilation and energy released.

metachronism (me-tak'rǫ-nizm). Error in computing time.

metallic poisoning. An occupational disability, of idiopathic, as distinguished from traumatic, origin. 58 Am J1st Workm Comp § 253.

metallum (me-tal'um). (Roman law.) A metal; a mine; a quarry.

metaphysical meaning. An artificial, overly-refined, or subtle meaning. 50 Am J1st Stat § 238.

metatus (me-tā'tus). A residence; a dwelling house.

metayer (me-tā'yėr). A person who worked a farm on shares; as, for half of the crops raised.

metecorn. Corn paid out for labor.

metegavel. Rent paid in victuals.

metempsychosis (me-temp-si-kō'sis). A belief that the souls of men, after death, pass into animals. Bonard's Will (NY) 16 Abb Pr NS 128, 182.

meteorological record. A record of weather or climate. 30 Am J2d Ev § 1001.

meteorological report. A weather report.

meteorological service. Furnishing information concerning the weather to be expected in a given area. A service expected of the Federal Aviation Agency. 49 USC § 1351.

meter. An installation made by a gas, electric, or water company for the purpose of measuring the amount of the product consumed in a particular house, place of business, or factory. A lineal measure of the metric system, equivalent to 39.37 inches.

See **parking meter; prepayment meter**.

meter charge. A charge made by a public utility for installing a meter. 43 Am J1st Pub Util § 55.

meter reader. An employee of an electric, gas, or water company, engaged in reading meters for the purpose of ascertaining and reporting to his employer the amount of the product consumed at particular houses, places of business, or factories.

meter rental. A service charge made by a public utility for the use or rental of one of its meters. 43 Am J1st Pub Util § 57.

metes and bounds (mēts and bounds). The boundary lines and marks of a piece of land. A means of description of land in a deed. 23 Am J2d Deeds § 228.

methanol (meth'ą-nol). Same as **methyl alcohol**.

metheglin (mę-theg'lin). A drink, otherwise known as mead, made from honey and malt, with yeast added. Marks v State, 159 Ala 71, 48 So 864.

method. Manner of accomplishing something. The way in which a thing is done.

As used in the Federal income tax statute providing that the taxpayer may make his returns in accordance with the "method" of accounting regularly employed in keeping the books of such taxpayer, the word "method" means the way of keeping the taxpayer's books according to a defined and regular plan. Huntington Securities Corporation v Bussey (CA6 Ohio) 112 F2d 368.

methomania (meth-ǫ-mā'ni-ą). A form of dipsomania. An abnormal craving for intoxicants. The befuddled condition of mind brought on by prolonged excessive use of intoxicants. State ex rel. Atty. Gen. v Savage, 89 Ala 1, 7 So 183.

methyl alcohol. Commonly known as wood alcohol; a narcotic poison rather than an intoxicating liquor. Obtained by the distillation of wood. 30 Am J Rev ed Intox L § 14.

metropolitan. Adjective: Pertaining to a metropolis, especially a large city such as New York. Noun: An archbishop.

metropolitan district. An entire center of population comprising a city and its suburbs.

mettre a large (mē'truh ah lärzh). To set free.

metus (me'tus). Fear; apprehension; dread; terror.

See **exceptio metus**.

meubles (mer'bluh). Same as **movables**.

See **biens meubles**.

Meum est promittere, non dimittere (mē'um est pro-mit'te-re, non di-mit'te-re). It is mine to promise, not to discharge.

meum et tuum (mē'um et tu'um). Mine and thine, my property and yours.

Mexican divorce. Literally a divorce obtained in Mexico, but often associated in the mind with a mail-order divorce. 24 Am J2d Div & S § 965.

See **mail-order divorce**.

Mexican grants. Land grants by the Mexican Government in areas later ceded to the United States.

Mexico Convention. A copyright treaty or convention to which the United States became a party. 18 Am J2d Copyr § 76.

meynour (mā-noor). Same as **mainour**.

mezzanine floor (mez'ą-nin flôr). A story of diminished height introduced between two main stories of a building, usually immediately above the ground floor. Biber v O'Brien, 138 Cal App 353, 32 P2d 425.

mfg. Abbreviation of "manufacturing." Seiberling v Miller, 207 Ill 443, 69 NE 800.

Michaelmas term (mik'l-mas tėrm). An English term of court held from November second to November twenty-fifth.

michel-gemote. One of the names of the general assembly, or general council or great council anciently held in England, which was the ancient predecessor of the body which finally developed into the modern parliament. See 1 Bl Comm 147.

michel-synod. Same as **michel-gemote**.

michel-synoth. Same as **michel-gemote**.

michery (mich'ėr-i). Trickery; larceny.

microphone. An instrumentality whereby sounds are intensified, in common use at the present time by public speakers and entertainers, and in radio and television.

microscopic blood test. See **microscopic examination**.

microscopic examination. A medical examination or analysis by a competent technician or other physician using a microscope to determine the condition of blood, urine, etc. Anno: 135 ALR 885; 23 Am J2d Dep § 220. An examination of blood stains with the aid of a microscope, particularly to ascertain if the blood was that of a human. State v Baker, 33 W Va 319, 370.

mid-air collision. A collision of aircraft, both of which are in flight.

mid-channel. The middle of a navigable stream. 56 Am J1st Wat § 177.

Grotius and Vattel speak of the middle of the river as the line of demarcation between two jurisdictions, but modern publicists and statesmen prefer the more accurate and more equitable boundary of the navigable mid-channel. If there be more than one channel of a river, the deepest channel is regarded as the navigable mid-channel for the purpose of territorial demarcation; and the boundary line will be the line drawn along the surface of the stream corresponding to the line of deepest depression of its bed. The islands on either side of the mid-channel are regarded as appendages to either bank; and if they have once been taken possession of by the nation to whose bank they are appendant, a change in the mid-channel of the river will not operate to deprive the nation of its possession, although the water-frontier line will follow the change of the mid-channel. Iowa v Illinois, 147 US 1, 9, 37 L Ed 55, 58, 13 S Ct 239.

middle lord. A mesne lord, standing in the middle, standing between his tenants who hold under him and the king or lord paramount under whom he holds. De Peyster v Michael, 6 NY 467.

middleman. One who buys from a manufacturer or supplier and sells to a consumer. An intermediary. One engaged, not to negotiate a sale or purchase, but simply to bring two parties together and permit them to make their own bargain. Synnott v Shaughnessy, 2 Idaho 122, 7 P 82; Banta v Chicago, 172 Ill 204, 50 NE 233; Moore v Turner, 137 W Va 299, 71 SE2d 342, 32 ALR2d 713; 12 Am J2d Brok § 173. An agent of an agent. State v Taberner, 14 RI 272.

middle name. The second Christian name of a person, intervening between the first Christian name and the surname; occasionally the name by which a person is called or which he uses.

An early rule, no longer closely adhered to, prevailed in some jurisdictions to the effect that both first and middle names were essential to a proper designation of a person. 38 Am J1st Name § 6.

middle of the river. See **middle of the stream**.

middle of the stream. The thread of a navigable river at mid-channel, generally equally distant from either bank. 56 Am J1st Wat § 177.

In international law, and by the usage of European nations, the term, as applied to a navigable river, is the same as the middle of the channel of the stream. By the language, "a line drawn along the middle of the river Mississippi from its source to the river Iberville," as there used, is meant along the middle of the channel of the river Mississippi. Iowa v Illinois, 147 US 1, 8, 37 L Ed 55, 57, 13 S Ct 239.

See **mid-channel**.

Middlesex. See **bill of Middlesex**.

middle thread. The middle or center line of a river, stream, way, street, or road. Ingraham v Wilkinson 21 Mass (4 Pick) 268.

See **middle of the stream**.

midget racing. A public attraction consisting of the driving by children of small or so-called "midget" automobiles propelled by two-horse power motors. Anno: 83 ALR2d 878.

midnight. Twelve o'clock at night. The opening of the civil day. Jones v German Ins. Co. 110 Iowa 75, 81 NW 188.

midnight deadline. With respect to a bank, midnight on the next banking day following the banking day on which the bank involved receives the relevant item or notice or from which the time for taking action commences to run, whichever is later. UCC §§ 4-104(1) (h).

midshipman. A student in the United States Naval Academy at Annapolis, Maryland. A young man in training for the purpose of receiving a commission in the Navy. Ranking above enlisted personnel of the Navy when serving aboard ship. United States v Cook, 128 US 254, 32 L Ed 464, 9 S Ct 108.

midway. Adjective: In the middle of a course, route, or journey. Noun: The section of a fair grounds devoted to entertainment and public amusements. The main channel of a navigable river; the deepest or most navigable channel of a river. Louisiana v Mississippi, 202 US 1, 50 L Ed 913.

midwife. A woman who assists another in childbirth. Banti v State, 163 Tex Crim 89, 289 SW2d 244. Sometimes regarded as a female obstetrician. Commonwealth v Porn, 196 Mass 326, 82 NE 31.

midwifery. The work of a midwife, that is assisting a woman in childbirth. Sometimes regarded more highly as the practice of obstetrics. Commonwealth v Porn, 196 Mass 326, 82 NE 31; State v Banti, 163 Tex Crim 89, 289 SW2d 247.

mieses (me-ess'es). (Spanish.) Grain crops.

migrant laborer. A laborer who travels from place to place, often with the seasons, for work, usually connected with the farm, particularly the cultivation and gathering of vegetables and the harvesting of fruit crops.

migration. Moving from one place to another, especially from one country to another. A movement by a group of people, for example, the Mormons to Utah in the Nineteenth Century. An ineffectual

attempt by a corporation to migrate to a sovereignty other than the state of its creation. 36 Am J2d For Corp § 11.
See **immigration**.

migratory birds. Birds which migrate with the change in season, sometimes many thousand miles. 35 Am J2d Fish § 32.

migratory divorce seeker. One who changes his residence or domicil to a state for the purpose of securing a divorce and residing in the state the required length of time for such purpose, but without any intention of remaining in the state permanently or indefinitely. 24 Am J2d Div & S § 252.

milch cow (milch kou). A dairyman's cow, a cow kept primarily for the milk she produces.

mile. A measure of distance equaling 5280 feet, and often referred to as the "land mile," because it is more common to landmen whose business is on land. Steamboat Co. v Fessenden, 79 Me 140, 146.
See **nautical mile**.

mileage. The distance between two points. The distance covered on a trip. The total of miles which a motor vehicle has been driven, as indicated by speedometer or odometer. An allowance to a public officer for expense of travel. 43 Am J1st Pub Of § 369. An allowance to a sheriff, constable, or similar officer, or the deputy of either, by way of compensation for the miles they travel in the performance of their duties. 47 Am J1st Sher § 100. An allowance to a juror calculated upon the number of miles traveled as required for attendance as a juror. 31 Am J Rev ed Jur § 65. An allowance of travel expense made to a witness in attendance at a trial. 58 Am J1st Witn § 878. An allowance of travel expense to an officer in the armed forces. 36 Am J1st Mil § 80.

mileage basis. A basis for the apportionment between states or taxing districts of taxes on the property of a transportation or communication company. 51 Am J1st Tax §§ 879 et seq.

mileage books. Small books of a size convenient for the pocket issued by railroad companies to be purchased and used by passengers as tickets for transportation, each page, or perforated section, good for a specified number of miles of travel, to be removed from the book and taken up by the train conductor as used.

Such books are frequently issued at a lower rate per mile than is charged for single trip tickets. 9 Am J2d Car § 811. The tickets contained in the book, being used on the basis of mileage covered, are to be distinguished from commutation tickets which are good for a specified number of trips between named stations or points. Pennsylvania R. Co. v Towers, 245 US 6, 62 L Ed 117, 38 S Ct 2.

mileage tickets. See **mileage books**.

miles (mī'lēz). A soldier; a knight. Singular of **milites**.

milieu (mē'lē-er). The middle.

militare. See **feudum militare**.

military. Pertaining to the Armed Forces, to war, to warfare. The Armed Forces.
See **martial law**.

Military Academy. The United States Military Academy at West Point. A classification given many private schools for boys, usually graduating students with the equivalent of a high school diploma, the classification being based upon military training given in the institution.

Military Appeals. See **Court of Military Appeals**.

military blockade. See **blockade**.

military bounty. A bounty paid for the purpose of inducing the enlistment of men in the military forces. 12 Am J2d Bount §§ 2, 4, 6.

military causes. Causes falling within the jurisdiction of military courts and tribunals.

military cemetery. A cemetery established in a foreign nation for the burial of members of the Armed Forces of the United States who were killed in action or died in the service of the United States in such country.
See **national cemetery**.

military commission. A tribunal for the trial and punishment of a military offense committed in time of war, for the trial of which no provision is made by statute. A commission of the state created under statutory authority to set up martial law in districts of the state in which insurrection and rioting exist, for the trial and punishment of offenders against such law in the district. 36 Am J1st Mil § 87.

military court. A court of the military; a **court-martial**.

military depot (dē'pō). See **military post**.

military draft. The enforcement by the government of its constitutional right to require all citizens of sufficient age and capacity to enter the military service of the country. Lanahan v Birge, 30 Conn 438, 443. A contingent or body of men for the armed forces called at one time under the selective draft.
See **selective draft**.

military enterprise. A martial undertaking, involving the idea of a bold, arduous, and hazardous attempt. Wiborg v United States, 163 US 632, 650, 41 L Ed 289, 296. Sometimes synonymous with **military expedition** but susceptible of a broader interpretation. 56 Am J1st War § 222.

military equipment. Supplies, facilities, accouterments, etc. of the Armed Forces. 36 Am J1st Mil § 16.

military establishment of the United States. The armed forces of the country represented by the army, navy, marine corps, and such other military bodies as Congress may see fit to establish. United States v Dunn, 120 US 249, 30 L Ed 667, 7 S Ct 507.

military expedition. A march or voyage of a body of men made with martial or hostile intentions or military in its character. United States v Ybanez (CC Tex) 53 F 536, 538. A journey or voyage by a company or body of persons, having the position or character of members of an armed service or services, for a specific warlike purpose; the body and the outfit or equipment of a body on a journey for a specific warlike purpose. 56 Am J1st War § 222.
See **military enterprise**.

military feuds (fūds). Feuds or fiefs held by knight-service under the feudal system.

military government. That government which is established by the military authorities upon the occupation of the enemy's territory, such government having the right to displace the pre-existing authority, and to assume to such extent as it may deem proper, the exercise by itself of all the powers and functions of government. 56 Am J1st War § 205.

military governor. The chief executive of a state, appointed by the President of the United States during a time of war and when the usual civil authority of that state cannot be duly maintained. 24 Am J1st Gov § 2.

military jurisdiction. Power and authority of a threefold character.

Under the Constitution of the United States, there are three kinds of military jurisdiction: one to be exercised both in peace and war; another to be exercised in time of foreign war without the boundaries of the United States, or in time of rebellion and civil war within states or districts occupied by rebels treated as belligerents; and a third to be exercised in time of invasion or insurrection within the limits of the United States, or during rebellion within the limits of states maintaining adhesion to the United States, when the public danger requires its exercise. The first may be called jurisdiction under military law, and is found in acts of Congress prescribing rules and articles of war, or otherwise providing for the government of the national forces. The second may be distinguished as military government, superseding, as far as may be deemed expedient, the local law, and exercised by the military commander, under the direction of the President, with the express or implied sanction of Congress. The third may be denominated martial law proper. Ex parte Milligan (US) 4 Wall 2, 18 L Ed 281.

Military Justice Code. See **Code of Military Justice.**

military lands. Areas of the public domain reserved for military or naval purposes. Pan American Petroleum & Transport Co. v United States, 273 US 456, 71 L Ed 734, 47 S Ct 416. Public lands held for allotment to veterans of the armed services as a reward for military service.

military law. The Code of Military Justice and other statutory provisions for the government of persons in the Armed Forces, to which may be added the unwritten or common law of the usages and customs of military service. 36 Am J1st Mil § 12.
See **martial law.**

military occupation. An incident of war; the occupation of hostile territory, displacing the pre-existing authority, and assuming, to such extent as may be proper, the exercise by the occupying power of all the powers and functions of government. Dooley v United States, 182 US 222, 45 L Ed 1074, 21 S Ct 762.

military offense. A violation or infraction of military law, such as desertion, sleeping on duty, etc. A violation of a rule prescribed by the commander of the forces of an occupying power.

military officer. See **officer of the armed forces.**

military or naval forces. Armed forces of the United States.

As to the meaning of the term as used in § 3 of the Federal Espionage Act, see Anno: 148 ALR 1445.

military outfit. See **outfit.**

military pension. See **pension.**

military personnel. Members of the Armed Forces.

military post. A place where troops are assembled; where military stores, animate or inanimate, are kept or distributed; where military duty is performed or military protection afforded; where something, in short, more or less closely connected with arms or war is kept or is to be done. 36 Am J1st Mil § 6.
See **military station.**

military quota. See **quota.**

military rank. See **rank.**

military reservation. A federal enclave established under authority of law as a land area to be devoted to military purposes. Burgess v Montana, 8 Mont 57, 19 P 558.

military search and seizure. Search and seizure by persons in military service.

During a state of war or after martial law has been declared, officers engaged in the military service may lawfully arrest anyone who, from information before them, they have reasonable cause to believe is engaged in opposing the Government, and may order a house to be forcibly entered and searched when there are reasonable grounds for supposing such person may be there concealed. No more force, however, can be used than is necessary to accomplish the purpose. 47 Am J1st Search § 5.

military service. Service in any of the armed forces of the United States in war or in peace. 36 Am J1st Mil §§ 20 et seq.

military state. A totalitarian nation, the existence of which depends upon the maintenance of armed forces to preserve the government by keeping the people in a state of subjection.

The army of the British Government is sometimes referred to as the "military state."

military station. A place or department where a military duty is to be discharged. The synonym of the word "depot," a place where military stores or supplies are kept, or troops assembled. United States v Caldwell (US) 19 Wall 264, 22 L Ed 114. A military post. 36 Am J1st Mil § 6.
See **military post.**

military tenure (ten'ūr). Land tenure by knight-service.

military testament. A soldier's or sailor's will; a will excepted from compliance with formalities required to be observed in the execution of wills generally. 57 Am J1st Wills § 661.

military training. The training of members of the armed forces. Training in military science and tactics given in a university or college which has accepted the benefits of a Federal Land Grant. 15 Am J2d Colleges § 24.

military tribunal. See **military court.**

military wedding. A slang term for a wedding under duress of threatened prosecution for seduction or bastardy.

milites (mī'li-tēz). Knights who formed a part of the royal army, in virtue of their feudal tenures. See 1 Bl Comm 404.

militia. A body of armed citizens trained to military duty, who may be called out in certain cases, but may not be kept in service, like standing armies, in time of peace. 36 Am J1st Mil § 42.
See **active militia; National Guard; state militia.**

militibus. See **de militibus.**

militus. See **feudum militus.**

milk. A food so vital that it has been the subject of regulation in all jurisdictions to preserve quality and purity of the product.

milk control. The regulation of the distribution of milk and the fixing of prices. 3 Am J2d Agri § 27.

milk co-operative. A co-operative association of milk producers. Elliott v Adeckes, 240 Minn 113, 59 NW2d 894.

milk cow. See **milch cow**.

milk dealer. One who buys and sells milk or one who sells milk obtained from his own cows. 22 Am J1st Food § 69.

milk depot. A place at which a dairy or milk dealer receives milk from the producer, sometimes where it is stored pending processing in a dairy. Anno: 31 ALR 187, s. 38 ALR 1506.

milk of magnesia. A proprietary medicine. State v F. W. Woolworth Co. 184 Minn 51, 237 NW 817, 76 ALR 1202.

mill. A factory or manufacturing establishment. 58 Am J1st Workm Comp § 117.
    By the conveyance of a "mill" eo nomine, no other land passes in fee except the land under the mill and its overhanging projections. But the term may include the free use of the head of water existing at the time of its conveyance, or any other easement which has been made with it, and which is necessary to its enjoyment. Morgan v Mason, 20 Ohio 344.

Mill Act. A statute providing for the appropriation of sites for the utilization of water power, upon payment of compensation for the taking. 56 Am J1st Wat § 21.

Millbank Prison (mil'bangk priz'n). A prison at Westminster, England, where persons who had been sentenced to be transported were temporarily confined.

milled money. Coined money.

Miller Act. A federal statute enacted in 1935, as a successor to the Heard Act of 1894, providing that before any contract, exceeding $2,000 in amount, for the construction, alteration, or repair of any public building or public work of the United States, is awarded to any person, such person shall furnish to the United States a performance bond for its protection and a payment bond for the protection of all persons supplying labor and material in the prosecution of the work provided for in the contract. 40 USC §§ 270a-270d.

Miller-Tydings Act. A federal statute, enacted in 1937, constituting an amendment to the Sherman Anti-Trust Act, declaring in effect that the fixing by agreement of the minimum resale price of commodities shall not be deemed unlawful by reason of anything contained in the anti-trust act, whenever such agreements are lawful where the resale is made. 15 USC § 1.

millimeter. A linear measure of the metric system, equivalent to 0.3937 inches.

milliner. One who designs, makes, or deals in ladies' hats. Woods v Keyes, 14 Allen (Mass) 236.

milling-in-transit. The privilege of a shipper of grain, particularly wheat, to have the shipment stopped for milling at some point upon the route as to which a through rate was determined, and have the shipment continued to destination under the through rate in the form of the flour produced by the milling of the grain. 13 Am J2d Car § 318.

mill man's lien. The common-law lien for his labor that one who saws logs of another into lumber or shingles has, on the general principle that persons who have bestowed labor upon an article or done some other act in reference to it by which its value is enhanced have a right to detain it until they are reimbursed for their expenditure and labor. 34 Am J1st Logs § 101.

mill race. An artificial channel conducting water to be utilized for power.

mill saw. A circular saw used in sawing logs into lumber. Batchelder v Shapleigh, 10 Me 135.

millsite location. The appropriation, under authority of law and the rules of the land department, of land for the accommodation and use of a mill or reduction works to be operated in connection with a mine. 36 Am J1st Min & M § 73.

mina (mī'na̯). An ancient measure of weight.

minable coal. Coal so situated that it may be mined profitably by judicious methods. Anno: 28 ALR2d 1031.

minae (mī'nē). Threats; menaces.

minare (mi-nā're). To mine.

Minatur innocentibus qui parcit nocentibus (minā'ter in-no-sen'ti-bus quī par'sit no-sen'ti-bus). He who spares those who are guilty menaces those who are innocent.

mind. The seat of reason. The ability to will, to direct, to permit, or to assent. McDermott v Evening Journal, 43 NJL 488, 492. The direction of one's thinking.

mind and memory. A term of art much used by the legal profession.
    At common law, "mind" and "memory" are convertible terms on the reasoning that without memory there can be no mind, and the person would be the mere recipient of a succession of present sensations, like the lowest type of animal life. Re Forman's Will (NY) 54 Barb 274, 286.
    See **sound mind and memory**.

mind reader. One who professes to know the unspoken and otherwise uncommunicated thoughts of another.

mine. An underground working for the excavation of minerals, consisting of pits, shafts, levels, tunnels etc. 36 Am J1st Min & M § 2. A term broad enough to include open cuts and quarries, by which substances such as coal, clay, ironstone, and limestone are extracted from the earth. 36 Am J1st Min & M § 2.
    But the word does not comprehend every possible excavation by which mineral matters are brought to the surface. It appears to be definitely settled, for example, that a gas well or an oil well cannot be regarded as a mine. Nor does a pile of tailings taken from another excavation constitute a mine. 36 Am J1st Min & M § 2.
    See **mining**.

mine development. Work in opening a mine for the purpose of removing minerals from the earth.

mine development costs. As a deduction from gross income, payments made, or debts incurred, for the development of a natural deposit of minerals after existence of minerals in commercially marketable quantities has been disclosed. Internal Revenue Code § 616.

mine dump. A pile of waste material removed from a mine in the process of taking out mineral, often of great size. 36 Am J1st Min & M § 179.

mine exploration costs. A deduction from gross income of costs paid or incurred in exploring for minerals other than oil or gas. Internal Revenue Code §§ 615, 617.

mine layout. A mining and railroad term for switching facilities for moving cars to and from the tipple. Raymond City Coal & Transp. Corp. v New York Cent. R. Co. (CA6 Ohio) 103 F2d 56.
See **tipple**.

mine patent. See **tunnel location**.

mine prop. A piece of timber in the form of a post, used in a mine as a support for the roof. 36 Am J1st Min & M § 147.

miner. One who mines, particularly one engaged directly in the occupation of extracting coal or ore from the earth. Anno: 11 ALR 155.
The meaning of the word "miner" must depend on the construction given in the particular jurisdiction. Watson v Lederer, 11 Colo 577, 19 P 602.
See **gin men**.

mineral. Broadly, a natural inorganic substance forming a part of the soil or crust of the earth. 36 Am J1st Min & M § 4. Any natural substance having sufficient value to be mined, quarried, or extracted for its own sake or its own specific use. 36 Am J1st Min & M § 4. Any inorganic substance which can be taken from the land, inclusive of oil and natural gas. Scott v Laws, 185 Ky 440, 215 SW 81, 13 ALR 369. A term inclusive of, not only coal and iron, but also oil and natural gas, diamonds, fluor spar, gypsum, granite, shale, freestone, and other substances, but not sand, gravel, or clay. 36 Am J1st Min & M §§ 5, 35.
In its ordinary and common meaning, the word is a comprehensive one and includes every description of stone and rock deposit, whether containing metallic or non-metallic substances; and where minerals are reserved in a conveyance, if the ordinary meaning of the word is to be changed or restricted, the language used must be reasonably clear to show that intent. Jeffrey v Spruce-Boone Land Co. 112 W Va 360, 164 SE 292, 86 ALR 866.
As to whether a conveyance or reservation of minerals is inclusive of minerals recoverable only by open pit mining, see Anno: 1 ALR2d 787.

mineral deed. A conveyance of a landowner's interest in minerals lying beneath the surface. 24 Am J1st Gas & O § 28. A conveyance by an owner of land of minerals therein, figuratively severing the minerals from the surface and vesting title to them in the grantee. 36 Am J1st Min & M § 32.

mineral industry. An industry in the production and fabrication of metals. 13 USC §§ 131, 132.

mineralizer. A substance which combines with a metal in the soil or crust of the earth to form ore. Armstrong v Lake Champlain Granite Co. 147 NY 495, 42 NE 186.

mineral land. Land made valuable by the deposits therein of mineral or minerals useful in the arts or essential in manufacturing. Northern P. R. Co. v Soderberg, 183 US 526, 47 L Ed 575, 23 S Ct 365.

mineral lease. See **mining lease**.

mineral reservation. The reservation in a deed of the minerals or a specific mineral in the land conveyed, in effect a reservation of a part of the fee. Kiersey v Hirsch, 58 NM 18, 265 P2d 346, 43 ALR2d 929.

mineral royalty (roi'al-ti). A royalty under a kind of lease recognized by the coal industry paid on the quantity of mineral mined, with the requirement that a stipulated amount be mined within a stated period of time, or, upon a failure to do so, to pay a certain amount of money equal to the income that would have been received by the landowner had the mineral been mined.
Such payments are royalties and are not to be considered as rentals. Logan Coal & Timber Asso. v Helvering (CA3) 122 F2d 848.
See **mining royalty**.

minerals in place. See **in place**.

minerator (mi-ne-rā'tor). A miner.

miner's inch. A unit of measurement of the rate of discharge of water, known in some of the Western states, being the amount of water that flows through an orifice one inch square in a vertical position and under a standard head prescribed by custom or by statute. New Brantner Extension Ditch v Kramer, 57 Colo 218, 141 P 498.
As fixed by California statute, the standard miner's inch of water shall be equivalent or equal to one and one-half cubic inches of water per minute measured through any aperture or orifice. This makes a miner's inch equivalent to one-fortieth of a second foot. Before the adoption of the statute a miner's inch was the quantity of water passing through an orifice one inch square under a four inch pressure, which would make the inch equivalent to one-fiftieth of a cubic foot per second. Lillis v Panoche Land & Water Co. 32 Cal App 668, 163 P 1040.

miners' rules and customs. A body of rules and customs developed by the miners of the western part of the country, constituting a large body of unwritten law to be given effect in all cases wherein they do not conflict with the statutes. 36 Am J1st Min & M § 76.

mingling. The mingling of the logs of one person with the logs of another in the course of a flood during floating operations. 34 Am J1st Logs § 101.
See **commingling of funds; commingling of goods**.

miniature golf course. A place of amusement consisting of a small area for the playing of golf in a modified form. Anno: 74 ALR 406.

miniature railroad. An amusement device, particularly appealing to children, consisting of a railroad of narrow gauge upon which rides may be had in small coaches pulled by a small locomotive. 4 Am J2d Amuse § 90.

Minima poena corporalis est major qualibet pecuniaria (mi'ni-ma pē'na kor-po-rā'lis est mā'jor quā'libet pe-kū-ni-ā'ri-a). The smallest corporal punishment is greater than any pecuniary one.

Minime mutanda sunt quae certam interpretationem habuerunt (mi'ni-mē mū-tan'da sunt kwē ser'tam in-ter-pre-tā-she-ō'nem hā-bu-ē'runt). Those matters shall least be changed which have attained a certain interpretation or construction.
The language of this maxim and certain other maxims which are related to it, carries the idea of an observance, an interpretation, a construction, and to some extent a judicial one, as evidenced by the word "interpretationem." O'Donnell v Glenn, 9 Mont 452, 23 P 1018.

miniments (min'i-ments). Same as **muniments**.

minimis non curat lex (mi'ni-mis non kū'rat lex). See **de minimis non curat lex**.

minimization of damages. The duty of the plaintiff to take reasonable action to avoid enhancing the damages caused by the defendant. 22 Am J2d Damg § 30. Taking advantage of such means or

opportunities as are reasonably available to an injured employee for the purpose of restoring earning capacity, which means co-operating with employer, physician, the industrial board or commission, and, if necessary, the courts. Anno: 105 ALR 1479.
See **mitigation of damages.**

minimum area restrictions. Provisions in zoning ordinances prescribing the minimum side or rear yard areas, the percentage of the area of a lot that may be occupied by the building, or the minimum area of lots to be occupied by residences in particular districts. 58 Am J1st Zon § 52.

minimum contacts test. A test of jurisdiction established by the United States Supreme Court under which a state court is permitted to acquire personal jurisdiction over a nonresident, although he is not personally served with process within the state, where he has had such a substantial connection with the forum state that traditional notions of fair play and substantial justice are not offended by exercise of the forum's jurisdiction over the case. International Shoe Co. v Washington, 326 US 310, 90 L Ed 95, 66 S Ct 154, 161 ALR 1057. The theory whereby the validity of a state tax on the income of a foreign corporation is to be determined according to whether it has certain minimum contacts with the taxing state, so that imposition of the tax does not offend traditional notions of fair play and justice. Anno: 67 ALR2d 1328; 3 L Ed 2d 1787.

minimum cost restriction. The amount fixed by a restrictive covenant as the lowest limit in cost of construction of any house to be erected upon the premises conveyed by the deed in which the covenant appears, thereby prohibiting the grantee or his successors in interest from erecting a house at a cost in a lesser amount. 20 Am J2d Cov §§ 260 et seq.

minimum damage limitation. Statutory provision prohibiting the allowance of damages in an amount lower than the prescribed amount for infringement of a copyright. 17 USC § 101(d).

minimum en route instrument flight rule altitude. An air traffic rule prescribed by the Federal Aviation Agency. 14 CFR §§ 600.1 et seq.

Minimum est nihilo proximum (mi'ni-mum est nihi'lo pro'xi-mum). The least or smallest is next to nothing.

minimum fee schedule. A schedule of fees for legal services adopted by a bar association, such constituting at least persuasive evidence of what constitutes a reasonable fee for such services. Anno: 143 ALR 719, s. 56 ALR2d 45, § 11[c].

minimum-height restriction. The restriction contained in a covenant of a deed to the effect that no structure less than a certain height prescribed will be erected upon the premises conveyed by the deed in which the covenant appears, thereby prohibiting the erection of a building of a height less than that prescribed. 20 Am J2d Cov § 265.

minimum jurisdictional amount. A constitutional or statutory limitation on jurisdiction which deprives a court of jurisdiction where the amount or value in litigation is less than a specified amount. 20 Am J2d Cts § 154.

minimum number. A limitation placed by statute upon the number of signers of a nominating petition. 25 Am J2d Elect § 171. A limitation placed by statute upon the number of signers of a petition for a special election. 26 Am J2d Elect § 189.

minimum premium. A premium in an amount fixed by the bylaws or board of directors of a building and loan association as the minimum of the charge to be made a member for the privilege of obtaining a loan from the association. 13 Am J2d B & L Assoc § 55.

minimum price. A price communicated by a landowner to his broker as the lowest price at which he will sell, irrespective of what the listing price may be. 12 Am J2d Brok § 110. A price, often referred to as an upset price, fixed by the court in a foreclosure proceeding below which the property may not be sold at the foreclosure sale. 37 Am J1st Mtg § 864. The minimum amount for which property must sell at an execution sale, being fixed by statute at a designated proportion of the appraised value. 21 Am J2d Exec § 227. A price, fixed as a condition of an auction sale, below which the property will not be sold. 7 Am J2d Auct § 18. A reserved price, which it is proper and not unusual in judicial sales, as in other sales at auction, for the court or trustee who conducts the sale to fix, which fixed minimum price must be equalled or exceeded by the highest bid in order that such bid may be accepted and reported. 30A Am J Rev ed Jud S § 93. A price regulation by law aimed at curbing harmful competition. Nebbia v New York, 291 US 502, 78 L Ed 940, 54 S Ct 505, 89 ALR 1469.

minimum rent. (Mining law.) Same as **minimum royalty.**

minimum residence. A requirement imposed as a condition of poor relief or welfare. 41 Am J1st Poor L §§ 23, 24. A requirement imposed as a condition of voting at an election. 25 Am J2d Elect § 66.

minimum sentence. The lightest sentence permitted by statute for one convicted of a particular offense or as an habitual criminal. State v Malusky, 59 ND 501, 230 NW 735, 71 ALR 190.

minimum share. An exemption from inheritance or succession taxation, based upon an amount fixed by statute, at or below which no tax is imposed. 28 Am J Rev ed Inher T § 296.

minimum wage laws. Statutes establishing a minimum for the amount of wages to be paid employees in certain industries and lines of work. 31 Am J Rev ed Lab §§ 813 et seq.

minimus (min'i-mus). The least; the smallest.

mining. Extracting coal or ore from the earth. The actual cutting or hewing of the mineral in a mine and its removal to the surface. Anno: 11 ALR 154. Including the ordinary treatment and processes normally applied by mine owners to obtain the commercially marketable mineral product. United States v Cannelton Sewer Pipe Co. 364 US 76, 4 L Ed 2d 1581, 80 S Ct 1581. A term sometimes deemed inclusive of the taking of clay, ironstone, and limestone from quarries, even the taking of such substances and coal from quarries or open pits. 36 Am J2d Min & M § 2.
By statute enacted in Indiana in the year 1889, it was declared that the word should be deemed to include the sinking of gas wells. See State of Indiana ex rel. Corwin v Indiana & Ohio Oil, Gas & Mining Co. 120 Ind 575, 22 NE 778.
See **miner; placer mining; right to coal.**

mining by outstroke. The hoisting or removal of ore from a mine through a shaft or opening in an adjoining mine. Speck v Cottonwood Coal Co. (CA9 Mont) 116 F2d 489.

mining claim. A parcel of public mineral land which has been appropriated under the statutes by a prospector who has discovered a precious metal or other valuable mineral thereon. 36 Am J1st Min & M § 69.

A mining claim, perfected under the law, is property in the highest sense of that term, which may be bought, sold and conveyed, and will pass by descent. Quigley v Gillett, 101 Cal 462, 469, 35 P 1040.

See **adverse claim; discovery; lode claim; mining location.**

mining district. A section of country usually designated by name and described or understood as being confined within certain natural boundaries, in which gold or silver or both are found in paying quantities, and which is worked therefor, under rules and regulations prescribed by the miners therein; as the White Pine mining district, the Humboldt mining district, etc. United States v Smith (CC Or) 11 F 487, 490.

mining land. See **mineral land.**

mining lease. A lease of land which grants to the lessee the right to mine and remove coal and minerals from the premises. 36 Am J1st Min & M §§ 39, 40. Sometimes difficult of distinction from a grant of minerals in place. 36 Am J1st Min & M § 43.

See **mineral deed.**

mining license. An incorporeal right to take ore or minerals from the land of another—a mere privilege, existing cotemporaneously with a like right in the grantor, carrying with it no estate or possessory right in the land. 36 Am J1st Min & M § 63.

mining lien. A special lien for the security of a person furnishing labor or materials toward the development of a mine. Berentz v Belmont Oil Mining Co. 148 Cal 577, 84 P 47.

mining location. Precisely, the act of appropriating a mining claim on the public domain. Often regarded and treated as a synonym of mining claim. 36 Am J1st Min & M § 69.

See **mining claim; tunnel location.**

mining partnership. A partnership formed between co-owners of mines or minerals in place for the development or working of the same or between parties having an interest merely in the operation of a mine, or in carrying on mining operations without actually owning the mine itself; a partnership of a special kind, having some of the features of a cotenancy. 36 Am J1st Min & M § 157.

mining penalty. A statutory penalty imposed on a mine owner for mining within a specified distance of the line of the adjoining owner. Wilson v Shrader, 73 W Va 105, 79 SE 1083. Any penalty imposed for the violation of a statute regulating the business of mining. 36 Am J1st Min & M § 156.

mining right. The right to enter upon and occupy a specific piece of ground for the purpose of working it, either by underground excavations or open workings, to obtain from it the minerals or ores which may be deposited therein.

By implication, the grant of such a right carries with it whatever is incident to or necessary to its beneficial enjoyment. See Smith v Cooley, 65 Cal 46, 2 P 880.

mining royalty. An amount payable by the lessee to the lessor under a mining lease, based upon the amount of mineral taken from the mine for the term of the lease or a period thereof. 36 Am J1st Min & M §§ 48 et seq.

See **mineral royalty.**

minis. See **de minis.**

minister. One who, having been ordained in the ministry, undertakes to perform certain services for another. First Presbyterian Church v Myers, 5 Okla 809, 50 P 70. A clergyman or pastor. The head of a department of the government of the United Kingdom.

See **public minister.**

ministerial. Subservient or subsidiary; mandatory as opposed to judicial or discretionary; pertaining to an act or duty performed in accordance with legal authority, rather than with regard to propriety, judgment etc. Antin v Union High School Dist. 130 Or 461, 280 P 664, 66 ALR 1271.

ministerial act. An act which does not involve the exercise of judgment. An act the performance of which involves nothing of discretion, official or otherwise, performance being required by direct and positive command of the law. 34 Am J1st Mand § 70. An act which a person performs under a given state of facts, in a prescribed manner, in obedience to the mandate of legal authority, and without regard to or exercise of his own judgment upon the propriety of the act being done. Galey v Board of Comrs. 174 Ind 181, 91 NE 593. An Act in the performance of a duty defined and prescribed by law with such precision and certainty as to leave nothing to the exercise of discretion or judgment. Rains v Simpson, 50 Tex 495.

ministerial duty. An official duty wherein the officer has no room for the exercise of discretion, official or otherwise, the performance being required by direct and positive command of the law. 34 Am J1st Mand § 70. A duty of an officer in respect to which nothing is left to his discretion; a duty absolute, certain, and imperative, involving merely execution of a specific act arising from fixed and designated facts. State ex rel. Sewer Dist. v Ellis, 163 Neb 86, 77 NW2d 809.

ministerial function. In one sense, a ministerial duty of a public officer. In another sense, a private function of a municipal corporation, as distinguished from a public or governmental function of such a body. Bedtke v Chicago, 240 Ill App 493, 498.

ministerial officer. An officer who is neither a judicial officer nor an executive officer and whose duties are mainly of a ministerial nature, that is, duties involving little or no discretion. 43 Am J1st Pub Of § 258.

ministerial powers. Powers of a public officer which require no exercise of judgment or discretion. Powers of a trustee which are directory, there being no scope for discretion in any of the details of their exercise. 54 Am J1st Trusts § 291.

ministerial trust. Same as **dry trust.**

minister of the gospel. See **minister.**

ministrant (min'is-trạnt). (Ecclesiastical law.) A party who cross-examined a witness.

ministri regis (mi-nis'trī rē'jis). Ministers of the king.

ministry. The work of a pastor or clergyman. The profession of a clergyman. The ministers, as heads of departments of the government of the United Kingdom considered collectively.

minor. An infant, a person who has not reached the age, usually 21 years, at which the law recognizes a general contractual capacity. 27 Am J1st Inf § 2.

minor aetas (mī'nor ē'tās). Under age; minority; infancy.

Minor ante tempus agere non potest in casu proprietatis, nec etiam convenire (mī'nor an'te tem'pus ā'je-re non po'test in kā'sū prō-pri-e-tā'tis, nek ē'-she-am kon-ve-nī're). A minor under age cannot act in the case of property, nor even enter into a contract.

minora regalia (mī-nō'ra rē-gā'li-a). Minor royal rights or prerogatives.

These were principally the rights and prerogatives of the king which had to do with his revenue. The British constitution vested these rights or prerogatives in the king in order to support his dignity and maintain his power, being a portion which each subject contributes of his property, in order to secure the remainder. See 1 Bl Comm 241, 281.

minori aetate. See **administration minori aetate; durante minore aetate.**

minor fault rule. See **major and minor fault rule.**

minority. A status created by law; the status of an infant. 27 Am J1st Inf § 2. The period during which one is an infant. The lesser of two factions in a political or other body of persons. A group or class of persons for whom the protection of the Bill of Rights is intended; persons of a race or religion other than the predominant race or religion in the state or political subdivision.

A characteristic feature of our constitutional system lies in the power of a single individual successfully to resist the claims of the whole community when he is in the right. McKeon v Bisbee, 9 Cal 137.

minority interest. Shares of stock in a corporation which are not sufficient in number to elect directors or otherwise control the action to be taken by the corporation. 18 Am J2d Corp § 496.

minority opinion. An opinion written or approved by one or more, but less than a majority, of the members of the court; to be distinguished from the opinion of the court. 20 Am J2d Cts § 71.

minority representation. A system of voting whereby a part of the voters, although constituting no more than a minority may nevertheless obtain representation by an officer of political principles to their liking, such representation being procured by methods of voting such as cumulative, limited, or restrictive voting. 26 Am J2d Elect §§ 273 et seq.

minority stockholders. Stockholders of a corporation insufficient in reference to the number of shares held in the aggregate to elect directors or otherwise control the management of the corporation. 18 Am J2d Corp § 496.

Minor jurare non potest (mī'nor jū-rā're non po'test). A minor cannot make oath.

Minor minorem custodire non debet; alios enim praesumitur male regere qui seipsum regere nescit (mī'nor mī-nō'rem kus-tō-dī're non de'bet; a'li-ōs e'nim prē-zu'mi-ter ma'le re'je-re quī sēp'sum re'je-re ne'-sit). A minor ought not to have the custody of a minor; because he is presumed to govern others poorly who does not understand how to govern himself.

Minor non tenetur respondere durante minori aetati; nisi, in causa dotis, propter favorem (mī'nor non te-nē'ter res-pon'dē-re du-ran'te mī-nō'rī ē-tā'tī; nī'sī, in kâ'za dō-tis, prop'ter fa-vō'rem). A minor is not held responsible during his minority, unless, by reason of grace or favor, in the matter of dower.

minor offenses. See **petty offenses.**

minor of tender years. Apparently, any minor; not the equivalent of child of tender years.

As the expression is used in pleadings in various connections, as in answers of guardians ad litem appointed for minors in probate proceedings, it may embrace as well minors of twenty years as twenty months. Meyer v King, 72 Miss 1, 16 So 245.

See **child of tender years.**

minor or major fault rule. See **major or minor fault rule.**

Minor, qui infra aetatem 12 annorum fuerit, utlagari non potest, nec extra legem poni, quia ante talem aetatem, non est sub lege aliqua, nec in decenna (mī'nor, quī in'fra ē-tā'tem 12 an-nō'rum fu'e-rit, ut-la-gā-rī non po'test, nek ex'tra lē'jem pō'nī, qui'a an'te tā'lem ē-tā'tem, non est sub lē'je a'li-qua, nek in de-sen'na). A minor who is under the age of twelve years cannot be outlawed, nor be placed outside the law, because before such age, he is not under any law, nor in a decennary.

Minor septemdecim annis non admittitur fore executorem (mī'nor sep-tem'de-sim an'nis non admit'i-ter fo're ex-e-ku-tō'rem). A person under the age of seventeen years is not permitted to be an executor.

mint. Verb: To coin money. Noun: A place for the coining of money; the United States Mint. Bronson v Rodes (US) 7 Wall 229, 247, 19 L Ed 141, 145. Any one of several aromatic plants used in medicines and flavoring extracts, such as peppermint. Adjective: New, particularly in the case of money or stamps.

See **assayer of the mint.**

mintage. A charge made for coining money.

mint julep. A refreshing and stimulating alcoholic beverage, prepared by combining whisky, sugar, and mint leaves, and served in glasses filled with chipped ice.

minus. Less; reduce by taking away a specific number.

Minus solvit, qui tardius solvit; nam et tempore minus solvitur (mī'nus sol'vit, quī tar'di-us sol'vit; nam et tem'po-re mī'nus sol'vi-ter). He does not pay who pays too late; for he is not discharged by lapse of time.

minus sufficiens in literatura (mī'nus suf-fi'she-enz in li-te-ra-tū'ra). Deficient in letters. See 1-Bl Comm 390.

minute. Noun: A division of time; one sixtieth part of an hour. Verb: To make a note of something said or done. Hinshaw v State, 147 Ind 334, 377, 47 NE 157.

See **minutes.**

minutes. A record of the proceedings of the court. 27 Am J2d Eq § 250. A memorandum of what happened or occurred in court during a proceeding in a particular case. 20 Am J2d Cts § 52. Short notes made by a clerk in the course of proceedings of the court, to be extended later in preparation of the record. Hoehne v Trugillo, 1 Colo 161; otherwise known as rough minutes or skeleton minutes. Johnson v Commonwealth, 80 Ky 377, 379. The record of the proceedings and testimony before the grand jury in a particular case. People v Quinn, 24 Misc 2d 111, 201 NYS2d 582. The record of a

MINUTE [805] MISCONDUCT

proceeding by an administrative agency acting judicially. 2 Am J2d Admin L §§ 441 et seq. The record of the business transacted at a meeting of the stockholders of a corporation. 18 Am J2d Corp § 174. The record of the acts of the board of directors of a corporation at a meeting. 19 Am J2d Corp § 1132. The record of the proceedings of an association or club. 6 Am J2d Asso & C § 58.
See **judge's minutes.**

minute book. A book in which the proceedings of a court are entered by the clerk of the court; a book in which the proceedings of a corporation's meetings are entered by the secretary. Any book or record containing minutes.
See **minutes.**

minute tithes (tī'thz). Small tithes.

minutio (mi-nū'she-ō). (Civil law.) A diminution; a reduction; a subtraction.

misa (mē'sah). Same as **mise.**

misadventure. An accident. Bad luck.
See **homicide by misadventure.**

misae (mi'sē). Costs of suit; expenses.

misallege (mis-a̧-lej'). To state, cite, or quote erroneously.

misapplication of funds. The conversion of funds. As a specific offense, the conversion by a bank officer of funds of the bank to the use of the officer or a third person, something beyond a mere act of official administration. 10 Am J2d Banks § 224.
See **misappropriation of funds.**

misapprehension. See **mistake.**

misappropriation. A conversion of property.

misappropriation of funds. An abstraction of cash, or a source of cash. 50 Am J1st Suret § 336. The failure of a person to account for or return a fund committed to him for a specific purpose. Anno: 17 ALR2d 1021.
The word is held not to apply to the payment of an extravagant price for services or materials properly appertaining to the business of the corporation. Dean v Shingle, 198 Cal 652, 246 P 1049.
See **misapplication of funds.**

misbehaviour. Improper conduct. Intentional wrongdoing rather than mere error in judgment. Smith v Cutler (NY) 10 Wend 589.

misbirth (mis-bėrth'). A miscarriage; an abortion.

misbranded. Characterizing an article which carries a false or misleading label, especially where the falsity is such as to defraud the public. United States v 90-5 Barrels, 265 US 438, 68 L Ed 1094, 44 S Ct 529.
See **misbranding.**

misbranding. An offering for sale of an article under the name of another article, the offering for sale of an imitation of another article, and the offering for sale in package form of an article which does not bear a label containing the name and place of business of the manufacturer, packer, or distributor and an accurate statement of the quantity of the contents in terms of weight, measure, or numerical count. 21 USC § 343; 35 Am J2d Food § 27.
A brand is a false brand whether it was intentionally erroneous or erroneous because of culpable negligence. Hatcher v Dunn, 102 Iowa 411, 71 NW 343.
See **mislabeling.**

miscarriage. Abortion; a premature birth. Anderson v Commonwealth, 19 Va 665, 58 SE2d 72, 16 ALR2d 942. The expulsion of the foetus at a period of utero-gestation so early that it has not acquired the power of sustaining an independent life. More precisely, the termination of pregnancy between the 16th and 28th week. 1 Am J2d Abort § 1. In reference to the application of the statute of frauds to an oral contract to answer for the miscarriage of another:—the default of a third person upon his debt or obligation for which the promisor had undertaken to answer. 49 Am J1st Stat of F § 65.

miscarriage of justice. A decision inconsistent with substantial justice. Kotteakos v United States, 328 US 750, 90 L Ed 1557, 66 S Ct 1239. The result of a case in which essential rights of a party were disregarded or denied. People v Musumeci, 133 Cal App 2d 354, 284 P2d 168.

miscasting. A mistake in the audit of an account.

miscegenation. The intermarrying, cohabiting, or interbreeding of persons of different races. A criminal offense under the statutes of a few jurisdictions, principally in the intermarriage of white persons with negroes or persons having a specified percentage of negro blood. 35 Am J1st Mar § 146; 36 Am J1st Misceg § 2.

miscegenetic marriage (mis''ȩ-je-net'ik mar'ạj). A marriage in violation of statute prohibiting the intermarriage of persons of certain different races, particularly persons of the white and black races.

mischarge. See **misdirection.**

mischief. Conduct resulting in injury or annoyance to another.
See **malicious mischief.**

miscognizant (mis-kog'ni-zant). Without knowledge of; ignorant of.

misconception. A misunderstanding. A mistake in interpretation of a statement. Walden v Skinner, 101 US 577, 25 L Ed 963.

misconduct. Improper conduct. A transgression of some established and definite rule of action, where no discretion is left, except what necessity may demand; a violation of definite law; a forbidden act. Citizens' Ins. Co. v Marsh, 41 Pa 386, 394. Intentional wrongdoing. Smith v Cutler (NY) 10 Wend 589.

misconduct in office. See **official misconduct.**

misconduct of attorney. Professional misconduct or misconduct outside professional dealings which shows one to be unfit for the profession and would have disqualified him from admission to the bar. 7 Am J2d Attys § 25. Immoral practices which demonstrate unfitness to practice law and would affect adversely the administration of justice. Re Gorsuch, 76 SD 191, 75 NW2d 644, 57 ALR2d 1355.
See **misconduct of counsel; professional misconduct.**

misconduct of counsel. The conduct of counsel for one party which prevents the adverse party from having a fair trial, consisting in improper remarks, comments, or arguments, wilfully and intentionally offering inadmissible evidence, propounding improper questions to witnesses, uncalled-for abuse of witnesses, etc. 39 Am J1st New Tr §§ 3 et seq.
See **professional misconduct of attorney.**

misconduct of judge. Improper or unjudicial conduct on the part of the judge in the course of the trial of a case, for example improper remarks tending to

MISCONDUCT [806] MISKENNING

prejudice the minds of the jury against one of the parties, absence from courtroom, etc. 39 Am J1st New Tr §§ 48 et seq.

misconduct of jury. Conduct on the part of the jury which impairs the trial from the standpoint of fairness and propriety, such as obtaining and acting upon information outside the evidence adduced at the trial, acting on the personal knowledge of a juror or jurors, expressions of prejudice, partiality, or antagonism toward one of the parties, separation without authority, etc. 39 Am J1st New Tr §§ 70 et seq.

misconduct of physician. Professional misconduct or conduct apart from the practice of the profession which demonstrates immorality, personal characteristics, and disposition rendering a person unfit for the practice of medicine. 41 Am J1st Phys & S §§ 49, 54, 57.
See **professional misconduct.**

miscontinuance. A continuance or postponement improperly ordered by the court.

misconveyance by carrier. See **misdelivery.**

miscreant (mis'krẹ-ạnt). An evil person. An unbeliever; a person who entertained doctrines subversive of moral obligation or the Christian religion.
A statute under William the Third provided that if any person with an understanding of Christianity wrote or taught or made speeches denying its truth he thereby rendered himself incapable of holding any office of trust; that for a second offense he should be unable to sue, act as guardian, executor, legatee or purchaser of land and suffer three years' imprisonment without bail. See 4 Bl Comm 44.

misdelivery. The delivery of goods by a carrier to some person other than the one to whom they were consigned. 13 Am J2d Car § 415.

misdemeanant (mis-dẹ-mē'nạnt). A person who has committed a misdemeanor.

misdemeanor. Customarily, an indictable offense not amounting to a felony, but sometimes including offenses not punishable by indictment. Commonwealth v Cano, 389 Pa 639, 133 A2d 800, cert den and app dismd 355 US 182, 2 L Ed 2d 186, 78 S Ct 267.
The distinction between misdemeanors and felonies now commonly adopted, frequently by statute, is that offenses punishable by death, or by imprisonment in the state prison or penitentiary, are felonies, whereas all others, including those punishable by imprisonment in the county jail, are misdemeanors. Roberson v United States (CA5 Ala) 249 F2d 737, 72 ALR2d 434, cert den 356 US 919, 2 L Ed 2d 715, 78 S Ct 704 (under Alabama law); Eckhardt v People, 126 Colo 18, 247 P2d 673. It is also to be observed that in some jurisdictions, there is a classification, particularly in reference to violations of the Motor Vehicle Law, where the breach is deemed, neither a misdemeanor nor a felony, but an "offense."

misdescription. An error in describing a party to an action; a matter of no consequence if the party is otherwise properly designated. 39 Am J1st Parties § 109. An error in a conveyance in respect of the description of the subject matter. 23 Am J2d Deeds §§ 155 et seq.

misdirection. An error on the part of the court in the charge or instructions given the jury.

mise (mīz). A plea of the general issue in a writ of right. 41 Am J1st Pl § 141. The costs or expenses of a litigation.

mise en escript (mēz ôn ĕs-krĭpt). Put in writing.

miserabile depositum (mi-se-rā'bi-le dē-pō'zi-tum). (Civil law.) A deposit made under stress of necessity; as, in the case of great peril such as fire or flood.

Misera est servitus ubi jus est vagum aut incognitum (mi'se-ra est ser'vi-tus u'bi jūs est va'gum ât in-kog'ni-tum). Wretched is the thraldom where the law is either uncertain or unknown. See 1 Bl Comm 416.

misericordia (mi-se-ri-kor'di-a). Mercy.

misericordia communis (mi-se-ri-kor'di-a ko-mū'nis). A fine imposed upon a community or a county.

misfeasance (mis-fē'zạns). The improper doing of an act which a person might lawfully do. Greenberg v Whitcomb Lumber Co. 90 Wis 225, 63 NW 93. The unlawful and injurious exercise of lawful authority, or the doing of a lawful act in an unlawful manner. Allas v Rumson, 115 NJL 593, 181 A 175, 102 ALR 648. The performance of a duty or act which one ought or has a right to do, but in a manner such as to infringe upon the rights of others. Anno: 20 ALR 104.

misfeasance in office (mis-fē'zạns in of'is). The performance by a public officer in his official capacity of a legal act in an improper or illegal manner. State ex rel. Hardie v Coleman, 115 Fla 119, 155 So 129, 92 ALR 988. A common-law offense, generally termed "official misconduct," and composed of the commission of a series of unlawful acts. State v Bolitho, 103 NJL 246, 261, 136 A 164, 172.

misfeasant (mis-fē'zạnt). A person guilty of misfeasance; a trespasser.

misfeasor. Same as **misfeasant.**

misfire. The failure of a cartridge to explode and propel the bullet when the trigger of the firearm is pulled. The ignition of the gas in the combustion chamber of an internal combustion engine at the wrong time or in an ineffective manner.

misfortune. Ill luck; ill fortune; calamity; the suffering of a loss. Anthony & Co. v Karbach, 64 Neb 509, 90 NW 243.

mishering. A freedom or exemption from amercement.

mishersing. Same as **mishering.**

misjoinder of causes of action. The impropriety in joining in one complaint, declaration, or petition distinct causes of action which should not be joined because of the want of consistency between them, because they do not affect all defendants named in the action, because they do not arise out of the same transaction, or because of other circumstance precluding joinder under the practice in the particular jurisdiction. 1 Am J2d Actions §§ 100 et seq. A term sometimes used to characterize the improper blending of two or more causes of action in one count of a complaint, declaration, or petition. 41 Am J1st Pl § 107.

misjoinder of parties. The defect of having made parties of record to an action persons who are neither necessary nor proper parties. 39 Am J1st Parties § 118.

miskenning (mis-ken'ing). An error in quoting or citing.

miskering. Same as **mishering.**

mislabeling. Affixing to an article offered for sale a label which is false or misleading in such particular as to deceive the public in reference to the weight, quantity, or measure of the article. 56 Am J1st Wts & L § 64. Affixing to a package of food a label which incorrectly states the identity, composition, quality, strength, or purity of the article. 22 Am J1st Food § 36. Affixing to the wrapper or container of a drug, or accompanying a drug with, a label which is false or misleading in any particular. 25 Am J2d Drugs § 30.
See **misbranding.**

mislaid goods. See **mislaid property.**

mislaid property. Property located in a place of which the owner has no recollection, although he put the property in such place voluntarily and intentionally. 1 Am J2d Aband § 2. Property placed by the owner in a location which he has forgotten, albeit he selected it intentionally as a place where he might later pick up the property. 34 Am J2d Aband § 3.

misleading. Leading into error. Deceiving.
As used in a statute forbidding corporations from taking a name so clearly resembling that of an existing corporation as to be misleading, the word is not synonymous with "confusing," but it means calculated to lead astray or lead into error persons who are contemplating or who are engaged in transactions with an existing corporation. Diamond Drill C. Co. v International Diamond Drill C. Co. 106 Wash 72, 179 P 120.

mismanagement. Improper management or inefficient management, particularly on the part of an officer, agent, trustee, or other person in a fiduciary capacity. Violation of the rules established by charter or bylaws or a culpable lack of prudence on the part of the officers of a corporation in whom the duty of management is vested. 19 Am J2d Corp § 1332.

misnomer. A mistake in a name; the giving of an incorrect name to a person in an accusation, indictment, pleading, or instrument. Culpepper v State, 173 Ga 799, 161 SE 623, 79 ALR 217. A mistake in the name of the plaintiff or defendant in a writ or process. Anno: 124 ALR 86 et seq. A mistake in the name of a party to an action, whether an individual or a corporation. 39 Am J1st Parties § 109. A mistake in the designation of a party or parties to a deed. 23 Am J2d Deeds § 51. In reference to a corporation, something more than a mere variation in words and syllables; such an interpolation, omission, or alteration of words as to constitute a failure to distinguish the corporation from all others. 18 Am J2d Corp § 144.

mispleading. The commission of essential error in pleading a cause of action or defense. Lovett v Pell (NY) 22 Wend 369, 375.

misprision (mis-prizh'ǫn). Contempt of the state, particularly in neglect of duty, obstruction of justice, or the concealment of crime. In loose usage, error or mistake. Merrill v Miller, 28 Mont 134, 72 P 423; Barone v Barone, 207 Or 26, 294 P2d 611.

misprision of felony or treason. The common-law offense of failure to inform the authorities as to a treason or felony that one has witnessed or that has come to his knowledge; the failure to prevent a felony from being committed. 21 Am J2d Crim L § 7. The federal offense of failure to disclose a felony coupled with some positive act of concealment, such as suppression of evidence, harboring of a criminal, intimidation of witnesses, or other positive act designed to conceal from the authorities the fact that a crime has been committed. Bratton v United States (CA10 Okla) 73 F2d 795. The concealment or failure promptly to disclose and make known to the President or some Judge of the United States, or to the Governor or some judge or justice of a particular state knowledge of the commission of any treason against the United States, such concealment or failure to disclose being that of one owing allegiance to the United States. 18 USC § 3.

misreading. The perpetration of a fraud upon a person who signs an instrument by purporting to read the contents to him, but by reading something very different. First Nat. Bank of Sturgis v Deal, 55 Mich 592, 593.

misrecital. A misstatement of a fact or facts.

misrepresentation. The statement of an untruth. A misstatement of fact, which, if accepted, leads the mind to an apprehension of a condition other and different from that which exists. 37 Am J2d Fraud § 2. In application for insurance:—a statement as a fact of something which is untrue, and which the insured states with the knowledge that it is untrue and with an intent to deceive, or which he states positively as true without knowing it to be true, and which has a tendency to mislead, where such fact in either case is material to the risk. 29 Am J Rev ed Ins § 698.

missed charge. An unexploded charge of explosive. 22 Am J2d Explos § 26.

missed hole. A hole drilled in a rock quarry or mine and charged with dynamite or other explosive, which has failed to explode. Stearns v Reidy, 33 Ill App 246, 247.

missile. A thrown object.

Missing Persons Act. Statute providing for the disposition of the property of a person by administration in the probate court where such person has been absent so long and under such circumstances pertaining to his disappearance and continued absence that he is reasonably and fairly presumed to be dead. 1 Am J2d Absent § 3. A federal statute relative to persons presumed to have been killed in action in the armed service and to certain other persons in government service. 50 USC Appx §§ 1001-1017.

missing ship. A ship which is presumed to have been lost because of her long absence without having been heard from.

missio (mi'she-ō). (Civil law.) A sending; a putting.

missio in bona (mi'she-ō in bō'na). (Civil law.) The putting a creditor in possession of his debtor's goods under an execution.

missio judicum in consilium (mi'she-ō jū'di-kum in kon-si'li-um). (Civil law.) The sending out of the judges to determine upon their decision.

missionary. One sent by a religious society to labor for the propogation of the faith, particularly in a foreign country or in a neglected field in this country. Anno: 17 ALR 1052. In a broader sense, a person who labors for a cause whether in the social, commercial, or political field.

Mississippi River flood control. See **flood control; Flood Control Act.**

missive. See letter; message.

Missouri Compromise. The provisions in the act of Congress passed in 1820 admitting the state of Missouri into the Union, whereby slavery was prohibited north of latitude 36° 30' n., excepting in that state.

misstaicus (mis-tā'i-kus). A messenger.

misstatement. A statement which is in error.

mistake. An erroneous mental conception which influences a person to act or omit to act. Nye v Sochor, 92 Wis 40, 65 NW 854. From the standpoint of relief in equity, some unintentional act, omission, or error, arising from ignorance, surprise, imposition, or misplaced confidence. Scurry v Cook, 206 Ga 876, 59 SE2d 371. As ground for relief by reformation of instrument, an unintentional act, omission, or error arising from ignorance, surprise, imposition, or misplaced confidence. Britton v Metropolitan Life Ins. Co. 165 NC 149, 80 SE 1072.
See **unilateral mistake.**

mistake of fact. An active mistake, consisting in the belief of existence of a matter or thing which is nonexistent, or vice-versa, or a passive mistake, consisting of unconsciousness, ignorance, or forgetfulness of a fact material to the transaction. Kowalke v Milwaukee Electric R. & Light Co. 103 Wis 472, 79 NW 762. A ground for cancellation of an instrument whether the instrument relates to an executory agreement or to one that has been executed, providing it affects the substance of the contract and is not a mere incident of the agreement. Steinmeyer v Schroeptel, 226 Ill 9, 80 NE 564. As ground for relief in equity by reformation of instrument:—(1) an unconscious ignorance or forgetfulness of a fact past or present and material to the contract; or (2) a belief in the present existence of a thing material to the contract which does not exist, or in the past existence of such a thing which has not existed. 45 Am J1st Reform Inst § 47. In the making of a payment:—a mistaken belief that the money was due the payee, when in truth it was neither legally nor morally due. 40 Am J1st Paym § 189.

mistake of law. An erroneous conclusion by one having a full knowledge of the facts as to their legal effect. Birkhouser v Schmitt, 45 Wis 316. An erroneous opinion or inference arising from an imperfect or incorrect exercise of the judgment upon the facts as they really are. Kowalke v Milwaukee Electric R. & Light Co. 103 Wis 472, 79 NW 762.

mistake of law and fact. A mistake of fact induced by a mistake of law, as in making a payment. 40 Am J1st Paym § 90.

mistery (mis'tėr-i). A trade; a calling; a business.

mistress. A woman who is the head of a household or of an institution such as an orphanage. A female who engages in sexual intercourse with a certain man for an extended period of time, sometimes receiving support money from him.

mistrial. The effect of prejudicial error which cannot be corrected or obviated by any action taken by the court. The equivalent of no trial; a nugatory proceeding.
Where a jury is discharged without a verdict, the proceeding is properly known as a mistrial; and where a verdict is set aside because it ought not to stand, the result is the same. The proceeding has miscarried, and the consequence is not a trial but a mistrial. Fisk v Henarie (CC Or) 32 F 417, 427.

misuse. See misuser.

misuser. The use of the privileges and franchises conferred upon a corporation in such manner as to defeat the ends for which the corporation was established. 19 Am J2d Corp § 1618. A wilful abuse or improper neglect of corporate privileges and franchises. 19 Am J2d Corp § 1619. The use of a franchise contrary to the conditions prescribed therein, 36 Am J2d Franch § 54, such as a refusal to comply with a rate ordinance. 36 Am J2d Franch § 18. The wrongful use or the failure to use a power. Erie & North-East Railroad Co. v Casey, 26 Pa 287, 318. The use of property for a purpose for which it was not designed. 18 Am J2d Conversion § 48. Use of dedicated land for any purpose other than that for which it was dedicated. 23 Am J2d Ded § 67.

mitigate. Verb: To lessen in severity or burden. To reduce: as, where the crime of murder may be reduced to manslaughter by the production of evidence of the defendant's insanity. See Sinclair v State, 161 Miss 142, 132 So 581, 74 ALR 241. Noun: The reduction of damages or punishment by reason of extenuating facts or circumstances.

mitigation of damages. Broadly, every fact tending to decrease the damages allowable in an action. 22 Am J2d Damg § 200. More precisely, those facts which tend to show that the conceded or assumed cause of action does not entitle the plaintiff to as large an amount of damages as otherwise would be recoverable. 22 Am J2d Damg § 200.
There are three typical situations within the more limited definition:—(1) that the plaintiff reasonably could have avoided a part or all the consequences of the defendant's wrongful act; (2) that the plaintiff received a benefit as a result of the defendant's wrongful act; and (3) that in cases where the defendant's conduct is material to the damages recoverable, his conduct was not as wrongful as plaintiff claims. 22 Am J2d Damg § 200.

mitigation of punishment. Lessening the punishment to be inflicted upon a convicted criminal out of consideration of circumstances such as former good behavior, the background of the defendant, the payment of damages by the defendant to the injured person, etc. 21 Am J2d Crim L §§ 584 et seq.

mitiori sensu. See in mitiori sensu.

mitior sensus (mi'she-or sen'sŭs). A more favorable meaning or interpretation.

Mitius imperanti melius paretur (mi'she-us im-pe-ran'tī me'li-us pa-rē'tėr). The more gently a person commands, the better he is obeyed.

mittendo tenorem recordi. See de mittendo tenorem recordi.

mitter (mit'tėr). To put; to send; to permit.

mitter à large (mit'tėr a lärj). To permit to go at large.

mitter avant (mit'tėr a-vant'). To set before; to produce, as, to produce in court.

mittere (mit'te-re). To send; to put; to permit; to discharge; to release.

mittere in confusum (mit'te-re in kon-fū'sum). To put into hotchpot.
See **hotchpot.**

mitter le droit (mit'tėr luh drwo). To pass a right; as if a man be disseised, and release to his disseisor all his right, the disseisor acquires a new right, which changes the quality of his estate, and renders that lawful which before was tortious or wrongful. See 2 Bl Comm 325.

mitter l'estate (mit'tėr l'is-tāt'). To pass an estate; as where one of two coparceners releases all her right to the other, thus passing the fee-simple of the whole. See 2 Bl Comm 324.

mittimus (mit'i-mus). A warrant of commitment to jail or prison. Biddle v Shirley (CA8 Kan) 16 F2d 566.

mixed action. An action appertaining in some degree to both real and personal actions, and therefore properly referable to neither of such classes. To illustrate, an action for the recovery of the possession of real property and damages for waste committed by the defendant. Thayer v Shorey, 287 Mass 76, 191 NE 435, 94 ALR 307.

mixed ambiguity. An ambiguity partaking of the nature of both a latent and a patent ambiguity. 30 Am J2d Ev § 1073.

mixed blood. Characterizing a person whose ancestors were of different races of men.

mixed blood Indian. Any Indian having an identifiable admixture, however small, of white blood. United States v First Nat. Bank, 234 US 245, 58 L Ed 1298, 34 S Ct 846.

mixed contract. A contract in which the values of the respective considerations are unequal.

mixed estate. A ground rent lease for ninety-nine years, renewable forever. Jones v McGruder (DC Md) 42 F Supp 193.

mixed gift. A gift in which there is included both real and personal property.

mixed government. A government partaking of the attributes of a democracy, a monarchy and an aristocracy at the same time.

mixed insurance company. An insurance company which embodies the characteristics of both a mutual company and a stock company. State v Willett, 171 Ind 296, 86 NE 68. An insurance company that has, at least in part, the nature of both stock and mutual companies, a certain portion of the profits being divided among the stockholders and a distribution of other accumulated funds made among the persons insured. Pink v Town Taxi Co. 138 Me 44, 21 A2d 656.

mixed jury. A jury composed of both men and women. 31 Am J Rev ed Jur § 101. A jury composed of persons of different races. 31 Am J Rev ed Jur § 99. An English jury which was composed of men half of whom were of the same nationality as the foreigner who was a party to the action and the other half Englishmen.

mixed larceny. Same as **compound larceny.**

mixed marine policy. A time and voyage policy wherein the voyage is designated by the policy, but the risk is limited to a specified time. 29 Am J Rev ed Ins § 324.

mixed marriage. A marriage between persons of different races.
See **miscegenation.**

mixed nuisance. A nuisance which is both public and private in its effects—public, because it violates public rights, and injures many persons, or all the community; and private, in that it also produces special injury to private rights. 39 Am J1st Nuis §§ 6, 7.

mixed penal law. A law concerned with both the thing to be declared a crime or offense and the punishment.

mixed powers. The mingling of powers normally divided between the executive, legislative, and judicial departments of government. The existence in one department of government of powers generally similar to those of another department, for example, the blending in the legislative powers of the United States of the judicial power of trying impeachments. 16 Am J2d Const L § 214.

mixed property. That kind of property which is not altogether real or altogether personal, but a compound of both, for example, heirlooms, tombstones, keys to a house, fixtures, etc. 42 Am J1st Prop § 28.

mixed question of law and fact. In loose usage, a question, the determination of which involves both law and fact.
There is really no such thing. What is sometimes so misnamed is a question which depends for its solution upon a question or questions of law and a question or questions of fact; but every such complicated proposition, when analyzed, is resolved into its elements of well-defined questions either of law or of fact, to be decided either by the judge or by the jury. State v Hayes, 162 La 917, 923, 111 So 327.

mixed tithes. Those tithes which consisted of natural products which had been nurtured and preserved in part by the care of man, such as of wool, milk, pigs, etc.
One tenth of these products had to be paid in gross, while in respect to personal tithes, only a tenth of the net gains or profits had to be paid. See 2 Bl Comm 24.

mixed train. A railroad train which combines both freight and passenger service. Arizona Eastern Railroad Co. v State, 29 Ariz 446, 242 P 870.

mixed war. A kind of war which can be carried on only between a nation on the one side and private individuals on the other. People v McLeod (NY) 1 Hill 377, 25 Wend 483.

mixing. See **commingling of funds; commingling of goods.**

mixtion (miks'chọn). Confusion,—the mingling of the goods of different owners.

M'Naghten Test. The right and wrong test of criminal responsibility, the terminology being taken from the title of an English Case. M'Naghten's Case, 10 Clark & F 200, 8 Eng Reprint 718.
See **right and wrong test.**

moat (mōt). A ditch filled with water surrounding a fortified town or castle, forming an added protection against invaders.

mob. A large and aggravated riot. Anno: 52 ALR 563. A riotous assemblage. An unorganized assemblage of many persons intent on unlawful violence either to persons or property. Anno: 13 ALR 770, s. 23 ALR 300, 44 ALR 1142, 52 ALR 563. Three or more persons assembled together with intent to do any unlawful act with force and violence against the person or property of another, or to do any unlawful act against the peace, or who, being lawfully assembled, shall agree with each other to do any unlawful act, and shall make any movement or preparation therefor. Blakeman v City of Wichita, 93 Kan 444, 144 P 816.

Blackstone defines the term as the riotous assembling of twelve persons, or more, and not dispersing upon proclamation. See 4 Bl Comm 142.

mobile home (mō′bil hōm). A house resting upon wheels, or so constructed that wheels may easily be placed under it, for easy transportation along the highway to another location.

mobile station. A radio-communication station capable of being moved. United States v Betteridge (DC Ohio) 43 F 53.

mobilia (mō-bi′li-a). Latin for **movables.**

Mobilia inhaerent ossibus domini (mō-bi′li-a in-hē′-rent os′si-bus do′mi-nī). Movables cling to the bones of their owner. Holbrook v Ford, 153 Ill 633, 39 NE 1091.

Mobilia non habent situm (mō-bi′li-a non hā′bent si′tum). Movables have no situs. Wyeth Hardware & Co. v H. F. Lang & Co. 127 Mo 242, 29 SW 1010.

Mobilia personam sequuntur (mō-bi′li-a per-sō′nam se-qu-un′ter). See **mobilia sequuntur personam.**

mobilia sequuntur personam (mō-bi′li-a se-qu-un′ter per-sō′nam). Movables follow the person.

Personal property, no matter how ponderous or unwieldly, in legal contemplation changes location with every change of the owner's domicil. 16 Am J2d Confl L § 29.

mob violence. The characteristic of mob action. See **mob.**

mock. To deride; to laugh at; to ridicule; to treat with scorn and contempt. State v Warner, 34 Conn 276, 279. To imitate in fun or jest.

mock marriage. A marriage performed by way of a jest, with no intention of entering into a contract of marriage or assuming the marital relationship, rights, and duties. Anno: 11 ALR 215.

mode. Manner or method, especially in reference to practice and procedure. Beers v Haughton (US) 9 Pet 329, 360, 9 L Ed 145, 157.

model. A style or design, especially of an automobile. A plan or design for the production and reproduction of works of art. 17 USC § 5(g). A copy or imitation of an object. State v Fox, 25 NJL 566, 602. Someone or something to be admired and imitated. One who wears clothing or jewelry by way of exhibiting it to prospective buyers.

model act. A statute proposed by the National Conference of Commissioners of Uniform State Laws for adoption in the various states as a uniform law.

For particular acts, see the concrete titles, such as **Administrative Procedure Act; Nuclear Facilities Liability Act.**

model training school. A school conducted in connection with a normal school or college of education for use in teacher training. School Dist. v Bryan, 51 Wash 498, 99 P 28.

moderamen inculpatae tutelae (mo-de-rā′men in-kul-pā′tē tū-tē′le). (Roman law.) The regulation of excusable protection; that is, lawful self-defense.

moderata misericordia (mo-de-rā′ta mi-se-ri-kor′di-a). A writ to prevent an excessive amercement or fine.

moderata misericordia capienda. See **de moderata misericordia capienda.**

Moderate castigavit (mo-de-rā′te kas-ti-gā′vit). He moderately chastised; that is, in a reasonable manner.

moderate speed. Speed, whether of a motor vehicle, train, or ship, which is not excessive under the circumstances or in violation of statute or ordinance. 8 Am J2d Auto § 716.

As applied to navigation, the rule by which to determine whether a given rate of speed is moderate or excessive, in view of the particular circumstances of the occasion, is that such speed only is moderate as will permit the steamer seasonably and effectually to avoid collision by slackening speed, or by stopping and reversing, within the distance at which an approaching vessel can be seen. Macham v New York (CC NY) 35 F 604, 609.

moderator. One who conducts a meeting, particularly one for discussion of propositions and courses of action to be taken, such as the synod or assembly of a religious body. Primarily, the presiding officer at a town meeting. Wheeler v Carter, 180 Mass 382, 386, 62 NE 471.

Modica circumstantia facti jus mutat (mo′di-ka ser-kum-stan′she-a fak′tī jūs mū′tat). A trifling circumstantial fact may change the law.

modicam castigationem adhibere (mo′di-kam kas-ti-gā′she-ō-nem ad-hi′be-re). To administer moderate chastisement. See 1 Bl Comm 445.

modification. See **alteration; amendment; change.**

modification of alimony. A modification of a judgment for alimony. 24 Am J2d Div & S § 655.

modification of award. A change effected by board, commission, or court of an award of workmen's compensation. 58 Am J1st Workm Comp § 499.

modification of contract. A change in the terms of a contract by a new or secondary agreement. 17 Am J2d Contr § 458.

modification of custody. The modification of an order awarding custody of a child or children to one of the parties in a suit for divorce. 24 Am J2d Div & S § 812.

modification of judgment. A change in the terms, rather than the reversal of, a judgment. 5 Am Jur 2d A & E § 937. Correcting a judgment to make it speak the truth of what was decided. Changing the terms of a judgment upon sufficient grounds presented therefor. 30A Am J Rev ed Judgm § 656.

modification of lease. A change in the conditions of a lease by agreement subsequent to the execution of the lease. 32 Am J1st L & T § 147.

modification of statute. See **amendatory statute.**

modification of support. The modification of a judgment or decree for support of spouse or child. 24 Am J2d Div & S §§ 655, 844.

modify. To change or vary, not to create.

A power given to modify or abolish implies the existence of the subject matter to be modified or abolished. When exercised to modify, it does not destroy identity, but effects some change or qualification in form or qualities, powers or duties, purposes or objects, of the subject matter to be modified, without touching the mode of creation. State v Lawrence, 12 Or 297, 7 P 116.

See expressions beginning **modification.**

modius (mō′di-us). A measure; a Roman dry measure equal to a little less than two imperial gallons.

MODO [811] MONETA

modo ad hunc diem. See **et modo ad hunc diem.**

modo decimandi. See **de modo decimandi.**

modo et forma (mō'dō et fôr'mạ). In the manner and form. Krause v Board of School Trustees, 162 Ind 278, 283, 70 NE 264.

modus (mō'dus). (Civil law.) Mode; manner; method; form; a measure.

Modus dat legem donationi (mō'dus dat lē'jem dō-nā-she-ō'nī). The form provides the law for the gift.

modus decimandi (mō'dus de-si-man'dī). Manner of tithing.
Any means whereby the general law of tithing was altered, and a new method of taking tithes was introduced, was called a "modus decimandi," or special manner of tithing. It was commonly called by the simple name of a "modus." See 2 Bl Comm 29.

modus de non decimando (mō'dus dē non de-si-man'dō). A manner or custom of not paying tithes.
Where particular persons or lands had become discharged or exempted by immemorial usage or custom from the payment of tithes they thus acquired a prescriptive immunity from such payment, which was called a "modus de non decimando." See 2 Bl Comm 29.

Modus de non decimando non valet (mo'dus dē non de-si-man'do non val'et). A modus or prescriptive exemption from the payment of tithes is not valid.
This was the rule as to lay tenants, but spiritual persons or corporations, such as monasteries, abbots, bishops, and the like were always capable of having their lands totally discharged of tithes by various means. See 2 Bl Comm 31.

Modus et conventio vincunt legem (mō'dus et konven'she-ō vin'kunt lē'jem). The form and the agreement control the law. Merchants' Bank v State Bank (US) 10 Wall 604, 19 L Ed 1008, 1018.

modus habilis (mō'dus ha'bi-lis). A proper manner.

modus injuriae (mō'dus in-jū'ri-ē). The means of injury. Terrell v Chesapeake & Ohio Railway Co. 110 Va 340, 66 SE 55.

Modus legem dat donationi (mō'dus lē'jem dat dō-nā-she-ō'nī). It is the form which gives validity to a gift. See 2 Bl Comm 310.

modus levandi fines (mō'dus le-van'dī fī'nēz). The manner of levying fines.

modus operandi (mō'dus o-pe-ran'dī). The method of operation.

modus tenendi (mō'dus te-nen'dī). The manner of holding,—the character of the tenure.

modus transferrendi (mō'dus trans-fe-ren'dī). The manner of transferring.

modus vacandi (mō'dus va-kan'dī). The manner of vacating or relinquishing.

modus vivendi (mō'dus vī-ven'dī). The mode of living.

moenia. See **intra moenia.**

moerda (mo-er'da). The ancient Teutonic word for murder. 4 Bl Comm 194.

Mohammedanism (mō-ham'e-dạn-izm). A religion founded by Mohammed, who is regarded by its followers known as Moslems as the true prophet, based upon a belief in one God, Allah, but accepting Jesus Christ as a prophet, although lesser than Mohammed. Hale v Everett, 53 NH 9.

moiety (moi'e-ti). A part; a fraction of a thing.
See **advowson of the moiety; taking by moieties; undivided interest.**

Moiety Act (moi'e-ti akt). An act of Congress providing for the forfeiture of smuggled goods and for an equal division of them between the informer and the government. United States v Auffmordt (DC NY) 19 F 893.

molding. An ornament on the cornice, eaves or surface of a building, becoming involved in litigation where it encroaches on the adjoining premises. 1 Am J2d Adj L § 123.

molendinum (mō-len-dī'num). A mill for grinding grain.

molestation. Interference with a church service or other meeting. Annoyance of, or interference with, a person, particularly where the victim is a child.

molestation clause. A provision in a separation agreement that the husband will not disturb, molest, or visit the home of the wife, except as business relations may require a visit. 24 Am J2d Div & S § 923. A comparable clause wherein the wife covenants that she will not molest, disturb, or speak disparagingly of the husband. Verdier v Verdier, 133 Cal App 2d 325, 284 P2d 94; Smith v Smith, 225 NC 189, 34 SE2d 148, 160 ALR 460.

molitura libera (mō-li-tū'ra li'be-ra). The liberty of having one's grain ground at a certain mill without cost.

molliter (mo'li-ter). Gently; softly; easily.

molliter manu (mo'li-ter ma'nū). Gently with the hand.

molliter manus imponere (mo'li-ter ma'nus im-po'nere). To lay hands gently. State v Durham, 141 NC 741, 53 SE 720.

Molliter manus imposuit (mo'li-ter ma'nus im-pō'zu-it). He gently laid hands upon him.

molutus (mō-lū'tus). Ground.

momentary delivery. A colorable delivery of property to vest title in the vendee. 37 Am J2d Frd Conv § 49.

momentary seisin. Seisin for an instant; sufficient to endow the wife of the man seized. 25 Am J2d Dow § 29

momentum (mō-men'tum). A moment of time; an instant. The product of the mass of a moving object and its linear velocity.

monarch (mon'ark). A king.

monarchy (mon'ạr-ki). A government entrusted in the hands of a single person. See 1 Bl Comm 49.

monasterium (mō-nas-te'ri-um). A monastery; a church.

monastery. A place of residence for monks and other persons who have retired from the world or desire for the time to lead the contemplative life.

moneta (mo-nē'ta). Coined metal; money, the term deriving from the temple of Juno Moneta wherein Roman money was coined.

Moneta est justum medium et mensura rerum commutabilium, nam per medium monetae fit omnium rerum conveniens, et justa aestimatio (mo-nē'ta est jus'tum mē'di-um et men-sū'ra rē'rum kom-mū-tā-bi'li-um, nam per mē'di-um mo-nē'tē fit om'ni-um rē'rum kon-ve'ni-enz, et jus'ta ēs-ti-mā'she-ō). Money is the just medium and measure of merchantable goods, for through the medium of money a convenient and proper estimate of all things is made.

Monetandi jus comprehenditur in regalibus quae nunquam a regio sceptro abdicantur (mo-nē-tan'dī jŭs kom-pre-hen'di-ter in rē-gā'li-bus kwē nun'quam ā rē'ji-ō sep'trō ab-di-kan'ter). The right of coining money is included among those royal prerogatives which are never renounced by the royal scepter.

monetary loss. A loss measurable in money.

money. Currency; current funds. Reese v First Nat. Bank (Tex Civ App) 196 SW2d 48, 171 ALR 516, error ref n r e. Cash or coin. Re Rogers, 91 NJ Eq 294, 109 A 16. Cash, including both coin and paper. 36 Am J1st Money § 2. In a specific sense, that which is coined or stamped by public authority as a medium of exchange and has its value fixed by public authority. 36 Am J1st Money § 2. The medium of exchange recognized by the custom of merchants and the laws of the country. 36 Am J1st Money § 2. In a general or comprehensive sense, wealth, commodities, everything transferrable in commerce. 36 Am J1st Money § 2. A generic term covering everything which by common concept represents property and passes currently from hand to hand without necessity for inquiry as to title. 11 Am J2d B & N § 11. A term of flexible meaning in a will, having either a restricted or a wide significance, according to the context of the will in which it occurs and those surrounding circumstances which the court is bound to consider in construction, sometimes meaning wealth or property, particularly personal property. 57 Am J1st Wills § 1349.

See **pin money; ready money; suit money.**

money claims. Claims or demands for money arising out of express or implied contracts. All rightful claims, whether founded upon contract, tort or penalties given by statute. Dittman Boot & Shoe Co. v Mixon, 120 Ala 206, 210, 24 So 847.

money counts. Money had and received, money lent, and money paid. 1 Am J2d Actions § 13.

money demand. See **money claims.**

money deposit. A deposit of money or its equivalent in check, draft, etc. National Surety Co. v Canon, 62 Colo 401, 163 P 284.

moneyed capital. Capital in money employed in a business the object of which is the making of a profit by the use of such money as money. 51 Am J1st Tax § 271.

moneyed corporation. A corporation organized for profit. Anno: 22 ALR2d 1026,§ 2. A commercial or business corporation rather than a charitable corporation. In the popular sense, a bank or finance company.

The term is defined by New York statute to mean every corporation having banking powers, or having the power to make loans upon pledges or deposits, or authorized by law to make insurances. Platt v Wilmot, 193 US 602, 611, 48 L Ed 809, 813, 24 S Ct 542.

money had and received. One of the common counts in assumpsit. 1 Am J2d Actions § 13.

An action originally for the recovery of debt, favored because more convenient and flexible than the common-law action of debt, has been gradually expanded as a medium for recovery upon every form of quasi-contractual obligation in which the duty to pay money is imposed by law independent of contract express or implied in fact. Stone v White, 301 US 532, 81 L Ed 1265, 57 S Ct 851.

money in court. See **deposit in court.**

money judgment. A judgment calling for the payment of a sum of money by one party to the other. A judgment which can be fully satisfied by a payment of money. Fuller v Aylesworth (CA6 Mich) 75 F 694, 700.

money land. Money held under trust to convert it to land.

money lender. A person who lends money as a business, particularly a person who makes small loans upon chattel security and salary assignments. 40 Am J1st Pawnb § 11.

money lent. One of the common counts in assumpsit. 1 Am J2d Actions § 13.

money made. Money collected by a sheriff or other officer under a writ of execution. In a more common sense, money earned by work or accumulated by way of taking a profit on an investment.

money of adieu. Earnest-money paid to bind a bargain, whereupon the parties bade each other adieu.

money of estate. A peculiar expression, the meaning of which may be explained by proof of a trade usage or custom. Howe v Hartness, 11 Ohio St 449.

money on hand. Sometimes including bank deposits, sometimes not. 57 Am J1st Wills § 1354.

money only. A phrase expressive of legal rather than equitable relief. Anno: 154 ALR 113.

money order. An instrument issued by an authorized officer of a bank and directed to another bank, evidencing the fact that the payee may demand and receive upon indorsement and presentation to the bank the amount stated on the face of the instrument, liability for payment resting solely on the issuing bank. 10 Am J2d Bks § 545. Broadly, any order for the payment of money, including a check or bank draft. McDougall v Lueder, 389 Ill 141, 58 NE2d 899, 156 ALR 1059. A telegraphed order for the payment of money, being a convenient method of transmitting money to a person at a distance.

See **post-office money order.**

money paid. One of the common counts in assumpsit. 1 Am J2d Actions § 13.

money paper. Commercial paper, investment paper, and commodity paper. UCC §§ 3-104, 7-104, 8-101, Comment 2.

money rent. Rent payable in money. 32 Am J1st L & T § 61.

moneys. The plural of money and nothing more. Mann v Mann (NY) 14 Johns 1.

Mongolian. A person of the yellow race. A native of Inner Mongolia or of Outer Mongolia.

monition (mō-nish'ǫn). A citation in a suit in admiralty. 2 Am J2d Adm § 153. A notice in a proceeding in rem for the forfeiture of property, citing the owners and all other persons claiming any right, title, or interest in the property seized to appear and show cause on or before a day named why forfeiture of the property should not be decreed in accordance with the prayer of the libel or information. 36 Am J2d Forf & P § 36. Notice of a proceeding in prize court, summoning all persons interested to show cause against the condemnation of the property as prize of war, such notice being issued and published upon the filing of the libel. 56 Am J1st War § 185.

monocracy (mō-nok'rā-si). A government with a single ruler.

monocrat (mon'ō-krat). The ruler of a monocracy.

monogamy (mō-nog'a-mi). The state or condition of a person who has but one spouse at a time.

monomachy (mō-nom'a-ki). Single combat; a combat between two persons; a duel.

monomania (mon-ō-mā'ni-ä). Partial or illusional insanity. People v Hubert, 119 Cal 216, 51 P 329; Commonwealth v Rogers, 48 Mass (7 Met) 500. Insanity upon one subject.

monomaniac (mon-ō-mā'ni-ak). A person insane on a particular subject, sane upon all other matters. 29 Am J Rev ed Ins Per § 3.

Monopolia dicitur, cum unus solus aliquod genus mercaturae universum emit, pretium ad suum libitum statuens (mo-no-pō'li-a di'si-ter, kum ū'nus sō'lus a'li-quod je'nus mer-ka-tū'rē ū-ni-ver'sum e'mit, pre'she-um ad su'um li'bi-tum sta'tu-enz). A monopoly is said to exist when one person alone buys the whole of some sort of merchandise, fixing the price to his own fancy.

monopolium (mo-no-pō'li-um). Same as **monopoly**.

monopoly. Broadly, the sole power of dealing in an article or doing a specified thing, either generally or in a particular place. 36 Am J1st Monop etc. § 2. A means of suppressing competition by the unification of interest or management or through agreement and concert of action. 36 Am J1st Monop etc. § 2.

monopoly of any part. An expression of the Federal Antitrust Act; a monopoly of any part of interstate or foreign trade or commerce. Lorain Journal Co. v United States, 342 US 143, 96 L Ed 162, 72 S Ct 181; United States v Paramount Pictures, 334 US 131, 92 L Ed 1260, 68 S Ct 915.

monopoly of trade. The acquisition of an exclusive right to, or the exclusive control of, a trade. 36 Am J1st Monop etc. § 2.

monoxide (mon-ok'sīd). See **carbon monoxide**.

monoxide poisoning. See **carbon monoxide poisoning**.

Monroe Doctrine. A principle established as a policy of the United States, asserting its right to resist any European interference with the affairs of the governments of the American republics.

The doctrine took its name from President Monroe, although it appears that John Quincy Adams, the Secretary of State in President Monroe's cabinet formulated the doctrine for enunciation.

monster. A plant or creature terribly deformed. A human-being by birth, but in some part resembling a lower animal.

"A monster ... hath no inheritable blood, and cannot be heir to any land, albeit it be brought forth in marriage; but, although it hath deformity in any part of its body, yet if it hath human shape, it may be heir." 2 Bl Comm 246.

monstrans de droit (mon'stranz duh drwo). A showing or setting forth of the right by the defendant in an action at common law under an information for trespass upon lands of the commonwealth. Commonwealth v Hite, 33 Va (6 Leigh) 588.

monstrans de faits (mon'stranz duh fā). A showing of deeds; a profert of deeds.

monstraverunt (mon-strä-vē'runt). See **writ of monstraverunt**.

monte (mon'tē). A game of chance played with cards of different colors, the gamble being on the color of a card to be dealt from a deck.

montes pietatis (mon'tēz pī-e-tā'tis). Rocks of benefaction,—pawn-shops.

They were probably so called because they were, as they still are, in many cases, patronized for the most part by poor persons.

month. A division of time, to be computed by the calendar, unless a contrary meaning is indicated by the statute or contract under construction. 52 Am J1st Time § 11. A calendar, rather than a lunar month. McGinn v State, 46 Neb 427, 65 NW 46 (constitutional provision respecting effective date of statute). For the purpose of computation of time of payment, a calendar month. 11 Am J2d B & N § 291; 40 Am J1st Paym § 13. As the term is used in a lease, a calendar month, as distinguished from a lunar month. 32 Am J1st L & T § 138. A calendar month for the purposes of a statute fixing the period of time for taking an appeal. 4 Am J2d A & E § 296.

monthly reporting policy. An insurance policy containing the requirement of monthly reports by the insured to the insurer of the value of the property covered under the policy, its exact location, and all other specific insurance in force on such property. Anno: 13 ALR2d 718; 29A Am J Rev ed Ins § 975.

monticolis Walliae. See **de monticolis Walliae**.

month to month tenancy. See **tenancy from month to month**.

monument. A tombstone. 31 Am J2d Ex & Ad § 322. A memorial to a deceased person, usually but not necessarily at his grave; a shaft or stone, not a building. Fancher v Fancher, 156 Cal 13, 103 P 206. Something more imposing than a mere gravestone. Fancher v Fancher, 156 Cal 13, 103 P 206. A marker of stone or metal of a point of historical interest, particularly a battlefield. 26 Am J2d Em D § 63. A physical object on the ground, natural or artificial, such as tree, stone, fence, etc., establishing or tending to establish a boundary line. Delphey v Savage, 227 Md 373, 177 A2d 249.

As the expression is used in a will providing for the erection of a "suitable monument" to the memory of the testator, the word "suitable" gives play to the discretion of the executors in the selection of the monument, its form and style, with reference to the amount of money set apart for the purpose. See Fancher v Fancher, 156 Cal 13, 103 P 206.

Monumenta quae nos recorda vocamus sunt veritatis et vetustatis vestigia (mo-nu-men'ta kwē nōs re-kor'da vo-kā'mus sunt ve-ri-tā'tis et ve-tus-tā'tis ves-ti'ji-a). Those monuments which we call records are the marks of truth and antiquity.

moonlighting. The pursuit by a public officer or public employee of employment or occupation apart from that of his public office or employment. Anno: 88 ALR2d 1235.

moonshine. An alcoholic liquor which has been illicitly, illegally, and clandestinely made. Everhart v State, 194 Tenn 272, 250 SW2d 368; State v Wills, 91 W Va 659, 114 SE 261, 24 ALR 1398. Whiskey which has been illicitly distilled or produced; whiskey unlawfully and illegally manufactured. State v Charette, 75 Mont 78, 242 P 343.

moor. To fasten and hold a vessel to anchor or pier by cable or chain. To tie floating logs to a structure, natural or artificial, on shore of the stream. 34 Am J1st Logs § 74.

moorage. A fee for the privilege of mooring a vessel. Wharf Case (Md) 3 Bland 361, 373.

moored vessel. A vessel at anchor or secured by cable.

Moore v Littel. A famous New York case, reported in 41 NY 33, holding that by virtue of a statute of the jurisdiction, where there is a person in being who would have immediate right to the possession of the land if the intermediate or precedent estate were presently terminated, the remainder is vested and not contingent, notwithstanding the estate may be defeated by subsequent events.

The specific holding is that under a conveyance to one for life and after his decease to his heirs and assigns forever, the remainder is vested. Moore v Littel, 41 NY 66.

mooring. A place to moor a vessel. See **moor.**

mooring in good safety. Placing a vessel in position to discharge her cargo. 29 Am J Rev ed Ins § 330.

moot case. A case involving only abstract questions; a case without relevancy to any controversy between the parties. Reserve Life Ins. Co. v Frankfather, 123 Colo 77, 225 P2d 1035, 39 ALR2d 146. See **moot question.**

moot court. A practice or simulated court where law students conduct fictitious suits.

moot question. An abstract or academic question. A hypothetical question. 1 Am J2d Actions § 56. A question which does not rest upon existing facts or rights; a question as to which in reality there is no actual controversy existing; a question which involves no right actually asserted and contested. 5 Am J2d A & E § 762. A question not arising on the facts presented in the case, but existing only in the light of hypothetical circumstances. Associated Press v NLRB, 301 US 103, 81 L Ed 953, 57 S Ct 650. A question which has lost significance because of a change in the condition of affairs between the parties, whether before or after the commencement of the action. 1 Am J2d Actions § 56. In another sense of the term, a debatable point which has never been decided, at least not in the jurisdiction.

mora (mō'rą̊). A delay; a pause; a hindrance. See **ex mora; in mora.**

mora debitoris. See **ex mora debitoris.**

moral. Adjective: Upright; virtuous, especially in matter of sex. Noun: A principle for determining that which is right and that which is wrong.

moral and social duty. See **moral obligation.**

moral certainty. See **proof to a moral certainty.**

moral character. See **bad moral character; character; good moral character.**

moral coercion. Importunity or overpersuasion in stressing the necessity of action or inaction, sometimes amounting to undue influence. 25 Am J2d Dur § 36. A form of duress. 13 Am J2d Canc Inst § 28. Imposition, oppression, undue influence or the taking of undue advantage of the business or financial stress or extreme necessity or weakness of another. Lafayette Dramatic Productions v Ferentz, 305 Mich 193, 9 NW2d 57, 145 ALR 1158.

moral compulsion. See **moral coercion.**

moral consideration. A consideration which is good only in conscience.

The idea that in every case where a person is under a moral obligation to do an act, as to relieve one in distress by personal exertions, or to spend money, a promise to that effect would bind him in law, is not supported by principle or precedent. It is a just rule of morality, sanctioned by the highest authority that a man should do towards others what he might reasonably expect from them under like circumstances. But a promise to fulfil the moral obligation created by this rule would not be enforced in any court of justice. Municipal laws will not decide what honor and gratitude ought to induce. It must be left to the forum of conscience. Cook v Bradley, 7 Conn 57.

moral duress. See **moral coercion.**

moral duty. See **moral obligation.**

moral eviction. The conduct of a landlord in rendering the premises unfit for the occupation of the tenant, without actually taking possession of any part of the land, as by introducing women of ill fame into other parts of the house. Campbell v Shields, 11 How Pr 365.

moral evidence. Evidence which is not demonstrative in character but of probative value in instructing the trier of the facts upon the issues of fact.

moral fraud. A fraud or deceit which involves moral wrong.

moral hazard. An expression of the insurance business; the chance or risk of the insured destroying the property, or permitting it to be destroyed, for the purpose of collecting the insurance.

In the law of fire insurance, the term is but another name for a pecuniary interest in the insured to permit the property to burn. Statistics, experience, and observation all teach that the moral hazard is least when the pecuniary interest of the insured in the protection of the property against fire is greatest, and that the moral hazard is greatest when the insured may gain most by the burning of the property. Syndicate Ins. Co. v Bohn (CA8 Neb) 65 F 165.

moral insanity. Such mental disease as destroys the ability to distinguish between right and wrong in a particular act; a perversion of the moral sense. 29 Am J Rev ed Ins Per § 3.

morality. That which teaches men their duty, and the reason of it; the rule which teaches us to live soberly and honestly. The virtues of justice, prudence, temperance, and fortitude. Lyon v Mitchell, 36 NY 235, 238.

moral law. The law, in a very broad sense of the term "law," of conscience.

Judge Dillon, in his Commentary on the Laws and Jurisprudence of England and America, says: "Not less wondrous than the revelations of the starry heavens, and much more important, and to no class of men more so than lawyers, is the moral law which Kant found within himself, and which is likewise found within, and is consciously recognized by, every man. This moral law holds its dominion by divine ordination over us all, from which escape or evasion is impossible. This moral law is the eternal and indestructible sense of justice and of right written by God on the living tablets of the human heart and revealed in his Holy Word." Moore v Strickling, 46 W Va 515, 33 SE 274.

morally wrong. See **wrong.**

moral mania (mor'ąl măn'ą̊). The same as moral insanity.

moral obligation. A duty arising from or connected with what was once a legal liability or from the receipt of benefit of a material or pecuniary nature. 17 Am J2d Contr §§ 132 et seq. An obligation arising from ethical motives, or a mere conscientious duty, unconnected with any legal obligation, perfect or imperfect, or (under the later cases) with the receipt of benefit by the promisor of a material or pecuniary nature. 11 Am J2d B & N § 219; 17 Am J2d Contr § 130. An obligation which, although lacking any foundation cognizable in law, springs from a sense of justice and equity that an honorable person would have, but not from a mere sense of doing benevolence or charity. People v Westchester County Nat. Bank, 231 NY 465, 132 NE 241, 15 ALR 1344.

As the term "moral and social duty" is used in the law pertaining to privileged communications, it has been defined as a duty recognized by English people of ordinary intelligence and moral principle, but at the same time not a duty enforceable by legal proceedings, whether civil or criminal. The question is "would the great mass of right-minded men in the position of the defendant have considered it their duty, under the circumstances, to make the communication." See Watt v Longsdon (Eng) 1 K. B. 130, 69 ALR 1005.

See **moral consideration.**

moral restraint. A restraint upon the actions of a person, not by the exertion of physical power or the giving of directions, orders, or commands, merely by his conformity to wishes or desires of another. 25 Am J1st Hab C § 24.

moral turpitude. Baseness, vileness, or depravity in the private and social duties which a man owes to his fellowmen or to society in general. Huff v Anderson, 212 Ga 32, 90 SE2d 329, 52 ALR2d 1310; Re Henry, 15 Idaho 755, 99 P 1054; State v Malusky, 59 ND 501, 230 NW 735, 71 ALR 190. Something immoral in itself, irrespective of the fact that it is punished by law. Ex parte Mason, 29 Or 18, 43 P 651.

The term "crime involving moral turpitude" as found in the Immigration Act connotes something more than "illegal" or "criminal". It implies an act which is contrary to the accepted and customary standard of right and duty between man and man prevailing in the United States. The test is not dependent upon a classification between felonies and misdemeanors nor upon a distinction between infamous and not infamous offenses. Jordan v DeGeorge, 341 US 223, 95 L Ed 886, 71 S Ct 703, reh den 341 US 956, 95 L Ed 1377, 71 S Ct 1011.

morandae solutionis causa (mo-ran'dē so-lu-she-ō'nis kâ'za). For the sake of delaying payment.

Mora reprobatur in lege (mō'ra re-prō-bā'ter in lē'je). Delay is disapproved in the law.

morari (mo-rā'rī). To delay; to hinder; to pause.

moratoria (mor'ạ-tō'ri-ạ). Plural of **moratorium.**

moratorium (mor-ạ-tō'ri-um). A period during which an obligor has a legal right to delay meeting an obligation. Anno: 137 ALR 1380. Legislation extending the time for payment of indebtedness. 3 Am J2d Agri § 30. Legislation providing in some manner for the temporary relief of debtors, particularly of those in the Armed Service, during the existence of war. Anno: 137 ALR 1380, 147 ALR 1311. The suspension of remedies against lessees. 32 Am J1st L & T § 1034.

moratory interest. Interest allowed in an action for breach of contract or tort for the unlawful detention of money found to be due. 22 Am J2d Damg § 179.

moratory statute. A statute granting a moratorium. Anno: 137 ALR 1380.

moratory tables. Same as **mortality tables.**

Moratur in lege (mo-rā'ter in lē'je). He delays or pauses in law; that is, he demurs.

morbosus (mor-bō'sus). Sickly; diseased; worn out.

morbus sonticus (môr'bus son'ti-kus). (Civil law.) An illness which incapacitated a person from attending to his business.

more colonico (mo're ko-lō'ni-kō). In a husbandlike manner.

more definite and certain. Relief sought by motion in reference to a pleading that is not sufficiently full, definite, and certain to enable the adverse party to prepare a responsive pleading or to prepare for trial, sought by the adverse party on motion addressed to the defective pleading. 41 Am J1st Pl § 359.

more necessary public use. A comparative presented in certain eminent domain cases.

Where land which has already been appropriated to a public use is sought to be condemned for "a more necessary public use," there are cases holding that the new use must be an absolute public necessity, but other cases hold that there may be a new taking if it be simply for a greater public good. Butte, Anaconda & Pacific Railway Co. v Montana Union Railway Co. 16 Mont 504, 41 P 232.

more or less. A phrase qualifying a statement of an absolute and definite amount, 46 Am J1st Sales § 155, for the purpose of providing against slight, accidental variations. M. W. Kellogg Co. v Standard Steel Fabricating Co. (CA10 Okla) 189 F2d 629, 26 ALR2d 1090. An expression used as an estimate of an otherwise designated quantity, to be interpreted broadly or narrowly according to the context in which it appears. 17 Am J2d Contr § 282. A term in a bill of lading leaving it open to the carrier to make a showing of the whole situation with respect to the quantity received for transportation and the quantity delivered, in determining the liability for deficiency at destination. Anno: 67 ALR2d 1043, § 5; 13 Am J2d Car § 283. Words, which, as applied to quantity of land, are intended to cover some slight or unimportant inaccuracy in description. 12 Am J2d Bound § 75. An expression used in connection with a designation of courses and distances in a boundary, to be disregarded if not controlled or explained by references to monuments, markers, or other expressions of intention, and to be given meaning and effect when so controlled and explained. Inglson v Olson, 199 Minn 422, 272 NW 270, 110 ALR 167; Sowles v Minot, 82 Vt 344, 73 A 1025. A term which, when included in a deed in describing the property conveyed according to a certain number of acres, serves to confine the land conveyed to land within boundaries designated in the description. 23 Am J2d Deeds § 240.

There is no doubt of the general proposition that where the words "more or less" are used as an estimate of an otherwise designated quantity and the object of the parties is the sale or purchase of a particular lot, as a pile of wood or coal, the cargo of a particular ship, or a certain parcel of land, the words used in connection with the estimated quantity are susceptible of a broad construction, and the contract will be interpreted as applying to the particular lot or parcel, provided it is otherwise sufficiently identified. Pine River Logging & Improv. Co. v United States, 186 US 279, 46 L Ed 1164, 22 S Ct 920. If the agreement is to manufacture, furnish, or deliver certain property not then in existence, or to be taken from a larger quantity, the addition of the words "more or less" will be given a narrow construction and held to apply only to such accidental or immaterial variations in quantity as would naturally occur in connection with such a transaction. Pine River Logging & Improv. Co. v United States, 186 US 279, 46 L Ed 1164, 22 S Ct 920.

more specific statement. Relief sought in reference to statement of cause of action or defense on a motion by the adverse party addressed to the pleading.

more than ordinarily legitimate. An anomalous expression which might well be dropped from the language of courts and lawyers.

A child is thus characterized by Blackstone, where, if a man dies and his widow soon marries, and then a child is born at such time that it might naturally be the child of either husband. In such a case, the child may, upon arriving at the age of discretion, choose either of the two men as his father. See 1 Bl Comm 456.

morganatic marriage (môr-ga-nat'ik mar'āj). Under the law of some countries, a man's marriage to a woman of lower rank who does not share his rank nor enjoy full legal rights as a wife.

morgangiva (mor'gan-gi-va). A gift made to a bride on the morning of her wedding.

Morgan Plan Company. A company which, while engaged in lending money, does so on a basis distinguishing it quite clearly from an institution operating in competition with a national bank. First Nat. Bank v Louisiana Tax Com. 289 US 60, 77 L Ed 1030, 53 S Ct 511, 87 ALR 840.

morgengeba (môr'gĕn-gä-bē). Same as **morgangiva**.

morgue (môrg). A place where the bodies of unidentified dead persons are kept and exposed to view for the purpose of identification or that they may be claimed by their friends. Koebler v Pennewell, 75 Ohio St 278, 288. Also the place where the body of a person whose death raises a suspicion of murder or foul play is kept pending an inquest.

Mormon. The name of a religious body founded by Joseph Smith in 1830, otherwise known as the Church of Jesus Christ of Latter-Day Saints. A member of the Mormon Church.

Mormon divorce. An invalid divorce consisting of an agreement by the parties to the marriage, with the consent of the church, to dissolve the marital relation. Hilton v Roylance, 25 Utah 129, 69 P 660.

Mormon marriage. A marriage by means of the sealing ceremony entered into before a proper official by members of the Mormon Church competent to contract marriage. Hilton v Roylance, 25 Utah 129, 69 P 660.

moron (mō'rŏn). Broadly, a person so retarded mentally as to be stupid. Technically, one whose mental performance is not above that of a child between the ages of seven and twelve. State v Driver, 88 W Va 479, 107 SE 189, 15 ALR 917, 921.

morphine. A principal alkaloid of opium; a narcotic, People v Clark, 7 Ill 2d 163, 130 NE2d 195, the two usual forms of which are morphine hydrochloride and morphine sulphate.

Morphine hydrochloride is a chemical combination of morphine and hydrochloric acid and morphine sulphate is a chemical combination of sulphuric acid and morphine. It is generally held that, in an indictment for selling such drugs, the word "morphine" is sufficiently specific to charge the selling of any of these compounds. Jefferson v State, 34 Okla 56, 244 P 460; Hoffman v United States (CA8 Minn) 20 F2d 328.

Morris Plan bank. A bank of a particular type, organized and operating for the primary purpose of enabling wage earners of good character to obtain credit on an instalment basis. Morris Plan Co. v Currie (Sup App T) 161 NYS 292. A company which, while engaged in lending money, does so on a basis distinguishing it quite clearly from an institution operating in competition with a national bank. First Nat. Bank v Louisiana Tax Com. 289 US 60, 77 L Ed 1030, 53 S Ct 511, 87 ALR 840.

Morris Plan Company. Same as **Morris Plan bank**.

mors (morz). Death.

Mors dicitur ultimum supplicium (morz di'si-ter ul'ti-mum sup-pli'she-um). Death is called the extreme penalty or the extremity of punishment.

Mors omnia solvit (morz om'ni-a sol'vit). Death dissolves, unbinds, or releases everything.

mort (môrt). Death.

mortal. Death-producing; coming to an end eventually by death. Man as a creature who must die. State v Baker, 122 Kan 552, 253 P 221.

mortality. The matter of being mortal. The death rate in a country, a state, a locality, or a family or other group of persons.

mortality tables. Statistical tables which show the probable expectancy or continuance of life of a normal person according to sex and age. 30 Am J2d Ev § 894.

mortal sin. A sin which exposes to death ultimately, unless forgiven. State v Baker, 122 Kan 552, 253 P 221.

mortal wound. A fatal wound. 26 Am J1st Homi § 265. A wound which is death-producing. State v Baker, 122 Kan 552, 252 P 221.

mort civile (môrt si'vĕl). Civil death,—the cessation of all of a person's legal rights and capacities.

mort d'ancestor (môrt d'an'ses-tor). The death of an ancestor; a writ of assize to recover land from an abator of which the demandant's father or mother, brother or sister, uncle or aunt, nephew or niece had died seised. See 3 Bl Comm 185.

Morte donantis donatio confirmatur (mor'te dō'nan-tis dō-nā'she-ō kon-fir-mā'ter). A gift is confirmed by the death of the donor.

mortgage. In the ancient sense, an estate in mortuo vadio or dead pledge. At common law, a qualified estate under a conditional conveyance given by way of security for the performance of an obligation, usually one for the payment of money. In the modern sense, a security or lien for the performance of an obligation. 36 Am J1st Mtg § 2. A conveyance of property to secure the performance of some obligation, the conveyance to be void on the due performance of the obligation. 36 Am J1st Mtg § 2.

mortgageable property. Property which can be subjected to a mortgage, the term usually being used

MORTGAGE-BOND [817] MOSQUITO

in reference to personal property and chattel mortgages. 15 Am J2d Chat Mtg § 21.

mortgage-bond. A bond which is secured by a mortgage.

mortgage clause. Same as **mortgagee clause**.

mortgage company. See **loan company**.

mortgage coupon bond. See **coupon bond**.

mortgage debentures. Debentures by which specific funds or property are pledged as security. Barton Nat. Bank v Atkins, 72 Vt 33, 45, 47 A 176. A paradoxical expression if the definition of debenture as a bond secured, at best, by a pledge of income be accepted.
See **debenture**.

mortgage deed. A deed given by way of security; a mortgage.

mortgagee (môr-gā̱-jē'). The person to whom a mortgage is made.
A mortgagee is held to be a "purchaser" within the meaning of a statute entitling the widow of a nonresident alien to the same rights in her husband's property as a resident, except as against a "purchaser" from her husband. Estate of Gill, 79 Iowa 296, 44 NW 553.

mortgagee clause. A clause in a policy of insurance covering property which provides for the payment of the proceeds of the policy in the event of a loss to the mortgagee under a mortgage on the insured premises, to the extent of the amount of the mortgage. 29 Am J Rev ed Ins § 728.

mortgagee in possession. A mortgagee in possession of the property mortgaged to him.
An expression adopted by courts and law writers as a convenient phrase to describe the condition of a mortgagee who is in possession of mortgaged premises under such circumstances as to make the satisfaction of his lien a prerequisite to his being dispossessed, even in jurisdictions where the mortgage itself can confer no possessory right either before or after default; but the authorities are in some confusion as to what these circumstances are. It has been said that the possession must be "lawfully" acquired, or "without force;" that it must be taken under the mortgage, and because of it; that it need not be under the mortgage, nor with a view thereto; that it must be with the consent of the mortgagor, express or implied, etc. But there is probably no case limiting the right of a mortgagee to hold property of which he is in lawful possession to a case where such possession was with the consent of the mortgagor. Stouffer v Harlan, 68 Kan 135, 74 P 610.

mortgage of goods. A chattel mortgage, a mortgage of personal property.

mortgage of patent. A mortgage of a patent right, the recording of which in the Patent Office, in accordance with the federal statute, is the equivalent of delivery of possession.

mortgagor (môr-gā̱j-o̱r'). A person who mortgages his property to another; the maker of a mortgage.

mortgage pool. A trust created by the owners of several or even many mortgages in transferring the instruments to a trustee to hold for the benefit of the transferrers. Anno: 107 ALR 1458.

mortgage tax. A tax imposed with reference to the recording of a mortgage. 51 Am J1st Tax § 1257.

morth. (Saxon.) Murder.

morthlaga. A murderer.

morthlage. Murder.

mortician. An undertaker.

mortification. Extreme embarrassment; humiliation. Mental suffering constituting an element of damages for false imprisonment. 32 Am J2d False Imp § 114. Decay, particularly of the body or a part thereof.

mortis causa (môr'tis kâ'zä̱). By reason of death; in expectation of death.

Mortis momentum est ultimum vitae momentum (môr'tis mo-mem'tum est ul'ti-mum vī'tē mo-men'-tum). The moment of death is the last moment of life. Terrill v Public Administrator, (NY) 4 Bradf 245, 250.

mortmain (môrt'mān). Literally, the dead hand. Property held out of circulation.
To alienate land in mortmain was to convey it to a corporation, aggregate, ecclesiastical or temporal. Perin v Carey, 65 US 465, 16 L Ed 701, 708.
At one time in England, all purchases of land by corporations were said to be purchases in mortmain. Various reasons have been advanced for this. One given by Blackstone is that purchases made by corporations were usually made by ecclesiastical corporations, the members of which having taken the vows of a religious order were reckoned as dead persons in law. See 1 Bl Comm 479.

mortmain statutes (môrt'mān stat'ūts). Statutes having the purpose of preventing an uneconomic accumulation of property in control of corporations, either lay or ecclesiastical. Perin v Carey (US) 24 How 465, 16 L Ed 701, 708. The British statutes, 15 Rich. II, ch. 5 (in Am J2d Desk Book Document 107) and 9 George II, ch. 36.
The purpose of the British mortmain act, 9 George 2, chap. 36, was to prevent property from falling into "dead" or unserviceable hands, such as a charitable use was deemed to be. Yates v Yates (NY) 9 Barb 324, 333.

mortua manu. See **in mortua manu**.

mortuary. A place to which dead bodies may be taken for keeping before burial or cremation. A kind of ecclesiastical heriot in the form of a customary gift claimed by and due to the minister in many parishes on the death of a parishioner. See 2 Bl Comm 425.

mortuary tables. Same as **mortality tables**.

mortuo vadio. See **estate in mortuo vadio**.

mortuum vadium (mor'tu-um va'di-um). Dead pledge. A landed security known to the common law; a feoffment on condition that the feoffor might re-enter if he paid to the feoffee a certain sum of money at a certain date. 36 Am J1st Mtg § 12.

mortuus (môr'tu-us). Dead.

Mortuus est (môr'tu-us est). He is dead.

Mortuus exitus non est exitus (mor'tu-us ex'i-tus non est ex'i-tus). A dead issue is not an issue; a child born dead is no child.

mortuus sine prole (mor'tu-us sī'ne prō'le). Dead without issue.

Moslem (moz'lem). See **Mohammedanism**.

mos pro lege (mōs prō lē'je). Custom instead of law.

mosquito regulation. A health regulation respecting

water in which the larvae of the mosquito may be nourished. Territory v Araujo, 21 Hawaii 56.

Mos retinendus est fidelissimae vetustatis (mōs re-ti-nen'dus est fī-de-lis'si-mē ve-tus-tā'tis). A custom of truest antiquity should be preserved.

most favored nation clause. The clause of a treaty between two nations under which either of the parties or its diplomatic or consular representative is entitled to all the rights and privileges of those of the nation most favored by a treaty made with it by the other party. 4 Am J2d Ambss § 19.

mostrencos (mos-tren'cos). (Spanish.) Estrays; waifs.

most significant contract theory. A recently formulated principle of conflict of laws, that in determining the law applicable to the execution, interpretation, validity, and performance of a contract, the court shall look to the law of the place which has the most significant contacts with the matter in dispute. 16 Am J2d Confl L § 42.

mote (mōt). A very small particle. (Saxon.) A meeting; a court; a popular assembly.

mot en mot. See **de mot en mot.**

motel. A structure in several separate units, located along the highway or close to a highway, at which motorists may obtain lodging with parking space and, in some instances, meals. A place of accommodation where lodgings are available for hire, with a minimum of personal service furnished by the proprietor. Schermer v Fremar Corp. 36 NJ Super 46, 114 A2d 757.

mothball fleet. Ships of the Navy taken out of service but held to await necessity for further service.

mother. The female parent.

mother country. In popular usage, England. More precisely, in reference to any part of the United States, the country from whose dominion such part was taken, for example, the status of Mexico in reference to California. 29 Am J2d Ev § 50.

mother-in-law. The mother of one's husband or of one's wife.

mother's natural guardianship. The succession of the mother to the guardianship of her natural children upon the death of her husband and their father, upon his abandonment of the family, or upon his removal from the guardianship of the children by the court. 25 Am J1st G & W § 7.

mother's pension. A means whereby mothers who are without means of support for their children may maintain the family relation not subject to the disgrace attendant on support furnished under the poor law; a provision for the payment of a definite sum, to be fixed by some public agency or court, for the mother and each child, leaving the mother free to spend the money in her own way. State ex rel. Stearns County v Klasen, 123 Minn 382, 143 NW 984.

mother state. The state from which the state of the forum was formed, for example, the status of Virginia in reference to West Virginia. Martin v Baltimore & O. R. Co. 151 US 673, 38 L Ed 311, 14 S Ct 533.

motion. The means of presenting a proposition in a meeting conducted according to parliamentary procedure. An application, normally incidental to an action, made to a court or judge for the purpose of obtaining an order or rule directing something to be done in favor of the applicant. 37 Am J1st Motions § 3.

For particular motions, see the specific relief demanded, such as **more specific statement; judgment on the pleadings, nonsuit,** etc.

motion costs. The cost pertaining to the bringing on and hearing of a motion. 20 Am J2d Costs § 9.

motion of court. See **own motion.**

motion picture. See **moving picture.**

motion day. A day appointed by the court for the hearing of motions.

motion man. The status of one working premises as a licensee under license granted by the owner, particularly one working a quarry. Rockport v Rockport Granite Co. 177 Mass 246, 254.

motion of course. A motion which the opposite party cannot resist without supporting affidavits.

motivation test. A test applied in determining the application of a guest statute to a paying passenger in a motor vehicle, according to whether or not the expectation of payment or compensation was "the" or "the sole" motivating factor for the furnishing of the transportation. McCann v Hoffman, 9 Cal 2d 279, 70 P2d 909.

motive. The reason which leads the mind to desire a result. Baker v State, 120 Wis 135, 97 NW 566. The moving cause which induces action, having wholly to do with desire. 26 Am J1st Homi § 36. The power which impels to action for a definite result; that which leads or tempts the mind to indulge in a criminal act. 21 Am J2d Crim L § 85. The object and purpose of contracting parties. 17 Am J2d Contr § 246.

motive power. The power to move something, such as a vehicle, a bus, a railroad train, or an airplane. 44 Am J1st RR § 402.

motor. A source of power; the engine of a motor vehicle.

motorboat. Literally a boat or small craft having a motor or engine for power. For the purposes of regulations prescribed by federal statute, every vessel propelled by machinery and not more than 65 feet in length, except tugboats or towboats propelled by steam, including a boat temporarily or permanently equipped with a detachable motor. 46 CFR § 24.10—17.

Motorboat Act. A federal statute regulating the operation of motorboats in order to promote safety in recreational boating and to encourage uniformity of regulation among the states and the federal government. 12 Am J2d Boats § 4.

See **Boating Act.**

motorbus. See **bus.**

motorcar. An automobile. A self-propelled car running on a railroad track.

motor carrier. A carrier by motor vehicle. A carrier operating one or more motor vehicles for the purpose of carrying passengers or freight or both, for hire and profit, over the public highways as a transportation roadbed. Barbour v Walker, 126 Okla 229, 259 P 552. The term includes both a common carrier by motor vehicle and a contract carrier by motor vehicle. Section 303(a) of the Motor Carrier Act of 1935; Interstate Commerce Com. (DC Okla) 41 F 268.

Motor Carrier Act. A comprehensive federal statute applicable to motor carriers transporting passengers or property in interstate or foreign commerce. 49 USC §§ 301 et seq.

motor carrier transportation agent. A person who acts as an intermediary between the public and a motor carrier in arranging for transportation. Francis v Allen, 54 Ariz 377, 96 P2d 277, 126 ALR 190.

motorcycle (mō'tor-sī-kl). A two-wheeled automotive vehicle having one or two riding saddles and sometimes having a third wheel for the support of a sidecar. 7 Am J2d Auto § 2. Not a motor-driven car. Anno: 138 ALR 420; 38 ALR2d 882.

motor-driven car. An automobile. An automobile having a body and cover for the convenience and protection of persons riding in it. 29A Am J Rev ed Ins § 1239.

motorman. A person who operates a streetcar, being in control of the motive power and brakes and under responsibility of maintaining a lookout for persons on the tracks.

motor number. The number given a motor vehicle by the manufacturer, such being normally embossed upon the engine or motor.

motor train. A railroad motorcar with or without trailers attached, but operated as a train. Anno: 45 ALR2d 438.

motor transportation. The business of carrying passengers or freight in powered vehicles.

motor transportation company. A corporation which provides or furnishes transportation service for hire for the public in general. Affiliated Service Corp. v Public Utilities Com. 127 Ohio St 47, 186 NE 703, 103 ALR 264.

motor truck. See **motor vehicle; truck.**

motor vehicle. An automobile; any vehicle powered by a motor, such as a truck or bus. State v Ridinger (Mo) 266 SW2d 626, 42 ALR2d 617. Any vehicle propelled by power, other than muscular power, except a traction engine or such motor vehicle as runs only upon rails or tracks. People v Smith, 156 Mich 173, 120 NW 581. For some purposes, a tool or implement. 31 Am J2d Exemp § 62.

Motor Vehicle Theft Act. A federal statute, commonly known as the Dyer Act, making it an offense to transport in interstate or foreign commerce a motor vehicle, knowing the same to have been stolen, or to receive, conceal, store, barter, sell, or dispose of a motor vehicle which constitutes interstate or foreign commerce, knowing the same to have been stolen. 7 Am J2d Auto § 305.

moulding. Same as **molding.**

mountain time. The time in one of the belts designated for the determination of standard time, such belt being characterized by the Rocky Mountains located therein.
See **standard time.**

mourant (moo-rôn'). Dying.

movable freehold. A term applied facetiously to land likely to be gained or lost to the owner by the recession or encroachment of the sea or by change in the course of a stream. Holman v Hodges, 112 Iowa 714, 84 NW 950.

movable rights. Rights in movables; rights in personal property.

movable property. Personal property, including negotiable instruments. 6 Am J2d Attach § 150.
See **movables.**

movables. Movable property which attends a man's person wherever he goes, such as money, clothing, furniture, boats, automobiles, etc. 42 Am J1st Prop § 24. Broadly, personal property.

move. To change position. To change the position of something. To change one's residence or domicil. Barstow v Stone, 10 Colo App 296, 52 P 48. To make a motion; to do whatever things are necessary to be done to obtain an order which the moving party desires that the court should make. O'Hanion v Great Northern Railway Co. 76 Mont 128, 245 P 518.
See **motions; removal.**

movement freedom. See **freedom of movement.**

movement of traffic. The movement of vehicles upon a street or highway. 25 Am J1st High §§ 204 et seq.

movent (mō'vent). A moving party, a party who makes a motion.

movie. A moving picture.

moving building. The operation of moving a building from one location to another, usually, but not necessarily, accomplished with the building remaining intact throughout the operation.
A building may be "removed," as a building, that is, as a standing building, intact, but that is not the only way. It may be "removed," within the common understanding, by taking the material and reconstructing, or rebuilding it at another locality. Board of Education v Townsend, 63 Ohio St 514, 59 NE 223.

moving company. A company engaged in the business of moving goods, particularly household goods and furniture, either short distances or long distances, the same company often being engaged also in the storage or warehouse business. Having the status of a common carrier where it holds itself out as engaged in the business for all who choose to employ it. 13 Am J2d Car § 17.

moving in commerce. Being transported or moved in commerce. Not inclusive of the holding of sheep at a commercial stockyard, not for immediate shipment, but for fattening and sale, either locally or at a distant place, at some future time. Kirk v St. Joseph Stock Yards Co. (CA8 Mo) 206 F2d 283, 40 ALR2d 980.

moving papers. The affidavits submitted in support of a motion. 37 Am J1st Motions § 14.

moving picture. A form of entertainment; a form of theatrical performance. The casting of photographs or other representations upon a screen in such rapid succession as to create the illusion of moving people or things, usually accompanied in present times by the reproduction of sound. 4 Am J2d Amuse § 2.

moving picture censorship. See **censorship.**

moving picture booker. One employed by a motion picture distributing agency to keep records of films sent from out of the state to the agency, to supervise the supplying of such films to exhibitors, and to direct their transportation. Republic Pictures Corp. v Kappler (CA8 Iowa) 151 F2d 543, 162 ALR 228, affd 327 US 757, 90 L Ed 991, 66 S Ct 523, reh den 327 US 817, 90 L Ed 1040, 66 S Ct 804.

moving picture license. A license required by a municipal corporation of one exhibiting moving pictures as a business. 4 Am J2d Amuse § 30.

moving picture show. An entertainment offered to the public by way of an exhibition of moving pictures. A place where motion pictures are exhibited for the purpose of amusement and entertainment; a public place of amusement. State v Morris, 28 Idaho 599, 155 P 296.

See **moving picture.**

moving picture rights. The right to reproduce in a moving picture, with or without sound, a substantial part of the story told in a literary work. Anno: 23 ALR2d 267.

moving picture theater. A theater in which the entertainment offered consists of moving pictures.

See **moving picture show.**

moyen (moi'en'). Same as **mesne.**

m.p. Abbreviation of melting point, used in scientific works.

M.P. Abbreviation of Military Police. Abbreviation of member of parliament.

m.p.h. Abbreviation of miles per hour.

Mr. Abbreviation of mister.

Mrs. The title preceding the name of a married woman.

ms. Abbreviation of manuscript.

MS. Abbreviation of motor ship.

M.S. Abbreviation of Master of Science.

M.S.T. Abbreviation of mountain standard time.

mud guards. Rear wheel protectors on motor vehicles, otherwise known as splash guards, to prevent so far as practicable, the throwing of dirt, water, or other materials on pedestrians and other vehicles, particularly the windshields of following vehicles. 7 Am J2d Auto § 159.

muffler. Equipment on the motor of a motor vehicle to prevent excessive noise from the exhaust. 7 Am J2d Auto § 158. Required equipment upon the engine of a motorboat, under some statutes. 12 Am J2d Boats § 12.

mugging (mug'ing). The practice of photographing persons arrested for crime. An assault by throwing an arm around the neck of the victim, usually upon an approach from behind, the purpose being to overpower the victim so that he can be robbed.

mulatto. In the popular sense of the term, a person with mixed white and Negro blood. Precisely, one born of a white parent and a Negro parent. Daniel v Guy, 19 Ark 121, 131.

It is contrary to the laws of nature for both parents of a mulatto to be persons of the white race. 10 Am J2d Bast § 43.

mulct (mulkt). Noun: A fine imposed for an offense; a penalty. Cook v Marshall County, 119 Iowa 384, 93 NW 378. Verb: To take by fraud or deceit.

Mulcta damnum famae non irrogat (mulk'ta dam'num fā'mē non ir'ro-gat). A fine does not inflict damage upon a person's reputation.

mulct tax (mulkt taks). A fine or penalty imposed for the purpose of suppressing certain trades or traffic in certain commodities upon which it is assessed, and as a punishment for engaging in such traffic; as where such a tax is laid on cigarettes in order to suppress the traffic in them. Cook v Marshall County, 119 Iowa 384, 93 NW 378. A tax imposed upon person and premises for selling intoxicating liquor in violation of law. 30 Am J Rev ed Intox L § 443.

mule. The hybrid offspring of a jackass and a mare of the horse family. An animal most valuable to the United States Army and to the American farmer prior to the advent of powered vehicles and implements.

See **hinny.**

mulier (mū'li-ėr). A matron. The status at common law of a woman after her marriage to the father of her son born out of wedlock. See 2 Bl Comm 248.

mulier puisne (mū'li-ėr pwē'nā). The status of the younger son born in wedlock of parents whose older son was born out of wedlock. 2 Bl Comm 248.

Muller Rule. The rule that if one with full knowledge of the evil propensities of a dog or other animal either wantonly excites it or voluntarily and unnecessarily puts himself in the way of the animal, he cannot recover from the harborer for an injury resulting from an attack by the dog or other animal. Anno: 66 ALR2d 930, 968; 4 Am J2d Ani § 107.

Multa conceduntur per obliquum quae non conceduntur de directo (mul'ta kon-sē-dun'ter per ob-li'quum kwē non kon-sē-dun'ter dē dī-rek'tō). Many things are permitted indirectly which are not permitted directly.

Multa fidem promissa levant (mul'ta fī'dem pro-mi'sa le'vant). Many promises weaken confidence. Brown v Castles, 65 Mass (11 Cush) 346, 350.

Multa ignoramus quae nobis non laterent si veterum lectio nobis fuit familiaris (mul'ta ig-nō-rā'mus kwē nō'bis non la'te-rent sī ve'te-rum lek'she-ō nō'bis fu'it fa-mi-li-ā'ris). We are ignorant concerning many things which would not be obscure to us if the reading of the ancients were familiar to us.

Multa in jure communi contra rationem disputandi pro communi utilitate introducta sunt (mul'ta in jū're kom-mū'nī kon'trā rā-she-ō'nem dis-pu-tan'dī prō kom-mū'nī ū-ti-li-tā'te in-trō-duk'ta sunt). Many things have been introduced into the common law which are contrary to logical reason, for the sake of the common welfare.

Multa multo exercitatione facilius quam regulis percipies (mul'ta mul'to ex-er-si-tā-she-ō'ne fa-si'li-us quam re-gū'lis per-si'pi-ēz). You perceive many things much more easily by practice than by rule.

Multa non vetat lex, quae tamen tacite damnavit (mul'ta non ve'tat lex, kwē ta'men ta'si-tē dam-nā'vit). There are many things which the law does not forbid, which it nevertheless tacitly condemns.

Multa transeunt cum universitate quae non per se transeunt (mul'ta trans'e-unt kum ū-ni-ver-si-tā'te kwē non per sē trans'e-unt). Many things pass with the whole which do not pass by themselves.

multifactual statement. A statement of two or more distinct facts, sometimes of fact, argument, and conclusion interwoven. Securities & Exchange Com. v Micro-Moisture Controls (DC NY) 21 FRD 164.

multifariousness. The joining or uniting in a declaration, bill, or complaint of two or more matters which are independent of, or unconnected with, one another. Roney v Chicago Title & Trust Co. 354 Ill 144, 188 NE 194. A term loosely applied to the joinder as defendants or plaintiffs of persons without a common interest in the litigation. Essen v Adams, 342 Mo 1196, 119 SW2d 773, 118 ALR 1393. The joining in a statute of dissimilar and discordant subjects. Boise City v Baxter, 41 Idaho 368, 238 P 1033.

multimember district. A legislative district entitled to two or more members of the legislative body. 25 Am J2d Elect § 25.

Multi multa; nemo omnia novit (mul′tī mul′ta; nē′mō om′ni-a nō′vit). Many persons know many things; no one knows all things.

multiphase. Operating in two or more phases, particularly a flow of electricity. Harrison v Detroit, Y. A. A. & J. R. Co. 137 Mich 78, 100 NW 451.

multiple agency. See **dual agency**.

multiple banking. Banking conducted by means of bank holding companies. 10 Am J2d Banks § 16.

multiple bill of exceptions. One bill embracing several exceptions. 4 Am J2d A & E § 428.

multiple damages. See **double damages; treble damages**.

multiple deeds. The deeds of two or more persons required in the fulfillment of the vendor's obligation under a land contract. 55 Am J1st V & P § 317.

multiple defendants. Two or more defendants in one action.

multiple dwelling. An apartment house; a flat. A tenement house. Any structure for the accommodation of two or more families or households in separate living units.
    Multiple dwelling as violation of restrictive covenant using word "house". See Anno: 14 ALR2d 1425.

multiple evidence. Evidence having probative value in more than one phase; sometimes admitted for one specific purpose to which it is confined. Green v Atlantic Coast Line Railroad Co. 136 SC 337, 343, 134 SE 385.

multiple family house. See **multiple dwelling**.

multiple interest. The penalty for usury; interest in twice the amount of the interest received from the victim. 55 Am J1st Usury § 144.

multiple issues. Two or more issues in one case.

multiple liability restriction. A clause in a contract for the renewal of a bond which limits the extent of the liability of the surety. 12 Am J2d Bonds § 46.

multiple libels. A method of proceeding for condemnation of misbranded drugs. 21 USC § 334(a).

multiple licensing. Licensing requirements respecting the same trade, imposed by both municipal and state authorities. 41 Am J1st Plumb § 5.

multiple parties. Two or more parties on one side.

multiple poinding (mul′ti-pl poin′ding). Double distress,—a Scotch proceeding akin to the modern interpleader, whereby a person in possession of money or goods may have the same distributed to the various claimants who are entitled thereto.

multiple proceedings. See **multiplicity of suits**.

multiple publication rule. The rule that there is a cause of action in favor of the defamed person in every state in which libel is published. Anno: 58 ALR2d 654 § 3.

multiple residence. See **multiple dwelling**.

multiple sclerosis. A disease of the nervous system evidenced by muscular weakness and tremors. Anno: 68 ALR2d 171-176.

multiple sentence. A sentence of one convicted as an habitual criminal, providing a penalty equal to double or treble the penalty imposed for the first offense. Anno: 58 ALR 99, s. 82 ALR 379, 116 ALR 236.

multiple signers. Two or more persons signing as makers of a promissory note.

multiple-stage taxes. Sales taxes applicable to the various transactions in the progress of goods from producer or manufacturer to ultimate consumer, such, for example, as sales by or to wholesalers. 47 Am J1st Sales T § 1.

multiple taxation. See **double taxation**.

multiple venue. The venue of a criminal prosecution for an offense which began in one district and ended in another. Anno: 5 L Ed 2d 974.

multiplex (mul′ti-plex). A newly-coined word for a multiple dwelling. The system by which two or even several telephone or telegraph messages may be transmitted over one wire at the same time.

Multiplex et indistinctum parit confusionem; et questiones quo simpliciores, et lucidiores (mul′ti-plex et in-dis-tink′tum pa′rit kon-fu-she-ō′nem; et questshe-ō′nēz quō sim-pli-she-ō′rēz, et lū-si-di-ō′rez). Multiplicity and indistinctness produce confusion; and the more simple questions are, the more lucid they are.

Multiplicita transgressione crescat poenae inflictio (mul-ti-pli′si-ta trans-gre-she-ō′ne kres′kat pē′nē in-flik′she-ō). The infliction of punishment should increase with the repetition of the offense.

multiplicates. Two or more copies of a document.

multiplication. The reproduction of copies of literary, artistic, or intellectual works. 18 Am J2d Copyr § 1.

multiplicity of suits. A ground of injunctive relief; something beyond the mere number of suits. 28 Am J Rev ed Inj § 50.
    The mere number of actions which might otherwise be brought does not, in and of itself, constitute a ground for equitable jurisdiction, nor is there any fixed number of actions which will constitute a multiplicity of suits so as to require or justify the assumption of equitable jurisdiction. In order for equity to act on the ground of avoidance of a multiplicity of actions, there must exist in the situation presented to the court something more than the mere number of actions to be avoided, such as the necessity of relief against repeated wrongs, and in any event there must be a community of right, interest, or issues in an action in equity. 27 Am J2d Eq § 48.

multiseller. A gambling device. 24 Am J1st Gaming § 28.

multistate corporation. A corporation incorporated under the laws of more than one state. Re Lyon, 144 App Div 104, 128 NYS 1004.

Multitudinem decem faciunt (mul-ti-tū′di-nem de′-sem fā′she-unt). Ten make a multitude.

Multitudo errantium non parit errori patrocinium (mul-ti-tū′dō er-ran′she-um non pa′rit er-rō′rī pa-trō-si′ni-um). The multitude of erring persons does not furnish an excuse for error.

Multitudo imperitorum perdit curiam (mul-ti-tū′dō im-pe-ri-tō′rum per′dit kū′ri-am). A multitude of unskillful practitioners ruin a court.

multitude of suits. A number of suits, but to be distinguished from multiplicity of suits from the standpoint of equity jurisdiction. 27 Am J2d Eq § 48.

multiversity. A word newly coined for a university containing many schools, colleges, and depart-

MULTI [822] MUNICIPAL

ments, and attended by an overwhelming number of students.

multi will. A will executed by more than one testator; a joint will.

multo fortiori (mul'tō for-she-ō'rī). With much more force; much more forcibly.

Multo utilius est pauca idonea effundere, quam multis inutilibus homines gravari (mul'tō ū-ti'li-us est pâ'ka i-dō'ne-a ef-fun'de-re, quam mul'tis in-ū-ti'li-bus hō'mi-nēz gra-vā'rī). It is much more useful to bring forth a few worthy things than that men should be burdened with many useless things.

multure (mul'tūr). A payment which was made in grain for the grinding of grain.

mund (mund). (Saxon.) Peace.

mundbrye. (Saxon.) A breach of the peace.

munera (mū'ne-ra). Plural of **munus**.

municeps (mū'ni-seps). (Roman law.) A citizen of a town; a person qualified to hold office.

municipal. Pertaining to the internal government of a state or nation; pertaining to a town or city or to its local government. 37 Am J1st Mun Corp § 3. Belonging to a city, town, or place; having the right of local government; belonging to or affecting a particular state or separate community; local; particular; independent.

The word is usually applied to what belongs to a city, but has a more extensive meaning, and is in legal effect the same as public or governmental, as distinguished from private. Cook v Portland, 20 Or 580, 27 P 263.

The word strictly applies only to what belongs to a city. The word is derived from the Latin word "municipium," meaning a city. In modern times, however, the word municipal has expanded in its meaning and it extends to that which pertains to the state as well as that which pertains to the city, as distinguished from that which is international. Winspear v Holman, 37 Iowa 542, 544.

municipal affairs. The internal business affairs of an incorporated town or city.

An exhaustive account of matters which have been held to come within this definition and of others which have been held not to come within it, will be found in the opinion of Timlin, J., in State, ex rel. Mueller v Thompson, 149 Wis 488, 137 NW 20.

municipal aid. The aid or assistance of a municipality given to a private enterprise, usually to cause it to locate therein. Aid formerly extended to a railroad company for the purpose of obtaining railroad service or connections. 44 Am J1st RR § 50.

municipal aid bonds. See **aid bonds; private object**.

municipal bond. A public security; a bond issued by a municipality. An evidence of indebtedness issued as one of a series of instruments issued at the same time by a city, town, or other corporate public body, negotiable in form, payable at a designated future time, and intended for sale in the market with the object of raising money for a municipal improvement the expense of which is beyond the immediate recourses of reasonable taxation, and payment of which of necessity or reason should be distributed over a period of years. 43 Am J1st Pub Sec § 6.

municipal bounty. See **local bounty**.

municipal bylaw. A term used in England and to some extent in this country for what is better known as a municipal ordinance. 37 Am J1st Mun Corp § 142.

municipal commissioners. See **commissioners of municipality**.

municipal contract. A public contract. A contract entered into by a municipal corporation. 38 Am J1st Mun Corp §§ 493 et seq.

municipal corporation. A body politic and corporate constituted by the incorporation of the inhabitants of a city or town for the purposes of local government thereof. A city or town or the local government thereof. Anno: 108 ALR 577 (within meaning of tax exemption statute.) A territorial or political subdivision established by the state for the purpose of administering local government. Lane v Minnesota State Agri. Soc. 62 Minn 175, 64 NW 382. The body politic created by organizing the inhabitants of a prescribed area, under the authority of the legislature, into a corporation with all the usual attributes of a corporate entity, but endowed with a public character by virtue of having been invested by the legislature with subordinate legislative powers to administer local and internal affairs of the community, and established as a branch of the state government to assist in the civil government of the state. 37 Am J1st Mun Corp § 3.

This term includes a county in that it also is a subdivision of the state. Williams v Wylie, 217 SC 247, 60 SE2d 586, 21 ALR2d 717.

See **municipal purposes**.

municipal corporation by prescription. A municipal corporation which has exercised its powers so long without objection upon the part of the state government that, although no charter is in existence, it is presumed that it was duly incorporated in the first place and that the charter has been lost. 37 Am J1st Mun Corp § 10.

municipal corporation de facto (de fak'to). The kind of municipal corporation which results when the people of a city, town or village have attempted to incorporate themselves under a statute which authorized such action, and have actually used and exercised the franchise of a municipal corporation by virtue of such proceedings, although the proceedings were so irregular that the validity of the corporation can be successfully attacked in a proceeding brought for that purpose by the state. 37 Am J1st Mun Corp § 13.

municipal corporation proper. A conventional municipal corporation, as distinguished from a municipal corporation de facto or a quasi municipal corporation.

municipal corporations acts. General laws under which cities and towns may be incorporated and governed.

municipal court. A local court created by statute, the jurisdiction of which is usually limited as to territorial ambit, and often as to the subject matter of litigation, sometimes being confined to that of a police court for the enforcement of municipal ordinances and regulations. State, ex rel. Stark v McArthur, 13 Wis 383, 386, but which may be extended, the state constitution permitting, to constitute general jurisdiction. 20 Am J2d Cts § 30.

municipal debt limit. See **limitation of indebtedness**.

municipal debt readjustment. A proceeding by an insolvent public debtor under the Bankruptcy Act to preserve assets and obtain a composition of indebtedness. 9 Am J2d Bankr §§ 1411 et seq.

municipal domicil. Domicil in a city or other municipality. 25 Am J2d Dom § 12.

municipal election. An election of municipal officers or of such municipal officers as are to be elected at one time.

municipal franchise. A franchise granted by a municipality.
See **franchise**.

municipal functions. Powers and duties bestowed and imposed upon a city for the specific benefit and advantage of the urban community embraced within the corporate boundaries. Lob v Jacksonville, 101 Fla 429, 134 So 205, 79 ALR 459.

municipal hospital. A hospital maintained by a municipality.

municipality. An incorporated city, village, or town.
See **municipal corporation**.

municipal judge (juj). The judge of a municipal court.

municipal law. In the most narrow sense of the term, the law pertaining to municipal corporations. In a more accurate sense, the law of a municipality, a state, even the nation, as distinguished from international law.

Strictly, this expression denotes the particular customs of one single municipium or free town, but it may with propriety be applied to any one state or nation, which is governed by the same laws and customs, and thus understood, it is properly defined to be a rule of civil conduct prescribed by the supreme power in a state, commanding what is right and prohibiting what is wrong. See 1 Bl Comm 44.
See **civil law**.

municipal lighting plant. A public utility owned or operated by a city, village, or town for the generation and sale of electric power.

municipal note. A note for money borrowed by a municipal corporation, usually payable and issued to a single investor and maturing at a date earlier than a bond issue. 43 Am J1st Pub Sec § 11.

municipal offense. An offense committed against a particular state of the Union or against a separate community. Cook v Portland, 20 Or 580, 27 P 263.

municipal officer. An officer whose duties and functions relate exclusively to the local affairs of a municipal corporation, and in whose conduct and administration of his office the municipality alone is interested. 37 Am J1st Mun Corp § 233. With less refinement, an officer elected or appointed as an officer of a municipality, albeit he has many duties involving the enforcement of state law. 42 Am J1st Pub Of § 21.

municipal order. Same as **municipal warrant**.

municipal ordinance. See **ordinance**.

municipal power. A matter of a grant of authority by the legislature, except as a degree of local sovereignty is granted by home rule provisions of the Constitution or where there prevails in the jurisdiction the principle of recognizing inherent right of local self-government with respect to municipal matters. 37 Am J1st Mun Corp § 111.

municipal purposes. Corporate purposes of a municipal corporation; purposes and activities designed primarily for the exclusive or principal benefit of the inhabitants of a particular municipality. 51 Am J1st Tax § 387. Public or governmental purposes, as contradistinguished from private purposes.

A corporation created for municipal purposes is a corporation created for public or governmental purposes, with political powers to be exercised for the public good in the administration of civil government, whose members are citizens, not stockholders. Cook v Portland, 20 Or 580, 27 P 263.
See **corporate act**.

municipal records. The books of record of the transactions of towns, city councils, and other municipal bodies, either executive or legislative in nature. 45 Am J1st Recds § 3.

municipal securities. Bonds issued by cities and towns.
See **municipal bond**.

municipal warrant. An order drawn by one municipal officer on another, in the disbursement of the funds of the municipality and payment of its indebtedness. A means of drawing money from the treasury. 43 Am J1st Pub Sec § 10.
See **warrant**.

municipal waterworks. A waterworks owned and operated by a municipal corporation. 56 Am J1st Watwk § 24.

municipia (mū-ni-si'pi-a). (Roman law.) Plural of **municipium**.

municipium (mū-ni-sip'i-um). (Roman law.) A town the inhabitants of which were Roman citizens, but were governed by their own magistrates and laws; a free town.

muniment (mū'ni-ment). The evidence or writing whereby a man is enabled to defend the title to his estate. United States v Lancaster (CC Ga) 44 F 885.

muniment of title. A document evidencing title. A title deed or other original document which, taken with other documents, shows a chain of title. 55 Am J1st V & P § 178.
See **title deeds**.

munitions. Supplies for waging war or equipping a military force, especially weapons and ammunition. 56 Am J1st War § 157.

munus (mū'nus). A gift; a feudal grant.

mur (mėr). A wall.

murage (mū'raj). A payment of money in lieu of **murorum operatio**.

mural monuments (mū'ral mon'u-ments). Monuments built in walls.

mural painting (mū'ral pān'ting). A painting on a wall or ceiling.

murder. A technical term or word of art which can be defined with particularity only by resort to the specific statute in the jurisdiction involved. Re Kirby, 162 Cal 91, 121 P 370. At common law, the killing of one human being by another with malice aforethought, either express or implied, that is, with deliberate intent or formed design to kill. 26 Am J1st Homi § 11; Wiley v State, 19 Ariz 346, 170 P 869; Commonwealth v Buzard, 365 Pa 511, 76 A2d 394, 22 ALR2d 846. The intentional killing of a human being without legal justification or excuse and under circumstances insufficient to reduce the crime to manslaughter. 26 Am J1st Homi § 11.

murder in the first degree. Murder with malice aforethought, the unique characteristic of which is deliberation or premeditation, a design or purpose to take life. 26 Am J1st Homi § 38.

MURDER [824] MUTILATE

murder in the second degree. The killing of a person by intent but without premeditation or deliberation, or, as otherwise stated, without malice aforethought or express malice. 26 Am J1st Homi § 38. Roughly stated, any offense of murder not in the first degree. Murder without express malice or a state of facts justifying or excusing the killing or reducing the offense to manslaughter. Often defined by statute as the killing of a person perpetrated by any act imminently dangerous to others and evidencing a depraved mind regardless of human life, although without any premeditated design to effect the death of any person. 26 Am J1st Homi § 43.

murdrare (mur-drā're). To murder.

murdre (mūr'druh). Murder.

murdritor (mur'dri-tor). A murderer.

murdrum (mėr'drum). The ancient Teutonic name which was applied to an amercement which the vill in which a moerda or secret killing was committed, was liable to pay; or, if the vill was too poor, the whole hundred was amerced. See 4 Bl Comm 194.

mure (mūr). Same as **mur.**

murorum operatio (mū-rō'rum o-pe-rā'she-ō). A feudal service consisting of labor in the repair and construction of walls and fortifications.

Murphy bed. A wall bed; a folding bed. Murphy Wall Bed Co. v Levin, 57 Ont LR 105, 14 BRC 395, [1925] 3 DLR 107.

murrey (mur'i). Blood color.

murthrum (mur'thrum). Murder.

musculoskeletal conditions (mus'kū-lō-skel'ẹ-tạl kon-dish'ọnz). Physical disabilities, such as those of shoulder, elbow, hip, knee, leg and foot. Anno: 2 ALR2d 309 § 4; 22 Am J2d Damg § 124.

museum. A place for the exhibition of articles of interest, whether by way of entertainment or instruction.

musical composition. A tune or melody represented in characters depicting notes, pitch, time, etc. on a staff which are to be followed by player of instrument or singer. A proper subject of copyright. 18 Am J2d Copyr § 36.
An intellectual creation which first exists in the mind of the composer; he may play it for the first time upon an instrument. It is not susceptible of being copied until it has been put in a form which others can see and read. The copyright law has not provided for the protection of the intellectual conception apart from the thing produced. White-Smith Music Publishing Co. v Appolo Co. 209 US 1, 17, 52 L Ed 655, 662, 28 S Ct 319.

musical instrument. A contrivance by which musical sounds are produced. Dunbar v Spratt-Snyder Co. 208 Iowa 490, 226 NW 22, 63 ALR 1016.

music broadcast. See **broadcasting.**

music school. A school for instruction in the use of musical instruments or in singing.

must. Indicating compulsion. Ordinarily a mandatory word. 50 Am J1st Stat § 28. In a statute, calling for substantial rather than literal compliance. Herron v Harbour, 75 Okla 127, 182 P 243, 29 ALR 905 (statute prescribing the form of an acknowledgment).
A statutory provision may be directory, rather than mandatory, in nature, notwithstanding use of the word "must." Re Johnson (ND) 75 NW2d 313, 55 ALR2d 1049.

muster. To bring together for a purpose, particularly that of military service or service as seamen on a vessel. The gathering together of men by military order at military camp for the purpose of selecting, and of subsequently training, those who on examination appear to possess the necessary qualifications for military service. Bannister v Soldiers Bonus Board, 43 RI 346, 112 A 422, 13 ALR 589. Precisely, the final selection of a person called for military duty as a person fit for service, and the actual enrollment of such person in the military service. 36 Am J1st Mil § 8.
Being derived from the Latin word "monstrare," meaning "to show," the word "muster" by itself may doubtless be applied to a parade of soldiers already enrolled, armed, and trained, but the addition of the preposition of motion removes all ambiguity, and "mustering into the service," or "mustering in," clearly implies that the persons mustered are not already in the service. Tyler v Pomeroy, 90 Mass (8 Allen) 480, 498.
A soldier is said to be "mustered into service" when he is actually called, or ordered, into actual military service. Such service begins on the date when the man is sworn in and becomes a soldier. Anno: 9 ALR 25.

mustered into federal service. Actual enrollment in the armed service of the United States Government; something more than being called for military duty and sent to a training camp for physical examination with the possibility of rejection as physically unfit for military service, without ever having been placed on a muster role. Bannister v Soldiers Bonus Board, 43 RI 346, 112 A 422, 13 ALR 589.

mustered into service. See **muster; mustered into federal service.**

mustering out. The discharge or separation of a person from service in the Armed Forces.

mustering-out pay. A lump-sum payment paid to a member of the Armed Forces upon his discharge or separation from the service. 56 Am J1st Vet & V A § 4.

muster-roll. A roll or list of the men mustered for service.

mustizo (mus-tē'zō). The issue of a Negro and an Indian. Miller v Dawson, 13 SC Eq (Dud) 174, 176. See **mestizo.**

mutation (mū-tā'shọn). A change; an exchange; a transfer; a conveyance. In biology, a change in inheritable characteristics, occurring suddenly, as by radiation.

mutation of libel. The amendment of the libel in an admiralty suit.

mutatio nominis (mū-tā'she-ō nō'mi-nis). (Civil law.) A change of name.

mutatis mutandis (mū-tā'tis mū-tan'dis). Those things being changed which should be changed; the respective differences taken into consideration; changed according to circumstances; with the necessary changes.

Mutato nomine de te fabula narratur (mū-tā'tō nō'mi-ne dē tē fā'bu-la nar-rā'ter). The story was told of you under a different name.

mute. Adjective: Silent. Noun: A person without the power of speech.
See **standing mute.**

mutilate. To tear or destroy in part; to render imperfect.

mutilated tickets. Railroad tickets which have been so handled or treated as to be deprived of some essential or material part. Young v Central of Georgia R. Co. 120 Ga 25, 47 SE 556.

mutilation of corpse. The wrong, for which civil liability is imposed, of wilfully, recklessly, wantonly, unlawfully, or negligently dismembering or disfiguring by cutting, scratching, or mishandling the body of a dead person. 22 Am J2d Dead B § 31. The criminal offense of dissecting or dismembering, without authority, the dead body of a person. 22 Am J2d Dead B § 49.

mutilation of instrument. Any physical act, falling short of the destruction of the instrument, whereby a written instrument is rendered imperfect. Woodfill v Patton, 76 Ind 575. Tearing or obliterating parts of a will. 57 Am J1st Wills §§ 493, 513.

mutiny. The usurpation by force, fraud, or intimidation of the command of a vessel from the master or other lawful officer in command, or the act of depriving him of authority and command on board, or the act of resisting or preventing him in the free and lawful exercise of his authority and command, or the act of transferring such authority and command to another not lawfully entitled thereto. 18 USC § 484.

The word is sometimes used as synonymous with the word "insurrection." McCargo v New Orleans Ins. Co. (La) 10 Rob 202.

Engaging in a sit-down strike and taking possession of the ship in defiance of the ship's officers are acts constituting at least prima facie evidence that the crew was guilty of mutiny. Peninsular & Occidental S.S. Co. v NLRB (CA5) 98 F2d 411.

mutual. The same on both sides of a transaction or relationship, whether it be a matter of affection, aversion, assistance, or advantage; reciprocal. Sharon v Sharon, 79 Cal 1, 16 P 345.

mutual account. An account in which items are debited and credited on both sides. 1 Am J2d Acctg § 5. With more elaboration, an account arising where there are mutual dealings between two persons and the account is allowed to run with a view to an ultimate adjustment of the balance; an account on which the items on either side belong and on which they operate to extinguish each other pro tanto, so that the balance on either side is the debt between the parties. 1 Am J2d Acctg § 5.

To render an account mutual within the meaning of the statute of limitations, there must be an alternate course of dealing between the parties, giving rise to cross demands upon which they might respectively maintain actions, and there must be a mutual agreement, express or implied, that the items of the account upon the one side and the other are to be set against each other. 34 Am J1st Lim Ac § 97.

mutual advantage rule. A rule for testing the status of a person in a particular situation.

Under this rule the true test of whether the user of an appliance is an invitee or licensee is whether the owner receives benefit or advantage from the permitted use; if so, the user is an invitee; if not, he is a licensee. Arthur v Standard Engineering Co. 89 App DC 399, 193 F2d 903, 32 ALR2d 408.

mutual assent. A meeting of the minds; consent. 17 Am J2d Contr § 18. Agreement. Martin v Thrower, 3 Ga App 784, 60 SE 825.

mutual benefit bailment. A bailment for compensation; a bailment in which the parties contemplate some price or compensation in return for benefits flowing from the fact of bailment. Armored Car Service, Inc. v First Nat. Bank (Fla App) 114 So 2d 431.

mutual benefit certificate. See **certificate of membership.**

mutual benefit society. A voluntary association or corporation formed and organized, aside from accompanying fraternal objectives, solely for the purpose of rendering financial aid or other assistance to their members, or certain designated beneficiaries of the latter, when visited by sickness, death, or other misfortune specifically designated. 36 Am J2d Frat O § 1.

The organization is commonly based upon the lodge system, with a graduated series of central or governing bodies, throughout which a representative form of government ordinarily prevails; that is, the directors, delegates, and other officers who have general charge and control of the property and business of the society and the management of its affairs are chosen by the members or their selected representative. 36 Am J2d Frat O § 1.

"Mutuality" is a term which designates payment for fraternal life insurance in exact proportion to its cost. If a fraternal benefit society lacks mutuality in payment for insurance afforded, it faces inevitable ruin. If some pay adequately and others do not, there is still want of mutuality and financial ruin of the society, though postponed, is none the less inevitable. Jenkins v Talbot (Ill) 170 NE 735.

mutual combat. A combat into which the parties enter willingly; a combat with the mutual intent to fight. State v Moss, 24 NM 59, 172 P 199.

mutual conditions. Concurrent conditions. Conditions such that the performance of one, which rests upon a party to a contract, is a condition precedent to the performance of the other as undertaken by the other party to the contract. 17 Am J2d Contr § 321.

mutual contract. A contract binding upon both parties, and which is capable of specific performance by each party against the other, or for damages for failure to perform the contract. Jordan v Indianapolis Water Co. (Ind App) 61 NE 12, 15.

Indeed, any valid contract is a mutual contract, since it is essential that it bind both parties.

mutual covenants. Covenants in the nature of mutual conditions, the performance of the one being a condition precedent to the obligation of performance of the other. 20 Am J2d Cov § 9.

mutual credit A knowledge on both sides of an existing debt due to one party, and a credit by the other party, founded on, and trusting to such debt, as a means of discharging it. This definition is not quite broad enough to cover all the cases, where there being a connection between the demands, equity acts upon it, and allows a setoff under particular circumstances. Courts of equity deviate from the strict rule of mutuality when the justice of the particular case requires it. Scott v Armstrong, 146 US 499, 507, 36 L Ed 1059, 1062, 13 S Ct 148.

See **mutuality of parties and demands.**

mutual demands. Reciprocal demands existing between the same persons at the same time. 20 Am J2d Countcl § 74.

See **mutual credit; mutuality of parties and demands.**

mutual easements. Servitudes arising upon the acceptance by the grantee of a deed containing a covenant binding both grantor and grantee. McFarland v Hanley (Ky) 258 SW2d 3.

mutual fund. Another term for **investment trust.**

mutual insurance. Insurance under the policies of a mutual insurance company, that is, one operating on a mutual basis rather than for the purpose of profits benefiting stockholders.
See **mutual insurance company; reciprocal insurance.**

mutual insurance company. A cooperative enterprise wherein the members constitute both insurer and insured, where the members all contribute, by a system of premiums or assessments, to the creation of a fund from which all losses and liabilities are paid, and wherein the profits are divided among themselves in proportion to their interests. 29 Am J Rev ed Ins § 89. Better known, as an insurance company which is not a stock insurance company, that is, one operating on a mutual basis rather than one operating for a profit to be paid to stockholders.

mutuality. The condition of being mutual, two persons bearing the same relationship toward each other in reference to a particular right or obligation; sharing a common burden or enjoying a common benefit on the same basis. The essential of a binding contract.

mutuality of consent. A meeting of the minds in assent. Caldwell v Cline, 109 W Va 553, 156 SE 55, 72 ALR 1211.

mutuality of contract. A meeting of the minds of the parties, that is, mutual assent. 17 Am J2d Contr § 18; 55 Am J1st V & P § 14.
See **mutuality of obligation.**

mutuality of demands. See **mutual credits; mutual demands; mutuality of parties and demands.**

mutuality of estoppel. The quality of reciprocity, neither party being bound unless the other party is bound.
An equitable estoppel operates neither in favor of, nor against, strangers, that is, persons who are neither parties nor privies to the transaction out of which the estoppel arose. 28 Am J2d Estop § 115.

mutuality of obligation. The characteristic of binding effect of a contract on both parties, 17 Am J2d Contr § 11; 46 Am J1st Sales § 61, or an undertaking on one side and a consideration on the other. 17 Am J2d Contr § 11; 49 Am J1st Spec Per § 34.
It is a rule of law that there must be mutuality in a contract; that is, it must be binding upon both parties at the same time, if it is to be deemed valid and enforceable as to either. Butterick Publishing Co. v Whitcomb, 225 Ill 605, 80 NE 247.

mutuality of parties and demands. A matter of demands between the same parties in the same capacity at the same time and mutuality as to the quality of the right. 20 Am J2d Countcl § 74.
The setoff or counterclaim must be such a demand that defendant, in his own name, or in the names of defendants sued, without bringing in the name of a stranger to the suit, may maintain an action upon it against a party, or all parties suing, as the case may be. Less than that is not mutuality. 20 Am J2d Countcl § 74.
Two persons are said to be mutually indebted when each of them owes a debt to the other. The debts may be simple contract, covenant or judgment,—but the demands must come under the classification of debts. A demand of damages for a tort is not a debt. Caldwell v Ryan, 210 Mo 17, 108 SW 533.

mutuality of remedy. Each party to a bilateral contract having the opportunity to compel performance of the promise to him. Philadelphia Ball Club v Lajoie, 202 Pa 210, 51 A 973. A doctrine asserted in cases of specific performance. The availability to both parties of the remedy of specific performance, or its equivalent in actual performance, at the time of the commencement of the suit or at the time of the decree. 49 Am J1st Spec Per §§ 35-37.

mutual life insurance company. A life insurance company which, while operating upon an old line basis with fixed premiums, cash surrender values, and policies issued strictly on an actuarial basis, has no stockholders, its insureds, as members, taking the place of stockholders, is operated on the distinctive basis that net profits from operation shall inure entirely to members or insureds in the form of annual dividends.
See **mutual benefit society.**

mutually indebted. See **mutual credits; mutual demands; mutuality of parties and demands.**

mutual mistake. A mistake which is reciprocal and common to all of the parties to a transaction. 27 Am J2d Eq § 33. A mistake of fact common to both parties to a contract, by reason of which each party has done what neither intended. Buol Machine Co. v Buckens, 14 Conn 639, 153 A2d 826. A mistake which is reciprocal and common to both parties to an instrument, each alike laboring under the same misconception in respect to the terms of the instrument. 45 Am J1st Reform Inst § 56. A mistake of all parties to an instrument, on account of which the instrument does not conform to or express their intention or agreement, as where by mistake some material part of a deed is omitted or the instrument is drawn to convey a different interest or a greater or lesser estate than was agreed upon by the parties. 23 Am J2d Deeds § 155.

mutual negligence. See **contributory negligence.**

mutual, open, and current account. A mutual account which has not been closed, settled, or stated, but in which the inclusion of further dealings between the parties is contemplated. 34 Am J1st Lim Ac § 96.

mutual promises. The promises of contracting parties, the promise by one party being the consideration for the promise by the other. 17 Am J2d Contr § 104.

mutual subscriptions. The promises of persons subscribing to a fund for the accomplishment of a common object which can only be accomplished through their aggregate efforts, the obligation of each constituting a sufficient consideration for the obligation of another. 50 Am J1st Subscr § 14.

mutual tax exemption. An exemption from taxation created by a contact between states relative to the property of the one state in the other state. Anno: 134 ALR 1417, 1423.

mutual telephone company. An association or corporation conducting a telephone business or maintaining and servicing certain telephone lines, not for profit, merely for the purpose of maintaining telephone service for its members. 52 Am J1st Teleg & T § 8.

mutual trust. See **reciprocal trust.**

mutual utility. See **co-operative utility.**

mutual wills. Sometimes called twin wills. Wills executed pursuant to an agreement between two or more persons to dispose of their property in a particular manner, each in consideration of the other. Anno: 169 ALR 12, 13. Wills executed with a common intention on the part of the testators, irrespective of whether there is a contract between them. Anno: 169 ALR 12, 13.

Mutual wills may be in separate instruments or in the same instrument. Anno: 169 ALR 13.

See **reciprocal wills.**

mutuant (mū'tu-ant). The person making a loan of the chattel under a mutuum.

See **mutuum.**

mutuari (mū-tu-ā'rī). To borrow.

mutuary (mū-tu-ā'rī). A term of the Roman or Continental law which applies to the person receiving a chattel or chattels delivered in the relation known as a mutuum. 8 Am J2d Bailm § 37. The person to whom the chattel is lent under a mutuum.

See **mutuum.**

mutuel (mü-tüel). See **pari-mutuel.**

mutuo. See **ex mutuo.**

mutus (mū'tus). Dumb; mute.

mutus et surdus (mū'tus et ser'dus). Dumb and deaf.

mutuum (mū'tụ̄-um). A relation known to the Roman or Continental law; a loan of a chattel for consumption or appropriation by the person receiving the article to his own use. 8 Am J2d Bailm § 37.

my creditors. A phrase inclusive of both individual and partnership creditors. Moody v Downs, 63 NH 50.

myelitis (mī-e-lī'tis). Inflammation of the spine. Wabash Western Railway Co. v Friedman, 41 Ill App 270, 273.

my estate. An expression having reference, as it appears in a will, to the estate of the testator in probate. 28 Am J1st Inher T § 504.

my hand. See **witness my hand.**

my hand and seal. See **witness my hand and seal.**

my just debts. See **just debts of decedent.**

mynute. Midnight.

my personal estate. The property owned personally by the person, without reference to whether it is real estate or personal property. Davison v Sparrow (App) 44 Ohio Ops 226, 58 Ohio L Abs 529, 97 NE2d 694.

myself. See **self.**

myself note. A promissory note payable to the maker's own self.

mystery. Something unknown; something kept secret. A person's trade, art, or occupation; such as merchant, mercer, tailor, painter, clerk, schoolmaster, husbandman, or the like. State v Bishop, 15 Me 122, 124.

mystic testament. A term apparently peculiar to the state of Louisiana, referring to a so-called secret will for the execution of which there are statutory requirements distinctive to such form of will, concerning the closing of the instrument by folding it or the placing of the instrument in an envelope and the signing, sealing, and attestation of the folded instrument or envelope. Lewis' Heirs v His Executor, 5 La 387, 393.

mythological name. A name taken from mythology, especially mythology of the ancient Greeks. Hygeia Distilled Water Co. v Hygeia Ice Co. 72 Conn 646, 45 A 957.

N

n. Abbreviation of noon. Abbreviation of north. Burr v Broadway Ins. Co. 16 NY 267, 271. Abbreviation of neutron.

naam (näm). (Saxon.) A taking; a distraining of goods.

nagging. Persisting in criticism, scolding, and complaints, sometimes constituting mental cruelty entitling the injured party to a divorce. Metcalf v Metcalf, 50 Wash 2d 167, 310 P2d 254. Irritating, disturbing, ruffling, or troubling the mind by persistent urging. Buchanan v Davis (Tex Com App) 12 SW2d 978.

naif. A person born a slave; a villein.

naivitas (nā′vi-tās). Villeinage,—the tenure or condition of a villein.

naked. Nude; unclothed; stripped of clothing; bare; incomplete; not full.
A person was held not to have been naked when he was stripped of clothing down to his waist. Commonwealth v Dejardin, 126 Mass 46.

naked confession. A confession which has not been corroborated.

naked possession. Actual possession without color of title. 3 Am J2d Adv P § 26.

naked power. A power of disposal accompanied by no interest or estate in the donee of the power. 41 Am J1st Pow § 5. A power of sale in a mortgage or deed of trust, accompanied by no interest, which can be executed only by the person designated. 37 Am J1st Mtg § 650.

naked trust. Same as **dry trust.**

nam. (Latin.) For; because.
See **naam.**

namare (na-mā′re). To take; to distrain.

namatio (na-mā′she-ō). A taking; a distress.

Nam de minimis non curat lex (nam dē mi′ni-mis non kū′rat lex). For the law does not pay attention to trifles.

name. The designation by which a person is known and called in the community in which he lives and is best known; the word or combination of words by which a person is distinguished from other individuals. 38 Am J1st Name § 2. The label or appellation which a person bears for the convenience of the world at large in addressing him, or in speaking of or dealing with him. Roberts v Mosier, 35 Okla 691, 132 P 678.

name and arms clause. The condition in a will, deed of gift, or deed of trust, that the person upon whom the property or beneficial interest is bestowed shall assume the name and arms or crest of the testator or settlor. Byng v Byng, 10 HL Cas 171, 11 Eng Reprint 991.

named insured. The person expressly designated in an automobile liability insurance policy as the person insured, as distinguished from other persons who may come within the protection of the policy by virtue of their relationship with the person thus named. Farley v American Auto. Ins. Co. 137 W Va 455, 72 SE2d 520, 34 ALR2d 933.

name index. An index of records of title by the names of grantor and grantee, mortgagor and mortgagee, etc.

name of corporation. See **corporate name.**

name of partnership. Except as otherwise required by statute, the name selected by the partners as a firm name. 40 Am J1st Partn § 10.

Nam ex antecedentibus et consequentibus fit optima interpretatio (nam ex an-te-se-den′ti-bus et kon-se-quen′ti-bus fit op′ti-ma in-ter-pre-tā′she-ō). For the best interpretation is made by examining the words which precede and those which follow; i. e., the context.

Nam feudum sine investitura nullo modo constitui potuit (nam fū′dum sī′ne in-ves-ti-tū′ra nul′lō mō′dō kon-sti′tu-ī po′tu-it). For a fee cannot be perfected in any manner without investiture. See 2 Bl Comm 311.

namium (na′mi-um). A taking; a distress of an owner's goods or cattle, either damage feasant, or by way of security for unpaid rent, overdue. See 3 Bl Comm 148.

namium vetitum (na′mi-um ve′ti-tum). A forbidden distress; that is, an improper or wrongful distress; as where goods or beasts have been distrained, under a pretense of their having done damage, and eloigned, or carried off to places unknown to their owner. See 1 Bl Comm 148.

Nam leges vigilantibus, non dormientibus, subveniunt (nam lē′jēz vi-ji-lan′ti-bus, non dor-mi-en′ti-bus, sub-ve′ni-unt). For the laws aid the vigilant, not those who slumber.

Nam nemo est haeres viventis (nam nē′mō est hē′rēz vī-ven′tis). For no one is the heir of a living person. See 2 Bl Comm 107.

Nam neque quies gentium sine armis, neque arma sine stipendis, neque stipendia sine tributis, haberi quent (nam ne′kwe qui′ēz jen′she-um sī′ne ar′mis, ne′kwe ar′ma si′ne sti-pen′dis, ne′kwe sti-pen′di-a sī′ne tri-bū′tis, ha-bē′rī kwent). For it is neither possible to have the peace of nations without armies, nor armies without pay, nor pay without taxes.

Nam omne testamentum morte consummatum est, et voluntas testatoris est ambulatoria usque ad mortem (nam om′ne tes-ta-men′tum mor′te kon-sum-mā′tum est, et vo-lun′tās tes-ta-tō′ris est am-bu-lā-tō′ri-a us′kwe ad mor′tem). For every testament is consummated by death, and the will of the testator is revocable up to his death. See 2 Bl Comm 502.

Nam qui facit per alium, facit per se (nam quī fā′sit per a′li-um, fā′sit per sē). For he who acts through another does the act himself.

Nam qui haeret in litera, haeret in cortice (nam quī hē′ret in li′te-ra, hē′ret in kor′ti-se). For he who clings to the letter keeps inside the rind; i. e., one who is too literal does not touch the meat or substance of the transaction.

Nam quilibet potest renunciare juri pro se introducto (nam quī′li-bet po′test rē-nun-she-ā′re jū′rī prō sē in-trō-duk′tō). For anyone may renounce a right introduced for his own benefit.

Nam qui non prohibet, cum prohibere possit, jubet (nam quī non pro′hi-bet, kum pro-hi-bē′re pos′sit jū′bet). For he who does not prevent when he can prevent, orders or sanctions. 1 Bl Comm 430.

Nam quod remedio destituitur, ipsa re valet, si culpa absit (nam quod re-mē'di-ō dē-sti-tū'i-ter, ip'sa rē va'let, sī kul'pa ab'sit). For that which lacks a remedy is the stronger by reason of that very fact, if it is without fault.

Quoting Lord Bacon, Blackstone says, "The benignity of the law is such, as when, to preserve the principles and grounds of law, it depriveth a man of his remedy without his own fault, it will rather put him in a better degree and condition than in a worse." See 3 Bl Comm 20.

Nam quod semel meum est, amplius meum esse non potest (nam quod se'mel me'um est, am'pli-us me'um es'se non po'test). For that which is once mine cannot be mine more fully.

Nam quo major vis est animi quam corporis, hoc sunt graviora ea, quae concipiuntur animo quam illa quae corporae (nam quō mā'jor vīs est a'ni-mī quam kor'po-ris, hōk sunt gra-vi-ō'ra ē'a, kwē kon-si-pi-un'ter a'ni-mō quam il'la kwē kor'po-rē). For, as the power of the mind is greater than that of the body, in the same way the sufferings of the mind are more severe than the pains of the body. Young v Western Union Tel. Co. 107 NC 370, 11 SE 1044.

Nam silent leges inter arma (nam si'lent lē'jēz in'ter ar'ma). For laws are silent among arms.

Nam verba debent intelligi cum effectu ut res magis valeat quam pereat (nam ver'ba de'bent in-tel'li-jī kum ef-fek'tū ut rēz mā'jis va'le-at quam per'e-at). For words ought to be understood in such a way that they may have some effect, so that the instrument may rather be valid than void.

naphtha (naf'thạ or nap'thạ). A highly inflammable and explosive liquid obtained by the distillation of petroleum. Standard Oil Co. v Wakefield, 102 Va 824, 47 SE 830. A product of petroleum intermediate between the associate products of gasoline and benzine. Gately v Taylor, 211 Mass 60, 97 NE 619.

naphtha fraction (nap'thạ frak'shọn). The elements taken together, more volatile than kerosene, which result from the first distillation of crude oil. United States v Gulf Refining Co. 268 US 542, 547, 69 L Ed 1082, 1086, 45 S Ct 597.

Napoleonic Code. See **Code Napoleon.**

naprapathy (na-prap'ạ-thi). A drugless system of treating human ailments by manipulation, based on an underlying theory that many human ailments are caused by a tightened or shrunken condition of a ligament. People v Witte, 315 Ill 282, 146 NE 178, 37 ALR 672.

narcotic. Singular of **narcotics.**

Narcotic Act. A federal statute which renders it unlawful for any person to purchase, sell, dispense, or distribute narcotics except in or from the original stamped package; or to sell, barter, give away, or otherwise transfer narcotics, except upon the written order on a prescribed form issued for a purpose; or for any unregistered person to have narcotic drugs in his possession or under his control, or to send, ship, carry, or deliver narcotics between the states or insular possessions or from or into the District of Columbia. 26 USC § 4724(b). A statute, known in its original form as the Harrison Narcotic Act, the manifest purpose of which is to require every person dealing in drugs to ascertain at his peril whether or not a product he sells comes within the inhibition of the statute, and to penalize any dealer who sells prohibited drugs, even though he may be ignorant of their character as such. 25 Am J2d Drugs §§ 34, 35.

Narcotic Drug Act. An act of Congress (38 Stat 785) which imposed a special tax on the manufacture, importation, and sale or gift of opium, cocoa leaves or their compounds or derivatives. United States v Doremus, 249 US 86, 63 L Ed 493, 39 S Ct 214. One of the uniform laws. 25 Am J2d Drugs § 18.
See **dealer.**

Narcotic Drugs Import and Export Act. A statute which makes it unlawful, with certain exceptions of narcotics necessary for medical and legitimate uses, to import any narcotic drug into the United States or any territory under its control or jurisdiction; and, with certain exceptions relating to the exportation of certain drugs for medical and scientific uses to countries that are parties to specified international conventions and agreements relating to the control of the traffic in narcotics, prohibits and prescribes punishment for the exportation of narcotic drugs from the United States or from any territory under the control or jurisdiction of the United States. 21 USC §§ 171 et seq.; 25 Am J2d Drugs § 34.

narcotics. Substances which directly induce sleep, allay sensibility and blunt the senses, and which, when taken in large quantities, produce narcotism or complete insensibility. 25 Am J2d Drugs § 2.

narr. An abbreviation of **narratio;** in the plural, "narrs."

narrare (nar-rā're). To narrate; to allege in a declaration or complaint; to allege as one of the counts of a declaration or complaint.

narratio (na-rā'shi-ō). A declaration or complaint; one of the counts of a declaration or complaint.

narrative. A statement of facts and events in the form of a running commentary.

narrative abstract of record. An abstract of record on appeal summarized in narrative form. 4 Am J2d A & E § 408.

narrative bill of exceptions. A bill of exceptions in narrative form as distinguished from a verbatim transcript of the evidence. 4 Am J2d A & E § 435.

narrative form in taking testimony. A method of receiving the testimony of a witness, the witness being asked to state the facts and then permitted to state them more or less in full in one long statement. Pumphrey v State, 84 Neb 636, 122 NW 19.

narrative transcript. A reporter's transcript in narrative form rather than a verbatim record. 4 Am J2d A & E § 412.

narratores. See **banci narratores.**

narrow construction. Rejecting the comprehensive sense, in favor of a narrow, contracted meaning, of words. Flaska v Dayton, 51 NM 13, 177 P2d 174. A technical construction. Clarke v Johnson, 199 Ga 163, 33 SE2d 425.
See **literal construction.**

narrow gauge railroad. A railroad having a width between the rails of less than the standard gauge.

narrow seas. A somewhat parochial term for waters of the ocean on the coast of England inside low-water mark. Commonwealth v Macloon, 101 Mass 1.

narrow view. The designation given the doctrine in reference to the right of a grantee to an easement in street or alley shown on a map or plat referred

NASCI [830] NATIONAL

to in the conveyance to him, that his private right of user is limited to the abutting street or alley and such others as are necessary to give him access to a public highway. 25 Am J2d Ease § 26.

nasci (na'sī). To be born.

nasciturus (na-si-tū'rus). A person to be born in the future.

nastre (năs'truh). To be born.

natale (nă-tā'le). The state or condition which a person inherits.

nati et nascituri (nā'tī et na-si-tū'rī). Persons already born or in being and those who are to be born in the future.

natio (nā'she-ō). A nation; a birthplace; a race of people.

nation. A body politic or society of men united together for the purpose of promoting their mutual safety and advantage by their combined strength, occupying a definite territory and politically organized under one government. 30 Am J Rev ed Internat L § 10.

The word presupposes or implies an independence of any other sovereign power more or less absolute, an organized government, recognized officials, a system of laws, definite boundaries, and the power to enter into negotiations with other nations. Montoyo v United States, 180 US 261, 45 L Ed 521, 21 S Ct 358.

See **sovereign state; state.**

national. Pertaining to the nation, that is, the United States.

See terms and expressions beginning **federal; national; United States.**

National Acts. Acts of Congress; federal statutes.
See particular terminology, such as **Labor Relations Act; Narcotic Act,** etc.

national agencies and instrumentalities. Agencies, departments, and instrumentalities of the United States.

See particular agency or instrumentality, such as **Interstate Commerce Commission; Labor Relations Board; State Department,** etc.

national bank. An instrumentality or agency of the Federal Government although, for the most part, similar in nature to, and governed by, the same rules as state banks insofar as their functions, powers, and liabilities are concerned. 10 Am J2d Bks § 5. A private banking corporation organized under United States statutes, and intended for public accommodation. Ryan v McLane, 91 Md 175, 46 A 340.

National Bank Act. A federal statute having the purpose of authorizing and regulating national banks. 10 Am J2d Bks § 14.

national banking association. A national bank.
As the term is used in the Judicial Code providing that for the purposes of suits against them, they are to be deemed citizens of the states in which they are respectively located, it does not include the Federal Reserve banks but is used to describe the ordinary commercial banks. American Bank & Trust Co. v Federal Reserve Bank, 256 US 350, 357, 65 L Ed 983, 989, 41 S Ct 499.

national bank notes. See **bank notes.**

national cemetery. A cemetery for which provision is made by Congress, administered by the National Park Service, Department of the Interior, and devoted as a place of burial for members of the Armed Forces, veterans of the Armed Forces, and the wives of such members and veterans. 24 USC § 281.

national citizenship. Citizenship in the United States as distinguished from citizenship of a state. 16 Am J2d Const L § 469.

The Fourteenth Amendment to the Constitution of the United States bridges the gap left by Article 4, § 2, so as to safeguard citizens of the United States against any legislation of their own states having the effect of denying equality of treatment in respect of the exercise of their privileges of national citizenship in other states. Colgate v Harvey, 296 US 404, 80 L Ed 299, 56 S Ct 252, 102 ALR 54, ovrld on another point Madden v Kentucky, 309 US 83, 84 L Ed 590, 60 S Ct 406, 125 ALR 1383.

national corporations. Corporations organized under the authority of acts of Congress.

national currency. That which is issued as money under the sanction of the nation. State v Gasting, 23 La Ann 609.

national debt. The debt of the United States and federal agencies held by the public. In other words, the debt of the United States plus the debts of the federal agencies less United States securities held by federal agencies and federal trust funds, and federal agency securities held by the United States Treasury and other federal agencies.

national defense. The military establishment of the United States and preparation for the defense of the nation against the enemy. Gorin v United States, 312 US 19, 85 L Ed 488, 61 S Ct 429, reh den 312 US 713, 85 L Ed 1144, 61 S Ct 617. A power of Congress under Clauses 11 to 16, inclusive, of Section 8 of Article I of the United States Constitution.

national domain (do-mān'). The public lands of the United States which are owned by the national government.

national domicil. Domicil in a nation. 25 Am J2d Dom § 12. The nation or country in which a person has his domicil, as distinguished from his state or local domicil.

national emergency. Any event which threatens peril to the nation or the people. An event of which cognizance must be taken if the safety of the nation and its people is to be preserved.

National Formulary. See **Formulary.**

national government. The federal government of the United States. The government of a single nation, united as a community by what is termed the social compact, and possessing complete and perfect supremacy over persons and things, so far as they can be made the lawful objects of civil government. Piqua Bank v Knoup, 6 Ohio St 342, 394.

National Guard. An organization of armed men, created and maintained under the United States Constitution, the federal statutes, and state constitutions and state statutes. 36 Am J1st Mil § 42. A primary reserve of the United States Army and Air Force, serving the states in disasters and civil disturbances, and subject to call to service of the United States in time of war or in anticipation of war.

While enrolled as soldiers of the state, the active militia or national guard, are neither " 'troops,' nor a 'standing army.' " State ex rel. Madigan v Wagener, 74 Minn 518, 77 NW 424.

nationality. Belonging and owing allegiance to a nation through being a citizen thereof by birth or naturalization. The national character of a ship as recognized by the law of nations, because it regularly carries the flag of the nation to which it belongs. 48 Am J1st Ship § 39. A term sometimes used incorrectly in referring to the national origin of an alien or naturalized citizen.

The fundamental principle of the common law with regard to English nationality was birth within the allegiance of the king. The principle embraced all persons born within the king's allegiance and subject to his protection. Such allegiance and protection were mutual, and were not restricted to natural-born subjects, or to those who had taken an oath of allegiance; but were predicable of aliens in amity, so long as they were within the kingdom. Children born of such aliens were therefore natural-born subjects. United States v Wong Kim Ark, 169 US 649, 655, 42 L Ed 890, 893, 18 S Ct 456.

Nationality Act. See **Immigration and Nationality Act.**

nationality of ship. See **nationality.**

nationalization. The taking over of an industry by a government, sometimes, although not necessarily, involving the confiscation of property.

nationalization loss. A loss incurred by the nationalization of property by a foreign government.

national origin. The descent or extraction of a person in reference to the nationality of his ancestors. Gonzales v Sheely (DC Ariz) 96 F Supp 1004.

National Prohibition. See **prohibition.**

national public policy. The public policy which prevails throughout the country as distinguished from the public policy of a locality. 17 Am J2d Contr § 176.

National Service Life Insurance. A special statutory type of life insurance for servicemen provided by the National Service Life Insurance Act of 1940. 29A Am J Rev ed Ins §§ 1970, 1980 et seq.

National Socialist. See **Nazi.**

national union. An association of local labor unions which is national in scope. 31 Am J Rev ed Lab § 42.

nativa (nā-tī'va). A naif; a female villein.

native. Noun: A person born within the jurisdiction. United States v Wong Kim Ark, 169 US 649, 42 L Ed 890, 18 S Ct 456. One of local birth. Adjective: Indigenous.

nativi (nā-tī'vī). Villeins; vassals.

nativitas (nā-ti'vi-tās). Same as **villeinage.**

nativity. Birth, particularly the place and surroundings.

Nativity. The birth of Jesus Christ.

nativo habendo (nā-ti'vō hā-ben'dō). A writ which a lord might have to recover a villein who had escaped and fled.

nativus (nā-tī'vus). A villein.

Natura appetit perfectum, ita et lex (nā-tū'ra ap'petit per-fek'tum, i'ta et lex). Nature seeks perfection, and so does the law.

Natura Brevium (nā-tū'ra brē'vi-um). An old collection of original writs which was compiled during the reign of Edward the Third.

Naturae vis maxima; natura bis maxima (nā-tū'rē vīs ma'xi-ma; nā-tū'ra bis ma'xi-ma). The force of nature is the most powerful; nature is doubly powerful.

Natura fide jussionis sit strictissimi juris et non durat, vel extendatur de re ad rem, de persona ad personam, de tempore ad tempus (nā-tū'ra fī'dē jūsshe-ō'nis sit strik-tis'si-mī jū'ris et non dū'rat, vel ex-ten-dā'ter dē rē ad rem, dē per-sō'na ad persō'nam, dē tem'po-re ad tem'pus). The nature of a suretyship is one of strictest law and does not endure or suffer an extension from one thing to another, from one person to another, or from one time to another.

natural. Occurring according to the usual course of nature or according to the operation of natural laws, which, in the particular case, may be unusual and extraordinary in common experience. Shafer v Keeley Ice Cream Co. 65 Utah 46, 234 P 300, 38 ALR 1523, 1527.

natural affection. That affection which a person's near relative is presumed to have for him.

natural allegiance (a-lē'jans). Allegiance to the sovereign or government of one's native state or country; allegiance by birth.

natural and probable consequence. A test of proximate cause. 38 Am J1st Negl § 57.

See **natural consequence; probable consequence.**

natural-born citizen. A citizen by birth, as distinguished from a citizen who has been naturalized.

natural boundary. See **natural monument.**

natural causes. Causes arising from the elements. Causes arising in the course of nature, not produced by man.

natural channel. The channel of a river or stream which has been formed by nature; the floor or bed on which the water flows and the banks on each side thereof as carved out by natural causes. Pima Farms Co. v Proctor, 30 Ariz 96, 245 P 369.

natural child. A child acquired by its lawful parents through birth rather than by adoption. A child born out of wedlock; an illegitimate child.

natural consequence. The consequence of an act which ordinarily follows it. 38 Am J1st Negl § 57. A result which reasonably might have been foreseen. McCann v Newark & South Orange Railway Co. 58 NJL 642, 34 A 1052. A consequence which might naturally be expected to follow; damages which would result in the usual course of things, as distinguished from accidental or collateral injury, or such as would spring from special circumstances not usually attendant upon such transactions. 22 Am J2d Damg § 56.

See **probable consequence; proximate result.**

natural day. The period of time elapsing between sunrise and sunset. Re Ten-Hour Law for Street Railway Corp. 24 RI 603, 54 A 602.

natural death. A death occurring other than through external violence or human agency. Slevin v Board of Police Pension Fund Comrs. 123 Cal 130, 55 P 785.

natural demand. A call of nature.

natural drainway. A natural means of drainage of surface water. A ravine, gorge, or similar depression, by means of which the surface water of a hilly or mountainous country is drained. Anno: 81 ALR

271. A depression or channel created by natural causes in which surface water flows at some season of the year. Tide Water Oil Sales Corporation v Shimelman, 114 Conn 182, 158 A 229, 81 ALR 256. A channel cut through the turf and into the soil by the flowing of water. Tide Water Oil Sales Corp. v Shimelman, 114 Conn 182, 158 A 229, 81 ALR 256. Any conformation of land which gives to surface water flowing from one tract to another a fixed and determinate course whereby it is discharged uniformly on the servient tract. 56 Am J1st Wat § 76.

natural easement. See **easement ex jure naturale.**

Naturale est quidlibet dissolvi eo modo quo ligatur (nă-tū-rā'le est quid'li-bet dis-sol'vī ē'ō mō'dō quō li-ga'ter). It is natural that any obligation should be released in the same manner in which it is made binding.

natural equity. Common honesty and right in a person's dealings with others.

naturales (na-tū-rā'lēz). (Roman law.) Illegitimate children born of a concubine.
See **fructus naturales.**

natural father. A real rather than a foster father; the father by birth in lawful wedlock rather than by legal adoption. The father of an illegitimate child.

natural flow of stream. See **natural state of stream.**

natural flow of surface water. That course which would be taken by surface water falling on the land of the upper proprietor or carried thereto from still higher land, and flowing or running therefrom onto the lands of the lower proprietor, undiverted and unaccelerated by any artificial interference therewith. Le Brun v Richards, 210 Cal 308, 291 P 825, 72 ALR 336.

natural fool. A person born without understanding; an idiot.

natural fruits. Also called fructus naturales,—the fruits and produce of perennial trees, bushes, and grasses. Crops produced by the powers of nature alone. 21 Am J2d Crops § 2.

natural gas. A mineral in the form of a vapor. 26 Am J2d Electr § 4. A gas, characterized by hydrocarbons in mixture, occurring naturally in the crust of the earth, obtained by drilling, and piped to cities and villages, industrial and commercial centers, for use in heating, illumination, and other purposes. 24 Am J1st Gas & O § 2. A commodity and property when reduced to possession. West v Kansas Gas Co. 221 US 229, 55 L Ed 716, 31 S Ct 564. For tariff purposes, crude bitumin or crude mineral. United States v Buffalo Natural Gas Fuel Co. 172 US 339, 43 L Ed 469, 19 S Ct 200.

Natural Gas Act. A comprehensive scheme of federal regulation of all sales of natural gas at wholesale in interstate commerce, whether by pipeline company or not, and whether occurring before, during, or after transmission by an interstate pipeline company. Northern Natural Gas Co. v State Corp. Com. 372 US 84, 9 L Ed 2d 601, 83 S Ct 646, reh den 372 US 960, 10 L Ed 2d 14, 83 S Ct 1011.

natural gas company. A company engaged in supplying natural gas for lighting, power, or other purposes to ultimate consumers. 26 Am J2d Electr § 4.
As used in the Natural Gas Act of June 21, 1938, a natural gas company means a person (including a corporation) engaged in the transportation of natural gas in interstate commerce or the sale in interstate commerce of such gas for resale. Illinois Natural Gas Co. v Central Illinois Public Service Co. 314 US 498, 86 L Ed 371, 62 S Ct 384.
See **gas companies.**

natural grade. The grade of a highway or street which has not been altered from that of the general lay of the land through which it runs.

natural guardian. See **guardian by nature; guardian by nurture.**

natural heirs. Heirs of the body, as distinguished from those entitled to succeed on intestacy. 23 Am J2d Deeds § 215. As the term is used in a will:— sometimes a term of limitation, sometimes the equivalent of issue or simply denoting certain individuals, sometimes meaning bodily heirs, the construction depending upon the context of the instrument and the surrounding circumstances. 57 Am J1st Wills § 1371. Sometimes meaning children, thereby excluding collateral heirs. 57 Am J1st Wills § 1368.

naturali laxitate. See **in naturali laxitate.**

natural impotency. Incurable impotency, not congenital incapacity for the sexual act. Jordan v Jordan, 93 Ill App 633 (ground of divorce); Cofer v Cofer (Tex Civ App) 276 SW2d 214.

natural increase of shares. An increase in the value of shares resulting from an increase in the earnings and profits of the corporation and a consequential increase in dividends. Miller v Guerrard, 67 Ga 284.

natural infancy. The state or condition of a child who is under seven years of age.

natural interruption. Under the civil law,—an interruption of a period of prescription, either by an entry into, and upon immovable things, or in taking away movables. Innerarity v Heirs of Mims, 1 Ala 660, 674.

naturalis possessio. See **possessio naturalis.**

naturalization. The conferring of the nationality of a state upon a person after birth, by any means whatsoever. 8 USC § 1101 (a) (23); Re Marques, 341 Mass 715, 172 NE2d 262. The act of adopting a foreigner and clothing him with the privileges of a native born citizen. Boyd v Nebraska, 143 US 135, 36 L Ed 103, 12 S Ct 375. An act involving the renunciation of a former citizenship and entrance into a similar relation towards a different body politic. Boyd v Nebraska, 143 US 135, 36 L Ed 103, 12 S Ct 375.

naturalization by marriage. The naturalization of an alien female upon her marriage to a citizen; the former rule in the United States, repealed by the Cable Act of 1922. 3 Am J2d Aliens § 116, note 5.

naturalization proceeding. A proceeding for the naturalization of an alien, which, while a judicial proceeding, is not an adversary proceeding, being merely a proceeding provided by statute for the administration of the naturalization laws in the case of an application for naturalization by an alien, wherein his fitness for citizenship may be determined. Rein v United States, 69 F2d 206.

naturalized citizen. A person who has been made a citizen of the United States under the authority of a federal statute. A citizen in truth, law, and fact; a citizen in every sense of the word. Osborn v Bank of the United States (US) 9 Wheat 739, 827, 6 L Ed 204, 225.

natural law. An abstract concept of law in accord with the nature of man. A rule which so necessarily agrees with the nature and state of man that, without observing its maxims, the peace and happiness of society can never be preserved. Borden v State, 11 Ark 519. Those fit and just rules of conduct which the Creator has prescribed to man, as a dependent and social being; and which are to be ascertained from the deductions of right reason, though they may be more precisely known, and more explicitly declared by divine revelation. Wightman v Wightman (NY) 4 Johns Ch 343, 348.

See **natural rights**.

natural liberty. A person's freedom to act as he may desire, excepting in so far as he is restrained or controlled by the laws of nature. See 1 Bl Comm 125.

natural life. A tautological expression.
The word "natural," in this connection, adds nothing to the meaning of the word "life," nor does it change it. Imprisonment for one's natural life is the same as imprisonment for life. The word "natural" may be rejected as surplusage. People v Wright, 89 Mich 70, 93, 50 NW 792.

naturally. In the usual course of things. Mitchell v Clarke, 71 Cal 164, 11 P 882.

natural monuments. Natural objects, such as trees, stones, and the like used in designating and describing land boundaries. 12 Am J2d Bound § 4.

natural objects of bounty. Those members of a testator's family entitled on the face of things to his bounty.

natural obligation. A moral obligation. Re Atkins' Estate (CA5) 30 F2d 761. An obligation which rests wholly in conscience and which is not enforceable under the laws of mankind.

See **moral obligation**.

natural parent. A real parent as distinguished from an adoptive parent or foster parent. The father of a child born out of wedlock.

natural person. An individual; a private person, as distinguished from an artificial person, such as a corporation.

natural phenomena. The powers, forces, and operations of nature, such as the movement of the heavenly bodies, the annual rainfall, gravity, etc. 29 Am J2d Ev § 100. Natural occurrences, such as storms.

natural pond. A small body of fresh water, created without the aid or interference of man.

See **great ponds**.

natural possession. See **possessio naturalis**.

natural premium plan. A form of insurance, also called the "assessment plan" wherein the insurance company limited its assessments or premiums to such a sum as was necessary to cover the actual cost of insurance from one renewal period to another. Westerman v Supreme Lodge, Knights of Pythias, 196 Mo 670, 94 SW 470.

natural presumption. A presumption which arises when a fact is proved, wherefrom by reason of the connection founded on experience, the existence of another fact is directly inferred. Gulick v Loder, 13 NJL 68.

natural resources. The land, waters, and mineral resources. Things of value existing in nature, such as minerals, waterpower, productive soil, etc.

natural result. See **natural consequence**.

natural right. A right which exists regardless of municipal or other law, if not repealed by legal fiat. Sult v Gilbert, 148 Fla 31, 3 So 2d 729. A right inherent in land, such as that of lateral support, of the right to the benefit of the flow of a stream of water, of the right of an owner of land to have the surface water discharged upon the lower land of his neighbor, etc. 25 Am J2d Ease § 6. An inherent political right, founded on a common necessity and interest, such as the right to appropriate the property of a person to the great necessity of the whole community. 26 Am J2d Em D § 1. A right which, in its primary and strictest sense, belongs to each person as a human being in a state of nature. Re Morgan, 26 Colo 415, 58 P 1071; Bednarik v Bednarik, 18 NJ Misc 633, 16 A2d 80. The right of self defense, a right which existed before the formation of society. 26 Am J1st Homi § 126. A fundamental right actually guaranteed by the constitution. 16 Am J2d Const L § 330. A right entitled to constitutional protection in addition to rights protected under the specific guaranty safeguarding a person in his life, liberty, or pursuit of happiness; for example the affection between parent and child, Lacher v Venus, 177 Wis 558, 188 NW 613, 24 ALR 403; for another example, the right to beget children. 16 Am J2d Const L § 330. According to some authority, a concept in the abstract, apart from constitutional rights. Henry v Cherry, 30 RI 13, 73 A 97.

natural science. See **science**.

natural state of stream. The condition of a stream of water under the ordinary operation of the physical laws which affect it. 56 Am J1st Wat § 19. The stage of water that ordinarily flows in the spring or other season of the year when the stream stands at the highest water mark. 56 Am J1st Wat § 19.

natural stream. See **natural watercourse**.

natural support. See **easement of natural support**.

natural use. The use of the water of a stream for purposes arising out of the necessities of life, such as household use and the watering of domestic animals. Cowell v Armstrong, 210 Cal App 218, 290 P 1036.

natural watercourse. Any well defined channel or arroyo in which surface waters flow in times of heavy rain, irrespective of the fact that the land is cultivated in dry seasons or that in certain places the water of the depression spreads out and no longer flows in a definite channel. Anno: 81 ALR 266. A river or other natural stream, as distinguished from an artificial channel. 56 Am J1st Wat § 6. A stream usually flowing in a particular direction, in a definite channel, and discharging into some other stream or body of water, exclusive of a course conducting surface water from a higher to a lower level. Lambert v Alcorn, 144 Ill 313, 33 NE 53.

A stream does not lose its character as a natural watercourse, because in times of drought the flow may be diminished, or temporarily suspended. It is sufficient if it is usually a stream of running water. Barkley v Wilcox, 86 NY 140, 143.

natural waters. A body or stream of water originating from natural as distinguished from artificial causes. 56 Am J1st Wat § 3.

natural year. A year comprising three hundred and sixty-five and one-fourth days. The period of time in which the earth completes one revolution around the sun.

Natura non facit saltum; ita nec lex (nā-tū′ra non fā′sit sal′tum; i′ta nek lex). Nature does not make any leaps; neither does the law.

Natura non facit vacuum; nec lex supervacuum (nā-tū'ra non fā'sit va'ku-um; nek lex su-per-va'ku-um). Nature does not make a vacuum, nor does the law do anything superfluous.

natura rei. See **ex natura rei.**

nature. The quality of a thing; the disposition of a person. The totality of the universe.

nauclerus (nâ-klē'rus). (Civil law.) A shipowner; a shipmaster.

naufragium (nâ-frā'ji-um). Shipwreck.

naught (nât). Bad, defective, or worthless.

naulage (nâ'lȧj). The freight of a ship's passengers.

naulum (nâ'lum). (Civil law.) Freight; fare; money paid for passage on a ship.

nauseam. See **ad nauseam.**

nauta (nâ'ta). A sailor; a seaman; a mariner; the charterer of a ship.

nautical assessors. The name applied to experienced shipmasters, two in number, called to the assistance of the admiralty court in all difficult cases involving negligence, who sit with the judge during the argument and give their advice upon questions of seamanship or the weight of testimony. The Empire (DC Mich) 19 F 558, 559.

nautical mile (nâ'ti-kạl mīl). A marine mile; a linear measure of distance on the sea, equivalent to approximately 6,080 feet, the name being taken from the knots in a ship's log line. Steamboat Co. v Fessenden, 79 Me 140, 146.

The International Nautical Mile is 1.150779 statute miles.

nautico foenere (nâ'ti-kō fē'ne-re). With marine interest,—that is, with interest at the very high rate which is charged on marine loans.

navagium (nạ-vā'ji-um). The service rendered by a tenant of carrying the goods of his lord by ship.

naval. Pertaining to the Navy.
See **Navy.**

Naval Academy. The United States Naval Academy at Annapolis, Maryland, for the education and training of cadets preparatory to their becoming officers of the Navy.

naval aircraft. Aircraft in the service of the Navy, in the Armed Services.

naval bounty. A bounty paid to induce enlistment in the Navy. 12 Am J2d Bount § 2. A bounty offered to the officers and crew of any ship of the Navy causing the destruction of an enemy vessel. Porter v United States, 106 US 607, 27 L Ed 286, 1 S Ct 539.

naval convoy. See **convoy.**

naval court martial. See **court martial.**

naval courts. English courts composed of naval officers and held in foreign countries to hear and determine cases involving the loss of English ships or grievances of their masters or crews.

naval lands. Areas of the public domain reserved for naval purposes. Pan American Transport Co. v United States, 273 US 456, 71 L Ed 734, 47 S Ct 416.

naval law. The rules and regulations governing officers and men of the Navy.
See **military law.**

naval officer. See **Navy.**

naval service. See **service in the Navy.**

naval station. A military station of the Navy. 36 Am J1st Mil § 6.

navigability. The quality of being navigable.
See **navigable waters.**

navigability in fact. The susceptibility of a river to use in its ordinary condition as a highway for commerce over which trade and travel are or may be conducted in the customary modes of trade and travel on water. Oklahoma v Texas, 258 US 574, 586, 66 L Ed 771, 42 S Ct 406, 411; Blackman v Mauldin, 164 Ala 337, 51 So 23.

navigable airspace. The air space above the minimum altitudes of flight prescribed by regulation issued under the Federal Aviation Act, including air space needed to insure safety in the takeoff and landing of aircraft. 49 USC § 1301 (24). The space above the space extending upward from the surface of land which is necessary for the full use and enjoyment of the land and the incidents of its ownership. 8 Am J2d Avi § 3.

navigable river. See **navigable waters.**

navigable waters. Rivers or other bodies of water used, or susceptible of being used in their ordinary condition, as highways for commerce, over which trade and travel are or may be conducted in the customary modes of trade and travel on water. Elder v Delcour, 364 Mo 835, 269 SW2d 17, 47 ALR2d 370. A stream or body of water having the capacity and suitability for the usual purpose of navigation, ascending or descending, by vessels such as are employed in the ordinary purposes of commerce, whether foreign or inland, and whether steam, sail, or other motive power. 56 Am J1st Wat § 179.

The test of navigability is whether the river, in its natural state, is used, or capable of being used, as a highway for commerce, over which trade and travel are or may be conducted in the customary modes of trade and travel on water. In the sense of the law, navigability is not destroyed because the watercourse is interrupted by occasional natural obstruction or portages; nor need the navigation be open at all seasons of the year, or at all stages of the water. Economy Light & Power Co. v United States, 256 US 113, 121, 65 L Ed 847, 854, 41 S Ct 409.

Navigability is a term of art, and often may be at variance with the usual and common conception of the meaning of the word. Under English common-law rules, waters were navigable which were salty or subject to the influence and flow of ocean tides, and all other waters were nonnavigable, irrespective of whether or not vessels of commerce or pleasure operated on them in fact. Anno: 47 ALR2d 385.

navigable waters of the United States. Those waters which are subject to the control of the Federal government for the regulation of commerce, and to which the Federal judicial power extends for the purpose of admiralty and maritime jurisdiction. The high seas and such lakes and streams as are navigable in fact, and which by themselves or their connection with other waters form a continuous channel or highway for commerce among the states or with foreign countries. 56 Am J1st Wat § 190.

navigate. To accomplish or participate in navigation.
See **navigation.**

navigation. The direction of a ship or aircraft in

movement; plotting a course and steering by the course plotted. The steering, directing, or managing of a vessel by a person or persons on board. Ryan v Hook (NY) 34 Hun 185, 191.

To navigate an aircraft. See 49 USC § 1301 (25)(26).

Navigation Act. An English statute enacted in the reign of Charles the Second, which prohibited other countries from trading with the colonies of England.

navigation district. An improvement district organized for the purpose of improvement of navigation upon a watercourse or body of water or a specified portion of a watercourse or body of water.

navigation rules. See **rules of navigation.**

navis (na'vis). A ship or vessel.

navis bona (nā'vis bō'na). A good ship; a vessel that is seaworthy.

Navy. A military body; one of the Armed Forces, inclusive of officers and men, ships, aircraft, and equipment. 36 Am J1st Mil § 4.

In connection with the transfer of the Navy of the Republic of Texas to the United States, the word was held to include the ships only, not the officers and men. Brashear v Mason (US) 6 How 92, 12 L Ed 357.

Navy Department. A part of the Department of Defense, having general supervision of the naval combat and service forces and such aviation as may be organic therein. 5 USC § 411a.

Navy personnel. Members of the Armed Forces in the United States Navy.

Navy Personnel Act. A federal statute enacted in 1899, providing primarily that commissioned officers of the line of the Navy and of the medical and pay corps should receive the same pay and allowances, except forage, as were or might be provided by or in pursuance of law for officers of corresponding rank in the Army. 36 Am J1st Mil § 69.

navy regulations. See **regulations of the navy.**

Navy yard. A place maintained and equipped for the construction or repair of vessels of the Navy.

naye. No. A negative vote in a legislative body.

nazeranna (na-ze-ran'na). A voluntary payment made to a government in recognition of the bestowal of a land grant or a public office.

Nazi (nät'sē). A contraction of the German term for National Socialist German Workers' Party headed by Adolph Hitler. A fascist or totalitarian in political belief. A derisive term.

N. E. Abbreviation of northeast. See **fraction of section.**

ne (nē). Not; lest.

ne admittas (nē ad-mit'tas). Not to admit. A prohibitory writ which forbade the bishop to admit any clerk to a particular living pending the suit of a clerk to determine his right to the living. See 3 Bl Comm 248.

neap tide. The tide which occurs when the difference between high tide and low tide is the smallest; the tide which occurs at moon's quadrature with the sun. Teschemacher v Thompson, 18 Cal 11, 21.

near. A relative term in speaking of distance. Kirkbride v Lafayette County, 108 US 208, 27 L Ed 705, 2 S Ct 501. A relative term, as it appears in the description in a deed, sometimes the equivalent of "at," at other times importing the sense of "along." 23 Am J2d Deeds § 243.

near beer. A malt liquor containing so little alcohol that it will not produce intoxication, even though consumed in quantity. State v Danenberg, 151 NC 718, 66 SE 301.

nearest blood. Usually regarded as tantamount to **next of kin.** 57 Am J1st Wills § 1398.

nearest blood kin. Usually same as **next of kin.** 57 Am J1st Wills § 1398. Ordinarily, words of purchase. Anno: 100 ALR2d 1073, § 2[a].

nearest blood relatives. Usually, although not necessarily, the same as **next of kin.** 57 Am J1st Wills § 1398. Ordinarily words of purchase. Anno: 100 ALR2d 1073, § 2[a].

nearest heirs. A term of art, ordinarily constituting words of limitation; words of purchase where it appears that the testator used them, not with technical accuracy, but inartificially to denote particular persons. 28 Am J2d Est § 118; 57 Am J1st Wills § 1398.

There is some conflict in the cases as to the effect of the word "nearest" when prefixed to "heir" or a similar term in a testamentary gift. Some of the cases hold that such a phrase includes all the heirs at law of the testator, while others take the view that the word "nearest" confines the gift to heirs at law of the class standing nearest in blood to the testator, excluding all others. However, the variation in the phrases construed and the context in which they are used make it impossible to formulate a definite rule from the decisions. Anno: 11 ALR 329.

nearest kin. Usually tantamount to **next of kin.** 57 Am J1st Wills § 1398. Often words of purchase. 28 Am J2d Est § 118.

nearest male heir. A term which, when appearing in a will, indicates the testator's nearest male relative. 57 Am J1st Wills § 1398.

nearest of blood. Same as **next of kin.** Anno: 11 ALR 329.

nearest of kin. Usually tantamount to **next of kin.** 57 Am J1st Wills § 1398. The nearest relatives by blood. Anno: 11 ALR 331.

nearest relatives. Next of kin. 57 Am J1st Wills § 1398. Words of purchase. 100 ALR2d 1073, § 2[a].

nearsightedness. A condition in the eyesight of a person whereby only near objects are seen by him distinctly. Not a local or constitutional disease. Anno: 96 ALR 429.

neat. Tidy; clean. Unmixed, especially in reference to a drink of an alcholic beverage. In an older sense, net, that is after deductions.

neat cattle. Cattle which have the cloven or split hoof and which also chew their cud.

A cow has both of these attributes, a hog has the first, only, and a horse has neither of them. The term includes all animals of the bovine species. Territory v Christman, 9 NM 582, 58 P 343.

neat profits. An old term, now rare, for **net profits.**

ne baila pas (nuh bī-lah pah). He did not deliver.

necation (nē-kā'shọn). A putting to death; a killing.

Nec curia deficeret in justitia exhibenda (nek kū'ri-a dē-fī'se-ret in jus-ti'she-a ex-hi-ben'da). Nor should the court be deficient in bestowing justice.

necessaries. In respect of a parent's liability:—such things as are necessary to supply the personal needs of the infant, suitable shelter, food, clothing, medical attention, and whatever else is essential to the health and comfort of the child, including education. 39 Am J1st P & C § 37. Within the rule that an infant may bind himself for necessaries:—those things which are reasonably necessary for the proper and suitable maintenance of the infant in view of his social position and situation in life, the customs of the social circle in which he moves, and the fortune possessed by him and by his parents, including, of course, such things as are obviously for the maintenance of existence. 27 Am J1st Inf § 17. Within the meaning of the liability of an insane person:—articles proper for the normal maintenance of the incompetent, the determination depending not merely on the nature of the articles but also upon their propriety and suitability for the incompetent, according to the circumstances and his condition of life. Belluci v Foss, 244 Mass 401, 138 NE 551. Within the meaning of a husband's duty to provide for his wife:—at common law, necessary food, drink, clothing, washing, medicine, instruction, and a suitable place of residence; with more liberality evidenced by more modern cases, looking to the means, ability, social position and circumstances of both husband and wife for the determination to be made in the particular case. 26 Am J1st H & W § 375. Repairs and supplies furnished a vessel, towage, use of dry dock or marine railway, for which the person furnishing is entitled to a maritime lien. 46 USC § 971.

A necessary article is one which the party actually needs. It is not enough to show that the article is per se classed as necessary, such as food and clothing. It must also be actually needed at the time. State v Thornton, 232 Mo 298, 134 SW 519.

Under the maritime law permitting the master of a ship to pledge the owner's credit for necessaries, the word does not import absolute necessity, but the circumstances must be such that a reasonably prudent owner, present, would have authorized the expenditures, and it is usually sufficient if they are reasonably fit and proper, having regard to the exigencies and requirements of the ship, for the port where she is lying and the voyage on which she is bound. 48 Am J1st Ship § 133.

Within the meaning of exemption statutes, what are necessaries must be largely a question of fact to be determined under the varying circumstances of each case. Goods furnished cannot be regarded as necessaries for the family of the debtor where he is unmarried, nor where they are merely the means by which payment is made for what is necessary, as where they are furnished him on credit and used by him to pay his board precisely as if he were paying it in money. The decisions do not confine the term to articles of commerce, but extend it to include, as well, services rendered even of a professional character, such as medical services or legal services. 22 Am J1st Exemp § 106.

Necessarium est quod non potest aliter se habere (ne-ses-sā′ri-um est quod non po′test a′li-ter sē hā-bē′re). That is necessary which it is not possible to be otherwise.

necessarily used. Reasonably required in the exercise of sound business prudence. Anno: 80 ALR 253.

necessarius (ne-ses-sā′ri-us). Necessary; unavoidable; inevitable.

necessary. Adjective: Essential; indispensable; unavoidable. Canton v Canton Warehouse Co. 84 Miss 268, 36 So 266; Abraham v Ins. Co. of N. A. 117 Vt 75, 84 A2d 670, 29 ALR2d 783. In an obsolete sense, appropriate; convenient; useful; essential. M'Culloch v Maryland (US) 4 Wheat 316, 4 L Ed 579. Noun: A necessary thing, usually found in the plural in court opinions and legal literature.
See **necessaries.**

necessary accommodations of carrier. Accommodations reasonably suitable and useful to the public. Chicago I. & L. Ry Co. v Baugh, 175 Ind 419, 94 NE 571.

necessary and indispensable party. See **indispensable party; necessary party.**

necessary and proper clause. Clause 18 of Section 8 of Article I of the United States Constitution, granting to Congress the power to make all laws which shall be "necessary and proper for carrying into execution" specific powers granted to Congress in preceding clauses of the section.

necessary and proper laws. As a matter of the constitutional authority of Congress to pass laws:—not only such measures as are absolutely and indispensably necessary, without which the powers granted must fail of execution; but all appropriate means conducive or adapted to the end to be accomplished, and which in the judgment of Congress will most advantageously effect it. Legal Tender Case, 110 US 421, 28 L Ed 204, 4 S Ct 122.

necessary business expense. An expense which is appropriate and helpful. Blackmer v Commissioner (CA2) 70 F2d 255, 92 ALR 982.
See **ordinary and necessary expense.**

necessary deposit. A deposit of something on a person's land or premises which has been made by or on account of some unavoidable cause or accident; as, by vis major or in the case of the salvage of goods from fire.

necessary diligence. That degree of diligence which men ordinarily engaged and acquainted with a certain business will use in conducting such business as one of their own affairs. Sanderson v Brown, 57 Me 308.

necessary domicil. A domicil which is established by operation of law; as in the case of a wife who acquires the domicil of her husband, regardless of her choice. 25 Am J2d Dom § 48.

necessary easement. An easement consisting of a servitude constituting the only reasonable means of enjoying the dominant tenement. Cherry v Brizzolara, 89 Ark 309, 116 SW 668.

necessary expense of business. See **necessary business expense.**

necessary expense of public body. An expenditure which a municipality is reasonably required to make in order to carry on its work and perform its duties. Anno: 113 ALR 1204. Such an expense as is incurred in procuring those things without which the peace and order of the community, its moral interests, and the protection of property would suffer. Fawcett v Mt. Airy, 134 NC 125, 45 SE 1029.

As to the meaning of the term as used within an exception to a provision requiring a vote of the people to authorize the debt of a political body, see Anno: 113 ALR 1202.

necessary for public use. Reasonably necessary for use in a reasonable time under the circumstances of the particular case. 26 Am J2d Em D § 111.
See **public necessity and convenience.**

necessary household furniture. Articles of household furniture which are indispensable or requisite for living in a convenient and comfortable manner. 31 Am J2d Exemp § 73.

necessary implication. A meaning derived from language as a matter of actual necessity or of so strong a probability of the intent of the writer or speaker that a contrary intent is not reasonably to be inferred. Detroit Citizens' Street Railway Co. v Detroit (CA6 Mich) 64 F 628.

necessary litigation. Unavoidable litigation. Litigation required for the protection of person or property.

Litigation is necessary in the sense of a statute providing that an executor or administrator shall be allowed reasonable attorneys' fees in any "necessary litigation" if such litigation is reasonable, useful and proper. Re Feehely, 182 Or 246, 187 P2d 156, 173 ALR 1334.

necessary municipal buildings. Buildings necessary to conduct the affairs of the city government. 26 Am J2d Em D § 40.

necessary party. A person without whom no judgment or decree determining the principal issues in the case can effectively be made; such a person as is necessary to a determination of the entire controversy. 39 Am J1st Parties § 5.

A party to the proceeding whose rights if not determined in that proceeding would be disturbed without due process of law; a party whose rights appear from the facts as they appear in the record to be involved in a determination of the issues before the tribunal. State v Pacific Tel. & Tel. Co. 144 Wash 383, 258 P 313. A person who must be joined as a party if he is within the jurisdiction. McAndrews v Krause, 245 Minn 85, 71 NW2d 153, 53 ALR2d 312. A party on appeal whose interests may be adversely affected by the decision on appeal. 4 Am J2d A & E § 276.

See **indispensable party.**

necessary repairs. Such repairs by a lessee as are necessary for the use of the leased premises by the tenant for the purposes for which they were leased. Anno: 45 ALR 24, s. 106 ALR 1361.

necessary rule. The rule of some jurisdictions in reference to the right of a grantee to an easement in a street or alley shown on a map or plat, where the conveyance to him is made with reference to such map or plat, that his right of user in the street or alley is limited to the abutting street or alley and such others as are necessary to give him access to a public highway. 25 Am J2d Ease § 26.

necessary tool. A tool or implement needed in the reasonable conduct of the debtor's trade, business, or profession. 52 Am J2d Exemp § 52.

necessary wearing apparel. Such articles of clothing or wearing apparel as are convenient and useful under the circumstances of the particular case. 31 Am J2d Exemp § 79. Clothing or dress which is convenient and comfortable, as distinguished from wearing apparel which is a luxury. Towns v Platt, 33 NH 345.

necessary work animal. A work animal which is indispensable, or merely reasonably necessary, convenient, or suitable, to the owner. 31 Am J2d Exemp § 70.

necessitas (ne-ses'si-tās). Necessity; that which is inevitable or unavoidable; need; penury; poverty.

necessitas culpabilis (ne-ses'si-tās kul-pā'bi-lis). Culpable necessity,—that necessity which excuses a man who kills another in self-defense. See 4 Bl Comm 187.

Necessitas est lex temporis et loci (ne-ses'si-tās est lex tem'po-ris et lō'sī). Necessity is the law of time and of place.

Necessitas excusat aut extenuat delictum in capitalibus, quod non operatur idem in civilibus (ne-ses'si-tās ex-kū'zat ât ex-te'nu-at dē-lik'tum in ka-pi-ta'li-bus, quod non o-pe-rā'ter ī'dem in si-vi'li-bus). Necessity excuses or extenuates the offense in capital crimes, but it does not operate in the same manner in civil cases.

Necessitas facit licitum quod alias non est licitum (ne-ses'si-tās fā'sit li'si-tum quod ā'li-as non est li'si-tum). Necessity makes lawful that which otherwise would be unlawful.

Necessitas inducit privilegium (ne-ses'si-tās in-dū'sit pri-vi-lē'ji-um). Necessity creates privilege.

Under this maxim, the common law excuses the commission of an act prima facie criminal if such act be done involuntarily, and under circumstances which show that the individual doing it was not really a free agent. Thus, if A by force take the hand of B, in which is a weapon, and therewith kill C, A is guilty of murder, but B is excused. Moral force, however, such as a threat of imprisonment will not excuse him. State v Dowell, 106 NC 722, 11 SE 525.

Necessitas inducit privilegium quoad jura privata (ne-ses'si-tās in-dū'sit pri-vi-lē'ji-um quō'ad jū'ra prī-vā'ta). Necessity creates privilege with respect to private rights.

Necessitas non habet legem (ne-ses'si-tās non hā'bet lē'jem). Necessity has no law. Heyfron v Mahoney, 9 Mont 497, 24 P 93.

Necessitas publica major est quam privata (ne-ses'si-tās pub'li-ka mā'jor est quam prī-vā'ta). Public necessity is more important than private.

The welfare of the public is considered in law superior to the interests of individuals, and, when there is a conflict between them, the latter must give way. Durham v Eno Cotton Mills, 141 NC 615, 54 SE 453.

Necessitas quod cogit, defendit (ne-ses'si-tās, quod kō'jit, dē-fen'dit). Necessity defends that which it compels.

Necessitas sub lege non continetur, quia quod alias non est licitum necessitas facit licitum (ne-ses'si-tās sub lē'je non kon-ti-nē'ter, quī'a quod a'li-as non est li'si-tum ne-ses'si-tās fā'sit li'si-tum). Necessity is not restrained by the law, because that which otherwise is not lawful necessity makes lawful.

Necessitas vincit legem (ne-ses'si-tās vin'sit lē'jem). Necessity supersedes law.

Necessitas vincit legem; legum vincula irridet (ne-ses'si-tās vin'sit lē'jem; lē'jum vin'ku-la ir'ri-det). Necessity supersedes law; it laughs at the fetters of the law.

necessitate. See **ex necessitate.**

necessitate legis. See **ex necessitate legis.**

necessitate rei. See **ex necessitate rei.**

necessities. See **necessaries; necessity.**

necessitous. Pressed by poverty; needy; unable to procure what is necessary for one's station. Destitute. Anno: 36 ALR 872.

necessitous circumstances. See **necessitous condition.**

necessitous condition. A condition of want of the necessaries of life. 27 Am J1st H & W § 436. Destitution. The condition of one without adequate, sufficient, or reasonable means of support. 23 Am J2d Desert §§ 13, 14. The condition of a child in need of the necessaries of life, which cover not only primitive physical needs, things absolutely indispensable to human existence and decency, but also those things which are in fact necessary to the particular person left without support; a condition of great need, extreme want, or poverty, or substantially the absence of means of securing the reasonable necessities of life, except through charity. 39 Am J1st P & C § 111. From the standpoint of a husband's liability for nonsupport, a relative term, the purpose of the statute under consideration and the conditions to which the husband and wife have been accustomed being determinative. 23 Am J2d Desert § 14.

necessity. A compulsion of natural forces or the forces of man. Less pompously, a toilet or water closet. Something necessary.
See **necessaries; public necessity; public necessity and convenience; way of necessity; work of necessity.**

necessity doctrine. A principle whereunder expressions of present pain are admissible in evidence on the issue of pain and suffering as an element of damages for personal injury, regardless of the person to whom they were made, notwithstanding their hearsay character. 22 Am J2d Damg § 309.

neck verse. A sentence in Latin required to be read by a convicted person in determining his right to the benefit of clergy.

Nec regibus infinita aut libera potestas (nek rē′ji-bus in-fi′ni-ta ât li′be-ra po-tes′tās). With kings, power should neither be unlimited nor free. See 1 Bl Comm 233.

Nec tempus nec locus occurrit regi (nek tem′pus nek lō′kus o-ker′rit rē′jī). Neither time nor place bars or affects the king.

Nec veniam effuso sanguine, casus habet (nek ve′ni-am ef-fū′sō san′gwi-ne, kā′sus hā′bet). Nor is there any occasion for indulgence where there is a shedding of blood.

Nec veniam, laeso numine, casus habet (nek ve′ni-am, lē′sō nū′mi-ne, kā′sus hā′bet). There is no occasion for indulgence where majesty has been affronted.

Nec vi, clam, aut precario (nek vī, klam, ât prē-kā′ri-ō). Neither forcibly, secretly, nor by sufferance.

ne deficiat justitia (ne dē-fi′she-at jus-ti′she-a). Lest justice fail.

Ne disseise pas (nuh dīs-says pah). He was not disseised.

Ne disturba pas (nuh dīs′toor-bah′ pah). He did not disturb,—the general issue pleaded in an action of quare impedit.

Ne dona pas (nuh dō-nah′ pah). He did not give,— the general issue pleaded in a writ of formedon, which was a writ of right to recover lands according to the form of the gift or grant in tail.

nee (nā). Born. A word conveniently used after the name of a married woman to indicate her maiden name, e.g. Esther Roe, née Doe.

need. A necessity. Something required but wanting.
As used in pension plans the term is a wholly relative term and there is no clear line of demarcation as to the requisite financial status of a particular recipient in order to justify the characterization of the benefit to him as charitable. Re Tarrant, 38 Cal 2d 42, 237 P2d 505, 28 ALR2d 419.
See **necessaries; needs of business.**

needful. Necessary.
As used in Article I, § 8, clause 17, of the Federal Constitution the term "needful buildings" has been held to embrace whatever structures are found to be necessary in the performance of the functions of the Federal Government. James v Dravo Contracting, 303 US 134, 82 L Ed 155, 58 S Ct 208, 114 ALR 318.

needless. Unnecessary, unjustifiable on the theory of necessity. Anno: 82 ALR2d 800, § 4.

needs of business. The amount of a product or material necessary for use in the business of a particular person. The requirements of a business in reference to a particular commodity. 46 Am J1st Sales § 135.

needy. Indigent, necessitous, very poor. Anno: 121 ALR 1007. Distressed by the want of means of living. Juneau County v Wood, 109 Wis 330, 333, 85 NW 387.

nee vife (nā vēf). Born alive.

ne exeat (nē ek′sẹ-at). A writ issued by a court of equity to restrain a person from going beyond the limits of the jurisdiction of the court, until he has satisfied the plaintiff's claim or has given bond for the satisfaction of the decree of the court. 38 Am J1st Ne Ex § 1.

Ne exeat regno (nē ek′sẹ-at reg′nō). Do not let him leave the realm.

Ne exeat republica (ne ek′sẹ-at rē-pub′li-ka). Do not let him leave the state,—the name given to the writ of ne exeat in some of the states of the Union.

nefas (nē′fas). A wrongful, sinful, wicked, unlawful, or criminal act.

negare (nē-gā′re). To negative; to deny.

Negatio conclusionis est error in lege (nē-gā′she-ō kon-klu-zhi-ū′nis est er′ror in lē′je). The denial of a conclusion is error in law.

Negatio destruit negationem, et ambae faciunt affirmationem (nē-gā′she-ō de-stru′it nē-gā-she-ō′nem, et am′bē fā′she-unt af-fir-mā-she-ō′nem). A negative destroys a negative, and both together they make an affirmative.

Negatio duplex est affirmatio (nē-gā′she-ō du′plex est af-fir-mā′she-ō). A double negative is an affirmative.

negative averments. See **negativing defenses.**

negative community. A term of art. Used in reference to the political economy as it was when those things which were common to all belonged no more to one than to the others, and hence no one could prevent another from taking of these common things that portion which he judged necessary to subserve his wants.
While he was using them others could not disturb him, but when he had ceased to use them, if they were not things which were consumed by the fact of use, the things immediately re-entered into the negative community and another could not use them. See Geer v Connecticut, 161 US 519, 525, 40 L Ed 793, 795, 16 S Ct 600.

NEGATIVE [839] NEGLECTED

negative condition. A condition against the occurrence of some event.

negative covenant. The usual form of restrictive covenant; a covenant which calls for refraining from certain acts or certain uses of property. 20 Am J2d Cov § 166.

negative easement. An easement, the effect of which is to preclude the owner of land subject to the easement from the doing of an act which if no easement existed, he would be entitled to do. Northwestern Improv. Co. v Lowry, 104 Mont 289, 66 P 792, 110 ALR 605. A true easement, the right granted being appurtenant to other land and not a mere personal right. 25 Am J2d Ease § 8.

negative evidence. Testimony that a fact did not exist or that a thing was not done, in other words testimony that denies rather than affirms. 30 Am J2d Ev § 1092. Testimony that one did not see or hear something, otherwise called testimony to negative knowledge. Union P. R. Co. v Burnham (CA10 Colo) 124 F2d 500.
"The trial judge practically told the jury that negative testimony was confined to that of a witness who, though present at a transaction, says that he did not see or hear." This is too limited a rule. Testimony which is positive in form may amount merely to negative testimony. Smith v Milwaukee Builders & Traders' Exchange, 91 Wis 360, 64 NW 1041.
The probative force of negative testimony depends largely upon circumstances. In some circumstances, its probative force may be so slight as to reach the vanishing point; in others, it may be more persuasive than the positive testimony of some witnesses. It is only when it is so clear that such testimony has no probative value whatever that reasonable men would not differ in their conclusions in reference thereto that courts are justified in disregarding it on the ground that it does not rise to the dignity of evidence. Union Pacific R. Co. v Burnham (CA10 Colo) 124 F2d 500.

negative finding. A finding expressly or by necessary implication against the existence of a certain fact. 53 Am J1st Trial § 1143.

negative knowledge. The failure of a witness to see and hear that which he would supposedly have seen or heard if it had occurred. Hoffard v Illinois Central Railroad Co. 138 Iowa 543, 110 NW 446.

negative order. Hardly an appropriate term of art, since an order may be affirmative in fact, although negative in form. Rochester Tel. Corporation v United States, 307 US 125, 83 L Ed 1147, 59 S Ct 754.

negative order doctrine. A rule, generally repudiated by the Supreme Court of the United States, that a federal court had no jurisdiction to review an order of an administrative agency by which the agency merely refused to grant the relief sought. 2 Am J2d Admin L § 574.

negative plea. The terminology of equity for a pleading by the defendant which does not bring new matter of defense into the record but seeks to destroy the efficacy of the plaintiff's case by denying some single critical fact stated in the bill. 27 Am J2d Eq § 204.

negative pregnant. A qualified denial pregnant with the admission of a substantial fact not squarely denied, characteristically in the very words of the allegation denied. 41 Am J1st Pl § 196.

Where the plaintiff alleges the defendant to be a corporation organized under the laws of a named state or country, a denial that it is a corporation organized under those laws is pregnant with an admission that it is a corporation. Wright v Fire Ins. Co. 12 Mont 474, 31 P 87.

negative prescription. (Civil law.) The loss or forfeiture of a right, by the proprietor's neglecting to exercise or prosecute it during the whole period which the law hath declared to be sufficient to infer the loss of it. Townsend v Jemison (US) 9 How 407, 417, 13 L Ed 194, 198.

negative servitude. See **negative easement.**

negative statute (staṭ'ūt). A statute which forbids or prohibits.

negative testimony. See **negative evidence.**

negative use. The use of a trademark for no purpose other than to prohibit another from using it. United Drug Co. v Theodore Rectanus Co. 248 US 90, 63 L Ed 141, 39 S Ct 48.

negativing defenses. Unnecessary anticipation of defenses, indicating want of skill in pleading a cause of action. 41 Am J1st Pl § 87. Usually unnecessary and inadvisable in drawing an indictment. 27 Am J1st Indict § 63.
In indictments, matters of defense need not, as a rule, be negatived, and where the statute creating the offense contains exceptions or provisos, not so incorporated with the clauses of the statute defining the offense that they enter into its description and are inseparable from it, the indictment need not set out that the defendants do not come within the exceptions or negative the provisos, but where the exceptions are stated in the clause which defines the offense, and are so incorporated with it that one cannot be read without the other, or, if embodied in a subsequent clause, section, or statute, they are so incorporated with the words used to define the offense that they become a part of the definition, it is necessary, in the absence of statute, to negative them, so that the description of the offense in the indictment may correspond with the description and elements in the statute. United States v Cook (US) 17 Wall 168, 21 L Ed 538.

negativing exceptions. See **negativing defenses.**

negatoire. See **action negatoire.**

negatum (nē-gā'tum). Denied.

Ne gist en le bouche (ne jist on le boush). It does not lie in the mouth,—it is not for one to say.

neglect. Verb: To omit to do or perform some work, act, or duty, required in one's business or occupation, or required as a legal obligation, such as that of making a payment. Noun: Omission to act or perform.
The word does not generally imply carelessness or imprudence, but simply an omission to do or perform some work, duty or act. Rosenplaenter v Roessle, 54 NY 262, 268.

neglected child. A child not cared for in the manner that the circumstances justly demand whether the failure lies in a wilful or unintentional disregard of duty, comprehending not alone a denial of that which is necessary to satisfy ordinary physical needs, but also the affection, guidance, and consideration required for the development of moral principles and ethical concepts in the mind of the child. 31 Am J Rev ed Juv Ct § 37.
A minor child who is not supplied with necessary medical and surgical care is "neglected" so as to

subject the parents to the penalties imposed by law therefor. Eggleston v Landrum, 210 Miss 645, 50 So2d 364, 23 ALR2d 696.

An infant prevented by its parents from receiving a blood transfusion necessary to save its life or to prevent a permanent mental impairment is a "neglected child" within the meaning of a statute defining such child as one who "has not proper parental care" and authorizing transfer of custody of the child to an appointed guardian, although the parents have not failed in their duty in other respects. People ex rel. Wallace v Labrenz, 411 Ill 618, 104 NE2d 769, 30 ALR2d 1132.

neglect of child. The want of reasonable care of a child by the parent, that is, the omission of such steps as a reasonable parent would take, such as are usually taken in the ordinary experience of mankind, provided the parent has such means as would enable him to take the necessary steps. 39 Am J1st P & C § 104.

See **wilful neglect of child.**

neglect of duty. The omission of one to perform a duty resting upon him. The neglect or failure on the part of a public officer to do and perform a duty or duties laid on him as such by virtue of his office or required of him by law. State ex rel. Hardy v Coleman, 115 Fla 119, 155 So 129, 92 ALR 988.

See **gross neglect of duty.**

neglect to prosecute. See **want of prosecution.**

negligence. A word of broad significance which may not readily be defined with accuracy. Jamison v Encarnacion, 281 US 635, 74 L Ed 1082, 50 S Ct 440. The lack of due diligence or care. A wrong characterized by the absence of a positive intent to inflict injury but from which injury nevertheless results. Haser v Maryland Casualty Co. 78 ND 893, 53 NW2d 508, 33 ALR 1018. In the legal sense, a violation of the duty to use care. Fort Smith Gas Co. v Cloud (CA8 Ark) 75 F2d 413, 97 ALR 833. The failure to perform an established duty which proximately causes injury to the plaintiff. Northern Indiana Transit v Burk, 228 Ind 162, 89 NE2d 905, 17 ALR2d 572. The failure to exercise the degree of care demanded by the circumstances; the want of that care which the law prescribes under the particular circumstances existing at the time of the act or omission which is involved. The omission to do something which a reasonable man, guided by those considerations which ordinarily regulate human affairs, would do, or doing something which a prudent and reasonable man would not do. 38 Am J1st Negl § 2. More particularly, the failure of one owing a duty to another to do what a reasonable and prudent person would ordinarily have done under the circumstances, or doing what such person would not have done, which omission or commission is the proximate cause of injury to the other 38 Am J1st Negl § 2.

A negligent act is one from which an ordinarily prudent person would foresee such an appreciable risk of harm to others as to cause him not to do the act, or to do it in a more careful manner. Haralson v Jones Truck Lines, 223 Ark 813, 270 SW2d 892, 48 ALR2d 248.

What constitutes "operation" or "negligence in operation" within statute making owner of motor vehicle liable for negligence in its operation. Anno: 13 ALR2d 378.

negligence as a matter of law. An undisputed fact or facts, so conclusive of negligence in conduct or omission in violation of a standard of care which is clear in its requirements and in its application to the case, that there is no question to be submitted to the jury and the court must declare that negligence is established. 38 Am J1st Negl § 344.

See **negligence per se.**

negligence of bailee. The failure of a bailee to exercise that degree of diligence and care in respect to the property in his possession under the bailment which the nature of his employment, the character of the bailment, and the attendant circumstances make it reasonable to expect of him. 8 Am J2d Bailm § 198.

negligence per se (neg'li-jens per sē). Literally, that which is negligence in itself. Negligence without question, negligence involving no debatable issue as to its existence, because the law, ordinarily the law in the form of statute or ordinance, has established the duty of the defendant toward the plaintiff which has been violated by the defendant to the injury of the plaintiff. 38 Am J1st Negl § 158.

Negligence per se results from a breach of a positive standard of conduct imposed by statute. Lavalle v Kaupp, 240 Minn 360, 61 NW2d 223.

negligent. Being guilty of negligence.
See **negligence.**

negligent escape. An escape occurring without the consent of, but through the carelessness of, the officer entrusted with the custody of the prisoner. Adams v Turrentine, 30 NC (8 Ired L) 147, 150.

negligent homicide. Causing the death of a person, without apparent intent to kill, but in doing an unlawful act or performing a lawful act in a careless or negligent manner, the danger of causing death being apparent. Barfield v State, 118 Tex Crim 394, 43 SW2d 106. The offense under modern statutes of the operation of a motor vehicle in reckless disregard of the safety of others, thereby causing the death of another. 7 Am J2d Auto § 291. Gross or culpable negligence in operating or driving a vehicle of any kind whereby a person is killed. 7 Am J2d Auto § 292.

See **manslaughter.**

negligentia (neg-li-jen'she-a). (Civil law.) Negligence; carelessness.

Negligentia semper habet infortunium comitem (neg-li-jen'she-a sem'per hā'bet in-for-tū'ni-um ko'mi-tem). Negligence always has misfortune for a comrade.

negligent waste. Same as **permissive waste.**

negotiability. A technical term derived from the usage of merchants and bankers in transferring bills of exchange and promissory notes. 11 Am J2d B & N § 2. The most vital and distinctive characteristic of a negotiable instrument, the term importing a transferable quality in the instrument to which it is applied; a quality of easy or simple transferability by any possessor; a quality of transferability which permits the transferee to take free of equities and defenses which could be asserted against the transferor of the instrument. 11 Am J2d B & N § 2. A quality turning entirely upon the form of the instrument and the terms in which it is expressed. 11 Am J2d B & N § 2.

negotiable. Having the quality and requisites of negotiability. 11 Am J2d B & N § 2.

negotiable bill of lading. A bill of lading in which it is stated that the goods are consigned or destined to the order of any person named in such bill. Uniform Bills of Lading Act §§ 4, 5. A bill of lading according to the terms of which the goods are to be delivered to bearer or to the order of a named person, or where recognized in overseas trade, if it runs to a named person or assigns. UCC § 7–104.

negotiable bonds. Bonds issued by private corporations, payable to order or bearer, whether the interest coupons are attached or detached. 12 Am J2d Bonds § 51. Bonds issued by the United States, the states, municipalities, and other political subdivisions which are payable to order or bearer. 43 Am J1st Pub Sec § 161.

negotiable coupons. The interest coupons attached to bonds upon the issuance of the bonds, payable to order or bearer upon their face without reference to any other paper. 12 Am J2d Bonds § 56. 43 Am J1st Pub Sec § 164.

negotiable instrument. Literally, an instrument having the transferable quality known as negotiability. An instrument, constituting a valid contract, for the payment of money in a certain, definite sum, to order or bearer, on demand, at sight, or in a certain time, or on the happening of an event which must occur, and payable absolutely, not on a contingency. 11 Am J2d B & N § 56. An instrument in writing signed by the maker or drawer; containing an unconditional promise or order to pay a sum certain in money; payable on demand, or at a fixed or determinable future time; payable to order or to bearer; and where addressed to a drawee, the latter is named or otherwise indicated with reasonable certainty. Uniform Negotiable Instruments Law § 1; Anno: 44 ALR2d 57, § 11. An instrument signed by the maker or drawer; containing an unconditional promise or order to pay a sum certain in money and no other promise, order, obligation, or power given by the maker or drawer except as authorized by statute; payable on demand or at a definite time; and payable to order or to bearer. UCC § 3–104(1). A bill of exchange, draft, check, promissory note, certificate of deposit, bearer bond, or other instrument to which there is extended the quality of negotiability by the Uniform Commercial Code or other statute. 11 Am J2d B & N § 6.

Negotiable Instruments Act. An attempt to codify the entire field of the law of negotiable instruments. One of the uniform acts. A uniform act specifically repealed by the Uniform Commercial Code. 15 Am J2d Com C § 6. A form of statute promulgated in 1896 by the National Conference of Commissioners on Uniform State Laws, based on the British Bills of Exchange Act of 1882, it being an outgrowth of many years of effort on the part of bar associations, jurists, publicists, bankers, and responsible men of business generally to secure uniformity in the law relating to negotiable instruments. Adopted over a period of about 30 years in all of the states—in the majority of them substantially, if not exactly, in the form promulgated by the commissioners. 11 Am J2d B & N § 41. Presently in force in all states except where it has been superseded by the Uniform Commercial Code.

negotiable note. A promissory note having all the requisites of negotiability. Graphically, "a courier without luggage, whose countenance is its passport."
See **negotiable instrument.**

negotiable paper. See **negotiable instrument.**

negotiate. To effect a negotiation. To attempt to effect the negotiation of a contract.
See **negotiation of contract; negotiation of instrument.**

negotiation of contract. The carrying on of a correspondence by letters and telegrams or the conducting of conversations in attempting to arrive at an agreement and contract. 17 Am J2d Contr § 25. The advertising and bids in the award of a public contract.

An order having authorized a finance committee to "negotiate" notes for the city's benefit, the word "negotiate" was held to be sufficient to include the entire transaction of asking for bids, or ascertaining the discount by private inquiry, and of deciding on the amounts, the rate, and the time on which the notes should be given. Brown v Newburyport, 209 Mass 259, 95 NE 504.

negotiation of instrument. The transfer of a negotiable bill or note by a first or subsequent holder to a successor holder. 11 Am J2d B & N §§ 309, 310. The transfer of a negotiable instrument from one person to another in such manner as to constitute the transferee the holder thereof. Uniform Negotiable Instruments Law § 30. To indorse and deliver a bill or note to another so that the right of action thereon shall pass to the indorsee or holder. Weckler v First Nat. Bank, 42 Md 581. The transfer of a negotiable instrument in such manner as to preserve independence of equities on the part of the holder receiving it. 11 Am J2d B & N § 312. The transfer of a bill, note or any instrument in such form that the transferee becomes a holder. UCC § 3–202(1), and Comment 1. The transfer of a negotiable instrument in due course. Edgar v Haines, 109 Ohio St 159, 141 NE 837, 38 ALR 795.

There can be no "negotiation" of a nonnegotiable instrument. Tool v Anderson, 116 Ind 88, 18 NE 445.

negotiant (nẹ-gō'shi-ạnt). Same as negotiator.

negotiator. One who negotiates for the purpose of entering into a contract or agreement, sometimes one who specializes in conducting negotiations for others for the same purpose. Banta v Chicago, 172 Ill 204, 50 NE 233. The person who negotiates a negotiable bill or note.

negotiorum gestor (ne-gō-she-ō'rụm jes'tor). (Civil law.) A person who does business,—a self-appointed agent who assumed the transaction of the business of another person, with no authority to do so.

negotium (ne-gō'she-um). (Roman law.) Business; occupation; employment; a business transaction; a money transaction; an affair.

Negro. A person of the black race dominating in equatorial Africa. In some jurisdictions a person of mixed blood descended from Negro ancestry from the third generation inclusive, although one ancestor of each generation may have been a white person. Frasher v State, 3 Tex App 263.

The word as used in a miscegenation statute that does not define it, has been construed to mean only negroes of the full blood, and not octoroons, mulattoes, and persons of mixed blood. 35 Am J1st Mar § 146.

As to negro or colored person within restrictive covenant, see Anno: 3 ALR2d 494.

NE. Abbreviation of northeast.

N. E. I. An abbreviation of **Non est inventus.**

neife (nēf). A female villein. See 2 Bl Comm 94.

neighbor. One who lives near another, especially where there are friendly relations between them.

neighborhood. A region, area, or territory of local significance, characterized by people living in it as neighbors; a local community. State v Hughes, 82 Mo 86, 89.

As the term is used in the common-law definition of trial by jury, the members of which were summoned from the visne or neighborhood, the word means the county where the act was committed. See People v Powell, 87 Cal 348, 25 P 481.

neighborhood benefit. A benefit accruing from a public improvement to a certain definite district by reason of its location in reference to the improvement. 27 Am J2d Em D § 367.

neighborhood road. Indiana terminology; a public highway, under the jurisdiction of the local authorities, opened and kept in repair by the public, for which land may be taken under the right of eminent domain. Kissinger v Hanselman, 33 Ind 80, 81.

neighborhood school policy. The policy of school authorities under which all children to be educated in public schools are required to attend a public school in their neighborhood. Taylor v Board of Education (CA2 NY) 294 F2d 36, cert den 368 US 940, 7 L Ed 2d 339, 82 S Ct 382.

neighboring property. Adjoining property or property in the immediate vicinity.

ne injuste vexes (nē in-jus'tē vek'sēz). You may not oppress unjustly; an ancient writ in the nature of a writ of right which lay where the tenant in fee simple and his ancestors had held of the lord by certain services, and the lord had obtained seisin of more or greater services than were due, to reduce them to their proper standard. See 3 Bl Comm 234. See also State v Commissioner of Roads, 8 SCL (1 Mill Const) 55.

neither (nē'thėr or nī'thėr). Not one or the other of two persons or things.

ne luminibus officiatur (nē lū-mi'ni-bus of-fi-she-ā'ter). (Civil law.) An easement or servitude which entitled its owner to receive unobstructed light in his house.

nem. con. An abbreviation of **nemine contradicente**.

nemine contradicente (nem'i-nē kon"trạ-di-sen'tē). No one saying the contrary; none dissenting.

Neminem laedit qui jure suo utitur (nē'mi-nem lē'dit quī jū're su'ō ū'ti-ter). One who makes a lawful use of his own property thereby injures no one. Graham v St. Charles Street Railroad Co. 47 La Ann 214, 16 So 806.

Neminem oportet esse sapientiorem legibus (nē'mi-nem o-por'tet es'se sa-pi-en-she-ō'rem lē'ji-bus). No one ought to be wiser than the laws.

nemo (nē'mō). No man; no one; nobody.

Nemo admittendus est inhibilitare seipsum (nē'mō ad-mit-ten'dus est in-hi-bi-li-tā're sē'ip'sum). No one is permitted to stultify himself. Coody v Coody, 39 Okla 719, 136 P 754.

Nemo agit in seipsum (nē'mō ā'jit in sē-ip'sum). No one acts against himself.

Nemo alienae rei, sine satisdatione, defensor idoneus intelligitur (nē'mō ā-li-ē'nē rē'ī, sī'ne sa-tis-dā-she-ō'ne dē-fen'sor i-dō'ne-us in-tel-li'ji-ter). (Roman law.) No one is regarded as a property protector of the property of another, without security.

Nemo alieno nomine lege agere potest (nē'mō ā-li-ē'nō nō'mi-ne lē'je ā'je-re po'test). (Civil law.) No one can sue in the name of another.

Nemo aliquam partem recte intelligere potest, antequam totum iterum atque iterum perlegerit (nē'mō a'li-quam par'tem rek'tē in-tel-li'je-re pō'test, an'te-quam tō'tum i'te-rum at'kwe i'te-rum per-le'je-rit). No one can rightly understand any part before he has read over the whole again and again.

Nemo allegans suam turpitudinem audiendus est (nē'mō al'le-ganz su'am ter-pi-tu'di-nem â-di-en'dus est). No one should be permitted to testify as to his own baseness or wickedness. The United States v Leffler (US) 11 Pet 86, 94, 9 L Ed 642, 645.

Nemo allegans turpitudinem suam, est audiendus (nē'mō al'le-ganz ter-pi-tū'di-nem su'am, est â-di-en'dus). No one asserting his own wickedness should be heard. A Roman-law maxim. People v Coffey, 161 Cal 433, 119 P 901.

Nemo beneficium suum perdat, nisi secundum consuetudinem antecessorum nostrorum et per judicium parium suorum (nē'mō be-ne-fi'she-um su'um per'-dat, nī'sī se-kun'dum kon-su-ē-tū'di-nem an-te-ses-sō'rum nos-trō'rum et per jū-di'she-um pā'ri-um su-ō'rum). No one shall lose his right, unless according to the custom of our ancestors, and by the judgment of his peers. See 3 Bl Comm 350.

Nemo bis punitur pro eodem delicto (nē'mō bis pū'ni-ter pro ē-ō'dem de-lik'tō). No one is twice punished for the same offense. See 4 Bl Comm 315.

Nemo bis vexari pro eadem cause (nē'mō bis ve-xā'rī prō e-ā'dem kâ'za). No one is to be twice tried for the same cause. State v Lee, 65 Conn 265, 30 A 1110.

Nemo bis vexari pro una et eadem cause (nē'mō bis ve-xā'rī prō ū'na et e-ā'dem kâ'za). No one shall be twice tried for one and the same cause. United States v Throckmorton (US) 8 Otto 61, 25 L Ed 93.

Nemo cogitationis poenam patitur (nē'mō ko-ji-ta-she-ō'nis pe'nam pa'ti-ter). No one shall suffer punishment by reason of his thoughts.

Nemo cogitur rem suam vendere, etiam justo pretio (nē'mō kō'ji-ter rem su'am ven'de-re, ē'she-am jus'tō pre'she-ō). No one is compelled to sell his property, even at a fair price.

Nemo contra factum suum venire potest (nē'mō kon'trā fak'tum su'um ve-nī're po'test). No one can go against his own act or deed. New York Continental Jewel Filtration Co. v Jones, 37 App DC 511.

Nemo damnum facit, nisi qui id fecit quod facere jus non habet (nē'mō dam'num fā'sit, nī'sī quī id fē'sit quod fā'se-re jūs non hā'bet). No one does harm except the person who does that which he has no right to do.

Nemo dare potest quod non habet (nē'mō da're po'-test quod non hā'bet). No one is able to give that which he has not.

Nemo dat qui non habet (nē'mō dat quī non hā'bet). No one gives who has not. Hendrie v Sayles, 98 US 546, 25 L Ed 176.

Nemo dat quod non habet (nē'mō dat quod non hā'bet). No one can give that which he has not. Mitchell v Hawley (US) 16 Wall 544, 21 L Ed 322, 324.

Nemo debet aliena jactura locupletari (nē'mō de'bet ā-li-ē'na jak-tū'ra lo-ku-plē-tā'rī). No one ought to be enriched by the loss of another.

Nemo debet bis puniri pro uno delicto (nē'mō de'bet bis pū-nī'rī prō ū'nō de-lik'tō). No one ought to be punished twice for one offense.

Nemo debet bis vexari eadem causa (nē'mō de'bet bis ve-xā'rī ē-ā'dem kâ'za). No one ought to be twice tried for the same cause.

Nemo debet bis vexari pro eadem causa (nē'mō de'bet bis ve-xā'rī prō ē-ā'dem kâ'za). No one ought to be twice tried for the same cause. Womach v St. Joseph, 201 Mo 467, 100 SW 443.

Nemo debet bis vexari pro una et eadem causa (nē'mō de'bet bis ve-xā'rī prō ū'na et ē-ā'dem kâ'za). No one ought to be twice sued for one and the same cause. Hunt v Darling, 26 RI 480, 59 A 399.

Nemo debet bis vexari si constet curiae quod sit pro una et eadem causa (nē'mō de'bet bis ve-xā'rī sī kon'stet kū'ri-ē quod sit prō ū'na et e-ā'dem kâ'za). No one ought to be sued twice if it appears to the court that it is for one and the same cause.

Nemo debet esse judex in propria causa (nē'mō de'bet es'se jū'dex in prō'pri-a kâ'za). No one ought to be a judge in his own case. People v O'Brien, 111 NY 1, 18 NE 692.

Nemo debet ex alieno damno lucrari (nē'mō de'bet ex ā-li-ē'nō dam'nō lu-krā'rī). No one ought to profit out of the loss of another.

Nemo debet immiscere se rei alienae ad se nihil pertinenti (nē'mō de'bet im-mi'se-re sē rē'ī ā-li-ē'nē ad sē ni-hil per-ti-nen'tī). No one ought to obtrude himself in the business of another which is of no concern to himself.

Nemo debet in communione invitus teneri (nē'mō de'bet in kom-mū-ni-ō'ne in-vī'tus te-nē'rī). No one ought to be kept in a partnership against his will United Ins. Co. v Scott & Seaman (NY) 1 Johns 106, 113.

Nemo debet locupletari aliena jactura (nē'mō de'bet lo-kū-plē-tā'rī ā-li-ē'na jak-tū'ra). No one ought to be made rich by another's loss. Green v Biddle (US) 8 Wheat 1, 83, 5 L Ed 547, 567.

Nemo debet locupletari ex alterius incommodo (nē'mō de'bet lo-ku-plē-tā'rī ex al-te'ri-us in-kom'-mo-dō). No one ought to be enriched at the expense of another. Berry v Stigall, 253 Mo 690, 162 SW 126.

Nemo debet rem suam sine facto aut defectu suo amittere (nē'mō de'bet rem su'am sī'ne fak'tō ât dē-fek'tu su'ō a-mit'te-re). No one ought to lose his property without any fault of his own.

Nemo de domo sua extrahi debet (nē'mō de dō'mō su'a ex-tra'hī de'bet). (Civil law.) No one ought to be dragged out of his own house.

Nemo duobus utatur officiis (nē'mō du-ō'bus ū-tā'ter of-fi'she-is). No one should occupy two offices.

Nemo ejusdem tenementi simul potest esse haeres et dominus (nē'mō e-jūs'dem te-ne-men'tī si'mul po'test es'se hē'rēz et do'mi-nus). No one can be the heir and the lord of the same tenement at the same time.

Nemo enim aliquam partem recte intelligere possit antequam totum iterum atque iterum perlegerit (nē'mō e'nim a'li-quam par'tem rek'te in-tel-li'je-re pos'sit an'te-quam tō'tum i'te-rum at'kwe i'te-rum per-le'je-rit). No one can rightly understand any part before he has read the whole over and over again.

Nemo est haeres viventis (nē'mō est hē'rēz vī-ven'tis). No one is the heir of a person who is alive. Heath v Hewitt, 127 NY 166, 27 NE 959.

Nemo est supra leges (nē'mō est su'pra lē'jēz). No one is above the laws.

Nemo ex alterius facto praegravari debet (nē'mō ex al-te'ri-us fak'tō prē-gra-vā'rī de'bet). No one ought to be oppressed by the act of another.

Nemo ex consilio obligatur (nē'mō ex kon-si'li-ō ob-li-gā'ter). No one is obligated by reason of giving advice.

Nemo ex dolo suo proprio relevetur, aut auxilium capiat (nē'mō ex dō'lō su'ō prō'pri-ō re-le-vē'ter, ât âk-zi'li-um kā'pi-at). No one is relieved by, or gains advantage from, his own fraud.

Nemo ex proprio dolo consequitur actionem (nē'mō ex prō'pri-ō dō'lō kon-se'qui-ter ak-she-ō'nem). No one by his own fraud or wrong acquires a right of action. Wright v Orange & Passaic Valley Railway Co. 77 NJL 774, 73 A 517.

Nemo ex suo delicto meliorem suam conditionem facere potest (nē'mō ex su'ō de-lik'tō me-li-ō'rem su'am kon-di-she-ō'nem fā'se-re po'test). (Civil law.) No one can make his situation better by his own wrongful act. Whitlock v Auburn Lumber Co. 145 NC 120, 58 SE 909.

Nemo in alium potest transferre plus juris quam ipse habet (nē'mō in a'li-um po'test trans-fer're plus jū'ris quam ip'se hā'bet). No one can transfer to another any better right or title than he himself has.

Nemo inauditus condemnari debet, si non sit contumax (nē'mō in-â'di-tus kon-dem-nā'rī de'bet, sī non sit kon-tū'max). No one ought to be condemned, without having been heard, unless he is contumacious.

Nemo in propria causa judex esse debet (nē'mō in prō'pri-a kâ'za jū'dex es'se de'bet). No one ought to be a judge in his own cause.

Nemo in propria causa testis esse debet (nē'mō in prō'pri-a kâ'za tes'tis es'se de'bet). No one ought to be a witness in his own cause. Sesler v Montgomery, 78 Cal 486, 19 P 656.

Nemo invitus compellitur ad communionem (nē'mō in-vī'tus kom-pel'li-ter ad kom-mū-ni-ō'nem). No one who is unwilling is forced into a joint possession. See 2 Bl Comm 185.

Nemo jus sibi dicere potest (nē'mō jūs si'bi dī'se-re po'test). No one can establish law for himself.

Nemo miles adimatur de possessione sui beneficii, nisi convicta culpa, quae sit laudanda per judicium parium suorum (nē'mō mī'lez ad-i-mā'ter dē po-ze-she-ō'ne su'ī be-ne-fi'she-ī, nī'sī kon-vik'ta kul'pa, kwē sit lâ-dan'da per jū-di'she-um pa'ri-um su-ō'rum). No soldier is to be deprived of the possession of his benefice, unless convicted of wrongdoing, which must be declared by the judgment of his peers. 2 Bl Comm 285.

Nemo militans Deo implicetur secularibus negotiis (nē'mō mi'li-tanz dē'ō im-pli'sē-ter se-kū-lā'ri-bus ne-gō'she-is). No one engaged in fighting for God should be bothered by secular business.

Nemo nascitur artifex (nē'mō na'si-ter ar'ti-fex). No one is the born master of an art.

Nemo patriam in qua natus est exuere, nec ligeantiae debitum ejurare possit (nē'mō pa'tri-am in quā nā'tus est ex-u'e-re, nek li-je-an'she-ē dē'bi-tum e-jū-rā're pos'sit). No one can renounce his native country, nor abjure his obligation of allegiance. Inglis v Trustees of Sailor's Snug Harbor (US) 3 Pet 99, 7 L Ed 617.

Nemo plus commodi heredi suo relinquit quam ipse habuit (nē'mō plus kom'mo-dī he'rē-dī su'ō re-lin'-quit quam ip'se hā'bu-it). (Civil law.) No one leaves behind a greater advantage for his heir than he himself had.

Nemo plus juris ad alienum transferre potest, quam ipse habet (nē'mō plus jū'ris ad ā-li-ē'num trans-fer're po'test, quam ip'se hā'bet). No one can transfer to another any greater right than he himself has.

Nemo plus juris in alium transferre potest quam ipse habet (nē'mō plus jū'ris in a'li-um trans-fer're po'test quam ip'se hā'bet). No one can convey a better title than he himself has. Wasserman v Metzger, 105 Va 744, 54 SE 893.

This was a maxim of the civil law, and it is a principle of the English common law that a sale out of market overt did not change the property from the rightful owner. Ventress v Smith (US) 10 Pet 161, 175, 9 L Ed 382, 387.

Nemo potest contra recordum verificare per patriam (nē'mō po'test kon'trā re-kor'dum ve-ri-fi-kā're per pa'tri-am). No one can prove by the country contrary to a record.

Nemo potest esse dominus et haeres (nē'mō po'test es'se do'mi-nus et hē'rēz). No one can be both owner and heir.

Nemo potest esse et dominus et tenens (nē'mō po'test es'se et do'mi-nus et te'nenz). No one can be both landlord and tenant. Liebschutz v Moore, 70 Ind 142.

Nemo potest esse simul actor et judex (nē'mō po'test es'se si'mul ak'tor et jū'dex). No one can be both the plaintiff and the judge at the same time.

Nemo potest esse tenens et dominus (nē'mō po'test es'se te'nenz et do'mi-nus). No one can be both the tenant and the landlord.

Nemo potest exuere patriam (nē'mō po'test ex-ū'e-re pā'tri-am). No one can renounce his country. Inglis v Trustees of Sailor's Snug Harbor (US) 3 Pet 99, 159, 7 L Ed 617, 638.

Nemo potest facere per alium quod per se non potest (nē'mō po'test fā'se-re per a'li-um quod per sē non po'test). No one can do through another that which he cannot do by himself.

Nemo potest facere per obliquum quod non potest facere per directum (nē'mō po'test fā'se-re per ob-lī'qu-um quod non po'test fā'se-re per dī-rek'tum). No one can do by circumlocution that thing which he is not permitted to do directly. Cummings v Missouri (US) 4 Wall 277, 18 L Ed 356, 363.

Nemo potest mutare consilium suum in alterius injuriam (nē'mō po'test mū-tā're kon-si'li-um su'um in al-te'ri-us in-jū'ri-am). No one can change his purpose to the injury of another.

Nemo potest patriam exuere (nē'mō po'test pā'tri-am ex-ū'e-re). No one can cast off his country. See 1 Bl Comm 370.

Nemo potest plus juris ad alium transferre quam ipse habet (nē'mō po'test plus jū'ris ad a'li-um trans-fer're quam ip'se hā'bet). No one can convey or transfer to another any greater right than he himself has.

Nemo potest sibi debere (nē'mō po'test si'bi de-bē're). No one can be indebted to himself.

Nemo praesens nisi intelligat (nē'mō prē'senz nī'sī in-tel'li-gat). No one is present unless he understands.

Nemo praesumitur alienam posteritatem suae praetulisse (nē'mō prē-zu'mi-ter ā-li-ē'nam pos-te-ri-tā'tem su'ē prē-tu-lis'se). No one is presumed to have preferred the posterity of another person to his own.

Nemo praesumitur donare (nē'mō prē-zu'mi-ter dō-nā're). No one is presumed to have made a gift. Haven v Foster, 9 Mass (9 Pick) 112.

Nemo praesumitur esse immemor suae aeternae salutis, et maxime in articulo mortis (nē'mō prē-zu'mi-ter es'se im'me-mor su'ē ē-ter'nē sa-lū'tis, et ma'xi-mē in ar-ti'ku-lō mor'tis). No one is presumed to be unmindful of his own eternal salvation, and especially at the point of death.

Nemo praesumitur ludere in extremis (nē'mō prē-zu'mi-ter lū'de-re in ex-trē'mis). No one is presumed to be jesting while at the point of death.

Nemo praesumitur malus (nē-mō prē-zu'mi-ter ma'-lus). No one is presumed to be wicked.

Nemo prohibetur plures negotiationes sive artes exercere (nē'mō pro-hi-bē'ter plū'rēz ne-gō-she-ā-she-ō'nēz sī've ar'tēz ex-er'sē-re). No one is prohibited from engaging in several or various businesses or arts.

Nemo prohibetur pluribus defensionibus uti (nē'mō pro-hi-bē'ter plū'ri-bus de-fen-she-ō'ni-bus u'tī). No one is prohibited from employing several defenses.

Nemo prudens punit ut praeterita revocentur, sed ut futura praeveniantur (nē'mō prū'denz pū'nit ut prē-te'ri-ta re-vō-sen'ter, sed ut fu-tū'ra prē-ve-ni-an'ter). No prudent person punishes in order that past transactions may be revoked, but he does so in order that future acts may be prevented.

Nemo punitur pro alieno delicto (nē'mō pū'ni-ter prō ā-li-ē'nō de-lik'tō). No one is punished for the crime of another.

Nemo punitur sine injuria, facto, seu defalta (nē'mō pū'ni-ter sī'ne in-jū'ri-a, fak'tō, sū dē-fal'ta). No one is punished without some wrong, act, or fault.

Nemo qui condemnare potest, absolvere non potest (nē'mō quī kon-dem-nā're po'test, ab-sol've-re non po'test). No one who can convict is unable to acquit.

Nemo sibi esse judex vel suis jus dicere debet (nē'mō si'bi es'se jū'dex vel su'is jūs dī'se-re de'bet). No one ought to be his own judge or to lay down the law for his own family.

Nemo sine actione experitur, et hoc non sine breve sive libello conventionali (nē'mō sī'ne ak-she-ō'ne ex-pe'ri-ter, et hōk non sī'ne brē've si've li-bel'lō kon-ven-she-ō-nā'lī). No one goes to law without a cause of action, and he does not do so without a writ or bill.

Nemo suo statuto ligatur necessitative (nē'mō sū'ō sta-tū'tō li-gā'ter ne-ses-si-tā-tī've). It is inevitable that no one can break his own statute. Kawananakoa v Polyblank, 205 US 349, 353, 51 L Ed 834, 836, 27 S Ct 526.

Nemo tenebatur prodere seipsum (nē′mō te-nē-bā′ter prō′de-re sē-ip′sum). No one was bound to appear against himself. See 4 Bl Comm 296.

Nemo tenetur ad impossibile (nē′mō te-nē′ter ad im-pos-si′bi-le). No one is bound to that which is impossible.

Nemo tenetur ad impossibilia (nē′mō te-nē′ter ad im-pos-si-bi′li-a). No one is bound to do things which are impossible.

Nemo tenetur armare adversarium contra se (nē′mō te-nē′ter ar-mā′re ad-ver-sā′ri-um kon′trā sē). No one is bound to arm his adversary against himself.

Nemo tenetur armare adversarium suum contra se (nē′mō te-nē′ter ar-mā′re ad-ver-sā′ri-um sū′um kon′trā sē). No one is bound to arm his adversary against himself. Larson v Salt Lake City, 34 Utah 318, 97 P 483.

Nemo tenetur divinare (nē′mō te-nē′ter di-vi-nā′re). No one is bound to divine the future.

Nemo tenetur edere instrumenta contra se (nē′mō te-nē′ter e′de-re in-stru-men′ta kon′trā sē). (Roman law.) No one is bound to produce instruments or writings which are against himself.

Nemo tenetur informare qui nescit, sed quisquis scire quod informat (nē′mō te-nē′ter in-for-mā′re quī ne′-sit, sed quis′quis sī′re quod in-for′mat). No one who is ignorant is bound to give information, but everyone is bound to know that concerning which he gives information.

Nemo tenetur jurare in suam turpitudinem (nē′mō te-nē′ter jū-rā′re in su′am ter-pi-tū′di-nem). No one is bound to give testimony in regard to his own turpitude.

Nemo tenetur prodere seipsum (nē′mō te-nē′ter prō′de-re sē-ip′sum). No one is bound to betray himself.

nemo tenetur seipsum accusare (nē′mō te-nē′ter se-ip′sum a-ku-zā′re). No one shall be compelled to accuse himself. 58 Am J1st Witn § 36.

Nemo tenetur seipsum infortuniis et periculis exponere (nē′mō te-nē′ter sē-ip′sum in-for-tū′ni-is et pe-ri′ku-lis ex-pō′ne-re). No one is bound to expose himself to misfortunes and dangers.

Nemo tenetur seipsum prodere (nē′mō te-nē′ter sē-ip′sum prō′de-re). No one is bound to betray himself. Ex parte Senior, 37 Fla 1, 19 So 652.

Nemo testis esse debet in propria causa (nē′mō tes′tis es′se de′bet in prō′pri-a kâ′za). No one ought to be a witness in his own cause. See 3 Bl Comm 371.

Nemo unquam judicet in se (nē′mō un′quam jū′di-set in sē). No one ever renders a decision in his own case.

Nemo unquam vir magnus fuit sine aliquo divino afflatu (nē′mō un′quam vir mag′nus fu′it sī′ne a′li-quō di-vi′nō af-flā′tū). No one was ever a great man without some divine inspiration.

Nemo videtur fraudare eos qui sciunt, et consentiunt (nē′mō vi-dē′ter frâ-dā′re ē′ōs quī si′unt, et kon-sen′she-unt). (Civil law.) No one is deemed to defraud those persons who have knowledge and give their consent.

nemy. Not

neon (nē′on). A colorless and inert gas.

neon sign (nē′on sīn). An advertising sign characterized by illumination by the use of tubes filled with neon.

nephew. The son of one's brother or sister. A relative in the third degree according to the civil-law method of computing degrees of kinship which prevails in most American jurisdictions. 23 Am J2d Desc & D § 48. As used in a will, sometimes, but not always, inclusive of a grandnephew. 57 Am J1st Wills § 1390.

nephews and nieces. The immediate male and female descendants of the brother or sister of the person named; not inclusive of grand-nephews and grand-nieces or more remote descendants. Estate of Woodward, 117 NY 522, 23 NE 120. Sometimes construed as inclusive, at other times as exclusive, of the half blood, the construction depending upon the context of the instrument in which the term appears. Anno: 49 ALR2d 1375.

ne plus ultra (nē plus ul′trā). Not to be exceeded. The highest. The greatest.

nepotism (nep′ọ-tizm). The appointment to public office or public position of a person related within a degree prescribed by statute to the appointing officer or his associate in office. 42 Am J1st Pub Of § 98.

Neque leges neque senatus consulta ita scribi possunt ut omnis casus qui quandoque in sediriunt comprehendatur; sed sufficit ea quae plaerumque accidunt contineri (nē′kwe lē′jēz nē′kwe se-nā′tus kon-sul′ta i′ta skrī′bī pos′sunt ut om′nis kā′sus kwī kwan-dō′kwe in sē-dī′ri-unt kom-prē-hen-dā′tur sed suf′fi-sit ē′a kwē plē-rum′quē ak′si-dunt kon-tin-ē′rī). Neither laws nor acts of a legislature can be so written as to include all actual or possible cases; but it is sufficient if they provide for those things which frequently or ordinarily may happen. State v Butts, 111 Fla 630, 149 So 746, 89 ALR 946.

Neque verbis praescriptis solemnibus vestitum est, neque facto aut datione rei transit in contractum innominatum (nē′kwe ver′bis prē-skrip′tis so-lem′-ni-bus ves-tī′tum est, ne′kwe fak′tō ât da-she-ō′ne rē′ī tranz′it in kon-trak′tum in-no-mi-nā′tum). That which has neither been clothed in prescribed, solemn words, nor by any act or matter of gift, passes into an implied contract. See 2 Bl Comm 445.

Ne quid respublica detrimenti capiat. (Latin.) That the state suffer no harm.

Ne quis plus donasse praesumatur quam in donatione expresserit (nē quis plus do-nās′se prē-zu-mā′ter quam in dō-nā-she-ō′ne ex-pres′se-rit). Lest anyone should be presumed to have given more than he expressed in his grant.

ne recipiatur (nē re-si-pi-ā′ter). Lest it should be received,—a caveat or caution given to an officer by one of the parties to an action instructing him not to receive the papers of an adverse party.

Ne Rector Prosternet Arbores (nē rek′tor pro-ster′-net ar-bo′rēz). The rector is not to fell trees,—the title of an English statute enacted in the reign of Edward the First, directed against the felling of trees in churchyards by parsons.

ne relesse pas (nuh rĕ-lĕss pah). He did not release.

nervous disorder. An affliction of the nervous system.

nervous shock. Agitation and emotional tension of an acute nature, for the time rendering one incapable of deliberate action, sometimes operating through parts of the physical organism to produce bodily illness. Dulieu v White & Sons (Eng) 2 KB 669, 17 Times L R 555.

net. Noun: A device woven from cord or string and used to catch fish. 35 Am J2d Fish § 47.That which remains after the deduction of all charges or outlay, as net profit. St. John v Erie Railway Company (US) 22 Wall 136, 22 L Ed 743. Adjective: Characterizing that which is left after deductions.

net balance. As applied to the proceeds of a sale, the balance of the proceeds after deducting the expenses incident to the sale. Evans v Waln, 71 Pa St 69, 74.

net capital stock. The difference between the total assets and the total liabilities of a corporation.
It may be in the form of three items: (1) Capital, which represents the original amount contributed in money or property or services; (2) surplus, which represents the earlier undistributed profits; and (3) undivided profits, which are the later, and usually smaller, undistributed profits. Anno: 45 ALR 1505.

net cash. Cash without the allowance of a discount. Dow Chemical Co. v Detroit Chemical Works, 208 Mich 157, 175 NW 269, 14 ALR 1200. The price of an article after discount deducted. The condition of payment by the purchaser before the seller is under obligation to deliver. 46 Am J1st Sales § 202.

net cash ten days. Payment due ten days from delivery of the goods to the purchaser. 46 Am J1st Sales § 202.

net earnings. The gross receipts of a business less operating expenses. A term often considered as the equivalent of net profits.
See **net profits**.

net estate. The estate of a decedent after deduction of debts, funeral expenses, and expenses of administration.
A statutory provision that the share of a testator's widow electing to take against the will shall not exceed one-third of his "net" personal estate, refers to that part of the estate which remains after payment of all charges against the entire estate including federal estate taxes. Re Uihlein's Will, 264 Wis 362, 59 NW2d 641, 38 ALR2d 961.
See **taxable estate**.

net gains. Profits; net earnings; the excess of receipts over expenditures. Connolly v Davidson, 15 Minn 519.

nether house of parliament (neth'ẽr hous of pär'lĭ-mẹnt). The lower house, the house of commons of the English parliament.

net income. Income by way of earnings, interest, or rent after the payment of taxes, insurance, expenses of maintenance and repairs, etc. Anno: 128 ALR 234.
See **taxable income**.

net income, proceeds, and profits. For most purposes, nothing more nor less than "net income." Dumaine v Dumaine, 301 Mass 214, 16 NE2d 625, 118 ALR 834.

net operating loss. A tax-law term for the excess of deductions, subject to certain statutory modifications, over the gross income. Mesaba-Cliffs Mining Co. v Commissioner (CA6) 177 F2d 201.

net operating loss carry over. A net operating loss sustained in one year used to reduce the taxable income of another year. IRC § 832(c)(10).

net premium. The amount of the premium on a life insurance policy less the dividend to which the insured is entitled. Technically, the cost of insurance; the premium charged less the loading for expenses and certain contingencies. Fox v Mutual Ben. Life Ins. Co. (CA8 Mo) 107 F2d 715.

net price. The price of real estate, stock, or grain, sold by a broker, in excess of the commissions of the broker and other expenses of sale.

net proceeds of sale. The proceeds of a sale less charges which may rightfully be deducted by the custodian or agent making the sale. Becker Steel Co. v Cummings, 296 US 74, 80 L Ed 54, 56 S Ct 15.

net profit. The difference between the end cost of a commodity or a security and the selling price after allowing for the expenses of sale. The gain which accrues on an investment after deducting expenses and losses. MacCulsky v Klosterman, 20 Or 108, 25 P 366. In the language of a bookkeeper, the balance which remains after deduction from gross earnings or profits. Harvey v Missouri Valley Electric Co. (Mo) 268 SW2d 820, 49 ALR2d 1124. The net earnings of a corporation applied to the payment of dividends to stockholders. 19 Am J2d Corp § 805.
The meaning of this term varies according to the context in which and the circumstances under which the words are used. Harvey v Missouri Valley Electric Co. (Mo) 268 SW2d 820, 49 ALR2d 1124.

net rental. Rental over and above all expenses. Perkins v Kirby, 39 RI 343, 97 A 884.

net rents, issues, income and profits. For most purposes, the same as net income. Ash v Ash, 126 NJ Eq 531, 10 A2d 150.

net return. Net income; net profit.
The "net return" of a bond purchased for a specified amount, is the interest paid on such bond increased or diminished by such an amount added or deducted at the time of each interest payment as will restore the purchase price to par at the maturity of the bond. Anno: 48 ALR 692.

net revenues. For most purposes, the same as net income. Re Joy, 247 Mich 418, 225 NW 878, 72 ALR 973. Tax collections less the cost of collection.

net succession. A term found in some inheritance tax statutes. The value of the property remaining for the beneficiary after the satisfaction of such charges and burdens as may be lawfully satisfied in due course of administration. Estate of Hite, 159 Cal 392, 113 P 1072.

net weight. The weight of a shipment of goods less the weight of containers, boxing, crating, chains, and the like. State ex rel. Washington Mill Co. v Great Northern Railway Co. 43 Wash 658, 86 P 1056.

net worth method. A method of calculating the income of a person whose records are inadequate; establishing a net worth of the person as of the beginning of a year, subtracting such amount from the amount established as his net worth at the end of the year, and repeating such calculation for each succeeding year of the period under examination. Holland v United States, 348 US 121, 99 L Ed 150, 75 S Ct 127.

ne unques accouple (nē un'quēz a-kou'pl). Never married.

ne unques administrator (nē un'quēz ad-mi'nis-trā-tor). No such administrator; an anciently recognized plea which put in issue the fact of administratorship. Roberts v White, 32 RI 185, 78 A 497.

ne unques executor. No such executor; an anciently recognized plea which put in issue the fact of executorship. Roberts v White, 32 RI 185, 78 A 497.

ne unques receivour (nē un'quēz re-sā-voer). No such receiver.

Ne unques seisie que dower (nē un'quēz sā'zē ke dow'er). He was never seised so that dower could attach.

Ne unques son receiver (nē un'quēz son re-sē'ver). He was never his receiver.

neurasthenia (nū-ras-thē'ni-ạ). A nervous condition characterized by depression, worry, and pains having no apparent cause. Colorado Springs & I. R. Co. v Nichols, 41 Colo 272, 92 P 691.
See **traumatic neurasthenia.**

neurological examination. A medical examination conducted by a neurologist. 23 Am J2d Dep § 299.

neurologist (nū-rol'ọ-jist). A specialist in the medical field of neurology.

neurology (nū-rol'ọ-ji). That branch of medicine which is concerned with the nervous system and diseases thereof.

neurosis (nū-rō'sis). A mental disorder characterized by unwarranted anxiety, sometimes by obsession; less than a pronounced disorganization. A mental affliction without serious derangement but which may constitute total disability. 29A Am J Rev ed Ins § 1525.

neutral. A country observing neutrality as to a war between two or more other nations. 56 Am J1st War §§ 217 et seq. The position of the gears in a motor vehicle at which the engine is disengaged so as not to be applying force in the movement of the vehicle.

neutrality. Taking no part in a dispute between others. Abstinence of a nation from any participation in a public, private, or civil war, and impartiality of conduct toward both parties. The Three Friends, 166 US 1, 41 L Ed 897, 17 S Ct 495.
While a neutral yields to other nations the unobstructed exercise of their sovereign or belligerent rights, her own dignity and security require of her the vindication of her own sovereign right to remain a peaceable and impartial spectator of the war. The Samtissima Trinidad (US) 7 Wheat 283, 5 L Ed 454.

neutralization of risk. Taking out an annuity contract and a life insurance contract in combination. Fidelity-Philadelphia Trust Co. v Smith, 356 US 274, 2 L Ed 2d 765, 78 S Ct 730.
See **hedging.**

neutral port. The port of a neutral nation in time of war between two or more other nations.

neutron (nū'tron). A particle of an atom.

ne varietur (nē va-ri-ē'ter). Lest it be changed. A mark or annotation placed on an instrument by a notary public by way of identification of the instrument. 11 Am J2d B & N § 193.

never indebted. The general issue pleaded in an action of debt on simple contract.

new. Newly made, recently manufactured; not previously used. Ajax Petroleum Products Co. v Blake (App) 70 Ohio L Abs 1, 126 NE2d 926.

new acquisition. A nonancestral estate; an estate acquired by purchase. Gray v Chapman, 122 Okla 130, 243 P 522.

new action. A subsequent action between the same parties and involving the same subject matter, brought following a prior dismissal.

new and further disability. A physical disability occurring after a period of disability. 58 Am J1st Workm Comp § 501.
A permanent disability, resulting after a period of temporary disability, has been held to constitute a "new and further disability" within the meaning of the provision permitting the filing of a claim for any new and further disability within a specified period. Cowell Lime & Cement Co. v State Industrial Com. 211 Cal 154, 294 P 703, 72 ALR 1118.

new and useful art. The subject of a patent to the same extent as a piece of machinery; a new and beneficial process of treating materials so as to produce a given result. O'Reilly v Morse (US) 15 How 62, 133, 14 L Ed 601, 632.
As the term is employed in the patent laws, it includes the word "method," which may be used interchangeably with the word "process." Honolulu Oil Corp. v Halliburton, 306 US 550, 83 L Ed 980, 59 S Ct 662.

new assignment. A repleading of the plaintiff's cause of action in different form to meet a plea which shows the declaration to be ambiguous; a restatement, with greater particularity and exactness, of the same cause of action already set up in the complaint or declaration. Bishop v Travis, 51 Minn 183, 185, 53 NW 461.

new building. A structure new from the ground up. A building, constructed in part from an older building but so entirely changed in plan, structure, dimensions, and general appearance as to become in a fair sense and according to the common understanding of men, another building. Mayville v Rosing, 19 ND 98, 123 NW 393.

new cause of action. A phrase applied in determining the application of a statute of limitations to an amended pleading. A cause of action based upon a state of facts different from those in the original pleading, a cause of action pleaded in behalf of parties not named in the original pleading, or a cause of action which embraces both such features. Love v Southern Railway Co. 108 Tenn 104, 65 SW 475.

new consideration. A consideration in addition to the consideration for the original contract, furnished on extension, renewal, or modification of the contract. 11 Am J2d B & N § 917; 17 Am J2d Contr § 460.

new contract. A contract which modifies or supersedes a prior contract. 17 Am J2d Contr § 459.

new domicil. A domicil acquired upon the relinquishment of a former domicil.

new edition. Copyrighted material to which new and original matter has been added. 18 Am J2d Copyr § 42.

New England town. A cluster of inhabitants dwelling near each other and possessing the power to manage their own prudential affairs. Hill v Boston, 122 Mass 344. Demonstrating democracy in action in its town meeting.

new enterprise. Within the meaning of a statute granting a tax exemption, a business or establishment created anew, not one which has merely come into the hands of a new owner or one which, although clothed in the dress of a new corporation, actually was built upon the ruins of an old corporation in liquidation and carries on the same business as the liquidated corporation. Continental Tobacco Co. v Louisville, 123 Ky 173, 94 SW 11.

new evidence. See **newly discovered evidence.**

new for old. See **one third new for old.**

new lease. A term of significance in the law of landlord and tenant.

Under an agreement among the executor of a lessor, the lessee, and one who desired to acquire the residue of the term, that the lessee should be released from liability, the lease surrendered, and a "new lease" executed for the residue of the term "on the same terms and conditions in all respects" as the original lease, the phrase "new lease" is referable to the document and not to the agreement creating the relation of landlord and tenant; hence, the new tenant is entitled to a lease containing the same option to purchase as was in the original lease. 32 Am J1st L & T § 308.

newly acquired vehicle. A term familiar in automobile insurance policies extending the coverage, within limitations, beyond the specific vehicle designated in the policy to a vehicle acquired after the inception of the policy. 7 Am J2d Auto Ins §§ 100 et seq.

newly discovered assets. Assets of a bankrupt coming to light after the closing of the estate in bankruptcy. Assets of a bankrupt which the bankrupt did not schedule, and which should have been administered for the benefit of the creditors. 9 Am J2d Bankr § 1273.

newly discovered evidence. Evidence discovered after verdict or decision. As ground for new trial:—evidence discovered since the trial, which could not have been discovered before the trial by the exercise of due diligence, and which is material to the issue, and not merely cumulative or impeaching. 39 Am J1st New Tr § 158.

"New proof," to be available in a bill of review, must be such as could not have been discovered before the hearing by the exercise of reasonable diligence. Ketchum v Breed, 66 Wis 85, 26 NW 271.

Facts or evidence forgotten at trial as newly discovered evidence which will warrant grant of new trial in civil case. Anno: 50 ALR2d 994.

new matter. That which, in defense, the defendant must plead affirmatively and prove. 29 Am J2d Ev § 129; 41 Am J1st Pl § 156. Acts, transactions, or happenings which occurred subsequent to those complained of by the plaintiff and which do not form a part of the original contract or transaction but are independent of it. 41 Am J1st Pl § 156. Whatever fact, if proved, would not tend to contradict the plaintiff's pleading, but would tend to establish some circumstance, transaction, or conclusion of fact not inconsistent with the truth of all the allegations in such pleading. Baldwin Locomotive Works v Edward Hines Lumber Co. 189 Ind 189, 125 NE 400, 127 NE 275, 13 ALR 1059.

new promise. A promise in addition to, or substituted for, the promise in an original agreement. 17 Am J2d Contr §§ 459 et seq. A promise made in writing by a debtor to his creditor after the cause of action is barred by the statute of limitations, to revive it, or before the action is barred, to keep it alive. Hellman v Kiene, 73 Iowa 448, 35 NW 516.

new proof. See **newly discovered evidence.**

news. Information, particularly information recently discovered or ascertained. Reports of recent occurrences of varied character, covering political, social, moral, religious, and other subjects, local or foreign, intended for the information of the general reader. Apparently authentic reports of current events of interest. 39 Am J1st Newsp § 2.

News is not always synonymous with facts, in the sense of verity. Much news ultimately proves fictitious, yet it is news notwithstanding. The word means no more (laying aside hoaxing and intentional falsehood) than apparently authentic reports of current events of interest. Associated Press v International News Service (CA2 NY) 245 F 244, 2 ALR 317, 318.

news company. A company engaged in the distribution of newspapers, magazines, other periodicals, and news sheets to stores which retail such publication.

new series. The continuation of a publication, such as the Atlantic Reporter or the American Law Reports, with new numbering of volumes and usually with some change in format.

new servitude. Same as **additional servitude.**

newspaper. A publication appearing at regular, or almost regular, intervals at short periods of time, as daily or weekly, usually in sheet form, and containing news, that is, reports of happenings of recent occurrence of a varied character, such as political, social, moral, religious, and other subjects of a similar nature, local or foreign, intended for the information of the general reader. 39 Am J1st Newsp § 2.

See **official newspaper.**

newspaper notice. A notice prepared for and published in a newspaper. The acclaim or criticism of the performance of an actor, musician, or dancer.

newspaper of general circulation. A newspaper of a state, county, city, or town, published for the dissemination of local or telegraphic news and intelligence of a general character, having a subscription list of paying subscribers, and established, printed, and published at regular intervals in such state, city, or town, and reaching all classes of the public. Anno: 68 ALR 547 (statutory definition). A newspaper which circulates at least to some extent among the general public, although it may be devoted to the interests of a particular class of persons and specialize in news and intelligence primarily of interest to that class. 39 Am J1st Newsp § 8. A newspaper which is not restricted to one county, or necessarily restricted to the state itself. State v Koen, 35 Neb 676, 53 NW 595.

A statute exempting "newspapers" from the operation of a sales tax has reference to the natural, plain, and ordinary significance of the word in general and common usage, and does not include magazines or periodicals. Gasson v Gay (Fla) 49 So 2d 525, 21 ALR2d 412.

Newspaper Publicity Law. The act of Congress requiring proprietors of newspapers, magazines, periodicals, etc., to file semi-annual sworn statements with the postmaster general and the local postmaster giving information as to the management, ownership, editorial department, the number of paying subscribers and other data, requiring publication of the statement and denying the use of the mails as a penalty for non-compliance. 39 Am J1st Newsp § 25.

newsstand. A small structure, sometimes not more than a table or desk, located in a hotel or public building, sometimes on the sidewalk in a downtown section, at which newspapers, magazines, racing forms, etc. may be purchased.

new style calendar. The modern calendar. The Gregorian calendar.

New Talys. See **Novae Narrationes**.

new trial. A re-examination of an issue of fact by the trial court with a view to correcting errors which have occurred in the course of the former trial. State v Burns, 312 Mo 673, 280 SW 1026, 44 ALR 848. A re-examination in the same court of an issue of fact after a verdict by a jury, a report of a referee or master, or a decision by the court. 39 Am J1st New Tr § 2. A remedy sought by motion made in the same action. 39 Am J1st New Tr § 186.

new trial on appeal. A new trial or trial de novo with limitations.
The normal review on appeal or by error proceeding is confined to consideration of the record below, with no new testimony taken or issues raised in the appellate court, the tendency being to limit appellate courts of final jurisdiction in their consideration of questions of facts. 4 Am J2d A & E § 1. The nearest approach to a complete trial de novo on appeal is in an appeal or error proceeding taken from a decree in equity, where the appellate court can make independent findings of fact, drawing its own conclusions from the evidence, but even in this instance the review is limited to a consideration of the record made in the lower court. 5 Am J2d A & E § 703.

new work. (Civil law.) Structures erected on land; improvements; alterations or additions which have been constructed on structures previously erected.
See **extra work**.

nexi (ne'xī). (Roman law.) Debtors who were held in bondage by their creditors as security for their debts.

next blood relations. Words of purchase, as synonymous with "children." McCann v McCann, 197 Pa 452, 47 A 743.

next business day. The secular or business day following a Sunday or a holiday. Uniform Negotiable Instruments L § 194. Within the meaning of the limitation of time for a drawee bank to determine whether or not it will pay a check presented for payment:—until midnight of the next business day following the day of presentment of the check. Rock Finance Co. v Central Nat. Bank, 339 Ill App 319, 89 NE2d 828.

next election. See **election to fill vacancy in office**.

next friend. The person through whom an infant maintains or defends a suit in the absence of a guardian or guardian ad litem. 27 Am J1st Inf §§ 113 et seq. Not a party to the action so as to be subject to interrogation under Rule 33 of the Federal Rules of Civil Procedure. Ju Shu Cheung v Dulles (DC Mass) 16 FRD 550.

next heirs. A term of art, ordinarily constituting words of limitation. Hamilton v Sidwell, 131 Ky 428, 115 SW 204; Price v Griffin, 150 NC 523, 64 SE 372; Davenport v Eskew, 69 SC 292, 48 SE 223.

next legal heirs. A term of art, ordinarily constituting words of limitation.
See **next heirs**.

next of kin. Those persons nearest in degree of blood relationship to whom the personal property of an intestate is distributed. 23 Am J2d Desc & D § 43. Strictly speaking, not synonymous with "heirs," who take the real estate of an intestate, although sometimes referred to as such. Tillman v Davis, 95 NY 17. Sometimes implying those persons who are entitled to the property of an estate whether they in fact bear any blood relationship or not. Wilcoxon v Owen, 237 Ala 169, 185 So 897, 125 ALR 539. As the term appears in a will:—the nearest blood relatives of the testator, except as the context of the will, properly construed in the light of the surrounding circumstances, indicates a broader significance, 57 Am J1st Wills § 1375; ordinarily inclusive of persons of the half blood. Anno: 49 ALR2d 1372. As used in a workmen's compensation act, nearest in degree of relationship. 58 Am J1st Workm Comp § 171. In respect to preference in appointment as administrator, ordinarily those persons who take the personal estate of the deceased under the statutes of distribution. 31 Am J2d Ex & Ad § 53.
The Massachusetts rule is that the term "next of kin," as used in a will, means the nearest blood relatives of the designated person, rather than those who would take under the statute of distributions, where the will contains nothing tending to show use of the words in a different sense. Agricultural Nat. Bank v Schwartz, 325 Mass 443, 91 NE2d 195, 32 ALR2d 289.

next-to-beer. Another name for near beer. 30 Am J Rev ed Intox L § 11.

nexum (nek'sum). (Roman law.) A formal contract between a debtor and his creditor whereby the debtor pledged his personal liberty as security for his indebtedness.

nexus theory (nek'sus thē'ọ-ri). Same as **minimum contacts test**.

N. F. Abbreviation of Norman French.

n/f. An abbreviation of no funds, stamped upon a check when payment refused for want of funds of the drawer.

N. G. Abbreviation of National Guard.

Nicene. (nī'sēn). The appellation given a religious creed promulgated in 325 A. D. at the first general council of Christians held at Nicea in Asia Minor.

niche. A hollowed space in a wall where a cinerary urn is or may be placed. 14 Am J2d Cem § 1.

nichil (nik'hil). Nothing.

nickel machine. An older term for **slot machine**.

nickname. Literally, a nicked name, a name snipped or whittled. A name applied to a person other than his true name, sometimes as a joke or in derision, at other times as a term of affection. 38 Am J1st Name § 8. A name given in contempt, derision, or sportive familiarity,—a familiar or opprobrious appellation. Ohlman v Clarkson Sawmill Co. 222 Mo 62, 120 SW 1155. As used in a will, sometimes, but not always, inclusive of a grandniece. 57 Am J1st Wills § 1390.
See **nephews and nieces**.

niece. The daughter of one's brother or sister. A relative in the third degree according to the civil-law method of computing degrees of kinship which prevails in most American jurisdictions. 23 Am J2d Desc & D § 48.
As the term is used in statutes relating to incest and prohibiting marriage between uncle and niece, it is confined to relationship by consanguinity and does not refer to relations by affinity. State v Tucker, 174 Ind 715, 93 NE 3.
See **nephews and nieces**.

niefe. Feminine of **naif.**

nient (nē). (Latin origin.) Not; nothing.

nient comprise (nē côm-prēz). Not included.

nient culpable (nē cûl-pah'bluh). Not guilty.

nient dedire (nē duh-dēr). Not to deny; to default.

nient le fait (nē luh fā). Not the deed.

nient seisi (nē say-zē). Not seized.

night. The hours of darkness. A manifestation of the natural phenomena of the rotation of the earth. 29 Am J2d Evi § 100.
See **nighttime.**

night auction. An auction sale at night, sometimes prohibited by law. 7 Am J2d Auct § 5.

night deposit. A bank deposit made after banking hours by placing the deposit and deposit slip in a bag or secure package and then placing the bag or package in a chute provided by the bank for receiving such deposits. 10 Am J2d Banks § 358.

night message. A classification of service by a telegraph company for which a reduced rate is charged, made according to the time of transmission. 52 Am J1st Teleg & T § 147.

night owl. See **owling.**

night season (nīt sē'zn). Same as **nighttime.**

nighttime. A time of day characterized by want of daylight or crepusculum sufficient to discern a man's face, moonlight not being considered. 13 Am J2d Burgl § 22. Sometimes defined by statute as the period between sunset and sunrise. Anno: 82 ALR2d 644, §§ 1 et seq.

nightwalker. See **nightwalking.**

nightwalking. The offense committed by a woman in strolling the streets at night for the unlawful purpose of picking up men for illicit intercourse, irrespective of expectation of gain. 42 Am J1st Prost § 1. Making a habit of being abroad at night for the purpose of committing some crime, of disturbing the peace, or doing some wrongful or wicked act. State v Dowers, 45 NH 543, 544.

Nigrum nunquam excedere debet rubrum (nī'grum nun'quam ex-sē'de-re de'bet ru'brum). The black should never depart from or go beyond the red, meaning that, the black ink text of the statute should not include matters which are not referred to in the red ink title.

nightwatchman. See **watchman.**

night work. Employment at night, a matter of permissible statutory regulation in reference to women and children, and in reference to particular industries, even of men. 31 Am J Rev ed Lab § 782.

nihil (nī'hil). Nothing; not; the return of a sheriff who has found nothing belonging to the defendant whereby he may be summoned, attached, or distrained. See 3 Bl Comm 282.

Nihil aliud potest rex quam quod de jure potest (nī'hil a'li'ud po'test rex quam quod dē jū're po'test). The king can do nothing other than that which he can do under the law.

Nihil capiat per billam (ni'hil kā'pi-at per bil'lam). Let him take nothing by his bill,—a formal expression which was used in a decree in equity in favor of the defendant.

Nihil capiat per breve (ni'hil kā'pi-at per brē've). Let him take nothing by his writ; a formal expression used in a judgment in favor of the defendant.

Nihil consensui tam contrarium est quam vis atque metus (ni'hil kon-sen'su-ī tam kon-trā'ri-um est quam vis at'kwe me'tūs). (Civil law.) Nothing is as much opposed to consent as force and fear.

Nihil dat qui non habet (ni'hil dat quī non hā'bet). He can give nothing who has nothing to give.

nihil debit. Same as **nil debit.**

Nihil de re accrescit ei qui nihil in re quando jus accresceret habet (ni'hil dē rē a-kre'sit ē'ī quī ni'hil in rē quan'dō jūs a-kre'se-ret hā'bet). Nothing accrues to a person in respect to a thing who, when the right accrues, has no interest in the thing.

nihil dicit (ni'hil di'sit). He says nothing.

Nihil enim aliud potest rex, nisi id solum quod de jure potest (ni'hil e'nim a'li-ud po'test rex, nī'sī id so'lum quod dē jū're po'test). For the king can do nothing, excepting only that which he is able to do lawfully. See 1 Bl Comm 238.

nihil est (ni'hil est). There is nothing. A sheriff's proper return on a summons where no service can be made.
Although non est inventus, he has not been found, is the more common form of such return, it is not as full as nihil est, there is nothing; which amounts to an averment that the defendant has nothing in the bailiwick, no dwelling house, no family, no residence, and no personal presence to enable the officer to make the service. Sherer v Easton Bank, 33 Pa 134, 138.

Nihil est enim liberale quod non idem justum (ni'hil est e'nim li-be-rā'le quod non ī'dem jus'tum). For there is nothing generous which is not at the same time just.

Nihil est magis rationi consentaneum quam eodem modo quodque dissolvere quo conflatum est (ni'hil est ma'jis rā-she-ō'nī kon-sen-tā'ne-um quam ē'ō-dem mō'dō quod'kwe dis-sol've-re quō kon-flā'tum est). Nothing is more agreeable with reason than to discharge anything in the same manner in which it was wrought or brought into being.

Nihil facit error nominis cum de corpore constat (ni'hil fā'sit er'ror nō'mi-nis kum dē kor'po-re kon'stat). (Civil law.) An error in the name is of no consequence when there is certainty as to the person.

nihil habet (ni'hil hā'bet). A sheriff's return on a scire facias as to a defendant whom he failed to serve. Sullivan v Johns (Pa) 5 Whart 366, 369.

Nihil habet forum ex scena (ni'hil hā'bet fō'rum ex sē'na). The forum holds nothing beyond the stage, meaning that the court or tribunal has nothing to do with what is not before it.

Nihil infra regnum subditos magis conservat in tranquilitate et concordia quam debita ligum administratio (ni'hil in'fra reg'num sub'di-tōs mā'jis kon-ser'vat in tran-qui-li-tā'te et kon-kor'di-a quam de'bi-ta lē'gum ad-mi-nis-trā'she-ō). Nothing better preserves the subjects of the realm in tranquillity and concord than the due administration of the laws.

Nihil iniquius quam aequitatem nimis intendere (ni'hil in-ī'qui-us quam ē-qui-tā'tem ni'mis in-ten'de-re). Nothing is more unfair than to stretch equity too far.

Nihil in lege intolerabilius est, eandem rem diverso jure censeri (ni'hil in lē'je in-to-le-rā-bi'li-us est, ē-an'dem rem dī-ver'sō jū're sen-sē'rī). Nothing is more intolerable in law than that the same matter should be decided differently by the court.

Nihil magis justum est quam quod necessarium est (ni'hil mā'jis jus'tum est quam quod ne-se-sā'ri-um est). Nothing is more just than that which is necessary.

Nihil nequam est praesumendum (ni'hil ne'quam est prē-zu-men'dum). Nothing bad or wicked should be presumed.

nihilo nil. See **de nihilo nil.**

Nihil perfectum est dum aliquid restat agendum (ni'hil per-fek'tum est dum a'li-quid re'stat ā-jen'dum). Nothing is perfect while something remains to be done.

Nihil peti potest ante id tempus, quo per rerum naturam persolvi possit (ni'hil pe'tī po'test an'te id tem'-pus, quō per rē'rum nā-tū'ram per-sol'vī pos'sit). (Civil law.) Nothing can be demanded before the time when in the nature of things it can be paid.

Nihil possumus contra veritatem (ni'hil pos'su-mus kon'trā ve-ri-tā'tem). We can do nothing against truth.

Nihil praescribitur nisi quod possidetur (ni'hil prē-skri'bi-ter nī'sī quod pos-si-dē'ter). There is no prescription except for that which is possessed or held in possession.

Nihil quod est contra rationem est licitum (ni'hil quod est kon'trā rā-she-ō'nem est li'si-tum). Nothing is lawful which is contrary to reason.

Nihil quod est inconveniens est licitum (ni'hil quod est in-kon-vē'ni-enz est li'si-tum). Nothing which is unconventional is lawful. See 1 Bl Comm 70.

Nihil simul inventum est et perfectum (ni'hil si'mul in-ven'tum est et per-fek'tum). Nothing is invented and perfected at the same time.

Nihil tam conveniens est naturali aequitati quam unumquodque dissolvi eo ligamine quo ligatum est (ni'hil tam kon-vē'ni-enz est nā-tū-rā'lī ē-qui-tā'tī quam ū-num-quod'kwe dis-sol'vi ē'ō li-gā'mi-ne quō li-gā'tum est). Nothing is so agreeable to natural equity as that anything should be released or discharged in the same manner in which it was made binding.

Nihil tam conveniens est naturali aequitati, quam voluntatem domini volentis rem suam in alium transferre, ratam haberi (ni'hil tam kon-vē'ni-enz est nā-tū-rā'lī ē-qui-tā'tī, quam vo-lun-tā'tem do'mi-nī vo-len'tis rem su'am in a'li-um trans-fer're, rā'tam hā-bē'rī). Nothing is so agreeable to natural equity as that the will of an owner who desires to convey or transfer his own property to another person should have validity.

Nihil tam naturale est, quam eo genere quidque dissolvere, quo colligatum est (ni'hil tam nā-tū-rā'le est, quam ē'ō je'ne-re quid'kwe dis-sol've-re, quō kol-li-gā'tum est). Nothing is so natural as that anything should be released or discharged in the same manner in which it was made binding.

Nihil tam proprium imperio quam legibus vivere (ni'hil tam prō'pri-um im-pe'ri-ō quam lē'ji-bus vī've-re). Nothing is so closely connected with government as to live in conformity with the laws.

nil (nil). A contracted form of **nihil.**

NIL. Abbreviation of Negotiable Instruments Act.

Nil agit exemplum, litem quod lite resolvit (nil ā'jit ex-em'plum, lī'tem quod lī'te re-sol'vit). A precedent which settles a controversy with a controversy does no good. Hatch v Mann (NY) 15 Wend 44, 49.

nil capiat. See **judgment of nil capiat.**

Nil capiat per billam (nil kā'pi-at per bil'lam). Same as **Nihil capiat per billam.**

Nil capiat per breve (nil kā'pi-at per brē've). See **judgment of nil capiat per breve.**

Nil debet (nil de'bet). He owes nothing. A plea of the general issue which may be asserted by the defendant in an action of debt on a simple contract, and in all other actions of debt which are not founded on a specialty or conclusive record. 41 Am J1st Pl § 141.

Nil dicit (nil dī'sit). He says nothing, meaning that he has not pleaded; that he has failed to interpose a plea or answer to the plaintiff's declaration or complaint. Wilbur v Maynard, 6 Colo 483, 485.

Nil facit error nominis si de corpore constat (nil fā'sit er'ror nō'mi-nis sī de kor'po-re kon'stat). Same as **Nihil facit error, etc.**

Nil frustra agit lex (nil frus'tra ā'jit lex). The law does nothing in vain. Doe, ex dem. Governeur's Heirs, v Robertson, (US) 11 Wheat 332, 355, 6 L Ed 488, 494.

Nil habuit in tenementis (nil hā'bu-it in te-ne-men'-tis). He has no interest in the tenement.

Nil sine prudenti fecit ratione vetustas (nil sī'ne prū-den'tī fē'sit rāshe-ō'ne ve-tus'tas). Antiquity did nothing without a wise or prudent reason.

Nil temere novandum (nil te'me-rē nō-van'dum). Nothing should be rashly changed or altered.

Nimia certitudo certitudinem ipsam destruit (ni'mi-a ser-ti-tu'dō ser-ti-tū'di-nem ip'sam de-stru'it). A certainty which is too certain destroys itself.

Nimia subtilitas in jure reprobatur (ni'mi-a su-ti'li-tās in jū're re-prō-bā'ter). Too much subtlety is discountenanced in the law.

Nimia subtilitas in jure reprobatur, et talis certitudo certitudinem confundit (ni'mi-a su-ti'li-tās in ju're re-prō-bā'ter et tā'lis ser-ti-tu'dō ser-ti-tū'di-nem kon-fun'dit). Too much subtlety is discountenanced in the law, and too much subtlety confuses certainty with certainty.

Nimium altercando, veritas amittitur (ni'mi-um al-ter-kan'dō, ve'ri-tās a-mit'ti-ter). The truth is lost by too much cross-examination.

nimmer (nim'ėr). A thief.

nine hundred ninety-nine year lease. A lease for a term of 999 years, valid in respect of the term in the absence of statute. 32 Am J1st L & T § 64.

Nineteenth Amendment. The amendment to the United States Constitution, the ratification of which was completed on August 26, 1920, the effect of which is to erase from the constitution and laws of each state every provision restricting the right of women to vote, and to make women legal voters to the same extent to which the right of suffrage has been conferred on men by the respective states. Anno: 71 ALR 1332.

ninety-nine year lease. A lease for a term of 99 years, valid in respect of the term, in the absence of statute. 32 Am J1st L & T § 64.

nisi (nī'sī). Unless; if not; except.

nisi convenissent in manum viri (nī'sī kon-vē-nis'sent in ma'num vī'rī). Unless they should come under the care of a husband.

Among the ancient Greeks and Romans women were never of age, but were subject to perpetual guardianship, unless when married. See 1 Bl Comm 464.

nisi decree. (nī'sī dẹ-krē'). See **decree nisi.**

nisi feceris (nī'sī fē'se-ris). Unless you should do it.

nisi judgment. (nī'sī juj'mẹnt). Nothing more than an order to show cause why judgment should not be rendered. Young v M'Pherson, 3 NJL 895, 897. See **decree nisi.**

nisi order. (nī'sī ôr'dėr). See **order nisi.**

nisi per legale judicium parium. See **pares regni.**

Nisi per legale judicium parium suorum vel per legem terrae (nī'sī per le-gā'le jū-di'she-um pā'ri-um su-ō'rum vel per lē'jem ter'rē). Unless by lawful judgment of his peers or equals, or by the law of the land.

It was in these famous words that Magna Charta guaranteed to every freeman the right of trial by jury, "the principal bulwark of our liberties," when his person or his property was at stake. See 3 Bl Comm 350.

nisi prius (nī'sī prī'us). Unless before. A trial before a single judge. An English court presided over by commissioners detailed on circuit from London to hold jury trials. In modern terminology, the trial, as distinguished from the appellate court, where both have exercised jurisdiction in a cause.

nisi prius court (nī'sī prī'us kôrt). The trial court.

nisi prius roll (nī'sī prī'us rōl). The record of the proceedings of the court in which a case was begun made up for the nisi prius court.

nisi prius writ (nī'sī prī'us rit). An old English writ which directed a sheriff to bring the jurors to Westminster unless before that time the justices of assize came into the county to try cases.

nisi rule (nī'sī rūl). See **rule nisi.**

nisi ubi leges cum justicia retrospicere possint (nī'sī u'bi lē'jēz kum jūs-tī'she-a re-trō-spī'se-re pos'sint). Unless where laws can relate back with justice. Pryor v Downey, 50 Cal 388, 402.

nitrate of soda. A mineral. 36 Am J1st Min & M § 5.

nitroglycerin. A substance which because of its nature as an explosive is dangerous at all times, in all places, and under all circumstances. 22 Am J2d Explos § 3. A substance compounded in a mixture of nitric acid, sulphuric acid and glycerin, which explodes even more readily when heated. Barnhardt v American Glycerin Co. 113 Kan 136, 213 P 663, 31 ALR 721.

nixie (niks'ē). A decoy or test letter; that is, a letter addressed to a fictitious person, or to a place where there is no postoffice. United States v Denicke (CC Ga) 35 F 407.

n. l. An abbreviation of **non liquet.**

NLRB. Abbreviation of National Labor Relations Board.

no. An abbreviation of number. Improper as an abbreviation of "north," "n." being the proper definition. Burr v Broadway Ins. Co. 16 NY 267, 271.

no action clause. A clause in an insurance policy purporting to indemnify or insure against loss from injuring the property or person of a third person, which provides in substance that no action shall be had on the policy to recover loss or expense, except as an action shall be brought by the insured for a loss or expense actually sustained and paid in money by the insured after the amount thereof has been fixed by final judgment or by agreement. 7 Am J2d Auto § 169; 29A Am J1st Ins § 1343.

no arrival, no sale. A stated condition in a contract of sale of goods, meaning that if the goods do not arrive at the destination indicated, the buyer acquires no property in the goods and does not become liable for the purchase price. Cundill v A. W. Millhauser Corp. 257 NY 416, 178 NE 680.

It has been held that a contract for goods "to be shipped" by a specified vessel at a price per pound "ex ship," with a provision for a fair allowance if "sea damaged," and saying "no arrival, no sale," does not make the arrival of the goods on the vessel named a condition precedent, where a portion of them are transhipped at an intermediate port because of a disaster to the vessel. See 46 Am J1st Sales § 201.

no award. A plea in an action upon an award which denies that an award was made.

nobile. See **feudum nobile.**

Nobiles magis plectuntur pecunia (nō'bi-lēz mājis plek-tun'ter pe-kū'ni-a). Persons of noble birth are more often punished in money; that is, by fines.

Nobiles magis plectuntur pecunia, plebes vero in corpore (no'bi-lēz mā'jis plek-tun'ter pe-kū'ni-a, plē'bēz vē'ro' in kor'po-re). Persons of noble birth are more often punished in money, but the common people in body; that is by corporal punishment.

Nobiles sunt qui arma gentilitia antecessorum suorum proferre possunt (no'bi-lēz sunt quī ar'ma jen-ti-li'she-a an-te-ses-sō'rum su-ō'rum pro-fer're pos'-sunt). Those persons are nobles who can produce the family arms of their ancestors.

Nobiliores et benigniores presumptiones in dubiis sunt praeferendae (no-bī-li-ō'rēz et be-nig-ni-ō'rēz pre-sump-she-o'nēz' in du'bīis sunt prē-fe-ren'dē). The more noble and charitable presumptions are to be preferred in doubtful cases.

Nobilitas est duplex, superior et inferior (no-bi'li-tas est du'plex, su-pe'ri-or et in-fe'ri-or). Nobility is twofold, superior and inferior.

nobility. The English class of persons of rank and title which includes dukes, marquesses, earls, viscounts, and barons.

All degrees of nobility and honor are derived from the king, and he may institute what new titles he pleases. Hence, these degrees are not of equal antiquity. See 1 Bl Comm 396.

no bill. An indorsement by a grand jury on an indictment, indicating "not found" or "not a true bill."

noblesse oblige (nō-bles' ō-blēj'). (French.) Literally, those of the higher rank or better class will be compelled. Inferentially, compelled to humane and proper conduct. The basis of the maxim that those persons who are in comfortable circumstances and possessed of means should set the example of obedience to the laws. State v Colonial Club, 154 NC 177, 69 SE 771.

nocent (nō'sẹnt). Guilty.

nocere (no'se-re). To hurt; to injure; to harm; to damage.

no collusion. See **affidavit of no collusion.**

no consideration. A form of plea or answer interposed in an action on a contract, advising the court that the contract sued on is not enforceable because it has no foundation to rest upon.

It has been often held that, under such a plea, the defense will fail if it is shown that there was any consideration whatever for the contract. The amount of it is immaterial. Shirk v Neible, 156 Ind 66, 75, 59 NE 281.

noctanter (nok-tan'ter). Nocturnally; by night.

nocumentum (no-ku-men'tum). Nuisance, or annoyance, signifying anything that works hurt, inconvenience, or damage. See 3 Bl Comm 215.

no damage clause. A provision in a contract precluding claims for damages due to delay in performance. Anno: 10 ALR2d 815; 22 Am J2d Damg § 50.

no evidence point. A point made on appeal asserting the absence of evidence to support a finding. Williston v Perkins, 51 Cal 554.

no eyewitness rule. The rule that where there was no eyewitness to a fatal accident, the presumption, or at least the inference, is, that, in the absence of circumstances indicating clearly to the contrary, the decedent exercised ordinary care for his own safety. 22 Am J2d Dth § 216.

no goods. A return, better known as a return of nulla bona, to a writ of execution in which the officer indicates a strict and diligent search by him but inability to find any property of the defendant liable to seizure under the writ. 30 Am J2d Exec § 562.

no immunity doctrine. The doctrine that an institution, which is not a part of the government, is not, merely because of its nature as a charity, immune from liability for damages in tort. 15 Am J2d Char § 158.

NOLCO. Abbreviation of net operating loss carry over, an income tax term.

nolens volens (nō'lenz vō'lenz). Willing or not willing; whether willing or not.

nolle (nol'e). To be unwilling.

no liability clause. A clause in a liability policy, providing that there shall be no liability in case the risk is covered by other valid or collectible insurance. 7 Am J2d Auto Ins § 201.

nolle prosequi (nol'e pros'e-kwī). A formal entry of record by the prosecuting attorney by which he declares unwillingness to prosecute a case or his intention not to prosecute the case further. 21 Am J2d Crim L § 512. An agreement not to proceed further in the suit as to a particular person or cause of action. 24 Am J2d Dism § 3. An entry made on the record by which the plaintiff declares that he will proceed no further. Steele v Beaty, 215 NC 680, 2 SE2d 854.

See **judgment of nolle prosequi.**

nolo contendere (nō'lō kǫn-ten'dę-rē). Literally, "I do not wish to contend." Substantially, though not technically, a plea of guilty; an implied confession; a quasi confession of guilt. 21 Am J2d Crim L § 497. A plea recognized in administrative proceedings. Re 17 Club, Inc. 26 NJ Super 43, 97 A2d 171.

It is difficult to define the exact nature of a plea of nolo contendere; regardless of the label attached, the plea for practical purposes is a plea of guilty, or the equivalent thereof. United States v Safeway Stores, Inc. (DC Tex) 20 FRD 451.

nol. pros. (nol pros). Abbreviation of **nolle prosequi.**

nolumus mutare (nol'u-mus mu-ta'ri). Not willing to change. Noble State Bank v Haskell, 219 US 104, 575, 55 L Ed 112, 341, 31 S Ct 186, 299.

nomen (nō'men). A name.

nomen collectivum (nō'men kol-lek-tī'vum). A collective name.

Nomen dicitur a noscendo, quia notitiam facit (nō'men dī'si-ter ā no-sen'dō, qui'a no-ti'she-am fā'sit). "Nomen" is so called from the word "noscendo," because it causes the thing to be known.

Nomen est quasi rei notamen (nō'men est quā'sī rē'ī no-tā'men). A name is, as it were, the distinguishing mark of a thing.

nomen generale (nō'men je-ne-rā'le). A general name; the name of a genus.

nomen generalissimum (nō'men je-ne-rā-lis'si-mum). A very general name.

A word or term which refers to a class or species is often referred to as nomen generalissimum. For example, the word horse is often used as a general term including mares, colts, stallions and geldings. State v Dunnavent, 5 SCL (3 Brev) 9.

nomen juris (nō'men jū'ris). A name or word of law; a law term.

Nomen non sufficit si res non sit de jure aut de facto (nō'men non suf'fi-sit sī rēz non sit dē jū're ât dē fak'tō). A name is not sufficient if the thing does not exist either in law or in fact.

nomina (no'mi-na). Plural of **nomen.**

nominal. Characterizing an existence in name only; without any actual, substantial existence. Park Amusement Co. v McCaughn (DC Pa) 14 F2d 553.

nominal capital. Capital employed in the conduct of a business which is not a material income-producing factor. Alexander & Garrett v United States (DC Ga) 21 F2d 547, term as found in Internal Revenue Act of 1917.

nominal consideration. A consideration in a nominal sum, such as "one dollar." 17 Am J2d Contr § 102; 23 Am J2d Deeds § 66.

nominal damages. An award to which the plaintiff is entitled, although he gives no evidence of any particular amount of loss, because the law infers damage from the breach of an agreement or the invasion of a right. Ferreira v Honolulu Star Bulletin Ltd. 44 Hawaii 567, 356 P2d 651, reh den 44 Hawaii 581, 357 P2d 112. Damages recoverable where a legal right is to be vindicated against an invasion that has produced no actual present loss of any kind or where, from the nature of the case, some compensable injury has been shown but the amount of that injury has not been proved. 22 Am J2d Damg § 5.

nominal holder. The holder of a negotiable bill or note who is not the beneficial owner and has no beneficial interest in the instrument. 12 Am J2d B & N § 1072.

nominal partner. A person who appears or is held out to the world as a partner, but who has no real interest in the firm or the business. Ditts v Lonsdale, 49 Ind 521, 529; Brown's Executor v Higginbotham (Va) 5 Leigh 583.

nominal party. One suing or defending for the use and benefit of another. A person who is the plaintiff in an action, but who is not the real party in interest. One joined as a party to comply with a technical rule of practice, not because he has an interest in the subject matter of the action.

nominal payee. The payee named in a negotiable instrument who is not the beneficial owner and has no beneficial interest in the instrument. 12 Am J2d B & N § 1073.

nominal plaintiff. See **nominal party**.

nominal right. A technical right; a right unimportant from the standpoint of substance. 27 Am J2d Eq § 13.

nominal trust. A dry trust; a passive trust. A trust in which the trustee has no duties to perform, the cestui que trust having the entire management of the estate. A trust of such nature that if the trustee does what he is directed to do, the result will be the same as if the trust were executed into a legal estate. 54 Am J1st Trusts § 13.

nominare (nō-mi-nā′re). To name; to nominate; to appoint; to accuse; to inform against.

Nomina si nescis perit cognitio rerum (nō′mi-na sī ne′sis per′it kōg-ni′she-ō rē′rum). If you do not know their names, the knowledge of things is lost.

Nomina sunt mutabilia, res autem immobiles (nō′mi-na sunt mū-ta-bi′li-a, rēz â′tem im-mō′bi-lēz). Names are mutable, but things are immutable.

Nomina sunt notae rerum (nō′mi-na sunt nō′tē rē′rum). Names are the distinguishing marks of things.

Nomina sunt symbola rerum (nō′mi-na sunt sim′bo-la rē′rum). Names are the symbols of things.

nominate. To name; to designate; to select or choose a person to be a candidate or proper person to hold an office or trust as an act preliminary to the person's appointment or election. Marbury v Madison (US) 1 Cranch 137, 167, 168, 2 L Ed 60, 70.

nominate contract. (Civil law.) A contract which falls under some special designation or name, such as a pledge, a sale, or a hiring.

nominatim (no-mi-nā′tim). (Civil law.) By name; expressly; particularly; each in turn.

nominating and reducing (nom-i-nā′ting and rē-dū′sing). An English method of impaneling jurors.

nomination. The act of nominating. A designation or selection. The designation of a candidate or candidates for public office or public offices, whether by a primary election, a convention, or a mere nominating petition. 25 Am J2d Elect § 128.

nomination of guardian. The selection of a guardian by an infant 14 years old or older. 25 Am J1st G & W § 28.

nominator (nom′i-nā-tor). One who names or appoints another to or for an office or trust.

nomine. See **eo nomine**.

nomine damni (nō′mi-ne dam′nī). Under the name or designation of "damages."

nominee. A person who has been chosen or selected as a candidate for an office. State v Hirsch, 125 Ind 207, 24 NE 1062.

nomine poenae (nō′mi-ne pē′nē). Under the name or designation of the word "penalty."

non (non). Not; no; by no means.

nonabatable nuisance. See **permanent nuisance**.

nonabatable structure. A structure which, if erected by an authority clothed with the power of eminent domain, could be made a lawful structure by condemning the property injured by it or the right infringed by it. Tulsa v Grier, 114 Okla 93, 243 P 753, 757.

See **permanent nuisance**.

nonability. The want of ability or capacity; legal incapacity.

nonacceptance. Want of acceptance.

See **dishonor by nonacceptance**.

Non acceptavit (non ak-sep-tā′vit). He did not accept.

nonaccess. Absence of sexual relations between husband and wife. The fact of the absence of the husband from the wife, in evidence for the purpose of establishing the absence of sexual relations between them for the period.

Non accipi debent verba in demonstrationem falsam, quae competunt in limitationem veram (non ak′si-pī de′bent ver′ba in de-mon-strā-she-ō′nem fal′sam, kwē kom′pe-tunt in li-mi-tā-she-ō′nem vē′ram). Words ought not to be taken in a false descriptive sense which are competent to describe a true limitation.

Non accrevit infra sex annos (non a-krē′vit in′fra sex an′nos). It did not accrue within six years,—a formal expression used in pleading the statute of limitations.

nonaction by Congress. See **inaction by Congress**.

nonae (nō′nē). Same as **nones**.

nonage. The condition of a person under the age of majority; **infancy**. Want of the requisite age to enter into a marriage or conduct a business transaction.

nonagency station. A station on the route of a common carrier without an agent in charge, so that the delivery of a shipment at such station occurs ordinarily when the goods are unloaded or set off thereat, under conditions which are not unreasonable. 13 Am J2d Car § 413.

nonagium (nō-nā′ji-um). Same as **nonage**.

Non alio modo puniatur aliquis, quam secundum quod se habet condemnatio (non a′li-ō mō′dō pū′ni-ā′ter a′li-quis, quam se-kun′dum quod sē hā′bet kon-dem-nā′she-ō). A person should not be punished in any other manner than that which the sentence of the court provides.

Non aliter a significatione verborum recedi oportet quam cum manifestum est, aliud sensisse testatorem (non a′li-ter ā sig-ni-fi-kā-she-ō′ne ver-bō′rum re-sē′dī o-por′tet quam kum ma-ni-fes′tum est, a′li-ud sen-sis′se tes-ta-tō′rem). (Civil law.) The ordinary meaning of the words ought not to be departed from unless it is manifest or clear that the testator intended otherwise.

non allocatur. See **et non allocatur**.

nonanalogous arts and uses. See **analogous arts and uses**.

nonancestral estate. An estate the title to which was acquired otherwise than by descent.

"There are but two characters of estate known to our jurisprudence. An estate is either ancestral or nonancestral. In some jurisdictions, the latter is termed 'new acquisition' or 'purchase.'" Gray v Chapman, 122 Okla 130, 243 P 522, 524.

nonancestral property. Property acquired otherwise than by descent. Gray v Chapman, 122 Okla 130, 243 P 522.

nonapparent easement. An easement which is not

obvious or susceptible of ascertainment by cursory inspection of the premises. 25 Am J2d Ease § 9.
See **noncontinuous easement**.

nonappearance. The failure of a defendant to enter an appearance in an action. The failure of a party or witness to appear in response to notice, process, or subpoena.

nonapportionable annuity. The ordinary annuity; an annuity not apportionable in respect of time, so that if the annuity dies before the day on which a payment becomes due, the personal representative of the annuitant is not entitled to a proportional part. 4 Am J2d Annui § 24.

non assumpsit (non a-sump'sit). A plea of the general issue in an action of assumpsit. 41 Am J1st Pl § 141.

Non assumpsit infra sex annos (non a-sump'sit in'fra sex an'nos). He did not undertake or promise within six years,—formal words used in pleading the statute of limitations in an action of assumpsit.

Non auditur perire volens (non â'di-ter per-ī're vo'-lenz). A person who desires to die is not to be listened to.

non bis in idem (non bis in ī'dem). Not twice for the same.

nonborrowing member. A member of a building and loan association who does not borrow from the association. Oklahoma City Federal Sav. & Loan Asso. v Swatek, 191 Okla 400, 130 P2d 514.

nonbusiness bad debt. A familiar term in income tax law, applying only to noncorporate taxpayers; a bad debt acquired otherwise than in the course of a taxpayer's trade or business. IRC § 166(d)(2).

noncancelable policy. A policy of insurance containing provisions which limit the right of the insurer to cancel the policy, particularly a policy of health and accident insurance restricting cancelation after an illness or accident occurring to the insured. Dudgeon v Mutual Ben. Health & Acci. Asso. 70 F2d 49.

non cepit (non sē'pit). A plea of the general issue in replevin. 41 Am J1st Pl § 142.

Non cepit modo et forma (non sē'pit mō'dō et for'ma). He did not take in the manner and form (alleged),—a formal expression used in pleading the general issue in an action of replevin.

nonclaim. The failure on the part of a claimant of property or rights to assert his claim against another who claims adversely to him.

nonclaim covenant. The equivalent of a covenant of warranty. 20 Am J2d Cov § 43.

nonclaim statute. A special statute of limitation on claims against a decedent's estate, providing, in general, that where a claim has been rejected or disallowed by the executor or administrator, the claimant must bring suit on it within a designated time, under penalty that otherwise the claim may be forever barred. 31 Am J2d Ex & Ad § 926. A statute requiring the presentation of a claim on the obligation of one since deceased to his executor or administrator, within a period of time prescribed by the statute, following the appointment of the executor or administrator. 31 Am J2d Ex & Ad § 270.

noncombatant. A civilian in time of war, especially a civilian in a war area. One in the armed services whose duties do not include engaging in combat with the enemy, such as a chaplain.

noncommercial partnership. Same as **non-trading partnership**.

noncommissioned officer. A person enlisted in the Armed Forces, who has some rank, but not a rank evidenced by a commission.
See **warrant officer**.

noncommittal answer. An answer by a witness which avoids a definite statement, such as "I could not say —possibly I did." Anno: 89 ALR2d 1261, § 1.

non-Communist affidavit. An affidavit negativing the connection of the affiant with the Communist Party by membership or affiliation. American Communications Asso. v Douds, 339 US 382, 94 L Ed 925, 70 S Ct 674, reh den 339 US 990, 94 L Ed 1391, 70 S Ct 1017.

noncommunity property. A term familiar in community property jurisdictions as property which is not a part of the community. Separate property of a spouse. 15 Am J2d Community Prop § 3.

non compos (non kom'pos). Same as **non compos mentis**.

non compos mentis (non kom'pos men'tis). Adjective: Mentally incompetent. Having a mental condition approximating total and positive incompetency; destitute of memory and understanding. Van Deusen v Sweet, 51 NY 378. Noun: A person of unsound mind. Beaumont's Case (Pa) 1 Whart 52.

non compotes mentis (non kom-pō'tēz men'tis). Plural of non compos mentis.

Non concedantur citationes priusquam exprimatur super qua re fieri decit citatio (non kon-sē-dan'ter si-tā-she-ō'nēz prī-us'quam ex-pri-mā'ter sū'per quā rē fī'e-rī dē'sit si-tā'she-ō). Citations ought not to be granted before it has been stated for what cause it is fitting that a citation should be made or issued.

non concessit (non kon-se'sit). He did not grant.

nonconforming use. A zoning law term; the use of a building or land that does not agree with the regulations applicable to the district in which the building or land is situated. Anno: 114 ALR 991.

nonconformists. Dissenters, persons who dissented from the forms of the orthodox English church.

Non consentit qui errat (non kon-sen'tit quī er'rat). He who errs or makes a mistake does not consent.

non constat (non kon'stat). It is not certain; it does not appear.

noncontestable clause. See **incontestability provision**.

noncontinuous easement. An easement the enjoyment of which can be had only by the interference of man, that is, one which has no means specially constructed or appropriated to its enjoyment and which is enjoyed at intervals, leaving between these intervals no visible sign of its existence, such as a mere right of way or a right to draw water. 25 Am J2d Ease § 10.

noncourt receiver. A receiver provided for in a contract in which one of the contracting parties is given the right to appoint a receiver of certain property upon the happening of a certain eventuality. A receiver appointed by a government official of the executive branch. 45 Am J1st Rec § 3.

non cul. An abbreviation of **non culpabilis**.

non culpabilis (non kul-pa'bi-lis). Not guilty.

noncumulative dividends. Dividends on preferred stock which do not cumulate upon omission of payment so as to require payment of a passed or omitted dividend of one year out of earnings of a following year. 19 Am J2d Corp § 878.

The term means that dividends on non- cumulative preferred stock, once passed or omitted, are dead; can never be made up. Guttmann v Illinois Cent. R. Co. (CA2) 189 F2d 927, 27 ALR2d 1066.

noncumulative option. An option provided the maker of a promissory note by the instrument, whereunder he may make payments of principal on dates for payment of interest, in advance of the stated maturity date. 11 Am J2d B & N § 288.

non damnificatus (non dam-ni-fi-kā'tus). See **plea of non damnificatus.**

Non dat qui non habet (non dat quī non hā'bet). He does not give who has not. Holland v Cruft, 69 Mass (3 Gray) 162, 178.

Non debeo melioris conditionis esse, quam auctor meus a quo jus in me transit (non de'be-ō me-li-ō'ris kon-di-she-ō'nis es'se, quam âk'tor mē'us ā quō jūs in mē trans'it). I ought not to be in any better condition than my ancestor from whom the right passed on to me.

Non deberet alii nocere quod inter alios actum esset (non de'be-ret a'li-ī no-sē're quod in'ter a'li-ōs ak'tum es'set). That ought not to prejudice a person which has been done between other persons.

Non debet actori licere, quod reo non permittitur (non de'bet ak-tō'rī lī'se-re, quod rē'ō non per-mit'-ti-ter). That which is forbidden the plaintiff ought not to be allowed the defendant.

Non debet adduci exceptio ejus rei cujus petitur dissolutio (non de'bet ad'dū-sī ex-sep'she-ō ē'jus rē'ī kū'jus pe'ti-ter dis-so-lū'she-ō). A plea of the very matter, the determination of which is sought, ought not to be interposed.

Non debet alii nocere, quod inter alios actum est (non de'bet a'li-ī no-sē're, quod in'ter a'li-ōs ak'tum est). That ought not to prejudice a person which has transpired between other persons.

Non debet alteri per alterum iniqua conditio inferri (non de'bet al'te-rī per al'te-rum in-ī'qua kon-di'-she-ō in-fer'rī). An inequitable condition ought not to be imposed by one person upon another.

Non debet cui plus licet, quod minus est non licere (non de'bet kī plus lī'set, quod mī'nus est non lī'se-re). A person to whom a greater license is given ought not to be forbidden that which is less.

Non debet dici tendere in praejudicium ecclesiasticae liberatatis quod pro rege et republica necessarium videtur (non de'bet dī'sī ten'de-re in prē-jū-di'she-um ē-klē-si-äs'ti-sē li-be-ra-tā'tis quod prō rē'je et rē-pub'li-ka ne-ses-sā'ri-um vi-dē'ter). That which is deemed necessary for the welfare of the king and the state ought not to be said to tend toward the prejudice of ecclesiastical liberty.

Non debet fieri, sed factum valet (non de'bet fī'e-rī, sed fak'tum va'let). It ought not to be done, but when it is done it is valid.

Non decet homines dedere causa non cognita (non de'set ho'mi-nēz de'dē-re kâ'za non kōg'ni-ta). No cause having been shown, it is unseemly to give men up. Re Washburn (NY) 4 Johns Ch 106, 114.

non decimando. See **de non decimando.**

Non decipitur qui scit se decipi (non de-si'pi-ter quī sit sē de'si-pī). A person is not deceived who knows that he is being deceived.

nondeclarant. See **alien nondeclarant.**

Non dedit (non de'dit). He did not grant.

Non definitur in jure quid sit conatus (non de-fī'ni-ter in jū're quid sit ko-nā'tus). What constitutes an attempt is not defined in the law.

nondelegable duty. The duty of a contractor which, under the terms of the contract, is to be performed by him personally. 27 Am J1st Ind Contr § 48.

nondelivery. A failure or omission to deliver.

non demisit (non dẹ-mī'sit). He did not demise,—the name given to a plea denying the demise, in an action for rent.

nondescript. Not such as to be classified. Babcock v Babcock & Wilcox Co. 137 Pa Super 517, 9 A2d 492.

non desidentia clerici regis. See **de non desidentia clerici regis.**

non detinet (non det'i-net). A plea of the general issue in an action of detinue.

non differunt quae concordant re, tametsi non in verbis iisdem (non dif'fe-runt kwē kon-kor'dant rē, tam-et'sī non in ver'bis ī-is'dem). Those matters do not differ which agree in substance although they are not in the same words.

nondisclosure. The failure to reveal a fact, with or without an intent to conceal it. State v Watson, 145 Kan 792, 67 P2d 515, 110 ALR 998; Tube Reducing Corp. v Unemployment Compensation Com. 1 NJ 177, 62 A2d 473, 5 ALR2d 855.

nondiscrimination clause. A provision in a public contract whereby the contractor agrees that he will not discriminate against any employee or applicant for employment because of race, creed, color or national origin, and also that he will take affirmative action to insure that job applicants are employed, and employees are treated during employment, without regard to their race, creed, color or national origin. Executive Order No. 10925, § 301(1) following 5 USC § 631.

nonenumerated article. An article not specifically enumerated in the tariff schedules. 21 Am J2d Cust D § 51.

non distringendo (non dis-trin-jen'dō). A writ which lay to prevent a distress.

Non dormientibus sed vigilantibus, leges subveniunt (non dor-mi-en'ti-bus sed vi-ji-lan'ti-bus, lē'jēz sub-ve'ni-unt). The laws do not assist slumberers, but only those who are vigilant. Friezleben v Shallcross, 14 Del (9 Houst) 1, 19 A 576.

Non dubitatur, etsi specialiter venditor evictionem non promiserit, re evicta, ex empto competere actionem (non du-bi-tā'ter, et'sī spe-she-ā'li-ter ven'-di-tor ē-vik-she-ō'nem non prō-mī'se-rit, rē ē-vik'ta, ex emp'tō kom-pe'te-re ak-she-ō'nem). It is not doubted that although the vendor has not specially promised, in the event of an eviction, an action on the contract of sale is competent. See Broom's Legal Maxims 768.

Non efficit affectus nisi sequatur effectus (non ef'fi-sit af-fek'tus nī'sī se-quā'ter ef-fek'tus). An intention is of no effect unless a result follows.

non ejusdem generis (non e-jūs'dem je'ne-ris). Not of the same kind. See 2 Bl Comm 512.

Non erit alia lex Romae, alia Athenis; alia nunc, alia posthac; sed et omnes gentes, et omni tempore, una lex, et sempiterna, et immortalis continebit (non e′rit a′li-a lex Rō′mē, a′li-a A-the′nis; a′li-a nunk, a′li-a post′hak; sed et om′nēz jen′tēz, et om′nī tem′-po-re, ū′na lex, et sem-pi-ter′na, et im-mor-tā′lis kon-ti-nē′bit). There will not be one law at Rome, another at Athens; one now and another afterward; but one law, eternal and immortal, shall bind all peoples together and for all time.

nones (nōnz). The ninth hour of the day after sunrise, or about 3 o'clock P. M.; a canonical hour at which was celebrated a religious rite. Rochester German Ins. Co. v Peaslee-Gaulbert Co. 120 Ky 752, 87 SW 3. Under the Roman Calendar, the seventh day of the months of March, May, July, and October, and the fifth day of the other months of the year. Rives v Guthrie, 46 NC (1 Jones L) 84, 87.

non est (non est). Is no. Is not.

Non est arctius vinculum inter homines quam jusjurandum (non est ark′she-us vin′ku-lum in′ter hō′-mi-nēz quam jūs-jū-ran′dum). There is no closer bond among men than an oath.

Non est certandum de regulis juris (non est ser-tan′-dum dē re-gū′lis jū′ris). There is no disputing about the rules of the law.

Non est disputandum contra principia negantem (non est dis-pu-tan′dum kon′trā prin-si′pi-a ne-gan′tem). There is no disputing with a person who denies established principles.

non est factum (non est fak′tum). A plea of the general issue in an action on a bond, a specialty, or a covenant, impeaching the instrument upon which suit is brought or denying the execution and signing thereof. Dilworth v Federal Reserve Bank, 170 Miss 373, 154 So 535, 92 ALR 1076. A method at common law of raising the issue of fraud in the making or act of execution of a deed. Kuczewski v De Magnussun, 242 Mich 296, 218 NW 657, 57 ALR 756; Dimmel v Morse, 36 Wash 2d 344, 218 P2d 334. A defense presented in equity by a plea in bar. Oliver v Persons, 30 Ga 391.

Non est in facultate mandatarii addere vel demere ordini sibi dato (non est in fa-kul-tā′tē man-da-tā′ri-ī ad′de-re vel de′me-re or′di-nī si′bi da′tō). It is not the function of a mandatary to add or subtract from the authority which has been given to him.

"He (the mandatary) was not authorized to exchange the lands for other property, or to accept the notes of the vendee as cash, or to accept personal security, or any form of security except that specified in the condition." Morrill v Cone (US) 22 How 75, 16 L Ed 253, 255.

Non est inventus (non est in-ven′tus). He has not been found—words that are used in an officer's formal return upon his unsuccessful attempt to arrest a defendant under a capias.

Non est inventus in balliva mea (non est in-ven′tus in bal-lī′va me′a). He has not been found in my bailiwick. A form of a sheriff's return on a capias, where he has been unable to find the defendant in his jurisdiction. See 3 Bl Comm 282.

Non est justum aliquem antenatum post mortem facere bastardum, qui tota tempore vitae suae pro legitimo habebatur (non est jus′tum a′li-quem an-te-nā′tum post mor′tem fā′se-re bas-tar′dum, quī tō′ta tem′po-re vī′tē su′ē prō le-ji′ti-mō hā-bē-bā′ter). It is not just to make anyone a bastard after his death who during his whole lifetime was regarded as legitimate.

Non est novum ut priores leges ad posteriores trahantur (non est nō′vum ut pri-ō′rez lē′jēz ad pos-te-ri-ō′rēz tra-han′ter). (Civil law.) It is not novel that earlier laws should give way to later ones. Broom's Legal Maxims 28.

Non est recedendum a communi observanti (non est re-se-den′dum ā kom-mū′nī ob-ser-van′tī). There should be no departing from common observance.

Non est regula quin fallat (non est re-gū′la quin fal′-lat). There is no rule which may not fail.

Non est reus nisi mens sit rea (non est rē′us nī′sī mēnz sit rē′a). There is no guilt unless there is a guilty intent.

Non est singulis concedendum, quod per magistratum publice possit fieri, ne occasio sit majoris tumultus faciendi (non est sīn′gu-lis kon-sē-den′dum, quod per ma-jis-trā′tum pub′li-se pos′sit fī′e-rī, ne o-kā′-she-ō sit mā-jō′ris tu-mul′tūs fā-she-en′dī). (Civil law.) That which can be done publicly through a magistrate is not to be conceded to individuals, lest it be the occasion of creating a greater disturbance.

nones y pares. A game of chance played on a billiard table. Anno: 135 ALR 124.

nonexclusive power of appointment. A power whereunder the donee has no right to exclude from the distribution any member of the class designated by the donor, grantor, or testator to be favored by the exercise of the power. Fidelity & Columbia Trust Co. v Barret, 166 Ky 411, 179 SW 396.

Non exemplis sed legibus judicandum est (non egzem′plis sed lē′ji-bus jū-di-kan′dum est). (Roman law.) Judgment should not be rendered from examples, but by the laws.

nonexistent person. A term of importance in reference to fictitious payee. 11 Am J2d B & N § 128. A person who does not exist, in the sense that he was not intended to be the payee by the drawer or maker. 11 Am J2d B & N § 129.

nonexisting bill. A concept involved in the principle that where a promise to accept a nonexisting bill is communicated to a particular person who, upon the face of the promise, takes for value a bill to which it is applicable and which is fairly within the scope of the promise, he is entitled to the benefits of such promise and may maintain an action thereon in his own name. 11 Am J2d B & N § 511.

nonexisting payee. An instrument payable to the order of a nonexisting person, such constituting an instrument payable to bearer where the fact of nonexistence was known to the person making the instrument so payable. 11 Am J2d B & N § 128.

Non ex opinionibus singulorum, sed ex communi usu, nomina exaudiri debent (non ex ō-pi-ni-ō′ni-bus singu-lō′rum, sed ex kom-mū′nī ū′sū, nō′mi-na ex-â-di′rī de′bent). (Civil law.) The names of things ought not to be learned from individual opinions, but from common usage.

nonexpert evidence. Testimony by one not qualified where particular qualifications are imposed as a prerequisite to the admission of testimony.

Non facias malum, ut inde veniat bonum (non fā′she-as ma′lum, ut in′de ve′ni-at bō′num). You should not do a wicked thing in order that good may come out of it.

NONFEASANCE

nonfeasance. The failure to act where duty requires an act. Of public officer:—neglect or refusal, without sufficient excuse, to do that which it is the officer's legal duty to do, whether wilfully, or through malice, ignorance, or oversight. State ex rel. Hardie v Coleman, 115 Fla 119, 155 So 129, 92 ALR 988. Of employee:—the failure to enter upon the performance of a duty which the contract of employment imposes upon an employee, Anno: 20 ALR 104 s. 99 ALR 409; the total omission or failure of an employee to enter upon the performance of some distinct duty or undertaking which he has agreed with his employer to do, Hagerty v Montana Ore Purchasing Co. 38 Mont 69, 98 P 643; the omission to do some act which ought to be performed. A matter of "not doing." 35 Am J1st M & S § 586. Of agent:—the total omission or failure of an agent to enter upon the performance of some distinct duty or undertaking which he has agreed with his principal to do. Anno: 20 ALR 104.

Non fecit (non fē'sit). He did not do it,—the name given to a plea which denied that the defendant was the maker of the instrument sued on.

Non fecit vastum contra prohibitionem (non fē'sit vas'tum kon'trä prō-hi-bi-she-ō'nem). He has not committed waste in violation of the prohibition,— a form of plea interposed by a tenant against whom a writ of estrepement had been brought. See 3 Bl Comm 226.

nonforfeiture provision. A provision of life insurance policy, or of a statute applicable to such a policy, that in the event of the lapse of the policy when it has a reserve value, the insured shall be entitled under options as follows: (1) to receive the cash surrender value; (2) to have the insurance policy continue in force for the full amount for such a period of extended insurance as the reserve, applied on the single-premium basis, will purchase; (3) or to have the policy become a paid-up policy for such amount as the reserve will purchase. 29 Am J Rev ed Ins § 620. The provision in a statute whereby a life insurance company is precluded from issuing a policy which provides for the forfeiture of the same upon failure of the insured to pay a loan on the policy or interest thereon, without reference to the fact, as it may be in a particular case, that the total indebtedness on the policy, principal and interest, is less than the loan value. Keeley v Mutual Life Ins. Co. (CA7 Ill) 113 F2d 633.

non-functional. Lacking in usefulness. See **functional.**

nongeneral power of appointment. See **special power of appointment.**

Non haec in foedera veni (non hēk in fē'de-ra vē'nī). I did not enter into this agreement. Smith v United States (US) 2 Wall 219, 17 L Ed 788, 792.

nonimmigrant. A person who enters the United States with the intent to spend some time therein but without any idea of becoming a citizen. An alien coming into the country in a status distinct from that of an immigrant, such as that of a student, crewman of a foreign vessel, accredited representative of a foreign government, etc. 8 USC § 1101(15).

Non impedit clausula derogatoria, quo minus ab eadem potestate res dissolvantur a quibus constituuntur (non im'pe-dit klâ'su-la dē-ro-ga-tō'ri-a, quō mī'nus ab ē-ā'dem po-tes-tā'te rēz dis-sol-van'ter ä qui'bus kon-sti-tu-un'ter). A derogatory clause does not prevent the dissolution of things by the same authority or power by which they were constituted. See Broom's Legal Maxims 27.

Non impedivit (non im-pe-dī'vit). He did not hinder or disturb; a plea of the general issue in an action under a writ of quare impedit. See 3 Bl Comm 249.

non implacitando aliquem de libero tenemento sine brevi (non im-pla-si-tan'dō a'li-quem dē li'be-rō tene-men'tō sī'ne brē'vī). A writ which lay to prevent officers of the law from interfering with a freehold without the king's writ.

Nonimportation agreement (non-im-por-tā'shǫn a̱-grē'ment). An agreement, made in protest against British taxation, between the American colonies to boycott all goods shipped from the British Isles and the West Indies.

Non infregit conventionem (non in-frē'jit konven-she-ō'nem). He did not break the covenant,— a plea which raises a substantial issue in an action for non-repair according to covenant whether there was a want of repairs or not.

Non in legendo sed in intelligendo leges consistunt (non in lē-jen'dō sed in in-tel-li-jen'dō lē'jēz konsis'tunt). The laws consist not in the reading of them, but in the understanding of them.

Non in regno Angliae providetur, vel est aliqua securitas major vel solennior, per quam aliquis statum certiorem habere possit, neque ad statum suum verificandum aliquid solennius testimonium producere, quam finem in curia domini regis levatum; quidem finis sic vocatur, ed quod finis et consummatio omnium placitorum esse debet, et hac de causa providebatur (non in reg'nō Ang'li-ē pro-vidē'ter, vel est a'li-qua se-ku'ri-tās mā'jor vel solen'ni-or, per quam a'li-quis sta'tum ser-she-ō'rem hä-bē're pos'sit, ne'kwe ad sta'tum su'um vē-ri-fikan'dum a'li-quid so-len'ni-us tes-ti-mō'ni-um prōdū'se-re, quam fī'nem in kū'ri-a do'mi-nī rē'jis levā'tum; quī'dem fī'nis sik vo-kā'ter, e'ō quod fī'nis et kon-sum-mā-she-ō om'ni-um pla-si-tō'rum es'se de'bet, et hāk dē kâ'za prō-vi-dē-bā'ter). In the kingdom of England there is not provided any greater or more solemn security by which one can have a more certain title, nor can any evidence more solemn be produced for confirming his title than by a fine levied in the king's court. It is called a fine because it is the finish and the consummation of all suits, and it was provided for that reason. See 2 Bl Comm 349.

nonintercourse laws. Laws prohibiting commerce with another nation. The closing of the ports of a nation to vessels of an offending state and the prohibition of the sailing of vessels from such ports to ports of the offender. 30 Am J Rev ed Internat L § 53.

Non interfui (non in-ter'fu-ī). I was not present.

nonintervention will. A will which provides in effect that no bond shall be required of the executor and that the executor is relieved from the duty of reporting his conduct of the administration of the estate to the court.

nonintoxicating liquor. A liquor which although containing some alcohol, will not produce intoxication, even though consumed in quantity. State v Danenberg, 151 NC 718, 66 SE 301.

nonissuable plea. A plea which raises no issue of fact; a plea which does not go to the merits, such as a plea in abatement.

nonjoinder of party. The omission of a necessary party to an action. 39 Am J1st Parties § 110.

See **necessary party**.

nonjudicial authorities. Boards and officers not vested generally with judicial powers.

nonjudicial day. Same as **nonjuridical day**.

nonjudicial foreclosure. The foreclosure of a chattel mortgage under a power of sale granted to the mortgagee by the terms of the mortgage. 15 Am J2d Chat Mtg § 214. The foreclosure of a mortgage or deed of trust, covering real estate, under a power of sale contained in the instrument or created by a separate instrument; a method of foreclosure infrequent in use but possible under the law of some jurisdictions. 37 Am J1st Mtg § 647.

nonjurable (non-jö'rạ-bl). Incapable of taking an oath.

nonjuridical day. A day upon which judicial proceedings shall not be conducted. Sunday, a day which should not be profaned by the tumult of forensic litigation. Vidal v Backs, 218 Cal 99, 21 P2d 952, 86 ALR 1134.

The courts do not regard statutory or legal holidays as nonjuridical days unless constrained to do so by the terms or the necessary effect of statutes, 50 Am J1st Sun & H § 77.

nonlegal investment. An investment by a trustee which does not qualify as a legal investment.
See **legal investment**.

non juridicus (non jö'ri'di-kus). Nonjuridical; not judicial; not legal.

nonjuror (non-jo'rọr). Any person living in England who refused to make the oath of allegiance to the government.

Non jus ex regula, sed regula ex jure (non jūs ex re-gū'la, sed re-gū'la ex jū're). The law does not come from the rule, but the rule comes from the law.

Non jus, sed seisina facit stipitem (non jūs, sed sē'si-na fā'sit sti'pi-tem). It is not the right, but seisin that makes the stock or root.

The meaning of the maxim is, that it is not the mere right to take possession of land, but the actual entry and assumption of possession which vests complete ownership, so as to enable the transmission of the inheritance. See 2 Bl Comm 312.

"(Counsel) rightfully claim that credit is due the courts of this state for repudiating one of the fruits of the feudal system, which has come down preserved to us in the common law maxim, 'Non jus sed seisina,' " etc. See Todd v Oviatt, 58 Conn 174, 20 A 440.

Non licet quod dispendio licet (non lī'set quod dispen'di-ō li'set). That is not permitted which can only be permitted with loss.

non licet verdict. See **verdict of non licet**.

nonlienable. Descriptive of an article not the subject of a mechanic's lien.

Non liquet (non lī'kwet). It is not clear.

nonlitigating party. A person joined as a party but who does not appear and actually litigate the controversy. Atty Gen v Pomeroy, 93 Utah 426, 73 P2d 1277, 114 ALR 726.

nonmailable matter. Matter which cannot lawfully be conveyed in the United States mails or delivered from any postoffice or by any letter carrier. United States ex rel. Milwaukee Social Democratic Publishing Co. v Burleson, 255 US 407, 410, 65 L Ed 704, 709, 41 S Ct 352. Not acceptable for transmission by mail.

nonmaritime contract. A contract which has some relation to or connection with a vessel but does not come within the classification of maritime contracts.
See **maritime contract**.

nonmaritime tort. A tort which does not classify as a maritime tort so as to come within the jurisdiction of admiralty.
See **maritime tort**.

Non memini (non mē'mi-nī). I do not remember.

non molestando (non mō-les-tan'dō). A writ which lay to protect a person from threatened unlawful molestation.

nonmoral (non-mor'ạl). Having no connection with morality or morals.

Non nasci, et natum mori, paria sunt (non na'sī, et nā'tum mō'rī, pa'ri-a sunt). To be born dead, and not to be born at all, are the same thing.

nonnavigable waters. Private waters; waters which are not navigable. 56 Am J1st Wat § 177.

nonnegotiability. The absence of the quality of negotiability in an instrument.

nonnegotiable bill of lading. Any bill of lading which is not negotiable according to the definition in the UCC § 7–104. A bill of lading in which the goods are consigned or destined to a specified person. Uniform Bills of Lading Act §§ 4, 5. Otherwise known as a straight bill of lading.

nonnegotiable chose in action. A right represented by an instrument which is not negotiable.

nonnegotiable instrument. According to a well-understood meaning in the law of bills and notes, a term of art which refers only to commerical paper. An instrument which is not negotiable, that is, any instrument which does not meet the requirements laid down to qualify an instrument as a negotiable one, or an instrument which in its inception was negotiable but has lost its quality of negotiability. Edgar v Haines, 109 Ohio St 159, 141 NE 837. An instrument which meets all requirements as to form of a negotiable instrument except that it is not payable to order or bearer. UCC § 3—805. An instrument which, according to the underlying theory of the Uniform Commercial Code, should be governed by all sections of the Code except as to matters concerned with holders in due course. 11 Am J2d B & N §§ 7, 47.

nonnegotiable paper. See **nonnegotiable instrument**.

Non obligat lex nisi promulgata (non ob'li-gat lex nī'sī pro-mul-gā'ta). A law is not binding unless it is promulgated.

Non observata forma, infertur adnullatio actus (non ob-ser-vā'ta for'ma, in-fer'ter ad-nul-lā'she-o ak'tus). When formality is not observed, it is inferred that the act is a nullity.

non obstante (non ob-stan'tē). Notwithstanding.

non obstante aliquo statuto in contrarium (non ob-stan'te a'li-quō sta-tū'tō in kon-trā'ri-um). Notwithstanding any statute to the contrary. See 1 Bl Comm 342.

non obstante veredicto (non ob-stan'te ve-re-dik'tō). Notwithstanding the verdict.
See **judgment notwithstanding the verdict**.

Non officit conatus nisi sequatur effectus (non of'fi-sit ko-nā'tus nī'sī se-quā'ter ef-fek'tus). An attempt works no injury unless a result follows.

Non omne damnum inducit injuriam (non om'ne dam'num in-dū'sit in-jū'ri-am). It is not every loss that produces the violation of a legal right.

Non omne, quod licet, honestum est (non om'ne, quod lī'set, ho-nes'tum est). Not all that is lawful is honorable.

The observation is that of Paulus, as quoted in the Digest; "and we have a similar observation from another Paul, who received inspiration from a purer source than the Roman law." (1 Cor. vi. 12.) See Howell v Baker (NY) 4 Johns Ch 118, 121.

Non omnium quae a majoribus nostris constituta sunt ratio reddi potest (non om'ni-um kwē ā ma-jō'ri-bus nos'tris kon-sti-tū'ta sunt rā'she-ō red'dī po'test). A reason cannot be given for all of those things which were established by our ancestors.

Non omnium, quae a majoribus nostris constituta sunt, ratio reddi potest; et ideo rationes eorum quae constituuntur inquiri non oportet; alioquin multa ex his quae certa sunt subvertuntur (non om'ni-um, kwē ā mā-jō'ri-bus nos'tris kon-sti-tū'ta sunt, rā'-she-ō red'dī po'test; et i'de-ō ra-she-ō'nēz e-ō'rum kwē kon-sti-tu-un'ter in-quī'rī non o-por'tet; a'li-o-quin mul'ta ex his kwē ser'ta sunt sub-ver-tun'ter). It is impossible to give reasons for all of the laws instituted by our ancestors and so it is not needful to inquire into the reasons; otherwise many of those which are established would be overturned. See 1 Bl Comm 70.

nonowned automobile clause. A clause in an automobile insurance policy extending the coverage to include the casual operation of a car other than that described in the policy. 7 Am J2d Auto Ins § 98.

nonpar stock. Same as **nonpar value stock.**

nonparticipating royalty. See **perpetual nonparticipating royalty.**

nonpartisan ballot. A form of ballot in an election, the most frequent use of which is in connection with the election of judges, wherein the names of candidates appear without party label or emblem. 26 Am J2d Elect § 211.

non-par value stock. Corporate stock, issued as statutes permit, without any nominal or par value. 18 Am J2d Corp § 223. Shares of stock issued by a business trust or Massachusetts trust similar to the no-par shares issued by a corporation. 13 Am J2d Bus Tr § 23.

nonpayment. The failure of an obligor to make payment on the maturity of the obligation. Failure to pay according to the terms of an obligation, the effect of which, in case of a bill or note, may be dishonor and protest.

See **dishonor by nonpayment; protest.**

nonpecuniary damages. Damages for injury of such nature that there is no money standard applicable in measurement of the amount of damages. Broughel v Southern New England Tel. Co. 73 Conn 614, 621. Damages the amount of which depends upon the enlightened judgment of an impartial court or jury, since it is not a matter of mathematical calculation, as illustrated in damages for pain, suffering, and defamation. L. W. Pomereae v White, 70 Neb 171, 97 NW 232.

nonpecuniary injury. See **nonpecuniary damages.**

nonperformance. A failure or omission to perform. The breach of a contract by failure to perform in accordance with the terms and conditions of the contract. 17 Am J2d Contr §§ 355 et seq.

Non pertinet ad judicem secularem cognoscere de iis quae sunt mere spiritualia annexa (non per'ti-net ad jū'di-sem se-ku-lā'rem kog-nō'se-re de ī'is kwē sunt me're spi-ri-tu-ā'li-a an-ne'xa). It does not belong to a secular judge to notice those matters which are purely spiritual.

nonplevin (non-ple'vin). The failure of a landowner, whose land had been taken by the king, to sue to recover it within fifteen days after the taking.

Prior to Magna Charta, such failure resulted in the owner's loss of his seisin in the land.

non ponendis in assisis et juratis (non pō-nen'dis in as-sī'sis et jū-rā'tis). A writ whereby a person was freed from assize and jury service.

Non possessori incumbit necessitas probandi possessiones ad se pertinere (non po-ze-sō'rī in-kum'bit ne-se'si-tas pro-ban'di po-ze-she-ō'nēz ad se per-ti-nē're). (Civil law.) The necessity or burden of proving that his possessions belong to him does not fall upon the possessor. See Broom's Legal Maxims 714.

non possumus (non pos'ŭ-mus). We are not able; we cannot.

Non potest adduci exceptio ejusdem rei cujus petitur dissolutio (non po'test ad-dū'sī ex-sep'she-ō ē-jus'-dem rē'ī kū'jus pe'ti-ter dis-so-lū'she-ō). A plea of the very matter the determination of which is sought cannot be interposed. See Broom's Legal Maxims 166.

Non potest probari quod probatum non relevat (non po'test prō-bā'rī quod pro-bā'tum fā'se-re kum in-jū'ri-a et dam'nō if it were proved would be irrelevant.

Non potest quis sine brevi agere (non po'test quis sī'ne brē'vī ā'je-re). No one can sue without a writ.

Non potest rex gratiam facere cum injuria et damno aliorum (non po'test rex gra'she-am fā'se-re kum in-jū'ri-a et dam'nō a-li-ō'rum). The king cannot grant an indulgence attended with injury and loss to others.

The meaning is that the king could not grant any pardon or immunity which would release the wrongdoer from a prosecution by appeal, since appeals were at the suit of the injured party and not of the king. See 4 Bl Comm 398.

Non potest rex subditum renitentem onerare impositionibus (non po'test rex sub'di-tum re-ni-ten'tem o-ne-rā're im-pō-zi-she-ō'ni-bus). The king cannot burden a protesting subject with impositions.

Non potest videri deisse habere, qui nunquam habuit (non po'test vi-dē'rī de-is'se hā-bē're, quī nun'quam hā'bu-it). (Civil law.) A person who never had cannot be deemed to have ceased to have.

nonpower boat. Sailboat. 12 Am J2d Boats § 77.

Non praestat impedimentum quod de jure non sortitur effectum (non prē'stat im-pe-di-men'tum quod de jū're non sor'ti-ter ef-fek'tum). That which is of no consequence in law offers no impediment.

nonprobate assets. Property left by a decedent not subject to administration by his personal representative.

non procedendo ad assisam. See **de non procedendo ad assisam.**

nonproduction of evidence. The failure of a party to testify, to call an available witness on a material issue, or to introduce documentary evidence within his control. 29 Am J2d Ev §§ 175 et seq.

nonprofit association. An association organized and operating without the purpose of making a profit, such as an association operating for a charitable purpose.

nonprofit corporation. A corporation ordinarily without stockholders, created for or devoted to charitable purposes or supported by charity; a charitable corporation. 18 Am J2d Corp §§ 10, 460.

nonprofit institution. See **charitable institution.**

nonprofit organization. See **nonprofit association; nonprofit corporation.**

non pros. Abbreviation of **non prosequitur.**

non prosequitur (non prǫ-sek′wi-tėr). An old form of judgment.
See **judgment of non prosequitur.**

non pros'd. Subjected to a **judgment of non prosequitur.** In modern usage, nonsuited.

Non quieta movere (non qui-ē′ta mo-vē′re). Not to disturb that which is settled. A good maxim in jurisprudence. Green v Hudson River Railroad Co. (NY) 28 Barb 9, 22.

Non quod dictum, sed quod factum est, inspicitur (non quod dik′tum, sed quod fak′tum est, in-spi′si-ter). Not what is said, but what is done, is regarded. Osborn v Cook, 65 Mass (11 Cush) 532, 536.

nonquota immigrant. An immigrant who is the child or the spouse of a citizen of the United States; an immigrant lawfully admitted for permanent residence who is returning from a temporary visit abroad; an immigrant born in Canada, Mexico, Cuba, Haiti, Dominican Republic, Canal Zone, or an independent country of central or South America, and a spouse or child of any such immigrant; an immigrant who was formerly a citizen of the United States and is applying for reacquisition of citizenship; an immigrant who was formerly a native-born or naturalized citizen of this country but who has lost his nationality by virtue of obtaining naturalization in a foreign state; an immigrant who is an established minister of a religious denomination and whose services are needed by such religious denomination having a bona fide organization in the United States and the spouse or child of any such immigrant; or an immigrant who is an employee or retired former employee of the United States Government abroad with a total of 15 years service, his accompanying spouse, and any child of his. 8 USC § 110(a)(27).

nonrecording insurance. Insurance designed, subject to certain exclusions or exceptions, to compensate a lender for losses resulting solely from the failure to file for public record an instrument securing a debt, usually a bill of sale, conditional sale contract, or chattel mortgage. American Aviation & General Ins. Co. v Georgia Telco Credit Union (CA5 Ga) 223 F2d 206, 51 ALR2d 316.

nonrecourse provision. The direction in a bill of lading whereby the consignor directs the carrier not to deliver the goods to the consignee until the carrier's charges are collected, thereby relieving himself from being compelled to pay any such charges, where the carrier delivers the goods to the consignee without collecting the charges as directed. New York Cent. R. Co. v Trans American Petroleum Corp. (CA7 Ill) 108 F2d 994, 129 ALR 206.

See **without recourse.**

Non refert an quis assensum suum praefert verbis, an rebus ipsis et factis (non re′fert an quis as-sen′-sum su′um prē′fert ver′bis, an rē′bus ip′sis et fak′-tis). It does not matter whether anyone expresses his assent by words or by acts and deeds.

Non refert quid ex aequipollentibus fiat (non re′fert quid ex ē-qui-pol-len′ti-bus fī′at). It does not matter which one of those things which are equivalent is done.

Non refert quid notum sit judici, si notum, non sit in forma, judicii (non re′fert quid nō′tum sit jū′di-sī, sī nō′tum non sit in for′ma, jū-di′she-i). It matters not what is known to the judge, if it is not known to him judicially. Riley v Wallace, 188 Ky 471, 222 SW 1085, 11 ALR 337, 340.

Non refert verbis an factis fit revocatio (non re′fert ver′bis an fak′tis fit re-vō-kā′she-ō). It does not matter whether a revocation is effected by words or by acts.

nonrefunding annuity contract. Same as **straight annuity.** 4 Am J2d Annui § 1.

nonregistered stockholder. A stockholder in fact who because of the failure of a corporate officer or transfer agent is not recorded as a stockholder on the books of the corporation. A term applied in the older period of superadded liability of stockholders to a stockholder who had his stock registered in a fictitious name or in the name of a person not financially responsible in order to avoid liability as a stockholder.

Non remota causa sed proxima spectatur (non rē-mō′ta kā′za sed pro′xi-ma spek-tā′ter). Not the remote cause, but the one which is proximate, is regarded.

nonresident. One who is in a place other than that of his domicil or residence.
See **domicil; residence.**

nonresident alien. A person who is neither a citizen nor a resident of this country. 3 Am J2d Aliens § 2. An alien who does not reside within the state. Estate of Gill, 79 Iowa 296, 44 NW 553.

nonresidentio pro clerico regis (non-re-si-den′she-ō prō kle′ri-kō rē′jis). A writ which lay to prevent the ouster of a clergyman for nonresidence, where he was absent in the king's service.

nonresident motorist. A status applied to a motorist involved in an accident, usually on a determination of the place of actual residence rather than domicil. 8 Am J2d Auto § 852.

nonresident pupil. A pupil at a public or high school who is not a resident of the school district. 47 Am J1st Sch § 154.

Non respondebit minor, nisi in causa dotis, et hoc pro favore doti (non re-spon-dē′bit mī′nor, nī′sī in kā′za dō′tis, et hōk prō fa′vō-re dō′tī). A minor shall not answer except in the case of dower, and this in favor of dower.

nonresponsible party. A person who has no property subject to levy for the enforcement of a judgment against him. A person who by reason of infancy or mental incompetency is not bound upon a contract which he has professed to make.

nonresponsive answer. An answer given by a witness upon examination in a trial or in the taking of a deposition which evades or does not relate to the question or interrogatory directed to him. 23 Am J2d Dep § 125; 58 Am J1st Witn § 575.

Non reus nisi mens sit rea (non rē'us nī'sī mēnz sit rē'a). There is no guilt unless there is a guilty intent.

non sanae mentis (non sā'nē men'tis). Not of sound mind.

nonsane memory (non'sān mem'ō-ri). Unsound memory; unsound mind.

nonscheduled airline. An airline operating only chartered flights, maintaining no flights on a fixed schedule of departures and arrivals.

nonscheduled airline passenger. A passenger on the aircraft of a nonscheduled airline. 29A Am J Rev ed Ins § 1261.

nonsense. Unintelligible matter which is contained in a writing.

non seq. An abbreviation of **non sequitur.**

non sequitur (non sek'wi-tėr). It does not follow.

Non sequitur clamorem suum (non sek'wi-ter kla-mō'rem su'um). He does not press his claim. See 3 Bl Comm 376.

Non solent quae abundant vitiare scripturas (non sō'-lent kwē a-bun'dant vi-she-ā're skrip-tū'rās). (Civil law.) Those matters which are superfluous do not ordinarily vitiate writings.

Non solum quid licet, sed quid est conveniens considerandum, quia nihil quod inconveniens est licitum (non sō'lum quid lī'set, sed quid est kon-vē'ni-enz kon-si-de-ran'dum, qui'a ni'hil quod in-kon-vē'ni-enz est li'si-tum). Not only that which is permitted, but that which is convenient or suitable is to be considered, because nothing which is inconvenient or unsuitable is lawful.

non solverunt (non sol-vē'runt). They have not paid, —a form of replication interposed upon a defendant's plea of payment. Ware v Hylton (US) 3 Dall 199, 202, 1 L Ed 568, 570.

nonstock corporation. A membership corporation. A corporation not organized for profit and operating under a charter which does not provide for the issuance of stock. American Aberdeen-Angus Breeders Asso. v Fullerton, 325 Ill 323, 156 NE 314; Missionary Baptist State Convention v State, 180 Kan 501, 305 P2d 846.

Non submissit (non sub-mis'sit). He did not submit, —the name given to a plea that the defendant did not submit to an arbitration.

non sui juris (non su'ī jū'ris). Legally incompetent to act for himself in making a contract or in appearing in a cause by himself or through an attorney. 27 Am J1st Inf § 140.

nonsuit. A method of taking the case from the jury for the insufficiency of the plaintiff's proof. 53 Am J1st Tr § 304. A determination that the evidence of the plaintiff is insufficient to support a judgment in his favor, wherefore the case should be taken from the jury. 53 Am J1st Tr §§ 304 et seq. A judgment given against the plaintiff on motion made by the defendant, such motion being in the nature of a demurrer to the plaintiff's evidence, whereby the defendant admits all that the plaintiff has proved to be true, but contends that in law this proof is nevertheless insufficient to entitle the plaintiff to a recovery. 24 Am J2d Dism § 4; 53 Am J1st Tr § 307. A judgment entered by the court when the plaintiff, being called, refuses to appear at the time when the jury is to deliver its verdict, or where the court decides that the plaintiff has given no evidence upon which a jury could find a verdict in his favor. Sandoval v Rosser, 86 Tex 682, 686, 26 SW 933. A judgment given against the plaintiff when he is unable to prove a case, or when he refuses or neglects to proceed to the trial of the cause after it has been put at issue. Deeley v Heintz, 169 NY 129, 132, 62 NE 158. For the purposes of the statute of limitations, a dismissal compelled by the court. 34 Am J1st Lim Ac § 282.

As used in a statute providing that when the plaintiff shall suffer a nonsuit, he may bring a new action within a prescribed time thereafter, it is generally held that the "nonsuit" need not be a technical one, and that the statute applies to a dismissal. The following have been held to be nonsuits within such a provision: a dismissal as to one of several defendants; a dismissal for failure to pay costs; a refusal to set aside an involuntary nonsuit and entry of judgment for the defendant; and, by some authority, the sustaining of a plea in abatement, and a voluntary dismissal by the plaintiff. The following, however, have been held not to be nonsuits within such a provision: the sustaining of a demurrer to a declaration, the exclusion of an item of account by a referee, and a judgment in bar of a claim, where the plaintiff has not pursued the proper remedy. 34 Am J1st Lim Ac § 282.

See **voluntary nonsuit.**

nonsuited. The condition of a plaintiff against whom a nonsuit has been entered.

See **nonsuit.**

Non sum informatus (non sum in-for-mā'tus). I am not informed,—a species of judgment by default which is given against a defendant when his attorney declares that he has no instruction to say anything in answer to the plaintiff, or in defense of his client. See 3 Bl Comm 397.

Non sunt longa ubi nihil est quod demere possis (non sunt lon'ga u'bi ni'hil est quod de'me-re pos'sis). Those matters are not prolix or superfluous wherein there is nothing which you can omit.

nonsupport. Failure to furnish support for a person, such as one's wife or child, whom he is obligated by law to support. The statutory offense of a husband who neglects or fails to provide his wife and children, or either, with the necessaries of life. Anno: 44 ALR2d 892. As ground for a divorce, the intentional failure of the husband to support his wife, without lawful excuse, when he had the ability to support her. Svanda v Svanda, 93 Neb 404, 140 NW 777.

Non suspicio cujuslibet vani et meticulosi hominis, sed talis qui possit cadere in virum constantem; talis enim esse metus, qui in se contineat vitae periculum, aut corporis cruciatum (non sus-pi'she-ō kū-jus'li-bet vā'nī et me-ti-kū-lō'sī ho'mi-nis, sed tā'lis quī pos'sit ka'de-re in vī'rum kon-stan'tem; tā'lis e'nim es'se me'tus, quī in sē kon-ti'ne-at vī'tē pe-ri'ku-lum, ât kor'po-ris kru-she-ā'tum). It must not be the apprehension of a foolish and fearful man, but such as would affect a courageous man; it should be such fear as would involve danger to life or bodily pain. See 1 Bl Comm 131.

Non temere credere, est nervus sapientiae (non te'me-re kre'de-re, est ner'vus sa-pi-en'she-ē). Not to believe rashly is the bowstring of wisdom.

Non tenuit (non ten'ū-it). He did not hold,—a name which was given to a pleading in actions of replevin

nontenure (non-ten'ur). The name given to a plea in a real action wherein the defendant denied his tenancy.

nonterm (non'term). A period between two terms of court.

nonterminus (non-ter'mi-nus). A period between terms of court.

nontestamentary assets. Property left by a testate decedent which does not pass under his will.

nontestamentary paper. An instrument not executed in such manner as to be entitled to probate as the will of a decedent.

nontrading firm. See **nontrading partnership**.

nontrading partnership. A partnership whose business does not involve buying and selling as a day to day activity. 40 Am J1st Partn § 12.

nonunion goods. Articles produced by a nonunion shop.

nonunion workers. Employees in a plant who do not belong to a labor union.

nonuser. Absence of user; want of user, as of an easement. 25 Am J2d Ease § 105. Failure to use premises for the purpose for which dedicated. Adams v Rowles, 149 Tex 52, 228 SW2d 849. The failure of a public body which has taken land for a public use to devote the property to such use within a reasonable time. 26 Am J2d Em D § 146. A possible method of abandoning a highway. 25 Am J1st High § 112. The failure to exercise a franchise within a reasonable time in accordance with the condition which inheres in the nature of the grant. The nonperformance by a corporation of conditions or requirements upon which its privileges and franchises were conferred. 19 Am J2d Corp § 1619.

Non valet confirmatio, nisi ille, qui confirmat, sit in possessione rei vel juris unde fieri debet confirmatio; et eodem modo, nisi ille cui confirmatio fit sit in possessione (non va'let kon-fir-mā'she-ō, nī'sī il'le, quī kon-fir'mat, sit in po-ze-she-ō'ne rē'ī vel jū'ris un'de fī'e-rī de'bet kon-fir-mā'she-ō; et ē-ō'dem mo'do, nī'sī il'le kī kon-fir-mā'she-ō fit sit in po-ze-she-ō'ne). A confirmation is not valid unless he who confirms is in possession of the thing or of the right whereof confirmation is to be made, and in the same manner, unless he to whom the confirmation is to be made is in possession.

Non valet exceptio ejusdem rei cujus petitur dissolutio (non va'let ex-sep'she-ō ē-jus'dem rē'ī kū'jus pe'ti-ter dis-so-lū'she-o). A plea of the very matter the determination of which is sought is not valid.

Non valet impedimentum quod de jure non sortitur effectum (non va'let im-pe-di-men'tum quod dē jū're non sor'ti-ter ef-fek'tum). An impediment or bar which has no effect in law will not avail.

Non verbis sed ipsis rebus, leges imponimus (non ver'bis sed ip'sis rē'bus, lē'jez im-pō'ni-mus). We do not impose laws upon words, but upon the things themselves.

Non videntur, qui errant, consentire (non vi-den'ter, quī er'rant, kon-sen-tī're). Those who err are not deemed to consent. A maxim is of universal application as well as of universal justice. Earle v De Witt, 88 Mass (6 Allen) 520, 543.

Non videntur rem amittere quibus propria non fuit (non vi-den'ter rem a-mit'te-re qui'bus pro'pri-a non fu'it). Persons to whom a thing did not belong are not deemed to lose it.

Non videtur consensum retinuisse si quis ex praescripto minantis aliquid immutavit (non vi-dē'ter kon-sen'sum re-ti-nu-is'se sī quis ex prē-skrip'tō minan'tis a'li-quid im-mū-tā'vit). Anyone is not deemed to have witheld his consent who has changed anything by the direction of a person who threatens him. See Broom's Legal Maxims, 278.

Non videtur perfecte cujusque id esse, quod ex casu auferri potest (non vi-dē'ter per-fek'tē kū-jus'kwe id es'se, quod ex kā'sū â-fer'rī po'test). (Civil law.) That is not deemed to belong to a person completely which can, upon occasion, be taken away.

Non videtur quisquam id capere, quod ei necesse est alii restituere (non vi-dē'ter quis'quam id kā'pe-re, quod ē'ī ne-ses'se est a'li-ī re-sti-tu'e-re). (Civil law.) Anyone is not deemed to recover that which he is obliged to give up to another.

Non videtur vim facere, qui jure suo utitur, et ordinaria actione experitur (non vi-dē'ter vim fā'se-re, quī jū're su'ō ū'ti-ter, et or-di-nā'ri-a ak-she-ō'ne ex-pe'ri-ter). (Civil law.) He is not deemed to use force who exercises his own right and sues in an ordinary action.

non vult contendere. See **plea of non vult contendere**.

Non vult contendere cum domina regina et posuit se in gratiam curiae (non vult kon-ten'de-re kum do'-mi-na rē-jī'na et po'su-it sē in grā'she-am kū'ri-ē). The defendant does not wish to contend with our mistress, the queen, but puts himself upon the mercy of the court. Commonwealth v Shrope, 264 Pa 246, 107 A 729, 6 ALR 690, 692.

non vult prosequi (non vult pro'se-quī). He will not prosecute. See 1 Bl Comm 268.

nonwaiver agreement. See **nonwaiver clause**.

nonwaiver clause. A clause in an insurance policy limiting the power of agents to waive conditions of the policy or restricting the manner in which a waiver of such condition may be made. 29A Am J Rev ed Ins § 1040.

nonwhite. A person not of the white race, such as a Mongolian or Negro.

noon. Twelve hours after midnight, the sun being at meridian. Abbreviated "M." The beginning of the sidereal day used by the astronomers. 52 Am J1st Time § 14. The middle of the day in common parlance.

noonday. Noon; midday.

noon hour. See **lunch hour**.

no-par shares. See **non-par value stock**.

No Popery Riots (nō pō'pėr-i rī'ots). Riots of unprecedented magnitude which occurred in London in June, 1780.

A mob of sixty thousand persons had control of the city for several days. The authorities were paralyzed. The cause of it was Lord George Gordon's petition to parliament for the repeal of Sir George Saville's act for the relief of Catholics. The riot spread throughout the kingdom. London was in a state of anarchy. On June sixth, thirty-six fires set by the mob were raging. The Fleet and King's Bench prisons were fired, and the prisoners released. All public buildings were threatened; many private homes were sacked and burned. More than four hundred and fifty persons were killed. The military finally subdued the mob. The courts held the respective hundreds liable for the losses in them. County of Allegheny v Gibson, 90 Pa 397.

no property found. A return of a writ of execution, somewhat wanting in perfection and completeness, but indicating the absence of property of the defendant upon which to make a levy. 21 Am J2d Exec § 478.

nor. A conjunction properly used in connection with "neither" in stating a negative proposition. State ex rel. Crow v St. Louis, 174 Mo 125, 73 SW 623.

no-raiding agreement. An agreement between rival labor unions that neither will solicit a member of the other for the purpose of inducing a change of membership. United Textile Workers v Textile Workers Union (CA7 Ill) 258 F2d 743.

no recourse. See **without recourse.**

normal school. A teachers' college. State Teachers College v Morris, 165 Miss 758, 144 So 374; Normal School Dist. v Painter, 102 Mo 464, 14 SW 938. A school particularly for the education and training of school teachers. 15 Am J2d Colleges § 4. Not a common or public school. 15 Am J2d Colleges § 1.

Norman Conquest (nôr'man kon'kwest). The conquest of England by the Normans in 1066, under William of Normandy.

Norman French. See **Law French.**

Norris-LaGuardia Act. A federal statute of 1932 which prohibits the issuance of injunctions in federal courts in cases involving or growing out of labor disputes, as therein defined, except in strict accord with the provisions of the statute. 29 USC §§ 101–115; 31 Am J Rev ed Lab §§ 541 et seq.
Statutes substantially the same as the Norris-LaGuardia Act have been enacted in a number of states, although some apply to the granting of ex parte and temporary injunctions only. 31 Am J Rev ed Lab § 541.

north. Due north, unless qualified or controlled by other words of the context in which it appears. 23 Am J2d Deeds § 248. A compass point; the direction of the north pole from any other point on the earth's surface.

Northampton table. A mortality table. 20 Am J2d Ev § 895.
See **mortality table.**

Northeastern Interstate Nuclear Compact. A compact similar to that of the Southern Interstate Nuclear Compact, proposed for and under consideration by northeastern states. 6 Am J2d Atomic E § 46.
See **Southern Interstate Nuclear Compact.**

northeast quarter. See **fraction of section.**

north one-half. See **fraction of section.**

Northwest Ordinance of 1787. An ordinance passed by Congress for the government of the Northwest Territory, the provisions of which were superseded by the adoption of the Constitution of the United States and are in force only as continued in force by acts of Congress after the adoption of the Constitution. 16 Am J2d Const L § 16.

northwest quarter. See **fraction of section.**

Northwest Territory. The public domain of the United States following the successful conclusion of the Revolutionary War and the making of a treaty of peace with England, lying west of the state of New York and north of the Ohio River. The domain from which the states of Ohio, Indiana, Illinois, Michigan, Wisconsin and part of Minnesota were formed. A territory of Canada extending from the northern boundaries of British Columbia, Alberta, Saskatchewan, and Manitoba beyond the Arctic Circle.

Noscitur a sociis (nō'si-ter ā sō'she-is). One is known by his companions.
The maxim is applied to the familiar rule of construction that the meaning of a word or expression may be gathered from the surrounding words, that is, from the context. 50 Am J1st Stat § 247.

Noscitur ex socio, qui non cognoscitur ex se (nō'si-ter ex so'she-ō, quī non kog-nō'si-ter ex sē). A person who may not be known by himself is known by his companion.

nota (nō'tạ). (Civil law.) A note; a memorandum; a distinguishing mark or sign; a brand.

notabilia. See **bona notabilia.**

not administered. Literally, assets of a decedent, sometimes his entire estate, not subjected to administration in a probate court.
At common law, goods, chattels, and credits "not administered," meant goods, chattels, and credits which had been the property of the decedent at his death, and remained in specie, unchanged and unconverted when the administrator de bonis non was appointed. Thus, money received by the former executor or administrator in his representative capacity, and kept by itself separate from his own money, is regarded as "not administered;" but if mixed and mingled with his own money, so that its identity is gone, it is regarded as converted, and so "administered," so far as the administrator de bonis non is concerned. Chamberlin's Appeal, 70 Conn 363, 39 A 734.

notare infamia (nō-tā're in-fā'mi-a). (Civil law.) To mark or brand a person as a mark of infamy.

notarial (nọ-tā'ri-ạl). Pertaining or relating to the office or functions of a notary; made or done by a notary.

notarial act. The execution of a deed or contract, such as a contract of adoption, before a notary public. Succession of Thomson, 221 La 791, 60 So 2d 411.

notarial seal. An official seal of a notary public which, when duly affixed, is at least prima facie evidence of the notary's official character and raises a presumption of the truth of statements made by the notary in such character.
The form of the seal is sometimes provided by law, but such a provision has been held merely directory. If a seal is required, he cannot use a private one, but must adopt an official seal inscribed as he may choose, but capable of making a definite and uniform impression on the paper authenticated or on some tenacious substance attached thereto. It is no longer necessary to use wax or some other adhesive substance on which the seal may be impressed and if the law does not positively prescribe otherwise, it is enough that the impress be made upon the paper itself in such manner as to be readily identified on inspection. 39 Am J1st Notary § 34.

notarius (nō-tā'ri-us). In old English law, a notary or conveyancer. (Roman law.) A rapid writer; a short-hand writer; an amanuensis.

notarizing. Certifying as a notary to the authenticity of a signature on a document.

notary (nō'tạ-ri). Same as **notary public**.

notary public (nō'tạ-ri pub'lik). An officer whose duty is to attest the genuineness of deeds or writings in order to render them available as evidence of the facts therein contained, 39 Am J1st Notary § 2, and who is authorized by statute to administer various oaths. 39 Am J1st Oath § 9.

notary's certificate. The certificate of a notary public living nearest the place of a fire, the loss under which is covered by an insurance policy, stating that he has examined the circumstances and believes that the insured has actually sustained loss to the amount specified in the certificate. 29A Am J Rev ed Ins § 1405. Broadly, any certification made by a notary public in an official capacity.

notary's record book. A record book which notaries are required in some jurisdictions to keep and to enter therein their notarial acts, which book must be deposited in a designated public office when the notary dies, resigns, or is removed from office, a certified copy of the record being made competent evidence. 39 Am J1st Notary § 45.

notary's seal. See **notarial seal**.

notation. A writing appearing upon an instrument but not in the regular formal order of the instrument. 17 Am J2d Contr § 263.
See **marginal notation**.

notch sensitive. A term applied to metals the useful life of which seems to be much more affected by stress than that of others. Northwest Airlines, Inc. v Glenn L. Martin Co. (CA6 Ohio) 224 F2d 120, 50 ALR2d 882, reh den 229 F2d 434, 50 ALR2d 897.

not due. See **not payable presently**.

note. A notation. A written promise to pay another a certain sum of money at a certain time. Grissom v Commercial Nat. Bank, 87 Tenn 350, 10 SW 774. A kind of commercial paper. UCC § 3–104(2). A negotiable promissory note. Uniform Negotiable Instruments L § 191. A term used interchangeably with promissory note. Shawano Finance Corp. v Julius, 214 Wis 637, 254 NW 355.

note an exception. A professional request, made with deference to the trial judge, but constituting the method of having made of record for use on appeal an exception to a ruling of the judge.

note in payment. A note given in satisfaction or extinguishment of a claim against the maker. 40 Am J1st Paym § 91.

note of a fine. An abstract of the writ of covenant, and the concord; naming the parties, the parcels of land, and the agreement, enrolled of record in the proper office in the process of alienating land by levying a fine. See 2 Bl Comm 351.

note of allowance. A note delivered by one of the masters of the court to a party to an action evidencing the right of the latter to prosecute a writ of error under the English practice.

note of hand. A name given generally by the unlearned, in common, to all those evidences of debts which are verified under the hand of the debtor, and which the creditor keeps.
It is not an apt legal term to describe a debt by judgment; nor is it ever used in that sense as its popular one. Perry v Maxwell, 17 NC (2 Dev Eq) 488, 496.

note of protest. A note of the fact of the protest of a negotiable instrument indorsed thereon by a notary at the time of its protest.
See **memorandum**; **municipal note**; **promissory note**; **public note**.

notes of stenographer. See **stenographer's notes**; **stenographic notes of court reporter**.

notes of the United States. See **United States notes**.

notes used in circulation. Notes issued by national banks and circulating as currency. United States v White (CC NY) 19 F 723. 724.

note to be renewed until paid in full. A provision in a note for indefinite renewal, but not to be construed as meaning that the maker has as much time as he desires to make payment of the principal sum, he being entitled to one renewal for the period specified in the original note, with no right to a renewal thereafter. Riepl v Sardino, 262 Wis 670, 56 NW2d 493, 35 ALR2d 1087.

not exempt by law. Not exempt under either federal or state law. 31 Am J2d Exemp § 7.

not found. The formal words which are indorsed on a bill of indictment by a grand jury upon its failure to indict the person named as accused in the bill. A form of return of a writ, summons, or notice, by which the officer holding the paper for service states the impossibility of making service due to inability to find the defendant or other person upon whom it should be served. A condition precedent under some statutes to service by publication. 42 Am J1st Proc § 89.
See **no property found**.

not guilty. See **plea of not guilty**.

not guilty verdict. See **verdict of not guilty**.

not hereinbefore disposed of. A familiar term in a residuary clause of a will, usually effective to determine that lapsed legacies and devises pass under the residuary clause. 57 Am J1st Wills § 1449.

nothus (no'thus). (Roman law.) Spurious; not genuine; an illegitimate; a bastard.

notice. In common parlance, information, intelligence, or knowledge. In law, actual notice, constructive notice, express notice or implied notice. 39 Am J1st Notice § 3. The acclaim or criticism in the press of the performance of an actor, musician, or dancer.
Whatever is sufficient to put a person upon inquiry is notice of all the facts to which that inquiry will lead when prosecuted with reasonable diligence and in good faith. Texas Co. v Aycock, 190 Tenn 16, 227 SW2d 41, 17 ALR2d 322.
See **actual notice**; **constructive notice**; **express notice**; **implied notice**; **personal notice**.

notice as soon as practicable. As required of an insured or a person protected by a fidelity bond in reference to a loss, notice within a reasonable time after discovery of the loss. Anno: 23 ALR2d 1083; 29A Am J Rev ed Ins § 1379.

notice in pais. A notice outside the record or writing; a notice not on the face of the record or writing.
For example, one who has signed a bond is not liable to the obligee thereon if the latter had notice either from the face of the bond or "in pais," that others were to sign it before delivery. 12 Am J2d Bonds § 18.

notice in person. Actual notice. Travelers' Ins. Co. v Farmers' Mut. Fire Ins. Asso. 211 Iowa 1051, 233 NW 153.
See **personal notice**.

notice in writing. Ordinarily a notice given in writing and subscribed by the person giving notice thereby.
A written notice may be a sufficient "notice in writing," although it is not signed, provided it purports to come from the person whose duty it is to give the notice. Cohn v Smith, 37 Cal App 764, 174 P 682.

notice of accident or claim. A notice required of the insured under a liability policy, to be given to the insurer respecting the occurrence of an accident or of a claim for damages resulting therefrom. 7 Am J2d Auto Ins § 141.

notice of action or proceeding. The formal notice required to confer jurisdiction; a summons or original notice.
A distinction is to be observed between knowledge of the pendency of an action or proceeding and notice thereof. If a defendant does not submit himself to the jurisdiction of the court, jurisdiction can be acquired in no other way than by actual or constructive notice, whatever he may know of the existence of the proceedings. National Metal Co. v Greene Consol. Copper Co. 11 Ariz 108, 89 P 535.

notice of appeal. The method of initiating a proceeding for appellate review, consisting of a notice as provided by statute, designating the court to which an appeal is taken, the judgment, order, or decree to be reviewed, stating the relief sought on appeal, the parties appealing, and the parties against whom relief is sought on appeal, such notice to be served and filed in accordance with statutory requirements. 4 Am J2d A & E §§ 316 et seq.

notice of appearance. The formal method of appearing in an action or proceeding. A written notice of appearance filed in the action or proceeding or a notice given orally in open court by a party or, in the usual case, by his attorney, stating that he appears. 5 Am J2d Appear § 14.
See **general appearance**; **special appearance**.

notice of arrival. A notice given by a common carrier to the consignee of a shipment of goods of the arrival of the goods at their destination. 13 Am J2d Car § 398.

notice of assignment. A notice of an assignment of a chose in action given to the debtor for the purpose of completing the assignment and vesting title in the assignee, especially for the purpose of precluding the debtor of the right to deal with the original creditor by making payment or otherwise in reference to the subject matter of the assignment. 6 Am J2d Assign § 96.

notice of attorney's lien. A notice of an attorney's special or charging lien upon a judgment recovered by him on behalf of his client, as such may be required by statute to be given the adverse party. 7 Am J2d Attys § 287.

notice of claim. A notice of claim for damages against a municipal corporation or other public body asserted for tortious injury to person or property, required by statute as a condition precedent to an action at law to recover on such claim. 38 Am J1st Mun Corp § 673. A notice of claim against a municipal corporation required by statute of a more comprehensive nature, embracing both ex contractu and ex delicto claims. 38 Am J1st Mun Corp § 677. A notice of the location of a mining claim. 36 Am J1st Min & M § 79.

notice of copyright. An indispensable part of the process by which the copyright of a published work is secured; a notice in form prescribed by statute, located in each published copy in the position prescribed by statute, and stated in the English language. 18 Am J2d Copyr § 56. For example, "Copyright (c) 1967 by Jurisprudence Publishers, Inc."

notice of defects. A notice of defects in a railroad fence or cattle guards required as a condition of the duty of the railroad company to repair such defects. 44 Am J1st RR § 163. A notice of the defective condition of a highway or street, required as a condition of municipal liability for injuries due to the defects. 25 Am J1st High § 441. A notice given by the purchaser to the seller of goods, wares, or merchandise of defects constituting a breach of warranty, sometimes required by a provision in the contract of sale, and always a matter of good practice before commencing an action for breach of warranty. 46 Am J1st Sales §§ 714 et seq.

notice of directors' meeting. A requirement where the meeting is a special one, calling for personal service, if practicable, upon every member of the board entitled to be present. 19 Am J2d Corp § 1133.

notice of discovery. A notice of location of a mining claim. 36 Am J1st Min & M § 79.
See **notice of location**.

notice of dishonor. A notice that a bill or note has been dishonored by nonacceptance or nonpayment. An essential of a cause of action of the holder against an indorser or drawer, unless waived or dispensed with, as where, under the circumstances, it cannot be given although due diligence be exercised in an attempt to give it. 11 Am J1st B & N § 801.

notice of dismissal. A notice filed by the plaintiff or served upon the defendant, as the statute may require, upon the voluntary dismissal of an action. 24 Am J2d Dism § 48.

notice of election. The notice, usually by publication, through which the voters are informed of the time, place, and purpose of an impending election. 26 Am J2d Elect § 193.

notice of excavation. A notice given by an owner of land to an adjoining owner of intent to make an excavation, thereby giving the adjoining owner opportunity to protect his premises against the excavation. 1 Am J2d Adj L § 51.

notice of exemption. A demand or claim that property seized under process for debt be released as exempt. 31 Am J2d Exempt §§ 142 et seq.

notice of forfeiture. A notice in a proceeding in rem for the forfeiture of property admonishing the owner and all other persons claiming any right, title, or interest in the property seized to appear and show cause on or before a day named why forfeiture of the property should not be decreed in accordance with the prayer of the libel or information. 36 Am J2d Forf & P § 36.

notice of infringement. See **notice of patent right**.

notice of intention to move for a new trial. A notice required by statute in some states to be served upon the adverse party by the party intending to move for a new trial, designating the statutory grounds upon which the motion will be made, and whether it will be made upon affidavits or the minutes of the court, or bill of exceptions, or a statement of the case. 39 Am J1st New Tr § 179.

notice of judgment. Notice to the party against whom a judgment has been rendered of the entry of the judgment, usually a matter of constructive notice from the docketing and indexing, but in a few instances required by statute as a matter of the giving of a formal notice. 30A Am J Rev ed Judgm § 98.

notice of lien. See **notice of attorney's lien; notice of mechanic's lien.**

notice of lis pendens. The common-law doctrine that a pending suit is notice to all the world, so that one who purchases property involved in the litigation takes it subject to, and is bound by, the judgment rendered therein. 34 Am J1st Lis P §§ 2, 3.
See **notice of pendency.**

notice of location. (Mining law.) A notice required by statute or local regulation in all, or nearly all, the mining states and territories to be posted on a mining claim sought to be located, containing the name of the locators, the name of the claim and the date of the location. 36 Am J1st Min & M § 79.

notice of loss. A notice of the occurrence of a loss, required to be given by insured to the insurer, as provided by the contract of insurance or statute, within a limited period of time. 29A Am J Rev ed Ins §§ 1373–1439.
See **proof of loss.**

notice of mechanic's lien. A notice required by statute in many jurisdictions to be given the owner of property by one claiming a mechanic's lien thereon, not for work performed or materials furnished under a contract with the owner, but for work on the premises performed in the capacity of a subcontractor or mechanic or for materials furnished under a contract with the principal contractor. 36 Am J1st Mech L § 125.

notice of motion. A means of bringing a motion on for hearing. A formal notice by one of the parties to an action that a motion described therein will be made before the court at the time and place stated in the notice.

notice of patent right. A notice given by a patentee or his assignee, if he makes or sells the article patented, of his patent right, either to the whole public by marking the article "patented" or to an infringer by informing him of the patent and of his infringement of it. 40 Am J1st Pat § 185.

notice of pendency. A notice filed in an action to recover a judgment affecting either title or possession, use or enjoyment of real property, for the purpose of giving notice on the record that there is a lien or claim outstanding and in force against the particular property, in effect a public announcement to beware of the title since it has a defect. A statutory requirement in states wherein the common-law doctrine of lis pendens has been modified, of a notice setting forth the style, number, and objective of an action, the court in which it is pending, a description of the property in controversy, and the names of the persons whose interests therein are sought to be affected, to be signed either by the party in whose behalf it is filed or by his attorney. 34 Am J1st Lis P § 24.
See **notice of lis pendens.**

notice of protest. See **protest.**

notice of stockholders' meeting. A statutory requirement in most jurisdictions to be observed according to the terms of the statute and, in the absence of a form prescribed by statute, to be met by any form of notice which informs stockholders that a meeting has been called and of its time and place, provided the hour as well as the day is specified, and, when necessary under the statute, a statement of the purposes of the meeting. 19 Am J2d Corp §§ 608 et seq.
Where notices are specific as to the time, place, and purpose of a meeting, and comply with the statute, substantial compliance with bylaws relating to the calling of stockholders' meetings is all that is required. Boericke v Weise, 68 Cal App 2d 407, 156 P2d 781.

notice of suit. See **notice of action or proceeding.**

notice of taking. A notice of the taking of a deposition, generally required by statute in order that the adverse party be afforded an opportunity to be present or to file cross-interrogatories. 23 Am J2d Notice § 34.

notice to perform. A method by which one party to a land contract may fix upon and assign a reasonable time for completing the contract, calling upon the party in default to perform according to the conditions of the contract. 55 Am J1st V & P § 115.

notice to plead (to plēd). A notice in writing served upon the defendant in an action by the plaintiff, apprising the defendant of the time within which he must plead.

notice to produce. A notice given to the adverse party to produce books or papers in his possession, the purpose of which is to permit the party giving notice to introduce parol or secondary evidence of contents on failure of the adverse party to produce in accordance with the terms of the notice. 29 Am J2d Ev § 842.

notice to quit. Notice terminating a tenancy. 32 Am J1st L & T § 993. A notice required under some circumstances as a condition precedent to an action for forcible entry and detainer. 35 Am J2d Forc E & D § 34. A notice usually required as a condition precedent to an action of ejectment where the defendant entered and held possession legally in the beginning. 25 Am J2d Eject § 56. A notice sometimes required as a preliminary to the execution of a writ of possession issued on a judgment in ejectment. 25 Am J2d Eject § 136.

notice to shore up. The notice to the adjoining landowner, which is required in most jurisdictions, to be given by the owner of land of his intention to make an excavation thereon, so that the adjoining owner may take the necessary precautions to protect the buildings on his land. 1 Am J2d Adj L § 51.

notified. Having been given notice.
In legal proceedings and in respect to public matters, the word is generally if not universally used as importing a notice given by some person whose duty it was to give it, in some manner prescribed, and to some person entitled to receive it, or be notified. Potwine's Appeal from Probate, 31 Conn 381, 384.

notified blockade. An established blockade of an enemy port, notice of which has been given to other governments. 56 Am J1st War § 172.

not impeachable for waste. See **unimpeachable for waste.**

not in consonance. Not in accord or agreement; inconsistent. Caldwell v Huffstutter, 173 Tenn 225, 116 SW2d 1017.

not in esse (not in es'se). Not in being.

noting protest. The memorandum, made on the instrument or on some other record, at the time of and embracing the principal facts attending dishonor, the purpose of which memorandum is to have a record from which the instrument of protest may be prepared, so that the notary will not be required to rely upon his memory as to the facts. Moreland v Citizens Sav. Bank, 114 Ky 577, 71 SW 520.

As soon as the presentment and demand of a negotiable instrument have been made, or at some seasonable hour during the same day, the notary makes a minute on the bill, or in his book of registry, consisting of his initials, the month, the day, the year, the refusal or acceptance of payment, and his charges of protest. This is the preliminary step towards the protest, which may be afterwards written out in full, "extended," as the elaboration of the minutes is termed, and it is called "noting." Bank of Ohio Valley v Lockwood, 13 W Va 392, 432, quoting Daniel on Negotiable Instruments.

notitia (nō-ti'she-a). Notice; knowledge; information.

Notitia dicitur a noscendo, et notitia non debet claudicare (nō-ti'she-a di'si-ter ā nōs-sen'dō, et nō-ti'she-a non de'bet klâ-di-kā're). Notice is so called from "noscendo," becoming known, and notice ought not to be defective.

not less than 10 years. A statutory clause expressing the statutory minimum sentence. Anno: 59 ALR2d 975.

not negotiable. Lacking the character of negotiability.

See **nonnegotiable instrument.**

not of inheritance. See **estate not of inheritance.**

notoriety. The state of being well known in the community; a matter of hearsay when offered to prove that which is reputed to exist. 29 Am J2d Ev § 503. The state or character of being well known, usually (and always when applied to crime) in an unfavorable sense. People v Salmon, 148 Cal 303, 83 P 42.

not original bill. See **bill not original.**

notorious. Unfavorably known to many persons. The open and general recognition of an illegitimate child by the father. 10 Am J2d Bast § 52.

A "notorious character" means a general character, and evidence of general character is admissible under an indictment using the term "notorious bad character." Leader v State, 4 Tex App 162.

notorious adultery. See **open and notorious adultery.**

notorious claim. A claim so well known in the community that one may be presumed to have had knowledge or notice thereof, including the extent of it. Watrous v Morrison, 33 Fla 261, 14 So 805.

notorious custom. A custom so generally known as to affect a contracting party with knowledge of it and raise the presumption that he dealt with reference to it. 21 Am J2d Cust & U § 17.

notorious possession. The possession of real property in a clearly defined and open manner. 25 Am J2d Eject § 43.

See **open and notorious possession.**

notorious recognition. See **general and notorious recognition.**

notorious resistance to lawful authority. A state of affairs so unusual and extraordinary that the usually constituted civil authorities are overpowered and consequently unable and inadequate for the time being successfully to contend therewith. Straus v Imperial Fire Ins. Co. 94 Mo 182, 6 SW 698.

not otherwise provided for. A common phrase in statutes, referring solely to the statute in which they occur. 21 Am J2d Cust D § 38.

not possessed. A name given to a plea in an action of trover which denied the possession of the plaintiff.

not proven. A form of Scotch verdict which acquitted the defendant of the charge against him, but left a suspicion upon him.

not satisfied. An irregular return of a writ of execution, intended as the equivalent of a return of "no goods" or "nulla bona". 30 Am J2d Exec § 562.

not served for want of property. An irregular return of a writ of execution, apparently intended as the equivalent of a return of "no goods" or "nulla bona." 30 Am J2d Exec § 562.

not to be performed within a year. See **agreement not to be performed within a year.**

not to interrupt. Words used in creating a covenant to stand seized.

A recital in a deed poll that the grantees are "not to interrupt" the grantor "during his lifetime, on the said premises," amounts to a covenant by the grantor to stand seized to his own use for life, with remainder to his grantees. 28 Am J2d Est § 348.

not to sue. See **covenant not to sue.**

n. o. v. Abbreviation of judgment notwithstanding the verdict.

nova (nọ'vạ). (Roman law.) New things; political changes; revolutions.

Nova constitutio futuris formam imponere debet, non praeteritis (nō'va kon-sti-tū'she-ō fu-tū'ris for'mam im-pō'ne-re de'bet, non prē-te'ri-tis). A new law ought to be prospective, not retrospective, in its operation. 50 Am J1st Stat § 478.

nova customa (nō'va kus'to-ma). New and increased customs duties, as distinguished from the ancient hereditary customs. See 1 Bl Comm 314.

Novae Narrationes (nō'vē nar-rā-she-ō'nēz). New Counts:—the title of a book on pleading published about 1350.

This book was also called The New Talys. See 3 Bl Comm 297.

Nova Statuta (nō'va sta-tū'ta). The New Statutes,—a name given to the statutes of England beginning with those enacted in the reign of Edward the Third, 1327.

novatio (nō-vā'she-ō). (Civil law.) A novation.

novation. The extinguishment of one obligation by another, a concept of the civil law introduced into common-law jurisprudence. 39 Am J1st Nov § 2. A contract that discharges immediately a previous contractual duty or a duty to make compensation and creates a new contractual duty, including as a party one who neither owed the previous duty nor was entitled to its performance. 2 Restatement, Contracts § 424. A mutual agreement among all parties concerned for the discharge of a valid existing obligation by the substitution of a new valid obligation on the part of the debtor or another, or a like agreement for the discharge of a debtor to his creditor by the substitution of a new creditor.

Greenwood Cotton Mill v Pace, 172 SC 531, 174 SE 423.

Novatio non praesumitur (nō-vā'she-ō non pre-zu'mi-ter). A novation will not be presumed. Morecraft v Allen, 78 NJL 729, 75 A 920.

novel. Adjective: New; recent. Noun: A narrative with plot in which the author has a property right and is entitled to copyright. 18 Am J2d Copyr §§ 10, 36.

See Novels.

novel assignment. Same as **new assignment**.

novel case. A case for which no precedent can be found. 52 Am J1st Torts § 8. A peculiar or extraordinary case arising in the complex and diversified affairs of men which cannot be classified under any of the distinct heads under which jurisdiction has theretofore been administered. 27 Am J2d Eq § 12.

novel design. See **novelty**.

novel disseisin (dis-sē'zin). New or recent disseisin,— a writ of assize which lay to recover land of which the demandant had been recently seised. See 3 Bl Comm 187.

novel impression. See **first impression**.

Novellae. Same as **Novels**.

Novellae Constitutiones (no-vel'lē kon-sti-tū-she-ō'nēz). Same as **Novels**.

Novels (no'vels). The New Constitutions—Novellae Constitutiones—which were laws promulgated by Justinian and his successors. See Mackeldey's Roman L §§ 80 et seq.

See **novel**.

novelty. An essential requisite of the patentability of an invention or discovery. A device or process unknown and unused by others prior to its invention or discovery by the applicant for a patent. 40 Am J1st Pat § 25.

As used in the patent law the term "novel design" means a thing of distinct and fixed individuality of appearance, a representation, a picture, a delineation, a device which addresses itself to the senses and taste, and produces pleasure or admiration in its contemplation. New York Belting & Packing Co. v New Jersey Car-Spring & Rubber Co. 137 US 445, 34 L Ed 741, 11 S Ct 195.

Noverint universi per praesentes (nō've-rint ū-niver'sī per prē-zen'tēz). Know all men by these presents.

novigild. (Saxon.) A ninefold compensation which was in certain cases exacted for injuries to property.

Novi operis nunciatio (nō'vī o'pe-ris nun-she-ā'she-ō). (Civil law.) An objection to or protest against a new work.

See **new work**.

Novis injuriis emersis nova constituere remedia (nō'vis in-jū'ri-is ē-mer'sis nō'va kon-sti-tu'e-re re-mē'di-a). New injuries having arisen, to establish new remedies for them. See 1 Bl Comm 148.

Novitas non tam utilitate prodest quam novitate perturbat (nō'vi-tās non tam ū-ti-li-tā'te prō'dest quam nō-vi-tā'te per-ter'bat). That which is new or novel does not benefit so much by its usefulness as it disturbs by its novelty.

Noviter ad notitiam perventa (nō've-ter ad nō-ti'she-am per-ven'ta). (Ecclesiastical law.) Matters which have recently come to one's notice.

Noviter perventa (nō'vi-ter per-ven'ta). Same as **noviter ad, etc.**

novo. See **de novo**.

novocain (nō'vō-kān). A local anesthetic but one which may result in disabling and painful consequences due to hypersusceptibility of the patient. 29A Am J Rev ed Ins § 1211.

novodamus (nō-vọ-dā'mus). We grant anew,—the granting clause in a renewal charter or franchise.

Novum judicium non dat novum jus, sed declarat antiquum (nō'vum jū-dī'she-um non dat nō'vum jūs, sed de-klā'rat an-tī'qu-um). A new judgment does not promulgate a new law, but declares the old law.

Novum opus (nō'vum ō'pus). (Civil law.) Same as **new work**.

novus homo (nō'vus hō'mo). A new man,—a man who has been pardoned of a crime.

now. At the moment; presently; contemporaneously. Pike v Kennedy, 15 Or 420, 15 P 637.

Where a lease is to commence in futuro and the covenant of the lessee is to redeliver the premises in the condition they "now are," without specific reference to the time intended, the tendency of the courts is to construe the phrase as relating to the condition of the premises at the time the term commences, not the time of the execution of the lease. Anno: 45 ALR 30, s. 106 ALR 1361.

now for then. See **nunc pro tunc**.

now standing. A term of a contract for the sale of standing trees, relating to trees in their size and condition at the time of the execution of the contract, rather than at the time of cutting and removal. Anno: 94 ALR 1420; 34 Am J1st Logs § 22.

noxa (nok'sa). (Civil law.) An injury committed on the person or property of a person by the slave, servant or animal of another.

noxal action (nok'sạl ak'shọn). Same as **noxalis actio**.

Noxalis actio (no-xā'lis ak'she-ō). (Civil law.) An action against the owner of a slave or an animal for injuries to persons or property committed by them.

Noxa sequitur caput (no'xa se'qui-ter ka'put). (Civil law.) The injury (committed by the slave or animal) follows the head (the master).

That is, the owner was liable for the acts of his slave or his animal. See Mackeldey's Roman L § 510.

noxia (nok'she-a). Same as **noxa**.

noxious business. See **offensive business**.

noxious fume. A gas which is sickening or discomforting. 39 Am J1st Nuis § 58. A gas which is destructive of life, whether animal or vegetable. Pennsylvania Lead Co.'s Appeal, 96 Pa 116.

noxious odor. A bad smell.

noxious substance. A substance which, when administered, is capable of destroying life, but which is not necessarily poisonous.

Pulverized glass, when administered in sufficient quantities, destroys life, but is not poisonous. People v Van Deleer, 53 Cal 147.

noysance (noi-zạns). Same as **nuisance**.

N. P. Abbreviation of "Notary Public." 1 Am J2d Abbr § 5.

NS. Abbreviation of new series.

nubibus (nū'bi-bus). See **in nubibus**.

nubile (nū'bil). Of sufficient age and physical development for marriage.

nubiles. See **anni nubiles**.

nubilis (nū'bi-lis). (Civil law.) Old enough to marry; of marriageable age; marriageable.

Nuclear Compact. See **Northeastern Interstate Nuclear Compact; Southern Interstate Nuclear Compact**.

nuclear explosion. An explosion incident to nuclear chain reaction. An explosion resulting from the development of energy by nuclear fission or nuclear fusion.

Nuclear Facilities Liability Act. A statute proposed by the National Conference of Commissioners on Uniform State Laws to be applied to the more hazardous types of atomic energy activities, such as those in nuclear reactor installations, wherein a potentiality of an uncontrolled nuclear chain reaction exists, providing in substance that a nuclear facility operator who has entered into an indemnification agreement with the Atomic Energy Commission shall be liable, without proof of fault, for injuries (except those compensable under workmen's compensation laws and injuries to the nuclear facility or to property located at the site and used in connection with the facility) arising out of or resulting from a nuclear incident caused by any reason other than an act of war. 6 Am J2d Atomic E § 47.

nuclear incident. An occurrence within the United States causing bodily injury, sickness, disease, or death, or loss of or damage to property, or for loss of use of property, arising out of or resulting from the radioactive, toxic, explosive, or other hazardous properties of source, special nuclear, or by-product material; provided, however, as to indemnification agreements in connection with a nuclear-powered ship, it shall mean any such occurrence outside the United States rather than within the United States. 42 USC § 2014(o).

nuclear reaction. The reaction consequent to the fission or fusion of atoms.

nuclear reactor. An apparatus, other than an atomic weapon, designed or used to sustain nuclear fission in a self-supporting chain reaction. 10 CFR § 50.2(k); 10 CFR Cum Supp § 115.3(h).

nuda (nū'dạ). Nude; bare; mere; naked; unclothed.

Nuda pactio obligationem non parit (nū'da pak'she-o ob-li-gā-she-ō'nem non pa'rit). A bare or naked promise does not effect a binding obligation. See Broom's Legal Maxims 745.

nuda patientia (nū'da pa-she-en'she-a). Mere sufferance.

nuda possessio (nū'da po-ze'she-ō). Mere or naked possession.

nuda propiedad (nū'da pro-pe'ay-dad). See **propiedad**.

Nuda ratio et nuda pactio non ligant aliquem debitorem (nū'da ra'she-o et nū'da pak'she-ō non li'gant a'li-quem de-bi-tō'rem). A bare or mere intention and a bare or mere promise do not bind any debtor.

nude (nūd). Naked; unclothed; bare; mere.

nude pact. Same as **nudum pactum**.

nudism. The criminal offense of indecent exposure of persons. 33 Am J1st Lewd etc § 7.

nudity. The unclothed state of a human being.

nudity in art. Representations of the unclothed human body in painting or sculpture. 33 Am J1st Lewd etc § 13.

nudum pactum (nū'dum pak'tum). Literally, a bare agreement. A promise not supported by a consideration. Todd v Weber, 95 NY 181.

Nudum pactum est ubi nulla subest cause propter conventionem; sed ubi subest causa fit obligatio, et parit actionem (nū'dum pak'tūm est u'bi nul'la sub'est kâ'za prop'ter kon-ven-she-ō'nem; sed u'bi sub'est kâ'za fit ob-li-gā'she-ō, et pa'rit ak-she-ō'nem). A nudum pactum is where there is no consideration on account of the promise; but where there is a consideration, an obligation is effected, and it supports an action. See Broom's Legal Maxims 745, 746.

Nudum pactum ex quo non oritur actio (nū'dum pak'-tum ex quō non ō'ri-ter ak'she-ō). A bare promise is one from which no action arises.

nuictander (nuīc-tän-dā'). Same as **nutander**.

nuire. (French.) To injure, hurt, or harm. Thornton v Dow, 60 Wash 622, 111 P 899.

nuisance. Anything that works hurt, inconvenience, or damage to another. Prior v White, 132 Fla 1, 180 So 347, 116 ALR 1176; Hofstetter v Myers, 170 Kan 564, 228 P2d 522, 24 ALR2d 188. Any- thing done by one which annoys or disturbs another in the free use, possession, or enjoyment of his property, or which renders its ordinary use or occupation physically uncomfortable. Jones v Trawick (Fla) 75 So 2d 785, 50 ALR2d 1319. That which has the effect of prejudicially and unwarrantably affecting the enjoyment of the rights of another. Sullivan v Waterman, 20 RI 372, 39 A 243. Anything done by one that works or causes injury, damage, hurt, inconvenience, annoyance, or discomfort to another in the legitimate enjoyment of his reasonable rights of person or property. District of Columbia v Potten, 55 App DC 312, 5 F2d 374, 40 ALR 1461, cert den 269 US 562, 70 L Ed 412, 46 S Ct 21. Anything which (1) annoys or disturbs the free use of another's property, or which renders its ordinary use or physical occupation uncomfortable, or (2) interferes with the rights of a citizen, either in person, property, the enjoyment of his property, or his comfort, or (3) materially lessens the enjoyment of property or the physical comfort of persons in their homes. Martin v Williams, 141 W Va 595, 93 SE2d 835, 56 ALR2d 756.

What may constitute a nuisance in a particular case depends upon many things, such as the type of neighborhood, the nature of the thing or wrong complained of, its proximity to those alleging injury or damage, its frequency or continuity, and the nature and extent of the resulting injury, damage, or annoyance; each case must, of necessity, depend upon particular facts and circumstances. Lehmkuhl v Junction City, 179 Kan 389, 295 P2d 621, 56 ALR2d 1409.

See **liquor nuisance; private nuisance; public nuisance**.

nuisance at law (nū'sạns at lå). Same as **nuisance per se**.

nuisance in fact. A nuisance arising, not from the essential nature of the operation or condition involved, but from the location of the premises, the surroundings, or the manner in which the operation is managed or conducted. 39 Am J1st Nuis § 7.

nuisance per accidens. See **per accidens nuisance.**

nuisance per se (pêr sē). An act, thing, omission, or use of the property which in and of itself is a nuisance, and hence is not permissible or excusable under any circumstances. State ex rel. Bradford v Stubblefield, 36 Wash 2d 664, 220 P2d 305, 17 ALR2d 1258. An act, occupation, or structure which is a nuisance at all times and under any circumstances, regardless of location or surroundings. Any act or omission or use of property or thing which is of itself hurtful to the health, tranquility, or morals, or which outrages the decency of the community. 39 Am J1st Nuis § 11.

nul (nul). No; no one; none.

nul agard (nul agard). No award.

nul assets ultra (nul as'sets ul'tra). No other assets.

nul disseisin (nul dis-sēz'in). A plea of the general issue in an action under writ of entry. 41 Am J1st Pl § 141.

Nul fait agard. No award was made.

null (nul). Nonexistent; void; of no legal effect.

nulla bona. (nul'ą bō'nạ). A return of a writ of execution signifying that the officer made strict and diligent search but was unable to find any property of the defendant liable to seizure under the writ, whereof to make a levy. 30 Am J2d Exec § 561. A plea by a garnishee denying that he holds property of, or is indebted to, the defendant.

Nulla curia quae recordum non habet potest imponere finem, neque aliquem mandare carceri, quia ista spectant tantummodo ad curias de recordo (nul'la kū'ri-a kwē re-kor'dum non hā'bet po'test im-po'ne-re fi'nem, ne'kwe a'li-quem man-dā're kar'se-ri, qui'a is'ta spek'tant tan-tum-mo'dō ad kū'ri-as dē re-kor'dō). No court which has not a record can impose a fine, nor can it order anyone to be imprisoned, because those matters belong only to courts of record.

Nulla emptio sine pretio esse potest (nul'la emp'she-o sī'ne pre'she-o es'se po'test). There can be no sale without a price. Brown v Bellows, 21 Mass (4 Pick) 179, 189.

Nulla impossibilia aut inhonesta sunt praesumenda; vera autem et honesta et possibilia (nul'la im-pos-si-bi'li-a ât in-ho-nes'ta sunt prē-zu-men'da; vē'ra â'-tem et ho-nes'ta et pos-si-bi'li-a). No impossible or dishonest things are to be presumed, but true, honest, and possible things are.

null and void (nul and void). That which binds no one; that which is incapable of giving rise to any rights or obligations under any circumstances; that which is of no effect.

But there are cases where the expression means voidable merely, that is, capable of being avoided. Ewell v Daggs, 108 US 143, 149, 27 L Ed 682, 684, 2 S Ct 408.

Nulla pactione effici potest ne dolus praestetur (nul'la pak'she-ō-ne ef'fi-sī po'test nē do'lus prē-stē'ter). It cannot be provided in any contract that fraud shall not be answered for. See Broom's Legal Maxims.

Nulle regle sans faute (nūl rē'gluh sôn fôt). No rule or government is free from fault.

Nulle terre sans seigneur (nūl tare sôn say-nyūr). There is no land without its lord.

Nulli enim res sua servit jure servitutis (nul'lī e'nim rēz sū'a ser'vit jū're ser-vi-tū'tis). For no one can reserve for his own property a servitude therein.

nullity. Something without legal effect, being null. A proceeding of no effect whatsoever because of a defect therein. Salter v Hilgen, 40 Wis 363, 365.

nullity suit. An action brought for the annulment of a marriage.

nullius filius (nul'li-us fi'li-us). Nobody's child; the status of an illegitimate child under the English common law. 10 Am J2d Bast § 146.

Nullius hominis auctoritas apud nos valere debet, ut meliora non sequeremur si quis attulerit (nul'li-us ho'mi-nis âk-to'ri-tās a'pud nos va'le-re de'bet, ut me-li-ō'ra non se-kwe'rē-mer sī quis at-tu-le'rit). No man's influence ought to prevail upon us not to follow better things, if any one presents them.

nullius in bonis (nul'li-us in bō'nis). In the property of no one; not property.

In the language of Lord Coke, the burial of the cadaver is nullius in bonis. Griffith v Charlotte, Columbia & Augusta Railroad Co. 23 SC 25.

nullius juris (nul'li-ūs ju'ris). Of no legal effect; without support in law.

Nulli vendemus, nulli negabimus, aut differemus, rectum vel justitiam (nul'lī ven-dē'mus, nul'lī ne-gā'bi-mus, ât dif-fe-rē'mus, rek'tum vel jūs-ti'she-am). We will sell to none, we will deny to none, we will delay to none, either right or justice. See 1 Bl Comm 141.

nullo est erratum (nul'lō est er-rā'tum). A plea to the assignment of errors in a coram nobis proceeding, equivalent to a demurrer, admitting the truth of the error assigned but insisting that in law it is not error. Chambers v State, 117 Fla 642, 158 So 153.

nullum arbitrium (nul'lum ar-bi'tri-um). No award.

Nullum crimen majus est inobedientia (nul'lum kri'-men mā'jus est in-ō-be-di-en'she-a). No crime is greater than disobedience.

Nullum crimen, nulla poena, sine lege (nul'lum kri'-men, nul'la pē'na, sī'ne lē'je). Without a law, there is no crime and no punishment. State v Burbee, 65 Vt 1, 25 A 964.

Nullum exemplum est idem omnibus (nul'lum eg-zem'plum est ī'dem om'ni-bus). No precedent or example is the same for all cases.

Nullum iniquum est praesumendum in jure (nul'lum in-i'qu-um est prē-zu-men'dum in jū're). Nothing iniquitous is to be presumed in law.

Nullum matrimonium, ibi nulla dos (nul'lum ma-tri-mō'ni-um, i'bi nul'la dōs). There is no dower where there is no marriage. If a marriage is dissolved, dower ceases. Wait v Wait (NY) 4 Barb 192, 202.

Nullum simile est idem (nul'lum si'mi-le est ī'dem). No similar thing is the same thing.

It must be the same case where you apply precedent. Lessee of Sweitzer v Meese (Pa) 6 Binn 500, 506.

Nullum simile quatuor pedibus currit (nul'lum si'mi-le qua'tu-or pe'di-bus ker'rit). Nothing which is similar runs on four feet. Lessee or Sweitzer v Meese (Pa) 6 Binn 500.

Nullum tempus occurrit ecclesiae (nul'lum tem'pus o-ker'rit e-klē'si-ē). No time runs against or bars the church. See 3 Bl Comm 103.

Nullum tempus occurrit regi (nul'lum tem'pus o-ker'-rit rē'jī). Time does not run against the king or sovereign. United States v Thompson, 98 US 486, 25 L Ed 194.

Nullum tempus occurrit reipublicae (nul'lum tem'pus o-ker'rit rē'ī-pub'li-sē). Time does not run against the state. Norrell v Augusta Railway & Electric Co. 116 Ga 313, 42 SE 466.

Nullus clericus nisi causidicus (nul'lus kle'ri-kus nī'sī kâ-si'di-kus). No clerk, unless a pleader; no one is a clergyman who is not also a lawyer. See 1 Bl Comm 17.

Nullus commodum capere potest de injuria sua propria (nul'lus kom'mo-dum kā'pe-re po'test dē in-jū'ri-a su'a prō'pri-a). No one can take advantage of his own wrong. Schmidt v Northern Life Asso. 112 Iowa 41, 83 NW 800.

Nullus debet agere de dolo, ubi alia actio subest (nul'lus de'bet ā'je-re dē do'lō, u'bī a'li-a ȧk'she-o sub'est). Where any other action exists, no one ought to sue in an action for deceit.

Nullus dicitur accessorius post feloniam sed ille qui novit principalem feloniam fecisse, et illum receptavit et comfortavit (nul'lus di'si-ter ak-ses-sō'ri-us post fe-lō'ni-am sed il'le quī nō'vit prin-si-pā'lem fe-lō'ni-am fē-sis'se, et il'lum re-sep-tā'vit et komfor-tā'vit). No one is called an accessory after the felony but the one who knew that the principal had committed the felony and who received and comforted him.

Nullus dicitur felo principalis nisi actor, aut qui praesens est, abettans aut auxilians actorem ad feloniam faciendam (nul'lus di'si-ter fe'lō prin-si-pā'lis nī'sī ak'tor, ât quī prē'senz est, a-bet'tanz ât âk-zi'li-anz ak-tō'rem ad fe-lō'ni-am fā-she-en'dam). No one is called a principal felon except the actor, or a person who is present, abetting or aiding the actor in the commission of the felony.

Nullus idoneus testis in re sua intelligitur (nul'lus i-dō'ne-us tes'tis in rē su'a in-tel-li'ji-ter). No person is deemed to be a qualified witness in his own behalf.

Nullus jus alienum forisfacere potest (nul'lus jūs ā-li-ē'num fo-ris-fā'se-re po'test). No person can forfeit the right of another.

Nullus liber homo aliquo modo destruatur nisi per legale judicium parium suorum, aut per legem terrae (nul'lus li'ber hō'mō a'li-quō mō'dō dē-stru-ā'ter nī'sī per lē-gā'le jū-di'she-um pā'ri-um su-ō'rum, ât per lē'jem ter'rē). No freeman shall in any manner be made to suffer corporal hurt save by the judgment of his peers or by the law of the land. See 1 Bl Comm 133.

Nullus liber homo capiatur vel imprisonetur (nul'lus li'ber hō'mō kā-pi-ā'ter vel im-pri-sō-nē'ter). No freeman may be taken or imprisoned. See 2 Bl Comm 93.

Nullus liber homo imprisonetur (nul'lus li'ber hō'mō im-pri-sō-nē'ter). No free man may be imprisoned. See Clark's Case (Eng) 5 Coke's Rep 64a.

Nullus recedat e curia cancellaria sine remedio (nul'lus re-sē'dat ē kū'ri-a kân-sel-lā'ri-a sī'ne re-mē'di-ō). No person departs from a court of chancery without a remedy.

Nullus simile est idem (nul'lus si'mi-le est ī'dem). A similar thing is not the same thing. Blake v Hamilton Dime Savings Bank, 79 Ohio 189, 87 NE 73.

Nullus videtur dolo facere, qui suo jure utitur (nul'lus vi-dē'ter dō'lō fa'se-re, quī su'ō jū're ū'ti-ter). No one is deemed to work a fraud who exercises his own right. Fisher, Brown & Co. v Fielding, 67 Conn 91, 34 A 714.

Nul ne doit s'enrichir aux depens des autres (nūl nuh dwa s'ôn're-shir' ō duh-pôn dāz ō'truh). No person ought to enrich himself at the expense of others.

Nul prendra avantage de son tort (nūl prôn-drah' äd'vän-täzh' duh sôn tôr). No one may take an advantage from his own wrongful act. Whitworth v Shreveport Belt Railway Co. 112 La 363, 36 S 414.

Nul sans damage avera error ou attaint (nūl sôn dahmäzh ah-vĕ-rah ĕr'ror oo ah-tân). No person shall have error or attaint, without damage.

nul tiel agard (nūl tī-ĕl ah-gard). No such award.

nul tiel corporation (nūl ti-el cor-por-ah'si-ôn). No such corporation,—a name given to a plea denying the existence of the defendant corporation.

nul tiel record. A common-law plea of the general issue when defendant intends to dispute the existence of the record upon which the action is based, whether it is a judgment or other record. 41 Am J1st Pl § 141. A plea in a proceeding on a bail bond or recognizance where the surety disputes the existence of the bond. 8 Am J2d Bail § 152.

nul waste (nul wāst). No waste,—a name given to the general issue in an action for waste.

nul waste fait (nul wāst fā). No waste was committed.

numbers. See **numbers game.**

numbers game. A form of lottery. 34 Am J1st Lot § 7. A lottery, conducted under a system devised with more or less ingenuity to disguise the character of the enterprise. A lottery scheme wherein the proprietor sells for a specific sum, usually a few cents, certificates or tickets which entitle the purchaser to some article of trifling value, such as a lead pencil, and also permit him to select certain numbers, say 3-9-13, which, if all drawn by a blindfolded person from a revolving wheel in which several numbers have been placed, entitle the purchaser of the ticket or certificate to a money prize much larger in amount than the sum which he has paid for the ticket or certificate. State ex rel. Kellogg v Kansas Mercantile Asso. 45 Kan 351, 25 P 984.

The "numbers game" in which each player places a bet, selects a number, and a winning number is determined by taking the first digit to the left of the decimal of the aggregate of prices paid for first, second, and third in each of the first three races at a certain race track, the holder of the winning number receiving a multiple of the amount of his play, is not a bet on a horse race, but a lottery, although the winning number is not determined by drawing. Forte v United States, 65 App DC 355, 83 F2d 612, 105 ALR 300.

Where one chooses a number and pays a certain sum, and the seller draws from a box an envelope containing a slip with numbers on it, and if the number chosen is on the slip, the buyer receives a multiple of the sum paid, greater or less according to agreement, and if not, he loses what he has paid, the transaction is a lottery. Commonwealth v Wright, 137 Mass 250.

A game in which the operator sells slips of paper containing three numbers with an agreement to pay a cash prize to holders of slips bearing numbers in sequence as they appear in a large number published daily in the press, such as the United States Treasury balance, is a lottery. Gilley v Commonwealth, 312 Ky 584, 229 SW2d 60, 19 ALR2d 1224.

numbers pool. Same as **numbers game.**

numeral. An arithmetical figure of Arabic or Roman origin. 29 Am J2d Ev § 92.

numerata pecunia (nu-me-rā′ta pe-kū′ni-a). Money which was enumerated or counted out, as distinguished from that which was weighed.

numerical index. An index of records of title according to the descriptions of land, the names of the parties to instruments, and the instruments themselves. 45 Am J1st Recds § 98.

Numerus certus pro incerto ponitur (nū′me-rus ser′-tus prō in-ser′tō po′ni-ter). A certain number is placed or put for an uncertain one.

nunciatio (nun-she-ā′she-o). (Civil law.) A protest; a proclamation; a declaration.

nuncio (nun′shi-ō). An ambassador of the Pope of Rome.

nuncius (nun′shi-us). An announcer; a messenger; a nuncio.

nunc pro tunc (nunk prō tunk). Literally, now for then.

nunc pro tunc amendment. (nunk prō tunk ą-mend′-męnt). An amendment or correction given retroactive effect by court order.
Thus, a defective jurat of an affidavit may be amended nunc pro tunc by leave of court. Beach v Averett, 106 Ga 73, 31 SE 806.

nunc pro tunc decree (nunk prō tunk dę-krē′). A decree in equity comparable to a **nunc pro tunc judgment.**

nunc pro tunc entry (nunk prō tunk en′tri). See **nunc pro tunc judgment; nunc pro tunc order.**

nunc pro tunc filing (nunk prō tunk fī′ling). The filing of a claim in bankruptcy after the expiration of the statutory period for filing claims. 9 Am J2d Bankr § 450. The filing of a pleading to take effect as of an earlier time. Galatis v Galatis (CA5 Fla) 55 F2d 571.

nunc pro tunc intervention (nunk prō tunk in-tėr-ven′shǫn). Intervention pursuant to leave of court by order, as of a prior stage of the action. 39 Am J1st Parties § 73.

nunc pro tunc judgment (nunk prō tunk juj′męnt). A method of amending the record of a judgment which is not in accord with that actually pronounced in the cause and rendered, so that the record will speak truthfully as of the date of entry, the amending judgment being literally "now for then." 30A Am J Rev ed Judgm § 591. A procedural device much employed in correcting defects in titles to real estate. Anno: 57 ALR 1462. A judgment in a criminal case entered pursuant to order as of the date of rendition. People v Lenon, 79 Cal 631, 21 P 967.

nunc pro tunc order (nunk prō tunk ôr′dėr). A method of amending a court record. 20 Am J2d Crts § 58. An order entered to take effect as of an earlier time. 37 Am J1st Motions § 30.

nuncupate (nung′kų-pāt). To make a nuncupative or verbal will.

nuncupative will (nung′kų-pą-tiv wil). A will declared orally by the testator before witnesses but dependent for validity under some statutes upon being reduced to writing and subscribed by the witnesses after the speaking of the testamentary words. 57 Am J1st Wills §§ 653, 660. Under the English Statute of Frauds and similar statutes in this country, except in the case of a soldier or seaman, the general rule is that a valid nuncupative will can be made only when the testator is in his last illness. 57 Am J1st Wills § 654. In some jurisdictions the validity of nuncupative wills is denied absolutely. 57 Am J1st Wills § 653.

nundinae (nūn′di-nē). Market-places; fairs; a fair.

nunquam (nun′kwam). Nowhere; on no occasion; never.

Nunquam crescit ex post facto praeteriti delicti aestimatio (nun′quam kre′sit ex post fak′tō prē-te′ri-tī dē-lik′tī ēs-ti-mā′she-ō). The degree of a past offense never increases from a subsequent act.

Nunquam decurritur ad extraordinarium sed ubi deficit ordinarium (nun′quam de-ker′ri-ter ad ex-tra-or-di-nā′ri-um sed u′bi de′fi-sit or-di-nā′ri-um). Resort is never made to the extraordinary until the ordinary has failed. See Broom's Legal Maxims 42.

Nunquam fictio sine lege (nun′quam fik′she-ō sī′ne lē′je). A fiction never exists without law.

nunquam indebitatus (nun′quam in-de-bi-tā′tus). Never indebted,—the name given to a plea in an action of indebitatus assumpsit whereby the defendant denies that he was ever indebted to the plaintiff.

Nunquam nimis dicitur quod nunquam satis dicitur (nun′quam ni′mis di′si-ter quod nun′quam sa′tis di′si-ter). That which is never said sufficiently is never said too much.

Nunquam praescribitur in falso (nun′quam prē-skri′-bi-ter in fal′so). A prescription never exists in the case of falsifying or forgery.

Nunquam res humanae prospere succedunt ubi negliguntur divinae (nun′quam rēz hū-mā′nē pros′pe-rē suk-sē′dunt u′bi ne-gli-gun′ter dī-vī′nē). Human affairs never prosper where divine things are neglected.

nuntio (nun′she-ō). Same as **nuncio.**

nuntius (nun′she-us). Same as **nuncius.**

Nuper de facto, et non de jure, reges Angliae (nu′per dē fak′tō, et non dē jū′re, rē′jēz Ang′li-ē). Recently kings of England in fact, and not of right. See 1 Bl Comm 204.

nuper obiitt (nū′per ō′bi-it). He recently died; an ancestral writ to establish an equal division of land, where, on the death of the ancestor, who had several heirs, one entered and held the others out of possession. See 3 Bl Comm 186.

nuptiae (nup′she-ē). Nuptials; marriage.

nuptiae secundae (nup′she-e se-kun′dē). A second or subsequent marriage after the first.

nuptial (nup′shąl). Adjective: Relating or pertaining to a marriage. Noun: A wedding; the ceremony of a wedding.

Nuptias non concubitus, sed consensus facit (nup′-she-ās non kon-ku′bi-tus, sed kon-sen′sus fā′sit). Not cohabitation, but consent, makes a marriage.

nurse. A person trained to take care of the sick, aged, wounded, or infirm and to assist a physician or surgeon; sometimes acting in the capacity of an independent contractor, at other times as an employee. Anno: 19 ALR 1189, s. 60 ALR 303.
Although the nurses on the staff of a hospital are the employees of the hospital for general purposes, they are not so for the purposes of surgery. When

assisting at an operation, they cease for the time being to be the employees of the hospital, inasmuch as they take their orders during that period from the operating surgeon alone, not from the hospital authorities. Anno: 19 ALR 1190, 1191, s. 60 ALR 303.

See **registered nurse**.

Nurse Corps. The Army Nurse Corps, Nurse Corps of the United States Navy and United States Naval Reserve, or the Air Force Nurse Corps, such being branches of the United States Military Service.

nursery. A room or apartment in a dwelling house set aside as a place for the care of an infant and as his place for sleeping; a room or apartment in a dwelling house set aside especially for the children of the family as a playroom or as living quarters for them. A place where trees, shrubs, plants, and so forth, are propagated from seed or otherwise for transplanting, for use as stock for grafting, and for sale. Needham v Winslow Nurseries, Inc. 330 Mass 95, 111 NE2d 453, 40 ALR2d 1450.

nursery school. A school for boys and girls under the age of kindergarten pupils.

nursery stock. Small trees, shrubs, or plants raised for transplanting or kept for sale to persons desiring them for transplanting. 3 Am J2d Agri § 50.

nursing home. A place at which sick or disabled persons may be cared for, fed, and housed. Not a hospital within the meaning of a hospitalization policy. Employers Casualty Co. v Givens (Tex Civ App) 190 SW2d 155.

nursing services. The services of a trained or practical nurse. Necessaries within the rule that an insane person may be held liable for necessaries. 29 Am J Rev ed Ins Per § 74.

nurture (nėr'tūr). To educate; to rear.

nurture guardian. See **guardian by nurture**.

nurture period. The period between an animal's birth and the time when it has been weaned, or should have been weaned according to the course of nature or the usual custom of those who raise domestic animals. Anno: 144 ALR 333; 15 Am J2d Chat Mtg § 71.

nusance (nū'sạns). An old form of the word **nuisance**.

nutander (nū-tän-dā). Nocturnally; in the nighttime; by night.

nutauntre. Same as **nutander**.

nute (nūt). Night.

nutricius. See **frater nutricius**.

nuyt. Night.

NW. Abbreviation of northwest.

nymphomania (nim-fọ-mā'ni-ạ). A morbid, uncontrollable sexual desire, but not insanity. Hill v Hill, 27 NJ Eq 214. A species of insanity or mental disease manifested in a morbid activity of the sexual propensity, sometimes amounting to irresistible impulse to perform the sexual act. Matchin v Matchin, 6 Pa 332.

O

o. An abbreviation for "son of" in ancient Irish surnames. From such derives the familiar prefix in names such as O'Hara; O'Mara; and O'Shea.

oath. A calling on God to witness what is averred as truth, accompanied expressly or impliedly with an invocation of God's vengeance or a renunciation of God's favor in the event of falsehood. 39 Am J1st Oath § 2. A solemn appeal to God, to a superior sanction, or to a sacred or revered person, to witness the inviolability of a promise or undertaking. People ex rel. Bryant v Zimmerman, 241 NY 405, 150 NE 497, 43 ALR 909. Any form of attestation by which a person signifies that he is bound in conscience to perform an act or to speak faithfully and truthfully. State ex rel. Braley v Gay, 59 Minn 6, 60 NW 676.

The word has been construed to include "affirmation" in cases where, by law. an affirmation may be substituted for an oath. 39 Am J1st Oath § 2.

oath decisory (dē-sī'sọ-ri). (Civil law.) A decisive oath,—an oath upon which the cause rested where one of the parties to the action elected to leave the issue to the oath of his adversary.

oath ex officio (ōth ex of-fi'she-ō). An oath made by an accused clergyman whereby he might swear his innocence (or others might do so for him) and thus escape the censure or punishment of the ecclesiastical court.

This practice of "canonical purgation," as it was called, continued until it was abolished by statute 13 Charles II, c. 12. See 3 Bl Comm 101.

oath in litem (ōth in lī'tem). (Civil law.) An oath as to the value of the thing in dispute.

oath of abjuration (ōth of ab-jö-rā'shọn). An oath made by a person upon his voluntary abandonment of his citizenship.

oath of allegiance. An oath, required to be taken in open court by a person seeking naturalization, that he will support the Constitution of the United States; that he entirely and absolutely renounces and abjures all allegiance and fidelity to any foreign prince, potentate, state, or sovereignty of which he was before a citizen or subject; that he will support and defend the Constitution and the laws of the United States against all enemies, foreign and domestic, and will bear true faith and allegiance to them; and that he will bear arms on behalf of the United States when required by law, or perform noncombatant services in the Armed Forces of the United States when required, or will perform work of national importance under civilian direction when required, depending upon his religious training and belief. 8 USC § 1448(a).

oath of calumny (of kal'um-ni). (Civil law.) An oath of good faith which was required of a plaintiff as a prerequisite of his right to sue.

oath of grand juror. A declaration, after having been duly sworn, that the grand jurors will diligently inquire and true presentment make of all such matters and things as shall be given them in charge; that they will keep secret the state's, their fellow jurors', and their own counsel; and that they will present no man for envy, hatred, or malice; neither will they leave any man unpresented for love, fear, favor, affection, or hope of reward, but will present things truly, as they come to their knowledge, according to the best of their understanding. Anno: 22 ALR 1357.

oath of juror. A statement under oath by a juror that he will do his duty as a juror, that he will well and truly try the issues joined, and a true verdict render according to the law and the evidence. Demato v People, 49 Colo 147, 111 P 703.

oath of loyalty. See **loyalty oath.**

oath of office. A qualifying oath, in a form prescribed by statute, of a public officer required, as an incident of office, upon assuming the office. 42 Am J1st Pub Of § 7. The qualifying oath of an administrator or executor. 31 Am J2d Ex & Ad § 106.

oath purgatory (pėr'gạ-tọ-ri). The oath made by a defendant in a trial by wager of law.

oath suppletory (sup'lē-tọ-ri). An oath which was administered to a party to an action who testified in his own behalf.

The rule of the law courts required two witnesses to supply full proof of a single fact, and hence it was held that the testimony of one witness supplied only half proof. And where one witness had testified to a single fact in a party's behalf, he was—contrary to the general rule—in order to make full proof, permitted to testify in his own behalf, and it was then that the suppletory oath was administered to him. See 3 Bl Comm 368, 370.

oathworthy (ōth-wėr'thi). Worthy of belief when testifying under oath; credible.

oats. An agricultural crop. A grain.

ob (ob). On account of; because of; by reason of; in consideration of.

Ob alterius culpam tenetur, sive servi, sive liberi (ob al-te'ri-us kul'pam te-nē'ter, sī've ser'vī, sī've li'be-rī). One is liable for the faults of others, if they are his servants, or if they are his children. See 1 Bl Comm 431.

ob causam aliquem a re maritima ortam (ob kâ'sam a'li-quem ā rē ma-ri'ti-ma or'tam). By reason of some cause or consideration arising out of a maritime matter.

ob continentiam delicti (ob kon-ti-nen'she-am dē-lik'tī). Because of, or by reason of, connection with the tort or the crime.

ob contingentiam (ob kon-tin-jin'she-am). Because or by reason of connection or relationship.

obedient. Submissive to authority, yielding compliance with commands, orders or injunctions; performing what is required, or abstaining from what is forbidden.

The word might with propriety be used to express the same meaning as the word "amenable," which is defined as liable to answer; responsible; answerable; liable to be called to account. Miller v Commonwealth, 62 Ky (1 Duv) 14, 17.

Obedientia est legis essentia (ō-be-di-en'she-a est lē'jis es-sen'she-a). Obedience is the essence of law.

ob favorem mercatorum (ob fa-vō'rem mer-ka-tō'rum). In favor of merchants; by reason of partiality toward merchants.

Ob infamiam non solet juxta legem terrae aliquis per legem apparentem se purgare, nisi prius convictus fuerit vel confessus in curia (ob in-fā'mi-am non sō'let jux'ta lē'jem ter'rē a'li-quis per lē'jem ap-paren'tem sē pur-gā're, nī'sī prī'us kon-vik'tus fu'e-rit vel kon-fes'sus in kū'ri-a). By reason of ill repute it is not customary according to the law of the land for anyone to purge himself by lex apparens, unless he was convicted or confessed in court.

obit (ō'bit). To reach the end in death.

obiter (ob'i-tėr). On the way; in passing; incidentally; cursorily.
See **dicta**.

obiter dicta (ob'i-tėr dik'tä). Same as **dicta**.

obiter dictum (ob'i-tėr dik'tum). Singular of obiter dicta.
See **dicta**.

Obit sine prole (ob'it sī'ne prō'le). He died without issue.

obituary (ō-bit'ū-ā-ri). A short resume of the life of a person who has just died, sometimes read at the funeral service, sometimes published in a newspaper.

object (ǫb-jekt'). Verb: To make an objection; to protest.

object (ob'jekt). Noun: A material thing. Any tangible thing, visible, or capable of discernment by the senses.
  As the word is used in an automobile collision insurance policy:—anything tangible and visible; not necessarily an automobile or other vehicle. Anno: 23 ALR2d 400, § 5; 7 Am J2d Auto Ins § 61.

objection. A protest against an act or omission. A statement of ground of opposition, for example, to the establishment of a highway. 25 Am J1st High § 25. A protest against a determination by the court, especially a ruling upon the admissibility of evidence. The ordinary method of raising in the trial court a question which would not otherwise appear upon the record, the matter being brought to the attention of the trial court for his ruling, and, when the ruling is adverse, followed with an exception thereto to be noted in the record. Calling attention in a proceeding before an administrative body to nonobservance or noncompliance with the provisions of the law. 2 Am J2d Admin L § 425.
See **exception; protest**.

objectionable business. See **offensive business**.

objectionable use. Such use of premises as is reprehensible, offensive, and deserving of disapproval. Theunissen v Huylers, Inc. 58 App DC 106, 25 F2d 530, 61 ALR 706.

objection to grand jury. An objection to the organization of a grand jury, including the matter of exclusion of persons because of race, color, sex, religious or political beliefs, even technical objections, except as a limitation is placed upon the latter by statute. 24 Am J1st Grand J §§ 26 et seq.

objective examination. A physical examination of a person made by a physician wherein he employs the ordinary use of his senses. Reeder v Thompson, 120 Kan 722, 245 P 127.

objective meaning of contract. Not what a promisor has in his mind, but what his promise is understood to mean by a reasonable man in the situation of the promisee. Lee v State Bank & Trust Co. (CA2 NY) 54 F2d 518, 85 ALR 216, cert den 285 US 547, 76 L Ed 958, 52 S Ct 395.

objective symptoms. Those symptoms which a physician by the ordinary use of his senses discovers from a physical examination. Reeder v Thompson, 120 Kan 722, 245 P 127.

objective test. The test in determining the adequacy of the performance of a building or construction contract. Anno: 44 ALR2d 1120, § 5[b].

objective standard of satisfaction. A matter of only operative fitness, quality, or mechanical utility. 17 Am J2d Contr § 367.

object of statute. The aim or purpose of a statute. For some purposes, the equivalent of subject of a statute. 50 Am J1st Stat § 191.

objects of a power (of a pou'ėr). Those persons belonging to a class who are eligible as appointees of a power.

objects of bounty. See **natural objects of bounty**.

oblata (ob-lā'ta). Offerings; gifts to the crown.

oblatio (ob-lā'she-ō). (Civil law.) An offer or tender of payment of a debt.

obligacion (o-ble-gah-she-on). An obligation.

Obligacion est un lien de droit (ōb-li-gä'si-on ät un li-en dē drwo). An obligation, is a bond of the law.

obligatio (ob-li-gā'she-ō). An obligation.

obligation. In an early and narrow sense, a bond or deed under seal wherein a person binds himself under penalty to do a thing. In the modern and popular sense, that which binds, as an oath, vow, promise, contract, or debt. Hargroves v Cooke, 15 Ga 321, 330.
  The word is derived from the Latin word "obligatio," tying up; and that from the verb "obligo," to bind or tie up; to engage by the ties of a promise or oath, or form of law; and obligo is compounded of the verb ligo, to tie or bind fast, and the preposition ob, which is prefixed to increase its meaning. Edwards v Kearzey, 96 US 595, 24 L Ed 793, 796.

obligation of contract. Simply, the binding effect of a contract. The law or duty which binds the parties to perform their agreement, being coeval with the undertaking to perform and consisting in the means which, at the time of the creation of the contract, the law affords for its enforcement, or, as otherwise stated, in the effective force of the law which applies to, and compels performance of, the contract, or a compensatory equivalent in damages for nonperformance. 16 Am J2d Const L § 435.

obligation of surety on bail bond. The undertaking that the accused shall appear in answer to the indictment, abide the orders and judgment of the court, and not depart without leave of the court. State v Benedict, 234 Iowa 1178, 15 NW2d 248.

obligations or liabilities outstanding in the state. A limitation, variously construed, on the effect of a service of process upon a foreign corporation through service upon an agent designated by the corporation or upon a statutory agent. 36 Am J2d For Corp § 484.

obligation under seal. See **specialty**.

obligatory bill (ob'li-gā-tō-ri). See **bill obligatory**.

oblige (ō-blēj'). See **noblesse oblige**.

obligee (ob-li-jē'). A promisee. The person to whom an obligation has been incurred. The person to whom a bond is made payable. The person entitled to enforce a guaranty. 24 Am J1st Guar § 30.

Within the meaning of the Uniform Reciprocal Enforcement of Support Act:—any person to whom a duty of support is owed, including a state or political subdivision. Uniform Reciprocal Enforcement of Support Act § 2(h).

obligor (ob'li-gôr). A promisor. One who has incurred an obligation to another. The person, natural or artificial, liable on a bond. Within the meaning of the Uniform Reciprocal Enforcement of Support Act:—any person owing a duty of support. Uniform Reciprocal Enforcement of Support Act § 2(g).

obliquus (ob-lī'kwus). Oblique; aslant; on the side; collateral; indirect: circumstantial.

obliterated monument. A monument marking the corners or boundary of a tract of land which has been obliterated by the action of the weather, farming operations, logging, mining, etc.

obliterate line. A boundary line obliterated by the action of the weather or by agricultural operations, logging, etc.

obliteration. A blotting out of letters, words, or figures on a written instrument. The effacing of a clause in a will by eraser or inking. 57 Am J1st Wills § 502.
The end may be accomplished by any erasure which shall be partial or complete. It may be done by drawing a pen through the words, or by burning or tearing, and it is not essential for obliteration that the words be rendered illegible, provided it is done with intent to cancel or revoke the instrument. Re Glass' Estate, 14 Colo App 377, 60 P 186.

oblivion (ọb-liv'i-ọn). Forgetfulness. In an unusual sense, an overlooking of a criminal offense, a pardon or amnesty.

obloquy (ob'lọ-kwi). Reprehension; blame; censure; reproach. Tonini v Cevasco, 114 Cal 266, 273, 46 P 103.

obreptio (ob-rep'she-ō). Same as **obreption**.

obreption (ob-rep'shọn). The obtaining of anything by false or fraudulent representations; the fraudulent obtaining of escheated property by false representations.

obrogare (ob-ro-gā're). (Civil law.) To amend, alter, or repeal a law by a new law.

obrogation (ob'rọ-gā'shọn). (Civil law.) The amendment, alteration, or repeal of an existing law by the adoption of a new one.

obscene. Offensive to decency or modesty. Expressing or presenting to the mind or view something which delicacy, purity, and modesty forbid to be expressed. United States v Bebout (DC Ohio) 28 F 522, 524.

obscene advertising. An advertisement which contains obscene language or obscene pictures.

obscene exhibition. See **obscenity**.

obscene language. Words calculated to corrupt morals or excite libidinous thoughts, irrespective of whether the words themselves are impure. 33 Am J1st Lewd etc. § 4. In reference to use of the mails: —offensive to chastity; foul and filthy so as to be offensive to a clear minded person. Anno: 76 L Ed 849; 41 Am J1st P O § 116.

obscene matter. See **obscenity**.

obscene picture. A picture which tends to excite lust. 33 Am J1st Lewd etc. § 9.

obscene publication. A book, magazine, pamphlet, etc., containing matter, the tendency of which is to deprave and corrupt those whose minds are open to corrupting influence and into whose hands such a publication may fall. 33 Am J1st Lewd etc. § 10. Any impure or indecent publication tending to corrupt the mind and to subvert the respect for decency and morality. Timmons v United States (CA6 Ohio) 85 F 204, 205.

obscene show. See **obscenity**.

obscenity. Something offensive to morality or chastity, indecent, or nasty. Commonwealth v Buckley, 200 Mass 346, 86 NE 910. That which shocks the ordinary and common sense of men as an indecency. State v Van Wye, 136 Mo 227, 37 SW 938. Any matter of a lewd, lascivious, or obscene tendency, which is calculated to corrupt and debauch the mind and morals of those persons into whose hands it may fall. See Swearingen v United States, 161 US 446, 40 L Ed 765, 16 S Ct 562.

observe. To see. To take notice of by appropriate conduct; to conform one's action or practice to; to keep; to heed; to obey; to comply with. Marshall County v Knoll, 102 Iowa 573, 580, 69 NW 1146.

obsession. Possessed of an idea or a desire which occupies the mind too fully for calm, deliberate, and effective contemplation. Not necessarily insanity or mental affliction relieving from legal responsibility for matrimonial misconduct. Anno: 19 ALR2d 152, 175, §§ 4, 14.

obsignare (ob-sig-nā're). (Civil law.) To affix a seal to a will or other document; to sign and seal an instrument.

obsolescence. A condition resulting from unforeseen changes in the art, which make the installation of new apparatus necessary. 43 Am J1st Pub Util § 145. The condition of a thing which has passed out of general use, is outmoded, and out of fashion. Re Stout, 151 Or 411, 50 P2d 768, 101 ALR 672. As a matter of deduction in computation of income for taxation, that which renders an asset economically useless, regardless of its physical condition, such as technological improvements, economic changes, and legislative or regulatory changes; functional depreciation. Real Estate-Land Title & Trust Co. v United States, 309 US 13, 84 L Ed 542, 60 S Ct 371.
Obsolescence is not necessarily confined to particular elements or parts of a plant; the whole may become obsolete. It may arise as the result of laws regulating or forbidding the particular use of the property as well as from changes in the act, the shifting of business centers, loss of trade, inadequacy, or other causes. Burnet v Niagara Brewing Co. 282 US 648, 75 L Ed 594, 51 S Ct 262. See **obsolete**.

obsolete. In a condition of **obsolescence**.

obsolete law. A statute never repealed but no longer enforced.

obstante (ob-stan'te). Obstructing; opposing; withstanding.

Obsta principiis (ob'stạ prin-sip'i-is). Withstand or resist the beginnings.
It is the duty of courts to be watchful for the constitutional rights of the citizen, and against any stealthy encroachments thereon. Legislatures are doubtless actuated by the same motives, but the vastness of their business sometimes prevents them, on a first presentation, from noticing objections

which become developed by time and the practical application of the objectionable law. Boyd v United States, 116 US 616, 635, 29 L Ed 746, 752, 6 S Ct 524.

obstetrician (ob-ste-trish'an). In the modern sense, a physician practicing obstetrics. In an older sense, inclusive of a midwife.

obstetrics (ob-stet'riks). The branch of medical science which has to do with the care of women during pregnancy and parturition. Stoike v Weseman, 167 Minn 266, 267, 208 NW 993.

obstinate desertion. A determined, fixed, and persistent desertion of one's spouse. 24 Am J2d Div & S § 99.

obstriction (ob-strik'shon). A bond or other obligation.

obstruct. To interpose obstacles or impediments; to hinder, impede, or in any manner, directly or indirectly, to intrude or prevent. 39 Am J1st Obst J § 10. To make difficult or to present obstacles to the accomplishing of a thing. Anno: 148 ALR 1446. To be or come in the way of, as, the bar in the harbor obstructs the passage of ships; clouds obstruct the light of the sun; to cut off the sight of (an object), as, the trees obstruct the distant hills. Silva v Waldie, 42 NM 514, 82 P2d 282.

obstructing easement. An unreasonable interference by the owner of the servient premises with the enjoyment of an easement. 25 Am J2d Ease § 89.

obstructing enlistments. Presenting obstacles to the obtaining of enlistments in the armed forces or simply making the recruiting of men difficult. Anno: 148 ALR 1446.

obstructing highway. Impeding, delaying, or obstructing traffic. 25 Am J1st High § 272. Impeding, embarrassing, or opposing the passage along and over a street or highway, but not necessarily to such an extent as to stop travel. Chase v Oshkosh, 81 Wis 313, 51 NW 560. Placing a structure in the street, or depositing waste material, so as to reduce the width of the way. United States v Republic Steel Corp. 362 US 482, 4 L Ed 2d 903, 80 S Ct 884, reh den 363 US 858, 4 L Ed 2d 1739, 80 S Ct 1605.

obstructing justice. The criminal offense under the common law, and by the statutes of many jurisdictions, of obstructing the administration and due course of justice. 39 Am J1st Obst J § 1.
See **obstruct**.

obstructing mails. An offense under federal statute in wilfully obstructing or retarding the passage of the mail or its carrier. 18 USC 324.

obstructing navigation. The offense, indictable at common law of obstructing a navigable water way; that is a water way navigable in fact.
Such an offense appears to be punishable as a public nuisance. To render such obstructions a nuisance, it is not necessary that they should actually have interfered with navigation and done it injury; it is sufficient if they rendered such navigation less convenient, less secure, and less expeditious. State v Narrows Island Club, 100 NC 477.

obstructing officer. Impeding a public officer in the performance of his duty by direct or indirect means. 39 Am J1st Obst J § 8.
The word includes any passive, indirect, circuitous impediments to the service or execution of process, such as hindering or preventing an officer by not opening a door or removing an obstacle or by concealing or removing property. 39 Am J1st Obst J § 10.
The word does not mean to oppose or impede the process with which the officer is armed, or to defeat its execution, but that the officer himself shall be obstructed. Davis v State, 76 Ga 721, 722.

obstruction. A blocking of passage, such as an object on or near a railroad track. An impediment.
See expressions beginning "obstructing."

obstruxit (ob-strū'xit). He obstructed.

Obstupare (ob-stu-pā're). To stop up.

Obstupavit et obstruxit (ob-stu-pā'vit et ob-stru'xit). He stopped up and obstructed.

obtaining by false pretense. See **false pretense**.

Obtemperandum est consuetudini rationabili tanquam legi (ob-tem-pe-ran'dum est kon-su-ē-tū'di-nī rā-she-ō-nā'bi-lī tan'quam lē'jī). Obedience is due or owing to a reasonable custom as much as to the law.

obtest. To call to witness.

Obtulit se (ob-tu'lit sē). He offered himself, he appeared,—a form of the record entry of a person's appearance in court.

ob turpem causam (ob tur'pem kâ'zam). For a base reason; for an immoral consideration.

obventio (ob-ven'she-ō). (Civil law.) Rent; revenue; income; yield; profits.

obvious danger. A danger which is observable or discoverable in the exercise of reasonable care which persons of ordinary intelligence may be expected to take for their own safety. Hardy v Chicago, R. I. & P. Ry. Co. 139 Iowa 314, 115 NW 8. A risk readily to be perceived either by the eye or by the intellect. Small v Travelers' Protective Asso. 118 Ga 900, 45 SE 706.

obvious defects. See **patent defects**.

obvious peril. See **obvious danger**.

obvious risk. See **obvious danger**.

ob vitae solatium (ob vī'tē sō-lā'she-um). Toward the comfort of life. Thurston v Carter, 112 Me 361, 92 A 295.

o. c. An abbreviation of "ope consilio,"—by the aid of counsel.

occasio (o-kā'zhe-ō). A feudal tribute exacted from tenants by the lord for his necessities.

occasion. An incident. In the strict sense, something which incidentally brings to pass an event, but not an efficient cause of the occurrence. Pennsylvania Co. v Congdon, 134 Ind 226, 33 NE 795. In ordinary use, a synonym of "cause." Williamsburgh City Fire Ins. Co. v Willard (CA9 Cal) 164 F 404.
See **privileged occasion**.

occasional. For the occasion; not regularly; pertaining to the cause; causal.

occasional contraband (kon'tra-band). Goods which are not actually contraband but which are treated as contraband by a belligerent.

occision (ok-sizh'on). A killing; a putting to death.

occult (o-kult'). Concealed; hidden; secret. Beyond the understanding of man. Of the mystic arts.

occultatio (o-kul-tā'she-ō). Concealment; hiding.

Occultatio thesauri inventi fraudulosa (o-kul-tā'she-ō the-sâ'rī in-ven'tī frâ-du-lō'sa). The concealment of discovered treasure is fraudulent.

occult crimes (krīms). Secret offenses; crimes committed by stealth.

occupacion. (Spanish.) A temporary taking of property by a competent tribunal or authority without compensation to the owner. The Navemar (DC NY) 24 F Supp 495.

occupancy. Possession in fact. The use of premises. 29A Am J Rev ed Ins § 895. The taking possession of those things which before belonged to nobody. 42 Am J1st Prop § 34. In reference to the rights of an occupying claimant:—such an occupancy as under the rules of the common law would entitle one to acquire a title by adverse possession, that is actual, open, and peaceable occupancy, but not necessarily occupancy as of one's dwelling place. 27 Am J1st Improv § 8.
"Physical occupancy" of property and legal possession of the same are not necessarily identical. A person may be held in law to be in actual possession of property, though at that time he be not physically upon it. State ex rel. Honey Island Land & Timber Co. v King, 110 La 961, 35 So 181.

occupancy agreement. An agreement carrying with it the right to occupy a specific apartment in a co-operative apartment building. 15 Am J2d Con Apt § 21.

occupant. One in enjoyment of the occupancy of premises. One in actual possession, the tenant as distinguished from the landlord who has possession but not occupancy. Parsons v Prudential Real Estate Co. 86 Neb 271, 125 NW 521.
For the purposes of the statutory requirement of notice of a proceeding for the establishment of a highway, the owner of a farm who is in the actual possession and control of it is the "occupant" thereof, although at the time he does not reside on the farm but in a village near by. A tenant who cultivates leased land is also an "occupant," although he does not reside thereon. 25 Am J1st High § 24.

Occupantis fiunt derelicta (o-ku-pan'tis fī'unt dē-re-lik'ta). Abandoned goods go to the first taker.

occupare (o-ku-pā're). (Civil law.) To occupy; to take possession of; to lay hold of; to seize.

occupatio (o-ku-pā'she-o). (Civil law.) An occupation; a seizure; a taking possession; a business, occupation or calling.

occupation. The enjoyment of real property. Ward v Crane, 118 Cal 676, 50 P 839. The taking and possessing of enemy territory in time of war. 56 Am J1st War §§ 204 et seq. A more or less continuous or habitual engagement in a certain line of employment or industrial or business activity. Anno: 50 ALR 1176; 106 ALR 1502. That which occupies or engages the time or attention; the principal business of one's life. Union Mut. Acci. Asso. v Frohard, 134 Ill 228, 25 NE 642. A profession, vocation, calling, employment, or trade. Stewart v Barber, 182 Misc 91, 43 NYS2d 560. For the purposes of the application of a diminished liability clause of an accident insurance policy:—the insured's principal vocation or pursuit. 29 Am J Rev ed Ins § 769. For the purposes of an exemption statute:—any employment in which the debtor is engaged to procure a living, or at which he habitually earns his living. 31 Am J2d Exemp § 3.

occupational disability clause. A provision in a health or accident insurance policy, or in a life insurance policy containing a disability provision, for the payment of periodic indemnity for total disability preventing the insured from performing any of the duties of his occupation, business, or profession. 29A Am J Rev ed Ins § 1516.

occupational disease. A disease which develops gradually and imperceptibly as a result of engaging in a particular employment and is generally known and understood to be a usual and natural incident or hazard of such employment. 58 Am J1st Workm Comp § 246. A disease caused by or especially incident to a particular employment. Iwanicki v State Industrial Acci. Com. 104 Or 650, 205 P 990, 29 ALR 682, 688. Something other than an accidental injury. But none the less a personal injury, the injury being regarded as sustained when the employee becomes unable to work. Iwanicki v State Industrial Acci. Com. 104 Or 650, 205 P 990, 29 ALR 682.

occupational prejudice. A prejudice against the occupation of a party, such as that of tending bar. 31 Am J Rev ed Jury § 178.

occupational restriction. A restriction contained in a covenant prohibiting the use of property in the pursuit of any occupation or certain prescribed occupations. 20 Am J2d Cov § 197.

occupation tax. A tax imposed for the purpose of revenue only on persons pursuing a certain occupation, vocation, or profession, such as that of practicing law, as distinguished from the charging of a license fee in the course of the regulation of an occupation, vocation, or profession. Royall v Virginia, 116 US 572, 29 L Ed 735, 6 S Ct 510. A tax upon the privilege of selling tangible personal property at retail, a tax sometimes regarded as included within the meaning of the term "sales taxes." 47 Am J1st Sales T § 1.

occupavit (o-ku-pā'vit). He took possession; a writ which lay to recover land which was lost in time of war.

occupied. Space, time, or even one's mind filled to the exclusion of anything else. Possessed in fact and used. As a warranty or representation in an insurance policy covering a building:—a substantial and practical use of the insured building for the purposes for which it is intended and as comtemplated by the policy. 29A Am J Rev ed Ins § 907.

occupy. To fill space; to take one's attention. To hold, to keep for use, or to possess, real estate. Missionary Soc. v Dalles City (US) 17 Otto 336, 27 L Ed 545, 2 S Ct 672.

occupying claimant. The terminology for one who seeks recovery for improvements made by him upon premises while he was in actual occupancy thereof in the belief that he had a good title.

Occupying Claimant's Acts. Statutes which provide a recovery by an occupying claimant, since dispossessed by the true owner, for improvements made by him while he was in actual occupancy of the premises in the belief that he had good title. 27 Am J1st Improv § 6.

occur. To happen. Johnson v Humboldt Ins. Co. 91 Ill 92.

occurrence. A happening; an event.
The time of the occurrence of an accident within the meaning of an indemnity policy is generally deemed to be the time when the complaining party was actually damaged, and not when the wrongful act was committed. Remmer v Glens Falls Indem.

Co. 140 Cal App 2d 84, 295 P2d 19, 57 ALR2d 1379.

occurrence witness. A witness having personal knowledge of an event from presence at its occurrence, especially a witness who observed an accident in which a personal injury or injuries were sustained. Krupp v Chicago Transit Authority, 8 Ill 2d 37, 132 NE2d 532.

ocean. The bounding main; the high sea.

ocean going steamer. A vessel equipped to sail the ocean, even including a large pleasure yacht. 12 Am J2d Boats § 1.

ochlocracy (ok-lok'ra̱-si). A government by a mob which has overturned the established order.

octabis (ok-tā'bis). Same as **octave**.

octave (ok'tāv). The eighth full tone above a given tone. The eighth day inclusive after a church feast day.

The first return day (the day on which original writs are made returnable) in every term is the first day in that term; as, for instance, the octave of St. Hilary, or the eighth day inclusive after the feast of that saint. See 3 Bl Comm 277.

octoroon (ok-tọ-rön'). The child of a white person and a quadroon; a person of one eighth Negro blood.

octo tales (ok'to tāls). A writ to summon men who shall supply a deficiency in the jury panel.

ocular refraction (ok'ụ-la̱r re-frak'shọn). The adaptation and accommodation of the light rays which enter the eye in keeping with optical principles, to secure proper focus and the formation of an accurate image on the retina. Abelson, Inc. v New York State Board of Optometrists, 5 NJ 412, 75 A2d 867, 22 ALR2d 929.

An applied arm of optical science, resting upon the work and discoveries of physicists and opticians through the ages, down to modern times. It does not treat the eye, whether in health or disease, but adapts the light waves which enter the eye, in accordance with optical principles, so as to produce focused and single vision with the least abnormal exertion on the part of the eye. Its distinction from medicine and its independence of medicine have been affirmed by the United States Supreme Court in every case in which the question has been brought up for adjudication. Silver v Lansburgh & Bro. (DC Dist Col) 27 F Supp 682.

oculist (ok'ụ-list). A physician who specializes in treating abnormalities and diseases of the eye. Black v Bearden, 167 Ark 455, 268 SW 27. One who practices medicine and surgery in the treatment of diseases of the eye. Anno: 141 ALR 884.

The practice of an oculist has relation to the practice of medicine and surgery in the treatment of diseases of the eye, and to the measurement of the powers of vision, and the adaptation of lenses for the aid thereof. Anno: 22 ALR2d 941.

odd lot. A transaction in stock negotiated by a broker involving less than one hundred shares.

Oderunt peccare boni, virtutis amore; oderunt peccare mali, formidine poenae (ō-dē'runt pe-kā're bō'nī, vir-tū'tis a-mō're; ō'dē-runt pe-kā're ma'lī, for-mi'di-ne pē'nē). By reason of their love of goodness, righteous men hate to sin; by reason of their fear of punishment, bad men hate to sin.

odhal or odhall. Allodial,—free; not held in subordination to another; opposed to feudal.

odio et atia. See **de odio et atia**.

Odiosa et inhonesta non sunt in lege praesumenda (ō-di-ō'sa et in-ho-nes'ta non sunt in lē'je prē-zumen'da). Odious and dishonest things are not to be presumed in law.

Odiosa non praesumuntur (ō-di-ō'sa non prē-zumun'ter). Odious or hateful things are not presumed.

odious plea. A plea that the plaintiff is an alien enemy. 3 Am J2d Aliens § 191.

odium (ō'di-um). Hatred or dislike, applied in the law particularly to hatred or dislike of a party to an action or of his cause of action or defense. Brow v Levy, 3 Ind App 464, 468.

odium spoliatoris. See **in odium spoliatoris**.

oeconomicus (ē-ko-no'mi-kus). An executor of the estate of a testator.

oeconomus (ẹ-kon'ọ-mus). An administrator; an advocate; a defender.

oecumenical (ē-ku-men'i-kal). Same as **ecumenical**.

odometer (ọ-dom'e-tėr). A device for recording the miles traveled by a vehicle.

odor. A refined word for smell. A nuisance when noxious. 39 Am J1st Nuis § 59.

oeps (oops or oos). Use.

oes (oos). Same as **oeps**.

of. Belonging to. Denoting possession or ownership. Davidson v Click, 31 NM 543, 47 ALR 1016, 249 P 100. Sometimes indicating origin, source, descent and the like. Stone v Riggs, 43 Okla 209, 142 P 298. As the word appears in a tariff schedule:—indicating an article wholly or primarily made from material designated. 19 USC § 1202, Headnote 9(f). Sometimes the equivalent of "in." Sisson v Board of Supervisors, 128 Iowa 442, 104 NW 454.

of a civil nature. See **suit of a civil nature**.

of age. The condition or state of a person who has attained his or her majority.
See **age of majority**.

of counsel. A phrase which indicates that the person named is assisting another lawyer in a cause or the trial of a case. A common designation for associate attorneys to distinguish them from the attorneys of record in a cause.

of course. See **as of course**.

offa execrata (of'fa ex-e-krā'ta). The morsel of execration, the corsned,—a piece of bread which, under the ancient Saxon law, was given to a person accused of crime to be eaten by him.

If it stuck in his throat, he was deemed guilty.

offal (of'ạl). Garbage; waste animal or vegetable matter; any filthy material. 37 Am J1st Mun Corp § 298. That which is permitted to fall away as of no value, for example, the chips in the dressing of a stone.

offend. To commit a public offense. To hurt the feelings.

offense. A crime. A felony, misdemeanor, or other infraction subject to prosecution. Osborne v Owsley (Mo) 264 SW2d 332, 38 ALR2d 1128. Agression. A hurt to the feelings.

This word in a clause of a contract of employment authorizing the employee's discharge may be given a broader meaning than crime and justify dismissal for conduct for which no one bothered to

OFFENSE [881] OFFICER

prosecute the offender, or something that is no legal crime at all. Twentieth Century-Fox Film Corp. v Lardner (CA9 Cal) 216 F2d 844, 51 ALR2d 728.

offense against the United States. See **federal offense.**

offense malum in se. See **mala in se.**

offense malum prohibitum. See **mala prohibita.**

offensive. Giving offense; causing displeasure or annoyance. Wounding the feelings. People v Whitman (Co Ct) 157 NYS 1107. Being aggressive.

offensive business. A business which is noxious or dangerous to the neighborhood. 20 Am J2d Cov § 198. A business which is noxious, unsanitary, unsightly, unusually noisy, or constituting a nuisance per se. Unity Builders Inc. v Scarborough (La App) 149 So 2d 141. A term of a restrictive covenant to be construed in accordance with the context of the covenant. Babcock v Laidlaw, 113 NJ Eq 318, 166 A 632.

offer. A proposal of terms made with the purpose of securing the acceptance thereof by another, thereby completing a contract. 17 Am J2d Contr § 31. A tender of performance.

offer and acceptance. Essentials in the formation of a contract; the means through which the minds of the parties meet. 17 Am J2d Contr § 31. The assent or meeting of the minds of the parties in completing a contract of guaranty. 24 Am J1st Guar § 34.

offered evidence. Evidence presented by a party on the trial of an action.
Such evidence may or may not be received. It is evidence adduced but it does not become evidence introduced unless it is admitted or received by the court. Tuttle v Story County, 56 Iowa 316, 317, 9 NW 292.

offer for the record. See **offer of proof.**

offering bribe. See **bribery.**

offering to do equity. A maxim which prescribes a condition of plaintiff's right to relief in equity. 28 Am J Rev ed Inj § 34.

offer of compromise. A concession by a party to a controversy, such as a reduction in claim, made for the purpose of settlement of the controversy. Daniels v U. S. Rubber Co. (Tex Civ App) 199 SW2d 533.

offer of evidence. Same as **offer of proof.**

offer of proof. Presenting evidence for admission or for a ruling upon admissibility. A formal offer by a party of proof, showing what testimony he proposes to adduce, and, when necessary, his intention to prove other facts which will render the evidence relevant or competent. Advising the court of the purpose for which apparently irrelevant or incompetent evidence is offered. Chambers v Minneapolis, St. Paul & S. Ste. M. R. Co. 37 ND 377, 163 NW 824, 954. The offer of testimony of a witness ruled incompetent by the trial court or of evidence ruled inadmissible by the trial court, such being an offer for the record, sometimes known as an avowal, the purpose being to present a good record on appeal by preserving the error in an adequate form. 53 Am J1st Trial § 99.

offer of tender. The physical act of offering the money in making a tender. 52 Am J1st Tend § 7.

offer to dedicate. The declaration of an owner of real estate of his purpose to dedicate the property to public use, made by him expressly or by act, by deed, or by plat. 23 Am J2d Ded § 18.

offer to guarantee. A step in the making of a contract of guaranty.
An offer to guarantee the obligation of a third party is not a guaranty. The assent of the parties is essential to a guaranty, and for such assent there must be an offer by one party and an acceptance of it by the other. An offer to guarantee is but a step in the negotiations leading up to the contract; the guaranty is the finished product of the negotiations. 24 Am J1st Guar § 34.

offer to restore. See **tender.**

office. A term of vague and variant import, the meaning of which varies necessarily with the context and the circumstances surrounding the use of the term. 42 Am J1st Pub Of § 2. A place wherein business is transacted. That function by virtue whereof a person has an employment in the affairs of another, whether public, private, or quasi-public and the right to such emoluments as accrue from the employment. 42 Am J1st Pub Of § 2. Purpose, for example, the office of a remedy.

office copy. A certified copy made by the officer in custody of the judicial records. State v Board of Public Works, 57 NJL 313, 316, 30 A 581.

office found. A finding of fact by inquest of office or other proceeding equivalent thereto that a certain individual is an alien.
At common law, until office found, an alien is competent to hold land against third persons, and no one has a right to complain in a collateral proceeding, if the sovereign does not enforce its prerogative. Phillips v Moore, 100 US 208, 25 L Ed 603.

office grant. A transfer or conveyance of land to a person entitled thereto by a public officer in certain cases where the owner cannot or will not execute it.

office hours. The period of time when a public or private office is open for the transaction of business.

Office of Alien Property. A division in the Department of Justice of the United States.

office of corporation. See **corporate officers; principal place of business.**

office of credit. Same as **office of honor.**

office of honor. An office which yields no profit. Alexander v Jenkins (Eng) LR 1 QB 797.

office of profit. A lucrative office; an office the incumbent of which is entitled to salary or other compensation. State v De Gress, 53 Tex 387, 400. A public office to which a compensation is attached. 42 Am J1st Pub Of § 23.

officer. A term of vague and variant import, the meaning of which varies necessarily with the context and the circumstances surrounding the use of the term. 42 Am J1st Pub Of § 2. A commissioned officer of the Armed Forces. 36 Am J1st Mil § 51. A policeman. One holding or inseparably connected with an office. Metcalf v Mitchell, 269 US 514, 70 L Ed 384, 46 S Ct 172. A person who holds an office, either public or private. 42 Am J1st Pub Of § 2.
An officer is distinguishable from a person who holds a place of trust or profit. Such places are not offices, and yet they occupy the same general level in dignity and importance. Members of the legislature are not officers. Their places are places of trust

and profit, but they are not offices of trust and profit. Doyle v Aldermen of Raleigh, 89 NC 133.
See **corporate officers; municipal officer; public officer**.

officer de facto. See **de facto corporate officer; de facto public officer**.

officer de jure (of'i-sėr de jö'ri). See **de jure officer**.

officer of the armed services. A commissioned officer. 36 Am J1st Mil § 51.
See **noncommissioned officer**.

officer of the United States. One who holds his office by virtue of appointment by the President, by one of the courts of justice, or by the head of a department authorized by law to make such appointment. 54 Am J1st U S § 11.

officer pro tempore (of'i-sėr prō tem'pō-re). See **pro tempore**.

officers of corporation. See **corporate officers**.

office work. Work in a business office; clerical work.

Officia judicialia non concedantur antequam vacent (of-fi'she-a jū-di-she-ā'li-a non kon-sē-dan'ter an'te-quam va'sent). Judicial offices are not granted or appointed before they become vacant.

official. In the capacity of an officer, especially a public officer. Formal.

While the word usually means pertaining to a public office, it is sometimes applied to persons holding fiduciary positions, to distinguish their transactions in such relations from their purely private business. Bissell v Wayne Probate Judge, 58 Mich 237, 238, 24 NW 886.

official act. An act done by an officer in his official capacity, under color and by virtue of his office.

An act need not be a lawful act that it may be an official one. If this were not so, the sureties on his official bond would never be responsible. Greenberg v People's use of Balaban, 225 Ill 174, 80 NE 100.

To constitute official action, it is not necessary that it shall be prescribed by statute nor that it be prescribed by a written rule or regulation. Duties are often established by settled practice. Whitney v United States (CA10 Okla) 99 F2d 327.

official ballot. A ballot prescribed by the legislature for use at an election, almost invariably being in a form modeled on what is known as the "Australian ballot system." 26 Am J2d Elect § 204.

official bond. A penal bond conditioned upon the performance of duties of office. A bond required of a public officer, in effect, a contract between the officer and the government, binding the officer to discharge the duties of his office, and binding the sureties to make good the defaults of the officer. 43 Am J1st Pub Of § 394.

official forms. Forms officially prescribed for use, for example, the official forms prescribed by the United States Supreme Court for use in bankruptcy proceedings. 9 Am J2d Bankr § 108.

official intermeddling. A matter of maintenance. Anno: 139 ALR 650.

official misconduct. An act constituting a breach of the good faith and right action impliedly required of all public officers. Etzler v Brown, 58 Fla 221, 50 So 416. Any act involving moral turpitude, or any act which is contrary to justice, honesty, principle, or good morals, if performed by virtue of authority of office. State v Examining & Trial Board, 43 Mont 389, 117 P 77. Any unlawful behavior in relation to the duties of his office, willful in its character, of any officer intrusted in any manner with the administration of justice, or the execution of the laws. Brackenridge v State, 27 Tex App 513, 11 SW 630.

official newspaper. A newspaper of a city or county in which public acts, resolutions, advertisements, and notices of the city or county are required to be published. Shelden v Butler County, 48 Kan 356, 29 P 759.

official notice. Another expression for **judicial notice**. The equivalent of judicial notice by an administrative agency. 2 Am J2d Admin L § 385.

official opinion. See **opinion**.

official oppression. The wrong of a public officer in exercising his official authority for his own selfish or vindictive reasons to the harm of another. Anno: 83 ALR2d 1008.

official records. Transcripts from books and records of the executive departments of the federal government which, when authenticated according to law, constitute evidence, by virtue of the federal official records statutes, concerning the matters of which they speak, if made by an officer or agent of the government in the course of the discharge by him of his official duty. Anno: 50 ALR2d 1197.
See **court record; public record**.

Official Records Statute. A federal statute providing that books or records of account, or minutes of the proceedings of any department or agency of the United States, are admissible to prove the act, transaction, or occurrence as a memorandum of which the same were made or kept. 28 USC § 1733(a).

Official Register. A publication compiled by the United States Civil Service Commission, showing persons occupying administrative and supervisory positions in the legislative, executive, and judicial branches of the Government of the United States and in the District of Columbia.

Official Reports as Evidence Act. One of the uniform laws. 30 Am J2d Ev § 994.

official rules. Rules governing the practice and procedure before an administrative agency. 2 Am J2d Admin L § 346.

official seal. The seal affixed to a document by a public officer. Kirksey v Bates (Ala) 7 Port 529. The instrumentality for affixing a seal that goes with a public office as part of the paraphernalia of office.

Such a seal must contain enough to show the official character of the officer and must be capable of making a distinct and uniform impression upon the paper upon which it is used, or on some tenacious substance such as wax attached thereto, capable of receiving an impression. A seal in the form of a scrawl of the pen does not fill the requirements of an official seal. 47 Am J1st Seals § 7.
See **great seal; seal of court**.

official trustee. An official trustee in bankruptcy under a former practice, now prohibited, of recognizing a particular corporation in the federal district as entitled to appointment as trustee in bankruptcy in all cases arising in the district requiring a trustee. 9 Am J2d Bankr § 621.

official use. An active use; that is, a use under which the feoffee to uses was required to perform active duties with reference to the property conveyed to him.

official visitors. See **visitors.**

Officia magistratus non debent esse venalia (of-fi'she-a ma-jis-trā'tus non de'bent es'se ve-nā'li-a). The offices of magistrates ought not to be the subjects of sale.

officiariis non faciendis vel amovendis (of-fi-she-ā'ri-is non fā-she-en'dis vel ā-mō-ven'dis). A writ which lay to stay the installation or removal of an officer of a corporation.

officina fraudis (of-fi-si'na frâ'dis). The workshop of fraud.

officina gentium (of-fi-si'na jen'she-um). The workshop of nations.

officina justitiae (of-fi-sī'na jūs-ti'she-ē). The workshop of justice, a term applied to the English Court of Chancery. Yates v People (NY) 6 Johns 337, 363.

officio. See **ex officio**; **functus officio.**

officio coronatoris. See **de officio coronatoris.**

officious will (ọ-fish'us wil). A will wherein the testator leaves his property to his family.

Officit conatus si effectus sequatur (of'fi-sit ko-nā'tus sī ef-fek'tus se-quā'ter). An attempt works an injury if the result follows.

officium (ọ-fish'i-um). An office.

Officium nemini debet esse damnosum (of-fi'she-um nĕ'mi-nī de'bet es'se dam-nō'sum). An office ought not to be a detriment to a person.

offset. A balancing or compensating factor. A printing process.
See **setoff**; **without offset.**

offset well. An oil well dug for the specific purpose of preventing drainage of oil to adjoining property. 24 Am J1st Gas & Oil § 43.

offspring. Children or issue. Anno: 23 ALR2d 842-845. Sometimes a word of limitation in grant or devise. Allen v Markle, 36 Pa 117.

offstreet parking. A parking lot. Parking places off the street provided for the purpose of relieving traffic congestion. 26 Am J2d Em D § 48.

off-the-road production. The production of materials used in highway maintenance. Thomas v Hempt Bros. 345 US 19, 97 L Ed 751, 73 S Ct 568.

of new (nū). Anew; over again.

of right. A matter of legal right.
See **as of course.**

Of two possible constructions, adopt the one which will save and not destroy. A canon of construction. Anniston Mfg. Co. v Davis, 301 US 337, 81 L Ed 1143, 57 S Ct 816.

ohm (ōm). The unit of electrical resistance; the resistance to a force of one volt in a current of one ampere. Peoria Waterworks Co. v Peoria R. Co. (CC Ill) 181 F 990.

oikeimania (oi-kei-ma'ni-a). A morbid state of a person's domestic affections, as an unreasonable dislike of his wife or child, without cause or provocation, turning love into hatred. Ekin v McCracken (Pa) 11 Phila 534, 540.

oil. A mineral. Scott v Laws, 185 Ky 440, 215 SW 81, 13 ALR 369.
See **crude oil.**

oil and gas lease. A grant of the sole and exclusive right to develop the land described in the lease for oil and gas or a demise for a designated term of years for the purpose of such development, subject to the conditions of a payment of royalty in the event of production, of the commencement of drilling operations on or before a specified date, and of the performance within a prescribed time of a certain amount of development work. 24 Am J1st Gas & O § 34.

oil and gas license. A distributor's license required because of the dangerous character of the product. 24 Am J1st Gas & O § 129. A license required for the storage or keeping of oil, gasoline, or other petroleum product. 24 Am J1st Gas & O § 154.

oil filings. Oil locations,—locations made on public lands of the United States and filed in the government land office pursuant to acts of Congress by persons in good faith claiming the land as oil land. Anthony Wilkinson Live Stock Co. v McIlquham, 14 Wyo 209, 83 P 364.

oil lease. See **oil and gas lease.**

oil license. See **oil and gas license.**

oil locations. Same as **oil filings.**

oil refinery. A plant wherein crude oil is refined by splitting it up into a number of commercial products by a process of fractional distillation. 24 Am J1st Gas & O § 123.

oil royalty. See **royalty.**

oil royalty pool. See **royalty pool.**

oil well. A well bored in the crust of the earth and the components thereof to a deposit of crude oil. A structure within the meaning of a lien law. 24 Am J1st Gas & O § 114. Not a mine. 36 Am J1st Min & M § 2.

oil well drilling. See **footage drilling**; **rotary drilling**; **turn-key drilling.**

oir. Same as **oyer.**

O.K. All right; correct. 1 Am J2d Abbr § 7. An abbreviation frequently used in the commercial world signifying the signer's approval of the instrument on which he indorses it.
The origin of the term "O.K." is obscure. While there are various explanations of the origin, none is well-grounded. It has, however, a well-defined meaning in common and commercial usage. Anything said to be "O.K." is understood to be all right or correct. Lithographical Printing Co. v Chase, 149 Mass 459, 21 NE 765; Morganton Mfg. Co. v Ohio River & C. R. Co. 121 NC 514, 28 SE 474.

OK bill of lading. A bill of lading bearing the written or stamped letters "OK," indicating that the goods were received by the carrier in good condition. Morganton Mfg. Co. v Ohio & Charleston Ry. Co. 121 NC 514, 28 SE 474.

old age. Advanced age; senility. Not mental incompetency in itself. Lindsey v Lindsey, 50 Ill 79; Westerbeck v Cannon, 5 Wash 2d 106, 104 P2d 918.

Old-Age and Survivors' Insurance. The system whereby employees and employers are taxed to provide for the payment of benefits to workers and their wives upon their reaching a stated age or suffering disability, popularly known as social security. 48 Am J1st Soc Sec § 9.

Old-Age and Survivors' Insurance Act. Federal statutes constituting a part of the Federal Social Security Act, providing a system of social security for employees. 26 USC §§ 1400 et seq.

old-age assistance. A provision made by state statute, complimentary to, and operating in conjunction with, the Federal Social Security Act, for benefits to persons in needy or indigent circumstances or without means of support, who have reached a specified age. 48 Am J1st Soc Sec §§ 39 et seq. In the broad sense, any aid granted by the public or by private persons to the elderly for support, maintenance, or medical care.

old-age exemption. A homestead exemption provided by statute for an aged person, even for an aged person who is not the head of a family. 26 Am J1st Home § 15.

Old Bailey (ōld bā'li). The name which was given to what was formerly the principal criminal court of London.

old line company. A life insurance company operating on a fixed-premium basis, as distinguished from a mutual benefit society or company issuing policies on an assessment basis, its policies having a cash surrender value after the first year.
See **old line policy.**

old line policy. A policy of life insurance in which the amount to be paid by the insured is fixed, the premiums to be paid are unalterable, and the liability incurred by the insurance company is also fixed, definite, and unchangeable. Clark v Metropolitan Life Ins. Co. 126 Me 7, 9, 135 A 357, 358.

Old Natura Brevium (nā-tū'ra brē'vi-um). A book or account compiled in the reign of Edward the Third, describing the writs in common use at that time.

old school. Having a conservative quality.

old school physician. One licensed to practice and practicing medicine according to the system approved by and taught in the leading medical schools. 41 Am J1st Phys & S § 85.

old style calendar. The calendar which was in use in England and America prior to the year 1752, when the "new style" or Gregorian calendar was adopted.

oleomargarine (o"lē-ọ-mar'ga-rin). A substance used as butter, made of vegetable oil and other ingredients, and fortified with vitamins. 35 Am J2d Food § 41.

oleo oil (ō'lẹ-ọ oil'). A food; a substance used in the preparation of oleomargarine. 35 Am J2d Food § 1.

Oleron. See **Laws of Oleron.**

oligarchy (ol'i-gär-ki). A government which is administered by a few persons.

olograph (ol'ọ-gràf). A **holographic will.**

olographic will (ol'ọ-graf-ik wil). Same as **holographic will.**

om (ōm). Same as **omme.**

ome bueno (om boo-ay-no). (Spanish.) A good or responsible man.

omissa vel male appretiate (o-mis-sa vel male ap-preti-at-e). Omissions or mistakes in understanding.

omissio (o-mi'she-ō). An omission.

Omissio eorum quae tacite insunt nihil operatur (o-mi'she-ō ē-ō'rum kwē ta'si-tē in'sunt ni'hil o-perā'ter). The omission of those things which are tacitly implied is of no importance.

omission. A leaving out. A failure to act. The failure to do something which ought to be done; not doing something required.
See **crime of omission.**

omissis omnibus aliis negotiis (o-mis'sis om'ni-bus a'li-is ne-gō'she-is). Putting aside all other business affairs.

omissus. See **casus omissus.**

omits to provide. A familiar phrase in statutes respecting the rights of pretermitted children.
As the expression is used in a statute providing that if a testator "omits to provide" in his will for his child, the child will take as if the testator had died intestate, it means simply an omission to make a provision for the child in the will, and has no reference to the pecuniary value of such provision, the object of the statute being merely to prevent the child from being overlooked. Allison v Allison, 101 Va 537, 44 SE 904.

omitted property. Property which has escaped taxation. Independent Pipe Line Co. v State Board of Equalization, 168 Okla 432, 33 P2d 797. Property of a decedent omitted in the assessment of inheritance tax. State v Brooks, 183 Minn 251, 236 NW 316. Lands omitted in the original assessment for a local improvement. St. Louis & K. C. Land Co. v Kansas City, 241 US 419, 60 L Ed 1072, 36 S Ct 647.

omme (um). A man; anyone.

Omne actum ab intentione agentis est judicandum (om'ne ak'tum ab in-ten-she-ō'ne ā-jen'tis est jū-dikan'dum). Every act is to be judged by the intention of the doer.

Omne crimen ebrietas, et incendit et detegit (om'ne kri'men ē-bri'e-tās, et in-sen'dit et dē-te'jit). Drunkenness both aggravates and lays bare every crime. See 4 Bl Comm 25.

Omne jus aut consensus fecit, aut necessitas constituit, aut firmavit consuetudo (om'ne jūs ât konsen'sus fē'sit, ât ne-ses'si-tas kon-sti-tu'it, ât firmā'vit kon-su-ē-tū'dō). (Civil law.) Consent created, necessity established, or custom confirmed every right.

Omne magis dignum trahit ad se minus dignum, quamvis minus dignum sit antiquius (om'ne mā'jis dig'num tra'hit ad sē mī'nus dig'num, quam'vis mī'nus dig'num sit an-ti'qui-us). Every worthier thing draws to itself the less worthy, although the less worthy be the more ancient.

Omne magis dignum trahit ad se minus dignum sit antiquius (om'ne mā'jis dig'num tra'hit ad sē mī'nus dig'num sit an-tī'qui-us). Every worthier thing draws to itself the less worthy, although it be older.

Omne magnum exemplum habet aliquid ex iniquo, quod publica utilitate compensatur (om'ne mag'-num eg-zem'plum hā'bet a'li-quid ex in-ī-quo, quod pub'li-ka u-ti-li-tā'te kom-pen-sā'ter). Every great example has something of unfairness, which is balanced by public advantage.

Omne majus continet in se minus (om'ne mā'jus kon'-ti-net in sē mī'nus). Every greater right or thing holds within itself the less.

Omne majus dignum continet in se minus dignum (om'ne mā'jus dig'num kon'ti-net in sē mī'nus dig'-num). Every more worthy thing contains the less worthy within itself.

Omne majus minus in se complectitur (om'ne mā'jus mī'nus in sē kom-plek'ti-ter). Every greater thing embraces the less within itself.

Omne principale trahit ad se accessorium (om'ne prin-si-pā'le tra'hit ad sē ak-ses-sō'ri-um). Every principal thing draws the accessory to itself. Parsons v Welles, 17 Mass 425.

Omne quod inaedificatur solo cedit (om'ne quod in-ē-di-fi-kā'ter sō'lō se'dit). Everything which is built into the soil goes with it. See Broom's Legal Maxims 401.

Omne sacramentum debet esse de certa scientia (om'ne sa-kra-men'tum de'bet es'se dē ser'ta sī-en'she-a). Every sworn statement ought to be of certain knowledge.

Omnes actiones in mundo infra certa tempora habent limitationem (om'nēz ak-she-ō'nēz in mun'dō in'fra ser'ta tem'po-ra hā'bent li-mi-tā-she-ō'nem). All actions in the world have limitation within certain periods of time.

Omnes homines aut liberi sunt aut servi (om'nēz hō'mi-nēz ât li'be-rī sunt ât ser'vī). All men are either freemen or slaves.

Omnes licentiam habere his quae pro se indulta sunt, renunciare (om'nēz lī-sen'she-am hā-bē're his kwē prō sē in-dul'ta sunt, re-nun'she-ā-re). (Civil law.) All are free to renounce those things which have been allowed for their benefit. See Broom's Legal Maxims 699.

Omnes prudentes, illa admittere solent quae probantur iis qui in arte sua bene versati sunt (om'nēz prū-den'tez, il'la ad-mit'te-re sō'lent kwē prōban'ter ī'is quī in ar'te su'a be'ne ver-sā'tī sunt). All prudent persons are accustomed to accept those things which have been approved by those who are well versed in their own art.

omnes res suas liberas et quietas haberet (om'nēz rēz su'as li'be-ras et qui-ē'tas hā-bē'ret). That he should retain all his property free and undisturbed. See 1 Bl Comm 291.

Omnes sorores sunt quasi unus haeres de una haereditate (om'nēz so-rō'rēz sunt quā'sī ū'nus hē'rēz dē ū'na hē-rē-di-tā'te). All sisters are, as it were, one heir of one inheritance.

Omne testamentum morte consummatum est (om'ne tes-ta-men'tum mor'te kon-sum-mā'tum est). Every will or testament is consummated or completed by death.

Omnia delicta in aperto leviora sunt (om'ni-a dē-lik'ta in a-per'to le-vi-ō'ra sunt). All offenses committed openly are less serious.

Omnia peccata sunt paria (om'ni-a pe-kā'ta sunt pā'ri-a). All crimes are alike.

omnia performavit (om'ni-a per-for-mā'vit). He has performed in all things. A defendant's plea in an action for breach of covenant. Bailey v Rogers, 1 Me 186, 189.

Omnia praesumuntur contra spoliatorem (om'ni-a prē-zu-mun'ter kon'tra spo-li-ā-tō'rem). All things are presumed against a suppressor of testimony. Western & Atlantic Railroad Co. v Morrison, 102 Ga 319, 29 SE 104.

Omnia praesumuntur legitime facta donec probetur in contrarium (om'ni-a prē-zu-mun'ter le-ji'ti-me fak'ta dō'nek pro-bē'ter in kon-trā'ri-um). All things are presumed to have been done lawfully until the contrary is proved. People ex rel. Copcutt v Yonkers, 140 NY 1, 35 NE 481.

Omnia praesumuntur rite et solemniter acta donec probetur in contrarium (om'ni-a prē-zu-mun'ter rī'tē et so-lem'ni-ter ak'ta do'nek prō-bē'ter in kon-trā'ri-um). All things are presumed to have been done regularly and with due formality until the contrary is proved. Robideaux v Herbert, 118 La 1089, 43 So 887.

omnia praesumunter rite et solemniter esse acta (om'ni-a prē-zu-mun'ter rī'tē et so-lem'ni-ter es'se ak'ta). All things are presumed to have been done regularly until the contrary is proved. 29 Am J2d Ev § 170.

Omnia praesumuntur rite et solemniter esse acta (om'ni-a prē-zu-mun'ter rī'tē et so-lem'ni-ter es'se ak'ta). All things are presumed to have been done correctly and with due formality.

Omnia praesumuntur rite et solemniter esse acta donec probetur in contrarium (om'ni-a prē-zu-mun'ter rī'tē et so-lem'ni-ter es'se ak'ta dō'nek prō-bē'ter in kon-trā'ri-um). All things are presumed to have been done correctly and with due formality until the contrary is proved. See Broom's Legal Maxims 944.

Omnia praesumuntur rite, legitime, solemniter esse acta, donec probetur in contrarium (om'ni-a prē-zu-mun'ter rī'tē, le-ji'ti-mē, so-lem'ni-ter es'se ak'ta, dō'nek prō-bē'ter in kon-trā'ri-um). All things are presumed to have been done correctly, lawfully and with due formality, until the contrary is proved.

Omnia praesumuntur solemniter esse acta (om'ni-a prē-zu-mun'ter so-lem'ni-ter es'se ak'ta). All things are presumed to have been done with due formality.

Omnia quae jure contrahuntur, contrario jure pereunt (om'ni-a kwē jū're kon-tra-hun'ter, kon-trā'ri-ō jū're per'e-unt). (Civil law.) All contracts which are entered into under a law, become void under a contrary law.

Omnia quae sunt uxoris sunt ipsius viri (om'ni-a kwē sunt u-xō'ris sunt ip'si-us vi'rī). All things which belong to the wife are the property of the husband.

Omnia rite acta praesumuntur (om'ni-a rī'tē ak'ta prē-zu-mun'ter). All things are presumed to have been regularly done. Fidelity & Casualty Co. v Eickhoff, 63 Minn 170, 65 NW 351.

Omnia rite esse acta praesumunter (om'ni-a rī'tē es'se ak'ta prē-zu-mun'ter). All things are presumed to have been done in due form. See Broom's Legal Maxims 944 n.

Omnia rite praesumuntur (om'ni-a rī'tē prē-zu-mun'ter). All things are presumed in favor of regularity.

omnibus (om'ni-bus). A coach or other large vehicle equipped for the carrying of many passengers, propelled in modern times by motor, in an earlier day by horses. (Latin.) Everything; all.
 See in omnibus.

Omnibus ad quos praesentes literae pervenerint, salutem (om'ni-bus ad quōs prē-zen'tēz li'te-rē per-ve'ne-rint, sa-lū'tem). To all to whom the present letters may come, greeting.

omnibus bill. A legislative bill covering various and miscellaneous subjects. A bill purporting to amend many sections of a code. Parkinson v State, 14 Md 184.

omnibus clause. A clause in an automobile liability insurance policy, providing that the term "insured" includes the named insured and also any other person while using the automobile and any person or organization legally responsible for the use thereof, provided the actual use of the automobile is by the

named insured or with his permission or consent. 7 Am J2d Auto Ins § 109.

omnibus count. A count of a declaration or complaint which combines in one all the money counts. Griffin v Murdock, 88 Me 254, 257.

omnibus legislation. See **omnibus bill.**

omnibus motion. A motion consisting of several motions in combination, including in some instances demands for relief of a different nature, depending on different facts and circumstances wholly unrelated. 37 Am J1st Motions § 6.

Omnibus qui reipublicae praesunt etiam mando, ut omnibus aequos se prebeant judices, perinde ac in judiciali libro scriptum habetur; nec quiquam formident quin jus commune audacter libereque dicant (om′ni-bus quī rē-ī-pub′li-sē prē′sunt ē′she-am man′dō, ut om′ni-bus ē′quos sē prē′be-ant jū′di-sēz, per-in′de ak in jū-di-she-ā′lī li′brō skrip′tum ha-bē′ter; nek quī′quam for′mi-dent quin jūs kom-mū′ne â-dak′ter li-be-rē′kwe dī′kant). To all those who govern the republic, I charge them to prove themselves to be fair judges as it is written in the Dome Book and boldly and freely to declare the common law. See 1 Bl Comm 65.

omni exceptione majores (om′nī ex-sep-she-ō′ne mā-jō′rēz). Above or superior to all criticism or exception.

Omnis actio est loquela (om′nis ak′she-ō est lo-kwē′la). Every action is a complaint.

Omnis conclusio boni et veri judicii sequitur ex bonis et veris praemissis et dictis juratorum (om′nis kon-klu′she-ō bō′nī et vē′rī jū-di′she-ī se′qui-ter ex bō′nis et vē′ris prē-mis′sis et dik′tis jū-rā-tō′rum). Every conclusion of a good and true judgment follows from good and true premises and the verdicts of jurors.

Omnis consensus tollit errorem (om′nis kon-sen′sus tol′lit er-rō′rem). Every consent removes error; error is cured by consent.

Omnis definitio in jure civili periculosa est, parum est enim ut non subverti possit (om′nis dē-fī-ni′she-ō in jū′re si′vi-lī pe-ri-ku-lō′sa est, pa′rum est e′nim ut non sub-ver′tī pos′sit). (Civil law.) Every definition in the civil law is dangerous, because there is little that cannot be subverted.

Omnis definitio in jure periculosa (om′nis dē-fī-ni′-she-ō in jū′re pe-ri-ku-lō′sa). Every definition in the law is dangerous. Brady v Bartlett, 56 Cal 350, 365. (But a good law dictionary is nevertheless a most valuable asset in a law library.)

Omnis definitio in jure periculosa est; parum est enim ut non subverti posset (om′nis dē-fī-ni′she-ō in jū′re pe-ri-ku-lō′sa est; pa′rum est e′nim ut non sub-ver′tī pos′set). Every definition in the law is dangerous, because there is little that cannot be subverted.

Omnis definitio in lege periculosa (om′nis dē-fī-ni′-she-ō in lē′je pe-ri-ku-lō′sa). Every definition in the law is dangerous.

Omnis exceptio est ipsa quoque regula (om′nis ex-sep′she-o est ip′sa quo′kwe re-gū′la). Every exception is itself also a rule.

Omnis indemnatus pro innoxis legibus habetur (om′-nis in-dem-nā′tus prō in-no′xis lē′ji-bus hā-bē′ter). Every uncondemned person is regarded by the law as innocent.

Omnis innovatio plus novitate perturbat quam utilitate prodest (om′nis in-no-vā′she-ō plus no-vi-tā′te per-ter′bat quam ū-ti-li-tā′te prō′dest). Every innovation causes more confusion by reason of its novelty than it benefits by its usefulness. Barden v Atlantic Coast Line Railway Co. 152 NC 318, 67 SE 971.

Omnis interpretatio si fieri potest ita fienda est in instrumentis, ut omnes contrarietates amoveantur (om′nis in-ter-pre-tā′she-o sī fī′e-rī po′test i′ta fi-en′da est in in-stru-men′tis, ut om′nēz kon-trā-ri-e-tā′tēz ā-mō-ve-an′ter). Every interpretation of instruments should be so made, if it can be so made, that all contradictions may be removed.

Omnis interpretatio vel declarat, vel extendit, vel restringit (om′nis in-ter-pre-tā′she-ō vel dē-kla′rat, vel ex-ten′dit, vel re-strin′jit). Every interpretation either declares, extends or restrains.

Omnis nova constitutio futuris formam imponere debet, non praeteritis (om′nis nō′va kon-sti-tū′she-ō fu-tū′ris for′mam im-pō′ne-re de′bet, non prē-ter′i-tis). Every new regulation ought to prescribe a form for the future acts, not for the past.

Omnis persona est homo, sed non vicissim (om′nis per-sō′na est hō′mō, sed non vi-sis′sim). Every person is a man, but not vice versa.

Omnis privatio praesupponit habitum (om′nis prī-vā′she-ō prē-sup-pō′nit ha′bi-tum). Every deprivation presupposes a prior enjoyment or possession.

Omnis querela et omnis actio injuriarum limitata est infra certa tempora (om′nis kwe-rē′la et om′nis ak′-she-ō in-ju-ri′ā-rum li-mi-ta′ta est in′fra ser′ta tem′-po-ra). Every complaint and every action for injuries is limited within certain times.

Omnis ratihabitio retrotrahitur, et mandato priori equiparatur (om′nis rā-ti-ha-bi′she-ō re-trō-tra′hi-ter, et man-dā′tō prī-ō′rī ē-qui-pa-rā′ter). Every ratification relates back, and is equivalent to a prior command. Fleckner v Bank of United States (US) 8 Wheat 338, 363, 5 L Ed 631, 637.

Omnis regula suas patitur exceptiones (om′nis re-gū′la su′as pa′ti-ter ex-sep-she-ō′nēz). Every rule is subject to its own exceptions.

omnium (om′ni-um). The aggregate.

omnium bonorum (om′ni-um bō-nō′rum). Of all the goods.

Omnium contributione sarciatur quod pro omnibus datum est (om′ni-um kon-tri-bu-she-ō′ne sar-she-ā′ter quod prō om′ni-bus dā′tum est). That which is given in behalf of all is restored by the contribution of all.

Omnium rerum quarum usus est, potest esse abusus, virtute solo excepta (om′ni-um rē′rum quā′rum ū′sus est, po′test es′se ab-ū′sus, vir-tū′te sō′lō ex-sep′ta). There can be abuse of all things of which there is use, virtue alone excepted.

on. In contact with the surface or upper part of a thing and supported by it. Rester v Moody & Stewart, 172 La 510, 134 So 690. Often used for "in," as on a train.

More definite in the description of real estate than "at," although sometimes meaning "in the vicinity of," as where the description refers to some geographic feature. 23 Am J2d Deeds § 243.

on acceptance. A condition in a draft making the instrument nonnegotiable. 11 Am J2d B & N § 141.

on account. Received on one's credit; to be charged.

A purchase of stock "on the account" imports a sale of stock to be delivered at a future time. Clews v Jamieson, 182 US 461, 45 L Ed 1183, 21 S Ct 845.

on account of. A common phrase in an order for the payment of money; not an indication of a particular fund for payment. First Nat. Bank v Lightner, 74 Kan 736, 88 P 59. A form of restrictive indorsement. 11 Am J2d B & N § 362.

on account of whom it may concern. An insurance term which is used to include all persons having an insurable interest in the property insured for whose benefit the policy is intended. Newsom v Douglas (Md) 7 Harr & J 417.

on a lay. A term characterizing the letting of a vessel to the master for operation on shares. 48 Am J1st Ship § 335.

on all fours. Precisely in point.
A case to be on all fours must be identical. Lessee of Sweitzer v Meese (Pa) 6 Binn 500, 506.

on a motor vehicle. See **in a motor vehicle.**

onanism (ō′nan-izm). Masturbation.

on a passage. A phrase used in marine insurance policies in prescribing the duration of the risk. At sea.

A vessel which is in port where she has put in to obtain the necessary clearance, water, and crew for her voyage is not "on a passage" within the meaning of the term as applied to a time policy continuing the risk if the vessel is "on a passage" at the end of the term. 29 Am J Rev ed Ins § 331.

on approval. See **sale on approval.**

on a public conveyance. See **in or on a public conveyance.**

on arrival. A term of instruction to collecting bank for presentation, giving the bank a reasonable time to await arrival of goods. 10 Am J2d Bks § 713.
See **sale on arrival.**

on call. On demand; when demanded; at any time called for. Bowman v McChesney, 63 Va (22 Gratt) 609, 612.

on call note. A note payable on demand. 12 Am J2d B & N § 1048.

once a highway, always a highway. An ancient maxim, the strength of which is weakened in modern times by exceptions and qualifications permitting the termination of even a public highway. 25 Am J1st High § 111.

once a mortgage, always a mortgage. A maxim often asserted in the application of the principle that if an instrument is a mortgage at its inception, it remains so with all the incidents thereof. 36 Am J1st Mtg § 3.

Once an Englishman always an Englishman. A phrase which sums up the early common-law doctrine of perpetual and unchangeable allegiance to the country of one's birth. Anno: 15 ALR2d 553 §§ 2–15.

once a week for four successive weeks. A familiar requirement for publication of a notice, having reference to publication so timed that not more than a seven-day interval shall occur between any two successive publications. 30A Am J Rev ed Jud S § 55.

once in jeopardy. Essentially the same as the defense of prior jeopardy, although a distinction is recognized by some authority.

A plea setting up a former jeopardy of the defendant who is now charged with the same offense. The justice of sustaining a plea of former acquittal or conviction is unquestioned and unquestionable, but a plea of "once in jeopardy" stands on narrower, more technical, and less substantial ground. It alleges only that there might have been a conviction or an acquittal if the judge trying the cause had not made a mistake in law which prevented a verdict. Commonwealth v Fitzpatrick, 121 Pa 109, 15 A 466.
See **prior jeopardy.**

on commission. The status of a salesman compensated by commissions rather than by salary. The status of goods placed in the hands of an agent for sale by him, his compensation to be in the form of a commission based upon a fixed percentage of the price received on sale.

on condition. See **condition.**

on demand. On an actual call or demand for payment. Crofoot v Thatcher, 19 Utah 212, 57 P 171.
See **demand paper; payable on demand.**

on demand after date. An expression in a promissory note indicating a demand instrument. 11 Am J2d B & N § 286.
See **demand paper.**

on duty. Actually engaged in work or services undertaken for another or charged with a present responsibility for the performance of such work or services should occasion for performance arise. United States v Denver & Rio Grande Railroad Co. (DC NM) 197 F 629, 631. Any person in the armed services not on leave or on furlough.

one bite rule. An old doctrine that every dog is entitled to one bite, such being enunciated as a basis for a rule that the owner of a vicious dog is not liable for an injury caused by the dog unless he knew or should have known of its dangerous propensities, which knowledge would not arise until after the dog had made at least one attack upon a person. 4 Am J2d Ani § 95.

one dollar. A recital of a nominal sum as consideration.

A sufficient statement of the consideration for a promise to answer for the debt of another, although the dollar is not in fact paid, if there is other good and valuable consideration for the promise. 49 Am J1st Stat of F § 373.

one dollar and other consideration. A common form of recital of consideration for a deed. 23 Am J2d Deeds § 65.

one dwelling. A phrase in a restrictive covenant subject to construction as against plurality of occupancy, or, according to some authority, as against plurality of houses. Koett v Tate, 248 Ky 135, 58 SW2d 374.

one-family house. A phrase exclusive of multiple dwellings. Virgin v Garret, 233 Ala 34, 169 So 711.

one free bite. Another term for the so-called **one bite rule.**

one half. See **half.**

one-man car. A streetcar without a conductor, the motorman at the front end performing the duties of a conductor as well as the duties of motorman. Sullivan v Shreveport, 251 US 169, 170, 64 L Ed 205, 208, 40 S Ct 102.

one-man corporation. A corporation, the stock of which is owned by one man or at least kept in close control by one man.

one man-one vote rule. A rule of legislative apportionment based on the principle of equality of representation lying at the foundation of representative government and requiring that no voter shall exercise, in the selection of the legislature, a greater voting power than other voters. Reynolds v Sims, 377 US 533, 12 L Ed 2d 506, 84 S Ct 1362.

oneness of husband and wife. The unity of husband and wife as it prevailed at common law, the entire legal existence of the wife being completely merged or incorporated in that of the husband, and as it prevails to a limited extent even in modern times under Married Woman's Enabling Acts. 26 Am J1st H & W § 3.

one-price policy. The doctrine opposed to discrimination between customers in reference to prices charged for goods or services. Shaw's Inc. v Wilson-Jones Co. (DC Pa) 26 F Supp 713.

onerando pro rata portione. See de onerando pro rata portione.

onerando pro rata portionis (o-ne-ran′dō prō rā′ta por-she-ō′nis). A writ for the relief of a joint tenant or tenant in common who had been compelled to pay more than his pro rata share of the rent.

onerari non (o-ne-rā′rī non). Should not be burdened or charged,—a name given to a plea in an action of debt denying that the defendant ought to be charged.

oneratio (o-ne-rā′she-ō). The load or cargo of a ship.

oneris ferendi (o′ne-ris fe-ren′dī). Of the burden of support,—an easement by which an adjoining neighbor was entitled to have his structure supported.

one residence. One dwelling.
Although the courts are in substantial agreement that a restriction in a covenant to "residence" purposes, standing alone, does not prohibit multiple dwellings, this unanimity disappears when the modifying term "one" is inserted before the word "residence." Anno: 14 ALR2d 1409.

one residence only. A phrase in a restrictive covenant, meaning that only one person or one person and his family shall reside on the land. Macy v Wormald (Ky) 329 SW2d 212; Gerstell v Knight, 345 Pa 83, 26 A2d 329.

onerous (on′ẹ-rus). Burdensome; not without consideration.

onerous cause. A good and legal consideration.

onerous contract. A contract supported by a valid consideration.

onerous deed. A deed which was executed by the grantor for a valuable consideration.

onerous gift. A gift which imposes some obligation upon the donee.

onerous title. A term used in Spanish-American land law signifying a title which was granted upon conditions which were onerous or burdensome to the grantee.

one third new for old. The familiar rule of marine insurance that in case of the partial loss of a vessel, there shall be deducted from the costs of repairs, chargeable to the insurer one third of the new materials replacing the old, on the theory that the new materials render the vessel that much more valuable than it was before the loss. 29A Am J Rev ed Ins § 1567.

one-way street. A street, the travel on which is restricted by ordinance or other regulation to vehicles moving in one direction. 25 Am J1st High § 216.

one-way ticket. The ticket of a passenger calling for transportation to destination only, not to destination and return.

One who institutes suit against another must be prepared to show a prior or superior equity in himself. A maxim of equity. 27 Am J2d Eq § 145.

One who invites another to ride is not bound to furnish a sound vehicle or a safe horse. Cleary v Eckart, 191 Wis 114, 210 NW 267, 51 ALR 576.

one-year clause. The clause in a statute of frauds respecting an agreement not to be performed within a year. 49 Am J1st Stat of F § 23.

on his behalf. For him and as authorized by him. State ex rel. La Follette v Kohler, 200 Wis 518, 228 NW 895, 69 ALR 348.

on information and belief. See upon information and belief.

only. Solely. In a colloquial sense, except for that.

on offer (on ôf′er). The state or condition of being for sale.

onomastic (on-ọ-mas′tik). Signed or subscribed in a handwriting other than that which appears in the body of the instrument.

on option. The status of property for the purchase of which an option has been granted. A term used by dealers in commercial paper, meaning that the purchaser has the right to return what he bought, or some of it, at any time within the option limit, to the broker, and get back from the broker the purchase price. Eames v H. B. Claflin Co. (CA2 NY) 239 F 631.

on or about. An allegation of time which lacks precision. A sufficient delegation of time in an indictment where precise time is not a material ingredient of the offense, although not where time is of the essence. 27 Am J1st Indict § 71.
An allegation that the arson charged occurred "on or about" a stated date is sufficient in respect of an allegation of the time of the offense. State v McDonald, 16 SD 78, 91 NW 447.
An allegation that the injury which caused death was inflicted "on or about" a specified time is sufficient as an allegation of time of the homicidal act in an indictment for homicide. 26 Am J1st Homi § 268.
Such phrase, as used in a contract of sale which calls for delivery "on or about" a specified date, admits only of a reasonable departure from the time specified. Arons v Cummings, 107 Me 19, 78 A 98.

on or about the person. A phrase familiar in statements of the offense of carrying a concealed weapon.
As used in a statute making it an offense to carry weapons concealed "on or about the person," the courts have interpreted the expression in two ways. Some courts have held that the words "on" and "about" are not synonymous, but have quite different meanings; the word "on" meaning attached to, and the word "about" meaning in close proximity to, or in easy reach of. However, other courts have held that the two words as used in the phrase are interchangeable, no added significance being given

to the use of the word "about." Anno: 50 ALR 1534.

on or before. A designation of time for performance of an agreement, giving to the promisor the right to perform at any time before the day specified. 52 Am J1st Time § 26.

on or in or about. A familiar phrase in workmen's compensation statutes constituting an elastic term, involving as a whole the idea of physical proximity in reference to a particular area constituting a place of work. 58 Am J1st Workm Comp § 86.

on or upon the death. A phrase in the limitation of a remainder having reference ordinarily to the right of possession and enjoyment of the property and not preventing the immediate vesting of the remainder. 28 Am J2d Est § 257.

on peut bien receivoir loy d'autruy, mais il est impossible par nature de se donner loy (ôn pur′bi-en′ re-sā-vuär loy dō-trū, mā′ĕl ăt am-pos-sĕblĕ par nätūr dĕ sĕ don-nā loy). One may well receive laws from another, but it is impossible in the nature of things for one to make laws for himself. Kawananakoa v Polyblank, 205 US 349, 353, 51 L Ed 834, 836, 27 S Ct 526.

onroerende and vast staat (ôn-roo′rĕn-dĕ and vahst staht). (Holland Dutch.) Land or real estate. Spraker v Van Alstyne (NY) 18 Wend 200, 208.

on sale. Being for sale. On hand and available for delivery when sold. Connecticut Paper Products v New York Paper Co. (DC Md) 39 F Supp 127.

on sight. Same as **at sight.**

onstand (on′stand). The payment of rent by an outgoing tenant to an incoming tenant for use and occupation during the harvesting of the outgoing tenant's crop.

The term has also been applied to the right of a workman, who has been employed to install an apparatus on the premises of another, to return thereto for the purpose of testing the sufficiency of the installation. Indermaur v Dames (Eng) LR 1 CP 274.

on the account. See **on account.**

on the body. See **in and on the body.**

on the death. A phrase in the limitation of a remainder having reference ordinarily to the right of possession and enjoyment of the property and not preventing the immediate vesting of the remainder. 28 Am J2d Est § 257.

on the front. At the front.

As used in a statute requiring automobiles during certain hours to display at least two lighted lamps "on the front," the phrase does not necessarily mean the very foremost part of the vehicle, but means such a point in front of the driver as will make the light visible in the direction in which the car is proceeding. State v Reed, 162 Iowa 572, 144 NW 310.

on the merits. See **judgment on the merits; merits of case.**

on the relation of. See **relator.**

on-the-spot broadcast. A broadcast directly from the event to the listener, not one from a tape or record previously made.

on trial. Literally, in the course of a trial before court and jury or the court without a jury. In one sense, listed for trial, as where the case appears on the trial docket or calendar.

The term as used in a statute providing that, whenever any criminal case shall be "on trial" at the end of any term, such term shall be continued until such case is finished, has been held to have its literal meaning, and requires that the case must be actually on trial before the court and jury at the end of the term. Commonwealth v MacLellan, 121 Mass 31.

See **sale on trial.**

onus (ō′nus). An English word of Latin origin. Burden. Also, burden of proof. In the Will of Lawrence Convey, 52 Iowa 197, 198.

onus probandi (o′nus prō-ban′dī). The burden of proof.

ope consilii (o′pe kon-si′li-i). By or with the aid of counsel.

ope et consilio (o′pe et kon-si′li-o). By or with aid and counsel.

open. Adjective: Characterizing that which is not secret or concealed. 33 Am J1st Lewd etc. § 2. Not closed, as an open gate. Verb: To make a breach or way in that which was closed. To make the opening statement in the trial of a case.

open account. An account the balance on which has not been ascertained; one which has not been closed, settled, or stated, and in which the inclusion of further dealings between the parties is contemplated. Anno: 1 ALR 1060 s. 39 ALR 369, 57 ALR 201. A transaction some of the terms of which have not been agreed upon, such as the price to be paid, or the time for payment. Anno: 1 ALR 1060, s. 39 ALR 369, 57 ALR 201.

open and continuous account. See **continuous account; running account.**

open and current account. An account based upon running or concurrent dealings between the parties, which has not been closed, settled, or stated, and in which the inclusion of further dealings between the parties is contemplated. Plunkett-Jarrell Grocery Co. v Terry, 222 Ark 784, 263 SW2d 229, 44 ALR2d 917.

See **current account; open account.**

open and gross lewdness. See **open lewdness.**

open and mutual account. See **mutual account; open account.**

open and notorious. Acts upon the land of another which are not in secret but of such a character as to be well calculated to notify the owner of the use made by such acts. 56 Am J1st Wat § 326.

open and notorious adultery. An offense predicated, not upon private immoral indulgence, but upon the publicity attendant upon the breach of the moral standard in such extent as to debase and demoralize society and degrade the institution of marriage. 2 Am J2d Adult § 9.

open and notorious insolvency. See **open insolvency.**

open and notorious possession. Possession evidenced by such acts and conduct as are sufficient to put a man of ordinary prudence on notice of the fact that the land in question is held by the claimant as his own. 3 Am J2d Adv P § 47. Possession of such openness as that the owner's knowledge of it and of the extent of it may be presumed. Watrous v Morrison, 33 Fla 261, 278.

open and visible easement. An apparent and obvious easement, one susceptible of ascertainment on a reasonable inspection of the premises by a person ordinarily conversant with the subject, such as a pathway or road. 25 Am J2d Ease § 9.

open bulk. Goods in the mass; exposed to view; not tied or sealed up. Re Sanders (CC NC) 52 F 802.

open competitive examination. An examination to determine the merits of applicants for a civil service position, open to applicants without reference to whether or not they are already in the service.

open concubinage. A concubinage that is plain and aboveboard, without secret, reserve, or disguise; not merely one that is notorious. Gauff v Johnson, 161 La 975, 977, 109 So 782.

open contract. A contract for the sale of land which contains no conditions relieving the vendor from producing evidence of title.

open corporation. A corporation the stock of which is widely held, the ownership of the shares not being confined to one man, a family, or persons in close association. A corporation in which all of the citizens or corporators have a vote in the election of the officers of the corporation. See McKim v Odom (Md) 3 Bland Ch 407, 416, footnote.

open court. A court in session. A public session of the court, as distinguished from a judge of the court in his chambers. Conover v Bird, 56 NJL 228, 230, 28 A 428. The constitutional guaranty that the courts shall always be open to all alike. 16 Am J2d Const L § 382.
See **public trial**.

open current account. See **open and current account**.

open danger. See **obvious danger**.

open doors. Hospitality. A name given to process which authorizes the officer to break doors if necessary to effect the service of the process.
See **opening door**.

open-end investment trust. An investment trust the capital structure of which is open to change during the life of the trust by the issuance of new shares and the retirement of existing shares.

open-end settlement. A settlement of a claim for workmen's compensation calling for payments to the injured employee but not fixing the period during which such payments are to continue, properly to be construed as fixing liability during the period that disability continues. Healey's Case, 124 Me 54, 126 A 21.

open fee. A common-law fee which, by reason of the lack of an heir, reverted, on the death of the person last seised, to the lord. See 2 Bl Comm 245.

open hearing. A hearing or investigation by an administrative agency which is open to the public. 2 Am J2d Admin L §§ 229, 258. An essential of a fair hearing before an administrative agency exercising judicial, quasi-judicial, or adjudicatory powers. 2 Am J2d Admin L § 412.
See **public trial**.

opening. A beginning. The participle of **open**.

opening a credit. Making an arrangement with a bank for a loan or with a store for a charge account. Coupled with prompt payment of the loan or regular payments upon the charge account, a good method of establishing a credit. To accept or pay the draft of a correspondent who has not furnished the drawee with funds to meet the draft.

opening a foreclosure. The effect of bringing action upon the mortgage debt after foreclosure in giving the mortgage a new right to redeem. Anno: 18 English Ruling Cases 173.
See **opening judgment**.

opening and closing. The right of the party holding the affirmative of the issue joined in the pleadings and who would be defeated if no evidence were given on either side, unless the trial court in its discretion, for some special reason, otherwise directs. 53 Am J1st Trial § 69.

opening bids. The act of opening the bids received following advertisement for bids in the letting of a contract, and upon the termination of the period for receiving bids as specified in the advertisement, for the purpose of determining the most favorable bid.

The phrase frequently occurs in the English books, and means that if after the biddings at a chancery sale are closed, anyone else comes in and offers a much higher price, the biddings may be opened and the additional offer accepted. It means no more than a suspension of the sale and a continuance of the property in the market. See Andrews v Scotton (Md) 2 Bland Ch 629, 644.

opening case. Making the opening statement. A further trial after decision for the introduction of new evidence or additional argument.
See **opening and closing; opening judgment**.

opening commission. An entering by the commissioners or commissioner upon the duties to be performed by them or him under a commission.

opening court. The formalities observed in the opening of a session of court.

opening default. Setting aside a default upon cause shown therefor by the defendant to permit him to appear and plead within a period of time fixed by the court.

opening door. A metaphorical expression for the situation in which a party becomes entitled to introduce evidence otherwise inadmissible by reason of the tender or introduction of similar or related evidence by his opponent. 53 Am J1st Tr § 97.

opening highway. The act whereby a highway is legally established. 25 Am J1st High § 19. To put in condition for use, or to place at the service or use of the public, a way which theretofore had a merely legal or paper existence, not having been used. 25 Am J1st High § 51. Removing obstructions. State v Hudson County Avenue Comrs. 37 NJL 12, 14. Clearing the way of snow. Sometimes inclusive of filling and grading. 25 Am J1st High § 67.

opening judgment. Bringing a judgment into view for the purpose of considering whether it should be corrected, modified, or vacated. 30A Am J Rev ed Judgm §§ 629, 630. The suspension of a judgment and of proceedings thereon. 30A Am J Rev ed Judgm § 728.
See **vacation of judgment**.

opening polls. The formal commencement of an election, at a time fixed by statute, when the polling place is opened for the reception of voters and the casting of ballots. 26 Am J2d Elect § 227.

opening record. See **searching record**.

opening rule. The changing back of a rule absolute to a rule nisi.

open insolvency. The insolvency of a person beyond his power to keep secret.

The term "open and notorious insolvency," as applied to the maker of a note, in connection with the rule that all the property of the maker, subject to the payment of debts, must be exhausted, before recourse can be had to the assignor, implies something more than when the term is used in common parlance. It implies, not the want of sufficient property to pay all of one's debts, but the absence of all property, within the reach of the law applicable to the payment of any debt. Hardesty v Kinworthy (Ind) 8 Blackf 304, 305.

open law. Trial by battle or trial by ordeal or by wager of law.

opening statement. A statement to the jury, or to the court in a trial without a jury, outlining the facts intended to be proved. State v Sibert, 113 W Va 717, 169 SE 410. A prefatory statement made in advance of the introduction of evidence, setting forth the nature of the controversy and its salient peculiarities, intended to indicate to court and jury the issues of fact involved. 53 Am J1st Trial § 454.

open lands. Unappropriated public lands open to entry as homesteads. 42 Am J1st Pub L § 19.

open letter. A letter addressed to a particular person but published so that its contents shall become known to the public.

open lewdness. At common law, acts of lewdness committed in public. Under statute, any lewdness not in secret, whether it be in the presence of one or several persons. 33 Am J1st Lewd etc. § 2.

The phrase "open and gross lewdness" is not equivalent to the phrase "gross lewdness in an open place." The word "open" has no reference to place at all, nor to number of people. It is used simply to define a quality of the act of lewdness. It is open lewdness as opposed to secret lewdness. It defines the same act, regardless whether it is committed in the presence of one or of many. The offense may be committed by the intentional act of exposing one's person indecently in the presence of one person, to whom it is offensive, as well as in the presence of many persons. It could not change the quality of the act that it was committed in the presence of a child of tender years,—too innocent to be offended by it. State v Juneau, 88 Wis 180, 59 NW 580.

See **gross lewdness.**

open mine. A mine dug or excavated so that the ore shows in the face of the mine. A mine in operation.

A mine lawfully leased to be opened is an "open mine" within the meaning of the rule that a tenant may, without being guilty of waste, continue to work mines or quarries that were open when the tenancy commenced, except as the contrary may appear by the terms or provisions of the lease or other instrument creating the estate. 56 Am J1st Waste § 25.

open mortgage clause. Same as **simple loss-payable clause.**

open policy. A policy of insurance covering property in which the value of the property insured is not fixed, but is left to be determined definitely in case of loss. 29A Am J Rev ed Ins § 1586. A term sometimes applied to a **running policy.** 29 Am J Rev ed Ins § 306.

open possession. Clearly defined and notorious possession, 25 Am J2d Eject § 43.

See **open and notorious possession.**

open primary. A primary election at which members of one political party are permitted to vote at the primary for candidates of a different political party, in other words, a primary in which a voter may "cross over" to a party other than his own and participate in the primary of that party. 25 Am J2d Elect § 148.

open running account. An account based upon a connected series of transactions, without break or interruption. Riffith v Portlock, 233 Iowa 492, 7 NW2d 199.

See **open account; running account.**

open season. The period prescribed by law or regulation during which fish or game, or certain species of fish or game, may be hunted and taken.

open shop. A place of employment in which union and nonunion men are employed without discrimination. 31 Am J Rev ed Lab § 95. A plan or policy of employers of labor the basic requirement of which is that there should be no discrimination for or against an employee on account of his affiliation or nonaffiliation with a labor union, except that at least one nonunion man in each craft should be employed on each particular job as an evidence of good faith. Industrial Asso. of San Francisco v United States, 268 US 64, 75, 69 L Ed 849, 852, 45 S Ct 403.

See **permit system.**

open theft. A larceny wherein the thief is caught red-handed.

open trial. See **public trial.**

open trust. An active trust, which may in some instances be a precatory trust. Anno: 49 ALR 64.

open venire. An order for the summoning of additional jurors in which the persons to be summoned are not indicated, their selection being left to the sheriff or other officer entrusted with the venire. 31 Am J Rev ed Jury § 91.

open, visible, and substantial change of possession. A change in the character of possession indicated by such outward, open, actual, and visible signs as can be seen by and known to the public or persons dealing with the property. Second Nat. Bank v Gilbert, 174 Ill 485, 51 NE 584.

open will. A term of the civil law for nuncupative will. Castro v Castro, 6 Cal 158, 160.

opera. A musical drama, consisting of airs, choruses, recitations, etc., usually enriched with magnificent scenery and costumes, representing the play of emotions, often acts prompted by passion. Bell v Mahn, 121 Pa 225, 15 A 523.

opera house. A theater, especially a theater wherein operas are performed. Egan v San Francisco, 165 Cal 576, 133 P 294; St. Louis Amusement Co. v St. Louis County, 347 Mo 456, 147 SW2d 667; Bell use of Commonwealth v Mahn, 121 Pa 225, 15 A 523.

operarii (o-pe-rā′ri-ī). Plural of **operarius.**

operarius (o-pe-rā′ri-us). A feudal tenant who held his land by manual labor for the lord of the manor.

operate. To perform surgery. To control the movement of a machine or instrumentality. To direct or superintend. Bosse v Marye, 80 Cal App 109, 118. To function.

As applied to a streetcar, the word is held not to be limited to a state of motion produced by the mechanism of the car, but includes at least ordinary stops upon the highway, and such stops are to be regarded as fairly incidental to its operation. Anno: 11 ALR 1228.

operating against the enemy. Operating in the field of hostilities, in the area where the enemy is to be found.

Troops in instruction camps across the ocean from the field of war are not "operating against the enemy" within the meaning of a statute giving officers serving with troops "operating against the enemy," when assigned to command above their rank, the pay appropriate to the command exercised. United States v Ferris, 265 US 165, 68 L Ed 161, 44 S Ct 487.

operating aircraft. Using an aircraft, including the navigation of aircraft, or causing or authorizing the operation of an aircraft, whether with or without the right of legal control. 49 USC § 1301(25).

As to what constitutes "operating aircraft" within the meaning of an exception of risk in a life insurance policy, see Anno: 47 ALR2d 1021.

operating automobile. See **operating motor vehicle.**

operating car. See **operating motor vehicle.**

operating charges. Costs of production, a matter of knowledge which can be acquired by observation on the part of persons dealing with the producing company. Lytle, Campbell & Co. v Somers, Fitler & Todd Co. 276 Pa 409, 120 A 409, 27 ALR 41.

operating expenses of carrier. All items of cost or expense incident to the actual handling and movement of traffic.

operating expenses of public utility. The cost of operation of the plant, general expenses, and cost of maintaining the property in such condition that its operating efficiency at the end is at least as great as it was at the beginning of the year. 43 Am J1st Pub Util § 141.

operating loss. See **net operating loss.**

operating motor vehicle. In common parlance, driving an automobile or other motor vehicle. Regulating and controlling the actual movements of the car, that is, having charge of it as a driver. 7 Am J2d Auto Ins § 42. Exercising control over the vehicle, although not at the time in the driver's seat. Anno: 51 ALR2d 928, § 5[a]; 7 Am J2d Auto Ins § 42. Any manipulation of the mechanical or electrical equipment of a motor vehicle, which would, alone or in sequence, set in motion the motive power. 7 Am J2d Auto § 256. Not limited to a state of motion produced by the mechanism of the vehicle, but including at least ordinary stops upon the highway, such stops being fairly incidental to operation. Commonwealth v Henry, 229 Mass 19, 118 NE 224.

A truck parked across a road for the purpose of unloading is in operation within the meaning of a statute in respect of lights. Hardware Mut. Casualty Co. v Union Transfer & Storage Co. 205 Ky 651, 266 SW 362.

A statutory provision that the "use and operation" by a nonresident of a motor vehicle within the state shall be deemed an appointment by him of the secretary of state as his attorney to receive service of process in any action growing out of such use is not confined in its operation to nonresidents personally operating motor vehicles within the state, but applies also to nonresidents, including foreign corporations and the individual members of nonresident partnerships, operating motor vehicles in the state through agents or employees who are also nonresidents. Jones v Pebler, 371 Ill 309, 20 NE2d 592, 125 ALR 451.

As to what constitutes "operation" within statute making owner of motor vehicle liable for negligence in its operation. See Anno: 13 ALR2d 378.

operating motor vehicle while intoxicated. Driving while intoxicated. Controlling the operation of the vehicle in any respect, such as starting the motor, while intoxicated. 7 Am J2d Auto § 256.

Some of the cases arising under statute prohibiting the operation of a motor vehicle while in an intoxicated condition hold that in order to constitute an operation, it is necessary for the vehicle to be in motion. Anno: 47 ALR2d 577, § 4[d].

operating receivership. A receivership in which the receiver operates a business, railroad, public utility, or manufacturing plant. 45 Am J1st Rec § 3.

operatio (o-pe-rā'she-ō). A single day's labor performed by an operarius for the lord of the manor.

operatio murorum. See **murorum operatio.**

operation of law. Through law, not by contract or otherwise by the act of a person.

operation of railroad. The movement of trains, including all acts necessary to permit movement, such as the loading and unloading of cars, the organizing of trains, and the handling of the locomotives and cars which make up a train. Arizona Eastern R.R. Co. v J. A. Matthews, 20 Ariz 282, 180 P 159, 7 ALR 1149; United States F. Ins. Co. v Northern P. R. Co. 30 Wash 2d 722, 193 P2d 868, 2 ALR2d 1065.

operative. Adjective: In working condition; in operation. Noun: One who operates machinery, as in a factory. Ward v Krinsky, 259 US 503, 527, 66 L Ed 1033, 1043, 42 S Ct 529.

operative property. Any property which may be reasonably necessary for use, in the operation and conduct of the particular kind or kinds of business in which such property is employed. Southern California Tel. Co. v Hopkins (CA9 Cal) 13 F2d 814.

operative trust. An active trust. A trust which maintains the legal estate in the trustee, to enable him to perform the duties devolved on him by the donor, and gives the cestui que trust only a right in equity to enforce the performance of the trust. 54 Am J1st Trusts § 13.

operative words. The words in an instrument which give it the character of a particular instrument, such as a deed, mortgage, release, etc. Agnew v Dorr (Pa) 5 Whart 131.

operator for hire. Any person who owns, controls, operates or manages any motor vehicle for hire for the transportation of persons or property on any public highway, or any person who engages in the business of leasing motor vehicles for a compensation for the transportation of persons or property upon the public highways. Louisville Taxicab & Transfer Co. v Blanton, 305 Ky 179, 202 SW2d 433, 175 ALR 1329 (statutory definition.)

operator of automobile. See **operating motor vehicle.**

operator's license. A license, issued by the Atomic Energy Commission to qualified individuals, for the manipulation of controls of production or facilities for the utilization of atomic energy. 42 USC § 2137. A license to operate a motor vehicle, required as a condition of the right to drive such a vehicle upon the public highway. 7 Am J2d Auto § 93.

operis novi nuntiatio (o'pe-ris no'vī nun-she-ā'she-ō). (Civil law.) Same as **novi operis nunciatio.**

ophthalmologist (of-thal-mol'ō-jist). A physician practicing the branch of medicine known as ophthalmology. Anno: 22 ALR 1177; 41 Am J1st Phys & S § 28.
See **ophthalmology**.

ophthalmology (of-thal-mol'ō-ji). The branch of medical science concerned with the eye. Harabedian v Superior Court of Los Angeles County, 195 Cal App 2d 26, 15 Cal Rptr 420, 89 ALR2d 994. The practice of medicine and surgery in the treatment of diseases of the eye, and in the measurement of the powers of vision, and the adaptation of lenses for the aid thereof. Anno: 22 ALR2d 941.

ophthalmoscope (of-thal'mō-skōp). An instrument used for the exploration of the interior of the eye. Atchison, Topeka & Santa Fe Railway Co. v Palmore, 68 Kan 545, 75 P 509.

opiate (ō'pi-āt). A narcotic drug containing opium or a derivative of opium. Any substance which tends to sooth. A drug administered to alleviate pain and quiet the sensibilities of the patient. Muller v St. Louis Hospital Asso. 5 Mo App 390, 393.

Opinio est duplex, scilicet, opinio vulgaris orta inter graves et discretios, et quae vultum veritatis, habet; et opinio tantum orta inter leves et vulgares homines absque specie veritatis (o-pi'ni-ō est dū'plex, si'li-set, o-pi'ni-ō vul-gā'ris or'ta in'ter grā'vēz et dis-krē'ti-os, et kwē vul'tum vē-ri-tā'tis, hā'bet; et o-pi'ni-ō tan'tum or'ta in'ter le'vēz et vulgā'rez ho'mi-nēz abs'kwe spe'she-ē vē-ri-tā'tis). Opinion is twofold, that is to say, common opinion springing from among serious and discreet persons, and which has the appearance of truth; and opinion arising among light-minded and ordinary men without the semblance of truth.

opinion. An inference or conclusion of fact which a person has drawn from facts which he has observed. Lipscomb v State, 75 Miss 559, 23 So 210. A belief rather than a representation of fact. 23 Am J2d Fraud § 45. As disqualification of juror, a prejudgment of the case. 31 Am J Rev ed Jury § 172.

opinion evidence. The testimony of a witness, given or offered in the trial of an action, that the witness is of the opinion that some fact pertinent to the case exists or does not exist, offered as proof of the existence or nonexistence of that fact. 31 Am J2d Ev § 764.
See **expert testimony; expert witness**.

opinion of administrative agency. A statement in writing by an administrative agency of the reasons which support its decision. 2 Am J2d Admin L § 511.

opinion of appellate court. See **opinion of court**.

opinion of court. A statement given by the court for its decision, usually presented in writing and published in a court report. 20 Am J2d Cts § 7. A statement in writing by an appellate court of the reasons for its decision or judgment. 5 Am J2d A & E § 901.
An opinion accompanying a decision is an opinion of the court only when it has been approved by the court making the decision, that is, where the court consists of more than one judge, by at least the majority required for a valid decision. 20 Am J2d Cts § 71.
The opinion of the court represents merely the reasons for its judgment, while the decision of the court is the adjudication. 20 Am J2d Cts § 70.
It is the "decision" rather than the "opinion" which is the subject of appellate review. Robertson v Vandergrift, 119 W Va 219, 193 SE 62.

opinion of the attorney general. An opinion prepared by the attorney general by way of advising the executive and administrative heads of the state government upon questions of law touching their official duties. 7 Am J2d Atty Gen § 8. The opinion of the Attorney General of the United States upon a question of law, required by the President or the head of any of the executive departments of the Federal Government. 5 USC §§ 303, 304.

Opinio quae favet testamento est tenenda (o-pi'ni-ō kwē fa'vet tes-ta-men'tō est te-nen'da). An opinion which favors a will is to be upheld.

opium. A narcotic. 25 Am J2d Drugs § 2. A drug used as an ingredient of certain medicines, also used to an extent, especially in the far east, as an intoxicant. State v Lee, 137 Mo 143, 147.

Opium Act. See **Harrison Narcotic Act**.

opium joint. A place to which opium addicts resort for the purpose of obtaining the drug and partaking thereof.

oportet (o-por'tet). It is necessary, fitting, or proper; it must be; it ought to be.

Oportet quod certae personae, terrae et certi status comprehendantur in declaratione usuum (o-por'tet quod ser'tē per-sō'nē, ter'rē et ser'tī stā'tus kom-pre-hen-dan'ter in de-kla-rā-she-ō'ne ū'su-um). It is necessary that certain persons, lands, and certain estates should be included in a declaration of uses.

Oportet quod certa res deducatur in donationem (o-por'tet quod ser'ta rēz dē-dū-kā'ter in dō-nā-she-ō'nem). It is necessary that a thing certain be brought into the gift.

Oportet quod certa res deducatur in judicium (o-por'tet quod ser'ta rēz dē-du-kā'ter in jū-di'she-um). It is necessary that a thing certain be brought to judgment.

Oportet quod certa sit res quae venditur (o-por'tet quod ser'ta sit rēz kwē ven'di-ter). It is necessary that anything which is sold should be a thing certain.

oppidum (op'i-dum). A town; a fortified town.

oppignerare (op-pig-ne-rā're). (Civil law.) To pledge; to pawn; to give in pledge.

opponent. An adversary. A party on the other side of the litigation; an opposing party or his counsel.

opportunity to be heard. See **day in court**.

opportunity to redeem. See **right of redemption**.

opposing officer. See **obstructing officer**.

opposing papers. Affidavits offered in resistance to a motion. 37 Am J1st Motions § 15.

Opposita juxta se posita magis elucescunt (op-pō'zi-ta jux'ta sē po'zi-ta mā'jis e-lū-ses'kunt). Things which are opposed are illumined more clearly when placed next to one another.

opposite party. An adversary in litigation.
Under the statutory rule that when a suit is prosecuted by the heirs, assigns, devisees, legatees or personal representatives of a decedent, the opposite party, if he testifies on his own behalf, cannot testify to matters which, if true, must have been equally within the knowledge of the decedent, the term

"opposite party" means the party in interest, the real party, and does not mean a defendant who is a mere nominal party such as an executor, who has no personal interest in the controversy. Penny v Croul, 87 Mich 15, 49 NW 311.

oppression. Bearing down on another or others in an oppressive manner. The exercise of unlawful power or other means, in depriving an individual of his liberty or property against his will. United States v Deaver (DC NC) 14 F 595, 597.

See **oppressive**.

oppressive. Cruel, severe, unduly dominating and exacting, exercising authority excessively. United States v Deaver (DCNC) 14 F 595, 597.

oppressive child labor. A condition of employment of children under a specified age in certain occupations, as proscribed by statute. 29 USC § 203(1).

oppressive legislation. Burdensome legislation against which, apart from constitutional provisions, the only protection is by an appeal to the people or their legislative representatives. 16 Am J2d Const L § 160.

oppressive litigation. Litigation for the purpose of harassing, annoying, and vexing an opponent, rather than for the adjudication of rights, being invoked, not for the attainment of justice, but to further or satisfy a malicious motive. Bridgeport Hydraulic Co. v Pearson, 139 Conn 186, 91 A2d 778.

oppressive use of process. Harassment by process with the malicious intent of injury or harassment. 1 Am J2d Abuse P § 9.

opprobrium (o-prō'bri-um). Infamy; **reproach**.

ops. Abbreviation of opinions.

optical illusion. Belief in a thing as seen when actually it is not there to be seen.

optician (op-tish'an). A person who makes or sells optical instruments, especially eyeglasses. 41 Am J1st Phys & S § 28. One who fills prescriptions of the oculist or optometrist, much in the same manner as the druggist carries out the direction and prescription of the physician. Anno: 22 ALR2d 941.

optic nerve. The nerve running between the brain and the eye. 58 Am J1st Workm Comp § 287.

optics (op'tiks). The science which treats of the nature and properties of light and vision. Abelson, Inc. v New York State Board of Optometrists, 5 NJ 412, 75 A2d 867, 22 ALR2d 929.

Optima enim est legis interpres consuetudo (op'ti-ma e'nim est lē'jis in-ter'pres kon-su-e-tū'dō). For custom is the best interpreter of the law. See Broom's Legal Maxims 931.

Optima est lex quae minimum relinquit arbitrio judicis (op'ti-ma est lex kwē mi'ni-mum re-lin'quit ar-bi'tri-o jū'di-sis). That law is best which leaves the least to the decision of the judge. See Broom's Legal Maxims 84.

Optima est lex quae minimum relinquit arbitrio judicis; optimus judex qui minimum sibi (op'ti-ma est lex kwē mi-ni'mum re-lin'quit ar-bi'tri-ō jū'di-sis); op'ti-mus jū'dex quī mi'ni-mum si'bi). That law is best which leaves the least to the decision of the judge; that judge is best who takes the least upon himself. See Broom's Legal Maxims 84.

Optimam esse legem, quae minimum relinquit arbitrio judicis; in quod certitudo ejus praestat (op'ti-mam es'se lē'jem, kwē mi'ni-mum re-lin'quit ar-bi'tri-ō jū'di-sis; in quod ser-ti-tū'dō ē'jus prē'stat). That law is best which leaves the least to the decision of the judge; this is because the certainty of it is manifest.

Optima statuti interpretatrix est ipsum statutum (op'ti-ma sta-tū'tī in-ter-pre-tā'trix est ip'sum sta-tū'tum). The best interpreter of a statute is the statute itself.

Optima statuti interpretatrix omnibus particulis ejusdem inspectis ipsum statutum (op'ti-ma sta-tū'ti in-ter-pre-tā'trix om'ni-bus par-ti'kū-lis e-jus'dem in-spek'tis ip'sum sta-tū'tum). The best interpreter of a statute, looking into all of its particulars or parts, is the statute itself.

Optimus interpres rerum usus (op'ti-mus in-ter'pres rē'rum ū'sus). Usage is the best interpreter of things. Destrehan v Louisiana Cypress Lumber Co. 45 La Ann 920.

Optimus interpretandi modus est sic leges interpretare ut leges legibus accordant (op'ti-mus in-ter-pre-tan'dī mō'dus est sik lē'jēz in-ter-pre-tā're ut lē'jēz lē'ji-bus a-kor'dant). The best manner of interpreting the laws is so to interpret the laws that the laws will accord with one another.

Optimus judex, qui minimum sibi (op'ti-mus jū'dex, quī mi'ni-mum si'bi). The best judge is the one who takes the least upon himself. See Broom's Legal Maxims 84.

Optimus legum interpres consuetudo (op'ti-mus lē'gum in-ter'pres kon-su-ē-tū'dō). The best interpreter of the laws is custom or usage.

option. An agreement by which one binds himself to perform a certain act, usually to transfer property, for a stipulated price within a designated time, leaving it to the discretion of the person to whom the option is given to accept upon the terms specified. 17 Am J2d Contr § 32. A continuing offer to sell at a price stipulated. Hirlinger v Hirlinger (Mo App) 267 SW2d 46, 44 ALR2d 1207. A stipulation not to revoke for a specified or reasonable time the offer therein made. Warner Bros. Pictures v Brodel, 31 Cal 2d 766, 192 P2d 949, 3 ALR2d 691. A future contract in which one of the parties has the right to insist on compliance with the terms of the contract, or to cancel the contract, at his election. A unilateral contract where given upon a contemporaneous consideration other than a promise. 17 Am J2d Contr § 5. A simple method of speculating in the rise or fall of the market price of commodities or stocks, no actual transaction by sale or purchase being contemplated. 24 Am J1st Gaming § 70. In the entertainment and professional athletic fields, an offer to perform as an actor, musician, etc., or as a baseball player, football player, etc. at a stipulated compensation within a designated time, leaving it to the person to whom the option is given to accept upon the terms specified. 17 Am J2d Contr § 32. The privilege which an archbishop had of nominating his bishop's clerk. See 1 Bl Comm 381.

See **stock option; stock-option plan.**

optional. Left to choice; discretionary.

optional agreement. An option, the essential feature of which always is that the person to whom it is granted is in position to choose whether or not he shall purchase on its terms. Johnson v Clark, 174 Cal 582, 163 P 1004.

See **option**.

optional bond. A bond which may be called for payment before maturity. 43 Am J1st Pub Sec § 8.

optional standard deduction. See **standard deduction.**

optional statutes. Workmen's compensation statutes open to acceptance or rejection by employee or employer. 58 Am J1st Workm Comp §§ 39 et seq.

optional writ. A common-law writ, designated as a praecipe, wherein the defendant was commanded to do a certain thing or, in the alternative, to show cause why he had not done it and should not be compelled to do it. See 3 Bl Comm 274.

optionee (op'shon-ē). The holder of an option. Phoenix Iron & Steel Co. v Wilkoff Co. (CA6 Ohio) 253 F 165, 1 ALR 1497, 1502.

option election. See **local option election.**

option of equivalent value. See **seller's option.**

option of forfeiture. A right or privilege of the lessor, under the provisions of the lease, upon breach of covenant by the lessee. 32 Am J1st L & T § 849.

option to purchase. A contract by which the owner of property agrees with another person that the latter shall have a right to buy the property at a fixed price within a certain time. 17 Am J2d Contr § 32; 46 Am J1st Sales § 56. The familiar provision in a lease, conferring upon the lessee the option to purchase the demised premises, it being supported, so far as consideration is concerned, by the payment of the reserved rent, so that it cannot be withdrawn by the lessor during the period specified for its continuance, and may be enforced specifically. 32 Am J1st L & T § 299.

option to purchase real property. A contract by which an owner of real estate agrees with another person that the latter shall have the privilege of buying the property at a specified price within a specified time, or within a reasonable time in the future, and imposes no obligation to purchase upon the person to whom it is given. 55 Am J1st V & P § 27.

option to rebuild, repair, or replace. The option of an insurer of property, provided by the policy issued by it, to replace, repair, or rebuild the property in the event of its destruction in whole or in part, in lieu of the satisfaction of insured's claim by a payment in money. 29A Am J Rev ed Ins § 1699.

option to renew. A right granted a lessee by the terms of the lease.

option to terminate. A provision in a lease giving the right or privilege to both parties, or one of them, to terminate the lease either at will or on the happening of some contingency, such as the destruction of or injury to the premises, or the decision of the landlord to sell, alter, or improve the property. Anno: 27 ALR 845, 35 ALR 519, s.116 ALR 931.

optometrist (op-tom'e-trist) One who practices optometry. One who exercises a degree of mechanical skill and experience in fitting glasses to the eye. Anno: 141 ALR 884.

optometry (op-tom-et-ri). The employment of any means other than drugs for the measurement of the power of vision and the adaptation of lenses for the aid thereof. McNaughton v Johnson, 242 US 344, 61 L Ed 352, 37 S Ct 178; Sage-Allen Co. v Wheeler, 119 Conn 667, 179 A 195, 98 ALR 897. Including, subject to same limitation as to means, diagnosis of any optical defect, deficiency, or deformity of the human eye, or visual or muscular anomaly of the visual system, but not including treatment of diseases of the eye. Anno: 141 ALR 890. More narrowly, the measurement of the range of vision. Anno: 141 ALR 883. Not the practice of medicine, being an applied arm of optical science resting upon the work and discoveries of physicists and opticians through the ages down to modern times. Silver v Lansburgh & Bro. 72 App DC 77, 111 F2d 518, 128 ALR 582; Abelson, Inc. v New York State Board of Optometrists, 5 NJ 412, 75 A2d 867, 22 ALR2d 929.

optulit (op'tu-lit). Same as **obtulit.**

opus (ō'pus). Work; labor; benefit; advantage. A written work or composition.

opus locatum (o'pus lo-kā'tum). Work let out to another.

opus magnificium (o'pus mag-ni-fi'she-um). Same as **opus manificium.**

opus manificium (o'pus ma-ni-fi'she-um). Work performed with the hands; manual labor.

opus novum (o'pus no'vum). Same as **new work.**

o. r. An abbreviation of **owner's risk.**

or. A conjunction normally in the disjunctive. A conjunction properly used with "either" in stating a proposition in the alternative. State ex rel. Crow v St. Louis, 174 Mo 125, 73 SW 623. Usually a word of substitution in a will. Re Boyle's Estate, 121 Colo 599, 221 P2d 357, 36 ALR2d 1106. In a deed, implying a disjunctive or alternative. 23 Am J2d Deeds § 218. The disjunctive form but to be interpreted in a copulative sense when necessary to the spirit and intent of the instrument in which it appears. 17 Am J2d Contr § 283. Subject to construction as "and" where the obvious intention appearing from the entire context of the instrument so requires. Davis v Vermillion, 173 Kan 508, 249 P2d 625. Subject to construction as "and" in a statute or municipal ordinance where such is in keeping with the intent of the statute or ordinance as such appears from the entire context. 37 Am J1st Mun Corp § 187; 50 Am J1st Stat § 282.

See **and/or.**

oraculum (o-ra'ku-lum). A Roman emperor's decision.

oral. By word of mouth; verbal; spoken, as opposed to written.

See expressions beginning "oral" which follow; also expressions beginning "parol."

oral chattel mortgage. A transaction which, while oral, contains all the essential elements of a written mortgage. 15 Am J2d Chat Mtg § 39.

oral contract. Same as **parol contract.**

oral defamation. Defamation by spoken words; slander.

oral demurrer. Same as **demurrer ore tenus.**

oral license. A license in real property conferred without a writing. 25 Am J2d Ease § 123.

oral trust. A trust in personal property, created and proved by parol. 54 Am J1st Trusts § 44.

oral will. A nuncupative will. The informal will of a soldier or sailor. 57 Am J1st Wills § 220.

See **nuncupative will.**

orator (or'ą-tor). A person who prays; a petitioner; a party who files or presents a petition to a court of justice; the complainant in an equity suit. A person skilled in the art of public speech.

oratrix (or'ā-triks). Feminine of **orator**.

or bearer. Words of negotiability. 11 Am J2d B & N § 105.

orchard. A tract of land, sometimes large, sometimes small devoted to the growing of trees which produce fruit or nuts good for food.
To constitute an orchard within the meaning of provisions in an eminent domain statute exempting orchards from condemnation, the number of fruit trees, within certain limits appears immaterial, but a few scattered or neglected and decayed trees are not considered an orchard. 26 Am J2d Em D § 109.

orchestra. A group of musicians who play together. The main floor of a theater.

orchestration (ôr-kes-trā'shọn). The arrangement of music for an orchestra. Anno: 19 ALR 970.

orcinus libertus (or'si-nus li-ber'tus). (Roman law.) A slave who was freed by a provision in the will of his deceased owner.

ordain. To constitute, to establish, to pass an ordinance. Kepner v Commonwealth, 40 Pa 124, 129. See **ordination**.

ordeal (ôr'dẹ-ạl). The most ancient species of trial for criminal offenses, founded upon the belief of the ancients that if a man were innocent, God would save him from death or injury when he was subjected to an ordeal. See 4 Bl Comm 342. See also Hurtado v California, 110 US 516, 529, 28 L Ed 232, 236, 4 S Ct 111.
See **cold-water ordeal; fire ordeal; hot-water ordeal; iron ordeal; trial by water**.

ordenamiento (or-day-nah-me-en-to). (Spanish.) An order issued by the crown; a royal order.

order. A command or direction. A list of goods or merchandise to be supplied by a dealer. A direction in writing by one person to another person for the payment of money to a third person. 11 Am J2d B & N § 139. The determination of an administrative body or agency. 2 Am J2d Admin L §§ 473 et seq.
See **order of court**.

order bill of lading. Same as **negotiable bill of lading**.

order for distribution. An order by the court having jurisdiction over the administration of a decedent's estate directing the administrator or executor to distribute the assets of the estate, such order normally being made after all claims of creditors of the estate have been determined for allowance or rejection, so that the amount of money or assets in kind available for distribution to those entitled to share in the estate is known.

order for publication. An order of court authorizing the service of process in a particular case by publication. 42 Am J1st Process § 94.

order nisi (ôr'der nī'sī). An order of court which is to become absolute and effective unless cause is shown why it should not become so, or unless some condition specified by the court shall not have been complied with or performed.

order nunc pro tunc (ôr'dėr nunk prō tunk). See **nunc pro tunc order**.

order of calls. The order of precedence which has been established as between different calls for the location of boundaries of land. 12 Am J2d Bound § 65.

order of continuance. An order of court continuing a case. 17 Am J2d Contin § 1

order of court. Broadly defined, the judgment or conclusion of a court on any motion or proceeding by which affirmative relief is granted or denied. 37 Am J1st Motions § 23. Precisely, a direction of a court or judge made in writing and not included in a judgment. State v Lindeman, 64 ND 518, 254 NW 276, 93 ALR 1442.

order of dismissal. An order of court required on an involuntary dismissal. 24 Am J2d Dism § 71. An order sometimes required for a voluntary dismissal. 24 Am J2d Dism § 50.

order of filiation (of fil-i-ā'shọn). An order of a competent court determining the paternity of a bastard child.

order of interpleader. An order in favor of the complainant in interpleader, directing that complainant pay the fund or property into court and be dismissed with his costs, and further that the defendants interplead and settle the controversy between themselves. 30 Am J Rev ed Interpl § 26.

order of reference. An order of court appointing a referee to hear or to hear and determine a matter pending before the court. Gerity v Seeger & Guernsey Co. 163 NY 119, 120.

order of repleader. See **repleader**.

Order of St. George. See **garter; knights of the garter**.

Order of the Bath. See **knights of the bath**.

Order of the Garter. See **garter; knights of the garter**.

Order of the Coif (ôr'dėr of the koif). An honorary fraternity of lawyers, membership being attained on the basis of exceptional work and standing as a student in a college of law.

order paper. A direction by one person to another person for the payment of money to a third person. 11 Am J2d B & N § 139.

order sua sponte. See **sua sponte**.

order taking. The taking of an order for goods to be furnished, as distinguished from a sale of the goods. A matter considered in determining whether a corporation is within the purview of statutes relative to foreign corporations transacting business in the state. 23 Am J1st For Corp § 381.

order to show cause. An order or rule of court made ex parte, citing an adverse party to appear before the court and show cause, if he can, why a certain thing shall not be done. 37 Am J1st Motions § 38. An alternative to notice of motion in bringing a motion on for hearing. A form of process. Hayward v Long, 178 SC 351, 183 SE 145, 114 ALR 1130.

ordinance. The act of the legislative body of a municipal corporation. A local law of a municipal corporation, of a general and permanent nature. 37 Am J1st Mun Corp § 142. A bylaw of a municipal corporation. 37 Am J1st Mun Corp § 142. A rule established for and in a municipal corporation by authority. State ex rel. Maxey v Swindell, 146 Ind 527, 45 NE 700. In a broader sense, a rule established by authority. State v Swindell, 146 Ind 527, 45 NE 700; Kepner v Commonwealth, 40 Pa 124, 130.
See **Northwest Ordinance of 1787**.

ordinandi lex (or-di-nan'dī lex). Adjective law,—the law regulating procedure in the courts.

Ordinarius ita dicitur quia habet ordinariam jurisdictionem, in jure proprio, et non propter deputa-

tionem (or-di-nā′ri-us i′ta di′si-ter qui′a hā′bet or-di-nā′ri-am jū-ris-dik-she-ō′nem, in jū′re prō′pri-ō, et non prop′ter de-pu-tā-she-ō′nem). An ordinary is so called because he has ordinary jurisdiction in his own right, and not by deputation or delegation.

ordinary. Adjective: Usual; normal; common. Hine v Wooding, 37 Conn 123, 126. Noun: An older term for a public house where food and lodging are furnished to the traveler at fixed rates, open to whoever may apply for accommodation, and having a bar. Talbott v Southern Seminary, 131 Va 576, 109 SE 440, 19 ALR 534. An officer with limited judicial powers, particularly a master or commissioner in equity.

A civil-law term applicable to any judge who had authority to take cognizance of causes in his own right, and not by deputation. In England, the ordinary was a judge of the ecclesiastical court. The goods of intestates were given to the ordinary by the crown. The title "ordinary" is also given to certain district judges in South Carolina. Hays v Harley, 8 SCL (1 Mills Const) 267, 268.

ordinary action. A civil action carried on by ordinary proceedings. 1 Am J2d Actions § 3.

ordinary and concise language. A phrase embodied in many modern codes to specify the manner in which pleadings shall be prepared and meaning simply that the pleading must be reasonably definite and certain, and not prolix. Harlan v Bernie, 22 Ark 217.

ordinary and necessary expense. A deduction in computation of taxable income where incurred as a common and accepted practice in the taxpayer's field of business, where it is appropriate and helpful in maintaining the taxpayer's business, and where it is not in violation of statute or public policy. Welch v Helvering, 290 US 111, 78 L Ed 212, 54 S Ct 8; Lilly v Commissioner, 343 US 90, 96 L Ed 769, 72 S Ct 497, 27 ALR2d 492; National Brass Works, Inc. v Commissioner (CA9) 182 F2d 526, 20 ALR2d 590.

See **necessary expense.**

ordinary bailment. A bailment for the sole benefit of the bailor, for the sole benefit of the bailee, or for the mutual benefit of both parties. 8 Am J2d Bailm § 6.

ordinary bailee. See **ordinary bailment.**

ordinary calling. A pursuit in business, trade, or employment which occupies at least a part of one's time with a degree of regularity. Ellis v State, 5 Ga App 615, 617.

ordinary care. A standard for the determination of negligence; the degree of diligence which one must observe in the performance of his common-law duty to use care to prevent injury to others. A relative standard; due care according to the circumstances of the case. 38 Am J1st Negl § 29. That degree of care that a man of ordinary prudence would exercise under the same or similar circumstances with reference to his own property. Smith v Maher, 84 Okla 49, 202 P 321. 23 ALR 270. In reference to pedestrians:—such care as persons of ordinary prudence and care, in driving and managing automobiles in the streets of a city, are accustomed to exercise and observe for the protection of persons traveling in the streets. Cincinnati Traction Co. v Harrison, 24 Ohio CCNS 1, 44 Ohio CC 435. As required of an officer or director of a corporation:—such care as a man of common prudence would take of his own affairs; more realistically, such care as a prudent man should exercise in like circumstances, not necessarily the care which such a person would show in the conduct of his own affairs of a similar kind. 19 Am J2d Corp § 1277. As required of a bailee:—such care as ordinarily prudent men, as a class, would exercise in caring for their own property under like circumstances, or, as it is sometimes expressed, when applied to bailees who make a business of keeping property for hire, that degree of care and diligence which may reasonably be expected from ordinarily prudent persons under similar circumstances, or that which capable and reasonably prudent persons engaged in the same business, and experienced and faithful in the particular department are accustomed to exercise when in the discharge of their duties. 8 Am J2d Bailm § 207.

ordinary conveyance. A voluntary deed as distinguished from a divesting of title by judgment of a court or a transfer directed by the court.

ordinary course of business. See **in the ordinary course of business.**

ordinary course of trade. See **in the ordinary course of business.**

ordinary diligence. That degree of care, attention, or exertion which, under the circumstances, a man of ordinary prudence and discretion would use in reference to the particular thing were it his own property, or in doing the particular thing were it his own concern. Anno: 15 ALR2d 856, § 13; 10 Am J2d Banks § 479.

ordinary dividend. A regular dividend paid by a corporation, as distinguished from an extra dividend or a stock dividend. 19 Am J2d Corp § 810.

ordinary flood. A flood the occurrence of which is reasonably to be anticipated, considering past experience in the weather and the topographical situation. Anno: 23 ALR2d 757. A flood in a series of floods occurring at intervals which are regular or irregular, frequent or infrequent. Cairo, Vincennes & Chicago R. Co. v Brevoort (CC Ind) 62 F 129.

ordinary flow. The usual volume of water in a watercourse at any given season.

The waters of a river flowing annually therein before, during and after the regularly occurring accretions, caused by melting snows, in the volume thereof constitute the usual and ordinary flow of the river, and are in no sense "storm" or "flood" or "vagrant" or "enemy" waters, as these terms are understood in law. Herminghaus v Southern Cal. Edison Co. 200 Cal 81, 252 P 607.

ordinary high-watermark. The line of the medium high tide between the spring and the neap tides. The average high-watermark. 12 Am J2d Bound § 13. The line along the banks of a river to which the water rises in the seasons of ordinary high water, or the line at which the presence of water is continued for such length of time as to mark upon the soil and vegetation a distinct character. Pacific Milling & Elevator Co. v Portland, 65 Or 349, 133 P 72.

ordinary income. Income from regularly recurring sources, such as earnings from work, interest, and dividends, as distinguished from a bonanza, winnings on a horse race, the prize won in a contest, or a capital gain realized on a sale of property. Sloane v Commissioner (CA6) 188 F2d 254, 29 ALR2d 580.

ORDINARY [898] ORGANIZATION

ordinary low-watermark. The average low-watermark at low tide. East Boston Co. v Commonwealth, 203 Mass 68, 89 NE 236.

ordinary luggage. Luggage which is personal to the passenger, and carried for his use or convenience, not something, such as merchandise, carried in pursuit of a trade or business. Yazoo & Mississippi Valley Railroad Co. v Blackmar, 85 Miss 7, 37 So 500; Oakes v Northern Pacific Railroad Co. 20 Or 392, 26 P 230.

ordinary negligence. The failure to exercise such care as the great mass of mankind ordinarily exercises under the same or similar circumstances. 38 Am J1st Negl § 46. The want of exercise of ordinary care.
See **ordinary care**.

ordinary occupation. See **ordinary calling**.

ordinary partnership. Any partnership other than a commercial partnership or a limited partnership. 42 Am J1st Partn § 11.

ordinary proceedings. The regular and usual method of carrying on a suit by due course at common law. 1 Am J2d Actions § 3.

ordinary prudent man. See **the ordinary prudent man**.

ordinary rainfall. Such rainfall as is not unprecedented and extraordinary. Cairo, Vincennes & Chicago R. Co. v Brevoort (CC Ind) 62 F 129.

ordinary repairs. Painting, papering or decorating, repairing plumbing fixtures or replacing plumbing, repairing the heating plant, etc. 33 Am J1st Life Est § 453.

ordinary risks of employment. Those perils, hazards, and dangers as are ordinarily and normally incident to or a part of the employment in question and of which the employee has knowledge, actual or implied, or of which it may be said that he is presumed to know. 35 Am J1st M & S § 299. Those dangers in the work which exist after the employer has done everything that he is bound to do for the purpose of securing the safety of the employee. Boatman v Miles, 27 Wyo 481, 199 P 933, 26 ALR 864.

ordinary skill. That degree of skill which men engaged in a particular work or art usually employed, not that skill which belongs to a few men of extraordinary endowment and capacity. Baltimore Baseball Club & Exhibition Co. v Tickett, 78 Md 375, 28 A 279.

ordinary travel. See **ordinary use of highway**.

ordinary use of highway. Use by motor vehicles, such having almost completely supplanted horse-drawn vehicles. 25 Am J2d High § 430.
In the absence of a specific regulation to the contrary, a bicycle is a vehicle of such nature that it properly may be used upon the highways and streets. 7 Am J2d Auto § 7.

ordinary wear and tear. See **wear and tear**.

ordination. The religious ceremony, celebration, and service at which a person is made a priest or minister of the Gospel.

ordinatione contra servientes (or-di-nā-she-ō'ne kon'trā ser-vi-en'tēz). A writ which lay for a master against his servant who left his service in violation of a statute or ordinance.

ordinatum est (or-di-nā'tum est). It is ordered.

ordine. See **ex ordine**.

Ordine placitandi servato, servatur et jus (or'di-ne pla-si-tan'dī ser-vā'tō, ser-vā'ter et jūs). By observing the order of pleading, the law is also observed. See Broom's Legal Maxims 188.

ordinis beneficium (or'di-nis be-ne-fi'she-um). (Civil law.) The benefit or privilege of order,—the right of a surety to have all of the creditor's remedies first exhausted against the principal, before resort might be had to him, the surety.

ordinum fugitivi (or'di-num fu-ji-tī'vi). Members of ancient English orders who renounced their adherence.

ordo attachiamentorum (or'dō at-ta-chi-ā-men-tō'rum). The order of attachments.

ordonnance (ôr'dọ-nạns). A compilation of international law on the subject of "prize."

ore. A natural combination of minerals; a natural compound of a mineral and some other substance, such as oxygen, sulphur, or arsenic, called its mineralizer, by which its usual properties are disguised or lost. Marvel v Merritt, 116 US 11, 29 L Ed 550, 6 S Ct 207.

oredelfe. The right to claim ore found in one's land.

Oregon boot. A heavy weight clasped about the ankle of a prisoner to prevent his escape.

ore-leave. The right to dig and take ore from a mine. See Ege v Kille, 84 Pa 333, 340.

ore tenus (o're tē'nus). By word of mouth; oral; orally.

orfgild (orf'gild). A compensation for, or a restoration of, property taken away, and applied particularly to cattle.

organic act. An act providing and establishing a government, for example the Act of 1878, providing a permanent form of government for the District of Columbia. 24 Am J2d D C § 4.

organic law. Constitutional law or, at least, law which carries a high degree of authority. St. Louis v Dorr, 145 Mo 466, 41 SW 1094, 46 SW 976. The basic law of a state or of a society, such as a mutual benefit society. 36 Am J2d Trat O § 9.

organization. A corporation, government or governmental subdivision or agency, business trust, estate trust, partnership or association, two or more persons having a joint or common interest, or any other legal or commercial entity. UCC § 1—201(28). Planning, arranging, and developing, as in organizing a corporation or a labor union. A term of practical politics; the leadership of a political party in a town, city, county, or state and those of the party, committeemen and others, who support the leadership.

organization costs. See **preconstruction costs; promotion expenses**.

organization of corporation. The process of forming and arranging into suitable disposition the parts of the body to be created and of defining the objects of such body. A process stopping short of the conferring of a franchise to be a corporation or charter. Hughes Co. v Farmers' Union Produce Co. 110 Neb 736, 194 NW 872, 37 ALR 1314, 1318. A process completed when the first meeting has been called, the act of incorporation accepted, officers elected, and bylaws providing for future meetings adopted. Roosevelt v Hamblin, 199 Mass 127, 85 NE 98.

organization tax. A term applied loosely to an incorporation fee. 18 Am J2d Corp § 41.

organization of board. The calling and holding of a meeting of a board or commission for the election of officers. Waterman v Chicago & Iowa Railroad Co. 139 Ill 658, 29 NE 689.

organized. See **organization**.

organized bar. See **bar association; integrated bar; state bar.**

organized labor. Union labor; the aggregate of labor unions and the members thereof.

organized territory. A territory of the United States having any form of autonomous government characterized by system. 49 Am J1st States § 4.

or his heirs. Words of limitation in the devise of a remainder, not preventing the creation of an indefeasible vested remainder. 28 Am J2d Est § 300.

oriel window (ō′ri-ęl win′dō). A bay window.

original. Adjective: Pertaining to the beginning or origin. Noun: The first or primitive form of a thing. An eccentric person. An instrument from which a copy or copies have been made.
See **duplicate; duplicate original.**

original asking price. The price at which a landowner lists his property for sale with a real estate broker. 12 Am J2d Brok § 111.

original bill. A bill in equity that begins an independent suit unconnected with any other previous or pending suit in the same court. 27 Am J2d Eq § 179.

original bill in the nature of a supplemental bill. A bill filed in a suit in equity when new parties, with new interests, arising from events which have transpired since the institution of the suit, are to be brought before the court. Whiting v Bank of United States (US) 13 Pet 6, 10 L Ed 33; Bowie v Minter, 2 Ala 406, 411.

original charter (chär′ter). The charter by which the first grant of the land was made by the superior to the vassal.

original construction of railroad. That construction of bridges, grades, culverts, rails, ties, docks, etc., that is prerequisite to the opening of the line for use in the operation of trains. Cleveland, Canton & Southern Railroad Co. v Knickerbocker Trust Co. (CC Ohio) 86 F 73, 76.

original contractor. Same as **principal contractor.**

original conveyances. A primary conveyance; that is, a conveyance by means of which the benefit or estate is created or first arises.
Such conveyances comprise the following: Feoffments, gifts, grants, leases, exchanges, and partitions. See 2 Bl Comm 309.

original cost. The amount expended in construction of a building or plant, as distinguished from present value or cost of reproduction. National Waterworks Co. v Kansas City (CA8 Mo) 62 F 853.

original cost theory. A theory of valuation of public utility property for rate-making purposes, based upon the idea that the utility is entitled to a return only on the actual sacrifice of funds made in creating the plant for service to the public. 43 Am J1st Pub Util § 105.

original damages. Damages arising from an injury to real estate of such nature that one recovery is all that is permitted by law, there being no basis for recovery from time to time as damages accrue. McHenry v Parkersburg, 66 W Va 533, 66 NE 750.

original deed. See **original conveyance.**

original entry. See **book of account; book of original entry.**

original evidence. Primary evidence, as distinguished from secondary evidence.

original jurisdiction. The jurisdiction conferred on or inherent in a court in the first instance. 20 Am J2d Cts § 98. The jurisdiction of a trial court, as distinguished from the jurisdiction exercised by an appellate court or a court with supervisory powers. 20 Am J2d Cts §§ 28, 98.

original negligence. A term pertinent to the last clear chance, referring to the negligence of the plaintiff in placing himself in the position of peril. 7 Am J2d Auto § 379.
See **primary negligence.**

original package. That package which, according to custom respecting the particular articles shipped, is usually delivered by the vendor to the carrier for transportation and delivered as a unit to the consignee. The package, as a unit, which is delivered by the shipper to the carrier at the initial place of shipment in the exact condition in which shipped. 15 Am J2d Com § 45. The unbroken package in the original form in which used by a shipper of intoxicating liquors for shipment and delivery into dry territory, provided the receptacle used is one ordinarily used by honest dealers in the same business and is recognized commercially as a usable receptacle. 30 Am J Rev ed Intox L § 40. A well-recognized method of selling patent or proprietary medicines. 25 Am J2d Drugs § 63. A restriction upon the right to purchase or sell narcotics under the Federal Narcotic Act. 26 USC § 4704(a). The denial of the power to impose a state or local tax upon goods imported from a foreign country while they remain the property of the importer, in his warehouse, in the original form or package in which they were imported. Brown v Maryland (US) 12 Wheat 419, 6 L Ed 678.
In the area of state taxation of goods transported from another state, the doctrine has been definitely rejected. Sonneborn Bros. v Cureton, 262 US 506, 67 L Ed 1095, 43 S Ct 643. Nor has the doctrine been a barrier to state regulation apart from taxation. 15 Am J2d Com § 44.

Original Packages Act. Another name for the Wilson Act of 1890, a federal statute respecting the transportation of intoxicating liquors from one state to another.
See **Wilson Act.**

original patent. Same as **basic patent.**

original plat. The first plat made of a town or village, as distinguished from a plat of the town or village in which additions made to the incorporated area are included.

original proceeding. See **principal action.**

original process. The process by which a suit or action is commenced. Hotchkiss' Appeal from Probate, 32 Conn 353, 355.

original promise. A promise not within the statute of frauds as a promise to answer for the debt of another, because it is made to subserve or promote an interest or purpose of the promisor and upon a consideration beneficial to him. 49 Am J1st Stat of F § 61. A promise, made at the time of or before the creation of the debt, in consideration of which the credit is given. Goldsmith v Erwin (CA4 NC) 183 F2d 432, 20 ALR2d 240.

original undertaking. See **original promise.**

original vein. The discovered vein of mineral relied upon in the location and perfection of a lode claim. 36 Am J1st Mines & M § 83.

original work. Work which an author has created by his own skill, labor, and judgment. Anno: 23 ALR2d 264, § 4.

original writ. The beginning or foundation of a common-law action. "It is a mandatory letter from the king in parchment, sealed with his great seal, and directed to the sheriff of the county wherein the injury is committed or supposed so to be, requiring him to command the wrongdoer or party accused, either to do justice to the complainant or else to appear in court and answer the accusation against him." See 3 Bl Comm 273.

In the United States, original writs, properly so-called, never existed, and while they have been abolished in England, their history and original functions are vital and instructive.
See **original process.**

originate. To give an origin or beginning to; to bring into existence; to take first existence; to have origin or beginning; to begin or exist or act. Dunbar v Spratt-Snyder Co. 208 Iowa 226 NW 22, 63 ALR 1016.

Origine propria nominem posse voluntate sua eximi manifestum est (o-ri'gi-ne prō'pri-a nō'mi-nem pos'se vo-lun-tā'te su'a ex'i-mī ma-ni-fes'tum est). It is manifest that no one can by his own will or wish free himself from his own origin. See Broom's Legal Maxims 77.

originis. See **forum originis.**

Origo rei inspici debet (ō'ri-gō rē'ī in'spi-sī de'bet). The origin of a thing ought to be regarded.

or in trust for. A form of restrictive indorsement of a bill or note. 11 Am J2d B & N § 362.

or lease. An oil lease obligating a lessee to drill a well within a certain time or pay delay rentals. 24 Am J1st Gas & O § 60.

ornamental fixtures. Articles removable by a tenant, although affixed to the premises, because brought on the premises by him and because of their nature as articles pertaining to his own pleasure, domestic comfort, and convenience. Raymond v Strickland, 124 Ga 504, 52 SE 619.

ornamental tree. A tree planted or kept for the beauty it adds to the premises.

or order. Words of negotiability. 11 Am J2d B & N § 105.

or other valuable effects. A term of art used in statutes prescribing the elements of the crime of false pretenses for extending the application of the statute in reference to the things obtained by the accused. 32 Am J2d False Pret § 42.

orphan. A minor child who has lost one or both of his or her parents. Heiss v Murphey, 40 Wis 276, 291.

orphanage part (ôr'fan-ąj pärt). The distributive share in his estate to which the children of an intestate are entitled by the custom of London.

By this custom their share is not fully vested in them until the age of twenty-one, before which they cannot dispose of it by will. If they die under that age, whether single or married, their share survives to the other children. But after the age of twenty-one, it is free from any orphanage custom and if they then die intestate it falls under the statute of distributions. See 2 Bl Comm 519.

orphanotrophi (ôr-fa-not'rō-fi). (Civil law.) Persons who had the charge or management of orphan asylums.

orphans' court. A probate court, 20 Am J2d Cts § 32, the name being suggested by the jurisdiction exercised in matters involving the care of orphans and their property.

orthopedic appliance (ôr-thō-pē'dik ą-plī'ąns). An appliance to be worn or used in the relief of a disease, injury, or deformity of bones and joints.

oscillation (os'i-lā'shǫn). Vibration.

osculation (os'kų-lā'shǫn). Close contact; kissing.

or to the use of. A form of restrictive indorsement of a negotiable instrument. 11 Am J2d B & N § 362.

O. S. Abbreviation of old style, particularly in reference to the calendar. Abbreviation of old series, also of ordinary seaman.

ostendit vobis (os-ten'dit vō'bis). It shows to you.

ostensible agency. An agency created by a course of conduct, for example, the agency of a wife to make purchases on the credit of the husband, arising from his acquiescence on many occasions in her thus binding him. 26 Am J1st H & W § 237. An agency existing when the principal intentionally, or by want of ordinary care, causes or allows a third person to believe another to be his agent. Armstrong v Barceloux, 34 Cal App 433, 167 P 895.

ostensible authority. Apparent authority, for example, such authority as an insurance company permits its agent to exercise, or which it holds him out to the public as possessing. 29 Am J Rev ed Ins § 146. Such authority as a principal, either intentionally or by want of ordinary care, causes or allows a third person to believe the agent to possess. Henry Cowell Lime & Cement Co. v Santa Cruz Nat. Bank, 82 Cal App 519, 255 P 881.

ostensible partner. One made known to the world as a member of a partnership and who in reality is a partner. Ditts v Lonsdale, 49 Ind 521, 529. One who, although not a partner by contract or agreement with the other member or members of the firm, is charged with liability as a partner because he has held himself out, or permitted himself to be held out, as being a member of the firm. 40 Am J1st Partn § 71.

ostensible partnership. See **ostensible partner.**

ostensurus (os-ten-sū'rus). To show.

ostentum (os-ten'tum). Same as **monster.**

osteoarthritis (os'tę-ō-är-thrī'tis). A type of arthritis; susceptible to aggravation by personal injury. Hanover Fire Ins. Co. v Sides (CA5 La) 320 F2d 437.

osteomyelitis (os'tę-ō-mī-ę-lī'tis). A disease of the bone. Merritt, Chapman & Scott Corp. v Fredin (CA9 Wash) 307 F2d 370.

osteopath (os'tę-ō-path). One who treats human ailments by osteopathy. A physician where licensed by the State Medical Board. State ex rel. Kester v North, 136 Ohio St 523, 17 Ohio Ops 159, 26 NE2d 1020. A physician within the meaning of a statute providing for the registration of births and deaths. Keiningham v Blake, 135 Md 320, 109 A 65, 8 ALR 1066.

osteopathy (os-tē-op'a-thi). A system of treatment of parts and tissues of the body by manipulations with the hands. State v Hopkins, 54 Mont 52, 166 P 304. A system of treatment of human ailments based on the theory that diseases are chiefly due to the deranged mechanism of bones, nerves, blood vessels, and other tissues, and can be remedied by manipulation. 41 Am J1st Phys & S § 2.

osteoporosis (os''tē-ō-pō-rō'sis). A disabling disease characterized by fragility of bones. Nelson v Twin City Motor Bus Co. 239 Minn 276, 58 NW2d 561.

oster. Same as **ouster**.

ostercus (os-ter'kus). Also called "austurcus,"—a goshawk used by falconers in hunting fowl; the modern chicken hawk.

ostium ecclesiae (os'ti-um e-klē'zi-ē). The door of the church,—the place where marriages were anciently solemnized.

Oswald's law (oz'wâlds lâ). The law by which compulsory celibacy was introduced into the priesthood in the tenth century.

other action pending. See **plea of another action pending**.

other country. See **foreign country**.

other hard incombustible material. Materials of the same kind as those specifically named. Odessa v Halbrook (Tex Civ App) 103 SW2d 223.

other insurance. Insurance on the same risk for the benefit of the same person.
See **contribution between insurers; double insurance; excess insurance**.

other insurance clause. The condition of an insurance policy against the existence or procuring of other insurance upon the same risk insured, without the consent of the insurer. 29A Am J Rev ed Ins § 954. A clause, common in fire insurance policies, the meaning of which is that if the assured has any other policy or insurance upon the property, by assignment or otherwise, by which the interest intended to be insured, is already either wholly or partially protected, he shall disclose that fact and have it indorsed on the policy, or the insurance shall be void. Aetna Fire Ins. Co. v Tyler (NY) 16 Wend 385.

othesworthe. Same as **oathworthy**.

oultre. See **en oultre**.

oultre le mere (ool'truh luh mare). Beyond seas.

oust. To effect an ouster.

ouster. A forced dispossession of real estate. A disseisin. The wrongful dispossession or exclusion from real property of a person entitled to the possession thereof. 25 Am J2d Eject § 47. The eviction of a foreign corporation from the state, prohibiting it from doing business. 36 Am J2d For Corp § 439.
See **eviction**.

ouster by abatement. Such an ouster as takes place where a person dies seised of an estate of inheritance, and before the heir or devisee enters, a stranger who has no right enters and gets possession of the freehold. Brown v Burdick, 25 Ohio St 260, 268.

ouster in pais (in pā). A dispossession or disseisin of a person in possession of land effected otherwise than by means of resort to legal proceedings.

ouster judgment. A judgment against the defendant in ejectment. 25 Am J2d Eject § 122. A judgment in forcible entry and detainer calling for the restitution of the premises to the plaintiff. 35 Am J2d Forc E & D § 53. A judgment in an election contest rendered against the contestee in possession of the office. 26 Am J2d Elect § 357.

ouster le main (le man). To remove the hand of the guardian. To cause a ward's lands to be delivered or released to him from the hands of the guardian upon the ward's attaining his majority. See 2 Bl Comm 68.

ousterlemain. Same as **ouster le main**.
See **livery**.

ouster le mer (le-măr). Beyond seas.

ouster of jurisdiction. Events occurring after the commencement of an action and the acquisition of jurisdiction causing a loss of jurisdiction. 20 Am J2d Cts §§ 147 et seq.

out. Away from, as out of store. Vernacular for a means of avoidance, as a condition under which one otherwise obligated is permitted to withdraw from the engagement. Cray, McFawn & Co. v Hegarty, Conroy & Co. (DC NY) 27 F Supp 93.

outage (ou'tāj). An inspection charge of two dollars per hogshead, fixed by a Maryland statute passed in 1872, to be paid by shippers of tobacco on tobacco shipped out of the state. Turner v Maryland (US) 17 Otto 38, 44, 27 L Ed 370, 373, 2 S Ct 44.

out and out conversion. The rule that real estate intended by partners to constitute a part of the firm property, or treated by them as belonging to the firm, is regarded in equity as converted into personalty for all purposes, as well for the purpose of the adjustment of the partnership debts and the claims of the partners between themselves as for the purpose of determining the succession as between the personal representative of a deceased partner and the heirs at law. 40 Am J1st Partn § 111.

outboard. A motorboat having the motor fastened on the outside at the stern of the craft. A powerboat. United States v Olson (DC Ky) 41 F Supp 433.

outbreak of war. The commencement of hostilities between two nations, with or without a declaration of war. 56 Am J1st War § 8.

outbuilding. A building on the same premises, usually made use of in connection with the dwelling house.
See **outhouse**.

outcome-determinative test. The rule that a federal court exercising jurisdiction solely because of the citizenship of the parties should apply a state law, although such is deemed a matter of "procedure" in one sense, where refusal to follow it will bring about a result impossible of attainment in a state court. Guaranty Trust Co. v York, 362 US 99, 89 L Ed 2079, 65 S Ct 1464, 160 ALR 1231.

outcrop. The exposure of a mineral vein above the surface of the earth or the point at which the vein comes the closest to the surface. Anno: 1 ALR 422.

outcry. The cry of a person imperiled by an assault, especially a female threatened by a sexual assault. 6 Am J2d Asslt & B § 156. The sound of an auctioneer's voice as he speaks or chants in offering an article for sale and invokes bidding.

outdoor advertising. Advertising appearing upon billboards and other structures in places observable

outer bar. The junior barristers or counsel, who sit outside the bar in an English court and in some other courts of the Commonwealth.

outer barrister. A barrister who pleads outside the bar; that is, otherwise than as sergeant or king's or queen's counsel.

Outer Continental Shelf. All submerged lands lying seaward and outside of the area of lands beneath navigable waters, and of which the subsoil and sea bed appertain to the United States and are subject to its jurisdiction and control. 43 USC § 1331(a).

Outer Continental Shelf Lands Act. A federal statute declaring and implementing the policy of the United States in reference to the subsoil and sea bed of the Outer Continental Shelf. 43 USC §§ 1313 et seq.

outer door. A door for ingress or egress to or from premises, as distinguished from a door leading from one portion of premises to another part of the same premises.
As to what constitutes an "outer door" within the rule which prohibits an officer from forcing or breaking the outer door for the purpose of serving process, see 42 Am J1st Proc § 42.

outer house. The name given to the lower branch of the Scotch court of sessions.

outfangthef (out'fang-thef). A thief who was captured outside the manor; a tenant who was arrested for larceny within a manor.

outfit. Equipment for work or activity, such as for plumbers, carpenters, or campers. Equipment for an expedition. The clothing, arms, and accouterments of a soldier. 36 Am J1st Mil § 16. A military unit, especially a division of the Army. An allowance made by the government to its foreign ministers and ambassadors.
See **ship and outfit**.

outhouse. A building, such as a barn, shed, or garage upon the same premises, and having a connection with the use of the dwelling house. A building adjacent to a dwelling house and subservient thereto, but distinct from the mansion itself. 5 Am J2d Arson § 20. An outside toilet or privy.

outhouse where people resort. A phrase appearing in statutes for the suppression of gambling, meaning any house on the premises standing apart from the house used as a dwelling house or place of business. 24 Am J1st Gaming § 29.

outland (out'lạnd). That part of a manor which was occupied by a tenant.

outlaw. In the modern sense of the term, a notorious criminal, especially when a fugitive from the law. At common law, one made defendant in an outlawry proceeding or judicially declared to be an outlaw in a regular proceeding brought for the purpose of such declaration. Dale County v Gunter, 46 Ala 118, 140.
An outlaw is one who is put out of the law; that is, deprived of its benefits and protection. In earlier times he was called a friendless man; one who could not, by law, have a friend. An outlaw was said caput genere lupinum, by which it was meant, that any one might knock him on the head as a wolf, in case he would not surrender himself peaceably when taken. He forfeited everything he had, whether it was in right or possession. All obligations and contracts were dissolved. But in modern times the word has a much less stringent meaning, importing, however, the forfeiture of property and civil rights. Drew v Drew, 37 Me 389, 391.

outlawed. In the earlier common law, the judicial determination and declaration that a named person was an outlaw. In the modern parlance of the layman and to some extent of the profession, barred by the statute of limitations. Drew v Drew, 37 Me 389, 391.

outlawry. A common-law doctrine, long since abolished or come into disuse in the United States, whereunder the property of one convicted of a crime was forfeited to the crown or state, he being placed, as it were, outside the law. United States v Hall, 198 F2d 726, 34 ALR2d 1088. A proceeding at common law under which by judgment a man was placed out of the protection of the law. A judgment declaring the defendant in such proceeding to be an outlaw. See 3 Bl Comm 284. See also Respublica v Doan (US) 1 Dall 86, 1 L Ed 47.
See **outlaw**.

outlay. An expense.

outlet. A way of escape for waters from a lake or a pond. 56 Am J1st Wat § 63. A place or means of disposal of particular articles of merchandise.

out of court. Not in or before the court; as, a settlement out of court. Having suffered nonsuit or dismissal.

out of employment. Not working. In a distinct sense, arising from employment. Gage v Connecticut General Life Ins. Co. (Mo App) 273 SW2d 761, 47 ALR2d 1234.

out-of-kilter (out-of-kil'tėr). A colloquial expression for out of order, not in condition for use, as a machine with broken working parts. Lonnecker v Borris, 360 Mo 529, 229 SW2d 524, 18 ALR2d 968.

out of my estate. A phrase in a clause of a will directing payment of an estate or succession tax, having reference to the residuary estate, that being sufficient, or the general estate of the testator. Anno: 37 ALR2d 111.

out of pocket. Spent; disbursed.

out-of-pocket expense. Expense which one is compelled to incur and pay.

out-of-pocket-loss rule. A rule of damages for fraud in misrepresentation of value, quality, or condition of property, that the defrauded party is entitled not to the benefit of the bargain, but only to the amount that he is "out-of-pocket" by reason of the fraud, which is the difference between the real value of the misrepresented property and the amount that he paid therefor. 37 Am J2d Fraud § 355; 55 Am J1st V & P § 573.

out of term. Between terms of court; at a time when no session of the court was held.

out of the state. Absent from the state. 34 Am J1st Lim Ac § 215.

out of time. Not on time; overdue; as a ship which has not arrived at the time expected. Appearing in the wrong generation; not in accord with modern customs, habits, and practices.

outparter (out'pärt-ėr). A cattle thief

out patient. A person who calls for medical treatment at a hospital, without becoming a room or ward patient.

outpeny (out'pen-i). The customary payment made

in the early period of the common law by a tenant upon the termination of the tenancy.

output. The production of a factory or plant for any given time. Anno: 1 ALR 1393.

outrage. An aggravated wrong. A bold or wanton injury to person or property; wanton mischief; gross injury. Mosnat v Snyder, 105 Iowa 500, 504, 75 NW 356. A rape.

outrage and indignity. A wrong capable of causing mental anguish in addition to bodily suffering. McKinley v Chicago & Northwestern Railroad Co. 44 Iowa 314.

outrageous battery. Malicious acts akin to mayhem. Clyde v Parillo, 25 NJ Misc 492, 55 A2d 810.

outre (ö-trā'). Outside; beyond.

outrefois acquit (ö-tr-foa a-ki). Same as **autrefois acquit**.

outre mere (ö-trā' mãr). Beyond the sea. Lands beyond the sea.

outrider (out'rī"dėr). A deputy sheriff who summoned persons at a distance to attend the county court; a highwayman. A rider on horseback who accompanies a carriage or coach.

outright gift. An absolute gift.

outroper (out'rō-pėr). A licensed auctioneer.

outside activities. Private employment or business pursued by a public officer or public employee. 43 Am J1st Pub Of § 265.

outside elevator. An elevator maintained in connection with the use of a building, but outside the building, such as an elevator reached through an opening in the sidewalk.

outside hazard. A hazard to a traveler on the highway, located on the margin, that is, outside the traveled portion. 25 Am J1st High § 528.

outstanding accounts. Unpaid accounts, both good and bad. 1 Am J2d Acctg § 2. Sometimes construed in accordance with custom as including accounts remaining after the bad accounts have been charged to profit and loss. McCulsky v Klosterman, 20 Or 108, 25 P 366.

outstanding and open account. An unpaid account not adjusted or reduced to a written obligation. 1 Am J2d Acctg § 2.

outstanding crop. A growing crop in the field, without reference to the state of growth. Sullins v State, 53 Ala 474, 476.

outstanding interest. The interest of a third party not directly involved in the transaction. So, an interest in mortgaged property other than that of mortgagor and mortgagee. 36 Am J1st Mtg § 199. An interest in property seized under execution other than that of the judgment debtor. 30 Am J2d Exec §§ 443 et seq. A claim of title in himself by a person who asserts such claim adversely to the ostensible owner of the land.

outstanding in the state. See **obligations or liabilities outstanding in the state.**

outstanding note. A note which is still a liability. Spring v Hill, 6 Cal 17.

outstandings. Debts outstanding against an applicant for credit insurance. 29A Am J Rev ed Ins § 1005. Uncollected debts; uncollected revenues. McCulsky v Klosterman, 20 Or 108, 25 P 366.

outstanding stock. Shares of corporate stock held as obligations of the corporation, as distinguished from treasury stock. Borg v International Silver Co. (CA2 NY) 11 F2d 147.

outstanding term. A lease for a term of years entitled to protection against grantees, heirs, and devisees of the lessor.

outstanding title. See **outstanding interest**.

outstroke mining. See **mining by outstroke**.

outsucken multures (out'suk"n mul'tụrs). Payments which were made by a tenant for having his grain ground at a mill at which his tenure did not bind him to have it ground.

outvote. To win an election. To cast more votes than are cast in an comparable precinct, district, or political subdivision.

outworker. Same as **homeworker**.

ouverte. Same as **overt**.

ovel. Equal. Same as **owel**.

ovelty. Same as **owelty**.

over. See **bind over; pleading over; remedy over**.

overboard. Out of the vessel and into the water.

overbreak. An engineering term signifying that portion of the material removed by a blast which was outside and beyond the slopes indicated by the slope stakes. Porter v State, 141 Wash 51, 250 P 449.

overcertification. The act of an officer or agent of a bank in certifying a check when the amount called for does not actually stand to the credit of the drawer on the books of the the bank. 10 Am J2d Banks § 229.

overcharge. An excessive charge. A charge of more than is permitted by law. Woodhouse v Rio Grande Railway Co. 67 Tex 416, 418. A charge made by a carrier for transportation services in excess of those applicable thereto under the tariffs lawfully on file with the Interstate Commerce Commission. 49 USC §§ 16(3) (g), 304(a) (5), 1006(a) (5).

The term "overcharge" as used by the Interstate Commerce Commission covers only cases where carriers have demanded and received a rate in excess of the published rate; it is not used in referring to cases where the published rate has been collected but is alleged, on one ground or another, to be an excessive rate. Miller v Davis, 213 Iowa 1091, 240 NW 743.

overcrowding. The act of a carrier in putting too many passengers in a conveyance.

overcyhsed. Same as **overcyted**.

overcyted. Found guilty; convicted.

overdraft. An overdrawing by a bank depositor. A payment by a bank from its funds of a check or draft drawn upon it by a depositor who does not have sufficient funds on deposit to pay the check or draft. American Surety Co. v First Nat. Bank (DC W Va) 50 F Supp 180.

An overdraft arises when, by check, draft, or order, a customer of the bank draws from that bank more money than is standing to his credit in his account with the bank. State v Jackson, 21 SD 494, 113 NW 880. The amount of an overdraft is not necessarily the sum drawn, but is the amount drawn less the amount to which the drawer, at the time, is entitled to a credit balance upon his ac-

OVERDRAW [904] **OVERREACHING**

count. Armstrong v Chemical Nat. Bank (CC NY) 41 F 234.

overdraw. See **overdraft.**

overdue. Past due. Having run beyond maturity.
Sometimes the term "overdue" is used in reference to a right of action against a drawer or indorser of a bill of exchange. In that connection a bill is not "overdue" until presented to the payee for payment, and payment refused. Sometimes the term is used in considering whether an indorser has been released by a failure of the holder to present the bill for payment, and to give the indorser notice of its dishonor within a reasonable time. The term is also applied to a bill which has come into the hands of an indorser, so long after its issue as to charge him with notice of its dishonor, and thus subject it in his hands to the defenses which the drawer had against it in the hands of the assignor. La Due v First Nat. Bank of Kasson, 31 Minn 33, 38.
See **maturity.**

overdue paper. An obligation for the payment of money not paid at maturity as fixed by the terms of the instrument or as extended by agreement of the parties.

overflow. To flow over; to flow over the bounds, over the brim; to cover with or as with water or other fluid; to spread over; to inundate: as, when one wrongfully diverts surface water and causes it to overflow another's land, causing damage. Miller v Letzerich, 121 Tex 248, 49 SW2d 404, 85 ALR 451.

overflowed lands. Lands which are covered by non-navigable waters, or are subject to such periodical or frequent overflows of water, salt or fresh (not including lands between high and low water marks of navigable streams or bodies of water, nor lands covered and uncovered by the ordinary daily ebb and flow of normal tides of navigable waters), as to require drainage or levees or embankments to keep out the water, and thereby render the lands suitable for successful cultivation. State of Florida ex rel. Ellis v Gerbing, 56 Fla 603, 47 So 353.
See **submerged lands.**

overflowing waters. See **flood waters.**

overhang. That part of a railroad car or streetcar which extends beyond the rails upon which the car is running. 14 Am J2d Car § 979.

overhanging roof. A roof extending over an adjoining property. Sometimes legalized as a continuous easement. Bubser v Ranguette, 269 Mich 388, 257 NW 845.

overhanging sign. A sign placed in such position that it overhangs the sidewalk or street. 3 Am J2d Advertg § 9.

overhanging structure. A structure with projections, particularly projections extending over an adjoining property.

overhaul. To repair completely; to recondition.

overhauling. Overtaking. Examining completely to determine needed repairs.
See **reconditioning.**

overhead. Wages and salaries, rent, telephone service, cost of office supplies, etc. 13 Am J2d Bldg Contr § 20. For the purpose of fixing the rates of a public utility, expenses for services of a nonproductive nature. Lytle, Campbell & Co. v Somers, Fitler, & Todd Co. 276 Pa 409, 120 A 409, 27 ALR 41, 43.
See **operating expenses of a public utility.**

overhead crossing. A highway elevated and crossing over a railroad track, thereby avoiding a grade crossing. One railroad elevated and crossing above another railroad. 44 Am J1st RR § 286. A highway elevated and crossing over another highway, common in modern highway systems.

overhead door. A door having hinged sections, engaged at the top with an overhead track to permit it to be pushed up and extended at some height in the building in opening it to permit ingress or egress; used extensively in garages, both public and private, and other places of business or work where vehicles are frequently driven in and out.

overhead expenses. Same as **overhead.**

overhead handrail. A handrail anchored in the top of a bus, upon which a standing passenger may seize in an emergency to prevent being thrown by a sudden movement or stopping of the bus. Fisher v Whitaker (Ky) 260 SW2d 651.

overhead rack. A rack on the side of a railroad car, bus, or airplane being located above the seated passengers, for wearing apparel and small articles of luggage. 14 Am J2d Car § 1034.

overhead through rate. Same as **through rate.**

overhead use. See **supersurface use.**

overinsurance. The existence of insurance upon the same risk in violation of the condition of the policy concerning other insurance unknown to the insurer or obtained without the consent of the insurer. 29A Am J Rev ed Ins § 954. A condition leading to fraud or carelessness on the part of the insured, there being less reason for him to desire the preservation of the property. 29A Am J Rev ed Ins § 954.
See **excess insurance.**

overissue. An issue of stock by a corporation in excess of the amount prescribed or limited by its charter. 18 Am J2d Corp § 230. An issue of bonds by a corporation in excess of the limit placed upon the amount of bonded indebtedness by the charter. 19 Am J2d Corp § 1061.

overloading. Crowding a passenger car or bus. Exceeding the license limit on the number of passengers, or the licensed weight, to be carried by an aircraft. Ziser v Colonial Western Airways, Inc. 10 NJ Misc 1118, 162 A 591. Violation of statute or regulation limiting the number of domestic animals to be carried in a single stock car in railroad transportation. Making an excessive charge for operating expenses or the maintenance of contingency reserves in calculating the amount of the premium to be charged for insurance.

overlord. A feudal superior; a master.

overpayment. A payment in excess of the amount of the obligation.
As the word is used in the Federal Revenue Act of 1932, Section 621(d), it is broad enough to include payments erroneously or illegally assessed as well as payments excessive in amount. D. Gottlieb & Co. v Harrison (DC Ill) 27 F Supp 424.

overplus. That which remains; a balance left over. An excess of acreage in a survey of public land. 12 Am J2d Bound § 62.

overreaching. Fraudulent conduct in taking unfair advantage.

overreaching clause. A clause in an indenture creating powers which refers for some powers to an extrinsic instrument, noting that such powers may be in excess of, that is, overreach the powers created by the indenture.

overriding royalty. A royalty, payable under an oil lease, consisting of a designated fraction or percentage of the working interest or of the total production. 24 Am J1st Gas & O § 87. Such fractional interest in the production of oil and gas as is created from the lessee's estate, whether by reservation when the original lessee transfers his interest by a sublease, or by grant when the original lessee conveys a fractional share to a third person. La Laguna Ranch Co. v Dodge, 18 Cal 2d 132, 114 P2d 351, 135 ALR 546.

overriding veto. The enactment of a statute or ordinance, after a veto of the measure by the executive, by the passage of the measure by a stated percentage, fixed by constitution or statute, of the votes of the legislative body. 37 Am J1st Mun Corp § 148; 50 Am J1st Stat § 112.

overrule. To refuse to grant; to deny, as where the court denies an objection by counsel; to set at naught; to annul.

overruling precedent. The nullification of a prior decision as a precedent by a constitutionally valid statute or the rendition of a decision by the same court or by a higher ranking court which establishes a different rule on the point of law involved. 20 Am J2d Cts § 231.

oversamessa. A fine imposed for a contempt of court or for permitting an escape.

over sea. Beyond the sea. Outside the jurisdiction.

overseas bill of lading. The form of a bill of lading provided by UCC § 2–323.

The provisions of the Uniform Commercial Code relating to bill of lading in overseas trade will not have frequent application, because bills of lading covering export are governed by the Federal Bills of Lading Act and federal regulations, while the negotiability of bills covered by exports is generally determined by the law of the foreign country in which the bill was issued.

overseers of highways. Officers charged with the duty of laying out and maintaining highways within their districts.

overseers of the poor. Local officials to whom is delegated the ministerial work in regard to the relief of the poor. 41 Am J1st Poor L § 15.

oversell. To sell a greater quantity than one can deliver.

oversize baggage. Baggage exceeding the dimensions given in the tariff filed by a carrier with the Interstate Commerce Commission. NAACP v Richmond Greyhound Lines, Inc. 246 NC 547, 99 SE2d 756, 68 ALR2d 1341.

oversman (ō'vėrz-mąn). An umpire chosen by arbitrators to settle a controversy upon the failure of the arbitrators to agree on a settlement.

overt (ō'vėrt). Open. Johnson v State, 125 Tenn 420, 143 SW 1134. Open to view. Admitting to direct evidence. Ashcraft v United States Fidelity & Guaranty Co. (Ky) 255 SW2d 485, 37 ALR2d 1078.

overt act. An act carrying an intent into effect. An open act; a physical act, as distinguished from an act of the mind; an act done pursuant to a formed intent, design, plan, or conspiracy. An act demonstrating a purpose and committed without attempt at concealment. In criminal assault:—a demonstration consisting of an attempt or offer to do injury to the person of another, 6 Am J2d Asslt & B § 22, exciting fear of immediate personal harm or disgrace. Merritt v Commonwealth, 164 Va 653, 180 SE 395. In homicide:—an open act, indicating a present purpose to do immediate great bodily harm. Johnson v State, 125 Tenn 265, 143 SW 1134. For the purposes of a conspiracy:—an act performed for the purpose of carrying out the conspiracy, a step toward its execution, and a manifestation that the conspiracy is at work. 16 Am J2d Consp § 11.

Although intent sometimes may make criminal an otherwise innocent act, the law is not concerned with mere guilty intention, unconnected with any overt act or outward manifestation. People v Belcastro, 356 Ill 144, 190 NE 301, 92 ALR 1223.

overtaking and passing. A manipulation of a motor vehicle whereby, upon coming up behind another vehicle, the former is turned into another lane of traffic, preferably a lane to the inside of the other vehicle, and additional motive power applied to enable the one vehicle to go by the other and return to its original lane of traffic. 8 Am J2d Auto §§ 778 et seq. A rule of navigation which places upon the overtaking vessel the responsibility of avoiding collision with the overtaken vessel. 48 Am J1st Ship § 259.

See **passing on the right**.

overtaking vessel. A vessel approaching another vessel from astern which continues to be an overtaking vessel until she has passed clear of the vessel overtaken. The Lackawanna (CA2 NY) 119 F2d 666.

See **overtaking and passing**.

overte. Same as **overt**.

over-the-counter market. A market in securities other than that existing in transactions through established stock exchanges. Fratt v Robinson (CA9 Wash) 203 F2d 627, 37 ALR2d 636. A market established by transactions directly between brokers and brokerage offices.

overtillage. Bad or inefficient husbandry in farming ground to the point of exhaustion of the soil. 56 Am J1st Waste § 17.

overtime. Work performed over and above the period of the regular working day. Work in addition to the regular hours for which compensation is calculated under the contract of employment. 35 Am J1st M & S § 66. Work after regular hours; sometimes work after hours fixed by contract at less than the statutory maximum hours; sometimes hours worked outside of a specified clock pattern without regard to whether previous work has been done, for example, Sunday or holiday labor. 31 Am J Rev ed Lab § 611.

overtime premium. Extra pay for overtime work. 31 Am J Rev ed Lab § 611.

overturning. Upsetting. As the word appears in a policy of automobile insurance:—loss of equilibrium and overbalancing to the extent of placing the vehicle beyond the power of those in charge to stop its movement. 7 Am J2d Auto Ins § 62.

A loaded truck the wheels of which sank in a soft shoulder, tipping the truck sufficiently to spill a considerable portion of the load, was held "overturned" within the meaning of a policy insuring against loss by overturning. Moore v Western Assur. Co. 186 SC 260, 195 SE 558.

oves (ō'vēz). Sheep.

ovesque (ō-vesk'). With.

ovis (ō'vis). (Latin.) Sheep.

owe. To be legally indebted. Succession of Guidry, 40 La Ann 671, 673, 4 So 893. To be under a political, moral, or social obligation.

owel (ō'el). Equal.

owele. Equal. Same as **owel**.

owel main (man). See **en owel main**.

owelty (ō'el-ti). Equality. A sum paid or secured, in the case of an actual partition of land in which the portions set off are not of equal value, by him who receives the more valuable portion to him who receives the lesser in value, for the purpose of equalizing the shares in value. Waller v George, 322 Mo 573, 16 SW2d 63.

owing. Due. United States v State Bank (US) 6 Pet 29, 8 L Ed 308.
See **owe**.

owler (ou'lẽr). A person who is guilty of owling.

owling (oul'ing). A crime which was so called from its being usually carried on in the night, and which consisted of transporting wool or sheep out of England.
The offense existed at common law, but was also made a statutory offense in the reign of Edward the Third. See 4 Bl Comm 154. Being out very late at night for pleasure, often for dissipation.

own. To be the owner of anything. State ex rel. Cole v District Court, 79 Mont 11, 254 P 863. To acknowledge; to admit.

own cousin. Same as **first cousin**.

owner. One who has complete dominion over particular property. 42 Am J1st Prop § 37. The person in whom the legal or equitable title rests. Anno: 2 ALR 779, s. 95 ALR 1086. In common understanding, the person who, in case of the destruction of property, must sustain the loss. 42 Am J1st Prop § 37.
As to the meaning of "owner" as used in statutes relating to the assessment and collection of taxes, see Anno: 2 ALR 792.
As to the meaning of the word "owner" as used in statutes penalizing unlawful cutting of timber, see Anno: 2 ALR 799.
As to the meaning of the term "owner" as used in statutes declaring who may redeem from sale under execution, see Anno: 2 ALR 794.
As to meaning of "owner" as used in real property statutes, see Anno: 2 ALR 778.
As to the meaning of the term "owner" as used in statutes relating to trespass or forcible entry and detainer, see Anno: 2 ALR 798.
See **landowner**.

owner identification sign. A requirement of statutes intended to prevent or limit the control of retail liquor dealers by distillers, wholesalers, and importers, the retail dealer being under duty to maintain a posted sign in his establishment showing the owner or owners thereof.

owner in fee. See **fee simple**.

owner of automobile. Not a technical term for the purposes of a registration statute; not confined to a sole owner or a person having an absolute right in the vehicle, and sometimes inclusive of a part owner or a conditional purchaser. 7 Am J2d Auto § 83.
A statute imposing liability on the "owner" of a car for damages resulting from its negligent operation by another extends to plural owners of a single automobile, so as to fasten liability on all of them. Sexton v Lauman, 244 Iowa 570, 57 NW2d 200, 37 ALR2d 353.

owner of land. See **landowner**.

owner of record. Same as **record owner**.

ownership. The rights of an owner. Title to property. Dominion over property. The right of possession and control of property, including the right to protect and defend such possession against the intrusion or trespass of others. 42 Am J1st Prop § 40. The right to dispose of a thing as one pleases, provided the rights of others are not thereby infringed or some law violated. See Higgins Oil & Fuel Co. v Guaranty Oil Co. 145 La 233, 82 So 206, 5 ALR 411, 414.
See **owner**; **title**.

ownership-in-place theory. The principle followed in a number of jurisdictions that oil and gas in place belong to the owner of the land and that he can convey and encumber them the same as any other mineral estate, subject, of course, to the possibility of their escape and resultant loss of title. 24 Am J1st Gas & O § 4.

owner's risk. A term employed by common carriers in bills of lading and shipping receipts to signify that the carrier does not assume responsibility for the safety of the goods. Morrison v Phillips & Colby Constr. Co. 44 Wis 405.

own motion. A disposition made in a pending case by the court, without application made therefor by either party, as where a case is continued without application made therefor, because the judge is needed immediately for the trial of a case of first importance in another division of the court.

own self. See **self**.

own up. Slang for admitting or confessing.

ox. Any animal within the class known as cattle, but particularly one of a type used in some parts of the world, formerly in this country, as a draft animal. A refined word for bull. Slang for a big boy or man.

oxen. Plural of **ox**.

oxfild (oks'fild). A restitution made by a hundred for an injury which was committed therein.

oxgang (oks'gang). The maximum quantity of land which was tillable by one ox; a quantity reckoned at between thirteen to fifteen acres.

ox-land. Same as **oxgang**.

oyer (ō'yr). To hear. The right to hear an instrument read. A hearing at common law on a bail bond. 8 Am J2d Bail § 154.

oyer and terminer (ō'yẽr and ter'mi-nẽr). A special or extraordinary commission which the king sometimes issued upon urgent occasions to try those criminal cases which stood in need of immediate prosecution. See 3 Bl Comm 270.

oyez (ō'yez). Hear ye.

oyster. A marine mollusk, relished as food by most people. Figuratively, a source of benefit or advantage.
See **shellfish**.

oystery (ois'tẽr-i). An oyster bed privately cultivated for the production of oysters commercially. A particular kind of fishing, included in a right of fishery Moulton v Libbey, 37 Me 472.

P

p. Abbreviation of page.

P. Roman numeral for 400.

p.a. Abbreviation of **per annum**.

paage. Same as **pedage**.

pacare (pa-kā're). To pay.

pacatio (pa-kā'she-ō). A payment.

pacato solo. See **in pacato solo**.

pace (pās). A linear measure of two and one-half feet. A step.

Paceatur (pa-se-ā'ter). Let him be released or discharged.

pace et imprisonamento. See **de pace et imprisonamento**.

pace et legalitate tuenda. See **de pace et legalitate tuenda**.

pace et plagis. See **de pace et plagis**.

pace et roberia. See **de pace et roberia**.

pace infracta. See **de pace infracta**.

pacific blockade. An interdiction of commerce with another nation, declared by way of retaliation or retorsion. 30 Am J Rev ed Internat L § 53.

Pacific Railroad Act. The federal statute of July 1, 1862, the purpose of which was to aid in the construction, maintenance, and operation of railroad and telegraph lines over routes specified, to promote the public interest and welfare, and to secure to the government the use of the same for postal, military, and other purposes. 52 Am J1st Teleg & T § 26.

Pacific time. One of the belts of standard time. See **standard time**.

pacifist (pas'i-fist). One opposed to war or the use of force against another nation or another people.
The word is also used and understood to mean one who refuses or is unwilling for any purpose to bear arms because of conscientious considerations and who is disposed to encourage others in such refusal. United States v Schwimmer, 279 US 644, 73 L Ed 889, 49 S Ct 448.

Paci sunt maxime contraria, vis et injuria (pa'sī sunt ma'xi-mē kon-trā'ri-a, vīs et in-jū'ri-a). Violence and injury are the greatest opponents of peace.

pack. Verb: To place together and prepare for transportation, as to make up a bundle or bale. State v Parsons, 124 Mo 436, 27 SW 1102. To put in a container. To admit more people into a place than it will hold comfortably. To fill a theater, auditorium, or other place of public exhibition or entertainment. Colloquially, in the Midwest, to carry a bundle, basket, or bag. Noun: A package; a bundle. The stores of an expedition carried in vehicles, on the backs of animals, or on the shoulders of men.

package. A bundle or parcel made up of several smaller parcels, combined or bound together in one bale, box, crate, etc. Commonwealth v Schollenberger, 156 Pa 201, 27 A 30. A bundle or bale made up for transportation, sometimes holding only a single article. State v Parsons, 124 Mo 436, 27 SW 1102. Something wrapped, boxed, or crated, rather than merely covered. Anno: 94 ALR2d 1419. Two things: (1) a receptacle of whatever form or character, and (2) the contents thereof. Mexican Petroleum Corp. v South Portland, 121 Me 128, 115 A 900, 26 ALR 965. In reference to misbranding or adulteration of food:—the immediate container of the article intended for consumption by the public. 35 Am J2d Food § 31. As the word appears in the statute respecting the labeling of drugs:—the immediate container of the drug, not the outside wrapping or box containing the parcels made up and intended for sale to the ultimate consumer. Seven Cases v United States, 239 US 510, 60 L Ed 411, 36 S Ct 190.
See **original package**.

package sale. A sale of liquor in a store in bottle or package, rather than by dispensed drinks.

packer. A person owning, operating, or managing a packinghouse. A corporation engaged in the marketing of meat food products and in the business of manufacturing meats or meat food products for sale or shipment in commerce. United Corp. v Federal Trade Com. (CA4) 110 F2d 473. One who processes and packs goods, particularly articles of food, for preservation and ultimate sale. One employed in placing merchandise or other articles in packages.

Packers and Stockyards Act. A federal statute, enacted in 1921, which imposes conditions upon the right to engage in business as commission men and livestock dealers in stockyards and provides for the regulation of such business in various respects. 7 USC §§ 181 et seq., 201 et seq.

packet. A small parcel. An old term of the postal laws for a written communication on four or more sheets of letter or correspondence-size paper. Williams v Wells, Fargo & Co. Express (CA8 Ark) 177 F 352.

packinghouse. A place where animals are slaughtered and their carcasses prepared and preserved for ultimate sale as meat products or other products obtained from the carcass. A place where vegetables and fruits are processed and canned.

packing jury. The employment of any means in violation of law for seating upon the jury in a particular case persons whose presence upon the jury is desired in preference to other persons. Strauder v West Virginia, 100 US 303, 309, 25 L Ed 664, 666.

packing price. Raising the price in order to obtain an outrageous profit. Plymouth Dealers Asso. v United States (CA9 Cal) 279 F2d 128.

pact (pakt). A compact; a contract; an agreement; a stipulation.

Pacta conventa quae neque contra leges, neque dolo malo inita sunt, omni modo observanda sunt (pak'ta kon-ven'ta kwē ne'kwe kon'tra le'jēz, ne'kwe dō'lō ma'lō in'i-ta sunt, om'ni mō'dō ob-ser-van'da sunt). Agreements which are neither contrary to the laws, nor fraudulently entered into, should be adhered to in every manner. See Broom's Legal Maxims 698.

Pacta dant legem contractui (pak'ta dant lē'jem kontrak'tu-i). The stipulations furnish the law for the contract.

Pacta privata juri publico derogare non possunt (pak'ta prī-vā'ta jū'rī pub'li-kō de-ro-gā're non pos'sunt). Private contracts cannot impair public law. Anderson v Eggers, 63 NJ Eq 264, 49 A 578.

Pacta privata non derogant juri communi (pak'ta prī-vā'ta non de'ro-gant jū'rī kom-mū'nī). Private agreements do not derogate from common right.

Pacta quae contra leges constitutionesque vel contra bonos mores fiunt, nullam vim habere, indubitati juris est (pak'ta kwē kon'tra lē'jĕz kon-sti-tu-she-ō-nes'kwe vel kon'tra bō'nos mō'rez fī'unt, nul'lam vim ha-bē're, in-du-bi-tā'ti jū'ris est). (Civil law.) It is unquestionably the law that agreements which are made contrary to the laws and the statutes or against good morals, are of no force in law.

Pacta quae turpem causam continent non sunt observanda (pak'ta kwē ter'pem kâ'sam kon'ti-nent non sunt ob-ser-van'da). Contracts which contain an unlawful consideration will not be enforced.

pact de non alienando (pakt de non a-li-en-an'do). A provision commonly contained in Louisiana mortgages whereby the mortgagee is relieved of making the holder of a subsequent mortgage a party to a suit to foreclose the prior mortgage.

The effect of such a provision in the mortgage is that the subsequent mortgagee must take notice of the proceedings at his peril. He may, however, apply to set aside the sale. 37 Am J1st Mtg § 552.

pacti conventi. See **exceptio pacti conventi.**

pactio (pak'she-ō). (Civil law.) A pact; a contract; an agreement; a bargain; a treaty; a covenant.

paction (pak'shon). A pact; a contract; a treaty.

Pactis privatorum juri publico non derogatur (pak'tis prī-vā-tō'rum jū'rī pub'li-kō non de-ro-gā'ter). Private contracts do not derogate from public law.

pactitious (pak-tish'us). Settled by a pact or contract.

Pacto aliquod licitum est, quid sine pacto non admittitur (pak'tō a'li-quod li'si-tum est, quid sī'ne pak'tō non ad-mit'ti-ter). By agreement a certain thing may be lawful which without the agreement would not be allowed.

pactum (pak'tum). (Civil law.) Same as **pactio.**

pactum de quota litis (pak'tum dē quō'ta lī'tis). (Civil law.) An agreement by which a person undertook to collect a debt in return for a specified share of the amount collected.

pactum vestitum (pak'tum ves-ti'tum). (Civil law.) A clothed or vested agreement,—an agreement or promise for which there was no consideration, but which was enforceable because of the formality of its execution. Aller v Aller, 40 NJL 446, 450.

pad. Verb: To fill out a hollow space. To make a cushion. To lengthen a speech or article by the inclusion of the nonessential. To increase an account fraudulently, particularly an expense account. Noun: A cushion. A foundation, as for launching a rocket. A tablet of sheets of paper for writing. A slang term for one's living quarters.

padder (pad'ẽr). A footpad; a highwayman on foot; a robber. Literally, one who pads.
See **pad.**

padding payroll. The act of a foreman or other employee in charge of a payroll in allowing unearned time to one or more employees. Anno: 41 ALR 235.

paddy. Rice; a rice field. An effigy of St. Patrick, used in certain parts of Pennsylvania to provoke a riot. Commonwealth v Haines (Pa) 4 Clark 17.

paddy wagon. A police vehicle used for taking arrested persons to jail or to court for arraignment.

padlock laws. Statutes which authorize the courts to order that premises constituting a liquor nuisance may not be occupied or used for any purpose for a specified period of time. 30 Am J Rev ed Intox L § 444.

paga (pah'gah). (Spanish.) Payment.

paganism (pā'gan-izm). The religion of all those persons who have not the true God, but worship idols. Robbin's Religions of All Nations. Hale v Everett, 53 NH 9. In the modern sense, one who does not believe, as do Christians, Moslems, and Jews, in one God.

page. One side of a leaf in a book, magazine, or newspaper.

page cost. An allowance for printing the record on appeal, according to a stated sum per page. 5 Am J2d A & E § 1021.

pagus (pā'gus). A county.

paid. Recompensed by an actual receipt of money or an equivalent in value. Canadian Car & Foundry Co. v American Can Co. (CA2 NY) 258 F 363, 6 ALR 1182, 1191.

paid and satisfied. Paid in fact.
See **satisfaction of judgment.**

paid reading matter. That part of the content of a newspaper for which money was paid to obtain right of publication. Anno: 35 ALR 12, s. 110 ALR 332.

paid-up addition. The amount of paid-up life insurance purchased, and added to the amount of insurance provided by the policy, by the use of the dividend to which insured was entitled as a single premium. 29 Am J Rev ed Ins § 648.

paid-up insurance. Life insurance under a policy which shall continue in effect for the full period of the insured's life, the premiums having been fully paid so as to call for no further payment by the insured to keep the policy effective against lapse. Lenon v Mutual Life Ins. Co. 80 Ark 563, 98 SW 117; Hamilton v Mutual Ben. Ins. Co. 109 Ga 381, 382. The amount of insurance which the existing cash surrender value of a life insurance policy will purchase, the same to remain in effect during the full period of the insured's life without payment of additional premiums. 29 Am J Rev ed Ins § 619.

paid-up stock. Corporate stock issued upon subscription therefor and full payment of the subscription price. A share in a building and loan association for which the holder has paid in full. 13 Am J2d B & L Assoc § 23.

pain. The sensation one feels when hurt. A protopathic sensation located in the nervous system. 22 Am J2d Damg § 105. Distress of the body or the mind.
See **mental anguish; physical suffering; suffering.**

paine forte et dure (pen fort ay dür). Same as **peine forte et dure.**

Paine's Age of Reason (pāns āj of rē'zon). A book written by Thomas Paine, an Englishman, published in 1794, containing statements denying the truth of the Scriptures and the story of Christ. Anno: 14 ALR 888.

pains. Plural of pain. Great effort to please or to accomplish in a most satisfactory manner.

pains and penalties. See **bill of pains and penalties.**

painter. An artisan. One who paints houses and other structures; a "laborer" for the purposes of an

exemption from execution. 31 Am J2d Exemp § 20. An artist. A rope for tying a boat to a wharf.

painters' colic. Same as **lead poisoning**.

painter's naptha (pān'tėrz nap'thạ). A product of successive distillation of crude oil. United States v Gulf Refining Co. 268 US 542, 547, 69 L Ed 1082, 1086, 45 S Ct 597.

paint stone. A mineral. Hartwell v Camman, 10 NJ Eq 128.

pairing. A practice followed in legislative bodies by members who will be absent from the body for necessity or convenience at a time when a measure is coming up for consideration and vote, whereby a member in favor of the measure and a member opposed to it each agree that in no event will he vote on the measure unless or until the agreement thus made has been terminated.

pairt. See **airt and pairt**.

pais (pā). The country; the jury; outside of court.
See **estoppel in pais; in pais**.

paix (pā). Peace.

palabra. See **de palabra**.

palace car. See **stock car**.

palace court (pal'ạs kōrt). An English court of justice which had jurisdiction in all personal actions which arose within twelve miles of the palace of the king.

palagium (pa-lā'ji-um). A duty which was imposed upon lords of manors for exporting and importing vessels of wine at any of their ports.

palam (pa'lam). (Civil law.) Openly; publicly; without concealment.

Palatinate (pạ-lat'i-nạt). A district in West Germany, the name deriving from former rulers known as count palatines.

palatine (pal'ạ-tin). Pertaining to a royal palace; possessing royal privileges.
See **counties palatine; courts of the counties palatine**.

palatium (pa-lā'she-um). A palace.

pallio cooperire (pal'li-ō ko-ō-pe-rī're). The marriage of the parents of an illegitimate child or children followed by a formal adoption of the child or children.

palm off. To palm off means to impose by fraud; to put off by unfair means. Hobart v Young, 63 Vt 363, 21 A 612.

palming off goods. The substitution by a dealer of his own or another's goods in the place of those called for by the purchaser, the substitution being made without the latter's consent. 52 Am J1st Tradem § 123.

palmistry. The practice of foretelling the fortune of a person by reading the lines which appear upon the palm of the hand. A crafty science whereby the simple minded are apt to be deceived. 36 Am J2d Fortunetelling § 2.

palm print. An impression left by the lines of the palm of the hand upon a smooth object. Proof of identity where authenticated and compared with other palm prints found at or near the scene of a crime. 29 Am J2d Ev § 770.

palpable (pal'pạ-bl). Easily perceptible; plain; obvious; manifest; as palpable error in the valuation of property. State ex rel. Pacific Power & L. Co. v Department of Public Works, 143 Wash 67, 254 P 839, 845.

palpable abuse of discretion. A clear, plain, or manifest abuse of discretion. 5 Am J2d A & E § 774.

Panama Canal Act. A federal statute granting powers to the Interstate Commerce Commission with respect to connections between rail and water transportation, whether by the Panama Canal or otherwise. 49 USC § 6(11)(a); 44 Am J1st R R § 281.

Panama Canal Zone. See **Canal Zone**.

Pandects (pan'dekts). The Digests or Pandects, a compilation of the Roman law under Justinian, which was published in the year 533 A. D.
See **Florentine Pandects**.

pander (pan'dėr). A pimp; a procurer.

pandering. The exploitation of the prostitution of females. 42 Am J1st Prost § 3. The acceptance of the earnings of a prostitute. Anno: 74 ALR 314, 320 et seq.

panel. A division of an administrative commission, the membership being divided, but each division having all the jurisdiction and powers of the commission itself. 2 Am J2d Admin L § 196. A list of jurors, comprising the entire number called for jury duty, a particular number required for a particular court, or the number, normally 12, filling the jury box in a particular case. 31 Am J Rev ed Jury § 74.
The word includes the jurors returned upon a special venire to fill out the deficiency after the regular panel has been exhausted. People v Coyodo, 40 Cal 586, 592.

panis (pan'is). A loaf; a loaf of bread.

pannellation (pan-e-lā'shon). The impaneling of a jury.

paper. See **accommodation paper; commercial paper; in paper; judgment paper; paper blockade; paper-book; paper days; paper money; paper office; paper title; ship's papers; valuable papers**.

paper-back. A book bound in paper rather than leather or cloth.

paper blockade. A blockade which has been duly proclaimed by the constituted authorities, but which has not been effectively enforced.

paper-book. A printed transcript of the record of a case in the trial court, prepared usually for the convenience of the apellate court.
See **paper-back**.

paper days. Those days during a term of court on which arguments were heard.

paper levy. The levy of a writ of attachment upon real estate without going on the land. Moore v Walker, 178 Tenn 218, 156 SW2d 439. The levy of an attachment without seizure or the taking of possession of the property intended to be bound by the levy. 6 Am J2d Attach § 296. The levy of an execution made by the mere indorsement thereof upon the writ. 30 Am J2d Exec § 239.
See **symbolic levy**.

paper money. Money created by public authority, that is, the government, in stamping paper as a medium of payment, indicating the value by denomination, and issuing it to circulate as money. 36 Am J1st Money § 17. Paper that circulates at par without discount. 11 Am J2d B & N § 975.

paper office (pā'pėr of'is). An office of the English government where state papers were kept.

paper patent. A term familiar in the fraternity of patent lawyers. A term applied in scorn or derision in the arguments of patent attorneys to the invention or discovery of the adverse party, meaning that it has never been put into commercial use, never been recognized by the trade, and its possessor has received no royalty for its license. Coltman v Colgate-Palmolive-Peet Co. (CA7 Ind) 104 F2d 508.

papers of ship. See **ship's papers.**

paper title. A title to real estate supported by a chain of conveyances. A title sufficient in support of a plaintiff in ejectment where consisting of a regular chain of title from the government or from some grantor in possession, or a regular chain of title back to the common source from which both plaintiff and his adversary claim. 25 Am J2d eject § 24. A plausible rather than a sound title.
See **color of title.**

Papist. A somewhat derogatory term for a Roman Catholic. 33 Am J1st L & S § 58.

par. Abbreviation of paragraph.

par (pär). Adjective: In the normal or usual condition, especially in reference to a person's health. Average. Noun: A standing of equal status. A fixed value of the money of one country in terms of the value of the money of another country, the exchange rate shifting above or below such fixed value according to the demand in the one country for the currency of the other.
See **par value.**

parade. A demonstration on street or highway in the marching of persons, the riding of horses, the driving of horses or of motor vehicles or vehicles loaded with instruments of war or peace.

paraffin (par'ạ-fin). A hydrocarbon mixture obtained primarily from the distillation of petroleum. 24 Am J1st Gas & O § 123.

paraffin wax. Paraffin in the solid state.

parage (pär'āj). Equality of rank, birth, or station; a bride's marriage portion.

paragium. Same as **parage.**

paragraph. A subdivision, normally indicated by an indent, of a written article, dealing with a particular point of the discussion and preferably unified. A distinct part of a discourse or writing; any section or subdivision of a writing or chapter which relates to a particular point, whether consisting of one or many sentences. Lehmann v Revell, 354 Ill 262, 188 NE 531. In the code pleading of some jurisdictions, a count or integral statement of a cause of action. Bailey v Mosher (CA8 Neb) 63 F 488, 490.

paragraph caption. A heading, appearing at the beginning of a paragraph, more or less indicating the content of the paragraph. Continental Casualty Co. v Trenner (DC Pa) 35 F Supp 643.

parallel. Adjective: Extended in the same direction, and in all parts equidistant; having the same direction or tendency; like; similar. Postal Tel. Cable Co. v Norfolk & Western Railroad Co. 88 Va 920, 926. Noun: A line parallel to the equator. A base line of the government survey of public lands.
See **base line.**

parallel parking. The parking of a motor vehicle close to and parallel with the curb or side of the highway or street. 7 Am J2d Auto § 232; 8 Am J2d Auto § 813.

parallel railroads. A word of art in statutes concerning the consolidation of railroads. Railroad lines, not necessarily equidistant from each other, but having the same general direction in the same section of the country and therefore likely to come in competition with each other. 44 Am J1st R R § 323.

paralysis (pạ-ral'i-sis). Loss of movement, sometimes of sensation, in a portion or all of the body. Klingbeil v Truesdell, 256 Minn 360, 98 NW2d 134.

paramount (par'ạ-mount). Above all. See 2 Bl Comm 59.

paramount force. See **government of paramount force.**

paramount right. A superior right.
See **eviction by title paramount.**

paramount title. A superior title.
See **eviction by title paramount.**

paramour (par'ạ-mör). A mistress. A lover with whom a woman carries on an illicit relationship. One having an illicit relationship, particularly with a married person. The third party in the triangle presented by infidelity. A word imputing want of chastity. 33 Am J1st L & S § 39.

paranoia (par-a-noi'a). A mental disorder characterized by delusions or hallucinations, 26 Am J1st Homi § 81, particularly delusions of grandeur or persecution. 29 Am J Rev ed Ins Per § 3.
A wife's paranoia which created an obsession that her husband was unfaithful to her is not a defense to an action for divorce based on her false accusations of adultery and continual nagging and arguments, where she was able to tell right from wrong. Dochelli v Dochelli, 125 Conn 468, 6 A2d 324.
See **insane delusion.**

parapherna (par-ạ-fèr'nạ). Same as **paraphernalia.**

paraphernalia (par"ạ-fèr-nä'li-ạ). At common and civil law, the apparel and ornaments of the wife, suitable and appropriate to her station, which, although being the property of the husband during his life and subject to the claims of his creditors for the satisfaction of such claims and subject to disposal by the husband except by his will, became, on his death, the exclusive property of the widow as against all persons other than the husband's creditors. 26 Am J1st H & W § 53. In equity and under statute, a separate property of the wife. 26 Am J1st H & W § 54.

paraphernal property (par-ạ-fèr'nàl prop'ẻr-ti). A term, particularly of the law of Louisiana, for that part or portion of the property of a married woman which forms no part of the dotal property. Hayes v Pratt, 147 US 550, 37 L Ed 276, 13 S Ct 495.

paraphrasing. Changing the words but reproducing the meaning. Eisenschiml v Fawcett Publications, Inc. (CA7 Ill) 246 F2d 598, cert den 355 US 907, 2 L Ed 2d 262, 78 S Ct 334.

paratum habeo (pa-rā'tum hā'be-ō). I have him ready.—Formal words used in a sheriff's return on a writ for the arrest of a defendant in a civil action.

Paratus est verificare (pa-rā'tus est ve-ri-fi-kā're). He is ready to verify; he is prepared to verify.

paravail. See **tenant paravail.**

parcel. A lot or tract of real estate. Ramsey County v Robert P. Lewis Co. 72 Minn 87, 75 NW 108. A package.

See **baggage; bill of parcels.**

parcella terrae (par-sel'la ter'rē). A parcel of land.

parcel post. The fourth class of mail matter, established with intent to provide for the public a means of transmission at moderate rates of articles formerly carried only by express companies at high rates. 41 Am J1st P O § 61.

parcel-post zone. An area prescribed by regulation for the purpose of determining the rate to be charged for a parcel mailed to be carried as parcel post, there being a number of such areas, each progressively farther from the office in which a parcel is mailed and numbered accordingly. 41 Am J1st P O § 61.

parcenary. Same as **coparcenary.**

parcener (pär'se-nėr). Same as **coparcener.**

parchment. The skin of an animal prepared as a surface for writing. A fine paper prepared in imitation of a parchment of skin. An instrument or document written on parchment.

parco fracto (par'ko frak'tō). Poundbreach; the breaking of a pound to permit impounded animals to escape.

parcus (par'kus). A park; a cattle pound.

par delictum (par dē-lik'tum). Equal wrong; equal fault.

pardon. Forgiveness, release, or remission. An act of grace proceeding from the power entrusted with the execution of laws, which exempts the individual on whom it is bestowed from the punishment the law inflicts for a crime he has committed. 39 Am J1st Pard § 4. A declaration on record by the chief magistrate of a state or country that a person named is relieved from the legal consequences of a specific crime. Biddle v Perovich, 274 US 480, 71 L Ed 1161, 47 S Ct 664, 52 ALR 832; Lime v Blagg, 345 Mo 1, 131 SW2d 583. A complete release from the control of the state imposed because of the offense. Re Anderson, 191 Or 49, 229 P2d 633, 230 P2d 770, 29 ALR2d 1051, 1073.

pardoning power. The power to grant pardons; an executive power, as it usually exists, but a power within the control of the people and to be conferred by them upon such officer or officers as they see fit. 39 Am J1st Pard § 12.

paree. See **execution paree.**

parens (pa'renz). (Roman law.) A parent; any relative in the direct ascending line.

Parens est nomen generale ad omne genus cognationis (pa'renz est no'men je-ne-rā'le ad om'ne je'nus kog-nä-she-ō'nis). "Parens" is a general name for every kind of relationship.

parens patriae (pa'renz pa'tri-ē). The parent of the country.

parens patriae doctrine (pa'renz pa'tri-ē dok'trin). The doctrine that all orphans, dependent children, and incompetent persons, are within the special protection, and under the control, of the state. 27 Am J1st Inf § 101.

parent. The father or mother. 39 Am J1st P & C § 2. In common parlance, the lawful father or mother by blood. Foreman v Henry, 87 Okla 272, 210 P 1026.
See **person in loco parentis.**

parentage. Parenthood, the state of being a parent. Descent. Family origin. The state of being in a direct ascending line of relationship.

parent corporation. A corporation which owns all or the majority of the stock of another corporation so that the latter stands in the relation to it of a subsidiary. 18 Am J2d Corp § 17.

parent country. See **mother country.**

parenthesis (pa-ren'the-sis). Additional words or clauses, marked off by commas, brackets, dashes, or curved lines, added to a sentence complete in grammatical construction by way of explanation or comment. In an earlier and narrower sense, a mark or sign used in punctuation, thus ( ), generally to indicate that the clause or words thus marked or included between such signs are not essential in the construction of the sentence. Early v Wilkinson & Hunt, 50 Va (9 Gratt) 68.

parenthetical statement. See **parenthesis.**

parenticide. Homicide in the killing of a parent. One who commits homicide in killing a parent.

parent of the country. See **parens patriae.**

parent state. The state of incorporation of a corporation which has the status of a foreign corporation in another or other states.
See **mother state.**

Parentum est liberos alere etiam nothos (pa-ren'tum est li'be-rōs a'le-re ē'she-am no'thos). It is the duty of parents to support their children, even the illegitimate ones.

pares (pa'rēz). Peers; equals; persons of equal rank, dignity or station.

pares curiae (pa'rēz kur'i-ē). Same as **pares curtis.** See 2 Bl Comm 54.

pares curtis (pā'rēz ker'tis). Peers of the court. Peers bound to attend court.

Pares debent interesse investiturae feudi, et non alii (pā'rēz de'bent in-ter-es'se in-ves'ti-tū-rē fū'dī, et non a'li-ī). The peers or vassals of the lord should be present at the investiture of a fee, and no others. See 2 Bl Comm 315.

paresis (par'e-sis). A general breaking down of the nervous system; a wasting away of the brain tissue from syphilis. Lins v Lenhardt, 127 Mo 271, 282.

pares regni (pa-rēz reg'nī). Peers of the realm, reaching the presence of the king. Hurtado v California, 110 US 516, 529, 28 L Ed 232, 236, 4 S Ct 111, 292.

Paria copulantur paribus (pa'ri-a ko-pu-lan'ter pa'ri-bus). Like things unite with like things.

Paribus sententiis reus absolvitur (paribus sen-ten'-she-is rē'us ab-sol'vi-ter). A defendant is acquitted by equal opinions; that is, where the same number of judges are for and against him

pari causa (pa'rī kâ'za). With equal right; on the same footing or basis.

pari delicto (pa'rī dē-lik'tō). In equal wrong; equally at fault.
See **in pari delicto.**

parientes (pah-re-en-tays). (Spanish.) Relatives.

paries (pā'ri-ēz). (Civil law.) The wall of a house.

paries communis (pa'ri-ēz kom-mū'nis). (Civil law.) A party-wall.

parietes. See **intra parietes.**

pari materia (pa'rī ma-te'ri-a). See **in pari materia.**

pari-mutuel. A method of wagering at race tracks, whereby those who bet on the winning horse share the total stakes less a percentage to the management. People v Monroe, 340 Ill 270, 182 NE 439, 85 ALR 605; Utah State Fair Asso. v Green, 68 Utah 251, 249 P 1016, 1028. Bookmaking by machine. 24 Am J1st Gaming § 25. A form of betting on horse races conducted by means of a machine which records the number of bets placed on a particular horse to win, place, or show, the owner of the machine receiving the wagers and giving the bettors tickets or certificates showing which horse they have chosen; the total amount received, less a commission to the owner of the machine, being divided among the winners. 24 Am J1st Gaming § 25. The machine used in pari-mutuel betting for recording the bets as they are placed and determining the odds from the bets placed. Commonwealth v Samuels, 79 Ky 618, 619.

Statutes have been passed in some states legalizing the pari-mutuel method of betting on horse races, while in others, statutes expressly forbidding such method have been enacted. 24 Am J1st Gaming § 25.

pari-mutuel betting. See **pari-mutuel.**

pari-mutuel machine. See **pari-mutuel.**

Par in parem imperium non habet (par in pa'rem im-pe'ri-um non hā'bet). An equal has no dominion over an equal.

pari passu (pā'rī pas'ū). Of the same grade; by equal steps; in equal degree.

pari ratione (pa'rī rā-she-ō'ne). For like reason; by the same reasoning.

Pari ratione eadem est lex (pā'rī rā-she-ō'ne e-ā'dem est lex). For a like reason the law is the same. State v Buchanan (Md) 5 Harr & J 317.

Paris Declaration. An international declaration of important points of maritime law made at Paris in 1856.

parish. A political subdivision in Louisiana, corresponding to a county. Re Supervisors of Election (CC Ill) 28 F 840. A corporation established solely for the purpose of maintaining public worship. Milford v Godfrey, 18 Mass (1 Pick) 90, 97. An administrative district of a religious society, headed by a priest or pastor. The members of a church in a parish, considered collectively.

The term in its generic legal sense does not denote any specific religious faith or denomination. Yanow v Seven Oaks Park, Inc. 11 NJ 341, 94 A2d 482, 36 ALR2d 639.

parish apprentices. Children of poor persons apprenticed out by the overseers of the poor to such persons as were thought fitting. See 1 Bl Comm 426.

parish child. A pauper child who is dependent upon the parish for support.

parish church. A local spiritual association or religious society; the building in which the public worship of the inhabitants of a parish is celebrated. Pawlet v Clark (US) 9 Cranch 292, 326, 3 L Ed 735, 747. A consecrated place having attached to it the rites of burial and the administration of the sacraments. 45 Am J1st Reli Soc § 2.

parish constable. A constable whose jurisdiction is confined to a parish.

parish court. A probate court. Simmons v Saul, 138 US 439, 34 L Ed 1054, 11 S Ct 369 (referring to parish court of Louisiana). An inferior English court the jurisdiction of which did not extend outside the parish in which it was held.

parish district. An ecclesiastical division of an English parish.

parish officers. Officers of a parish as a political subdivision; officers of a parish in the sense of a religious district or body. Officers of an English ecclesiastical parish, consisting of constables, churchwardens, and overseers.

paris-mutuel. Same as **pari-mutuel.**

parity. A yardstick for measuring the prosperity of the farmer, the measurement taken being relative, the purpose being to have the prices of farm products at such levels that such products will have the same purchasing power in terms of goods and services that they had in the so-called base period from 1910 to 1914. 3 Am J2d Agri § 28.

Parium eadem est ratio idem jus (pa'ri-um ē-ā'dem est rā'she-ō ī'dem jūs). In similar cases the reason is the same, the law is the same.

parium judicium (pa'ri-um jū-di'she-um). The judgment of one's peers,—the verdict of a jury of one's peers.

park. A tract of land acquired by a city, town, or other public authority, for ornament, and as a place for the resort of the public for recreation and amusement. 39 Am J1st Pks & S § 2. A tract set apart by the federal government for the enjoyment, health, and comfort of the people, particularly lands of scenic value.

In England, the word, when applied to an inclosed tract of land in the country, signifies that the lands inclosed are the private grounds of the proprietor. In London, however, as well as in any city in England, the term "park" signifies an open space intended for the recreation and enjoyment of the public, such signification being the same whether the word be used alone, or with some qualifying term, as "Hyde Park," or "Regent's Park." Archer v Salinas City, 93 Cal 43, 28 P 839.

See **parking.**

park board. See **park commission.**

park commission. A local, state, sometimes an interstate, administrative body exercising powers in reference to the opening and maintenance of public parks. New York Water Service Corp. v Palisades Interstate Park Com. 14 App Div 2d 794, 220 NYS2d 489; 39 Am J1st Pks & S § 16.

park commissioner. A member of a park commission or park board.

park district. A public corporation or authority established and operating in the acquisition, development, and maintenance of a park. 39 Am J1st Pks & S § 3.

parked. See **parking.**

parking. A park strip in the street, sometimes between the curb and the sidewalk, sometimes in the middle of the street. The assembling or leaving of things in a place, for example, artillery, vehicles of war, automobiles, or railroad cars, when they are not in use. New Orleans v Lenfant, 126 La 455, 52 So 575. The voluntary act of leaving a vehicle on the street unattended, also the stopping or standing of a vehicle on the street, even though occupied and attended, for a length of time inconsistent with a reasonable use of the street. 7 Am J2d Auto § 231.

The term "parked" is not susceptible of a mean-

PARKING [913] PARODY

ing of momentary hesitation in changing direction of a vehicle. Hartsock v George, 59 Ohio App 249, 12 Ohio Ops 523, 27 Ohio L Abs 65, 17 NE2d 667.

parking area. A place set apart close to an industrial plant, place of business, hospital, stadium, etc. where customers, employees, and visitors may park their automobiles.

parking facility. See **parking area; parking lot.**

parking lot. A place for the parking of motor vehicles, usually for a charge. Ex parte Mobile Light & Railroad Co. 211 Ala 525, 101 So 177, 34 ALR 921, 923. A place off the streets where automobiles may be parked, that is, left under the care of the proprietor of the place. A place where automobiles may be driven, left parked or standing, and removed by the owner at pleasure, normally operated for compensation in the form of a fee for the privilege of parking. 24 Am J1st Garag § 3.

parking meter. A meter placed along the curb of a street or in a public parking place wherein coins may be inserted for the purpose of paying for parking space for a time measured and demonstrated automatically by the instrumentality. 7 Am J2d Auto § 238.

parking on the highway. The voluntary act of leaving an automobile on the highway when not in use. A wrecked car, with passengers in it and the outside wheels in the ditch, is not so parked. Kastler v Tures, 191 Wis 120, 124, 210 NW 415, 417.
See **parking.**

parking place. See **parking area; parking lot.**

parking station. A parking lot operated for compensation in the form of payments in amounts scaled according to the time the parked car is left at the station.
See **parking lot.**

park strip. A portion of a street or other public way, either between the curb and the sidewalk or in the middle of the way, in which grass, flowers, bushes, even small trees may be grown, for the purpose of ornamentation. 25 Am J1st High § 72. A comparatively narrow strip of land, lying within the borders and part of a single street, withdrawn from travel and ordinary street uses and devoted to ornamental purposes and perhaps in a small degree to those of rest and recreation. Kupelian v Andrews, 233 NY 278, 135 NE 502.

parkway. A boulevard. A highway designed especially for travel for pleasure and recreation, although not limited to such use in the absence of express regulation to that effect. 25 Am J1st High § 6. A term sometimes used for **park strip.**

Parle hill (pärl hil). A hill where English courts were anciently held.

parler le ment (pär′lā le môn). To speak the mind. See 1 Bl Comm 146.

Parliament (pär′li-ment). The legislative department of the English government, consisting of the House of Lords and the House of Commons.

parliamentary (pär-li-men′ta̞-ri). Relating or pertaining to the English parliament; relating or pertaining to legislation or to a legislature.

parliamentary agents. Professional lobbyists, in the employ of private persons and corporations, who exert themselves among the members of parliament in the interest of legislation favorable to their constituents, but in a strictly lawful manner.

parliamentary bill. A draft or skeleton of a statute.

parliamentary divorce. A divorce granted by an act of the legislature. Cooper v Telfair (US) 4 Dall 14, 1 L Ed 721. A divorce granted by the British Parliament. Closson v Closson, 30 Wyo 1, 215 P 285, 29 ALR 1371.

parliamentary law. The body of law which governs the conduct of the meeting of a legislative body.

Such rules are quite different from constitutional provisions which the people have set up as defining and limiting the powers and duties of the legislature. The former are subject to revocation and modification at the pleasure of the body creating them, while the latter are the law of its being, and prescribe the terms upon which it has power to act at all. See Landes v State, 160 Ind 479, 489, 67 NE 189.

parliamentary rules. The rules adopted by an organization to control the conduct of its meetings, such as those applicable to the annual meeting of a religious body, to the conduct of the convention of a veterans' organization, or to a literary society.
See **parliamentary law.**

parliamentary taxes (tak′ses). Taxes which are imposed by a direct statutory act of the English parliament.

parliamentary will. The so-called will of one who has made no will at all, that is, the so-called intestate laws which provide for the passing of title to the property of one who died without leaving a will to such person or persons as the lawmakers, in their judgment and wisdom, have thought best entitled thereto. Kohny v Dunbar, 21 Idaho 258, 121 P 544.

parliament of dunces (of dun′ses). A name which was given to the parliament of 1404, in the reign of Henry the Fourth, and from which all lawyers were excluded.

parliamentum indoctum (par-li-a-men′tum in-dok′-tum). Same as **parliament of dunces.**

parliamentum insanum (par-li-a-men′tum in-sā′num). Same as **mad parliament.**

parlor car. A car upon a train for the accommodation of first-class passengers, where beverages and like refreshments may be obtained.

paroche (pa-rosh′). A parish. Same as **parochia.**

parochia (pa-rō′ki-a). A parish.

Parochia est locus quo degit populus alicujus ecclesiae (pa-rō′ki-a est lō′kus quō de′jit po′pu-lus a-li-kū′jus e-klē′si-ē). A parish is the place in which the people of a certain church reside.

parochial. Of or pertaining to a parish; confined or restricted to a parish, without reference to any specific religious faith or denomination. Yanow v Seven Oaks Park, Inc. 11 NJ 341, 94 A2d 482, 36 ALR2d 639. Provincial.

parochial church. Same as **parish church.**

parochial school. A school maintained by a church or religious body, coupling religious instruction with instruction as given in the public schools. Yanow v Seven Oaks Park, Inc. 11 NJ 341, 94 A2d 482, 36 ALR2d 639.
See **sectarian school.**

parody. A reproduction or representation of a literary or dramatic work in structure with changes in the names of characters, also in the situations represented, usually for the sake of comedy. 18 Am J2d

Copyr § 105. The reproduction of a musical work with changes intended to create humor.

par of exchange (pär of eks-chānj'). The value of the money of one country in that of another; the relative melting value of the gold coins of each of two nations. Murphy v Kastner, 50 NJ Eq 214, 220, 24 A 564.

parol. Oral; by word of mouth. Extrinsic to a writing.
See terms and expressions following which begin **parol**; also words and expressions beginning **oral**.

parol agreement. See **parol contract**.

parol assignment. An assignment of a claim, right, or chose in action made without a writing. 6 Am J2d Assign § 84.

parol authority. The authority of an agent conferred without a writing. 3 Am J2d Agency § 70.

parol contract. In the usual and more simple sense of the term, a contract not in writing; an oral contract. In a technical sense, a simple contract, that is, a contract which, although it may be in writing, is not under seal, is not a specialty. Perrine v Cheeseman, 11 NJL 174; Ballard v Walker (NY) 3 Johns Cas 60, 65.

parol contract of insurance. A contract which is complete in its terms and complies with all the requirements imposed by law in the making of a contract of insurance, except that it is not in writing as may be required by charter provision or statute. 29 Am J Rev ed Ins § 189.

parol demur; See **demurrer ore tenus; the parol demur**.

parole. The release of a prisoner of war upon condition, particularly that he will not, unless exchanged, engage in the armed forces against the country which had taken him prisoner, during the pendency of the war. The release of a convict from imprisonment upon certain conditions to be observed by him. Crooks v Sanders, 123 SC 28, 115 SE 760, 28 ALR 940.
Parole is not an act of clemency, but a penological measure for the disciplinary treatment of prisoners who seem capable of rehabilitation outside of prison walls. It does not set aside or affect the sentence; the convict remains in the legal custody of the state and under the control of its agents, subject at any time, for breach of condition, to be returned to the penal institution. Re Anderson, 191 Or 49, 229 P2d 633, 230 P2d 770, 29 ALR2d 1051, 1073.

parole board. An administrative board provided by statute for considering applications for parole and, according to the terms of the statute, granting or denying a parole or making recommendation to the Governor as to the disposition of the application. 39 Am J1st Pard § 86.

parole system. The system whereby the policy of paroling prisoners is administered, usually based in part upon statutory provisions for indeterminate sentences.
See **indeterminate sentence**.

parol evidence. The oral or verbal testimony of a witness. See 3 Bl Comm 369. Precisely, evidence of matters not contained in the writing, whether oral utterance or other writing, offered as proof of terms and conditions of a contract in writing. 30 Am J2d Ev § 1016.

parol evidence rule. The rule which excludes evidence of prior or contemporaneous oral agreements which would vary a written contract. Garrett v Ellison, 93 Utah 184, 72 P2d 449, 129 ALR 666.
The rule that the intention of the parties as evidenced by the legal import of the language of a valid written contract cannot ordinarily be varied by parol proof of a different intention. The rule, correctly regarded as a matter of substantive law, that the purposeful act of embodying all the terms of an agreement in a writing produces the contract of the parties, a single and final memorial of the understanding of the parties which must stand in exclusion of prior or contemporaneous negotiations. 30 Am J2d Ev § 1016.

parol gift. A gift of personal property made without incorporation of terms in a written instrument, evidenced by the manual delivery of the property. 24 Am J1st Gifts § 24. A gift of land without deed or other conveyance. Burris v Landers, 114 Cal 310, 46 P 162. A gift of land rendered ineffective by the statute of frauds, except as the delivery of possession to, and the making of valuable and permanent improvements by, the donee render the gift enforceable notwithstanding its parol character. 24 Am J1st Gifts § 68.

parol lease. A lease not in writing signed by the lessor. 32 Am J1st L & T § 36.

parol license. An authority given to do some act or a series of acts on the land of another, without passing any interest in the land. Hicks Brothers v Swift Creek Mill Co. 133 Ala 411, 31 So 947.

parol may demur (mā dē-mėr). See **the parol demur**.

parol partition. A division of lands by common consent by coparceners or tenants in common without any writing. Before the statute of frauds was enacted (1677) such a partition was valid and binding, and tenants in common might make partition by parol if it were accompanied with livery of seisin in severalty, and parceners might make partition by parol generally. The authorities are in conflict as to whether such a partition is valid under the statute of frauds. In some states statutes specifically require a writing. 40 Am J1st Partit § 18.

parol representation. A representation by words, acts and conduct, by arts or artifices. 23 Am J1st Fraud § 24.

Parols font plea (pạ-rōls' font plē). Words make the plea.

parol will. A nuncupative will. The informal will of a soldier or sailor. 57 Am J1st Wills § 220.
See **nuncupative will**.

par oneri (par o'ne-rī). Equal to the burden.

parricide (par'i-sīd). The murder of one's parent; a person who is guilty of the murder of his parent.

parricidium (par-ri-sī'di-um). (Civil law.) The murder of a parent or any near relation.

pars (pärz). A part; a party; a party to an action; a function; a duty.

Parsee (pär'sē). One of a religious sect, the members of which are to be found for the most part in India, which constitutes a remnant of the followers of the ancient religion of Persia established by Zoroaster. Wadia v United States (CA2 NY) 101 F2d 7.

pars ejusdem negotii (parz ē-jus'dem ne-gō'she-ī). A part of the same transaction or business.

pars enitia (parz e-ni'she-a). The part or share of the eldest.

pars fundi (parz fun'dī). A part of the soil.

pars gravata (parz gra-vā'ta). The party aggrieved.

Pars illa communis accrescit superstitibus, de persona in personam, usque ad ultimam superstitem (parz il'li kom-mū'nis a-kre'sit sū-per-sti'ti-bus, dē per-sōn'na in per-sō'nam, us'kwe ad ul'ti-mam sū-per-sti'tem). That common part accumulates to the survivors from person to person, down to the last survivor. See 2 Bl Comm 184.

pars judicis (parz jū'di-sis). The part, function, or duty of a judge.

parson. A pastor; a minister of the gospel or clergyman in charge of a church or parish. A man who, under the English ecclesiastical system had full possession of all the rights of a parochial church.

He was called parson, persona, because by his person the church, an invisible body, was represented; and he is in himself a body corporate, in order to protect and defend the rights of the church, which he personates, by a perpetual succession. He is sometimes called the rector, or governor, of the church. See 1 Bl Comm 384.

parsonage (pär'son-āj). A dwelling house occupied by the pastor of a church, ordinarily owned by the church. 45 Am J1st Relig Soc § 30.

When a church has acquired all the ecclesiastical rights it becomes, in the language of law, a rectory or parsonage, which consists of a glebe, tithes, and oblations established for the maintenance of the parson or rector to have cure of souls within the parish. Pawlet v Clark (US) 9 Cranch 292, 326, 3 L Ed 735, 747.

parsonage tithes. Tithes belonging to the rector of a parish.

parson imparsonee. Same as **persona impersonata**.

pars pro toto (pärs prō tō'tō). A part for the whole. Jennings v Insurance Co. of Pennsylvania (Pa) 4 Binn 244.

pars rationabilis (parz rā-she-ō-nā'bi-lis). A reasonable part or share. See 2 Bl Comm 491.

pars rea (parz rē'a). A party defendant.

pars viscerum matris (parz vi'se-rum mā'tris). Part of the insides of the mother,—that is, not yet born.

part. A portion; a share; a side; a faction. A division of a court established for cases of a distinct character, as equity part.

part and pertinent (pėr'ti-nent). Appurtenant; belonging to.

parte (par'te). One side; one party.

parte inaudita (par'te in-â'di-ta). One party not having been heard; ex parte.

Partem aliquam recte intelligere nemo potest antequam totum iterum atque iterum perlegerit (par'tem a'li-quam rek'te in-tel-li'je-re nē'mō po'test an'te-quam tō'tum i'te-rum at'kwe i'te-rum per-le'je-rit). No one can properly understand a part of anything until he has read over the whole again and again.

parte materna. See **ex parte materna**.

parte non comparente (par'te non kom-pa-ren'te). A party not appearing,—that is, a party in default.

parte paterna. See **ex parte paterna**.

Parte quacumque integrante sublata tollitur totum (par'te quā-kum'kwe in-te-gran'te sub-lā'ta tol'li-ter tō'tum). An integral part having been taken away, the whole disappears.

partes (par'tēz). Parties.

Partes finis nihil habuerunt (par'tēz fī'nis nī'hil ha-bu-ē'runt). The parties to the fine had no interest; a plea used to defeat a fine levied by a stranger. See 2 Bl Comm 357.

partial. Biased; prejudiced. Affecting or relating to a part.
See **pro tanto**.

partial acceptance. An acceptance of a bill of exchange by which the drawee accepts for part only of the amount for which the bill is drawn; a qualified acceptance. 11 Am J2d B & N § 517. An acceptance of a part of the property offered for dedication, the remainder being rejected. 23 Am J2d Ded § 46.

partial ademption. See **pro tanto ademption**.

partial appointment. The exercise of a power of appointment in reference to a fund without exercising the whole power at one time, applying the power to a portion of the fund or property. 41 Am J1st Pow § 73.

partial assignment. An assignment by a debtor of a part of his property for the benefit of creditors. 6 Am J2d Assign § 39. The splitting of an entire claim or debt arising out of a single transaction and making a part of the claim or debt the subject of an assignment, such being valid at common law only with the consent of the debtor, since he has a right to pay his debt in one lump sum and to refuse to be subjected to suits by more than one claimant. 3 Williston, Contracts 3d ed § 442; 6 Am J2d Assign § 76.

The reasons obtaining at common law for refusing to enforce a partial assignment do not apply in equity, or in jurisdictions with modern practice acts or rules, where the procedure contemplates that all interested persons be made parties and their rights determined by a single decree. 6 Am J2d Assign § 77.

partial breach. The result of a party's failure to perform fully or substantially. 17 Am J2d Contr § 446.

partial condemnation. The taking of a part of a tract or lot of land under the power of eminent domain. 27 Am J2d Em D § 269.

partial custody. Part-time custody of a child awarded in an action for divorce.

partial delivery. A delivery or tender by the seller of only a part of the goods or commodities constituting the subject matter of sale. 46 Am J1st Sales § 218.

partial dependency. The status of a person who depends upon another for part of his support and maintenance. The status of a person who has some means but not sufficient for his support. Utah Fuel Co. v Industrial Com. 80 Utah 301, 86 ALR 858, 15 P2d 297.

partial disability. A disability resulting in only a partial loss of earning power, the claimant still being capable of performing remunerative employment. 58 Am J1st Workm Comp § 283. Physical power in part only or physical inability in part of injured member. Fidelity Union Casualty Co. v Munday (Tex Civ App) 26 SW2d 676. A physical disability less than total; in contradistinction to total disability. 29A Am J Rev ed Ins § 1515.

partial disclosure. A fraud where accompanied with the wilful concealment of material and qualifying facts. 23 Am J1st Fraud § 86.

partial dismissal of appeal. A dismissal of appeal as to some of the parties or some of the issues. 5 Am J2d A & E § 923.

partial distribution. An interim distribution by an executor or administrator, that is, a distribution made of funds available for distribution without waiting until the entire estate is available and ready for distribution. 31 Am J2d Ex & Ad § 555.

partial emancipation. The act of a parent in authorizing his minor child to make its own contract of service, and to collect and spend its wages, but retaining custody and control of the child. Lufkin v Harvey, 131 Minn 238, 154 NW 1097. The release of a minor child by the parent as to a part of the period of minority or a part of the rights of the parent in reference to care, custody, and control of the minor. Porter v Powell, 79 Iowa 151, 44 NW 295.

partial embargo. See **embargo.**

partial eviction. An eviction of a tenant from a part of the premises. 32 Am J1st L & T § 480.

To constitute a partial eviction which will operate as a suspension of rent, there must be either an actual expulsion of the tenant, or some act of a permanent character, done by the landlord with the intention and effect of depriving the tenant of the enjoyment of some part of the demised premises, to which he yields, abandoning possession within a reasonable time. Bartlett v Farrington, 120 Mass 284.

partial failure of consideration. The failure of a party to a contract to receive all that was due him under the terms of the contract. A defense pro tanto; an excuse for nonperformance by the other party where there is no substantial consideration left in support of the promise of the other party. 17 Am J2d Contr § 100. Recognizable only as the part is determinable. 11 Am J2d B & N § 658.

See **partial want of consideration.**

partial illegality. See **partial invalidity.**

partial incapacity. See **partial disability; partial insanity.**

partial insanity. A condition of mind characterized by some derangement. A condition wherein the mind is haunted or weakened, but is not entirely incapable of remembering, reasoning or judging. State v Jones, 50 NH 369. Another term for insane delusion. 21 Am J2d Crim L § 41. A concept without basis from the standpoint of the right and wrong test of criminal responsibility. 21 Am J2d Crim L § 40.

The doctrine has been advanced by some text writers that partial insanity may be a mitigating element in determining the degree of homicide of which the accused may be convicted. The general rule, however, appears to be that insanity, when interposed as a defense in a criminal prosecution is either a complete defense or none at all. 26 Am J1st Homi § 105.

partial integration rule. The rule that where the entire agreement has not been reduced to writing, parol evidence to prove the part not reduced is admissible although not admissible as to the part reduced to writing. 12 Am J2d B & N § 1243; 30 Am J2d Ev § 1043. The merger or extinguishment of the provisions of a land contract in the deed executed in the performance of the contract by the vendor, subject to covenants and stipulations not intended to be incorporated in the deed or not necessarily performed and satisfied by the execution and delivery of the conveyance. 55 Am J1st V & P § 328.

partial intestacy. The condition of the estate of a testate decedent in reference to property owned by him but not disposed of by the will.

partial invalidity. The invalidity of a part of a municipal ordinance, such being sufficient to invalidate the entire ordinance where it has a general influence over the rest of the ordinance. 37 Am J1st Mun Corp § 167. The characteristic quality of a statute which is constitutional in part and unconstitutional in another part. 50 Am J1st Stat § 474. The unconstitutionality of a statute in part, the effect of which upon the remainder of the statute depends upon the severability of the invalid part from the remainder. 16 Am J2d Const L § 181. The characteristic quality of a contract which contains an illegal provision among legal provisions. 17 Am J2d Contr § 230.

See **divisible contract; severability of statute.**

partiality. Bias; prejudice.

partial law. A law which embraces within its provisions only a portion of those persons who exist in the same state and are surrounded by like circumstances. Hatcher v State, 80 Tenn (12 Lea) 368.

partial liquidation. Literally, a liquidation which does not dispose of all the property or wind up all the affairs of a corporation or an insolvent. Technically, a proceeding involving the surrender by a corporation of a portion of its capital. Smith v Dana, 77 Conn 543, 60 A 117.

partial loss. A loss of the use of a member of the body for some purposes. Partial disability in health, mind, or person. 22 Am J2d Damg § 117. The destruction of a part of insured property. The loss at sea of a part of the cargo.

See **general average; particular average.**

partially disclosed principal. The principal, for whom an agent acts, whose identity is not known to the person who deals with the agent, such person knowing or having reason to know that the person with whom he deals is or may be acting for a principal. Dodge v Blood, 299 Mich 364, 300 NW 121, 138 ALR 822; Williston, Contracts 3d ed § 283; Restatement, Agency 2d ed § 4.

partial manufacture. A term pertaining to the imposition of customs duties. A mere stage in the development of material toward an ultimate and predestined product. Tide Water Oil Co. v United States, 171 US 210, 43 L Ed 139, 18 S Ct 837.

partial negotiation. An attempt to transfer, by indorsement of a bill or note, a part only of the amount payable, or an attempt to transfer the instrument to two or more indorsees severally. 11 Am J2d B & N § 320.

partial pardon. A pardon which remits only a portion of the punishment or absolves the convicted person from only a portion of the legal consequences of the crime. Warren v State, 127 Tex Crim 71, 74 SW2d 1006.

partial payment. A payment of a part of the obligation owing. An instalment payment.

A payment of interest is a "partial payment" within the provisions of a statute barring partial payments from tolling or extending the limitation period for mortgage foreclosure. Weekes v Rumbaugh, 144 Neb 103, 12 NW2d 636, 150 ALR 129.

partial performance. See **part performance.**

partial probate. The probate of only the valid portions of a will which contains invalid clauses. 57 Am J1st Wills § 782.

partial release. A release of the condition upon which an estate was granted, superficially a partial release, but having effect under the rule in Dumpor's Case, to eliminate the condition entirely. 28 Am J2d Est § 169.

partial restraint of trade. See **restraint of trade.**

partial restraint on alienation. A restraint on alienation other than an unqualified restraint, such as a restriction upon alienation to a particular person or persons or within a certain period of time. 41 Am J1st Perp § 75.

partial reversal. A reversal on appeal as to less than all the parties or as to less than all the issues. 5 Am J2d A & E §§ 949, 950, 953.

partial unconstitutionality. See **partial invalidity.**

partial verdict. A verdict in a criminal case prosecuted under an indictment containing several counts, wherein the accused is found guilty on some of the counts, without mention of the remaining counts. Jolly v United States, 170 US 402, 42 L Ed 1085, 18 S Ct 624.

partial waiver. A waiver of the condition upon which an estate was granted, superficially a partial waiver, but having the effect under the rule in Dumpor's Case, to eliminate the condition entirely. 28 Am J2d Est § 168.

partial want of consideration. The situation where an instrument is given in part for a valuable consideration and in part as a gift. Anno: 161 ALR 1372, 1378; 11 Am J2d B & N § 244.
See **partial failure of consideration.**

partial zoning. Zoning ordinances applicable to only a part of the entire area within the limits of the municipality. 58 Am J1st Zon § 34.

partible (pär'ti-bl). Capable of being separated, divided, partitioned, or portioned out.

particeps criminis (pär'ti-seps krim'i-nis). A party to the crime. One who participated in some manner in the commission of a crime.

The term, which, in common acceptation, means an act that may be visited by an indictment, or other criminal prosecution, applies also to other transactions contrary to good morals, whether they be immoral per se, or prohibited by statute under a penalty, or by a simple prohibition, or as militating against the policy of a statute, or fraud, or other corrupt contract. Johnson v Cooper, 10 Tenn (2 Yerg) 524.

particeps doli (par'ti-seps do'lī). A party to the fraud.

Particeps plures sunt quasi unum corpus in eo quod unum jus habent et oportet quod corpus sit integrum, et quod in nulla parte sit defectus (par'ti-seps plū'rēz sunt quā'sī ū-num kor'pus in ē'ō quod ū'num jūs hā'bent et o-por'tet quod kor'pus sit in'te-grum, et quod in nul'la par'te sit de-fek'tus). Many parceners are, as it were, one body, in this respect; that they have one right and it is necessary that the body be perfect, and that there be no defect in any part.

participate. To receive or have a part or share of; to partake of; to experience in common with others; to have or enjoy a part or share in common with others; to partake; as to participate in a discussion; to take part in; as to participate in joys and sorrows.

Bew v Travelers' Ins. Co. 95 NJL 533, 112 A 859, 14 ALR 983, 984.

Participating and assenting both imply affirmative action of some sort, as distinguished from mere silence and inaction. See Mason v Moore, 73 Ohio St 275, 76 NE 932.

participating in aeronautics. Managing and controlling an airplane in flight or making the decisions regarding the flight and directing another or others directly in control of the plane. 29A Am J Rev ed Ins § 1265.

While the earlier cases held that a passenger "participates in aeronautics" within the meaning of an aviation exclusion clause in a life or accident insurance policy, the modern trend of authority is distinctly to the contrary. Anno: 45 ALR2d 462; 29A Am J Rev ed Ins § 1265.

participating in crime. See **participation in crime.**

participating policy. A policy of insurance which entitles the holder to share in the profits of the insurer by way of dividends.

participating share. A share in a security or securities constituting a single investment of funds of several individual trusts. 54 Am J1st Trusts § 396.

participation. The act or fact of partaking, having or forming part of; the fact or condition of sharing in common with others; associating or sharing with others in some act or matter. Smith v Mutual Ben. Health & Acci. Asso. 175 Kan 68, 258 P2d 993, 45 ALR2d 456.

participation agreement. An agreement in the trust instrument or bylaw of a business trust organized for the purpose of producing oil, entitling the holder to a certain share of the oil produced. 13 Am J2d Bus Tr § 23.

participation in aeronautics (pär-tis-i-pā-shọn a''ër-ọ-nât-iks). See **participating in aeronautics.**

participation in crime. Engaging in the commission of a criminal offense as a principal or as an accessory, aider, or abettor. 21 Am J2d Crim L §§ 115 et seq.

participation in labor dispute. As disqualification for unemployment compensation, an active involvement, such as picketing. Tube Reducing Corp. v Unemployment Compensation Com. 136 NJL 410, 56 A2d 596, affd 1 NJ 177, 62 A2d 473, 5 ALR2d 855.

participation rights. See **rights.**

particula (par-ti'ku-la). A small parcel of land.

particular agent. An agent authorized by his principal to do one or two particular things. Ruby v Talbott, 5 NM 251, 21 P 72.
See **special agent.**

particular average. A term used in contradistinction to general average, denoting a loss on vessel, cargo, or freight, to be borne by the owner of the particular subject or interest upon which it happens. 48 Am J1st Slip § 621. A term generally regarded as synonymous with "partial loss" when used in a limitation of liability in a marine insurance policy. 29A Am J Rev ed Ins § 1585.

See **free from average unless general; free from particular average.**

particular averment (ạ-vėr'mẹnt). An allegation or pleading of a particular fact.

particular custom. A custom confined to a county, city, town, parish, or other locality, its existence to be determined as a matter of fact upon proof. Bodfish v Fox, 23 Me 90.

particular estate. A term of art in the law of estates for a life estate or estate for years which precedes a future estate or interest, especially where the future estate is a remainder. 28 Am J1st Est § 208.

particular lien. A charge upon a particular piece of property, by which it is held for the payment or discharge of a particular debt or duty. 33 Am J1st Liens § 5.

particular malice. Ill will; grudge; a desire to be revenged on a particular person. State v Long, 117 NC 791, 799, 23 SE 431.

particular pardon. Same as **special pardon.**

particular power. See **particular agent; special power of appointment.**

particular preceding estate. See **particular estate.**

particulars. The items of an account.
See **bill of particulars.**

particular services. Services rendered by a person in his particular or peculiar profession, art, trade or calling. Buchman v State, 59 Ind 1, 13.

particular strike. A strike against a particular employer rather than against all employers in an industry or territory. 31 Am J Rev ed Lab § 369.

particular tenant. The holder of a particular estate. See **particular estate.**

partido agreement. An agreement of bailment of cattle containing a condition respecting the right to the increase of the cattle during the period of the bailment. Allen v Whiting, 58 Ariz 273, 119 P2d 240; Bowers v Western Livestock Co. (ND) 103 NW2d 109.

parties. See **party.**

parties' books. Books of original entry, also called "shopkeepers' books," or "shopbooks." 30 Am J2d Ev § 918.

parties to contract. See **party; third parties.**

parties to a judgment. Strictly speaking, only persons named as parties in the record who are properly served with process or enter their appearance. 30A Am J Rev ed Judgm § 396. For the purposes of the application of the principle of res judicata:—all persons having a direct interest in the subject matter of the suit and having a right to control the proceedings, defend, examine the witnesses, and take an appeal if the case is appealable. Vane v C. Hoffberger Co. 196 Md 450, 77 A2d 152, 22 ALR2d 1450.

partisan feeling. See **partisanship.**

partisanship. Favoritism toward a party to an action. Prejudice disqualifying a judge. 30A Am J Rev ed Judges § 104.
See **bias; political activity; prejudice.**

partition. The division made between two or more persons of lands, tenements, hereditaments, or goods and chattels belonging to them as co-owners. Technically, the division of real estate made between coparceners, tenants in common, or joint tenants. 40 Am J1st Partit § 2. The action or proceeding through which co-owners of property cause it to be divided into as many shares as there are owners, according to their interests therein, or, if that cannot be done equitably, to be sold for the best obtainable price and the proceeds distributed.

Michael v Sphier, 129 Or 413, 272 P 902, 73 ALR 1.

partition commissioners. Commissioners appointed by the court in partition proceedings, whose duty it is to examine the premises, make a preliminary or advisory partition and report back to the court. 40 Am J1st Partit § 76.

partition deed. A deed executed and delivered in effecting a partition of real estate.
See **partition.**

partitione facienda. See **de partitione facienda.**

partition fence. A fence erected on the boundary line between the lands of adjoining owners, where there is no road, alley, or the like between the lands. 35 Am J2d Fenc § 6. A common fence, that is, one of which each of the adjoining owners may make use in connection with the use made by him of his premises.

The term does not apply to such fences as may be erected by each proprietor on his own land, though near and parallel to the boundary line. Jeffries v Burgin, 57 Mo 327, 329.

partition sale. A sale of a vessel ordered by an admiralty court. 2 Am J2d Adm § 101. A sale ordered and made in an action for the partition of real estate, where a division of the land into shares according to the several interests of the parties cannot be done equitably, such sale to be made for the best possible price and the proceeds divided in accord with the several interests. Michael v Sphier, 129 Or 413, 272 P 902, 73 ALR 1.

partition wall. A wall which is merely a fence.
"Partition wall" is not a phrase which in legal technology is used to designate a wall used by owners as a party wall. A party wall is such by agreement. Western Granite & Marble Co. v Knickerbocker, 103 Cal 111, 116, 37 P 192.

partner in commendam (pärt'nėr in kom-men'dam). A term of the Louisiana law for limited partner. Tatum v Acadian Production Corp. (DC La) 35 F 40.
See **limited partnership.**

partners. The members of a partnership. Persons who contribute either property or money to carry on a joint business for their common benefit, and who own and share the profits thereof in certain proportions. 40 Am J1st Partn § 2.

partner's equity. See **equity of partner.**

partnership. An association of two or more persons to carry on as co-owners a business for profit. Uniform Partnership Act § 6. A combination, effected by two or more persons, of capital or personal services for the purpose of conducting a business for their common benefit. The contract of two or more competent persons to place their money, effects, labor, and skill, or some or all of them, in lawful commerce or business, and to divide the profit and bear the loss in certain proportions. 40 Am J1st Partn § 2. But, strictly speaking, a relation or status rather than a contract. Spaulding v Stubbings, 86 Wis 255, 56 NW 469. A distinct legal entity according to some authority; a legal entity for some purposes only, according to other authority. 40 Am J1st Partn § 18. For federal income tax purposes, inclusive of a syndicate, group, pool, join venture, through or by means of which any business, financial operation, or venture is carried on, and which is not a corporation, an association taxable as a corporation, or a trust or estate. Internal Revenue Code § 761.

See **general partnership; limited partnership; ostensible partner; quasi partner; silent partner.**

Partnership Act. One of the uniform laws.

partnership assets. All assets of a partnership applicable to the payment of the partnership debts, under the well-defined principles for the administration of the affairs of insolvent partnerships under the direction of a court of equity. Thayer v Humphrey, 91 Wis 276.

partnership association. A business organization exclusively a creature of statute; a type of artificial person standing halfway between a limited partnership and a corporation. 40 Am J1st Partn § 518. An association in the form of a kind of partnership but departing from a general partnership characterized by unlimited liability of partners, all partners being special partners. 40 Am J1st Partn § 504. An association organized under laws making the capital subscribed alone responsible for the debts of the association; a corporation for the purposes of an ajudication in bankruptcy. 11 USC § 1(8); Bankruptcy Act § 1(8).

partnership goodwill. The advantage which the partnership business has from its establishment or from the patronage of its customers, over and above the mere value of its property and capital.

It rests in the probability that the old customers of the partnership will continue their custom and commend it to others, and it may include the advantages which may be derived from the partners holding themselves out as carrying on the business identified with the name of a particular firm. 40 Am J1st Partn § 109.

partnership inter sese (pärt'ner-ship in'ter sē'sē). A real partnership, a partnership characterized by a community of losses, as well as of profits. See Germer v Donaldson (CA3 Pa) 18 F2d 697.

partnership name. The designation or name of a partnership under which it transacts its business.

Such a name may be the name of one or all the members of the firm, or it may be a fictitious name, but the statutes of many jurisdictions required the filing of a certificate setting forth the fact if the names of all the partners are not disclosed in the firm name. 40 Am J1st Partn § 10.

partnership property. That jointly owned property in whatever form which represents the contributions of the several partners toward the capital employed by the firm in its business, plus the earnings, and less the losses, of the firm in its operations. Whitcomb v Converse, 119 Mass 38.

partner's lien. (pärt'nẻrs lē'en). The lien which each member of a partnership may assert upon property belonging to the partnership for the amount of his interest in the partnership, and for advances made by him for the use of the firm. Allen v Hawley, 6 Fla 142. Another term for the equity of a partner. 40 Am J1st Partn § 404.

See **equity of partner.**

partner's share. The balance to which a partner is entitled after the payment of all the partnership debts and the adjustment of the partnership account between himself and his co-partners. Taft v Schwamb, 80 Ill 289, 300.

See **equity of partner.**

part owner. One of two or more persons who own property as co-owners. Sexton v Lauman, 244 Iowa 570, 57 NW2d 200, 37 ALR2d 353.

The term is not properly applied to partners, but is in common use in the law to denote a class of persons distinct from partners. Breck v Blair, 129 Mass 127, 128.

See **cotenancy; joint tenancy; tenancy in common.**

part performance. Performance by a party to a contract which is less in extent than full or substantial performance as measured by the conditions of the agreement. 17 Am J2d Contr §§ 379 et seq. The doctrine that part performance of an oral contract for the sale of real estate has the effect, subject to certain conditions concerning the nature and extent of the act constituting performance and the right to equitable relief generally, of taking such contract from the operation of the statute of frauds, so that equity may decree it specific performance or grant other equitable relief. 49 Am J1st Stat of F § 419. Within the meaning of the equitable doctrine that part performance takes an oral contract out of the operation of the statute of frauds:—such acts as change the plaintiff's position and would result in a fraud, injustice, or hardship upon him, if the contract were not executed or enforced. 49 Am J1st Stat of F § 427.

parts in a set. See **bills in a set.**

part-time worker. See **casual employee.**

parturition (pär-tụ-rish'on). Giving birth to a child.

partus (pär'tus). Issue; a child; offspring.

Partus ex legitimo thoro non certius noscit matrem quam genitorem suam (par'tus ex le-ji'ti-mō tho'rō non ser'she-us nō'sit mā'trem quam je-ni-tō'rem su'am). The child or offspring of a legitimate marriage does not know his mother any more certainly than his father.

partus sequitur ventrem (par'tus se'qui-ter ven'trem). The offspring follows the mother. 4 Am J2d Ani § 10.

party. A person who has engaged in a transaction or made an agreement. UCC § 1—201(29). One of the opposing litigants in a judicial proceeding—a person seeking to establish a right or one upon whom it is sought to impose a corresponding duty or liability, including any person by whom or against whom a suit, either at law or in equity, is brought. 39 Am J1st Parties § 4. For the purposes of a right to appeal, persons named as parties in the original pleadings and persons who subsequently come or are brought into the action for the purpose of seeking relief or of being subjected to relief. 4 Am J2d A & E §§ 174, 175. For some purposes, a person interested in the litigation, as well as a party of record, for example, the disqualification of a judge. Anno: 10 ALR2d 1312, or incompetency to testify to a transaction had with a person since deceased. 58 Am J1st Witn § 283. For the purpose of the rule of res judicata, any person who has a direct interest in the subject matter of the suit and has a right to control the proceedings, defend, examine the witnesses, and appeal if an appeal lies. Vane v C. Hoffberger Co. 196 Md 450, 77 A2d 152, 22 ALR2d 1450.

As to who is a party for the purposes of the application of a statute or rule of practice authorizing a physical or mental examination of a party. 23 Am J2d Dep § 226.

See **indispensable party; necessary party; political party; proper party.**

party affiliation. Adherence to a political party and support of its candidates for election. 25 Am J2d Elect § 159.

party aggrieved. See **aggrieved party.**

party candidate. A candidate for election nominated by a political party and running as the candidate of such party. Putnam v Kozer, 119 Or 535, 250 P 625.

party convention. See **convention.**

party defendant. See **defendant.**

party in default. See **default.**

party injured. See **injured party.**

party in interest. A party to an action who has an actual interest in the controversy, as distinguished from a nominal party.
See **interested person.**

party interested. See **interested person; party in interest.**

party jury. Same as **jury de medietate linguae.**

party litigant. A person named as a party to an action or suit. For some purposes, a party who will really litigate the controversy, as distinguished from one defaulting in the action or consenting to judgment. National Bank v McCrillis, 15 Wash 2d 345, 130 P2d 901, 144 ALR 1197.

party of record. A person formally designated as a party to an action or an appeal, as distinguished from a person who has an interest in the subject matter involved.

party plaintiff. See **plaintiff.**

party rate. A reduced fare charged by a carrier for persons in a prescribed number traveling as a party, that is, as a group at the same time.

party square. A square on an election ballot which permits the voting of a straight party ticket by one mark only, that is, a mark in the square. 26 Am J2d Elect § 210.

party to a judgment. See **parties to a judgment.**

party to be charged. A familiar expression in the statute of frauds, meaning the party against whom the contract is sought to be enforced. 49 Am J1st Stat of F § 384.

party wall. A dividing wall for the common benefit and convenience of the tenements which it separates. Lederer v Colonial Invest. Co. 130 Iowa 157, 106 NW 357; Coumas v Transcontinental Garage, Inc. 62 Wyo 99, 230 P2d 748, 41 ALR2d 539. A wall located upon or at the division line between adjoining premises and used, intended to be used or available to be used by both owners of such premises in the construction or maintenance of improvements on their respective tracts. 40 Am J1st Part W § 2.

In order to constitute such a wall, the structure need not stand partly on the land of each adjoining landowner; it may rest entirely on the land of one owner and still have the legal characteristics of a party wall. 40 Am J1st Part W § 2.

Parum cavet natura (pa′rum ka′vet nā-tū′ra). Nature takes but little precaution.

Parum cavisse videtur (pa′rum ka-vis′se vi-dē′ter). (Roman law.) He seems to have taken but little care or precaution.

Parum differunt quae re concordant (pa′rum dif′ferunt kwē rē kon-kor′dant). Those things differ but little which accord in substance.

Parum est latam esse sententiam nisi mandetur executioni (pa′rum est lā′tam es′se sen-ten′she-am nī′sī man-dē′ter ex-e-ku-she-ō′nī). A sentence is not sufficiently comprehensive unless it is committed to execution.

Parum proficit scire quid fieri debet, si non cognoscas quomodo sit facturum (pa′rum pro′fi-sit sī′re quid fī′e-rī de′bet, sī non kog-nōs′kas quō-mō′dō sit fak-tū′rum). It profits but little to understand what ought to be done if you do not know in what manner it should be done.

par value. The value of an instrument for the payment of money as determined by the face of the instrument. The face value of a bond. An amount fixed as the nominal value of a share of corporate stock, such amount indicating the sum of money or value of property or services which a subscriber is represented as having contributed to the corporation in exchange for such share. Randle v Winona Coal Co. 206 Ala 254, 89 So 790, 19 ALR 118; Fort Edward v Fish, 156 NY 363, 370, 371, 50 NE 973.

A sale of bonds at par is a sale at the rate of one dollar in money for one dollar in bonds. This is the accepted meaning in the mercantile world. Ft. Edwards v Fish, 156 NY 363, 50 NE 973.

Par value and the actual value of issued stock are not synonymous; there is often a wide disparity between them. 18 Am J2d Corp § 222.
See **nonpar value stock.**

parva proditio (par′va prō-di′she-o). Petit treason, the killing of a master by a servant; of a husband by a wife; of a superior by an ecclesiastic.

parva serjeantia (par′va ser-je-an′she-a). Same as **petit sergeanty.**

parvum cape (par′vum kāp). A judicial writ to recover possession of land in a real action in which the tenant had appeared but had made default.

parvum servitium regis (par′vum ser-vi′she-um rē′jis). Small service of the king; petit sergeanty.

pas (pä). Precedence; the right to precede.

Pascha (pas′ka). Easter.

pascua silva (pas′ku-a sil′va). (Civil law.) A wooded pasture.

pass. Noun: A short leave of absence for a person in military service. A license to enter a government office, industrial plant, military establishment, or reservation. Permission or license to ride on the conveyance of a carrier without payment of fare. 14 Am J2d Car § 843. A slang expression for attempting familiarity with a female. Verb: To vest in heir or devisee upon death of owner. Estate of Kennedy, 157 Cal 517, 108 P 280.

passage for logs. A passageway over or around a dam whereby logs may be floated and transported. Crookston Waterworks, P. & L. Co. v Sprague, 91 Minn 461, 98 NW 347, 99 NW 420.

passage money. Compensation for the carriage of a passenger on a ship. The Main v Williams, 152 US 122, 129, 38 L Ed 381, 384, 14 S Ct 486.

passage of act. See **passage of statute.**

passage of statute. The date the act secures the approval of the two houses of the legislature. State v Mounts, 36 W Va 179, 14 SE 407. The date of the approval of the act by the chief executive, or in the absence of his approval, the date of final passage over the veto. 50 Am J1st Stat § 504. Sometimes construed as the effective date of the statute. Consolidated Motors v Skusen, 56 Ariz 481, 109 P2d

41, 132 ALR 1040 (relative to exception of delinquent taxes from interest).
See **final passage.**

passageway. A way for entrance or exit. A hallway. A way used for public passage. 25 Am J1st High § 3.

passagio (pas-sā'ji-o). A writ to compel the officers of a port to allow a person who held the permission of the king to depart across the sea.

passagium (pas-sā'ji-um). A passage; a voyage.

passator (pas-sā'tor). A person having the control of passage on a river.

passbook. A book carried by the customer of a bank in which the teller enters the amount and date of a deposit made. 10 Am J2d Bks § 347. A small account book carried by a shareholder in a building and loan association, showing the state of his account, at least the deposits made by him. Broadly, a book of buyer, customer, or borrower in which the seller, banker, or creditor enters their mutual transactions.

passed dividend. An omitted dividend; a dividend not declared at the time for the declaration of the dividend under former practice of the corporation, especially where the dividend is one payable regularly on preferred stock.

passenger. One riding in a conveyance, as distinguished from one in control of the operation of the vehicle. One who travels in a public conveyance by virtue of contract, express or implied, with the carrier as to payment of fare or that which is accepted as the equivalent of a cash fare. A person whom a common carrier has contracted to carry from one place to another, and has in the course of the performance of that contract received under his care, either upon the means of conveyance, or at the point of departure of that means of conveyance. 14 Am J2d Car § 740. One transported for hire or under a contract with the carrier as distinguished from one riding a train or other conveyance for the purpose of rendering service in connection with the journey. 29A Am J Rev ed Ins § 1253. A person being carried in an elevator or riding on an escalator. 26 Am J2d Elev §§ 23-32, 79.
See **guest in aircraft; guest in motor vehicle.**

passenger agent. An agent of a railroad company in charge of the passenger business generally or in a particular city or locality. Anno: 113 ALR 87.

passenger car. A railroad car used for the transportation of passengers.
An old passenger car which has been converted into a pay car and is used on the railroad as such is in no sense a passenger car any more than a baggage or mail car could be so considered. Travelers' Ins. Co. v Austin, 116 Ga 264, 42 SE 522.
See **passenger motor vehicle.**

passenger depot. See **depot.**

passenger elevator. An elevator for carrying passengers as distinguished from a freight elevator. 26 Am J2d Elev § 2. An elevator so constructed as to be usable only for the carriage of passengers. 29A Am J Rev ed Ins § 1236. An elevator commonly used for the carriage of passengers, whatever the nature of the construction may be and irrespective of whether or not the conveyance is used for both freight and passenger service. Anno: 96 ALR 1411.

passenger motor vehicle. A motor vehicle which, in manner of construction, as well as use, is a vehicle for carrying passengers rather than goods or merchandise. Poncino v Sierra Nevada Life & Casualty Co. 105 Cal App 671, 286 P 729.
See **private passenger automobile.**

passenger train. A railroad train which carries passengers, their baggage, mail, and express only. Arizona Eastern Railroad Co. v State, 29 Ariz 446, 242 P 870.

pass for cause. To let a juror go unchallenged for cause, leaving open the opportunity for peremptory challenge.

passim (pas'im). Here and there; indiscriminately.

passing indictment to files. Holding the charge in abeyance; postponement of trial. 27 Am J1st Indict § 23.

passing of act. See **passage of statute.**

passing of property. See **succession; transfer.**

passing of title. A transfer of title, voluntary or involuntary.

passing on the right. An offense committed in the operation of a motor vehicle under some statutes and ordinances. 7 Am J2d Auto § 224.

passing vehicle. To go by a vehicle.
As used in a statute requiring motor vehicles to come to a stop before "passing" any school bus which has stopped for the purpose of taking on or discharging school children, the term means to go by, regardless of whether the school bus and the motor vehicle are traveling in the same direction or in the opposite direction at the time when the school bus comes to a stop. Thus a statute contemplates the stopping of motor vehicles approaching from an opposite direction as well as those traveling in the same direction. Fisher v J. H. Sheridan Co. 182 SC 316, 189 SE 356, 108 ALR 981.
See **overtaking and passing.**

passing vessel. See **overtaking and passing.**

passion. An intensity of emotion. Hate or love. Sexual desire. Moved by feelings, emotions, or sympathy, without conscious violation of duty. Alabama Gas Co. v Jones, 244 Ala 413, 13 So 2d 873. As an element characterizing the degree of the offense of homicide, rage, anger, resentment, fear, excitement, or nervousness, but of sudden development. 26 Am J2d Homi § 44.
See **sudden passion.**

passive. Inactive; quiescent; not active; permissive.

passive bond. A noninterest-bearing bond the holder of which is by its terms to have some future advantage or profit from it.

passive concealment. Silence without active suppression of a fact. 37 Am J2d Fraud § 145.

passive connivance. Conduct of the complaining spouse which smoothed the path of the other to the adulterous bed. Vinton v Vinton, 264 Mass 71, 161 NE 817.

passive debt. A debt which bears no interest.

passive indulgence. Failure to proceed against a debtor at a time when the means of collecting against collateral security exists. 50 Am J1st Suret § 115.

passive negligence. Negligence which lies in the failure to act, that is, to do something which one is under a legal obligation to do. 38 Am J1st Negl § 3.

passive participation. Something more than a merely passive attitude toward a conspiracy; a passive consent to the object of the conspiracy and concurring with the purposes of the other conspirators, although actually standing by while the others put the conspiracy into effect. O'Neil v State, 237 Wis 391, 296 NW 96, 135 ALR 719.

passive receivership. A receivership in which the receiver merely preserves the property, collects the assets, and reports to the court. State Bank v Domestic Sewing Machine Co. 99 Va 411, 39 SE 141.

passive trust. A trust whereof the trustee has no active duties to perform; a trust in which the beneficiary has the entire management of the estate and the retention of legal title is not essential to the performance of any duty imposed upon the trustee. 54 Am J1st Trusts § 13.
See **dry trust.**

passive use. Same as **permissive use.**

passive waste. Same as **permissive waste.**

passport. A formal document issued by a competent officer of a sovereign state or nation to a citizen or subject of the state or nation, certifying his citizenship or allegiance, addressed to foreign powers, and requesting that the bearer of it pass freely and safely. 40 Am J1st Pass § 1. As issued by the United States Secretary of State, a political document by which the bearer is recognized in foreign countries as an American citizen, and which by usage and the law of nations is received as evidence of the fact. Urtetiqui v D'Arbel (US) 9 Pet 692, 699, 9 L Ed 276, 278. A document issued in time of war, under the authority of the government of one of the belligerents, entitling the person to whom it is issued to pass through the country of that belligerent. A document issued in time of war, under the authority of a government which is neutral, entitling a vessel to sail on a proposed voyage to the country of one of the belligerents. The Amiable Isabella (US) 6 Wheat 1, 5 L Ed 191.

past consideration. A consideration given before the making of a promise and without reference to it.
As to sufficiency of a past consideration in support of a promise, see 17 Am J2d Contr §§ 125 et seq.

past due. Overdue. Having run beyond maturity.
See **overdue paper.**

paster. A small, gummed piece of paper carrying a name, for use in an election in voting for the person named on the paper by inserting the paper in a blank space on the ballot or, as sometimes authorized by statute, by placing the paper over a printed name appearing on the ballot. 26 Am J2d Elect § 269.

pasteurization (pas″tĕr-i-zā'shọn). The exposure of milk or beer to high temperature for the purpose of destroying noxious bacteria. Pfeffer v Milwaukee, 171 Wis 514, 177 NW 850, 10 ALR 128. A heating of raw milk to the boiling point for the purpose of purification. People ex rel. Empire v Sohmer, 218 NY 199, 112 NE 755.

Pasteur treatment. A method of preventing disease, especially rabies, by inoculation, the name deriving from Louis Pasteur, a French bacteriologist, who first employed it. Buck v Brady, 110 Md 568, 73 A 277.

pastor. A clergyman; a minister of the gospel in charge of a church. An ordained minister of the gospel who has been installed according to the usage of a Christian denomination in charge of a specific church or body of churches. First Presbyterian Church v Myers, 5 Okla 809, 50 P 70.

pasturage. See **agistment.**

pasture. Verb: To take the cattle or other grazing animals of another on one's land for grazing. Noun: Grass land devoted to the grazing of cattle and other grazing animals.
See **admeasurement of pasture; ancient pasture; common of pasture.**

pasture bred. Sire unknown.

pastus (pas'tus). Customary provision which was made by feudal tenants for the lord of the manor upon the occasion of his visit to the land.

Pateat universis per praesentes (pa'te-at ū-ni-ver'sis per prē-zen'tēz). Know all men by these presents.

patens. See **ambiguitas patens.**

patent. Adjective: Obvious, evident. Open to view on ordinary inspection. Miller v Moore, 83 Ga 684, 10 SE 360. Noun: A commission evidencing a right, such as a commission entitling one to a public office. A conveyance or grant of public lands, particularly to one who has made a homestead entry and complied with the statutory conditions respecting settlement, residence, cultivation, and payment. 42 Am J1st Pub L § 31. A grant of mineral rights in public lands. 36 Am J1st Min & M § 25. The right of monopoly secured by statute to those who invent or discover new and useful devices and processes. The exclusive right of manufacture, sale, or use secured by statute to one who invents or discovers a new and useful device or process. 40 Am J1st Pat § 2. Verb: To obtain a patent upon an invention.
See **patent right.**

patentable. Possessing the requisites of utility, novelty, and invention which entitle one to a patent. 40 Am J1st Pat § 21. Referring to a result, together with ingenuity in bringing it about. National Cash Register Co. v Boston Cash Indicator & Recorder Co. 156 US 502, 39 L Ed 511, 15 S Ct 434.
The machine, process or product is but its material reflex and embodiment. It must be new and shown to be of practical utility in order to be patentable. Smith v Nichols (US) 21 Wall 112, 22 L Ed 566.

patentable invention. See **patentability.**

patentable novelty. A new device produced by the exercise of inventive power and skill. General Electric Co. v DeForest Radio Co. (DC Del) 7 F2d 90.

patentable process. A new and useful method of treatment of certain materials to produce a particular result or product. Holland Furniture Co. v Perkins Glue Co. 277 US 245, 72 L Ed 868, 48 S Ct 474.

patent ambiguity. An uncertainty appearing on the face of an instrument, such that the court, reading the language in the light of all the facts and circumstances referred to in the instrument, is unable to derive therefrom the intention of the parties. 23 Am J2d Deeds § 251. In will:—an ambiguity appearing upon the face of the instrument, for example, a bequest to "some" of the six children of the testator's brother. 57 Am J1st Wills § 1042.

Patent Compensation Board. A board established by the Atomic Energy Act of 1954 to advise the Atomic Energy Commission in reference to the determination of royalty fees, compensation, or awards for the owner of a patent dealing with atomic energy. 42 USC § 2187(a).

patent danger. An obvious peril. 38 Am J1st Negl § 91.

patent defects. Defects in a subject matter of sale so obvious that a purchaser dealing in person necessarily must see them.

patented claim. A claim to a homestead upon government land upon which a patent has been issued and delivered. A claim to mineral rights in public lands upon which a patent has been issued and delivered. 36 Am J1st Min & M § 25.
See **placer claim patent.**

patentee. The person to whom letters patent are issued by the government.

patent inside. Content of the inside pages of a newspaper, usually a weekly newspaper, not pertaining to local events or gathered by reporters on the paper, but obtained from an external editorial source. 39 Am J1st Newsp § 8.

patent matter. Same as **patent inside.**

patent medicine. A medicine compounded by a manufacturer according to his own formula. 25 Am J2d Drugs § 3.
The term does not convey the idea that the medicine is a "patented" medicine. Jacobs v Beecham, 221 US 263, 55 L Ed 729, 31 S Ct 555.

Patent Office. A federal bureau located in Washington D. C., headed by the Commissioner of Patents, wherein the merits of an application for a patent are considered and where all records, drawings, models, specifications, and other papers and things pertaining to patents are required by law to be kept and preserved. 40 Am J1st Pat § 10.

patent of precedence (of prē-sē'dẹns). Letters patent granted to certain English barristers as a mark of distinction, and entitling them to certain prerogatives.

patent right. A right under a patent obtained for an invention, held by the patentee or an assignee.
In its usual signification, the term means, a privilege granted by the government to the first inventor of a new and useful discovery or mode of manufacture that he also shall be entitled, during a limited period, to the exclusive use and benefit thereof. In the granting of patents, the Federal Government has never sought to do more, and in fact has never exercised greater authority, than to extend protection to the privilege, such as that granted by a patent for an invention, against the infringement of those who seek to invade it. Crown Cork & Seal Co. v Maryland, 87 Md 687, 40 A 1074.

patent right note. A note given for a patent right. 11 Am J2d B & N § 189.

patent rolls (pat'ẹnt rōlz). English records of letters patent.

patent writ (rit). An open or unsealed writ.

pater (pā'ter). A father.

Pater aut mater defuncti, filio non filiae haereditatem relinquent. . . . Qui defunctus non filios sed filias relinquerit, ad eas omnis haereditas pertineat (pā'ter ȧt mā'ter dē-funk'tī, fī'li-ō non fī'li-ē hē-re-di-tā'tem re-lin'quent. . . . Quī dē-funk'tus non fī'li-os sed fī'li-as re-lin'kwe-rit, ad e'ās om'nis hē-re'di-tās per-ti'ne-at). A father or mother having died leave their inheritance to their son, not to their daughter. . . . Whoever dying shall leave no sons, but daughters, to them the whole inheritance shall belong. See 2 Bl Comm 213.

Pater est quem nuptiae demonstrant (pā'ter est quem nup'she-ē de-mon'strant). He is the father whom the marriage indicates. 10 Am J2d Bast § 11.

paterfamilias (pā"ter-fā-mil'i-as). The father of a family.

paternal (pạ-ter'nạl). Belonging to, or proceeding from, the father.

paternal fee. See **feudum paternum.**

paternal inheritance (in-her'i-tạns). An inheritance from or through the father.

paternal power. That parental authority which a father has over his children.

paternal property. That property which has descended from one's father, or from the stock of the father.

paterna paternis (pa-ter'na pa-ter'nis). Paternal property descends to paternal descendants.

paternity. The state or condition of being a father; fatherhood.
See **presumption of paternity.**

paternity proceeding. A proceeding, otherwise known as a bastardy or filiation proceeding, to establish the paternity of a child born out of wedlock and to compel the father to contribute to its support. 10 Am J2d Bast § 74.

paternity test. A scientific test in determining the paternity of a child. A blood-grouping test. 23 Am J2d Dep § 211.

Pater Noster. The Lord's Prayer.

paternum. See **feudum paternum.**

pater patriae (pā'ter pa'tri-ē). Same as **parens patriae.**

path. A trail. A way worn by many footsteps. A course taken in traveling. A course of conduct.
See **bicycle paths.**

pat hand. A hand of draw poker obtained upon the original deal and retained by the player without discard or replacement. An advantage in a prospective controversy.

pathological condition (path-ō-loj'i-kạl kon-dish'ọn). A diseased condition of the body. Stedmen v United States Mut. Acci. Asso. 123 NY 304, 25 NE 399.

pathological fracture. A bone fracture resulting primarily from a diseased condition.

pathology (pạ-thol'ō-ji). The branch of medicine concerned with the nature of disease and the changes in body, bones, and tissues produced by a particular disease. Anno: 135 ALR 885.

pathometer (pa-thom'e-ter). An instrument for measuring electrical impulses of the human body, employed as a lie detector.

patibulated (pạ-tib'ụ-lā-ted). Hanged on a gallows or gibbet.

patibulum (pa-ti'bu-lum). A gallows; a gibbet.

patiens (pa'she-enz). A patient; a person who suffers something to be done.

patient. Noun: One being cared for as sick, disabled, or diseased, by physician or nurse. One receiving dental care or undergoing dental work. A person may be a patient without his consent, when the facts tend to show that through bodily suffering his mind has partially lost its hold, for under such circumstances it may still be the professional duty of the physician to treat him. Meyer v Supreme Lodge Knights of Pythias, 178 NY 63, 70 NE 111. Adjective: Forbearing. Tolerating delay or inefficiency.

patient forbearance rule. The rule that cohabitation with one's spouse is not condonation of a marital offense consisting of acts of cruelty or indignities, where the injured spouse hopes that the other will mend his or her ways and the marriage be saved by patient forbearance. Anno: 32 ALR2d 13.

patria (pā'tri-ą). The country; a country; a neighborhood; a jury.
See **bona patria**.

Patria laboribus et expensis non debet fatigari (pa'tri-a la-bō'ri-bus et ex-pen'sis non de'bet fa-ti-gā'rī). A jury ought not to be troubled with labors and expenses.

patriam. See **ad patriam**.

patria potestas (pā'tri-ą pọ-tes'tās). (Roman law.) Paternal power.

Patria potestas in pietate debet, non in atrocitate, consistere (pa'tri-a po-tes'tās in pī-e-tā'te de'bet, non in a-trō-si-tā'te, kon-sis'te-re). Paternal power should consist of kindness, not of cruelty. See 1 Bl Comm 452.

patricide (pat'ri-sīd). A person who kills his father; the crime of murdering one's own father.

patricius (pa-tri'she-us). (Civil law.) A title of the highest honor, conferred on those who enjoyed the chief place in the emperor's esteem. Wharton's Law Dictionary.

patrimonial (pat-ri-mō'ni-ąl). Paternal; parental; pertaining to patrimony; pertaining to property inherited from a father or from a paternal ancestor.

patrimonium (pat-ri-mō'ni-um). (Civil law.) Property inherited from or through a father; patrimony.

patrimony (pat'ri-mọ-ni). An inherited estate; property inherited from a father or from an ancestor on the father's side.

patrinus (pa-tri'nus). A godfather.

patriotic association. A voluntary association, sometimes a corporation, organized for the promotion of patriotic purposes, the teaching of love of country, and giving the respect to her leaders past and present which they deserve.

patrocinium (pa-trō-si'ni-um). (Roman law.) Patronage; protection; a defense in a court of justice.

patron. A customer. One who supports an enterprise or activity such as an art gallery or museum. In a technical sense, a person who possesses the right of presentation to a benefice.

patronage. Resorting to a store, shop, office, or service establishment for obtaining goods, merchandise, services, etc. The right of nominating the minister of a church. See 2 Bl Comm 21. Support and favor.
 To state that a certain prostitute is under the "patronage" of a man is held equivalent to stating that she is his kept mistress. Moore v Bennett, 48 NY 472, 475.

patronage dividend. A dividend distributed by a cooperative association, not because of any interest in the cooperative owned by the distributee, but because of his patronage of the business conducted by the association. Internal Revenue Code § 116 (b) (2) (A). A dividend, otherwise known as a patronage refund, paid to members out of the profits of a cooperative association in an amount determined by the use made of the facilities of the association by the patron. 18 Am J2d Coop Asso § 14.

patronage refund. See **patronage dividend**.

patronatus (pa-trō-nā'tus). Same as **patronage**.

patronize. To give or bestow patronage. To act in a condescending manner.
See **patronage**.

Patronum faciunt dos, aedificatio, fundus (pa-trō'num fā'she-unt dōs, ē-di-fi-kā'shė-ō, fun'dus). An endowment, a building, and a parcel of land, make a patron.

patronymic (pat-rọ-nim'ik). A person's surname. The family name derived from one's father.

patroon (pą-trön'). The lord of a manor in Dutch colonial New York.

patruelis (pa-tru'e-lis). (Civil law.) A cousin on the father's side; a paternal first cousin.

patruus (pa'tru-us). A paternal uncle; an uncle on the father's side.

pattern bargaining. Bargaining by a labor union for a number of labor contracts based on the example of one contract considered desirable. Anno: 9 L Ed 2d 1051.

patting down. Same as frisking.
See **frisk**.

Paul VI. His Holiness, the Pope, Bishop of Rome, Sovereign of the State of Vatican City, and spiritual leader of the Roman Catholic Church, since 1963.

pauper. A poor person; an indigent person. One receiving public aid, eating the public bread. 41 Am J1st Poor L § 4.

pauperis. See **in forma pauperis**.

pauper settlement. See **settlement of pauper**.

pave. To cover the ground, especially in street or highway, with a hard substance.
See **pavement**.

pavement. A hard substance applied to the surface of the ground, especially the substance, usually cement or asphalt, applied to street or highway so as to make a convenient surface for travel. Cedar Rapids v Cedar Rapids & Marion City Railway Co. 108 Iowa 406, 409 (holding that the word does not include the flooring of a bridge).
 A pavement is not limited to uniformly arranged masses of solid material, as blocks of wood, brick, or stone; but it may be as well formed of pebbles or gravel, or other hard substance, which makes a compact, even, hard way or floor. Belcher's Sugar Refining Co. v St. Louis Grain Elevator Co. 101 Mo 192, 13 SW 822.

paviage (pā'vi-ąj). A paving or highway tax.

pavilion. A building used for public entertainments and exhibitions, often in a park or public ground, sometimes open on the sides. Phelps v Winch, 309 Ill 158, 140 NE 847. An ornamental structure, often found on the grounds whereon a mansion or large dwelling house is located. A structure on hospital or sanitarium grounds wherein patients may relax and be benefited.

paving. See **pavement**.

pawn. Verb: To pledge personal property as security for payment of a debt. Noun: A bailment of personal property as security for a debt or obligation, redeemable upon certain terms and with the implied power of sale on default. 40 Am J1st Pawnb § 2.

pawnbroker. A person whose business or occupation it is to take or receive, by way of pledge or pawn, any goods, wares, merchandise, or other kind of personal property, as security for the repayment of money lent thereon. 40 Am J1st Pawnb § 2. A person who keeps a shop for the purchase or sale of goods, and takes goods by way of security for money advanced thereon. Levinson v Boas, 150 Cal 185, 88 P 825.

pawnbroker's license. A license required of one permitted to carry on the business of a pawnbroker. 40 Am J1st Pawnb § 7.

pawnee (pâ-nē'). A person to whom goods are pawned or pledged.

pawnor (pâ'nọr). A person who makes a bailment of personal property by way of pledge or pawn.

pawnshop. A place at which the business of a pawnbroker is carried on. Asakura v Seattle, 265 US 332, 342, 68 L Ed 1041, 1045, 44 S Ct 515.

pax (paks). Peace.

pax ecclesiae (pax e-klē'si-ē). The peace of the church.

pax regis (paks rē'jis). The peace of the king.

pax Roma (paks Rō'mä). The peace of Rome.

pax vobiscum (paks vō-bis'kūm). Peace be with you.

pay. Verb: To recompense another in satisfaction of a debt, by way of a reward, or for goods, other property, or services received from or rendered by him. To discharge a debt; to deliver a creditor the value of a debt, either in money or goods, to his acceptance, by which the debt is discharged. Beals v Home Ins. Co. 36 NY 522, 527. Constituting an order to pay, as it appears in a bill of exchange. 11 Am J2d B & N § 139. Noun: That which is received by way of recompense, particularly for work and services.
See **salary; wages.**

payable. Due or to be paid. Eckel v Jones, 8 Pa 801. To be paid, rather than "may be paid." 40 Am J1st Paym § 58. A word which in itself leaves no option or privilege as to time or manner of payment. Johnson v Dooley, 65 Ark 71, 44 SW 1032; Farmers Bank v Johnson, 134 Ga 486, 68 SE 85. Likely or able to yield a profit; profitable; as, payable wash dirt; a payable commercial undertaking. Guaranty Trust Co. v Henwood (CA8 Mo) 98 F2d 160.

payable as convenient. Some indulgence in extension of credit but nevertheless an acknowledgment of a debt to be paid. Black v Bachelder, 120 Mass 171, 173.

payable at. Designation of bank upon instrument for payment of money, the authorities being in conflict upon the question whether the designation is the equivalent of an order to the bank to pay from any funds of the maker or drawer available for payment. 11 Am J2d B & N § 111.

payable in advance. Due in advance. 30 Am J Rev ed Int § 12.

payable in kind. See **in kind.**

payable in trade. Payable in such articles as are dealt in by the party who is thus to make payment. Dudley v Vose, 114 Mass 34, 36.

payable on demand. See **demand paper.**

payable only to himself. Words negativing negotiability. 11 Am J2d B & N § 108.

payable through. A form of designation for collection. UCC, Comment to § 3-120; 11 Am J2d B & N § 11.

payable to bearer. A bearer instrument. 11 Am J2d B & N §§ 106, 124.

payable to bills payable. Designation of an impersonal payee in creating a bearer instrument. 11 Am J2d B & N § 124.

payable to cash. A designation creating a bearer instrument. 11 Am J2d B & N § 106.
See **pay cash or order.**

payable to holder. Words of negotiability. 11 Am J2d B & N § 105.

payable to order. Words of negotiability. 11 Am J2d B & N § 105.

payable upon return of this instrument properly endorsed. A phrase insufficient in itself to create an order instrument. 11 Am J2d B & N § 107.

pay and divide rule. Same as **divide and pay over rule.**

pay any bank. An indorsement upon a check or similar item delivered for collection. 10 Am J2d Bks § 694. A form of restrictive indorsement. 11 Am J2d B & N § 362.
Under the provisions of the Uniform Commercial Code, after an item has been indorsed with the words "pay any bank" or the like, only a bank may acquire the rights of a holder until (a) the item has been returned to the customer initiating collection; or (b) the item has been specially endorsed by a bank to a person who is not a bank. UCC § 4–201(2).

pay cash or order. Not the equivalent of an order to pay to a specified person or to bearer so as to constitute the instrument a bill of exchange. Orbit Mining & Trading Co. v Westminster Bank, Ltd. [1962] 3 All Eng 565 (CA).
A promissory note, payable to "cash or order," and indorsed in blank by the maker thereof, is in effect "payable to bearer." Hale v State, 120 Ga 138, 47 SE 547.

pay check. A check given in payment of wages. 31 Am J Rev ed Lab §§ 822-826.

payee. A person to whom a payment is made or who is designated in a bill or note as the person to whom payment is to be made.
The Commercial Code purports to settle the long-continued conflict over the status of the payee as a holder in due course by declaring that a payee may be a holder in due course. UCC § 3–302(2), and Comment 2; 11 Am J2d B & N §§ 415–419.

payer. One who pays or is obligated to make a payment. An essential of a negotiable instrument, the person obligated thereby.

pay in full. To discharge an obligation completely. A direction respecting a legacy sufficient to exonerate it from the burden of taxes. Re Caswell's Estate, 239 App Div 694, 268 NYS 691.

paying. Making a payment. Profitable, such as a "paying" business.

paying quantities. See **in paying quantities.**

paying teller. See **teller.**

payment. The discharge of an obligation by the delivery and acceptance of money, or of something equivalent to money, which is regarded as such at the time by the person to whom the payment is due. State v Tyler County State Bank (Tex Com App) 277 SW 625, 282 SW 211, 42 ALR 1347. The performance of the consideration clause of a contract, or the satisfaction of a liability imposed by law, the term implying a debt from him who pays to him who is to receive, and further that when the payment is complete the debt will be discharged. United States Fidelity & Guaranty Co. v State, 169 Okla 59, 36 P2d 47.

payment by mistake. See **payment under mistake of fact**; **payment under mistake of law.**

payment for honor. A former practice of the commercial world, sometimes known as payment supra protest, now obsolete because of existing facilities for quick communication, whereunder, a bill of exchange or promissory note having been protested for nonpayment, a third party would pay in order to protect the credit of the drawer or maker which otherwise would suffer during the period of delay ensuing before the latter could be notified of the protest and take steps of his own to protect his credit. 11 Am J2d B & N § 506.

payment for transportation. The fare paid by a passenger on train, bus, plane, or taxicab.
The "payment" for transportation which will take one out of the category of "guest," the motorist's liability to whom is restricted to cases of wilful or wanton misconduct, must be made under such facts and circumstances as will raise an inference of the acquiescence of the motorist in the assumption of liability for mere negligence. Hasbrook v Wingate, 152 Ohio St 50, 87 NE2d 87, 10 ALR2d 1342.

payment in cash or its equivalent. See **cash or its equivalent.**

payment in due course. Payment at or after the maturity of the instrument to the holder thereof in good faith and without notice that his title is defective. 11 Am J2d B & N § 964.
For effect of the Commerical Code upon the requirement of a payment in due course for the discharge of a negotiable instrument, see Comment 3 to UCC § 3–603.

payment in good faith. See **payment in due course.**

payment into court. A deposit in court, of money or property capable of delivery, made through the clerk of the court, pursuant to an order of the court rendered upon an application therefor, to be disposed of ultimately as the rights of the interested parties may appear. 23 Am J2d Funds & D § 2. A requirement imposed upon the plaintiff in interpleader. 30 Am J Rev ed Interpl § 26. A deposit made with the clerk of court of an amount of money which the depositor admits to be due his adversary in an action pending in the court. Dirks v Juel, 59 Neb 353, 80 NW 1045.

payment of check. The act of the drawee bank in handing over money, in the amount in which the check is drawn, to the payee or indorsee, or in giving the payee or indorsee something in lieu of cash, often a credit in his account at the bank in the amount of the check, accepted unconditionally by the payee or indorsee. 10 Am J2d Bks § 543.
While the phrase "to pay" in ordinary parlance may seem to connote only payment to a third party, as a matter of law a bank does "pay" a check drawn on it in its own favor; that is to say, it charges the same against the account of the depositor and causes that check to augment the bank's own funds. Colby v Riggs National Bank, 67 App DC 259, 92 F2d 183, 114 ALR 1065.

payment supra protest. Same as **payment for honor.**

payment under mistake of fact. A payment made by one person to another on the mistaken supposition of the existence of a specific fact which would entitle the other to the money, where the money would not have been paid if it had been known to the payer that the fact was otherwise. 40 Am J1st Paym § 187.

payment under mistake of law. A payment made by a person who having full knowledge of the facts comes to an erroneous conclusion as to their legal effect. 40 Am J1st Paym § 207.

payment under protest. See **protest.**

pay no money to agents. A statement made in rendering a bill.
As the expression appears on a bill rendered by a corporation for goods sold, it is the equivalent of a notice not to pay to an unauthorized agent; it is not a notice of limitation on the ostensible authority of the agent who made the sale to receive payment. American Sales Book Co. v Cowdrey, 100 Ark 325, 140 SW 134.

pay only through clearing house. The usual form of indorsement of a check made by a collecting bank in sending the check to a clearing house, such being sufficient to transfer the instrument from the indorsing bank to the redeeming bank. 10 Am J2d Banks § 840.

pay off. To eliminate an obligation by paying the obligee. To pay a confederate for his assistance in committing a fraud or crime. To recompense one for his keeping silent respecting the commission of a crime or the perpetration of a fraud.

payoff. A slang expression for time of reckoning or settlement, also for an unexpected occurrence of importance.

payor. Same as **payer.**

pay over. See **divide and pay over**; **pay off.**

payroll. A list of employees, sometimes inclusive even of corporate officers and executives, entitled to wages or salary for a period of working time, normally a week, and of the respective amounts due such persons for the period. The amount of money required to fund the list.

payroll check. A check representing the wages of an employee upon a payroll. 10 Am J2d Banks § 512.

pays. Same as **pais.**
See **pay.**

P. C. Abbreviation of **Privy Council.**

p.c. An abbreviation of **pleas of the crown.** Also, an abbreviation of **privy council.**

pd. Abbreviation of paid.

peace. The tranquility enjoyed by members of a community where good order reigns. 12 Am J2d Breach P § 4. That invisible sense of security which every person feels so necessary to his comfort, and for

which all governments are instituted. Miles v State, 30 Okla Crim 302, 236 P 57, 44 ALR 129. The termination of a war, of hostilities between nations. 56 Am J1st War § 13.
See **time of peace.**

peaceable entry. An entry upon real estate without the use of force to obtain entry.

peaceable possession. An uncontested and unresisted possession. Such possession of land as is continuous and not interrupted by adverse suit to recover the estate. Stanley v Schwalbe, 147 US 508, 37 L Ed 259, 13 S Ct 418.

peace bill. See **bill of peace.**

peace bond. See **bond to keep the peace.**

peace foundation. See **World Peace Foundation.**

peaceful assembly. See **right of assembly.**

peaceful persuasion. Persuasion without threat or intimidation.

peaceful picketing. Picketing without violence, intimidation, physical obstruction, or misrepresentation of facts. Anno: 120 ALR 347, s. 124 ALR 773, 127 ALR 887. Absence, not only of violence, but of any unlawful act. Senn v Tile Layers Protective Union, 301 US 468, 81 L Ed 1229, 57 S Ct 857.

peace justice. See **justice of the peace.**

peace officer. A public officer, such as a sheriff, deputy sheriff, marshal, policeman, or constable.

peace of the king. The protection of the king, as extending over the locality where an offense was committed. State v Jones, 1 Miss (Walk) 83, 85, or to the victim of an alleged offense. State v Dunkley, 25 NC (3 Ired L) 116.

peat. A material consisting of decayed plants which grew in swamp or bog in the geological past. Valuable for covering ground, even used as fuel in certain parts of the world. 27 Am J2d Em D § 279.

peat moss. The form in which peat is sold and used as a ground cover.

pecans. Nuts grown on trees in several of the southern states, edible and nutritious, and constituting an important agricultural crop. Superior Oil Co. v Griffin (Okla) 357 P2d 987, 87 ALR2d 224.

Peccata contra naturam sunt gravissima (pe-kā'ta kon'trä nā-tū'ram sunt gra-vis'si-ma). Crimes against nature are the lowest.

peccatum (pe-kā'tum). A sin; a crime; an offense; a fault.

Peccatum peccato addit qui culpae quam facit patrocinium defensionis adjungit (pe-kā'tum pe-kā'tō ad'dit quī kul'pē quam fā'sit pa-trō-si'ni-um defen-she-ō'nis ad-jun'jit). A person adds a crime to a crime who connects a wrong which he has committed with his defense.

peck. A unit of dry measure, consisting of eight quarts, one fourth of a bushel.

pecora (pek'ō-rā). Plural of **pecus.**

pectore judicis. See **in pectore judicis.**

pecudes (pe-ku'dēz). Plural of **pecus.**

pecudum. See **fructus pecudum.**

peculation (pek-ụ-lā'shọn). The betrayal of an official trust by embezzlement or other fraud committed by a public officer in misapplying public property. Bork v People, 91 NY 5, 16.

peculator (pek'ụ-lā-tọr). A defaulter; an embezzler.

peculatus (pe-ku-lā'tus). (Civil law.) Peculation; the embezzlement of public moneys.

peculiar. Adjective: Eccentric; strange. Noun: An English parish which is independent of the ordinary.

peculiar benefits. An expression of the law of eminent domain for benefits from an improvement to property of the condemnee by reason of the direct relationship of the property to the improvement. 27 Am J2d Em D § 368.

Peculiar People. A religious sect whose belief in prayer as a cure for disease resembles that of the Christian Scientists. Regina v Senior (Eng) 19 Cox, CC 219.

peculiars court. See **court of peculiars.**

peculium (pẹ-kū'li-um). (Roman law.) The private property belonging to a son or a slave, independently of the father or the master.

peculium castrense (pe-ku'li-um kas-tren'se). (Roman law.) The private property of a son which he acquired while he was a soldier or in a military camp.

pecunia (pe-kū'ni-a). Money. Property, especially property in cattle.

Pecunia dicitur a pecus, omnes enim veterum divitiae in animalibus consistebant (pe-kū'ni-a di'si-ter ā pe'kus, om'nēz e'nim ve'te-rum di-vi'she-ē in a-nima'li-bus kon-sis-tē'bant). "Pecunia" is so called from the word "pecus" (an animal of the bovine species), because all the wealth of our forefathers consisted of animals.

pecunial (pē-kū'ni-ạl). Pertaining to money; pecuniary.

pecuniae non numeratae. See **exceptio pecuniae non numeratae.**

pecunia non numerata (pe-kū'ni-a non-nu-me-rā'ta). (Civil law.) Money not paid.

pecunia numerata (pe-kū'ni-a nu-me-rā'tā). Money counted out or paid.

pecuniary. Involving money or money's worth. Financial; pertaining or relating to money; capable of being estimated, computed, or measured by money value.

pecuniary ability. The ability to pay one's debts.

pecuniary benefit. A benefit which can be valued in money. Dallas R. & Terminal Co. v Moore (Tex Civ App) 52 SW2d 104.

pecuniary causes. Certain causes which were cognizable in the ecclesiastical courts; those causes which arose either from the withholding of ecclesiastical dues, or the commission or omission of some act relating to the church, whereby some damage accrued to the plaintiff. See 3 Bl Comm 88.

pecuniary condition. The wealth of a person and his income, whether from property or his earnings. See **financial condition.**

pecuniary damages. See **pecuniary injury; pecuniary loss.**

pecuniary injury. An injury, the damages from which are measurable in money. Such an injury as can be, and usually is, without difficulty, estimated by a money standard. Broughel v Southern New England Tel. Co. 73 Conn 614, 621.

pecuniary interest in action. A direct interest in the result of a particular case. Robinson v State, 86 Ga App 375, 71 SE2d 677. As necessary to sustain a right to appeal:—a substantial and immediate interest, a future, contingent, or merely speculative interest ordinarily being insufficient. 4 Am J2d A & E § 180.

pecuniary interest of judge. Such an interest in the event or subject matter of the suit that the judge will be directly affected by realizing a pecuniary gain or suffering a pecuniary loss. Anno: 10 ALR2d 1320.

pecuniary legacy. A legacy which is to be paid out of the general assets of the testator's estate when they shall be converted into money. Humphrey v Robinson, 52 Hun 200, 203, 5 NYS 164.

pecuniary loss. A loss of money or of something by which money or something of money value may be acquired. Dow v Legg, 120 Neb 271, 231 NW 747, 74 ALR 5; Green v Hudson River Railroad Co. (NY) 32 Barb 25, 33.
As this term is used in death statutes allowing the "pecuniary damages" resulting to the beneficiaries to be recovered in an action, the words are not used in a sense of the immediate loss of money or property, but they look to the prospective advantages of a pecuniary nature which have been cut off by the premature death of the person from whom they have proceeded. 22 Am J2d Dth § 123.

pecuniary profit. Financial gain.
A corporation which is operated for "pecuniary profit" is one which is operated for the pecuniary profit of its stockholders or members. Santa Clara Female Academy v Sullivan, 116 Ill 375, 387.

pecuniary resources. See **pecuniary condition.**

pecunia sepulchralis (pe-kū'ni-a se-pul-krā'lis). Money which was paid to a priest for prayers at the opening of a grave.

pecunia trajectitia (pe-kū'ni-a tra-jek-ti'she-a). (Civil law.) Money which was carried across (the sea); a loan in money or in wares which the debtor purchased with the money to be sent by sea, and whereby the creditor assumed the risk of loss from the day of the departure of the vessel until her arrival at the port of destination. See Mackeldey's Roman Law § 433.

pecus (pe'kus). (Roman law.) An animal of the bovine species; a beast; a domestic animal; a herd; a flock.

pecus vagans, quod nullus petit, sequitur, vel advocat (pe'kus vā'ganz, quod nul'lus pe'tit, se'qui-ter, vel ad'vo-kat). Wandering cattle, which no one seeks, follows, or calls. See 1 Bl Comm 298.

ped. A bag.

pedage (ped'āj). A toll paid by pedestrians for the use of certain roads.

pedagium (pe-dā'ji-um). Same as **pedage.**

pedaneus (pē-dā'nẹ-us). (Roman law.) At the foot; inferior; of lower rank or status.

pedaulus (pe-dâ'lus). A Roman judge of lower rank who tried trivial causes.

peddler. One who goes from house to house carrying in a bag goods exposed by him for sale and delivery to whomever may be prevailed on to buy. Crawley v State, 57 Ga App 376, 195 SE 453. In a more modern sense, one who goes from place to place and from house to house carrying for sale and exposing to sale goods, wares, and merchandise which he carries. An itinerant, solicitant vendor of goods who sells and delivers to purchasers the identical goods which he carries with him. 40 Am J1st Ped § 3.

peddler's license. A license required of a peddler primarily as a means of regulation and avoidance of sharp practices and impositions upon the public. 40 Am J1st Ped § 30.

peddler's note. A promissory note which recites the consideration for which given. 11 Am J2d B & N § 189.

pedem ponere (pe'dem pō'ne-re). To place the foot upon; to enter upon and take possession of land.

pede pulverosus (pe'de pul-ve-rō'sus). Dusty-foot; a huckster or peddler who attended fairs.

pederasty (ped'ẹ-ras-ti). Unnatural intercourse between males; more particularly between a man and a boy.

pedestrian. Noun: A person walking on sidewalk street, or highway.
As to who is a "pedestrian" with respect to rights given, and duties imposed, by traffic rules and regulations, see Anno: 30 ALR2d 866.

pedestrian use. The use of a public way by pedestrians. Home Laundry Co. v Louisville, 168 Ky 499, 182 SW 645. In a distinct sense, a use lacking interest, of little appeal to the imagination.

pedigree. Ancestry. A record of ancestry; family tree. The descent of a pure-bred animal as it appears in a registry.
See **tradition.**

pedigree evidence. Proof of ancestry, descent, birth, age, race, relationship, and cognate matters, by general reputation, oral and written declarations, admissible under an exception to the hearsay rule, as well as by direct evidence. 29 Am J2d Ev § 508.
See **tradition.**

pedigree exception. See **pedigree evidence.**

pedis abscissio (pē'dis ab-si'she-ō). An ancient punishment for crime by cutting off a foot.

pedis positio (pe'dis pō-zi'she-ō). The placing of the foot,—the physical act of stepping on the land to effect an entry and an assumption of possession.

pedis possessio (pe'dis po-ze'she-ō). Possession by a foothold; a momentary personal presence on land. Monroe v Rawlings, 331 Mich 49, 49 NW2d 55. In one sense, an actual possession by occupancy of the whole of the entire tract under consideration, as distinguished from virtual possession. Wheeler v Clark, 114 Tenn 117, 85 SW 258.

pedlar (ped'lar). An old form of the word **peddler.**

Peeping Tom. The lout who looked at Lady Godiva as she rode unclad. One who derives a sexual satisfaction from observing others in the nude or dishabille.

peer. An equal.
A man's equals in rank are his peers. At common law a nobleman was entitled to be tried in a criminal case by a jury composed of his peers or equals. Bishops, however, although lords of parliament, held their baronies by right of the church, and were not of noble blood, and hence, were not so entitled. Peeresses did not have this right at common law, but statute 20 Henry VI, c. 9, gave it to them. See 1 Bl Comm 401.

peerage (pēr'ąj). The right or dignity of a member of the English nobility.
The right was originally territorial, annexed to lands, cattles, manors, and the like, but later it became personal, and was confined to the lineage of the party ennobled. In Blackstone's time peers were created by writ or by letters patent. See 1 Bl Comm 400.

peeress (pēr'es). A lady of the nobility. 1 Bl Comm 401.

peers. See **peer.**

pee-wee golf. See **miniature golf course.**

peine (pān). Punishment.

peine forte et dure (pĕn fôrt ay dür). A cruel and relentless punishment,—the torturing punishment which was anciently inflicted on a defendant accused of felony who refused to plead, as a penalty for his obstinacy. State v Woodward, 68 W Va 66, 69 SE 385; 4 Bl Comm 325.

pejorative (pē'jō-rą-tiv). Disparaging.

pejorem partem. See **in pejorem partem.**

pelex (pē'leks). (Roman law.) The mistress of a married man; a concubine.

pellex. Same as **pelex.**

pellagra (pe-lag'rą). A disease caused by dietary deficiency, characterized by stomach and intestinal pains and nervous disorders. Anno: 68 ALR2d 171-176.

pen. Noun: An instrument for writing with ink. A slang term for penitentiary or state prison. Verb: To write. To confine.

penal. An elastic term but strictly and primarily denoting punishment, whether corporal or pecuniary, imposed and enforced by the state for a crime or offense against its laws. 36 Am J2d Forf & P § 2.

penal action. An action founded entirely upon a statute which subjects a wrongdoer to a liability in favor of a person wronged as a punishment for the wrongful act, without limiting such liability to the actual damages suffered. 1 Am J2d Actions § 42. In a very broad sense, inclusive of a criminal prosecution.

penal bill. Same as **penal bond.**

penal bond. A bond conditioned upon the performance of duties of office, or other obligations undertaken by the principal obligor in the bond or collateral things to be done by him. 12 Am J2d Bonds § 1. A bond conditioned upon the forfeiture of a penalty for its breach, as distinguished from a bond providing for liquidated damages. Carey v Mackey, 82 Me 516, 20 A 84.

penal code. A division of the statutory law of a jurisdiction comprehensive of crimes and criminal proceedings. A model code proposed by the American Law Institute.

penal farm. A correctional institution to which persons convicted of misdemeanors are sent, instead of to the county jail. Summers v State, 198 Ind 241, 243, 151 NE 615, 616. A farm maintained as a part of the correctional system of a state to which prisoners may be sent for rehabilitation by work, whether at agricultural pursuits or industrial plants maintained on the land.

penal law. See **penal code; penal statute.**

penal statute. A statute which defines and prescribes the punishment for a criminal offense. A statute which provides a penalty enforceable in a civil action. A statute, such as a wrongful death statute, providing for an assessment of damages with reference to the degree of culpability of the defendant. 22 Am J2d Dth § 5. A statute which imposes a penalty for transgressing its provisions. A statute that imposes a penalty or creates a forfeiture as the punishment for the neglect of some duty, or the commission of some wrong, that concerns the good of the public, and is commanded or prohibited by law. 50 Am J1st Stat § 16.

penal sum. The amount of the penalty specified in a bond or undertaking for its breach or non-fulfilment.

penalty. In the broad sense of the term, the consequences visited by law upon the heads of those who violate the law, particularly provisions of the criminal law and police regulations. A punishment for the nonperformance of an act or for the performance of an unlawful act, the character of the imposition not being changed by the manner in which it is inflicted, whether by civil action or criminal prosecution. 36 Am J2d Forf & P § 2. In a narrower sense, an extraordinary liability to which the law subjects a wrongdoer in favor of the person wronged, such liability not being limited to the damages suffered. 36 Am J2d Forf & P § 2. A statutory penalty which an individual is allowed to recover against a wrongdoer as a satisfaction for the wrong or injury suffered, without reference to the actual damage sustained. Nordling v Johnston, 205 Or 315, 283 P2d 420, 48 ALR2d 1369. An agreement to pay a stipulated sum on a breach of contract, irrespective of the damage sustained. A sum inserted in a contract, not as the measure of compensation for a breach, but rather as a punishment for default, or by way of security for actual damages which may be sustained by reason of nonperformance, and involving the idea of punishment. Management, Inc. v Schassberger, 39 Wash 2d 321, 235 P2d 293. An additional payment for a privilege such as that of payment of principal prior to due date. Anno: 70 ALR2d 1334.

penalty adjudged to be paid. A pecuniary penalty, not a penalty by imprisonment. 36 Am J2d Forf & P § 2.
See **fine.**

penalty for nonpayment of taxes. A penalty, often in the form of imposition of interest charges, on the amount in which a taxpayer is delinquent in payment. 51 Am J1st Tax § 970.

penance (pen'ąns). Punishment for an ecclesiastical offense.

pen and ink levy. Same as **paper levy.**

pence. In British usage, the plural of penny.
See **Peter's pence.**

pencil. Noun: A slender rod of wood with a core of material which will make marks on a smooth surface, used for writing. Verb: To affix a signature by pencil. 23 Am J2d Deeds § 25.
See **writing.**

pendant. See **auter action pendant.**

pendency (pen'den-si). The state or condition of being undecided or pending.

pendency of action. The status of an action or suit from the time it is commenced until its final determination by judgment or order. McDowell v Blythe Bros. Co. 236 NC 396, 72 SE2d 860. The period of life of an action from the time of its commence-

ment to its final determination. 1 Am J2d Actions § 91.
See **commencement of action; lis pendens; notice of pendency; pending action.**

pendency of another action. See **plea of another action pending.**

pendency of criminal prosecution. The status of a criminal prosecution from the time it is commenced by (1) the filing of a formal complaint of affidavit, (2) the return of an indictment or the filing of an information, (3) the issuance of a warrant to an officer for service, or (4) the arrest and commitment of the accused, until the final determination made by judgment. 21 Am J2d Crim L § 3.

pendens (pen'denz). Same as **pending.**
See **lis pendens.**

pendente. Pending. Suspended.

pendente absentia (pen-den'tē ab-sen'she-a). See **administrator of absentee.**

pendente lite (pen-den'tē lī'tē). During the pendency of the suit, action, or litigation; while the suit, action, or litigation is pending.

pendente lite administrator (pen-den'tē lī'te ad-min'-is-trā-tor). A special or temporary administrator appointed where the appointment of a general representative is delayed for any reason, particularly the existence of a will contest. 31 Am J2d Ex & Ad § 650.

pendente lite alimony (pen-den'tē lī'tē al'i-mọ-ni). Same as **temporary alimony.**

pendente lite allowance (pen-den'tē lī'te a-lou'ạns). Allowance to a wife of temporary alimony, maintenance, suit money, and attorneys' fees ordered for her maintenance pending litigation and to enable her to prepare her case in a suit for divorce or for alimony, support, separate maintenance, independent of any proceeding for divorce. 27 Am J1st H & W § 414.
See. **temporary alimony.**

pendente lite injunction. See **preliminary injunction; temporary injunction; temporary restraining order.**

pendente lite nihil innovetur (pen-den'tē lī'te ni'hil in-no-vē'ter). Nothing should be changed during the pendency of an action. 34 Am J1st Lis P § 2.

pendente lite purchaser (pen-den'te lī'tē per'chạs-er). A purchaser of property involved in litigation concerning its ownership or liens claimed against it, who buys while the litigation is pending. Ward v Lockwood, 234 Ky 160, 27 SW2d 692; Newman v Chapman, 23 Va (2 Rand) 93.

pendente lite receivership. A receivership in which a receiver is appointed by the court to hold certain property during the pendency of an action in which the property is involved. 45 Am J1st Rec § 3.

pendente minoritate executoris. See **administrator pendente minoritate executoris.**

pendente placito. See **estrepement pendente placito.**

pendentes (pen-den'tēz). (Civil law.) Things that are suspended or hanging; unplucked crops.

pending. Undecided. In suspense.

pending action. An action which has been commenced and has not been terminated by a final judgment or order.
Under statutes providing for removal of causes, it may be said in general that whatever the form of proceeding to bring the defendant into court, the suit is pending when he is subject to judicial orders. 32 Am J2d Fed Proc § 464.
See **commencement of action; pendency of action.**

pending litigation. See **pending action.**

pending prosecution. See **pendency of criminal prosecution.**

penes me (pe'nez me). In my possession.

penetration. The entry of the private part of the male, at least to some extent, in the private part of the female. 44 Am J1st Rape § 3.

penetration per anum (pėr ạn'um). Penetration through the external terminus of the alimentary canal. 48 Am J1st Sod § 2.

penetration per os (pėr os). Penetration in the mouth, —words used in describing certain unnatural practices which according to the weight of modern authority are held to amount to the crime of sodomy, although it was formerly held otherwise in England. 48 Am J1st Sod § 2.

penicillin (pen-i-sil'in). A drug used in the prevention of infection, but to which some people are susceptible so as to endure painful disorders upon treatment with it. Johnson v National Life & Acci. Ins. Co. 92 Ga App 818, 90 SE2d 36.

penis. The male organ. Mutual Ben. Health & Acci. Asso. v Blaylock 163 Miss 567, 143 So 406, 87 ALR 679.

penitentiary. A place of imprisonment in which convicts sentenced to hard labor are confined by authority of law. 41 Am J1st Pris & P § 2. In some jurisdictions, a county or other local prison, as distinguished from a state prison; a prison for confinement under relatively short sentences or under civil process.

penny. A cent in United States or Canadian money, the coin of lowest denomination. A British coin equaling one twelfth of a shilling.
See **averpenny; bord-halfpenny; festing penny; God's penny; hundred-penny; inpeny; outpenny; pence.**

pensa (pen'sạ). A weight.

pensata (pen-sā'ta). Weighed.

pensio (pen'she-ō). (Civil law.) A payment; a payment for the rent or hire of a thing.

pension. A gratuity paid by the government in recognition of past services in the Army or Navy. Dismukes v United States, 297 US 167, 80 L Ed 561, 56 S Ct 400, reh den 297 US 728, 80 L Ed 1011, 56 S Ct 594. A bounty or gratuity bestowed as a token of the government's benevolence. Anderson v United States (CA9 Wash) 205 F2d 326, 40 ALR2d 639. A regular allowance paid to an individual by government in consideration of services rendered, or in recognition of merit, civil or military. 40 Am J1st Pens § 3. A payment made to a widow, the children, or the dependents of a deceased serviceman. 40 Am J1st Pens § 12. A gratuitous payment made to an aged person. 40 Am J1st Pens § 7. A stated allowance or stipend made in consideration of past services or of the surrender of rights or emoluments, to one retired from service. Kneeland v Administrator, Unemployment Compensation Act, 138 Conn 630, 88 A2d 376, 32 ALR2d 896. A periodical payment of a fixed amount made to retired public and private employees by way of retirement pay, often from a fund accumulated by joint contributions of employer and employees.

As to what constitutes a "pension" within meaning of federal statutes excluding actions on claims for pensions from jurisdiction of federal courts, see Anno: 40 ALR2d 646.

See **mother's pension; teachers' pensions.**

Pension Bureau. A former federal agency the duties of which are within the functions of the present Veterans' Administration.

pensioner. The recipient of a pension; a person who is supported by the bounty of another.

pension fund. A fund provided and accumulated for the payment of pensions to retired employees. Clarke v Ireland, 122 Mont 191, 199 P2d 965.

pension money. Money due, or to become due, to pensioners. 31 Am J2d Exemp § 98.

Pentecost (pen'tḝ-kost). The seventh Sunday after Easter.

pent road. A highway which is closed at the terminal points. Public Utilities Com. v Jones, 54 Utah 111, 179 P 745. Wolcott v Whitcomb, 40 Vt 40, 41. A road which, having gates and bars at certain points, is not an open highway. Bridgman v Hardwick, 67 Vt 132, 134, 31 A 33.

pentway. A road which furnishes access to lands not reached by a highway, but open for use by anyone who desires to use it. Latah County v Peterson, 3 Idaho 398, 29 P 1089.

peon (pē'ọn). A debtor who is compelled to work for his creditor until his debt is paid. Bailey v Alabama, 219 US 219, 242, 55 L Ed 191, 201, 31 S Ct 145.

peonage (pē'ọn-ạj). The status or condition of compulsory service based upon the indebtedness of the peon to the master. 48 Am J1st Slav § 5. The criminal offense of holding a person to service or labor in liquidation of a debt or obligation. 18 USC § 444. A violation of the acts of Congress which were passed pursuant to the enforcement clause of the Thirteenth Amendment to the United States Constitution. United States v Reynolds, 235 US 133, 59 L Ed 162, 35 S Ct 86.

peonia (pḝ-ō'ni-ạ). (Spanish.) The portion granted to a foot soldier of spoils taken, or lands conquered in a war. Strother v Lucas (US) 12 Pet 410, 442, footnote, 9 L Ed 1137, 1151, footnote.

people (pē'pl). The state; the nation; any consolidated political body. United States v Three Friends, 166 US 1, 41 L Ed 897, 17 S Ct 495. The subjects or inhabitants of a nation. The Pizarro (US) 2 Wheat 227, 246, 4 L Ed 226, 231.

"The popular leaders, who in all ages have called themselves the people," etc. See 4 Bl Comm 438.

people of the state. The representatives of the state itself; the state itself, as where a criminal prosecution is entitled as by "The People of the State."

As the expression is used in some connections, such as with reference to enjoyment of the public waters within the state, it includes all people lawfully within the state, whether of the state, in the sense of being residents thereof or otherwise. Rossmiller v State, 114 Wis 169, 89 NW 839.

people of the United States. The sovereign people. Citizens. Boyd v Nebraska, 143 US 135, 36 L Ed 103, 12 S Ct 375.

peppercorn (pep'ẽr-kõrn). A pepper berry. A term often used in the past in expressing the consideration of a contract in which no more than a nominal consideration was intended.

per (pẽr). By; through; in; by means of; on; with; under. A word used to indicate agency. Indicating signature affixed in the execution of an agency. 11 Am J2d B & N § 558.

A signing by which the name of the principal appears "per" the agent is uniformly regarded as a proper method of executing the agency so as to impose liability upon the principal and, conversely, no personal liability upon the agent. Restatement, Agency 2d § 156, Comment a.

In proceeding under a writ of entry, if the intruder or disseisor has conveyed to a third person, or the land has descended to his heir, the writ must allege the fact, because the action must be against the tenant the defect of whose title must be set forth, whether it arose from his own wrong or that of his predecessor in possession. One such alienation or descent makes the first degree, which is called the "per," because in such case the form of the writ is that the tenant had no right but "by" the original wrongdoer who aliened to him or from whom it descended to him. A second alienation or descent makes another degree called the "per and cui," because in such case the form of the writ is that the tenant had no title to enter but "by" or "under" a prior alienee, "to whom" the intruder demised it. See 3 Bl Comm 181.

per accidens nuisance (per ak'si-denz nū'sạns) An act, occupation, or structure not a nuisance per se, but one which may become a nuisance by reason of circumstances, location, or surroundings. 39 Am J1st Nuis § 11.

per accident clause. A clause in a liability insurance policy limiting the liability of the insurer to a specified amount for each accident or occurrence. Anno: 55 ALR2d 1301.

per aes et libram (per ēs et li'bram). (Roman law.) By the brass or copper money and the scales,—a form which was used in certain sales.

per alluvionem (per al-lu-vi-ō'nem). (Civil law.) By alluvion,—by the solid material which is gradually washed up on a person's land by action of the water.

Per alluvionem id videtur adjici, quod ita paulatim adjucitur, ut intelligere non possumus quantum quoque memento temporis adjiciatur (per al-lu-vi-ō'nem id vi-dē'ter ad'ji-sī, quod i'ta pâ-la'tim ad-ju'si-ter, ut in-tel-li'je-re non pos'su-mus quan'tum quo'kwe mo-men'tō tem'po-ris ad-ji-she-ā'ter). That material is deemed to be added by alluvion which is so accumulated little by little that we are unable to perceive how much is added at any certain moment of time.

per ambages (per am-ba'jēz). By evasions; by circumlocution.

perambulation (pẽr-am-bū-lā'shọn). Visitation for making an inspection.
See **visitation.**

perambulatione facienda. See **de perambulatione facienda.**

per and cui (per and kī). By and to whom.

per annulum et baculum (per an'nu-lum et ba'ku-lum). By the ring and staff.

Prior to the time of Pope Gregory VII, in the eleventh century, all bishops were appointed by the king, the usual method of investiture being a delivery by the king to the bishop of a ring and pastoral staff or crosier. This was known as investiture per annulum et baculum. See 1 Bl Comm 378.

per annum (per an'num). By or for a year.
In a contract providing for the payment of interest at a certain rate per annum, the words are held by the authorities to mean that interest is to be computed and paid at the rate specified for the duration of the contract period, and not to mean that interest is payable annually. 30 Am J Rev ed Int § 11.

per anus (pėr ā'nus). Characterizing an examination or treatment of a human body through the opening at the lower end of the alimentary canal.
See **penetration per anum**.

per autre vie (per ō'ter vē). For the lifetime of another person.

per aversionem (per av-er-she-ō'nem). See **sale per aversionem**.

per bouche (pėr boush). With the mouth; orally; verbally.

per breve de privato sigillo (per brē've dē pri-vā'tō si-jil'lo). By writ of privy seal.
"The sign manual is the warrant to the privy seal, and the privy seal is the warrant to the great seal; and in this last case the patent is subscribed, 'per breve de privato sigillo.'" See 2 Bl Comm 347.

per capita (per ka'pi-ta). By the head or individual. Wagner v Wagner, 303 Ky 140, 197 SW2d 86. Sharing by heads, that is, share and share alike. Anno: 126 ALR 159; 23 Am J2d Deeds § 200; 57 Am J1st Wills § 1291. Sharing by the heads throughout an entire class, for example the ten grandchildren of A taking share and share alike, albeit the ten grandchildren are children of three sons of A, one son having two children, one son three, and one son five. The characterization of a vote in a stockholders' meeting where each stockholder has one vote irrespective of the number of shares owned by him. 19 Am J2d Corp § 635.
Anno: Taking per stirpes or per capita under will. 13 ALR2d 1023.

percennarius (per-sen-nā'ri-us). A parcener.

percentage. A part or portion. Precisely, a portion stated in terms of a part of one hundred, as six per cent is six out of one hundred or three out of fifty.

percentage commission. The commission of a broker calculated upon a certain percentage of the price obtained for the customer in a transaction negotiated by the broker. 12 Am J2d Brok § 161.

percentage compensation. An allowance to the trustee of a business trust by way of compensation of a certain percentage of the profits of the business. Anno: 156 ALR 141.

percentage depletion. A specified percentage of a taxpayer's gross income from oil and gas wells, other natural deposits, or timber lands. W. D. Haden Co. v Commissioner (CA5) 321 F2d 169.

percentage of alcohol. A criterion for determining the character of a beverage as intoxicating liquor. 30 Am J Rev ed Intox L § 6.

percentage of safety. A margin, to be observed by a trustee in investing trust funds, between the value of the security and the amount of the investment. 54 Am J1st Trusts § 426.

percentage of vote. The size of the vote cast for the candidates of a political party, or for any one candidate, calculated according to the percentage of total vote cast at the election. 29 Am J2d Elect § 162.

percentage payments. See **progress payments**.

per centum (pėr sen'tum). By the hundred.

perception. The faculty of comprehension. Acquisition of knowledge. As derived from the Latin "perceptio," a receiving or taking of possession.

perceptional insanity. A mental derangement characterized by illusion or hallucination. 26 Am J1st Homi § 78.

perception-reaction distance. The distance in which an automobile traveling at a stated speed may be stopped.
For chart of driver stopping distances, see Am J2d Desk Book, Document 176.

perch. A unit of lineal measure, the same as a rod. A unit of cubic measure for stone, equalling in most jurisdictions twenty-four and three fourths cubic feet. Baldin Quarry Co. v Clements, 38 Ohio St 587. A roost for a bird. A kind of fish.

per clerum et populum (per kle'rum et po'pu-lum). By the clergy and the people.

percolating waters (pėr-kō-lā'ting wâ'tėrs). Waters which ooze, seep, filter, or percolate through the ground under the surface without a definite channel, or in a course that is uncertain or unknown and not discoverable from the surface without excavation for that purpose. 56 Am J1st Wat § 111. Waters which filter through the ground and collect in underground cavities, forming springs, or in what are commonly known as wells. Erickson v Crookston Waterworks, Power & Light Co. 105 Minn 182, 117 NW 435.

percolation. The movement of a liquid through a porous substance, as water below the surface of the ground.
See **percolating waters**.

per consequens (per kon'se-quenz). In consequence.

per considerationem curiae (per kon-si-de-rā-she-ō'nem kū'ri-ē). By the consideration of the court.

per contra (pėr kon'tra). To the contrary. On the other hand.

per corpus (pėr kôr'pus). By the body; that is, by trial by battle or by ordeal.

per cur. An abbreviation of **per curiam**.

per curiam (per kū'ri-am). By the court; by the court as a whole.

per curiam opinion (per kū'ri-am ō-pin'yun). An opinion of the court in which the judges or justices are all of one mind and the question involved is so clear that the opinion is not elaborated by an extended discussion of the supporting reasons. 20 Am J2d Cts § 72.
"It is true this (decision) is criticised as only a per curiam opinion, but why it should have less weight for that reason is not clear." Western Union Tel. Co. v Houghton, 146 Pa 561, 23 A 248.

per day. By the day.
See **per diem**.

per defaltam (pėr dī-fal'tam). By default.

per descent. By descent.
See **assets per descent**.

per diem (pėr dī'em). The compensation of a public officer in the form of an allowance for days actually spent in the performance of official duty. 43 Am J1st Pub Of § 358. Not a fee, but an emolument for a clerk of court, being payable for attendance at court irrespective of whether or not court business is transacted. 15 Am J2d Clk Ct § 13. A fee paid a witness for each day's attendance in a case. 20 Am J1st Costs §§ 53-56.

The term, signifying "per day," is sometimes used by some courts held to be included in the term "fees," and sometimes otherwise. The two terms are not always synonymous. See Anderson v Beadle County, 51 SD 6, 211 NW 968, 969.

per diem fee or compensation. See **per diem.**

perdonatio utlagariae (per-do-nā'she-o ut-la-ga'ri-ē). A pardon for a person who had been outlawed for contempt of court.

perduellio (per-du-el'li-ō). (Civil law.) Treason; a hostile attempt against the state.

perdurable (pėr'dū-ra-bl). Everlasting; enduring forever.

peregrine (per'ē-grin). A stranger; a foreigner; an alien; a resident without civil rights. A falcon.

peregrini (pe-re-gri'nī). (Civil law.) A stranger; a foreigner; an alien; an alien enemy; a slave.

peremptoria. See **exceptio peremptoria.**

peremptorius (per-emp-tọ'ri-us). (Civil law.) That which permanently destroys.

peremptory (per'emp-tọ-ri). Final; positive; conclusive.

peremptory challenge. A challenge to a juror to be exercised by a party to a civil action or criminal prosecution without assignment of reason or cause. Bufford v State, 148 Neb 38, 26 NW2d 383. A challenge to a judge without assignment of reason or cause. Austin v Lambert, 10 Cal 2d 73, 77 P2d 849, 115 ALR 849.

peremptory defense. A defense which denies the right of the plaintiff to sue.

peremptory exception. An answer which merely raises an issue of law, the legal effect of which is the same as that of a demurrer. Lambeth v Turner, 1 Tex 364, 367.

peremptory instruction. The direction of a verdict.

peremptory mandamus. Same as **peremptory writ of mandamus.**

peremptory mandate. Same as **peremptory writ of mandamus.**

peremptory nonsuit. A judgment for the defendant rendered upon the failure of the plaintiff to establish a prima facie case. Jacques v Fourthman, 137 Pa 428, 429, 20 A 802.

peremptory plea. A plea which sets up the defense that the plaintiff has no right to sue.

peremptory rule. Same as **rule absolute.**

peremptory writ of mandamus. A writ of mandamus requiring the party to do the thing absolutely, as distinguished from an alternative writ which requires him to do the thing, or show cause why he should not in his answer. 35 Am J1st Mand § 380.

perennial. Lasting throughout the entire year or for a long time.

perennial crop. A crop grown from perennial plants, grasses, bushes, or vines, albeit labor and fertilizer may be required. Twin Falls Bank & Trust Co. v Weinberg, 44 Idaho 332, 257 P 31, 54 ALR 1527; Superior Oil Co. v Griffin (Okla) 357 P2d 987, 87 ALR2d 224.

perennial grasses. See **perennial crop.**

per equipollens (per e-qui-pol'lenz). By an equivalent.

peresewar. Same as **pursuer.**

per eundem (per ē-un'dum). By the same.

per expressum (pėr eks-pres'sum). By expression; expressly.

per extensum (pėr ek-sten'sum). At length; fully.

Per extraneam personam nihil nobis acquiri potest (per ex-tra'ne-am per-so'nam ni'hil no'bis ac-kwi'rī po'test). Through a stranger we can acquire no rights.

Although this maxim of the Roman law is not in form found in our law, yet its principle is at the foundation of all our rules as to the privity of contract and estate, and as to matters inter alios acta. Kyle v Wells, 17 Pa 286.

per fas et nefas (per fas et ne'fas). By right or wrong.

perfect. Free from error or mistake; complete.

perfected. Completed; fully performed; executed.

perfect fool. The man who is his own lawyer.

perfecting bail. Same as **justifying bail.**

perfecting lien. The filing or service of notice of a mechanic's lien. 36 Am J1st Mech L § 167. The completion of the creation of a lien so that it will be effective against the creditors of the lienee in his bankruptcy.

perfecting transfer. A familiar term in the law of bankruptcy, referring to the completion of a transfer of assets so that it will be good against the creditors of the transferor in his bankruptcy.

perfection of appeal. The completion of compliance with all of the steps outlined by statute for obtaining a review of a judgment or decree. 4 Am J2d A & E § 295.

perfection of entry. The performance by an entryman upon public lands of the conditions requisite to perfect his entry and obtain the right to a patent. 42 Am J1st Pub L § 23.

perfection of reason. An encomium given the common law. 1 Bl Comm 70.

perfect obligation. An obligation the performance of which is not dependent upon the will or conscience of the obligor but is a matter of legal right. Edwards v Kearzey, 96 US 595, 24 L Ed 793.

perfect ownership. A perpetual ownership, unencumbered by any real rights in a person other than the owner. Maestri v Board of Assessors, 110 La 517, 34 So 658.

perfect right. A right under the law, not merely a moral right or one dependent upon the conscience of the obligor. Edwards v Kearzey, 96 US 595, 24 L Ed 793.

perfect title. A title that is clear, there being no reasonable doubt as to any fact or point of law upon which validity depends. 55 Am J1st V & P § 149. A title free from litigation, palpable defects, or grave doubts, consisting of both legal and equitable title fairly deducible of record. Pearce v Freeman, 122 Okla 285, 254 P 719. A title uniting in one and the same person the possession, the right of possession, and the right of property. Donovan v Pitcher, 53 Ala 411. As a feature of the implied obligation of the vendor under a contract for the sale of real estate, synonymous with marketable title. 55 Am J1st V & P § 149.

A perfect title must be one that is good and valid beyond all reasonable doubt. To be good, it should be free from litigation, palpable defects and grave doubts; should consist of both legal and equitable titles, and should be fairly deducible of record. Turner v McDonald, 76 Cal 177, 180, 18 P 262.

perfect trust. An executed trust.

Perfectum est cui nihil deest secundum suae perfectionis vel naturae modum (per-fek'tum est kī ni'hil de'est se-kun'dum su'ē per-fek-she-ō'nis vel na-tu'rē mo'dum). That is perfect which lacks nothing according to the measure of its perfection or nature.

perfect war. A war formally declared. A war formally declared in which one whole nation is at war with another whole nation. 56 Am J1st War § 4.

perfidy (pėr'fi-di). A breach of faith, trust or confidence.

perform. To act for the purpose of accomplishment. In the usual and ordinary legal sense, to act in complete accomplishment of one's obligation. Wooldridge v Stern (CC Mo) 42 F 311.

per formam doni (per for'mam dō'nī). By the form of the gift.

Tail-general is so called, because however often the donee in tail shall marry, his issue in general by all and every such marriage is, in successive order, capable of inheriting the estate-tail, per formam doni. See 2 Bl Comm 113.

performance. Such a thorough fulfillment of a duty as puts an end to obligations by leaving nothing more to be done. Reid v Field, 83 Va 26, 32. The doing of the acts required by a contract at the time and place therefor and in the manner stipulated. 17 Am J2d Contr § 355. Nothing less than complete performance for the purposes of the exception from the requirements of the statute of frauds of a contract not to be performed within a year. 49 Am J1st Stat of F § 35. The giving of a show; the rendition of a musical or dramatic work in public.

See **part performance; specific performance.**

performance bond. A type of contractors' bond; a bond which guarantees that the contractor will perform the contract, and usually provides that if the contractor defaults and fails to complete the contract, the surety can itself complete the contract or pay damages up to the limit of the bond. 17 Am J2d Cont Bond § 1.

performance for profit. The exclusive right of the proprietor of a copyright of a musical composition or his assignee. 18 Am J2d Copyr § 24.

A performance for profit may exist, even though no admission fee is charged or no profit actually made. The performance of a copyrighted musical composition in a restaurant or hotel, without charge for admission to hear it, infringes the exclusive right of the owner of the copyright to perform the work publicly for profit. The performance is a part of a total for which the public pays, and the fact that the price of the whole is attributed to a particular item is not important. 18 Am J2d Copyr § 120.

performance on contract. See **performance.**

performance test. A test of the subject matter of a contract in the manner provided by a provision of the contract by way of determining whether or not there has been such performance of the contract as to entitle the party to the payment of money or other consideration called for by the contract. 17 Am J2d Contr § 372.

performed within a year. See **agreement not to be performed within a year.**

perform the duties required of him by law. A term apt in stating the condition of the bond of an executor or administrator, extending to all duties in reference to the due administration of the estate, including the payment of debts and the distribution of the net assets among those entitled by law to receive them. 31 Am J2d Ex & Ad § 127.

per fraudem (pėr frâ'dem). By means of fraud; by fraud; by deceit.

pericarditis (per"i-kär-dī'tis). An inflammation of the membranous sac which encloses the heart.

periculi imminentis evitandi causa (pe-ri'ku-lī im-mi-nen'tis ē'vi-tan'di kâ'za). For the purpose of avoiding imminent danger. Barnard v Adams (US) 10 How 270, 304, 13 L Ed 417, 431.

periculo petentis (pe-ri'ku-lo pe-ten'tis). At the risk of the petitioner.

Periculosum est res novas et inusitatas inducere (pe-ri-ku-lō'sum est rēz no'vas et in-us-i-ta'tās in-du'se-re). It is dangerous to introduce new and untried things.

Periculosum existimo quod bonorum virorum non comprobatur exemplo (pe-ri-ku-lō'sum eg-zis'ti-mō quod bō-nō'rum vi-rō'rum non kom-prō-bā'ter eg-zem'plō). I believe that that which is not approved by the example of worthy men is dangerous.

periculosus (per-i-ku-lō'sus). Perilous; fraught with peril or danger; dangerous.

periculum (pē-rik'ū-lum). Peril; danger; risk.

Periculum rei venditae, nondum traditae, est emptoris (pe-ri'ku-lum rē'ī ven'di-te, non'dom tra'di-tē, est emp-tō'ris). The risk of a thing sold, but not yet delivered, is that of the buyer.

peril. Exposure to injury, loss, or destruction; imminent or impending danger, risk, hazard, or jeopardy. Terre Haute & Indianapolis Railroad Co. v Brunker, 128 Ind 542, 552, 26 NE 178.

perils of inland waters. See **perils of river, lake, or canal.**

perils of river, lake, or canal. A term analogous to and of like import with perils of the sea; risks arising from natural accidents peculiar to river, canal or lake which do not happen by the intervention of man and are not avoidable by human prudence. 48 Am J1st Ship § 455.

perils of the sea. Natural and inevitable accidents occurring upon the sea. 48 Am J1st Ship § 454. Accidents peculiar to the sea which do not happen by the intervention of man and are not preventable or avoidable by human prudence. 48 Am J1st Ship § 454. Extraordinary occurrences of the elements at sea; lightning, tempests, rocks, and violent stress of weather, winds, and waves. 29A Am J Rev ed Ins § 1310. Sometimes inclusive of capture by pirates. 48 Am J1st Ship § 454.

A clause of a motor carrier liability policy insuring against perils of the seas, lakes, rivers, or inland waters, while on ferries contemplates a loss arising during the course of transportation by water. Long Motor Lines v Home Fire & Marine Ins. Co. 220 SC 335, 67 SE2d 512.

perils of the street. See **street perils.**

per incuriam (per in-kū'ri-am). Through carelessness; through inadvertence; through lack of care.

perinde valere (per-in'de val-ē're). To be equally valid,—a dispensation whereby a clerk or clergyman who was not qualified was nevertheless admitted to a benefice.

per industriam (per in-dus'tri-am). By industry.

per industriam hominis (per in-dus'tri-am ho'mi-nis). By the industry of man. See 2 Bl Comm 391.

per infortunium (per in-for-tu'ni-um). By misfortune; by misadventure; accidentally.

per interim charge d'affairs. See **charge d'affairs.**

period. A stage in history or, as in geology, in natural processes. An interval of time.
    The word has its etymological meaning, but it also has a distinctive signification according to the subject in connection with which it may be used. It may mean any portion of complete time, from a thousand years, or less, to the period of a day; and when used to designate an act to be done, or to be begun, though its completion may take an uncertain time, as, for instance, the act of exportation, it must mean the day on which the exportation commences, or it would be an unmeaning and useless word in its connection. Sampson v Peaslee, (US) 20 How 571, 579, 15 L Ed 1022, 1027.

periodical. Adjective: Occurring at regular intervals. Noun: A magazine or other publication appearing at regular intervals of time, usually weekly or monthly. Houghton v Payne, 194 US 88, 97, 48 L Ed 888, 890, 24 S Ct 590.

periodical appropriation. An annual appropriation of public funds.
    See **appropriation.**

periodical rests. See **rest.**

periodic apportionment. The apportionment of legislative districts from time to time as provided by constitution or statute, usually following the taking of the federal census, for the purpose of making the apportionment conform to changes in population. 25 Am J2d Elect § 15.

periodic employee. See **casual employee.**

periodic insanity. Intermittent insanity; insanity interrupted by lucid intervals.

periodic payments. See **instalment payments.**

period of gestation (jes-tā'shon). The period of time elapsing between a child's conception and its birth, which is, normally, nine months. 23 Am J2d Desc & D § 88.

period of nurture. See **nurture period.**

period of prescription. See **prescriptive period.**

period of woman. See **menses.**

periphrasis (pe-rif'ra̧-sis). Circumlocution; verbosity.

per ipsum regem et totum consilium in parliamento (per ip'sum rē'jem et tō'tum kon-si'li-um in par-li-a-men'tō). By the king himself and the whole council in parliament.

Perishable Agricultural Commodities Act. A federal statute passed under the Commerce Clause of the United States Constitution to facilitate the flow of perishable agricultural commodities in commerce by licensing dealers, commission merchants, and brokers, and by prohibiting unfair practices. Rothenberg v Rothstein & Sons (CA3 Pa) 183 F2d 524, 21 ALR2d 832.

perishable cargo. A ship's cargo subject to deterioration from inherent causes. Perry v Cobb, 88 Me 435, 34 A 278.

perishable goods. See **perishable property.**

perishable property. Property subject to decay, deterioration, or depreciation. Anno: 3 ALR3d 595 § 1. Precisely, property which by its inherent nature is subject to immediate decay, Anno: 3 ALR3d 597-604, to decay in a short time. Illinois Cent. Railroad Co. v McClellan, 54 Ill 58. Broadly, any property which will materially depreciate in value, whether by natural decay or from other causes. Anno: 3 ALR3d 608. For some purposes, as for a sale in bankruptcy, property likely to deteriorate in value, even though physical deterioration is not reasonably to be expected. Re Pedlow (CA2 NY) 209 F 841.

peritonitis (per"i-tǫ-nī'tis). A disease characterized by inflammation of the lining of the abdomen.

Perjurii poena divina, exitium; humana dedecus (per-jū'ri-ī pe'na di-vī'na, ex-i'she-um; hu-mā'na dē-de'kus). The divine punishment of perjury is death; the human punishment, disgrace. See 4 Bl Comm 139.

Perjuri sunt qui servatis verbis juramenti decipiunt aures eorum qui accipiunt (per-jū'rī sunt quī ser-vā'tis ver'bis jū-ra-men'tī de-si'pi-unt â'rēz ē-ō'rum quī ak-si'pi-unt). They are perjured who, by preserving the words of the oath, deceive the ears of those who receive it.

perjury. Wilful and corrupt false swearing or affirming, after an oath lawfully administered, in the course of a judicial or quasi-judicial proceeding as to some matter material to the issue or point in question. 41 Am J1st Perj § 2. In a broader sense, wilful false swearing in regard to any matter or thing respecting which an oath is required or even authorized by law. State v Miller, 26 RI 282, 58 A 882.
    False statements of a witness, made in open court are not the subject of perjury, where they have been corrected before the case was submitted. State v Ledford, 195 Wash 581, 81 P2d 830.

per laudamentum parium suorum (per lâ-dā-men'tum pā'ri-um su-ō'rum). By the declaration of his peers.

per laudamentum sive judicium parium (per lâ-dā-men'tum sī've jū-di'she-um pā'ri-um). By the verdict or judgment of his peers.

per legale judicium parium (per le-ga'le jū-di'she-um pa'ri-um). By the lawful judgment or verdict of his peers.

per legem Angliae (per le'jem An'gli-ē). By the law of England.

per legem terrae (per lē'jem ter'rē). According to the law of the land. 16 Am J2d Const L § 542.

per legem terrae et per communem legem terrae (per lē'jem ter'rē et per kom-mū'nem lē'jem ter'rē). By the law of the land and by the common law of the land. Hurtado v California, 110 US 516, 525, 28 L Ed 232, 235, 4 S Ct 111, 292.

per le gree ou sans le gree (per le grē ou sôn le grē). With consent or without it.

permanent. To continue indefinitely; to continue until a change shall be made.
    Not, however, to continue forever, nor perpetually, nor for life, nor for any fixed or certain period. Lord v Goldberg, 81 Cal 596, 601, 22 P 1126, 1128; Newton v Commissioners of Mahoning County (US) 10 Otto 548, 25 L Ed 710, 712.

permanent abode. A domicil or home. Anderson v Pifer, 315 Ill 164, 146 NE 171, 37 ALR 134.

A home, which a party may leave as interest or whim may dictate, but which he has no present intention to abandon. Sullivan v Detroit, Ypsilanti & Ann Arbor Railway Co. 135 Mich 661, 98 NW 756.

permanent alimony. Alimony awarded by final judgment in an action for the annulment of a marriage. 4 Am J2d Annul § 102. An allowance which a court compels the husband to pay to his wife for her support and maintenance where there exists between them a legal separation or divorce. 24 Am J2d Div & S § 600. Permanent in the sense that it is a final provision for the maintenance of the wife, contained in a judgment either decreeing that she is entitled to separate maintenance or granting her a divorce limited or absolute. Huffman v Huffman, 47 Or 610, 86 P 593.

Alimony is never permanent in the absolute sense, usually terminating upon the death of either one of the parties to the divorce. 24 Am J2d Div & S § 515. In some jurisdictions, a woman entitled to alimony may lose the right to receive it by misconduct. 24 Am J2d Div & S § 685.

permanent building and loan association. A building and loan association which issues its stock, not all at once, nor in series, but at any time when application is made therefor. Cook v Equitable Bldg. & Loan Asso. 104 Ga 814, 821.

Permanent Court of International Justice. The judicial branch of the League of Nations, established in 1920 under the auspices of the league, succeeded by the International Court of Justice established as the judicial branch of the United Nations. 30 Am J Rev ed Internat L § 54.

permanent damages. Literally, lasting injury to person or property. Technically, injury to real estate which is permanent in character, so that all the damages, whether present, past, or prospective must be recovered in a single action. 22 Am J2d Damg § 28.

permanent disability. Narrowly defined, a disability remaining to the end or during the lifetime of the person involved. 29A Am J Rev ed Ins § 1529. More broadly defined, a disability which, with reasonable probability, will continue for some indefinite period of time, there being no present indication of recovery. Stuhlbarg v Metropolitan Life Ins. Co. 73 Ohio App 355, 29 Ohio Ops 72, 39 Ohio L Abs 525, 53 NE2d 828, affd 143 Ohio St 390, 28 Ohio Ops 343, 55 NE2d 640.

Under a policy of war risk insurance a person's disability is permanent when it is based upon conditions which render it reasonably certain at the time that it will continue throughout the life of the insured. Adams v United States (CA7 Ill) 116 F2d 199.

permanent employment. Steady employment, a steady job, a position of some permanence, as contrasted with a temporary job or temporary employment. Arentz v Morse Dry Dock & Repair Co. 249 NY 439, 164 NE 342, 62 ALR 231. Employment for an indefinite period, which, in the absence of some special consideration, may be terminated at any time by either party. Dicks v Clarence L. Boyd Co. 205 Okla 383, 238 P2d 315, 28 ALR2d 870.

Under special circumstances the term has been construed to mean continuous or indefinite employment, not terminable at the will of either party. Sullivan v Detroit, Ypsilanti & Ann Arbor Railway Co. 135 Mich 661, 98 NW 756.

permanent franchise. See **perpetual franchise.**

permanent government. An expression connoting substitution for a former temporary or provisional government. Eckloff v District of Columbia, 135 US 240, 34 L Ed 120, 10 S Ct 752.

permanent improvement. Something done to or put on land which cannot be removed or carried away, either because it has become physically impossible to separate it from the land or because, in contemplation of law, it has been annexed to the soil and is therefore to be considered a part of the freehold. 27 Am J1st Improv § 19.

permanent injunction. An injunction granted after final hearing on the merits, as distinguished from a temporary injunction granted by way of provisional relief. Riggins v Thompson, 96 Tex 154, 157, 71 SW 14.

permanent injury. An injury, the future effect of which as a complete or partial disability appears with reasonable certainty. 22 Am J2d Damg § 117. Within the meaning of the risk assumed by an insurer, a lasting or continuous injury. Rom v Republic Coal Co. 94 Mont 250, 22 P2d 157.

An injury by pollution of well waters may be permanent in a legal sense, though not perpetual, unending, or unchangeable. Haveman v Beulow, 36 Wash 185, 217 P2d 313, 19 ALR2d 763.

See **permanent disability.**

permanent insurance. A policy of insurance under which the insurer agrees to be and remain forever liable to the insured, his heirs and assigns. Marshall v Franklin Fire Ins. Co. 176 Pa 628, 35 A 204. The policy issued after consideration of an application for insurance, as distinguished from a binder or temporary insurance.

permanent insurance fund. A fund established pursuant to federal statute for insuring deposits in banks insured by the Federal Deposit Insurance Corporation. 12 USC § 1821; 10 Am J2d Bks § 427.

See **state insurance fund.**

permanent leasehold. See **perpetual leasehold.**

permanent location. For purposes of taxation of tangible personal property, a more or less permanent location, as distinguished from a transient or temporary location. Not a location in the sense that real estate has a location, or a location fixed beyond any present intention of ever removing the property. 51 Am J1st Tax § 454.

The expression does not mean that to be so located the goods must remain in the place indefinitely, or until they are worn out. Hopkins v Baker Bros. & Co. 78 Md 363, 28 A 284.

permanent monument. A marker of a boundary line of more or less permanency, at least one not of a perishable nature.

Stakes and posts referred to in the recorded location of a mining claim, may or may not be permanent monuments and their permanency presents a question for the determination of a jury under the evidence produced. J. E. Riley Invest. Co. v Sakow (CA9 Alaska) 98 F2d 8.

permanent nuisance. A nuisance of such a character and existing under such circumstances that it will be presumed to continue indefinitely, being at once necessarily productive of all the damage which can ever result from it. 39 Am J1st Nuis § 131.

permanent receivership. A receivership established by the court after judgment, Decker v Gardner, 124

NY 334, 26 NE 814, as distinguished from a receivership had by way of provisional relief.

permanent repairs. For practical purposes, improvements. 33 Am J1st Life Est § 454.

permanent residence. Domicile. Re Gape, [1952] Ch 743, [1952] 2 All Eng 579, 35 ALR2d 380.
See **domicil**; **residence.**

permanent road. A road surfaced with crushed rock, gravel, macadam, brick, concrete, asphalt-macadam, or any other hard surfacing material. Pine v Baker, 76 Okla 62, 184 P 445 (statutory definition).

permanent scholarship. The tuition of one pupil in perpetuo, that is, the right to send any fit person within the option of the holder to college, as a pupil, to be educated, subject to the usual regulations of the institution, free of tuition. Howard College v Turner, 71 Ala 429.

permanent statute. See **perpetual statute.**

permanent support order. An order for the permanent support of wife or of a child. 23 Am J2d Desert §§ 49, 112, 118.

permanent trespass (tres'pas). A trespass of a permanent nature, where the injury is continually renewed; as where a man's cattle are habitually permitted to trespass and spoil and consume the herbage. See 3 Bl Comm 212.

per medietatem linguae (per me-di-e-tā'tem lin'gwē). See **jury de medietate linguae.**

per metas et bundas (per me'tas et bun'das). By metes and bounds.

per minas (per mi'nas). By threats.
See **duress per minas.**

per minas duress (per mi'nas dū-res'). Same as **duress per minas.**

per mis (per mē). In two parts; in half.

per misadventure (per mis-ad-ven'tūr). By misfortune; by accident; accidentally.

per mis et per tout (per mē et per tou). By the half, and by all.

permissible levy. The maximum levy of taxes permitted by law. 38 Am J1st Mun Corp § 427.

permission. Leave; license; sufferance.

permission of court. See **leave of court.**

permission of insured. The consent of the owner of an automobile covered by an insurance policy to the use of the car by another. Anno: 5 ALR2d 608.
See **consent of insured.**

permissive. Permitted; allowed; suffered to continue.

permissive constitutional provision. A provision of a constitution in such permissive terms that reasonably, it is not to be construed as mandatory. 16 Am J2d Const L § 91.

permissive counterclaim. A counterclaim constituting an essentially independent action, having no relation to the subject matter of the plaintiff's cause of action. Big Cola Corp. v World Bottling Co. (CA6 Tenn) 134 F2d 718. Any claim against an opposing party not arising out of the transaction or occurrence that is the subject matter of the opposing party's claim. Rule 13 (b), Federal Rules of Civil Procedure.

permissive franchise. A franchise to be exploited only as the grantee thereof sees fit to exploit it, except as he is influenced toward exploitation by the right of the municipality which granted the franchise to forfeit it for nonuser. Murray v Roberts (CA2 NY) 103 F2d 889.

permissive party. See **proper party.**

permissive possession. A term loosely applied to the occupation of real property by one person with the consent of the owner or the person entitled to possession, for example, occupation of premises by a licensee. Jeffers v Edge (Okla) 295 P2d 787.
A tenancy at will may arise as a result of the taking possession of land by permission, "permissive possession," as it is called, without any understanding as to the duration of the possession; and this tenancy may, by reason of the reservation or payment of rent, be changed into a periodic tenancy. Smith v Royal Ins. Co. (CA9 Cal) 111 F2d 667.

permissive use. A use of premises which is not hostile or adverse to the owner. The use of premises by express or implied permission or license granted by the owner. 25 Am J2d Ease § 54. The use of the premises of another with his consent or sufferance. The use of premises by the public under, and in connection with, its use by the owner in any manner desired by him. Anno: 58 ALR 240; 23 Am J2d Ded § 29. An interest in real property, recognized only in equity prior to the statute of uses, arising where the legal title was conveyed to one person for the use or benefit of another.

permissive use of highway. The use of street or highway for purposes other than that of travel and transportation. 25 Am J High § 168.

permissive waste. Waste by a tenant, otherwise known as negligent waste or passive waste, in failing to exercise the ordinary care of a prudent man for the preservation and protection of the estate, such as permitting a house to remain uncovered, whereby the timbers become rotten. 56 Am J1st Waste § 4.

permit. Verb: To give permission; to license. To grant leave or liberty; to allow to be done by giving consent or by not prohibiting. Wilson v State, 19 Ind App 389, 46 NE 1050. To tolerate. Cowley v People, 83 NY 464. Noun: A permission granted in writing, such as a building permit. A license.

permit system. A system or practice of employers of labor, adopted to enforce the "open shop" plan, the object of which was to limit sales of certain specified kinds of materials to builders who supported the plan.
To render this restriction effective, the person concerned was required to obtain a permit from the builders' exchange, specifying the kinds and quantities of materials to be furnished and the particular job on which they were to be used. Industrial Asso. of San Francisco v United States, 268 US 64, 75, 69 L Ed 849, 852, 45 S Ct 403.

permittere. (Latin.) To permit.

per mitter le droit (per mit'ā le drwoi). By the release of the right,—one of the modes in which releases operated at common law, as where a person who has been disseised releases to the disseisor, his heir or feoffee.
By the release, the right which was in the releaser is added to the possession of the releasee, and the two combined perfect the estate. Miller v Emans, 19 NY 384, 387.

per mitter l'estate (per mit'ā l'es-tat'). By the release of the estate,—one of the modes in which releases operated at common law.

As where two or more are seised, either by deed, devise or descent, as joint-tenants or coparceners of the same estate, and one of them releases to the other, this is said to enure by way of mitter l'estate. Miller v Emans, 19 NY 384, 388.

permitting gambling. Knowingly acquiescing in the use of one's property or premises, or of property or premises under one's control, as a place to gamble. 24 Am J1st Gaming § 42. Licensing gambling. 24 Am J1st Gaming § 10.

permit to run at large. Intentionally or negligently permitting one's animals to run at large. Pongetti v Spraggins, 215 Miss 397, 61 So 2d 158, 34 ALR2d 1277.

permutatio (per-mu-tā'she-o). (Civil law.) Same as **permutation.**

permutation (pėr-mū-tā'shọn). An exchange or barter of goods.

per my et per tout (per mē et per tou). By the half or moiety, and by all.

The phrase describes the seisin of joint tenants, in whom there must be unity of possession. They each of them have the entire possession (not merely half), as well of every parcel as of the whole. See 2 Bl Comm 182.

pernancy (pėr'nạn-si). The taking, perception, or receipt of the rents, profits, or other advantages arising from an estate in real property. See 2 Bl Comm 163.

pernor (pėr'nọr). A receiver; a taker; a recipient.

pernor of profits (of prof'its). A person who enjoys the profits or advantages arising out of an estate in real property; a cestui que use.

pernour (per-noor'). Same as **pernor.**

per omnes (per om'nēz). By all persons.

per pais (per pā). By the country.
See **trial by the county.**

per patriam (per pā'tri-äm). By the country, by means of a jury of the vicinage.

perpetration of felony. The commission of a felony.
Under the usual statutory provision that homicide committed in the perpetration of a felony is murder in the first degree, where the homicide is committed within the res gestae of the felony charged, it is committed in the perpetration of, or attempt to perpetrate, the felony. Conrad v State, 75 Ohio St 52, 78 NE 957.
See **attempt.**

perpetrator. One who perpetrates. A principal in the first degree; that is the person who actually commits the criminal act, as distinguished from one who aids or abets in its commission. Myers v State, 19 Okla Crim 129, 197 P 884, 18 ALR 1057.

perpetual. Everlasting or eternal. Continuous; without interruption.
Which of the above variant meanings is to apply in the particular case is to be determined according to the subject to which the adjective is applied. Scanlan v Crawshaw, 5 Mo App 337, 339.

perpetual annuity. An annuity granted in fee. Anno: 54 ALR2d 373 § 6. An annuity to continue for an unlimited time without interruption; one to be enjoyed longer than the lifetime of the first taker or beneficiary. 4 Am J2d Annui § 7.

perpetual care. The obligation of the proprietor of a cemetery, imposed by statute or by contract with a purchaser of lots, for the upkeep of the lots and graves thereon in sodding, cutting grass, planting shrubbery, etc. 14 Am J2d Cem § 20.

perpetual contract. A contract without limit as to duration. 17 Am J2d Contr § 486.

perpetual curacy (kur'ạ-si). A curacy where all the tithes are appropriated, and no vicarage is endowed, but instead thereof, the perpetual curate is appointed by the appropriator. See 1 Bl Comm 393.

perpetual easement. An easement to continue in operation and be enforceable forever. 25 Am J2d Ease § 99.

Perpetua lex est, nullam legem humanam ac positivam perpetuam esse; et clausula quae abrogationem excludit ab initio non valet (per-pe'tu-a lex est, nul'-lam le'jem hu-mā'nam ak po-zi-tī'vam per-pe'tu-am es'se; et klā'su-la kwē ab-ro-gā-she-ō'nem ex-klu'dit ab in-i'she-ō non va'let). The law is perpetual that no human and positive law is to be perpetual; and a clause which excludes or precludes abrogation or repeal is void from the beginning.

perpetual existence of corporation. The immortality of a corporation as spoken of in the Dartmouth College Case. Dartmouth College v Woodward (US) 4 Wheat 518, 4 L Ed 629.
See **perpetual succession.**

perpetual franchise. A franchise to endure forever, at least so long as the state refrains from interfering to terminate it. Anno: 2 ALR 1109; 35 Am J2d Ferr § 44; 36 Am J2d Franch § 44; 56 Am J1st Watwk § 5.

perpetual injunction. Same as **permanent injunction.**

perpetual lease. A lease for a yearly rental to one for as long as he shall comply with the contract and pay the rent. The equivalent of a conveyance in fee reserving the rent, 32 Am J1st L & T § 1039; creating a qualified, base, or determinable fee. Smith v Improvement District, 108 Ark 141, 156 SW 455; Piper v Meredith, 83 NH 107, 139 A 294, 55 ALR 148.

perpetually. See **perpetual; in perpetuum.**

perpetual non-participating royalty. A right to royalties on oil and gas produced which is reserved or granted before any oil and gas lease is executed, granting or reserving no right to participate in the making of future leases. Denver Joint Stock Land Bank v Dixon, 57 Wyo 523, 122 P2d 842, 140 ALR 1270.

perpetual rate. A rate for public utility service fixed as for all time, displacing the power of the municipality to fix reasonable rates. Mobile Electric Co. v Mobile, 201 Ala 607, 79 So 39.

perpetual restriction. A restriction by covenant unlimited in respect of time. 20 Am J2d Cov § 180.

perpetual statute. A statute which, not being by its terms limited in its operation to a particular period of time, will continue in force until duly altered or repealed by competent authority. 50 Am J1st Stat § 513.

perpetual succession. Continuous and uninterrupted succession of a corporation so long as it shall continue to exist as a corporation. 18 Am J2d Corp § 65. In the case of a life insurance company, an existence which may run beyond the period for which the corporation may legally exist, so far as existence is necessary to give effect to the obligations assumed under policies issued by the company. State ex rel. Major v German Mut. L. Ins. Co. 224 Mo 84, 123 SW 19.

perpetual tax lien. An expression loosely applied to the lien of an assessment which, as provided by statute, shall stand with priority as against future and recurring liens for ad valorem taxes. Altman v Kilburn, 45 NM 453, 116 P2d 812, 136 ALR 554.

perpetuam rei memoriam. See **in perpetuam rei memoriam.**

perpetuation of testimony. Preserving testimony for possible use in future litigation by taking the deposition of the witness, thus guarding against the possible loss of his testimony by death or incompetency. 23 Am J2d Dep § 8.

perpetuity. Literally, something that lasts forever. In an artificial sense of the term, as used in the law of property, a limitation of a contingent future interest in violation of the rule against perpetuities. A limitation, whether executory or by way of remainder, of either real or personal property, which is not to vest until after expiration of, or will not necessarily vest within, the period fixed and prescribed by law for the creation of future estates and interests, and which is not destructible by persons for the time being entitled to the property subject to the future limitation, except with the concurrence of the individual interested under that limitation. 41 Am J1st Perp § 7.

See **rule against perpetuities.**

perpetuity of the king. The attribute of absolute immortality which the law of England ascribes to the king, in his political capacity.

Henry, Edward, or George may die, but the king survives them all. For, immediately upon the decease of the reigning prince, in his natural capacity, his kingship or imperial dignity, by act of law, without any interregnum or interval, is vested eo instanti in his heir. See 1 Bl Comm 249.

perpetuum rei testimonium. See **in perpetuum rei testimonium.**

per power of attorney. By power of attorney.
See **power of attorney.**

per pro (pėr prō). An abbreviation of **per procuration.** Giles v Newton (DC NY) 21 F2d 484.

per proc. An abbreviation of **per procuration.**

per procuration (per prok-ū-rā'shon). By proxy. An expression used by an agent in executing a note or other contract on behalf of his principal, which indicates that the authority of the agent is special and limited.

per quae servitia (per kwē ser-vi'she-a). By which services,—a writ by which the cognizee in a fine of lands could have the tenant attorn to him.

perquirere (per-qui're-re). To acquire; to purchase.

perquisites (per'kwi-zits). Emoluments or profits accruing to a public officer beyond the salary payable to him. 43 Am J1st Pub Of § 359. Fees, allowances, privileges or compensation beyond those of his ordinary salary or wages, which an officer or employee may receive with propriety. Cantling v Hannibal & St. Joseph Railroad Co. 54 Mo 385.

perquisitio (per-qui-zi'she-o). An acquisition; a purchase.

perquisitor (pėr-kwiz'i-tor). Same as **purchaser.**

perquisitum (pėr-kwiz'i-tum). A purchase; an acquisition.

per quod (per kwŏd). By which; by means of which.

per quod actio accrevit (per quod ak'she-o a-krē'vit). By means of which an action accrued.

per quod consortium amisit (per kwod kon-sor'she-um a-mi'sit). Through or by means of which, he has lost the consortium. 27 Am J1st H & W § 501.

per quod defamatory (per kwod dĕ-fam'a-tō-ri). See **libelous per quod; slanderous per quod.**

per quod matrimonium amisit (per kwod ma-tri-mō'-ni-um a-mī'sit). Through or by which he has lost his marriage. Harrison v Cage (Eng) 5 Mod 411.

per quod servitium amisit (per kwod ser-vi'she-um a-mi'sit). By or through which he lost his services.

Per rationes pervenitur ad legitimam rationem (per ra-she-ō'nēz per-ve'ni-ter ad le-ji'ti-mam ra-she-ō'nem). By reasoning one arrives at the legal or proper reason.

Per rerum naturam, factum negantis nulla probatio est (per re'rum na-tu'ram, fak'tum ne-gan'tis nul'-la pro-ba'she-ō est). In the nature of things, a person who denies a fact is held to no proof.

per saltum (pėr sal'tum). By a leap or bound, that is, quickly; speedily.

per sceptrum (per sep'trum). By the sceptre; by the sword.

per se (pėr sė). By itself. By or through itself; simply; as such; in its own relations. Burr v Winnett Times Publishing Co. 80 Mont 70, 258 P 242.

persecutio (per-se-kū'she-ō). (Civil law.) The act of prosecuting or proceeding against a person in either a civil or a criminal action.

per se defamatory. See **libelous per se; slanderous per se.**

per se negligence (pėr sė neg'li-jęns). See **negligence per se.**

per se nuisance (pėr sė nū'sạns). See **nuisance per se.**

per se slander. See **slander per se.**

persistent refusal of sexual intercourse. A ground of divorce in some jurisdictions; constant and continuous refusal. Goucher v Goucher, 82 Cal App 449, 255 P 892.

persistent violator. An habitual criminal. 25 Am J1st Habit Cr § 11.

In some jurisdictions, the term is used to signify that a person charged with a given criminal offense has previously been convicted of a similar offense, and in such states the persistent violator is guilty of an aggravated offense. State v Bruno, 69 Utah 444, 256 P 109.

person. An individual or an organization. UCC § 1–201(30). An individual man, woman, or child or, as a general rule, a corporation. 18 Am J2d Corp § 20. Inclusive of bodies politic and corporate. Waterbury v Board of Com. 10 Mont 515, 26 P 1002. As used in the Bankruptcy Act, inclusive of corporations, officers, partnerships, and women, except where otherwise specified. Bankruptcy Act § 1(23); 11 USC § 1(23). Under the negotiable Instruments Law, an individual or a body of persons whether incorporated or not. Uniform Negotiable Instruments Law § 191. As used in the anti-trust laws, inclusive of corporations and associations. 36 Am J1st Monop etc § 186. Inclusive of corporations where used in a statute imposing a license tax. 33 Am J1st Lic § 49. Usually inclusive of corporations in a tax statute, 51 Am J1st Tax § 318. Inclusive of corporations where used in a statute relating to the sale of commodities by weight or measure. 56 Am J1st W & L § 5. Inclusive of corporations in a pure food law. State v Belle Springs Creamery Co.

83 Kan 389, 111 P 474. For the purposes of the due process clause, either a citizen or an alien. 3 Am J2d Aliens § 8. For the purposes of extradition, either a citizen or an alien. 31 Am J2d Extrad § 17.

A corporation is deemed a "person" within the meaning of the statute of limitations, and consequently, the statute ordinarily runs against corporations and domestic corporations are generally included within the class of persons who may plead the statute, and they may, as a general rule, acquire title by adverse possession for the statutory period in the same manner and to the same extent as an individual. 34 Am J1st Lim Ac § 372. A municipal corporation is a "person" within the meaning of the statute of limitations. 34 Am J1st Lim Ac § 397.

Liquor license laws may either expressly permit, or be held susceptible of a construction which authorizes corporations to be licensed thereunder, and the word "person," as used in such legislation, is usually held to embrace a corporation, irrespective of whether there is an express provision to that effect in the license law or in general law. 30 Am J Rev ed Intox L § 126.

The word "person," where used in statutes defining crimes, is usually construed to include a corporation, so as to bring corporations within the prohibition of the statute. 19 Am J2d Corp § 1436.

Dependent upon the entire context of the instrument, the word "person," as used in a will, may or may not include a corporation. 57 Am J1st Wills § 1326.

persona (pėr-sō'nạ). (Civil law.) A person.

personable. Having a good appearance. In an unusual sense, competent to incur obligations enforceable at law.

Persona conjuncta aequiparatur interesse proprio (per-sō'na kon-junk'ta ē-qui-pa-rā'ter in-ter-es'se prō'pri-ō). The fact of a person's being connected by ties of blood is equivalent to his having a personal interest.

persona ecclesiae (per-sō'na e-kle'si-ē). (Eccles.) Person of the church; a parson.

Persona est homo, cum statu quodam consideratus (per-sō'na est hō'mō, kum sta'tū quō'dam kon-si-de-rā'tus). A person is a man when considered with reference to a certain status.

Personae vice fungitur municipium et decuria (per-sō'nē vī'se fun'ji-ter mu-ni-si'pi-um et de-kū'ri-a). A town or a borough acts as a person. Warner v Beers (NY) 23 Wend 103, 144.

person aggrieved. See **aggrieved; aggrieved party.**

persona impersonata (pėr-sō'na im-per-sō-nā'ta). A parson who has been inducted into and put into possession of a benefice. See 1 Bl Comm 391.

personal. Pertaining to the person. Terre Haute Electric Railway Co. v Lauer, 21 Ind App 466, 475. Springing from or belonging to one's self; affecting or relating to one individually. Genung v Best, 100 NJ Eq 250, 253, 135 A 514, 516.

personal actions. Action brought for the specific recovery of goods and chattels, or for damages or other redress for breach of contract or other injuries, of whatever description, the specific recovery of lands, tenements, and hereditaments only excepted. 1 Am J2d Actions § 38. As to form, either ex contractu or ex delicto; as to place of trial, local or transitory; as to object, in personam or in rem. 1 Am J2d Actions § 38.

personal ailment. A sickness, but not inclusive of confinement in childbirth. 29 Am J Rev ed Ins § 758.

personal assets. The personal property of a person. Personal property of a decedent vesting in his executor or administrator as assets available for the payment of the decedent's debts, consisting of goods, chattels, money, credits, unpaid legacies, and corporate stock. 31 Am J2d Ex & Ad § 197.

personal benefit. For the benefit of a person individually.

As the term is used in a testamentary gift, the words do not limit the beneficiary to so much as is necessary for his support. The word benefit is much broader than the word support. But it is not so broad as to include any purpose to which the absolute owner of property can devote it. Re Robinson, 101 Vt 464, 75 ALR 59.

personal bias. See **bias.**

As a cause for the disqualification of a judge to sit in the trial of a case, "personal bias" must amount to personal prejudice against the party. Such bias cannot be shown by a judicial opinion formed on legal evidence offered in open court in the hearing of a case, however adverse or severe it may be upon the party concerned. Parker v New England Oil Corp. (DC Mass) 13 F2d 497.

personal chattel. Any article of tangible personal property.

An account receivable is not a personal chattel. Plunkett-Jarrell Grocery Co. v Terry, 222 Ark 784, 263 SW2d 229, 44 ALR2d 917.

See **personal effects; personal things.**

personal contract. See **personal service contract.**

personal covenant. A covenant which does not run with the land so as to bind the heirs, personal representative, or transferee of the covenantor, but binds only the covenantor personally. 20 Am J2d Cov § 29.

personal earnings. Earnings by physical or mental labor, unaided by capital, except in so far as may be necessary to supply the means of performing such labor as a necessary incident of the same, such, for instance, as the ax of a wood cutter, or the pen, ink, and paper of a writer. Kerr v Tyler Guaranty State Bank (Tex Civ App) 283 SW 601, 603.

personal easement. Same as **easement in gross.**

personal effects. Clothing, jewelry, ornaments, and other articles carried or worn upon the person. See **effects.**

personal estate. Every species of property not of a freehold nature, including not only goods and chattels, but rights and credits. Bullowa v Gladding, 40 RI 147, 100 A 249.

As to what passes under term "personal estate" in will, see Anno: 53 ALR2d 1059.

See **my personal estate.**

personal execution. See **execution against the person.**

personal exemption. See **exemption; tax exemption.**

personal holding company. A corporation subjected to a special federal income tax in order to avoid the use of the organization by an individual in a high tax bracket for tax avoidance purposes. IRC § 451.

A corporation at least 80 per cent of the income of which in one year was derived from interest, and at least fifty per cent of the outstanding stock of which was owned by not more than five persons, was a personal holding company as defined in Section 351(b) (1) of the Revenue Act of 1934. O'Sullivan Rubber Co. v Commissioner (CA2) 120 F2d 845.

Personalia personam sequuntur (per-so-nā'li-a per-sō'nam se-qu-un'ter). Personal property follows the person. Flanders v Cross, 64 Mass (10 Cush) 514, 516.

personal immunity. See **immunity; privacy.**

personal indignity. A ground for divorce, consisting of an act insulting or humiliating to the victim, evidencing hate or estrangement of the offender from the innocent spouse, as a result of which the victim finds further cohabitation intolerable. 24 Am J2d Div & S § 156. Conduct that renders life burdensome and intolerable without being so violent as to endanger life. Sharp v Sharp, 106 Pa Super 33, 161 A 453.

personal injury. An injury to the body of a person. Smith v Buck, 119 Ohio St 101, 162 NE 382, 61 ALR 1343; Rheudasil v Clower (Tenn) 270 SW2d 345, 46 ALR2d 1083. A personal wrong; an invasion of a personal right; an injury which pertains to the person, the individual. People v Quanstrom, 93 Mich 254, 53 NW 165. As the subject of an action:—an injury to the person, whether the action is based upon contract or tort. 34 Am J Rev ed Lim Ac § 103. Any actionable injury to the individual himself, whether or not it involves physical contact. Bennett v Bennett, 116 NY 584, 23 NE 17. Any injury causing actual physical pain, discomfort, or disability to any person, which occasions loss or damage either to such person or to any other person entitled to the benefit of the services of the injured person. White v Safe Deposit & Trust Co. 140 Md 593, 118 A 77, 24 ALR 482, 485 (alienation of spouse's affections); sometimes inclusive of an injury affecting the reputation, character, conduct, manner, and habits of a person. Tisdale v Eubanks, 180 NC 153, 104 SE 339, 11 ALR 374. As the term is used in venue statutes:—a physical or bodily injury. 56 Am J1st Ven § 15. As the term is used in workmen's compensation acts:—any lesion or change in the structure of the body, causing harm thereto and a lessened facility of its natural and normal use. 58 Am J1st Workm Comp § 194.

There are two classes of personal injuries: those that are fatal, and those that are not fatal. The term naturally includes injuries of both classes because no one of either class is not an injury. The obvious and ordinary meaning of the term is all injuries, whether fatal or not. Hendel v State Farm Mut. Auto. Ins. Co. (CA7 Ind) 97 F2d 777.

A right of action exists in favor of a child permanently injured through the negligence of another prior to its birth but after it had become a viable child, under a constitutional provision affording a remedy to every "person" for injury done him in his person. Williams v Marion Rapid Transit, 152 Ohio St 114, 87 NE2d 334, 10 ALR2d 1051.

personalis actio (per-sō-nā'lis ak'she-ō). (Civil law.) A personal action; an action against a person.

personaliter (per-so-nal'i-ter). Personally.

personality The law which appertains or relates to, or deals with, persons. Identity; individuality.

personality conflicts. See **incompatibility.**

personal judgment. A matter of personal taste or feeling. 17 Am J2d Contr § 367.
See **judgment in personam.**

personal jurisdiction. See **jurisdiction in personam.**

personal knowledge. One's own knowledge. With more accuracy, knowledge derived from the exercise of one's own senses. Little v Massachusetts N. E. St. R. Co. 223 Mass 501, 112 NE 77. A person's direct knowledge of anything, as distinguished from that which he learns by hearsay.

personal law. The law which follows the person, as distinguished from the law of the place where the person may be.

personal liability. An obligation attaching to the person, as distinguished from an obligation enforceable against property. A liability of an agent or fiduciary imposed on a personal basis for something done by him in the course of the agency or administration of the trust.
See **stockholder's liability.**

personal liberty. That liberty of the individual which consists in the power of locomotion, of changing situation, or removing his person to whatsoever place his own inclination may direct, without imprisonment or restraint, unless by due course of law.

Next to personal security, the law of England regards, asserts, and preserves the personal liberty of individuals. See 1 Bl Comm 134.
See **life, liberty, and property.**

personal luggage. Whatever the passenger takes with him for his personal use and convenience, according to the habits or wants of the particular class to which he belongs, either with reference to the immediate necessities or to the ultimate purposes of the journey. This would include not only articles of apparel, whether for use or ornament, but also the gun-case or fishing apparatus of the sportsman, the easel of the artist on a sketching tour, or the books of the student, and other articles of analogous character, the use of which is personal to the traveler, and the táking of which has arisen from the fact of his journeying. Oakes v Northern Pacific Railroad Co. 20 Or 392, 26 P 230.

personally acquainted with. A statement of knowledge of identity, common to certificates of acknowledgment. 1 Am J2d Ack § 70.

personally appeared. A phrase common in certificates of acknowledgment, sometimes accepted as the equivalent of "personally known." 1 Am J2d Ack § 69.

personally known to me. A statement of knowledge of identity common to certificates of acknowledgment. 1 Am J2d Ack § 68.

As the words are used in a notary's certificate of acknowledgment stating that the party acknowledging the instrument is "personally known to me" to be the person whose name is subscribed thereto, such knowledge involves such an acquaintance, derived from association with the person in relation to other people, as establishes his identity with at least reasonable certainty. Such an acquaintance cannot depend upon the word of one or two or three individuals, but must be based upon a chain of circumstances surrounding the person, all of which tend to show that he is what he purports to be. Something affirmative in the nature of evidence of identity must appear during the course of the acquaintanceship. Anderson v Aronsohn, 181 Cal 294, 184 P 12, 10 ALR 866, 869.

personal notice. Actual notice. Travelers' Ins. Co. v Farmers' Mut. Fire Ins. Asso. 211 Iowa 1051, 233

NW 153. Notice given individually to the person concerned. Notice communicated directly to a person, not through another. 39 Am J1st Notice § 11.

personal property. Money, goods, and movable chattels. Ralston Steel Car Co. v Ralston, 112 Ohio St 306, 147 NE 513, 39 ALR 334. Goods, chattels, things in action, evidences of debt, and money. All objects and rights which are capable of ownership except freehold estates in land, and incorporeal hereditaments issuing thereout, or exercisable within the same. 42 Am J1st Prop § 23.

The ultimate test in determining what particular items pass under a testamentary gift of "personal property" is the intention of the testator. While it is clear that the term is sufficiently broad in its accepted technical significance to include all forms of property other than land or interests in land, if the testator intended that it should embrace so much, in a majority of cases the courts have, in view of the actual intention of the testator as disclosed by the language of the will and the circumstances surrounding its execution, construed the term as carrying a restricted rather than a broad signification. In some instances, it has been held that the term passed only personal or household effects. In other instances, the term has been construed as including only intangibles or as excluding certain kinds of tangible property, such as growing crops. 57 Am J1st Wills § 1339.

personal-property loan broker. One who makes a business of making small loans on the security of chattel mortgages on personal property. 40 Am J1st Pawnb § 9.

personal property tax lien. A lien for unpaid taxes on personal property, usually extending to the real as well as the personal property of the taxpayer, and sometimes a lien only upon the real estate. 51 Am J1st Tax §§ 1011, 1018.

personal release. A release of one co-obligor with the consent of the other co-obligors. Any release of one co-obligor given under circumstances which operate to prevent it from effecting a release of all the co-obligors. 45 Am J1st Rel § 34.

Personal replevin. Ill-chosen terminology for the writ of habeas corpus.

personal representative. Ordinarily, the executor or administrator of a decedent's estate. 31 Am J2d Ex & Ad § 1. For some purposes, an heir, next of kin, assignee, trustee, receiver, etc. 12 Am J2d Bonds § 24; 29A Am J Rev ed Ins § 1656; 36 Am J2d Frat O § 154. For the purpose of protection against testimony by party or interested person:—the executor or administrator of a deceased person, or a person or party who has succeeded to the right of the deceased, whether by purchase, descent, or operation of law. 58 Am J1st Witn § 237. As a proper party plaintiff to recover for the death of an employee under the Federal Employers' Liability Act: —an executor or administrator only. 35 Am J1st M & S § 474.

personal rights. A classification of the rights which a person has in relation strictly to the duties owed to him by others and the wrongs consequent to the breach or violation of such duties. Duffies v Duffies, 76 Wis 374, 45 NW 522.

See **rights of person.**

personal security. The security of the debtor's personal promise to pay the debt, as distinguished from property pledged, mortgaged, or held in trust. Merrill v National Bank of Jacksonville, 173 US 131, 43 L Ed 640, 19 S Ct 360. Security in the promise or undertaking of a guarantor or surety, as distinguished from property pledged, mortgaged, or held in trust. A person's legal and uninterrupted enjoyment of his life, his limbs, his body, his health, and his reputation. See 1 Bl Comm 129.

See **life, liberty, and property.**

personal service contract. A contract for the furnishing of services by the promisor only, that is, services to be performed by no person other than the promisor.

Illustrations of such contracts ordinarily given are: a master's contract to instruct his apprentice; an author's contract to compose a particular work; a contract of a physician or an attorney at law to render professional services. Janin v Browne, 59 Cal 37, 44.

personal service corporation. A corporation whose earnings are primarily from the services rendered by its principal stockholders. Thomas E. Basham Co. v Lucas (DC Ky) 21 F2d 550.

personal service of process. The actual or direct delivery of the summons or notice, or a copy thereof, to the person to whom it is directed or to someone who is authorized to receive it in his behalf. 42 An J1st Proc § 48.

personal services. The work and labor of a certain person. For some purposes, inclusive of the services of an instrumentality, such as a team of horses. 34 Am J1st Logs § 107. Work performed in reference to the person, such as by the valet of a man or the personal maid of a woman.

See **personal service contract.**

personal servitude. See **servitude in gross; slavery.**

personal statute. A statute affecting the status and condition of a person, such as one which determines the age of majority. Saul v His Creditors (La) 5 Mart 569.

personal tax. Broadly, the burden imposed by government on its own citizens for the benefits which that government affords by its protection and its laws. United States v Erie Railroad Co. (US) 16 Otto 327, 333, 27 L Ed 151, 155, 1 S Ct 223. In a narrower sense, a poll or head tax.

personal things. Personal effects. Not inclusive of securities, money, or real property. Re Klewer's Estate. 124 Cal App 2d 219, 268 P2d 544, 41 ALR2d 941.

As to what passes under a bequest of "personal things," see Anno: 41 ALR2d 941.

personal tithes (tīthz). Tithes which were paid in the products of manual labor or manufacture.

personal tort. A wrong against the person. A wrong to the person, such as an assault; also a wrong affecting the feelings and reputation, such as libel, slander, and malicious prosecution. Slauson v Schwabacher, 4 Wash 783, 31 P 329.

A tort which is not an injury to property is a personal tort. Gray v Blight (CA10 Colo) 112 F2d 696.

personal trademarks and tradenames. Trademarks and tradenames which indicate to the public that the personal care and skill of a certain individual have been exercised in the selection or production of the goods in connection with which the mark or name is used. 52 Am J1st Tradem § 33.

personalty (pėr'sọn-ạl-ti). Same as **personal property.**

personal use trust. A trust which is for a specific personal use, the consequence being that the interest of the beneficiary is inalienable and not liable for his debts. 54 Am J1st Trusts § 161.

personam (pėr-sō'nam). See **in personam; in personam action.**

persona non grata (per-sō'na non gra'ta). A person who is not acceptable.

persona praedilecta (per-sō'na prē-di-lek'ta). A highly favored person.

persona standi in judicio (per-sō'na stan'dī in jū-di'-she-ō). Capacity of standing in judgment; capacity to sue or to be sued.

personation. Assuming the identity of another. See **impersonation.**

person beyond the seas. See **beyond the seas.**

persone (per-so'ne). A parson; a rector.

personero (per-so-nay-ro). (Spanish.) An attorney.

person in authority. Sheriff, constable, police or peace officer making an arrest and having the prisoner in custody, jailer, prosecuting attorney or district attorney, authorized investigator, a prosecuting witness, an examining magistrate, an interpreter, or the agent of any of the foregoing. 29 Am J2d Ev § 564 (discussing confession made under promise of immunity by "person in authority").

person indemnified. The person with whom an indemnity agreement is executed. 42 USC § 2014(r) (statutory definition of Atomic Energy Act of 1954).
See **indemnity.**

person in loco parentis (per'son in lo'ko pā-ren'tis). One who has taken a position in reference to a child of that of a lawful father, assuming the office of a father and the obligation of supporting the child, assuming a parental character and discharging parental duties, although not the parent. Brinkerhoff v Merselis' Executors, 24 NJL 680, 683. One who takes a child into his home and treats it as a member of his own family, educating and supporting it as if it were his own child. 39 Am J1st P & C § 61.

person non compos. See **non compos mentis.**

person of color. See **colored person.**

person or party interested. See **interested person; party in interest.**

person primarily liable. A person whose name appears on the face of a negotiable instrument. as a maker or one obligated by the instrument. 11 Am J2d B & N § 120.

persons meeting. See **meeting; meeting each other.**

Perspicua vera non sunt probanda (per-spi'ku-a ve'ra non sunt pro-ban'da). Evident facts need not be proved. Pollard's Estate, 18 Pa Dist 636, 638.

per stirpem (per ster'pem). By representation.
See **per stirpes.**

per stirpes (per ster'pēz). Per class, particularly distribution by the class. 23 Am J2d Deeds § 200. Taking together the share that a parent would have taken. Anno: 126 ALR 159; 57 Am J1st Wills § 1291. By representation; taking a share which a deceased ancestor would have taken had he survived the intestate. 23 Am J2d Desc & D § 65.

Sometimes a per stirpes distribution has been defined in such a manner as to include, in the definition, the proposition that the number of stocks or roots, into which an estate is originally to be divided is to be determined by reference to the oldest generation which is represented by a living member. Thus, it has been said that in a stirpital distribution the number of stocks in the distribution is determined by the number of the nearest class of blood relatives who survived the decedent and the number of such class who have died leaving issue surviving the decedent. Re McKeon's Estate, 25 Misc 2d 850, 199 NYS2d 158.

Taking per stirpes or per capita under will. Anno: 13 ALR2d 1023.

persuade. To induce. To incline the will, to prevail upon by argument, advice, expostulations, or reasons. Wilson v State, 38 Ala 411, 413.

persuasive authority. See **judicial dicta; precedent.**

per subsequens matrimonium (per sub'se-quenz ma-tri-mō'ni-um). By a subsequent marriage.

pertaining to more hazardous occupation. Accident insurance policy provisions for diminution of indemnity where insured engages in, or does act pertaining to, a more hazardous occupation. Anno: 8 ALR2d 481.

pertenencia (per-te-nen'she-a). A land measure used in Spanish-American land grants, being a square of two hundred varas, or five hundred and fifty feet. Castillero v United States (US) 2 Black 1, 17 L Ed 360.

per testes (per tes'tēz). By witnesses. Nobles v Georgia, 168 US 398, 406, 42 L Ed 515, 518, 18 S Ct 87.

pertinens (per'ti-nenz). Appurtenant; belonging to.

pertinent. Having a bearing upon a matter at hand, particularly evidence bearing upon the issues made by the pleadings.

pertinent hypothesis. An hypothesis which, if sustained, would logically influence the issue. Graham v State, 125 Tex Crim Rep 210, 67 SW2d 296.

pertinentiae (per-ti-nen'she-ē). Appurtenances; things which are appurtenant, or belong to, or are incident to.

per totam curiam (per tō'tam kū'ri-am). By the whole court,—by all the judges of the court.

per tot. cur. An abbreviated form of **per totam curiam.**

per totum tempus praedictum (per to'tum tem'pus prē-dik'tum). During the whole of the time aforesaid.

per tout (per tou). By all.

per tout et non per my (pėr tou et non pėr mē). By all and not by the half.

If an estate in fee be given to a man and his wife, they are neither properly joint tenants, nor tenants in common, because the two being considered as one person in law, they cannot take the estate by moieties, but both are seised of the entirety, per tout et non per my; the consequence of which is, that neither of them can dispose of any part without the assent of the other, but the whole must remain to the survivor. See 2 Bl Comm 182, note.

perturbation (pėr-tėr-bā'shọn). A disturbance; a breach of the peace.

perturbator (pėr'tėr-bā-tọr). A person who broke the peace.

perturbatrix (pėr'tėr-bā-triks). A female who broke the peace.

per universitatem (per ū-ni-ver-si-tā'tem). (Civil law.) As a whole; as an entirety.

per usucaptionem (per u-su-kap-she-ō'nem). By continuous use.

per vadium (per va'di-um). By pledge; by way of pledge.

per vadium et salvos plegios (per va'di-um et sal'vos ple'ji-os). By gage and safe pledges.

Per varios actus, legem experientia facit (per va'ri-os ak'tus, lē'jem ex-pe-ri-en'she-a fa'sit). By various acts, experience makes the law.

per verba de futuro (per ver'ba de fu-tu'rō). In words of the future tense. See 1 Bl Comm 439.

per verba de futuro cum copula (per ver'ba de fu-tu'rō kum ko'pu-la). See **marriage per verba de futuro cum copula**.

per verba de praesenti (per ver'ba de prē-zen'tī). In words of the present tense. See 1 Bl Comm 439. See **marriage per verba de praesenti**.

per verba de praesenti tempore (per ver'ba dē prezen'tī tem'po-re). By words of the present tense.

perversion of legal remedy. Abuse of process; malicious prosecution; false arrest; false imprisonment.

Per vinum delapsis capitalis poena remittitur (per vī'num de-lap'sis ka-pi-tal'is pe'na re-mit'ti-ter). The punishment for a capital offense committed while intoxicated is remitted. A rule of the Roman law which the common law never adopted. See 4 Bl Comm 26.

per visum ecclesiae (per vi'sum e-kle'si-ē). By or under the supervision of the church.

per visum juratorum (per vi'sum jū-rā-tō'rum). By the viewing of the jury.

per vivam vocem (per vi'vam vo'sem). By the living voice.

Pervolvat quo planeta suum circulum annus mora motus est (per-vol'vat quō pla-nē'ta (su'um ser'kulum an'nus mo'ra mō'tus est). A year is the duration of the movement in which a planet revolves through its orbit.

per year. Annually. Curtiss v Howell, 39 NY 211, 213.

pesage (pe-zäzh'). A toll charged for weighing commodities.

peseta (pe-sā'tą). The monetary unit of Spain.

peso (pā'sō). The monetary unit of the Philippines and some Latin-American countries. A silver coin current and legal tender in the island of Puerto Rico until September, 1900, in which year an act of Congress provided for the redemption of all the coins then in circulation in the island, at the rate of sixty cents in American coins for each peso. Serralles v Esbri, 200 US 103, 111, 50 L Ed 391, 395, 26 S Ct 176.

pessimi exempli (pes'si-mī eg-zem'plī). Of the worst example.

pest. An animal or insect which preys upon crops.

pest house. A building for the detention and care of persons inflicted with communicable disease.

pestilence. A contagious disease, often fatal; a raging of such a disease in epidemic proportions. Sings v Joliet, 237 Ill 300, 86 NE 663; Prichard v Morganton, 126 NC 908, 36 SE 353.

petens (pe'tenz). A suitor; a plaintiff; a demandant.

petere (pe'te-re). (Civil law.) To seek; to sue; to petition; to demand; to claim; to sue for; to bring an action.

Peter's pence (pē'tėrs pėns). An ancient tax which was levied upon every dwelling house in England, and upon most of the religious houses as well, and which was paid over to the pope.

petit (pet'it). Small; petty; little.

petit auxilium. See **et petit auxilium**.

petit cape (pe'tit kāp). Same as **parvum cape**.

petite assize (pe-tēt' ạ-sīz'). A jury which was empaneled to try the fact of possession.

petitio (pe-ti'she-ō). A petition; a demand; a claim. In the civil law, a plaintiff's statement of his cause of action in an action in rem.

petition. A formal request in writing addressed to one in a position of authority or to a body, such as a municipal council, usually signed by a number of persons. An application. The name given in some jurisdictions to the pleading by which the plaintiff in a civil action, whether in law or equity, sets forth his cause of action and invokes the jurisdiction of the court. 41 Am J1st Pl § 73. In some jurisdictions, the pleading by the plaintiff in a special proceeding. The pleading which seeks condemnation of property in a proceeding in eminent domain. 27 Am J2d Em D § 395.

petition de droit (de drwoi). A petition of right, by which property in the possession of the crown is recovered in the English court of chancery.

petitioner. One seeking relief by a petition. See **petition**.

petition for certiorari. An application for a writ of certiorari, a pleading in effect, the purpose of which is to set the proceeding in motion. Hall v Hood, 121 Misc 572, 201 NYS 498.

petition for highway. An application by property owners for the opening of a highway. 25 Am J1st High § 22.

petition for improvement. A property owner's petition for the formation of a local improvement district, the ultimate purpose being the construction of a public improvement, the cost to be defrayed by a special assessment. 48 Am J1st Spec A § 129.

petition for redress of grievances. See **redress of grievances**.

petition for referendum. See **referendum petition**.

petition for rehearing. A request for a rehearing. See **rehearing**.

petition in bankruptcy. A document filed in a court of bankruptcy or with a clerk thereof initiating a proceeding under the Bankruptcy Act. Bankr Act § 1(24); 11 USC § 1(24). A pleading in effect. Royal Indem. Co. v American Bond & Mortgage Co. 289 US 165, 77 L Ed 1100, 53 S Ct 551.

petitioning creditor. A creditor who institutes proceedings against his debtor in a court of bankruptcy.

petition in insolvency. A petition, voluntary or involuntary, for the adjudication of a person as an insolvent, to the purpose that insolvency proceedings may ensue, wherein such assets as the insolvent has may be distributed according to law. 29 Am J Rev ed Insolv § 14.

petition in intervention. See **intervention.**

petition of rights. A declaration of the liberties of the people by the English parliament in the reign of Charles the First, in the year 1629.

petitio principii (pẹ-tish'i-ō prin-sip'i-ī). Begging the question. Leache v State, 22 Tex Crim 279.

petit judicium (pe'tit jū-di'she-um). He prays or demands judgment.

petit juror. A trial juror.
See **juror.**

petit jury (pet'it jö'ri). A trial jury; otherwise known as a traverse jury or a common jury. 31 Am J Rev ed Jur § 2.
See **jury.**

petit larceny (pet'it lär'sen-i). Larceny in the taking of property of small value, a misdemeanor, rather than a felony under modern statutes. 32 Am J1st Larc § 3.

Under the common law, larceny where the value of the property stolen was twelve pence or under. If the value exceeded twelve pence, the crime was grand larceny. Both offenses were felonies and were distinguished by the punishments inflicted, that of grand larceny being death, and of petit larceny whipping or some other corporal punishment. 32 Am J1st Larc § 3.

petit mal (pe-tē' mal'). A mild form of epilepsy.

petitor (pet'i-tọr). A petitioner; a plaintiff; a claimant; a demandant.

petitory action (pet'i-tọ-ri ak'shọn). A proceeding at law for the recovery of real property, corresponding to the common-law action of ejectment, and which can only be maintained where the plaintiff shows a legal title to the property in himself, as distinguished from an equitable title. Gilmer v Poindexter (US) 10 How 257, 267, 13 L Ed 411, 415.

petitory suit (pet'i-tọ-ri sūt). A suit in admiralty brought to try title.

petit sergeanty (sär' or sėr'jẹn-ti). Holding lands of the king by the service of rendering to him annually some small implement of war, as a bow, a sword, a lance, an arrow, or the like, with no personal service. See 2 Bl Comm 82.

petit treason (tre'zn). The killing of a husband by a wife; of a lord or master by a servant; of his lord or ordinary by an ecclesiastic.

These were called petit "treason" because they were breaches of the lower allegiance of private and domestic faith. See 4 Bl Comm 75.

peto (pē'tō). I seek; I pray; I demand; I claim.

petrol (pe-trōl' or pet'rọl). The term used in England for gasoline. Minerals Separation v Butte & Superior Mining Co. 250 US 336, 343, 63 L Ed 1019, 1023, 39 S Ct 496.

petroleum. An oil of natural origin formed beneath the surface of the earth. Kelley v Ohio Oil Co. 57 Ohio St 317, 49 NE 399. A solution of hydrocarbons; the product of an oil well in the form in which it comes to the surface or is extracted.
See **crude oil.**

petroleum products. Oils having a preferential affinity for metalliferous matter. Minerals Separation v Butte & Superior Mining Co. 250 US 336, 343, 63 L Ed 1019, 1023, 39 S Ct 496.
See **gasoline; kerosene; naphtha.**

pettifogger (pet'i-fog-ėr). A lawyer whose practice is of a small or petty character; a lawyer of little importance.

pettifogging shyster (pet'i-fog-ing shīs'tėr). An unscrupulous practitioner of the law who disgraces his profession by doing mean work, and resorts to sharp practice to do it. Bailey v Kalamazoo Publishing Co. 40 Mich 251, 256.

petty average (pet'i ạv'ẹ-rạj). The necessary expenses laid out by the master of a ship, such as towage, wharfage, etc.

petty bag office. (pet'i bag of'is). An office in the English court of chancery where original writs were issued which related to the interests of the crown.

Those writs that related to a subject were originally kept in a hamper and those which related to the interests of the crown were kept in a little bag. Hence arose the distinction between the "hanaper office" and the "petty bag office." These offices were at all times open to the subject, who might, at any time have on demand any writ for which he might call. Yates v People (NY) 6 Johns 337, 363.
See **clerk of the petty bag.**

petty chapmen (chap'men). Persons traveling from town to town with goods and merchandise. Emmons v Lewiston, 132 Ill 380, 24 NE 58.

petty constable (kon'stạ-bl). Inferior officers in every town and parish, subordinate to the high constable of the hundred.

The office combined the ancient office of head borough, tithingman, or borsholder and the modern office of constable merely. See 1 Bl Comm 356.

petty jury. Same as **petit jury.**

petty larceny. Same as **petit larceny.**

petty offense. A minor criminal offense, triable by a magistrate without a jury. People v Grogeran, 260 NY 138, 183 NE 273, 86 ALR 1266. In some jurisdictions, inclusive of misdemeanors, at least a misdemeanor not amounting to an indictable offense. 21 Am J2d Crim L § 22.

petty officer. A noncommissioned officer of the Navy, either petty officer first class, petty officer second class, or petty officer third class, the latter ranking immediately above seaman and petty officer first class immediately below chief petty officer.
See **chief petty officer; senior chief petty officer.**

petty sessions. A justice's court of summary jurisdiction.

petty treason. Same as **petit treason.**

pew. A seat in a church. A property right; the right to a particular seat in a church. 45 Am J1st Reli Soc §§ 85, 86.

pew holder. One having the right to a particular pew or seat in a church. Massachusetts Baptist Missionary Soc. v Bowdoin Square Baptist Soc. 212 Mass 198, 98 NE 1045.

pew right. See **pew.**

peyote (pạ-yō'tạ). A drug obtained from a cactus plant, having toxic, deleterious, intoxicating, and hallucinating effects. People v Woody (Cal App) 35 Cal Rptr 708.

Pfc. Abbreviation of Private First Class.

pfd. Abbreviation of preferred.

P.G. Abbreviation of postgraduate.

PHA. Abbreviation of Public Housing Administration.

pharmacist. One qualified to practice pharmacy. An apothecary. 25 Am J2d Drugs § 4.
See **pharmacy.**

pharmacopoeia (fär"mạ-kọ-pē'iạ). See **United States Pharmacopoeia.**

pharmacy. The profession of compounding, preparing, and dispensing drugs, medicines, and poisons. State v Wood, 51 SD 485, 215 NW 487, 54 ALR 719. A drug store.

Pharm. D. Abbreviation of doctor of pharmacy.

phase. A stage in the development of something of a progressive nature. A stage of a movement in cycles, particularly an alternating current of electricity.

phenobarbital (fē-nọ-bär'bi-tal). A sedative drug; not a poison. Equitable Life Assur. Soc. v Heminover, 100 Colo 231, 67 P2d 80, 110 ALR 1270.

philanthropic. Benevolent. Anno: 115 ALR 1133. Pertaining to philanthropy. Charitable. Rotch v Emerson, 105 Mass 431, 434.

philanthropic purpose. See **philanthropy.**

philanthropy (fi-lan'thrọ-pi). Acts or gifts prompted by good will or kind feeling. Not necessarily the equivalent of charity. 15 Am J2d Char § 61.

Philippines. A nation of the far east, occupying territory, formerly known as Philippine Islands, ceded to the United States by Spain under the Treaty of Paris, December 10, 1898, independence having been proclaimed on July 4, 1946, in accordance with the Tydings-McDuffie Act passed by Congress in 1934.

photograph. An image produced by photography.

photographer. One whose occupation is photography; an artist, as distinguished from an artisan or mechanic. New Orleans v Robira, 42 La Ann 1098, 8 So 402.

Photographic Copies of Business and Public Records as Evidence Act. One of the uniform laws. 30 Am J2d Ev § 1012.

photographic copy. A copy of a written instrument made by the process of photographing the original, the copy produced sometimes being reduced in size. Enelow v New York Life Ins. Co. (CA3 Pa) 83 F2d 550, 105 ALR 493, cert den 298 US 680, 80 L Ed 1401, 56 S Ct 948.
A photograph of a document is but a copy of that document, and its admission in evidence as a document is governed by the rules pertaining to copies. Maclean v Scripps, 52 Mich 214, 218.

photography. The art and process of producing images upon a sensitive surface by employing the chemical action produced by light or radiation.

photostat. See **photostatic copy.**

photostatic copy. A copy of a written instrument made by a photostat, an instrument or device for rapid and inexpensive reproduction by photograph. Enelow v New York Life Ins. Co. (CA3 Pa) 83 F2d 550, 105 ALR 493, cert den 298 US 680, 80 L Ed 1041, 56 S Ct 948.

photo-traffic camera. A camera which provides the basis for a mathematical computation of the rate of speed of a motor vehicle by taking two photos at a set-time interval apart. People v Hildebrandt, 308 NY 397, 126 NE2d 377, 49 ALR2d 449.

PHS. Abbreviation of Public Health Service.

p. h. v. An abbreviation of **pro hac vice.**

physical abuse. See **abuse.**

physical and incurable incapacity for marriage. Incapacity to consummate the marriage; impotency. 35 Am J1st Mar § 121.

physical coercion. See **coercion.**

physical condition. See **health; physical defect.**

physical cruelty. As ground for divorce:—actual personal violence, or such a course of physical treatment as endangers life, limb or health, and renders cohabitation unsafe. Brown v Brown, 215 SC 502, 56 SE2d 330, 15 ALR2d 163.

physical defect. A condition of the body, resulting from accident or sickness, which impairs bodily function, particularly in movement. Something that materially impairs, weakens, or undermines the constitution, tends to reduce powers of resistance, and thereby enhances the risk of death. 29A Am J Rev ed Ins § 1211.

physical delivery. Manual delivery; a delivery from hand to hand. 23 Am J2d Deeds § 91.

physical depreciation. Deterioration due to age and wear, a constant factor, resulting from use, decay, and the action of the elements. Central Railroad of New Jersey v Martin (DC NJ) 30 F Supp 41.

physical disability. See **physical defect; total physical disability.**

physical examination. An examination of a person by a physician for the purpose of determining his physical condition, sometimes required of a litigant, involving, not only observation of the body, but also an inquiry by questions and answers as to the cause and character of a disability. 23 Am J2d Dep §§ 210 et seq.
See **medical examination.**

physical fact. A fact which is perceived by the senses.

physical fact rule. The principle that the testimony of a witness which is physically impossible and unbelievable, being irreconcilable with, or contrary to, physical facts and common observation and experience, is to be striken or disregarded as being without evidentiary value, even though uncontradicted by other evidence. 30 Am J2d Ev § 1085; 53 Am J1st Tr § 149. The principle that a reviewing court need not accept findings of fact which are inconsistent with well-known physical laws or with other facts or circumstances so well settled as to be the proper subject of judicial notice. 5 Am J2d A & E § 827.

physical force. The power of the body, or of a source of power, applied by man.
The term, as used in relation to assaults, is synonymous with the term "violence," and the two terms are used interchangeably. State v Wells, 31 Conn 210.
See **force.**

physical impossibility. Impossibility of accomplishment under the state of science and mechanics of the day. A concept which varies from age to age, even from decade to decade, illustrated by the inaptness of the stock example given not so many years ago of traveling from New York to London in one day. Le Roy v Jacobosky, 136 NC 443, 48 SE 796.

physical impossibility doctrine. See **physical fact rule.**

physical impotency. See **impotency**.

physical inability to work. As the clause appears in the regulations of a railway relief department:—inability to perform such labor as the injured member was engaged in at the time of his injury, or similar labor which will enable him to earn wages equally remunerative. Keith v Chicago, Burlington & Q. R. Co. 82 Neb 12, 116 NW 597.

physical infirmity. A condition of the body, resulting from accident or sickness, which impairs bodily function, particularly in movement. Something that materially impairs, weakens, or undermines the constitution, tends to reduce powers of resistance, and thereby enhances the risk of death. 29A Am J Rev ed Ins § 1211.

physical injury. A personal injury. In reference to property, an injury which interferes with an owner's right of dominion, use, enjoyment, and disposition, such as a blocking of ingress or egress, or an injury which directly harms the physical property, such as the destruction of a building. Rigney v Chicago, 102 Ill 64.

physical interference. Broadly, any physical obstruction of movement. In a technical sense, an injury to or a disturbance of land from a physical aspect, as distinguished from a disturbance constituting annoyance or other discomfort of a mental nature and personal to the owner. Annoyances from smoke and noise are of a mental nature. An obstruction to an owner's access to his property is physical. Austin v Augusta Terminal Railway Co. 108 Ga 671, 34 SE 852.

physically incapacitated for marriage. The condition of a person who is unable, by reason of incurable physical imperfection or malformation, to accomplish copulation or coition, the consummation of marriage. Anonymous, 89 Ala 291, 7 So 100.

physical medicine. See **physiotherapy**.

physical occupancy. See **occupancy**.

physical ouster. See **ouster**.

physical possession. The taking hold of property, exercising dominion over it. Galbraith v Buffalo Vegetable Marketing Co. 128 Misc 77, 79, 217 NYS 764.
See **occupancy**.

physical shock. See **shock**.

physical suffering. Pain, particularly prolonged pain indicating a physical derangement or unhealthy condition of the body. 22 Am J2d Damg § 105.

physical therapy. Same as **physiotherapy**.

physical violence. Force violently applied.
As a ground for divorce, "physical violence" may consist in many acts, each slight in its character, and none producing marks of violence upon the person, and yet, considered as a whole, they may be ground for divorce; certainly so when from them the court is able to say the life of the wife is endangered. Thompson v Thompson, 186 Iowa 1066, 173 NW 55, 5 ALR 710, 711.
See **physical force; violence**.

physical welfare. See **health**.

physician. Broadly, one who practices the art of healing disease and preserving health. 41 Am J1st Phys & S § 2. A person skilled in the art of healing. State v Borah, 51 Ariz 318, 76 P2d 757, 115 ALR 254. One who is proficient in the art of healing by means of the application of physics or medicine to the patient. 41 Am J1st Phys & S § 2. One who prescribes remedies for sickness and disease. Travelers Ins. Co. v Bergeron (CA8 Iowa) 25 F2d 680, 58 ALR 1127, cert den 278 US 638, 73 L Ed 553, 49 S Ct 33. Technically, one legally qualified for, and engaged in, the practice of medicine. Joyner v State, 181 Miss 245, 179 So 573, 115 ALR 954. For the purposes of privilege in communications between "physician" and patient:—only one lawfully engaged in the practice of medicine under authority duly granted to pursue that profession. 58 Am J1st Witn § 411.

The word is derived from the Greek word "phusis," meaning nature, and in a restricted sense means one who administers medicine to cure diseases, but, in its proper sense, it has a broader signification, and means one who by a knowledge of the nature and structure of the human system, and of the nature and properties of substances, cures the injuries and diseases to which it is subject. The word includes not only doctors, who administer medicine and physic, but surgeons who, by a knowledge of the human system, are able to amputate an injured and diseased limb, or to extract a bullet with skill and as much safety to life and as little pain as the case admits of. Re Hunter, 60 NC 372.

The word "physician," as used in a statute authorizing the registration of any person who was a reputable resident physician of good moral character and who, on a date designated by the statute, was engaged in the actual practice of medicine within the state, and who submitted a diploma or other credential or evidence of his qualification, was construed as including any person of whatever school, and whether belonging to any known school, engaged in good faith in treating human ills by any remedy or remedies, however simple, so as to be known among the people as a physician, and not limited to such persons as possess that technical knowledge of the human system and the knowledge of the drugs and other remedies, and how to administer them, commonly supposed to be possessed by members in good standing of the great schools of medicine. Anno: 4 ALR2d 684.

physician and patient. The relation whereunder a physician administers professionally to another, essentially consensual. 41 Am J1st Phys & S § 71.

The relation between a surgeon performing an autopsy and the body of the dead person is not the relation of physician and patient. Carmody v Capital Traction Co. 43 App DC 245. But the relation may exist between a hospital patient and an intern who is a graduate of a medical school, with a doctor's degree, though, it may be, not licensed to practice his profession in the ordinary way by so holding himself out to the public. Eureka-Maryland Assur. Co. v Gray, 74 App DC 191, 121 F2d 104.

physician's certificate. A death certificate. 29A Am J Rev ed Ins § 1937.

physician's liability insurance. A form of liability insurance, now in common use, which insures a physician against liability from acts or omissions while practicing his profession. Insurance against malpractice, error, or mistake. 29A Am J Rev ed Ins § 1358.

physician's license. A license to practice the healing art. 41 Am J1st Phys & S § 15.

physiognomy (fiz-i-og'nō-mi). The practice of purporting or trying to ascertain the character and aptitudes of a person by examining features of the cranium and face. Anno: 43 LRA NS 203, 204. The facial features of a person.

physiotherapist (fiz"i-ō-ther'a-pist). One who practices physiotherapy.

physiotherapy (fiz"i-ō-ther'a-pi). The treatment of disease or physical disability by massage, heat, exercise, or other physical means, rather than by drugs. Anno: 86 ALR 631, 632.

pia fraus (pī'a frâs). Pious fraud:—the name was given to the practices of the church in its defeat of the statutes of mortmain by circumvention.

piazza (pi-az'ä). A public square. A porch. 13 Am J2d Burgl § 11.

picaroon (pik-a-rön'). A robber.

piccage (pik'aj). A charge which was made for a booth concession at a fair.

pickery (pik'ėr-i). Petty larceny; small thievery.

picket. A sentry. One engaged in picketing.
See **picketing**.

picketing. A method of promoting a strike or boycott. The establishment and maintenance of an organized esponiage upon the works of an employer and upon persons going to and from them. Thomas v Indianapolis, 195 Ind 440, 145 NE 440, 35 ALR 1194. The stationing of men for observation, or for the purpose of attempting to influence workers to quit their employment or intending workers not to seek employment, or for the purpose of apprising the public of the dispute with the employer and influencing them to withhold their patronage. The acts of the men so stationed in fulfillment of such a purpose, sometimes, although not necessarily, accompanied by acts of coercion or intimidation. 31 Am J Rev ed Lab § 432.
See **peaceful picketing**.

pickpocket. A thief who secretly steals from the pockets of his victims.
See **pocket picking**.

pick-up service. The service of the carrier involved in calling for and collecting freight, and receipting therefor, from a dock, platform, or doorway directly accessible to highway vehicles, at the consignor's warehouse, factory, store, or similar place of business; and including transportation therefrom to the premises of the carrier's freight depot. Southern Ry. Co. v Acme Fast Freight, Inc. 74 App DC 390, 124 F2d 229. A service undertaken under special contract by a motor carrier, whereby the carrier becomes a delivering carrier under the Interstate Commerce Act. Keystone Motor Freight Lines v Drannon-Signaigo Cigar Co. (CA5 Tex) 115 F2d 736.

pick-up truck. A motor vehicle with small truck body, handy for the transportation of packages and other light articles, being also available for use as an ordinary one-seated automobile. Anno: 38 ALR2d 877.

pie. A pastry. Jumbled printing type. As derived from the Latin "pes," a foot.

piece. A weapon, particularly a firearm.
See **bail piece; committitur piece; satisfaction piece**.

piece basis See **piecework**.

piecemeal appeals. Successive appeals taken from the same decision. 4 Am J2d A & E § 49.

piecemeal construction. The construction of a municipal building or other improvement a part at a time, particularly for the purpose of avoiding violation of debt-limit provisions. 38 Am J1st Mun Corp § 428.

piecemeal zoning. Same as **partial zoning**.

piecework. Work performed for compensation according to the number of articles produced, sometimes at home. A basis of compensation of census takers. 14 Am J2d Census § 3.

piepoudre court. See **pie-powder court**.

pie-powder court. An ancient court of England.
The curia pedis pulverizati or court of dusty feet which was said to have been so called from the dusty feet of its suitors, or as Coke thought, because justice was as swift there as dust falling from the feet, or possibly from the French "pied puldreaux," a peddler. It was the lowest and the most expeditious court in England and was a court of record presided over by the steward of each fair or market. See 3 Bl Comm 32.
In the often quoted language of Chief Justice Shaw of Massachusetts: "If a pie-powder court could be called on the instant and on the spot, the true rule of justice for the public would be to pay the compensation with one hand, while they apply the ax with the other." Old Dominion Land Co. v United States, 269 US 55, 65, 70 L Ed 162, 165, 46 S Ct 39.

pier. A structure built out over the water of a harbor at which a vessel may be tied, for use in loading and unloading cargo and for the convenience of passengers boarding the vessel or going ashore therefrom. 56 Am J1st Whar § 2. A projection of the land, and for purposes of jurisdiction to be so treated. The Haxby (DC Pa) 94 F 1016.

pierage (pēr'aj). A toll charged for the use of a pier.

piercing the veil of corporate entity. See **disregarding corporate entity**.

pig. A casting of iron; pig iron. An animal otherwise known as a hog, especially a young hog.
See **hog; pig iron**.

pigeon shooting. Shooting pigeons after they are liberated from a trap, with the purpose of demonstrating or improving one's marksmanship. Anno: 82 ALR2d 818 et seq; § 6.

piggery. A pigpen; a place where pigs are raised.

pightel (pī'tl). A small inclosed parcel of land.

pig iron. Crude iron, the original basis for the manufacture of steel and forms of iron, produced in a blast furnace. Carnegie Steel Co. v Cambria Iron Co. 185 US 403, 410, 46 L Ed 968, 975, 22 S Ct 698.

pignoratio (pig-no-rā'she-ō). (Civil law.) A contract of pledge.

pignoratitia actio (pig-no-rā-ti'she-a ak'she-ō). (Civil law.) An action founded upon a contract of pledge.

pignorative contract (pig'nō-ra-tiv kon'trakt). A contract of pledge.

pignori acceptum (pig-nō'rī ak-sep'tum). Delivered and taken in pledge or pawn.

pignoris captio (pig-nō'ris kap'she-ō). (Civil law.) The taking of a pledge to secure the payment of a demand.

pignus (pig'nus). (Civil law.) A pledge of goods in which they were delivered by the pledgeor to the

pledgee. A contract of pledge or pawn. 41 Am J1st Pldg & Col § 2.
See **hypothecation**; **pledge**.

pigsty. A pigpen.
See **piggery**.

pigtle. Same as **pightel**.

piissima regina conjunx divi imperatoris (pi-is'si-ma re-ji'na kon'junks di'vi im-per-a-tō'ris). The most pious queen consort of the sacred emperor. See 1 Bl Comm 218.

pilfer (pil'fẽr). To steal. Becket v Sterrett (Ind) 4 Blackf 499, 500. To ruin by depredation. Anno: 38 ALR 1125.

pilferage (pil'fer-ạj). Larceny or stealing, particularly stealing something of small value. Anno: 48 ALR2d 20. Filching or taking a small part only, rather than the whole. 32 Am J1st Larc § 2. Ruin by depredation. Anno: 38 ALR 1125.

pillage (pil'ạj). The plundering, ravaging, or carrying off of goods, commodities, or merchandise, by open force or violence. American Ins Co. v Bryan & Maitland (NY) 26 Wend 563, 573.

pillory (pil'ọ-ri). A contrivance which was used as a means of punishment for crime, consisting of a wooden board, affixed to a post, through which the head and arms of the culprit protruded.

pilot. A person taken on board a ship at a particular place for the purpose of conducting the ship through a river, road, or channel, or from or into a port. Hobart v Drogan (US) 10 Pet 108, 9 L Ed 363. The steersman, a person entrusted with the helm and direction of the vessel on her voyage. Atlee v Northwestern Union Packet Co. (US) 21 Wall 389, 22 L Ed 619. In aviation:—one who flies or is qualified to fly, an airplane, airship, or balloon. 8 Am J2d Avi § 33.

pilotage. The services of a pilot. That branch of maritime law dealing with the protection and regulation of pilots. 48 Am J1st Ship § 197. The fees, compensation, and charges of a pilot for his services rendered or tendered a vessel entering port or departing therefrom. 48 Am J1st Ship §§ 195, 210.

pilotage lien. See **pilot's lien**.

pilot laws. Statutes providing for and regulating pilotage, and the appointment, qualifications, duties, conduct, compensation, and employment of pilots.

Pilot laws are regulations of navigation and are therefore regulations of commerce, but they are within the class of regulations which may be prescribed by the states until Congress sees fit to act, and are then superseded only to the extent that they are in actual conflict with Federal regulations. 48 Am J1st Ship §§ 197 et seq.

pilot light. A small burner on gas stove or furnace, kept lighted for the purpose of igniting a larger burner. Baldridge v Wright Gas Co. 154 Ohio St. 452, 43 Ohio Ops 369, 96 NE2d 300. An electric light kept burning at night to indicate the location of a particular thing, such as stairway, bathroom, or electric switch.

pilot plant. An industrial, but more often a utility, plant, built and operated on an experimental basis, primarily for the purpose of determining costs of production and the charges which must be made for goods or services in order to show a profit in operation.

pilots' association (ạ-sō-si-ā'shọn). A local association, usually unincorporated, formed for their common benefit by pilots, who ordinarily deposit their fees in a common fund, which, after deducting expenses therefrom, is distributed to the several members according to the number of days they were respectively on the active list. 48 Am J1st Ship § 196.

pilot's license. A license authorizing the licensee to operate and fly an aircraft. A license authorizing the licensee to act as a pilot of vessels. 48 Am J1st Ship § 200.

pilot's lien. A pilot's maritime lien for his services, as performed or tendered, in conducting a vessel into or from port. 48 Am J1st Ship § 195.

pimp. A term of opprobrium, a pimp being the lowest of men, one who obtains customers for a whore. Butte v Peasley, 18 Mont 303, 45 P 210.

pimping. Obtaining customers for a prostitute. Sharing in the earnings of a prostitute.

To constitute the statutory offense of pimping, the defendant must be a male person; he must have knowledge that a certain person is a prostitute; there must be earnings from the prostitution; the defendant must derive his support in whole or in part from such earnings, knowing them to have been the proceeds from prostitution. People v Fuski, 49 Cal App 4, 192 P 552.

See **pandering**.

pimp tenure (ten'ụr). An ancient land tenure in which the tenant rendered services as a procurer.

pin money. An allowance, particularly by husband to wife, for small needs. An allowance made by a husband to his wife, payable during cohabitation, in money or in granting her the use of his property for profit, in appreciation of her services as a housekeeper. 26 Am J1st H & W § 52. A doctrine peculiar to English equity jurisdiction, under which a husband was allowed to give his wife the privilege of working for herself, acting as a free trader, and of acquiring profits by her earnings and savings which neither he nor his creditors could reach. 26 Am J1st H & W § 52.

pin-money doctrine. See **pin money**.

pioneer patent. Same as **basis patent**.

pious uses. An ancient term. Religious uses. Religious uses under the control of the king, as where a vehicle or other article which had caused the death of a person was forfeited to pious uses. Fields v Metropolitan Life Ins. Co. 147 Tenn 464, 249 SW 798, 36 ALR 1250, 1251.
See **deodand**.

pipe. A tube of metal, wood, plastic, concrete, or other material through which a liquid is conveyed. A tube for making sounds of a musical character.

pipe line. A line of pipe, usually of steel, sometimes of lead or even of plastic, running over or beneath the surface of the earth for the transportation of water, oil, or other liquid. 24 Am J1st Gas & O § 131. An instrumentality of commerce within the meaning of the commerce clause of the United States Constitution. 15 Am J2d Com § 48.

The term evidently means something different from "pipes," and conveys the idea of a line of pipe running upon or in the earth, carrying with it the right to the use of the soil in which it is placed. Dietz v Mission Transfer Co. 95 Cal 92, 100, 30 P 380.

pipe-line system. The main transmission line and a network of gathering lines leading to various oil

PIPE-ROLL [950] PLACE

wells being served. Alexander v Cosden Pipe Line Co. 290 US 484, 78 L Ed 452, 54 S Ct 292.

pipe-roll (pīp-rōl). A treasury account which was kept in the English exchequer.

pipowder court. Same as **piepowder court.**

piracy. A term for the infringement of a copyright or a taking of literary property without permission. The crime of being a pirate, an offense against humanity and all mankind. 41 Am J1st Pir § 1. Robbery on the high seas. 41 Am J1st Pir § 3. The committing of depredations against ships on the high seas out of a spirit of malevolence, with or without the taking of plunder. United States v The Brig Malek Adhel (US) 2 How 210, 11 L Ed 239. Robbery, murder, or other acts of hostility against the United States or citizens thereof on the high seas under color of commission from a foreign state, or under pretence of such authority. 18 USC § 495.

Congress has also declared a seaman who raises violent hands upon his commander, thereby hindering and preventing his fighting in defense of his vessel or goods entrusted to him, and those who, while engaged in a piratical cruise or enterprise, or being members of any such crew or enterprise, land from the vessel and commit robbery on the shore, to be pirates and subject to punishment as such. 18 USC §§ 484, 493; 41 Am J1st Pir § 3.

Pirata est hostis humani generis (pi-rā′ta est hos′tis hu-mā′nī je′ne-ris). A pirate is the enemy of the human race.

pirate. An enemy of the human race. One who roves the sea in an armed vessel without commission or passport from any government, solely on his own authority, and for the purpose of seizing by force, and appropriating to himself without discrimination whatever ships or vessels he may choose to plunder. 41 Am J1st Pir § 1. One guilty of piracy.
See **piracy.**

piratical. Acting in aggression unauthorized by the law of nations, hostile in character, wanton and criminal in commission, and utterly without sanction from any public authority or sovereign power. United States v The Brig Malek Adhel (US) 2 How 210, 232, 11 L Ed 239, 248. In short, acting as a pirate.
See **piracy; pirate.**

piscaria (pis-kăr′iä). Fisheries of all kinds. Moulton v Libbey, 37 Me 472, 490.

piscary (pis′ka̧-ri). Same as **piscaria.**

pistareen (pis-ta̧-rēn′). A Spanish silver coin which in 1835 passed current in the United States for twenty cents, or one fifth of a dollar, although purporting to be a quarter of a dollar or twenty-five cents; so that its real value, as well as its current value, was uncertain.

Upon a charge of counterfeiting such a coin, it was held that it was not a coin made current by the laws of the United States. United States v Gardner (US) 10 Pet 618, 9 L Ed 556.

pistol. A firearm with short barrel, to be held with one hand in firing; a deadly weapon. 56 Am J1st Weap § 3.

Pistol Act. One of the uniform statutes. 56 Am J1st Weap § 5.

pistol range. A place for training in or testing of marksmanship by pistol or revolver. A place of public amusement. Anno: 140 ALR 415.

pit. A hole or cavity in the ground. A mine, particularly a coal mine. A cavity dug in mining by way of reaching the ore. 36 Am J1st Min & M § 182. A hole dug in the ground and filled with water in which female thieves were drowned, instead of hanging them.

pitfall. A dangerous condition on premises. 38 Am J1st Negl § 105. A trap to ensnare the unwary. Hall v Manson, 99 Iowa 698, 68 NW 922.

pix (piks). Same as **pyx.**

pix-jury. Same as **pyx-jury.**

P. J. An abbreviation of **presiding judge.**

pk. Abbreviation of park or peck.

placard. A printed or written notice for display in a public place.

placarding. Publicizing by exhibition of placards, an activity often engaged in by strikers. 31 Am J Rev ed Lab §§ 427-429.

place. Verb: To come in second in a race, particularly a horse race. To give position to something. Holicer Gas Co. v Wilson, 45 So 2d 96. Noun: A location. A public square. Indian Rocks Beach South Shore, Inc. v Ewell (Fla) 59 So 2d 647, 32 ALR2d 940. A highway. Carlin v Chicago, 262 Ill 564, 104 NE 905. A street. 25 Am J1st High § 7. A structure devoted to a particular use, such as an arsenal or dockyard. United States v Bevans (US) 3 Wheat 336, 390, 4 L Ed 404, 417. A building, even a vessel moored at a wharf. 30 Am J Rev ed Intox L § 460. A region. Wilder v State, 34 Okla Crim 291, 246 P 660. A locality, situation or site. Indian Rocks Beach South Shore, Inc. v Ewell (Fla) 59 So 2d 647, 32 ALR2d 940. An occupied estate. Indian Rocks Beach South Shore, Inc. v Ewell (Fla) 59 So 2d 647, 32 ALR2d 940.
See **situs.**

place for repentance. The opportunity which a man engaged in the commission of a crime may have to withdraw before its consummation, without incurring criminality. Hyde v United States, 225 US 347, 56 L Ed 1114, 32 S Ct 793.

placeman. A person who, for the time, is serving the state in the performance of a duty required of him as a citizen such as a juror or election inspector, although not in the capacity of a public officer. Worthy v Barrett, 63 NC 199, 202.
See **place of trust or profit.**

placement. The act, particularly that of an employment agency, in obtaining employment for a person. The act of a carrier by rail in putting a car in location on a sidetrack for loading of goods by a consignor or unloading by a consignee.
See **constructive placement of cars.**

place name. The name of a place incorporated in a trademark or tradename. 52 Am J1st Tradem § 66.

place of abode. A place where one lives permanently, rather than temporarily. A domicil; a home; a place of residence. Sanders v Greenstreet, 23 Kan 425, 431.
See **domicil; home; residence; usual place of abode.**

place of amusement. A place to which people resort for diversion or pleasure, some being exhibitive and others participative, the former being represented by theaters, stadiums, and so forth and the latter by skating rinks, bowling alleys, and so forth. 4 Am J2d Amuse § 1.

place of burial. A cemetery; a burial plot; sometimes the open sea. Brambir v Cunard White Star Ltd. (DC NY) 37 F Supp 906, affd (CA2) 119 F2d 419.

place of business. A place actually occupied, either continually or at regular periods, by a person or his clerks, in the pursuit of a lawful employment which occupies his time, attention, and labor. Stephenson v Primrose (Ala) 8 Port 155.

See **place of doing business; principal place of business; usual place of business.**

place of contract. The place in which a contract is made, completed, or executed. 16 Am J2d Confl L § 36. The place in which a contract is performed or, according to a most modern view, the place where the contract is of the most significance. 16 Am J2d Confl L §§ 38, 40.

The place where a contract is made is the place where, by acquiescence or final agreement of the minds of the parties, the contract is concluded. Mutual Life Asso. v Harris, 94 Tex 25, 57 SW 635.

If the parties to a prospective contract are in different jurisdictions, the place where the last act is done which is necessary to complete the contract and give it validity is regarded as the place in which the contract is made. 16 Am J2d Contr § 36.

place of delivery. The place where the goods were sold unless the nature of the article, the usage of trade, a condition of the contract, or the previous course of dealing between buyer and seller requires delivery to be made elsewhere. Hatch v Standard Oil Co. (US) 10 Otto 124, 134, 25 L Ed 554, 557. The place specified in a contract for the sale of personal property at which the seller is to make delivery to the purchaser. The place of final delivery of a shipment by the carrier to the consignee. 14 Am J2d Car § 587.

place of destination. See **destination.**

place of doing business. Any place at which the particulars of a corporate enterprise are conducted. 18 Am J2d Corp § 160.

See **principal place of business.**

place of election. See **polls.**

place of holding court. An essential to the conception of a "court;" an appropriate place for the administration of justice. 20 Am J2d Cts § 1.

See **venue.**

place of meeting. The place fixed for the meeting of the board of directors of a corporation. 19 Am J2d Corp § 1124. The place fixed by statute, charter, bylaw, or determination of the board of directors for a stockholders' meeting. 19 Am J2d Corp § 601.

place of most significant contracts. The place which has the most significant contracts with a dispute concerning a contract, the law of which should govern the resolving of the controversy, according to a newly-formulated principle of conflict of laws. 16 Am J2d Confl L § 42.

place of payment. The place fixed by a contract for the payment of money, or by the parties in a subsequent agreement, as the place where the payment is to be made. The place, often a bank, designated in a promissory note, as the place where the maker is to pay the obligation. 11 Am J2d B & N § 187. A house, bank, counting room, store, or place of business, where the holder can present the note, where the maker can deposit or provide funds to meet it, and where a legal offer to pay can be made. 11 Am J2d B & N § 972. In the absence of a designation of place in the note, the place of residence of the maker. 11 Am J2d B & N § 89. In the absence of a designation in the contract or an agreement of the parties to the contrary, the residence of the debtor, where the payment is one to be made in property. 11 Am J2d B & N § 972.

place of performance. The place fixed by the terms of the contract in express terms. The place which, as determined by fair inference in construction of the contract, is to be the place of performance in accordance with the intention of the parties. In instances where there is neither express nor implied agreement as to the place of performance, the place where the contract was made. 17 Am J2d Contr § 331.

See **place of contract; place of payment.**

place of resort. Literally, a place to which people resort for pleasure and recreation. In the usual legal sense, a place to which people resort for gambling and other illegal activities. Lynn v State, 247 Tex Civ App 590, 11 SW 640.

place of trial. Venue.

See **change of venue; venue.**

place of trust or profit. A term comprehensive in the broad sense of public officers, fiduciaries, even corporate officers, but having a particular application in reference to ineligibility for a public office. A position which, although not a public office, occupies the same general level in dignity and importance.

As an office has some relations to the public, so must places of trust and profit involve the exercise of functions affecting the public, in order to constitute a disqualification for other similar places. Doyle v Aldermen of Raleigh, 89 NC 133.

See **placemen.**

place of work. See **working place.**

place of worship. A church. A place set apart for rites or services of any kind which express reverence for a deity. People v Stanley, 81 Colo 276, 255 P 610.

The use of the Bible in a public school does not make the school a place of worship. Hackett v Brooksville School Dist. 120 Ky 608, 87 SW 792.

placer claim. A mining claim covering property wherein the valuable mineral is found, not in veins, lodes, or ledges within the rock, but in a loose condition in the softer materials making up the surface of the earth. 36 Am J1st Min & M § 71.

placer claim patent. A patent issued by the federal government covering the surface and minerals to found in placer form thereunder, also known veins sought to be covered by the patent, and all unknown veins thereafter discovered by the patentee. 36 Am J1st Min & M § 124.

placer location. The marking of the boundaries of a placer claim.

See **placer claim.**

placer mines. Mines in which the mineral is generally found in the softer material which covers the earth's surface, and not among the rocks beneath. Reynolds v Iron Silver Mining Co. 116 US 687, 695, 29 L Ed 774, 777, 6 S Ct 601.

placer mining. Taking the soft earthy matter in which the particles of mineral are loosely mingled, and, by filtration, separating the one from the other. Reynolds v Iron Silver Mining Co. 116 US 687, 695, 29 L Ed 774, 777, 6 S Ct 601.

place to work. See **working place.**

placita (pla'si-ta). Marginal titles. The convening order of the court.

It was a vital requirement of the common law that the record should contain a "placita." Fifty-three cases were reversed at one term of the Supreme Court of Illinois because the record in each of them failed to contain a "placita." Planing Mill Lumber Co. v Chicago, 56 Ill 304, 305.

placitabile (pla-si-tā'bi-le). Pleadable; capable of being pleaded.

placita communia (pla'si-ta kom-mū'ni-a). Common pleas; that is, pleas or suits including all civil actions between subject and subject. See 3 Bl Comm 40.

placita coronae (pla'si-ta ko-rō'nē). Pleas of the crown; English criminal actions.

placita juris (pla'si-ta jū'ris). Pleas or rules of law.

placitamentum (pla-si-tā-men'tum). Pleading.

Placita negativa duo exitum non faciunt (pla'si-ta ne-ga-tī'va du'ō ex'i-tum non fa'she-unt). Two negative pleas do not make an issue.

placitare (pla-si-ta're). To plead.

placitator (pla'si-tā-tor). A pleader.

placitum (plas'i-tum). Singular of placita.

plaga (plā'gą). A wound; a stroke.

plagiarii (pla-ji-ā'ri-ī). (Civil law.) Persons who committed the crime of plagium, which corresponded to the common-law offense of kidnapping. See 4 Bl Comm 219.

plagiarism (plā'ji-ą-rizm). Copying or adopting the literary, musical, or artistic composition or work of another and publishing or producing it as one's own original composition or work. 18 Am J2d Copyr §§ 98 et seq.

plagiarius (plā-ji-ā'ri-us). Singular of **plagiaru.**

plagis et mahemio. See **de plagis et mahemio.**

plagium (plā'ji-um). (Civil law.) The offense of spiriting away and stealing men and children. See 4 Bl Comm 219.

plaideur (pla-dur'). A pleader.

plain error. Palpable error, as in a valuation of property. State v Department of Public Works, 143 Wash 67, 254 P 839.

plain homage (plān hom- or om'ąj). In feudal tenure, the service of fidelity alone.

plaint (plānt). The original or first process, setting forth the cause of action at large, by which an action was begun in an inferior court at common law. Shaw v Dutcher & Harris (NY) 19 Wend 216, 219. A private memorial tendered in open court to the judge, wherein the party injured set forth his cause of action.

In small actions, involving less than forty shillings, which were brought in the court-baron or in the county court, no royal writ was necessary and the suit was not begun by original writ, but by plaint. See 3 Bl Comm 273.

plaintiff. The party complaining in an action or proceeding. A person who brings a suit, action, bill, or complaint. See 3 Bl Comm 25. Any natural or artificial person who institutes an action in his own name or who is joined of record with another or with others who are maintaining an action or proceeding. 39 Am J1st Parties § 4.

plaintiff in error (in er'ǫr). The unsuccessful party to the action who prosecutes a writ of error in a higher court.

plan. A project, program, design, or scheme. A proposed arrangement, readjustment, or reorganization of a debtor's affairs in a proceeding in the bankruptcy court. A draft, outline, or drawing of a building or other structure. A product of architectural services. 5 Am J2d Arch § 3.

See **plans and specifications.**

plank in a shipwreck. A graphic expression used to characterize the saving of a junior equity by acquiring the legal title. 27 Am J2d Eq § 151.

plank road. A road of a kind no longer in use but familiar in the early days of the country, characterized by the use of planks or slabs of timber as a surface of the traveled portion of the way in marshy sections otherwise impassable.

planned development. See **land development.**

plano. See **de plano.**

plan of doing business. A formulated scheme for the accomplishment of the purpose or purposes for which a business is conducted. N. R. Bagley Co. v Cameron, 4 Pa D & C 81.

plans and specifications. The outline or drawing representing a building or other structure to be erected, together with the particulars or details of construction. 13 Am J2d Bldg Contr § 12. A product of architectural services. 5 Am J2d Arch § 3.

plant. A factory or place where an industry is conducted, inclusive of the machines and instrumentalities therein contained. 35 Am J1st M & S § 424. An establishment where machinery or mechanical power is utilized in connection with the employment of the individual. 58 Am J1st Workm Comp § 117. The place of generation of electricity, plus the wires, poles, and other appliances necessary for the transmission of the current to users. Brown v Gerald, 100 Me 351, 61 A 785.

In its ordinary sense, the word includes whatever apparatus is used by a business man in carrying on his business,—not his stock in trade, which he buys or makes for sale, but goods or chattels, fixed or movable, alive or dead, which he keeps for permanent employment in his business. Gulf States Steel Co. v Jones, 203 Ala 450, 83 So 356, 23 ALR 702, 704.

The plant of an employer is that part of his fixed property over which he has exclusive control. But the term does not include a place over which the employer has no oversight or method of protecting the employee from the negligent or wrongful acts of third persons. Carlson v Mock, 102 Wash 557, 173 P 637.

plantation. A place brought under cultivation and planted with crops or trees. A large farm. Atty. Gen. v S. B. Judges, 38 Cal 291, 295. A large area of land, cultivated by workers who live upon the land, usually devoted to the raising in quantity of one or two crops, such as cotton, sugar cane, or rice, often given special character by the owner's mansion upon the premises.

For discussion of the construction of a devise of a "plantation," see 57 Am J1st Wills § 1342.

plantation crossing. Same as **farm crossing.**

plant checker. An employee whose duties consist primarily in compiling reports of production, determining standards of production in reference to the time consumed, and calling attention of his superiors to deviations from job descriptions or standards. NLRB v Armour & Co. (CA10) 154 F2d 570, 169 ALR 421, cert den 329 US 732, 91 L Ed 633, 67 S Ct 92.

plant guard. A person privately employed, acting as a guard at a factory or industrial plant.

plant protection personnel. See **plant guard.**

plaque. A thin piece of metal, wood, or plaster with a face suitable for carrying an inscription, so as to be usable as a memorial. 15 Am J2d Char § 60.

plaster cast. A cast made of plaster, but especially a cast placed upon a member to keep a fractured bone in place after it has been set. United States v Telles (DC Cal) 226 F Supp 670.

plasterer. One who follows the mechanical pursuit of coating walls and ceilings of rooms with plaster. 33 Am J1st Lic § 39. An artisan; a mechanic. Merrigan v English, 9 Mont 113, 22 P 454.

plastic surgery. A surgical operation for the repair or restoration of an injured or destroyed part of the body, especially a part of the face or head, for the purpose of correcting a disfigurement. 22 Am J2d Damg § 103.

plat. A representation on a flat surface of a tract of land, depicting the boundaries by indicating monuments, markers, and lines, natural or artificial. A showing of the subdivisions and lots of a city, town, or village. A map or diagram upon which an owner of land lays it off into blocks and streets and sells lots with reference thereto. 23 Am J2d Ded §§ 23 et seq.
Land is said to be "platted" when it is laid out in lots, blocks, and streets, which are so designated on a map or plat thereof. "The mere fact of platting, taken by itself, is rather a circumstance looking to annexation. It is an attempt to impress upon the territory an urban character." Forsyth v Hammond, 142 Ind 505, 40 NE 267, 41 NE 950.
See **original plat.**

plate. A sheet of metal of uniform thickness and even surface. Sonken-Galamba Corp. v Atchison, T. & S. F. Ry. Co. (DC Mo) 33 F Supp 814. A dish constituting a part of a table service. Metal dishes or ware coated with silver. A holder of false teeth fitted to the mouth and gum.

plate glass insurance. Insurance covering particularly the windows of a building against loss or breakage by perils stated. Vorse v Jersey Plate Glass Ins. Co. 119 Iowa 555, 93 NW 569.

platform scales. A weighing scales so constructed that vehicles, loaded or unloaded, may be weighed thereon. A weighing scales with a platform upon which the barrel, bag, or other receptacle to be weighed may be conveniently placed. 35 Am J2d Fixt § 97.

platted. See **plat.**

play. A dramatic work of either a humorous or a serious nature to be performed or presented to the public on stage, by television, or by motion picture. A form of literary property; a subject of copyright. 18 Am J2d Copyr § 10. Recreation; sport; fun.

play around. To be unfaithful to one's spouse.

playground. A place for recreation, especially a place for children to play. A region for recreation.

playhouse. A theater. A small structure for children to play in.
See **theater.**

playing cards. Sometimes a diversion, sometimes gambling, dependent upon whether or not wagers are made upon the outcome of the game. Cards used in a game.

playing policy. See **numbers game.**

playright. A term suggested for the right to represent or produce a literary or musical composition. 18 Am J2d Copyr § 1.
See **playwright.**

play street. A street which, for the benefit and the protection of children playing therein, is completely closed to traffic, except such as is within the requirements of the abutting owners. Tamburrino v Sterrick Delivery Corp. 241 App Div 221, 271 NYS 765.

playwright. A writer of plays.
See **playright.**

plea. The answer required by law of one formallly accused of crime. 21 Am J2d Crim L § 458. The pleading by way of answer to a petition, declaration, or complaint. 41 Am J1st Pl § 115. In equity, a special answer to all or some part of the bill, but on a single issue, setting up, in lieu of a detailed reply to all the allegations of the bill, as in an answer, some particular fact or facts as a cause for dismissing, delaying, or barring the suit as a whole. 27 Am J2d Eq § 204.

plead. To draft and serve or file a pleading, particularly a pleading by defendant. To raise a defense. Farm Bureau Auto. Ins. Co. v Martin, 97 NH 196, 84 A2d 823, 29 ALR2d 811.

pleader. A person who prepares a pleading or pleadings; a party who files or serves a pleading.

pleading. A formal statement by a party to an action or proceeding of the operative facts, as distinguished from evidentiary facts, which constitute the respective claim or defense. McMillan v Plymouth Electric Light & Power Co. 70 Ind App 336, 123 NE 446. The allegation made by a party to an action or proceeding for the purpose of presenting or joining the issue to be tried and determined, whether such issue is of law or of fact. 41 Am J1st Pl § 2. The science and course of allegation whereby a party in court presents his demand or defense against the demand of the other party to be made a matter of record. Kansas City v O'Connor, 36 Mo App 594, 599.

pleading a counterclaim. See **counterclaim.**

pleading a setoff. See **setoff.**

pleading a statute. Formally setting forth the terms of the statute. Stating the facts which bring the case within the statute, even without taking formal notice or even a mention of the statute itself. Hart V Baltimore & Ohio Railroad Co. 6 W Va 336, 348.

pleading in haec verba. Pleading a written instrument in the same words as the instrument.

pleading over. Serving or filing an amended pleading after an attack by one's adversary upon one's pleading. Pleading to the facts after demurrer overruled. 41 Am J1st Pl § 250. A pleading by the defendant in a criminal case after the overruling of a plea by him not going to the merits of the case, such as a plea in abatement. 21 Am J2d Crim L § 466.

pleading to the jurisdiction. See **plea to the jurisdiction.**

pleading to the merits. Raising and developing the issues between the parties or bringing forward whatever defenses the defendant may have which he wishes to interpose in bar of the plaintiff's claim. 41 Am J1st Pl § 131.

plea in abatement. A dilatory plea in a criminal case, challenging irregularities in procedure occurring before arraignment, but setting up no facts going to the real merits of the case. 21 Am J2d Crim L § 468. A plea in a civil action bringing to the attention of the court some fact or circumstance, not disclosed on the face of the record, which will defeat the particular action without absolutely and forever precluding or excluding right of recovery in the plaintiff. 41 Am J1st Pl § 124.

plea in bar. A pleading interposed by the defendant in an action as a complete defense, designed to defeat the action for all time. 41 Am J1st Pl § 115. A plea by an accused in a criminal case, asserting any matter in confession and avoidance not admissible under the plea of not guilty. 21 Am J2d Crim L § 464.

plea in confession and avoidance. A plea which admits the cause of action alleged by the plaintiff, to the extent at least of giving color to the matter, and sets up other matter in avoidance of the same. 41 Am J1st Pl § 158.

plea in discharge. A form of plea in confession and avoidance in which the defendant admits the existence at one time of a cause of action but alleges that, before the action, the defendant satisfied and discharged plaintiff's claim by payment. Nichols v Cecil, 106 Tenn 455, 61 SW 768.

plea of another action pending. A form of plea in abatement interposing the objection that a former action between the same parties for the same cause is still pending. 1 Am J2d Abat & R § 38.

plea of former jeopardy. See **plea of prior jeopardy.**

plea of guilty. A voluntary plea by an accused admitting the commission of the act charged as a criminal offense, generally permitted except in capital cases. 21 Am J2d Crim L § 484. In a criminal case, an admission or confession of guilt, a submission without contest, a waiver of defense, as conclusive as a verdict of a jury, admitting all material averments of fact in the accusation, leaving no issue for the jury, except in those instances where the extent of a punishment is to be imposed or found by the jury. 21 Am J2d Crim L § 495.

plea of liberum tenementum (plē of li'be-rum te-ne-men'tum). A plea of freehold; a plea which in some jurisdictions is allowed to be interposed by the defendant in an action of trespass. Fort Dearborn Lodge v Klein, 115 Ill 177, 3 NE 272.

plea of limitations. A pleading which invokes the protection of the statute of limitations in a civil case. 34 Am J1st Lim Ac § 428. A special plea of the statute of limitations in a criminal case. 21 Am J2d Crim L § 160.

plea of ne unques administrator (plē of nē un'quĕz ad-mi'nis-trā-tor). See **ne unques administrator.**

plea of nil debit (plē of nil de'bet). See **nil debit.**

plea of nolo contendere (plē of nō'lō kọn-ten'dẹ-rē). See **nolo contendere.**

plea of non assumpsit (plē on non a-sump'sit). See **non assumpsit.**

plea of non cepit (plē of non sē'pit). See **non cepit.**

plea of non damnificatus (plē of non dam-ni-fi-kā'-tus). Literally, a plea of not injured. A proper pleading by the defendant in an action on a covenant to indemnify and save harmless. 27 Am J1st Indem § 33. A plea interposed in an action of debt on a bond, which is equivalent to a plea setting up the defendant's fulfillment of his obligation. State Bank v Chetwood, 8 NJL 1, 25.

plea of non detinet (plē of non det'i-net). See **non detinet.**

plea of non possumus (plē of non pos'ū-mus). A plea of want of capacity.

plea of non vult contendere (plē of non vult kon-ten'de-re). A plea similar to nolo contendere. The defendant will not contest. Re 17 Club, Inc. 26 NJ Super 43, 97 A2d 171.
This is not a confession of guilt, because an accused person might find himself without witnesses to establish his innocence, from their death, absence, or other cause, and hence waive a fruitless contest. Commonwealth v Shrope, 264 Pa 246, 107 A 729, 6 ALR 690, 692.

plea of not guilty. A plea in a criminal case which denies and controverts the existence of every fact essential to constitute the crime charged or to establish the accused's guilt, placing in issue every essential element of the offense charged. 21 Am J2d Crim L § 467. The plea of the general issue in an action for conversion of personal property. 18 Am J2d Conversion § 149. A plea of the general issue in tort actions and ejectment. 25 Am J2d Eject § 85; 41 Am J1st Pl § 141. A plea of the general issue in an action of trespass. 41 Am J1st Pl § 141. A plea of the general issue in an action of trespass on the case. 1 Am J2d Actions § 42.

plea of pregnancy. A plea interposed in a criminal prosecution whereby the execution of a pregnant woman is sought to be stayed by reason of her pregnancy.

plea of prior jeopardy. A special plea in bar, required in some jurisdictions, although not in others, to present the defense of former jeopardy. 21 Am J2d Crim L § 473.
See **prior jeopardy.**

plea of reconvention. A pleading interposing a counterclaim in the answer. McLeod v Bertschy, 33 Wis 176.

plea of sanctuary (sangk'tụ̄-ạ-ri). A plea anciently allowed in criminal cases under which the defendant, accused of any crime except treason or sacrilege, might set up the privilege of sanctuary.
That is, he might flee to a church or churchyard, and within forty days thereafter go into sackcloth, confess himself guilty before a coroner, state the circumstances of the offense, take oath that he abjured the realm and would quit the kingdom and never return without the king's leave. This privilege of sanctuary was much abridged in 1535, and in 1623 was altogether abolished. See 4 Bl Comm 332.

plea puis darrein continuance (plē pwē där-rān kôn-tin-ū-ôns). A plea alleging matters of defense arising after the commencement of the action and after issue joined. 41 Am J1st Pl § 168. A plea which impugns the right of further prosecution, not the right of an action altogether. Heirn v Carron, 19 Miss 11 (Smedes & M) 361.

please pay. In form a courteous request; in legal effect an order to pay. 11 Am J2d B & N § 139.

plea side. The civil side or department of a court as distinguished from the criminal department.

pleas of the crown (plēz of the kroun). Criminal cases, so called in England, because the majesty of the whole community centers in the king, who by law is supposed to be the person injured by every infraction of the public rights. See 4 Bl Comm 2.

pleas roll. The record of a case which contains the pleadings which were filed in the action.

pleasure and business purposes. A familiar term in automobile insurance policies; a term usually defined by the terms of the policy.
Whether a particular activity is within the policy definition is to be determined from the particular facts in each case. 7 Am J2d Auto Ins § 31.
See business use; commercial use.

pleasure drive. See boulevard; parkway.

pleasure resort. See resort.

pleasure use. See pleasure and business purposes.

plea to the jurisdiction. A plea in a criminal case strictly limited to the question of jurisdiction, of necessity preceding a plea of not guilty. 21 Am J2d Crim L § 463. A plea in a civil case where the want of jurisdiction is to be shown by evidence. 41 Am J1st Pl § 129.

plea to the merits. See pleading to the merits.

plebeian (plę-bē′ạn). One of the common people, as distinguished from a member of the patrician class.

plebiscita (pleb-i-sī′ta). The decrees of the Roman people which went into effect without the concurrence of the senate, and which were simply laws established by popular vote.

plebiscite (pleb′i-sit or -sēt). A popular vote on a proposed law or on any question submitted to the people.

plebiscitum (pleb-i-sī′tum). Singular of plebiscita.

plebity (pleb′ị-ti). (Roman law.) The plebes; the plebeians; the common people.

plebs (plebz). (Roman law.) A plebeian; one of the common people.

pledge. A bailment of personal property as security for a debt or obligation, redeemable upon terms, and with the implied power of sale on default. 41 Am J1st Pldg & Col § 2.
The Roman name applicable to a contract of pledge or pawn was pignus or vadium. The difference between a pignus and a hypothecation consisted in this: in the former, the possession of the thing pledged passed to the pledgee; in the latter, it did not. 41 Am J1st Pldg & Col § 2.

pledgee (ple-jē′). A person to whom personal property is pledged by a pledgor.

pledgee's lien. The lien which a pledgee acquires in the thing pledged to the extent of the indebtedness secured, and which is usually held to continue as long as he retains the possession thereof either actual or symbolic and the debt which it was pledged to secure remains unpaid. 41 Am J1st Pldg & Col § 28.

pledgeholder. A third person to whose custody pledged property is entrusted instead of to that of the pledgee.

pledgery. Suretyship. An undertaking to answer for the obligation of another. Gloucester Bank v Worcester, 27 Mass 528, 531.

pledge of affiliation. A pledge of adherence to a particular political party and of support of its nominees, sometimes required as a condition of voting in a primary election. 25 Am J2d Elect § 159.

pledge of rents and profits. Broadening the security of a mortgage by including rents and profits of the mortgaged real estate. 36 Am J1st Mtg § 36.

pledges. Persons who became sureties to answer for the obligation of another. Plural of pledge.

pledges to restore. The sureties on a defendant's redelivery bond in an action of replevin.

pledgor (plej′or). A person who makes a pledge of personal property to a pledgee.

plee (plē). A plea; an action.

plegiabilis (ple-ji-ā′bi-lis). Personal property which may be lawfully pledged.

plegii de prosequendo (ple′ji-i de prō-se-quen′dō). Pledges to prosecute.
Under the ancient action of replevin to recover cattle or goods alleged to have been wrongfully taken in distress, the plaintiff was required to find pledges which should be security to try the right of distress. See 3 Bl Comm 146.

plegii de prosequendum (ple′ji-ī dē prō-se-quen′dum). Same as plegii de prosequendo.

plegii de retorno habendo (ple′ji-ī dē re-tor′nō hā-ben′dō). Pledges to have the return.
Under the ancient action of replevin to recover cattle or goods alleged to have been wrongfully taken in distress, the plaintiff was bound to find such pledges as security for his return of the thing distrained to the distrainor, if the right should be determined against the plaintiff. See 3 Bl Comm 147.

plein age. See de plein age; plena aetas.

plein vie. See en plein vie.

plena aetas (plē′na ē′tas). Full age; majority.

Plena et celeris justitia fiat partibus (plē′na et se′le-ris jus-ti′she-a fī′at par′ti-bus). Let full and speedy justice be done to the parties.

plena fides (plē′na fī′dēz). Full faith; full confidence.

plena forisfactura (plē′na fo″ris-fak-tū′ra). A full or complete forfeiture; a forfeiture of all one's property.

plena probatio (plē′na pro-bā′she-ō). (Civil law.) Full proof,—proof by two witnesses, or by a public document. See 3 Bl Comm 370.

plena propiedad (play-nah pro-pe-ay-dahd). See propiedad.

plenarie (ple-nā′ri-e). Fully.

plenarty (plē′nạr-ti). The condition of a church as being full, after a clergyman had once been instituted in it, whether his induction had been rightful or not. See 3 Bl Comm 243.

plenary (plē′nạ-ri). Full and complete. Commonwealth v Breakwater Co. 214 Mass 10, 100 NE 1034. Unabridged.

plenary action. A suit or action, independent of any other proceeding, in which the merits of the cause are fully inquired into and determined, as distinguished from a summary proceeding in which formalities are less strict and which are usually merely ancillary to some other action or proceeding. May v Henderson, 268 US 111, 115, 69 L Ed 870, 873, 45 S Ct 456.

plenary power. Power as broad as equity and justice

require. London v Joslovitz, 279 App Div 280, 110 NYS2d 58.

plenary suit. Same as **plenary action.**

plena vita. See **in plena vita.**

plene administravit (plē'nē ad-mi-nis-trā'vit). A plea of an executor or administrator, in an action against him on a debt of his decedent, setting forth the fact that he has fully administered the estate. Wilkins v Gibson, 113 Ga 31, 38 SE 374.

plene administravit praeter (plē'nē ad-mi-nis-trā'vit prē'ter). A plea of an executor or administrator in an action against him on a debt of his decedent, alleging that he has fully administered the estate, excepting as to assets which are insufficient to meet the plaintiff's claim.

plene computavit (plē'nē kom-pū-tā'vit). He has fully accounted,—a plea in an action of account alleging that the defendant has already rendered a full account.

plenipotentiary (plen″i-pō-ten'shi-ạ-ri). A person who is fully empowered or commissioned to act for his constituent. An ambassador.

pleno comitatu. See **in pleno comitatu.**

pleno jure (plē'nō jū'rē). With full right.

pleno lumine. See **in pleno lumine.**

plenum dominium (plē'num dō-min'i-um). (Civil law.) Full ownership, the right of property in a thing coupled with the right to its use and enjoyment.

plenum rectum (plē'num rek'tum). Full, complete, or absolute right.

pleurocentesis (plö″rō-sen-tē'sis). Draining the chest cavity. Breaux v All State Ins. Co. (La App) 86 So 2d 132.

plevina (ple-vī'na). Security; the liability or undertaking of a surety.

Plimsoll line. A line marked on the side of a merchant ship as a gauge to prevent overloading, the line marking the limit of safe submergence.

Plimsoll mark. Same as **Plimsoll line.**

pl'it'm. An abbreviation of **placitum.**

plot. The scheme of a dramatic or literary work. An area of ground marked off. A diagram.

plottage. The added value that accrues to two or more lots in one ownership, where the entire plot can be improved to better advantage than the individual lots. Re New York, 127 Misc 710, 729, 217 NYS 544.

plough-land (plou'land). As large a tract of land as could be ploughed by one plough in a year. Arable land.

plough silver. Money paid by a feudal tenant to the lord of the manor in lieu of service by ploughing.

plow. A farm implement used to cut and turn over the soil in preparation of a seed bed.

plowbote (plou'bōt). A tenant's common-law right of estovers consisting of a sufficient amount of the timber necessary in making or repairing all instruments, tools, and implements used in husbandry. Anderson v Cowan, 125 Iowa 259, 101 NW 92.

plow horse. A work horse, particularly one used in farm work.

plow-land (plou'land). Same as **plough-land.**

plowman's fee (plou'mạns fē). An ancient customary descent in equal shares to the sons of the decedent, varied by larger shares to the oldest or the youngest son.

plow silver. Same as **plough silver.**

plugging well. A conservation measure required by statute in some jurisdictions upon the abandonment of an oil well. 24 Am J1st Gas & O § 148.

Water, if not plugged off when a well is abandoned, may migrate through the oil sand to adjacent producing wells and eventually ruin them. Gas sands may also be flooded and gas wasted if gas is allowed to escape into the air. All wells should be plugged if they are abandoned. Forbes v United States (CA9 Mont) 125 F2d 404.

plumber. An artisan who works in fitting and repairing waterpipes, bathroom installations, and the like. 41 Am J1st Plumb § 2.

plumbing. Work connected with the system of pipes, traps, sinks, bowls, etc. whereby water is conducted into, through, and out of a building. Blegman v Winkler, 120 Misc 483, 198 NYS 758. The system itself.

plumbism (plum'bizm). Lead poisoning. 58 Am J1st Workm Comp §§ 252, 253. A disease common among painters, usually caused by inhaling lead fumes from the paint. Anno: 29 ALR 694.

plumbum (plum'bum). Lead.

plunder. Verb: To take the property of others by force. To take the property of others by any means, whether force or fraud. To pilfer, to swindle. Carter v Andrews, 33 Mass (16 Pick) 1, 9. Noun: Property acquired by criminal or fraudulent act. The fruits of a crime.

plunderage (plun'dẹr-āj). Embezzlement committed aboard a ship.

plural. Consisting of more than one.

Pluralis numerus est duobus contentus (plū-rā'lis nu'me-rus est du'ō-bus kon-ten'tus). The plural number is contented or satisfied with two.

pluraliter (plū-rā'li-ter). Plurally; in the plural number.

plurality. A plural condition or state, being in excess of one. The excess of one number over another.

plurality estate. See **estate in plurality.**

plurality of subject matter. A characterization of the content of a statute embracing more than one subject. 50 Am J1st Stat § 192.

plurality of trust. The situation where separate and several trusts, to be administered by the same trustee, are created by the same instrument. 54 Am J1st Trusts § 16.

plurality vote. The largest vote received as between candidates for an office at an election; the winning vote, except where a majority of votes cast is required by constitutional provision or statute. 26 Am J2d Elect § 309.

plural marriage (mar'āj). A marriage of a person who already has one or more living spouses. A bigamous or polygamous marriage.

plural patents. A patent for an entire combination or process and another patent or patents for such part or parts of the combination or process as are new and useful. 40 Am Jist Pat § 83.

Plures cohaeredes sunt quasi unum corpus, propter unitatem juris quod habent (plū'rēz ko-hē're-dēz sunt quā′sī ū′num kor′pus, prop′ter ū-ni-tā′tem jū′ris quod hā′bent). Several coheirs are one body, as it were, because they have unity of right.

Plures participes sunt quasi unum corpus, in eo quod unum jus habent (plū′rēz par-ti′si-pēz sunt quā′sī ū′num kor′pus, in e′ō quod ū′num jūs hā′bent). Several parceners are one body, as it were, in this, that they have one right.

pluribus unum. See **E Pluribus Unum.**

pluries writs (plū′ri-ēz rits). Multiple or successive writs of attachment or execution issued in the same action or upon the same judgment. 6 Am J2d Attach § 278; 30 Am J2d Exec § 84.
    At common law, a writ of execution issued after the second or alias writ was a pluries writ. Bigelow v Renker, 25 Ohio St 542. So was a writ of attachment issued after an alias writ had been returned "nothing found." See 3 Bl Comm 283.

pluris petitio (plū′ris pe-ti′she-ō). A demand for too much, that is, for more than is owing.

plus. Added to. In Latin, more.

Plus exempla quam peccata nocent (plus eg-zem′pla quam pe-kā′ta no′sent). Examples do more harm than offenses.

Plus peccat auctor quam actor (plus pe′kat âk′tor quam ak′tor). The instigator sins more than the actual perpetrator.

plus petitio (plus pe-ti′she-ō). (Roman law.) A demand of too much, that is, of more than is due or owing.

Plus valet consuetudo quam concessio (plus va′let kon-su-e-tu′dō quam kon-se′she-ō). Custom is more powerful than grant.

Plus valet unus oculatus testis, quam auriti decem (plus va′let ū′nus o-ku-lā′tus tes′tis, quam â′ri-tī de′sem). One eye-witness is worth more than ten ear-witnesses.

Plus vident oculi quam oculus (plus vi′dent o′ku-lī quam o′ku-lus). Eyes see more than an eye sees,— several see more than one.

ply. To perform in repetition acts of the same kind.
    A reference to plying a business at a certain place ordinarily imports that such place is a seat of the business. New York, New Haven & Hartford Railroad Co. v Scovill, 71 Conn 136, 41 A 246.

P.M. Abbreviation of postmaster, also of Principal Meridian.

p.m. Abbreviation of post meridiem, after noon.

pneumatic tire. A rubber tire for a motor vehicle, inflated with compressed air. 7 Am J2d Auto § 70.

pneumoconiosis (nu″mō-kō-nē-ō′sis). A diseased condition of the lungs caused by the inhalation of dust particles such as a stonecutter may be subjected to. Sullivan's Case, 265 Mass 497, 164 NE 457, 62 ALR 1458; Schmidt v Merchants Despatch Transp. Co. 270 NY 287, 200 NE 824, 104 ALR 450, reh den 271 NY 531, 2 NE2d 680, 104 ALR 462.

pneumonia. A disease of the lungs characterized by a severe inflammation of the tissues. Nashville v Reese, 138 Tenn 471, 197 SW 492. A serious disease of the lungs in which the tissues become inflamed and hardened, rendering breathing difficult and painful. Young v New York Life Ins. Co. 360 Mo 460, 228 SW2d 670. A common disease but sometimes classified as an accidental injury for the purposes of workmen's compensation. 58 Am J1st Workm Comp § 244.

P. O. An abbreviation of "postoffice."

poaching (pōch′ing). Trespassing upon land for the purpose of killing and taking game there.

poblador (po-blah-dor). A term used in certain Spanish-American grants and signifying a person who undertook to bring together a certain number of families or settlers, and build a town. Hart v Burnett, 15 Cal 530, 538.

pocket judgment (pok′et juj′m̧ent). A bond given to secure an obligation; a statute merchant.
    See **statute merchant.**

pocket picking. Taking from another's pocket. A form of larceny. 32 Am J1st Larc § 44.
    Picking another's pocket, exercising only such force as is necessary to lift and remove the property from the pocket, is not robbery. However, if the thief jostles his victim for the purpose of diverting attention in order to pick his pocket, the force is sufficient to constitute robbery. Duluth St. R. Co. v Fidelity & D. Co. 136 Minn 299, 161 NW 595.

pocket-sheriff (pok′et-sher″if). A sheriff appointed by the king without the customary nomination of the judges. See 1 Bl Comm 342.

pocket veto. A veto of a legislative bill effected by the retention of the bill by the executive, his return of the measure as approved or rejected within the time fixed by law being prevented by the adjournment of the law-making body. 50 Am J1st Stat § 121.

pod net. See **Dutch net.**

poena (pē′na). A punishment; a penalty; a compensation.

Poena ad paucos, metus ad omnes perveniat (pe′na ad pâ′kos, me′tus ad om′nēz per-ve′ni-at). Punishment for the few means that fear comes to all.

poena corporalis (pe′na kor-po-rā′lis). Corporal punishment.

Poenae potius molliendae quam exasperandae sunt (pē′nē po′she-us mo-li-en′dē quam ex-as-per-an′dē sunt). Punishments should rather be softened than aggravated.

Poenae sint restringendae (pē′ne sint restrin-jen′dē). Punishments should be restrained.

Poena ex delicto defuncti, haeres teneri non debet (pē′na ex de-lik′to de-funk′ti, hē′rēz te-nē′ri non de′bet). The heir ought not to be bound by a penalty imposed for the wrong done by the deceased.

poenalis (pe-nā′lis). (Civil law). Penal; carrying or imposing a penalty.

poenam. See **in poenam.**

Poena non potest, culpa perennis erit (pe′na non po′test, kul′pa pe-ren′nis e′rit). Punishment cannot be everlasting, but error or sin will be.

poena pilloralis (pē′na pi-lo-rā′lis). Punishment in the pillory.
    See **pillory.**

Poena suos tenere debet actores et non alios (pē′na su′os te-nē′re de′bet ak-to′rēz et non a′li-os). The punishment ought to belong to the actual perpetrators and not to others.

Poena tollit potest, culpa perennis erit (pē′na to′lit po′test, kul′pa pe-ren′nis e′rit). The punishment can be removed, but the sin or error will be perpetual.

poenitentia (pē-ni-ten'she-a). Repentance; altered intent.

poetic justice. Rewards for virtue; punishment for sin. A satirical expression for idealistic, rather than practical attempts to regulate the conduct of men and women.

poin. See **en poin**.

poinding (pün'- or pin'ding). A distress; an attachment of goods.

point of destination. See **destination**.

point of impact. A term of conflicts of laws, meaning the point at which the tortious acts of the defendant impinged upon the rights of the complaining party. Ettore v Philco Television Broadcasting Corp. (CA3 Pa) 229 F2d 481, 58 ALR2d 626.
See **place of most significant contacts**.

point of law. A matter of law, as distinguished from a matter of fact, involved in a case or controversy.
See **precedent**.

point of production. Within the meaning of a statute exempting from a vehicle tax motor vehicles used exclusively in delivering dairy or other farm products:—the farm where the livestock was prepared for disposal and where milk was produced and agricultural products raised, or where dairy farm products were made. State ex rel. Wisconsin Allied Truck Owners Asso. v Public Service Com. 207 Wis 664, 242 NW 668.

point reserved. See **reserved point**.

points. The propositions to be presented in a brief. Afflerbach v Yorktown Independent School Dist. (Tex Com App) 289 SW 1003, 1005. Facts, Kent v State, 64 Ark 247, 251, especially circumstances which give the character of excellence, as the "points" of a prize winning animal at a fair.
See **terms and expressions beginning point**.

point system. A system provided by statute or regulation in some jurisdictions for the purpose of singling out habitual or persistent motor-vehicle-law violators, whereby points are charged against a driver's record for violation, and his license suspended or revoked upon his accumulating a specified number of such points. 7 Am J2d Auto § 112.

poison. A substance which when taken will destroy life or be seriously injurious to health. Anno: 110 ALR 1277, s. 131 ALR 1061; 29A Am J Rev ed Ins § 1226. Any substance which, where introduced into the system, either directly or by absorption, produces violent, morbid, or fatal changes, or which destroys living tissue with which it comes in contact. Watkins v National Electrical Products Corp. (CA3 Pa) 165 F2d 980. Any substance which, when applied to the body or introduced into the system, without acting mechanically but by its own inherent qualities, is capable of destroying life. People v Van Deleer, 53 Cal 147. A substance of such properties as to be capable of destroying life when taken in small doses. 29A Am J Rev ed Ins § 1226. Any substance which ordinarily has such a harmful or deadly effect on the body that it ought not to be taken internally without technical familiarity or medical direction. 25 Am J2d Drugs § 6.

poisoning. A specific felony under the statutes of some jurisdictions, usually committed by mixing a lethal potion with food or drink served the victim. 26 Am J1st Homi § 604.

poker. A game of chance played with cards, almost invariably for money so as to constitute gambling. 24 Am J1st Gaming § 20.
See **draw poker; stud poker**.

polar star rule. The principle that a written document which is ambiguous is to be construed according to the intent of the maker, grantor, or devisor as gathered from the four corners of the instrument. Hanks v McDanell, 307 Ky 243, 210 SW2d 784, 17 ALR2d 1.

pole. A slender piece of wood or metal of such strength and length as to serve to support a line, a tent, even a roof of a barn. A linear measure, the equivalent of a rod, sixteen and one half feet.

pole-raising. An indictable offense in the early days of the country, where symbolizing dissatisfaction with the government, because of the tendency to incite violence. Pennsylvania v Morrison (Pa) 1 Addison 274, 275.

pole tax. A license fee imposed on a telegraph or telephone company according to the number of poles erected and maintained in the municipality. 52 Am J1st Teleg & T § 51.
See **poll tax**.

police. Verb: To keep order. To keep clean, particularly the ground around buildings of the military. Noun: The law-enforcing department of a state or local government having the duty of maintaining order, detecting crimes, and making arrests. Peace officers. In the broadest sense, inclusive of both administrators and magistrates. State ex rel. Walsh v Hine, 59 Conn 50, 21 A 1024.

police court. A local court. 20 Am J2d Cts § 30. A municipal court for the summary trial of petty offenders and violators of city ordinances.

police department. The department of a municipal government, consisting of a head, usually known as the chief of police, captains, lieutenants, inspectors, sergeants, detectives, patrolmen, traffic officers, and other officers within the broad category of policemen, which has the duty of maintaining order, detecting crime, and making arrests.

police force. See **police department**.

police judge. A magistrate. The judge of a police court.

police justice. A magistrate whose jurisdiction extends only to criminal cases and is the same in such cases as that of a justice of the peace. Wenzler v People (NY) 2 Cow Crim 72, 74.

police magistrate. See **police judge; police justice**. State v Evans, 161 Mo 95, 61 SW 590.

policeman. A peace officer. 47 Am J1st Sher § 5. An officer of the police department, having such powers as are conferred upon him by statute or municipal ordinance.

police power. A term impossible of abstract, and incapable of complete, definition. Berman v Parker, 348 US 26, 99 L Ed 27, 75 S Ct 98. In one sense, the whole power of government to which all other powers are only incidental and ancillary; nothing more or less than the powers of government inherent in every sovereignty to the extent of its dominions. A.F.L. v American Sash & Door Co. 67 Ariz 20, 189 P2d 912, affd 335 US 538, 93 L Ed 2d 222, 69 S Ct 258, 6 ALR2d 481. An attribute of sovereignty, comprehending the power to make and enforce all wholesome and reasonable laws and regulations necessary to the maintenance, upbuilding, and advancement of public weal and protection of public interests. State ex rel. Whetsel v Wood, 207 Okla 193, 248 P2d 612, 34 ALR2d 1321. That power in government which restrains individuals from transgressing the rights of others, and restrains them in their conduct so far as is necessary to protect the rights of all. State v Dolan, 13 Idaho 693, 92 P 995. The domestic order of the state, whereby the individuals thereof, like members of a well-governed family, are bound to conform their general behavior to the rules of propriety, good neighborhood, and good manners, and to be decent, industrious, and inoffensive in their daily lives. Hunter v Green, 142 Fla 104, 194 So 379. The vast residual power of the state, comprising that portion of the sovereignty of the state not surrendered by the terms of the United States Constitution to the Federal Government. 16 Am J2d Const L § 262.

police precinct. A subdivision of the area of a municipality to which a part of the force of the city—officers and men—are assigned for duty, normally having a station house.

police problem. A pressing element of emergency arising from impending danger to the community and demanding urgent attention to abate or avoid it. Greenberg v Lee, 196 Or 157, 248 P2d 612, 35 ALR2d 567. One who is a persistent violator of laws.

police record. A court record of the conviction or convictions of a person. Any record kept by police as to persons apprehended by them and the charges against such persons. People v Yates, 339 Ill 421, 171 NE 557.

police regulations. Statutes and ordinances dealing with the health, safety, and morals of the people. Mitchell v Cumberland Tel. & Tel. Co. 188 Ky 263, 221 SW 547, 10 ALR 946, 949.
See **police power.**

police sergeant. See **police department.**

policy. Expedience. A course of action. Principle. On a much lower scale, the numbers game.
See **numbers game; policy of insurance; public policy.**

policy game. Same as **numbers game.**

policy loan. See **loan on life insurance policy.**

policymaking. A superior discretionary power or duty. Commonwealth ex rel. Meredith v Frost, 295 Ky 137, 172 SW2d 905.

policy racket. See **numbers game.**

policy of insurance. The parlance of the insurance business, the contract between the insured and the insurer. State ex rel. Sheets v Pittsburgh, Cincinnati, Chicago & St. Louis Ry. Co. 68 Ohio St 9, 67 NE 93.
The formal document in which a contract of insurance appears. London Assur. Corp. v Paterson, 106 Ga 538, 32 SE 650.
See **annual dividend policy; assessment policy; blanket policy; deferred dividend policy; fire policy; life policy; old line policy; paid-up policy; running policy; term policy; tontine policy; valued policy; voyage policy; wager policy.**

policy of the law. The reason for and the principle of the law.

The expression is synonymous with the term "public policy." See Billingsley v Clelland, 41 W Va 234, 245, 23 SE 812.
See **public policy.**

polio (pol'i-ō). A colloquial term for **poliomyelitis.**

poliomyelitis (pol''i-ō-mī-ẹ-li'tis). A disease which attacks the gray matter of the spinal cord, often causing paralysis. Cunningham v State, 18 Misc 2d 367, 186 NYS2d 146, revd on other grounds 10 App Div 2d 751, 197 NYS2d 542, affd 11 NY2d 808, 227 NYS2d 253, 181 NE2d 852. An infectious disease, especially of children, now well under control by virtue of medical and scientific research supported by funds obtained from well-founded charity.

political activity. Serving on a political committee, holding office in a party organization, making partisan speeches or campaigning for candidates. 30A Am J Rev ed Judges § 56.

Politiae legibus, non leges politiis adaptandae (poli'she-e le'ji-bus, non le'jēz po-li'she-is ad-aptan'dē). Politics should be adapted to the laws, not the laws to politics.

politic. Expedient, especially in reference to the effect of a course of action upon others.
See **body politic; body politic and corporate.**

political. Pertaining to the government. Re Kemp, 16 Wis 359, 396. Pertaining to the establishment of a form of government. Commonwealth v McCarthy, 281 Mass 253, 183 NE 495, 85 ALR 1141. Pertaining to the activity of, or work for, a political party; pertaining to anything connected with candidacy for office or the support of a candidate for office.

political body. A body of government, such as a legislature or municipal commission. A body established as a source or administrator of governmental power, such as a state, a county, a municipality. Not the same as a political party. Brown v Finnegan, 369 Pa 609, 133 A2d 809.

political compact. A treaty between two or more nations. 52 Am J1st Treat § 3. A compact establishing a government.
See **Mayflower Compact.**

political committee. Any committee or combination of three or more persons co-operating to aid or promote the success or defeat of a political party. Anno: 125 ALR 1031. The organized force of a political party in the nation as the national committee, in the state as the state committee, and locally as a county or town committee, consisting of committeemen, elected in a primary election and leaders known as chairmen or executive committeemen, maintaining an office and staff of workers, particularly in the six months preceding an election.

political convention. See **convention.**

political corporation. Same as **public corporation.**

political crime. An offense against the government. Activity in a political uprising without reference to guilt of any specific offense. Anno: 94 ALR 1493; 31 Am J2d Extrad § 23.

political division. See **political subdivision.**

political economy. A word displaced by the modern term **economics.**

political equity. Those principles to be followed by states or nations in adjusting matters or controversies between them, such to be distinguished from the equity administered by a court of equity. Rhode

Island v Massachusetts (US) 12 Pet 657, 738, 9 L Ed 1233, 1266.

political liberty. See **civil liberties.**

political newspaper. A newspaper published by a political party; a newspaper which adheres to and supports one political party over others.

political offender. See **political crime.**

political office. Any office of the civil government not connected with the administration of justice. United States v Fitzpatrick (US) 13 Wall 568, 20 L Ed 707, 708. Any office filled by a popular election. Any public office not within the civil service system, that is, one whose occupant is not protected in his tenure by civil service laws.

political party. A number of persons united in opinion and organized in the manner usual to the then existing political parties. State ex rel. Howells v Metcalf, 18 SD 393, 100 NW 923. An unincorporated association of persons sponsoring certain ideas of government or maintaining certain political principles or beliefs respecting governmental policy, formed for the purpose of urging the adoption and execution of such principles in governmental affairs through officers of like beliefs. 25 Am J2d Elect § 116. An organization which has polled a sufficiently large number of votes at the preceding general or municipal election to entitle it to nominate all its candidates for office and to elect all its party officers at primaries, under the provisions of the election law. Brown v Finnegan, 389 Pa 609, 133 A2d 809.

political power. That power which a sovereign or state exerts by his or its own authority. Rhode Island v Massachusetts (US) 12 Pet 657, 738, 9 L Ed 1233, 1266. The power of a political party, a group of persons, or even an individual to influence an election.

political propaganda. See **propaganda.**

political purpose. A purpose to influence the exercise of political rights. Commonwealth v McCarthy, 281 Mass 253, 183 NE 495, 85 ALR 1141.

political question. A question, the determination of which is a prerogative of the legislative or executive branch of the government, so as not to be appropriate for judicial inquiry or adjudication. 20 Am J Cts § 80.

It would be difficult to draw a clear line of demarcation between political and non-political questions, but among the questions which have been recognized as political rather than judicial in nature, none comes more clearly within the former classification than those which involve the propriety of acts done in the conduct of the foreign nations with our government. Z. & F. Assets Realization Corp. v Hull, 72 App DC 234, 114 F2d 464.

political revolt. The existence of war in a material sense rather than in a legal sense. Three Friends, 166 US 1, 41 L Ed 897, 17 S Ct 495. A turning away from the leaders of a political party theretofore recognized.

See **Young Turks.**

political rights. The power to participate directly or indirectly in the establishment or management of government. People v Washington, 36 Cal 658, 662. Constitutional rights, particularly the right of assembly, suffrage, and the right to be a candidate for and to hold public office.

political subdivision. A subordinate political body. A county, township, or municipal corporation. A territorial division to the electors of which there is committed to some extent the power of local government. State v Corker, 67 NJL 596, 52 A 362.

politics. The science of government. In a practical sense, political activity.
See **political activity.**

polity (pol'i-ti). A society with an organized government. An established government.

poll. Verb: To cut off, for example, the horns of a steer. To vote. To receive votes in an election. To canvass the electorate for the purpose of forecasting the result of an election. Noun: A head. An individual among several persons. A list of persons, particularly, a list of jurors or of voters. More precisely, a list of persons who voted at an election. Citizens & Taxpayers of De Soto Parish v Williams, 49 La Ann 422, 21 So 647.

See **catchpoll; challenge to the poll; deed poll; polls.**

pollicitation (po-lis-i-tā'shon). A sort of contract recognized in the civil law which arises from a promise made by one party only, without any consent or acceptance by the other.

This peculiar kind of obligation exists only from an individual towards a body politic or government. M'Culloch v Eagle Ins. Co. 18 Mass (1 Pick) 278, 283.

polling jury. Examining the jurors individually to ascertain whether they are unanimous in support of the verdict. 53 Am J1st Trial § 1015. A procedure whereby each juror is asked individually the finding at which he has arrived, creating individual responsibility by requiring each juror to answer for himself, and affording the court an opportunity to ascertain with certainty that a unanimous verdict has in fact been reached and that no juror has been coerced or induced to agree to a verdict to which he has not fully assented. 21 Am J2d Crim L § 371.

polling place. See **polls.**

polls. One of the places where the votes are cast at an election. The place of holding an election within a district, precinct, or other territorial unit. 26 Am J2d Elect § 228.
See **poll.**

poll tax. A tax of a fixed amount imposed upon all the persons, or upon all the persons of a certain class, resident within a specified territory, without regard to their property or the occupations in which they may be engaged. 51 Am J1st Tax § 38. A tax imposed upon each man of a certain age for road purposes, payable in cash or in services rendered in work upon the roads. 25 Am J1st High § 84. Abolished absolutely as a prerequisite to voting in federal elections by the Twenty-Fourth Amendment to the United States Constitution. 25 Am J2d Elect § 81.

pollution. See **air pollution; water pollution.**

polo. A game played by teams of four men each, mounted on horses, the object of which is to score by driving a small wooden ball with an instrument known as a mallet, through the goal of the opponents. Douglas v Converse, 248 Pa 232, 93 A 955.

po. lo. suo. An abbreviation of **ponit loco suo.**

polyandry (pol-i-an'dri). The state or condition of a woman who has more than one living husband.

polycythemia (pol″i-sī-thē'mi-ạ). A chronic condition of slow, insidious development, in which the red blood cells increase to exceed the maximum normal count of 5 million per cubic millimeter and the hemoglobin content of the blood increases to exceed the maximum normal of 85 per cent. Miller v Lykes Bros.-Ripley S. S. Co. (CA5 La) 98 F2d 185.

Polygamia est plurium simul virorum uxorumve connubium (po-li-ga′mi-a est plu′ri-um si′mul vi-rō′rum u-xōr′um-ve kon-nu′bi-um). Polygamy is the marriage with several husbands or wives at the same time.

polygamy (pō-lig′a̯-mi). The offense or practice of marrying again by one who has a spouse living. Reynolds v United States (US) 8 Otto 145, 25 L Ed 244, 250. Popularly known as the practice of having several wives.

polygarchy (pol′i-gär-ki). A government by several rulers.

polygraph (pol′i-gràf). A machine for making copies of written instruments. An instrument which records the pulse of the heart in tracings.

polymania (pol-i-mān′i̯a̯). The form of insanity which amounts to general mental alienation. Re Russell (NY) 1 Barb Ch 38, 41.

polyphase (pol′i-fāz). See **multiphase**.

polytechnic (pol-i-tek′nik). Pertaining to applied science and engineering.

pomoeria (po-moe′ri-a). The bounds. See 1 Bl Comm 30.

pond. A small body of water substantially at rest in its natural state, that is, without a substantial current. 56 Am J1st Wat § 50. A small body of water artificially created by impounding a stream or draining surface water to a depression. A confined or stagnant body of fresh water. Rockland Water Co. v Camden & Rockland Water Co. 80 Me 544, 15 A 785.

See **great ponds**.

Ponderantur testes, non numerantur (pon-de-ran′ter tes′tēz, non nu-me-ran′ter). Witnesses are weighed, not counted. Bakeman v Rose (NY) 14 Wend 105, 109.

pondus (pon′dus). Same as **poundage**.

pondus regis (pon′dus rē′jis). The king's weight, a standard weight established by parliament. See 1 Bl Comm 276.

pone (pō′ne). See **de pone; writ of pone**.

ponendo sigillum ad exceptionem. See **de ponendo sigillum ad exceptionem; ponendum sigillum ad exceptionem**.

ponendum in ballium (pō-nen′dum in bal′li-um). A writ which lay to admit a person to bail.

ponendum sigillum ad exceptionem (pō-nen′dum si-jil′lum ad ex-sep-she-ō′nem). A writ which lay to compel the judges to place the seal of the court upon exceptions to rulings made at the trial of a case.

pone per vadium et salvos plegios (pō′ne per va′di-um et sal′vos ple′ji-os). Put by gage and safe pledges.

A writ which was issued after the return of the original writ and the nonappearance of the defendant, ordering the sheriff to attach the defendant by taking gage, that is, certain of his goods, to be forfeited if he did not appear, or by making him find safe pledges or sureties to be amerced in the event of his nonappearance. See 3 Bl Comm 280.

ponere (pō′ne-re). (Latin.) To place. To put.

poniard. A dagger. People v Ruiz, 88 Cal App 502, 263 P 836.

Ponit loco suo (pō′nit lō′kō su′ō). He put him in his place or stead.

Ponit se super patriam (pō′nit sē sū′per pa′tri-am). He puts himself upon the country,—he leaves the matter for the jury to decide, that is, he pleads not guilty. See 4 Bl Comm 341.

pontage (pon′tāj). A tax levied for the maintenance of a bridge; a toll charged for the use of a bridge.

pontibus reparandis (pon′ti-bus re-pa-ran′dis). A writ directing the repair of a bridge.

pontium reparatio (pon′she-um re-pa-rā′she-ō). The reparation of bridges.

This was a part of the trinoda necessitas which was an obligation falling on all freemen or at least on all free householders and to which their estates were subject, whatever other immunities they might enjoy. No rank or dignity could exempt a man from the service of rendering aid in the construction and repair of bridges and highways. Butler v Perry, 240 US 328, 60 L Ed 672, 36 S Ct 258.

pontoon. A float supporting a bridge or other structure. A vessel for the purposes of admiralty jurisdiction. The Mackinaw (DC Or) 165 F 351.

pony-truck. The truck of a locomotive resting on the small wheels which are in front of the driving wheels. Eker v Pettibone (CA7 Ind) 110 F2d 451.

pool. An association of persons engaged in buying or selling a certain commodity or commodities. Kilbourn v Thompson, 103 US 168, 26 L Ed 377. A contract or combination between competing producers or dealers in commodities, particularly those of prime necessity, whereby the parties effect an illegal restraint of trade by agreement to refrain from competition and to divide profits from their respective businesses in fixed proportions. 36 Am J1st Monop etc. § 18. An arrangement between carriers for division of traffic. 44 Am J1st R R § 360. An agreement between carriers for a division of earnings. United States v Trans-Missouri Freight Asso. (CA8 Kan) 58 F 58. A cumulation of the products of members of a co-operative association for sale of the entire amount. Texas Farm Bureau Cotton Asso. v Stovall, 113 Tex 273, 253 SW 1101. An agreement to unite resources for the accomplishment of a particular purpose, as where the banks of a locality joined in a plan for aiding another bank in financial difficulty. 10 Am J2d Bks § 334. One of several related games of billiards, played by two or more persons on a table with pockets, with numbered balls, a tapered stick known as a cue ball, the object being to drive the balls into the pockets in the order of the numbers, Recreation Club Inc. v Miller, 192 Miss 259, 5 So 2d 678; a game sometimes played as a gambling game. 24 Am J1st Gaming § 21. A combination of persons, each staking a sum of money on the success of a horse in a race, or a contestant in a game, the money to be divided among the successful bettors according to the amount put in by each. 24 Am J1st Gaming § 23. In the most simple sense, a small body of water, such as a swimming pool.

See **car pool**.

pooling. Commingling the funds of several trusts for investment in one or more securities. 54 Am J1st Trust § 396. Forming a pool. Texas Farm Bureau Cotton Asso. v Stovall, 113 Tex 273, 253 SW 1101.

POOLING

See **pool**.

pooling agreement. See **pooling contract**.

pooling commissions. An objectionable practice by brokers severally representing the parties to a transaction in dividing the commissions on an even basis. 12 Am J2d Brok § 174.

pooling contract. A contract made in effecting a pool, an illegal contract where the pool is illegal. United States v Trans-Missouri Freight Asso. (CA8 Kan) 58 F 58.

See **pool**; **voting agreement**; **voting trust**.

pooling royalties. An arrangement whereby the owners of separate tracts of land share proportionately in the sum obtained by the payment of royalties on production of all oil wells within the entire area comprehended. 24 Am J1st Gas & O § 66.

poolroom. A room open to the public and equipped with tables, cues, etc. for the playing of pool or billiards, a charge being made the players by the keeper. 4 Am J2d Amuse § 24. A turf exchange; that is, a room or place where money is received, won, and lost on horse races, and where tickets for pools on horse races run, or to be run, at divers race courses, are bought, sold, and cashed. State v Vaughan, 81 Ark 117, 98 SW 685.

pool selling. A form of gambling; the receiving from several persons of wagers on the same event, especially a horse race, the total sum of which is to be divided among the winners, subject to the commission or charge exacted by the seller of the pool. 24 Am J1st Gaming § 24. A kind of gambling, but not a lottery. Commonwealth v Kentucky Jockey Club, 238 Ky 739, 38 SW2d 987.

pool table. "Apparatus" for the purposes of an exemption from execution. Anno: 2 ALR 821.
See **pool**.

pool ticket. A ticket issued by the person conducting a pool by way of gambling.
See **pool selling**.

poor. Destitute and helpless, lacking in ability to support oneself and without means of support. Busser v Snyder, 282 Pa 440, 128 A 80, 37 ALR 1515.
See **poor person**.

poor debtors' acts. Statutes whereunder a person arrested under body execution may obtain his discharge from custody by showing inability to satisfy the judgment.

poor debtor's oath. See **poor man's oath**.

poor farm. A farm lacking in productivity. A farm operated in connection with a poorhouse. 41 Am J1st Poor L § 33.

poorhouse. A place for the care of destitute persons who are unable to support themselves.
See **alms house**; **county farm**.

poor laws. See **welfare laws**.

poor man's oath. An oath taken by a person arrested under a body execution, whereby he may be discharged. 30 Am J2d Exec § 875. An affidavit, made by a plaintiff who, having a just cause of action against the defendant, is, by reason of his poverty, unable to give security for costs, stating that such is the fact. Cole v Hoeburg, 36 Kan 263, 13 P 275.

poor man's will. A name applied, preferably with tongue in cheek, to a joint bank account. 10 Am J2d Bks § 369.

poor officers. Overseers of the poor. Public officers whose duties pertain to the administration of public relief for poor and destitute persons. 41 Am J1st Poor L § 15.

poor or poorest. An ineffectual designation of the objects of one's bounty.
Whenever the term "poor" or the term "poorest" has been used to describe a beneficiary in a bequest or devise, it has been held to be insufficient for uncertainty. McDonough's Executors v Murdoch (US) 15 How 367, 398, 14 L Ed 732, 746.

poor person. A pauper; an indigent or destitute person. 41 Am J2d Poor L § 4. Any person in immediate need of means for obtaining food, clothing, shelter, or medical care, without reference to whether or not he has relatives liable for his support. Goodale v Lawrence, 88 NY 513.

poor rate. A tax levied to raise money for the relief and care of the paupers living in the district.

poor relations. As a designation of beneficiaries of a will, those persons entitled to take under the statute of distribution, without reference to the adjective "poor." Anno: 57 ALR 1185.

poor relief. Support provided the poor and destitute by a public body, better known in the present as welfare.
See **welfare**; **welfare laws**.

poor risk. A risk which an insurer does not want to cover.

Pope (pōp). The head of the Roman Catholic Church.

Pope Clement. See **Clementines**.

Pope Gregory. See **Gregorian calendar**.

Pope John. See **John XXIII**.

Pope Paul. See **Paul VI**.

populaire. See **action populaire**.

popular action. An action to recover a penalty, the cause being given by law to the people in general. 23 Am J2d Forf & P § 61. An action to recover a penalty, prescribed by statute and given to any informer, that is, to any such person as will bring suit for the penalty. Miami Copper Co. v State, 17 Ariz 179, 149 P 758.

popular courts. Old courts in England such as the hundred courts and the borough courts.

popular government. A government wherein the body of the nation keeps in its own hands the empire, or the right of command. Representative democracy, as in the United States. McGowen v Stark, 10 SCL (1 Nott & M'c) 387.

popularity contest. A contest conducted at a gathering of people, such as the audience in a theater, wherein votes are taken to determine the person to be acclaimed as the most popular. A facetious term applied to an election campaign wherein the candidates do not discuss principles.

popular sense. The meaning of a word or phrase according to contemporary usage. Franklin Light and Power Co. v Southern Cities Power Co. 164 Tenn 171, 47 SW2d 86.

popular use. Public use, inclusive not only of a use to which the public is entitled by law, but of occasional and precarious enjoyment of property by members of society in their individual capacities, had without the power to enforce such enjoyment at law.

populated area. An area along a street or highway wherein so many people reside that a motorist must not drive at a high, excessive, or unwarranted rate of speed. 7 Am J2d Auto § 445.

population. The inhabitants of a place, a state, or a country. Ludwig v Board of County Comrs. 170 Neb 600, 103 NW2d 839.

populiscitum (po-pu-li'si-tum). (Roman law.) Same as **plebiscitum.**

populus (pop'ū-lus). (Roman law.) The people, including all citizens of every class and rank.

porch. An extension of a building beyond the main wall, sometimes enclosed, sometimes open, providing a place of recreation and enjoyment, often, where situated on a level with the second floor, a place for sleeping. 20 Am J2d Cov § 251.

porpoise (pôr'pus). A cetacean. A mammal of the ocean; a whale rather than a fish, although called a fish royal.
See **fish royal.**

port. A place urban in character, contiguous to navigable waters, with facilities, for the loading, unloading, surfacing, outfitting, and provisioning of vessels. 38 Am J1st Ship § 223. Any place from which merchandise can be shipped for importation or at which merchandise can be imported. 19 USC § 232. In loose usage, a harbor; a safe station for ships. Wharf Case (Md) 3 Bland 361, 369. In a distinct sense, that side of a ship on one's left hand when facing the bow. In a more appealing sense, a dark red wine.
See **cinque ports; close port; foreign port; home port; public port.**

portable steps. Steps carried by a porter and put in place for use by passengers in boarding or departing a car. 14 Am J2d Car § 1010.

Portal-to-Portal Pay Act. A federal statute covering the matter of compensation of an employee for time spent on the employer's premises in reaching the place where his services are to be rendered in preparing to start actual work, and other nonproductive activities. 31 Am J Rev ed Lab § 633.

portatica (por-tā'ti-ka). Port duties.

port authority. A state or local administrative authority vested with powers respecting the establishment and maintenance of a port, sometimes of an airport. Estrada v Parking Associates Corp. 37 Misc 2d 1033, 236 NYS2d 403.

port charges. Charges imposed against a vessel for services received at a port, such as charges for fumigation required under quarantine regulations. Dampskibs Aktieselskabet Jeanette Skinner v Munson S.S. Line (CA2 NY) 20 F2d 345.
See **port toll.**

port district. The area contiguous to a port. A port authority.
See **port authority.**

porter. An alcoholic beverage made from browned malt from which it derives color. 30 Am J Rev ed Intox L § 10. One who carries luggage of passengers at an airport, railroad station, etc. One in attendance upon the passengers in a sleeping car on a train. An officer of an English court who carried a white rod before the justices.

portgreve (pōrt'grēv). The chief magistrate of an English seaport town.

portion. A part or share. In a narrow sense, the part of a parent's estate, or of the estate of one standing in the place of a parent, which is given to a child. Dickison v Dickison, 138 Ill 541, 544.

portman. An inhabitant of one of the so-called cinque ports of England.
See **cinque ports.**

portmote (pōrt'mōt). An ancient court which was held in certain English seaports and in certain towns inland as well.

port of arrival. See **port of entry.**

port of call (of kâl). A seaport at which ships usually stop on a given voyage or route.

port of departure. The port from which a vessel clears upon the commencement of a voyage.
The port of departure of a ship sailing from the port of a foreign country to a port of the United States, is the foreign port from which she clears and departs. If the vessel puts in at another foreign port after so clearing and before her departure for the United States, the port at which she thus stops is not her port of departure. United States v The Dago (CA4 Md) 61 F 986, 989.

port of destination. Taking into account, the whole of the outward voyage contemplated at the time a vessel clears, the port at which such voyage is to terminate. Cole v Union Mut. Ins. Co. 78 Mass (12 Gray) 501, 503.

port of deportation. The port from which an alien is deported. 3 Am J2d Aliens § 95.

port of discharge. Any place at which it is usual for ships to discharge cargo and to which a ship is destined for the purpose of discharging cargo. Bramhall v Sun Ins. Co. 104 Mass 510, 513.
See **safe port of discharge.**

port of entry. A port designated as one of entry for purposes of collecting custom duties. 21 Am J2d Customs § 6. Any place designated by executive order of the President, by order of the Secretary of the Treasury, or by Act of Congress, at which a customs officer is assigned with authority to accept entries of merchandise, to collect duties, and to enforce the various provisions of the customs and navigation laws. 19 CFR § 1.1(d). The port at which immigrants arrive. 8 USC § 1221.

port of unlivery. The port in which a vessel is to discharge its cargo. The Two Catherines (CC RS) F Cas No 14288.

portoria (por-tō'ri-a). Plural of **portorium.**

Porto Rico. See **Puerto Rico.**

portorium (por-tō'ri-um). (Civil law.) Customs duty; a tax levied on exported and imported goods.

portrait painting. The profession or occupation of painting the portraits of persons.

port risk. The risk carried by an insurer upon a vessel while it is in port. Nelson v Sun Mut. Ins. Co. 71 NY 453, 459.

portsale (pōrt'sāl). A public auction.

port toll. A toll charged for landing goods from a ship at a port.
See **port charges.**

port to port. The status of merchandise arriving at the port of entry for immediate transportation to another port of entry. 21 Am J2d Cust D §§ 72, 76.
See **voyage policy.**

port watch. See **watch**.

position in life. See **social position**; **standard of living**.

positive. Absolute; certain. Coleman v Roberts, 1 Mo 97, 100.

positive fraud. Actual, as distinguished from constructive, fraud. 37 Am J2d Fraud § 4.

positive community. The community of interest existing where several persons own a thing, each having a particular and definite portion of the whole. Geer v Connecticut, 161 US 519, 525, 40 L Ed 793, 795, 16 S Ct 600, quoting Pothier.

positive condition. A condition which must happen to bring into existence a right or to bring about a defeasance.

positive evidence. The testimony of an eyewitness. Commonwealth v Webster, 59 Mass (5 Cush) 295. Testimony to the affirmative of a proposition, that is, that a certain event did occur in the sight or hearing of the witness, as distinguished from testimony in the negative, that is, that the witness did not see or hear any such happening. 30 Am J2d Ev § 1092.

positive fraud. Actual, as distinguished from constructive fraud. Intentional deception. 37 Am J2d Fraud § 4.

positive law. The rules of conduct established by tacit acquiescence or by the legislature, and which derive their force and authority from such acquiescence or enactment, and not because they are the dictates of natural justice, and as such, of universal obligation. Commonwealth v Aves, 35 Mass (18 Pick) 193, 212.

positive prescription. (Civil law.) The Roman usucapio, which is the acquisition of property, real or personal, immovable or movable, by the continued possession of the acquirer for such a time as is described by the law to be sufficient. Townsend v Jemison (US) 9 How 407, 417, 13 L Ed 194, 198.

positive representation. A statement made without qualification express or implied. 37 Am J2d Fraud § 203.

positive right. An unqualified right—one which is not dependent upon, and which in fact does not admit of any exercise of, discretion. Chapman v Dorsey, 230 Minn 279, 41 NW2d 438, 16 ALR2d 1015.

positive testimony. See **positive evidence**.

positivi juris (po-zi-tī'vī jū'ris). Of positive law.

Posito uno oppositorum negatur alterum (po'zi-tō ū'nō op-po-zi-tō'rum ne-gā'ter al'te-rum). By the establishment of one of two opposing propositions, the other one is denied.

positus (pos'i-tus). (Latin.) Placed.

posse (pos'se). Noun: A body of men, even a single man, summoned by a sheriff or other peace officer to assist him in making an arrest. The power or force of the county. Verb: (Latin.) To be able; to be possible.

posse comitatus. The body of men summoned by a sheriff or other peace officer to assist him in making an arrest. Better known in modern usage as a posse. See **posse**.

possess. To have possession.

possessed. Mad; under the control of evil spirits. Having possession. Seized. Flowers v Flowers, 89 Ga 632, 635.

The term is a variable one in the law, and has different meanings as it is used in different circumstances. It sometimes means a temporary interest in lands; as we say a man is possessed, in contradistinction to being seized. It sometimes implies the corporal having; as we say a man is seized and possessed. But it sometimes implies no more than that one has a property in a thing; that he has it as owner; that it is his. In this sense it may be used even though an intruder may have excluded the owner for the time being. And there is never any impropriety in making use of the term when the only possession the intruder has is apparently subordinate to that of the general owner. Mayor of Detroit v Park Com. 44 Mich 602, 603.

possessio (pos-ze'she-ō). (Civil law.) That condition in which a person exercises his power over a corporal thing at his pleasure, to the exclusion of all others. The physical relation between a person and a thing which forms the basis of every notion of possession. See Mackeldey's Roman Law § 238.

possessio bonae fidei (pos-ze'she-ō bō'nē fī-dē'ī). (Civil law.) Possession in good faith,—the possession of one who believes that no other person has a better right to the possession than himself. See Mackeldey's Roman Law § 243.

possessio bona fide (pos-ze'she-ō bō'na fī'de). Possession in good faith.

possessio bonorum (pos-ze'she-ō bō-nō'rum). (Civil law.) The possession of goods. An official installation into the estate of a decedent in consequence of a petition therefor which the praetor granted. See Mackeldey's Roman Law § 657.

possessio civilis (pos-ze'she-ō si'vi-lis). (Roman law.) Civil possession,—a possession under a claim of ownership; a possession which anticipated the acquisition of ownership by prescription. See Mackeldey's Roman Law §§ 241, 285.

Possessio est quasi pedis positio (pos-ze'she-ō est quā'sī pē'dis po-zi'she-ō). Possession is, as it were, the position or placing of the foot.

possessio fratris (pos-ze'she-ō fra'tris). The possession or seisin of the brother.

Possessio fratris de feodo simplici facit sororem esse haeredem (pos-ze'she-ō fra'tris dē fū'dō sim'pli-sī fā'sit so-rō'rem es'se hē're-dem). The possession or seisin of the brother in fee simple, makes the sister the heir. See 2 Bl Comm 227.

Possessio fratris facit sororem esse haeredem (pos-ze'she-ō fra'tris fā'sit so-rō'rem es'se hē're-dem). The possession of the brother makes the sister the heir. See 2 Bl Comm 227.

possessio malae fidei (pos-ze'she-ō ma'lē fī-dē'ī). Possession in bad faith,—the possession of a person who knows that he is not entitled to the possession. See Mackeldey's Roman Law § 243.

possession. Occupancy and exercise of dominion over property. 42 Am J2d Prop § 42. The exercise of dominion over land, even without a residence thereon. Morrison v Kelly, 22 Ill 610. A holding of land legally by one's self or through another, such as a lessee, under title, estate, or interest of any kind. Whithed v St. Anthony & Dakota Elevator Co. 9 ND 224, 83 NW 238.

Respecting real property, possession involves exclusive dominion and control such as owners of like property usually exercise over it. The existence of such possession is largely a question of fact dependent on the nature of the property and the surrounding circumstances. 35 Am J2d Forc E & D § 20.

To constitute possession, within the meaning of a reconveyance act requiring a tax title holder, in order to preserve his interest against redemption, to take possession or institute a proceeding to secure possession within the time provided, the land must be appropriated to the individual use in such a manner as to apprise the community that it is in the exclusive use and enjoyment of the person so appropriating it. Pickens v Adams, 7 Ill 2d 283, 131 NE2d 38, 56 ALR2d 605.

What amounts to possession and what to mere custody in the law of larceny cannot be determined according to any settled formula, but the question in any particular case must depend largely upon the capacity in which the accused was given access to or dominion over the property taken, and upon the powers or duties which the owner gave or imposed upon him with respect thereto. For example, one to whom property is delivered by the owner for some limited, special, or temporary purpose may be regarded as having its custody only, and as capable of committing larceny thereof. Hence, if the owner gives property to another to take to the owner's house, and such other person wrongfully sells it, he is guilty of larceny, although he conceived the intent and purpose so to dispose of it after he had received it. 32 Am J1st Larc § 56.

possessio naturalis (pos-ze'she-ō na-tū-rā'lis). (Roman law.) Natural possession.
Every other kind of possession not qualified for usucapion, whether mere detention or juridical possession, in contradistinction to *civilis possessio,* was termed *naturalis possessio.* See Mackeldey's Roman Law § 241.

possession by inclosure. An actual adverse possession by inclosing or fencing premises, accompanied by other acts evidencing claim of ownership. Faulks v Schrider, 72 App DC 308, 114 F2d 587.

possession in deed. Same as **possession in fact.**

possession in fact. Actual possession, sometimes called possession in deed,—an actual and continuous occupancy or exercise of full dominion.
This may be either, first, an occupancy in fact of the whole that is in possession, which is ordinarily called pedis possessio, and may be called substantial possession, or, second, an occupancy of part thereof in the name of the whole, where there is sufficient evidence of the bounds of the whole that is claimed as one entirety, and the circumstances are such that the law extends the possession of the part that is occupied to these bounds. 42 Am J1st Prop § 42.

possession in law. A constructive possession as distinguished from possession in deed, or in fact, by way of actual occupancy; that possession which the law annexes to title. 42 Am J1st Prop § 42.

possession of burglars' tools. A criminal offense, especially where the possession is with intent to use the tools for the purpose of effecting a burglary. 13 Am J2d Burgl § 74.

possession of game. As a criminal offense, the possession of game taken during the closed season. 35 Am J1st Fish § 50.

possession of land. See **possession.**

possession of liquor. Having personal charge of or exercising the right of ownership, management, or control over liquor. 30 Am J Rev ed Intox L § 59.

possession of liquor-making materials. As a criminal offense, an actual possession with control of the goods and an intent to violate the law. 30 Am J Rev ed Intox L § 59.

possession or enjoyment provision. A statutory provision taxing transfers intended to take effect in possession or enjoyment at or after death. 28 Am J Rev ed Inher T § 159.

possessions. Technically referring to personalty, but subject to construction, where it appears in a will, as including real estate. 57 Am J1st Wills § 1338.

Possessio pacifica pour anns 60 facit jus (po-ze'she-ō pa-si'fi-ka pör än six'ti fa'sit jūs). Peaceable possession for sixty years establishes a right.

possessio pedis (pos-ze'she-ō pe'dis). See **pedis possessio.**

possessio vaut titre (po-ze'she-ō vō tē'tr). Possession is as valuable as title.

possessor. One who possesses. The person in possession.

possessor bona fide. See **bona fide possessor.**

possessor in bad faith. A person who possesses as owner, but who well knows that he has no title to the thing, or that his title is vicious and defective. Gaines v Hennen (US) 24 How 553, 16 L Ed 770, 775.

possessor malae fidei (pos-ze'sor ma'lē fī-dē'ī). (Civil law.) A possessor who knows that he is not entitled to the possession.

possessory action. An action brought to recover possession of property. An action to recover possession of real estate, such as **ejectment.** An action to recover possession of personal property, such as **replevin.**
In Louisiana, an action to recover the possession of personal property is called a possessory action. Preston v Zabrisky, 2 La 226, 227.

possessory interest. A temporary, qualified property in the things of which the mere possession is delivered to a person. 8 Am J2d Bailm § 71.

possessory judgment. A judgment which establishes the right to possession. In Scottish law, a judgment giving a party the right to possession until the question of possession be decided in due course of law.

possessory lien. A lien which continues only during the possession of the lienor.

possessory proceeding. See **possessory action; summary possessory proceeding.**

possessory warrant. A process resembling a search warrant used in criminal proceedings, but differing in that it is a civil process under which the property is to be delivered to the person from whom it was violently or fraudulently taken or enticed away or in whose peaceable and lawful possession it last was. Claton v Ganey, 63 Ga 331, 332.

possibilitas (pos-si-bi'li-tās). A possibility.

possibility. That which is not contrary to the nature of things and can be accomplished; that which is capable of being conceived or thought of. Topeka City Railway Co. v Higgs, 38 Kan 375, 16 P 667. A mere or bare possibility, such as an expectancy. A real possibility in the sense of a potentiality.
See **expectancy.**

possibility of death. The possibility of the occurrence of death in an unexpected manner. The possibility of death before termination of the normal span of life. The expectation of death which must come ultimately to all men.

possibility of issue. See **possibility of issue extinct.**

possibility of issue extinct. A contingency affecting the character of an estate as vested or contingent, as continuing or as terminated. 28 Am J2d Est § 319. A concept to be denied, both American and English authorities being in accord upon the proposition that, for the purpose of determining whether there is a violation of the rule against perpetuities, the possibility of issue is never considered extinct as long as a person lives. 41 Am J1st Perp § 26.

The courts have declined to fix a period in a woman's life beyond which she cannot have children, or to assert that there is an age limit beyond which they will feel justified in declaring that a woman cannot give birth. United States Fidelity & Guarantee Co. v Douglas, 134 Ky 374, 120 SW 328.

The law does not assume that there is an impossibility of issue at any age, however great, so that a remainder to the children of a woman who has an estate for life is not extinguished until her death, although she may be very old and childless. 28 Am J2d Est § 319.

Although it is a recognized legal presumption that the possibility of issue is never extinct as long as a person lives, the courts nevertheless have on occasion sanctioned distribution of a testamentary gift prior to the death of the woman on whose failure of issue or further issue it was conditioned, upon the theory that, because of her age or physical condition, the improbability of her having children or more children has been established to such a degree that distribution should be permitted. Anno: 67 ALR 542, 543.

As to the doctrine of possibility of issue, see Anno: 98 ALR2d 1285.

possibility of performance. See **impossibility of performance.**

possibility of reverter. A type of future interest, if it may be properly designated as an interest, which remains in a grantor by deed or his successor in interest or in a testator's heirs or devisees where, by grant or devise, there has been created an estate in fee simple determinable or an estate in fee simple conditional, the fee automatically reverting upon the occurrence of the event by which the estate is limited. Anno: 16 ALR2d 1247; 28 Am J2d Est § 182.

There is a difference between a true possibility of reverter and a power of termination which consists of a right of entry for condition broken retained by the grantor of a fee upon a condition subsequent. Donehue v Nilges (Mo) 266 SW2d 553, 45 ALR2d 1150. Some authorities, however, designate the right of reentry for condition broken or the power of termination which remains in the grantor or his successors in interest or in the heirs or devisees of a testator, where an estate on condition subsequent has been created, as a "possibility of reverter." 28 Am J2d Est § 182.

possibility on possibility. A fatal defect at common law in limitations of future interests. 41 Am J1st Perp § 5. Illustration: a limitation for the life of an unborn person with a limitation after his death to his unborn children. Greenleaf v Greenleaf, 332 Mo 402, 58 SW2d 448.

possible. Liable to happen or come to pass; capable of existing or of being conceived or thought of; capable of being done; not contrary to the nature of things. Topeka City Railway Co. v Higgs, 38 Kan 375, 383, 16 P 667, 674.

See **possibility.**

post. Noun: A military establishment where a body of troops is permanently on duty. United States v Caldwell (US) 19 Wall 264, 268, 22 L Ed 114, 116. The area assigned to a sentry for the performance of his duty. An upright support, such as in a fence or porch. Verb: To make entries in a ledger from entries previously made in day book or journal. Arnold v Barner, 100 Kan 36, 163 P 805. To put a letter in the mail. To keep another informed. To keep one's self informed. To attach a written notice or bulletin to a wall, post, or board, so that the contents will be displayed to the public for the information of the public. Iowa-Missouri Grain Co. v Powers, 198 Iowa 208, 196 NW 979, 33 ALR 1268, 1270. Adverb: After; afterward.

See **posting.**

post act (pōst'akt). A subsequent act; an act done afterwards.

postage. The charge imposed by the mail service for carrying matter by mail.

See **postage stamp.**

postage stamp. An adhesive stamp in various convenient denominations, purchased at a post office or through some other instrumentality of the post office department, and affixed to matter placed in the mail by way of prepayment of the postage upon such matter. United States v One Zurnstein Briefmarken Katalog (DC Pa) 24 F 516.

postal card. A card for mailing, produced by the post office department and sold through its instrumentalities, used for brief messages, and sent as first class mail.

See **post card.**

postal certificates. Instruments issued to postal savings depositors which could be surrendered in exchange for United States bonds. Pimpel v Pimpel (Ky) 253 SW2d 613, 35 ALR2d 1092.

post card. A card for mailing, privately produced and sold, usually containing a picture or words of greeting or congratulation on one side. Sent as first class mail.

See **postal card.**

postal clerk. See **mail clerk.**

postal inspector. A position in the United States postal service involving inspection and investigation in all phases of the postal service. 39 USC § 3523(a).

postal laws. The laws pertaining to the United States mail.

See **mail.**

postal money order. See **post-office money order.**

postal note. A post-office money order not exceeding ten dollars in amount. 39 USC § 5105.

See **post-office money order.**

postal officers. Federal officers whose duties pertain to the mails and post offices.

postal savings. A system once provided by the United States Postal Service whereby persons might open and maintain savings accounts with the Service, discontinued by Act of March 28, 1966; 80 Statutes at Large 92.

postal service. The handling of the mails.

See **mail.**

postal zones. See **parcel-post zone.**

post conquestum (post kon-ques'tum). After the Conquest.
See **Norman Conquest.**

post conspicuously. To post a notice prepared in such a manner and posted in such a place that it is easily observed and easily read. R.S. Oglesby Co. v Lindsey, 112 Va 767, 72 & E 672.

Post-conviction Procedure Act. A uniform law which provides that a person convicted of a crime and incarcerated under sentence of death or imprisonment who claims that his sentence was imposed in violation of the United States Constitution or the Constitution or laws of the state, or that the sentencing court had no jurisdiction, or that the sentence exceeds the authorized maximum, or that the sentence is otherwise subject to collateral attack upon any ground of error previously available under a writ of habeas corpus or of coram nobis or other common-law or statutory remedy, may institute a proceeding under the act to set aside or correct the sentence, which proceeding comprehends and takes the place of all other common-law and statutory remedies previously available and is to be used exclusively in lieu thereof. 18 Am J2d Coram Nobis § 30.

postdate. To place a future date, as the date of its execution, upon an instrument which is presently executed.

postdated check. A check carrying a date later than the date of actual execution, such being held to be payable at sight, or upon presentment thereof at the bank, at any time on or after the day of its date as such appears on the instrument. 11 Am J2d B & N § 287.

postdated instrument. An instrument for the payment of money dated as of a day after the execution and delivery of the instrument. 11 Am J2d B & N § 208.
See **postdated check.**

post diem (post dī'em). After the day.

post disseisin (pōst dis-sē'zin). After the disseisin, a disseisin following a recovery of seisin, committed by the same disseisor.

post disseisinam (pōst dis-sē'zin-am). Same as **post disseisin.**

postea (pōs'tē-ą). An indorsement on the record, made in the trial court, reciting all the proceedings had in the trial court after the cause was ready for trial. 27 Am J2d Eq. § 243.

posted notice. See **post; posting.**

post entry. An entry added to an account or list previously completed, such as the manifest of a ship. 19 USC § 1440.

Posteriora derogant prioribus (pos-te-ri-ō'ra de'rogant pri-ō'ri-bus). Later things derogate from earlier ones.

posteriores (pos-te-ri-ō'rēz). (Roman law.) Descendants who follow in a direct line beyond the sixth degree.

posteriority (pos-tē-ri-or'į-ti). The state or condition of anything which follows in point of time.

posterity. Descendants, inclusive of children, grandchildren, even of the remotest of generations in the descending line. In modern usage, the generations to follow the one which comprises the present social order, God help them. Breckinridge v Denny & Faulkner, 71 Ky (8 Bush) 523, 527.

post exchange. A mercantile establishment conducted on a military reservation or military camp for patronage by members of the armed forces and their families.

post facto (pōst fak'tō). After the fact; after the commission of the crime.
See **ex post facto.**

post-factum (pōst-fak'tum). An after act; an act which is done afterward.

post fine (pōst'fīn). See **king's silver.**

postgraduate institution. An educational institution, usually styled a university, having courses of instruction for college graduates leading to doctorate, master-of-arts, or professional degrees. 15 Am J2d Colleges § 1.

post hoc (pōst hōk). After this. Indicating in reference to an accident or other distinct event, that which happened after the event. Reynolds v Texas & P. Railroad Co. 37 La Ann 694.

posthumous (pos'tu-mus). Literally, after burial. In common usage, after death, particularly the death of the father.

posthumous child. A child born after the death of the parent. A child in being from the time of conception, for the purpose of the rule of descent, provided he or she is born alive with reasonable assurance of continuing to live. 23 Am J2d Desc & D § 88. A child living within the meaning of a bequest to "children living." Hall v Hancock, 32 Mass (15 Pick) 255.

posthumous work. The product of an author whose death occurred before publication. Shapiro, Bernstein & Co. v Bryan (CA2 NY) 123 F2d 697.

Posthumus pro nato habetur (post'u-mus prō na'tō hā-bē'ter). A posthumous child is regarded as born before the death of the father.
Where a gift is to "children born," it is doubtful whether this maxim of the civil law would be followed. Nevertheless, a child en ventre sa mere is to be considered a child living, so as to take under a bequest to "children living." Hall v Hancock, 32 Mass (15 Pick) 255.

posting. A method of publication, for example, the posting of an ordinance in one or more places within the municipality. Simpson v Highwood, 372 Ill 212, 23 NE2d 62, 124 ALR 1459. The giving of notice by posting a written or printed copy in one or more places as the statute may require. 39 Am J1st Notice § 31. A method of service of process. 42 Am J1st Proc § 102. Mailing. Making entries in a ledger from entries previously made in day book or journal.
See **post.**

post letter. A letter put into the mail.
While there are English cases holding the other way, the general rule of decision in this country is that a letter may be a post letter even though it is directed to a fictitious address, and that whether it can be delivered or not is of no consequence. Goode v United States, 159 US 663, 40 L Ed 297, 16 S Ct 136.

postliminary. The antonym of preliminary. McComb v C. A. Swanson & Sons (DC Neb) 77 F Supp 716.

postliminary activities. An expression of the Portal-to-Portal Pay Act, referring to necessary activities of an employee following the work shift. 31 Am J Rev ed Lab § 637.

postliminium (pōst-li-min'i-um). Same as **postliminy**.

Postliminium fingit eum qui captus est in civitate semper fuisse (post-li-mi'ni-um fin'jit e'um quī kap'-tus est in si-vi-tā-te sem'per fu-is'se). (Civil law.) Postliminy conceives him who was captured always to have been within the state.

postliminy (pōst-lim'i-ni). The law under which property, if taken by an enemy in time of war, is restored to its former state, upon coming again under the power of the nation to which it formerly belonged. Herbert v Moore (Tex) 1 Dall 592, 593. The resumption by a prisoner of war of his civil rights after his release; the restoration of property captured in war to its owner, after recapture. Leitensdorfer v Webb, 1 NM 34, 44.

post litem motam (post lī'tem mō'tam). After the commencement of the action, suit, or litigation.

postman. A mailman making deliveries on a route, particularly a city route. In the court of exchequer, two of the most experienced barristers, called the postman and the tub-man (from the places in which they sit), have a precedence in motions. See 3 Bl Comm 28, note.

postmaster. One holding a public office established for the benefit of the public in the operation of a post office, the receipt and distribution of the mails from such office, and such other matters as are prescribed by statute for performance by the incumbent. 41 Am J1st P O § 12.

Postmaster General. The head of the Post Office Department of the United States Government and a member of the Cabinet of the President. 41 Am J1st P O § 9.

post meridian. After noon.

post-mortem (pōst-môr'tem). After death.

post-mortem examination (pōst-môr'tem eg-zam-i-nā'shọn). See **autopsy**.

post mortem inquisitio (pōst môr'tem in-qui-zi'shē-ō). An inquisition after death,—an inquest, held before a jury of the county, which was instituted to inquire (at the death of any man of fortune) the value of his estate, the tenure by which it was held, and who, and of what age his heir was; thereby to ascertain the relief and value of the primer seisin, or the wardship and livery which should thereupon accrue to the king. See 2 Bl Comm 68.
See **inquest**.

postnati (post-nā'tī). Plural of **postnatus**.

postnatus (pōst-nā'tus). A person born in the country subsequently to a great political event occurring in that country. Dawson's Lessee v Godfrey (US) 4 Cranch 321, 2 L Ed 634.

post-note. A note issued by a bank, but distinct from a bank note, which formerly passed as currency, since payable at a future time.

postnuptial. After marriage.

postnuptial agreement. See **marriage settlement; property settlement; separation agreement**.

postnuptial settlement. See **marriage settlement; property settlement**.

post obit bond. See **bond post obit**.

post obit note (pōst ō'bit nŏt). A promissory note payable a specified time after the death of the maker. 11 Am J2d B & N § 172.

post office. A particular building or place for the receipt, handling, and delivery of mail matter, or the transaction of other business in connection with the postal service. 41 Am J1st P O § 2.
See **branch post office; mail**.

post-office clerk. A federal employee in the mail service, his duties, performed in a post office, consisting in handling, distributing, and delivering mail, and in transacting with patrons of his office such business as they may have in reference to the mails and the office.

Post Office Department. A department of the federal government charged with the establishment and maintenance of post offices and post roads, the transmission, distribution, and delivery of the mail. 54 Am J1st U S § 53.

post office inspector. See **postal inspector**.

post-office money order. An order for the payment of money issued by a postmaster in accord with a money order system of the United States Postal Service established for convenience and safety in the remission of funds. 39 USC § 5101. An order for the payment of money to the payee named therein, drawn by one post office upon another under authority of an act of Congress and departmental regulations. 11 Am J2d B & N § 32; 41 Am J1st P O § 44.

postoperative treatment. Treatment of a patient after surgery. 41 Am J1st Phys & S § 98.

postpone. To defer. "To delay." Boies v Henney, 130 Ill 130, 146. To delay one creditor by granting a preference to another.

postponement. Deferment. Delay. Often used as synonymous with continuance, but preferably in the sense only of a delay in trial by putting the trial over to another day of the term or to a later hour of the same day. 17 Am J2d Contin § 1.

postponement of enjoyment. See **rule against postponement of enjoyment**.

postponement of lien. The subordination of a lien to another lien on the same property entitled to priority. 9 Am J2d Bankr § 562.

postponement of limitations. The suspension or interruption of the running of a statute of limitations. 34 Am J1st Lim Ac §§ 186 et seq.

postponement of trial. See **postponement**.

post prolem suscitatam (post prō'lem su-si-tā'tĕm). After issue born.

post rem (pōst rem). After the transaction; after the closing of the transaction; after the occurrence of the act.

postremo-geniture (pos-tre'mō-jen'i-tur). Another name for borough-English, which was a custom attached to burgage tenure whereby the youngest, and not the eldest, son succeeded to the tenement on the death of his father. See 2 Bl Comm 83.

post rem statement (pōst rem stāt'mẹnt). A statement or declaration made after the act or the completion of the transaction. 29 Am J2d Ev § 605.

post road. A road over which the mail is carried.
See **post routes**.

post routes. All public roads and highways while kept up and maintained. 39 USC § 482. All the waters of the United States during the time the mail is carried thereon, all the railroads or parts of railroads and all air routes which are now, or hereafter may be, in operation; all canals and plank roads during the time the mail is carried thereon; the road on which mail is carried to supply any court house which may be without a mail; the road on which mail is carried under contract made by the Postmaster General for extending the line of post to supply mails to post offices not on any established route, during the time such mail is carried thereon; and all letter-carrier routes established in any city or town for the collection and delivery of mail matter. 39 USC § 481.

postscript. An addition to a letter appearing after the signature. Something added by the author at the end of a book or article.

post-terminal sittings (póst-tèr'mi-nal sit'ings). Sessions of the court which are held after the expiration of the term.

post terminum (post tèr'mi-num). After the term.

post-town. Any town containing a post office.

postulatio (pos-tu-lā'she-ō). (Roman law.) An application or petition which was presented to the praetor for leave to accuse a person of having committed a crime.

postulatio actionis (pos-tu-lā'she-ō ak-she-ō'nis). (Roman law.) An application or petition which was presented to the praetor for leave to institute an action.

post-verdict proceedings. Literally, any proceeding in a case after verdict returned. Specifically, proceedings after verdict rendered in the jury trial of an equity suit. 27 Am J2d Eq § 243.

pot. A cooking vessel of metal, earthenware, or glass. Slang for the abdomen of a person, also for marijuana.

potable. Capable of being used as a drink. See **drinkable.**

potability. Capability for use as a beverage. Anno: 91 ALR 518.

potentate (pō'tẹn-tāt). A very powerful ruler or sovereign.

potentia (po-ten'she-a). Power; ability; authority; supremacy; a possibility.

Potentia debet sequi justitiam, non antecedere (po-ten'she-a de'bet se'quī jūs-ti'she-am, non an-te-sē'de-re). Power ought to follow justice, it ought not to precede it.

Potentia est duplex, remota et propinqua; et potentia remotissima et vana est quae nunquam venit in actum (po-ten'she-a est dū'plex, re-mō'ta et pro-pin'-qua; et po-ten'she-a re-mo-tis'si-ma et vā'na est kwē nun'quam vē'nit in ak'tum). Possibility is double, remote and near; that which never comes into action is a power the most remote and vain.

Potentia inutilis frustra est (po-ten'she-a in-u'ti-lis frus'tra est). Useless power is vain.

potential. Latent. Endowed with energy. Unrealized. Undeveloped, as in the case of the possibility of disability from a hernia. Ashworth v Calcasieu Paper Co. (La App) 85 So 2d 681, 684.

potential existence. An existence which, while not in actuality, is to come as a natural product of something which is in actual existence. Dickey v Waldo, 97 Mich 255, 56 NW 608. As characterizing the subject matter of a sale:—the natural product or the expected increase of something already belonging to the seller. O'Hare v Peacock Dairies, 26 Cal App 2d 345, 79 P2d 433.

potentially (pọ-ten'shạl-i). In possibility not in act, not positively; in efficacy, not in actuality. Long v Hines, 40 Kan 220, 19 P 796.

potential possession. A characterization of the principle whereunder the owner of land is able to sell future crops to be grown thereon, the owner of cows to dispose of their future offspring, and a lessee under an oil and gas lease to transfer effectively a percentage interest in his production. 24 Am J1st Gas & O § 94.

Potentia non est nisi ad bonum (po-ten'she-a non est nī'sī ad bō'num). Power does not exist, except for good.

potentia propinqua (po-ten'she-a prō-pin'qua). A near or common possibility, such as death without issue. See 2 Bl Comm 169.

potentia remotissima (po-ten'she-a re-mō-tis'si-ma). A possibility the least likely to come to fruition in occurrence.

potestas (pọ-tes'tās). (Civil law.) Power; authority; official authority; magistracy.

Potestas delegata non potest delegari (po-tes'tās de-le-gā'ta non po'test de-le-gā'rī). Delegated power or authority cannot be delegated. Warner v Martin (US) 11 How 209, 223, 13 L Ed 667, 672.

Potestas regis est facere justitiam (po-tes'tās rē'jis est fa'se-re jūs-ti'she-am). The power of the king is to execute justice.

Potestas regis juris sit, non injuriae (po-tes'tas rē'jis jū'ris sit, non in-jū'ri-ē). The power of the king is of right, not of injury.

Potestas stricte interpretatur (pō-tes'tās strik'te in-ter-pre-tā'ter). Power is to be strictly interpreted.

Potestas suprema seipsum dissolvere potest, ligare non potest (pō-tes'tās sū-prē'ma sē-ip'sum dis-sol've-re po'test, li-gā're non po'test). Supreme power can dissolve itself; it cannot bind itself.

potestate parentis. See **in potestate parentis.**

Potest quis renunciare pro se, et suis, jus quod pro se introductum est (po'test quis re-nun-she-ā're prō sē, et su'is, jūs quod prō sē in-trō-duk'tum est). Anyone can renounce for himself and his (successors) a right which has been created in his behalf.

pot hunting. Killing game indiscriminately. More precisely, hunting for the purpose of marketing game. 35 Am J2d Fish § 34.

Potior conditio defendentis (po'she-or kon-di'she-ō de-fen-den'tis). The position of the defendant is the stronger.
    Where there is turpitude, the law will help neither party. The maxim applies in such a case. Burke v Child (US) 21 Wall 441, 22 L Ed 623.

Potior est conditio defendentis (po'she-or est kon-di'she-ō de-fen-den'tis). The position of the defendant is the stronger.

Potior est conditio possidentis (po'she-or est kon-di'she-ō pos-si-den'tis). The situation of the party in possession is the stronger. Magoun v Lapham, 38 Mass (21 Pick) 135, 140.

pot shot. An easy shot by a hunter; a shot at a sitting bird or reclining game animal without arousing it so as to give it a chance for its life.

Pott's fracture (pots frak'tụr). A fracture consisting of the breaking of one bone of the lower leg between the knee and ankle joints, and a severance of the malleolus process of the other one so as to effect a complete solution of the continuity of both bones. Peterson v Modern Brotherhood, 125 Iowa 562, 101 NW 289.

potwallopers (pot wol″ọp-ėrs). The voters of certain English boroughs who were qualified by reason of the fact that they cooked their own food.

Poultry Counter (pōl'tri koun'tėr). A name which was given to one of the ancient prisons in London.

pound. A place for confinement of strays and other animals found running at large illegally, maintained by public authority or maintained by a private agency through contract or arrangement with public authority. Massachusetts Society for Prevention of Cruelty to Animals v Commissioner of Public Health, 339 Mass 216, 158 NE2d 487; Harriman v Fifield, 36 Vt 341, 345. A unit of weight, sixteen ounces avoirdupois, twelve ounces troy. The monetary unit of Great Britain, equalling twenty shillings.

poundage. Fees to which a sheriff is entitled for official services. Commissions or fees to which a trustee or officer of the court is entitled for making a judicial sale. 30A Am J1st Jud S § 46.

poundage fees. See **poundage**.

pound-breach (pound'brēch). The forcible taking of animals from a pound, after they have been actually impounded there. See 3 Bl Comm 146.

poundmaster. A municipal officer in charge of an animal pound. 4 Am J2d Ani § 48.

pound net. See **Dutch net**.

pour autrui stipulation. Same as **stipulation pour autrui**.

pour compte de qui il appartient (pör kont de kē ēl ạ-pär'tē-en). For account of whom it may concern.

pourparler (pör-pär'lā). (French.) Negotiations leading up to an agreement, contract, or treaty.

pourparty. Same as **partition**.

pourpresture. Same as **purpresture**.

pourprise. See **purpresture**.

pour seisir terres (pör sā'zēr tärs). A writ which lay for the seizure by the crown of lands held in dower by the widow of a tenant in capite, if she re-married without the consent of the king.

poursuivant (pör-swi'vänt). A messenger of the king.

pourveyor. Same as **purveyor**.

poustie (pūs'tē). Power.

poverty. Absence of assets. Bowersox's Appeal, 100 Pa 434. The condition of being poor, that is, lacking means sufficient for comfortable living.
See **poor**; **poor person**.

poverty affidavit. See **poor man's oath**.

poverty and immorality. By no means synonymous. Edwards v California, 314 US 160, 86 L Ed 119, 62 S Ct 164.

powder mark. A mark on the skin of a person or object hit by a bullet from a gun fired at close range. Aetna Life Ins. Co. v Milward, 118 Ky 716, 82 SW 364.

power. The ability to act, regarded as latent or inherent; the faculty of doing or performing something; capacity for action or performance. Bradley v State ex rel. Hill, 111 Ga 168, 36 SE 630. Authority in the sense of jurisdiction or the exercise of jurisdiction. Kendall v United States (US) 12 Pet 524, 622, 9 L Ed 1181, 1220. Authority, as the authority of an agent. Capability of acting to bind one's self or another. In some contexts, a permissive or discretionary term. Wadsworth v Eau Claire County, 102 US 534, 26 L Ed 221. A power of appointment. Physical force. A term exclusive of hand power in workmen's compensation statutes. 58 Am J1st Workm Comp § 117.

Power Act. A comprehensive federal statute setting forth a complete plan for the development and improvement of navigation and for the development, transmission, and utilization of electric power in any of the streams or other bodies of water over which Congress has jurisdiction under its commerce powers, and upon the public lands and reservations of the United States under its property powers. 16 USC §§ 791(a) et seq.

power appendant. A power of appointment existing under the circumstances that it is given to a person having an estate in the property and the estate to be created by the power is to take or may take effect in possession, during the continuance of the estate to which the power is annexed, as a power to a life tenant in possession to make leases. 41 Am J1st Pow § 5.

power appurtenant. Same as **power appendant**.

powerboat. A boat which is propelled by power other than man-power. United States v Olson (DC Ky) 41 F Supp 433.
See **motorboat**; **outboard**.

power collateral. Same as **collateral power**.

Power Commission. A commission created by the Federal Power Act, consisting of five members appointed by the President, by and with the consent of the Senate, to carry out the provisions of the act, including the regulation of electric utility companies engaged in interstate commerce. 43 Am J1st Pub Util § 236.

power coupled with an interest. A power conferred by a writing which vests in the agent an interest or property in the subject of the agency, not merely an interest in the proceeds or results of the exercise of the agency. Cox v Freeman, 204 Okla 138, 227 P2d 670, 28 ALR2d 430. A power of appointment coupled with an interest in the thing itself, that is to say, a power engrafted on the estate in the thing, not on the product of the exercise of the power. 41 Am J1st Pow § 5.

power district. An improvement district organized to establish and administer a project for the creation and distribution of electric power to consumers, or a district created as a special assessment district to function in the making and collection of special assessments for funds to build a power plant to be administered by a municipality or county. 48 Am J1st Spec A § 114. Sometimes regarded as a governmental subdivision. Platt Valley P. P. & I. Dist. v Lincoln County, 144 Neb 584, 14 NW2d 202, 155 ALR 412.

power-driven vessel. A vessel propelled by power transmitted through machinery, rather than by sail. 12 Am J2d Boats § 1.

powered aircraft. Aircraft having an engine or mechanical means of propulsion of some sort; not a mere glider. 29A Am J Rev ed Ins § 1263. Any airplane other than a glider. Anno: 17 ALR2d 1067; 54 ALR2d 415.

power in gross. A power of appointment given to a person having an estate in the property, where the estate to be created under or by virtue of the power is not to take effect in possession until after the determination of the donee's estate. 41 Am J1st Pow § 5.

power in trust. See **trust power.**

power line. An electric line of high voltage, particularly a cross-country line carrying electricity from place of production to cities, towns, and industrial plants. An instrumentality of commerce with the meaning of the commerce clause of the United States Constitution. 26 Am J2d Electr § 14.

power of agent. An ability on the part of an agent to produce a change in a given legal relation by doing or not doing a given task; also a limitation upon the ability of the agent to bind the principal, such ability resting only on his actual or apparent authority. 3 Am J2d Ag § 68.

power of alienation. The right and capacity to convey property.
See **rule against suspension of power of alienation.**

power of appointment. Authority enabling one person to dispose of an interest which is vested in another. Re Zanatta, 99 NJ Eq 339, 131 A 515. A liberty or authority reserved by, or limited to, a person to dispose of real or personal property for his own benefit, or for the benefit of others, and operating on an estate or interest, vested either in himself or in some other person, such liberty or authority, however, not being derived out of such estate or interest, but overreaching or superseding it, either wholly or partially. 41 Am J1st Pow § 2.
See **general power of appointment; special power of appointment.**

power of attorney. A written instrument, known as a power of attorney, letter of attorney, or warrant of attorney, People v Smith, 112 Mich 192, 70 NW 466, by which one person, as principal, appoints another as his agent and confers upon him the authority to perform certain specified acts or kinds of acts on behalf of the principal. Arcweld Mfg. Co. v Burney, 12 Wash 2d 212, 121 P2d 350. A written instrument authorizing an attorney at law to appear in an action on behalf of the maker or to confess judgment against him. Treat v Tolman (CA2 NY) 113 F 892.

A power of attorney may be general, as where it confers authority to sell property without specification of particular property, or special, as where it authorizes a sale to a particular person. 3 Am J2d Ag § 23.

A power of attorney creates an agency relationship, with the giver of the power remaining the legal owner of any property involved. Smith v United States (DC Hawaii) 113 F Supp 702.

power of attorney to confess judgment. A power or warrant of attorney which confers the authority to confess judgment against the grantor of the power upon an instrument evidencing an obligation. 30A Am J Rev ed Judgm § 170.

power of consumption. The power to use principal, particularly for support, maintenance, and comfort. Anno: 36 ALR 1186, 1195.

power of disposal. An expression used in reference to the power of one other than the owner of property to dispose of it by will.
See **power of appointment; power of sale.**

power of eminent domain. See **eminent domain.**

power of sale. A provision in a chattel mortgage for the enforcement of the lien of the mortgage by sale, without the necessity of resort to judicial proceedings. 15 Am J2d Chat Mtg §§ 127 et seq. A provision in a real estate mortgage, or in a separate instrument, whereunder a sale may be had by way of enforcement of the mortgage upon default of the mortgagor. 37 Am J1st Mtg § 652. A power given a life tenant to dispose of the estate for the purposes of obtaining means of support, maintenance, education, etc. 28 Am J2d Est § 86. Authority conferred upon an agent for the sale of property of the principal. 3 Am J2d Ag §§ 99 et seq.
See **testamentary power of sale.**

power of termination. The interest which remains in the grantor or his successors, or the successors of a testator, where an estate on condition subsequent has been created, such being a right of re-entry for condition broken. 28 Am J2d Est §§ 188 et seq.

power of the county. A posse comitatus.
See **posse.**

powers of corporation. See **corporate powers.**

powers of sale and exchange. Literally, inclusive of any power conferred upon another to effect either a sale or exchange of property.

In the English law, the term has a definite meaning and implies that the proceeds of the sale are to be reinvested in another estate of the same character, and to be settled to the same uses. In practice they are often exercised in aid of, and not to interfere with, the ultimate limitations, and to carry out the intention of the parties. Rail v Dotson, 22 Miss (14 Smedes & M) 176, 184.

powers that be. Same as **constituted authorities.**

power to modify. See **modify.**

power to defeat the corpus. See **power of consumption.**

power to sell. Authority to sell.

Generally speaking, a fiduciary's "power to sell" means the authority given by statute, or by the instrument creating the trust, or the capacity inherent in the functioning of his office, as distinguished from his "right to sell," which is used in the sense of doing that which is proper or correct, in adherence to duty and necessity. Virginia Trust Co. v Evans, 193 Va 425, 69 SE2d 409, 32 ALR2d 769.
See **powers of sale and exchange.**

poynding. Same as **poinding.**

Poynings' Laws (poi′nings lâs). A set of statutes enacted in the 10 Henry VII. (1494), so called because Sir Edward Poynings was then lord deputy, restraining the powers of the Irish parliament, and making English statutes then in force effective in Ireland. See 1 Bl Comm 102, 103.

pp. Abbreviation of **pages.**

p.p. Abbreviation of **per procuration.** Abbreviation of **propria persona.**

p.p.a. Abbreviation of **per power of attorney.**

practicable. Feasible; workable; usable.
See **if practicable.**

practical. That which pertains to actual practice or the doing of things, as distinguished from abstract theory.

practical construction. A construction of an instrument by the parties in interest while in interest. 23 Am J2d Deeds § 171. The construction of a contract, which is ambiguous, in accord with the presumption that the parties contracted with reference to fair, reasonable, and practical results. Ture-man v Altman, 361 Mo 1220, 239 SW2d 304, 26 ALR2d 729. An administrative construction of a statute enacted for the regulation of a department of government. Bloxham v Consumers' Electric Light & Street Railroad Co. 36 Fla 519, 18 So 444.

practical joke. An act committed against a person with the idea of causing the victim embarrassment, even with the possibility of some real pain and discomfort. 6 Am J2d Asslt & B § 116. The playing of a prank, especially one of a boisterous or rather violent nature, upon a fellow employee. 58 Am J1st Workm, Comp § 268.

practical location. An actual designation by the parties upon the ground of the monuments and bounds called for by the deed. Wells v Jackson Iron Mfg. Co. 47 NH 235.

practice. A custom, usage, or habit. 21 Am J2d Cust & U § 1. Adjective, as distinguished from substantive, law. Those legal rules which direct the course of proceeding to bring parties into court and the course of the court after they are brought in. Kring v Missouri (US) 17 Otto 221, 231, 27 L Ed 506, 510, 2 S Ct 443. The method of procedure whereby a case is started, parties brought in, and the case conducted to judgment or prior termination, even to and through an appeal. Kansas City v O'Connor, 36 Mo App 594, 599. All that relates to the manner in which a case shall be conducted and tried, from its inception to final judgment and execution. Wright v State, 5 Ind 290.
See **procedure.**

practice act. A statute regulating and prescribing procedure in courts of justice, sometimes in a comprehensive form, at other times supplemented by rules of practice. Helvering v Continental Oil Co. 63 App DC 5, 68 F2d 750.
See **rules of practice.**

practice court. A court which is attached to the king's bench court and which hears ordinary matters and disposes of common motions.
See **moot court.**

practice of dentistry. The treating of diseases or lesions of the human teeth, or of jaws, or correction of malpositions thereof. State v Brown, 37 Wash 97, 79 P 635. In short the practice of the profession of dentistry.
See **dentist; dentistry.**

practice of law. Rendering the services peculiar to the profession. The work of an attorney at law in the preparation of pleadings and other papers incident to actions and special proceedings, the management of such actions and proceedings on behalf of clients before judges and courts, the preparation of legal instruments of all kinds, and, in general, advising clients and taking action for them in matters connected with law. 7 Am J2d Attys § 1. Inclusive of counseling as well as trial work. 30A Am J Rev ed Judges § 11. The giving of such advice or the rendition of such service as requires the use of any degree of legal knowledge or skill. Anno: 111 ALR 23. Not a business open to all, since it is limited to qualified individuals. Re Co-operative Law. Co. 198 NY 479, 92 NE 15.

practice of medicine. The practice of the art of healing disease and preserving health. Anno: 86 ALR 623. The treatment of a human being by another person for the purpose of relieving an ailment, with a public profession on the alleged doctor's part of the ability to cure and heal. State v Stoddard, 215 Iowa 435, 245 NW 273, 86 ALR 616. Diagnosing, prescribing, and treating persons who are sick and afflicted. People v T. Wah Hing, 79 Cal App 286, 249 P 229.
See **physician; surgery.**

practicing dentistry. See **practice of dentistry.**

practicing law. See **practice of law.**

practicing lawyer. A person who customarily and habitually holds himself out to the public as a lawyer and who demands compensation for his services rendered as such. State v Bryan, 98 NC 644, 647, 4 SE 522.
A retired lawyer who conducts but one suit in court for a friend or neighbor, without fee or reward, is not a "practicing lawyer." McCargo v State (Miss) 1 So 161.
See **practice of law.**

practicing medicine. See **practice of medicine.**

practitioner. A lawyer who is engaged in the practice of his profession; a physician who is similarly engaged. Any person who is practicing a profession. A Christian Science healer.

prados (prä'dos). A term encountered in Spanish-American land grants, signifying fields. See Vernon Irrigation Co. v Los Angeles, 106 Cal 237, 247, 39 P 762.

prae (prē). Before.

praebenda (prē-ben'da). Same as **prebend.**

praeceptores (prē-sep-to'rēz). Masters in chancery.

praecipe (prē'si-pe). An order; a command; a writ ordering a person to do some act or to show cause why he should not do it. An application addressed to the clerk of court for the issuance of a summons. McMillon v Harrison, 66 Fla 200, 63 So 427. An order by a judgment creditor to the clerk of court for the issuance of a writ of execution. Yazoo & M. V. R. Co. v Clarksdale, 257 US 10, 66 L Ed 104, 42 S Ct 27. A demand by an appellant of the clerk of court for the inclusion of designated papers in the transcript. 4 Am J2d A & E § 405.

praecipe in capite (prē'si-pe in ka'pi-te). A writ of right which lay when one of the king's immediate tenants in capite was deforced. See 3 Bl Comm 195.

praecipe quia dominus remisit curiam (prē'si-pe qui'a do'mi-nus re-mī'sit kū'ri-am). A writ because the lord has waived his court.
A writ of right thus called was formerly used for the same purpose as the later praecipe in capite to oust the lord of his jurisdiction by suing out this writ in the king's court, instead of by writ of right in the court-baron of the lord. See 3 Bl Comm 195.

praecipe quod reddat (prē'si-pe quod red'dat). Command him to restore; the name of a writ employed in a common recovery commanding the defendant to restore possession. See 2 Bl Comm 358.

praecipe quod teneat conventionem (prē'si-pe quod te'ne-at kon-ven-she-ō'nem). The name of the writ which commenced the action of covenant in fines, which were abolished by 3 & 4 William IV, c. 74. See Jones' Blackstone, 1188, note.

praecipitium (prē-si-pi'she-um). An ancient form of punishment wherein the culprit was hurled from some high place head foremost.

praeco (prēkō). (Roman law.) A court crier; a herald.

praecogitata malicia. See **ex praecogitata malitia.**

praecognita (prē-kog'ni-ta). Matters to be understood beforehand, as a prerequisite to the understanding of other matters.

praecognitum (prę-kog'ni-tum). Singular of **praecognita**.

praed. An abbreviation of **praedictus**.

praedia (prē'di-a). Things which partake of the realty; things or rights which pertain to land. See 2 Bl Comm 428.

praedia bella (prē'di-a bel'la). Same as **praedia bellica**.

praedia bellica (prē'di-a bel'li-ka). Goods captured in war; booty.

praedial (prē'di-ạl). From the soil; out of the land. Pertaining to land or real estate.

praedial servitude (ser'vi-tūd). A servitude or easement in the land of another.

praedial tithes (tīthz). Tithes which were products of the soil.

praedia rustica (prē'di-a rus'ti-ka). Plural of **praedium rusticum**.

praedia stipendiaria (prē'di-a stī-pen-di-ā'ri-a). (Civil law.) Provincial lands belonging to the Roman people.

praedia tributaria (prē'di-a tri-bu-tā'ri-a). (Civil law.) Provincial lands of the Roman emperor.

praedia volantia (prē'di-a vo-lan'she-a). Volatile estates; that is, movables of a solid character such as beds, tables and heavy furniture which seem fixed to the house and are therefore considered as a part of the building. See 2 Bl Comm 428.

praedicta (prē-dik'ta). Same as **praedictus**.

praedictum (prē-dik'tum). Same as **praedictus**.

praedictus (prē-dik'tus). Said; aforesaid; stated before.

praedictus X similiter. See **et praedictus X similiter**.

praedium (prē'di-um). Singular of **praedia**.

praedium dominans (prē'di-um do'mi-nanz). The dominant tenement of an easement. Morgan v Mason, 20 Ohio 401.

Praedium domini regis est directum dominium, cujus nullus est author nisi Deus (prē'di-um do'mi-nī rē'jis est dī-rek'tum do-mi'ni-um, kū'jus nul'lus est â'thor nī'sī Dē'us). The estate of the king is direct ownership of which God alone is the author.

praedium rusticum (prē'di-um rus'ti-kum). (Roman law.) A rural estate.

praedium serviens (prē'di-um ser'vi-enz). The servient tenement of an easement. Morgan v Mason, 20 Ohio 401.

Praedium servit praedio (prē'di-um ser'vit prē'di-ō). Land may be subject to an easement in land.

praedium urbanum (prē'di-um ur-bān'um). (Civil law.) A city estate.

praef. An abbreviation of **praefatus**.

praefatus (prē-fā'tus). Said; aforesaid; stated before.

praefectus (prē-fek'tus). Same as **prefect**.

praefectus praetorio (prē-fek'tus pre-tō'ri-ō). A pretorian prefect,—a high judicial officer in the Roman occupation of England.

praefine (prē'fīn). The primer fine, or a noble for every five marks of land sued for, being one-tenth of the annual value, due the king, by ancient prerogative, upon commencing a suit for the alienation of land by fine. See 2 Bl Comm 350.

praejudicialis (prē-jū-di-she-ā'lis). (Civil law.) Prejudged; adjudicated beforehand or in advance.

praejudicium (prē-jū-di'she-um). Prejudgment; prejudice.

praejuramentum (prē-jū-ra-men'tum). A preliminary oath of innocence required of an accused under Saxon law.

praelatus (prē'la-tus). Same as **prelate**.

praemissae (prē-mis'sē). The premises. See **ex praemissis**.

praemissorum fidem. See **inpraemissorum fidem**.

praemissorum ignarus (prē-mis-sôr'um ig-nä'rus). Not ignorant of the premises. Gerard v Dickenson (Eng) 2 Coke Rep. Part IV, 18.

praemium (prē'mi-um). A compensation; a reward; a price.

praemium concubinati (prē'mi-um kon-ku-bi-nā'tī). The price of concubinage; the price of the loss of chastity.

praemium pudicitiae (prē'mi-um pū-di-si'she-ē). The price or value of chastity.

praemium pudoris (prē'mi-um pu-dū'ris). The price of shame.

praemunire (prē-mụ-nī'rē). The offense, which was not a capital one, of obeying other authority in preference to that of the crown.

It originated from the exorbitant power claimed and exercised in England by the pope of Rome, and it took its name from the words of the writ which initiated a prosecution for the offense, "praemunire facias," etc., "Cause A to be forewarned that he appear before us to answer the contempt with which he stands charged." See 4 Bl Comm 103.

praenomen (prę-nō'men). A name preceding the surname or family name; a Christian name. Laflin & Rand Powder Co. v Steytler, 146 Pa 434, 23 A 215. The first of the three names which every Roman had.

praepositus (prē-po'si-tus). A presiding officer; a sheriff.

praepositus ecclesiae (prē-po'si-tus e-klē'si-ē). A church-warden.

praepositus villae (prē-po'si-tus vil'lē). A town constable.

Praepropera consilia raro sunt prospera (prē-prō'pe-ra kon-si'li-a ra'rō sunt pros'pe-ra). Precipitate or rash counsels are rarely prosperous.

praerogativa regis (prē-ro-ga-tī'va rē'jis). The prerogative of the king.

praescriptio (prē-skrip'she-o). (Civil law.) The mode of acquiring property by uninterrupted possession.

Praescriptio est titulus ex usu et tempore substantiam capiens ab auctoritate legis (pre-skrip'she-ō est ti'tu-lus ex ū'sū et tem'po-re sub-stan'she-am ka'pi-enz ab âk-to-ri-tā'te lē'jis). Prescription is title taking its essence from use and time by authority of law.

Praescriptio et executio non pertinent ad valorem contractus, sed ad tempus et modum actionis instituendae (prē-skrip'she-ō et ex-e-kū'she-ō non per'ti-nent ad va-lō'rem kon-trak'tus, sed ad tem'-pus et mō'dum ak-she-ō'nis in-sti-tu-en'dē). Prescription and execution do not affect the validity of a contract, but they go to the time and manner of instituting an action.

praescriptio fori (prē-skrip'she-ō fō'rī). An objection to the forum or the jurisdiction.

praesens in curia (pre'senz in ku'ri-a). Present in court.

Praesentare nihil aliud est quam praesto dare seu offere (prē-zen-tā're ni'hil a'li-ud est quam prē'stō da're sū of-fer're). To present is nothing other than to give or offer forthwith.

praesentes. See **inter praesentes.**

praesenti. See **in praesenti.**

praesentia. See **in praesentia.**

Praesentia corporis tollit errorem nominis (prē-zen'-she-a kor'po-ris tol'lit er-rō'rem no'mi-nis). The presence of the substance cures an error in the name of it. Smoot v United States, 237 US 38, 42, 59 L Ed 829, 830, 35 S Ct 540.

Praesentia corporis tollit errorem nominis; et veritas nominis tollit errorem demonstrationis (prē-zen'she-a kor'po-ris tol'lit er-rō'rem no'mi-nis; et ve'ri-tās no'mi-nis tol'lit er-rō'rem de-mon-strā-she-ō'nis). The presence of the person cures an error in his name; and the accuracy of the name cures an error of description.

praesentia diversorum. See **in auditu; in praesentia diversorum.**

praesentiam mariti. See **extra praesentiam mariti.**

praeses (prē'sēz). A Roman governor.

praestare (prē-stā're). (Roman law.) To perform; to fulfil; to execute; to guarantee; to become surety for; to answer for; to be responsible for; to excel.

Praestat cautela quam medela (prē'stat kâ-tē'la quam me-de'la). Caution is better than cure.

praestatio (prē-stā'she-ō). Same as **prestation.**

praestation. Same as **prestation.**

Praesumatur pro justitia sententiae (prē-zu'mā-ter prō jūs-ti'she-a sen-ten'she-ē). A presumption exists in favor of the justice of a sentence.

Praesumitur pro legitimatione (prē-zu'mi-ter prō le-ji-ti-mā-she-ō'ne). There is a presumption in favor of legitimacy.

Praesumitur pro negante (prē-zu'mi-ter prō ne-gan'te). There is a presumption in favor of a negation.

Praesumitur pro reo (prē-zu'mi-ter pro re'ō). There is a presumption in favor of a defendant. Culpepper v State, 4 Okla Crim 103, 111 P 679.

praesumptio (prē-zump'she-ō). (Latin.) Presumption. A bold intrusion.

Praesumptio ex eo quod plerumque fit (prē-zump'-she-ō, ex ē'ō quod ple-rum'kwe fit). A presumption (arises) from that which usually happens.

praesumptio fortior (prē-zump'she-ō for'she-or). A stronger presumption.

praesumptio hominis (prē-zump'she-ō ho'mi-nis). A human or natural presumption.

praesumptio juris (prē-zump'she-ō jū'ris). A presumption of law; a rebuttable presumption; a prima facie presumption.

praesumptio juris et de jure (prē-zump'she-ō jū'ris et dē jū're). A presumption of law as to the law; a conclusive or irrebuttable presumption.

Praesumptio juris plena probatio (prē-zump'she-ō jū'ris plē'na pro-bā'she-ō). A presumption of law amounts to full proof.

Praesumptiones sunt conjecturae ex signo verisimili ad probandum assumptae (prē-zump-she-ō'nēz sunt kon-jek-tu're ex sig'nō ve-rī-si'mi-lī ad pro-ban'-dum as-sump'tē). Presumptions are conjectures from probable indication which are assumed for purposes of proof.

Praesumptio valet in lege (prē-zump'she-ō va'let in lē'je). A presumption prevails in law.

Praesumptio violenta, plena probatio (prē-zump'she-ō vi-ō-len'ta, plē'na prō-bā'she-ō). A violent or strong presumption amounts to full proof.

Praesumptio violenta valet in lege (prē-zump'she-ō vi-ō-len'ta va'let in lē'je). A violent or strong presumption prevails in law.

praeteritorum memoria eventorum (prē-ter-i-tō'rum me-mō'ri-a ē-ven-tō'rum). The memory of past events. See 1 Bl Comm 69.

Praetextu liciti non debet admitti illicitum (prē-tex'tū li'si-tī non de'bet ad-mit'tī il-li'si-tum). An unlawful thing ought not to be permitted under a pretext of legality.

praetor (prē'tor). One of the two high Roman officers who performed judicial functions.

praetor fidei commissarius (prē'tor fī-de'ī kom-mis-sā'ri-us). (Civil law.) A praetor who was specially appointed to decide cases which involved trusts.

praetorian law (prē-tōr'i̯an lâ). The law made by the Roman praetors, as distinguished from the civil law which was made by the people.

praevaricator (prę-var'i-kā-to̧r). (Civil law.) A person who committed a breach of trust.

pragmatic (prag-mat'ik). Practical. Pertaining to the civil or ecclesiastical affairs of a community. In a distinct sense, overly officious.

prairie (prā'ri). Land characteristic of the Mississippi Valley, gently rolling, bearing few trees, except along streams, having a deep fertile soil, and covered with grass until broken for cultivation. A meadow or tract of grass land, especially a so-called natural meadow. Interstate Galloway Cattle Co. v Kline, 51 Kans 23, 28, 32 P 628, 629.

prairie fire. A grass fire covering an area, often a large area, of open or agricultural lands. Rogers v Parker, 159 Mich 278, 123 NW 1109.

Prather speed device. Same as **speed watch.**

prava consuetudo (pra'va kon-su-e-tu'dō). A depraved or wicked custom; a perverse custom.

Praxis judicum est interpres legum (pra'xis jū'di-kum est in-ter'prez lē'gum). The practice of the judges is the interpreter of the laws.

prayer. A supplication addressed to God. That part of a pleading which designates and asks for the relief sought by the party.

The prayer is no part of a plaintiff's cause of action and it cannot aid in curing a defective complaint, but it may serve to show what kind of a case the plaintiff supposes he has made and the kind of relief to which he conceives himself to be entitled, and may indicate the object which he seeks to accomplish. See 41 Am J1st Pl §§ 109 et seq.

An appropriate prayer should be incorporated in a bill or petition for equitable relief. 27 Am J2d Eq. § 182.

prayer for alternative relief. See **prayer in the alternative.**

prayer for process. A technical requirement of a bill in equity that the plaintiff, as the last formal part of his bill, name the defendant, so that he may be brought into court. 27 Am J2d Eq. § 182.

prayer for relief. See **prayer.**

prayer healing. A purported healing of disease by prayer alone. 41 Am J1st Phys & S § 30.

prayer in aid (in ād). In real actions, the tenant may pray in aid; that is, he may call for assistance of another to help him to plead because of the feebleness or imbecility of his own estate.
Thus, a tenant for life may pray in aid of him that hath the inheritance in remainder or reversion, and an incumbent may pray in aid of the patron and ordinary; that is, that they shall be joined in the action and help to defend the title. See 3 Bl Comm 300.

prayer in the alternative. A prayer in a pleading by a plaintiff in doubt as to the specific relief to which he is entitled, being in the alternative, so that if one kind of relief be denied, another may be granted, each kind being consistent with the case made by the complaint or bill. 27 Am J2d Eq. § 182; 41 Am J1st Pl § 111.

preacher. See **minister; pastor.**

preamble. A prefatory statement most aptly illustrated by the fifty-two words at the beginning of the Constitution of the United States. A clause in a statute, following the title and preceding the enacting clause, explanatory of the reasons for the enactment and the objects sought to be accomplished. 50 Am J1st Stat § 152. A statement at the beginning of a municipal ordinance by way of a finding of fact by the council and the reasons, purpose, or occasion of or for the enactment. Continental Oil Co. v Santa Fe, 25 NM 94, 177 P 742, 3 ALR 398.
The preamble to the Constitution of the United States indicates the general purposes for which the people ordained and established the Constitution, but the preamble itself has never been regarded as the source of any substantive power conferred on the Federal Government or on any of its departments. Although one of the declared objects of the Constitution, as stated in the preamble, was to secure the blessings of liberty to all under the jurisdiction and authority of the United States, no power can be exerted to that end by the United States unless, apart from the preamble, it is found in some express delegation of power or in some power to be properly implied therefrom, in the body of the Constitution. Jacobson v Massachusetts, 197 US 11, 49 L Ed 643, 25 S Ct 358.

preamble of constitution. See **preamble.**

preamble of statute. See **preamble.**

preappointed evidence (prē-a-poin'ted ev'i-dens). Evidence the form and character of which are prescribed by law.

pre-audience (prē-â'di-ens). The right which the crown may grant by letters patent to such barristers as it may think proper to honor as a mark of distinction, by which right those barristers were entitled to be heard before others; sometimes next after the king's attorney general, but usually following his majesty's counsel. See 3 Bl Comm 28.

prebend (preb'end). The office of a prebendary. See 1 Bl Comm 383.

prebendary (preb'en-dạ-ri). An ecclesiastical officer subordinate to a bishop.
The dean and chapter are the assistants or council of the bishop. The chapter, consisting of canons or prebendaries, are sometimes appointed by the king, sometimes by the bishop, and sometimes elected by the prebendaries themselves. See 1 Bl Comm 383.

precariae (pre-kā'ri-ē). Day-works, which the tenants of certain manors were bound to give their lords in harvest time.
Magna precaria was a great or general reaping day.—Wharton's Law Dictionary.

precarious circumstances (prẹ-kā'ri-us sẻr'kum-stans-ẹs). A desperate financial condition. A financial condition approaching insolvency or bankruptcy.
The circumstances of an executor are said to be "precarious" only when his conduct and character present such evidence of improvidence or recklessness in the management of the trust estate, or of his own, as in the opinion of prudent and discreet men, endangers its security. Shields v Shields (NY) 60 Barb 56, 61.

precarious right. A granted right which is revocable at the will of the person who granted it.

precarium (prẹ-kā'ri-um). (Civil law.) A convention whereby one person allowed another the use of a thing or the exercise of a right gratuitously till revocation. See Mackeldey's Roman Law § 447.

precatory (prek'ạ-tō-ri). Beseeching. Entreating.

precatory trust. A term of dual meaning: (1) a trust which is not enforceable for the reason that the words of entreaty or permission relied upon to create a trust are not to be construed as words of command or direction so as effectively to create a trust; (2) a trust employing precatory words which can be construed as words of command or direction effective to create a valid trust. 54 Am J1st Trusts §§ 54 et seq.

precatory words. Words of request, recommendation, suggestion, or expectation. Re Bernheim, 82 Mont 198, 266 P 378, 57 ALR 1169. Words whose ordinary significance imports entreaty, recommendation, or expectation, rather than mandatory direction, such as, "desire," "request," "beg," "wish," etc., but which, in a proper context, may be construed as words of command. 57 Am J1st Wills § 1180.

precedence. The right or privilege of preceding in time, rank, or order.

precedent. A decision or determination of a point of law made by a court in a case to be followed by a court of the same rank or of a lower rank in a subsequent case presenting the same legal problem, although different parties are involved in the subsequent case. 20 Am J2d Cts § 183. The decision of an administrative agency. 2 Am J2d Admin L § 241.
As to the effect of a decision of a court of one state in a court of a sister state, see 20 Am J2d Cts § 203.
As to the effect of a decision of a court in a foreign country as a precedent, see 20 Am J2d Cts § 200.
See **stare decisis.**

precedent condition. See **condition precedent.**

preceding estate. An estate after which a future interest is limited. 28 Am J2d Est § 208.

prece partium (pre'se par'she-um). By the prayer of the parties.

precept. An order or direction. A warrant; an order in writing. A writ or process. Adams v Vose, 67 Mass (1 Gray) 51, 58.

precept of clare constat (pre'sept ov kla're kon'stat). The deed of a superior confirming title in the heir of a deceased vassal.

precept of sasine (pre'sept ov sā'zĕn). The order of a superior that his vassal be invested with seisin.

preces (prē'sēz). Same as **precariae.**

precinct. See **election district; magisterial precinct; police precinct.**

precipe (pres'i-pē). Same as **praecipe.**

precipitate (prẹ-sip'i-tąt). Impetuous. Acting in a hurry.

precipitate (prẹ-sip'i-tāt). To hurl downward. To form and fall, as rain.

precium (pre'she-um). Same as **pretium.**

precluded. Prevented. Made impossible. Coffin v Fidelity-Philadelphia Trust Co. 374 Pa 378, 97 A2d 857, 39 ALR2d 625. Estopped. Baskett v Ohio Valley Banking & Trust Co. 214 Ky 41, 45, 281 SW 1022.

Precludi non debet (pre-klu'dī non de'bet). He ought not to be barred.

precognition (prē-kog-nish'ọn). A preliminary examination of witnesses by the prosecuting attorney before the trial of a criminal case.

precognosce (prē-kog-nos'). To pre-examine.

preconceived malice (prē-kon-sēvd' mal'is). Same as **malice aforethought.**

precondition. A condition precedent; a condition which must happen before either party to a contract is bound by it. A redundancy for "condition," to put in shape, as a boxer for a contest.

preconstruction costs. Engineering and superintending expenses; contractors' profits; interest on the cost of plant during construction; insurance and taxes during construction; promotion expenses; and legal expenses connected with the organization of the company. 43 Am J1st Pub Util § 117.

precontract (prē-kọn'trakt). A contract which a person has previously entered into and by which he has incapacitated himself from entering into a second contract of the same kind.

precox paranoia. See **dementia precox paranoia.**

predated instrument. An antedated instrument, that is, an instrument for the payment of money dated as of a day prior to the execution and delivery of the instrument. 11 Am J2d B & N § 208.

predating. Dating a contract as of a date earlier than the date of execution. 17 Am J2d Contr § 69.

predatory animal. An animal which preys upon the livestock of farmers.

predecessor. In its common acceptation, the word means a person who goes before or precedes another in a given state, position, or office.

The word does not necessarily express any relation of legal privity. One person may be a predecessor of another without the relation of contractual succession. P. Lorillard Co. v Peper (CC Mo) 65 F 597, 598.

predestination (prē-des-ti-nā'shọn). Destiny. In theology, foreordination of events by God.

See **absolute predestination; limited predestination.**

predial (prē'di-ạl). Same as **praedial.**

predial servitude. Same as **praedial servitude.**

predial tithes. Same as **praedial tithes.**

predicate (pred'i-kāt). To use as a basis or ground of an action, defense, or argument.

predominant (prẹ-dom'i-nạnt). Greater or superior in power and influence.

Thus, a predominant motive, when several motives may have operated, is one of greater force and effect, in producing the given result, than any other motive. See Matthews v Bliss, 39 Mass (22 Pick) 48, 53.

pre-emption (prẹ-emp'shọn). The act of buying anything before or ahead of others.

An entry made upon unappropriated public lands for homestead purposes. 42 Am J1st Pub L § 19. The right granted by act of Congress to settlers on public lands of the United States to cultivate, improve and acquire title thereto. United States v Fitzgerald (US) 15 Pet 407, 10 L Ed 785; Nix v Allen, 112 US 129, 28 L Ed 675, 5 S Ct 70. The right, otherwise known as a first-refusal option, of a unit owner in a condominium to purchase at a predetermined price, or meet any offer of purchase by a matching offer, in the event another unit owner desires to sell. 15 Am J2d Con Apt § 17. The act of a nation in detaining property of foreigners brought within her boundaries, so that her own residents may have opportunity to purchase it.

pre-emption entry. An entry made upon unappropriated public lands for homestead purposes. Hartman v Warren (CA8 Minn) 76 F 157, 161.

pre-emption laws. Federal statutes beginning with the Act of September 4, 1841, under which a settler upon public lands of the United States, surveyed and subject to private entry, might acquire title.

The pre-emption laws differ from the homestead law in that under the former, claims might be initiated prior to record notice, three months being allowed the settler within which to file his declaratory statement with the register of the proper district, while under the homestead law, the rights of the settler only attached to the land from the date of the entry in the proper land office. St. Paul, M. & M. R. Co. v Donohue, 210 US 21, 52 L Ed 941, 28 S Ct 600; Maddox v Burnham, 156 US 544, 39 L Ed 527, 15 S Ct 448.

pre-emption of field. Action taken by Congress in passing legislation in a field theretofor open to state legislation. 16 Am J2d Confl L § 8; 15 Am J2d Com § 23.

pre-emption of land. See **pre-emption.**

pre-emption of way. The failure of a motorist to give right of way to another vehicle.

pre-emptive rights of stockholders. See **rights.**

pre-existing debt. See **antecedent debt.**

pre-existing obligation. See **antecedent debt.**

prefabricated house. A house constructed of materials cut and fit before they are brought upon the premises. Community Home Builders, Inc. v Town Council of North Kingstown, 83 RI 409, 117 A2d 544.

prefects. Administrative officers, as known to history and, in some places, even in modern times.

Functionaries well known in the Roman law, and under the empire clothed with extensive powers, both judicial and administrative. With the decline of the empire they seem to have lost their importance and finally to have disappeared; but hundreds of years later, the office was revived in the French Republic in 1800, and was bestowed upon the heads of departments into which the country had been divided by the national assembly in 1790. These prefects were assisted by a council of prefecture. The prefect was charged with the administration of local affairs, and was practically the representative of the central government in public matters. The title was carried into several states of the Union whose legislation was framed upon the Code Napoleon, but until the establishment of the Republic, was apparently unknown in Mexico. It seems to have been recognized there prior to 1836, being mentioned in the constitutional law of that year. Crespin v United States, 168 US 208, 213, 42 L Ed 438, 440, 18 S Ct 53.

preference. The right of one person over other persons, to be appointed administrator, for example, the right of a surviving spouse. 31 Am J2d Ex & Ad §§ 50 et seq. A right given to a stockholder of a corporation to subscribe at a stated price for shares of a new issue in proportion to the shares already held by him. Miles v Safe Deposit & Trust Co. 259 US 247, 66 L Ed 923, 42 S Ct 483. A provision in a succession or inheritance tax statute which for the purposes of exemptions and rates divides recipients into classifications based upon relationship to decedent. 28 Am J Rev ed Inher T § 302. A term often confused with "priority," but distinguishable by considering a priority as legal and a preference as something which the law may make voidable. The act of a debtor in preferring one or more of his creditors to others by paying him or them without favoring the others with payment. 37 Am J2d Frd Conv § 89.

See **fraudulent preference; preferential transfer; tariff preference; voidable preference.**

preference shares. Same as **preferred stock.**

preference to ports of one state. A restriction upon the power of Congress under the commerce clause of the United States Constitution, but having no effect upon the states in the regulation of their domestic affairs, and restraining Congress in the enactment of legislation only in reference to positive legislation looking to a direct privilege or preference. 15 Am J2d Com § 81.

preferential assignment. An assignment for the benefit of creditors wherein the assignor gives a preference to certain of his creditors. 6 Am J2d Assign for Crs § 69. Broadly, any assignment which prefers one creditor over another.

See **voidable preference.**

preferential dividend. See **preferred dividend.**

preferential primary. A form of primary election, such as is now held in New Hampshire, Oregon, and some other states in reference to presidential candidates, which, while not conclusive of nomination, gives the members of a political party, who are qualified to vote at the primary, an opportunity for expressing their choice, and gives a candidate the opportunity of testing his appeal to the voters.

preferential tariff. See **tariff preference.**

preferential transfer. A transfer of property made by an insolvent debtor to one creditor to the exclusion of others. 29 Am J Rev ed Insolv § 82. An act of bankruptcy; a transfer of any of the property of a creditor for or on account of an antecedent debt, made or suffered by such debtor while insolvent and within four months before the filing by or against him of a petition initiating a proceeding under the Act, the effect of which transfer will be to enable such creditor to obtain a greater percentage of his debt than some other creditor of the same class. Bankruptcy Act § 60(a)(1); 11 USC § 9-6(a)(1); 9 Am J2d Bankr § 146.

See **voidable preference.**

preferential voting. A term used to describe various systems under which a voter is permitted or required to express more than one choice for the same office. 26 Am J2d Elect § 275.

preferred. Having a preference. Having an advantage which another person does not have. In the case of a thing, having an advantage attached which another thing of the same character does not have. State ex rel. Thompson v Cheraw & Chester Railroad Co. 16 SC 524, 530.

preferred beneficiaries. Beneficiaries under wrongful death statutes classified according to natural dependency on the deceased. 22 Am J2d Dth § 48.

preferred creditor. See **preference.**

preferred dividend. A dividend declared and paid on preferred stock. A dividend payable by virtue of contract to one class of stockholders in priority to that to be paid to another class. 19 Am J2d Corp § 809.

preferred legacy. A legacy which, by the terms of the will, is to be paid before other legacies. 57 Am J1st Wills § 1458.

preferred maritime lien. A lien arising prior in time to the recording and indorsement of a preferred ship mortgage; or a lien for damages arising out of tort, for wages of a stevedore when employed directly by the owner, operator, master, husband, or agent of the vessel, for wages of the crew of the vessel, for general average, or for salvage, including contract salvage. 46 USC § 953 (a).

preferred share. A share of a business trust carrying a preference in the payment of dividends. 13 Am J2d Bus Tr § 23.

See **preferred stock.**

preferred ship mortgage. A mortgage of a vessel given a preferred status by the Ship Mortgage Act, subject to conditions respecting the size of the vessel and compliance with registration and other provisions of the Act. 2 Am J2d Adm § 122.

preferred stock. A part of the capital stock of a corporation, the peculiar and distinctive characteristic of which is that it is entitled to a priority over other stock in the distribution of profits. Sometimes called guaranteed stock. Corporate stock given a preference over common stock in the distribution of capital assets upon a dissolution of the corporation. 18 Am J2d Corp § 213. Building and loan association stock to which a preference in payment of dividends or in distribution of assets upon insolvency is attached. 13 Am J2d B & L Assoc § 23.

The holder of preferred stock is a shareholder in the corporation. He is not a corporation creditor, and has no rights as such. His rights are those of the common shareholder, except as those rights are limited by the statute and the contract and the

prefiled. A legislative bill filed before the opening of the legislative session.

additional right to have his dividends paid out of earnings and his stock redeemed out of assets in preference to the common shareholder. Oklahoma Hotel Bldg. Co. v Houghton, 202 Okla 591, 216 P2d 288, 16 ALR2d 1307.

prefiled. A legislative bill filed before the opening of the legislative session.

prefix. Something added at the beginning of a word to create a new word, for example, "pre" to "filed" for "prefiled." A title preceding a name, for example, "Mr." or "Mrs." Feldman v Silva, 54 RI 202, 171 A 922.

pregnancy. The physical state of a mother in whose womb gestation has begun. Commonwealth v Parker, 50 Mass (9 Metc) 263, 267.

Pregnancy is neither an ailment, a condition of unsound health, nor a disease. Rasicot v Royal Neighbors of America, 18 Idaho 85, 108 P 1048.

See **sickness.**

pregnant. With child; bearing a fetus. Anno: 16 ALR2d 951.

See **affirmative pregnant; negative pregnant; quick with child.**

pre-incorporation services. Services in promoting and organizing a corporation.

prejudge. See **prejudice.**

prejudgment interest. Interest allowed by way of damages, as for the unlawful detention of money found to be due the plaintiff in action for breach of contract or tort. 22 Am J2d Damg § 179.

prejudice. In one sense, detriment, as where one has changed his position in reliance upon the promise of another. Suffering an invasion of one's legal right. Having one's pecuniary interest affected by a judgment. Gloss v People, 259 Ill 332, 102 NE 763. In another sense, partiality; bias. Preconceived opinion. An opinion formed before the facts are known or in disregard of facts. Hudgins v State, 2 Ga 173, 176.

See **dismissal without prejudice; dismissal with prejudice; local influence; local prejudice.**

prejudice of judge. Pertaining to the mental attitude toward a party to the litigation, not the view entertained regarding the subject matter involved. 30A Am J Rev ed Judges § 170. A hostile feeling or spirit of ill will, or undue friendship or favoritism, directed against or for one of the litigants. Haslam v Morrison, 113 Utah 14, 190 P2d 520.

prejudice of juror. A leaning of the mind, a propensity or prepossession toward a view, so that the mind is not indifferent; a prejudgment of the case, not necessarily a matter of enmity or ill will against either party. 31 Am J Rev ed Jury § 172.

prejudicial. Detrimental or derogatory to a party. Naturally, probably, or actually bringing about a wrong result. State v Farrar, 103 Kan 774, 176 P 987.

prejudicial alteration. Such an alteration of an instrument as materially affects the rights of a party thereto. 4 Am J2d Alt Inst § 8.

prejudicial error. Reversible error. 5 Am J2d A & E § 783. Error of such substance that, upon a review of the record, it appears that the rights of the complaining party have been injuriously affected by the error, or that he has suffered a miscarriage of justice. 5 Am J2d A & E § 783.

prejudicial evidence. In the sense of evidence inadmissible because prejudicial, evidence which has no purpose other than to prejudice the minds of the jury. 29 Am J2d Ev § 260. In another sense, evidence so material to the issues or having such tendency to arouse the sympathy or passions of the jury that its admission, if in error, is ground for reversal on appeal. 5 Am J2d A & E § 801.

prelate (prel'ăt). A superior ecclesiastical officer who does not act vicariously; as, a bishop or an archbishop.

preliminary alimony. See **temporary alimony.**

preliminary arrest. An arrest made before charges preferred against the person taken into custody; an arrest made without a warrant. 5 Am J2d Arr § 22.

preliminary estimate. A statement of value made on filing a declaration of taking under the power of eminent domain. Jacksonville Expressway Authority v Bennett (Fla App) 158 So 2d 821.

preliminary examination. A judicial inquiry to determine whether there is "probable cause" for an accusation of crime, the nature of which offense is thereby made known to the accused, the primary purpose being to ascertain whether there is reasonable ground to believe that a crime has been committed and whether there is just cause to believe that the defendant charged by the accusation committed it. 21 Am J2d Crim L § 443.

See **preliminary hearing.**

preliminary hearing. The hearing to which an accused is entitled on preliminary examination, leading to his commitment, his release on bail if the offense is bailable, or his discharge from custody for want of evidence to bind him over. 21 Am J2d Crim L §§ 449, 450. Not a "trial" within the meaning of a statute providing grounds for change of venue. State ex rel. Hale v Marion County Municipal Court, 234 Ind 467, 127 NE2d 897. A hearing in an eminent domain proceeding for the determination of questions respecting the right of the petitioner to maintain the proceeding. 27 Am J2d Em D § 401.

preliminary injunction. An injunction granted prior to a hearing on the merits, being in no way dependent upon such hearing, its purpose being merely to preserve the status quo until the final hearing on the merits. 28 Am J Rev ed Inj § 12.

In some jurisdictions, the term "injunction" means a preliminary, as distinguished from a final, injunction, the latter being considered merely as a decree in equity.

See **temporary injunction.**

preliminary mandatory injunction. An injunction in a form rarely granted, it being granted only on a clear showing of necessity of preventing irreparable or serious injury, the injunction calling for the performance of some act on the part of the party against whom it is granted. 28 Am J Rev ed Inj § 22.

preliminary activity. See **Portal-to-Portal Pay Act.**

preliminary statement. See **opening statement.**

preliminary term insurance. Term insurance provided during the earlier period of the coverage of a life insurance policy, no net value or reserve being built up during the period of the term, the policy to continue as a regular life insurance policy after the expiration of the preliminary term. 29 Am J Rev ed Ins § 623.

premarital. A characterization of conduct, particularly sexual relations, prior to marriage.

See **antenuptial.**

PREMATURE [979] PREMIUM

premature action. An action commenced before the accrual of the cause of action sought to be enforced. Sullivan v Arkansas Valley Bank, 176 Ark 278, 2 SW2d 1096, 57 ALR 296; Broyles v Commonwealth, 309 Ky 837, 219 SW2d 52. An action for divorce commenced before the existence of the ground for divorce. 24 Am J2d Div & S § 184.

premature birth. A birth occurring before the expiration of the natural period of pregnancy. Sullivan v Old Colony Street R. Co. 197 Mass 512, 83 NE 1091.
See **miscarriage.**

premature delivery. A delivery by the seller of goods in advance of the time of delivery as fixed by the contract of sale. 46 Am J1st Sales § 232.
See **premature birth.**

premature execution. A writ of execution issued in advance of the time prescribed by law for the issuance of execution. 30 Am J2d Exec § 49.

premature judgment. A judgment by default entered before return day. 30A Am J Rev ed Judgm § 205.

premature labor. Labor as characteristic in childbirth but occurring before the usual time, unexpectedly early.
See **miscarriage.**

premature return. The return of an execution at a time prior to that fixed by law. 30 Am J2d Exec § 555.

premature sale. An execution sale made before the day fixed by the notice of sale. King v Cushman, 41 Ill 31. An execution sale at a time in advance of the time prescribed by law. 30 Am J2d Exec § 332.

premature tender. A tender made before maturity of the obligation. 52 Am J1st Ten § 17.

premeditate. To meditate in advance of action; to form a clear intent.
For example, a robber with a dirk or pistol turns a corner and meets a bank messenger with a roll of bills. In a moment he determines to get it. In the next moment he shoots or stabs the messenger dead, takes the package and flees. His malice was deliberately premeditated though it occupied but a few seconds. Commonwealth v Tucker, 189 Mass 457, 76 NE 127.

premeditated (prę-med'i-tā-ted). Thought of beforehand for any space of time, however short. State v Landgraf, 95 Mo 97, 8 SW 237.

premeditation. Forethought. Thinking and reflecting, having sufficient volition to make a choice, and by the use of mental powers, to refrain from a homicidal act. People v Barberi, 149 NY 256, 43 NE 635. Thinking beforehand for any time, however short. State v Marsh, 171 Mo 523, 528, 71 SW 1003.

premier serjeant (prē'mi-ėr sär'jent). The first in rank of the king's serjeants, so constituted by letters patent and having the first right to pre-audience. See 3 Bl Comm 28, note.

premises. The grounds of an argument or dissertation. In an instrument, something written before in the same instrument. Alaska Improv. Co. v Hirsch, 119 Cal 249, 255, 47 P 124, 51 P 340. A formal part of a deed, otherwise known as the caption, preceding the habendum clause, containing recitals of the grantor's motive for the conveyance, the names and designations of the parties, the consideration expressed for the deed, words of grant, and the description of the property conveyed. 23 Am J2d Deeds § 33. The part of a bill in equity which embraces the real substance of the suit, setting out all the essential facts on which the plaintiff relies as grounds of relief. 27 Am J2d Eq § 181. Real estate, particularly real estate with buildings. Meador v Blonde, 34 Wyo 397, 244 P 222.

The word "premises," within the meaning of a clause in an insurance policy prohibiting the keeping of certain articles upon the premises, refers to the insured building, and is not inclusive of buildings not connected with the one insured or of the yard of the building insured. 29A Am J Rev ed Ins § 920.

The word as used in a provision prohibiting the sale of liquor to be drunk on the "premises," is sufficiently broad to include a bench which touches the wall of a house just outside the street door, which is under the control of the house owner, but does not include an independent building not under his control, or the adjoining highway. 30 Am J Rev ed Intox L § 20.

premises liability. The liability of the owner, lessee, occupant, contractor, or other person for a personal injury sustained on the property.

premises liability insurance. Insurance protecting an owner or occupant of real property against liability to a person injured by reason of a defective condition of the premises.
See **public liability insurance.**

premium. A premium is a reward or recompense for some act done. Alvord v Smith, 63 Ind 58. An amount offered by way of a prize to a successful competitor in a contest. 24 Am J1st Gaming §§ 100 et seq. A purse, prize, stake or sweepstake; some valuable thing offered by a person for the doing of something by others, into the strife for which he does not enter. Harris v White, 81 NY 532. Something given a purchaser of merchandise in addition to the article or commodity purchased. 52 Am J1st Trad St § 11. An amount paid above par value because of quality or of demand. An advance payment of rent in a lump sum, calculated on the basis of present worth of sums to be paid in the future. A sum paid to the master under a contract of apprenticeship, to cover instruction and maintenance. An amount paid by a borrower for the privilege of receiving a loan in preference to other applicants. 13 Am J2d B & L Assoc § 54.
See **bond premium; insurance premium.**

premium earned. An accounting term in the insurance business, meaning the pro rata portion of a premium, in force during the accounting period, applicable to the expired period of the policy. That part of the premium paid by a borrowing member of a building and loan association which is proportionate to the time which has elapsed upon a premature severance of their relation. 13 Am J2d B & L Assoc § 121.

Since a premium is paid in advance to cover a definite period of time, the company is said to have "earned" the premium in direct proportion to the amount of time that has elapsed since the policy was placed upon the books.

premium loan provision. The provision frequently found in life insurance contracts that upon the failure of the insured to pay a premium within a time stipulated for payment, the insurer, without more, will pay the premium in insured's behalf and charge it as a loan against the policy, provided the reserve value is sufficient. 29 Am J Rev ed Ins § 551.

premium note. A note given to an insurance company, particularly a life insurance company, for a premium due upon a policy of insurance. 29 Am J Rev ed Ins § 542.

premium pudicitiae. Same as **praemium pudicitiae**.

premium pudoris. Same as **praemium pudoris**.

premium rate. The premium charged for insurance. 29 Am J Rev ed Ins §§ 503 et seq. The rate at which the premium on an insurance policy is calculated.

premium receipt. The receipt given by an insurance company upon receiving payment of a premium upon a policy.
See **interim receipt**.

premium reserve. See **unearned premium reserve**.

premiums written. An accounting term in the insurance business, meaning the amount of premiums for insurance written during the accounting period, subject to deductions for premiums returned to policyholders and risks reinsured.

premunire. Same as **praemunire**.

prenatal injury. An injury occurring to a child in the womb.

prender. See **in prender**.

prender de baron (pren'dėr de bar'on). To take a husband; to marry.

prenomen (prē-nō'men). A first name; a given name.

prenuptial. See **antenuptial**; **premarital**.

prenuptial agreement. See **antenuptial contract**.

prenuptial settlement. See **antenuptial settlement**.

preoccupation. Engrossed in one's thoughts, a mental condition sometimes so pronounced as to constitute unawareness of surroundings, even danger.

prepaid. Paid in advance.
See **prepayment**.

prepaid stock. See **paid-up stock**.

preparation. That which is prepared; something made, equipped, or compounded for a particular purpose. Anno: 77 ALR2d 1246. A drug. A patent medicine. An element considered in determining the offense of an attempt to commit a crime. Devising or arranging the means or measures necessary for the commission of the offense, as distinguished from an attempt which is the direct movement toward commission after the preparations are made. 21 Am J2d Crim L § 111.

No definite line can be drawn between an "attempt" and "preparation" to commit a crime, but the question is one of degree. The accused has frequently been held to have passed beyond "preparation," although interrupted before the last of his intended steps. United States v Coplon (CA2 NY) 185 F2d 629, 28 ALR2d 1041.

prepayment. Payment before the maturity of the obligation.

prepayment meter. An instrumentality containing a slot for money, the placing of which in the slot sets in motion a mechanism whereby a determined amount of gas is released for consumption in house or place of business. 43 Am J1st Pub Util § 58.

prepay station. A station at which the carrier delivers freight to the consignee, directly and without the intervention of a local agent, and to which consignments are accepted only upon the condition of charges for transportation being prepaid by the shipper. Bird v Railroads, 99 Tenn 719.

prepense (prẹ-pens'). Planned ahead; premeditated. Sullivan v State, 100 Wis 283, 293.
See **premeditated**.

preponderance of evidence. The weight, credit, and value of the aggregate evidence on either side; the greater weight of the evidence; the greater weight of the credible evidence. In the last analysis, the probability of the truth; evidence more convincing as worthy of belief than that which is offered in opposition thereto. 30 Am J2d Ev § 1164.

The expression does not mean the mere numerical array of witnesses; it means weight, credit, and value. Willcox v Hines, 100 Tenn 524, 45 SW 781.

preprimary convention. The convention of a political party held prior to a primary election for the purpose of nominating candidates, the names of which are to be placed on the primary ballot as convention candidates. State ex rel. Palmer v Miller, 74 NM 129, 391 P2d 416.

prerogativa regis (prē-ro-gā-ti'va rē'jis). The prerogative of the king.

prerogative. Precedence. A prior right or privilege. In an older day, that power, pre-eminence, or privilege which the king hath or claimeth over and beyond other persons, and above the ordinary course of the common law, in right of his crown. Atty. Gen. v Eau Claire, 37 Wis 400, 443. In modern times, the inherent and paramount power of the people. Bignell v Cummins, 69 Mont 294, 222 P 797, 36 ALR 634, 637.

prerogative court. A probate court. Robinson v Fair, 128 US 53, 86, 32 L Ed 415, 423.

prerogative cy pres. See **cy pres**.

prerogative law. The law of royal prerogative.

prerogative of purveyance and pre-emption (of pėr-vā'ạns and prē-em'shọn). A right enjoyed by the crown of buying up provisions and other necessaries, by the intervention of the king's purveyors, for the use of his royal household, at an appraised valuation, in preference to all others, and even without the consent of the owner; and also of forcibly impressing the carriages and horses of the subject, to do the king's business on the public roads, in the conveyance of timber, baggage, and the like, however inconvenient to the proprietor, upon paying him a settled price. See 1 Bl Comm 287.

prerogative remedial legislation. A name given by Judge Cooley in his Constitutional Limitations to a species of legislation not obnoxious to the law, based upon the recognized power of the legislature, as parens patriae, to pass proper rules and regulations for superintendence, disposition, and management of the property of infants, lunatics, and others under disability.

Within the legitimate scope of such legislation is the power which may be conferred upon one standing in a fiduciary relation to a minor or incompetent, to change the character of the estate, and even to dispose of its proceeds, when it is to the interest of the minor or incompetent. Rider v Regan, 114 Cal 667, 678, 46 P 820.

prerogative writs. Writs issued in cases of public right and those affecting the sovereignty of the state, its franchises and prerogatives, or the liberties of its people. State ex rel. Goodwin v Nelson County, 1 ND 88, 45 NW 33; Atty. Gen. v Railroad Co. 35 Wis 513. Writs under which extraordinary remedies are made available.
See **extraordinary remedies**.

pres. See **cy pres.**

Pres. Abbreviation of "president." 1 Am J2d Abbr § 5.

presbyter (pres'bi-tėr). An elder in the church; a delegate representing a local church in presbytery. A priest or minister.

Presbyterian Church. A protestant church. The United Presbyterian Church in the United States of America.

See **General Assembly; presbytery; synod.**

Presbyterianism. See **Calvinism.**

presbytery (pres'bi-ter-i). The governing body of the United Presbyterian Church in the United States of America in a district of the church. The district itself.

prescribable (prē-skrī'ba-bl). Capable of, or subject to, being acquired by prescription.

prescribe. To lay down beforehand as a rule of action; to ordain, appoint, define authoritatively. To impose as a peremptory order; to dictate, appoint, direct, ordain. Sevier v Riley, 198 Cal 170, 175, 244 P 323. To give law. State v Seattle Nat. Bank, 130 Wash 69, 226 P 259, 33 ALR 1206, 1209. To give a prescription.

prescribed by law. Made law by actual legislation. Exline v Smith & McFarland, 5 Cal 112. Broadly, made law by any authorized body.

prescribing in a que estate. Prescription in a man and all those persons whose estate he has. 25 Am J2d Ease § 58.

prescription. The acquisition of an easement by adverse user under claim of right for the prescriptive period. The acquisition of incorporeal hereditaments by adverse user. Plaza v Flak, 7 NJ 215, 81 A2d 137, 27 ALR2d 324. A presumption of grant from long possession and exercise of right. 25 Am J2d Ease § 39. In the broad sense of modern times, the gaining of a title by adverse possession. 3 Am J2d Adv P § 4. A direction in writing prepared by a physician, to be presented by the patient to a druggist, setting forth the drug or medicine to be furnished the patient by the druggist and the manner in which it shall be prepared, and directions for its use by the patient. 25 Am J2d Drugs § 5. Any direction to a patient for the use or application by him of any drug for the cure of any bodily disease; even an oral direction for the use of a drug. State v Baker, 229 NC 73, 48 SE2d 61.

While it has been contended that the term refers only to medical provision for human beings, there seems to be no reason why a recipe or formula for the treatment of animals may not be called a "prescription," from whatever source it may proceed. Ray v Burbank, 61 Ga 505.

See **municipal corporation by prescription; negative prescription; positive prescription; presumed grant.**

prescription acts. Statutes establishing the respective periods of time within which various rights or titles may be acquired by prescription.

prescriptive easement. An easement arising, created, or acquired by prescription.
See **prescription.**

prescriptive license. A license in real property acquired by prescription. 33 Am J1st Lic § 97. An anomalous concept, since use under a license, being permissive, cannot ripen into a prescriptive right.

Los Angeles Brick & Clay Products Co. v Los Angeles, 60 Cal App 2d 478, 141 P2d 46.

prescriptive period. The period of time necessary to acquire an easement by prescription. 25 Am J2d Ease § 50.

prescriptive title. See **title by prescription.**

prescriptive way. See **way by prescription.**

presence. The bearing or personality of a person. The fact of being at a place at a particular time.

The meaning of the word depends upon the circumstances. No one can accurately define it. It implies an area which has no metes and bounds. Anything done within the four walls of a room which is free from outside interference is usually done in the presence of all who are in the room whether it is seen or not. But proximity and consciousness may create presence. Nock v Nock's Exrs. 51 Va (10 Gratt) 106, 117.

See **constructive presence.**

presence of accused. The fundamental principle of criminal procedure that after indictment found, nothing shall be done in the absence of the prisoner and the correlative right of the accused to be present at his own trial. 21 Am J2d Crim L § 271. The right of the accused to be present at all stages of his trial, applicable in all capital cases, in fact, in all felonies; also applicable in prosecutions for misdemeanors to the extent that the accused undoubtedly has the right to be present, although in some jurisdictions authority to proceed in his absence is recognized where only a misdemeanor is involved. 21 Am J2d Crim L § 272.

presence of officer. When an offense is committed so as to justify an arrest without a warrant:—being in such a position that the commission of the offense is on view or that knowledge of the commission of the offense may be acquired by him through any of his senses, including the sense of hearing or smell. 5 Am J2d Arr § 31.

Under the usual statutory provision authorizing a peace officer to arrest without warrant where an offense is committed in his "presence," the words do not necessarily mean within his sight, but it is held sufficient if the officer arrives on the scene immediately after the encounter, attracted by the noise of it. Porter v State, 124 Ga 297, 52 SE 283.

presence of the court. A phrase to be given a liberal interpretation as it appears in a statute defining contempt of court.

The court consists not of the judge, the courtroom, the jury, or the jury room individually, but all of these combined, so that the court is present wherever any of these constituent parts is engaged in the prosecution of the business of the court according to law. Anno: 42 ALR2d 970; 17 Am J2d Contpt § 7.

A court in session is considered present where its officers, jurors, and witnesses are required to be in the performance of their several duties, so that an assault, threat, or act of intimidation against such a person while attendant upon the court is a direct contempt. State v Goff, 28 SC 17, 88 SE2d 788, 52 ALR2d 1292.

Since the grand jury is an arm of the United States District Court, proceedings before the grand jury are to be regarded as being proceedings in the court. Hence, contempts occurring in the presence of the grand jury are to be treated as taking place in the presence of the court and are therefore subject to be punished summarily by the court, without indictment. Camarota v United States (CA3 NJ) 111 F2d 243.

presence of the testator. See **in the presence of the testator.**

present. Noun: A gift; a gratuity; to make a gift or gratuity. Adjective: Being at a place at a particular time.
See **presence.**

presentation. An offering by one entitled to do so of a qualified person to be installed in a benefice.

presentation of bill. The delivery of a bill passed by the legislature to the executive for his approval or veto. State ex rel. State Pharmaceutical Asso. v Michel, 52 La Ann 936, 27 So 565.
See **presentation of claim; presentment for acceptance; presentment for payment.**

presentation of claim. A notification by a creditor to the debtor of the existence of the claim, sometimes accompanied with an itemized statement, and usually given for the purpose of inducing payment. The filing of a claim, for example, the filing of a claim for workmen's compensation with the administrative board or commission. 58 Am J1st Workm Comp § 407. The filing of a claim against a decedent so as to make it a matter of record in court. 21 Am J1st Ex & Ad § 371. The furnishing of a statement or notice of claim against a municipal corporation to the corporation for the purpose of audit and allowance, such being a condition precedent to an action against the municipality upon the obligation comprehended by the claim. 38 Am J1st Mun Corp § 673.

presentation of motion. The making of a motion in court or to a judge at a time when the party making the motion has the right to have it heard by the court.

presentative. See **advowson presentative.**

present danger doctrine. See **clear and present danger.**

presented. See **presentation** and expressions beginning **presentation.**

presentee (prẹ-zen'tē'). The person to whom a presentation to a benefice was made.
See **presentation.**

present estate (prez'ẹnt es-tāt'). An estate which is presently vested.

present fact. A fact presently existing. 37 Am J2d Fraud § 47.

present heirs. A man's heirs as determined on the day of his death. In some connections, the heirs apparent. Fountain County Coal & Mining Co. v Beckleheimer, 102 Ind 76, 1 NE 202.

presenting bank. Any bank presenting an item except a payor bank. UCC § 4–105(e).

presenting question in lower court. A fundamental condition of right to review; the raising of objections and the taking of exceptions in the lower court. 5 Am J2d A & E §§ 545 et seq.

present interest. An interest which is presently vested.
As used in the Federal Gift Tax statute, a gift of income beginning at once and lasting for life or for a period of years is a gift of a present interest, and a gift of principal at a future date is a gift of a future interest. These rules are to be followed whether the two sorts of gifts are to different persons or to the same person. Charles v Hassett (DC Mass) 43 F Supp 432.

presently. At once; now; immediately; forthwith.

presentment. An informal accusation, made by the grand jury on its own knowledge, to be used by the prosecutor as the basis for a true bill or indictment. Bennett v Kalamazoo Circuit Judge, 183 Mich 200, 150 NW 141. Precisely, an accusation by the grand jury made on its own motion. Anno: 22 ALR 1367, s. 106 ALR 1388, 120 ALR 437; 27 Am J1st Indict § 4.
The words "presentment" and "indictment" have come to be substantially interchangeable terms. Coons v State, 191 Ind 580, 134 NE 194, 20 ALR 900.

presentment for acceptance. The presenting of a bill of exchange to the drawee therein named for his acceptance and agreement to pay the bill, usually at some time in the future. 11 Am J2d B & N § 730. Any act which amounts to a notification of the holding of a bill of exchange with a request to accept, accompanied by the bill. 11 Am J2d B & N § 734.
Where the acceptance of the bill is in writing, the word "seen," or the word "accepted," or the word "presented," written on the bill itself, or on any other paper relating to the transaction, will amount to an acceptance of the bill. Barnet v Smith, 30 NH 256.

presentment for payment. The method by which it is determined whether a person primarily liable on an instrument will pay or whether it will be necessary to resort for payment to persons secondarily liable. A demand for payment; a personal or face-to-face demand accompanied by a readiness to make actual presentment or exhibition of the instrument and its surrender upon payment. 11 Am J2d B & N § 738.

presentment of bill of exchange. See **presentment for acceptance; presentment for payment.**

presentment of Englishry. A relic of the Conquest. In England, under Norman rule, Englishry was said to be presented when it was proved that a murdered man was an Englishman, and thus the county was saved from an amercement which otherwise would have been imposed upon it. See 4 Bl Comm 195.

present prices. As the term is used in a contract to purchase a commodity, the prices prevailing at the time of the making of the contract. Flash v Rossiter, 116 App Div 880, 102 NYS 449.

presents. See **these presents.**

present use. A new use of an old instrumentality. 40 Am J Pat § 45. A use immediately in existence so as to be operated upon forthwith by the statute of uses. 28 Am J2d Est §§ 340 et seq.

present value. The value under present conditions, as distinguished from the original cost. National Water Works v Kansas City (CA8 Mo) 62 F 853.

present worth. The value, to be ascertained by computation using a stated rate of assumed interest, of a sum to be paid in the future. Commissioner v State St. Trust Co. (CA1) 128 F2d 618, 142 ALR 943.
In reference to the allowance of damages for decreased earning capacity, the jury should be instructed that, in determining the amount of recovery for this item of damage, it should reduce

such damages to their present worth. 22 Am J2d Damg § 349.

preservation of self. See **self-preservation.**

preservative. A substance placed in foodstuff to enable it to resist decomposition or fermentation. 22 Am J2d Food § 46.

preserve. See **game preserve; private preserve.**

preserving tender. See **keeping tender good.**

presidential election. An election at which a President of the United States is elected, albeit indirectly by the election of presidential electors. 25 Am J2d Elect § 9.

presidential electors. Persons chosen at a presidential election, comprising what is known as the electoral college, each state being entitled to as many as the total number of United States Senators and Representatives of such state in the Congress, entitled to elect a President and Vice President of the United States but in actual practice voting in accord with the vote cast in their respective states.

president. A chief officer of many corporations, associations, and societies. The presiding officer at a meeting of a body.

presidential trade agreement. An agreement concluded between the President of the United States and the representatives of a foreign country, intended to promote trade between the two countries and usually containing conditions respecting the granting of tariff preferences. 21 Am J2d Cust D § 11.

president judge. The title in some states of the ranking judge of a court having two or more judges.

president of corporation. A corporate officer, having powers which vary according to statute or the charter and bylaws of the corporation, but who, in the absence of statute, charter, or bylaw to the contrary, is the general manager of corporate affairs with authority to act for the corporation in its business. 19 Am J2d Corp § 1169.

president of the council (of the koun'sil). A member of the king's council or cabinet having precedence next after the lord chancellor and the lord treasurer. See 1 Bl Comm 230.

President of the United States. The chief executive officer of the federal government, the executive power being vested in him by the Constitution of the United States. Article 2, § 1. That officer of the United States Government upon whom the Constitution has conferred the executive power of the government; whom it has made the commander-in-chief of the army and navy; whom it has authorized, by and with the consent of the senate, to make treaties, and to appoint ambassadors, ministers and consuls; and whose duty it has made to take care that the laws be faithfully executed. See 54 Am J1st U S § 36.

President's Committee on Equal Employment Opportunity. A federal agency charged with duties intended to prevent discrimination in employment because of race, creed, color, or national origin.

presiding judge. The judge who presides at the trial of a case. Tucker v Yandow, 100 Vt 169, 135 A 600, 601.

press. Verb: To insist; to importune; to force. Noun: A tool or instrument which applies pressure in an industrial operation. A form of punishment by torture. State v Woodward, 68 W Va 66, 69 SE 385. Newspapers and other publications considered collectively.

See **freedom of speech and of the press.**

press association. An organization engaged in gathering news of events occurring throughout the country and over the world and distributing reports thereof to newspapers. 39 Am J1st Newsp § 26.

press freedom. See **freedom of speech and of the press.**

pressing of seamen. See **impressment.**

pressure gauge. A gauge showing the pressure of steam in a boiler or of gas in a chamber.

prest (prest). Ready.

prestation (pres-tā'shon). A feudal rent paid by the tenant to the lord either in services or in the yield of the land.

presume. To assume. To take for granted, on the basis of human experience or of facts in evidence, although the precise thing assumed is not proved. Morford v Peck, 46 Conn 380, 385.

presumed bias. The bias of a juror conclusively presumed on account of his relation to a party or to the cause. United States v Wood, 299 US 123, 81 L Ed 78, 57 S Ct 177, reh den 299 US 624, 81 L Ed 459, 57 S Ct 319.

presumed compulsion. See **legal compulsion.**

Presumed Decedent's Act. A statute which provides for the disposition of the property of a person presumed dead because of an unexplained absence for a stated number of years. 1 Am J2d Absent § 3.

presumed dereliction (prē-zūmd' der-e-lik'shon). The doctrine that a thing is presumed to have been abandoned when it so appears by acts or circumstances, as when it is thrown away in any public place where it cannot be taken up, or where another is suffered to possess it without contradiction, or where possessory acts have long been abstained from. Rhodes v Whitehead, 27 Tex 304.

presumed grant. A theoretical basis of the acquisition of title by adverse possession or of a prescriptive right by adverse possession or adverse user. 3 Am J2d Adv P § 3; 25 Am J2d Ease § 39.

presumed malice. See **malice in law.**

presumitur pro reo (pre-zu'mi-ter prō re'ō). It is presumed in favor of the defendant. Culpepper v State, 4 Okla Crim 103, 111 P 679.

See **presumption of innocence.**

presumptio (pre-zump'she-ō). Same as **presumption.**

Presumptio, ex eo quod plerumque fit (prē-zump'she-ō, ex ē'ō quod ple-rum'kwe fit). A presumption arises from that which occurs many times. Post v Pearsall (NY) 22 Wend 425, 475.

presumptio juris et de jure (pre-zump'she-ō jū'ris et dē jū're). Same as **presumption de juris et de jure.**

presumption. A rule of law that attaches definite probative value to specific facts or draws a particular inference as to the existence of one fact, not actually known, arising from its usual connection with other particular facts which are known or proved. 29 Am J2d Ev § 160. The assumption or taking for granted of the existence of a fact, permitted or required under the law as a self-evident result of human reason and experience. Ward v Metropolitan Life Ins. Co. 66 Conn 227, 238, 33 A 902. An effect of an evidentiary fact from which the trier of fact must find the existence of another fact unless and until evidence is introduced which will support a finding of its nonexistence. UCC § 1-201(31). A rule of law attaching definite probative value to a specific fact, as distinguished from an inference which is a permissive conclusion by a trier of fact, unaided by any rule or theory of law directly applicable. People v Hillebrandt, 308 NY 397, 126 NE2d 377, 49 ALR2d 449; Stumpf v Montgomery, 101 Okla 257, 226 P 65, 32 ALR 1490, 1496.

See **conclusive presumption; conflicting presumptions; legal presumption; mixed presumption; presumption; rebuttable presumption; violent presumption.**

presumption juris et de jure (prē-zump'shǫn jū'ris et dē jū're). A presumption of law and from law; that is, a **conclusive presumption.**

presumption of access. The presumption of sexual intercourse between husband and wife having opportunity for intercourse. The presumption of access between husband and wife for sexual relations which prevails until the contrary is plainly proved. 10 Am J2d Bast § 12.

presumption of coition (of kō-i'shǫn). The presumption that married persons have co-habited. Whitney v Whitney, 169 Cal App 2d 209, 337 P2d 313.

presumption of death. The presumption that the death of a certain person has occurred, where his survival to the pertinent date is contrary to the ordinary course of nature, or opposed to the common experience of mankind. Young v Shulenberg, 165 NY 385, 59 NE 135. A presumption arising upon proof that a person disappeared and has not been heard of for a long period of time, usually 7 years, without explanation of the purpose or reason of his absence. 1 Am J2d Absent § 1. The presumption arising from the continued and unexplained absence of a person from his home or place of residence, without intelligence from or concerning him, for a period of seven years. 22 Am J2d Dth § 304.

presumption of fact. A logical and reasonable conclusion of the existence of a fact in a case, not presented by direct evidence as to the existence of the fact itself, but inferred from the establishment of other facts from which by the process of logic and reason, based upon human experience, the existence of the assumed fact may be concluded by the trier of the fact. 29 Am J2d Ev § 161. An inference arising from the commonly accepted experiences of mankind. Meares v Meares, 256 Ala 596, 56 So 2d 661.

presumption of guilt. An anomalous expression except as it be understood to mean something which authorizes but does not require conviction. 13 Am J2d Burgl § 54.

See **presumption of innocence.**

presumption of innocence. The presumption in a criminal prosecution that the accused is innocent until he is proved guilty, a presumption which places upon the state the burden of proof of guilt and, according to some authority, is of evidentiary value in favor of the accused. 29 Am J2d Ev §§ 225, 226. A presumption which applies, not only in criminal cases, but in civil cases where the commission of a crime is in issue. 29 Am J2d Ev § 224.

presumption of law. An assumption made by the law itself, compelling the court to a resulting conclusion, which may or may not have a logical or reasonable foundation in basic fact. 29 Am J2d Ev § 163. A presumption which derives its force from the law of the jursidiction, not from logic or probability as such, but is usually founded upon public policy, social convenience, and safety. Indianapolis v Keeley, 167 Ind 516, 79 NE 499.

There are two kinds of presumptions of law, irrebuttable or conclusive presumptions and rebuttable or disprovable presumptions. 29 Am J2d Ev § 163.

See **conclusive presumption; rebuttable presumption.**

presumption of law and fact. See **mixed presumption.**

presumption of legitimacy. The presumption that a child born in wedlock is legitimate. 10 Am J2d Bast § 11. The presumption that a child was born in lawful wedlock, such prevailing, in the absence of proof to the contrary, upon the broad principles of natural justice and the supposed virtue of the mother. 10 Am J2d Bast § 10.

presumption of marriage. The very strong presumption that a marriage, once shown, is legal and valid. 35 Am J1st Mar § 192. The presumption, where legitimacy is in issue, that the relations between a man and woman who produced offspring were lawful rather than meretricious. 10 Am J2d Bast § 10.

If a former marriage is necessary to sustain the presumption of legitimacy, such marriage will be assumed until proof to the contrary is forthcoming. Re Mathew's Estate, 153 NY 443, 47 NE 901.

presumption of paternity. The presumption that a child born in wedlock is the child of the husband, except as it be proved that the husband did not have access to the wife. 10 Am J2d Bast § 12.

See **presumption of access.**

presumption of payment. The presumption that a transfer of money or property by a debtor to the creditor is a payment of the debt rather than a gratuity. 40 Am J1st Paym § 238. The presumption that a debt evidenced by a writing has been paid where such written evidence is in the possession of the obligor. 40 Am J1st Paym § 240. The presumption, arising as a matter of convenience and of sound public policy, that after a great lapse of time between the creation of an obligation and an attempt to enforce it, usually twenty years but a lesser period in some jurisdictions, the debt is presumed to have been paid. 40 Am J1st Paym §§ 243 et seq.

presumption of regularity. The presumption, subject to rebuttal, that a public officer has performed his duty, acting in a regular and lawful manner. The rebuttable presumption that regulations, decisions, or orders of an administrative agency acting within the limits of the jurisdiction conferred upon it by law are regular and valid. 2 Am J2d Adm L § 748.

presumption of sanity. The presumption, holding until satisfactory proof to the contrary is presented, that a man is sane, capable of managing his own affairs, competent to enter into contracts, and capable of understanding the nature and effect of his own acts. 29 Am J2d Ev § 203. The presumption that every man is sane and fully competent until satisfactory proof to the contrary is presented; the presumption, in the absence of proof to the contrary, that a man is capable of understanding the nature and effects of his contracts, and that he comprehends the effect and result of legal proceedings. First Christian Church v McReynolds, 194 Or 68, 241 P2d 135.

presumption of survivorship. The presumption that a person shown to be alive at a given time remains alive until the contrary is shown by some sufficient

proof, or, in the absence of such proof, until a different presumption arises. 22 Am J2d Dth § 294.
As to survivorship as between persons who died in a common disaster, see 22 Am J2d Dth §§ 295 et seq.

presumptive. Founded upon or resting upon a presumption.

presumptive damages. Another term for punitive or exemplary damages. 22 Am J2d Damg § 236.

presumptive evidence. A term of variable meaning. Evidence to be considered as proof of a point unless rebutted. Circumstantial evidence; that is, evidence which shows the existence of one fact by proof of the existence of others from which the first may be inferred. State v Kornstett, 62 Kan 221, 61 P 805. Evidence which is not conclusive but subject to rebuttal or explanation.

presumptive heir. See **heir presumptive.**

presumptive title. A title appearing from nothing more than occupancy of the premises. The naked possession of a disseisor. 3 Am J2d Adv P § 236.

presumptive trust. Same as **resulting trust.**

pretenced (prē'tenst). Pretended.

pretended. Sham; fictitious; make-believe.

Pretended Title Statute (tī'tl stat'ūt). The statute 32 Henry VIII., c. 9, providing that no one shall sell or purchase any pretended right or title to land unless the vendor has received the profits thereof for one whole year before such grant, or has been in actual possession of the land, or of the reversion or remainder, on pain that both purchaser and vendor shall each forfeit the value of the land to the king and the prosecutor. See 4 Bl Comm 135.

pretense. See **false pretense; pretext.**

pretensed (prē-tenst'). Pretended.

preterition (pret-e-rish'on). (Civil law.) The failure of a testator to make some provision in his will for an heir who would be entitled to succeed to his estate or some portion of it in the absence of a will.

pretermission (prē-tėr-mish'on). The act of pretermitting. The condition of being pretermitted.
See **pretermit.**

pretermit (prē-tėr-mit'). To fail to take note of a person. To omit a person, particularly one's child from one's will. 57 Am J1st Wills § 573.

pretermitted child. See **pretermitted heir.**

pretermitted heir. One who as a child or descendant of another would have shared in the estate of the latter if the latter had died intestate but who is not named in or provided for by the will left by such ancestor.
As to statutes respecting right of pretermitted children, see 57 Am J1st Wills § 573.

pretext (prē'tekst). An ostensible reason or motive assigned or assumed as a color or cover for the real reason or motive; false appearance; pretense. State v Ball, 27 Neb 601, 604.

pretium (prē'shi-um). Price; value; reward; pay.

pretium affectionis (prē'shi-um a-fek-shi-ō'nis). The price or value of affection.
The term is applied to that rule for the estimation of damages for the loss of things having peculiar personal value to the owner, such as a family portrait or a pleasure yacht wherein the measure of damages is the actual value to the owner, taking into account its cost, the practicability and expense of replacing it, and such other considerations as in the particular case affect its value to the owner. The H. F. Dimock (CA1 Mass) 77 F 226, 233.

pretium feudi (pre'she-um fū'dī). The price of a fief or fee. See 4 Bl Comm 96.

pretium periculi (pre'she-um pe-ri'ku-lī). The price of peril or risk; the compensation paid or the charge made for assuming a marine insurance hazard.

Pretium succedit in locum rei (pre'she-um suk-sē'dit in lō'kum re'ī). The price or value of a thing takes the place of it.

pretor (prē'tor). Same as **praetor.**

pretorian prefect (prē-tor'i-an prē'fekt). See **praefectus praetorio.**

pretorium (prē-tō'ri-um). The official residence of a Roman praetor; a court room.

pretrial conference calendar. A court calendar, in addition to the trial calendar, listing the cases wherein a pretrial conference has been called and the time therefor. Union Oil Co. v Hanes, 27 Cal App 2d 106, 80 P2d 516; State ex rel. Kennedy v District Court, 121 Mont 320, 194 P2d 256, 2 ALR2d 1050.

pretrial deposition. See **deposition.**

pretrial discovery. See **discovery.**

pretrial procedure. Provision made by statute or rule of court for a conference between court and counsel to consider simplification of the issues, the necessity or desirability of amendment of the pleadings, the possibility of obtaining admissions to avoid unnecessary proof, limitation on the number of expert witnesses, a preliminary reference, and such other matters as may aid in the disposition of the action. 53 Am J1st Trial § 11. An informal proceeding before an administrative agency for the submission and consideration of facts, arguments, offers of settlement, and proposals of adjustment. 5 USC § 1004 (d).
See **deposition; discovery.**

prevailing party. The party who is successful or partially successful in an action, so as to be entitled to costs. 20 Am J2d Costs §§ 14, 15.
To be a prevailing party does not depend upon the degree of success at different stages of the suit; but upon whether at the end of the suit or other proceeding, the party, who has made a claim against the other, has successfully maintained it. If he has, he is the prevailing party. Bangor & Piscataquis Railroad Co. v Chamberlain, 60 Me 285, 286.

prevailing party on appeal. The party who obtains a reversal or a modification of judgment substantially favorable to him. 5 Am J2d A & E § 1015.
In eminent domain proceedings instituted by the state wherein an appeal is taken to the District Court from an award of the commissioners, the "prevailing party", entitled by statute to an award of costs and disbursements, is the litigant who prevails with respect to the particular issues raised and determined by the appeal, rather than the litigant who ultimately prevails in the condemnation proceeding. State v Miller Home Development, 243 Minn 1, 65 NW2d 900, 50 ALR2d 1377.

prevailing rate of wages. The wages received generally by those who are working at the same trade or occupation. People ex rel. Rolf v Coler, 58 App Div 347, 68 NYS 1101. The average, rather than the highest or lowest, wages paid for a legal day's work in the same trade or occupation. Anno: 93 ALR 1255.

prevailing wages. See **prevailing rate of wages.**

prevarication. A lie. (Civil law.) A breach of trust.

prevent. To hinder; to obstruct; to intercept.
 A person who is "induced" by means of representations or promises to delay a suit, is not thereby "prevented" from suing. Burr v Williams, 20 Ark 171, 185.

prevention. The act of preventing. The means of preventing. (Civil law.) The right of a judge to take cognizance of an action over which he has concurrent jurisdiction with another judge.
 See **writ of prevention.**

prevention of cruelty to animals. See **society for the prevention of cruelty to animals.**

preventive injunction. An injunction in the ordinary form, one directed against an act or acts, rather than one in the affirmative requiring the performance of an act. An injunction which commands the party against whom it is directed to refrain from doing a specified act or acts. Lakesville Woolen Mills v Spray Water Power & Land Co. 183 NC 511, 112 SE 24.

preventive justice. Requiring security to keep the peace. 12 Am J2d Breach P § 41. Any relief, such as an injunction, which prohibits or restrains certain acts.

preventive remedies. Those remedies in equity by which a violation of a primary right is prevented before the threatened injury is done, or by which the further violation is prevented after the injury has been partially effected, so that some other relief for the wrong actually accomplished can be granted.
 The injunction is a familiar example. See 1 Pomeroy's Equity Jurisprudence § 112.

previous. Prior; preceding; earlier in point of time; former.
 See words and phrases beginning **prior.**

previous chaste character. A familiar expression characterizing the victim of seduction.
 As the expression is used in the ordinary statutory definition of seduction under promise of marriage, as seducing and having illicit connection with an unmarried female of "previous chaste character," it does not mean purity of mind, nor purity of heart, but merely purity of body; that is, that the female has never sustained illicit relations with anyone prior to the alleged offense of the defendant. State v Holter, 32 SD 43, 142 NW 657.

previous experience. See **experience.**

previous indorsements guaranteed. See **prior indorsements guaranteed.**

previous insurance. See **other insurance; other insurance clause; prior application, rejection, or cancellation.**

previously. An adverb of time, used in comparing an act or state named, to another act or state, subsequent in order of time, for the purpose of asserting the priority of the first. Lebrecht v Wilcoxon, 40 Iowa 93, 94.

price. The consideration furnished or to be furnished by a buyer of property. 46 Am J1st Sales § 60; 55 Am J1st V & P § 23.
 The consideration for a sale, whether of personalty or realty. 46 Am J1st Sales § 60; 55 Am J1st V & P § 334. The consideration for services rendered. The amount charged or asked for property or services.

price book. A book carried by a traveling salesman, showing the current price for the merchandise he sells.

price control. The control and regulation by the government, state, or federal, of the prices at which commodities may be marketed. Charles Uhden, Inc. v Greenough, 181 Wash 412, 43 P2d 983, 98 ALR 1181. Relieving farmers from unfavorable economic conditions by maintaining a price for a farm product or products by government purchases, government loans, or a planned and accomplished reduction of acreage devoted to a particular crop or crops. 3 Am J2d Agri §§ 26, 27. The exercise of the war powers of Congress in providing an effective means for the control of prices of commodities, thus preventing unbridled price inflation. 56 Am J1st War § 39. The exercise of the legislative power in fixing prices of motor vehicles, particularly maximum-price allowances for used cars. 7 Am J2d Auto § 34. Partaking of a judicial nature in some aspects, of a legislative character in others. 1 Am J2d Admin L § 181.

price discrimination. Charging one customer more than another for the same article or service.
 Accepting the doctrine that it is unlawful for anyone engaged in interstate commerce to discriminate in price between customers, we would accept the further doctrine that selling to one at a price and refusing to sell to another at any price is a price discrimination, there being no other reason for the refusal to sell. The "one price" policy, although now accepted as sound, wise, and just is of comparatively recent adoption. It has however been written into the amendments to what we know as the Sherman Anti-Trust Act. Shaw's Inc. v Wilson-Jones Co. (DC Penn) 26 F 713.

price fixing. The product of an unlawful combination where perfected by an agreement between manufacturers or dealers to maintain specified prices. 36 Am J1st Monop etc. § 7.
 See **price control.**

price quotations. See **market quotations.**

Price v Neal. A case known for the doctrine that, as between equally innocent persons, the drawee who pays money on a check or draft the signature to which was forged cannot recover the money from the one who received it; in other words, a drawee who has paid a bill of exchange or check cannot recover the payment from a holder in good faith for value and without fault. 3 Burr 1354, 97 Eng Reprint 871.

pride gavel (prīd gav′el). A rent or tribute. —Wharton's Law Dictionary.

prier. See **age prier.**

priest. A clergyman, particularly a clergyman of the Roman Catholic or other Catholic Church.

Priestly v Fowler. An English Case sometimes said to have been the source of the doctrine of assumption of risk by an employee. 3 Mees & W 1, 150 Eng Reprint 1030, 19 ERC 102.

primae impressionis (prī′mē im-pre-she-ō′nis). Of first or novel impression; without a precedent; involving a point not previously decided.

prima facie (prī′mạ fā′shi-ē). At first sight. In reference to evidence, adequate as it appears, without more.

prima facie case (prī'mą fā'shi-ē kās). A case supported by sufficient evidence to warrant submission to the jury or trier of the fact and the rendition of a verdict or finding in accord therewith. A cause of action or defense sufficiently established by a party's evidence to justify a verdict in his favor, provided the other party does not rebut such evidence. Atlas Bank v Doyle, 9 RI 78.

prima facie evidence (prī'mą fā'shi-ē ev'i-dęns). Evidence which if unexplained or uncontradicted, is sufficient to carry the case to the jury and to sustain a verdict or finding in favor of the side of the issue which it supports, but which may be contradicted by other evidence. McKenzie v Standard Acci. Ins. Co. 198 SC 109, 16 SE2d 529

That is prima facie just, reasonable, or correct which is presumed to be just, reasonable, or correct until the presumption has been overcome by evidence which clearly rebuts it. Atchison, Topeka & Santa Fe Railway Co. v State, 23 Okla 210, 100 P 11.

prima facie presumption. A presumption which holds good until overthrown by proof; a rebuttable presumption; a presumption which is not conclusive.

primage (prī'mąj). A small compensation paid by a shipper to the master of a ship for his trouble and care bestowed on the shipper's goods and which the master is entitled to retain, in the absence of an agreement to the contrary with the owners of the vessel. Peters v Speights, 4 Md Ch 375, 381.

prima materia. See materia prima.

Prima pars aequitatis aequalitas (prī'ma parz ē-qui-tā'tis ē-qua'li-tās). The prime or foremost feature of equity is equality.

primaria ecclesia. (Latin.) The main or mother church of the faith.

primariae preces (prī-mā'ri-ē prē'sēz). First prayers or suits,—the imperial prerogative of the emperor of Rome whereby he always exercised the right of naming a person to fill the office of prebendary in the first prebend to become vacant after his accession. See 1 BL Comm 381.

primaries. See primary election.

primarily engaged. Substantially engaged in an enterprise, even though less than one half of one's time or efforts are expended upon it. Federal Reserve System v Agnew, 329 US 441, 91 L Ed 408, 67 S Ct 411.

primarily for sale to customers. An income-tax law term signifying property held by a dealer for sale to customers in the ordinary course of business. Anno: 46 ALR2d 639.

primarily liable. See primary liability.

primary. Adjective: First in order of time or development; original; preparatory to something higher. State of Indiana v Hirsch, 125 Ind 207, 24 NE 1062. Noun: Any convention, caucus, or meeting of voters, or a primary election, for choosing candidates for public office or selecting delegates to a convention.

See **primary election,** also words and phrases beginning "principal."

primary administrative jurisdiction. See primary jurisdiction doctrine.

primary boycott. A boycott applied directly and alone to the offending person by withdrawing from him all business relations on the part of the organization that initiated the boycott. Booker & Kinnaird v Louisville Board of Fire Underwriters, 188 Ky 771, 224 SW 451, 21 ALR 531. A combination to refrain from dealing with an employer, or to advise, or by peaceful means persuade, his regular customers to refrain. 31 Am J Rev ed Lab § 462.

primary cause. An efficient cause; a proximate cause. 38 Am J1st Negl § 50.

See **proximate cause.**

primary contract. A contract which has been superseded or modified by a later contract called the secondary contract. 17 Am J2d Contr § 459. A building or construction contract between the owner of the premises and a building contractor, as distinguished from a contract made by the latter in subletting a part of the work.

primary conveyance. See original conveyance.

primary easement. An easement to which a secondary easement is appendant, as an easement in a ditch attached to which there is a secondary easement of access over the servient premises for the purpose of cleaning out and repairing the ditch. Carson v Gentner, 33 Or 512, 52 P 506.

primary election. A nominating device of a political party; the selective mechanism by which the members of a political party express their preference in the selection of the party's candidates for public office. 25 Am J2d Elect § 148. An election conducted as a party affair for the selection of candidates to be placed on the official ballot at an election. Wagner v Gray (Fla) 74 So 2d 89.

primary evidence. The best evidence of which the case in its nature is susceptible. 29 Am J2d Ev § 448. That evidence which suffices for the proof of a particular fact until contradicted or overcome by other evidence. Cross v Baskett, 17 Or 84, 21 P 47.

primary franchise. The franchise of corporate existence; the result of a grant of special privileges to the incorporators which enables them to act for certain designated purposes as a single individual and exempts them, unless otherwise specially provided, from individual liability. 18 Am J2d Corp § 66.

primary jurisdiction. The power of a court to hear and adjudicate a case brought before it. State ex rel. Barker v Assurance Co. of America, 251 Mo 278, 158 SW 640.

primary jurisdiction doctrine. The principle that the courts can not or will not determine a controversy involving a question which is within the jurisdiction of an administrative tribunal, prior to the decision of that question by the administrative tribunal, (1) where the case demands the exercise of administrative discretion, requiring the special knowledge, experience, and services of the administrative tribunal, to determine technical and intricate matters of fact; and (2) where uniformity of ruling is essential to comply with the purposes of the regulatory statute administered. 2 Am J2d Admin L § 788.

primary legal right. A right with which the law invests a person and for the infringement of which he is entitled to a remedy. Granahan v Celanese Corp. of America, Plastics Div. 3 NJ 187, 69 A2d 572; Norwood v McDonald, 142 Ohio St 299, 27 Ohio Ops 240, 52 NE2d 67.

primary liability. The liability of the person who, by the terms of the instrument of obligation, is absolutely required to pay the same. 11 Am J2d B &

N § 525. The liability of a maker or principal, as distinguished from that of a guarantor, indorser, or other person under secondary liability. Winkle v Scott (CA8 Mo) 99 F2d 299. The liability of personal property, left by a decedent, for his debts before resorting to real estate, left by him, for the satisfaction of such obligations. 23 Am J2d Desc & D § 137. The liability of a person causing an injury to another who because of his relation to the injured person and the legal obligation to such person should bear the responsibility in damages rather than another person also liable to the injured person but under a different relationship and different character of legal obligation. Builders Supply Co. v McCabe, 366 Pa 322, 77 A2d 368, 24 ALR2d 319; Schaefer v Fond du Lac, 99 Wis 333, 341.

primary material. Raw material.

primary meeting. A political convention; an organized assemblage of electors or delegates representing a political party or principle.
 The usual purpose of such a meeting is the nomination of candidates to be voted for at a general election. Price v Lush, 10 Mont 61, 24 P 749.

primary negligence. The original, as distinguished from the subsequent, negligence of the defendant. 7 Am J2d Auto § 379.

primary obligation. An obligation imposed by law in consequence of a person's voluntary undertaking, or by the law on the ground of public policy or utility; as, for example to perform one's contract or to refrain from committing a trespass. See 8 Harvard L Rev 200.
 See **primary liability.**

primary patent. Same as **basic patent.**

primary powers. Main or principal powers, as distinguished from incidental, implied, or mediate powers.

primary purpose. The principal motivation for a course of conduct. State v Erickson, 44 SD 63, 182 NW 315, 13 ALR 1189.

primary receivership. A receivership to which another receivership, usually in another jurisdiction, is ancillary. 45 Am J1st Rec § 420.

prima seisina (prī'mā sē'zi-na). Same as **primer seisin.**

primate (prī'māt). One of the most highly developed animals; ape or man. (Ecclesiastical.) A presiding archbishop in the Church of England.

prima tonsura (prī'ma ton-sū'ra). The first cutting,— the right to the first crop.

prime. First class. First in quality.

prime (pr ī'ma). (French.) Premium. Bonus.

prime minister. In a parliamentary system, such as that in Great Britain, the head of the government, subject to the will of parliament.

primer (prī'mėr). (French.) To lead. To surpass.

primer election (prī'mėr ē-lek'shọn). The first choice; the first selection.

primer fine. A sum which by ancient prerogative was due the king upon the suing out of the writ or praecipe at the commencement of a suit to levy a fine.
 This sum was a noble for every five marks of land sued for; that is, one tenth of the annual value. See 2 Bl Comm 350.

primer seisin (sē'zn). A feudal burden, only incident to the king's tenants in capite, and not to those who held of inferior or mesne lords.
 It was a right which the king had, when any of his tenants in capite died seised of a knight's fee, to receive of the heir, provided he was of age, one whole year's profits of the lands, if they were in immediate possession; and half a year's profits, if the lands were in reversion expectant on an estate for life. See 2 Bl Comm 66.

primes. See **en primes.**

prime serjeant. Same as **premier serjeant.**

primis. See **in primis.**

primitiae (prī-mish'i-ē). First fruits; the first year's profits of a clergyman's benefice, which were claimed by and went to the pope. See 2 Bl Comm 67.

Primo excutienda est verbi vis, ne sermonis vitio obstruatur oratio, sive lex sine argumentis (prī'mō ex-kū-she-en'da est ver'bī vis, ne ser-mō'nis vi'she-ō ob-stru-ā'ter o-rā'she-ō, sī've lex sī'ne ar-gu-men'-tis). The force of a word should be weighed in the beginning, lest the sentence be stifled by the fault of expression or the law be without reason.

primogeniture (prī-mọ-jen'i-tụr). The condition or state of the child who is the first born. The principle of descent of real estate to the eldest son of the decedent. 23 Am J2d Desc & D § 6.

primogenitus (prī-mọ-jen'i-tus). The child first born.

primo venienti (prī'mō ve-ni-en'tī). To the first person who comes.

Primum coram comitibus et viatoribus obviis, deinde in proxima villa vel pago, postremo coram ecclesia vel judicio (prī'mum kō'ram ko-mi'ti-bus et vī-a-tō'ri-bus ob'vi-is, dē'in-de in pro'xi-ma vil'la vel pā'gō, pos-trē'mō kō'ram e-klē'si-a vel jū-di'she-ō). First before the inhabitants and the casual travelers, then in the nearest town or village, lastly before the church or court house. See 1 Bl Comm 297.

primum decretum (prī'mum de-krē'tum). A preliminary or provisional decree which was granted in ecclesiastical and admiralty suits.

primus inter pares (prī'mus in'tėr pā'rēz). First among one's peers or equals.

prince. A ruler; a sovereign. As in Great Britain, the son of a king or queen. In a democracy, a person of eminence, a person of quality, an engaging personality.

prince consort (kon'sōrt). The husband of a reigning queen, as Prince George of Denmark was to Queen Anne. See 1 Bl Comm 222.

Prince of Wales. The oldest son of a British sovereign and, as such, first in line of succession.

princeps (prin'seps). (Civil law.) A chief; a leader; a prince; a ruler; the Roman emperor.

Princeps et respublica ex justa causa possunt rem meam auferre (prin'seps et rēs-pub'li-ka ex jus'ta kā'za pos'sunt rem me'am â-fer're). The sovereign and the state can take away my property for a justifiable cause.

Princeps legibus solutus est (prin'seps lē'ji-bus so-lū'tus est). The ruler or sovereign is exempt from the law.

principal. Adjective: Of first importance. In the first rank. Noun: The head of a high school or grade school. The amount of an original indebtedness as distinguished from interest accruing. The corpus of an estate in property. In an agency relationship, the person for whom another acts and from whom he derives authority to act. 3 Am J2d Agency § 1. In bail and recognizance:—the person released on bail. 8 Am J2d Bail § 1. The party to a suretyship who enters into the main contract with the obligee, the one who is directly interested in and benefited by the main contract, and the one to whom or from whom the consideration for the main obligation flows. 50 Am J1st Suret § 3. In guaranty, the person whose obligation is covered by the undertaking of the guarantor. 24 Am J1st Guar § 29. In crime:— one actually or constructively present, and abetting the commission of the offense, that is, doing some act at the time of the commission of the crime that is in furtherance of the offense. 21 Am J2d Crim L § 120.

Under Federal statutes, he who, in the commission of an illegal act with others, such as maintaining an illicit still, conducting a burglary or a holdup, arms and instructs his confederates to kill if obstructed in the attempt, with the purpose and intent that they do so, is in law a principal in any wilful killing which results from carrying out those instructions. Young v United States (CA5 Tex) 97 F2d 200. See, also **principal D**, 1010.

principal action. An action in which or from which an auxiliary, ancillary, or provisional remedy develops or arises.

principal administration. The administration of the estate of a decedent in the jurisdiction of his domicil, as distinguished from ancillary administration in another jurisdiction where there are assets left by the decedent which require administration. 31 Am J2d Ex & Ad § 681.

principal cause. See **challenge for principal cause.**

principal challenge. See **challenge for principal cause.**

principal contract (kon'trakt). A contract entered into by the principals themselves, as distinguished from a contract in which one or both or all the principals are represented by an agent, or by agents.

principal contractor. The contractor standing in direct relation to the owner and responsible to him, but ordinarily permitted by the nature of his contract to perform the contract by subletting to others, if he sees fit. 36 Am J1st Mech L § 51.

principal debt. The original debt, as distinguished from liability enhanced by accruing interest. The primary liability. The obligation of a principal in a transaction. The obligation of a principal debtor, as distinguished from the obligation of his surety, guarantor, or indemnitor. An indebtedness or liability, as distinguished from a promise to pay such indebtedness or liability. London & San Francisco Bank v Bandmann, 120 Cal 220, 52 P 583.

See **primary liability; principal.**

principal debtor. A debtor whose obligation is covered by a guaranty or contract of suretyship.

principal defendant. The defendant in an action as distinguished from a debtor served with a notice of garnishment in the action.

principal employment or business. The occupation or business on which the debtor chiefly relies for a livelihood, and which engrosses most of his time and attention, not for a day, a week, or a month, but throughout the year. Smalley v Masten, 8 Mich 529.

principal fact. The main or chief fact at issue in a cause.

principal in first degree. One who commits a criminal act either in person or through an innocent agent. State v Wilson, 235 Iowa 538, 17 NW2d 138; State v Minton, 234 NC 716, 68 SE2d 844, 31 ALR2d 682; Red v State, 39 Tex Crim 667, 47 SW 1003.

principal in second degree. One present at the commission of a criminal act, lending countenance, aid, encouragement, or other mental assistance, while another commits the act. Red v State, 39 Tex Crim 667, 47 SW 1003. One present at the time a crime is committed, lending countenance, aid, or encouragement, or one keeping watch at some convenient distance while another person performs the actual criminal act. Brown v Commonwealth, 130 Va 733, 107 SE 809.

principalis (prin-si-pā'lis). A principal.

Principalis debet semper excuti antequam perveniatur ad fideijussores (prin-si-pā'lis de'bet sem'per ex-kū'tī an'te-quam per-ve-ni-ā'ter ad fī-de"i-jus-sō'rēz). The principal debtor should always be exhausted before resort is had against the sureties.

principally engaged. See **principal employment or business.**

principal meridian. A north and south line, running as any meridian of longitude, established and numbered in connection with the government survey of public lands for the purpose of numbering townships laid out by the survey, a township being given a range number according to the tier of townships in which it appears east or west of such meridian, which number, taken in connection with a number similarly recognized in reference to an east and west or base line, serves to locate the township in the vast area surveyed. Meas v Whitener-London Realty Co. 119 Ark 301, 178 SW 390.

See **base line; range.**

principal obligation. See **principal debt.**

principal office. The principal place of business of a corporation, the activities of which extend over a wide area, sometimes over state lines, even into foreign countries. 18 Am J2d Corp § 160.

principal officer or agent. An agent of a foreign corporation upon whom service of process may be made in an action against the corporation; a chief officer or agent. 36 Am J2d For Corp § 556.

principal place of business. The criterion of the residence or nonresidence of a corporation. 36 Am J2d For Corp § 38. As a venue for the adjudication of a debtor in bankruptcy, the place where the debtor's personal business affairs are conducted, notwithstanding his principal income is from a business conducted elsewhere. Re Knox (CA6 Tenn) 11 F2d 743.

The principal place of business of a corporation is that place which has been designated by the corporation in compliance with, and in the manner prescribed by, statute. That place is often the principal or main office of the company in the case of a domestic corporation, but obviously the principal place of business as here defined is not necessarily the office of the corporation. State v Vincent, 144 Wash 246, 257 P 849.

Principia data sequuntur concomitantia (prin-si'pi-a da'ta se-qu-un'ter kon-kom-i-tan'she-a). The principles given, the concomitants follow.

Principia probant, non probantur (prin-si'pi-a pro'-bant, non pro-ban'ter). Principles prove; they are not proved.

Principiis obsta (prin-si'pi-is ob'stā). Oppose or withstand beginnings; nip trouble in the bud.

principio. See **in principio.**

Principiorum non est ratio (prin-si-pi-ō'rum non est rā'she-ō). A reason for principles does not exist; there is no reason for principles.

principium (prin-sip'ī-um). The beginning; the outset.

Principium est potissima pars cujusque rei (prin-si'pi-um est po-tis'si-ma parz kū-jus'kwe re'ī). The beginning is the strongest part of anything.

principium et fons (prin-si'pi-um et fonz). The origin and source.

principle. The cause, source, or origin of anything; that from which a thing proceeds, as the principle of motion, the principles of action; ground, foundation, that which supports an assertion, an action, or a series of actions, or of reasoning; a general truth; a law comprehending many subordinate truths; as the principles of morality, of law, of government. People v Stewart, 7 Cal 140, 143.

print. See **printing.**

printed form. See **form.**

printed matter. See **printing.**

printed scroll (skrōl). The common modern and valid form of a seal. 47 Am J1st Seals § 4.

printing. Putting words, figures, or characters on paper by the use of type and ink. Arthur v Moller, 97 (US) 7 Otto 365, 24 L Ed 1046, 1047; Forbes Lithograph Mfg. Co. v Worthington, 132 US 655, 660, 33 L Ed 453, 454, 10 S Ct 180. Writing in letters used in printing rather than in the script of ordinary handwriting.

prior. Preceding. Having precedence.
See expressions which follow, beginning "prior;" also expressions beginning "former" or "previous."

prior acquittal. See **prior jeopardy.**

prior action pending. See **pendency of action; pending action; plea of another action pending.**

prior adjudication. A previous judgment in which the same matter in a dispute between the same parties was, or might have been put in issue and tried. Cromwell v Sac County (US) 4 Otto 351, 24 L Ed 195.
See **res judicata.**

prior application, rejection, or cancellation. A matter of information sought by an insurance company of an applicant for insurance respecting prior history of his experience in obtaining or being rejected for insurance.

prior appropriation. The doctrine which prevails in some American jurisdictions that the person who first diverts and applies to a beneficial use the waters of a stream of public right has a prior right of continued use to the extent of his appropriation. Wyoming v Colorado, 259 US 419, 66 L Ed 999, 42 S Ct 552. The doctrine of the western states concerning the use of water for irrigation. 30 Am J Rev ed Irrig § 18.

prior conviction. As a prerequisite to punishment as a subsequent offender, a conviction which denotes the establishment of guilt according to some legal mode, whether it be by judgment on plea or verdict. 25 Am J1st Habit Cr § 10.
See **prior jeopardy.**

prior decision. See **precedent.**

prior equity. A superior equity required as a condition of equitable relief. Jefferson County v McGrath, 205 Ky 484, 266 SW 29, 41 ALR 586.

prior estate. See **preceding estate.**

priori. See **a priori.**

prior indorsements guaranteed. A guaranty of the genuineness of the indorsements and no more. Johnston v Schnabaum, 86 Ark 82, 109 SW 1163.

Prior in tempore, potior in jure (prī'or in tem'po-re, pō'she-or in jū're). First in time, superior in right. He has the better title who was first in point of time. See Broom's Legal Maxims 353.

priority. The attribute or quality of that which is earlier or previous in point of time. Precedence. Of lien:—a superiority of security over other liens either in point of time or as declared by law from considerations of public policy. Of claim:—the right to have one's claim against a decedent's estate satisfied out of estate assets before other claimants are permitted to resort to such assets, 21 Am J1st Ex & Ad §§ 393 et seq; the status of a claim in insolvency proceedings which calls for payment of it before any payment is made on other claims, 29 Am J Rev ed Insolv §§ 46 et seq; in bankruptcy, distribution in order determined by classes of debts of funds not subject to lien in the hands of the trustee in bankruptcy as assets of the estate in bankruptcy. 9 Am J2d Bankr § 528.
See **preference.**

priority of attachment. Priority of an attachment in reference to another attachment of the same property, as determined by order of levy or by order of issuance of the writs. 6 Am J2d Attach § 468. The priority of an attachment in reference to other liens. 6 Am J2d Attach §§ 464 et seq.

priority of exercise. The principle that in a case of concurrent jurisdiction, the court which first exercises jurisdiction acquires exclusive jurisdiction to proceed further in the case. Scott v Industrial Acci. Com. 46 Cal 2d 76, 293 P2d 18.

prior jeopardy (prī'or jep'är-di). A defense, otherwise known as double jeopardy or former jeopardy, based upon a provision of the United States Constitution found in the Fifth Amendment or a similar provision of a state constitution, deriving from a principle of the common law that a man shall not be brought into danger of his life or limb more than once for one and the same offense; a rule prohibiting a second punishment for the same offense and, as well, a second trial for the same offense. 21 Am J2d, Crim L § 165.
The test is not whether the defendant has already been tried for the same act, but whether he has been put in jeopardy for the same offense. See Gavieres v United States, 220 US 338, 55 L Ed 489, 31 S Ct 421.
See **identity of offenses.**

prior lien. See **priority.**

prior losses. A matter of information sought by an insurance company of an applicant for insurance respecting the experience of the applicant in reference to losses of his property covered by insurance.

prior mortgage. A mortgage entitled to satisfaction out of the mortgaged property before other liens or mortgages on such property are to be satisfied.
See **priority.**

prior negligence. Negligence so remote from the time of the injury as not to constitute a proximate cause. Holwerson v St. Louis & Suburban Railway Co. 157 Mo 216, 57 SW 770.

prior petens (prī'or pe'tenz). The first applicant; the earlier claimant. A plaintiff who sues first, that is, before the defendant sues him. Conant v Conant, 10 Cal 239, 245.

Prior possessio cum titulo posteriore melior est priore titulo sine possessione (prī'or po-ze'she-ō kum ti'tu-lō pos-te-ri-ō're me'li-or est prī-ō're ti'tu-lō sī'ne po-ze-she-ō'ne). Prior possession with subsequent title is better than prior title without possession.

prior recovery. See **prior adjudication.**

Prior tempore, potior jure (prī'or tem'po-re, pō'she-or jū're). First in time, superior in right.

prior tenant. Same as **casual ejector.**

prior testimony. Testimony given at a former trial, admitted under an exception to the hearsay rule upon a showing of necessity arising from the death or incompetency of the witness or his unavailability for the instant case, provided certain conditions such as identity of parties and issues, opportunity for cross examination in the former case, an authenticity of reproduction are met. 21 Am J2d Crim L § 343; 29 Am J2d Ev §§ 738 et seq.

prior title. A title which will prevail in law or equity as against another asserted title, lien, or interest.

prior use principle. The rule that property devoted to a public use is not subject to condemnation under the power of eminent domain for the same use, since no public use or public necessity can be served by such a taking. 26 Am J2d Em D § 93.

priory (prī'or-i). A religious house presided over by a prior and next in dignity after an abbey.

prisage (prī'zāj). The king's right to share in a prize; his right of taking two tons of wine from every ship importing into England 20 tons or more.
Under Edward I, this was changed into a duty of 2s. for every ton imported by merchant strangers and called butlerage, because paid to the king's butler. See 1 Bl Comm 315.

prise (prīz). A capture, but not necessarily a lawful taking by a belligerent in a lawful war. Dole v New England Mut. Marine Ins. Co. 88 Mass (6 Allen) 373, 388.
See **prize.**

prisel en auter lieu (prē-sel ôn ō-tā lyuh). A taking in another place.

priso (prī'zō) A prison; a prisoner; a prisoner of war.

prison. A generic term comprising places maintained by public authority for the detention of persons confined under legal process, whether criminal or civil, and whether the imprisonment is for the purpose of insuring the production of the prisoner to answer in future legal proceedings, or whether it is for the purpose of punishment for an offense of which the prisoner has been duly convicted and sentenced. 41 Am J1st Pris & P § 2.

prison bounds. See **liberties of the jail.**

prison breach. A criminal offense, at common law and by statute in some jurisdictions, in breaking from prison with or by the exertion of force, in contrast to an escape by stratagem. Anno: 96 ALR2d 525-527, §§ 6-8.

prison breaking. Same as **prison breach.** 27 Am J2d Escape § 2.

prisoner. A person deprived of his liberty by virtue of a judicial or other lawful process. 41 Am J1st Pris & P § 2.

prisoner of war. A person who has been captured by hostile troops while engaged in warfare and who is held by them as a prisoner.

prison rule. A rule whereunder the conduct of a prisoner is regulated and controlled.
See **liberty of the rules.**

prisoner's domicil. See **domicil of a prisoner,** supra.

prison warden. See **warden.**

prist (prist). **Ready.**

Prius vitiis laboravimus, nunc legibus (prī'us vi'she-is lā-bo-ra'vi-mus, nunk lē'ji-bus). First we labored with the vices, now with the laws.

privacy. The right to be left alone, that is, to be free from unwarranted publicity and to live without unwarranted interference by the public in matters with which the public is not necessarily concerned. Prents v Morgan, 221 Ky 765, 299 SW 967, 55 ALR 964. The so-called right, founded upon the claim that a man has the right to pass through this world, if he wills, without having his picture published, his business enterprises discussed, his successful experiments written up for the benefit of others, or his eccentricities commented upon either in handbills, circulars, catalogues, periodicals, or newspapers; and, necessarily, that the things which may not be written and published of him must not be spoken of him by his neighbors, whether the comment be favorable or otherwise. Roberson v Rochester Folding Box Co. 171 NY 538, 64 NE 442. The right of a person to demand that his private affairs be not scrutinized in public without his consent. Annos: 138 ALR 22; 168 ALR 446; 14 ALR2d 750. A right premised upon the individual's right to the pursuit of happiness. Barsky v United States, 83 App DC 127, 167 F2d 241, cert den 334 US 843, 92 L Ed 1767, 68 S Ct 1511, reh den 339 US 971, 94 L Ed 1379, 70 S Ct 1001. An independent legal right of the individual, the violation of which constitutes a tort. 41 Am J1st Priv § 2.
The theory that everyone has a right to privacy, and that the same is a personal right growing out of the inviolability of the person. The right to one's person may be said to be a right of complete immunity, to be let alone. That a person is entitled to relief at law or in equity for an invasion of this right, is generally understood to have been first publicly advanced in an article entitled "The Right to Privacy," in 4 Harvard Law Review, 193 (December, 1890), wherein some of the necessities for involving such relief are set out. Henry v Cherry, 30 RI 13, 73 A 97.

private. Adjective: Belonging to an individual or group of persons. Not for the public or open to the public. Noun: An enlisted man in the Army of the lowest, or next to the lowest, rank.

private act. A statute which is confined in operation and effect to particular individuals, associations, or corporations, not affecting the community at large, and must be pleaded and proved by a party who relies upon it. 50 Am J1st Stat § 12.

private alley. A narrow way not open to public use, the use being confined legally to a certain owner or owners of property. 25 Am J1st High § 8.

private attorney. Same as **attorney in fact.** Hall v Sawyer (NY) 47 Barb 116, 119.

private bank. An unincorporated bank. 10 Am J2d Banks § 13.

private banker. The proprietor of an unincorporated bank. A person or firm engaged in receiving deposits, discounting commercial paper, selling bills of exchange, and doing a banking business without special privileges or authority from the state. Perkins v Smith, 116 NY 441, 446, 23 NE 21. A person or firm engaged in the banking business under authorization by the state, subject to the general requirements of supervision and inspection. Ex parte Wisner, 36 Mont 298, 92 P 958.

According to most authorities, the legislature may prohibit all private banking and restrict the right to conduct a banking business to corporations. The term "bank" as used in some statutes does not include a private banker. 10 Am J2d Banks § 13.

private bill office. An office in the British parliament where private acts are framed.

private boarding house. See **boarding house.**

private bonded warehouse. A bonded warehouse but under bond only for the storing of such merchandise as shall belong or be consigned to the owner or proprietor. 19 USC § 1555.
See **bonded warehouse.**

private capacity. The capacity in which a municipal corporation operates where not engaged as an arm of the state in a governmental capacity. The capacity in which a municipal corporation operates where it enters into the business of furnishing water, lights, power and sewerage, or passenger transportation by streetcar. J. B. McCrary Co. v Winnfield (DC La) 40 F Supp 427.

private car. A railroad passenger car owned or engaged by a certain person or persons only.

private carrier. One who transports only for those with whom he sees fit to contract. Ace High Dresses v J. C. Trucking Co. 122 Conn 578, 191 A 536, 112 ALR 86. One who, without making it a vocation, or holding himself out to the public as ready to act for all who desire his services, undertakes, by special agreement in a particular instance only, to transport property or persons from place to place either gratuitously or for hire. 13 Am J2d Car § 8.
See **contract carrier by motor vehicle.**

private carrier by motor vehicle. A carrier who is neither a common carrier or a contract carrier by motor vehicle but which transports property of which it is the owner, lessee, or bailee for the purpose of sale, rent, or bailment, or in furtherance of a commercial enterprise. Interstate Commerce Com. v A. W. Stickle & Co. (DC Okla) 41 F Supp 268 (definition in § 305(a) of the Motor Vehicle Carrier Act of 1935).

private cemetery. A cemetery devoted to one family or a small part of the community. 14 Am J2d Cem § 2.

private college or university. A college or university supported by private funds or privately endowed. 15 Am J2d Colleges § 2.

The fact that a private institution of learning receives aid from the state or federal government does not of itself make it a public corporation. 15 Am J2d Colleges § 2.

private communication. See **privileged communication.**

private convenience yields to the convenience of the public. An equitable principle. North Hill Memorial Gardens v Hicks, 230 Ark 787, 326 SW2d 797.

private corporation. A corporation created for private as distinguished from purely public purposes. Miller v Davis, 136 Tex 299, 130 SW2d 973, 136 ALR 177.

The character of a corporation as public or private is determined by the terms of its charter and the general law under which it was organized, not upon the character of its stockholders or the number of persons engaged in the enterprise. Macon County Tel. Co. v Bethany Mut. Tel. Asso. 270 Ill 183, 110 NE 334.

private court. Not at all a court in the usual and proper sense of the term; merely a body set up by a private organization for its internal purposes. State ex rel. Henderson v Boone County Court, 50 Mo 317.

private credit to seal. See **seals of private credit.**

private crossing. An overhead crossing erected and maintained by a private person for passageway across a highway. 25 Am J1st High § 295. A passage across, under, or over a railroad track running across a farm, for the use and convenience of the proprietor or tenant of the farm. Wheeler v Rochester & Syracuse Railroad Co. (NY) 12 Barb 227, 230.

private duty. A duty owed by an individual under particular circumstances. The duty of a municipality operating in a private capacity.
See **private capacity.**

private dwelling. A dwelling house. A room or rooms used and occupied, not transiently, but as a residence, in an apartment house, hotel, or boarding house. Carroll v United States, 267 US 132, 143, 69 L Ed 543, 547, 45 S Ct 280 (definition in statute establishing National Prohibition).

private dwelling house. A dwelling house for a single family. 20 Am J2d Cov § 196.

A majority of courts have reached the conclusion that the term when used in a restrictive covenant prohibits the use of property for a duplex or double house. Anno: 14 ALR2d 1395.

private easement. An easement which confers a benefit upon certain individuals only.
See **private way.**

private eleemosynary corporation (el-ḝ-mos′i-nạ-ri kôr-pō-rā′shọn). A corporation created for the administration of a public or private charity, the endowments of which have been received from individuals. 15 Am J2d Char § 43.

private enterprise. Cultivating the soil, manufacturing articles for sale, dealing in merchandise, and the pursuit of numerous and various other activities which enlist individual energy. Dodge v Mission Tp. (CA8 Kan) 107 F 827. In the language of the ultraconservative, something undefiled by governmental regulation or participation.

As used in a provision of a state constitution forbidding the state to be interested in any "private or corporate enterprise," the term has been held not merely to forbid the state to become interested in private enterprise carried on by individuals and corporations, but also to prohibit the state from itself engaging in private enterprises ordinarily undertaken only by private promoters. State ex rel. Wilkinson v Murphy, 237 Ala 332, 186 So 487, 121 ALR 283.

privateer (prī-vā̱-tēr'). A private armed vessel commissioned by a belligerent to capture vessels of the enemy. 56 Am J1st War § 169. A vessel owned and manned by private persons, acting under a commission or letters of marque from a recognized government, and equipped to plunder the maritime commerce of the enemy of the country granting the commission. 41 Am J1st Pir § 2.

privateering. Operating a vessel as a privateer. 41 Am J1st Pir § 2.
See **privateer.**

private ferry. The means maintained by individuals for personal use in crossing a stream.
Such a ferry is mainly for the use of the owner, and although he may take pay for ferriage, he does not follow it as a business. His ferry is not open to the public at its demand. He may, or may not keep it going. 35 Am J2d Ferr § 2.

private first class. An enlisted man of the Army, ranking immediately above a private.

private function. The function of a municipal corporation in the exercise of powers conferred upon it, not primarily or chiefly from considerations connected with the government of the state at large, but for the private advantage of the compact community which is incorporated as a distinct legal personality, particularly the function in reference to the property or contracts of the municipality. 37 Am J1st Mun Corp § 114. In a broader sense, any activity in a private as distinguished from a public capacity.
See **private capacity; private enterprise.**

private gain. A gain accruing to the benefit of an individual, not to the benefit of the public or of a charity.
Under Federal statute exempting the property of educational institutions from taxation in the District of Columbia, provided the property is not used for private gain, as so used, the term has reference only to gain realized by any individual or stockholder who has a pecuniary interest in the corporation, and not to profits realized by the institution, but turned back into the treasury or expended for permanent improvements. District of Columbia v Mt. Vernon Seminary, 69 App DC 251, 100 F2d 116.

private garage. A building or structure appurtenant to a private residence or apartment house, etc., designed for the housing or storage of a motor vehicle by the owner, tenant, or other person. Anno: 61 ALR 312.

private injury. See **private wrong.**

private international law. The subject of conflict of laws, that which regulates the comity of states in giving effect in one to the municipal laws of another relating to private persons, or concerns the rights of persons within the territory and dominion of one state or nation, by reason of acts, private or public, done within the dominion of another, being based on the broad general principle that one state or country will respect and give effect to the laws of another so far as can be done consistently with its own interests. 16 Am J2d Confl L § 1.

privately stealing. Committing larceny from the person by picking pocket, cutting away a purse, etc. Larceny in taking property directly from the person of the owner, as by snatching it from his hands, albeit the taking is in a public place. 32 Am J1st Larc § 44.

private market. An anomaly since any market, as properly defined, is public in character. 35 Am J1st Mark & M § 2. A market kept by an individual for his personal use and advantage, without letting out of stalls to others. State v Natal, 41 La Ann 887, 890, 6 So 722.

private motor carrier. See **private carrier.**

private nuisance. A nuisance which threatens injury to one or a few persons. McFarlane v Niagara Falls, 247 NY 340, 160 NE 391, 57 ALR 1. A nuisance which violates only private rights and produces damages to one or to no more than a few persons. Riggins v District Court, 89 Utah 183, 51 P2d 645.
See **nuisance.**

private passenger automobile. An automobile kept for use by the owner or members of his family, not for carrying passengers for hire as a business. A four wheeled vehicle; a vehicle other than a motorcycle. Paupst v McKendry, 187 Pa Super 646, 145 A2d 725.
See **passenger motor vehicle.**

private pass way. See **private way.**

private person. An individual who acts as such, as distinguished from one who acts officially or on behalf of the public.

private pond. A pond above land privately owned and subject to private control only.
To fall within the meaning of the term, the pond must be essentially private. It must be a sheet of water covering exclusively the land of its owner, and must be such as no one could forbid him its use, any more than the cultivation of the soil underneath, if it was free from water. A body of water covering 1040 acres, 1000 acres of which covers land of one owner and forty acres of which covers the land of an adjoining owner, is not a private pond. Peters v State, 96 Tenn 682, 36 SW 399.
For cases holding certain ponds or lakes to be private, see Anno: 15 ALR2d 755.

private powers. The powers of a municipality exercised for the advantage of the inhabitants of the municipality as such, and of itself as a legal personality, not powers exercised in a governmental capacity as a political subdivision of the state. Winona v Botzet (CA8 Minn) 169 F 321.
See **private capacity.**

private preserve. An area set apart on one's own premises as a game or fish preserve. A natural or artificial pond for the culture of fish, privately owned and maintained. State v Theriault, 70 Vt 617, 41 A 1030.
See **game preserve.**

private property. The property of a person as distinguished from the property of a government or a governmental body. Inclusive of property privately owned, although devoted to a public purpose. 42 Am J1st Prop § 12.
See **right of private property.**

private prosecutor. One appointed to assist the state in a particular criminal case or requested to appear by the regular prosecutor. 24 Am J1st Grand J § 43.
See **relator.**

private publication. See **limited publication.**

private purpose. A building up of a private fortune; the redress of a private wrong; the improvement of private property; the promotion of private enterprise, except where such is incident to the public benefit. 51 Am J1st Tax § 321.

private railroad. A railroad confined to the transportation of one's own property, not open to public use.
See **private track.**

private residence. A residence for one family only. Anno: 18 ALR 460.
See **private dwelling house.**

private right of way. The privilege which one person or particular class of persons have of passing over the land of another in some particular line. 25 Am J2d Ease § 7.
See **private way.**

private rights. Rights which a person is entitled to exercise as an individual, such as ownership and enjoyment of property, the right to travel, to communicate, privacy, etc. Such rights, when applied to property, as persons may possess unconnected with, and not essentially affecting, the public interest, or growing out of a public institution of society. Rugh v Ottenheimer, 6 Or 231.

private road. A road maintained and open on one's own premises for his own use, the use of his tenant, or the use of their licensees, invitees, or guests; not open to the public. A road which, although public in the sense of being open to use by the public, actually subserves the convenience of such a limited number of persons that it falls within a separate classification in respect to establishment, maintenance, and repair. Sherman v Buick, 32 Cal 242, 252.
See **private railroad; private track; private way.**

private sale. A sale negotiated and completed otherwise than by auction upon notice. 30 Am J2d Exec § 342; 31 Am J2d Ex & Ad §§ 343, 378, 445; 30A Am J Rev ed Jud S § 67.

private school. A school organized and maintained by a private person or corporation. State v Counort, 69 Wash 361, 124 P 910. A school organized and managed by individuals, and not by the public as an institution of the state. Livingston v Davis, 243 Iowa 21, 50 NW2d 592, 27 ALR2d 1237.
As to what constitutes "private school" within statute making attendance at such a school compliance with compulsory school attendance law, see Anno: 14 ALR2d 1369.

private secretary. A person employed for the rendition of services for one or a few persons, as distinguished from one employed to render services, as such may be required, for any executive, manager, officer, or employee of a business. A "laborer" for the purposes of an exemption from execution. Abrahams v Anderson, 80 Ga 570, 5 SE 778.

private session. A hearing or investigation by an administrative agency not open to the public. 2 Am J2d Admin L §§ 229, 258. A hearing in chambers. A session of court during which the public is excluded from the courtroom by order of the court. 24 Am J2d Div & S § 334.

private statute. See **private act.**

private stream. See **private waters.**

private track. A railroad track maintained for the convenience of one or more persons or of one or more industries, not open to public use. A railroad track not constructed or used for general traffic or devoted to public use, as a spur track used by a railroad merely for the purpose of reaching its roundhouse. 44 Am J1st R R § 227.

private trust. Any trust which has been created for a purpose other than a public or charitable purpose. 15 Am J2d Char § 6.

private use. The use of public funds, public property, or the powers of government for such a purpose or in such a manner that it is not a public use.
Under the settled doctrine that a municipal corporation cannot use its funds to promote a private commercial enterprise, a management and use of land as a street to promote the interests of merchants and traders who might occupy it, and to furnish better facilities for doing business and making profits, is not a public, but a private use of the land. Re Opinion of Justices, 197 NY 58, 91 NE 405.
See **public use.**

private warehouseman. A person maintaining a warehouse for his own use or under conditions such that the function of maintenance is not of any public interest. 56 Am J1st Wareh § 4.

private waters. Waters above land privately owned and subject to private control only. A stream to the bed of which a riparian owner can show title deraigned from the United States or from the state. Webb v Board of Comrs. 124 Kan 38, 257 P 966.

private way. A road or way intended for the exclusive use and benefit of one or more particular persons. 25 Am J1st High § 4. A means of passage for one or more individuals from some place to some other place. Seery v Waterbury, 82 Conn 567, 74 A 908. A way for travel over the surface of land, even over an artificial passageway or stairway. 25 Am J2d Ease § 7. An incorporeal hereditament of a real nature, being the right of going over another man's ground. The privilege which one person or particular class of persons have of passing over the land of another in some particular line. 25 Am J2d Ease § 7.
See **way of necessity.**

private way appurtenant. An incorporeal right of passage over the land of another, which is annexed to and belongs with another distinct tenement. 25 Am J2d Ease § 11.

private way in gross. The merely personal right or privilege of passing over the land of another in a specified line.
Such a right being personal to the one who is entitled to its enjoyment cannot be transferred by deed, assignment or otherwise, but it ceases to exist upon his death. Kripp v Curtis, 71 Cal 62, 11 P 879.

private wharf. A wharf for private use only, not open to the use of the public. 56 Am J1st Wharves § 3.

private wrong. An infringement or violation of a right belonging to an individual as an individual, in distinction from the violation of a duty to the nation, to a state, or to the community considered as a community. A violation of a duty due from one person to another, for the breach of which the law provides a right of action. Rhobidas v Concord, 70 NH 90, 47 A 82.

Privatio praesupponit habitum (pri-vā′she-ō prē-su-pō′nit hā′bi-tum). A deprivation presupposes something held or possessed.

Privatis pactionibus non dubium est non laedi jus caeterorum (prī-vā′tis pak-she-ō′ni-bus non dū′bi-um est non lē′dī jūs sē-te-rō′rum). (Roman law.) There is no doubt that the rights of others are not prejudiced by private agreements. See Broom's Legal Maxims 697.

Privatorum conventio juri publico non derogat (prī-vā-tō'rum kon-ven'she-ō jū'rī pub'li-kō non de'ro-gat). An agreement of private persons cannot derogate from public right.

Privatorum pacta non derogant juri communi (prī-vā-tō'rum pak'ta non de'ro-gant jū'rī kom-mu'nī). The agreements of private persons cannot derogate from common right.

Privatum commodum publico cedit (prī-vā'tum kom'mo-dum pub'li-kō sē'dit). Private convenience must yield to public welfare.

Privatum incommodum publico bono pensatur (prī-vā'tum in-kom'mo-dum pub'li-kō bo'nō pen-sā'ter). Private inconvenience is compensated by the public welfare. The interest of the individual will not be permitted to stand in the way where the public good is concerned. Daniels v Homer, 139 NC 219, 51 SE 992.

privement enceinte. Pregnant in the first stages. Pregnancy not observable on a passing glance.

privies. See **privy.**

privigna (prī-vig'na). (Civil law.) A step-daughter.

privignus (prī-vig'nus). (Civil law.) A step-son.

privilege. A right peculiar to an individual or body. Ripley v Knight, 123 Mass 519. An advantage held by way of license, franchise, grant, or permission, not possessed by others. Special enjoyment of a good, or exemption from an evil or burden. Wisener v Burrell, 28 Okla 546, 118 P 999. An immunity existing under the law. For tax purposes, any occupation or business which the legislature may declare to be a privilege and tax as such. Seven Springs Water Co. v Kennedy, 156 Tenn 1, 299 SW 792, 56 ALR 496. (Civil law.) A tacit hypothecation of a thing without any transfer of the possession of it or of the right to possession. The Glide, 167 US 606, 42 L Ed 296, 17 S Ct 930.

See **immunity; special privilege; writ of privilege.**

privilege against self-incrimination. A privilege of one who is accused of a crime, existing under the Fifth and Fourteenth Amendments to the Federal Constitution, as well as under the constitutions of most of the states, not to be compelled to give self-incriminating testimony. 21 Am J2d Crim L § 349. The privilege of a witness, based upon the Fifth Amendment to the Constitution of the United States, a provision of a state constitution, 58 Am J1st Witn § 36, or a principle of the common law, Allen v State, 183 Md 603, 39 A2d 820, 171 ALR 1138; State v Cdanowicz, 69 NJL 619, 55 A 743. To refuse to answer any question that will incriminate or tend to incriminate himself. 58 Am J1st Witn § 36.

The wisdom of the exemption has never been universally assented to since the days of Bentham, many doubt it today, and it is best defended not as an unchangeable principle of universal justice, but as a law proved by experience to be expedient. Twining v New Jersey, 211 US 78, 53 L Ed 97, 29 S Ct 14.

The privilege of immunity from self-incrimination under the Fifth Amendment to the United States Constitution, to be available, must be invoked by the witness. The privilege of silence is solely for his benefit and is deemed waived unless invoked. The Fifth Amendment affords no immunity to a witness against the use of his voluntary testimony against him. United States v Mary Helen Coal Corp. (DC Ky) 24 F Supp 50.

See **self-incrimination.**

privileged communication. A communication between persons in such a confidential relationship, be it attorney and client, physician and patient, or confessor and penitent, that public policy prohibits the disclosure thereof by the person to whom it was made, as a witness testifying in an action or proceeding, upon objection thereto by the person who made it. 58 Am J1st Witn §§ 363 et seq. Communications between husband and wife, declared privileged in encouragement of the utmost confidence between the spouses, thus aiding in the preservation of the marital status, so that neither spouse is competent to testify to a confidential communication, made to him or her by the other spouse, in a civil action, whether or not the husband or wife is a party, or in a criminal prosecution against one of the spouses, apart from actions or prosecutions excepted by statute or which are such that the exclusion of the testimony would not be in fulfilment of the principle of the privilege. 58 Am J1st Witn §§ 375 et seq. Within the meaning of the law of defamation:—a statement uttered or published which, by reason of its character or the occasion upon which it was made, is to be deemed, absolutely or conditionally, wanting in respect of the essential element of the tort or offense of libel or slander, 33 Am J1st L & S § 124; a communication which would be defamatory and actionable, except for the occasion on which, or the circumstances under which, it was made. Mullens v Davidson, 133 W Va 557, 57 SE2d 1, 13 ALR2d 887.

As to the effect of an act as a confidential communication between husband and wife, see Anno: 10 ALR2d 1389.

privileged copyholds (kop'i-hōlds). Copyholds held in ancient demesne, called "privileged" because, although they could not be conveyed by feoffment, but had to pass by surrender to the lord or his steward, in the manner of common copyholds, yet they were not to be held at the will of the lord, but according to the custom of the manor. See 2 Bl Comm 100.

privileged debts. Obligations entitled to a priority or preference.

See **preference; priority.**

privileged occasion. An occasion the circumstances of which are such as to make privileged a statement otherwise defamatory, thereby rendering the statement wanting in respect of the essential element of the tort of libel or slander. Blakeslee v Carroll, 64 Conn 223, 29 A 473.

See **privileged communication.**

privileged relation. A relation of such nature that communications between the parties thereto are protected against disclosure by one of the parties, as a witness testifying in an action or proceeding, upon objection thereto by the other party. 58 Am J1st Witn §§ 363 et seq.

See **privileged communication.**

privileged vessel. Same as **favored vessel.**

privileged villeinage. Same as **villeinage socage.**

privileged will. A civil-law term for nuncupative will. Castro v Castro, 6 Cal 158, 160.

privilege fee. An occupation tax.

The sales tax of Michigan is said to be a privilege fee imposed upon persons doing business at retail. It is not imposed upon the consumer, but upon those engaged in the business of making sales at retail. It is left optional with the retailer whether he will absorb the tax himself or collect it from his customers. Miles Laboratories v Simon (DC Mich) 33 F Supp 962.

privilege from arrest. See **immunity from arrest.**

privilege in defamation. See **privileged communications.**

privilege of five years. A privilege of extension of the term of a lease, granted by a clause in the lease. 32 Am J1st L & T § 961.

privilege of renewing one year more. A privilege of extension of the term of a lease, granted by a clause in the lease. 32 Am J1st L & T § 961.

privilege of return. The right to return a mare for breeding without payment of an additional breeding fee, where the previous service by the stallion has proved to be fruitless. 4 Am J2d Ani § 77.

privilege of sanctuary. See **sanctuary.**

privilege of telegraph company. Absence of liability in transmitting a defamatory message, except where the transmitting agent of the telegraph company happened to know that the message was spurious or that the sender was acting, not in the protection of any legitimate interest, but in bad faith and for the purpose of traducing another. O'Brien v Western Union Tel Co. (CA1 Mass) 113 F2d 543.

privileges and appurtenances. An apt word in a conveyance carrying easements. 25 Am J2d Ease § 95.

privileges and immunities. Synonymous terms in reference to the guarantee of the United States Constitution. 16 Am J2d Const L § 476. Of citizens of the several states within the meaning of the guarantee under Article IV § 2 of the United States Constitution:—the fundamental privileges and immunities belonging of right to the citizens of all free governments, which have at all times been enjoyed by citizens of the several states of the Union from the time of their becoming free, independent, and sovereign states; protection by the government, with the right to acquire and possess property of every kind, and to pursue and obtain happiness and safety, subject to such restraints as the government may prescribe for the general good of the whole people. 16 Am J2d Const L § 477.
See **immunity; privilege.**

privileges and immunities clause. Section 2 of Article IV of the United States Constitution and a clause of the 1st section of the Fourteenth Amendment to the United States Constitution.
See **privileges and immunities.**

privileges and immunities of citizens. See **privileges and immunities.**

privilege tax. A tax upon the pursuit of an occupation or the conducting of a business. Bank of Commerce & Trust Co. v Senter, 149 Tenn 574, 577, 579, 260 SW 144.
When a statute authorizes the levy and collection of taxes upon taxable property, and to license, tax and regulate certain businesses and "all other privileges" taxable by the state, the word "privileges" does not mean such things as are technically privileges, and cannot ever be enjoyed or exercised in England except through the prerogative of the crown or under act of parliament, or, in this country, by authority of law, but to denote other occupations and business of the kind mentioned. Jacksonville v Ledwith, 26 Fla 163, 7 So 885.
See **occupation tax.**

privilegia (prī-vi-lē′ji-a). (Roman law.) Private laws.

privilegia favorabilia (prī-vi-lē′ji-a fa-vō-rā-bi′li-a). A private law enacted for the benefit of an individual or a corporation. Christ Church v Philadelphia (US) 24 How 300, 16 L Ed 602.

privilegium (pri-vi-lē′ji-um). An advantage or favor granted by law but not possessed under the common law.

privilegium clericale (pri-vi-lē′ji-um kle-ri-kā′le). The clerical privilege,—benefit of clergy. See 3 Bl Comm 365.

Privilegium contra rempublicam non valet (pri-vi-lē′-ji-um kon′tra rem-pub′li-kam non va′let). Privilege as against the state is of no avail.

Privilegium est beneficium personale et extinguitur cum persona (pri-vi-lē′ji-um est be-ne-fi′she-um per-so-nā′le et ex-tin′gwi-ter kum per-sō′na). A privilege is a personal benefit and is extinguished with the person.

Privilegium est quasi privata lex (pri-vi-lē′ji-um est quā′sī prī-vā′ta lex). A privilege is, as it were, a private law.

Privilegium non valet contra rempublicam (pri-vi-lē′-ji-um non va′let kon′tra rem-pub′li-kam). A privilege is of no avail as against the state.

privily (priv′i-li). Privately or secretly. Coombes v Thomas, 57 Tex 321, 322.

privity (priv′i-ti). An elusive term. In general, an identity of interest between persons, so that the interest of the one is measured by the same legal right as that of the other. Fleming v Cooper, 225 Ark 634, 284 SW2d 857, 58 ALR2d 694. The relation between two titles where one derives from the other or both derive from a common source. Jax Ice & Cold Storage Co. v South Florida Farms Co. (Fla) 109 So 212, 218. Continuity of interest; successive relationships to the same rights of property, as between decedent and heir, intestate and administrator, testate and executor, and grantor and grantee. Zaragosa v Craven, 33 Cal 2d 315, 202 P2d 73, 6 ALR2d 461. For the purposes of the doctrine of res judicata, such an identity in interest that one person represents the same legal right as another, as a consequence of which, the judgment is binding as to a subsequent grantee, transferee, or lienor of property. 30A Am J Rev ed Judgm § 399. For the purposes of estoppel by judgment, one who has an interest in the subject matter through a party to the action. Seymour v Wallace, 121 Mich 402, 80 NW 242. In reference to the scope and effect of an injunction, mutual or successive relationship to the rights of property. 28 Am J Rev ed Inj § 296. As an element of admissibility of former testimony of a witness since become unavailable:—a relationship arising from connection with a decedent's estate or out of interest in property, or the relationship of principal and surety or of successive plaintiffs in actions for wrongful death, the word being used in somewhat the same sense as in the field of property law. Re Silvies River, 115 Or 27, 237 P 322.

privity in law. Identity of interest between persons, so that the interest of one is measured by the same legal right as that of the other. Fleming v Cooper, 225 Ark 634, 284 SW2d 857, 58 ALR2d 694. Successive relationships to the same right of property.

privity of contract. A material interest in the performance of a contract of one who did not join in the making of the contract. The impact of a contract upon a person from or to whom the consideration moves. 17 Am J2d Contr § 297.

privity of estate. A connection between the estate of one and the estate of another, for example, as between lessor and lessee. Davidson v Minnesota Loan & Trust Co. 158 Minn 411, 197 NW 833, 32 ALR 1418. A succession in rights. Vineberg v Hardison (Fla App) 108 So 2d 922; Helman v Pittsburgh C. C. & St. L. R. Co. 58 Ohio St 400, 50 NE 986.
See **privity**.

privity of possession. A continuity of actual possession, as between prior and present occupant, the possession of the latter succeeding the possession of the former under deed, grant, or other transfer, or by operation of law. Vance v Wood, 22 Or 77, 29 P 73.

privy (priv'i). One in privity with another. Shew v Call, 119 NC 450, 26 SE 33. One connected with another by reason of their having a mutual interest in the same action or thing. Western Loan & Sav Co. v Silver Bow Abstract Co. 31 Mont 448, 78 P 774. An outside toilet. Monroe v Gerspach, 33 La Ann 1011.
See **privity; privy vault**.

Privy Council (priv'i koun'sil). Advisers of the crown.

privy examination (priv'i eg-zam-i-nā'shọn). The examination of a married woman, separately from her husband, in taking her acknowledgment to the execution of a deed or other instrument in which she joins with her husband. Henderson v Smith, 26 W Va 829.

privy in estate. See **privity of estate**.

privy in representation. The executor of a testator, or the administrator of an intestate.

privy to an action. See **privity**.

privy seal (sēl). A seal which is affixed to royal grants or letters patent which are to pass under the great seal.
The sign manual is the warrant to the privy seal and the privy seal is the warrant to the great seal. See 2 Bl Comm 347.

privy signet (sig'net). A seal which was always in the custody of the principal secretary of state and was affixed to royal grants and letters patent after the king's own sign manual had been superscribed. See 2 Bl Comm 347.

privy vault. The walled-in space below an outdoor privy. Not a water closet, since no supply of water is maintained for flushing it. Commonwealth v Roberts, 155 Mass 281, 29 NE 522.

privy verdict. A verdict delivered to the judge out of court, relieving the jury from their confinement in case of agreement after the judge has adjourned court, to be affirmed by an oral verdict given publicly in court upon resumption of the session. 53 Am J1st Tr § 1010.

prize. A sum offered by way of reward for the winner of a contest, without opportunity for the person offering it to compete for the purpose of gaining back the thing offered or any part thereof. 24 Am J1st Gaming § 100. That which is offered and is to be won in a lottery. 34 Am J1st Lot § 5. Property legally captured in time of war. 56 Am J1st Wars § 180.

prize candy. A lottery scheme involving the sale of candy in boxes, each box being represented to contain a prize of money or jewelry and the purchaser selecting his box in ignorance of its contents. 34 Am J1st Lot § 7.

prize contest. A contest in which a prize is given as a matter of grace and favor and as a reward for skill or quality of endeavor. 24 Am J1st Gaming § 100. A guessing or puzzle contest; a voting or popularity contest. 34 Am J1st Lot §§ 12, 17. A lottery where tickets are sold, some to draw prizes, some to draw nothing as blanks. 34 Am J1st Lot § 7.

prize court. A court which administers prize law, adjudicating the right to property as prize of war. An anomaly in jurisprudence as a domestic court administering law of the nations. 56 Am J1st War § 182.
Having taken goods of the enemy, the captors have a right to proceed against them as belligerent property in a court of prize; for in no other way, and in no other court can the questions presented on a capture jure belli be properly and effectually examined. The Schooner Adeline & Cargo (US) 9 Cranch 244, 284, 3 L Ed 719, 733.

prize fight. A pugilistic encounter or boxing match for a prize or wager. 4 Am J2d Amuse §§ 81, 86. Engaging in any fight for a prize, stake, or reward, whether in public or private and however conducted, in which the contestants intend to inflict some degree of bodily harm on each other. People v Taylor, 96 Mich 576, 56 NW 27; Seville v State, 49 Ohio St 117, 30 NE 621.

prize goods. See **prize of war**.

prize law. A body of international law under which the right to movable property and claimed a prize of war is determined. 56 Am J1st War § 180.

prize money. A sum of money offered by way of a reward to the winner of a contest or as the stake in a lottery. The purse or stake in a prize fight. The proceeds of the sale of a vessel or goods taken as prize of war.
Under the federal prize statutes the net proceeds of all property condemned as prize are to be decreed to the United States and be ordered by the court to be paid into the Treasury of the United States. 56 Am J1st War § 201.

prize of war. Goods or movables in the hands of the enemy, used, or intended to be used, for hostile purposes, captured by land or naval forces in time of war. 56 Am J1st War § 180.

prize package. A scheme of lottery whereby a person who pays a certain price for a package of candy, tea, or other merchandise is entitled to select it from a number of packages, some of which, in addition to the commodity, contain a ticket which entitles the purchaser to a prize, while other packages contain nothing but the commodity. 34 Am J1st Lot § 7.

prize proceeding. A proceeding for the condemnation of property as constituting prize of war. 56 Am J1st War § 181.

prize ring. The so-called "squared circle," enclosed by ropes, where boxing contests and prize fights are held.

prize ring rules. The rules of a prize fight.
See **London Prize Ring Rules**.

pro (prō). For; before; on behalf of; in favor of; in place of; in consideration of; in proportion to; as; by way of.

pro aetate probanda. See **commission pro aetate probanda.**

proavo. See **de proavo.**

proavus (pro'a-vus). A great grandfather.

probabilis causa litigandi (pro-ba'bi-lis kâ'za li-ti-gan'dī). A probable cause of litigation.

probability. Likelihood, but coupled with some uncertainty, of occurrence.
To instruct the jury that they may act on probabilities means simply that they may act on less than convincing evidence, or without that moral certainty required by law. People v O'Brien, 130 Cal 1, 8, 62 P 297, 299.
See **in all probability.**

probable. Likely to occur, but involving an element of uncertainty. Green v Catawaba Power Co. 75 SC 102, 55 SE 125. With a greater weight of evidence in support than against. State v Trout, 74 Iowa 545, 38 NW 405.

probable cause. Reasonable cause as shown by the circumstances of the case. Goldstein v Sabella (Fla) 88 So 2d 910, 58 ALR2d 1418.

probable cause for a prosecution. A reasonable ground for suspicion, supported by circumstances sufficiently strong in themselves to warrant a cautious, or as some courts put it, a prudent man, in believing that the party charged is guilty of the offense with which he is charged. The existence of such facts and circumstances as would excite belief in a reasonable mind, acting on the facts within the knowledge of the prosecutor, that the person charged is guilty of the offense for which he is prosecuted. Such facts and circumstances as, when communicated to the generality of men of ordinary and impartial minds, are sufficient to raise in them a belief or real, grave suspicion of the guilt of the person charged. 34 Am J1st Mal Pros § 47.

probable cause for arrest. A reasonable ground of suspicion, supported by circumstances sufficiently strong in themselves to warrant a cautious man in believing the accused to be guilty. In substance, a reasonable ground for belief in guilt. Brinegar v United States, 338 US 160, 93 L Ed 1879, 69 S Ct 1302, reh den 338 US 839, 94 L Ed 513, 70 S Ct 31.

probable cause for attachment. A reasonable belief in the existence of facts necessary to sustain an attachment. The actual existence of facts necessary to sustain an attachment. 6 Am J2d Attach § 599.

probable cause for capture. The existence of circumstances such as to warrant a reasonable ground of suspicion that the vessel is engaged in an illegal traffic. 56 Am J1st War § 198.

probable cause for issuance of a search warrant. A reasonable ground of suspicion, supported by circumstances sufficiently strong in themselves to warrant a prudent and cautious man in the belief that the person accused is guilty of the offense with which he is charged. 47 Am J1st Search § 22.

probable cause for statement otherwise tortious as defamatory. A reasonable ground of suspicion, supported by circumstances sufficient to warrant a cautious man in believing in the truth of the statement pleaded as the basis of a cause of action for defamation. Coates v Wallace, 4 Pa Super 253, 257.

probable cause to hold accused for trial. Reasonable ground to believe that a crime has been committed and just cause to believe that the defendant committed it. State ex rel. Stevenson v Jameson, 78 SD 431, 104 NW2d 45.

probable consequence doctrine. A test of proximate cause according to whether or not the injury was reasonably foreseeable by a person of ordinary intelligence and prudence. 26 Am J2d Electr § 48.

probable consequences. Those consequences which are more likely than not to follow the use of a given means. Western Commercial Travelers' Asso. v Smith (CA8 Mo) 85 F 401. A result which, when viewed in retrospect, appears to be the reasonable rather than the extraordinary consequences of a wrong. Brown v Rhoades, 126 Me 186, 137 A 58, 53 ALR 834. Those consequences which a person of average competence and knowledge being in the situation of a person whose conduct is in question, and having the same opportunities of observation, might be expected to foresee as likely to follow such conduct. 38 Am J1st Negl § 57.

probable evidence. Same as **presumptive evidence.**

probable expectancy. Such a thing as one has the right to expect as a concomitant of civilized society, for example, the right to a reasonably free labor market. L. D. Wilcutt & Sons v Driscoll, 200 Mass 110, 85 NE 897.
See **expectation of life; mortality tables.**

Probandi necessitas incumbit illi qui agit (pro-ban'dī ne-se'si-tās in-kum'bit il'lī quī ā'jit). The necessity of proving, the burden of proof, lies upon him who sues.

probandum. See **factum probandum.**

probans. See **factum probans.**

probata. See **allegata et probata.**

probate. The judicial act whereby an instrument is adjudged a valid will and ordered to be recorded; the statutory method of establishing the proper execution of the instrument and giving notice of its contents. 57 Am J1st Wills § 743. Broadly, a characterization of functions of the probate court, whether it be the probate of a will, the approval of the accounts of an administrator of a decedent's estate, or any other judicial act within the province of the court. Johnson v Harrison, 47 Minn 575, 578. In older usage, the equivalent of acknowledgment, 1 Am J2d Ack § 1; relating to proof.

probate code. The body or system of law relating to the estates of deceased persons and of persons under guardianship. Johnson v Harrison, 47 Minn 575, 579.

probate court. A court exercising jurisdiction in probating wills and in matters of administration of decedents' estates, guardianships, absentees, etc. 20 Am J2d Cts § 32.
It is generally considered that probate, orphans' and surrogate courts are courts of special and limited jurisdiction, but instances are not lacking to sustain the statement that such courts have general jurisdiction. 20 Am J2d Cts § 32.

probate duty. A duty to be treated as an expense of administration of a decedent's estate. The earliest form of death duty in England. 28 Am J Rev ed Inher T § 4. An estate tax.

probate estate. The estate of a decedent in probate.

probate fee. See **probate duty.**

probate homestead. Premises of a decedent set apart to the surviving spouse and minor children, to be held by them exempt from liability for the debts of the decedent. 26 Am J1st Home § 185.

probate in common form. A survival of probate procedure under ecclesiastical law; an ex parte proceeding instituted by the executor or other proponent of a will to obtain the admission of the propounded instrument to record as a valid will.
It is distinguished from the other form of probate, known as solemn probate, by its ex parte character, no opportunity being given for a contest. 57 Am J1st Wills § 758.

probate in solemn form. A proceeding by the executor or other proponent of a will to obtain the admission of the propounded instrument to record as a valid will, under summons to interested parties calling upon them to witness the proceeding and to take whatever part therein they see fit. An adversary proceeding upon notice or citation in which parties in interest opposed to the will have the opportunity to contest its validity. 57 Am J1st Wills § 758.

probate judge. The judge who presides in a probate court.

probate jurisdiction. A special jurisdiction for the probate of wills, the appointment of executors, administrators, guardians, and committees, the approval of the accounts of such fiduciaries, etc., sometimes exercised by a separate court, at other times by a separate division of a court of general jurisdiction. 20 Am J2d Cts § 32.

probate law. In common understanding,—as distinct and clearly defined a branch of the law as is criminal law or corporation law; in popular signification including all matters of which probate courts generally have jurisdiction, among which are estates of deceased persons. Johnson v Harrison, 47 Mich 575, 579.

probate matters. Matters within the jurisdiction of a probate court. Re Mortenson, 248 Ill 520, 94 NE 120.
See **probate jurisdiction.**

probate of will. See **caveat; probate.**

probate proceeding. A proceeding in the probate court, usually upon notice of motion or order to show cause. Sometimes upon summons or other formal process as in the probate of a will in solemn form. A "civil action" for the purpose of a statute which disqualifies a judge in a civil action for causes specified in the statute. 30A Am J Rev ed Judges § 95.

probate research. A matter of searching for heirs of a particular decedent or in finding evidence to substantiate the claim of a person made as an heir. Cochran v Zachery, 137 Iowa 585, 115 NW 486.
See **heir hunter.**

probate sale. A sale, such as an executor's or administrator's sale, had under order of court in a proceeding in probate.

probate tax. See **probate duty; estate tax.**

probatio (pro-bā'she-ō). Proof; a trial; an examination.

probatio mortua (pro-bā'she-ō mor'tu-a). Dead proof; that is, proof by writings or by things or objects offered in evidence.

probation. A trial or test, particularly of the fitness of a person for a position. Also a period for the observance of a person under a suspended sentence for crime with reference to the advisability of giving him opportunity to resume his place in society without undergoing confinement in prison. A matter of action taken before the prison door is closed, being the suspension of sentence or suspension of execution of sentence prior to commitment, for the purposes of education and rehabilitation of the accused. 21 Am J2d Crim L §§ 562 et seq. A discharge from commitment as an insane person upon condition of remaining in a condition of sanity, to be recommitted summarily upon insanity appearing. Metaxos v People, 76 Colo 264, 230 P 608.

probationary custody. An award of the custody of a child of divorced parents, made upon the granting of the divorce, but with the expectation that an application for a final award will be made and heard at a later date. 24 Am J2d Div & S § 809.

probationary discharge. See **probation.**

probationary status. A person having a period of probation in a civil service position by way of a further test of his qualifications for appointment. 15 Am J2d Civ S § 24. The status of a person convicted of a crime during the period of suspension of sentence, or suspension of execution of sentence, as ordered by the court to afford opportunity for his rehabilitation. 21 Am J2d Crim L §§ 562 et seq.

Probationes debent esse evidentes, id est, perspicuae et faciles intelligi (pro-bā-she-ō'nēz de'bent es'se e-vi-den'tēz, id est, per-spi'ku-ē et fa'si-lēz in-tel'li-jī). Proofs ought to be evident; that is, they ought to be plain and easily understood.

probation officer. An officer, usually attached to a juvenile court, who is charged with the care of juvenile delinquents, and in some jurisdictions with the superintendence of convicts who are at large on probation or suspended sentence.

probatio plena (prō-bā'she-ō plē'na). (Civil law.) Full proof; that is, proof by two witnesses, or by a public document. See 3 Bl Comm 370.

probatio semi-plena (pro-bā'she-ō se-mī-ple'na). (Civil law.) Half proof; that is, proof by one witness only. See 3 Bl Comm 370.

probatio viva (pro-bā'she-ō vī'va). Living proof; that is, proof by a living witness or witnesses.

Probatis extremis, praesumitur media (prō-bā'tis ex-trē'mis, prē-zu'mi-ter me'di-a). When the extremes have been proved, those things which lie between are presumed.

probative (prō'bạ-tiv). Having a tendency to prove or establish.

probative facts (prō'bạ-tiv fakts). Evidentiary facts. Facts which tend to prove ultimate facts. 41 Am J1st Pl § 8.

probative value. The weight as evidence of evidentiary facts. Wilson v Haughton (Ky) 266 SW2d 115, 41 ALR2d 950.
See **weight of evidence.**

probator (prō-bā'tọr). Also called an "approver" or "prover,"—a person who, after having been indicted for treason, or other felony, and arraigned for it, confesses his guilt before pleading guilty or not guilty and accuses the persons who were his accomplices of the same crime, in order to obtain a pardon for himself. See 4 Bl Comm 330.

probi et legales homines (prō'bī et lē-ga'lēz ho'mi-nēz). Plural of **probus et legalis homo.**

pro bono et malo (prō bō'nō et ma'lō). For good and evil.

pro bono publico (prō bō'nō pub'li-kō). For the public good or welfare.

probus et legalis homo (prō'bus et lē-ga'lis hō'mō). A true and lawful man; that is, a man who can serve upon a jury, be a witness, or bring an action to recover lands or money due him. See 3 Bl Comm 102.

procedendo (prō-sẹ-den'dō). An order or writ issued by an appellate court commanding a court of inferior jurisdiction to proceed to judgment in a case pending before it, but not attempting to control the inferior court as to what the judgment should be. State ex rel. Davey v Owen, 133 Ohio St 96, 12 NE2d 144, 114 ALR 686. An order issued by a court of review on the decision of a cause on appeal or writ of error, directing the action to be taken or disposition to be made of the cause by the lower court. State v Banning, 205 Iowa 826, 218 NW 572; Yates v People (NY) 6 Johns 337, 403.

procedendo ad judicium (prō-se-den'dō ad ju-di'sheum). A remedy under early English common-law and chancery practice to compel an inferior tribunal to proceed to judgment in a given case where the judge of such court was delaying the proceeding, but without directing any particular judgment. Re Press Printers & Publishers (CA3 NJ) 12 F2d 660.

procedendo de loquela (pro-se-den'dō de lo-kwē'la). A king's writ which directed the court to proceed in a tenant's real action, in response to the latter's aid prayer.

The aid prayer was a call for assistance to plead because of the feebleness or imbecility of the estate of the tenant himself. See 3 Bl Comm 300.

procedendo on aid prayer (pro-se-den'dō on aid prayer). See **procedendo de loquela.**

procedural due process. A regular course of justice, which is not unreasonable or arbitrary, upon notice and hearing, in pursuance of an efficacious remedy secured by the law of the state. 16 Am J2d Const L § 549. An orderly proceeding appropriate to the case or adapted to its nature, just to the parties affected, and adapted to the ends to be attained; one in which a person has an opportunity to be heard, and to defend, enforce, and protect his rights with the assistance of counsel before a competent and impartial tribunal legally constituted to determine the right involved. 2 Am J2d Admin L § 353.

procedural law. The law which governs the manner in which rights are enforced and wrongs rectified. Hardie v Bryson (DC Mo) 44 F Supp 67. The law which prescribes the procedure to be followed in a case.

procedure. The means adopted, that is the practice followed, whereby a court adjudicates controversies within its jurisdiction and properly presented to it, as distinguished from the substantive principles according to which rights and wrongs are determined. Green v Board of Comrs. 126 Okla 300, 259 P 635; Nordling v Johnston, 205 Or 315, 283 P2d 994, 48 ALR2d 1369.

See **practice.**

procedure extra ordinem (ex'tra or'di-nem). (Civil law.) An informal proceeding before a magistrate terminating in a decision which could not be enforced without a further action to secure execution.

proceeding. In ordinary usage, including all methods of invoking the action of courts and applicable generally to any step taken by a suitor to obtain the interposition or action of a court. 1 Am J2d Actions § 3. An action. More particularly, any application to a court of justice, however made, for aid in the enforcement of rights, for relief, for redress of injuries, for damages, or for any remedial object. 1 Am J2d Actions § 3. In reference to the restriction upon federal courts of granting an injunction to stay proceedings in state courts:—any step taken, or which may be taken, in the state court or by its officers, from the institution of the action to the termination of final process. Hill v Martin, 296 US 393, 80 L Ed 293, 56 S Ct 278. In one peculiar sense, the equivalent of special proceeding. In a broad sense, inclusive of an inquiry before a grand jury. Hale v Henkel, 201 US 43, 66, 50 L Ed 652, 662, 26 S Ct 370, even of the conduct of a matter before an executive department or administrative agency. Bowers v New York & Albany Lighterage Co. 273 US 346, 71 L Ed 676, 47 S Ct 389.

See **action; ancillary proceeding; practice; procedure; special proceeding; summary proceeding.**

proceeding according to the course of the common law. A rhetorical statement, pleasing to the ear but leaving no definite impression upon the understanding. Hahn v Kelly, 34 Cal 391, 411.

proceeding for information of title. See **information of title.**

proceeding in admiralty. See **admiralty.**

proceeding in bankruptcy. In the broad sense, any invoking of the jurisdiction of the bankruptcy court; in a technical sense, a summary proceeding in a court of bankruptcy. 9 Am J2d Bankr §§ 68 et seq.

proceeding in court. See **proceeding.**

proceeding in error. A proceeding by writ of error for the removal of a cause to a higher court for review. State v Scott, 34 Wyo 163, 242 P 322.

proceeding in insolvency. Any assignment for the benefit of creditors or other proceeding intended to liquidate or rehabilitate the estate of the person involved. UCC § 1–201(22). A proceeding wherein a person may be adjudicated insolvent and the assets of his estate be distributed according to law. 29 Am J Rev ed Insolv §§ 14 et seq.

State insolvency statutes sometimes provide for the discharge of the debtor from his debts, but discharge under state laws is subject to material exceptions or limitations. 29 Am J Rev ed Insolv § 88.

proceeding in personam. See **in personam action.**

proceeding in rem. See **in rem action.**

proceeding quasi in rem. See **quasi in rem action.**

proceeding supplementary to execution. See **supplementary proceeding.**

proceeds. That which is received for something, whether in cash or other thing of value. Phelps v Harris (US) 11 Otto 370, 380, 25 L Ed 855, 858.

The term as used in a statute requiring labor claims to be first paid out of the "proceeds of sale" of property of an insolvent means, in case of a receivership, what remains after payment of the costs and expenses of the receivership necessary to the carrying out of the trust by the receiver as the hand of the court. Sloan & Z. Co. v Lyons Ref. Co. 290 Pa 442, 139 A 133, 55 ALR 275.

As used in a will or other trust instrument the term, used alone, is generally regarded as equivocal, meaning either (1) the income, product or profits from property, or (2) the fund arising upon the sale of property; its meaning in the particular case is to be determined primarily from the context of the instrument in which it is used and the subject matter to which it is applied. Anno: 1 ALR2d 194.

proceeds and avails of insurance. For the purposes of exemption from execution, the amount collected from an insurance company under a contract of insurance. Le Blanc's Succession, 142 La 27, 76 So 223.

proceeds of sale. See **proceeds.**

proceeds receivable by the executor. Funds in the hands of the executor where he is named as beneficiary, where the proceeds are subject to estate obligations, or where there is a legal obligation on the part of the executor to use them for the benefit of the estate. Anno: 80 L Ed 174, s. 85 L Ed 1012, 1013.

proceres (pros'ẹ-rēz). Chiefs; nobles; princes; municipal magistrates.

process. A method of producing something from raw material. Producing by chemical action, by the operation or application of some element or power of nature, or by adding one substance to another. Corning v Burden (US) 15 How 252, 267, 14 L Ed 683, 690. A series of actions, motions, or occurrences; progressive act or transaction; continuous operation or treatment; a method of operation or treatment. Martin v Minerals Separation North American Corporation (DC Md) 29 F Supp 146. In patent law, a manner of treatment of certain materials to produce a given result; an act or series of acts performed upon the subject matter to transform and reduce it to a different state or thing. Cochrane v Deener, 94 US 780, 24 L Ed 139. In a broad sense, all of the acts of the court from the beginning to the end of an action or proceeding. Blair v Maxbass Secur. Bank, 44 ND 12, 176 NW 98. The means by which the purposes of the law may be applied and executed as between private litigants or as between the state and an accused. In a technical sense, the means of compelling a defendant to appear in court, whether in a civil or criminal case. A writ, warrant of arrest, or other means of subjecting person or property to the jurisdiction of the court. 42 Am J1st Proc § 2.
See **due process of law; service of process.**

processing materials. Applying a process to materials. Materials used in manufacturing; raw materials. Anno: 30 ALR2d 1439.
See **process.**

process in rem. A process, as that of a court of admiralty, adapted to the establishment and enforcement of a right in a thing, as distinguished from the enforcement of a personal liability. State v Voorhies, 39 La Ann 499, 2 So 37.

procession. A line of persons on foot or in vehicles, proceeding in an orderly manner, as in bearing the body of a friend or relative to place of burial. 25 Am J1st High § 212.
See **parade.**

processioned. See **processioning.**

processioner. A person appointed upon the application of the owner or owners of land, the boundaries of which are in doubt, to determine the correct boundary. 12 Am J2d Bound § 94.

processioning proceeding. A special statutory proceeding for the determination of a boundary in dispute. Andrews v Andrews, 252 NC 97, 113 SE2d 47. A proceeding invoked by a landowner who desires a survey whereby the boundary lines of his tract may be surveyed, established, and marked anew, being in the nature of preventive relief. Watson v Bishop, 69 Ga 51, 53.

process of attaint. See **attaint.**

process of garnishment. See **garnishment.**

process of gavelet. See **gavelet.**

process of law. See **due process of law; process; service of process.**

process of manufacturing. In the broad sense, manufacturing something from raw material. Making an article entirely by hand or machinery into a new form capable of being used and designed to be used in ordinary life. 21 Am J2d Cust D § 43.

process of mining. The obtaining of mineral from an excavation in the earth, which necessarily implies two things: First, the actual cutting or hewing of the mineral; and, second, its removal to the surface. Anno: 11 ALR 154.
See **strip mining.**

process of outlawry. See **attainder by process of outlawry; outlawry.**

processor. One who receives material, particularly grain, fruit, or other product of the farm, and converts it to a form suitable for consumption or use.
See **process.**

process regular on its face. See **regular on its face.**

process roll. A record wherein process was entered to interrupt the running of the statute of limitations.

process tax. An excise imposed on the processing rather than on the product. Glenn L. Martin Co. v United States (DC Md) 23 F Supp 262.

processum continuando (prō-ses'um kọn-tin-ụ-an'dō). For continuing the process,—the name given to a writ which lay to keep process of the court alive and in force beyond the time of its normal life.

Processus legis est gravis vexatio, executio legis coronat opus (pro-se'sus lē'jis est gra'vis ve-xā'she-ō, ex-e-kū'she-ō lē'jis ko-rō'nat ō'pus). The process of the law is a grave vexation; the execution of the law crowns the work.

process verbal. A detailed account of the proceedings held before a public officer and the result thereof, formally attested by him as true and correct. Hall v Hall, 11 Tex 526, 539.

procès-verbal (pro-sā'ver-bal'). (French.) An official report.

prochain (pro'shen). (French.) Same as prochein.

prochein (pro'shen). Nearest; next.

prochein ami (pro'shen a-mi'). (French.) Same as **next friend.**

prochein amy. Same as **prochein ami.**

prochein avoidance (ạ-voi'dạns). The next vacancy.

procheyn. Same as **prochein.**

procheyn heir (pro'shen är). The next heir.

proclaimed rate. A rate of customs duty proclaimed by the President. 19 USC § 1202, Headnote 9(d).

proclamare (pro-kla-mā're). To call out; to proclaim; to warn.

proclamation. An announcement made on behalf of the government. Lapeyre v United States (US) 17 Wall 191, 21 L Ed 606. An official announcement

of a matter of great and vital public interest, such as the ratification of an amendment to the United States Constitution. 16 Am J2d Const L § 25. As made by the President of the United States, a public act of which all courts of the United States are bound to take notice and to which they must give effect. Panama Refining Co. v Ryan, 293 US 388, 79 L Ed 466, 55 S Ct 241.
See **writ of proclamation.**

proclamation of a fine. A statutory requirement.
By 1 Richard III, c. 7 (Fines, 1483), confirmed and enforced by 4 Henry VII, c. 24 (Fines, 1488), the fine, after engrossment, was required to be openly read and proclaimed in court sixteen times (four in the term in which it was made, and four in each of the three succeeding terms), but this requirement was reduced to once each term by 31 Elizabeth, c. 2 (Fines, 1588), and these proclamations were indorsed on the back of the record. See 2 Bl Comm 352.

proclamation of election. The notice of an election to be held for the election of officers or passing upon propositions submitted to the voters. The formal statement made by an election officer at the opening of the polls, usually:—"Hear ye, hear ye, the polls are now open."

proclamation of peace. A proclamation by the President of the United States announcing the end of war and the return of peace. 56 Am J1st War § 13.

proclamation of the President. See **proclamation.**

proclamation on exigent (on ek'si-jent). In outlawry proceedings, the sheriff's proclamation that the defendant will be outlawed if he does not surrender.
If a non est inventus is returned upon a capias, an alias writ, and a pluries writ, successively, a writ of exigent is sued out requiring the sheriff to cause the defendant to be proclaimed, required, or exacted, in five county courts successively, to render himself; and, if he does, then to take him, but if he does not appear, and is returned required for the fifth time, he is to be outlawed by the coroners of the county. See 3 Bl Comm 283.

pro concilio (prō kon-si'li-ō). For advice.

pro confesso (prō kon-fes'ō). See **confession of judgment; decree pro confesso.**

pro correctio et salute animae (prō kor-rek'she-ō et sa-lū'te a'ni-mē). For the cure and welfare of the soul.

procreation. The production of offspring.
See **words of procreation.**

proctor (prok'tor). An officer of the ecclesiastical court corresponding to an attorney at law in the courts of the common law. See 3 Bl Comm 25. One licensed to practice admiralty law. One who stands in the relationship to a litigant in admiralty as the attorney of a party in an ordinary civil action. Jackson v Ore Navigation Corp. (DC Md) 159 F Supp 935. One, familiar to generations of law students, who supervises examinations.
See **divorce proctor.**

procul dubio (prō'kul dū'bi-ō). Without doubt.

procuracy (prok'ū-rā-si). The written authority of a procuratur which empowers him to act for his principal.

procurador del comun (pro-cou-rah-dor day co-moon). A solicitor-general. The title of an officer of the Spanish government frequently encountered in Spanish-American grants in certain districts.

He was an officer appointed to make inquiry, put the petitioner in possession of the land prayed for, and execute the lieutenant-governor's and commandant's orders relative to the premises. Lecompte v United States (US) 11 How 115, 13 L Ed 627.

procuratio (prok-ū-rā'she-ō). Procuration; management; administration; a letter of attorney; an attorney in fact; an attorney; an agent.

procuration (prok-ū-rā'shon). Every power or authority given by one person to another by means of an instrument in writing. Williams v Conger, 125 US 397, 422, 31 L Ed 778, 789, 8 S Ct 933. (Ecclesiastical.) An annual payment made by a parish priest to the bishop or archdeacon.

procuration money. Charges of a scrivener or broker for procuring loans. See 4 Bl Comm 157.

procurator (prok'ū-rā-tor). The donee of a procuration; a proctor.
See **procuration; proctor.**

procurator fiscal (fis'kal). A public prosecutor; a prosecuting attorney.

procuratorium (prok-ū-rā-tō'ri-um). The written authority or proxy of a proctor.

procurator litis (prok-ū-rā'tor li'tis). (Civil law.) A person who performed services in a litigation or lawsuit corresponding to those of a modern attorney.

procurator negotiorum (prok-ū-rā'tor ne-go-she-ō'rum). (Civil law.) A manager of affairs; a business manager; an attorney in fact.

procure. To bring into possession; to obtain. Mighell v Dougherty, 86 Iowa 480, 53 NW 402. To cause to occur. To bring about, especially an event fraught with evil. United States v Richmond (CA3 Pa) 17 F2d 28.

procurer (prō-kūr'er). One who uses means to bring anything about, especially one who does so secretly and corruptly. United States v Richmond (CA3 Pa) 17 F2d 28. One who seduces females into prostitution. A pimp.
See **pandering; pimp.**

procuring breach of contract. A tort, in interfering with the right of another, under the doctrine of Lumley v Gye, 118 Eng Reprint 749, 1 ERC 706.

procuring cause. The act which effects a sale or transaction. 12 Am J2d Brok § 189.
As the basis of a broker's right to his commissions, the term refers to the cause originating from a series of events that without break in their continuity results in the prime object of the employment of the broker. Roth v Thomson, 40 Cal App 208, 215; Smith v Preiss, 117 Minn 392, 136 NW 7.

pro defectu (prō dē-fek'tū). For failure of; because of the lack or want of.

pro defectu emptorum (prō dē-fek'tū emp-tō'rum). For want or failure of buyers.

pro defectu exitus (prō dē-fek'tū ex'i-tus). For failure of issue.

pro defectu haeredis (prō dē-fek'tū hē-rē'dis). For want or failure of an heir.

pro defectu justitiae (prō dē-fek'tū jus-ti'she-ē). For defect or want of justice.

pro defendente (prō dē-fen-den'te). For, or in favor of, the defendant.

pro derelicto (prō de-re-lik'tō). For a derelict; as abandoned property.

prodigal (prod'i-gal). A spendthrift; an unthrift.
Under the Roman law, if a man by notorious prodigality was in danger of wasting his estate, he was looked upon as non compos, and committed to the care of curators or tutors by the praetor. But under the common law, when a man on an inquest of idiocy has been returned an "unthrift," and not an idiot, no further proceedings are had. See 1 Bl Comm 305.
See **spendthrift trust.**

pro dignitate regali (prō dig-ni-tā'te rē-gā'lī). For or because of the royal dignity.
Pro dignitate regali, no man can marry a queen dowager, without special license from the king, on pain of forfeiting his lands and goods. See 1 Bl Comm 223.

prodigus (pro'di-gus). (Roman law.) A prodigal; a spendthrift; an extravagant person.

prodition (prō-dish'ọn). Treason.

proditor (prod'i-tọr). A traitor; a person who has committed treason.

proditorie (prō-di-tō'ri-e). Traitorously; treasonably.

pro diviso (prō di-vī'sō). As divided, that is, in severalty.

pro domino (prō dō'mi-nō). As master.

pro donato (prō dō-nā'tō). As a gift; by way of gift.

pro dote (prō do'te). (Civil law.) As a dowry; by way of dowry.

produce (prọ-dūs'). Verb: To give being or form to; to manufacture; to make. Mighell v Dougherty, 86 Iowa 480, 53 NW 402. (prod-ūs'). Noun: In the broad sense, anything grown or manufactured, whether by hand or machinery. In a more limited sense, products of the farm, particularly those marketed daily or at least weekly, such as milk, other things from the dairy, fruits, and vegetables.

produce broker. A broker who negotiates for the sale or exchange of the produce of others. Banta v Chicago, 172 Ill 204, 50 NE 233.

producent (prọ-du'sẹnt). A party who produces or offers a person as a witness.

producer. One who produces whether by farming or manufacturing, although used more commonly to denote a person who raises crops or puts crops in condition for marketing. Allen v Smith, 173 US 389, 399, 43 L Ed 741, 744, 19 S Ct 446.

producers' bounties. Bounties allowed to producers for the purpose of stimulating manufacturing. 12 Am J2d Bount § 3.

product. That which is produced in manufacturing or farming. The result of a course of conduct. The result of a chemical change. The number obtained upon multiplying one number by another.
See **by-product.**

product and profit of labor. A term of art.
As the expression is used in a statute prohibiting the product and profit of convict labor, the words do not refer to articles of property, but to the net value of labor. A manufactured article is not known in common parlance, in law or in political economy, as the product of labor. Labor enters into its production, but is often an insignificant element. The article is the product of raw material and labor combined, or, as it is commonly expressed, labor and capital. People v Hawkins, 157 NY 1, 51 NE 257.

production. A bringing forth. The output of a factory; the grain, produce, fruit, and increase in number or weight of animals realized on a farm. A painting, a literary or musical composition. Dano v Mississippi O. & R. R. R. Co. 27 Ark 564, 567.

production and subsistence loans. Loans for agricultural purposes where production or economic disaster has caused need of farmers for credit not otherwise available. 7 USC §§ 1007-1009; 12 USC § 1148a-2.

production certificate. A certificate issued by the Administrator of the Federal Aviation Agency authorizing the production of duplicates of an aircraft, aircraft engine, propeller, or appliance for aircraft. 49 USC § 1423(b).

production facility. Any equipment or device determined by rule of the Atomic Energy Commission to be capable of the production of special nuclear material in such quantity as to be of significance to the common defense and security, or in such manner as to affect the health and safety of the public; or any important component part especially designed for such equipment or device as determined by the Commission. 42 USC § 2014(t).
For other definitions contained in the regulations of the Atomic Energy Commission see 10 CFR §§ 50.2(a) (1) (2), 10 CFR Cum Supp § 50.2(a) (3).

production of documents. Relief under statute or according to principles of equity by a discovery. 23 Am J2d Dep §§ 164 et seq.
See **subpoena duces tecum.**

production of goods for commerce. Manufacturing, mining, handling, or working on goods in any other manner. Borden Co. v Borella, 325 US 679, 89 L Ed 1865, 65 S Ct 1223, 161 ALR 1258.

production of suit. An old term for making a case in the first instance.
Anciently, at common law, a defendant was not required to answer the charge made by the plaintiff until the plaintiff had, by his witnesses, made out at least a probable case, and this was called the "production of the suit." But this practice was discontinued and has not been followed since the reign of Edward the Third. See 3 Bl Comm 295.

production payment. A right to a specified sum of money or a specified amount of minerals, payable out of an agreed share of minerals produced or of proceeds from sale of minerals.
If the right must continue over the entire term of a mineral lease, it is a royalty, not a production payment. United States v Morgan (CA5 Miss) 321 F2d 781.

production tax. A tax upon the production or severance from the soil of natural resources such as timber, oil, gas, and the like. 51 Am J1st Tax § 1259.
See **gross production tax.**

productio sectae (pro-duk'she-ō sek'tē). Same as **production of suit.**

productivity of land. Cropping value; the ability to produce in terms of specified amounts, such as a stated number of bushels of grain per acre. 55 Am J1st V & P § 84.

products liability. The liability of the manufacturer or seller of an article for an injury caused to person or property by a defect in or condition of the article sold. 46 Am J1st Sales § 799. The liability of a manufacturer or packer of drugs or poisonous substances to an ultimate consumer injured as a result of defects in, or mislabeling of, the product consequent to his want of exercise of due care in the preparation and marketing of the product. 25 Am J2d Drugs § 49. The liability of a druggist for an injury resulting to another from the use of a drug compounded or dispensed by the druggist, where the injury is chargeable directly to a want of due or ordinary care on the part of the druggist in the compounding or dispensing of the drug. 25 Am J2d Drugs §§ 52 et seq.

products liability insurance. A contract or policy of insurance specifically designed to protect the producer, manufacturer, or seller of goods against liability arising by reason of injury to the person or property of others caused by the use of his products. 29A Am J Rev ed Ins § 1360.

product test. The test of criminal responsibility according to whether or not the unlawful act was the product of either mental disease or mental defect. 21 Am J2d Crim L § 39.

pro emptore (pro emp-tō're). (Civil law.) As a purchaser.

pro eo quod (prō ē'ō quod). For this, that.

pro et durante (prō et du-ran'te). For and during.

pro facti (prō fak'ti). As a fact.

pro falso clamore (prō fal'sō kla-mō're). For false claim.

pro falso clamore suo (prō fal'sō kla-mō're su'ō). For or by reason of his own false claim.

profane (prō-fān'). Adjective: Common rather than sacred. Irreverent toward or contemptuous of sacred things. Verb: To desecrate. To put to an ignoble or improper use.

profane language. See **profanity**.

profanity (prō-fan'i-ti). Calling for or implying divine vengeance or divine condemnation, with or without directly employing the name of the Deity. Gaines v State, 75 Tenn (7 Lea) 410.
See **blasphemy**; **cursing**.

profanity in presence of female. A distinct crime or offense in some jurisdictions. Ray v State, 113 Ga 1065, 39 SE 408.

profectitium peculium (prō-fek-ti'she-um pe-kū'li-um). That property which children make out of the property of their father.
All they acquire in this way, belongs entirely to their father, who has them under his power. Sparks v Spence, 40 Tex 694, 700.

profectitus (pro-fek'ti-tus). (Civil law.) Inheritable property.

profer. Same as **profert**.

profert (prō'fert). An offer made formally in a pleading to produce a particular document relied upon by the pleader by way of cause of action or defense. 41 Am J1st Pl § 60. The production of, or offer to produce, a document, made by a party to an action for the purpose of enabling his adversary to read and examine the document. A means of getting a bail bond before the court for action. 8 Am J2d Bail § 154.

profert ad curiam (pro'fert ad kū'ri-am). Same as **profert in curia**.

profert and oyer (pro'fert and ō'yėr). The production of a document for reading by the adverse party. 41 Am J1st Pl § 60.

profert in curia (pro'fert in kū'ri-a). Producing a document in court for reading or attaching a copy thereof to the pleading. Germain v Wilgus (CA9 Cal) 67 F 597, 599.

profession (prō-fesh'on). A statement or declaration, especially a declaration of religious faith or belief. A vocation or employment in preparation for which specialized education and training is required, as in law, medicine, or engineering. Cummings v Pennsylvania Fire Ins. Co. 153 Iowa 579, 134 NW 79. A vocation characterized by the use of specialized knowledge or attainments. Ocean Acci. & Guarantee Corp. v Herzberg's, Inc. (CA8 Neb) 100 F2d 171. A vocation wherein one puts his specialized knowledge to use for the benefit of others, not confining its use to study, to the enhancement of knowledge, or to the accomplishment of an abstract purpose. Edwards v Bates County, 163 US 258, 266, 41 L Ed 151, 155, 16 S Ct 998. For the purposes of an exemption statute, the employment in which the debtor habitually earns his living. 22 Am J1st Exemp § 35.

professional. One engaging in a profession in accordance with the standards of conduct required of one in such profession. One who has made a career, engaging for pay or prize money, out of an activity others follow for diversion or pleasure, such as a professional football player or professional golfer. One who has concentrated his efforts upon performing an art for pay as a means of subsistence, as distinguished from the amateur who engages for the sake of the art or his own pleasure.

professional adviser. One advising upon matters purportedly within the scope of his professional capacity. 37 Am J2d Fraud § 52.

professional bailee. One who makes it his business to act as a bailee and deals with the public on a uniform basis, such as a common carrier, the proprietor of a parking lot, or a warehouseman. 8 Am J2d Bail § 131.

professional baseball. A sport conducted for profit in charging admissions. A business for some purposes. Anno: 56 ALR 813.

professional capacity. A function or status characterized by the employment of the specialized knowledge and skill of a particular profession in attending upon another.
Within the statutory rule which prohibits a physician from testifying as to facts learned while attending his patient in a "professional capacity," a physician who was called as a physician, attended the patient as a physician, diagnosed the case as a physician, and administered remedies as a physician, acted in a professional capacity. And he so acted even though called in by a third party and against the protests of the patient. Meyer v Supreme Lodge Knights of Pythias, 178 NY 63, 70 NE 111.

professional corporation. A corporation formed for the purpose of practicing a profession. 18 Am J2d Corp §§ 31, 32.
As a general rule a corporation cannot lawfully engage in the practice of law, or in the practice of medicine, surgery, or dentistry. Some statutes, however, permit persons engaged in other professions to form corporations or associations for the practice of their professions. 19 Am J2d Corp § 1052.

professional employee. Broadly, any employee whose duties call for the practice of a profession. For the

professional purposes of the Fair Labor Standards Act, an employee whose primary duties consist of the performance of work requiring knowledge of an advanced type in the field of science or learning, or original and creative in character in a recognized field of artistic endeavor, and whose work requires the consistent exercise of discretion and judgment in its performance, is predominantly intellectual and varied in character, and is generally compensated on a salary or fee basis in a specified amount. 29 USC Appx § 5431.3.

professional ethics. See **ethics; judicial ethics; legal ethics.**

professional expert. A person who is skilled in a professional occupation, the word professional being here used as it generally is, to distinguish classes of professional persons from those who are engaged in the various occupations of business or trade.

We speak of the professions of medicine, law, and divinity as the learned professions, and also of the profession of arms. And the term has come to be applied to other occupations or callings, all of which require learned and special preparation in the acquirement of scientific knowledge and skill, necessary to a proper understanding and successful management of such occupations; for example the professional occupation of a civil engineer. Commonwealth ex rel. Hensel v Fitler, 147 Pa 288, 23 A 568.

See **expert witness.**

professional gambler. A person who makes his living or a substantial portion thereof in pursuing the business or practice of unlawful gambling by the use of cards, dice, or other gambling device, with the purpose of thereby winning money or other property, or who conducts, either as owner or employee, a place for gambling. 24 Am J1st Gaming § 46.

professional journal. A publication devoted to the special interests of the members of a particular profession, such as a medical journal or a publication for members of the bar. 39 Am J1st Newsp § 9.

professional judgment. The judgment exercised by a professional man in a bona fide manner and in reference to a matter within the scope of his profession. 41 Am J1st Phys and S § 103.

professional liability insurance. A policy protecting insured, a professional man, against liability arising from his acts or omissions in the practice of his profession. 29A Am J Rev ed Ins § 1358.

professional misconduct. Conduct of an attorney at law which shows him to be unfit or unsafe to manage the business of others in the capacity of a lawyer. 7 Am J2d Attys § 25. Conduct that tends to bring reproach on the legal profession or to injure it in the favorable opinion of the public. Wernimont v State, 101 Ark 210, 142 SW 194. The conduct of a physician which is dishonorable or disreputable in connection with the practice of his profession, which demonstrates incompetency and unfitness for such practice, or is substantially in conflict with the ethics of the profession. 41 Am J1st Phys & S § 49.

See **misconduct of attorney; misconduct of physician.**

professional partnership. A nontrading partnership; a partnership for the practice of a profession, such as a partnership between attorneys at law. 40 Am J1st Partn § 12.

professional services. Services rendered in a professional capacity.

professional society. An organization of the members of a particular profession, for their mutual benefit, the benefit of the profession, and the benefit of the public, on a local, statewide, or national basis, one of the outstanding examples of which is the American Bar Association.

proffer (prof'ėr). To offer.
See **offer of proof; profert.**

profile. A side view represented in a plan prepared by an architect. 27 Am J2d Em D § 424.

pro fine. See **capias pro fine.**

profit. See **profit à prendre; profits; transaction for profit.**

profit apprendre. Same as **profit à prendre.**

profit à prendre (prō'fe ah prôn'druh). A right exercised by one person in the soil of another, accompanied with participation in the profits of the soil or right to take a part of the produce of the land. 25 Am J2d Ease § 4. The power and privilege to acquire through severance ownership of some part of the physical substances included in the possession of land. United States v Gossler (DC Or) 60 F Supp 971.

Examples of profit à prendre are the right to take timber from the land of another, or coal, or to fish in water belonging to another. 25 Am J2d Ease § 4.

profit à rendre (prō'fē ah rôn'druh). The produce of the soil of his land which the tenant yielded up or rendered to him who had a profit à prendre in the land.

profit corporation. A business corporation, organized with a view toward realizing gains to be distributed among its members. Anno: 16 ALR2d 1347.

profiteering. Any conduct or practice involving the acquisition of excessive profits. Mount v Welsh, 118 Or 568, 247 P 815, 822.

profits. Gains. The excess of gross sales over cost of goods plus expenses of operation. McDaniel v State Fair (Tex Civ App) 286 SW 513, 516. The excess of receipts over expenditures. Connolly v Davidson, 15 Minn 519. For some purposes, the equivalent of income. Anno: 24 ALR 17; 130 ALR 512. The return to capital rather than earnings from labor performed or services rendered. Columbus Mining Co. v Ross, 218 Ky 98, 101, 290 SW 1052.

See **mesne profits; net profits; undivided profits.**

profit-sharing plan. An arrangement in a corporation whereby the compensation of officers, agents, or employees is in part dependent upon or payable out of profits of the business. 19 Am J2d Corp §§ 1413 et seq.

pro forma (prō fôr'mą). As a matter of form.

progeny. Children, descendants, offspring.

prognosis (prog-nō'sis). A statement by a physician concerning the probable course of a disease or the duration of an injury and the possibility or probability of recovery. 37 Am J2d Fraud § 82.

progress certificate. A certificate issued by an architect or engineer during the course of construction of a building or other improvement, prepared for the information of the owner concerning performance by the contractor, particularly in reference to payments to be made during the course of construction. 13 Am J2d Bldg Contr §§ 32-40.

progressive capacity. The capacity of an infant increasing from babyhood to the age of majority. 27 Am J1st Inf § 7

progressive tax. Strictly, a tax which, as in the case of the federal income tax, applies higher rates progressively as the taxable amount increases. State ex rel. Foot v Bazille, 97 Minn 11, 106 NW 93. An excise or license tax on retail merchants computed on their gross sales at a percentage which increases with the volume of the taxpayer's business. Stewart Dry Goods Co. v Lewis, 294 US 550, 79 L Ed 1054, 55 S Ct 525, reh den 295 US 768, 79 L Ed 1709, 55 S Ct 652. Inclusive in the broad sense, of a graduated tax.

See **graduated tax.**

progress payments. Payments made to a contractor during the performance of the work, usually calculated in amount according to the percentage of work accomplished. Anno: 22 ALR2d 1344; 17 Am J2d Contr § 348.

pro hac vice (prō hak vī'se). For this occasion. McNeal v Braun, 53 NJL 617, 23 A 687.

Prohibetur ne quis faciat in suo quod nocere possit alieno (pro-hi-bē'ter nē quis fa'she-at in su'ō quod no-sē're po'sit ā-li-ē'nō). It is prohibited to do on one's own property that which may injure another's. Conrad v Baltimore & Ohio Railroad Co. 64 W Va 176, 61 SE 44.

prohibit. To forbid, To prevent.

prohibited goods. Goods, merchandise, and other articles, the importation of which into the United States is prohibited. 21 Am J2d Cust D § 22.

prohibitio de vasto, directa parti (pro-hi-bi'she-ō dē vas'tō, dī-rek'ta par'tī). A writ which lay to prohibit the tenant from committing waste during the pendency of an action.

prohibition. A remedy the purpose of which is to prevent a tribunal possessing judicial or quasi-judicial powers from exercising jurisdiction over matters not within its cognizance, or exceeding its jurisdiction in matters of which it has cognizance. Anno: 77 ALR 246. A total restraint on traffic in intoxicating liquors. Ex parte Meyer, 84 Tex Crim 288, 207 SW 100. National prohibition under the act of Congress passed in 1919 (41 Statutes at Large, 305), known as the Volstead Act prohibiting the manufacture, sale, transportation, and exportation of intoxicating liquors for beverage purposes, for the enforcement of the Eighteenth Amendment to the United States Constitution. National Prohibition Cases, 253 US 350, 64 L Ed 946, 40 S Ct. 486, 588.

See **writ of prohibition.**

For repeal of Eighteenth Amendment, see **Twenty-first Amendment.**

prohibition agent. A federal officer in the hierarchy for the enforcement of the former National Prohibition Act. Not an internal revenue officer. United States v Parzah, (DC Pa) 18 F2d 1003.

prohibition commissioner. The Commissioner of Internal Revenue in his capacity of officer for administration of the National Prohibition Act. Gnerich v Rutter, 265 US 388, 390, 68 L Ed 1068, 1069.

See **prohibition.**

prohibition director. A federal officer in the hierarchy for the enforcement of the National Prohibition Act.

See **prohibition.**

prohibition of waste. See **writ of prohibition of waste.**

prohibitive. Tending to prohibit or prevent or to exclude or bar.

prohibitive impediments. Those impediments or restrictions which do not make a marriage void, but which render the parties liable to punishment.

prohibitive license. A license required as a condition of doing business, the fee for which is so high as to be prohibitive of engaging in the business. 52 Am J1st Trad St § 14.

prohibitory injunction. Same as **preventive injunction.**

prohibitory writ. See **injunction; writ of prohibition.**

prohibitum. See **malum prohibitum.**

pro ignorantia literarum (prō ig-nō-ran'she-a li-te-rā' rum). Through ignorance of letters; by reason of inability to write.

pro illa vice (prō il'la vī'se). For that occasion.

proinde (prō-in'de). Therefore; accordingly.

pro indefenso (prō in-de-fen'sō). As undefended.

pro indiviso (prō in-di-vī'sō). As undivided.

pro interesse suo (prō in-ter-es'se su'ō). In proportion to his own interest.

projecting load. A load on a vehicle on the highway, part of which projects beyond the body of the vehicle, sometimes to the side but more often to the rear. 25 Am J1st High § 234.

projectio (pro-jek'she-ō). Alluvion, or the gradual washing up of the sand and earth so as to increase the quantity of land owned by a riparian proprietor.

projection. An overhang.

projection of the shore. An extension of the land by wharf or pier. The Russell No. 6 (DC NY) 42 F Supp 904.

projectoscope (prō-jek'tọ-skōp). An instrumentality for displaying a photographic impression by throwing an enlargement upon a screen. Anno: 72 ALR2d 316, § 6[a].

projet (prō-zhā'). The draft of a proposed treaty between two or more nations.

pro laesione fidei (prō lē-she-ō'ne fī-dē'ī). For a breach of faith.

In the reign of Stephen, the clergy tried to turn their ecclesiastical courts into courts of equity by entertaining suits pro laesione fidei, as a spiritual offense against conscience, in case of nonpayment of debts or breaches of contract generally, until this attempt was checked by the Constitutions of Clarendon. See 3 Bl Comm 52.

prolapsus uteri (prō-lap'sus u'te-rī). Falling of the womb. Cole v Cole, 37 Tenn (5 Sneed) 57.

prolatum (prō-lā'tum). An extra judicial opinion, given in or out of court; a saying not to be accepted as an opinion. Thorne v San Francisco, 4 Cal 127, 156.

pro legato (prō le-gā'tō). As a legacy.

proles (prō'lēz). Issue; offspring; descendants; posterity.

Proles sequitur sortem paternam (prō'lez se'qui-ter sor'tem pa-ter'nam). The child follows the lot of the father. Lynch v Clarke (NY) 1 Sandf 583, 660.

proletarius (pro-le-tā'ri-us). (Civil law.) A person who had no property to be taxed, but paid a tax only on account of his children.—Wharton's Law Dictionary.

prolicide (prō'li-sid). The killing by a parent of his offspring.

prolixity. Verbosity, particularly in a pleading. 41 Am J1st Pl § 27. Excessiveness in wording. 27 Am J1st Indict § 51.

prolocutor (prō-lok'ū-tor). (Ecclesiastical.) The presiding officer in a convocation or assembly of the English clergy.

prolongation. An extension of the time within which an act is required to be done or within which an obligation is to be performed.

pro lucrari (prō lu-krā'rī). For the sake of gain.

pro majori cautela (prō ma-jō'rī kâ-te'la). For greater caution; for greater security.

promenade (prom-e-näd'). A public place for strolling or walking for pleasure. Appleton v New York, 219 NY 150, 114 NE 73, 7 ALR 629.

promise. Verb: To engage. To pledge one's self to performance. To assure the performance of a particular act. To pledge by contract. Knecht v Mutual Life Ins. Co. 90 Pa 118. Noun: An assurance, in whatever form of expression used, that a thing will or will not be done. Baehr v Penn-O-Tex Oil Corp. 258 Minn 533, 104 NW2d 661. Something more than an acknowledgement of an obligation. UCC § 3-102(1)(c), and Comment 2. A declaration which gives to the person to whom it is made a right to expect or claim the performance or non-performance of some particular thing. Taylor v Miller, 113 NC 340, 342, 18 SE 504. An undertaking which binds the promisor for the happening of a future event, provided it is supported by a consideration. 17 Am J2d Contr § 2.

promisee. The person to whom a promise is made.

promise of immunity. A promise, made by a person in authority in obtaining a confession, that the accused shall be immune in whole or in part from prosecution or punishment. 29 Am J2d Ev § 563.

promise of marriage. An engagement of marriage to the promisee.
As the words are used in the statutory offense of seduction under promise of marriage, the promise need not be expressed in any set form, or in any particular words. It is enough if language is used which implies such a promise, and is intended to convey that meaning, and is in fact so understood by the prosecutrix. State v Brinkhaus, 34 Minn 285, 286.
See **breach of promise**.

promise to answer for the debt, default, or miscarriage of another. An undertaking by a person not before liable, for the purpose of securing or performing the same duty for which the original debtor continues to be liable. Dillaby v Wilcox, 60 Conn 71, 22 A 491.

promise to pay. An undertaking to pay. UCC § 3-102(1)(c).

promise to pay the debt of another. See **promise to answer for the debt, default, or miscarriage of another**.

promise to pay when able. An acknowledgment sufficient for the purpose of creating a stated account only where there is an absolute assent to the amount. Kaunitz v Wheeler, 344 Mich 181, 73 NW2d 263.

promisio (prōm-ish'i-o). See **stipulatio**.

pro misis et custagiis (prō mi'sis et kus-tā'ji-is). For his costs and charges.

promisor (prom'i-sor). A person who makes a promise to another; a person who promises.

promissory estoppel. A new name for an established doctrine. The principle that an estoppel may arise from the making of a promise, even though without consideration, if it was intended that the promise should be relied upon and in fact it was relied upon, and if a refusal to enforce it would be virtually to sanction the perpetration of fraud or would result in other injustice. 28 Am J2d Estop § 48.
A promise which the promisor should reasonably expect to induce action or forbearance of a definite and substantial character on the part of the promisee and which does induce such action or forbearance is binding if injustice can be avoided only by the enforcement of the promise. Fried v Fisher, 328 Pa 497, 196 A 39, 115 ALR 147.

promissory note. A contract in writing for the payment of money, usually with the added feature of negotiability. Annis v Pfeiffer, 278 Mich 692, 271 NW 568; Sabine v Leonard (Mo) 322 SW2d 831. A term used interchangeably with note. Shawano Finance Corp. v Julius, 214 Wis 637, 254 NW 355. A term well understood as indicating a negotiable note. Road Improv. Dist. v Southern Trust Co. 152 Ark 422, 239 SW 8.
See **negotiable note; note**.

promissory oath. A solemn appeal to God, or, in a wider sense, to some superior sanction or a sacred or revered person (as the temple, the altar, the blood of abel, the Koran, a tribal superior, etc.) in witness of the inviolability of a promise or undertaking. People ex rel. Bryant v Zimmerman, 241 NY 405, 150 NE 497, 43 ALR 909, 913.

promissory representation. A representation as to something which will be or is intended to be done in the future. 37 Am J2d Fraud § 57. In the law of insurance, an allegation as of something to happen during the existence of the insurance. 29 Am J Rev ed Ins § 698.
As the basis of estoppel, see **promissory estoppel**.

promissory statement. See **promissory representation**.

promissory warranty. An absolute undertaking by an insured, contained in a policy of insurance or in a paper properly incorporated by reference, that certain facts or conditions pertaining to the risk shall continue, or that certain things with reference thereto shall be done or omitted. 29 Am J Rev ed Ins § 709.

promontory (prom'on-tō-ri). A headland; a high point of land jutting into sea or lake. United States v Otley (DC Or) 34 F Supp 182.

promote. To give a start to something, perchance the organization of a corporation. To forward. To contribute to growth and enlargement. Bank of Italy v Johnson, 200 Cal 1, 251 P 784, 792.

promoter. A person who undertakes to bring about the incorporation and organization of a corporation, procures for it the rights and capital by which it is to carry out the purposes set forth in its charter, and establishes it as able to do business, bringing together the person interested in the enterprise, aiding in procuring subscriptions to stock, and setting in motion the machinery which leads to the formation of the corporation. 18 Am J2d Corp § 106. One who performs in like manner in the organization of a co-operative apartment association. 15 Am J2d Con Apt § 21. In a less well-known sense, an informer, one who is responsible for the starting of a criminal prosecution. In the broadest sense, one who promotes, be it nothing more than a game of cards.

promotion. The advancement of an employee from one position in the work to a position of more significance and better compensation. The advancement of a person in the civil service to a higher position on the basis of qualifications. 15 Am J2d Civ S § 20. The work in organizing and establishing a corporation in business, bringing together persons interested in the enterprise, aiding in procuring subscriptions to stock, and doing other work leading to the formation of the corporation. 18 Am J2d Corp § 106. Any activity by a person in the status of a promoter.
See **promoter.**

promotional examination. A civil service examination given persons in the service as the basis of determining merit for promotion. 15 Am J2d Civ S § 10.

promotion expenses. Necessary expenses incurred by promoters before incorporation of the company being organized with their aid. 18 Am J2d Corp § 108.

prompt. Adjective: Punctual. Expeditious; quick. Pearson v Washingtonian Pub. Co. 68 App DC 373, 98 F2d 248. Prepared beforehand. Tobias v Lissberger, 105 NY 404, 12 NE 13. Verb: To urge. To cue an actor.

promptly. Expeditiously. 46 Am J1st Sales § 163. With reasonable diligence. having regard to the circumstances. Bowles v Mutual Ben. Health & Acci. Asso. (CA4 Va) 99 F2d 44, 119 ALR 756.

prompt-note (prompt-nōt). A notice given to one who has bought on credit of the due date of his obligation to pay.

prompt notice. Notice given within a reasonable time. Anno: 76 ALR 59; 41 ALR2d 853 (notice of breach of warranty). Notice given with reasonable dispatch. Black & W. Cab. Co. v New York Indem. Co. 108 W Va 93, 150 SE 521 (notice of accident as required by insurance policy).

promptu. See **in promptu.**

promulgate (prō-mul'gāte). To give notice to the public of the enactment of a law or the prescribing of a rule of court.

promulgation (prō-mul-gā'shọn). Making known to the public the enactment of a statute or the prescribing of a rule of court. To publish a statute or rule of court. 20 Am J2d Cts § 83.

promutuum (pro-mu'tu-um). A quasi contract whereby a person to whom money had been paid under a mistake, became bound to repay it.

pro non scripto (prō non skrip'tō). As though not written; as though it had never been written.

pronouncement of judgment. The rendition of judgment by the court. 30A Am J Rev ed Judgm § 49. The rendition of judgment and direction for the entry thereof. People v Walker, 76 Cal App 192, 200, 244 P 94, 98.

pronouncement of sentence. The judgment of a court of criminal jurisdiction. Kennedy v Reid, 101 App DC 400, 249 F2d 492. The act of a court of criminal jurisdiction in formally declaring to the accused the legal consequences of the guilt which he has confessed or of which he has been convicted. State v Fedder, 1 Utah 2d 117, 262 P2d 753.

proof. Evidence. More precisely, the effect of evidence; the establishment of a fact by evidence. 29 Am J2d Ev § 2. A matter of conviction or persuasion resulting from a consideration of the evidence. Dege v Produce Exchange Bank, 212 Minn 44, 2 NW2d 423.

proof beyond reasonable doubt. See **reasonable doubt.**

proof gallon. A gallon of proof spirits or the equivalent thereof. 26 USC § 5002(a)(8).
See **proof spirits.**

proof of claim. A written and verified statement of a claim against a decedent, presented for payment by filing in the probate court or serving the same upon the personal representative as the statute may require. 31 Am J2d Ex & Ad §§ 298 et seq. In bankruptcy, a demand against a fund in possession of the court for distribution. 9 Am J2d Bankr § 428. A statement in writing, signed and verified by the creditor, with caption and title as prescribed by Order 21 of the General Orders in Bankruptcy, setting forth a claim against the estate in bankruptcy, the consideration therefor, whether any and, if so, what securities are held therefor, whether any and, if so, what payments have been made thereon, and declaring that the claim is justly owing from the bankrupt to the creditor. Bankruptcy Act § 57(a); 11 USC § 93(a); 9 Am J2d Bankr § 439. A sworn statement of subject matter and amount of a claim against an insolvent in insolvency proceedings, made for the purpose of participating in the distribution of assets to creditors. 29 Am J Rev ed Insolv § 31.

proof of death. Evidence of death. 22 Am J2d Dth §§ 299 et seq. The proof of loss under a life insurance policy.
See **death certificate.**

proof of loss. A statement in writing, usually under oath, of a loss sustained by an insured, required by policy provision or statute to be submitted to the insured within the time prescribed by the policy or statute, stating the amount of the loss and the manner in which it occurred. 29A Am J Rev ed Ins §§ 1373-1439.
See **due proof of loss.**

proof of publication. An affidavit or certificate of publication made by the publisher of a newspaper or his authorized agent as proof of the publication of a notice, summons, order, and so forth. 39 Am J1st Newsp § 14.

proof of service. See **return of process.**

proof per testes (per tes'tēz). Proof of a disputed will by the persons who witnessed its execution.

proof spirits. A liquid which contains one-half its volume of ethyl alcohol of a specific gravity of .7939 at 60 degrees Fahrenheit referred to water at 60 degrees Fahrenheit as unity. 26 USC § 5002(a)(7).

proof to a moral certainty. The equivalent of proof beyond a reasonable doubt, signifying such proof as satisfies the judgment and conscience of the jury, as reasonable men, that the defendant is guilty of the crime charged. 30 Am J2d Ev § 1171.

pro omni servitio (prō om'nī ser-vi'she-ō). In lieu of all service.

pro opere et labore (prō ō'pe-re et la-bō're). For work and labor. See 1 Bl Comm 471.

prop. A support.
See **mine prop.**

propaganda. (prop-a-gan'dä). Ideas communicated for the purpose of influencing the thoughts of another, especially, in the modern sense, distorted principles intended to deceive. An antisocial activity insofar as it advocates the destruction of organized government, of mass industrial revolts against municipal government, and revolutionary mass action for the final destruction of government. 47 Am J1st Sedit Etc § 13.

The term "political propaganda," for the purposes of the Foreign Agents Registration Act, is defined at length in such statute. 22 USC §§ 611-616.

One of the qualifications which charitable organizations generally must meet in order that a gift to them may be deductible for gift tax purposes is that carrying on "propaganda" or otherwise attempting to influence legislation shall not constitute a substantial part of their activities. IRC 1954 § 2522; 26 USC 2522.

propane gas (prō'pān gas). A chemical combination of carbon and hydrogen, about 1-1/2 times heavier than air, odorless, colorless, invisible, and highly inflammable. 26 Am J2d Electr § 5.

pro patria (prō pā'tri-ạ). For one's country.

proper. Fitting. Conforming to an accepted standard. Decent.

proper action. A technical term of very limited usage for an action brought in the name of the county. Richardson v Stuesser, 125 Wis 66, 103 NW 261.

proper books of account. The books of account of a merchant or trader kept in such a manner, however inartistic or unprofessional it may be, that the real condition of the financial affairs of the business may be ascertained and determined upon an examination thereof. Siegel v His Creditors, 95 Cal 409, 414, 30 P 559.

proper burial. See **decent burial; respectable burial.**

proper care. See **standard of care.**

proper district. The federal district to which a cause removed from state court should be brought; the district which includes the county or place where the suit is pending at the time of removal. General Invest. Co. v Lake Shore & N. S. R. Co. 260 US 261, 67 L Ed 244, 43 S Ct 106.

proper election. See **election to fill vacancy in office.**

proper evidence. See **admissible evidence.**

proper feud (fūd). A military fee or feud.

proper independent advice. Advice by a competent and disinterested person. Zwirtz v Dorl, 123 Okla 284, 253 P 75.

proper indorsement. An indorsement of a bill or note, embracing the signature of the indorser and in such form as to transfer title to the instrument and warrant payment by the maker to the indorsee. Thompson v Farmers' State Bank, 159 Iowa 662, 140 NW 877.

The signature of an indorser without additional words is a sufficient indorsement to effect an assignment or negotiation, as the case may be, of a bill or note, when the assignment or negotiation is completed by such delivery as is requisite. Such is the customary or usual indorsement. Additional words, however, may be employed to express the intent to negotiate or assign, as the case may be. 11 Am J2d B & N § 351.

proper lookout. See **lookout.**

proper name. The first or Christian name of a person. 38 Am J1st Name § 4.

proper parental care. Such care as an ordinarily prudent parent would exercise over the child for its welfare under the same or similar circumstances. Mitchell v Davis (Tex Civ App) 205 SW2d 812, 12 ALR2d 1042.

proper party. A person who may but need not be joined. McAndrews v Krause, 245 Minn 85, 71 NW2d 153, 53 ALR2d 312. A person without whom a judgment or decree may be rendered in the action, but not a judgment or decree which shall completely settle all the questions which may be involved in the controversy and conclude the rights of all the persons who have an interest of some kind in the subject matter of the litigation. Serr v Biwabik Concrete Aggregate Co. 202 Minn 165, 278 NW 355, 117 ALR 1009. Any person materially interested, either legally or equitably, in the subject matter of the litigation, such person, having been joined, being bound by the judgment or decree rendered in the action. 39 Am J1st Parties § 5.

proper person. A person whose condition entitles him to be carried as a passenger by a common carrier, the carrier having the right to refuse transportation to a person who is disorderly, intoxicated, afflicted with a contagious disease, or in such condition otherwise as to render his presence dangerous to the lives or health of passengers. Bogard v Illinois Central Railroad Co. 144 Ky 649, 139 SW 855.

proper purpose of inspection. A lawful purpose, not contrary to the interests of the corporation, whereby a stockholder in good faith seeks information bearing upon the protection of his interest and that of other stockholders in the corporation, as distinguished from a purpose to be vexatious, to gratify curiosity, or to use the information obtained for speculation. Sawyers v American Phenolic Corp. 404 Ill 440, 89 NE2d 374, 45 ALR2d 1.

proper title. A title sufficient to comply with the vendor's obligation under contract of sale. 56 Am J1st V & P § 166.

Within the meaning of the Puerto Rican law that allows a ten-year prescription, a "proper" title does not mean a perfect title. If the title is good on its face, and the possessor under it has no notice of any extrinsic defect, it will found a good title in ten years. Fernandez & Bros. v Ayllon Y Ojeda, 266 US 144, 146, 69 L Ed 209, 211, 45 S Ct 52.

See **good title; marketable title.**

proper tool or implement. For the purposes of an exemption of a debtor, a tool or implement adapted to the trade or business in which he is engaged. Baker v Maxwell, 183 Iowa 1192, 168 NW 160, 2 ALR 814.

property. In a popular sense, a chattel or tract of land. 42 Am J1st Prop § 3. Inclusive of both real estate and personalty. Anno: 115 ALR 553; 57 Am J1st Wills § 1338. Inclusive of both tangibles and intangibles; that which is corporeal and that which is incorporeal. Bouse v Hutzler, 180 Md 682, 26 A2d 767, 141 ALR 843. Strictly, that dominion or indefinite right of user, control, and disposition which one may lawfully exercise over particular things or objects. 42 Am J1st Prop § 2. The right and interest which a man has in lands and chattels to the exclusion of others. Ralston Steel Car Co. v Ralston, 112 Ohio St 306, 147 NE 513, 39 ALR

334. The right of a person to possess, use, enjoy, and dispose of a thing. Willcox v Penn Mut. Life Ins. Co. 357 Pa 581, 55 A2d 521, 174 ALR 220. The free use, enjoyment, and disposal of a person's acquisitions without control or diminution save by the law of the land. Department of Financial Institutions v General Finance Corp. 227 Ind 373, 86 NE2d 444, 10 ALR2d 436. Not the material object itself, but the right and interest or domination rightfully obtained over such object, with the unrestricted right to its use, enjoyment, and disposition. Howlett v Doglio, 42 Ill 311, 82 NE2d 708, 6 ALR2d 790; Akron v Chapman, 160 Ohio St 382, 116 NE2d 697, 42 ALR2d 1140. A species of title, inchoate or complete, legal or equitable, embracing rights which lie in contract, executory or executed. Smith v United States (US) 10 Pet 326, 9 L Ed 442.

As the term is used in the guarantee of the Fourteenth Amendment:—the right to acquire, possess, and enjoy particular things and objects in any way consistent with the equal rights of others and the just exactions and demands of the state. Wright v Hart, 182 NY 330, 75 NE 404; Ives v South Buffalo R. Co. 201 NY 271, 94 NE 431; all valuable interests which a man may possess outside of himself—outside of his life and liberty—being more than that which a person owns. 16 Am J2d Const L § 364. As the term appears in constitutional provisions respecting taking of property:—a word of most general import, extending to every species of right and interest, capable of being enjoyed as such, upon which it is practicable to place a money value. 26 Am J2d Em D § 173.

As used in a statutory provision authorizing a corporation to receive "property" in payment for its stock, the term is not used in its broad sense which includes anything susceptible of ownership, but is limited to that which may readily be applied to the debts of the corporation. 18 Am J2d Corp § 258.

Property Act. A uniform law drawn primarily to abolish anachronisms in the law of property, to abolish many out of date characteristics which have come down from the early feudal law of England, and which are out of place in the law of today, in effect to make the law a much more modern and effective instrument and to free courts and lawyers of the present from being compelled in cases involving the title to real property, to wander in a labyrinth of ancient learning. Ellingrod v Trombla, 168 Neb 264, 95 NW2d 635.

property covered. Property within the coverage of an insurance policy; property within the terms of any instrument, particularly an instrument which purports to create a lien.

property damage. A part of the coverage of an automobile liability policy. 7 Am J2d Auto Ins § 80.

property dividend. A dividend on corporate stock paid in real or personal property. 19 Am J2d Corp § 809.

property held for sale. See **sale in ordinary course of business.**

property in custodia legis (prop'er-ti in kus-tō'di-a lē'jis). Property in custody of the law.
See **custody of the law.**

property in estate in bankruptcy. Inclusive of both legal and equitable interests, embracing everything that has exchangeable value or goes to make up a man's wealth, and every interest or estate which the law regards of sufficient value for judicial recognition. 9 Am J2d Bankr § 848.

property insurance. Insurance in which the risk is that of the loss of property, as from fire, flood, windstorm, etc A contract of insurance whereby the insurer becomes bound, for a consideration in the form of a premium or premiums, to indemnify the insured for actual loss, in whole or in part, not exceeding title to real property, to wander in a labyrinth policy as insured. 29 Am J Rev ed Ins § 4.

property not administered. See **not administered.**

property per industriam (prop'er-ti per in-dus' tri-am). A term of art for the qualified right of property acquired in a wild animal by capturing, confining, taming, and domesticating it. 4 Am J2d Ani § 17.

property propter impotentiam (property prop'ter im-po-ten'she-am). Property by reason of its inability.
The term is applied to that qualified property which a person may have in animals ferae naturae which are too young to stray; such as young conies in a burrow, or young birds in a nest. State v Theriault, 70 Vt 617, 41 A 1030.

property propter privilegium (property prop'ter pri-vi-lē'ji-um). Property by reason of privilege.
The term is applied to that qualified property which a person may have in animals ferae naturae, by reason of his exclusive right or privilege of hunting them. See 2 Bl Comm 394.

property ratione impotentiae (property ra-she-ō'ne im-po-ten'she-ē). Same as **property propter impotentiam.**

property ratione soli (property ra-she-ō'ne sō'lī). Property by virtue of ownership of the soil, for example, fish in private waters. 4 Am J2d Ani § 18; 35 Am J2d Fish § 3.

property rights. Economic interests supported by the law. United States v Willow River Power Co. 324 US 499, 89 L Ed 1101, 65 S Ct 761.
See **property.**

property settlement. An agreement between husband and wife settling property rights in anticipation of the breaking up of the marital union: (1) determining the rights of the parties in jointly owned property and stating the disposition to be made of it; (2) settling all claims of each spouse in the property of the other and claims of each spouse to title to property held in the name of the other; (3) mutually releasing all past and present claims except as established by the agreement; (4) waiving and releasing all future rights as spouse in the property of each other; (5) surrendering the rights of each on the death of the other, including rights of inheritance, homestead, dower, and the right to administer the estate of the other and to have exemptions and allowances from the estate; and (6) agreeing that each will execute all documents necessary or desirable to carry out the purposes of the agreement. Anno: 35 ALR2d 712, § 2; 24 Am J2d Div & S § 883.

property tax. A tax on the ownership of property, without reference to the particular name by which the tax is designated. 51 Am J1st Tax § 29. A tax assessed on all property or on all property of a certain class located within a certain territory on a specified date in proportion to its value, or in accordance with some other reasonable method of apportionment, the obligation to pay which is absolute and is not based upon any voluntary action of the person assessed. 51 Am J1st Tax § 29. A tax on things tangible or intangible, as distinguished from a tax on a right to use or transfer things, or on the proceeds of a business in which the use of things is essential. Anno: 103 ALR 20.

Property taxes are not personal debts; they are enforced contributions to the state or taxing unit and unless otherwise provided are collectible only from the property assessed. Maricopa County v Trustees of Arizona Lodge, 52 Ariz 329, 80 P2d 956.

property tort. An unlawful interference by one person with the enjoyment by another of his private property. 52 Am J1st Torts § 40.

propiedad (pro-pe-ay-dahd). A term found in Spanish-American grants signifying the right to enjoy and dispose freely of things which are ours, so far as the law forbids not.

Commonly, the dominion which is not accompanied by the usufruct is called "propiedad" or "nuda propiedad," and the dominion which is accompanied by the usufruct is called "plena propiedad." Castillero v United States (US) 2 Black 1, 17 L Ed 360, 400.

Propinquior excludit propinquum; propinquus remotum; et remotus remotiorem. (pro-pin'qui-or ex-klū'dit pro-pin'qu-um; pro-pin'qu-us rē-mō'tum; et rē-mō'tus re-mō-she-ō'rem). The one who is nearer excludes the one who is near; the near excludes the remote; and the remote excludes the more remote.

propinquity (prǭ-ping'kwi̯-ti). Relationship; consanguinity. Nearness in point of time or place.

propinquus (pro-pin'qu-us). A near relative; next of kin; a kinsman.

propios (pro'pe-os). (Spanish.) Land reserved for public buildings.

When a town was founded in Spanish America, certain portions of ground termed "propios" were laid off and reserved as the inalienable property of the town, for the purpose of erecting public buildings, markets, etc., or to be used in any other way, under the direction of the municipality for the advancement of the revenues or the prosperity of the place. They were not held for specific purposes, but the municipality might convert them to the uses which it should judge most convenient. Strother v Lucas (US) 12 Pet 410, 442, footnote, 9 L Ed 1137, 1150, footnote.

propone (prǭ-pōn'). To propound; to proffer; to offer as, to propone a will for probate; to make a motion.

proponent (prǭ-pō'nent). A party who propones or who alleges; a person who offers a will for probate; a party who makes a motion.

proportion. A part; a share. Equality between ratios. See **apportionment.**

proportional rate. One carrier's part of a through rate over the lines of two or more carriers. Hocking Valley R. Co. v Lackawanna Coal & Lumber Co. (CA4 W Va) 224 F 930.
See **pro rata freight charge.**

proportional representation. A generic term for various involved systems of voting, similar in essentials, but varying in details, usually having reference in particular to the election of a legislative body, the underlying theory being that the conventional system of election by a majority or plurality of the votes cast does not result in the election of a body as representative of the people as it is possible to obtain by a more scientific system. 26 Am J2d Elect § 273.

See **apportionment; Hare system; list system.**

proportional system. Taxation at a fixed and uniform rate in proportion to the amount of taxable property based upon a cash valuation. State ex rel. Foot v Bazille, 97 Minn 11, 106 NW 93.

See **apportionment; proportional representation.**

proportionate negligence. Same as **comparative negligence.**

proportionate recovery clause. Same as **pro rata clause.**

proportum (pro-por'tum). Purport; meaning; import; signification.

proposal. An offer. An offer of marriage. The introduction of a measure in a legislative body. An expression of intention. Taylor v Miller, 113 NC 340, 342, 18 SE 504. Precisely, a suggestion to induce negotiations or offers by others. Williston, Contracts 3d ed § 27; Restatement Contracts § 25; 17 Am J2d Contr § 33.

proposition. A proposed law submitted to the voters at an election. The statement on the ballot in submitting a question of a bond issue to the vote of the people at an election. 43 Am J1st Pub Sec § 88. A proposal or offer inviting an acceptance. Perry v Dwelling House Ins. Co. 67 NH 291, 33 A 731. A proposal to a female that she submit to an illicit relation.

proposition of law. A point of law presented in assignments of error or brief on appeal. 5 Am J2d A & E §§ 661, 684 et seq.

Propositum indefinitum aequipollet universali (pro-po'zi-tum in-de-fi-nī'tum ē-qui-pol'let ū-ni-ver-sā'lī). An indefinite proposition is equivalent to a general one.

propositus (pro-po'zi-tus). The person proposed; the person from whom all the degrees of relationship are computed in a tree or table of consanguinity. See 2 Bl Comm 203.

Pro possessione praesumitur de jure (prō po-ze-she-o'ne prē-zu'mi-ter dē jū're). A presumption of law arises from possession.

pro possessore (prō po-ze-sō're). As a possessor.

Pro possessore habetur qui dolo injuriave desiit possidere (prō po-ze-sō're hā-bē'ter quī dō'lō in-jū-ri-ā've dē'si-it pos-si-dē're). A person is deemed to be a possessor who has been dispossessed by fraud or injury.

pro posse suo (prō pos'se su'ō). According to his own ability.

propound. To propose. To set forth. To offer a will for probate.

propres (prō'prĕz). See **res propria est quae, etc.**

propria causa. See **in propria causa.**

propria manu (prō'pri-a ma'nū). By his own hand.

Propria manu pro ignorantia literarum signum sanctae crucis expressi et subscripsi (prō'pri-a ma'nū prō ig-nō-ran'she-a li-te-rā'rum sig'num sank'tē kru'sis ex-pres'sī et sub-skrip'sī). On account of ignorance of letters I have impressed and subscribed the sign of the sacred cross with my own hand. See 2 Bl Comm 305.

propria persona. See **in propria persona.**

propriedad (prō-pri-ay-dahd'). (Spanish.) Property.

proprietary. Adjective: In the capacity of an owner. Being a proprietor. Noun: A proprietor. An owner. Trustees of New Castle Common v Gordy (Sup) 33 Del Ch 334, 93 A2d 509, 40 ALR2d 544. A certain owner. Ferguson v Arthur, 117 US 482, 487, 29 L Ed 979, 981, 6 S Ct 861.

proprietary function. The function of a municipal corporation which it exercises with respect to its private rights as a corporate body. 37 Am J1st Mun Corp § 114. The function of a municipal corporation in which it acts and contracts for the private advantage of the inhabitants of the city and of the city itself. Omaha Water Co. v Omaha (CA8 Neb) 147 F 1.

proprietary lease. A lease by a co-operative apartment association which carries with it the right to occupy a specific apartment. 15 Am J2d Con Apt § 21.

proprietary medicine. A medicine compounded of various single ingredients. De Forest (US), 13 How 274, 14 L Ed 143. More precisely, a medicine compounded by a manufacturer according to his own formula. 25 Am J2d Drugs § 3.

proprietary powers. The powers of a municipal corporation in exercising proprietary functions, as distinguished from its public or governmental powers. High Point v Duke Power Co. (CA4 NC) 120 F2d 666.

See **proprietary function.**

proprietas (pro-prī'e-tās). (Civil law.) Property; that which is peculiarly one's own; ownership.

proprietas nuda (prō-prī'e-tās nū'da). Naked property; property in which the owner has title without the use.

proprietas plena (pro-prī'e-tās plē'na). Full property; that is, property in which the owner has both the title and the use.

Proprietas totius navis carinae causam sequitur (prō-prī'ē-tās tō-shē'us nā'vis ka'rī-nē kâ'zam se'qui-ter). The property in the whole ship follows that of the keel. Glover v Austin, 23 Mass (6 Pick) 209, 220.

Proprietas verborum est salus proprietatum (pro-prī'e-tās ver-bō'rum est sa'lus pro-prī-e-tā'tum). The propriety or aptness of words is the salvation of property.

proprietate probanda. See **de proprietate probanda.**

Proprietates verborum observandae sunt (pro-prī-e-tā'tēz ver-bō'rum ob-ser-van'dē sunt). The proprieties of words should be preserved.

proprietor. An owner of premises. An owner of property. Turner v Cross, 83 Tex 218, 18 SW 578. The owner of a business. Cady v Kerr, 11 Wash 2d 1, 118 P2d 182, 137 ALR 713.

proprietor of subject of copyright. The author or one to whom he assigns his right to the work. 18 Am J2d Copyr §§ 28, 32.

propriis manibus (pro'pri-is man'i-bus). With his own hands.

proprio jure (prō'pri-ō jū're). In his own right.

proprio motu. See **ex proprio motu.**

proprio nomine (prō'pri-ō no'mi-ne). In his own name.

proprios (prō'pri-ōs). (Spanish.) Same as **propios.**

proprio vigore (prō'pri-ō vi-gō're). Of its own force; by its own force; automatically.

proprium. See **feudum proprium.**

propter (prop'tėr). On account of; by reason of; because of; for.

propter adulterium (prop'ter a-dul-te'ri-um). By reason of adultery.

propter affectum. See **challenge propter affectum.**

propter commodum curiae (prop'ter kom'mo-dum kū'ri-ē). For the convenience or accommodation of the court.

propter consuetudinem (prop'tėr kon-su-ē-tū'di-nem). Property by reason of the tendency of a wild animal to come on a person's land. Hannam v Mockett, 2 Barn & C 934, 107 Eng Reprint 629.

propter curam et culturam (prop'ter kū'ram et kul-tū'ram). For care and cultivation.

propter defectum (prop'ter dē-fek'tum). For failure of; because of the lack or want of.
See **challenge propter defectum.**

propter defectum sanguinis (prop'ter dē-fek'tum san'gwi-nis). Through failure of blood; that is, through failure of issue.
If the tenant dies without heirs, it is a cause for the escheat of the land to the lord. See 2 Bl Comm 245.

propter delictum (prop'ter dē-lik'tum). On account of a crime, wrong, or fault.
See **challenge propter delictum.**

propter delictum tenentis (prop'ter dē-lik'tum te-nen'tis). Through the fault of the tenant.
It was a cause for escheat of the land to the lord if the blood of the tenant was attainted. He who was attainted suffered an extinction of blood as well as he who died without heirs. See 2 Bl Comm 245.

propter hoc (prop'ter hōk). On account of this; because of this. Reynold v Texas & P. Railroad Co. 37 La Ann 694.

propter honoris respectum. See **challenge propter honoris respectum.**

propter impotentiam (prop'ter im-po-ten'she-am). On account of inability.
See **property propter impotentiam.**

propter majorem securetatem prop'ter ma-jō'rem se-kū-ri-tā'tem). For greater security.

propter nuptias. See **donatio propter nuptias.**

propter odium delicti (prop'ter ō'di-um dē-lik'tī). By reason of the wickedness of the offense.

propter privilegium (prop'ter prī-vi-lē'ji-um). By reason of his privilege.
A man may have a qualified property in wild animals because of his privilege (propter privilegium). That is, he may have the privilege of hunting and killing them to the exclusion of other persons. See 2 Bl Comm 394.
See **property propter privilegium.**

propter rem ipsam non habitum (prop'ter rem ip'sam non ha'bi-tum). Because he could not recover the thing itself.

propter saevitiam (prop'ter sē-vi'she-am). Because, or by reason of, cruelty.

pro quer. An abbreviation of **pro querente.**

pro querente (prō kwe-ren'te). For the plaintiff.

pro rata. In proportion; proportionately according to the share, interest, or liability of each person concerned. Home Ins. Co. v Continental Ins. Co. 180 NY 389, 73 NE 65. in proportion to some rate or standard, fixed in the mind of the person speaking or writing, manifested by the words spoken or written, according to which rate or standard the allowance is to be made or calculated. Rosenberg v Frank, 58 Cal 387, 406.

For the meaning of "pro rata" as the term appears in contracts of sale, see Anno: 74 ALR 995.

See **apportionment**, also terms commencing **pro rata; prorating**.

pro rata clause. A clause in an insurance policy, otherwise known as a proportionate recovery clause, to the effect that the insurer shall not be liable for any greater proportion of any loss which may occur than the amount named in the policy shall bear to the entire amount of insurance upon the property. 29A Am J Rev ed Ins § 1707. The provision in an automobile liability insurance policy that if the insured has other insurance against a loss covered by the policy, the insurer shall not be liable for a greater proportion of such loss than the applicable limit of liability stated in the policy bears to the total applicable limit of liability of all valid and collectible insurance against such loss. 7 Am J2d Auto Ins § 200.

pro rata contribution. Contribution between several co-obligors so that no one of them will be compelled to bear the whole, or more than his just share, of the common burden or obligation. 18 Am J2d Contrib §§ 19 et seq.

pro rata distribution. See **pro rating claims**.

pro rata freight charge. A charge for delivery of shipment short of destination.

Pro rata freight is sometimes allowed a carrier when transportation has been interrupted or delayed by stress of weather or other cause. In such case, if the freighter or his consignee is willing to dispense with the performance of the whole voyage, and voluntarily accept the goods before the end of the voyage, a proportionate amount of freight will be due as freight "pro rata itineris." 13 Am J2d Car § 465; 48 Am J1st Ship § 432.

See **proportional rate**.

pro rata itineris (prō rā′ta i-ti′ne-ris). See **pro rata freight charge**.

pro rata itineris peracti (prō rā′ta i-ti′ne-ris per-ak′tī). In proportion to the voyage performed.

See **pro rata freight charge**.

prorate (prō-rāt′). To divide or distribute proportionately; to assess pro rata. Rosenberg v Frank, 58 Cal 387, 405.

prorating attachments. Placing all attaching creditors on an equality in point of precedence, each one sharing in the property attached in the proportion which his claim bears to the total of claims of attaching creditors. 6 Am J2d Attach § 467.

prorating claims. A distribution of assets to creditors in proportion to the size of their respective claims where there are insufficient assets for payment of all claims in full. 31 Am J2d Ex & Ad § 314. The rule in bankruptcy as between claims of equal standing and priority. 9 Am J2d Bankr § 1262.

prorating taxes. A division of the burden of taxes upon real estate as between vendor and purchaser. Thompson v Crains, 294 Ill 270, 128 NE 508, 12 ALR 931.

proration. Apportionment.

See **apportionment; pro rata**.

proration allowance. The allowance, made an oil producer as his share of the total production of oil within a given area, in the course of limiting production to prevent economic waste. Champlin Refining Co. v Corporation Com. 286 US 210, 76 L Ed 1062, 52 S Ct 559, 86 ALR 403.

proration of production. An economic measure in oil production to avoid a flooding of the market.

The usual type of statute in this field imposes upon a regulatory body the duty of determining from time to time the reasonable market demand for gas and oil, limiting the total production to the amount of demand, and prorating that among the several producers. Thompson v Consolidated Gas Utilities Corp. 300 US 55, 81 L Ed 510, 57 S Ct 364.

proration statute. A statute providing that the amount of estate taxes shall be paid out of the estate before its distribution and shall be equitably prorated among the persons interested in the estate to whom benefit accrues, except as the testator directs otherwise in his will. Anno: 26 ALR2d 927; 37 ALR2d 203.

See **proration of production**.

pro rege (prō rē′je). For the king; for the crown.

pro rege et republica necessarium (prō rē′je et rē-pub′li-ka ne-ses-sā′ri-um). Necessary for the king and the commonwealth.

pro re nata (prō rē nā′tạ). For the occasion as it arises; for the immediate occasion; according to circumstances.

pro retorno habendo (prō re-tor′nō ha-ben′dō). That he have a return.

See **judgment pro retorno habendo**.

pro rigore justitiae (prō ri-gō′re jūs-ti′she-ē). For greater strictness of justice. Hurtado v California, 110 US 516, 529, 28 L Ed 232, 237, 4 S Ct 111, 292.

prorogue (prǫ-rōg′). To terminate a legislative session.

pro salute animae (prō sa-lu′te a′ni-mē). For the welfare of his soul; for the salvation of his soul.

pro salute animae ejus, ecclesiae consilio (prō sa-lū′te a′ni-mē e′jus, e-klē′si-ē kon-si′li-ō). For the salvation of his soul, by direction of the church.

pro salute animarum (prō sa-lū′te a-ni-mā′rum). For the salvation of souls.

proscribed. Forbidden. (Civil law.) Outlawed; sentenced to civil death.

pro se (prō sē). For one's self. Appearing for one's self in an action or criminal prosecution. 5 Am J2d Appear § 10; 21 Am J2d Crim L § 310.

prosecute. To proceed against judicially. Brooks v Bates, 7 Colo 576, 580. To maintain rather than to commence or begin an action. Anno: 75 ALR 461, 465 et seq. To maintain a criminal proceeding.

prosecuted with effect. A phrase to be found in appeal bonds.

The weight of authority holds that the expression means more than a mere prosecution of the appeal to a final determination and that it requires a final determination in favor of the appellant. But other authorities hold that the phrase merely means a prosecution of the appeal is to be conducted with due diligence to a final determination, whether favorable or unfavorable to the appellant. 5 Am J2d A & E § 1030.

prosecuting attorney. A public officer elected or appointed, as provided by constitution or statute, to conduct suits, generally criminal, on behalf of the state in his jurisdiction. 42 Am J1st Pros Atty § 2.

Broadly, any attorney at law who represents the state or political body under which a criminal prosecution is waged. The officer attending on grand jurors with matters on which they are to pass, aiding in the examination of witnesses, and giving such general instructions as they may require, but under duty to retire while the jury is deliberating on the evidence or voting on a matter under investigation. 24 Am J1st Grand J § 43.

prosecuting officer. A prosecuting attorney. The sheriff or other peace officer who makes the affidavit or signs the information under which a criminal prosecution is begun.

prosecuting witness. The witness upon whose complaint a prosecution, particularly a prosecution for rape, is begun.

Prosecutio legis est gravis vexatio; executio legis coronat opus (pro-se-kū'she-ō lē'jis est gra'vis vexā'she-ō; ex-e-kū'she-ō lē'jis ko-rō'nat ō'pus). The prosecution of the law is a grave vexation; the execution crowns the work.

prosecution. In the usual sense, a criminal proceeding at the suit of the government. Tennessee v Davis (US) 10 Otto 257, 269, 25 L Ed 648, 652. Broadly, the maintaining of an action or proceeding, whether civil or criminal.
See **prosecute.**

prosecution of a common purpose. The distinctive element of a joint enterprise. The equivalent of a joint enterprise. Rodgers v Saxton, 305 Pa 479, 158 A 166, 80 ALR 280.

prosecutor. A prosecuting attorney; a prosecuting officer; a prosecuting witness.
The plaintiff or petitioner for a writ of certiorari is called a prosecutor in some jurisdictions. State, Cape May etc., Railway Co. v Cape May, 59 NJL 396, 36 A 696.

prosequi (prŏ'se-quī). To follow; to pursue; to prosecute.
See **nolle prosequi.**

pro socio (prō sō'she-ō). For a partner; in behalf of a partner.

pro solido (prō sō'li-dō). As a bulk; in bulk.

prospect. Something in anticipation, as the prospect of a crop or of a victim to be fleeced. (Mining law.) An undeveloped mine. See Kelly v Clark, 21 Mont 291.

prospecting. Looking over the field and taking samples for analysis to determine where there is mineral in paying quantities.
Used with reference to annual labor to be expended upon a mining claim, the word is not used in the sense of exploration and discovery, which are necessary before a valid location can be made, but rather in the sense of development and demonstration, that the value of the ledge may be determined, as distinguished from the ascertainment of its existence. Anno: 14 ALR 1465.

prospective (prŏ-spek'tiv). Looking to the future.

prospective damages. Same as **future damages.**

prospective heir. See **heir apparent; heir presumptive.**

prospective statement. See **promissory representation.**

prospective statute. A statute without retrospective effect, having no application to transactions which occurred, or rights which accrued, before it became operative. 50 Am J1st Stat § 476.

prospectus. A brochure describing property offered for sale. 55 Am J1st V & P § 81. A statement giving information respecting securities offered for sale or to be issued. 47 Am J1st Secur A § 8. A proposal upon which negotiations by offer and acceptance may be based. 17 Am J2d Contr § 34. A statement, usually in the form of a printed brochure, of the advantages of taking shares in a corporation to be organized. 18 Am J2d Corp § 332.

prosthetic appliance (pros-thet'ik a-pli'ans). A replacement of a missing limb or other part of the body.

prostitute. One who practices prostitution. A whore. Anno: 14 ALR 1502.
See **prostitution.**

prostitution. The practice of a female in offering her body to indiscriminate sexual intercourse for pay. 42 Am J1st Prost § 1. In a more general sense, the selling of one's self or devoting to infamous purposes that which is in one's power. State v Gardner, 174 Iowa 748, 156 NW 747, ovrld on other grounds State v Frey, 206 Iowa 981, 221 NW 445.

pro suo (prō su'ō). As his own.

pro tanto (prō tan'tō). For so much; for as far as it goes; to such an extent.

pro tanto acquittance (prō tan'tō a-kwit'ans). A receipt for part of a demand. State v Shelters, 51 Vt 102.

pro tanto ademption (prō tan'tō a-demp'shon). The destruction or alienation of a part of the subject of a legacy or bequest, the remainder still passing to the devisee or legatee. 57 Am J1st Wills § 1581.

pro tanto validation (prō tan'tō val-i-dā'shon). The validation of an assignment for the benefit of creditors by assent thereto given by only a part of the creditors. Smith v Leavitts, 10 Ala 92.

protect. To cover, shield, or defend against injury, harm or danger of any kind.
As the word is used in a statute giving a lien for materials used for the "protection" of machinery in a mill, the furnishing of lubricating oil is not a protection within the meaning of the statute, although it may preserve the machinery and keep it from wearing out. Standard Oil Co. v Lane, 75 Wis 636, 44 NW 644.

protecting commercial paper. Making sure that it is paid. Equitable Trust Co. v First Nat. Bank, 275 US 359, 72 L Ed 313, 48 S Ct 167, 168.

protection personnel. See **plant guard.**

protection order. An order of court made for the protection of the property of a wife upon her husband's desertion of her.

protection writ. See **writ of protection.**

Protectio trahit subjectionem, et subjectio protectionem (prō-tek'she-ō trā'hit sub-jek-she-ō'nem, et sub-jek'she-ō prō-tek-she-ō'nem). Protection draws to itself allegiance, and allegiance, protection. United States v Wong Kim Ark, 169 US 649, 655, 42 L Ed 890, 893, 18 S Ct 456.

protective agency. A detective or investigating agency. Burns v Johnson, 174 Tenn 615, 130 SW2d 89, 123 ALR 1022. An agency which furnishes protection personnel for industrial plants, mercantile establishments, public institutions, etc.

protective devices. See **safety appliances.**

protective jurisdiction. Jurisdiction to entertain preventive remedies.
See **preventive remedies.**

protective tariff. A tariff maintained at such a high rate as to discourage importation, thereby relieving an American industry of competition from abroad.

protective theory. A theory sometimes applied in determining the amount of property which can be taken in condemnation proceeding, the theory being that more can be taken than that which is barely necessary, since if the condemner owned the adjacent land, it could sell it under restrictions preserving the beauty of the project, thus facilitating an increase in the value of the surrounding private properties. Cincinnati v Vester (CA6 Ohio) 33 F2d 242, 68 ALR 831, affd 281 US 439, 74 L Ed 950, 50 S Ct 360.

protective trust. Similar to a spendthrift trust, the indenture of trust protecting against alienation and liability for debts of the beneficiary by providing conditions for the termination or forfeiture of the trust estate, by giving the trustee discretion to be exercised in making disbursements to beneficiaries, or by similar devices. 54 Am J1st Trusts §§ 147, 148.

protector. Literally, one who protects, as a king may be a "protector of the faith."

protectorate (prọ-tek′tọr-ặt). Government by a protector. A country which the United States has taken under its protection but not with the intent to assume sovereignty over it. Pearcy v Stranahan, 205 US 257, 51 L Ed 793, 27 S Ct 545.

protectory (prọ-tek′tọ-ri). An institution for the education and care of destitute or homeless boys, especially those in danger of becoming delinquent. Duggan v Slocum (CC Conn) 83 F 244, 246.

pro tem. Abbreviation of pro tempore.

pro tem. clerk. A person appointed and serving as clerk of court during the absence of the regular clerk, when he is unable or unwilling to attend to the duties of the office, or during such period of time as he may be under disqualification to act. 15 Am J2d Clk Ct § 8.

pro tem. officer. A person serving in an office during the absence of the duly appointed or elected officer.

pro tempore (prō tem′pọ-re). For the time; temporarily; during the inability or absence of the regular or standing officer. Cutter v Tole, 3 Me 38, 41.

pro tempore judge (prō tem′pọ-re juj). A judge selected to act in the absence, disability, or disqualification of the regular judge, or temporarily under other circumstances, as provided by constitution or statute. 30A Am J Rev ed Judges § 237.

pro termino vitarum suarum (pro ter′mi-nō vī-tā′rum su-ā′rum). For the term of their own lives.

protest. A remonstrance. A technical term for a proceeding to cancel or defeat an entry of public lands. 42 Am J1st Pub L § 31. A notice, preferably in writing, given at the time a payment is paid, to the person who made the demand, that the person making the payment does not acquiesce in the legality of the demand or surrender any right he may have to recover back the money paid. Meyer v Clark (NY) 13 Daly 497, 509. An objection to the payment of a customs duty; a distinct and clear specification of each substantive ground of objection to the payment of the duty. 21 Am J2d Cust D §§ 91 et seq. An objection within limitations of time fixed by law to an administrative rule or regulation. 2 Am J2d Admin L § 288. A formal objection to the proposed action of a city council or other authority in making a local improvement. 48 Am J1st Spec A § 153. The procedure of a taxpayer who questions his liability to the tax assessed against him or the validity of the statutes or proceeding pursuant to which it was assessed, thereby making a basis for the recovery back of the money paid by showing that payment was not voluntary. Jaynes v Heron, 46 NM 431, 130 P2d 29, 142 ALR 1191.

The expression "under protest" has a well-known meaning in the business world and when written upon a receipt imports that the person writing it intends to enforce his rights. The words ordinarily signify that the receiptor objects to receiving the thing in its condition, or under the circumstances, but does so, under compulsion of circumstances, to prevent still further loss, but at the same time retaining all his rights of action against the other party. Anno: 1 ALR 904.

See **marine protest; objection; protest of negotiable instrument; remonstrance.**

protestando (prō-tes-tan′dō). A notice or statement by which a party to an action preserves his right of disputing the fact protested against, in some other suit or proceeding. State v Beason, 40 NH 367, 372.

Protestants. Christians but not Roman Catholics or members of the Eastern Orthodox Church.

In consequence of the protest against the decree of the Diet of Spires (or Spire or Speiers), held in Germany, under the Emperor Charles V, in 1529, the followers of Luther were denominated Protestants, a general term which was applied alike to all who adopted the principles of the Reformation in opposition to the Catholic Church, and which has continued to the present time. Hale v Everett, 53 NH 9.

protestation. A formal part of a plea in equity, no longer required or in general use, wherein the defendant negatived any confession or acknowledgment by him of all or any part of the matters contained in the bill. 27 Am J2d Eq § 207. A manner of pleading whereby the party interposes an oblique allegation or denial of some fact, protesting that such a matter does or does not exist, and at the same time avoiding a direct affirmation or denial, its purpose being to save the party from being concluded as to some fact, which cannot be directly affirmed or denied without falling into duplicity of pleading, and which if he did not thus protest, he might be deemed to have tacitly waived or admitted. See 3 Bl Comm 311.

protest for nonacceptance. See **protest of negotiable instrument.**

protest of negotiable instrument. The formal certificate, notice, declaration, or memorandum, drawn up and signed by a notary public, that he presented the instrument for acceptance or for payment and that it was refused. In loose usage, an act or series of acts in presenting the instrument for acceptance or payment, noting the fact of dishonor by nonacceptance or nonpayment, and the making of the formal certificate, declaration, memorandum, or notice of protest by the notary. 11 Am J2d B & N § 789.

For contents and formal requisites of protest or certificate thereof, see 11 Am J2d B & N § 798.

prothonotary (prō-thon'ō-tā-ri). A clerk of court, particularly a chief or principal clerk. A ministerial officer of the court, having the custody of its records and seals, with power to certify to the correctness of transcripts from such records, and possessing authority to perform certain acts of a judicial nature incidental to his ministerial duties.

pro timore mortis, et recesserunt quam cito potuerunt (pro tim'ō-rē môr'tis, et reses'er-unt kwam sī'tō po-tū'e-rŭnt). In fear of death, and they ran away as quickly as they could. McGrowther's Case, Fost CL 13, 168 Eng Reprint 8.

protocol (prō'tō-kol). A record; a register; a rough or preliminary draft of a contract or a treaty. Ceremonial forms, particularly those governing conduct toward heads of state or their diplomatic representatives.

protocollum (prō-to-kol'lum). (Civil law.) A memorandum made by a notary of an official transaction.

protocolo. (Spanish.) The original draft of a document which is retained by the notary.

protonotary (prō-ton'ō-tā-ri). Same as **prothonotary**.

protutor (prō-tū'tọr). (Civil law.) A person who acted as a guardian when he was not one, or who was really a guardian and acted as one without knowing it.

prout (prō'ut). According as; as; as charged.

prout eis visum fuerit, ad honorem coronae et utilitatem regni (prō'ut e'is vi'sum fu'erit, ad ho-nō'rem ko-rō'nē et u-ti-li-tā'tem reg'nī). As it should appear to them to the honor of the crown and the advantage of the kingdom. See 1 Bl Comm 408.

prout moris est (prō'ut mo'ris est). As is the custom, usage, or practice.

prout patet per recordum (prō'ut pā'tet per rē-kor'-dum). As it appears by the record. Philpot v McArthur, 10 Me 127, 134.

provable claim. See **provable debt**.

provable debt. A debt susceptible of proof against a bankrupt estate. Davis v Aetna Acceptance Co. 293 US 328, 79 L Ed 393, 66 S Ct 151. A claim provable against an estate in bankruptcy within the meaning of § 63 of the Bankruptcy Act (11 USC § 103). 9 Am J2d Bankr § 390.

prove. To establish a fact by the requisite degree of evidence, whether it be an affirmative or a negative, one which the plaintiff must establish as a part of his case or a defense to be established affirmatively by the defendant. People v Winters, 125 Cal 325, 328, 57 P 1067.

proved. See **prove; legally proved**.

prover (prō'vėr). Same as **probator**.

pro veritate (prō ve-ri-tā'te). For the truth; as true.

provided. Upon condition. Clausen v Title Guaranty & Surety Co. 168 App Div 569, 153 NYS 835, affd 222 NY 675, 119 NE 1035. An apt word in the creation of a condition subsequent. 28 Am J2d Est § 144. An apt and appropriate word in the creation of a contingent remainder. 28 Am J2d Est § 265.

It does not always follow that a clause operates as a proviso in a technical sense, merely because it is preceded by the word "provided." Whether it is a proviso in effect, or merely a conjunction equivalent to the word "and" or the word "but," must in part be determined from the context and from all the provisions relating to the same subject matter. Radil v Morris & Co. 103 Neb 84, 170 NW 363, 7 ALR 539, 541.

providentia. (Latin.) Forethought. Divine will.

province. A duty or function. A colony. A political subdivision of Canada comparable to a state in the United States. A region removed from the center of government and culture. The circuit of an archbishop's jurisdiction. 1 Bl Comm 111.

province of court and jury. The separate and distinctive functions characteristic of a system of jurisprudence derived from the common law, the province of the court being to determine and decide questions of law presented at the trial and to state the law to the jury, the province of the jury being to decide or determine the facts of the case from the evidence adduced, in accordance with the instructions given by the court. 53 Am J1st Trial § 156.

provincial constitutions. The decrees of provincial synods, held under the bishops of Canterbury province, from Stephen Langton in the reign of Henry III (1216-1272) to Henry Chichele in the reign of Henry IV (1399-1413), and adopted also by the province of York in the reign of Henry VI (1422-1461). See 1 Bl Comm 83.

provision. See **heir of provision; provided; provisions**.

provisional. That which is merely temporary, or for the time being, or for the occasion, excluding the idea of permanency. De Haro v United States (US) 5 Wall 599, 18 L Ed 681, 688.

provisional appointment. An appointment to a civil service position made in an emergency where there is no appropriate eligible list for the position, being made in anticipation of an examination, with a view to the appointee's qualifications to serve for the period of an emergency and pending the promulgation of an eligible list. 15 Am J2d Civ S § 25.

provisional assignee. A receiver.

provisional courts. Courts which were established during the Civil War in insurgent territory occupied by national forces, under the authority of the President as Commander-in-chief of those forces. Mechanics' & Traders' Union Bank v Union Bank of Louisiana (US) 22 Wall 276, 22 L Ed 871.

provisional government. A government temporarily established, in anticipation of, and to exist and continue until, another shall be instituted and organized in its stead. Chambers v Fisk, 22 Tex 504, 535.

provisional injunction. See **temporary injunction**.

provisional judgment. A judgment to be made absolute on motion, unless cause is shown against judgment. 30A Am J Rev ed Judgm § 119.

provisional order. An order made during the course of an action or proceeding, not constituting a final adjudication. The temporary order of an administrative agency. 2 Am J2d Admin L § 466.
See **interim order; interlocutory order**.

provisional policy. Same as **monthly reporting policy**.

provisional receivership. A term sometimes confused with ancillary receivership, but standing for that which is substantially a pendente lite receivership.
See **pendente lite receivership**.

provisional remedy. A remedy of a party to an action, not intended as a means of reaching a determination and adjudication of the issue or issues, but as a means whereby the party who invokes it successfully prevents the adverse party from taking steps during the course of the action which would

thwart the enforcement of a judgment obtained in the action. Not a special proceeding, but a merely collateral proceeding permitted only in connection with a regular action, and as one of its incidents. Snavely v Abbott Buggy Co. 36 Kan 106, 12 P 522.
See **attachment; injunction.**

provisional revocation. See **dependent relative revocation.**

provisione hominis. See **ex provisione hominis.**

provisione legis (pro-vi-zhe-ō'ne lē'jis). By provision of law.

provisione mariti. See **ex provisione mariti.**

provisione viri (pro-vi-zhe-ō'ne vī'rī). By provision of the husband.

Provisions of Oxford (prō-vizh'ǫnz of oks'ford). Those enactments of the English Parliament passed to prevent Henry the Third from interfering with the enforcement of Magna Charta.

provisions. Food for men or animals. 31 Am J2d Exemp §§ 77-79.

proviso (prō-vī'zō). A clause which imposes a condition.
See **provided.**

Proviso est providere praesentia et futura, non praeterita (prō-vī'sō est pro'vi-dē're prē-zen'she-a et fu-tū'ra, non prē-ter'i-ta). A proviso is to provide for the present and the future, but not for the past.

proviso in statute (prō-vi'zō in staṭ'ūt). A clause in a statute which limits, restrains, or determines in some particular the application of the statute. 50 Am J1st Stat § 435.

In determining whether a given provision in a statute is an exception or a proviso, the true test is to be found, not in whether the qualifying words are prefaced by the term "except" or "provided," but in the nature or meaning of the qualifying words themselves. 50 Am J1st Stat § 430.

A proviso is not always limited in its effect to the part of the enactment with which it is immediately associated; it may apply generally to all cases within the meaning of the language used. McDonald v United States, 279 US 12, 73 L Ed 582, 49 S Ct 218.

provisor (prō-vī'zǫr). A candidate for a bishopric or a living nominated by the Pope before there was a vacancy. See 4 Bl Comm 111.

provocation. A defense in a divorce case based upon physical violence, verbal abuse, or other course of conduct on the part of the plaintiff likely to lead to retaliation by the defendant, thereby inducing the conduct of the defendant complained of as a ground of divorce. 24 Am J2d Div & S § 174. As an element of voluntary manslaughter as distinguished from murder:—an act, the natural tendency of which is to produce passion in ordinary men, and which, the jury are satisfied, did produce it in the case before them. 26 Am J1st Homi § 25.

It is generally agreed that in the determination of whether the provocation is sufficient or reasonable, ordinary human nature, or the average of men recognized as men of fair average mind and disposition, should be taken as the standard, unless, indeed, the person whose guilt is in question is shown to have some peculiar weakness of mind or infirmity of temper, not arising from wickedness of heart or cruelty of disposition. 26 Am J1st Homi § 25.

provoke. To excite; to stimulate; to arouse, to make angry. State v Warner, 34 Conn 276, 279.

See **provocation.**

provoking a difficulty. Making trouble with a purpose.

An assault or the menace of one, by an overt act, with intent to inflict death or great bodily harm in the event it is resisted, made maliciously to bring about that result and enable the provoking party to wreak his vengeance on the assailant, is an "aggression," or "fault," and a "provoking of a difficulty," within the legal sense and meaning of the terms. Foutch v State, 95 Tenn 711, 34 SW 423.

provocative language. See **offensive language.**

provoked error. See **invited error.**

provost (prov'ǫst). The chief executive officer in certain corporations, principally educational institutions.
In Scotland, a magistrate.

provost court. A military court in occupied territory.

provost marshal (marsh'ạl). An officer of the military in charge of military police or having custody of prisoners.

prox. An abbreviation of **proximus.**

proximate cause. As an element of tort liability:—that cause, which, in natural and continuous sequence, unbroken by any efficient intervening cause, produces the injury, and without which the result would not have occurred. The primary moving cause, or the predominating cause, from which the injury follows as a natural, direct, and immediate consequence, and without which it would not have occurred. 38 Am J1st Negl § 50. That act or omission which immediately causes or fails to prevent the injury. Stacy v Williams, 253 Ky 353, 60 SW2d 697. The efficient cause; the one that necessarily sets the other cause in motion, and brings about the result without the intervention of any force started and working actively from a new and independent source. 38 Am J1st Negl § 50. Such cause, not necessarily the last cause or the act nearest to the injury, but such act as actually aided in producing the injury as a direct and efficient cause. Milton Bradley Co. v Cooper, 79 Ga App 302, 53 SE2d 761, 11 ALR2d 1019. As element of liability for wrongful death:—an act which produces the injury and death in a natural and continuous sequence, unbroken by any new, independent cause. 22 Am J2d Death § 31.

As an element of recoverable damages in tort cases:—legal cause, something beyond mere cause in fact, something other than a remote cause. That cause which in natural and continuous sequence, unbroken by an efficient intervening cause, has produced the injuries for which damages are sought to be recovered. 22 Am J2d Damg § 20. As an element of damages in contract cases:—a requirement that gives way to the doctrine of foreseeable or anticipated consequences. 22 Am J2d Damg § 20.

Proximate cause has a different meaning in insurance cases than it has in tort cases. In insurance cases the concern is not with the question of culpability or why the injury occurred but only with the nature of the injury and how it happened. If the nearest efficient cause of the loss is one of the perils insured against, the court looks no further. In such cases, the insurer is not relieved from responsibility by showing that the property was brought within the peril insured against by a cause not mentioned in the contract. 29A Am J Rev ed Ins § 1134.

See **concurrent cause; contributory cause; efficient cause; immediate cause; natural and probable** consequences; primary cause; producing or inducing cause.

promixate consequences. See **proximate cause; proximate result.**

proximate legal cause. See **proximate cause.**

proximate result. A result traceable directly to an act or omission, without the occurrence of another culpable and efficient agency intervening. McMann v Newark & South Orange Railway Co. 58 NJL 642, 34 A 1052.

See **proximate cause.**

proximation doctrine. See **cy pres; equitable approximation doctrine.**

proximity (prok-sim′i̯-ti). Nearness in space, time, distance, kinship, etc.

proximo gradu. See **in proximo gradu.**

proximus (prok′si-mus). The nearest; the next.

Proximus est cui nemo antecedit; supremus est quem nemo sequitur (pro′xi-mus est kī nē′mō an-te-sē′dit; su-prē′mus est quem nē′mō se′qui-ter). He is next whom no one precedes; he is last whom no one follows.

proximus haeres (pro′xi-mus hē′rēz). The nearest heir; the next heir.

proximus sequente (pro′xi-mus se-quen′te). The next following.

prox. seq. An abbreviation of **proximus sequente.**

proxy. An authorization, usually given in writing, under which one person acts for another. An authority given in writing by the holder of corporate stock to another to exercise the voting rights to which he is entitled as a stockholder. Commissioner of Banks v Cosmopolitan Trust Co. 253 Mass 205, 148 NE 609, 41 ALR 658. An authority given by one delegate to another whereunder the latter votes in place of the other at a political convention. 26 Am J2d Elect § 235. An authority given by a creditor whereunder another votes in the place of him at a creditors' meeting in a proceeding in bankruptcy. 9 Am J2d Bankr § 593. The person who holds an authorization to act in the place of another. 9 Am J2d Bankr § 593; 19 Am J2d Corp §§ 669 et seq.

proxy holder. See **proxy.**

proxy signature. A signature affixed for another.

prudence. The matter of being **prudent.**

prudent. Sensible, cautious, exercising judgment.
There may be an infinitesimal shade of difference between "cautious" and "prudent," but a reasonably prudent person and a reasonably cautious person are substantially the same, and possess identical significance for all practical purposes. Certainly, the words "cautious" and "prudent" are used interchangeably in defining negligence. Malcolm v Mooresville Cotton Mills, 191 NC 727, 730, 133 SE 7.

prudent investment theory. The theory, sometimes applied in the earlier days of public utility rate regulation, that a public utility is entitled to a return based only on its actual sacrifice, represented by the amount of capital prudently put into the business. 43 Am J1st Pub Util § 105.

See **safe investment rule.**

prudent man. See **the ordinary prudent man.**

prudent man rule. The rule that one taking a negotiable instrument from the payee or prior endorsee is put upon inquiry as to infirmity or defect in the instrument by circumstances calculated to arouse the suspicions of a prudent man, so as to be charged with constructive notice of the infirmity or defect by his failure to make inquiry with reasonable diligence. 11 Am J2d B & N § 431.

prudent operator rule. The rule that a stipulation in an oil and gas lease on a royalty basis that development shall be at the discretion of the lessee does not leave development to the uncontrolled will of the lessee, he being required to do by way of development that which a prudent operator would deem just and proper under the circumstances. 24 Am J1st Gas & O § 62.

See **the ordinary prudent man.**

Prudenter agit qui praecepto legis obtemperat (pruden′ter ā′jit quī prē-sep′tō lē′jis ob-tem′pe-rat). He acts prudently who is obedient to the precept of the law.

p. s. An abbreviation of **public statutes;** abbreviation of **postscript.**

pseudo-corporation. An income-tax term for a closely held corporation.

psoriasis (sō-rī′a̯-sis). A chronic inflammatory skin disease. Sawyer v Department of Labor & Industries, 48 Wash 2d 761, 296 P2d 706,709.

psychiatric examination. See **mental examination.**

psychiatrist (sī-kī′a̯-trist). A doctor of medicine who specializes in psychiatry.

psychiatry (sī-kī′a̯-tri). The practice of medicine in the study and treatment of disorders of the mind.

psychic healer. One who professes to treat disease by the application of forces beyond the physical world. Post v United States (CA5) 135 F 1022.

psychopath (sī-ko̯-path). A person afflicted with a psychopathic condition.

See **psychopathic; sexual psychopath.**

psychopathic (sī-ko̯-path′ik). Characterized by emotional instability, impulsiveness of behavior, lack of customary standards of good judgment, or failure to appreciate the consequences of one's act. Ditrich v Brown County, 215 Minn 234, 9 NW2d 510.

See **sexual psychopath.**

psychopathic personality (sī-ko̯-path′ik pėr-so̯-nal′i̯-ti). See **psychopathic; sexual psychopath.**

ptomaine poisoning (tō′ma̯-in poi′zning). A stomach disorder caused by the eating of food containing toxic bacilli. Newsoms v Commercial Cas. Ins. Co. 147 Va 471, 137 SE 456, 52 ALR 363.

pubertas (pu-ber′tās). In the civil law, the age of a child from fourteen years upward. See 4 Bl Comm 22.

puberty (pū′bėr-ti). The age under the common law at which a person may lawfully marry, twelve for girls and at fourteen for boys. See 1 Bl Comm 436.

pubic (pū′bik). Characterizing the lower part of the abdomen, the part covered with hair.

public. Adjective: Belonging to the entire community. Unrestricted in participation. Noun: The people. The populace; the community. "That vast multitude, which includes the ignorant, the unthinking, and the credulous, who, in making purchases, do not stop to analyze, but are governed by appearance and general impressions." J. W. Collins Co. v F. M. Paist Co. (DC Pa) 14 F2d 614.

It is conceded that the public does not mean all

the people in the state or in any county or town. The public is a term used to designate individuals in general without restriction or selection. Garkane Power Co. v Public Service Co. 98 Utah 466, 100 P2d 571, 132 ALR 1490.

The word sometimes has the meaning of international, sometimes national, and sometimes state. See Morgan v Cree, 46 Vt 773.

public accommodation. A place open to serve the public. An inn. A hotel. A restaurant. A place to obtain food and lodging, rather than a place of amusement. 4 Am J2d Amuse § 1.

public accountant. One who furnishes accounting or auditing service, on a fee basis, per diem, or otherwise, for more than one employer. Frazer v Shelton, 320 Ill 253, 150 NE 696, 43 ALR 1086.

One who comes into the offices of a company one or two days a month for the purpose of auditing and balancing its books, reconciling its bank account with its books, checking and totaling the bookkeeper's records of the payroll checks, and who also prepares the income tax returns of the company, performs the services of a public accountant rather than those of a bookkeeper. Jaeger Mfg. Co. v Maryland Casualty Co. 231 Iowa 151, 300 NW 680.

See **certified public accountant.**

public acknowledgment of paternity. Holding a child out to relatives, friends, acquaintances, and the world as one's own. Estate of Jessup, 81 Cal 408, 21 P 976, 22 P 742.

public act. A statute. 16 Am J2d Const L § 588. An act which concerns the whole community. A statute which concerns the whole community, the public at large. An act which applies equally to all persons within the territorial limits of its operation, even though it applies to a particular locality alone. 50 Am J1st Stat § 12. For some purposes, a statute of another state. Anno: 134 ALR 1472.

public adjuster. One whose business is the adjustment of claims for insurance, employed, not regularly for full time by one person or company, but by members of the public, insureds or insurers, as their need of an adjuster arises. Larson v Lesser, (Fla) 106 So 2d 188.

public administrator. A public officer who administers the estates of decedents where no one else qualifies to act as a personal representative. 31 Am J2d Ex & Ad § 61.

public affair. A matter relating to government. State v Mitchell, 210 Wis 381, 245 NW 640, 86 ALR 1361. An assemblage thrown open to the public. An event much talked about. A scandal constituting an item of conversation for many persons.

public aid. See **farm aid; railroad aid; welfare.**

public aircraft. An aircraft used exclusively in the service of any government or of any political subdivision thereof, including the government of any state, territory, or possession of the United States, or the District of Columbia, but not including any government-owned aircraft engaged in carrying persons or property for commercial purposes. 49 USC § 1301(30).

public alley. A highway, usually a narrow way bisecting a city block, existing through dedication to the public or acquisition by the municipality. 25 Am J1st High § 8.

publican (pub'li-kạn). One who serves food or drink prepared for consumption on the premises. Friend v Childs Dining Room Hall Co. 231 Mass 65, 120 NE 407, 5 ALR 1100. An innkeeper. A saloonkeeper. (Civil law.) A tax collector.

public and domestic tranquillity. Public peace.

The expression means nothing more than the public peace, which is made up of the aggregate of individual peace and domestic peace, and is nothing more than a subdivision of the one and an aggregation of the other. One cannot lawfully disturb the quiet of domestic life by that same kind of offensive and tumultuous carriage which would anywhere constitute a breach of public peace, although no one but the family of which he is a member is present. Anno: 1 ALR 591.

publicanus (pub-li-kā'nus). (Civil law.) Same as **publican.**

publication. A newspaper or magazine; a book. Dissemination of information by notice given the public. State, ex rel. Torryson, v Gray, 21 Nev 378, 32 P 190. The issuance of a newspaper or magazine from the place where it has been printed. Re Monrovia Evening Post, 199 Cal 263, 248 P 1017. The composing, printing, issuance, and distribution of a newspaper to its subscribers and the public. Age-Herald Publishing Co. v Huddleston, 207 Ala 40, 92 So 193, 37 ALR 898, 905. The printing of a notice in a newspaper of general circulation and distribution. 39 Am J1st Notice § 30. A means of service of process where authorized by statute. 42 Am J1st Proc §§ 89 et seq. In reference to copyright and the law of literary property, those acts of an author which evidence a dedication of his work to the public and on which depends the loss of his common-law copyright, the acquisition of his statutory copyright, or both. American Visuals Corp. v Holland (CA2 NY) 239 F2d 740. In the law of libel and slander:—the communication of defamation to one or more persons other than the person defamed. 33 Am J1st L & S §§ 90 et seq. In criminal libel, a communication to anyone at all, even to the person defamed. 33 Am J1st L & S § 311.

publication date. The earliest date when copies of the first authorized edition are placed on sale, sold, or publicly distributed by the proprietor of a copyright or under his authority. 17 USC § 26.

publication of forgery. Asserting expressly or impliedly that a forged instrument is genuine. People v Bradford, 84 Cal App 707, 258 P 660.

publication of marriage bans. The announcement made in church of an intended marriage. 35 Am J1st Mar § 24.

publication of newspaper. See **publication.**

publication of process. See **service by publication.**

publication of summons. See **service by publication.**

publication of will. The communication by the testator to the attesting witnesses at the time they attest of his intention that the instrument which they are called upon to attest shall take effect as his will. 57 Am J1st Wills § 283.

public attorney. An attorney at law.

public auction. See **auction; public sale.**

public authority. An agency created for the construction and maintenance of a public work or public improvement, such as a port authority, power authority, etc. In the most general sense, the authority of government, the power of the nation, state, or political subdivision.

public benefit. See **public use.**

public blockade. A naval blockade of a port, established in fact and publicized by notice given to other governments. 56 Am J1st War § 172.

public body. A governmental body. A public corporation.

public bond. A bond issued by a state, municipality, or other public body, usually, although not necessarily, under seal, constituting a promise binding the obligor to pay a sum of money to the holder thereof or to bearer, and, where made payable to order, or to bearer, having all the qualities of commercial paper. 43 Am J1st Pub Sec § 6.

public bonded warehouse. A warehouse bonded for the storage of imported merchandise generally. 19 USC § 1555.

public bridge. A bridge which forms a part of a public highway and which has been erected for the use of the public. First Nat. Bank v Malheur County, 30 Or 420, 45 P 781.

public building. A building owned by a public body, particularly if it is used for public offices or for other public purpose. Anno: 19 ALR 543.
See **public improvement.**

public business. The business affairs of the government. The business of a public body. The business of a public service corporation in its relations with the public. Minnesota Canal & Power Co. v Pratt, 101 Minn 197, 112 NW 395.

public calamity. See **calamity.**

public carrier. A common carrier. A carrier which holds itself out in its dealings and course of business with the public as being ready and willing for hire to perform the services rendered by it and within the field of its operations for the public generally. State v Washington Tug & Barge Co. 140 Wash 613, 250 P 49.
See **common carrier.**

public cemetery. A cemetery available for use by the general community, a neighborhood, or a church, the characteristic being public use rather than title to the ground. 14 Am J2d Cem § 2.

public character. Same as **public personage.**

public charge. A person who cannot support himself, has no means of support, has no one to furnish him support, and accordingly must look to a public body or public welfare agency for his maintenance and care. Ex parte Fragoso (DC Cal) 11 F2d 988.

public charity. Any real charity, the word "charity" implying public interest or welfare. 15 Am J2d Char § 6. A charity for the benefit of an indefinite number of persons. 51 Am J1st Tax § 601.

public college or university. A college or university founded or taken over and supported by the state or a political subdivision thereof.
The fact that a college or university founded by the state is given or accepts donations from private persons does not alter the nature of its foundation or change the character of the corporation. 15 Am J2d Colleges § 2.

public contract. A contract for the construction of a public improvement or for the furnishing of supplies to a public body. 43 Am J1st Pub Wks § 10.

public contractor's bond. See **contractor's bond.**

public convenience. That which is fitted or suited to the public need. Milwaukee Co. of Jehovah's Witnesses v Mullen, 214 Or 281, 330 P2d 5, 74 ALR2d 347, app dismd and cert den 359 US 436, 3 L Ed 2d 932, 79 S Ct 940 (zoning ordinance.)
See **public necessity and convenience.**

public conveyance. A vehicle used for carrying passengers for compensation. 7 Am J2d Auto Ins § 35. A conveyance the proprietor of which makes a public offer of conveyance at a fixed fare to all persons. Stanley v American Motorists Ins. Co. 195 Md 180, 73 A2d 1, 30 ALR2d 268; Anderson v Fidelity & Casualty Co. 228 NY 475, 127 NE 584, 9 ALR 1544, 1550. In one sense, a vehicle, such as a passenger elevator, which is open for service to the public, even without payment of a fare. Davis v Colorado Sav. Bank, 78 Colo 509, 242 P 985.
Contract carriers who may not be compelled to become common carriers but who may be subjected to many of the same regulatory requirements as common carriers may be within the term "public or livery conveyances." Stanley v American Motorists Ins. Co. 195 Md 180, 72 A2d 1, 30 ALR2d 268.

public corporation. A municipal or political corporation. A corporation with political powers. Phillips v Baltimore, 110 Md 431, 72 A 902. A corporation created for public purposes only, connected with the administration of the government, the interests and franchises of which are the exclusive property and domain of the government itself. Dartmouth College v Woodward (US) 4 Wheat 518, 4 L Ed 629.
A corporation may have a double aspect according to the nature of the powers granted and exercised. If they were granted and exercised for public purposes exclusively, they belong to the corporate body in its public, political, or municipal character. If the grant was for purposes of private advantage and emolument, though the public may derive a common benefit therefrom, the corporation, quoad hoc, is to be regarded as a private company. 18 Am J2d Corp § 8.

public credit. The value of a thing, the worth of a performance, in the opinion of the public.
See **seals of public credit.**

public dance. A dance to which the public is admitted, and which is held for profit, direct or indirect. 4 Am J2d Amuse § 3. A place of amusement. 4 Am J2d Amuse § 1.

public danger. See **public peril.**

public debt. In a narrow sense, national or state obligations; in a broader sense, national obligations, state obligations, county obligations, town obligations, in fact the obligations of any public body. 43 Am J1st Pub Sec § 3.

public debtor. Broadly, the nation, a state, county, town, municipal corporation, or political subdivision obligated under outstanding indebtedness. A municipal corporation, school district, local improvement district, county, or other political subdivision eligible for relief by the composition of its indebtedness under provisions of the Bankruptcy Act. 9 Am J2d Bankr § 1416.

public decency. See **disorderly conduct; indecency; obscenity.**

public defender. An attorney at law appointed to aid indigent persons accused of crime, becoming in the individual case in which he acts counsel for the accused to the same extent as if retained by the accused regularly and for all purposes of the case. 21 Am J2d Crim L § 323.

public depositary. A bank or other institution authorized to receive deposits of public moneys. United States Fidelity & Guaranty Co. v Kansas, 81 Kan 660, 106 P 1040.

public disorder. See **disorderly conduct; insurrection; riot.**

public dispensary. A liquor store conducted by the state or municipality. 30 Am J Rev ed Intox L § 204.

public dock. See **public wharf.**

public documents. Official papers. Documents on file in a public office. All publications printed by order of Congress, or either house thereof. McCall v United States, 1 Dak 307, 314.

public domain. The public lands of the United States or of a state. Barker v Harvey, 181 US 481, 490, 45 L Ed 963, 968, 21 S Ct 690; People v Shearer, 30 Cal 645, 658. Literary, musical, or dramatic compositions so dedicated to the public as not to be subject to copyright. 18 Am J2d Copyr § 42. A device or process so well known and in such common use as not to be patentable. 40 Am J1st Pat § 25.

public duty. A duty owed the public, whether by a public officer or employee or by one who comes in contact with the public.
See **governmental functions.**

public easement. A public right of way. 25 Am J2d Ease § 7. The right of the public to use a highway; an easement which embraces every reasonable and proper use of the way in the transportation of persons or property not prohibited by law. 25 Am J1st High § 166.

public eating house. A restaurant. 29 Am J Rev ed Innk § 9.

public emergency. An unusual exigency bearing directly upon the public welfare, the determination of which is primarily a legislative function. 16 Am J2d Const L §§ 270, 300. Any emergency so affecting the public health and safety that summary relief by restriction of the offending thing is necessary. 39 Am J1st Nuis § 187.

public employee. A federal or state employee. An employee of any public body. Inclusive of public officer only by express stipulation or where such construction is the only reasonable one under the circumstances. Anno: 5 ALR2d 415.

public enemy. A nation with which the country is at war or a subject or citizen of a nation with which the country is at war. A pirate on the high seas. 14 Am J2d Car § 523.

public escheator. A public officer or public body upon whom rests the duty of bringing actions for escheat or for a sale or conveyance of escheated property. 27 Am J2d Esch § 32.

public exigency (pub'lik ek'si-jen-si). A sudden and unexpected happening, an unforeseen occurrence or condition, a perplexing contingency or complication of circumstances, or a sudden or unexpected occasion for action. Good Roads Machinery Co. v United States (DC Mass) 19 F Supp 652. An occurrence which bears directly upon the public welfare.
See **public emergency.**

public flag. See **flag.**

public footway. A footway in public use, independent of a highway.

public fund. Money belonging to the United States, an agency of the United States, a state or subdivision thereof, or a municipal corporation. Smyer v United States, 273 US 333, 71 L Ed 667, 47 S Ct 375; Pinal County v Hammons, 36 Ariz 36, 243 P 919; Beckner v Commonwealth, 174 Va 454, 5 SE2d 525. Money raised by the operation of law for the support of the government or the discharge of its obligation. 42 Am J1st Pub F § 2.

public garage. An automobile repair place or business open for service to the public generally; a garage which accepts cars for parking or storage. 24 Am J1st Garag § 2.

As used in a restrictive convenant the term has been given various meanings. According to some interpretations, it is restricted to places for the storage of automobiles. According to others, it includes every phase of the business, including storing, hiring, sales, servicing, and repairs. Anno: 54 ALR 666; 99 ALR 543.

public grant. A conveyance or grant of land by the United States or a state.

public ground. Ground in which the general public has a common use; streets, alleys, commons, and the like. Patrick v Young Men's Christian Asso. 120 Mich 185, 191.

public health. See **health** and expressions beginning "health."

Public Health Service. A federal agency of the Department of Health, Education, and Welfare.

public hearing. A hearing or investigation by an administrative agency which is open to the public. 2 Am J2d Admin L § 229.
See **public trial.**

public highway. A way for the use of the public; a highway. For the purposes of an accident insurance policy which contains a provision for compensation for injuries received on a public highway:—any way used by the public in going from one place to another, such as a platform at a railroad depot used by the public for the purpose of going to and from trains. Rudd v Great Eastern Casualty & Indem. Co. 114 Minn 512, 131 NW 633.

public hospital. A hospital open to the public generally for the rendition of its services, especially where operated without purpose of financial gain, albeit charges are made for its services. Hibbing v Commissioner, 217 Minn 528, 14 NW2d 923, 156 ALR 1294.

public house. An inn, hotel, or other place of public accommodation. A restaurant. 29 Am J Rev ed Innk § 9. A house commonly open to the public, either for business, pleasure, religious worship, the gratification of curiosity, or the like, and including all houses made public by the occupation of them, as taverns or inns, or in any other way. Cole v State, 28 Tex App 536, 13 SW 859.

public housing. Housing provided by public funds in slum clearance and the construction of low-cost housing in the interest of people of limited means. 42 Am J1st Pub H L § 1.

Public Housing Administration. A federal agency assisting local housing authorities in building low-rental public housing for low-income families, making contributions and making or backing up loans to finance such housing.

public ignominy (pub'lik ig'nō-min-i). Infamy, reproach, dishonor. Public hatred or detestation. Mahanke v Cleland, 76 Iowa 401, 405. Public disgrace;

public dishonor. Brown v Kingsley, 38 Iowa 220, 221.

publici juris (pub'li-sī jū'ris). Of public right.

public improvement. Things planned, established, or constructed by public bodies for the use of the public, such as a library, schoolhouse, park, etc. 43 Am J1st Pub Wks § 2. Original construction or substantial reconstruction, as distinguished from repair. Hazard v Main Street Realty Co. (Ky) 262 SW2d 87, 41 ALR2d 609.

As used in connection with municipal government, the term must be taken as applying to those improvements which are the proper subject of police and municipal regulation—such as gas, water, almshouses, hospitals, etc.,—and cannot be extended to subjects foreign to the object of incorporation, and beyond its territorial limits. Low v Marysville, 5 Cal 214, 215.

See **public works**.

public indebtedness. See **public debt**.

public institution. One which is created and exists by law or public authority, such as an asylum, charity, college, university, hospital, schoolhouse, etc. Henderson v Shreveport Gas, Electric Light & Power Co. 134 La 39, 63 So 616.

public interest. Matters of general right or interest, such as state or municipal boundaries, the existence or location of a highway, the existence of a private right or privilege in public land, and so forth. 29 Am J2d Ev § 506. Something more than an interest on the part of many members of the public, each from the standpoint of an individual. Anno: 132 ALR 1188.

public international law. The law of nations, being that law which regulates the political intercourse of nations with each other or concerns questions of rights between nations. 16 Am J2d Confl L § 1.

publicist. A writer, particularly a writer on political and international law subjects. 30 Am J Rev ed Internat L § 2. A publicity agent.

publicity. See **publication**.

public land. Land of the United States or a state, particularly land open to public sale or other disposition under general laws. 42 Am J1st Pub L § 13. A term of varying senses, depending largely on the context in which it appears and the special circumstances of the case. Kindred v Union Pacific R. Co. 225 US 582, 56 L Ed 1216, 32 S Ct 780.

public-land-grant rates. See **land-grant rates**.

public land survey. See **governmental survey**.

public laundry. A laundry which distributes the products of its work to the public. Van Zandt's Inc. v Department of Labor, 129 Misc 747, 222 NYS 450.

public lavatory. A lavatory maintained by the municipality or other public body for public use, often with direct access from street or public way.

public law. The part of the law which is concerned with the state in its sovereign capacity, including international law and criminal law. A statute which concerns the public, as distinguished from a private act.

public laws. Statutes.
See **public law**.

public liability insurance. Insurance protecting the insured against liability to a member or members of the public.

See **automobile liability insurance; liability insurance; premises liability insurance**.

public library. A general library for the use of inhabitants of a city, village, or political subdivision. A charitable purpose. 15 Am J2d Char § 47.

public market. A place designated by municipal authority for the sale of articles necessary or convenient for the subsistence of men and domestic animals. 35 Am J1st Mark & M § 2. Any market open to the public.

"It may well be doubted whether the term 'public market' is one which is known to our law. Markets overt, such as exist in England, are unknown here; nor is it usual in this country to grant to private parties the franchise or liberty of keeping or holding a fair or market, as is done in England. Our statute authorizes municipal corporations to establish markets and market houses, and to provide for the regulation and use thereof. But we are not aware that any class of markets in this country, not established by municipal authority, or by virtue of a market franchise granted by the state, has been held, merely because of the magnitude of the business carried on therein, to be impressed with a public use, so as to be held by the courts to be public markets, in that sense." American Livestock Com. Co. v Chicago Live Stock Exchange, 143 Ill 210, 32 NE 274.

See **market**.

public mill. A water, steam, wind, or other mill whose owner or tenant grinds or offers to grind, grain for toll or pay. Howard Mills Co. v Schwartz Lumber & Coal Co. 77 Kan 599, 95 P 559.

public minister. A diplomatic representative serving his government in a foreign country. 4 Am J2d Ambss § 1. A member of the cabinet and head of a department of government in Great Britain.

public money. See **public fund**.

public necessity. An exigency or expediency which justifies the taking of property for a public use. 26 Am J2d Em D §§ 111 et seq.

See **public use**.

public necessity and convenience. Need for the services of a carrier to operate upon the highway sufficient to justify the public authority in granting franchise, license, or permission for operation. 13 Am J2d Car § 82. Ground for the improvement of a highway, existing in use by the public rather than for the benefit of one or a few individuals. 25 Am J1st High § 60. The convenience of the public prompting state or municipality in authorizing special, permissive, or incidental use of a highway, always in subordination to the use of the way for travel and transportation. 25 Am J1st High §§ 168 et seq.

The public necessity, which is a statutory condition precedent in many states to the granting of a franchise to a public service corporation, does not mean indispensable to the public. An urgency less pressing will suffice. The expression means a public need without which the public is inconvenienced to the extent of being handicapped in the pursuit of business or wholesome pleasure, or both—without which people generally of the community are denied, to their detriment, that which is enjoyed by other people generally, similarly situated. Chicago, Rock Island & Pacific Railway Co. v State, 126 Okla 48, 258 P 874.

See **certificate of public necessity and convenience**.

public note. A note for money borrowed by a public body, usually payable and issued to a single investor and maturing at a date earlier than a bond issue. 43 Am J1st Pub Sec § 11.

public notice. A notice given to the public either by posting the notice in a public place or by its publication in a newspaper.

public nuisance. A violation of a public right, either by a direct encroachment upon a public right or property or by doing some act which tends to a common injury, or by omitting to do some act which the common good requires, and which it is the duty of a person to do, which results in injury to the public. A common nuisance, that is, the doing of, or the failure to do, something that injuriously affects the safety, health, or morals of the public, or works some substantial annoyance, inconvenience, or injury to the public. 39 Am J1st Nuis § 8. A condition of things which is prejudicial to the health, comfort, safety, property, sense of decency or morals of the citizens at large, resulting either from an act not warranted by law, or from neglect of a duty imposed by law. Nuchols v Commonwealth, 312 Ky 171, 226 SW2d 796, 13 ALR2d 1478.

public offenses. Actions or omissions in violation of law for which punishment is provided by law. State ex rel. Streit v Justice Court, 45 Mont 375, 123 P 405. All crimes and misdemeanors, not merely those constituting breaches of the peace. Oleson v Pincock, 68 Utah 507, 251 P 23.

public office. A term of vague and variant import, the meaning of which varies necessarily with the context and the circumstances surrounding the use of the term. 42 Am J1st Pub Of § 2. A public agency or trust created in the interest and for the benefit of the people. 42 Am J1st Pub Of § 8. An office the duties of which partake in some degree of the sovereign powers of the state or are imposed upon the incumbent by authority of the law. 42 Am J1st Pub Of § 4. An office the duties of which are not merely clerical or those only of an agent or employee but are performed in the execution or administration of the law. 42 Am J1st Pub Of § 4.

public officer. An incumbent of a public office invested with certain powers and charged with certain duties pertinent to sovereignty. State ex rel. Newman v Skinner, 128 Ohio St 325, 191 NE 127, 93 ALR 331. Such an officer as is required by law to be elected or appointed, who has a designation or title given him by law, and who exercises functions concerning the public, assigned to him by law. 42 Am J1st Pub Of § 2.

See **de facto public officer**; **de jure officer**.

public park. See **park**.

public parking. See **parking lot**.

public passage. A public way over land or water.

public peace. That invisible sense of security, which every man feels so necessary to his comfort, and for which all governments are instituted. State v Benedict, 11 Vt 236.

See **public and domestic tranquillity**.

public performance. See **performance**; **performance for profit**.

public peril. A term pertinent to a discussion of workmen's compensation, referring to a peril to which the public is exposed rather than a peril peculiar to the employment. 58 Am J1st Workm Comp § 257.

See **public emergency**.

public personage. A person who, by his accomplishments, fame, or mode of life, or by adopting a profession or calling which gives the public a legitimate interest in his doings, has rendered his affairs and his character matters of public interest, thereby relinquishing at least a part of his right of privacy. 41 Am J1st Priv § 18.

public place. A place commonly open to the general public. Pugh v State, 55 Tex Crim 462, 117 SW 817. A place where the public resorts. Armstrong v New La Paz Gold Mining Co. (CA9 Cal) 107 F2d 453. Within a requirement as to the posting of notices: —a place to which the public resorts, so that a notice in such a place may be expected to be seen by persons who are interested in or affected by the subject of the notice. Anno: 2 ALR 1008; 30A Am J Rev ed Jud S § 52. Within the meaning of statutes defining the criminal offense of exposure of person: —a place where acts performed are likely to be seen by a number of casual observers, for example, a public highway or bus. 33 Am J1st Lewd etc § 7.

public policy. The policy of the law; the policy in relation to the administration of the law. Practically synonymous with public good or public welfare. National Bank of Commerce v Greenberg, 195 Tenn 217, 258 SW2d 765, 38 ALR2d 1337. The policy of promoting the public welfare and opposing that which is at war with society and in conflict with the moral principles of the period. 17 Am J2d Contr § 175. The protection and promotion of public welfare, including public health and morality. Hanks v McDanell, 307 Ky 243, 210 SW2d 784, 17 ALR2d 1. That principle of law which holds that no subject or citizen can lawfully do that which has a tendency to be injurious to the public or against the public good. Consumers' Oil Co. v Nunnemaker, 142 Ind 560, 41 NE 1048. A will-o'-the-wisp of the law which varies and changes with the interests, habits, needs, sentiments, and fashions of the day. Wallihan v Hughes, 196 Va 117, 82 SE2d 553. Not a matter of principle to be laid down by the court, although the court may be called upon to determine what the public policy is in a particular respect, as for example, where it must determine whether a contract is or is not invalid because it is contrary to good public policy. 20 Am J2d Cts § 64.

public port. A complex subject, consisting of something that is natural, as a convenient access from the sea, a safe situation against winds, and a shore upon which vessels may well unlade; something that is artificial, as keys, wharves, and warehouses; and something that is civil, as privileges and regulations given to it by the government.

It often includes more than the bare place where ships may lade or unlade; it is sometimes extended many miles, including several places as members of the port; designating one as a port of entry and another as a port of delivery. Wharf Case (Md) 3 Bland 361, 369.

public proceedings. The proceedings of an administrative board.

See **public hearing**.

public property. Property owned by the government or a governmental body. Property owned by the public as such in a governmental capacity. 42 Am J1st Prop § 12. Property belonging to the state or a political subdivision thereof, such as a county, city, town, and the like, used exclusively for a public purpose. Anoka County v St. Paul, 194 Minn 554, 261 NW 588, 99 ALR 1157 (tax exemption).

See **public land.**

public prosecutor. See **prosecuting attorney; prosecuting officer.**

public purpose. A classification distinguishing objectives for which the government is to provide from those which are left to private inclination, interest, or liberality. The support of government, or a recognized object of government, or promotion of the welfare of the community. 51 Am J1st Tax § 326.

To conserve and develop water resources, for domestic use, for irrigation, and for power and light, are all common public purposes or uses. Gallardo v Porto Rico Railway, Light & Power Co. (CA1 Puerto Rico) 18 F2d 918.

A use of public property for any public purpose, to warrant exemption from taxation, must be an exclusive use by the public, open to all the people on a basis of equality to such extent as the capacity of the property admits, or an exclusive use by some public or quasi-public agency on behalf of the public. Cleveland v Board of Tax Appeals, 153 Ohio St 97, 91 NE2d 480, 16 ALR2d 1354.

See **public use.**

public record. A record required by law to be kept, or necessary to be kept, in the discharge of a duty imposed by law, or directed by law to serve as a memorial and evidence of something written, said, or done. 45 Am J1st Recds § 2. Inclusive of a legislative, judicial, or executive record. 45 Am J1st Recds § 3. Inclusive of a record of title. 45 Am J1st Recds § 4.

public relations. A term of frequent usage in modern times, often over-worked, concerned with informing the public of activities and creating favorable public opinion, whether such is sought by a public body, a charitable organization, a corporation, or business enterprise.

public relief. See **relief; welfare.**

public report. See **report; repute.**

public revenue. See **taxation.**

public river. A navigable river.

public road. A way open to all the people, without distinction, for passage and repassage at their pleasure. Sumner County v Interurban Transportation Co. 141 Tenn 493, 213 SW 412, 5 ALR 765,
 Same as a **highway.**

public room. A room in an inn or hotel, such as the lobby, to which guests or visitors are admitted indiscriminately.

public sale. A sale at auction to the highest bidder at which the public is given the opportunity to bid. Offredy v Huhla, 135 Conn 20, 60 A2d 779, 4 ALR2d 572. A sale at auction, made upon notice or invitation to the public so that the public be given the opportunity to engage in competitive bidding, and held at a place to which the public have access. 30A Am J Rev ed Jud S § 67.
 See **auction.**

public school. A primary, elementary, intermediate, grammar, or high school, organized and maintained as an institution of the state or a political subdivision of the state, and open to all on equal terms. Yanow v 7 Oaks Park, Inc. 11 NJL 341, 94 A2d 482, 36 ALR2d 639.

public seal. See **official seal.**

public securities. The bonds issued by a state, municipal corporation, or other public body. In a broader sense, including United States bonds, but usually referring to state and local obligations.

public service. Service rendered as a public officer or employee; service rendered in any capacity for or on behalf of the government, national, state, or local. Utility service, such as the furnishing of gas or electricity. The public service that may entitle certain individuals, including private corporations, to privileges and immunities not enjoyed by the public generally, is a public service that carries with it some measure of public control and supervision; and the right of public control and authority must precede or accompany the grant of the privilege, and be so much a part of it that the privilege cannot be exercised without incurring the responsibility and liability that attaches to the performances of public duties. The beneficiary of the grant must be, in some degree, the servant of the public, and subject to the control and authority of some public agency. This is the test to which the right to the enjoyment of special privileges by individuals and private corporations must be subjected, and by this standard their right to privileges and immunities not allowed to the general public must be adjudged. Louisville Railway Co. v Louisville Fire & Life Protective Asso. 151 Ky 644, 152 SW 799.

public service commission. A state agency to which the state or state legislature has delegated the power to regulate public utilities. 43 Am J1st Pub Util § 193.

public service company. See **public service corporation; public utility.**

public service corporation. A quasi-public corporation, operating for the purpose of supplying gas or electricity to users, carrying passengers or freight, or otherwise as a public utility. 18 Am J2d Corp § 9.
 See **public utility.**

public sewer. See **sewer.**

public square. See **square.**

public statute. See **public act.**

public stocks. Government or municipal bonds or obligations; public securities.

public store. Any premises owned or leased by the government and used for the storage of merchandise for the final release of which from customs custody a permit has not been issued. 19 USC § 1561.

public streams. Same as **navigable waters.**

public swearing. Profane swearing, or cursing, or taking the name of God in vain, in the presence and hearing of other persons and in a public place. Commonwealth v Linn, 158 Pa 22, 27 A 843.

public tax. A general federal, state, or municipal tax. J. W. Perry Co. v Norfolk, 220 US 472, 55 L Ed 548, 31 S Ct 465. A tax for a general public purpose, as distinguished from an assessment to obtain funds to expend for a purpose of special or particular benefit to the property of the taxpayer. Schulz v Dixon County, 134 Neb 549, 279 NW 179, 119 ALR 1294.

public toilet. A toilet maintained by the municipality or other public body for public use, often with direct access from street or public way.

public track. A railroad track whereon cars are placed for loading or unloading by shippers or consignees of carload lots. Illinois Cent. R. Co. v Crawford, 244 Miss 300, 140 So 2d 90, 143 So 2d 427.

A comparatively short railroad track connecting an industry with the main line of a railroad, used principally by the industry but open to other shippers. Wolfard v Fisher, 48 Or 479, 84 P 850, 87 P 530.

public transportation. Service in transportation of passengers or freight for hire, available to the public, and rendered without discrimination. Rutledge Co-op. Asso. v Baughman, 153 Md 297, 138 A 29, 56 ALR 1042.

public trial. A trial which is not secret; a trial open for attendance by the public, except as a limitation upon number attending, imposed without partiality or favoritism, is necessary to prevent overcrowding or disorder or to obtain the testimony of a witness emotionally disturbed. People v Jelke, 308 NY 56, 123 NE2d 769, 48 ALR2d 1425; State v Hensley, 75 Ohio St 255, 79 NE 462.

See **open court.**

public trust. A charitable trust. A public office. See **charitable trust.**

publicum jus (pub'li-kum jūs). (Civil law.) Public law.

public urinal. See **public toilet.**

public use. The use of premises by the public at large, that is, the general, unorganized public, rather than by one person, a limited number of persons, or a restricted group. 23 Am J2d Ded § 5. In patent law, a use in public as distinguished from a secret or experimental use. Electric Storage Battery Co. v Shimadzu, 307 US 5, 83 L Ed 1071, 59 S Ct 675, reh den. 307 US 650, 83 L Ed 1529, 59 S Ct 675.

For the purpose of exercise of the power of eminent domain, a matter of public employment or public advantage dependent upon the view taken in the particular jurisdiction involved. Employment or use by the public involving a right on the part of the public, or some portion of it, or some public or quasi-public agency on behalf of the public; to use the property after it is condemned. From the opposite standpoint, public advantage, convenience, or benefit, anything which tends to enlarge the resources, increase the industrial energies, and promote the productive power of any considerable number of the inhabitants of a section of the state, or which leads to the growth of towns and the creation of new resources for the employment of capital and labor, thereby contributing to the general welfare and prosperity of the whole community. 26 Am J2d Em D § 27.

It is a well-established doctrine that, where the owner of property has devoted it to a use in which the public has an interest, he in effect, grants to the public an interest in such use, and must, to the extent of that interest, submit to be controlled by the public for the common good, so long as such use is maintained. People v Steele, 231 Ill 340, 83 NE 236.

See **more necessary public use; public purpose.**

public utilities commission. Same as **public service commission.**

public utility. That which is of use and of service to the public. A corporation or business rendering, and devoting its property to, a public use or service. Nevada-California Power Co. v Borland, 76 Cal App 519, 245 P 209. That which serves, or stands ready to serve, an indefinite public which has a legal right to demand and receive its services or commodities. 43 Am J1st Pub Util § 2. Including every common carrier, gas, electric, telephone, telegraph, water, and heat corporation, and warehousemen, where the service is performed for, or the commodity delivered to, the public generally. Garkane Power Co. v Public Service Com. 98 Utah 466, 100 P2d 571, 132 ALR 1490.

public utility franchise. See **franchise.**

public verdict. A verdict delivered by the jury in open court. 53 Am J1st Tr § 1010.

public vessel. A vessel of the government or of a foreign government. The Navemar, 303 US 68, 82 L Ed 667, 58 S Ct 432; 2 Am J2d Adm § 120.

Public Vessels Act. A federal statute which provides that a libel in personam may be brought against the United States in admiralty, or the United States may be impleaded in admiralty, for damages caused by a public vessel of the United States, and for compensation for towage and salvage service, including contract salvage, rendered to a public vessel of the United States. 46 USC § 781; 2 Am J2d Adm § 120.

public war. Any contention by force between two nations, in external matters, under the authority of their respective governments. 56 Am J1st War § 2.

public warehouseman. The proprietor of a warehouse the services of which are offered on a compensated basis to the public without discrimination. A warehouseman subject to regulation by the government as performing a function of interest to the public. 56 Am J1st Wareh § 4.

public waters. Navigable waters.

public way. A highway.

public weigher. A public officer, weighing grain or other commodities at terminal elevators or other public warehouses. 56 Am J1st Wareh § 18.

public welfare. A variety of interests, spiritual, monetary, physical and aesthetic. The primary social interests of safety, order, and morals. That condition of the public in which it best enjoys the advantages of life as offered by nature to which man must and has oriented himself. 16 Am J2d Const L § 307.

See **general welfare.**

public wharf. A wharf open to public use in the docking of vessels and the loading and unloading of cargo.

Whether a wharf or landing is public or private depends on the ownership of the soil, the purposes for which it was built, the authority by which it was erected, the uses to which it has been applied, and the nature and character of the structure. If the land on which it is constructed is vested in the public, or if built by public authority on land condemned, or if it be at the terminus of a public highway, and practically forms a part thereof, or has been dedicated by the owner to the use of the public, it may be regarded as a public wharf or landing. See 56 Am J1st Whar § 3.

public works. All works of a fixed nature, such as highways, canals, waterworks, docks, etc., constructed by public bodies for public use, protection, or enjoyment. 43 Am J1st Pub Wks § 2.

See **public contract; public improvements.**

public worship. Church services. Worship conducted by religious societies constituted according to their own notions of ecclesiastical authority and ritual propriety, opening their places of worship and admitting to their religious services such persons and upon such terms and subject to such regulations as they may choose to designate and establish.

public writings. The acts of public functionaries, in the executive, legislative, and judicial departments of government, including the transactions which official persons are required to enter in books or registers, in the course of their public duties, and which occur within the circle of their own personal knowledge and observation. (Greenleaf on Evidence, section 470.)
See **public record**.

public wrongs. Crimes and misdemeanors, breaches and violations of the public rights and duties, due to the whole community, considered as a community, in its social aggregate capacity. Anno: 23 ALR 529.

publish. To make or effect a publication. To give publicity.
See **publication**.

publisher. A person who publishes or makes anything known. One whose business is the publishing of a newspaper or periodical.
See **publication**.

pudendum (pū-den'dum). The external female genitals. The vulva. State v Wisdom, 122 Or 148, 257 P 826.

pudicity (pū-dis'i-ti). Chastity; personal purity.

pueblo (pöeb'lō). A large structure made of stone or adobe, housing a village of Southwestern Indians living on a communal basis. United States v Chavez, 290 US 357, 78 L Ed 360, 54 S Ct 217.
In its original signification, the term means people or population, but it is used in the sense of the English word "town." It has the indefiniteness of that term, and like it, is sometimes applied to a mere collection of individuals residing at a particular place, a settlement or village, as well as to a regularly organized municipality. Trenouth v San Francisco, 100 US 251, 25 L Ed 626.

Pueblo dwellers. Indians of the southwest, sedentary rather than nomadic in inclination, and disposed to peace and industry. United States v Chavez, 290 US 357, 78 L Ed 360, 54 S Ct 217.
See **pueblo**.

pueblo right (pöeb'lō rīt). The right of a pueblo under Mexican law to the use of so much of the waters of a stream flowing through it as is necessary for municipal purposes and for the supply of its inhabitants; a right superior to those of riparian proprietors which prevails in modern times in favor of cities which are the successors of the Mexican pueblos. 56 Am J1st Watwk § 45.

puer (pū'er). (Civil law.) A boy; a child; an unmarried man.

puerility (pū-e-ril'i-ti). (Civil law.) The condition of boys from the ages of seven to fourteen, inclusive, and that of girls from the ages of seven to twelve, inclusive.

Pueri sunt de sanguine parentum, sed pater et mater non sunt de sanguine puerorum (pu'e-rī sunt dē san'-gwi-ne pa-ren'tum, sed pa'ter et ma'ter non sunt dē san'gwi-ne pu-er-ō'rum). Children are of the blood of the parents, but the father and the mother are not of the blood of the children.

pueritia (pu-e-ri'she-a). (Civil law.) The age of childhood; that is, from seven to fourteen years. See 4 Bl Contm 22.

puerperal (pū-ėr'pe-ral). The condition of a woman in the labor of child birth. Relating to childbirth.

puerperal insanity (pū-ėr'pe-ral in-san'i-ti). A form of insanity arising from some peculiar transitional condition of the system. Leache v State, 22 Tex Crim 279.

Puerto Rico (pwer'to rē'kō). An island lying between the Atlantic Ocean on the north and the Caribbean Sea on the south; a free commonwealth associated with the United States under an act of Congress approved by President Truman, July 3, 1952.

pues. Same as **puis**.

puffer. One who exaggerates, especially in respect of the quality of goods offered for sale by him. A ficticious bidder at an auction, engaged as such by the person conducting the sale. 7 Am J2d Auct § 26.
See **puffing**.

puffing. The talk of a seller or trader in expounding the merits of his property, so much to be expected of him as not to amount to fraud. Curby v Mastenbrook, 288 Mich 676, 286 NW 123, or a warranty. 46 Am J1st Sales § 326. Making ficticious bids at an auction sale, under employment by the seller or proprietor of the sale, to increase the competition among bidders, thereby enhancing the price at which a bona fide bidder purchases, the ficticious bidder being protected by an understanding with the seller or proprietor of the sale that he shall not be bound by his bids. 7 Am J2d Auct § 26; 30 Am J2d Exec § 365; 31 Am J2d Ex & Ad § 380; 30A Am J Rev ed Jud S § 97.

pug. A small dog with a snub nose. Slang for pugilist.

pugilist (pō'ji-list). One who has made an occupation out of boxing or prize fighting.

puis darrein continuance. (pwē där-rān kôn-tin-ū-ōns). See **plea puis darrein continuance**.

puisne (pū'ne). Younger; junior in point of time, right, or rank.
See **mulier puisne**.

puisne judge (juj). An associate judge.

puis que (pwi ke). After that.

puissance (pū'i-sans). Power; authority.

pulley. A mechanical contrivance of rope or cable running over a grooved wheel, convenient in lifting weights in its most simple state and a means of increasing the effect of applied power when employed in combinations. A machine for tariff purposes. Nord Light, Inc. v United States, 49 Cust & Pat App 12.

Pullman. See **sleeping car company**.

Pullman porter. An employee of a sleeping car company who serves passengers as an attendant.

pulmonary embolism (pul'mō-na-ri em'bō-lizm). The plugging up of an artery in a lung by a blood clot. Anno: 20 ALR 81.

puncheon (pun'chon). A punch. A tool used by counterfeiters for stamping out counterfeit coins. Ridgeley's Case (Eng) 1 East PC 171. A barrel or cask. A short post.

punctuation. The use of certain marks, such as a comma, colon, semicolon, bracket or parenthesis, in a sentence to give it clarity. A minor, not a decisive or controlling, element in the construction of a statute. 50 Am J1st Stat § 253. Not of controlling significance in the construction of a will. 57 Am J1st Wills § 1155. Subordinate to the text in the construction of a contract. 17 Am J2d Contr § 279.

punctum temporis (pungk'tum). A point of time; a moment; an instant.

pundbrech. Same as **pound breach.**

punish. To impose punishment. To impose and inflict a penalty. Bradley v State ex rel. Hill, 111 Ga 168, 36 SE 630.
See **punishment.**

punishable. Liable to punishment.
Where statute makes an offense "punishable" in a certain manner, the use of the word is held to make it a matter of discretion as to whether or not the court will impose the designated punishment. Ex parte Mills, 135 US 263, 34 L Ed 107, 10 S Ct 762.

punishment. Physical or mental distress inflicted. The penalty for a transgression of the law. Orme v Rogers, 52 Ariz 502, 260 P 199. The suffering or confinement inflicted on a person by authority of law and the judgment or sentence of a court for some crime or offense committed by him. Washington v Dowling, 92 Fla 601, 109 So 588. Synonymous with "penalty," "liability," and "forfeiture," as such terms are used in penal provisions. United States v Reisinger, 128 US 398, 32 L Ed 480, 9 S Ct 99.

punitive damages. Damages which are allowed as an enhancement of compensatory damages because of the wanton, reckless, malicious, or oppressive character of the acts of which the plaintiff complains. 22 Am J2d Damg § 236. Damages awarded to punish the defendant for a wilful act and to vindicate the rights of a party in substitution for personal revenge, thus safeguarding the public peace. Winkler v Hartford Acci. & Indem. Co. 66 NJ Super 22, 168 A2d 418.

punitive statute (pū'ni-tiv stat'ūt). A statute which creates a forfeiture or imposes a penalty. Peterson v Ball, 211 Cal 461, 296 P 291, 74 ALR 187.

punitory damages (pū'ni-tō-ri). Same as **punitive damages.**

pupil. One in attendance to receive instruction at a private or public school. (Civil law.) A minor; a ward under guardianship.

pupil assignment laws. The laws governing the assignment of students to the public schools, particularly in reference to the elimination of race segregation. 15 Am J2d Civ R § 42.

pupillaris substitutio (pu-pil-lā'ris sub-sti-tū'she-ō). (Civil law.) Pupillary substitution, which consists in a father or paternal grandfather nominating an heir for an impubescent child immediately subject to his paternal power, in the event that such child should die after his father or grandfather, in his impubescence. A testament which one makes for his impubescent child, because his child, while impubescent, cannot testamentate.—Mackeldey's Roman Law § 721.

pupillarity (pū-pi-lar'i-ti). The age of a child's puerility; minority.

Pupillus pati posse non intelligitur (pu-pil'lus pā'tī pos'se non in-tel-li'ji-ter). A ward or minor is not considered as being able to suffer prejudice.

pur (pör). For; during; by.

pur autre vie (pör ō'tre vē). For the life of another.
See **estate pur autre vie.**

pur cause de vicinage (cōz duh vee'cee-nagh). See **common because of vicinage.**

pur ceo que (pör sĕ kuh). Forasmuch as; inasmuch as.

purchase. To acquire title otherwise than by descent. 23 Am J2d Desc & D § 2. To acquire title by the voluntary act of another. For the purposes of recording laws, a purchaser acquiring legal title, or, under some statutes, a person acquiring an equitable title, even a mortgagee. 45 Am J1st Recds § 147. To take as owner, mortgagee, or pledgee. Uniform Warehouse Receipts Act § 58. Including a taking by sale, discount, negotiation, mortgage, pledge, lien, issue or reissue, gift, or any other voluntary transaction creating an interest in property. UCC § 1–201 (32).
See **buyer; words of purchase.**

purchase money. Money paid by the purchaser upon a purchase or in satisfaction of a debt to the seller or vendor created by the purchase. Austin v Underwood, 37 Ill 438.

purchase-money judgment. A judgment for purchase money due the vendor or seller entered after the conveyance of title to the purchaser. Coke's Appeal, 23 Pa 186.

purchase-money mortgage. A mortgage executed to secure the purchase money or a part thereof by a purchaser of property, contemporaneously with the acquisition of the title thereto, or afterward, but as a part of the same transaction. 36 Am J1st Mtg § 15.

purchase-money paper. A note or draft given the vendor or seller in payment of the purchase price of real or personal property purchased by the maker.
See **purchase-money mortgage.**

purchase on margin. See **marginal purchase.**

purchase option rider. Same as **guaranteed insurability rider.**

purchase price. See **price; purchase money; total contract price.**

purchaser. A person who takes by purchase. UCC § 1–201(33).
See **buyer; purchase.**

purchaser for value. A purchaser under a contract based upon a valuable consideration. 17 Am J2d Contr § 85.
A person who acquires property in consideration of the complete satisfaction and discharge of an antecedent debt is a purchaser for value, according to the weight of numerical authority. Noe v Smith, 67 Okla 211, 169 P 1109.

purchaser in bad faith. An inexact terminology for a purchaser who does not qualify as a bona fide purchaser because of notice of defects in title and outstanding equities. Forbes v First Nat. Bank, 21 Okla 206, 95 P 785.

purchaser in good faith. See **bona fide purchaser.**

purchaser of note or bill. Either an indorsee, assignee, or transferee of a bill or note.

purchaser pendente lite (per'cha-ser pen-den'te li'te). See **pendente lite purchaser.**

purchaser's risk. See **buyer's risk.**

purchaser without notice. See **bona fide purchaser.**

purchasing agent. An agent whose duties consist in purchasing supplies and materials needed in the operation of an industrial plant. Not a managing agent within the meaning of a statute concerning

PURE [1028] PURPOSE

the service of process upon a foreign corporation. Anno: 113 ALR 78.

pure accident. An accident involving two or more persons but no negligence or fault on the part of any one of them. 38 Am J1st Negl § 6.

pure and wholesome water. Water reasonably clean and free from dirt, discoloration, and odor, and reasonably free from bacteria and coli, or any other infection and contamination rendering the water unfit for domestic use and unsafe and dangerous to individuals. 56 Am J1st Watwk § 75.

pure bill of discovery. A bill wherein the only relief sought is a discovery, no demand being made for the recovery of damages or the accomplishment of anything other than a disclosure by the defendant. 23 Am J2d Dep § 141.

pure bill of review. A bill of review in equity to obtain a review and reversal of the decree for error apparent, that is, error or defect on the face of the proceeding. 27 Am J2d Eq § 257.

pure-blooded livestock. See **purebred livestock.**

purebred livestock. Livestock of one breed only, so kept over years and generations by careful selection of sires and dams for mating.

pure chance. A happening by the hand of fate alone, without control or direction.

pure chance doctrine. The principle followed, particularly in England and Canada that a lottery is characterized by winning or losing entirely by chance; that there is no lottery where merit or skill play any part in determining the distribution to be made. 34 Am J1st Lot § 6.

pure charity. An undertaking for a charitable purpose only. The relief of poverty, advancement of education, advancement of religion, promotion of health, the obtaining of good government, and the accomplishment of that which is beneficial to the community in any other respect. 15 Am J2d Char § 57.

pure democracy. A form of government under which the laws are made, not by elected representatives of the people, but by the people in assembly.

pure endowment insurance. See **endowment insurance.**

pure food laws. Statutes intended primarily to protect the public from fraud in the sale of food and to secure the general health. 35 Am J2d Food § 2. See **Food, Drug, and Cosmetic Act.**

purely. Completely; closely; unqualifiedly. White v Smith, 189 Pa 222, 42 A 125.

purely public charity. See **pure charity.**

pure obligation. An obligation with respect to which no condition precedent remains which has not been performed.

pure plea. An affirmative plea in equity, consisting entirely of new matter in defense. 27 Am J2d Eq § 204.

pure tax. An obligation, which is not a debt, imposed on property or persons alike for the support of the government or other public purpose. Dressman v Farmers' & Traders' National Bank, 100 Ky 571, 38 SW 1052.

pure villeinage. Same as **purum villenagium.**

purgation. Getting rid of the undesirable. Elimination of contents of stomach or bowels. Cleansing.

purgation by oath. The ancient practice whereby the defendant cleared himself of a criminal charge by a denial of it under oath or by the aid of compurgators who swore to his innocence. The filing in a contempt proceeding of a verified categorical denial of a charge of criminal contempt, thereby disposing of the case in contempt, but leaving the accused punishable for perjury in the event his oath is false. Osborne v Purdome (Mo) 244 SW2d 1005, 29 ALR2d 1141, cert den 343 US 953, 96 L Ed 1354, 72 S Ct 1046, reh den 343 US 988, 96 L Ed 1375, 72 S Ct 1072.

purgatory (pėr'ga-tọ-ri). A state of suffering after this life, in which those souls are for a time detained who depart this life, after their deadly sins have been remitted as to the stain and guilt, and as to the everlasting pain that was due to them, but who have, on account of those sins, still some debt of temporal punishment to pay; as also those souls which leave this world guilty only of venial sins.
In purgatory these souls are purified and rendered fit to enter into heaven, where nothing defiled enters. (Catholic Belief, Lambert.) Harrison v Brophy, 59 Kan 1, 51 P 883.

purge by the hot iron (pėrj). See **ordeal.**

purge by water. See **ordeal.**

purge of wrong. An adequate and effective renunciation and repudiation by a person of his prior unconscionable or wrongful conduct. Dickerson v Murfield, 173 Or 662, 147 P2d 194. The assumption of responsibility for a tortious act committed by another person.

purgery (pėr'jėr-i). A room in which hogsheads full of sugar are placed in a standing or upright position for the purpose of being drained of the molasses contained in the sugar. V. & A. Meyer & Co. v Queen Ins. Co. 41 La Ann 1000, 6 So 899.

purging contempt. To free one's self from guilt of contempt of court.
See **purgation by oath.**

purging tort (pėr'jing tōrt). See **purge of wrong.**

purging usury. Removing the taint of usury, as by abandoning the usurious agreement and the execution of a new obligation for the amount of the actual debt, free from the usury, and bearing legal interest. 55 Am J1st Usury § 97.

purlieu (pėr'lū). Land which was near a royal forest and which had previously formed a part of the forest itself.

purloin (pėr-loin'). To pilfer; to steal; to filch.

pur moyen (poor mwah'yėn). By means of.

purpart (pėr'pärt). That part of an estate, which, having been held in common, is by partition allotted to anyone of the parties to it. Seiders v Giles, 141 Pa 93, 101, 21 A 514.

purparty (pėr'pär-ti). Same as **purpart.**

purport (pėr'pōrt). That which appears on the face of an instrument. The United States v Turner (US) 7 Pet 132, 136, 8 L Ed 633, 635. The apparent, but not necessarily the legal, import of the instrument. Lacy v State, 33 Okla 161, 242 P 296.

purport clause. A clause in an indictment, setting forth the substance of a written instrument, not purporting to give the precise terms. 27 Am J1st Indict § 85.

purpose. An aim. A design or plan. An intention.

purposely. Intentionally; designedly. Fahnestock v State, 23 Ind 231, 262.

purpose of legislative bill. The general intent of the bill, not the details through and by which such intent is manifested and effectuated. Allied Mut. Ins. Co. v Bell, 353 Mo 891, 185 SW2d 4, 158 ALR 415.

purpose of statute. The object, aim, design, or motive of the statute; the end in view. 50 Am J1st Stat § 303.

purposes of corporation. See **corporate purposes.**

purpresture (pėr-pres'tůr). An obstruction of or encroachment on a highway, made without right or proper authorization. 25 Am J1st High § 273. A structure obstructing a navigable water. 56 Am J1st Whar § 10. An encroachment on or appropriation of lands or waters which are common or public. People ex rel. McCormick v Western Cold Storage Co. 287 Ill 612, 123 NE 43, 11 ALR 437. Sometimes known as "pourpresture."

purprisum (pur-prī'sum). An enclosure; a close.

purq. Same as **purquoi.**

purquoi (pėr-kwà). Wherefore; why.

purse. A pocket book. The handbag of a woman. Something valuable offered by way of a prize for the winner of a contest. Stone v Clay (CA7 Ill) 61 F 889, 890 (horserace). A wager if the person offering it stands a chance of winning it back in competition. 24 Am J1st gaming § 100.

purser (pėr'sėr). An officer of a ship, particularly a ship carrying passengers, in charge of the accounts of the vessel and transactions with passengers. A ship's officer who represents the owners of the vessel as their fiscal agent. Spinette v Atlas Steamship Co. (NY) 14 Hun 100, 105. Not a "clerk" within the meaning of a bequest to clerks. Anno: 38 ALR 789, 790.

purse snatching. A form of larceny. 32 Am J1st Larc § 44.

pursuant to (pėr-sū'ạnt tö). Acting or done in consequence or in prosecution (of anything); hence, agreeable; conformable; following; according. Old Colony Trust Co. v Commissioner, 301 US 379, 81 L Ed 1169, 57 S Ct 813.

pursue. To follow for the purpose of overtaking. To cause a person's prosecution for crime; to prosecute. To follow as a profession or occupation.

pursuer (pėr-sū'ėr). The complainant in a suit in the ecclesiastical courts.
The plaintiff is so designated in the law courts of Scotland.
See **pursue.**

pursuit. A following after one for the purpose of overtaking him. Engaging in something as a profession, an occupation, or a recreation. Cook v Massey, 38 Idaho 264, 220 P 1088, 35 ALR 200, 206.
See **fresh pursuit.**

pursuit of happiness. See **life, liberty, and pursuit of happiness.**

pursuit of principal debtor. The taking of measures for the collection of a debt from the principal debtor before seeking payment by the guarantor. 24 Am J1st Guar § 108.

pur tant que (poor tôn kuh). Because; forasmuch as.

purum villenagium (pū'rum vil-le-nā'ji-um). Absolute or pure villeinage, wherein the service was base in its nature and uncertain as to time and quantity. See 2 Bl Comm 62.

purus (pu'rus). Pure; clear; absolute.

purus idiota (pū'rus i-di-ō'ta). An absolute idiot. See 1 Bl Comm 303.

purveyance (pėr-vā'ạns). An ancient prerogative of the English crown in making purchases of provisions and necessities.
It was regulated by Magna Charta and later abolished altogether. By virtue of it, the crown enjoyed the right of buying up provisions and other necessaries for the use of the royal household at an appraised valuation, and in preference to all others, even without the consent of the owner. Re Barre Water Co. 62 Vt 27, 20 A 107.

purveyance and pre-emption (and prē-emp'shọn). The royal prerogative often referred to as **purveyance.** See 1 Bl Comm 287.

purveyor (pėr-vā'ọr). A provider; a royal officer who purchased articles for the king at his own price.

purview (pėr'vū). The subject matter of a statute in contradistinction to the other parts of it, such as the preamble, the saving, and the proviso. The San Pedro (US) 2 Wheat 132, 4 L Ed 202. All that portion of a statute following the preamble—the whole scope of the enactment. McNeeley v South Penn Oil Co. 52 W Va 616, 44 SE 508.

pus. Suppuration from an infection.
See **puis.**

push car. A small vehicle propelled by manpower, frequently used in handling baggage at air and railway terminals.

put. An option to sell, particularly corporate stock, securities, or commodities, at a stipulated price, on or before a specific future date or within a specified future period of time, such as 30, 60, or 90 days. An option of the class of future contracts in which one of the parties has a right to insist on compliance with the terms of the contract, or to cancel the contract, at his election. More precisely, the privilege of delivering or not delivering things sold. Anno: 83 ALR 573; 36 ALR2d 1397.

putative (pū'tā-tiv). Reputed; supposed; assumed; believed.

putative father. The man charged as the father of an illegitimate child.

putative marriage. A marriage which, although invalid on account of some impediment, is nevertheless contracted in good faith by both or one of the parties. 35 Am J1st Mar § 52.

put in fear. Intimidated.
When a robbery is alleged to have been committed by putting in fear, this does not imply any great degree of terror or fright in the victim. It is sufficient if so much force or threatening by word or gesture, be used as might create an apprehension of danger; or induce a man to part with his property without, or against, his consent. See 4 Bl Comm 243.

put in issue. To raise an issue by the denial of an allegation or the allegations of one's adversary.
To put an alleged fact or matter in issue is to plead by way of plea or answer in such manner as to show that the said fact or matter is in issue, and, if the statute requires, to verify such plea or answer. Johnson v Greenen, 98 Ind App 612, 188 NE 796.

put in suit (in sūt). To bring an action upon; to sue upon; as, to put a promissory note in suit.

put in ure (put in ur'e). To put into use or practice.

put out of court. The status of the case after a decision which is final for the purpose of appeal, that is, a decision which places it beyond the power of the court, after expiration of the term, to place the parties back in their original condition. 4 Am J2d A & E § 56. Having sustained the direction of a verdict unfavorable to one's case.

puts. Options.
See **put.**

putting witnesses under the rule. Excluding subpoenaed or proposed witnesses from the courtroom during the examination of a witness. 53 Am J1st Tr § 31.

put to answer (put to an'ser). Held for trial on a criminal charge.

put to a right. Having a mere right to property, without either possession or even the right of possession. 2 Bl Comm 197.

put upon. To submit to trial.

puys. Same as **puis.**

puz. Same as **puis.**

puzzle. A difficult problem. A toy which presents a problem, such as a jig-saw picture, the solution of which requires ingenuity. White v Aronson, 313 US 16, 82 L Ed 20, 58 S Ct 95.

puzzle contest. A contest in the working of a puzzle, a prize being awarded to the winner, the question whether such constitutes a lottery being best determined according to whether or not the prize is won by chance or by skill. 34 Am J1st Lot § 12.

pyelogram (pī'e-lō-gram). An X-ray picture taken with the use of an injected solution necessary to make a picture. Klein v Yellow Cab Co. (DC Ohio) 7 FRD 169.

pykerie. Same as **pickery.**

pyramiding (pir'a-mid-ing). Building up to a peak. Merging corporations in a complex form with a holding corporation at the top. Controlling prices in a stock or commodity market by a series of operations.

Pyramiding occurs when a producer authorizes several persons to sell the same coal, and they may in turn offer it for sale to other dealers. In consequence the coal competes with itself, thereby resulting in abnormal and destructive competition which depresses the market price for all coals in the market. Appalachian Coals v United States, 288 US 344, 77 L Ed 825, 53 S Ct 471.

pyromania (pī-rō-mā'ni-a). An uncontrollable passion or mania for burning buildings. Smith v Commonwealth, 62 Ky (1 Duv) 224, 231, ovrld on other grounds Shannahan v Commonwealth, 71 Ky (8 Bush) 463.

pyx (piks). A receptacle in a mint where sample coins are placed for testing.

pyx-jury (piks'jö"ri). A jury composed of goldsmiths, formed to test the English coinage.

Q

Q. B. An abbreviation of **Queen's Bench.**

Q. C. An abbreviation of **Queen's Counsel.**

q. c. f. An abbreviation of **quare clausum fregit.**

q'd. An abbreviation of quod.

qua (kwä). As; in what manner; how; in the office, rôle, or capacity of; as, qua guardian, qua executor.

quack. One who pretends to have more knowledge or skill in a science or profession, especially medicine, than he possesses in fact. An ignorant or fraudulent pretender to medical skill. Brinkley v Fishbein (CA5 Tex) 110 F2d 62. An incompetent physician. Burk v Foster, 114 Ky 20, 69 SW 1096.

quack medicine. A remedy or specific the composition of which is kept secret, and which is sold to be used by the purchaser without the advice of a regular or licensed physician. Kohler Mfg. Co. v Beeshore (CA3 Pa) 59 F 572, 574.

qua cunque via data (quä kun′kwe vī′a da′ta). Whichever way it is considered. Westcott v Cady (NY) 5 Johns Ch 334.

quadragesima (kwod-ra-jes′i-mạ). The first Sunday in Lent, which falls about forty days before Easter Sunday.

Quadragesms. A name which was given to the collection of Year Book reports of the years 40-50 Edward III, and which appeared as volume 3 of the 1678-80 edition (better known as the "Folio" or "Vulgate" edition) of the Year Books.

quadrans (kwod′ranz). A one-fourth part.

quadrantata terrae (quad-ran-tā′ta ter′rē). An ancient land measure equal to about one-fourth of an acre.

quadripartite (kwod-ri-pär′tīt). Being apportioned into four parts; having four parties.

quadroon (kwod-rön′). A person of mixed race, being the child of a mulatto and a white. State v Treadway, 126 La 300, 323, 52 So 500.

quadruplicatio (quad-rup-li-kā′she-ō). A Roman law pleading corresponding to the common-law rebutter, being the defendant's reply to the actor's triplicatio. See 3 Bl Comm 310.

quadruplication (kwod-rö-pli-kā′shọn). Same as quadruplicatio.

Quae ab hostibus capiuntur, statim capientium fiunt (kwē ab hos′ti-bus ka-pi-un′ter, stā′tim ka-pi-en′she-um fī′unt). Whatever things are taken from enemies immediately become the property of the captors.

Quae ab initio inutilis fuit institutio, ex post facto convalescere non potest (kwē ab in-i′she-ō in-u′ti-lis fu′it in-sti-tū′she-ō, ex post fak′tō kon-va-le′se-re non po′test). (Civil law.) An institution which was void from the beginning cannot be made valid by a subsequent act.

Quae ab initio non valent, ex post facto convalescere non possunt (kwē ab in-i′she-ō non va′lent, ex post fak′tō kon-va-le′se-re non pos′sunt). Those things which are not valid in the beginning cannot be made valid by a subsequent act.

Quae accessionum locum obtinent extinguuntur cum principales res peremptae fuerint (kwē ak-se-she-ō′num lō′kum ob′ti-nent ex-tin-gu-un′ter kum prin-si-pā′lēz rēz per-emp′tē fu′e-rint). When the principal things have been extinguished or destroyed, those things which hold the position of incidents to them are also extinguished or destroyed. See Broom's Legal Maxims 496.

Quae ad unum finem loquuta sunt, non debent alium detorqueri (kwē ad ū′num fī′nem lo-ku-u′ta sunt, non de′bent a′li-um de-tor-kwē′rī). Those things which have been said to one purpose ought not to be twisted into another.

Quae cohaerent personae a persona separari nequeunt (kwē ko-hē′rent per-sō′nē a per-sō′na se-pa-rā′rī ne′kwē-unt). Those things which are connected with the person ought not to be separated from the person.

Quae communi lege derogant stricte interpretantur (kwē kom-mū′nī lē′je dē′ro-gant strik′te in-tėr-pre-tan′ter). Those (statutes) which derogate from the common law are strictly interpreted.

Quae contra rationem juris introducta sunt, non debent trahi in consequentiam (kwē kon′tra ra-she-ō′nem jū′ris in-trō-duk′ta sunt, non de′bent trā′hī in kon-se-quen′she-am). Those things which have been introduced contrary to the reason of the law ought not to be drawn into precedent. Precedents against law or reason must be set aside. George Jonas Glass Co. v Glass Bottle Blowers' Asso. 77 NJ Eq 219, 79 A 262.

Quaecunque intra rationem legis inveniuntur intra legem ipsam esse judicantur (kwē-kun′kwe in′tra ra-she-o′nem lē′jis in-ve-ni-un′ter in′tra lē′jem ip′-sam es′se ju-di-kan′ter). Whatever comes within the reason of the law is adjudged to be within the law itself.

quaedam nova consuetudo (kwē′dam nō′va kon-su-ē-tū′dō). A certain new custom.

quae de minimis non curat (kwē dē mi′ni-mis non kū′rat). Which (the law) does not regard trifles.

Quae dubitationis causa tollendae inseruntur communem legem non laedunt (kwē du-bi-tā-she-ō′nis kâ′za tol-len′de in-se-run′ter kom-mū′nem lē′jem non lē′dunt). Those things which are interpolated for the purpose of removing doubt do not offend the common law.

Quae dubitationis tollendae causa contractibus inseruntur, jus commune non laedunt (kwē du-bi-tā-she-ō′nis tol-len′dē kâ′za kon-trak′ti-bus in-se-run′ter, jūs kom-mū′ne non lē′dunt). (Civil law.) Those matters which are inserted in contracts for the purpose of removing doubt do not offend the common law.

quae est eadem (kwē est ē-ā′dem). Which is the same matter.

Quae fieri non debent, facta valent (kwē fī′e-rī non de′bent, fak′ta va′lent). Those things which ought not to be done may nevertheless be valid when they have been done.

Quae incontinenti vel certo fiunt inesse videntur (kwē in-kon-ti-nen′tī vel ser-tō fī′unt in-es′se vi-den′ter). Those things which are done directly and certainly are deemed to be included.

Quae in curia acta sunt rite agi praesumuntur (kwē in kū′ri-a ak′ta sunt ri′te ā′jī prē-zu-mun′ter). Those things which have been done in court are presumed to have been done correctly.

Quae in curia regis acta sunt rite agi praesumuntur (kwē in kū′ri-a rē′jis ak′ta sunt ri′te ā′jī prē-zu-mun′ter). Those things which have been done in the king's court are presumed to have been done correctly.

Quae in partes dividi nequeunt solida a singulis praestantur (kwē in par′tēz di-vi′dī ne′kwe-unt sō′li-da a sin′gu-lis prē-stan′ter). Those things which cannot be divided into parts are performed by each person as a whole.

Quae inter alios acta sunt nemini nocere debent, sed prodesse possunt (kwē in′ter a′li-ōs ak′ta sunt ne′mi-nī no-sē′re de′bent, sed pro-des′se pos′sunt). Those things which are done between others ought not to prejudice a person, but they can benefit him.

Quae in testamento ita sunt scripta ut inteligi non possint, perinde sunt ac si scripta non essent (kwē in tes-ta-men′tō i′ta sunt skrip′ta ut in-tel′li-jī non pos′sint, per-in′de sunt ak sī skrip′ta non es′sent). Those things which are so written in a will that they cannot be understood are just as if they had not been written.

quae ipso usu consumuntur (kwē ip′sō ū′sū kon-sū-mun′ter). Which were consumed for his own use. Westcott v Cady, 5 Johns Ch 334.

Quae legi communi derogant non sunt trahenda in exemplum (kwē lē′jī kom-mū′nī dē′ro-gant non sunt trā-hen′da in eg-zem′plum). Those things which derogate from the common law ought not to be drawn into precedent.

Quae legi communi derogant stricte interpretantur (kwē lē′jī kom-mū′nī dē′ro-gant strik′te in-ter-pre-tan′ter). Those things which derogate from the common law are strictly interpreted or construed.

Quaelibet concessio domini regis capi debet stricte contra dominum regem, quando potest intelligi duabus viis (kwē′li-bet kon-se′she-ō do′mi-nī rē′jis ka′pī de′bet strik′tē kon′tra do′mi-num rē′jem, quan′dō po′test in-tel′li-jī du-ā′bus vī′is). Every grant of our lord the king ought to be taken strictly against our lord the king, when it can be understood in two ways.

Quaelibet concessio fortissime contra donatorem interpretanda est (kwē′li-bet kon-se′she-ō for-tis′si-mē kon′tra dō-nā-tō′rem in-ter-pre-tan′da est). Every grant is to be interpreted or construed most strictly against the grantor. Courtis v Dennis, 48 Mass (7 Met) 510, 516.

Quaelibet jurisdictio cancellos suos habet (kwē′li-bet jū-ris-dik′she-ō kan-sel′lōs su′ōs hā′bet). Every jurisdiction has its own limits.

Quaelibet pardonatio debet capi secundum intentionem regis, et non ad deceptionem regis (kwē′li-bet par-do-nā′she-ō de′bet ka′pī se-kun′dum in-ten-she-ō′nem rē′jis, et non ad dē-sep-she-ō′nem rē′jis). Every pardon ought to be interpreted or construed agreeably with the intention of the king and not for the deception of the king.

Quaelibet poena corporalis, quamvis minima, major est qualibet poena pecuniaria (kwē′li-bet pē′na kor-po-rā′lis, quam′vis mi′ni-ma, ma′jor est qua′li-bet pē′na pe-ku-ni-ā′ri-a). Every corporal punishment, even the least, is greater than any pecuniary punishment.

Quae mala sunt inchoata in principio vix bono perguntur exitu (kwē ma′la sunt in-ko-ā′ta in prin-si′pi-ō vix bo′nō per-gun′ter ex′i-tū). Things which are bad in principle at the outset are rarely completed with good at the end.

quae nihil frustra (kwē ni′hil frus′tra). Which (the law) (requires) nothing in vain.

Quae non fieri debent, facta valent (kwē non fī′e-rī de′bent, fak′ta va′lent). Those things which ought not to be done may nevertheless be valid when they have been done.

Quae non valeant singula juncta juvant (kwē non va′le-ant sin′gu-la junk′ta ju′vant). Things which are void severally may be valid when joined.
That is, words or expressions which are inoperative when taken singly may often be made effective when construed in conjunction with the words or expressions which accompany them. Breasted v Farmers' Loan & Trust Co. 8 NY 299.

quae plura (kwē plu′ra). An ancient writ whereby an escheator was ordered to ascertain what other or additional land the decedent held at his death besides the land disclosed by the inquisition.

Quae praeter consuetudinem et morem majorum fiunt neque placent neque recta videntur (kwē prē′ter kon-su-ē-tū′di-nem et mō′rem mā-jō′rem fī′unt ne′kwe pla′sent ne′kwe rek′ta vi-den′ter). Those things which are done contrary to the custom and manner of our ancestors neither please nor seem right.

Quae propter necessitatem recepta sunt, non debent in argumentum trahi (kwē prop′ter ne-se-si-ta′tem re-sep′ta sunt, non de′bent in ar-gu-men′tum trā′hī). Those things which are allowed by reason of necessity ought not to be drawn into argument.

Quaeras de dubiis legem bene discere si vis (kwē′ras de du′bi-is lē′jem be′ne di′se-re sī vis). You should inquire concerning doubtful matters if you wish to understand the law well.

quaere (kwē′rē). Query; it is a question.

Quaere de dubiis, quia per rationes pervenitur ad legitimam rationem (kwē′re de du′bi-is, qui′a per ra-she-ō′nēz per-ve′ni-ter ad le-ji′ti-mam ra-she-ō′nem). Inquire concerning doubtful matters, because through reasonings the legal reason is arrived at.

Quae regio in terris nostri non plena laboris (kwē rē′ji-ō in ter′ris nos′trī non plē′na la-bō′ris). What region on earth is not filled with our works (Vergil.) From Webster's argument in Gibbons v Ogden (US) 9 Wheat 1, 158, 6 L Ed 1, 61.

quae relicta sunt et tradita (kwē rē-lik′ta sunt et tra′di-ta). Which have been left and handed down.

quaerens (kwē′renz). He who complains; a plaintiff.

Quaerens nihil capiat per billam (kwē′renz ni′hil ka′-pi-at per bil′lam). Let the plaintiff take nothing by his bill.

Quaerens non invenit plegium (kwē′renz non in-vē′nit ple′ji-um). The plaintiff has not found a pledge, or security.

Quaerere dat sapere quae sunt legitima vere (kwē′re-re dat sa′pe-re kwē sunt le-ji′ti-ma ve′re). Inquiry gives knowledge as to what things are truly lawful.

Quae rerum natura prohibentur nulla lege confirmata sunt (kwē rē′rum na-tū′ra pro-hi-ben′ter nul′la lē′je kon-fir-mā′ta sunt). Those things which are prohibited in the nature of things are confirmed by no law.

quaeritur (kwē′ri-ter). It is doubted.

QUAE [1033] QUALIFIED

Quae singula non prosunt, juncta juvant (kwē sin'gu-la non prō'sunt, junk'ta ju'vant). Those things which are of no consequence severally may be valid jointly.

quaesta (kwēs'tą̊). An indulgence or remission of punishment for sin granted by the Roman Catholic Church, or by the Pope.

quaestio (kwest'she-ō). In the Roman law, an inquest or investigation into an alleged offense made by a commission. In medieval law, an inquisition by torture.

quaestio facti (kwest'she-ō fak'tī). A question of fact.

quaestio juris (kwest'she-ō jū'ris). A question of law.

quaestiones perpetuae (quest-she-ō'nēz per-pe'tū-ē). (Roman law.) Permanent commissions which were established to investigate crimes.

quaestor (kwēs'tor). A Roman magistrate.

quaestus (kwēs'tus). An estate acquired by purchase, as distinguished from one acquired by inheritance.

Quae sunt minoris culpae sunt majoris infamiae (kwē sunt mi-nō'ris kul'pē sunt ma-jō'ris in-fa'mi-ē). Those things which are less culpable may be more infamous.

Quae temporalia sunt ad agendum perpetua sunt ad excipiendum (kwē tem-po-rā'li-a sunt ad ā-jen'dum per-pe'tu-a sunt ad ek-si-pi-en'dum). Things which afford a ground of action, if raised within a certain time, may be pleaded at any time, by way of exception. Buty v Goldfinch, 74 Wash 532, 133 P 1057.

Quaker marriage. A marriage not solemnized by an ordained minister or judicial officer but valid under statute as in accord with the religious belief of the Quakers. 35 Am J1st Mar § 25.

quale jus (qua'le jūs). What kind of right,—a writ which ordered an investigation of a judgment in favor of a clergyman for the purpose of preventing an evasion of the statutes of mortmain.

qualification. A limitation or modification; a condition which limits. A quality that fits a person for a position. A condition prescribed either by constitutional provision or legislative enactment for holding public office. 42 Am J1st Pub Of § 37. Competency to act in a particular capacity, such as executor or administrator. 31 Am J2d Ex & Ad § 67. Taking an oath and providing a bond as conditions of acting in a particular capacity, for example, as executor or administrator. 31 Am J2d Ex & Ad §§ 106, 107. A technical term for the process of analyzing the nature of the question before the court for the purpose of determining the law applicable as between the laws of two or more jurisdictions. 16 Am J2d Confl L § 3.

See **eligible to an office; oath of office; official bond.**

qualification of candidate. The possession of qualifications to fill the office sought in the election. 25 Am J2d Elect § 174. In a primary election, the possession of qualifications prescribed by statute or by party rules and regulations. Robert v Cleveland, 48 NM 226, 149 P2d 120, 153 ALR 635.

qualification of elector. The existence of certain conditions respecting citizenship, residence, age and etc., prescribed by constitutional provision or statute. 25 Am J2d Elect § 58. For the act of voting itself, the additional qualification of registration.

While a statue providing for a local option election may require that a signer of a petition for such an election be a registered voter, to be a "qualified elector" within the meaning of such statute, it is not necessary that one be registered. Anno: 100 ALR 1309, 1310.

See **registration of voters.**

qualification of grand juror. The elements of citizenship and residence and the absence of bias, prejudice, or interest. 24 Am J1st Grand J §§ 7 et seq.

qualification of juror. The possession of the qualifications prescribed by constitution or statute, such as age, mental competency, literacy, citizenship, residence, character, and in rare instances the ownership of property and the payment of taxes. 31 Am J Rev ed Jury § 67.

qualification of voter. See **qualification of elector.**

qualified. Having fitness or capacity. Having taken the official oath and having given an official bond in preparing to accept a public office to which one has been elected or appointed. Archer v State, 74 Md 443, 22 A 8.

qualified acceptance. A conditional acceptance of an offer; an acceptance which modifies the terms of the offer. In effect, a counteroffer. 17 Am J2d Contr § 62. An acceptance of a bill of exchange which varies the effect of the bill as drawn. 11 Am J2d B & N § 515.

qualified dedication. A dedication of land for some public purpose, such as a street or highway which is made subject to limitations, conditions, restrictions or reservations. 23 Am J2d Ded § 37.

qualified denial. A denial insufficient as a pleading for want of positivism. 41 Am J1st Pl §§ 148, 192.

qualified discharge. A discharge in bankruptcy which excepts from the operation thereof debts which were provable in a prior proceeding in bankruptcy involving the same bankrupt wherein a discharge was denied the bankrupt. Anno: 156 ALR 857; 9 Am J2d Bankr § 741.

qualified elector. A person who is qualified to vote at an election but may or may not exercise his franchise or privilege of voting. Bergevin v Curtz, 127 Cal 86, 89, 59 P 312.

See **qualification of elector; qualified voter.**

qualified estate. See **qualified fee; qualified interest.**

qualified fee. An estate limited to a person and his heirs, with a qualification annexed to it providing that the estate must determine whenever that qualification is at an end.

Because the estate may last forever, it is a fee; because it may end on the happening of an event, it is called a qualified or determinable fee. 28 Am J2d Est § 22.

qualified indorsement. See **conditional indorsement.**

qualified interest. An interest in property under which control falls short of the absolute, the property not being objectively and lawfully appropriated to one's use in exclusion of all other persons. Griffith v Charlotte, Columbia & Augusta Railroad Co. 23 SC 25.

See **qualified fee.**

qualified majority decision. A court decision concurred in by the requisite number of justices to make it binding, such number being fixed by statute at more than a simple majority. State ex rel. Mason v Baker, 69 ND 488, 288 NW 202.

qualified nuisance. Anything lawfully but so negligently or carelessly done or permitted as to create a potential and unreasonable risk of harm which, in due course, results in injury to another. Taylor v Cincinnati, 143 Ohio St 426, 55 NE2d 724, 155 ALR 44.

qualified owner. The owner of a qualified interest in a thing.
See **qualified interest**.

qualified privilege. See **conditionally privileged communication**.

qualified property. Same as **qualified interest**.

qualified refusal. A refusal to deliver up a chattel on demand of the person lawfully entitled thereto, not amounting to a conversion of the chattel because accompanied by a reasonable qualification or requirement, such as insistence upon payment of charges for which one has a lien. 18 Am J2d Conv § 44.

qualified right. A right, the exercise of which depends upon a justification. Harding v Ohio Casualty Ins. Co. 230 Minn 327, 41 NW2d 818. A common right.
See **common right**; **qualified interest**.

qualified salvage. A reward in the nature of salvage made to members of the crew of the vessel saved. 47 Am J1st Salv § 20.

qualified stock option. An option under which an employee of a corporation may buy stock in the corporation, its parent company, or a subsidiary. Internal Revenue Code § 422(b).

qualified survivor. A technical term of community-property law in some jurisdictions, referring to a status acquired by the surviving spouse pursuant to a statutory procedure in order to have the right to dispose of the part of the community property that he does not own. 15 Am J2d Community Prop § 107.

qualified voter. A person qualified as an elector, being entitled to vote, and who actually votes. Carroll County v Smith, 111 US 556, 565, 28 L Ed 517, 520, 4 S Ct 539; Bergevin v Curtz, 127 Cal 86, 89, 59 P 312.
See **qualified elector**.

qualify. See **qualification**; **qualified**.

qualifying clauses. Provisions in a contract or conveyance containing conditions.

Qualitas quae inesse debet, facile praesumitur (qua'li-tãs kwē in-es'se de'bet, fa'si-le prē-zu'mi-tēr). A quality which ought to belong to a thing is readily presumed.

qualitative rule of evidence. A rule by which the admissibility of evidence is determined.

quality. A state or condition, particularly of goods or merchandise. Uniform Sales Act § 76(1); 46 Am J1st Sales § 343.

quamdiu (quam-di'ū). As long as; so long as; until.

quamdiu bene se gesserint (quam-di'u be'ne sē je'se-rint). As long as they properly conduct themselves; during good behavior.

quamdiu se bene gesserit (quam-di'ū sē be'ne je'se-rit). As long as he shall behave himself. That is, during good behavior. See 1 Bl Comm 267.

Quam legem exteri nobis posuere, eandem illis ponemus (quam lē'jem ex'te-rī nō'bis po-su'e-re, e-an'dem il'lis po-ne'mus). Whatever law foreigners have imposed upon us, we will impose the same law upon them. See 1 Bl Comm 260.

Quam longum debet esse rationabile tempus, non definitur in lege, sed pendet ex discretione justiciariorum (quam lon'gum de'bet es'se rā'she-ō-nā'bi-le tem'pus, non de-fī'ni-ter in lē'je, sed pen'det ex dis-kre-she-ō'ne jus-ti-she-a-ri-ō'rum). How long a reasonable time ought to be is not defined by law, but depends upon the discretion of the judges.

Quamvis aliquid per se non sit malum, tamen si sit mali exempli, non est faciendum (quam'vis a'li-quid per sē non sit ma'lum, ta'men sī sit ma'lī ek-zemp'lī non est fa-she-en'dum). Although anything may not be bad or evil in itself, yet if it is of bad example, it should not be done.

Quando abest provisio partis, adest provisio legis (quan'dō ab'est prō-vī'zhe-o par'tis, ad'est prō-vi'zhe-ō lē'jis). When the provision of the party is lacking, the provision of the law supplies it.

quando acciderint (quan'dō ak-si'de-rint). When they shall come in.

Quando aliquid conceditur, conceditur id sine quo illud fieri non possit (quan'dō a'li-quid kon-sē'di-ter, kon-sē'di-ter id sī'ne quo il'lud fī'e-rī non pos'-sit). When anything is granted, that without which it cannot be effective is also granted.
The grant of a dam overflowing the grantor's land at the time of the grant, following the maxim, carries with it to the grantee the right to continue the overflow. Troup v Hurlbut (NY) 10 Barb 354, 359.

Quando aliquid mandatur, mandatur et omne per quod pervenitur ad illud (quan'dō a'li-quid man-dā'ter, man-dā'ter et om'ne per quod per-ve'ni-ter ad il'lud). When anything is commanded, everything by which it can be accomplished is also commanded.

Quando aliquid per se non sit malum, tamen si sit mali exempli, non est faciendum (quan'dō a'li-quid per sē non sit ma'lum, ta'men si sit ma'lī ek-zemp'lī, non est fa-she-en'dum). When anything is not bad or evil in itself, yet if it is of bad example, it should not be done.

Quando aliquid prohibetur ex directo, prohibetur et per obliquum (quan'dō a'li-quid prō-hi-bē'ter ex di-rek'tō, prō-hi-bē'ter et per ob-li'qu-um). When anything is prohibited directly, it is also prohibited indirectly. Re Co-operative Law Co. 198 NY 479, 92 NE 15.

Quando aliquid prohibetur, prohibetur et omne per quod devenitur ad illud (quan'dō a'li-quid prō-hi-bē'ter, et om'ne per quod de-ve'ni-ter ad il'lud). When anything is prohibited, every means by which the thing may be accomplished is also prohibited.
When the thing done is substantially that which was by the statute prohibited, it falls within the statute, simply because, according to the true construction of the statute, it is the thing thereby prohibited. State, ex rel. Matthews, v Forsyth, 147 Ind 466, 44 NE 593.

Quando aliquis aliquid concedit, concedere videtur et id sine quo res uti non potest (quan'dō a'li-quis a'li-quid kon-sē'dit, kon-sē'de-re vi-dē'ter et id sī'ne quō rēz u'tī non po'test). When anyone grants anything, he is deemed to grant also that without which the thing granted cannot be used. See 3 Kent's Comm 421.

Quando charta continet generalem clausulam posteaque descendit ad verba specialia quae clausulae generali sunt consentanea, interpretanda est charta secundum verba specialia (quan'dō kar'ta kon'ti-net je-ne-rā′lem klâ′su-lam post-e-ā′kwe de-sen′dit ad ver′ba spe-she-ā′li-a kwē klâ′su-lē je-ne-rā′li sunt kon-sen-tā′ne-a, in-ter-pre-tan′da est kar′ta se-kun′dum ver′ba spe-she-ā′li-a). When a deed contains a general clause, and afterward comes down to special words, which are consistent with the general clause, the deed is to be construed according to the special words.

quandocumque (quan-dō-kum′kwe). Whenever; as often as.

Quando de una et eadem re, duo onerabiles existunt, unus pro insufficientia alterius de integro onerabitur (quan′dō dē ū′na et e-ā′dem rē, du′ō ō-ne-rā′bi-lēz eg-zis′tunt, ū′nus prō in-suf-fi-she-en′she-a al-te′ri-us dē in′te-grō ō-ne-rā′bi-ter). When two persons are chargeable with one and the same thing, one of them is chargeable with the whole thing, upon the failure of the other.

Quando dispositio referri potest ad duas res, ita quod secundum relationem unam vitiatur et secundum alteram utilis sit, tum facienda est relatio ad illam ut valeat dispositio (quan′dō dis-po-zi′she-ō re-fer′rī po′test ad du′as rēs, i′ta quod se-kun′dum re-lā-she-ō′nem ū′nam vi-she-ā′ter et se-kun′dum al′te-ram ū′ti-lis sit, tum fa-she-en′da est re-lā′she-ō ad il′lam ut va′le-at dis-po-si′she-ō). When a disposition can refer to two things, so that according to one relation it would be void, and according to the other it would be valid, then the relation must be made so that the disposition will be valid.

Quando diversi desiderantur actus ad aliquem statum perficiendum, plus respicit lex actum originalem (quan′dō di-ver′sī de-si-de-ran′ter ak′tus ad a′li-quem sta′tum per-fi-she-en′dum, plus re′spi-sit lex ak′tum o-ri-gi-nā′lem). When different acts are required to perfect a certain estate, the law regards the original act as most important.

Quando duo jura concurrunt in una persona, aequum est ac si essent in diversis (quan′dō du′ō jū′ra kon-ker′runt in ū′na per-sō′na, ē-qu-um est ak sī es′sent in di-ver′sis). When two rights concur in one person, it is just as if they were in different persons.

The maxim is applied in the rule that where there are two separate rights of entry in one person, the loss of one of the rights by lapse of time does not impair the other. Kissinger v Wilson, 53 Ark 400.

Quando hasta vel aliud corporeum quidlibet porrigitur a domino se investituram facere dicente; quae saltem coram duobus vasallis solemniter fieri debet (quan′dō has′ta vel a′li-ud kor-po′re-um quid′li-bet por-ri′ji-ter ā do′mi-nō sē in-ves-ti-tū′ram fa′se-re dī-sen′te; kwē sal′tem kō′ram du-ō′bus va-sal′lis so-lem′ni-ter fī′e-rī de′bet). When a spear, or some other tangible thing, is presented by the lord saying that he thus made investiture; and this thing ought to be done solemnly in the presence of at least two vassals. See 2 Bl Comm 367.

Quando jus domini regis et subditi concurrunt, jus regis praeferri debet (quan′dō jūs do′mi-nī rē′jis et sub′di-tī kon-ker′runt, jūs rē′jis prē-fer′rī de′bet). When a right of our lord the king and that of a subject come into conflict, the right of the king ought to be preferred.

Quando jus domini regis et subditi insimul concurrunt, regis praeferri debet (quan′dō jūs do′mi-nī rē′jis et sub′di-tī in′si-mul kon-ker′runt, rē′jis prē-fer′ri de′bet). When a right of our lord the king comes into conflict, that of the king ought to have preference.

Such maxim should apply to the state, and her revenues should be protected with as much solicitude as those of the British King. State v Foster, 5 Wyo 199, 38 P 926.

Quando lex aliquid alicui concedit, concedere videtur id sine quo res ipsa esse non potest (quan′dō lex a′li-quid a′li-kī kon-sē′dit, kon-sē′de-re vi-dē′ter id sī′ne quō rēz ip′sa es′se non po′test). When the law grants anything to anyone, it is deemed also to grant that without which the thing itself cannot exist.

Quando lex aliquid alicui concedit, conceditur et id sine quo res ipsa esse non potest (quan′dō lex a′li-quid a′li-kī kon-sē′dit, kon-se′di-ter et id sī′ne quō rēz ip′sa es′se non po′test). When the law grants anything to anyone, that is also granted without which the thing itself cannot exist.

Quando lex aliquid alicui concedit, omnia incidentia tacite conceduntur (quan′dō lex a′li-quid a′li-kī kon-sē′dit, om′ni-a in-si-den′she-a ta′si-te kon-sē-dun′ter). When the law grants anything to anyone, all things which are incident thereto are tacitly granted.

Quando lex aliquid alieni concedit, conceditur et id sine quo res ipsa esse non potest (quan′dō lex a′li-quid ā-li-e′nī kon-sē′dit, kon-sē′di-ter et id sī′ne quō rēz ip′sa es′se non po′test). When the law grants anything to another, that is also granted without which the thing itself cannot exist. People v Hicks (NY) 15 Barb 153, 160.

Quando lex aliquid concedit, concedere videtur et illud, sine quo res ipsa esse non potest (quan′dō lex a′li-quid kon-sē′dit, kon-sē′de-re vi-dē′ter et il′lud sī′ne quō rēz ip′sa es′se non po′test). When the law grants anything, it appears to grant that also without which the thing itself cannot exist. Re McDonald, 2 NY Crim 82, 97.

Quando lex est specialis, ratio autem generalis, generaliter lex est intelligenda (quan′dō lex est spe-she-ā′lis, rā′she-ō â′tem je-ne-rā′lis, je-ne-rā′li-ter lex est in-tel-li-jen′da). When a law is special, but the reason for it is general, the law is to be understood in a general sense.

Quando licet id quod majus, videtur licere id quod minus (quan′do lī′set id quod mā′jus, vi-dē′ter lī-sē′re id quod mī′nus). When that which is greater is allowed, that which is less is deemed to be allowed.

Quando plus fit quam fieri debet, videtur etiam illud fieri quod faciendum est (quan′dō plus fit quam fī′e-rī de′bet, vi-dē′ter e′she-am il′lud fī′erī quod fa-she-en′dum est). When more is done than ought to be done, certainly that will be deemed to have been done which ought to have been done.

Quando quod ago non valet ut ago, valeat quantum valere potest (quan′dō quod ā′gō non va′let ut ā′gō va′le-at quan′tum va-lē′re po′test). When that which I do is not valid as I do it, let it have as much validity as it can have.

Upon this principle, it has been determined, that a deed which was intended to operate as a lease and release, but could not take effect in that manner, was good as a covenant to stand seised. Jackson ex dem. Troup v Blodget (NY) 16 Johns 172, 178.

Quando res non valet ut ago, valeat quantum valere potest (quan′dō rēz non va′let ut ā′gō, va′le-at quan′tum va-lē′re po′test). When the thing is not valid as I do it, let it have as much validity as it can have.

It is a growing doctrine that wherever a party has

the power to do a thing, and means to do it, the instrument he employs shall, if possible, be so construed as to give effect to his intention. Bond v Bunting, 78 Pa 210, 219.

Quando verba et mens congruunt, non est interpretationi locus (quan'dō ver'ba et menz kon'gru-unt, non est in-ter-pre-tā-she-ō'nī lō'kus). When the words and the intention agree, there is no room for interpretation.

Quando verba statuti sunt specialia, ratio autem generalis, generaliter statutum est intelligendum (quan'dō ver'ba sta-tū'tī sunt spe-she-ā'li-a, rā'she-ō â'tem je-ne-rā'lis, je-ne-rā'li-ter sta-tū'tum est in-tel-li-jen'dum). When the words of the statute are special, yet the reason for it is general, the statute is to be understood in a general sense.

Quant beastes savages le roye aler hors del forrest, le property est hors del roy (kônt best sä-väzh' lĕ ruä' alā' ôr del for-rest, lĕ prŏ-per-ti ā ôr del ruä'). When the king's wild beasts go out of the forest, the property in them is out of the king.

quantes fois (känt fwah). How many times.

quanti minoris (quan'tī mī-nō'ris). A form of action in Louisiana for the reduction of the price, in consequence of a defect in the thing sold. Millaudon v Soubercase (La) 3 Mart NS 287, 288.

quantitative rule of evidence. A rule for evaluating evidence as to probative value.

quantity discount. A discount on the regular price allowed for a purchase in large quantity.

quantity of. A descriptive phrase akin to "diverse" and "sundry." 27 Am J1st Indict § 83.

quantum (kwon'tum). Quantity or amount. So much. How much. Connelly v Western Union Tel. Co. 100 Va 51, 40 SE 618.

quantum counts (kwon'tum kounts). The counts of quantum meruit and quantum valebant in general assumpsit. 1 Am J2d Actions § 13.

quantum damnificatus (quan'tum dam-ni-fi-kā'tus). How much was he damaged,—the name given to the submission to a jury in a suit in equity of the amount of the damages suffered by the plaintiff.

quantum indemnificatus (quan'tum in-dem-ni-fi-kā'tus). To what amount he should be indemnified.

quantum meruit (kwon'tum me'ru-it). As much as it is worth. The amount deserved. A common count of general assumpsit. 1 Am J2d Actions § 13. A common count of assumpsit for work and labor.

quantum sufficit (kwon'tum su-fis'it). As much as sufficeth; sufficient.

quantum valebant (kwon'tum va-lē'bant). As much as it is worth. A common count of general assumpsit. 1 Am J2d Actions § 13. A common count of assumpsit for materials furnished.

quantus (kwon'tus). See **quantum**.

quarantine. The privilege given a widow to use certain portions of her husband's estate until dower is allotted; her right to remain in and use the mansion house temporarily. 25 Am J2d Dow § 171. The comparable right of a widower in a jurisdiction in which his right in his deceased wife's real estate is similar to dower. 25 Am J2d Dow § 171.

Health regulations providing for the isolation of persons having contagious or infectious diseases; health regulations which prohibit persons so affected from entering a designated area of the state or municipality; regulations which prohibit the transportation of infected goods into the jurisdiction of the regulatory board. 25 Am J1st Hlth § 32. A prohibition by law of the removal of livestock or plant life from a section afflicted with a disease. Anno: 65 ALR 526. The detention of a vessel in port, before permitting the landing of passengers or the unloading of cargo, as a protection against contagion from abroad. 48 Am J1st Ship § 21. The place where a vessel is detained because suspected of carrying persons afflicted with a contagious disease or infected cargo.

quarantine regulations. See **quarantine**.

quarantine station. A building provided for the care of persons held under quarantine. The position of a vessel in quarantine.
See **pesthouse; quarantine**.

quare (kwā'rē). Wherefore; why; on which account; because.

quare clausum fregit (quā'rē klâ'sum frē'jit). Because he broke the close.
See **trespass quare clausum**.

quare ejicit infra terminum (quā'rē ē'ji-sit in'fra ter'-mi-num). Because he ousted him during the term. The name of an ancient writ which lay for a tenant against his landlord for ejecting him from the leasehold premises. See 3 Bl Comm 206.

quare impedit (kwā'rē im'pe-dit). Because he has hindered; an action or writ which lay for a patron against a disturber of his right of presentation to a benefice to recover it. See 3 Bl Comm 245.

quare incumbravit (quā'rē in-kum-brā'vit). Because he has encumbered; a special action which lay for a patron against a bishop to recover the presentation and for damages for admitting a clerk pending a quare impedit. See Bl Comm 248.

quare non admisit (quā'rē non ad-mi'sit). Because he did not admit; a writ for a patron against a bishop for damages for not admitting a clerk upon a writ ad admittendum clericum. See 3 Bl Comm 250.

quare non permittit (quā'rē non per-mit'tit). A writ which lay against a patron who refused to present a nominated clergyman to a church.

quarentina habenda. See **de quarentina habenda**.

quare obstruxit (quā'rē ob-strü'xit). A writ which lay against a person who obstructed a way.

quarreling. The indulging by two or more persons in an altercation, dispute, brawl, or angry contest.
It takes two to make a quarrel. A quarrel cannot be ex parte. Carr v Conyers, 84 Ga 287.

quarry (kwor'i). Verb: To remove building stone from a bed of rock. Noun: Game pursued by a hunter or by dogs. A bed or ledge from which stone is taken.

A quarry is similar to a mine, in the sense that the material removed, be it mere rock, or stone, or valuable marble, is removed because of its value for some other purposes, and in the sense that it is not removed for the purpose of improving the property from which it is taken. It is distinguished from a mine in the fact that it is usually open at the top and front, and in the ordinary acceptation of the term, it is further distinguished in the character of the material extracted. Re Kelso, 147 Cal 609, 82 P 241.

quarter. Mercy granted to a disabled or surrendering adversary. One fourth. A United States coin having

QUARTER [1037] QUASI

the value of one fourth dollar. A quarter section of land.
See **quarter section**.

quarter chest. A measure of tea, about twenty-five pounds.

quarter days (kwâr'tėr dās). In England, those days when quarterly rent generally fell due and when leaseholds generally expired.
These days were March 25th, June 24th, September 29th, and December 25th.

quartering. Dismemberment. A cruel and unusual punishment for crime. 21 Am J2d Crim L § 612.

quartering soldiers. Assigning soldiers to a place for living accommodations, particularly in the dwellings of residents. See the Third Amendment to the Constitution of the United States.

quarterly (kwâr'tėr-li). Every three months, or quarter yearly. Leonard v St. Clair, 27 Idaho 568, 149 P 1058.

quarterone (kwâr-tẹ-rōn'). A term of the West Indies for a person of mixed white and Negro blood, specifically a person who is the issue of a white person and a tercerone. Daniel v Guy, 19 Ark 121, 131.
See **tercerone**.

quarteroon (kwâr-tẹ-rön'). Same as **quarterone**.

quarter seal (kwâr'tėr sēl). A seal which was kept in the Scotch chancery and which made the impression of a quarter segment of the great seal.

quarter section. A square piece of land, one hundred sixty acres in area, constituting one fourth of a section laid out by the government survey, being the Northwest, Northeast, Southeast, or Southwest quarter of such a section. McCartney v Dennison, 101 Cal 252, 35 P 766. Any single tract of one hundred sixty acres.

quarter sessions of the peace. See **court of quarter sessions of the peace**.

quarter to quarter. See **tenancy from quarter to quarter**.

quarter year (yēr). Ninety-one days; the odd six hours being disregarded.

quarto die post (quar'tō dī'e post). On the fourth day after.
A defendant when summoned by a writ to appear, had three days of grace beyond the return of the writ within which to make his appearance; and if he appeared on the fourth day inclusive, "quarto die post," it was sufficient. See 3 Bl Comm 278.

Quarto Edition. An edition of Year Books which came out in ten volumes around the end of the 16th century or the beginning of the 17th century.
See **Year Books**.

quartz. A crystalline mineral, sometimes gold-bearing. Ferguson v Ray, 44 Or 557, 77 P 600.

quartz mill. A plant for the extraction of valuable minerals from quartz. 36 Am J1st Min & M § 73.

quash. See **quashing**.

quashal. A quashing, for example, a quashing of a writ of certiorari. 14 Am J2d Certiorari §§ 52, 53.
See **quashing**.

quashing. Suppressing. Vacating or setting aside. Annulling.

quashing array. A setting aside or withdrawal of the entire array or list of persons called for jury service. 31 Am J Rev ed Jury § 102. A remedy on motion by way of raising an objection to the array or panel on the ground of a prejudicial defect or irregularity in the selecting and summoning of jurors which affects the integrity of the entire panel. 31 Am J Rev ed Jury § 105.

quashing criminal prosecution. A remedy had upon motion directed against a defective indictment, information, or other accusatory pleading. 21 Am J2d Crim L § 172. A remedy for defect in the grand jury, including the disqualification of particular jurors or defective procedure in summoning or impaneling the jury. 24 Am J1st Grand J § 29.

quashing habeas corpus (kwosh'ing hā'be-as kor'-pus). A remedy against a writ of habeas corpus improperly or fraudulently obtained. 25 Am J1st Hab C § 136.
In habeas corpus proceedings, a motion to quash the writ is held to amount to the same thing as a demurrer to the petition. Bleakley v Barclay, 75 Kan 462, 89 P 906.

quashing indictment or information. See **quashing criminal prosecution**.

quashing panel. Same as **quashing array**.

quashing prosecution. See **quashing criminal prosecution**.

quashing venire (kwosh'ing vẹ-nī'rē). Same as **quashing array**.

quasi (kwā'sī). As if; as it were. Relating to or having the character of. People v Bradley, 60 Ill 390, 402.

quasi admission. An admission by inconsistent statement. 30 Am J2d Ev § 1082.

quasi affinity (ạ-fin'ị-ti). That relationship which exists between a person who is engaged to marry and the relatives of the person to whom he or she is affianced.

quasi agnum lupo committere ad devorandum (quā'sī ag'num lū'pō kom-mit'te-re ad dē-vo'ran-dum). As a sheep given to a wolf to be devoured. Hall v Perkins (NY) 3 Wend 626, 630.

quasi arbitrator. A person whose professional duties as an accountant, architect, engineer, etc. call for the settlement of controversies, although he is not designated or selected as an "arbitrator." Anno: 54 ALR2d 335, § 7.

quasi bailment. A constructive bailment; an involuntary bailment.

quasi commons. Uninclosed lands in jurisdictions where the rule is that an owner of cattle incurs no liability by permitting his cattle to range at will over uninclosed lands or over lands not guarded by such a fence as is prescribed by law. 4 Am J2d Ani § 49.

quasi-community property. Property that would have been community property had it been acquired while the spouses were domiciled in the particular community property jurisdiction concerned with the controversy. 15 Am J2d Community Prop § 3.

quasi contract. An obligation imposed by law, on grounds of justice and equity, usually to prevent unjust enrichment. A fiction of the law, adopted to achieve justice and enforce legal duties by means of an action ex contractu where no true contract exists. 58 Am J1st Wk & L § 2.

quasi contractus (kon-trak'tus). (Civil law.) An obligation similar in character to that of a contract, but which arose not from an agreement of parties, but from some relation between them or from a volun-

tary act of one of them, or, stated in other language, an obligation springing from voluntary and lawful acts of parties in the absence of any agreement.
See **quasi contract**.

quasi corporation. A body which exercises certain functions of a corporation but which has not been created a corporation by or under any act, general or special, of the legislature. School Dist. v St. Joseph Fire & Marine Ins. Co. 103 US 707, 26 L Ed 601. A term sometimes applied to a county, township, or other political subdivision not regarded as a true municipal corporation. Snider v St. Paul, 51 Minn 466, 53 NW 763.

quasi crime. An act not of a nature making it a subject of criminal prosecution but for which a forfeiture or penalty may be imposed. An act subject to prosecution in a bastardy proceeding or in quo warranto. People v Bradley, 60 Ill 390, 402; Wiggins v Chicago, 68 Ill 372, 375.

quasi-delict (dẹ-likt'). A tort in which there is an absence of malice; as, an unintentional trespass.

quasi-deposit (dẹ-poz'it). That kind of a bailment which results from the finding of goods which have been lost.

quasi derelict. A vessel which, although not technically a derelict, is in such circumstances of peril that services performed in saving it must be deemed highly meritorious and accordingly compensable under principles of salvage. 47 Am J1st Salv § 5.

quasi easement. A condition of apparent servitude, such as the existence of a worn path over premises, not constituting a real easement because of unity of ownership as between the premises benefited and the premises used.

quasi estoppel. A legal bar, analogous to estoppel in pais in some respects, based upon the doctrine of election, the principle which precludes a party from asserting to another's disadvantage, a right inconsistent with a position previously taken by him. 28 Am J2d Estop § 29.

quasi ex contractu (quā'sī ex kon-trak'tu). See **quasi contract; quasi contractus**.

quasi-fee (kwā'sī-fē). An estate gained by wrong.—Wharton's Law Dictionary.

quasi feme sole (quā'sī fem sōl). A term, out of use since the enactment of Married Women's Acts, for a married woman employing her separate equitable estate in a business and subjecting it to indebtedness incurred in the business. Djett v North American Coal Co. (NY) 20 Wend 570.

quasi guardian (kwā'sī gär'di̯an). A person who, without legal appointment or qualification, assumes the functions of guardian by exercising control over the person, or estate, or both, of a minor. Zeideman v Molasky, 118 Mo App 106, 94 SW 754.

quasi individual. A corporate entity. State v Haun, 7 Kan App 509, 54 P 130.

quasi in rem action (quā'sī in rem ak'shon). An action which, although conventional in the sense of having named persons as parties, has the direct object of reaching and disposing of property or of some interest therein; an action in which the judgment deals with the status, ownership, or liability of particular property and operates only as between the particular parties to the proceeding. 1 Am J2d Actions § 41. An action in which the adjudication, involves a thing in the sense of a personal status, such as an action for divorce, 24 Am J2d Div & S § 245, or a proceeding for the adoption of a child, 2 Am J2d Adopt § 48, but also involves an element not found in an action strictly in rem where parties are not designated and the adjudication involves only a thing. Joiner v Joiner, 131 Ga 217, 62 SE 182.

quasi in rem judgment (quā'sī in rem juj'ment). See **judgment quasi in rem**.

quasi in rem jurisdiction. See **jurisdiction quasi in rem**.

quasi in rem proceeding. Same as **quasi in rem action**.

quasi-judicial. The characterization of an adjudicatory function of an administrative agency. 1 Am J2d Admin L § 138. The characterization of an act partially judicial, such as the issuance of a warrant of arrest by a clerk of court. 15 Am J2d Clk Ct § 22. The characterization of a power reposed in an officer or board involving the exercise of discretion, judicial in its nature, in connection with and as incidental to the administration of matters assigned or intrusted to such officer or board. Green v Board of commissioners, 126 Okla 300, 259 P 635.

Where the administrative tribunal is under a duty to consider evidence and apply the law to the facts as found, thereby exercising a discretion of judgment judicial in nature on evidentiary facts, the function is ordinarily quasi-judicial and not ministerial. Handlon v Belleville, 4 NJ 99, 71 A2d 624, 16 ALR2d 1118.

The acts of an officer which are executive or administrative in their character and which call for the exercise of that officer's judgment and discretion are not ministerial acts and his authority to perform such acts is quasi-judicial. American Casualty Ins. & Secur. Co. v Fyler, 60 Conn 418, 22 A 494; Langenberg v Decker, 131 Ind 471, 31 NE 190.

quasi-judicial confession. A confession made on a preliminary examination before a magistrate, at a coroner's inquest, or before a grand jury. Matthews v State, 55 Ala 187.

quasi-judicial function. See **quasi-judicial**.

quasi-judicial office. A public office the incumbent of which exercises quasi-judicial functions. A characterization of the office of attorney at law, he being an officer of the court. 7 Am J2d Attys § 3.
See **quasi-judicial**.

quasi-judicial power. The power under which quasi-judicial functions are exercised.
See **quasi-judicial**.

quasi-judicial tribunal. See **quasi-judicial**.

quasi-legislative. The characterization of a power which is legislative in nature but exercised by an administrative agency. 1 Am J2d Admin L § 92.

quasi-lien. A lien not arising under contract or directly under statute, but existing by way of provisional relief obtained in an action, such as an attachment lien. Meyers v C. I. T. Corp. 132 Conn 284, 43 A2d 742.

quasi-municipal corporation. See **quasi corporation**.

quasi-negotiable instrument. An instrument which possesses some, but not all, of the elements of negotiability. 11 Am J2d B & N § 4.

quasi office. The position of a candidate who has been nominated for an office, but has not yet been elected to that office. State ex rel. Rinder v Goff, 129 Wis 668, 109 NW 628.

quasi partners. Tenants in common.
See **joint stock company.**

quasi party. A party by implication from interest, such as the state in an action for divorce. 24 Am J2d Div & S § 44. A person of a class represented in a class suit who is not named specifically as a party. 39 Am J1st Parties § 44.

quasi-public corporation. A public service corporation; a corporation affected with a public interest. 18 Am J2d Corp § 9. A private corporation which has been given certain powers of a public nature, such as the power of eminent domain. Philadelphia Rural Transit Co. v Philadelphia, 309 Pa 84, 159 A 861. A corporation having an appropriate franchise from the state to provide for a necessity or convenience of the general public incapable of being furnished by private competitive business. Atty. Gen. v Haverhill Gaslight Co. 215 Mass 394, 101 NE 1061.

quasi-public use. The use of premises by a public utility. 23 Am J2d Ded § 5.

quasi realty (kwā-sī rē'ạl-ti). Movable property, such as title deeds and heirlooms, which pass to the heir.

quasi tenant (kwā-sī ten'ạnt). A subtenant who is permitted by the reversioner to hold over after the expiration of the tenant's lease.

quasi trademark. The brand used by a manufacturer for the purpose of designating a certain grade of his product. 52 Am J1st Tradem § 47. A trade name. Vonderbank v Schmidt, 44 La Ann 264, 10 So 616.

quasi trustee (kwā'sī trus-tē'). A person who derives a benefit from a breach of trust.

qua supra (quā sū'pra). As appears above.

quatenus (quā'te-nus). As; how far; how long; in so far as; since.

quater cousin. A cater cousin, a fourth cousin.

quatuor maria. See **extra quatuor maria; intra quatuor maria.**

quatuor maria rule (qua'tu-or ma'ri-a rūl). The early common-law rule in England that if a wife had issue while her husband was within the four seas, that is, within the jurisdiction of the King of England, such issue was conclusively presumed to be legitimate, except upon proof of the husband's impotence. 10 Am J2d Bast § 11.

quatuor parietes. See **inter quatuor parietes.**

quatuor pedibus currit (qua'tu-or pe'di-bus ker'rit). It runs on all-fours with; it exactly corresponds; it is precisely in point.

quay (kē). A wharf. A vacant space between the first row of buildings and the water's edge used for the reception of goods and merchandise imported or to be exported. New Orleans v United States (US) 10 Pet 662, 715, 9 L Ed 573, 594.

quayage (kē'ạj). A charge or toll exacted for the use of a quay or wharf. Rowan's Executors v Portland, 47 Ky (8 B Mon) 232, 253.
See **wharfage.**

quean (kwēn). A lewd woman.
See **Elizabeth II.** See also words and phrases commencing **king** or **king's.**

queen. A female sovereign or ruler; a king's consort.

Queen Anne's Bounty (ạns boun'ti). The grant of Queen Anne by her royal charter, whereby all the revenue of first-fruits and tenths, which had anciently gone to the pope and later to the king, was vested in trustees to form a perpetual fund for the augmentation of poor livings. See 1 Bl Comm 286.

queen consort (kọn'sôrt). The wife of the reigning king of England.
As queen consort, by virtue of her marriage, she possesses various prerogatives above all other women of the kingdom. See 1 Bl Comm 218.

queen dowager. See **dowager queen.**

queen-gold (kwēn'gōld). The aurum reginae or royal revenue belonging to every queen consort during her marriage to the king. See 1 Bl Comm 219.

queen mother (kwēn muth'ér). A dowager queen who is also the mother of the sovereign.

queen regent (rē'jent). The queen regent, regnant, or sovereign, is she who holds the crown in her own right, with all the same powers, prerogatives, rights, duties, and dignities, as if she had been a king. See 1 Bl Comm 218.

queen regnant. See **queen regent.**

queen's counsel. A title conferred upon barristers of good standing and proved ability in England and Canada.

queen's bench. See **court of king's bench.**

queen's evidence. Same as **state's evidence.**
See **dowager queen.**

queen sovereign. See **queen regent.**

Queen's Prison (priz'n). An English prison which was formed by uniting the queen's bench prison, the Fleet, and the Marshal-sea.

queen's silver. See **silver.**

que estate (kwe es-tāt'). Which estate; whose estate. See **prescribing in a que estate.**

que est le mesme (ke ā le mām). Which is the same.

Quemadmodum ad quaestionem facti non respondent judices, ita ad quaestionem juris non respondent juratores (quem-ad-mō'dum ad kwēst-she-ō'nem fak'tī non re-spon'dent jū'di-sēz, i'ta ad kwēst-she-ō'nem jū'ris non re-spon'dent jū-rā-tō'rēz). Just as judges do not answer questions of fact, so jurors do not answer questions of law.

quem redditum reddit (quem red'di-tum red'dit). Let it be rendered to whom it should be rendered,—an old writ which lay where a rent-charge, or other rent which was not rent-service, was granted by fine, holding of the grantor.

quer. An abbreviation of **querens.**

querela (kwẹ-rē'lạ). A complaint; an action; a suit. See **audita querela; duplex querela.**

querela inofficiosi testamenti (kwe-rē'la in-of-fi-she-ō'sī tes-ta-men'tī). Complaint of an undutiful will.
The Roman law upon such a complaint permitted a will to be set aside if it left nothing to a child who thus complained, but the common law of England furnishes no such ground for avoiding a will. See 2 Bl Comm 502. In the United States, the common-law rule has been changed by statute in most jurisdictions.
See **pretermitted heir.**

querens (kwe'renz). A complaining party; a plaintiff.

Queretaro Treaty. See **Guadalupe Hidalgo Treaty.**

quest (kwest). An inquiry.
See **inquest.**

questa (kwes'ta). An inquisition; an inquest.

question. The point in controversy. The point to be decided.

A question to be decided implies something in controversy, or which may be the subject of controversy. There is no "question" before a judge who merely makes a formal order for the hearing of a matter. McFarlane v Clark, 39 Mich 44, 46.

"Our conclusion is that this history of the convention (of the framers of the United States Constitution) shows a settled purpose to include within the Federal jurisdiction all questions which involve the national peace and harmony, and that the word 'questions' includes every issue capable of a judicial determination." King v M'Lean Asylum of Massachusetts General Hospital (CA1 Mass) 64 F 331, 339.

question certified. See **certification of question.**

question in chief. A question asked a witness on his direct examination.

questionnaire. A list of questions submitted to persons interviewed by a taker of the census. 14 Am J2d Census §§ 2, 9.

question of fact. A question for the jury in a trial by jury or for the court in a trial to the court. A question of the truth to be decided upon conflicting evidence.

question of law. A question for the court. A question arising in a case in court as to the terms of the law by which the case is to be adjudicated.

A matter may be a "matter of law," although it is not purely a question of law, if it involves a matter of legal inference, notwithstanding, that it involves a matter of fact. Lovinier v Pearce, 70 NC 167, 171.

questions of law and fact. Questions for the court and questions for the jury. 53 Am J1st Tr § 156.

See **mixed question of law and fact; province of court and jury.**

questio vexata (kwest'she-o ve-xa'ta). A troublesome question,—a term often applied to a question of law which has perplexed the courts.

questus (kwes'tus). Same as **quaestus.**

questus est nobis (kwes'tus est nō'bis). A writ of nuisance which lay against a person who had acquired land with a nuisance thereon which he suffered to continue.

qui (kwi). Who; which; what.

quia (qui'a). Because.

Qui abjurat regnum amittit regnum, sed non regem; patriam, sed non patrem patriae (quī ab-jū'rat reg'num ā-mit'tit reg'num, sed non rē'jem; pā'tri-am, sed non pā'trem pā'tri-ē). He who abjures the realm, leaves the kingdom, but not the king; the country, but not the father of the country.

Qui accusat integrae famae sit et non criminosis (quī a-kū'sat in'te-grē fa'mē sit et non kri-mi-nō'sus). Let him who accuses be of honest reputation and not a criminal.

Qui acquirit sibi acquirit haeredibus (quī ak-qui'rit si'bi ak-quī'rit hē-re'di-bus). He who acquires for himself acquires for his heirs.

quia datum est nobis intelligi (qui'a da'tum est nō'bis in-tel'li-jī). Because it has been given to us to understand.

Qui adimit medium dirimit finem (quī ad'i-mit me'dium di'ri-mit fī'nem). He who takes away the means destroys the end.

quia dominus remisit curiam. See **praecipe quia dominus remisit curiam.**

Quia dominus rerum non apparet ideo cujus sunt incertum est (qui'a do'mi-nus rē'rum non ap'pa-ret i'de-ō kū'jus sunt in-ser'tum est). Where it is not apparent who is the owner of goods, on that account it is not certain whose they are.

Quia Emptores (qui'a emp-tō'rēz). See **statute quia emptores.**

quia erronice emanavit (qui'a er-ro'ni-se e-ma-nā'vit). Because it issued erroneously.

Quia eventus est qui ex causa sequitur, et dicuntur eventus quia ex causis eveniunt (qui'a ē-ven'tus est quī ex kâ'za se'qui-ter, et di-kun'ter ē-ven'tus qui'a ex kâ'zis ē-ve'ni-unt). Because the event is that which follows from the cause, and they are called events because they come out of the causes.

Quia impotentia excusat legem (qui'a im-po-ten'she-a ex-kū'sat lē'jem). Because the performance is impossible, it releases the obligation. 17 Am J2d Contr § 404.

Quia interest reipublicae ut sit finis litium (qui'a in'ter-est rē-i-pub'li-sē ut sit fī'nis li'she-um). For it is in the interest of the state that there should be an end of strife.

Quia juris civilis studiosos decet haud imperitos esse juris municipalis, et differentias exteri patriique juris notas habere (qui'a jū'ris si'vi-lis stu-di-ō'sōs de'set hâd im-pe'ri-tos es'se jū'ris mu-ni-si-pā'lis, et dif-fe-ren'she-as ex'te-rī pā-tri-ī'kwe jū'ris nō'tas hā-bē're). For students of the civil law should not be ignorant of the municipal law and of the noteworthy differences between the laws of foreign countries and those of their own. See 1 Bl Comm 16.

Qui alienum fundum ingreditur, venandi aut aucupandi gratia, potest a domino prohiberi ne ingrediatur (quī ā-li-ē'num fun'dum in-gre'di-ter, ve-nan'dī ât â-ku-pan'dī grā'she-a, po'test ā do'mi-nō pro-hi-bē're nē in-gre-di-ā'ter). (Roman law.) He who comes into the estate of another in order to hunt or catch birds can be prohibited by the owner from coming in. See 2 Bl Comm 412.

Qui aliquid statuerit parte inaudita altera, aequum licet dixerit, haud aequum fecerit (quī a'li-quid sta-tu'e-rit par'te in-â'di-ta al'te-ra, ē'qu-um lī'set di'xe-rit, hâd ē'qu-um fe'se-rit). He who decides anything without having heard the other side, although he may decide correctly, has by no means acted justly. See 4 Bl Comm 283.

Qui alterius jure utitur, eodem jure uti debet (quī al'te-ri-us jū're u'ti-ter, e-ō'dem jū're u'tī de'bet). A person who uses the right of another ought to enjoy the same right.

Quia non sua culpa, sed parentum, id commisisse cognoscitur (qui'a non su'a kul'pa, sed pa-ren'tum, id kom-mi-si'se kog-no'si-ter). Because she is regarded as having committed it, not through her own fault, but that of her parents. See 1 Bl Comm 438.

Qui approbat non reprobat (quī ap'pro-bat non re'pro-bat). He who approves or ratifies cannot repudiate.

Quia quando aliquid prohibetur, prohibetur et id per quod pervenitur ad illud (qui'a quan'dō a'li-quid prō-hi-bē'ter, prō-hi-bē'ter et id per quod per-ve'ni-ter ad il'lud). Because, when anything is prohibited, that by which it is accomplished is also prohibited.

qui arma gerit (quī ar'ma je'rit). One who bears arms.

quia timet (qùi'a ti'met). Because he fears.
See **bill quia timet; quieting title**.

Qui bene distinguit, bene docet (quī be'ne dis-tin'-gwit, be'ne do'set). He who distinguishes well teaches well.

Qui bene interrogat, bene docet (quī be'ne in-ter'ro-gat, be'ne do'set). He who questions well teaches well.

Qui cadit a syllaba cadit a tota causa (quī ka'dit ā sil'la-ba ka'dit ā tō'ta kâ'za). He who loses by a syllable loses in his whole cause.

Qui cito dat bis dat (quī si'tō dat bīs dat). He who gives quickly gives twice. Louisiana v New Orleans, 102 US 203, 207, 26 L Ed 132, 133.

quick (kwik). Rapid. Prompt. Pregnant.

quick dollar. A profit in a transaction quickly consummated.

quickening (kwik'ning). The first movement of the fetus felt by a pregnant woman.
See **vitalized**.

quick hemiplegy. See **hemiplegy**.

quick sale statute. A statute permitting a judicial sale of perishable property under terms intended to expedite the sale. Anno: 3 ALR3d 596-604.

quick with child. The state of pregnancy in which the fetus shows signs of life by appreciable movement.
See **vitalized**.

Qui concedit aliquid, concedere videtur et id sine quo concessio est irrita, sine quo res ipsa esse non potuit (quī kon-sē'dit a'li-quid, kon-sē'de-re vi-dē'ter et id sī'ne quō kon-se'she-ō est ir'ri-ta, sī'ne quō rēz ip'sa es'se non po'tu-it). He who grants anything is deemed to grant also that without which the grant is idle, without which the thing itself is worthless.

Qui confirmat nihil dat (quī kon-fir'mat ni'hil dat). He who merely confirms gives nothing. Branham v San Jose, 24 Cal 585, 605.

Qui contemnit praeceptum, contemnit praecipientem (quī kon-tem'nit prē-sep'tum, kon-tem'nit prē-si-pi-en'tem). He who contemns a precept contemns the preceptor.

Quicquid acquiritur servo, acquiritur domino (quik'-quid ak-quī'ri-ter ser'vō, ak-quī'ri-ter do'mi-nō). Whatever is acquired by the servant is acquired by the master.

Quicquid demonstratae rei additure satis demonstratae frustra est (quik'quid de-mon-strā'tē rē'ī ad'di-ter sa'tis de-mon-strā'tē frus'tra est). Whatever is added to the description of a thing which is already sufficiently described is superfluous. See Broom's Legal Maxims 630.

Quicquid est contra normam recti est injuria (quik'-quid est kon'tra nor'mam rek'tī est in-jū'ri-a). Whatever is contrary to the rule of right is wrong.

Quicquid in excessu actum est, lege prohibetur (quik'quid in ex-ses'sū ak'tum est, lē'je prō-hi-bē'ter). Whatever is done in excess is prohibited by law.

Quicquid judicis auctoritati subjicitur, novitati non subjicitur (quik'quid jū'di-sis âk-to-ri-tā'tī sub-ji'si-ter, nō-vi-tā'tī non sub-ji'si-ter). Whatever is subjected to the authority of a judge is not subjected to novelty or innovation.

Quicquid plantatur solo, solo cedit (quik'quid plan-tā'ter sō'lō, sō'lō sē'dit). Whatever grows in the soil is a part thereof. King v Morris, 74 NJL 810, 68 A 162.

Quicquid recipitur, recipitur secundum modum recipientis (quik'quid re-si'pi-ter, re-si'pi-ter se-kun'dum mō'dum re-si-pi-en'tis). Whatever is received is applied according to the wish of the recipient.

Quicquid solvitur, solvitur secundum modum solventis (quik'quid sol'vi-ter, sol'vi-ter se-kun'dum mō'-dum sol-ven'tis). Whatever is paid is applied according to the wish of the person making the payment.

Quicquid solvitur, solvitur secundum modum solventis; quicquid recipitur, recipitur secundum modum recipientis (quik'quid sol'vi-ter, sol'vi-ter se-kun'-dum mō'dum sol-ven'tis; quik'quid re-si'pi-ter, re-si'pi-ter se-kun'dum mō'dum re-si-pi-en'tis). Whatever is paid is applied according to the wish of the person who pays; whatever is received is applied according to the wish of the recipient.

Qui cum alio contrahit, vel est vel debet esse non ignarus conditionis ejus (quī kum a'li-ō kon'tra-hit, vel est vel de'bet es'se non ig-nā'rus kon-di-she-ō'nis ē'jus). He who contracts with another is not, or ought not to be, ignorant of his condition.

Qui cum aliter tueri se non possunt, damni culpam dederint, innoxii sunt (quī kum a'li-ter tu-ē'rī sē non pos'sunt, dam'nī kul'pam de'de-rint, in-no'xi-ī sunt). (Civil law.) Those who, when they cannot otherwise defend themselves, assume the responsibility of causing damage, are deemed innocent. See 4 Bl Comm 185.

Quicunque habet jurisdictionem ordinariam est illius loci ordinarius (quī-kun'kwe hā'bet jū-ris-dik-she-ō'nem or-di-nā'ri-am est il-lī'us lō'sī or-di-nā'ri-us). Whoever has ordinary jurisdiction is the ordinary of that place.

Quicunque jussu judicis aliquid fecerit non videtur dolo malo fecisse, quia parere necesse est (qui-kun'kwe jus'sū jū'di-sis a'li-quid fe'se-rit non vi-dē'ter dō'lō ma'lō fe-sis'se, qui'a pa-rē're ne-ses'se est). Whoever does anything by the order of a judge is not deemed to have acted with an evil motive, because it is necessary to obey.

quid (kwid). What.

Qui dat finem, dat media ad finem necessaria (quī dat fī'nem, dat mē'di-a ad fī'nem ne-ses-sā'ri-a). He who provides the end provides the means necessary to the end.

Qui destruit medium, destruit finem (quī dē'stru-it me'di-um, dē'stru-it fī'nem). He destroys the end who destroys the means to the end.

quid juris clamat (quid jū'ris kla'mat). What right he claims,—a writ which lay to compel the holder of the particular estate to attorn to the grantee of the reversion or remainder.

Qui doit inheriter al pere, doit inheriter al fitz (kē duä' an-ėr-ē-tā al pär, duät' an-er-ē-tā al fitz). He who should inherit from the father should inherit from the son. See 2 Bl Comm 250.

quid pro quo (kwid prō kwō). The consideration for a contract. That which is supplied by one party in consideration of that which is supplied by the other party. 17 Am J2d Contr § 85.

Quidquid enim sive dolo et culpa venditoris accidit in eo venditor securus est (quid'quid e'nim sī've dō'lō et kul'pa ven-di-tō'ris ak'si-dit in ē'ō ven-di'-tor se-kū'rus est). For as to anything which happens without deceit or fault of the vendor, as to that, the vendor is secure.

Quid sit jus, et in quo consistit injuria, legis est definire (quid sit jūs, et in quō kon-sis'tit in-jū'ri-a, lē'jis est de-fi-nī're). What is a right, and in what an injury consists, it is for the law to define or determine.

Quid turpi ex causa promissum est non valet (quid ter'pī ex kâ'za pro-mis'sum est non va'let). A promise which is founded upon an immoral consideration is not binding.

quieta clamantia (qui-ē'ta kla-man'she-a). A quitclaim.

quieta non movere (qui-ē'ta non mō-vē're). Not to disturb that which is quiescent.

quietantia (qui-ē-tan'she-a). An acquitance; a discharge.

quietare (qui-e-tā're). To acquit; to exonerate; to discharge; to free; to release.

quiete clamare (qui-ē'te kla-mā're). To quitclaim.

quiet enjoyment. See **covenant of quiet enjoyment.**

quieting title. An action or suit in court designed to effect a removal of a cloud or clouds on title to real property, known in older times as a bill qui timet. Sharon v Tucker, 144 US 533, 36 L Ed 532, 12 S Ct 720. A remedy, originating in equity, enlarged and supplemented in many jurisdictions by statute, having for its purpose an adjudication that a claim of title to or an interest in property, adverse to that of the plaintiff, is invalid, so that the plaintiff and those claiming under him may be forever afterward free from any danger of the hostile claim. 44 Am J1st Quiet T § 1.

quieti reditus (qui-ē'tī re'di-tus). Same as **quit rents.**

quietum clamare (qui-ē'tum kla-mā're). To quitclaim.

quietus (kwī-ē'tus). A process of the probate court of the state of Rhode Island whereby an administrator might be fully discharged. White v Ditson, 140 Mass 351, 4 NE 606.

quietus redditus (qui-ē'tus red'di-tus). Singular of **quieti redditus.**

Qui evertit causam evertit causatum futurum (quī e-ver'tit kâ'zam e-ver'tit kâ-zā'tum fu-tū'rum). He who destroys a cause destroys its future effect.

Qui ex damnato coitu nascuntur, inter liberos non computentur (quī ex dam-nā'tō ko-ī'tū nas-kun'ter, in'ter li'be-ros non kom-pu-ten'ter). Those who are born of an unlawful union are not counted among the children. See Broom's Legal Maxims 519.

Qui facit id quod plus est, facit id quod minus est, sed non convertitur (quī fā'sit id quod plus est, fa'sit id quod mī'nus est, sed non kon-ver'ti-ter). He who does that which is more does that which is less, but it cannot be turned around.

Qui facit per alium facit per se (quī fā'sit per a'li-um fā'sit per sē). He who acts through another acts by or for himself. A fundamental maxim of agency. Stroman Motor Co. v Brown, 116 Okla 36, 243 P 133. A maxim often stated in discussing the liability of employer for the act of employee. 35 Am J1st M & S § 543.

If in the nature of things the master is obliged to perform the duties by employing servants, he is responsible for their act in the same way that he is responsible for his own. Anno: 25 ALR2d 67.

Qui habet jurisdictionem absolvendi, habet jurisdictionem ligandi (quī hā'bet jū-ris-dik-she-ō'nem ab-sol-ven'dī, hā'bet jū-ris-dik-she-ō'nem li-gan'dī). He who has jurisdiction to free or release, has jurisdiction to bind.

Qui haeret in litera, haeret in cortice (quī hē'ret in li'te-ra, hē'ret in kor'ti-se). He who clings to the letter, keeps inside the rind; meaning that too literal an interpretation does not reach the heart or core of the transaction. Riggs v Palmer, 115 NY 506, 22 NE 188.

Qui ignorat quantum solvere debeat, non potest improbus videre (quī ig-nō'rat quan'tum sol've-re de'be-at, non po'test im-prō'bus vi-dē're). He who does not know how much he ought to pay, cannot seem dishonest (if he refuses to pay).

Qui illi temporalibus, episcopo de spiritualibus, debeat respondere (quī il'lī tem-po-rā'li-bus, e-pis'ko-pō dē spi-ri-tu-ā'li-bus, de'be-at rē-spon-dē're). Who should answer to him in temporal matters, to the bishop in spiritual matters. See 1 Bl Comm 387.

Qui in jus dominiumve alterius succedit jure ejus uti debet (quī in jūs do-mi-ni-um've al-te'ri-us suk-se'-dit jū're ē'jus u'tī de'bet). He who succeeds to the right or ownership of another, ought to enjoy the rights of that other. See Broom's Legal Maxims 473.

Qui in utero est, pro jam acto nato habetur quoties de ejus commodo quaeritur (quī in u'te-rō est, prō jam ak'tō nā'tō ha-bē'ter quō'ti-ez dē ē'jus kom'mo-dō kwē'ri-ter). He who is in the womb is regarded as actually born whenever his advantage or benefit is sought. See 1 Bl Comm 130.

Qui jure suo utitur neminem laedit (quī jū're su'ō u'ti-ter ne'mi-nem lē'dit). He who uses his own legal right injures no one. American Press Asso. v Daily Story Publishing Co. (CA7 Ill) 120 F 766.

Qui jure suo utitur nullum damnum facit (quī jū're su'ō u'ti-ter nul'lum dam'num fa'sit). One who makes use of his own legal right does no injury. Knoedler v Glaenzer (CA2 NY) 55 F 895.

Qui jussu judicis aliquod fecerit non videtur dolo malo fecisse, quia parere necesse est (quī jus'sū jū'di-sis a'li-quod fe'se-rit non vi-dē'ter dō'lō ma'lō fe-sis'se, qui'a pa-re'-rē ne-ses'se est). He who does anything by the order of a judge is not deemed to have acted with an evil motive or design, because it is necessary to obey.

quilibet ignem suum salve (quī'li-bet ig'nem su'um sal've). See **quod quilibet ignem,** etc.

Quilibet potest renunciare juri pro se introducto (quī'li-bet po'test re-nun-she-ā're jū'rī prō sē in-tro-duk'tō). Anyone may waive a right asserted in his behalf. Burgettstown Nat. Bank v Nill, 213 Pa 456, 63 A 186.

Quilibet renunciare potest beneficium juris pro se introductum (quī'li-bet re-nun-she-ā're po'test be-ne-fi'she-um jū'ris prō sē in-trō-duk'tum). Anyone may waive a right introduced for his own benefit. People v Van Rensselaer, 9 NY 291, 333.

Quilibet renunciare potest juri pro se introducto (quī'li-bet re-nun-she-ā're po'test jū'rī prō sē in-trō-duk'tō). Anyone may waive a right asserted in his behalf. Miles v Boyden, 20 Mass (3 Pick) 213, 218.

Qui male agit, odit lucem (quī ma'le ā'jit, ō'dit lū'-sem). He who does wrong hates the light.

Qui mandat ipse fecissi videtur (quī man'dat ip'se fe-si'se vi-dē'ter). He who orders or commands is deemed to have done the thing himself.

Qui melius probat, melius habet (quī me'li-us pro'-bat, me'li-us hā'bet). He who proves more recovers more.

Qui molitur insidias in patriam id facit quod insanus nauta perforans navem in qua vehitur (quī mo'li-ter in-si'di-as in pa'tri-am id fā'sit quod in-sā'nus nâ'ta per'fo-ranz nā'vem in quā ve'hi-ter). He who lays snares against his country acts as did the crazy sailor who bored holes in the ship in which he sailed.

Qui nascitur sine legitimo matrimonio, matrem sequitur (quī na'si-ter sī'ne le-ji'ti-mō ma-tri-mo'ni-ō, ma'trem se'qui-ter). He who is born out of lawful wedlock succeeds his mother.

Qui non cadunt in constantem virum, vani timores sunt aestimandi (quī non ka'dunt in kon-stan'tem vī'rum, vā'nī ti-mō'rēz sunt ēs-ti-man'dī). Those fears are considered as groundless which do not affect a man of firmness.

Qui non habet, ille non dat (quī non hā'bet, il'le non dat). He who has not cannot give.
A man cannot grant what he does not own, actually or potentially. Zartman v First Nat. Bank, 189 NY 267, 82 NE 127.

Qui non habet in aere luat in corpore, ne quis peccetur impune (quī non hā'bet in ē're lū'at in kor'po-re, nē quis pek-sē'ter im-pū'ne). He who has no money must suffer corporal punishment, lest someone who offends may go unpunished.

Qui non habet in crumena luat in corpore (quī non hā'bet in kru'me-na lū'at in kor'po-re). Who has nothing in his purse, let him suffer in body; i. e., if he cannot pay the fine or amercement which has been imposed upon him. See 4 Bl Comm 380.

Qui non habet potestatem alienandi habet necessitatem retinendi (quī non hā'bet po-tes-tā'tem ā-li-en-an'dī hā'bet ne-ses-si-tā'tem re-ti-nen'dī). A person who has not the power of alienating is under the necessity of retaining.

Qui non improbat, approbat (quī non im'pro-bat, ap'prō-bat). He who does not disapprove or repudiate, approves or affirms.

Qui non libere veritatem pronunciat proditor est veritatis (quī non li'be-re ve-ri-tā'tem prō-nun-she-at prō'di-tor est ve-ri-tā'tis). He who does not freely speak the truth is a traitor of the truth.

Qui non negat, fatetur (quī non ne'gat, fa-tē'ter). He who does not deny, admits.

Qui non obstat quod obstare potest facere videtur (quī non ob'stat quod ob-stā're pō'test fa'se-re vi-dē'ter). He who does not prevent what he can prevent is deemed to do the act.

Qui non prohibet cum prohibere possit, jubet (quī non prō'hi-bet kum prō-hi-bē're pos'sit, jū'bet). He who does not forbid when he can forbid, orders or commands.

Qui non prohibet quod prohibere potest, assentire videtur (quī non prō'hi-bet quod pro-hi-bē're po'-test, as-sen-tī're vi-dē'ter). He who does not forbid that which he can forbid, is deemed to assent.

Qui non propulsat injuriam quando potest, infert (quī non prō-pul'sat in-jū'ri-am quan'dō po'test, in'fert). He who does not repel an injury when he can, causes it.

quinquennial census. A federal census of manufacturers, mineral industries, and other businesses, taken every five years. 13 USC §§ 131, 132.

quinquepartite (kwin-kwę-pär'tīt). Five-sided; having five parts or five parties.

quinque portus (quin'kwe por'tus). The five ports.

quinterone (kwin-tę-rōn'). A term of the West Indies for a person of mixed white and Negro blood, specifically a person who is the issue of a white person and a quarterone. Daniel v Guy, 19 Ark 121, 131.
See **quarterone.**

quinto exactus (quin'to egs-ak'tus). In outlawry proceedings, the sheriff's return after the fifth proclamation, or summons.
"But if he does not appear, and is returned quinto exactus (required for the fifth time), he shall then be outlawed by the coroners of the county." See 3 Bl Comm 283.

Qui obstruit aditum, destruit commodum (quī ob-strū'it a'di-tum, dē'stru-it kom'mo-dum). He who obstructs an approach, or way, destroys a convenience.

Qui omne dicit, nihil excludit (quī om'ne di'sit, ni'hil ex-klū'dit). He who says all excludes nothing; he who tells all omits nothing.

Qui parcit nocentibus innocentes punit (qui par'sit no-sen'ti-bus in-no-sen'tēz pū'nit). He who spares those who are guilty punishes those who are innocent.

Qui peccat ebrius, luat sobrius (quī pe'kat ē'bri-us, lū'at sō'bri-us). He who offends while drunk suffers punishment when sober. See Broom's Legal Maxims 17.

Qui per alium facit per seipsum facere videtur (quī per a'li-um fā'sit per sē-ip'sum fā'se-re vi-dē'ter). He who acts through another is deemed to do the act himself.

Qui per fraudem agit, frustra agit (quī per frâ'dem ā'jit, frus'tra ā'jit). He who acts fraudulently acts vainly, or to no purpose.

Qui potest et debet vetare jubet (quī po'test et de'bet vē-tā're ju'bet). He who can and ought to forbid (by his silence), commands. New York & New England Railroad Co. v New York, New Haven & Hartford Railroad Co. 52 Conn 274, 283.

Qui potest et debet vetare, tacens, jubet (quī po'test et de'bet ve-tā're, ta'senz, jū'bet). He who can and ought to forbid, and is silent, orders or commands.

Qui primum peccat ille facit rixam (quī prī'mum pe'kat il'le fā'sit ri'xam). He who offends first is the one who makes the quarrel.

Qui prior est in tempore, potior est in jure (quī prī'or est in tem'po-re, pō'she-or est in jū're). He who is first in time is first in right. Walton v Hargroves, 42 Miss 18.

Qui prior est in tempore, prior est in jure (quī prī'or est in tem'po-re, prī'or est in jū're). He who is first in point of time is first in right.

Qui prior est tempore, potior est jure (quī prī'or est tem'po-re, pō'she-or est jū're). He who is first in time is first in right. Lancashire Ins. Co. v Corbetts, 165 Ill 592, 46 NE 631.

Qui prior in tempore, potior in jure (quī prī'or in tem'po-re, po'she-or in jū're). He who is first in time is stronger in right.

Qui pro me aliquid facit, mihi fecisse videtur (quī prō mē a'li-quid fā'sit, mi'hi fe-sis'se vi-dē'ter). He who does anything in my behalf is deemed to have rendered it to me.

Qui providet sibi, providet haeredibus (quī prō'vi-det si'bi, pro'vi-det hē-re'di-bus). He who provides for himself provides for his heirs.

Qui rationem in omnibus quaerunt, rationem subvertunt (quī ra-she-ō'nem in om'ni-bus kwē'runt, rā-she-ō'nem sub-ver'tunt). They who seek a reason for everything subvert reason. See Broom's Legal Maxims 157.

Qui sciens solvit (scil. indebitum) donandi consilio id videtur fecisse (quī si'ens sol'vit (sil in-de'bi-tum) dō-nan'dī kon-si'li-ō id vi-dē'ter fe-sis'se). One who knowingly pays what is not due is deemed to have done it with the intention of making a gift. Walker v Hill, 17 Mass (17 Tyng) 380, 388.

Quis custodiet custodes? (quis kus-tō'di-et kus-tō'-dēz). Who was to watch the guards? Briscoe v Bank of Kentucky (US) 11 Pet 257, 349, 9 L Ed 709, 745.

Qui semel actionem renunciaverit, amplius repetere non potest (quī se'mel ak-she-ō'nem re-nun-she-ā've-rit, am'pli-us re-pe'te-re non po'test). He who has once renounced an action cannot assert it again.

Qui semel malus, semper praesumiter esse malus in eodem genere (quī se'mel ma'lus, sem'per prē-zu'-mi-ter es'se ma'lus in e-ō'dem je'ne-re). He who has once been bad is always presumed to be bad in the same way.

Qui sentit commodum sentire debet et onus (quī sen'-tit kom'mo-dum sen-tī're de'bet et ō'nus). He who secures the benefit ought to assume the burden. Pennington v Todd, 47 NJ Eq 569, 21 A 297.

Qui sentit onus, sentire debet et commodum (quī sen'tit ō'nus, sen-tī're de'bet et kom'mo-dum). He who assumes the burden ought to secure the benefit. Pennington v Todd, 47 NJ Eq 569, 21 A 297.

Qui serius solvit, minus solvit (quī se'ri-us sol'vit, mī'nus sol'vit). He who pays late, pays less. Louisiana v New Orleans, 102 US 203, 207, 26 L Ed 132.

Quisquis est qui velit jurisconsultus haberi, continuet studium, velit a quocunque doceri (quis'quis est quī ve'lit jū-ris-kon-sul'tus hā-bē'rī, kon-ti'nu-et stu'di-um, ve'lit ā quō-kun'kwe do-sē'rī). Anyone who wishes to be regarded as one learned in the law should continue his study and should wish to be taught by whomsoever.

Quisquis praesumitur bonus; et semper in dubiis pro reo respondendum (quis'quis prē-zū'mi-ter bō'nus; et sem'per in dū'bi-is prō re'ō re-spon-den'dum). Everyone is presumed to be honest; and in doubtful cases it should be resolved in favor of the defendant.

quit. To terminate an employment. 35 Am J1st M & S § 26. To vacate premises. To be acquitted. To be exonerated. To be released or discharged.

Qui tacet consentire videtur (quī ta'set kon-sen-tī're ve-dē'ter). He who is silent is deemed to consent. See Broom's Legal Maxims 138.

Qui tacet consentire videtur ubi tractatur de ejus commodo (quī ta'set kon-sen-tī're vi-dē'ter u'bi trak-tā'ter dē ē'jus kom'mo-dō). He who is silent is deemed to consent when his advantage is drawn into question. Thalheim v State, 38 Fla 169, 192, 20 So 938.

Qui tacet non utique fatetur, sed tamen verum est eum non negare (quī ta'set non u-tī'kwe fa-tē'ter, sed ta'men ve'rum est e'um non ne-gā're). (Civil law.) He who is silent certainly does not confess, but it is nevertheless true that he does not deny.

qui tam (quī tam). Who also share.

qui tam action (quī tam ak'shọn). An action to recover a penalty brought by an informer in the situation where one portion of the recovery goes to the informer and the other portion to the state. Williams v Wells, F. & Co. (CA8 Ark) 177 F 352.

qui tam pro domino rege, etc., quam pro se ipso in hac parte sequitur (quī tam prō do'mi-nō rē'je, etc., quam prō sē ip'sō in hāk par'te se'qui-ter). Who prosecutes this suit as well for the king, etc., as for himself. 36 Am J2d Forf & P § 79.

Qui tardius solvit, minus solvit (quī tar'di-us sol'vit, mī'nus sol'vit). He who pays too tardily pays too little.

quitclaim. A deed in the words of "remise, release, and quitclaim," manifesting the intention of the grantor to convey his present interest, whatever it may be, to the grantee. 23 Am J2d Deeds § 36. A deed which conveys whatever interest the grantor has in the property, as distinguished from a grant of the fee or other estate with warranty of title. 23 Am J2d Deeds § 291.

Qui timent cavent et vitant (quī ti'ment ka'vent et vi'tant). They who fear take care and avoid.

Qui totum dicit nihil excipit (quī to'tum di'sit ni'hil ek'si-pit). He who tells all reserves nothing, or holds nothing back.

quit-rents. Rents of assize of freeholders and of copyholders, the terminology deriving from the fact that upon paying them, the tenant was free of all other services to the lord of the manor. See 2 Bl Comm 42.

quittance (kwit'ạns). An acquittance; a discharge; a release; an exoneration.

Qui vi rapuit, fur improbior esse videtur (quī vī ra'pu-it, fer im-prō'bi-or es'se vi-dē'ter). (Civil law.) One who seizes by force seems to be the more wicked thief. See 4 Bl Comm 242.

Quivis praesumitur bonus donec probetur contrarium (quī'vis prē-zu'mi-ter bō'nus dō'nek prō-bē'ter kon-trā'ri-um). Anyone is presumed honest until the contrary is proved.

Qui vult decipi, decipiatur (quī vult de'si-pī, dē-si-pi-ā'ter). Let him be deceived who wishes to be deceived. If a person refuses to protect himself by lending his attention, it is of his own choice that he is misled. Roseman v Canovan, 43 Cal 110, 117.

quoad (kwō'ad). As to; as long as; as far as; until.

quoad hoc (kwō'ad hok). As to this matter; up to this time.

quoad omnia (kuō'ad om'ni-ạ). As to all things; in respect to all things.

quo animo (kuō an'i-mō). With what intent.

The expression is sometimes used synonymously with the word "intent;" as, "evidence has been allowed to prove the quo animo." Kennedy v Gifford (NY) 19 Wend 296, 300.

quocunque modo velit, quocunque modo possit (quo-kun'kwe mō'dō ve'lit, quō-kun'kwe mō'dō pos'sit). In whatever way he wishes, in whatever way he can. Executors of Clason v Bailey (NY) 14 Johns 484, 492.

quod ab aedibus non facile revellitur (quod ab ē'dibus non fā'si-le re-vel'li-ter). That which cannot easily be severed from a building. See 2 Bl Comm 428.

Quod ab initio non valet, tractu temporis non convalescit (quod ab in-i'she-ō non va'let, trak'tū tem'po-ris non kon-va-le'sit). That which is not valid at the outset is not cured by lapse of time.

Lapse of time cannot render an act valid, which was originally void. Holyoke v Haskins, 22 Mass (5 Pick) 20, 27.

Quod ad jus naturale attinet, omnes homines aequales sunt (quod ad jūs na-tū-rā'le at'ti-net, om'nēz ho'mi-nēz ē'quā-lēz sunt). (Civil law.) It holds good, according to natural law, that all men are equal.

Quod aedificatur in area legata cedit legato (quod ē-di-fi-kā'ter in a're-a lē-gā'ta sē'dit lē-gā'tō). That which is erected upon a tract which has been devised, goes with the devise. See Broom's Legal Maxims 424.

Quod alias bonum et justum est, si per vim vel fraudem petatur, malum et injustum efficitur (quod a'li-as bō'num et jus'tum est, sī per vim vel frâ'dem pe-tā'ter, ma'lum et in-jus'tum ef-fi'si-ter). That which is otherwise good and just becomes wicked and unjust if sought by fraud or force.

Quod alias non fuit licitum necessitas licitum facit (quod a'li-as non fu'it lī'si-tum ne-ses'si-tās lī'si-tum fā'sit). Necessity renders that lawful which would otherwise be unlawful.

quodam ignoto. See **de quodam ignoto.**

quodam modo (quō'dam mō'dō). In a certain manner.

Quod approbo non reprobo (quod ap'pro-bō non re-prō'bō). That which I approve or confirm, I cannot repudiate. See Broom's Legal Maxims 712.

Quod a quoque poenae nomine exactum est id eidem restituere nemo cogitur (quod ā quō'kwe pē'nē no'mi-ne egs-ak'tum est id e-ī'dem re-sti-tu'e-re nē'mō ko'ji-ter). (Civil law.) No one is compelled to restore that which has been exacted from anyone as a penalty.

Quod attinet ad jus civile, servi pro nullis habentur non tamen et jure naturali, quia quod ad jus naturale attinet, omnes homines aequali sunt (quod at'ti-net ad jūs si'vi-le, ser'vī prō nul'lis ha-ben'ter non ta'men et jū're na-tu-rā'lī, qui'a quod ad jūs na-tu-rā'le at'ti-net, om'nēz ho'mi-nēz ē-quā'lī sunt). (Civil law.) As it pertains to the civil law, slaves are regarded as nobodies, not so, however, by natural law; for as pertains to natural law, all men are equal.

quod billa cassetur (quod bil'la kas-sē'ter). That the bill be quashed.

quod breve cassetur (quod brē've kas-sē'ter). That the bill be quashed.

quod cepit et asportavit (quod se'pit et as-por-tā'vit). Because he took and carried away. A formal expression used in indictments for larceny. Ward v People (NY) 6 Hill 144, 147.

quod computet (quod kom'pu-tet). That he account.

quod concessum fuit (quod kon-ses'sum fu'it). Which was conceded.

Quod constat clare, non debet verificari (quod kon'stat kla're, non de'bet ve-ri-fi-kā'rī). That which clearly appears is not required to be proved.

Quod constat curiae opere testium non indiget (quod kon'stat kū'ri-ē o'pe-re tes'ti-um non in'di-jet). That which is clear to the court does not require the exertion of witnesses.

Quod contra juris rationem receptum est, non est producendum ad consequentias (quod kon'trā jū'ris rā-she-ō'nem re-sep'tum est, non est prō-du-sen'dum ad kon-se-quen'she-ās). (Civil law.) That which has been accepted against the reason of the law should not be drawn into precedent.

Quod contra legem fit, pro infecto habetur (quod kon'tra lē'jem fit, prō in-fek'tō ha-bē'ter). That which is done contrary to the law is regarded as not having been done.

quod cum (quod kum). For that. Whereas. An expression used in introducing matter of inducement in a pleading, that is, matter in explanation of the claim alleged. Spiker v Bohrer, 37 W Va 258.

quod cum ad specialem instantiam (quod kum ad spę-shē-al'em in-stan'shi-am). That at the special instance. See Yelverton (Eng) 40.

Quodcunque aliquis ob tutelam corporis sui fecerit jure id fecisse videtur (quod-kun'kwe a'li-quis ob tu-tē'lam kor'po-ris su'ī fe'se-rit jū're id fe-sis'se vi-dē'ter). Whatever anyone has done for the defense of his person is deemed to have been done lawfully.

quod curia concessit (quod kū'ri-a kon-ses'sit). Which the court granted.

Quod datum est ecclesiae, datum est Deo (quod da'tum est e-klē'si-ē, da'tum est Dē'ō). That which is given to the church is given to God.

Quod demonstrandi causa additur rei satis demonstratae, frustra fit (quod de-mon-stran'dī kâ'za ad'di-ter re'ī sa'tis de-mon-strā'tē, frus'tra fit). That which is added to anything by way of description, which is already sufficiently described, is superfluous.

Quod dubitas ne feceris (quod du'bi-tās ne fe'se-ris). You should not do that about which you are in doubt. Re Cowdery, 69 Cal 32, 61, 10 P 47.

quod eat inde quietus (quod e'at in'de qui-ē'tus). That he go hence acquitted,—formal words in a judgment of acquittal on a charge of crime. State v Buchanan (Md) 5 Harr & J 317.

quod ei deforceat (quod e'ī de-for'she-at). That he deforced him.

The name of the writ authorized by the statute 13 Edward I, c. 4, for persons whose lands had been recovered against them by default. It was not strictly a writ of right, but so far partook of the nature of one that it could restore the right to one who had been unwarily deforced by his own default. See 3 Bl Comm 193.

Quod enim ante nullius est, id naturali ratione occupanti conceditur (quod e'nim an'te nul-li'us est, id na-tu-ra'lī rā-she-ō'ne o-ku-pan'tī kon-se'di-ter). For that which previously belonged to no one becomes by natural reason the property of an occupant. Livermore v White, 74 Maine 452.

Quod enim semel aut bis existit, praetereunte legislatores (quod e'nim se'mel ât bis eg-zis'tit, prē-te're-unt le-jis-lā-tō'rēz). For legislators overlook or ignore that which has only happened once or twice.

Quod est ex necessitate nunquam introducitur nisi quando necessarium (quod est ex ne-ses-si-tā'te nun'quam in-tro-du'si-ter nī'sī quan'dō ne-ses-sā'ri-um). That which exists from necessity is never introduced excepting when it is necessary.

Quod est inconveniens, aut contra rationem non permissum est in lege (quod est in-kon-ve′ni-enz, ât kon′tra ra-she-ō′nem non per-mis′sum est in lē′je). That which is inconvenient or against reason is not permitted in the law.

Quod est necessarium est licitum (quod est ne-sessā′ri-um est li′si-tum). That which is necessary is lawful.

Quod factum est, cum in obscuro sit, ex affectione cujusque capit interpretationem (quod fak′tum est, kum in ob-skū′rō sit, ex af-fek-she-ō′ne kū-jūs′kwe ka′pit in-ter-pre-tā-she-ō′nem). (Civil law.) When it is doubtful as to what has been done, the act should take its explanation from the disposition or character of the person who did it.

Quod fieri debet facile praesumitur (quod fī′er-ī de′bet fa′si-le prē-zu′mi-ter). That which ought to be done is easily presumed.

Quod fieri non debet, factum valet (quod fī′e-rī non de′bet, fak′tum va′let). That which ought not to be done may be valid when done. See Broom's Legal Maxims 182.

quod fieri potest (quod fī′er-ī po′test). What can be done; as much as possible.

quod fuit concessum (quod fu′it kon-ses′sum). Which was granted; which was conceded.

Quod habeant et teneant se semper bene in armis et equis ut decet et oportet; et quod sint semper prompti et bene parati ad servitium suum integrum nobis explendum et peragendum, cum semper opus adfuerit, secundum quod nobis debent de foedis et tenementis suis de jure facere (quod ha′be-ant et te′ne-ant sē sem′per be′ne in ar′mis et e′quis ut de′set et o-por′tet; et quod sint sem′per promp′tī et be′ne pa-rā′tī ad ser-vi′she-um su′um in′te-grum nō′bis ex-plen′dum et per-ā-jen′dum, kum sem′per ō′pus ad-fu′e-rit, se-kun′dum quod nō′bis de′bent dē fē′dis et te-ne-men′tis su′is dē jū′re fa′se-re). That they hold and keep themselves well equipped in arms and horses as is fit and proper, and that they be always ready and well prepared to discharge and render their whole service to us when there shall be need, according to what they ought to do for us by reason of their fees and tenements and by reason of the law. See 1 Bl Comm 410.

Quod id certum est quod certum reddi potest (quod id ser′tum est quod ser′tum red′dī po′test). That is certain which can be rendered certain. Elterich v Leicht Real Estate Co. 130 Va 224, 107 SE 735, 18 ALR 441, 448.

Quod inconsulto fecimus, consultius revocemus (quod in-kon-sul′tō fe′si-mus, kon-sul′she-us re-vosē′mus). That which we do without consideration or rashly, we should recall or revoke upon further consideration.

Quod initio non valet, tractu temporis non valet (quod in-i′she-ō non va′let, trak′tū tem′po-ris non va′let). (Civil law.) That which is not valid at the beginning does not become valid by lapse of time.

Quod initio vitiosum est non potest tractu temporis convalescere (quod in-i′she-ō vi-she-ō′sum est non po′test trak′tū tem′po-ris kon-va-le′se-re). (Civil law.) That which is void in the beginning cannot become valid by lapse of time.

Quod in jure scripto "jus" appellatur, id in lege Angliae "rectum" esse dicitur (quod in jū′re skrip′tō "jūs" ap-pel-lā′ter, id in lē′je An′gli-ē "rek′tum" es′se di′si-ter). That which in the civil law is called "jus," is called "rectum" in the law of England.

Quod in minori valet, valebit in majori; et quod in majori non valet, nec valebit in minori (quod in mī-nō′rī va′let, va-lē′bit in ma-jō′rī; et quod in majō′rī non va′let, nek va-lē′bit in mī-nō′rī). That which is valid in the greater will be valid in the less; and that which is not valid in the greater will not be valid in the less.

Quod in uno similium valet, valebit in altero (quod in ū′nō si-mi′li-um va′let, va-lē′bit in al′te-rō). That which is valid in one of two similar things is valid in the other.

Quod ipsis, qui contraxerunt, obstat, et successoribus eorum obstabit (quod ip′sis, quī kon-traxē′runt, ob′stat, et suk-ses-sō′ri-bus e-ō′rum obstā′bit). (Civil law.) That which bars those who have themselves contracted will also bar their successors.

Quod jussu alterius solvitur pro eo est quasi ipsi solutum esset (quod jus′sū al-te′ri-us sol′vi-ter prō e′ō est quā′sī ip′sī so-lū′tum es′set). (Civil law.) That which is paid by the order of another is as to him just as if it had been paid to himself.

quod libera sit cujuscunque ultima voluntas (quod li′be-ra sit kū-jus-kun′kwe ul′ti-ma vo-lun′tās). That the last will of everyone be free. See 2 Bl Comm 499.

Quod meum est sine facto meo vel defectu meo amitti vel in alium transferri non potest (quod me′um est sī′ne fak′tō me′ō vel dē-fek′tū me′ō a-mit′tī vel in a′li-um trans-fer′rī non po′test). That which is mine cannot be transferred to another without either my act or my default. See Broom's Legal Maxims 465.

Quod meum est, sine facto sive defectu meo amitti seu in alium transferri non potest (quod me′um est, sī′ne fak′tō si′ve de-fek′tū me′ō a-mit′tī sū in a′li-um trans-fer′rī non po′test). That which is mine cannot be transferred to another without either my act or my default.

Quod meum est sine me auferri non potest (quod me′um est sī′ne me â-fer′rī non po′test). That which is mine cannot be taken away without me (consenting).

Quod minus est in obligationem videtur deductum (quod mī′nus est in ob-li-gā-she-ō′nem vi-dē′ter deduk′tum). That which is the lesser sum is deemed to be incorporated in the contract.

Quod naturalis ratio inter omnes homines constituit, vocatur jus gentium (quod na-tu-ra′lis rā′she-ō in′ter om′nēz ho′mi-nēz kon-sti′tu-it, vo-kā′ter jūs jen′she-um). (Civil law.) That rule which natural reason has established among all men is called the law of nations. See 1 Bl Comm 43.

Quod necessarie intelligitur id non deest (quod ne-ses-sā′ri-e in-tel-li′ji-ter id non de′est). That which is necessarily understood is not lacking.

Quod necessitas cogit, defendit (Quod ne-ses′si-tās ko′jit, dē-fen′dit). Necessity defends or protects that which it compels.

Quod non apparet non est (quod non ap-pa′ret non est). The fact not appearing is presumed not to exist. Shepherd v The Schooner Clara, 102 US 200, 202, 26 L Ed 145, 146.

Quod non apparet non est, et non apparet judicialiter ante judicium (quod non ap-pa′ret non est, et non ap-pā′ret ju-di-she-ā′li-ter an′te ju-di′she-um). That which does not appear does not exist, and nothing appears judicially prior to judgment.

Quod non capit Christus, capit fiscus (quod non kă'pit kris'tus, kă'pit fis'kus). That which the Church does not take, the treasury takes.

quod non fuit negatum (quod non fu'it ne-gā'tum). That which was not denied.

Quod non habet principium non habet finem (quod non hă'bet prin-si'pi-um non hă'bet fī'nem). That which has no beginning has no end.

Quod non legitur, non creditur (quod non le-ji'ter, non kre'di-ter). That which is not read is not credited or believed.

Quod non valet in principali, in accessorio seu consequenti non valebit; et quod non valet in magis propinquo, non valebit in magis remoto (quod non va'let in prin-si-pā'lī, in ak-ses-sō'ri-ō sū kon-sequen'tī non va-lē'bit; et quod non va'let in ma'jis pro-pin'quō, non va-lē'bit in ma'jis re-mō'tō). That which is not valid as to the principal matter will not be valid as to the accessory or consequential matter; and that which is not valid as to the more proximate matter will not be valid as to the more remote matter.

quod nota (quod nō'ta). Which note; of which take notice.

Quod nullius esse potest, id ut alicujus fieret nulla obligatio valet efficere (quod nul-lī'us es'se po'test, id ut a-li-kū'jus fī'e-ret nul'la ob-li-gā'she-ō va'let ef-fī'se-re). (Civil law.) No agreement is effective to bring it about that that which can belong to no one shall be the property of someone.

Quod nullius est, est domini regis (quod nul-lī'us est, est do'mi-nī rē'jis). That which belongs to no one is the property of our lord the king. See Broom's Legal Maxims 354.

Quod nullius est, id ratione naturali occupanti conceditur (quod nul-lī'us est, id rā-she-ō'ne na-tū-rā'lī o-ku-pan'tī kon-sē'di-ter). That which belongs to no one is by natural reason granted to the occupant thereof. See 2 Bl Comm 258.

Quod nullum est, nullum producit effectum (quod nul'lum est, nul'lum prō-dū'sit ef-fek'tum). That which is a nullity produces no effect.

Quod omnes tangit, ab omnibus debet supportari (quod om'nēz tan'jit, ab om'ni-bus de'bet sup-por-tā'rī). That which affects all ought to be supported by all.

quod partes replacitent (quod par'tēz re-pla'si-tent). That the parties replead.

quod partitio fiat (quod par-ti'she-ō fī'at). That a partition be made.

Quod pendet, non est pro eo, quasi sit (quod pen'det, non est prō e'ō, quā'sī sit). (Civil law.) That which is pending, or undecided, is just as if it did not exist.

Quod per me non possum, nec per alium (quod per mē non pos'sum, nek per a'li-um). That which I cannot do myself, I cannot do through another.

quod permittat (kwod pėr-mit'at). That he permit,— a writ which lay to permit a plaintiff to enjoy his common as he ought. See 3 Bl Comm 240.

quod permittat prosternere (quod pėr-mit'tat prō-ster'ne-re). That he permit to abate,—the name of an ancient writ which lay at common law in relief of an individual who had sustained injury by reason of a nuisance. 39 Am J1st Nuis § 117.

Quod per recordum probatum, non debet esse negatum (quod per re-kor'dum pro-bā'tum, non de'bet es'se ne-gā'tum). That which is proved by the record ought not to be denied.

Quod populus postremum jussit, id jus ratum esto (quod po'pu-lus pos-trē'mum jus'sit, id jūs rā'tum es'tō). What the people have last commanded, let that be the settled law.

"The general rule is everywhere admitted, that a statute passed by the highest law-making power authorized to legislate upon the subject repeals all previous inconsistent laws." Flaherty v Thomas, 94 Mass (12 Allen) 428, 433.

Quod primum est intentione ultimum est in operatione (quod pri'mum est in-ten-she-ō'ne ul'ti-mum est in o-pe-rā-she-ō'ne). That which is first in intention is last in operation.

Quod principi placuit, legis habet vigorem (quod prin'si-pī pla'ku-it, lē'jis hă'bet vi-gō'rem). That which is agreeable to the prince, hath the force of law.

The common law has proved to be a system replete with vigorous and healthy principles, eminently conducive to the growth of civil liberty; and it is in no instance disgraced by such a slavish political maxim as that which the Institutes of Justinian have introduced, "Quod principi," etc. Clark v Allaman, 71 Kan 206, 80 P 571.

Quod principi placuit legis habet vigorem, cum populus ei et in eum omne suum imperium et potestatem conferat (quod prin'si-pī pla'ku-it lē'jis hă'bet vi-gō'rem, kum po'pu-lus e'ī et in e'um om'ne su'um im-pe'ri-um et po-tes-tā'tem kon'fe-rat). That which pleases the ruler has the force of law, since the people have conferred all authority and power upon him. 1 Bl Comm 74.

Quod principi placuit, legis habet vigorem, ut pote cum lege regia, quae de imperio ejus lata est, populus ei et in eum omne suum imperium et potestatem conferat (quod prin'si-pī pla'ku-it, lē'jis hă'bet vi-gō'rem, ut po'te kum lē'je rē'ji-a, kwē dē im-pe'ri-ō ē'jus la'ta est, po'pu-lus e'ī et in e'um om'ne su'um im-pe'ri-um et po-tes-tā'tem kon'fe-rat). That which is pleasing to the ruler has the force of law; since, by the royal law which has been promulgated concerning his supreme power, the people have conferred upon him all of its authority and power.

Quod prius est verius est; et quod prius est tempore potius est jure (quod pri'us est ve'ri-us est; et quod pri'us est tem'po-re po'she-us est jū're). That which is first is more true, and that which is first in time is the stronger in law.

Quod pro minore licitum est, et pro majore licitum est (quod prō mī'nō-re li'si-tum est, et prō mā-jō're li'si-tum est). That which is lawful in respect to a lesser thing is lawful as to a greater one.

quod prostravit (quod pros-trā'vit). That he abate,— a judgment commanding the abatement of a nuisance.

Quod pure debetur praesenti die debetur (quod pu're de-bē'ter prē-zen'tī dī'e de-bē'ter). That which is entirely due is due on the present day.

Quodque dissolvitur eodem modo quo ligatur (quod'kwe dis-sol'vi-ter e-ō'dem mō'dō quō li-gā'ter). A thing is released or discharged in the same manner in which it is made binding.

Quod quilibet ignem suum salve (quod qui'li-bet ig'-nem su'um sal've). That every person should make reparation for his own fire. Cincinnati, New Orleans & Texas Pacific Railroad Co. v South Fork Coal Co. (CA6 Tenn) 139 F 528.

Quod quis ex culpa sua damnum sentit, non intelligitur damnum sentire (quod quis ex kul'pa su'a dam'num sen-tīt, non in-tel-li'ji-ter dam'num sen-tī're). (Civil law.) Anyone who incurs loss from his own fault, is not deemed to have incurred any loss.

Quod quisque populus ipse sibi jus constituit, id ipsius proprium civitatis est, vocaturque jus civile, quasi jus proprium ipsius civitatis (quod quis'kwe po'pu-lus ip'se si'bi jūs kon-sti'tu-it, id ip-sī'us prō'pri-um si-vi-tā'tis est, vo-kā-ter'kwe jūs si'vi-le, quā'sī jūs prō'pri-um ip-sī'us si-vi-tā'tis). That which people have decreed as law for themselves is peculiar to that state, and is called the civil law, as being peculiar to that particular state.

Quod quisquis norit in hoc se exerceat (quod quis'-quis nō'rit in hok sē ex-er'se-at). Let everyone employ himself in that which he understands.

Quod quis sciens indebitum dedit hac mente, ut postea repeteret, repetere non potest (quod quis si'enz in-de'bi-tum de'dit hak men'te, ut pos'te-a re-pe'te-ret, re-pe'te-re non po'test). (Civil law.) A person cannot recover that which he has given, knowing that it is not due, with the intention that he will afterward recover it.

quod recuperet (quod re-ku'pe-ret). That he recover.

quod redeat inde quietus in perpetuum, et quaerens in misericordia (quod re'de-at in'de qui-ē'tus in per-pe'tu-um, et kwē'renz in mi-se-ri-kor'di-a). That he go hence forever exonerated, and that the plaintiff be in mercy.

Quod remedio destituitur ipsa re valet si culpa absit (quod re-me'di-ō de-sti-tu'i-ter ip'sa rē va'let sī kul'pa ab'sit). That which is without a remedy avails of itself, if there be no fault in the party seeking to enforce it. See Broom's Legal Maxims 212.

quod rex non debet esse sub homine, sed sub Deo et lege (kwod rex non de'bet es'se sub ho'mi-ne, sed sub Dē'ō et lē'jē). Because the king ought not to be subservient to man, but under God and the law. Prohibitions del Roy, 12 Coke's Reports, 63.

quod salvum fore receperint (quod sal'vum fo're re-sē'pe-rint). Which they had received for safe-keeping.

Quod semel aut bis existit praetereunt legislatores (quod se'mel ât bis eg-zis'tit prē-ter'e-unt le-jis-la-to'rēz). The lawmakers overlook or ignore that which has happened but once or twice.

Quod semel meum est amplius meum esse non potest (quod se'mel mē'um est am'pli-us me'um es'se non po'test). That which is once mine cannot be mine more completely.

Quod semel placuit in electione, amplius displicere non potest (quod se'mel pla'ku-it in ē-lek-she-ō'ne, am'pli-us dis-pli'se-re non po'test). One cannot be displeased with that which has once satisfied him in making his election.

quod si contingat (quod sī kon-tin'gat). Which, if it happens.

Quod solo inaedificatur solo cedit (quod sō'lō in-ẹ-di-fi-kā'ter sō'lō sē'dit). (Civil law.) That which is built into the soil goes with the soil. See Mackeldey's Roman Law § 275.

quod stet prohibitio (quod stet pro-hi-bi'she-ō). That the prohibition stand.

Quod sub certa forma concessum vel reservatum est, non trahitur ad valorem vel compensationem (quod sub ser'ta for'ma kon-ses'sum vel re-ser-vā'tum est, non trā'hi-ter ad va-lō'rem vel kom-pen-sā-she-ō'nem). That which is granted or reserved under a certain form, cannot be twisted into a valuation or compensation.

Quod subintelligitur non deest (quod sub-in-tel-li'ji-ter non de'est). That which is understood is not wanting, or left out.

Quod tacite intelligitur deesse non videtur (quod ta'-si-te in-tel-li'ji-ter de-es'se non vi-dē'ter). That which is impliedly understood is not deemed to be wanting, or left out.

Quod talem eligi faciat, qui melius et sciat et velit et possit, officio illi intendere (quod tā'lem ē'li-jī fā'she-at, quī me'li-us et si'at et ve'lit et pos'sit, of-fi'she-ō il'lī in-ten'de-re). That he cause such a person to be chosen who knows most and who is both willing and able to hold that office. See 1 Bl Comm 347.

quod tota curia concessit (quod tō'ta kū'ri-a kon-se'sit). Which the whole court concedes or grants.

Quod vanum et inutile est, lex non requirit (quod va'num et in-u'ti-le est, lex non re-quī'rit). The law does not require that which is vain and useless.

Quod vero contra rationem juris receptum est, non est producendum ad consequentias (quod ve'rō kon'tra ra-she-ō'nem jū'ris re-sep'tum est, non est prō-du-sen'dum ad kon-se-quen'she-as). That which in truth has been received or accepted against the reason of the law, is not to be extended into precedent.

quod vide (kwod vī'dē). Which see; usually abbreviated, "q. v."

Quod voluit non dixit (quod vo'lu-it non di'xit). He did not say that which he wished to say.

quoins (kwoins). Wedges placed between casks stowed in the hold of a ship to keep the casks from rolling. Thomas v Ship Morning Glory, 13 La Ann 269. The squared stones used in constructing the corner of a building.

quo jure (kwō jö'rē). By what right; by which right.

Quo ligatur, eo dissolvitur (quō li-gā'ter, e'ō dis-sol'vi-ter). By that means by which it is made binding, it is released or discharged.

Quo magis nesciunt eo magis admirantur (quō mā'jis ne'si-unt e'ō mā'jis ad-mi-ran'ter). They admire most that of which they know the least.

quo minus (kwō mī'nus). By which the less; a writ wherein the plaintiff is alleged to be the king's farmer or debtor and that by the injury done to him by the defendant, of which he complains, he is less able to pay what he owes the king.

By this fiction the plaintiff secured the jurisdiction of the exchequer. See 3 Bl Comm 45, 286.

Quo modo quid constituitur, dissolvitur (quō mō'dō quid kon-sti-tu'i-ter, dis-sol'vi-ter). A thing may be released or discharged in that manner by which it was created.

Quo modo quid constituitur eodem modo dissolvitur (quō mō'dō quid kon-sti-tū'i-ter e-ō'dem mō'dō dis-sol'vi-ter). In that manner in which a thing was constituted or created, it may be dissolved.

Quomodo quo quid constituitur, dissolvitur (quo-mō'dō quō quid kon-sti-tu'i-ter, dis-sol'vi-ter). In that manner in which a thing was constituted or created, it may be dissolved.

quondam (kwon'dam). Former. The former incumbent of an office.

quorum. The number of members of a body required to be present in order for the body to transact business. As applied to courts, the requirement that a certain number of judges must be present in order to render a valid decision, such requirement being imposed by constitutional or statutory provision. 20 Am J2d Cts § 68. Of grand jury:—the least number of grand jurors necessary to concur in an indictment. 24 Am J1st Grand J § 15. As applied to Congress, a majority of each House. US Const Art 1 § 5 cl 1. As applied to a legislative body of the state, a municipality, or other political subdivision, the number of members prescribed by constitution or statute. In a political committee, a majority. 25 Am J2d Elect § 125. In a political convention, the number of delegates actually assembling. 25 Am J2d Elect § 122. Of a board of directors:—a sufficient number for the exercise of the powers of the board, being a majority unless a different number is expressly prescribed. 19 Am J2d Corp § 1126. Of stockholders:—a sufficient number of stockholders for the transaction of business at a stockholders' meeting, a matter now usually governed by statute, by charter provision, or by the bylaws of the corporation, provided they do not contravene provisions of the charter or statute. 19 Am J2d Corp § 620. At common law, any number of shareholders present at a duly called meeting. Applequist v Swedish Evangelical Lutheran Gethsemane Church, 154 Wash 351, 282 P 224.

quorum aliquem vestrum A. B. C. D., etc., unum esse volumus (quō'rum a'li-quem ves'trum A. B. C. D., etc., ū'num es'se vo'lu-mus). Of whom we will that some one of you, A. B. C. D., etc., be one. See 1 Bl Comm 351.

quota. A fixed amount, for example a quota under the Taft Inter-American Coffee Agreement fixing the amount of coffee to be imported into the United States from coffee-producing countries of the Western Hemisphere. 21 Am J2d Cust D § 11. A particular amount of a commodity fixed by statute in reference to the sale, shipment and distribution of such commodity. 35 Am J1st Mark & M § 30. A limitation upon the acreage in a certain crop, imposed upon a producer as a condition of his right to parity payments or other protection under an agricultural adjustment act. 3 Am J2d Agri § 28. A limitation of the number of immigrants from a particular country which will be admitted to the United States in a particular year. 3 Am J2d Aliens § 53. The number of men to be called to military service at a particular time under statutory provisions for compulsory service. Taber v Board of Supervisors (Sup) 14 NYS 211, 213.

quota immigrant. Any immigrant who is not a nonquota immigrant. 8 USC § 1101(a)(32).
See **nonquota immigrant.**

Quota Law. A statute which prescribes a quota system for immigration to the United States whereunder a limitation is placed upon the number of immigrants from particular countries to be admitted into the country in one year. 8 USC §§ 1151-1157.

quota litis. See **de quota litis.**

quota system. See **Quota Law.**

quotations. See **market quotations.**

Quotiens dubia interpretatio libertatis est, secundum libertatem respondendum erit (quō'she-enz dū'di-a in-ter-pre-tā'she-ō li-ber-tā'tis est, se-kun'dum li-ber-tā'tem re-spon-den'dum e'rit). Whenever the construction or interpretation of liberty is in doubt, it shall be resolved in favor of liberty.

Quotiens idem sermo duas sententias exprimit, ea potissimum accipiatur, qui rei gerendae aptior est (quō'she-enz ī'dem ser'mō dū'as sen-ten'she-as ex-pri'mit, e'a po-tis'si-mum ak-si-pi-ā'ter, quī re'ī je-ren'dē ap'she-or est). Whenever the same language expresses two meanings, that is to be accepted as preferable which is more apt for carrying out the subject matter.

quotient award. An award of arbitrators arrived at by dividing the aggregate of the several amounts of individual estimates of the arbitrators by the number of arbitrators and accepting the quotient as the amount of the award to be made, regardless of individual judgment as to the propriety of the amount. 5 Am J2d Arb & A § 135.

A quotient award is not more lawful for arbitrators than is a quotient verdict for jurors. Schreiber v Pacific Coast Fire Ins. Co. 195 Md 639, 75 A2d 108, 20 ALR2d 951.

quotient verdict. The verdict rendered in a civil action in pursuance of an agreement by the jurors to determine the amount of damages by adding the several estimates of the jury and dividing the aggregate amount by the number of jurors, without the assent of the individual jurors to the amount thus computed as representing actual damages suffered by the plaintiff. 53 Am J1st Tr § 1030.

Quoties in stipulationibus ambigua oratio est, commodissimum est id accipi quo res de quo agitur in tuto sit (quō'she-es in sti-pu-lā-she-ō'ni-bus am-bi'-gu-a o-rā'she-ō est, kom-mo-dis'si-mum est id ak'si-pī quō rēz dē quō ā'ji-ter in tu'tō sit). (Civil law.) Whenever in stipulations the language is ambiguous, it is most correct to accept it in that sense by which the matter with which it deals may be protected.

Quoties in verbis nulla est ambiguitas, ibi nulla expositio contra verba expressa fienda est (quō'she-es in ver'bis nul'la est am-bi-gu'i-tas, i'bi nul'la ex-po-zi'she-o kon'tra ver'ba ex-pres'sa fī-en'da est). Whenever there is no ambiguity in the words, then no explanation contrary to the expressed words should be made.

quousque (quo-us'kwe). Until; how long; how far.

quovis modo (quō'vis mō'dō). In whatever way or manner.

quo warranto (kwō wo-ran'tō). Literally, by what authority. A high prerogative writ at common law. A writ of inquiry as to the warrant for doing the acts of which complaint is made. The remedy or proceeding by which the sovereign or state determines the legality of a claim which a party asserts to the use or exercise of an office or franchise and ousts the holder from its enjoyment, if the claim is not well founded, or if the right to enjoy the privilege has been forfeited or lost. 44 Am J1st Quo W § 2. A demand made by the state upon an individual or corporation to show by what right such individual or corporation exercises some franchise or privilege appertaining to the state which, according to the constitution and laws of the land, cannot be legally exercised in the absence of a grant or authority from the state. State v Perkins, 138 Kan 899, 28 P2d 765. The common-law remedy for contesting an election. 26 Am J2d Elect § 316.

quum (qu'um). When; whenever; as often as. See **cum**.

Quum de lucro duorum quaeratur, melior est conditio possidentis (qu'um de lu'krō du-ō'rum kwē-rā'ter, me'li-or est kon-di'she-ō pos-si-den'tis). (Civil law.) Whenever the advantage of one of two persons is sought, the position of the one in possession is the better.

Quum duo inter se repugnantia reperiuntur in testamento, ultimum ratum est (qu'um du'ō in'ter sē re-pug-nan'she-a re-pe-ri-un'ter in tes-tā-men'tō, ul'ti-mum rā'tum est). When two repugnant matters are found in a will, the latter one is confirmed. Jackson, ex dem. Livingston v Robins (NY) 16 Johns 537, 547.

Quum in testamento ambigue aut etiam perperam scriptum est, benigne interpretari et secundum id quod credibile est cogitatum credendum est (qu'um in tes-tā-men'tō am-bi'gu-e ât e'she-am per'pe-ram skrip'tum est, be-nig'ne in-ter-pre-tā'rī et se-kun'-dum id quod kre-di'bi-le est ko-ji-tā'tum kre-den'-dum est). Where an ambiguous or even an erroneous expression occurs in a will, it should be construed liberally, and in accordance with the testator's probable meaning. See Broom's Legal Maxims 568.

Quum principalis causa non consistit ne ea quidem quae sequuntur locum habent (qu'um prin-si-pā'lis kâ'za non kon-sis'tit nē e'a qui'dem kwē se-quun'ter lō'kum hā'bent). When the principal cause does not stand, neither do those which follow it have a place. Broom's Legal Maxims 496.

Quum quod ago non valet ut ago, valeat quantum valere potest (qu'um quod ā'gō non va'let ut ā'gō, val'le-at quan'tum va-lē're po'test). Whenever what I do is not valid as I do it, it may nevertheless have as much validity as it can have.

q. v. An abbreviation of **quod vide**.

R

R. An abbreviation of **range.**

R. A. Abbreviation of rear admiral, also of regular army.

rabid dog. A dog afflicted with rabies.

rabies (rā′bi-ēz). A disease of flesh-eating animals, including man, affecting the nervous system and characterized by violent convulsions.
See **Pasteur treatment.**

race. A contest of speed, whether of man, animals, or machines. A division of mankind on the basis of distinctive characteristics of color, size, hair, etc.
See **dog racing; horse race.**

race discrimination. See **discrimination.**

race horse. A horse bred and trained for racing. A horse entered and ridden or driven in horse races.

race meeting. An assembly or meeting of persons coming together upon notification for the purpose of witnessing any trial of speed of horses, whether running or trotting. State ex rel. Duensing v Roby, 142 Ind 168, 41 NE 145 (statutory definition.)

race segregation. See **segregation.**

race track. A place of amusement; a place for horse racing or automobile racing; also, in the broad sense of the term, a track where athletes contend in racing and other events.

raceway. An artificial waterway or canal dug in the earth; a channel cut in the ground. 56 Am J1st Wat § 150.

rachater (rah″cha-tay′). To redeem; to ransom; to buy back.

rachetum (rah′che-tum). A redemption; a ransom; a repurchase.

racial discrimination. See **discrimination.**

racial restriction. A provision in a deed or real estate contract forbidding the sale or transfer of the property to, or occupancy thereof by, persons of a certain race or religious faith. 20 Am J2d Cov § 184.
See **discrimination.**

racing. Reckless driving. 7 Am J2d Auto § 277.
See **race.**

rack (rak). An instrument of torture upon which the body of the victim was stretched by means of jackscrews for the purpose of extorting a confession from him.

racket. Any kind of sharp or unlawful practice operated for profit; as, the **numbers game.**

racketeer. Using one's position, especially a position as officer of a labor union, to extort or obtain money by fraud. Hazelton v Murray, 21 NJ 115, 121 A2d 1. The organized use of threats, coercion, intimidation, and violence to compel the payment for actual or alleged services of arbitrary or excessive charges under the guise of membership dues, protection fees, royalties, or service rates. United States v McGlone (DC Pa) 19 F Supp 285, 286.

rack-rent (rak′rent). A rent amounting to the full value of the tenement or near it. See 2 Bl Comm 43.

rack vintage. Wine made from the dregs of the barrel or vat.

radar (rā-där). An instrument for detecting the distance and position of an object through sending radio waves against it and receiving them upon their being reflected from the object. Equipment possessed by police for measuring the speed of motor vehicles. 7 Am J2d Auto § 327.

radar speed meter. A device for measuring the speed of a moving vehicle. 7 Am J2d Auto § 327.

radiation. Any or all of the following:—alpha rays, beta rays, gamma rays, x-rays, neutrons, high-speed electrons, high-speed protons, and other atomic particles; but not sound or radio waves, or visible, infrared, or ultra-violet light. 10 CFR Cum Supp § 20.3(a) (12).

radiation council. An agency established to consult with scientific experts and to advise the President of the United States as to radiation matters, including programs of co-operation with the states. 42 USC § 2021(h).

radio. An instrumentality whereby sounds or signals are converted into waves which are transmitted through space to receivers without the use of wires. 44 Am J1st Rad § 2. The industry of transmission by radio, whether it be the dissemination of news, a cultural or scientific program, a drama, or a comedy.

radioactive material. Any material or combination of material that spontaneously emits ionizing radiation. 18 USC § 831.

radioactive substance. A substance which emits ionizing radiation. 15 USC § 1261(m).

Radio Act of 1927. A federal statute regulating radio communication, superseding a federal statute of 1912, and in turn repealed by the Communications Act of 1934. 47 USC §§ 151 et seq.

radio broadcasting. See **broadcasting.**

radio communication. The transmission by radio of writing, signs, signals, pictures, and sounds of all kinds, including all instrumentalities, facilities, apparatus, and services (among other things, the receipt, forwarding, and delivery of communications) incidental to such transmission. 47 USC § 153.

radiogram. A message by wireless, that is by radio.

radiograph. An x-ray picture. 29 Am J2d Ev § 799.

radioisotope (rā″di-ọ-ī′sọ-tōp). A byproduct; radioactive material yielded in or made radioactive by exposure to radiation incident to the process of producing or utilizing special nuclear material. 42 USC § 2014(e); 10 CFR § 37.3(f).

radiologist (rā-di-ol′ọ-jist). A doctor of medicine qualified as an expert in the employment of the x-ray and its use in the diagnosis and treatment of disease.

radius. A term used in prescribing limits of distance or area. Sacks v Legg, 219 Ill App 144. A term used in prescribing the efficacy of automobile lights. Anno: 31 ALR2d 1424. A straight line extending from the center of a circle or sphere to its circumference or surface. Mead v Anton, 33 Wash 2d 741, 207 P2d 227, 10 ALR2d 588; Anno: 29 ALR2d 517.

In construing the word "radius" as contained in a restrictive covenant against competition within a radius of a designated distance from a restaurant

sold to the covenantees, the ordinary meaning of the term, namely, a right line extending from the center of a circle to the curve thereof, will be applied, to the exclusion of a suggested meaning that the specified distance should be measured along existing streets and sidewalks. Mead v Anton, 33 Wash 2d 741, 207 P2d 227, 10 ALR2d 588.

For meaning of term "radius" as employed in contract, statute, or ordinance as descriptive of area, location or distance, see Anno: 10 ALR2d 588.

radmans. Same as **redmen.**

raencon (răn'sôn). A ransom.

raffle. A form of lottery. 34 Am J1st Lot § 11. A form of gambling, the participants paying for so called chances, the winner taking the amount in play subject to a deduction for the benefit of the person conducting the game. 24 Am J1st Gaming § 20.

raffling. See **raffle.**

raft. A platform of logs or boards floating on water. A vessel for the purposes of admiralty jurisdiction. Re Eastern Dredging Co. (DC Mass) 138 F 942.

rafting logs. The moving of logs by floating them on a stream, the logs being bound together sufficiently to keep them from scattering.

ragpicking. The occupation of going from door to door to obtain old clothing, discarded linen, or bedding to be used in the making of rugs or used in the manufacture of paper. Commonwealth v Hubley, 172 Mass 585, 51 NE 558.

rail fence. A fence constructed of wooden rails, sometimes roughly-hewed rails, alternating from section to section slightly in direction, thereby presenting a worm-like feature.

A Virginia worm rail fence projecting equally on the land of each adjoining owner is, by immemorial usage, a good division fence. 35 Am J2d Fen § 17.

railing. See **handrail.**

railroad. A road of metallic rails to which cars are adapted and on which they can and do operate. O'Malley v Riley County, 86 Kan 752, 121 P 1108. A transportation facility operating on rails, engaged in the transportation of freight and passengers for substantial distances and making stops at regular stations for the receipt and discharge of freight and passengers. 44 Am J1st RR § 3. In its popular meaning, a facility used commercially for the transportation of both passengers and freight, 35 Am J1st M & S § 394, or a company engaged in maintaining and operating such as a facility. International & G. N. R. Co v Dawson, 111 Tex 247, 232 SW 279, 15 ALR 1367.

For comprehensive definition in the Interstate Commerce Act, see 49 USC § 1(3).

See **carrier; common carrier; street railway.**

railroad aid. The use of public money, the public credit, or the taxing power in aid of the construction, maintenance, or operation of railroads. 44 Am J1st RR § 56.

railroad aid bonds. Bonds issued on the public credit in obtaining funds for railroad aid. 43 Am J1st Pub Sec § 64.

railroad bond. A bond issued by a railroad corporation. 12 Am J2d Bonds § 51.

railroad bridge. A bridge or viaduct constructed for the use of railroad transportation.

railroad car. In common usage, a vehicle running on a railroad track and used for the transportation of persons or goods, merchandise, and other articles. Precisely, any vehicle adapted to the rails of a railroad track, whether a passenger car, freight car, locomotive, work car, caboose, terminal car, or even a handcar. 44 Am J1st RR § 272.

railroad commission. An administrative agency regulating the operation of railroads and often other utilities.

See **public service commission.**

railroad company. A railroad corporation, an association of persons, even a natural person, engaged in the operation of a railroad facility. International & G. N. R. Co v Dawson, 111 Tex 247, 232 SW 279, 15 ALR 1367. For the purposes of reorganization under provisions of the Bankruptcy Act:—any common carrier by railroad engaged in the transportation of persons or property in interstate commerce, except a street, a suburban, or interurban electric railway which is not operated as a part of a general railroad system or which does not derive more than 50 percentum of its operating revenues from the transportation of freight in standard railroad freight equipment. Bankruptcy Act § 77(m); 11 USC § 205(m).

railroad corporation. Ordinarily, a public service corporation. A corporation organized for and engaged in the operation of a railroad.

See **railroad company.**

railroad crossing. In the most common usage, the crossing of a highway or street over, under, or above a railroad. In one sense, the intersection of one railroad by another.

See **farm crossing; grade crossing; intersection; overhead crossing.**

railroad depot. See **depot.**

railroad engine. See **locomotive.**

railroad equipment. Necessary adjuncts such as cars, locomotives, and other movable property, but not everything necessary to the operation of the railroad, not machine shops, roundhouses, etc. 44 Am J1st RR § 272.

railroad fences. Fences which statutes almost universally require railroads to construct and maintain on either side of their tracks for the purpose of preventing injuries to horses, cattle, and other livestock. 44 Am J1st RR §§ 151 et seq.

See **cattle guard.**

railroad fire. A fire caused by operation of a railroad or originating on railroad premises. 35 Am J2d Fires §§ 10, 21.

railroad grant. A grant of public lands to a railroad for right of way or by way of aid in railroad construction, the purpose being to encourage settlement on public lands through providing railroad facilities for settlers. 42 Am J1st RR § 46.

railroad hazard. Broadly, any danger in connection with the operation of a railroad. A term of art for the hazard in the employment of railroading by reason of which workers in such employment are exempted from the application of the fellow servant rule by statute. 35 Am J1st M & S § 392.

railroad hospital. A hospital maintained by a railroad company wherein injured or sick employees may receive care. 26 Am J1st Hospit § 15.

railroad intersection. See **intersection.**

railroad land grants. See **railroad grants.**

railroad line. See **railroad route.**

railroad property. Property essential to the operation of a railroad.

The term includes the road-bed, right of way, tracks, bridges, stations, rolling-stock, and such like property; but it does not include land owned by the railroad and held for sale by it, for profit, in no way connected with the use and operation of the railroad. Northern Pacific Railroad Co. v Walker, (CC ND) 47 F 681, 685.

As to what is railroad property for the purpose of taxation, see Anno: 80 ALR 252.

See **railroad equipment.**

railroad receiver. A receiver appointed by the court under its equitable powers or as authorized by statute, to take possession of the lines and property of a railroad and operate them.

railroad relief fund. See **relief association; relief fund.**

railroad reorganization. A readjustment of existing interests in equity, particularly in a federal court, necessitated by a failing financial condition of the corporation. 19 Am J2d Corp § 1517. A reorganization of a railroad company under provisions of the Bankruptcy Act. 9 Am J2d Bankr §§ 1442-1492.

railroad right of way. The strip of land upon which a railroad line is maintained and operated. 44 Am J1st RR § 74. A right of crossing another's land. Anno: 132 ALR 183; 44 Am J1st RR § 74. The substantial, corporeal land upon which a railroad is built, with the rights incident to its enjoyment, rather than an easement of way or right to cross the land. 51 Am J1st Tax § 891.

The words "right of way" used in a statute making a railroad liable for fires communicated from its right of way have no reference to the title of the railroad company to the land, but simply designate the locality where the fire must originate to make the company liable. 35 Am J2d Fires § 8.

railroad rolling stock. See **rolling stock.**

railroad route. The course of a railroad line between its terminals. 44 Am J1st RR § 202.

railroad shop. The place or structure where locomotives and other railroad rolling stock of a railroad are repaired and serviced.

railroad signals. Signals given in the operation of railroad trains by way of bell, whistle, lights, etc., especially at railroad crossings. 44 Am J1st RR § 385. Hand or light signals given by trainmen and switchmen to one another for the purpose of directing the moving of train or cars.

railroad station. A place maintained by a railroad company as a stopping place for trains and for the accommodation of passengers, shippers, and persons receiving freight, including not only the building, but also passageways, walkways, and platforms prepared for passengers in boarding and leaving trains and for the accommodation of persons having business at the station. 44 Am J1st RR § 254.

The word is used synonymously with the term "passenger depot," meaning the place, the grounds and the buildings prepared for and used by the traveling public at such point in waiting for, taking, and leaving the trains, and by the company in operating the road at that point. As to just what constitutes a passenger depot or station at a particular place is a question of fact. State v Indiana & Illinois Southern R. Co., 133 Ind 69, 32 NE 817.

See **depot; union station.**

railroad stock. Outstanding stock issued by a railroad corporation.

railroad system. Broadly, the aggregation or network of railroads of the United States physically connected for the interchange of business. Texas & Pacific R. Co. v Gulf, C. & S. F. R. Co. 270 US 266, 70 L Ed 578, 46 S Ct 263. In another sense, an operating relationship and unity of railroad routes, lines, branches, and trackage involving common control, common management, something more than mere physical connections and through-traffic arrangements. 44 Am J1st RR § 203.

railroad ticket. See **ticket.**

railroad tie. See **tie.**

railroad time. An old term, now in disuse, for standard time. 52 Am J1st RR § 3.

railroad track. The rails, ties, and ballast upon which the trains run. 44 Am J1st RR § 227. A way for the transportation of freight or passengers. A track used or intended for the purpose of transporting or moving produce, freight, or passengers in connection with the business of the owner or operator. 35 Am J1st M & S § 428. For tax purposes, railroad right of way in use as such. 51 Am J1st Tax § 889.

The meaning of the word "track" as applied to a railroad, depends on circumstances and context, but the word as ordinarily understood is not synonymous with railroad, the latter word having a more extended significance. However, the word track as sometimes used, is synonymous with and means roadway or right of way. In any case, a railroad track is inseparable from the right of way and is an incident to it; the right of way is the principal thing although it is of no practical use without a superstructure and rails, since the track is necessary to the use and enjoyment of the right of way. 44 Am J1st RR § 227.

railroad train. See **train.**

railroad unemployment insurance account. An account to be maintained by the Secretary of the Treasury in the unemployment trust fund established by the Social Security Act. 45 USC § 360.

Railroad Unemployment Insurance Act. A federal statute which sets up a comprehensive plan for the payment of unemployment insurance benefits to persons defined in the act as employees of railroads, and other specified employees engaged in or intimately connected with carriage by rail. 45 USC §§ 351 et seq.; 48 Am J1st Soc Sec § 12.

railroad yard. An area containing shops, switch tracks, sidings, freight depot, and sometimes the main station of a railroad.

railway. Same as **railroad.** 44 Am J1st RR § 3.

Railway and Canal Traffic Act. An act passed by Congress in 1854, which prohibited any limitation of a carrier's liability unless the contract containing it was signed by the parties and the stipulation itself was such "as should be adjudged by the court or judge before whom any question relating thereto shall be tried to be just and reasonable." 14 Am J2d Car § 537.

railway company. Same as **railroad company.** 44 Am J1st RR § 3.

railway cut. An excavation, having definite upper and outer edges and sloping sides, made in a right of way for the purpose of keeping the road bed on the level or, at any rate, avoiding a steep grade. Newton v Louisville & N. R. Co. 110 Ala 474, 19 So 19.

Railway Labor Act. A federal statute intended to provide means for the peaceful settlement by agreement or arbitration of labor controversies between interstate carriers, including carriers by air, and their employees. 45 USC §§ 151 et seq.; 31 Am J1st Lab § 345.

railway mail service. The transportation and handling of the mail on mail cars on railroads. 39 USC §§ 521 et seq.

railway postal clerks. Mail clerks who sort and distribute the mail in railway post offices or post office terminals and transfer offices, and perform other duties pertaining to the railway mail service. 41 Am J1st P O § 33.

railway post office. The car in which railway postal clerks perform their duties.

rainfall. See **ordinary rainfall; rainwater.**

rain water. Water, as it falls from the clouds, before it has entered the soil, river, lake, or sea.

rainy days. For the purposes of a stipulation excusing delay in unloading of cargo, only those days on which, considering the facilities of the port, cargo could not be landed with safety. Kerr v Schwaner (CA9 Or) 177 F 659.

raise. To produce; to present; to rear. To move to a higher level. To increase in size or amount.

raise a rate. To levy a tax. To increase a rate, e.g. the rate for utility service.

raised. Reared. A male reared to the age of twenty-one. Shoemaker v Stobaugh, 59 Ind 598, 600. Elevated. Increased. Produced as crops.

raised check. A check altered by raising the amount of the sum payable. United States Fidelity & Guaranty Co. v First Nat. Bank (CA5 Tex) 172 F2d 258.

raised instrument. An alteration in an instrument for the payment of money which raises the amount payable. 36 Am J2d Forg § 18.
See **raised check.**

raised crops. Crops which have matured and are in condition to be harvested, but which as yet have not been harvested in fact. McNally v Dean, 154 Wash 110, 281 P 9, 66 ALR 1417.

raised way. An elevated street or highway.

raising amount of instrument. Forgery in changing the true amount of a check or other instrument for the payment of money to a larger amount. Crocker-Woolworth Nat. Bank v Nevada Bank, 139 Cal 564, 73 P 456.

raising money. Collecting or procuring a supply of money for use, as, in the case of a municipal corporation, by taxation, or perhaps by means of a loan. Childs v Hillsborough Electric Light & Power Co. 70 NH 318, 324.

raising revenue. Levying taxes. Anno: 4 ALR2d 975.

raison d'être (rā-zôn' dā'tr). The reason or cause of being or existing.

rake-off. The amount taken out of money in play by the person conducting the game. 24 Am J1st Gaming § 20. A share in the proceeds of an illegal enterprise. A share of the proceeds of crime given a law-enforcement officer for his forbearance.

rambling. Wandering about. 55 Am J1st Vag § 7.

ramp. A passageway between two levels.

ran (ran). (Saxon.) Robbery.

ranching. The raising of livestock, particularly cattle, in large numbers, on an extensive acreage. A form of agriculture. 3 Am J2d Agri § 1.

random (ran'dum). See **at random.**

range. A cook stove, rueled by wood, coal, gas, or electricity, usually attached to the premises. 35 Am J2d Fixt § 91. Grazing land of large area, often on the public domain. Big Butte Horse & Cattle Asso. v Anderson, 133 Or 171, 289 P 503, 70 ALR 399. A feature of the government survey of public lands, being a designation of a township laid out by the survey in terms of a number corresponding to the number of the tier of townships, in which the township appears, east or west of an established principal meridian and another number corresponding to the tier of townships, in which the township appears, north or south of an established base line, the intersection of the tiers thus affording a means of locating a township in a vast area surveyed. Meas v Whitener-London Realty Co. 119 Ark 301, 178 SW 390.

For example of a description of a quarter section or 160 acres in a square:—The Northwest (NW) Quarter of Section Twenty-eight (28) in Township Seventy-five (75) North, Range Twenty-six (26) West of the 5th Principal Meridian.
See **base line; principal meridian.**

range levy. A levy upon livestock in a pasture or on a range without taking possession of the animals, the officer describing the animals by brands or marks, designating the number thereof, as nearly as possible, and giving notice to the defendant owner. 30 Am J2d Exec § 258.

range stock. Livestock feeding and living upon the open range. Livestock that roam and feed upon the open and unenclosed tracts of land in the state. Wightman v King, 31 Ariz 89, 250 P 772.

rank. The standing of an officer or enlisted man of the Armed Forces relative to other officers and enlisted men. 36 Am J1st Mil § 55.

ransom. A price or consideration paid or demanded for the redemption of a captured person or persons —a payment that releases from captivity. Keith v State, 120 Fla 847, 163 So 136. A sum of money paid to release a person or property captured in war; a heavy fine; a sum paid for a pardon; a sum paid to release a person from unlawful imprisonment or detention.

ransom-bill (ran'sum-bil). A contract to pay for property captured in naval warfare, and providing for its safe conduct.

ransom bond. A bond given to procure the discharge of property or persons captured in time of war. 56 Am J1st War § 111.

rape. The having of unlawful carnal knowledge by a man of a woman, forcibly and against her will. The unlawful carnal knowledge of a female by force and without her consent. 44 Am J1st Rape § 2.

In some counties in England, an intermediate division between a shire or county and a hundred, each containing about three or four hundreds, as the rapes in Sussex. In Kent, these divisions were called lathes. Each rape had its rape-reeve, and each lathe had its lathe-reeve, corresponding to the shire-reeve or sheriff of the shire or county. See 1 Bl Comm 116.

See **statutory rape.**

rape of the forest (of the for'est). A trespass with force or violence committed within a park or forest.

rape-reeve. See **rape.**

rapid. Very swift, advancing with haste or speed. People v Grogan, 260 NY 138, 183 NE 273, 86 ALR 1266.

rapina (ra-pī'na). Robbery.

rapist (răp'ist). A person who commits rape; a ravisher.

raptim et sparsim (rap tim et spar sim). Hastily and spasmodically.

raptor (rap'tor). Same as **rapist.**

raptu haeredis. See **de raptu haeredis.**

raptus (ra'tus). Rape.

raptu virginum. See **de raptu virginum.**

rapuit (ra'pu-it). He raped; he ravished.

rare. Exceptional. Scarce; found most infrequently. Lacking density. Partially raw.

rascal (răs'kal). A scoundrel, except as used with a light touch, as it often is, e.g., "you little rascal." The words, "he was a damned rascal," although a vulgar expression, are, perhaps, the strongest in use to convey our ideas of moral turpitude. Brown v Mims, 9 SCL (2 Mill Const) 235, 236.

rasura (ra-zū'ra). Same as **rasure.**

rasure (rā'zūr). An erasure; an alteration in a written instrument. Ruby v Talbott, 5 NM 251, 21 P 72.

rasus (rā'zus). Erased.

rat. A rodent. A mean fellow; a paltry fellow, one to be treated with contempt. A scab.
See **rat-proofing; scab.**

ratable (rā'ta-bl). Taxable; subject to taxation. State v Camp Sing, 18 Mont 128, 44 P 516. That which can be estimated. Proportional.
See **pro rata.**

ratable distribution. As in bankruptcy, a distribution on all claims, of equal priority, as proved or established by adjudication, on one rule of proportion applicable to all alike. Merrill v National Bank of Jacksonville, 173 US 131, 143, 43 L Ed 640, 645, 19 S Ct 360.

ratable estate (es-tāt'). Taxable estate; the real and personal property that the legislature has designated as taxable. Marshfield v Middlesex, 55 Vt 545, 546.

ratable polls (pōls). Taxable persons.

ratable property (prop'ėr-ti). Property in its quality and nature capable of being rated; that is, appraised or assessed for purposes of taxation. Coventry Co. v Assessors of Taxes, 16 RI 240, 241.

ratable value (val'ū). The ratable value of property is its appraised or assessed value for purposes of taxation. Coventry Co. v Assessors of Taxes, 16 RI 240, 241.

ratably. On a ratable basis. Proportionally.
See **ratable.**

ratam rem habere (ra'tam rem hā-bē're). To consider the matter or transaction as ratified.

rate. Verb: To estimate value or capability; to classify. A price or valuation. A unit by which a calculation is made, as rate of interest; rate of speed; rate of growth; or rate of exchange. The charge imposed by a common carrier. 13 Am J2d Car §§ 105 et seq., 461 et seq. The price stated or fixed for a public utility service, that is, the price stated or fixed for some commodity or service of general need or utility supplied to the public, measured by a specified unit or standard. 43 Am J1st Pub Util § 82. A local property tax; a special or local assessment for a public improvement. 48 Am J1st Spec A § 3.

rate fixing. See **rate making.**

rate for freight. See **freight rate.**

rate making. The process of determining a rate to be charged, particularly a rate subject to government control, as where it is for service by a public utility. A function which is purely legislative in its character, whether it is exercised directly by the legislature itself or by some subordinate or administrative body, to whom the power of fixing rates in detail has been delegated. Prentis v Southern R. Co. 211 US 210, 53 L Ed 150, 29 S Ct 67.
See **fair return.**

rate of assessment. The amount of a special assessment per stated amount of valuation.
See **assessments of mutual benefit society; tax rate.**

rate of duty. A tariff rate; a rate on a particular item of property being imported from a foreign country, even a free rate, as enacted by Congress or proclaimed by the President. 19 USC § 1202, Headnote 9(d).

rate of exchange. The rate according to which the money of one country is exchanged for the money of another, for example, the number of American dollars to be received for an English pound.

rate of fare. See **fare.**

rate of interest. A certain percent of the principal sum charged by way of interest per year. 30 Am J Rev ed Int § 26.
See **legal interest.**

rate of premium. See **premium rate.**

rate of tax. See **tax rate.**

rate of wages. The wage scale as fixed by contract or collective bargaining.
See **prevailing rate of wages.**

rate tithes (rāt tīths). Tithes which were charged ratably on the property within the parish.

rate war. A sudden and violent fluctuation in rates charged by competing railroads for the transportation of freight or passengers. United States v Trans-Missouri Freight Asso. (CA8 Kan) 58 F 58.

rate zone. See **zone.**

rat hole. A boring for oil made by a drill or small bore. Honolulu Oil Corp. v Halliburton, 306 US 550, 83 L Ed 980, 59 S Ct 662.

ratification. Giving effect by approval. Treating as good or authorized an act which otherwise might be disavowed or even treated as a tort. 18 Am J2d Conv § 73. A confirmation of an act already performed, not an authorization of an act to be performed. Barker v Chesterfield, 102 Mass 127, 128. An express promise or a promise implied from conduct by which a party to a contract otherwise voidable accepts it and undertakes to be bound by it. Crawford v Gordon, 88 Wash 553, 153 P 363. Accepting the benefits of a transaction with knowledge of fraud inducing the same by the other party. 37 Am J2d Fraud §§ 332 et seq. The affirmance by a person, upon reaching his majority, of a contract made by him during his infancy. 27 Am J1st Inf §§ 11 et seq. In the law of agency:—the adoption or affirmance by a person of a prior act which did not bind him, but which was done or professed to be done on his account, thus giving effect to the act, as to some or all persons, as if originally authorized. Rogers v Beiderwell, 175 Kan 223, 262 P2d 814, 45 ALR2d 578; Gulf Refining Co. v Travis, 201 Miss 294, 30 So 2d 398.

The essence of ratification is approval. Jordan v Beaumont (Tex Civ App) 337 SW2d 115, error ref n r e. To ratify the act of an agent means to approve and sanction, and presupposes knowledge or at least some alerting circumstantial information of the unauthorized act. MacLeod v Ajax Distributing Co. 22 NJ Super 121, 91 A2d 635, 34 ALR2d 504.

To ratify is to give validity to the act of another, and implies that the person or body ratifying has at the time power to do the act ratified. A county board could not ratify a subscription without a vote of the county because they could not make a subscription in the first instance without such an authorization. Norton v Shelby County, 118 US 425, 452, 30 L Ed 178, 189, 6 S Ct 1121.

Ratification of an unauthorized act is equivalent to an original grant of authority. Rogers v Beiderwell, 175 Kan 223, 262 P2d 814, 45 ALR2d 578.

ratification of forgery. The ratification of an unauthorized or forged signature, giving effect to the instrument to which it is appended. Wilson v Hayes, 40 Minn 531, 42 NW 467.

ratification of marriage. A method of validating a voidable marriage. An affirmance of a voidable marriage by living together as husband and wife with full knowledge of facts constituting an impediment to the marriage. 4 Am J2d Annul § 45.

ratification of treaty. A ratification by the United States Senate of a treaty negotiated by the President, such requiring a vote of two thirds of the Senators present concurring with the treaty. 52 Am J1st Treat § 11.

ratified. See **ratification.**

Some confusion has arisen as to the use of the word "ratified," and as to whether ratification is a fact or a conclusion of law arising from the facts. As the term is applied to principal and agent it is a fact and not a legal conclusion, but when it is used in a sense akin to estoppel, it is a conclusion of law. Minnich v Darling, 8 Ind App 539, 544, 36 NE 173.

ratify. To give approval. To confirm. To make a ratification.
See **ratification.**

ratihabitio (ra-ti-ha-bi'she-ō). Same as **ratification.**

Ratihabitio mandato aequiparatur (ra-ti-ha-bi'she-ō man-dā'tō ē-qui-pa-rā'ter). A ratification is equivalent to a command. Dempsey v Chambers, 154 Mass 330, 28 NE 279.

Ratihabitio mandato comparatur (ra-ti-ha-bi'she-ō man-dā'tō kom-pa-rā'ter). Ratification is to be compared with a command.

This maxim of the Roman law has been changed to "Ratihabitio mandato aequiparatur" (Ratification is equivalent to a command), ever since the days of Lord Coke. It has never been doubted that a man's subsequent agreement to a trespass done in his name and for his benefit amounts to a command so far as to make him answerable. Dempsey v Chambers, 154 Mass 330, 28 NE 279.

ratihabition (rat″i-hā-bish'on). Same as **ratification.**

Ratihabitio priori mandato aequiparatur (ra-ti-ha-bi'-she-ō prī-ō'rī man-dā'tō ē-qui-pa-rā'ter). A ratification is equivalent to a previous command. "A maxim borrowed from the Roman law, and now an element in the jurisprudence of every civilized nation." Palmer v Yates, 5 NY Super Ct (3 Sandf) 137, 151.

rating. An evaluation of something, such as the credit of a man or a television program, usually made on a purported scientific basis. The grading of candidates for civil service positions by written examinations. 15 Am J2d Civ S § 11. The determination of the relative state or condition of a vessel in reference to its insurable quality. 29 Am J Rev ed Ins § 504. Rank in the military.

See **Hooper rating; horsepower ratings; rate making.**

rating bureau. An organization of insurance companies or insurance agents for the purpose of promoting the business, welfare, and convenience of the parties thereto and to secure uniformity in the business, particularly in reference to premium rates. 29 Am J Rev ed Ins § 109. An organization engaged in examining particular premises for the purpose of determining the premium rate to be applied in insuring the property.

ratio (rā'shiō). The relation between two numbers or two magnitudes of the same kind; the relation between two similar magnitudes in respect to quantity; the relation between two similar quantities in respect to how many times one makes so many times of the other; especially the relation expressed by indicating the division of one quantity by the other, or by the factor that multiplied into one will produce the other. Relative amount; proportion. Re Klock, 30 App Div 24, 41, 51 NYS 897.

ratio (rā'she-ō). (Latin.) A reckoning. Computation; calculation. Reason; motive.

ratio decidendi (rā'she-ō de-si-den'dī). The reason for deciding; the reasoning or principle, or ground upon which a case is decided.

Ratio est formalis causa consuetudinis (rā'she-ō est for-mā'lis kā'za kon-su-e-tu'di-nis). Reason is the molding cause of custom or usage.

Ratio est legis anima; mutata legis ratione mutatur et lex (rā'she-ō est lē'jis a'ni-ma; mu-tā'ta lē'jis ra-she-ō'ne mu-tā'ter et lex). Reason is the spirit or soul of the law; by a change in the reason of the law, the law is also changed.

Ratio est radius divini luminis (rā'she-ō est rā'di-us di-vī'nī lu'mi-nis). Reason is a ray of divine light.

Ratio et auctoritas duo clarissima mundi lumina (rā'she-ō et âk-to'ri-tās du'o kla-ris'si-ma mun'dī lu'mi-na). Reason and authority are the two most shining lights in the world.

ratio impertinens (rā'she-ō im-per'ti-nenz). An impertinent reason, an argument not pertaining to the question. Wilmington & Weldon Railroad Co. v Board of Railroad Comrs. (CC NC) 90 F 33, 34.

Ratio in jure aequitas integra (rā'she-ō in jū're ē'qui-tās in'te-gra). Reason in law is impartial equity.

ratio law. A statute providing that the number of liquor licenses to be granted in a particular area shall not exceed a specified ratio to the number of inhabitants. 30 Am J Rev ed Intox L § 137.

ratio legis (rā'she-ō lē'jis). The reason of the law; the reason underlying the law; the reason for the existence of the law.

Ratio legis est anima legis (rā'she-ō lē'jis est a'ni-ma lē′jis). The reason of the law is the spirit or soul of the law.

ration. Noun: A term familiar in the armed service, being food for one man for one day. Verb: To distribute or divide food on a calculated basis in time of scarcity.

rationabili parte. See **de rationabili parte.**

rationabili parte bonorum. See **de rationabili parte bonorum.**

rationabilis (rā-she-ō-nā′bi-lis). Reasonable; rational.

rational (rash′on-al). Capable of reasoning; sane.

rational basis. A reasonable basis in the law; the criterion in the review of an administrative order by the court. The application of the law in a just and reasoned manner. 2 Am J2d Admin L § 619.

rational doubt. Same as **reasonable doubt.**

rationale (rash-o-nā′lē). Rational basis; the reasoning in support of a proposition.

rationalibus divisis. See **de rationalibus divisis.**

rational intent. An intent founded on reason, as a faculty of the mind, and opposed to an irrational purpose. Supreme Lodge v Gelbke, 198 Ill 365, 370, 64 NE 1058.

rational interpretation. A term which has been applied to a doctrine sometimes followed in the interpretation of written instruments, whereby language held to be lacking is supplied by the court, and language held to be superfluous is disregarded, in an effort to give effect to the intention of the maker of the instrument.

The same doctrine has been employed in the construction of statutes. The doctrine is a dangerous one because of its tendency toward judicial legislation. Shellenberger v Ransom, 41 Neb 631, 59 NW 935.

rational volition (vō-lish′on). Volition, attended by the powers of reason, to consider and judge the act done in all its relations—moral as well as physical. Daniels v New York, New Haven & Hartford Railroad Co. 183 Mass 393, 67 NE 424.

ratione contractus (rā-she-ō′ne kon-trak′tus). By reason of the contract.

ratione impotentiae (ra-she-ō′ne im-po-ten′she-ē). By reason of impotence.

ratione loci (ra-she-ō′ne lō′sī). By reason of the place or locality.

ratione materiae (ra-she-ō′ne ma-tē′ri-ē). By reason of the matter in hand.

ratione personae (ra-she-ō′ne per-sō′nē). By reason of the person concerned.

ratione prescriptionis (rā-she-ō′ne prē-skrip-she-ō′nis). By reason of a prescriptive right or duty.

ratione privilegii (ra-she-ō′ne pri-vi-le′ji-ī). By reason of privilege.

rationes (rā-she-ō′nēz). The pleadings in an action.

ratione soli (rā-she-ō′ne sō′lī). On account of the soil; by reason of one's ownership of the soil.
See **property ratione soli.**

ratione tenurae (ra-she-ō′ne te′nu-rē). By reason of one's tenure.

ratione tenurae or prescriptionis (ra-she-ō′ne te′nu-rē or pre-skrip-she-ō′nis). By reason of a right or duty of tenure or prescription. State ex rel. Roundtree v Board of Comrs. 80 Ind 478.

ratione tenurae suae (rā-she-ō′ne te′nu-rē su′ē). By reason of his own tenure.

rationing. Placing a limitation upon the amount of certain necessities of life which can be purchased, as in time of war, when such commodities are in short supply. 56 Am J1st War §§ 46 et seq.
See **ration.**

Ratio non clauditur loco (rā′she-ō non klâ′di-ter lō′kō). Reason is not confined to place or locality.

ratio of safety. A margin, to be observed by a trustee in investing trust funds, between the value of the security and the amount of the trust investment. 54 Am J1st Trusts § 426.

ratio pertinens (rā′she-ō per′ti-nenz). A pertinent reason, a reason pertaining to the question. Wilmington & Weldon Railroad Co. v Board of Railroad Comrs. (CC NC) 90 F 33, 34.

Ratio potest allegari deficiente lege, sed vera et legalis et non apparens (rā′she-ō po′test al-le-gā′rī de-fi-she-en′te lē′je, sed ve′ra et lē-gā′lis et non ap-pa′-renz). Where the law is deficient, the reason can be alleged, but it must be true and lawful and not merely apparently so.

rat proofing. Constructing a building in such manner and of such materials that rats cannot gain entrance. 13 Am J2d Bldgs § 29.

rattening (rat′ning). The practice of concealing the tools of a workingman for the purpose of compelling him to join a labor union, a statutory offense in some jurisdictions.

ratum (rā′tum). Rated as valid; deemed or recognized as valid.

raunsom. Same as **ransom.**

raunsome. Same as **ransom.**

ravine. A deep gully or gorge; a natural drainway for surface water. Anno: 81 ALR 271; 56 Am J1st Wat § 76.

As used in an indictment for rape, the word has been held to imply a want of consent and that by reason of employing the word "ravish," the indictment need not aver specifically that the rape was committed against the woman's will. There is also authority to the contrary. See 44 Am J1st Rape § 57.

ravish (rav′ish). To rape. To seize and carry away with force. To enrapture.

ravishment (rav′ish-ment). Being ravished. Ravishing.
See **ravish.**

ravishment de gard. The abduction of a ward.

razor. An instrument with a sharp cutting edge for shaving a man's face.

It is an article of common domestic use, and while no one could be held guilty of the offense of carrying a dangerous and deadly weapon concealed about his person, simply because he so carried a razor, yet, if surrounding circumstances would tend to show that he carried it as a weapon of offense, he might become liable to the charge, because a razor, when thus used, is notoriously a weapon dangerous to life. See Brown v State, 105 Miss 367, 62 So 353.

R. C. L. An abbreviation of **Ruling Case Law,** q. v.

re (rē). In the case of; in the matter of; in regard to. See **in re**.

R. E. A. Abbreviation of **Rural Electrification Administration**.

rea. See **mens rea; reus**.

reaching full age. See **majority**.

reacknowledgment. An acknowledgment of an instrument intended to correct a prior acknowledgment of the same instrument. Bernhardt v Brown, 122 NC 587, 29 SE 884.

reaction time. The time required for response to a stimulus, especially in an emergency. 8 Am J2d Auto § 893.

reactor. See **nuclear reactor**.

read. To ascertain the contents of a writing, a document, or printed matter from the words and signs thereof. New Orleans v Brooks, Connor & Norton, 36 La Ann 641, 642.

readily accessible. Available for immediate use in an emergency.
Life preservers placed in the bunk of each member of the crew of a fishing trawler are "readily accessible," within the meaning of a statute which requires life preservers to be so placed as to be readily accessible. Noble v Moore-McCormack Lines, Inc. (DC Mass) 96 F Supp 369.

readily realizable market value. A value existing where property is readily to be converted into cash or its equivalent in such manner as to realize the fair value of the property. Clark v Welch (DC Cal) 46 F2d 563.

reading ability. See **literacy**.

reading bill. A requirement of the constitution in the legislative consideration of a bill that before final passage, the bill shall be read at length, section by section, a certain number of times, in each house. 50 Am J1st Stat § 79.

reading indictment or information. A step in the arraignment of one accused of crime. People v Goldenson, 76 Cal 328, 19 P 161; Rule 10, Federal Rules of Criminal Procedure.

reading ordinance. A step in the enactment of a municipal ordinance, the requirement being for the reading of the ordinance one or more times, as the statute may provide, before the council. 37 Am J1st Mun Corp § 144.

readings. Lectures on ancient English statutes. Coke on Littleton 280.

readjustment of debts. Various forms of relief under the Bankruptcy Act. Compromise settlements.

read law. See **to read law**.

readmission. Authorizing a foreign corporation to do business in the state after a withdrawal of the corporation from the state. 36 Am J2d For Corp § 315.

ready. Prepared at the moment. Tobias v Lissberger, 105 NY 404, 12 NE 13. Able and willing to proceed, as with performance of a contract. Smith v Keeler, 51 Ill App 267.
See **readily realizable market value**.

ready, willing, and able customer. A customer, found by a broker for his client, who is ready and willing to contract and able to complete the contract.

ready, able, and willing buyer. A buyer who desires to make the purchase and has at hand the money to meet the cash payment required, without resort to or dependence upon third persons for funds, and without raising the money upon property. Anno: 1 ALR 528.

ready money. Cash; current money.

reaffiliation. A renewal of membership after a lapse, suspension, or expulsion. See 36 Am J2d Frat O §§ 74 et seq.

reagent. A chemical term for a substance which by reason of its capacity to cause reaction is used to detect, measure, or convert other substances. Martin v Minerals Separation North American Corp. (DC Md) 29 F Supp 146.

real (rē'ạl). Regal; royal; pertaining to the crown; pertaining to realty. Not fictitious or a product of the imagination.

real actions. Those actions which are brought for the specific recovery of lands, tenements or hereditaments, some being founded on the seizure or possession, and some on the property or right. 1 Am J2d Actions § 38.

real advancement. An advancement made by a conveyance of real property. Williams v Stonestreet, 24 Va (3 Rand) 559, 561.
See **advancements**.

real assets. Real estate left by a decedent which is subject to payment of his debts. 31 Am J2d Ex & Ad § 196. Broadly, real property.

real chattel. See **chattels real**.

real chymin (chi'min). A royal road.

real claim. A claim which is good under the law or asserted in good faith as good under the law, rather than one concocted of fraud or overly-vivid imagination. Rue v Meirs, 43 NJ Eq 377, 380, 12 A 369.

real composition. A composition of tithes, an agreement whereby the landowner discharged his land for liability for tithes.

real contract. A contract concerning real property; in the civil law, a contract which had some specific thing for its subject matter.
See **land contract**.

real controversy. An actual, as distinguished from a simulated controversy, moot case, hypothetical case, or abstract question. 20 Am J2d Cts §§ 80, 81; 27 Am J2d Equity § 14.

real covenant. A covenant having for its object something annexed to, inherent in, or connected with, land or real property—one which relates to, touches, or concerns the land granted or demised and the occupation or enjoyment thereof. 20 Am J2d Cov § 29. A covenant which runs with the land, binding not only the heirs and personal representatives of the covenantor, but his grantees as well. Hawkins v Whayne, 198 Okla 400, 179 P2d 138.

real estate. Land or real property. Land and the grass or other crop growing thereon. Croasdale v Butell, 177 Kan 487, 280 P2d 593, 49 ALR2d 1112.
As defined for purposes of taxation, see Anno: 57 ALR 869.
See **estate for years; life estate; real property**.

real estate agent. See **real-estate broker**.

real estate and rental guide. A publication largely taken up with transactions concerning real property and constituting an advertising medium for real estate owners and realtors. 39 Am J1st Newsp § 8.

real-estate broker. An agent who, for a commission or brokerage fee, bargains or carries on negotiations in behalf of his principal as an intermediary between the latter and a third person in transacting business relative to the sale or purchase of real estate. 12 Am J2d Brok § 1. One whose business is to procure the purchase or sale of lands, acting as middleman or negotiator between potential vendors and purchasers to bring them together and arrange the terms. Quinn v Phipps, 93 Fla 805, 113 So 419, 54 ALR 1173.

real estate broker's lien. A lien in support of the broker's right to compensation by way of sharing in the purchase money. 12 Am J2d Brok §§ 242, 243.

real estate contract. See **land contract; real contract.**

real estate corporation. A corporation authorized to buy and sell real estate in the normal and regular course of its business. Eisen v Post, 3 NY2d 518, 169 NYS2d 15, 146 NE2d 779; Tuttle v Junior Bldg. Corp. 227 NC 146, 41 SE2d 365.

real estate investment trust. A trust formed by a group of people pooling their capital for the purpose of investing in real estate.

real-estate partnership. A partnership formed for the purpose of buying and selling land generally or for speculation on a single venture, or for the purchase, sale, improvement, and leasing of real property for profit. 40 Am J1st Partn § 13.

real-estate pool. Same as **real estate syndicate.**

real estate syndicate. An organization having the purpose of pooling the funds of members to invest in real estate or to deal in it as a commodity of traffic. Kilbourn v Thompson, 103 US 168, 195, 26 L Ed 377, 388.

real-estate tax. The most common form of direct property tax, being a tax levied upon real estate, without reference directly to the use made of the property but according to an assessed valuation. 51 Am J1st Tax § 31.

real evidence. Evidence addressed directly to senses of the court or jury without interposing the testimony of witnesses other than as required in laying the basis for such evidence, 29 Am J2d Ev § 769, involving the production or exhibition in court of something directly connected with the incident out of which the cause of action arose, such as the injured parts of the body in an action to recover for a personal injury. Smith v Ohio Oil Co. 10 Ill App 2d 67, 134 NE2d 526, 58 ALR2d 680.

real fixture. A fixture which becomes a part of the land at annexation to the freehold because of the intent with which it is affixed. Capen v Peckham, 35 Conn 94.

re aliena. See **in re aliena.**

real injury. An injury resulting from or caused by an act, as distinguished from an injury caused by words.

realize. To understand. To bring to fruition. To obtain the advantage or benefit of a thing, as taking a profit on an investment.

To realize means to bring into actual possession. It is ordinarily used in contrast to hope, or anticipation. A man may hope to sell his property for a certain sum, but until he actually sells it and receives the money, or its equivalent, he cannot be said to have "realized" either his hopes or his profits. Lorillard v Silver, 36 NY 578, 579.

Under section 22 of the Revenue Act of 1934, realization of income is the taxable event, rather than the right to receive it, and realization is not deemed to occur until the income is paid. But the decisions and regulations have consistently recognized that receipt in cash or property is not the only characteristic of realization of income to a taxpayer on the cash receipts basis. Where the taxpayer does not receive payment in money or property, realization may occur when the last step is taken by which he obtains the fruition of the economic gain which has already accrued to him. Helvering v Horst, 311 US 112, 85 L Ed 75, 61 S Ct 144.

realizing income. See **realize.**

realizing on security. Foreclosure by action or sale under a power of sale.

realm (relm). A region. A state; a sovereignty. Carr v Lewis Coal Co. 96 Mo 149, 8 SW 907.

real party in interest. The person to be benefited by, or entitled to receive the benefits of, the suit. More precisely, that person who can discharge the claim upon which suit is brought and control the action brought to enforce it, usually but not necessarily the person beneficially interested in the cause of action. 39 Am J1st Parties § 17.

For the purpose of res judicata the courts will look beyond the nominal party whose name appears formally upon the record and will treat as the real party him whose interests are involved in the litigation. Gibson v Solomon, 136 Ohio St 101, 16 Ohio Ops 36, 23 NE2d 996, 125 ALR 903.

real property. Land. Such things as are permanent, fixed, and immovable; lands, tenements, and hereditaments of all kinds, which are not annexed to the person or cannot be moved from the place in which they subsist. 42 Am J1st Prop § 13. In a strictly technical sense, such an interest as one has in land; a right, interest, or ownership, existing in the soil, and consisting of an estate in fee or for life. Callihan v Martin, 3 Cal 2d 110, 43 P2d 788, 101 ALR 871.

The term has been frequently defined by statute to be coextensive with lands, tenements, and hereditaments, and covers all that goes to make up the earth in its natural condition, including petroleum as found in its natural state, unmined coal, sand or gravel in its original bed, subterraneous water not flowing in a definite course, but percolating through the earth, a room in a house, a toll bridge over a navigable river, and the tolls authorized by law, and mining claims. 42 Am J1st Prop § 13.

See **fixture.**

real property arrangement. A matter of relief provided by Chapter XII of the Bankruptcy Act so that a debtor can pay his creditors over a period of time while retaining his real property. Re Dick (CA7 Wis) 296 F2d 912. A proceeding in the bankruptcy court to obtain a modification or alteration of the indebtedness of an individual which is secured by a lien or liens on real property. 9 Am J2d Bankr § 1350.

real release. A release wherein the creditor declares that he considers the debt as acquitted.

It is equivalent to a payment, and renders the thing no longer due. Booth v Kinsey, 49 Va (8 Gratt) 560, 568.

real representative. The heir or devisee of a decedent who left real property. Louisville Trust Co. v Kentucky Nat. Bank (CC Ky) 87 F 143, 145.

real security. Security in property rather than in the undertaking of a surety or guarantor. Merrill v National Bank of Jacksonville, 173 US 131, 158, 43 L Ed 640, 650, 19 S Ct 360.

real service. Same as **service real**.

real servitude. See **service real**.

real statute (stat'ūt). A statute which regulates property within the state where it is in force, as distinguished from a personal statute which follows and governs the party subject to it wherever he goes. Saul v His Creditors (La) 5 Mart NS 569.

real things. See **things real**.

realty (rē'al-ti). Same as **real property**.

real value. The market value under fair competition, and under normal market conditions. International Harvester Co. v Kentucky, 234 US 216, 221, 58 L Ed 1284, 1287, 34 S Ct 853.

real wrong. An injury to real property.

reaming (rē'ming). Enlarging the bore. An operation in the care and maintenance of an oil well. Anno: 55 ALR 1564.

As used by oil-well drillers the word means the enlargement of a smaller hole to its bottom. The reaming ceases when the bottom of the small hole is reached, although the larger hole may be continued below that point. Clarke v Blue Licks Springs Co. 184 Ky 827, 213 SW 222, 4 ALR 234, 239.

Ream linguam non facit nisi mens rea (rē'am lin'-gwam non fā'sit nī'sī menz rē'a). The tongue is not guilty unless the mind is guilty.

reapportionment. A change in legislative or congressional districts, sometimes periodically, for the purpose of providing equality of representation, particularly after a population change. 25 Am J2d Elect § 15.

reappointment. The reinstatement of a civil service employee. 15 Am J2d Civ S § 42. The appointment to public office of a person presently serving in the same office.

reappraisement. A computation of customs duties following a protest. 21 Am J2d Cust D § 94.

rear admiral. A commissioned officer of the Navy, of a rank comparable to major general of the Army.

rear-end collision. A common form of traffic accident, one vehicle striking another in the rear, as when the vehicle in the lead stops suddenly. 8 Am J2d Auto § 770.

reargument. A rehearing of a motion. 37 Am J1st Motions § 18. A rehearing in an appellate court. 5 Am J2d A & E §§ 978 et seq.

rear light. See **tail light**.

rear-line restriction. A restriction established by covenant against the erection of building nearer than a specified distance to the rear line of the lot. 20 Am J2d Cov § 240.

rear lines. See **back lines**.

rearraignment (rē-a-rān'ment). An arraignment of the accused after amendment of the accusatory pleading or the substitution of an indictment or information for one which has been lost. 21 Am J2d Crim L § 455.

rearrest. The retaking of a prisoner following his escape from custody. 5 Am J2d Arr § 78.

reason. The ability to think and draw conclusions. Cause; justification. Good sense; good judgment.

Lawyers are copious in their encomiums on the reason of the common law. They tell us that the common law is the perfection of reason; that it always intends to conform thereto, and that what is not reason is not law. But every particular reason of every rule in the law cannot at this distance of time be precisely accounted for, and it is sufficient that there be nothing flatly contradictory to reason, and then the law will presume it to be well founded. See 1 Bl Comm 70.

See **by reason of**.

reasonable. Not extreme. Not arbitrary, capricious, or confiscatory. Public Service Com. v Havemeyer, 296 US 506, 80 L Ed 357, 56 S Ct 360.

"What is reasonable depends upon a variety of considerations and circumstances. It is an elastic term which is of uncertain value in a definition." Sussex Land & Live Stock Co. v Midwest Refining Co. (CA8 Wyo) 294 F 597, 34 ALR 249, 257.

reasonable basis in law. See **rational basis**.

reasonable belief. A belief begotten by attendant circumstances fairly creating it, and honestly entertained. Howard v State, 110 Ala 92, 20 So 365.

reasonable care. A relative term; care required by the circumstances of the case. Due care under the circumstances. 38 Am J1st Negl § 29.

reasonable cause. For prosecution:—the existence of a reasonable ground of presumption that the charge is or may be well founded. Wood v United States (US) 16 Pet 342, 366, 10 L Ed 987, 996. A reasonable amount of suspicion, supported by circumstances sufficiently strong to warrant a cautious man in believing that the accused is guilty. Tucker v Cannon, 32 Neb 444, 446. For failure to file tax return on time—inability to file on time notwithstanding the exercise of ordinary business prudence; such cause as reliance on Treasury publication; sometimes oversight of one's attorney or accountant. Estate of Fisk v Commissioner (CA6) 203 F2d 358.

A taxpayer's failure to file an income tax return is due to reasonable cause within a statutory exemption from penalty where failure is due to reasonable cause, where the taxpayer has acted with ordinary business care and prudence in the matter. Orient Invest. & Finance Co. v Commissioner, 83 App DC 74, 166 F2d 601, 3 ALR2d 612.

See **probable cause**; **reasonable excuse**.

reasonable charge. See **reasonable rate**.

reasonable compensation. Just compensation. Sweet v Rechel, 159 US 380, 404, 40 L Ed 188, 198, 16 S Ct 43.

See **reasonable rate**.

reasonable diligence. A relative term. Diligence as required by the circumstances of the case. 38 Am J1st Negl § 29.

In any business involving the personal safety and lives of others, reasonable diligence is nothing less than the most watchful care and the most active diligence; anything short of this is negligence and carelessness. Stanley v Steele, 77 Conn 688, 60 A 640.

See **reasonable time**.

reasonable doubt. As militating against the sufficiency of the evidence:—an actual and substantial doubt of the defendant's guilt arising from the evidence, or from a want of evidence, as distinguished from a vague apprehension. A fair doubt based upon reason and common sense and growing out of the testimony in the case. A doubt arising from a candid and impartial investigation of all the evidence, being such as, in an ordinary transaction of life, would cause a reasonable and prudent man to hesitate and pause. That state of mind which, after a fair comparison and consideration of all the evidence in the case, both for the state and for the defense, leaves the minds of the jury in such a condition that they cannot say they feel an abiding conviction to a moral certainty of the truth of the charge. Saunders v State, 4 Okla Crim 264, 111 P 965.

As a reason for a decision in favor of the constitutionality of a statute or municipal ordinance:—want of certainty that the statute or ordinance is so plainly and culpably violative as to offend the constitution. Ours Properties, Inc. v Ley, 198 Va 848, 96 SE2d 754.

reasonable excuse. A relative term; an excuse which is reasonable under the circumstances of the particular case. Anno: 31 ALR 632.

See **reasonable cause.**

reasonable facilities. A relative term; facilities required of a carrier which are reasonable in relation to all the surrounding circumstances and in the light of conditions existing at the time. Atchison, T. & S. F. R. Co. v State, 71 Okla 167, 176 P 393, 11 ALR 992. Station facilities:—such facilities as may fairly be demanded by patrons and prospective patrons, regard being had, among other things, to the size of the place, the extent of the demand for transportation, the cost of furnishing the additional accommodations asked for, and all other facts which would have a bearing upon the questions of convenience and use. Atlantic Coast Line R. Co. v Wharton, 207 US 328, 52 L Ed 230, 28 S Ct 121.

reasonable ground for prosecution. See **reasonable cause.**

reasonable hour. See **reasonable time.**

reasonable man rule. The rule that in review of an administrative determination, the court will not substitute its judgment or discretion for that of the agency, but will deem the evidence in support of the order sufficient where it is such that a reasonable man considering it would make the same determination. 2 Am J2d Admin L § 686.

reasonable means of conveyance. Any means of conveyance which can be employed upon a public highway with reasonable regard for the safety and convenience of the public, and without inflicting upon the owner of the fee an injury differing in kind from that imposed by use and improvement for ordinary public travel. 25 Am J1st High § 165.

The public is not confined to the use of vehicles in common use at the time when the highway or street was established, but may use such other reasonable means of conveyance as may be discovered in the future, provided they do not exclude the proper use of the highway by other kinds of vehicles, or tend to destroy it as a means of passage and travel common to all. McClintock v Richlands Brick Corp. 152 Va 1, 145 SE 425, 61 ALR 1033.

reasonable use of highway. Use of the highway in such a manner as not unnecessarily or unreasonably to impede the exercise of the same right by others. 25 Am J1st High § 164.

See **reasonable means of conveyance.**

reasonable parts. Those parts of a decedent's personal estate to which his widow and lineal descendants were entitled at common law, notwithstanding the dispositions made by him in his will. See 2 Bl Comm 491.

reasonable police regulation. See **reasonable regulation.**

reasonable probability. The degree of proof required in civil cases to support a conclusion of fact; not proof beyond a reasonable doubt or proof to a moral certainty, only evidence which tends with reason to prove the essential facts in a case, either directly, indirectly, or by permissible inferences. 30 Am J2d Ev § 1163.

reasonable provocation. Anything the natural tendency of which is to produce passion in ordinary men, and which the jury are satisfied did produce it in the case before them. 26 Am J1st Homi § 25.

reasonable prudence. Same as **ordinary care.**

reasonable rate. A rate charged by a carrier in such amount as to provide a reasonable compensation for its services and no more. 13 Am J2d Car § 106. A rate charged by a public service company which is not oppressive to those served or confiscatory from the standpoint of the company; a rate which provides the company a fair return on its investment and no more. Brymer v Butler Water Co. 179 Pa 231, 36 A 249.

See **fair return.**

reasonable regulation. A regulation which is a proper exercise of the legislative power in protecting the public and providing safeguards for its interest, considering the nature of the condition sought to be remedied, the purpose of the regulation, the means of regulation adopted, and the relation between the purpose and the means. 16 Am J2d Const L §§ 278 et seq.

reasonable restraint rule. The rule that in granting or devising a vested estate, a restraint upon alienation may be imposed for a reasonable period of time, but not beyond the life of the grantee or devisee. Cities Service Oil Co. v Taylor, 242 Ky 157, 45 SW2d 1039, 79 ALR 1374.

reasonable return. See **fair return.**

reasonable skill. Such skill as is ordinarily possessed and exercised by persons of common capacity, engaged in the same business or employment. Mechanics Bank v Merchants Bank, 47 Mass (6 Met) 13, 26.

reasonable time. A period consistent with reasonable dispatch and without unreasonable delay. 37 Am J2d Fraud § 417. A time that is reasonable considering the nature, purpose, and circumstances of the relevant act. UCC § 1–204(2). A time for presentment of a check for payment that is reasonable from the standpoint of the nature of the instrument, the usage of the trade or business, and the facts of the particular case. 11 Am J2d B & N § 764. For performance of contract in absence of condition as to time, a time which is reasonable from the standpoint of the subject matter of the contract, the situation of the parties, their intention, what they contemplated at the time the contract was made, and the circumstances attending performance. 17 Am J2d Contr § 330.

reasonable time for delivery. A delivery by a seller of goods during usual business hours where the purchaser is a merchant; a delivery at any hour of the day designated for delivery, provided there is still sufficient light, time, and opportunity for the purchaser properly to inspect and care for the goods. 46 Am J1st Sales § 167. A delivery by a carrier within business hours and under such circumstances that the consignee may receive and put away his goods in a manner consistent with their safety. 13 Am J2d Car § 410.

See **reasonable time for transportation.**

reasonable time for transportation. Of passenger:— transportation in time according with published timetable or schedule as due care in accord with the circumstances of the case permits. 14 Am J2d Car § 881. Of freight:—transportation in such time as the mode of conveyance, the distance, the nature of the goods, the season of the year, the character of the weather, and the ordinary means for transportation under the control of the carrier. 13 Am J2d Car § 365.

The meaning of the term as contemplated by a provision of a bill of lading that claims for loss, in case of failure to deliver, must be made within a specified time after the lapse of a "reasonable time for delivery," depends upon the circumstances of the particular case and means such time as is necessary conveniently to transport and make delivery of the shipment in the ordinary course of business, in the light of the circumstances and conditions surrounding the transactions. Chesapeake & O. R. Co. v Martin, 283 US 209, 75 L Ed 983, 51 S Ct 453.

reasonable use doctrine. The maxim of the common law that the use of one's own property must be such as not unreasonably to injure others in depriving them of the lawful use and enjoyment of their properties. 38 Am J1st Negl § 15; 39 Am J1st Nuis § 16. A rule in respect of the use of percolating water by a landowner, restricting each landowner to a reasonable exercise of his own rights and a reasonable use of his own property in view of the similar rights of others. 56 Am J1st Wat § 114. The rule that a riparian proprietor may use or detain the water of the stream for purposes necessary for the use and enjoyment of his abutting property, qualified only by the correlative rights of other riparian owners, certain rights of the public, and the condition that the use be had in such manner as not to injure others in the enjoyment of their rights. 56 Am J1st Wat §§ 18, 274.

reasonable user. The use of property by a co-owner which is not capricious, irresponsible, or malicious, but in one of the ordinary methods of reaping profits from property of like character and in like circumstances. 20 Am J2d Coten § 37.

Where two persons own a motor vehicle as tenants in common, the limitation of the right of each is that he is bound so to exercise his rights in the property as not to interfere with the rights of his cotenant. State ex rel. Fohl v Karel, 131 Fla 305, 180 So 3.

See **reasonable use doctrine.**

reasonably cautious. See **reasonable care.**

reasonably prudent person. See **prudent;** the **ordinary prudent man.**

reasonably safe. Safe according to the usages, habits, and ordinary risks of the business.

A master performs his duty when he furnishes those appliances of ordinary character and reasonable safety, and the former is the test of the latter; for, in regard to the style of implement or nature of the mode of performance of any work, "reasonably safe" is to be tested by the foregoing definition. Chrismer v Bell Tel. Co. 194 Mo 189, 92 SW 378.

reasonably satisfy the jury. Convince the jury as reasonable men that it is worthy of belief. Anno: 147 ALR 383.

reasoning creature. Man. State v Jones, 1 Miss (Walk) 83, 85.

reassignment. An assignment made by an assignee. An assignment made by the assignee of an insurance policy. 29 Am J Rev ed Ins § 687. An assignment by an assignee back to the assignor. A new calendar of cases necessitated by exigencies such as unexpected settlements, continuances, voluntary dismissals, or unexpected prolongation of certain trials.

reassignment of homestead. The practice under the statutes of many of the states of the Union fixing a maximum for the value of real property which shall be exempt from levy and sale under execution, of causing the homestead to be selected or assigned again, that is, reassigned, where the homestead originally assigned has so increased in value as to exceed in value the limit fixed by the statute. 26 Am J1st Home § 44.

reassurance. Restoration of confidence.
See **reinsurance.**

reattachment. An attachment of a defendant's person subsequently to his release from a previous attachment in the same action.
See **alias writ.**

reattestation. An attestation of a previously attested instrument, following an alteration thereof. 4 Am J2d Alt Inst § 24. The attestation of a will upon re-execution or republication of the instrument. 57 Am J1st Wills § 625.

rebate. A giving back. A deduction. A discount for prompt payment. State v Schwarzchild, 83 Me 261, 265, 22 A 164. A distribution made by a corporation to stockholders in proportion to the amount of business done with the corporation. Uniform Printing & Supply Co. v Commissioner (CA7 Ill) 88 F2d 75, 109 ALR 966. The act of an insurance company in charging an insured less than the prevailing rate; a matter of discrimination. 29 Am J Rev ed Ins § 506. A deduction made by a common carrier from the rate or charge specified in the tariff schedule. A refunding or repayment by a common carrier of any portion of the rate, fare, or charge made to it in accord with the tariff schedule for the services of the carrier in transporting freight or passengers. 13 Am J2d Car § 114. An allowance made to the purchaser of a municipal bond for the purpose of overcoming the effect of a minimum price fixed by statute. 43 Am J1st Pub Sec § 145.

rebating. See **rebate.**

rebellion. An insurrection against lawful authority which is void of all appearance of justice. 30 Am J Rev ed Insurr § 2. The open and active opposition of a number of citizens or subjects of a country or state to its government. 56 Am J1st War § 2. A term incorrectly applied to the war between the states, otherwise known as the Civil War. 30 Am J Rev ed Insurr § 2.

Rebellion does not constitute a war in a legal sense prior to the recognition of the participants as belligerents by the existing domestic government or by foreign nations. 30 Am J Rev ed Insurr § 2.
See **insurrection.**

rebels. Persons who resist authority. Persons in rebellion against the government. A term loosely but incorrectly applied to the personnel of the Confederate Forces engaged in the Civil War. 30 Am J Rev ed Insurr § 2.

rebouter (re′bôu-tay″). To rebut; to repel; to bar.

rebroadcast. An exact reproduction of a radio program. Lobe v Turner (Tex Civ App) 257 SW2d 800.
See recreation.

rebuild. To build up again; to build or construct after having been demolished.
The term is not in meaning restricted to the erection of a new structure on the site of the old one. Hence, if a building is blown down by a storm, it is possible to rebuild it on a new site. Board of Education v Townsend, 63 Ohio St 514, 59 NE 223.

rebuilding covenant. See covenant to rebuild.

rebus. See de rebus; in rebus.

rebus sic stantibus (rē′bus sic stan′ti-bus). While things thus stand.

rebut (rę-but′). To deny; to contradict; to avoid.

rebuttable (rę-but′ạ-bl). Capable of being rebutted.

rebuttable presumption. A presumption which is not conclusive but may be overcome by opposing evidence. 30 Am J2d Ev § 1165. A provisional procedural assumption of a fact which is prescribed by a rule of a substantive law. Simpson v Simpson, 162 Va 621, 175 SE 320, 94 ALR 909. An assumption of facts made because common experience has established that they ordinarily exist where the basic facts from which the assumption arises have been established, but which may, in truth and fact, not exist at all. Wyatt v Baughman, 121 Utah 98, 239 P2d 193.

rebuttal. Contradiction or refutation. The speech of a debater in refutation of the statements made by his opponent.

rebuttal evidence. Evidence answering or disputing that given by the opposite party. 53 Am J1st Trial § 120. That evidence which is offered and introduced to explain, repel, counteract, or disprove testimony or facts introduced by or on behalf of the adverse party, including not only evidence which contradicts the witnesses on the opposite side but also evidence in denial of any affirmative fact which the adverse party has endeavored in any manner to prove. 29 Am J2d Ev § 250.

rebuttal of presumption. The adducing of evidence which meets a presumption and dispels it. 29 Am J2d Ev § 165.
See rebuttable presumption.

rebutter (rę-but′ėr). A pleading by the defendant in response to plaintiff's surrejoinder. 41 Am J1st Pl § 181.

rebutting evidence. See rebuttal evidence.

recall. To call back. To remember. To set aside; to vacate; to remove from office.

recalling witness. The act of a party, with the permission of the court, in calling a witness for further examination or cross-examination after a previous calling and examination or cross-examination of the witness in the same case. 58 Am J1st Witn § 561. Having a witness return to repeat his testimony in order to settle a dispute raised between jurors in their deliberations. 53 Am J1st Trial § 936.

recall of judicial decision. The reversal or annulment of a judicial decision by a vote of the electors in a proceeding instituted for such purpose. People v Western Union Tel. Co. 70 Colo 90, 198 P 146, 15 ALR 326; 28 Am J Rev ed Init & R § 52.

recall of mandate, writ, or order. The quashing or setting aside by an appellate court of a remittitur, mandate, or other writ or order issued by it. 5 Am J2d A & E § 1008.

recall of public officer. The removal of a public officer by direct action of electors, that is by the vote of bona fide electors. 28 Am J Rev ed Init & R § 53. The removal of an elective municipal officer by vote of the people at an election called for the purpose by a specified number of citizens. 37 Am J1st Mun Corp § 247.

recall of pardon. The revocation or cancellation of a pardon before its delivery and acceptance, by the officer or body which granted it. 39 Am J1st Pard § 47.

recall of witness. See recalling witness.

recant. To change one's testimony as given at a former trial because it is untruthful. State v D'Onofrio, 221 Md 20.

recantation. The admission by a witness that his testimony as given at a prior trial was mistaken or false. 39 Am J1st New Tr § 169.

recanvass. A review by a canvassing board or other election officers of the returns of the election made by them. 26 Am J2d Elect § 303.

recapitalization. A change in the capitalization of a corporation, especially upon reorganization, by increase or decrease in number of shares of stock or of a particular issue of stock, sometimes providing for preferred stock, at other times, eliminating preferred in favor of common, or by other method of altering the capital structure. 9 Am J2d Bankr § 1590; 18 Am J2d Corp §§ 211 et seq., 1518. For income tax purposes, see Bazley v Commissioner, 331 US 737, 91 L Ed 1782, 67 S Ct 1489, 173 ALR 905.
Refunding of municipal bonds is not a "recapitalization" within Federal income tax law provision that no taxable gain shall be recognized on exchange of securities incident to a corporate "recapitalization." Emery v Commissioner (CA2) 166 F2d 27, 1 ALR2d 409.

recaption. See recapture; reprisal.

recapture. The retaking and returning to custody of an escaped prisoner. 27 Am J2d Escape § 26. The retaking of property taken as prize of war. 56 Am J1st War § 180. The taking of a vessel from pirates or an enemy who has taken it without right. 47 Am J1st Salv § 10. The retaking of waters which have escaped from artificial confinement, before they have reached a stream. 56 Am J1st Wat § 176.
See reclamation.

Receditur a placitis juris potius quam injuriae et delicta maneant impunita (re-se′di-ter ā pla′si-tis jū′ris pō′she-us quam in-jū′ri-ē et de-lik′ta ma′ne-ant im-pu′nī-ta). Settled law will be departed from rather than that wrongs and crimes shall remain unpunished.

receipt. The acceptance of property upon a delivery thereof. The acceptance of money offered by way of payment or gift. An acknowledgment in writing of the receipt of money. Glickman v Weston, 140 Or 117, 11 P2d 281, 12 P2d 1005. Written evidence of the discharge of an obligation.
No receipt can have the effect of destroying per

se any subsisting right; it is only evidence of a fact. It is not a release. A receipt "in full," however, given knowingly and without fraud, has been accorded the conclusive effect of a formal release, but such cases are usually those of compromise of disputed claims or receipts for unliquidated damages. Ryan v Ward, 48 NY 204.

A mere receipt for money does not import a promise, obligation, or liability and hence is not within the statute of limitations governing contracts, but if it recites that the money received is to be applied to the account of the person from whom it was received, it partakes of both a receipt and a contract and becomes subject to the statute of limitations applicable to contracts. 34 Am J1st Lim Ac § 85.

See **interim receipt; trust receipt; warehouse receipt**.

receipt for transportation. In effect, a **bill of lading**. Empire Transp. Co. v Wallace, 68 Pa 302.

If the payment was not by way of compromise or settlement of a disputed claim, such a receipt is no bar to a recovery of any balance actually due the creditor. Ryan v Ward, 48 NY 204.

receipt in full. A receipt acknowledging payment in full. A release for some purposes. Dreyfus v Roberts, 75 Ark 354, 87 SW 641.

receipting for property. A recognized practice wherein the lien of an attachment or execution is continued in force without the necessity of continued physical custody of the property by the officer who served the writ, such being accomplished by delivering the property to a third person who gives his receipt to the officer and becomes responsible for the safekeeping of the property during the pendency of the action. 6 Am J2d Attach § 550.

receipt of the exchequer (of the eks-chek'ẽr). That division of the exchequer which managed the royal revenues, and the other, which was the court or judicial part of it. See 3 Bl Comm 44.

receiptor. A person who receipts for property delivered into his custody by a sheriff who has seized the property in making a levy under a writ of attachment or execution.

See **receipting for property**.

receivable accounts. See **accounts receivable**.

receivable bills. See **bills receivable**.

receive. To take into one's possession, e.g., a letter, a gift, one's salary, or earnings. Hallenbeck v Getz, 63 Conn 385, 388; Commissioner v Williston, 315 Mass 638, 54 NE2d 43, 151 ALR 1395.

As the words "receive" and "accept" are used in the statute of frauds, the authorities generally agree that they do not mean the same thing, although they are ordinarily synonymous. To "receive" seems to imply taking into possession by the buyer, while "accept" means an assumption of ownership on the part of the buyer, treating the goods as his own. Mack Co. v Bear River Milling Co. 63 Utah 565, 227 P 1033, 36 ALR 643, 646.

In computing income taxes, although there is authority to the contrary, the general view is that where a dividend is declared in one year, but not paid or payable to the stockholder until a subsequent year, it is "received" and taxable in the later rather than the earlier year. But actual receipt is not necessary, and a dividend may be taxed in the year in which it was constructively received by being made unqualifiedly subject to his demand. Anno: 120 ALR 1282.

received. See **receive; value received**.

receiver. A person appointed to take custody of property in a receivership. A person appointed by the court to receive and preserve the property or fund in litigation, and receive its rents, issues, and profits, and apply or dispose of them at the direction of the court, sometimes having the additional duty of operating a business in order to maintain it as a going concern. 45 Am J1st Rec § 3. Any receiver of an estate in bankruptcy. Bankruptcy Act § 1(31); 11 USC § 1(31). An instrumentality for intercepting and disseminating radio communications by sound or signal. An instrumentality for receiving telephonic communications.

See **bank receiver; equity receiver; pendente lite receivership; temporary receiver**.

receiver general of the public revenue (jen'ẹ-rạl of the pub'lik rev'ẹ-nū). A county tax collector in England.

receiver in bankruptcy. See **receiver**.

receiver of stolen property. A person who receives into his possession or under his control with felonious intent any stolen goods or chattels with knowledge that they have been stolen. Watts v People, 204 Ill 233, 240, 68 NE 563.

See **receiving stolen property**.

receiver pendente lite (rẹ-sē'vẽr pen-den'te li'te). See **pendente lite receivership**.

receiver's certificate. A certificate or evidence of indebtedness, issued under order of the court by a receiver in possession of property in payment for goods or services purchased or engaged by the receiver, payable out of a particular fund in the receivership, and usually constituting a first lien on the property in the receivership. 45 Am J1st Rec § 366.

receivership. The means of reaching a legitimate end through the exercise of the equitable power of the court or under statutory authorization by appointing one known as a receiver with property to seize and take custody of property. An ancillary remedy, sometimes in the nature of a provisional remedy, whereby the preservation of property in litigation is accomplished by placing it in the possession of a receiver appointed by the court. Pereira v Wulf, 83 Mont 343, 272 P 532. An equitable remedy for the dissolution or reorganization of a corporation in financial distress.

receivership in aid of execution. A receivership in proceedings supplemental to execution in a case where the right to such remedy is appropriate under circumstances such as the refusal of the judgment debtor to apply his property to the judgment debt, the necessity of collecting future earnings of the judgment debtor, etc. 30 Am J2d Exec § 852.

receivership in foreclosure. A receivership in an action for the foreclosure of a mortgage or lien. 45 Am J1st Rec § 3. A proceeding in aid of an action for the foreclosure of a mortgage on real estate, wherein a receiver is appointed to take possession of the mortgaged property, collect the rents and profits, pay the expenses of the receivership, insurance, and taxes, account for the surplus proceeds, and turn them over to the court for application on the mortgage debt or, if not required for satisfaction thereof, to the mortgagor. 37 Am J1st Mtg § 912.

receiving a bribe. See **bribery.**

receiving a prize. See **draw a prize.**

receiving deposits while insolvent. The wrong, usually constituting a criminal offense, of a director or officer of a bank in permitting deposits to be made, knowing that the bank is insolvent. 10 Am J2d Banks §§ 198, 242 et seq.

receiving stolen goods. Same as **receiving stolen property.**

receiving stolen property. A criminal offense in receiving stolen goods, knowing them to have been stolen in some jurisdictions a substantive crime, indictable and punishable as an offense separate and distinct from the larceny itself. In other jurisdictions an accessorial offense, the receiver being subject to indictment and punishment as an accessory to the theft or larceny. 45 Am J1st Rec St P § 2.

receiving teller. See **teller.**

recens insecutio (rē'senz in-se-kū'she-ō). Same as **recens secta.**

receiving value therefor. Receiving payment or reward, in some manner, for the particular and specific act of signing an instrument for the payment of money. Gaspard v Lachney (La App) 92 So2d 277.

recens secta (rē'senz sek'ta). Fresh suit; fresh pursuit. "And if the party robbed do his diligence immediately to follow and apprehend the thief (which is called making fresh suit), or do convict him afterwards, or procure evidence to convict him, he shall have his goods again." See 1 Bl Comm 297.

recent. New or fairly new. Characterizing the period of time immediately preceding the present moment.
In the law of larceny, under the rule that the possession of stolen property must be recent after the theft in order to afford a just basis for an inference of guilt on the part of the possessor, the word "recent" in this connection is incapable of exact definition. Except perhaps in extreme cases, no definite time can be fixed as to when, as a matter of law, possession is or is not recent. What is recent possession varies, within a limited range, with the conditions and surrounding circumstances of each case, and is, within such range, to be determined by the jury upon the facts of the particular case. The particular period of time involved is an important element to be considered, but it is not the only one. The circumstances and character of the goods, their salability, and whether they are cumbersome or easily portable, are also among the factors to be considered. 32 Am J1st Larc § 142.
"We think that 'recent transactions' to which this Court has declared a tax law may be retroactively applied, Cooper v United States, 280 US 409, 411, 74 L Ed 516, 50 Sup Ct Rep 164, must be taken to include the receipt of income during the year of the legislative session preceding that of its enactment." Welch v Henry, 305 US 134, 83 L Ed 87, 59 S Ct 121.

recently. Lately.
As the word is used in connection with the probative value of evidence that stolen goods were recently in the possession of the defendant, it refers to the defendant's possession soon after the theft and not to possession immediately before prosecution. See State v Wiley, 53 Mont 84, 164 P 84.
Possession of the fruits of crime recently after its commission justifies the inference that the possession is guilty possession, and though only prima facie evidence of guilt, may be of controlling weight unless explained by the circumstances or accounted for in some way consistent with innocence. Wilson v United States, 162 US 613, 619, 40 L Ed 1090, 1095, 16 S Ct 895.

recent transaction. See **recent.**

reception of verdict. The declaration of the verdict by the foreman of the jury in open court, all other members of the panel being present for questioning in reference to their adherence to the verdict thus declared. 53 Am J1st Trial § 1020.

receptus (rē-sep'tus). (Civil law.) An arbitrator.

recess. A short break in the course of a morning or afternoon session of court. A time when court is not in session due to an adjournment of the session. 20 Am J2d Cts §§ 47-50. A break in the session of a legislative body; a temporary suspension or interruption of a session or meeting rather than an adjournment sine die. Anno: 28 ALR 1157. An interval of time between sessions of a religious body. Ellis v State, 10 Ala App 252, 65 So 412.

recession (rę-sesh'ọn). A granting back of property by the grantee to his grantor. A diminution in business activity.

recessus (rę-ses'us). An exit; a going out; an egress.

recessus maris (rē-ses'sus ma'ris). The receding of the sea.
See **reliction.**

recetour (re'ce-toor"). A person who received or harbored a felon or an outlaw.

recettement (re-cet'môn). The receiving or harboring of a felon or an outlaw.

recettour. Same as **recetour.**

rechate. A ransom.

rechater (re'chah-tay"). To ransom.

recidivist (rę-sid'i-vist). One who has relapsed into crime after having been once convicted and punished. An **habitual criminal.**

recidivism (rę-sid'i-vizm). The relapse into crime of one once convicted and punished for a crime.
See **habitual criminal.**

reciprocal (rē-sip'rō-kal). Operating on two sides, the operation on the one side being in return for the operation on the other side.

reciprocal accounts (rę-sip'rō-kal a-kounts'). Same as **mutual accounts.**

reciprocal contract (rē-sip'rō-kal kon'trakt). A bilateral contract, a contract in which the promise of each party forms the consideration for the promise of the other party.

reciprocal covenants (rē-sip'rō-kal kuv'ę-nants). See **mutual covenants.**

reciprocal demands. Demands between two persons, one against the other and the other against the one, as in mutual accounts. 1 Am J2d Acctg § 5.
See **mutuality of parties and demands.**

reciprocal demurrage (rē-sip-rō-kal dę-mėr'āj). A charge imposed against a carrier for the detention of loaded cars beyond a specified period by way of recompense to the shipper for the inconvenience resulting to him from the detention. 13 Am J2d Car § 492.

reciprocal distress. A second distress taken when the first failed because the property was taken out of the jurisdiction to defeat it. 3 Bl Comm 148.

reciprocal easements. See **mutual easements**.

reciprocal exemption. An exemption from inheritance or succession tax of the intangible personal property of residents of other states, conferred by statute in favor of property left by decedents resident in a state which confers a similar exemption to residents of the state in which the statute was enacted. Anno: 42 ALR 333, 394, s. 86 ALR 741, 760; 69 ALR 949, s. 139 ALR 1062. An exemption from inheritance or succession tax granted on a reciprocal basis to foreign charitable institutions. Bendheim's Estate, 100 Cal App 2d 398, 223 P2d 874; Uihlein's Estate, 247 Wis 476, 20 NW2d 120.

reciprocal insurance. A system whereby individuals, partnerships, or corporations, engaged in a similar line of business, undertake to indemnify each other against a certain kind or kinds of losses by means of a mutual exchange of insurance contracts, usually through the medium of a common attorney in fact appointed for that purpose by each of the underwriters, under agreements whereby, as among themselves, each member separately becomes both an insured and an insurer with several liability only. 29 Am J Rev ed Ins § 102.

reciprocal insurance association. An association providing reciprocal insurance to its members. 29 Am J Rev ed Ins § 102.
See **reciprocal insurance**.

reciprocal libel or slander. Defamation of the defendant by the plaintiff arising out of the same transaction as that in which the plaintiff asserts defamation of him by the defendant. 20 Am J2d Countcl § 41.

Reciprocal Enforcement of Support Act. One of the uniform laws. 23 Am J2d Desert § 125. A statute enacted for the purpose of avoiding difficulties in the enforcement of an obligation of support where the person owing the duty has departed from the state in which the dependent resides.

reciprocal mistake. See **mutual mistake**.

reciprocal negative easement. An easement arising from restrictions by covenant limiting the use of land to residential purposes for the benefit of the entire tract, being created on the division of the tract and conveyance in severalty to different grantees of the entire tract. Allen v Detroit, 167 Mich 464, 133 NW 317.

reciprocal remainders. See **cross remainders**.

reciprocal states. Within the meaning of the Uniform Insurers Liquidation Act, states which have adopted the Act. Martin v General American Casualty Co. 226 La 481, 76 So2d 537, 46 ALR2d 1178.

reciprocal statute. A limitation statute of one state which provides that when an action arising in another state is barred therein by limitation, no action thereon shall be brought in the former state except by a citizen thereof who has held the cause of action from the time it accrued. 34 Am J1st Lim Ac § 370.
See **reciprocal exemption; retaliatory statute.**

reciprocal tariff, commerce, or navigation. A matter of stipulation by treaty or trade agreement between nations whereby the one agrees with the other and, in reverse, the other with the one, that either one of them shall have every advantage or favor in reference to customs duties, commerce, and navigation that the other has granted to any other nation. 21 Am J2d Cust D § 10.

reciprocal trusts. Trusts existing where A creates a trust for B and B creates a similar trust for A, A and B usually being husband and wife or members of the same family. Anno: 139 ALR 526; 38 ALR2d 522; 98 L Ed 21.

reciprocal wills. Wills in which the testators name each other as beneficiaries under similar testamentary plans. Anno: 169 ALR 13.
Wills may be strictly reciprocal, each testator leaving his or her entire estate to the survivor, and they may depart from strict reciprocity by including bequest to third persons, without losing their character as "reciprocal" wills. 57 Am J1st Wills § 681.

reciprocity. Interchange of privileges and advantages.
See terms and expressions beginning **reciprocal** or **reciprocity**; also see **mutuality**.

reciprocity between states or nations. An arrangement between states which permits an attorney at law moving from one state to another to be admitted to practice in the latter state without examination. Anno: 51 ALR2d 1198. A matter of relationship between states or nations whereby the recognition in one state or nation of a right under the laws of another state or nation is to be considered in determining whether the latter shall recognize a similar right arising under the laws of the former. Hart v Oliver Farm Equipment Sales Co. 37 NM 267, 21 P2d 96, 87 ALR 962.
No doctrine of comity, in the sense of reciprocity, governs absolutely the action of a court with regard to the enforcement of a foreign right; no foreign right should be refused enforcement merely because it arose in a state, the courts of which do not enforce similar rights created abroad. Restatement, Conflict of Laws § 6, Comment a.
The "reciprocity" rule, whereby a judgment of a foreign country will be given such effect in an American court as the courts of that country would accord to an American judgment, may not be invoked where plaintiffs are not citizens of the United States. Bata v Bata (Sup) 39 Del Ch 258, 163 A2d 493, rearg den 39 Del Ch 548, 170 A2d 711, cert den 366 US 964, 6 L Ed 2d 1255, 81 S Ct 1926.
See **reciprocal tariff, commerce, or navigation.**

reciprocity statute. See **reciprocal statute.**

recital. Detailed statement of fact. The statement in a deed denoting the operative effect of the instrument. A statement of jurisdictional facts appearing in a judgment. 30A Am J Rev ed Judgm § 40. A fault in pleading, the statement being indirect and not positive. 41 Am J1st Pl § 37.

recite. To set forth in detail.
The statute requiring a sheriff's deed to recite the execution is not fulfilled by referring to such execution. Ogden v Walters, 12 Kan 282, 285.

reciting a statute. Quoting or stating in detail the contents of a statute. Hart v Baltimore & Ohio Railroad Co. 6 W Va 336, 348.

reckless. Careless. Disregard or indifference to consequences under circumstances involving danger to life or safety of others. State v Custer, 129 Kan 381, 282 P 1071, 67 ALR 909; State v Mills, 181 NC 530, 106 SE 677.

When applied to negligence, the word has no legal significance which imports other than simple negligence or a want of due care. But in the use of the word in connection with averments of facts to which it refers and explains, it may imply more than mere heedlessness or negligence. Louisville and Nashville Railroad Co. v Anchors, 114 Ala 492, 22 So 279.
See **recklessness**.

reckless driving. A criminal offense; a basis of liability for injury to the person or property of another. Driving under circumstances showing a reckless disregard of the consequences; driving carelessly and heedlessly in wilful or wanton disregard of the rights or safety of others, or without due caution and circumspection and at a speed or in a manner endangering person or property. 7 Am J2d Auto § 263; 26 Am J1st Homi § 215.

recklessness. Indifference to consequences; indifference to the safety and rights of others. Wantonness; more than ordinary negligence. Harrington v Los Angeles Railway Co. 140 Cal 514, 74 P 15; Kansas Pacific Railway Co. v Whipple, 39 Kan 531, 542.
See **reckless**; **reckless driving**.

reckless statement. A statement sufficient in support of an action for fraud and deceit, as made with indifference as to the truth of the representation. 37 Am J2d Fraud § 12.

reclaim. To demand or effect a reclamation.
See **reclamation**.

reclaimed animal. A wild animal taken into possession, custody, and control, such being rendered effective by taming, domesticating, or confining it. 4 Am J2d Ani § 17.

reclaimed land. See **made land**; **reclamation**.

reclamation. Making land fit for cultivation, as by draining swamps, 25 Am J2d Drains § 3, or irrigating arid land. The taking of a wild animal into possession. Anno: 49 ALR 1498; 4 Am J2d Ani § 17. Demanding and obtaining the return of one's property in the possession of another. The retaking of property once abandoned, lost, or mislaid. 1 Am J2d Aband §§ 24, 25, 28, 30, 32. A proceeding in bankruptcy whereby the real owner of property obtains it from the trustee in the estate in bankruptcy. 9 Am J2d Bankr § 1194.

Reclamation Act. A federal statute providing a plan for the reclamation by means of irrigation of arid lands, and for the entry of the reclaimed lands by homesteaders. 43 USC §§ 371 et seq.

reclusion. An involuntary withdrawal from society. Forced confinement. Punishment in being confined in a prison at hard labor, carrying civil degradation. Phelps v Reinarch, 38 La Ann 547, 551.

recognition. Taking notice of. Acknowledgment; admission. Identification from circumstances in one's knowledge. Becoming bound by a **recognizance**.

recognition of bastard (bas′tȧrd). See **recognition of paternity**.

recognition of belligerency (rē″kog-nish′ǫn of be-lij′e-ren-si). The recognition by one country of a state of war as existing between two other countries. The recognition by a government of a force within the country contending with arms against it, thereby rendering that which might have been an insurrection or rebellion a civil war. 56 Am J1st War § 2. An accordance by the political and executive departments of a foreign government of belligerent rights to a body or mass of people engaged in civil war, by which such mass or body are granted the rights and immunities of civilized warfare and assume the burdens thereof. See The Ambrose Light (DC NY) 25 F 408, 412.

recognition of government. Acknowledging the existence as a sovereign nation of a revolting state or province upon its having manifested the ability to sustain its new status as a nation. 30 Am J Rev ed Internat L § 13.

recognition of paternity. Words, acts, or conduct indicating that a child born out of wedlock is one's child. 10 Am J2d Bast § 29.

recognition of superior title. Words, acts, or conduct subordinating one's possession to, or admitting the existence of, a superior title, thereby effectively negativing the character of one's possession as adverse to the holder of such title. 3 Am J2d Adv P § 82.

recognitors (rẹ-kog′ni-tǫrs). Jurors impaneled on an assize of nuisance. Barnet v Ihrie (Pa) 17 Sarg & R 174.

recognizance. An obligation entered into before a court of record or duly authorized magistrate, containing a condition to do some particular act, usually to appear and answer a criminal accusation. A term used interchangeably with **bail bond** in many statutes and court opinions. 8 Am J2d Bail § 2.

recognize. To give recognition.
See **recognition**.

recognizee (rẹ-kog-ni-zē′). The person to whom the promise is made in a recognizance.

recognizor (rẹ-kog′ni-zǫr or rẹ-kon′i-zǫr). A person who binds himself by a recognizance.

recommend. To speak with favor. To advise in favor of a course of action to be taken. In the context of a will, usually the equivalent of a direction to be followed by the executor. Pembroke Academy v Epsom School Dist. 75 NH 408, 75 A 100. A word of command or direction effective to create a precatory trust. Anno: 107 ALR 897. To commit; to entrust; to consign; to give in charge. Ex parte Seward, 299 Mo 385, 253 SW 356, 31 ALR 665, 668.

recommendation for credit. A representation in commendation of another person's credit.
Such a recommendation does not create contractual relations between the parties thereto and the recommending party is not liable for the default of the person whose credit he recommends unless he fraudulently makes the recommendation in order to induce the giving of a credit. See 24 Am J1st Guar § 7.

recommendation for employment. See **service letter**.

recommendation of mercy. A statement by the jury accompanying a verdict of guilty recommending the defendant to the mercy of the court in the sentence to be imposed. 53 Am J1st Trial § 1061.

recommendatory words. See **precatory words**.

recommit. To make a recommitment.
See **recommitment**.

recommittal. See **recommitment**.

recommitment. Returning a convict to prison upon his breach of the terms or conditions of parole. Badgley v Morse, 132 Kan 544, 296 P 344, 74 ALR 1115. Returning a convict to prison upon his violation of the terms of a pardon issued subject to conditions, the effect of the violation being to nullify the pardon, making the situation the same as if no pardon had taken effect. 39 Am J1st Pard § 73. The resubmission of a case to a master or referee, as where his report or decision has been set aside. A. T. Stearns Lumber Co. v Howlett, 260 Mass 45, 157 NE 82, 52 ALR 1125.

recompensation. A Scottish term for the plaintiff's pleading in response to defendant's plea of compensation, that is, a plea of setoff.

recompense (rek'ǫm-pens). A reward; a compensation; a remuneration; a payment for services rendered.

recompense of recovery in value (of rę̄-kuv'ėr-i in val'ū). Judgment for the demandant in a common recovery where the vouchee has disappeared, being for the recovery of lands of equal value. 2 Bl Comm 358.

reconcile (rek'ǫn-sīl). To effect a reconciliation.
See **reconciliation.**

reconciliation. A composing of differences. A resumption of cohabitation by spouses previously living apart. Construing a contract so as to give effect to provisions apparently contradictory or conflicting. Jurors harmonizing their views in deliberations. 53 Am J1st Trial § 911.
"It is quite probable that etymologically the two words ('harmonize' and 'reconcile') are not synonymous, but, as commonly used, they are so nearly equivalent that we are satisfied that the jury have understood the rule of their duty as to conflicting evidence precisely the same whether they were told to harmonize or to reconcile such evidence." Holdridge v Lee, 3 SD 134, 138, 52 NW 265.

reconditioned automobile. An automobile which has been restored, so far as possible, to its original condition by repairs and the replacement of wornout and defective parts.
Where a dealer in secondhand motor vehicles undertakes to overhaul and recondition such vehicles for subsequent sale to the general public, he has the same duty as the manufacturer to exercise reasonable care with reference to the equipment of the vehicle and with respect to ascertainment of its condition, so that it may kept under control and not become a menace to life and limb. Bock v Truck & Tractor, 18 Wash 2d 458, 139 P2d 706.

reconditioning. Restoring an appliance, vehicle, or machine, to its original condition, so far as possible, by repairs and the replacement of wornout and defective parts.

reconduction (rē-kǫn-duk'shǫn). (Civil law.) The renewal of a lease.

reconsideration. The taking up for renewed consideration that which has been passed or acted upon previously. People ex rel. Lawrence v Board of Supervisors, 48 App Div 428, 432, 63 NYS 317. A rehearing. A discussion and consideration in a meeting of a matter previously considered and decided. 19 Am J2d Corp § 628 (meeting of stockholders); 37 Am J1st Mun Corp § 150 (meeting of council of municipality).
See **rehearing.**

reconsideration of bill. The action of a grand jury in considering a charge after having once voted not to indict, after an indictment has been quashed or set aside, or after a new trial has been granted. 27 Am J1st Indict §§ 17-20. The reconsideration by a body of the legislature of a bill which it has passed, the right to which, in the absence of a special rule to the contrary, continues so long as the bill remains in the custody or under the control of the body proposing reconsideration. 50 Am J1st Stat § 89.

reconstruction. The process by which the seceding southern states were reorganized after the War between the States, otherwise known as the Civil War. A rebuilding. A complete rebuilding. The act of constructing again. Goodyear Shoe Machinery Co. v Jackson (CA1 Mass) 112 F 146. Work done upon a structure which has been demolished in whole or in part. Vincent v Frelich, 50 La Ann 378, 23 So 373.
Under statutes authorizing special assessments for the "reconstruction" of street improvements, the word presupposes the nonexistence of the thing to be reconstructed, as an entity; that the thing before existing, has lost its entity. The fact that some of the material or parts which entered into the composition of the original entity are used does not negative the character of an operation as a reconstruction. 48 Am J1st Spec A § 604.
In patent law, the reconstruction of a machine is the rebuilding of it, as distinguished from its repair or replacement. Goodyear Shoe Machinery Co. v Jackson (CA1 Mass) 112 F 146.

Reconstruction Acts (rē-kǫn-struk'shǫn akts). Two acts of Congress passed shortly after the Civil War, in 1867, providing a plan for the re-organization of the state governments of those states of the Union which had seceded from it. Texas v White (US) 7 Wall 700, 19 L Ed 227.

Reconstruction Amendments. Amendments XIII, XIV, and XV to the United States Constitution.

Reconstruction Finance Corporation. A one-time federal corporate body exercising various functions in reference to loans and advances for financing projects under federal state, or municipal law and the rendering of financial assistance to business enterprises, which functions have been transferred to other federal agencies and instrumentalities. 15 USC § 601, note.

recontinuance (rē-kǫn-tin'ū-ạns). The recovery back of an incorporeal hereditament which has been tortiously divested.

reconvene (rē-kon-vēn'). In the civil law, to interpose a counterclaim.

reconvenire (re-kon-ve-nī're). (Civil law.) To plead a cross-demand.

reconventio (re-kon-ven'she-ō). (Civil law.) A cross demand. A counterclaim.

reconvention (rē-kǫn-ven'shǫn). A cross demand. The civil-law equivalent of a counterclaim. 20 Am J2d Countcl § 5.

reconversion. The abandonment, prevention, or frustration of equitable conversion.
After there has been an equitable conversion of land into money or money into land, and before any actual conversion has taken place, that fiction may be abandoned and the property again considered in equity according to its actual character as realty or personalty as the case may be, as a result of the election of the person entitled to the property to take it in its unconverted form. 27 Am J2d Eq Conv § 17.
See **double conversion.**

reconveyance. A conveyance by the grantee under a former conveyance to the grantor in such conveyance.

recoop (rē-köp'). Same as **recoupe**.

Recopilacion (rä-co-pe-lah-the-ón). A compilation of the laws of Spain for the government of the Indies made in 1661 by order of Philip IV.

It is the only authentic collection of the ordinances and decrees governing Spanish-America prior to the year 1860. See Ponce v Roman Catholic Apostolic Church, 210 US 296, 315, 52 L Ed 1068, 1076, 28 S Ct 737.

record. Noun: A memorial and evidence of something written, said, or done. 45 Am J1st Recds § 2. A plate, tape, or wire containing impressions from which sounds are reproduced.

Under the ancient authorities the word signified a roll of parchment upon which the proceedings and transactions of a court were entered and drawn up by its officers. Blackstone gives substantially the same definition. But in the United States, paper has universally supplied the place of parchment as the material for the record. Nugent v Powell, 4 Wyo 13, 33 P 23.

See **court record; index; public record.**

record (rē-kǫrd'). Verb: To recite or repeat in writing; to transcribe; to enter upon a book provided for that purpose. Montgomery Beer Bottling Works v Gaston, 126 Ala 425, 28 So 497. To make a record, to spread the contents of an instrument upon a public record, for example, the copying of an instrument filed for record in a book kept for the purpose in a public office. 45 Am J1st Recds § 65. To file for record in a proper office, as in the case of chattel mortgages and conditional sale contracts. 15 Am J2d Chat Mtg § 81; 45 Am J1st Recds § 67. Making an impression upon plate, tape, or wire of sounds for reproduction by record player or for television.

recordari (rek-ôr-dā'rī). A substitute for an appeal from a judgment of a court not of record, where the appeal has been lost by fraud or accident. Critcher v McCadden, 64 NC 262, 263.

recordari facias loquelam (rek-ôr-dā'rī fā'shi-as lō-kwē'lam). That you cause the plaint to be recorded. See 3 Bl Comm 34.

Recorda sunt vestigia vetustatis et veritatis (re-kor'da sunt ves-ti'ji-a ve-tus-tā'tis et ve-ri-tā'tis). Records are the marks of antiquity and truth.

recordation of verdict. The formal reception of a verdict by the clerk of the court and his entry of the same upon the records of the court with the assent, express or implied, of the jury, thus ending the trial. 53 Am J1st Trial § 1027.

recordatur (re-kor-dā'ter). Let it be entered of record.

record court. See **court of record.**

record date. The date specified in the declaration of a dividend on corporate stock as of which one must be a stockholder of record in order to be entitled to the dividend, the specification of date being for the purpose of determining the right to the dividend as between successive owners of stock. 19 Am J2d Corp § 892.

recorded. See **record.**

recorder. A public officer in charge of the public records of instruments and instruments filed for record, having the duty of making a public record, or of filing as a public record, instruments presented to him for record. An elective county officer in some jurisdictions. In other jurisdictions, a subordinate officer in the office of county clerk or clerk of court.

recorder's court. An inferior court of limited jurisdiction established under legislative authority in a city or town with a jurisdiction which is usually similar to that of justices' courts in civil matters and to that of police courts in criminal cases. Colton v Superior Court, 84 Cal App 303, 257 P 909.

recording. See **record.**

recording acts. See **recording laws.**

recording laws. Statutes which provide for the recording of instruments, particularly instruments affecting title to real estate, and prescribe the manner in which the record is to be made. 45 Am J1st Recds § 65.

recording machine. A machine for recording the words of a person on a wax plate, a steel tape, or wire for later reproduction in sound. 23 Am J2d Dep § 59.

recording officer. See **recorder.**

recording patent. The recording of a patent in the Patent Office, together with the specifications, by way of giving constructive notice to all the world of their existence. Sontag Chain Stores Co. v National Nut Co. 310 US 281, 84 L Ed 1204, 60 S Ct 961, reh den 311 US 724, 85 L Ed 471, 61 S Ct 53.

recording tax. A tax imposed upon the recording of a mortgage, contract, or other instrument relating to real property. 51 Am J1st Tax § 1257.

record notice. Constructive notice of a matter of public record, especially of an instrument of title or mortgage. 45 Am J1st Recds § 85.

recordo et processu mittendis. See **de recordo et processu mittendis.**

record of conviction. A judicial record of the ascertainment of the guilt of a person accused of crime and judgment thereon by the court, implying not only the record of a verdict, but also the record of the court's judgment or sentence thereon. Commonwealth v Minnich, 250 Pa 363, 95 A 565.

See **recordation of verdict.**

record of corporation. See **corporate records.**

record of court. See **court record.**

record of nisi prius (nī'sī pri'us). A transcript of the pleadings in a case handed to the judge who is to preside at the trial.

record on appeal. Those papers and only those papers which the trial court is required to transmit or certify to the appellate court and on which the latter court decides the cause. 4 Am J2d A & E § 397.

record on removal. The copy of the record of the suit in the state court to be filed on removal of the cause to the federal court, consisting of the copies of the process, pleadings, depositions, testimony, and any other proceedings of record in the state court, including the petition for removal. 28 USC § 76; Carson v Dunham, 121 US 421, 30 L Ed 992, 7 S Ct 1030.

record owner. The owner of premises under either a legal or equitable title as such ownership appears from the public records of title. Godwin v Gerling, 362 Mo 19, 239 SW2d 352, 40 ALR2d 1250.

See **title of record.**

record player. An instrument for the reproduction of sounds recorded by impression upon wax plate, wire, or steel tape, much used in the enjoyment of music.

record proper. Those papers, documents, files, minutes and other records which the law requires to form the record of a case, and no others. Hodges v State, 38 Okla Crim 259, 259 P 1056.
See **judgment roll; strict record.**

records and books of account. The serial, continuous, and permanent memorials of a concern's business and affairs, chronologically and systematically kept and arranged. Cudahy Packing Company v United States (CA7 Ill) 15 F2d 133.

record title. See **title of record.**

recordum (re-kor'dum). A record.

record warranty. The warranty by the insured under a policy of insurance upon stocks of goods or merchandise, that he will make and keep inventories and books of account to be kept in an iron or other fireproof safe, or other secure place, and will, upon demand, produce such books and inventories for the inspection of the insurer. 29A Am J Rev ed Ins § 939.

recount. A second canvass of the votes cast at an election for a particular office. 26 Am J2d Elect § 295. An inspection and recounting of votes in a contest of an election. 26 Am J2d Elect § 355.

recoup (rẹ-köp'). Same as **recoupe.**

recoupe (rẹ-kö-pā'). To plead a **recoupment.**

recoupment (rẹ-köp'mẹnt). Literally, a cutting back. Davenport v Hubbard, 46 Vt 200. A deduction from a money claim whereby cross demands arising out of the same transaction are allowed to compensate one another, the balance only to be recovered. National Cash Register Co. v Joseph, 299 NY 200, 86 NE2d 561, 12 ALR2d 812. The right of a defendant, in the same action, to cut down the plaintiff's demand either because the plaintiff has not complied with some cross obligation of the contract on which he sues or because he has violated some duty which the law imposes on him in the making or performance of that contract. 20 Am J2d Countcl § 1.
Recoupment, as distinguished from the offsetting of one transaction against another, means a deduction from a money claim whereby cross demands arising out of the same transaction are allowed to compensate one another and the balance only to be recovered. National Cash Register Co. v Joseph, 299 NY 200, 86 NE2d 561, 12 ALR2d 812.

recoupment theory. A theory sometimes applied in determining the amount of property subject to condemnation under the power of eminent domain, the theory being that if the public body is permitted to take somewhat more than that which is barely necessary for the improvement, it will be able to dispose of parts not needed at favorable prices, thereby recouping much of the cost of the improvement. Cincinnati v Vester (CA6 Ohio) 33 F2d 242, 68 ALR 831, affd 281 US 439, 74 L Ed 950, 50 S Ct 360.

recourse. A seeking of aid or assistance. Resort to a person for satisfaction of a demand. In ordinary legal and commercial usage, resort by creditor or obligee to a surety, guarantor, or indorser for payment, after the default of the principal debtor or person under primary liability. Industrial Bank & Trust Co. v Hesselberg (Mo) 195 SW2d 470.
See **without recourse.**

recourse to law. Invoking the jurisdiction of a court by commencing an action or proceeding.

recousse (rẹ-kös'). Same as **recaption.**

recover. To become well after suffering sickness or disability. To acquire by means of litigation; to acquire as the result of a formal judgment or decree of a court. To receive; to come into possession of. Standidge v Chicago Railways Co. 254 Ill 524, 533, 98 NE 963, 966.
To recover, in law, is to recover anything, or the value thereof, by judgment; as if a man sue for any land, or other thing, movable or immovable, and have a verdict or judgment for him. See Norton v Winter, 1 Or 47.

recoverable. Susceptible of being recovered or regained.
The bankruptcy law provides alternately for the regaining of preferential payments by the trustee, first by visiting the creditor with the danger of a penalty—the disallowance of any portion of his claim; and secondly, in case of the knowing creditor, the right on the part of the trustee to bring suit. In either case the payments are gotten back,—there is a recovery, and in both—whether under stress of the penalty or by virtue of a suit—it is the law that makes them recoverable. Peterson v Nash Brothers (CA8 Minn) 112 F 311.

recoveree (rẹ-kuv-ėr-ē'). A person who suffered a common recovery.

recoverer (rẹ-kuv'ėr-ėr). A demandant who recovered a judgment in a proceeding by common recovery.

recovery. The amount which a claimant ultimately receives under or in consequence of a judgment. United States v Konstovich (CA4 Va) 17 F2d 84. In the usual sense, the amount of damages awarded. In a broader sense, the effect of any judgment rendered in favor of one asserting a cause of action. Receiving or coming into possession of something.
In its general use, the word signifies a recovery had by process and course of law; though in a special case it may mean collected or obtained without suit. It has its ordinary and popular meaning of payment compelled by action in the revenue laws of the state. People v Reis, 76 Cal 269, 279, 18 P 309.
See **common recovery; prior adjudication.**

recovery back. The recovery of a payment made to a person from the person himself. 11 Am J2d B & N §§ 991 et seq.

recovery by double voucher (by dub'l vou'chėr). A form of common recovery wherein the writ was brought against a person to whom a conveyance was made as a matter of form and who vouched the real tenant, the latter vouching the common vouchee.

recovery of judgment. The rendition of judgment in favor of a party, whether plaintiff or defendant. In one sense, obtaining payment or satisfaction of a judgment. Hackett v Hyson, 72 RI 132, 48 A2d 353, 166 ALR 1096, 1098.

recreant (rek'rẹ-ạnt). A disloyal person. One unmindful of duty. A coward.
In the course of a trial by wager of battle, a champion was said to prove "recreant" when he yielded to his adversary and pronounced the "horrible word of craven," which signified disgrace and obloquy, rather than anything determinate in meaning. See 3 Bl Comm 340.

recreation (rē'krē-ā-shon). A radio broadcast dramatizing actual events taken from a prior broadcast. Lobe v Turner (Tex Civ App) 257 SW2d 800; Anno: 15 ALR2d 793.

recreation (rek-rē-a'shon). Amusement, play, or other form of relaxation, by way of refreshment of mind or body.

recreational area or center. A place for indulging in sports, hunting, fishing, photography, or the enjoyment of nature. Sometimes a place of public accommodation. 15 Am J2d Civ R § 29.

A city making large expenditures and receiving only nominal fees in maintaining an indoor community recreational center is engaged in a governmental function. Ramirez v Ogden City, 3 Utah 2d 102, 279 P2d 463, 47 ALR2d 539.

recreational center. See **recreational area or center.**

recredentials (rek-rē-den'shäls). See **letter of recredentials.**

recrimination. A defense in an action for divorce, consisting of the plaintiff's guilt of misconduct which in itself is a ground of divorce. 24 Am J2d Div & S § 226.

re-cross-examination. The re-examination of a witness by the other party after the party who called him has re-examined him following his cross-examination.

It is proper to limit the re-cross-examination of a witness who has been examined and fully cross-examined and subsequently recalled and re-examined in chief, to the matters testified to by the witness on such re-examination. 58 Am J1st Witn § 563.

recruiting. Obtaining persons to strengthen a force, particularly for the armed forces.

Recruiting heretofore usually having been accomplished by getting volunteers, the word is apt to call up that method only in our minds. But recruiting is gaining fresh supplies for the forces, as well by draft as otherwise. See Schenck v United States, 249 US 47, 53, 63 L Ed 470, 474, 39 S Ct 247.

recruiting against the United States. The offense prescribed by federal statute of recruiting soldiers or sailors within the United States to engage in armed hostility against the United States. 52 Am J1st Treas § 11.

recruiting and enlistment service. The service of obtaining recruits and inducting them into the armed forces, coupled with the means, agencies, and instrumentalities adopted for use in the performance of such service. O'Hare v United States (CA8 ND) 253 F 538.

rectatus (rek-tā'tus). Same as "arrectatus," a person who was accused or suspected of crime.

recte (rek'tē). Rightly; properly; correctly; suitably; favorably; duly; well.

rectifier (rek'ti-fī-ėr). One who purifies spirits in any manner, or who mixes them with anything else and sells them under any name.

rectify. To make right. To correct; to amend. To distill. Anno: 108 ALR 1075, 1077-1079. To distill again and again.

To rectify distilled spirits is not to manufacture such spirits. See Commonwealth v Giltinan, 64 Pa 100, 105.

recto (rek'to). See **de recto.**

recto de advocatione. See **de recto de advocatione.**

recto de dote. See **de recto de dote.**

recto deficere. See **de recto deficere.**

recto patens. See **de recto patens.**

rector (rek'tor). A minister of the gospel or priest in charge of a parish.
See **parson.**

rectorial tithes (rek'tor-i-al tīths). Great tithes; tithes of grain, hay, or wood.

rector provinciae (rek'tor pro-vin'she-ē). A Roman provincial governor.

rectory (rek'tor-i). Same as **parsonage.**

recto sur disclaimer (rek'tō sėr dis-klā'mėr). An old writ which lay for the lord of the manor against his tenant upon the tenant's disclaimer of tenure.

rectum (rek'tum). Right; that which is right.
See **anus.**

rectum esse (rek'tum es'se). To be right.

rectum rogare (rek'tum ro-gā're). To pray or petition for that which was right.

rectus in curia (rek'tus in kū'ri-a). Right in court; in good standing in the eyes of the court. Exonerated. Union Bank v Powell's Heirs, 3 Fla 175.

Recuperatio, i. e., ad rem per injuriam extortam sive detentam, per sententiam judicis restitutio (re-kū-pe-rā'she-ō, i. e., ad rem per in-jū'ri-am ex-tor'tam si've de-ten'tam, per sen-ten'she-am jū'di-sis re-sti-tū'she-ō). Recovery, that is, restitution through the judgment of a court of a thing wrongfully extorted or withheld.

recuperatores (re-kū-pe-rā-tō'rēz). Roman judges.

Recurrendum est ad extraordinarium quando non valet ordinarium (re-ker-ren'dum est ad ex-tra-or-di-nā'ri-um quan'dō non va'let or-di-nā'ri-um). Resort or recourse must be had to the extraordinary when the ordinary does not succeed.

recurrent insanity (rē-kur'ent in-san'i-ti). Insanity temporary in character and returning from time to time, resulting from some peculiar transitional condition of the system. Leache v State, 22 Tex Crim 279, 3 SW 539.

recurrent nuisance. A nuisance characterized by injury to another or others of a recurring nature, the harm not being inflicted all at one time. 39 Am J1st Nuis § 131.

recurring employment. Employment to perform a particular service or class of service, somewhat regularly from time to time and with a fair expectation of repetition for a reasonable period. 58 Am J1st Workm Comp § 93.

recusable (rē-kū'za-bl). Open to rejection.
See **irrecusable.**

recusant (rek'ū-zant or rē-kū'zant). A person who refused to admit the ecclesiastical supremacy of the king of England or to attend the English church.

recusatio judicis (re-ku-zā'she-o jū'di-sis). (Civil and ecclesiastical law.) An exception to a judge for suspicion of partiality. See 3 Bl Comm 361.

recusation (rek-ū-zā'shon). Challenging a judge for prejudice or bias. Challenging a judge for disqualification, including a challenge on the judge's own motion. State ex rel. Miller v Aldridge, 212 Ala 660, 103 So 835, 39 ALR 1470. Challenging an administrative officer, or member of an administrative board, conducting a hearing on the ground of disqualification to act. 1 Am J2d Admin L § 67.

recusatio testis (re-ku-zā'she-ō tes'tis). (Civil law.) The rejection of a witness by reason of his incompetency to testify.

red. A primary color. The color at the lower end of the spectrum. In modern parlance, a characterization of a communist or one who favors the creation of a socialist state such as prevails in Russia and its satellite countries. A term susceptible to construction as a person who believes in disobedience to the laws of private property and the appropriation of all such property by the state. Toomey v Jones, 124 Okla 167, 254 P 736, 51 ALR 1066.

red book of the exchequer (red bùk of the ekschek'ėr). A very old record of the English exchequer in which holders of lands were registered.

red cap. A porter at a station of a carrier to assist passengers, especially with their luggage.

Red Cross. A nationwide charitable corporation operating under a charter conferred by Congress, supported by contributions by members and other people of good will, serving the armed forces, and standing ready to furnish relief in disasters, such as hurricanes, earthquakes, and so forth, performing community services such as the collection of blood donations, and also rendering international services of a charitable nature.

Reddendo singula singulis (red-den'dō sin'gu-la sin'-gu-lis). Separate things or matters to be assigned or rendered to separate things or matters. A maxim of construction, meaning that where the sense requires it, and furtherance of the legislative intention, words or clauses in a statute are to be taken distributively. 50 Am J1st Stat § 267.

reddendum (re-den'dum). A clause in a deed used to effect a reservation of an estate in the land granted, for example, the reservation of a life estate. Freudenberger Oil Co. v Simmons, 75 W Va 337, 83 SE 995.

reddere (red'de-re). To return; to render; to come in as revenue or rent.

reddidit se (red'i-dit se). He has surrendered himself, —a form of indorsement on a bail piece when the proper officer has certified that the defendant is in custody.

redditarium (red-di-tā'ri-um). Rent; rental.

reddition (re-dish'ǫn). A surrender; a restoration.

redditus (red'di-tus). A return; a return or compensation for the possession of land; rent.
Under the feudal system, this render, reditus, return or rent, consists in chivalry principally of military services; in villeinage, of the most slavish services; and in socage, it usually consists of money, though it may consist of services still, or of any other certain profit. See 2 Bl Comm 299.

redditus albi (red'di-tus al'bī). Same as **white rents**.

redditus assisus (red'di-tus as-sī'sus). A fixed rent.

redditus capitales (red'di-tus ka-pi-tā'lēz). Chief rents, rents which were paid by a freeholder in full discharge of all service.

redditus nigri (red'di-tus ni'grī). Same as **black rents**.

redditus quieti (red'di-tus qui-ē'tī). Same as **quit-rents**.

redditus siccus. A dry rent; a rent seck. 32 Am J1st L & T § 1040.

See **rent seck**.

red dog. A mining-law term for a by-product of bituminous coal mining.
It is taken out with the coal and dumped and discarded near the pit mouth, where it often takes fire from spontaneous combustion. Used in combination with cement for making fireproof brick and hollow tile. Toupet-Taylor Engineering Co. v Red Dog Mfg. & Supply. Co. (CA3 Pa) 16 F2d 454.

redeem. To make a redemption.
See **redemption**.

redeemable bond. A bond which may be called for payment before its maturity. Fales v Multnomah County, 119 Or 127, 248 P 151.

redelivery. A second delivery of a deed which was invalid on the first delivery, after the cause of invalidity has been removed. 23 Am J2d Deeds § 87. The return of a property seized in replevin to the defendant upon his giving a redelivery bond. 46 Am J1st Replev § 85. A delivery back or restoration of the possession of property which has been delivered up or taken out of a person's possession.
See **covenant to redeliver; reissuance; renegotiation**.

redelivery bond. Same as **delivery bond**.

redemise (rē-dē-mīz'). See **demise and redemise**.

redemption. A recovery back of property by payment of money or performance of other condition. A regaining of property taken from one, as under a mortgage, by paying what is due. Miller v Ratterman, 47 Ohio St 141, 156, 24 NE 496. The obtaining of pledged property by the pledgor from the pledgee upon payment, or tender of payment, of the debt secured by the pledge. 41 Am J1st Pldg & Col § 103. A right granted by statute to the owner, junior lienor, or other person interested in property sold at judicial sale of regaining the property from the purchaser by payment or performance of other conditions prescribed by the statute. 30A Am J Rev ed Jud S §§ 232 et seq. The obtaining by the debtor in execution, lienor, or other person interested of property sold under the writ upon compliance with the conditions prescribed by statute, especially the payment of the amount paid by the purchaser with interest thereon. 30 Am J2d Exec § 522. The equitable right of the mortgagee under a chattel mortgage, or one in privity with him, to obtain the property upon satisfaction of the debt secured, even after condition broken. 15 Am J2d Chat Mtg § 239. The obtaining of one's impounded animal upon payment of the damages caused by it to the property of another and the expenses of impounding and care of the animal. 4 Am J2d Ani § 44.
The right to redeem from a mortgage after a foreclosure sale thereunder is purely statutory, and can be exercised only by those to whom it is given by the statute, and in the method prescribed by the statute conferring the right. 37 Am J1st Mtg § 823.
See **equity of redemption**.

redemptioner. A person redeeming property. A person entitled to redeem, e.g., a junior lienor. Sharp v Miller, 47 Cal 82, 85.

redemptiones (re-demp-she-ō'nēz). Redemptions; ransoms; briberies; heavy fines.

redemption from execution sale. See **redemption**.

redemption from foreclosure sale. A statutory right of the mortgagor, junior lienor, or other person interested in the property, to recover the mortgaged property sold on foreclosure by payment of the price paid by the purchaser at the sale, interest, and other charges, and the performance of other conditions prescribed by the statute. 37 Am J1st Mtg §§ 823 et seq.

redemption from tax sale. An opportunity and procedure provided whereby a former owner, his successors in interest, or anyone having substantial interest in the premises, may defeat a tax sale, although it has been valid and regular in every respect, and revest himself with title as complete and as unqualified as it was before the tax was assessed, by repayment of the amount which the purchaser paid for the property, with interest and costs. 51 Am J1st Tax § 1097.

redemption of bond. See **redeemable bond**; **retirement of securities**.

redemption of money. Paying money of the country for foreign money. Paying current money for bills or coin taken out of circulation.

redemption of pledge. See **redemption**.

redemption of stock. A purchase of its own stock by a corporation and its cancellation of the shares. 18 Am J2d Corp § 282.

redemption of securities. See **retirement of securities**.

redemption on foreclosure. See **redemption**; **redemption from foreclosure sale**.

red flag. A sign of danger. The emblem of revolutionaries who favor the creation of a socialist state such as prevails in Russia and its satellite countries. A symbol of ideas hostile to established order and opposed to organized government. A display which under particular circumstances constitutes a breach of the peace. People v Burman, 154 Mich 150, 117 NW 589.

red-flag legislation. A statute prohibiting the display of a red flag, banner, or device of any color or form whatsoever, in any public place, or in any place of public assembly, or from or on any house, building, or window, as a sign, symbol, or emblem of opposition to organized government, as an invitation to anarchy, or as an aid to propaganda of a seditious character. 47 Am J1st Sedit Etc § 14.

red-handed. In the act of committing the crime.

redhibition (red-hi-bish'ọn). The avoidance of a sale on account of some vice or defect in the thing sold, which renders it either absolutely useless, or its use so inconvenient and imperfect that it must be supposed that the buyer would not have purchased it had he known of the vice. Andrews v Hensler (US) 6 Wall 254, 18 L Ed 737, 739 (referring to statutory definition).

redhibitory defect (red-hib'i-tō-ri dē-fekt'). Such a defect in an article which has been sold as would warrant the purchaser in returning it to the seller.

redhibitory vice (vīs). Same as **redhibitory defect**.

redirect examination. The examination of a witness by the party who called him, after the cross-examination of the witness by the other party, for the purpose of having the witness explain his testimony on cross-examination, his expressions, and motives in using them, the scope of the examination to be confined as a general rule to matters referred to in the cross-examination. 58 Am J1st Witn § 562.

rediscounting paper. A function of banks, particularly federal reserve banks, in taking at a discount the discounted paper of other banks. 10 Am J2d Banks §§ 5, 690. Ordinarily, involving an indorsement as well as a taking at a discount. Dorsey v United States (CA8 Neb) 101 F 746, 749.

redisseisin (rē-dis-sē'zin). A repeated disseisin.

redisseisina. See **de redisseisina**.

redistricting. See **reapportionment**.

reditus. Same as **redditus**.

reditus albi. Same as **white rents**.

reditus assisus. Same as **redditus assisus**.

reditus capitales. Same as **redditus capitales**.

reditus nigri. Same as **black rents**.
See **white rents**.

reditus quieti. Same as **quit-rents**.

reditus siccus. Same as **redditus siccus**.

red light. A stop signal on street or highway.

red-light abatement acts (red-līt ạ-bāt'mẹnt akts). Statutes providing for the abatement of houses of prostitution.

red-light district. The district in a city where houses of prostitution are situated.
See **vice district**.

red man. An American Indian.

redmans (red'mạns). Same as **redmen**.

redmen. Tenants who rendered customary feudal services of riding with or for the lord of the manor.

redobatores (re-do-ba-tō'rēz). Thieves who dyed cloth a different color for the purpose of concealing their thefts.

redocketing. Bringing on an indictment, once held in abeyance, for trial. 27 Am J1st Indict § 23. Restoring to calendar or trial docket a case once dropped from calendar or docket.

redraft (rē-drȧft'). The drawing of a new bill of exchange on the drawer or indorser of a bill which has been protested, by the holder of the original bill. The making of a second draft in the preparation of a will or other instrument.

redraw (rē-drȧ'). To make a redraft.
See **redraft**.

redress (rẹ-dres'). Remedy. Compensation; reparation.

redress of grievances. A matter of constitutional right of assembly and petition. The demand, made by people in assembly, of the legislative body to obtain a change in the laws, the enactment of new laws, or for anything else connected with the powers or duties of the government. 16 Am J2d Const L §§ 353 et seq.

redtape. Forms and routines followed in official business. The panoply of bureaucracy.
"Redtape is order carried to fastidious excess—system run out into trivial extremes; but while no department of practical life should be subject to that infliction, there is scarcely anything in which a due degree of order can be neglected without grave dangers." Webster v Thompson, 55 Ga 432, 434.

redubbers (rẹ-dub'ẽrs). Same as **redobatores**.

reduce. To lessen. To break a thing down into its various elements. To analyze a problem so that it can be solved. To impoverish. To bring to want. Anno: 2 ALR 1265.

reduce a decree. In Scotland, the recall of a decree.

The difference between reponing a decree and having it reduced, appears to be, that on reponing, the pursuer in the original process, must show that the decree was well founded; but when it is not reponed, the defender must show that the decree was ill founded. In both instances, the proceeding to effect the object is the same, by a libel or claim founded upon the original suit and seeking to invalidate its effect. See Monroe v Douglas (NY) 4 Sand Ch 126, 201.

reduced fare. A fare charged a passenger by a carrier at less than the rate fixed by the tariff schedule. A legal fare but less than the regular fare, as one upon an excursion or family ticket.

reduced rate. A charge made by a carrier of freight which is less than that fixed by the tariff schedule. See **reduced fare**.

reductio ad absurdum (rẹ-duk'shi-ō ad ab-sėr'dum). A leading back to an absurdity; an absurd conclusion.

reduction of capitalization. A reduction in the nominal capitalization of a corporation by retiring a portion of the authorized shares, reducing the nominal or par value of the outstanding shares, or the surrender of shares by the stockholders. 18 Am J2d Corp §§ 233 et seq.

reduction of par value. See **reduction of capitalization**.

reduction of sentence. The correction of an excessive sentence. 21 Am J2d Crim L § 536. Amending a sentence to reduce the punishment, even to the extent of placing the defendant on probation. 21 Am J2d Crim L § 571.

See **good behavior**.

reduction of stock. See **reduction of capitalization**.

reduction plant. A place where the bodies of dead animals are taken for the purpose of saving whatever is in them of value, such as hide, tallow, etc.

reduction to possession. The act of taking possession. The act of a husband in reference to his wife's property; some act on the part of the husband evidencing intent to acquire the property to the exclusion of the wife, to divest the right of the wife, and to make the property his own absolutely. 26 Am J1st H & W § 61. Changing an intangible into a tangible, as by collecting a debt.

reduction to practice. The completion of a discovery by putting the product thereof, an invention, to use or practice. 40 Am J1st Pat § 27.

In patent interference proceedings, the law pertaining to a successful reduction to practice is not satisfied by demonstrations which indicate that if subjected to a practical test a device might work, but rather requires the submission of evidence establishing that the device was subjected to a practical test and that it did, in fact work. Jacke v Long, 27 Cust & Pat App 1147, 111 F2d 184.

It is academic that the question of what constitutes reduction to practice in the sense of the patent laws may depend in a large part on the inherent nature of the article under scrutiny, together with the consideration of the use for which it is designed. As, where tests of a metal fishing rod conducted in casting tournaments, were held to establish a reduction to practice though no fish was ever caught with a rod embodying the invention. Heddon v Cowdery, 26 Cust & Pat App 743, 100 F2d 426.

reduction to present worth. See **present worth**.

redundancy (rẹ-dun'dạn-si). Excess, particularly in words. Matter in a pleading not essential to the statement of cause of action or defense. 41 Am J1st Pl § 350. Needless repetition of averments. Including details of evidence by which facts are established. Carpenter v Reynolds, 58 Wis 666, 671, 17 NW 300.

redundant matter (rẹ-dun'dạnt mat'ėr). See **redundancy; surplusage**.

re-energizing. Turning electric current into wires not then energized or following an interruption of service. 26 Am J2d Electr § 111.

re-enter (rẹ-en'tėr). To make or effect a re-entry. See **re-entry**.

re-entry. The return of one previously in the country as a resident alien after a period of voluntary absence from the country, however brief. Bonetti v Rogers, 356 US 691, 2 L Ed 2d 1087, 78 S Ct 976 (32 Tulane L Rev 778). A formal entry upon the leased premises by the lessor upon a declaration by him of a forfeiture of the lease. 32 Am J1st L & T § 870. The resumption of possession pursuant to a right reserved when the former possession was parted with. A remedy given by the feudal law for non-payment of rent, but so ancient that its origin has never been traced.

"If," runs the old law, "a man makes a feoffment, gift, or lease reserving rent, with a condition that if the rent be behind, it shall be lawful for the feoffor and his heirs to re-enter, if the rent be behind, the feoffor or lessor may enter into the lands and hold them in his former estate." Michaels v Fishel, 169 NY 381, 388, 62 NE 425.

See **re-entry for condition broken**.

re-entry for condition broken. The interest which remains in the grantor or his successors, or the successors of a testator, where an estate on condition subsequent has been created. 28 Am J2d Est §§ 188 et seq. Actually, a power of termination rather than a substantial estate. 28 Am J2d Est § 189.

re-establishment of highway. The establishment of a highway previously abandoned or vacated, entailing the same acts and proceedings necessary to create a highway in the first instance. 25 Am J1st High § 127.

reeve (rēv). See **borough reeve; church reeve; land-reeve; shire-reeve; tithing-reeve; trithing-reeve**.

re-exchange. A matter of indemnity to the holder of a bill for the loss he sustains by the failure of the drawee to pay the amount at the time and place, and in the money, called for in the bill. Furness, W. & Co. v Rothe (CA4 Va) 286 F 870, 27 ALR 1185. The amount which the holder of a dishonored bill of exchange would have to pay, in the currency of the country where the original bill was drawn, for a good bill payable where the original bill was payable and for the same amount of money plus the expense of protest. Pavenstedt v New York Life Ins. Co. 203 NY 91, 96 NE 104.

re-execution. The execution of a will previously altered or revoked. 57 Am J1st Wills § 625.

re-execution of lost instrument. See **restoration of lost instrument**.

re. fa. lo. An abbreviation of **recordari facias loquelam**.

refalo. Same as **re. fa. lo.**

refection (rẹ-fek'shọn). Refreshment. Food. A light meal. (Civil law.) Restoration; restitution; redress.

refer. To make a reference. To submit a case to a referee for his decision or report.
To refer a matter imports a reference in the common form; that is, to empower referees to decide, in case of necessity, by a majority, and to proceed upon hearing one party, if the other, being duly notified, shall fail to be present. Billington v Sprague, 22 Me 34, 45.

refer by rule of court. To order a reference.
"An authority to prosecute or defend a suit implies a power to refer it by rule of court, that being a legal mode of prosecuting or defending." See Buckland v Conway, 16 Mass 396.

referee. A person appointed by a court to perform certain offices in the progress of a case pending in the court of his appointment, sometimes trying the issues or part of the issues and reporting findings of fact, at other times trying the case and rendering a decision therein. 45 Am J1st Ref § 3. An officer of the court, sometimes a general officer, at other times a special officer appointed for a particular case. 20 Am J2d Cts § 4. An officer conducting preliminary or original hearings upon claims for workmen's compensation. 58 Am J1st Workm Comp § 454. A term sometimes loosely applied to an auditor appointed to examine accounts or to a person appointed to make a partition or conduct a sale in a partition action.
See **report of referee.**

referee in bankruptcy. A judicial officer invested by the Bankruptcy Act, subject always to review by the judge, with most extensive jurisdiction in bankruptcy matters, judicial as well as administrative duties being delegated to him for the purpose of conserving the time of the judge for other work of the court. 9 Am J2d Bankr § 91. Acting, in his capacity as a referee, as the court, not as a special master, except in respect of a limited number of matters in which determination is restricted to the judge of the court. The court for most purposes in bankruptcy. 9 Am J2d Bankr § 92.

referee in case of need. A person whose name is inserted in a bill of exchange by the drawer or any indorser, as a person to whom the holder may resort in case of need, that is to say, in case the bill is dishonored by nonacceptance or nonpayment.
It is in the option of the holder to resort to the referee in case of need or not, as he may see fit. Uniform Negotiable Instruments L § 131.

referee's report. See **report of referee.**
Sometimes a trial and determination for report of findings to the court, at other times a trial and determination with a decision by the referee. 45 Am J1st Ref § 3.

reference. A trial and determination of issues or questions arising in civil cases by some person appointed for that purpose by the court in which the cause is pending. The act of the court in submitting the issues in a case to the referee.
See **referee.**

reference on consent. The practice of referring by consent of the parties under a rule of the court an action pending therein to a referee appointed by the court to hear and determine the issues in the action and report his decision or findings to the court. Shain v Peterson, 99 Cal 486, 33 P 1085.

reference statute. A statute which refers to an older statute, purporting to make it a part of the new legislation. 50 Am J1st Stat § 36. A statute which declares that a certain designated statute of the United States, such as the Volstead Act, or of another state, shall be the law of the state. Ex parte Burke, 190 Cal 326, 212 P 193; State v Armstrong, 31 NM 220, 243 P 333.

reference to arbitration. See **submission to arbitration.**

referendarius (re-fe-ren-dā'ri-us). A Roman officer who laid the causes of petitioners before the emperor.

Referendo singula singulis (re-fe-ren'dō sin'gu-la sin'gu-lis). The words or expressions should be construed distributively, as distinguished from a collective construction.

referendum (ref-ẹ-ren'dum). The power reserved to the people at their own option to approve or reject at the polls an act of the legislature. 28 Am J Rev ed Init & R § 2. The power of the residents of a municipality to approve or reject at the polls any act of the municipal legislative body. 37 Am J1st Mun Corp § 204. The determination of questions as to certain existing or proposed legislation by reference to a vote of the people, employed in determining questions covering wide ranges, among the more general of which are the adoption of municipal charters, the location of county seats and the incurring of municipal indebtedness. State ex rel. Birchmore v State Canvassers, 78 SC 461, 59 SE 145. The submission of an act of the legislature to the people for approval or rejection in an election. The submission of a foreign ambassador to his government of a proposition in reference to which he requires further authority from his government in order to act in the particular matter.
Provision made by a state legislature for a convention to pass upon a proposed amendment to the Federal Constitution is not a legislative act, and is therefore not within the provisions of the state Constitution for a referendum of any act of the legislature. State ex rel. Tate v Sevier, 333 Mo 662, 62 SW2d 895, 87 ALR 1315.

referendum measure. A measure which has been enacted in due form by the state legislature and thereafter referred to and adopted by the people in whole or in part at an election held for that purpose. Tesoriere v Second Judicial Dist. 50 Nev 302, 258 P 291.

referendum petition (ref-ẹ-ren'dum pẹ-tish'ọn). A petition by a specified number of electors requesting that proposed or enacted legislation, as the case may be, be submitted to the people for their approval or rejection.

refiling. The filing of a pleading previously withdrawn. 41 Am J1st Pl § 318. A requirement in reference to a chattel mortgage, under statute, after a certain period of time, if the mortgage is to be maintained as effective against third persons. 15 Am J2d Chat Mtg § 109.
See **reinscription.**

refinement. Elaboration of statement. Verbiage, frequently found in indictments, in setting forth what is not essential to the constitution of the offense, and therefore not required to be proved on the trial. State v Gallimore, 24 NC (2 Ired L) 372, 377.

refinery (rẹ-fīn'er-i). A plant where raw material is prepared for use, sometimes by separation of ele-

ments, at other times by removing impurities and changing the form of the product.
See **oil refinery**.

refining distilled spirits. The removal, chemical change, or modification of objectionable soluble matter in distilled spirits to alter, in some degree at least, the character or quality of the entire volume of the spirits. Mayes v Paul Jones & Co. (CA6 Ky) 270 F 121.

refining oil. The operation whereby crude oil is split up into a number of commercial products by a process of fractional distillation. 24 Am J1st Gas & O § 123.

reform. To make better by change and correction. To make improvements in the law by legislative acts. To eliminate vice. To become a better person. To proceed for and with the reformation of an instrument. Sullivan v Haskin, 70 Vt 487, 490, 41 A 437.

Reformation. The revolution which took place in the sixteenth century against certain doctrines and practices of the Roman Catholic church, starting out as an attempt to reform the church, but ending with the establishment of Protestant churches. The revolutionary religious movement in the reign of Henry the Eighth in which the Protestants separated themselves from the Roman church.
   The Reformation "opens an entirely new scene in ecclesiastical matters; the usurped power of the pope being now forever routed and destroyed, all his connections with the island cut off, the crown restored to its supremacy over men and spiritual causes, and the patronage of bishoprics being once more indisputably vested in the king." See 4 Bl Comm 430.

reformation of instrument. A remedy of an equitable nature afforded to the parties and the privies of parties to written instruments which import a legal obligation, to reform or rectify such instruments whenever they fail, through accident, mistake, or fraud, or a combination of fraud and mistake, to express the real agreement or intention of the parties. 45 Am J1st Reform Inst § 2.

reformation of policy. The action of the court in changing the terms of an insurance contract or policy to make it express the real agreement or intention of the parties. 29 Am J Rev ed Ins § 338.

reformatory (rẹ-fôr'mạ-tọ-ri). A penal institution, sometimes a state institution, intended as a place of imprisonment or confinement of persons convicted of crimes of a less serious nature who appear to be of a type subject to reformation by a proper course of treatment, education, and discipline during confinement. A penal institution adapted to the reformation of young persons who have committed small offenses or are likely to become outcasts in society. See McAndrews v Hamilton County, 105 Tenn 399, 403, 58 SW 483.
See **house of correction; reform school**.

reform school. An institution, commonly known in modern times as an industrial school, for the reception and care of wayward, incorrigible, or vicious youths, male or female, and to a certain extent, in some jurisdictions, of youths whose parents are incapable or unworthy, in surroundings where they may be taught to be moral and industrious and where they may be freed from the corrupting influence of bad associates. 26 Am J1st House of C § 2.

refraction. See **ocular refraction**.

refresh (rẹ-fresh'). To revive; to stimulate.

refresher (rẹ-fresh'ẹr). One of a series of fees paid to an English barrister at intervals during the progress of a litigation. A course of instruction in a subject previously studied, as often had in preparing for bar examinations.

refreshing memory. Directing the attention of a witness to some particular circumstance, conversation, or declaration that may cause him to recall and relate facts temporarily confused or forgotten. The act of a witness giving testimony in referring to writings or memoranda as an aid to his memory. 29 Am J2d Ev § 876; 58 Am J1st Witn § 578.
   Refreshing of memory by writings or memoranda may be classified into two groups: (1) where the use of the memoranda revives the present recollection of the witness and he testifies therefrom; and (2) where past recollection is recorded in the memoranda but the witness has no independent recollection of the facts and circumstances and is unable, after reference to the memoranda, to recall any distinct recollection thereof, but is able to testify that he once knew the facts and correctly applied them. Anno: 125 ALR 22.

refreshing recollection. See **refreshing memory**.

refreshment stand. A place selling soft drinks, cigars, cigarettes, ice cream, sandwiches, etc., but not meals as such.

refrigerated car. A railroad car cooled by ice or mechanically to render it suitable for transportation of fruit or other products perishable in heat. 13 Am J2d Car § 343.

refrigeration. See **cold storage; refrigerated car**.

refuge. A place of safety. The other state to which a fugitive from justice flees. Ex parte Stanley, 25 Tex App 372, 8 SW 645.
See **house of refuge**.

refugee. A person who, being domiciled in one place, seeks refuge in another country or in another jurisdiction to save his life and property from the destructive consequences of war, revolution, or dictatorship. 25 Am J2d Dom § 47.
See **fugitive from justice**.

Refugee Organization. See **International Refugee Organization**.

Refugee Relief Act. A federal statute of 1953 authorizing the issuance of special nonquota immigrant visas in specified numbers to certain groups of aliens seeking to enter the United States as immigrants. 50 USC Appx §§ 1971-1971q.

refund. Noun: A repayment, as where a public utility returns a part of a rate collected to its customers. The refinancing of an indebtedness. Verb: To return money which a person has received from another to that person. Hayner v Trott, 4 Kan App 679, 684.
See **rebate; refunding bonds**.

refund annuity. An annuity under a contract which provides that upon the death of the annuitant prior to receiving the entire principal in periodical annuities, the balance remaining shall be paid to the estate of the annuitant or designated beneficiary. 4 Am J2d Annui § 1.

refunding bonds. The replacement of one obligation with another, including the selling of new securities for the purpose of redeeming those outstanding. 43 Am J1st Pub Sec § 156. Bonds issued in replacement of outstanding bonds, constituting obligations in themselves for what they purport to be on their face and under the statutes pursuant to which they are issued, being organized extensions and continuations of the obligations replaced. Folks v Marion County, 121 Fla 17, 163 So 298, 102 ALR 659. A form of bond given to obtain the release of attached property from the custody of the officer who served the writ but not from the lien of the attachment. 6 Am J2d Attach § 523. Bonds sometimes required of and given by the legatees and distributees of a decedent's estate in order to protect an executor or administrator from loss arising out of a subsequently occurring deficiency of assets. 31 Am J2d Ex & Ad § 556.

refusal. The denial of a request or demand. The rejection of an offer or of property sought to be delivered. The rejection of an offer of possession.

Although, in its ordinary usage, the word usually imports that a demand has been made upon a person and that in some manner he has signified that he declines to comply with that demand, it is frequently used in the law as signifying a simple failure or neglect to perform a legal duty, and in such case, a failure or neglect to act is held to be a "refusal" to act. Sherman v Credit Finance Corp. 78 Colo 330, 241 P 722.

A tortious refusal to return a check, on the part of the drawee, to the holder or collecting bank, is not necessary to render the drawee liable thereon under the provisions of the Negotiable Instruments Law that where the drawee refuses to return the bill within twenty-four hours, he will be deemed to have accepted it; but mere passive neglect to return is sufficient. See Wisner v First Nat. Bank, 220 Pa 21, 68 A 955.

See **qualified refusal; vexatious refusal.**

refusal of performance. The refusal of the obligee under a contract to accept obligor's performance as constituting compliance with the contract.

Whether or not the owner as party to a building and construction contract is entitled to refuse to accept the performance made by the contractor is to be determined according to objective criteria or, at least, the claim of dissatisfaction must be made in good faith. 13 Am J2d Bldg Contr § 30.

refusal of premises. The right of a lessee under a lease which provides him an option of renewal. Anno: 26 ALR 1416.

refusal to cohabit. See **persistent refusal.**

refusal to plead. Standing mute. 21 Am J2d Crim L § 462.
See **default.**

refusal to receive telegram. See **wilful refusal.**

refuse (rē-fūz'). Verb: To reject. To deny a request or demand. To fail to comply with a demand, as to refuse to pay money when demanded. See Kimball v Rowland, 72 Mass (6 Gray) 224, 225.
See **refusal.**

refuse (ref'ūs). Noun: That which is refused or rejected. Matter or things discarded or thrown away. Useless things. Trash. Matter unfit for use; matter unfit for food. Pantlind v Grand Rapids, 218 Mich 18, 177 NW 302, 15 ALR 280, 285.
See **garbage; offal.**

regalem potestatem in omnibus (re-gā'lem po-tes-tā'tem in om'ni-bus). Regal power in all matters. See 1 Bl Comm 117.

regal fishes (rē'gal fish'es). Same as **royal fishes.**

regalia (re-gā'li-a). Royalties; royal prerogatives. See 1 Bl Comm 241. Insignia and robes of rank. Finery in wearing apparel.

regalia majora (re-gā'li-a mā-jō'ra). Greater royalties or prerogatives; that is, those royalties or prerogatives of the kingdom which appertain to dignity of station. See 1 Bl Comm 241.

regalia minora (re-gā'li-a mī-nō'ra). The lesser royalties or prerogatives; that is, those which are inferior to the regalia majora and which immediately concern the acquisition of money; these are properly fiscal, and relate to the rights of the king's revenue. See 1 Bl Comm 241.

regard. Concern. Kind feeling toward another.
See **court of regard.**

regardant (re-gär'dant). Attached to land so as to pass with a conveyance of land as an incident thereof.
See **villein regardant.**

rege inconsulto (rē'je in-kon-sul'tō). The king not having been advised,—a writ which lay to stay proceedings in any matter which might affect the king's interests, until he could be advised.

regency (rē'jen-si). Rule by a regent. The status of the government or the executive branch of the government during the rule of a regent. The period of the rule of a regent, as demonstrated in expressions such as "regency architecture," "regency painting," etc.

regent (rē'jent). Acting in the place of a king where the king is under mental disability or is too young to rule.
See **regents.**

regents. Officers constituting a board in the control and government of a state college or university. 15 Am J2d Colleges § 11.
See **regent.**

Reges ex nobilitate, duces ex virtute sumunt (rē'jēz ex no-bi-li-tā'te, dū'sēz ex vir-tū'te sū'munt). They chose the kings for their nobility, and the leaders for their bravery. See 1 Bl Comm 409.

reg. gen. An abbreviation of **regula generalis;** and also of **regulae generales.**

Regia dignitas est indivisibilis, et quaelibet alia derivativa dignitas est similiter indivisibilis (rē'ji-a dig'ni-tās est in-di-vi-sī'bi-lis, et kwē'li-bet a'li-a de-ri-va-ti'va dig'ni-tās est si-mi'li-ter in-di-vi-si'bi-lis). Royal power is indivisible, and whatever other power is derived from it is likewise indivisible.

Regiam Majestatem (rē'ji-am maj-es-tā'tem). The "most ancient and authentic book" of Scotland, "containing the rules of their common law." See 1 Bl Comm 95.

regia via (rē'ji-a vī'a). A royal road.

regicide (rej'i-sīd). A person who killed a king or a queen; the crime of killing a king or queen.

regidor (ray-he-dor). A term encountered in Spanish-American grants, signifying a member of the "regimiento," or municipal council of the capital, or seat of administration, of a division or province.

The regidores of a council or regimiento never exceeded twelve in number and held their offices for life. Strother v Lucas (US) 12 Pet 410, 442, note, 9 L Ed 1137, 1149, note.

regimiento (re-ji-mi-en'tō). See **regidor.**

region (rē'jon). An area of the country or of the

world, as the area surrounding the Great Lakes or the valley of Amazon river.

regional banks. A class of banks authorized and organized by the Governor of the Farm Credit Administration, known as "banks for co-operatives," the lending power of which is prescribed by statute, pertaining primarily to the making of loans to co-operative associations. 12 USC § 1134c.

regis. See **forum regis.**

register. Verb: To enroll; to record. To enter one's name as a voter or as a guest at a hotel. To indicate, as by facial expression or movement of a member of the body. Noun: A record. An official record. Re Plumb (Sup) 7 NYS 492. A list of names, such as names of registered voters. People ex rel. Stapleton v Bell, 119 NY 175, 181, 23 NE 523. A device for counting, such as a cash register.
See **federal register; record; registration.**

registered bond. A bond made payable to a particular person whose name is registered on the books of the issuer. Benwell v Newark, 55 NJ Eq 260, 264, 36 A 668.
See **registered security.**

registered letter See **registered mail.**

registered mail. A class of mail established for the transmission of valuable mail matter. A letter properly stamped for registration—that is, having fixed to it stamps representing the established charge for that service as well as the necessary postage—for which upon delivering it to the postmaster, the sender is entitled to a receipt in return, and to have the letter marked with a number, and entered in an appropriate book of record as registered on that day and by that number. 41 Am J1st P O § 43.

registered nurse. A nurse accepted, after an examination, as qualified by education and training, and registered as such.

registered security. A bond or security which specifies a person entitled to the security or to the rights it evidences and the transfer of which may be registered upon books maintained for that purpose by or on behalf of an issuer. UCC § 8—102(1)(c).

registered ship. See **registration of vessel.**

registered stocks. Stocks issued by a state, county, or municipality transferable only on the public record books of the states or municipalities issuing them. Bonaparte v Appeal Tax Court, 104 US 592, 26 L Ed 845.
See **registered security.**

registered tonnage (tun'ăj). The cubical contents of a ship expressed in tons, or the amount of weight which she will carry as entered upon some official record. The carrying capacity of a ship, measured in tons, as stated in the ship's papers under which she is sailing. See Reck v Phenix Ins. Co. 130 NY 160, 164.

registered voter. A person who has been lawfully registered, and who has the present right to vote.
The term does not include persons who may have been entitled to be registered, nor those who have been lawfully registered and are not registered voters at a given time thereafter because, since their registration, they have for some reason become disqualified to vote. Daniel v Claxton, 35 Ga App 107, 108, 132 SE 411.
See **registration of voters.**

register of letters. A book kept in each United States postoffice in which every registered letter received by the office is entered of record by its number on the day of its registration, which book has the character of an official record authorized by law, is therefore admissible in evidence. 30 Am J2d Ev §§ 999, 1000.

register of original writs. An English record of original writs issued.

register of wills. A clerk of the probate court in some jurisdictions.

register's court. The name for a probate court in some states.

Registra Brevium (re-jis'trą brē'vi-um). The registry of writs, an office connected with the English chancery in which were kept the precedents of all the writs. See 1 Pomeroy's Equity Jurisprudence § 21.

registrar. One having the duty of registering a transfer of corporate stock. 18 Am J2d Corp § 408. The functionary of a college, university, or other institution in charge of the enrollment of students. Broadly, any person whose duty it is to keep a register.

registrarius (re-jis-tra'ri-us). An officer in civil-law jurisdictions corresponding to a notary public. 39 Am J1st Notary § 3.

Registrar of Copyrights. The incumbent of a federal office provided by the Copyright Law, vested with duties in keeping and preserving the records of the copyright office, the registration of copyrights, and the deposits of money received as copyright fees. 17 USC §§ 201-208.

registration. The act of registering. The act of a guest at a hotel in signing his name and giving his address upon engaging accommodations. Anno: 19 ALR 533, s. 53 ALR 988; 29 Am J Rev ed Innk § 17.
See **filing; recording; register,** also phrases beginning "registration"

registration for military service. The enrollment of a person subject to call under statutes rendering military service compulsory. 36 Am J1st Mil § 24.

registration of alien. A federal, sometimes a state, requirement, accompanied often with a requirement of fingerprinting, for the purpose of having a record of aliens in the country or the state and a means of identifying them. 3 Am J2d Aliens §§ 111 et seq.
See **Alien Registration Act.**

registration of animal. The entry of an animal, kept as a breeding animal, upon the books of the breeders' association, such entry being for the authentication of the animal as pure-blooded. The entry of a male animal, kept for breeding purposes, on the records of a designated public office as a condition of permission to advertise the animal for service as a sire. 4 Am J2d Ani § 76.

registration of claim to copyright. A step in the perfecting of a copyright, such being accomplished in the office of the Registrar of Copyrights and accompanied by the deposit of two copies of the work. 18 Am J2d Copyr § 55.

registration of criminal. See **criminal registration act.**

registration of land titles. A system for the registration of titles to land, whereby the official certificate of title always shows the state of the title and the person in whom it vested, dispensing with cumbersome abstracts of title and extensive searches of the record. 45 Am J1st Reg L T § 2.

REGISTRATION [1079] REGULA

The system is often called the Torrens system, such name deriving from that of Sir Robert Torrens, who drafted the first registration of title law, enacted in South Australia in 1858. The system spread to the other Australian states, to British possessions, and to England itself. With various modifications it has been adopted in some of the states in this country, the Philippines, and several of the Canadian provinces. 45 Am J1st Reg L T § 2.

registration of patent. See **recording patent.**

registration of stock transfer. The entry of a transfer of shares of corporate stock upon the books of the corporation or of its registrar or transfer agent. 18 Am J2d Corp § 408.

registration of trademark. The registration, under federal statutes, of trademarks used in commerce with foreign nations, or among the several states, or with Indian tribes, and of certain foreign or international trademarks. 52 Am J1st Tradem § 39.

registration of vessel. The entry of a vessel upon a register provided for by federal statute for the purpose of declaring her nationality when engaged in trade with foreign nations and to enable her to assert that nationality wherever found. 46 USC §§ 11 et seq.; 48 Am J1st Ship § 47.
See **enrollment of vessel; registered tonnage.**

registration of voters. A method of determining beforehand who is eligible to vote at any given election. State ex rel. Walker v Bridges, 27 NM 169, 199 P 370. A process in which applicants furnish information respecting age, residence, literacy, and any other matter affecting the qualification for voting, and sign their names in the book in which such information is recorded by way of authentication of the information and as a means of identification when they appear on election day to vote. 25 Am J2d Elect § 105.

registration receipt card. A card given to an alien upon his registration as required by law, which card he must at all times carry with him and have in his personal possession. 3 Am J2d Aliens § 112.

registration tax. Same as **recording tax.**

registrum librum (re-jis'trum li'brum). The register book of the English chancery court.

registrum omnium brevium (re-jis'trum om'ni-um brē'vi-um). A register of all writs; the register of such writs as were suable out of the king's courts. See 3 Bl Comm 183.

registry. See **register; registration.**

registry of ship. The registration of a vessel in the foreign trade which endows it with national character. 48 Am J1st Ship §§ 46 et seq.
See **registration of vessel.**

reg. lib. An abbreviation of **registrum librum.**

Regnal years of British Sovereigns:
William I, Oct. 14, 1066 to Sept. 9, 1087.
William II, Sept. 26, 1087 to Aug. 2, 1100.
Henry I, Aug. 5, 1100 to Dec. 1, 1135
Stephen, Dec. 26, 1135 to Oct. 25, 1154.
Henry II, Dec. 19, 1154 to July 6, 1189.
Richard I, Sept. 23, 1189 to Apr. 6, 1199.
John, May 27, 1199 to Oct. 19, 1216.
Henry III, Oct. 28, 1216 to Nov. 16, 1272
Edward I, Nov. 20, 1272 to July 7, 1307.
Edward II, July 8, 1307 to Jan. 25, 1327.
Edward III, Jan. 25, 1327 to June 21, 1377.
Richard II, June 22, 1377 to Sept. 30, 1399.
Henry IV, Sept. 30, 1399 to Mar. 20, 1413.
Henry V, Mar. 21, 1413 to Aug. 31, 1422.
Henry VI, Sept. 1, 1422 to Mar. 4, 1461.
Edward IV, Mar. 4, 1461 to Apr. 9, 1483.
Edward V, Apr. 9, 1483 to June 26, 1483.
Richard III, June 26, 1483 to Aug. 22, 1485.
Henry VII, Aug. 22, 1485 to Apr. 21, 1509.
Henry VIII, Apr. 22, 1509 to Jan. 28, 1547.
Edward VI, Jan. 28, 1547 to July 6, 1553.
Mary, July 6, 1553 to Nov. 17, 1558.
Elizabeth, Nov. 17, 1558 to Mar. 24, 1603.
James I, Mar. 24, 1603 to Mar. 27, 1625.
Charles I, Mar. 27, 1625 to Jan. 30, 1649.
The Commonwealth, Jan. 30, 1649 to May 29, 1660.
Charles II, May 29, 1660 to Feb. 6, 1685.
James II, Feb. 6, 1685 to 1688.
William III and Mary, Feb. 13, 1689 to Mar. 8, 1702.
Anne, Mar. 8, 1702 to Aug. 1, 1714.
George I, Aug. 1, 1714 to June 11, 1727.
George II, June 11, 1727 to Oct. 25, 1760.
George III, Oct. 25, 1760 to Jan. 29, 1820
George IV, Jan. 29, 1820 to June 26, 1830.
William IV, June 26, 1830 to June 20, 1837.
Victoria, June 20, 1837 to Jan. 22, 1901.
Edward VII, Jan. 22, 1901 to May 7, 1910.
George V, May 7, 1910 to Jan. 20, 1936.
Edward VII, Jan. 20, 1936 to Dec. 11, 1936.
George VI, Dec. 11, 1936 to Feb. 6, 1952.
Elizabeth II, Feb. 6, 1952 to —.

regnant (reg'nạnt). Same as **regent.**

regnum ecclesiasticum (reg'num e-klē-si-ās'ti-kum). The ecclesiastical kingdom.

Regnum non est divisibile (reg'num non est di-vi-si'bi-le). The kingdom is not divisible.

reg. orig. Abbreviation of **register of original writs.**

regrant. To grant again property once granted but returned to the grantor by forfeiture or otherwise by operation of law.

regrating (re-grāt'ing). Manipulation in buying and selling a commodity for the purpose of controlling the price. Precisely, the buying of a commodity in a market and selling it in the same market, or within four miles of the place, for the purpose of controlling the price. 36 Am J1st Monop etc § 20.

regress (rḗ'gres). A returning; a going back. A reentry. A privilege of re-entry or return.

regula (reg'ụ-lạ). A rule.

regula Catoniana (re-gū'la kā-tō-ni-ā'na). (Roman law.) The rule of Cato regulating the testamentary disposition of property.

regulae generales (re-gū'lē je-ne-rā'lēz). General rules and orders of the English courts.

regulae juris (re-gū'lē jū'ris). Rules of law.

Regula est, juris quidem ignorantiam cuique nocere, facti vero ignorantiam non nocere (re-gū'la est, jū'ris qui'dem ig-no-ran'she-am kī'kwe no-sē're, fak'tī ve'rō ig-no-ran'she-am non no-sē're.). The rule is that a person's ignorance of the law may render him guilty, but that his ignorance of fact will not.

regula generalis (re-gū'la je-ne-rā'lis). Singular of **regulae generales.**

Regula pro lege, si deficit lex (re-gū'la prō lē'je, sī de'fi-sit lex). In default of the law, the maxim rules.
This maxim applies in determining whether a widow, under the circumstances of the case, was entitled to dower. Chrisman v Linderman, 202 Mo 605, 100 SW 1090.

regular. Conforming to an established rule, principle, or custom. Myers v Rasback (NY) 4 How Pr 83, 85. Consistent. Following a fixed procedure or schedule. Acting or happening at uniform intervals. Guillara v Liquor Control Com. 121 Conn 441, 185 A 398, 105 ALR 563.

See **irregular; regularly.**

Regular Army. The part of the Armed Forces maintained as a permanent establishment for service on land in both war and peace.

As used in a benefit certificate providing that, if the insured shall engage in the occupation of a soldier in the "regular army" in time of war, the insurer should be liable only for a limited sum, the term was held to mean all soldiers in the military service of the United States in time of war, and to include a member of the National Guard while he was in the service of the United States in time of war; and that the term was not to be construed with reference to the Federal statutes classifying the military organizations of the United States. Anno: 15 ALR 1283.

regular care of physician. Continuous medical care considering the nature of the injury and the progress of the patient, not necessarily indicating medical treatment during all that time. 29A Am J Rev ed Ins § 1534.

regular clergy. Members of the clergy who belonged to some monastery or religious house, as distinguished from members of the secular clergy who did not.

regular dealer in securities. A person or corporation licensed to deal and actually dealing with the general public in the purchase and sale of securities. Trading Associates Corp. v Magruder (CA4 Md) 112 F2d 779. A merchant of securities, whether an individual, partnership, or corporation, with an established place of business, regularly engaged in the purchase of securities and their resale to the public. Internal Revenue Code § 1236(c).

regular deposit. A bailment, the agreement being to return the very thing deposited.

regular dividend. The ordinary dividend paid by a corporation, as distinguished from an extra dividend or a stock dividend. 19 Am J2d Corp § 810.

regular election. For most, although not all, purposes the same as a **general election.**

The expression does not necessarily mean general election, or township election, or any state, county, city, or district election. It simply means the regular election prescribed by law for the election of the particular officer to be elected. People v Budd, 114 Cal 168, 45 P 1060.

The words "regular general election" may mean an election at which officers are to be regularly elected or "regular" may be used merely to exclude special elections, or it may be used synonymously or interchangeably with the word "general." Allen v State, 14 Ariz 458, 130 P 1114.

regular employment. Employment for a definite and more or less extended period of time; or of a continuing nature, although for no definite period. 58 Am J1st Workm Comp § 92. The consistent employment of a working force by an industry over a given period of time. Jones v Cochran, 46 Ga App 360, 167 SE 751. The consistent employment of a given number of persons. Anno: 81 ALR 1233.

See **regularly employed.**

regular general election. See **regular election.**

regular indorsement. An indorsement of a bill or note for the purpose of transferring title to the instrument.

See **irregular indorsement.**

regulariter (re-gū-lā'ri-ter). Regularly; according to some rule or regulation.

Regulariter non valet pactum de re mea non alienanda (re-gu-lā'ri-ter non va'let pak'tum dē rē me'a non ā-li-ē-nan'da). According to rule, an agreement that I shall not alienate my property is not valid.

regularity of official acts. The validity, reasonableness, and correctness of the act of an administrative agency. 2 Am J2d Admin L §§ 748 et seq.

See **presumption of regularity.**

regularly. In a regular manner; in a way or method accordant to rule or established mode; in uniform order; methodically; in due order. Belleville v Citizens' Horse Railway Co. 152 Ill 171, 38 NE 584.

See **regular.**

regularly employed. Employed on a permanent rather than a special or temporary basis. Customarily employed.

See **regular employment.**

regularly organized bank. A bank organized either under state law or under an act of Congress. Not inclusive of a private bank. 42 Am J1st Pub F § 12.

regular meeting. A stated meeting of the directors of a corporation or of the stockholders, that is, a meeting at a time and place provided by charter, bylaw, or statute. Such a meeting of a board or other body as the law requires to be held at a stated time and place. State, ex rel. Cline, v Wilkesville Township, 20 Ohio St 288, 293. The stated meeting of an association, club, society, or fraternal body.

regular on its face. A negotiable instrument without defect appearing on the instrument itself. 12 Am J2d B & N § 1198.

Process is said to be regular on its face when it proceeds from a court or body having authority of law to issue process of that nature, and which is legal in form and contains nothing to notify or fairly apprise anyone that it is issued without authority. Pankewiscz v Jess, 27 Cal App 340.

regular panel. The panel of jurors called for service during a term of court. 31 Am J Rev ed Jury § 74.

See **panel.**

regular party. See **proper party.**

regular passenger train. A train engaged in carrying passengers, running regularly upon an advertised time card of the company, and equipped as are all other passenger trains. Illinois Central Railroad Co. v People, 143 Ill 434, 33 NE 173.

regular proceeding. An action, whether given by the common law or provided by statute, which is prosecuted by and against proper parties and according to the established form of proceeding and rules of practice. Myers v Rasback (NY) 4 How Pr 83, 85.

regular rate. For the purposes of the provision of the Fair Labor Standards Act relating to overtime compensation, the hourly rate actually paid for the normal nonovertime work week. Walling v Helmerich & Payne, 323 US 37, 89 L Ed 29, 65 S Ct 11.

regulars. Soldiers in the Regular Army. (Ecclesiastical.) Persons who were attached to, and followed, the rites of some religious order.

regular session. A session of a legislative or other body required by law to be held, or an adjournment thereof. Waterville v County Comrs. 59 Me 80, 88.

regular term. A term of court begun at the time appointed by law, and continued, at the discretion of the court, to such time as it may appoint, consistent with law. Wightman v Karsner, 20 Ala 446, 452.

regular use of automobile. The use of an automobile which is not casual or incidental, but consistent. Allowing for variation in time, place, and purpose on the particular occasions upon which the car was driven. Pacific Auto. Ins. Co. v Lewis, 56 Cal App 2d 597, 132 P2d 846.

As to "regular use" within the meaning of a clause of an automobile insurance policy excluding from coverage under a drive-other-cars clause an automobile owned or hired by, or furnished to, the named insured for regular use, see 7 Am J2d Auto Ins § 106.

regulate. To replace confusion with order. To control or direct. To place and enforce limitations and restrictions upon conduct. Nichols v Yandra, 151 Fla 87, 9 So 2d 157, 144 ALR 1351; Thielen v Kostelecky, 69 ND 410, 287 NW 513, 124 ALR 820. To foster, protect, control and restrain. 15 Am J2d Com § 64 (regulation of commerce.)

The power to regulate does not include the power to prohibit. "To regulate" is not synonymous with "to prohibit." People v Gadway, 61 Mich 285, 28 NW 101.

regulation. Control or direction by restriction or rule of something permitted or suffered to exist. 30 Am J Rev ed Intox L § 22. Any rule for the ordering of affairs, public or private, whether by statute, ordinance, or resolution. Kepner v Commonwealth, 40 Pa St 124, 129. The control by authority of a public service corporation in reference to service, charges, and other matters in its operations involving public interest. Boston & M. R. Co. v Hooker, 233 US 97, 58 L Ed 868, 34 S Ct 526. Madison v Southern Wisconsin R. Co. 156 Wis 352, 146 NW 492, 10 ALR 910. A qualification, restriction, or limitation modifying or destroying the original act with which it is connected, or defeating, terminating, or enlarging an estate granted. See Re Russell, 163 Cal 668, 126 P 875.

See **police power.**

regulation charge. The fee imposed for a license required under the police power, as distinguished from a license tax. 33 Am J1st Lic § 43.

regulation of commerce. Regulation of interstate and foreign commerce by Congress under Article I, section 8, clause 3 of the United States Constitution by way of protection, control, and restraint, with appropriate regard for the welfare of those who are immediately concerned and of the public at large. Second Employers' Liability Cases, 223 US 1, 56 L Ed 327, 32 S Ct 169.

It is sometimes difficult to define the distinction between that which affects or influences and that which regulates commerce. Hannibal and St. Joseph Railroad Co. v Husen, 95 US 465, 470, 24 L Ed 527, 530. A plenary power of Congress, complete in itself, as broad as the economic needs of the nation, and subject to no limitations except the prohibitions and limitations of the United States Constitution and the amendments thereto. 15 Am J2d Com § 8.

regulations of the Navy (reg-ū-lā′shǫns ov the nā′vi). Rules governing the officers and men of the United States navy, established by the secretary of the navy with the approval of the President, under authority of the Congress. Ex parte Reed, 100 US 13, 22, 25 L Ed 538, 539.

regulatory license. A license required as a matter of promoting public health, safety, or welfare, rather than as a revenue measure.

rehabere facias seisinam (re-ha-bē′re fā′she-as sē′sinam). You cause him to have back his seisin,— a writ which lay to compel a sheriff to repossess a plaintiff after the sheriff had seised the defendant of more land than he should under a habere facias seisinam.

rehabilitate (rē-hạ-bil′i-tāt). To effect a rehabilitation.

See **rehabilitation.**

rehabilitation. The restoration of a sick or disabled person to health and good physical condition. The restoration of a drug addict to abstinence and useful life. 25 Am J2d Drugs § 74. The restoration of one convicted of a crime to a respected and useful position in society, often by putting him on probation. Logan v People, 138 Colo 304, 332 P2d 897; State v Summers, 60 Wash 2d 702, 375 P2d 143. The restoration of a failing business to a sound financial position, as by composition, arrangement, reorganization, or readjustment of indebtedness. 9 Am J2d Bankr §§ 1279 et seq.

See **vocational rehabilitation.**

rehearing. A new hearing and a new consideration of the case by the court in which the suit was originally heard, and upon the pleadings and depositions already in the case. Read v Patterson, 44 NJ Eq 211, 10 A 385. A hearing granted by an appellate court wherein there may be presented errors of law or fact, or both, asserted to have been committed by it, to the end that it may revise its own action erroneously or mistakenly taken and modify or set aside its own judgment. 5 Am J2d A & E § 978. A second consideration of a motion by the court. 37 Am J1st Motions § 18. A reconsideration by an administrative agency of a determination previously made by it. 2 Am J2d Admin L §§ 520 et seq.

See **new trial.**

rehearing on appeal. See **rehearing; trial de novo.**

rei (re′ī). Plural of **reus.**
See **forum rei.**

rei adjudicatae. See **exceptio rei adjudicatae.**

Rei depositae proprietas apud deponentem manet, sed et possessio (re′ī de-po′zi-tē prō-prī′e-tās a′pud de-pō-nen′tem ma′net, sed et po-ze′she-ō). The property and also the possession in a thing deposited remain in the depositor.

rei gestae. See **forum rei gestae.**

reimburse. To place in a treasury, as an equivalent for what has been taken, lost, or expended; to refund; to pay back; to restore; as to reimburse the expenses of a war. State ex rel. Sayre v Moore, 40 Neb 854, 59 NW 755. To replenish the funds of a person after payments made by him. To make good losses suffered.

See **contribution; indemnify; restitution.**

reindictment. An indictment on a charge covered by prior indictment which has been quashed or set aside by the court or after the granting of a new trial. 27 Am J1st Indict §§ 18, 19.

reine (rēn). A queen.

reinlistment. See **enlistment.**

re-inscription. The recording of a mortgage within a certain number of years, as provided by statute, from the date of its original inscription or recording, or from the date of the maturity of the obligation secured. 45 Am J1st Recds § 50.

reinstate. To effect a reinstatement.
See **reinstatement.**

reinstatement. Restoration of a person or a thing from a position from which he or it has been removed. South v Commissioners of the Sinking Fund, 86 Ky 186, 190, 5 SW 567. The act of an employer in taking back an employee previously discharged. Restoration of a civil service employee to his former position following his removal, suspension, or transfer to another position. 15 Am J2d Civ S § 42. Restoration to membership in a body, such as a labor union. 31 Am J1st Lab §§ 67, 68. The restoration of membership in a mutual benefit society following a lapse, suspension, or expulsion. 36 Am J2d Frat O § 74. An order for the continuation of an action following a dismissal or nonsuit, 24 Am J2d Dism § 79, leaving the case in the position in which it stood prior to the dismissal or nonsuit.

To reinstate a case means simply to place again in the position enjoyed prior to dismissal. An order of court granting a motion to reinstate the case does not say that the plaintiff shall be permitted to file a new complaint, or that he shall be entitled to a new trial. United States v Green (CA9 Mont) 107 F2d 19.

reinstatement of action. See **reinstatement.**

reinstatement of appeal. The restoration of a case to the appellate court calendar following a dismissal of the appeal. 5 Am J2d A & E § 928.

reinstatement of bankruptcy proceeding. A remedy of a creditor not given notice of an application for the dismissal of an involuntary proceeding for adjudication, upon which application a dismissal was ordered. 9 Am J2d Bankr § 266. The restoration of an ordinary bankruptcy proceeding upon the failure of a reorganization or arrangement proceeding obtained in the original bankruptcy proceeding.

reinstatement of case. See **reinstatement.**

reinstatement of employee. See **reinstatement.**

reinstatement of indictment. Proceeding under an indictment following a dismissal of the prosecution, such being allowed under special circumstances, as where the order of dismissal remains within the control of the court. 27 Am J1st Indict § 22. Bringing on for trial an indictment previously passed to the files. 27 Am J1st Indict § 23.

reinstatement of member. See **reinstatement.**

reinstatement of policy. The revival of a policy of insurance after it has lapsed or become forfeited, especially a forfeiture for the nonpayment of premiums, pursuant to a provision for revival contained in the policy and the performance of such conditions as are imposed by such provision, or pursuant to the agreement of the parties. 29 Am J Rev ed Ins § 368.

There is a difference of opinion whether the reinstatement of an insurance policy constitutes a new contract. 29 Am J Rev ed Ins § 369.

reinsurance. A contract whereby one party, the reinsurer, agrees to indemnify another, the reinsured, either in whole or in part, against loss or liability which the latter may sustain or incur under a separate and original contract of insurance with a third party, the original insured. A term inclusive, in its broad sense of a contract between two insurers by which one assumes the risk of the other and becomes substituted to its contract, so that on the assent of the original policy holder the liability of the first insurer ceases and that of the second is substituted. A contract by which an insurance company, in consideration of the transfer of the policies or assets of a company which is insolvent or wishes to retire from business, assumes all or certain liabilities of the latter company, or a contract by which, as the result of the consolidation or merger of two or more companies, the surviving company assumes the risk of its predecessors. 29A Am J Rev ed Ins § 1747.

reinsurance reserve. A fund required by statute of an insurance company for the protection of its policyholders, such to be applied in the event of the insolvency or dissolution of the company to the reinsurance of outstanding risks carried by the company. 29 Am J Rev ed Ins § 56.

rei interventus (rē'ī in-ter-ven'tus). An intervening circumstance; a circumstance creating an estoppel against one of the parties.

Reipublicae interest voluntates defunctorum effectum sortiri (re-ī-pub'li-sē in'ter-est vo-lun-tā'tēz dēfunk-tō'rum ef-fek'tum sor-tī'rī). It is of interest to the state that the wishes of those who are dead should receive their effect.

rei sitae. See **forum rei sitae.**

reissuable notes. Bank notes capable of reissue for circulation as money after they had once been paid.

reissuance of instrument. The issuance of a bill or note by the maker or acceptor who has acquired the instrument by its renegotiation back to him. 11 Am J2d B & N § 527.

reissuance of patent. The issuance of new letters patent upon surrender of the old. 40 Am J1st Pat § 108.

A patent is granted to secure certain rights to inventors for a limited time. A reissued patent is one which merely secures those rights more definitely in some particular wherein the original patent was defective. A reissued patent has the same standing in law as an original patent. See Ingersoll v Holt (CC Cal) 104 F 682, 683.

reissued abstract. An abstract of title prepared for one person but issued and delivered to another person. Phoenix Title & Trust Co. v Continental Oil Property, 43 Ariz 219, 29 P2d 1065.

reissued patent. See **reissuance of patent.**

Rei turpis nullum mandatum est (rē'ī ter'pis nul'lum man-dā'tum est). (Civil law.) The mandate of an immoral thing is a nullity.

rei venditae et traditae. See **exceptio rei venditae et traditae.**

reject. To throw away; to discard; to refuse to receive; to refuse to grant, as to reject a prayer or request. Preston v Fidelity Trust & Safety Vault Co. 94 Ky 295, 302, 22 SW 318.

A claim of a creditor is said to have been rejected when, after having been presented in due form to the proper officer for allowance or approval as a valid claim, it has been disallowed by that officer in the manner provided by law. Such rejection is often made a condition precedent to the maintenance of an action to establish the claim. Fidelity & Deposit Co. v State Bank of Portland, 117 Or 1, 242 P 823.

rejection of call. The rejection by the court of a call of a boundary where there is another call with which it can not be reconciled. 12 Am J2d Bound § 66.

rejection of claim. The disallowance of a claim.

rejection of offer. Any act or word of the offeree indicating that he declines the offer or justifying the offeror in inferring that the offeree intends not to accept the offer or give it further consideration. 17 Am J2d Contr § 39.

rejoin (rē-join'). To file a rejoinder to a plaintiff's replication. See 3 Bl Comm 310.

rejoinder. A pleading by the defendant in response to the plaintiff's replication or reply. 41 Am J1st Pl § 181.

rejoining allegation (rē-join'ing al-ē-gā'shọn). The pleading in an ecclesiastical testamentary cause corresponding to the common-law replication.

rejoining gratis (rē-join'ing grā'tis). The pleading of a rejoinder without notice or demand from the plaintiff.

rel. Abbreviation of **relatione**.
See **ex rel.**

related. Having a relationship, whether by blood or consanguinity, or in a business or professional capacity.
As employed in a provision permitting persons "related to" a member of a benefit society to be named as beneficiaries in a benefit certificate of the society, the words were held to include relatives by affinity as well as by blood. Bennett v Van Riper, 47 NJ Eq 563, 22 A 1055.
See **relations; relatives.**

related claims. Claims resting upon facts substantially identical. Landstrom v Thorp, 189 F2d 46, 26 ALR2d 1170.

related taxpayers. Taxpayers so related by blood, business, corporate, trust, or fiduciary connections, as such are prescribed specifically by statute, that one of them, as an accrual basis taxpayer, is not entitled to take a deduction from earnings for items of expense due the other as a cash basis taxpayer. Internal Revenue Code § 267 (a) (2).

Relatio est fictio juris et intenta ad unum (rē-lā'she-ō est fik'she-ō jū'ris et in-ten'ta ad ū'num). Relation is a fiction of the law and is intended for one purpose.

relation. See **related; relations; relatives.**

relation back. The principle by which an act done at one time is considered by a fiction of the law to have been done on a preceding date. Operative effect of a deed as of a date prior to execution and delivery of the instrument. 23 Am J2d Deeds § 286. The doctrine that the final delivery of an instrument in escrow relates back to and takes effect at the time of the original deposit in escrow. 28 Am J2d Escr § 29. The principle that where a person takes by execution of a power of appointment, he takes, under the authority of the power, as if the power and the instrument executing the power had been incorporated in one instrument, the title resting on the act creating the power and taking effect as of the date of the instrument which conferred the power. 41 Am J1st Pow § 70. The principle that the recording of an instrument is deemed in law to have been done on the day the instrument was filed for record in the recorder's office, although he did not actually copy the instrument upon the record until several days later. Gibson v Chouteau (US) 13 Wall 92, 20 L Ed 534. A principle unsuccessfully asserted as the basis of guilt of burglary where the entry, as by an employee servant, or lodger, was lawful but an intent to steal was formed in the mind of such a person after gaining entrance. 13 Am J2d Burgl § 9.
See **retrospective operation.**

relatione. See **ex relatione.**

relation of debtor and creditor. See **debtor and creditor relation.**

relation of physician and patient. See **physician and patient.**

relations. Family connections. Business, professional, or social connections.
When used in wills, the word is ordinarily construed as including relatives by consanguinity, and excluding relatives by affinity, unless a contrary intention is manifested. The term "relations" or "blood relations" in wills generally means such persons as take under the statute regarding the distribution of estates of intestates, but it may include those who actually are related by blood although they could not inherit from him because of the disqualification of illegitimacy. 57 Am J1st Wills § 1391.
As to who are "relations" with the meaning of an anti-lapse statute, see Anno: 19 ALR 2d 1159; 57 Am J1st Wills § 1442.
See **degrees of kinship; industrial relations; relatives.**

relations by affinity. See **affinity.**

relations by blood. Persons related by having the blood of a common ancestor. Anno: 10 ALR 864.
See **collateral kinsmen; consanguinity; kin; nearest bloodkin; nearest blood relatives.**

relationship. See **affinity; blood; cognates; cognation; consanguinity; relation; relations.**

relations of the half blood. See **half blood.**

Relatio semper fiat ut valeat dispositio (re-lā'she-ō sem'per fi'at ut va'le-at dis-pō-zi'she-ō). Reference should always be so made that a testamentary disposition may be effective.

relative. Adjective: Dependent upon or to be considered with reference to something else. Relevant; pertinent. Noun: A relation by blood or affinity.
See **relations; relatives.**

relative confession. A confession where the accused confesseth and appealeth others thereof, thereby to become an approver.
If on this appeal the approver is successful, he receives pardon; if he is not successful he is convicted upon his confession, that is, upon his testimony against himself. State v Willis, 71 Conn 293, 309, 41 A 820.

relative convenience doctrine. The principle that upon an application for injunction, the court shall consider and weigh the relative convenience and inconvenience and the comparative injuries to the parties and to the public which would result from the granting or refusal of the injunction sought, the essential concept being that the court is not bound to make a decree which will do more mischief and wreak greater injury than the wrong which it is asked to redress. 28 Am J Rev ed Inj § 52.

relative fact. A circumstance; a fact which relates to another fact.

relative impediment (im-ped'i-ment). A bar to the marriage of certain related persons to each other, because of their relationship.

relative powers (pou'ėrs). Powers which relate to land.

relative revocation. See **dependent relative revocation**.

relative rights. The right of one person considered in reference to the right of another, most vividly illustrated in reference to the use of the highway by particular persons or by particular vehicles. 25 Am J1st High §§ 218 et seq.

relatives. Relations either by blood or affinity. As persons excluded from voting in a creditors' meeting for the election of a trustee in bankruptcy:—persons related to the bankrupt by affinity or consanguinity within the third degree, as determined by the common law, and the spouse of the bankrupt. Bankruptcy Act § 1(27); 11 USC § 1(27).

The word "relatives" when used in a contract has no such fixed and definite meaning as will thwart the express intention of a party thereto. Bennett v Van Riper, 47 NJ Eq 563, 22 A 1055.

The rule is quite universal in the state jurisdictions that the word embraces the persons who would take under a statute of distribution and descent in case of intestacy. Thus, by virtue of the right to take under the statute of distribution and descent in New York, an illegitimate child and its mother are not only relatives, but are parent and child within the meaning of the statute. See Middleton v Luckenbach S.S. Co. (CA2 NY) 70 F2d 326.

See **degrees of kinship; relations; relations by blood.**

relatives by affinity. See **affinity.**

relatives by blood. See **relations by blood.**

relatives of the half blood. See **half blood.**

Relativorum cognito uno, cogniscitur et alterum (re-la-ti-vō'rum kog'ni-tō ŭ'nō, kog-no'si-ter et al'te-rum). When one of two related things is known, the other is also known.

relator. A person beneficially interested on whose behalf an action is maintained by the state or sovereign power, the action being, as it is said, an ex rel action, brought on the relation of a person having a beneficial interest. 35 Am J1st Mand § 319; 44 Am J1st Quo W § 73. The informer in a qui tam action. 36 Am J2d Forf & P § 79.

relatrix (rẹ-lā'triks). Feminine of **relator.**

relaxare (rē-la-xā're). To release; to free; to discharge.

relaxatio (rē-la-xā'she-ō). A release.

relaxavi (rē-la-xā'vī). I have released.

relay station. An intermediary in broadcasting. 47 USC § 153.

release. The giving up or abandoning of the claim or right to the person against whom the claim exists or the right is to be enforced or exercised. The discharge of a debt by the act of a party in distinction from an extinguishment which is a discharge by operation of law. 45 Am J1st Rel § 2. Of interest of witness:—anything that divests the witness of all interest in the event of the suit. Anno: 28 ALR 15, 16. A discharge from duty or from confinement as a prisoner.

When the word "released" is stamped or written across the face of a bill of lading, it signifies that the carrier is exempt from his common-law liability as an insurer. Morganton Mfg. Co. v Ohio River & Charleston Ry. Co. 121 NC 514, 28 SE 474.

See **discharge; lease and release.**

release bond. A bond given to obtain the release of property held by an officer under levy of a writ of attachment or execution. 6 Am J2d Attach § 523; 30 Am J2d Exec § 277. A bond given to obtain the release of property under levy by releasing it, not merely from the custody of the officer who made the levy, but from the lien of the levy. 6 Am J2d Attach § 523; 30 Am J2d Exec §§ 277, 280.

release by estoppel. A release executed by a party under such circumstances that he is precluded by his own negligence from asserting that it is not legal and binding upon him; as where a person who signed a release could read it and did not although he had full opportunity to do so before signing it. Wallace v Chicago, St. Paul, Minneapolis & Omaha Railway Co. 67 Iowa 547, 549.

release by way of enlarging an estate. See **release deed.**

release by way of passing an estate. See **release deed.**

release deed. A deed of quitclaim. 23 Am J2d Deeds § 16.

Formerly, the term seems to have been applied only to deeds conveying all the right, title and interest of the grantor to a grantee who already had some estate in possession in the land released, but in modern usage it is not one of the essentials of a release deed that the grantee shall already have some right, title or interest in the property released. The term is therefore now synonymous with the term quitclaim deed. Anno: 44 ALR 1269.

Blackstone calls such a conveyance a "release" and says that releases may inure either by way of enlarging an estate; as where a life tenant receives a release of all his right from a remainderman, thus giving the life tenant an estate in fee; or releases may be by way of passing an estate; as where one of two coparceners releases all her right to the other, thus passing a fee simple of the whole. See 2 Bl Comm 324.

released. See **release.**

releasee (rē-lē-sē'). A person who is released; a person to whom a release is executed.

release of claim. See **release.**

release of curtesy. A release of a husband's right of curtesy by due execution of a formal release as a part of the spouse's deed of conveyance or encumbrance, or through a joint conveyance by husband and wife, duly executed and acknowledged. 25 Am J2d Dow § 115.

release of debt. See **release.**

release of dower. The extinguishment of a wife's inchoate right of dower by due execution of a formal release as part of the spouse's deed of conveyance or encumbrance, or through a joint conveyance by husband and wife, duly executed and acknowledged. 25 Am J2d Dow § 115.

release of expectancy. The assignment of the expectancy of an heir apparent, either to his ancestor or to another potential heir or distributee. 23 Am J2d Desc & D § 165.

release rate. A rate charged by a carrier which is less than the regular rate but operating to release or

reduce the liability of the carrier for loss of or damage to the goods in transit.
 Neither the marking of a bill of lading, "released," nor the making of a "release rate" will have the legal effect of releasing or reducing the liability of the carrier for loss of or damage to the goods, where no effort was made to place or fix a valuation of the goods when shipped, although the shipper understood that the "release rate" was lower when the bill of lading was marked "released." See Central of Georgia Railroad Co. v Hall, 124 Ga 322, 52 SE 679.

release to uses. A conveyance to one for the use of another, effected by deed of lease and release.
 See **lease and release.**

release under seal. See **technical release.**

releasor (rȩ̄-lē'sǫr). A person who releases; a person who executes a release.

relegatio (re-le-gā'she-ō). (Civil law.) A kind of exile in which the person exiled retained his civil rights.

relegation (rel-ȩ̄-gā'shǫn). A temporary banishment.

reletting. A definite letting of the same premises by the lessor under a prior lease upon the forfeiture of such lease or the failure of the lessee to take possession.
 The term was held not to apply to a holding over by the tenant even if such subsequent occupation amounted to a tenancy at will. Moseley v Allen, 138 Mass 81, 83.
 See **sublease.**

relevamen (re-le-vā'men). Same as **relief.**

relevancy. The logical relation between evidence offered and a fact to be established. State v Knox, 236 Iowa 499, 18 NW2d 716, 29 Am J2d Ev § 252.

relevant evidence. Any matter of fact the effect, tendency, or design of which, when presented to the mind, is to produce a persuasion concerning the existence of some other matter of fact—a persuasion either affirmative or disaffirmative of its existence. Edmonds v State, 163 Neb 323, 79 NW2d 453. Concisely, evidence of one fact rendering the existence of the fact in issue probable or improbable, according to the common course of events. People v Nitzberg, 287 NY 183, 754, 38 NE2d 490, 40 NE2d 40, 138 ALR 1253; Barnett v State, 104 Ohio St 298, 135 NE 647, 27 ALR 351; Masterson v Harris County Houston Ship Dist. (Tex) 15 SW2d 1011.
 Whatever testimony is offered which will assist in knowing which party speaks the truth of the issue, is relevant, and when to admit it does not override other formal rules of evidence, it ought to be received. Moran v Abbey, 58 Cal 163, 168.

relevium (re-le'vi-um). See **relief.**

reliance. Dependence. Trust or confidence, particularly in promises and representations. As an element of actionable fraud or deceit:—an inducement to action or injurious change of position on the part of the plaintiff. 37 Am J2d Fraud § 223.

reliance interest. A term of art in the law of damages for breach of contract. Expenditures made, or property transferred or consumed, by the party not in default in reliance on the contract. Anno: 17 ALR2d 1300.

relict (rel'ikt). A widow or widower. Spitler v Heeter, 42 Ohio St 100.

relicta (re-lik'ta). An abandonment by the defendant of his plea or defense to an action.

relicta verificatione (re-lik'ta ve-ri-fi-kā-she-ō'ne). See **confession relicta verificatione.**

reliction (rȩ̄-lik-shǫn). The withdrawal of waters, exposing as land that which was previously under water. The recession of waters from an existing bed. Anno: 54 ALR2d 645. An addition to land caused by the permanent withdrawal of the water by which it was previously covered. 56 Am J1st Wat § 476.
 See **submergence.**

relief. The objective of an action, proceeding, or motion; an award of damages or a judgment, decree, or order requiring an adversary to perform as directed or to refrain from specified conduct. As defined in the Federal Administrative Procedure Act:—the whole or part of any agency (1) grant of money, assistance, license, authority, exemption, exception, privilege or remedy; (2) recognition of any claim, right, immunity, privilege, exemption, or exception; or (3) taking any other action upon the application or petition of, and beneficial to, any person. 5 USC § 1001(f). Public aid to persons who are destitute and unable to support and maintain themselves. 41 Am J1st Poor L §§ 13 et seq.
 Anciently called "relevium,"—an incident to every feudal tenure, by way of fine or composition with the lord for taking up the estate, which was lapsed or fallen in by the death of the last tenant. Although reliefs originated while feuds were only life estates, they continued after feuds became hereditary, and hence were justly regarded as one of the heaviest grievances of tenure; especially when they were, as at first, merely arbitrary and at the will of the lord; so that if he demanded an exorbitant relief, the heir was disinherited. See 2 Bl Comm 65.
 "The relation of the heriot to the relief has been one of the chief battle-fields on which the fight of different theories of the early law has been waged. The date of the origin of the heriot has been material only as bearing upon this; and most of those who have studied the subject do not doubt their identity, or at least that it was upon the plan of the heriots that the Norman Conqueror fashioned his plan of relief, as Blackstone says." (Cf. 2 Bl Comm 423.) See Hammond's Blackstone.
 See **poor person; welfare.**

relief acts. See **farm relief; Soldiers' and Sailors' Civil Relief Acts; welfare.**

relief association. An association of the employees of a large corporate employer, particularly a railroad company, organized and acting for the purpose of making provision for employees or their representatives in the event of illness, injury, or death. 35 Am J1st M & S § 116.

relief benefits. Fringe benefits provided by a corporation for sick or injured employees. 19 Am J2d Corp § 1055.
 See **relief fund.**

relief fund. A fund administered by the officers of a relief association with the aid of the employer, contributed to usually by employer and employees, and used to pay benefits to employees or their representatives in the event of illness, injury, or death. 35 Am J1st M & S § 116.

relief worker. See **work relief.**

religion. A belief had or sought by man to explain the meaning of his existence. A person's understanding of his relation to the Creator and of the obligations of reverence and obedience imposed by such relation. Reynolds v United States, 98 US 145,

162, 25 L Ed 244, 249; Davis v Beason, 133 US 333, 33 L Ed 637, 10 S Ct 299; Nicholls v Lynn, 297 Mass 65, 7 NE2d 577, 110 ALR 377. Some system of faith and practice, resting on the idea of the existence of one God, the Creator and Ruler, to whom his creatures owe obedience and love. Knight's Estate, 159 Pa 500, 502, 28 A 303. An individual's belief in a relation to a Supreme Being, involving duties superior to those arising from any human relation, and not including essentially political, sociological, or philosophical views or a merely personal moral code. 8 USC § 1448(a) (relative to release of alien from obligation of military service). The belief in a relation to a Supreme Being involving duties superior to those arising from any human relation. (Selective Service Act of 1948 § 6(j).) Belief in the existence of superior beings exercising power over human beings by volition, and imposing rules of conduct, with future rewards and punishments. McMasters v State, 21 Okla Crim 318, 207 P 566, 29 ALR 292. All the different systems of faith and worship to be found in the world. Simpson v Welcome, 72 Me 496.

See **establishment clause.**

Religio sequitur patrem (re-li′ji-ō se′qui-ter pa′trem). The religion follows the father; that is, the child is deemed to adopt the religion of his father.

religious assembly. An assembly of religious persons, whether engaged in religious worship or not. State v Fisher, 25 NC (3 Ired L) 111, 114.

religious belief. See **religion.**

religious books. Books such as teach or inculcate religion. Simpson v Welcome, 72 Me 496.

religious corporation. A membership corporation, organized for the purpose of maintaining religious worship and spreading the faith. 45 Am J1st Reli Soc §§ 5 et seq. In older times, a bishop, dean, parson, or vicar having title to religious property. 18 Am J2d Corp § 7.

In England ecclesiastical or religious corporations were those in which the members composing it were altogether spiritual persons, such as bishops, parsons, deans and chapters, and were erected for the furtherance of religion and perpetuating the rites of the church, but in this country church corporations are generally classed as religious corporations even though the trustees or other persons who represent the corporation are wholly composed of laymen. Mackenzie v Trustees of Presbytery, 67 NJ Eq 652, 61 A 1027.

See **religious society.**

religious delusion. An idea concerning the application of religious belief to life's affairs so misconceived as to be incredible to a sane person. Insanity constituting a defense in a criminal case, provided it arises from mental disease rather than mere religious belief. State v Di Paolo, 34 NJ 279, 168 A2d 401, cert den 368 US 880, 7 L Ed 2d 80, 82 S Ct 130.

A delusion that the act charged as a crime was one commanded by God has been held a defense on the ground that, under such circumstances, the defendant could not have known that the act was wrong, although he may have known that it was illegal. There is some authority, however, that knowledge that the act was in violation of law is a sufficient predicate for responsibility and therefore for denying the defense. 21 Am J2d Crim L § 41.

religious denomination. Same as **religious sect.**

religious freedom. See **freedom of religion.**

religious journal. A newspaper or magazine published by a religious society.

religious liberty. See **freedom of religion.**

religious meeting. An assemblage for religious worship irrespective of the particular nature and form of worship. A meeting for the promotion of religious worship or the propagation of the faith. An assemblage of people met for the purpose of performing acts of adoration to the Supreme Being, or to perform religious services in recognition of God as an object of worship, love, and obedience, without reference to the faith with respect to the Deity entertained by the persons so assembled. Cline v State, 9 Okla Crim 40, 130 P 510.

An assembly, if lawful and decent, which meets for public divine service comes within the purview of a statute prohibiting the disturbance of any assemblage met for religious worship. 24 Am J2d Disturb M § 2.

religious men. Men who lived in monasteries; monks.

religious principles. Those sentiments, concerning the relations between God and man, which may influence human conduct.

Of these, perhaps the most influential hitherto has been the view entertained as to the probability that God would punish vice. A person's sentiments on that subject, whether of belief, disbelief, or doubt, must be deemed part of his religious principles. Percey v Powers, 51 NJL 432, 17 A 969.

religious purpose. The advancement of religion. The propagation of the faith. Maintaining religious worship.

An association formed for the purpose of exercising some ecclesiastical control over its members, or prescribing some form of worship for them, or subjecting those of its members who fail to conform to its rules to ecclesiastical discipline, is formed for a "religious purpose." But a Young Men's Christian Association formed to promote growth in grace and Christian fellowship among its members, and aggressive Christian work, especially by and for young men, and to seek out and aid the worthy poor, is not formed for a "religious purpose." Hamsher v Hamsher, 132 Ill 273, 23 NE 1123.

See **religion.**

religious sect. A body or number of persons, united in tenets, but constituting a distinct organization or party holding sentiments or doctrines different from those of other bodies. 45 Am J1st Reli Soc § 2. A body of persons distinguished by peculiarities of faith and practice from other bodies adhering to the same general system. Evans v Selma Union High School Dist. 193 Cal 54, 222 P 801, 31 ALR 1121. A religious denomination; the aggregate of those persons who adhere to, profess, or entertain the same religious creed, persuasion, or opinions. Hale v Everett, 53 NH 9. People believing in the same religious doctrines, who are more or less closely associated or organized to advance such doctrines and increase the number of believers therein. State ex rel. Weiss v District Board of School Dist. 76 Wis 177, 44 NW 967. A denomination of religious persons having a common system of faith, either written or traditional. See State v Trustees, 7 Ohio St 58, 64.

religious seminary. See **seminary.**

religious society. A body of persons organized for the purpose of maintaining religious worship, usually meeting in some stated place for the worship of God and for religious instruction. Anno: 17 ALR 1063, s. 28 ALR 864, 81 ALR 1184. More elaborately, a voluntary organization whose members are associated together not only for religious exercises, also for the purposes of maintaining and supporting its ministry, providing the conveniences of a church home, and promoting the growth and efficiency of the work of the main church body of which it forms a coordinate part. First Presbyterian Church v Dennis, 178 Iowa 1352, 161 NW 183.

This term as it is used in the contemplation of a constitutional provision providing for exemption from taxation is to be taken in its ordinary acceptation as meaning an assocation or body of communicants or a church usually meeting in some stated place for worship or for instruction, or organized for the accomplishment of religious purposes, such as instruction or dissemination of some tenet or particular faith or otherwise furthering its teaching. Mordecai F. Ham Evangelistic Asso. v Matthews, 300 Ky 402, 189 SW2d 524, 168 ALR 1216, 1221.

religious teacher. A minister of the gospel. Pfeiffer v Board of Education, 118 Mich 560, 77 NW 250. Broadly, any person engaged in a sincere attempt to teach the principles of any religious sect or faith, whether or not ordained as a minister.

religious test. An appraisal of a person according to the religion in which he believes. "No religious test shall ever be required as a qualification to any office or public trust under the United States." US Const, Art VI, cl 3.

religious training. Training in the principles of religion and religious belief.
See **religion**; **religious belief**.

religious tribunal. See **church judicatory**.

religious uses. See **charitable uses**.

religious worship. See **worship**.

relinquishment. An abandonment; a yielding up of all claim to a thing.
See **release**; **renunciation**.

reliqua (rel'i-kwä). A balance of account.

reliquidation. The recalculation and reassessment of a customs duty following a protest. 21 Am J2d Cust D § 94.

relocatio (rē-lo-kā'she-ō). (Civil law.) The renewal of a lease without making any change in its terms.

relocation. The selection of a new location, as for an office or place of business. A change in location, as of a railroad station. 44 Am J1st RR § 261.

relocation center. A place for the detention during time of war of citizens or subjects of hostile nations or of citizens of the United States of hostile origin or association. 56 Am J1st War § 28.

relocation of claim. The location of a claim to mining ground previously covered by a location of claim which was invalid or which, if valid, has come to an end by abandonment, forfeiture for nonperformance of assessment work, or other means. 36 Am J1st Min & M § 99.

relocation of route. A change in the location or intended location of a railroad. 44 Am J1st RR § 208.

relocation of way. A change in the location or route of a highway, to be accomplished only by competent authority and in the manner prescribed by law. 25 Am J1st High § 106.

rem. See **in rem**; **post rem**; **res**.

remain. To stay in a place. To be left after others or other things have departed or been taken away.

remainder. An estate, whether in real or personal property, limited to take effect in possession immediately after the expiration of a prior estate known as the particular estate, created at the same time and by the same instrument. 28 Am J2d Est § 195.

The word is relative and implies a prior disposition of some part of the estate, but the particular estate and the remainder constitute one whole, are carved out of the same inheritance, and may both vest at the same time and subsist together. Moore v McKinley, 246 Iowa 734, 69 NW2d 73.

The essence of a remainder is that it is to arise immediately on the determination of the particular estate by lapse of time or other determinate event, and not in abridgement of it. 28 Am J2d Est § 196.

Though, strictly speaking, a remainder is not the same as reversion, the term "remainder," as used in a particular statute, such as the income tax law, may be construed to include what, in a strict common-law sense, is a "reversion." Commissioner of Corp. & Taxation v Bullard, 313 Mass 72, 46 NE2d 557, 146 ALR 772.

See **alternative remainders**; **contingent remainder**.

remainder after remainder. A permissible limitation where the remainders are in the alternative so that one takes effect if the other does not. 28 Am J2d Est § 216.

remainder limited by way of use. A use which was so qualified that it was given effect as a remainder. 28 Am J2d Est § 337.

remainderman. One entitled to an estate in remainder.

Under a statute providing that as respects the passing and limitation over of real or personal property dependent, under the terms of any instrument, on the foster parent dying without heirs, the minor adopted child is not deemed the child of the foster parent so as to defeat the rights of remaindermen, the term "remaindermen" was held to include all those persons who might ultimately be entitled to take the estate, whether they were technically remaindermen under the definition of the common law or otherwise. Re Leask, 197 NY 193, 90 NE 652.

See **remainder**.

remainders on a contingency with a double aspect. Alternative remainders so limited that the second takes effect in lieu of the first, and only in case the first never takes effect at all. 28 Am J2d Est § 216.

As an illustration, a limitation to A for life, and after A's death, if he have children, to them in fee simple, and if he have no children, then to B in fee simple. In such case, in one alternative the remainder in favor of the children vests, and in the other alternative the remainder in favor of B vests. First Nat. Bank v Pointer, 174 Tenn 472, 126 SW2d 335.

remainder on a double contingency. See **remainders on a contingency with a double aspect**.

remainders on a single contingency with a double aspect. Same as **remainders on a contingency with a double aspect**.

remand. The return of a case by an appellate court to the trial court for entry of a proper judgment, further proceedings, or for a new trial. 5 Am J2d A & E §§ 962 et seq. The return of a cause, by the reviewing court on certiorari, to the tribunal to which the writ was directed. 14 Am J2d Certiorari § 74. The return of a case to an administrative agency after a review by the court of a determination or decision of such agency. 2 Am J2d Admin L § 764. The disposition made of a petitioner denied relief in a habeas corpus proceeding, he being sent to the custody or restraint from which he was taken under the writ. 25 Am J1st Hab C § 154. The sending back to the state court by the federal court of a cause previously removed from the state court to the federal court. 28 USC § 1447(c).

See **mandate; procedendo; reversed and remanded.**

remand for further proceedings. See **remand.**

remanentia (re-ma-nen'she-a). Same as **remainder.**

remanentiam. See **adremanentiam.**

Remanent pro defectu emptorum (re-man'ent pro de-fek'tu emp-to'rum). They remain for want of purchasers; that is, goods offered for sale by a sheriff.

remanere (rē-ma-nē're). To remain; to continue; to demur.

remanet (rem'a-net). A cause which is ready for trial, but which must await the next term of court.

Rem domino vel non domino vendente duobus in jure est potior venditione prior (rem do'mi-nō vel non do'mi-nō ven-den'te du-ō'bus in jū're est po'she-or ven-di-she-ō'ne prī'or). One, whether owner or not, having sold a thing to two persons, he to whom it was first sold is the stronger in right.

remarriage. The marriage of a surviving spouse or of a divorced spouse. The marriage of a divorced spouse to husband or wife under the marriage dissolved by the divorce.

remarriage table. A table of chances of remarriage of a surviving spouse, taking into account such a known factor as age, usable particularly in calculating the value of a life estate terminable upon remarriage. Re Keenan's Estate, 302 NY 417, 99 NE2d 219, 25 ALR2d 1459.

remediable (rę-mē'di-a-bl). Capable of being remedied or redressed.

remediable right (rę-mē'di-a-bl rīt). A right enforceable by resort to law and the invoking of an appropriate remedy. Ebner v Haverty Furniture Co. 138 SC 74, 78, 136 SE 19.

remedial (rę-mē'di-al). Providing a remedy or means of redress; pertaining to remedy or redress.

remedial act (akt). Same as **remedial statute.**

remedial action. A civil action for recovery of damages for the benefit of the injured party as compensation, the purpose being to indemnify the plaintiff rather than punish the defendant. 1 Am J2d Actions § 42.

An action is remedial where it is brought by the party injured, but it is penal when it is brought by a common informer. O'Keefe v Weber, 14 Or 55, 12 P 74.

remedial cases. Those cases wherein the remedy is afforded through certain extraordinary writs, such as prohibition, mandamus, certiorari and quo warranto. State v St. Paul & Sioux City Railroad Co. 35 Minn 222, 223, 28 NW 245.

remedial law. The law of practice. The law which provides a remedy for the enforcement of rights and the redress of grievances and sets forth the rules whereby the remedy is applied.

remedial legislation. See **remedial statute.**

remedial statute. A statute to be construed liberally as one intended to reform or extend existing rights or to correct defects and eliminate mischief in a pre-existing statute. 50 Am J1st Stat §§ 14, 15. A statute pertaining to matters of practice and procedure rather than matters of substantive law. 50 Am J1st Stat § 15.

See **prerogative remedial legislation.**

remedy. The means employed to enforce a right or redress an injury. Paulsen v Reinecke, 181 La 917, 160 So 629, 97 ALR 1184. The means or method whereby a cause of action or corresponding obligation is effectuated and by which a wrong is redressed and relief obtained. Jewett v City Transfer & Storage Co. 129 Cal App 556, 18 P2d 351. The appropriate legal form of relief by which a remediable right may be enforced. Ebner v Haverty Furniture Co. 138 SC 74, 78, 136 SE 19. Any remedial right to which an aggrieved party is entitled with or without resort to a tribunal. UCC § 1—201(34).

remedy by due course of law. Reparation for injury ordered by a tribunal having jurisdiction, in due course of procedure, after a fair hearing. Hanson v Kreheiel, 68 Kan 670, 75 P 1041.

See **due course of law; due process of law.**

remedy over. Recourse against a third person to recover a sum which one has been compelled to pay to another.

See **third party action.**

Rem in bonis nostris habere intelligimur, quotiens ad recuperandum eam actionem habeamus (rem in bō'nis nos'tris hā-bē're in-tel-li'ji-mer, quō'she-enz ad re-ku-pe-ran'dum e'am ak-she-ō'nem hā-be-ā'mus). We are supposed to have a property in our goods whenever we have an action to recover them. See 2 Bl Comm 397.

remise (rę-mīz'). A surrender; a release; a reconveyance.

remise, release and quitclaim (rę-mīz', rę-lēs' and kwit'klām). Operative words of a quitclaim deed. 23 Am J1st Deeds § 16.

remission (rę-mish'on). A release; a pardon; an exoneration. A remitting. The forgiving of a pecuniary penalty or forfeiture. 23 Am J1st Forf & P §§ 24, 53. An act of the chief executive of a state in forgiving a fine under his power to pardon. 39 Am J1st Pard § 26.

remission for jurisdiction (for jö-ris-dik'shon). See **remittitur for jurisdiction.**

remission of assets. The transfer of assets of a decedent's estate by an ancillary representative to the representative at the domicil of the decedent.

remission of damages. See **remittitur.**

remission of fine, forfeiture, or penalty. See **remission.**

remission of punishment. See **commutation of sentence; pardon; remission.**

Remissius imperanti melius paretur (rę-mis'sus im-pe-ran'ti me'li-us pa-rē'ter). He who commands the more gently is the better obeyed.

Remissum magis specie, quam vi; quia, cum venditor pendere juberetur, in partem pretii emptoribus ac-

crescebat (re-mis'sum mā'jis spe'she-ē, quam vī; qui'a, kum ven'di-tor pen-dē're ju-bē-rē'ter, in par'tem pre'she-ī emp-tō'ri-bus a-kre-sē'bat). Remitted rather in appearance than in fact; because when the vendor was ordered to pay he increased the price to the buyers in proportion. See 1 Bl Comm 317.

remit. To effect a remission as by a pardon or forgiveness of a forfeiture. To transmit or forward money, especially by way of payment of a debt. Nicoletti v Bank of Los Banos, 190 Cal 637, 214 P 51, 27 ALR 1479, 1483; Colvin v United States Mut. Acci. Asso. (NY) 66 Hun 543, 545, 21 NYS 734; 40 Am J1st Paym § 36.
See **remission**.

remittance. The transmitting of money. Money transmitted. A payment sent by mail or other means of transmission.

remittance man. A stipendiary. In popular usage, a dissolute member of the family sent afar to live on a remittance without further blemishing the family name.
See **stipendiary**.

remittee (rē-mit-ē'). A person to whom a remittance is sent or made.
A person who remits. There is a practice of procuring a check to be drawn by a third party to be used in paying a debt due from the person procuring the check to the person to whom the debtor has had the check made payable. This practice is recognized in the case of foreign bills of exchange, and the person procuring the bill is known technically as the "remitter" of it. And in such case the payee of the bill, who takes it from the remitter for value, is held to be a bona fide purchaser for value. Boston Steel & Iron Co. v Steuer, 183 Mass 140, 66 NE 646.
The doctrine that where a man has a right to lands, but is out of possession, afterward has a freehold cast upon him by some subsequent defective title, and enters by virtue of that title, in such case he is remitted, or sent back, by operation of law, to his ancient and more certain title.
The right of entry, which he gained by a bad title, is ipso facto annexed to his own inherent good title; and his defeasible estate is utterly defeated and annulled, by the instantaneous act of the law, without his participation or consent. See 3 Bl Comm 19.

remittere (rē-mit'te-re). To release; to relinquish.

remittit damna. He remits damages;—a plaintiff's record entry of a remission or waiver of a part of the damages awarded by the verdict of the jury in his favor. Van Alen v Rogers, 1 Johns Cas 281.

remittitur (rē-mit'i-tėr). A reducing of a verdict because of the excessiveness of the award, often required of a plaintiff as a condition of affirmance of the judgment entered upon the verdict. 22 Am J2d Damg § 366. The remanding of a case by an appellate court to the trial court from which the appeal taken.
See **mandate; remand**.

remittitur for jurisdiction (rē-mit'i-tėr for jō-ris-dik'shǫn). The reduction by the plaintiff of his claim by a voluntary credit in order to bring the claim within the jurisdictional maximum limit of the court. 20 Am J2d Cts § 165.

remittitur of record. See **remand**.

remittor (rē-mit'ǫr). Same as **remitter**.

remnant rule. The rule that whenever in subdividing a line or space, the surveyor declares the dimensions he has given to each subdivision except the last and there leaves an irregular space without designating its dimensions, he is presumed to have thrown all the remainder, much or little into such irregular and unmeasured portion. Pereles v Gross, 126 Wis 122, 105 NW 217; Anno: 97 ALR 1232.

remnants and surpluses (rem'nants and sėr'pluses). A technical expression used in the registry of the admiralty and applied to the residue which remains after the satisfaction of claims for seamen's wages, for bottomry bonds, for salvage services, and for supplies of materialmen, where a ship has been sold to satisfy such claims. China Mut. Ins. Co. v Force, 142 NY 90; 36 NE 874.

remnant theory. A theory sometimes applied in determining the amount of property subject to condemnation under the power of eminent domain, the theory being that if only such property as is barely necessary for the improvement is taken, there will be left fragments of property of such size and shape as to be separately valueless, the result being that the public body condemning will be required to pay for the whole, notwithstanding it only took a part. Cincinnati v Vester (CA6 Okla) 33 F2d 242, 68 ALR 831, affd 281 US 439, 74 L Ed 950, 50 S Ct 360.

remonstrance. A protest. An objection. An objection, for example, to the establishment of a highway. 25 Am J1st High § 25.
The distinction between a remonstrance and an appeal is clear. A remonstrance is interposed in opposition to the act or proceeding and is made before action is taken, while an appeal is made after the act or proceeding, usually upon the ground that the law has not been adhered to. Girvin v Simon, 127 Cal 489, 494, 59 P 945.

remote. Distant in relationship, as a remote cause. A matter of time between two events, such as the occurrence of an accident and the date of the trial of the action arising out of the accident. Anno: 85 ALR2d 516.

remote cause. A speculative rather than a direct cause of injury, consequently no basis for the recovery of damages. 22 Am J2d Damg § 21. A cause which is not sufficiently proximate as to constitute the foundation of an action for negligence. 38 Am J1st Negl § 53. A cause so remote in efficiency in reference to injury or cause of loss as to be dismissed from consideration by the court. Mahoney v Beatman, 110 Conn 184, 147 A 762, 66 ALR 1121.
If two distinct causes are successive and unrelated in their operation, they cannot be concurrent. One of them must be the proximate and the other the remote cause, and the law will regard the proximate as the efficient and responsible cause, disregarding the remote cause. 38 Am J1st Negl § 67.

remote damages. Damages from an injury not occurring directly from and as a natural result of the wrong complained of; damages of an unusual and speculative nature. Braun v Craven, 175 Ill 401, 51 NE 657.
As a legal ground for the exclusion of damage in a tort action, "remoteness" means, not severance in point of time, but the absence of direct and natural causal sequence—the inability to trace in regard to the damage the propter hoc in a necessary or natural descent from the wrongful act. See Dulieu v White & Sons, 2 K. B. (Eng.) 669, 17 Times L. R. 555.

remote indorsee. The status of an indorsee holding a bill or note in reference to an indorser under an indorsement made prior to the one under which he received the instrument. 11 Am J2d B & N § 639.

remote materialman. A materialman furnishing materials for construction work whose only relationship to the principal contractor is that he has furnished materials to a subcontractor. 17 Am J2d Cont Bond § 91.

Remoto impedimento emergit actio (rē-mō'tō im-pe-di-men'tō, ē-mer'jit ak'she-ō). The impediment or bar being removed, the action emerges or comes to life.

removable cloud on title. A cloud on the title to property which, although apparently valid, is in fact invalid. 44 Am J1st Quiet T § 11.

removal. A moving of something. A change of residence. A change of domicil. Barstow v Stone, 10 Colo App 296, 52 P 48. A person's departure to and settlement in a foreign country. Jones v McMasters (US) 20 How 8, 22, 15 L Ed 805, 810.
See **move**.

removal for cause. The removal of a public officer from office for reasons which the law and sound public policy recognize as sufficient warrant for removal, that is, legal cause, not merely cause which the appointing power in the exercise of discretion may deem sufficient. 43 Am J1st Pub Of § 205.

removal from office. Divesting an incumbent of the powers and emoluments of office. An incident of the sovereign power which creates an office, the title to office being held subject to the conditions imposed by the sovereign power in constitution or statute. 43 Am J1st Pub Of §§ 181, 182. The divesting of the power, authority, and position of a person as an executor or administrator of a decedent's estate. 31 Am J Ex & Ad § 109.
As used in a constitutional provision providing that an officer unless "removed" holds office until his successor qualifies, the word refers to ouster from office under the statute authorizing removals for misconduct, and does not refer to ouster by quo warranto proceedings, which are invoked only where a person is usurping an office to which he has no legal title. See Haymaker v State ex rel. McCain, 22 NM 400, 163 P 248.
Removal from office also applies to corporate officers, removal being accomplished as provided for and regulated by statute or provision of the charter of the corporation. 19 Am J2d Corp § 1105.
See **removal for cause**.

removal of body from grave. A disinterment, sometimes compelled, sometimes voluntary for purpose of changing place of interment. 22 Am J2d Dead B §§ 22 et seq.

removal of building. See **moving building**.

removal of cause. In the usual sense of the term, the transfer of a case from a state to a federal court, made on the petition of a defendant or defendants. Shamrock Oil & Gas Corp. v Sheets, 313 US 100, 85 L Ed 1214, 61 S Ct 868. In the broad sense of the term, any transfer of a case from one court to another.
See **change of venue**.

removal of cloud on title. See **cloud on title; quieting title**.

removal of officer. See **removal from office**.

removal of property from jurisdiction. A ground of attachment, whether an actual physical removal or a constructive removal by assignment or transfer of the property to a nonresident, with intent to hinder or delay creditors or, under some statutes, irrespective of intent. 6 Am J2d Attach §§ 243, 244.

removal rider. A permit issued by an insurance company to an insured, authorizing him to remove his insured goods to a new location. Anno: 38 ALR 1520.

removal tax. A tax levied upon the removal from one country to another of property acquired by succession or testamentary disposition. Re Peterson, 168 Iowa 511, 151 NW 66, affd Duus v Brown, 245 US 176, 62 L Ed 228, 38 S Ct 111.

remove. To effect a removal.
See **move; removal**.

remover (rē-mō'vėr). The transfer of a cause to another court from the one wherein it is pending, by writ of error, certiorari, review, etc.

rem proceeding. See **in rem action**.

rem suam. See **in rem suam**.

rem versum. See **in rem versum**.

remuneration. Compensation. Salary; wages. Russell v Ely & Walker Dry Goods Co. 332 Mo 645, 60 SW2d 44, 87 ALR 953.

renal colic (rē'nạl ko'lik). A serious illness arising from malfunction of the kidneys or urinary system. 29 Am J Rev ed Ins § 745.

renant (rē-nahn'). Denying.

rencounter (ren-koun'tėr). A sudden fight, without deliberation.

render (ren'dėr). To give; to furnish; to present; to deliver.
Mailing a statement which is to be rendered by a certain date is not a rendering of it unless it is received by that date. Peabody v Satterlee, 166 NY 174, 59 NE 818.

rendered account (ren'dėrd ạ-kount'). Same as **account rendered**.

rendered and satisfied. See **judgment rendered and satisfied**.

rendering decision. Decision-making, consisting in both fact finding and application of the law, although where a case is tried by a court with a jury, the fact finding is generally the exclusive province of the jury. Fasplund v Hannett, 31 NM 641, 249 P 1074, 58 ALR 573.

renders (ren'dėrs). See **services**.

rendition of judgment (ren-dish'ọn of juj'mẹnt). The act of the court in orally pronouncing a judgment in apt language which finally determines the rights of the parties to the action, and leaves nothing more to be done except the ministerial act of the clerk in entering the judgment. American Surety Co. v Mosher, 48 Ariz 552, 64 P2d 1025; Seisser v Oregon S. L. R. Co. 33 Idaho 291, 193 P 731.
See **date of rendition of judgment**.

rendition warrant. A warrant of extradition. 31 Am J2d Extrad § 61.
See **extradition warrant**.

renegade (ren'ẹ-gād). A deserter from a cause, faith, or political party.

renegotiation. The negotiation of a negotiable instrument by a prior party to whom the instrument has been negotiated back. 11 Am J2d B & N § 527.

Renegotiation Act. A federal statute providing for the renegotiation of war contracts and the recapture of excessive profits realized under contracts for the supply of war matériel. 50 USC Appx §§ 1191 et seq.

renegotiation of war contract. The modification of a contract for military needs made in time of national emergency and war, after the termination of hostilities, for the purpose of preventing an excessive buildup of military stores and matériel and protecting the government against excessive profits disrupting national economy. 56 Am J1st War § 49.

renew. To make over; to rebuild; to re-establish. Quinn v Valiquette, 80 Vt 434, 68 A 515. To refresh, revive, or rehabilitate an expiring or declining subject. Bright v Dayton (CA5 Ga) 107 F2d 153. To confirm a contract made under the disability of infancy or mental incompetency. Minnich v Darling, 8 Ind App 539, 544, 36 NE 173.

renewable insurance. Insurance which can be extended in duration by a mere notice from the insured, without the making of a new contract. Continental Casualty Co. v Trenner (DC Pa) 35 F Supp 643.

renewable term insurance. Term insurance with a provision for renewal without an additional medical examination.

renewal. Renewing; being renewed.
See **renew**; **successive renewals**.

renewal commission. A commission, calculated on a renewal premium, to which an insurance agent is entitled by virtue of having obtained the application for the policy by solicitation of the insured.

renewal note. A new promissory note given by way of renewing the obligation under a prior note.
As applied to promissory notes, in commercial and legal parlance, the word "renewal" or "renewed" means more than the substitution of another obligation for the old one. It means to re-establish a particular contract for another period of time. It means to restore to its former conditions an obligation on which the time of payment has been extended. Kedey v Petty, 153 Ind 179, 54 NE 798, 800.

renewal of chattel mortgage. See **refiling**.

renewal of contract. The extension or continuation of a contract for an additional term following the expiration of the contract according to its terms. 17 Am J2d Contr § 464.

renewal of copyright. An extension under the Copyright Law of the period of a copyright as provided by the statute. Miller Music Corp. v Charles N. Daniels, Inc. 362 US 373, 4 L Ed 2d 804, 80 S Ct 792.

renewal of indebtedness. The substitution of a new obligation for a pre-existing indebtedness. An extension of time of payment. 34 Am J1st Lim Ac § 368. Neither borrowing of money nor effecting a loan. State v Love, 170 Miss 666, 150 So 196, 90 ALR 506.

renewal of insurance. See **renewal of policy**.

renewal of lease. A creation of a new lease rather than an extension of an old lease. 32 Am J1st L & T § 956.
See **extension of lease**.

renewal of motion. A motion submitted following the denial of a similar motion. 37 Am J1st Motions § 19.

renewal of patent. An extension of the life of a patent pursuant to statute under a right which is as much an incident of the invention as the right to obtain a patent. 40 Am J1st Pat § 103.

renewal of policy. The continuance of insurance in force by the payment of a new premium, sometimes under a provision for renewal contained in the contract of insurance.
A renewal of insurance by the payment of a new premium and the issuance of a receipt therefor, where there is no provision in the policy for its renewal, is a new contract on the same terms as the old, but where the renewal is in pursuance of a provision to that effect, it is not a new contract but an extension of the old. 29 Am J Rev ed Ins § 357.
See **renewable insurance**.

renewal until paid. A provision for the renewal of a note contained in the instrument.
The courts appear to be in complete agreement that a "renewal until paid" or similar provision in a note authorizes, not an indefinite number of renewals thereof, but one renewal. Riepl v Sardino, 262 Wis 670, 56 NW2d 493, 35 ALR2d 1087.

reniant. Same as **renant**.

renounce (rē-nouns'). To waive or relinquish; as, to renounce a right.
The term as used in the Uniform Limited Partnership Act providing that a person erroneously believing himself to be a limited partner is not liable as a general partner "provided that on ascertaining the mistake he promptly renounces his interest in the profits of the business," means the giving up of a right or claim; the object of the provision is to put creditors in the position they would have occupied if there had been no limited partner at the time their debts were contracted. Gilman Paint & Varnish Co. v Legum, 197 Md 665, 80 A2d 906, 29 ALR2d 286.
See **renunciation**.

renounce probate. To decline to act as executor.
See **retractation**.

renovare (rē-no-vă′re). To renew.

rent. Verb: To obtain possession of premises under a lease. To let premises. Noun: Compensation in money, provisions, chattels, or services, paid or given in exchange for the use and occupation of real estate. 32 Am J1st L & T § 428. A sum stipulated to be paid for the use and enjoyment of land, liability for which becomes absolute when it accrues upon the occupation of the premises for which it is to be paid. Ambrozich v Eveleth, 200 Minn 473, 274 NW 635, 112 ALR 269. The return to the lessor under a mining lease. 36 Am J1st Min & M § 48. The return to the lessor under a gas or oil lease. 24 Am J1st Gas & O § 65. The return to a bailor under a bailment for hire. 8 Am J2d Bailm § 225.
The word is derived from the Latin word "redditus." De Haven v Sherman, 131 Ill 115, 22 NE 711.
The term as used in a statute giving a landlord a lien for unpaid rent, may not be so construed as to include taxes which the tenant has covenanted to pay, in the absence of a clear intention of the parties to that effect expressed in the lease. Lamoine Mott Estate v Neiman, 77 F2d 744, 99 ALR 1097.
The term within the meaning of price control regulations includes any commission paid by a tenant for obtaining a lease. Anno: 156 ALR 1463.
See **accustomed rent**; **ancient rent**; **assart rent**; **assize rent**; **black-mail**; **black rents**; **chief rents**;

corn-rents; dead rent; delay rentals; distress for rent; double rent; dry rent; extinguishment of rent; fee farm rent; firma alba; forehand rent; gale; gavelbred; ground rent; irredeemable ground rent; meal rent; maiden rents; quarter days; quit-rents; rack-rent; redditus; royalty; table rents; wayleave rent; white farm; white rents.

rental. A charge made by way of rent. A sum total of rents accruing from particular premises for a year or other definite period of time. Fremont, Elkhorn & Missouri Valley Railroad Co. v Bates, 40 Neb 381, 393. Another term for **rent roll**.

rental agent. An agent who simply lets premises and collects rents thereon. St. Paul v Clark, 84 Minn 138, 140, 86 NW 893.

rental guide. See **real estate and rental guide**.

rental value. The amount for which premises will let; not a conjectural, but a fair, value to be ascertained by evidence of what the premises will rent for in the open market or evidence of other facts from which the fair value may be determined. Brewington v Loughran, 183 NC 558, 112 SE 257, 28 ALR 1543. The measure of recovery for a wrongful withholding of plaintiff from possession of real property. 22 Am J2d Damg § 132.

The term as applied to lands covered with a growing crop, means, not what the lands may be rented for in the vicinity for ordinary purposes, but the value of the use for the purpose of maturing and harvesting the crop; of necessity, the value of the crop in the condition at which it exists at the time of the injury is the prime factor in the ascertainment of the value of the use. Anno: 19 ALR 495.

rent charge. A charge upon land, created by deed or will, for the payment of sum due periodically, collectible by distraint, constituting a hereditament which will pass to the heirs and devisees of him in whose favor it was created, unless disposed of by him during his lifetime. 32 Am J1st L & T §§ 1039, 1040.

See **tithe rent-charge**.

rent days. Days commonly fixed for the payment of rents, determined in ancient times according to ecclesiastical festivals or holidays.

renting automobiles. A business, of great proportions in modern times, for the furnishing of automobiles to customers at airports, railroad stations, bus stations, hotels, etc. under leases providing for the payment of a fixed rental, the automobile to be driven by the lessee.

A business consisting mainly in furnishing automobiles from a central garage on orders generally by telephone is not an agency for public use or a public utility. Terminal Taxicab Co. v District of Columbia, 241 US 252, 60 L Ed 984, 36 S Ct 583.

See **hired automobile clause**.

rent in kind. Crop rent. 32 Am J1st L & T § 61.

rent insurance. A contract of insurance indemnifying the insured owner or lessor of premises against loss of rent under certain specified conditions, such as the premises becoming untenantable because of fire or other casualty. Anno: 17 ALR2d 1228. A species of guaranty insurance; a contract whereunder the insured landlord is guaranteed a specified fixed revenue from his lands. Anno: 17 ALR2d 1230. A contract of insurance indemnifying a tenant for any loss which accrues to him by reason of having to pay rent for a period during which the rented premises are untenantable from fire or other cause specified in the contract. Anno: 17 ALR2d 1231.

rent laws. Statutes protecting tenants against exorbitant rents and from dispossession so long as they pay the agreed rent or a reasonable rent, enacted during a housing shortage, especially one resulting from war conditions. 32 Am J1st L & T § 1036.

rent loss insurance. See **rent insurance**.

rent, mortgage, and repair. As a phrase in a delegation of powers, referring to real estate rather than personalty. Caracci v Lillard, 7 Ill 2d 382, 130 NE2d 514, 53 ALR2d 1053.

rent roll. A list of a person's tenants and the rents due under their leases.

rents and profits. See **rents, issues, and profits**.

rent sec (rent'sek). Same as **rent seck**.

rent seck (rent'sek). A ground rent, reserved by the grantor upon an alienation of the fee, but without a right of distraint for collection. 32 Am J1st L & T § 1040.

rent service. A ground rent, a rent charge, payable in corporeal service and some pecuniary medium, arising upon an alienation of the fee with a reservation of rent and the right to distrain for nonpayment, constituting an estate remaining in the grantor and passing upon his death the same as the land would have passed in the absence of an alienation. 32 Am J1st L & T § 1040.

Rent service arising upon conveyances in fee simple seems to have been abolished by the Statute of Quia Emptores (1290) prohibiting subinfeudations. 32 Am J1st L & T § 1040.

rents, issues, and profits. The income or net income from land or an estate therein. People v Savings Union, 72 Cal 199, 203, 13 P 498. A kind of estate growing out of the land for life, or years, producing an annual or other rent. Bruce v Thompson, 26 Vt 741, 746.

rents of assize (of a-sīz'). Immutable fixed rents of freeholders and copyholders of ancient manors.

renunciation. A definite giving up or casting off of something. A legal act by which a person abandons a right acquired, but without transferring it to another. Johnston's Estate, 186 Wis 599, 203 SW 376. A disclaimer of interest by succession made after the ancestor's death, which, if effective, relates back to the time of death and avoids the succession. Bostian v Milens, 239 Mo App 555, 193 SW2d 797, 170 ALR 424. Refusal to accept a gift. Gottstein v Hedges, 210 Iowa 272, 228 NW 93, 67 ALR 1218. A method of discharging a negotiable instrument consisting of the holder's express disclaimer of rights in the instrument. 11 Am J2d B & N § 948. The refusal by a person designated trustee to act as such. 15 Am J2d Char § 40. The refusal of one entitled to appointment as an executor or administrator to accept the appointment. 31 Am J2d Ex & Ad § 77. An agent's termination of the agency relationship. 3 Am J2d Agency § 40.

See **repudiation**.

renunciation by surviving spouse. A refusal of dower or statutory share of a surviving spouse in the estate of a decedent in order to take under his or her will; a rejection of provisions of a will in order to take dower or the statutory share of a surviving spouse. 25 Am J2d Dow § 162.

renunciation of citizenship. See **expatriation; oath of allegiance**.

renunication of executorship. See **renunciation**.

renunciation of legacy or devise. A declination of a legacy or devise by positive act or statement of the beneficiary. 57 Am J1st Wills §§ 1566, 1571.

renunciation of property. A dereliction. An abandonment of property.

Renunciation or dereliction of property requires both the intention to abandon and external action. This is true of property at sea as well as on land. Even the title of the owner to property lying at the bottom of the sea is not necessarily divested. Murphy v Dunham (DC Mich) 38 F 503. There must be a voluntary intention to abandon, or evidence from which such intention may be presumed. Belcher Oil Co. v Griffin (CA5 Fla) 97 F2d 425.

See **renunciation**.

renunciation of will. See **renunication by surviving spouse**; **renunciation of legacy or devise**.

renvoi (ren'voi). (French.) A dismissal; a sending back, particularly of a diplomatic officer. The doctrine in the field of conflict of laws that in determining the question before it, the court of the forum must take into account the whole law of the other jurisdiction, including not only the local law of such other jurisdiction, but also its rules as to conflict of laws, and then apply the law as to the actual question which the rules of the other jurisdiction prescribe, which law may be the law of the forum. 16 Am J2d Confl L § 2. Rejected as putting the court on the course of a never-ending circle. Haumschild v Continental Casualty Co. 7 Wis 2d 130, 95 NW2d 814.

The doctrine of renvoi has generally been repudiated by the American authorities. 16 Am J2d Confl L § 2.

reo absente (re'ō ab-sen'te). The defendant being absent; in the absence of the defendant.

reopening account. A review or reconsideration of an account, such as a guardian's account, had after a purported final settlement. 25 Am J1st G & W § 172. The reconsideration of a trustee's account after settlement thereof by decree or order of court. 54 Am J1st Trusts § 511.

reopening case. Permitting either party to present further evidence after the parties have rested. 53 Am J1st Trial § 123. Action on the part of a police department in resuming investigation upon the disclosure of an item of new evidence in a case previously closed for want of evidence of guilt.

See **new trial**.

reopening estate. A matter with which bankruptcy courts are expressly invested with jurisdiction, such courts being empowered to reopen closed estates for cause shown, Bankruptcy Act § 2(a) (8); 11 USC § 11(a) (8), as for the administration of assets of substantial value which the bankrupt did not schedule. 9 Am J2d Bankr § 1273. The resumption of administration of a decedent's estate, after an order discharging the executor or administrator and the approval of his final account of distribution, because of the existence of newly discovered assets. 31 Am J2d Ex & Ad § 124.

An administration should be reopened to permit prosecution of an action, not barred by limitations, against the estate. Re Miles' Estate, 262 NC 647, 138 SE2d 487.

reorganization of bank. See **bank reorganization**.

reorganization of corporation. See **corporate reorganization**.

repair. Verb: To restore to a sound condition that which is decayed, dilapidated, injured, or partially destroyed. 48 Am J1st Spec A § 47. To restore by renewal or replacement of subsidiary parts of a whole. Hammond v El Dorado Springs, 362 Mo 530, 242 SW2d 479, 31 ALR2d 1367. Noun: The act of restoration to a sound, good, or complete state after decay, injury, dilapidation or partial destruction. Goodyear Shoe Machinery Co. v Jackson (CA1 Mass) 112 F 146.

It would be in violation of a proper construction of the term "repair" to hold that it included an original improvement, or work of a different character from that previously done. Santa Cruz Rock Pavement Co. v Broderick, 113 Cal 628, 633, 45 P 863.

In a contract of sale a covenant to repair, and to replace defective parts of the article contemplates a restoration to the original condition, but does not contemplate the employment of experts to experiment with the article and redesign and reconstruct it. Allegheny County v Maryland Casualty Co. (DC Pa) 42 F Supp 672.

Work which may be considered "repairs" within the meaning of a provision of an instrument which creates a trust and charges the cost of making repairs on the trust property to the income therefrom includes expenditures for modernizing buildings by putting in new fronts, reconstructing a barn, digging a well, the repairing or replacing of roofing and plumbing, cleaning flues, repairing old or installing new heating equipment, painting and papering rooms, and whatever else is reasonably necessary to keep up a house. Anno: 128 ALR 255 et seq.

See **covenant to repair**; **good condition and repair**; **good repair**; **habitable repair**; **necessary repairs**.

repair and replace. See **repair**.

reparable injury (rep'a-ra-bl in'jö-rē). An injury the damage from which is merely in the nature of pecuniary loss, and can be exactly and fully repaired by compensation in money. Puckette v Hicks, 39 La Ann 901, 2 So 801.

reparanda. See **domo reparanda**.

reparation. The making good of a wrong or injury caused another. Amends or compensation for an injury; redress. The return of an unlawful exaction, especially a wrongful and unlawful charge made by a common carrier. Payments made by a country defeated in a war under obligation imposed by the treaty of peace.

reparatione. See **de reparatione**.

reparatione facienda. See **de reparatione facienda**.

reparationem et sustentationem. See **ad reparationem, etc.**

reparatio pontium (re-pa-rā'she-ō pon'she-um). The repair of bridges.

repartiamento (re-pär-tia-men'tō). A term encountered in Spanish-American grants signifying a partition of common property among the several owners.

All the lands in the kingdom of Spain were divided into "territoria." The "territorium" was divided into "proprios," "solares," "ejidos," "pastos," "dehesas," and "monte." The "proprios" belonged to the town as its proper severalty. The "solares" belonged to their respective owners in severalty. The residue of the "territorium"—"ejidos," "pastos," and "dehesas"—was the community property of the members of the community. When the necessity ceased, the system was changed and about the time of the discovery of America (1492). It was determined to reduce these community lands to private ownership. This was done through various officers and commissioners of the government. The act was never called or characterized as a grant or a concession, but as a partition among the owners of common property, giving to each his share in severalty. This act was called "repartiamento." Steinbach v Moore, 30 Cal 498, 501.

repatriation (rę-pā-tri-ā'shǫn). The restoration of a person to citizenship previously lost by expatriation. A return to the country of one's birth and citizenship of origin. To replace an existing pavement on a street or highway with a new pavement. Ten Eyck v Albany, 65 Hun 194, 198, 20 NYS 157.

repave. To reconstruct the paving of a street or highway. Anno: 41 ALR2d 614.

repay. To compensate for something received. To make return in money or of goods in kind. Grant v Dabney, 19 Kan 388.

repeal. To revoke or recall. Oakland Paving Co. v Hilton, 69 Cal 479, 11 P 3.

repeal by implication. See **implied repeal.**

repeal of constitution. An express, implied, or constructive repeal of a provision of a constitution by the adoption of an amendment to the constitution. 16 Am J2d Const L § 27.

repeal of franchise. The termination of a franchise by the exercise of a reserved power of revocation or repeal. 23 Am J1st Franch § 26.

repeal of statute. The termination of the effect of a statute as existing law by a later statute or constitutional provision. 50 Am J1st Stat §§ 516 et seq. The annulment of a statute, whereby it ceases to have any existence, accomplished directly or expressly through a later statute or constitutional provision, or indirectly or impliedly by the enactment of a statute or the adoption of a constitutional provision which is repugnant to or inconsistent with the statute. Oakland Paving Co. v Hilton, 69 Cal 479, 485, 11 P 3.
See **implied repeal.**

repeated. Reiterated. Told as heard, as where a slanderous statement is told to a third person by the person to whom it was first communicated. Performed again. Occurring again.
The word is to be distinguished from "continued." A "repeated" violation of a statute may be one which has ceased for a substantial period of time prior to the institution of a proceeding to enjoin it, whereas a "continued" violation would charge violation up to the time of filing suit. Re Mauch Chunk Brewing Co. (DC NH) 43 F Supp 205.

repeated transactions. Transactions undertaken and performed one after another. Anno: 87 ALR 97.

repeated trespasses. A succession of wrongs of the same kind, each sufficient in itself to constitute a tort.
See **continuing trespass.**

repeater. See **recidivist.**

Repellitur a sacramento infamis (re-pel'li-ter ā sa-kra-men'tō in-fā'mis). He who is infamous is denied the right to be sworn or to make oath.

Repellitur exceptione cedendarum actionum (rē-pel'-li-ter ek-sep-she-ō'ne sē-den-dā'rum ak-she-ō'num). He is defeated in his plea that the actions were assigned.

repentance. Sorrow for one's own wrongdoing.
See **locus penetentiae.**

repetition (rep-ę-tish'ǫn). (Civil law.) A claim and demand to recover back a payment made under a mistake on a condition which had not been performed.
See **repeated.**

repetito namio (re-pe'ti-tō na'mi-ō). A second or reciprocal distress, in lieu of a first one which was eloigned.
Hence, it is a command to the sheriff to take other goods of the distrainor, in lieu of the distress formerly taken, and eloigned, or withheld from the owner. It is one distress taken to answer another, by way of reprisal. See 3 Bl Comm 148.

repetundarum crimen (re-pe-tun-dā'rum krī'men). (Roman law.) Bribery; the crime of bribery or extortion committed by a public officer.

replace. To restore to a former position. To substitute. To provide an equivalent, as in building a house to take the place of one destroyed by fire.
See **repair; reproduction.**

replacement cost. See **reproduction cost.**

replead. To serve or file a new pleading.
See **pleading over.**

repleader (rē-plē'dėr). An order or judgment awarded by the court after verdict requiring the parties to replead from that stage of the pleadings where there appears to have been the first error in the pleadings.
Such an order is usually made where by misconduct or inadvertence the issue has been joined on an immaterial fact or where a finding on the issue made would be inconclusive. See 3 Bl Comm 395.

replegiare (rē-ple-ji-ā're). To receive back by way of pledge; to replevin.
See **de replegiare.**

replegiare de averiis (rē-ple-ji-ā're dē a-ve'ri-is). A writ which lay to replevin cattle which had been taken by distress.

Replegiare est, rem apud alium detentam cautione legitima interposita, redimere (re-ple-ji-ā're est, rem a'pud a'li-um de-ten'tam kâ-she-ō'ne le-ji'ti-ma in-ter-po'zi-ta, re-di'me-re). To replevin is to redeem with lawful security, a thing detained by another. See 3 Bl Comm 146.

replegiari facias (re-ple-ji-ā'rī fā'she-ās). That you cause to be replevied;—a writ which issued out of chancery, commanding the sheriff to deliver distrained goods to their owner. See 3 Bl Comm 146.

repleviable (rę-plev'i-ạ-bl). Subject to an action of replevin; capable of being replevined.

replevin (rē-plev'in). An action in which the owner or one who has a general or special property in a thing taken or detained by another seeks to recover possession in specie, and sometimes the recovery of damages as an incident of the cause. 46 Am J1st Replev § 2. The writ authorizing the seizure of the property by the officer to whom it is directed. In some jurisdictions a written requisition subscribed by the plaintiff's attorney directing the sheriff to seize certain described property. 46 Am J1st Replev § 79.

replevin bond. The bond required of the plaintiff in an action in replevin in obtaining a writ or requisition for the seizure of the property by an officer during the course of the proceeding and before judgment in the action, conditioned for the prosecution of the action, for the return of the property if return thereof is adjudged, and for the payment of such sum as may for any cause be recovered in the action against the plaintiff, the bond being primarily for the protection of the defendant in the event the plaintiff does not prevail. 46 Am J1st Replev § 75.

replevin in the cepit (rē-plev'in in the sē'pit). An action of replevin for goods which have been wrongfully taken, as distinguished from replevin to recover goods which have been wrongfully withheld.

replevisable (rę̄-plev'i-sạ-bl). Capable of being recovered by an action of replevin.

replevish (rę̄-plev'ish). To replevin.

replevisor (rę̄-plev'i-sǫr). The plaintiff in an action of replevin.

replevy (rę̄-plev'i). To secure the possession of personal property by means of an action of replevin.

replevy bond. A form of bond given upon obtaining the release of attached property from the custody of the officer who made the levy. 6 Am J2d Attach § 523.
See **delivery bond; replevin bond.**

repliant (re-plī'ant). A plaintiff who pleads a replication in answer to a defendant's plea.

replicatio (re-pli-kā'she-ō). A Roman law pleading corresponding to the replication of the common law and being the actor's reply to the defendant's exceptio. See 3 Bl Comm 310.

replication. Same as **reply.**

reply. An additional pleading by the plaintiff as such may be required or permitted to meet or avoid matters in the answer. 41 Am J1st Pl § 174. Plaintiff's answer to a setoff or counterclaim. 20 Am J2d Countcl § 148. In equity, a pleading by the plaintiff addressed to the allegations of fact in the defendant's plea. 27 Am J2d Eq § 208. The argument of the plaintiff following, and by way of answer to the argument of the defendant in the trial of an action.

reply brief. A brief filed by the appellant in response to the points made by the respondent, it being improper to raise new points or assignments in such a brief. 5 Am J2d A & E § 689.

repone (rę̄-pōn'). See **reduce.**

report. Verb: To give information, as where an officer reports the result of an investigation to his superior. Noun: Repute. A presentation of facts, sometimes in formal detail, as in the case of the statement of an executor, administrator, guardian, trustee, or receiver, accompanying his account, and setting forth the circumstances of his administration of the estate. The statement of the financial condition of a corporation and the amount of business transacted for the period, furnished to stockholders and public officers having supervision over corporate affairs at regular periods or sometimes at irregular periods, as in the case of special reports.

A citation requiring a guardian to make a report of his administration is construed as equivalent to a direction to him to render an account. See Heisen v Smith, 138 Cal 216, 71 P 180.

See **referee's report; rumor.**

reportare (rē-por-tā're). To report.

report by grand jury. A report made by a grand jury respecting the character of conduct of public officers or citizens, without including an indictment or presentment against such officers or persons. 24 Am J1st Grand J § 36.

reported cases. See **court reports.**

reporter. One who gathers information and writes reports of events of interest for publication in a newspaper.
See **court reporter.**

reporter's transcript. See **transcript.**

reporting policy. See **monthly reporting policy.**

report of accident. See **accident report.**

report of decision. See **court reports; report of referee.**

report of market. See **market quotations.**

report of referee. The report of a referee to whom a case has been referred, made and returned to the court which ordered the reference, showing the proceedings had before him, his findings of fact and conclusions of law, and in some jurisdictions in certain cases, the decision of the referee upon the whole case. 45 Am J1st Ref §§ 29 et seq.

reports of cases. See **court reports.**

repose statute. A statute of limitation. 34 Am J1st Lim Ac § 10.

reposition of the forest (rē-pō-zish'ǫn of the for'est). The reinclusion of a purlieu; that is, the reincorporation of land in a forest which was near the forest and which had formerly been a part of it.

repossession. A taking of possession after a relinquishment of possession. A remedy of the vendor upon default by the buyer under a conditional sale contract. 47 Am J1st Sales § 951. The remedy of the holder of a trust receipt in retaking possession of the subject matter of the receipt upon default of the debtor. 53 Am J1st Tr Rec § 10.
See **re-entry.**

reprendre. (French.) To take back; the source of the English word "reprieve."

represent. To state as a fact. To act for. To stand in the place of.

The proceeds of an insurance policy stand to the owner in the place of the property lost; it is the value of the house paid by the insurance company, not because it acquires the property, but because it agreed to pay so much for the house if destroyed by fire. Hence, if the house was exempt from execution, so also is the insurance. Chase v Swayne, 88 Tex 218, 30 SW 1049.

representation. A statement of a fact, truthful or untruthful. Within the meaning of the law of fraud: —anything short of a warranty, proceeding from the words, act, or conduct of the party charged, which is sufficient to create upon the mind a distinct impression of fact conducive to action. Pocatello Secur. Trust Co. v Henry, 35 Idaho 321, 206 P 175, 27 ALR 337. In the law of insurance:—an oral or written statement by the insured or his authorized agent to the insurer or its authorized agent, made prior to the completion of the contract, giving information as to some fact or state of facts with respect to the subject of the insurance, which is intended or necessary for the purpose of enabling the insurer to determine whether it will accept the risk, and at what premium. 29 Am J Rev ed Ins § 698.

The principle of descent to the eldest son of an eldest son in prejudice of proximity of blood. 23 Am J2d Desc & D § 6. The doctrine under which a court of equity with jurisdiction to sell property may, in a proper case, alienate the contingent title or interest of unborn remaindermen, or even the contingent title of interested persons in esse whose names and addresses are unknown, provided all the parties are before the court who can be brought before it, and the rights of the nonexistent or as yet unascertained parties will be represented and sufficiently defended by those who are made parties and who have motives of self-interest and affection to make such defense. 31 Am J Rev ed Jud S § 13.

See **class action; class suit; implied representation; per stirpes; right of representation; virtual representation.**

representation by counsel. Having legal counsel, especially in an action, proceeding, or criminal prosecution. The constitutional right of a person accused of crime to be assisted by counsel in his defense. 21 Am J2d Crim L §§ 309 et seq.

representation work. (Mining law.) The annual labor or "assessment work," as it is often called, required by statute providing that on each mining claim, until a patent is issued for it, there shall be annually expended in labor or improvements a specified sum of money, and that upon failure to do so, the claim shall be open to relocation in the same manner as if no location was ever made. De Noon v Morrison, 83 Cal 163, 23 P 374.

representative. An agent, an officer of a corporation or association, a trustee, executor, or administrator of an estate, or any other person empowered to act for another. UCC § 1—201(35). A member of the House of Representatives in Congress or a state legislature. A person who stands in the place of another, as heir, or in the right of succeeding to an estate of inheritance; one who takes by representation; a person who occupies another person's place and succeeds to his rights and liabilities. Lee v Dill (NY) 39 Barb 516, 520. A person who sues or defends in the interest of the estate of a decedent as his personal representative, heir, devisee, legatee, or distributee. 29 Am J2d Ev § 679.

See **labor representative; legal representative; personal representative; real representative.**

representative action. Same as **class action.**

representative capacity. The capacity in which one acts on behalf of some person or estate, not for himself personally.

When a party sues or is sued in such capacity, it is necessary that the capacity in which he sues or is sued should appear in the title, to show the relation between the party and the estate represented, and that he is in court, not for himself, but for the estate he represents. Van Brunt & Davis Co. v Harrigan, 8 SD 96, 98, 76 NW 984.

representative democracy. A government by representatives elected by the people. A representative form of government.

See **pure democracy.**

representative form of government. A government conducted and constituted by the agency of representatives, delegates, or deputies chosen by the people in regularly recurring elections.

The definition is held to express fairly the modern American idea of such a government. "A fraternal benefit association must have a representative form of government. This requires that the directors or other officers who have general charge and control of the property and business of the society and the management of its affairs shall be chosen by the membership thereof." Lange v Royal Highlanders, 75 Neb 188, 106 NW 224, 110 NW 1100.

representative in interest. See **representative.**

representative of a deceased person. The executor or administrator of a deceased person, or a person or party who has succeeded to the right of the deceased, whether by purchase, descent, or operation of law. 58 Am J1st Witn § 237. A person appointed, not by a testator in his will, but by the law, to represent an ancestor, and upon whom the law casts the inheritance. Bowen v Hackney, 136 NC 187, 48 SE 633.

See **personal representative.**

representative of nonresident motorist. A designated state official for the purpose of service of process. 8 Am J2d Auto § 849.

representative or article of value. An unusual and rather inept expression.

As used in a statute prohibiting any slot machine or mechanical device, as the result of the operation of which any merchandise or money is won or lost, this phrase refers to a material or tangible thing of value and does not include free games automatically won on a pinball machine so as to render such a machine subject to seizure and destruction as a gambling device. Gayer v Whelan, 59 Cal App 2d 255, 138 P2d 763.

representative peers (pērs). Those members of the house of lords of the English parliament who are elected to represent Scotland and North Ireland.

representative suit. Same as **class suit.**

repressive license. A license required as a condition of doing business, the fee for which is so high as to be prohibitive. 52 Am J1st Trad St § 14.

reprieve (rę̄-prēv'). A word derived from the French, "reprendre," to take back. The postponement of the execution of a sentence for a definite time, or to a day certain, not defeating the ultimate execution, merely delaying it temporarily. 39 Am J1st Pard § 7.

reprieve ex arbitrio judicis (ex ar-bi'tri-ō jō'di-sis). A reprieve the power to grant which belongs of common right to every tribunal which is invested with authority to award execution. 39 Am J1st Pard § 7.

reprieve ex mandatio regis (ex man-dā'she-ō rē'jis). A reprieve from the mere pleasure of the Crown. 39 Am J1st Pard § 7.

reprieve ex necessitate legis (ex ne-ses-si-tā'te lē'jis). A reprieve required by law to be granted under certain circumstances, as when a woman convicted of a capital offense alleges pregnancy of a quick child in delay of execution, or when a prisoner has become insane between the time of sentence and the time fixed for execution. 39 Am J1st Pardon § 7.

reprimand (rep'ri-mȧnd). A severe and solemn reproach or censure for disobedience or wrongdoing; as the reprimand of an attorney by the court for unprofessional conduct.

reprisal (rę̄-prī'zal). A form of retorsion, being the act of a sovereign state, taken short of war, in retaliation against another nation for what it deems to be a wrong committed against it by the other nation, as where a nation seizes property of another nation which has refused to pay a debt to it, to repair an injury, or give adequate satisfaction for it, such property to be finally confiscated for want of satisfaction of the debt or the giving of compensation for the injury. 30 Am J Rev ed Internat L § 53. A remedy, also known as "recaption," by the mere act of the party injured, where another person has wrongfully deprived him of his goods or chattels, or wrongfully detains his wife, child, or servant.

In such case, the owner of the goods, or the husband, parent, or master may lawfully claim and retake them wherever he happens to find them, provided he does so in a manner not riotous, and without a breach of the peace. Prigg v Pennsylvania (US) 16 Pet 539, 613, 10 L Ed 1060, 1088.

See **letters of marque and reprisal.**

reprises (re-pri'zes). Such deductions as are required to be made from gross income in order to ascertain the clear or net profit of land.

The term does not include deductions for bad management, or personal shortcomings of the holder of the land, or from fire or flood or similar casualty, but deductions for burdens incident to the land as such, taxes, charges and impositions of all kinds which attach to the land itself, are included in the meaning of the term. Delaware & Hudson Canal Co. v Von Storch, 196 Pa 102, 105, 46 A 375.

reproach (rē-prōch'). Shame; disgrace. Obloquy. Bettner v Holt, 70 Cal 270, 11 P 713.

Reprobata pecunia liberat solventem (re-pro-bā'ta pe-kū'ni-a li'be-rat sol-ven'tem). Money refused releases the person who pays; that is, who tenders.

reprobatur (re-pro-bā'ter). A Scotch action the purpose of which was to convict a witness of perjury.

reproduction. A repetition of production. The act of reproducing an article in violation of a patent right. Goodyear Shoe Machinery Co. v Jackson (CA1 Mass) 112 F 146.

reproduction cost. A relevant factor in determining the present value of a public utility plant for rate-making purposes. According to one view, the cost of construction of a plant identical with the plant appraised; according to another view, the cost of construction of a plant of equal efficiency, capacity, and durability.

According to still another view, neither the cost of reproducing the existing plant or system nor the cost replacing an existing system or plant by an equivalent one is final as determining the new or present value of a public service property, but both may be of evidential effect in determining the actual fair value thereof. 43 Am J1st Pub Util § 113.

re propria. See **in re propria.**

republic (rē-pub'lik). A country with a **republican form of government.**

republican form of government. A government constructed on the principle that the supreme power resides in the body of the people. See Chisholm v Georgia (US) 2 Dall 419, 457, 1 L Ed 440, 456. A government which derives all its powers directly or indirectly from the people and which is administered by persons holding their offices for a limited period or during good behavior. 16 Am J2d Const L § 390. Not to be confused with the Republican Party.

Within the meaning of the provision of section 4 of article 4 of the United States Constitution that "the United States shall guarantee to every state in this Union a republican form of government," the term signifies a government of a state of the Union which has been recognized by Congress as being a government republican in form. Pacific States Tel. Co. v Oregon, 223 US 118, 56 L Ed 377, 32 S Ct 224.

republican government. See **republican form of government.**

republication. The repetition of a slanderous statement by the person to whom it was originally communicated. 33 Am J1st L & S § 95. A publication of a will previously altered or revoked. 57 Am J1st Wills § 625.

Ordinarily, when a codicil is said to "republish" a will, it is meant that a will, then valid, is republished as of the date of the codicil. Anno: 33 ALR2d 928.

Prior to the statute of frauds, a will devising real property could be republished by parol in the same manner as a will bequeathing personalty, but since the enactment of the statute of frauds and the statute of wills a revoked will cannot be revived by an oral declaration of the testator, or otherwise than by a re-execution or republication or by a codicil. Where a statute makes no provision for a republication, but simply requires that in the original execution and publication of the will certain solemnities must be observed relative to the signing of the will by the testator and by subscribing witnesses, the weight of authority and the better rule is that the republication must be made with like solemnity as the execution of the original will and an oral republication is insufficient; nor can the republication be shown by mere parol evidence. 57 Am J1st Wills § 625.

republication of will. See **republication.**

repudiation. A denial of validity or of authority. Refusal to recognize an obligation asserted as binding one. A denial of responsibility or obligation. State Sav. Bank v Black, 91 Iowa 490, 59 NW 282. A certain, definite, unequivocal, and timely denial by one person of the authority of another who has purported to act for him as his agent in incurring a liability. Sullivan v Bennett, 261 Mich 232, 246 NW 90, 87 ALR 791.

See **anticipatory repudiation; renunciation.**

repudiation of contract. Refusal to recognize the existence of a contract or the doing of something inconsistent with its existence; renunciation of liability under a contract. 17 Am J1st Contr § 443. A refusal or declination to perform in accordance with the contract. Lane v Chantilly Corp. 251 NY 435, 167 NE 578, 68 ALR 653.

repudiation of gift. The avoidance of a gift made by an infant donor, after becoming of age. 24 Am J1st Gifts § 17.

See **renunciation.**

repudium (rē-pū'di-um). (Roman law.) The breach of a contract to marry.

repugnance (rē-pug'nans). Repugnancy.

repugnancy (rē-pug'nan-si). Inconsistency. Swan v United States, 3 Wyo 151, 9 P 931. Inconsistency or contradiction in allegations of material facts. 27 Am J1st Indict § 110; 41 Am J1st Pl § 47.

In pleading, the common-law doctrine of repugnancy relates to inconsistent matters of substance which are alleged in the same count or plea. Counts and pleas, however, which are merely inconsistent with one another are not for that reason repugnant in a legal sense. 41 Am J1st Pl § 48.

repugnancy doctrine. A doctrine stated in reference to the construction of repugnant provisions in a will that the law favors the first taker; that the first taker in a will is presumed to be the favorite of the testator; that an absolute gift in a will cannot be cut down by subsequent inconsistent language of doubtful or ambiguous significance, it being necessary before such a result will be permitted that the language indicating an intention to cut down the gift be as clear, plain, and unequivocal as that used in the gift itself; that the presumption is that the first taker receives a fee in spite of subsequent words casting doubt on such result; that in case of doubt as to the quantity of an estate devised, the general rule is that an absolute rather than a qualified estate was intended; and that where a devise of an absolute interest is made, subsequent limitations attempting to deprive the estate of any of the incidents appertaining to it are repugnant and void. 57 Am J1st Wills § 1320.

repugnant allegations. See **repugnancy.**

repugnant provisions. Inconsistent provisions, as in a deed or will. 23 Am J2d Deeds §§ 237-239, 250, 267.
See **repugnancy doctrine.**

repugnant remedies. See **inconsistent remedies.**

reputable (rep'ū-ta-bl). In good repute. Worthy of repute.
The term as used in a statute authorizing the registration of any person who was a reputable resident physician of good moral character, who on the first day of July 1897 was engaged in the actual practice of medicine within the state, was construed as referring to any person who is regarded as honorable and praiseworthy as a member of the medical profession, of whatever school, or whether classed with any particular school, by any reason of the character of his work and his conduct professionally and not limited to physicians and surgeons who are graduates from some reputable medical school, or belonged to some incorporated medical society. Anno: 4 ALR2d 685.

reputable dog. A dog with no record of doing mischief or of viciousness. Williams v Moray, 74 Ind 25; Blair v Forehand, 100 Mass 136.

reputable physician. See **reputable.**

Reputatio est vulgaris opinio ubi non est veritas (re-pu-tā'she-ō est vul-gā'ris o-pi'ni-ō u'bi non est ve'-ri-tās). Reputation is common opinion where there is no actual fact.

reputation. Repute. People v Belcastro, 356 Ill 144, 190 NE 301, 92 ALR 1223. The repute in which a man is held by his neighbors. Anno: 10 ALR 9.
See **character**; **crime of reputation**; **general reputation**; **repute.**

repute. The esteem or opinion held by the public, the community, or neighborhood in respect of a person or a thing. People v Belcastro, 356 Ill 144, 190 NE 301, 92 ALR 1223.
See **good repute.**

reputed children. A term designating illegitimate children. Anno: 34 ALR2d 49, § 11.

reputed owner. A person who by supposition or opinion derived from outward appearances, appears to be the owner of the property in question. Santa Cruz Rock Paving Co. v Lyons, 5 Cal Unrep 260, 266, 43 P 599.

request. To ask or express a wish for something. Philomath College v Wyatt, 27 Or 390, 31 P 206, 216. Sometimes to direct or command, although in a delicate manner. In other words, a precatory word, subject to construction in a proper case as a mandatory term. Coulson v Alpaugh, 163 Ill 298, 45 NE 216; Shaver v Weddington, 247 Ky 248, 56 SW2d 980.
Under some circumstances, a request is the same as a command and has the same meaning. A request from a person in authority is understood to be a mere euphemism. It is in fact a command in an inoffensive form. See State ex rel. Freeman v Scheve, 65 Neb 853, 91 NW 846.
The words "request," "hope," "not doubting," that the executor will conduct in a specified manner, when they come from a testator who has power to command, are to be construed as commands in his will, clothed merely in the language of civility, and they impose on the executor a duty which courts have in repeated instances enforced. Pembroke Academy v Epsom School Dist. 75 NH 408, 75 A 100.
The word may be employed in a will as an entreaty, depending upon the context in which the word is inserted and the circumstances attendant upon its use. Marx v Rice, 1 NJ 574, 65 A2d 48, 9 ALR2d 584.

request for instruction. A request directed to the court by a party for an instruction to the jury, upon the general issues or upon particular phases of the case, in order that the points of law and the case may be fully presented to the jury by the instructions. 53 Am J1st Tr § 512.

request note. A notice to a person having dutiable goods in his possession, requiring him to secure a permit for their removal.

require. To need; to call for; to make necessary; to demand. 17 Am J2d Contr § 281; 46 Am J1st Sales § 135.
The word is derived from the Latin "requiro," compounded of "re" and "quiro"—to seek for, or to seek to get back. Although it may undoubtedly be used in the sense of the word "need," that is neither its primary nor its usual signification. According to all the lexicographers, and in common parlance, it means to command; to ask by right and by authority. Duhamel v Port Angeles Stone Co. 59 Wash 171, 176, 109 P 597.
When used in a statute the word "required" may be equivalent to the word "commanded;" as where commissioners were by statute not only authorized, but "required" to levy a yearly tax. Taylor v Commissioners of Newberne, 55 NC (2 Jones Eq) 141.

required. See **require.**

required medical treatment. Necessary medical treatment. Scott v State, 90 Tex Crim 100, 233 SW 1097, 16 ALR 1420.

requirement contract. A contract which calls for the one party to furnish all of the supply of a certain material required for the operation of the business of the other party for a prescribed time, and for the latter to purchase all of such required supply from the former. 28 Am J Rev ed Inj § 121.
The essence of a requirements contract is that the amount of the commodity needed by the purchaser cannot be exactly defined at the beginning of the year and it is for this reason that a contract of this type which deals for future needs is entered into. William C. Atwater Co. v Terminal Coal Corporation (DC Mass) 32 F Supp 178.

requirements of the business. As a designation of quantity of goods purchased:—the quantity which is actually needed in the buyer's business as distinguished from the quantity ordered or desired by the buyer, provided there is good faith and no fraud. 46 Am J1st Sales § 158.

Under an agreement to fill the buyer's requirements, the obligations of the parties are governed by the needs of the business even though those needs increase or decrease because of varying conditions to which the business is ordinarily subject, for such conditions may be said to be within the contemplation of the parties. Loudenback Fertilizer Co. v Tennessee Phosphate Co. (CA6 Tenn) 121 F 298.

requisition. An authoritative demand, for example, the demand of the government for military supplies. The taking of private property for use by the government in the waging of a war. International Paper Co. v United States, 282 US 399, 75 L Ed 410, 51 S Ct 176. A substitute for a writ of replevin in some jurisdictions, accomplishing the same purpose, although subscribed and issued by plaintiff's attorney. 46 Am J1st Replev § 79.

A request issued by the President of the United States as the chief executive of the Federal Government, requiring a quota or detachment of militia to be furnished or held in readiness for the service of the United States. A requisition, which is a mere courteous request, is to be distinguished from an "order" made by the President as commander-in-chief of the militia, which is a mandatory act. Mills v Martin (NY) 19 Johns 7, 26.

requisitions on title (rek-wi-zish'ons on tī'tl). Objections indicated by the solicitor of the vendee to apparent flaws in the title of the vendor.

requisitory letter (rę-kwiz'i-tǫ-ri let'ėr). Same as **letter rogatory.**

re-recording. See **re-inscription.**

reregistration. A periodic registration, required in some states, following an original registration for voting in the same district. 25 Am J2d Elect § 107. See **re-inscription.**

rerum natura. See **in rerum natura.**

Rerum ordo confunditur, si unicuique jurisdictio non servetur (re'rum or'dō kon-fun'di-ter, sī ū-nī-kī'kwe jū-ris-dik'she-ō non ser'vė-ter). The order of things is confused if everyone does not give heed to his own jurisdiction.

Rerum progressu ostendunt multa, quae in initio praecaveri seu praevideri non possunt (re'rum progres'sū os-ten'dunt mul'ta, kwē in in-i'she-o prē-kavē'rī sū prē-vi-dē'rī non pos'sunt). In the progress of things many matters appear which could not be prevented or provided for in the beginning.

Rerum suarum quilibet est moderator et arbiter (re'rum su-ā'rum quī'li-bet est mo-de-rā'tor et ar'biter). Everyone is the manager and master of his own affairs or his own property.

res. Abbreviation of **resolution,** also of **reserve.**

res (rēz). (Latin.) The thing. The real thing. A transaction. An affair. The subject matter of a trust in a sense of the property held under trust. The subject matter of an action in the sense of the property or status involved.
See **in rem.**

res accendent lumina rebus (rēz ak-sen'dent lu'mi-na re'bus). Things shed their light upon things. One thing illuminates or clarifies another. Keisselbrack v Livingston Ch (NY) 4 Johns 144, 149.

res accessoria (rēz ak-ses-sō'ri-a). An accessory thing.

Res accessoria non ducit, sed sequitur suum principale (rēz ak-ses-sō'ri-a non dū'sit, sed se'qui-ter su'um prin-si-pā'le). The accessory thing does not lead, but it follows its principal thing. See Broom's Legal Maxims 493.

Res accessoria sequitur rem principalem (rēz ak-ses-sō'ri-a se'qui-ter rem prin-si-pā'lem). The accessory thing follows the principal thing. See Broom's Legal Maxims 491.

Res accrescit domino (rēz a-kre'sit do'mi-nō). The thing goes to increase the principal thing. That is, anything annexed or added to a principal thing becomes a part of it. See argument of counsel in Banks v Ogden (US) 2 Wall 57, 17 L Ed 818.

res adjudicata. Same as **res judicata.**

resale. A sale at retail following a purchase at wholesale. A second sale by of the same goods or property by a seller. Banks v Pann, 82 Cal App 20, 254 P 937. A remedy of the seller under an executory contract of sale where the buyer refuses to receive or take the goods, or repudiates the contract. 46 Am J1st Sales § 566. A remedy of the seller of goods under an executed contract of sale where title has passed to the buyer but the seller has retained his lien by the retention of possession or by the exercise of the right of stoppage in transitu. 46 Am J1st Sales § 568. A remedy of the vendor under a conditional sales contract upon retaking the property for the default of the vendee. 47 Am J1st Sales § 966. A judicial sale, following a prior sale of such nature, where the purchaser fails to comply with his bid or where the sale is vacated. 30A Am J Rev ed Jud S §§ 270 et seq.

resale at purchaser's risk. One of the modes of proceeding in a court of equity when a purchaser at a judicial sale, after confirmation, fails or refuses to complete his purchase.

Under this mode of procedure, the court may order a resale of the property, holding the purchaser responsible for any deficiency. Hammond v Cailleaud, 111 Cal 206, 215, 43 P 607.

resale price. See **price control.**

res aliena (rēz-ā-li-ē'na). The property of another.

res caduca (rēz ka-dū'ka). (Civil law.) A fallen thing; escheated property.

resceit. The ancient English practice of permitting a person who was not a party to the action to come into it and plead a right of his own.

resceu. Same as **rescue.**

rescind (rę-sind'). To effect a rescission.
See **rescission.**

rescissio (re-si'zhe-ō). (Civil law.) A rescission; a repeal; an abrogation.

rescission. The termination of a contract through its abrogation or annulment by word or act of the parties or by a judgment or decree of the court. The termination of a contract by mutual consent of the parties or pursuant to a condition contained in the contract, or for fraud, failure of consideration, or a material breach or default. Maytag Co. v Alward, 253 Iowa 455, 112 NW2d 654, 96 ALR2d 162. The termination of the contract, and restoration of the contracting parties substantially to their status quo. Anno: 94 ALR 1240.

Treating a contract as broken and desisting from further performance, where the other party to the contract has been guilty of a breach of it, is an abandonment of the contract, but it is not a "rescission" technically speaking. It is merely the acceptance of the situation which the wrongdoing of the other party has brought about. Anvil Mining Co. v Humble, 153 US 540, 552, 38 L Ed 814, 818, 14 S Ct 876.

As the word is applied to contracts, to "rescind" in some cases means to terminate the contract as to future transactions, while in others it means to annul the contract from the beginning. Hurst v Trow Printing & Bookbinding Co. 2 Misc 361, 366, 22 NYS 371.

See **cancellation**.

rescission in pais (rę-sizh'ọn in pā). The setting aside of an instrument outside of court by the act of a party as distinguished from a rescission in equity. McCall v Superior Court of Imperial County, 1 Cal 2d 527, 36 P2d 642, 95 ALR 1019.

rescissory action (rę-sis'ọ̄-ri ak'shọn). An action to rescind a contract or other written instrument.

res communes (rēz kom'mu-nēz). (Roman law.) Things which are common property.

The human race having multiplied, men partitioned among themselves the earth and the greater part of those things which were on its surface. That which fell to each one among them commenced to belong to him in private ownership, and this process is the origin of the right of property. Some things, however, did not enter into this division, and remain therefore to this day in the condition of the ancient and negative community. These are the things which the jurisconsults called "res communes." Among them are the air, the water which runs in the rivers and the sea. Wild animals, ferae naturae, have also remained in the ancient state of negative community. Geer v Connecticut, 161 US 519, 525, 40 L Ed 793, 795, 16 S Ct 600.

res controversa (rēz kon-tro-ver'sa). (Civil law.) The matter in controversy; the thing in dispute.

res coronae (rēz ko-rō'nē). The property of the crown.

res corporales (rēz kor-po-rā'lēz). (Civil law.) Corporeal property; tangible property.

rescous. Same as **rescue**.

rescript (rē'skript). A statement in writing delivered by a court announcing its decision or conclusions of law; the decision of a Roman emperor on a doubtful point which was submitted to him for his determination.

rescue. Saving a person exposed to peril. The crime committed where a person, other than the official custodian, either directly or indirectly, unlawfully aids another person to escape from proper custody. 27 Am J2d Escape § 3. Unlawfully taking away and setting at liberty a distrained animal, whether by force, by threat, or in a peaceful manner. Hamlin v Mack, 33 Mich 103, 105. At common law rescue and pound breach were both actionable and indictable wrongs. "The writ of rescous lieth where a man doth distrain for rent or service, or for damage feasant, and would impeach or impound the cattle, and the other party doth rescue them or take them from him, he shall have the writ of rescous." See Newell v Clark, 46 NJL 363, 376.

rescue clause. A clause, sometimes called a "sue and labor" clause, in a marine insurance policy, enabling the insured to take every measure necessary for the preservation and recovery of the property, without losing his right to abandon, and making it his duty to take such action. 29A Am J Rev ed Ins § 1568. A clause in a marine insurance policy which authorizes the insured to sue, labor, and travel for the safety of the subject-matter of the insurance, or any part thereof, without prejudice to the insurance. St. Paul Fire & Marine Ins. Co. v Pacific Cold Storage Co. (CA9 Wash) 157 F 625.

rescue doctrine. The doctrine that where one person is exposed to peril of life or limb by the negligence of another, the latter will be liable in damages for injuries received by a third person in a reasonable effort to rescue the person so imperiled. Marshall v Nugent (CA1 NH) 222 F2d 604, 58 ALR2d 251; 38 Am J1st Negl § 80. The same principle applied to injuries received in saving property exposed to peril by negligence. 38 Am J1st Negl § 81. The principle that one is justified in exposing himself to risks in the protection of human life which otherwise he could not assume without charging himself with contributory negligence. Hammonds v Haven, (Mo) 280 SW2d 814, 53 ALR2d 992.

See **saving property doctrine**.

rescussit (res-kus'sit). He rescued.

rescussor (res-kus'ọr). A person who committed a rescue; a rescuer.

rescussu. See **de rescussu**.

rescussus (res-kus'sus). A rescue.

rescutere (res-ku'te-re). To rescue.

rescyt. The receiving or harboring of a person who had committed a felony and had been convicted thereof.

Res denominatur a principaliori parte (rēz de-no-mi-nā'ter ā prin-si-pā-li-ō'rī par'te). A thing receives its name from its principal part.

res derelicta (rēz de-re-lik'ta). Abandoned property; property from which the mind has withdrawn affection, and which has thus fallen back into the natural state of res nullius, the property of no one, and is again susceptible of becoming the property of the occupant. Rhodes v Whitehead, 27 Tex 304.

resealing. Correcting or giving renewed effect to a writ.

research organization. See **heir hunter**.

resentence. Pronouncing sentence for a criminal offense after revision, modification, or vacation of judgment, during the term at which the judgment was entered. 21 Am J2d Crim L §§ 569 et seq. Pronouncing sentence after a reversal on appeal because of error of the trial court in imposing sentence, whether by the appellate court or the trial court upon remand of the case. 5 Am J2d A & E § 976.

reservation. The engaging of a room at a hotel or a table in a restaurant in advance of the service to be rendered or the accommodation to be had. Often used as a term interchangeable with "exception." Stephan v Kentucky Valley Distilling Co. 275 Ky 705, 122 SW2d 493. In one sense a grant by a grantee back to the grantor. Precisely, the creation in behalf of the grantor of a new right issuing out of the thing granted. 23 Am J2d Deeds § 262.

A reservation is to be distinguished from an "exception," which is of a part of the thing granted and of something in esse at the time. Winston v Johnson, 42 Mich 398, 401, 54 NW 958.

See **condition; exception; Indian reservation; military reservation.**

reservation Indians. Indians living on Indian reservations.

While they are so living, the jurisdiction of the Federal Government over their tribes, and over the members of such tribes, is exclusive, and they cannot be controlled or governed by the laws of the state within which the reservations are located, except as such laws are specifically authorized by Congress or clearly do not interfere with federal policies concerning Indian reservations. Warren Trading Post v Arizona State Tax Com. 380 US 685, 14 L Ed 2d 165, 85 S Ct 1242.

See **Indian reservation.**

reservation of easement. The creation in behalf of the grantor of a new right, issuing out of the same grant, of an easement appurtenant to the grantor's remaining land. 25 Am J2d Ease § 21.

Reservatio non debet esse de proficuis ipsis, quia ea conceduntur, sed de redditu novo extra proficua (re-zer-vā′she-ō non de′bet es′se dē pro-fi′ku-is ip′sis, qui′a e′a kon-se-dun′ter, sed dē red′di-tū nō′vō ex′-tra pro-fi′ku-a). A reservation ought not to be of the profits themselves, because they are granted, but it should be of a new rent aside from the profits.

reserve. Verb: To appropriate to a particular purpose. To exclude. To set aside. To set apart from that which has been granted. To make a reservation. Meigs v M'Clung's Lessee (US) 9 Cranch 11, 17, 3 L Ed 639, 641. Noun: An organization of the Armed Forces, holding men for training without serious disruption of their civilian activities, but subject to call of active service. A fund or sum of money retained for a special purpose. A fund of a bank, known as a legal reserve, being required by law in an amount proportioned to the deposits by way of assurance to depositors of opportunity to withdraw cash as they need or desire it. State v Brewer, 202 NC 187, 162 SE 363, 81 ALR 1424. In insurance, a sum of money variously computed or estimated, which, with accretions from interest, is set aside, as a fund with which to mature or liquidate, either by payment or reinsurance with other companies, future unaccrued and contingent claims, and claims accrued but contingent and indefinite as to amount or time of payment. Maryland Casualty Co. v United States, 251 US 342, 64 L Ed 297, 40 S Ct 155. In the distinctive meaning in respect of life insurance maintained on the level-premium basis:—the accumulated saving upon a policy which results from the fact that the amount of the premium is greater than the mortality cost during the early years of the insurance and less than the mortality cost in later years, such amount constituting the source of the nonforfeiture value of the policy upon lapse. Williams v Union Central Life Ins. Co. 291 US 170, 78 L Ed 711, 54 S Ct 348, 92 ALR 693. The amount of money or assets necessary for a life insurance company to have at any given time to enable it, with interest gained and premiums paid as they shall mature, to meet all claims on the insurance policies then in force as they shall become due according to the particular mortality table accepted; to be reckoned as a liability, and calculated on net premiums; theoretically, the difference between the present value of the total insurance and the present value of the future premiums on the insurance. Anno: 13 ALR 187.

See **loss and loss expense reserve; mean reserve; terminal reserve; unearned premium reserve.**

Reserve Act. The Federal Statute of 1913 under which the federal reserve system was established. 12 USC §§ 341 et seq.

See **reserve banks; reserve system.**

reserve an exception. To cause an objection of a party to be entered of record during the progress of a trial or other proceeding in a court.

See **reserving question in lower court.**

reserve an objection. To reserve, with the permission of the court, the right to make an objection at a later time in the trial.

reserve banks. Banks, incorporated under the act of Congress known as the Federal Reserve Act of 1913 and statutes amendatory thereof, and which are members of the Federal reserve system. American Bank & Trust Co. v Federal Reserve Bank, 256 US 350, 65 L Ed 983, 41 S Ct 499, 25 ALR 971, 975, 976. Banks operating under the supervision of the Federal Reserve Board to act as government depositories and fiscal agents of the government; to receive and maintain the legal reserves of banks in the federal reserve system; to discount notes, drafts, and bills of exchange arising in actual commercial transactions; to make short term advances to member banks upon their promissory notes, and, subject to rules and regulations prescribed by the Federal Reserve Board, to engage in open market operations. 10 Am J2d Banks § 272.

Reserve Board. The agency of the United States which acts with primary authority in supervising banks in the Federal Reserve System. 10 Am J2d Banks § 272. A board of governors of the Federal Reserve System, composed of seven members appointed by the President with the consent of the President, empowered to exercise general supervision over federal reserve banks, and granted specific authority in reference to the rediscount of commercial paper and the rates of discount. 10 Am J2d Banks § 5.

reserve clause. A term, in popular use in reference to the contracts of professional athletes, especially baseball players, whereunder the services of the athlete are reserved for the club, although not engaged for more than one year at a time.

See **reserved option.**

reserved. Set apart for a purpose or for a person, as a part of a subdivision set apart for a community theater or a suite of rooms held for a person.

This word in a plat may operate, in the light of the circumstances under which it is used, to show a dedicatory intention. 23 Am J2d Ded § 27.

See **case reserved; crown cases reserved; reservation.**

reserved lands. Lands in the public domain withdrawn from sale, entry, settlement, or other manner of acquisition by the public. 42 Am J1st Pub L § 12. Tracts of public land lawfully appropriated by the government to any purposes and thereby severed from the mass of public lands, so that no subsequent law or proclamation will be construed to embrace them or operate upon them, although no exception be made of them.

The rule is general that no entry or sale of any land can be made which has been reserved for the use of the United States, or one of the states, but they may be restored to the public domain, as, for example, where a military post is abandoned by the government. 42 Am J1st Pub L § 19.

reserved option. Broadly, any option provided a party under the terms of a contract. In common usage, an option contained in the terms of a contract permitting a party to rescind or cancel. 17 Am J2d Contr §§ 495-498.

reserved point. A point not decided by the appellate court in the disposition of a case, being expressly reserved from decision. Re Monaghan's Estate, 70 Ariz 349, 220 P2d 726, affd 71 Ariz 334, 227 P2d 227. A point of law which is decided by the court in the course of a trial, but conditionally only, and subject to reargument.

See **reserving question in lower court.**

reserved powers of the state. Powers which are not delegated to the Federal Government or prohibited to the states by the United States Constitution. United States v Darby, 312 US 100, 85 L Ed 609, 61 S Ct 451, 132 ALR 1430. Powers which proceed, not from the people of America, but from the people of the several states, remaining the same after, as before the acceptance of the United States Constitution, except as they may be abridged by that instrument. United States v Appalachian Electric Power Co. 311 US 377, 85 L Ed 243, 61 S Ct 291, reh den 312 US 712, 85 L Ed 1143, 61 S Ct 548.

reserved price. Same as **minimum price.**

reserved question. See **certification of question; reserved point.**

reserved way. A way newly created by a grantor by means of a reservation. Winston v Johnson, 42 Minn 398, 401, 54 NW 958. Sometimes an implied way as a way of necessity in reference to land retained by the grantor.

See **way of necessity.**

reserve for loss claims. See **loss and loss expense reserve; reserve.**

reserve fund. See **reserve.**

reserve method. A method of bookkeeping elected by a taxpayer under the federal income tax law, whereby he sets up a reserve for bad debts, with or without the maintenance of a reserve fund, adding such additions to the reserve as will make the balance large enough to absorb expected bad debts. Internal Revenue Code § 166(c)(d).

Reserve System. A system of banks, operating under supervision of advisory and regulatory agencies, provided by Act of Congress in 1913 for the purposes of promoting sound banking practices and facilitating a flow of credit and money essential to the economic growth of the country. 10 Am J2d Banks § 5.

See **Advisory Council; Governors of the Federal Reserve System; Reserve Act; reserve banks.**

reserving. Making a reservation.
See **reserve.**

reserving question in lower court. A fundamental condition of right to review; the raising of objections and the reservation of exceptions to rulings. 5 Am J2d A & E §§ 545 et seq.

See **reserved point.**

reservoir (rez'ẽr-vwor). A place where water collects naturally, or is stored for use when wanted, as to supply a fountain, a canal, or a city, or for any other purpose. Howell v Big Horn Basin Colonization Co. 14 Wyo 14, 81 P 785.

Res est misera ubi jus est vagum et incertum (rēz est mi'se-ra u'bi jūs est va'gum et in-ser'tum). It is a sorry affair when the law is vague and uncertain.

reset (rē-set'). The receiving or harboring of an outlaw. The harboring of an outlaw.

res fungibles (rēz fun'ji-blēz). (Civil law.) Fungible property,—property which was consumable by use and returnable in kind, such as wine.

res furtivae (rēz fer'ti-vē). Things which had been stolen.

Res generalem habet significationem, quia tam corporea, quam incorporea, cujuscunque sunt generis naturae sive speciei, comprehendit (rēz je-ne-rā'lem hā'bet sig-ni-fi-kā-she-ō'nem, qui'a tam kor-pō're-a, quam in-kor-pō're-a, kū-jus-kun'kwe sunt je'neris na-tū'rē sī've spe-she'ē-ī, kom-pre-hen'dit)."Thing" has a general meaning, because it includes the corporeal as well as the incorporeal, of whatever kind, nature or species the things may be.

res gestae (rēz jes'tē). A matter incidental to the main or principal fact, and explanatory thereof; acts or words through which a main event speaks. Cummings v Illinois Cent. R. Co. 364 Mo 868, 269 SW2d 111, 47 ALR2d 513. Acts and words which are spontaneous and so related to the transaction or occurrence in question as reasonably to appear to be evoked and prompted by it. 29 Am J2d Ev § 708.

resiance (rez'i-ans). Same as **residence.**

resiant (rez'i-ant). Residing.

reside. To dwell in a place. To be a resident. Kelsey v Green, 69 Conn 291, 37 A 679.

residence. A term of dual meaning, sometimes meaning a temporary, permanent, or transient character of abode; at other times meaning one's fixed abode or domicil. 25 Am J2d Dom § 4. Sometimes a mere physical presence in a place; at other times an abiding in a place with intent to make it one's home. Manufacturers' Mut. Ins. Co. v Friedman, 213 Ark 9, 209 SW2d 102, 1 ALR2d 557; People ex rel. Heydenreich v Lyons, 374 Ill 557, 30 NE2d 46, 132 ALR 511; Dixie Fire Ins. Co. v McAdams (Tex Civ App) 235 SW2d 207, 41 ALR2d 714. Sometimes a temporary, at other times an actual or permanent, abiding place. 2 Am J2d Adopt § 52. A word having a variety of meanings dependent upon the context in which it is employed as well as the subject matter involved, Hughes v Illinois Public Aid Co. 2 Ill 2d 374, 118 NE2d 14, 43 ALR2d 1421, sometimes meaning domicil, at other times not. State v Garford Trucking, 4 NJ 346, 72 A2d 851, 16 ALR2d 1407. A dwelling house.

Under the provision of the Uniform Negotiable Instruments Act for sending notice of dishonor of a bill or note to the residence of an indorser, the term "residence" is not used in a strict sense as necessarily implying a permanent, exclusive, or actual abode in the place, but it may be satisfied by a temporary, partial, or even constructive residence. 11 Am J2d B & N § 856.

As to requisite residence for purposes of old age assistance, Anno: 43 ALR2d 1427. As to relationship between "residence" and "domicil" under venue statutes, see Anno: 12 ALR2d 757.

See **domicil; inhabitancy; legal residence; one residence; one residence only.**

residence of bankrupt. The domicil of the bankrupt. 9 Am J2d Bankr § 40.
See **domicil.**

residence of corporation. Residence only as declared by law in the state of incorporation. 18 Am J2d Corp § 159.

For purposes of venue, a corporation is a "resident" of the county designated in its articles of association, its certificate of registered agent, and its annual reports regularly filed, and its place of doing business and its offices; and an action against the corporation transitory in its nature may properly be brought in that county even though the corporation's principal and only office is in fact located over the county line in an adjoining county. Higgins v Hampshire Products, 319 Mich 674, 30 NW2d 390, 175 ALR 1083.

Within the meaning of a state statute making the county in which the defendant resides a proper county for the trial of the action, the county in which lies the place designated by a foreign corporation as its principal office and place of business within the state in the papers filed by it with the secretary of state and the county clerk as a condition precedent to its doing business in the state, is its residence. Anno: 129 ALR 1289.

residence of debtor. Sometimes, but not always, the equivalent of domicil. 31 Am J2d Exempt § 17.
See **domicil**; **residence of bankrupt**.

residence of decedent. The domicil of the decedent. Re Glassford's Estate, 114 Cal App 2d 181, 249 P2d 248, 34 ALR2d 1259 (purposes of ancillary administration of decedent's estate); 31 Am J2d Ex & Ad § 32; 57 Am J1st Wills § 766 (purposes of jurisdiction for probate of will).
See **domicil**.

residence of foreign corporation. See **residence of corporation**.

residence of infant. See **domicil by operation of law**.

residence of voter. The domicil of the voter; his home; his place of permanent abode. The place where he is habitually present, and to which, when he departs, he intends to return. The home to which, whenever absent, he intends to return. 25 Am J2d Elect § 66.

residence of ward. The domicil of the ward. 25 Am J1st G & W § 25.
See **domicil**.

residence of wife. See **domicil by operation of law**.

resident. One who resides in a place. One having either legal residence or domicil. Stadtmuller v Miller (CA2 NY) 11 F2d 732, 45 ALR 895, 897. A physician, usually a younger man, employed for the practice of his profession in a hospital, acquiring proficiency in a speciality or gaining experience for later general practice.
See **domicil**; **residence**.

resident agent. An agent of a foreign corporation in residence either permanently or temporarily for the purpose of the agency, the term being exclusive of a mere transient. Anno: 113 ALR 84.

resident alien. An alien having the status of a resident and accordingly in a separate classification. 3 Am J2d Aliens § 2. An alien who has come into the United States from a foreign country with the purpose of abandoning his residence abroad and of making his home here. People ex rel. Dobson v McClay, 2 Neb 7, 9.

resident freeholder. A resident of the place who is the owner of a freehold interest in lands situated therein. See Damp v Dane, 29 Wis 419, 427.

residential district. A district characterized by a predominance of structures used as dwelling places or residences. 58 Am J1st Zon § 36.

residential district ordinance. A zoning ordinance dealing with isolated blocks or districts, not enacted for the purpose of adopting a comprehensive plan for the municipality. 58 Am J1st Zon § 34.

residential restriction. A covenant limiting the erection or use of buildings on premises to residences or residential purposes, or limiting the type of dwellings or residences which can be erected on the premises. 20 Am J2d Cov §§ 189 et seq. A zoning ordinance which limits the construction of building in a stated district to residences or residential purposes. 58 Am J1st Zon §§ 36 et seq.

resident sales agent. A local agent of a foreign corporation. 36 Am J2d For Corp § 563.

residuary (rē-zid′ū-ā-ri). The residuary estate of a testate decedent. A legatee or devisee under a legacy or devise of the residuary estate or a part thereof. Estate of Vanuxem, 212 Pa 315, 61 A 876, 878.
See **residuary estate**.

residuary bequest. Same as **residuary gift**.

residuary clause. A clause in a will which purports to dispose of that part of the estate which is left after other legacies and devises have been paid and all legal claims against the estate discharged. 57 Am J1st Wills § 1415.

The term seems to contemplate the former provisions in the will to carry into effect the wishes of the testator as to the disposition of his estate, and is used to cover all that remains after such former dispositions of property have been carried out. Morgan v Huggins (CC Ga) 48 F 3, 5.

The phrase "rest, residue, and remainder" is frequently used in wills to devise and bequeath all of the property of the testator which he has not by his will specifically devised or bequeathed. " 'All the rest, residue, and remainder of my property, both real and personal,' expresses no intent to limit or exclude from the residuum anything personal or real, anything whatever which for any reason might prove to be ineffectually disposed of. It expresses a clear intent on the part of the testator to make a full and complete disposition of his property." Wilson v Sanger, 57 App Div 320, 322, 68 NYS 30.

As a rule, an enumeration of specific articles in a residuary clause will not make the bequest specific as to such articles unless they are designated in such a way as to differentiate them from the residue. A bequest of all a man's personal property is a residuary and not a specific legacy, since its import is the same as is expressed by the words, "rest and residue." But a devise of "all the residue of the testator's real estate and personal property not hereinbefore enumerated, as hereinafter described," is a specific bequest of the subsequently enumerated property, and does not entitle the beneficiary to take as a residuary legatee the lapsed legacies and property not enumerated in the bequest to him. 57 Am J1st Wills §§ 1415 et seq.

residuary devise. See **residuary clause**; **residuary gift**.

residuary devisee. One favored by a residuary devise.

residuary estate. That part of an estate of a testate decedent which remains after discharging all legal and testamentary claims of the estate or, in other words, that which is left after the payment of charges, debts, and particular legacies and devises.

57 Am J1st Wills § 1415. The final residuum which remains of the estate of a testator after the payment of all his bequests and devises. Wetmore v St. Luke's Hospital (NY) 56 Hun 313, 320, 9 NYS 753.

residuary gift. A legacy or devise bequeathed by the residuary clause of a will. A legacy or devise of the residuary estate or of a part of the residuary estate. 57 Am J1st Wills § 1415.
 See **residuary clause; residuary estate.**

residuary legacy. See **residuary clause; residuary gift.**

residuary legatee. One favored by a **residuary legacy.**

residue of estate. Same as **residuary estate.**

residuum (rē-zid'ū-um). The part which is left. Something left over. Buffington v Mason, 327 Mass 195, 97 NE2d 538, 37 ALR2d 1.
 See **residuary estate.**

residuum of the residuum (rē-zid'ū-um of the rē-zid'ū-um). That which remains of a testator's estate after the payment of a specifically devised portion of the residuary estate.
 "While strictly speaking, the phrase may imply a contradiction, it expresses what was intended by" "all the rest and residue of my said residuary estate not herein otherwise disposed of." United States Trust Co. v Black, 9 Misc 653, 655, 30 NYS 453.

residuum rule (rē-zid'ū-um rūl). The principle that, even though an administrative agency is not bound by the rules of evidence binding upon a court, and even though the agency may in its discretion accept any evidence that is offered, still in the end there must be a residuum of legal evidence to support the finding of the agency. Carroll v Knickerbocker Ice Co. 218 NY 435, 113 NE 507; Doca v Federal Stevedoring Co. 308 NY 44, 123 NE2d 632, reh den 308 NY 744, 125 NE2d 102.

resign (rē-zīn'). See **resignation.**

Resignatio est juris proprii spontanea refutatio (re-zig-nā'she-ō est jū'ris prō'pri-ī spon-tā'ne-a re-fu-tā'she-ō). A resignation is a spontaneous giving up of one's own right.

resignation. A voluntary withdrawal of an officer of the Armed Forces from the service. 36 Am J1st Mil § 60. The voluntary relinquishment of his position by a civil service employee. 15 Am J2d Civ S § 34. The relinquishment of the office of executor or administrator under conditions prescribed by statute. 31 Am J2d Ex & Ad § 119.

resignation of public office. A well recognized right. 43 Am J1st Pub Of § 166. A relinquishment of a part of the term of a public office with intent accompanied by an act of relinquishment. 43 Am J1st Pub Of § 165. To give up, to give back the office with intent to relinquish it.
 A prospective resignation may, in point of law, amount but to a notice of intention to resign, since it is not accompanied by a giving up of the office; possession is still retained and may not necessarily be surrendered till the expiration of the legal term of the office, because the officer may recall his resignation,—may withdraw his proposition to resign. State ex rel. Ryan v Murphy, 30 Nev 409, 97 P 391, 720.

resignee (rē-zī-nē). A person in whose favor another person tenders his resignation.

resilire (re-zi-lī're). To refuse to enter into a contract.

res immobiles (rēz im-mō'bi-lēz). (Civil law.) Immovable corporeal things, consisting of land and that which is connected therewith either by nature or art, such as trees and buildings. See Mackeldey's Roman Law § 160.

res in re (rēz in rē). The entering of the male organ in that of the female. Mere penetration. 44 Am J1st Rape § 3.

res integra (rēz in'te-gra). An untouched matter; a point without a precedent; a case of novel impression.

res inter alios (rēz in'ter a'li-os). Matters between others; the acts of strangers or third parties.

res inter alios acta (rēz in'ter a'li-os ak'ta). The acts and declarations either of strangers, or of one of the parties to the action in his dealings with strangers. Chicago & Eastern Illinois Railroad Co. v Schmitz, 211 Ill 446, 456, 71 NE 1050.
 The recitals of an instrument are not ordinarily admissible against third persons as proof of the facts recited, being as to them res inter alios acta. 29 Am J2d Ev § 841.

Res inter alios acta alteri nocere non debet (rēz in'ter a'li-os ak'ta al'te-rī no-sē're non de'bet). Transactions between certain parties ought not to prejudice third parties.
 "The general rule is that a person's books of account cannot be used as evidence upon issues between third persons, that entries in such books as to such third persons are res inter alios acta, and cannot be used against persons not parties to them." State ex rel. Pabst Brewing Co. v Carpenter, 129 Wis 180, 108 NW 641.

Res inter alios judicatae nullum aliis praejudicium faciunt (rēz in'ter a'li-os jū-di-kā'tē nul'lum a'li-is prē-jū-di'she-um fā'she-unt). (Civil law.) Matters which are adjudged as between certain persons effect no prejudice as to others; matters determined in a case do not prejudice those not parties thereto.

res ipsa loquitur (rēz ip'sa lo'qui-ter). The thing speaks for itself. The rule that proof that the thing which caused the injury to the plaintiff was under the control and management of the defendant, and that the occurrence was such as in the ordinary course of things would not have happened if those who had its control or management had used proper care, affords sufficient evidence, or, as sometimes stated by the courts, reasonable evidence, in the absence of explanation by the defendant, that the injury arose from, or was caused by, the defendant's want of care. 38 Am J1st Negl § 295.
 The three essential elements of the doctrine of res ipsa loquitur are: (1) the instrumentality must be under the control or management of the defendant; (2) the circumstances, according to common knowledge and experience, must create a clear inference that the accident would not have happened if the defendant had not been negligent; and (3) the plaintiff's injury must have resulted from the accident. Lewis v Wolk, 312 Ky 536, 228 SW2d 432, 16 ALR2d 974.
 The term means "the thing speaks for itself," and that means the thing or instrumentality involved speaks for itself. It clearly does not mean the accident speaks for itself. It means that when the initial fact, namely what thing or instrumentality caused the accident has been shown then, and not before, an inference arises that the injury or damage occurred by reason of the negligence of the party who had it under his exclusive control. The inference of negligence arising from the initially established fact

compels the defendant, in order to relieve himself of liability, to move forward with his proof to rebut the inference of negligence. Travelers Ins. Co. v Hulme, 168 Kan 483, 213 P2d 645, 16 ALR2d 793.

resist. To make **resistance.**

resistance. Opposition by direct, active, forcible, or quasi-forcible means. State v Welch, 37 Wis 196, 201. The criminal offense in resisting orders issued by lawful authority. 39 Am J1st Obst J § 5.

resisting officer. A criminal offense at common law and also by force of statute in resisting a public officer in the performance of his duties or opposing him by interposing obstacles or impediments to hinder, impede, or prevent him from performing his duties. 39 Am J1st Obst J §§ 8 et seq.

Under a statute penalizing under the single term "resist," it is not enough that the performance of a duty is opposed, obstructed, interrupted, hindered, or prevented; the officer must be resisted, and the resistance must be active and direct toward him. 39 Am J1st Obst J § 8.

res judicata (rēz jū-di-kā′ta). Literally, the thing has been decided, been adjudicated. State v Wear, 145 Mo 162, 192, 46 SW 1099. The principle that an existing final judgment rendered upon the merits, without fraud or collusion, by a court of competent jurisdiction, is conclusive of rights, questions, and facts in issue, as to the parties and their privies, in all other actions in the same or any other judicial tribunal of concurrent jurisdiction. 30A Am J Rev ed Judgm § 324.

The effect of a judgment as res judicata appears in at least three aspects, viz. merger of cause of action, bar, and estoppel. Anno: 49 ALR2d 1038.

A difference exists between the effect of a judgment as a bar to a second action between the same parties upon the same claim or demand and its effect in another action upon a different cause of action; in the former case, the judgment on the merits constitutes an absolute bar to the second action, being a finality, not only as to every matter which was offered and received to sustain or defeat the claim or demand, but also as to any other admissible matter which might have been offered for that purpose; in the latter case, the judgment is a bar only as to the matters actually litigated and determined in the former action, and not as to what might have been litigated and determined therein. Smith v Smith, 235 Minn 412, 51 NW2d 276, 32 ALR2d 1135.

Res judicata facit ex albo nigrum, ex nigro album, ex curvo rectum, ex recto curvum (rēz jū-di-kā′ta fā′sit ex al′bō ni′grum, ex ni′grō al′bum, ex ker′vō rek′tum, ex rek′tō ker′vum). When anything has been adjudicated, it makes white black, black white, curved straight and straight curved.

Res judicata pro veritate accipitur (rēz jū-di-kā′ta prō ve-ri-tā′te ak-si′pi-ter). (Civil law.) A matter which has been adjudicated is accepted or received as true.

Res judicata pro veritate habetur (rēz jū-di-kā′ta prō ve-ri-tā′te hā-bē′ter). An adjudicated matter shall be deemed correct. O'Donnell v Glenn, 9 Mont 452, 23 P 1018.

res mancipi (rēz man′si-pī). (Roman law.) Things that were the subject of mancipium; things capable of being sold by the mancipium.

res mobiles (rēz mō′bi-lēz). (Civil law.) Corporeal movable things, whether they were self-moving or not. See Mackeldey's Roman Law § 160.

res nova (rēz no′va). A new matter; a case, point, or matter without a precedent; a point of law which has not been decided.

res nullius (rēz nul-lī′us). The property of no one. See **res derelicta.**

Res nullius naturaliter fit primi occupantis (rēz nul′lī-us na-tū-rā′li-ter fit pri′mī o-ku-pan′tis). The property of no one naturally becomes that of the first occupant.

resolution. An expression of the opinion or mind of a municipal counsel concerning some matter of administration and providing for the disposition thereof, being less formal than an ordinance and requiring no set form of words. Sawyer v Lorenzen, 149 Iowa 87, 127 NW 1091. An expression of any legislative department of government other than by statute. A proposition of law declared in a case, e.g. the **first resolution in Wild's Case.**

See **joint resolution.**

resolutive (rez′ō̱-lū-tiv). Same as **resolutory.**

Resoluto jure concedentis, resolvitur jus concessum (re-zo-lū′tō jū′re kon-sē-den′tis, re-zol′vi-ter jūs kon-ses′sum). By the extinction of the right of the grantor, the right granted is extinguished. See Broom's Legal Maxims 467.

resolutory (rez′ō̱-lū-tō̱-ri). Determinative.

resolutory condition. A condition in a contract which permits the obligation to take effect immediately but subject to being nullified or defeated upon the happening of a certain event. New Orleans v Texas & Pacific R. Co. 171 US 312, 43 L Ed 178, 18 S Ct 875 (quoting from the Louisiana Civil Code which is said to be similar to the Code Napoleon in such respect).

reson. Right; justice; reason.

resort. Verb: To have recourse. To turn to one for aid or assistance. To use, as to resort to arms. To go to a place, even to go once. State v Ah Sam, 15 Nev 27. A place of frequent assembly. Re Sic, 73 Cal 142, 152, 14 P 405 (place for smoking opium).

Noun: A place operated for the health or pleasure of its patrons, not for the entertainment of transients. 29 Am J Rev ed Innk § 10.

See **dernier resort; joint.**

resorter (re-zôr′ta). To return; to go back.

resort to courts. See **access to courts.**

resources. Assets; means; income.

The word does not necessarily mean money in hand. A debtor may have ample resources to pay all his debts as they become due, and yet have no money in his pocket or in bank. Sacry v Lobree, 84 Cal 41, 23 P 1088.

respect. Honor; esteem. Concern; consideration.

"Respect is the voluntary tribute of the people to worth, virtue, and intelligence, and while these are found on the judgment seat, so long and no longer, will courts retain the public confidence." Carter v Commonwealth, 96 Va 791, 32 SE 780.

respectable (rē̱-spek′ta̱-bl). Worthy of respect; decent; proper.

respectable burial. A decent and proper burial, considering the financial, religious, social, and political standing of the deceased, and, to a certain extent, of his relatives. Seaton v Commonwealth, 149 Ky 498, 149 SE 871.

respective. Having reference to a single thing or a single person among several, as the respective abilities of the partners in a law firm. A word in a will indicative of a stirpital distribution where used in reference to legatees or devisees. Anno: 16 ALR 28, s. 78 ALR 1392, 126 ALR 165.

respectus (rę-spek'tus). Respite; delay.

Res periit domino (rēz per'i-it do'mi-nō). The thing is lost to the lord.
The destruction of a thing is the owner's loss. Krause v Crothersville School Trustees, 162 Ind 278, 70 NE 264.

Res periit domino suo (rēz per'i-it do'mi-nō su'ō). A thing which has been destroyed is lost to its owner. See Broom's Legal Maxims 238.

Res perit domino (rēz per'it do'mi-nō). Property destroyed is lost to its owner. Krause v Crothersville, 162 Ind 278, 70 NE 264.

Res perit suo domino (rēz per'it su'ō do'mi-nō). Property destroyed is lost to its owner. Osborn v Nicholson (US) 13 Wall 654, 20 L Ed 689, 695.

Res per pecuniam aestimatur, et non pecunia per res (rēz per pe-kū'ni-am ēs-ti-mā'ter, et non pe-kū'ni-a per rēz). Property is valued by the standard of money, and not money by the standard of property.

Respiciendum est judicanti, nequid aut durius aut remissius constituatur quam causa deposcit; nec enim aut severitatis aut clementiae gloria affectanda est (re-spi-she-en'dum est jū-di-kan'tī, ne-quid ât du'ri-us ât rē-mis'sus kon-sti-chu-ā'ter quam kâ'za de-po'sit; nek e'min ât se-ve-ri-tā'tis ât kle-men'she-ē glo'ri-a af-fek-tan'da est). It should be observed by one adjudicating that nothing should be construed either more harshly nor more mildly than the cause warrants, for neither the glory of severity nor clemency should be affected.

respite (res'pit). A temporary suspension of the execution of a sentence; a delay; a forbearance or continuation of time. Mishler v Commonwealth, 62 Pa 55, 60.

respond. To be responsible for; to answer. The Mary F. Barrett (CA3 Pa) 279 F 329, 24 ALR 148, 152.

respondeat ouster (re-spon'de-at ous'ter). Let him answer over.
See **judgment of respondeat ouster**.

Respondeat raptor, qui ignorare non potuit quod pupillum alienum abduxit (re-spon'de-at rap'tor, quī ig-no-rā're non po'tu-it quod pu-pil'lum ā-li-ē'num ab-dū'xit). Let the ravisher answer, he who could not be ignorant of the fact that he has traduced the ward of another.

respondeat superior (re-spon'de-at su-pe'ri-or). The doctrine under which liability is imposed upon an employer for the acts of his employees committed in the course and scope of their employment. 35 Am J1st M & S § 543.
The tort liability of a principal for the act of his agent is based, not on the agency relationship, but on the relation of employer and employee, and is expressed by the maxim "respondeat superior." 3 Am J2d Agency § 261.

respondent. The party against whom an appeal is taken to a higher court, being the successful party in the lower court. The defendant in an action. The defendant in a suit in equity. Brower v Nellis, 6 Ind App 323, 33 NE 672. A defendant in certain special proceedings, such as mandamus. 35 Am J1st Mand § 327.

respondentia bond (res-pon-den'shi-ạ bond). A maritime hypothecation, technically of cargo, but sometimes covering both ship and cargo, given ordinarily in a foreign port by the master of a vessel by way of security for advances made to supply the necessities of the ship. O'Brien v Miller, 168 US 287, 42 L Ed 469, 18 S Ct 140.

Respondera son soveraigne (res-pōn'de-ra son sō-ver-ēn'). His superior shall answer.

respondes oustre (res-pon'dēz ous'ter). Same as **respondeat ouster**.

responsalis (re-spon-sā'lis). A person who answered for another; an attorney; a proctor.

responsa prudentum (re-spon'sa pru-den'tum). Opinions of learned lawyers. 1 Bl Comm 80.

responses. See **book of responses**.

responsibility. Duty; bounden duty. Obligation; liability. Crockett v Barre, 66 Vt 269, 272, 29 A 147.

responsibility for crime. See **criminal capacity**.

responsibility laws. See **financial responsibility laws**.

responsible. Under obligation. 8 Am J2d Bailm § 140. Under liability. Lattin v Gillette, 95 Cal 317, 30 P 545. Legally responsible. Anno: 72 ALR 1414. Answerable, legally or morally, for the discharge of a duty, trust, debt, service, or other obligation; accountable, as to a judge, master, creditor, ruler, or rightful superior; subject to obligations; bound. The Mary F. Barrett (CA3 Pa) 279 F 329, 25 ALR 148, 152. Reliable and able to pay.
See **criminal capacity**.

responsible bidder. A bidder in the letting of a contract for a public work or improvement who has financial responsibility and also the judgment, skill, ability, capacity, and integrity to complete the improvement. O'Brien v Carney (DC Mass) 6 F Supp 761; Kelling v Edwards, 116 Minn 484, 134 NW 221; State ex rel. Eaves v Rickards, 16 Mont 145, 40 P 210.
See **lowest responsible bidder**.

responsio (re-spon'si-ō). An answer; the response of a witness to a question asked him.

Responsio unius non omnino auditur (re-spon'si-ō ū-nī'us non om-nī'nō â-dī'ter). (Roman law.) The testimony of a single witness is not to be heard at all.

responsive allegation (rę-spon'siv al-ę-gā'shọn). The pleading in an ecclesiastical testamentary cause corresponding to the plea at common law; an answer.

responsive pleading. An answer responding to the allegations of the complaint; a reply responding to the allegations of a counterclaim.

res privatae (rēz pri-vā'tē). (Civil law.) Private property; property belonging to individuals. See Mackeldey's Roman Law § 170.

Res propria est quae communis non est (rēz prō'pri-a est kwē kom-mu'nis non est). That is one's own which does not belong to the community.
Under the Civil law, the goods "propres" are those which belong to the wife personally, and of which the fruits and revenues only enter into the community; the "conquets" are all those of which the principal or capital, as well as the fruits and income which they produce, enter the community. The fruits and income of the "propres," as well of the husband as of the wife, are also called "conquets", because they form a portion of the goods of the community. Le Breton v Miles (NY) 8 Paige Ch 261, 269. (Civil law.) Public things; things which belong to the public; things which are free to every

member of the state. See Mackeldey's Roman Law § 170.

res publica (rēz pub'li-ka). The republic; the government; the state.

Res quae intra praesidia perductae nondum sunt, quanquam ab hostibus occupatae, ideo postliminii non egent, quia dominum nondum mutarunt ex gentium jure (rēz kwē in'tra prē-si'di-a per-duk'tē non'-dum sunt, quan'quam ab hos'ti-bus o-ku-pā'tē, i'de-o post-li-mi'ni-i non e'jent, qui'a dō'mi-num non'dum mu-tā'runt ex jen'she-um ju're). Things which have not yet been brought into camp, although in the possession of the enemy, do not require postliminy on that account, because by the law of nations they have not yet changed their ownership.

res quotidianae (rēz quo-ti-di-ā'nē). Common, everyday matters.

res religiosae (rēz re-li-ji-ō'sē). Religious matters; cemeteries.

res sacrae (rēz sak'rē). (Civil law.) Sacred things; consecrated things.

Res sacra non recipit aestimationem (rēz sāk'ra non rē'si-pit ēs-ti-mā-she-ō'nem). (Civil law.) A sacred thing does not admit of valuation.

res sanctae (rēz sangk'tē). (Civil law.) Sacred, holy, or inviolable things.

resseiser (re-sēz'er). The retaking of the possession of land by a person who had been disseised.

Res sua nemini servit (rēz su'a ne'mi-nī ser'vit). No one can have a servitude in his own land.

rest. See **residue; rests**.

Restatement of the Law. A statement of rules of law in certain subjects, adopted and promulgated by the American Law Institute, the statement of a rule being entitled to weight as a product of expert opinion and as the expression of the law by the legal profession. Poretta v Superior Dowel Co. 153 Mo 308, 137 A2d 361, 71 ALR2d 898.

restaurant. An eating house; an establishment where meals and refreshments are served. Anno: 122 ALR 1399. A place where a customer goes to satisfy his immediate need of food and where he, rather than the proprietor, selects the particular food he wants at a price fixed for that food by the proprietor. Ford v Waldorf System, 57 RI 131, 188 A 633. A place to which a person resorts for the temporary purpose of obtaining a meal or something to eat. State v Shoaf, 179 NC 744, 102 SE 705, 9 ALR 426, 427.

restaurant keeper. One who keeps a place for serving meals to suit the taste of his patrons. State v Shoaf, 179 NC 744, 102 SE 705, 9 ALR 426, 427.

restitutio in integrum (res-ti-tū'shi-ō in in'tē-grum). The restitution of a thing in its entirety; that is, restoring the thing to its original state.

The maxim is a leading one in admiralty in collision cases, where repairs are practicable, the rule being that the damages assessed shall be sufficient to restore the injured vessel to the condition in which she was at the time when the injury was inflicted upon her. Phoenix Ins. Co. v The Atlas, 93 US 302, 23 L Ed 863.

restitution. The restoration to a person of that of which he has been wrongly deprived. Relief against the unjust enrichment of one person at the expense of another. Relief for one who has been compelled to pay money under a judgment since reversed. 5 Am J2d A & E §§ 997 et seq. The restoration of property of which one has been deprived under a judgement since reversed. 5 Am J2d A & E § 1004. The ordinary form of judgment for the plaintiff in an action for forcible entry and detainer, awarding restitution of the premises to him, with costs. 22 Am J1st Forc E & D § 48. In the modern sense of the term, compensation, reimbursement, indemnification or reparation for benefits derived from, or for loss or injury caused to another. Holloway v People's Water Co. 100 Kan 414, 167 P 265, 2 ALR 161.

See **restoration rule; unjust enrichment; writ of restitution**.

restitutione temporalium (re-sti-tū-she-ō'ne tem-po-rā'li-um). A writ which lay for a bishop to have his temporalities restored to him.

See **temporalities**.

restitution interest. A term of art in the law of damages for breach of contract, being the interest of the nondefaulting party in the benefit which he conferred on the defaulter pursuant to the contract and prior to its breach. Restatement, Contracts § 347; Restatement, Restitution § 107.

restitution of consortium (res-ti-tū'shon of kon-sôr'-she-um). The enforcement of a husband's duty to cohabit with his wife and treat her as a spouse. 26 Am J1st H & W § 17.

restitution of conjugal rights (of kon'jō-gal rīts). An ecclesiastical suit to compel a husband or wife who had deserted the other spouse to return and live with the spouse who had been deserted.

See **restitution of consortium**.

restitutor (res'ti-tū-tor). The restorer. 1 Bl Comm 66.

restoration. The re-establishment of a monarchy. The enthronement of Charles II following the Rule of Cromwell. Bringing back to a former condition, as a restoration of health. Giving back that which was previously taken away.

To put a new bridge in place of one destroyed is in effect nothing more than a restoration. State ex rel. Roundtree v Board of Commissioners, 80 Ind 478.

See **restitution**.

restoration in kind. See **repay**.

restoration of capital. Correcting an impairment of capital of a bank.

restoration of destroyed instrument. The re-execution of an instrument which has been destroyed, sometimes by the voluntary act of maker or obligor, sometimes compelled by action. 34 Am J1st Lost Papers § 9.

restoration of lost instrument. The re-execution of a lost instrument, sometimes by the voluntary act of maker or obligor, sometimes compelled by action. 34 Am J1st Lost Papers § 9.

restoration of record. The restoring of a lost or destroyed public record through procedure prescribed by statute. 34 Am J1st Lost Papers §§ 27 et seq. The replacement of a judicial record which has been lost, stolen, or destroyed, also the replacement in its original condition of a judicial record improperly altered. 20 Am J2d Cts § 63.

restoration of status quo (res-tō-rā'shon of stā'tus quo). The act of the plaintiff in a suit for cancellation of an instrument in restoring, the defendant to the position he occupied before the transaction in question. 13 Am J2d Canc Inst § 37. The placing of the other party to the contract in the position in which he was at the time of entering into the contract, as an essential part of the rescission of a contract. 17 Am J2d Contr § 512.

restoration rule. The rule that the plaintiff in an action for an injury to his real property is entitled to recover the cost of repairing the real estate so as to restore it to its condition immediately prior to the injury. Cattin v Omaha, 149 Neb 434, 31 NW2d 300.

restoration to competency. The return of an incompetent person to a state of sanity or competency to manage his own affairs. An adjudication under which a person confined as insane is discharged from custody or under which a person placed under guardianship is released therefrom. 29 Am J Rev ed Ins Per § 27.

restorative remedies (rẹ-stōr'ạ-tiv rem'e-dēs). Those remedies in equity by which the plaintiff is restored to the full enjoyment of the right, property, or estate to which he is entitled, but which use and enjoyment have been hindered, interfered with, prevented, or withheld by the wrongdoer. See 1 Pomeroy's Equity Jurisprudence § 112.

restore. To bring back. To return a thing. To accomplish a restoration.
See **restoration.**

rest period. See **coffee break.**

rest stop. A stopping place on the route of a motor carrier for the refreshment and convenience of the passengers.

restrain. To prohibit, limit, confine, or abridge a thing or a person, either temporarily or permanently, for a day only, or for all time. Re Charge to Grand Jury (DC Ill) 62 F 828, 831.

restraining order. Broadly, any injunction other than a mandatory injunction. In common legal usage, an order granted without notice to the adverse party, intended only as a restraint on him until the propriety of granting a temporary injunction can be determined, having no effect other than that of preserving the status quo until hearing upon application for a preliminary or temporary injunction. Rogers v Kendall, 173 Wash 390, 23 P2d 862. A cease and desist order by an administrative agency. 2 Am J2d Admin L § 467.

restraining statutes. A term of art. The statutes, also called "disabling" statutes, passed in the reign of Elizabeth, which curbed the leasing of lands by the church and by eleemosynary corporations, excepting on certain conditions, and which resulted in the turning over to Elizabeth of much valuable land by the prelates, for which she paid nothing. See 3 Bl Comm 320.

restraint. Suppression, a holding back, a deprivation of liberty, by affirmative conduct. National Labor Relations Board v Grower-Shipper Vegetable Asso. (CA9 Cal) 122 F2d 368; Anno: 123 ALR 622; 83 L Ed 691. Reserve. Keeping one's emotions under control.

restraint of alienation. See **restraint on alienation.**

restraint of marriage. A provision in a contract, deed, or will which operates as a positive or probable, absolute or partial, prohibition of marriage. 35 Am J1st Mar §§ 247 et seq.

restraint of trade. Combinations and practices interfering unreasonably with the normal production and supply of commodities by the suppression of competition therein, or by other means; an instrument of monopoly. 36 Am J1st Monop etc § 2. A contractual restriction upon the right of a person to engage in a trade, business, or profession. 36 Am J1st Monop etc §§ 50 et seq.

Contracts, associations, and combinations which are only in partial and reasonable restraint of trade are generally regarded as valid. 36 Am J1st Monop etc § 8.

restraint on alienation. A fetter or restriction upon the transfer of property sought to be imposed by a grantor or testator who seeks to convey or dispose of property and at the same time exercise control over its alienation. 41 Am J1st Perp § 66.

See **partial restraint on alienation; rule against suspension of power of alienation.**

restraint on use. A restraint on the use of property imposed by testator or grantor which is inconsistent with the estate devised or granted. 41 Am J1st Perp § 69.

restraints and detainments of all kings, princes, and people of what nation, condition, or quality soever. A familiar clause in marine insurance policies by way of an extension of the coverage and in bills of lading and charter parties by way of stating an excuse for nonperformance of the contract. Anno: 137 ALR 1241; 29A Am J Rev ed Ins § 1323. Restraints in a sovereign rather than a civil capacity. Bradlie v Maryland Ins. Co. (US) 12 Pet 378, 9 L Ed 1123. Captures and detentions by the commissioned agents of a lawful government. 29A Am J Rev ed Ins § 1323.

The term "restraint" is not limited to cases where the limitation, restriction, or confinement is imposed by those in possession of the person or thing which is limited, restrained, or confined, but includes a restriction created by the application of external force. Olivera v Union Ins. Co. (US) 3 Wheat 183, 4 L Ed 365.

restraints of kings. A clause in a marine insurance policy extending the coverage to captures, seizures, and detentions by the commissioned officers and agents of a sovereign or sovereign power. McCargo v New Orleans Insurance Co. (La) 10 Rob 180.

See **restraints and detainments of all kings, princes, and people of what nation, condition, or quality soever.**

restraints of princes. A clause in a marine insurance policy extending the coverage to loss by an exercise of the sovereign or governmental power controlling and divesting the dominion or authority of the owner over the ship. Baker Castor Oil Co. v Insurance Co. of North America (CA2 NY) 157 F2d 3, cert den 329 US 800, 91 L Ed 684, 67 S Ct 494.

See **restraints and detainments of all kings, princes, and people of what nation, condition, or quality soever.**

Res transit cum suo onere (rēz trans'it kum su'ō ō'ne-re). The property passes with its burden.

rest, residue, and remainder. See **residuary clause.**

restrict. To limit. To keep within limits.

restricted allotment. Conditions imposed in the allotment of tribal lands to individuals, particularly conditions against alienation by the allottee, intended to safeguard and conserve the property for the Indians. United States v Ramsey, 271 US 467, 470, 70 L Ed 1039, 1041, 46 S Ct 559.

restricted data. All data concerning (1) design, manufacture, or utilization of atomic weapons; (2) the production of special nuclear material; or (3) the use of special nuclear material in the production of energy; but not including data declassified pursuant to the Atomic Energy Act. 42 USC § 2014(w).

restricted land. Lands allotted to Indians, the alienation of which is subjected to restrictions imposed by Congress to protect the Indians from their own incompetency. Kenny v Mills, 250 US 58, 61, 63 L Ed 841, 845, 39 S Ct 417.
See **reserved lands.**

restricted publication. Same as **limited publication.**

restriction. A limitation, for example, a limitation imposed in dedicating land, 23 Am J2d Ded §§ 37 et seq. or by a zoning ordinance.
See **videlicet.**

restriction of liability. See **limitation of liability.**

restrictive covenant. A covenant restricting or regulating the use of real property or the kind, character, and location of buildings or other structures that may be erected thereon, usually created by a condition, covenant, reservation, or exception in a deed, but susceptible of creation by contract not involving transfer of title to land and by implication. 20 Am J2d Cov §§ 165 et seq.

restrictive indorsement. An indorsement of a negotiable instrument which either prohibits the further negotiation of the instrument, or constitutes the indorsee the agent of the indorser, or vests the title in the indorsee in trust for or to the use of some other person. Uniform Negotiable Instruments Law § 36. An indorsement which either is conditional, or purports to prohibit further transfer of the instrument, or includes the words "for collection," "for deposit," "pay any bank," or like terms signifying a purpose of deposit for collection, or otherwise states that it is for the benefit or use of the indorser or of another person. UCC § 3—205.

restrictive interpretation. A narrow construction of a statute, particularly a narrow construction adopted for the purpose of permitting the statute to be upheld as constitutional. 16 Am J2d Const L § 147.

restrictive prescription (pre-skrip'shọn). A prescription by which a remedy or right is lapsed. 25 Am J2d Ease § 43.

restrictive voting. Voting restricted to a smaller number of candidates than there are offices to be filled, as where five judges of a municipal court are to be elected, the restriction being imposed for the purpose of assuring minority representation. 26 Am J2d Elect § 276. A strategy in practical politics known as the single shot.
See **single shot.**

rest-room. A toilet; a customary accommodation in a gasoline filling station. Anno: 116 ALR 1208.

rests. Those periods at certain intervals when balances in an account are struck in order that accrued interest may be added to the principal and thus bear interest from that time. 30 Am J Rev ed Int § 60. A word of art indicating that a party has no more evidence to offer at the particular stage of the trial. Refreshment by sleep or by taking one's ease.

resubmission. An order of reference after the report of a referee under prior submission in the same case has been set aside either in whole or in part. 45 Am J1st Ref § 46.

resubmission of bill. The submission to a grand jury of a charge previously considered and rejected by them. 27 Am J1st Indict § 17.

See **reconsideration of bill.**

result. A consequence. That which has happened. The determination made in an action. The consequence of an accident.
See **natural consequence.**

resulting power. A power or authority of the United States fairly deducible from the powers specified in the Constitution, though neither expressly specified nor deducible from any one specified power or ancillary to it alone, but growing out of the aggregate of powers conferred upon the government, or out of sovereignty instituted.
The power of the Federal Government to issue treasury notes and to make them legal tender for the payment of debts thereafter incurred, is such a power. Knox v Lee & Parker Davis (Legal Tender Cases) (US) 12 Wall 457, 534, 20 L Ed 287, 307.

resulting trust. A trust, sometimes called a presumptive trust, but a real trust raised by operation, implication, or presumption of law from acts, relations, or the situation of the parties from which an intent to create a trust appears. Dunn v Zwilling Bros. 94 Iowa 233, 237; Swon v Huddleston (Mo) 282 SW2d 18, 55 ALR2d 205. A trust arising in a transaction whereby one person thereby becomes invested with legal title but is obligated in equity to hold such title for the benefit of another, the intention of the person acquiring the legal title to hold in trust for the other being implied or presumed as a matter of law, although no intention to create or hold in trust has been manifested expressly and there is an absence of fraud actual or constructive. Farmers & T. Bank v Kimball Milling Co. 1 SD 388, 47 NW 402. A trust arising where property is transferred under circumstances giving rise to an inference that the person who made the transfer or caused it to be made did not intend the transferee to take the beneficial interest in the property. Moses v Moses, 140 NJ Eq 575, 53 A2d 805, 173 ALR 273. A trust arising where title to real or personal property is taken in the name of one other than the person advancing the consideration. Arneman v Arneman, 43 Wash 2d 787, 264 P2d 256, 45 ALR2d 370.

resulting use. A term, unfamiliar in modern times, for resulting trust.

resummons (rē-sum'ọns). A second summons, issued where for some reason the original summons has become ineffective.
See **alias summons.**

res universitatis (rēs ū-ni-ver-si-tā'tis). (Civil law.) Things in common,—things which belong to a community. See Mackeldey's Roman Law § 170.

resurface. To apply to a street or highway a top covering or layer of durable material of substantial depth or thickness. Anno: 84 ALR 1158. A reconstructing of a street for the purposes of a special assessment. Anno: 41 ALR2d 616.

resurrender (rē-sur-ren'dèr). The reconveyance of copyhold land to the mortgagor upon the payment of the mortgage debt.

resurvey. The survey of a tract of land according to a former plat or survey, the duty of the surveyor being to relocate, upon the best evidence obtainable, the courses and lines at the same place where originally located by the first surveyor. 12 Am J2d Bound § 61.

retail. See **sale at retail.**

retail dealer. Same as **retailer**.

retailer. A person engaged in the business of making sales of goods or merchandise at retail. Anno: 171 ALR 698.

retailer maintaining place of business in this state. One maintaining a place of business in the state for the sale of goods or merchandise at retail, whether in person or through an agent. State Tax Com. v General Trading Co. 233 Iowa 877, 10 NW2d 659, 153 ALR 602.

retailer method of pricing inventory. Applying an arbitrary standard or rule in fixing an approximate value of merchandise in stock. Anno: 66 ALR2d 837.

retail excise tax. See **sales tax**.

retail price control. See **price control**.

retail sales tax. See **sales tax**.

retail store. The ordinary store kept for the sale of goods and merchandise, as distinguished from a wholesale place which furnishes goods and merchandise only to dealers.

retain (rē-tān′). To continue to hold; to keep. Richardson v Seevers' Adm'r. 84 Va 259, 269. To hire; to employ, particularly, to hire an attorney at law.

retained life interest. An interest to continue for the life of the grantor, retained by him in the property conveyed. 26 USC § 2036(a).

retained percentage. A percentage of the contractor's current earnings under a building and construction contract retained for the time by the owner. 43 Am J1st Pub Wks § 55.

retainer. The act of a person in engaging an attorney at law professionally, whether by express agreement or impliedly by seeking and obtaining his advice and assistance. 7 Am J2d Attys § 91. A preliminary fee given to counsel to secure his services or to prevent the opposite side from engaging them. 7 Am J2d Attys § 208. A term loosely used for the right of an executor or administrator to deduct indebtedness due from a distributee. 31 Am J2d Ex & Ad § 567. Precisely, the right of an executor or administrator, who is himself a creditor of the estate, to retain the amount of such debt out of the funds of the estate in his hands. 31 Am J2d Ex & Ad § 567.

See **general retainer**; **special retainer**.

retaining fee. The fee of an attorney at law under a general retainer. Anno: 60 ALR2d 1014 § 3.
See **retainer**.

retaining lien. The lien of an attorney at law of common law origin but existing under statute in some jurisdictions, attaching to all papers, books, documents, securities, moneys, and property of the client coming into the possession of the attorney in the course of and with reference to his professional employment, thereby permitting him to hold them as security for the general balance due him from the client for professional services and disbursements. 7 Am J2d Attys §§ 273, 276.

retaining wall. A wall erected for the purpose of preventing a slide of earth from the premises.

retains. A word of art for the handling charges of a co-operative association. Ozona Citrus Growers Asso. v McLean, 122 Fla 188, 165 So 625.
See **retain**.

retaking. See **recapture**; **repossession**.

retaliation (rḛ-tal-i-ā′shǫn). Reprisal; retorsion. An offensive rather than a defensive act. Phoenix v Carey (La App) 108 So 2d 268. The principle which would require such a sentence upon a person convicted of crime as would inflict upon him the same hurt he has done to his neighbor, as, if a man put out his neighbor's eye, he should lose one of his own; but if his neighbor had but one eye, he should lose both of his. See 4 Bl Comm 12.
See **recrimination**.

retaliatory argument. Argument of counsel which, although otherwise objectionable as appealing to racial, religious, or social prejudice, is to be accepted because in reply to an improper line of argument by opposing counsel. 39 Am J1st New Tr § 61.

retaliatory statute. A statute of one state, the purpose of which is to be as onerous to the citizens or corporations of another state as a statute of the latter is to citizens or corporations of the former, for example, a statute imposing upon foreign corporations the same taxes, fees, and penalties as are imposed by the home state of the corporation upon corporations of the taxing state. Anno: 49 ALR 754, s. 77 ALR 1497; 83 ALR 469; 91 ALR 798; 16 Am J2d Const L § 247; 36 Am J2d For Corp § 267: A statute providing that whenever the laws of a particular state impose greater burdens and limitations upon insurance companies organized in the enacting state, and doing business in such other state, than are imposed by the laws of the enacting state upon foreign insurance companies doing business in that state, then the same burdens and prohibitions imposed by the foreign state shall be imposed by the enacting state upon such insurance companies of the foreign state. 29 Am J Rev ed Ins § 71. Statutes providing that where the laws of another state provide for the levy of taxes upon liquor products manufactured outside the state and sold and dispensed within the state, in excess of the taxes, fees, and charges on the liquor products of manufacturers of such state, the same or additional taxes, fees, and charges are to be levied upon the liquor products of manufacturers of such state. 30 Am J Rev ed Intox L § 203.

retaliatory taxes. Taxes imposed by a retaliatory statute.
See **retaliatory statute**.

retallia (re-tal′li-a). Retail; dividing a commodity into parts.

retare (re-tā′re). To charge a person with the commission of a crime; to accuse; to suspect.

retaxation of costs. A correction of an erroneous taxation of costs. 20 Am J2d Costs § 93.
A retaxation of costs either affirms, modifies or corrects the taxation had. A new taxation necessarily implies that the former taxation is vacated or annulled. Baker v Codding, 3 Misc 512, 513, 23 NYS 5.

retention of title as security. The right of the vendor under an executory contract for the sale of land, holding the legal title in trust for the purchaser, subject to the payment of the purchase money in accordance with the terms of the contract. 55 Am J2d V & P § 355.

retire. To terminate employment and acquire a status of retirement, receiving retirement benefits. To sever relations with a business and acquire a status of retirement. To withdraw negotiable paper from circulation. To take up or pay an obligation voluntarily.

"A man as sanguine as Micawber might describe his bankruptcy as a retirement of his obligations, but a merchant seeking credit who spoke in such euphemisms might find himself in trouble later. Where creditors receive a petty dividend on the collapse of their debtor, their claims may be extinguished but are hardly retired." Thomson v Commissioner (CA2 NY) 108 F2d 642.

See **retirement.**

retired. See **retire; retirement.**

retirement. Voluntarily taking up and paying an obligation. The status of one who has ceased to work or engage in business. A termination of employment under conditions entitling one to retirement benefits. The antithesis of a discharge or forced resignation. Brown v Little Brown & Co. 269 Mass 102, 66 ALR 1284, 168 NE 521. The severance of a member of the armed forces from the service under conditions entitling him to pension or retirement benefits. 36 Am J1st Mil § 36.

retirement benefit. Broadly, any benefit received upon retiring from employment, under a formal or informal benefit plan. A benefit payable to a designated beneficiary upon the death of one retired under a retirement plan calling for the payment of amounts periodically by way of pension or retirement money. Re Simpson's Estate, 43 Cal 2d 594, 275 P2d 467, 47 ALR2d 991.

See **pension; Social Security.**

retirement from the Armed Forces. Separation from service in the Armed Forces for physical disability or because of length of service. 10 USC §§ 1201 et seq.

retirement fund. See **pension fund; teachers' retirement funds.**

retirement of bond. See **retirement of securities.**

retirement of jury. The jury proceeding to the jury room for their deliberation following the reception of evidence, arguments of counsel, and instructions by the court.

retirement of partner. The withdrawal of a partner from the firm, resulting in a dissolution of the partnership. 40 Am J1st Partn § 242.

retirement of securities. The calling and redemption of a bond by payment. The voluntary payment of a bond. A repurchase of its own stock by a corporation and the cancellation of the repurchased shares, destroying all rights adhering to them. 18 Am J2d Corp § 282. The elimination of shares of stock in a building and loan association by paying off the shareholder. 13 Am J2d B & L Assoc § 27.

Under section 117(f) of the Revenue Act of 1934, dealing with the retirement of securities, the word is not used in an artificial sense. In common understanding and according to the dictionaries, the word "retirement" is broader in scope than the word "redemption." McClain v Commissioner, 311 US 527, 85 L Ed 319, 61 S Ct 373.

See **redeemable bond.**

retirement of stock. See **retirement of securities.**

retirement pay. See **pension; retirement benefit.**

retonsor (rē-ton'sor). A shaver or clipper of coins.

retorna brevium (re-tor'na brē'vi-um). The returns of writs; the term day for the return of a writ. See 3 Bl Comm 278.

retorno habendo (re-tor'nō hā-ben'dō). A writ in aid of a successful defendant in an action of replevin, whereby the goods taken from him under the writ of replevin are returned to him. See 3 Bl Comm 149.

retorsion (rẹ-tôr'shọn). The adoption of forcible measures by a sovereign state, which deems that it has been wronged by another nation, in order to compensate it for past injury or to restrain further wrongful acts.

Among the different measures which are included in the meaning of the term are reprisals, blockade, interdiction of commercial intercourse, the detention of vessels, and embargo. 30 Am J Rev ed Internat L § 53.

retortion (rẹ-tôr'shọn). Same as **retorsion.**

retouching. Adding details to a painting or photograph. Removing blemishes on a picture.

retour sans frais (rē-toor'sòn frā). To return without charges,—an instruction given by the drawer of a bill of exchange in the event of the dishonor of the bill by the drawee.

retour sans protet (re-toor' sôn prō'tay). To return without protest,—an instruction given by the drawer of a bill of exchange in the event of the dishonor of the bill by the drawee.

retractation (rē-trak-tā'shọn). The withdrawal of a renunciation of the office by the person named as executor in a will.

retraction. A statement of such a nature and published in such a manner as to manifest an honest intention to repair the harm done to the injured reputation by a defamatory statement. 33 Am J1st L & S § 123. Withdrawal of bid by a bidder at an auction sale. 7 Am J2d Auct § 30; 30A Am J Rev ed Jud S § 96.

See **retractation.**

retractus aquae (re-trak'tus a'kwē). The ebbing of the tide.

retrahere (re-tra'he-re). To draw back; to withdraw.

retransfer. See **reassignment; renegotiation.**

retraxit (rẹ-trak'sit). An open and voluntary renunciation of his suit made by plaintiff in open court, being the act of the plaintiff, performable by counsel only under special authority. 24 Am J2d Dism § 3. A voluntary renunciation by the plaintiff in open court of his suit and the cause thereof, through which he forever loses his action. Virginia Concrete Co. v Board of Supervisors, 197 Va 821, 91 SE2d 415, 56 ALR2d 1283.

See **judgment of retraxit.**

retreat. A place for contemplation, especially for the religious. Withdrawal from an encounter. The rule that a person when attacked by another, except in his own house, shall seek to withdraw from the encounter by giving ground, before taking the life of his assailant. 26 Am J1st Homi § 150.

retreat to the ditch. A principle similar to **retreat to the wall.** 26 Am J1st Homi § 151.

retreat to the wall. The principle that a person who is assailed elsewhere than in his own dwelling is not justified in taking the life of his assailant so long as there is a safe avenue of escape from the attack. 26 Am J1st Homi § 150.

retroactive (rē-trō-ak'tiv). Acting on things that are past. Simpson v City Savings Bank, 56 NH 466.

See **relation back; retrospective operation.**

retroactive amnesia (rē-trō-ak'tiv am-nē'si-ạ). See amnesia.

retroactive decision. A court decision which makes and applies a new rule of law, and attaches another and unforeseen liability to a contract after its execution. Clancy v Barker (CA8 Neb) 131 F 161.

retroactive legislation. See retrospective legislation.

retroactive operation. See relation back; retrospective operation.

retrocession (rē-trō-sesh'ọn). A term of the civil law, meaning the restitution of an ancient title to a true owner.
Such an act confers no new title; it merely recognizes and confirms a previously existing title in another. Amet v Boyer, 43 La Ann 562, 578, 9 So 622.

retrospective (ret-rō- or rē-trō-spek'tiv). Looking backward or upon things that are past. Simpson v City Savings Bank, 56 NH 466.

retrospective effect. See relation back; retrospective operation.

retrospective laws. See retrospective legislation; retrospective operation.

retrospective legislation. Laws which take away or impair vested rights acquired under existing laws, or create a new obligation, impose a new duty, or attach a new disability in respect of transactions or considerations already passed. 16 Am J2d Const L § 413. A statute which changes or impairs a present right by going behind it to give to anterior circumstances an efficacy which they did not have when the right accrued, or which relates back to and gives to a previous transaction a legal effect different from that which it had under the law when it was completed. International Mortgage Trust Co. v Henry, 139 Kan 154, 30 P2d 311; Clark Implement Co. v Wadden, 34 SD 550, 149 NW 424.
A statute is not rendered retroactive merely because the facts or requisites upon which its subsequent action depends, or some of them, are drawn from a time antecedent to the enactment. See Reynolds v United States, 292 US 443, 78 L Ed 1353, 54 S Ct 801.
A statute which does not change the legal effect of prior facts or transactions is not unconstitutionally retrospective merely because it relates thereto, or because it relies thereon to aid in fixing the present status of a person, or because some requisites for its action are drawn from a time antecedent to its passage. State ex rel. Sweezer v Green, 360 Mo 1249, 232 SW2d 897, 24 ALR2d 340.

retrospective operation. The operation of a statute as of a time prior to enactment or effective date. 16 Am J2d Const L § 413. The effect sometimes given a predated contract. 17 Am J2d Contr § 69.
See retroactive decision; retrospective legislation.

retrospective statute. See retrospective legislation.

rettare. Same as retare.

rette (ret). Same as rettum.

rettum (ret'tum). A charge or accusation of the commission of a criminal offense.

return. Verb: To come back to a place. To yield a profit. To make statement of one's activities, as where an officer returns process directed to him for service. Noun: A coming back. Profit or earnings. A statement in writing of what one has done in the performance of a duty or duties. An account, particularly for tax purposes.

See tax return.

returnable (rē-tėr'nạ-bl). (1) Capable of being returned; (2) (law) legally required to be returned. Daniels v Lewis, 7 Colo 430, 4 P 57.

returnable process. Process upon which the officer who is to execute it is required to certify his doings under the process. Utica City Bank v Buell (NY) 9 Abb Pr 385, 391.

returnable writ. Same as returnable process.

return day. The time specified in a writ or process for the defendant to appear and defend. 42 Am J1st Proc § 14. The day fixed by law for a defendant to appear and answer following the service of process upon him. Carlson v Burt, 111 Cal 129, 43 P 583. The last day for the return of a writ of execution. 21 Am J Exec §§ 471 et seq.

return day of an election. The day following an election upon which the board or other body legally authorized to canvass the returns of an election, is required by law to commence the canvass of the returns. Carlson v Burt, 111 Cal 129, 43 P 583.

return flow. Water, drawn from a stream and impounded or used in irrigation, which subsequently arrives again at the stream from which it was initially abstracted. United States v Warm Springs Irrigation Dist. (DC Or) 38 F Supp 239.

return in certiorari. See return to writ.

return in mandamus. See return to writ.

return not found. See not found.

return nulla bona (rē-tėrn' nul'ạ bō'nạ). The return of an execution which states a search by the execution officer for property whereof to make a levy and the absence of any such property. 30 Am J2d Exec § 562.

return of attachment. The act of the sheriff or other officer to whom a writ of attachment is directed. The indorsement on the writ of what the officer has done thereunder, and the filing of the writ as indorsed with the clerk of the court out of which the writ issued. 6 Am J2d Attach § 316. A statement on the back of a writ of attachment noting the levy thereof upon real estate, describing the property, and noting the date and time of day of the levy. 6 Am J2d Attach § 312.

return of execution. A showing by the execution officer of the things done by him under the writ of execution. The sheriff's indorsement upon a writ of execution of the levy made by him under the writ, the disposition of the property seized under the levy, and the disposition of the proceeds of the sale, if any, made by him under the writ. 30 Am J2d Exec §§ 551 et seq.

return of indictment. A bringing of an indictment into open court—that is, while the judge is presiding. 27 Am J1st Indict § 31.

return of inquisition. A finding whether the individual subject of the inquisition is or is not mentally incompetent. 29 Am J Rev ed Ins Per § 22.

return of premium. Any payment by an insurer to insured made on the basis of a premium paid by the insured but unearned. 29 Am J Rev ed Ins § 593.

return of process. A short account in writing made by an officer in respect to the manner in which he has executed a writ or process; his official statement of the acts done by him under the writ in obedience to its direction and in conformity with the requirements of law. 42 Am J1st Proc § 117.

See **tarde; undue return.**

return of warrant. A return of a warrant for the arrest of a person, by the officer to whom it was given for service, showing substantially all that the officer did within the scope of proper execution. Gibson v Holmes, 78 Vt 110, 62 A 11.

return of writ. See **return of attachment; return of execution; return of process; return to writ.**

returns of election. See **election returns.**

return ticket. See **round-trip ticket.**

return to state. A coming back to the state after an absence therefrom. For the purposes of starting the running of a statute of limitations, a return by one in a manner so public, open, and notorious that his creditor may find him and serve him with process by the exercise of reasonable diligence. 34 Am J1st Lim Ac § 226.

return to writ. A response to a writ or process, as where a sheriff or other officer having the custody of a prisoner responds to a writ of habeas corpus by stating in form prescribed by statute the material facts respecting the detention of the prisoner. 25 Am J1st Hab C §§ 137 et seq. The response of the court or officer to whom a writ of certiorari is directed; a certification of the record of the proceedings sought to be reviewed. 14 Am J2d Certiorari § 47. The response or answer by the officer to whom a petition or writ of mandamus is directed, answering the allegations of fact in the petition or writ. 35 Am J2d Mand § 354.
See **return of process.**

reus (rē'us). A defendant; a person who is guilty of a criminal offense; a party to a contract; a party to an action.

Reus excipiendo fit actor (re'us ex-si-pi-en'dō fit ak'-tor). The defendant by his plea may make himself a plaintiff.

Reus laesae majestatis punitur, ut pereat unus ne pereant omnes (re'us lē'sē ma-jes-tā'tis pū'ni-ter, ut per'e-at u'nus nē per'e-ant om'nez). A defendant guilty of treason is punished, so that one may die lest all may perish.

reus promittendi (re'us prō-mit-ten'dī). (Civil law.) A party to a contract who makes a promise therein; a promisor.

reus stipulandi (re'us sti-pu-lan'dī). (Civil law.) A party to a contract to whom a promise is made; a promisee.

reve (rēv). Same as **reeve.**

revealed law. See **divine law.**

reve mote (rēv mōt). A court which was presided over by a shire-reeve or sheriff.

revendication (rē-ven-di-kā'shọn). The right which an unpaid vendor had, under the civil law, upon the insolvency of the vendee, to reclaim, in specie, such part of the goods as remained in the hands of the vendee entire, and without having changed their quality. See Benedict v Schaettle, 12 Ohio St 515, 520.

revenge. Verb: To take vengeance, to retaliate. Noun: Retaliation; vengeance. A malicious injury inflicted in return for an injury. People v Pierson, 2 Idaho 76, 3 P 688.

revenue. Return from property. Bates v Porter, 74 Cal 224, 239, 15 P 732. Income produced without impairment of capital. Re Ratcliffe, 139 La 996, 72 So 713. The income of the government, state or national, arising from taxation, duties, fees, and the like. 42 Am J1st Pub F § 2. Precisely, the total income of the government, state or national, derived from all sources, subject to be applied to public purposes. Fergus v Brady, 277 Ill 272, 115 NE 393.

revenue act. See **revenue law.**

revenue bill. A bill introduced in Congress for the raising of revenue for the support of the government and the payment of the expenses incurred in governmental activities. A bill for levying taxes in the strict sense of the term, as distinguished from a bill for a purpose which incidentally may include the raising of revenue. Annotation: 4 ALR2d 976, 980 et seq; a bill which must originate in the House of Representatives. US Const Art I § 7, cl 1.

"Mr. Justice Story (1 Story, Const § 880) has well said that the practical construction of the Constitution and the history of the constitutional provision in question (article 1, section 7) proves that revenue bills are those that levy taxes in the strict sense of the word, and are not bills for other purposes which may incidentally create revenue." Twin City Nat. Bank v Nebeker, 167 US 196, 202, 42 L Ed 134, 136, 17 S Ct 766.

revenue bond. A bond issued by a public body payable solely from a special fund arising from the revenues accruing from operation of an enterprise or project for the construction, operation, and maintenance of which the bond was issued. 43 Am J1st Pub Sec § 8.

revenue law. A tax statute. A law passed under the power granted to Congress by § 8 of Article I of the United States Constitution "to lay and collect taxes, duties, imposts, and excises." California ex rel. McColgan v Bruce (CA9 Nev) 129 F2d 421, 147 ALR 782.

As the term is used in connection with the jurisdiction of the United States courts, it means a law imposing duties on imports or tonnage, or a law providing in terms for revenue; that is, a law which is directly traceable to the power granted to Congress by section 8 of article 1 of the Federal Constitution, "to lay and collect taxes, duties, imposts, and excises." United States v Hill, 123 US 681, 31 L Ed 275, 8 S Ct 308.

A law passed for the purpose of authorizing the levy and collection of taxes in some form. The term does not include laws which are passed for other purposes although they may incidentally create revenue. The National Prohibition Act, passed for the purpose of carrying out the provisions of the Eighteenth Amendment, is not a revenue law. United States v McConnell (DC Pa) 10 F2d 973.
See **Internal Revenue Code.**

revenue officers. Officers of the United States for the administration and enforcement of the Internal Revenue Code.
See **Internal Revenue Service.**

revenue stamps. The means of collecting many of the taxes imposed by the federal government, the requirement of the law being that a stamp be attached to an article subject to tax and canceled, or posted and displayed as prescribed by statute, such stamps being available for purchase from the government. The evidence of payment of a tax. United States v

Chamberlain, 219 US 250, 55 L Ed 204, 31 S Ct 155.

Re, verbis, scripto, consensu, traditione, junctura vestes sumere pacta solent (rē, ver'bis, skrip'tō, kon-sen'sū, tra-di-she-ō'ne, junk-tū'ra ves'tēz su'me-re pak'ta so'lent). Compacts are accustomed to take their clothing from the subject matter, the words, the writing, the delivery and the consent or joining together.

reversal. An overthrowing; a setting aside. An annulling; an avoiding. Cowdery v London, 139 Cal 298, 303, 73 P 196; Laithe v McDonald, 7 Kan 255, 268. The act of an appellate court in setting aside, annulling, or vacating the judgment or order, entered by the court below. 5 Am J2d A & E § 948.

As the word is used in connection with judgments, its usual meaning contemplates only a reversal by an appellate court; that is, by any court authorized to set aside the judgment. See Manfull v Graham, 55 Neb 645, 649.

reverse. See **reversal.**

reverse bars. Angle irons curved in the reverse arc to the frames of a steel or iron ship and fastened with one flat side against one side of the projecting flange of the frames, strengthening the hull of the vessel and constituting a part of it. The President Roosevelt (CA2 NY) 116 F2d 420.

reversed and remanded. A familiar expression meaning that the appellate court has set aside the judgment rendered in the trial court and that the case goes back to the trial court for a new trial. Myers v McDonald, 68 Cal 162, 8 P 809.

reverse direction rule. The well-settled principle that if a difficulty arises in running the line of a survey of lands in one direction, and all the known calls are met by running them in the reverse direction, the latter is a proper procedure. 12 Am J2d Bound § 60.

reverser (rę-vėr'sėr). Same as **reversioner.**

reverse turn. See **u-turn.**

reversible error. Prejudicial error. Error in the court below which has injuriously affected the appellant or by which he has suffered a miscarriage of justice. 5 Am J2d A & E § 783.

reversion. A future estate in either real or personal property arising by operation of law to take effect in possession in favor of a grantor, lessor, or transferor, or his heirs, distributees, devisees, or legatees, after the termination of a prior particular estate granted, demised, or devised. 28 Am J2d Est § 171. An estate arising from the failure to dispose of an ultimate interest, or from the failure of an attempted but invalid disposition of an ultimate interest. 28 Am J2d Est § 173. The returning of property to the grantor or his heirs or devisees upon the exhaustion or running out of the grant, in other words, the returning of the property after the grant is over. Norman v Horton, 344 Mo 290, 126 SW2d 187, 125 ALR 531. The estate of a landlord during the existence of the outstanding leasehold estate. 32 Am J1st L & T § 76. An estate in praesenti, vested in the sense of a present fixed right of enjoyment in futuro, Norman v Horton, 344 Mo 290, 126 SW2d 187, 125 ALR 531; an estate dependent in respect of possession on the determination of the particular estate granted or devised. Metcalfe v Miller, 96 Mich 459, 56 NW 16.

A reversion may exist, under the view taken in some jurisdictions, as a repository for the "fee" or "inheritance" to be taken under ultimate contingent interests during the pendency of present interests. For instance, a reversion is sometimes stated to exist where an ultimate remainder in fee is contingent. Until it vests, there is a reversion in the grantor or devisor and his heirs. 28 Am J2d Est § 173.

The words "revert" and "reversion" are sometimes loosely used to describe an interest different from a reversion in the true sense of the term. A reversion does not become a remainder or a remainder a reversion because it is so called in the instrument creating it. The words should be construed in the light of the intent of the testator or grantor. Brown v Guthery, 190 NC 822, 130 SE 836.

See **possibility of reverter; reverter.**

reversionary. In or by way of reversion; relating or pertaining to a reversion.

reversionary interest. A reversion.

reversionary lease (lēs). A lease the term of which is to begin at a future time.

reversioner. A person entitled to an estate in reversion.

See **reversion.**

reversor (rę-vėr'sǫr). A reversioner; in Scotch law, a debtor who made a wadset or mortgage.

revert (rę-vėrt'). To turn backward. To come back to a former owner. Pearce v Lott, 101 Ga 395, 399, 29 SE 276. To operate by way of a reversion; to come back to a grantor or lessor. Sometimes loosely used as the equivalent of "go to." Mastellar v Atkinson, 94 Kan 279, 14 P 367.

See **reversion.**

Revertendi animum videntur desinere habere tunc, cum revertendi consuetudinem deseruerint (re-verten'dī a'ni-mum vi-den'ter de-si'ne-re hā-bē're tunk, kum re-ver-ten'dī kon-su-ē-tū'di-nem de-se-ru'e-rint). They are then considered as having ceased to have the intention or returning, when they have abandoned the habit of returning. A maxim of the civil law. See 2 Bl Comm 392.

reverter. The restoration of the use of property to a donor in dedication upon the termination of the use for which dedicated. 14 Am J2d Cem § 24.

See **formedon in the reverter; possibility of reverter; reversion; revert.**

reverter doctrine. The rule that one returning to his domicil of origin from his domicil of choice may reacquire the domicil of origin while on the return trip. 25 Am J2d Dom § 36.

revest. To vest again in the same person. To return to a grantor after the termination of a particular estate granted by him. McPheeters v Wright, 124 Ind 560, 24 NE 734.

See **reversion.**

review. A consideration by an appellate court of the decision of an inferior court, contemplating the affirmance, reversal, or modification of such decision in accordance with the law. 4 Am J2d A & E § 1. A proceeding expressly authorized by statute in some state, distinct from review on appeal or in error proceeding. 46 Am J1st Rev § 2. A proceeding in the nature of a new trial of the issues tried before, except as leave be granted to amend the pleadings. 46 Am J1st Rev § 3. A review by a court of the decision or determination made by an administrative agency. 2 Am J2d Admin L §§ 553 et seq.

See **bill of review; certiorari; judicial review; scope of review**.

reviewability. The question whether an issue in its nature is one proper for consideration by an appellate court. 4 Am J2d A & E § 17.
See **appealability**.

review on appeal. See **review; scope of review**.

revise. To make a revision.
See **revision**.

revised statutes. A familiar term in many jurisdictions, denoting a code based upon a prior code with alterations and additions necessary to bring the code up to date.

revision. Looking over a thing, such as an article or a schedule of public utility rates, and reviewing it carefully for the purpose of making changes, additions, and corrections, if such be deemed advisable. Goodwin v Prime, 92 Me 355, 363, 42 A 785.
In local assessment proceedings, the words "revision" and "correction" refer to the fact that the board may be called upon to review that which has been done, and to make the proceedings conform to the law. Hutcheson v Storrie, 92 Tex 685, 51 SW 848.
To revise is to review or re-examine for correction, and when applied to a statute, the word contemplates the re-examination of the same subject matter contained in the prior statute, and the substitution of a new, and what is believed to be, a still more perfect rule. Casey v Harned, 5 Iowa 1.

revival. Restoration of strength. Restoration to a condition of activity.

revival of action. The procedure by which a proper party, personal representative, heir, distributee, legatee, or devisee, is substituted for a deceased party and the action continued in name of the substituted party. Grant v McAuliffe, 41 Cal 2d 859, 264 P2d 944, 42 ALR2d 1162. A procedure at common law and under some statutes by writ of scire facias but more commonly, under modern statutes, by motion. 1 Am J2d Abat & R § 117.
The revival is not a new suit; it is still the same suit, in which both parties are entitled to the benefit of all former proceedings. Havens v Seashore Land Co. 57 NJ Eq 142, 149, 41 A 755.

revival of cause. The revival of a cause of action barred by the statute of limitations. 34 Am J1st Lim Ac §§ 289-336.
According to the weight of authority in this country, the term "revived cause of action" has two distinct meanings. One refers to a cause of action barred by the statute of limitations, and brought to life again in the manner provided by statute, as by a new promise in writing signed by the debtor. The other meaning refers to a cause of action the statutory life of which has been revived or restored in the same manner, but before the cause of action has become barred by the statute. Bullard v Lopez, 7 NM 561, 37 P 1103.

revival of corporation. The revival of corporate existence after expiration of the corporate charter, such being permissible only as authorized by statute. 18 Am J2d Corp § 69. The revival of a dissolved corporation, as permitted by statute. 19 Am J2d Corp § 1651.

revival of easement. The revival, upon rebuilding, of an easement once extinguished by the destruction of the servient structure. 25 Am J2d Ease § 114.

revival of judgment. Giving new life to a dormant judgment, whether by a writ or without a writ, as the statute permits. 30A Am J Rev ed Judgm §§ 571 et seq.

revival of offense. Subsequent conduct of the offender which permits the assertion of an offense previously condoned as a ground of divorce. 24 Am J2d Div & S § 221.

revival of policy. The reinstatement of a policy of insurance after it has lapsed or become forfeited, especially where forfeited for the nonpayment of premiums, pursuant to a provision for reinstatement contained in the policy and the performance of such conditions as are imposed by such provision, or pursuant to the special agreement of the parties. 29 Am J Rev ed Ins § 368.
There is a difference of opinion whether the reinstatement of an insurance policy constitutes a new contract. 29 Am J Rev ed Ins § 369.

revival of will. The act of a testator in giving testamentary effect to a will previously revoked by a new testamentary act in re-executing or republishing the will. 57 Am J1st Wills § 615. Giving renewed effect to an earlier will previously revoked by a later will by a still later will revoking the intermediate will. 57 Am J1st Wills § 619.
It is held in many cases that a revoked will or codicil can be revived by a subsequent codicil. Anno: 33 ALR2d 925.

revive. To come back to the vigor of life. To bring back to the vigor of life. To effect a revival.
The primary meaning of the word is "to give life to again." If it is a creative act to give life to dead matter once, it is no less a creative act to give life again to the same matter when it becomes dead. The syllable "re" in the word indicates the use of old matter, and the syllable "vive" means "to give life to," which is one of the primary meanings of the word "create." The quality of the act inheres in the giving of life, not in the material that is to be vivified. Nor is the quality of the act changed by repetition. See Re Bank of Commerce v Wiltsie, 153 Ind 460, 53 NE 950.
See **revival**.

revived cause. See **revival of cause**.

revivor. A proceeding for the revival of an action abated by the death of a party. 1 Am J2d Abate etc § 117.
See **bill of revivor; revival of action**.

revivor and supplement. See **bill of revivor and supplement**.

revocable license. See **simple license**.

revocability. The quality or condition of being subject to revocation. The distinctive characteristic of a will; absent in a deed. 23 Am J2d Deeds § 6.
See **revocation**.

revocation. A nullification; a cancellation; a putting to naught. A withdrawal; a recall. The nullification of an offer by the offeror before acceptance of the offer. 17 Am J2d Contr § 35. A spouse exercising his or her right to disregard a condonation of an offense by the other spouse, because of subsequent conduct of the offender, thereby asserting the once condoned offense as a ground of divorce. 24 Am J2d Div & S § 221.

revocation clause. A clause contained in a will, purporting to revoke an earlier will or wills. 57 Am J1st Wills § 466.

revocation of agency. The termination of the relationship of principal and agent by the principal or by the agent. 3 Am J2d Agency §§ 37 et seq.

revocation of franchise. The termination of a franchise by exercise of a reserved power of termination. 36 Am J2d Franch § 50.

revocation of gift. The avoidance of a gift by the donor because of incompleteness of the transaction, a condition in the transaction, or other peculiar circumstance. 24 Am J1st Gifts §§ 53 et seq.

revocation of guaranty. The termination by the guarantor of a continuing guaranty or of his offer to guarantee an obligation to be incurred at a future time. 24 Am J1st Guar § 64.

revocation of letters. The nullification of the letters of an executor or administrator for invalidity of the appointment or upon the removal of an executor or administrator by the court. 31 Am J2d Ex & Ad §§ 102, 109.

revocation of license. The termination of a license in real property, provided the right to revoke exists. 25 Am J2d Ease § 128. The termination of the privilege bestowed upon the licensee by a license granted by a public body for the conducting of a particular business or the following of a certain occupation. 33 Am J1st Lic § 65. The termination of a liquor license upon a ground provided by statute. 30 Am J Rev ed Intox L § 174.

revocation of offer. See **revocation.**

revocation of probate. The rendition by a probate court of a decree vacating and annulling a prior decree admitting a will to probate. 57 Am J1st Wills § 967.

revocation of will. The annulment of a will, making it speak for nought in whole or in part, by a clause in a later valid will, by an inconsistent disposition of property in a later valid will or codicil, or by tearing, cutting, burning, obliterating, erasing and defacing the instrument with intent to annul or cancel it. 57 Am J1st Wills §§ 455 et seq.

The revocation of a will consists of two things, —the intention of the testator, and some outward act or symbol of destruction. A defacement, obliteration, or destruction, without the animo revocandi, is not sufficient. Neither is the intention—the animo revocandi—sufficient, without some act of obliteration or destruction. Cutler v Cutler, 130 NC 1, 40 SE 689.

The difference between a revocation and an alteration of a will is that if what is done simply takes away what was given before, or a part of what was given before, then it is a revocation; but if it gives something in addition, or gives something else, then it is more than revocation, and cannot be done by mere obliteration. When by obliteration of certain words a different meaning is imparted, there is not a mere revocation. There is something more than the destruction of that which has been antecedently done. There is a transmutation by which a new clause is created. See Miles' Appeal, 68 Conn 237, 36 A 39.

See **dependent relative revocation; implied revocation.**

revocatur (re-vō-kā'ter). It is recalled or set aside.

revoke. To withdraw, cancel, or annul. To set at nought. To effect a revocation.
See **revocation.**

revolt. An insurrection. A rising against authority. The act of a seaman in unlawfully and forcefully, or by fraud or intimidation, usurping command of the vessel or depriving the master or other officer in command of his command, or resisting or preventing him from exercising his command, or transferring such authority to another not lawfully entitled thereto. 18 USC § 481. The endeavor of the crew of a vessel, or any one or more of them, to overthrow the legitimate authority of her commander, with intent to remove him from his command, or against his will to take possession of the vessel by assuming the government and navigation of her, or by transferring their obedience from the lawful commander to some other person. The United States v Tappan (US) 11 Wheat 417, 6 L Ed 508.

See **insurrection.**

revolution. A sudden, radical, and fundamental change in the government or political system, usually effected with violence or at least some acts of violence, sometimes after prolonged struggle between armed forces, and prompted ordinarily by internal conditions oppressive to the people. The overthrow of an established government, generally accompanied by far-reaching social changes. State v Diamond, 27 NM 477, 202 P 988, 20 ALR 1527, 1532.

revolver. A firearm with short barrel, to be held in firing with one hand; a deadly weapon. 56 Am J1st Weap § 3.

revolving capital fund. A fund accumulated by a co-operative association by way of capital by the retention of all or a portion of the operating profit of the association, each member being credited with his proportionate part on the books and usually issued a certificate showing such credit. 18 Am J2d Coop Asso § 15.

revolving door. A door, consisting of four parts or vanes hung on an axle, which swings in a complete circle, thereby permitting entrance or exit by one who walks into the space between two vanes and on through a half circle of the revolution. Anno: 20 ALR2d 34.

reward. A sum of money or other recompense offered by the government, a natural person, an association, or a corporation to the members of the public generally, or to persons of a particular class, for the performance of a particular service, such as the finding of a lost article of property, locating a missing person or a lost child, or the giving of information leading to the arrest of a person for a crime recently committed, and paid to a person for the performance of such service in accord with the offer and the conditions imposed in the offer. Zwolane v Becker Mfg. Co. 150 Wis 517, 137 NW 769.

The words "reward," and "bounty" are nearly allied in meaning. Reward is said to be the appropriate term to apply the case of a single service, which can be only once performed, and, therefore, will be earned only by the person or co-operating persons who succeed while others fail, while the term bounty applies where the services or action of many persons are desired, and each who acts upon the offer may entitle himself to the promised gratuity without prejudice from or to the claims of others. Ingram v Colgan, 106 Cal 113, 39 P 437.

rewriting contract. A derogatory term for a judicial decision which adds or subtracts terms from a contract in construction. 17 Am J2d Contr § 242.

rex (reks). A king.

Rex debet esse sub lege, quia lex facit regem (rex de'bet es'se sub lē'je, qui'a lex fā'sit rē'jem). The king ought to be under the law because the law makes the king. See 1 Bl Comm 239.

Rex est caput et salus reipublicae, et a capite bona valetudo transit in omnes (rex est ka'put et sa'lus re-i-pub'li-sē, et ā ka'pi-te bō'na va-le-tū'dō tranz'it in om'nĕz). The king is the head and safety of the state, and from a worthy head prosperity comes to all.

Rex est legalis et politicus (rex est lē-gā'lis et po-li'ti-kus). The king is both a legal and a political person.

Rex est lex vivens (rex est lex vī'venz). The king is the living law.

Rex est major singulis; minor universis (rex est mā'-jor sin'gu-lis; mī'nor ū-ni-ver'sis). The king is greater than any individual person, but less than all of them together.

Rex est vicarius et minister Dei in terra: omnia quidem sub eo est, et ipse sub nullo, nisi tantum sub Deo (rex est vī-kā'ri-us et mi-nis'ter Dē'ī in ter'ra: om'ni-a qui'dem sub e'ō est, et ip'se sub nul'lō, nī'sī tan'tum sub Dē'ō). The king is the vice-gerent and minister of God on earth: everything is under him and he is under no one except God alone. See 1 Bl Comm 241.

Rex hoc solum non potest facere quod non potest injuste agere (rex hŏk sō'lum non po'test fā'se-re quod non po'test in-jus'te ā'je-re). This thing alone the king cannot do; that is, he is unable to do an injustice.

Rex non debet esse sub homine, sed sub Deo et lege (rex non de'bet es'se sub ho'mi-ne sed sub Dē'ō et lē'je). The king ought not to be subordinate to man, but he should be under God and the law.

Rex non debet esse sub homine, sed sub Deo et lege, quia lex facit regem (rex non de'bet es'se sub ho'mi-ne, sed sub Dē'ō et lē'je, qui'a lex fā'sit rē'jem). The king ought not to be subordinate to man, but he should be under God and the law, because the law makes the king. See Broom's Legal Maxims 47.

Rex non potest fallere nec falli (rex non po'test fal'le-re nek fal'lī). The king can neither deceive nor can he be deceived.

Rex non potest peccare (rex non po'test pe-kā're). The king can do no wrong. Mills v Stewart, 75 Mont 429, 247 P 332, 47 ALR 424, 427.

Rex nunquam moritur (rex nun'quam mo'ri-ter). The king never dies.

An attribute of the king's majesty is his perpetuity. The law ascribes to him, in his political capacity, absolute immortality. Immediately upon the death of the reigning king, in his natural capacity, his kingship or imperial dignity, by act of law, without any interregnum or interval, is vested at once in his heir, who is from that moment king to all intents and purposes. See 1 Bl Comm 239.

RFC. Abbreviation of **Reconstruction Finance Corporation.**

RFD. An abbreviation of **rural free delivery,** customarily used in addressing mail to a person on a rural mail route.

r.g. An abbreviation of **regulae generales.**

rhinoscope (rī'nō-skōp). An instrument used by physicians for the exploration of the nasal cavities. Atchison, Topeka & Santa Fe Railway Co. v Palmore, 68 Kan 545, 75 P 509.

Rhodian law (rō'di-ạn lâ). An ancient compilation of maritime law by the people of the commercially prosperous island of Rhodes, appearing about 900 B. C.

Rhodian law of jettison. See **lex Rhodia de jactu.**

ribaldus (rib'ạl-dus). A vagrant; a vagabond.

ribaud (rē-bō'). A rogue; a vagrant; a whoremonger; a person given to all manner of wickedness.— Wharton's Law Dictionary.

ribbon copy. The first or original instrument typed or written where a carbon copy or copies were made by the same typing. 29 Am J2d Ev § 488.

Richard I. Richard the First, who was the king of England from September 23rd, 1189, until April 6th, 1199.

Richard II. Richard the Second, who was the king of England from June 22nd, 1377, until September 30th, 1399.

Richard III. Richard the Third, who was the king of England from June 26th, 1483, until August 22nd, 1485.

ricochet (rik-ọ-shā' or -shet'). The rebounding of a hurled object caused by striking a flat surface. The deflection of the course of a bullet upon striking a hard object.

Riddleberger Act. A Virginia statute passed in 1882, whereby it was proposed to reduce the bonded indebtedness of the state, because West Virginia had been carved out of it; and West Virginia flatly declined to assume any portion of the debt, chiefly because its people claimed that all the money had been spent in the other state.

ride. To sit on and be carried. To be carried, as in a vehicle. To be carried but at the same time to be in control, as in riding a horse or motorcycle. Silverstein v Commercial Casualty Ins Co. 237 NY 391, 143 NE 231, 35 ALR 32, 33.

rider. Literally one who rides, whether on a horse or in a vehicle. In legal usage, a sheet or sheets containing written, typewritten, or printed matter, attached to an instrument and intended to be considered a part thereof, the most frequent use thereof being in contracts of insurance. A part of the policy or contract of insurance, if incorporated, attached, or referred to in the instrument in so clear a manner as to leave no doubt of the intention of the parties in such respect. 29 Am J Rev ed Ins § 268. A new and unrelated enactment or provision included in a proposed legislative measure, usually intended to "ride" or slip through.

"A still more objectionable practice (than the passage of omnibus bills and logrolling) grew up, of putting what is known as a 'rider' on the appropriation bills, and thus coercing the executive to approve obnoxious legislation, or bring the wheels of the government to a stop for want of funds." Commonwealth ex rel. Elkin v Barnett, 199 Pa 161, 48 A 976, 55 LRA 882.

ridgling (rij'ling). A horse with one testicle removed, the other one being undescended and hanging so high in the belly as not to be reached in the ordinary castration. Douglass v Moses, 89 Iowa 40.

riding. Taking a ride. A division of a county or shire in England, particularly the county of York, being a corrupt form of the word "trithing." 1 Bl Comm 116.

riding horse. A horse that is ridden rather than driven. A horse that carries a mount rather than pulls a vehicle.

A saddled and bridled horse on which the insured was riding, and from which he was thrown, receiving fatal injuries, was held not a vehicle within the meaning of an accident policy covering loss of life sustained by the wrecking or disablement of any vehicle in which the insured was riding, or by being accidentally thrown therefrom. Riser v Federal L. Ins. Co. 207 Iowa 1101, 224 NW 67, 63 ALR 292.

riding on platform. Accepting the platform for the time as the means of conveyance. Something more than being temporarily on the platform for a necessary or proper purpose. 29A Am J Rev ed Ins § 1257.

riding skimmington (rī'ding skim'ing-ton). A mock ceremony for shaming conjugal seducers, once common in parts of England.

The usual practice was to place effigies of the persons on a pole, in a cart or on a donkey and carry them through the public streets amid the jeers of the populace. See Cropp v Tilney (Eng) 3 Salkeld 225.

riding with or accompanied by a licensed driver. Accompanied by a person licensed to drive a motor vehicle, under such conditions and in such proximity that he can maintain supervision necessary for safety, and render assistance, if need be, with reasonable promptness. 7 Am J2d Auto § 105.

rien (ri-en'). (French.) Nothing; not.

rien culp (kulp). Not guilty.

rien culpable. See **de rien culpable.**

rien dit (dē). He says nothing.

rien en arrere (on a-rēr'). Nothing in arrears.

rien luy doit (lū-i' dwä). He owes him nothing.

Rien passa par le fait (pas'a pär le fāt). Nothing passed by the deed.

riens. Same as **rien.**

riens en arriere (ri-en' ôn är-rare'). Nothing in arrears.

riens lour deust (ri-en' loor doost). Not their debt.

riens per descent (ri-en' per des-sôn'). A plea in an action of ejectment raising the issue whether the plaintiff was seized of the land by inheritance. Wood v Jackson (NY) 8 Wend 9.

rifle range. An area equipped for training in and testing of marksmanship. A public place of amusement. 52 Am J1st Amuse § 64.

rigger. One who installs or repairs rigging.

rigging. Scaffolding and staging used in the construction of a building. Jones v Russell, 224 Ky 390, 6 SW2d 460. Equipment of a vessel, that is, ropes, cables, etc., by which the masts are supported and the sails handled. 48 Am J1st Ship § 71.

right. Adjective: Correct; fitting. In accord with law, morality, and justice. The opposite of left. Conservative. Noun: That to which a person has a just and valid claim, whether it be land, a thing, or the privilege of doing something or saying something, such as the right of free speech. Property, interest, power, prerogative, immunity, and privilege. Shaw v Proffitt, 57 Or 192, 109 P 584. In the broad sense, inclusive of remedy. UCC § 1—201(36).

"The word is one of the most deceptive of pitfalls; it is so easy to slip from a qualified meaning in the premise to an unqualified one in the conclusion. Most rights are qualified. A man has at least as absolute a right to give his own money as he has to demand money from a party that has made no promise to him; yet if he gives it to induce another to steal or murder, the purpose of the act makes it a crime." American Bank & Trust Co. v Federal Reserve Bank, 256 US 350, 65 L Ed 983, 41 S Ct 499, 25 ALR 971, 977.

When we speak of a person having a right, we must necessarily refer to a civil right as distinguished from the elemental idea of rights absolute. We must have in mind a right given and protected by law, and a person's enjoyment thereof is regulated entirely by the law which creates it. If we were to consider these rights as absolute, nothing but chaos could result. See Nickell v Rosenfield, 82 Cal App 369, 255 P 760.

See **equitable right; legal right.**

right ad rem (ad rem). A right against a thing; a right against the property as distinguished from a right against the person.

right and wrong test. A test, applied in determining responsibility for an act otherwise constituting criminal homicide, according to the ability or capacity of the accused to distinguish between right and wrong. 26 Am J1st Homi § 79. The test of criminal responsibility of a mentally deficient person according to whether the accused was laboring under such a defect of reason from disease of the mind as not to know the nature and quality of the act he was doing; or, if he did know it, that he did not know he was doing what was wrong. 21 Am J2d Crim L § 33. The test of criminal responsibility of an infant according to whether or not he knew that the act constituting the offense was wrongful. 21 Am J2d Crim L § 27. A matter of moral right and wrong or, according to other authorities, right or wrong within the intendment of law. 21 Am J2d Crim L § 35. A test according to whether the accused knows the difference between right and wrong, can understand his relation to others, and that which others bear to him, and has knowledge of the nature of his act so as to perceive its consequences to himself and others. 21 Am J2d Crim L § 34.

right arm of the law. A graphic expression denoting an injunction. DeWitt v Hays, 2 Cal 463, 469.

right by prescription. See **prescription.**

right close. See **writ of right close.**

rightful (rīt'fůl). By right; lawful; proper.

rightful subjects of legislation. Lawful, rather than proper or expedient, subjects. Territory ex rel. McMahon v O'Connor, 5 Dak 397, 41 NW 746.

right-hand lane. A traffic lane to the right, as a driver moving forward sees it, of the median line of highway or street.

right-hand side. The traffic rule of driving on the right side of the highway. 25 Am J1st High §§ 205 et seq. An illustration of a rule of the road. Reipe v Elting, 89 Iowa 82, 56 NW 285.

right heirs. Those persons on whom the law casts the real estate of a decedent or admits to participate in the distribution of his personal estate. 57 Am J1st Wills § 1371.

Before the abolition of estates tail, the term was used to distinguish the preferred heir, to whom the estate was limited, from the heirs in general, but

RIGHT

since such abolition, the term is equivalent to "heirs." Brown v Wadsworth, 168 NY 225, 237, 61 NE 250.

right in personam (in per-sō'nam). A right against the person.

right in rem (in rem). A right in a thing, whether by ownership of the whole or of an interest.

right of access. See **access; access to courts.**

right of action. The right to bring suit in a particular case. A present right to commence and maintain an action at law to enforce the payment or collection of a debt or demand. Hibbard v Clark, 56 NH 155. A remedial right affording redress for the infringement of a legal right belonging to some definite person. Fielder v Ohio Edison Co. 158 Ohio St 375, 49 Ohio Ops 265, 109 NE2d 855, 35 ALR2d 1365. Precisely, the right of the plaintiff to sue, the essentials of which are (1) a good cause of action; (2) the performance of all conditions precedent; and (3) the existence of the right to maintain the action in the plaintiff unaffected by circumstances which will constitute in law a bar to the maintenance of the suit. 1 Am J2d Actions § 46.

right of alienation. The right to alienate or dispose of one's property in any lawful manner. The right to make any disposition of one's property not interfering with the existing rights of others, subject only to such limitations as are prescribed by law. 42 Am J1st Prop § 52.

right of appeal. The right to invoke the jurisdiction of an appellate court to obtain a review of a judgment, existing, not as an inherent or inalienable right, but as a right conferred by law under proper authority. 4 Am J2d A & E §§ 172 et seq.

right of approach. The right of a belligerent to visit a ship at sea to determine her nationality.

The right to visit and search merchant ships on the high seas, whatever be the ships, the cargoes, the destinations, is an incontestable right of the lawfully commissioned cruisers of a belligerent nation, but it should be exercised with as much regard to the safety of the vessel detained as is consistent with a thorough examination of her character and voyage. 56 Am J1st War § 152.
See **access.**

right of assembly. See **assembly.**

right of bench. The right of a particular judge to sit on an elevated seat.

right of being a corporation. See **franchise.**

right of burial. The right to the custody of the dead body of a person for the purpose of burial, such as the right of surviving spouse or child of the decedent. 22 Am J2d Dead B § 7. The privilege or license of the owner of a burial lot in a cemetery, the same to be enjoyed so long as the place continues to be used as a burial ground, subject to municipal regulation and control, and legally revocable whenever the public necessity requires. 14 Am J2d Cem § 31.

right of common. See **common.**

right of conquest. See **conquest.**

right of conscience (of kon'shens). Liberty in religious belief and observance. State v Cummings, 36 Mo 363, 375.

right of curtesy. See **curtesy.**

right of dower. See **dower.**

right of discussion. See **freedom of speech and of the press.**

right of drainage. The jus aqueductus or easement which gives the owner of land the right to bring down water through or from the land of another, either from its source or from any other place. Nellis v Munson, 108 NY 453, 459, 15 NE 739.

right of drip. See **easement of drip; eavesdrip.**

right of election. See **election.**

right of eminent domain. See **eminent domain.**

right of entry. The right to the possession of certain land. See Cecil v Clark, 44 W Va 659, 666, 30 SE 216.
See **re-entry; re-entry for condition broken.**

right of first publication. See **first publication.**

right of fishery. See **fishery.**

right of habitation. The right of a person to occupy the house of another without charge.

right of homestead. See **homestead; homestead exemption.**

right of indefinite user. An essential quality or attribute of absolute property. Eaton v Boston, C. & M. R. R. 51 NH 504.

right of inspection. See **inspection; inspection of records.**

right of interrogatory. See **interrogating; interrogatories.**

right of lien. See **lien.**

right of personal security. See **personal security.**

right of possession (pō-zesh'on). A person's right to occupy and enjoy property. See 2 Bl Comm 196.

right of pre-emption. See **pre-emption.**

right of privacy. See **privacy.**

right of private property. A right which consists in the free use, enjoyment and disposal of all acquisitions, without any control or diminution, save only by the laws of the land. Evans v Reading Chemical Fertilizing Co. 160 Pa 209, 218, 28 A 702.
See **property.**

right of probable expectancy. See **probable expectancy.**

right of property. See **property.**

right of protest. See **protest.**

right of redemption. See **equity of redemption; redemption.**

right of re-entry. See **re-entry for condition broken.**

right of representation. The right to take by descent as a representative of the decedent on the basis of ancestry. 23 Am J2d Desc & D §§ 54 et seq. The equivalent of "per stirpes." Johnson v Huntley, 39 Wash 2d 499, 236 P2d 776.
See **representation.**

right of retainer. See **retainer.**

right of search. See **search; search and seizure.**

right of self-defense. See **self-defense.**

right of sepulture. Same as **right of burial.**

right of setoff. See **retainer; setoff.**

right of suffrage. See **suffrage.**

right of suit. Same as **right of action.**

right of support. See **lateral support; support of building; support of person.**

right of survivorship. See **survivorship.**

right of user. See **user.**

right of vending. See **vending.**

right of visit and search. See **visit and search.**

right of visitation. See **visitation.**

right of way. A matter of the law of the road, a relative matter, existing only in reference to other persons using the highway, comprehending the right to proceed at a particular place or point in street or highway to which other persons must at such time and place defer. 25 Am J1st High §§ 204 et seq. The right of the driver of a vehicle to proceed on the way, it being the duty of other drivers in other vehicles on the way, under the circumstances, to permit him to proceed. 7 Am J2d Auto §§ 198 et seq. The right of a vehicle to proceed uninterruptedly in a lawful manner in the direction in which it is moving in preference to another vehicle approaching from a different direction into its path. Heidle v Baldwin, 118 Ohio St 375, 161 NE 44, 58 ALR 1186. The right of a vessel to proceed on course, to which other vessels must defer. 48 Am J1st Ship §§ 250 et seq. A boating regulation. 12 Am J2d Boats §§ 14 et seq. A right of passage, an easement. The right of one person, of several persons, or of the community at large, to pass over the land of another. Kurz v Blume, 407 Ill 383, 95 NE2d 338, 25 ALR2d 1258.

See **private way; railroad right of way.**

right of way by custom. A right of way acquired by custom, particularly by customary use by the inhabitants of a particular locality, recognized by the common law of England, although ordinarily not recognized by the American common law. 25 Am J2d Ease § 19.

right of way by grant (of wā bī grạnt). A right of way granted in express terms by a deed. 25 Am J2d Ease § 20.

right of way by necessity. A right of way founded upon an implied grant or implied reservation, the implication arising from the necessity of a way for use of premises granted or premises retained by the grantor. 25 Am J2d Ease § 34.

right of way by reservation. A right of way created by a deed reserving in the premises conveyed an easement therefor. 25 Am J2d Ease § 21.

right of way ex vi termini (rīt of wā ex vī ter'mi-nī). A right of way over the land of another confined to a particular line. Crosier v Brown, 66 W Va 273, 66 SE 326.

right of way in gross. See **easement in gross.**

rights. The pre-emptive rights of stockholders of a corporation in reference to a new issue of stock; the right to subscribe to shares of the new issue, in preference to persons who are not present stockholders, on equal terms with other existing stockholders, that is, in the proportion that the number of shares of his existing stock bears to the total number of outstanding shares of existing stock. 18 Am J2d Corp § 275.

rights in action. Representatives of money and of personal things included in the term "choses in action." State v Tower, 122 Kan 165, 251 P 401.

rights of accused. The constitutional, statutory, or common-law rights of one accused of crime, such as due process, equal protection, fair and impartial trial, speedy trial, the assistance of counsel, public trial etc. 21 Am J2d Crim L §§ 218 et seq.

rights of persons. In the broad sense, the equivalent of personal rights. In a technical sense, physical rights, such as the right to travel from place to place, to see, and to hear the manifestations of nature. Duffies v Duffies, 76 Wis 374, 45 NW 522.

See **personal rights.**

rights of things. Such rights as a man may acquire over external objects, or things unconnected with his person. See 1 Bl Comm 122.

right, title, and interest. A term of art sometimes employed in accomplishing a levy of an execution on real estate for the purpose of securing under the writ whatever title the debtor may have in the land, as a fee simple, an estate for life or for years, a right of redemption, etc. 30 Am J2d Exec § 250.

A term descriptive of the operation of a quitclaim deed in reference to the interest conveyed. 23 Am J2d Deeds § 291.

right to alluvion (rīt to a̤-lū'vi-ọn). See **alluvion.**

right to appeal. See **right of appeal.**

right to bear arms. A right under the Second Amendment to the United States Consitution; the right to bear arms as they are borne by a well-regulated militia in battle. Strickland v State, 137 Ga 1, 72 SE 260. Not a constitutional right to carry weapons on one's person as a civilian. Hill v State, 53 Ga 473, 480.

right to coal. See **coal.**

right to counsel. See **assistance of counsel.**

right to day in court. See **day in court.**

right to fish. See **fish; fishery.**

right to fair trial. See **fair trial.**

right to follow a trade, business, or occupation. The right to earn a livelihood in a trade or occupation, a right within the guaranties of the Fourteenth Amendment. New State Ice Co. v Liebmann, 285 US 262, 76 L Ed 747, 52 S Ct 371. A property right of which one is not to be deprived without due process of law. 16 Am J2d Const L § 371.

right to full hearing. See **full hearing.**

right to go extra viam (rīt to go ex'tra vī'am). See **extra viam rights.**

right to jury trial. See **trial by jury.**

right to lateral support. See **lateral support.**

right to liberty. See **liberty.**

right to marry. A natural right, subject to such restrictions as the legislature may impose in the interest of morality and the social order. 35 Am J1st Mar § 10.

right to office. See **title to office.**

right to open and close. See **opening and closing.**

right to operate automobile. A privilege in the sense of being subject to a license requirement, but a common right in the sense of the right to make use of the highways for travel and the transportation of property. 7 Am J2d Auto § 6.

right to privacy. See **privacy.**

right to redeem. See **equity of redemption; redemption.**

right to rely. As an element of actionable fraud or deceit, calling for a representation made to the complaining party directly or indirectly and of such nature that it was reasonably calculated to deceive him and induce him to do that which otherwise he would not have done. Emery v Third Nat. Bank, 314 Pa 544, 171 A 881.

right to speedy trial. See **speedy trial.**

right to travel. See **travel.**

right to trial by jury. See **jury trial.**

right to surcharge and falsify. See **surcharge and falsify.**

right to vend. See **vending.**

right to vote. See **suffrage.**

right to work. See **right to follow a trade, business, or occupation.**

right-to-work law. A statute or provision of a state constitution that no one shall be denied an opportunity to attain or retain employment because he is or is not a member of a labor organization, prohibiting employers from entering into contracts obligating themselves to exclude persons from employment because they are or are not labor union members. 31 Am J1st Lab § 3.

right turn. An act in the operation of a motor vehicle wherein the vehicle is turned to the right at an intersection for the purpose of proceeding to the right on the intersecting street, usually regulated by statutes, ordinances, or rules of the road so as to require the driver to keep as close as practicable to the right hand curb or edge of the highway. 8 Am J2d Auto § 803.

rigore juris. See **de rigore juris; ex rigore juris.**

rigor juris (rī'gor jū'ris). The strictness of the law; strict law.

rigor mortis (rī'gor môr'tis). The stiffness of death; the stiffness of a dead body.

ring. A band of metal. A small band of precious metal worn on the finger as an ornament or to symbolize a marriage or betrothal. Anno: 92 ALR 608. A circle, such as the place in a tent for performance of acts of a show. A combination of persons associated together for illegal or otherwise improper purposes. Schomberg v Walker, 132 Cal 224, 228, 64 P 290.
See **prize ring.**

ring dropping. A kind of larceny by trick.

ring fight. See **prize fight.**

ringing off. Same as **ringing up.**

ringing out. Same as **ringing up.**

ringing the change. The offense of persuading a buyer to believe that he has given a bad coin and thereby inducing him to give another good one.

ringing up. A method by which a group of dealers on a board of trade discharge contracts for future delivery before delivery is due by a system of offsets, cancelations and adjustments of differences in lieu of actual delivery of the commodity sold; a more complex case of setoff. Lyons Mill Co. v Goffe & Carkener (CA8 Kan) 46 F2d 241, 83 ALR 501.

In not less than three fourths of the transactions in the grain pit there is no physical handing over of any grain, but there is a settlement, either by the direct method, so called, or by what is known as ringing up. Chicago Board of Trade v Christie Grain & Stock Co. 198 US 236, 246, 49 L Ed 1031, 1037, 25 S Ct 637.

ring settlement. See **ringing up.**

rink. See **skating rink.**

riot. A tumultuous disturbance of the peace by three or more persons assembling of their own authority, with an intent mutually to assist one another against anyone who shall oppose them in the execution of some enterprise of a private nature, and afterward actually executing such purpose in a violent and turbulent manner, to the terror of the people, whether the act intended was of itself lawful or unlawful. Adamson v New York, 188 NY 255, 80 NE 937. The acts or conduct of a body of men —three or more—in committing an unlawful act or breach of the peace in a tumultuous manner, or in the doing of a lawful act in a violent tumultuous manner. Anno: 121 ALR 251; 29A Am J Rev ed Ins § 1302. A tumultuous meeting of three or more persons upon some common purpose, to do an unlawful act, which they actually execute with violence. Date v Sumner, 29 SCL (2 Speers) 599.

rioter. Anyone who encourages, incites, promotes, or takes part in a riot. 46 Am J1st Riot § 14.
See **riot.**

riotose. In a riotous manner; riotously.

riotous (rī'ot-us). Tumultuous in disturbance of the peace. Partaking of the nature of a riot. The substantial equivalent of the word "violent." State v Kutter, 59 Ind 572, 574.

riotous assembly. A group of persons engaged in a riot.
See **mob.**

ripa (rī'pạ). The banks or shore of a river.

riparia (ri-pā'ri-a). Water flowing between banks; a river.

riparian (rī-pā'ri-ạn). Belonging to the bank of a river. 56 Am J1st Wat § 278.

riparian land. Land bounded or traversed by a natural stream of water. 56 Am J1st Wat § 273. Land in actual contact with the water. 56 Am J1st Wat § 277.

Riparian land is, in any event, limited in its extent by the watershed of the stream; in other words, lands beyond the watershed cannot be regarded as riparian. 56 Am J1st Wat § 278.

riparian owner. Same as **riparian proprietor.**

riparian proprietor. An owner of land which is bounded or traversed by a natural stream. In loose usage, inclusive of an owner of land on the shores of the sea or of a lake. 56 Am J1st Wat § 273.

riparian rights (rī-pā'ri-ạn rīts). Rights existing as natural and inherent incidents of the ownership of riparian land. 56 Am J1st Wat § 274. The rights of an owner of land bounded or traversed by a natural stream of water in the use of the stream or the water therein. The right to the flow of the stream in its natural course and in its natural condition in respect of both volume and purity, except as affected by reasonable use by other proprietors, the right of access to and use of the stream or water, and the right to accretions. 56 Am J1st Wat § 273.

riparian waters (rī-pā'ri-ạn wả'tẻrs). The waters of the ordinary flow and underflow of a stream.

When such waters rise above the line of highest ordinary flow, they are to be regarded as flood waters. Motl v Boyd, 116 Tex 82, 111, 286 SW 458.

riparius (rī-pā'ri-us). (Latin.) Belonging to the bank of a river. 56 Am J1st Wat § 273.

Riparum usus publicus est jure gentium sicut ipsius fluminis (ri-pā'rum ū'sus pub'li-kus est jū're jen'she-um sik'ut ip-sī'us flu'mi-nis). (Civil law.) The public use of the banks is, by the law of nations, just the same as that of the river itself.

ripe. Fully matured; ready; in proper condition. Hosmer v Hoitt, 161 Mass 173, 175, 36 NE 835.

ripe for judgment. Brought to a final determination, everything having been done that ought to be done before entry of a final adjudication. Kelly v Foley, 284 Mass 503, 188 NE 349.

ripe for review. The status or condition of administrative determination in reference to judicial relief by way of review. 2 Am J2d Admin L § 583.

riser. The board which determines the height of a step in a stairway. Anno: 25 ALR2d 372, § 4.

risicum (ri'si-kum). An insurance risk or hazard.

rising. A growing. An advancing. An upward movement. A revolt or insurrection.

rising of the court. The court's final adjournment; the last day of the term of court. State v Weaver, 11 Neb 163, 165, 8 NW 385.

risk. The chance of injury or loss. The peril of loss or injury to the insured which is protected by an insurance policy. Physicians' Defense Co. v Cooper (CA9 Cal) 199 F 576.
See **assumption of risk.**

risk and causes of loss. The coverage of an insurance policy. 29A Am J Rev ed Ins §§ 1132 et seq. The peril or contingency against which the insured is protected, such as fire, flood, sickness, etc. 29 Am J Rev ed Ins § 192.
See **attachment of risk.**

risk assumed. See **assumption of risk.**

risk of buyer. See **buyer's risk.**

risk of seller. See **seller's risk.**

risk of war. A risk resulting in an injury of which war, and not some other risk or hazard was the proximate cause. Dennehy v United States (DC NY) 15 F2d 196.

risks incurred. Risks assumed. Risks which an insurer undertakes to cover in a policy or contract of insurance. American Surety Co. v Ryan, 185 La 678, 170 So 34.
See **assumption of risk**; **risks and causes of loss.**

risks of employment. See **ordinary risks of employment.**

risks of navigation. Inclusive of any risk in the movement of a vessel. A broader term than "perils of the sea."
"There is no case holding that risk of navigation means the same thing as perils of navigation, and there is no authority that I have been able to find, defining or fixing the meaning of this term." Hartford Fire Ins. Co. v Baker, 127 Okla 166, 260 P 6.

rite (rī'tē). Rightly; properly; with due formality. A ceremonial act, as observed at a wedding.

ritual. A prescribed form for the conduct of a meeting of a lodge or fraternal benefit society. 36 Am J2d Frat O § 28.

rivage (riv'āj). A toll which was collected for navigating certain rivers of England.

rival unions. Labor unions competing in obtaining applications for membership and the right to represent the employees of a particular industry or plant in collective bargaining.

river. A large inland stream of water flowing into the sea, a lake, or another river. Chamberlain v Hemingway, 63 Conn 1, 27 A 239.

river bed. The area which is kept practically bare of vegetation by the wash of the waters in their onward course from year to year, although parts of it may be dry at times. 56 Am J1st Wat § 448. That portion of the soil which is alternately covered and left bare, as there may be an increase or diminution in the supply of water, and which is adequate to contain it at its average and mean stage during the entire year, without reference to the extraordinary freshets of the winter or spring, or the extreme droughts of the summer or autumn. Alabama v Georgia (US) 23 How 505, 16 L Ed 556, 560. The banks and the permanently submerged soil. State v Faudre, 54 W Va 122, 46 SE 269.
The shores of a navigable river are the spaces between high and low-water marks, and the bed of a river includes the shores. See State ex rel. Ellis v Gerbing, 56 Fla 603, 47 So 353.

river boat. In the broad sense, a boat or vessel on a river. In the popular sense, a large vessel to be navigated on a river, which may carry some freight, but is primarily for passengers, particularly persons traveling for pleasure. A place of amusement, also of entertainment. Shannon v Streckfus Steamers, Inc. 279 Ky 649, 131 SW2d 833.

river boundary. A natural boundary of lands in private ownership, the exact location of which must depend upon whether the title to the bed of the river is in the state or the riparian owners and the view taken in the particular jurisdiction concerning the ownership between high and low-water mark. 12 Am J2d Bound § 20. Sometimes a state boundary.
Where statute makes a great river the common boundary between two states, it means only the well-defined and unmistakable stream, and does not also include the interlacing unnavigable water belts, streams, and streamlets which, in the level alluvial bottom lands through which the river flows, emerge here and there from such main body. Little v Green, 144 Iowa 492, 123 NW 367.

river thread. See **thread of stream.**

riviation (riv-i-ā'shọn). The use of rivers for fishing.

rivulet (riv'ū-let). A natural watercourse in the form of a small stream. 56 Am J1st Wat § 6.

rixa (rik'să). An angry dispute; a quarrel.

rixatrix (rik-sā'triks). A scold. The word is confined to the feminine gender. See 4 Bl Comm 168.

R.N. Abbreviation of registered nurse; abbreviation of Royal Navy.

r'na. An abbreviation of "regina," the queen.

road. Any strip of land used or appropriated for travel, whether by an individual, a corporation, or the public. 25 Am J1st High § 3. Often used synonymously with highway. 25 Am J1st High § 3.

roadbed. The part of a railroad upon which the tracks are laid. San Francisco v Central P. R. Co. 63 Cal 467. The foundation, located on the right of way, on which the super structure of rails, ties, ballast, etc., rests. 44 Am J1st RR § 227. Not confined to the space occupied by ties, but extending to such a distance as puts one in danger of collision with a passing train. 29A Am J Rev ed Ins § 1259 (exception of risk of injury received while on roadbed). The foundation of a highway or street, of crushed stone, tailings from a mine, cinders, etc.

road brand. A brand required by statute to be placed upon cattle before they are removed from the county where they are gathered to a market beyond the state line.
    Such a brand is to be recorded in the county from whence the cattle are driven. Crowell v State, 24 Tex App 404, 6 SW 318.

road camp. A place where prisoners detailed to work on highways are detained, fed, and housed when not working.

road district. An improvement district established for the construction and maintenance of a highway. 25 Am J1st High § 606. A quasi corporation. 37 Am J1st Mun Corp § 6.

road engine. An ordinary locomotive used by a railroad for pulling a train, rather than for switching purposes. Prosser v Montana Central R. Co. 17 Mont 372, 43 P 81.

road grader. A machine, self-powered in modern times, equipped with a broad heavy blade to smooth the road and bring it to the proper pitch or level. For some purposes a motor vehicle. Anno: 77 ALR2d 947.

roadhouse. An inn or tavern; sometimes a place of accommodation by the service of food and drink only. Anno: 19 ALR 526, s. 53 ALR 988; 29 Am J Rev ed Innk § 9.

road rules. See **rules of the road.**

roadstead. A place close to shore at which ships may anchor, although not a harbor. Cole v Union Mut. Ins. Co. 78 Mass (12 Gray) 501.

road stock. Stock in a turnpike company. Holbrook v Union Bank (US) 7 Wheat 553, 5 L Ed 521.

road test. Driving a motor vehicle on the highway to determine need for repairs, the nature of repairs needed, or the condition of the vehicle after repairs made. Kenner v Century Indem. Co. 320 Mass 6, 67 NE2d 769, 165 ALR 1463. An examination given an applicant for a driver's license to ascertain his ability to operate an automobile on highway or street. 7 Am J2d Auto § 108.

roadway. The part of a street or highway intended for use by vehicles and animals. 25 Am J1st High § 3. Road; a roadbed. The right of way of a railroad. 44 Am J1st RR § 74. The roadbed of a railroad and the space of ground that the railroad is allowed by law in which to construct its roadbed and lay its track. San Francisco v Central P. R. Co. 63 Cal 467.

road work. Broadly, work performed in the construction or maintenance of highways. Labor performed by convicts upon highways. Work done under statute requiring labor to be performed by the male citizens or inhabitants of a specified age, without compensation, on the public roads for a certain number of days each year, or to pay a certain sum in money for each day's labor thus required. 25 Am J1st High § 84.

rob. To commit the crime of robbery. In loose usage, to steal from or defraud.

robaria (ro-bā′ri-a). Robbery.
    It is said that originally the offense consisted in the taking by force from a person of his "robe" or clothing.

robator (ro-bā′tor). A robber.

robber (rob′ẽr). A person who commits the crime of robbery. In loose usage, one who steals from or defrauds another.

robbery. The felonious taking of money or goods of value from the person of another or in his presence, against his will, by force or by putting him in fear. 46 Am J1st Rob § 2.
    The gist of the offense of robbery both at common law and under the Illinois statute is the force or intimidation employed in taking from the person of another, and against his will, property belonging to him or in his care, custody, or control. People v Casey, 399 Ill 374, 77 NE2d 812, 11 ALR2d 865.
    An intent to deprive an owner of his property and to convert it to the use and benefit of the accused is an essential element of the offense of robbery. People v Gallegos, 130 Colo 232, 274 P2d 608, 46 ALR2d 1224.

robbery insurance. Insurance covering a loss by robbery, that is by a crime containing all the elements of the offense of robbery. Anno: 48 ALR2d 19. A coverage of the felonious and forcible taking of the property of the insured by violence inflicted upon the custodian of the property, by putting such person in fear of violence, or by any overt felonious act committed in the presence of such person and of which he was actually cognizant at the time. 29A Am J Rev ed Ins § 1338.

robbour. A robber.

roberia (ro-be′ri-a). Same as **robaria.**

Roberts' Rules of Order. A compilation and discussion of parliamentary rules.
    See **parliamentary rules.**

robin. See **round robin.**

robour. A robber.

Rochdale store. A store operated by a co-operative association or society, the name deriving from the city of Rochdale, England in which one of the earliest co-operative societies was organized.

rock. Stone in the mass or in pieces. The crust of the earth. As used in construction and excavation contracts, not necessarily the meaning of the term in geology. Chicago v Duffy, 117 Ill App 261, aff'd 218 Ill 242, 75 NE 912.

rock and roll. The movement of a vessel, especially a small craft upon a rough sea. A peril to small watercraft. 12 Am J2d Boats §§ 38, 52. A form of modern music, characterized by a rhythmic beat.

rock in place. Rock that is inclosed and embraced in the general mass of the mountain, as distinguished from float soil and débris on the surface.

Rockefeller Foundation. A trust chartered for the broad purpose of promoting the well-being of mankind throughout the world, the practical objectives being the advancement of knowledge and the application of knowledge to human interests and needs, particularly by studies in reference to the world's food supply, overpopulation, educational opportunities, and cultural activities. Anno: 34 ALR 686, s. 62 ALR 339, 108 ALR 301.

rodent. Broadly, any small mammal with teeth adapted for nibbling. In popular usage, such a mammal with destructive tendencies, such as a rat or mouse.

rodeo (rọ-dā′ō). A place of amusement wherein the entertainment consists in exhibitions developed from the activities of the cattle ranches of the West, consisting of riding bucking horses, roping cattle, etc.

Roentgen ray. See **X-ray.**

rogare (ro-gā're). (Roman law.) To ask; to demand; to propose the enactment of a law; to offer a candidate for election.

rogatio (ro-gā'she-ō). (Roman law.) An asking; a request; the proposal of a law for enactment.

rogationes, quaestiones, et positiones debent esse simplices (ro-gā-she-ō'nēz, quēst-she-ō'nēz, et po-zi-she-ō'nez de'bent es'se sim'pli-sēz). Demands, questions and claims ought to be simple.

rogation-week (rō-gā'shon-wēk). A week in each year during which the boundaries of English parishes and manors were surveyed.

rogatio testium (ro-gā'she-ō test'she-um). An essential of a valid nuncupative will, being a request by the testator to some person or persons present at the time the testamentary words are spoken, to bear witness that such constitute his will. 57 Am J1st Wills § 658.

rogatory letter (rog'a-tō-ri let'ėr). See **letter rogatory.**

rogo (ro'gō). I ask; I request; I demand. See 1 Bl Comm 239.

rogue (rōg). A scoundrel. A mischievous person, not necessarily a mean person. McClurg v Ross (Pa) 5 Binn 218, 219. A term often applied with affection to a person, particularly a child or old person. An old male elephant which stays apart from the herd.

rogues' gallery (rōgs gal'ę-ri). A collection of photographs of persons convicted of crime, preserved and exhibited in a police department or prison for the future identification of such persons. 41 Am J1st Privacy § 27.

roiaume (roi'ōm). The realm; the kingdom.

roigne (roin'yā). The queen.

roll. Verb: To move a thing by turning it over and over. A slang term in police circles and the underworld for robbing a person who is drunk or helpless. Lasecki v State, 190 Wis 274, 275, 208 NW 868, 869. Noun: A parchment; a record.
See **enroll; enrolled bill; enrolled order; judgment roll; jury list.**

rolled-up plea. A plea or answer by the defendant in an action for libel or slander in which he combines the defenses of truth and fair comment, alleging in effect the truth of the matters of fact stated in the publication, that such facts are proper matters of public interest and concern, and that the published comments thereon are justified. Lothrop v Adams, 133 Mass 471; Kinsley v Herald & Globe Asso. 113 Vt 272, 34 A2d 99, 148 ALR 1164.

roller coaster. An amusement device consisting of a track having abrupt inclines and declines on which the open cars in which the patrons ride are carried with great speed. Kehoe v Central Park Amusement Co. (CA3 Pa) 52 F2d 916.
A structure upon which rests a track several hundred feet long, on which wooden cars are run at a high rate of speed. The cars are elevated by a cogwheel attachment, so that the track is a considerable distance from the ground at the highest place. It is built on a general incline, with slight elevations intervening from that point to the end of the track, where it comes to the surface of the ground near the place of starting. The cars are run from the highest point by force of gravity, and are operated as a matter of amusement to those who take rides, and incidentally for the pecuniary profit of the proprietors. Re Hull, 18 Idaho 475, 110 P 256.

roller skating. An amusement or sport in which the participants move on skates having small wheels known as rollers.
See **skating rink.**

rolling credit. A continuous and ever-extending credit up to a certain specified limit. Tobler v Willis, 59 Tex 80, 85.

rolling door. See **overhead door; revolving door.**

rolling mill. A machine for rolling out bars and sheets of metal. A plant in which such machines are operated.

rolling stock. The locomotives and cars of a railroad company. 44 Am J1st RR § 272. Any wheeled vehicle of a carrier of freight or passengers.
The term embraces the movable property belonging to a railroad company, and is declared personal property for purposes of taxation. By movable property is meant such property as in its ordinary use is taken from one part of the line to another, such as cars, locomotives and their attachments and usual accompaniments. Ohio & Missouri Railroad Co. v Weber, 96 Ill 443, 448.

Roman calendar. See **Gregorian calendar; Julian calendar.**

Roman Catholic. A Christian who acknowledges the authority of the Pope of Rome. Hale v Everett, 53 NH 9. A member of the Roman Catholic Church.

Roman Catholic Church. A Christian church, originating in the very early days of Christianity, governed by a supreme pontiff, the Pope of Rome, and a hierarchy.

Roman law. That law which comprehends the laws which prevailed among the Romans, without regard to the time of their origin.
The term is in a strict sense limited in its application to the laws of the Romans which prevailed until the compilation of the civil law under Justinian in 530 A. D. See Mackeldey's Roman Law §§ 18, 20, 70.

Roman pound. See **usurae centesimae.**

romescot (rōm'skot). Same as **Peter's pence.**

Romney-marsh (rom'nē-marsh). A tract in the county of Kent, containing twenty-four thousand acres, governed by certain ancient and equitable laws of sewers, composed by Henry de Bathe, a venerable judge in the reign of King Henry the Third, from which laws all commissioners of sewers in England may receive light and direction. See 3 Bl Comm 73, and note.

rondeau (ron'dō). The same as **rondo.**

rondo (ron'dō). A variety of billiards, sometimes played as a gambling game. Anno: 60 ALR 349.

roof. The outside covering of a building, sometimes of wooden shingles, more frequently in modern times of prepared or composition shingles. A top limit, as a roof placed on prices or wages.
See **overhanging roof.**

roof sign. A sign painted or erected on the roof of a building. 3 Am J2d Advertg § 15.

room. A part of a building, bounded or enclosed by walls. Leominster Fuel Co. v Scanlon, 243 Mass 126, 137 NE 271, 24 ALR 1459.

The word includes a description of the perpendicular as well as the horizontal planes which bound the parcel of the house described by it, and excludes the outside of lateral walls, at least when they constitute the walls of another room, as clearly as the words "first floor" exclude the flooring of the story above it. Leominster Fuel Co. v Scanlon, 243 Mass 126, 137 NE 271, 24 ALR 1459, 1460.

rooming house. A house where bedrooms as such are furnished paying guests. Cedar Rapids Invest. Co. v Commodore Hotel Co. 205 Iowa 736, 218 NW 510, 56 ALR 1098.
See **lodging house.**

root. A stock of descent,—an ancestor in whom a succession of inheritance begins.

rooter. An instrumentality used to cut away and remove roots in sewers. State v Gootstein, 206 Minn 246, 288 NW 221, 125 ALR 715. A term in popular, if not the best, usage for one who supports and encourages an athletic team in its contests.

root of title. The conveyance or instrument which begins the chain of a land title.

roster (ros'tėr). A roll or list of names. A list of names of persons in a unit of the armed forces. A word which is used instead of the word "register," and which comprehends a list of all military officers, connected with the regiment, brigade or division, and is kept as are records of orders and official communications. Matthews v Bowman, 25 Me 157, 167.

rota (rō'ta). A court.

rotary drilling. Drilling a well by the rotation of a bit. A method frequently used in boring for oil. Boring is done by rotation of a bit attached to a steel pipe, which, when so used is called a "drill stem." A smaller bore, called a "rat hole," sometimes precedes, and is reamed out to obtain the full-sized hole. To aid operation, drilling fluid (mud laden water) is pumped into the upper end of the drill stem and escapes into the well at high velocity through holes in the bit. It rises through the space between the pipe and the earth walls of the well and carries to the surface cuttings made by the bit. It holds back and seals the penetrated formations. Hydrostatic pressure of the drilling fluid is very great and the fluid in a penetrated formation will not flow into the well unless it is under greater pressure. Honolulu Oil Corp. v Halliburton, 306 US 550, 83 L Ed 980, 59 S Ct 662.

rotation. The movement of the earth on its axis. Regular and recurring succession. The appropriation of water for irrigation purposes during a certain number of hours a day, a certain number of days a week, or a certain number of weeks a year, leaving the water free during the remaining time for appropriation for the use of other persons. 30 Am J Rev ed Irrig § 32.

rotation of names. A system employed in the preparation of ballots for an election in which the names of the candidates appear in a different order from district to district or precinct to precinct, even from county to county, the practice being employed to assure that no candidate has the advantage of being first on the ballot in every voting place. 26 Am J2d Elect § 207.

rotted. Spoiled and in a condition unfit for consumption. Robert L. Berger Co. v National Fire Ins. Co. 331 Ill App 102, 72 NE2d 727 (vegetables).

rotten boroughs (rot'n bur'ōs). Small English boroughs which, notwithstanding their decline in population, returned members to parliament.

rotten clause. A clause in a marine insurance policy the usual form of which provides that if the ship is unseaworthy on a regular survey, by reason of being rotten or unsound, the underwriters are discharged. Janney v Columbian Ins. Co. (US) 10 Wheat 411, 6 L Ed 354.

roturier (rō-tü-ri-ā'). In old French law—one not noble. A free commoner; one who did not hold his land by homage and fealty, yet owed certain services.

rough minutes. Unofficial memoranda, made by the clerk of the court for his own convenience, of orders as they are announced by the court.
Such memoranda are made by the clerk for his own guidance in entering the orders of the court on the register and in the minutes of the court, and do not constitute an official record of the court, although they are sometimes useful as evidence. The book in which such memoranda are made by the clerk is often referred to as a "blotter." Brownell v Superior Court of Yolo County, 157 Cal 703, 109 P 91.

rough shadowing. A practice, sometimes resorted to by detectives, of openly and publicly following and watching a person, usually as a means most effective to prevent his going away from the place.
Such actual surveillance and pursuit may constitute an actionable wrong as suggestive of criminality, fatal to public esteem, and productive of public contempt or ridicule. Shultz v Frankfort Marine Acci & Plate Glass Ins. Co. 151 Wis 537, 139 NW 386.

roulette (rö-let'). A gambling game characterized by the use of a wheel for the determination of the winner.

roundhouse. A railroad shop, often having a turntable.

round trip. A trip by carrier which includes return to the point of departure.

round-trip ticket. A ticket for transportation by carrier to a specific destination and return to point of original departure, sometimes at a reduced rate. 14 Am J2d Car § 845.
See **excursion; excursion rate.**

roundup (round'up). A general gathering together of the cattle on a range which is had by the custom of cattlemen, for the purpose of branding calves and separating or "cutting out" the cattle of the several respective owners. Hebberd v Southwestern Land & Cattle Co. 55 NJ Eq 18, 27, 36 A 122.

roup (roup). A disease of chickens. Hoarseness. An auction sale.
See **articles of roup.**

rout. A criminal offense consisting in the moving forward of an unlawful assembly toward the execution of its unlawful design. 46 Am J1st Riot § 7. A disorderly crowd, especially one fleeing in terror.

route. The course or location of a highway. 25 Am J1st High §§ 9 et seq. The course of a railroad line between its terminals. 44 Am J1st RR § 202. The line or course followed by a vessel proceeding from one port to another. 48 Am J1st Ship §§ 393 et seq. The course followed by a mail carrier or a route salesman. The course of a shipment of goods on the line or lines of a carrier or carriers. 13 Am J2d Car § 323.

See **en route; through route.**

route salesman. A salesman who follows a regular route in making sales to customers. 28 Am J Rev ed Inj § 103.

routing by carrier. Selection by the carrier of the route of transportation of a shipment of goods, it being obligatory upon the carrier to select the route with due regard to the rights and interests of the shipper. 13 Am J2d Car § 323.

routously (rout'us-li). See **riotously.**

roving commission rule. The rule that where an employee's duties require him to circulate in a general area with no fixed place or hours of employment, or to go to and from his home to various outside places of work, and his employer furnishes him with a motor vehicle to use in his work, it can be found that he continues in the service of his employer, for the purposes of the liability of his employer for an injury resulting from his negligence, until he actually reaches home. Anno: 52 ALR2d 365, § 7.

rowboat. A boat designed and constructed to be propelled by oars. Not a vessel within the meaning of a rule of navigation. Fischer v Camden etc. Ferry Co. 124 Pa 154, 16 A 634.

roy (riä). The king.

royal amercement. See **amercement royal.**

royal family. In a larger sense, all those persons who are by any possibility inheritable to the crown. In a narrower sense, only those who are within a certain degree of propinquity to the king.
After that degree is past, they fall into the rank of ordinary subjects, and are seldom considered any further, unless called to the succession upon failure of the nearer lines of consanguinity. See 1 Bl Comm 224.

royal fish. See **fish royal.**

royal fishery. An exclusive right of fishing in a navigable river. Arnold v Mundy, 6 NJL 1.

royal fishes. The grand fishes of the sea, such as whales and sturgeons.
These fishes belonged to the king by his royal prerogative, and no subject could take them without the king's special grant. Arnold v Mundy, 6 NJ L 1.

royal forest. A forest of the king, stocked with beasts of the chase.

royal fowls. Wild swan on the sea and arms of the sea.

royal franchise. A privilege, such as that of fishing in a navigable river, granted by the king. Arnold v Mundy, 6 NJL 1.

royal grant. A grant made by the king.
Such grants were always matters of public record and whether they were of lands, honors, liberties, franchises, or other matters, they were by charter or letters patent and usually directed or addressed by the king to all his subjects at large. See 2 Bl Comm 346.

royal mines. Gold and silver mines owned by the king at common law as within his prerogative, although on private property.
At common law, mines of gold and silver were by the prerogative of the sovereign, the property of the crown, though discovered in the land of private owners. They were termed "royal mines," and belonged to the sovereign wherever they were found. The prerogative is supposed to have originated as a necessary incident of the king's right of coinage in order to supply him with materials; metals in which there was no gold or silver, however, belonged to the proprietor of the soil. 36 Am J1st Min & M § 6.

royal prerogative (prẹ-rog'ạ-tiv). Those rights and capacities which the king enjoys alone, in contradistinction to others, and not those which he enjoys in common with any of his subjects. See 1 Bl Comm 239.
A New Jersey chancellor has defined the term as "that special pre-eminence which a sovereign has over all other persons, and out of the course of the common law, by right of regal dignity." In Great Britain the royal prerogative includes the right of sending and receiving ambassadors, of making treaties, and (theoretically) of making war and concluding peace, of summoning parliament, and of refusing assent to a bill, with many other political, judicial, ecclesiastical, etc., privileges. See Aetna Casualty & Surety Co. v Bramwell (DC Or) 12 F2d 307.

royal river. Any navigable river of England so far as the tide ebbs and flows.
It is said to be a branch of the sea, so far as it flows, and the sea is under the dominion of the king. See Arnold v Mundy, 6 NJL 1.
"Lord Hale says that, as the common highways upon the land are the common land passage, so these kinds of rivers, whether fresh or salt, that bear boats or barges, are highways by water; and as the highways by land are called the 'king's highways,' so these public rivers for public passage are called 'royal streams,' not in reference to the propriety of the river, but to the public use." See New England Trout & Salmon Club v Mather, 68 Vt 338, 35 A 323.

royal stream. See **royal river.**

royalty. The consideration payable by the lessee to the lessor under an oil or gas lease. 24 Am J1st Gas & O § 65. The right to share in production of oil or gas. Anno: 4 ALR2d 497. Compensation for the privilege of drilling and producing gas and oil, consisting of a share of the product or of money representing such share. Alexander v King (CA10 Okla) 46 F2d 235, 74 ALR 174, cert den 283 US 845, 75 L Ed 1455, 51 S Ct 492. A fractional interest in the production of oil or gas created by the owner of the grant, either by reservation when an oil and gas lease is entered into, or by direct grant to a third person. La Laguna Ranch Co. v Dodge, 18 Cal 2d 132, 114 P2d 351, 135 ALR 546. A payment made by the lessee under a mining lease to the lessor, based on the output of the mine. 36 Am J1st Min & M § 48. A payment made for the privilege of using a patented invention. Carbice Corp. v American Patents Development Co. 283 US 27, 75 L Ed 819, 51 S Ct 334. The compensation to which an author is entitled for the use of his work under license. 18 Am J2d Copyr §§ 92 et seq. The status of a king, queen, or princess, even of one of nature's noblemen.
With respect to damages recoverable from an innocent trespasser who extracts coal or other solid mineral from the land, the terms "royalty" and "value" should not be regarded as synonymous but as alternative measures of recovery. Hughett v Caldwell County, 313 Ky 85, 230 SW2d 92. 21 ALR2d 373.

ROYALTY [1127] RULE

Royalty, when used in connection with a license under a patent, means the compensation paid by the licensee to the licensor for the use of the licensor's patented invention. This is substantially Webster's definition except that the latter adds "usually at a certain rate for each article manufactured, used, sold, or the like." The word rate itself does not define or designate the "unit." There have been various units used in license contracts under patents such as "device manufactured," "period of use," or "device sold." Royalty provisions frequently provide for the payment of a fixed amount per device manufactured, sold, sold or used, or for fixed payments per unit of time. Hazeltine Corporation v Zenith Radio Corp. (CA7 Ill) 100 F2d 10.

royalty interest. See **royalty**.

royalty oil. Oil severed and set apart for the payment of the obligation to render royalty. Anno: 4 ALR2d 497.

royalty pool. An arrangement created by an agreement between landowners binding each of them to turn into a common fund or pool any oil found and produced on his land or royalties therefrom, such owners to share in certain proportions in the fund or pool thus accumulated, after payment of expenses of management. Hathaway v Porter Royalty Pool, 296 Mich 90, 295 NW 571, 138 ALR 955, amd 296 Mich 733, 299 NW 451, 138 ALR 967.

royalty tax. A tax upon rents or royalties received.

Roy est l'original de touts franchises (riä′ ay l'o-ri′-zhi-nal de too frän-shĕs′). The king is the origin of all franchises.

Roy n'est lie per ascun statute, si il ne solt expressement nosme (riä n'ay lē per äs-cŭn′ stä-tūt, sē il ne suät ex-pres′môn nŏs′me). The king is not bound by any statute, if he be not expressly named to be so bound. See Broom's Legal Maxims 72.

r.s.v.p. Please reply; an abbreviation of the French "réspondes s'il vous plaît."

rubber check. See **bogus check**.

rubber processing. See **vulcanization**.

rubber stamp. A stamp of rubber used for affixing a signature or memorandum. A facetious term for one who does nothing of importance except at the direction of another.

rubber-stamp signature. A signature affixed to bill, note, 11 Am J2d B & N § 210, or will 57 Am J1st Wills § 248, by rubber stamp.

rubbish. Refuse. Waste materials collected by a municipality. 38 Am J1st Mun Corp § 614. Nonsense.

rubbish dump. See **dump**.

rubric (rö′brik). A chapter or section heading, deriving from the Latin "ruber," meaning red, because of the early practice or custom of setting headings in red.

rudder. The instrumentality on a vessel by which the craft is steered. A comparable device on an aircraft.

rudely. In a rude manner; coarsely; uncivilly; violently. State v Lawrence, 19 Neb 307, 314.

rule. A statement of law appearing in an opinion of the court in support of the decision rendered in the case. An order of court; a specific direction or requirement of a court, made in a particular matter or proceeding, with respect to the performance of some act incidental thereto. 37 Am J1st Motions § 20. That which is prescribed or laid down as a guide to conduct; that which is settled by authority or custom; a regulation; a prescription; a minor law; a uniform course of things. South Florida Railroad Co. v Rhoads, 25 Fla 40, 5 So 633.

rule absolute. The rule or order of court granted upon a rule or order to show cause, where sufficient cause is not shown. 37 Am J1st Motions § 38.

rule absolute for a new trial. An abbreviated form of entry of an order for a new trial.
The order of the court formerly entered would be "judgment vacated, verdict set aside and new trial granted." Fisher v Hestonville, Mantua & Fairmount Passenger Railway Co. 185 Pa 602, 605, 40 A 97.

rule against accumulations (a-genst′ a-kū-mū-lā′-shọns). A rule based on the English statute known as the Thelluson Act or on equivalent laws enacted in other jurisdictions rendering nugatory provisions for the accumulation of the rents and profits of property beyond a certain period provided by the statute. 41 Am J1st Perp § 44. A statutory rule against the adding of interest or income to a fund, pursuant to the provisions of a deed or will, for the purpose of preventing the expenditure thereof, beyond a limited number of years. 41 Am J1st Perp § 48.

rule against perpetuities. The rule which prohibits the creation of future interests or estates which by possibility may not become vested within a life or lives in being at the time of the testator's death or the effective date of the instrument creating the future interest, and twenty-one years thereafter, together with the period of gestation when the inclusion of the latter is necessary to cover cases of posthumous birth. 41 Am J1st Perp § 3.

rule against possibility on a possibility. The rule of the common law that in the grant or devise of property there could not be a possibility on a possibility, and which applied to prevent a limitation for the life of an unborn person with a limitation after his death to his unborn children to take as purchasers. 41 Am J1st Perp § 5.

rule against postponement of enjoyment. A rule of public policy which forbids unreasonable restrictions on the enjoyment of property.
The principle has become established that no restriction on the use and enjoyment of property will be enforced by the courts where the restriction is such that it is inconsistent with the interest or estate which has been granted or devised. 41 Am J1st Perp § 69.

rule against restraint on alienation. The principle that since one of the incidents of property is the right to convey it, the law does not permit a grantor or testator to fetter the ownership of grantee or devisee by imposing a restraint on alienation by him, thereby seeking to maintain control over alienation or use of the property. 41 Am J1st Perp § 66. A rule giving force to the principle that the conveyance of a title in fee simple carries with it as a necessary incident the right of free and unlimited alienation. 41 Am J1st Perp § 79.

rule against suspension of power of alienation. A rule under statute, distinct from the rule against perpetuities, which prohibits the imposing of conditions in rendering property inalienable beyond a period fixed by the statute. 41 Am J1st Perp § 2.

rule day. Return day. The day on which a defendant served by process is required to appear. The day on which an order or rule to show cause to made returnable.

rule in Dumpor's Case. See **Dumpor's Case.**

rule in Shelley's Case. In the classic statement of the rule as made in the case from which it derived its name:—when the ancestor by any gift or conveyance takes an estate of freehold, and in the same gift or conveyance an estate is limited, either mediately or immediately to his heirs in fee or in tail, the word "heirs" is one of limitation, not of purchase. 1 Coke 93b, 104b, 76 Eng Reprint 206, 234. In terms in which it is usually stated:—the principle that when a person takes an estate of freehold, legal or equitable, under a deed, will, or other writing, and in the same instrument there is a limitation by way of remainder, either with or without the interposition of another estate, of an interest of the same legal or equitable quality, to his heirs or heirs of his body, as a class of persons to take in succession from generation to generation, the limitation to the heirs entitles the ancestor to the whole estate. 28 Am J2d Est § 102. The rule that if one makes a limitation to another for life, with a remainder over mediately or immediately to his heirs, or the heirs of his body, the heirs do not take remainders at all, but the word "heirs" is regarded as defining or limiting the estate which the first taker has, and his heirs, if they take at all, take by descent, and not by purchase. Lytle v Hulen, 128 Or 483, 275 P 45, 114 ALR 587.

A grant or devise to a man "during his natural life, and then to his heirs, in a jurisdiction where the rule in Shelley's Case is in force, gives an absolute estate to the grantee or devisee, but in those jurisdictions where the rule in Shelley's Case is not in force, the grantee or devisee takes only a life estate. Doyle v Andis, 127 Iowa 36, 102 NW 177.

rule in Wild's Case. See **first resolution in Wild's Case; second resolution in Wild's Case.**

rulemaking. A judicial power in respect of promulgating rules regulating the practice in cases coming before the court. 20 Am J2d Cts § 82. Legislative power in fact but one of the functions exercised by an administrative agency. 1 Am J2d Admin L §§ 92 et seq.

rule nisi (rōl nī'sī). A rule or order of court granted ex parte on the motion of one party, directing the other party to the action or proceeding to show cause why the rule should not be made absolute, such ex parte rule becoming absolute unless such cause is shown. 37 Am J1st Motions § 38.

rule of capture. See **capture.**

rule of court. A rule governing procedure or practice promulgated by a court. 20 Am J2d Cts § 82. A term used in some jurisdictions for an order of court. 37 Am J1st Motions § 20.

rule of descent. See **canons of descent.**

rule of ejusdem generis (rōl of e-jus'dem je'ne-ris). See **ejusdem generis.**

rule of intendment. A rule of pleading that a verdict will aid a defective statement of a cause, though not the statement of a defective cause. Neufield v United States, 73 App DC 174, 118 F2d 375.

rule of presumption. The rule under which a presumption arises from a certain fact or facts, the same to stand until proof to the contrary is forthcoming, in other words a rule which shifts the burden of proof in the sense of going forward with the evidence. State ex rel. Robertson v Lane, 126 Minn 78, 147 NW 951.

See **presumption.**

rule of property. A rule of law determinative of title.

rule of reasonable restraint. See **reasonable restraint rule.**

rule of shifting descents. See **shifting descents.**

rule of stare decisis. See **stare decisis.**

rule of the prison. See **prison rule; liberty of the rules.**

rule of triennial cohabitation. See **triennial test.**

ruler. A strip of wood or metal, having a straight edge, marked in inches and fractions of inches, and used in drawing a straight line and in measuring length. A king, queen, or other sovereign.

rulers of England. See **regnal years.**

rules. A very technical term for the times when motions are heard by the court, either in vacation, between regular terms of court, or during such terms. Southall's Admr. v Exchange Bank, 53 Va (12 Gratt) 312.

See **rule; rule day.**

Rules Enabling Act. The federal statute of June 19, 1934, empowering the Supreme Court to prescribe rules of practice for the federal courts, subject to the condition that the court shall not abridge, enlarge or modify substantive rights in the guise of regulating procedure. 28 USC §§ 723b, 723c.

rules of civil procedure. The official terminology in many jurisdictions for rules of practice in civil cases.

See **Federal Rules of Civil Procedure; rules of practice.**

rules of criminal procedure. The official terminology in many jurisdictions for rules of practice in criminal cases.

See **Federal Rules of Criminal Procedure; rules of practice.**

rules of descent. See **canons of descent.**

rules of evidence. Principles which express the mode or manner of proving the facts and circumstances upon which a party relies to establish a fact in dispute. Kring v Missouri, 107 US 221, 27 L Ed 506, 2 S Ct 443. Rules provided by statute or by the agency itself in respect of the admissibility of evidence in a hearing before an administrative agency. 2 Am J2d Admin L § 377.

rules of navigation. The rules and regulations prescribing the manner in which vessels shall be controlled in operation generally or under particular circumstances and conditions. 48 Am J1st Ship §§ 244 et seq. Navigation rules for small watercraft. 12 Am J2d Boats § 14.

The rules which govern the steering and sailing of vessels of the United States and whch are designed to indicate exactly what two vessels approaching with risk of collision shall do to avoid each other. They are based largely upon two fundamental principles, viz.: (1) Vessels meeting should generally keep to the right, other things being equal; and (2) the vessel better able to control her movements should give way to the other. The latter rule is all the more clearly applicable where the other vessel is not under control at all, or is in a crippled condition. 48 Am J1st Ship § 250.

Rules of Oleron. See **Laws of Oleron.**

rules of practice. In the broad sense, rules, whether of the common law, under statute, or prescribed and promulgated by the court, which govern the procedure in a case. Adjective law. In common usage, procedural rules promulgated by the courts, sometimes in comprehensive form, at other times as supplementary to a practice act.

See **Federal Rules of Civil Procedure; Federal Rules of Criminal Procedure; Federal Rules of Equity Practice.**

rules of procedure. See **rules of practice.**

rules of the prison. See **prison rule; liberty of the rules.**

rules of the road. The law of the road, as established by statute or long-continued custom or usage, regarding the rights of vehicles and persons meeting or passing in a highway, the purpose being to prevent or minimize collisions and other accidents. Packard v O'Neill, 45 Idaho 427, 262 P 881, 56 ALR 317. Navigation rules for small watercraft. 12 Am J2d Boats § 14.

See **traffic regulations.**

rule to plead. An order of court requiring a party to plead within the time specified in the order.

rule to show cause. Same as **order to show cause.**

ruling. A determination made by the court during the course of a trial, for example, a determination of the admissibility of particular evidence. State v O'Brien, 18 Mont 1, 43 P 1091. In some connections, the final decision in a case.

Ruling Case Law. The predecessor of American Jurisprudence, abbreviated in citation to R. C. L. See **American Jurisprudence.**

rum. A spiritous liquor, distilled from a "wine" made by the fermentation of molasses. 30 Am J Rev ed Intox L § 12.

rumor (rö'mor). Popular report; a current story passing from one person to another without any known authority for the truth of it.

"Report" is a synonym for the word; another is "hearsay," and another, "story." State v Culler, 82 Mo 623.

rump parliament (rump pär'li̇-mȩnt). The English parliament under the Commonwealth, from 1648 to 1660.

run. Verb: To move fast. To operate. Noun: A stream; a creek. Watts v Lindsey's Heirs (US) 7 Wheat 158, 162, 5 L Ed 423, 424.

A vessel is said to be "running" when it is engaged in actual employment or when it is commercially engaged. The word is thus used in contradistinction to the condition of a vessel which is laid up and out of use and is not making trips upon the water. See Canton Ins. Office v Independent Transp. Co. (CA9 Wash) 217 F 213.

run at large. See **running at large.**

runaway. A horse out of control of driver or rider.

runaway plane. An aircraft without a pilot at the controls. Southern Air Transport v Gulf Airways, Inc. 215 La 366, 40 So 2d 787.

runaway shop. An anti-union tactic on the part of an employer in the removal or threat to remove the plant to another location by way of manifesting economic power over his employees. 29 USC § 8 (a) (1).

run into money. To amount to a considerable amount of money.

A phrase used to describe the condition of a note after it had matured where the note was by its terms made payable in money or in specific property, at the option of the maker. Perry v Smith, 22 Vt 301, 306.

runner. A traveling salesman. An agent employed by an attorney at law to solicit legal business and stir up litigation. 7 Am J2d Attys § 40. An employee of bank or broker, having a variety of duties but especially that of delivering funds or securities to customers.

running. See **run.**

running account. An open account. An account without break or interruption by settlement or adjustment. Riffith v Portlock, 233 Iowa 492, 7 NW2d 199. An account of running or current dealings between the parties kept unclosed with the expectation of the addition of further transactions. Connor Livestock Co. v Fisher, 32 Ariz 80, 255 P 996, 57 ALR 196. An organized statement of purchases of goods at intervals or other transactions with the credits for payments at intervals set out. Harper v Barton, 2 La App 317.

When all the items in the account relate to one continuous transaction between the same parties, although the goods were delivered on separate orders, and at different dates, within short intervals of each other, and the dealings of the parties indicate an expectation to continue such business relations, the transactions constitute a continuous running account. William M. Graham Oil & Gas Co. v Oil Well Supply Co. 128 Okla 201, 244 P 591.

running a corner. Acquiring a corner on the market. See **corner.**

running at large. The running or wandering of animals not under restraint of fence or other inclosure. 4 Am J2d Ani § 90.

running board. A part of the structure of older automobiles, most infrequently found on modern cars, being, in effect, a step running between the front and rear fenders.

running covenant. See **covenant running with the land.**

running days. Successive days. A term pertinent in determining liability for demurrage, meaning all days on which the ship could run. 48 Am J1st Ship § 608.

running lines. Determining boundary lines, reference being had to the calls in the grant and to the field notes carried into the grant or the map or plan with reference to which the conveyance is made. 12 Am J2d Bound § 55.

running policy. A policy of insurance, particularly marine insurance, whereby successive insurances are contemplated, such to be defined as to subject, place, and amount by indorsements and additions to the instrument agreed upon by the parties. 29 Am J Rev ed Ins § 306.

running privilege. The right of a railroad company to use the tracks of another railroad company. 44 Am J1st RR §§ 375 et seq.

running switch. Same as **flying switch.**

running time. The period of time required for a train to cover a specific part of its line, or the entire line, according to schedule. 44 Am J1st RR § 367.

run over. To exceed the capacity of a container. To go beyond a limit. To ride or drive over a person or an object.

As to the meaning of the term "run over," as it appears in an accident insurance policy. Anno: 138 ALR 411.

running with the land. Included in and going with the land.
See **covenant running with the land.**

rupture (rup'tŭr). A breaking down or bursting asunder, splitting apart. Travelers' Indem. Co. v P & P Ice & Coal Co. 248 Ky 443, 58 SW2d 640. A splitting apart of a steam boiler, as distinguished from a bursting or explosion. Cleveland Drop Forge Co. v Travelers' Indem. Co. 114 Ohio St 549, 553, 151 NE 671, 672. A break in official or personal relations. Another term for **hernia.**

rural credit acts. Statutes which employ the credit or taxing power of the government to assist owners of agricultural lands by lending money upon the land as security. 3 Am J2d Agri § 25.

Rural Electrification Administration. An agency of the United States Department of Agriculture, performing duties respecting the extension of electrical service to farms and farmers, particularly by the organization of co-operative associations. Anno: 56 ALR2d 413.

rural free delivery. The delivery of mail on routes extending beyond city or village limits, particularly in rural areas.

rural homestead. Land constituting a homestead exempt from execution, located outside the limits of city or village. 26 Am J1st Home § 33.

rural land. Land devoted to the pursuit of agriculture, irrespective of its location with reference to a municipality.

rural way. A road or highway in a pastoral region.

rush. To move swiftly. To push or drive with speed or violence. To make a sudden assault. To assault a person by rushing at him from behind and violently pushing him forward. A dangerous and unlawful sport. Markley v Whitman, 95 Mich 236, 54 NW 763.

rust. A plant disease caused by fungi, especially destructive of wheat. A coating caused by oxidation. A reddish or brownish color.
As used in bills of lading exempting the carrier from damage to the goods by rust, the word is usually held to include rust caused by sea water, as well as rust resulting from atmospheric dampness. Broderick & Bascom Rope Co. v Luckenbach S.S. Co. 139 Wash 444, 247 P 937.

rusticos. See **inter rusticos.**

rusticum judicium (rus'ti-kum jū-di'she-um). Same as **rusticum jus.**

rusticum jus (rus'ti-kum jūs). Rustic or simple justice.
"The application of an equal division of damages (in cases of marine collision) is said to be the 'rusticum jus.' That is to say, it is an application of that sense of fair dealing and of justice imbedded in our nature, the conclusions of common sense, of a mind 'abnormis sapiens' (one of nature's philosophers)." The Victory (CA4 Va) 68 F 395, 400.

rut. An elongated and comparatively narrow depression in the surface of a highway. 25 Am J1st High § 488. A fixed, although not necessarily the best, routine or course of practice. Sexual excitement of the male deer, goat, or sheep at regular periods.

ruta (rö'tä). (Civil law.) Things which have been dug out of the soil, such as rock, coal and the like.

rye. A grain used in the making of flour and whisky. A short term for rye whisky.

Rylands v Fletcher. An English Case which has given its name to the principle that a person who, for his own purposes, brings on his land and collects and keeps there anything likely to do mischief if it escapes, must keep it on his own premises at his peril, and is prima facie liable for all the damage which is the natural consequence of its escape. (Eng) LR 3 HL 330.

S

s. An abbreviation for **scilicet,** although the more common abbreviation is "ss."

S ½ Abbreviation of south one half, used particularly in describing land according to the government survey, applying to a section or part of a section.

Sabbath (sab'ạth). Sunday,—the one day of the week commonly set apart and observed in Christian countries as a day of public worship, relaxation, and refreshment. State v Williams, 26 NC (4 Ired L) 400, 402.

The word is not strictly synonymous with the word "Sunday;" Sabbath signifies Saturday, the seventh day of the week, the Jewish Sabbath; Sunday signifies the first day of the week, commonly called the Lord's Day. But by common usage, the terms are used indiscriminately to denote the Christian Sabbath, to wit, Sunday. See State v Drake, 64 NC 589, 591.

See **Sunday law.**

Sabbath breaking. Working, engaging in business, or the pursuit of other activity forbidden on the Sabbath. State v Popp, 45 Md 432, 437.

See **Sunday law.**

sabbatical leave (sạ-bat'i-kạl lēv). A year or more absence permitted a member of a college or university faculty for study, writing, or travel, usually with continuing pay or part pay. State ex rel. West Virginia Board of Education v Sims, 139 W Va 802, 81 SE2d 665.

Sabbatum (sab-ạ'tum). The Sabbath; Sunday.

sabotage (sa-bō'taj). Wilful and malicious physical damage or injury to physical property. Burns v United States, 274 US 328, 71 L Ed 1077, 47 S Ct 650; State v Moilen, 140 Minn 112, 167 NW 345, 1 ALR 331. The malicious damage or injury to the property of an employer by an employee. State v Moilen, 140 Minn 112, 167 NW 345, 1 ALR 331, 332. Wilful, malicious, and intentional acts of force and violence or unlawful methods of terrorism which retard or slow up work by employees or others, or of any deliberate attempt to reduce profits of an employer as a means of accomplishing a change in industrial ownership or control or to effect any political end. 47 Am J1st Sedit etc § 3.

sac (sak). The jurisdiction of an ancient court-baron or manor court; the privilege of holding such a court within a manor.

sacaburth (sak'ạ-bėrth). A person who entered upon a fresh pursuit of his goods after they had been stolen.

saccabor. Same as **sacaburth.**

saccularii (sa-ku-lā'ri-ī). (Roman law.) Cutpurses. Both the Romans and the Athenians punished such offenders more severely than common thieves. By analogy it is observed that pickpockets in England were denied benefit of clergy. See 4 Bl Comm 242.

sack. A bag. Plunder. A fund in hand to be used for purposes of corruption.

"This meaning was doubtless first given to the word by vile and corrupt persons, engaged in distributing and receiving such funds, and, when first used in that sense, might well have been regarded as a slang expression, of the meaning of which courts would not then have taken judicial notice, but it is now so frequently used to convey this particular meaning, that it can hardly be considered, when employed for that purpose, as simply the language of slang and understood only by the vulgar." See Edwards v San Jose Printing & Pub. Soc. 99 Cal 431, 436, 34 P 128.

sacquier (sä-kē-ay'). An arrameur or officer of a port who directed the proper loading and stowage of cargoes aboard ships.

sacra (sā'krạ). The right of a Roman to participate in sacred celebrations.

sacramentales (sa-kra-men-tā'lēz). Compurgators or persons who in a trial by wager of law swore to the innocence of the defendant.

sacramentum (sa-kra-men'tum). (Roman law.) An oath.

sacramentum decisionis (sa-kra-men'tum de-si-zhe-ō'nis). (Civil law.) The oath of decision; the voluntary and decisive oath whereby the suit could be decided, if the other party, not being able to prove his charge, offered to refer the decision to the oath of his adversary.

If the latter refused, the charge was taken as confessed by him. See 3 Bl Comm 342.

sacramentum fidelitatis (sa-kra-men'tum fī-de-li-tā'tis). The oath of fealty.

Sacramentum habet in se tres comites, veritatem, justitiam et judicium; veritus habenda est in jurato, justitia et judicium in judice (sa-kra-men'-tum hā'bet in sē trēz ko'mi-tēz, ve-ri-tā'tēm, jūs-ti'she-am et jū-di'she-um; ve'ri-tās hā-ben'da est in jū-rā'tō, jus-ti'she-a et jū-di'she-um in jū'di-se). An oath has within itself three concomitants, truth, justice, and judgment; truth should be observed in the person making oath and justice and judgment in the judge.

Sacramentum si fatuum fuerit, licet falsum, tamen non committit perjurium (sa-kra-men'tum sī fa'tu-um fu'e-rit, lī'set fal'sum, ta'men non kom-mit'tit per-ju'ri-um). A foolish oath, although it be false, does not convict one of perjury.

sacrifice. Giving up something for the sake of saving something else. The destruction of property to save other property from impending peril. The Roanoke (DC Wis) 46 F 297, 298.

See **voluntary sacrifice.**

sacrilege (sak'ri-lej). The larceny of sacred things; as, from a church. Desecration. Mistreatment of things held sacred by others.

Sacrilegii instar est rescripto principis obviari (sa-kri-le'ji-ī in'star est re-skrip'tō prin'si-pis ob-vi-ā'rī). It is sacrilege to oppose the ruler's rescript. 1 Bl Comm 74.

sacrilegium (sa-kri-le'ji-um). (Civil law.) Same as **sacrilege.**

sacrilegus (sa-kri'le-gus). A sacrilegious person; a thief who stole sacred things.

Sacrilegus omnium praedonum cupiditatem et scelera superat (sa-kri'le-gus on'mi-um prē-dō'num ku-pi-di-ta'tem et se'le-ra su'pe-rat). A sacrilegious person exceeds the cupidity and wickedness of all robbers.

sacristan (sak'ristạn). A sexton or caretaker of a church.

sadism (säd'izm). The obtaining of satisfaction, even sexual pleasure, from hurting another. A species of insanity or mental disease in which the sexual instinct of the patient is abnormal or perverted. State v Petty, 32 Nev 384, 391, 108 P 934.

saeculare. See **forum saeculare.**

Saepe constitutum est, res inter alios judicatas aliis non praejudicare (sē'pe kon-sti-tū'tum est, rēz in'ter a'li-os ju-di-kā'tas a'li-is non prē-jū-di-kā're). It has often been decided that things adjudged as between others (than the parties before the court) do not prejudice.

Saepenumero ubi proprietas verborum attenditur, sensus veritatis amittitur (sē-pe-nu'me-rō u'bi propri'ē-tās ver-bō'rum at-ten'di-ter, sen'sus ve-ri-tā'tis ā-mit'ti-ter). When the propriety of the language is given attention, the true meaning is very often lost.

Saepe viatorem nova non vetus orbita fallit (sē'pe vi-ā'tō'rem no'va non ve'tus or'bi-ta fal'lit). The new or fresh wheel mark or road often deceives the traveler, not the old one.

saepius requisitus (sē'pi-us re-qui'zi-tus). Often requested or demanded.

saevitia (sē-vi'she-a). Cruelty constituting a cause for a decree of separation in an ecclesiastical court. Ring v Ring, 118 Ga 183, 44 SE 861.

safe. Noun: A repository for valuables, often proof against burglary as well as fire. Adjective: Not in danger; out of harm's way.
See **adequately safe; reasonably safe.**

safe bill. Such a bill of exchange as would be honored and paid by the drawee on using proper diligence. Warder v Whitall, 1 NJL 84.

safe-conduct. Protection against harm while traveling. Guided in safety. Taken through a locality or region with safety to the person.
See **letters of safe-conduct.**

safe-deposit box. A metal box, coming in various convenient sizes, with lock, usually a double lock, for the keeping of valuable papers in one's home or office or, as is often the case, in the vault of a bank or safe-deposit company.

safe-deposit business. Maintaining a fire and burglar proof vault wherein the safe-deposit boxes of customers may be deposited, subject to access at convenient times, under leases calling for the payment of rent, normally an annual rent, such business being engaged in by banks and safe-deposit companies.

safe-deposit company. Any person, bank, or corporation offering, for remuneration, to furnish on its premises, for the safekeeping of the personal property of others, safe-deposit boxes, access to contents of which involve the use of a key obtained by the individual depositor.

safeguard. A safety device, especially an appliance to minimize or obviate danger from electrical appliances and equipment. 26 Am J2d Electr § 46.

safe investment rule. A rule applied in the computation of the present worth of a decedent's expected future earnings.
Under the so-called "safe investment rule," the jury, in determining the present value of the decedent's expected future earnings, should use that rate of interest which, in the jury's considered judgment, is reasonable, just, and right under the circumstances, taking into consideration the evidence presented, the jury's knowledge of the prevailing interest rates within the limits prescribed by law in the area, and what rate of interest could fairly be expected from safe investments as made by a person of ordinary prudence, but without particular financial experience or skill. 22 Am J2d Dth § 125.
See **prudent investment theory.**

safekeeping. A deposit of money or other personal property whereunder a duty rests upon the person who receives the money or other property to keep it and return it intact upon demand. In effect, a special deposit. Wright v Payne, 62 Ala 340.

safe landing. The responsibility of a carrier in reference to the act of a passenger in alighting from the carrier's conveyance. Harries v Atlantic Greyhound Corp. 243 NC 346, 90 SE2d 710, 58 ALR2d 939.

safe-place statutes or ordinances. Statutes or municipal ordinances enacted to provide for the safety of buildings and premises devoted to public amusements or entertainments by imposing strict duties of maintenance and repair upon owners and proprietors. Anno: 126 ALR 1251; 4 Am J2d Amuse § 58.

safe place to work. See **safe working place.**

safe-pledge (sāf'plej). A surety for a person's appearance in court.

safe port of discharge. A familiar condition in charter parties. A port which a vessel can enter safely with her cargo or at least a port having an anchorage where the vessel can lie and discharge her cargo afloat. 48 Am J1st Ship § 324.

safe return. See **stipulation for safe return.**

safety appliance. A thing constituting a guard against danger or calculated to reduce the peril in a dangerous instrumentality. 38 Am J1st Negl § 90.

Safety Appliance Acts. Federal statutes designed to safeguard and protect railroad employees from injury or death from the hazards of their employment by requiring the railroads to equip their locomotives and cars with various safety devices, and imposing liability for death or injury predicated on failure to observe the requirements of such statute. 35 Am J1st M & S § 228. Statute regulating railroads in respect of the safety of their appliances and equipment for the protection of persons and property transported. 44 Am J1st RR § 274.

safety device. A thing constituting a guard against danger or calculated to reduce the peril in a dangerous instrumentality. 38 Am J1st Negl § 90.
See **Safety Appliance Acts.**

safety of way. The condition of street or highway considered in reference to use without danger to person or property from defects, obstructions, nuisances, and other sources of peril. 25 Am J1st High §§ 342 et seq.

safety statutes. Statutes intended to protect employees against death or injury in the course of employment by requiring the observance of precautions on the part of employers in reference to the condition of the working place and the instrumentalities of the work. Statutes meant to protect all types of employees, not being limited to those engaged in hazardous employment. Hillman v Northern Wasco County Peoples' Utility Dist. 213 Or 264, 323 P2d 664.
See **Safety Appliance Acts.**

safety zone. A portion of street or highway set apart for the use of pedestrians, vehicular traffic being excluded, one of the most common of which is a zone established for pedestrians awaiting a bus or other public conveyance. 25 Am J1st High § 265. A zone for the safety and convenience of persons entering and leaving public conveyances, vehicular traffic being excluded. 7 Am J2d Auto § 197.

safe working place. The measure of the employer's duty in reference to the condition of the working place. A standard of care required of an employer in the terms of care exercised by prudent employers in similar circumstances, the degree depending upon the dangers attending the particular employment. 35 Am J1st M & S § 183.

The place in which an employee is directed to work is "safe," within the meaning of the law, when all the safeguards and precautions which ordinary experience, prudence, and foresight would suggest have been taken to prevent injury to the employee while he is himself exercising reasonable care in the service which he undertakes to perform. Peterson v Chicago, Rock Island & Pacific R. Co. 149 Iowa 496, 128 NW 932.

sages de la ley (sä′jez de lä lä). Persons learned in the law.

sag hole. A depression of small area in which surface waters collect. 56 Am J1st Wat § 72.

sagging wire. A wire strung from pole to pole, particularly a wire carrying an electric current, which has dropped so far from level as to constitute a danger to pedestrians or drivers of vehicles.

sagibaro. A shrewd person; a judge.

said (sed). Aforesaid; before mentioned; above mentioned.

sail. Verb: To put to sea. To start a voyage. To leave port with the intent to proceed on a voyage. Noun: A piece of canvas spread out from the mast of a vessel or boat to catch the wind, thereby applying the force of the wind to the moving of the craft through the water.
See **under sail.**

sailboat. Small watercraft propelled by the power of the wind upon a sail. Not a vessel within the meaning of a regulation governing places of anchorage. 12 Am J2d Boats § 1.

sailing instructions. Directions in writing carried by each master of a vessel sailing with others in a fleet or convoy, whereby the course, the meaning of signals, and havens in case of storm or distress, etc. are communicated to all persons in command of vessels.

sailing rules. Navigation rules for small watercraft. 12 Am J2d Boats § 14.
See **rules of navigation.**

sailor. A seaman. One of the crew of a vessel. An enlisted man in the Navy, an ordinary seaman in the merchant service, a commissioned officer of the Navy or a ship's officer. 57 Am J1st Wills § 662 (For the purposes of a statute relaxing the requirements of a statute in reference to the formalities of a will.)

sailor-mongers (sā′lor-mon″gėrs). Persons employing or operating with other lawless persons who board vessels upon entering a port, and by the help of intoxicants and the use of other means, often savoring of violence, get the crews ashore and sell them to outgoing vessels at an enormous price. United States v Sullivan (CC Or) 43 F 602, 604.

sailor's will. See **seaman's will.**

Saint Vitus' Dance. An affliction of the nervous system. Braun v Craven, 175 Ill 401, 51 NE 657.

sairement (sār′ment). An oath.

saisina (sā′zi-na). Same as **seizin.**

salable. See **merchantable.**

salable value. See **market value.**

Saladine tenth. See **tenths.**

salarium (sal-ạ′ri-um). (Civil law.) Salary; pay; wages; an allowance for provisions.

salary. Compensation for personal service. Papeay v Nolan, 157 Tenn 222, 7 SW2d 815, 60 ALR 408; compensation for services in a position or office. 35 Am J1st M & S § 63. Compensation for personal services, as distinguished from profits realized in commercial dealings, returns from capital, or returns from the labor of others. 31 Am J2d Exemp § 39. Compensation paid periodically for services. State ex rel. Murray v Riley (Sup) 45 Del 192, 70 A2d 712, 14 ALR2d 630. A fixed annual or periodical payment for services, depending upon the time, and not upon the amount, of services rendered. 43 Am J1st Pub Of § 357.

In many situations, the words "wages" and "salary" are synonymous. In other instances, a distinction is recognized, "salary" connoting compensation for services more important than those for which "wages" are paid and also compensation on a basis more fixed and permanent than that of wages. 35 Am J1st M & S § 63.

salary-loan broker. One who engages in the business of making small loans on the security of wage assignments. 40 Am J1st Pawnb § 9.

sale. A transfer of the property in a chattel for a consideration. Edward v Ioor, 205 Mich 617, 172 NW 620, 15 ALR 256. A transfer of personal property at a fixed money price payable in cash or in goods. Hartwig v Rushing, 93 Or 6, 182 P 177. A transfer of the title to personal property for money. 46 Am J1st Sales § 2. For tax purposes, a bona fide transfer of property for an amount of money or a money equivalent which is fixed or determinable. Gregory v Helvering, 293 US 465, 79 L Ed 596, 56 S Ct 266, 97 ALR 1355. A transfer of the general or absolute, as distinguished from a special, property in a thing, for a price in money. Union Secur. v Merchants' Trust & Sav. Co. 205 Ind 127, 185 NE 150, 95 ALR 1189. But sometimes inclusive, as in the case of a conditional "sale," of a transaction which does not effect an absolute transfer of title. Carter v Slavick Jewelry Co. (CA9 Cal) 26 F2d 571, 58 ALR 1043. A term inclusive of the sale of securities. People v Gillett, 243 Ill App 41. A term also applied very frequently to the transaction under a land contract as well as to a conveyance by deed for a consideration. Fox v Adrian Realty Co. 327 Mich 89, 41 NW2d 486, 15 ALR2d 1037.
See **bulk sale; conditional sale; futures.**

sale against the box. A short sale of stock by one who owns shares of the same stock.
If the stock declines, the seller can cover at a profit; if it increases in value, he can avoid loss by delivering the shares which he owns. Du Pont v Commissioner (CA3) 110 F2d 641, cert den 311 US 657, 85 L Ed 421, 61 S Ct 11.
See **short sale.**

sale and exchange. See **power of sale and exchange.**

sale as is. A sale without express or implied warranty. 46 Am J1st Sales § 319. A sales term in the used car business. 8 Am J2d Auto § 654.

Where an article is sold "as is," the use of the expression implies that the buyer takes a chance in making the purchase. It implies that he is taking delivery of a thing in some way defective and upon the express condition that he trust to his own examination of it. In effect, the seller says "You look the article over, and, if you buy it, you do so at your risk." It imports a purchase and acceptance without guaranties. Ferguson v Koch, 204 Cal App 342, 261 P 489, 491.

sale at auction. See **auction.**

sale at retail. A sale to a customer for his own use, or the use of his family, rather than for resale by him in the course of business. Anno: 139 ALR 376. A transfer of title to tangible personal property, made in the ordinary course of the transferer's business, for consumption or use by the purchaser or for any other purpose except that of resale by him in the ordinary course of business. Boyer-Cambell Co. v Fry, 271 Mich 282, 260 NW 165, 98 ALR 827.

A legislative definition of the phrase appearing in a sales tax statute will prevail over definitions which may be found in the dictionary, and render immaterial the question whether a transaction on which a tax is levied meets the technical requisites of a sale at common law or the meaning of the same phrase as used in other enactments. Anno: 139 ALR 373, 374.

sale at wholesale. See **wholesale.**

sale by agent. A term of art; an actual sale made and completed on behalf of a principal; producing for the principal a purchaser able, ready, and willing to buy on the terms of the principal. Walker v Russell, 240 Mass 336, 134 NE 388.

sale by executor or administrator. A sale by a personal representative of assets of the decedent's estate. 31 Am J2d Ex & Ad §§ 341 et seq.

sale by inch of candle. See **sale by the candle.**

sale by sample. A sale of goods under an executory contract in which the goods are unidentified other than by express or implied representation that they correspond to an exhibited sample. Anno: 12 ALR2d 528; 46 Am J1st Sales § 214.

See **warranty in sale by sample.**

sale by the acre. The sale of a specific area of land. 55 Am J1st V & P § 127.

A contract of sale by the acre is one wherein a specified quantity is material. Under such a contract the purchaser does not take the risk of any deficiency and the vendor does not take the risk of any excess. Anno: 153 ALR 7 et seq.

sale by the candle. Also called "sale by inch of candle,"—a form of auction sale consisting of offering the property for sale for such a length of time as would suffice for the burning of an inch of candle. Anderson v Wisconsin G. R. Co. 107 Minn 296, 120 NW 39.

sale by the tract. A sale of land designated as a particular tract, without particular reference to the number of acres contained therein. 55 Am J1st V & P § 127.

A sale by the tract or in gross is one wherein the boundaries are specified, but quantity is not specified, or if specified, the existence of the exact quantity specified is not material; each party takes the risk of the actual quantity varying to some extent from what he expects it to be. Newman v Kay, 57 W Va 98, 49 SE 926.

sale en masse (sāl en mas'). Sale of several things in one lot for one sum. A judicial sale of real estate where the property is sold without division and sale by parcels. 30A Am J Rev ed Jud S § 85. An execution sale of several distinct parcels of real estate, or several articles of personal property, together for a single gross sum. Anniston Pipeworks v Williams, 106 Ala 324, 18 So 111.

sale f.o.b. See **free on board.**

sale f.o.b. cars. See **free on board cars.**

sale for cash. See **cash sale.**

sale for debt. An execution sale. A sale by an administrator or executor to pay a debt or debts of the decedent. Bashore v Whisler (Pa) 3 Watts 490, 494.

sale for taxes. A sale of property to enforce the payment of taxes assessed thereon. 51 Am J1st Tax § 1022. A sale of a delinquent taxpayer's property after seizure in the collection of federal taxes, interest, and penalties. Internal Revenue Code §§ 6321, 6331.

sale in bulk. See **bulk sale.**

sale in gross. See **sale by the tract; sale en masse.**

sale in inverse order of alienation. The doctrine of inverse order of alienation. 35 Am J1st Marsh A § 32.

See **inverse order of alienation.**

sale in ordinary course of business. See **in the ordinary course of business.**

sale in parcels. An execution sale of personal property consisting of various articles in which each article is offered and sold separately. 30 Am J2d Exec § 343. An execution or judicial sale of real property consisting of separate tracts, or susceptible of division into separate tracts, in which the tracts are offered and sold separately. 30 Am J2d Exec § 344; 30A Am J Rev ed Jud S § 85.

sale in partition. See **partition sale.**

sale note. A note given by the purchaser at an auction sale to cover the price of his purchase.

See **bought and sold notes.**

sale of bond at par. See **par.**

sale of goods to arrive. See **sale on arrival.**

sale of intoxicant. See **sale of liquor.**

sale of land. An actual transfer of title to the land from grantor to grantee by an appropriate instrument of conveyance executed for a consideration in money or the equivalent of money. Keogh v Peck, 316 Ill 318, 147 NE 266, 38 ALR 1151. An effective transfer of the equitable title to real estate from vendor to vendee under a contract of sale. 55 Am J1st V & P § 356.

See **land contract.**

sale of liquor. The transfer of title to intoxicating liquor from one person to another by agreement and for a consideration, or, according to some authority a transfer by what is known as barter or exchange, even a transfer by way of a loan. 30 Am J Rev ed Intox L § 210.

The weight of authority is that where several persons contribute to a fund and with it one of their number purchases liquor, which is divided among them in proportion to their several contributions, it is not a sale by the one to the others, but merely the division of the fruits of a joint and lawful enterprise. 30 Am J Rev ed Intox L § 218.

sale of real estate. See **sale of land.**

sale of security. Any agreement whereby a person transfers, or agrees to transfer, either the ownership of or an interest in a security. A broad term, as used in Securities Acts, inclusive of an exchange of securities, a subscription for corporate stock, an extension of the maturity of investment certificates, and a contract by a corporation to dispose of shares rendered available upon an increase in the number of shares by proper action taken. 47 Am J1st Secur A § 19.

sale on approval. A sale of personal property, sometimes called a sale on trial, which is subject to a condition precedent, namely the approval of the buyer, the latter having the right to reject the property as not suitable to his needs upon timely notice given to the seller following a trial period. Smith v Clews, 114 NY 190, 21 NE 160. A bailment with an option to buy. Osborne v Francis, 38 W Va 312, 18 SE 591.

sale on arrival. A sale of goods to be shipped to the buyer from a distance which is conditional upon the arrival of the goods at the point where the buyer is to receive them.

A sale of goods "to arrive" or "on arrival," per or ex a certain ship, has been construed to be a sale subject to a double condition precedent, namely, that the ship arrives in port and that when she arrives, the goods are on board, and if either of these conditions fails, the contract becomes nugatory. 46 Am J1st Sales § 201.

sale on condition. An executory contract of sale, otherwise mutual and binding, the duty to perform which is subject to the happening of an event, upon which, if it does happen, the duty to perform becomes binding on both parties. 46 Am J1st Sales § 38.

See **conditional sale; sale on arrival.**

sale on contingency. Same as **sale on condition.**

sale on execution. See **execution sale.**

sale on option. See **option; sale on approval.**

sale on trial. See **sale on approval.**

sale or exchange. A transfer of property from one man to another in consideration of some price or recompense in value. 2 Bl Comm 446.

A mortgagor's conveyance of the realty to the mortgagee in consideration of a cash payment and cancellation of the mortgage and bond constitutes a sale within the terms of the mortgagor's contract with a broker giving the latter an exclusive right to sell and a right to compensation upon a "sale or exchange" of the property before a specified date. Whiteman v Fidei, 176 Pa Super 142, 106 A2d 644, 46 ALR2d 1113.

sale or exchange of capital asset. A method of realizing gain or loss for tax purposes, involving a complete, bona fide, and permanent transfer of an ownership interest, in other words, a transfer of economic reality. Gregory v Helvering, 293 US 465, 79 L Ed 596, 55 S Ct 266, 97 ALR 1355.

sale or return. A sale defeasible upon condition subsequent, title to the goods passing to the purchaser, subject to being divested out of him and revested in the seller by a return of the goods according to the terms of the contract. Anno: 52 ALR 596; 46 Am J1st Sales § 480.

sale per aversionem (sāl per a-ver-sheō′nem). As defined by the Civil Code of Louisiana,—a sale of land "from one fixed boundary to another fixed boundary, when the object is designated by the adjoining tenements."

A sale by measurement is not such a sale. Minor v Daspit, 128 La 33, 38, 54 S 413. To constitute such a sale, there must be certain limits, or a distinct object described, as a field enclosed, or an island, because it is presumed that the parties have their attention fixed rather on the boundaries than the enumeration of the quantity. State v Buck, 46 La Ann 656, 670, 15 So 531.

Sales Act. A comprehensive statute covering sales of personal property. One of the Uniform Laws. 46 Am J1st Sales § 3. A uniform act specifically repealed by the Commercial Code. 15 Am J2d Com C § 6.

sales agent. A salesman. A soliciting agent of an insurance company.

salesbook. The record of sales made at an auction. 7 Am J2d Auct § 41. A day book in a retail business, kept under a system of bookkeeping employed very little in modern times.

sales contract. See **contract to sell; executed contract of sale; executory contract of sale; land contract.**

salesclerk. A salesman in a department store.

sales guaranteed. An expression used by merchants to mean that if the goods purchased by the buyer are not sold, or if they prove to be hard to sell, the buyer may return them to the seller and take credit for their value. Newell v Nicholson, 17 Mont 389, 43 P 180.

salesman. One engaged in making sales, usually for another but sometimes in his own business. One trained in the work or art of salesmanship and having the ability to sell. A person or company employed, appointed, or authorized by dealer to sell, offer for sale or delivery, or solicit subscriptions to or orders for, or dispose of inquiries about, or deal in any manner in, securities within the state, whether by direct act or through subagents. Commonwealth v Boyle, 108 Pa Super 598, 165 A 521. A laborer for the purposes of a statutory exemption from execution. Hamberger v Marcus, 157 Pa 133, 27 A 681.

See **broker; traveling salesman.**

sales manager. The head of the sales department of a business. A managing agent of a foreign corporation within the meaning of a statute concerning the service of process upon foreign corporations. 36 Am J2d For Corp § 560. A laborer for the purposes of an exemption from execution. Shriver v Carlin & F. Co. 155 Md 51, 141 A 434, 58 ALR 767.

Sales of Reversions Act (of rẹ̄-vẽr′shọns akt). An English statute passed in 1867, providing in effect that no purchase, made bona fide and without fraud or unfair dealing, of any reversionary interest in real or personal estate, should be set aside merely on the ground of undervalue. McAdams v Bailey, 169 Ind 518, 82 NE 1057.

sales tax. A tax upon a sale or the receipts of a sale. 47 Am J1st Sales T § 1. A tax levied on, with respect to, or measured by, sales of tangible personal property. Polar Ice Cream & Creamery Co. v Andrews, 375 US 361, 11 L Ed 2d 389, 84 S Ct 378. A tax imposed on the sale of certain articles by the Internal Revenue Code. Internal Revenue Code §§ 4001, 4011, 4021, 4031, 4041. Sometimes a tax

SALE [1136] SALVAGE

upon the sale of a luxury, such as jewelry, liquor, and so forth, while in other instances a tax upon the sale of commodities, even necessities. A tax variously construed, under the terms of the particular statute establishing it, as imposed upon the retailer, the consumer, the sale or transaction itself, or the business of selling goods. 47 Am J1st Sales T § 2. An excise rather than a property tax. 47 Am J1st Sales T § 2.

sale to arrive. Same as **sale on arrival.**

sale under power. A method of foreclosing a mortgage on real estate without resort to the court. 37 Am J1st Mtg § 647. A method of enforcing a chattel mortgage without the necessity of resort to judicial proceedings. 15 Am J2d Chat Mtg §§ 127 et seq. Broadly, any sale under a power of sale.
See **power of sale.**

sale with option. See **option; sale on approval.**

sale with strings. A sale with a right of repurchase or of obtaining a lease back.

Salic Law (sal′ik lâ). The earliest barbarian code, in use by a Teutonic tribe in the fifth century. The law of the Franks.

saline springs. Salt springs.

Salique law (sal′ik or sa-lēk′lâ). Same as **Salic law.**

saliva test. A test for intoxication, sometimes applied to the driver of an automobile, the purpose being to determine by chemical analysis the alcoholic content of his blood. 7 Am J2d Auto § 259.

salon (så-lôn). A large room for the reception of guests. In modern usage, a place for the reception of customers, especially in establishments for the sale of wearing apparel for women. A beauty parlor. A place for the exhibition and sale of works of art.

saloon (sạ-lön′). A room or place where intoxicating liquors are sold and drunk, commonly without meals. 30 Am J Rev ed Intox L § 20.
See **barroom.**

saloonkeeper. The proprietor of a saloon.

saloon type body (sạ-lön′ tīp bod′i). The usual sedan or closed body of an automobile. Smith v Kliesrath, 28 Cust & Pat App 1293, 120 F2d 1015.

salting samples. The act of the vendor of mining property in mixing gold or other minerals in with samples of ore taken from the property, for exhibition to a prospective purchaser. Loaiza v Superior Court, 85 Cal 11, 24 P 707.

salt meadows. Meadows over which the ordinary tides do not flow, but which are overflowed by unusually high tides. Church v Meeker, 34 Conn 421, 423.

salt silver. An ancient tax or fee paid by tenants to the lord of the manor for the privilege of receiving salt from his larder.

salt springs. Springs of water heavy in content of salt.
See **salt well.**

salt well. A well characterized by the salty content of the water taken therefrom. Williamson v Jones, 43 W Va 562, 27 SE 411. A well from which salt brine is procured and used for the purpose of making salt. Clifton v Montague, 40 W Va 207, 21 SE 858.

salus (sa′lus). Health; safety; welfare.

Salus populi est suprema lex (sa′lus po′pu-lī est su-prē′ma lex). The welfare of the people is the highest law.

Salus populi suprema lex est (sa′lus po′pu-lī su-prē′ma lex est). The welfare of the people is the highest law; a maxim constituting the foundation of all civil government and an age-old ruling principle of jurisprudence. Ruona v Billings, 136 Mont 554, 323 P2d 29.
On this maxim rests the principle that one may not so use his property as unreasonably to injure others. Cook County v Chicago, 311 Ill 234, 142 NE 512, 31 ALR 442, 445.

Salus populi suprema lex esto (sa′lus po′pu-lī su-prē′ma lex es′tō). Let the welfare of the people be the highest law.

Salus reipublicae suprema lex (sa′lus re-ī-pub′li-sē su-prē′ma lex). The welfare of the state is the highest law.
The idea that in effect the morality of corporations is opportunism pure and simple was anciently embodied in the maxim, and its doctrine should be very sparingly resorted to by a state which has a written constitution or by a business corporation created by a written charter. Cook v American Tubing & Webbing Co. 28 RI 41, 65 A 641.

Salus ubi multa consilia (sa′lus u′bi mul′ta kon-si′li-a). There is safety in many counsels.

Salus ubi multa consiliarii (sa′lus u′bi mul′ta kon-si-li-ā′ri-ī). There is safety in many counselors.

salutem (sạ-lū′tĕm). Greeting.

salute. An act of greeting. A gesture of respect.

salute to flag. See **flag salute.**

salvage. A reward for services successfully rendered in saving property from maritime danger by one under no obligation or duty to render the services. Three States Lumber Co. v Blanks (CA6 Tenn) 133 F 479. The compensation allowed to persons by whose voluntary assistance a ship at sea, or her cargo, or both, have been saved in whole or in part from impending sea peril, or in recovering such property from actual peril or loss, as in cases of shipwreck, derelict or recapture. 47 Am J1st Salv § 2. Property of some value obtained from the remains of properties subjected to catastrophe, such as fire or flood. Springfield Fire & Marine Ins. Co. v Hays, 57 Okla 266, 156 P 673. A comparatively small amount recovered from an investment which has gone dead. Anno: 103 ALR 1286, s. 116 ALR 1356, 1357.

salvage corps. An organization, normally maintained by private enterprise, the purpose of which is to have members in attendance at a fire for the particular purpose of saving property and preserving it from the elements until the owner or owners can assume care of it.

salvage lien. The lien of the salvors upon ship or cargo saved from a peril of the sea, such securing the payment of salvage to them. 47 Am J1st Salv § 29. A maritime lien of the highest rank.

salvage loss. A marine insurance term signifying a total loss of the property insured diminished by salvage, which takes place in relation to goods when there is either an absolute or a constructive total loss of the subject insured but some remains of the property have been recovered by the insured. Devitt v Providence Washington Ins. Co. 61 App Div 390, 401, 70 NYS 654.

SALVAGE [1137] SANCTION

salvage measured by wages. A reward in nature of salvage made to members of the crew of the vessel saved. 47 Am J1st Salv § 20.

salvage services. Services entitling to salvage; useful services of any kind rendered to vessel or cargo exposed to imminent peril from dangers of the sea. 47 Am J1st Salv § 9.

salva guardia. See **de salva guardia.**

salvian interdict (sal'vi-an in-ter'dikt). (Roman law.) A foreclosure of a pledge of the goods of a tenant given by him to secure the payment of his rent.

Salvation Army. An international organization engaged in religious worship of the Christian faith and maintaining centers for social rehabilitation, engaged particularly in offering shelters for transients who are destitute or of very limited means, the care of unmarried mothers, treatment for alcoholism, etc. Anno: 17 ALR 1054, s. 168 ALR 1259.

Salvation Army meeting. A religious meeting when the purpose is religious worship. 24 Am J2d Disturb M § 2.

salvo (sal'vō). Saving; excepting.

salvo conducto. See **de salvo conducto.**

salvo jure cujuslibet (sal'vo jū're kū-jus'li-bet). Saving the rights of each one; that is, without prejudice.

salvo me et haeredibus meis (sal'vo mē et hē-rē'di-bus me'is). Excepting me and my heirs.

salvo pudore (sal'vō pu-dō're). Decency being observed. See 4 Bl Comm 213.

salvor (sal'vor). One who renders or performs salvage service. 47 Am J1st Salv § 2.
See **cosalvor; salvage.**

salvor's lien (sal'vors lē'en). Same as **salvage lien.**

salvus plegius (sal'vus plē'ji-us). A safe-pledge.

same. Adjective: Alike in all respects. Identical. Pronoun: The above-mentioned; the before-mentioned.
The word does not always mean "identical," "not different," or "not other." It frequently means of the kind or species, though not the specific thing. It is often used as a substitute for that which was used before, and is employed in the sense of a pronoun. In this sense it is very frequently used in pleadings and in legal documents. To deliver policies and receive premiums upon the same is equivalent to, to deliver policies and receive premiums upon them, or, substituting the noun for its representative pronoun, to deliver policies and receive premiums on policies. Crapo v Brown, 40 Iowa 487, 493.

same case. See **s. c.**

same contract or transaction. For the purpose of joinder of causes of action, one transaction having a substantial unity with another or other transactions. 1 Am J2d Actions § 107. A preponderating doctrine in the law of larceny, that the larceny of articles belonging to different owners, if committed at the same time and place, constitutes but one offense; and that while the state can, if it chooses, include all these offenses in one indictment, yet if it chooses to indict the thief for stealing only one of the articles belonging to one of the owners, it cannot subsequently be allowed to indict for the larceny of any other of the articles so taken, for it was taken in the same transaction and that would be double jeopardy for the same offense. Dean v State, 9 Ga App 571, 71 SE 932. For the purposes of a counterclaim, the contract or transaction which is the foundation of plaintiff's suit. Benton County State Bank v Nichols, 153 Or 73, 54 P2d 1166.

In actions ex contractu, a counterclaim, to be one arising out of the same contract or transaction, must be a cause of action in favor of a defendant against a plaintiff which might have arisen out of the original transaction, in view of the parties, and which, at the time the contract was made, they could have intended might, in some event, give one a claim against the other for compliance or noncompliance with its provisions. Krausse v Greenfield, 61 Or 502, 123 P 392.

Such a "transaction" is not limited to the facts set forth in the complaint, but includes the entire series of acts and mutual conduct of the parties in the business or proceeding between them which formed the basis of the transaction. 20 Am J2d Countcl § 67.

same invention. The invention for which a patent will be reissued, being the identical invention covered by the original patent. 40 Am J1st Pat § 114.

same offense. An identical or similar offense, for the purposes of enhancement of punishment under habitual criminal statutes. 25 Am J1st Habit Cr § 15.
See **indentity of offenses; prior jeopardy; same contract or transaction.**

same parties. See **mutuality of parties and demands.**

same quality, height and fitness. A term of comparison in a building contract, applicable to the entire structure of the standard. 13 Am J2d Bldg Contr § 10.

same transaction. See **same contract or transaction.**

sample. An article or a portion taken from a large number or bulk as a fair representative of the whole quantity; a specimen. See Brantley v Thomas, 22 Tex 270.
See **sale by sample.**

sanae mentis (sā'nē men'tis). Of sane mind; of sound mind.

sanatorium (san-a-tō'ri-um). A place where an invalid may rest and receive medical care in pleasant and healthful surroundings, particularly a place for a person afflicted with tuberculosis. An institution for the recuperation and treatment of persons suffering from physical or mental disorders. United Cerebral Palsy Asso. v Zoning Board, 382 Pa 67, 114 A2d 331, 52 ALR2d 1093.

sanctio (sangk'she-ō). (Civil law.) Same as **sanction.**

Sanctio justa, jubens honesta et prohibens contraria (sangk'she-ō jus'ta, jū'benz ho-nes'ta et pro'hi-benz kon-trā'ri-a). (Civil law.) A just sanction, commanding that which is honorable and forbidding the contrary.

sanction. Approval. Authority. Something giving force and authority. A coercive measure. That part of a law which signifies the evil or penalty which will be incurred by the wrongdoer for his breach of it. 50 Am J1st Stat § 151. As used in the Federal Administrative Procedure Act:—the whole or part of any agency (1) prohibition, requirement, limitation or other condition affecting the freedom of any person; (2) withholding of relief; (3) the imposition of any form of penalty or fine; (4) destruction, taking, seizure or withholding of property; (5) assessment of damages, reimbursement, restitution, compensation, cost, charges or fees; (6) the requirement, revocation, or suspension of a license; or (7) the taking of other compulsory or restrictive action. 5 USC § 1001(f).

sanction of oath. A belief that God will punish falsehood, whether in this world by remorse of conscience or other method or by a means reserved for the future state of being in the next world. 39 Am J1st Oath § 5.

sanctuary (sangk'tū-ā-ri). A sacred place where in older times a person who had committed a crime was immune from arrest. A church or temple. That part of a church in which the main altar is located.

sand. A species of stone. Wright v Carollton Gravel & Sand Co. (Ky) 242 SW2d 751, 26 ALR2d 1449. Disintegrated rock.
See **gravel**.

sanding. The duty of a carrier to sprinkle sand upon snowy or icy spots on steps or platforms on its premises. 14 Am J2d Car § 1054. The process of putting sand on icy or snowy street or highway. Smoothing a board by rubbing it with sandpaper. Removing old paint or varnish.

sand pit. A digging upon land where sand in salable quantities is obtainable. Williamson v Jones, 43 W Va 562, 27 SE 411.

Sandwich Islands. The name by which the islands which comprise the present state of Hawaii were formerly known.

sane. Possessed of sanity.
See **sanity**.

sane memory. Good memory; sound understanding. See **sound mind and memory**.

sane or insane clause. A clause in a life insurance policy extending the exception of suicide to intentional self-destruction by an insane as well as by a sane person, regardless of the moral or criminal quality of the act. 29A Am J Rev ed Ins § 1147.

sang. (French.) Blood; consanguinity.

sangue. See **demi-sangue**.

sanguinem emere (san'gwi-nem e'me-re). To buy one's blood—a redemption or purchase by a villein of his blood or tenure that he might become a freeman.

Sanguinis conjunctio benevolentia devincit homines et caritate (san'gwi-nis kon-junk'she-ō be-ne-vo-len'she-a de-vin'sit ho'mi-nēz et ka-ri-tā'te). The tie of kinship overcomes men through benevolence and affection.

sanguis (sang'gwis). Blood; blood-relationship; consanguinity.

sanipractor (san-i-prak'tor). One who practices a system of healing without drugs. Anno: 86 ALR 631, 632.

sanis (san'is). A form of punishment for crime which at one time prevailed among the Greeks, and which consisted in fastening the culprit to a piece of wood.

sanitarium. Same as **sanatorium**.

sanitary. The absence of source of infection or disease. In a state of sanitation. In the interest of sanitation. For the preservation of health by removing sources of infection and disease. Re Theresa Drainage Dist. 90 Wis 301, 305, 63 NW 288.

sanitary district. An improvement or assessment district established with reference particularly to improvements, such as sewers and sewage disposal plants, in the interest of sanitation and health. 48 Am J1st Spec A § 35. A municipal corporation organized to secure, preserve, and promote the public health. People ex rel. Longenecker v Nelson, 133 Ill 565, 579.

sanitary regulations. Building regulations imposed in the interest of health. 13 Am J2d Bldgs §§ 29, 30. Regulations intended to prevent the spread of communicable diseases. 25 Am J1st Hlth § 25.

sanitation. The practical application of science in protecting health by eliminating sources of contagion and disease-producing conditions; hygienic measures in sewage disposal and drainage projects. Oakland County Drain Comrs. v Royal Oak, 325 Mich 298, 38 NW2d 413, 11 ALR2d 1122.

sanity. Soundness of mind; mental competency.
A person is sane when he is of sound mind; when he is possessed of a mind which is not that of an imbecile and which is healthy. See Robinson v Adams, 62 Me 369.
Sanity is not an ingredient of crime. It is a condition precedent of all intelligent action, as well benevolent as nefarious. It is a quality of the actor, not an element of the act. It is a pre-existing fact which may be taken for granted as implied by law and general experience. We do not infer sanity from the criminal act as we do malice and premeditation. Sanity is a premise, not a conclusion. The sanity of a human being is an assumed fact, never depending upon evidence until it is disputed. State v Quigley, 26 RI 263, 58 A 905.
See **insanity; presumption of sanity**.

sapling. A tree too small to be useful for any good purpose when cut; a part of the undergrowth in a forest. 34 Am J1st Logs § 2.

sans (sanz). Without.

sans ceo que (sôn se ke). Without this, that.

sans impeachment de wast (sanz im-pēch'ment de wäst). Without impeachment of waste,—a clause in a deed or lease signifying that the grantee or lessee shall not be liable for waste. See 2 Bl Comm 283.

sans jour (sanz jör). Without day.

sans nombre (sanz nôm'br). Without number.

sans recours (sanz rē-kour'). Without recourse.

sanus (san'us). Sane; whole; sound; in a healthful state, whether mind or body. Den v Vancleve, 5 NJL 695, 775.

sapiens (sā'pi-enz). (Latin.) Wise; sensible.

Sapiens incipit a fine, et quod primum est intentione, ultimum est in executione (sā'pi-enz in'si-pit ā fī'ne, et quod pri'mum est in-ten-she-ō'ne, ul'ti-mum est in ex-e-ku-she-ō'ne). A wise man begins at the end, and that which is first in intention is last in execution.

Sapiens omnia agit cum consilio (sā'pi-enz om'ni-a ā'jit kum kon-si'li-ō). A wise man does everything with deliberation.

sapientes, fideles, et animosi (sa-pi-en'tēz, fī-dē'lēz, et a-ni-mō'sī). Wise, faithful, and brave. See 1 Bl Comm 408.

sapientia (sā-pi-en'she-a). (Latin.) Wisdom; prudence.

Sapientia legis nummario pretio non est aestimanda (sā-pi-en'she-a lē'jis num-mā'ri-ō pre'she-ō non est ēs-ti-man'da). The wisdom of the law is not to be estimated or computed in money value.

Sapientis judicis est cogitare tantum sibi esse permissum, quantum commissum et creditum (sa-pi-en'tis jū′di-sis est ko-ji-tā′re tan′tum si′bi es′se per-mis′-sum, quan′tum kon-mis′sum et kre′di-tum). A wise judge should only permit himself to think in so far as a matter is committed and intrusted to him.

sart (särt). Wooded land which has been converted into arable land.

sasine (sā′sin). Same as **seizin**.

satisdare (sa-tis-da′re). (Civil law.) To give "satisdatio."
See **satisdatio**.

satisdatio (sa-tis-da′she-ō). (Civil law.) A security given by the defendant in an action for the payment of any judgment that may be rendered against him. See 3 Bl Comm 291.

satisfaction. The discharge of an obligation; the payment of a debt. A fulfillment of needs. A performance of the terms of an accord. Harrison v Henderson, 67 Kan 194, 72 P 875.
See **accord and satisfaction; discharge; release**.

satisfaction by legacy. The discharge of an inter vivos obligation by bequest made by the will of the obligor in favor of the obligee, as where a legacy satisfies a covenant contained in a marriage settlement. Anno: 26 ALR2d 15.

satisfaction contract. A contract which provides in terms that performance by the one party must be satisfactory to the other. United States Heat & Power Corp. v Lachman, 235 Mich 75, 209 NW 187.
See **satisfaction with performance**.

satisfaction in fact. See **technical release**.

satisfaction of judgment. Compliance with or fulfillment of the mandate, such ordinarily being the payment of the money due thereunder. 30A Am J Rev ed Judgm § 990. The release of a judgment as "paid" or "satisfied."
As used in a clause of a liability insurance policy requiring action to be brought against the insurer within a certain time after the judgment against the insured has been paid and satisfied, the word "satisfied" is synonymous with the word "paid." It means satisfaction in fact, the payment of the judgment in full, and not the entry of that satisfaction upon the record. 29A Am J Rev ed Ins § 1798.

satisfaction of mortgage. The payment of a mortgage. 36 Am J1st Mtg § 406.

satisfaction of the court. Convincing the court. Removing doubt from the mind of the court.
Where a fact is to be established to the satisfaction of the court, the words "to the satisfaction of the court" do not mean simply the sufficiency of the proof, but go to the quieting of the mind of the judge, —go to the freedom to act according to his judgment on the question, and this is particularly the case where he is to judge as to his own bias and prejudice. State v Chapman, 1 SD 414, 47 NW 411.

satisfaction of the jury. Convincing the jury; removing doubt from the minds of the jurors.
To prove a thing to the satisfaction of a jury means that the jury must be satisfied that the thing existed. To satisfy the mind, according to the common notion of mankind, is to free it from doubt, to set it at rest. This is the primary meaning of the word, according to all the lexicographers, when used in this connection. To accomplish this result —to "satisfy" a body of men of the truth of a disputed fact—requires much more than a preponderance of the evidence. Clear and convincing evidence must be adduced in its favor. Kelch v State, 55 Ohio St 146, 45 NE 6.

satisfaction piece. A warrant signed by the party in whose favor a judgment has been rendered and acknowledged as required by law, or, in England, signed by an attorney for that purpose authorized, directing the officer of the court having charge of the record to enter a satisfaction of the judgment on the roll. Lownds v Remsen (NY) 7 Wend 35, 40.

satisfaction with performance. A determination to be made by objective criteria; the question whether the owner, as a reasonable man, should have been satisfied with the work. Anno: 44 ALR2d 1120, § 5[b]; 13 Am J2d Bldg Contr § 30. A determination entirely subjective, the owner or contracting party entitled to performance having the right to pass on the performance and determine whether or not it is satisfactory, without the necessity of disclosing the reasons for the determination made by him, provided he acts in good faith. United States Heat & Power Corp. v Lachman, 235 Mich 75, 77, 209 NW 187.
The word "satisfactory" is employed in two different senses when applied in contracts to make or supply something to the "satisfaction" of a person, or a thing "satisfactory" to him. If the article to be made or supplied is one which involves personal taste or feeling, such as a dress or a portrait, the person to be satisfied is the sole judge, and the article must conform to his peculiar taste or feelings; but if it does not involve such taste or feelings, as a keg of nails, or a piece of machinery, the article need only be "reasonably" satisfactory. Pennington v Howland, 21 RI 65, 41 A 891.

satisfactory deal. A transaction by a broker which his principal, as a reasonable man, should accept; a transaction negotiated by a broker which his principal can not refuse so as to preclude liability to the broker for the commission to which the latter is otherwise entitled under the terms of the contract between them. Mullally v Greenwood, 127 Mo 138, 29 SW 1001.

satisfactory evidence. Same as **satisfactory proof**.

satisfactory goods. See **satisfaction with performance**.

satisfactory indorser. An indorser for accommodation who is satisfactory to the payee, subject to the qualification that the payee is not to reject capriciously. Cutter v Cutter, 48 NY Super Ct (16 Jones & S) 470, 475.

satisfactory note. A promissory note given by a person of undoubted solvency or supported by surety or indorser of undoubted solvency. 46 Am J1st Sales § 179.

satisfactory performance. See **satisfaction with performance**.

satisfactory proof. Convincing evidence. Sufficient evidence. Evidence such as to satisfy an unprejudiced mind of the truth. 30 Am J2d Ev § 1080.
To be satisfied of the truth of anything implies the absence of a reasonable doubt, but it does not imply the absence of belief that there is a possibility that the thing is not true. The jury may believe there is a possibility of the defendant's innocence, and yet properly convict him; for although it may be possible he was innocent, yet they may be entirely satisfied that he was guilty. People v Phipps, 39 Cal 326, 334.

In cases involving statutes requiring "satisfactory" proof of genuineness of handwriting offered for comparison, it has generally been held that the proof required is such as would require the court to find as a fact that the writing was genuine. Anno: 41 ALR2d 578.

See **satisfaction of jury.**

satisfactory proof of loss. A proof of loss made to an insurer, sufficient to make out a prima facie case and to enable the insurer to form an intelligent estimate of its rights and liabilities. 29A Am J Rev ed Ins § 1403.

satisfactory title. A title to real estate which is satisfactory to the other party to a contract, subject only to the limitation that he must act in good faith in considering the state of the title. Anno: 47 ALR2d 457; 52 Am J1st Exch P § 23. A title to real estate which is satisfactory by objective standards, being a good or marketable title; such a title that no reasonable objection can be made thereto. Anno: 47 ALR2d 457.

satisfied. Paid. Philadelphia Pickling Co. v Maryland Casualty Co. 89 NJL 330, 98 A 433. Approving of performance, having received satisfaction.

See **satisfaction; satisfactory proof.**

satisfied encumbrance. A mortgage or other lien standing of record as security for a debt which has since been paid.

satisfy. To make satisfaction.
See **satisfaction; satisfied.**

Satius est petere fontes quam rivulos (sa'she-us est pe'te-re fon'tēz quam ri'vu-los). It is more satisfactory to seek the spring or source than the little rivulets.

Satius est petere fontes quam sectari rivulos (sa'she-us est pe'te-re fon'tēz quam sek-tā'rī ri'vu-lōs). It is more satisfactory to seek the spring than to follow the little rivulets.

The maxim expresses the advice of Lord Coke that in deciding cases the ancient sources of the law should be consulted. Dyson v Rhode Island Co. 25 RI 600, 57 A 771.

Saturday. The seventh and last day of the week by the calendar. The Sabbath under the religion of the Jews. 50 Am J1st Sun & H § 10. A juridical day. 50 Am J1st Sun & H § 77.

sault (sâlt). An assault.

sausage. A food composed of meat, salt, and spices. Armour v State Dairy & Food Com. 159 Mich 1, 123 NW 580.

sauvement (sâv'mont). Safely.

savanna (sạ-van'ạ). A natural open meadow in tropical or semitropical region having abundant rainfall.

A savanna is not absolutely constant in its state and extent, but from the constitution of the soil, or its humidity, or other natural quality, not well understood, there takes place in savannas but little change, and they may be considered nearly permanent, unless disturbed by cultivation. See Stapleford v Brinson, 24 NC (2 Ired L) 311, 312.

save harmless. See **to indemnify and save harmless; to save harmless.**

save the statute. To prevent the bar of the statute of limitations against a plaintiff's cause of action by suing before the statutory period has elapsed.

savin (sav'in). A juniper tree, also called juniperus sabina. A drug obtained from the juniper tree.

saving clause. A clause in a statute stating that the valid provisions will be enforced in spite of any judicial determination that certain parts of the action are unconstitutional. 16 Am J2d Const L § 187. A restriction in a repealing act, saving rights, pending proceedings, penalties, etc., from the annihilation which would result from unrestricted repeal. State ex rel. Crow v St. Louis, 174 Mo 125, 73 SW 623.

saving life doctrine. See **rescue doctrine.**

saving property doctrine. The proposition that a defendant who by his negligence has endangered the property of another is liable for personal injuries incurred by the owner, or person in charge of such property, in an effort to save it, if the effort is impelled by the necessity of the occasion, and is reasonably prudent under the circumstances. 38 Am J1st Negl § 81. The rule that it is not contributory negligence per se for one to expose himself to some danger in an endeavor to save his own property, the property of his employer, or the property of a third person. 38 Am J1st Negl § 230.

savings account. An account of a savings bank customer. An account between a savings bank and a depositor, which differs from an ordinary account in a commercial bank in two respects: (1) the amount on deposit bears interest, subject to conditions as to the time of deposit, and (2) the right of withdrawal may be subject to an advance notice of a prescribed number of days, weeks, or months. An account in a commercial bank under conditions respecting interest and withdrawals which distinguish it from the ordinary account in such a bank.

savings and loan association. An association chartered by the Federal Home Loan Bank Board to encourage thrift and promote the ownership of homes by accepting deposits to bear interest and making loans for home financing. 13 Am J2d B & L Assoc § 10.

See **building and loan association.**

Savings and Loan Insurance Corporation. A corporation created by Congress to insure the accounts of all federal savings and loan associations and the accounts of building and loan, savings and loan, homestead associations, and co-operative banks organized and operating under state law or the laws of a district, territory, or possession in which they are chartered. 13 Am J2d B & L Assoc § 12.

savings bank. A term of dual meaning. A banking institution in the hands of disinterested persons, the profits of which inure wholly to the benefit of the depositors in dividends or in a reserve surplus for their greater security. A bank in which the depositor becomes a creditor of the bank for the amount of the deposit and receives such interest on the deposit as the trustees or directors of the bank may agree to pay, and in which the profits belong to the corporation and its stockholders. In a sense known throughout the country, a bank which accepts and pays interest on deposits of savings, subject to whatever conditions may be prescribed as to the time such savings remain on deposit. 10 Am J2d Banks § 4.

savings bank check. An anomaly of words, being nothing more than a slip denoting a withdrawal of funds from a savings account.

savings bond. A United States bond payable to a designated person, sometimes with an alternative payee, payable in progressively larger amounts the longer it is held.

SAVINGS [1141] SCANDAL

savings deposit. A deposit in a savings bank or with a building and loan association.
See **Christmas club deposit.**

saving to suitors clause. A qualification in the federal statute which vests original jurisdiction of civil cases in admiralty in the federal district courts, exclusive of the courts of the state, saving to suitors in all cases all other remedies to which they are otherwise entitled. 28 USC § 1333.
For jurisdictional effect of the clause, see 2 Am J2d Adm §§ 105 et seq.

saw logs. Logs which can be sawed into lumber. Anno: 72 ALR2d 738.

saw-log timber. Same as **saw timber.**

saw-mill timber. Same as **saw timber.**

saw timber. Trees of such size, shape, and kind as to be susceptible of conversion to lumber. Anno: 72 ALR2d 740. Trees of all varieties from which suitable articles can be made, or which can be used to advantage in any class of manufacture or construction. Teachout v Clough, 143 Mo App 474, 127 SW 672.

say, about. A term used by a seller when he makes no representation as to quantity of subject matter. Anno: 1 ALR 1395.

s. c. An abbreviation of the words "same case," often employed in briefs and law writings where the same case is cited several times for different points. An abbreviation of the Latin word "scilicet," but not employed as frequently as **"ss."**

scab. A worker who is opposed to a labor union, who refuses to strike, or who takes the place of a striking employee, becoming a strike breaker. Paltry fellow, especially from the standpoint of union labor. State v Christie, 97 Vt 461, 123 A 849, 34 ALR 577, 579.

scab shop. A place of employment for nonunion men only.

scabies (skā'bi-ēz). A contagious disease of the skin caused by burrowing mites; sometimes transmitted between animals in close confinement in railroad car or truck. Nichols v Atchison, T. & S. F. Ry. Co. 180 Kan 101, 299 P2d 52.

scaccario. See **de scaccario.**

scaccarium (ska-kā'ri-um). The court of exchequer. See 3 Bl Comm 44.

scaffold. A framework of wood or metal upon which to stand and place materials in working upon a building; sometimes known as staging. Anno: 59 ALR 1090. Inclusive of staging both inside and outside of a building upon which work is performed. 58 Am J1st Workm Comp § 98. The raised platform from which a person is dropped in executing the death penalty by hanging.

scaffolding. Same as **scaffold.**

scale (skāl). To cut down; to proportion.
See **scales.**

scaleboard. A board or shingle upon which a weigher at a scales marks the weights of single loads weighed by him, the entry for his scalebook being made from the tally of the figures on the scaleboard. Crane Lumber Co. v Otter Creek Lumber Co. 79 Mich 307, 44 NW 788.

scalebook. A book of entries made by a weigher, showing the weights of loads weighed by him. Crane Lumber Co. v Otter Creek Lumber Co. 79 Mich 307, 44 NW 788.

scale-down agreement. An agreement by the creditors of a single debtor under which they undertake to accept reduced sums in full satisfaction of their claims. Anno: 147 ALR 744.

scales. An instrumentality for weighing.

scale ticket. A ticket made out by the weigher at a scales and handed to the driver of a load weighed, showing the weight of the load. Chicago & A. R. Co. v American Strawboard Co. 190 Ill 268, 60 NE 518.

scale tolerance (tol'e-rans). The normal variation between different scales in the weighing of carloads of coal.
Under the rules of the Interstate Commerce Commission, scale tolerance beyond one hundred pounds is not to be permitted. Smith v Louisville & Nashville R. Co. 202 Iowa 292, 295, 209 NW 465, 466.

scaling timber. Measuring or estimating the number of board feet of lumber a log or tree will produce. Kennedy v South Shore Lumber Co. 102 Wis 284, 288.

scalp. A short deal or transaction, that is, one which is intended to be closed out promptly with a profit. McCormick v Nichols, 19 Ill App 334. The skin on the top and back of the head.

scalper (skal'pėr). See **scalping; ticket scalping.**

scalping. Removing the scalp or a part of the scalp of a person. The making of a short-term profit by an adviser in respect of investments through taking advantage of the market reaction to advice given by him. Securities & Exchange Com. v Capital Gains Research Bureau, Inc. 375 US 180, 11 L Ed 2d 237, 84 S Ct 275. Taking advantage of a customer in charging him an excessive price. Any form of business practice in seeking an unmerited profit.
See **ticket scalping.**

scandal. An act or condition which leads to disgrace as shocking to the community or offensive to the feelings of the public. Defamation.
See **scandalous matter.**

scandalous matter (skan'dal-us mat'ėr). Allegations in a pleading which are both impertinent and reproachful. Woods v Morrell (NY) 1 Johns Ch 103, 106. Impertinent allegations which are damaging to the reputation of the person aspersed. 27 Am J2d Equity § 187.
The rule is sometimes stated that no person is obliged to reanswer matter of "scandal" in responding to a bill of discovery, but the term "scandal" has a limited and technical meaning in this connection, referring only to scandal and infamy arising from crime. Skinner v Judson, 8 Conn 528.

scandalum magnatum (skan'da-lum mag-nā'tum). The slander of great men.
The term was used in early English law to designate words spoken in derogation of a peer, a judge, or other great officer of the realm. Such slander was considered a more heinous offense than the slander of a common person. The doctrine of scandalum magnatum, however, has long been obsolete in England, being finally abolished by statute. It is said to by unknown in the United States. 33 Am J1st L & S § 3.

scandalmonger. One who maliciously repeats and disseminates scandal. 33 Am J1st L & S § 45.

scandal sheet. A newspaper mainly devoted to the detailing of violations of moral obligations through crime, acts of lawless violence, or conduct induced by lust, especially one in which the stories and articles are illustrated, or purport to be illustrated, by pictures. 33 Am J1st Lewd etc § 12.

scan. mag. An abbreviation of **scandalum magnatum.**

scapegoat. One who bears the blame, sometimes taking the punishment, for another person's offense.

scapellare. To haggle.

scar. A mark, sometimes a disfigurement, resulting from a cutting of the skin. Houston Lighting & Power Co. v Reed (Tex Civ App) 365 SW2d 26, error ref n r e.

scarlet fever. A communicable disease, particularly of children, characterized by a rash and fever, usually accompanied by sore throat. 25 Am J1st Hlth § 25.

scattering votes. Votes cast at an election for persons whose names do not appear on the printed ballot but which have been written in by the voters. State ex rel. Ragan v Junkin, 85 Neb 1, 122 NW 473.

scavage (skav'ăj). A toll exacted of foreign merchants by town officers for showing or exposing goods for sale in the town. See 1 Bl Comm 316.

scavenger (skav'en-jer). A person employed to remove filthy matter, particularly one who cleans out privy vaults. State ex rel. Moriarity v McMahon. 69 Minn 265, 72 NW 79.

scenario (se-nä'ri-o). A complete plot for a moving picture, reduced to writing, with the addition of essential details for acting the play. Anno: 23 ALR2d 275, § 7.

scene of accident. Place of accident.

scenic railway. An amusement device; a roller coaster; a miniature railway for children.
See **roller coaster.**

scenic road. A pleasure drive.

schedule (sked'ūl). Noun: A small scroll; a writing additional or appendant; an inventory. A writing to be sworn to and filed by a bankrupt, showing the amount and kind of his property, the location thereof and its money value, in detail; a list of all his creditors, showing their residences or places of business, if known, or if unknown, that fact to be stated, the amount due to or claimed by each of them, the consideration thereof, the security held by them, if any, and what claims, if any, are contingent, unliquidated, or disputed; and a claim for such exemptions as he may be entitled to—all in triplicate, one copy for the clerk, one for the referee, and one for the trustee. 9 Am J2d Bankr § 367. A list of assets and liabilities to be filed by an insolvent in insolvency proceedings. 29 Am J Rev ed Insolv § 15. Verb: To prepare a list or inventory.
See **time schedule; time table.**

schedule in bankruptcy. See **schedule.**

schedule injuries. Injuries compensable under a workmen's compensation statute for specific sums, regardless of the fact that the workman has not been incapacitated to perform his accustomed duties and has suffered no loss of earnings or earning capacity. 58 Am J1st Workm Comp § 287.

schedule of exempt property. The list of property selected by a debtor as that which he claims exempt from execution. 31 Am J2d Exemp § 146. A part of the schedule to be filed by a bankrupt. 9 Am J2d Bankr § 367.

scheme (skēm). A plan or artifice; a plot. A combination of thoughts, theories, or the like, connected and adjusted by design; a systematic plan; a system. Weiss v United States (CA5 La) 120 F2d 472. An outline of an article, for example, 9 Am J2d Bankr page 1.

scheme to defraud. A plan designed or concocted for perpetrating a fraud.
As the term is used in the Federal statutes making criminal the use of the mails for the purpose of executing a scheme to defraud, if the scheme or artifice in its necessary consequence is one which is calculated to injure another, to deprive him of his property wrongfully, then it is to defraud within the meaning of the statute. See Horman v United States (CA6 Ohio) 116 F 350.

schireman (shīr'man). An earl.
An earl is a title of nobility so ancient that its origin cannot be clearly traced. Among the Saxons they were called ealdormen (elder men) with the same meaning as the word senior or senator among the Romans. And the Saxons called them "schiremen" because they had each of them the civil government of a several division or shire. See 1 Bl Comm 398.

schism (sizm). A division of the membership of a society respecting the conduct of the organization or the principles which it espouses. A breach of unity among people of the same religious faith. 45 Am J1st Reli Soc § 65. A separation of a religious society into parts, without change of faith or ulterior relations. McKinney v Griggs, 68 Ky (5 Bush) 401.

schismaticus inveteratus (skiz-ma'ti-kus in-ve-te-rā'tus). Persistently opposed to orthodox religious beliefs. See 1 Bl Comm 389.

schizophrenia (skiz-ọ-frē'ni-ạ). A mental disorder, not necessarily an impairment of intelligence, characterized by hallucinations, indifference, and delusions of omnipotence and persecution. Not necessarily insanity constituting a defense in an action for divorce. 24 Am J2d Div & S § 409.

scholarship. Demonstrated ability to acquire knowledge. A gift of money or other aid, as by a grant of free tuition, to help a particular student maintain the financial burden of attending college or university, sometimes under conditions, such as services of the donee in teaching or as a laboratory assistant or participation by the donee in athletics. 15 Am J2d Colleges § 18.

scholarship record. A public record of the progress and grades of pupils in public schools. Valentine v Independent School Dist. 187 Iowa 555, 174 NW 334, 6 ALR 1525. The rating of a student according to his grades or other attainments. 15 Am J2d Colleges § 27.

scholastic rating (skọ-las'tik rā'ting).
See **scholarship record.**

school. A place for systematic instruction in any branch or branches of knowledge; a place where instruction is imparted. 47 Am J1st Sch § 2. A place where instruction is imparted, irrespective of the number of persons being taught. People v Levisen, 404 Ill 574, 90 NE2d 213, 14 ALR2d 1364; Livingston v Davis, 243 Iowa 21, 50 NW2d 592, 27 ALR 2d 1237. A term sometimes limited to a public or common school. 47 Am J1st Sch § 2. In usual sense, exclusive of university, college, business college, or other institution of higher education. 47 Am J1st Sch § 2.

The word as used in a constitutional provision exempting from taxation such property as may be used for school purposes means a place where systematic instruction in useful branches is given by methods common to schools and institutions of learning, as distinguished from schools conducted for teaching, dancing, writing, deportment, and other things, which are not schools in the ordinary sense. People ex rel. McCullough v Deutsche E. L. J. Gemeinde, 249 Ill 132, 94 NE 162.

The word "school" as used in a statute requiring denial of a liquor license for a location within five hundred feet of a school is not subject to a more restricted definition than the definition of the word in building restriction cases. Boys' Club of Detroit v Pajula, 342 Mich 150, 69 SW2d 348, 49 ALR2d 1097.

See **parochial school; private school; public school.**

school board. An administrative body, composed of a number of directors, commissioners, or trustees, charged with the duty of administering public schools within a city, town, or district. 47 Am J1st Sch § 29. A special commission within a constitutional provision prohibiting the legislature from delegating the power to tax to any special commission. Wilson v Philadelphia School Dist. 328 Pa 225, 195 A 90, 113 ALR 1401.

school building. See **schoolhouse.**

school census. A census taken of pupils in the schools as of a particular date, showing ages and attainments according to grade. 14 Am J2d Census § 11.

school children. In common usage, children receiving elementary instruction in public, parochial, and private schools.

In common acceptation, the term refers to young people in attendance upon educational institutions of a subordinate character, places of primary instruction, and, ordinarily, and without something to indicate a wider meaning to be intended, it will not be taken to include pupils in attendance upon such higher institutions of learning as colleges or universities, or institutions for the teaching of trades, professions or business. State ex rel. Seattle v Seattle Electric Co. 71 Wash 213, 128 P 220.

school directors. See **school board.**

school district. A local administrative authority with fixed territorial limits created by the legislature, and subordinate to its will, as an agent of the state for the sole purpose of administering the state's system of public education. 47 Am J1st Sch § 12. A subordinate agency, subdivision, or instrumentality of the state, performing the duties of the state in the conduct and maintenance of the public schools. State ex rel. McKittrick v Whittle, 333 Mo 705, 63 SW2d 100, 88 ALR 1099. A public corporation. 18 Am J2d Corp § 8.

See **centralized district; consolidation of school districts; independent school district.**

school fund. A fund created for the promotion and maintenance of a common or public school system provided for by the constitution and statutes of the various states. 47 Am J1st Sch § 83.

school house. A building which houses a school. Any building which is appropriated for a use prescribed or permitted by the law to public schools. Alexander v Phillips, 31 Ariz 503, 254 P 1056, 52 ALR 244. The entire school plant, including main building, playground, gymnasium, stadium, and other structures for competitive athletic games and sports, and other buildings appropriated to uses prescribed or permitted by law to a public school. Alexander v Phillips, 31 Ariz 503, 254 P 1056, 52 ALR 244.

school lands. Lands set apart from the public domain, the proceeds from the sale of which can be used only for educational purposes. 47 Am J1st Sch §§ 62 et seq. Lands reserved for the puspose of being applied to schools in the territories of New Mexico, Utah, Colorado, Dakota, Arizona, Idaho, Montana, and Wyoming and in the states and territories carved out of them, by section 1946 of the Revised Statutes of the United States, providing that sections 16 and 36 in each township should be thus reserved. Pike v State Board of Land Comrs. 19 Idaho 268, 277, 113 P 447.

school nurse. A nurse employed by the school authorities for rendition of professional services in a public school. 47 Am J1st Sch § 190.

school of law. A law college.

school of medicine. A medical college. A system of medical treatment, such as homeopathy or allopathy. 41 Am J1st Phys & S § 85.

school placement laws. The laws governing the assignment of students to public schools, particularly in reference to the elimination of race segregation. 15 Am J2d Civ R § 42.

school preference law. A statute authorizing boards of education to provide separate schools for white and Negro children whose parents voluntarily elect that their children shall attend a school with members of their own race. 15 Am J2d Civ R § 45.

school purpose. See **educational purpose.**

school taxes. Taxes imposed and levied particularly for the purposes of the establishment, construction, and maintenance of schools. 47 Am J1st Sch §§ 76 et seq.

school prayer. A prayer given in school, usually as a part of morning exercises. 47 Am J1st Sch § 210.

schoolteacher. See **teacher.**

schoolteacher's pension. See **teacher's pension.**

school township. A territorial subdivision for school purposes. A township comprising one school district, being divided into subdistricts for the administration of the several schools of the district. W. H. Dreves, Inc. v Oslo School Township, 217 Ind 388, 28 NE2d 252, 128 ALR 1405.

See **centralization of schools.**

school trustees. See **school board.**

sciagraph (sī'a̱-gra̱f). Same as **skiagraph.**

Sciant praesentes et futuri (si'ant prē-zen'tēz et fu-tū'rī). Know all men present and in future.

science. Knowledge derived from study, observation, and experimentation and arranged for use in system and form. Study in a branch of knowledge conducted abstractly but also with observation and experimentation.

sciendum est (si-en'dum est). It should be known.

sciens et prudens (si'enz et pru'denz). Knowing and intending.

scienter (sī-en'tēr). Knowledge, particularly knowledge which charges with guilt or liability. Knowledge of an owner of an animal concerning the viciousness of the beast. 4 Am J2d Ani § 86. Knowledge on the part of a person making a representation, at the time when the representation is made, that it is false. 37 Am J2d Fraud § 197. An element of liability for interference with the performance of a contract, consisting in knowledge of the existence of the contract. 30 Am J Rev ed Interf § 42. An element of the crime of incest, consisting in knowledge that the person with whom one engages in sexual intercourse is within the prohibited degree of relationship. 27 Am J1st Incest § 7.

scienti (sī-ęn'tī). To him who has knowledge.

"Scienti is not equivalent to 'volenti.' It cannot be said that where a man is lawfully engaged in work, and is in danger of dismissal if he leaves his work, that he wilfully incurs any risk which he may encounter in the course of such work." Thrussell v Handyside (Eng) LR 20 QB Div 359.

Scientia sciolorum est mixta ignorantia (sī-en'she-a si-ō-lō'rum est mix'ta ig-no-ran'she-a). The knowledge of superficial persons is scrambled ignorance.

Scientia utrinque par pares contrahentes facit (sī-en'she-a u-trin'kwe par pa'rēz kon-tra-hen'tēz fa'-sit). Knowledge on both sides makes the contracting parties equal. See Broom's Legal Maxims 772.

Scientia utriusque par pares contrahentes facit (sī-en'she-a u-tri-us'kwe par pa'rēz kon-tra-hen'tēz fa'-sit). Knowledge on both sides makes the contracting parties equal.

Scienti et volenti non fit injuria (sī-en'tī et vo-len'tī non fit in-jū'ri-a). No injury is done to a person who understands and consents.

scientific books. Publications of the writings of experts in medicine, surgery, mechanics, chemistry, nuclear science, and other fields of specialized learning.

See **books of exact science.**

scientific institution. An institution devoted to teaching or research in science or a particular field of science.

As to what is a scientific institution within the meaning of an exemption from property tax, see Anno: 34 ALR2d 1221.

scientific journal. A publication devoted to the special interests of some branch of science. 39 Am J1st Newsp § 9.

scientific organization. An organization exempt from federal income tax because of the scientific nature of its activities, its refraining from prohibited transactions, and also from an unreasonable accumulation of income. Internal Revenue Code § 503.

scienti non fit injuria (sī-en'tī non fit in-jū'ri-a). No injury is done to a person who has knowledge of the facts.

"In discussing the question as to whether the plaintiff assumed the risk by continuing at work (with knowledge of his danger), the judges called attention to the fact that the maxim upon which the assumption of risks was based was not Scienti non fit injuria, bue Volenti non fit injuria. A majority of them therefore concluded that the mere fact that the servant remained at work after discovering the danger to which he was exposed did not authorize the court to say, as a matter of law, that he consented to assume the risk. They held that whether he did so or not was a question for the jury. The justness of his decision has been recognized by some of the American courts." Choctaw, Oklahoma & Gulf R Co. v Jones, 77 Ark 367, 375, 92 SW 244.

sci. fa. An abbreviation of **scire facias.**

scil. An abbreviation of **scilicet.**

scilicet (sil'i-set). Towit; that is to say, abbreviated "ss.," "s.," or "scil." An allegation of fact in a pleading in form dispensing with proof of the precise circumstance alleged. Lindekugel v Spokane, P. & S. R. Co. 149 Or 634, 42 P2d 907, 99 ALR 721.

scintilla juris (sin-til'ą jör'is). A particle of right; a spark of interest.

scintilla of evidence (sin-til'ą of ev'i-dęns). The least particle of evidence, a mere trifle of evidence. Offutt v Columbian Exposition, 175 Ill 472, 476, 51 NE 651.

scintilla rule. The rule, now very generally rejected or abandoned in most jurisdictions, that a verdict is never directed for a party if there is any evidence, slight though it may be, in favor of the other party. 53 Am J1st Trial § 356. The rule that if there is any evidence presenting a conflict, at least evidence of some substance, not mere vague, uncertain or irrelevant matter, the case must be submitted to the jury. Nugent v Nugent, 281 Ky 263, 135 SW2d 877.

Scire debes cum quo contrahis (sī're de'bez kum quō kon-tra'his). You ought to know the person with whom you contract.

Scire et scire debere aequiparantur in jure (sī're et sī're de-bē're ē-qui-pa-ran'ter in jō're). To know and to be bound or to be deemed to know are equivalent in the law.

scire facias (sī'rē fā'shi-as). A writ of statutory origin (13 Edward I, chapter 45) used both as an original writ to obtain a judgment where none has before existed and as a writ of execution or continuation of a judgment previously entered. 47 Am J1st Sc F §§ 3, 4. A writ requiring the defendant to appear and show cause why the plaintiff should not be permitted to take some step wherein he has the advantage of a public record. 47 Am J1st Sc F § 2. A writ founded on a matter of record, such as a recognizance or judgment, on which it lies to obtain execution or for other purpose, such as to hear errors. 47 Am J1st Sc F § 2. A writ for the revival of a judgment. 47 Am J1st Sc F § 17. A proceeding for the enforcement of an execution against a garnishee, generally limited to cases where the garnishee defaults, and where there has been no specific property garnished, so that it is necessary to discover and identify the property of the defendant in the possession of the garnishee. Parker, Peeples & Knox v El Saieh, 107 Conn 545, 141 A 884, 59 ALR 1424. A remedy for the enforcement of a bail bond or recognizance on forfeiture. 8 Am J2d Bail § 145.

The term "scire facias" applies not only to a certain writ, but also to the action or proceeding instituted under the writ. 47 Am J1st Sc F § 1.

scire facias ad audiendum errores (sī're fā'she-ās ad â-di-en'dum er-rō'rēz). A common-law writ available to a plaintiff in error who had assigned errors, to compel the executors or administrators of the deceased defendant in error to join in error. United States Mut. Acci. Asso. v Weller, 32 Fla 210, 215.

scire facias quare executionem non (sī're fā'she-ās quā're ex-e-kū-she-ō'nem non). A common-law writ available to the executors or administrators of a defendant in error, to compel the plaintiff in error, who had not assigned errors, to do so. United States Mut. Acci. Asso. v Weller, 32 Fla 210, 215.

Scire facias quare restitutionem habere non debet (sī're fā'she-ās quā'rē re-sti-tū-she-ōn'em hā-bē're non de'bet). Make it known why he ought not to have restitution.—A process in the nature of an order to show cause which issued as a preliminary to the issuance of a writ of restitution where a satisfied judgment was reversed on appeal and the record failed to show the amount paid or lost by the appellant. Bank of United States v Bank of Washington (US) 6 Pet 8, 8 L Ed 299.

scire facias sur mortgage (sī're fā'she-ās sur môr'gāj). A writ for the enforcement of a mortgage upon default of the mortgagor.

Scire feci (sī're fe'sī). I have made known; I have given notice; I have notified.

scire fieri inquiry (sī're fī'e-rī in-kwī'rī). A writ which lay to inquire into the disposition of his goods made by the defendant.

sciregemot (sci're-ge-mōt''). (Saxon.) A court held within a shire or county; a county court.

Scire leges non hoc est verba earum tenere, sed vim et potestatem (sī're lē'jēz non hok est ver'ba e-ā'rum te-nē're, sed vim et po-tes-tā'tem). (Civil law.) To know the laws is not to grasp their words alone, but their force and power as well.

Scire proprie est rem ratione et per causam cognoscere (sī're prō'pri-ē est rem rā-she-ō'nē et per kâ'zam kog-no'se-re). To know properly is to know the thing by reason and through the cause of it.

scite (sīt). A site; a situation; a location. (Latin.) Informed; knowing.

sclerosis. See **arterio sclerosis.**

scold. To rebuke or find fault with another. A person, especially a woman, who scolds.
See **common scold; cuckingstool; scolding.**

scolding (skōl'ding). Mere clamor, railing, personal reproof.
Argument dignifies the orator and instructs and convinces the auditor. Scolding relieves somewhat the hysteria of the scolder, but only amuses or irritates the hearer. Argument is the professional weapon of the lawyer; scolding is that of the communis rixatrix (common scold). Rahles v J. Thompson & Sons Mfg. Co. 137 Wis 506, 118 NW 350.
See **scold.**

scope of authority. The authority of an agent, conferred by his principal, for the performance of acts which are either proper for the accomplishment of the end or object for which the agent was appointed or are such acts as are usual in matters of the kind. First Nat. Bank v Nelson, 38 Ga 391.
As applied to the duty of a public officer, the "scope" of his duty is his design, aim, or purpose; his intention; and it is not to be confused with "scope of authority," which includes only such acts as he may perform with lawful authority. Linblom v Ramsey, 75 Ill 246, 251.

scope of employment. Line of duty; course of the service; pursuit or transaction of the employer's business; furtherance of the employer's interest. 35 Am J1st M & S § 554. Doing for the employer that which one has been directed to do by the employer. Rolfe v Hewitt, 227 NY 486, 125 NE 804, 14 ALR 125. A relative term comprehending consideration of the surrounding circumstances, including the character of the employment, the nature of the wrongful deed, and the time and place of its commission. Horton v Jones, 208 Miss 257, 44 So 2d 397, 15 ALR2d 824.
Any act which can fairly and reasonably be deemed to be an ordinary and natural incident, or a natural, direct, and logical result of the employment is within the meaning of the phrase "scope of employment." Rolfe v Hewitt, 227 NY 486, 125 NE 804, 14 ALR 125. Acts are said to be within the scope of the employee's employment when they are incidental to his regular duties as such an employee and are of some benefit to the employer and not personal to the employee. Myers v Industrial Acci. Com. 191 Cal 673, 218 P 11.
See **in the course of the employment.**

scope of review. The matters proper for consideration by an appellate court upon review of a lower court decision. 5 Am J2d A & E § 702. The matters proper for consideration when properly presented upon the review by the court of a determination of an administrative agency. 2 Am J2d Admin L § 610. A variable in appellate practice, ranging from a trial de novo on appeal to a determination of no more than the question whether there was substantial error producing a miscarriage of justice in the trial court, the scope of review in the particular case depending upon constitutional and statutory provisions. 5 Am J2d A & E § 702.
See **trial de novo.**

scot. See **bi-scot; church-scot; scot and lot; soul-scot.**

scot and lot (skot and lot). A customary contribution laid upon all subjects according to their ability; duties the payment of which was a prerequisite to the right to vote. In the frame or Code for the province of Pennsylvania, compiled by William Penn, it was provided that every inhabitant of the province who paid scot and lot to the government should be deemed a freeman of the province and should be capable of electing or being elected a member of the provincial council or general assembly of the province. Frieszleben v Shallcross, 14 Del (9 Houst) 1, 19 A 576.

Scotch peers (skoch pērs). Those members of the English house of lords who hail from Scotland.

Scott v Sanford. See **Dred Scott Case.**

Scottish Rite. A modern Masonic order.

scoured wool. Wool cleaned and freed of dirt and grease; an agricultural commodity exempted from the general coverage of the Federal Motor Carrier Act. Interstate Commerce Com. v Wagner (DC Tenn) 112 F Supp 109.

scow. A watercraft with a flat bottom, propelled usually by a tugboat and used for carrying freight.

scrambling possession. A condition where two or more persons are struggling for the possession of land, or at least where one person has unlawfully entered upon the possession of another without his knowledge, or without opportunity on his part to determine whether he will submit to the possession of the other or not. 35 Am J2d Forc E & D §18.

scramming contract (skram'ing kon'trakt). A mining contract which confers the right to mine and gather such ore as may be left within the limits of a mine or pit, the same having been opened and mined before.
Such a contract does not contemplate breaking through the walls of the mine or pit, and mining in a newly discovered vein of ore. Davie v Lumberman's Mining Co. 93 Mich 491, 53 NW 625.

scrap. Tobacco sweepings and bits torn from leaves, used in the manufacture of cigars and cigarettes.

Latimer v United States, 223 US 501, 56 L Ed 526, 32 S Ct 242. Metal from worn out machines and vehicles, particularly automobiles, of value only for reprocessing or as an ingredient in the making of steel. Clawson & Bals v Harrison (CA7 Ill) 108 F2d 991. Clippings and pictures placed in a scrapbook. Brief memoranda.

scrapbook. A book in which pictures, clippings from newspapers, and other items of personal interest have been pasted or otherwise attached.

scrap iron. The waste from the manufacture of boilers, the erection of bridges, etc. Schlesinger v Beard, 120 US 264, 30 L Ed 656, 7 S Ct 456. Metal, otherwise known as "scrap" from worn out machines and vehicles, especially automobiles.
See **scrap.**

scrap turpentine. That part of the turpentine which, on exuding from the tree has trickled down the trunk and continues to adhere thereto. Griffith v Hulyon, 90 Fla 582, 107 So 354.

scratch sale. A term of the cotton exchange for a sale offset by a purchase at the same price on the same day. Dupont v United States, 300 US 150, 81 L Ed 570, 57 S Ct 391.

scratch sheet. A printed sheet devoted to horse racing generally or to the races to be run on the day of publication, giving the names of the horses entered, the jockeys up on each horse, facts as to the ownership, pedigree, age, and weight of the horses, the distance of the several races, the condition of the track, predictions as to the winners, and notations as to the horses once entered but "scratched," that is, withdrawn from a race, the latter presumably being the feature from which the name of the publication derives. Anno: 153 ALR 463.

scrawl (skrâl). Shapeless or illegible handwriting. A mark with a pen serving as a seal.

screen credit. The right of an author of a play, produced as a motion picture or by television performance, to have his name appear as author upon the screen or in the televised broadcast. Anno: 23 ALR2d 311-313, § 20. The publicity given the name of the author in accord with such right. Credit given the producer, director, actors, etc. in a moving picture or televised production by listing the names on the screen.

screening. Obstructing the view. 25 Am J1st High § 67. Protecting by a screen, either literally, as by placing a screen to protect patrons in a stadium against batted balls, or figuratively, as where a public figure is protected by guards who keep crowds at a distance. Investigating persons, particularly persons seeking employment in positions of trust and responsibility.

screening coal. Putting coal through a screen for the purpose of removing the extremely small pieces, dirt, and other impurities.

scribere est agere (skrī'be-re est ā'je-re). To write is to act. That is, writing is the doing of an act.
Therefore, a bare writing with no publication of it may amount to a crime; as if the writer indicts treasonable matter. See 4 Bl Comm 80.

scrinio judicis. See **in scrinio judicis.**

scrip. A document representing fractional shares in a stock dividend. An order on the state treasurer to pay the sum named whenever available funds are in the treasury. Hays v McDaniel, 130 Ark 52, 58, 196 SW 934. A credit entered in a public land office entitling the holder or his assignee to select and appropriate a certain number of acres of public land in a given locality. Wait v Commissioner of State Land-Office, 87 Mich 353, 356, 49 NW 600. A substitute for money in the form of certificates of indebtedness, employed in various parts of the country during the extremity of the Great Depression, particularly during the days of enforced closing of the banks.

scrip coupon ticket. A railroad ticket good over connecting lines and interchangeable as between carriers. 49 USC § 22(1).

scrip dividend. A dividend on corporate stock consisting of a scrip or certificate entitling stockholders who receive it to the privileges and rights specified therein, sometimes a right to distribution of accumulated earnings at a later date, at other times a right to additional stock, bonds, or other obligations of the corporation. Staats v Biograph Co. (CA2 NY) 236 F 454. A certificate issued by a corporation to its stockholder evidencing the holder's title to the same extent of interest in the property and franchise as a stock dividend, except that the corporation has the right to pay the scrip dividend out of future earnings, and except also that the scrip dividend confers no right to vote. Bailey v New York Cent. & HRR Co. (US) 22 Wall 604, 22 L Ed 840. A stock dividend, represented by a certificate or scrip, of fractional shares.

script (skript). An original written instrument, as distinguished from a duplicate. The manuscript or typed copy of a play.

Scriptae obligationes scriptis tolluntur, et nudi consensus obligatio contrario consensu dissolvitur (skrip'te ob-li-gā-she-ō'nēz skrip'tis tol-lun'ter, et nu'dī kon-sen'sus ob-li-gā'she-ō kon-trā'ri-ō kon-sen'su dis-sol'vi-ter). Written obligations are released or discharged by writings, and an obligation of mere consent is dissolved or discharged by a consent to the contrary.

scriptis olim visis. See **ex scriptis olim visis.**

scriptum (skrip'tum). A written instrument; a writing.
See **script.**

scriptum indentatum (skrip'tum in-den-tā'tum). An indented writing; an indenture.

scriptum obligatorium (skrip'tum ob-li-gā-tō'ri-um). A writing obligatory; an instrument under seal; a bond.

scrivarius (skrī-vā'ri-us). An officer under the civil law who was also designated as registrarius and as actuarius and whose duties were similar to those of a modern notary public; anciently, a scribe, who only took notes or minutes, and made short drafts of writings and instruments, both public and private. 39 Am J1st Notary § 3.

scrivener (skriv'nėr). One who has drafted an instrument, for example, a will. One who follows the occupation of drafting instruments. A copyist; a scribe; a clerk; a conveyancer.

scroll (skrōl). A writing rolled up or designed to be rolled up. A scrawl or flourish intended as a seal.

scruple (skrö'pl). Doubt or hesitancy respecting action to be taken, for example, reluctance to take an oath.

scrutator (skrö-tā'tor). An officer whose duty it was to search the shores of a river for flotsam, jetsam, wreck, and the like and to guard the rights of the king therein.

scuffle (scuf'l). A disorderly pushing or struggle by two or more persons; a fight.

scupper (skup'ẽr). An opening in a bulkhead on a ship, made to permit water to run off the deck. The Wildwood (DC Wash) 41 F Supp 956.

scurrilous (skur'i-lus). Vulgar, indecent, or abusive. 33 Am J1st L & S § 54.

scurvy. A disease to which sailors were particularly susceptible in the past, resulting from deficiency in diet, particularly a deficiency in vitamin C.

scutage (skū'tāj). Money paid by the tenant to his lord in lieu of knight service. See 2 Bl Comm 74.

scutagio habendo. See **de scutagio habendo.**

scutagium (skū-tă'ji-um). Same as **scutage.**

scutifer (skū'ti-fẽr). The attendant of a knight; an esquire.

scuttling. Sinking a ship by opening holes below the water line. 48 Am J1st Ship § 636.

Scylla and Charybdis. See **between Scylla and Charybdis.**

s.d. Abbreviation of **sight draft.**

scutum (skū'tum). A large quadrangular wooden shield covered with hide; in feudal times signifying money paid in lieu of military service. See 2 Bl Comm 74.

Scylla and Charybdis. See **between Scylla and Charybdis.**

se (sē). Himself; themselves; itself; the very person; the very thing.
See **inter se; per se.**

S.E. Abbreviation of southeast.

SE ¼ An abbreviation of the southeast quarter of a section of land according to the government survey or of a lesser but square or rectangular portion of a section.

sea. The ocean. A salt-water arm of the ocean, even a river in which the tide ebbs and flows. Pacific Milling & Elevator Co. v Portland, 65 Or 349, 133 P 72. In the broader sense, any body of water of considerable size, whether fresh water or salt water.
See **at sea; four seas; perils of the sea.**

sea battery (bat'ẽr-i). A battery committed on the person of a seaman on the high seas.

sea brief (sē brēf). Same as **sea letter.**

sea burial. See **burial at sea.**

sea damaged. Damaged by exposure to a peril or perils of the sea.
A clause in a contract for the purchase of goods to be shipped by water, "sea damaged, if any, to be taken at a fair allowance," contemplates the risk of damage to the goods by perils of the sea, and does not restrict to any particular ship the subsequent transportation of the goods to their destination. Harrison v Fortlage, 161 US 57, 64, 40 L Ed 616, 619, 16 S Ct 488.

sea duty. See **sea service.**

seal. A symbol of authenticity. An impression made by means of an instrument or device, such as an engraved metallic plate, on wax or wafer affixed to an instrument, or directly upon the instrument itself. A scroll or other distinguishing mark placed upon an instrument as a seal. The word "seal" placed upon an instrument. The abbreviation "L.S." placed upon an instrument as a legal seal. 47 Am J1st Seals § 4. An essential of a deed at common law and under some statutes, 23 Am J2d Deeds §§ 1, 18, but disappearing from the requirements of the law with the expansion of literacy and the corresponding ability of a grantor to affix his own signature with legibility sufficient to authenticate the instrument as one representing his own act and deed. 47 Am J1st Seals § 8.
See **official seal; sealed and delivered.**

sea laws. A term sometimes applied to the sailing regulations which were founded in ancient usage and sanctioned by the adjudications of admiralty and prize courts, and which until comparatively recent times furnished the principal rules of navigation. 48 Am J1st Ship § 244.

sea lawyer. A term applied facetiously to a sailor who talks volubly of the legal rights of sailors, also to a person in another walk of life but contentious in respect of legal rights.

sealed. Having a seal affixed; under seal.
See **sealing ceremony.**

sealed and acknowledged. The equivalent of "sealed and delivered" in a certificate of acknowledgment. 1 Am J2d Ack § 75.

sealed and delivered. A phrase in a certificate of acknowledgment reciting the execution of the instrument by the person acknowledging. 1 Am J2d Ack § 75.
The intention to seal, whether expressed or implied, does not make a seal. The recital "signed, sealed and delivered," or the words "whereunto we have affixed our seals," do not make a sealed instrument, if as a fact nothing is affixed to the signatures which the law recognizes as a seal. Empire Trust Co. v Heinze, 242 NY 475, 478, 152 NE 266.

sealed contract. See **contract under seal; specialty.**

sealed grain. Grain in a field warehouse or granary, particularly grain pledged for the payment of a government loan made in a price-support program.
See **field warehousing; sealing up.**

sealed instrument. See **seal; sealed.**

sealed verdict. A verdict reached by agreement during a recess of the court, signed and sealed, to be presented and affirmed by the jury at the next opening of the court. 58 Am J1st Trial § 1010.

sealer. A public officer having the duty of inspecting scales or other measuring devices and placing a seal upon such as are found to be accurate. 56 Am J1st Wts & L § 21.

sea-letter. A ship's passport furnished by the customhouse, under the signature of the President of the United States and the secretary of state and usually issued only in time of war. Sleght v Rhinelander (NY) 1 Johns 192, 203.

sea level. The level of the sea, midway between high and low tide; the point from which heights on land are indicated.

sealing ceremony. The form of solemnization of marriages required of its members by the Mormon Church, the same being sufficient to constitute a valid marriage between persons competent to enter into a marriage, assuming that requirements imposed by law other than the matter of ceremony are met. Hilton v Roylance, 25 Utah 129, 69 P 660.

sealing up. Affixing a seal, usually a metal seal, to the door of a building or the cover of a container in such position that the seal must be broken in order to open the door or raise the cover. An act

SEALING [1148] SEARCH

of dominion over a safe sufficient to perfect a levy upon the contents thereof. 30 Am J2d Exec § 242.

sealing valve. A valve on a gas meter with so close a bearing as absolutely to stop the flow of gas when adequately closed. Gill v Eakin, 203 Miss 204, 33 So 2d 821.

seal of corporation. See **corporate seal.**

seal of court. An instrument authenticating by imprint or otherwise the process and writs issued by the court. 42 Am J1st Proc § 12. A requirement in the case of a court of record. Aikman v Edwards, 55 Kan 751, 42 P 366; Van Norman v Gordon, 172 Mass 576, 53 NE 267.

seal of the United States. The great seal of the Federal Government of which the secretary of state is the custodian.

The signature of the President is the warrant for affixing the great seal to an instrument executed by the President and is only to be affixed to an instrument which is complete. It attests by an act supposed to be of public notoriety, the verity of the presidential signature. Marbury v Madison (US) 1 Cranch 137, 158, 2 L Ed 60, 67.

seal of the United States Supreme Court (sēl ov thē ū-nī'ted stāts sụ̄-prēm' kọrt). The arms of the United States on a piece of steel the size of a dollar, with the words in the margin "The Seal of the Supreme Court of the United States." Rule 1, adopted at the February term, 1790. 1 L Ed 432.

seals of private credit. Seals used by private persons or private corporations. 47 Am J1st Seals § 3.

seals of public credit. Seals kept and used by public authority. Kirksey v Dates (Ala) 7 Port 529. The Great Seal of the United States; the Great Seal of a state, the seals of courts of record, and other seals of which judicial notice is taken.

In England, such seals are those of the king and of his ancient and public courts of justice, the great seal of the United Kingdom, the great seals of England, Scotland, and Ireland and the seal of the Corporation of London. 47 Am J1st Seals § 3.

seam. The line where pieces of cloth are joined with thread. A layer of coal or other mineral underground; a fissure carrying ore or other valuable mineral. 36 Am J1st Min & M § 83.

A term often used synonymously with the word "stringer," and commonly understood by miners to be a crack or crevice filled by mineral deposit, and occurring in the country rock, and by means of which the prospector anticipates being led to an ore body or deposit of commercial value. Oftentimes, a "discovery" is made on a "seam," and if so made, the location is valid in law. McShane v Kenkle, 18 Mont 208, 44 P 979.

seaman. An enlisted man of the Navy, ranking immediately above seaman apprentice and immediately below petty officer, third class. Broadly, a person whose occupation is to assist in the management of a vessel at sea. Holt v Cummings, 102 Pa 212. A member of the crew of a ship; a mariner. Scharrenberg v Dollar S.S. Co. 245 US 122, 127, 62 L Ed 189, 193, 38 S Ct 28. A common sailor and, for some purposes, any person performing a maritime service, such as a mate, pilot, purser, steward, etc. 48 Am J1st Ship § 144. In one sense, including master, a ship's officer, ship's surgeon, as well as a member of the crew. 47 Am J1st Salv § 20 (as person entitled to salvage).

The term as used in various statutes, is a flexible term, the meaning of which depends upon the circumstances in which it is used and the purpose of a particular statute in which it occurs. Anno: 161 ALR 832.

See **mariner.**

seaman apprentice. An enlisted man of the Navy, ranking immediately above a seaman recruit and immediately below a seaman.

seaman at sea. For the purposes of executing a valid seaman's will, on board a vessel which has left the wharf and is being navigated for the purposes of the voyage upon which he shipped as a member of the crew, not withstanding the vessel is still in a river, perhaps in a harbor, rather than on the open sea. 57 Am J1st Wills § 663.

seaman recruit. An enlisted man of the Navy, of the lowest rank.

seaman's lien. The lien which a seaman has on the ship for his wages, which he may enforce either in a court of admiralty or a court of common law. 48 Am J1st Ship §§ 161, 162.

seaman's will. The informal will of a seaman, whether oral or in writing, rendered valid, where the will of a person of another occupation would be invalid, under an exception from compliance with the formalities required to be observed in the execution of wills generally, recognized because of the dangers, diseases, disasters, and the possibility of sudden death constantly besetting a seaman and the inability of such a person to find the time or the means to make a deliberate and written testamentary disposition. 57 Am J1st Wills § 661.

sea mile. Same as **nautical mile.**

seance (sā'äns). A demonstration in which a medium purports to communicate with departed spirits. McMasters v State, 21 Okla Crim 318, 207 P 566, 29 ALR 292.

sea pay. Increased pay because of performance of sea duty. 36 Am J1st Mil § 71.

See **sea service.**

sea perils. See **perils of the sea.**

seaplane. An aircraft constructed and equipped for landing upon water; a vessel or marine object for some purposes, particularly the rules of navigation and the law of salvage. 8 Am J2d Avi § 20.

A seaplane is a mechanical device for aerial navigation, within the meaning of provision in accident policy exempting insurer from liability for injuries, fatal or nonfatal, sustained by insured while in or on any vehicle or mechanical device for aerial navigation, or in falling therefrom or therewith or while operating or handling any such vehicle or device. Wendorff v Missouri State Life Ins. Co. 318 Mo 363, 1 SW2d 99, 57 ALR 615.

sea port. See **port.**

search. A matter of invasion and quest, implying some sort of force, actual or constructive, much or little. State v Quinn, 111 SC 174, 97 SE 62, 3 ALR 1500. A quest by an officer of the law, secret, intrusive, or accompanied by force. Hale v Henkel, 201 US 43, 80, 50 L Ed 652, 668, 26 S Ct 370. An examination or inspection, by authority of law, of one's premises or person, with a view to the discovery of stolen, contraband, or illicit property, or of evidence of guilt to be used in the prosecution of a criminal action for some crime or offense with which one is charged. Newberry v Carpenter, 107 Mich 567, 65 NW 530. The right of a belligerent to search a merchant ship of a neutral nation at sea,

or its papers, for contraband or for enemy subjects. 56 Am J1st War § 152. Inspection of a home by a health officer. District of Columbia v Little, 85 App DC 242, 178 F2d 13, 13 ALR2d 954.
See **search and seizure; title search.**

search and seizure. Means for the detection and punishment of crime; the search for and taking custody of property unlawfully obtained or unlawfully held, such as stolen goods, property forfeited for violation of the law, and property the use or possession of which is prohibited by law, and the discovery and taking into legal custody of books, papers, and other things constituting or containing evidence of crime.
See **search warrant; unreasonable search and seizure.**

searching record. The familiar rule that a demurrer or its equivalent in a motion searches the whole record, is carried back to the first substantial defect, and that judgment is to be given against the party who committed the first fault in pleading, for him who, upon the whole record, appears entitled to judgment. 41 Am J1st Pl § 232.

search warrant. A form of criminal process which may be invoked only in furtherance of a public prosecution. An order in writing, in the name of the people, the state, or the commonwealth, according to the local practice, signed by a magistrate, and directed to a peace officer, commanding him to search for personal property and bring it before a magistrate. 47 Am J1st Search § 3. An examination or inspection, by authority of law, of one's premises or person, with a view to the discovery of stolen, contraband, or illicit property, or some evidence of guilt to be used in the prosecution of a criminal action for some crime or offense with which he is charged. 47 Am J1st Search § 4.
See **blanket search warrant.**

sea service. Service in the Navy performed at sea under the orders of a department, and in vessels employed by authority of law. 36 Am J1st Mil § 71

seashore. See **shore.**

season. A division of the year, as spring, summer, fall, or winter, recognized because of distinctive condition of the weather, the number of hours of daylight, the growth, and maturity of plants. The business year in theatrical, recreational, or entertainment ventures and in winter and summer resorts. A period wherein the taking of particular game or fish is permitted or not permitted, depending upon whether the designation is that of an open or closed season.
See **closed season; open season.**

seasonable appearance. An appearance within season; that is, a defendant's appearance in an action within the time allowed by law, after the service of the summons upon him.

seasonable motion. A motion made in good time, that is, timely in reference to the situation of the adverse party, each case being controlled by the particular circumstances, if not by express statute. Layton v Lee (Del) 196 A2d 578.

seasonably. Acting at or within the time agreed, or if no time is agreed, at or within a reasonable time. UCC § 1—204(3).

seasonably turn. A term often employed in a rule of the road, meaning that the operators of vehicles proceeding in the opposite direction shall, upon meeting in the highway, turn to the right in such time that neither shall be retarded in his progress by reason of the other occupying the half of the way which the law has assigned to his use, when he may have occasion to use it in passing. Cupples Mercantile Co. v Bow, 32 Idaho 774, 189 P 48, 24 ALR 1296, ovrld on another point Hamilton v Carpenter, 49 Idaho 629, 200 P 724; Neal v Rendall, 98 Me 69, 56 A 209. Turn in season to prevent a collision. Bragdon v Kellogg, 118 Me 42, 105 A 433, 6 ALR 669, 671.

seasonal. Of or pertaining to the season. To be expected of the season at hand, as a seasonal sickness or seasonal weather. Lincoln Gas & Electric Co. v Watkins, 113 Neb 619, 204 NW 391.

seasonal conditions. Conditions of the weather peculiar to a particular season of the year. Layman v State Unemployment Compensation Com. 167 Or 379, 117 P2d 974, 136 ALR 1468. Any condition of temperature, health of persons or animals, or the growth of plants reasonably to be expected during a particular season of the year.
See **seasonal.**

seasonal employment. Employment in occupations which can be carried on only at certain seasons or fairly definite portions of the year. Hogsett v Cinek Coal & Feed Co. 127 Neb 393, 255 NW 546, 93 ALR 305.

seasonal flood. A flood normally to be expected to occur in a stream at certain seasons or at other regular intervals due to the usual manifestations of nature in precipitation of water at such times. 56 Am J1st Wat § 91.

seasonal industry. An industry whose activities for the most part are confined to a particular season or particular seasons of the year, for example, the packing or processing of fruits and vegetables. 31 Am J Rev ed Lab § 699.

seasonal service. Service by a carrier during the harvesting season when additional cars are required for the moving of crops. 13 Am J2d Car § 157.

seasonal stream. A stream which flows only during that part of the year when rains occur. 56 Am J1st Wat § 9.

seasonal use. The use of real property, not continuous but seasonal, as for crop-raising, fishing, logging, taking off ice, etc. 3 Am J2d Adv P § 57.

sea stores. The supplies of different articles provided for the subsistence and accommodation of the ship's crew and passengers. United States v Hawley & Letzerich (DC Tex) 160 F 734.

seat. To place a person in a seat, literally or figuratively, as to seat one elected or appointed to an office. In a rare sense, to settle upon land. Hawkins v Barney's Lessee (US) 5 Pet 457, 468, 8 L Ed 190, 194.
See **seated land.**

seat belt. A requirement in a passenger aircraft; a contrivance of heavy bands with buckles for fastening one's person to the seat or floor as a protection in case of a sudden movement in the air or an unexpected but possible occurrence fraught with peril upon takeoff or landing. The requirement of such a contrivance now made by statute in most jurisdictions in respect of automobiles, intended as a protection against injury in collisions, upsets, skids, and sudden stops.

seated land. Occupied or cultivated land; land producing a revenue. Stoetzel v Jackson, 105 Pa 562, 567.

seat of county. See **county seat.**

seat of court. The place of holding court, usually fixed by constitution or statute. 20 Am J2d Cts § 37.
See **county seat.**

seat of government. The place where the primary instrumentalities of government are located, especially the legislative and executive branches. The capital city of a state. The District of Columbia. 24 Am J2d D C § 1.

seat of justice. See **county seat; seat of court.**

seat on exchange. A term of art for membership in a stock or commodity exchange, constituting a right to do business on the exchange, subject to the rules thereof. Sometimes regarded as property, at other times as a mere personal license or privilege, but in any event a thing of value, often of great value. 50 Am J1st Stock Ex § 11.

sea watch. A ship's lookout composed of one or two men designated to perform that duty while half of the ship's crew is on duty at sea. O'Hara v Luckenbach S.S. Co. 269 US 364, 371, 70 L Ed 313, 317, 46 S Ct 157.
See **watch.**

seaweed. Vegetation grown in the sea but cast upon the shore by the action of the water. Carr v Carpenter, 22 RI 528, 48 A 805.
See **kelp.**

seaworthy. Able to withstand the forces of the sea. Fireman's Fund Ins Co. v Compania de Navegacion (CA5 La) 19 F2d 493. Reasonably fit, from the standpoint of a vessel, to perform the service which she has undertaken to perform. Tight, staunch, strong in the hull, well furnished and victualed, and in all respects equipped in the usual manner for the service in which she is engaged, including a crew, adequate in number and sufficient and competent for the voyage, and a master of skill, competence, sound judgment and discretion. 48 Am J1st Ship § 44. The condition of a ship staunch and sound, of sufficient materials and construction, with sufficient sails, tackle, rigging, cables, anchors, stores, and supplies, commanded by a master of competent skill and capacity, worked by a competent and sufficient crew, and generally, in every respect, fit for the voyage contemplated. 29A Am J Rev ed Ins § 999.

A ship which is badly stowed is unseaworthy. The Malcolm Baxter, Jr. French Overseas Corp. v French Republic (CA2 NY) 20 F2d 304.

seaworthiness. See **seaworthy.**

sebastomania (sē-bas-tō-mā'ni-ą). Religious mania.

se bene gerendo. See **de se bene gerendo.**

SEC. Abbreviation of Securities and Exchange Commission.

sec. An abbreviation of security. Harrison v Cravens, 25 Tenn App 215, 155 SW2d 873.

The letters "sec." appearing after the name of a signer on a promissory note are to some extent indicative that the relation of principal and surety existed between such signer and the other signers. Koblegard Co. v Maxwell, 127 W Va 630, 34 SE2d 116.

secession. A withdrawal from membership in an organized group. The attempted but ineffectual withdrawal of eleven southern states from the Union established by the United States Constitution.

The attempt of a state to withdraw from the United States. The Union of states is perpetual and indissoluble, and no state has the right to secede therefrom, nor will its attempt to separate itself from the Union destroy its identity as a state, or free it from the binding force of the Federal Constitution. 49 Am J1st States § 16.
See **schism.**

seck (sek). Without the right or remedy of distraining.
See **rent seck.**

seclusion. A withdrawal from society. A voluntary confinement. Phelps v Reinach, 38 La Ann 547, 551.

secondarily liable. See **secondary liability.**

second arrest. See **rearrest.**

secondary agreement. Same as **secondary contract.**

secondary boycott. A boycott applied with the purpose of bringing an alleged offender to terms by refusing to have any business relations with persons dealing with such offender, until he has yielded to the demand for terms. 31 Am J Rev ed Lab § 463; 36 Am J1st Monop etc § 27. A combination, not merely to refrain from dealing with a person, or to advise or by peaceable means persuade his customers to refrain, but to exercise coercive pressure upon such customers, actual or prospective, in order to cause them to withhold or withdraw patronage from him through fear of loss or damage to themselves should they deal with him. Duplex Printing Press Co. v Deering, 254 US 443, 65 L Ed 349, 41 S Ct 172, 16 ALR 196. A combination of many to injure one in his business by coercing third persons against their will to cease patronizing him by threats of similar injury. Truax v Corrigan, 257 US 312, 66 L Ed 254, 42 S Ct 124, 27 ALR 375, per opinion of Chief Justice Taft. An attempt by a labor organization or its agents to exercise coercive pressure upon an employer, not directly concerned in a labor dispute, by inducing or encouraging his employees to engage in a strike or concerted refusal to work in an effort to bring about some adverse action by such employer against an employer with which the labor organization has a labor dispute. Anno: 96 L Ed 284.

secondary contract. A contract which modifies or supersedes a prior contract known as the primary contract. 17 Am J2d Contr § 459.
See **subcontract.**

secondary conveyances. Same as **derivative conveyances.**

secondary distribution value. The value of a comparatively large block of corporate stock, calculated on the assumption that the most prudent method of disposal calls for marketing a part of the stock from time to time rather than throw the entire block on the market. Newberry v Walsh, 20 NJ 484, 120 A2d 242.

secondary easement. An easement appurtenant or incident to the principal or primary one.

Every easement includes secondary easements; that is, the right to do such things as are necessary for the full enjoyment of the easement itself. But this right is limited and must be exercised in such a reasonable manner as not injuriously to increase the burden upon the servient tenement. The burden of the dominant estate cannot be enlarged to the manifest injury of the servient estate by any alteration in the mode of enjoying the former. The owner must not trespass upon the servient tenement beyond the limits fixed by the grant or use. North Fork Water Co. v Edwards, 121 Cal 662, 54 P 69.

secondary evidence. Evidence which is not the primary or best evidence of which the case is susceptible. Evidence admissible of necessity, although not primary evidence, because of the impossibility of producing the primary evidence, as where an instrument pertinent to a case has been lost or destroyed without fault on the part of the party who otherwise would produce it in evidence, in which case, a true copy or oral evidence of the contents is admissible. 29 Am J2d Evi §§ 448 et seq.

secondary franchise. The powers granted to a corporation by the sovereign and specified in its charter or by statute. 18 Am J2d Corp § 66. Any of those franchises of a corporation other than its right or franchise to be a corporation, which is the primary franchise. Virginia Cañon Toll Road Co. v People ex rel. Vivian, 22 Colo 429, 45 P 398.

secondary liability. The liability on an instrument of any person who is not primarily liable thereon. 11 Am J2d B & N § 525. The liability of one of two tortfeasors liable to the same injured person of such nature in reference to the liability of the other tortfeasor that he is entitled to assert a liability over the other tortfeasor for indemnification as to payment required to be made by him to the injured person. The liability of an employer for injury to a third person caused by the act of the employee. Schubert v August Shubert Wagon Co. 249 NY 253, 164 NE 42, 64 ALR 293.

Primary and secondary liability, essential for a right of indemnity, are not based on a difference in degrees of negligence or on any doctrine of comparative negligence, but on a difference in the character or kind of wrongs which cause the injury, and in the nature of the legal obligation owed by each of the wrongdoers to the injured person. Builders Supply Co. v McCabe, 366 Pa 322, 77 A2d 368, 24 ALR2d 319.

secondary meaning. A meaning of a word or phrase additional to its primary meaning, for example, the meaning of the word "sheep" as a timid person. A special or trade meaning acquired by usage in connection with one's goods, services, or business. Anno: 150 ALR 1068; 23 ALR2d 260.

secondary obligation. See **secondary liability.**

secondary party. A party to an instrument but under a secondary liability.

A guaranty of payment endorsed on a note, while creating an absolute obligation to pay, does not make the guarantor a primary party, and since his liability is secondary, he is released by an extension of time to the maker of the note. Winkle v Scott (CA8 Mo) 99 F2d 299.

secondary school. A high school. 47 Am J1st Sch § 4.

secondary service wire. A line supplying electric current to a household, place of business, or factory. Anno: 40 ALR2d 1322, § 8.

second class mail. Newspapers and other periodical publications. 41 Am J1st P O § 57.

second cousin. The same as first cousin once removed. Re O'Mara's Estate, 106 NJ Eq 311, 151 A 67. The child of a first cousin. Anno: 54 ALR2d 1011. A relative in the fifth degree according to the civil law method of computing degrees of kinship which prevails in most American jurisdictions. 23 Am J2d Desc & D § 48.

The children of one's first cousins are sometimes popularly called his second cousins, but are, more properly, his first cousins once removed. Culver v Union & N. H. Trust Co. 120 Conn 97, 179 A 487, 99 ALR 663.

second cousin once removed. The child of a second cousin. A relative in the sixth degree according to the civil law method of computing kinship which prevails in most jurisdictions. Anno: 54 ALR2d 1012, § 1(b). Often called a third cousin.

second degree burglary. A daytime burglary. The breaking and entering of an uninhabited dwelling house or apartment, or a dwelling house or apartment not actually occupied at the time, with intent to commit a felony. 13 Am J2d Burgl § 28.

second degree manslaughter. See **manslaughter.**

second degree murder. See **murder in the second degree.**

second degree principal. See **principal in second degree.**

second degree relationship. A degree of kinship, including brothers, sisters, grandparents and grandchildren, according to the civil law method of computing degrees of kinship which prevails in most American jurisdictions. 23 Am J2d Desc & D § 48.

See **degrees of kinship.**

second deliverance. The remedy of a nonsuited plaintiff in replevin.

In an action of replevin, the statute of Westm. II c 2 (1285), restrained a plaintiff, when nonsuited, from suing out a fresh replevin, but allowed him a writ of second deliverance by means of which he could again secure possession of the goods by giving security as before. See 3 Bl Comm 150.

second delivery. The delivery by a depositary in escrow pursuant to the terms of the deposit. 28 Am J2d Escr § 10.

See **redelivery.**

second distress. A new distress which was levied where the first one was not sufficient to satisfy or secure the demand of the plaintiff.

secondhand. Any material or article of which prior use has been made. Weaver v Palmer Bros. Co. 270 US 402 409, 70 L Ed 654, 656, 46 S Ct 320.

secondhand automobile. A used car. 47 Am J1st Sec H D § 11.

secondhand dealer. A dealer in secondhand goods. 47 Am J1st Sec H D § 2.

secondhand dealer's license. A license required of a secondhand dealer as a regulatory measure. 47 Am J1st Sec H D § 3.

secondhand evidence. Hearsay.

secondhand goods. Goods of which prior use has been made. Weaver v Palmer Bros. Co. 270 US 402, 70 L Ed 654, 46 S Ct 320.

secondhand store. Any store in which any kind of secondhand goods are dealt in, for example, secondhand furniture or secondhand books. 47 Am J1st Sec H D § 2.

secondhand value. The value of a used article, taking account of the inability to reflect the merely personal regard of the owner for such items as household goods and clothing in estimating the value. 22 Am J2d Damg § 150.

second indictment. See **reindictment.**

second jeopardy. See **prior jeopardy**.

second lieutenant. A commissioned officer of the Army, holding the lowest rank of commissioned officers. A commissioned officer of the Marine Corps of comparable rank.

second mortgage. A junior mortgage, a mortgage to which another mortgage is prior.

second of exchange. The second of a set of bills of exchange, drawn in duplicate or triplicate, the honor of any one of which avoids the others. Bank of Pittsburgh v Neal (US) 22 How 96, 16 L Ed 323.

second of exchange, first unpaid. A notation appearing on the face of a bill of exchange for the purpose of indicating that it is one of a set of the same bill. 11 Am J2d B & N § 61.

second resolution in Wild's Case. A principle declared in a famous English decision (Wild's Case, 6 Coke 16d, 77 Eng Reprint 227):—where there is a devise to one and his or her children, and there are children in existence, it will be presumed, in the absence of any contrary indication in the context, that the parent and children were intended to take a fee concurrently. Anno: 161 ALR 629 et seq; 28 Am J2d Est § 69.

seconds. Those persons who attend upon the respective combatants in the fighting of a duel and who attend to the requisite formalities, before and after the combat. Those persons who attend upon the participants in a boxing match or prize fight. Articles of merchandise with some defects or imperfections, but nevertheless of value.

The terms "firsts" and "seconds" are terms of quality, common in mercantile usage. See Iselin v United States, 271 US 136, 138, 70 L Ed 872, 873, 46 S Ct 458.

second surcharge (sėr'chärj). A writ issued against a person who had surcharged a common after there had been an admeasurement of pasture. See 3 Bl Comm 239.

secret. Undisclosed. That which is not communicated or disclosed.
See **trade secret**.

secretary. A person employed to take care of correspondence and records in an office, sometimes vested with responsibility in the management of the office.

secretary of corporation. A corporate officer, sometimes having no function other than that of keeping a record of the business transacted at stockholders', directors', and committee meetings, but ordinarily possessing inherent or implied power to perform certain acts necessary to the transaction of the business of the corporation. 19 Am J2d Corp § 1172.

Secretary of State. The head of the United States State Department and ranking member of the Cabinet. A state office, ordinarily created by constitutional provisions.

As a rule his duties are such as those of countersigning and affixing the great seal of the state to commissions, official acts, and other instruments issued or executed by the governor; the certifying to state measures; the filing of petitions under initiative and referendum laws; the filing of certificates of nomination under certain laws; the canvassing of returns of state elections; and the keeping of public state records. 49 Am J1st States § 53.
See **State Department**.

secret assault. An assault made in such a manner that the person assailed is prevented from seeing who his assailant is and from repelling the assault. State v Jennings, 104 NC 774, 776, 10 SE 249.

secret ballot. A method of election essential to the preservation of the integrity of the election. A secret method of voting at an election. Johnson v Clark (DC Tex) 25 F Supp 285.

secrete (sę̇-krēt). To conceal. To hide property; to put property where an officer of the law will probably be unable to find it. 6 Am J2d Attach § 236. To hide in some place of secrecy. Darneal v State, 14 Okla Crim 540, 174 P 290.

secret formula. A formula for the production of a substance or article; a formula of value in improvement of product or in stepping up production. 52 Am J1st Tradem § 138.

secret hearing. See **closed trial or hearing**.

secret lien. A lien which does not appear of record or in any other manner so as to be noticed by purchasers and encumbrancers. Palmer v Howard, 72 Cal 293, 13 P 858.

secret partnership. A partnership composed of persons one or more of whom is not disclosed to the public as a member of the firm. Winship v Bank of the United States (US) 5 Pet 529, 561, 8 L Ed 216, 228.

secret process. A mechanical or industrial process of value as an improvement of product or in an increase of production per unit of time. 52 Am J1st Tradem § 138.

Such a method of manufacture or operation in the production of a commercial product as is understood to constitute a process under the patent laws; a mode of treatment of certain materials to produce a given result. It is a conception of the mind seen only by its results. Thus, where the ingredients used in the manufacture of an article were well known, but by combining them by a different method from any other in use the result is a product of a different character from that produced by the ordinary method of combining them, the method of mixing the ingredients and so treating them is a secret process. Taylor Iron & Steel Co. v Nichols, 133 Am St Rep 760.

The difference between a secret process and a patent is that the owner of a patent has a monopoly against all the world, while the owner of a secret process has no right except against those who have contracted, expressly or by implication, not to disclose the secret, or who have obtained it by unfair means. The jurisdiction of equity to protect such trade secrets is founded upon trust and confidence. The court fastens the obligation upon the conscience of the party, and enforces it against him in the same manner as it enforces against a party to whom a benefit is given, the obligation of performing a promise on the faith of which the benefit has been conferred. Whether the subject matter is patentable or not, if the designer discovers and keeps secret a process of manufacture, though he will not have an exclusive right to it as against the public, after he shall have published it, or against those who in good faith acquire knowledge of it, yet he has a property right, which a court of chancery will protect against one who in bad faith and breach of confidence undertakes to apply it to his own use. Smoley v New Jersey Zinc Co. (DC NJ) 24 F Supp 294.

secret profit. A profit or advantage obtained by a promoter, director, or officer of a corporation by reason of his official position without bringing the transaction to the attention of the stockholders. 18 Am J2d Corp §§ 111-117; 19 Am J2d Corp § 1281.

A profit is not secret or unlawful if all the parties having a direct interest know of it and assent to it, or do not repudiate it. Hays v The Georgian, 280 Mass 10, 181 NE 765, 85 ALR 1251.

secret society. A society whose meetings are for the most part closed to the public, limited strictly to members, employing signs and ritual which are secret, being protected against disclosure by an obligation under oath taken by each member.
See **lodge**.

secrets of state. See **state secret**.

secrets of trade. See **trade secrets**.

secret testament. Same as **mystic testament**.

secret trust. A term frequently applied to any express or implied arrangement or understanding between a testator and a legatee whereby the latter is to take ostensibly as an ordinary legatee under the will of the testator, but is thereafter to apply the bequest or a part of it toward some charitable purpose; the real design of the bequest being to circumvent the statute limiting charitable bequests and devises. 15 Am J2d Char § 28.

secret vote. The ordinary election by ballot as conducted in the United States. 26 Am J2d Elect § 234.
See **secret ballot**.

sect (sekt). See **religious sect**.

secta (sek'tạ). Suit in court. The followers of the plaintiff in an ancient common-law action, who accompanied him to court to support the averments of his declaration. See 3 Bl Comm 295.

secta ad curiam (sek'ta ad kū'ri-am). A writ which lay against a party who refused to perform his suit at the county court or court-baron.—Cowell.

secta ad furnum (sek'ta ad fer'num). Suit at the furnace. See **secta ad molendinum**. See 3 Bl Comm 235.

secta ad molendinum (sek'ta ad mo-len-dī'num). A writ to compel the defendant to grind his corn at the plaintiff's mill.

The writ lay where the plaintiff enjoyed this right by custom or prescription. Likewise, a man had a writ of secta ad furnum, secta ad torrale, et ad omnia alia hujusmodi (his suit at the oven, his suit at the kiln and all others of the same kind;) for their suit or service due to his public oven, his bake house or his kiln. See 3 Bl Comm 235.

secta ad torrale (sek'ta ad tor-rā'le). Suit at the bake house.
See **secta ad molendinum**.

secta curiae (sek'ta kū'ri-ē). A tenant's attendance at court, as an incident of certain feudal tenure.

Secta est pugna civilis, sicut actores armantur actionibus, et quasi, accinguntur gladiis, ita rei (e contra) muniuntur exceptionibus, et defenduntur, quasi, clypeis (sek'ta est pug'na si'vi-lis, sik'ut aktō'rēz ar-man'ter ak-she-ō'ni-bus, et quā'sī, ak-singun'ter gla'di-is, i'ta re-ī (e kon'tra) mū-ni-un'ter ex-sep-she-ō'ni-bus, et de-fen-dun'ter, quā'sī, kli'pe-is). A suit is a civil fight, and just as the plaintiffs are armed with actions and, as it were, girded with swords, so the defendants are, on the other hand, fortified with pleas and defended, as it were, with shields.

Secta quae scripto nititur a scripto variari non debet (sek'ta kwē skrip'to ni'ti-ter a skrip'to va-ri-ā'rī non de'bet). A suit which is founded upon a writing ought not to vary from the writing.

sectarian (sek-tā'ri-ạn). Pertaining to some one of the various religious sects. People ex rel. Vollmar v Stanley, 81 Colo 276, 255 P 610.

Those religious doctrines are sectarian which are the doctrines of one religious sect and are not shared in common with other religious sects. State ex rel. Weiss v District Board of School Dist. 76 Wis 177, 44 NW 967.

sectarian book. A book which shows that it teaches the peculiar dogmas of a religious sect as such.

A book is not sectarian which merely comprehends the dogmas as interpreted by a part of the adherents of a sect; nor is a book sectarian merely because it was edited or compiled by a person of a particular sect. It is not the authorship or the mechanical composition, but the contents which give the book its character. Hackett v Brooksville School Dist. 120 Ky 608, 87 SW 792.

sectarian college or university. A college or university maintained by a church or religious sect. 15 Am J2d Colleges § 31.

sectarian instruction. As prohibited in public schools by constitutional provision, an instruction in religious doctrine, particularly a doctrine believed by some religious sects and rejected by others. State ex rel. Freeman v Scheve, 65 Neb 853, 91 NW 846, 93 NW 169.

sectarianism. Teaching or publicizing religious belief in a public institution, especially a public school. 47 Am J1st Sch § 208.

sectarian purpose. A purpose in aid or futherance of some religious sect or denomination. People ex rel. Vollmar v Stanley, 81 Colo 276, 255 P 610.

sectarian school. A school maintained by a church or religious body, usually giving sectarian instruction. A school which fosters and, in its instruction, to some extent, propagates the belief and doctrine of some particular religious sect. Hackett v Brooksville School Dist. 120 Ky 608, 87 SW 792.

To constitute a sectarian school or sectarian institution which may not lawfully be maintained at public expense, it is not necessary to show that the school is wholly devoted to religious or sectarian instruction. Knowlton v Baumhover, 22 Iowa 691, 166 NW 202, 5 ALR 841.
See **parochial school**.

sectarian teaching. See **sectarian instruction**.

sector (sek-tā'tọr). A suitor; a tenant who owed to his lord the service of secta curiae, that is, of attendance at court.

section. A numbered area of 640 acres in a square, according to the governmental survey of public lands. In common usage, an area of 640 acres according to the government survey in any combination of parts. A region contained in a much larger area. A distinct part of a book or article. A subdivision of a chapter, indicated by the character "§". A subdivision or paragraph of a statute or code. See Lehmann v Revell, 354 Ill 262, 188 NE 531; State v Babcock, 23 Neb 128, 133.

sectional prejudice. Local prejudice. Anno: 78 ALR 1456.

section boss. An employee of a railroad who directs the work of section hands, having duties comparable to those of a foreman in an industry.

section hand. A railroad worker employed in the maintenance of roadbed and track.

section number. The number given a section of land laid out by the government survey. See **township.**

sectores (sek-tō'rēz). (Roman law.) The successful bidders or buyers at a public auction.

secular (sek'ū-lạr). Temporal; pertaining to temporal things, things of the world; worldly; distinguished from the holy or spiritual. Allen v Deming, 14 NH 133, 139.

secular business. An engagement in secular things, such as the giving of a note. Allen v Deming, 14 NH 133, 139.

secular clergy (klėr'ji). Those members of the clergy who did not belong to any monastery or religious house, as distinguished from the regular clergy who did.

secular day. A day other than Sunday. A day for the transaction of business generally. State v Duncan, 118 La 702, 43 So 283.

secundum (sẹ-kun'dum). According to; in accordance with; in favor of. Following; coming close behind.
See **Corpus Juris Secundum.**

secundum aequum et bonum (se-kun'dum ē'qu-um et bō'num). According to justice and right.

secundum allegata (se-kun'dum al-le-gā'ta). According to the allegations; that is, according to the allegations contained in the pleadings. See 3 Bl Comm 142.

secundum allegata et probata (se-kun'dum al-le-gā'ta et prō-bā'ta). According to the pleadings and the proofs.

secundum consuetudinem manerii (se-kun'dum kon-su-e-tū'di-nem ma-ne'ri-ī). According to the custom of the manor.

secundum formam chartae (se-kun'dum for'mam kar'tē). According to the form of the deed or charter.

secundum formam doni (se-kun'dum for'mam dō'nī). According to the form of the gift.

secundum formam statuti (se-kun'dum for'mam sta-tū'tī). According to the form of the statute.

secundum legem communem Angliae (se-kun'dum lē'jem kom-mū'nem ang'li-ē). According to the common law of England.

secundum legem et consuetudinem Angliae (se-kun'-dum lē'jem et kon-su-e-tū'di-nem an'gli-ē). According to the law and custom of England. See 4 Bl Comm 262.

secundum naturam (se-kun'dum na-tū'ram). According to the nature; according to nature; natural.

Secundum naturam est, commoda cujusque rei eum sequi, quem sequentur incommoda (se-kun'dum na-tū'ram est, kom'mo-da kū-jus'kwe re'ī e'um se'quī, quem se-quen'ter in-kom'mo-da). It is according to nature that he who has the benefit of the thing should have the burden.

secundum normam legis (se-kun'dum nor'mam lē'jis). According to the rule of law.

secundum probata (se-kun'dum prō-bā'ta). According to the proofs; that is, according to the evidence brought out at the trial.

secundum regulam (se-kun'dum re-gū'lam). According to rule.

secundum regulas (se-kun'dum re-gū'lās). According to the rules. See 1 Bl Comm 387.

secundum subjectam materiam (se-kun'dum sub-jek'tam ma-te'ri-am). According to the subject matter. See 1 Bl Comm 229.

secundum usum mercatorum (se-kun'dum ū'sum mer-ka-tō'rum). According to the custom of merchants; that is, according to the "law merchant."

secure. Adjective: Stable; unlikely to fail or fall. Free from worry. Not exposed to peril. Verb: To protect. To keep in a position not exposed to peril. To make certain of payment, guaranteeing against the possibility of nonpayment. Scholbe v Schuchardt, 292 Ill 529, 127 NE 169, 13 ALR 247, 250. To give assurance or guaranty against a risk or hazard of some kind. Scholbe v Schuchardt, 292 Ill 529, 127 NE 169, 13 ALR 247.

secured creditor. A creditor under an obligation secured as to payment by lien or incumbrance upon property of the debtor or a third person. In bankruptcy, a creditor who has security for his debt upon the property of a bankrupt of a nature to be assignable under the Act or who owns a debt for which some indorser, surety, or other person secondarily liable for the bankrupt has such security upon the bankrupt's assets. Bankruptcy Act § 1(28); 11 USC § 1(28).

secured debt. See **secured creditor**; **secured transaction.**

secured transaction. An obligation secured by a mortgage or other lien.
See **secured creditor**; **security interest.**

securitas (se-kū'ri-tās). Security; a surety; a release; a discharge.

securitate pacis (se-ku-ri-tā'te pā'sis). A writ which lay to cause a person to give security to keep the peace.

securities. See **security.**

Securities Act of 1933. A federal statute controlling and regulating the issuance and sale of securities in the interest of the investing public. 15 USC §§ 77a et seq. 47 Am J1st Secur A § 1.

securities acts. Statutes controlling and regulating the issuance and sale of securities for the purpose of protecting the investing public. 47 Am J1st Secur A § 1.

Securities and Exchange Commission. An agency provided by the Federal Securities Exchange Act, invested with powers and duties in the administration and enforcement of the Federal Securities Exchange Act. 50 Am J1st Stock Ex § 15.

securities exchange. A stock exchange; an exchange for transactions in securities.

Securities Exchange Act. A federal statute enacted in 1934, embodying a comprehensive plan for the regulation of securities exchanges. 15 USC §§ 78 et seq.; 50 Am J1st Stock Ex § 15.

Securities Valuation Reserve. See **Mandatory Securities Valuation Reserve.**

security. A stock certificate, bond, or evidence of secured indebtedness. Anno: 47 ALR2d 229. A share of stock. Anno: 52 ALR 1098 (term as used in a will). A stock, bond, or other contract wherein an investment is made for the purpose for securing

SECURITY [1155] SEDUCE

income or profit. 47 Am J1st Secur A § 16. Any instrument issued or offered to the public by any company, evidencing or representing any right to participate or share in the profits or earnings or the distribution of assets of any business carried on for profit. People v McCalla, 63 Cal App 783, 220 P 436. An instrument issued in bearer or registered form of a type commonly dealt in upon securities exchanges or markets or is commonly recognized in any area in which it is issued or dealt in as a medium for investment; an instrument evidencing a share, participation, or other interest in property or in an enterprise or evidences an obligation of the issuer. UCC § 8—102(1)(a).

Protection of citizen, resident, or transient against attack directed against his person or property. Protection of the nation against attacks from abroad and subversion from within. A mortgage, lien, encumbrance, deposit, or pledge for the payment of a debt or the performance of an obligation. In the broad sense, inclusive of "surety." 50 Am J1st Suret § 3.

Security is that which makes the enforcement or promise more certain than the mere personal obligation of the debtor or promisor, whatever may be his possessions or financial standing. It may be a pledge of property, or an additional personal obligation; but it means more than the mere promise of the debtor with property liable to general execution. It is true that the greater the possessions of the promisor, the more certain the enforcement of his promise, and in a sense, the creditor is more secure; but such is not the security known and expressed in the law. First Nat. Bank v Hollingsworth, 78 Iowa 575, 43 NW 536.

See **realizing on security.**

security agreement. An agreement which creates or provides for a security interest. UCC § 9—105(1)(h).

security deposit. See **security.**

security deed. A term probably confined to the state of Georgia and there meaning a deed conveying the legal title to land as security for the payment of a debt.

Upon default in payment, the holder of the debt reduces it to judgment, and the holder of the legal title to the land makes and places of record a quitclaim conveyance to the debtor, reinvesting him with the legal title. The land may then be levied upon and sold to satisfy the judgment. Scott v Paisley, 271 US 632, 633, 70 L Ed 1123, 1124, 46 S Ct 591.

See **deed of trust; mortgage.**

security for costs. A bond, undertaking, or deposit required of a plaintiff to secure the payment of costs in the action or the unpaid costs of a prior action. 20 Am J2d Costs §§ 37 et seq.

security for good behavior. See **security to keep the peace.**

security interest. An interest in personal property or fixtures which secures payment or performance of an obligation. 15 Am J2d Com C § 7. In the broad sense, an interest in security of any form.

security on appeal. See **appeal bond.**

security regulations. Regulations in the interest of preserving the country against subversive activities and of protecting it against attacks from abroad.

security requirements. See **financial responsibility laws; security regulations.**

security to keep the peace. A bond, undertaking, or deposit as security against committing a breach of the peace. 12 Am J2d Breach P §§ 41-51.

Securius expediuntur negotia commissa pluribus, et plus vident oculi quam oculus (se-kū'ri-us ex-pe-di-un'ter ne-gō'she-a kom-mis'sa plū'ri-bus, et plūs vi'dent o'ku-li quam o'ku-lus). Matters which are committed to several persons are executed more surely, because eyes see more than an eye sees.

securus (se-kū'rus). Safe; secure; sure.

secus (se'kus). Otherwise; not so.

sed (sed). But; however; yet.

sedato animo (se-dā'tō a'ni-mō). With settled intent.

sed contra (sed kon'trā). But otherwise. See 3 Bl Comm 417.

se defendendo (sē dē-fen-den'dō). In defending himself; in self-defense.

sedente curia (se-den'te kū'ri-a). The court sitting; during a session of the court.

sederunt (sē-dē'runt). A session of court.

sedes (sē'dēz). (Latin.) Seat.

sedge (sej). See **sedge-flats.**

sedge-flats (sej'flats). Tracts of land lying below ordinary high water mark, which are covered by every tide, and grow a coarse or long sedge, which cattle will not eat, and which like seaweed, is valuable only for bedding and manure. Church v Meeker, 34 Conn 421, 429.

sedition. A commotion, or the raising of a commotion, in the state, not amounting to an insurrection. Exciting discontent against the government, or resistance to lawful authority. To attempt by word, deed or writing to promote public disorder or induce riot, rebellion, or civil war. State v Shepherd, 177 Mo 205, 76 SW 79. The wilful and knowing utterance, writing, or publication of disloyal, scurrilous, or abusive matter against the United States or a state, or the flag, military forces, or uniform of the Armed Forces, which matter is designed and calculated to bring them into contempt, matter which aggregates, incites, fosters or encourages antagonism, opposition, and hostility to organized government, or matter which obstructs or interferes with recruiting or enlistment services strengthening the Armed Forces. 47 Am J1st Sedit etc § 2.

During the presidency of John Adams, Congress passed a sedition act making it an offense to libel the government, the Congress, or the President, and there were four prosecutions under it, but it was unpopular and was soon repealed. State v Shepherd, 177 Mo 205, 221, 76 SW 79.

seditious agitator (sẹ-dish'us aj'i-tā-tor). One who attempts by word, deed, or writing to induce riot, rebellion, or civil war. One who is a disturber of the public peace and order, a subverter of just law, and a bad citizen. Wilkes v Shields, 62 Minn 426, 64 NW 921.

sed non allocatur (sed non al-lo-kā'ter). But it is not allowed.

sedo (sē'dō). (Mexican.) I grant.

sed per curiam (sed per kū'ri-am). But by the court (it was held).

seduce. To lead astray. Putnam v State, 29 Tex App 454, 16 SW 97. To accomplish a seduction.

See **seduction.**

seduced (sę-dūsd'). Corrupted; drawn aside from the path of virtue. Seduction accomplished.
See **seduction**.

seduction. The act of leading astray. Being lead astray. In the ordinary legal sense, the act of a man in inducing a woman to surrender her chastity. Morehead v Commonwealth, 194 Ky 592, 240 SW 93. The act of a man in inducing a chaste woman to have unlawful sexual intercourse with him. 47 Am J1st Seduc § 2. The act of persuading or inducing a woman of previous chaste character to depart from the path of virtue by the use of any species of arts, persuasion, or wiles which are calculated to have and do have that effect, and result in her ultimately submitting her person to the sexual embraces of the person accused. 47 Am J1st Seduc § 2.

To seduce a woman is to corrupt, deceive, and draw her aside from the path of virtue which she was pursuing, by such acts and wiles as are calculated to operate upon a virtuous female. State v Eckler, 106 Mo 585, 590.

In some instances, particularly in a case where a wife sues as wronged by the defendant in an alleged seduction of plaintiff's husband, the word "seduction" has reference to the misconduct of a woman toward a man. 27 Am J1st H & W §§ 522 et seq.

sed vide (sed vi'de). But see.

see. Noun: The dignity or the jurisdiction of a bishop. Verb: To observe with the eyes. To obtain a mental impression or understanding. Seaboard Air Line R. Co. v Myrick, 91 Fla 918, 109 So 193. To perceive and obtain knowledge by the use of the eyes. Tracey v Standard Acci. Ins. Co. 119 Me 131, 109 A 490, 9 ALR 521.

The word "see" and the word "hear," when used in a negative statement, are often used to express the negation of apprehension or conscious knowledge. A person may hear or see and yet not observe; that is, he may not have a conscious knowledge of the object or noise he actually sees or hears, and, ordinarily, when questioned as to the fact, he will say that he did not see or hear. See Seaboard Air Line R. Co. v Myrick, 91 Fla 918, 109 So 193, 195.

seed grain. Grain purchased or saved from a prior crop to plant.

seed grain loans. Loans by the federal government or a state to needy farmers for the purchase of seed grain. William Deering & Co. v Peterson, 75 Minn 118, 120.

seeding cloud. See **cloud seeding**.

seed laws. Statutes designed to protect the public from adulterated or unsuitable seeds and setting up reasonable regulations in furtherance of such purpose. 3 Am J2d Agri § 50.

seed relief. The furnishing of agricultural seeds to persons needing, but without means to obtain, them. 3 Am J2d Agri § 33.

seen. Past participle of **see**. A word of art for the acceptance of a bill of exchange. Barnet v Smith, 30 NH 256.

seepage. The loss of water from a watercourse or a body of water, natural or artificial, by its slow movement through the ground or wall of the reservoir. 56 Am J1st Wat § 29.

seesaw. Same as **teeter-totter**.

segregation. Separation, as where goods are separated for purposes of identification. An enforced separation of races, particularly the white and colored races, as under statutes and constitutions providing for the separate education of colored and white children. 47 Am J1st Sch § 216.
See **de facto segregation**; **discrimination**.

segregation of dower. See **assignment of dower**.

seigneur (sē'nyǫr). A lord; a master.

seigniory (sē'nyǫr-i). The dominion and authority of the lord of the manor. A lordship; a manor.

seigniory in gross (in grōs). A lordship which was not attached to any manor.

seine (sān or sēn). Noun: A large fish net. Verb: To take fish from a body of water by the use of a net. 35 Am J2d Fish §§ 47, 54.

seing. See **blank seing**.

seipsum absentare (sīp'sum ab-sen-ta'rē). To absent one's self.

seise. See **seize**.

seised. Having **seisin**. Having been subjected to **seizure**.

seised in fee (sēzed in fē). See **in fee**.

seised in his demesne as of fee (in his de-mēn' as of fē). Clothed with seisin as owner in fee; seised in fee simple.

seised to uses. Holding title for the use or benefit of another.
See **covenant to stand seized to uses**.

seisi. Same as **seised**.

seisin (sē'zin). The possession of a freehold estate by the owner. 42 Am J1st Prop § 45. The possession of land coupled with the right to possess it and a freehold estate therein, practically the same thing as ownership. Holt v Ruleau, 83 Vt 151, 74 A 1005. For the purpose of dower, the force of possession under some title or the right to hold the title, either a seisin in deed or a seisin in law. 25 Am J2d Dow § 26.

A person is said to be "seised" or "seized" of personal property when he has the ownership of it, his ownership of it carrying with it the right of possession. Burdett v Burdett, 26 Okla 416, 109 P 922.
See **covenant of seisin**; **livery of seisin**.

seisina facit stipitem (se-zī'na fa'sit sti'pi-tem). Seisin makes the stock.

seisin by hasp and staple (sē'zn bī hasp and stā'pl). The investiture of a person of seisin by the feoffee's taking hold of the hasp of the door of the house and then bolting himself in.

seisin in deed. A seisin in fact. An actual corporeal seisin which, existing in the husband, is a subject to which common-law dower or its statutory equivalent attaches. 25 Am J2d Dow § 26.

seisin in fee. See **in fee**.

seisin in law (sē'zin in lä). The right to immediate possession of land under a freehold title. The right to make immediate seisin, which, existing in a husband during coverture, is a subject to which common-law dower or its statutory equivalent attaches. 25 Am J2d Dow § 26.

Although the law passed an inheritance to the heir immediately on the death of his ancestor, the heir thereby acquired only a seisin in law, and this, alone, did not enable him to transmit the inheritance to his heirs. He must have obtained an actual seisin or possession or seisin in fact, which is the kind of seisin to which the maxim refers, as distinguished from seisin in law. Such was the rule at common law under the first canon of descent, generally repudiated in the United States. 23 Am J2d Desc & D § 69.

seize. To grasp; to catch. To take prisoner. To take possession, particularly of land. To make a seizure.

seizin. Same as **seisin.**

seizing in transitu (sē′zing in tran′zi-tu). See **stoppage in transitu.**

seizing of heriots (sē′zing of her′i-ǫts). The taking by the lord of the manor of his heriots upon the death of his tenant in copyhold. See 2 Bl Comm 97.

seizure. The taking of a thing into possession, the manner of taking and whether such taking is actual or constructive depending upon the nature of the thing seized. 36 Am J2d Forf & P § 30. Arresting and taking as a prisoner.
See **search and seizure.**

seizure and capture. The taking of the ships, goods, and effects of the enemy upon the high seas in time of war. 56 Am J1st War § 151.

seizure and confiscation. The taking and using of the property of the enemy in time of war, wherever it may be found and without compensation. 56 Am J1st War § 72.

selecti judices (se-lek′tī jū′di-sēz). (Roman law.) Chosen judges,—judges chosen by the praetor, of whom those who were to serve were appointed by lot. See 3 Bl Comm 366.

selection of appraiser. See **appointment of appraiser.**

selection of exempt property. The act of a debtor in choosing the property he wishes to retain, as against an execution, where he has more than the number or value of chattels allowed by law as exempt. 31 Am J2d Exemp § 146.
See **designation of homestead.**

selection of grand jurors. The drawing of a list of persons to serve on the grand jury, usually closely regulated by statute. 24 Am J1st Grand J § 18.

selection of guardian. A matter committed largely to the discretion of the appointing court, but subject to a right of nomination by a ward who has reached a certain age, ordinarily that of 14 years, the paramount consideration, however, being the best interests of the ward. 25 Am J1st G & W §§ 26 et seq.

selection of homestead. See **designation of homestead.**

selection of jurors. The preparation of a list of names of persons for jury service; the depositing of names on such list in a jury wheel or box; a drawing from the jury wheel or box of the names of persons to serve as jurors at a certain trial term of court; the drawing from the names of persons summoned as jurors for a trial term of names of persons to serve as jurors in a particular case; and finally the impaneling of a jury in a particular case after examination of the several jurors on voir dire and the exercise of challenges. 31 Am J Rev ed Jury § 76.

selection of remedy. See **election of remedies.**

selective adoption. A basic principle that only so much of the English common law should be adopted as is compatible with our views of liberty and sovereignty, or as is adaptable to the peculiar conditions and circumstances of each state or to the wants and necessity of its people, or in harmony with the genius, spirit, and objects of its institution. Fuchs v Goe, 62 Wyo 134, 163 P2d 983, 166 ALR 1329.

selective draft. The process, machinery, and agencies in selecting and inducting into military service the persons who are subject to call for such service under a compulsory service act. 36 Am J1st Mil § 24.

selective draft act. See **Selective Service Act.**

selective logging operation. A term of the timber trade having reference to the provision in a contract for the sale and purchase of standing timber which reserves the privilege of designating the timber to be removed by the purchaser and the order of removal. Anno: 79 ALR2d 1243.

selective sales tax. A sales tax confined to a particular commodity or a limited number of commodities, such as taxes upon sales of intoxicating liquors, cigarettes, gasoline, and other petroleum products. 47 Am J1st Sales T § 1.

selective service. A form of compulsory military service. 36 Am J1st Mil § 22.
See **selective draft; Selective Service Act.**

Selective Service Act. A federal statute authorizing a draft for military service, that is, imposing compulsory military service and providing the means for calling men to the service. 50 USC Appx §§ 451 et seq.

selectmen. The members of a town board, especially in the New England states. Municipal officers. 37 Am J1st Mun Corp § 224.

selectus judex (se-lek′tus jū′dex). Singular of **selecti judices.**

self. One's own self, as where a note is made payable to "self."

self-abuse. See **masturbation.**

self-crimination. Same as **self-incrimination.**

self-defense. A right founded upon the law of nature but deemed necessary even in organized society to personal safety and security and as not incompatible with the public good. 26 Am J1st Homi § 126. The use of force by a person against another to protect himself from bodily harm or an offensive contact, which he believes will result from conduct apparently intended to cause injury or offensive contact, or which is such as to put him in apprehension thereof. 6 Am J2d Asslt & B § 158. That which the law deems justified as the defense of one's person by such force and in such manner as is reasonably necessary when put under the necessity or apparent necessity of defending oneself without any fault on one's part, in order to protect against the peril of death or serious bodily injury at the hands of another. 26 Am J1st Homi § 125.

self-degradation. Putting oneself in a degrading position. Testimony of a witness not exposing him to any criminal prosecution or rendering him liable to any penalty or forfeiture, yet having a direct tendency to degrade his reputation. 58 Am J1st Witn § 35.

self-destruction. Literally, death by one's own hand or act, whether intentional or accidental. The equivalent of suicide for the purposes of an exception in a life insurance policy. 29A Am J Rev ed Ins § 1145.
As the terms are frequently employed in policies of life insurance, "suicide" and "self-destruction"

are held to be legally synonymous, and both mean an intended voluntary taking of one's own life. Connecticut Mut. Life Ins. Co. v Akens, 150 US 468, 37 L Ed 1148, 14 S Ct 155.

self-disserving evidence. Evidence which is unfavorable to the party who offers it.

self-employed. Working, but not for an employer. Conducting one's own trade or business as sole proprietor or as a partner.

self-employed retirement plan. A retirement plan of a professional man, proprietor of a business, partner, or other self-employed person whereby he sets aside a specified part of his current earnings for use as a retirement fund in the future, which plan, if qualified under the tax law, permits to a limited extent the deduction of his contributions in determining his net income for tax purposes. Internal Revenue Code § 401(c)(1).

self-employment income. Net earnings from self-employment, subject to certain specific limitations fixed by statute. Internal Revenue Code § 1402(b).

self-employment tax. A tax paid by self-employed persons to finance their coverage under the social security system.
See **self-employment income.**

self-executing forfeiture. The termination of a franchise by the operation of a forfeiture clause in the grant without more. 36 Am J2d Franch § 46.

self-executing provision. A provision of a constitution which is effective without legislation, no action by the legislature being required to put it in operation. 16 Am J2d Const L § 94.
A constitutional provision may be said to be self-executing when it takes immediate effect and ancillary legislation is not necessary to the enjoyment of the right given, or the enforcement of the duty imposed. In short, if a constitutional provision is complete in itself, it executes itself. Lanigan v Gallup, 17 NM 627, 131 P 627.

self-executing treaty. A treaty with a foreign nation that operates of itself without the aid of legislation. 52 Am J1st Treat § 2.

self-help. A controverted doctrine in reference to escaping from the custody of an officer which is unlawful. 27 Am J2d Escape §§ 7, 12.
See **self-preservation.**

self-incrimination. The giving of testimony, the furnishing of evidence, or a demonstration by act, by which a witness incriminates himself because it is such or tends to be such as will convict him of a crime. 58 Am J1st Witn §§ 57 et seq.
See **privilege against self-incrimination.**

self-inflicted. Upon oneself by oneself.
Under a compensation statute which excludes only those injuries which are purposely self-inflicted, it is not enough that the employee merely disregards some rule, regulation, or order of the master, since such conduct may constitute nothing more than ordinary negligence on the part of the employee, and mere negligence does not destroy the right to compensation. But an accident resulting from a disobedience of express orders may be one intentionally produced within the meaning of the statute. Anno: 23 ALR 1172.

self-inflicted injury. For definition particularly in reference to use of intoxicants and drugs within the meaning of disability provision of insurance policy, see Anno: 166 ALR 834.

self-insurance. An employer engaging to make compensation payments directly to the injured employee in lieu of carrying insurance, he being required, as a condition of dispensing with an insurance carrier to furnish satisfactory proof of financial ability, file a bond, or make a deposit of securities as a guaranty of compensating his injured employees. 58 Am J1st Workm Comp § 546.
See **reciprocal insurance.**

self-insurer. An employer under workmen's compensation who is permitted, under the conditions respecting self-insurance, to dispense with an insurance carrier. Sheehan Co. v Shuler, 265 US 371, 373, note, 68 L Ed 1061, 1062, note, 44 S Ct 548.
See **self-insurance.**

self-murder. An expression equivalent to suicide. Connecticut Mut. Life Ins. Co. v Groom, 86 Pa 92.

self-pollution. See **masturbation.**

self-preservation. The instinct of protecting one's self against danger. The desire to live; the instinct which generally prompts men to acts of care and caution when approaching or in the presence of danger. Wabash R. Co. v De Tar (CA8 Iowa) 141 F 932. The instinct from which the presumption of due care for one's own protection arises. 38 Am J1st Negl § 337.

self-proving instrument. A written instrument admissible in evidence without preliminary proof of genuineness. 29 Am J2d Ev § 853.

self-regarding. See **self-disserving evidence**; **self-serving declaration.**

self-serving declaration. A statement, made out of court, favorable to the interest of the declarant. 29 Am J2d Ev § 621.
The vital objection to the admission of this kind of evidence is its hearsay character; the phrase "self-serving" does not establish an independent ground of objection. Wachovia Bank & Trust Co. v Wilder, 255 NC 114, 120 SE2d 404.

sell. To make a sale.
See **sale.**

sell and dispose of. Depending upon the context in which it appears, a term which may mean disposal by sale only or disposal by sale, barter, or exchange. Killmer Paint & Glass Co. v Davenport-Bethell Co. 136 Okla 252, 277 P 653, 63 ALR 997.

seller. One who sells property of his own. The vendor in a land contract or the party to a contract of sale of personal property who is making a sale of his property. Inclusive in the broader sense of the term of one who makes a sale for another, such as a broker. Anno: 50 ALR2d 1228 (involving civil liability under the Securities Exchange Act).

seller's lien. See **vendor's lien.**

seller's option. The option of a seller of a commodity upon an exchange to deliver the same at any time within a month. Pixley v Boynton, 79 Ill 351. The option of the vendor in a contract of sale of personalty to accept money or something else of equivalent value if offered to him. Lee Lumber Co. v Hotard, 122 La 850, 48 So 286.
See **put.**

seller's risk. The risk of loss of the goods pending delivery thereof or the passing of title thereto to the buyer. 46 Am J1st Sales §§ 279, 280.

seller's talk. A seller's remarks respecting the quality of the goods offered for sale. 46 Am J1st Sales § 89. Statements which, although exaggerated as to value, quality, etc., are such as to be expected of a seller under universal commercial practices and reasonably to be understood as expressing no more than the opinion of the seller. 37 Am J2d Fraud § 54; 46 Am J1st Sales § 326; 55 Am J1st V & P § 67.

selling against the box. See **sale against the box.**

selling short. See **short sale.**

selling titles. See **bracery.**

semaphore (sem'a-fōr). A system of signaling by the use of flags. An arrangement of lights, flags, and wooden, metal, or plastic arms, supported by a standard, near a railroad track, operated for the giving of signals to trains. Wagner v Chicago & A. R. Co. 265 Ill 245, 106 NE 809, affd 239 US 452, 60 L Ed 379, 36 S Ct 135.

semb. An abbreviation of **semble.**

semble (sem'bl). It seems; a dictum holds.
See **come semble; et semble.**

semblement. Similarly.

Semel civis semper civis (se'mel si'vis sem'per si'vis). Once a citizen, always a citizen.

Semel malus semper praesumitur esse malus in eodem genere (se'mel ma'lus sem'per prē-zū'mi-ter es'se ma'lus in e-ō'dem je'ne-re). Once bad, a person is always presumed to be bad in the same way.

semestria (se-mes'tri-a). (Civil law.) Collected decisions of the Roman emperors.

semicolon. A punctuation mark.
The comma and the semicolon are both used for the same purpose, namely, to divide sentences and parts of sentences, the only difference being that the semicolon makes the division more pronounced than the comma; but at the last it is the sense of the words, taken together, that dictates where the punctuation marks are to be placed, and what they shall be. Holmes v Phenix Ins. Co. (CA8 Mo) 98 F 240.

semidetached houses. Houses with separate entrances and separate approaches or sidewalks but having a wall in common so as to be in violation of a covenant restricting the premises to detached dwelling houses. Liedman v Hall, 110 Misc 365, 180 NYS 514.

semi-matrimonium (se-mi-mat-ri-mō'ni-um). (Civil law.) Half-marriage; concubinage.

seminary (sem'i-nạ-ri). An educational institution, particularly one for the education of ministers of the gospel. Church v Bullock, 104 Tex 1, 109 SW 115. A private school, especially for young women.

Seminoles. See **five civilized tribes.**

semiplena probatio (se-mī-plē'na prō-bā'she-ō). In translation, **half-proof.**

semitontine policy (sem-i-ton'tĕn pol'i-si). An endowment policy of life insurance.
See **tontine policy.**

semi-trailer. A vehicle of the trailer type so used in conjunction with a motor vehicle that some part of its own weight and that of its load rests upon or is carried by another vehicle. Maryland Casualty Co. v Cross (CA5 Tex) 112 F2d 58.

semper (sem'per). Always; at all times.

Semper in dubiis benigniora praeferenda sunt (sem'per in dū'bi-is be-nig-ni-ō'ra prē-fe-ren'da sunt). (Civil law.) In doubtful cases more liberal constructions are always to be preferred.

Semper in dubiis id agendum est, ut quam tutissimo loco res sit bona fide contracta, nisi quum aperte contra leges scriptum est (sem'per in du'bi-is id ā-jen'dum est, ut quam tu-tis'si-mō lō-kō rēz sit bō'na fi'de kon-trak'ta, nī'sī qu'um a-per'te kon'tra lē'jēz skrip'tum est). (Civil law.) In doubtful matters it should always be arranged so that a bona fide contract is in the safest situation, excepting when the writing is plainly contrary to law.

Semper in obscuris quod minimum est sequimur (sem'per in ob-skū'ris quod mi'ni-mum est se'qui-mer). In obscure matters we always following the construction which is least obscure. Sturges v Crowninshield (US) 4 Wheat 122, 150, 4 L Ed 529, 537.

Semper in stipulationibus et in caeteris contractibus id sequimur quod actum est (sem'per in sti-pu-lā-she-ō'ni-bus et in sē'te-ris kon-trak'ti-bus id se'-qui-mer quod ak'tum est). (Civil law.) In stipulations and in other contracts, we always follow that which has been agreed upon.

Semper ita fiat relatio ut valeat dispositio (sem'per i'ta fi'at re-lā'she-ō ut va'le-at dis-pō-zi'she-ō). A reference should always be made so that the disposition will be valid.

semper necessitas probandi incumbit ei qui agit (sem'per ne-ses'si-tās prō-ban'di in-kum'bit e'i qui a'jit). The burden of proof always lies upon him who alleges.

semper paratus (sem'per pa-rā'tus). Always prepared; always ready.

Semper praesumitur pro legitimatione puerorum, et filiatio non potest probari (sem'per prē-zū'mi-ter prō le-ji-ti-ma-she-ō'ne pu-er-ō'rum, et fi-li-ā'she-ō non po'test prō-bā'rī). A presumption always exists in favor of the legitimacy of children, because filiation cannot be proved.

Semper praesumitur pro matrimonio (sem'per prē-zū'mi-ter prō ma-tri-mō'ni-ō). A presumption always exists in favor of matrimony; that is, in favor of the validity of the marriage. See 35 Am J1st Mar § 303.

Semper praesumitur pro negante (sem'per prē-zū'mi-ter prō ne-gan'te). A presumption always exists in favor of a person who denies; that is, a defendant.

Semper praesumitur pro sententia (sem'per prē-zū'mi-ter prō sen-ten'she-a). A presumption always exists in favor of a sentence.

Semper, qui non prohibet pro se intervenire, mandare creditur (sem'per, qui non prō'hi-bet prō sē in-ter-ve-nī're, man-dā're kre'di-ter). One who does not forbid another to act in his stead is always deemed to have authorized him to do so.
The maxim is one of equity applicable to the ratification by a principal of the unauthorized act of an agent by silence or acquiescence. See Philadelphia, W. & B. R. Co. v Cowell, 28 Pa 329.

Semper sexus masculinus etiam foeminum continet (sem'per se'xus mas-ku-lī'nus ē'she-am fe-mi'num kon'ti-net). (Civil law.) The masculine sex of gender always includes the feminine also.

Semper specialia generalibus insunt (sem'per spe-she-ā'li-a je-ne-rā'li-bus in'sunt). (Civil law.) Special expressions or provisions are always included in general ones.

Semper ubique et ab omnibus (sem'per ū'bī'kwē et ab om'ni-bus). At all times, everywhere, and by everyone.

"Considerable latitude must be allowed for differences of view as well as for possible peculiar conditions which this court can know but imperfectly, if at all. Otherwise, a constitution, instead of embodying only relatively fundamental rules of right, as generally understood by all English-speaking communities, would become the partisan of a particular set of ethical or economical opinions, which by no means are held semper ubique et ab omnibus." Otis v Parker, 187 US 606, 47 L Ed 323, 23 S Ct 168.

Senate. One of the two bodies of the Congress of the United States, composed of two Senators from each state. United States Constitution, Article 1, § 3, Clause 1. One of the houses of a state legislature. 49 Am J1st States § 28.

senator. A member of the senate; a member of the king's council.

Senatores sunt partes corporis regis (se-na-tō'rēz sunt par'tēz kor'po-ris re'jis). The senators are a part of the body of the king.

senatus consulta (sē-nā'tus kon-sul'tạ). Acts of the Roman senate. 1 Bl Comm 86.

senatus consultum (se-nā'tus kon-sul'tum). A public act of the Roman senate. See 1 Bl Comm 86.

senatus consultum ultimae necessitatis (se-nā'tus kon-sul'tum ul'ti-me ne-ses-si-tā'tis). The act of the senate in particular emergency. See 1 Bl Comm 136.

senatus decreta (se-nā'tus de-krē'ta). The private acts of the Roman senate. See 1 Bl Comm 86.

senescallus (se-ne-skal'lus). Same as **seneschal.**

seneschal (sen'e-shạl). The steward of a manor.

senile dementia (sē'nil dẹ-men'she-ạ). A weakened condition of the mind due to old age. 57 Am J1st Wills § 100. A form of insanity marked by weakness indicating a mental breaking down in advance of bodily decay. Hiett v Shull, 36 W Va 563, 565, 571, 15 SE 146.

senility (sẹ-nil'ị-ti). Old age. The mental state or condition of a very old person. The weakness attendant upon old age, whether of mind or body. Equitable Life Assur. Soc. v Garrett, 25 Ala App 446, 148 So 338.

senior. Higher in rank; prior or superior in force or effect; longer in service; older. One of a senior class.
When the word is added to a man's name, it indicates merely that he is the father of a man of the same name; it is not a part of the legal name, but is simply descriptio personae. Ferguson v Dillon, 3 Mo 59, 60.

senior chief petty officer. A noncommissioned officer of the Navy, ranking immediately above chief petty officer and immediately below master chief petty officer.

senior class. The most advanced class in high school or undergraduate college.

senior high. See **high school.**

seniority. The principle in labor relations that length of employment determines the order of layoffs, rehirings, and advancements. Anno: 142 ALR 1055.

senior mortgage (môr'gāj). A mortgage, the lien of which is entitled to or priority over that of a junior mortgage or other incumbrance.

senior widow. A widow claiming dower in lands of her deceased husband who was the ancestor of a decedent whose surviving spouse is a dower claimant in respect of the same lands. 25 Am J2d Dow § 87.

sensu. See **lato sensu.**

sensu et re ipsa. See **in sensu et re ipsa.**

sensu honesto (sen'su ho-nes'tō). By or according to its fair or proper sense or meaning.

Sensus verborum est anima legis (sen'sus ver-bō'rum est a'ni-ma lē'jis). The meaning of the words is the spirit of the law.

Sensus verborum est duplex, mitis et asper, et verba semper accipienda sunt in mitiore sensu (sen'sus ver-bō'rum est dū'plex, mi'tis et as'per, et ver'ba sem'per ak-si-pi-en'da sunt in mi-she-ō're sen'su). The meaning of words is twofold, mild and harsh, and words should always be taken in their milder sense.

Sensus verborum ex causa dicendi accipiendus est, et sermones semper accipiendi sunt secundum subjectam materiam (sen'sus ver-bō'rum ex kâ'za di-sen'dī ak-si-pi-en'dus est, et ser-mō'nēz sem'per ak-si-pi-en'dī sunt se-kun'dum sub-jek'tam ma-tē'ri-am). The meaning of words is to be taken from the occasion of their utterance, and conversation should always be understood according to their subject matter.

sentence. A judgment in a criminal case denoting the action of the court in formally declaring to the accused the legal consequences of the guilt which he has confessed or of which he has been convicted. State v Fedder, 1 Utah 2d 117, 262 P2d 753.
See **punishment.**

sentence of nullity. A judicial declaration of the nullity of a marriage.

sententia (sen-ten'she-a). (Civil law.) An opinion; a decision; a judgment; the meaning or sense of a word or sentence.

Sententia a non judice lata nemini debet nocere (sen-ten'she-a a non jū'di-se lā'ta ne'mi-nī de'bet no-sē're). A sentence or judgment rendered by a person who is not a judge ought not to harm anyone.

Sententia contra matrimonium nunquam transit in rem judicatam (sen-ten'she-a kon'tra ma-tri-mō'ni-um nun'quam tran'zit in rem jū-di-kā'tam). A sentence or judgment which is in contravention of marriage never becomes a thing adjudged.

Sententia facit jus, et legis interpretatio legis vim obtinet (sen-ten'she-a fa'sit jus, et lē'jis in-ter-pre-tā'she-ō lē'jis vim ob'ti-net). A judgment makes law, because the interpretation of the law has the force of law.

Sententia facit jus, et res judicata pro veritate accipitur (sen-ten'she-a fa'sit jus, et rēz jū-di-kā'ta prō ve-ri-tā'te ak-si'pi-ter). A judgment makes law, because a thing adjudged is received as the truth.

Sententia interlocutoria revocari potest, definitiva non potest (sen-ten'she-a in-ter-lo-ku-tō'ri-a re-vo-kā'ri po'test, de-fi-ni-tī'va non po'test). An interlocutory judgment can be recalled or revoked, but a final one cannot.

Sententia non fertur de rebus non liquidis (sen-ten'-she-a non fer'ter de rē'bus non li'qui-dis). A judgment is not rendered upon matters which are not clear.

sentimental value. The value of an article upon considerations other than the true value or market value. 22 Am J2d Damg §§ 136, 150.

separable (sep'a-ra-bl). Severable; capable of being separated or divided into component parts.

separable contract. See **divisible contract; severability of contract.**

separable controversy. A term of significance in reference to the removal of an action or suit from state to federal court. A cause of action, included in an action or suit in which more than one cause of action is asserted, which can be disentangled and separated from the other cause or causes of action and fully adjudicated separately. Anno: 110 ALR 189; 19 ALR2d 748. Necessitating a suit capable of separation into parts, so that in one of the parts a controversy may be presenting by one party and fully decided and determined without the presence of the other parties on the same side with him before the removal of the cause. Anno: 110 ALR 189.

A separable controversy is no longer an adequate ground for removal of a case from a state to a federal court unless it also constitutes a separate and independent claim or cause of action. The concept of "separate cause of action" restricts removal more than the concept of "separable controversy." In a suit covering multiple parties or issues based on a single claim there may be only one cause of action and yet be separable controversies. American Fire & Casualty Co. v Finn, 341 US 6, 95 L Ed 702, 71 S Ct 534, 19 ALR2d 738.

separali. See **in separali.**

separate (sep'a-rāt). Verb: To divide; to disunite. To place in different places; to keep apart.

separate (sep'a-rāt). Adjective: Divided; distributed. Merrill v Pepperdine, 9 Ind App 416, 36 NE 921. Disconnected; independent; not a part of something else; distinct.
See **joint.**

separate acknowledgment. An acknowledgment by a married woman apart from the acknowledgment by her husband. 1 Am J2d Ack § 2.

separate action. An action brought by a single plaintiff, as distinguished from an action in which two or more persons join as plaintiffs.

separate and apart. A characterization of a status in the relations between husband and wife in which there has been, not merely a discontinuance of sexual relations, but a living apart for such a period and in such a manner that the fact that they are not living together is open to observation. Anno: 51 ALR 768; 97 ALR 988; 111 ALR 871.

separate and independent cause of action. See **separable controversy.**

separate business of wife. A business carried on by a married woman on her sole account. 27 Am J1st H & W §§ 463 et seq.

separate but equal. A doctrine, since repudiated, which justifies the segregation of races, particularly the white and black races in the public schools, where the accommodations and facilities provided are equal in service and comfort. Anno: 38 ALR2d 1188; 94 L Ed 1135; 98 L Ed 882.

separate cause of action. See **separate counts.**

separate controversy. See **separable controversy.**

separate counts. Two or more charges of distinct offenses in an indictment or information, each count being in contemplation of the law a separate indictment. 27 Am J1st Indict § 129. Divisions of a complaint, petition, bill, or declaration wherein the plaintiff pleads a single cause of action in more than one count, that is, in as many ways as he sees fit, in order to meet any possible phase of the evidence; divisions of a complaint, petition, bill, or declaration wherein the plaintiff states two or more causes of action, each being separately set forth. 41 Am J1st Pl §§ 106 et seq.

Under the rule of pleading that separate counts are required for separate and distinct causes of action, separate and distinct causes of action must be such as are both separable from each other, and separable by some distinct line of demarcation. Chaft Refrigerating Machine Co. v Quinnipiac Brewing Co. 63 Conn 551, 29 A 76.

separate defense. A defense in an action against two or more persons asserted by only one of the defendants. 41 Am J1st Pl § 119.

separate domicil. The domicil of a wife apart from that of her husband, being chosen by her, under circumstances which render it appropriate, necessary, or proper for her to have a separate domicil. 25 Am J2d Dom § 53.

separate estate of wife. A property owned, held and controlled by a married woman free from the dominion or control by the husband, as provided in equity or by Married Woman's Acts. 26 Am J1st H & W §§ 34 et seq. A property placed by law in the ownership, management, and control of a married woman. Cross v Benson, 68 Kan 495, 75 P 558.

separate examination. An examination of a married woman in taking her acknowledgment of her signature, made privately and apart from her husband, with respect to whether her signature was affixed voluntarily and without fear or compulsion of her husband. 1 Am J2d Ack § 2.

separate-general verdict (jen'e-ral vėr'dikt). A finding by the jury upon any of the issues in favor of the plaintiff or the defendant.

The meaning of the expression is that the verdict is separate as to the particular issue as distinguished from any other issue in the case, and that it is general as to the particular issue. It is only applied in cases where there is more than one issue. It is not to be confused with a special verdict, which is a finding of facts by the jury. Witty v C. O. & S. W. Railroad Co. 83 Ky 21, 29.

separate maintenance. Provision made by a husband for the support of his wife living apart from him. The condition or status of a married woman who is living apart from her husband and is being supported by him, but without being divorced from him. An action which in some jurisdictions may be maintained by a married woman who is compelled through her husband's fault to live apart from him, by which action she is allowed separate maintenance or permanent alimony without being forced to seek a divorce. 27 Am J1st H & W §§ 401 et seq.

separate offenses. Criminal offenses so distinct that the evidence necessary to establish one differs from the evidence necessary to establish the other. 21 Am J2d Crim L § 8.

separate opinion. An opinion by one of the judges or justices of a court consisting of more than one judge or justice which is not approved by a majority of the members of the court, whether it be a concurring or a dissenting opinion. 20 Am J2d Cts § 71.

separate property. An estate in a community property jurisdiction held, both in its use and in its title, for the exclusive benefit of either the husband or the wife. 15 Am J2d Community Prop § 3.

See **separate estate of wife.**

separate trials. Separate trials of issues appearing in the same action upon a severance of the issues. 53 Am J1st Trial § 53. Separate trials of joint defendants in a criminal prosecution. 21 Am J2d Crim L § 127.

separatim (se-pa-rā'tim). Separately; severally; distinctly.

separation. The act by which something is separated. The condition or status of being separated, particularly that of husband and wife. A cessation of cohabitation of husband and wife by mutual agreement. Anno: 111 ALR 869. As a ground for divorce:—a physical separation of husband and wife with the intent to sever the marital status, at least an intent not to resume marital relations, sometimes, in the terms of the statutory requirement, beyond any reasonable expectation of reconciliation. 24 Am J2d Div & S § 148.

The word has been used as synonymous with the word "divorce" with both legislative and judicial sanction, and when so used is applied to both a mere divorce a mensa et thoro as well as to a divorce a vinculo matrimonii; this is, it applies to all kinds of judicial separation of man and wife. Butler v Washington, 45 La Ann 279, 814, 818, 12 So 356.

See **judicial separation.**

separation agreement. An agreement made between husband and wife in prospect of the breaking up of the marital union, stipulating that it shall be lawful for the parties to live separate and apart until, by mutual agreement, the separation is ended, customarily containing a provision for support of the wife and children, if there be children of the union, and sometimes a stipulation that neither party will interfere with the other, such an agreement having a proper function even though the parties do not own property of consequence. 24 Am J2d Div & S § 883.

separation from service. The release of a member of the armed forces from active service, sometimes subject to obligations to the branch of which he was a member. 56 Am J1st Vet & V A § 4.

separation of grades. The elimination of grade crossings by providing overhead and underground crossings.

separation of jury. The separation of one or more jurors from their fellow jurors. The dispersal of a jury, the jurors going to their several homes or about their businesses or pleasures. 53 Am J1st Trial § 861.

The term implies the failure of the officer in charge of the jury to keep them together after they have retired for deliberation. Such separation is in some states in itself ground for a new trial. In other states it is ground for a new trial unless it is affirmatively established that no prejudice resulted therefrom. People v Adams, 143 Cal 208, 76 P 954.

separation of powers. The separation of executive, legislative, and judicial powers, a fundamental characteristic of the United States Government and the state governments as well. 16 Am J2d Const L § 210.

See **division of powers.**

separation of spouses. See **divorce; judicial separation; separate maintenance; separation.**

separation wage. Another term for **dismissal compensation.**

separatists (sep'a-rā-tists). A religious sect which seceded from the Church of England.

separator. See **threshing machine.**

septicemia (sep-ti-sē'mi-a). Blood poisoning.

septic tank. A tank placed underground as a sanitary disposal system, that is, for the treatment and disposal of sewage. Sanitation Dist. No. 1 v Campbell (Ky) 249 SW2d 767.

sepulcher (sep'ul-kėr). A burial place; a grave; a tomb. A place for the keeping of religious relics.

sepulture (sep'ul-tūr). Burial. Interment.
See **burial.**

seq. See **et seq.**

Sequamur vestigia patrum nostrorum (se-quā'mer ves-ti'ji-a pa'trum nos-trō'rum). Let us follow in the footsteps of our fathers.

sequela (se-kwē'la). A suit; a process; a prosecution.

sequela curiae (se-kwē'la kū'ri-ē). Suit of court.

sequester (sē-kwes'tėr). To seize property under a writ of sequestration. (Civil law.) To renounce or relinquish a right or claim; to disclaim.
See **sequestration.**

sequestrari facias (se-kwe-strā'ri fā'she-as). A writ of execution against a beneficed rector, whereunder the bishop was ordered to withhold the profits and income of the benefice for the plaintiff.

sequestration (sek'wes or sē-kwes-trā'shon). An equitable writ or process and the remedy thereunder by which property is taken into the possession of the court in order to assure obedience to a decree. 47 Am J1st Seques § 2. Equitable relief in aid of a party to an action of ejectment by a seizure of the rents and profits for preservation during the pendency of the action. 25 Am J2d Eject § 78. The seizure of the husband's property as a remedy in a matrimonial action in order to prevent a delinquent husband or father from escaping his liability for alimony or support by leaving the state. Smith v Smith, 255 App Div 652, 9 NYS2d 188. A doctrine of equity which originated in the doctrine of equitable election, and under which, when the widow elects to take against the will of her husband, the general rule is that the property given to her by such instrument will be sequestered for the benefit of those whose gifts under the will are disturbed by the action of the widow in electing to take against it. 57 Am J1st Wills § 1552.

sequestration receivership. A receivership established in a sequestration proceeding against a corporation. 45 Am J1st Rec § 3.

sequestrator (sek'wes or sē'kwes-trā-tor). A party at whose instance a sequestration proceeding is prosecuted in a court of equity.

Sequi debet potentia justitiam, non praecedere (se'-qui de'bet po-ten'she-a jū-sti'she-am, non prē-sē'de-re). Power ought to follow justice, not to precede it.

sequitur. See **et sequitur.**

serenade (ser-en-ād'). See **charivari.**

serf (sėrf). A person who, under the feudal system, was bound to the soil of his birth-place to perform menial service for the lord of the manor.

sergeant. A noncommissioned officer of the Army, ranking immediately above a corporal and immediately below a staff sergeant.

sergeant-at-arms. An officer of a legislative body or society who is appointed to enforce its rules and orders of procedure and decorum for the conduct of a meeting.

sergeant first class. A noncommissioned officer of the Army, ranking immediately above staff sergeant and immediately below master sergeant.

sergeant major. A noncommissioned officer of the Army, holding the highest rank of any noncommissioned officer.

serial bonds. Bonds issued by a public body payable at different times. 43 Am J1st Pub Sec § 8. Bonds of a corporation or municipality which are issued in a series of which different parts are redeemable at different specified dates. Fales v Multnomah County, 119 Or 127, 248 P 151.

serial building and loan association (bil'ding and lōn a-sō-si-ā'shon). A building and loan association whose stock is divided into series, each series being issued separately. Cook v Equitable Bldg. & Loan Asso. 104 Ga 814, 821, 30 SE 911.

serial number. The number placed upon a bond in issuance of the instrument. An identifying number placed upon the vehicle by the manufacturer of an automobile. An identifying number given to a person in the armed forces.

seriatim (sē-ri-ā'tim). Successively; in succession; severally.

seriaunt. Same as **serjeant**.

series of notes. Several promissory notes of different dates but given in a series of transactions over a period of time between the same parties.

serious. Important; weighty; momentous and not trifling. Lawlor v People, 74 Ill 228, 231.

serious ailment. A grave, if not dangerous, affliction of the body. French v Fidelity & Casualty Co. 135 Wis 259, 115 NW 869.

serious and wilful misconduct. Deliberate misconduct, something more than mere negligence or even gross or culpable negligence. Conduct to which moral blame attaches; the intentional doing of something either with the knowledge that it is likely to result in serious injury or with a wanton and reckless disregard of its probable consequences. 58 Am J1st Workm Comp § 200.

serious bodily harm. See **serious bodily injury**.

serious bodily injury. An injury which gives rise to apprehension; an injury which is attended with danger. (Webster's Dictionary.) George v State, 21 Tex App 315, 317.

The word "serious," when used to define the degree of bodily harm or injury apprehended, requires or implies as high a degree as the word "great," and the latter word means high in degree, as contradistinguished from trifling. Lawlor v People, 74 Ill 228, 231.

serious illness. A grave, important, weighty trouble. An illness attended by danger, giving rise to apprehension. Eminent Household of Columbian Woodmen v Prater, 24 Okla 214, 103 P 558. An illness which permanently or materially impairs, or is likely permanently or materially to impair, the health or constitution. Anno: 153 ALR 717; 29 Am J Rev ed Ins § 745.

serious injury. See **serious bodily injury**.

serious misconduct. Improper conduct of a grave and serious nature. Gonier v Chase Co. 97 Conn 46, 115 A 677, 19 ALR 83, 88 (term appearing in workmen's compensation statutes).

As the term is used in workmen's compensation acts, Bevan in his work on Workmen's Compensation says, page 401: "To constitute serious misconduct, it is probable that the legislature intended to signify conduct that an average workman, in being guilty of, would either know, or ought to know, if he turned his mind to consider the matter, to be conduct likely to jeopardize his own and his fellow workmen's safety." Horst Co. v Industrial Acci. Com. 184 Cal 180, 193 P 105, 16 ALR 611, 617.

See **serious and wilful misconduct**.

serjeant (sär' or sėr'jent). British for **sergeant**. The title of the highest rank attainable in England in the profession of the common law.

See **ancient serjeant; common serjeant; King's premier serjeant; premier serjeant**.

serjeant-at-law. Same as **serjeant**.

Serjeants' Inn (sär'jents in). The name of one of the English inns of court of which the serjeants-at-law were members.

serjeanty. See **grand serjeanty; petit sergeanty**.

Sermo index animi (ser'mō in'dex a'ni-mī). Discourse is the index of the mind.

Sermones semper accipiendi sunt secundum subjectam materiam, et conditionem personarum (ser-mō'nēz sem'per ak-si-pi-en'di sunt se-kun'dum subjek'tam ma-tē'ri-am, et kon-di-she-ō'nem per-so-nā'rum). Conversations are always to be understood according to the subject matter and the condition of the person.

serological blood test (sē-rō-loj'i-kal blud test). A blood test to determine type or group, of a special value in cases of disputed paternity because, although it cannot indicate with precision that a particular person is the father of the child whose paternity is in issue, in many instances it can establish that an alleged father could not have been the sire. Anno: 46 ALR2d 1003, § 1(b).

servage (sėr'vāj). The feudal service of furnishing one or more workingmen for the lord of the manor.

Servanda est consuetudo loci ubi causa agitur (ser-van'da est kon-su-e-tu'do lo'sī u'bi kâ'za a'ji-ter). The custom or usage of the place where the action is brought should be observed.

The maxim is one of the civil law. Decouche v Savetier, 3 Johnson's Ch (Md) 190.

servant. In older usage, a menial or domestic. In modern times, an employee performing any particular sort of service, at least service which is directed so as not to require the exercise of discretion or executive ability. 35 Am J1st M & S § 2. A person employed to perform personal service for another in his affairs and who, in respect of his physical movements in the performance of the service, is subject to the other's control or right to control. American Nat. Co. v Denke, 128 Tex 229, 95 SW2d 370, 107 ALR 409. Definitely, one who is not an independent contractor. 27 Am J1st Ind Contr § 2. As a person whose claim is entitled to priority under the Bankruptcy Act:—one who served the bankrupt in a more or less subordinate position. Re Ko-Ed Tavern (CA3 NJ) 129 F2d 806, 142 ALR 357.

Within the meaning of embezzlement statutes, a servant is any person who is in the employ of another and who, in the discharge of his duties, is subject to the immediate control and direction of his employer. Private house servants or domestics, day laborers engaged to carry vegetables to market for sale and bring back the proceeds, and solicitors engaged for a salary to collect debts have been held to be such servants. 26 Am J2d Embez § 25.

For meaning of the term "servant" as it appears in a designation of a beneficiary under a will, see Anno: 38 ALR 786.

servants' pay. The pay, rations, and clothing of a private soldier, or money in lieu thereof, which are allowed to an army officer for each private servant which he is authorized to keep. 36 Am J1st Mil § 79.

servato juris ordine (ser-va'tō jö'ris or'di-ne). In keeping with the order of the court. See 4 Bl Comm 179.

serve. To make or effect a service of the process of a court; as, to serve a subpoena or a summons. To perform a duty. To be a servant.

servi (ser'vī). (Roman law.) Persons who were employed in husbandry and manufactures. Ex parte Meason (Pa) 5 Binney 167, 180.

service. Work performed. Employment by another. A contraction of military service. A breeding.

A person is in the "service" of another when he is so occupied that during the continuance of the relation he is bound to submit his will to the direction and control of that other in the prosecution of that occupation. Cameron v State Theatre Co. 256 Mass 466, 467, 152 NE 880, 881.

The term as used in a provision of the Social Security Act defining employment as any service performed by an employee for his employer, means, not only work actually done, but the entire employer-employee relationship for which compensation is paid to the employee by the employer. Social Secur. Board v Nierotko, 327 US 358, 90 L Ed 718, 66 S Ct 637, 162 ALR 1445.

As used in the statutes and otherwise in connection with military and naval affairs, the word is an ambiguous one which is used in many senses. When used coupled with the word "active," referring to times of war or national emergency, it has a limited and immediately understandable meaning, but it may be used in a larger and more comprehensive sense, as where a statute refers to a severance of connection with "service" of an officer connected with a particular branch or department of the naval establishment, in which case the naval service as a whole may be signified. 36 Am J1st Mil § 20.

See **continuous service; military service; public service; services of wife.**

service association. An association the primary purpose, or one of the primary purposes, of which is to render services of special benefit to the members, such as an automobile association, an automobile dealers' association, an apple growers' association, etc. An association for the purpose of community improvement.

See **service organization.**

service by mail. Service of process or notice by mailing copy to the party to be served at his last known address where actual personal service cannot be obtained. 42 Am J1st Proc § 60.

service by publication. Service of process by publishing it in a newspaper in compliance with terms and conditions prescribed by statute. 42 Am J1st Proc §§ 89 et seq.

service charge. A percentage added to the bill for meal or drinks in hotel or restaurant.

Service charges collected by proprietors of hotels and restaurants and distributed among their waiters and other employees in accordance with a prearranged plan, or at the discretion of the employers, are wages subject to unemployment tax acts to the extent that an employer is required to pay unemployment taxes or contribute to such payment. Anno: 83 ALR2d 1024.

service club. See **service association.**

service company. A company performing service in maintaining an instrumentality, such as an elevator, in condition for good and safe operation, under contract with the owner or occupant of the premises.

See **public service corporation; service organization.**

service contract. A contract whereby one of the parties undertakes to perform services for the other.

service corporation. See **public service corporation.**

service del roy. See **essoin service del roy.**

service fee. The fee to which a sheriff, constable, or other officer of the law is entitled for service notice, summons, or other process or paper. The sum charged for the service of a male breeding animal. 4 Am J2d Ani § 78.

service in aumone (ser'vis in â-mō'ne). A gift of lands for church services to be performed for the welfare of the soul of the donor.

service letter. A letter of recommendation or character reference given by an employer to his employee upon the termination of the employment. 35 Am J1st M & S § 39.

Service Letter Act. A statute requiring employers generally or employers of particular classes to give employees upon termination of their employment letters setting forth the nature and duration of the services rendered and the cause of leaving. 31 Am J Rev ed Lab § 758.

service lien. A lien for work and labor performed. A common-law or statutory lien for service by a male breeding animal, sometimes on the female served, sometimes on both the female and the resulting foal. 4 Am J2d Ani § 78.

servicemen. Persons in, or who have been in, the armed forces. The terminology for certain employees of a business or industry, such as those who repair machines and appliances in the possession of customers.

Servicemen's Indemnity Act. A federal statute, enacted in 1951, under which all men in the armed forces were provided protection by life insurance without payment of premiums on the part of the servicemen. 29A Am J Rev ed Ins § 1970.

servicemen's insurance. Insurance provided by the government and issued to persons in the armed services. 29A Am J Rev ed Ins § 1970.

service of execution. Every act and proceeding necessary to be taken by the sheriff or execution officer to make the money required for satisfaction of the judgment and execution, including a sale of the property where necessary. Fallows v Continental & C. Trust & Sav. Bank, 235 US 300, 59 L Ed 238, 35 S Ct 29.

service of notice. The communication of the contents of a notice to the person entitled to receive it or intended to receive it in such manner that, as provided by law, he is charged with having received it, whether by mailing, posting, the delivery of a copy, etc. 39 Am J1st Notice §§ 27 et seq.

service of pleading. A common requirement under modern rules of pleading and practice, consisting in the delivery of a true copy to the adverse party or his attorney of record. 41 Am J1st Pl § 317.

service of process. The delivery or other communication of a summons, writ, or other process to the opposite party, or other person entitled to receive it, in such manner that, as provided by law, he is charged with having received it, whether by reading the paper to him, delivering a true copy to him, mailing a copy to him, leaving a copy at his place or residence, or publication. 42 Am J1st Proc § 23.

As applied to process of courts, the word ordinarily implies something in the nature of an act or proceeding adverse to the party served, or of a notice to him. United States v McMahon, 164 US 81, 87, 41 L Ed 357, 360, 17 S Ct 28.

See **service by mail**; **service by publication**; **substituted service**.

service of summons. See **service of process**.

service of the ship. Acts done by a seaman for the benefit of the ship or in the actual performance of his duty, even including some acts on shore leave. 48 Am J1st Ship § 169. Working in the course of employment as a seaman, not in the course of a private pursuit. Barlow v Pan Atlantic S.S. Corp. (CA2 NY) 101 F2d 697.

service organization. An agency for the purpose of procuring help, employment, or engagement in service for a fee, sometimes temporary or emergency employment. State ex rel. Weasmer v Manpower of Omaha, Inc. 161 Neb 387, 73 NW2d 692.

See **service association**.

service pipe. A pipe running from the main of a public utility, usually in the street or highway, to abutting premises, for use in supplying water or gas to the premises.

service real (sėr'vis rēl). A term of the civil law meaning a service servitude which one estate owes to another, or the right of doing something or having privilege in one man's estate for the advantage and convenience of the owner of another estate. Karmuller v Krotz, 18 Iowa 352, 357.

The estate unto which the service is due is called "praedium dominans," or the ruling estate; and the other estate, which suffers or yields the service, is called "praedium serviens," or an estate subject to a privilege or service. Morgan v Mason, 20 Ohio 401.

services. A term applied to those acts or "renders," as they were called, which were due to the lords from their tenants under the old system of feudal tenure. See 2 Bl Comm 60.

See **service**.

services and labor. As the term appears in Married Woman's Acts:—pertaining to manual efforts as distinguished from business ventures carried on by the wife in her own name. 27 Am J1st H & W § 466.

services of wife. A term of art.

In connection with the right of a husband to maintain an action for the loss of his wife's "services," the word has come down to us from times in which the action originated, and it fails to express to the common mind the exact legal idea intended by it. The word, as so used, implies whatever of comfort, aid, assistance, and society the wife would be expected to render to or bestow upon her husband, under the circumstances and in the condition in which they may be placed, whatever those may be. (Cooley on Torts.) See Womach v St. Joseph, 201 Mo 467, 100 SW 443.

See **services and labor**.

service station. See **gasoline filling station**.

service wire. A line of wire supplying electric current to a household, place of business, or industry. Anno: 40 ALR2d 1322, § 8.

servidumbre (ser-ve-doom'bray). A word found in Spanish-American grants, signifying a "servitude." Mulford v Le Franc, 26 Cal 88, 106.

serviens ad legem (ser'vi-enz ad lē'jem). A sergeant-at-law. Same as **serjeant**.

serviens narrator (ser'vi-enz nar-rā'tor). A sergeant-at-law. Same as **serjeant**.

servientes ad legem (ser-vi-en'tēz ad lē'jem). Plural of **serviens ad legem**.

servient estate (sėr'vi-ęnt es-tāt). Same as **servient premises**.

servientis ad legem (ser-vi-en'tis ad lē'jem). Of a serjeant-at-law. 1 Bl Comm 24.

servient premises. Land owned by one person which is subject to an easement in another. A tenement or estate upon which an easement in the form of a charge or burden is placed for the benefit of a dominant estate or tenement.

See **easement**.

servient tenement. Same as **servient premises**.

Servile est expilationis crimen; sola innocentia libera (ser-vī'le est ex-pi-la-she-ō'nis krī'men; sō'la in-nō-sen'she-a lī'be-ra). The crime of plundering or robbing is servile; innocence alone is free.

servile labor (sėr'vil lā'bor). Menial labor. State v Stout, 43 Okla Crim 19, 276 P 795. Labor requiring physical rather than mental effort. State v Smith, 19 Okla Crim 184, 198 P 879. Secular, everyday business.

"A sheriff may race his horse after a fugitive debtor, and find the exercise servile enough; and, I think, common sense would say it was also secular." Per Brainard, J., in Gladwin v Lewis, 6 Conn 49.

servile tenure. See **furca et flagellum**.

Servi nascuntur (ser'vī nas-kun'ter). They are born slaves. 1 Bl Comm 424.

Servitia personalia sequuntur personam (ser-vi'she-a per-sō-nā'li-a se-qu-un'ter per-sō'nam). Personal services follow the person.

servitia servientium et stipendia famulorum (ser-vi'she-a ser-vi-en'she-um et sti-pen'di-a fa-mu-lō'rum). The services of servants and the wages of slaves. See 2 Bl Comm 511.

servitio regis. See **ession de servitio regis**.

servitium (sėr-vi'she-um). Service; feudal service; service rendered by the tenant to the lord of the manor under the feudal system.

servitium foedale et praediale (ser-vi'she-um fē-dā'le et prē-di-ā'le). A personal service which was due on account of land held in fee.

servitium forinsecum (ser-vi'she-um fo-rin'se-kum). Service which was due the king and which was foreign or aside from that due the lord of the manor.

Servitium in lege Angliae, regulariter accipitur pro servitio quod per tenentes dominis suis debetur ratione feodi sui (ser-vi'she-um in lē'je Ang'li-ē, re-gulā'ri-ter ak-si'pi-ter prō ser-vi'she-o quod per tenen'tez do'mi-nis su'is de-bē'ter ra-she-o'ne fe'o-di su'i). The word "servitium" is regularly taken in the law of England to mean the service which is due their lord from the tenants by reason of their fee.

servitium intrinsecum (ser-vi'she-um in-trin'se-kum). Service which was due the chief lord from the tenant.

servitium liberum (ser-vi'she-um lī'be-rum). Free service, the service rendered by freemen, as distinguished from that which was rendered by serfs and vassals.

servitium militare (ser-vi'she-um mi-li-ta're). Same as **knight-service.**

servitium regale (ser-vi'she-um re-gā'le). Royal service, service which was due the king in the exercise of his prerogative rights.

servitium scuti (ser-vi'she-um skū'ti). Service money; scutage or money paid by the tenant to his lord in lieu of knight service. See 2 Bl Comm 74.

servitium sokae (ser-vi'she-um sō'kē). Service of the plow. Same as **socage.**

servitude. The term of the civil law for easement. The right of the owner of one parcel of land, by reason of his ownership, to use the land of another for a special purpose of his own, not inconsistent with the general property in the other person. Korricks Dry Goods Co. v Kentall, 33 Ariz 325, 264 P 692, 58 ALR 145. Bondage.
See **easement; involuntary servitude.**

servitude in gross. See **easement in gross.**

servitude of drip. See **easement of drip.**

servitus (sėr'vi-tus). (Civil law.) The condition of a slave; slavery; servitude; an easement; a servitude.

servitus actus (ser'vi-tūs ak'tus). Same as **servitus itineris.**

servitus altius non tollendi (ser'vi-tūs al'ti-us non tollen'di). (Civil law.) The easement or servitude of not being free to build any higher than the buildings of one's neighbor.

servitus aquae ducendi (ser'vi-tus a'kwē du-sen'dē). (Civil law.) The servitude or easement of running water across the land of another.

servitus aquae hauriendae (ser'vi-tus a'kwē hâ-rien'dē). (Civil law.) The servitude or easement of drawing water from a well or spring on the land of another.

servitus cloacae mittendae (ser'vi-tus klo-ā'sē miten'dē). (Civil law.) The servitude or easement of transmitting sewage across the land of a neighbor.

servitus fumi imittendi (ser'vi-tūs fu'mi im-mitten'dī). (Civil law.) The servitude or easement of conveying smoke through the chimney of a neighbor, or over his land.

servitus itineris (ser'vi-tus i-ti'ne-ris). (Civil law.) The servitude or easement of passing over a neighbor's land on horseback, by carriage or on foot.

servitus luminum (ser'vi-tus lu'mi-num). (Civil law.) The servitude or easement of having the light come unobstructed to a certain part of one's premises or through certain windows or openings.

servitus ne luminibus officiatur (ser'vi-tus ne lu-mi'-ni-bus of-fi-she-ā'ter). (Civil law.) A servitude or easement under which one's light was not to be obstructed by his neighbor.

Servitus non ea natura est, ut aliquid faciat quis, sed ut aliquid patiatur aut non faciat (ser'vi-tus non e'a na-tū'ra est, ut a'li-quid fā'she-at quis, sed ut a'li-quid pa-she-ā'ter ât non fā'she-at). (Civil law.) It is not in the nature of a servitude or easement that a person should do something, but that he should suffer something or should not do something.

servitus oneris ferendi (ser'vi-tus ō'ne-ris fe'ren-dī). (Civil law.) The servitude or easement of furnishing support for a neighbor's building.

servitus pascendi (ser'vi-tus pa-sen'dī). (Civil law.) The servitude or easement of pasturing cattle on the land of a neighbor.

servitus pecoris ad aquam adpulsam (ser'vi-tus pe'ko-ris ad a'quam ad-pul'sam). (Civil law.) The servitude or easement of driving cattle to water on the land of a neighbor.

servitus praedii urbani (ser'vi-tus prē'di-ī ur-bā'ni). (Civil law.) An urban servitude; any servitude or easement which was appropriate to a city estate.

servitus praediorum (ser'vi-tus prē-di-ō'rum). (Civil law.) A praedial servitude; a servitude or easement in the land of another.

servitus projiciendi (ser'vi-tus prō-ji-she-en'dī). (Civil law.) The servitude or easement of projecting one's building over the land of another.

Servitus servitutis esse non potest (ser'vi-tus ser-vi-tū'tis es'se non po'test). There cannot be an easement upon an easement.

servitus stillicidii (ser'vi-tus sti-li-si'di-ī). (Civil law.) The servitude or easement of permitting the rain water to drip from the eaves of one's house upon the land of a neighbor.

servitus tigne immittendi (ser'vi-tus tig'ne im-mitten'dī). (Civil law.) The servitude or easement of inserting a beam in the wall of one's neighbor.

servitus viae (ser'vi-tus vī'ē). (Civil law.) The servitude or easement of a right of way over the land of a neighbor.

servus (ser'vus). A slave; a servant.

Servus facit, ut herus det (ser'vus fā'sit, ut he'rus det). The servant performs that the master may give.
A maxim of the civil law illustrating the reward or consideration of a contract of employment. See 2 Bl Comm 445.

sess (ses). An assessment or tax.

sessio (se'she-ō). A session; a meeting; a sitting.

session. The time during which a legislative body, other assembly, or court meets for the transaction of business. People v Auditor of Accounts, 64 Ill 82, 86. The meeting of an administrative board, agency, or commission. 2 Am J2d Admin L §§ 227 et seq. The meeting of any organized body or group. A meeting of a legislative body for a day; the entire period during a particular year in which a legislature assembled for business, as the 45th session of the General Assembly of Iowa.

session laws (lâs). The collected laws which have been enacted at the successive sessions of a state legislature.

session of court. Broadly, a term of court. Precisely, a time during a term of court when the court actually sits for the transaction of business. 20 Am J2d

Cts § 44. The time during which the court is in fact holding court at the place appointed, and engaged in business. Re Gannon, 69 Cal 541, 545, 11 P 240.

sessions of the peace (of the pēs). A court of record held before two or more justices of the peace for the execution of the authority given them by their commission and certain acts of Parliament. People v Powell (NY) 14 Abb Pr 91, 93.

set. Adjective: Fixed or established. Verb: To put in place. To mark down; to put on paper.
See **articles of set**.

set apart. To divide for a purpose, sometimes for identification, as in setting apart a homestead.
Under a divorce statute authorizing the court to decree that the separate property of the husband be "set apart" for the support and maintenance of the wife, the words include authority to decree the transfer of absolute title to such property to the wife. Powell v Campbell, 20 Nev 232, 20 P 156.

set aside. See **setting aside**.

setback lines. See **building lines**.

setback restriction. See **building lines**.

set fire to. To make burn. 5 Am J2d Arson § 43.
In the law of arson it has been held that the terms "burn" and "set fire to" are synonymous, and that the use of the latter term does not vary the common-law rule that burning is necessary to the offense. Anno: 1 ALR 1164.

set for trial. See **setting case for trial**.

set of bills. See **bills in a set**.

set of exchange. See **bills in a set**.

setoff. A discharge or reduction of one demand by an opposite demand. Malle v Harrell, 118 Tex 149, 12 SW2d 550. A defense or an independent demand made by the defendant to counterbalance that of the plaintiff, in whole or in part. Mack v Hugger Bros. Constr. Co. 153 Tenn 260, 283 SW 448, 46 ALR 389. The right which exists between two persons, each of whom under an independent contract, express or implied, owes an ascertained amount to the other, to set off their mutual debts by way of deduction so that in an action brought for the larger debt, the residue, only after such deduction, may be recovered. Teeters v City Nat. Bank, 214 Ind 498, 14 NE2d 1004, 118 ALR 383. A counter demand which a defendant holds against a plaintiff, arising out of a transaction extrinsic to the plaintiff's cause of action. 20 Am J2d Countcl § 2. A money demand independent of and unconnected with the plaintiff's cause of action. Pekofsky v State, 15 Misc 2d 358, 180 NYS2d 930. In the broad sense, the discharge or reduction of one demand by an opposite one, or the right one party has against another to use his claim in full or partial satisfaction of what he owes to the other. 20 Am J2d Countcl § 2. Simply a mode of defense whereby the defendant acknowledges the justice of the plaintiff's demand on the one hand, but, on the other, sets up a demand of his own to counterbalance it, either in whole or in part. Peacock Hotel v Shipman, 103 Fla 633, 138 So 44; Steck v Colorado Fuel & Iron Co. 142 NY 238, 37 NE 1. In relation to transactions in futures, the method by which a contract to purchase is set off against a contract to sell without the formality of an exchange of warehouse receipts or actual delivery of the commodity, being in legal effect a delivery. Lyons Mill Co. v Goffe & Carkener (CA10 Kan) 46 F2d 241, 83 ALR 501. In respect of a decedent's estate:—the right of an executor or administrator, who is himself a creditor of the estate, to retain the amount of such debt out of the funds of the estate in his hands. A term used loosely for the right of an executor or administrator to deduct indebtedness due from a distributee. 31 Am J2d Ex & Ad § 567.

setoff of benefits. Deducting the benefit to remaining property from a public improvement in ascertaining damages for property taken in eminent domain. 27 Am J2d Em D § 357.

setoff of judgments. A right of an equitable nature, arising as an incident of the general jurisdiction of the court over its suitors, whereby the satisfaction of a judgment may be wholly or partly produced by compelling a judgment creditor to accept in payment a judgment to which he is subject. 30A Am J Rev ed Judgm § 1011.

set on foot. To arrange; to place in order; to set forward; to put in the way of being ready. United States v Ybanez (CC Tex) 53 F 536, 538.

set out. To start on a journey. To commence work upon a project to be accomplished. To set forth. To allege verbatim; to recite the very words of a document in a pleading. First Nat. Bank of Chadron v Engelbercht, 58 Neb 639, 641, 79 NW 556.

setting aside. Vacating, annulling; making void. A remedy on attack against an indictment for insufficiency, error, defect, or irregularity. 27 Am J1st Indict §§ 137 et seq.
"When it is said that such a voluntary deed is void or set aside, these terms must be understood as meaning only that the conveyance, while good against all others, shall not operate to defeat the equity of the creditors of the grantor." Steinmeyer v Steinmeyer, 64 SC 413, 42 SE 184.
See **quashing; vacation; vacation of judgment**.

setting case for trial. Fixing a certain day upon or after which the case may be called for final disposition or trial. 53 Am J1st Trial § 9.
"At the time the cause is first set upon the trial calendar," has been held to be synonymous with the words, "at the time the case is set for trial." Mutual Bldg. & Loan Asso. 220 Cal 282, 30 P2d 509.

settle. To take up residence in a place. To arrange or put in order. To pay a bill or account. To adjust differences; to eliminate controversy. To make a determination. To establish title or estate in a person.
When used with relation to pending litigation, the word has not acquired such a well defined meaning as would enable courts to interpret the intent of the parties in making use of it in connection with the ending of the litigation, without the aid of extrinsic evidence. Recourse must be had to the context of the agreement of the parties, to the circumstances under which the agreement was made, including the state and the various phases of the litigation referred to, and the conferences and correspondence between the parties pending the negotiation of the agreement. Setzer v Moore, 202 Cal 333, 260 P 550.
A written agreement "to settle" is not equivalent to an agreement to pay. It is not a recognition of the debt claimed; it is an offer to adjust matters and may be rather a denial of any indebtedness. Parker v Carter, 91 Ark 162, 120 SW 836.
When applied to a liquidated demand, "to settle" means to pay it. When applied to an unliquidated demand, the word means to effect a mutual adjust-

SETTLED [1168] SEVERABILITY

ment between the parties and to agree upon the balance. State v Staub, 61 Conn 553, 568.

settled account. An account which has been paid. 1 Am J2d Acctg § 21. In loose usage, an account stated.

settled insanity. Insanity caused by abstinence from alcoholic beverages by one whose system has been broken down by long-continued or habitual drunkenness.

It is called settled insanity to distinguish it from temporary insanity or drunkenness, directly resulting from drink. Sanders v McMillian, 31 Tex Crim 318, 20 SW 744.

settlement. The ending of a controversy by agreement. The determination of an issue or of the correctness of an account. The payment of an obligation. The order made upon a trustee's account, determining the amount of the trust in the hands of the trustee and his liability therefor, decreeing distribution to the parties entitled thereto, and in the case of a continuing trust, re-awarding the body of the trust to the trustee for further administration. 54 Am J1st Trusts § 511. An administrative determination of the amount due from the United States upon a public contract. Illinois Surety Co. v United States, 240 US 214, 221, 60 L Ed 609, 614, 36 S Ct 326.

The actual occupation of lands by a pre-emptor for the purpose of obtaining title thereto from the government. 42 Am J1st Pub L § 22.

As a prerequisite to the acquisition of public lands of the United States, the term is used as comprehending acts done on the land by way of establishing or preparing to establish an actual personal residence—going thereon and, with reasonable diligence, arranging to occupy it as a home to the exclusion of one elsewhere. The law makes it plain that there must be a definite purpose in good faith to obtain a home by proceeding faithfully and honestly to comply with all the requirements. See Great Northern Railway Co. v Reed, 270 US 539, 545, 70 L Ed 721, 724, 46 S Ct 380.

A settlement on public lands of the United States with a view to pre-empt is made by a person who inhabits and improves such land and erects a dwellinghouse thereon, in good faith and with a view and intent of obtaining title to the same by complying with the provisions of the pre-emption law of the United States. See Peterson v First Division St. Paul & Pacific Railroad Co. 27 Minn 218, 222.

See **compromise and settlement; equity for a settlement; family settlement; marriage settlement; property settlement.**

settlement in pais (in pā). A settlement or adjustment of differences between the parties themselves, out of court.

settlement of a minister. A term of art, of little significance in modern times.

In colonial times in New England it was the general practice of parishes not having parsonages to grant a sum of money or other property to the minister, exclusive of his annual salary, which is emphatically called his settlement. This name was derived from the uses to which it was intended the money should be applied by him. That is, he was expected to establish a permanent home among his people and be conveniently situated to perform his duties. 45 Am J1st Reli Soc § 29.

settlement of bill of exceptions. See **settlement of case.**

settlement of case. A settlement of a bill of exceptions by a determination that it is correct, made by the trial judge where the parties to the appeal are unable to agree to the correctness of the bill. 4 Am J2d A & E § 444.

settlement of pauper. The place where a poor person has a legal right to support as a pauper. The residence, home, or dwelling place, rather than the domicil, of the pauper. 41 Am J1st Poor L § 23. Sometimes both residence and domicil. Re Quale, 213 Minn 421, 7 NW2d 153 (condition of right to old-age assistance).

settlement option. An option provided for the insured under a life insurance policy, respecting the method and time of payment of the proceeds of the insurance. An option provided the annuitant under an annuity contract in reference to taking a straight annuity, an annuity with refund to a designated beneficiary, or an annuity with a contingent beneficiary. A similar option under a pension or retirement plan.

settler. One who has made a settlement upon public lands. A pioneer in a new country or a region newly opened to settlement in an older country.

settlor. The creator of a trust. One who has conveyed or transferred property to another who is to hold the same as trustee for the benefit of a third person or persons. The person who furnishes the consideration for the trust, even though in form the trust is created by another person, as where a decedent by paying a quid pro quo has caused another person to make a transfer of property with enjoyment subject to change by the exercise of such power by the decedent. Lyman v Commissioner (CA2 NY) 109 F2d 99.

seven bishops. See **Case of the Seven Bishops.**

Seventh Amendment. An amendment to the United States Constitution, contained in the Bill of Rights, preserving the right of trial by jury in suits at common law where the value in controversy exceeds $20, and providing further that no fact tried by a jury shall be otherwise re-examined in any court of the United States than according to the rules of the common law.

seven years' absence. Absence from which there arises a presumption of death where it has continued as an unexplained absence of a person from his home or place of residence without any intelligence from or concerning him for the period of seven years. 22 Am J2d Dth § 304.

sever. To cut in two; to divide.
See **severance.**

severability. The quality of being susceptible to division, leaving parts independent of each other.

severability clause. Same as **saving clause.**

severability of contract. The quality in a contract in contrast with entirety. The quality which renders the contract susceptible to division into sets to be performed, each set embracing a performance on the one side which is an agreed exchange for performance on the other. Restatement, Contracts § 266, Comment e. A quality which renders enforceable a valid part, it availing pro tanto, although another part may be invalid. 17 Am J2d Contr § 230. A quality which characterizes an agreement reached by the parties through negotiations wherein each item or some of the items were regarded as units, as distinguished from an agreement whereof the items were regarded from no point of view other than that in which they were regarded as a whole, as an entirety without divisibility. A quality to be determined according to the intention of the parties as determined by a fair construction of the contract itself, by the subject matter to which it has reference, or the circumstances of the particular transaction giving rise to the question. 17 Am J2d Contr § 325.

As a general rule a severable contract is one in its nature susceptible of division and apportionment. Whether a contract is entire or separable is a question very largely of intention, which intention is to be determined from the language the parties have used and the subject matter of the agreement. The divisibility of the subject matter or the consideration is not necessarily conclusive, though of aid, in arriving at the intention. Where it reasonably appears from the language of the contract or from its terms that the parties intended that a full and complete performance should be made with reference to the subject matter of the contract by one party, in consideration of the obligation of the other party, to the contract, it is said to be entire. Quarton v American Law Book Co. 143 Iowa 517, 121 NW 1009.

A contract may be severable as to some of its terms, or for certain purposes, but indivisible as to other terms or for other purposes. Simmons v California Institute of Technology, 34 Cal 2d 264, 209 P2d 581.

In construing a contract to determine whether it is entire or severable, many of the courts have regarded the singleness or apportionability of the consideration as an important test—that is, if the consideration is single, the contract is entire, but if the consideration is expressly or by necessary implication apportioned, the contract is severable. 17 Am J2d Contr § 326.

A plaintiff can sue once; he must then set up his whole cause of action. He cannot sue in successive actions for different parts of the same thing. But separate independent agreements may be included under one contract, and if they are divisible, suit upon one agreement does not preclude suit upon the other. The usual test of severability is whether the consideration is so segregated that it may be severally applied to each independent covenant in the contract. Hospelhorn v Circle City Coal Co. (CA6 Ky) 117 F2d 166.

severability of deposition. The quality of being susceptible to division, leaving parts independent of each other; a quality upon which the right to use only a part of a deposition upon a trial is based. 23 Am J2d Dep § 108.

severability of statute. A concept applicable when a part of a statute is unconstitutional, the question being whether severability permits the saving of the part not unconstitutional in itself. The quality of a statute in the respect that a part of it has meaning and can stand by itself. A matter to be determined according to the apparent intent of the legislative body which enacted the legislation. 16 Am J2d Const L § 182.

If it is impossible to tell what part of a statute is intended to be operative when some of its provisions are unconstitutional, it is wholly invalid. Woolf v Fuller, 87 NH 64, 174 A 193, 94 ALR 1067.

severable contract. See **divisible contract; severability of contract.**

severable deposition. See **severability of deposition.**

severable judgment. A judgment consisting of separate, distinct, and unrelated parts, the disposition of one of which on appeal will not affect the other, as where a judgment is on different causes of action pleaded in separate counts, or severed by the court, so that they stood independently for the purpose of an award of judgment. 4 Am J2d A & E § 254.

severable statute. See **severability of statute.**

several. Separate and distinct, implying diversity or division. Merrill v Pepperdine, 9 Ind App 416, 36 NE 921. Lunt v Post Printing & Publishing Co. 48 Colo 316, 110 P 203. More than two, but not a multitude. Sometimes deemed to include as many as seven. Tift v Harden, 22 Ga 623.

several actions. Actions which are separate, as distinguished from those which are joint.

several covenant. A covenant made with two or more covenantees which contains words of severalty, or whereby the covenantees take separate interests in the fruits of the covenant.

A covenant by more than one person must be regarded as several, where the interest of the covenantors is separate and performance cannot be made jointly, unless the intention of the parties appears to have been that each should be bound for the performance of the other. 20 Am J2d Cov § 10.

several defenses. Separate defenses by joint defendants. 41 Am J1st Pl § 119. Two or more defenses pleaded by one defendant. 41 Am J1st Pl §§ 161 et seq.

several fishery. An obsolete term for an exclusive fishery.
See **exclusive fishery.**

several inheritance. A characteristic of descent, heirs taking moieties as tenants in common. 23 Am J2d Desc & D § 50.

several liability. The individual liability of two or more persons in reference to claimant's demand. Pruyn v Black, 21 NY 300, 303.
See **joint and several liability.**

severally. Distinctly; separately; apart from others. State Nat. Bank v Reilly, 124 Ill 464, 471.

severally liable. See **several liability.**

several ownership (ō'nėr-ship). Ownership by a single person, as distinguished from ownership as tenant in common or joint tenant.

severalty. See **estate in severalty; in severalty; tenant in severalty.**

severance (sev'ėr-ạns). The act of severing, dividing, or separating; the state of being disjoined or separated. Anno: 18 ALR 1342. The act or fact of so removing anything attached or affixed to land, or a part of the land itself, so as to change its character from being a part of the real property to personal property. Buckout v Swift, 27 Cal 433. A graphic expression for separation of the ownership of minerals from the ownership of the land. 36 Am J1st Min & M § 29. A conveyance of land with an exception or reservation of mineral rights or a conveyance of the mineral rights or of the surface alone. 24 Am J1st Gas & O § 17. The termination of a joint tenancy or tenancy in common. 20 Am J2d Coten §§ 15, 31.
See **harvest.**

severance of action. The splitting of a cause of action by a pleader. The severance of issues for separate trials. A method of granting separate trials to sepa-

rate defendants in a civil action. 53 Am J1st Trial § 55.
See **severance of criminal prosecution; severance of issues; splitting cause of action.**

severance of criminal prosecution. Separate trials of the defendants in a criminal case because of antagonistic defenses, admission or confession by one, etc. 53 Am J1st Trial §§ 56 et seq.

severance of issues. The separation of issues appearing in a trial for a separate trial of a particular issue or issues, especially where there are equitable issues to be tried to the court and issues at law to be tried to a jury. 53 Am J1st Trial § 53.

severance of member. The amputation or physical separation of arm, leg, hand, etc. Anno: 18 ALR 1342; 29A Am J Rev ed Ins § 1511.

severance of statute. The separation by judicial construction of those provisions of the statute which are constitutional from those which are unconstitutional, and striking the latter from the statute. Ballard v Mississippi Cotton Oil Co. 81 Miss 507, 34 So 533.
See **severability of statute.**

severance pay. A payment made by an employer to an employee upon termination of the employment, otherwise known as dismissal compensation or separation wage.
See **dismissal compensation.**

severance tax. A tax directed against the production, or severance from the soil, of natural resources such as timber, oil, natural gas etc. 51 Am J1st Tax § 1259. A tax on the skin of a fur-bearing animal taken within the state. 35 Am J2d Fish § 41.

severe. Serious; grave. Harsh; strict.
See **intolerable severity.**

severe disease. A disease causing a severe illness. Anno: 153 ALR 717. A disease which permanently or materially impairs, or is likely to impair permanently or materially, the health or constitution. 29 Am J Rev ed Ins § 745.

severe gale. A wind of great velocity, having the capacity of wreaking great destruction. Missouri Pacific Railroad Co. v Columbia, 65 Kan 390, 69 P 338.

severe illness. An illness which permanently or materially impairs, or is likely to impair permanently or materially, the health or constitution. Anno: 153 ALR 717; 29 Am J Rev ed Ins § 745.

severing. See **sever; severance.**

sewage. Filth and waste matter carried away in sewers and drains. 25 Am J2d Drains § 1. Excrement, as well as waste, refuse or foul matter, carried off in sewers and drains, whether open or closed, by the water flowing therein. Durham v Eno Cotton Mills, 144 NC 705, 57 SE 465.

sewage disposal plant. See **disposal plants.**

sewer. An underground conduit or covered drain which carries away filth and waste matter, or, as in the case of a storm sewer, surface water and street wash. Anselmi v Rock Springs, 53 Wyo 223, 80 P2d 419, 116 ALR 1250; 25 Am J2d Drains § 1.
That which is a "drain" in rural and agricultural communities may be called a "sewer" in an urban community. 25 Am J2d Drains § 1.

sewerage. The sewer system of a municipality or other political subdivision. The removal of sewage. Sewage.

sex. Character as male or female. Comprehensive in the modern sense of the term of anything connected with the attraction of one sex for the other in a physical way and sexual intercourse.
See **asexualization.**

sexagenarian (sek"sa-je-nā'ri-an). A person over sixty but less than seventy years of age.

sex deviate (seks dē-vi-at). See **homosexual; lesbian.**

sextery lands (seks'tėr-i lands). Lands which were donated to a church for the support of its sexton.

Sextus Decretalium (sex'tus dē-krē-tā'li-um). The sixth decretal which was added to the decretals of Gregory IX., by Boniface VII., about 1298. See 1 Bl Comm 82.

sexual assault. The indecent conduct of a man toward a woman or child or of a man toward another man, accompanied by the threat or danger of physical suffering or injury or inducing fear, shame, humiliation, and mental anguish. 6 Am J2d Asslt & B § 24. The act of a man in taking indecent liberties with a woman, as where he indecently fondles her without her consent. Walker v State, 132 Ala 11, 31 So 557. The act of a man in placing a woman in fear of an attack by him upon her chastity. 6 Am J2d Asslt & B § 119.
See **assault with intent to rape; indecent assault.**

sexual commerce. Same as **sexual intercourse.**

sexual disease. Same as **venereal disease.**

sexual intercourse. The actual contact of the sexual organs of a man and a woman, and an actual penetration into the body of the latter. State v Frazier, 54 Kan 719, 725, 39 P 819.
The term does not comprehend intercourse which is partial or imperfect, as in cases where that is impossible because of malformation, sensitive repugnance, or impotence. 4 Am J2d Annul § 32.

sexual psychopath (sek'sū-al sī'kō-path). One affected with a form of psychopathic personality which disposes him to the commission of sexual offenses. A person who, by a habitual course of misconduct in sexual matters, has evidenced an utter lack of power to control his sexual impulses, and who, as a result, is likely to attack or otherwise inflict injury, loss, pain, or other evil on the objects of his uncontrolled and uncontrollable desires. State ex rel. Pearson v Probate Court, 205 Minn 545, 287 NW 297, affd 309 US 270, 84 L Ed 744, 60 S Ct 523, 126 ALR 530. A person in whom there is combined emotional instability and impulsiveness of behavior or inability to appreciate the consequences of his acts, so that he is unable to control his sexual desires and thereby dangerous to other persons. Ditrich v Brown County, 215 Minn 234, 9 NW2d 510. A person adjudicated to be a "sexual psychopath." Anno: 24 ALR2d 373, § 9.

shackles. Iron bands fastened on the legs or arms of a prisoner and joined by a chain.
See **handcuffs; manacles.**

shadow. To trail a person from place to place, observing his activities and associates, usually with the intent to prevent him from becoming aware of the surveillance.
See **rough shadowing.**

shadow area. The part of a field of controversy which is indefinite as to the exact nature of the questions presented. An area in which questions of law and questions of fact coalesce. 5 Am J2d A & E § 829.

shaft. A part of a mine; a vertical or slanting passage way from which lateral diggings reach the mineral. A heavy rod by which power is applied to a moving part of a machine.
See **discovery shaft.**

Shakers. A religious society known particularly for condemning marriage contracted with unworthy motives. Waite v Merrill, 4 Me 102.

shale. A mineral. Anno: 17 ALR 167, s. 86 ALR 990.
Rock formed by the consolidation of clay, mud, or silt, having a finely stratified or laminated structure.
It presents almost endless varieties of texture and composition, passing, on the one hand, into clays, or, where much indurated into slates and argillaceous schists; on the other into flagstones and sandstones; or again through calcareous gradations into limestone, or through ferruginous varieties into clay ironstone, and through bituminous kinds into coal. R. J. Funkhouser & Co. v Fiske & Co. (CA3 Pa) 106 F2d 679.

shall. Providing generally, but not always, a mandate, where appearing in a constitutional provision. 16 Am J2d Const L § 92. Ordinarily, a word of mandate, the equivalent of "must," where appearing in a statute. Stanfield v Willoughby (Ky) 286 SW2d 908, 53 ALR2d 925; State ex rel. McKittrick v Wymore, 343 Mo 98, 119 SW2d 941, 119 ALR 710; Saba v Homeland Ins. Co. 159 Ohio St 237, 112 NE2d 1, 44 ALR2d 841. Construed as "must" in a statute providing for increased punishment for a subsequent offender. People v Gowasky, 244 NY 451, 155 NE 737, 58 ALR 9. Sometimes meaning "may," as where used in a statute providing that when property owners petition for the improvement of a street, the municipal authorities "shall" cause the work to be done. Rockwell v Junction City, 92 Kan 513, 141 P 299.
The word "shall" may be held to be merely directory when no advantage is lost, when no right is destroyed, when no benefit is sacrificed, either to the public or to any individual, by giving it that construction. Montgomery v Henry, 144 Ala 629, 39 So 507.

shall become due and payable. Due and payable at the option of the holder of the instrument in which the clause appears. Nickell v Bradshaw, 94 Or 580, 183 P 12, 11 ALR 623.

shall go. The equivalent of "shall vest" where used in a statute of descent. Plass v Plass, 121 Cal 131, 53 P 448.

sham (sham). Adjective: False, counterfeit, pretended, feigned, unreal. Noun: Deception; any trick or fraudulent device that disappoints; a make-believe imposition; a humbug. Williams v Territory, 13 Ariz 27, 108 P 243.

sham answer. See **sham pleading.**

sham bidder. One who bids at an auction for the purpose of inflating the price for the benefit of the owner of the property or other person interested in the sale; a puffer.
See **puffer.**

sham conviction. A conviction in a sham or collusive proceeding under which the defendant pleads guilty to a minor offense in order to avoid an anticipated prosecution on a more serious charge based on the same facts. Anno: 75 ALR2d 691, § 4.

sham defense. See **sham pleading.**

sham gift. A gift in form but not in fact, there being no intent or understanding on the part of the purported donor or purported donee that the former should divest himself of control over the subject matter. Richardson v Smith (CA2 Conn) 102 F2d 697, 125 ALR 774.

sham marriage. A marriage ceremony performed in jest. A marriage entered into by one of the parties in good faith but illegal because of intentional acts or omissions on the part of the other party. Lee v State, 44 Tex Crim 354, 72 SW 1005.

sham pleading. Allegations pleaded in bad faith. A pleading which is false in fact to the knowledge of the pleader, whatever it may be in form. 41 Am J1st Pl § 50. A pleading palpably and manifestly false on its face. Commonwealth ex rel. Meredith v Murphy, 295 Ky 466, 174 SW2d 681.
See **frivolous answer.**

shape-up. A labor-law term for a system of hiring a crew for a particular job.
The particular needs of an employer are communicated to the union which, together with the employer, shares the responsibility for posting information at various places, and the employer then employs a hiring boss, both for the purpose of recruiting a specific crew from among those applicants who appear at a predesignated "shape-up" point, and for the purpose of acting thereafter as crew foreman until the work is completed. Anno: 38 ALR2d 414.

share. A word of different connations. 57 Am J1st Wills § 1327. The portion of a testator's estate given to a particular beneficiary. 57 Am J1st Wills § 1327. The portion of an intestate estate to which one of two or more heirs or distributees is entitled. A share of corporate stock. The proportional equitable ownership of a shareholder in a business trust. Schumann-Heink v Folsom, 328 Ill 321, 159 NE 250, 58 ALR 485.
See **distributive share; share of stock.**

share and share alike. Ordinarily, but not necessarily, a phrase of severance which negatives the creation of a joint tenancy. Anno: 46 ALR2d 532, 537. Ordinarily, but not necessarily, indicative of a per capita distribution. Anno: 126 ALR 159; 57 Am J1st Wills §§ 1265, 1297.

share-a-ride arrangement. See **car pool.**

sharecropper. One whom a landowner engages under a sharecropping arrangement. 21 Am J2d Crops § 35.

sharecropping. An arrangement whereby a landowner hires a person to cultivate the land and raise a crop thereon and to receive for his labor a share of the crop which he works to make and harvest. 21 Am J2d Crops § 35.

shareholder. A stockholder. A participant in a business trust, occupying a relation to the trust similar to the relation of a stockholder in a corporation to the corporation. 13 Am J2d Bus Tr § 30. Broadly, one who holds or is entitled to a share in any form of enterprise or property.
As to the several classes of persons who are included in the term shareholder as it is used in the Federal statute authorizing an assessment of one hundred per cent against a shareholder of a national bank, for the benefit of creditors of the bank, see McCandless v Haskins (DC SD) 20 F2d 688.
See **stockholder; treasury shares.**

shareholder's derivative suit. See **derivative action.**

share lease. A lease providing for the payment of grain or crop rent.
See **share rent; share tenant.**

share lien. The lien of a building and loan association upon shares of its stock for any indebtedness of the shareholder to the association. 13 Am J2d B & L Assoc § 26.

share of stock. A unit of interest in a corporation. The property interest of a stockholder in the corporation. 18 Am J2d Corp § 209.
The tangible property of a corporation and the shares of stock therein are separate and distinct kinds of property and belong to different owners, the first being the property of the artificial person —the corporation—the latter the property of the individual owner.
A share of stock merely represents, or is a fractional part of, some other property. Millar v Mountcastle, 161 Ohio St 409, 119 NE2d 626, 49 ALR2d 381.
Shares of stock are to be distinguished from the certificates which merely represent ownership of the stock. State v Crawford, 159 Or 377, 80 P2d 873.

share rent. A rent payable in a share of the crop produced upon the demised premises. 32 Am J1st L & T § 468.

share-ride arrangement. See **car pool.**

share tenant. A tenant who holds land under a lease which provides that he is to share the crops produced with his landlord. Louisiana Farm Bureau Cotton Growers' Co-op. Asso. v Bannister, 161 La 958, 962, 109 So 776.
See **share rent.**

share warrant. A warrant or certificate issued by a corporation evidencing the right of its holder to receive a specified number of paid-up shares of the stock of the corporation.

shave. To cut away. To strip or pillage. To oppress by extortion. To deceive, defraud, or overreach. Bronson v Wiman (NY) 10 Barb 406, 428. To make a profit by taking an unconscientious advantage of another. To exact a discount at an unconscientious rate. Stone v Cooper (NY) 2 Denio 293, 295.

she. The nominative form of the feminine pronoun, applicable to a woman, girl, female animal, or ship.

sheathing. A covering, particularly of a wall. 13 Am J2d Bldgs § 13. The covering of a roof, the shingles resting thereon.

sheath knife. See **bowie knife.**

shed. An outbuilding, especially on farm premises. A shelter for animals. A part of the freehold. Roden v Williams, 100 Neb 46, 158 NW 360.

sheep. A mammal. A domestic animal kept for the production of wool, which is taken from the shorn fleece, and for meat known as mutton.

sheep range. See **range.**

sheer (shēr). Verb: To deviate from a course. Adjective: Transparent. Unmixed. Perpendicular.
In nautical language, the word means a deviation from the line of the course in which a vessel should be steered, and though it may occur from causes unpreventable by the most skilful seamanship, it more often happens from an unsteady helmsman; as where he is not watchful enough of the state of the tide when advancing to a dock. Camden & Amboy Railroad Co. v Brady (US) 1 Black 62, 17 L Ed 84, 88.

sheet. See **balance-sheet; charge-sheet.**

sheeting. See **sheathing.**

shelf lands. See **Outer Continental Shelf.**

Shelf Lands Act. See **Outer Continental Shelf Lands Act.**

shell eggs. Ordinary chicken eggs as distinguished from eggs which have been powdered or otherwise processed; an agricultural commodity within the meaning of the exemption of such commodity from the general coverage of the Federal Motor Carrier Act. 13 Am J2d Car § 41.

Shelley's Case. See **Rule in Shelley's Case.**

shellfish. Oysters, clams, and other aquatic animals without the power of locomotion. A subject of private ownership where planted in a place, marked by posts or otherwise, where none of the kind have been growing naturally. 35 Am J2d Fish § 5.

shellfishery. A place for gathering shellfish, such as oysters and clams; or in a broader sense, the right to take shellfish which may be found on the bed of a particular stretch of water. 35 Am J2d Fish § 13. A matter of private right where shellfish have been planted in a marked place in which none of the kind have been growing naturally. 35 Am J2d Fish § 5.

shelter. Housing. A local term for housing and care of dependent or delinquent children. A place wherein domestic animals are protected against rain, snow, and cold.

sheriff. A public officer; an officer having the dual character of a peace officer and a ministerial officer. 47 Am J1st Sher § 3. A county officer representing the executive or administrative power of the state within his county. 47 Am J1st Sher § 2. An officer for the execution of criminal and civil process.
The office of sheriff is one of the oldest known to the common law. It is inseparably associated with the county. The name itself signifies keeper of the shire or county. The office is said to have been created by Alfred when he divided England into shires, but Coke believed it to have been of Roman origin. In England the sheriff was the immediate officer of the king within the shire, the conservator of the peace within the county, keeper of the county jail and commander of the posse comitatus, and he served and enforced the processes of the state. In the United States his functions are similar and he is the chief executive officer of the state in his county. He obeys the mandate of the state not only when issued to him by the courts of his county, but he executes writs directed to him by the courts of other counties. State ex rel. Beach v Finn, 4 Mo App 347, 352.

sheriffalty (sher'if-al-ti). Same as **shrievalty.**

sheriff's certificate of sale. See **certificate of sale.**

sheriffs' courts (kōrts). The principal courts of the city of London.
They were held before their steward or judge, and from them a writ of error lay to the court of hustings, before the mayor, recorder and sheriff. See 3 Bl Comm 81, note.

sheriff's deed. The deed given by the sheriff who conducts an execution sale of real estate to the purchaser. 30 Am J2d Exec § 393. The deed given to the purchaser at a judicial sale conducted by the sheriff under an order directing him in his official capacity to conduct the sale. 30A Am J Rev ed Jud S § 172.

sheriff's indemnity (in-dem'ni-ti). The statutory right which a sheriff has in many jurisdictions to demand and receive indemnity for enforcing an execution where he entertains a doubt as to the title to the property to be levied on. 47 Am J1st Sher § 143. The bond which indemnifies the sheriff directed to seize and hold property under a writ of execution, where such property is claimed by one other than the defendant in the execution. 30 Am J2d Exec § 752.

sheriff's inquest. See **inquest of office; inquest of title.**

sheriff's jury. A jury impaneled to inquire into and render verdict as to the ownership of personal property seized under execution. 30 Am J2d Exec § 119.

sheriff's sale. See **execution sale; judicial sale.**

sheriffwick (sher'if-wik). Same as **shrievalty.**

Sherman Act. The federal antitrust act which denounces contracts, combinations, and conspiracies in restraint of trade or commerce, supplemented by the Wilson Tariff Act and the Clayton Act. 15 USC §§ 1 et seq; 36 Am J1st Monop etc. § 141.

Sherrer Case. An important decision by the United States Supreme Court on the effect of a foreign judgment of divorce as res judicata on the issue of jurisdiction where the defendant, a nonresident, appeared in the action but did not contest on the issue of jurisdiction. Sherrer v Sherrer, 334 US 343, 92 L Ed 1429, 68 S Ct 1087, 1 ALR2d 1355.

shewage. Same as **scavage.**

shewer (shō'ér). A person appointed by the court during the progress of a trial to conduct a viewing by the jury.

shifting. Changing position. Varying. Passing from one person to another.

shifting burden of tax. Employing a condition in a will whereunder certain bequests are to bear the burden of an inheritance or estate tax, thereby relieving from payment of such tax a bequest which otherwise would be chargeable therewith. Anno: 117 ALR 126; 37 ALR2d 110.

shifting descents. The rule of the English common law that a descent of land, once vested, is liable to be defeated by the later birth of an heir, even a remote heir who, however, is in a nearer degree of kinship than the heir in whom the descent first vested. 23 Am J2d Des & D § 89.

shifting of burden of proof. The passing of the burden of proof in the sense of the duty of producing evidence to meet the evidence produced, or the prima facie case made by one's adversary, from side to side as the trial of the case progresses and evidence is introduced by the respective parties. 29 Am J2d Ev § 124.

The ultimate burden of proof, that is, the burden of establishing the truth of a given proposition by the quantum of proof required by law never shifts. 29 Am J2d Ev § 124.

shifting risk. See **blanket policy.**

shifting severalty. An estate in land of limited duration.

shifting stock. The ordinary stock of merchandise which from day to day is depleted by sales and restored by purchases.

shifting uses. Estates in futuro, known as executory interests, created by conveyances to uses, recognized in equity and validated by the Statute of Uses, but invalid under the early common law as in contravention of the rigid rules against a limitation of a fee on a fee or the taking effect of a future estate by the cutting short of a prior estate. 28 Am J2d Est § 333.

shilling. An English coin, amounting in value to twelve pence or the one-twentieth part of a pound.

shin-plaster. A piece of paper money much depreciated in value.

Shinto (shin'tō). A religion of the Japanese.

ship. Verb: To deliver goods and merchandise to a carrier for transportation. State v Carson, 147 Iowa 561, 126 NW 698. To load upon car, truck, or ship for transportation. State v Carson, 147 Iowa 561, 126 NW 698. To transport. Noun: A marine structure intended for transportation of goods or passengers. 48 Am J1st Ship § 36.

The word, as applied to a vessel, embraces her boats, tackle, apparel, and appurtenances, because part of the ship as a going concern, and for the same reason, "ship or vessel of war" includes her armament, search lights, stores,—everything, in short, attached to or on board the ship in aid of her operations. United States v Dewey, 188 US 254, 268, 47 L Ed 463, 471, 23 S Ct 415.

As to what constitutes a ship subject to salvage, see 47 Am J1st Salv § 3.

A contract "to ship by" a certain vessel for a particular voyage ordinarily means to put on board and does not include the subsequent carriage. Harrison v Fortlage, 161 US 57, 40 L Ed 616, 16 S Ct 488.

See **vessel.**

ship and outfit. A term stating the subject of marine insurance effected for the purposes of a fishing voyage, consisting principally in the apparatus and instruments necessary for the taking of fish, seals, etc., and the disposing of them when taken, in such a manner as to bring home the produce of the voyage, but not including "goods" in the ordinary sense of the term. 29 Am J Rev ed Ins § 304.

ship broker. An agent for the transaction of business between owners of ships and charterers or shippers. A person who negotiates the purchase and sale of ships and the business of freighting vessels. Little Rock v Barton, 33 Ark 436, 446.

shipbuilding lien. A lien which has been very generally provided by statute in various states for labor and materials furnished toward the original construction of vessels.

It is in no sense a maritime lien and cannot be enforced in an admiralty court. 48 Am J1st Ship § 554.

ship-chandler. A dealer in supplies and provisions for ships.

shipmaster. See **master of ship.**

shipment. The delivery of goods on board a carrier. 46 Am J1st Sales § 168. Goods consigned for transportation.

A shipment was held to have been made by placing goods on board a vessel bound for the intended destination and engaged in an honest effort to obtain a cargo for that port. Mora Y Ledon v Havemeyer, 121 NY 179, 24 NE 297.

shipment by freight. Shipment by railroad.

ship mortgage. A mortgage covering a vessel, governed by the law of chattel mortgages generally and by statutory provisions. 48 Am J1st Ship § 72.

Ship Mortgage Act. A federal statute regulating mortgages covering vessels registered or enrolled as United States vessels. 46 USC §§ 911 et seq. A statute which provides for a maritime lien enforceable by suit in rem in favor of any person furnishing repairs, supplies, towage, use of drydock, marine railway, or other necessaries to a vessel upon the order of the owner or of a person authorized by the owner. 46 USC § 971.

shipowner's lien. The lien of a shipowner for demurrage, freight, or other maritime service or obligation. 48 Am J1st Ship § 562.

shipper. The consignor of a shipment. The person who entrusts goods to a carrier for transportation and delivery.

shipper's lien for loss. The lien which shippers have by the maritime law, upon the vessel employed in the transportation of their goods and merchandise from one port to another, reciprocal to the ship's lien for freight, as a security for the fulfilment of the contract of the carrier that he will safely keep, duly transport and rightly deliver the goods and merchandise shipped on board, as stipulated in the bill of lading or other contract of shipment. 48 Am J1st Ship § 334.

shipper's weight, load, and count. A phrase inserted in a bill of lading by the carrier to place the responsibility for the manner of loading, the accuracy of the description of the goods in the bill, and the accuracy of the bill as to the number of articles in the shipment, upon the shipper. 13 Am J2d Car § 292.

shipping. Delivering goods or merchandise to a carrier for transportation. The business of transportation, especially by water. The instrumentalities of transportation by water, their regulation, ownership and employment and the rights and liabilities connected with or growing out of them.

shipping agent. An agent of a common carrier having general authority to make all reasonable contracts of carriage. 13 Am J2d Car § 227. An employee of an industry charged with duties respecting the obtaining of transportation for shipments of the products of his employer. A managing agent within the meaning of statutes concerning the service of process upon foreign corporations. Anno: 113 ALR 78, 79.

shipping articles. A formal agreement entered into between the master of a vessel and the members of the crew respecting the terms of employment, the voyage to be made, and other matters. 48 Am J1st Ship §§ 148 et seq.

shipping commissioner. A federal officer provided by statute for each port of entry which is also a port of ocean navigation to superintend the employment and discharge of seamen. 46 USC §§ 541 et seq.

shipping instructions. The instructions given by a shipper to the carrier concerning the nature of the shipment and the attention required to preserve it against damage or loss. 13 Am J2d Car § 316.

shipping order. An order given to the seller of goods by the buyer for the transportation of specific goods by carrier.

shipping receipt. A bill of lading. 13 Am J2d Car § 265.

ship receipt. The written acknowledgment of a ship receiving cargo, acknowledging the receipt of goods on board the vessel, describing them by the marks upon them or the packages. People v Bradley (NY) 4 Park Crim 245, 247.

ship's bill. That copy of a bill of lading executed in triplicate which is kept by the master for his own information as to the nature of his undertaking.

ship's company. The officers and crew of a ship.

ship's course. See **course of vessel.**

ship's doctor. A qualified medical practitioner carried on a ship to administer to crew and such passengers as may be carried. 48 Am J1st Ship § 356.

ship's husband. A person appointed by part owners of a ship to act as the general agent of all the owners in respect of the ship, with authority to contract for necessary supplies, repairs, equipment, and services, and to hire officers and crew. 48 Am J1st Ship § 104.

shipside. A familiar term in charter-parties and contracts of carriage.

In the case of a contract for the shipping of cotton to a port, consigned to the order of the shipper, shipside, the word "shipside" does not put the carrier on notice that the shipper had made a special contract with a steamship company in regard to carrying the cotton, so that special damages would be caused by delay in transportation. Lee v Railroad, 136 NC 533, 48 SE 809.

See **alongside.**

ship's papers. The registration or enrollment of a vessel and other papers required by law to be carried by a vessel as the primary and best evidence of national character and of the ownership of vessel and cargo. 48 Am J1st Ship § 218.

ship's service. See **service of the ship.**

ship's stores. See **stores.**

shipwreck. See **wreck.**

shipwrecked goods. Such goods as after a shipwreck are cast upon land, and left there, by the sea. 48 Am J1st Ship § 647.

shire (shēr or shir). Another word for county, derived from the Saxon, particularly a county of England having a name ending in "shire." State ex rel. Milton v Dickenson, 44 Fla 623, 33 So 514.

shire clerk (shīr' klėrk). The clerk of an English county court.

shire-mote (shīr'mōt). An English county court.

shire-reeve (shīr'rēv). Same as **sheriff.**

shock. A concussion or violent jarring. A sudden agitation of body or mind; a physical or mental manifestation of disturbance. A severe disturbance of the mind from distress or surprise. A disorder in the system of blood circulation, resulting from injury or onset of illness, and indicated by a decrease in blood pressure, weakness, often by unconsciousness. Haile v Texas & Pacific R. Co. (CA5 La) 60 F 557. The effect of an electric current passing through the body.

See **nervous shock.**

shocking evidence. Gruesome evidence. 29 Am J2d Ev § 260.

shock wave. See **sonic boom.**

shoddy (shod'i). Any material which has been spun into yarn, knit or woven into fabric, and subsequently cut up, torn up, broken up, or ground up.

Weaver v Palmer Bros. Co. 270 US 402, 409, 70 L Ed 659, 661, 46 S Ct 318. Cheap and inferior merchandise.

shoes of assignor. An assignee standing in the same position as his assignor. 6 Am J2d Assign § 102.

shoe track. A footprint.

shoot. To employ a firearm. To project a missile, arrow, or bullet by gun, bow, or sling. To use an explosive.
The word is frequently, perhaps usually, employed synonymously with the word "kill." Shooting a person naturally means that a person was hit by the substance with which the gun or pistol was loaded. Bader v New Amsterdam Casualty Co. 102 Minn 186, 112 NW 1065.

shooting a person. See **shoot.**

shooting craps. The same as throwing dice. 24 Am J1st Gaming § 20.

shooting gallery. A public place of recreation in the practice of marksmanship. 4 Am J2d Amuse § 40.

shooting match. A test of marksmanship, becoming illegal as gambling only where wagers are placed. 24 Am J1st Gaming § 28.

shooting oil well. The use of explosives in releasing the oil so as to make the well productive. Clark v E. I. Du Pont D'Nemours Powder Co. 94 Kan 268, 146 P 320.

shop. A place of employment. A working place, especially one which has machinery or mechanical power to be utilized in connection with the employment of the individual. 58 Am J1st Workm Comp § 117. A place where goods are sold at retail, especially wearing apparel. Commonwealth v Annis, 81 Mass (15 Gray) 197, 199.
A restaurant is a shop or store within the protection of a burglary statute. State v Charette, 98 NH 477, 103 A2d 192, 43 ALR2d 827.
A house used for the purpose of manufacturing woodwork has been regarded as a "shop," within the meaning of the word as used in a statute defining the subjects of arson. State v Arthur, 151 NC 653, 65 SE 758.
See **bucket shop; closed shop; open shop; pawnshop.**

shopbook. The account book of a tradesman or shopkeeper.
See **books of account.**

shopbook rule. The rule of evidence under which the books of account of a party are rendered admissible as evidence of goods sold and delivered or of services performed, it being the rule in the great majority of the states to admit entries in books made in the ordinary course of business at or near the time of the transaction to which they relate, where properly authenticated according to the requirements of the particular jurisdiction. 30 Am J2d Ev § 918.

shopcard. See **union shopcard.**

shopkeeper. One who keeps a shop; a storekeeper. See **shop.**

shopkeepers' books. See **shopbook; shopbook rule.**

shoplifting. The stealing of goods from a store or a shop. 32 Am J1st Larc § 45.

shopping center. A new category of business district differing in substantial respects from other groupings of retail establishments, being characterized by off-street parking facilities and a uniform plan or scheme of development. Anno: 76 ALR2d 1173.
See **supermarket.**

shop-right rule. The rule that an employee who, during his hours of work and while working with his employer's materials and appliances, or with the assistance of helpers provided by the employer, conceives and perfects an invention which he patents, must accord to his employer a right or license to use the invention. United States v Dubilier Condenser Corp. 289 US 178, 77 L Ed 1114, 53 S Ct 554, 85 ALR 1488.

shop steward. The representative of a labor union in a factory or industrial plant, his primary duty being to see that union rules are followed and attention given to the grievances of employees. A labor union representative whose duty it is to keep a record of all non-union men on works where he is employed and to present their names at the branch meeting. State v Dyer, 67 Vt 690, 704, 32 A 814.

shore. The margin of the sea; that space of land which is alternately covered and left dry by the rising and falling of the tide; the space between high and low-water mark. 56 Am J1st Wat § 448. The area lying between the lines of high water and low water, over which the tide ebbs and flows. 12 Am J2d Bound § 13. Beach. The space between high and low water marks of a watercourse. State ex rel. Ellis v Gerbing, 56 Fla 603, 47 So 353.
As applied to inland waters, the word "shore" generally has application only to large bodies of water, as lakes and large rivers, and means the land adjacent thereto. Axline v Shaw, 35 Fla 305, 17 So 411.
See **by the shore.**

shore lands. The area known as the **shore.**
As applied to lands along the margin of a tideless body of water, below the ordinary high-water mark but without any defined outer boundary, the term "shore lands," has been construed as including the land to the line of navigability. Seattle v Oregon & W. R. Co. 255 US 56, 65 L Ed 500, 41 S Ct 237.

shore leave. Leave granted a sailor or seaman to go ashore for recreation.

shore line. The margin of the shore. The **shore.** Peoria v Central Bank, 224 Ill 43, 79 NE 296.

shore of watercourse. See **shore.**

shore pay. Pay for service in the Navy other than sea service. 36 Am J1st Mil § 71.

shoring up. Bracing; supporting a building with props. Supporting a vessel out of water with props. Covering an opening in granary, railroad car, or bin to prevent contents from spilling. Supporting the sides of an excavation with boards, masonry, or props.
See **notice to shore up.**

short. Not extensive in length, whether of distance or time. The condition of one who has sold short. Lacking funds, particularly funds which one should have according to a record or book of account.
The word "short" may not always impute dishonesty or criminality, but it may be so used. Where a person is employed to sell merchandise and collect therefor and turn in his collections to his employer, to charge that he is "short" is to impute dishonesty. Swift & Co. v Gray (CA9 Cal) 101 F2d 976.
See **short sale.**

short bill. See **short form.**

short cause. A cause the trial of which will presumably be brief.

short-cause calendar. A trial calendar of cases which will not require for trial a period of time exceeding a prescribed limit. 53 Am J1st Trial § 6.

short complaint. See **short form.**

short deal. See **scalp**; **short sale.**

short entry. A term of art used by bankers for the notation made in a customer's bank book respecting a note deposited by the customer for collection, indicating that the amount of the note is not to be carried to the general balance of the customer until collection has been made. 10 Am J2d Banks § 411.

shortest and best route. In reference to locating a highway, the shortest practicable way, not necessarily a way on a straight line. Anno: 63 ALR 516, 518.

short form. A relatively simple form of indictment prescribed by statute. 27 Am J1st Indict § 53. A form of pleading authorized by statute or rule of practice in stating a cause of action upon a promissory note, bill of exchange, or other instrument for the unconditional payment of money only. 12 Am J2d B & N § 1100. A bill in equity filed in a United States court which alleges only the ultimate facts of the plaintiff's cause of action. Mumm v Jacob E. Decker & Sons, 301 US 168, 81 L Ed 983, 57 S Ct 675.

shorthand. A writing in characters specially designed for speed.

short haul charges. A matter of discrimination by a common carrier in charging or receiving a greater compensation in proportion for a shorter than for a longer distance of transportation over the same line or route in the same direction. 13 Am J2d Car § 205.

shortly after. As the phrase appears in an extension of time of payment of a note, within a reasonable time after the date specified. Trinley & Sons v Golter, 93 NH 268, 41 A2d 243.

short measure. The offense of a seller of goods or merchandise of a particular measure in delivering a short measure for the full price. 56 Am J1st Wts & L § 46.

short notice. See **short summons.**

short order. An order of court the time for serving which has been shortened by the court. A simple meal to be prepared and served quickly at a restaurant.

short period year. A year for which a tax return is filed, which actually is a period of less than one year but treated as a full tax year, under certain conditions such as a change by a taxpayer of his annual accounting. Internal Revenue Code § 443(a).

short sale. A sale of that, usually corporate stock, which the seller does not at the time possess, but which, by the future date or time agreed upon for its delivery to the purchaser under the terms of the contract, the seller must in some way acquire for the purpose of such delivery. Provost v United States, 269 US 443, 70 L Ed 352, 46 S Ct 152.

In a short sale, ordinarily the customer does not actually produce the stock for delivery; the broker borrows the securities or furnishes his own. The broker charges the price of the borrowed stock to the customer, and the account is carried until the customer orders the broker to repurchase the securities, after which an adjustment is made between the broker and customer on the difference between the selling and purchasing price. 12 Am J2d Brok § 116.

The margin in such case is the sum of money deposited with the broker to protect him from any loss he might be subjected to by reason of a subsequent rise in the market price of the stock.

short sale against the box. See **sale against the box.**

short statute of limitations. A statute of limitations which prescribes a very short limitation period for reasons of public policy, as in the case of a statute fixing the period of time within which the validity of a tax sale may be questioned. 51 Am J1st Tax § 1155.

short summons. A summons in which the time within which the defendant is required to appear and answer is shorter than the time which is usually required.

short-swing profit. A profit made on the sale of securities held for only a short time after purchase.

short swing speculation. The purchase and sale, or sale and purchase, of corporate stock within a period of less than six months. 15 USC § 78p(b) (involving unfair use of information by corporate "insiders".)

short ton. The usual ton of 2000 pounds as distinguished from the long ton of 2240 pounds. 19 USC § 1202, Headnote 9(e).

short weight. The offense of a seller of goods or merchandise of a particular weight in delivering a short weight for the full price. 56 Am J1st Wts & L § 46.

shotgun quarantine. A quarantine maintained by means of an armed force. Wilson v Alabama G. S. R. Co. 77 Miss 714, 28 So 567.

shotgun wedding. A slang term for a wedding under duress of threatened prosecution for seduction or bastardy.

shoulder of highway. The part of a highway between the paving or traveled part of the way and the gutter or drainage ditch. The part of a highway immediately adjacent to and lending support to the paved or surfaced portion.

should or could test. The two types of questions presented to a court upon review of an administrative determination: (1) questions relating to whether the particular type of act could be done by the particular type of agency in the manner in which it was done—that is, does the law permit the act which was done; and (2) questions relating to whether the act should have been done—that is, questions whether the conclusions of the agency were correct, whether its act was proper or justified, and whether the facts or evidence warrant it. 2 Am J2d Admin L § 611.

show. Noun: An exhibition by way of public entertainment, whether in drama on the stage or in a motion picture, a musical comedy, burlesque, ballet, etc. A circus. Verb: To demonstrate. To make apparent or clear, either to the eye or to the understanding or to both, by display, by evidence, by illustration, or by other means. Kenyon v Crane, 28 Cust & Pat App (Pat) 1208, 120 F2d 380. To come in third in a race, particularly a horse race.

As the noun is used in connection with amusements, it has been held to apply only to out-of-doors sports, and to be inapplicable to a moving picture exhibition. State v Chamberlin, 112 Minn 52, 127 NW 444.

show boat. A vessel used primarily for entertainment purposes but nevertheless within admiralty jurisdiction. 2 Am J2d Adm § 30.

show cause. To comply with a rule or order of the court to show cause by offering law and facts to influence the court in its decision of the point before it.

show cause order. See **order to show cause.**

showering. The practice of sprinkling and cooling livestock with a spray of water when they are shipped in freight cars.
This is usually done by holding a pipe from an elevated tank, with one end of the pipe flattened, so that the water is thrown through the openings in the cars as they slowly pass. Peck v Chicago Great Western Railway Co. 138 Iowa 187, 115 NW 1113.

shower room. A room in an inn or hotel, furnished and equipped as a place where patrons may enjoy a shower bath. Anno: 18 ALR2d 976, 977.

showroom. A room in a hotel wherein a traveling salesman may display his samples to customers. 29 Am J Rev ed Innk § 47.

shrew. A small mammal, having a reputation for malignancy. A common scold. 15 Am J2d Com S § 2.

shrievalty (shrē'val-ti). The office or jurisdiction of a sheriff; the period of a sheriff's term of office.

shrinkage. Contraction in weight or bulk. A loss of weight or bulk of a shipment while in transit. 14 Am J2d Car § 526.

shrub. A bush, being distinguished from a tree in having two or more stems in place of a single trunk. A kind of nursery stock. 39 Am J1st Nurs § 1.

shuffle board. A game in which discs are propelled by a cue toward squares with numbers whereby the scoring is accomplished.

shun pike (shun pīk). A road intended merely to enable travelers to evade a tollgate. 54 Am J1st Turn & T R § 17.

shunt. To move something, especially to the side; to divert an electric current. Weston Electrical Instrument Co. v Empire Electrical Instrument Co. (CC NY) 131 F 82.

shunting cars. Switching railroad cars. 35 Am J1st M & S § 233.
See **kicking cars.**

shutdown. Termination of work of production in a factory.
A mill or works is shut down when its machinery is not being operated, although its employees may be engaged in loading its product for shipment. McKenzie v Scottish Union & Nat. Ins. Co. 112 Cal 548, 44 P 922.

shut-in royalty. A royalty paid by the lessee under an oil and gas lease to keep the lease in force in the absence of production. Anno: 96 ALR2d 348.

shut-off valve. A valve for cutting off gas supply to stove or furnace. 26 Am J2d Electr § 236.

shyster (shī'stėr). A trickish knave, one who carries on a business, especially a legal business, in a dishonest manner. Gribble v Pioneer Press Co. 34 Minn 342, 343. An unethical and unscrupulous lawyer.

si (sī). (Latin.) If; although; provided that; as if; whether.

si (se). (Spanish.) Yes.

Si a jure discedas, vagus eris et erunt omnia omnibus incerta (sī ā jọ're di-sē'dās, va'gus e'ris et e'runt om'ni-a om'ni-bus in-ser'ta). If you depart from the law, you will be a wanderer, and everything will be uncertain to everyone.

Si alicujus rei societas sit, et finis negotio impositus est, finitur societas (sī a-li-kū'jus re'ī so-si-e'tas sit, et fī'nis ne-gō'she-ō im-po'zi-tus est, fī'ni-ter so-si-e'tas). If a matter is a partnership affair, when the transaction or business is concluded, the partnership is at an end. Griswold v Waddington (NY) 16 Johns 438, 488.

Si aliquid ex solemnibus deficiat, cum aequitas poscit subveniendum est (sī a'li-quid ex so-lem'ni-bus de-fi'she-at, kum ē'qui-tās po'sit sub-ve-ni-en'dum est). If anything is deficient in formal requisites, when equity requires it, it should be supplied.

si aliquid sapit (sī a'li-quid sa'pit). If he knows anything; if he has understanding.

Si antiquitatem spectes, est vetustissima; si dignitatem, est honoratissima; si jurisdictionem, est capacissima (sī an-ti-qui-tā'tem spek'tēz, est ve-tus-tis'si-ma; sī dig-ni-tā'tem, est ho-nō-rā-tis'si-ma; sī jū-ris-dik-she-ō'nem, est kā-pā-sis'si-ma). If you regard its antiquity, it is most venerable; if its dignity, it is most honorable; if its jurisdiction, it is very wide. See 1 Bl Comm 160.

Si assuetis mederi possis nova non sunt tentanda (sī as-su-ē'tis me-dē'ri pos'sis no'va non sunt ten-tan'da). If you can be cured by customary remedies, new ones should not be tried.

sib. A contraction of **sibling.**

sibling (sib'ling). Kin, especially a brother or sister. Precisely, one of two or more persons having the same parents, born at different times.

sic (sik). So; thus; simply; in this manner.
See **et sic.**

sic ad judicium. See **et sic ad judicium.**

sic ad patriam. See **et sic ad patriam.**

Sic enim debere quem meliorem agrum suum facere, ne vicini deteriorem faciat (sik e'nim de-bē're quem me-li-ō'rem ag'rum su'um fā'se-re, nē vī-sī'nī de-tē-ri-ō'rem fā'she-at). (Roman law.) Everyone ought so to improve his own land that he may do no injury to his neighbor.

sic fecit. See **et sic fecit.**

sic hic (sik hik). So here.

Sic interpretandum est ut verba accipiantur cum effectu (sik in-ter-pre-tan'dum est ut ver'ba ak-si-pi-an'ter kum ef-fek'tu). An expression or provision should be so construed that the words may have effect.

sic jubeo (sik jū'be-ō). I so order or command.

sick. Adjective: Affected with or suffering from physical or mental disorder; more or less disabled by disease or bad health; indisposed; ill. Nauseated. Upset. Noun: Persons who are sick, considered as a class.
See **sickness.**

sick benefits. Payments made under a policy of health insurance; payments made under a mutual benefit certificate providing health insurance.

Fringe benefits provided by a corporation for its employees. 19 Am J2d Corp § 1055.

sick leave. A leave of absence granted a civil service officer or employee, sometimes with pay, on account of his sickness or physical disability. 15 Am J2d Civ S § 30.

sickness. The condition of being sick. A condition interfering with one's usual activities. Manhattan Life Insurance Co. v Francisco, 84 US (17 Wallace) 672, 21 L Ed (US) 698. Any affection of the body which deprives it temporarily of the power to fulfill its usual functions. Doody v Davie, 77 Cal App 310, 246 P 339. A diseased condition which has advanced far enough to incapacitate. Milam v Norwich Union Indem. Co. 107 W Va 574, 149 SE 668.
See **illness**; **last sickness**; **serious illness**; **sick**.

sick pay. Pay received by an employee under a wage continuation plan, for time when sickness rendered work by him impossible. 19 Am J2d Corp § 1055.

si constet de persona (sī kon'stet de per-sō'na). If it clearly appears as to the person.

si contingat (sī kon-tin'gat). If it happens.

sic pendet. See **et sic pendet**.

sic subscribitur (sik sub-skrī'bi-ter). It is so subscribed.

sic ulterius. See **et sic ulterius**.

sicut alias (sik'ut a'li-as). As on another occasion.

sic utere tuo ut alienum non laedas (sik u'te-re tu'ō ut ā-li-ē'num non lē'das). So use your own property as not to injure that of another. A maxim of the common law. 38 Am J1st Negl § 15. A maxim applicable to adjoining landowners and to a large extent governing in determining the rights, duties, and liabilities of adjoining landowners in respect of each other. 1 Am J2 Adj L § 2. A principle constituting to a large extent the foundation of the police power. 16 Am J2d Const L § 267.

sic uti suo ut non laedat alienum (sic ū'tī sū'ō ut non lē'dat al-i-ē'num). To use his own in such manner that he does not injure another. Rylands v Fletcher (Eng) LR 3 HL 330.

sicut me Deus adjuvet (sik'ut mē Dē'us ad-jū'vet). So help me God.

Sicut natura nil facit per saltum, ita nec lex (sik'ut na-tū'ra nil fā'sit per sal'tum, i'ta nek' lex). Just as nature does nothing by a leap, so neither does the law.

sic volo (sik vo'lō). I so will it; I will it thus.

side. Margin, edge, or border. An area or field in a graphic sense, as equity side.
See **civil side**; **equity side**; **plea side**.

side-bar reports. Reports of opinions of trial courts.

side-bar rules. A term of older English practice for rules or orders rendered by the court without application therefor formally made, for example, a rule to plead within a prescribed time.

sidecar. A small car attached to the side of a motorcycle for carrying a passenger, the same being supported by a third wheel. Neighbors v Life & Casualty Ins. Co. 182 Ark 356, 31 SW2d 418.

side judge (sīd juj). An associate judge.

side lights. Lights on the side of a motor vehicle of more than normal width, marking the extreme left side of the vehicle, required by statute in some jurisdictions. Anno: 21 ALR2d 77-84, §§ 24-26.

side lines. The margins of something, such as a highway. 12 Am J2d Bound § 52. Lines on building lots established, sometimes by municipal regulation, but more often by restrictive covenants, to mark the limits of construction in the direction of either side of the lot. 20 Am J2d Cov § 238. The boundary lines of a mining claim which do not cross the vein, running on each side of it. 36 Am J1st Min & M § 90.

sidereal day (sī-dē'rẹ-ạl dā). A day measured by the transit of certain stars. A day which begins at the noon or middle of the "day," in common parlance. 52 Am J1st Time § 14.
A mean sidereal day is 23 hours, 56 minutes, 4.091 seconds of mean solar time. Rochester German Ins. Co. v Peaslee's Gaulbert Co. 120 Ky 752, 87 SW 1115, 89 SW 3.

sidereal month (sī-dē'rẹ-ạl mùnth). A month as determined by changes in the position of the moon relative to certain stars. Guaranty Trust & S.D. Co. v Buddington, 27 Fla 215, 9 So 246.

side restriction. Provisions in zoning ordinance stipulating the minimum side area of the yard or lawn, or the percentage of the area of a lot that may be occupied by the building thereon. 58 Am J1st Zon § 52.

side street. A street intersecting a main or other street with heavy traffic.

sidetrack. A railroad track used for loading, unloading, reloading, storing, and switching railroad cars. 44 Am J1st R R § 231. A railroad track upon which one train is switched to permit another train to pass on the main track. A spur track for the benefit of a factory or industrial plant. Anno: 4 ALR 530.
See **spur track**.

sidewalk. A walkway along the margin of a street or other highway, designed and prepared for the use of pedestrians, to the exclusion of vehicles. 25 Am J1st High § 7.
As the word is used in the United States, it does not mean a walk or way constructed of any particular kind of material, or in any special manner, but ordinarily it means that part of the street of a municipality which has been set apart and is used for pedestrians, as distinguished from that portion set apart and used for animals and vehicles. Graham v Albert Lea, 48 Minn 201, 205.

sidewalk elevator. See **outside elevator**.

sidewalk stand. A booth or small structure standing upon the sidewalk for commercial or other purpose calling for contact with persons using the way. 25 Am J1st High § 306.

siding. The covering of the outer surface of the wall of a house or other structure. A **sidetrack**.

Si duo in testamento pugnantia reperientur, ultimum est ratum (sī du'ō in tes-ta-men'tō pug-nan'she-a re-pe-ri-en'ter, ul'ti-mum est rā'tum). If in a will two repugnant clauses are found, the latter one controls.

siens (si-ens'). Scions; descendants.

Si equam meam equus tuus pregnantem fecerit, non est tuum sed meum quod natum est (sī ē'quam me'am e'qu-us tu'us preg-nan'tem fē'se-rit, non est tu'um sed me'um quod nā'tum est). If your horse shall cause my mare to be with foal, the offspring is not yours, but mine.

si fecerit te securum (sī fe'se-rit tē se-kū'rum). If he shall have given you security,—an original writ di-

sight. The power to see. The faculty of vision. Act of seeing; perception of objects by the instrumentality of the eyes; view. Tracey v Standard Acci. Ins. Co. 119 Me 131, 109 A 490, 9 ALR 521, 529. A grand or spectacular view. Something worth seeing. Spoken in satire, something not pleasing to the sight. The observation of a bill of exchange or draft by the drawee upon presentation for acceptance.

See **after sight**; **at sight**; **loss of sight**.

sight bill. Same as **sight draft**.

sight draft. A bill of exchange or draft payable upon presentation to the drawee. The equivalent of a check payable upon demand. Mt. Vernon Nat. Bank v Canby State Bank, 129 Or 36, 276 P2d 262, 63 ALR 1133.

A draft payable at or after sight can never become due until after it has been accepted. Musson v Lake (US) 4 How 262, 11 L Ed 967.

sigillare (si-jil-lā′re). To affix a seal; to seal.

sigillum (si-jil′lum). A seal.

Sigillum est cera impressa, quia cera sine impressione non est sigillum (si-jil′lum est sē′ra im-pres′sa, qui′a sē′ra sī′ne im-pre′she-ō-ne non est si-jil′lum). A seal is the wax which has been impressed, because the wax without the impression is no seal. See 2 Bl Comm 306.

sigla (sig′lạ). (Roman law.) Abbreviations.

sign. Verb: To append one's name to a document. To subscribe in one's own handwriting. Knox's Estate, 131 Pa 220, 230. To execute or adopt any symbol with present intention to authenticate a writing. UCC § 1—201(39). Noun: A billboard. A placard or board bearing advertising or a public notice. 3 Am J2d Advertg § 13. A symbol, such as a ditto mark indicating repetition of the matter immediately above it. 1 Am J2d Abbr § 9. An indication, such as a condition of the sky indicating the approach of bad weather.

signa (sig′na). (Civil law.) Evidence addressed to the senses, as by exhibits offered in court.

signal. A means of communication. An incitement to action or to the avoidance of danger. An indication of an act to follow. A demonstration by a motorist, with hand, light, or mechanical device, to warn other users of his intended movement, such as backing, left turn, etc.

See **railroad signals**.

signalman. A man employed in giving signals, particularly a railroad employee giving signals to trains. 35 Am J1st M & S § 389.

signal post. A post along a railroad track indicating the necessity of giving a signal at that point, especially a whistle for a railroad crossing.

signal torpedo. A cartridge or explosive detonated by the wheel of a locomotive or railroad car when placed on the rail, used by trainmen as a signal. 31 Am J2d Explos § 8.

signare (sig-nā′re). To sign; to seal.

signatorius annulus (sig-nā-tō′ri-us an′nu-lus). (Civil law.) A seal ring; a signet ring.

signatory (sig′nạ-tọ-ri). A person who signs a contract or other instrument as a party thereto, or as an agent of a party thereto. A nation which has become a party to a treaty.

signature. The name of a person appended by him to an instrument. The execution of any symbol upon a writing with intent to authenticate the instrument as one made or put into effect by him. UCC § 1- 201(39). The authentication of a deed by the grantor's act in writing his name upon the instrument at such a place on the instrument that it will appear as having been affixed for the purpose of authentication. 23 Am J2d Deeds §§ 23 et seq. The affixing of the name of the maker or drawer of a negotiable instrument upon the instrument by such maker or drawer or by his agent or representative. 11 Am J2d B & N §§ 209 et seq. The appending of his name, by a party to a contract in writing, upon the instrument as a manifestation of intent to enter into the contract represented by the instrument. 17 Am J2d Contr § 70. The affixing of a name or mark to an instrument for the purpose of authenticating it as a testamentary disposition of property. 57 Am J1st Wills § 244.

The words "written signature" in a statute requiring such a signature must be construed as requiring that the signature shall be in one's own handwriting, or if he is unable to write, his mark. Irving v Goodimate Co. 320 Mass 454, 70 NE2d 414, 171 ALR 326.

signature by mark. The use, normally by an illiterate person, of a mark, such as a cross, even a fingerprint or thumbprint, as a substitute for a complete signature of one's name. A valid signature when witnessed as required by statute. 17 Am J2d Contr § 72; 23 Am J2d Deeds § 25; 57 Am J1st Wills §§ 250-252.

See **his mark**.

signature by proxy. A signature affixed by a proxy. See **per proc.**; **proxy**.

signature card. A card containing the signature of a depositor given to a bank as a means of authenticating signatures on paper presented to the bank purporting to be those of the depositor. A card filed with a bank by a depositor, requiring the signatures of certain persons on instruments presented for the purpose of withdrawing funds from the account. 10 Am J2d Banks § 494.

signed. Executed by the affixing of one's signature. Bensimer v Fell, 35 W Va 15, 12 SW 1078.

See **sign**; **signature**.

signed, sealed, and delivered. An expression in a certificate of acknowledgment which states, in effect, the execution of the instrument. 1 Am J2d Ack § 75.

signet (sig′net). A seal.

See **clerk of the signet**; **privy signet**.

signet ring. A ring with the wearer's signet or seal upon it.

significant contact. See **most significant contact theory**.

significavit (sig″ni-fi-kā′vit). (Ecclesiastical law.) A writ for the recaption of a person who had been excommunicated.

signify. To make known by signs or words; express; communicate; announce; declare. State v Klein, 94 Wash 212, 162 P 52.

signing. See **sign**; **signature**.

sign manual. A signature. The signature of a monarch on an official document. See 2 Bl Comm 346.

signum (sig'num). A sign; a signature; a mark intended as a signature.

Si in chartis membranisve tuis carmen vel historiam vel orationem Titius scripserit, hujus corporis non Titius sed tu dominus esse videris (sī in kar'tis membrā-nīs've tu'is kar'men vel his-tō'ri-am vel ō-rā-she-ō'nem ti'she-us skrip'se-rit, hu'jus kor'po-ris non ti'she-us sed tu dō'mi-nus es'se vi-dē'ris). (Civil law.) If Titius shall have written a poem, a history or a speech on your paper or parchment, not Titius, but you, are deemed to be the owner of the whole. See 2 Bl Comm 406.

si ita est (sī i'ta est). If it is true. An expression used in writs of mandamus which issued out of the English court of chancery to compel an inferior court to sign a bill of exceptions, and commanding the judge to seal it, if the fact alleged be truly stated. Ex parte Crane (US) 5 Pet 190, 193, 8 L Ed 92, 93.

Si judicas, cognosce (sī jū'di-kas, kog-no'se). If you judge, first understand.

silage (sī'lăj). See **silo**.

silence. Refraining from speech. The absence of speech; not a concealment or representation in itself. 37 Am J2d Fraud § 144.
Mere silence, as a general rule does not amount to an assent, but, taking it together with other circumstances, there are many cases in which silence or acquiescence will warrant a conclusive presumption that assent has been given. Myers v Cook, 87 W Va 265, 104 SE 593.
Silence operates as a waiver only when there is an obligation to speak. Dunbar v Farnum, 109 Vt 313, 196 A 237, 114 ALR 996.
See **estoppel by silence**.

silence of Congress. A doctrine of frequent application in determining whether a state may enact regulations in a field of legislation in the absence of any direct expression of the will of the Federal Government, the rule being that when the subjects of a power are in their nature national or admit of one uniform system or plan, exclusive regulation by Congress is presumed to be required, and the failure of Congress to exercise the power of regulation is deemed to be an expression of its will that the subject should remain free from restrictions or impositions upon it by the several states. 16 Am J2d Const L § 209.

Silent leges inter arma (sī'lent lē'jēz in'ter ar'ma). The laws are silent in warfare.
"The maxim expresses a fact, and a necessary fact, rather than a sentiment or principle." See argument of counsel in Prize Cases (US) 2 Black 635, 17 L Ed 459, 465.

silent partner. Same as **dormant partner**.

silent partners. Persons not known to be partners and not appearing to the public as partners, but who are nevertheless partners, as by partaking of profits, to all intents and purposes or, at least, in respect of third persons. 40 Am J1st Partn § 15.

silent policeman. A mechanical device placed at an intersection of streets for controlling traffic. Aaronson v New Haven, 94 Conn 609, 110 A 872, 12 ALR 328.

silica (sil'i-kä). A mineral found in quartz and sand. 36 Am J1st Min & M § 5.

silicosis (sil-i-kō'sis). A chronic and serious disease of the lungs, caused by the inhalation of dust, especially dust of silica. Anno: 68 ALR2d 196.

silo (sī'lō). A pit or structure in a cylindrical form, especially one used for the storing of a green crop and the curing of such into a form known as silage, of special value as feed for livestock.

silva caedua (sil'va sē'du-a). Wood or timber preserved for annual cutting.

silver. A precious metal used in the coining of money, and in various arts, crafts, and industries.
See **ale-silver; aver silver; bullion; green silver; herring silver; king's silver; plough silver**.

silver certificates. Certificates issued by the United States Government to circulate as money and secured by silver in the treasury.

silver coin. Money coined in part at least from silver; specie. Belford v Woodward, 158 Ill 122, 41 NE 1097.

silver coinage. The coinage of silver as provided by statute and with the amount of silver in particular coins as provided by statute. Bronson v Rodes (US) 7 Wall 229, 19 L Ed 141.

silver fox. A fox noted for the value of its pelt. A fox which can be bred, raised, and pelted in captivity. Fromm Bros. v United States (DC Wis) 35 F Supp 145.

sim (sim). Contraction of similis. Resembling; similar.
See **et sim**.

Si meliores sunt quos ducit amor, plures sunt corrigit timor (sī me-li-ō'rez sunt quōs du'sit a'mor, plū'rēz sunt kor'ri-jit ti'mor). Although love guides those who are better, fear corrects more.

similar. Having a resemblance in many respects to, nearly corresponding with, is somewhat like, or has a general likeness to, some other thing. Japan Import Co. v United States, 24 Cust & Pat App 167, 86 F2d 124; Fletcher v Interstate Chemical Co. 94 NJL 332, 110 A 709, 17 ALR 92, affd 95 NJL 543, 112 A 887, 17 ALR 92. Something less than being an exact duplicate of something else. 13 Am J2d Bldg Contr § 10. Sometimes, depending upon the context in which it appears, meaning identical or exactly alike. Anno: 17 ALR 94.

similarly. In like manner. In manner substantially the same. General Motors Corp. v Read, 294 Mich 558, 293 NW 751, 130 ALR 429.

simile materia. See **in simile materia**.

similis (si'mi-lis). (Latin.) Resembling. Similar.
See **et sim**.

similiter (si-mil'i-tėr). The like. A formal statement in writing whereby a party expresses his acceptance of an issue tendered by the pleading of his adversary.
A similiter is not in strictness a part of a pleading, but common-law practice regarded it as a vital formality. Huling v Florida Sav. Bank, 19 Fla 695, 705.

similiter dicere (si-mi'li-ter di'se-re). To say the like; to homologate. Hecker v Brown, 104 La 524, 527, 29 So 232.

similitude provisions. Provisions in tariff schedules intended to charge articles not enumerated therein with the duty applicable to articles which they most resemble. 21 Am J2d Cust D § 51.

Similitudo legalis est casuum diversorum inter se collatorum similis ratio; quod in uno similium valet, valebit in altero. Dissimilium dissimilis est ratio (si-mi-li-tū'dō lē-gā'lis est ka'su-um di-ver-sō'rum in'ter sē kol-la-tō'rum si'mi-lis rā'she-ō; quod in ū'nō si-mi'li-um va'let, va-lē'bit in al'te-rō. Dis-si-mi'li-um dis-si'mi-lis est rā'she-ō). Legal similarity is a similar reason of different cases compared with one another, and what prevails in one similar case prevails in another. The reason of dissimilar cases is dissimilar.

simonia (si-mō'ni-a). Same as **simony**.

simony (sim'ọ-ni). The crime of buying or selling ecclesiastical preferment, or the corrupt presentation of anyone to an ecclesiastical benefice for money or reward. State v Buswell, 40 Neb 158, 58 NW 728.

The word derives from Simon Magus, who was found to have purchased holy orders. It was not a common-law offense, but was wholly an ecclesiastical one. See 2 Bl Comm 278.

Si mortuo viro uxor ejus remanserit, et sine liberis fuerit, dotem suam habebit—si vero uxor cum liberis remanserit, dotem quidem habebit, dum corpus suum legitime servaverit (sī mor'tu-ō vi'rō u'xor e'jus re-man'se-rit, et sī'ne li'be-ris fu'e-rit, dō'tem su'am hā-bē'bit—sī vē'rō u'xor kum li'be-ris re-man'se-rit, dō'tem qui'dem hā-bē'bit, dum kor'pus su'um le-ji'ti-me ser-vā've-rit). If upon her husband's death his wife shall survive him, and she shall be without children, she will have her dower —but if she shall survive him with children she shall have dower while she lives in propriety. See 2 Bl Comm 133.

simple. Free of complexity. Easily understood. Unmixed. Not aggravated.
See **fee simple**.

simple annuity. Same as **straight annuity**.

simple assault. An attempt to do bodily harm to a person which fails, falls short of doing the harm, touching the body or doing the battery. For instance, striking at another within striking distance, but not striking him. State v Lightsey, 43 SC 114, 115, 20 SE 975.

simple average. Same as **particular average**.

simple blockade (blok-ād'). A blockade which may be established by a naval officer, acting upon his own discretion or under direction of superiors, without governmental notification.

In the case of a simple blockade, captors are bound to prove its existence at the time of the capture; while in the case of a public blockade, the claimants are held to proof of discontinuance in order to protect themselves from the penalties of attempted violation. Hunter v United States (US) 2 Wall 135, 17 L Ed 796.

simple bond. An obligation whereby the obligor binds himself, his heirs, executors, and administrators to pay a certain sum of money to a named obligee on demand or on a day certain. Burnside v Ward, 170 Mo 531, 71 SW 337.

simple confession. A plea of guilty in a criminal prosecution. State v Willis, 71 Conn 293, 309, 41 A 820.

simple contract. A parol contract; an oral contract; a written contract not under seal. Perrine v Cheeseman, 11 NJL 174. Any contract other than a specialty or a contract of record. Western Union Tel. Co. v Taylor, 84 Ga 408, 11 SE 396.

simple homage (sim'pl om'ąj). A mere acknowledgment of tenure. See 1 Bl Comm 367.

simple interest. Interest computed on principal only. 30 Am J Rev ed Int § 2. The straight interest computed on the principal sum from the time when by the terms of the contract interest is to commence, to the time of payment or judgment. Hovey v Edmison, 3 Dak 449, 460, 22 NW 594.

simple larceny. A plain theft unaccompanied by any other atrocious circumstance. 32 Am J1st Larc § 3. The felonious taking and carrying away by man or woman of the personal goods of another, neither from the person, nor by night in the house of the owner. State v Chambers, 22 W Va 779.

simple license (lī'sėns). The grant of authority, without reward or consideration, to do a particular act, or series of acts, on another's land, without passing any interest or estate in the soil.

Such a license is revocable at the pleasure of the licensor, but not to make the licensee responsible in trespass or otherwise for acts done on the land in pursuance of the license. Neither is it revocable where the grantee has been induced to expend his means or money towards its enjoyment, without reimbursing him for what has been thus expended. Wynn v Garland, 19 Ark 23.

simple loss payable clause. A clause in a policy of insurance on property subject to mortgage or lien, covering loss by fire, windstorm, flood, or other peril, providing for the payment of the proceeds of the insurance in the event of a loss to the named mortgagee or lienor as his interest may appear, but without conditions serving to give the mortgagee or lienor a right of recovery greater than that of the mortgagor or lienee, so that a breach of a condition of the policy by the mortgagor or lienee which precludes him from recovering against the insurer likewise precludes a recovery by mortgagee or lienor. Collinsville Sav. Soc. v Boston Ins. Co. 77 Conn 676, 60 A 647.

simple negligence. Negligence which is neither gross nor wanton; the failure to use ordinary care. Differing from gross negligence in degree, but not in kind. See Semons v Towne, 285 Mass 96, 188 NE 605.

simple obligation. See **simple bond**; **simple contract**.

simple socage (sok'ąj). Free socage; that is, land tenure by services which were certain, free, and honorable.

simple trust. A simple conveyance of property to one upon trust for another, without further specifications or directions.

In such case the law regulates the trust and the cestui que trust has the right of possession and of disposing of the property, and he may call upon the trustee to execute such conveyances of the legal estate as are necessary. (Perry on Trusts.) Cone v Dunham, 59 Conn 145, 20 A 311.

simplex (sim'pleks). (Latin.) Simple. Not complex.
See **feudum simplex**.

Simplex commendatio non obligat (sim'pleks kom-men-dā'she-ō non ob'li-gat). Mere commendation is not binding.
See **seller's talk**.

simplex dictum (sim'plex dik'tum). A mere allegation.

Simplex et pura donatio dici poterit ubi nulla est adjecta conditio nec modus (sim'plex et pū'ra do-nā'she-ō dī'sī pō'te-rit ū'bi nu'la est ad-jek'ta kon-di'she-ō nek mō'dus). A gift can be said to be pure and simple when no condition or modification is annexed to it.

simplex justitiarius (sim'plex ju-sti-she-ā'ri-us). Simple justice.

simplex loquela (sim'plex lo-kwē'la). A mere allegation or matter of complaint.

simplex obligatio (sim'plex ob-li-gā'she-ō). A simple obligation.
See **simple bond**; **simple contract**.

simplex peregrinatio (sim'plex pe-re-grī-nā'she-ō). Simple pilgrimage.

Simplicitas est legibus amica, et nimia subtilitas in jure reprobatur (sim-pli'si-tās est lē'ji-bus a-mī'ka, et ni'mi-a sub-ti'li-tās in jö're re-pro-bā'ter). Simplicity is a friend to the law and too much subtlety is disapproved in the law.

simpliciter (sim-plis'i-tėr). Simply.

Simplification of Fiduciary Security Transfers. One of the uniform statutes. Am J2d Deskbook, Document 129.

simulated (sim'ū-lā-ted). Counterfeited; feigned; pretended.
If the general impression which the article makes when seen alone is such as is likely to lead the ordinary purchaser to believe it to be the original article, there is an unlawful simulation amounting to unfair competition. Chesebrough Mfg. Co. v Old Gold Chemical Co. (CA6 Tenn) 70 F2d 383.

simulatio latens (si-mu-lā'she-ō lā'tenz). Simulated or feigned illness.

simulation. See **simulated**.

simul cum (sī'mul kum). Together with.

simul et simul (sī'mul et sī'mul). Together and at the same time.

simultaneous death (sim-ul-tā'nę-us deth). A death so contemporaneous with the fatal injury as to be instantaneous in the sense that the victim endured no pain and suffering. Moffett v Baltimore & Ohio R. Co. (CA4 W Va) 220 F 39. The death of two or more persons in a common disaster under circumstances such that it is impossible to determine the first to die or the last to survive. 57 Am J1st Wills § 1617. The death of ancestor and heir apparent occurring under such circumstances that there is no evidence as to which survived the other. 23 Am J2d Desc & D § 103.

Simultaneous Death Act. A uniform law which provides that where title to or the devolution of property depends upon priority of death and there is no sufficient evidence that the persons have died otherwise than simultaneously, the property of each person shall be disposed of, except as otherwise provided in the act, as if he had survived. 9C ULA 160; Anno: 20 ALR2d 236, § 1; 22 Am J2d Dth § 297.

simultaneously (sim-ul-tā'nę-usly). Occurring together; occurring at the same time. Anno: 20 ALR2d 235.
The word does not necessarily mean at the very same instant, but may, and often does mean at substantially the same time. Cloyes v Middlebury Electric Co. 80 Vt 109, 66 A 1039.
The word as used in the Uniform Simultaneous Death Act means at the same instant rather than at substantially or approximately the same time. Anno: 20 ALR2d 237.

simultaneous sentences. Sentences for more than one offense, running concurrently. 21 Am J2d Crim L § 547.

simultaneous trusts. Reciprocal trusts.

since. Adverb: After. Not always limited to the time between the present and a past event, or to a space of time between two certain past events, and some times embracing a future time. 52 Am J1st Time § 27. Preposition: During; at a time after; from and after. 52 Am J1st Time § 27.

sincere. Without guile; without pretense; without fraud or deceit.

sine (sī'ne). Without.

sine animo remanendi (sī'ne a'ni-mō re-ma-nen'dī). Without intent to remain.

sine animo revertendi (sī'ne a'ni-mō re-ver-ten'dī). Without an intention of returning; without intending to return.

sine assensu capituli (sī'ne as-sen'sū ka-pi'tu-lī). A writ for a church corporation to recover its lands which had been wrongfully conveyed.

sine brevi. See **debitum sine brevi**.

sine consideratione curiae (sī'ne kon-si-de-rā-she-ō'ne kū'ri-ē). Without having been considered or passed upon by the court.

sine cura (sī'ne kū'ra). Without care; charged with no duty.

sinecure (sī'nę-kūr). A position of profit entailing little, if any, effort or responsibility. A benefice without cure of souls.

sine damno. See **injuria sine damno**.

sine day adjournment. See **adjournment sine die**.

sine decreto (sī'ne de-krē'tō). Without judicial sanction.

sine die (sī'ne dī'ē). Without day; finally; without any time set for further consideration.

sine hoc quod (sī'ne hōk quod). Without this, that.

sine injuria. See **damnum sine injuria**.

sine liberis (sī'ne li'be-ris). Without children.

sine numero (sī'ne nu'me-rō). Without number or limit.

Sine possessione usucapio procedere non potest (sī'ne po-ze-she-ō'ne u-su-kā'pi-ō pro-sē'de-re non po'-test). Prescription cannot exist without possession.

sine prole (sī'ne prō'le). Without issue.

sine qua non (sī'ne kwā non). Without which it is not; an indispensable requisite.

Sine scripto jus venit, quod usus approbavit, nam diuturni mores consensu utentium comprobati legem imitantur (sī'ne skrip'to jūs vē'nit, quod ū'sus appro-ba'vit, nam di-u-ter'nī mō'rēz kon-sen'sū u-ten'she-um kom-pro-bā'tī lē'jem i-mi-tan'ter). Law comes without any writing, that which usage has established, for long established customs sanctioned by the consent of those adopting them represent law. See 1 Bl Comm 74.

sine spe revertendi (sī'ne spē re-ver-ten'dī). Without the hope of returning.

sine spe revertendi et sine animo revertendi (sī'ne spē re-ver-ten'dī et sī'ne a'ni-mo re-ver-ten'dī). Without the hope of returning and without the intention of so doing.

sine vi aut dolo (sī'ne vī ât dō'lō). Without force or fraud.

single. Standing alone. One only. Unmarried. Hill v

Moore, 85 Tex 335, 341, 119 SW 162. A room in hotel or motel for one person.

single adultery. Adultery committed where only one of the parties to the offense is a married person. Hunter v United States (Wis) 1 Pinney 91.

single bill. Same as **bill obligatory.**

single bond. Same as **single bill.**

single combat (kom'bat). A duel; a battel.

single creditor. A term of art in marshaling assets; a creditor having a lien upon only one fund or item of property. Newby v Norton, 90 Kan 317, 133 P 890.

single dwelling house. A dwelling house for a single family. 20 Am J2d Cov § 196.

single dwelling restriction. A restriction in a covenant contained in a deed or land contract which limits construction upon the premises to single dwellings, that is one-family dwellings, as distinguished from apartment houses and other multiple dwellings. 20 Am J2d Cov § 196.

single family. See **family.**

single letter. An older term of the postal laws for a letter consisting of one sheet. Williams v Wells, Fargo & Co. Express (CA8 Ark) 177 F 352.

single man. A man of marriageable age who has never been married. A man of marriageable age presently unmarried.

single-member district. A legislative district having one representative in the legislature. 25 Am J2d Elect § 25.

single original. An instrument not in duplicate.

single premium annuity contract. An annuity contract for which the purchaser pays a single premium, that is, a premium in one lump sum. 4 Am J2d Annui § 1.

single publication rule. The principle that an injury occurs and a cause of action arises from a single publication of a defamatory article. 16 Am J2d Confl L § 72.
Under the single publication rule, any single integrated publication, such as one edition of a newspaper or magazine, or one broadcast, is treated as a unit, giving rise to only one cause of action of defamation, invasion of privacy, or similar tort. Hartmann v Time, Inc. (CA3 Pa) 166 F2d 127, 1 ALR2d 370.

single shot. In the vernacular of practical politics, the strategy whereby in an election where several judges of a court or several members of a board are to be elected, a minority may succeed in electing one judge or one member by voting for their candidate and no others.

single-story dwelling. A dwelling house having only one floor level. Anno: 92 ALR2d 886, § 5(a).

single subject. One subject.
As the term is used in the common constitutional provision requiring that a statute shall contain but one subject which shall be clearly expressed in its title, where all the provisions of the statute fairly relate to the same subject, have a natural connection with it, or are the incidents or means of accomplishing it, then the subject is "single," and if it is sufficiently expressed in the title, the provision is satisfied. State v Smith, 233 Mo 242, 135 SW 465.

single tax. The theory that all revenue for the support of government should be derived from a tax on a single subject, that is, real property.

single tax club. An organization devoted to the promotion of the theory of single tax. Anno: 138 ALR 460.

single woman. A female of marriageable age who has never been married. A woman of marriageable age presently unmarried. Devinney v State (Ohio) Wright 564.

singular. One of a kind. Unique. Denoting one only. See **all and singular.**

singulariter (sin-gu-la'ri-ter). Singly; one at a time.

Singuli in solidum tenentur (sin'gu-lī in so'li-dum te-nen'ter). Each one is bound or obligated for the whole.

sink. A fixture in a dwelling house, factory, office building, or other structure, constituting a part of the plumbing, wherein water may be run and discharged as desired. 35 Am J2d Fixt § 123. A depression in land wherein surface water is collected, sometimes becoming a swamp or bog.

sinking fund. A fund accumulated by a debtor, usually a corporation or public body, and invested in such a manner that its gradual accumulations will enable it to meet and wipe out the debt at maturity thereof. Huron v Second Ward Sav. Bank (CA8 SD) 86 F 272. A fund arising from particular taxes, imposts, or duties which is appropriated toward the payment of the interest accruing on a public debt and for the gradual payment of the principal. 43 Am J1st Pub Sec § 4. A cumulative security for the payment of the debt with which it is connected, and especially earmarked for the extinction of the debt. Clark v Philadelphia, 328 Pa 521, 196 A 384, 115 ALR 212. A public fund maintained by the state for the purpose of guaranteeing the reimbursement of the state, county, township, municipal, school corporation or other public agency in the event of the loss of public funds caused by the failure of the depository. 42 Am J1st Pub F § 18.

sinking fund tax. A tax which is raised to be applied to the payment of the principal and interest of a public debt or obligation. Brooks v Brooklyn, 146 Iowa 136, 124 NW 868.

Si non appareat quid actum est, erit consequens ut id sequamur quod in regione in qua actum est frequentatur (sī non ap-pā're-at quid ak'tum est, e'rit kon-se'quenz ut id se-quā'mer quod in re-ji-ō'ne in qua ak'tum est fre-quen-tā'ter). If it does not appear what was done, the consequence will be that we shall follow that which is commonly done in the locality in which it was done.

si non omnes (sī non om'nēz). A writ which lay to assemble the justices, under which two or more of the justices were empowered to hold court if all the justices of the court were not present.

Si nulla sit conjectura quae ducat alio, verba intelligenda sunt ex proprietate, non grammatica sed populari ex usu (sī nu'la sit kon-jek-tū'ra kwē du'kat a'li-ō, ver'ba in-te-li-jen'da sunt ex prō-pri-e-tā'te, non gram-ma'ti-ka sed po-pu-lā'ri ex u'su). If there is no conjecture which leads to a different conclusion, words are to be understood according to their proper sense or meaning; and not according to a grammatical usage, but according to a popular one.

**Si plures conditiones ascriptae fuerunt donationi conjunctim omnibus est parendum; et ad veritatem copulative requiritur quod utraque pars sit vera, si divisim, quilibet vel alteri eorum satis est obtem-

perare; et disjunctivis, sufficit alteram partem esse veram (sī plu'rēz kon-di-she-ō'nēz a-skrip'tē fu-ē'runt do-na-she-ō'ni kon-junk'tim om'ni-bus est pa-ren'dum; et ad ve-ri-tā'tem ko-pu-lā'ti-ve re-qui'ri-ter quod u-trā'kwe parz sit vē'ra, sī di-vī'-sim, qui'li-bet vel al'te-rī e-ō'rum sa'tis est ob-tem-per-a're; et dis-junk-tī'vis, suf'fis-sit al'te-ram par'-tem es'se ve'ram). If several conditions of a gift have been written in the conjunctive, they must all be performed; and, as to their truth, it is required that each part shall be true taken jointly; if they are separately written, it is sufficient to comply with any one or other of them, and as they are disjunctive, it is sufficient if either part be true.

Si plures sint fidejussores, quotquot erunt numero, singuli in solidum tenentur (sī plū'rēz sint fī-de-jus-sō'rēz, quot'quot e'runt nū'me-rō, sin'gu-lī in so'li-dum te-nen'ter). If there are several sureties, however great their number, each one is jointly bound for the whole.

si prius (sī prī'us). If before.

Si quidem in nomine, cognomine, praenomine, agno-mine legatarii testator erraverit, cum de persona constat nihilominus valet legatum (sī qui'dem in nō'-mi-ne, kog-nō'mi-ne, prē-nō'mi-ne, ag-nō'mi-ne lē-gā-tā'ri-ī tes-tā'tor er-ra've-rit, kum de per-sō'na kon'stat ni-hil-o-mī'nus va'let lē-gā'tum). (Civil law.) If any testator shall have erred in the name, the cognomen, the praenomen or title of a legatee, the legacy will nevertheless be valid when the person intended is made clear.

Si quid universitati debetur, singulis non debetur; nec, quod debet universitas, singuli debent (sī quid u-ni-ver-si-tā'ti de-bē'ter, sin'gu-lis non de-bē'ter; nek, quod de'bet u-ni-ver'si-tās sin'gu-lī de'bent). If anything is owing a corporation, it is not due each member; nor do the individuals owe what the corporation owes. See 1 Bl Comm 484.

si quis (sī' kwis). If anyone. A term of art for a public notice, of an ecclesiastical matter particularly.

Si quis cum totum petiisset partem petat, exceptio rei judicatae vocet (sī quis kum tō'tum pe-ti-is'set par'tem pe'tat, ek-sep'she-ō rē'ī ju-di-kā'tē vo'set). If anyone sue for a part when he should have sued for the whole, the judgment is res adjudicata. Faurie v Pitot (La) 2 Mart 83.

Si quis custos fraudem pupillo fecerit, a tutela remo-vendus est (sī quis kus'tos frâ'dem pu-pil'lō fe'se-rit, ā tū-tē'la re-mo-ven'dus est). If any guardian commits a fraud against his ward, he should be removed from his guardianship.

Si quis praegnantem uxorem reliquit, non videtur sine liberis decessisse (sī quis prēg-nan'tem u-xō'rem re'li-quit, non vi-dē'ter sī'ne li'be-ris de-sessis'se). (Civil law.) If anyone has left his wife while she was pregnant, he is not deemed to have died without children.

Si quis rem dat et partem retinet, illa pars quam retinet semper cum eo est, et semper fuit (sī quis rem dat et par'tem re'ti-net, il'la parz quam re'ti-net sem'per kum e'ō est, et sem'per fu'it). If anyone grant anything and reserve a part, that part which he reserves is in him, and always will be. Greenleaf's Lessee v Birth (US) 6 Pet 302, 310, 8 L Ed 406, 409.

si quis sine liberis decesserit (sī quis sī'ne li'be-ris de-ses'se-rit). If anyone shall have died without children.

Si quis unum percusserit, cum alium percutere vellet, in felonia tenetur (sī quis ū'num per-kus'se-rit, kum a'li-um per-ku'te-re vel'let, in fe-lō'ni-a te-nē'ter). If anyone kill one man when he intended to kill another, he is held for felony.

sirup. Another spelling for **syrup.**

sister. A woman or girl related to one by having been born of the same parents. A relative in the second degree according to the civil law method of computing degrees of kinship which prevails in most American jurisdictions. 23 Am J2d Desc & D § 48.
See **half sister.**

sister-in-law. The wife of one's brother or the sister of one's spouse. In common usage, also inclusive of the wife of one's husband's or wife's brother.

sister state. Another state of the United States.

Si suggestio non sit vera, literae patentes vacuae sunt (sī sug-jest'she-ō non sit ve'ra, li'te-rē pa-ten'tēz va'ku-ē sunt). If the suggestion is not true, the letters patent are void.

sit (sit). To preside as a judge. To be open for the business of the court.
See **sitting of court.**

sit-down strike. A strike wherein the employees do not leave the plant but refrain from work. Anno: 123 ALR 656; 83 L Ed 691.

site (sīt). A place where something stood in the past, as the site of Carthage. A prospective location for something, particularly a public building or industrial plant.
See **county site.**

si te fecerit securum (sī tē fe'se-rit se-kū'rum). If he shall have made you secure; if he give you security. See 3 Bl Comm 274.

sit in banc (sit in bangk). Same as **sit in bank.**

sit in bank (in bangk). To hold a session of a court at which all of the judges of the court are present.

sit in camera (in kạm'ėr-ạ̈). To hold a session of court in chambers or privately.

sit in misericordia (in mi-se-ri-cor'di-a). Let him be in mercy,—meaning, let him be amerced or fined. See 4 Bl Comm 379.

sitio. See **sitio ganado mayor.**

sitio ganado mayor (sē'te-o gah-nah'do mah'yor). A technical Spanish and Mexican legal term, well established, defined, and known as a section or township in the surveys of the United States.
It was a square, the four sides of which each measured five thousand varas. A conveyance of a "sitio" deeded as certain a form and quantity of land as a conveyance of a section. United States v Cameron, 3 Ariz 100, 21 P 177.

Sit quilibet homo dignus venatione sua, in silva, et in agris, sibi propriis, et in dominio suo; et abstineat omnis homo a venariis regiis, ubicunque pacem eis habere voluerit (sit quī'li-bet hō'mō dig'-nus ve-nā-she-ō'ne su'a, in sil'va, et in a'gris, si'bi prō'pri-is, et in do-mi'ni-ō su'ō; et ab-sti'ne-at om'-nis hō'mō a ve-na'ri-is rē'ji-is, u-bi-kun'kwe pa'sem e'is hā-bē're vo-lu'e-rit). Let every man be strict in his hunting in his own woods and fields and within his own manor; and let every man abstain from the royal hunting preserves if he should wish to have peace. See 2 Bl Comm 415.

sitting. See **sit; post-terminal sittings; sitting of court.**

sitting in bank. See **sit in bank.**

sitting of court. A session of court. A term of court.
"The district judges in their sittings in the several counties, for the trial of issues of fact, attended as they were by clerks, sheriffs, juries, and all the paraphernalia of courts of record, were holding district courts, and the duration of each of those sittings was a term of court." See Gird v State, 1 Or 308, 311.

situated. Located. Located physically.
Personal property is "situated" wherever it happens to be for the time being. County of Allegheny v Gibson, 90 Pa 397, 421.

situs (sī'tus). The place of the occurrence or the location of property involved in an action. 16 Am J2d Confl L § 11. Location of property in a physical sense. Location of property in a legal or fictional sense, as the situs of personal property for taxation.
See **business situs.**

situs for taxation. A place within the jurisdiction of the taxing authority. For real property, the place wherein the property is situated. For a license tax, the place wherein the acts which require a license are performed. 51 Am J1st Tax § 441. For a personal property tax, the county, city, town, or other taxing district in which the owner lives or has his domicil, except as the property has acquired a definite situs elsewhere, or unless other provision is made by statute. 51 Am J1st Tax § 448. For a tax on intangibles, the domicil of the owner, except as intangible property may have lost that situs under an exception such as that of "business" or "commercial situs." 51 Am J1st Tax § 463. For a personal or poll tax, the domicil of the person taxed. 51 Am J1st Tax § 447.

situs of assets. The location of assets left by a decedent, determinative of jurisdiction for administration. 31 Am J2d Ex & Ad § 38.

si universitas ad unum redit (sī u-ni-ver'si-tās ad ū'-num re'dit). If a corporation be reduced to one member. See 1 Bl Comm 469.

Si vasallus feudum dissipaverit, aut insigni detrimento deterius fecerit, privabitur (sī va-sal'lus fū'dum dis-si-pā've-rit, ât in-sig'nī dē-tri-men'tō dē-te'ri-us fē'se-rit, pri-vā'bi-ter). If a vassal shall have wasted the fee, or shall have made it less valuable by any extraordinary injury, he shall be deprived of it. See 2 Bl Comm 282.

sive sit masculus sive foemina (sī've sit mas'ku-lus sī've fē'mi-na). Whether (the heir) be male or female. See 2 Bl Comm 71.

Sive tota res evincatur, sive pars, habet regressum emptor in venditorem (sī've to'ta rēz e-vin-kā'ter, sī've parz, hā'bet re-gres'sum emp'tor in ven-di-tō'rem). Whether evicted altogether or partly, the vendee has his remedy against the vendor. See Broom's Legal Maxims 678.

Six Carpenters' Case. A celebrated case holding that refusal to pay for refreshment at a public tavern did not render a patron liable in an action of trespass as for an unlawful entry, because he had committed no trespass, and holding by way of dictum that the doctrine of trespass ab initio applied only where an entry was made under a license given by law, and not by permission of the party, and was not by permission of the party, and was followed by a trespass committed upon the premises. 8 Coke 146a.

six clerks in chancery (siks klėrks in chạn'sėr-i). The clerks in whose office a bill in equity was filed. Originally these clerks were all clergymen or priests and it was not until the English constitution began to change that a statute was enacted which permitted them to marry. See 3 Bl Comm 443.

six months' rule. The doctrine whereby the superior equity of claims based on operating expenses is extended to claims for material furnished or services and labor rendered within six months, or some other reasonable period, previous to the appointment of a receiver. 45 Am J1st Rec § 301.

Sixteenth Amendment. An amendment to the United States Constitution granting Congress the power to lay and collect taxes on incomes, from whatever sources derived, without apportionment among the several states, and without regard to any census or enumeration.

Sixth Amendment. An amendment to the United States Constitution contained in the Bill of Rights, providing that in all criminal prosecutions, the accused shall enjoy the right to a speedy and public trial by an impartial jury of the state and district wherein the crime shall have been committed, to be informed of the nature and cause of the accusation, to be confronted with the witnesses against him, to have compulsory process for obtaining witnesses in his favor, and to have the assistance of counsel for his defense.

sixth degree. A degree of relationship, that of the children of one's second cousins, according to the civil law method of computing degrees of kinship which prevails in most American jurisdictions. 23 Am J2d Desc & D § 48.

skates. Metal runners or blades attached to the shoes, or in a frame convenient for attaching to shoes, upon which one may propel himself in a gliding movement over ice. Slang for old horses or old men.
See **roller skating.**

skating rink. A public place of amusement, usually equipped with freezing elements maintaining a good surface of ice. Inglis v Rymer, 113 Fla 732, 152 So 4. A place for skating whether on ice skates or roller skates, often a public place where a charge is made for admission.
See **roller skating.**

skeleton bill of exceptions. A bill of exceptions which does not contain the evidence or rulings, but instead contains directions to the clerk of the trial court as to the parts of the transcript which are to be copied into the record for the appellate court. 4 Am J2d A & E § 434.

skeleton minutes. Minutes or short notes made by the court of the business transacted by the court during his sitting, the same to be extended later by the clerk of the court in the proper book of record. Johnson v Commonwealth, 80 Ky 377, 379.

sketch. A drawing or design with little, if any, detail. An outline of story or article to be written. A story told briefly, with little detail. A product of architectural services. 5 Am J2d Arch § 3.

skiagraph. Same as **radiograph.**

skid. An uncontrolled movement of a motor vehicle in sliding forward or to the side, caused by application of brakes or defective balance in the vehicle.

skid marks. The marks on the paving or ground left by the tires of a skidding motor vehicle. Anno: 70 ALR 544, s. 94 ALR 1192; 7 Am J2d Auto § 339.

skiff. A long and narrow rowboat, sometimes equipped with a sail. Quinette v Bisso (CA5 La) 136 F 825, cert den 199 US 606, 50 L Ed 330, 26 S Ct 746.

skill. Ability; proficiency. Knowledge coupled with the ability to apply it.

See **ordinary skill; reasonable skill; utmost care and skill.**

skilled witness. See **expert witness.**

skimmington. See **riding skimmington.**

skip-tracing. Services in locating debtors who have disappeared.

skip-tracing agency. An agency which assists creditors in locating delinquent debtors, either indirectly by giving advice and mailing materials or directly by uncovering information concerning the whereabouts of the delinquent ones.

Such a service or agency is to be distinguished from a collection agency in the respect that it does not directly attempt to collect the debt from the debtor. Rothschild v Federal Trade Com. (CA7) 200 F2d 39, cert den 345 US 941, 97 L Ed 1367, 73 S Ct 832; Wachsman v United States (Mun Ct App Dist Col) 175 A2d 789.

skylarking. Boisterous play, especially by employees who should be working. 35 Am J1st M & S § 201; 58 Am J1st Workm Comp § 268.

sky sign. A sign on the roof of a building. 3 Am J2d Advertg § 15.

slacker. One who evades a duty, particularly the duty of rendering military service in time of war.

The word is not found in lexicons published prior to World War I, but had its genesis as to use and meaning in the conditions following our entrance into such war, and in the exigencies of its successful prosecution. During the war it was unquestionably a term of the severest reproach, well understood by all men, and calculated to subject its bearer to hatred and contempt in practically every community in the land. Choctaw Coal & Mining Co. v Lillich, 204 Ala 533, 86 So 383, 11 ALR 1014, 1016.

slack lime. Lime to which water has been applied in the course of preparing it for use in making mortar.

slack statute. A state statute enacted for the purpose of taking advantage of the credit allowed against the federal estate tax for death taxes paid to any state or territory. Re Gallagher, 57 NM 112, 255 P2d 317, 37 ALR2d 149.

slag. Refuse taken from a furnace. 49 Am J1st Stat of F § 156.

slander. In modern usage, the speaking of base and defamatory words which tend to prejudice another in his reputation, office, trade, business, or means of livelihood. 33 Am J1st L & S § 3.

The term "slander" was formerly used as including both written and spoken defamation. Fenstermacher v Indianapolis Times Pub. Co. 102 Ind App 189, 1 NE2d 655.

See **fair comment; privileged communication; privileged occasion.**

slander of great men. See **scandalum magnatum.**

slander of property. Words or conduct which tend to disparage or reflect upon the quality, condition, or value of particular property. Paull v Halferty, 63 Pa 46.

slander of title. Words, written, printed, or uttered, which bring or tend to bring in question the right or title of another to real or personal property. 33 Am J1st L & S § 344. A false and malicious statement, oral or written, made in disparagement of a person's title to real or personal property, or some property right of his. Landstrom v Thorpe (CA8 SD) 189 F2d 46, 26 ALR2d 1170.

Slander of title is a false and malicious statement, oral or written, in disparagement of a person's title to real or personal property, causing him special damage, and the essential elements of a cause of action therefor are the uttering and publication of the slanderous words by defendant, the falsity of the words, malice, and special damages. Cawrse v Signal Oil Co. 164 Or 666, 103 P2d 729, 129 ALR 174.

slanderous per quod (slan'dėr-us pėr quod). Spoken words possibly of a noxious quality in respect of causing injury to another by prejudicing him in reputation, office, or means of livelihood, but actionable only as their injurious effect is established by due allegation and proof. Elkins v Roberts (Ky) 242 SW2d 994, 38 ALR2d 159.

slanderous per se (slan'dėr-us pėr sē). Spoken words of such nature as to be presumed by law actually and necessarily to damage the person of and concerning whom they are spoken, so as to be actionable without extrinsic proof of their injurious character. Elkins v Roberts (Ky) 242 SW2d 994, 38 ALR2d 159.

slattern (slat'ėrn). A woman untidy in appearance and habits.

See **slut.**

slaughterhouse. A building or plant where the business of butchering animals is conducted. 48 Am J1st Slaughter § 1.

Slaughter-House Cases. Cases responsible for a famous decision of the United States Supreme Court upholding a statute which rendered an exclusive franchise to a slaughterhouse company, the point at issue being the reasonableness of the classification made by the statute. (US) 16 Wall 36, 21 L Ed 394.

slaughtering. The killing of an animal for food. Shain v Armour & Co. (DC Ky) 50 F Supp 977. Killing brutally or in large numbers, whether of people or animals.

slave. A person owned by, and bound to, another. 48 Am J1st Slav § 4.

slave master. The owner of a slave.

slavery. Bondage. Involuntary servitude. An institution where one man is owned by and bound to another. 48 Am J1st Slav § 4.

The term implies involuntary servitude—a state of bondage; the ownership of mankind as a chattel, or at least the control of the labor and services of one man for the benefit of another, and the absence of a legal right to the disposal of his own person, property, and services. Plessy v Ferguson, 163 US 537, 542, 41 L Ed 256, 257, 16 S Ct 1138.

slave trade. The holding or transportation of human beings for sale as slaves. 48 Am J1st Slav § 1.

slay. To kill.

The word adds nothing to the force and effect of the word "kill," when used with reference to the taking of human life. It is particularly applicable to the taking of human life in battle; and when it is not used in this sense, it is synonymous with the word "kill." The man that is slain is killed; and the

sled. man that is killed by the hand of his fellow man is slain. State v Thomas, 32 La Ann 349, 351.
See **slaughtering**.

sled. A low vehicle mounted on runners, used by children, occasionally by adults, in coasting on snow or ice.
See **sleigh**.

sleep. To delay action to secure one's rights. To rest in both body and mind without conscious thought and a minimum of movement.

sleeper. One who is asleep. A horse in a race or a man in a contest, unknown before but winning or rating high in the race or contest. A beam which supports a building, placed horizontally on the foundation. A sleeping car.

sleeping car company. A public service corporation which under a contract with a railroad company, operates in a more or less independent manner its own cars as component parts of passenger trains for the purpose of furnishing to passengers sleeping facilities at night and special accommodations during the day, together with services incidental thereto, for which certain charges over and above the regular railroad fare are made for the benefit of the company operating the cars. 48 Am J1st Sl Car Co. § 1. Facetiously characterized as "flying nondescripts."

sleeping on rights. Laches. 27 Am J2d Equity § 130.

sleeping partner. Same as **dormant partner**.

sleeping porch. See **porch**.

sleepwalking. See **somnambulism**.

sleigh. A vehicle equipped with runners, for use on snow or ice. 25 Am J1st High § 165.
See **sled**.

slide. An amusement device, particularly for children, usually found in parks, wherein a child may slide on his backside. Chardon v Alameda Park Co. 1 Cal App 2d 18, 36 P2d 136. To coast in a sled.
See **skid**.

slight. Inconsiderable. Unimportant. Janesville v Carpenter, 77 Wis 288, 46 NW 128.

slight care. An attempted but very difficult classification. Care exercised in a particular situation less than that called for by ordinary and common prudence. Litchfield v White, 7 NY 438. Care so slight in degree that the failure to exercise it must be deemed gross negligence. Merchant's Nat. Bank v Guilmartin, 93 Ga 503, 21 SE 55.

slight diligence. Same as **slight care**.

slight negligence. A classification as impracticable as any classification according to a concept of degrees of negligence. 38 Am J1st Negl § 45. An absence of that degree of care and vigilance which persons of extraordinary prudence and foresight are accustomed to use; not sufficient as the foundation of an action or as a defense in a negligence action. 38 Am J1st Negl § 45.

sling. A weapon, consisting of a piece of rope or leather for throwing a stone from a pouch at the end. The weapon used by David against Goliath.
See **slingshot**.

slingshot. A weapon consisting of a small stick of wood with prongs or arms to which elastic bands are attached to furnish a means of compulsion of a small stone or piece of metal with force; sometimes classed as a deadly weapon. 56 Am J1st Weap § 3. A sling such as David used against Goliath.

See **sling**.

slip. A landing for a ferry. A place for mooring a vessel. 48 Am J1st Ship § 263. A rider attached to a contract, particularly a contract of insurance. 29 Am J Rev ed Ins § 268. A memorandum constituting a contract in itself, as a binding slip. A technical term for a great quantity of dust blown out of a blast furnace.

The escape of dust from blast furnaces into the atmosphere is, and always has been, incident to their operation. It escapes at all times, but in larger quantities when what is known as a "slip" occurs. In the operation of all blast furnaces "slips" occur from time to time. These are occasioned by the caking or incrusting of the ore in the stack of the furnace, and the falling away of the ore, fuel, and limestone beneath the crust by reason of continued combustion and the liquefaction of the iron, thus forming a chamber or vacant space into which the incrusted ore drops, occasioning an explosion, the violence of which depends upon the extent of the cavity produced and the amount of gas accumulated therein. See Sullivan v Jones & Laughlin Steel Co. 208 Pa 540, 57 A 1065.

See **binder; rider**.

slip of the tongue. Language different from that which the person who uttered the words intended to say.

slop stand. A sink. Leonard Bros. v Zachary (Tex Civ App) 94 SW2d 509.

slot machine. A coin-operated machine so operated that small amounts are put at hazard to win a larger amount. 34 Am J1st Lot § 16. An automatic vending machine; any machine requiring the deposit of money or metal chips therein before operating. 33 Am J1st Lic § 11.

slough (sluf). A depression; a marsh or swamp. Anno: 40 ALR 852. Sometimes considered a natural drainway of surface water. 56 Am J1st Water § 75. In an unusual sense of the term, one of the waterways which separate islands in a river from one another or from the mainland. Dunlieth & Dubuque Bridge Co. v County of Dubuque, 55 Iowa 558, 565.

slowdown. A concerted slowing down of production on the part of employees in an industrial plant. Kennedy v Westinghouse Electric Corp. 16 NJ 280, 108 A2d 409, 47 ALR2d 1025. A direction posted on a sign or communicated by signalman or traffic officer in controlling the movement of trains on a railroad or vehicles on a highway.

slow-moving vehicle. A vehicle which is not maintaining the pace of other vehicles on the highway or in the same lane of the highway, assuming that the other vehicles are not operated in excess of the speed limit.

slow sign. A sign on the highway calling for a reduction in speed of vehicle. A sign along a railroad track calling for a reduction in speed of train.

sluiceway (slös'wā). Artificial watercourse, usually constructed for taking water from a natural watercourse for use in mining or industry.

A sluiceway over reclaimed flats, through which the tide ebbs and flows, is not a watercourse. Chamberlain v Hemingway, 63 Conn 1, 27 A 239.

slum. A section of a city wherein poor and underprivileged persons are housed in inferior and dilapidated dwellings, flats, apartment houses, and tenements.

slum clearance. The improvement of housing for people of limited means by tearing down dilapidated and inferior structures and erecting new buildings, particularly apartment houses or other multiple dwellings, to be leased at moderate rentals. A public purpose. 26 Am J2d Em D § 42.

slush fund. Money collected for a corrupt use. Boehm v United States (CA8 Mo) 123 F2d 791.

slut. A slattern; a bold woman; in some connections, an unchaste woman. 33 Am J1st L & S § 39. A woman too careless and lazy to keep herself or her home in a condition of cleanliness, but not necessarily an unchaste woman. Cooper v Seaverns, 81 Kan 267, 105 P 509. A bitch; a female dog.

small average. Same as **petty average.**

small beer. A beer of low alcholic content. 30 Am J Rev ed Intox L § 10.

small brew. Near beer; a nonintoxicating malt beverage. 30 Am J Rev ed Intox L § 11.
 A term used in certain liquor statutes synonymously with "malt beverage" and "near beer" and classed with mixtures, preparations and liquids in which alcohol appears in varying proportions with other ingredients, and which may or may not contain alcohol in such proportion with the other ingredients that the stomach can bear enough of the mixture to produce intoxication. Commonwealth v Henry, 110 Va 879, 65 SE 570.

Small Business Act. A federal statute which declares and implements the policy of aiding, counseling, assisting, and protecting the interests of small business concerns in order to preserve free competitive enterprise. 15 USC § 631.

Small Business Administration. A federal agency created to carry out the policy declared by statute to aid, counsel, assist, and protect small business concerns. 15 USC § 633(a).

small business concern. A business independently owned and operated and not dominant in its field. 15 USC § 632.

small business corporation. A corporation which, although small in capitalization and the number of persons employed, may be a vital economic asset of the community.
 For definition of small business corporation for tax purposes, see Internal Revenue Code § 1244(c).

Small Business Investment Act. See **small business investment company.**

small business investment company. An investment company licensed and operated under the Federal Small Business Investment Act of 1958, particularly for the supplying of long-term equity capital to small business concerns.

small claims court. A tribunal, sometimes existing independently, at other times constituting a separate division of a court of general jurisdiction, being provided for the general purpose of providing a summary procedure, less costly and less protracted than the ordinary procedure, for the litigation of small claims, that is, claims not exceeding a certain specified amount. Superior Wheeler Cake Corp. v Superior Court, 203 Cal 384, 264 P 488.

small damages. Damages which, although small in the amount awarded, were calculated and allowed as compensation for an actual loss.
 See **nominal damages.**

small debtors' court.

small employer. An employer of five or less workmen in the same industry or business, or in the case of an employer with different businesses, five or less workmen in one single and distinct business. Moore v Isenman, 127 Me 370, 143 A 462, 61 ALR 898.

small loan act. A statute regulating the business of those who make small loans on conditional sale contracts, chattel mortgages, pledges, or assignments of wages. A statute regulating the business of pawnbrokers. 40 Am J1st Pawnb §§ 8, 9. A uniform statute regulating the small loan business. Madison Personal Loan v Parker (CA2 NY) 124 F2d 143.

small loan company. A company making loans in comparatively small amounts, usually secured by chattel mortgage, conditional sale contract, or pledge.

smallpox. A communicable disease characterized by fever, vomiting, and eruptions which sometimes leave scars. 25 Am J1st Hlth § 25.

Small Reclamation Projects Act. A federal statute supplementing the Federal Reclamation Act. 43 USC §§ 422a-422k.
 See **Reclamation Act.**

small tithes (smâl tīths). Praedial tithes, other than great tithes, and also mixed tithes and personal tithes.

smart money. In the modern sense of the term, the same as **punitive damages.** 22 Am J2d Damg §§ 236 et seq.
 It is interesting, as well as instructive, to observe that in colonial days the term smart money was employed in a manner entirely different from the modern signification which it has obtained, being then used as indicating compensation for the smarts of the injured person, and not as now, money required by way of punishment and to make the wrongdoer smart. Murphy v Hobbs, 7 Colo 541, 5 P 119.

smell. One of the senses.
 "We do know that the olfactory nerves are just as efficient as the optic or auditory nerves. The difficulty lies in the fact that our conscious use of them is so less frequent. To put it another way, we may smell as we see or hear, but we do not sniff nearly as frequently as we look or listen. The problem is not one of sensitivity but rather of selectivity. Consequently, skill in the art of detection through the sense of smell comes from experience rather than aptitude." United States v Commercial Creamery Co. (DC Wash) 43 F Supp 714.

smeller. One able to test products, such as cheese and alcoholic beverages, by smelling a sample.

smelting. The process of developing metal from ore by the removal of other substances and impurities.
 By its derivation, the term is synonymous with the word "melting," but in metallurgy and commercial manufacture it has come to have a more contracted meaning. In his treatise on Metallurgy, Frederick Overman says: "When metallic ores are exposed to heat, and such reagents as develop the metal, we call it smelting, in contradistinction from the mere application of heat, causing the ore to become fluid, which is called 'melting.' " Lowrey v Cowles Electric Smelting & Aluminum Co. (CC Ohio) 68 F 354, 369.

Smith Act. A federal statute which makes it unlaw-

the overthrow of the government by force. 18 USC § 2385.

smog. A mixture of smoke and fog; any mixture in the air which impairs vision or is discomforting to a person in his breathing.

smoke. Noun: The visible exhalation, vapor, or substance that escapes or is expelled from a burning body—especially from burning vegetable matter, as wood, coal, peat, or the like. St. Paul v Haugbro, 93 Minn 59, 100 NW 470. Verb: To give off matter constituting vapor interspersed with small particles of carbon produced by the burning of some substance. To use tobacco by drawing the smoke therefrom into the mouth, sometimes by inhaling it into the lungs, accomplished by the employment of cigar, cigarette, or pipe.

smoke farthings. An ancient tax.
As early as the Norman Conquest mention is made in Domesday Book of "fumage" or "fuage," vulgarly called "smoke farthings," which were a tax or duty paid by custom to the king for every chimney in the house. See 1 Bl Comm 324.

smokehouse. A place where cigars, cigarettes, and tobacco in other forms are sold. In older usage, an outbuilding used on occasion for smoking meat.

smokeless coal. A term of the coal business, not intended as a precise expression of a scientific concept.
A trade or commercial term applied to a grade of soft coal in which the volatile matter runs from sixteen to twenty-one per cent. The volatile matter in hard coal is a much smaller percentage. Ordinarily soft coal contains from thirty-two to forty per cent volatile matter and its tendency is to produce a dense smoke. State v Chicago, Milwaukee & St. Paul Railway Co. 114 Minn 122, 130 NW 545.

smuggling. The criminal offense of knowingly and wilfully, with intent to defraud the United States, clandestinely introducing into the United States any merchandise which should have been declared for customs duty. 21 Am J2d Cust D § 119.

snap judgment. A judgment by default. See Nation v Savely, 127 Okla 117, 260 P 32, 34. A conclusion reached without deliberation.

snatching. A form of larceny; robbery where accompanied by force. 46 Am J1st Rob § 21.
See **body snatching**.

snatching purse. A form of larceny. 32 Am J1st Larc § 44.

sneak. A person who acts in a contemptible underhand manner. A furtive fellow.
See **area-sneak**.

snodder (snod'er). A rope attached to a fish net and used for hauling in the net. Nolan v General Seafoods Corp. (CA1 Mass) 112 F2d 515.

snowbed stream. A watercourse having its source in a snowbed in the mountains which forms regularly at a certain season of the year. 56 Am J1st Wat § 8.

snow chains. Chains fitted to the rear tires of an automobile to give traction on snow and ice and reduce the likelihood of skidding.

snow job. A slang term for activity in investigation or prosecution intended to cover and hide offenses of a much more serious nature.

snuff. A pulverized form of tobacco, the consumers of which usually sniff it through the nose although it is also plastered on the gums and thus absorbed rather than chewed. State v Olson, 26 ND 304, 144 NW 661.

so. Abbreviation of **south**.

s. o. Abbreviation of **seller's option**.

soap box derby. A well organized contest and exhibition, operated under rules established by a national organization, wherein the participants, boys of limited age, race against time in vehicles of their own design and construction which may be described as coasters on wheels. Cummings v General Motors Corp. 146 Conn 443, 151 A2d 884, 72 ALR2d 1129.

s.o.b. An abbreviation of clear and unmistakable import.
A wife's statement, to those present at the husband's place of business, that the allegations in his petition for a divorce were lies and that he was a "s-o-b" for making them, is not public defamation in itself. McKoin v McKoin, 168 La 32, 121 So 182, the court characterizing the statement as nothing more than disgusting and senseless abuse.

sober. Temperate or sparing in use of intoxicating liquor. 29 Am J Rev ed Ins § 774. Not under the influence of liquor or drugs. Having self-control.
A statutory requirement that a juror shall be sober refers only to the time in which the juror sits, and his qualification is not affected by his habits in regard to intoxicating liquor at other times, unless they have gone so far as to make him of unsound mind at all times. Anderson v State, 54 Ariz 387, 96 P2d 281, 126 ALR 501.

soca (so'ka). An ancient Latin word meaning a plough. See 2 Bl Comm 80.

socage (sō'kāj). Land tenure by nonmilitary service.
See **common socage; free socage; guardian in socage; simple socage**.

socage tenure (sō'kāj ten'yūr). See **socage**.

socagium (so-kā'ji-um). Socage.

Socagium est servitium socae (so-kā'ji-um est servi'she-um sō'sē). Socage is the service of the plough. See 2 Bl Comm 81.

socer (so'ser). A father-in-law.

social club. A term of art, embracing a variety of organizations other than business, philanthropic, or educational associations. Duquesne Club v Bell (CA3 Pa) 127 F2d 363, 143 ALR 1377. As an organization exempt from federal income tax, a club not organized for profit or for the benefit of private shareholders. Internal Revenue Code § 50-1(c)(7).
As the term is used in the Federal income tax law, if any material, that is, important part of the club's activities (but not as much as a moiety thereof) are social as contradistinguished from the remaining non-social activities, it is a social club. Town Club of St. Louis v United States (CA8 Mo) 68 F2d 620.
Within the meaning of the Federal statute imposing a tax on the fees or dues of such a club, it is in general a club that has for its primary purpose the cultivation of companionable relations. However, no exact definition can be given for such a club and whether the fees or dues of a particular club or organization are subject to tax as a social club is primarily a question of fact. The issue is to be determined according to the predominant purpose of the organization, and social features which are

merely incidental to the general activities of an organization will not characterize it as a social club. But if the predominant purpose of an organization is social, it is a social club, notwithstanding the fact that other activities may be important, or that the activating motive of the members in joining was to make business contacts. Anno: 80 ALR 1297, s. 143 ALR 1382; 86 L Ed 633.
See **athletic club; club; country club; fraternal order or society.**

social duty. See **moral obligation.**

social guest. See **guest.**

social insurance. Those forms of insurance intended primarily to enable an old or disabled person to live without resort to a public welfare agency.

socialism. A much abused term, standing at one time for an economic system calling for increased participation by the government in the affairs of the people, meaning public ownership and operation of public utilities, the absorption of industrial plants by the government, looking toward a day when private ownership of property might be eliminated, except for the most personal things; applied in more recent times as a cloak for totalitarian governments and dictatorships.
See **communism.**

social position. The rank of one as a member of the social order as indicated by standard of life, companions, degree of culture, regard for the amenities, and etc.

Social Security. In the broadest sense, the welfare of the people with ample means of subsistence and enjoyment of life under the protection of the Government. In the popular sense, the system which provides old-age and survivors' insurance benefits. 48 Am J1st Soc Sec § 2.

Social Security Act. A federal statute providing for the establishment of a nation-wide federal and state system of old age assistance, old age and survivors' insurance benefits, and unemployment insurance or compensation, plus some incidental benefits. 42 USC §§ 301 et seq.

Social Security Board. The federal agency which operates the social security system. 48 Am J1st Soc Sec § 9.

social standing. Same as **social position.**

societas (so-si′e-tās). (Roman law.) A partnership. Hagget v Hurley, 91 Me 542, 40 A 561.

societe anonyme (sō-sē′ä-tā″ ä′nō-neem″). An association the liability of the members of which is limited.

society. The community. The people of the community or considered as a whole in state or nation. The associates which one has. A voluntary association, sometimes a corporation, organized and existing for the mutual benefit of its members in patriotic, religious, charitable, or professional pursuits or for providing benefits in case of illness or disability of a member or for his widow or children in the event of his death.
See **association; club; mutual benefit society; social club.**

Society for Prevention of Cruelty to Animals. An organization, recognized as charitable in purpose, which teaches kindness and consideration for dumb animals, advocates legislation penalizing cruelty to animals, and urges by appropriate acts the enforcement of such legislation. Anno: 12 ALR2d 874, § 5; 15 Am J2d Char § 88.

society of wife. A right of the husband known by the legal term "consortium."
As the word is used in connection with a husband's right to recover damages for the loss of his wife's "society," it means such capacities for usefulness, aid, and comfort as a wife, which she possessed at the time of the injury which she suffered by the act or omission of the defendant. Golden v Greene Paper Co. 44 RI 231, 116 A 579, 21 ALR 1514, 1516.
See **consortium.**

socii (so′shē-ī). Associates; partners; members of a partnership. Williams v Milton, 215 Mass 1, 102 NE 355.

Socii mei socius meus socius non est (so′she-ī mē′ī so′she-us mē′us so′she-us non est). (Civil law.) The partner of my partner is not my partner.

sociopath (sō′shi-ọ-path). Another term for sexual psychopath.

socman (sok′man). A tenant in socage.
See **sokemans.**

sod. Turf. A layer of the surface taken from lawn, meadow, or pasture, with the grass growing thereon as supported by the roots therein.

sodding. Covering the surface of the ground with sod brought from another place, normally for the purpose of obtaining a good grass cover quickly. Holmes v Heeter, 146 Ky 52, 142 SW 210. Creating a grass lawn by laying thereon sod cut from a grass meadow or from a plot specially adapted to the growing of grass for sod making. 36 Am J1st Mech L § 66.

sodomy. Broadly, unnatural sexual relations as between persons of the same sex, or with beasts, or between persons of different sex but in an unnatural manner. 48 Am J1st Sod § 1. Perverted sexual practice. 48 Am J1st Sod § 2. In the narrow sense, sexual connection between two human beings of the male sex. Ausman v Veal, 10 Ind 355.
A common-law crime deriving its name from the Biblical city of Sodom.

soft drink stand. A place, sometimes on the sidewalk, where soft drinks, candy, and other small items of food or confection are obtainable. Re Henery, 124 Iowa 358, 100 NW 43.

softening of the brain. A disease of the brain which gradually obliterates the memory and mental faculties. Holden v Meadows, 31 Wis 284, 296.

soil. The surface layer of earth; the layer which produces plant life and is tilled in the raising of crops.
See **common in the soil.**

Soil Bank Act. A federal statute designed to assist farmers in diverting a portion of their crop-land from production, thereby avoiding the accumulation of excessive agricultural commodities, and to promote soil conservation, by providing for payments to them in consideration of their putting a certain amount of their crop-land in "soil bank," that is taking it out of production, at least out of production of certain crops. United States v Maxwell (CA8 Iowa) 278 F2d 206.

soil bank payment. See **Soil Bank Act.**

soile. See **en autre soile.**

SOIT [1191] SOLE

Soit baile aux commons (swah bīl ō cōm'môn). Let it be delivered to the commons.

Soit droit fait al partie (swah drwo fāt al par-tee'). Let right be done to the party.

Soit fait comme il est desire (swah' fā côm ēl ā dā-zēr'). Let it be as it is desired. 1 Bl Comm 184.

sojourne (sō'jėrn). To stay in a place for a short time.

soke (sōk). The right to hold court and do justice, with the franchise to receive certain fees or fines arising from it; jurisdiction more or less wide over certain territory, or over certain men, or the right to exercise such jurisdiction; the duty of submitting to such jurisdiction; a jurisdiction or franchise; the district over which such jurisdiction extended. (Webster's Dictionary.)

sokemanries (sōk-man'riz). See **sokemans**.

sokemans (sōk'mạns). Socmen, tenants in socage. Britton, because of their freedom from base services, calls them "sokemans," and their tenure "sokemanries;" which he describes to be lands and tenements which are not held by knight service, nor by grand serjeanty, nor petit, but by simple services, being lands enfranchised by the king or his predecessors from their ancient demesne. See 2 Bl Comm 100.

soken (sō'kn). A district held by socage tenure.

soke-reeve (sōk'rēv). A rent gatherer in a soken.

Sola, ac per se, senectus donationem, testamentum aut transactionem non vitiat (so'la, ak per sē, senek'tus do-nā-she-ō'nem, tes-ta-men'tum ât transak-she-ō'nem non vi'she-at). Old age alone and of itself will not vitiate a gift, a will, or a transaction. Van Alst v Hunter (NY) 5 Johns Ch 148, 159.

solar day (sō'lạr dā). From sunrise to sunset. By solar time, one rotation of the earth.

solares. A term frequently occuring in Spanish-American land grants and meaning house lots of a small size, upon which dwellings, shops, stores, and the like were to be built. Hart v Burnett, 15 Cal 530, 554.

solar month (sō'lạr munth). A calendar month.

solar time. Time as measured by what appears to be the daily transit of the sun, caused by the rotation of the earth. 52 Am J1st Time § 2.
See **local sun time; mean solar time; standard time; sun time or standard.**

solar year. The time which elapses from the sun's appearance on one of the tropics to its return to the same; commonly 365 days, and in leap years, 366 days; unless the context or other indications show a different intent, it means a year consisting of twelve calendar months. See 52 Am J1st Time § 10.

solatium (sō-lā'shi-um). Compensation or damages for sorrow, mental anguish, or wounded feelings. Morgan v Southern Pacific Co. 95 Cal 510, 30 P 603; Marshall v Consolidated Jack Mines Co. 119 Mo App 270, 95 SW 972.

sold. Past tense of sell. A word used by an auctioneer in accepting a bid as being the highest one made and completing the sale. 7 Am J2d Auct § 31. A slang expression for succumbing to trick, deception, or fraud.
As used in conversation, and even by law writers, the word may signify only, that a bargain or contract to sell has been made, or that there has been such a contract, and delivery of the goods, or that such a contract has been made and completed by the payment of the price. The meaning will usually be clearly ascertained by the words used in connection with it, or by the circumstances developed. An example of the first sense would be, "if goods are sold upon condition to be performed at the time of delivery, and the goods are delivered, but the conditions are not performed," and where it is said, "the vendor has a lien for the price of goods sold." An example of the second sense is where we speak of "an action for goods sold." An example of the third is where we say, "if the purchaser neglects to remove goods sold within a reasonable time, the seller may charge him with storage." Hathaway v Burr, 21 Me 567.

soldier. One of the Army as a private, noncommissioned officer, musician, technician, artificer, or other enlisted man. 36 Am J1st Mil § 5. Either an enlisted man or a commissioned officer for the purpose of making a "soldier's will." 57 Am J1st Wills § 662.

Soldiers' and Sailors' Civil Relief Act. A federal statute providing for a stay of an action or proceeding in any court in which a person in military service is involved as a party plaintiff or defendant at any stage thereof, either on the court's own motion, or upon application by the person in military service or some person on his behalf, unless, in the opinion of the court, the ability of the plaintiff to prosecute the action or of the defendant to conduct his defense is not materially affected by reason of his military service. 50 USC appx § 521; 37 Am J1st Mtg § 907; 56 Am J1st War § 26.

soldier's bounty. See **military bounty.**

soldiers' homes. See **veterans' homes.**

soldier's will. The informal will of a soldier, whether oral or in writing, rendered valid, where the will of a person in another occupation would be invalid, under an exception from formalities required to be observed in the execution of wills generally, recognized because of the dangers, diseases, disasters, and the possibility of sudden death constantly besetting a soldier and the inability of such a person to find the time or the means to make a deliberate and written testamentary disposition. 57 Am J1st Wills § 661.

sold notes. See **bought and sold notes.**

sole (sōl). As one only. Single. Not joint. Exclusive. See **feme sole.**

sole actor doctrine. The principle that the knowledge of a corporate officer or agent is imputed to the corporation notwithstanding it has reference to a transaction in which the officer or agent is acting fraudulently or adversely to the corporation, where it appears that the officer or agent is the sole representative of the corporation in the transaction in question. 19 Am J2d Corp § 1267.

sole and unconditional ownership. Ownership of such dominion that no one else has any interest in the property as an owner and the quality of the estate is not limited or effected by any condition. The ownership of an estate or property without outstanding interest or condition attached which would cause the loss of the property, if it should occur, to fall upon another person. 29A Am J Rev ed Ins § 791.
The clause in an insurance policy requiring sole and unconditional ownership has to do, not with questions of title to be precisely determined, but with beneficial and practical ownership. Libby

Lumber Co. v Pacific States Fire Ins. Co. 79 Mont 166, 255 P 340, 60 ALR 1.

An insurance policy's condition as to "sole and unconditional ownership" refers to the real owner and is not broken by the mere fact that the record title is, for purposes of convenience, in another for a time. American Indem. Co. v Southern Missionary College, 195 Tenn 513, 260 SW2d 269, 39 ALR2d 714.

As the expression is used in fire insurance policies requiring the insured to be the sole and unconditional owner of the insured property, a purchaser in possession under a contract whereby the former owner agrees to sell and the buyer absolutely binds himself to purchase and to pay an agreed price for the property, is almost universally held to be the unconditional owner, because the loss from an injury to or destruction of the property falls upon him. Phenix Insurance Co. v Kerr (CA8 Neb) 129 F 723.

See **sole ownership; unconditional ownership.**

sole corporation. Same as **corporation sole.**

sole discretion of trustee. The broadest measure of permissible discretion, but not an unbridled or unlimited discretion, since such would negative the existence of a trust. 54 Am J1st Trusts § 36.

sole efficient cause. The proximate cause of an accident. 7 Am J2d Auto § 376.

sole judge. One coming to a conclusion or reaching an opinion uncontrolled by others. Prudential Ins. Co. v Nelson (CA6 Tenn) 101 F 2d 441.

solely. Acting alone. Standing alone. Without another.

solemnitas (so-lem'ni-tās). Solemnity; formality.

Solemnitates juris sunt observandae (so-lem-ni-tā'tēz jö'ris sunt ob-zer-van'dē). The formalities of the law should be observed.

solemnization of marriage. The performance of the formal act or ceremony by which a man and woman contract marriage and assume the status of husband and wife. 35 Am J1st Mar § 25. As a requirement of the law, any celebration or ceremony which gives utterance to and public evidence of the contract of marriage. Howard v Kelly, 111 Miss 285, 71 So 391.

solemn form. See **probate in solemn form.**

solemn oath (sol'ẹm ōth). Same as **corporal oath.**

solemn occasion for advisory opinion. A situation where the executive or legislature is in doubt as to its power or authority or the authority of a subordinate under its direction and the elimination of such doubt is necessary to enable it to act legally and intelligently upon a pending question. Re Opinion of Justices, 269 Mass 611, 168 NE 536, 66 ALR 1477.

solemn war. A war declared in form and of the perfect kind. 56 Am J1st War § 4.

See **perfect war.**

solemn will. A civil law term for a written will. Castro v Castro, 6 Cal 158, 160.

Solent foeminarum ductu bellare, et sexum in imperiis non discernere (so'lent fē-mi-nā'rum duk'tū bel-lā're, et se'xum in im-pe'ri-is non dis-ser'ne-re). They are accustomed to wage war under the leadership of women, and they make no sex distinctions in matters of government. See 1 Bl Comm 194.

sole ownership. Exclusive ownership. An ownership so complete that no other person has any interest in the property. See **sole and unconditional ownership.**

sole possession. Exclusive possession.

sole representative doctrine. Same as sole actor doctrine. 19 Am J2d Corp § 1267.

See **sole actor doctrine.**

sole tenant (sōl ten'ạnt). A tenant whose ownership is entire; that is, neither joint nor in common.

solicit. To importune, entreat, implore, ask, attempt, or try to obtain an order. 30 Am J Rev ed Intox L § 272. To invite a business transaction, for example, the issuing of a policy of insurance. Maryland Casualty Co. v McTyler, 150 Tenn 691, 266 SW 767, 48 ALR 1168. To commit the offense of **solicitation.**

solicitation. An act of soliciting. The substantive offense of inciting or soliciting another to commit a crime. 21 Am J2d Crim L § 114. The act of a prostitute in seeking patronage on the street or in a public place, railroad station, bus terminal, etc. 42 Am J1st Prost § 1.

See **indirect solicitation.**

solicitation of adultery. The expression of a desire and a willingness on the part of one person to commit adultery with another and an effort to obtain that person's consent. State v Butler, 8 Wash 194, 35 P 1093.

solicitation of bribe. Corruptly offering to receive a bribe, or expressing a willingness to receive one; an offense at common law and under various statutes, although something less than bribery or even an attempt to receive a bribe. 12 Am J2d Brib § 11.

solicitation of business. Seeking orders for goods or services. A matter considered in determining whether a corporation is within the purview of statutes relative to foreign corporations transacting business in the state. 36 Am J2d For Corp § 246. An unethical practice by an attorney at law constituting ground for disbarment or suspension from practice, whether conducted personally or through the employment of an agent or runner. 7 Am J2d Attys § 40.

See **solicit.**

solicitation of order. See **solicit; solicitation of business.**

solicitation of proxies. The solicitation of stockholders of a corporation to obtain proxies to vote at a stockholders' meeting. 19 Am J2d Corp § 678. Any request for a proxy, whether or not accompanied by or included in a form of proxy; any request to execute, not to execute, or to revoke a proxy; or the furnishing of a form of proxy or other communication to security holders under circumstances reasonably calculated to result in the procurement, withholding, or revocation of a proxy. Anno: 12 L Ed 2d 1240, 1246.

solicitation of votes. Requesting a vote for a particular candidate or candidates of an election; a criminal offense where conducted at restricted times and places on election day. 26 Am J2d Elect § 374.

soliciting agent. An agent who solicits orders for goods or services to be furnished by his principal. Sometimes, but not invariably, regarded as a managing agent for the purpose of statutes concerning the service of process upon a foreign corporation. 36 Am J2d For Corp § 560. An agent of an insurance company empowered to solicit, receive,

SOLICITOR

and report applications, but ordinarily without authority to accept an application on behalf of the company and complete the making of a contract of insurance. 29 Am J Rev ed Ins § 193. A special agent of an insurance company, having authority only to solicit insurance, submit applications therefor to the company, and to perform such acts as are incidental to that power. Turner v Supreme Lodge K. P. 166 Okla 286, 27 P2d 612, 93 ALR 647.

In the absence of special circumstances, including statutory or contractual provisions, an agent of the insurer who solicits or effects insurance is not the agent of the insured. 29 Am J Rev ed Ins § 136.

solicitor. A person who, going from person to person or from house to house, seeks orders, subscriptions, contributions, or any other kind of support, or who, without necessarily having the intention of making a direct sale, distributes literature, pamphlets, hand bills, samples, and the like for the purpose of information, advertising, or for other purposes such as the furtherance of public, political, economic, religious, or social beliefs, systems, projects, or doctrines. 40 Am J1st Ped § 6. Inclusive of a soliciting agent. Not inclusive of a peddler. Anno: 9 ALR2d 737. An attorney at law acting as the head of the law department of a municipal corporation or other division of government. In England, a person trained in the law who prepares briefs, drafts pleadings and legal instruments, consults with and advises clients, but is not heard in court, at least not in the superior courts.

English attorneys-at-law have been called "solicitors" since the Judicature Act of 1873 took effect. They are not members of the bar and are not heard in the superior courts; and the power of admitting them to practice, and striking them off the roll, has not been given to the inns of court. Re Ricker, 66 NH 207, 29 A 559. This decision contains a most valuable account of the qualifications, functions, privileges, and duties of barristers, serjeants, solicitors and attorneys-at-law.

Solicitor General. An officer learned in the law in the Department of Justice, assisting the Attorney General in the performance of the duties of the latter, appointed by the President of the United States, by and with the advice and consent of the Senate. 5 USC § 293. In England, a barrister of high rank next in precedence after the attorney general, with whom he is associated in the performance of his duties, and permitted to sit within the bar of the respective courts with the king's counsel. See 3 Bl Comm 28 and note.

solido. See **in solido.**

solidos legales (so'li-dos lē-gā'lēz). Lawful shillings. See 2 Bl Comm 509.

solidum (sol'i-dum). The whole.
See **in solidum.**

solitary confinement. A special condition of imprisonment. 21 Am J2d Crim L § 615. A punishment for crime consisting of the complete isolation of the prisoner from all human society and his confinement in a cell where he has no direct intercourse with or sight of any human being, and no employment or instruction; it is the complete exclusion from human associations. Re Medley, 134 US 160, 33 L Ed 835, 10 S Ct 384.

The term is to be distinguished from **close confinement.**

SOLVENCY

solo (sō'lō). Performed by one.
See **in solo.**

Solo cedit quod solo implantatur (sō'lō sē'dit quod sō'lō im-plan-tā'ter). (Civil law.) That which is planted in the soil belongs to the soil.

Solo cedit quod solo inaedificatur (sō'lō sē'dit quod sō'lō in-ē-di-fi-kā'ter). (Civil law.) That which is built into the soil belongs to the soil.

solo flight. The first air flight of a student pilot without an instructor in the plane with him. De Rienzo v Morristown Aircraft Corp. 28 NJ 231, 146 A2d 127.

so long as. Technical words used to create a determinable fee. Consolidated School Dist. v Walter, 243 Minn 153, 66 NW2d 881, 53 ALR2d 218.

In most instances in which the language of disposal does not include a use of the expression "for life", or a similar one, but gives or grants the premises "for so long as" the conveyee shall occupy the same as a home, or in similar terms, the conclusion reached has been that a life estate was given. The question is affected, and may of course be controlled, by peculiarities of the particular instrument. Anno: 45 ALR2d 707.

solo proprio. See **in solo proprio.**

solum (sō'lum). Soil; ground.

solum et fundum (sō'lum et fun'dum). The bottom and the soil.

A grant solum et fundum of a river is a grant of the bottom of the river and the soil beneath. Arnold v Mundy, 6 NJL 1.

Solum rex hoc non facere potest, quod non potest injuste agere (sō'lum rex hōk non fā'se-re po'test, quod non po'test in-jus'te ā'je-re). This alone the king cannot do, he cannot act contrary to law.

Solus Deus haeredem facit (sō'lus Dē'us hē-rē'dem fā'sit). God alone makes an heir.

solutio (sō-lū'she-ō). (Civil law.) Payment; settlement.

solutio indebiti. See **indebiti solutio.**

Solutio pretii emptionis loco habetur (sō-lū'she-ō pre'she-ī emp-she-ō'nis lō'kō hā-bē'ter). The payment of the price is regarded as taking the place of a sale.

Title acquired by the conversion of a chattel takes effect from the time of the conversion. This rests upon the maxim, which presumes that the wrongdoer is in possession of the property and has not voluntarily parted therewith to a third party. Third National Bank v Rice (CA8 Mo) 161 F 822.

solutum. See **in solutum.**

solutus (sō-lū'tus). (Civil law.) Free; freed; released; free from debt or mortgage; unincumbered; paid.

solvency. The condition of a person having sufficient assets to meet his obligations as they mature in the ordinary course of business. Ability to pay one's debts, not a mere disposition to pay. Janes v Scott, 59 Pa 178. A word which implies as well the present ability of the debtor to pay out of his estate all his debts, as also such condition of his property as that it may be reached and subjected by process of law, without his consent, to the payment of such debts. 29 Am J Rev ed Insolv § 2.

Solvency is to be distinguished from the state of a person who possesses the ability to secure further credit and thus incur further indebtedness. The lat-

SOLVENCY [1194] SOUND

ter state may be one of insolvency. Baily v Hornthal, 154 NY 648, 49 NE 56.
See **actuarial solvency.**

solvency policy. A policy of credit insurance.
See **credit insurance; guaranty policy.**

Solvendo esse nemo intelligitur nisi qui solidum potest solvere (sol-ven'dō es'se nē'mō in-tel-li'ji-ter nī'sī quī so'li-dum po'test sol've-re). (Civil law.) No one is regarded as solvent except a person who can pay in full.

solvendum in futuro (sol-ven'dum in fu-tū'rō). To be paid in the future. See 2 Bl Comm 513.

solvent (sol'vent). Adjective: In a condition of solvency. Noun: A substance which operates to dissolve another substance.
See **solvency.**

solvent credit. See **solvent debt.**

solvent debt. A debt which can promptly be enforced and realized. Ward v Pittsburgh, 321 Pa 414, 184 A 240, 105 ALR 682. An obligation which is collectible by the creditor in the ordinary course of business, resort to suit or execution not being required. Stillman v Lynch, 56 Utah 540, 192 P 272, 12 ALR 552, 559.

solvent debtor. See **solvency.**

solvere (sol've-re). To pay; to release.

solvit (sol'vit). He paid.

Solvit ad diem (sol'vit ad dī'em). He paid at the day.

Solvitur adhuc societas etiam morte socii (sol'vi-ter ad'huk so-si'e-tās e'she-am mor'te so'she-ī). (Civil law.) A partnership is also dissolved by the death of a partner.

Solvitur eo ligamine quo ligatur (sol'vi-ter e'ō li-gā'-mi-ne quō li-gā'ter). A person is released in the same manner in which he is bound. Livingston v Lynch (NY) 4 Johns Ch 573, 582.

solvit vel non (sol'vit vel non). Whether he has paid or not.
Although the jury must pass upon the issue of solvit vel non, they are to be governed, as the court directs, by the law as to the presumption of payment from lapse of time. Gulick v Loder, 13 NJL 68.

Sommersett's Case. A celebrated English case decided in 1772, holding a Negro slave to be a freeman on English soil.

somnambulism (som-nam'bū-lizm). Walking in one's sleep. 21 Am J2d Crim L § 29. Characterized by one authority as a species of mental unsoundness connected with sleep which destroys moral agency during the period of its existence. Fain v Commonwealth, 78 Ky 183.

somnolentia (som-nō-len'she-a). The lapping over of a profound sleep into the domain of apparent wakefulness.
This condition is said to produce a state of involuntary intoxication, which for the time destroys moral agency. Fain v Commonwealth, 78 Ky 183 quoting Wharton & Stille.

son. One's male child. One's male child born in wedlock. Wilkinson v Adam, 1 V. & B. 422, 35 Eng Reprint 163. A word which is not a technical legal term having a fixed and definite meaning, but one which is flexible and subject to construction to give effect to the intention of the maker of the instrument in which it appears. Conner v Gardner, 230 Ill 258, 82 NE 640.

sonans. See **idem sonans.**

son assault. Same as **son assault demesne.**

son assault demesne (son a-sâlt' de-mēn'). His own assault. The plea of self-defense. See 3 Bl Comm 308.

son damage. See **en son damage.**

son done. See **de son done.**

son gree. See **de son gree.**

sonic boom (son'ik böm). A byproduct of the "jet age"; a mechanical phenomenon of the air consisting of pressure waves and sound waves generated by an object moving through the air at a speed equal to or exceeding that of sound. 8 Am J2d Avi § 99. A disturbance or shock caused by a jet airplane flying at a speed in excess of the speed of sound. Anno: 74 ALR2d 755.

son of a bitch. See **s. o. b.**

son tort. See **de son tort.**

sorcery (sôr'ser-i). See **witchcraft.**

sore feet. A slang appellation for a child born a matter of days or weeks after the marriage of his parents.

sorghum (sôr'gum). A plant cultivated for the production of molasses, such being rendered from the sweet juice pressed out of the stalk. The molasses or syrup produced from such plant.

sortitio (sor-ti'she-ō). A casting lots; deciding by casting lots.

sortito (sor-tī'tō). An adverb meaning by lot; as jurors are chosen. See 3 Bl Comm 366.

soul-scot (sōl'skot). A part of a man's property set apart at his death for the church for the welfare of his soul. See 2 Bl Comm 425.

sound. Adjective: Healthy; free from disease or disability. Verb: To gauge the depth of a stream or body of water by dropping a weighted line. Noun: A body of water between two larger bodies, or between an island and the mainland. 12 Am J2d Bound § 13.

Sound. In eastern states, Long Island Sound. 12 Am J2d Bound § 13.

sound amplifier. See **amplifier.**

sound and disposing mind and memory. A matter of the possession of sanity. Campbell v Campbell, 130 Ill 466, 22 NE 620.
A testator is of sound and disposing mind and memory, if, at the time of making his will, he has sufficient mental capacity to be able to understand the act he is doing, to understand and recollect the nature and situation of his property, and to remember and understand his relations to the persons who have claims upon his bounty and whose interests are affected by the provisions of the instrument. Re Smith's Estate, 200 Cal 158, 252 P 325.
See **disposing mind; sound mind.**

sound animal. An animal without organic defect or infirmity which renders it unfit for immediate, present, usual, and reasonable use. 46 Am J1st Sales § 396.

sound barrier. Pressure waves which build up ahead of an object moving through the air at a speed equal to or exceeding that of sound. 8 Am J2d Avi § 99.
See **sonic boom.**

sound discretion. See **judicial discretion.**

sound health. Good health. A physical condition characterized by the absence of any grave, important, or serious disease; freedom from any ailment seriously affecting the health. 29 Am J Rev ed Ins § 746.

As the term is generally used in life insurance policies providing that the insured must be in "sound health" at the date of the policy, it means good health. It is not to be taken literally. It does not mean perfect health, or imply absolute freedom from bodily infirmity or tendency to disease, but means generally the absence of any vice or disease in the constitution of a serious nature, or that has a direct tendency to shorten life, as contradistinguished from a temporary ailment or indisposition. Anno: 40 ALR 662.

sound horse. See **sound animal.**

sounding in damages. Capable of being accurately measured in money. For damages only, as an action sounding in damages.

sound memory. See **sound and disposing mind and memory; sound mind.**

sound mind. The mind of a person who is sane and mentally competent. Characterizing ability of a testator to understand in a general way the nature and extent of his property, his relation to those who naturally have a claim to benefit from the property left by him, and the practical effect of the will as executed. Re Wilmoott's Estate (Fla) 66 So 2d 465, 40 ALR2d 1399; Re Hagan, 143 Neb 459, 9 NW2d 794, 154 ALR 573.

The term is commonly synonymous with "sane" as distinguished from "insane," and is itself as plainly descriptive of its meaning as any other definition would be. People v Brisbane, 295 Ill 241, 248, 129 NE 185, 188.

sound mind and memory. See **sound and disposing mind and memory.**

sound physical condition. Sound health; not necessarily perfect health. Not negatived by a mere temporary indisposition. French v Fidelity & Casualty Co. 135 Wis 259, 115 NW 869.

See **sound health.**

sound price. See **warranty of soundness from sound price.**

sound signals. Signals by sound prescribed by statutory and administrative rules to control the navigation of ships and small watercraft. 12 Am J2d Boats § 18; 48 Am J1st Ship § 261.

sound title. A marketable title; a title not open to a reasonable doubt. 30A Am J Rev ed Jud S § 189; 56 Am J1st V & P § 167.

sound track. A tape or other contrivance upon which speech, song, and other sounds are imprinted for reproduction synchronized with a motion picture film. Foreign & Domestic Music Corp. v Licht (CA2 NY) 196 F2d 627.

sound truck. A motor vehicle equipped with a loudspeaker, used for advertising or the making of announcements upon the streets. 25 Am J1st High § 194.

sound value. An estimated value of securities not dealt in sufficiently to establish a market value by resort to market quotations. Anno: 133 ALR 1068. Permissibly the par value of long-term securities which are held, not for sale on the market, but as investments, where there has been no default in payment of interest or of instalments of principal and there is absent any appraisal or offer for sale or other circumstance which indicates their value to be less. 9 Am J2d Bankr § 165. As used in a policy of insurance, the actual cash value of the property in its undamaged state or condition. 29A Am J Rev ed Ins § 1546.

sound vessel. The condition of a vessel on its first voyage. Lynch v Postlethwaite (La) 7 Mart 69.

source material. (1) Uranium, thorium, or any other material which is determined by the Atomic Energy Commission to be source material; or (2) ores containing one or more of the foregoing materials in such concentration as the Commission may by regulation determine from time to time. 42 USC § 2014(x).

sources of the law. The origins of legal principles in the legislative and judicial processes. Reported cases, authoritative textbooks, comprehensive text treatments, such as American Jurisprudence 2d, constitutions and statutes.

south. A word indicating a point on the compass, being due south, unless qualified or controlled by other words. 23 Am J2d Deeds § 248.

southeast quarter. See **fraction of section.**

Southern Interstate Nuclear Compact. A compact between several southern states for the purpose of providing the instrument and framework for a cooperative effort between the states to improve the economy of the South through the proper employment of nuclear energy. 6 Am J2d Atomic E § 46.

south one-half. See **fraction of section.**

South Sea Bubble. A ten million pound scheme for monopolizing the trade of England with Spanish-America, which was given form in 1711 and failed in 1720.

southwest quarter. See **fraction of section.**

souvent (sū'vänt). Often.

sovereign (suv'- or sov'e-rān). A ruler; a king; the supreme power in a government. A gold coin of Great Britain, equivalent in value to one pound.

"To the Constitution of the United States the term sovereign is totally unkown. There is but one place where it could have been used with propriety. But, even in that place it would not, perhaps, have comported with the delicacy of those who ordained and established that Constitution. They might have announced themselves 'sovereign' people of the United States: But, serenely conscious of the fact, they avoided the ostentatious declaration." Chisholm v Georgia (US) 2 Dall 419, 454, 1 L Ed 440, 455.

sovereign and inherent power. See **inherent power; sovereign power.**

sovereign immunity. The principle that the sovereign cannot be sued in its own courts or in any other court without its consent and permission; a principle which applies with full force to the several states of the Union. 49 Am J1st States § 91. The principle that the United States is immune from suit except where it consents thereto, as by a statute such as the Federal Tort Claims Act. 28 USC §§ 1491 et seq.; 20 Am J2d Cts § 152. The principle that a sovereign state is bound to respect the independence of every other sovereign state, so that the courts of one country will not sit in judgment on the acts of the government of another, done within its own territory. 20 Am J2d Cts § 152.

sovereign nation. See **sovereign state.**

sovereign people. See **people of the state; people of the United States.**

sovereign power. The power to make and enforce laws.

"By the sovereign power is meant the making of laws; for wherever that power resides, all others must conform to, and be directed by it, whatever appearance the outward form and administration of the government may put on. For it is at any time in the option of the legislature to alter that form and administration by a new edict or rule, and to put the execution of the laws into whatever hands it pleases; by constituting one or a few, or many executive magistrates, and all the other powers of the state must obey the legislative power in the execution of their several functions, or else the constitution is at an end." See 1 Bl Comm 49.

See **inherent power.**

sovereign prerogative. See **royal prerogative.**

sovereign right. A right which the state alone, or some of its governmental agencies, can possess. City of St. Paul v Chicago, Milwaukee & St. Paul Railway Co. 45 Minn 387, 397, 48 NW 17.

See **prerogative.**

sovereign state. A people permanently occupying a fixed territory, bound together by common laws, habits, and customs into one body politic, exercising through the medium of an organized government, independent sovereignty and control over all persons and things within its boundaries, capable of making war and peace, and of entering into international relations with other communities. 30 Am J Rev ed Internat L § 10.

In the United States, each state constitutes a distinct and independent sovereignty, and consequently the laws of one state do not operate of their own force in any other state. 16 Am J2d Confl L § 4.

sovereignty (sov'ę-ren-ti). The power to govern; supreme political authority. That public authority which commands in civil society, and orders and directs what each citizen is to perform to obtain the end of its institution.

s.p. An abbreviation of **sine prole.**

space. The distance between things. Room for persons or things. The boundless expanse in all directions from the earth.

See **Aeronautics and Space Act.**

space of intersection. A term found in the federal statute respecting priorities as between mining claims where two or more veins intersect or cross each other. 30 USC § 41.

Some courts take the view that the phrase, "space of intersection," refers to intersection of the veins only, but others assume that it may mean intersection of the veins or of the claims themselves, depending upon the facts of the particular case. 36 Am J1st Min & M § 112.

spado (spā'dō). (Civil law.) A person without capacity to reproduce; an impotent person.

spadones (spȧ-dō-nēz). Plural of **spado.**

Spanish land grant. A grant made by the government of Spain of land formerly within its dominions but now within the territorial limits of the United States. Bryan v Kennett, 113 US 179, 28 L Ed 908, 5 S Ct 407.

span of horses. A term of horses, not merely a pair of horses. Ames v Martin, 6 Wis 361.

spare tire. An extra tire carried on a motor vehicle for possible use consequent to a puncture or other imperfection occurring in one of the tires. 24 Am J1st Garag § 26.

spark arrester. A device upon a chimney, sometimes required of the proprietor of an industrial plant in order to obviate or lessen the danger of fires ignited by sparks. Anno: 25 ALR 994.

sparring. Boxing, usually with gloves, without attempting to land a heavy blow.

See **boxing match; prize fight.**

sparsim (spär'sim). Sparsely; rarely.

spaying (spā'ing). The practice of removing the ovaries of a female animal, usually to prevent propagation. Sterilization of a female to prevent propagation.

S.P.C.A. Abbreviation of the **Society for the Prevention of Cruelty to Animals.** Siemens' Estate, 346 Pa 610, 31 A2d 280, 153 ALR 483, cert den 320 US 758, 88 L Ed 452, 64 S Ct 66.

spe. See **in spe.**

speaking demurrer. A demurrer which should be overruled as setting up a ground dehors the record, or a ground which to be sustained requires reference to facts not appearing on the face of the pleading attacked. 41 Am J1st Pl § 209.

speaking order. An order of court, such as an order granting a new trial, which contains matter which is explanatory and illustrative of the direction which is given by the order. Duff v Duff, 101 Cal 1, 35 P 437.

speaking with prosecutor. Making an arrangement for leniency in sentence.

special. Belonging to a certain or specific class, kind, genus or species; peculiar; particular; opposed to general.

special acceptance (ak-sep'tạns). An acceptance of a bill of exchange which specifies the place of payment.

See **qualified acceptance.**

special account. An account opened in a bank for a special purpose as the result of a special understanding and creating the relationship of trustee or bailee of the fund deposited on the part of the bank. City Nat. Bank v Brink, 98 Ind App 275, 187 NE 689.

See **special deposit.**

special act. See **private act; special legislation.**

special action. A statutory action.

See **extraordinary remedies.**

special action on the case. Same as **trespass on the case.**

special administration. The administration of the estate of a deceased person by a special administrator.

special administrator. An administrator of a decedent's estate appointed by the probate court to take charge of the property of the estate pending a contest or other delay in the appointment of an executor or administrator, the purpose of the appointment being to prevent loss of assets occurring in the absence of an authorized agent to collect debts due the decedent and to preserve the assets of the estate pending the appointment of a regular administrator or executor and the beginning of a regular administration. State ex rel. Hamilton v Guinotte, 156 Mo 513, 57 SW 281.

See **special letters of administration.**

special agent. One authorized to do one or more specific acts in pursuance of particular instructions, to act in a particular transaction, or in a particular way. Southern States Fire Ins. Co. v Kronenberg, 199 Ala 164, 74 So 63.

special agreement. Same as **special contract.**

special appearance. An appearance for the sole purpose of objecting to the jurisdiction of the court, not operating as a submission of defendant's person to the jurisdiction of the court. Re Blalock, 233 NC 493, 64 SE2d 848, 25 ALR2d 818. An appearance testing the jurisdiction of the court over the defendant's person, including the question of sufficiency of the process or manner of service, or, in some jurisdictions, testing jurisdiction of the subject matter. 5 Am J2d Appear § 2.

special assessment. A local assessment; the levy of a burden upon property within a limited area for the payment for a local improvement supposed to be for the benefit of all property within the area. 48 Am J1st Spec A § 3.

The word "tax" as it is used in a statute is usually construed to have reference to taxation for general purposes, and not to local assessments. McIlroy v Ugitt, 182 Ark 1017, 33 SW2d 719, 73 ALR 1223. Local assessments do not come within the meaning of the word "tax" as used in the constitutional provision exempting lands of the state from taxation. Re Simpson, 43 Cal 2d 594, 275 P2d 467, 47 ALR2d 991.

In their ordinary sense, local assessments are not taxes, but they are taxes in the more general signification that they are a charge put upon property by authority of the lawmaking power. The general distinction is taken between taxes and local assessments that the former are forced contributions levied by the government alike upon all property, for the purpose of raising revenue for the support of the government without reference to the special benefits that will inure to the property thus taxed, while the latter are also forced contributions which are levied by the government, but upon certain particular property, with a view of raising revenue for certain designated purposes, having direct reference to the special benefits that will inure to the property thus taxed. Shreveport v Prescott, 51 La Ann 1895, 26 So 664; Altman v Kilburn, 45 NM 453, 116 P2d 812, 136 ALR 554.

special assessment bond. Same as **improvement bond.**

special assessment district. Same as **improvement district.**

special assessment lien. A statutory lien on property charged with a special or local assessment to secure the payment of the assessment. 48 Am J1st Spec A § 196.

special assumpsit. Assumsit upon an express contract or promise. 1 Am J2d Actions § 15.

special attorney. See **attorney special**; **special counsel**; **special prosecutor.**

special authority. See **special power.**

special bail. See **bail below.**

special bailiffs (bā'lifs). "Mean persons" employed by sheriffs to aid bailiffs of hundreds and to serve writs and executions and make arrests. See 1 Bl Comm 345.

special bailment. A bailment affecting the public interest in such a way that the law has imposed on the bailee a liability more stringent than that of an ordinary bailee. Anno: 93 ALR 834; 8 Am J2d Bailm § 6.

special bastard. A bastard who was born before the marriage of his parents who intermarry thereafter.

This was not bastardy by the ecclesiastical law, but by the common law, it is. See 3 Bl Comm 335.

special benefits. Benefits deductible in ascertaining the amount of damages to be awarded in eminent domain, as resulting from the improvement for which land is taken and peculiar to condemnee's property or interest, not being shared by all the property in the vicinity. 27 Am J2d Em D § 368.

special case. A term corresponding in English practice with "agreed case." Germano v Gresham Fire & Acci. Ins. Soc. (Australia) [1924] Vict LR 592. A case reserved for decision by the judges in bank or by a higher court. A proceeding unknown to the common law, arising under statute.

See **extraordinary remedies.**

special census. A census taken by the Bureau of the Census upon request or for a particular purpose. 14 Am J2d Census § 2.

special charter. A charter granted a corporation by special act of the legislature. 18 Am J2d Corp § 26. A charter of a municipal corporation granted by or under a statute other than one providing for the incorporation of municipal corporations generally.

special charter city. See **special charter.**

special commission. An administrative agency for a special purpose. Wilson v Philadelphia School Dist. 328 Pa 225, 195 A 90, 113 ALR 1401.

As the term was used in a constitutional prohibition against a legislative delegation of municipal functions to any "special commission," the object of the provision was held to be to prevent the state legislature from interfering with local governments by the appointment "of its own special commissions for the control of purely local matters." And it was held also that the aggregate body of qualified electors could not be regarded as a "special commission" within the meaning of the prohibition. Ex parte Pfahler, 150 Cal 71, 88 P 270.

special constable (kon'stạ-bl). A civilian sworn in to aid a constable in preserving the peace.

special contract. A contract under seal; a specialty.

The term has often been defined as being synonymous with the word specialty, meaning a contract under seal. Other authorities have treated it as a simple contract either written or parol. McManus v Cassidy, 66 Pa 260.

See **specialty.**

special counsel. An attorney at law employed by an attorney general of a state to assist him in the discharge of his official duties. 7 Am J2d Atty Gen § 3. An attorney at law employed by the Attorney General of the United States in connection with the functions of the Department of Justice or, where the public interest so requires, as an assistant to a United States District Attorney in a particular case. 7 Am J2d Atty Gen § 4.

See **special prosecutor.**

special court. A court created by legislative act. State v Allen, 117 Ohio St 470, 159 NE 591.

special court-martial. One of three kinds of court-martials, intermediate, a general court-martial and a summary court-martial, conducted before a body of at least three commissioned officers, and limited in jurisdiction generally to noncapital offenses.

special custom. A local or particular, as distinguished from a general, custom. 21 Am J2d Cust & U § 6.

special damages. Such compensatory damages as arise from the special circumstances of the case, that is, the peculiar circumstances of the case, and may, if properly pleaded, be added to the general damages. 22 Am J2d Damg § 15. The natural, but not the necessary, result of an injury. 22 Am J2d Damg § 15. Damages for breach of contract arising naturally but not necessarily from the breach. Parker v Harris Pine Mills, 206 Or 187, 291 P2d 709, 56 ALR2d 382. Damages sustained by a plaintiff beyond the mere loss of his property. Sarkesian v Cedric Chase Photographic Laboratories, 324 Mass 620, 87 NE2d 745, 12 ALR2d 899. In the law of libel and slander, loss of a temporal or material advantage of any kind, such as loss of an emolument, a favorable marriage, a profitable employment, or even substantial hospitality. 33 Am J1st L & S § 204.

The distinction between general and special damage arising from breach of contract are not absolute, but relative; in other words, damage which is general in relation to a contract of one kind may be classified as special in relation to another. Kerr S.S. Co. v Radio Corp. of America, 245 NY 284, 157 NE 140, 55 ALR 1139, cert den 275 US 557, 72 L Ed 424, 48 S Ct 118.

special demurrer. A demurrer aimed at a particular defect in a pleading, which must be assigned as the ground of demurrer. 41 Am J1st Pl § 225. A demurrer which lies only for defects in form and adds to a general demurrer a specification of the particular ground of exception. 41 Am J1st Pl § 206. A demurrer directed to a matter of form rather than substance, being concerned with matters in abatement, ambiguity, uncertainty, and the like. 41 Am J1st Pl § 204.

special deposit. A deposit delivered into the possession of a bank to be kept separate and distinct from the general assets of the bank and to be returned or delivered intact on demand, the title to the thing deposited remaining in the depositor. 10 Am J2d Banks § 360. The placing of specific money or property in the possession of a bank under terms such that the bank is under obligation to return the identical thing deposited to the depositor, Keyes v Paducah & I. R. Co. (CA6 Ky) 61 F2d 611, 86 ALR 203, no relation of debtor and creditor between the bank and the depositor being created. Bassett v City Bank & T Co. 115 Conn 1, 160 A 60, 81 ALR 1488.

The state courts do not agree as to whether a deposit made in a bank for special purposes constitutes a trust fund in the hands of the bank, but the federal courts hold that if the deposit is made as a general deposit, the fact that it is made for the purpose of providing a credit which is to be used thereafter for a special purpose does not give it the status of a trust fund in the hands of the bank. Santee Timber Corporation v Elliott, 7 F2d 179.

See **special account.**

special deputy sheriff. A deputy sheriff who is an officer pro hac vice (for the particular occasion); to execute a particular writ on some certain occasion.

He acts under a specific, not a general appointment and authority. See Allen v Smith, 12 NJL 159, 163.

special election. An election arising from some exigency or special need, such as filling a vacancy in office or submitting to the electors a measure or proposition for adoption or rejection. 25 Am J2d Elect § 3.

special emergency. Something more pressing than the usual emergency, exigency, crisis, or predicament; a sudden, acute, and taut situation not foreseeable in time to deliberate and exercise judgment or discretion. People v Uncapher, 207 Misc 960, 141 NYS2d 377.

special errand rule. The rule that where an employee's duties require him to circulate in a general area with no fixed place or hours of employment, or to go to and from his home to various outside places of work, and his employer furnishes him with a motor vehicle to use in his work, it can be found that he continues in the service of his employer, for the purposes of the liability of his employer for an injury resulting from his negligence in the operation of the vehicle, until he actually reaches home. Anno: 52 ALR2d 365, § 7.

special estate tail. An estate in tail under a limitation to one and certain specified heirs of his body, as the heirs of his body begotten of a certain wife. 28 Am J2d Estates § 45.

special exception. An exception directed to a matter of form rather than substance.

See **special demurrer.**

special execution. An execution upon a judgment which specifies the particular property to be sold. 21 Am J2d Exec § 17.

special exemption from taxation. An exemption from taxation granted to a particular class of persons, such as veterans, old persons, or persons of limited means without earning power. Eyers Woolen Co. v Gilsum, 84 NH 1, 64 ALR 1196, 146 A 511. An exemption from taxation granted by contract. 51 Am J1st Tax § 507.

special fee conditional. A fee simple conditional limited to one and the heirs of the body by a particular spouse. Anno: 114 ALR 604; 28 Am J2d Est § 38.

special finding. An answer made by the jury to an interrogatory, being distinguished from a special verdict in the fact that it always accompanies a general verdict and further in the fact that it need not cover all the material issues. 53 Am J1st Trial § 1005. A finding of fact made by the court in a trial to the court. Not a mere report of the evidence, but a statement by the court of the ultimate facts on which the law of the case must determine the rights of the parties; a finding of the propositions of fact which the evidence establishes, and not the evidence on which those ultimate facts are supposed to rest, such finding having the same effect as the verdict of a jury. Rhodes v United States Nat. Bank (CA7 Ill) 66 F 512.

special franchise. A franchise distinct from the franchise to be a corporation or the franchise in the sense of the powers granted in the charter. 18 Am J2d Corp § 66. A right to do something in a public street or place which, except for the grant under which it is exercised, would be a trespass. People ex rel. New York C. & H. R. R. Co. v Gourley, 198 NY 486, 92 NE 398; People ex rel. Harlem River & Port Chester Railroad Co. v State Board of Tax Comrs. 215 NY 507, 109 NE 569.

The right to be a corporation is frequently called a "franchise," as it is in one sense, but not in the sense that a grant of a right to build a railroad in a public street is a franchise; and it is unfortunate that the same word is used with widely different meanings, for it leads to confusion unless qualified by an appropriate adjective, such as "general" or "special." The right to be a corporation, or the corporate right of life, is inseparable from the corporation itself. It is part of it, and cannot be sold or assigned. That franchise is general and dies with the corporation, for it cannot survive dissolution or repeal. On the other hand, grants to do something in the public streets, or special franchises, are not part of the corporation. They can be made to an individual with the same legal force or effect as to a corporation. Unless there is some legislative restriction, they can be mortgaged and sold. They are no part of corporate life if owned by a corporation, any more than they are no part of corporate life if owned by an individual. Lord v Equitable Life Assur. Soc. 194 NY 212, 87 NE 443.

special fund doctrine. The principle that a commitment of a municipal corporation is not subject to debt limit provisions where the obligation is payable out of a special fund and the municipality is not liable to pay the obligation out of its general funds in the event the special fund proves insufficient, and the transaction by which the indebtedness is incurred cannot in any event deplete the general resources of the municipality. 38 Am J1st Mun Corp § 468.

special grand jury. A grand jury summoned where there has been a failure to draw or summon a regular grand jury or where the regular grand jury has been discharged. 24 Am J1st Grand J § 17.

special guaranty. A guaranty which names certain definite persons as obligees. 24 Am J1st Guar § 15. A guaranty limited to the person to whom it is addressed, usually contemplating a trust or reposing a confidence in that person. Tidioute Sav. Bank v Libbey, 101 Wis 193, 71 NW 182.

special guardian. A guardian appointed to protect the interests of an infant or incompetent in a proceeding already instituted.

A guardian ad litem is appointed for the purpose of prosecuting or defending an action; a special guardian is appointed merely to protect the interests of the ward by inquiring into the proceedings and seeing to it that the ward is not prejudiced by anything which is done in the proceedings.

special healing. A purported treatment of sickness or healing of disease by methods other than those practiced by physicians. 41 Am J1st Phys & S § 31.

special heir. See **heir special.**

Specialia generalibus derogant (spe-she-al'i-a je-ne-ra'li-bus de'ro-gant). Special words or provisions restrict or modify general ones.

"A statute which treats of persons of an inferior rank cannot by any general word be so extended as to embrace a superior; the class first mentioned is to be taken as the most comprehensive." Lewis v Fisher, 80 Md 139, 30 A 608.

speciali gratia. See **ex speciali gratia.**

special imparlance (im-par'lans). An imparlance reserving execeptions and objections.

special income tax. A tax on a special type of income, particularly income previously escaping taxation. Welch v Henry, 305 US 134, 83 L Ed 87, 59 S Ct 121, 118 ALR 1142, reh den 305 US 675, 83 L Ed 437, 59 S Ct 250.

special indorsement. An indorsement of a negotiable instrument which specifies the person to whom or to whose order the instrument is to be payable. 11 Am J2d B & N § 361.

special injunction. A term of the early English practice for an injunction to prevent irreparable injury in a case where the preventive aid of the court of equity was the ultimate and only relief sought, being distinguished in this respect from the common injunction which was granted in aid of or as secondary to another equity. 28 Am J Rev ed Inj § 10.

special inquiry officer. An officer of the immigration service charged with duties in the determination of admission or exclusion of an alien. 8 USC § 1226(a).

special interrogatories. Interrogatories contained in or referred to in a bill in equity, constituting a definite part of such a bill according to traditional equity practice. 27 Am J2d Equity § 181. Interrogatories directed to the jury upon a request for a special verdict or special findings. 53 Am J1st Trial § 1005.

special issue. A plea denying some one material and traversable allegation in the declaration, and concluding to the contrary.

Such a plea never advances new matter, but merely denies some particular material and traversable allegation, the denial of which is, in effect, a denial of the entire right of action. Kimball v Railroad Co. 55 Vt 95, 97.

See **special pleading.**

specialist. A physician who confines his practice to specific diseases or disabilities. A physician who holds himself out as having special knowledge and skill in the treatment of a particular organ or disease and who is bound to bring to the discharge of his duty to patients employing him as a specialist that degree of skill and learning ordinarily possessed by physicians who devote special attention and study to such organ or disease, having regard to the present state of scientific knowledge. 41 Am J1st Phys & S § 90. In the broad sense, any person who concentrates in practice upon a division of a profession, occupation, or calling.

specialized court. See **court of limited jurisdiction.**

special judge. A judge selected to act in the absence, disability, or disqualification of the regular judge, or under other circumstances, as provided by constitution or statute. 30A Am Rev ed Judges § 237.

Some courts make a distinction between a judge pro tem and a special judge, saying that the former is appointed for a term of court or some part thereof, during which time he exercises all the functions of the regular judge, while a special judge is appointed to act in a particular case. 30A Am J1st Judges § 238.

special judgment. Same as **judgment in rem.** Smith v Colloty, 69 NJL 365, 368, 55 A 805.

special jurisdiction. See **court of limited jurisdiction.**

special jury. Same as **struck jury.**

special law. See **private act; special legislation.**

special legislation. A statute which does not have a uniform operation, relating to particular persons or things of a class, either particularized by the express terms of the act, or separated by any method of selection from the whole class to which the law might, but for such limitations, be applicable. 50 Am J1st Stat § 7. A statute which by force of a stated or inherent limitation arbitrarily excludes some persons, places, or things upon which otherwise it would operate. Iowa Motor Vehicle Asso.

v Board of Railroad Comrs. 207 Iowa 461, 221 NW 364, 75 ALR 1. A statute making a classification not based on any reasonable ground. Nicholls v Spokane Public School District, 195 Wash 310, 80 P2d 833. See **special legislation, D,** 1219.

special letter of credit. A letter of credit addressed exclusively to an individual therein named. 24 Am J1st Guar § 22.

special letters of administration. The letters granted to a special administrator.
See **special administrator.**

special license. A license required of certain kinds of dealers, such as peddlers and hawkers, as well as of those who deal in certain kinds of merchandise, such as retailers of intoxicating liquors or medicines. 33 Am J1st Lic § 51.

special lien. A charge upon a particular piece of property, by which it is held for the payment or discharge of a particular debt or duty. 33 Am J1st Liens § 5.
If a lien extends to everything, acquired and to be acquired, it is not special merely because it was created by a mortgage or other express contract. Green v Coast Line Railroad Co. 97 Ga 15, 24 SE 814.

special lien for services. The lien of an artisan or mechanic upon the personal property of another for services rendered upon the same.
See **charging lien; mechanic's lien.**

special limitation. See **conditional limitation.**

specially appear. See **appear specially.**

special master. One to whom a matter is referred by a court of bankruptcy to hear and report his findings of fact and conclusions of law. 9 Am J2d Bankr § 107.

special meeting. A meeting of the directors, or of the stockholders, of a corporation other than the annual meeting of stockholders or a regular meeting of the board of directors.

special mobile equipment. Equipment of an automobile for a special purpose, such as a rack for the display of garments by a salesman, not connected with the actual operation of the vehicle in reference to driving it upon the highway.

special motion. Any motion which must be brought on for hearing upon supporting papers. A motion which affects substantial rights and is not to be granted ex parte. 37 Am J1st Motions § 14.

special nuclear material. (1) Plutonium, uranium enriched in the isotope 233 or in the isotope 235, and any other material determined by the Atomic Energy Commission to be special nuclear material, exclusive of source material; or (2) any material artificially enriched by any of the foregoing, exclusive of source material. 42 USC § 2014(y).

special occupant. The status of an heir in possession, but under the terms of a grant, not by right of inheritance. See 2 Bl Comm 259.

special owner. Some person holding the property with the consent and as the representative of the actual owner.
The term is applied to personal property only. See Frazier v State, 18 Tex App 434, 441.

special paper. See **clean paper.**

special partner. A partner in a limited partnership protected against general liability for the firm debts. 40 Am J1st Partn § 511.

special partnership. Same as **limited partnership.**

special place. A certain bank, store, or other building within a city or town, as distinct from the city or town itself.

special plea. A plea by the accused in a criminal case other than a plea of guilty or not guilty. 21 Am J2d Crim L §§ 458 et seq.
See **special pleading.**

special pleading. A pleading required for presentation of special matters of defense, that is, matters going beyond a mere denial of plaintiff's allegations. 41 Am J1st Pl § 144. A pleading in excuse or justification; a pleading in confession and avoidance. Gelston v Hoyt (US) 3 Wheat 246, 327, 4 L Ed 381, 401.
Special matters of defense should be specially pleaded. 41 Am J1st Pl § 150.

special police. Extra police engaged for duty on an extraordinary occasion, such as a celebration attended by a large crowd of people, some of whom are likely to be persons over whom there should be police surveillance.

special power. The authority of an agent to do only a specific act or acts in pursuance of particular instructions, or with restrictions necessarily implied from the act to be done. 3 Am J2d Agency § 6.
See **special power of appointment; special power of attorney.**

special power of appointment. A power of appointment under which the donee of the power is restricted to passing on the property to certain individuals or class of individuals designated or described in the instrument which creates the power. Marx v Rice, 1 NJ 574, 65, A2d 48, 9 ALR2d 584.
Under statute a special power in trusts exists:—(1) when the disposition which it authorizes is limited to be made to any particular person other than the grantee of such power; (2) when any person or class of persons, other than the grantee, is entitled to any benefit from the disposition or charge authorized by the power. Re Uihlein's Will, 264 Wis 362, 59 NW2d 641.

special power of attorney. A power couched in specific rather than general terms, as a power to sell, not any land owned by the principal, but specified land of the principal; a power to sell to a particular purchaser, not any purchaser; or a power to sell on specified terms, not on any terms. White v Breen, 106 Ala 159, 19 So 59.

special power in trust. See **special power of appointment.**

special privilege. A right, power, franchise, immunity, or privilege granted to or vested in a person or class of persons, to the exclusion of others and in derogation of common right. Plattsmouth v Nebraska Telephone Co. 80 Neb 460, 114 NW 588.

special proceeding. A civil remedy other than an ordinary action. Hazelton-Moffit Special School District v Ward (ND) 107 NW2d 636. Inclusive of every special statutory remedy which is not in itself an action. Sullivan v Storz, 156 Neb 177, 55 NW2d 499, 34 ALR2d 1142. A proceeding instituted for the appointment of an ancillary receiver or for the exercise of summary jurisdiction. Knauth v Latham, 242 US 426, 61 L Ed 404, 37 S Ct 139. A proceeding before an administrative agency. Ames v Department of Labor & Industry, 176 Wash 509, 30 P2d 239, 91 ALR 1392. A proceeding characterized by commencement upon petition and notice, rather than upon service of summons or other form of regular process.

Nearly thirty years prior to the adoption of the California Constitution of 1879, special cases and special proceedings had been defined by the state supreme court as something entirely different, as new cases, the creation of statute, and the special proceedings under which were unknown to the general framework or courts of law and equity, and as not including any class of cases for which courts of general jurisdiction had always supplied a remedy. See Bixler's Appeal, 59 Cal 550, 555.

special property. An interest in property other than full ownership, such as that of a bailee in possession, a lienor, a mortgagee, etc.

special prosecutor. Counsel employed to assist the prosecuting attorney in the conduct of a criminal prosecution. 42 Am J1st Pros Atty § 10.

special rate. A railroad rate granted specially for a particular shipment of goods. 13 Am J2d Car § 185.

special reason. A term of art for a circumstance calling for a variance in the application of a zoning regulation. 58 Am J1st Zon § 196.

special receiver. A receivership, as in a mortgage foreclosure, wherein the receiver takes custody only of particular property. 45 Am J1st Rec § 3.

special registration. A registration of voters required for and effective only in reference to a particular election, for example, a local option election. 30 Am J Rev ed Intox L § 97.

special relief. Specific relief prayed for in a complaint, bill, or petition in equity. 27 Am J2d Equity § 182.

special replication. A replication or reply setting up new matter in avoidance of the defenses pleaded in the answer. 41 Am J1st Pl § 178.

special retainer. A fee paid to an attorney preliminary to a particular case or litigation.

special rule of court. An order of court adopting a rule of practice or a method of procedure in the particular cause before the court, as a departure from the usual practice or procedure.

"If under the stipulation, the judge was to abdicate for a time, and proceed as an arbitrator, to hear and decide the facts and the law, and upon such findings was again to proceed as a court to pronounce judgment, this was an adoption of that method of trying the cause. The submission was thus made a special rule of court, and was not revocable." Hastings v Jones (CA7 Ill) 18 F2d 833.

special salvage. A reward in the nature of salvage made to members of the crew of the vessel saved. 47 Am J1st Salv § 20.

special seal. A seal adopted by a corporation different from its corporate seal, for a special occasion. 18 Am J2d Corp § 154.

special session. Any session of a legislative body which is lawfully held and which is not a regular session or a part or an adjournment of a regular session. People ex rel. Carter v Rice, 135 NY 473, 31 NE 921.

See **sessions of the peace.**

special statutory proceeding. See **extraordinary remedies; special proceeding.**

special stop. A stopping place on the line of a carrier not noted in its schedule or posted as a stop.

special statute. See **private act; special legislation.**

special tax. A tax levied for a particular governmental purpose. 48 Am J1st Spec A § 3. A tax levied for a special public purpose.

A special assessment for local improvement is not such a tax. Illinois Central Railroad Co. v Decatur, 126 Ill 92, 18 NE 315.

special taxing district. A district fixed by legislative determination, without reference to town, county or regular taxing district lines, as a district which is to receive a special benefit and to bear the expense of a local improvement by means of a local assessment. 48 Am J1st Spec A § 115.

special term. A term of court, contra-distinguished from a regular or adjourned term, appointed by the presiding officer or officers, held at an unusual time, for the transaction of some particular business. Wightman v Karsner, 20 Ala 446, 452. In some jurisdictions, a term for the transaction of court business other than jury trials.

special territorial jurisdiction. See **extraterritoriality.**

special ticket. A ticket issued by a carrier good only upon certain trains and for a limited time, and to be used only in accordance with terms prescribed therein. 14 Am J2d Car §§ 813, 814.

special traverse (spesh'al trav'ĕrs). A form of denial at common law, the design of which is to explain or qualify the denial, commencing with the words "absque hoc" or the English equivalent "without this, that," then pursuing the material portion of the words of the allegation which it denies. 41 Am J1st Pl § 190.

special trust. An active or real, as distinguished from a dry, trust.

specialty. An instrument under seal wherein an obligation is embodied. Mutual Trust & Dep. Co. v Boone (Ky) 267 SW2d 751, 45 ALR2d 962. A contract under seal. A designation sometimes given to a bond, that is an obligation under seal, as distinguished from a promissory note or other simple contract. Commonwealth v Smith, 92 Mass (10 Allen) 448. The practice of a specialist in a profession.

Certain decisions have denominated statutes as specialties which give a right to an ascertained or readily ascertainable money liability upon which an action of debt may be maintained. Williamson v Columbia Gas & Electric Corp. (DC Pa) 27 F Supp 198.

See **special contract; specialist.**

specialty debt. See **specialty.**

specialty hauler. A carrier which confines its transportation service to a special class or classes of property. Carolina Freight Carriers Corp. v United States (DC NC) 38 F Supp 549, affd 315 US 475, 86 L Ed 971, 62 S Ct 722.

special use of highway. The use of street or highway for purposes other than those of travel and transportation. 25 Am J1st High § 168.

special venire. A venire issued by the court to summon jurors after the general panel has become exhausted and additional jurors are required to complete a trial jury. Additional jurors called in case of a deficiency in or exhaustion of the regular jury panel. 31 Am J Rev ed Jury § 91.

special venireman (vē-ni'rē-man). See **special venire.**

special verdict. A verdict finding the facts, in response to interrogatories submitted to it, without a conclusion as to the party prevailing in the case, such being left to the determination by the court upon the application of the law to the facts as found by the jury. 53 Am J1st Trial § 1005.

special warranty. A covenant of warranty contained in a deed, which is limited or restricted to certain persons or claims. In its most usual form, a warranty only against claims held by, through, or under the grantor. Central Life Assur. Soc. v Impelmans, 13 Wash 2d 632, 126 P2d 757. An implied warranty on the sale of a chattel ordered by the purchaser for a special purpose that the chattel is fit for that purpose. 46 Am J1st Sales § 346.

special warranty deed. A deed which contains a covenant of special warranty rather than a covenant of general warranty.
See **special warranty.**

specie (spē'shē). Gold or silver coins of the coinage of the United States. Belford v Woodward, 158 Ill 122, 41 NE 1097.

species (spē'shēz). A sort, a kind, a class subordinate to a genus, which is a class embracing many species.
The expression "an animal of the horse species" would, therefore, only include the animals known as stallions, geldings, mares, fillies and colts. Smythe v State, 17 Tex App 244, 251.

species facti (spe'she-ēz fak'tī). The kind or character of the act.

specific. Definite. Explicit.

specification. A statement in detail. A statement of grounds of opposition to the discharge of a bankrupt. 9 Am J2d Bankr § 718. The doctrine under which a change made by one person in the species of a substance or article belonging to another, passes title from the owner to him who wrought the change. 1 Am J2d Access § 1. The technical name of that part of the formal charge made against a defendant in court-martial proceedings which sets forth the acts or omissions of the accused relied upon as the legal constituents of the offense. 36 Am J1st Mil § 98.

specification of error. The setting forth in an assignment of error on appeal the alleged error committed by the lower court which is relied upon as a ground of reversal. 5 Am J2d A & E § 648.

specifications. A product of architectural services. A statement in detail of the manner in which a building or other improvement is to be constructed, including the materials to be used. 5 Am J2d Arch § 3; 13 Am J2d Bldg Contr § 12. A written description of an invention and the discovery thereof to be filed with an application for a patent. 40 Am J1st Pat § 85.
The purpose of the statutory requirement that an application for a patent shall contain a written description of the invention and discovery, and, in the case of a machine, the principle thereof, and shall particularly point out and distinctly claim the part, improvement, or combination which the applicant claims as his invention or discovery is not only that any person skilled in the art to which it pertains may construct and use it after the expiration of the patent, but also to inform the public during the life of the patent of the limits of the monopoly asserted, so that it may be known which features may be safely used or manufactured without a license, and which may not. 40 Am J1st Pat § 85.

specific bequest. See **specific devise; specific legacy.**

specific criminal intent. See **specific intent.**

specific denial. A denial by the defendant in his answer addressed to a specific substantive fact alleged by the plaintiff in his pleading. 41 Am J1st Pl § 150.

specific deposit. A deposit of money or other property for some specific and particular purpose; as where a note is deposited for collection, or money is deposited to pay a particular note. Officer v Officer, 120 Iowa 389, 94 NW 947.
See **special deposit.**

specific devise. A devise of real estate specifically described, or a portion or share thereof, or a devise of all the testator's "right, title and interest" in real estate specifically described. 57 Am J1st Wills § 1404.

specific devisee. One named in a will as the recipient of a **specific devise.**

specific gravity. The ratio of the weight of a substance to that of an equal volume of another substance used as a standard. Ohio Oil Co. v Conway, 281 US 146, 74 L Ed 775, 50 S Ct 310.

specific insurance. Insurance against a specific peril or in a specific amount. Anno: 13 ALR2d 725. Insurance under a policy covering particular property specifically, as contrasted with insurance under a blanket policy.

specific intent. The intent to commit the very forbidden act charged as the offense in a criminal prosecution. 21 Am J2d Crim L § 82.
Specific intent is present when from the circumstances the offender must have subjectively desired the prohibited result. State v Daniels, 236 La 998, 109 So 2d 896.

specific legacy. A bequest of a particular, individualized chattel, fund, or portion of the testator's personal estate, which is set apart from the balance of his property and which is differentiated from all other articles or funds of the same or a similar nature; a bequest which may be satisfied only by delivery of the specific object, fund, or portion designated, and not by the receipt of some equivalent in money or property. Henderson v First Nat. Bank, 189 Ga 175, 5 SE2d 636, 128 ALR 816; Gorham v Chadwick, 135 Me 479, 200 A 500, 117 ALR 805.

specific legatee. One named in a will as the beneficiary of a **specific legacy.**

specific lien. A special lien. 33 Am J1st Liens § 5.

specific performance. The actual accomplishment of a contract by the party bound to fulfill it. Guadulupe County Board of Education v O'Bannon, 26 NM 606, 195 P 801. The remedy by which a party to a contract is compelled to do precisely what he ought to have done without being coerced by a court. Edwards v Tobin, 132 Or 38, 284 P 562, 68 ALR 152. The equitable remedy of compelling performance of a contract as distinguished from an action for damages at law for breach through nonperformance. Acme Food Co. v Older, 64 W Va 255, 61 SE 235.

specific taxes. Taxes of a fixed amount by the head or number, or by some standard of weight or measurement and requiring no assessment other than a listing or classification of the subjects to be taxed.
Poll taxes are invariably specific taxes and excises are commonly specific, although the modern tendency is toward ad valorem taxation even in case of

excises, as being more consonant with justice. See 51 Am J1st Tax § 26.

specific traverse (trạ'vẻrs). See **special pleading; specific denial.**

specified person. A term of art in the law of negotiable instruments, having reference to an existing person capable of indorsing the instrument and of being a party to a contract. Bergman v Avenue State Bank, 284 Ill App 516, 1 NE2d 432.

specify. To mention with particularity. To make a specification.
See **specification; specifications.**

spectacles. Eyeglasses. Sights which are impressive.

speculate. To take the risk of loss in view of possible gain. Arentsen v Moreland, 122 Wis 167, 99 NW 790. To buy or sell with the expectation of profiting by rise or fall in price; often to engage in hazardous business transactions for the chance of unusually large profits. Clucas v Bank of Montclair, 110 NJL 394, 166 A 311, 88 ALR 302.

speculative damages. Damages not proved with reasonable certainty, the trier of the fact being left to speculate as to the actual damages suffered by the plaintiff. 22 Am J2d Damg § 24.
Damages are not speculative merely because they cannot be computed with mathematical exactness, if under the evidence they are capable of reasonable approximation. Hawkinson v Johnston (CA8 Mo) 122 F2d 724.
"So long as the jury are considering the material pecuniary injury, and the physical pain, their inquiry relates to what are termed actual damages; but when authorized by a vicious intent of the wrongdoer, they turn to the realm of mental anguish, public indignity, wounded sensibility, etc., the damages may more appropriately be described as presumptive, speculative, or imaginary." Murphy v Hobbs, 7 Colo 541, 5 P 119, 123.

speculative or trading value. The value of securities based upon a possibility or probability, depending upon the future happening of certain contingencies respecting the affairs of the company issuing the securities, that they would in the future acquire a substantial cash market value. Haight v Stewart, 36 Cal App 514, 172 P 769.

speculative security. A stock, bond, or other security the value of which materially depends on proposed or promised future promotion or development. Anno: 87 ALR 81.
The term has been defined by a state blue sky law as including a stock, bond, note, contract, or other security, which shall, in subscription, issuance, sale, transfer, negotiation, or distribution, be represented to yield a profit to the purchaser or other transferee of more than eight per cent on the price at which it is offered. Superior Producing & Refining Co. v Handlan, Hearne & Co. 100 W Va 547, 548, 131 SE 857.

speculator. See **speculate; ticket speculator.**

speech freedom. See **freedom of speech and of the press.**

speed. Rapidity of motion. Application of Reo Motor Car Co. 57 App DC 9, 16 F2d 349.
See **moderate speed.**

speeding. The offense of exceeding a speed limit.

speed laws. Statutes and ordinances regulating the speed of vehicles upon street or highway in the interest of public safety. 7 Am J2d Auto §§ 180 et seq.

speed limit. A restriction by statute or ordinance upon the speed at which a motor vehicle may be operated upon highway or street, usually a maximum, but sometimes a minimum, limit. 7 Am J2d Auto §§ 180 et seq. A restriction imposed by statute or ordinance upon the speed at which a motorboat may be operated upon public waters. 12 Am J2d Boats § 15.

speed meter. See **radar speed meter.**

speedometer. An instrumentality in a motor vehicle, in view of the driver, which indicates the speed at which the vehicle is being driven.

speed trap. A watch maintained, whether in person or through an instrumentality, for the particular purpose of detecting violations of speed laws in a particular section of street or highway. 39 Am J1st Obst J § 16.

speed-watch. A means of measuring speed of a motor vehicle, consisting of two rubber hoses set across the highway at a measured distance, and so equipped and constructed that when the front wheels of a vehicle strike the first hose, a clock is set in operation, and when the wheels strike the second hose, the clock stops, so that a reading of the speed of the vehicle in miles per hour is recorded. People v Duskin, 11 Misc 2d 945, 174 NYS2d 527.

speedy trial. A right of an accused. 21 Am J2d Crim L § 241. A trial conducted according to fixed rules, regulations, and proceedings of law, free from vexatious, capricious, and oppressive delays. State v Jackson, 228 Or 371, 365 P2d 294, 89 ALR2d 1225; Gerchman v State, 206 Tenn 109, 332 SW2d 182.
The constitutional and statutory right of one accused of a criminal offense to a speedy trial is a right which is personal to the accused alone and one in which the state has no special interest, and it has been held without question that he may waive his right in that respect. Anno: 129 ALR 574.

Spencer's Case. A leading English case on the law of covenants. 5 Coke 16a, 77 Eng Reprint 72.
The first resolution in Spencer's Case, if regarded alone, implies that a covenant cannot run with the land if it relates to a thing not in esse. The second resolution, however, makes it clear that a covenant relating to a thing not in esse may run with the land if the thing to be done relates to and touches, and is not merely collateral to, the land, and if the intention of the parties that the covenant should run with the land is shown by the covenant. 20 Am J2d Cov § 30.

spendthrift. One so prodigal, profligate, or drunken, that there is need for the appointment of a guardian. 25 Am J1st G & W § 20. In common usage, a careless spender; one who does not know the value of money.

spendthrift trust. A trust created to provide a fund for the maintenance of the beneficiary which shall be secure against his improvidence or incapacity. Huestis v Manley, 110 Vt 413, 8 A2d 644. A trust which restrains either voluntary or involuntary alienation by the beneficiary of his interest in the trust, or which, in other words, bars such interest from seizure in satisfaction of his debts. Keelers' Estate, 334 Pa 225, 3 A2d 413, 121 ALR 1301.

spe recuperandi (spē re-kū-pe-ran'dī). In the hope of recovering.

spermatozoa (spėr"mạ-tọ-zō'ạ). Seminal fluid. State v Perry, 41 W Va 641, 646.

spes (spēz). Hope.

spes accrescendi (spēz a-kre-sen'di). The hope of surviving.

Spes est vigilantis somnium (spēz est vi-ji-lan'tis som'ni-um). Hope is the dream of the vigilant man.

Spes impunitatis continuum affectum tribuit delinquendi (spēz im-pu-ni-tā'tis kon-tin'u-um a-fek'tum trī'bu-it de-lin-quen'dī). The hope of impunity offers a constant temptation to delinquency.

spes recuperandi (spēz re-ku-pe-ran'dī). The hope of recovering; the expectation of receiving compensation or indemnity. Aetna Fire Ins. Co. v Tyler (NY) 16 Wend 90.

spiffs (spifs). A mercantile term for goods which are not in demand. Anderson v Burg & Sons, 170 Minn 53, 55, 212 NW 9.

spike mike. An electronic listening device consisting of a microphone attached to a foot-long spike, with an amplifier, a power pack, and earphones, used by police by inserting the spike through a wall separating an observation post from premises suspected of being used for criminal purposes, until the spike contacts a heating duct serving the suspect premises, so that conversations throughout the premises are audible to police officers listening with earphones. Silverman v United States, 365 US 505, 5 L Ed 2d 734, 81 S Ct 679.

spill (spil). A gate, also called a waste gate, through which the waste or superfluous water in an irrigation ditch is allowed to run off. Howell v Big Horn Basin Colonization Co. 14 Wyo 14, 81 P 785.

spillway. A channel to carry off water from a reservoir.
See **spill**.

spinal block. Anesthesia by desensitizing the nerve roots at the point where they reach the spine. Anno: 53 ALR2d 158.

spinal puncture. A means of obtaining a sample of a bodily component for chemical analysis in aid of a physical examination. 23 Am J2d Dep § 226.

spin-off. The divesting by a corporation of its stock in another corporation, sometimes required by the judgment or decree in a suit under the Anti-trust Act.

spinster. An unmarried female some years past marriageable age.

spirit of Constitution. The true meaning of a provision of the Constitution, although not explicit, because in accord with the general purpose of the provision. 16 Am J2d Const L § 71.

spirits. See **ardent spirits**; **spiritous liquor**.

spiritual. Pertaining to the soul rather than the physical body of man. The higher as distinguished from the material or carnal nature of man. The relation between man and God.
As the word is used to define hopes and fears which may be held out to a person charged with crime when a confession is sought, it has been held to mean that which pertains to the soul or higher endowments of the mind in its relation to the Spirit of God, the Holy Spirit, and that which pertains to our holy religion. The spiritual nature of man would be his higher self, not the carnal. Johnson v State, 107 Miss 196, 65 So 218.

spiritual corporation. A church or ecclesiastical corporation, such as a bishop of the Episcopal Church. An incorporated religious society.

spiritual courts (kōrts). Ecclesiastical courts.

spiritualism (spir'i-tụ-ạl-izm). A belief that the spirits of the dead can communicate with the living through the agency of persons called "mediums," who, under such belief, are credited with the possession of qualities or gifts not possessed by mankind in general. Middleditch v Williams, 45 NJ Eq 726, 17 A 826.
See **medium**; **seance**.

spiritualities (spir-i-tụ-ạl'i-tēs). A bishop's income or revenue.

spiritual lords. See **lords spiritual**.

spirituous liquor. A liquor composed, in whole or in part, of alcohol extracted by a process of distillation. 30 Am J Rev ed Intox L § 12.

spital (spit'ạl). A hospital, especially one for patients having loathsome diseases.

spite fence. A fence of no beneficial use to an owner of premises, but erected and maintained by him for the purpose of annoying his neighbor. 1 Am J2d Adj L § 106.

spite structure. A structure which is of no beneficial use or pleasure to the owner but was erected and is maintained by him for the purpose of annoying his neighbor or with the malicious motive of injuring the neighbor by depriving the latter's premises of light, air, or view. Racich v Mastrovich, 65 SD 321, 273 NW 660.
See **spite fence**.

splash dam. A dam erected for the purpose of making a stream capable of floating logs. 34 Am J1st Logs § 72.

splash guard. A flap or apron attached to the fender of a motor vehicle so as to minimize the spray or splash of water or mud to the rear of the vehicle. People v Kiser, 112 Cal App 2d 903, 254 P2d 1125.

split convention. A political convention held by a faction of the party. A political convention from which a large group of delegates, although a minority, has withdrawn. 25 Am J2d Elect § 166.

split decision. A decision to which there are dissents by a minority of justices.
See **equally divided court**.

split-level house. A house with floor on different levels, violating a covenant confining structures to single-story dwellings. Anno: 92 ALR2d 886, § 5[a].

split-off. Same as **spin-off**.

split of stock. See **stock split**.

split sentence. Imposing a fine and imprisonment but suspending the sentence, although collecting the fine. Ex parte Bosso (Fla) 41 So 2d 322.

split switch. A term used in railroading referring to an occurrence, often serious in its consequences, wherein the wheels of one truck of a car remain on the main or straight track and the wheels of the other truck take the switch.
This is sometimes caused by a failure to open the switch all the way. Simone v Rhode Island Co. 28 RI 186, 66 A 202.

splitting appeal. Taking successive appeals from the same decision. Jolley v Martin Bros. Box Co. 90 Ohio App 415, 48 Ohio Ops 99, 107 NE2d 259.

splitting causes of action. Bringing separate actions upon separate and distinct causes of action against the same person in lieu of joining all of such causes in one action. The practice, not permitted, of splitting one cause of action and maintaining successive suits for different parts. 1 Am J2d Actions § 127.

In applying the rule to the case of a contract twice broken, it has been facetiously observed that it is not permitted to make two suits out of one pair of breeches.

splitting commission. A reprehensible practice on the part of an agent or broker in dividing his commission with the other party to the transaction or the agent or broker for the other party. 3 Am J2d Agency § 254; 12 Am J2d Brok §§ 174 et seq.

splitting fees. See **division of fees**.

split-up. See **spin-off**; **stock split**.

spoiled ballot. A ballot cast at an election containing erasures, delineations, stricken names of candidates, or distinguishing marks. 26 Am J2d Elect §§ 266, 270.

spoils system. A system under which appointment to public office is a reward for political work, with resulting evils of inefficiency, extravagance, interruption of public business by office seekers, corruption of the electoral franchise, and political assessments. Civil Service Com. v Auditor General, 302 Mich 673, 5 NW2d 536. The system replaced by the merit system under civil service. 15 Am J2d Civ S § 1.

spoken slander (spō'kn slan'dėr). See **slander**.

spoliation (spō-li-ā'shon). A material, but unauthorized, alteration of an instrument by a stranger without privity with any of the parties to the instrument, such being without effect upon the validity of the instrument if it can be shown by evidence what the language was as it originally stood. 4 Am J2d Alt Inst § 14. Alterations made in a will by a stranger to the instrument, without the knowledge of the testator. 57 Am J1st Wills § 513. A plundering or devastation, as by an invading force. Pillaging, plundering, and robbing. Wichita Royalty Co. v City Nat. Bank (CA5 Tex) 109 F2d 299.

spoliation claims. See **French spoliation claims**.

spoliator (spo-li-ā'tor). See **in odium spoliatoris**; **spoliation**.

Spoliatus debet ante omnia restitui (spo-li-ā'tus dē'-bet an'te om'ni-a re-sti'tu-ī). One who has been despoiled ought to have restitution before all things.

Spoliatus episcopus ante omnia debet restitui (spo-li-ā'tus e-pi'sko-pus an'te om'ni-a dē'bet re-sti'tu-ī). A bishop who has been despoiled ought to have restitution before all things.

spondeo (spon'de-ō). I promise.

Spondet peritiam artis (spon'det pe-ri'she-am ar'tis). He promises the skill of his art.

sponging-house (spun'jing-hous). A house where persons arrested for debt were kept for a day in order that their friends might have opportunity to keep them from going to prison by paying their debts.

sponsalia (spon-sā'li-a). (Civil law.) Mutual promises to marry.

sponsio (spon'si-ō). (Latin.) A solemn promise. An engagement.

sponsio judicialis (spon'si-ō ju-di-she-ā'lis). (Roman law.) A feigned issue; a fictitious issue of fact.

spontaneous exclamation. Words uttered without thought, such as an involuntary utterance indicating present pain. 22 Am J2d Damg § 309. For the purpose of admissibility notwithstanding hearsay character, words which are spontaneous and so related to the transaction or occurrence in question as reasonably to appear to be evoked and prompted by it. 29 Am J2d Ev § 708.

What constitutes a spontaneous utterance such as will bring it within the exception to the hearsay rule depends necessarily upon the facts peculiar to each case. Beausoliel v United States, 71 App DC 111, 107 F2d 292.

See **dying declaration**.

sponte oblata (spon'te ob-lā'ta). A gift to the king.

Sponte virum fugiens mulier et adultera facta, doti sua careat, nisi sponsi sponte retracta (spon'te vī'rum fu'ji-enz mu'li-er et a-dul'te-ra fak'ta, do'tī su'a ka're-at, nī'sī spon'sī spon'te rē-trak'ta). A woman who runs away from her husband and commits adultery loses her dower, unless she is voluntarily taken back by her husband.

sport. A game. Pastime or diversion.

sporting house. An old term for house of prostitution.

sporting woman. A prostitute. Johnson v Weedin (CA9 Wash) 16 F2d 105.

sportula. (Latin.) A gift or present. Remuneration of a worker in excess of the agreed-upon compensation.

spot cash. Cash on delivery of the goods. McIver v Williamson-Halsell-Frazier Co. 19 Okla 454, 92 P 170.

spot sales. A brokerage term denoting sales contemplating immediate delivery to the purchaser of the commodities or securities purchased. United States v New York Coffee & Sugar Exchange, 263 US 611, 616, 68 L Ed 475, 476, 44 S Ct 225. A term used by grain brokers denoting sales of grain already in the city where the sale is made in railroad cars or elevators for immediate delivery by order on carrier or transfer of warehouse receipt. Board of Trade v United States, 246 US 231, 236, 62 L Ed 683, 686, 38 S Ct 242.

spotter (spot'ėr). A paid informer. A private detective employed to keep a person under surveillance and report unlawful, immoral, or suspicious conduct. An employee given the additional duty of observing the conduct of fellow workers and reporting violations of working rules to the employer.

spotting cars. Shifting railroad cars to place on siding, spur track, or industrial track where they can be loaded or unloaded conveniently by shipper or consignee.

A voluntary service of uniform practice in railroading, and included in a line-haul rate, which rate is usually made to or from an area within which the carrier holds itself out as agreeing to deliver freight in its freight depot or at team tracks or on sidings or private spur-tracks. This service consists, in delivering a car on a team track, of spotting the car at a point where merchandise of the class contained in the car is usually and most conveniently unloaded. United States v American Sheet & Tin Plate Co. 301 US 402, 81 L Ed 1186, 57 S Ct 804.

spotting service. See **spotting cars**.

spot zoning. A provision of a zoning ordinance, creating a small area within the limits of the zone prescribed by the ordinance in which are permitted uses inconsistent with those permitted in the larger area. Anno: 128 ALR 740, s. 149 ALR 292. A carving out of one or more properties located in a given use district and reclassifying them in a different use district. Chayt v Maryland Jockey Club, 179 Md 390, 18 A2d 856.

An attempt to erect a manufacturing plant in a district zoned for and occupied by first class single residences only might be properly held to be spot zoning and unreasonable and arbitrary, but this can hardly be said of buildings of public utilities devoted to public service and promotive of public welfare. Higbee v Chicago B. & Q. R. Co. 235 Wis 91, 292 NW 320, 128 ALR 734.

spousals (spou'zạls). Mutual promises to marry.

spouse (spouz). A husband or wife.

spouse-breach (spouz'brĕch). Adultery.

spouted. A term familiar in the operation of grain elevators.

Grain is said to be "spouted" when it is caused to go from a grain elevator by force of gravity into box cars standing on railway tracks. W. W. Cargill Co. v Minnesota ex rel. Railroad & Warehouse Com. 180 US 452, 461, 21 S Ct 423.

S. P. Q. R. An abbreviation of **senatus, populusque Romanorus,** the senate and the Roman people.

sprain (sprān). A violent straining or wrenching of the ligaments or muscles of a joint without dislocation of the bones.

spraying crops. Applying poisonous substances in liquid by spray to growing crops, sometimes by the use of aircraft, to eradicate insect pests. 3 Am J2d Agri § 47.

spring. The season of the year which succeeds winter and in which plants start to grow. Water issuing by natural forces out of the earth at a particular place. Furner v Seabury, 135 NY 50, 31 NE 1004. A place where water by natural forces usually issues from the ground. Magoon v Harris, 46 Vt 264. A place where the water issues from the earth by the operation of natural forces, although it may have been artificially opened. Proprietors of Mills v Braintree Water Supply Co. 149 Mass 478, 21 NE 761.

spring branch. A small creek forming the outlet of a spring. Wooton v Redd's Executor, 53 Va (12 Gratt) 196, 198.

spring gun. A weapon installed on premises to fire or discharge automatically upon the intrusion of a trespasser, so as to kill or incapacitate him. United Zinc & Chemical Co. v Britt, 258 US 268, 66 L Ed 615, 42 S Ct 299, 36 ALR 28.

springing uses. Estates in futuro, known as executory interests, created by conveyances to uses, recognized in equity and validated by the Statute of Uses, but invalid under the early common law as in contravention of the rigid rules against a limitation of a fee on a fee or the taking effect of a future estate by the cutting short of a prior estate. 28 Am J2d Est § 333.

spring scales. A scales for weighing which measures the weight in ounces or pounds according to the pressure exerted against a spring. 56 Am J1st Wts & M § 22.

spring shot. A shot so arranged in blasting that it simply makes a chamber at the bottom of the drilled hole; whereas, a blast proper is a stronger charge, and both tears and throws the earth and rock. Spokane v Patterson, 46 Wash 93, 89 P 402.

spring tide. The increased tide at new moon or full moon.

sprinkler discharge or leakage insurance. Insurance against loss or damage by reason of the accidental discharge of leakage of an automatic sprinkler or sprinkler system maintained for fire extinguishment purposes. 29A Am J Rev ed Ins 1370.

sprinkler system. An overhead arrangement of water pipes and sprinklers, constructed and maintained in a building as a protection against fire, water being turned on automatically upon a rise in temperature consequent to the starting of a fire.

sprinkler truck. A motor truck of the public works department of a municipality equipped with sprinkler for the sprinkling of streets. Healy v Philadelphia, 321 Pa 488, 184 A 124.

sprinkling street. Artificial sprinkling of streets with water, sometimes in the course of cleaning the streets, but often for the purpose of preventing the blowing of dust accumulating on the way. 25 Am J1st High § 69.

spudded in. A technical term of oil-well drillers.

As the phrase is employed and understood among oil operators, it denotes the first abrasion of the soil by the drill, or that of first entrance of the drill into the ground. Scheel v Harr, 27 Cal App 2d 345, 80 P2d 1035.

spur. See **spurs; spur track.**

spurii (spū'ri-ī). (Roman law.) Illegitimate children born of a prostitute.

The Roman law distinguished between such children and "naturales" who were the children of a concubine and had the right of inheritance from the mother and of support from the father, while spurii had no legal rights either of inheritance or **support.** Dickinson's Appeal, 42 Conn 491.

spurious. Counterfeit; fake.

spurious bill. A bank bill either signed by persons who are not officers of the bank whence it purports to have issued, or by the names of fictitious persons.

A bill may be both counterfeit and forged, or both counterfeit and spurious, but it cannot be both forged and spurious. Farris v State, 1 Ohio St 185, 187.

spurius (spū'ri-us). (Roman law.) Singular of **spurii.**

spurs. Metal spikes attached to the heels of telephone or telegraph linemen, tree surgeons, and other persons whose duties include the climbing of wooden poles or trees, by which the foot carrying the weight of the climber may be anchored to the tree. Small metal prods worn on the heels of horsemen, used in urging the horse to greater speed or in directing the movements of a trained horse.

spur track. A short railroad track leading from a line of railway and connected with it at one end only. 44 Am J1st R R § 231. A railroad track running off a main line, usually to a mine or an industry. A connection with some railroad affording communication with market. Anno: 4 ALR 530.

spy. A person who has committed the offense of being a spy, an offense which is not known to the civil or statute law and which is one of a purely military character, cognizable only in time of war, and before a tribunal having its life, existence and authority, continued and defined by purely military power. Re Robert Martin (NY) 45 Barb 142, 144. One who obtains national defense information and communicates it to a foreign nation in time of war

Rosenberg v United States, 346 US 273, 97 L Ed 1607, 73 S Ct 1152. One guilty of espionage.
See **espionage**.

square. An open area in a city, usually at the intersection of several streets, frequented by the public and sometimes kept in condition similar to that of a park. 23 Am J2d Ded § 4. A tract set apart for the free and common use of the public. Re Third Street, 177 Minn 146, 225 NW 86, 74 ALR 561. Ground devoted to public use, either for purposes of free passage, or to be ornamented and improved for a pleasure ground. 39 Am J1st Pks & S § 2. A place set apart as a place for the erection of a court house or other county buildings. Logansport v Dunn, 8 Ind 378, 382. A representation of a plane with four sides of equal length and four right angles. An instrument having two sides joined so as to be usable by carpenter or other artisan in laying out or determining a right angle. A slang term, in common use by teenagers, for a person deemed to be old fashioned in ideas, manners, or dress.
See **party square**.

square inch of water. A stream of water with a cross section area of one square inch measured at right angles with its flow, taking account of the velocity of whatever head is acting upon it.

squatter (skwot'ẽr). A term of American origin applied to settlers on public lands of the United States who have not complied with the regulations of the land office. Glasgow v Hortiz (US) 1 Black 595, 17 L Ed 110, 113.

Squib Case (skwib kās). The celebrated case of Scott v Shepherd, 2 W Bl 892, 1 Smith Leading Cas 797, wherein the defendant was held liable to the plaintiff for putting out his eye, as a result of having thrown a lighted squib into a market whence several persons successively picked it up and threw it from them until it exploded and put out the plaintiff's eye. 38 Am J1st Negl § 77.

squire. A magistrate. A title of office and courtesy frequently, but not exclusively, given to a justice of the peace. Anno: 38 ALR2d 186.

SS. Abbreviation of steamship.

ss. Abreviation of **scilicet**, used most often in the caption of affidavits, for example:

State of New York } ss:
County of Monroe

stab. To wound with a pointed instrument. State v Patza, 3 La Ann 512, 514.

stabilization of prices. Various activities of the federal government in the effort to keep prices of certain farm products stable, particularly in making payments to farmers for keeping land out of production of certain crops.

stabilization programs. The various activities and efforts on the part of the federal government in stabilizing the prices of grain and other farm products.

Stabit praesumptio donec probetur in contrarium (sta'bit prē-zump'she-ō dō'nek pro-bē'ter in kon-trā'ri-um). A presumption stands until there is proof to the contrary.
"And it seems reasonable that presumption, which is not founded on the basis of certainty, should yield to evidence, which is the test of truth." Davenport v Mason, 15 Mass (15 Tyng) 85, 90.

Stabit presumptio pro veritate (sta'bit prē-zump'she-ō prō ve-ri-tā'te). Presumption stands for truth. Defreese v Lake, 109 Mich 415, 67 NW 505.

Stabitur praesumptioni donec probetur in contrarium (stā'bi-ter prē-zump'she-ō-ni dō'nek pro-bē'ter in kon-trā'ri-um). A presumption stands until the contrary is proved. Marquet v Aetna Life Ins. Co. 128 Tenn 213, 159 SW 733.

stable. A barn. A building, sometimes only a shed, to shelter livestock or provide a place for storing feed for animals and farm machinery. Culp v Firestone Tire & Rubber Co. 303 Pa 257, 154 A 479.
See **livery stable**.

stable-stand. Standing ready, as evidence of intent to kill a deer in a forest.

stack. Verb: To arrange things in a pile or heap. To cheat at cards by secretly arranging them in the pack. Noun: A large pile of hay, straw, etc., arranged with some order. A chimney of a factory.

stack sheet. A memorandum showing the quantity of straw in a stack, made out in the ordinary course of business from scale tickets. Anno: 83 ALR 815.

stadium. A place for sports and outdoor performances, constructed usually with elevated tiers of seats encircling the playing or exhibition field. Alexander v Phillips, 31 Ariz 503, 254 P 1056, 52 ALR 244.
A stadium is not a school building within the meaning of a statute authorizing the use of money from a special fund for school buildings; neither is it within the meaning of a statute authorizing a bond issue for school buildings. Board of Education v Williams (Ky) 256 SW2d 29.

staff judge advocate. The legal adviser and counsel of a commanding general or officer of equal rank.

staff sergeant. A noncommissioned officer of the Army, ranking immediately above a sergeant and immediately below sergeant first class.

stage. See **auto stage**.

stagecoach. A vehicle for public transportation, pulled by horses, common in the earlier days of the country.

stage line. A bus line of a common carrier by bus or motor coach. Bruce Transfer Co. v Johnston, 227 Iowa 50, 287 NW 278.

staging. See **scaffold**.

stagnum (stag'num). A pond.
"A pool doth consist of water and land; and therefore by the name of stagnum or a pool the water and land shall pass also." Johnson v Rayner, 72 Mass (6 Gray) 107, 110.

stains. See **blood stains**.

stairway. A flight of stairs, a series of steps ascending or descending to a different level. Montgomery Ward & Co. v Snuggins (CA8 Minn) 103 F2d 458.

stake. The amount put up by way of wager or bet. Money or other property which, under the terms of a bet or wager is to become the property of the winner of the bet or wager upon the happening of the event. 24 Am J1st Gaming § 14.

stakeholder. One with whom money or property is deposited to abide the result of a gambling contract or transaction. Martin v Francis, 173 Ky 529, 191 SW 259.
He is a mere depositary of both parties for the money deposited by them respectively, with a

naked authority to deliver it over on the proposed contingency. If the authority is actually revoked before the money is paid over, it remains a naked deposit to the use of the depositor. The stakeholder is in no proper sense a party to the illegal contract, nor is he in pari delicto with the parties. Ball v Gilbert, 53 Mass (12 Met) 397, 402.

stale check. A check held for an unreasonable time before indorsement or presentation for payment. Home Sav. Bank v Bentley, 5 Wis 2d 19, 92 NW2d 377, 67 ALR2d 1450.

stale claim. A claim subject to the defense of laches or limitation of action.

stale equity. Same as **stale claim**.

stall. A small inclosed place in a building. An inclosed place in a public market for use by a farmer or dealer in selling his products. An inclosed place in a barn, where one horse may be kept conveniently.

stallage (stâ'lāj). The liberty of maintaining a market stall.

stalled vehicle. A vehicle disabled so as not to be movable under its own power, particularly a vehicle in such condition on the highway.

stallion. A male horse, uncastrated, and kept for breeding purposes.
See **killyth-stallion; standing a stallion**.

stamp. See **postage stamp; revenue stamps; rubber stamp; stamp taxes; trading stamps**.

stamp acts. Statutes which impose stamp taxes. English statutes of such nature which constituted one of the primary causes of the American revolution.

stampeding. Frightening livestock into running. 8 Am J2d Avi § 100. Delegates at a political convention suddenly giving overwhelming support to a candidate for nomination.

stamping. Affixing stamps, such as postage stamps, or revenue stamps, as required. Making a mark or impression with a stamp.

stamp tax. In the narrow but generally accepted sense of the term, a tax charged on written instruments as such, collected by means of stamps impressed or affixed to the instrument charged, the latter being important in the enforcement of legal rights. 23 Am J2d Deeds § 21; 49 Am J1st Stamp T § 2. In the broad sense, any tax collected by requiring the affixing of stamps to an article, such stamps to be obtained from the tax or revenue office.
See **revenue stamps**.

stand. A structure, usually in a public place, for the accommodation of particular persons, such as the members of a band or other entertainers.
See **grandstand; leave standing**.

standard. A flag or emblem. A determined means of comparison or evaluation, e.g., a **building standard**.
A specimen of undisputed handwriting of a person offered for comparison with handwriting alleged to be his but denied by him. 36 Am J2d Forg § 49.

standard deduction. An optional deduction allowed the taxpayer in computing net income for federal income tax. Internal Revenue Code § 141. A similar deduction in computing net income for state income tax.

standard fire policy. See **standard policy**.

standard form. See **standard policy**.

standard gauge. A railroad the tracks of which are laid with a distance of four feet, eight and one-half inches between the rails.

standardized high school. A high school which complies with established standards and conditions for receiving state aid. State ex rel. Mannes v Alquist, 59 ND 762, 231 NW 952, 72 ALR 494.

standard liability policy. An automobile liability policy in the form required by statute or regulation having the force of law.

standard man. See **the ordinary prudent man**.

standard mortality tables. Life expectancy tables of standard authority, such as the American table and other tables appearing in the statutes, although the courts are inclined to favor the latest tables, because the facts upon which they are calculated are much more complete.
At various times and to some extent at the present time, the Wigglesworth, a table prepared in the United States, and the Northhampton and Carlisle tables, which were prepared in England, have been accepted by courts as standard. 29 Am J2d Ev § 895.

standard mortgagee clause. A loss payable clause for the protection of the interest of a mortgagee of the insured property, in a form prescribed by statute. 29 Am J Rev ed Ins. § 731.
See **union mortgage clause**.

standard of care. The standard according to which negligence in a particular situation is determined. The care which an ordinary prudent person would exercise under like circumstances. The supposititious course of an ordinary prudent and careful person under the same circumstances. 38 Am J1st Negl § 30.
See **the ordinary prudent man**.

standard of comparison. See **standard**.

standard of living. The manner of living in reference to amenities, comforts, and luxuries, as well as the necessities of life.

Standard Oil Trust. See **trust**.

standard policy. An insurance policy in a form prescribed by or complying with statute. 29 Am J Rev ed Ins § 257.

Standards Bureau. The national bureau or office of Standard Weights and Measures, established for the facilitation of the administration of federal laws and regulations pertaining to the adoption and enforcement of standard weights and measures. 15 USC § 271.

standard sizes and weights. Sizes or weights for specified products, or the size or capacity of containers of such products, as prescribed by statute or ordinance. 56 Am J1st Wts & L § 35.

standard sun time. See **standard time**.

standard time. Time measured by a standard adapted to mean solar time to convenient use in commerce, business and the ordinary affairs of life, the country being divided into time zones, each zone having as an accepted time, the actual sun time at the middle degree of longitude of the zone. 52 Am J1st Time § 3.
Where statute has designated the time of day at which an act shall be done, such as the time for holding court, the decisions are not uniform as to whether the statute is to be construed as meaning

sun time or as referring to standard time. 52 Am J1st Time § 6.

standard weights. See **standard sizes and weights.**

stand by. See **standing by.**

standing. The position of a person in reference to his capacity to act in a particular instance, for example, the standing of a person to maintain a derivative action. 19 Am J2d Corp § 559.

See **credit rating; social position; standard of living; stopping or standing.**

standing army. A military force of persons engaged full time in the service, maintained in times of peace as well as of war.

See **regular army.**

standing a stallion. Keeping a stallion for service in breeding mares, fees being charged by way of compensation for such service.

standing by. Awaiting opportunity for the necessity of action, as a master of a vessel remaining in position and readiness to respond to duty. 48 Am J1st Ship § 118. Ready to respond with assistance, comfort, or support for another. For the purposes of equitable estoppel, silence or inaction where one ought to speak or act. 28 Am J2d Estop § 53.

As applied to the equitable principle of estoppel, a person "stands by," not merely by being actually present, but by having knowledge under such circumstances as render it his duty to communicate such knowledge. Gaddes v Pawtucket Institution for Sav. 33 RI 177, 192, 80 A 415.

standing in loco parentis (lō'kō pā-ren'tis). See **loco parentis.**

standing jack. A male jackass kept for the purpose of breeding, particularly for breeding mares of the horse family, such breeding being productive of a mule, a hybrid but very good work animal.

standing juror aside. A provisional exercise of a peremptory challenge. 31 Am J Rev ed Jury § 230.

standing master. A master in chancery appointed to serve as a regular officer of the court, rendering services as a master in any case in which a master is needed. 27 Am J2d Equity § 225.

standing mute. An accused in a criminal case refusing to plead. 21 Am J2d Crim L § 462. The equivalent of a plea of not guilty. Anno: 58 ALR 79, s. 82 ALR 369, 116 ALR 231.

standing of member. The status of a member of a fraternal order or society in reference to the payment of dues, attendance at meetings, and engaging in the work and activities of the order or body.

See **good standing.**

standing order. An order of court applicable generally to actions, its effect not being confined to a particular case, for example, an order made at the close of a term of court, that all actions not disposed of are continued. 37 Am J1st Motions § 25.

See **General Orders in Bankruptcy.**

standing seised. See **seised; seised to uses.**

standing timber. Live trees in their natural state. Anno: 72 ALR2d 740. A part and parcel of the land in which rooted. 42 Am J1st Prop § 19.

standing to sue. Broadly, capacity to maintain an action as plaintiff. 39 Am J1st Parties § 12. In the usual legal sense, the capacity to sue where more than one's own interest is involved, as in a taxpayer's action or in a derivative action. 19 Am J2d Corp § 559.

standing trees. See **standing timber.**

standing trustee. Same as **official trustee.**

standing vehicle. See **leave standing; stalled vehicle; stopping or standing.**

standpipe. A cylindrical tank for storing water, usually of sufficient height to create water pressure.

stand seised to the use of. Technical words proper to create a covenant to stand seised. 28 Am J2d Est § 348.

See **seised to uses.**

stannary courts (stan'a-ri kôrts). Courts established for the tinners of Devonshire and Cornwall.

staple (stā'pl). See **estate by statute staple; law of the stable; mayor of the staple.**

staple crops (stā'pl krops). Such productions of the soil as have an established and defined character in the commerce of the country.

Among them amy be included wheat, rye, oats, buckwheat, beans, corn, barley, potatoes, etc. Keeran v Griffith, 34 Cal 580.

stapula (sta'pu-la). Staple.

starboard (stär'bōrd or bėrd). That side of a ship on one's right hand when facing the bow.

starboard watch (stär'bōrd wach). See **watch.**

star-chamber (stär'chäm"bėr). See **court of star-chamber.**

stare ad rectum (stā're ad rek'tum). To stand trial; to abide by the judgment of the court.

stare decisis (stā're de-sī'sis). The doctrine or principle that decisions should stand as precedents for guidance in cases arising in the future. A strong judicial policy that the determination of a point of law by a court will generally be followed by a court of the same or a lower rank in a subsequent case which presents the same legal problem, although different parties are involved in the subsequent case. 20 Am J2d Cts § 183.

The great principle, stare decisis, so fundamental in our law, and so congenial to liberty, is peculiarly important in popular governments, where the influence of passions is strong, the struggles for power are violent, the fluctuations of party are frequent, and the desire of suppressing opposition, or of gratifying revenge under the forms of law and by the agency of the courts, is constant and active. Ex parte Bollman (US) 4 Cranch 75, 89, 2 L Ed 554, 559.

An opinion rendered by a court of a foreign country, especially a British court, although having no effect by stare decisis in this country, may well be persuasive on an American court, particularly where the foreign court deals in its opinion with a question of law common to all civilized nations. 20 Am J2d Cts § 200.

The decision of a court of one state does not have effect as stare decisis in the court of another state, although it may be considered and even followed by the court of the sister state because its reasoning is persuasive. 20 Am J2d Cts § 203.

While even a single adjudication of the court, upon a question properly before it, is not to be questioned or disregarded except for the most cogent reasons, and then only in a case where it is plain that the judgment was the result of a mistaken view of the condition of the law applicable to the question, the doctrine of stare decisis is not without exceptions. It does not apply where it can be shown that the law has been misunderstood or misapplied, or where the former determination is evidently contrary to reason. Rumsey v New York & New England Railway Co. 133 NY 79, 30 NE 654.

stare decisis et non quieta movere (stā're de-sī'sis et non qui-ē'ta mo-vē're). To stand by the decisions and not to disturb settled points.

stare in judicio (stā're in ju-di'she-ō). To stand in judgment; to submit to the jurisdiction of the court.

star pages. Pages of a second or later edition of a book, particularly a law book, marked with a star at a certain line or word and indicating at such point a page number of the earlier edition, thereby correlating the pagination of the later edition with the earlier.

starr (stär). A term which was applied by the Jews in England to all contracts, deeds, or other obligations.

state. A body politic or society of men united together for the purpose of promoting their mutual safety and advantage by their combined strength, occupying a definite territory, and politically organized under one government. McLaughlin v Poucher, 127 Conn 441, 17 A2d 767. People, territory, and government considered in combination. Texas v White (US) 7 Wall 700, 19 L Ed 227, ovrld on other grounds 113 US 476, 28 L Ed 1044, 5 S Ct 588. A complete body of free persons united together for their common benefit, to enjoy peaceably what is their own, and to do justice to others. Chisholm v Georgia (US) 2 Dall 419, 1 L Ed 440.

Under the United States Constitution:—a political community of free citizens, occupying a territory of defined boundaries, and organized under a government sanction and limited by a written constitution, and established by the consent of the governed. Coyle v Smith, 221 US 559, 55 L Ed 853, 31 S Ct 688. For the purposes of the Fair Labor Standards Act, any state of the United States, the District of Columbia, or any territory or possession of the United States, 29 USC § 203(c).

See **sovereign state.**

state agency. A department, commission, board, committee, or body of any form operating as an instrumentality of the state government.

state aid. Financial aid given by the state to city, town, or county, one of the older examples of which is the giving of funds for construction of highways. 25 Am J1st High § 610. The distribution of state funds to local bodies for use in the construction of school buildings or the maintenance of public schools on a basis provided by statute, sometimes in proportion to the number of persons of school age or the number in attendance at the public schools. Aid by public funds of the state granted to private and sectarian colleges and universities. 15 Am J2d Colleges §§ 2, 31. Support or assistance furnished by the state to institutions, organizations, or individuals for a public purpose, and, as applied particularly to individuals, in a use of state funds to support its needy citizens. Beach v Bradstreet, 85 Conn 344, 353, 82 A 1030.

See **welfare.**

state aid highway. A highway constructed and maintained by a county or other political subdivision with financial aid furnished by the state. A road built at the joint expense of the state and the county. See De Witt County v Greene, 320 Ill 491, 493, 151 NE 372.

state antitrust laws. State statutes of the same general character as the Sherman Act, but differing in scope and detail, and state constitutional inhibitions against trusts and monopolies, with directions to pass appropriate suppressive legislation, and forbidding the legislative grant to any corporation of the power to enter into such combinations. 36 Am J1st Monop etc § 119.

state auditor. A state officer whose office is a branch of the executive department of the state and whose duties relate almost exclusively to the fiscal affairs of the state, of which he has a general superintendence. 49 Am J1st States § 55.

state bar. All the persons admitted to practice law in the state. In a technical sense, an organization, membership in which is a prerequisite to the privilege of practicing law in the state. Anno: 151 ALR 617.

See **integrated bar.**

state bonds. Obligations of the state, issued according to the method provided by law for using the state's credit to obtain money for accomplishing a governmental purpose, the instruments issued being instrumentalities of government. 43 Am J1st Pub Sec § 16.

state census. A census taken under state law, sometimes covering all the population, at other times a particular class of the population, such as legal voters. 14 Am J2d Census § 5.

state classification rule. The principle that the character of a corporation is to be determined for the purposes of adjudication in bankruptcy by the classification in which the corporation was placed by the statutes of the state in which it was organized. Re Union Guarantee & Mortgage Co. (CA2 NY) 75 F2d 984, cert den 296 US 594, 80 L Ed 421, 56 S Ct 142.

state college. A college maintained by the state, sometimes with, sometimes without, the imposition of charges for tuition against residents of the state.

state commission. An agency of the state government.

See particular commission, such as **highway commission; public service commission,** etc.

state constitution. A compact made by and between the citizens of a state to govern themselves in a certain manner, constituting the paramount and supreme law of the state so far as consistent with the United States Constitution. 16 Am J2d Const L § 2. A fundamental act of legislation by the people of the state acting in their sovereign capacity. Sage v New York, 154 NY 61, 47 NE 1096. An act of extraordinary legislation by which the people establish the structure and mechanism of their government. Ellingham v Dye, 178 Ind 336, 99 NE 1, app dismd 231 US 250, 58 L Ed 206, 34 S Ct 92.

state courts. See **courts.**

stated account. See **account stated.**

stated case. See **agreed case.**

State Department. One of the executive departments of the United States government, headed by the Secretary of State, principally charged with the management of foreign affairs and foreign trade relations. 54 Am J1st US § 48.

state department. See **State Department; state agency.**

stated meeting. Same as **regular meeting.**

stated term. A regular term of court.

state election. An election wherein state officers are elected. 25 Am J2d Elect § 10.

state experience factor. See **experience.**

state fund. See **state funds; state insurance fund.**

state funds. Public funds belonging to the state. 42 Am J1st Pub F § 2. Moneys of which the state has taken possession pursuant to law, even though such moneys may be held by the state for special purposes. Lawrence v American Surety Co. 263 Mich 586, 249 NW 3, 88 ALR 535.
See **public funds.**

state governor. See **governor.**

state hospital. A hospital maintained by the state, particularly a hospital for the care of the insane.

state institution. See **institution.**

state insurance fund. A fund managed and administered by the state for the payment of workmen's compensation awards and the defrayment of the expense of administering the workmen's compensation laws, employers contributing to the fund as assessed, the arrangement taking the place of conventional insurance. 58 Am J1st Workm Comp §§ 552-554. A fund for the insurance of crops. 21 Am J2d Crops § 6.

state jail. A state reformatory, penitentiary, or prison. Ex parte Mills, 135 US 263, 271, 34 L Ed 107, 110, 10 S Ct 762.

state lands. See **public lands.**

statement. An allegation, recitation, or presentation, verbally or on paper. Montague v Thomason, 91 Tenn 168, 173.

statement of affairs. A filing required of a bankrupt, the purpose of which is to render information concerning the bankrupt's financial affairs available to the creditors and trustee in bankruptcy. 9 Am J2d Bankr § 380.

statement of case. An informal statement required of a plaintiff in a small claim's court in lieu of a formal complaint, bill, or declaration. A statement required in some states on motion for a new trial.
A party moving for a new trial on the ground that the findings of fact are against the evidence should specify in the statement each particular finding which in his opinion is against the evidence. Where the motion is based on the ground that the evidence is insufficient to support the verdict, a statement which contains substantially all the evidence given at the trial need not specify the particulars in which it is insufficient. 39 Am J1st New Tr § 199.

statement of claim. See **claim; statement of demand.**

statement of confession. See **confession; confession of judgment; power of attorney to confess judgment.**

statement of cost of property. A filing which a bankruptcy court may require of a bankrupt. 9 Am J2d Bankr § 381.

statement of defense. The pleading of an affirmative defense in an answer.

statement of demand. A statement in writing setting forth the demand, showing its nature and character and the amount due and owing thereon. Brennan v Swasey, 16 Cal 141.

statement of facts. In some jurisdictions, the equivalent of agreed case. 3 Am J2d Agr C § 1. The primary essential of a pleading, such statement, however, to be confined to the ultimate facts.

state militia (mi-lish'ạ). An organization comprised of men who come from the body of the citizens, and when not engaged at stated periods in drilling, and other exercises, they return to their usual vocations, as is usual with militia, and are subject to call when the public exigencies demand it. 36 Am J1st Mil § 42.

state moneys. See **state funds.**

state officer. In a popular sense,—an officer whose jurisdiction is coextensive with the state. In a more enlarged legal sense,—one who receives his authority under the laws of the state, and performs some of the governmental functions of the state. 49 Am J1st States § 52.

state of mind. The mental operation of a person; knowledge, belief, or intent. 29 Am J2d Ev § 355.

state of war. See **war.**

state penitentiary. See **state prison.**

state police power. See **police power.**

state prison. The ordinary prison for the confinement of persons convicted and under sentence of confinement for felonies or misdemeanors where the sentence is for an extended duration, at least for a year, known in some jurisdictions as a state penitentiary. United States v Smith (CC Va) 40 F 755, 759.

state reports. See **court reports.**

stateroom. A cabin or room for the accommodation of a passenger or ship's officer on a vessel. 48 Am J1st Ship § 354. A bedroom on a sleeping car.

state's attorney. See **attorney general; county attorney; district attorney; prosecuting attorney.**

state secret. A matter of government or of a department of the government protected against disclosure by a witness in ordinary judicial proceedings. 58 Am J1st Witn § 535.

state's evidence. Testimony in a criminal prosecution which implicates the witness as a participant in the offense but given voluntarily in the hope of avoiding prosecution of self or of receiving a light sentence. 58 Am J1st Witn § 525.

state's immunity from suit. See **immunity from suit.**

state superintendent of public instruction. An administrative officer having duties which vary as between jurisdictions, but ordinarily serving to coordinate the activities in the educational process of the public schools.

state tax. In one sense, any tax levied under a general state law; in another sense, any tax levied for general state purposes. Youngblood v Sexton, 32 Mich 406.

state treasurer. See **treasurer.**

state university. A university maintained by the state, sometimes with, sometimes without, the imposition of tuition charges against residents of the state.

statim (stā'tim). Immediately.

stating part. The narrative part of a bill in equity, otherwise known as the premises, embracing the real substance of the suit.
The state part must set out all the essential facts on which the plaintiff relies as a ground of relief. 27 Am J2d Equity § 181.

statio iterve navigio (sta′she-ō i-ter′ve nā-vi′ji-ō). A navigable place or route. See Note: Ann Cas 1914B 1068.

station. See **bus terminal; military station; railroad station.**

station agent. An employee of a railroad company in charge of a specific station on the line of the company. A resident agent of a foreign railroad company. 36 Am J2d For Corp § 563.

stationer's form. A form often foisted upon unsophisticated persons upon the representation that the user need only fill in the blanks in order to produce a legal instrument, such as a will. 57 Am J1st Wills § 634.

station grounds. Grounds including such territory surrounding a railroad depot or station as may be required to satisfy the reasonable convenience and necessity of the public while engaged in transacting business with the railroad company, and which is actually used for such purpose. 44 Am J1st RR § 169.

station in life. See **social position; standard of living.**

station in life rule. The rule that the amount and character of the benefits to which one for whose support provision is made in a testamentary instrument is entitled must be determined according to his station in life. Anno: 101 ALR 1499 et seq. A similar rule which prevails in determining the amount of alimony to which a divorced wife is entitled. 24 Am J2d Div & S § 635.

station license. A license for the operation of a radio or television station. 44 Am J1st Rad § 6.

station platform. The platform maintained by a carrier for use by its patrons in boarding and leaving its cars or vehicles. Garcia v New York City Transit Authority, 19 App Div 2d 530, 240 NYS2d 275.

statist (stāt′ist). A statistician. An obsolete term for statesman.

statistics. See **vital statistics.**

Stat nominis umbra (stat no′mi-nis um′bra). But the shadow of the name remains. That is, the thing has become a mere name in the place of that which formerly existed. Briscoe v Bank of Kentucky (US) 11 Pet 257, 349, 9 L Ed 709, 745.

Stat pro ratione voluntas (stat pro rā-she-ō′ne vo-lun′tās). The purpose stands for the consideration. Aller v Aller, 40 NJL 446, 451.

Stat pro ratione voluntas populi (stat prō ra-she-ō′ne vol-lun′tas po′pu-lī). The will of the people takes the place of reason.

"With the wisdom or expediency of a constitutional provision, the judges have no concern." People v Draper (NY) 25 Barb 344, 376.

statu liber (sta′tū li′ber). A free person, as distinguished from a slave.

The manumission or freeing of a slave makes him a "statu liber." Valsain v Cloutier, 3 La 170, 176.

statu quo. See **in statu quo; restoration of status quo.**

status. Position or rank. A legal personal relationship or condition, not temporary in its nature nor terminable at the mere will of the parties, with which third persons and the state are concerned. Re Davidson, 223 Minn 268, 26 NW2d 223, 170 ALR 215. An existing state of affairs.

"The very meaning of the word 'status,' both derivative and as defined in legal proceedings, forbids that it should be applied to a mere relation (such as that of marriage). 'Status' implies relations, but it is not a mere relation." De La Montanya v De La Montanya, 112 Cal 101, 44 P 345.

See **crime of status.**

status of the ship. A status acquired by being a member of a ship's company or doing a seaman's work and incurring a seaman's hazards. Kermarec v Compagnie Generale Transatlantique, 358 US 625, 3 L Ed 2d 550, 79 S Ct 406.

status quo (stā′tus quō). The settled condition or state. The state of affairs before change or alteration.

See **in statu quo; restoration of status quo.**

Status reipublicae maxime judicatis rebus continetur (sta′tus rē-ī-pub′li-sē ma′xi-mē jū-di-kā′tis rē′bus kon-ti-nē′ter). The stability of the state is best maintained by matters adjudicated.

The United States Supreme Court "has contributed its share to that stability which results from a respect for things adjudicated." Beauregard v New Orleans (US) 18 How 497, 15 L Ed 469, 472.

Statuta pro publico commodo late interpretantur (sta-tu′ta prō pub′li-kō kom′mo-dō la′tē in-ter-pre-tan′ter). Statutes enacted for the public welfare are to be liberally construed.

Statuta suo clauduntur territorio, nec ultra territorium disponunt (sta-tū′ta su′ō klâ-dun′ter ter-ri-tō′ri-ō, nek ul′tra ter-ri-tō′ri-um dis-pō′nunt). Statutes are confined to their own territory; they do not govern outside their territorial limits. New York Foundling Hospital v Gatti, 9 Ariz 105, 79 P 231.

statute. An act of the legislature as an organized body. Washington v Dowling, 92 Fla 601, 109 So 588. The written will of the legislative department, expressed according to the form necessary to constitute it a law of the United States or of the state, and rendered authentic by certain prescribed forms and solemnities. In a broader sense, inclusive of an act of the legislature, an administrative regulation, or any enactment, from whatever source originating, to which the state gives the force of law. 50 Am J1st Stat § 2.

statute against common right. A statute in derogation of a right supported by the common law. Coral Gables v Christopher, 108 Vt 414, 189 A 147, 109 ALR 474.

Statute de Donis. An early English statute (13 Edw I) passed primarily to prevent certain evils of alienation prevalent under the pre-existing estate of fee simple conditional, having the effect of giving existence to estates in fee tail. 28 Am J2d Est § 45.

For text of the statute, see Am J2d Desk Book, Document 104.

Statute de Donis Conditionalibus. Same as **Statute de Donis.**

Statute de Mercatoribus. See **De Mercatoribus.**

statute in pari materia. See **in pari materia.**

statute merchant. See **De Mercatoribus; estate by statute merchant.**

statute mile. The mile of 5,280 feet, as legalized in England and adopted in the United States. Steamboat Co. v Fessenden, 79 Me 140.

Statute of Acton Burnel. See **Acton Burnel.**

statute of amendment. A statute which permits the correction of certain omissions and imperfections in pleadings. State ex rel. Smith v Trimble, 315 Mo 166, 175, 285 SW 729.

Statute of Anne. An English statute (3 & 4 Anne ch 9) by which promissory notes were put upon the same footing as inland bills of exchange in accordance with the custom of merchants or general business usage. 11 Am J2d B & N § 38.

Statute of Charitable Uses (stat'ūt ov char'i-ta̱-bl ū'ses). An act of parliament passed in 1601 to protect the property of charitable institutions and placing them under the general supervision of the lord chancellor. 43 Elizabeth, ch 4.

For text of statute, see Am J2d Desk Book, Document 113.

Statute of Circumspecte Agatis. See **Circumspecte Agatis.**

statute of distribution. A statute which provides a system of succession to the personal property left by a decedent or, as is frequently the case, for the descent and distribution of both real estate and personal property. 23 Am J2d Desc & D § 9.

Statute of Enrolments. An English statute (1536;27 Hen. v III ch 16) which required all deeds of bargain and sale to be enrolled in order to be valid. 28 Am J2d Est § 346.

For text of the statute, see Am J2d Desk Book, Document 110.

statute of entail. Same as **Statute de Donis.**

Statute of Fines. An English statute enacted in 1540, providing for the barring of an entail by levying a fine.

statute of frauds. A statute which requires certain classes of contracts to be in writing. Sometimes called a statute for the prevention of frauds and perjuries. 49 Am J1st Stat of F § 1. A term sometimes applied in England to statutes affording relief against transfers of property designed to hinder and defraud creditors. 37 Am J2d Frd Conv § 2.

Statute of Gloucester. An English statute (6 Edw I ch 5, 1278) providing a penalty for waste.

For text of statute, see Am J2d Desk Book, Document 102.

The statute 6 Edward I, ch. 1, which gave costs in all cases when the plaintiff recovered damages. The statute originated costs de incremento, that is, costs awarded by the court and added to the damages assessed by the jury. Day v Woodworth (US) 13 How 362, 14 L Ed 181.

Statute of Hue and Cry. An English statute enacted in 1285, which provided for immediate hue and cry upon the commission of a robbery or other felony and that the people of the hundred where a robbery was committed should be held liable for it unless they captured the robber. 13 Edw I, chs 1, 2; 4 Bl Comm 293.

statute of jeofails. (stat'ūt of jef'āls). See **jeofails.**

statute of limitations. See **limitation of actions.**

Statute of Malefactors in Parcis (mal-ē-fak'torz in par'kis). An English statute for the protection of game preserves against poachers.

Statute of Marlborough. The statute (1267) 52 Henry III, ch 23, confirming Magna Charta and Charta de Foresta and regulating certain tenures and matters of procedure. Sometimes called Statute of Marlbridge after the place where parliament was sitting at the time of the enactment.

Statute of Marlbridge. Same as **Statute of Marlborough.**

Statute of Merton. The English statute, so called, of 20 Henry III, ch 9 which is, in fact, not a statute, but a mere entry on the minutes of Parliament of a refusal by the English lords to assimilate the law of England to that of other civilized countries by affirmatively declaring that the marriage of the parents subsequent to the birth rendered the child legitimate. See 10 Am J2d Bast § 146.

statute of nonclaim. See **nonclaim statute.**

statute of the state. Any enactment, from whatever source originating, to which the state gives the force of law. Atlantic Coast Line R. Co. v Goldsboro, 232 US 548, 58 L Ed 721, 34 S Ct 364.

Statute of Uses. An English statute of 1536 (27 Henry VIII ch 10), generally recognized as a part of the common law of states of the United States, which gave a legal status to so-called "uses" theretofore recognized only in equity, providing that the legal title should follow the beneficial interest and vest in the "cestuis que use" after such quality, manner, form and condition as they had before in or to the use, confidence or trust that was in them. 28 Am J2d Est § 344. A statute, the most significant effect of which was to validate executory interests theretofore recognized only in equity. 28 Am J2d Est § 333.

For text of statute, see Am J2d Desk Book, Document 109.

Statute of Westminster. An act of the English Parliament in 1285 (13 Edw I, ch 34), providing that "if a wife willingly leave her husband and go away and continue with her advouterer" she shall be barred of dower, unless her husband later forgives her and takes her back.

Statute of Westminster I. The name given to a statute enacted in 1275 in the reign of Edward the First, providing for many reforms. See 4 Bl Comm 425.

Statute of Westminster II. Same as **Statute de Donis.**

Statute of Westminster III. Same as **Statute Quia Emptores.**

Statute of Wills. An English statute (1540; 32 Henry VIII ch 1) often said to have been the foundation of the modern English law of wills, being of most significance in its giving validity to devises of real estate not theretofore recognized at common law. 57 Am J1st Wills § 3. An English statute (34 & 35 Henry VIII ch 5; 1542, 1543) supplementing the earlier statute.

For text of the statutes, see Am J2d Desk Book, Documents 111, 112.

Statute of Winchester. Same as **Statute of Hue and Cry.**

Statute Quia Emptores. An act of Parliament in 1290 (18 Edw I ch 1), prohibiting sub-infeudation as by providing that upon all sales or feoffments of lands, the feoffee shall hold the same, not of the immediate feoffor, but of the chief lord of the fee, of whom such feoffor himself held it, the object of the Act being to remove feudal restraint upon the alienation of land. 28 Am J2d Est § 3. A statute which had the effect of abolishing rent service. Van Rensselaer v Hays, 19 NY 68.

For text of statute, see Am J2d Desk Book, Document 105.

Statutes at Large. See **United States Statutes at Large.**

statutes of laborers. English statutes concerning laborers, servants, and apprentices.

statutes of mortmain. See **mortmain statutes.**

statutes of repose (of rē-pōz'). Statutes of limitation. Atchison, Topeka & Santa Fe Railroad Co. v Burlingame Township, 36 Kan 628, 14 P 271.
See **limitation of actions.**

statutes personal. Terminology of the continental or civil law.
See **statutes real.**

statutes real. Terminology of the continental or civil law.
The Spanish and French laws touching community property, and those of California and Texas and other states derived from them, are held to be, in the vocabulary of the civilians, statutes real and not statutes personal; that is to say, they apply to things within a country's jurisdiction rather than to persons wherever they may be or go. Commissioner v Skaggs (CA 5 Tex) 122 F2d 721.

statute staple. See **estate by statute staple.**

statute to prevent frauds and perjuries. See **statute of frauds.**

statuto. See **ex statuto.**

statuto mercatori. See **de statuto mercatori.**

statutory. Created or existing under or by virtue of a statute.

statutory acre. An acre the area of which was fixed by statute as distinguished from the customary acre.
See **customary acre.**

statutory action. A remedy provided by statute which does not exist at common law or a remedy for the enforcement of a particular right more effective than that existing at common law. A private right of action predicated upon the violation of a statute. 1 Am J2d Actions § 73.

statutory bond. A bond required by statute. A bond which either literally or substantially meets the requirements of statute. Southern Surety Co. v. United States Cast Iron Pipe & Foundry Co. (CCA) 13 F2d 833.
A distinction is made between a common-law bond and a statutory bond in that the latter is one which conforms to a statute, while the former does not, although it may have been so intended. Mt. Vernon v Brett, 193 NY 276, 86 NE 6, 10.

statutory copyright. A copyright to which an author is entitled by statute, as distinguished from the so-called "copyright at common law" or right of literary property. 18 Am J2d Copyr § 1.

statutory dedication. A dedication of land to public use made according to statute and operating by way of grant. 23 Am J2d Ded § 3.

statutory discovery. The remedy of discovery as provided by statute, the authorities being in conflict on the question whether the statutory remedy supersedes the equitable remedy of discovery. 23 Am J2d Dep § 142.

statutory emancipation (ē-man-si-pā'shǫn). A proceeding authorized by statute in some states whereby courts are empowered to remove the disabilities of an infant on a proper application and proof of his capacity.
This is not a true emancipation, since its result is to remove the general disabilities of infancy, rather than the father's right to the child's services. 39 Am J1st P & C § 64.

statutory exposition. The inclusion in a statute of the construction made by the courts of an earlier statute on the same subject.

statutory felony. See **felony.**

statutory foreclosure. The foreclosure of a lien or mortgage without suit, but by notice and sale pursuant to statute.

statutory form. A form of pleading, process, indictment, or instrument which meets statutory requirements. A form set forth in a statute, e.g., a form of deed.
See **short form.**

statutory guardian. A guardian appointed by will pursuant to statute. 25 Am J1st G & W § 12. In a broader sense, any guardian appointed pursuant to and in accord with the statutes.

statutory interest. See **lawful interest.**

statutory interpleader. The remedy of interpleader as provided by statute, such being analogous to the remedy in equity by bill of interpleader, and concurrent with and cumulative of the equitable remedy, the latter remaining available in a proper case notwithstanding the statutory remedy. 30 Am J Rev ed Interpl § 18.

statutory investment. See **legal investment.**

statutory jurisdiction. In effect, jurisdiction as conferred by legislation enacted pursuant to the constitution of the sovereignty on behalf of which the court functions. 20 Am J2d Courts § 91. Jurisdiction in equity as granted by statute apart from the inherent jurisdiction of a court of chancery. Kelly v Conner, 122 Tenn 339, 123 SW 622.

statutory liability. See **liability created by statute.**

statutory lien. A lien resting on statute. 9 Am J2d Bankr § 960. A lien existing under the common law and declared by statute, sometimes with modification of its incidents, or a lien created by statute for a situation where no right of lien existed at common law. 33 Am J1st Liens § 24.

statutory pardon. A pardon granted by an act of the legislature. 39 Am J1st Pard § 21.

statutory penalty. See **penalty.**

statutory rape. Carnal knowledge of a female under a stated age, with or without her consent. 44 Am J1st Rape § 17.

statutory receiver. A receiver appointed by a court acting under statutory authority. 45 Am J1st Rec § 3.

statutory reprieve. A reprieve granted by an act of the legislature. 39 Am J1st Pard § 21.

statuto stapuli. See **de statuto stapuli.**

Statutum affirmativum non derogat communi legi (sta-tū'tum af-fir-ma-tī'vum non dē'ro-gat kom'mu-nī lē'gi). An affirmative statute does not derogate from the common law.

Statutum de Militibus (sta-tū'tum dē mi-li'ti-bus). The statute concerning soldiers. See 1 Bl Comm 347.

Statutum generaliter est intelligendum quando verba statuti sunt specialia, ratio autem generalis (sta-tū'tum je-ne-rā'li-ter est in-tel-li-jen'dum quan'dō ver'ba sta-tū'tī sunt spe-she-ā'li-a, rā'she-ō â'tem je-ne-rā'lis). When the words of a statute are special, but the reason is general, the statute is to be understood generally.

STATUTUM [1215] STEEL

Statutum Mercatoribus (sta-tū'tum mer-ka-tō'ribus). See **De Mercatoribus**.

Statutum speciale statuto speciali non derogat (statū'tum spe-she-ā'le sta-tū'tō spe-she-ā'lī non de'rogat). A special statute does not derogate from a special statute.

stay. Verb: To put a stop to further proceedings, usually temporarily. Noun: A postponement of an action or proceeding.
See **moratorium; supersedeas**.

stay of action. The postponement of proceedings in a case until the happening of a contingency, regardless of the time or the term of court at which such contingency happens. Simmons v Superior Court of Los Angeles County, 96 Cal App 2d 119, 214 P2d 844, 19 ALR2d 288. Restraint by injunction of the institution or prosecution of an action. 28 Am J Rev ed Inj §§ 200 et seq.

stay of arbitration. An injunction against arbitration proceedings for fraud or duress practiced against one of the parties, or on the ground of the absence of a bona fide dispute. 5 Am J2d Arb & A § 83.

stay of execution. An order issued by the court, upon cause shown, against the issuance or the enforcement of an execution.

Stays of execution are of three classes: (1) those which are ordered by the court in which judgment is rendered, but not as the result of any appellate proceeding, and which proceed upon the ground that for some cause, the execution of the judgment ought to be postponed to some subsequent date, or, perhaps, ought not to take place at all; (2) those which result from statutes or rules of court granting the defendant a further time in which to satisfy the judgment upon his giving security therefor; and (3) those which are a consequence of, or attend, appellate proceedings. 30 Am J2d Exec § 692.
See **supersedeas**.

stay on appeal. See **stay of execution; supersedeas**.

stay statute. See **moratorium**.

steady course. The course of a vessel unchanging as to the direction in which headed and such that her future position may be calculated from present position and speed. Commonwealth v Dominion Line (CA2 NY) 20 F2d 729.

steal. Verb: To commit larceny. Daugherty v Thomas, 174 Mich 371, 140 NW 615. To take without right or leave, with intent to keep wrongfully, the goods of another. Grooms v State, 85 Fla 413, 96 So 296. Noun: A taking by larceny or theft. In the broad sense, any conversion or embezzlement. Anno: 55 ALR 836. A colloquial term for the obtaining of property for an inadequate consideration.

Having no common-law definition to restrict its meaning as an offense, the word "stealing" is commonly used to denote any dishonest transaction whereby one person obtains that which rightfully belongs to another and deprives the owner of the rights and benefits of ownership, but may or may not involve the element of stealth usually attributed to the word purloin. Crabb v Zerbst (CA5 Ga) 99 F2d 562.
See **intent to steal; larceny; stolen**.

stealing. See **steal**.

stealing child. See **kidnapping**.

stealth. Acting in such manner as to not to disclose the act. Furtive action.

Where a person is accused of taking property from another by stealth, the word necessarily connotes lack of knowledge on the part of the victim. Spencer v United States, 73 App DC 98, 116 F2d 801.
See **steal**.

steamboat. Watercraft propelled by the power of steam, that is, by a steam engine. 12 Am J2d Boats § 1.
See **steamship**.

steamboat channel. A term sometimes employed in establishing a boundary in a river, signifying the deepest part of the stream. Louisiana v Mississippi, 202 US 1, 49, 50 L Ed 913, 930, 26 S Ct 408, 571.

steamboat company. A corporation, company, association, joint stock association, partnership, or person, their lessees, trustees or receivers appointed by any court whatsoever, owning, controlling, leasing, operating or managing any vessel over and upon public waters. State ex rel. Stimson Timber Co. v Kuykendall, 137 Wash 602, 243 P 834, 55 ALR 954, affd 275 US 207, 72 L Ed 241, 48 S Ct 41.

steamboat debts. All existing debts contracted for repairs, supplies, and running expenses for and on account of the steamboat, for which the owner is liable. Moran v Prather (US) 23 Wall 492, 23 L Ed 121, 123.

steam boiler. A boiler used for producing steam and holding it under pressure; an inherently dangerous instrumentality. Rosenfeld v Albert Smith & Son, Inc. 180 App Div 691, 168 NYS 214, affd 227 NY 613, 125 NE 924.

steam company. A company engaged in producing steam and holding it under pressure for distribution to users through mains and pipes, primarily for heating dwelling houses, office buildings, and industrial plants. 26 Am J2d Electr § 25.

steam dredge. See **dredge**.

steam engineer. The operator of a steam engine. A mechanical pursuit for the purpose of a tax exemption. 51 Am J1st Tax § 548. One who has a watch in the engine room and stokehole of a steamship. Baggaley v Aetna Ins. Co. (CA7 Ill) 111 F2d 134.

steam-roller. A vehicle equipped and running upon heavy rollers, used in pressing loose materials upon the ground into a compact form with smooth surface, particularly in paving streets and highways.

steamship. A ship propelled by the power of steam, that is by steam engine. In loose usage, a ship propelled by power other than that of wind on sail.

steamship agent. A ship broker. A managing agent within the meaning of statutes concerning the service of process upon foreign corporations. Anno: 113 ALR 78, 79.

steam vessel. See **steamboat; steamship**.

steel. A hard metal produced from iron and an alloy of carbon and metals such as nickel and chromium.

The working and hardening of steel were common three thousand years ago in Greece and it probably required a number of centuries for it to reach the stage it had then arrived at in Greece. Damascus steel was produced in Oriental countries in very remote periods. United States v Aluminum Co. of America (DC NY) 44 F Supp 97.

steel mill. A mill for the production of steel and the shaping of the metal into various forms for use by manufacturers.
See **all-pull mill**.

steer (stĕr). Verb: To control a vehicle or vessel in respect of the direction of movement. Noun: A castrated male of the cattle family, kept primarily for the production of beef by rapid growth superinduced through intensive feeding.

steerage. The lowest classification of a ship's accommodations for passengers.

steering rules. Navigation rules for small watercraft. 12 Am J2d Boats § 14.
See **rules of navigation.**

stellionate (stel'yọn-āt). Fraud committed in entering into a contract for the sale of property which the vendor has previously sold.

stenographer. One who takes notes of dictation in shorthand and transcribes them in typewriting. In loose usage, a typist. A "laborer" for the purposes of an exemption from execution. 31 Am J2d Exempt § 20. A "worker" within the meaning of some labor laws. 31 Am J Rev ed Lab § 1.
See **court reporter.**

stenographer's notes. The notes written in shorthand upon the taking of a deposition. Scott v Missouri-Pacific R. Co. 333 Mo 374, 62 SW2d 834.

stenographically reported. See **stenographic notes of court reporter.**

stenographic notes of court reporter. The court reporter's notes, taken in shorthand, of the testimony in a case in the form of questions propounded to a witness by counsel or court and the answers or responses of the witness, objections by counsel, the rulings thereon, exceptions to rulings, the colloquy between court and counsel or between counsel pertaining to the case, and in some jurisdictions the instructions given by the court to the jury. 53 Am J1st Trial § 563.

A trial in a Federal court is not "stenographically reported" unless the reporter was one appointed under the Federal Rules of Civil Procedure or was agreed upon by the parties. The rule does not contemplate that one party shall employ a stenographer of his choice to report for him, without the authority of the court or the adversary. Middleton v Hartford Acci. & Indem. Co. (CA5 Tex) 119 F2d 721.

stepchild. A son or daughter of one's spouse by a former spouse. Re Smith's Estate, 49 Wash 2d 229, 299 P2d 550, 63 ALR2d 299. A son or daughter of one's spouse, born to him or her before the marriage to one, and not one's own child. Not a child within the meaning of a statute providing for inheritance by "children" of the intestate. 23 Am J2d Desc & D § 55.

One does not cease to be a stepchild within the meaning of an inheritance tax statute prescribing the rate of taxation on legacies to stepchildren, upon the death of the natural parent, even where there are no surviving issue of the marriage which created the relationship. Re Bordeaux' Estate, 37 Wash 561, 225 P2d 443, 26 ALR2d 249.

stepfather. The relationship of a man to his stepchild.
See **stepchild.**

Stephen (stē'fn). The king of England from December 26th, 1135, until October 25th, 1154.

stepmother. The relationship of a woman to her stepchild.
See **stepchild.**

stepparent. A stepmother or a stepfather. Department of Welfare v Siebel, 6 NY2d 536, 190 NYS2d 683, 161 NE2d 1, app dismd 361 US 535, 4 L Ed 2d 538, 80 S Ct 586. Not a parent within the meaning of a statute providing for the descent of property to a parent. 23 Am J2d Desc & D § 57.
See **stepchild.**

stepping stone. A block of stone, sometimes wood, frequently used in former times when vehicles were higher, for alighting from carriage or other means of conveyance. A means of advancement in position or situation.

stepping up or stepping down current. See **transformer.**

A rate so determined is known as a "current cost rate." Jenkins v Talbot, 338 Ill 441, 170 NE 735, 80 ALR 638.

step rate method. A recognized method of fixing rates of fraternal life insurance based on the principle that the insured pays only so much as the society may require to meet its death losses for that year in the membership age of the insured.

stereotype (ster'ē-ọ-tīp). A plate for printing press, cast in type metal.

stereotype matter (ster'ē-ọ-tīp mat'ẽr). Content of a newspaper produced by persons other than those writing particularly for such paper. Anno: 68 ALR 550.

sterility (ste-ril'i-ti). Incapability of producing offspring. Vileta v Vileta, 53 Cal App 2d 794, 128 P 376. Inability to beget or bear children, not necessarily associated with loss of power of copulation. 24 Am J2d Div & S § 80.

sterilization (ster'-il-i-zā'shọn). The process by which an article is rendered free from disease germs, such as the disinfection of secondhand goods to prevent the spread of contagious diseases. 47 Am J1st Sec H D § 5. Ridding clothing and other articles, particularly milk bottles, of microbes by exposure to great heat or chemical action. 25 Am J1st Hlth § 31. The operation of removing the organs of reproduction or rendering them ineffective, sometimes authorized by statute in reference to certain criminals. 21 Am J2d Crim L § 612. An operation upon a mental defective to deprive him or her of the power of procreation. 29 Am J Rev ed Ins Per § 33. An operation upon a man for the purpose of protecting his wife from conception and the dangers attendant upon childbirth. Anno: 93 ALR 573.

sterling (stẽr'ling). Adjective: Standard quality, particularly in reference to silver. Made of silver of standard quality. Noun: Silver of standard quality. English money. Precisely, the standard of fineness of English money.

stet processus (stet prọ-ses'us). An entry of the dismissal of an action voluntarily made by the plaintiff.

stevedore (stē'vẹ-dōr). One who works in the loading and unloading of ships. 27 Am J1st Ind Contr § 17; 48 Am J1st Ship § 211.

A stevedore is not a seaman. Zarowitch v F. Jarka (DC NY) 21 F2d 187.

stevedore's lien (stē'vẹ-dōrs lē'en). A maritime lien for services rendered in loading or unloading a vessel lying in navigable waters. 48 Am J1st Ship § 212.

steward. An employee of ship or airline attending to the personal needs of passengers. One in management of the services of a social club in reference to

providing meals, other refreshments, and rooms for lodging.
See **lord high steward; shop steward.**

steward and marshal. See **court of the steward and marshal.**

steward of chiltern hundreds. An honorary office in England.

steward of the king's household. See **court of the steward of the king's household.**

stewardess. A female steward. Best known in modern times as an attendant serving the personal needs of passengers upon an air liner.

sticker. A small gummed piece of paper carrying a name, for use in an election in voting for the person named on the paper by inserting the paper in a blank space on the ballot or, as sometimes authorized by statute, by placing the paper over a printed name appearing on the ballot. 26 Am J2d Elect § 269.

stifling bids. Acts or statements intended to prevent bidding at an auction. 30A Am J Rev ed Jud S § 98. Any conduct, artifice, agreement, or combination, which prevents open, free, and competitive bidding at an auction. 7 Am J2d Auct § 28.
See **chilling bids.**

stifling competition. See **stifling bids; suppression of competition.**

stick up. Same as **hold up.**

stickler (stik'lėr). An obstinate and uncompromising person.

stiletto (stil-e'tō). See **dagger.**

still. Equipment for the distillation of liquor, especially alcoholic liquor. Any instrument or device capable of separating alcohol from any liquid containing alcohol; a still worm, which is any vessel capable of being used for the purpose of distilling. State v Scott, 119 Or 446, 249 P 817.

still beer. A substance made of corn meal and molasses, designed for the purpose of, and to be used for, distilling whisky.
It is alcoholic and will produce intoxication if drunk to excess. Where it has been found to be in such physical state that it could be actually drunk as a beverage, it has been held to be such. Patterson v State, 24 Ga App 239.

stillborn child. A child without life at the moment of birth; dead when born. Western Union Tel. Co. v Cooper, 71 Tex 507, 9 SW 598.

stillicidium (stil-i-sid'i-um). A servitude of eaves-drip.
See **eaves-drip.**

Stillwell Act. A New York statute passed in 1831, relative to imprisonment for debt.

still worm. The coil of pipe in a still.
See **still.**

stint. Limit; restriction. An allotment. Blackstone says that a right of common of pasture which has not been admeasured is erroneously called a "common without stint." See 3 Bl Comm 239.

stipend (stī'pend). A salary or other periodic or regular payment.

stipendiary (stī-pen'di-ạ-ri). A person who receives a remittance regularly. A person receiving compensation regularly for services. A magistrate compensated by a salary.

stipendiary estate. An estate granted for military services.

stipulate. To enter into a stipulation or agreement.

stipulated damages. Same as **liquidated damages.**

stipulatio (sti-pu-lā'she-ō). (Roman law.) An undertaking or security given by the plaintiff in an action for the prosecution of the action and the payment of costs if he loses the cause. See 3 Bl Comm 291.

stipulation. In admiralty, the equivalent of a bond furnished in a proceeding. 2 Am J2d Adm § 157. An agreement, admission, or concession made in a judicial proceeding by the parties thereto or their attorneys, in respect of some matter incident to the proceeding, for the purpose, ordinarily, of avoiding delay, trouble, and expense. 50 Am J1st Stip § 2. A method of voluntary dismissal of action. 24 Am J2d Dism § 7.
Stipulations differ in their character, some being mere admissions of fact, simply relieving a party from the inconvenience of making proof, while others embody all the essential characteristics of a contract. Thayer v Federal Life Ins. Co. 217 Wis 282, 258 NW 489.

stipulation for exchange. A provision, usually written "with exchange" after the amount, in a promissory note which obligates the maker to pay exchange where payment of the note is made in foreign money. 11 Am J2d B & N § 165.

stipulation for judgment. A consent to the entry of the judgment.
A consent to a judgment is a waiver of errors by a party consenting thereto and a judgment entered by consent or stipulation will not be disturbed on appeal. See Morrow v Learned, 76 Cal App 538, 245 P 442.

stipulation for safe return. A bond given by one set of owners of a vessel in order to employ her when the others dissent, to secure the safe return of the vessel, or in case of her loss to pay to the dissenting owners the value of their shares. 48 Am J1st Ship § 102.

stipulation of facts. An agreement by the parties to an action on certain particular facts, thus avoiding the need to present evidence regarding them but not eliminating the court's function of drawing inferences from the stipulated facts and others shown by evidence. 3 Am J2d Agr C § 5. The equivalent in some American jurisdictions of agreed case. Northwestern Mut. Life Ins. Co. v Tone, 125 Conn 183, 4 A2d 640, 121 ALR 993; Pryor v Briggs Mfg. Co. 312 Mich 476, 20 NW2d 279, 161 ALR 699.

stipulation pour autrui (sti-pū-lā'si-ôn pūr ō'trū-ē). A stipulation, so called in the civil law, made by the parties to a contract in favor of a third person, he remaining a third person and a stranger to the contract until, by accepting the stipulation, he becomes a party. Allen & Currey Mfg. Co. v Shreveport Waterworks Co. 113 La 1091, 37 So 980.

stipulatio sponsalitia (sti-pu-lā'she-ō spon-sā-li'she-a). Same as **sponsalia.**

stipulator. A promisor. A surety on a bond or stipulation filed in an admiralty suit. 2 Am J2d Adm § 157. Broadly, one who enters into a stipulation.

stirps (stėrps). Same as **stirpes.**

stirpes (ster'pēz). The person from whom a family or branch of a family is descended. A branch of a family.
See **per stirpes.**

stirpital distribution (stèr'pi-tạl dis-tri-bū'shọn). See **per stirpes**.

stock. The capital, shares of stock, or certificates of stock issued by a corporation. The sum of all the rights and duties of shareholders in a corporation. 18 Am J2d Corp § 208. Shares in a joint stock company. 30 Am J Rev ed Jnt-Stk Co § 10.

The word is sometimes used in statutes as a generic term referring to livestock, and when so employed it means such animals as horses, mules, and cattle, but as the word was used in a bequest of "all my notes, bonds, stock, and money," the court held that it was "in the wrong stable" to be construed as meaning livestock, but that it meant dead stock, choses, bonds, evidence of an interest in the capital stock of some incorporated or joint-stock company. Capehart v Burrus, 122 NC 119, 29 SE 97.

See **capital stock; livestock; nursery stock; public stocks**.

stock and bond broker. Same as **stockbroker**.

stock and bond plan. A method of computing the aggregate market value of a taxpayer's capital stock. 51 Am J1st Tax § 834.

stock and carriers. An old term of art in the postal laws for horses and men. 41 Am J1st P O § 89.

stock assessment. A demand or request made of stockholders or of subscribers to corporate stock for contribution proportionate in amount to the number of shares held or subscribed for to replace a loss of capital. A method of enforcing the superadded liability of a stockholder in bank or other corporation. The evaluation of corporate stock for taxation. 51 Am J1st Tax § 834.

stock association. Same as **joint-stock company**.

stock bailout. Preferred stock issued as a nontaxable stock dividend. IRC § 305.

stock bin. A bin in a steel plant holding one or two days' supply of ore for a furnace. Youngstown Sheet & Tube Co. v Bowers, 358 US 534, 3 L Ed 2d 490, 79 S Ct 383.

stockbook. A corporate record of the stockholders of a corporation, showing the amount of stock held by each, the numbers of the stock certificates issued to the particular stockholders, etc. 18 Am J2d Corp § 470.

See **subscription book**.

stockbroker. An agent, who, for a commission or brokerage fee, bargains or carries on negotiations in behalf of his principal as an intermediary between the latter and third persons in transacting business relative to the sale or purchase of corporate stock, bonds, and other securities. Banta v Chicago, 172 Ill 204, 50 NE 233; 12 Am J2d Brok § 1. A person employed in buying and selling stocks. Banta v Chicago, 172 Ill 204, 50 NE 233, 40 LRA 611, 615. One who engages in the business of selling, offering for sale, or negotiating for the sale of, any security. Anno: 87 ALR 71. A person engaged for all or part of his time in the business of buying and selling securities who, in the transaction concerned, acts for, or buys a security from or sells a security to, a customer. UCC § 8—303. One who deals in stock of moneyed corporations and other securities. Little Rock v Barton, 33 Ark 436, 446, 447.

stockbroker's lien. See **broker's lien**.

stock car. A railroad car built to carry livestock, sometimes called, for no good reason, a palace car. In racing parlance, an automobile built for ordinary use, as distinguished from one built for racing only.

stock certificate. A written instrument signed by the proper officers of a corporation, stating or acknowledging that the person named therein is the owner of a designated number of shares of its stock. Whitehead v Gormley, 116 Okla 287, 245 P 562, 47 ALR 171; 18 Am J2d Corp § 245. Evidence of the ownership of intangible property interests in the corporation. Millar v Mountcastle, 161 Ohio St 409, 119 NE2d 626, 49 ALR2d 381. Not a mere evidence of a stock but, in effect, the stock itself, under the Uniform Stock Transfer Act and the Uniform Commercial Code. 6 Am J2d Attach § 39.

Stock certificates are frequently spoken of as securities but they are not securities in the strict legal significance of that term, since they are not evidences of indebtedness. Nelson v Owen, 113 Ala 372, 21 So 75.

stock company. A corporation. A company or association which has issued shares of stock representing ownership of proportionate interests in the enterprise. A company organized to present a repertoire of plays in one city, ordinarily in one theater.

See **joint-stock company; stock insurance company**.

stock control. See **control of corporation**.

stock corporation. The ordinary private corporation with a capital stock divided into shares. People ex rel. Winchester v Coleman, 133 NY 279, 31 NE 96.

See **stock insurance company**.

stock district. A district established under statute with the purpose and effect of requiring the owners of livestock within the district to keep their livestock restrained against trespassing upon the premises of other persons in order that crops may be cultivated on unfenced premises. 4 Am J2d Ani § 51.

stock dividend. A dividend paid by a corporation in stock of the corporation or in stock which the corporation holds in another corporation. Liebman v Auto. Strop Co. 241 NY 427, 150 NE 505. A corporate dividend payable in stock instead of cash, the declaration of which involves the creation and issuing of new stock to be distributed pro rata to the shareholders as evidence of the contemporaneous transfer of an equivalent amount of the surplus earnings or profits to the capital fund of the corporation. 19 Am J2d Corp § 812. An increase in the number of shares, the increased number representing the same property that was represented by the smaller number of shares. Booth v Gross K. & Co. 30 NM 465, 238 P 829, 41 ALR 868.

Far from being a realization of profits of the stockholder, such a dividend tends rather to postpone such realization, in that the fund represented by the new stock has been transferred from surplus to capital, and is no longer available for actual distribution. Eisner v Macomber, 252 US 189, 64 L Ed 521, 40 S Ct 189.

As to what constitutes a stock dividend under the rules governing allocation of stock dividends between income and principal in a trust estate. See Anno: 44 ALR2d 1297.

stock exchange. See **exchange**.

stock exchange certificate. A certificate of membership in a stock exchange. Anno: 44 ALR2d 947, § 16.

stock grazers. Persons who make use of their land in pasturing livestock. Persons who make a business of producing livestock for the market.

stock grazers' bounty. A bounty paid for the protection of interests of stock grazers; a bounty on predatory animals.

stockholder. The owner of one or more shares of stock in a corporation which has a capital stock. 18 Am J2d Corp § 460. One who appears on the books of the corporation as a holder of stock issued by the corporation. A person distinct from the corporate entity. J. F. Parkinson v Building Trades Council, 154 Cal 581, 98 P 1027.

Persons become stockholders either by original subscription, by direct purchase from the corporation, or by subsequent transfer from the original holders.

The purchase of stock of a corporation is not a loan to that corporation of the amount of such stock. None of the elements of debtor and creditor exist. Oklahoma Hotel Bldg. Co. v Houghton, 202 Okla 591, 216 P2d 288, 16 ALR2d 1307.

stockholder's derivative suit. See **derivative action**.

stockholder's liability. A liability for debts of the corporation, once imposed to a limited extent upon stockholders by constitutional or statutory provisions, since eliminated except for certain classes of debts, such as wages or obligations incurred before the prescribed amount of capital stock was subscribed for or paid in, and, of course, liability upon unpaid shares. 10 Am J2d Banks § 73; 19 Am J2d Corp § 775.

See **superadded liability**.

stockholders' meeting. A meeting of the stockholders of a corporation called for the purpose of electing directors and transacting other business requiring the action or consent of the stockholders, such as, amendment of the articles or certificate of the corporation, sale or mortgage of corporate assets, consolidation and merger, etc. 19 Am J2d Corp § 599.

stockholder's primary liability. The liability of a stockholder directly to a creditor of the corporation under former statutes, such liability attaching immediately upon the contracting of the debt by the corporation.

See **stockholder's liability**.

stockholder's secondary liability. The liability of a stockholder to a creditor of the corporation under former statutes, such liability arising upon the exhaustion of all remedies against the corporation for the collection of the debt, at least not before the return unsatisfied of an execution taken out upon a judgment obtained against the corporation upon the debt.

See **stockholder's liability**.

stockhouse. A place in a steel mill wherein one or two days' supply of ore for a furnace is kept. Youngstown Sheet & Tube Co. v Bowers, 358 US 534, 3 L Ed 2d 490, 79 S Ct 383.

stocking. An item of knit goods. Vietor v Arthur, 104 US 498, 26 L Ed 633. Adding to a stock of merchandise or replacing articles sold from such stock.

stock insurance company. An insurance company organized and operating as a private business corporation rather than as a mutual insurance company or mutual benefit society. An incorporated insurance company in which the initial capital investment is made by subscribers to the stock, and the business is thereafter conducted by a board of directors elected by the stockholders, and, subject to state statutes, the distribution of earnings and profits as between stockholders and policy holders is determined by the board. Atlantic Life Ins. Co. v Moncure (DC Va) 35 F2d 360, affd (CA4) 44 F2d 167, cert den 283 US 823, 75 L Ed 1438, 51 S Ct 346. An insurance corporation which has a capital stock owned by its stockholders, and whose capital is the basis of its business, out of which the losses and expenses are paid, with those insuring in such company paying premiums as the basis of their contract. An insurance company wherein the stockholders contribute all the capital, stand all the losses and take all the profits. State v Willett, 171 Ind 296, 86 NE 68.

stock in trade. That form of property owned by a craftsman upon which he exercises his art, skill, or workmanship, and upon which he uses the tools of his trade or business, including raw materials and the manufactured goods themselves. 31 Am J2d Exemp § 113. A merchant's stock of goods.

See **stock of merchandise**.

stock of descent. An ancestor in whom a succession of inheritance begins.

stock of goods. See **stock in trade**; **stock of merchandise**.

stock of merchandise. The stock in trade of a merchant. The goods or chattels which a merchant holds for sale. Swift & Co. v Tempelos, 178 NC 276, 101 SE 8, 7 ALR 1581, 1584.

stock-option. An option for the purchase or sale of corporate stock. 18 Am J2d Corp § 299. Often having reference to an option held by an officer of or key employee of the corporation for the purchase of stock from the corporation or from some source provided by a definite plan.

See **call**; **put**.

stock-option plan. A plan for granting options to corporate officers or employees for the purchase of stock in the corporation, usually limited in respect of the number of shares and specific in reference to the price. 18 Am J2d Corp § 299.

stock rights. See **rights**.

stocks (stoks). A contrivance employed in former times for the discipline or punishment of a prisoner, consisting of a board through holes in which his feet and arms protruded.

stock split. An increase in the number of shares evidencing the ownership of a corporation without altering the amount of capital, surplus, or segregated earnings. 19 Am J2d Corp § 808. A mere dividing up of the outstanding shares of a corporation into a greater number of units without disturbing the stockholder's original proportional participating interest in the corporation; a matter of form not of substance. Re Hormann's Estate, 3 App Div 2d 5, 157 NYS2d 704; Re Hogan's Estate, 24 Misc 2d 449, 138 NYS2d 864.

stock subscription. See **subscription to stock**.

stock subscription book. See **subscription book**.

stock subscription note. A note covering the liability of a subscriber to corporate stock upon his subscription contract. Crofoot v Thatcher, 19 Utah 212, 57 P 171.

stock range. See **range**.

stock transfer. The process of transferring the ownership of a share or shares of corporate stock.

STOCK [1220] STOPPING

Stock Transfer Act. One of the uniform laws. A comprehensive statute respecting the transfer of corporate stock and the rights of transferees. 18 Am J2d Corp § 376. A uniform law specifically repealed by the UCC. 15 Am J2d Com C § 6.

stock transfer agent. See **transfer agent.**

stock transfer tax. An excise tax on the transfer of shares of corporate stock. A stamp tax on both the issuance and transfer of shares of corporate stock. 50 Am J1st Stk Tr Tax § 2.

stockyard. A place with facilities for the reception and care of livestock in connection with the transportation or marketing thereof. 50 Am J1st Stocky § 1. A place conducted for profit as a public market, with pens in which livestock are received and kept for sale or shipment. Stafford v Wallace, 258 US 497, 513, 66 L Ed 735, 740, 42 S Ct 397, 23 ALR 229.

stockyard corporation. A corporation engaged in maintaining and operating a stockyard as a business enterprise. 50 Am J1st Stocky § 1.

Stockyards Act. See **Packers and Stockyards Act.**

stolen. Obtained by larceny or theft. In a broader sense, obtained by larceny or any manner of conversion or embezzlement. Anno: 45 ALR 836.

The word "stolen", as used in the National Motor Vehicle Theft Act (18 USC § 2312), making it a criminal offense for one to transport, in interstate or foreign commerce, a motor vehicle knowing it to have been stolen, is not limited to a taking which amounts to common-law larceny, but includes an embezzlement or other felonious taking with intent to deprive the owner of the rights and benefits of ownership. United States v Turley, 352 US 407, 1 L Ed 430, 77 S Ct 397, 56 ALR2d 1300.

stolen automobile. See **stolen.**

stolen goods. See **receiving stolen goods; stolen.**

stolidity. Want of emotion or excitement. Greenfield v People, 85 NY 75.

stomach pump. A device operating by suction and used for removing the food content of the stomach for gastric analysis. 23 Am J2d Dep § 226.

stone. A rock. A mineral found in rock. Wright v Carollton Gravel & Sand Co. (Ky) 242 SW2d 751, 26 ALR2d 1449.

stonecutter's disease. A disease of the lungs to which stonecutters are subject, the cause being the lodging of tiny particles of stone in the lungs. Sullivan's Case, 265 Mass 497, 164 NE 457, 62 ALR 1458.

stone quarry. See **quarry.**

stoning to death. See **lapidation.**

stool. A seat supported by three or four legs, having no back.
See **cucking-stool.**

stool pigeon. A person used as a decoy for the purpose of apprehending persons suspected of crime. One who gains the confidence of another for the purpose of spying upon him and becoming an informer against him. A despicable character.

stop. Verb: To come to an end. To halt; to cease movement. To obstruct. To prevent movement. Noun: A place for stopping, as on the line or route of a carrier.

stop box. A box enclosing the valve in a gas line by which service to a house or place of business is controlled. 26 Am J2d Electr § 217.

stop cock. A valve by which the movement of a fluid or gas is stopped or regulated. A valve by which gas service to a house, place of business, or industrial plant is turned on or turned off.

stopgap ordinance. A zoning ordinance enacted in contemplation of the later adoption of a comprehensive zoning ordinance, and intended to preserve the status quo of a particular section of the municipality pending the adoption of the permanent regulations. 58 Am J1st Zon § 137.

stop, look, and listen rule. The rule adopted in some jurisdictions, known sometimes as the Pennsylvania rule, that it is the duty of a traveler approaching a railroad crossing to stop, look both ways and listen to ascertain if a train is approaching. Dunning v Bond (CC Miss) 38 F 813. A rule sometimes imposed upon bus drivers, particularly the drivers of school buses, by bus company or school authority.

stop loss order. See **stop order.**

stop order. An order by a public service commission which requires a carrier to stop for passengers or freight at a certain point on route or line. A direction given by a customer to his broker to the effect that if a designated stock or commodity owned by the customer touches the price named in the order, the broker shall sell it at the best available price; sometimes known as a "stop loss order," the purpose being to provide a measure of protection of the customer against loss beyond a certain point in a fluctuating market. 12 Am J2d Brok § 129.
See **stop payment order.**

stopover privilege. A privilege granted under the ticket of a passenger by common carrier whereby he may stop at a point or points intervening the place of departure and the destination specified in the ticket. 13 Am J2d Car § 318.

stoppage. An obstruction or hindrance to the doing of a particular thing. The Cogne (DC Va) 20 F2d 698.

stoppage in transitu (stop'aj in tran'zi-tu). A right which a seller of goods on credit has to recall them or retake them while they are in the possession of a carrier or other middleman who received them for delivery to the buyer, on the discovery of the insolvency of the buyer. 46 Am J1st Sales § 526.

stoppage of work. A cessation of the work and operations in a place of employment.

The phrase, as used in the amended provision of the Unemployment Compensation Act disqualifying an employee for benefits for unemployment due to a stoppage of work existing because of a labor dispute in the establishment in which he is or was last employed, refers to the work and operations of the employer's establishment and not to the work of the individual employee, and does not operate to disqualify employees who participate in a strike which does not result in the stoppage of the employers' work. Lawrence Baking Co. v Unemployment Comp. Com. 308 Mich 198, 13 NW2d 260, 154 ALR 660.
See **strike.**

stop payment order. An unequivocal notice from the drawer of a check to the drawee that the check is not to be paid by the bank. 10 Am J2d Banks § 641.

stopped. See **stop; stopping or standing.**

stopping distance. The distance within which a motor vehicle may be brought to a complete stop, such varying with the rate of speed. 8 Am J2d Auto § 987.

For charts of stopping and braking distances, see Am Jur 2d Desk Book, Documents 174-176.

stopping or standing. A vehicle motionless in street or highway, whether or not parked. Modern Indiana Transit, Inc. v Burk, 228 Ind 162, 89 NE2d 905, 17 ALR2d 572.

stopping payment. The closing of a bank upon its insolvency. The act of the drawer of a check in revoking or cancelling the check, before it has been certified, accepted, or paid by the bank upon which it is drawn, by giving an unequivocal direction or instruction to the bank that the check is not to be paid. 10 Am J2d Banks § 641.

See **stop payment order.**

stopping well. Same as **plugging well.**

stop sign. A sign upon highway or street requiring a stop by the driver of any vehicle using the street, particularly signs calling for a stop at an intersection with another street or highway. 7 Am J2d Auto § 196. A sign placed along a railroad track calling for the stopping of a train at that point.

stop signal. A signal given by the driver of a vehicle on the highway, by hand, light, or mechanical device, to warn other drivers, particularly one following immediately behind, of his intention to stop. A red traffic light. 78 Am J2d Auto § 195. A signal by a traffic officer or other person to a motorist, calling for a stop. 7 Am J2d Auto §§ 746, 747. A red light, mechanical, or hand signal given to the engineer or other employee of the railroad in charge of the movement of a train that the train is to stop.

storage. See **cold storage; dead storage; live storage; warehouse.**

storage battery. A battery for generating electric current, especially current for the ignition of an internal combustion engine.

storage lien. A maritime lien for the storage of watercraft. 12 Am J2d Boats §§ 30, 31. A lien for the storage of an automobile. 24 Am J1st Garag §§ 48 et seq.

See **warehouseman's lien.**

store. Verb: To lay away; to put in storage. Noun: A place where goods are kept on deposit, especially in large quantities—a warehouse; and also, a place where goods are kept for sale in large or small quantities. Pitts v Vicksburg, 72 Miss 181, 184. A place where goods and merchandise are kept and sold.

An establishment for the sale of merchandise is a "store" notwithstanding all sales are confined to residents of the plantation owned by the storekeeper. 33 Am J1st Lic § 47.

See **department store; public store; secondhand store.**

store account. A book account kept by the keeper of a store for goods sold on credit. Salomon v Pioneer Co-operative Co. 21 Fla 374.

See **book account.**

stored or kept. Warehoused or deposited for safekeeping. 29A Am J Rev ed Ins § 921 (involving condition in insurance policy that certain articles shall not be "stored or kept" upon the premises.)

See **storing or keeping.**

store furniture. See **furniture; trade fixtures.**

storehouse. A warehouse. A repository for the storage of goods. Steele v State, 80 Neb 9, 113 NW 798.

See **entrepot; magazine; warehouse.**

stores. The supplies of different articles provided for the subsistence and accommodation of the ship's crew and passengers. United States v Hawley & Letzerich (CC Tex) 160 F 734.

See **store.**

storing or keeping. Warehousing or depositing for safekeeping.

As used in the Federal Fair Labor Standards Act of 1918, the word is defined as meaning the placing of agricultural or horticultural commodities in storage rooms or other places where the commodities are to be held prior to further preparation or shipment, or the taking care of the commodities while they are being so held. Gordon v Paducah Ice Mfg. Co. (DC Ky) 41 F Supp 980.

See **stored or kept.**

storm. A manifestation of the operation of natural forces in the fall of rain, hail, or snow, especially when accompanied by wind. A high wind blowing at the rate of from sixty to eighty miles an hour. The Snap (DC Va) 24 F 292.

See **cyclone; tornado.**

storm sewer. See **sewer.**

storm waters. Enemy waters,—freshet and flood waters of a river, as distinguished from its ordinary and usual flow. Herminghaus v Southern California Edison Co. 200 Cal 81, 252 P 607.

See **flood waters.**

story. A habitable space between two floors of a building; a set of rooms on the same floor or level. Biber v O'Brien, 138 Cal App 353, 32 P2d 425. All the rooms on one level of a building; a horizontal section of a building. 32 Am J1st L & T § 1662. A term commonly used in expressing a maximum-height restriction in a covenant contained in a deed or land contract. Hobson v Cartwright, 93 Ky 368, 20 SW 281. The relating of an event or series of events, real or imaginary, in words uttered orally or written. A literary work.

As used in a lease describing the demised premises as a "story" or a "floor," such term includes the outside of the walls inclosing such story or floor as a part of the premises demised, for it is the apparent intention in such cases to separate a section of the building as a distinct tenement. The words "story" and "floor" define the lower and upper boundaries of this, but there is nothing to fix the lateral boundaries except the boundaries of the building. 32 Am J1st L & T § 166.

See **rumor; upper story.**

stowage. The placing of cargo on a ship.

See **broken stowage.**

stowaway. A person on a ship at sea without status as ship's officer, seaman, or passenger. A person who conceals himself on board a vessel about to leave port in order to obtain a free passage. United States v Sandrey (CC La) 48 F 550, 551.

straddle. Noun: A transaction whereby a person protects himself against either a rise or fall of the price of a stock or commodity by obtaining options to purchase or to sell. A combination of a "put" and a "call," in which one party is either to sell and deliver to the other the commodity or stock at a specified price or to demand it from the other at a specified price, incurring no legal liability if he does neither. Anno: 83 ALR 573. Verb: To drive over the median line of the highway. 8 Am J2d Auto § 952.

straddle year. A fiscal year adopted by a corporation for tax purposes, a part of which comes before a tax rate change and part after such change.

straight annuity. An annuity payable under a contract which provides for the termination of all payments upon the death of the annuitant. 4 Am J2d Annui § 1. An annuity under which the payments to be made by the insurance company terminate upon the death of the annuitant, without refund of any part of principal or interest to a third person. Bartle v Pennsylvania R. Co. 51 Ohio L Abs 161, 78 NE2d 410, mod on other grounds 150 Ohio St 387, 38 Ohio Ops 237, 82 NE2d 853.

straight bill of lading. A nonnegotiable bill of lading; a bill of lading in which it is stated that the goods are consigned or destined to a specified person. 13 Am J2d Car § 265.

straight life. The most common form of life insurance; ordinary life insurance. Life insurance which matures and calls for payment by the insurer only upon the death of the insured, containing no endowment or other feature calling for payment of the proceeds of the insurance prior to that time.

straight line depreciation. A deduction in calculating net income subject to tax, computed by dividing the adjusted basis of the property at the beginning of the year, less the estimated salvage value, by the number of years of estimated useful life remaining at the time. Internal Revenue Code § 167.

straight party ticket. A ballot whereon the candidates voted for are all of one party. A ballot facilitated by a provision for a party square or circle on the ballot whereby, if marked, the entire party ticket is voted without more. 26 Am J2d Elect § 260.

strait jacket. An instrument of discipline or restraint, consisting of a stout tight jacket which binds the arms firmly against the body, used in restraining violent criminals and mentally unbalanced persons.

stramineus (strạ-min'ẹ-us). (Latin.) Straw.

stramonium (strā-mō'ni-um). A narcotic poison the effects of which, taken internally, are intoxication, delirium, loss of sense, drowsiness, a sort of madness and fury; loss of memory, convulsions, spasms, paralysis of the limbs, cold sweats and excessive thirst. Pitts v State, 43 Miss 472, 485.

strand (strand). Shore; that portion of the land lying between ordinary high and low water marks. Stillman v Burfeind, 21 App Div 13, 15, 47 NYS 280, 281.

stranded logs. Logs intended to be floated to a destination on a stream but remaining on the land after washing ashore. 34 Am J1st Logs § 76.

stranded vessel. See **stranding.**

stranding. A peril of the sea. Lanasa Fruit Steamship & I. Co. v Universal Ins. Co. 302 US 556, 82 L Ed 422, 58 S Ct 371. The striking of a vessel upon a rock, bank, reef, or the like. Strong v Sun Mutual Ins. Co. 31 NY 103. A ship running aground or taking ground, not in the ordinary course of navigation, but by accident, or the force of the wind or sea, and remaining stationary for some time. 29A Am J Rev ed Ins § 1318. Being left in a helpless position; being left without funds in a strange city.

In the law of marine insurance, the term implies a stopping of a vessel's progress and a resting for a longer or a shorter period. Lehigh & Wilkes-Barre Coal Co. v Globe & Rutgers Fire Ins. Co. (CA2 NY) 6 F2d 736, 43 ALR 215, 218.

See **voluntary stranding.**

stranger. One who was not a party to a transaction. One not in interest. As a depositary of an escrow: —one not a party to the instrument; one so free from any personal or legal identity with the parties to the instrument as to leave him free to discharge his duty as a depositary to both parties without involving a breach of duty to either. 28 Am J2d Escr § 12.

As used in a statute making absolutely void the attornment of a tenant to a "stranger," the word has been held to signify a person between whom and the landlord there is no privity, and whose title or right of possession is not derived from the landlord but is hostile to his title. See O'Donnell v McIntyre, 118 NY 156, 164, 23 NE 455.

Within the meaning of an inheritance tax statute, the term has been construed as intended to exhaust the whole category of persons who might be called to the inheritance, whether by will or ab intestato; so construed, the term applies to all who have not the status of legitimate ascendants, descendants, or collateral relations, and thus includes a widow. Baker's Succession, 129 La 74, 55 So 714.

stranger to judgment. One neither a party to the action nor in privity with a party. 30A Am J Rev ed Judgm § 393.

stranger to the blood. One not related by blood. A relative by affinity, not by blood, such as wife, daughter-in-law, or son-in-law. Campbell v California, 200 US 87, 50 L Ed 382, 26 S Ct 182.

strangulation. Causing death by cutting off the breath, as by squeezing the throat with hands or a cord. 26 Am J1st Homi § 436.

strappado (stra-pä'dō). A form of punishment or torture inflicted by raising the victim with a rope and then letting him drop with an ensuing painful jerk.

straw. The product left from a cutting of mature wheat, oats, barley, etc. after the grain has been removed therefrom by threshing.

straw bail. See **straw bond.**

strawberries. A vine crop. 21 Am J2d Crops § 4.

straw bond. A bail bond with sureties who are financially irresponsible. A bail bond in which the surety or sureties are fictitious persons. People v Bogart (NY) 3 Park Crim 143, 172.

straw man. A dummy. An irresponsible bondsman or surety. One made to appear as the owner of record who in fact holds title for another.

straying animal. See **estray.**

stream. A river, brook, or rivulet, anything in fact that is liquid and flows in a line or course. French v Carhart, 1 NY 96, 107. A steady current in a river or in the sea, especially the middle or most rapid part of a current or tide; as the gulf stream. A continued course or current.

The distinction between a stream and a pond or lake is that in one case the water has a natural motion or current, while in the other the water in its natural state is substantially at rest. The fact that there may be some current in a body of water is not alone sufficient to make it a stream, nor will the swelling out of a stream into broad water sheets make it a lake. Illinois Cent. Railroad Co. v Chicago, 173 Ill 471, 50 NE 1004.

See **bed of stream; channel; thread of stream.**

streamline. A shape or design calculated to decrease wind resistance, particularly in reference to aircraft, motor vehicles, railroad cars, and watercraft.

Streamline in the planning of bodies of airplanes, boats, automobiles, and railroad cars, is a design which will result in uninterrupted flow of the air or water about the body, instead of an eddying or turbulent motion. A streamlined body offers the least possible resistance to the fluid, and permits the current which it breaks simply to reunite in its wake, without the retarding or dragging eddies and turbulence created by partial vacuum in the wake of a non-streamlined body. The streamline design is typically a long ellipse, tapering to a point; it is illustrated in the cross-section of an airplane wing, and in a bird's and a fish's body. Forman v American Express Co. (DC NY) 37 F Supp 82.

street. A highway or public thoroughfare in an urban community, such as a city, town, or village. 25 Am J1st High § 7. A kind of highway, the public having the right to use it for purposes of travel. Chicago Motor Coach Co. v Chicago, 337 Ill 200, 169 NE 22, 66 ALR 834; Graff v Casper, 73 Wyo 486, 281 P2d 685, 52 ALR2d 254.

While the term does not include the mere private way, it does include all the public roads or ways within the municipality over which it has jurisdiction and as to which it owes the public the duty of exercising reasonable care to keep them and maintain them in reasonably safe condition for public use. Indian Rocks Beach South Shore, Inc. v Ewell (Fla) 59 So 2d 647, 32 ALR2d 940.

The term is not applicable to rural highways. Some authorities take the view that the term is generic, embracing all urban ways which can be, and are generally, used for ordinary purposes of travel. Others limit the application of the term to thoroughfares in the built-up portions of the urban territory. 25 Am J1st High § 7.

There are cases pro and con on the question whether a statutory regulation of "highway" traffic is applicable to traffic upon a "street." 7 Am J2d Auto § 170.

The word means more than the surface; it means the whole surface and as much of the depth as is, or can be, used, not unfairly, for the ordinary purpose of a street. It comprises a depth which authorizes the urban authority to do that which is done in every street, namely, to raise the street, and lay down sewers, and also to lay down gas and water pipes. Cornwall v Garrison, 59 Idaho 287, 81 P2d 1094.

A street may include a dock or a part of a dock; as where a private dock is built on a public street on the shore of navigable waters, the dock becomes a part of the street, and the public has a right to travel over it. Pan-Pacific Constr. Co. v Meadows, 85 Cal App 775, 260 P 355.

"Lot" and "street" are two separate and distinct terms, and have separate and distinct meanings. The term "lots" in its common and ordinary meaning, includes that portion of the platted territory measured and set apart for individual and private use and occupancy, while the term "streets" means that portion set apart and designated for the use of the public. Earl v Dutour, 181 Cal 58, 183 P 438, 6 ALR 1163, 1164.

streetcar. A large coach or car for the transportation of passengers, propelled over fixed tracks to which the wheels are adapted. Montgomery v Santa Ana Westminster R. Co. 104 Cal 186, 37 P 786. A vehicle for some purposes. Foster v Curtis, 213 Mass 79, 99 NE 961.

streetcar track. That part of the right of way or street on which the rails and ties are laid; the ties, spikes, rails, and switches. Detroit Citizens Street R. Co. v Detroit, 125 Mich 673, 85 NW 96, 86 NW 809.

street crossing. See **crossing**.

street fair. A fair conducted on the streets of a municipality, such usually being considered an improper use of the streets. 25 Am J1st High § 196.

street grade. See **grade**; **grade line**.

street improvement. A public improvement. See **front foot plan**; **fronting and abutting**; **special assessment**.

street intersection. See **intersection**.

street number. The number given a street by way of designating it, such as 20th Street, Parkersburg, West Virginia. 25 Am J1st High § 614. The number of a house on a particular street, constituting a part of an address. A listing of names of voters of a precinct or election district by street, address, party affiliation not appearing.

street perils. Perils peculiar to the use of a street or other public way. 58 Am J1st Workm Comp § 226.

street railroad. Same as **street railway**.

street railway. A railroad upon tracks laid on and along the streets of a municipality, primarily for the accommodation of passengers going from one point to another in such municipality or to and from the suburbs. Highland Ave. & Belt R. Co. 119 Ala 105, 24 So 114. A common carrier whether of goods or passengers. 13 Am J2d Car § 12. Operated ordinarily for the transportation of passengers only. Not a railroad in the ordinary sense. 44 Am J1st RR § 6.

Within the provisions of the Bankruptcy Act a street railway is considered a railroad. The word railroad when considered in its generic sense includes street railways; that is to say, that where there is nothing to indicate that the word is used in a restricted sense the same should be given its broad meaning. Columbia R. Gas & E. Co. v State (CA4 SC) 27 F2d 52, 59 ALR 665.

See **streetcar**; **streetcar track**.

street risks. See **street perils**.

streetwalker. A prostitute who solicits patronage on the streets. 42 Am J1st Prost § 2.

streetwalking. The offense committed by a prostitute in soliciting patronage on the street. The offense of a common prostitute offering herself for sale on the streets at unusual or unreasonable hours, endeavoring to induce men to follow her for the purpose of prostitution. Pinkerton v Verberg, 78 Mich 573, 44 NW 579.

strict construction. A narrow or literal construction. A narrow construction of a contract, especially a literal or technical construction of an isolated or special clause which defeats the true meaning of the contract as such is apparent from all its provisions. Sindlinger v Department of Financial Institutions, 210 Ind 83, 199 NE 715, 105 ALR 501. A narrow construction of a statute, confining its operation to matters affirmatively, definitely, irresistibly, or specifically pointed out by its terms, and to cases which fall fairly within its letter, or the clear, plain, obvious, or natural import of the language used. 50 Am J1st Stat § 388.

STRICT [1224] STRIKING

strict foreclosure. The foreclosure of a mortgage without a sale of the mortgaged property, being accomplished by a suit in equity and a decree rendered therein extinguishing the mortgagor's equity of redemption, such decree calling for payment of the debt secured within a reasonable period of time fixed by the court and further providing that upon failure of the defendant or defendants to make such payment within the time prescribed, all the right, title, and interest, both legal and equitable, of the defendant or defendants shall be vested absolutely and forever unconditionally in the plaintiff. 37 Am J1st Mtg § 529.

In England and in some jurisdictions in this country, the rights of the vendor of land where the contract is executory may be enforced by a decree in the nature of a strict foreclosure. Such a decree has sometimes been called a decree for cancellation of the contract; time is given and, if it expires without the money being paid, the contract is canceled by the decree or judgment of the court, and the vendor again becomes the owner of the estate. 55 Am J1st V & P § 455.

stricti juris (strik'tī jū'ris). Of strict right; of strict law; of strictly legal interpretation without aid from principles of equity. See 2 Bl Comm 108.

strictissimi juris (strik-tis'si-mī jū'ris). Of strictest right.

strict liability. Same as **absolute liability**.

strictly accountable. Absolutely liable without deduction.

strictly confidential. Not to be divulged.

The generally accepted elements of a strictly confidential relationship, position or office are enumerated as secrecy, integrity, trust, confidence, skill, and competence in the performance of the duties imposed upon the appointing officer and by him delegated to the one holding such relationship. Klatt v Akers, 232 Iowa 1312, 5 NW2d 605, 146 ALR 808.

strictly construed. See **strict construction**.

strictly ministerial. A characterization of a duty which is specific, imperative, and ministerial, without scope for exercise of discretion. 34 Am J1st Mand § 66.

stricto jure. See **in stricto jure**.

strict performance. A literal performance of the stipulations of a contract. 17 Am J2d Contr § 370.

strict priority. The principle, first enunciated in equity receivership cases, carried over to railroad reorganization cases under § 77 of the Bankruptcy Act, reaffirmed and re-enunciated in corporate reorganization cases under Ch X of the Bankruptcy Act, that in order to win the approval of the court as fair and equitable, a plan of reorganization must preserve for the holders of the several interests the advantage of their respective priorities, except as otherwise provided in the Bankruptcy Act. 9 Am J2d Bankr § 1586. A rule which gives creditors secured or unsecured the right to exclude stockholders entirely from the reorganization plan when the debtor is insolvent. Helvering v Alabama Asphaltic Limestone Co. 314 US 598, 86 L Ed 504, 62 S Ct 540.

strict record. The record proper in an action, consisting of the pleadings, the process, the verdict, and the judgment.

Where a question of law is raised upon the strict record, no exception is necessary to place such question before the United States Circuit Court of Appeals. Montgomery v Erie Railroad Co. (CA3 NJ) 97 F2d 289.

strict settlement. The entailing of an estate. See **entail**.

strife. Altercation. Conflict; a quarrel.

Strife and contention do not necessarily imply blows. They may be evidenced by passionate words, looks and gestures. State v Warner, 34 Conn 276, 279.

strike. Verb: To eliminate; to expunge. To administer a blow. To act in concert with other employees in refusing to work. Noun: A discovery of valuable ore. Coming upon oil in quantity in drilling. A simultaneous cessation or quitting of work by a body of workmen acting in combination for the purpose of coercing their employer to accede to some demand they have made upon him which he has refused. 31 Am J Rev ed Lab § 369. A cessation of work by employees in an effort to obtain for themselves more desirable terms of employment or a general concerted refusal by workmen to work in consequence of an alleged grievance. Anno: 11 ALR 1006, s. 35 ALR 722. A cessation of work by all or part of the employees acting in concert. 29 Am J Rev ed Ins § 1371 (definition found in insurance policy). A cessation of work by employees in an effort to get for themselves more desirable terms. Anno: 28 ALR2d 298 (for purposes of Unemployment Compensation Act).

See **general strike; legal strike; lockout; picketing**.

strike benefits. Payments by a labor union to members on strike.

strike breaker. See **scab; strike breaking**.

strike breaking. Overcoming a strike or the effect of a strike. Entering employment in an industrial plant wherein a strike is in progress. Taking the place of a striking employee.

strike clause. A provision frequently inserted in executory contracts for the sale of goods whereby the seller is to be excused in case his performance of the contracts is prevented by strikes. 46 Am J1st Sales § 238.

strike fund. A fund of a labor union accumulated and held for the purpose of paying members of the union on strike.

strike insurance. See **labor dispute insurance**.

strike misconduct. Misconduct arising out of, developed by, or closely connected with, a strike by employees in a labor dispute. NLRB v Industrial Cotton Mills (CA4) 208 F2d 87, 45 ALR2d 880.

strike off. See **strike out; struck off**.

strike out. To expunge, by ruling of the court from a record or pleading, immaterial, scandalous or superfluous matter. In terminology adopted from baseball, the failure to succeed in a particular endeavor.

strike suit. A derivative action instituted by a minority of stockholders for the purpose of oppressing the majority and involving the corporation itself in disaster for selfish purposes and for reasons not always revealed. 19 Am J2d Corp § 560.

striking a docket (strī'king a dok'et). An English expression for the entry of the petition, bond and affidavit of a petitioning creditor in an involuntary proceeding for an adjudication in bankruptcy.

striking a jury. See **struck jury.**

striking conterclaim. The expunging of a counterclaim upon motion. 20 Am J2d Countcl § 147.

striking distance. The position of one's assailant at such point that it is lawful to use force to repel the attack, the assailant being close enough to one as to lead one to believe that physical injury will be inflicted upon him by the assailant unless the latter is subjected to force. 6 Am J2d Asslt & B § 71.

striking employee. The status of an employee participating in a strike. Tedesco v Turner & Seymour Mfg. Co. 19 Conn Supp 192, 110 A2d 650.

striking evidence. A remedy to exclude improper evidence from the consideration of the jury, as where a witness has answered a question before time to interpose an objection or after an objection has been sustained, or evidence admitted upon assurance of counsel that its relevancy will appear, where such relevancy never appears. 53 Am J1st Trial § 149. Eliminating from the record a nonresponsive or objectionable answer by a witness. 58 Am J1st Witn § 575.

striking pleading. A remedy against immaterial, irrelevant, redundant, scandalous and impertinent matter in a pleading. 41 Am J1st Pl §§ 349 et seq. A remedy against a pleading considered as a whole, as where the pleading is sham or frivolous or is clearly and irremediably defective and states no cause of action or defense. 41 Am J1st Pl §§ 346-348.

stringer. A crack or crevice appearing in rock which is filled with a mineral deposit, by means of which a prospector is led to a body of ore of commercial value. McShane v Kenkle, 18 Mont 208, 44 P 979.

strip. To remove clothing. To become nude. To take away parts from an automobile or machine for use in other vehicle or machine. To clear ground of vegetation. To farm land to exhaustion, depriving it of fertility.

strip mining. A method of mining coal by uncovering the vein instead of reaching it by shaft and laterals.

stripper. A term of show business for a girl who removes her apparel or the most of it during her routine.

stripper well. An oil well which produces less than ten barrels of crude oil per day. St. John v Brown (DC Tex) 38 F Supp 385.

stroke. A sudden onset of disease, especially apoplexy or paralysis. 1 Am J2d Act of God § 10.
See **heat stroke.**

strong-arm clause. The provision of the Bankruptcy Act that the trustee in bankruptcy, as to all property, whether or not coming into possession or control of the court, upon which a creditor of the bankrupt could have obtained a lien by legal or equitable proceedings at the date of bankruptcy, shall be deemed vested as of such date with all the rights, remedies, and powers of a creditor than holding a lien thereon by such proceeding, whether or not such a creditor actually exists. Bankruptcy Act § 70(c); 11 USC § 110(c); 9 Am J2d Bankr § 857.

strong arm of equity. Injunctive relief. 28 Am J Rev ed Inj § 3.

strong beer. Ordinary American beer, as made from malt and hops.
This term, though practically obsolete as recently as 1906, was once in familiar use as the name of beer made of malt and hops, and so called to distinguish it from "small beer," which was compounded of molasses and yeast with the addition of either ginger or spruce, and which contained a very small percentage of alcohol. Strong beer was rich in the intoxicating principle, analysis showing eight per cent alcohol. The courts had no difficulty in determining that it was an intoxicating liquor. Potts v State, 50 Tex Crim 368, 97 SW 477.

strong hand. See **with strong hand.**

struck down. See **knocked down; struck off.**

struck jury. A jury chosen from a panel drawn for a particular case, not from the regular panel, sometimes called a special jury. A jury drawn by the exercise of strikes, each party being entitled to strike a certain number of names of persons appearing as qualified jurors on a special venire drawn and summoned for the case. 31 Am J Rev ed Jury § 90. A jury selected by an officer authorized by law, as a jury commissioner, instead of being drawn from the wheel, as in the case of common jurors. State v Withrow, 133 Mo 500, 513.

struck off. The acceptance of a bid and the completion of a sale of an article at auction. 7 Am J2d Auct § 31.
In the language of the auction room, and in common parlance, property is said to be "struck off" or "knocked down," when the auctioneer, by the fall of his hammer, or by any other audible or visible announcement, signifies to the bidder that he is entitled to the property on paying the amount of his bid, according to the terms of the sale. Sherwood v Reade (NY) 7 Hill 431, 439.

structural alteration. Such an alteration of a building as changes the physical structure so materially as to create a different building. Kinston Cotton Mills v Liability Assur. Corp. 161 NC 562, 77 SE 682.

structural defect. A condition in the structure itself which renders it not reasonably safe for the use for which it was intended. Krooner v Waterbury, 105 Conn 476, 479, 136 A 93, 94.

structure. In the broad sense, any construction or piece of work composed of parts joined together in some definite manner; in a restricted sense, a building of any kind, particularly one of size. 20 Am J2d Cov § 194. Any form or arrangement of building or construction materials involving the necessity or precaution of providing proper support, bracing, tying, anchoring, or other protection against the pressure of the elements. St. Louis Park v Casey, 218 Minn 394, 16 NW2d 459, 155 ALR 1128 (as defined in a zoning ordinance). An edifice for any use; that which is built, as a dwelling house, church, shed, store, etc. Favro v State, 39 Tex Crim 452, 46 SW 932.
While a building is always a structure, all structures are not buildings. Katsoff v Lucertini, 141 Conn 74, 108 A2d 812.

strumpet (strum'pet). A prostitute; a female given to indiscriminate lewdness.

strychnine (strik'nin). An alkaloid. A poison. Riley v Interstate Businessmen's Acci. Asso. 184 Iowa 1124, 169 NW 448, 2 ALR 57.

stub. A part of an instrument, especially the statement of an account, torn off and retained as a memorandum.

stub line. A small branch line of railroad. Arizona Eastern Railroad Co. v State, 29 Ariz 446, 242 P 870.

stub of check. That part of the sheet which remains in a checkbook after a check has been written and pulled from the book, such part normally being used to indicate the state of the bank account by adding deposits and subtracting the amount of the checks written. Screenland Magazine v National City Bank, 181 Misc 454, 42 NYS2d 286.

stud. A male horse, uncastrated, and kept for breeding purposes.
See **studding.**

stud book. A book kept by the owner of a stallion in which is entered the mares bred, with date of the service. A register of thoroughbred horses.
When a horse entered in the English Stud Book is exported, it is customary to send with it a document called an export certificate, issued by the keepers of the stud book, by means of which a foreign purchaser is enabled to register the horse in the stud book of his country. Halbronn v International Horse Agency & Exchange, High Court of Justice (Eng) [1903] 1 KB 270.

studding. A two-by-four or two-by-six piece of lumber, placed upright in a building, upon which the boards making up the sides of the building are nailed and to which the laths of the inside walls are attached.

studendum et orandum. See **ad studendum et orandum.**

student. A person in attendance at a college or university. One receiving instruction in a public or private school.

student driver. A person receiving instruction in the driving of an automobile, usually by letting him operate the vehicle under the direction of a person accompanying him.

student pilot. A person receiving instruction in the flying of aircraft.

students' union. An organization of the entire body of students at a college or university; a building maintained by such an organization for student activities.

stud horse. See **stud.**

stud poker. A variety of the game of poker, characterized by the fact that some of the cards in the hands are dealt face up.

study expense. A preliminary expense of a local improvement project, sometimes incurred without being followed by the construction of the improvement tentatively contemplated. 48 Am J1st Spec A § 53.

stuff gown. The gown worn by a barrister who has not attained the rank of queen's counsel.

stuffing ballot box. Illegal voting by inserting in the ballot box ballots marked by other than qualified and legal voters. Ex parte Siebold, 100 US 371, 25 L Ed 717, 720.

stultify (stul'ti-fī). To plead one's own insanity or other want of capacity, in his own suit to set aside his own deed or other contract, or in an action against him to enforce the contract.
The ancient rule that a man shall not stultify himself is no longer law either in England or in the United States. See 2 Kent Comm 451.

stumpage (stum'pāj). The sum by agreement to be paid an owner for trees standing (or lying) upon his land, the party purchasing being permitted to enter upon the land and to cut and remove them. The price paid for a license to cut.
Stumpage on lumber is somewhat of the nature of a percentage paid on copyright, or of a royalty for the use of a patent, or a duty paid on mineral productions. Blood v Drummond, 67 Me 476, 478.

stump measurement. The measurement of the trunk of a tree at the point where it would normally be cut for commercial purposes. Anno: 39 ALR 1316.

stuprum (stū'prum). The debauching or rape of a previously chaste woman.

sturgeon (ster'jon). See **fish royal.**

style of cause. The caption and heading of process and pleading.

style of firm. See **firm name and style.**

style of writ or process. The designation of the person or government from whom the command on the face of the writ appears to emanate; thus "The People of the State of Michigan to the Sheriff of the County of Wayne, Greeting." 42 Am J1st Proc § 9.

suability (sū-a-bil'i-ti). See **suable; sue.**

suable (sū'a-bl). Being subject to suit, that is capable of being sued. Liable to be sued.
" 'Suable' and 'suability' are words not in common use, but they concisely, correctly convey the idea annexed to them." Chisholm v Georgia (US) 2 Dall 419, 470, 1 L Ed 440, 462.

suable cause. A cause of action; a matured cause of action.

suapte natura (su-ap'te na-tū'ra). In its own nature.

sua sponte (su'a spon'te). Upon his own responsibility; of his own motion.
See **own motion.**

sub. A prefix meaning under; subordinate to. A contraction of submarine.

subagent. A person employed by an agent to assist him in conducting the affairs of the principal. 3 Am J2d Agency § 7. The agent of an agent.
If his appointment is expressly or impliedly authorized, he becomes the agent of the principal. 3 Am J2d Agency § 149.

subagency. See **subagent.**

subbailment. A bailment by a bailee to a third person. A delegation by a bailee to a third person to whom he delivers the property involved in his undertaking.
Of course, the bailee cannot relieve himself of responsibility by subbailment, without the consent of or authorization, express or implied, by the original bailor. 8 Am J2d Bailm § 190.

sub bois (sub bwa). Underwood; underbrush.

sub colore juris (sub ko-lō're jū-ris). Under color of right.

sub colore officii (sub ko-lō're o-fi'she-ī). Under color of office.

sub conditione. On condition.
One of the three phrases by which, without more, a conditional estate may be created. It is the first one named by Littleton, and Coke says of it: "This is the most express and proper condition in deed, and therefore our author beginneth with it." Clapp v Wilder, 176 Mass 332, 57 NE 692.

subcontract. An undertaking employed chiefly in the building and construction field whereby one, who has assumed the status of a principal contractor by entering into a contract with an owner of premises

SUBCONTRACTOR

or public body for the construction of a building or improvement for such owner or public body, enters into a contract with a third person, called a subcontractor, whereunder the latter undertakes to perform some part of the work which the principal contractor has agreed to perform under his contract with the owner or public body or to furnish and supply materials needed in the performance of such contract. Anno: 112 ALR 824; 36 Am J1st Mech L § 50.

subcontractor. A person who takes a portion of a contract from the principal contractor. Fox v Dunning, 129 Okla 228, 255 P 582. One who agrees under contract with a principal or original contractor to construct for him some part of the structure which the principal contractor has engaged to construct under his contract with an owner of premises or public body, or to furnish and supply materials needed for the performance of such contract. Anno: 112 ALR 824. A person whose relation to the principal contractor is substantially the same as to a part of the work as the latter's relation to the owner. 36 Am J1st Mech L § 51.

It is generally held that a person performing individual labor on a structure for the contractor is not a subcontractor. But it has been held that a laborer is in a sense a subcontractor, and he may fall within the statutory definition. 36 Am J1st Mech L § 51.

sub cura mariti (sub kū'ra ma'ri-tī). Under the care of the husband.

sub curia (sub kū'ri-a). Under the court; under the law.

sub disjunctione (sub dis-junk-she-ō'ne). In the disjunctive.

subdivide. To divide a tract of land into lots before developing or improving the tract. Gill v Saunders, 182 Ark 453, 31 SW2d 748.

subdivision. A land development; an area divided into building lots.
See **political subdivision; subdivide.**

subdivision bond. A bond issued by a township, county, or other political subdivision.

subfeudation (sub-fū-dā'shon). Same as **subinfeudation.**

subflow. See **underground stream.**

subfluvial (sub-flō'vi-al). Beneath a river or stream.

subhastian (sub-has'ti-an). A sale subhastio.
See **subhastio.**

subhastio (sub-has'ti-ō). At the foot of the spear.
In ancient Rome, military spoils were disposed of at the foot of the spear—subhastio—by auction, or increase. Balesh v Hot Springs, 173 Ark 661, 293 SW 14.

subinfeudation (sub-in-fū-dā'shon). The feudal system of land tenure according to which tenants under the king, who was styled the "lord paramount," rented out portions of their lands to persons inferior to them, becoming lords with respect to these inferior persons, new feudal relations being created with each grant. De Peyster v Michael, 6 NY 467. The carving out of small estates to tenants by inferior lords, to be held of themselves.

This practice under the feudal system grew until the superior lords observed that they were losing all their feudal profit of wardship, marriage, and escheat and it was first checked by Magna Charta, and later abrogated by the Statute of Quia Emptores. See 2 Bl Comm 91.

subirrigation. Irrigation by conducting water underground in porous pipes.

subjacent support. A right of an adjoining landowner. The support of the surface by the underlying strata of the earth, or the support of the upper floors of a building by the part below.

The surface, in this connection, means not merely the geometrical superficies without a thickness, but includes all above the subjacent stratum in question and therefore includes a higher stratum as well as the actual surface of the soil, and the owner of the higher stratum is entitled to the same rights as the actual surface owner. It has been held, however, that the word "surface," when used in this connection in a deed without a qualifying phrase, signifies only the superficial part of the land, and therefore one having such grant is entitled to subjacent support of the superficial part of his land only. 1 Am J2d Adj L § 77.

subject. A citizen. An inhabitant. A person domiciled in a country and enjoying the protection afforded by it under sovereign power. The Pizarro (US) 2 Wheat 227, 245, 4 L Ed 226, 231.
See **subject to.**

subjecting property to debts. See **execution sale; judicial sale; levy.**

subjecting to debts in inverse order of alienation. See **inverse order of alienation.**

subjective examination. A medical examination in which the physician obtains the information necessary to form a conclusion as to the condition of the patient from the facts as related to him by the patient. Reeder v Thompson, 120 Kan 722, 245 P 127.

subjective impossibility of performance. Impossibility of performance personal to the promisor, not inhering in the nature of the act to be performed. 17 Am J2d Contr § 415.

subjective standard of satisfaction. A matter of taste, fancy, or sensibility determining satisfaction with performance of a contract. Gerish v Herold, 82 NJL 605, 83 A 892.

subjective symptoms. Those symptoms which a physician learns from the expressions of the patient. Reeder v Thompson, 120 Kan 722, 245 P 127.

subjective test. See **subjective standard of satisfaction.**

subject matter of act. Same as **subject matter of statute.**

subject matter of action. See **jurisdiction of the subject matter; subject of the action.**

subject matter of contract. Property or services of a wide range, the reported cases indicating that almost every conceivable form of property or services has been involved. 17 Am J2d Contr § 14.

subject matter of statute. In general, the same as **subject of statute.**

If there is any difference between "subject of statute" and "subject matter of statute," it is in respect to the offices which they respectively perform, the word "subject" indicating the chief thing to which the statute relates, and "matter" the things which are secondary, subordinate, or incidental. 50 Am J1st Stat § 191.

subject of act. Same as **subject of statute.**

subject of bankruptcy. The subject of the relations between an insolvent, nonpaying, or fraudulent debtor and his creditors, extending to his and their relief. Wright v Union Cent. Life Ins. Co. 304 US 502, 82 L Ed 1490, 58 S Ct 1025, reh den 305 US 581, 80 L Ed 411, 56 S Ct 92.

subject of statute. The matter or thing forming the groundwork of the statute, the chief thing or matter to which it relates and with which it deals. The matter to which the statute in question relates and with which it deals, as distinguished from its object which is the aim or purpose of the enactment. 50 Am J1st Stat § 191.

As the word is employed in a constitutional provision requiring the subject of a statute to be expressed in its title, the word is used in a broad and extended sense, and is the thing forming the generic head of the matter submitted. It may include numerous minor subjects relating, germane to, and having a mutual connection with, the subject proper. See Kemp v State, 35 Okla Crim 128, 248 P 1116.

It is a very indefinite expression. A phrase may state the subject in a very general or indefinite manner, or with minute particularity. It is impossible to prescribe any standard of particularity for the legislature and the matter is left to legislative discretion. State ex rel. Bragg v Rogers, 107 Ala 444, 19 So 909.

See **single subject.**

subject of the action. The primary right of the plaintiff and a wrong in violation of such right, whereby a remedial right arises in his favor. Studebaker Corp. v Hanson, 24 Wyo 222, 157 P 582, 160 P 336. Not something relating to the thing itself about which the controversy has arisen, but rather the origin and ground of the plaintiff's right to recover or obtain the relief asked. Collier v Ervin, 3 Mont 142. Either the property which is sought to be recovered or alleged to be injured, or a substantive right which has been violated, to enforce or maintain which the action is brought. 20 Am J2d Countcl § 70.

subject to. Words of qualification. Consolidated Coal Co. v Peers, 166 Ill 361, 46 NE 1105. Words of qualification of the estate granted by a deed. 23 Am J2d Deeds § 217. Words of condition; sufficient to destroy the negotiability of the instrument where serving to subject the instrument to the terms of another agreement. 11 Am J2d B & N § 143. A phrase which, appearing in a contract, usually indicates that a promise is not to be performed except upon a condition or the happening of a stated event. Jones v Palace Realty Co. 226 NC 303, 37 SE2d 906. A phrase insufficient in itself to constitute the assumption of a mortgage. Anno: 101 ALR 284; 37 Am J1st Mtg § 998.

A provision in the assignment of a lease that it is "subject to" the agreements of the lessee contained in the lease does not constitute a contract obligating the assignee unqualifiedly to perform the duties imposed upon the lessee, so as to render him liable to reimburse the lessee, on account of rents which the lessee was compelled to pay and which accrued after the assignee resigned the term, as the words "subject to" are words of qualification and not words of contract. 32 Am J1st L & T § 350.

The words "subject to the terms of said lease" do not impose contractual liability on an assignee to a lessor to carry out the covenants of the lease. Coles Trading Co. v Spiegel (CA9 Ariz) 187 F2d 984, 24 ALR2d 702.

subject to final payment. A familiar condition in the banking business.

Where checks received by a bank from a depositor are credited to his account "subject to final payment," which provision is sometimes printed in the depositors' pass books as applying to out-of-town checks, the meaning of the provision is that if such a check is not paid upon its presentation to the drawee bank, the amount of it will be charged back to the depositor's account. See Douglas v Federal Reserve Bank, 271 US 489, 493, 70 L Ed 1051, 1053, 46 S Ct 554.

subject to restriction. A clause in a deed having reference to restrictions set forth in some other deed or instrument. 20 Am J2d Cov § 169.

subject to terms of. See **subject to.**

subject to the jurisdiction thereof. A phrase made familiar by inclusion in the Fourteenth Amendment.

As these words are used in the first section of the Fourteenth Amendment of the Federal Constitution, providing for the citizenship of all persons born or naturalized in the United States and subject to the jurisdiction thereof, the purpose would appear to have been to exclude by the fewest words (besides children of members of the Indian tribes, standing in a peculiar relation to the National Government, unknown to the common law), the two classes of cases, children born of alien enemies, in hostile occupation, and children of diplomatic representatives of a foreign state,—both of which, by the law of England and by our own law, from the time of the first settlement of the English colonies in America, had been recognized exceptions to the fundamental rule of citizenship by birth within the country. United States v Wong Kim Ark, 169 US 649, 682, 42 L Ed 890, 902, 18 S Ct 456.

sub judice (sub jö'di-sē). Before the court for its consideration and determination.

sub jugum matrimonii (sub jū'gum ma-tri-mō'nē-ī). Under the yoke of matrimony; the state of being married. Macfarland v Heim, 127 Mo 18.

Sublata causa tollitur effectus (sub-lā'ta kā'za tol'li-ter e-fek'tus). By removing the cause, the effect is removed.

Sublata veneratione majistratuum, respublica ruit (sub-lā'ta ve-ne-rā-she-ō'ne ma-ji-strā'tu-um, rĕz-pub'li-ka ru'it). The state is ruined by the loss of respect for magistrates.

Sublato fundamento, cadit opus (sub-lā'tō fun-da-men'tō, ka'dit ō'pus). With the removal of the foundation, the structure falls.

Sublato principali, tollitur adjunctum (sub-lā'tō prin-si-pā'lī, tol'li-ter ad-junk'tum). By the removal of the principal thing, the adjunct is removed.

sublease. A grant by a lessee of an interest in the demised premises, or a part thereof, less than his own, a reversion remaining in him. 32 Am J1st L & T § 392.

Where the sublease is for the whole term, it is, in law, an assignment, as between the original lessor and the sublessee, but may be given effect as a contract, as between the sublessor and sublessee. Davidson v Minnesota Loan & Trust Co. 158 Minn 411, 197 NW 833, 32 ALR 1418.

See **underlease.**

sublessee. A tenant who holds under a lease made by a sublessor.

See **sublease.**

sublessor. A lessee who has made a sublease.
See **sublease.**

subletting. Making a sublease. 32 Am J1st L & T § 393.
See **sublease.**

sublimation (sub li-mā'shon). Refining or purifying. The elimination of unwanted matter from alcoholic beverages. Commonwealth v Giltinan, 64 Pa 100, 105.

submarine. A vessel which can operate both on the sea and when submerged therein. A vessel for the purpose of admiralty jurisdiction. United States v Woodbury (CA1 Mass) 175 F2d 854.

submerged fen (sub-mėrjd' fen). A swamp or marsh covered with water for the time. Webber v Pere Marquette Boom Co. 62 Mich 626, 635.

submerged lands. Lands, particularly privately owned lands, covered by waters. Lands, once lying above water, since submerged. Mulry v Norton, 100 NE 426, 3 NE 581.
See **lands beneath navigable waters.**

Submerged Lands Act. A federal statute dealing with rights, titles, and interests in lands beneath navigable waters within state boundaries and Outer Continental Shelf Lands. 43 USC §§ 1301 et seq.

submergence. The disappearance of land under water and the formation of a navigable body of water over it, so that the submerged land is lost to the owner, except and until it be restored to him by reliction. Mulry v Norton, 100 NY 426, 3 NE 581.
See **subsidence.**

submission. A surrender or yielding, as to an arrest or a command. Referring a matter to another for consideration and decision, e.g., the act of the court in instructing the jury and sending them out to return a verdict.
See **final submission.**

submission agreement. See **agreement for submission.**

submission of controversy. The equivalent in some American jurisdictions of "agreed case." New York Tel. Co. v Siegel-Cooper Co. 202 NY 502, 96 NE 109.

submission to arbitration. Resort to arbitration for the settlement of a controversy.
See **agreement for submission; arbitration.**

submission to nonsuit. The act of the plaintiff in taking a voluntary nonsuit. Hartquist v Tamiami Trail Tours, 139 Fla 328, 190 So 533, 79 ALR 688.

submit. To be submissive. To make a submission.
See **submissive.**

sub modo (sub mō'dō). Subject to a modification or qualification; after a fashion; in some manner. See 2 Bl Comm 291.

subnormal intelligence. See **subnormal mentality.**

subnormal mentality. Weakness of intellect; deficiency in mental function. 21 Am J2d Crim L § 28. A possible defense to a criminal charge. State v Roy, 40 NM 397, 60 P2d 646, 110 ALR 1.

subordinate body. A local lodge or benefit society which owes allegiance to a state or national organization of the lodge or society. 36 Am J2d Frat O § 35.

subordinate fact. See **subsidiary fact.**

suborn (sub-ôrn'). To engage in subornation.
See **subornation.**

subornation (sub-ôr-nā'shọn). The crime of procuring another person to commit a crime. The procurement of the commission of an unlawful act.

subornation of perjury. The crime of procuring another to commit perjury by inciting, instigating, or persuading. 41 Am J1st Perj § 74. In a proper sense, the equivalent of perjury itself. United States v Silverman (CA3 Pa) 106 F2d 750.

suborner (sub-ôr'ner). One who suborns.
See **subornation.**

subpartnership. A so-called partnership formed between a member of a partnership and a third person for a division of the profits coming to him from the partnership enterprise, by an agreement of such a character as to disclose the essentials necessary to a partnership between the partner and the third person.

Such third person does not become a member of the first partnership nor is he liable for its debts. 40 Am J1st Partn § 14.

subpoena. The ordinary process by which the attendance of a witness in court is compelled, being issued by the clerk of court. 58 Am J1st Witn § 13. A writ or process in equity, equivalent to a summons in an action at law, through which a party is subjected to the jurisdiction of the court. Commercial Bank of Rodney v State, 12 Miss (4 Smedes & M) 439, 515.

subpoena ad testificandum (sub-pē'na ad tes-ti-fi-kan'dum). A writ to bring a witness into court to testify; a subpoena for a witness. See 3 Bl Comm 369.

subpoena duces tecum (sup-pē'na dū'sēz tē'kum). An ancient writ, having for its object the production of evidence to be used, so far as admissible, in a trial. In the modern sense, a subpoena which, in addition to the usual clauses requiring the attendance of the witness in court to testify, contains clauses directing him to produce at the same time for use as evidence in the litigation certain described books, papers, records, and documents. 58 Am J1st Witn §§ 20 et seq. A subpoena ordering the witness to bring with him the books, documents, or other evidence described in the subpoena. Langenberg v Decker, 131 Ind 471, 31 NE 190.

subpoena ticket. A ticket issued by a prosecuting attorney under which in some jurisdictions a witness is summoned to court to give his testimony in a criminal prosecution.

sub potestate (sub po-tes-tā'te). Under the protection.

sub potestate parentis (sub po-tes-tā'te pa-ren'tis). Under the protection of a parent. See 1 Bl Comm 465.

sub potestate viri (sub po-tes-tā'te vi'rī). Under the control of her husband.

Generally, at common law a woman can do no act to bind herself; she is said to be sub potestate viri, and subject to his will and control. Her acts are not voidable, but are void ab initio. Elliot v The Lessee of Peirsol (US) 1 Pet 328, 339, 7 L Ed 164, 169.

subreption. The fraudulent securing of escheated property by concealment of the truth.

subrogation. The substitution of one person in the place of another with reference to a lawful claim or right against a third person. The principle that when one person has been compelled to pay a debt which ought to have been paid by another, he becomes entitled to exercise all the remedies which the creditor possessed against that other person. 50 Am J1st Subro § 2. Sometimes referred to as the doctrine of substitution.

It is a device adopted or invented by equity to compel the ultimate discharge of a debt or obligation by him who in good conscience ought to pay it. It is the machinery by which the equity of one man is worked out through the legal rights of another. 50 Am J1st Subro §§ 2 et seq.

This is a substitution of another person in place of the creditor to whose rights he succeeds in relation to the debt, and gives to the substitute all the rights, priorities, remedies, liens, and securities of the person for whom he is substituted. The principle of subrogation is broad enough to cover every instance in which one person is required to pay a debt for which another is primarily answerable, and which in equity and good conscience ought to be discharged by the latter. United States Fidelity & G. Co. v Bramwell, 108 Or 261, 217 P 332, 32 ALR 829.

See **conventional subrogation; legal subrogation.**

subrogation by contract. See **conventional subrogation.**

subrogation of cotenant (sub-rọ-gā'shọn of kō-ten'-ạnt). The principle that a cotenant who has paid off or satisfied a debt secured by a mortgage or lien on the common property is entitled to assert the rights of the mortgagee or lienholder and to enforce the mortgage or lien as against his cotenant or cotenants to the extent that they should contribute to the satisfaction of the mortgage or lien. 20 Am J2d Coten § 67.

subrogation of insurer (sub-rō-gā-shọn of in-shör'ėr). The right of an insurer on payment of a loss to be subrogated pro tanto to any right of action which the insured may have had against any third person whose wrongful act or neglect caused the loss insured against by the insurer. 29A Am J Rev ed Ins § 1719.

Subrogatum tenet locum subrogati (sub-ro-gā'tum te'net lō'kum sub-ro-gā'tī). A subrogation takes the place of that which is subrogated.

The axiom should be understood as applicable, when the thing has been changed into something else by the owner, he having received the other thing in its place. Place v Norwich & New York Transp. Co. 118 US 468, 30 L Ed 134, 145, 6 S Ct 1150.

subrogee (sub-rō-jē'). A person who by subrogation acquires the rights of another person.

subrogor (sub-rō-gor'). One whose rights are acquired by another through subrogation.

sub rosa (sub rō'zạ). Under the rose; secretly; privately; clandestinely.

sub salvo et securo conducto (sub sal'vö et se-kū'rō kon-duk'tō). Under safe and secure conduct.

subscribe. To sign. To sanction. To agree to take and pay for corporate stock on the issuance thereof or for a newspaper or magazine to be issued periodically. To agree to take and pay for, as for corporate stock on the issuance thereof or for a newspaper or magazine to be issued periodically. To lend support to a charitable, religious, educational, theatrical, musical, or recreational organization by agreeing to contribute certain amounts thereto. 50 Am J1st Subscr § 1.

subscribed. Signed. Signed at the end of the instrument. Stone v Marvel, 45 NH 481.

subscribed and sworn to before me. An expression which, followed by the date and signature of the officer administering the oath, constitutes the jurat of an affidavit. 3 Am J2d Affi § 16.

subscriber. One who has subscribed to something. See **subscription to stock.**

subscribing witnesses. Attesting witnesses. 57 Am J1st Wills §§ 308 et seq.

subscription. A signature. A signature at the end of an instrument. 23 Am J2d Deeds § 24. The signing of one's name by way of giving sanction or effect to a document. 57 Am J1st Wills §§ 243, 336. An undertaking, either written or oral, to give or pay money or its equivalent, or to give property, in the furtherance and promotion of some object or undertaking, generally, an object or purpose for the promotion of which numerous persons are uniting their means and efforts. 50 Am J1st Subscr § 1. A promise in writing of a donation to a university or college. 15 Am J2d Colleges § 33. An application for a share or shares of a business trust. 13 Am J2d Bus Tr § 24.

subscription book. A record of the subscriptions made to an issue of corporate stock. 18 Am J2d Corp § 370.

subscription contract. A promise or undertaking to subscribe based upon a sufficient consideration, sometimes the promises of other subscribers. 50 Am J1st Subscr §§ 10 et seq. See **subscription to stock.**

subscription to newspaper. An agreement to accept the numbers of a newspaper as they are issued and to pay therefor, either in one sum for a year or in lesser sums for periods of a year.

To become a subscriber for a newspaper includes some voluntary act on the part of the subscriber, or something which is in effect an assent by him to the use of his name as a subscriber. A person to whom a paper is sent without his knowledge or consent, either expressed or implied, is not a subscriber. Ashton v Stoy, 86 Iowa 197, 64 NW 804.

subscription to stock. An agreement to subscribe for or take stock to be issued by a corporation. 18 Am J2d Corp § 291.

The legislature may prescribe the manner and mode of creation of a subscription contract and declare what shall amount to such a contract or what shall be evidence that the party proposing to take stock has completed the contract on his part. 18 Am J2d Corp § 292.

See **call.**

subscribing witness. Same as **attesting witness.**

subsequent. Coming after, whether in time, place, or order.

subsequent condition. See **condition subsequent.**

subsequent creditor. One who becomes a creditor following a transaction by the debtor brought up for consideration, such as a conveyance made to defraud or delay creditors.

subsequent negligence. Negligence operating at the time an injury is sustained and as the cause thereof, as distinguished from negligence operating prior to the accident but in some degree connected therewith. Negligence which is the proximate, as distinguished from the remote, cause of an injury.

subsequent offender. See **habitual criminal.**

Holwerson v St. Louis & Suburban Railway Co. 157 Mo 216, 57 SW 770.

subsequent purchaser. A purchaser under a later purchase of the same premises from the same grantor or one in the chain of record title running from such grantor.
While not including a purchaser from an apparent stranger to the title of the grantor in the unrecorded deed, the term does include not only the purchaser from the grantor himself, but every subsequent purchaser from one who appears from the records to be the owner of, or to be authorized to convey, the title and interest that the grantor had when he made a deed which has not been recorded. 45 Am J1st Recds § 149.

subsequent purchaser for value. See **bona fide purchaser.**

subsequent purchaser in good faith. See **bona fide purchaser.**

subservient possession. See **permissive possession.**

subsidence. The sinking of land, as where support has been removed by mining. Anno: 35 ALR 1137; 36 Am J1st Min & M § 184. A shifting, falling, slipping, seeping, or oozing of the soil from its natural position, caused by the removal of support. Levi v Schwartz, 201 Md 575, 95 A2d 322, 36 ALR2d 1241.
See **submerged lands; submergence.**

subsidiary. A corporation, all or the majority of the stock of which is owned by another corporation, so that the latter is in the relation to it of a parent corporation. A corporation which is controlled by another corporation by reason of the latter company's ownership of at least a majority of the shares of the capital stock. 18 Am J2d Corp § 17.

subsidiary corporation. See **subsidiary.**

subsidiary fact. A fact indeterminate of an issue in itself, although of some weight in the determination of the ultimate fact. Baumgartner v United States, 322 US 665, 88 L Ed 1525, 64 S Ct 1240.

subsidiary trust. A trust auxiliary to a business trust. Beilin v Krenn & Dato, 350 Ill 284, 183 NE 330.

subsidium. See **in subsidium.**

sub sigillo (sub si-jil'lo). Under seal. State v Buchanan (Md) 5 Harr & J 317.

sub silentio (sub sī-len'she-ō). Silently.

subsistence. A means of support. Wall v Williams, 93 NC 327. An allowance to an enlisted man of the armed forces for living expenses, made under certain circumstances. 36 Am J1st Mil § 34. An allowance for a defendant wife in an action for divorce, brought against her in a state other than that of her domicil, to cover her living expenses while in the state for the purpose of defending the suit. State ex rel. Pearce v Superior Court, 34 Wash 2d 768, 209 P2d 906.

subsistence allowance. See **subsistence.**

subsistence loans. See **production and subsistence loans.**

sub spe reconciliationis (sub spē re-kon-si-li-ā-she-ō'nis). In the hope of reconciliation.

substance. Essentials. The antithesis of "form." State v Japone, 202 Iowa 450, 455, 209 NW 468, 471.

substance of indictment. The essential allegations.
When an indictment is adjudged to be insufficient in substance, it is because it lacks something essential to make a legal charge of crime. Certain portions of an indictment are formal and some substantial. The statement or body of the indictment must set forth all the ingredients of the offense, and charge the defendant directly and positively with the commission of it. This is the substance of the charge, because essential to it. State v Burgdoerfer, 107 Mo 1, 17 SW 646.

substance over form. A determination of the effect of a transaction according to the substance of the matter rather than the particular form or label adopted in designating it. Re Smiley, 35 Wash 2d 863, 216 P2d 212.

substantial adverse claim. A claim which is real and actual, as distinguished from one which is merely colorable. A claim disclosing a contested matter of right involving at least a fair doubt and reasonable room for controversy in matters of law or fact. Harrison v Chamberlin, 271 US 191, 70 L Ed 897, 46 S Ct 467 (claim sufficient to deprive court of bankruptcy of constructive possession of property).

substantial breach. Same as **material breach.**

substantial claim. See **substantial adverse claim.**

substantial compliance. See **substantial performance.**

substantial consummation of reorganization plan. The occurrence of each of the following events:(1) transfer, sale, or other disposition of all or substantially all of the property dealt with by the plan pursuant to the provisions of the plan; (2) assumption of operation of the business and management of all or substantially all of the property dealt with by the plan by the debtor or by the corporation used for the purpose of carrying out the plan: and (3) commencement of the distribution to creditors and stockholders, affected by the plan, of the cash and securities specified in the plan. Bankruptcy Act § 229(a); 11 USC § 629(a).

substantial destruction. As a condition relieving a tenant from liability for rent:—an effective destruction of the building so complete that the building is untenantable and restoration will amount in effect to the construction of a new building. 32 Am J1st L & T § 506.

substantial error. An error which upon the trial works harm and from which a party sustains substantial injury. People v Perlman, 128 Misc 68, 71, 217 NYS 662, 665. An error of the trial court which operates in the impairment of a substantial right of the accused. 5 Am J2d A & E § 778.

substantial evidence. Evidence beyond a scintilla; evidence affording a substantial basis of fact from which the fact in issue can reasonably be inferred. 31 Am J Rev ed Lab § 338. Such relevant evidence as a reasonable man would accept as adequate to support the conclusion sought to be drawn from it. Anno: 123 ALR 647; 83 L Ed 691. Such evidence as will convince reasonable men and on which such men may not reasonably differ as to whether it establishes a case or defense. Morton v Mooney, 97 Mont 1, 33 P2d 262.
Substantial evidence means more than a mere scintilla. It is of substantial and relevant consequence and excludes vague, uncertain, or irrelevant matter. It implies a quality of proof which induces conviction and makes an impression on reason. It means that one weighing the evidence takes into consideration the facts presented to him and all reasonable inferences, deductions and conclusions

to be drawn therefrom and, considering them in their entirety and relation to each other, arrives at a fixed conviction. NLRB v Union Pacific Stages (CA9) 99 F2d 153.

substantial evidence rule. The rule that a determination of fact by an administrative body should be upheld unless arbitrary or clearly wrong; that a ruling based on findings supported by substantial evidence shall be sustained unless they rest on erroneous legal foundations. NLRB v Babcock & Wilcox Co. 351 US 105, 100 L Ed 975, 76 S Ct 679.

substantialibus. See **in substantialibus.**

substantial justice rule. The rule that a judgment shall not be reversed if it appears that there has been no error in reference to substantive principles, that substantial justice has been done, and that such error as occurred in the lower court was technical. West v State, 24 Ariz 237, 208 P 412.

substantially. In the main. Essentially.

substantially as set forth. Words of reference to another document. Sufficient in a claim of a patent to import into the claim the particulars of the specifications. Westinghouse v Boyden Power Brake Co. 170 US 537, 42 L Ed 1136, 18 S Ct 707.

These words in the claim of a patent, do not limit the patentee to the exact mechanism described in his specifications, or prevent recovery against infringers who have adopted mechanical equivalents for such mechanism. 40 Am J1st Pat § 93.

substantially prevailing party. The party entitled to costs on appeal where the judgment of the lower court is affirmed in part and reversed in part. 5 Am J2d A & E § 1014.

substantially reversed. A modification on appeal so inclusive of the whole judgment that there is an entire rather than a partial reversal. 5 Am J2d A & E § 1032.

substantial performance. Performance of a contract which, while not a full performance, is performance in good faith, and in compliance with the contract except perhaps for minor and relatively unimportant deviations. 17 Am J2d Contr § 378. Performance of all the essentials necessary to the full accomplishment of the purposes of the contract. 13 Am J2d Bldg Contr § 43. Performance short of full performance but sufficient to substantiate a recovery of the contract price less a deduction for want of completion of the work. 58 Am J1st W & L § 52. Such an approximation to complete performance of a building contract that the owner obtains substantially what was called for by the contract, although it may not be the same in every particular, and although there may be omissions and imperfections on account of which there should be a deduction from the contract price. Handy v Bliss, 204 Mass 513, 90 NE 864. In one sense, full performance according to the fair intent of the contract. In another sense, performance distinctly short of full performance. 46 Am J1st Sales § 213.

substantial performance doctrine. The principle that where there has been a breach of one of several promises, the question whether there has been a failure of consideration, a complete failure or a partial failure, is determined according to whether or not there has been a substantial performance of the contract. 11 Am J2d B & N § 244.

See **substantial performance.**

substantial possession. Actual possession in the sense of actual occupancy of the entire tract under consideration. Wheeler v Clark, 114 Tenn 117, 85 SW 258.

substantial right. An essential, as distinguished from a technical, right. Sullivan v Storz, 156 Neb 177, 55 NW2d 499, 34 ALR2d 1142. That which concerns the subject matter of the action or proceeding.

The fact that a matter is discretionary does not prevent it from being a matter affecting a substantial right. Re Engebretson, 68 SD 255, 1 NW2d 351, 142 ALR 1454.

substantive due process. Freedom from arbitrary action coupled with the equal operation of the laws. 16 Am J2d Const L § 550.

substantive law. That part of the law which creates, defines, and regulates rights, as distinguished from the part which prescribes the remedies and the procedure for the enforcement of rights. Hardie v Bryson (DC Mo) 44 F Supp 67; Mix v Board of County Comrs. 18 Idaho 695, 112 P 215.

A statute or other rule of law will be characterized as substantive or procedural according to the nature of the problem for which a characterization must be made. Grant v McAuliffe, 41 Cal 2d 859, 264 P2d 944, 42 ALR2d 1162.

substitute. One who, or that which, stands in the place of another; that which stands in lieu of something else. State v Fargo Bottling Works Co. 19 ND 396, 124 NW 387. (Civil law.) A person to whom an "institute" appointed by will is by the will directed to transfer property which is by the will devised to him.

See **institute; substituted.**

substitute bill of lading. A bill of lading issued in place of a bill which has been lost, stolen, or destroyed. 13 Am J2d Car § 421.

substituted. One person or one thing acting, serving, or occupying the place of another.

The word describes a replacement of one thing by another and, in most of its ordinary uses, implies the removal or elimination of the thing replaced. But this definition is not reliable when one is dealing with legal relations as when concrete objects are in mind. For example, we have the common case of a substituted trustee, in which the original trustee ceases to act and have the powers of a trustee, but he continues to be liable as a trustee for his acts while in office. Fidelity-Philadelphia Trust Co. v Hale & Kilburn Corporation (DC Pa) 24 F Supp 3.

substituted administrator. See **administrator de bonis non.**

substituted automobile. See **substituted vehicle.**

substituted bequest. See **substitution by will.**

substituted executor. See **substitutionary executor.**

substituted legacy. See **substitution by will.**

substituted party. See **substitution of parties.**

substituted service. Service of process by leaving a copy of the summons or writ with a suitable person at the residence, dwelling house, or place of abode of the party to be served. 42 Am J1st Proc § 60. In some jurisdictions, the equivalent of actual or personal service. Grant v Lawrence, 37 Utah 540, 108 P 931. A term applied in some jurisdictions to **service by mail** or **service by publication.**

substituted shipment. A substitution of goods for the goods specified in a bill of lading. 13 Am J2d Car § 373.

substituted tax return. The replacement of one income tax return by another as a matter of right of the taxpayer within the period allowed by statute for filing returns or within such extended time as the commissioner may grant under the statute. J. E. Riley Invest. Co. v Commissioner (CA9) 110 F2d 655.

substituted trustee. A trustee who, when appointed, steps into the place of the old trustee, charged with the trust, and with all the powers and duties of the old trustee. 54 Am J1st Trusts § 133.

Although the original trustee ceases to act and have the powers of a trustee, he continues to be liable as a trustee for his acts while in office. Fidelity-Philadelphia Trust Co. v Hale & Filburn Corp. (DC Pa) 24 F Supp 3.

substituted vehicle. A familiar term in the field of automobile insurance; a vehicle temporarily used by the insured, where the automobile described in the policy is withdrawn from use because of breakdown, repair, servicing, loss, or destruction. 7 Am J2d Auto Ins § 103.

substitute judge. A judge selected to act in the absence, disability, or disqualification of the regular judge, or under other circumstances, as provided by constitution or statute. 30A Am J Rev ed Judges § 237.

substitute juror. See **alternate juror**.

substitute paper. An instrument for the payment of money given by way of substitution for a lost, destroyed, or mutilated instrument, of the same tenor. 11 Am J2d B & N § 59.

See **substitute bill of lading**.

substitution. Putting one person or one thing in the place of another. Subrogation.

As the term is used in the law of wills, to create a substitution is to bequeath property to one or more persons, to be succeeded in the enjoyment thereof by others designated by the testator. Succession of Meunier, 52 La Ann 79, 26 So 776.

See **subrogation; substitution by will**.

substitutional gift. See **substitution by will**.

substitutional remainders. See **alternative remainders**. 28 Am J2d Est § 216.

substitutionary bequest. See **substitution by will**.

substitutionary executor (sub-sti-tū′shǫn-ā-ri eg-zek′-ū-tǫr). A person nominated by a will to act as executor in the event of the death, inability, or refusal to act, of the person first named. Edwards' Estate (Pa) 12 Phila 85.

substitution by will. The effect of a clause in a will whereby the testator provides for the replacement of the beneficiary of a particular bequest by another person, or the replacement of a bequest to a designated beneficiary by another bequest to or in favor of the same beneficiary, under circumstances set forth in the clause. 57 Am J1st Wills § 1181. A gift over, that is, a gift to a charity to take effect in the event a designated gift does not take effect. Re Harrington's Estate, 151 Neb 81, 36 NW2d 577. A gift by later will or codicil in substitution for a gift made to the same beneficiary by the original will. Anno: 37 ALR2d 17, 48.

A testamentary gift is substitutional where the testator provides that someone shall take it in event of the death of the original beneficiary before the period of distribution. One taking by substitution can take only under the terms of the will, subject to the same conditions as are attached to the gift. Re Waring, 293 NY 186, 56 NE2d 543, 157 ALR 1101.

substitution clause in policy. A provision in an automobile liability policy whereby coverage is extended to the use of an automobile driven by the insured by way of substitution for the vehicle designated in the policy of insurance. 7 Am J2d Auto Ins § 103.

substitution clause in will. See **substitution by will**.

substitution doctrine. Another term for **subrogation**. 50 Am J1st Subro § 2.

substitution of attorney. The change made by a party in his attorney of record in a pending case, such substitution of one attorney for another being a matter of right, except where the original attorney has an interest in the subject matter of the suit, and accomplished under accepted procedure by an order of substitution obtained on motion. 7 Am J2d Attys § 148.

substitution of debtor. A novation. 39 Am J1st Nov § 13.

See **imperfect delegation**.

substitution of parties. A change of parties by the substitution of a new plaintiff or defendant for the original plaintiff or defendant, accomplished by an amendment of the pleading and process as permitted by an order of court, such order being granted only where a new cause of action is not introduced by the amendment. 39 Am J1st Parties § 98. The revival of an action upon the death of a party by the personal representative, heir, or devisee. 1 Am J2d Abat & R §§ 120 et seq. A novation by the substitution of a new debtor for an old one. 39 Am J1st Nov § 13.

A substitute defendant in the true sense of the term is one who takes the place of another defendant in the same suit or controversy, not one who is sued upon an entirely different cause of action. McCann v Bentley Stores Corp. (DC Mo) 34 F Supp 231.

sub suo periculo (sub su′ō pe-ri′ku-lō). At his own risk.

subsurface entry. An entry upon land made below the surface thereof, for example, by excavation in the course of mining. 52 Am J1st Tresp § 14.

subsurface use. The use of space below a highway by abutting owners for private purposes. 25 Am J1st High § 198.

subtenant. The lessee under a sublease. A person who rents all or a portion of leased premises from the lessee for a term less than the original one, leaving a reversionary interest in the first lessee. 32 Am J1st L & T § 392.

subterfuge (sub′tẽr-fūj). Something resorted to for concealment. Foster-Fountain Packing Co. v Haydel, 278 US 1, 73 L Ed 147, 49 S Ct 1. A plan or scheme to escape or avoid responsibility for one's acts.

subterranean stream (sub-tẹ-rā′nẹ-ạn strēm). A definite and known channel in which subterranean waters flow. 56 Am J1st Water § 103. Underground waters flowing in a distinct, well-defined and permanent channel, as distinguished from percolating waters which spread in every direction through the earth. Tampa Waterworks Co. v Cline, 33 Fla 586, 20 So 780.

subterranean waters (sub-tẹ-rā′nẹ-ạn wâ′ters). Underground bodies or streams of water flowing in

subtraction. The process of taking one number from a larger number to find the difference. The neglect to perform a suit, duty, custom, or service which a person owes to another.

It was a wrong which had chiefly to do with those duties and services, arising out of land tenure, which a tenant owed his landlord, and included the duty or service of paying rent. See 3 Bl Comm 230.

suburb. A township, village, or other municipality adjacent to a city, having an identity because of the number of residents or the business or industrial operations therein conducted.

subversion. Subversive activities.
See **subversive**.

subversive (sub-vĕr'siv). Noun: One who seeks to undermine and overthrow established authority of the government. An organization that teaches and advocates the overthrow of government by force or violence. Adler v Board of Education, 342 US 485, 96 L Ed 517, 72 S Ct 380, 27 ALR2d 472. Adjective: Undermining the foundation of government.

Mere personal abstention from violence, or even from violent language, does not secure immunity from deportation as a subversive alien, if the result of the gentlest and most guarded speech is to advocate or teach that subversion which is condemned by statute. The "philosophic" anarchist is an anarchist nevertheless. United States ex rel. Georgian v Uhl (CA2 NY) 271 F 676, cert den 256 US 701, 65 L Ed 1178, 41 S Ct 623.
See **sedition; treason**.

subversive alien. See **subversive**.

sub voce (sub vō'sē). Under the word or title.

subway. An underground way or passage. A means of public transportation below the surface of the street, particularly an underground electric railway or bus line. 25 Am J1st High § 200.

successful party. See **prevailing party**.

succession. Following another; succeeding to the rights of another, as where a new corporation which is a reorganization of another corporation takes the rights of the old corporation. 19 Am J2d Corp § 1524. The passing of property in possession or enjoyment, present or future, and dispositions of property by will, deed, or laws of descent, by reason whereof any person shall become entitled in possession or expectancy to property upon the death of any other person. Wright v Blakeslee, 101 US 174, 25 L Ed 1048.

The word is one of technical meaning in the law and signifies the taking of property by inheritance or will from the estate of a decedent, or by operation of law; and it is a word which clearly excludes those who take by deed, grant, gift, or any form of purchase or contract. Quarles v Clayton, 87 Tenn 308, 10 SW 505.
See **descent; hereditary succession; intestate succession; perpetual succession; universal succession**.

succession ab intestato (suk-sesh'on ab in-tes-tā'tō). (Civil law.) The descent or inheritance of property from one who has died without leaving a will. See 2 Bl Comm 490.

succession duty. A succession tax.

Successionis feudi talis est natura, quod ascendentes non succedunt (suk-se-she-ō'nis fū'dī tā'lis est na-tū'ra, quod a-sen-den'tēz non suk-sē'dunt). The nature of feudal succession is such that persons in the ascending line do not inherit. See 2 Bl Comm 211.

succession tax. An excise on the privilege of taking property by will, inheritance, or succession in any other form, upon the death of the owner. A tax upon the right to receive property from the estate of the decedent. McLaughlin v Green, 136 Conn 138, 69 A2d 289, 15 ALR2d 1210; Chase v Commissioner of Taxation, 226 Minn 521, 33 NW2d 706, 6 ALR2d 214. A tax imposed upon a legacy, devise, or distributive share of the estate of a decedent, not upon the estate. Re Rath, 10 Cal 2d 399, 75 P2d 509, 115 ALR 836; Re Daniels' Estate, 159 Ohio St 109, 50 Ohio Ops 79, 111 NE2d 252. Sometimes used loosely as inclusive of an estate tax on the theory that it is a duty or tax upon the transmission of a decedent's property, that is, his whole estate.

succession words. See **words of inheritance**.

successive. In succession; following in a regular sequence.

A grant of the right to "successive renewals" of a lease does not grant a right to renew indefinitely, since the word "successive" imports concatenation, and not duration. Geyer v Lietzan, 230 Ind 404, 103 NE2d 199, 31 ALR2d 601.

successive assignees. Persons who have acquired the same claim by a succession of assignments, one assignee assigning to another, the latter to still another, etc. Persons who have in succession acquired the same claim from the same assignor. 6 Am J2d Assign § 113. Two assignees for the benefit of creditors, one being appointed upon the death, disability, or removal from office of the other. 6 Am J2d Assign for Crs § 92.

successive disabilities. One personal disability succeeded by another, as where mental incompetency follows infancy. 34 Am J1st Lim Ac § 210. Disabilities of different persons where an estate passes by descent, devise, or purchase from one person under disability to another person under disability. 34 Am J1st Lim Ac § 211.

successive indictments. See **reindictment**.

successive renewals. See **successive**.

successive transactions. See **repeated transactions**.

successive trespasses. See **repeated trespasses**.

successor. One who assumes a public office upon expiration of term, retirement, resignation, or removal of a prior incumbent. One who follows another, as an heir follows the ancestor. One who follows another in interest. Inclusive of an executor. West Shore R. Co. v Wenner, 70 NJL 233, 57 A 508, reaffirmed 71 NJL 682, 60 A 1134.

A corporation may be considered the "successor" of another, although both corporations retain their corporate identity, dependent upon the facts and surrounding circumstances, and this status may exist in the absence of either an amalgamation, merger, or technical consolidation. North Texas Nat. Bank v Thompson (Tex Civ App) 23 SW2d 494.
See **hereditary successor; representative**.

successors. A term in a contract indicating assignability. 6 Am J2d Assign § 10.

The use of the word in an order of the National Labor Relations Board has been upheld by the United States Supreme Court, although the court

has indicated that the liability of such a successor in regard to carrying out a board order is dependent more on the nature of the transaction between the parties than on the wording of the order. Regal Knitwear Co. v NLRB, 324 US 9, 89 L Ed 661, 65 S Ct 478, affg (CA2) 140 F2d 746.
See **successor**.

successors and assigns. Words of limitation in a deed to a corporation.

successors in interest. Successive owners.
As used in a statute affecting transfers of property with intent to defraud creditors and making such transfers void as against all creditors and their "successors in interest," the term was held to include the assignees of such creditors. Windhaus v Bootz, 3 Cal 351, 25 P 404.

successor trustee. Same as **substitute trustee**.

Succurritur minori; facilis est lapsus juventutis (suker'ri-ter mī-nō'rī; fa'si-lis est lap'sus ju-ven-tū'tis). A minor should be favored; youth errs easily.

sucesión legitima. (Spanish.) Lawful issue. Ortiz De Rodriguez v Vivoni, 201 US 371, 376, 50 L Ed 792, 794, 26 S Ct 475.

suction (suk'shon). A sucking force. Displacement waves sometimes caused by large and powerful vessels when they are propelled at a high rate of speed.
The liability of the vessel and her owner for damage resulting to other properly handled craft from this source, is well settled. See 48 Am J1st Ship § 280.

sudden (sud'n). Hasty. Unforeseen; unexpected.

sudden anger. See **sudden passion**.

sudden emergency. An occurrence fraught with danger which is unexpected and occurs so abruptly as to be unnoticed before the peril is presented. Booth v Price, 183 Ark 975, 39 SW2d 717, 76 ALR 957.

sudden emergency doctrine. The principal of the law of negligence that one placed in a position of sudden emergency or peril other than by his own negligence may be held free from negligence or contributory negligence, although he would be charged with negligence if he had been given sufficient time for thought and reflection. 38 Am J1st Negl § 41.

suddenly. Happening without previous notice, or with very brief notice; coming unexpectedly; rapid and unforeseen; hastily prepared, employed, made, or done; unexpected, unusual, abrupt; unlooked for. Anno: 122 ALR 840.

sudden passion. Characteristically of sudden development.
In the definition of manslaughter as homicide committed without premeditation but under the influence of "sudden passion," the words mean any intense and vehement emotional excitement of the kind prompting to violent and aggressive action, as rage, anger, hatred, furious resentment or terror. State v Linville, 148 Kan 142, 79 P2d 869.

sudden peril. See **sudden emergency**.

sue (sū). To prosecute; to make legal claim; to seek for in law.
The word appears to be properly applicable to civil actions and suits and to criminal prosecutions as well. Bacon says, "An indictment is defined as an accusation at the suit of the king." See United States v Moore (CC NH) 11 F 248, 251.
See **covenant not to sue; put in suit**.

sue and labor clause. Same as **rescue clause**.

sue out. To obtain writ, process, or order of court upon an application therefor. Anno: 27 ALR2d 267.
Process is "sued out" when it has been issued and delivered to a person qualified and authorized to serve it. Maddox v Humphries, 30 Tex 494, 497.

suertes (soo-err-tay). A term found in Spanish-American grants, meaning plots of ground within the limits of a city, pueblo, or town, for sowing grounds, of a larger size than "solares," for cultivating or planting, as gardens, vineyards, orchards, etc. Hart v Burnett, 15 Cal 530, 555.

sue upon. See **sue; put in suit**.

suffer. To feel or endure mental or physical pain or distress. To endure. To authorize or permit by approval or acquiescence in an act or course of conduct. New York Life Ins. Co. v Calhoun (CA8 Mo) 97 F2d 896.
To suffer implies not merely nonresistance to that which is done, but also an approval of, or at least an acquiescence in, it, with an ability to prevent it. Purinton v Jamrock, 195 Mass 187, 80 NE 802.

sufferance (suf'ėr-ans). Endurance of pain or distress, physical or mental. Toleration; acquiescence.
See **bill of sufferance; estate by sufferance; tenancy at sufferance**.

suffer a nonsuit. To be subjected to a nonsuit. Having one's case taken out of court by an order of court. 24 Am J2d Dism § 72; 34 Am J1st Lim Ac § 282.

suffering. Physical pain; mental anguish.
There is no adequate definition of pain; the best that can be done is to describe a reaction to pain. This reaction is the body's awareness of unpleasant changes or activities that call attention to a particular region of the body. Pain is thus a protopathic sensation located in the nervous system. Recognition of the possible danger resulting from this sensation is "suffering," as distinguished from the initial and continuing pain. Sometimes courts refer to this type of pain and suffering as physical pain and suffering. 22 Am J2d Damg § 105.
The word "suffering" in a policy of insurance on an animal against destruction "necessary in order to immediately relieve incurable suffering" means conscious pain, so acute as to demand action without delay in order to put the animal out of its misery. Abraham v Insurance Co. of N. A. 117 Vt 75, 84 A2d 670, 29 ALR2d 783.

suffering a prisoner to escape. A criminal offense, sometimes a basis of civil liability, on the part of the custodian of a prison in voluntarily permitting a prisoner to escape. 27 Am J2d Escape § 21.

suffer to run at large. Intentionally or negligently permitting one's animals to stray from one's premises upon the premises of others or the highway. Serr v Biwabik Concrete Aggregate Co. 202 Minn 165, 278 NW 355, 117 ALR 1019.

sufficient. Adequate. So much as is needed. Equal to the purpose proposed. Pensacola & Atlantic Railroad Co. v State, 25 Fla 310, 5 So 833.

sufficient bail. See **sufficient sureties**.

sufficient consideration. That which is actually given, suffered, or accepted for a promise, whether slight or significant, and whether reducible or not to a pecuniary value, provided it is a present consideration or within one of the judicial or statutory exceptions to the requirement of a present consideration. 17 Am J2d Contr § 92.

sufficient deed. See **good and sufficient deed.**

sufficient description. That description which will enable third persons, aided by inquiries which the instrument itself indicates and directs, to identify the property. Sandwich Mfg. Co. v Robinson, 83 Iowa 567, 49 NW 1031 (requisite of description of mortgaged property in a chattel mortgage).

sufficient evidence. Abstractly, evidence of such probative value as to support the verdict of the jury or a finding of fact by the court. Practically, evidence such as will satisfy an unprejudiced mind of the truth of that which the court or jury has found to be the fact. Re Cruson, 189 Or 537, 221 P2d 892, 20 ALR2d 219.

Where a statute provides that the schedule of rates fixed by the commissioners shall be "sufficient" evidence that the rates thus fixed were just and reasonable, the word "sufficient" does not mean "conclusive." Pensacola & Atlantic Railroad Co. v State, 25 Fla 310, 5 So 833.

sufficient fence. Nothing less than a fence which meets the requirements of the law or the agreement of the parties in respect of its character. 22 Am J2d Fen § 23.

sufficient possession. As the basis of an action of forcible entry and detainer in case of dispossession: —an actual, quiet, and peaceable possession. Schwinn v Perkins, 79 NJL 515, 78 A 19. To support a claim of adverse possession:— possession, under a claim of right or title, for the whole period prescribed by the statute, which is actual, open, visible, notorious, continuous, and hostile to the true owner's title and to the world at large. 3 Am J2d Adv P § 6.

sufficient provocation. See **reasonable provocation.**

sufficient sureties. Sureties on a bail bond of financial ability to respond in payment of the amount of the bond and of sufficient vigilance to secure the appearance and prevent the absconding of the accused. 8 Am J2d Bail § 82.

suffix (su-fiks). Something added to a word to give a distinctive meaning. A word or abbreviation following a name, such as "Sr." 38 Am J1st Name § 9.

suffocation. See **asphyxiation.**

suffragan (suf'ra-gan). An assistant bishop.

suffrage. The right to vote; a political right or privilege as distinguished from a civil right, property right, or right of person. A conventional right, subject to regulation by the legislature to any extent not prohibited by the express or implied provisions of state of federal constitutions; a right which does not exist except as granted by the constitution and laws enacted pursuant thereto. 25 Am J2d Elect § 53. A privilege rather than a right, being dependent upon public policy as expressed in constitution or statute. Chamberlin v Wood, 15 SD 216, 88 NW 109.

sugar bounty. A bounty provided for in 1890 by act of Congress on the production of all kinds of sugar in the United States.

After the sugar producers, in reliance upon the act, had made extensive and costly preparations, by enlarging their plants, to profit by the bounty, Congress, believing the legislation to be unconstitutional, as it probably was, repealed it. A later act of Congress, in 1895, provided for financial relief of those who had suffered by the repeal of the act of 1890, and this later act was upheld by the Supreme Court. United States v Realty Co. 163 US 427, 41 L Ed 215, 16 S Ct 1120.

Sugar Trust (shŭg'ạr trust). See **trust.**

suggest. To bring an idea to the attention of another for consideration. A word which may or may not be precatory, depending upon the context in which it appears and the circumstances under which it occurs.

Where the word is used in a will, without any qualifying or explanatory words or circumstances to affect its ordinary meaning, it has been held merely to place a matter before another for consideration, and, under ordinary circumstances, in no wise to carry with it an expression of desire, will or entreaty. When so used, it is not a precatory word and is insufficient to create a trust. Williams v Baptist Church of Baltimore, 92 Md 497, 48 A 930.

suggested price. A retail price suggested or recommended to a dealer by the producer or manufacturer. 52 Am J1st Tradem § 185.

suggestio falsi (su-jes'ti-ō fal'sī). A suggestion of that which is false or untrue; a misrepresentation. 37 Am J2d Fraud § 144.

suggestion award. An award made by a corporation or other business enterprise to an employee for a suggestion respecting possible new products, improvement of product, saving in cost of production, etc.

suggestion of death. Calling the death of a party to the attention of a court and making it a matter of record, such being a step in the revival of an action abated by the death of a party. 1 Am J2d Abat & R § 118.

suggestive matters. Matters relative to the issue, whether preceding or following the commission of a civil wrong or criminal act. 29 Am J2d Ev §§ 270 et seq.

suicide. Death by one's own hand intentionally lifted against himself. 29A Am J Rev ed Ins § 1145.

By statute in Missouri, "every person deliberately assisting another in the commission of self-murder shall be deemed guilty of manslaughter in the first degree." State v Webb, 216 Mo 378, 115 SW 998.

By the early common law of England, suicide was ranked as an infamous crime and was held to be a "species of felony" punishable by a forfeiture to the king of the goods and chattels of the felo de se, and an ignominious burial in the highway with a stake driven through his body. Suicide has never been classed as a crime in the United States, but there are cases holding attempted suicide to be an offense, even in the absence of statute. 26 Am J1st Homi §§ 84-86.

suicide pact. A mutual agreement to commit suicide. 26 Am J1st Homi § 85.

suicide, sane or insane. See **sane or insane clause.**

sui generis (sū-i jen'ẹ-ris). Of its own kind, peculiar, for example, a statutory proceeding for declaratory judgment, neither legal nor equitable. Moss v Moss, 20 Cal 2d 640, 128 P2d 526, 141 ALR 1422.

sui juris (sū'ī jō'ris). Of full capacity. In his own right; capable of entering into a contract. See 1 Bl Comm 443.

For definition of the term as it pertains to contributory negligence of children see Anno: 107 ALR 161.

suit. An action; a legal proceeding of a civil kind. Re Oliver, 77 Ohio St 474, 83 NE 795. Any proceeding in a court of justice by which a person pursues therein that remedy which the law affords him. Upshur County v Rich, 135 US 467, 34 L Ed 196, 10 S Ct 651. A term broader than "action," since it is inclusive of all judicial proceedings whether actions or not. 1 Am J2d Actions § 4. Not inclusive of a proceeding in continuation of an original action, such as a proceeding for modification of a decree. Anno: 143 ALR 414. Not inclusive of a criminal prosecution. Anno: 40 ALR2d 1397. Inclusive of a criminal prosecution, since an indictment or information is an accusation at the "suit" of the sovereign. United States v Moore (CC NH) 11 F 248, 251.

"It must be conceded that the word, as applied to legal controversies, both by the legal profession and others, is now used and recognized as a generic term of broad significance, often understood and used, even by legislatures and courts, to designate almost any proceeding in a court, even, though rarely, being applied to a criminal prosecution in certain connections." Patterson v Standard Acci. Ins. Co. 178 Mich 288, 144 NW 491.

Historically, "action" is more properly applied to a legal remedy only, whereas "suit" is more properly applied to an equitable remedy only, but this distinction is no longer regarded as important. 1 Am J2d Actions § 4.

To do suit was a feudal service of the tenant to follow the lord in his courts in time of peace and in his armies or warlike retinue in time of warfare. See 2 Bl Comm 54.

For particular suits, see definitions commencing **actio; action.**

suitable monument. See **monument.**

suitable watch. See **constant watch.**

suit against the state. See **action against the state.**

suit at common law. See **action at common law.**

suitcase. A flat traveling bag.
See **baggage.**

suit club. A scheme devised for the distribution of clothes by chance; a form of lottery. 34 Am J1st Lot § 13.

suit for discovery. A bill wherein the only relief sought is a discovery, no demand being made for the recovery of damages or the accomplishment of anything other than a disclosure by the defendant. 23 Am J2d Dep § 141.

suit for partition. See **action in partition.**

suit in condemnation. See **eminent domain.**

suit in equity. An action in equity. A suit prosecuted and tried in accordance with the modes of procedure known to courts of equity. 27 Am J2d Equity § 177.

Under modern statutes in most jurisdictions, an action in equity is an ordinary civil action. It is still important, however to determine whether the case is one at law or in equity, since the character of the case may determine such matters as the method of review, the right to a jury trial, etc. 1 Am J2d Actions § 7.

An action involving an alleged infringement of trademark and seeking an injunction against the defendants and an accounting of their profits is in the nature of an old action in equity, and, as such, is triable before a court without a jury. Folmer Graflex Corp. v Graphic Photo Service (DC NY) 41 F 319.

suit money. The money necessary to enable a married woman to carry on or defend a matrimonial action. Rubin v Rubin, 233 Md 118, 195 A2d 696, 99 ALR2d 256.

suit of a civil nature. Any action or suit traditionally cognizable by courts of law or equity, not involving criminal prosecution or punishment for crime. Milwaukee County v White Co. 296 US 268, 80 L Ed 220, 56 S Ct 229. A proceeding in a court of justice by which a person pursues a remedy afforded him for the redress of a private wrong, as distinguished from a criminal prosecution. Milwaukee County v M. E. White Co. 296 US 268, 80 L Ed 220, 56 S Ct 229.

suit of local nature. See **action of a local nature.**

suitor (sū′tǫr). A litigant; a party to an action or suit.

suitors' fund. A fund in the English chancery court made up of sums paid in as costs.

suits pro laesione fidei (sūts prō lē-zhe-ō′ne fī-dē′ī). Suits for breach of faith.

In the reign of Stephen, the clergy attempted to turn their ecclesiastical courts into courts of equity by entertaining such suits as for spiritual offenses against conscience, in cases of nonpayment of debt or indeed any breach of contract. But this attempt was frustrated by the Constitutions of Clarendon in 1166. See 3 Bl Comm 52.

suit to quiet title. See **quieting title.**

suit to remove cloud. See **quieting title.**

sulfur (sul′fẻr). Another spelling of **sulphur.**

sulphur (sul′fẻr). A chemical element. A mineral. 36 Am J1st Min & M § 5.

sum. The result of an addition of numbers. An amount or quantity of money, large or small. United States v Van Auken, 96 US 366, 24 L Ed 852.

sum at risk. The maximum amount of insurer's liability under a policy; in the case of a valued policy, the valuation placed upon the property by the policy itself. 29A Am J Rev ed Ins § 1586. A term used in marine insurance policies meaning the valuation placed upon the insured property by the policy itself. Standard Marine Ins. Co. v Nome Beach Lighterage & Transp. Co. (CA9 Cal) 133 F 636.

summa. See **in summa.**

Summa caritas est facere justitiam singulis et omni tempore quando necesse fuerit (sum′ma ka′ri-tās est fā′se-rē ju-sti′she-am sin′gu-lis et om′nī tem′po-re quan′dō ne-ses′se fu′e-rit). The greatest charity is to do justice to everyone and at all times when it shall be needed.

Summa est lex quae pro religione facit (sum′ma est lex kwē prō re-li-ji-o′ne fā′sit). The highest law is that which makes for religion.

summa injuria (sum′ma in-jū′ri-a). The greatest injury. See 1 Bl Comm 62.

Summam esse rationem quae pro religione facit (sum′mam es′se ra-she-ō′nem kwē prō re-li-ji-o′ne fā′sit). The highest reason is that which makes for religion. See Broom's Legal Maxims 19.

summa providentia (sum′ma pro-vi-den′she-a). The greatest prudence. See 1 Bl Comm 461.

Summa ratio est quae pro religione facit (sum'ma rā'she-ō est kwē prō re-li-ji-ō'ne fā'sit). The highest reason is that which makes for religion. See Broom's Legal Maxims 19.

summarily. Expeditiously; dispensing with formalities which merely delay action.

A statute giving the orphans' court the power "summarily" to direct payment of the prorated portions of an estate tax will be construed as not dispensing with the essential elements of due process as regards notice and opportunity to be heard. Moreland's Estate, 351 Pa 623, 42 A2d 63, 1 ALR2d 972.

summary. Short, concise. Reduced into a narrow compass or into a few words. Treese v Ferguson, 120 Okla 235, 251 P 91.

summary abatement. The abatement of a nuisance without judicial proceeding, even without notice or hearing, often by a destruction of the offending thing or structure. 39 Am J1st Nuis § 183 et seq.

summary contempt proceeding. A proceeding for an adjudication of contempt for a direct contempt in the immediate presence of the court, without pleading, affidavit, or formal charges, albeit the accused may be entitled to a hearing or at least opportunity to make an explanation of his conduct under oath. 17 Am J2d Contpt §§ 86-88.

summary conviction. Convicting an accused without giving him the benefit of a trial.
See **summary contempt proceeding.**

summary court-martial. The lowest in the rank of courts-martial, conducted before one commissioned officer, limited in jurisdiction to offenses of a minor or petty nature of which enlisted men, not commissioned officers, stand accused.

summary dismissal. A dismissal of a civil service employee without giving him opportunity to defend himself or a hearing of any kind. Anno: 131 ALR 396.

summary forfeiture. A forfeiture to the state of property without giving the owner opportunity to be heard. Anno: 17 ALR 574.

summary judgment. A judgment in a summary proceeding, as one rendered pursuant to statute against the sureties on a bond furnished in an action. 50 Am J1st Suret § 209. A judgment in certain actions specified in the statute providing the remedy, rendered upon plaintiff's motion, usually with supporting affidavits, upon the failure of the defendant to controvert the motion by filing an affidavit of defense or his failure to file an affidavit of defense or affidavit of merits sufficient to show the existence of a genuine issue of fact. 41 Am J1st Pl § 340.

A motion for summary judgment is not a trial; on the contrary it assumes that scrutiny of the facts will disclose that the issues presented by the pleadings need not be tried because they are so patently insubstantial as not to be genuine issues at all. Consequently, as soon as it appears upon such a motion that there is really something to "try," the judge must at once deny it and let the cause take its course in the usual way. Cohen v Eleven West 42nd Street (CA2 NY) 115 F2d 531.

summary jurisdiction. A jurisdiction exercised by summary proceedings, as in a bankruptcy court. 9 Am J2d Bankr § 68.

summary possessory proceeding. A proceeding, summary in character, to which a landlord may resort for the recovery or possession of leased premises when he becomes entitled to possession. 32 Am J1st L & T § 1016.

summary proceeding. A proceeding by which a controversy is settled, case disposed of, or trial conducted in a prompt, simple manner without the aid of a jury and without observance of requirements which prevail in a plenary action in reference to commencement of action, service of papers, etc. Western & A. R. Co. v Atlanta, 113 Ga 537, 38 SE 996. A proceeding in the Bankruptcy Court upon petition and answer at a day set for hearing upon notice or order to show cause against the relief proposed. 9 Am J2d Bankr § 69. A proceeding before an administrative body, requiring notice and hearing, but not requiring a full compliance with the rules governing trials of civil actions. Emerson v Hughes, 117 Vt 270, 90 A2d 910, 34 ALR2d 539.

Summary proceedings are not conducted without proper investigation of the facts, or without notice, or an opportunity to be heard by the person alleged to have committed the acts, or whose property is sought to be affected. The term summary proceedings is also applied to proceedings which are taken lawfully, but without resort to the courts, such as the physical abatement of a nuisance, or the recaption of goods. Western & Atlantic Railroad Co. v Atlanta, 113 Ga 537, 38 SE 996.

summary trial. A trial of a person on a criminal charge, without a jury. A trial in a summary proceeding.

summation. The concluding argument of counsel, made after the introduction of evidence has been completed, counsel summarizing the points in favor of his client. A term sometimes applied to the court's statement of salient points in the evidence in his charge to the jury.

summing up. See summation.

summo jure. See in summo jure.

summoneas (sum-mō'ne-ās). A summons.

summons. In ordinary usage of the term, original process upon a proper service of which an action is commenced and the defendant therein named brought within the jurisdiction of the court, although sometimes regarded as process only when issued by the clerk or other officer of the court. 42 Am J1st Proc § 2. In convening a grand jury, a venire, precept, or such process or writ as is prescribed for the purpose by statute. 24 Am J1st Grand J § 21.

summum jus (sum'mum jūs). The highest right; the strictest or most rigid law.

Summum jus est summa injuria (sum'mum jūs est sum'ma in-jū'ri-a). Rigid law is the greatest injustice. Ogden v Saunders (US) 12 Wheat 213, 283, 6 L Ed 606, 630.

Summum jus summa injuria (sum'mum jūs sum'ma in-jū'ri-a). Rigid law is the greatest injustice, or, more freely translated, "too strict an interpretation of the law is frequently productive of the greatest injustice."

The maxim has its counterpart in the maxim, "Right too rigid hardens into wrong." Caldwell v Ryan, 210 Mo 17, 43, 108 SW 533.

sum payable. The amount payable by the obligor under a bill, note, or contract.

sumptuary laws (sump'tū-ā-ri lâs). Statutes restraining luxury and extravagant expense in dress, diet, and the like.

The sumptuary law of 1336, still in force in the time of Blackstone, provided that no man should be served at dinner or supper with more than two courses, except upon certain important specified holy days, when he might be served with three courses. See 4 Bl Comm 170.

Sunday. The first day of the week. 50 Am J1st Sun & H § 2. A holy day set apart as the Christian Sabbath, the observance of which as a day of rest is generally provided for by statute. The seventh day of the Jewish week. 50 Am J1st Sun & H § 2.

A statutory declaration that a certain day shall be a legal holiday does not indicate an attempt to elevate its status to that of Sunday. 50 Am J1st Sun & H § 2.

The observance of Sunday as a Sabbath or day of ceremonial rest was first enjoined by the Emperor Constantine as a civil regulation in conformity with the practice of the Christian church. Hence it is a maxim of the civil law, "Diebus dominicis mercari, judicari vel jurari non debet." On the Lord's Days it is not fitting to transact business, to decide cases nor to make an oath. Richardson v Goddard (US) 23 How 28, 16 L Ed 412, 417.

When the word is used in a statute which does not in any of its provisions indicate that some other meaning is intended, Sunday is construed as meaning the entire day from midnight of Saturday until midnight of Sunday. 50 Am J1st Sun & H § 2.

Sunday edition. The edition of a daily newspaper which comes out on Sunday; not a weekly newspaper. 39 Am J1st Newsp § 4.

Sunday law. A statute or municipal ordinance, sometimes known as a "blue law," which prohibits, with some necessary exceptions, the performance of labor or the engaging in a business, occupation, sport, or amusement enterprise on Sunday or during certain hours on Sunday. Petit v Minnesota, 177 US 164, 44 L Ed 716, 20 S Ct 666.

In its enactment, the legislature has given the sanction of law to a rule of conduct, which the entire civilized world recognizes as essential to the physical and moral well-being of society. One day in seven is the rule founded in experience and sustained by science. Hennington v Georgia, 163 US 299, 41 L Ed 166, 16 S Ct 1086.

Sunday Law of Charles the Second. The statute, 29 Car. II, c. 7, sec. 1, which provided that "no person whatsoever shall do or exercise any worldly labor, business, or work of their ordinary calling, on the Lord's Day."

This is not the prohibition of all worldly business or work, but only of one's "ordinary calling" so that one having no ordinary calling cannot come under the statute. In the United States, Sunday laws generally omit this limitation. Lovejoy v Whipple, 18 Vt 379.

Sunday school. A school providing religious instruction on Sunday, usually conducted in a church. A religious meeting within the meaning of a statute denouncing the disturbance of such a meeting. 24 Am J2d Disturb M § 2.

Sunday walking. Taking a walk for exercise, or recreation, not within a Sunday law which prohibits unnecessary walking on Sunday. Sullivan v Maine Central R. Co. 82 Me 196, 19 A 169.

sun parlor. A glass-inclosed room, often a porch, exposed to the sun. 20 Am J2d Cov § 257.

sunstroke. A severe disturbance of the body, caused by excessive exposure to the sun or even to artificial heat, resulting in convulsion and coma. Anno: 117 ALR 740; 36 ALR2d 1105.

An exhaustive search of the authorities appears to make it clear that the term may be applied with propriety to a condition produced by artificial heat as well as by the heat of the sun, and that the best usage warrants it; that such condition is comprehended within the ordinary meaning of the word wherever it is used with care and precision, whether in technical scientific treatises, or in works designed for the general reader. Continental Casualty Co. v Johnson, 74 Kan 129, 85 P 545.

sun time. Same as **solar time.**

suo genere. See **in suo genere.**

suo nomine (su'ō nō'mi-nē). In his own name.

suo periculo (su'ō pe-ri'ku-lō). At his own risk.

super (sū'pėr). Prefix: Over; above; higher in rank. Noun: One having a nonspeaking part in a play. Slang for superior, also for superintendent.

superadded liability. A personal liability, otherwise known as double liability, once imposed quite generally in this country by constitutional or statutory provisions upon stockholders in banks or business corporations, such being a liability of a stockholder for debts or obligations of the banking or other corporation to the extent of the par value of the stock held by him. 10 Am J2d Banks § 73; 19 Am J2d Corp § 778.

At the present time, in practically all American jurisdictions, constitutional and statutory provisions imposing such liability for the general debts incurred by corporations, including banking corporations, either have been abolished or a constitutional or statutory provision declares that stockholders shall not be individually liable as such otherwise than for the unpaid shares owned by them. 19 Am J2d Corp § 775.

super altum mare (sū'per al'tum ma're). On the high sea.

superatione pasturae. See **de superatione pasturae.**

supercargo (sū-pėr-kär'gō). A person employed by a commercial company or merchant to take charge of a cargo exported by the company or merchant to a foreign country or countries, to sell the goods there to the best advantage, and to purchase proper commodities to relade the ship on its return voyage. 48 Am J1st Ship § 484.

superconception (sū"pėr-kǫn-sep'shǫn). Conception by a woman already pregnant; also known as "superfoetation."

superficiarius. (Latin.) A term of the civil law for tenant under a lease for ground rent.

superficies (sū-pėr-fish'iēz). (Civil law.) The surface; anything erected upon and attached to the soil so as to become a part of the land.

See **in superficie.**

Superficies solo cedit (su-per-fish'i-ēz sō'lō se'dit). (Civil law.) Anything built into the land goes with the land.

Superflua non nocent (su-per'flu-a non nō'sent). Superfluous things do not harm; superfluity does not prejudice.

superfluous allegations. See **surplusage.**

superfoetation (su-per-fē-tā'shon). Same as **superconception.**

superhuman. Above man. Having powers beyond those of man.

See **irresistible superhuman cause.**

superintend. To act as a superintendent. To exercise the power of superintendence.

superintendence. Oversight, inspection, supervision. Moffitt v Asheville, 103 NC 237, 9 SE 695. Care and oversight for the purpose of direction, and with authority to direct. The act of superintending.
"The word seems properly to imply the exercise of some authority or control over the person or thing subjected to oversight." Dantzler v De Bardeleben Coal & Iron Co. 101 Ala 309, 14 So 10.

superintendent. A corporate officer usually in charge of one of the several departments of the business. 19 Am J2d Corp § 1174. A representative of an employer, whose principal duty is that of superintendence of the workmen.

superintendent of banks. A state officer appointed and invested with power to license banks, supervise the conduct of the banking business within the jurisdiction, and liquidate failed banks. 10 Am J2d Banks § 17.

superintendent of highways. A state or municipal officer having and exercising powers and duties in reference to the establishment, construction, and maintenance of highways and streets.

superintendent of hospital. The person in charge of the operation of a hospital. 26 Am J1st Hospit § 8.

superintendent of public instruction. See **state superintendent of public instruction; superintendent of schools.**

superintendent of schools. An officer employed by a board of education, in charge of the work of the public schools in a city. In some jurisdictions, a county officer who maintains a general supervision over the public schools of the county.
See **state superintendent of public instruction.**

superintendent of streets. A municipal officer in charge of work upon the streets, whether construction or maintenance.

superintending control. Same as **supervisory jurisdiction.**

superior body. The body to which a local lodge or benefit society owes allegiance. 36 Am J2d Frat O § 35.

superior court. A term applied to courts of general jurisdiction generally. In some jurisdictions, the title of a court of general jurisdiction; in others, the title of an appellate court; in still others, the title of a municipal or county court.

superior force. An act of God. A fortuitous event. A force majeure. A force which man is not able to resist, in fact, a force which man can neither foresee nor prevent. Lehman, Stern & Co. v Morgan's Louisiana & Texas Railroad & S.S. Co. 115 La 1, 38 So 873 (definition in Louisiana Code of 1825).

superior lien. A prior lien. Gilman v Jones, 87 Ala 691, 5 So 785, 7 So 48.

superior servant rule. The common-law rule that an employee assumes the risk of the negligence of his superior fellow servant in directing employees, the operation of machinery, and the conduct of the work, to the same extent that he assumes the risk of the negligence of fellow laborers employed with him in the performance of the work. 35 Am J1st M & S § 364.
As promulgated by the supreme court of Ohio, the rule was that, where one servant was placed, by his master, in a position of subordination to another, and subjected to his orders and control, and such inferior servant, without fault, and while engaged in the discharge of his duties, was injured by the negligence of the superior servant, the master was liable for such injury; and this was true even though, at the time of the injury, the superior servant was performing the duties of a common workman. Moore v Dublin Cotton Mills, 127 Ga 609, 56 SE 839.

superior title. A title which will prevail in law or equity as against another asserted title, lien, or interest.

superior use. The principle under which property devoted to one public use is subject to condemnation for another of superior rank in respect of public necessity. 26 Am J2d Em D § 90.

supermarket. A business establishment, essentially of the modern age, consisting of a large, sometimes gigantic, store stocked with food of all kinds and varieties, quantities of all items of goods and merchandise found in ordinary grocery stores, some articles of hardware, even some articles of clothing, and operating under a self-help plan, the customers taking the packages and articles from the shelf or bin, and paying for them at a place near the exit known as a check-out.

supernatural (sū-pėr-nat'ū-ral). That which occurs beyond the experience, knowledge, comprehension, and understanding of man. That which occurs beyond the powers of nature as such are known to man.

superonerare (su-per-ō-ne-ra're). To surcharge. See **surcharge.**

superoneratio (su-per-ō-ne-rā'she-ō). A surcharging. See **surcharge.**

supersede (sū-pėr-sēd'). To remove in making way for another. To drop from use and replace.

supersedeas (sū-pėr-sē'dē-as). A suspension of the power to issue an execution on a judgment or decree from which an appeal or proceeding in error has been taken; or, if a writ of execution has issued, a prohibition emanating from the appellate court against the execution of the writ, in other words, an auxiliary process designed to supersede the enforcement of the judgment of the court below brought up for review. 4 Am J2d A & E § 364. The effect of an appeal, writ of error, or certiorari, in suspending the enforcement of the judgment against which the appeal, writ of error, or certiorari is directed.

supersedeas bond. A bond required upon obtaining supersedeas, conditioned to protect the interest of the appellee or defendant in error. 4 Am J2d A & E § 369. A bond given by a party appealing from a judgment to stay execution thereon pending the appeal.

superseded pleading. A pleading replaced by an amended or substituted pleading. 41 Am J1st Pl § 202.

supersedendo. See **de supersedendo.**

supersedere (sū"pėr-se-dē'rē). To supersede; to stay.

superseding cause. Same as **intervening cause.**

super se susceperunt (sū'per sē su-sē-pē'runt). They supported, defended, or undertook.

superstitious uses (sū-pėr-stish'us ū'ses). Uses such as those providing for masses for the welfare of the souls of the dead, which were held not to be strictly charitable uses. See 2 Bl Comm 273. See also, Harrison v Brophy, 59 Kan 1, 51 P 883.

supersurface use. The use of the space above a highway by abutting owners for private purposes. 25 Am J1st High § 198.
See **airspace.**

Supervacuum esset leges condere, nisi esset qui leges tueretur (su-per-va'ku-um es'set lē'jēz kon'de-re, nī'sī es'set qui lē'jēz tu-ē-rē'ter). It would be superfluous to make laws, unless those laws, when made, were to be enforced. Chisholm v Georgia (US) 2 Dall 419, 464, 1 L Ed 440, 460.

supervening cause. See **intervening cause.**

supervening negligence. See **intervening cause; last clear chance.**

supervise. To exercise oversight. To keep under inspection.
See **superintendence.**

supervising commissioner. The person before whom a deposition is taken, acting under a commission. 23 Am J2d Dep § 91.

supervising officer. The person before whom a deposition is taken, including a person acting under a commission as well as an independent public officer. 23 Am J2d Dep § 91.

Supervision of Trustees for Charitable Purposes Act. One of the uniform laws. 9 CULA Supp; 15 Am J2d Char § 114.

supervisor. In some jurisdictions, the title of a member of a county board. As defined by the Labor Management Relations Act, an individual having authority, in the interest of the employer, to hire, transfer, suspend, layoff, recall, promote, discharge, assign, reward, or discipline other employees, or responsibility to direct them, or to adjust their grievances, or effectively to recommend such action if, in connection with the foregoing the exercise of such authority requires the use of independent judgment. 29 USC § 152(3)(11); 31 Am J Rev ed Lab § 205.
See **board of supervisors.**

supervisor of highways. A state or local officer in charge of construction and maintenance of highways.

supervisory employee. A superintendent, foreman, or supervisor.

supervisory jurisdiction. A kind of original jurisdiction frequently conferred upon appellate courts, especially the highest court of the jurisdiction, in the nature of superintending control over inferior courts, exercised sometimes by making rules for inferior courts and enforcing those rules, and at other times by compelling or prohibiting action by the inferior court. 20 Am J2d Cts §§ 111 et seq. The control exercised in some jurisdictions by a court over executive or administrative officers and boards who exercise judicial functions incidentally. 1 Am J2d Admin L § 21.

supervisory writ. A writ such as certiorari, mandamus, or prohibition issued by a court having constitutional power to exercise a superintending control over inferior tribunals in order to keep such inferior tribunals within the bounds of their proper jurisdiction.
See **supervisory jurisdiction.**

super visum corporis (su'per vī'sum kor'po-ris). On a view of the body. 18 Am J2d Corn § 11.

super visum vulneris (su'per vī'sum vul-ne'ris). Upon a view of the wound.

supper money. An allowance made an employee working overtime.

supplement. (sup'lē-mẹnt). Verb: To add to a published work for the purpose of giving additional and later material. Noun: A publication, usually issued periodically, supplying additional and later material to an original publication.

supplemental (sup-lē-men'tạl). Added to supply a deficiency, or defect.

supplemental account. An account required of a guardian for the correction of errors in his prior accounting. 25 Am J1st G & W § 160.

supplemental act. Same as **supplemental statute.**

supplemental affidavit. An affidavit filed by the creditor in attachment in addition to the affidavit upon which the writ was issued, setting forth further facts in support of the application for the writ. 6 Am J2d Attach § 275.

supplemental answer. See **supplemental pleading.**

supplemental assessment. An additional special assessment for the payment of a local improvement, required because of the insufficiency of the original assessment. 48 Am J1st Spec A § 150.

supplemental bill. A pleading in equity which is supplemental or additional to, and filed in aid or support of, an original bill or complaint. Rebelo v Cardoso, 81 RI 360, 103 A2d 80. A pleading in equity which has the function of supporting the cause of suit existing when the original bill was filed. Bethlehem Fabricators v H. D. Watts Co. 286 Mass 556, 190 NE 828, 93 ALR 1124.

supplemental brief. An additional brief on appeal filed by consent of court or pursuant to rules of court. 5 Am J2d A & E § 690.

supplemental complaint. See **supplemental pleading.**

supplemental deed. A deed to the purchaser at a tax sale in substitution for an original which is defective or invalid. 51 Am J1st Tax § 1087.

supplemental injunction. An injunction issued in aid of an action before the court for the purpose of protecting its jurisdiction or making its judgment effective. 28 Am J Rev ed Inj § 15. An injunction granted by way of aiding an action or proceeding in another court in preserving the existing status until the case has been disposed of in the other court. 28 Am J Rev ed Inj § 16.

supplemental levy. A levy made by the officer to whom a writ of attachment is directed, after a prior levy by him under the writ, such additional levy being necessary to satisfy the writ. 6 Am J2d Attach § 294.

supplemental petition. A petition asserting matters arising subsequent to the filing of the petition, for example, matters arising after the filing of a petition for certiorari. Lavore v Industrial Acci. Com. 28 Cal App 2d 488, 82 P2d 738.

supplemental pleading. A pleading of new matter in support of an original complaint, bill, declaration, or petition. Jenkins v International Bank, 127 US 484, 32 L Ed 189, 8 S Ct 1186. A pleading bringing to the notice of the court matters occurring since the filing or service of the original pleading. 41 Am J1st Pl § 261.

An answer consisting merely of an addition to the original answer of the defendant, which original

SUPPLEMENTAL [1242] SUPPRESS

answer had contained all the denials necessary to put in issue the material allegations of the complaint, was a supplemental answer and not an amended one. Yeatman v Patrician, 144 Wash 241, 257 P 622.
See **supplemental bill.**

supplemental proceeding. See **supplementary proceeding.**

supplemental remedy. See **extraordinary remedies; supplementary proceeding.**

supplemental statute. A statute intended to improve an existing statute by adding something thereto without changing the original text. 50 Am J1st Stat § 3.

supplemental surety. One who stands as surety for another who is himself only a surety. 50 Am J1st Suret § 5.

supplemental tax. An additional inheritance tax imposed by way of correcting error in the omission of property made in calculating the amount of the tax. Anno: 64 ALR 1283.

supplementary (sup-lẹ-men'tạ-ri). Same as **supplemental.**

supplementary proceeding. A proceeding for the enforcement of a judgment where the ordinary means of enforcement by execution is unavailable or unavailing, sometimes regarded as a proceeding in the original action, at other times as a civil action or proceeding in itself, whereunder the plaintiff is enabled to examine the judgment debtor and third persons for the purpose of obtaining information concerning property owned by the debtor which may be applied in payment of the judgment. 30 Am J2d Exec §§ 774 et seq.

suppletory oath. See **oath suppletory.**

supplicate. To petition in an earnest and humble manner.

supplicatio (sup-pli-kā'she-ō). (Civil law.) Same as **duplicatio.**

supplicavit (sup-li-kạ'vit). He hath supplicated.
See **writ of supplicavit.**

supplicium (sup-pli'she-um). (Civil law.) The death penalty.

supplies. Available aggregate of things needed or demanded; anything yielded or afforded to meet a want. Anderson v United States Fidelity & G. Co. 44 NM 483, 104 P2d 906, 129 ALR 1084 (word appearing in performance bond).

supply. Verb: To furnish. To meet a need. Noun: A substitute serving temporarily, particularly in teaching school.
See **bill of supply; supplies.**

support. Verb: To carry the weight of something. To comfort and sustain. To furnish the necessities of life for maintenance in a proper manner, not merely the necessities for a bare maintenance. Anno: 13 ALR 689 (term appearing in workmen's compensation statute). To provide the means of maintenance of a person. 50 Am J1st Sup Per § 2. Noun: Articles for the sustenance of a person, as food, clothing, and other conveniences, even medicines and medical services. 50 Am J1st Sup Per § 2. Maintenance, subsistence, or income for the sustenance of one person or a family. Wall v Williams, 93 NC 327. As used in a statute exempting from execution food necessary for the "support of the debtor and his family" for a specified period:—provisions on hand sufficient to provide for the necessary use of the family for the prescribed period; usually not inclusive of such provisions as are necessary to provide for persons the debtor is under no obligation to support. 31 Am J2d Exemp § 78.
See **lateral support; subjacent support.**

support bond. See **bond for support.**

supporting affidavit. An affidavit in support of a motion, for example, a motion for a continuance. 17 Am J2d Contin § 44. An affidavit in support of an application for injunction, particularly a preliminary or temporary injunction. 28 Am J Rev ed Inj § 264.

supporting papers. Affidavits in support of a motion. 37 Am J1st Motions § 14.

support of building. A right of an owner and a corresponding liability of an adjoining owner under grant, express or implied, or under reservation, sometimes existing as a prescriptive right, although not included in the right of lateral support and confined to the condition of things at the time of the acquisition of the right. 1 Am J2d Adj L §§ 40-42.
See **lateral support; subjacent support.**

support of child. A moral obligation; a principle of natural law, as well as the common law, to maintain and care for one's minor child. 39 Am J1st P & C § 35.

Support of Dependents Act. One of the uniform laws. 23 Am J2d Desert § 125.

support of family. The duty of a husband, arising out of the marital relationship and imposed by law, to provide wife and family with a place of abode, the necessities and comforts of life, which are suitable when considered in reference to the particular estate, social rank, and condition of the husband and wife, and the means and earning power of the husband. 26 Am J1st H & W §§ 337, 338.

support of land. See **lateral support; subjacent support.**

support of person. See **support.**

support of wife. A duty arising out of the marital relationship and imposed by law which continues during the existence of the relationship. 26 Am J1st H & W § 338.
See **support of family.**

support order. An order for support of wife or child, especially an order under the Uniform Desertion and Nonsupport Act. 23 Am J2d Desert §§ 48 et seq. An allowance, in addition to alimony, granted a divorced wife, for the maintenance of children placed in her custody by the judgment or decree of divorce. 24 Am J2d Div & S § 827.

support trust. A protective trust wherein the interest of the beneficiary is protected against his grantees or assignees and against his creditors by limiting his interest to that which is necessary for his support and education. 54 Am J1st Trusts § 163.

supposition. Something regarded as true, without proof.
In the law of evidence, an inference is a deduction from the facts proved and differs widely from a "supposition," which requires no such premise for its justification. Continental Casualty Co. v Paul, 209 Ala 166, 95 So 814, 30 ALR 802, 804.

suppress. To restrain. To put down by force.
To suppress means to prevent, and does not mean

SUPPRESSIO [1243] SURETY

to license or sanction the act to be suppressed. Schwuchow v Chicago, 68 Ill 444, 448.
See **suppression.**

suppressio mensis (sup'pre'she-ō men'sis). Suppression of the menses.

suppression. The subduing of a movement by force. Restraint. Concealment. Abolition.
There is a distinction between the suppression of a fact and mere silence. Where there is an obligation to speak, a failure to speak will constitute the suppression of a fact; but, where there is no obligation to speak, silence cannot be termed suppression. Chicora Fertilizer Co. v Dunan, 91 Md 144, 46 A 347.

suppression of bids. See **chilling bids; stifling bids.**

suppression of competition. A form of monopolistic practice. 36 Am J1st Monop etc § 6.

suppression of deposition. A remedy obtained on motion raising an objection to the use of a deposition on the ground of defects or irregularities in the proceeding for and the taking of a deposition. 23 Am J2d Dep § 130.

suppression of evidence. Relief obtained upon motion in preventing evidence illegally secured from being introduced in a case. 29 Am J2d Ev § 425. The failure of a party to testify or to produce available witnesses, his destruction or spoliation of evidence. 29 Am J2d Ev §§ 175 et seq.
To determine whether there has been a suppression of evidence, by the state in a criminal prosecution, it is necessary to consider the facts and circumstances in each case in which the question arises. If the evidence in question has no probative value, is merely cumulative, or is equally available to the accused, there can certainly be no duty on the prosecution to disclose such evidence to the accused in order to avoid what would otherwise amount in practical effect to concealment or suppression. Re Curtis (DC Dist Col) 36 F Supp 408.

suppression of the menses. Stopping of the menses. Sometimes the exciting cause of temporary insanity. Smith v Smith, 47 Miss 211, 217.

suppression of will. The failure of a person having the will of another in his custody to produce it for probate on notice of the death of the testator. The failure of a person having the custody of a will because of the delivery of the instrument to him for custody and safekeeping, to produce the instrument for probate after the testator's death or within a certain time thereafter, provided he has notice of the death. 57 Am J1st Wills § 750.

suppressio veri (su'pre'she-ō ve'rī). Suppression of the truth.

Suppressio veri, expressio falsi (sup-pre'she-ō vē'rī, ex-pre'she-ō fal'sī). The suppression of that which is true amounts to the expression of that which is false. Addington v Allen (NY) 11 Wend 374, 417.

Suppressio veri, suggestio falsi (su-pre'she-ō ve'rī, su-jest'she-ō fal'sī). The suppression of truth is the expression of falsehood. Paul v Hadley (NY) 23 Barb 521, 525.

sup pro. Abbreviation of **supplementary proceeding.**

supra (sū'prạ). Above; above mentioned; in addition to.
See **ubi supra.**

supra dictus (sū'prạ dik'tus). As stated above; as before stated.

supra protest. See **acceptance for honor; acceptance supra protest; payment for honor.**

supremacy. See **act of supremacy; supremacy clause.**

supremacy clause. The provision in Article VI, Clause 2, of the United States Constitution that "this Constitution and the laws of the United States which shall be made in pursuance thereof and all treaties made, or which shall be made, under the authority of the United States, shall be the supreme law of the land, and the judges in every state shall be bound thereby, anything in the Constitution or laws of any state to the contrary notwithstanding.

suprema voluntas (su-prē'ma vo-lun'tas). The last will.

Supreme Court. In some jurisdictions the highest appellate court; in other jurisdictions a court of general jurisdiction.

Supreme Court of the United States. See **United States Supreme Court.**

supreme executive power. Such power as will secure an efficient execution of the laws, which is the peculiar province of the executive department, to be accomplished, however, in the manner and by the methods and within the limitations prescribed by the constitution and statutes of the state. State ex rel. Stubbs v Dawson, 86 Kan 180, 119 P 360.

supreme law of the land. See **supremacy clause.**

sur (sėr). On; upon.

surcharge a common. To disturb a common by putting more cattle therein than the pasture and herbage will sustain, or more than one so doing has a right to do.
The other owners are thereby injured by being deprived of their respective portions, or by contracting them into a smaller compass. See 3 Bl Comm 237.

surcharge (sėr-chärj'). An additional amount added to the usual charge. An exaction.

surcharge and falsify. To disprove a stated account in respect of particular items by showing the inclusion of an item by error (surcharging) and by showing error respecting the amount of an item. (Falsifying.) Rehill v McTague, 114 Pa 82.

surcharging guardian. Holding a guardian responsible for money or property of the ward lost by reason of negligence or failure of duty, or which the guardian might have recovered and received by the exercise of reasonable diligence and ordinary prudence, also for his failure to invest funds of the ward so as to obtain income therefrom. 25 Am J1st G & W § 174.

sur disclaimer (sėr dis-klā'mėr). On disclaimer. See 3 Bl Comm 233.

surety. A person who engages under a contract of suretyship to answer for the debt, default, or miscarriage of another. 50 Am J1st Suret §§ 2, 3. For some purposes, inclusive of a guarantor. UCC § 1 —201(40).
As applied to persons, the word has an established and well-known meaning in the minds of most people, and indicates an obligation to stand for the sum absolutely, unless discharged by the supine negligence of the obligor after notice. It is in broad contrast with the word "guaranty" which imports a conditional liability, that is, liability if due steps are taken against the principal debtor. Marberger v Pott, 16 Pa 9.
See **suretyship.**

surety company. A corporation engaged in the business of acting as a surety or guarantor on bonds, undertakings, or contracts, for compensation known as a premium. 50 Am J1st Suret § 312.

surety company agent. The agent of a surety company, comparable in reference to the scope of his authority to the agent of an insurance company. 50 Am J1st Suret § 314.

surety company contract. A contract wherein the surety is a compensated surety, that is, a surety company. 50 Am J1st Suret § 313.

surety contract. A contract of suretyship. See **suretyship**.

surety of the peace (of the pēs). A bond or undertaking to keep the peace.

suretyship. A contractual relation, resulting from a primary, original, absolute, and unconditional engagement, whereby one person, the surety, engages to be answerable for the debt, default, or miscarriage of another, the principal. Madison County Farmers Asso. v American Employers' Ins. Co. (CA8 Ark) 209 F2d 581, 42 ALR2d 1153; Welch v Walsh, 177 Mass 555, 59 NE 440.

While the contract of a surety is, in a sense, accessory or collateral to a valid principal obligation contracted by another person, either contemporaneously or previously, his obligation to the creditor or promisee of the principal is direct, primary, and absolute. 50 Am J1st Suret § 2.

It is the essence of the contract that there be a subsisting valid obligation of a principal debt. Without a principal there can be no surety. First Nat. Bank v Boxley, 129 Okla 159, 264 P 184, 64 ALR 588.

The vital difference between the contract of a surety and that of a guarantor is that a surety is charged as an original promisor, while the engagement of the guarantor is a collateral undertaking. A surety is a party to the principal obligation, undertaking together with the principal debtor that it shall be performed, while the guarantor is not a party to the principal obligation. 24 Am J1st Guar § 11.

surface. Verb: To apply to street, highway, or driveway a top covering or layer of durable material of substantial depth or thickness. Anno: 84 ALR 1158. Noun: The superficial part of the land; the part of land capable of being used for agricultural purposes. Anno: 31 ALR 1530. Within the meaning of the right to subjacent support:—any stratum above the subjacent stratum in question, including any higher stratum as well as the actual surface of the soil. 1 Am J2d Adj L § 77. In mining law, the soil lying over the minerals. Not merely a geometrical surface, but whatever earth, soil, or land lies above and superincumbent on a mine. Clinchfield Coal Corp. v Compton, 148 Va 437, 139 SE 308, 55 ALR 1376. A somewhat elastic term, as it appears in an oil lease, the meaning of which is to be determined according to such collateral matters as the situation of the parties, the business in which they are engaged, the purposes to be accomplished, and etc. Ramage v South Penn Oil Co. 94 W Va 81, 118 SE 162, 31 ALR 1509.

surface deed. A deed designed to convey the surface of the land alone, not carrying the minerals below the surface. 36 Am J1st Min & M § 31. A matter of reservation or exception of mineral rights. 24 Am J1st Gas & O § 29.

surface measurement. Following the surface of the ground in measuring land; running the chain or tape at the surface up and down hill, without stretching it from the top of one acclivity to the top of another. 12 Am J2d Bound § 58. A method to be compared with **horizontal measurement**.

surface of land. See **surface**.

surface stream. A stream which flows in a permanent, distinct, and well-defined channel from the lands of one owner to those of another. Tampa Waterworks Co. v Cline, 37 Fla 586, 20 So 780.

surface water. Water derived from falling rain or melting snow, or rising to the surface in springs, and diffused over the surface of the ground. 56 Am J1st Water § 65. Inclusive of flood water severed from the main current and spreading out over lower ground. 56 Am J1st Water § 92.

surgeon (sėr'jon). A person who heals by means of manual operations. 41 Am J1st Phys & S § 2. A physician who specializes in surgery.

surgery. A specialized branch of the art of healing, limited to manual operations performed with instruments or appliances, by a legally qualified physician. Joyner v State, 181 Miss 245, 179 So 573, 115 ALR 954. Therapy of a distinctly operative kind. Stewart v Raab, 55 Minn 20, 56 NW 256.

See **medical or surgical treatment**.

surgical aid. A resident physician or interne assisting the surgeon in performing an operation. "Relief pertaining to surgery or used in surgery."

In its ordinary significance, the term is not limited to the personal service of the surgeon, but includes all the means and instrumentalities used in surgery which will help to effect a cure. Olmstead v Lamphier, 93 Conn 20, 104 A 488, 7 ALR 542, 544.

surgical nurse. See **nurse**.

surname (sėr'nām). A person's last name. The family name. 38 Am J1st Name § 3. The name continued from parent to child.

Originally there were no surnames but the insufficiency of a given name to distinguish an individual led necessarily to the adoption of surnames. In the fourth year of Edward IV (1464), the first statute requiring the use of surnames came into existence. 38 Am J1st Name § 3.

surplus. That which is not needed; that which is left over. Lawrence v American Surety Co. 263 Mich 586, 249 NW 3, 88 ALR 535. A fund constituting part of the capitalization of a corporation, accumulated by profits, earnings, and other increments. A fund constituting part of the capital structure of a bank, built up by earnings. The property or fund which a corporation has in excess of its capital stock, and above all its debts and liabilities. State v Yard, 42 NJL 357, 359. The amount to be divided between the survivors under the tontine plan of insurance, comprising the funds remaining after the payment of benefits, expenses, and the intermediate apportionment of profits. 29 Am J Rev ed Ins § 16. As applied to a trust fund: —an amount in excess of the capital or corpus of the trust. Alvis v Bank of America Nat. Trust & Sav. Asso. 95 Cal App 2d 118, 212 P2d 608, 36 ALR2d 1209.

surplusage. Words in an instrument which add nothing to the force and legal effect of the instrument. 11 Am J2d B & N § 198. Superfluous or unnecessary allegations or words in an indictment or information. 27 Am J1st Indict § 109. Matter included in a pleading which is not essential to the statement of a cause of action or defense. 41 Am J1st Pl § 51.

surplusage does not vitiate. A maxim. State v Richards, 32 W Va 348, 9 SE 245.

Surplusagium non nocet (ser-plū-sā'ji-um non no'-set). Surplusage does not harm; surplusage does not prejudice.

surplus earnings. An amount owned by a corporation, over and above its capital and actual liabilities. People ex rel. Manhattan Fire Ins. Co. v Commissioners of Taxes, 76 NY 64, 74.

surplus fund. A fund remaining after the accomplishment of the purpose for which an appropriation of public funds was made. Anno: 70 ALR 431. Funds not necessary to be kept on hand in cash for immediate use or ordinary demands have been held to be surplus funds of the state. See Lawrence v American Surety Co. 263 Mich 586, 249 NW 3, 88 ALR 535.

surplus line broker. An insurance broker whose business activities embrace variable risks and kinds of insurance. 29 Am J Rev ed Ins § 77.

surplus money proceeding. A proceeding in a mortgage foreclosure to determine rights in the part of the proceeds of foreclosure sale not required for satisfaction of the mortgage and payment of costs. 37 Am J1st Mtg § 873.

surplus personal estate. That part of the personal property in the estate of a decedent which remains after the payment of expenses of administration and debts, including taxes, for which the decedent was liable or for which the estate is liable. Weinberg v Safe Deposit & Trust Co. 198 Md 539, 85 A2d 50, 37 ALR2d 188.

surplus proceeds. That part of the proceeds of a sale on execution not required in satisfaction of the judgment. Anno: 97 ALR 1003.
See **surplus money proceeding.**

surplus property. An excess of property seized under a writ of attachment or execution over the amount required to satisfy the indebtedness of the defendant. 6 Am J2d Attach § 145; 30 Am J2d Exec § 230. Goods purchased for use by the armed forces, the need for which has disappeared with the termination of hostilities and the release or discharge of military personnel.

surplus water. A supply of water in excess of that to which a canal proprietor is lawfully entitled for purposes of navigation. 13 Am J2d Can § 16. Water flowing over lands from adjoining premises upon which it had been spread for irrigation purposes. 30 Am J Rev ed Irrig § 26.

surprise. Astonishment by the unexpected. Aroused by the unusual. The condition in which a party to an action finds himself, contrary to his reasonable expectation, through no fault or neglect of his own, and to his probable injury. Gidionsen v Union Depot Railway Co. 129 Mo 392, 401, 31 SW 800. A ground for relief only where accompanied by fraud or circumvention. Citizens' National Bank v Branden, 19 ND 489, 126 NW 102; McDaniels v Bank of Rutland, 29 Vt 230.

surrebutter (sur-ē-but'ėr). A plaintiff's pleading in response to the defendant's rebutter. 41 Am J1st Pl § 181.

surrejoinder (sur-ē-join'dėr). A pleading by the plaintiff in response to the defendant's rejoinder. 41 Am J1st Pl § 181.

surrender. Yielding possession. A yielding up of an estate for life or years, to him who has the immediate estate in reversion or remainder, wherein the estate for life or years may drown by the mutual agreement. Schieffelin v Carpenter (NY) 15 Wend 400, 405. A giving up of something, as where a subscriber gives back to the corporation stock for which he has not paid the subscription price. Anno: 101 ALR 232. The relinquishment of one's right to an invention, thereby dedicating it to the public. 40 Am J1st Pat § 61. A condition of recovery of payment upon an instrument. 12 Am J2d B & N § 1025 (surrender of instrument.) A yielding of one's person as where an accused surrenders to an officer of the law.

surrender by bail. The turning over or delivery of a prisoner who had been released on bail to the custody of the law, by his bondsmen or sureties.

surrender by operation of law. A surrender by a tenant which results from acts which imply mutual consent independently of the expressed intention of the parties that their acts shall have that effect.
Such a surrender is by way of estoppel; and the relinquishment of possession by the tenant and the resumption of possession by the landlord operate, as a general rule, as a surrender by operation of law. 32 Am J1st L & T § 905.
See **surrender in law.**

surrender charge. A charge imposed by a life insurance company in determining cash-surrender value, or the amount of paid-up, or extended insurance. 29 Am J Rev ed Ins § 626.

surrender clause. The provision in an oil or gas lease whereby the lessee is given the privilege of surrendering his rights and terminating his liability upon the giving of a stipulated notice or the payment of a designated sum of money, or, in some cases, without either of these formalities. 24 Am J1st Gas & O § 78. The clause of a life insurance policy which provides certain options for the insured upon his surrender of the policy. 29 Am J Rev ed Ins § 619.

surrenderee (su-ren-dėr-ē'). The cestui que use; that is, the person for whose use a surrender was made by a tenant to his lord. See 2 Bl Comm 366.

surrenderer (su-ren'dėr-ėr). One who surrenders. A tenant who surrendered his copyhold estate to his lord.
"Till the admittance of the cestui que use, the lord taketh notice of the surrenderer as his tenant." See 2 Bl Comm 368.

surrender in deed (in dēd). A surrender effected by means of a deed from the surrenderer to the surrenderee.

surrender in fact. A surrender by tenant for life or years to the remainderman or reversioner, according to the apparent intent of the parties. Schieffelin v Carpenter (NY) 15 Wend 400, 405.
The effect is to pass the estate of the tenant to the landlord, extinguishing the rent reserved. It is a contractual act which occurs only through the consent of both parties, evidenced by express agreement or an unequivocal act which implies that they have agreed to consider the surrender as being made. To show acceptance of surrender of a leasehold by implication, there must be evidence of acts so inconsistent with the terms of the lease that the relation of landlord and tenant established by reletting could not be enforced under the terms of the

first lease. Ralph v Deiley, 293 Pa 90, 141 A 640, 61 ALR 763.

surrender in law. A surrender of a lease to the reversioner by accepting from the latter a new lease of the same premises or a part thereof. Schieffelin v Carpenter (NY) 15 Wend 400, 405.
See **surrender by operation of law.**

surrender of charter. The dissolution or termination of the existence of a corporation by a formal act on the part of the corporation in yielding its charter to the sovereignty under which the corporation was created and the acceptance of the same by the government. 19 Am J2d Corp § 1591.

surrender of franchise. The termination of a franchise by its voluntary surrender by the grantee, even a surrender presumed from circumstances indicating abandonment. 36 Am J2d Franch § 47.
See **surrender of charter.**

surrender of policy. The cancellation of an insurance policy completed upon delivery of the instrument by the insured to the insurer. 29 Am J Rev ed Ins § 400.

surrender of preference. The yielding by the creditor of a bankrupt to the trustee in bankruptcy of a conveyance, assignment, lien, transfer, or encumbrance, which is void or voidable under the Bankruptcy Act, as a condition of the allowance of the claim of such creditor. 9 Am J2d Bankr § 485.

surrender of tenancy. A yielding of a tenancy to the owner of the reversion or remainder, the effect being an extinguishment of the tenancy. 32 Am J1st L & T § 900.

surrenderor. See **surrenderer.**

surreptitious (sur-ep-tish'us). Clandestine. Secret. Kept secret, especially for a fraudulent purpose.

surrogate (sur'ō-gāt). A deputy chancellor who presides in English ecclesiastical courts; the title of the judge who presides in a probate court in certain states of the Union.

surrogate's court. A probate court. 20 Am J2d Cts § 32.
See **probate court.**

surrounding circumstances. The circumstances surrounding a transaction, an act, or an accident involved in an action or proceeding.
The surrounding circumstances, which, in connection with the happening of an accident, may permit an inference of culpability on the part of defendant under the rule of res ipsa loquitur, refer, not to circumstances directly tending to show lack of care, but only to neutral matters of control and management by defendant which, when explained, may appear to be entirely consistent with due care. Plumb v Richmond Light & R. Co. 233 NY 285, 133 NE 504, 25 ALR 685.

sursisa (ser-sī'sa). Same as **sursise.**

sursise (sėr-sīz'). Negligence; default.

sursumredditio (ser-sum-re-di'she-ō). A surrender, the yielding up of a copyhold estate by the tenant into the hands of the lord. See 2 Bl Comm 365.

surtax. An additional tax imposed on income already taxed. A tax at an increased rate on income exceeding a specified amount. Van Dyke's Appeal, 217 Wis 528, 259 NW 700, 98 ALR 1332.

surveillance (sėr-vāl'ans). Oversight. Observation, especially of a person suspected of criminal activities.

survey. The determination of the boundary or boundaries of land. Bunger v Grimm, 142 Ga 448, 83 SE 200. The map, plat, or other memorandum of the determination of a land boundary by a surveyor. 12 Am J2d Bound § 99. An architect's examination of premises in making recommendations for construction, preliminary sketches, and layouts. 5 Am J2d Arch § 3. An examination of a vessel taken as a prize of war for the purposes of an appraisal leading to a sale before an adjudication in a court of prize. 56 Am J1st War § 181.
The word "survey" and the word "map" or "profile" are sometimes used as convertible terms, but a distinction has been made between books of surveys and maps or draughts of land. And generally, when the term "survey" is used in relation to the location of proprietary rights, it is understood to mean a description, in words and figures, of the lands located. See Atty. Gen. v Stevens (NY) 1 Saxton Ch 369.
See **call; Congressional Survey; course; range.**

surveyor. An officer in the customs service. 21 Am J2d Cust D §§ 64, 65. A person who engages in the occupation of measuring land surfaces, establishing land boundaries, etc. Doe v Jones, 327 Ill 387, 158 NE 703, 55 ALR 303.

surveyor of the port. See **surveyor.**

survival. Continuation of life.

survival acts. Statutes which provide for the survival of a cause of action notwithstanding the death of a party. 1 Am J2d Abat & R §§ 51 et seq.

survival of cause of action. A cause of action remaining effective notwithstanding death of plaintiff or defendant. 1 Am J2d Abat & R §§ 51 et seq.

survive. To outlive another person or live beyond a designated date or the happening of a designated event. 57 Am J2d Wills § 1396.
See **survival of cause of action.**

survive to the remaining children. Words of purchase.
The expression as used in a testamentary provision that in the event of death of any of the testator's children for whose benefit a trust is created, without issue living at the time of such child's death, the share of such child in the income and capital of the trust shall survive to the remaining children above named share and share alike, imports that the accretion upon the death of one without issue living goes to the children then living, to the exclusion of the issue of a deceased child. Marbury v Bouse, 187 Md 106, 48 A2d 582, 166 ALR 1272, 1275.

surviving. See **survival; survive; survivor.**

surviving children. A familiar designation of beneficiaries under will or deed of trust.
In the absence of qualifying words, the term "surviving children" in a deed of trust to provide for the grantor's surviving children means all who survive the grantor or other designated person. Frosch v Walter, 228 US 109, 57 L Ed 750, 33 S Ct 494; Nass' Estate, 320 Pa 380, 182 A 401, 114 ALR 1.

surviving wife. A widow. For definition of term as it pertains to the rights of a woman, who married an injured workman, to compensation as his "surviving wife," under workmen's compensation acts, see Anno: 98 ALR 994.

survivor. One who outlives another person or persons of a group of which he was a part, or lives

SURVIVORSHIP [1247] SUSPENSION

beyond a designated date or the happening of a designated event. 57 Am J1st Wills § 1396.

The vested or contingent character of a remainder to survivors frequently depends upon whether the survivorship relates to the death of the testator or grantor or to some other. Obviously, if words of survivorship relate to the period of distribution, generally the death of the life tenant, the remainder is contingent, since who will survive such time in order to take the remainder is uncertain until the time of the life tenant's death or other event. Survivorship is then a condition precedent to the vesting of a gift, and a remainder subject to a condition precedent is contingent. If the words of survivorship are held to refer to the time of the grant or of the death of the testator, or, in other words, to the time when the deed or will takes effect, the remainder may be vested, either absolutely or defeasibly, or the conditions of the limitation, other than survivorship, may render the remainder contingent, even though the persons who are to take are definitely ascertained. 28 Am J2d Est § 266.

survivorship. The fact of being a survivor, of outliving another person or other persons. A right incident to an estate in joint tenancy whereunder the entire estate, upon the death of a joint tenant, remains in the survivor or survivors. 20 Am J2d Coten § 3. A right incident to an estate by the entireties, so that upon the death of one of the spouses, the whole of the estate remains in the survivor. 26 Am J1st H & W § 82.

See **presumption of survivorship; survivor; wife's right of survivorship.**

survivorship annuity. An annuity for joint lives of two persons and for the life of the survivor. 4 Am J2d Annui § 6.

survivorship of joint tenants. See **survivorship.**

susceptible. Ready to be persuaded. Easily influenced.

suspect. Verb: To entertain a suspicion of guilt. To hold a faint belief. To believe something, knowing the lack of proof to sustain the belief. Noun: One under suspicion of guilt of a crime.

suspends. A word of bad portent, quite familiar during the Great Depression, meaning that a bank has failed, that an examiner or other public officer has been appointed to take it over, or that it ceases or refuses to make payments in the ordinary course of business. UCC § 4—104(1)(k).

suspence. A state of uncertainty.
See **en suspence.**

Suspendatur per collum (sus-pen-dā'ter per ko'lum). Let him be hanged by the neck.

These Latin words in their abbreviated form "sus. per coll.," were written opposite the name of a convict sentenced to be hanged in the calendar or list of all the prisoners' names, with their separate judgments in the margin. See 4 Bl Comm 403.

suspended. Temporarily inactive or inoperative; held in abeyance.

Such is its meaning in the constitutional provision that the privilege of the writ of habeas corpus shall never be suspended. See Wisener v Burrell, 28 Okla 546, 118 P 999.

suspended sentence. See **suspension of sentence.**

suspension. A termination of an employee's service by the employer, usually for the purpose of an investigation to determine whether or not the employee should be retained in service. A break in the relationship of employer and employee consequent upon the employee's deviation from the employer's business. 35 Am J1st M & S § 555. A temporary but forced withdrawal of a civil service employee. 15 Am J2d Civ S § 34.

suspension of action. The status of an action following the death of a party but prior to the substitution of the representative of the deceased party or other person who succeeds to his interest. 1 Am J2d Abat & R § 47.

suspension of interest. The stopping of the running of interest on an obligation by tender which is refused or by something preventing the payment of the obligation other than the fault of the debtor. 30 Am J Rev ed Int § 51.

suspension of judgment. See **opening judgment; stay of execution.**

suspension of liquor license. A temporary deprivation of rights or privileges under a license to sell or deal in alcoholic beverages. 30 Am J Rev ed Intox L § 174.

suspension of member. A temporary deprivation of the rights and privileges of membership in a society. 36 Am J2d Frat O § 62. The lifting for the time of the name of a member of a non-profit corporation from the membership list and the annulment for the time of his rights as a member. 18 Am J2d Corp § 473.

suspension of payment. Failure to pay obligations because of want of financial ability.

The expression means something more than a failure of the maker of commercial paper to seek the holder and pay him. Business men well understand its meaning; there is the idea in it of a failure to pay from an inability to do so. It has been held in effect that a suspension of payment occurs where a person indebted to others is unable to meet his engagements with and to pay his creditors in full. McCormick & Co. v Gem State Oil & Products Co. 38 Idaho 470, 222 P 286, 34 ALR 867, 871.

See **moratorium; suspends.**

suspension of performance. An interruption in the performance of a contract whether by agreement of the parties or caused by supervening circumstances.

suspension of policy. The ineffectiveness of a policy of insurance for a period, such as for the time during which a forfeiture, later avoided, is in existence. 29 Am J Rev ed Ins § 734.

suspension of power of alienation. See **rule against suspension of power of alienation.**

suspension of pupil. Denying a school pupil the right of attendance, not permanently but for a stated period of time. 47 Am J1st Sch § 177.

suspension of sentence. The suspension of imposition of sentence after conviction or plea of guilty for determinate and reasonable period. 21 Am J2d Crim L § 552. Postponement of the judgment of the court temporarily or indefinitely, the conviction and the disabilities arising therefrom remaining and become operative when judgment is rendered. Ex parte Bates, 20 NM 542, 151 P 698; Buchanan, 146 NY 264, 40 NE 883, 886. Staying the execution of a sentence imposed upon plea of guilty or conviction of a criminal offense. 21 Am J2d Crim L § 558.

suspension of statute of limitations. The lifting of a statute of limitations from a cause of action because of certain circumstances such as disability of the plaintiff, the absence of the defendant from the state, concealment of cause of action, etc. 34 Am J1st Lim Ac §§ 186 et seq.

suspensive condition. A term of a contract whereby the obligation is not to take effect until the happening of a certain event. New Orleans v Texas & Pacific R. Co. 171 US 312, 43 L Ed 178, 18 S Ct 875 (quoting from the Louisiana Civil Code which is said to be similar to the Code Napoleon in such respect). In effect, a **condition precedent.**

suspenso. See **in suspenso.**

sus. per coll. See **suspendatur per collum.**

suspicion. The imagination of the existence of something without proof, upon very slight evidence or upon no evidence at all. Gulf, Colorado & Santa Fe Railway Co. v Shieder, 88 Tex 152, 30 SW 902.

sustain. To uphold. To provide support. To endure; to undergo.
Within the meaning of the Federal income tax statute losses are "sustained" when the events definitely occur which give rise thereto. Brooks v United States (DC Pa) 32 F Supp 158.

sustaining demurrer. Upholding a demurrer. Deciding in favor of the demurrant.
A demurrer is sustained when an order of court is made to the effect that the demurrer is sustained and the order is entered upon the docket. See Kaufman v Buckley, 285 Mass 83, 188 NE 607.

sustenance (sus'tĕ-nans). That which supports life; food; victuals; provisions; that necessary food and drink which is sufficient to support life and maintain health. Groves v State, 116 Ga 516, 42 SE 755.

Suum cuique incommodum ferendum est, potius quam de alterius commodis detrahendum (su'um ki'kwe in-ko-mo'dum fe-ren'dum est, pō'she-us quam dē al-te'ri-us ko'mo-dis dē-tra-hen'dum). Each one must suffer his own inconvenience rather than take away the convenience of another. See 4 Bl Comm 31.

suum cuique tribuere (su'um kī'kwe tri-bū'e-re). Unto each shall be rendered that which is his.

suus (sū'us). His own.

s. v. An abbreviation of **sub voce.**

SW⁴. An abbreviation of a kind found in descriptions of real estate according to the government survey, standing for the Southwest Quarter, whether of a section or a quarter section of land.

swale (swāl). A depression in the ground, often wet or marshy. 56 Am J1st Water § 76.

swamp. Verb: To overcome; to overwhelm. To sink because filled with water. Noun: A marsh; a tract of wet land, usually partially covered by shallow waters. An area of land which is wet or marshy because depressed so as to receive the flow of surface waters or because of underground waters coming to the surface in spring. 56 Am J1st Water § 7.
As distinguished from overflowed lands, swamp lands are lands which require drainage to dispose of needless water or moisture on or in the lands, in order to make them fit for successful and useful cultivation. State ex rel. Ellis v Gerbing, 56 Fla 603, 47 So 353.

swampland. See **swamp.**

swap. A trade or exchange of property. 30 Am J2d Exch P § 1.

swear. To put a person under oath, that is, to administer an oath. To take an oath, that is, to put one's self under oath. To take God's name in vain; to curse.
As the word is used in the law of perjury, to swear means to state a fact or facts under the sanctity of an oath or affirmation administered by some duly qualified officer having authority to administer the oath in the particular proceeding or investigation in which the statement of the affiant is to be made. State v Dallagiovanna, 69 Wash 84, 124 P 209.
See **cursing; false swearing; oath; public swearing.**

swear in. To administer an oath to a person; to administer the oath of office to a person appointed to that office. Thalheim v State, 38 Fla 169, 189, 20 So 938.
See **oath of office.**

swearing the peace (swăr'ing the pēs). Making a statement under oath of facts warranting the granting by the court of a supplicavit.
See **supplicavit.**

swearing witness. Putting a witness under oath. 58 Am J1st Witn § 549.

sweatbox. A prolonged and unremitting questioning of an accused, especially when accompanied by deprivation of refreshment, rest, or relief, for the purpose of extorting a confession from him. 29 Am J2d Ev § 550.

sweat cloth. A facetious expression for a gaming table, especially one used for throwing dice. United States v Smith (CC Dist Col) Cranch cc 659, F Cas No 16329.

sweating. The nefarious practice of abusing prisoners or persons suspected of possessing information to force them to confess or to tell what they know.
See **sweatbox; third degree.**

sweepstakes. A contest, especially a horse race, or game of chance in which the winner "sweeps in" or takes all the stakes wagered.
As defined by the American racing rules, a sweepstakes or stake is a race publicly declared open to all complying with its conditions, for which the prize is the sum of the stakes which the subscribers agree to pay for each horse nominated; and, if an additional sum of money, cup, plate, or other reward is offered to the winner, the race is still a sweepstakes, whatever may be the name given to such addition. Three subscribers, unless otherwise stipulated in its conditions, make a sweepstakes, and the race is not void so long as there is a horse qualified to start. Stone v Clay (CA7 Ill) 61 F 889, 890.

sweet cider. A nonintoxicating beverage made from the juice of apples.

swein (swīn). A freeholder in one of the king's forests. See 3 Bl Comm 72.

sweinmote court (swīn'mōt kort). A forest court held three times in each year before the verderors of the forest as judges and with sweins or freeholders of the forest as jurors, to inquire into grievances committed by forest officers and to try presentments certified from the court of attachments. See 3 Bl Comm 72.

swell. Verb: To increase in volume or size. To cause an increase, e.g. an increase in the damages for an injury. To be filled with emotion or the sense of one's own importance. Noun: A wave, particularly a large wave.

swimming pool. A pool, especially an artificial, pool of water for the immersion of human beings; in plain words, a place for swimming. Gopalangio v Chicago, 23 Ill 2d 570, 179 NE2d 663, 92 ALR2d 1276. Sometimes a public place. 4 Am J2d Amuse § 50.

swindler. One who swindles.
See **swindling**.

swindling. The acquisition of property or an instrument representing a valuable right by means of some device or fraudulent representation with intent to appropriate such property or instrument or to destroy or impair the right of the owner therein. 32 Am J2d False P § 2.

As the words "swindling" and "cheating" are ordinarily used, they import a fraudulent causing of pecuniary or property loss. See United States v Cohn, 270 US 339, 346, 70 L Ed 616, 619, 46 S Ct 251.

The word is of German origin and of indefinite meaning. It does not import an indictable offense and is held to mean no more than the word "cheating," which does not impute a crime. Stevenson v Hayden, 2 Mass (2 Tyng) 406, 408.

The word has no legal or technical meaning, but it commonly implies that there has been recourse to petty and mean artifices for obtaining money, which may or may not be strictly illegal. The disappointed and vexed creditor not infrequently will apply the term "swindler" to a delinquent debtor, and an absconding debtor is not infrequently spoken of as having swindled his creditors. Hence the word does not per se import a crime. Cunningham v Baker, 104 Ala 160, 171, 16 So 68.

swine. Another term for hog.

swinging claim. The act of the owner of a mining claim in appropriating ground not within the limits of his claim. 36 Am J1st Min & M § 89.

swinging door. See **revolving door**.

switch. Verb: To change course. To change opinion or preference. To change the position of something. To move railroad cars from one track to another or from one place in a train to another place in a train. Noun: An instrumentality for opening or closing an electric circuit. Thomson-Houston Electric Co. v Nassau Electric R. Co. (CA2 NY) 107 F 277. A switch track of a railroad. A section of railroad track which may be moved a short distance by a lever so as to permit a train or cars to move from such track to another track.

See **flying switch; frog; gravity switch; kicking cars; running switch; split switch**.

switch box. A receptacle for electric switches, usually placed on a wall. 43 Am J1st Pub Util § 41.

switch connections. Switches available for moving the cars of one railroad line to another railroad line.

switch engine. A locomotive used only for switching and purposes incidental to the maintenance and operation of a railroad yard.

The distinction between a road engine and a switch engine, as they are known in railroading, is this: The road engine has a pilot in front. A yard or switch engine has a footboard, both front and rear, upon which the brakemen and switchmen step and stand while switching cars. A road engine is heavier, too heavy for switching conveniently and has no footboards. Prosser v Montana Cent. R. Co. 17 Mont 372, 43 P 81.

switching operations. See **switch; switching service**.

switching service. Also called transfer service,—the service rendered by a railroad company in switching cars for special benefit of shipper or consignee, either preceding or following a transportation service.

The term applies only to a shipment on which legal freight charges have already been earned, or are to be earned. It is an incident to a line haul and may be rendered preceding the line haul, during a line haul, as in transferring cars to a connecting road, or after the end of the line haul. Cummings Sand & Gravel Co. v Minneapolis & St. Louis Railroad Co. 182 Iowa 955, 166 NW 354.

Use of a locomotive to push cars from an industrial plant along main line tracks of another railroad company running through a city to the company's own switchyards does not constitute "switching operations," excepted from the operation of the statute requiring a lookout ahead on locomotives. Alabama G. S. R. Co. v Brookshire (CA6 Tenn) 166 F2d 278, 1 ALR2d 612.

switchman. A railroad employee who operates switches. 35 Am J1st M & S § 435.

switch stand. An upright piece of metal upon which the lever which operates a railroad switch is mounted.

switch target. A device so adjusted to a railroad switch stand that the switch cannot be opened or closed without shifting the targets, the white to a right angle position to the main track when the switch is closed, and the red to a similar position when the switch is open. Chicago, Indianapolis & Louisville Railway Co. v Barker, 169 Ind 670, 83 NE 369.

switch track. A railroad track used for switching cars as incidental to a regular train haul, also made use of at times for loading, unloading, and storing cars. 44 Am J1st RR § 231.
See **sidetrack**.

swoon. To faint.

sword. A hand weapon having a long sharp blade. A deadly weapon. 56 Am J1st Weap § 3.

sword cane. A sword carried in a walking stick or cane; a deadly weapon. Anno: 30 ALR 816.

sworn. See **duly sworn; legally sworn; mainsworn; swear**.

sworn copy. A copy proved by oral evidence to have been compared with the original document and to correspond exactly therewith. Verified under oath.
See **certified copy**.

sworn evidence. Testimony given under oath.
An affidavit stating facts of which the affiant purports to have knowledge is "sworn evidence." See Ex parte Germain, 258 Mass 289, 298, 155 NE 12, 15.

sworn to. Verified before a proper officer. Hocking Power Co. v Harrison, 20 Ohio App 135, 139, 153 NE 155, 157. Stated under oath.

syb and som. (Saxon.) Peace and security.

syllabi (sil'a-bī). Headnotes of reported cases. 20 Am J2d Cts § 77.
See **headnotes**.

syllabis et verbis. See **in syllabis et verbis**.

syllabus (sil'a-bus). Singular of **syllabi**.

syllabus rule (rūl). The rule that the syllabus of a

decision, as printed in the cases contained in the state reports, alone constitutes the law of the case. Walsh v E. G. Shinner & Co. (CA3 Del) 20 F2d 586. Such rule is established in Ohio as a rule of court applicable to the decisions of the Supreme Court of Ohio, Baltimore & O. R. Co. v Baileeie, 112 Ohio, St 567, 148 NE 233.

syllogism (sil'ọ-jizm). A logical reasoning, consisting of a major premise, a minor premise and a conclusion. For example: All men are human; Smith is a man. Therefore Smith is a human being.

Every action at law to redress a wrong or enforce a right, if properly instituted, is a syllogism of which the major premise is the proposition of law involved, the minor premise is the proposition of fact, and the judgment the conclusion. Lamphear v Buckingham, 33 Conn 237.

sylva (sil'vạ). A wood.

sylva caedua. Same as **silva caedua.**

sylvestres (sil-ves'trēz). Frequenters of wooded land. See 2 Bl Comm 39.

symbol (sim'bol). A mark, object, or letter that stands for something, such as © standing for copyright or a ditto mark indicating a repetition. 1 Am J2d Abbr § 9; 18 Am J2d Copyr § 58.

symbolic delivery. A transaction wherein physical custody is retained by the party who in the reality of the situation should not have possession. A constructive change of possession. 15 Am J2d Chat Mtg § 137. A delivery of goods of such a nature or so situated as to make actual manual delivery impossible. 24 Am J2d Frd Conv § 43. The act of a purchaser or mortgagee of a chattel in merely touching the chattel and declaring his ownership of it. Sloan v National Surety Co. 74 App Div 417, 77 NYS 428. The delivery of the key to a warehouse containing the subject matter in question; the delivery of a bill of lading or warehouse receipt in lieu of the property itself. 41 Am J1st Pldg & Col § 14; 56 Am J1st Wareh § 39. The completion of a gift of property of such nature that an actual manual delivery is impossible, such as an unequivocal declaration of gift, accompanied by a delivery of the only means by which possession of the article can be obtained, by delivery of an instrument making an appropriation of the property to the donee, or other act indicating unmistakably an intent to transfer the property to the donee. 24 Am J1st Gifts § 27.

symbolic levy. A levy of a writ of attachment without taking actual possession of the property, as in the case of a levy upon a judgment. Edwards v Tracy, 203 Iowa 1083, 212 NW 317.

See **paper levy.**

symbolic possession. The constructive possession of goods which is exercised by a person who holds a warehouse receipt or other indicia of their ownership.

symmetry (sim'e-tri). Harmony as between parts of a structure. Correspondence of parts in shape and size.

symbolum animae (sim'bo-lum a'ni-mē). The symbol of the soul. See 2 Bl Comm 425.

sympathetic illness. An illness resulting from a mental or emotional disturbance caused by the observance of the suffering of another from injury or illness. 52 Am J1st Torts § 70.

sympathetic strike (sim-pạ-thet'ik strīk). A strike in support of another existing strike of other employees. Anno: 83 ALR 458; 71 L Ed 261.

A strike instigated in aid of a secondary boycott is such a strike. In essence it is a threat to inflict damage upon the immediate employer, between whom and his employees no dispute exists, in order to bring him against his will into a concerted plan to inflict damage upon another employer who is in dispute with his employees. Duplex Printing Press Co. v Deering, 254 US 443, 474, 65 L Ed 349, 360, 41 S Ct 172.

synagogue (sin'ạ-gog). A place used by Jews for religious worship and study. Olhack v Temple Anshe Sholom, 184 Misc 1071, 56 NYS2d 598.

synchronize (sing'krọ-nīz). To adjust the movement of parts of a machine so that they relate properly, one to the other.

syndic (sin'dik). A corporate agent. A trustee appointed to represent the creditors of the estate of an insolvent person under the law of Louisiana. Bank of Tennessee v Horn (US) 17 How 157, 15 L Ed 70.

The word appears in Spanish-American grants but is not contained in the recapilacion or official compilation of the laws of the Indies. The Spanish Dictionary of the Academy, and the French authors on Jurisprudence, agree in defining it to mean the person charged with the care, defense, and advancement of the interests of a community. In France, the trustee who holds the property of a bankrupt, is styled "le syndic." See Strother v Lucas (US) 12 Pet 410, 442, note, 9 L Ed 1137, 1150, note.

syndicalism (sin'di-kạ lism). Any doctrine or precept advocating, teaching, or aiding and abetting the commission of crime, sabotage, or unlawful acts of force and violence or unlawful methods of terrorism, as a means of accomplishing a change in industrial ownership or control, or effecting any political change. Burns v United States, 274 US 328, 71 L Ed 1077, 47 S Ct 650.

syndicate (sin'di-kāt). An association of individuals formed for the purpose of conducting and carrying out some particular business transaction, ordinarily of a financial character, in which the members are mutually interested. Hathaway v Porter Royalty Pool, 296 Mich 90, 295 NW 571, 138 ALR 955, amd 296 Mich 733, 299 NW 451, 138 ALR 967. Sometimes but not necessarily a partnership. 40 Am J1st Partn § 3. A system, plan, or arrangement whereunder the writings of a columnist are distributed to newspapers throughout the country for publication.

syngraph (sing'gráf). Singular of **syngrapha.**

syngrapha (sing'gráf-ạ). A term of the canonists for what the lawyers called "chirographa."

See **chirographa.**

synod (sin'ọd). A church board. The council of a religious society. Roshi's Appeal, 69 Pa 462 (German Reformed Church). An intermediate governing body or judicatory of a Protestant church, particularly a Presbyterian church.

There are in the Presbyterian system of ecclesiastical government, in regular succession, the presbytery over the session or local church, the synod over the presbytery, and the general assembly over all. These are called, in the language of the church organs, "judicatories," and they entertain appeals from the decisions of those below, and prescribe corrective measures in other cases. Watson v Jones (US) 13 Wall 679, 727, 20 L Ed 666, 676.

synonym (sin'ō-nim). A word which expresses the same, or much the same, idea as another.

synopsis (si-nop'sis). A summary of the contents of an article.
See **syllabi**.

syphilis (sif'i-lis). An infectious venereal disease, having severe consequences if not treated successfully. Beard v Royal Neighbors, 53 Or 102, 99 P 83.

syphilis test. A test of the blood or other content of the body by chemical analysis to determine the existence of syphilitic infection. 23 Am J2d Dep § 226.
See **Wasserman test**.

syrup. A thick sweet liquid; a heavy solution of sugar in water. An article of food for table use. McDermott v State, 143 Wis 18, 126 NW 888, revd on another point 228 US 115, 57 L Ed 754, 33 S Ct 431.

system. Plan or arrangement, particularly in conducting an operation. An organization.

system of railroad. See **railroad system**.

systolic pressure (sis-tol'ik presh'ūr). Blood pressure. A matter of significance in reference to the employment of a lie detector.
See **lie detector**.

T

t. Abbreviation of ton, of teste, of termino.

taberna (tạ-bẻr′nạ). A tavern.

tabernaculum (tab-ėr-nak′ū-lum). A tavern.

table. A compilation of information, particularly scientific information, such as a mortality table, a remarriage table, a table of weights, etc. 29 Am J2d Ev § 889. A piece of household furniture or of furnishing of an office or place of work, consisting of a flat top supported by legs.

See **experience table; gaming table; mortality table; tax table.**

table of surrender values. A tabulated list in a life insurance policy showing the increasing cash-surrender value from year to year or from one period of years to another period of years.

table rents. (Ecclesiastical.) Rents which were collected to supply the bishop's table.

tables of life expectancy. See **mortality table.**

tablet. Sheets of writing paper bound together.

table top. Literally, the top of a table. A device employed in loading and unloading ships. "The defendants provided a wooden platform, called a 'table top,' between the ship and the quay, which was fastened at one end to the ship's gunwale by ropes, the other end unfixed upon the quay. In the course of their duty, the stevedores would have to go upon this 'table top.'" Loader v London & India Docks Joint Committee (Eng) 8 LT 5.

tabula in naufragio (ta′bu-la in nâ-fra′ji-ō). Literally, a plank in a shipwreck. A graphic expression applied to the saving of a junior equity by acquiring the legal title. 27 Am J2d Equity § 151.

tabularius (ta-bu-lā′ri-us). A notary.

tachograph (tak′ọ grȧf). The record of the speed of an object as registered by a tachometer. 8 Am J2d Auto § 949.

tachometer (tak-ẹ-om′e-tėr). A device for measuring speed, whether it be a vehicle, the current of a stream, the blood in a human vessel, etc.

tacit (tas′it). Silent; not expressed; implied.

Tacita quaedam habentur pro expressis (ta′si-ta kwē′dam hā-ben′ter prō ex-pre′sis). Certain things which are tacit are regarded as expressed.

tacite (ta′si-te). Tacitly; silently; impliedly.

tacit hypothecation (hī-poth-ẹ-kā′shọn). A hypothecation which is implied by law for the security of a creditor.

tacit law (lȧ). That law which arises out of the silent consent and the customs and usages of the people.

tacit mortgage. The security for the performance by a parent of his duty and obligation as guardian of his child, his entire estate being bound in effect for the proper discharge of the trust. 25 Am J1st G & W § 47.

tacito et illiterato hominum consensu et moribus expressum (ta′si-tō et il-li″te-rā′tō ho′mi-num konsen′sū et mo′ri-bus ex-pres′sum). Expressed by the silent and unwritten consent and customs of men. 1 Bl Comm 64.

tacking. Changing the course of direction of a sailboat by changing the position of the sails. Adding. A doctrine which permits an adverse possessor to add his period of possession to that of a prior adverse possessor in order to establish a continuous possession for the period prescribed by statute for the ripening of adverse possession into title. Fagan v Grady, 101 NH 18, 131 A2d 441. An attempt on the part of a creditor having two liens of different priorities to join them so as to perfect priority over the lien of a third person intervening the two liens. 30A Am J Rev ed Judgm § 529. A long established rule of the English court of chancery that where property is subject to successive mortgages, and the third mortgagee had advanced his money without notice of the second mortgage, he may take an assignment of the first mortgage and require the second mortgagee to redeem from both of the other mortgages before the property can be subjected to the second mortgage. 36 Am J1st Mtg § 203.

tacking disabilities. Adding the period of time within which a plaintiff was under one disability, for example, infancy, to the period of a succeeding disability suffered by him, for example, insanity, for the purpose of determining whether or not the statute of limitations has run against his cause of action. 3 Am J2d Adverse Possession § 132; 34 Am J1st Lim Ac § 210.

tackle. The rigging and pulleys employed on a vessel in operating the sails; a part of the ship as a going concern. 48 Am J2d Ship § 36. Equipment for an expedition or outing, such as a fishing trip.

See **block and tackle.**

Taft-Hartley Act. See **Labor Relations Acts.**

tag. See **dog tag; label.**

tailage (tā′lạj). Burdens, charges, or impositions, put or set upon persons or property for public uses. Anno: 17 ALR 1059.

tail estate. See **fee tail.**

tail female. See **fee tail female.**

tailgate. Noun: The door at the rear end of a truck, to be opened or entirely removed in unloading cargo at the rear. Inter-Southern Life Ins. Co. v Bowyer, 90 Ind App 494, 169 NE 65. Verb: To drive a motor vehicle closely behind another vehicle. 8 Am J2d Auto § 773.

tail general. See **fee tail general.**

tailings. Refuse, particularly from mining operations. Ore which has been taken out of a mine and from which all of the valuable mineral content has not been extracted. Commissioner of Internal Revenue v Kennedy Mining & Milling Co. (CA9 Cal) 125 F2d 399.

taillight. A light, required by statute, to be carried at the back of a vehicle on a public highway, as a warning to vehicles approaching in darkness or at a time when natural light is deficient. 8 Am J2d Auto § 153.

tail male. See **fee tail male.**

tailor's suit club. See **suit club.**

tail special. See **fee tail special; special estate tail.**

tailzie (tal-ye). A term of the Scottish law comparable to the English "entail." Hubbell v Hubbell, 135 Iowa 637, 113 NW 512.

taini. Freeholders.

taint. See **attainder; taint of usury.**

taint of usury. The illegality in a usurious transaction attaching to all consecutive obligations or securities growing out of the transaction. 55 Am J1st Usury § 96.

take. To lay hold of, to seize or grasp in some manner. 32 Am J1st Larc § 12. To receive either by descent or by purchase. Re Billings' Estate v Hauver, 65 Cal 593, 4 P 639. To acquire; to obtain; to procure. Hallenbeck v Getz, 63 Conn 385, 388.

There may be a taking of property although there is no actual entry within its bounds and no artificial structure erected upon it. Milhous v State Highway Dept. 194 SC 33, 8 SE2d 852, 128 ALR 1186.

Conditions so burdensome may be imposed that they constitute an outright "taking" of property, within the meaning of the Fourteenth Amendment to the Federal Constitution, although the title to the property and some vestiges of its uses remain in the owner. East Coast Lumber Terminal, Inc. v Babylon (CA2 NY) 174 F2d 106, 8 ALR2d 1219.

take an exception. Same as **note an exception.**

take effect. To become effective. Anno: 76 ALR 646.
See **effective date.**

take his own life. To commit suicide; to destroy one's own life voluntarily and intentionally. Dickerson v North Western Mut. L. Ins. Co. 200 Ill 270, 65 NE 694, affg 102 Ill App 280.

Defined as it pertains to the applicability of a suicide clause in a life insurance policy in Anno: 35 ALR 160.

take-home pay. The weekly wages or salary of an employee less deductions by way of withholding for taxes, payment made into pension fund, Social Security tax, group insurance premium, etc.

taken for public use. Possessed, occupied, used, and enjoyed by a public body or public agency for public purposes. Pontiac Improv. Co. v Cleveland Metropolitan Park Dist. 104 Ohio St 447, 135 NE 635, 23 ALR 866. A term broad enough to include cases in which access to the abutting premises is obstructed by a change of grade of a highway, or where there is such physical injury to property as results in destruction or substantial impairment of its usefulness. White v Southern R. Co. 142 SC 284, 140 SE 560, 57 ALR 634.
See **taking for public use.**

take-nothing judgment. A judgment that plaintiff take nothing; a judgment that plaintiff take nothing under a designated count or counts of his declaration or complaint. Goldfarb v Bronston, 154 Fla 180, 17 So 2d 300.

take-off. The amount taken out of money in play by the person conducting the game. 24 Am J1st Gaming § 20. The movement of an aircraft in leaving the ground and becoming air-borne. An imitation of a public character for comic effect.

take testimony. To receive the evidence of sworn witnesses either in a court or before an officer or body authorized to receive it.

take-up statute. A state tax statute enacted for the purpose of absorbing the credit given in computing the federal estate tax for death taxes paid to a state or territory. Anno: 63 ALR 1096, s. 147 ALR 467.

taking. See **take.**

taking abstract. Making an abstract or summary of an article or instrument, e.g., noting the important features, such as date, description of property, time of recording, etc. from the public record of a deed, conveyance, or mortgage. Anno: 80 ALR 772.

taking bill pro confesso. See **decree pro confesso.**

taking by eminent domain. See **eminent domain; taking for public use.**

taking by moieties (tā′king bī moi′e-tēs). Taking as tenants in common.

taking by right of representation. See **per stirpes.**

taking case from jury. Directing a verdict. The result of various motions testing the sufficiency of the evidence to sustain a judgment in favor of the party against whom the motion is made, where the court grants the motion. 53 Am J1st Trial §§ 293 et seq.

taking effect. See **take effect.**

taking for public use. Entering upon private property for more than a momentary period and, under the warrant or color of legal authority, devoting it to a public use, or otherwise informally appropriating or injuriously affecting it in such a way as substantially to oust the owner and deprive him of all beneficial enjoyment thereof. 26 Am J2d Em D § 157. An actual interference with, or disturbance of, property rights, as distinguished from injuries and interferences which are merely consequential, incidental, trivial, insignificant. Noble State Bank v Haskell, 219 US 104, 55 L Ed 112, 31 S Ct 186; Bonnett v Vallier, 136 Wis 193, 116 NW 885.

Within the meaning of a constitutional provision that private property shall not be taken for public use without just compensation, the term includes any action, the effect of which is to deprive the owner of all or most of his interest in the subject matter, such as destroying or damaging it. United States v General Motors Corp. 323 US 373, 89 L Ed 311, 65 S Ct 357, 156 ALR 390.

Diminution in value of a business made less prosperous as a result of regulation does not constitute a "taking" of property within the due process clause of the constitution. California State Auto. Asso. Inter-Insurance Bureau v Maloney, 341 US 105, 95 L Ed 788, 71 S Ct 601.
See **taken for public use.**

taking from the person. An element of robbery.

In robbery, taking from the person does not mean that the property must be in contact with the person, or even that it must be in his actual or immediate presence, but that it must be so in the possession or under his control that violence or putting him in fear was the means used by the robber to take it. See 46 Am J1st Rob § 7.
See **larceny from the person.**

taking off. See **take-off.**

taking per capita. See **per capita.**

taking per stirpes. See **per stirpes.**

taking poison. See **poison.**

taking, stealing, and carrying away. Allegation of the asportation in an indictment for larceny. State v Donahue, 75 Or 409, 144 P 755, 147 P 548, 5 ALR 1121.

taking-unconscionable advantage. Taking advantage of the condition, circumstances, or necessities of the other party in making a contract with him that no honest man would accept and that no sane person in the position of the other party would make. 37 Am J2d Fraud § 23.

taking without compensation. See **taking for public use.**

tale. Something related. A story. A tally, count, or enumeration. Pickering v Moore, 67 NH 533, 32 A 828. An ancient term for a plaintiff's declaration, narratio or count, the pleading in which he sets forth his cause of action. See 3 Bl Comm 293.

talent scout. One who finds a person of possible talent as an actor or entertainer and introduces him to a producer, usually under agreement to receive a percentage of earnings. 27 Am J2d Employ Ag § 9. A person who, having found a person with possible talent as an actor or entertainer, introduces the latter to an employment agency under agreement to receive a percentage of all commissions received by the agency on the earnings of the person thus introduced. Warner v Marchetti, 52 Cal App 2d 172, 125 P2d 838.

tales. Same as **talesmen**.

tales de circumstantibus (tāls dē ser-kum-stan′ti-bus). Jurors from the bystanders, that is, jurors empaneled from bystanders in the court room to form a jury, where a sufficient number of qualified jurors are not available for the trial of a case. 31 Am J Rev ed Jury § 3. For so many of the bystanders,—an old writ for directing the addition of a sufficient number of persons from those present in the court room to make up the jury of twelve. See 3 Bl Comm 365.

tales-juror. Same as **talesmen**.
See **talesmen**.

talesmen (tālz′men). Jurors, sometimes called tales-jurors, returned, often from bystanders, to complete a jury panel when because of challenge or other cause, there is not a petit jury to determine a civil or criminal case. 31 Am J Rev ed Jury § 3. In occasional usage, a synonym of jurors. 31 Am J Rev ed Jury § 3.

When talesmen are summoned for use in a particular case after the regular panel has been exhausted, it is not necessary that the talesmen be actually in the courtroom when summoned. They are no less bystanders because they were summoned in advance to be there for use when needed. Morgan v Sun Oil Co. (CA5 Tex) 109 F2d 178.

talio (tā′li-ō). (Civil law.) A punishment in kind, on the principle, "an eye for an eye, a tooth for a tooth," etc.

Talis interpretatio semper fienda est, ut evitetur absurdum, et inconveniens, et ne judicium sit illusorium (tā′lis in-ter-pre-tā′she-ō sem′per fi-en′da est, ut e-vi-tē′ter ab-ser′dum, et in-kon-ve′ni-enz, et nē ju-di′she-um sit il-lu-sō′ri-um). Such an interpretation should always be made that absurdity and inconvenience may be avoided, and lest the judgment be illusory.

talisman (tal′is-man). A good luck charm, often constituting the subject matter of schemes to defraud. Anno: 34 ALR 1292.

Talis non est eadem, nam nullum simile est idem (tā′lis non est e′a-dem, nam nul′lum si′mi-le est i′dem). That which is like is not the same, for nothing which is merely similar is the same.

talis qualis (tā′lis quā′lis). As much as; such as.

taliter (tā′li-ter). Thus; in such a manner; so.

Taliter processum est (tā′li-ter pro-ses′sum est). In such manner it proceeds.

talking machine. A phonograph or other device by which the human voice is reproduced by mechanical means. Edmunds v Duff, 280 Pa 355, 124 A 489, 33 ALR 7, 19.

tallagium (tal-la′ji-um). Same as **talliage**.

talliage (tal′li-aj). A tax of the same nature as scutage, but levied upon the inhabitants of cities and burghs.

The tax was not imposed upon property, but upon persons, according to the value of their estates. Aliens were assessed at a double rate. See 1 Bl Comm 310.

talliatum. See **feudum talliatum**.

tallies of loan (tal′ēz of lōn). Bills of credit which were issued by the officers of the English exchequer when a temporary loan was necessary to meet the exigencies of government.

They were first termed "tallies of loans and orders of repayment," charged on the credit of the exchequer in general, and made assignable from one person to another. Baldwin's Views on Cases (US) 11 Pet 120; Views on Brisco v Commonwealth Bank of Kentucky, 9 L Ed 931.

tally. Verb: To count. Noun: A count or reckoning, particularly of the number of votes cast for a candidate in an election. 26 Am J2d Elect § 291.

Taltarum's Case. An ancient English case out of which common recoveries arose. Yearb. 12 Edw IV 19-21; 28 Am J2d Est § 47.

talweg. Same as **thalweg**.

talzie. Same as **tailzie**.

tam (tam). So; to such extent or degree; so much.

tame animal. A domestic animal; an animal associated with family life or accustomed to live in or near the habitations of men. Commonwealth v Flynn, 285 Mass 136, 188 NE 627, 92 ALR 206.

tamen (tā′men). However; yet; nevertheless; notwithstanding.

tam facti quam animi (tam fak′ti quam a′ni-mī). As much in deed as in intent.

tam immensus aliarum super alias ascervatarum legum cumulus (tam im-men′sus a-li-ā′rum sū′per ā′li-ās as-ser-vā-tā′rum lē′gum ku′mu-lus). Such an immense accumulation of laws heaped one upon the other. 1 Bl Comm 81.

tamper. See **tampering**.

tampering (tam′pėring). Meddling; interfering. Making corrupting or perverting changes. Foolish or trifling experimentation. United States v Tomicich (DC Pa) 41 F Supp 33.

The word does not necessarily imply the commission of a criminal act. Keefe v Donnell, 92 Me 151, 159, 42 A 345.

tampering with jury. Contacting a member or members of a jury for the purpose of influencing their action as jurors, sometimes including bribery or corruption. 39 Am J1st New Tr § 105.

tampering with motor vehicle. Meddling with a motor vehicle, particularly with controls or equipment. State v Ridinger (Mo) 266 SW2d 626, 42 ALR2d 617.

As to what constitutes offense of "tampering" with motor vehicle or contents, see Anno: 42 ALR2d 624.

tamping. Pressing or pounding upon material put in as filling to give it solidity. Leo F. Piazza Paving Co. v Bebeck & Brkich, 141 Cal App 2d 226, 296 P2d 368, 369, footnote.

tam quam (tam quom). As much as; as well as.

tangible (tan'ji-bl). Capable of being possessed or realized; readily apprehensible by the mind; real; substantial; evident. Williams v Board of Comrs. 84 Kan 508, 114 P 858.

tangible property. Property of material substance. Property which can be possessed physically, such as goods, wares and merchandise. Re Arbib's Estate, 127 Misc 820, 216 NYS 522.

tango (tang'gō). An intricate ball-room dance of South American origin. A game of chance. Anno: 60 ALR 347.

tanistry (tan'is-tri). An ancient Irish land tenure wherein the land descended to the oldest and most worthy man of the blood and name of the deceased ancestor.

tank bottoms. A term of the trade for the sediment which is deposited in crude oil tanks during their use for oil storage. Insurance Co. v Crude Oil Contracting Co. (DC Okla) 32 F Supp 116.

tank car. A railroad car the body of which consists of a large tank for the transportation of liquids, such as oil, gasoline, syrup, etc.

tank-car company. A company which owns and holds for leasing to others tank cars for the transportation of liquid substances, such as oil, gasoline, syrup, etc. General American Tank Car Corp. v El Dorado Terminal Co. 308 US 422, 84 L Ed 361, 60 S Ct 325, reh den 309 US 694, 84 L Ed 1035, 60 S Ct 465.

tannery. A place where raw hides or skins are tanned. Anno: 32 ALR 1358.

Tanquam prescriptum quod possessum (tan'quom prē-skrip'tum quod po-zes'sum). Prescription extends only so far as possession.

tanquam testamentum inofficiosum (tan'quom tes"-ta-men'tum in-of-fi"she-ō'sum). As an improvident will, i.e., a will in which the nearest relatives of the testator have been overlooked. See 1 Bl Comm 448.

tantrum. An unrestrained display of anger by act and word.

tantum. See **in tantum.**

Tantum bona valent, quantum vendi possunt (tan'-tum bō'na va'lent, quan'tum ven'di pos'sunt). Goods are worth as much as they can be sold for.

Tantum habent de lege, quantum habent de justitia (tan'tum hā'bent dē lē'je, quan'tum hā'bent dē jŭ-sti'she-a). Matters are important in law in so far as they possess justice.

tantus (tan'tus). As much; so much; so great.

tape. A tape measure. A narrow strip of cloth or paper. A magnetized strip upon which sounds are recorded and from which they are reproduced.

tape measure. A narrow strip, graduated in inches, feet, yards, rods, meters, etc., used in making linear measurements.

tape record. A record of the speed of a vehicle as recorded on a tachograph. Sound recorded upon a narrow band of metal for reproduction.

tap line. A service line supplying electric current to a household, place of business, or factory. Anno: 40 ALR2d 1322, § 8.

tapping wire. See **wire tapping.**

tarde (tär'di). The return of a sheriff or other officer stating that he received the process too late for service.

tardiness. Arriving late at school. 47 Am J1st Sch § 173. The matter of being late for any event or appointment for which a definite time has been set.

tardy objection. An objection to a pleading delayed in the making until after issues are joined, or after the introduction of evidence, or after judgment. 41 Am J1st Pl § 67.

tare (târ). An allowance made in determining weight for the outside or covering of an article, whether it is a box, barrel, bag, bale, crate, or other form of covering or container. Napier v Barney (CC NY) 5 Blatchf 191 (allowance in imposing customs duties).

target. The object of an attack. The object shot at in rifle practice. In modern usage, a definite goal, an objective, as such an amount of machines to be produced in a month.
See **switch target.**

tariff. A customs duty upon an imported article. A table or catalog containing the names of several kinds of merchandise with the duties or customs to be paid thereon upon importation. 21 Am J2d Cust D § 1. A schedule or tabulated list of railroad or public-utility rates.
See **protective tariff.**

tariff preference. A concession made to a foreign country in permitting an article shipped from such country to be received in this country upon the payment of a customs duty less than that charged upon the same article from another country or to be received duty free where the same article coming from another country is dutiable.

tariff schedule. A schedule contained in 19 USC § 1202, effective August 31, 1963, presenting tariff classifications in detail, with co-ordinating provisions. 21 Am J2d Cust D § 32. A schedule of the rates of a carrier. 13 Am J2d Car § 107. A schedule of the charges of a public service company.

tart. A prostitute, particularly one who solicits on the street.

tauri liberi libertas (tâ'ri lī'be-ri-lī-ber'tās). A bull for the free and common use of the tenants of the manor.

Taurus (tâ'rus). A bull.

tautology (tâ-tol'ō-ji). The quality of excessiveness in wording. 27 Am J1st Indict § 51.

tavern. A public place where accommodations of food and lodging are furnished to the traveling public for compensation. Anno: 19 ALR 519, s. 53 ALR 988. A place where intoxicating liquor is sold in small quantities to be drunk on the spot. 30 Am J Rev ed Intox L § 20.

taverner (tav'ér-nėr). The proprietor or keeper of a tavern.

tavern keeper. The proprietor or keeper of a tavern. A publican.

tax. A forced burden, charge, exaction, imposition, or contribution assessed in accordance with some reasonable rule of apportionment by authority of a sovereign state upon the persons or property within its jurisdiction to provide public revenue for the support of the government, the administration of the law, or the payment of public expenses. 51 Am J1st Tax § 3. Any payment exacted by the state or its municipal subdivisions as a contribution toward the cost of maintaining governmental functions, where the special benefit derived from their performance is merged in the general benefit. State ex rel. Fargo v Wetz, 40 ND 299, 168 NW 835, 5 ALR 731. A charge upon persons or property imposed by or under authority of the legislature for public purposes. Yosemite Lumber Co. v Industrial Acci. Com. 187 Cal 774, 204 P 226, 20 ALR 994.

Taxes are the enforced proportional contribution of persons and property, levied by the authority of the state for the support of the government and for all public needs, and so long as there exist public needs just so long exists the liability of the individual to contribute thereto. The obligation of the individual to the state is continuous and proportioned to the extent of the public wants. Patton v Brady, 184 US 608, 619, 46 L Ed 713, 719, 22 S Ct 493.

A tax is not regarded as a debt in the ordinary sense of the term, for the reason that a tax does not depend upon the consent of the taxpayer, and there is no express or implied contract to pay taxes. Taxes are not contracts between party and party, either express or implied; they are the positive acts of the government, through its various agents, binding upon the inhabitants and enforceable against them without reference to their personal or individual consent to be bound. Tax Com. v National Malleable Casting Co. 111 Ohio St 117, 144 NE 604, 35 ALR 1448.

The word "taxes," as used in the priority provision of the Bankruptcy Act, is not to be construed in a limited sense, but as including all obligations imposed by the state or political subdivisions under their respective powers for governmental or public purposes. It includes any pecuniary burden laid upon individuals or property for the purpose of supporting the government or undertakings authorized by it, irrespective of the name given the imposition, or the method of collection. No distinction is observed between impositions under the police power and impositions under the taxing power. 9 Am J2d Bankr § 543.

The difference between a tax and a penalty is sometimes difficult to define, and yet the consequences of the distinction in the required method of their collection often are important. Where the sovereign enacting the law has power to impose both tax and penalty, the difference between revenue production and mere regulation may be immaterial, but not so when one sovereign can impose a tax only, and the power of regulation rests in another. They do not lose their character as taxes because of the incidental motive. But there comes a time in the extension of the penalizing features of the so-called tax when it loses its character as such and becomes a mere penalty, with the characteristics of regulation and punishment. Bailey v Drexel Furniture Co. 259 US 20, 66 L Ed 817, 42 S Ct 449.

See **special assessment.**

taxable. Subject to a tax; liable to taxation.

taxable costs. Those costs and expenses of the party prevailing in an action or suit which may properly be included in the judgment of the court. American Nat. Bank v Cooper, 44 Idaho 288, 256 P 372.

taxable credit. Any obligation or contract which creates an enforceable indebtedness on the part of the obligor or promisor.

A contract to pay money is such an obligation, but a mere option is not, since it creates no indebtedness. Re Assessment of Shields, 134 Iowa 559, 111 NW 963.

taxable estate. The net estate of a decedent for the assessment of an estate, inheritance, or succession tax. The estate less the deductions allowed by law. 26 USC §§ 2051 et seq.; United States v Kombst, 286 US 424, 76 L Ed 1201, 52 S Ct 616; Hampton v Hampton, 188 Ky 199, 221 SW 496, 10 ALR 515.

taxable gain. See **capital gain.**

taxable gifts. Broadly, gifts subject to statutory gift taxes. Precisely, completed gifts by conveyance, assignment or transfer of money, property or property rights vesting legal or equitable title in the donee, a relinquishment of dominion and control over the property by the donor, the absence of a full and adequate consideration, the absence of a disclaimer or renunciation by the donee, and competence on the part of the donor to make the gift. Internal Revenue Code § 2501 (a).

taxable income. Adjusted gross income less deductions, whether itemized deductions or the standard deduction, plus the personal and dependency exemptions. Internal Revenue Code § 63. In another distinct sense, income which is not tax-exempt.

taxable property. Property which is liable to taxation; property which is not exempt from taxation.

taxable transfer. A transfer of property subject to gift tax.

See **taxable gifts.**

taxable value. The value at which property is assessed for taxation which is usually only a percentage of its actual or real value. 51 Am J1st Tax § 696.

For taxable value of taxpayer's capital or capital stock, see 51 Am J1st Tax § 834.

tax anticipation note. A note issued by a public body, payable only out of a special fund, in anticipation of tax collections creating or replenishing the fund. 43 Am J1st Pub Sec § 13.

tax anticipation warrant. A warrant issued by a public body payable only out of a special fund in anticipation of tax collections creating or replenishing the fund. 43 Am J1st Pub Sec § 13.

taxatio (ta-xā'she-ō). (Civil law.) An order made by the judge reducing the amount of damages claimed by the plaintiff in an action.

taxatio expensarum (ta-xā'she-ō ex-pen-sā'rum). The taxation of costs.

taxation. The assessment and collection of taxes, a power and process by which the sovereign raises revenue to defray the necessary expenses of government, apportioning the cost of government among those who in some measure are privileged to enjoy its benefits and must bear its burdens. Messer v Lang, 129 Fla 546, 176, 113 ALR 1073. An act of sovereignty to be performed, so far as it conveniently can be, with justice and equality to all. Union Pass. R. Co. v Philadelphia, 101 US 528, 25 L Ed 912. Graphically, but realistically stated, obtaining the greatest amount of feathers with the least squawking.

See **tax.**

taxation and representation. Concomitants under the American system of government. The rallying cry of the framers of the Federal Constitution.

The principle was that the consent of those who were expected to pay the tax was essential to its validity. Hence, the Constitution provided that representatives and direct taxes should be apportioned among the states according to numbers, Article I, Section 2, and that all duties, imports, and excises should be uniform throughout the United States,

Article I, Section 8. Pollock v Farmers' Loan & Trust Co. 157 US 429, 158 US 601, 39 L Ed 759, 1108, 15 S Ct 673, 912.

taxation of costs. The act of entering the various costs and the amounts thereof against the party or parties against whom costs have been awarded or allowed by the court. A ministerial function to be performed in a court of record by the clerk of the court, except as the court may be called upon to determine an objection to the manner in which the function has been performed by the clerk. 20 Am J2d Costs § 89.

tax avoidance. A legal method of lessening the tax burden, as by taking advantage of legal deductions in calculating net income for taxation.
See **tax evasion.**

tax benefit rule. The rule that the recovery by a taxpayer of any item previously deducted on his income tax return is taxable in the year of recovery to the extent that the original deduction or credit reduced his income tax liability in a prior year or years. Internal Revenue Code § 111.

tax bracket. The category in which a taxpayer appears in a tax computation table, such depending upon the amount of his taxable income.

tax calendar. A series of dates noted throughout an entire calendar year upon each of which dates the taxpayer shall take the action indicated by the calendar opposite such date.

tax certificate of sale. A certificate evidencing the sale of real property for unpaid delinquent taxes. Nelson v Central Land Co. 35 Minn 408, 410, 29 NW 121.

tax clause. A clause in a will intended to alleviate the burden of estate or inheritance taxes.

tax collector. A public officer, elected or appointed, acting in a ministerial capacity in the collection of taxes. 51 Am J1st Tax § 996.

tax commission. An administrative agency engaged in the administration of tax laws.

tax compromise. An agreement whereby the United States Government agrees to accept payment of less than the determined liability for federal tax.

tax computation table. A table prepared by the Internal Revenue Service for the use of taxpayers, the tabulation showing the amount of income tax to be paid on taxable income according to the amount of the income and the type of return as a single return, joint return of husband and wife, or a return made by a taxpayer as head of a household.

Tax Court. A special federal court taking the place of the body formerly known as the Board of Tax Appeals, available to a taxpayer against whom the Treasury Department claims a deficiency upon compliance with the prescribed procedure. Internal Revenue Code § 6213.

tax credit. A credit against income tax itself, as distinguished from a deduction which applies only to reduce the income. The sum owing a taxpayer for overpayment. Internal Revenue Code § 6402(a).

tax deduction. See **deduction.**

tax deed. A deed evidencing the conveyance of title to premises sold at a sale for the nonpayment of taxes assessed thereon, which is ordinarily executed by the tax collector and by him delivered to the purchaser at the sale.
In some jurisdictions the deed is executed and delivered immediately after the sale and the title conveyed is subject to defeasance by the redemption of the property; in others the deed is not delivered until the period of redemption has expired. 51 Am J1st Tax § 1082.

tax district. Same as **taxing district.**

taxes. See **tax; taxation.**

tax evasion. Fraud in representation or concealment in attempting to avoid payment of a tax legally due, as in the case of an income tax, the filing of a return fraudulently understated in a willful attempt to evade payment. Willingham v United States (CA5 Tex) 289 F2d 283; Swallow v United States (CA10 Colo) 307 F2d 81, cert den 371 US 950, 9 L Ed 2d 499, 83 S Ct 504, reh den 372 US 925, 9 L Ed 2d 731, 83 S Ct 718. A felony punishable by a fine of not more than $10,000 or up to five years imprisonment, or both. Internal Revenue Code § 7201.

tax exempt income. Income exempt from income tax; nontaxable income, such as interest on state and municipal bonds, compensation for injuries or sickness, proceeds of life insurance, etc. Funds accruing as income in the broad sense of the term, but not taxable as income.

tax exemption. A personal exemption of a fixed amount, as determined by statute, to be deducted from gross income in determining the taxable income of a person. Internal Revenue Code § 151. A dependent constituting a personal exemption in computation of taxable income.
See **exemption from taxation; tax exempt income; tax-exempt organization.**

tax-exempt organization. An organization which, because of its character, particularly as religious, charitable, or educational, is exempt from taxation.

tax ferret. A public employee of a taxing body, usually a county, directed to ascertain property or other source of taxation omitted from assessment or levy and place it upon the rolls for assessment, levy, and the collection of taxes thereon. Ingram v Chappell, 127 Okla 135, 260 P 20.

tax-free income. See **tax exempt income.**

tax-free property. Property exempt from taxation. See **exemption from taxation.**

taxi. Noun: Same as **taxicab.** Verb: To control the movement of an aircraft upon the ground under its own power.

taxicab. An automobile used in the transportation of passengers for hire. A motor-driven passenger conveyance held for public hire at certain places where the driver may be reached by telephone or radio communication, charging upon a time or distance basis, and carrying passengers to destinations without following a fixed route. Columbia v Alexander, 125 SC 530, 119 SE 241, 32 ALR 746; Memphis v State, 133 Tenn 83, 179 SW 631; Anderson v Yellow Cab Co. 179 Wis 300, 191 NW 748, 31 ALR 1197, 1200.

taxicab company. A company operating taxicabs, furnishing automobiles for transportation with driver on order, and, as such, a common carrier. Terminal Taxicab Co. v Kutz, 241 US 252, 60 L Ed 984, 36 S Ct 583.

taxicab service. The continuous or intermittent service, as required, provided by taxicab companies at airports, railroad stations, and bus stations.

taxing district. The political division or subdivision throughout which a particular tax is levied and col-

lected. An incorporated governmental agency of the state. 37 Am J1st Mun Corp § 6.
See **special taxing district**.

taxing power. A power inherent in sovereignty and unlimited in the absence of constitutional restrictions, but subject in its exercise to the discretion of the authorities in whom it is reposed, the principal check against its abuse resting in the responsibility of the members of the legislature to their constituents. 51 Am J1st Tax § 39. A power of the state which is one of the attributes of sovereignty inherent in every form of government whether or not it is authorized by a constitution. People ex rel. Scott v Pitt, 169 NY 521, 62 NE 662.
See **the power to tax is the power to destroy**.

taxing unit. A public body assessing, levying, and collecting taxes, such as the state, the county, or a city.
See **tax district**.

tax levy. See **levy**.

tax lien. A lien imposed by constitution or statute as security for the payment of a tax. A security established by statute of which the collecting body may avail itself in default of payment of taxes, being against the property itself, not on the interest of the person assessed, its primary purpose being to allow the property to be taken or sold for nonpayment of taxes. 51 Am J1st Tax § 1010.
See **personal property tax lien**.

tax limit. Provisions of state constitutions expressly limiting the rate at which taxes may be levied. A limit usually, if not invariably, based upon the valuation of the taxable property within the taxing unit, sometimes restricting taxes to a certain percentage of the valuation, at other times restricting them to a designated amount of taxes per stated amount of valuation. 51 Am J1st Tax § 138.

tax list. A list of a taxpayer's property as given by him to the assessor or as made by the assessor. A listing of all the taxable property in the taxing unit. The official list or book containing the descriptions of property and the names of persons who are liable to assessment. A schedule of the polls and ratable estate of the inhabitants upon which taxes are to be assessed. Wilson v Wheeler, 55 Vt 446, 452.
See **tax rolls**.

tax on income. See **income tax**.

tax on property. See **property tax**.

taxpayer. One who has paid a tax. One who pays taxes regularly.
One who pays under protest an income tax due from another with the view to minimizing possible liability is a taxpayer and as such entitled to the benefit of a statute authorizing the recovery back of any sum in any manner wrongfully collected. Parsons v Anglim (Ca9 Cal) 143 F2d 534, 154 ALR 153.

taxpayer's action. An action supported by the financial interest of the plaintiff as a taxpayer in a municipality or other public body receiving a tax, not in his individual right, but as the representative of the municipality or other public body whose interests are alleged to be jeopardized by the inefficiency or maladministration of its officers. 52 Am J1st Taxp Act § 1. An action maintained by a taxpayer singly or in a class suit to restrain unlawful municipal action which leads, directly or indirectly, to taxation. 52 Am J1st Taxp Act §§ 2, 3. A remedy granted by a court of equity or a court exercising equity powers to prevent the consummation of an act on the part of a public body or agency or of public officers involving an illegal expenditure of public money or the creation of an illegal debt. 43 Am J1st Pub Wks § 220.

taxpayer's remedy. See **taxpayer's action**.

tax power. See **taxing power**.

tax purpose. The ultimate use and object for which a fund is raised by taxation, which, as a support for the imposition, can be nothing other than a constitutionally valid public purpose. 51 Am J1st Tax § 321.

tax rate. The rate of levy; the fraction or decimal of the assessed value to be paid as a tax. The graduated rate at which an income, estate, or gift tax is imposed.
The provision that state taxation of national bank shares shall not be at a greater rate than that assessed on other moneyed capital has reference to the entire process of assessment, and includes the valuation of the shares as well as the percentage charged on the valuation. Anno: 59 ALR 19.
See **tax limit**.

tax receipt. A receipt given by tax collector for payment of taxes. 51 Am J1st Tax § 959.

tax return. A written statement of one's income for the taxable year, accepted by the taxing authority as verified under oath, showing income from all sources, such as dividends, interest, rents, earnings, etc. and the amount of income taxable as calculated, taking account of deductions and exemptions. A sworn list required of a taxpayer, showing his personal property subject to taxation, such to be presented to the assessor in time for the making up of the tax list. 51 Am J1st Tax § 667. In a broader sense, any statement or report made to the taxing authority of property, income, gift, estate, or inheritance subject to taxation.

tax rolls. The original extensions of the levies made by the proper authorities, including state, county, township, and school taxes. Smith v Scully, 66 Kan 139, 71 P 249.
See **tax list**.

tax sale. See **sale for taxes**.

tax table. A simplified method of computing income tax available to taxpayers having less than $5000 of adjusted gross income who choose to take the standard deduction. Internal Revenue Code § 3. A table prepared by the Internal Revenue Service or taxing authority wherein the amount of the income tax due on taxable income as reported in a return is calculated for the taxpayer in brackets established according to the nature of the return as joint or single, the number of personal exemptions, the amount of taxable income, etc.

tax title. The title acquired by the purchaser at a tax sale. 51 Am J1st Tax §§ 1055, 1060 et seq. A title dependent alone upon the validity of a tax sale. 51 Am J1st Tax § 1078. A title dependent in some jurisdictions upon the title of the person assessed. 51 Am J1st Tax § 1081.

tax warrant. A compulsory process for the collection of taxes, authorizing sale of the delinquent taxpayer's property.

tax year. The calendar year or the fiscal year of the taxpayer, in either event a period of 12 months. The annual accounting period of the taxpayer; such accounting period being the annual period (including a 52-53 week year) on the basis of which the taxpayer regularly computes his income in keeping his books. Internal Revenue Code § 44(c).

tb. Abbreviation of tuberculosis.

tb hospital. A hospital caring for patients afflicted with tuberculosis.
See **sanatorium.**

teach. To give instruction. To give lessons. To impart knowledge.
The word as used in the standard form of teacher's contract prescribed by the school law, refers to general instruction within the fields embraced by the teacher's certificate, including all incidents and subdivisions thereof. Ganaposki's Case, 332 Pa 550, 2 A2d 742, 119 ALR 815.

teacher. A person who is employed to teach in a public or private school. One in the special occupation or profession of teaching in schools. 47 Am J1st Sch § 108. An employee rather than a public officer in connection with the public schools. 47 Am J1st Sch § 108.

teacher's certificate. A revocable personal privilege granted by a board or officer under legislative authority to a person qualified to teach in the public schools and under such restrictions as may be reasonably imposed. 47 Am J1st Sch § 110.

teachers' college. An educational institution of college rank, established by constitutional provision or statute for the education and training of school teachers. 15 Am J2d Colleges § 4.

teachers' institute. A meeting of teachers for the purpose of receiving professional instruction. 47 Am J1st Sch § 123.

teacher's license. Same as **teacher's certificate.**

teacher's pension. A pension provided by way of retirement pay for schoolteachers, usually from a fund accumulated by contributions made by the school district and the teacher. 40 Am J1st Pens § 17.

teachers' retirement fund. A fund provided and accumulated in accordance with statute, usually by contributions made thereto by teachers and the school district or unit, for the payment of pensions to retired teachers. 40 Am J1st Pens § 17.

teachers' tenure. See **tenure statutes.**

team. A number of persons constituting one side in a game, as a football team. A number of persons who work in harmony to accomplish a task.

team and wagon. A team of horses and a wagon such as was formerly in common use as a vehicle for hauling goods, merchandise, harvested crops, etc.
See **team of horses; wagon.**

team of horses. In common usage, a pair of horses worked together. Broadly, as in an exemption statute, a pair of horses worked together or one horse worked by himself. 31 Am J2d Exemp § 71.
As used in a statute exempting from execution the team of a householder used in and about his business, the word was held to include any team of animals which might or could be so used, whether the number of animals composing the team consisted of one, two, three, four, or more. See Wilcox v Hawley, 31 NY 648, 655.

teamster. One who drives a team. In a more limited sense, one who drives a team in hauling goods for others. 31 Am J2d Exemp § 22. Inclusive for some purposes of a driver of a truck.

team work. The performance of work by two or more persons with good co-ordination of their respective efforts.
As the term is used in an exemption statute exempting from execution horses used in team work, it means work done by a team as a substantial part of a man's business, as in farming, staging, express carrying, drawing of freight, peddling, the transportation of material used or dealt in as a business. Tishomingo Sav. Institution v Young, 87 Miss 473, 40 So 9.

tear (târ). To render assunder. A colloquial expression for moving with haste. State v Helgerson, 247 Iowa 651, 75 NW2d 227, 231.
Tearing is inclusive of "cutting," for the purposes of the revocation of a will. Anno: 115 ALR 717.

tear gas (tĕr'gas). A gas which irritates the eyes, even to the extent of causing temporary blindness. Sometimes employed by police to quell a riot or subdue a person resisting arrest with force.

tear gas gun. A weapon wherein tear gas is employed as the offensive or defensive charge. Anno: 92 ALR 1098.

tearing. See **tear.**

tea room. A restaurant, especially one where light lunches are served.

teazer (tē'zėr). A railroad operated at a loss. Reagan v Mercantile Trust Co. 154 US 418, 38 L Ed 1030, 14 S Ct 1062 (Texas terminology.)

technical. Pertaining, relating or belonging to some particular art or science. Pertaining to mechanical arts or applied sciences. Involved in a detail rather than a principle.

technical agreed case. The submission of facts to the court for the determination of a controversy without the institution of an action. 3 Am J2d Agr C § 2.

technical conversion. Such a conversion as takes place where one sells the personal property of another innocently, in good faith, and with no intent to ignore the rights of the owner.
The term is synonymous with "innocent conversion." Plack v Baumer (CA3 Pa) 121 F2d 676.

technical error. Immaterial error. An error committed in the course of a trial, but without prejudice to a party. 5 Am J2d A & E § 780. An error committed in the trial of a case which is purely abstract and harmless for practical purposes. Epps v State, 102 Ind 539, 556.

technical estoppel. An estoppel by record or by deed. 28 Am J2d Estop § 2.

technical malice. The intentional doing of a harmful or injurious act without justification or excuse, although without ill will or spite. 30 Am J Rev ed Interf § 45.

technical release. An instrument under seal, or some other form of satisfaction which legally imports full payment.
As a technical release was always under seal, and the consideration could not be inquired into, it was regarded as conclusive, even though given without consideration in fact. The difference between a technical release and satisfaction in fact was that in the one case the law regarded the claim as paid, and would not allow the party to deny by proof, while in the other, the claim was in fact paid. Ryan v Becker, 136 Iowa 273, 111 NW 426.

technical total loss. See **constructive total loss.**

technical trust. The legal relationship existing where the legal title is in one person and the equitable ownership in another, or where there are rights, titles, and interests in property distinct from the legal ownership. 54 Am J1st Trusts § 4.

teeter-totter. An amusement device for children, often found in public parks or on playgrounds, consisting of a plank mounted upon a bar for support and alternately rising and falling at each end when used in play. 39 Am J1st P & S § 41.

teinds (tēnds). An ancient Scotch word for **tithes.**

telecast (tel'ē-kast). A broadcast by television. Norman v Century Athletic Club, Inc. 193 Md 584, 69 A2d 466, 15 ALR2d 777.
See **television.**

Telechron. A trademark. Telechron, Inc. v Telechron Corp. (CA3 Del) 198 F2d 903.

telegram. A message or dispatch transmitted by telegraph. Western Union Tel. Co. v Hill, 163 Ala 18, 50 So 248. A message transmitted by radio, teletype, telegraph wire, cable, or any mechanical method of transmission, or the like. UCC § 1—201(41).

A received telegram is a writing within the meaning of the Statute of Frauds; a writing may be made with a steel pen an inch long or with a copper wire a thousand miles long. Walton v Mandeville, 56 Iowa 588, 9 NW 894.

telegraph. Noun: An apparatus used to transmit intelligence to a distant point by means of electricity. 52 Am J1st Teleg & T § 4. Verb: To send a telegram.

"Without this section making the provisions of the chapter relating to telegraph companies expressly applicable to telephone companies, we think the term 'telegraph,' as a mode of transmitting messages or other communications, is sufficiently comprehensive to embrace the telephone." Cincinnati Inclined Plane Railway Co. v Telegraph Asso. 48 Ohio St 390, 27 NE 890.

telegraph company. A company, almost invariably a corporation, engaged in the business of sending communications by telegram and furnishing services allied to such communication business. A company exercising a quasi public employment, chartered for public purposes, clothed with the power of eminent domain, bound to serve the people impartially, carefully and in good faith and in several of the states of the Union held to be a common carrier and subject to liability as such. Strong v Western Union Tel. Co. 18 Idaho 389, 109 P 910.

telegraphing money. The transmission of money or credit to a person at a distance by an order upon a bank in the place where he is at the time, sent by telegram, directing the bank to furnish him with funds or credit in the amount stated in the order. 10 Am J2d Banks § 308.
See **cable transfer of exchange.**

telephone. An instrument for transmitting or receiving articulate speech electrically. Richmond v Southern Bell Tel. & Tel. Co. 174 US 761, 43 L Ed 1162, 19 S Ct 778. An apparatus for the transmission of human speech or other sounds over distances greater than the ordinary limits of audibility. 52 Am J1st Teleg & T § 4.

telephone answering service. A service on behalf of business and professional men, especially physicians, whereby calls are answered at such times as the client is absent from his office and relayed to him at a fixed or appropriate time and place.

telephone business. The furnishing of telephone service, even by a mutual company to subscribers who pay assessments in lieu of fixed charges. Anno: 21 ALR 1167.

telephone company. A company, usually a corporation, engaged in the business of furnishing for compensation the means of communication by telephone and rendering services allied with such communication business.

The term embraces all corporations, associations, and individuals owning or operating any telephone line or exchange in the state. Anno: 21 ALR 1171.

telephone connection. A connection of telephone wires, particularly the wires of different telephone companies or telephone systems, necessary for communication other than local.

As used in a statute requiring telephone companies to supply all applicants for telephone connection, the words obviously mean that for which patrons of the telephone customarily apply. No such persons can be excluded, provided they are willing to comply with reasonable regulations, but the words do not confer any right upon one telephone company to insist upon a physical connection of its system with that of another company. Oklahoma-Arkansas Tel. Co. v Southwestern Bell Tel. Co. (CA8 Ark) 45 F2d 995, 76 ALR 944.
See **telephone exchange.**

telephone directory. A listing in print of all subscribers to telephone service in a particular city, village, town, metropolitan area, or other locality by names, telephone numbers, and street addresses. A facility within the meaning of a regulation that telephone subscribers shall not use any mechanical apparatus or device in connection with the facilities furnished by the company, without the consent of the company. Anno: 63 ALR2d 1098.

telephone exchange. A building or part of building equipped with instrumentalities for connecting telephone lines so that a call made on one will be transmitted over such line and a connecting line so as to reach a phone on the latter. State ex rel. Synod of Ohio v Joseph, 139 Ohio St 229, 39 NE2d 515, 138 ALR 1274.

telephone line. A wire, carried overhead on poles or underground in a conduit, over which articulate speech is transmitted and received.

A statute defines the term as including every sort of property used, operated, controlled, or owned by any telephone corporation to facilitate the business of affording telephonic communication. State ex rel. Buffum Tel. Co. v Public Service Com. 272 Mo 627, 199 SW 962.

telephone token. A small flat piece of metal placed in a slot in a public telephone to activate the instrument for use.

telephonic system. A system for the transmission of intelligence and news.

It is, perhaps, in a limited sense, and yet in a strict sense, a common carrier, and it must be equal in its dealings with all citizens in every department of business. Commercial Union Tel. Co. v New England Tel. & Tel. Co. 61 Vt 241, 17 A 1071.

telephony (tel'ę-fō-ni). The art or process of reproducing sounds at a distance, as by telephone. Dunbar v Spratt-Snyder Co. 208 Iowa 490, 226 NW 22, 63 ALR 1016.

televise (tel'ē-viz). To broadcast by television. Norman v Century Athletic Club, Inc. 193 Md 584, 69 A2d 466, 15 ALR2d 777.

television (tel-ē-vizh'on). An electronic process whereby scenes or views are transmitted by radio, wire, or cable, through the conversion of light rays into radio waves by a transmitting instrument and the reconversion of such waves by a receiving instrument into beams which produce pictures upon projection onto a screen, such operation normally being accompanied by radio communication in sound.

television station. A place equipped and manned for the transmission of scenes or views and accompanying sounds by the process known as television.

teller. A clerk in a bank who transacts business with customers by way of receiving and paying out money. 10 Am J2d Banks § 154. An election officer, engaged particularly in the counting of votes. Wheeler v Carter, 120 Mass 382, 62 NE 471. One who counts or assists in counting the votes at a corporate election.

telltale. A tale bearer. A gossip. A series of strips, usually of leather, hung above a railroad track for the purpose of warning a trainman on top of a car of a bridge or other instrumentality having a structure over the tracks so low as to strike the trainman if he remains standing on top of a car, the warning being necessary in hours of darkness and given by the harmless brushing of the strips against the face or head of the trainman. 35 Am J1st M & S § 224.

temere (te'me-rē). Rashly; by chance; accidentally.

temperance. The quality or condition of being temperate. The movement toward the prohibition or control of the traffic in intoxicating liquors.

See **temperate**.

temperance union. A society organized for the purpose of teaching and promoting temperance, particularly temperance in the use of alcoholic beverages.

See **Women's Christian Temperance Union**.

temperate. Moderate. Self-restrained. Habitual moderation in regard to the indulgence of the natural appetites and passions. People v Dashaway Asso. 84 Cal 114, 123, 24 P 277. Restrained in the use of intoxicating liquors, although not necessarily totally abstaining. 29 Am J Rev ed Ins § 774.

temperate damages. Damages allowed in cases of a certain class, without proof of actual or special damage, where the wrong done must in fact have caused actual damage to the plaintiff, though, from the nature of the case, he cannot furnish independent, distinct proof thereof. 22 Am J2d Damg § 16.

tempest. A violent wind, especially one accompanied by rain; an act of God. 1 Am J2d Act of God § 5.

Templars (tem'plärs). An order of religious knights which was organized in England in the twelfth century. A modern Masonic order, called the Knight Templars.

temporalis actio (tem-po-rā'lis ak'she-ō). (Civil law.) An action which had to be brought within a certain limited time, if it was brought at all.

temporalities (tem-pō-ral'i-tēs). The revenues of a parish of the Roman Catholic Church which are derived from pew rents, Sunday and other collections, graveyard charges, school fees and donations.

The pastor of the parish as the administrator and agent of the archbishop, who is considered as the owner of the church property, is in charge of the temporalities. Barabasz v Kabat, 86 Md 23, 30, 37 A 720.

temporal lords. See **lords temporal**.

Tempora mutantur et leges mutantur in illis (tem'po-ra mu-tan'ter et lē'jēz mu-tan'ter in il'lis). Times change and laws change with them. State v Soward, 83 Ark 264, 103 SW 741.

temporarily. Not permanently; for a time only. Worthington v McDonald, 246 Iowa 466, 68 NW2d 89, 47 ALR2d 135.

temporary. Lasting for a short time only. United States ex rel. Lesto v Day (CA2 NY) 21 F2d 307. Lasting for a time only; existing or continuing for a limited time; not of long duration; not permanent; transitory; changing. Young v Povich, 121 Me 141, 116 A 26, 29 ALR 48.

temporary administrator. An administrator of a decedent's estate appointed for some cause, such as the pendency of a will contest, whereby regular administration is delayed, the property being exposed in the meantime to waste and loss in the absence of an authorized agent to collect the debts and preserve the assets. 31 Am J2d Ex & Ad § 649.

temporary ailment. A disability or sickness of such short duration as not to negative the existence of sound health or sound physical condition. French v Fidelity & Casualty Co. 135 Wis 259, 115 NW 869.

temporary alimony. An allowance made by the court, otherwise known as alimony pendente lite or alimony ad interim, to be paid by the husband for the maintenance of the wife during the pendency of a matrimonial action either by or against her. Richardson v Richardson, 218 Minn 42, 15 NW2d 127, 154 ALR 526; Davis v Davis, 15 Wash 2d 297, 130 P2d 3, 55.

temporary allowance. An award by the court to be paid by the party against whom it is directed during the pendency and before final determination of the action, as in the case of an award of temporary alimony or of child support.

temporary appropriation. A temporary taking of property for a public purpose. 27 Am J2d Em D § 351.

temporary child support. An award against the husband as a party to an action for divorce, directing payment for the support of a child of the union sought to be severed by the divorce. 24 Am J2d Div & S § 836.

temporary commitment. The temporary restraint of an insane person without an adjudication of his insanity, properly to prevent either self-destruction or injury to other persons by his acts. 29 Am J Rev ed Ins Per § 39.

temporary condemnation. Same as **temporary appropriation**.

temporary court. A court created to exist for a specified period of time or for the duration of a certain situation, usually an emergency. 20 Am J2d Cts § 1.

temporary custody. A disposition made by the court of the custody of a child to continue pending trial of a divorce suit between the parents. 24 Am J2d Div & S § 809.

See **temporary commitment**.

TEMPORARY [1262] TEMPUS

temporary damages. Damages for injury to, or trespass on, real property, otherwise known as continuing damages, awarded on the basis that the wrong is continuing in character and that successive actions may be required to make the plaintiff whole, the amount of the recovery being limited to those damages which have accrued to date of suit. 22 Am J2d Damg § 28.

temporary disability. A disability of the person from which he has or will recover. A disability which is not permanent and which is to last for a limited time only, as distinguished from a disability which is perpetual or indefinite in its duration. See Lawrence v State Industrial Com. 120 Okla 197, 251 P 40. A physical disability which, although it may be total for the time, is not such a disability as is reasonably probable to continue for an indefinite period of time. 29A Am J Rev ed Ins § 1529. For the purpose of workmen's compensation, a condition that exists until the injured workman is as far restored as the permanent character of the injuries will permit. 58 Am J1st Workm Comp § 283.

temporary employee. See **casual employee.**

temporary injunction. An injunction pendente lite or provisional injunction which is to operate pending a hearing of the suit on its merits, or until the final decree of the court shall have been entered. An order issued, not in pursuance of the final determination of any controverted right, but merely to prevent a threatened wrong, or any further perpetration of injury, or the doing of any act thereafter whereby the right to a thing may be embarrassed or endangered, or whereby its value may be materially lessened or the thing itself totally lost, and by such prevention to maintain things in the condition in which they are at the time, and protect the property or rights involved from further injury until the issues and equities can be determined after a full examination and hearing. 28 Am J Rev ed Inj § 12.

See **restraining order.**

temporary insanity. A temporary derangement of the mind which may result from any transient condition, as, for example, intoxication. 29 Am J Rev ed Ins Per § 3.

temporary insurance. Insurance according to the terms and conditions of a standard form of policy commencing upon application being made for a policy and continuing, subject to a limitation of reasonable time, until either the policy can be written or its issuance approved or disapproved by authorized representatives of the insurer, or some other temporary impediment to the complete and formal contract of insurance may be removed. 29 Am J Rev ed Ins § 205.

A temporary contract of life insurance is usually in writing. It may take the form of a provisional policy, a rider attached to a policy, or a binding slip or receipt. It may also be made orally by an authorized agent or officer of the insurer. Anno: 2 ALR2d 952.

temporary judge. A special or substitute judge. 30A Am J Rev ed Judges § 237.

temporary loan. A loan to a municipal corporation which is to be paid with and by the taxes of a current fiscal year. People ex rel. Peene v Carpenter, 31 App Div 603, 608, 52 NYS 781.

temporary nuisance. A nuisance resulting from a condition which is not fixed and indeterminable, lasting for a limited time only. 39 Am J1st Nuis § 131. A nuisance arising from negligence in the maintenance of a structure or the operation of a business or industry. Shelley v Ozark Pipe Line Co. 327 Mo 238, 75 ALR 1316, 37 SW2d 518.

temporary obstruction. The obstruction of a highway for a limited period of time, incidental to a lawful use of the way, or to serve some public purpose, such as the repair of the way itself or the construction of other public improvements, excavations for installation of public utility pipes and wires, etc. 25 Am J1st High § 302.

temporary order. A provisional or interim order by an administrative agency. 2 Am J2d Admin L § 466.

See **restraining order; temporary injunction.**

Temporary Organic Act. An Act of Congress of June 20, 1874 in reference to municipal government of the District of Columbia. 24 Am J2d D C § 3.

temporary receiver. A receiver appointed to take custody of property and hold it pending the appointment of a permanent receiver. 45 Am J1st Rec § 3.

temporary restraining order. A restraining order which in terms indicates or contemplates that a further hearing on the application is to be had before the application is finally acted on. State v Baker, 62 Neb 840, 847, 88 NW 124.

See **restraining order.**

temporary severance. Detaching a fixture from the real estate for a temporary purpose, not involving a change in the character of the article. 35 Am J2d Fixt § 26.

temporary statute. A statute which, by its terms, is to remain in force for a limited time only or a statute operative only during the continuance of the emergency which prompted enactment. 50 Am J1st Stat § 514.

temporary suit money. An interim or preliminary allowance of counsel fees to the wife made during the pendency of an action for divorce. 24 Am J2d Div & S § 576.

temporary support. See **temporary alimony; temporary child support.**

tempore (tem'po-re). (Latin) At the right time. Seasonably.

See **ex tempore.**

tempore et loco (tem'po-re et lō'kō). In time and place.

temporis. See **exceptio temporis.**

temporis exceptio (tem'po-ris ex-sep'she-ō). (Civil law.) A plea which set up lapse of time as a defense to the action.

temptation. Allurement or inducement.

Temptation is not always invitation. As the common law is understood by the most competent authorities, it does not excuse a trespasser because there is a temptation to commit, or hold property owners bound to contemplate the infraction of property rights because the temptation to untrained minds to infringe them might have been foreseen. Wilmot v McPadden, 79 Conn 367, 65 A 157.

tempus (tem'pus). Time.

tempus continuum (tem'pus kon-ti'nu-um). (Civil law.) A continuous time; a period of time which was uninterrupted by holidays, absences, or other causes. See Mackeldey's Roman Law § 195.

Tempus enim modus tollendi obligationes et actiones, quia tempus currit contra desides et sui juris contemptores (tem′pus e′nim mo′dus tol-len′di ob-li-ga-she-ō-nēz et ak-she-ō′nez, qui′a tem′pus kur′rit kon-tra dē′si-dēz et su′i ju′ris kon-temp-tō′rez). For time is a means of dissipating actions and obligations, because time runs against the slothful and those who are careless of their own right.

tempus exceptio (tem′pus ek-sep′she-ō). Same as **temporis exceptio.**

tempus regis Edwardi (tem′pus re′jis Ed-war′di). In the time of King Edward; that is, of Edward the Confessor who was king of the West Saxons from 1042 until 1066.

tempus utile (tem′pus ū′ti-lē). (Civil law.) A time of advantage, a time which only begins to run against him who is affected by it after his knowledge thereof. See Mackeldey's Roman Law § 195.

tenancy. The occupancy of a tenant. Possession under right or title.

A tenancy exists where one has let real estate to another, to hold of him as landlord. When duly created and the tenant put into possession, he is the owner of an estate for the time being, and has all the usual rights and remedies to defend his possession. But a tenancy does not necessarily imply a right to complete and exclusive possession; it may be created with implied or express permission of a right to possession on the part of the landlord, for all purposes not inconsistent with the privileges granted to the tenant. Morrill v Mackman, 24 Mich 279.

See **cotenancy; entire tenancy; general tenancy; joint tenancy; privy; re-entry; tenant; use and occupation.**

tenancy at sufferance. The tenancy of one who continues in possession after his right to possession has terminated, his original entry having been lawful. 32 Am J1st L & T § 75. The tenancy of a lessee holding over the term of his lease without objection on the part of the landlord. 32 Am J1st L & T § 938.

A tenancy at sufferance is of such a nature as necessarily implies an absence of *any agreement* between the owner and the tenant, and if express assent is given by the owner to such possession, the tenancy is thereby instanter converted into a tenancy at will, or from year to year, according to the circumstances. Willis v Moore, 59 Tex 628.

See **estate by sufferance.**

tenancy at will. A tenancy to continue for so long as continuation is in accord with the wishes and desires of both parties. An estate which confers a right to the possession of the premises demised for an indefinite period of time, its duration and ultimate termination depending upon the joint wills of the parties, either being able to effect a termination without incurring liability to the other. 32 Am J1st L & T § 66. According to some authorities, the tenancy which arises where a lessee holds over the term of his lease with the express or implied consent of the landlord. 32 Am J1st L & T § 939.

tenancy by elegit. See **estate by elegit.**

tenancy by entireties. See **estate by entireties.**

tenancy by sufferance. See **tenancy at sufferance.**

tenancy for life. See **life estate; life tenant.**

tenancy for years. An interest arising from a lease, contract, or agreement for the possession of lands or tenements for a definite period of time. A tenancy under a lease whereby the landlord contracts to grant the possession and enjoyment of land, or hereditaments of a demisable nature, for a period of years certain; and in most cases the tenant agrees to render to the landlord a rent in money, or any other kind of payment, at the end of stated periods of a year or more during the term. 32 Am J1st L & T § 61.

tenancy from month to month. A tenancy where no definite time is agreed upon and the rate is fixed at so much per month. Thompson v Baxter, 107 Minn 122, 119 NW 979. A tenancy created by a holding over after the expiration of a lease for months. 32 Am J1st L & T § 941. An estate less than freehold. 28 Am J2d Est § 130.

tenancy from quarter to quarter. A tenancy under a lease which does not prescribe the duration but fixes the rental at a certain sum per quarter or three months period. 32 Am J1st L & T § 71. A tenancy created by a holding over after the expiration of a lease for one or more quarters of a year. 32 Am J1st L & T § 941.

tenancy from week to week. A tenancy where no definite time is agreed upon and the rent is fixed at so much per week. 32 Am J1st L & T § 71. A tenancy created by a holding over after the expiration of a lease for weeks. 32 Am J1st L & T § 941.

tenancy from year to year. A tenancy where no definite time is agreed upon and the rent is fixed at so much per year. Thompson v Baxter, 107 Minn 122, 119 NW 797. A tenancy created by a holding over after the expiration of a term for years and the continued payment of the yearly rent reserved. 32 Am J1st L & T § 940. An estate evolving from an estate at will, being one of the estates from period to period, an estate less than a freehold. 28 Am J2d Est § 130.

tenancy in common. That tenancy whereby two or more persons are entitled to land in such manner that they have an undivided possession, but several freeholds or interest. 20 Am J2d Coten § 22. A tenancy characterized by a single essential unity—that of possession, or of the right to possession, of the common property. 20 Am J2d Coten § 23.

A tenancy in common of personal property is essentially similar to such a tenancy of real property, each tenant in common owning and possessing an undivided interest in the whole property. Re Engel's Estate, 413 Pa 475, 198 A2d 505.

tenancy in fee. A tenancy under a lease for a term, renewable forever, but subject to termination for nonpayment of the rent reserved, the interest of the lessee being that of a base, qualified, or determinable fee. Smith v Improvement Dist. 108 Ark 141, 156 SW 455.

See **fee simple.**

tenancy in tail. See **fee tail.**

tenancy in tail after possibility of issue extinct. See **fee tail after possibility of issue extinct.**

tenant. One who occupies the premises of another in subordination to that other person's title and with his assent express or implied. 32 Am J1st L & T § 2. Broadly, any person having a tenancy.

A tenant, although having exclusive possession, charge, and control, is not an owner of the land within a statute making it unlawful for any person to hunt on the land of another without first having obtained permission of the owner. Anno: 2 ALR 799, s. 95 ALR 1099.

See **sole tenant; tenancy; untenant.**

tenantable premises. Premises which are habitable, fit to be lived in. 32 Am J1st L & T § 654.
For meaning of the phrase "good tenantable condition," as such appears in a covenant by a tenant to make repairs, see Anno: 45 ALR 12.

tenant at sufferance. See tenancy at sufferance.

tenant at will. See tenancy at will.

tenant by elegit. See estate by elegit.

tenant by entirety. See estate by entireties.

tenant by statute merchant. See estate by statute merchant.

tenant by statute staple. See estate by statute staple.

tenant by the curtesy. See curtesy; curtesy consummate; curtesy initiate.

tenant for life. See life tenant.

tenant for years. See tenancy for years.

tenant from month to month. See tenancy from month to month.

tenant from week to week. See tenancy from week to week.

tenant from year to year. See tenancy from year to year.

tenant in bordage. See bordage.

tenant in capite. See in capite.

tenant in chivalry. See knight service.

tenant in common. One of two or more owners of property who hold under a tenancy in common. See tenancy in common.

tenant in dower (in dou'ėr). A widow who holds land by virtue of her dower. See dower.

tenant in fee. See fee simple.

tenant in fee simple. See fee simple.

tenant in fee tail. See fee tail.

tenant in free socage. See free socage.

tenant in mortgage (in mor'gáj). The feoffee in a common-law mortgage or mortuum vadium, as it was called, which consisted of a feoffment on the condition that the feoffer might re-enter if he paid to the feoffee a certain sum of money at a certain date. 36 Am J1st Mtg § 12.

tenant in possession. A lessee in possession under the terms of the lease. In a broader sense, one who maintains possession legally by himself or through another under title, estate, or interest of any kind.
The definition of the term embraces, within the natural and usual meaning of the words, a judgment debtor as well as his lessee. The owner in fee is no less, in legal contemplation, a tenant, than the man who occupies under him, since the definition of tenant is one that holds or possesses lands or tenements by any kind of title, either in fee, for life, years, or at will. Whithed v St. Anthony & Dakota Elevator Co. 9 ND 224, 83 NW 238.

tenant in severalty (in sev'ėr-ąl-ti). A sole tenant; a person who holds lands or tenements in his own right only, without any other person being joined or connected with him in point of interest, during his estate therein. 2 Bl Comm 953.

tenant-like manner. Characterizing the occupation by a tenant as reasonable and proper in reference to the care and treatment of the premises. 32 Am J1st L & T § 779.

tenant paravail (par-ba-vāl). The tenant of a tenant.
Under the feudal system, if the king granted a manor to A, and A granted a portion of the land to B, then B was said to hold of A, and A, of the king. In other words, B held his lands immediately of A, but mediately of the king. The king was therefore styled lord paramount; A was both tenant and lord, or was mesne lord; and B was called tenant paravail, or the lowest tenant; being he who was supposed to make avail, or profit of the land. See 2 Bl Comm 60.

tenant pur auter vie (ten'ạnt pėr ōtr vē). A tenant holding for the life of another; a tenant having an estate for the life of another. See 2 Bl Comm 120, 124.

tenant right. A word of art for the lessee's right to a renewal of the tenancy.

tenant without impeachment of waste. See without impeachment of waste.

tender. Noun: The small car attached to a locomotive, wherein fuel and water are carried. 35 Am J1st M & S § 229. A boat or small vessel carrying freight, passengers, or supplies to or from a larger vessel. An unconditional offer of payment, consisting in the actual production, in current coin of the realm or other lawful money, of a sum not less than the amount due on a specific debt or obligation. 52 Am J1st Ten § 2. An offering of that which a person received under a contract made as a condition of the right to rescind. 17 Am J2d Contr § 512. Verb: To offer to pay or perform an obligation.
In a literal sense, the word is equivalent to the word "offer". 6 Eng Rul Cas 589.
See legal tender.

tender of amends (ten'dėr ov a-mends'). An offer to settle a claim arising out of tort or contract.

tender of issue (of ish'ö). The concluding phrase of a plea offering to submit the controversy to the court or to the jury. For practical purposes, the raising of an issue by a pleading responsive to the pleading of the adverse party.

tender of payment. See tender.

tender of performance. An offer by the obligor to perform a contract according to its terms and conditions. An offer of performance, one of the effects of which is to place the other party unjustifiably refusing it in default, and to permit the party making the tender to exercise his remedies for breach of contract. Walker v Houstin, 215 Cal 742, 12 P2d 952, 87 ALR 937. An offer by the vendor in a contract to sell real estate to convey in full compliance with the terms of the contract. 55 Am J1st V & P § 324. A presentation of goods by the seller to the purchaser under a contract of sale in the course of a delivery or attempted delivery of the goods.
The word "tender," as used in connection with mutual and concurrent promises, does not mean the same kind of offer as when it is used in reference to the payment or offer to pay an ordinary debt due in money; it means only a readiness and willingness, accompanied with an ability on the part of one of the parties, to do the acts which the agreement requires him to perform, provided the other party will concurrently do the things which he is required by the contract to do, and a notice by the former to the latter of such readiness. Robins v Mack International Motor Truck Corp. 113 NJL 377, 174 A 551.

tender years. The years of infancy, particularly the earlier years.

tending bar. See **bartender.**

tenement (ten'ē-ment). A house. Polson v Parsons, 23 Okla 778, 104 P 336. Real property; inclusive of any incorporeal hereditament which issues out of corporeal property or which is annexed thereto. Hertz v Abrahams, 110 Ga 707, 36 SE 409.

In its most extensive signification, the word comprehends everything which may be holden, provided it be of a permanent nature. In a more restricted sense, it is a house or building. Oskaloosa Water Co. v Board of Equalization, 84 Iowa 407, 51 NW 18.

Within the meaning of a statute authorizing proceedings to try questions concerning unlawful detention of lands or "tenements" and providing that if the same is held unlawfully, restitution shall be had, a house upon land to which its owner has no title, but in which he claims and enjoys the right of peaceable possession, which house is occupied by one leasing from such owner, is a "tenement." 32 Am J1st L & T § 1017.

tenemental lands (ten-ē-men'tal lands). Lands which were distributed by the lords among their tenants.

These tenemental lands included both bookland, or charterland, and folkland. See 2 Bl Comm 90.

tenement house. A multiple dwelling, ordinarily housing people of very limited means or persons on welfare, usually several stories high, and containing many separate apartments or tenements, usually involving the use of bath and toilet facilities in common by the tenants of several tenements. Lignot v Jeakle, 72 NJ Eq 233, 65 A 221. A building, the different rooms or parts of which are let for residence purposes by the possessor to others, as distinct tenements, so that each tenant, as to the room or rooms occupied by him, would sustain to the common landlord the same relation that the tenant occupying a whole house would sustain to his landlord. See Rose v King, 49 Ohio St 213, 30 NE 267.

A building containing three separate apartments on separate floors, each rented by the owner to a separate family, is a "tenement house" within the meaning of a statute providing that the owner of every tenement house shall provide for the lighting of all public halls at night. Gibson v Hoppman, 108 Conn 401, 143 A 635, 75 ALR 148.

tenementum (te-ne-men'tum). A tenement; an estate held by a tenant.

tenendum (tē-nen'dum). A clause formerly appearing in deeds, setting forth the tenure of the grantee, that is, the kind of tenure on which the land was to be held. 2 Bl Comm § 408.

tenendum per servitium militare, in burgagio, in libero socagio (te-nen'dum per ser-vi'she-um mi-li-tā're, in bur-gā'ji-ō, in li'be-rō so-kā'ji-ō). To hold by military service, in burgage, in free socage. See 2 Bl Comm 299.

tenens (te'nenz). A tenant.

tener (te'nä). To hold; to keep.

tenere (te-nē're). To hold; to keep; to understand; to grasp.

teneri (te-nē'ri). That part of a bond in which the maker states that he is held and firmly bound, etc.

tenet (ten'et). Something held or possessed. A principle, especially one pertaining to religious faith.

tenir in socage (te-nēr' in sō-käj'). To hold in socage.

Tennessee Valley Authority. An agency of the United States Government, employing almost 18,000 persons, established to develop the Tennessee river for the production of electric power and for other purposes connected with flood control, the improvement of navigation, chemical engineering research, aiding regional development, conservation of natural resources, and to construct other facilities for the production of electric power. United States ex rel. Tennessee Valley Authority v An Easement & Right-of-Way (DC Ky) 246 F Supp 263.

tenor. The exact words. A copy of an instrument setting forth the very words and figures. 36 Am J2d Forg § 37. The general meaning or purport.

tenore praesentium (te-nō're prē-zen'she-um). By the tenor of these presents.

Tenor est qui legem dat feudo (te'nor est qūi lē'jem dat fū'do). It is the true intent or meaning which gives validity to the fee or grant. See 2 Bl Comm 310.

Tenor investiturae inspiciendus (te'nor in-ves-ti-tū'rē in-spe-shi-en'dus). The character of the investiture must be regarded. A maxim of the law of feuds resulting from the variety of the prescribed services to be rendered by the tenant.

tenor of a will. The purport, rather than the exact words, of the instrument. It is enough to prove the tenor or substance of a lost will, without proving the precise statement of the language terms used in it. Jones v Casler, 139 Ind 382, 38 NE 812.

tenor of bill of exchange. The terms of time and manner of payment of a bill of exchange. Lindley v First Nat. Bank of Waterloo, 76 Iowa 629, 41 NW 381.

ten pins. A game of skill, akin to bowling. Anno: 60 ALR 352.

tentative allowance. A provisional allowance. An allowance not to be accepted as final.

As the term is used with reference to deductions in the Federal income tax law, it means the original allowance proposed by the taxpayer in his return and accepted automatically and without investigation by the Commissioner; and after he has completed his investigation of the claimed deduction and passed upon the question of amortization, his allowance is no longer tentative but becomes final as can any allowance of a deduction. Fifth Ave. Uniform Co. v Commissioner (CA2) 70 F2d 677.

tentative finding. A finding by an administrative officer whose function is to hear and report, his recommendation not being binding upon the board or officer having the deciding authority. 2 Am J2d Admin L § 427.

tentative trust. See **Totten Trust.**

Tenterden's Act. See **Lord Tenterden's Act.**

tenths (tenths). Temporary aids issuing out of personal property, and granted by parliament to the king.

They were the actual tenth or fifteenth part of all of each subject's movable property. Tenths were first granted under Henry the Second to pay the expense of a Palestine crusade against the Saracen emperor, Saladine; whence this levy was called the Saladine tenth. See 1 Bl Comm 308.

tent show. A circus; a dramatic performance produced in a tent.

tenure (ten'ūr). A term of extensive significance, meaning the mode by which one holds an estate in land and importing also any kind of holding, from mere possession to the owning of an estate of inheritance. 28 Am J2d Est § 3. The right of certain public officers and public employees to be retained in employment, subject only to removal for certain enumerated causes and in a prescribed manner. 47 Am J1st Sch § 127. Term of public office or public employment. People v Waite (NY) 9 Wend 58.

In its technical sense, the word means the manner whereby lands or tenements are holden, or the service that the tenant owes to his lord. In the latter case, there can be no tenure without some service, because the service makes the tenure. The word is also used as signifying the estate in the land. The most common tenure by which lands are held in the United States is "fee simple," which is an absolute tenure of land to a man and his heirs forever, without rendering service of any kind. Bard v Grundy's Devisees, 2 Ky 168, 169.

See **fixed tenure; tenancy.**

tenure by divine service. A land tenure in which the tenants were to perform some certain expressly defined and prescribed special divine service; such as to sing so many masses, to distribute a fixed sum in alms.

After the Statute of Quia Emptores (1290) only the king could grant lands to be held by this tenure. See 2 Bl Comm 102.

tenure by free alms. Same as **tenure in frankalmoign.**

tenure in ancient demesne (in ān'shent de-mēn'). A tenure embracing all those lands or manors, which, though subsequently granted out to private subjects, were actually in the hands of the crown in the time of Edward the Confessor, or William the Conqueror, and are recorded as so being in the Domesday Book. See 2 Bl Comm 99.

tenure in burgage. See **burgage tenure.**

tenure in capite (in ka'pi-te). A land tenure wherein the tenant held his land directly of the crown or chief lord, with no lord intervening.

tenure in chief. Same as **tenure in capite.**

tenure in frankalmoign. Same as **frankalmoign tenure.**

tenure in gavelkind. See **gavelkind.**

tenure of office. The right to hold office for a prescribed term. 43 Am J1st Pub Of § 149. The possession of an office. The length of time an office is held.
See **tenure statutes; term of office.**

tenure of schoolteacher. See **tenure; tenure statutes.**

tenure of trustee. The continuance of one's status as trustee until he resigns, is discharged, dies, becomes incompetent, or the trust terminates. 54 Am J1st Trusts § 127.

tenure statutes. Statutes granting to public officers or employees the right to be retained in employment indefinitely, subject only to removal for enumerated causes and in a manner prescribed by law. Statutes wherein specific tenure rights are attached to the position of teaching in the public schools, particularly the right to be retained in employment indefinitely, subject only to removal for certain enumerated causes and in a prescribed manner. 47 Am J1st Sch § 127.

terce (tėrs). The widow's third; dower.

tercerone (ter'se-rōn). A person of mixed blood, the issue of a white person and a mulatto. Daniel v Guy, 19 Ark 121, 131.

term. A portion of an agreement relating to a particular matter. UCC § 1—201(42). An estate for years; an estate the duration of which is limited and determined. Delaware L. & W. R. Co. v Sanderson, 109 Pa 583, 1 A 394.

termagant (tėr'mạ-gant). A common scold. 15 Am J2d Com S § 2.

term annuity. An annuity the payments of which are terminable by the voluntary act of the annuitant. Bodine v Commissioner (CA3) 103 F2d 982.

term bailment. A bailment for a prescribed period of time. 8 Am J2d Bailm § 277.

term bill of exceptions. A bill of exceptions showing matters which occurred prior to the trial. Robinson v Field, 342 Mo 778, 117 SW2d 308.

term bonds. Bonds issued at one time and all falling due at one time. Fales v Multnomah County, 119 Or 127, 248 P 151.

term for years. See **estate for years; tenancy for years.**

terminable interest. For estate tax purposes, an interest which terminated on or before the death of the one whose estate is sought to be taxed. Goodman v Granger (CA3 Pa) 243 F2d 264, cert den 355 US 835, 2 L Ed 2d 47, 78 S Ct 57.

As to failure of terminable interest to qualify for marital deduction, see Internal Revenue Code § 2523, subds (b), (d).

terminal. A point on a railroad line which is either the beginning or destination of traffic. 44 Am J1st RR § 241. The station or depot of a carrier. An airport. The landing place used by a ferry.

terminal car. A railroad car kept at a particular station for use in the yards.

terminal carrier. The carrier which makes the final delivery of the goods, either delivering the goods itself to the consignee, or through another carrier acting as its agent. 14 Am J2d Car § 662.

terminal facilities. Instrumentalities at the terminal of a railroad provided to implement the handling of traffic. 44 Am J1st RR § 241. Passenger station, freight station, and other facilities rendered available by a carrier for its customers.

terminal illness. Last illness.

terminal railroad. A railroad which as an instrumentality assists railroad transportation companies in the collection, transfer, and distribution of traffic at a place which is a terminal of different railroad lines. 44 Am J1st RR § 241. A railroad rendering terminal services, switching and delivering railroad cars from one carrier to another or from the carrier to the consignee of the shipment. 13 Am J2d Car § 13.

terminal railway company. A company operating a terminal railroad. Delt R. Co. v United States (CA7 Ill) 168 F 542, cert dismd 223 US 743, 56 L Ed 638, 32 S Ct 532.
See **terminal railroad.**

terminal reserve. A reserve, appearing on the books of a life insurance company, maintained by it against its liability on a life insurance policy or annuity contract issued by it and outstanding.

terminal services. Services rendered by a carrier at its station or in its yards in loading and unloading

freight, switching, elevator service, refrigeration etc. 13 Am J2d Car § 470.
See **terminal railroad**.

terminating building and loan service. A building and loan association in which all of the stock matures at the same time.
Upon such maturity, the face value of the stock is paid to the members, and the association comes to an end. Cook v Equitable Bldg. & Loan Asso. 104 Ga 814, 821.

termination. An end of something in space or time.
See **cancellation**.

termination in plaintiff's favor. An end to a criminal prosecution or civil proceeding in favor of he who is the plaintiff in an action for malicious prosecution, however such end is reached, provided the end is such that the prosecutor must institute proceedings anew if he desires to continue further with his purpose of prosecution. 34 Am J1st Mal Pros § 31.
As the word is used in the rule requiring a termination of the prosecution as one of the essential prerequisites of an action for malicious prosecution, a criminal prosecution is "terminated" (1) where there is a verdict of not guilty; (2) where the grand jury ignore a bill; (3) where a nolle prosequi is entered; and (4) where the accused has been discharged from bail or imprisonment. Graves v Scott, 104 Va 372, 51 SE 821.

termination of corporation. See **dissolution of corporation**.

termination of criminal prosecution. See **termination in plaintiff's favor**.

termination of employment. A termination of the relationship between employer and employee. Emerick v Connecticut General L. Ins. Co. 120 Conn 60, 179 A 335, 105 ALR 413.

termination of highway. A discontinuance or vacation of the way.

termination of lease. The efflux of the term, the happening of a condition subsequent and re-entry, by way of conditional limitation, by operation of law, as in the case of the merger of the tenancy in the reversion, or by cancellation of the lease. 32 Am J1st L & T § 824.
See **expiration of term**.

termination of offer. The expiration of the period of time during which the offer is to remain in effect, whether such be a definite period as fixed by the terms of the offer or by custom or usage of trade, or the reasonable period of time during which an offer remains in effect in the absence of a definite time limit; the withdrawal or revocation of the offer before it has been accepted; the death of the offeror or offeree; or the rejection of the offer by the offeree. 17 Am J2d Contr §§ 35 et seq.

termination of partnership. See **dissolution of partnership**.

termination of risk. A phrase familiar in the law of insurance, signifying the termination of the coverage provided by the policy by the expiration of the term for which the policy was issued, by breach of warranty or condition, or by the cancellation, rescission, or surrender of the policy to the insurer. 29 Am J Rev ed Ins § 317.

termination of trust. The termination of the relationship of trustee and beneficiary in accordance with the limitations or conditions of the trust, although not before the trustee has accounted to the beneficiary and the latter has received all the property and funds due him. 54 Am J1st Trusts § 70.
The expression includes not only the final transfer of a trust estate to the beneficiary, but also the resignation or discharge of the trustee named in the deed and the transfer of the trust fund by it to a new trustee. Haas v Hudson County Nat. Bank, 115 NJ Eq 311, 170 A 611, 94 ALR 1099.

termination of war. The exchange of peace treaties or the ratification of a peace treaty, or the recognition of the termination of the contest by the branches of government having the war power. 56 Am J1st War § 13.

terminer. See **court of oyer and terminer; oyer and terminer**.

termini. See **ex vi termini; terminus**.

terminis terminantibus. See **in terminis terminantibus**.

term insurance. Life insurance under a contract providing protection for a stated number of years, subject to the payment of premiums, sometimes renewable without an additional medical examination, sometimes convertible to other forms of life insurance written by the insurer. A policy of insurance under which the insurance contracted for covers only losses occurring before the expiration of a term stated in the policy. Aetna Casualty & Surety Co. v Commercial State Bank of Rantoul (DC Ill) 13 F2d 474.

terminus (tėr'mi-nus). A term; an estate for years; an estate the duration of which is limited and determined. Delaware L. & W. R. Co. v Sanderson, 109 Pa 583, 1 A 394. A boundary; an end; a limit.
See **terminal**.

Terminus ac foedum non possunt constare simul in una eademque persona (ter'mi-nus ak fē'dum non pos'sunt kon-stā're si'mul in ū'na e-ā-dem'kwē per-sō'na). A term and the fee cannot at the same time vest in one and the same person.

terminus ad quem (ter'mi-nus ad quem). The termination or end of a private right of way.
See **terminus a quo**.

Terminus annorum certus debet esse et determinatus (ter'mi-nus an-nō'rum ser'tus de'bet es'se et de-ter-mi-nā'tus). A term for years ought to be certain and determinate.

terminus a quo (ter'mi-nus ā quō). The end from which, as matter of point, place, or time.
To every private right of way, there are two essential requisites, first, the "terminus a quo," or the point or place from which the grantee is to set out in order to use the way, and the "terminus ad quem," the place where the way is to end; and second, that the grantor has the right, not the mere revocable permission of setting out from the terminus a quo, and proceeding to and entering the terminus ad quem. Garrison v Rudd, 19 Ill 558, 563.

terminus juris (ter'mi-nus jō'ris). The time within which an appeal could be determined in the ecclesiastical courts.

termite (tėr'mīt). A wood-boring insect capable of causing much damage to wooden structures and furniture. Kirkley v Merrimack Mut. Fire Ins. Co. 232 NC 292, 59 SE2d 629.

term of court. The period of time appointed by law during which a court may, and is supposed to, perform its judicial functions. The time in which a court is open for the trial of causes or the transaction of other official business. 20 Am J2d Cts § 44. Sometimes defined as the space of time during which the court holds a session. Parrott v Wolcott, 75 Neb 530, 106 NW 607.

The expression is sometimes used in statutes as synonymous with the term "session of court," and does not necessarily refer to the beginning of the statutory term of the court. See Nation v Savely, 127 Okla 117, 260 P 32, 35.

See **adjourned term; appearance term; equity term; special term; trial term; vacation.**

term of lease. That period which is granted for the lessee or tenant to occupy and have possession of the premises. The duration of a lease in years, months, weeks, or days. The estate or interest which the lessee has in the premises under and by virtue of the lease. 32 Am J1st L & T §§ 61 et seq.

term of office. A fixed and definite period of time during which the incumbent of an office is to hold it. Collison v State, 39 Del 460, 2 A2d 97, 119 ALR 1422. The time during which one regularly chosen by election or appointment and inducted into office is entitled to hold the same, perform its functions and enjoy its privileges and emoluments. State v Knight, 76 Mont 71, 245 P 267.

See **tenure of office.**

term of patent. The duration of the patent and of the rights of the patentee thereunder. Diamond Match Co. v Adirondack Match Co. (CC Vt) 65 F 803.

term of years. A period of years. As used in a statute providing for increased punishment of any person upon a conviction after a previous conviction for an offense punishable by imprisonment for a "term of years," a minimum of two years. 25 Am J1st Habit Cr § 2.

See **tenancy for years.**

termor (tėr'mor). The owner of an estate for life or for years.

term policy. See **term insurance.**

terms good firms. A commercial or mercantile expression.

The acceptance of an offer to purchase a commodity on the condition "terms good firms" was held to mean that the commodity was to be weighed at its destination by responsible business men, and that the seller did not bind himself to accept weights made by unreliable people. Anno: 1 ALR 1509.

terms net cash. A condition in a contract of sale requiring the purchaser to pay the price before being entitled to delivery of the goods. 46 Am J1st Sales § 202.

See **net cash; net cash ten days.**

terra (ter'ạ). Land.

terra affirmata (ter'ra af-fir-mā'ta). Farmed land; land which let to be farmed.

terracing. Changing the contour of a tract of real estate so as to have successive ascending and descending levels.

terra culta (ter'ra kul'ta). Cultivated land.

terra debilis (ter'ra dē'bi-lis). Barren land.

terrae (ter'rē). Lands.

See **frustrum terrae.**

terrae dominicales (ter'rē do-mi-ni-kā'lēz). Demesne lands, lands reserved by the lord of the manor for his own use and that of his family. See 2 Bl Comm 90.

terrae dominicales regis (ter'rē do-mi-ni-kā'lēz re'jis). The king's demesne lands. See 1 Bl Comm 286.

terrae tenementales (ter'rē te-ne-men-tā'lēz). Lands which the lord of the manor distributed among his tenants. See 2 Bl Comm 90.

terra excultabilis (ter'ra ex-kul-tā'bi-lis). Land which could be ploughed.

terra firma (ter'ra fir'ma). Firm land; dry land.

terra frisca (ter'ra fris'ka). Fresh land; uncultivated land.

terra hydata (ter'ra hy-dā'ta). Land which was subject to hidage, which was a tax levied on each hide of land.

terra lucrabilis (ter'ra lu-krā'bi-lis). Reclaimed land.

Terra manens vacua occupanti conceditur (ter'ra ma'nenz va'ku-a o-kū-pan'ti kon-sē'di-ter). Land remaining vacant is granted to the occupant.

terra Normanorum (ter'ra nor-man-ō'rum). Land of the Normans, land which was held under Norman tenure.

terra nova (ter'ra no'va). New land, land which had been recently cleared.

terra putura (ter'ra pu-tū'ra). Forest land which was held by the service of victualing the keepers of the forest.

terra sabulosa (ter'ra sa-bu-lō'sa). Sandy land; land covered with gravel.

terra sancta. See **essoin de terra sancta.**

terra testamentalis (ter'ra tes"ta-men-tā'lis). Land which could be transferred by will.

Terra transit cum onere (ter'ra tran'zit kum ō'ne-re). Land passes with its burdens.

terra vestita (ter'ra ves-tī'ta). Planted or seeded land.

terra wainabilis (ter'ra wā-nā'bi-lis). Tillable land.

Terra Walliae cum incolis suis, prius regi jure foedali subjecta, jam in proprietatis dominium totaliter et cum integritate conversa est, et coronae regni Angliae tanquam pars corporis ejusdem annexa et unita (ter'ra wal'li-ē kum in'ko-lis su'is, prī'us rē'ji jū're fē-dā'li sub-jek'ta, jam in prō-pri-ē-tā'tis do-mi'ni-um to-tā'li-ter et kum in-teg-ri-tā'te kon-ver'sa est, et ko-rō'nē reg'nī ang'li-ē tan'quom parz kor'po-ris e-jus'dem an-ne'xa et u-nī'ta). The country of Wales, with its inhabitants was formerly subject to the king under feudal law; now it is wholly converted into a principality and annexed to and united with the crown of England as a part of the same body. See 1 Bl Comm 94.

terra warrenata (ter'ra war-re-nā'ta). Land in which there was free warren or the franchise of hunting and preserving game in a warren.

terre (tār). Land.

terre seynte. See **essoin de terre seynte.**

terre-tenant (tār'ten"ạnt). A person who is a purchaser, mediately or immediately, from a judgment debtor, while the land purchased is bound by the judgment. An owner of real property which is subject to the lien of a judgment against another person. Not a "debtor" within the meaning of a statute exempting a certain amount out of the proceeds of land. Eberhart's Appeal, 39 Pa 509.

terrible. Exciting terror. Frightful or dreadful. Denver & Rio Grande Railroad Co. v Roller (CA9 Cal) 100 F 738.

territorial. Pertaining or belonging to a territory of the United States.

territorial court. A court in the judicial system of a territory of the United States. 49 Am J1st States §§ 107, 131.

Although the judicial system set up in a territory of the United States is part of the federal jurisdiction, the phrase "court of the United States," when used in a federal statute, is generally construed as not referring to territorial courts. International Longshoremen's & Warehousemen's Union v Wirtz (CA9 Hawaii) 170 F2d 183, cert den 336 US 919, 93 L Ed 1082, 69 S Ct 641, reh den 336 US 971, 93 L Ed 1121, 69 S Ct 936.

territorial governor. The chief executive of a territory of the United States. New York ex rel. Kopel v Bingham, 211 US 468, 53 L Ed 286, 29 S Ct 190.

territorial judge. The judge of a court of a territory of the United States. McAllister v United States, 141 US 278, 39 L Ed 982, 15 S Ct 889.
See **territorial court.**

territorial jurisdiction. The limits of the geographical boundaries of a district within which a judge or other judicial officer has jurisdiction to act judicially, and outside of which his judicial acts are null and void. Phillips v Thralls, 26 Kan 780, 781. The jurisdiction of a court in reference to the area in which the process of the court is affective. Jurisdiction subject to territorial limitations.

The jurisdiction of a court cannot extend beyond the territory belonging to the sovereignty on behalf of which it functions, and its jurisdiction may be further limited territorially, by constitutional or statutory provisions, to a part only of the territory of the sovereignty to which it belongs. 20 Am J2d Cts § 153.

territorial limitation. A charter limitation in reference to the territorial scope of the operations of the corporation. 36 Am J2d For Corp § 87. A limit upon the exercise of judicial power. Lynde v Winnebaco County (US) 16 Wall 6, 21 L Ed 272. Limitation of jurisdiction to territory within certain definite boundaries. 20 Am J2d Cts § 153. A limitation on the operation of a statute to territory within the boundaries of a particular district or political division or subdivision. 50 Am J1st Stat § 485.

territorial possessions. All lands acquired by the United States by treaty or purchase which have not become an integral part of the United States, in other words, territory that has not been incorporated into the United States. Rassmussen v United States, 197 US 516, 49 L Ed 862, 25 S Ct 514.

territorial waters. See **three mile limit.**

territorium. See **extra territorium.**

territory. An area, especially one of significance from a particular aspect, as in the case of a salesman's territory or of good hunting territory. A region which, although not a state, has an organized system of government. People of Porto Rico v Rosaly y Castillo, 227 US 270, 33 S Ct 352, 57 L Ed 507.

As the word is used in the phrase "the United States and all territory subject to the jurisdiction thereof," it means the regional areas—of land and adjacent waters—over which the United States claims and exercises dominion and control as a sovereign power. It refers to areas or districts having fixity of location and recognized boundaries. Cunard Steamship Co. v Mellon, 262 US 100, 67 L Ed 894, 43 S Ct 504, 27 ALR 1306, 1315.

See **territorial possessions; unincorporated territory; unorganized territory.**

territory adjacent. See **adjacent territory.**

territory of the United States. See **territory.**

terrorem. See **in terrorem.**

terrorem populi. See **in terrorem populi.**

terroristic act (ter-rǫr-is′tik akt). Act of vandalism or violence. Anno: 116 ALR 507.

tertia (tėr′shạ). The third part; dower. See 2 Bl Comm 129.

tesmoignance. See **entesmoignance.**

test. See **performance test; triennial test; tuberculin test; Wasserman test; wild beast test.**

testable (tes′tạ-bl). The state or condition of a person who is possessed of testamentary capacity.
See **testamentary capacity.**

Test Act. An act of parliament of 1672, directing all officers, civil and military to take oaths and make the declaration against transubstantiation in any of the king's courts at Westminster, or at the quarter sessions, within six calendar months after their admission. See 4 Bl Comm 58.

testacy (tes′tạ-si). The condition of a deceased person who died leaving a valid will.

testament (tes′tạ-ment). Historically, a disposition of personal property effective upon the death of the testator, but in modern usage, a will disposing of either real or personal property, or both kinds of property. 57 Am J1st Wills § 2.

In common usage, the words, will, testament, and last will are synonymous. Occidental L. Ins. Co. v Powers, 192 Wash 475, 74 P2d 27, 114 ALR 531.

See **adulterinum testamentum; ex testamento.**

Testamenta latissimam interpretationem habere debent (tes-ta-men′ta la-tis′si-mam in-ter-pre-ta-she-ō′nem ha-bē′re de′bent). Wills ought to have the broadest interpretation or construction.

testamentary (tes′tạ-men′tạ′ri). See **testamentary character.**

testamentary arbitrator. A person appointed by a testator in his will to interpret and settle difficulties between beneficiaries growing out of dispositions made by the will. Anno: 104 ALR 362, 363.

testamentary capacity. The capacity to accomplish the purpose of making a valid will as determined objectively from the standpoint of the purpose. The capacity of a person making a will to know the natural objects of his bounty, to comprehend the kind and character of his property, to understand the nature and effect of his act, and to make a disposition of his property according to some plan formed in his mind. Re Hagan, 143 Neb 459, 98 NW2d 794, 154 ALR 573.

A testator is of sound and disposing mind and memory, and hence, competent, if at the time of making his will, he has sufficient mental capacity to understand the nature of the act he is doing, to understand and recollect the nature and situation of his property, and to remember and understand his relations to persons who have claims upon his bounty and whose interests are affected by the provisions of the instrument. In re Smith's Estate, 200 Cal 152, 252 P 325.

Testamentary capacity includes a recollection of

the persons related to him by ties of blood and affection, and of the nature of the claims of those who are excluded from participating in his estate. 57 Am J1st Wills § 51.

testamentary character. See **testamentary instrument.**

testamentary class. Persons included and comprehended under some general description in a will, bearing a certain relation to the testator, having a common relation to each other, sustaining the same relation to the bequest, or included together in a grouping made by the testator. 57 Am J1st Wills § 1259.

testamentary disposition. The disposition of property by deed, will, or otherwise, in such a manner that it shall not take effect unless or until the grantor dies. Chestnut Street Nat. Bank v Fidelity Ins. Trust & Safe Deposit Co. 186 Pa 333, 40 A 486.
See **testamentary instrument.**

testamentary expenses. Expenses of administration. Construed in some instances, although not in others, as inclusive of estate taxes or duties, as the phrase appears in a direction by the testator to the executor for the payment by the latter of "testamentary expenses." Anno: 51 ALR 466.

testamentary guardian. A guardian appointed by the deed or the last will of the parent of the ward. 25 Am J1st G & W § 12.

testamentary heir. See **heir testamentary.**

testamentary instrument. An instrument such that, from the language used, it is apparent that the maker intended to make a disposition of his property or some part thereof, to be effective at his death. 57 Am J1st Wills § 8. An instrument manifesting a donative intent, but neither conferring nor evidencing an intent to confer, upon the donees any property, right, or benefit during the life of the maker, having no binding effect during his life, and remaining revocable by him at his pleasure. 57 Am J1st Wills § 7.

An instrument is testamentary when it is written or made so as not to take effect until after the death of the person making it, and to be revocable and to retain the property under his control during his life, although he may have believed that it would operate as an instrument of a different character. Benson v Benson, 125 Okla 151, 256 P 912, 62 ALR 935.

testamentary power. The power to make a will existing under the law as a matter of privilege. Hamilton v Morgan, 93 Fla 311, 112 So 80.

Convicts may have the capacity and yet be denied the power to make a will. 57 Am J1st Wills § 51.
See **testamentary capacity.**

testamentary power of sale. A power of sale of real or personal property of a decedent conferred upon the executor of the estate of the decedent by his will. 31 Am J2d Ex & Ad § 437.

Where a power of sale is given to an executor by virtue of his office, and not to him as an individual, the presumption is that it was given for the purpose of being executed in the interest of the estate and not for his own benefit. Sweeny v Warren, 127 NY 426, 28 NE 413.

testamentary trust. A trust created by will.
See **precatory trust.**

testamentary trustee. A trustee appointed by the court to execute a trust created by a will, either nominated by the will itself or not so nominated. See Re Hazard (NY) 51 Hun 201, 4 NYS 701.

testamento (tes-ta-men'to). A last will or testament.

testamentum (tes-ta-men'tum). A last will or testament.

Testamentum est voluntatis nostrae justa sententia de eo, quod quis post mortem suam fieri velit (tes-ta-men'tum est vo-lun-tā'tis nos'trē jus'ta sen-ten'she-a, dē eo', quod quis pōst mor'tem su'am fī'e-ri vē'lit). A will is the legal declaration of a man's intentions, which he wills to be performed after his death. See 2 Bl Comm 499.

testamentum inofficiosum (tes-ta-men'tum in-of-fi-she-ō'sum). Same as **unofficious will.**

Testamentum omne morte consummatum (tes-ta-men'tum om'ne mor'te kon-sum-mā'tum). Every will is consummated or perfected by death.

testate (tes'tāt). A deceased person who died leaving a will; the condition of a person who dies leaving a will.

testatio mentis (tes-tā'she-ō men'tis). A bearing witness of the mind; a testament; a will. See 2 Bl Comm 499.

testation (tes-ta'shon). Same as **attestation.**

testator (tes-tā'tor). A deceased person who died leaving a valid will.

Testatoris ultima voluntas est perimplenda secundum veram intentionem suam (tes-ta-tō'ris ul'ti-ma vo-lun'tas est per-im-plen'da se-kun'dum vē'ram in-ten-she-ō'nem sū'am). The last will of a testator is to be fulfilled according to his true intention.

testator's presence. See **in the presence of the testator.**

testatrix (tes-tā'triks). Feminine of **testator.**

testatum (tes-tā'tum). Testified.

testatum capias (tes-tā'tum kā'pi-as). A writ or process issued in a civil action for the arrest of a defendant when the return of a previously issued process showed that he could not be found within the county. See 3 Bl Comm 283.

testatum clause (tes-tā'tum klâz). Same as **testimonium clause.**

testatum writ (tes-tā'tum rit). A writ of fieri facias issued from a court which renders a judgment for the purpose of subjecting property of the judgment debtor in another county to the satisfaction of the judgment. 30 Am J2d Exec § 60.

testatus (tes-tā'tus). Testate; a testator.

test case. A case involving an actual controversy but brought for the purpose of determining the law upon the point presented. 1 Am J2d Actions § 56.

A "test case" is not necessarily a moot case, and where a case is one of fact or right, there is no principle of law or policy which will deprive a party of a determination, simply because his motive in the assertion of such a right is to secure such a determination. It is a matter of common practice. Indeed, most of the cases of trespass to try title are of this sort. See Adams v Union Railroad Co. 21 RI 134, 42 A 515.

teste (tes'tē). Verb: To bear witness. Richbourg v Rose, 53 Fla 173, 44 So 69. Noun: A formal declaration bearing witness to the official character and time of issuance of a judicial writ. 42 Am J1st Proc § 9.

teste clause (tes'te klâz). Same as **testimonium clause**.

tested (tes'ted). Witnessed; attested; executed in the presence of witnesses who certify to the fact. Given a test; subjected to a test.

Teste meipso (tes'te mē-ip'so). I, myself bear witness.

teste of a deed. See **testimonium clause**.

teste of writ (tes'tē of rit). See **teste**.

Testes ponderantur, non numerantur (tes'tez pon-de-ran'ter, non nu-me-ran'ter). Witnesses are weighed, not counted.

test explosion. A nuclear explosion detonated on an experimental basis. 6 Am J2d Atomic E § 48.

Testibus deponentibus in pari numero dignioribus est credendum (tes'ti-bus dē-pō-nen'ti-bus in pā'ri nu'me-ro dig-ni-or'i-bus est krē-den'dum). Where the witnesses have testified in equal numbers (on each side), the more worthy of them are to be believed.

testify (tes'ti-fī). To give one's testimony under oath as a witness.

In an action by a seller's personal representative against the buyer upon a book account, the representative's offer in evidence of the decedent's books of account is not such a "testifying" by the representative as to constitute a waiver, within the meaning of a statute relating to testimony as to transactions with the decedent, so as to permit the surviving opponent to take the stand against him. Johnson v Hoffman, 7 NJ 123, 80 A2d 624, 26 ALR2d 1001.

testimonia (tes'ti-mō'ni-a). Testimony; evidence.

testimonial admission. An informal judicial admission whereby a party may bar his claim or defense by his own testimony. Rosbottom v Hensley, 61 Ill App 2d 198, 209 NE2d 655.

Testimonia ponderanda sunt, non numeranda (tes-ti-mō'ni-a pon-de-ran'da sunt, non nu-me-ran'da). Testimony is to be weighed, not counted (by the number of witnesses).

testimonio. A word found in Spanish-American grants and signifying the first copy of the expediente of such a grant.

An expediente is a complete statement of every step taken in the proceedings. A grant of final title papers is attached to the testimonio and delivered to the grantee as evidence of title, and entry is made at the time in a book called the Toma de Razon, which identifies the grantee, date of the grant, and property granted. The dictionaries define tomas razon as meaning to register; to take a memorandum of; to make a record of a thing, and toma de razon, they define as meaning a memorandum book. Ainsa v United States, 161 US 208, 219, 40 L Ed 673, 677.

testimonium (tes-ti-mo'ni-um). See **testimonium clause**.

testimonium clause (tes-ti-mo'ni-um klâz). The clause in a written instrument, otherwise known as a testatum clause, such as "in witness whereof," by which the act and date of execution is directed to the writing. Arrington v Arrington, 122 Ala 510, 26 So 152. An attestation clause. 13 Am J2d Bonds § 12.

In the case of a corporation grantor, the testatum clause recites that the corporation has caused its corporate seal to be affixed and its corporate name to be signed by its duly authorized officers. Kelly v Calhoun, 95 US 710, 24 L Ed 544.

See **attestation clause**.

testimony. The words of a witness upon the stand. 29 Am J2d Ev § 3. In loose usage, the evidence in a case. Roberts v Carlson, 142 Neb 851, 8 NW2d 175.

Testimony is one thing and evidence is another; testimony is the words heard from the witnesses in court, and evidence is what the jury considers it worth. Schultz v Bower, 57 Minn 493, 59 NW 631.

testis (tes'tis). A witness.

Testis de visu praeponderat aliis (tes'tis dē vī'su prē-pon'de-rat a'li-is). An eyewitness outweighs other witnesses.

Testis nemo in sua causa esse potest (tes'tis nē'mo in su'a kâ'za es'se pō'test). No one can be a witness in his own cause.

Testis oculatus unus plus valet quam auriti decem (tes'tis o-ku-lā'tus ū'nus plūs va'let quam â-rī'ti de'-sem). One eyewitness is worth more than ten ear-witnesses.

test letter. A decoy letter, that is, an imitation of a genuine letter, usually marked and directed to a fictitious person, placed in the mails by postal inspectors or officers of the department of justice for the purpose of detecting a post-office employee who is suspected of appropriating letters or their contents; or a letter sent through the mails by such officers to a person suspected of sending prohibited matter through the mails, for purpose of detecting him in such violation of the law. Montgomery v United States, 162 US 410, 40 L Ed 1020, 16 S Ct 797; Goode v United States, 159 US 663, 40 L Ed 297, 16 S Ct 136.

Testmoignes ne poent testifie le negative mes l'affirmative (test-mwa'nyä nuh pē tes'ti-fi-ay" luh ne-ga-tēv may l'af-fir-ma-tēv). Witnesses cannot testify to a negative, but they may testify to an affirmative.

test oath. An oath required as an assurance of a person's loyalty to the nation and government. 39 Am J1st Oath § 7.

test of insanity. The principle applied in determining whether a person is afflicted with such mental infirmity as to be unable to bind himself by contract, as to render him irresponsible for acts otherwise criminal, or as to require his commitment to an institution. 29 Am J Rev ed Ins Per § 2.

See **right and wrong test**.

test order. A provisional or temporary order by an administrative agency. 2 Am J2d Admin L § 466.

test pilot. A pilot who flies new or repaired aircraft by way of testing the safety and control of the craft.

test run. Taking out a ship or smaller watercraft for the purpose of testing its performance. Gilreath v Silverman, 245 NC 51, 95 SE2d 107.

tetanus (tet'a-nus). An infectious disease characterized by contractions of muscles, especially the muscles of the jaw, so that the disease is often known as lockjaw. Pitman v Commercial Travelers' Eastern Acci. Asso. 284 Mass 467, 188 NE 241.

Texas fever. A contagious or infectious disease of cattle. 4 Am J2d Ani § 38.

textbook. A book of instruction in a particular subject, particularly a book for use in schools, colleges, and universities. 47 Am J1st Sch § 202. A law book covering a particular subject, such as insurance, municipal corporations, admiralty, etc.

textile design. A design of a pattern of color of cloth. H. M. Kolbe v Armgus Textile Co. (CA2 NY) 315 F2d 70, 99 ALR2d 390.

text-writer. The author of a text book or treatise upon some branch of the law or scientific subject.

thaini. Freeholders.

thalweg (täl'väch). The deep way or most navigable channel; the middle, deepest, or most navigable channel. State of Iowa v Illinois, 147 US 1, 8, 37 L Ed 55, 57, 13 S Ct 239. The name given to the principle of the law of nations that where nations are divided by a navigable river, each should hold for commercial reasons to the center thread of the main channel or current along which vessels in the carrying trade pass, in other words to the channel of commerce, not the shallow water of the stream. 30 Am J Rev ed Internat L § 16.

Thanksgiving Day. A holiday as designated by the proclamation of the governor of a state or by the President of the United States. State v Hirsch, 125 Ind 207, 24 NE 1062.

that is to say. A phrase of art used as a videlicet. See **videlicet**.

theater. A building especially adapted to dramatic, operatic, or spectacular representations; a playhouse. Asa G. Candler, Inc. v Georgia Theater Co. 148 Ga 188, 96 SE 226. A room, hall, or other place so arranged that a body of spectators can have an unobstructed view of the platform where dramatic or musical entertainment is presented. 4 Am J2d Amuse § 2. Literally, as derived from the Greek, a place for seeing. Asa G. Candler, Inc. v Georgia Theater Co. 148 Ga 188, 96 SE 226.

theater license. A license required by a municipal corporation of one operating a theater.
See **theater ticket**.

theater ticket. A ticket entitling to admission to a performance in a theater, ordinarily entitling the holder to a seat reserved for him and noted upon the ticket.

A license issued by the proprietor, pursuant to the contract, as convenient evidence of the right of the holder to admission to the theater at the date named, with the privilege specified, subject, however, to his observance of any reasonable condition appearing on the face thereof. The license, though granted for a consideration, is revocable for a violation of such condition by the holder of the ticket in the manner specified therein. The ticket is not the contract, although to some extent it is evidence thereof. The contract is implied from the circumstances, and is an agreement on the part of the proprietor, for the consideration mentioned, to admit the holder of the ticket, upon presentation thereof, to his theater at the date named, with the right to occupy the seat specified, subject, however, to his observance of any reasonable condition appearing on the face thereof. Collister v Hayman, 183 NY 250, 76 NE 20.

theater ticket speculator. See **ticket speculator**.

theatrical agency. An employment agency specializing in actors and entertainers of stage, screen, radio, and television. 27 Am J2d Employ Ag § 9.

theatrical exhibition. See **theatrical performance**.

theatrical performance. A dramatic, operatic, or spectacular representation. 4 Am J2d Amuse § 2.

theatricals. An unseemly demonstration in court, usually for the purpose of exciting the sympathy of court or jury. Tom Reed Goldmines Co. v Berd, 32 Ariz 479, 260 P 191, 57 ALR 55.
See **theatrical performance**.

The Bold Buccleugh. A celebrated English admiralty case decided in 1852 by the judicial committee of the privy council, establishing the rule that the privilege or claim of a maritime lien constitutes a present right of property in the ship, a jus in re, to be afterwards enforced in admiralty by process in rem; and that from the moment when the claim or privilege attaches, it is inchoate, and when carried into effect by legal process, by a proceeding in rem, it relates back to the period when it first attached.

This claim or privilege travels with the vessel into whatsoever possession it may come, even that of a bona fide purchaser; and it is not divested by the death or insolvency of the owner. The John G. Stevens, 170 US 113, 42 L Ed 969, 18 S Ct 544.

theft. Larceny. A broader term than larceny, including other forms of wrongful deprivation of the property of another. 32 Am J1st Larc § 2.

The word is defined as a fraudulent taking of corporeal personal property belonging to another from his possession, or from the possesssion of some person holding the same for him, without his consent, with intent to deprive the owner of the value of the same, and to appropriate it to the use or benefit of the person taking. The taking must be wrongful, so that if the property came into the possession of the person accused of theft by lawful means, the subsequent appropriation of it is not theft, but if the taking, though originally lawful, was obtained by any false pretext, or with any intent to deprive the owner of the value thereof, and appropriate the property to the use and benefit of the person taking, and the same is so appropriated, the offense of theft is complete. Anno: 30 ALR 663.
See **theft insurance**.

theft bote (theft bōt). The common law offense of an owner in receiving the property from one who took it by theft, under an agreement not to prosecute or to prosecute but in a fainthearted manner. State v Hodge, 142 NC 665, 55 SE 626.

theft insurance. Insurance against the risk of loss by theft. 29A Am J Rev ed Ins § 1333. A contract to indemnify against loss by thieves. Anno: 46 LRA (NS) 562; 47 LRA (NS) 296.

Where the word "theft" is used in an insurance policy, without definition, it should be interpreted as liberally as possible to protect the insured. American Ins. Co. v Burson (CA5 Fla) 213 F2d 487, 48 ALR2d 1.

The word "theft" in a policy insuring against loss by burglary, larceny, or "theft", is a broader term than "larceny," including wrongful deprivation of property by embezzlement or swindling. Fidelity & Casualty Co. v Wathen, 205 Ky 511, 266 SW 4, 41 ALR 844.

The word "theft" is ordinarily synonymous with the word larceny. But even in jurisdictions where the act of the taker constitutes statutory larceny, it is usually held that there is no "theft," as the word is used in policies of insurance against theft, unless there is an intent to deprive the owner, not temporarily but permanently, of his property. Anno: 46 ALR 536.
See **automobile theft insurance**.

theft loss. A deduction of loss by theft in computation of taxable income, "theft" being broadly defined in this connection to include larceny, robbery, embezzlement, even a wrongful withholding by a trustee. Internal Revenue Code § 165; Vincent v Commissioner (CA9) 219 F2d 228. A deduction in determining the taxable estate of a decedent for estate tax purposes of losses incurred by theft during the settlement of the estate. Internal Revenue Code 1954 § 2054; 26 USC § 2054.

thegn (thăn). A tenant in capite.
See **tenant in capite.**

Thellusson Act. An English statute by which all persons are prohibited from settling property by deed or will so that the rents and profits shall be wholly or partially accumulated for a longer term than the life of the settlor, or 21 years after his death, or during the minority of a person or persons living at the time of the death of the settlor, or during the minority or respective minorities only of a person or persons who, if of full age, would have been absolutely entitled under the settlement. Act of 39 and 40 Geo III, Ch 98; 41 Am J1st Perp § 44.

theme. The underlying thought of an article or discourse. In the law of copyright, the underlying thought presented in an original way, characterized by novelty or embellishment, so that it becomes the literary property of the author in the exclusive use of which he is entitled to protection. Roe-Lawton v Hal E. Roach Studios (DC Cal) 18 F2d 126.

then. At that time. Next in the order of events. Accordingly. As used in a will, subject to construction as an adverb of time, having its ordinary grammatical acceptation in meaning, or as a word of reasoning connecting a consequence with a premise, in other words, the equivalent of "in that event." 57 Am J1st Wills § 1332. A word sometimes postponing the ascertainment of a class until the time to which it has reference. 57 Am J1st Wills § 1283. In a limitation of a remainder, ordinarily relating to the time of enjoyment rather than the time of vesting. Anno: 103 ALR 599.

A will providing that, at the expiration of a life estate, the testator "then" gives the remainder to his children "absolutely and forever," uses the word "then" as an adverb of time to be construed as relating solely to the time of enjoyment of the estate, and not to the time of its vesting in interest. Re Kroos, 302 NY 424, 99 NE2d 222, 47 ALR2d 894.

In an indictment, where the time when an act was done is alleged as "then," and time is not an issuable fact in the case, the word "then" means any time within the period of the statute of limitations. State v Archer, 32 NM 319, 255 P 396, 399.

then and there. See **did then and there.**

then cash value. The amount of money the property involved would produce, if offered and sold for cash in the open market upon the relevent date. Re Woolsey, 109 Neb 138, 190 NW 215, 24 ALR 1038.

thence. From a stated place.
The phrase "thence up the river" as used in field notes describing the boundary of a survey of public land, must be read with the declaration that the survey is on the southern bank of the river, in the light of the drawing or plat representing the river as the northern boundary. Oklahoma v Texas, 268 US 252, 69 L Ed 937, 45 S Ct 497.

Insurance on a ship to a port, "thence" to another, and "thence" to a third, is the same as from the first to the last with liberty to stop at the intermediate ports. When applied to an intermediate port, the words "thence" or "from" have not the same exclusive sense as when used with regard to the commencement of a voyage. Bradley v Nashville Ins. Co. 3 La Ann 708.

then living. Characterizing survivorship referred to the termination of a life estate or other intervening estate. 28 Am J2d Est § 269. A phrase in a will operating to preclude application of rule that a class is to be determined as of the time of death of the testator. 57 Am J1st Wills § 1284.

theocracy (thẹ-ok′rạ-si). A government which recognizes God as its ruler.

Theodoric. See **Edictum Theodorici.**

theological seminary (thē-ọ-loj′i-kạl). See **seminary.**

theolonium (the-o-lō′ni-um). Toll.

the ordinary prudent man. The standard man; the average prudent individual; the reasonable and prudent man or the careful and diligent man. An abstract man of ordinary mental and physical capacity, but an ideal man in the sense that his conduct is in every case the gauge of due care under the circumstances, notwithstanding the precautions attributed to him are not those of usage and custom. 38 Am J1st Negl § 30.

theoretical inch. A term referred to in discussions of measurement of water.
In water measurement, the theoretical inch is founded upon the theory that water spouting from the side of a flume with a certain head, say four feet, will have the same velocity as if it fell the same distance through the air, and, as this velocity is fixed and certain, the amount of water referred to in the theoretical inch is fixed and certain. But the theory is not true in actual practice. Janesville Cotton Mills v Ford, 82 Wis 416, 52 NW 764.

theory of case. The design or principle on which a party maintains his alleged cause of action or defense. A necessary statement in a bill in equity. O'Brien v People, 216 Ill 354, 75 NE 108.
The theory of the case should be presented with sufficient allegations of fact to give basis and point to the charges, but if the allegations develop too much theory, the door will be open to the criticism of stating mere conclusions of law or of being too abstract. O'Brien v People, 216 Ill 354, 75 NE 108.
As a general rule, a reviewing court considers the case only upon the theory upon which it was tried in the court below. 5 Am J2d A & E § 546.

theosophy (thẹ-os′ọ-fi). A philosophy, perhaps a religion, which teaches the obtaining of insight in divine principle through contemplation and revelation. Anno: 12 ALR2d 872, § 4.

the parol demur. An old common-law expression for a stay to await the expiration of time removing the disability of a party.
When the heir was sued upon a specialty obligation of the ancestor chargeable on the inheritance, if he was an infant he might pray that "the parol demur" until he should reach his majority. See 27 Am J1st Inf § 157.

the people. Citizens. Anno: 68 L Ed 266, 267.
See **people of the state; people of the United States.**

The power to tax is the power to destroy. A famous declaration of Chief Justice Marshall in McCulloch v State of Maryland, 4 Wheat (US) 431, 4 L Ed 579.
A striking instance of the truth of this proposition is seen in the fact that the existing tax of ten per cent, imposed by the United States on the circulation of all other banks than national banks, drove

therapy (ther'a-pi). The treatment of disease, whether by the administration of drugs or surgery. Stewart v Raab, 55 Minn 20, 21, 56 NW 256.
See **drugless therapeutics; physiotherapy.**

thereafter. After a certain event. In a limitation of a remainder, ordinarily relating to the time of enjoyment rather than the time of vesting. 28 Am J2d Est § 257.

thereafter clause. A term familiar to oilmen, being a clause in an oil or gas lease intended to establish rights in the lessee notwithstanding termination of the primary term of the lease, where production is maintained. Anno: 100 ALR2d 901.

thereby. Because of; by reason of. Hornbrook v Elm Grove, 40 W Va 543, 21 SE 851.

there is hereby granted. Words importing a grant in praesenti and an immediate transfer of interest. Okanogan County v Cheetham, 37 Wash 682, 80 P 262.

theretofore. Before a certain time or the time of the occurrence of a known event. Hamilton v State, 129 Fla 219, 176 So 89, 112 ALR 1013.

thereunto. An elliptical form of expression for the phrase "to do that."
Hence, an agent "thereunto authorized in writing" is an agent who must be authorized in writing "to do that;" that is, for example, to execute a written contract for his principal. Anno: 27 ALR 612.

thereupon. Without delay or lapse of time. Putnam v Langley, 133 Mass 204, 205.

thesaurus inventus (thē-sâ'rus in-ven'tus). Found treasure; treasure-trove.

Thesaurus regis est vinculum pacis et bellorum nervus (thē-sâ'rus rē'jis est vin'ku-lum pa'sis et bel-lō'rum ner'vus). The treasury of the king is the bond of peace and the sinew of war.
"These maxims, it is said, should apply to the state, and her revenues should be protected with as much solicitude as those of the British king." State v Foster, 5 Wyo 199, 38 P 926.

these presents. Formal words for "this instrument," "this very instrument."

thesmothete (thes'mō-thēt). A law giver.

thief. A person who has committed the crime of larceny. One guilty of theft.

thimblerig (thim'bl-rig). To cheat by means of prestidigitation.

thimbles and balls. A game of chance played with thimbles and a ball, success depending on designating the thimble under which the ball has been placed. 24 Am J1st Gaming § 28.

thing. See **things.**

thing appendant (thing a-pen'dant). A thing which is affixed or belongs to some more important thing.

thing in action. Same as **chose in action.**

thing of value. Something having a monetary value. 17 Am J2d Contr § 95.
As the term is used in the law of larceny, it includes any tangible thing which the law recognizes as being property. Columbus Railroad Co. v Woolfolk, 128 Ga 631, 58 SE 152.
The term is defined, as it pertains to the subject of gambling, as any thing affording the necessary lure to indulge the gambling instinct. Painter v State, 163 Tenn 627, 45 SW2d 46, 81 ALR 173.

things. Inanimate objects. Gayer v Whelan, 59 Cal App 255, 139 P2d 763. As the subject matter of a bequest, effects, goods, assets, or property, dependent upon the intent of the testator as such appears from the will. Arnolds Estate, 240 Pa 261, 87 A 590.
See **rights of things.**

things personal. Goods, money, and all other movables, which may attend the owner's person wherever he cares to go. Transcontinental Oil Co. v Emmerson, 298 Ill 394, 131 NE 645, 16 ALR 507, 512.

things real (rēl). Such things as are permanent, fixed, and immovable, which cannot be carried out of their place, as lands and tenements. Transcontinental Oil Co. v Emmerson, 298 Ill 394, 131 NE 645, 16 ALR 507, 512.

think. See **I think.**

Third Amendment. An amendment to the Constitution of the United States, one of the Bill of Rights, forbidding the quartering of soldiers in time of peace in any house without the consent of the owner, and in time of war except as in a manner prescribed by law.

third arbitrator. An arbitrator called in by two original arbitrators to act in conjunction with them and thus break a deadlock.
He is not an umpire, because he does not act alone. 5 Am J2d Arb & A § 85.

third-class mail. Circulars and books, and other printed matter not in first or second class; merchandise; seeds, bulbs, and plants. 41 Am J1st P O § 60.

third cousin. The child of a second cousin. A relative in the sixth degree according to the civil-law method of computing degrees of kinship which prevails in most American jurisdictions. Anno: 54 ALR2d 1012, § 1(b). Sometimes known as a second cousin once removed.

third degree. The employment of coercion, mental or physical, in obtaining a confession. People v Loper, 159 Cal 6, 112 P 720.

third degree relative. Under the civil-law method of computing degrees of kinship which prevails in most American jurisdictions, an uncle, aunt, nephew, niece, and great grandparent. Anno: 55 ALR2d 645, § 1[b].
See **degrees of kinship.**

third house. A facetious name for that which is nothing more nor less than an organized lobby. Common Council of Detroit v Rentz, 91 Mich 78, 51 NW 787.

third parties. All persons who are not parties to the contract, agreement, or instrument of writing, by which their interest in the thing conveyed is sought to be affected. Morrison v Trudeau (La) 1 Mart NS 384, 387. Persons other than original plaintiff or defendant but brought into the action.
See **bystander; third person.**

third-party action. A concept and the application thereof in modern practice under statute or rule of practice whereby the defendant in an action brings into the action a third person under allegation in an appropriate pleading that the third person is liable over to the defendant in reference to the cause of action asserted by the plaintiff, so that there may

third-party beneficiary. The beneficiary of a contract made between two other persons. 17 Am J2d Contr § 302.

third-party beneficiary contract. A contract for the benefit of a third person. 17 Am J2d Contr § 302.

third-party claim. A claim to property held under attachment as the property of the defendant in the action, made by a person not a party to the action. 6 Am J2d Attach §§ 572 et seq.

third-party complaint. The pleading of the defendant against a third person whom he seeks to bring into the action as a party because of an alleged liability over to the defendant.
See **third-party action.**

third-party contract. See **third-party beneficiary contract.**

third-party plaintiff. The defendant in an action who assumes the status of a plaintiff in bringing a third person into the action as one liable over him.
See **third-party action.**

third-party practice. A principle found in modern practice statutes and rules of practice whereby a defendant is permitted to bring into the action a person or persons who are liable over to the defendant, the efficacy and justice being that the several issues between the plaintiff and the defendant and between the defendant and the third person brought into the action will be determined at one time and by the same jury or trier of the fact.
See **impleader.**

third-party summons. A summons or notice by which a person not originally a party to an action is summoned to answer a third-party complaint.

third-party technique. Giving propaganda actually circulated by a party in interest the appearance of being spontaneous declarations of independent groups. Eastern R. Presidents Conference v Noerr Motor Freight, Inc. 365 US 127, 5 L Ed 2d 464, 81 S Ct 523.

third person. One not involved. A bystander. As a depositary of an escrow:—a stranger to the instrument, not a party to it; a person so free from personal or legal identity with the parties to the instrument as to leave him free to discharge his duty as a depositary to both parties without involving a breach of duty to either. 28 Am J2d Escr § 12.
The dictation of a letter otherwise libelous by the president of a corporation to his stenographer, in the course of the business of the corporation, is not a communication to a third person. Globe Furniture Co. v Wright, 49 App DC 315, 265 F 873, 18 ALR 772.
As the expression is used in the generally recognized rule that the acts of a de facto officer are valid as to "third persons," it means those persons having business of an official character with such officer, and not third persons in the usual legal sense in which the term is used. State ex rel. Brockmeier v Ely, 16 ND 569.
See **third parties.**

third possessor. One who buys mortgaged property without assuming to pay the mortgage.
If one buys real estate, and does not assume the payment of the first mortgage, he is bound only as a third possessor. He must either give up the property, or pay the amount for which it was mortgaged. This is the full extent of his responsibility as a purchaser. See Thompson v Levy, 50 La Ann 751, 752, 23 So 913.

third rail. An extra rail of an electric railroad, particularly a subway or elevated railroad, through which electric current for the propulsion of the car or train is supplied. Riedel v West Jersey & S. R. Co. (CA3 Pa) 177 F 374.

thirlage (thėr'lăj). The servitude of being required to have the grain raised on the land ground at a particular mill for which a certain payment was to be made.

Thirteenth Amendment. The Amendment to the United States Constitution which abolished slavery and established universal freedom in the United States. Civil Rights Cases, 109 US 3, 27 L Ed 835, 3 S Ct 18.

tholonium (tho-lō'ni-um). Toll.

thorium (thō'ri-um). A radioactive element. 42 USC § 2098(a).

thorough. Complete. Painstaking.
See **toll thorough.**

thoroughfare (thur'ọ̄-far). A passage through; a street or way open at both ends and free from any obstruction. Mankato v Warren, 20 Minn 144. A highway.
See **main thoroughfare.**

thorough repair. Sufficient repair; repair sufficient to make the premises tenantable. 32 Am J1st L & T § 789.

thousand. Ten hundred; abbreviated "M."

thousand-year lease. A lease for a term of 1,000 years, a valid lease, except as terms are restricted by statute. 32 Am J1st L & T § 64.

thread of stream. The mean center line of the main channel of a stream or river. Buttenuth v St. Louis Bridge Co. 123 Ill 535, 17 NE 439. The middle line between the shores, irrespective of the depth of the channel, taking it in the natural and ordinary stage of the water, at its medium height, neither swollen by freshet nor diminished by drought. 12 Am J2d Bound § 28. Noting, however, that according to some authority, the thread of a nonnavigable river is to be ascertained from the measurement of the water at its lowest stage. Hardt v Orr, 142 Neb 460, 6 NW2d 589.

threat. Words or conduct intended to intimidate. A means of duress. Allen v Plymouth, 313 Mass 356, 47 NE2d 284; Fox v Piercey, 119 Utah 367, 227 P2d 763.
In law, a threat is a declaration of an intention or determination to injure another person by the commission of some unlawful act. An intimidation is the act of making another person timid or fearful by such a declaration. If the act intended to be done is not unlawful, then the declaration is not a threat in law, and the effect thereof is not intimidation in a legal sense. Payne v Western & Atlantic Railroad Co. 81 Tenn (13 Lea) 507.
As to the effect of a threat as a breach of the peace, see 12 Am J2d Breach P § 12.

threat by mail. The indictable offense of using the mails for the transmission of threatening matter. 41 Am J1st P O § 111.

threatened cloud. An anticipated cloud on the title to property such as equity will take cognizance of in a suit to quiet title. 44 Am J1st Quiet T § 17.

three days' grace. See **days of grace.**

threefold damages. See **treble damages.**

three-fourths clause. A provision in a policy of insurance that the insurer shall not be liable for an amount greater than a stated part or percentage, usually three-fourths, of the actual cash value of the property insured. 29A Am J Rev ed Ins § 1547.

three-judge court. Any appellate court sitting with three justices in accordance with law. Any court having three qualified judges or justices, albeit court is actually held in one place and at one time by only one judge. In the most common sense of the term, a federal district court of three judges sitting on one case, as required in certain cases, particularly where an injunction is sought to restrain the enforcement of a statute or administrative order on the ground of unconstitutionality. 28 Am J Rev ed Inj § 252.

three-judge federal district court. See **three-judge court.**

three-mile belt. Same as **three-mile limit.**

three-mile limit. The territorial waters of a state on the sea coast are often so designated since they include a strip three nautical miles wide off shore. The width of the strip had its origin in the ordinary range of an ancient coast-defense cannon, estimated to be a marine league, that is, three nautical miles.

three-mile zone. Same as **three-mile limit.**

thresher's lien. A statutory lien for the value of services in threshing grain. 3 Am J2d Agri § 14.

threshing machine. A machine which separates grain from the straw, often called a separator. A machine, which, in its most complete form, beats the grain from the ears of cereals, separates the grain from the straw, and winnows it from the chaff. Cook v Massey, 38 Idaho 264, 220 P 1088, 35 ALR 200, 205.

threshing outfit. A term familiar in the past but losing significance with the introduction of the combine. Engine, separator, and water wagon. See **combine.**

thrift payment. A payment made to an employee pursuant to a thrift or savings plan. 31 Am J Rev ed Lab § 616.

thrithing (thrī'thing). A riding. See **riding.**

through (thrö). By way of. From end to end.
The word does not always mean from one end or side to the other end or side, but frequently means simply within; as I walked through the wilderness. See Provident Life & Trust Co. v Mercer County, 170 US 593, 602, 42 L Ed 1156, 1160, 18 S Ct 788.

through an agent. Acting by another. Anno: 45 ALR2d 587, § 3.

through bill of lading. A bill of lading whereunder a carrier agrees to transport the goods from the point of delivery by the shipper to a designated point of destination, although such transportation extends over the line of a connecting carrier. 13 Am J2d Car § 265.

through carriage. See **through route.**

through error. By mistake. Application of Byers, 43 Cust & Pat App (Pat) 803, 230 F2d 451, 457.

through freight. See **through bill of lading; through freight contract; through train.**

through freight contract. A contract between shipper and carrier for the shipment of goods from the initial point to the point of final destination, at a through rate, where such transportation extends over the line of a connecting carrier. Toledo, P. & W. R. Co. v Merriman, 52 Ill 123.

through highway or street. A public way at which vehicles approaching on intersecting highways or streets must stop before entering.

through passenger. See **through ticket; through train.**

through passenger train. See **local through train.**

through rate. The rate of a carrier for a shipment from point of receipt by the carrier to the ultimate destination, although the destination may be one which can be reached only by the employment of a connecting carrier. 13 Am J2d Car § 206. The rate from an originating point to the final destination, or to a gateway like Chicago, via a particular point.
Thus, on a shipment of grain from Enid, Oklahoma, to Chicago via Kansas City, the overhead through rate was 38.5 cents per hundred pounds. Board of Trade v United States, 314 US 534, 86 L Ed 331, 62 S Ct 366.
Through carriage implies a "through rate." This "through rate" is not necessarily a joint rate. It may be an aggregation of separate rates fixed independently by the several carriers forming the "through rate," as where the "through rate" is "the sum of the locals" on the several connecting lines, or is the sum of lower rates otherwise separately established by them for through transportation. See St. Louis Southwestern Railway Co. v United States, 245 US 136, 139, note, 62 L Ed 199, 205, note, 38 S Ct 49.

through route. The route for the continuous carriage of goods from the originating point on the line of one carrier to destination on the line of another. St. Louis Southwestern Railway Co. v United States, 245 US 136, 139, note, 62 L Ed 199, 205, note, 38 S Ct 49.
See **through rate.**

through ticket. A railroad ticket which entitles the holder, not only to passage over the line of the company issuing it, but also over other connecting lines over which it is necessary to pass in order to reach his destination. A through ticket does not require the passenger to make a continuous trip over all the lines without stopping. Louisville & Nashville Railroad Co. v Klyman, 108 Tenn 304, 67 SW 472.
See **coupon ticket; stopover privilege.**

through train. A train, whether a freight or passenger train, which makes stops at only certain selected and definite stations. Arizona Eastern R. Co. v State, 29 Ariz 446, 242 P 870.

through transportation. Transportation undertaken by a common carrier where the destination of the shipment is one to be reached by connecting carrier, being beyond the line of the contracting carrier. 14 Am J2d Car § 689.
See **through ticket.**

thrown from vehicle. A method of sustaining personal injury, particularly in reference to the coverage of an accident insurance policy. A hurling of the insured from the car so that thereafter the person and the car are on independent orbits of action and momentum, and the result is that the person is no longer within the vehicle. Jones v Federal Life Ins. Co. 124 Colo 106, 234 P2d 615, 24 ALR2d 1450.

As to scope of clause of insurance policy covering injuries sustained from being "accidentally thrown from" a vehicle, see Anno: 24 ALR2d 1454.

thrown into bankruptcy. Adjudicated a bankrupt by a court of competent jurisdiction. Wilcox v Toledo & Ann Arbor Railroad Co. 45 Mich 280, 282, 7 NW 892. Adjudicated a bankrupt in an involuntary proceeding.

thrown out of vehicle. See **thrown from vehicle.**

thru. Same as **through.**

thumbing a ride. See **hitchhiker.**

thumbing the nose. An historic and present-day sign of contempt.

thumbprint. A mark in a signature by mark. Anno: 114 ALR 1116.
See **fingerprints.**

tick. A blood-sucking insect which prays on cattle and sheep, and sometimes upon man, often responsible for the communication of disease. 4 Am J2d Ani § 32.

ticker. An instrumentality of a broker's officer upon which market quotations are received. 24 Am J1st Gaming § 36.

ticker tape. A tape running out of a recording device, consisting of news items, racing results, boxscores of baseball games, market quotations, local, national, and international news, etc. National Tel. News Co. v Western U. Tel. Co. (CA7 Ill) 119 F 294.

ticket. The entire list of candidates of a particular political party. 26 Am J2d Elect § 207. The means of admission to a theater or other place of amusement. 4 Am J2d Amuse § 5. A railroad ticket, amounting, according to some authority to a mere receipt or token, but, according to other authority, to a contract between the holder and the carrier. 14 Am J2d Car § 811. A maritime contract for the transportation of a person on a ship. 48 Am J1st Ship § 351. A document evidencing a transaction commonly known in the stock-brokerage business as the "loan" of shares of stock and the return by the borrower to the lender of shares of stock "borrowed." Provost v United States, 269 US 443, 449, 70 L Ed 352, 353, 46 S Ct 152.
See **coupon ticket; general ticket; one-way ticket; round-trip ticket; subpoena ticket; theater ticket; through ticket.**

ticket agency. A place where tickets to theaters, stadiums, and other places of amusement and recreation may be purchased. An office maintained by two or more carriers wherein tickets for transportation of passengers upon any of their lines may be purchased.

ticket agent. An employee of a common carrier, serving primarily in selling tickets to prospective passengers at a station of the carrier. An employee of a ticket agency.

ticket broker. See **ticket agency; ticket scalping.**

ticket office. An office maintained by a carrier wherein prospective passengers may purchase tickets. 14 Am J2d Car § 800.
See **ticket agency.**

ticket of leave. Probation granted to a person convicted of crime, whereby he is permitted to go at large.

ticket scalping. The practice of buying a large number of tickets to a forthcoming athletic or theatrical event, with the purpose, often accomplished, of selling them at a profit. The business of buying and selling the return ends of excursion railroad tickets and tickets which have been partially used. Ford v East Louisiana Railroad Co. 110 La 414, 34 So 585. Brokerage in railroad tickets. Hoffman v Northern Pacific Railroad Co. 45 Minn 53, 55, 47 NW 312.

Dealing in railway tickets in the manner commonly known as "ticket scalping" is not against public policy, and a ticket so sold and purchased is not thereby rendered invalid, in the absence of a statute or of a rule or regulation, of which the purchaser is chargeable with knowledge, prohibiting such transfer. Knecht v Cleveland, C. C. & St. L. R. Co. 18 Ohio Dec 202, 6 Ohio NP NS 13.

ticket speculator. A person who sells theater or other tickets at an advance over the price charged by the management.

Speculation of this kind frequently leads to abuse, especially when the seating capacity is filled and but few tickets are left, so that extortionate prices may be exacted. Collister v Hayman, 183 NY 250, 76 NE 20.

tickler. An appointment book. A pad for memorandums made to aid the memory. Another term for **telltale.**

tidal test. A common-law test of navigability, the rule being that only those waters in which the tide ebbs and flows are to be classified as navigable waters. 56 Am J1st Water § 178.

tidal waters. Waters in which the tide ebbs and flows. Chamberlain v Hemingway, 63 Conn 1, 27 A 239. Perhaps all salt waters. Water coming in from the sea because of the rising tide. Waters which rise and fall with the tides of the sea.

It is the rise and fall of the water, and not the proportion of salt water to fresh, that determines whether a particular portion of a stream is within tide water. Atty. Gen. v Woods, 108 Mass 436, 439.

tide. The ebb and flow of the sea upon the shore due to the attraction of the moon and sun.
See **flood-tide; high tide; low tide; mean high tide; mean low tide; neap tide.**

tidelands. Lands at the margin of tidal waters which are alternately covered and uncovered by the rise and fall of the tide, between the lines of mean high tide and mean low tide, or, as sometimes provided by statute, extreme low tide. 56 Am J1st Water § 448.

Tidelands are not divested of their classification or character as such by the mere fact that title thereto may have passed from the sovereign to the individual. State v Van Vlack, 101 Wash 503, 172 P 563.

tide water. See **tidal waters.**

tideway (tīd'wā). Land between high and low-water mark on the shore where the tide ebbs and flows. Re New York, 217 App Div 587, 591, 217 NYS 359, 363.

tie. Noun: One of the wooden timbers upon which the rails of a railroad track are laid. Something that binds. A necktie. Verb: To fasten things together, as with a string, cord, or wire. To equal another in a contest in reference to points, scores, etc. To equal another candidate in number of votes received in an election.

As applied to an appointment by election, the word signifies a state of equality between two or more competitors for the same position. A tie is that which is tied. It is a knot. Hence, the object of providing for a casting vote, in case of a tie, is to untie the knot. Wooster v Mullins, 64 Conn 340, 30 A 144.

tied-house evil. A term characterizing the control of retail liquor dealers by manufacturers, wholesalers, and importers. 30 Am J Rev ed Intox L § 38.

tiel (tel). Such.

tiempo inhabil. (Spanish.) A period of disability; a period of insolvency.

tiends. See **annuity of tiends.**

tierce (tērs). Same as **terce.**

tiers (tērz). Rows of seats or other objects, particularly at different heights.
See **terce.**

tie slash. The tops of trees the bodies of which have been used for making railroad ties. Caldwell v United States, 250 US 14, 18, 63 L Ed 816, 817, 39 S Ct 397.

tie slashing (tī slash'ing). See **tie slash.**

tie vote. An even vote in a legislative body. The exigency occurring when rival candidates for an elective office receive an equal number of votes. 26 Am J2d Elect § 315.

tiger. A large flesh-eating mammal of the cat family, native to Asia, tawny in general color, but having black stripes.
See **blind tiger.**

tigni immittendi (tig'ni im-mit-ten'di). (Civil law.) The servitude or easement of projecting the beams of one's building into the wall of a neighbor.

tignum (tig'num). (Civil law.) Building material.

Tilden Act (til'den akt). A New York statute passed in 1875 which authorized the bringing of actions by the state to recover unlawful gains made by the holders of state, county and city offices.

till. As a limit of time, the same as until. 52 Am J1st Time § 25.

tillage (til'āj). The cultivation of land.

timber. A word of varied meanings, the meaning in a particular case to be ascertained from the entire context of the contract. 34 Am J1st Logs § 2. Standing trees. 34 Am J1st Logs § 2. Lumber, such as beams, rafters, planks, and other boards sawed from standing trees. Alcutt v Lakin, 33 NH 507. That sort of wood proper and suitable to be used for the construction of buildings, furniture, ships, etc. 34 Am J1st Logs § 2.
See **log timber; saw timber.**

timber culture entry (tim'bėr kul'tūr en'tri). A settlement of an entryman on public lands of the United States under the provisions of an act to encourage the growth of timber on western prairies, approved March 3, 1873, and the various amendments thereto. Hartman v Warren (CA8 Minn) 76 F 157, 160.

timberland. Land covered with growing timber, especially land in the public domain. 42 Am J1st Pub L §§ 13, 14.

timber license. A license to enter upon land and to cut and remove timber. 34 Am J1st Logs §§ 43 et seq.

timber measure. A measurement of the circumference of a standing tree, the bark being included in the measurement. 34 Am J2d Logs § 23.
See **board foot.**

timbering mine. Placing timbers in a mine to support the roof of a tunnel or chamber.

timber suitable for turpentine purposes. Any timber, of whatever size, that is ordinarily used for the taking of turpentine, the size being determined by custom if one is shown to be applicable. Dorsey v Clements, 202 Ga 820, 44 SE2d 783, 173 ALR 509.

time. A concept related to motion, as one day for the complete rotation of the earth, a year for the complete revolution of the earth around the sun. A period of history. A period within the lifetime of a person, as a term of apprenticeship, even of imprisonment. A matter for computation according to rules of law. 52 Am J1st Time § 15.
See **reasonable time.**

time and one-half. Special compensation for extra work, rather than the regular rate of compensation. State ex rel. Murray v Riley, 45 Del 192, 70 A2d 712, 14 ALR2d 630.

time bargains. Gambling transactions by parties who never intend to buy or sell, but merely to speculate upon the future price of stocks or commodities by compounding for differences. 24 Am J1st Gaming §§ 66 et seq.

time bill of exchange. Same as **time draft.** 11 Am J2d B & N § 13.

time certificate. A memorandum evidencing wages earned.

time certificate of deposit. An instrument issued by a bank reciting that the person named therein has deposited in the bank the sum specified, payable to the order of himself on the return of the certificate properly indorsed, with interest, the sum to be left a stated period of time, usually six months or one year, and not to bear interest after the expiration of such period. 10 Am J2d Banks § 455.

time draft. An unconditional order in writing addressed by one person to another, signed by the person giving it, requiring the person to whom it is addressed to pay at a fixed or determinable future time a sum certain in money to order or bearer. Uniform Negotiable Instruments Law § 126; UCC § 3—104(2)(a); 11 Am J2d B & N § 13.

time immemorial. Beyond the time of legal memory. An ancient time.

time is of the essence. The condition of performance of a contract within the time limited for performance by the terms of the contract. 17 Am J2d Contr § 332.
When it is said that time is of the essence, the proper meaning of the phrase is that performance by one party at the time specified in the contract or within the period specified in the contract is essential in order to enable him to require performance from the other party. It does not mean that delay will not give rise to a right of action against him. A breach of any promise in a contract, whether of vital importance or not will do that; nor does the phrase mean merely that time is a material matter, but that it is so material that exact compliance with the terms of the contract in this respect is essential to the right to require counter performance. Williams v Shamrock Oil & Gas Co. 128 Tex 146, 95 SW2d 1292, 107 ALR 269.

timely. Within the time required by contract or statute. Wm. B. Scaife & Sons Co. v Commissioner (CA3) 117 F2d 572.

timely amendment. An amendment of an income tax return filed by the taxpayer within the statutory period allowed for filing returns or within such extended time as the Commissioner may grant under the statute. J. E. Riley Invest. Co. v Commissioner (CA9) 110 F2d 655. An amendment of a pleading filed or served upon the adverse party within the time permitted for amendments by statute or rule of court, or, in the case of an amendment by leave of court, within the time fixed by the court. 41 Am J1st Pl §§ 289, 296.

time marine policy. See **time policy.**

time of legal memory. Within the period of recorded history, as distinguished from a remote period the events of which are unrecorded and accordingly unknown. For some purposes, in England, the beginning of the reign of Richard the First in 1189. 21 Am J2d Cust & U § 4 (involving duration of custom.)

time of memory. Same as **time of legal memory.**

time of peace. The period commencing with the legal end of a war, that is, with the exchange of peace treaties or the ratification of a peace treaty. 56 Am J1st War § 13.
In the United States, following a war, the time of peace begins when the President has by his proclamation announced that hostilities are at an end, and when Congress by its legislation has recognized the same fact. McElrath v United States, 102 US 426, 26 L Ed 189.
See **armistice.**

time of war. See **war.**

time option. An option which is to continue in force for a certain specified time.

time out of mind. See **time immemorial.**

time paper. An instrument for the payment of money at a time fixed by the instrument.
See **time draft.**

time policy. A policy of marine insurance which insures no specific voyage, but covers any voyage within the prescribed time of the policy, and the loss and damage the ship may sustain by the perils insured against within the limited period. Wilkins v Tobacco Ins. Co. 30 Ohio St 317.

time schedule. See **timetable.**

time study. Observing the carrying on of work in an industry with the idea of perfecting plans to perform the same work in a lesser number of man hours.

timetable. A time schedule of trains or other vehicles of a carrier, showing the time of arrivals and departures of particular trains, busses, or airplanes.

time zone. A belt of the earth's surface running from pole to pole created by an artificial division for the purpose of applying the system of standard time throughout the world, each belt or zone covering one hour of time, the time registered throughout an entire zone to be the same. 52 Am J1st Time § 3.

timid. Lack of confidence in one's self. Easily put in fear.
See **cautious.**

Timores vani sunt aestimandi qui non cadunt constantem virum (ti-mō'rēz vā-ni sunt ĕs-ti-man'di qui non kă'dunt kon-stan'tem vī'rum). Fears are to be regarded as groundless which do not affect a man of firmness.

tin. A metal much used as an alloy. Pots, pans, and other utensils of the kitchen.

tincture (tingk'tūr). A drug in solution, as tincture of iodine.

tip. A gratuity given for personal service, as to a porter, table waiter, steward, etc. A part of the earnings of an employee where it is within the contemplation of the parties to the employment that it shall be retained by the employee as part of his compensation. 58 Am J1st Workm Comp § 314. A part of gross income for tax purposes.
It would seem that a tip may range from a pure gift of benevolence or friendship, to a compensation for a service measured by its supposed value but not fixed by an agreement. Most often the term is applied to what is paid a servant in addition to the regular compensation for his service, to secure better service, or in recognition of it. Williams v Jacksonville Terminal Co. (CA5 Fla) 118 F2d 324.

tipple (tip'l). Verb: To indulge in alcoholic beverages. Noun: A place where open or gondola type railroad cars may be tipped by a mechanical device so that the contents fall out, the cars being thereby emptied and unloaded. A place where cars of coal brought to the pit mouth of a mine are loaded onto railroad cars or motor trucks. 36 Am J1st Min & M § 178.

tippling house. A place where intoxicating liquor is sold in small quantities to be drunk on the premises. 30 Am J Rev ed Intox L § 20. A barroom; a saloon; a grog-shop. Leesburg v Putnam, 103 Ga 110, 114.

tipstaff (tip'stăf). A bailiff.

tire marks. The marks made by the tires of a vehicle as it is driven, often material evidence as to the speed or manner of operation of the vehicle. 8 Am J2d Auto § 958.

tithable (tī'thạ-bl). Subject to being taxed for tithes; liable for tithes; capable of yielding tithes.

tithe rent-charge (tīth rent'chärj). A rent-charge which was substituted by the Statutes 6 & 7, William IV, c. 71, for tithes.

tithes (tīthz). Tenths; a species of incorporeal hereditaments, being the tenth part of the increase, yearly arising and renewing from the profits of lands, the stock upon lands, and the personal industry of the inhabitants, due the church for the support of the clergy. See 2 Bl Comm 24.
See **commutation of tithes; composition of tithes; great tithes; infeudation of tithes; jactitation of tithes; mixed tithes; modus decimandi, et seq.; parsonage tithes; personal tithes; praedial tithes; rate tithes; rectoral tithes; small tithes.**

tithing (tī'thing). A tenth of a hundred. A hundred was made up of ten tithings, each of which was composed of ten families, and it constituted a governmental district. See 1 Bl Comm 115.

tithing-man (tī'thing-man). Same as **tithing-reeve.**

tithing-reeve (-rēv). The chief or constable of a tithing.

title. The legal estate in fee, clear of all valid claims, liens, and encumbrances whatsoever, or expressed differently, the ownership of land without any rightful participation by any other person in any part of it. Porter v Noyes, 2 Me 22. The union of all the elements which constitute ownership, at common law divided into possession, right of possession and right of property, the last two now, however, being considered essentially the same. Carroll v Newark, 108 NJ 323, 158 A 485, 79 ALR 509. The foundation of ownership; the basis of a person's right or the extent of his interest. The means whereby an owner is enabled to maintain or assert his possession and enjoyment. 42 Am J1st Prop § 36. The right of an owner considered with reference either to the manner in which the property has been acquired or its capacity of being effectually transferred. 42 Am J1st Prop § 36.

Under the Uniform Stock Transfer Act, title means legal title and does not include a merely equitable or beneficial ownership or interest. Lyons v Freshman, 124 Mont 485, 226 P2d 775, 23 ALR2d 1165.

See **equitable title; legal title; ownership.**

title bond. A bond given to the purchaser of real property as security for the transfer to him of a good title to the property. Goodman v Moore, 22 Ark 191, 194.

title by accession. See **accession.**

title by adverse possession. See **adverse possession.**

title by alluvion. See **alluvion.**

title by bankruptcy. The title of the trustee in bankruptcy to assets of the estate in bankruptcy available for administration in bankruptcy and for distribution by payment of costs and expenses of the proceeding and distribution to creditors. Re Lesser (DC NY) 100 F 433, 436.

title by cession (bī sesh'ọn). The complete and unqualified title to all property possessed by the grantor vested in a nation under a treaty ceding territory to such nation, by which cession all real property passes to the grantee together with all buildings erected thereon by the grantor or by others with the grantor's permission—except such as belong to individuals who have acquired and preserved a right of removal. 30 Am J Rev ed Internat L § 44.

title by conquest (bī kon'kwest). Title to territory acquired by one nation from another in open war. Caldwell v State (Ala) 1 Stew & P 327, 333.

title by descent. Title acquired by succession or inheritance upon the death of an owner.
See **descent.**

title by discovery and occupation. The title acquired by a nation when its citizens or subjects, in its name and by its authority or with its assent, take and hold actual, continuous and useful possession of territory unoccupied by any other government or its citizens. 30 Am J Rev ed Internat L § 42.

title by limitation. See **adverse possession; title by prescription.**

title by prescription (bī prē-skrip'shọn). A title which may be acquired by use and time.

The elements of such a title are open, visible, and continuous use under a claim of right, adverse to and with the knowledge of the owner. While a title by prescription does not rest upon statutes of limitation, the courts incline to consider a prescriptive period as analogous to the time fixed by the law of the state as to limitations for commencing actions for the recovery of real property. See F. C. Ayres Mercantile Co. v Union P. R. Co. (CA8 Colo) 16 F2d 395, 399.

See **adverse possession; prescription; presumed grant.**

title by purchase. A title under any mode of acquiring an estate, except that of inheritance. Delaney v Salina, 34 Kan 532, 9 P 271, 276.

title by record. A title under judicial or other public record. A land title derived from the state; the title of a patentee of land or the immediate or remote vendee of a patentee. Shaw v Robinson, 111 Ky 715, 724, 64 SW 620.

Title by patent from the United States is title by record; and delivery of the instrument to the grantee is not essential to pass the title as in the conveyances by private persons. Jesse v Chapman, 68 Okla 199, 173 P 1044.

See **title of record.**

title covenants. Covenants ordinarily inserted in conveyances, being required by the purchaser as protection against insufficiency of title obtained by him from the vendor. 20 Am J2d Cov § 43. Covenants for title appearing in a lease.

A lessor's covenant for title must either be an express agreement or words must be used from which such an agreement can be implied; it has been held that the covenant does not arise from the mere relation of landlord and tenant. 32 Am J1st L & T § 268.

See **covenant against encumbrances; covenant for further assurance; covenant of good right to convey; covenant of quiet enjoyment; covenant of seisin; covenant of warranty.**

title deed. A deed constituting a part of the chain of title to real estate. 55 Am J1st V & P § 179.

title document. See **document of title.**

title guaranty company. A company engaged in the business of guaranteeing or insuring titles to real estate.

title in fee simple. Full and unconditional ownership.

Real property deeded to a person by warranty deed, but in fact for security only, would not be held by him by title in fee simple. First Nat. Bank v Moon, 102 Kan 334, 170 P 33.

See **fee simple.**

title insurance. A contract whereby the insurer for a valuable consideration agrees to indemnify the insured in a specified amount against loss through defect of title to real estate wherein the latter has an interest either as purchaser or otherwise. Foehrenbach v German-American Title & T. Co. 217 Pa 331, 66 A 561.

A policy of title insurance has been said to be a contract in the nature of a covenant against incumbrances. It differs, however, from a covenant of warranty and the rules applicable to such a warranty do not apply to the policy. Ordinarily no liability arises under such a policy except for actual loss sustained, but one already in possession claiming to be the owner when such a policy issues to him may recover thereon though he expends nothing, and hence suffers no loss in reliance on the policy, his loss occurring from a defect in the source of his title. 29A Am J Rev ed Ins § 1372.

title note. A promissory note given by the purchaser of personal property, containing a provision whereunder title to the property is reserved to the seller until the note is paid. 11 Am J2d B & N § 202.

title of record. Title to real estate appearing from an examination of the records of title and judicial records which have reference to the property or any part thereof. Sufficient in support of a plaintiff in ejectment where consisting of a regular chain of title from the government or some grantor in possession, or of a regular chain of title back to the common source from which both plaintiff and his adversary claim. 25 Am J2d Eject § 24.

It has usually been held that where a purchaser of land contracts for good record title, he will not be required to accept a title which depends upon

adverse possession not disclosed by record, even though such a title might be otherwise marketable. Anno: 46 ALR2d 570.
See **title by record.**

title of statute. A heading in words given a statute for the purpose of calling attention to the subject matter of the act. The first part of a statute, often expressing the name by which it is to be known or cited and usually expressing the subject or object of the statute.
Formerly, the title of a statute was of little consequence, but since the adoption of state constitutional provisions requiring the subject or object of every act to be expressed in the title, the title has become not only a necessary part of the statute, but an important one. 50 Am J1st Stat §§ 159 et seq.

title paramount. A superior title. A better title.
See **eviction by title paramount.**

title reservation contract. A contract of sale whereby title to the property sold is reserved by the seller as security for the payment of the purchase price or such part of the purchase price as remains unpaid.

title retaining note. Same as **title retention note.**

title retention note. A note given by the purchaser of property, one of the terms of which provides for the retention of title in the seller until payment of the note. 11 Am J2d B & N § 202.

title search. An abstract of title. An examination of the abstract of title to premises and of records of title and judicial records pertinent to the property made by the attorney for a purchaser prior to the closing of the deal.

title to office. The right to exercise the functions of a public office and to receive the emoluments of the office.

title to property. See title.

titulo (ti'tu-lō). A word commonly found in Spanish-American grants, which is a nomen generalissimum, applied as well to title papers, which convey title, in the usual acceptation of the term, as to those which confer a mere right of occupancy. De Haro v United States (US) 5 Wall 599, 18 L Ed 681, 688.

Titulus est justa cause possidendi id quod nostrum est (ti'tu-lus est ju'sta kâ'za pos-si-den'di id quod nos'-trum est). Title is the just cause of possessing that which is ours.

t-junction. An intersection at which one of the highways meets the other but does not cross it. Anno: 53 ALR2d 861, § 5(b).

to. Toward. Until. 52 Am J1st Time § 25. Either inclusive or exclusive of the date or event which follows it, according to the intention manifest from the entire context. Conway v Smith Mercantile Co. 6 Wyo 327, 44 P 940. In describing a boundary, usually but not necessarily exclusive of the thing, such as a stream or highway, to which it has reference. 12 Am J2d Bound §§ 26, 52.
It is generally defined to be a word of exclusion, unless by necessary implication it must be held to be used in an inclusive sense. Thus, the word to, as used in a contract stipulating that deliveries of property were to be made up to a stated date, or in an order extending time to a certain day, is a term of exclusion. 52 Am J1st Time § 25.

to advance money or materials. See **advance.**

to answer damages on another's behalf. To pay debts of another. Smolka v James P. Chandler & Son, 41 Del 255, 20 A2d 131, 134 ALR 629.

to arrive. A term inserted in a contract for sale of goods, effective in making the contract conditional or contingent upon arrival. 46 Am J1st Sales § 201.

to assume. See **assume.**

to assume and pay and save harmless. Two distinct stipulations in a conveyance of mortgaged property, one for assumption of the mortgage by the grantee and the other for the indemnification of the grantor respecting such mortgage. 37 Am J1st Mtg § 999.

tobacco. A plant, the leaves of which are used by man, ordinarily after processing, for chewing, smoking, or snuffing. Not a drug. 25 Am J2d Drugs § 1. Not a food. Gundling v Chicago, 176 Ill 340, 52 NE 44.

tobacco market. A town having one or more tobacco warehouses is known as a market. Townsend v Yeomans, 301 US 441, 81 L Ed 1210, 57 S Ct 842.

to be able. To have the means, particularly the means of making payment. Anno: 1 ALR 530.

to be performed. See **performance.**

to be the sole judge. See **sole judge.**

toboggan. A sled without runners, coasting or being towed on the boards or other material which makes its bottom. Illingworth v Madden, 135 Me 159, 192 A 273, 110 ALR 1090.

toboggan slide. A steep hill or artificially constructed slide for toboggans, being put in use only when covered with snow. Barrett v Lake Ontario Beach Improv. Co. 174 NY 310, 66 NE 968.

toft (tôft). A vacant space of ground where a house formerly stood.

toftum (tof'tum). Same as **toft.**

toga virilis (tō'ga vi-rī'lis). The gown of manhood of the Romans.
Before the young men acquired this robe they were not permitted to bear arms, but were regarded as part of the father's household. Having acquired the robe, they were regarded as part of the community. See 1 Bl Comm 404.

together with. And also.
The expression is commonly used in descriptions of property in a deed, and when so used it imports a close and inseparable union between the preceding description and that which follows the expression. Mitchell v D'Olier, 68 NJL 375, 53 A 467.
The use of such words in designating particular property in a residuary clause of a will, generally distinguishes the designated property from the residue so as to make the legacy or devise of such property specific. Anno: 128 ALR 840.

to have and to hold. Formal words used in the habendum clause of a deed.
As used in a will, the words were construed to manifest an intention that the legatee named receive the property bequeathed into her custody and retain the same during the period named in the bequest. Scott v Scott, 137 Iowa 239, 114 NW 881.

toilet. A water closet; a bathroom.

to indemnify and save harmless. An engagement of indemnity, also effective in some contexts as an assumption of a mortgage debt. 37 Am J1st Mtg § 999.

token (tō'kn). A symbol that betokens something; that is, that carries within itself that which it signifies. Shelton v Erie Railroad Co. 73 NJL 558, 66 A 403. A symbol of value purchased for money and used in place of money in payment of bus fare, telephone call, or charge for parking a motor vehicle.

For definition of the word as it pertains to slot machines played for amusement, see Anno: 148 ALR 894.

See **false token; railroad ticket**.

to knowingly misrepresent. To represent that which is not true with knowledge that the representation is false and with an intent to cause another to act to his prejudice upon such misrepresentation. Hyde v United States, 119 F 610, 119 CCA 493.

tolerance. A variation from a prescribed standard permitted by law in certain instances, particularly in reference to weights and measures. 56 Am J1st Wts & M § 49. Giving respect to the views and opinions of others, not so much in accepting them as sound, as in recognition of the right of another person to have views and opinions.

to lie. The note on an execution duly issued under signature of the clerk and ready for service, but not delivered to an officer for levy. Davis v Roller, 106 Va 46, 55 SE 4.

See **lie**.

toll. Verb: To suspend or interrupt the running of the statute of limitations. 21 Am J2d Crim L § 158; 34 Am J1st Lim Ac §§ 186 et seq. To lead away or entice, as to toll a hog with a sack of corn. Noun: A charge, as for milling or telephone service, and particularly for the use of a turnpike, toll road, or toll bridge. 54 Am J1st Turn & T R § 10. The charge of a ferryman. 35 Am J2d Ferr § 1. A charge for services of a public utility. A charge exacted for towage. Compensation for the use of another's property and of improvements thereon. People ex rel. Curren v Schommer, 392 Ill 17, 63 NE2d 744, 167 ALR 1347.

See **port toll**.

tollage (tō'lăj). Toll; the payment of toll; the exaction of toll.

toll bridge. A bridge for the use of which a toll is collected. As a private instrumentality, a bridge built and maintained under public authority as a portion of the highway with which it is connected, dedicated to public use, subject only to the right of the proprietors to exact reasonable toll for such use.

Aside from the right of the company to collect tolls, a toll bridge does not differ from the ordinary highway constructed and maintained by the inhabitants of the district through which it passes. Pittsburgh & West End Passenger Railway v Point Bridge Co. 165 Pa 37, 41

See **pontage**.

tollere (tol'le-re). (Civil law.) To raise; to lift up; to elevate; to take away; to carry away; to defeat.

Tolle voluntatem et erit omnis actus indifferens (tol'-le vo-lun-tā'tem et e'rit om'nis ac'tus in-dif'fe-renz). Take away the will and every act will be indifferent.

toll gate. A gate erected upon a turnpike or toll road at which toll is collected from passing travelers; so constructed as effectively to bar passage when closed. 54 Am J1st Turn & T R § 6.

toll house. A house erected at or near a toll gate for the use and accommodation of the toll gatherer. 54 Am J1st Turn & T R § 6.

tolling. See **toll**.

tolling statute. The suspension or interruption of the statute of limitations by reason of circumstances such as absence of the defendant from the state, concealment to avoid the service of process, etc. 21 Am J2d Crim L § 158; 34 Am J1st Lim Ac §§ 186 et seq.

toll road. A highway for the use of which a toll is collected. 54 Am J1st Turn & T R § 2.

toll service. Telephone service in long distance communication for which a toll is charged.

toll the entry. To bar or defeat the right of entry.

toll the statute. See **tolling statute**.

toll thorough (thur'ō). A toll demandable by an express grant, by custom or prescription on a public highway, in a public port, or for the use of public property.

It is so called because the party claiming it is presumed to have had no original right to the place where he demands toll. Charles River Bridge v Warren Bridge (US) 11 Pet Baldwin's Views 152, 9 L Ed 938, 947.

toll traverse (tra-vèrs'). A toll demanded for passing on or over the private property of the claimant, or using it in any other way. Charles River Bridge v Warren Bridge (US) 11 Pet Baldwin's Views 152, 9 L Ed 938, 947.

toll turn (tèrn). A toll charged for bringing back unsold cattle from a market.

tolnetum (tol-nē'tum). Toll.

tolt (tōlt). A precept from the sheriff whereby the proceedings on a writ of right might be removed from a court-baron into the county court.

It was called a tolt because it tolled or took away and removed the cause from the court-baron. See 3 Bl Comm 34.

tolta (tol'ta). A wrong; an extortion.

toma de razon (to'mah day rah-thone'). See **testimonio**.

to make one's law. To deny under oath a criminal charge or accusation.

A litigant was anciently said to make his law when he was successful in a trial by compurgation.

tomar razon (to-mar' rah-thone'). See **testimonio**.

tomb. A chamber or vault, formed wholly or partly in the earth or entirely above ground, for the reception of the dead. Re Byrne's Estate, 98 NH 300, 100 A2d 157, 47 ALR2d 591.

tombstone. A stone raised at a grave or in a cemetery lot as a memorial to the person or persons buried there. 14 Am J2d Cem § 33.

to mine. See **mining**.

to my use. A phrase employed in a restrictive endorsement. 11 Am J2d B & N § 362.

ton. A unit of avoirdupois weight commonly understood as 2000 pounds, although technically such is a so-called short ton, the long ton being 2240 pounds. 21 Am J2d Cust D § 33.

ton-mile tax. A form of tax imposed in some jurisdiction upon contract motor carriers and private motor carriers for hire.

tonnage. The capacity of a vessel in respect of the amount of cargo which it can carry. Any measure in tons.

In commercial designation, the word means the

number of tons burden a ship or vessel will carry, as estimated and ascertained by the official admeasurement and computation prescribed by public authority. The term has long been an official one intended originally to express the burden that a ship would carry, in order that the various dues and customs which are levied upon shipping might be levied according to the size of the vessel, or rather in proportion to her capability of carrying burden. Hence, the term has become almost synonymous with the word "size." Mobile Trade Co. v Lott (US) 12 Wall 221, 20 L Ed 376, 377.

tonnage duty. A charge on a vessel, according to its tonnage, as an instrument of commerce, for entering or leaving a port, or navigating the public waters of the country; any tax for the bare privilege of entering a port and navigating the navigable waters of the state. 51 Am J1st Tax § 108. A tax levied upon a railroad at a specified rate per ton of all goods carried. 51 Am J1st Tax § 108. A tax or duty imposed on vessels as such, usually at a specified rate per ton of capacity or weight of registered tonnage, computed according to prescribed rules of admeasurement. 48 Am J1st Ship § 650.

tonnage tax. Same as **tonnage duty.**

tonsillectomy (ton'si-lek'tō-mi). The removal of tonsils by surgery. Carroll v Missouri Power & Light Co. 231 Mo App 265, 96 SW2d 1074.

tonsura (ton-sū'ra). Tonsure.

tonsure (ton'sur). The shaving of the hair from the crown of a man's head.
Originally it was the law that no man should be admitted to the privilege of the clergy who had not the clerical habit and tonsure. See 4 Bl Comm 366.

tontine company (ton-tēn' kum'pan-i). A company or association the members of which received life rents or annuities for life and the survivors prorated the share of each deceased member among them.

tontine insurance (in-shör'ans). See **tontine policy.**

tontine policy (ton-tēn' pol'i-si). Life insurance with the distinguishing characteristic of a survivorship provision, the policy being based upon an agreement whereby the survivor of a class of persons who contribute to a common fund and persist as paying members become, at the end of a specified period, entitled to divide the "surplus," the funds remaining after the payment of benefits, expenses, and the intermediate apportionment of profits. 29 Am J Rev ed Ins § 16.
The term is said to have come from the name of Tonti, an Italian, who originated tontine insurance in the seventeenth century.

to occupy. See **occupy.**

tool. A usable article employed as a means to effect a purpose in the execution of a design or the production of some result. Anno: 2 ALR 821. Confined, according to some courts, but not by others, to instruments worked by muscular power. 31 Am J2d Exemp § 51.
As to whether a motor vehicle is exempt from execution as a "tool," see Anno: 37 ALR2d 720.

tools of trade. Instruments or implements used in the trade, occupation, business, or profession of the owner. 31 Am J2d Exemp §§ 51 et seq.
As to whether a motor vehicle is exempt from execution as a "tool of a trade, calling, business, or profession," see Anno: 37 ALR2d 720.

tooth. A member of the body. High v State, 26 Tex App 545.

top. The highest part.
In mining law, the "apex" of a vein is sometimes called the "top." It is the top or terminal edge of the vein, on the surface, or the nearest point to the surface; it is the top of the vein proper, rather than of a spur or feeder, just as the highest point in the roof of a house would be taken to be the apex of the house, and not the chimney or flagstaff. Anno: 1 ALR 419.

topography (tō-pog'ra-fi). The characteristics of land in respect to surface features such as hills, streams, valleys, etc. 42 Am J1st Pub L § 59.

to procure a purchaser. See **procuring cause.**

to read law. To prepare for the profession.
"To read law," while not strictly a technical term to which a certain meaning must attach to the exclusion of all others, is yet an expression with a meaning known to lawyers. Among lawyers the expression means to take up the study of the law with the purpose of being admitted to the bar and practicing the profession. Its meaning is not confined to the preparatory course; but properly includes that reading of cases and textbooks of which every lawyer does more or less after his admission. Benson's Estate, 169 Pa 602, 604, 32 A 654.

to regulate. See **regulate.**

tornado (tôr-nā'dō). A violent storm distinguished by the vehemence of the wind. A windstorm featured by cyclonic or whirling winds of tumultuous force. 29A Am J Rev ed Ins § 1329. A violent windstorm, usually accompanied by a funnel-shaped cloud; an act of God. 1 Am J2d Act of God § 5. Not to be confused with the widely extended rotary storm known as a **cyclone.** Queen Ins. Co. v Hudnut Co. 8 Ind App 22, 26, 35 NE 397. Not to be confused with a **hurricane.**
It appears that for the purposes of insurance, the terms "hurricane," "tornado," and "windstorm" are often treated as synonymous. See **windstorm insurance.**

tornado insurance. See **windstorm insurance.**

torpedo (tôr-pē'dō). Noun: A projectile loaded with explosive employed against ships in war. Verb: To hit a ship with a projectile loaded with explosive. To lower and detonate a cartridge of explosive in an oil well for the purpose of releasing the oil from a pocket. 24 Am J1st Gas & O § 114. Slang: To prevent agreement by injecting new considerations.
See **signal torpedo.**

torpedo doctrine. Another expression for the doctrine of **attractive nuisance.** 38 Am J1st Negl § 142.

Torrens Acts. Statutes adopting the Torrens System of registration of land titles. 45 Am J1st Reg L T § 2.

Torrens System. A system for the registration of titles to land, whereby an official certificate always shows the state of the title and the person in whom it is vested, the name deriving from Sir Robert Torrens who drew the first Registration Act, such having been adopted in South Australia in 1858. 45 Am J1st Reg L T § 2.
The system spread to the other Australian states and territories, to other British possessions, and to Great Britain itself. With various modifications it has been adopted in several of the states in the United States, in several of the Canadian provinces, and in the Philippines. 45 Am J1st Reg L T § 2.

tort. A wrong. Hayes v Massachusetts Mut. Life Ins. Co. 125 Ill 626, 18 NE 322. A wrong independent of contract. International Ocean Tel. Co. v Saunders, 32 Fla 434, 14 So 148. A breach of duty which the law, as distinguished from a mere contract, has imposed. Western Union Tel. Co. v Taylor, 84 Ga 408, 11 SE 396. An injury or wrong committed, either with or without force, to the person or property of another.

Such injury may arise by the nonfeasance, by the malfeasance, or by the misfeasance of the wrongdoer. Gindele v Corrigan, 129 Ill 582, 22 NE 516.

In a general way, a tort is distinguished from a breach of contract in that the latter arises under an agreement of the parties, whereas the tort, ordinarily, is a violation of a duty fixed by law, independent of contract or the will of the parties, although it may sometimes have relation to obligations growing out of, or coincident with a contract, and frequently the same facts will sustain either class of action. Busch v Interborough Rapid Transit Co. 187 NY 388, 80 NE 197.

Although the same act may constitute both a crime and a tort, the crime is an offense against the public pursued by the sovereign, while the tort is a private injury which is pursued by the injured party. 52 Am J1st Torts § 2.

tortfeasor. One guilty of a tort. A person who commits a tort; a wrongdoer.

See **joint tortfeasors.**

tortious. Partaking of the nature of a tort; wrongful; injurious. Characterizing conduct, whether of act or omission which is of such character as to subject the actor to liability under the principles of the law of torts. Restatement, Torts, Vol 1 § 6.

See **tort.**

tortious conveyance. A conveyance of the whole fee and not merely the right or estate which the grantor had the right to convey. Orndoff v Turman, 29 Va (2 Leigh) 200.

torture. The infliction of severe pain as a means of persuasion. Anno: 16 ALR 372. Torment by means of the rack, or other contrivances for inflicting physical pain, employed for the purpose of extorting confessions. See 4 Bl Comm 32.

to save harmless. An expression in an engagement of indemnity. Foster v Atwater, 42 Conn 244, 252.

See **to indemnify and save harmless.**

to secure. See **secure.**

to settle. See **settle.**

to ship by. See **ship.**

tot (tot). Noun: A word written opposite an item in an account to indicate an approval of it. Verb: To total.

tota curia (tō'ta kū'ri-a). The whole court, the court with all the justices present.

total. Noun: The whole amount; the entire quantity. Adjective: Constituting the whole of a thing. Complete; absolute; utter; entire. Verb: To ascertain an amount by addition. To equal a certain amount, considered in entirety.

total and permanent disability. See **permanent disability; total disability.**

total breach. An entire breach, a material breach, a breach of contract which goes to the whole consideration. 17 Am J2d Contr § 446.

total contract price. The entire amount paid, or agreed to be paid, by the purchaser.

The amount of a mortgage assumed by a purchaser of realty on an instalment sale must be excluded from the basis used for determining the proportion of the gain which is taxable in a given year. Burnet v S. & L. Bldg. Corp. 288 US 406, 77 L Ed 861, 53 S Ct 428.

total dependent. A person who has no means whatever by which to support himself. Utah Fuel Co. v Industrial Com. 80 Utah 301, 15 P 2d 297, 86 ALR 858.

total destruction. See **total loss.**

total disability. As an occurrence insured against, such a disability as renders the insured unable to perform all the substantial and material acts necessary to the prosecution of his trade, business, or occupation in a customary and usual manner, irrespective of the fact that he is not reduced to a state of absolute helplessness. 29A Am J Rev ed Ins § 1517. For the purpose of workmen's compensation, a disability or incapacity which completely destroys the claimant's earning power so that he is not capable of performing any remunerative employment, subject however to the rule in some jurisdictions that the fact that an injured employee may be able to perform light work, or that some usefulness remains in an injured member, does not preclude a finding of total disability. 58 Am J1st Workm Comp § 283.

An insurer's liability for the payment of benefits for total disability rendering insured unable to engage in any occupation or perform any work for compensation is tested by whether insured is incapacitated to earn in any occupation to which he may reasonably be fitted and whether his remaining earning capacity bears a substantial relation to his natural or previous capacity to earn. Patton v Prudential Ins. Co. 181 Tenn 138, 178 SW2d 760, 1 ALR2d 750.

As the term is used in a health policy, it does not mean absolute physical disability on the part of the insured to transact any kind of business pertaining to his occupation. It may exist although the insured is able to perform occasional acts if he is unable to do any substantial portion of the work connected with his occupation. Brotherhood of Locomotive Firemen & Enginemen v Aday, 97 Ark 425, 134 SW 928.

The term must of necessity be relative in its signification, which depends largely upon the occupation and employment in which the disabled person is engaged. A person who labors with his hands might be so disabled by a severe injury to one hand as not to be able to labor at all at his usual occupation, whereas a merchant or a professional man might by the same injury be only disabled from transacting some kinds of business pertaining to his occupation. Lobdill v Laboring Men's Mut. Aid Asso. 69 Minn 14, 71 NW 696.

total disability clause. A clause in a health or accident policy, sometimes in a life insurance policy, providing for the payment of benefits in the event of the occurrence of the total disability of the insured. 29A Am J Rev ed Ins § 1504. A provision in a life insurance policy for waiver of premiums during the total or permanent disability of the insured. 29 Am J Rev ed Ins § 581.

total disability for work. Such disability as incapacitates one from performing the usual tasks of a workman in such a manner as to enable him to procure and retain employment. Anno: 67 ALR 786.

See **total disability**; **total loss of business time**.

total failure of evidence. The utter absence of all evidence. The failure to offer proof, either positive or inferential, to establish one or more of the many facts, the establishment of all of which is indispensable to the finding of the issue for the plaintiff. Cole v Hebb (Md) 7 Gill & J 20, 28.

total incapacity. See **total disability**.

total loss. The complete destruction of the property covered by an insurance policy. The complete destruction of a building as a building, although not necessarily the extinction of all its parts as materials or such destruction that no part is left standing. 29A Am J Rev ed Ins § 1536. In marine insurance, a total and actual loss to the insured of the subject matter of the insurance; a destruction of the thing in specie, even though some of its component elements or parts may remain. 29A Am J Rev ed Ins § 1570.

There can be no "total loss" so long as the remnant of the structure standing is reasonably adapted for use as a basis upon which to restore the building to the condition in which it was before the injury; and whether it is so adapted depends upon whether a reasonably prudent owner, uninsured, desiring such a structure as the injured one was before the injury, would, in proceeding to restore the building to its original condition, utilize such remnant as such basis. Royal Insurance Co. v McIntyre, 90 Tex 170, 182, 37 SW 1068.

A building is "wholly destroyed" within the meaning of a statute providing that when an insured structure shall be wholly destroyed the amount of the policy shall be conclusive of the true value of the property when insured and of the true amount of the loss, where it has lost its specific character and ceased to exist as a building, although a portion of the foundation remains which might be used in rebuilding. Grandview Inland Fruit Co. v Hartford F. Ins. Co. 189 Wash 590, 66 P2d 827, 109 ALR 1472.

As the term is used in fire insurance, it means the complete destruction of the insured property by fire, so that nothing of value remains of it, as distinguished from a partial loss, where the property is damaged, but not entirely destroyed. This does not mean that the materials of which the building was composed were all utterly destroyed or obliterated, but that the building, though some part of it may be left standing, has lost its character as a building, and, instead thereof, has become a broken mass, or so far in that condition that it cannot properly any longer be designated as a building. When that has occurred, then there is a total destruction or loss. A total loss does not mean an absolute extinction. Corbett v Spring Garden Ins. Co. 155 NY 389, 50 NE 282.

See **constructive total loss**.

total loss of business time. Inability to work at one's specific occupation, regardless of ability to do other work. Continental Casualty Co. v Wagner (CA8 Mo) 195 F2d 936, 31 ALR2d 1216.

See **total disability for work**.

total loss of eyesight. A complete loss of eyesight; a loss of eyesight to the extent that one cannot distinguish colors or objects one from another in good light, although he can distinguish between light and darkness; in some contexts, loss of eyesight which disables one from pursuing his usual and customed occupation. 29A Am J Rev ed Ins § 1513.

totally or substantially destroyed. An effective destruction of buildings as such, not necessarily a complete annihilation. 32 Am J1st L & T § 506.

total mental disability. The state of a person whose mental faculties are entirely suspended. Anno: 24 ALR 214. More realistically, a **total disability**.

total permanent disability. See **permanent disability**; **total disability**.

total physical disability. The state of a person who has lost the power to move. Anno: 24 ALR 214. More realistically, a **total disability**.

total repudiation doctrine. The doctrine that a party to a contract who has repudiated the contract is precluded from asserting an arbitration clause in the contract. Anno: 3 ALR2d 394, § 4.

toted (tō'ted). See **tot**.

to the account. See **on account**.

to the country whence they came. To the country from which aliens last entered the United States; to the country in which is located the foreign port at which aliens last embarked for the United States or for foreign territory contiguous to the United States. 8 USC § 1253(a); 3 Am J2d Aliens § 94.

to the credit of. A form of restrictive indorsement. Werner Piano Co. v Henderson, 121 Ark 165, 180 SW 495.

to the diligent belongs the reward. A maxim supplanted in bankruptcy by the principle that equality is equity. Re Wisconsin Co-operative Milk Pool (CA7 Wis) 119 F2d 999.

to the order of. Words of negotiability. 11 Am J2d B & N § 105.

totidem verbis (tot'i-dem vėr'bis). In so many words.

toties quoties (tō'shi-ēz kwō'shi-ēz). As often as it shall happen.

toto. The whole.

toto genere (tō'tō je'ne-re). In all of its kind.

Totten Trust. A trust created by a bank deposit made by one person of his own money in his own name as trustee for another, such being a tentative trust merely, revocable at will, until the depositor dies or completes the gift in his lifetime by some unequivocal act or declaration, such as delivery of the passbook or notice to the beneficiary. Anno: 38 ALR2d 1244 et seq.; 10 Am J2d Banks § 392; Restatement, Trusts 2d § 58.

A savings account deposit by one person of his own money in his own name as trustee for another, standing alone, is a tentative trust, revocable at will until the depositor dies or completes the gift in his lifetime. Re Rodgers' Estate, 374 Pa 246, 97 A2d 789, 38 ALR2d 1238.

totum (tō'tum). The whole.

Totum praefertur unicuique parti (tō'tum prē-fer'ter ū-ni-kī'kwē par'ti). The whole is preferred to any one part.

touch at port. To stop a vessel at a port. Audenreid v Mercantile Mut. Ins. Co. 60 NY 482.

touching. Arousing emotion. Contiguous.
See **contiguous**.

toujours et uncore prist (too-zhoor' et un-kōr prē). Now and always ready.

tour (tör). A long trip, especially a trip for pleasure. A trip across and around the country in performance of duty or by way of following an occupation

TOURIST [1286] TOWNSHIP

or profession, as in the case of a trip by an entertainer, an orchestra, or a theatrical company. A trip taken by persons in a group for the pleasure of travel, for instruction, or religious inspiration.

tourist camp. A place where wayfarers, particularly tourists traveling in motor vehicles, are provided a place to camp, with water, connections to electric lines, and toilet facilities, for compensation.

tourist card. A requirement made in some countries in lieu of a visa for a visitor from a foreign country making a short stay.

tourist house. A residence or dwelling wherein wayfarers, primarily tourists traveling in motor vehicles, are given lodging or lodging with breakfast.

tourist's policy. A policy of insurance covering personal effects usually carried by tourists and travelers. Tibbils v Federal Ins. Co. (Mun Ct App Dist Col) 119 A2d 114. A policy of insurance covering the luggage and personal effects of tourists against risk of loss by fire, lightning, and perils of navigation or transportation. Anno: 55 ALR 804.

to use. See **use**.

to use and control as he thinks proper. A phrase in a lease authorizing acts or conduct of the tenant which would otherwise constitute waste. 56 Am J1st Waste § 7.

tous mes effets (tö māz ef-āz'). (French.) All my effects.
See **effets**.

Tout ce que la loi ne defend pas est permis (tö sē kē lä luä' nē dā-fon'pä ā per-mē'). Everything which the law does not prohibit is allowed or permitted.

tout temps prist (tö tôn pree). He has always been ready. The common-law form of averring readiness to pay, in pleading a tender of payment. See 3 Bl Comm 303.

to utter. See **utter**.

to utter and publish. See **uttering and publishing counterfeit**.

tout un sound (tö un sound). All one sound.

tow (tō). Verb: To draw something along a course, particularly a vessel. Ryan v Hook (NY) 34 Hun 185, 191. To pull a motor vehicle along a highway or street. 8 Am J2d Auto § 839. Noun: One or more vessels being towed or drawn. 48 Am J1st Ship § 488. An automobile or two or more automobiles in tandem being drawn on the highway.
Within the meaning of a clause in an automobile liability policy exempting the insurer from liability while the vehicle is being towed, a trailer attached to a truck is being towed although the vehicles have come to a temporary stop in the course of their journey. Maryland Casualty Co. v Cross (CA5 Tex) 112 F2d 58.

towage (tō-āj). The supplying of power by a vessel to tow or draw another. 48 Am J1st Ship § 488. A charge exacted for towing a vessel.

towage lien. A maritime lien for services rendered in towing the vessel. 2 Am J2d Adm § 124.

towage service (tō-āj sėr'vis). The employment of one vessel to aid in the propulsion or to expedite the voyage of another, when there is no circumstance of peril, and nothing more is required than the acceleration of her progress. Stevens v The White City, 285 US 195, 76 L Ed 699, 52 S Ct 347.

toward. Facing.

The word is of very comprehensive signification, for it means in the direction of. To shoot at a person means to shoot toward him; to shoot in the general direction of the person. Both "toward" and "at" are words of somewhat indefinite meaning and their general significance is usually controlled by the context in which they are used. State use of Johnston v Cunningham, 107 Miss 140, 65 So 115.

towboat. Same as **tugboat**.

towed. See **tow**.

towel service. See **laundry supply service**.

towing. See **tow**.

to wit. That is to say; namely. A videlicet.
See **videlicet**.

towline. The hawser, table, or rope by which a vessel is towed by a tug. 48 Am J1st Ship § 503. Any rope or chain used for towing.

town. A word with varied popular as well as technical meanings. Historically, a collection of houses enclosed by a wall, the word deriving from the Anglo-Saxon "tun." An incorporated municipality of limited population. 37 Am J1st Mun Corp § 5. In some jurisdictions, particularly the New England and northeastern states, the political subdivision known elsewhere as a township. 37 Am J1st Mun Corp § 5. In a popular sense, an urban community or the section of a city where the retail stores, hotels, theaters, etc., are located, as illustrated by the familiar expression: "Go downtown."
See **township**.

town apprentice (a-pren'tis). A person articled as an apprentice by the town authorities to keep him from becoming a charge upon the town.

town board. A board of supervisors or trustees vested with various powers in reference to the government of a town. 52 Am J1st Towns § 9.

town council (toun koun'sil). Same as **town board**.

town farm. A poor farm.

town hall. A building wherein town officers are located and wherein town meetings are held.

Town Hall. A term capable of acquiring a secondary meaning as the title of a literary work or theatrical performance. Anno: 23 ALR2d 308.

town meeting. A meeting of the electors of a town for the purpose of determining such matters pertaining to the prudential affairs of the town as they may lawfully determine; often referred to as the most effective demonstration of democracy in action. 52 Am J1st Towns § 11.

town order. See **warrant**.

town pauper (pâ'pėr). A pauper supported by a town.

town recorder. See **magistrate**.

township. A political subdivision vested with certain powers of local government. 52 Am J1st Towns § 2. A territorial subdivision for school purposes, known as a school township. W. H. Dreves, Inc. v Oslo School Township, 217 Ind 388, 28 NE2d 252, 128 ALR 1505. A territory six miles square surveyed by the government for the purpose of entry and sale as public lands, often called a congressional township. 52 Am J1st Towns § 2. In some states, the equivalent of town. 37 Am J1st Mun Corp § 5.
See **town**.

township board. A board of supervisors or trustees

vested with various duties in the government of a town. 52 Am J1st Towns § 9.

township trustee. One of the public officers in charge of the affairs of a town. 52 Am J1st Towns § 15. A member of the town or township board. 52 Am J1st Towns § 9.

townsite. A tract of land segregated from the public domain under proper authority and by proper procedure as the site for a proposed town. Rice v Colorado Smelting Co. 28 Colo 519, 66 P 894. The reservation from public lands of space for a town on the shores of harbors, at the junction of rivers, important portages, or any natural or prospective center of population. 43 USC § 711. Broadly, the location selected for a proposed town.

town warrant. See **warrant.**

town way (wā). Any street, lane, alley, road, or other highway in a town or city, which the public has a right to use, irrespective of the origin of the way. Parks v Boston, 25 Mass (8 Pick) 218.

toxicologist (tok-si-kol'ō jist). A physician having special knowledge relative to poisons and treatment of sickness caused by a poison. Anno: 135 ALR 885. A person versed in the science of toxicology. State v Cook, 17 Kan 392, 394.

toxicology (tok-si-kol'ō-ji). A science which includes the effect of poisons upon the human system. State v Cook, 17 Kan 392, 394.

tp. An abbreviation of **township.**

T. R. Abbreviation of tons registered, having reference to a vessel.

traced copy. A copy made by placing transparent paper over a signature or other writing and tracing the signature or other writing thereon. Howard v Russell, 75 Tex 171, 12 SW 525. A mechanical copy or facsimile of an original map, document, or drawing, produced by following its lines, with pen or pencil, through a transparent medium, called tracing paper. Chapman v Ferry (CC Or) 18 F 539, 540.

tracing funds. Following or identifying particular funds after such have been mingled with other funds.
See **following trust fund or property.**

tracing heirs. See **heir hunter.**

tracing person. See **heir hunter; trailing.**

tracing trust fund. See **following trust fund or property.**

track. An imprint left by the foot of a person, or by the wheel of a vehicle, on the ground, even at times, upon payment. 29 Am J2d Ev § 377.
See **railroad track; sidetrack; streetcar track; trackage.**

trackage. The tracks of a railroad or railroad system, considered in their entirety.
The word is sometimes used as referring to the right to construct and operate railroad tracks on the streets or other public grounds of a city. St. Paul v Chicago, Milwaukee & St. Paul Railway Co. 63 Minn 330, 63 NW 267, 65 NW 649, 68 NW 458.

trackless trolley. A means of public transportation operating, with electric power conveyed through an overhead line as in the case of streetcars, but not on rails, the vehicle being able to move from the thread of the street to the curb line for the convenience of passengers boarding and departing.

tract. A brochure. An area of real estate. A lot or parcel of land. Ramsey County v Robert P. Lewis Co. 72 Minn 87, 75 NW 108.

Tractent fabrilia fabri (trak'tent fa-bri'li-a fa'brī). Let smiths perform smithcraft.

tract index. An index of records of title according to the description of the property conveyed, mortgaged, or otherwise encumbered. 45 Am J1st Recds § 78.

traction engine. A means of motive power seldom seen in the present day, being a steam engine used to pull plows or heavy loads on the highway.
See **tractor.**

tractor. A motor-powered vehicle with cab for the driver, used for hauling vans or trailers. An engine having traction, powered by gasoline or diesel fuel, used for moving heavy objects and in pulling plows and other implements of agriculture.
A farm tractor is not a motor vehicle within the meaning of a statute providing for constructive or substituted service on a nonresident motorist. Anno: 48 ALR 1284.

tractor-trailer. A vehicle on the highway consisting of tractor and trailer in combination.

tradas in ballium (trā'das in bal'li-um). Deliver you to bail,—a writ which lay to admit to bail a person who had been found under a writ de odio et atia to have been maliciously imprisoned.
See **de odio et atia.** In its broadest significance, any bargain or sale. See May v Rice, 101 US 231, 239, 25 L Ed 797, 800.

trade. An exchange of one commodity, article, or piece of real or personal property for another, sometimes including the addition on the one side of an amount of money known as boot. 30 Am J2d Exch P § 1. An occupation or calling; any ordinary occupation or business whether manual or mercantile. State v Cuthrell, 235 NC 173, 69 SE2d 233. Any occupation or business carried on for subsistence or profit. Re Pinkney, 47 Kan 89, 27 P 179; Campbell v Motion Picture Machine Operators' Union, 151 Minn 220, 186 NW 781, 27 ALR 631. Any employment in which one is engaged to procure a living or in which he habitually earns his living. 31 Am J2d Exemp § 51. A term implying a more or less continuous or habitual engagement in certain lines of industry, employment, or activity. 58 Am J1st Workm Comp § 82.
Commerce generally. May v Sloan, 101 US 231, 25 L Ed 797. Exchange or dealing of any kind, but more especially the barter or purchase and sale of goods, wares and merchandise, either by wholesale or retail. Anno: 76 L Ed 1210. Buying and selling, even a sale of land. May v Sloan, 101 US 231, 25 L Ed 797.
The term as used in the Sherman Anti-Trust Act is not synonymous with the word "commerce," "trade" being of more restricted import than the word "commerce." 36 Am J1st Monop etc § 157.
Commerce relates to dealings with foreign nations; trade, on the contrary, means mutual traffic among ourselves, or the buying, selling, or exchanging of articles between members of the same community. Hooker v Vandewater (NY) 4 Denio 349.
The word "trading" is the equivalent of the word "dealing" as applied to goods, wares, merchandise, and commodities, which words, in mercantile language, are always used with reference to corporeal substances, and never to mere choses in action. Fleckner v Bank of the United States (US) 8 Wheat 338, 353, 5 L Ed 631, 634.

trade acceptance. Commercial paper. Continental Nat. Bank & Trust Co. v Stirling, 65 Idaho 123, 140 P2d 230, 149 ALR 314. A draft or bill of exchange, drawn by the seller on the purchaser of goods sold, and accepted by such purchaser, the purpose of the transaction being to enable the seller to raise money upon the paper before the obligation of the purchaser matures under the terms of sale. Legal Discount Corp. v Martin Hardware Co. 199 Wash 476, 91 P2d 1010, 129 ALR 420. A form of obligation revived in this country under the regulations of the Federal reserve bank board. Atterbury v Bank of Washington Heights, 241 NY 231, 239, 149 NE 841.

trade agreement. See **collective labor agreement.**

trade association. A classification of voluntary unincorporated associations; an association organized for the purposes of trade. 6 Am J2d Asso & C § 2. An association of persons in the same trade or industrial operation for the purpose of gathering and disseminating information useful to their members, particularly in the stabilization of production and prices. 36 Am J1st Monop etc § 86.

trade building. A structure used in carrying on any trade or manufacture.

trade combination. See **monopoly; restraint of trade.**

Trade Commission. A federal agency established by the Federal Trade Commission Act and empowered and directed by such Act to prevent the use of methods, acts or practices declared unlawful by the Act. 52 Am J1st Tradem § 198. An agency established by the Federal Trade Commission Act as an agency for the enforcement of such statute, including the gathering and compiling of information concerning, and the investigation of the organization, conduct, practices, and management of, certain corporations, and the administration and enforcement of the Federal Antitrust Laws. 52 Am J1st Tradem § 203. A quasi-judicial tribunal, the orders of which are administrative orders as distinguished from judicial decrees. National Candy Co. v Federal Trade Com. (CA7 Ill) 104 F2d 999.

Trade Commission Act. A federal statute, enacted in 1914, establishing the Federal Trade Commission, declaring unfair methods of competition and unfair or deceptive acts or practices in commerce to be unlawful, and empowering the Trade Commission to prevent the use of such methods, acts, or practices. 15 USC §§ 41 et seq.; 52 Am J1st Tradem § 198. The act of February 9, 1893, passed by Congress to prevent persons, partnerships, or corporations from using unfair methods of competition in commerce between the states and with foreign nations, between the District of Columbia and any state, territory, or foreign nation and within the District of Columbia. Federal Trade Com. v Klesner, 274 US 145, 71 L Ed 972, 47 S Ct 557.

trade custom. See **trade usage.**

trade discount. A discount allowed a dealer because of his status as a dealer.

trade dispute. A controversy between an employer and his employees as to terms and conditions of the employment. 31 Am J Rev ed Lab § 369.

As to meaning of the term as it appears in provisions of the Social Security or Unemployment Compensation Acts relative to disqualification for benefits, see Anno: 154 ALR 672.

Trade Expansion Act. A federal statute of 1962 the purpose of which is to stimulate the economic growth of the United States and maintain and enlarge foreign markets for the products of United States agriculture, industry, mining, and commerce, such stimulation to be accomplished through trade agreements with foreign countries. 19 USC §§ 1801-1991; 21 Am J2d Cust D § 19.

trade fair. See **trade show.**

Trade Fair Act. A federal statute of 1959 providing for the granting of certain privileges relative to the trade fair to be held in the United States, particularly the admission into the United States from a foreign country of articles to be exhibited at such fair, without the imposition of customs duty or internal revenue tax upon such article. 19 USC §§ 1751-1756.

trade fixture. An article annexed by a lessee to the real estate to aid him in carrying on his trade or business on the premises. Ray v Young, 160 Iowa 613, 142 NW 393. A structure or chattel annexed to the freehold for the purpose of trade or manufacture. In re Shelar (DC Pa) 21 F2d 136; Ward v Town Tavern, 191 Or 1, 228 P2d 216, 42 ALR2d 662. An article annexed to the realty by a tenant for the purpose of carrying on a trade or business, not exclusively agricultural. Frost v Schinkel, 121 Neb 784, 238 NW 659, 77 ALR 1381. Property which a tenant has placed on the rented real estate to advance the business for which the realty is leased, and which may, as against the lessor and those claiming under him, be removed at the end of the term. John P. Squire & Co. v Portland, 106 Me 230, 76 A 679. Such a chattel as merchants usually possess and annex to the premises which are occupied by them in order to enable them the better to store, handle, and display their goods and wares, such as counters, shelves, showcases, scales, etc. 37 Am J2d Frd Conv § 254.

trade-in. An old or used article or machine turned in as part of the purchase price of a new article or machine, particularly in the automobile and home appliance business. 30 Am J2d Exch P § 3.

trade-in allowance. The amount allowed by an automobile or appliance dealer to a purchaser for his automobile or appliance turned in as part payment of the purchase price of a new automobile or appliance.

trade information. Information interchanged between persons engaged in the same trade or industrial operation.

trade-in value. See **blue book; trade-in allowance.**

trade journal. See **trade publication.**

trade libel. False words published of and concerning a person which tend to prejudice him in his business, profession, occupation, or employment in such manner and to such extent that, as a necessary consequence, they prevent him from obtaining therefrom that pecuniary reward which, probably, he otherwise would have obtained. 33 Am J1st L & S § 63.

trademark. A sign, device, or mark by which the articles produced or dealt in by a particular person or organization are distinguished or distinguishable from those produced or dealt in by others. 52 Am J1st Tradem § 2. A mark entitled to registration under the federal statute relating to the registration of trademarks, whether registered or not. 15 USC § 108.

trademark infringement. See **infringement of trademark.**

tradename. A name, word, or phrase employed by one engaged in business, as a means of identifying his products, business, or services, and of establishing good will. A name involving the individuality of the producer of or dealer in goods, used by him for protection in trade, to avoid confusion in business, and to secure the advantages of a good reputation as a producer or dealer. 52 Am J1st Tradem § 3. Sometimes referred to as a quasi-trademark. Vonderbank v Schmidt, 44 La Ann 264, 10 So 616. A part or all of a firm name or corporate name or abbreviation thereof, serving to some extent the same purpose as a trademark. 52 Am J1st Tradem § 3.

tradename infringement. See **infringement of tradename.**

trade publication. A publication of special interest to the members of a particular trade or industry, such as printing, the making of clothing, the manufacture of automobiles, the milling of flour, etc. 29 Am J2d Ev § 892.

trader. One who sells goods substantially in the form in which he bought them and who has not converted them into another form of property by his skill and labor. 51 Am J1st Tax § 320. A person who makes it his business to buy merchandise, goods, or chattels and sell the same at a profit. State v Rosenbaum, 80 Conn 327, 68 A 250.
See **feme sole trader**; **treaty trader.**

trade route. A route followed by a dealer, such as a milk dealer, in delivering the product to regular customers. 28 Am J Rev ed Inj § 103.

trade secret. Information respecting the business or process of production of a dealer or producer, of special value to him in reference to competitors. 52 Am J1st Tradem § 118. Secrets of any character peculiar and important to the business of the employer which have been communicated to an employee of the employer in the course of a confidential employment. 35 Am J1st M & S § 96. Information relative to an industrial process or the conduct of a business, known only to the owner and those of his employees to whom it is necessary to confide if the fact known is to be made of value or, at any rate, not available to the trade generally. 28 Am J Rev ed Inj § 72.

trade show. An exhibition of local, state, or national, or international, scope, wherein the manufacturers or dealers exhibit their products of a particular line such as automobiles, motorboats, computers, etc.
See **Trade Fair Act.**

trade slander. Same as trade libel except that the defamatory words are spoken instead of published. 33 Am J1st L & S § 63.
See **trade libel.**

tradesman. A man who follows a particular trade. A man engaged in business, as distinguished from a professional man.
In England, the word would seem to be principally used as expressive of a person engaged in traffic, as a small shopkeeper; but in this country, it embraces a much larger class. Here it is seldom applied to persons engaged in the business of buying and selling, but is generally accepted as signifying mechanics and artisans of every kind whose livelihood depends upon the labor of their hands. Richie v McCauley, 4 Pa 471, 472.

trade slogan. A slogan employed as a trade name. Yellow Cab Co. v Sachs, 191 Cal 238, 216 P 33, 28 ALR 105. Apt words identifying a business by reference to the activities therein.

trade talk. Same as **seller's talk.**

trade terms. Words, phrases, and expressions having a meaning peculiar to a particular trade, for example, the term "working a street," familiar in the parlance of door-to-door salesmen. Re Curtis, 64 Conn 501, 30 A 769.
See **trade-name.**

trade trust. A monopoly or unlawful combination in the form of a trust for the control of prices in a particular business or trade. 36 Am J1st Monop § 19.

trade union. Broadly, a labor union, an association of workers which exists for the purpose, in whole or in part, of bargaining on behalf of workers with employers about the terms or conditions of employment. Restatement, Torts § 778. In a restricted sense, a labor union organized on a craft basis, composed of workers engaged in a common occupation, although often employed by different employers. 31 Am J Rev ed Lab § 13.

trade usage. A uniform course of conduct followed in a particular trade, calling, occupation or business. Any practice or method of dealing having such regularity of observance in a place, vocation, or trade as to justify an expectation that it will be observed with respect to the transaction in question. UCC § 1—205(2).

tradidi (trā'di-dī). I have leased.

trading. See **trade.**

trading bank. A commercial, as distinguished from, a savings bank.

trading contract. A business contract. A contract between persons engaged in business.

trading corporation. A kind of business corporation. A corporation the chief business of which is to buy and sell for profit goods and chattels.
The following have been held not to be trading corporations: a warehouse company, a company to buy and sell stocks and bonds, a fire insurance company, a building and loan association, a water company, a laundry company, a transportation company, a forwarding company, a public library, a social club, a mining company. See United States Hotel Co. v Niles (CA6 Ohio) 134 F 225.

trading firm. See **trading corporation**; **trading partnership.**

trading in dormant titles. A form of maintenance of which cognizance has been taken by statute, the first statute on the subject being that of 32 Henry VIII, chapter 9. 14 Am J2d Champ § 11.

trading partnership. A commercial partnership; a partnership organized for the purpose of trade or commerce.
If the business of a partnership, according to the usual mode of conducting imports, in its nature, the necessity of buying and selling, the firm is properly regarded as a trading or commercial partnership, otherwise it is nontrading or noncommercial. 40 Am J1st Partn § 12.

trading stamp. A stamp given by way of a premium upon the purchase of merchandise, redeemable in merchandise according to a previously arranged plan. A memorandum in writing given by a merchant to a customer upon the purchase of and payment for goods in cash, which expresses in money value a small percentage of the price of the goods bought and paid for, and entitles the recipient, after he has accumulated a certain number of such memorandums, often known as coupons, to use them, to the extent of their designated value, in payment for any other goods of the merchant which he may afterward desire, or goods of some other person or trading company that has undertaken to redeem the coupons. 52 Am J1st Trad St § 2.

In its ultimate analysis the use of trading stamps by a merchant is simply a form of advertising, resorted to for the purpose of increasing trade; merely an instrumentality or incident of a business, not a business in itself in the commercial sense. 52 Am J1st Trad St § 3.

trading-stamp license. An exaction upon trading stamps or trading stamp schemes for the purpose of regulation, revenue, or both. 52 Am J1st Trad St § 12.

trading value. See **blue book**; **speculative or trading value**; **trade-in allowance**.

trading with the enemy. Commercial intercourse with a subject of a nation with whom the United States is at war, whether proximate or remote, direct and personal, as between principal and principal, or through the intervention of an agent. 56 Am J1st War § 108. Carrying on commercial intercourse in time of war with a subject of enemy nationality or a loyal or neutral subject voluntarily residing in hostile territory or carrying on business therein. 3 Am J2d Aliens § 174.

Trading With the Enemy Act. A federal statute interdicting trading and commercial intercourse with enemies and allies of enemies, except with license of the President. 50 USC Appx §§ 1 et seq.; Propper v Clark, 337 US 472, 93 L Ed 1480, 69 S Ct 1338, reh den 338 US 841, 94 L Ed 514, 70 S Ct 33.

traditio brevis manus (trā-di'she-ō brē'vis ma'nus). (Civil law.) The delivery of goods by mere consent, unaccompanied by any physical act. See Mackeldey's Roman Law § 284.

traditio clavium (trā-di'she-ō klā'vi-um). (Civil law.) The delivery of the keys,—that is a symbolic delivery of a thing by a tradition of the key to its enclosure. See Mackeldey's Roman Law § 284.

Traditio loqui facit chartam (trā-di'she-ō lo'quī fā'sit kar'tam). Delivery gives voice to a deed.

tradition. Knowledge, belief, or practices transmitted orally from father to son, or from ancestors to posterity.

When applied to pedigree, some authorities treat "tradition," "repute" and "reputation" as convertible terms. They mean such declarations and statements respecting the pedigree as have come down from generation to generation from deceased relatives in such a way that even though it cannot be said or determined which of the deceased relatives originally made them, or was personally cognizant of the facts therein stated, yet it appears that such declarations and statements were made as family history ante litem motam, by a deceased person, connected by blood or marriage with the person whose pedigree is to be established. Re Estate of Hurlburt, 68 Vt 366, 35 A 77.

The word "tradition" as used in the civil law means "delivery." Keepers v Fidelity Co. 56 NJL 302, 28 A 585.

traditional law. The common law.

Traditionibus dominia rerum, non nudis pactis, transferuntur (tra-di-she-ō'ni-bus do-mi'ni-a rē'rum, non nū'dis pak'tis, trans-fe-run'ter). The ownership of things is transferred by delivery, not by naked promises. See 2 Bl Comm 312.

traditio nihil aliud est quam rei corporalis de persona in personam, de manu in manum, translatio aut in possessionem inductio; sed res incorporales, quae sunt ipsum jus rei vel corpori inhaerens, traditionem non patiuntur (tra-di'she-ō ni'hil a'li-ud est quam rē'ī kor-po-rā'lis dē per-sō'na in per-sō'nam, dē ma'nū in ma'num, trans-lā'she-ō āt in po-ze-she-ō'nem in-duk'she-ō; sed rēz in-kor-po-rā'lez, kwē sunt ip'sum jūs rē'i vel kor'po-rī in-hē'renz, tra-di-she-ō'nem non pa-ti-un'ter). Livery is nothing but the transfer or the induction into possession of a corporeal hereditament from person to person, from hand to hand; but an incorporeal hereditament, which is the right itself to a thing or inherent in the person does not permit of livery. See 2 Bl Comm 317.

Traditio nihil amplius transferre debet vel potest ad eum qui accipit, quam est apud eum qui tradit (trā-di'she-ō ni'hil am'pli-us trans-fer're dē'bet vel po'-test ad ē'um quī ak'si-pit, quam est a'pud ē'um quī trā'dit). (Civil law.) Delivery ought to and can transfer nothing more to him who receives it than is in the possession of him who delivers.

traditio rei (tra-di'she-ō rē'ī). The delivery of the thing.

traditor (trad'i-tor). A traitor, a person who commits treason.

traditur in ballium (tra'di-ter in bal'li-um). He is delivered to bail.

traffic. The movement of vehicles upon the highways and streets. The operations of a carrier in transporting freight and passengers. Buying and selling; commercial intercourse. The passing of goods or commodities from one person to another for an equivalent in goods or money. Williams v Fears, 110 Ga 584, 35 SE 699.

See **liquor traffic**.

traffic car. A vehicle powered by a motor, having three wheels, two in the rear joined by an axle, with a single wheel in front, and a chassis upon which a body is installed like that of an ordinary small truck, the driver occupying a saddle and being protected from the weather in front by a windshield. Womack v Life & Casualty Ins. Co. (La App) 184 So 357.

traffic circle. An intersection, sometimes involving several streets, intended to facilitate traffic in moving from one street to another by being arranged and posted for movement of vehicles one way and in a circle. 7 Am J2d Auto § 203.

traffic contract. A contract between railroad companies respecting the operations of the one in reference to the operations of the other, often granting the privilege to the one of running its trains over the tracks of the other. 44 Am J1st RR § 375.

traffic control devices. Signal lights, stop signs, caution signs, etc. on street or highway.

traffic court. A municipal or police court exercising jurisdiction over traffic offenses. A court having special jurisdiction over traffic offenses. Johnson v Virginia, 373 US 61, 10 L Ed 2d 195, 83 S Ct 1053.

traffic infraction. The violation of a statute or ordinance respecting traffic on street or highway, usually of a minor nature. Ando v Woodberry, 8 NY2d 165, 203 NYS2d 74, 168 NE2d 520.

traffic lanes. Longitudinal divisions of a highway or street made to separate traffic moving in opposite directions, and in the case of four lanes, to separate fast moving from slow moving traffic in the same direction.

traffic offense. A violation of a statute or ordinance in reference to the manner of operation of vehicles upon street or highway. 7 Am J2d Auto §§ 168 et seq. A public offense. Smith v Hubbard, 253 Minn 215, 91 NW2d 756.

traffic officer. A policeman or other officer of the law posted particularly for the purpose of controlling traffic on street or highway and arresting persons who violate traffic laws.

traffic pool. See **pool.**

traffic regulations. Regulations prescribed by statute or ordinance for the operation of automobiles and other vehicles upon the public highways. 7 Am J2d Auto §§ 168 et seq. Rules and regulations prescribed by law regarding the rights of vehicles and persons meeting or passing in a highway. 25 Am J1st High § 205. Regulations prescribed by law for the operation or navigation of boats. 12 Am J2d Boats §§ 14-19.
See **air traffic rules; rules of the road.**

traffic rules. See **traffic regulations.**

traffic violation. A violation of a statute or ordinance regulating the operation of motor vehicles.
See **traffic infraction.**

trahens (tra'henz). One drawing; the drawer of a bill of exchange.

trahere (tra'he-re). To draw.

trail. Noun: A path or track. A way, road, or path suitable for the purpose of driving cattle over or along on their way to a market. United States v Andrews, 179 US 96, 99, 45 L Ed 105, 106, 21 S Ct 46. A course marked by footprints. Verb: To follow behind. To follow a person by his footprints or other sign left by him. To use blood hounds to follow the scent of one suspected of the commission of a crime, for the purpose of apprehending him. 26 Am J1st Homi § 331.

trailer. A car attached to a streetcar and operated with the latter. A vehicle used for transportation of freight on the highway, being towed by a tractor or another powered vehicle. Waddey v Maryland Casualty Co. 171 Tenn 112, 100 SW2d 984, 109 ALR 654. A vehicle having a large and commodious body, which can be towed upon the highway but is usually parked and used as living quarters; sometimes called a house trailer. A building within the meaning of a building code, where set up as a stationary home. Lower Merion Township v Gallup, 158 Pa Super 572, 46 A2d 35, app dismd 329 US 669, 91 L Ed 591, 67 S Ct 92. Not a motor vehicle within the meaning of a statute providing for constructive or substituted service upon a nonresident motorist. Anno: 48 ALR2d 1284.

A freight trailer falls into the category of trade equipment within the Michigan rule that damages for the loss of use of tools and trade equipment are recoverable in replevin, where the plaintiff's source of livelihood consisted of hiring out his trailer and tractor with himself as driver. Steel Motor Service v Zalke (CA6 Mich) 212 F2d 856, 48 ALR2d 1045.

trailer coach. A large vehicle carrying passengers but pulled by another vehicle, such as a tractor. McNown v Pacific Freight Lines, 50 Cal App 2d 221, 122 P2d 582.

trailer park. An area, usually adjacent to a highway, wherein house trailers are parked and used as living quarters, the area being equipped with electric, water, and gas lines, for the accommodation of the inhabitants of the trailers. Vissers v Jordon (Fla App) 131 So 2d 754.

trailing. See **trail.**

train. An aggregation of cars drawn by an engine or engines. La Mere v Railway Transfer Co. 125 Minn 159, 145 NW 1068. Engine and cars assembled and coupled together for a run or trip on a railroad. United States v Erie R. Co. 237 US 402, 59 L Ed 1019, 35 S Ct 621.

A train pulled by a small engine called a "dummy," although exclusively engaged in carrying passengers, is a railroad train, within the meaning of a statute prescribing precautions to be observed by railroads. Birmingham Mineral Railroad Co. v Jacobs, 92 Ala 187, 9 So 320.

Within the air-brake provision of the Federal Safety Appliance Act, a train consists of an engine and cars which have been assembled and coupled together for a run or trip along the road. When a train is thus made up and is proceeding on its journey it is within the operation of the air-brake provision. But it is otherwise with the various movements in railroad yards whereby cars are assembled and coupled into outgoing trains, and whereby incoming trains which have completed their run are broken up. These are not train movements but are mere switching operations, and so are not within the air-brake provision. United States v Southern Pacific Co. (CA9 Cal) 100 F2d 984.

A locomotive with one or more cars attached to it, with or without passengers or freight, in motion upon a railroad from one point to another by means of power furnished by the locomotive, would undoubtedly constitute a train. Caron v Boston & Al. R. 164 Mass 523, 527, 42 NE 112.

See **accommodation train; local freight train; mixed train; passenger train; regular passenger train; wild train.**

trained nurse. See **nurse; registered nurse.**

trainee. One undergoing training in a shop or factory for the purpose of qualifying as an employee.

training expenses. Expenses incurred by an employer in training employees in production and salesmen.

training school. See **industrial school; model training school.**

train schedule. See **timetable.**

train wreck. The smashing, breaking or other damage to the cars of a railroad train which stop its journey, occurring by running off the track or by collision with another train or car of a train. Anno: 51 ALR 1331.

A term used in a policy of accident insurance providing double indemnity for death resulting from a train wreck does not contemplate or intend a total destruction of a train of cars, or even of one of the cars constituting a component part of a train. Mochel v Iowa State Traveling Men's Asso. 203 Iowa 623, 213 NW 259, 51 ALR 1327.

traitor (trā'tor). A person who has committed treason. One who has betrayed his country.
See **treason.**

trajectu. See **in trajectu.**

tram (tram). An open car used in mines for hauling coal or ore. The word in Great Britain for streetcar.

tramp. A vagrant; a nonresident vagrant. 55 Am J1st Vag § 1. A person who wanders from place to place begging or doing occasional jobs for a living. Slang for a girl leading a dissolute life.

tramp corporation. A corporation receiving its charter to act as a corporation in one state with no intention of doing business in that state, but with intent to do business in another state or other states. State v Georgia Co. 112 NC 34, 17 SE 10.

tramp's joint. A place frequented by persons engaged in evil and secret practices, usually illegal practices. State v Shoaf, 179 NC 744, 102 SE 705, 9 ALR 426.

tramp vessel. A ship operating without schedule and not as a component of a fleet of a shipping company, picking up cargo as it finds it.

tramway (tram'wā). Track for a tram; a railway in a mine. O'Malley v Riley County, 86 Kan 752, 121 P 1108. A streetcar line in Great Britain.

tranquility. Serenity; a state of undisturbed emotions.

See **public and domestic tranquility.**

transacting business. Doing business. Engaging in business.

It has been held that entering into a contract to transact business is, in the unlimited meaning of the term, "transacting business," but that such was not the meaning of the term as contemplated in a statute requiring foreign corporations to perform certain acts as a prerequisite to transacting business within the state. Tri-state Amusement Co. v Forest Park Highlands Amusement Co. 192 Mo 404, 90 SW 1020.

See **doing business; engaging in or transacting business.**

transacting business within the state. See **doing business in state.**

transaction. A matter of dealing between parties, the word implying action, consent, knowledge, or acquiescence on the part of both of them. Blount v Blount, 158 Ala 242, 48 So 581. The carrying on or through of any matter or affair by two parties in concert, the word implying mutuality. 58 Am J1st Witn § 238. The doing or performing of some business between parties, or the management of any affair, for the benefit or detriment of one or both of the parties. Re Wind, 27 Wash 2d 421, 178 P2d 731, 173 ALR 1276 (transaction with decedent). An act or agreement, or several acts or agreements having some connection with each other, in which two or more persons are concerned and by which legal relations between them are altered. 1 Am J2d Actions § 108.

As the word is employed in codes of pleading, it means something which has taken place whereby a cause of action has arisen. It must therefore consist of an act or an agreement, or several acts or agreements having some connection with each other, in which more than one person is concerned, and by which the legal relations of such persons between themselves are altered. Craft Refrigerating Machine Co. v Quinnipiac Brewing Co. 63 Conn 551, 29 A 76.

See **repeated transactions.**

transaction for profit. Any business activity productive of income. Re Kansas City Star Co. 346 Mo 658, 142 SW2d 1029, 130 ALR 1168.

transactions connected with same subject of action. A phrase applicable to a given state of facts wherefrom the plaintiff seeks different kinds of relief, but all of which kinds of relief spring from the same state of facts, and therefore are connected with the same subject of action. 1 Am J2d Actions § 109.

transaction with person since deceased or incompetent. A transaction between a witness and a person who has since died or become incompetent, so conducted that the latter, if living, could contradict the witness should he testify falsely. 58 Am J1st Witn § 238.

transcript. A written or typewritten copy. A typewritten transcript of the court reporter's stenographic notes taken on trial. A deposition reduced to writing. A complete record of the case filed on appeal, including all material matters. 4 Am J2d A & E § 404.

In the absence of statute or rule of court, a reporter's transcript is not, as such, part of the record, but must be made so, if it is to be available on appeal, by embodying it in a bill of exception, although once it is made a part of the bill of exceptions, the trial judge may adopt it as a correct statement of the evidence given on the trial. 4 Am J2d A & E § 411.

transcripted judgment. A judgment entered in a county other than that in which rendered, so as to perfect a judgment lien upon real estate in the other county, upon the filing of a transcript of the judgment record in such county. 30A Am J Rev ed Judgm § 124. A judgment of a justice of the peace made a judgment of a court of record by filing a transcript of the record of the judgment in the court of the justice of the peace with the clerk of the court of record.

transcription. A copy of a writing; the act of making a copy.

See **transcript.**

transcript of the evidence. A record of the evidence as prepared by the court reporter. Blair v Greene, 246 Ala 28, 18 So 2d 668.

Transeat in exemplum (trans'e-at in eg-zem'plum). Let it pass into an example or precedent.

transfer. Verb: To place property in the hands of another. Culbertson v Cabeen, 29 Tex 247. To pass title. New Home Bldg. Supply Co. v Nations, 259 NC 681, 131 SE2d 425. For some purposes, to transfer legal title. Lyons v Freshman, 124 Mont 485, 226 P2d 775, 23 ALR2d 1165 (under the Uniform Stock Transfer Act). Noun: A delivery of possession. A passing of title or ownership. A bill of sale; a deed. A sale. An assignment. Every means and manner by which property can pass from the ownership and possession of one person to the ownership and possession of another, either by act of the parties or by operation of law, or both. 42 Am J1st Prop § 54. Under the Bankruptcy Act, the sale and every other and different mode, direct or indirect, of disposing of or of parting with property or with an interest therein or with the possession thereof, or of fixing a lien upon property or upon an interest therein, absolutely or conditionally, voluntarily or involuntarily, by or without judicial proceedings, as a conveyance sale, assignment, payment, pledge, mortgage, lien, encumbrance, gift, security, or otherwise, including the retention of a security title to property delivered to a debtor. Bankruptcy Act § 1(30); 11 USC § 1(30).

A ticket or token given by a carrier to a passenger

TRANSFER [1293] TRANSIENT

which entitles him to transportation upon another line of the carrier.

transfer agent. A person having the duty of registering a transfer of corporate stock. 18 Am J2d Corp § 408. Not a managing agent within the meaning of a statute concerning the service of process upon a foreign corporation. Anno: 113 ALR 79.

transfer by indorsement (bī in-dōrs'mẹnt). The indorsement and delivery of a negotiable instrument to the indorsee.

Such delivery may be actual, as where it is manually handed by one to the other, or it may be constructive, as where the indorser puts the instrument in the power or under the control of the indorsee. Clark v Sigourney, 17 Conn 510, 524.

transfer by operation of law. An automatic transfer of title or ownership, being effected without voluntary action by either party directed particularly toward accomplishing a transfer. Dodier Realty & Invest. Co. v St. Louis Nat. Baseball Club, 361 Mo 981, 238 SW2d 321, 24 ALR2d 683.

transfer company. A motor carrier. A company engaged primarily in hauling goods from terminal of a common carrier to the place of business or residence of consignee. A railroad company which makes a business of shifting cars delivered to it by a carrier to a siding, house track, or unloading track of the consignee. 14 Am J2d Car § 663.

transferee. One to whom a transfer is made.

transfer in contemplation of death. A transfer of property, usually to spouse or child, impelled by the thought of death. United States v Wells, 283 US 102, 75 L Ed 867, 51 S Ct 446. Inclusive of a gift inter vivos, as well as a gift causa mortis, provided it is made in contemplation of death. Anno: 7 ALR 1030, s. 21 ALR 1337, 75 ALR 549, 120 ALR 188, 148 ALR 1056.

transfer of cases. The transfer of a case by one court to another.
See **removal of cause.**

transfer of exchange. See **cable transfer; telegraphing money.**

transfer of jurisdiction. The passing of jurisdiction from state court to federal court upon proper proceedings taken for removal of the cause, subject to jurisdiction of the state court being restored on remand. See 32 Am J2d Fed Pract § 510.

transfer of order paper. The negotiation of a negotiable instrument.

transfer of property. See **transfer.**

transferor. One who makes a transfer.

transferred intent. The principle whereunder one acting with a wrongful intent is held criminally responsible for an ensuing wrong which was not intended by him. State v Griego, 61 NM 42, 294 P2d 282. The doctrine that where one intends to assault a certain person, and by mistake or inadvertance assaults another in his stead, the act is nevertheless a crime, the intent being transferred from the party intended to the person actually assaulted. People v Rothrock, 21 Cal App 2d 116, 68 P2d 364.

transferred judgment. An assigned judgment. A judgment transcripted to another county. 30A Am J Rev ed Judgm § 124. A judgment of a justice of the peace transcripted to a court of record.

transferred sale. A singular term of the cotton exchange for a sale offset by a purchase at the same price on the same day. Dupont v United States, 300 US 150, 81 L Ed 570, 57 S Ct 391.

transfer service (tráns'fėr sėr'vis). See **switching service; transfer company.**

transfer tax. A tax on the transfer of or succession to property. Colorado v Harbeck, 232 NY 71. A tax in the nature of an excise tax on the transfer of property. Cole v Nickel, 43 Nev 12, 177 P 409, 185 P 565.

The state tax on inheritance has been called a transfer tax and the Federal tax, an estate tax, but both have been imposed as excises on the transfer of property from a decedent and both to take effect at the instant of transfer. Frick v Pennsylvania, 268 US 473, 69 L Ed 1058, 45 S Ct 603, 42 ALR 316.

See **gift tax; inheritance tax; stock transfer tax; succession tax.**

transformer. A device for changing the voltage of an electric current, particularly from the voltage of a high line to the voltage appropriate for residential use. Brooklyn Edison Co. v Davidson, 269 NY 48, 198 NE 627.

transgressio (trans-gre'she-ō). A trespass.

transgressione. See **trespass.**

Transgressione multiplicata, crescat poenae inflictio (trans-gre-she-ō'ne mul-ti-pli-kā'ta, kres'kat pē'nē in-flik'she-ō). Upon the multiplication of transgression, let the infliction of punishment increase.

transgressive trust (trȧns-gres'iv trust). A trust which by its terms transgresses or violates the rule against perpetuities.

Nothing is denounced as a perpetuity that does not transgress this rule, and equity follows this rule by way of analogy in dealing with executory trusts; and those trusts which transgress the rule are called transgressive trusts, being in equity the substantial equivalent of what in law are called perpetuities. Pulitzer v Livingston, 89 Me 359, 364, 36 A 635.

transhipment (trȧn-ship'mẹnt). Same as **transshipment.**

transient. A person passing through a place or staying there only temporarily.

transient alien. An alien in the country temporarily or one merely passing through the country. Anno: 32 ALR 8, s. 48 ALR2d 813, 836-840, §§ 7, 17.

transient dealer. One who establishes himself in business in a locality with the intention and determination to remain there for a short period of time only, whether such period is a definite or indefinite one, such as a period of weeks or months, or until a particular stock of merchandise is disposed of, or until the local market for the commodity handled by the dealer has been exhausted, and who for such limited period engages or occupies a building or other place for the exhibition and sale of his goods or wares. 40 Am J1st Ped § 4. Sometimes called a transient merchant. Carrolton v Bazette, 159 Ill 284, 42 NE 837. Distinguished from a peddler in the respect that he has a definite place for the exhibition and sale of his goods, however temporary his stay at such place may be. Anno: 94 ALR 1083.

The term relates rather to the character of the business carried on by the merchant than to the residence of the individual merchant. Ottumwa v Zekind, 95 Iowa 622, 64 NW 646.

transient foreigner. Same as **transient alien.**

transient merchant. See **transient dealer.**

transient pauper. A pauper without a settlement in the place where aid for him is sought. 41 Am J1st Poor L § 28.

transient property. Personalty merely temporarily within the limits of the state. Anno: 110 ALR 723; 51 Am J1st Tax § 453.

transire (trans-ī'rē). A customs permit for the passage of goods.

transit. See **in transit.**

Transit in rem judicatam (trans'it in rem ju-di-kā'tam). It passes into, or is merged into a judgment.
"If there be any one principle of law settled beyond all question, it is this, that whensoever a cause of action in the language of the law, transit in rem judicatam, and the judgment thereupon remains in full force unreversed, the original cause of action is merged and gone forever." United States v Leffler (US) 11 Pet 86, 101, 9 L Ed 642, 647.

transit number. A number stamped upon a check by a bank by way of identifying the check as paper going through the bank. Bohlig v First Nat. Bank, 233 Minn 523, 48 NW2d 445.

transitory. Fleeting. Not permanent.
See **chose transitory.**

transitory action. An action upon a cause of action that could have arisen in any place whatsoever, having no such reference to one place as to render it a local action. 56 Am J1st Venue § 3.

transitory crime. A crime the venue for the prosecution of which may, by force of statute, be laid in a county other than that in which the offense may have been committed. Watt v People, 126 Ill 9, 18 NE 340.

transitory seisin. Seisin for the instant or for the moment, as where the person seised is a mere conduit of title for passing an estate. 25 Am J2d Dow § 29.

transit privileges. Stopover, milling-in-transit, and similar privileges granted a shipper by a carrier. 13 Am J2d Car § 318.

Transit terra cum onere (trans'it ter'ra kum ō'ne-re). The land passes with its burden or encumbrance. The maxim presupposes a transfer of the land, and when that actually takes place, it forms the medium of a privity between the assignees. See Mygatt v Coe, 124 NY 212, 26 NE 611.

transitu. See **in transitu.**

transitus (tran'si-tus). Transit; a passing over or through; a conveyance.

transit visa (tran'sit vē'zạ). A visa limited by its terms and conditions to a continuous trip through the country.
See **visa.**

transivit in rem judicatam (tran-siv'it in rem jūd-i-ka'tem). It has been merged into the judgment. Kendall v Hamilton (Eng) 4 App Cas 504.

translado (trans-lah'tho). (Spanish.) A transcript; a copy.

translate. To make a translation.
See **translation.**

translation. Giving the equivalent of a written or spoken statement in the words of another language or dialect. Rasmussen v Baker, 7 Wyo 117, 50 P 819. A change from one condition to another, as from the physical to the spiritual.
See **interpreter.**

translator. See **translation.**

transmission. A sending, conveying, or passing. A devolution of property by will or by law. Rogers v Commissioner (F) 1 T Ct 629. The remission of funds by one bank to another. 10 Am J2d Banks § 308. The instrumentality of a motor vehicle whereby the power of the motor is applied to the wheels for moving the vehicle. 8 Am J2d Auto § 649.

transmission for collection. The sending of commercial paper to a bank for collection. 10 Am J2d Banks § 308.

transmission of assets. The act of an ancillary representative in remitting assets of the estate in his control to the domiciliary representative. 31 Am J2d Ex & Ad § 706. The sending of assets in an ancillary receivership to the primary receiver. Anno: 45 ALR 633.

transmission of funds. See **transmission.**

transmission of intelligence. Communication.
The Supreme Court has held that the transmission of intelligence is commerce. The court said: "Other commerce deals only with persons, or with visible and tangible things. But the telegraph transports nothing visible and tangible; it carries only ideas, wishes, orders and intelligence." Western Union Tel. Co. v Pendleton, 122 US 347, 30 L Ed 1187, 7 S Ct 1126.

transmutation. The change of one thing into another. A graphic expression applied to agreements between spouses concerning the status and disposition of their property, particularly in reference to status as community property. Chavez v Chavez, 56 NM 393, 244 P2d 781, 30 ALR2d 1236.

transom. (tran'som). A crosspiece or crossbar. A panel, usually of glass, over a door, which may be raised or lowered in control of ventilation. Slane v Curtis, 41 Wyo 402, 286 P 372, 288 P 12, 69 ALR 906.

transport. Verb: To carry from one place to another. To convey, as by truck, train, ship, wagon, cart, etc. United States v Sheldon (US) 2 Wheat 119, 120, 4 L Ed 199, 200. As required of a carrier:—to deliver at the final destination. 14 Am J2d Car § 691. Noun: A ship employed for carrying soldiers or military supplies.

transportation. The carriage of persons or property from one point to another. Removing a person from the country by way of punishment upon his conviction of an offense against the laws of the country. Fong Yue Ting v United States, 149 US 697, 709, 37 L Ed 905, 911, 13 S Ct 1016. As used in the Interstate Commerce Act:—not only the physical instrumentalities, but all services in connection with the receipt, delivery, elevation, transfer in transit, ventilation, refrigeration or icing, storage, and handling of the property transported. 49 USC § 1(3).
The word is used in constitutional provisions and statutes relating to intoxicating liquor in its ordinary sense. It comprehends any real carrying about, from one place to another, or a substantial movement of liquor from one place or vicinity to another, whether on the person or in a vehicle. 30 Am J Rev ed Intox L § 40.
Under the Interstate Commerce Act authorizing

the Interstate Commerce Commission to adjust rates to meet "transportation conditions," such conditions may and should include conditions other than mere operating conditions. Board of Trade v United States (DC Mo) 36 F Supp 865.
See **facility of transportation.**

Transportation Act. A federal statute regulating railroads and motor carriers. 13 Am J2d Car § 36.

transportation agent. See **shipping agent.**

transportation company. A carrier. A transfer company.

transportation conditions. See **transportation.**

transportation expenses. Freight on shipment of goods or other property. The fare for the transportation of a passenger. As a deduction in calculation of net income for tax purposes, only the travel cost, not including meals and lodging. IRS Pub. No. 463 (10/65) p 1.
See **mileage; travel expense.**

transportation in bond. The transportation in the United States of imported articles entered under bond without payment of customs duties. 21 Am J2d Cust D § 76.

transportation of liquor. See **transportation.**

transportation of pupils. The modern practice of carrying school pupils in busses to a central or consolidated school. A practice sometimes invoked to alleviate a so-called de facto segregation of races in the public schools by carrying pupils from districts predominantly white to districts predominantly colored and vice-versa.

transportation ticket. See **ticket.**

transship. See **transshipment.**

transshipment. Moving cargo from one vessel to another. A violation of a contract of affreightment, except as authorized by the contract or required of necessity. 48 Am J1st Ship §§ 404-406.

transubstantiation. (tran-sub-stan-shi-ā'shọn). The theological doctrine that the consecration of the bread and wine in the sacrament of communion make them the actual body and blood of Christ.

trap. To catch and take game by the use of a trap. 35 Am J2d Fish § 6. Noun: A hidden danger on premises, the peril of which would be avoidable if the existence of the thing were known. O'Shea v Lavoy, 175 Wis 456, 185 NW 525, 20 ALR 1008. Any very dangerous construction or condition designedly arranged to do injury. Moffat v Kenny, 174 Mass 311, 315, 54 NE 850.
"A trap is a figure of speech, not a formula. It involves the idea of concealment and surprise, of an appearance of safety under circumstances cloaking a reality of danger." Latham v Johnson, Ltd. (Eng) 1 K B 398.
See **entrapment; speed trap.**

trapdoor. A door in ceiling or floor for occasional access to upper or lower story.

trassatus (tra-sā'tus). The drawee of a bill of exchange.

traumatic (trâ'mat'ik). Originating in a violent application of force to the body.

traumatic disease (trâ-mat'ik di-zēz'). A disease resulting from a physical injury.
A claim for workmen's compensation based upon disability arising from traumatic disease should specify the time when, and the place where, the accident occurred. Iwanicki v State Industrial Acci. Com. 104 Or 650, 688, 205 P 990, 29 ALR 682.

traumatic mental depression (trâ-mat'ik men'tạl dẹ-presh'on.) A condition of mental depression caused by worry following the sustaining of a personal injury, often worry pertaining to financial stress resulting from disability. Wilson v Home Gas Co. 267 Minn 162, 125 NW2d 725.

traumatic neurasthenia (nū-ras-thē'ni-ạ). The technical name of a disease of the nervous system whereby it has become so weakened that there is a lack of power in the nerve centers to perform their functions properly.
The disease usually results from a wound or injury. Colorado Springs & Interurban Railway Co. v Nichols, 41 Colo 272, 92 P 691.

travail (trav'ạl). The labor and pains of childbirth. State v Watzek, 158 Minn 351, 197 NW 669. The condition of a mother in giving birth to a child, from the beginning of pains until delivery. "That perilous crisis, when, if ever, the mind will be most fearful of uttering a falsehood." Bacon v Harrington, 22 Mass (5 Pick) 63.

travel. Verb: To go from one place to another. To make a trip. To pass over a public way for the purpose of business, convenience, or pleasure. 25 Am J1st High § 427. To make such use of a way as the occasion may require legitimately. Caddo Electric Cooperative v Bollinger (Okla) 285 P2d 200, 55 ALR2d 172. Noun: A constitutional right under the Fifth Amendment to the United States Constitution. Aptheker v Secretary of State, 378 US 500, 12 L Ed 2d 992, 84 S Ct 1659. The act of taking a trip. Ex parte Archy, 9 Cal 147, 164.
To travel is to pass or make a journey from place to place, whether on foot, on horseback, or in any conveyance. Traveling is the act of making a journey; change of place; passage. The word "traveling," as used in some penal statutes, may have a narrow meaning; but, in order to maintain an action against a city or town for a defect in a highway, one need be a traveler only in the general sense above indicated. Hendry v North Hampton, 72 NH 351, 56 A 922.
A person is still "traveling" while delayed for a short time by an unforeseen accident. See Ex parte Archy, 9 Cal 147, 164.

travel agency. The business of making reservations on behalf of clients or customers with carriers by ship, rail or air, hotels, theaters, etc., booking tours, and advising people in reference to trips in prospect. The business of bringing together members of the traveling public and the operators of passenger automobiles who are not engaged in business as regularly licensed common or private carriers of passengers for hire. Francis v Adams, 54 Ariz 377, 96 P2d 277, 126 ALR 190.

travel bureau. A state or municipal agency promoting travel to the place from other states or foreign countries.

traveled part of highway. Same as **traveled part of the road.**

traveled part of the road. That part of the road which is prepared for travel, not merely the most traveled part. Winter v Harris, 23 RI 47, 49 A 398.

traveled road. A road actually used and traveled as a public highway, irrespective of whether it has been legally established and laid out or dedicated as such. Czech v Great Northern Railway Co. 68 Minn 38, 70 NW 791.

See **traveled part of the road.**

traveler. One who is traveling. One who spends much time in traveling. One using a public way. One who travels in any way, even for a short distance and in the city, town, or village of his residence. Leon v Kitchen Bros. Hotel Co. 134 Neb 137, 277 NW 823, 115 ALR 1078. As one for whom a public way must be kept reasonably safe, anyone rightfully using the way viatically or who has occasion to pass over the way for the purpose of business, convenience, or pleasure. 25 Am J1st High § 427. As a person entitled to carry a concealed weapon, one who travels such distance from his home that he goes beyond the circle of his general acquaintances, among strangers with whose habits, conduct, and character he is not acquainted. 56 Am J1st Weap § 15.

A radio repairman sitting in a customer's car parked in the street outside his shop, when his work on the car was interrupted by a rainstorm, is not a "traveler" on the highway, within a statute imposing on cities the duty to keep the highway safe for "travelers." Wershba v Lynn, 324 Mass 327, 86 NE2d 511, 14 ALR2d 179.

See **travel; wayfarer.**

traveler's check. An instrument, usually one of a set, purchased from a bank or other financially responsible institution, as a source of ready money on cashing the instrument, while traveling in the country or abroad, without identification other than the signature of the purchaser. 10 Am J2d Banks § 546. An instrument constituting a complete purchase and sale of credit, having the characteristics of a cashier's check where issued by a bank, and constituting a foreign bill of exchange. 11 Am J2d B & N § 17.

The instrument usually provides and is in such form that the check must be signed by the purchaser when obtained and countersigned again by him when he receives payment. It is the second signature which is the instrument's final currency. Paulink v American Express Co. 265 Mass 182, 163 NE 740, 62 ALR 506.

travel expense. A deduction in calculation of income tax purposes, when incurred while traveling away from home in pursuit of a trade or business. Internal Revenue Code § 162(a). A deduction in calculation of income for tax purposes, when incurred while traveling away from home for the production or collection of income, or the management, conservation, or maintenance of property held for the production of income, or in connection with the determination, collection, or refund of any tax. Internal Revenue Code § 212.

See **mileage; travel pay.**

travel fee. See **mileage.**

traveling. See **travel.**

traveling abroad. Traveling in a foreign country. While the usual meaning of the expression signifies travel in a foreign country, and an officer is understood to be traveling "abroad" when he goes to a foreign port or place under orders to proceed to that place, or from a foreign port to a home port, yet he is not so traveling when going from one place to another in the United States by the shortest route although it may take him into a foreign country such as Canada, or upon the high seas. United States v Hutchins, 151 US 542, 38 L Ed 264, 14 S Ct 421.

traveling man. See **traveling salesman.**

traveling salesman. One who travels from place to place, selling to retailers alone. Upchurch v LaGrange, 159 Ga 113, 125 SE 47. Often called a commercial traveler or commercial salesman. Known in an older day as a "drummer." A person who is employed to travel from one place to another to sell goods for his employer.

Such a person is not a "day laborer" although by his contract with his employer he is paid by the day. Briscoe v Montgomery & Co. 93 Ga 662.

traveling way. That part of the underground workings of a mine used exclusively for purpose of travel and transportation. 35 Am J1st M & S § 215.

See **traveled part of the road.**

travel pay. An allowance for travel expense, especially where made to persons in the armed forces. 36 Am J1st Mil § 80.

See **travel expense; mileage.**

travel time. Time spent by an employee in coming to and leaving his place of employment.

traversable (trav'ẽr-sạ-bl). Subject to being traversed or denied.

See **traverse.**

traverse (trav'ẽrs). Verb: To contest or deny an allegation. Noun: A denial of the facts alleged in the pleading of an adverse party. 41 Am J1st Pl § 190.

traverse jury (trav'ẽrs jö'ri). A petit jury, that is, a trial jury. 31 Am J Rev ed Jury § 2. A jury impaneled to sit on the trial of an action. United States v Taylor, 147 US 695, 698, 37 L Ed 335, 337, 13 S Ct 479.

traverser (trav'ẽr-sẽr). A party to an action who pleads by way of denial. Commonwealth v Hite, 33 Va (6 Leigh) 588.

See **traverse.**

t. r. e. An abbreviation of **tempus regis Edwardi.**

tread. Verb: To walk; to step. Noun: The part of a shoe which makes contact with the ground. The part of a tire which makes contact with the surface of the way, grooved to provide traction. The top board of a step in a stairway. Anno: 25 ALR2d 372, § 4.

treason. Levying war against the United States or adhering to the enemies of the United States, giving them aid and comfort. US Const Art 3 § 3. A breach of allegiance. United States v Wiltberger (US) 5 Wheat 76, 5 L Ed 37. A criminal attempt to destroy the existence of the government. Respublica v Chapman (Pa) 1 Dall 53, 1 L Ed 33.

treason, felony, or other crime. A phrase found in Article IV, section 2, clause 2, of the United States Constitution, relative to extradition for crime, embracing every act forbidden and made punishable by a law of a state. See Kentucky v Dennison (US) 24 How 66, 16 L Ed 717.

treasurer. A state or municipal officer whose duties are to receive and take custody of the public moneys, and to pay them out on warrants. 37 Am J1st Mun Corp § 406; 49 Am J1st States § 54.

The state treasurer is not a trustee of moneys in the state treasury, but holds them only as the agent of the state. 49 Am J1st States § 54.

treasure-trove. Any gold or silver in coin, plate, or bullion found concealed in the earth or in a house or other private place, but not lying on the ground, the owner of such discovered treasure being unknown. 1 Am J2d Aband § 4.

treasury. The accumulation of funds of the nation, state, or other public body. An accumulation of valuables. A place for the safekeeping of funds or valuables.

Money is said to be in the treasury whenever and wherever it is in the official custody of the treasurer or subject to his direction and control. People v McKinney, 10 Mich 53, 88.

Treasury Department. An executive department of the United States Government, headed by the Secretary of the Treasury, and charged with the duties of the management and collection of revenue and the support of the public credit. 5 USC §§ 241 et seq; 54 Am J1st US § 49.

treasury note. A note issued by the United States Treasury and constituting legal tender.

treasury shares. Corporate stock which has been subscribed and paid for, but has thereafter been reacquired by the corporation by purchase, donation, forfeiture, or other means. 18 Am J2d Corp § 216.

treasury stock. Same as **treasury shares.**

treasury warrant. See **warrant.**

treat. To bestow by way of gift. To furnish by way of giving pleasure, as, for instance, drinks, cigars, food, and lodging. To bargain or negotiate with another. To act or behave toward another in a certain manner, for example, to act toward a child born out of wedlock as if it were one's own child, thereby acknowledging paternity. 10 Am J2d Bast § 52. To alleviate or seek to alleviate a condition, as to treat a wound. To perform work upon a material or a thing in order to render it fit for a purpose, as in treating metal.

treatise (trē'tis). A discussion of principles and the application thereof in a field of interest or concern, such as science, religion, law, government, or politics. 29 Am J2d Ev §§ 887 et seq.

treatment. The manner in which a person or a thing is treated. The behaviour of one spouse toward the other spouse. Robinson v Robinson, 66 NH 600, 23 A 362.

See **cruel and inhuman treatment.**

treatment endangering health or reason. A ground for divorce in some jurisdictions, consisting of conduct such as to result in actual injury to the health of the complaining spouse or such as to make it probable that an impairment of health or reason will result if the conduct is continued. 24 Am J2d Div & S § 38.

treatment endangering life. A ground for divorce in some jurisdictions, consisting of a course of conduct, whether violent or not, which, under the circumstances of the case, endangers life. Anno: 5 ALR 713.

treaty. A written contract between nations executed with the formality customary in dealings and transactions between nations, although not necessarily in a particular and prescribed form. A contract between nations for which the consent of the contracting parties is given expressly or tacitly, verbally or in writing. 52 Am J1st Treat § 5. A contract of reinsurance.

treaty power. The power to make treaties with foreign nations, such being given by the United States Constitution to the President acting with the advice and consent of the Senate, any treaty requiring the concurrence of two-thirds of the senators present. 52 Am J1st Treat § 7.

By the United States Constitution, the several states are prohibited from entering into any treaty, alliance, or confederation, and they shall not, without the consent of Congress, enter into a compact with another state or with a foreign power. US Const Art 1 § 10.

treaty trader. An alien entitled to enter the United States solely to carry on trade under and in pursuance of the provisions of an existing treaty between the country of which he is a national and the United States. Susuki v Harris (DC Tex) 29 F Supp 46.

treble costs. A term of art.

Where a statute gives "treble costs," they are to be calculated thus: 1. The common costs; 2, half of these; and then half of the latter. Van Auken v Decker, 2 NJL 108, 111.

treble damages. Multiple damages awarded under statutory authority for certain classes of wrongs, some courts regarding the excess of the award over the amount of injury actually sustained as an extraordinary liability imposed by way of penalty, others regarding it as an extraordinary liability imposed under a statute which is remedial and nonpunitive. 22 Am J2d Damg §§ 267, 268.

treble penalty. A sentence imposed upon one convicted as an habitual criminal equal to three times that imposed for a first offense. Anno: 58 ALR 99, s. 82 ALR 379, 116 ALR 236.

trebucket (trē'buk-et). Same as **ducking stool.**

tree. A woody plant with a trunk or stem from which branches spring. 34 Am J1st Logs § 2. A part and parcel of the land in which rooted. 42 Am J1st Prop § 19. An interest in real estate, except as to a tree growing in a nursery and raised to be sold and transplanted. 49 Am J1st Stat of F § 155. A piece of timber suitable for building and like purposes. Nettles v Lichtman, 228 Ala 52, 152 So 450, 91 ALR 1455.

See **boundary trees; bounded tree; line tree; nursery; timber.**

tree warden. A public functionary having care and control of the trees on the public grounds of a town. Markham v Middletown, 102 Conn 571, 129 A 524, 44 ALR 1475.

trench. A ditch. A long ditch prepared and used for concealment and cover by soldiers in combat.

trench digger. A man who digs trenches. A machine used in digging trenches, being equipped with motor for power. Wood v Food Fair Stores, Inc. 49 NJ Super 352, 139 A2d 805.

tres (trēz). Three.

tresayle (tres'āl). The grandfather of a person's grandfather; that is a person's great-great-grandfather. See 3 Bl Comm 186

Tres faciunt collegium (trēs fā'she-unt kol-le'ji-um). Three make a corporation; that is, three persons may form a corporation.

By the maxim, the Roman law required three persons to form a corporation, but after it was formed, it might continue to exist as a corporation although the members were reduced to one. See 1 Bl Comm 469.

tresor trouvé (trā'zor' trōvä'). Treasure trove.

trespass. A misfeasance, transgression, or offense which damages another's person, health, reputation, or property. Cox v Strickland, 120 Ga 104, 47 SE 912. In the widest application of the term, any transgression or offense against the laws of nature or society whether relating to person or property. Grunson v State, 89 Ind 533. The equivalent of tort or wrong. Bichenor v Hayes, 41 NJL 193. An unauthorized entry on another's property. Heller v New York, N.H. & H.R. Co. (CA2 NY) 265 F 192, 17 ALR 823, 825. A common-law form of action which lies for the recovery of damages inflicted by the direct application of force. An action which lies whenever an injury is the immediate result of the force originally applied by the defendant, and the plaintiff is injured thereby. 52 Am J1st Tresp § 2.

In its widest signification, trespass means any violation of law. In its most restricted sense, it signifies an injury intentionally inflicted by force either on the person or property of another. But still it has a signification in law much more narrow than the first, and more enlarged than the second meaning given, and embraces all cases where injury is done to the person or to property, and is the indirect result of wrongful force. Hill v Kimball, 76 Tex 210, 13 SW 59.

trespass ab initio (tres'pas ab i-ni'she-ō). A trespass from the beginning. A trespass by retrospective operation, the principle being that where an entry, authority, or license is conferred by law under which conduct otherwise constituting a trespass may be justified, an abuse of such authority will destroy the privilege and render the act done in excess of authority, a trespass from the beginning, that is, from the time of the entry. 52 Am J1st Tresp § 19.

trespass de bonis. Same as **trespass de bonis asportatis.**

trespass de bonis asportatis (tres'pas dē bō'nis aspor-tā'tis). The common-law form of action for the recovery of damages resulting from the taking of chattel property from the possession of the plaintiff. 52 Am J1st Tresp § 2.

trespass de uxore abducto (tres'pas dē u-xō're abduk'tō). An action of trespass for the abduction of the wife of the plaintiff. See 3 Bl Comm 139.

trespasser. A person who enters the premises of another without license, invitation, or other right, and intrudes for some definite purpose of his own, or at his convenience, or merely as an idler with no purpose apparent, other than, perhaps, to satisfy his curiosity. 38 Am J1st Negl § 109. A person who enters upon the land of another and who is neither suffered nor invited to enter. Anno: 36 ALR 37. In the broadest aspect of the term, one who has committed a trespass of any kind or nature.

trespass for mesne profits. A form of action supplemental to ejectment, brought against one wrongfully in possession to recover damages for the disturbance of the plaintiff's possession together with the profits which accrued during the wrongful possession. 52 Am J1st Tresp § 2.

trespass on the case. A common-law form of action, otherwise known as "case" and "action on the case," for an injury resulting from a wrongful act other than physical force, or for an injury resulting from nonfeasance or negligence, or for an injury which is consequential, as distinguished from a direct or immediate, result of the wrongful act. 52 Am J1st Tresp § 5. A remedy devised by the courts in remote times when actions were so carefully classified that a mistake in name was generally fatal to the case, its purpose being to cover new wrongs as they might occur so as to prevent a failure of justice.

1 Am J2d Actions § 22. Inclusive in the broad sense of the term of an action of assumpsit. 52 Am J1st Tresp § 6. More precisely, the remedy confined to actions for the redress of torts, the gravamen of the charge being the tort or wrong of the defendant, notwithstanding such tort or wrong may be also a breach of an express or implied contract. 1 Am J2d Actions § 22.

See **vis impressa.**

trespass per quod consortium amisit (tres'pas per quod kon-sor'she-um a-mī'sit). An action of trespass which lay where the defendant had assaulted or ill-used the wife whereby the plaintiff husband was deprived of her society. See 2 Bl Comm 140.

trespass per quod servitium amisit (tres'pas per quod ser-vi'she-um a-mī'sit). An action of trespass which lay where the defendant had assaulted or ill-used a servant of the plaintiff whereby plaintiff was deprived of his services. See 3 Bl Comm 142.

trespass quare clausum. Same as **trespass quare clausum fregit.**

trespass quare clausum fregit (tres'pas quā're klâsum frē'jit). The common-law remedy for the recovery of damages for the wrong of intruding upon the real property of another. 52 Am J1st Tresp § 2.

trespass to try title. An action to recover possession of real property and damages for any trespass committed upon such property by the defendant. 52 Am J1st Tresp § 2. An action displacing or supplementing the common-law action of ejectment in some jurisdictions. 25 Am J2d Eject § 4.

trespass vi et armis (tres'pas vī et ar'mis). The common-law remedy for the recovery of damages inflicted by the direct application of force. 52 Am J1st Tresp § 3.

See **vis impressa.**

trestle (tres'l). A wooden frame used by a carpenter or woodworker in combinations of two or more to support the boards upon which he works. A support of a bridge.

tret (tret). A deduction which is made for dust in weighing certain commodities.

triable (trī'a-bl). Capable of being tried; within the jurisdiction of the court.

trial. In common parlance, a test of one's physical or mental strength; a burden to be born; a test. In law, a judicial investigation and determination of the issues between the parties to an action. 53 Am J1st Trial § 2. An examination before a competent tribunal, according to the law of the land, of the facts or law put in issue in a cause, for the purpose of determining such issue. Finn v Spagnoli, 67 Cal 330, 332, 7 P 746. Technically, that step in an action by which issues or questions of fact are decided; often signifying a judicial examination of issues, whether of law or of fact. Columbus Packing Co. v State, 106 Ohio St 469, 140 NE 376, 37 ALR 1525. Sometimes inclusive of hearings upon motions attacking process or jurisdiction, as well as hearings upon motions attacking pleadings. 53 Am J1st Trial § 2. In its most comprehensive sense in reference to a criminal prosecution, inclusive of all the proceedings down to the acquittal or conviction of the accused. State v Hudson, 55 RI 141, 179 A 130, 100 ALR 313.

As to the stage of a trial at which the plaintiff may take a voluntary nonsuit or dismiss without prejudice, see Anno: 89 ALR 13.

The hearing of evidence after default in a divorce

proceeding is not a "trial," as that term is used in statutory provisions for new trial. Hamblin v Superior Court, 195 Cal 364, 233 P 337, 43 ALR 1509.

See **mistrial; public trial; summary trial.**

trial anew. Same as **trial de novo.**

trial at nisi prius. See **nisi prius.**

trial balance. A recapitulation of debit and credit balances of all open accounts of the business. Rosenthal v Dickerman, 98 Mich 208, 57 NW 112.

trial by battel. Same as **trial by wager of battel.**

trial by certificate (bī ser-tif'i-kāt). A form of trial which was allowed in cases where the evidence of the person certifying was the only proper criterion of the point in dispute.

Such trials were permitted to save trouble and circuity in cases where the evidence must have been conclusive if submitted to a jury. See 3 Bl Comm 333.

trial by court. See **trial by the court.**

trial by fire. An ancient form of trial in criminal cases, in which the accused was required to carry in his hand a piece of red-hot iron weighing from one to three pounds, or else to walk barefoot and blindfold over nine red-hot plough-shares, laid lengthwise at equal distances.

If he escaped unhurt, he was acquitted, but if otherwise, as was usually the case, he was adjudged guilty. See 4 Bl Comm 342.

trial by inspection. A trial by the judges, not by a jury, of some single matter which was obvious to sight. Roberts v Ogdensburgh & Lake Champlain Railroad Co. (NY) 29 Hun 154, 156.

In former times, the English courts of common law might, if they saw fit, try by inspection or examination, without a jury, the question of the infancy, or of the identity of a party; or, on an appeal of mayhem, the issue of mayhem or no mayhem; and, in an action of trespass for mayhem, or for an atrocious battery, might after a verdict for the plaintiff, and on his motion, and upon their own inspection of the wound, super visum vulneris, increase the damages at their discretion. In each of those exceptional cases, it was not thought necessary to call a jury to decide it, because the fact, from its nature, was deemed evident to the court, either from ocular demonstration or other irrefragible proof. The inspection was not had for the purpose of submitting the result to the jury; the question was thought too easy to require such submission. Union Pacific Railway Co. v Botsford, 141 US 250, 35 L Ed 734, 737, 11 S Ct 1000.

trial by jury. A trial in which the jurors are the judges of the facts and the court is the judge of the law. State ex rel. Rhodes v Saunders, 66 NH 39, 25 A 588. A matter of constitutional or statutory right to a trial by a legal, proper, fair, and impartial jury drawn from a cross section of the community. 31 Am J Rev ed Jury §§ 7 et seq.

A constitutional right to trial by jury "in all cases in which it has been heretofore used," does not extend to a suit in equity, even where, as incidental to the main relief sought, the complainant asks money damages. Jamaica Sav. Bank v M. S. Investing Co. 274 NY 215, 8 NE2d 493, 112 ALR 1485. The Seventh Amendment providing that in suits at common law where the value in controversy shall exceed $20 the right of trial by jury shall be preserved, has no application to cases where the recovery of money damages is an incident to equitable relief, even though damages might have been recovered in an action at law. NLRB v Jones & L. Steel Corp. 301 US 1, 81 L Ed 893, 57 S Ct 615, 108 ALR 1352.

See **jury.**

trial by ordeal (bī ôr'dēl). See **ordeal.**

trial by proviso. A proceeding whereby the defendant in an action undertakes to bring the cause to trial upon the failure of the plaintiff to do so.

trial by purgation (per-gā'shọn). See **corsned; purgation.**

trial by record (bī rek'ọrd). The trial of an issue arising on the record of an action, without a jury and without taking any testimony.

trial by the country. A trial of an accused by a jury of his peers.

See **jury of the country.**

trial by the court. A trial held before one or more judges without a jury. Air-way Electric Appliance Corp. v Day, 266 US 42, 70, 69 L Ed 162, 169, 45 S Ct 18.

See **trial by inspection.**

trial by the iron. Same as **trial by fire.**

trial by wager of battel (bī wā'jer of bat'l). A duel or combat which in ancient times was sanctioned by law as a form of trial, in which champions, in civil actions, represented the parties, under the superstition that the right would triumph.

The last trial by battel on record was in 1638. See 3 Bl Comm 337, et seq.

trial by wager of law (of lâ). A species of trial anciently used in civil actions, wherein the defendant gave pledges or sureties that he would wage his law; that is, that he would appear at the time set when he would make oath as to his innocence and would produce compurgators, witnesses in his behalf, who would swear that they believed his oath. See 3 Bl Comm 341.

trial by water (bī wâ'ter). A trial by water-ordeal, which was performed either by plunging the defendant's bare arm up to the elbow in boiling water, or by casting him into a pool of water.

If he escaped harm from the boiling water, or sank in the plunge, he was deemed innocent and acquitted, but if he was scalded by the hot water, or if he floated when thrown into the pool, he was adjudged guilty. See 4 Bl Comm 343.

trial counsel. A trial lawyer. A lawyer assisting the attorney of record in the trial of a case. The prosecuting counsel in a general or special court-martial.

trial de nova. (trī'al dē nō'vō). A new trial; a new trial on appeal. 4 Am J2d A & E § 2. A trial on appeal from a justice of the peace to a court of general jurisdiction. 31 Am J Rev ed J P § 129. Trying anew the matter involved in an administrative determination the same as if it had not been heard before and as if no decision had been previously rendered, the hearing being upon the record made before the administrative agency and such further evidence as either party may see fit to produce. 2 Am J2d Admin L § 698.

See **new trial; new trial on appeal.**

trial examiner. A hearing officer of an administrative agency, comparable to an auditor or special master of a court. Annotation: 89 ALR 426, s. 171 ALR 782; 2 Am J2d Admin L § 407. An officer of the National Labor Relations Board who conducts

hearings and receives evidence in proceedings under the National Labor Relations Act. 31 Am J Rev ed Lab § 297.

trial judge. A judge who presides at the trial of a cause.

trial jury. A jury for the trial of a case, as distinguished from a grand jury which returns an indictment. 31 Am J Rev ed Jury § 2.
See **jury.**

trial marriage. A marriage entered into under agreement that either or both parties shall have the option of annulling it. 4 Am J2d Annul § 7. A concept incidentally elucidated in "The Monastery" by Sir Walter Scott.

trial minutes. See **minutes.**

trial per pais (trī'al pėr pā). A term of ancient usage for trial by the peers of the party accused. 31 Am J Rev ed Jury § 7. Trial by jury.

trial per testes (per tes'tēz). A trial by witnesses testifying before the court, without a jury.

trial record. The record of the proceedings in a case in the trial court.

trial term. That part of the business of a court which is devoted to jury trials.

trial to begin anew. To begin again the examination of the matter of fact in issue in the trial. 31 Am J Rev ed Jury § 128.

triare (trī-ā're). To try.

triatio (trī-ā'she-ō). A trial.

Triatio ibi semper debet fieri, ubi juratores meliorem possunt habere notitiam (trī-ā'she-o i'bi sem'per dē'-bet fī'e-ri; u'bi ju-ra-tō-rēz me-li-ō'rem pos'sunt hā-bē're no-ti'she-am). A trial ought always to be had where the jury can have the better information.

tribe. See **Indian tribe.**

Tribonian. A lawyer of Rome, who, with other lawyers, under the auspices of the Emperor Justinian compiled the present body of civil law, about 533 A.D. See 1 Bl Comm 81.

tribunal. A court. The seat or bench for the judge or judges of a court.

tributary. A stream which empties into or feeds another stream, as in the case of the Missouri River and the Mississippi River.
In a general sense a stream is tributary to a river when the stream empties into another river which empties into that river. Miller v Insurance Co. 12 W Va 116.

tribute (trib'ūt). A tax which is imposed by a sovereign upon his subjects; a tax which is imposed by one nation upon another nation.

trichinosis (tri-kīnō'sis). A disease centered in the intestine, usually resulting from the eating of pork insufficiently cooked to be purified of means of infection. Mouren v Great Atlantic & Pacific Tea Co. 1 App Div 2d 767, 148 NYS2d 1.

trick. An artifice.
See **larceny by trick.**

tricycle. A small vehicle having three wheels and propelled by foot power, used as a plaything by children, preferably on the sidewalk. 7 Am J2d Auto § 4.

triennial cohabitation. See **triennial test.**

triennial test (trī-en'i-al test). The old rule of the English ecclesiastical courts known as the rule of triennial cohabitation, which required a husband and wife to live together for three years, and if at the end of that time the marriage remained unconsummated, or the wife appeared to be a virgin, impotence was presumed.
In modern times in England the rule has been held not to apply where the court is satisfied of the husband's impotence by other evidence. Anno: 28 ALR2d 514, § 6.
There is some American authority expressly rejecting, and other American authority, expressly adopting, the triennial test. Anno: 28 ALR2d 514, § 6; 24 Am J2d Div & S § 358.

triens (trī'enz). The third part; dower. See 2 Bl Comm 129.

trientes (trī-en'tēz). Four per cent per annum.
The Romans at one time allowed centesimae, one per cent monthly, or twelve per cent per annum, to be taken as interest for common loans; but Justinian reduced this to trientes, or one third of the centesimae, that is four per cent. But he allowed a higher rate to be taken from merchants because of the greater hazard. See 2 Bl Comm 462.

triers (trī'ėrs). Persons appointed by the court to try a challenge for favor. The respective functions of court and jury. 53 Am J1st Trial § 156.

trifling. Verb: Making play of another's affections. Adjective: Trivial. Paltry. Of little value; of little moment.
Under the rule that an injunction will be denied where the injury complained of is of a trifling character which may be readily compensated by the allowance of damages, the word "trifling" means trifling per se and not trifling as compared with the injury which would result to the defendant from the granting of the injunction. Anno: 61 ALR 925.
Under the principle that an injured party is required to prevent or lessen his damages if he can do so at a reasonable cost, or as commonly stated: "He must protect himself if he can do so at trifling expense," the word "trifling" has reference to the situation of the parties. It means a sum which is trifling in comparison with the consequential damages which the plaintiff seeks to recover in the particular case. So, a property owner is not required to make expenditures, which in proportion to the injury threatened are considerable, for the purpose of protecting his property. It seems that want of sufficient funds will excuse his absence of effort to lessen damages. 22 Am J2d Damg § 32.

trigamist (trig'a-mist). See **trigamus.**

trigamus (trig'a-mus). A trigamist; a person who has been lawfully married to three different wives, one at a time.

trim. Verb: To put in order; to make neat. To balance a load or cargo. To decorate. To clip. To castrate. Noun: Woodwork around the windows and doors of a building. A position in which stage lights are placed for most effective and appropriate illumination.
As applied to a canal boat, "trimming" is shoveling the grain from one place to another on the boat, and this is done by longshoremen with scoops or shovels. "Trimming" a ship's cargo when loading is stowing it and securing it for the voyage. See Budd v New York, 143 US 517, 530, 36 L Ed 247, 250, 12 S Ct 468.

trimming trees. Cutting branches off trees to improve the appearance or to prevent interference with telephone or electric wires.

trim ship (trim ship). See **trim.**

trina admonitio (trī'na ad-mo-ni'she-ō). The third warning.
This was the final warning given to a prisoner who stood mute, before putting him on the rack to compel him to confess his crime. See 4 Bl Comm 325.

Trinity. The Father, Son, and Holy Spirit or Holy Ghost. The first Sunday following Pentecost.
The three series of annotated state reports, comprising American Decisions in one hundred volumes, covering the period from 1765 to 1869, American Reports in sixty volumes, covering the period from 1869 to 1887, and American State Reports in one hundred and forty volumes, covering the period from 1887 to 1911.

Trinity term (tėrm). An English term of court beginning May 22nd and ending June 12th.

trinket (tring'ket). An ornament or plaything, rather than a thing of utility.
Bracelets, shirt pins, rings, and brooches,—they are clearly articles of personal decoration and adornment, and literally fall within the description of trinkets. See Ocean S.S. Co. v Way, 90 Ga 747, 17 SE 57.

trinoda necessitas (trī-nō'da ne-ses'si-tas). The threefold necessity. The three burdens to which all free householders, if not all freemen were subject under the ancient laws of England.
These were the duty of rendering military service against an enemy, the duty of assisting in the construction of castles or forts, and the duty of keeping bridges in repair. Butler v Perry, 240 US 328, 331, 60 L Ed 672, 674, 36 S Ct 258.

triode (trī'ōd). A vacuum tube employed in the amplification of radio waves. Lewis v Smith (CA7 Ill) 228 F2d 926.

triors (trī'ors). Same as **triers.**

trip. A journey, voyage, or excursion. A stumble.
See **round trip.**

tripartite (trip'är-tīt or trī-pär'tīt). In three parts; having three parties, as, a tripartite contract.

tripartite contract (trī-pär'tīt kọn'trakt). A contract having parties of the first, second, and third parts.
See **third-party beneficiary contract.**

triple damages. See **treble damages.**

triple letter. A letter of three sheets. Williams v Wells, Fargo & Co. Express (CA8 Ark) 177 F 352.

triplicatio (trip-li-kā'she-ō). A Roman law pleading corresponding to the common law sur-rejoinder, being the actor's reply to the defendant's duplicatio. See 3 Bl Comm 310.

triplication (trip-li-kā'shọn). An ecclesiastical law pleading corresponding to a common law rejoinder.

trip permit. A temporary license for the operation of a vehicle as a motor carrier. 7 Am J2d Auto § 90.

trithing (trī'thing). Old terminology for a division of a county or shire.
Where a county or shire was divided into three intermediate jurisdictions, they were called trithings and were anciently governed by a trithing-reeve. Having survived in the county of York, their name became corrupted into "ridings;" the north, the east, and the west riding. See 1 Bl Comm 116.

trithing-reeve (trithing-rēv). See **trithing.**

triverbial days (tri-vėr'bi-al dās). The twenty-eight judicial days in each year which the Roman law allowed to the praetor for deciding cases. These days were called triverbial because upon them the praetor was permitted the use of the three words "Do dico, addico," I give judgment, I expound the law, I execute the law. See 3 Bl Comm 424, and footnote.

trivial error. Immaterial error; harmless error. 5 Am J2d A & E § 776.

trolley. A streetcar; a streetcar line. Any railway propelled by electric power and running over a route limited in length, often between a city and its suburbs or neighboring cities.

trolley pole. A pole upon which the electric wires which carry the current for propelling a streetcar or trolley are affixed and carried.

tronage (tron'ạj). An ancient toll charged for the weighing of wool.

troops. Soldiers; officers and men in any branch of the military forces. Louisville & N. R. Co. v United States, 258 US 374, 66 L Ed 668, 42 S Ct 337.
In 1850 the word had, and it has ever since had an established meaning:—namely, "soldiers collectively,—a body of soldiers." Contemporary legislation draws a clear distinction also between "troops," that is, those having the status of soldiers, and those who once had been in, or were seeking to enter the military service. United States v Union Pacific Railroad Co. 249 US 354, 357, 63 L Ed 643, 645, 39 S Ct 294.

trophy (trō'fi). Something taken as a symbol of victory, for example, the football used in a football game. In an older time, the head of a defeated opponent.

tropical year. The interval between two consecutive returns of the sun to the vernal equinox.

trove (trōv). Found.
See **treasure-trove.**

trover (trō'vėr). The common-law action for the recovery of damages for the conversion of personal property. 18 Am J2d Conversion § 1.

troy weight (troi wāt). The measure employed in weighing gold, silver, and precious jewels, characterized by grains, pennyweight, and ounces troy, twelve of such ounces making one pound troy.

truancy. The act of a child of school age in wilfully avoiding attendance at school. The act of a child in deserting his home or place of abode. 31 Am J Rev ed Juv Ct § 36. Neglect of work.

truant. Broadly, one who is in a state of truancy. A pupil absent from school without the permission of his parent. Holmes v Nester, 81 Ariz 372, 306 P2d 290, 62 ALR2d 1322.
The cases present differing views as to what constitutes a truant from school. Anno: 62 ALR2d 1328.
See **truancy.**

truant officer. See **attendance officer.**

truce (trös). An agreement made between belligerents that they will temporarily cease hostilities.

Truce of God. An armistice proclaimed by the church in medieval times.

truck. A large vehicle used in the transportation of goods, propelled by motor. A low platform on wheels used in factories and warehouses for carrying goods, especially heavy articles. Garden produce.
See **pick-up truck.**

Truck Acts. Statutes regulating the medium in which wages are payable. 31 Am J Rev ed Lab § 822.

As early as the fourteenth century, laws in England prohibited the payment of wages, in certain trades, in anything but lawful money of the realm; and in 1831, all of these laws were consolidated into what is known as the Truck Act, embracing nearly all classes of trades. The purpose of this legislation was the abolition of what was known in that country as the Truck System, that is to say, the payment of wages to laborers in goods or by truck. Similar legislation in the United States has been held constitutional.

trucker. One who drives a truck. A company engaged in the business of hauling goods for others. One engaged in truck farming.

truck farming. The growing of vegetables, a kind of agriculture. 58 Am J1st Workm Comp § 97.

truckman. See **trucker**.

Truck System. See **Truck Acts**.

true. In accord with fact, with the actual state of things. Honest; sincere. Reliable. Moulor v American Life Ins. Co. 111 US 335, 345, 28 L Ed 447, 451, 4 S Ct 466. Real, genuine, as a true plumber. Andrews v Peck, 83 Conn 666, 78 A 445.
See **half truth**.

true admission. A judicial admission, that is, an admission made by a party in the course of judicial proceedings. 29 Am J2d Ev § 597.

true bill. An indictment found by the concurrence of the requisite number of grand jurors, as indicated by the indorsement of the words "true bill" on the instrument. 27 Am J1st Indict § 30.

true cash value. The value which property has, as used, and by reason of its use. Pittsburg, Cincinnati, Chicago & St. Louis Railway Co. v Backus, 154 US 421, 430, 38 L Ed 1031, 1037, 14 S Ct 1114.
See **actual cash value**.

true construction. The rule of construction in ascertaining the intent of the parties as revealed in the language of the instrument and, as necessary in a proper case, in interpreting such language in the light of the surrounding circumstances.

In construing contracts, recourse must first be had to the language of the instrument. A true construction of the words or phrases used is the touchstone of legal right. They are to be interpreted according to their strict and primary acceptation unless from the context of the instrument and the intention of the parties to be collected from it as they appear to be used in a different sense, the cardinal rule always being to give effect to the intention of the parties in the light of the surrounding circumstances. Prudential Ins. Co. v Nelson (CA6 Tenn) 101 F2d 441.

true copy. An exact copy of a written instrument.

true estate. The estate of a decedent for local probate purposes, not necessarily the estate for federal estate tax purposes. Hooker v Drayton, 69 RI 290, 33 A2d 206, 150 ALR 723.

true in every spot and place. A broad warranty of soundness, particularly in reference to a horse. Andrews v Peck, 83 Conn 666, 78 A 445.

true man doctrine. The rule that one subjected to a felonious assault which produces imminent danger to him of death or great bodily harm is not required to retreat but may stand his ground, repel force by force, and if, in the reasonable exercise of his right of self-defense, he kills his assailant, he is justified. 26 Am J1st Homi § 151.

true meridian (trö me-ri'di-an). A great circle of the earth running through the geographical poles. A meridian according to which the boundary lines of public lands of the United States are to be run in surveying. 43 USC § 751; 12 Am J2d Bound § 10.

true party in interest. Same as **real party in interest**.

true value. See **full and true value**.

true verdict. A verdict which represents the conclusion of the jury as reached where each juror has given honest consideration to the rights of the parties litigant, or the accused, as the case may be, and has exercised his best judgment, guided by the law and the weight of the evidence introduced at the trial. 53 Am J1st Trial § 1028.

truly. In a true manner. Faithfully.
See **fairly; true**.

trunk line. The main line of a railroad. The main line of a public utility.
See **trunk railway**.

trunk line sewer. A sewer having lateral branches.

trunk railway. A commercial railway connecting towns, cities, counties, or other points within the state or in different states, which has the legal capacity, under its charter or the general law, of constructing, purchasing, and operating branch lines or feeders connecting with its main stem or trunk, the main or trunk line bearing the same relation to its branches that the trunk of a tree bears to its branches, or the main stream of a river to its tributaries. Diebold v Kentucky Traction Co. 117 Ky 146, 77 SW 674.

trust. Noun: A fiduciary relationship; a matter of confidence. 54 Am J1st Trusts § 4. A confidential relationship involving a trustee, beneficiary, and a res consisting in property. 54 Am J1st Trusts § 4. The legal relationship between one person having an equitable ownership in property and another person owning the legal title to such property, the equitable ownership of the former entitling him to the performance of certain duties and the exercise of certain powers by the latter, which performance can be compelled in a court of equity or a court which follows equitable principles. 54 Am J1st Trust § 4. The separation of the same estate into parts, legal and equitable, the owner of either part being entitled to the aid of the court in establishing and enforcing his rights. McDonogh v Murdoch (US) 15 How 367, 14 L Ed 732. A monopoly. State ex rel. Watson v Standard Oil Co. 49 Ohio St 137, 30 NE 279. Verb: To have confidence in a person; to extend credit to a person. Putnal v Inman, 76 Fla 553, 80 So 316, 3 ALR 1580.

The word is often employed in law, as well as in popular language, in a sense which is much broader than its ordinary technical significance, as denoting or as synonymous with confidence, fiduciary relationship, etc., and it is often used in reference to the confidential aspect of any kind of a bailment or possession by one person of the property of another. In its literal significance the word "trust" implies nurturing and sheltering of a sacred confidence. In its more technical significance, the word still implies such confidence in a relationship which involves a trustee, beneficiary, and a res. 55 Am J1st Trusts § 4.

As the word is used in the law pertaining to unlawful combinations and monopolies, a "trust" in its original and typical form is a combination formed by an agreement among the stockholders in a number of competing corporations to transfer their shares to an unincorporated board of trustees, and to receive in exchange trust certificates in some agreed proportion to their stockholdings. By popular development the word has come to signify any combination, whether of producers or vendors of a commodity, for the purpose of controlling prices and suppressing competition, so that all contracts, agreements, and schemes whereby those who are competitors combine to regulate prices are called "trusts." 36 Am J1st Monop etc § 19.

trust allotment to Indians. See **restricted allotment.**

trust company. A corporation, usually engaged in a general banking business, and in particular as a compensated trustee of funds or property. A bank for purposes of regulation. 10 Am J2d Banks § 11.

trust deed. See **deed of trust; trust.**

trust deposit. A deposit in a bank in trust for the benefit of a person other than the depositor.

trust de son tort (trust de son tôrt). See **trustee de son tort.**

trustee. That person in a trust relationship who holds the legal title to the property subject to the trust, for the benefit of the beneficiary or cestui que trust, with certain powers and subject to certain duties imposed by the terms of the trust, principles of equity, or statutory provision. 54 Am J1st Trusts § 112. The person to whom property is conveyed by a deed of trust given by way of security. The title of some public officers, such as township trustees and members of the board of a state, county, or municipal college or university. 15 Am J2d Colleges § 11.

Every man to whom a business is entrusted by another has a trust to perform; and every man is a trustee who is to advise concerning, or to operate, the business of another. Quinn v Thipps, 93 Fla 805, 113 So 419, 54 ALR 1173.

trustee de son tort (trus-tē de son tôrt). A trustee by reason of one's own wrong. Morris v Joseph, 1 W Va 256. One charged as a constructive trustee by reason of his own wrong. 54 Am J1st Trusts § 218. In effect, a **trustee ex maleficio.**

trustee ex delicto (trus-tē ex de-lik'tō.) One charged as constructive trustee because of his own wrong. 54 Am J1st Trusts § 218.

See **trustee de son tort; trustee ex maleficio; trustee in invitum.**

trustee ex maleficio (ex ma-le-fi'she-ō). A trustee from wrongdoing; the trustee of a trust arising by operation of law from a wrongful acquisition. A person charged as a constructive trustee because without right he has entered into possession or assumed the management of property belonging to another. Morris v Joseph, 1 W Va 256.

See **constructive trust.**

trustee in bankruptcy. One to whom the administration of a bankrupt estate is delegated and confided. 9 Am J2d Bankr § 621.

The Bankruptcy Act specifies either one or three trustees for a bankrupt estate, and there is nothing in the Bankruptcy Act or the General Orders which supports the appointment of two or more than three trustees for an estate. Whenever three trustees have been appointed, the concurrence of at least two of them is necessary to the validity of their acts concerning the administration of the estate. 9 Am J2d Bankr § 623.

See **official trustee.**

trustee of express trust. A trustee duly appointed or designated, as distinguished from a trustee de son tort or a trustee under a constructive trust.

The term includes a person with whom, or in whose name, a contract is made for the benefit of another. Muncie Natural Gas Co. v Muncie, 160 Ind 97, 66 NE 436.

trustee process. A remedy akin to garnishment, that is, a proceeding whereby property, money or credits of a debtor in possession of another, the garnishee, are applied to the payment of the debts by means of process against the debtor and garnishee. Pennsylvania Railroad Co. v Rogers, 52 W Va 450, 44 SE 300. The remedy of garnishment. 6 Am J2d Attach § 2.

truster. The maker or creator of a trust. Sometimes applied to the person upon whom a trust is conferred. Interallied Commercial Co. v Standard Beryllium Corp. 39 Misc 2d 269, 240 NYS2d 433.

trust estate. The res of a trust. The fund or property held by the trustee for the benefit of the cestui que trust.

The expression seems to be used with some confusion in the books. Sometimes it is employed to express the estate of the trustee, and sometimes that of the cestui que trust. Cooper v Cooper, 6 NJ Eq 9, 12.

trust ex delicto. See **trustee ex delicto.**

trust ex maleficio (trust ex ma-le-fi'she-ō). See **trustee ex maleficio.**

trust for value. A trust created by the trustor in return for a valuable and adequate consideration.

trust fund. A fund held in trust by a trust company or other trustee.

See **following trust fund or property; special deposit.**

trust fund doctrine. The principle, commonly known as the American doctrine, that the property of a corporation must be appropriated to the payment of debts before any assets are distributed among stockholders. Wood v Dummer (CC Me) 3 Mason 308, F Cas No 17944; Hospes v Northwestern Mfg. & Car Co. 48 Minn 174, 50 NW 1117. Sometimes stated broadly as meaning that the assets of a corporation constitute a trust fund for the benefit of its creditors. 19 Am J2d Corp § 1021. The equitable principle that the assets of an insolvent corporation become, from the date of its assured insolvency, a trust fund for equal distribution among its creditors, so that thereafter none of them can obtain priority by levy of or by recovering a judgment and levying an execution against the corporation. 19 Am J2d Corp § 1579. The principle that the capital stock of a corporation, at least, of an insolvent corporation, is in equity a trust fund for the payment of its creditors, regardless of whether it has been paid into the company or exists in the form of unpaid instalments upon stock subscriptions. 19 Am J2d Corp § 722. The doctrine under which subscribers to stock in a corporation are liable for a balance due on their unpaid subscriptions after the dissolution of the corporation, although the subscriptions were obtained fraudulently and although the charter of the corporation was annulled, revoked, and cancelled for fraud practiced on the state in securing the articles of incorporation. State ex rel. Havner v Associated Packing Co. 216 Iowa 1053, 90 ALR 1339, 249 NW 761.

As to whether the insolvency of the corporation precludes the rescission of a subscription contract on the ground of fraud practiced upon the subscriber, see 18 Am J2d Corp § 336.

trust fund immunity. The principle that while a charity is not immune from liability in tort or from suit where it is sought to impose a tort liability upon it, the trust property or funds by which it is supported or maintained cannot be reached by execution under a judgment obtained against it in an action to recover damages for a tort. 15 Am J2d Char § 157.

trust fund theory. See **trust fund doctrine; trust fund immunity.**

trust indenture. An instrument which states the terms and conditions of a trust, such as a pension trust or a trust created by way of security for a bond issue.

Trust Indenture Act. A federal statute of 1939 having a purpose comparable to that of other federal securities legislation, namely to afford the public protection in connection with securities. 15 USC §§ 77aaa etc.

trusting. In some contexts, a precatory word operating in the creation of a trust. Anno: 49 ALR 81.

trusting and believing. In some contexts, a precatory expression operating in the creation of a trust. Anno: 49 ALR 82.

trusting and confiding. In some contexts, a precatory expression operating in the creation of a trust. Anno: 49 ALR 81.

trust in invitum (in in-vī'tum). A trust raised by operation of law without the consent of the trustee.

Such a trust arises where goods have been stolen or converted to the use of the taker and sold, with respect to the proceeds, whether such proceeds are in the form of money or other property purchased therewith, and equity will in such cases enforce a trust in invitum in the original taker or in his assignee with notice. Likewise, where a trustee or other fiduciary has misapplied trust funds a like trust will be raised. Lightfoot v Davis, 198 NY 261, 91 NE 582.

See **trustee de son tort.**

trust inter vivos (trust in'ter vī'vos). A trust which becomes effective during the life of the settlor; in other words, a living trust. 54 Am J1st Trusts § 5.

trustor (trus'tor). The grantor, creator, maker, or settlor of a trust.

trust patent to Indians. See **restricted allotment.**

trust power. A power of appointment or disposal to be exercised by the donee of the power for the benefit of one other than himself. 41 Am J1st Pow § 3.

Trust powers are imperative and their performance may be compelled in equity. In every case where the trust is valid as a power, the lands to which the trust relates remain in or descend to the person otherwise entitled, subject to the execution of the trust as a power. Tilden v Green, 130 NY 29, 28 NE 880.

trust pursuit rule. The following of trust property wrongfully converted by the fiduciary for the purpose of compelling restitution to the beneficiary. 54 Am J1st Trusts § 248.

See **following trust fund or property.**

trust receipt. A security transaction intended to aid in financing importers and retail dealers who do not have sufficient resources to finance the importation or purchase of merchandise, and who may be unable to acquire credit except through utilization as collateral of the merchandise imported or purchased. 53 Am J1st Tr Rec § 1. A comparatively modern instrument of security protecting a bank or finance company for money advanced or credit given for the purchase of goods by a dealer, the bank or finance company receiving title from the manufacturer and taking from the dealer a statement that he holds the goods in trust for the bank or finance company, it being contemplated by the transaction that the dealer will resell the goods and repay the bank or finance company, and that the ultimate buyer or consumer will obtain clear title. 47 Am J1st Sales § 838; 53 Am J1st Tr Rec § 2.

Trust Receipts Act. One of the uniform statutes. Repealed by the Commercial Code. 15 Am J2d Com C § 6.

trust relationship. See **fiduciary relation; trust.**

truth. The state of being true.
See **true.**

truth drug. Same as **truth serum.**

truth serum (tröth sē'rum). A drug used with some success in testing an accused on the question of insanity or sex deviation but not as yet determined to be a reliable and accurate means of ascertaining truth or deception. 29 Am J2d Ev § 830.

try a case. See **trial.**

try and decide. See **hear and determine.**

tuberculin test. A method of testing cows for tuberculosis, provided by statute as a health measure for insuring a pure supply of milk. 22 Am J1st Food § 72.

tuberculosis (tu̇-bėr-kụ-lō'sis). A serious disease, involving the formation of nodules in tissues of the body, particularly of the lungs, but yielding to modern medical treatment commenced before it has reached an advanced stage. 29 Am J Rev ed Ins § 745.

tubman (tub'man). A barrister of experience in the court of exchequer. See 3 Bl Comm 28, note.

Tucker Act. A federal statute in reference to jurisdiction of certain actions brought against the United States. 28 USC § 1346.

tug. Same as **tugboat.**

tugboat. A watercraft used to tow or accelerate the progress of another vessel in some manner. 48 Am J1st Ship § 488. A small but powerful vessel employed for towing other vessels. See Phoenix Ins. Co. v The Atlas, 93 US 302, 23 L Ed 863. A vessel employed for pushing as well as pulling other vessels.

tuition. A fee charged a student at a college or university for the privilege of attendance at the institution. 15 Am J2d Colleges § 18. A charge sometimes imposed on a pupil in a public school because of his nonresidence, and sometimes paid by the district of his residence. 47 Am J1st Sch § 154.

tulit (tū'lit). He brought.

tumbrel (tum'brel). A cart. Another term for **ducking stool.**

tumult (tū'mult). An uproar. Commotion or confusion, usually involving noise.

tumultuous assembly. An assembly conducted with disorder, noise, and confusion.
    An assemblage of a thousand people in the main street of a city, obstructing the use of the street, discharging bombs, skyrockets, Roman candles, and other missiles loaded with powerful explosives, at private property, endangering life and preventing the use of the street for purposes of business, is a tumultuous assembly. Madisonville v Bishop, 113 Ky 106, 67 SW 269.

tumultuous petitioning. An offense in the nature of a riot, in violation of the statute 13 Charles II, st. 1, c. 5 (1661) providing that not more than twenty names shall be signed to any petition to the king or either house of parliament for any change in the laws, unless previously approved by the public officers named in the statute. See 4 Bl Comm 147.

tun (tun). The Anglo-Saxon word from which our word "town" derived.

tunc (tunk). Then; at that time.
    See **nunc pro tunc.**

tunnel. An underground way. The excavation made in a mine for the purpose of exploring for or reaching a vein or lode of mineral. 36 Am J1st Min & M § 72.

tunnel location. A term of mining men. The right to drive a tunnel beneath the surface in making an exploration for the discovery of minerals, and, in the event of the discovery of mineral in such manner, to appropriate veins or lodes thereof, not previously known to exist, within a limited distance from the tunnel. 36 Am J1st Min & M § 72.

turbary (tèr'bạ-ri). See **common of turbary.**

turbulence (tèr'bū-lęns). Air in violent motion creating a condition of concern to an air pilot. 8 Am J2d Avi § 93.

turf (tèrf). Sod. A layer of earth with grass growing upon it and the roots of the grass matted within it. A track for horse racing.
    See **common of turbary.**

turf and twig (tèrf and twig). A clod of turf, or a twig or bough growing on the land, the usual symbolic means by which livery of seisin was effected, one of these being delivered on the land by the feoffor to the feoffee. See 2 Bl Comm 315.

turf exchange. A place where patrons congregate and bet on horse races run at another place. James v State, 4 Okla Crim 587, 112 P 944.

turn. A gate or bar on a turnpike or toll road at which tolls are collected. 54 Am J1st Turn & T R § 2. A change in the direction of movement. A development.

turning. The manipulation of a motor vehicle in changing direction. 7 Am J2d Auto § 216.

turning lights. Lights on a motor vehicle to be used as signals in turning. 7 Am J2d Auto § 157.

turning out by the heels. A jocular term for physical ouster from possession of real estate. 3 Am J2d Adv P § 174.

turning signal. The signal to be given by the driver of a vehicle upon the highway in advance of making a turn, as a warning to approaching or following vehicles. 7 Am J2d Auto § 217.

turning state's evidence. Voluntarily giving testimony against those with whom one participated in the commission of a crime, the testimony implicating one's self, but given in the hope of avoiding prosecution of self or of receiving a light sentence. 58 Am J1st Witn § 525.

turn-key drilling. See **turn-key job.**

turn-key job. An expression of the construction industry, meaning a complete house, one ready for occupancy by the owner as a dwelling. 13 Am J2d Bldg Contr § 10. A term with a fixed and definite meaning in the oil industry.
    On such a job the driller of an oil well undertakes to furnish everything and does all the work required to complete the well, place it on production, and turn it over ready to "turn the key" and start the oil running into the tanks. Walker v Chitty (CA6 Ohio) 112 F2d 79; Retsal Drilling Co. v Commissioner (CA5 Tex) 127 F2d 355.

turnout (tèrn'out). A siding or sidetrack branching out from the main line or track of a railroad. Appeal of River Front Railroad, 133 Pa 134, 19 A 356, 357.

turnover. A business term for the employment of assets in a series of acts, as buying a stock of particular merchandise, such as shoes, selling it out, and then replenishing the stock by another purchase. Park Amusement Co. v McCaughn (DC Pa) 14 F2d 553.

turnover order. An order rendered in a proceeding supplementary to judgment and execution requiring the judgment debtor to turn over for application to the satisfaction of the judgment property subject to execution, in his possession or under his control, disclosed in the supplementary proceeding. 30 Am J2d Exec § 838. An order in a turnover proceeding in bankruptcy, the terms of which call for the delivery of property of the bankrupt to the trustee in bankruptcy. 9 Am J2d Bankr § 1150.

turnover proceeding. A summary proceeding in a court of bankruptcy brought for the purpose of summarily retrieving for the trustee in bankruptcy, who is entitled thereto, assets concealed and diverted from him, the efficacy of such proceeding appearing in the fact that the withholding of such assets pending the outcome of plenary suits to recover them would intolerably obstruct and delay administration of the bankrupt estate. 9 Am J2d Bankr §§ 1137 et seq.

turnpike. A highway for the use of which a toll is charged; a highway which is distinctive in the respect that one who refuses to pay the toll may be turned back as of right. 54 Am J1st Turn & T R § 2. In loose usage, an improved highway.

turnpike corporation. A private corporation engaged in operating a turnpike or toll road.

turnpike road. Same as **turnpike.**

turnstile. (tèrn'stīl). A revolving post with bars, placed in a fence to permit a passage of persons but precluding passage of animals; a device of similar construction placed at an entrance to a theater, subway, etc. to restrict entrance to one person at a time. Gascoigne v Metropolitan Westside Elevated R. Co. 239 Ill 18, 87 NE 883. Sometimes released for movement by placing a coin in a slot.

turntable. A revolving platform, found in railroad shops and terminals, upon which a locomotive is turned around.

turntable cases. Cases involving an injury to a child on a turntable which elucidate the doctrine of attractive nuisance. 38 Am J1st Negl § 143.
See **attractive nuisance.**

turntable doctrine. The principle of liability for attractive nuisance as applied in cases involving an injury to a child sustained while playing upon a turntable. 38 Am J1st Negl § 143.
See **attractive nuisance.**

turpentine. A tree crop classified as fructus industriales. Richbourg v Rose, 53 Fla 173, 44 So 69. An ingredient of paints and varnishes, made from matter exuded from a pine tree.

turpentine timber. See **timber suitable for turpentine purposes.**

turpis (tėr′pis). Bad; base; immoral; wicked; dishonorable.

turpis contractus (ter′pis kon-trak′tus). A dishonorable contract.

Turpis est pars quae non convenit cum suo toto (ter′-pis est parz kwē non kon-vē′nit kum su′ō tō′tō). That part is bad which does not correspond with its own whole.

turpitude (tėr′pi-tūd). Depravity.
See **moral turpitude.**

turris (tur′ris). A tower.

tuta (tū′ta). Safe; secure.

Tuta est custodia quae sibimet creditur (tū′ta est kus-tō′di-a kwē si′bi-met krē′di-ter). That custody or guardianship is safe which is intrusted to itself alone.

tutela (tū-tē′la). (Civil law.) A guardianship or tutelage.

tuteur. (French.) Guardian or protector.

Tutius erratur ex parte mitiori (tū′she-us er-rā′ter ex par′te mi-she-ō′rī). It is safer to err on the side of leniency.

Tutius semper est errare in acquietando, quam in puniendo; ex parte misericordiae quam ex parte justitiae (tū′she-us sem′per est er-rā′re in a-qui-e-tan′do, quam in pu-mi-en′dō; ex par′te mi-se-ri-kor′di-ē quam ex par′te ju-sti′she-ē). It is always safer to err in acquitting than in punishing; on the side of mercy rather than on the side of justice. See Broom's Legal Maxims 326.

tuto. See **in tuto.**

tutor (tū′tor). A guardian. A person who under the Roman law occupied practically the same position with reference to his minor charge as a guardian of the person of an infant occupies toward his ward, under our laws. See 1 Bl Comm 460. A teacher engaged privately. A teacher instructing one pupil at a time.
See **protutor.**

tutorship. The position, duties, and authority of a tutor.
See **dative tutorship; tutor.**

tutrix (tū′triks). Feminine of **tutor.**

T. V. A. Abbreviation of Tennessee Valley Authority.

Twelfth Amendment. An amendment to the Constitution of the United States, prescribing the manner of choosing a President and Vice President.

twelve-man jury. The common law jury; the jury required by statute in many jurisdictions. 31 Am J Rev ed Jury § 121.

Twentieth Amendment. An amendment to the Constitution of the United States which fixes the date of the commencement of the terms of President, Vice President, United States Senators, and members of the House of Representatives, and the filling of vacancy in the office of the Presidency or Vice Presidency due to death before the time fixed for the beginning of term, failure to qualify, or failure to elect.

Twenty-eight Hour Law. A federal statute, applicable to the interstate transportation of livestock, which provides that a carrier shall not keep livestock confined in cars for a period longer than twenty-eight consecutive hours without unloading for rest, water, and feeding, for a period of at least five hours, unless the unloading is prevented by storm or other unavoidable causes which cannot be anticipated or avoided by the exercise of due diligence and foresight, but permitting the extension of the period of permissible confinement to thirty-six hours upon the written consent of the owner or person in charge of the shipment. 45 USC §§ 71-74; 13 Am J2d Car § 356.

Twenty-first Amendment. An amendment to the Constitution of the United States repealing the Eighteenth Amendment relative to traffic in intoxicating liquors.

Twenty-fourth Amendment. An amendment to the United States Constitution barring payment of poll tax as a qualification in federal elections.

Twenty-second Amendment. An amendment to the Constitution of the United States limiting Presidential terms of office.

Twenty-third Amendment. An amendment to the Constitution of the United States providing a Presidential vote for the District of Columbia.

twice in jeopardy. See **prior jeopardy.**

twig. See **turf and twig.**

Twine's Case (twīns kās). A famous English case involving conveyances in fraud of creditors, reported in 8 Coke 80.

twin wills. Same as mutual wills. Anno: 169 ALR 12, 13.
See **mutual wills.**

twisting. The efforts of an agent representing an insurance company to induce a person to drop insurance already held by him in some other insurance company and take out insurance in the company represented by the agent, especially where characterized by misrepresentations. 29 Am J Rev ed Ins § 63.

two-courts rule. The principle followed by a higher appellate court in not interfering with a finding of facts made by the trial court if such finding has been affirmed by an intermediate appellate court. 5 Am J2d A & E § 828.

two-dismissal rule. The rule in some jurisdictions that a notice of voluntary dismissal of an action shall operate as an adjudication upon the merits when filed by a plaintiff who has once dismissed an earlier action based on or including the same claim. 24 Am J2d Dism § 76.

two-donee statute. A statute providing that a person may make a conveyance or a devise of lands to a succession of donees, then living, not exceeding two, and to the heirs of the body of the remainderman, and in default thereof to the right heirs of the donor in fee simple. 41 Am J1st Perp § 11.

two-for-one rule. The rule that where a carrier does not furnish a car of the dimensions or weight-carrying capacity ordered by a shipper, but for reasons of convenience furnishes a car of different dimensions or weight-carrying capacity which is thereupon loaded to capacity, and the balance of the shipment is taken in another car, the entire shipment is subject to carload minimum weight rates applicable to the car of the dimensions or weight-carrying capacity ordered. Atchison, T. & S. F. R. Co. v Judson Freight Forwarding Co. (DC Cal) 49 F Supp 789.

two-innocent-persons principle. The principle of equity that when one of two innocent persons—that is, persons each guiltless of an intentional moral wrong—must suffer a loss, it must be borne by that one of them who, by his conduct, has rendered the injury possible, or who could have prevented it. 28 Am J2d Estop § 62. The maxim that as between one of two innocent persons who must suffer from the fraud of a third, he who furnishes the means to commit the fraud, or whose negligence enables the third person to commit it, must bear the loss. 37 Am J2d Fraud § 306.

two-issue rule. The rule that where there are two or more distinct defenses upon which the parties are at issue, a general verdict will stand on appeal if it can be supported on the basis of any one of them, regardless of error in the charges to the jury pertaining to the others. 5 Am J2d A & E § 787. A rule of some courts that if the case presents two separate issues, and if one issue, complete in itself as a cause of action or defense, is submitted to the jury free from error, and the jury returns a general verdict and there is nothing to indicate upon which issue the general verdict is grounded, the issue which presents the claimed error may be disregarded. McCrate v Morgan Packing Co. (CA6 Ohio) 117 F2d 702.

For limitations upon the two-issue rule, see 5 Am J2d A & E § 787. See also McCrate v Morgan Packing Co. (CA6 Ohio) 117 F2d 702.

two-level appellate system. A system prevailing in some states under which there are two levels of courts to or through which an appeal may be taken. 4 Am J2d A & E § 3.

two-step appeal. An appeal taken in a state having a two-level structure of appellate courts, the appeal going first to an intermediate court and from thence to the higher court of appeals. 4 Am J2d A & E § 3.

two universities. See **courts of the two universities.**

two-witness rule. A rule provided by statute in some jurisdictions which requires for conviction in a capital case the testimony of at least two witnesses. State v Palko, 122 Conn 529, 191 A 320, 113 ALR 628, affd 302 US 319, 82 L Ed 288, 58 S Ct 149. The rule in certain cases which requires two witnesses or one witness and corroborating circumstances to prove a fact. 41 Am J1st Perj § 78. The rule that the testimony of two witnesses or its equivalent is required to overcome the weight of defendant's answer in equity as evidence. 30 Am J2d Ev § 1100.

tymbrella (tim-brel′la). Same as **tumbrel.**

type certificate. A certificate issued by the Administrator of the Federal Aviation Agency for aircraft, aircraft engines, and propellers. 8 Am J2d Avi § 22.

type restriction. A restriction by covenant limiting the erection or construction of buildings upon the premises involved to a certain type of structure, particularly a dwelling house or residence. 20 Am J2d Cov § 190.

typhoid fever. A common infectious disease, but sometimes classified as an injury or personal injury for the purposes of an award of workmen's compensation. 58 Am J1st Workm Comp § 244.

typographical error. The error of a printer in setting type. Thompson v Alexander City Cotton Mills Co. 190 Ala 184, 67 So 407. In loose usage, the error of a stenographer in typing.

tyranny (tir′a-ni). The rule of a despot or tyrant; absolutism.

tyrant (tī′rant). See **despot; tyranny.**

Tyrrel's Case. An ancient English case before the statute of uses, which held that a use upon a use could not be sustained, reported in Dwyer 155a.

U

U. Abbreviation of University, also of Union.

uberrima fides (u-ber′ri-ma fī′dēz). Utmost good faith, as required of one who contracts with another to whom he stands in a fiduciary relationship. 37 Am J2d Fraud § 15.
Insurance policies are traditionally contracts uberrimae fidei. Stipcich v Metropolitan Life Ins. Co. 277 US 311, 72 L Ed 895, 48 S Ct 512.

Ubi aliquid conceditur, conceditur et id sine quo res ipsa esse non potest (u′bi a′li-quid kon-sē′di-ter, kon-sē′di-ter et id sī′ne quō rēz ip′sa es′se non po′-test). Where anything is granted, that is also granted without which the thing itself cannot exist. See Broom's Legal Maxims 483.

Ubi aliquid impeditur propter unum, eo remoto, tollitur impedimentum (u′bi a′li-quid im-pe′di-ter prop′ter ū′num, e′ō re-mō′tō, tol′li-ter im-pe-di-men′tum). Where anything is impeded by reason of one thing, with the removal of that, the impediment is removed.

Ubi cessat remedium ordinarium ibi decurritur ad extraordinarium (u′bi ses′sat re-mē′di-um or-di-nā′ri-um i′bi de-kur′ri-ter ad ex-tra-or″di-nā′ri-um). Where an ordinary remedy is useless, then resort must be made to an extraordinary one.

Ubi culpa est, ibi poena subesse debet (u′bi kul′pa est, i′bi pē′na sub-es′se de′bet). Where the fault is, there the punishment ought to be visited.

Ubicunque est injuria, ibi damnum sequitur (u-bi-kun′kwe est in-ju′ri-a, i′bi dam′num se′qui-ter). Wherever there is a legal wrong, there damage follows.

ubicunque fuerimus in Anglia (u-bi-kun′kwe fu-e′ri-mus in Ang′li-a). Wherever we may be in England.

Ubi damna dantur, victus victori in expensis condemnari debet (u′bi dam′na dan′ter, vik′tus vik-tō′rī in ex-pen′sis kon-dem-nā′rī de′bet). Where damages are awarded, the unsuccessful party ought to be adjudged to pay the costs of the successful party.

Ubi eadem ratio, ibi idem jus (u′bi e-ā′dem rā′she-ō, i′bi ī′dem jūs). Where the transaction is the same, the law is the same.
"The object of these liens being the same, their effect must be the same." See Ames v Palmer, 42 Me 197.

Ubi eadem ratio, ibi idem jus; et de similibus idem est judicium (u′bi e-ā′dem rā′she-ō, i′bi ī′dem jūs; et dē si-mi′li-bus ī′dem est jū-di′she-um). Where the reason is the same, the law is the same, and in similar cases the judgment is the same.

Ubi est forum, ibi ergo est jus (u′bi est fō′rum, i′bi er′go est jūs). Where the forum or place of jurisdiction is, there the law is accordingly.

Ubi et dantis et accipientis turpitudo versatur, non posse repeti dicimus; quotiens autem accipientis turpitudo versatur, repeti posse (u′bi et dan′tis et ak-si-pi-en′tis ter′pi-tu-dō ver-sā′ter, non pos′se re′pe-tī dī′si-mus; quō′she-enz a′tem ak′sī″pi-en′tis ter′pi-tu-dō ver-sā′ter, re′pe-ti pos′se). When there is turpitude in both the giver and the receiver, we say the thing cannot be recovered, but that whenever the turpitude is in the receiver only, it can be recovered. Mason v Waite, 17 Mass 560, 562.

Ubi factum nullum, ibi fortia nulla (u′bi fak′tum nul′lum, i′bi for′she-a nul′la). Where there is no fact, there can be no force.

ubi jus ibi remedium (u′bi jūs i′bi re-mē′di-um). Wherever the law gives a right, it also gives a remedy. 1 Am J2d Actions § 47.

Ubi jus incertum, ubi jus nullum (u′bi jūs in-ser′tum, u′bi jūs nul-lum). Where the law is uncertain, there there is no law.

Ubi lex aliquem cogit ostendere causam, necesse est quod causa sit justa et legitima (u′bi lex a′li-quem kō′jit os-ten′de-re kâ′zam, ne-ses′se est quod kâ′za sit jus′ta et lē-ji′ti-ma). Where the law compels anyone to show cause, it is necessary that the cause be just and lawful.

Ubi lex est specialis, et ratio ejus generalis generaliter accipienda est (u′bi lex est spe-she-ā′lis, et rā′-she-ō e′jus je-ne-rā′lis je-ne-rā′li-ter ak-si-pi-en′da est). Where the law is special, but the reason of it is general, it should be construed generally.

Ubi lex non distinguit, nec nos distinguere debemus (u′bi lex non dis-tin′gu-it, nek nōs dis-tin-gu′e-re de-bē′mus). Where the law does not distinguish, we ought not to distinguish.

Ubi major pars est, ibi totum (u′bi mā′jor parz est, i′bi tō′tum). Where the greater part is, there is the whole.

Ubi matrimonium, ibi dos (u′bi ma-tri-mō′ni-um i′bi dos). Where there is a marriage, there is dower.

Ubi non adest norma legis, omnia, quasi pro suspectis habenda sunt (u′bi non ad′est nor′ma lē′jis, om′-ni-a quā′sī prō sus-pek′tis hā-ben′da sunt). Where there is no rule of law, everything should be regarded, as it were, with suspicion.

Ubi non est annua renovatio, ibi decimae non debent solvi (u′bi non est an′nu-a re-no-vā′she-ō, i′bi de′si-mē non de′bent sol′vī). Where there is no annual renovation, there tithes ought not to be paid.

Ubi non est condendi auctoritas, ibi non est parendi necessitas (u′bi non est kon-den′dī āk-tō′ri-tas i′bi non est pa-ren′dī ne-ses′si-tās). Where there is no authority to command, there is no need of obeying.

Ubi non est directa lex, standum est arbitrio judicis, vel procedendum ad similia (u′bi non est di-rek′ta lex, stan′dum est ar-bit′ri-ō ju′di-sis, vel pro′se-den′dum ad si-mi′li-a). Where there is no direct law, the decision of the judge is to be supported, or reference made to similar cases.

Ubi non est lex, ibi non est transgressio quoad mundum (u′bi non est lex, i′bi non est trans-gre′she-ō quo′ad mun′dum). Where there is no law, there is no transgression as far as worldly matters are concerned.

Ubi non est manifesta injustitia, judices habentur pro bonis viris, et judicatum pro veritate (u′bi non est ma-ni-fes′ta in-jus-ti′she-a, jū′di-sēz ha-ben′ter pro bō′nis vir′is, et ju-di-kā′tum pro ve-ri-tā′te). Where there is no manifest injustice, judges ought to be regarded as honest men, and their judgment as truth.

Ubi non est principalis, non potest esse accessorius (u′bi non est prin-si-pā′lis non pō′test es′se ak-ses-sō′ri-us). Where there is no principal, there can be no accessory.

Ubi nulla est conjectura quae ducat alio, verba intelligenda sunt ex proprietate non grammatica sed populari ex usu (u'bi nul'la est kon-jek-tū'ra kwē dū'kat ā'li-ō, ver'ba in-tel-li-jen'da sunt ex pro-pri-e-tā'te non gram-ma'ti-ka sed po-pu-lā'rī ex ū'su). Where there is no inference which would lead to another conclusion, words are to be understood according to their proper sense, not in their grammatical signification, but according to their popular usage.

Ubi nullum matrimonium, ibi nulla dos (u'bi nul'lum ma-tri-mō'ni-um, i'bi nul'la dos). Where there is no marriage, there no dower is due. See 2 Bl Comm 130.
  If a marriage be dissolved, dower ceases. Wait v Wait (NY) 4 Barb 92, 202.

Ubi pars est ibi est totum (u'bi parz est i'bi est tō'tum). Where the greater part is, there is the whole.

Ubi periculum, ibi et lucrum collocatur (u'bi pe-ri'ku-lum, i'bi et lū'krum kol-lo-ka'ter). Where the hazard is, there the profit should accrue.

Ubi pugnantia inter se in testamento juberentur, neutrum ratum est (u'bi pug-nan'she-a in'ter se in testa-men'to ju-be-ren'ter, nū'trum rā'tum est). (Civil law.) Where directions repugnant to one another are given in a will, neither of them is valid.

Ubi quid generaliter conceditur, inest haec exceptio, si non aliquid sit contra jus fasque (u'bi quid je-ne-rā'li-ter kon-sē'di-ter, in'est hēc ex-sep'she-ō, sī non a'li-quid sit kon'tra jūs fas'kwē). Where anything is granted generally, this exception is implied, that nothing shall be contrary to law and right.

Ubi quis delinquit ibi punietur (u'bi quis de-lin'quit i'bi pu-ni-ē'ter). Where a person commits a crime, there he is to be punished.

ubi re vera (u'bi rē vē'ra). Where, in truth; when, in reality.

ubi supra (ū'bī sū'prạ). "Where above mentioned." A term sometimes used following the title of a case to indicate that the volume and page of the case will be found where the same case has been cited shortly before.

Ubi verba conjuncta non sunt, sufficit alterutrum esse factum (u'bi ver'ba kon-junk'ta non sunt, suf'fi-sit al-ter-ut'rum es'se fak'tum). (Civil law.) Where words are not in the conjunctive, it is sufficient that either of them be executed or complied with.

u-drive it. See **drive-it-yourself system.**

ukase (ū-kās'). An official order or decree.
  An imperial order of the czar of Russia was so called.

ULA. Definition of Uniform Laws Annotated.

ullage (ul'āj). The amount by which a cask, particularly a cask of wine, falls short of being full.

ulna (ul'nạ). An arm; the ancient ell, corresponding to the modern yard measure. See 1 Bl Comm 275.

ulnage (ul'nāj). Same as **alnage.**

ulnager (ul'nāj-ėr). Same as **alnager.**

ulterior estate (ul-tē'ri-ọr es-tāt'). The estate created by a gift over, to take effect upon the determination of a particular estate; that is, an estate in remainder. Johnston's Estate, 185 Pa 179, 39 A 879. A future interest, that is, an estate limited after a preceding estate. 28 Am J2d Est § 208.

ulterior purpose. An undisclosed purpose; a purpose not revealed by what is expressed or implied.
  The rule that a stockholder will not be permitted to inspect corporate books for an "ulterior purpose" seems to be merely another mode of stating that the inspection must be for purposes germane to the stockholder's status as such. Anno: 15 ALR2d 29.

ulterius concilium (ul-tē'ri-us kon-si'li-um). Further consideration or argument.

ultima ratio (ul'ti-ma rā'she-ō). The last reason; the last resort.

ultimate burden of tax. The burden of payment of a tax, such as a sales tax, as passed along to one who did not pay it in the first instance.

ultimate fact. A fact upon the existence or nonexistence of which liability is to be determined. Anno: 146 ALR 134. The final and resulting fact reached by processes of legal reasoning from the detailed or probative facts, as distinguished from evidentiary facts and conclusions of law. 41 Am J1st Pl § 7.
  As the term pertains to workmen's compensation statutes, it is defined as a fact upon the existence or nonexistence of which liability depends according to the language used in the statute. Anno: 146 ALR 134.

ultimate finding. A finding of an ultimate fact or facts.

ultimate payment. Final payment. Payment of the obligation as it stands after any and all substitutions, renewals, or extensions. National Exchange Bank v Gay, 57 Conn 224, 17 A 555.

ultimatum (ul-ti-mā'tum). A final proposition. A final offer. A final statement of terms in diplomatic negotiations for the settlement of a dispute.

ultima voluntas (ul'ti-ma vo-lun'tās). A last will.

Ultima voluntas testatoris est perimplenda secundum veram intentionem suam (ul'ti-ma vo-lun'tās tes-ta-tō'ris est per-im-plen'da se-kun'dum vē'ram inten"she-ō'nem su'am). The last will of a testator is to be fulfilled according to his true intent.

ultimum supplicium (ul'ti-mum sup-pli'she-um). (Civil law.) The extreme punishment; the death penalty.

Ultimum supplicium esse mortem solam interpretamur (ul'ti-mum sup-pli'she-um es'se mor'tem sō'lam in-ter-pre-tā'mer). (Civil law.) We regard death alone as being the extreme punishment.

ultimum tempus pariendi (ul'ti-mum tem'pus pa-rien'dī). The extreme time or period of gestation.

ultimus haeres (ul'ti-mus hē'rēz). The last heir; the lord; the king.

ultra (ul'trạ). Beyond; outside of; more than; in excess of.

ultra fines mandati (ul'trạ fī'nēz man-dā'tī). Beyond or outside the scope of authority.

ultrahazardous activity. An activity which necessarily involves a risk of serious harm to the person, land or chattels of others which cannot be eliminated by the exercise of the utmost care, and is not a matter of common usage. Anno: 54 ALR2d 776.

ultra mare (ul'trạ ma're). Beyond the sea; beyond seas.

ultra petita (ul'trạ pe'ti-ta). Beyond that which was sought or prayed for.

Ultra posse non potest esse et vice versa (ul'trạ pos'se non po'test es'se et vī'se ver'sa). That which is beyond possibility cannot be, and vice versa.

ultra reprises (ul'trạ re-prī'sēz). Net; after deductions.

ultra vires (ul'trạ vī'rēz). Beyond the powers. Characterizing a contract, act, or transaction of a corporation which is beyond the express or implied powers of the corporation under any circumstances or for any purpose. Randall v Mickle, 103 Fla 1229, 138 So 14, 86 ALR 804. Foreign to the nature and design of the corporation involved. 10 Am J2d Banks § 276; 19 Am J2d Corp § 963. Characterizing a contract entered into by a public body which is without power or authority to bind itself by such an agreement. 43 Am J1st Pub Wks § 13. Characterizing an act beyond the powers conferred by a franchise so substantial and continued as to amount to a clear violation of the condition upon which the franchise was granted. 36 Am J2d Franch § 54.

The terms "illegality" and "ultra vires" represent totally different and distinct ideas. Whether a contract is illegal or not is determined by its quality; whether it is ultra vires or not is determined from the consideration of the powers expressly conferred upon the corporation by the instrument of its creation, together with those other powers employed in the purposes of its creation and in the powers expressly granted. 19 Am J2d Corp § 964.

ultra vires act. See **ultra vires.**

umbilical cord (um-bil'i-kạl kōrd). The cord which connects the body of the mother with that of her unborn child, and through which the blood circulation of the mother passes into the body of the child.

umpirage (um'pīr-ạj). The award of the umpire alone, in an arbitration where a reference is made to two arbitrators, and in case of a disagreement, to an umpire alone, and the arbitrators have failed to agree and make an award. Powell v Ford, 72 Tenn (4 Lea) 278, 288.

umpire (um'pīr). A person selected by arbitrators, pursuant to the authority of the submission, to decide the matter in controversy when the arbitrators are unable to agree, and standing by virtue of his selection as the sole arbitrator of the issue originally submitted to the arbitrators. 5 Am J2d Arb & A § 84. One chosen to decide the issue or issues in an arbitration when the arbitrators are in deadlock, and having the power to settle the matter by his sole award. Chandos v American Fire Ins. Co. 84 Wis 184, 54 NW 390. A person selected by referees to participate in the decision on the inability of the referees to come to agreement on the decision. 45 Am J1st Ref § 27. An official in a game or sport, such as baseball, who applies the rules of the game and settles disputes.

unable. See **inability.**

unable to proceed under its own power. Unable to proceed under the same conditions and in the same manner as before, without help or repairs, giving due regard to safety of the operation. 29A Am J Rev ed Ins § 1245.

unaccrued royalty. An expression criticized as inept and self-contradictory.

It would seem that the expression is a contradiction in terms; and in fact the right to share in oil that may be produced accrues immediately upon delivery of the lease. Apparently what is meant by "unaccrued royalty" is a supposed interest in unpossessed oil in the ground, which is, of course, real estate. Upon principle, however, it cannot be said that one has any title to oil in the ground simply because, as beneficiary of an oil contract, he may become entitled to a share of oil reduced to possession. To say that a lessor has title to oil in the ground by reason of his royalty interest is to confound his title as landowner with his rights under the lease. Anno: 90 ALR 771.

una cum (ū'na kum). Together with.

una cum omnibus aliis (u'na kum om'ni-bus a'li-is). Together with all other things.

unadjusted debt. A debt uncertain in amount, not settled or agreed upon as to amount. Richardson v Woodbury, 43 Me 206, 214.

unalienable (un-āl'yen-ạ-bl). Same as **inalienable.**

unanimous. Complete in approval or concurrence.

The decision or vote of a judicial or legislative body is unanimous when it is concurred in by all the members who are present, if the members present constitute a quorum, even though one or more members are absent. Such a body, with a quorum present, proceeds ordinarily as if every member were sitting in his place, and exercises all the powers with which it is invested. Harroun v Brush Electric Light Co. 152 NY 212, 46 NE 291.

unanimous decision. A decision in which all the judges or justices hearing the case concur.

unanimous verdict. A verdict in which all the jurors concur. 31 Am J Rev ed Jury § 10.

una parte. See **de una parte; ex una parte.**

Una persona vix potest supplere vices duarum (u'na per-sō'na vix po'test sup-plē're vī'sēz du-ā'rum). One person can scarcely supply the places of two.

unattached. The state or condition of property upon which no attachment has been levied. Unfettered by the bonds of matrimony. Neither married nor engaged.

unattended. See **attendant.**

unattested instrument. An instrument which does not bear the signatures of attesting or subscribing witnesses.

unauthorized connection. A connection to the station or line of an individual subscriber to telephone service, made without the authorization of the subscriber and the telephone company.

Both the subscriber and the telephone company must consent if the connection is to be deemed anything else but unauthorized. Anno: 74 ALR2d 858.

Unauthorized Insurer's Act. One of the uniform laws. 29 Am J Rev ed Ins § 67.

unauthorized practice of law. Conducting the practice of law without the license required by law. 7 Am J2d Attys § 73.

una voce (u'na vō'se). With one voice; with one accord; unanimously.

unavoidable accident. An occurrence of an unusual, unexpected, or extraordinary character, usually occurring without any direct participation by man. French v Pirnie, 240 Mass 489, 134 NE 353, 20 ALR 1098. Something beyond human foresight and control. 32 Am J1st L & T § 796. Such an occurrence, as under all the circumstances, could not have been foreseen, anticipated, or avoided in the exercise of ordinary care. McBride v Woods,

UNAVOIDABLE [1311] UNCONSTITUTIONAL

124 Colo 384, 238 P2d 183, 29 ALR2d 101. An inevitable accident which could not have been foreseen and prevented by the exercise of that degree of diligence which reasonable men would exercise under like conditions, and which resulted without any fault attributable to the persons sought to be held responsible. 31 Am J Rev ed Lab § 823. Such an occurrence or happening as, under all attendant circumstances and conditions, could not have been foreseen or anticipated in the exercise of ordinary care. 7 Am J2d Auto § 350.

See **inevitable accident**.

unavoidable casualty. An occurrence of an unusual, unexpected, or extraordinary character, usually occurring without any direct participation by man. French v Pirnie, 240 Mass 489, 134 NE 353, 20 ALR 1098. Something beyond human foresight and control. 32 Am J1st L & T § 796.

See **unavoidable accident**.

unavoidable cause. An accidental cause; a cause which cannot be avoided by the exercise of due diligence and foresight; a cause which reasonably prudent and cautious men under like circumstances do not and would not ordinarily anticipate and whose effects under similar circumstances they do not and would not ordinarily avoid. Chicago, Burlington & Quincy Railroad Co. v United States (CA2 NY) 194 F 339, 344.

unavoidable delay. A delay occurring by unavoidable cause, by unavoidable accident, or unavoidable casualty.

Unavoidable delay in the performance of a contract, to amount to an excuse by custom or usage, must be confined to delays due to causes originating after the contract has been entered into. Lima Locomotive & Machine Co. v National Steel Castings Co. (CA6 Ohio) 155 F 77.

unavoidable occurrence. An **unavoidable accident** or **unavoidable casualty**.

For definition of term as it appears in a condition of a contract of sale providing for relief from the obligation under certain circumstances, see Anno: 51 ALR 1010.

unavoidably prevented. Prevented without fault attributable to any person. Anno: 31 ALR 631.

unblocked frog. A frog in a railroad switch which has not been blocked or filled in such manner as to prevent a person's foot or shoe from being caught and wedged in the frog. Southern Pacific Co. v Seley, 152 US 145, 150, 38 L Ed 391, 393, 14 S Ct 530; Union Pacific Railway Co. v James, 163 US 485, 41 L Ed 236, 16 S Ct 1109.

unborn child. A child in the womb of the mother. A child not yet delivered from the womb. One of a generation to come.

In some jurisdictions, statutes relating to the crime of abortion or related offenses, although speaking in terms of "a woman" or "any woman", contain further language referring to such woman's "child" or "unborn child", as by providing that the criminal acts must be done with the intent to destroy an unborn child. It would appear that under enactments of this kind, proof of pregnancy is essential to a conviction. Anno: 46 ALR2d 1406.

See **in being**.

unbroken package. See **original package**.

uncertainty. Lacking in **certainty**.

As applied to pleadings, the word does not include "ambiguity," although the leading English dictionaries give the word "uncertain" as one of the meanings of the word "ambiguous." See Kraner v Haney, 82 Cal 209, 212, 22 P 1137.

unchaste. Lacking in virtue and chastity. 35 Am J1st Mar § 134.

unchaste woman. A woman who is sexually impure; a loose woman; a woman of loose character. Foster v Hanchett, 68 Vt 319.

unchastity. See **unchaste**; **unchaste woman**.

unciae (un'she-ē). See **usurae centesimae**.

uncle. A brother of one's father or mother. A relative in the third degree according to the civil-law method of computing degrees of relationship which prevails in most American jurisdictions. Anno: 55 ALR2d 645, § 1[b].

As to the meaning of the term in reference to war risk life and disability insurance, see Anno: 55 ALR 584.

unclean hands doctrine. See **clean hands doctrine**.

uncollectible. Not to be realized for want of assets subject to execution. Not to be paid voluntarily. Not to be collectible without suit or threat of suit.

A creditor's claim is said to be uncollectible when he has failed to receive the amount due after exhausting every effort to collect it, short of sending it to an attorney for collection. Globe & Rutgers Fire Ins. Co. v Lesher, Whitman & Co. 126 Misc 874, 215 NYS 225, 229.

unconditional. Without conditions; without restrictions; absolute. Columbia Water Power Co. v Columbia Electric Street R. Co. 172 US 475, 491, 43 L Ed 521, 527, 19 S Ct 247.

unconditional credit. A credit, given by the drawee bank upon its books for a check forwarded to it for collection, which is not subject to revocation. First Nat. Bank v Universal C. I. T. Credit Corp. 132 Ind App 353, 170 NE2d 238.

unconditional heirs (ārs.) In Louisiana, heirs who inherit property without any reservation, or without making any inventory.

unconditional ownership. Title where the quality of the estate is not limited or affected by any condition. 29A Am J Rev ed Ins § 791.

See **sole and unconditional ownership**.

unconscionable (un-kon'shon-a-bl). Morally reprehensible.

unconscionable advantage. See **taking unconscionable advantage**.

unconscionable bargain. See **unconscionable agreement**.

unconscionable agreement. An agreement, usually made when one of the parties was in a position of disadvantage, which is oppressive, especially one which unreasonably restricts the liberty of a party to exercise his calling or earn his living, or imposes an extortionate rate of interest. 17 Am J2d Contr § 192.

unconscious plagiarism (un-kon'shus plā'ji-a-rizm). Using the literary work of another in one's own work without realizing that it is actually the work of another, the ideas and concepts used having been implanted in the mind by a previous and forgotten study made of the work of the other person. Anno: 23 ALR2d 341.

unconstitutional law. See **unconstitutional statute**.

unconstitutional statute. A self-contradictory expression, since a statute in conflict with the constitution is not law but is wholly void and as inoperative in legal contemplation as if it had never been passed, notwithstanding it has the form and name of law. 16 Am J2d Const L § 177.

When a statute is adjudged to be unconstitutional, it is as if it had never been. Rights cannot be built up under it. Contracts which depend upon it for their construction are void. It constitutes a protection to no one who has acted under it, and no one can be punished for having refused obedience to it before the decision was made. And what is true of an act void in toto is true also as to any part of an act which is found to be unconstitutional, and which consequently is to be regarded as having never at any time been passed and in legal effect. Re Rahrer (CC Kan) 43 F 556.

As used in the United States Code, the term "unconstitutional" has reference to the United States Constitution, not to a state constitution. Anno: 83 L Ed 1195.

uncontrollable. Out of control. Not subject to control. Irresistible.

uncontrollable event. An irresistible occurrence. An occurrence which can neither be restrained nor prevented. Lehman, Stern & Co. v Morgan's Louisiana & Texas Railroad & S.S. Co. 115 La 1, 38 So 873.

uncontrollable impulse. See **irresistible impulse.**

uncontrolled discretion. Discretion given a trustee which is not subject to judicial rectification.

The court should not tolerate an abuse of discretion on the part of a trustee, even though the trust instrument purports to give him uncontrolled discretion. Anno: 27 ALR2d 1337.

uncore (un'kor). Again; now.

uncore prist (un'kor prist). He is still ready.

The expression was used in the formal pleading of a tender, wherein the pleader alleged that he has always been ready (tout temps prist), and still is ready (uncore prist), to pay. See 3 Bl Comm 303.

uncuth (un-kuth'). (Saxon.) Unknown; a stranger.

unde (un'de). Whence; from where; from what.

undefended (un-dẹ-fen'ded). Without defense; no defense being interposed, as when a defendant is in default.

unde nihil habet (un'de ni'hil hā'bet). Whence he has nothing.

unde petit judicium (un'de pe'tit ju-di'she-um). Whereof he demands judgment.

under a certain age. A status terminating when the person passes the anniversary of such age. Anno: 73 ALR2d 874, 875.

under a designated age. See **under a certain age.**

under and subject to the payment of. A stipulation in a conveyance of mortgaged property ineffective as an assumption of the mortgage debt.

Such a stipulation does not with sufficient clearness import an intention by the grantor to create, and by the grantee to assume, a personal obligation to pay the mortgage debt. 37 Am J1st Mtg § 998.

underbid. To bid less than another bidder.

undercharge. A charge imposed by a carrier for the transportation of a passenger or property which is less than the rate, fare, or charge applicable to such transportation as set forth in the published tariff schedule. 13 Am J2d Car § 108.

under consideration by the grand jury. Inclusive of all proceedings had in the grand jury room insofar as they include the reception of evidence and the ultimate action taken upon it. Anno: 4 ALR2d 398.

under control. See **control; control of vehicle.**

under conviction. Having a strong belief. Under sentence not yet executed.

While the sentence stands unexecuted, a person who has been found guilty of crime and sentenced is said to be "under conviction"; he stands "under" it, it rests upon his head; but when he has suffered the penalty, he has paid the debt, the sentence has spent its force, and no longer hovers over him. See Osborne v Kanawha County Court, 68 W Va 189, 69 SE 470.

underground conduit. A tube laid below the surface of the ground in which electric, telegraph and telephone wires may be strung. 52 Am J1st Teleg & T § 50.

underground circuit. A telephone, telegraph, or electric wire strung in a conduit below the surface of the ground. 52 Am J1st Teleg & T § 50.

underground stream. A stream of water which flows in a fixed or definite channel, the existence and location of which is known or ascertainable from surface indications or other means without subsurface excavations. 56 Am J1st Water § 108.

underground water. An underground stream, an underground pool, or water percolating below the surface.

See **percolating water; subterranean waters; underground stream.**

under his care. A familiar term in embezzlement statutes, of broader meaning than the term "possession."

A person may have money or property of another "under his care," although it is in the actual possession of another. 26 Am J2d Embez § 15.

under his hand. Denoting a signature in one's own handwriting; not inclusive of a rubber-stamp signature. Anno: 37 ALR 87. A formal phrase indicating a signature, as by a justice of the peace upon a warrant issued by him. Salazar v Taylor, 18 Colo 538.

underlease. A lease by a lessee of a part of his unexpired term. Bedford v Terhune, 30 NY 453. A lease by a lessee of a part of the premises demised to him. 32 Am J1st L & T § 403.

underletting. See **underlease.**

under own power. Moving by force of a power contained therein; not in tow.

under protest. See **protest.**

under sail. Underway with sails set.

The expression is not synonymous with the expression "carrying sail," which means simply equipped with sails. Thus, a steamer may be under way and carrying sail and yet not be under sail. Belden v Chase, 150 US 674, 695, 37 L Ed 1218, 1225, 14 S Ct 264.

under seal. With seal affixed.

See **seal.**

undersheriff. An officer on the staff of a sheriff; a deputy sheriff. 47 Am J1st Sher § 154. A general deputy sheriff,—a deputy sheriff who, by virtue of his appointment, has authority to execute all the ordinary duties of the office of sheriff. Allen v Smith, 12 NJL 159, 162. In old England, an officer immediately subordinate to the sheriff, or high-sheriff, as he was often called.

The undersheriff usually performed all the duties of the office of sheriff; the personal presence of the sheriff himself was seldom necessary. Statute limited the term of the office of the undersheriff to one year. See 1 Bl Comm 345.

In some jurisdictions, a distinction is made between a deputy sheriff and an undersheriff, although both are subordinate to the sheriff.

undersigned. The person whose name is signed, or the persons whose names are signed, at the end of a document; the subscriber or subscribers. Farmers' Exchange Bank v Sollars, 353 Ill 224, 187 NE 289, 89 ALR 398.

understand. To have full and clear knowledge of; to have full comprehension of; to comprehend. Fox v Shaeffer, 131 Conn 439, 41 A2d 46, 157 ALR 132.

understanding. The mental quality of discernment. An interpretation. Agreement.

"Understood" is synonymous with the word "agreed". Phoenix Iron & Steel Co. v Wilkoff Co. (CA6 Ohio) 253 F 165, 1 ALR 1497.

"The words 'understood' and 'agreed' may be used synonymously." Mount v Montgomery County, 168 Ind 661, 80 NE 629.

While, in a sense, the word may be said to involve a conclusion, it is an ambiguous word, and is sometimes used as synonymous with the word "agreement." While a witness should not be asked what "understanding" was arrived at, if such testimony is admitted without objection, or cross-examination, it should go to the jury with a view to ascertaining what was meant by the word. Sykes v City Sav. Bank, 115 Mich 321.

understood. See **understanding.**

undertaker. A person engaged in the business of caring for the bodies of deceased persons and the disposition of them by burial or otherwise. 54 Am J1st Und & E § 2. One whose business it is to arrange for burying the dead and to oversee funerals. State ex rel. Kempinger v White, 177 Wis 541, 188 NW 607, 23 ALR 67, 69.

An undertaker is not necessarily an embalmer. State ex rel. Kempinger v White, 177 Wis 541, 188 NW 607, 23 ALR 67, 69.

undertaker's license. A license required of an undertaker by the state under its police power. 54 Am J1st Und & E § 5.

undertaking. Broadly, that which one has agreed to do. Technically, an obligation in writing binding the signatories to pay such an amount as shall be adjudged due. General American Industries, Inc. v County Court of Clear Creek County, 136 Colo 86, 316 P2d 565.

Although the essential purpose of an undertaking is the same as that of a bond, and an undertaking with security is in common usage and in the language of the law, a bond, the dissimilarity in terms is fundamental. An undertaking has to do with amounts to be determined, whereas a bond has to do with liquidated amounts. 12 Am J2d Bonds § 1.

The distinction between a bond and an undertaking is that the principal should sign the former and that he is not required to sign the latter. Russell v Chicago, B. & Q. R. Co. 37 Mont 1, 94 P 488, 501.

undertaking for costs. See **security for costs.**

undertaking to keep the peace. See **bond to keep the peace.**

under-tenant. A tenant who holds under an underlease or sublease. Bedford v Terhune, 30 NY 453.

See **underlease.**

under the age limit fixed by law. A familiar term in exclusion clauses in policies of automobile insurance, having reference to the operation of the vehicle covered by the policy in violation of statute or ordinance which prescribes a regulation in reference to the age of drivers. 7 Am J2d Auto Ins § 38.

under the influence of an intoxicant. Under so much influence from intoxicant as impairs the ability of the subject to care for himself. Kuroske v Aetna Life Ins. Co. 234 Wis 394, 291 NW 384, 127 ALR 1505 (clause in accident insurance policy excluding from coverage injuries sustained while under the influence of an intoxicant).

See **driving while intoxicated.**

under the influence of intoxicating liquor. Affected by the taking of intoxicating liquor, irrespective of a specific degree of intoxication. 7 Am J2d Auto § 257. Intoxicated. 29A Am J Rev ed Ins § 1230. So affected by intoxicating liquor as not to have the full use of one's physical and mental powers as such are present when one is in a normal condition. Grinnell v General Acci. Co. 80 Vt 526, 68 A 655 (clause appearing in an exception in a policy of accident insurance).

See **driving while intoxicated.**

under the law. In conformity with law. Subject to the law.

"We are under the laws of the United States—that is, we are subject to those laws. We live under a certain jurisdiction—that is, we are subject to it." Mills v Stoddard (US) 8 How 345, 366, 12 L Ed 1107, 1115.

under the peace. In the king's peace; under the protection of the king; within the jurisdiction and protection of the state. Commonwealth v Macloon, 101 Mass 1.

See **bond to keep the peace.**

under the rule. See **rule.**

under-tutor (un'der-tū-tor). (Civil law.) A person appointed by a court to act for a minor when his tutor's interests are in conflict with his own. Welch v Baxter, 45 La Ann 1062, 1064, 13 So 629.

underway. In progress. Moving.

A vessel is underway when she is not at anchor, not made fast to the shore, and not aground. A steam vessel which is being towed is underway, within the definition. The Scandinavia (DC NY) 11 F2d 542.

underwriter. One who has incurred an obligation by executing his signature to an instrument, particularly an insurance contract. One who insures another under a contract or policy of insurance. Childs ex rel. Smith v Firemen's Ins. Co. 66 Minn 393, 69 NW 141. One who has agreed to take an entire stock or bond issue or so much of a stock or bond issue as is not taken by the public. Re Hackett, Hoff & Thiermann (CA7 Wis) 70 F2d 815; Rauer's Law & Collection Co. v Harrell, 32 Cal App 45, 162 P 125.

An underwriter's contract is not an agreement to lend money. See Re Hackett, Hoff & Thiermann (CA7 Wis) 70 F2d 815.

An underwriting contract is not a contract to make a loan, but is one to insure the sale of bonds. It is a contract to insure the sale of the bonds subscribed, and, in case they are not sold before the instalments fall due, then to purchase and pay for them at par. It is an underwriting and not an agreement to loan money. Stewart v Miller & Co. 161 Ga 919, 132 SE 535, 45 ALR 559, 565.

See **board of fire underwriters.**

underwriters' association. A voluntary association organized by insurance companies or insurance agents for the purpose of promoting the business, welfare, and convenience of the parties thereto, and to secure uniformity in the business. 29 Am J Rev ed Ins § 109.

underwriters' rules. Rules established by insurance companies relative to the classification of risks in reference to the type and manner of construction of buildings, electric wiring, etc. 29A Am J Rev ed Ins § 1893.

underwriting contract. See **underwriter.**

underwriting ratio. See **expense ratio; loss ratio.**

undique (un'di-kwe). In all directions; on all sides.

undisbursed income. Income retained in the estate by executor or trustee.

Under a provision in a will that "any undisbursed income" should be paid to the residuary estate after the death of the life tenant, the words will be taken to mean any income not actually paid out to the life tenant, and will not be restricted in their meaning to include only that income accruing during the period between the death of the life tenant and the distribution to the residuary estate. Rhode Island Hospital Trust Co. v Otis, 77 RI 296, 75 A2d 210.

undisclosed agency. A situation where one who is in fact an agent for another deals with a third person in the character of a principal, his status as an agent being unknown to the third person. 3 Am J2d Agency § 307.

undisclosed assets. Assets of a bankrupt not disclosed by him to his trustee in bankruptcy or otherwise coming to the notice of the trustee. 9 Am J2d Bankr § 860.

undisclosed principal. A principal whose identity is unknown to a third person who deals with his agent, knowing that the latter is acting for some principal. The principal in an undisclosed agency. 3 Am J2d Agency § 307.

See **undisclosed agency.**

undisposed of. See **undisbursed income.**

undisputed. Not contested.

undistributed profits. See **undivided profits.**

undivided interest. A fractional interest in property. 23 Am J2d Deeds § 290. An interest which has not been segregated. The nature of the title held by a tenant in common or a joint tenant.

undivided profits. Profits of a corporation which have neither been distributed as dividends nor carried to surplus account. Edwards v Douglas, 269 US 204, 70 L Ed 235, 46 S Ct 85.

Surplus and undivided profits are the property of the corporation. As their names indicate, they are not capital stock, but are something besides capital stock. First Nat. Bank v Moon, 102 Kan 334, 170 P 33.

undocumented vessel. Any vessel which is not required to have, and does not have, a valid marine document issued by the Bureau of Customs. 46 USC § 527(1).

undres. Minors; persons under age.

undressed lumber. Boards which have not been processed and fashioned for use as building materials.

undrinkable. Not potable. Not suitable for drinking. Anno: 11 ALR 1237.

undue influence. A species of fraud or constructive fraud whereby means brought to bear upon a person his free agency is destroyed and the will of another person substituted therefor. 25 Am J2d Dur §§ 35, 36. A species of constructive fraud which the court will not undertake to define particularly less the very definition itself should furnish a guide by which its consequences may be evaded. 23 Am J2d Deeds § 148. As invalidating a will, influence which substitutes the wishes of another for those of the testator; such influence as overcomes the free volition of the testator and substitutes the purposes of another. 57 Am J1st Wills §§ 350, 351.

Strictly speaking, there is a difference between fraud and undue influence as grounds of a caveat. Undue influence may, in a general way, be characterized as fraudulent; but not all fraud amounts to undue influence in the meaning of the law. To constitute undue influence within the meaning of the law, there must be mental constraint, moral coercion, the substitution of external for internal agency. Franklin v Belt, 130 Ga 37, 60 SE 146.

undue means. An inappropriate, unsuitable, and unjust means.

A statute providing for the vacation of an award of arbitrators procured by "undue means" does not apply merely because an award is made by two arbitrators after the resignation of the third and before the expiration of the three-day period claimed to be established by the arbitration agreement for appointing a successor. Amalgamated Asso. v Connecticut Co. 142 Conn 186, 112 A2d 501, 49 ALR2d 891.

undue return. An officer's false, defective or inaccurate return of a writ or process placed in his hands for execution.

To make return according to law is not only to return the precept to the authority that issued it, but to return with it a statement by the officer of his doings in executing it. That statement must contain all of his doings within the scope of proper execution; otherwise the return will be undue, and may be essentially false. Gibson v Holmes, 78 Vt 110, 62 A 11.

unearned income. Income from property or an investment, as distinguished from income received from a trade, profession, or employment. New York ex rel. Cohn v Graves, 300 US 308, 81 L Ed 666, 57 S Ct 466, 108 ALR 721.

unearned premium. An insurance premium or part of such premium to which the insurance company is not entitled because of not having carried the risk. That portion of the premium paid by a borrower to a building and loan association which is proportionate to the unexpired part of the period for which the loan was made, upon a premature severance of their relation. 13 Am J2d B & L Assoc § 121.

unearned premium reserve. A reserve required by modern statutes of insurance companies to assure the return of unearned premiums. 29 Am J Rev ed Ins § 56. A reserve which comes into being as the natural result of collecting premiums in advance for insurance to extend over a stated period of time in the future. The estimated aggregate amount which an insurance company would be obliged to tender to its policyholders as returned premiums for the unexpired terms, should it wish to cancel every policy in force.

The premium reserve, so-called, of a life insurance company, represents the insurer's debt at any given time on the policies it has issued and which are in force, and, hence, the corresponding fund which, in addition to general assets, it should have in reserve to meet such indebtedness. Anno: 13 ALR 187.

unemployment compensation. See **unemployment insurance.**

unemployment insurance. A form of social security, under state statutes complementary to the Federal Social Security Act, which provides for the payment of benefits to unemployed persons, subject to terms and conditions. 48 Am J1st Soc Sec § 10. Compulsory, state-imposed insurance, carried at the expense of employers, or employers and employees jointly, by which the financial burden of unemployment is transferred from the taxpayers generally to the industry in which unemployment exists or to industry as a whole. Insurance against loss arising from unemployment, voluntarily procured by an employee at his own expense from an insurer carrying such risks. 29 Am J Rev ed Ins § 17.

A subsistence allowance paid by the United States to a veteran attending school, under the provisions of the Servicemen's Readjustment Act, is within the provision of a previously enacted state statute disqualifying, for unemployment benefits, anyone receiving "unemployment allowances or compensation granted by the United States ... to ex-servicemen." Hannan v Administrator, Unemployment Compensation Act, 137 Conn 240, 75 A2d 483, 21 ALR2d 1068.

Before an individual may be deemed "unemployed" for any week, within the meaning of the unemployment compensation statute, two things must exist: (1) he must perform no service during the week and (2) he must be paid no wages for the week. Ackerson v Western Union Tel. Co. 234 Minn 271, 48 NW2d 338, 25 ALR2d 1063.

See **railroad unemployment insurance act.**

unemployment relief arrangement. An arrangement by an association for the sale of contracts to employed persons by way of compensation for them in the event they become unemployed. 29 Am J Rev ed Ins § 17.

unemployment trust fund. A trust fund established by the Social Security Act into which is required to be paid all moneys received in the statutory unemployment funds of the several states. 48 Am J1st Soc Sec § 11.

unequivocal. Certain. Not doubtful. Without ambiguity. Clear, sincere; plain. Molyneux v Twin Falls Canal Co. 54 Idaho 619, 35 P2d 651, 94 ALR 1264.

unerring. Incapable of error or failure; certain; sure; infallible. Gardner v State, 27 Wyo 316, 196 P 750, 15 ALR 1040.

unethical. Wanting in observance of ethical principles.

See **ethics.**

unexpected. Not expected; coming without warning; sudden. Bachus v Ronnebaum, 98 Ind App 603, 186 NE 386.

unexpected injury. An injury to an employee not intended or expected to be the result of what he was doing on the particular occasion. 58 Am J1st Workm Comp § 196.

unexpended. Not spent.

The word as it is used in a will may carry with it a clear and unambiguous purpose on decedent's part to give his beneficiaries unrestricted power to spend such part of the corpus of his estate as they see fit. Anno: 114 ALR 952.

unfair comment. The antithesis of fair comment. Comment actuated by malice as inferred from false statements exceeding the limits of fair and reasonable criticism, made recklessly in disregard of the rights of one who may be injured by them. 33 Am J1st L & S § 162.

unfair competition. The unjust appropriation of, or injury to, the goodwill or business reputation of another. 52 Am J1st Tradem §§ 86, 93 et seq. Acts done or practices employed for the purpose of pirating the trade of a competitor. The simulation by one person of the name, symbols, or devices employed by a business rival, so as to induce the purchase of his goods under a false impression as to their origin or ownership and thus secure for himself benefits properly belonging to his competitor. 52 Am J1st Tradem § 86. The repetition of words of a competitor in business in such a way as to convey a misrepresentation materially injuring the person who first used them, by appropriating credit of some kind which the first user has earned. International News Service v Associated Press, 248 US 215, 63 L Ed 211, 39 S Ct 68, 2 ALR 293.

Practices opposed to good morals, because characterized by deception, bad faith, fraud, and oppression, are unfair methods of competition. Consolidated Book Publishers v Federal Trade Com. (CA7) 53 F2d 942.

Unfair competition in the use of names or marks consists in the use of a name or mark by the defendant which tends to delude the public into believing the defendant's business is in some way connected with that of the plaintiff. The test is, whether the use of the name or mark would breed confusion in the minds of the public. Martha Washington Candies Co. v Goldstein (DC Pa) 28 F Supp 861.

unfair labor practice. An act, whether by employer or employee, in violation of the regulations and prohibitions of a labor relations act. 31 Am J Rev ed Lab §§ 224 et seq.

As the word is employed by labor organizations, it has the technical and well-understood meaning, as applied to an employer, not that he has been guilty of any fraud, breach of faith, or dishonorable conduct, but that he has refused to comply with the conditions upon which union men would consent to remain in the employ or handle materials supplied by the employer. J. F. Parkinson Co. v Building Trades Council, 154 Cal 581, 98 P 1027.

unfair list. A listing of names frequently used as the means of promoting a boycott. 31 Am J Rev ed Lab § 480.

See **boycott.**

unfair products. For the purposes of a boycott, the products of an employer deemed to be unfair to union labor. Anno: 6 ALR 957, s. 116 ALR 513.

unfair to organized labor. A familiar expression in times of labor unrest, appearing on the placards or banners of pickets. 31 Am J Rev ed Lab § 428.

unfair trade practice. See **unfair competition.**

UNFAITHFULNESS [1316] UNIMPEACHABLE

unfaithfulness. See **adultery.**

unfavorable signal. A traffic signal halting traffic. 8 Am J2d Auto § 743.

unfit for food. Adulterated; consisting in whole or in part of filthy, decomposed, or putrid substances. Anno: 45 ALR2d 861.

unfit premises. See **untenantable condition.**

unforeseen clause. An undiscovered cause or a cause not discovered in time to prevent injurious effects from its operation. A cause which could not have been foreseen as likely to occur. Viterbo v Friedlander, 120 US 707, 30 L Ed 776, 7 S Ct 962.

ungeld (un'geld). (Saxon.) An outlaw.

unguarded shaft. An open elevator shaft.

uniform. Noun: Clothing of a prescribed color and tailoring, as worn by members of the Armed Forces, pupils in certain schools, and employees in certain trades and occupations. Adjective: Without variation. Conforming to a standard.

As the word is used in the first paragraph of section 8, article I, of the United States Constitution, providing that all duties, imposts and excises shall be uniform throughout the United States, this word is to be understood in what has been termed its "geographical" sense, or as meaning uniformity as to all the taxpayers similarly situated with regard to the subject matter of the tax. Nicol v Ames, 173 US 509, 521, 43 L Ed 786, 794, 19 S Ct 522. That is to say, wherever a subject is taxed anywhere, it must be taxed everywhere throughout the United States, and at the same rate. Knowlton v Moore, 178 US 41, 84, 44 L Ed 969, 987, 20 S Ct 747.

See **act of uniformity.**

uniform acts. See **uniform statutes.**

Uniform Commercial Code. See **Commercial Code.**

Uniform Code of Military Justice. See **Code of Military Justice.**

uniformity. A condition characterized by absence of variation between two or more things or activities. See **uniform.**

Uniformity of Process Act (of pro'ses akt). An English statute, 2 William IV Ch 39, making original process uniform for the courts of Westminster.

uniformity of taxation. A requirement of the United States Constitution in reference to federal duties, imposts, and excises. Art I § 8 cl 1. A general principle that taxes should be levied in accord with some reasonable system of apportionment. 51 Am J1st Tax § 151.

As this clause is used in Article I, § 8 of the Constitution, providing that all duties, imposts, and excises shall be uniform throughout the United States, it means that such taxes may only be levied with geographical uniformity. See United States v Doremus, 249 US 86, 63 L Ed 493, 39 S Ct 214.

The uniformity required by the provision of the United States Constitution that excises imposed by the United States must be uniform throughout the United States is not an intrinsic uniformity relating to the inherent character of the tax as respects its operations on individuals, but is merely a geographical uniformity requiring the same plan and the same method to be operative throughout the United States. Fernandez v Wiener, 326 US 340, 90 L Ed 116, 66 S Ct 178, reh den 327 US 814, 90 L Ed 1038, 66 S Ct 525.

uniform laws. See **uniform statutes.**

uniform operation of laws. An embodiment of the guaranty of equal protection of the laws. 16 Am J2d Const L §§ 488, 489.

A law which applies alike to all the subjects upon which it acts, which applies equally to all persons or things within a legitimate class to which, alone, it is addressed, complies with a constitutional provision requiring laws of a general nature to have a uniform operation. The word uniform, in this connection, does not mean universal. The provision intends simply that the effect of general laws shall be the same to and upon all persons who stand in the same relation to the law,—that is, all the facts of whose cases are substantially the same. See Re Sohncke, 148 Cal 262, 82 P 956.

uniform state laws. See **uniform statutes.**

uniform statutes. Statutes drafted by a commission on Uniform Laws, or by a committee appointed by State Boards of Commissioners for promoting Uniformity of Legislation, and recommended to the legislatures of the various states for adoption, the purpose being to provide statutes on the subjects involved which, upon being adopted as recommended, will render the statutory provisions and rules uniform in terms and operation throughout the country. 50 Am J1st Stat §§ 40 et seq. Published in Uniform Laws Annotated.

For particular uniform statute, see the specific subject, such as **Commmercial Code; Negotiable Instruments Act; Warehouse Receipts Act,** etc.

uniform tax. See **uniformity of taxation.**

unilateral (ū-ni-lat'e-ral). One-sided.

unilateral contract. A contract in which there is a promise on one side only, the consideration therefor being an act or something other than another promise. 17 Am J2d Contr § 5.

The term "unilateral" has also been used to describe what is sometimes denominated a contract but which is in reality merely an offer to contract, as, for example, a promise to pay one for services if he should perform them, the latter being under no obligation to perform such services. 17 Am J2d Contr § 5.

unilateral mistake. A mistake on the part of only one of the parties to a transaction. Peterson v Paulson, 24 Wash 2d 166, 163 P2d 830. A mistake in the expression of the intention of one of the parties to a contract. 17 Am J2d Contr § 146.

A unilateral error is not, in itself, a ground of avoidance of a contract. If accompanied by other facts, however, such as hardship amounting to injustice, coupled with knowledge on the part of the one party that the other was laboring under a mistake, a unilateral mistake is ground for avoidance of a contract. Anno: 59 ALR 815.

unilateral rescission. A rescission of a contract by one party for cause. 17 Am J2d Contr § 501.

unimpeachable for waste. A phrase, such as "without impeachment of waste," in an instrument which creates a tenancy, which legalizes or authorizes acts or conduct that would otherwise constitute waste on the part of the tenant. 56 Am J1st Waste § 7.

The phrase "without impeachment of waste" is, in equity, so restrained in its meaning that it will not permit the tenant for life to commit malicious waste so as to destroy the estate, and a court of equity will sometimes, when there is no remedy at law, interpose when the tenant "without impeachment of waste" does something affecting the inheritance in an unreasonable way, or seeks maliciously or unconsciably to destroy it. Derham v Hovey, 195 Mich 243, 161 NW 883, 21 ALR 999.

unimproved land. Land in relation to which nothing has been done, either on or off the land, the direct and proximate tendency of which was to enhance its value in the market. Vandall v South San Francisco Dock Co. 40 Cal 83, 90. Land without buildings or other improvements. Land in a state of nature.

uninclosed land. Land which is not fenced. Graves v Ashburn, 215 US 331, 54 L Ed 217, 30 S Ct 108.

unincorporated association. See **association**.

unincorporated territory. A territory, organized or unorganized, belonging to the United States but not incorporated into the United States. 49 Am J1st States § 4.

uninhabitability. See **untenantable condition**.

uninhabited premises. Real property not presently occupied by persons who actually live or abide thereon. Shepherd v Board of Supervisors, 137 Cal App 421, 30 P2d 578.

uninsured motorist clause. A clause in an automobile insurance policy intented to protect the insured who is injured in person or in property through the fault of a motorist who is not himself insured or is a hit-and-run driver. 7 Am J2d Auto Ins § 135.

unintelligible (un-in-tel′i-ji-bl). Incapable of being understood; not expressing any meaning.

Union. The inseparable United States of America. Coyle v Oklahoma, 221 US 559, 55 L Ed 853, 31 S Ct 688. A one-time disputed merger of Great Britain and Ireland.
See **Act of Union; Articles of Union.**

union. A labor union. 31 Am J Rev ed Lab § 13. A trade union. Tracy v Banker, 170 Mass 266, 49 NE 308. Consolidation or merger, especially of churches. 45 Am J1st Reli Soc § 78.

union button. A button to be worn on the lapel, indicating labor-union membership. 31 Am J Rev ed Lab § 230.

union depot. Same as **union station.**

union-depot company. A company which maintains and operates a station for two or more carriers, being a corporation separate and apart from the several carriers. 44 Am J1st RR § 268.

unionizing. Organizing a union of employees of a particular shop or business; inducing the employees of a particular shop or business to join a labor union. 31 Am J Rev ed Lab § 54. In fine distinction, not the inducing of employees to become members of a labor union, but inducing the employer to enter into a collective labor agreement with the union. Per Opinion of Brandeis, J., dissenting in Hitchman Coal & Coke Co. v Mitchell, 245 US 229, 62 L Ed 260, 38 S Ct 65.

union label. A part of the workings of trade unions; a label which shows that the goods which bear it are made by the labor of members of the union. 31 Am J Rev ed Lab § 73. A quasi trademark indicating the origin of a manufactured product in union labor. Anno: 42 ALR2d 718.

union mortgage clause. A clause in a policy of insurance covering property, which, in addition to a provision for payment of the proceeds of insurance to a mortgagee as his interest may appear, contains terms for the additional protection of the mortgagee, providing that the interest of the mortgagee in the proceeds shall not be invalidated by the act or neglect of the mortgagor or owner of the insured property, or, less frequently, that no act or default of any person other than the mortgagee or those claiming under him shall affect his right to recover in case of loss. 29 Am J Rev ed Ins § 731.

union of students. See **students' union**.

union rules. The rules and regulations provided and promulgated by a labor union for the conduct of its members. 31 Am J Rev ed Lab § 36.

union-security contract. A collective labor agreement establishing a union shop. Pacific Fire Rating Bureau v Book Binders and Bindery Women's Union, etc. 115 Cal App 2d 111, 251 P2d 694.
See **agency-shop agreement.**

union shop. A place of work where membership in a labor union is a condition of remaining in employment, even though not a condition precedent to employment. 31 Am J Rev ed Lab § 95.

union shop card. A card or placard identifying a shop or place of employment as one in which only union labor is employed. Di Leo v Daneault, 329 Mass 590, 109 NE2d 824.

union station. A railroad station used jointly by two or more railroads. 44 Am J1st RR § 268.
See **union-depot company.**

unique value. A special value based upon an unusual or appealing nature of an article, the scarcity of articles of such kind, or a sentimental consideration arising from the personal use and personal associations involved.

unissued stock. Corporate stock which has been authorized but is not outstanding.

unit. One single thing. One single person. One single group of persons, as a squad, platoon, or company of men in a military force. An apartment in a condominium. 15 Am J2d Con Apt § 1.
See **employing unit.**

unitary award. An award for alimony and child support combined. Anno: 2 ALR3d 599, § 3.

unitary business (ū′ni-tạ-ri biz′nes). A descriptive term meaning that the concern to which it is applied is carrying on one kind of business—a business the component parts of which are to closely connected and necessary to each other to justify division or separate consideration as independent units. State v Kent-Coffey Mfg. Co. 204 NC 365, 168 SE 397, 90 ALR 476.

unitary domicil (ū′ni-tạ-ri dom-i-sil). The matrimonial domicil, the domicil resulting where the domicil of a married woman is merged by fiction in that of her husband. 24 Am J2d Div & S § 257.

unitary transaction rule. See **Kimbell-Diamond doctrine.**

unitas personarum (ū′ni-tās per-sō-nā′rum). The merger of two legal persons into one.

unit assessment. A separate assessment for taxation of parts or parcels of land belonging to the same owner. 51 Am J1st Tax § 686. The assessment for taxation of the property of transportation and communication companies owning, or operating upon, a continuous line of property, such as tracks or wires, extending into or through several states, or several counties or other taxing districts of a single state, as a homogenous unit representing a single profit-earning business, as an alternative to assessing separately so much of the line as lies within the

state or smaller taxing unit in question, assuming that such portion of the entire assessment representing the share referable to the particular taxing district in question is set aside by a proper and reasonable method of apportionment. 51 Am J1st Tax § 877.

See **unit valuation rule**.

united in interest. See **unity of ownership**.

United Kingdom (ū-nī′ted king′dum). Great Britain and Northern Ireland.

United Nations. A governmental agency of international status created by nations of the world to deal with questions of an international character. 30 Am J Rev ed Internat L § 9.

The overlying purpose of the United Nations is the maintenance of peaceful relations between nations by providing a forum wherein differences may be discussed and adjusted without resort to arms, although collateral thereto are activities in economic, social, cultural, educational, health, and related matters.

United Nations Charter. The Charter of the United Nations, an exercise of the treaty-making power of the United States so far as participation by the United States is concerned. Rice v Sioux City Cemetery, 349 US 70, 99 L Ed 897, 75 S Ct 614. Drawn up at the United Nations Conference on International Organizations at San Francisco, California, April 25—June 26, 1945.

united nuisance. Same as a **mixed nuisance**. 39 Am J1st Nuis §§ 6, 7.

United Press. A well-known organization for the gathering and dissemination of news, serving newspapers in its membership throughout the world.

United States. The Union of several states, each equal in power, dignity, and authority, brought into being by the Constitution, emanating from and adopted by the people in whom the sovereignty resides. M'Culloch v Maryland (US) 4 Wheat 316, 4 L Ed 579. A body politic and corporate, capable of attaining the objects for which it was created, by the means which are necessary for their attainment. Van Brocklin v Tennessee, 117 US 151, 29 L Ed 845, 6 S Ct 670. A person for the purpose of a pretrial deposition under Federal Rule 26(a) of the Federal Rules of Civil Procedure. 23 Am J2d Dep § 242. Inclusive in reference to transactions with foreign nations of all territories subject to the jurisdiction of the Federal Government, wherever located. Downes v Bidwell, 182 US 244, 45 L Ed 1088, 21 S Ct 770.

A Federal government was created in 1777 by the union of thirteen colonies of Great Britain in "certain articles of confederation and perpetual union," the first one of which declared that "the stile of this confederacy shall be the United States of America." Each member of the confederacy was denominated a "state." The confederacy, owing to well-known historical reasons, having proven a failure, a new Constitution was formed in 1787, by "The people of the United States" "for the United States of America," as its preamble declares. Downes v Bidwell, 182 US 244, 249, 45 L Ed 1088, 1092, 21 S Ct 770.

See expressions following which begin with "United States," also terms and expressions beginning "federal" or "national."

United States agency. See **federal agency**.

United States Attorney General. See **Attorney General of the United States**.

United States Cemeteries. National cemeteries; military cemeteries in foreign countries; a congressional cemetery. 14 Am J2d Cem § 3.

United States Circuit Court (sėr′kit kōrt). A United States court of original jurisdiction which was abolished in 1911, and the jurisdiction of which was taken over by the United States District Court.

United States Circuit Court of Appeals (ov a-pēls′). A United States court which was created in 1891, with three judges for each circuit, and hearing appeals from the United States district courts and formerly, appeals from the United States Circuit Court. Succeeded by the United States Court of Appeals.

See **court of appeals**.

United States citizen. The antithesis of alien. A person born or naturalized in the United States and subject to the jurisdiction thereof. US Const Art 14, cl 1. One who by birth, naturalization, or other means is a member of the independent political society of the United States of America. 3 Am J2d Aliens § 1.

United States Code. The codification of the federal statutes.

United States Commissioner. An officer of the federal district court, vested with certain duties in reference to arraignment of persons accused of federal offenses, admission to bail, etc. Not to be classified as a judge of a United States court. Todd v United States, 158 US 278, 39 L Ed 982, 15 S Ct 889.

United States Constitution. The fundamental document of the American system of government, constituting the supreme law of the land, as adopted by the people of the United States through their representatives in the Convention of 1787 and ratified by conventions in the states, and as amended in compliance with provisions regarding amendments contained in the document. 16 Am J2d Const L §§ 11, 18 et seq.

United States Court of Appeals. See **court of appeals**.

United States Courts. Courts upon which the judicial power of the United States is conferred by the third article of the United States Constitution. American Ins. Co. v Canter (US) 1 Pet 511, 7 L Ed 242; Federal Trade Com. v Klesner, 274 US 145, 71 L Ed 972, 47 S Ct 557. The United States Supreme Court and courts inferior to it, commonly known as federal courts, ordained and established by Congress in the exercise of its constitutional powers. 20 Am J2d Cts § 6.

For the purpose of enforcing Federal law applicable to the whole country and therefore applicable to the District of Columbia, the courts of the District are held to be Federal courts. Federal Trade Com. v Klesner, 274 US 145, 71 L Ed 972, 47 S Ct 557.

United States District Attorney. An officer appointed in each federal judicial district whose duty it is to prosecute therein all delinquents for crimes and offenses cognizable under the authority of the United States and all civil actions in which the United States is concerned, under the general superintendence and direction of the Attorney General. 42 Am J1st Pros Atty § 2.

United States District Courts. The trial courts of the federal system, one for each federal judicial district, the jurisdiction of such courts and the venue of actions brought therein being prescribed by the United States Code. 20 Am J2d Cts § 11.

United States Government Life Insurance. Life Insurance provided by the government and made available to veterans of World War I by way of conversion of their level-premium term insurance known as United States War Risk Insurance. 29A Am J Rev ed Ins § 1970.

United States homeopathic pharmacopoeia. An official publication listing drugs and medicines, adapted to the homeopathic school of medicine. 25 Am J2d Drugs § 1.

United States judge. A judge of a court of the United States. Fong Yue Ting v United States, 149 US 698, 37 L Ed 905, 13 S Ct 1016.

United States Land Office. See **General Land Office.**

United States Marshal. A ministerial officer through whom the commands of the Judicial Department of the United States must be executed, although belonging to the executive department of the government. Re Neagle, 135 US 1, 34 L Ed 55, 10 S Ct 658.

Marshals are mere ministers of the law to execute the orders of the Federal courts, with no authority in their official characters to do any act that shall expressly or impliedly bind anyone by warranty. If a marshal steps out of his official duty and does what the law has given him no authority to do, he is usually personally liable to the injured party. The Monte Allegre (US) 9 Wheat 616, 645, 6 L Ed 174, 181.

United States Mint. See **mint.**

United States notes. Notes issued by the United States under the authority of Congress, intended to circulate as money and with the national bank notes to constitute the credit currency of the country.

They were obligations of the United States and each one was an engagement to pay to the bearer a certain number of gold or silver dollars. People ex rel. Bank of New York v Supervisors of New York (US) 7 Wall 26, 19 L Ed 60.

See **bank note; treasury note.**

United States of America. See **United States.**

United States Pharmacopoeia (ū-nī'ted stāts fär''mȧ-kọ̈-pē'iạ̈). An official list of drugs and medicines, noting their properties. 25 Am J2d Drugs § 1.

United States Rule. An old and indeterminate appellation for the principle that a partial payment, in the absence of an agreement or statute to the contrary, should be applied first to the interest due.

For discussion of application of the principle, see 30 Am J Rev ed Int § 49.

United States Statutes at Large. An official publication of the federal statutes, concurrent resolutions of Congress, treaties, international agreements other than treaties, proclamations by the President, and proposed or ratified amendments to the Constitution of the United States.

United States Supreme Court. The highest of the courts of the federal court system, established by the Constitution of the United States, and having both original and appellate jurisdiction. US Const Art 3; 20 Am J2d Cts §§ 6, 9. Occupying a singular position within the dual system of federal and state jurisdiction to the extent that certain decisions of the highest court of a state are reviewable and may be set aside by it. 20 Am J2d Cts § 9.

United States treasury notes. See **treasury note.**

United States Treaties and other International Agreements. A compilation of treaties and international agreements entered into by the United States. 1 USC § 112(a).

See **treaty.**

United States vessel. See **vessel of the United States.**

unit owner. The owner, singular or plural, of an apartment in a condominium. 15 Am J2d Con Apt § 1.

unit-price contract. A contract under which payment of compensation is to be made at specified unit rates for different kinds of work performed or materials furnished or both. 17 Am J2d Contr § 346.

unit prices. Prices at which the various articles in the inventory of a public utility plant are taken in the valuation of the plant for rate-making purposes. 43 Am J1st Pub Util § 114.

unit rates. The rates specified in a contract for different kinds of work performed or materials furnished or both. 17 Am J2d Contr § 346.

unit rule. The rule applied in some political conventions that the entire vote of a delegation shall be cast as a unit, the proposition or candidate for whom it is to be cast being determined by a majority vote of the delegation.

See **unit assessment; unit valuation rule.**

unit rule in taxation. See **unit assessment; unit valuation rule.**

unit valuation rule. The rule that the value of shares of corporate stock for death tax purposes is ascertained by multiplying the total number of shares to be valued by the sale price of one share sold on an exchange. Citizens Fidelity Bank & Trust Co. v Reeves (Ky) 259 SW2d 432.

See **unit assessment.**

unity of husband and wife. See **unity of spouses.**

unity of interest. See **unity of ownership.**

unity of ownership. By the whole, not by the half or other part. The identity of the interests of joint tenants, whereby each joint tenant is entitled to the same period of duration or quantity of interest in lands. See 2 Bl Comm 181.

unity of possession. One of the essential elements of a joint tenancy, meaning that each of the joint tenants has the entire possession of the property, as well of every parcel of it as the whole.

That is, no one of them has the sole possession of any part. See 2 Bl Comm 181.

unity of seisin (ov sē'zn). The merger of one seisin in another, as where the owner of a servient tenement acquires the dominant tenement also.

See **unity of possession.**

unity of spouses. The concept of the common law whereby husband and wife become by marriage one person, the entire legal existence of the wife being completely merged or incorporated in that of the husband. 26 Am J1st H & W § 3.

It has been said that a husband and wife are considered separate persons in equity, in divorce proceedings, and in proceedings brought for the annulment of a divorce obtained by fraud. Usen v Usen, 136 Me 480, 13 A2d 738, 128 ALR 1449.

unity of time. One of the essential properties of a joint tenancy whereby the estates of the joint tenants must be vested at one and the same time. See 2 Bl Comm 181.

unity of title. One of the essential properties of a joint tenancy, under which the estates of the joint tenants must be created by one and the same act, whether legal or illegal; as by one and the same grant, or by one and the same disseisin. See 2 Bl Comm 181.

See **unity of ownership.**

Uniuscujusque contractus initium spectandum est et causa (ū-nī′us-kū-jus′kwe kon-trak′tus i-ni′she-um spek-tan′dum est et kâ′zā). (Civil law.) The beginning and the consideration of every contract should be scrutinized.

Unius responsio testis, omnino non audiatur (ū-nī′us re-spon′si-ō tes′tis, om-nī′nō non â-di-ā′ter). The evidence of one witness may never be admitted.

This was the ancient rule of the civil law, which the early common law adopted and which Blackstone characterized as absurd. See 3 Bl Comm 370.

universal. Not limited in application. Pertaining to all, without exception. Koen v State, 35 Neb 676, 53 NW 595.

universal agent. An agent authorized to transact all the business of his principal of every kind and do all delegable acts for him. Baldwin v Tucker, 112 Ky 282, 65 SW 841.

A principal can have only one universal agent. Baldwin v Tucker, 112 Ky 282, 65 SW 841.

Universal Copyright Convention. An international copyright agreement ratified by the United States Senate in 1954, effective for the United States September 16, 1955. 18 Am J2d Copyr § 76.

Universalia sunt notiora singularibus (u-ni-ver-sā′li-a sunt no-ti-ō′ra sin-gu-lā′ri-bus). Universal matters are better known than particular ones.

universal military service. Military service required by law of every able-bodied citizen or national. 36 Am J1st Mil §§ 22, 23.

universal partnership. A partnership in which each individual partner has contributed all of his property to the partnership.

universal succession (ū-ni-vėr′sal suk-sesh′ǫn). The artificial continuance of the person of a deceased by an executor, heir, or the like, so far as succession to rights and obligations is concerned.

It is a fiction, the historical origin of which is familiar to scholars, and it is this fiction that gives whatever meaning it has to the saying **mobilia sequuntur personam.** Blackstone v Miller, 188 US 189, 47 L Ed 439, 23 S Ct 277.

universitas (u-ni-ver′si-tās). (Latin.) The whole. The total.

As the term was used in the civil law it meant a corporation: that is one whole entity formed out of many individuals. See 1 Bl Comm 469.

universitas bonorum (u-ni-ver′si-tās bo-nō′rum). All of a person's goods; all of a person's estate.

Universitas vel corporatio non dicitur aliquid facere nisi id sit collegialiter deliberatum, etiamsi major pars id faciat (u-ni-ver′si-tās vel kor-po-rā′she-ō non di′si-ter a′li-quid fā′se-re nī′si id sit kol-lē″ji-ā′li-ter dē-li-be-rā′tum, e-she-am′si mā′jor parz id fā′shē-at). A university or a corporation is said not to do anything unless it is deliberated upon collectively, even though a majority of the members should act upon it.

university. Precisely, an aggregation or union of colleges. An educational institution in which the teaching covers a broad, if not universal, field, instructing in many branches of the arts and sciences, reaching out to cover all manner of higher learning, and possessing the power to confer degrees indicating proficiency in the branches taught. 15 Am J2d Colleges § 1.

A university is a "scientific institution" within the meaning of a statutory provision for exemption from personal property taxes. District of Columbia v Catholic Education Press, Inc. 91 App DC 126, 199 F2d 176, 34 ALR2d 1214.

universum jus (u-ni-ver′sum jūs). An entire right; sole ownership.

universus (u-ni-ver′sus). All; the whole; whole; entire.

unjust. Unfair. Contrary to justice.

All human actions are either just or unjust as they are in conformity to or in opposition to law. Borden v State, 11 Ark 519.

unjust discrimination. See **discrimination.**

unjust enrichment. The circumstances which give rise to the obligation of restitution, that is, the receiving and retention of property, money, or benefits which in justice and equity belong to another. Herrmann v Gleason (CA6 Mich) 126 F2d 936; Straube v Bowling Green Gas Co. 360 Mo 132, 227 SW2d 666, 18 ALR2d 1335.

See **restitution.**

unkerjay (un′kėr-jā). A morphine addict.

unknown contents. See **contents unknown.**

unknown motorist clause. A clause of an automobile insurance policy protecting the insured in reference to injury in person or in property by a hit-and-run driver, the conditions of the accident being such that it is impossible to ascertain whether or not the offending driver has insurance. 7 Am J2d Auto Ins § 135.

unknown parties. Persons within the meaning of statutes authorizing actions to be prosecuted against unknown persons.

Proceedings against unknown persons are of two classes: (1) those brought against that class of claimants to property who are known to exist, but whose names are unknown; and (2) those brought against that class of claimants whose names are not known, and who may or may not exist. 39 Am J1st Parties § 7.

unkouth. Same as **uncuth.**

unlade (un-lād′). To relieve a vessel of the burden of cargo.

In some cases the word means to transship cargo from one vessel to another. See The Cherie (CA1 Me) 13 F2d 992, 995.

unlage. (Saxon.) An unjust law.

unlaw (un-lâ′). A property qualification which was required of witnesses.

unlawful. Contrary to law. Not allowed or permitted by law. Not in the manner required by law. State v Campbell, 217 Iowa 848, 251 NW 717, 92 ALR 1176; State v Falkner, 182 NC 793, 108 SE 756, 17 ALR 987.

See **illegal; illicit; invalid; ultra vires.**

unlawful ab initio. Unlawful from the beginning.

In cases of total divorce, the marriage is declared null, as having been absolutely unlawful ab initio (from the beginning); and the parties are therefore separated pro salute animarum (for the welfare of their souls). See 1 Bl Comm 440.

See **trespass ab initio.**

unlawful accumulation. An accumulation of an estate in violation of the rule against perpetuities or in violation of statutes comparable to the Thellusson Act of England. 41 Am J1st Perp § 44.

See **Thellusson Act**.

unlawful act. See **unlawful**.

unlawful arrest. See **false arrest**; **false imprisonment**.

unlawful assembly. A gathering of persons, usually three or more, with a common intent, formed before or at any time during the meeting, to attain a purpose, lawful or unlawful, which will interfere with the rights of others, by committing disorderly acts in such a manner as to cause sane, firm, and courageous persons in the neighborhood to apprehend a breach of the peace. Anno: 58 ALR 751, s. 93 ALR 737; 46 Am J1st Riot § 2.

Each charge of unlawfully assembling largely and necessarily depends upon the object and character of the meeting, and whether or not the overt acts done by the participants therein pursuant to a common understanding are of such a nature as to incite well grounded fear in persons of reasonable firmness and courage, of a riot, rout, affray, or other breach of the peace. State v Butterworth, 104 NJL 579, 142 A 57, 58 ALR 744.

See **mob**; **riot**.

unlawful belligerent. An enemy not entitled to the protection of the laws of war, because of the want of a lawful war or of the violation by it of the laws of war. 56 Am J1st War §§ 3 et seq.

unlawful cohabitation (kō-hab-i-tā′shon). The living together as husband and wife by a man and woman who are not married to each other. Ex parte Nielsen, 131 US 176, 33 L Ed 118, 121, 9 S Ct 672.

unlawful combination. An agreement in restraint of trade.

See **monopoly**; **restraint of trade**.

unlawful conspiracy. A criminal offense, indictable at common law where two or more persons confederate and combine together, by concerted means, to do that which is unlawful or criminal, to the injury of the public, or portions or classes of the community, or even to the rights of an individual. Beck v Railway Teamsters' Protective Union, 118 Mich 497, 77 NW 13.

See **conspiracy**.

unlawful contract. A contract wherein a person undertakes to do an act which the law forbids, or to omit an act which the law enjoins, and for that reason unenforceable.

It is distinguishable from a void contract which is a contract which has no legal force, and which, for that reason, cannot be enforced. King v King, 63 Ohio St 363, 59 NE 111.

See **illegal contract**.

unlawful detainer. The unlawful withholding or detention of real property after the acquisition of a peaceable and actual, but unlawful, possession. 35 Am J2d Forc E & D § 32.

unlawful entry. A trespass. A going upon the property of another without right or authority. As an element of burglary, the intrusion of any part of the body for the purpose of committing a felony upon the premises. Anno: 23 ALR 289; 13 Am J2d Burgl § 10.

unlawful injury. An **actionable wrong**.

Giving to the term the broadest meaning possible under the authorities, it can include no injury that is not of such a character that it would constitute an actionable wrong,—an injury for which an action for the resultant damages could be maintained against the perpetrator; or which, if merely threatened, could be enjoined in equity if the remedy at law were deemed inadequate. People v Schmitz, 7 Cal App 330, 369, 94 P 419.

unlawful killing. See **homicide**; **manslaughter**; **murder**.

unlawfully. Illegally; illicitly. In a manner contrary to law. A technical word in an indictment of information. 27 Am J1st Indict § 67.

The term implies that an act is done, or not done, as the law allows or requires. State v Falkner, 182 NC 793, 108 SE 756, 17 ALR 986, 990.

See **unlawful**.

unlawful order. An order rendered without jurisdiction. An erroneous order.

Every erroneous order is unlawful, and for that reason may be reversed on appeal. Ex parte Cohen, 5 Cal 494.

unlawful picketing. Picketing which is not in furtherance of a legitimate interest of labor or is not carried on peacefully. 31 Am J Rev ed Lab §§ 433 et seq.

unlawful possession of intoxicating liquor. Maintaining custody or exercising the right of ownership, management, or control over intoxicating liquor when possession of such article is in violation of law. 30 Am J Rev ed Intox L § 59.

unlawful trust. See **trust**.

unlearned parliament. Same as **parliament of dunces**.

unless lease. An oil or gas lease containing a provision that a default by the lessee in the prosecution of exploratory work shall terminate his rights unless on or before a day set there shall be paid the agreed computation for the period specified, with like payments for like successive periods. 24 Am J1st Gas & O § 60.

unliquidated claim. A claim in respect to which the exact amount which the claimant is entitled to recover has not been ascertained. Dycus v Brown, 135 Ky 140, 121 SW 1010.

unliquidated damages. Damages not stipulated by the parties or otherwise determined as to amount thereof. 22 Am J2d Damg § 212. Not an existing indebtedness within the meaning of attachment statutes. Craig v Gaddis, 171 Miss 379, 157 So 684, 95 ALR 1494.

A claim for unliquidated damages is not included within the expression "goods, effects, or credits." Wilde v Mahaney, 183 Mass 455, 67 NE 337.

unliquidated demand. See **unliquidated claim**; **unliquidated damages**.

unlisted stock. Shares of stock not listed on a stock exchange.

unlivery (un-liv′ĕr-i). Discharge of cargo from a vessel. The Two Catherines (CC RI) 2 Mason 319, F Cas No 14288.

unloading. See **loading and unloading**.

unloading clause. See **loading and unloading clause**.

unmailable. Same as **nonmailable**.

unmarried. Not presently under the bonds of matrimony, irrespective of prior status. Myers v Denver & R. G. R. Co. 61 Colo 302, 157 P 196. Estate of Kaufman, 131 NY 620, 30 NE 242. In some contexts, the equivalent of never having been married. Anno: 7 ALR2d 1386.

unmeasured right of common (un-mezh′ŭrd rit ov kom′on). A commoner's right of common before

it was admeasured or apportioned under a writ of admeasurement of pasture.
The uncertainty of this right caused it to be called erroneously a "common without stint or sans nombre." See 3 Bl Comm 239.

unnatural offense. Same as **crime against nature.**

unnatural will. A will in which the testator fails to provide for spouse or children, the natural objects of his bounty, or makes a provision for them which is inadequate from the standpoint of the size of the estate and their financial circumstances. 57 Am J1st Wills §§ 149, 150.

unnecessary cruelty. Torture or abuse of an animal; the infliction of pain without need. 4 Am J2d Ani § 28.

unnecessary exposure. The failure to use ordinary care for one's own safety, that is, contributory negligence. Shevlin v American Mut. Acci. Asso. 94 Wis 180, 68 NW 866.
Unnecessary exposure to danger is the equivalent of voluntary exposure to unnecessary danger. 29A Am J Rev ed Ins §§ 1174, 1175.
See **indecent exposure.**

unnecessary exposure to danger. See **unnecessary exposure.**

unnecessary hardship. An imprecise term appearing in some zoning ordinances.
It is recognized that the term does not lend itself to precise definition automatically resolving every case. The criterion of unnecessary hardship is whether the use restriction, viewing the property in the setting of its environment, is so unreasonable as to constitute an arbitrary and capricious interference with the basic right of private property. The fact that the enforcement of zoning regulation in question would deprive the applicant of any practical economic use of his property, without any commensurate advantage to other properties in the neighborhood, was held to constitute an unnecessary hardship within the operation of the zoning ordinance. Anno: 168 ALR 26 et seq.

Un ne doit prise advantage de son tort demesne (ŭn ne duä prēs äd-vän-täzh' de sôn tor de-māne'). A person ought not to take advantage of his own wrong.

Uno absurdo dato, infinita sequuntur (ū'nō ab-ser'do da'tō, in-fĭ'ni-ta se-qu-un'ter). If one absurdity is allowed, an infinite number will follow.

uno actu (ū'nō ak'tū). By one act.

unoccupancy. See **unoccupied building.**

unoccupied building. A building without animate occupants. 29A Am J Rev ed Ins § 907.
See **vacant and unoccupied.**

unoccupied vehicle. A vehicle which is unattended so that there is no one to move or to see to the moving of it in case traffic conditions require removal. McLaurine v Birmingham, 247 Ala 414, 24 So 2d 755, 163 ALR 962.

unoffered lands. Those public lands of the United States which have not been offered for sale or settlement. Northern Pacific Railway Co. v De Lacey, 174 US 622, 628, 43 L Ed 1111, 1113, 19 S Ct 791.

unofficial notes. Notes of the testimony of a witness taken by one other than the official reporter. 29 Am J2d Ev § 765.

unofficial opinion. An opinion of a court commissioner or referee which has not been confirmed by the court and accordingly is of no value as a precedent. Flint v Chaloupka, 72 Neb 34, 99 NW 825.
See **unofficial report.**

unofficial primary. A caucus called for the purpose of nominating candidates of a political party. 25 Am J2d Elect § 145.

unofficial publication. A publication of laws or court reports by a private publisher.

unofficial report. A court report published by a private publisher. Ex parte Griffiths, 118 Ind 83, 20 NE 513.

uno flatu (ū'nō flā'tū). In one breath.
"Yet it (the code) is to be considered as one homogeneous whole, established uno flatu." Central of Georgia Railway Co. v State, 104 Ga 831, 31 SE 531.

unopened way. A way used by the public which has never been officially and formally opened to public use. Klepper v Seymour House Corp. 246 NY 851, 158 NE 29, 62 ALR 955.

unorganized territory. A territory of the United States without a government in an elaborate form. 49 Am J1st States § 4.

unperfected. See expressions beginning "imperfect."

unpermitted. See **unlawful.**

unpleaded (un-plē'ded). Not alleged in a pleading; not pleaded.

unprecedented. Without precedent. Unknown to history or record of past events.

unprofessional conduct. See **professional misconduct.**

unpossessed. Not held in possession; unoccupied.

unqualifiedly subject to the demands of the shareholder. The actual receipt of a dividend by a shareholder or an entry of the amount of the dividend to the credit of the shareholder in his account with the corporation. Anno: 158 ALR 1432.

unques (un'kwes). Yet; still; always.

unques prist (un'kwes prist). Always ready.

unreasonable. Not rational or reasonable.

unreasonable rates. Rates of a public service corporation which are so low as to be noncompensatory, or those which are so much higher than simply compensatory rates that they are exorbitant. Homestead Co. v Des Moines Elec. Co. (CA8 Iowa) 248 F 439, 12 ALR 390.

unreasonable restraint of trade. See **restraint of trade.**

unreasonable search. An examination or inspection without authority of law of one's premises or person, with a view to the discovery of stolen, contraband, or illicit property, or for some evidence of guilt, to be used in the prosecution of a criminal action. 47 Am J1st Search § 52.

unreasonable search and seizure. A seizure of property discovered on an unreasonable search. 47 Am J1st Search § 52.
A literal "search" and "seizure" is not required to constitute an unreasonable search and seizure. The surreptitious removal from his office of incriminating documents belonging to the accused by an officer making a supposedly friendly visit constitutes an unreasonable search and seizure. 47 Am J1st Search § 52.

unreasonable seizure. A seizure of one's property or

effects without authority of law. 47 Am J1st Search § 52.
See **unreasonable search and seizure.**

unreasonable time. See **reasonable time.**

unrecorded. The state or condition of a document which has neither been filed for record nor placed of record on the public records.

unrelated business income. Income of a tax exempt organization from a trade or business not substantially related to the purpose of the organization which exempts it from income tax. Internal Revenue Code § 512(b)(12).

unresponsive answer. An answer by a witness which avoids or fails to meet the question or interrogatory propounded.

unrestricted. Without restrictions; without conditions; absolute. Columbia Water Power Co. v Columbia Street Railway, etc. Co. 172 US 475, 491, 43 L Ed 521, 527, 19 S Ct 247.

unrestricted district. A district established by a zoning law but not restricted thereby in reference to the use to be made of premises therein. 58 Am J1st Zon § 33.

unruly animal. An animal difficult, if not impossible, to control. 4 Am J2d Ani § 49.

unsafe bank. A bank which is insolvent or approaching insolvency.

unsafe driver. An incompetent or inexperienced driver of a motor vehicle.

unsafe speed. The speed of a motor vehicle at such a rate as to render it impossible to control the course of the vehicle or to stop it in time to avoid a collision with other vehicles or objects along the way. Robinson v LeSage, 145 Me 300, 75 A2d 447.

unsatisfactory title. A title to real estate so defective as not to be a marketable title.
See **marketable title.**

unseated land. Land which is neither occupied nor cultivated.
Land which has not been farmed or cultivated, or which has not been cleared, or which, after having been cultivated has not been used for a long period of time. Keating v Williams (Pa) 5 Watts 382, 384.

unseaworthy. Not seaworthy.
See **seaworthy.**

unscheduled assets. Assets of a bankrupt not listed in the schedule of his property. 9 Am J2d Bankr § 860.

unset diamond. A diamond of a nature to be worn as a jewel which has not been mounted upon a ring or other article of jewelry. 29 Am J Rev ed Ins § 298.

unsettled pauper. A poor person who has not gained a residence.
See **settlement of pauper.**

unsolemn admissions. Admissions which have been acted upon, or have been made to influence the conduct of others, or to derive some advantage to the party, and which cannot afterwards be denied without a breach of good faith. Metcalf v Hart, 3 Wyo 513, 31 P 407.

unsolemn war. A war in which there has been no solemn or formal declaration of war by either belligerent.

unsound animal. An animal having an organic defect or infirmity which renders it unfit for immediate, present, usual, and reasonable use. 46 Am J1st Sales § 396.

unsound memory. An imperfect memory. A memory which has failed in situations where there should have been a recollection.
"That men may and do have what is denominated unsound memories, although otherwise of sound mind, is a matter of common knowledge. It is most generally observable in persons of old age, who have lost the power to remember past events; but no one would class them as insane persons. That such a person might do an act and be perfectly conscious of it, and of its moral and legal effect, and yet forget it, is not open to dispute." State v Coyne, 214 Mo 344, 114 SW 8.

unsound mind. The mind of an insane or mentally deficient person.
As used in a statute providing for the appointment of a guardian of the property and minor children of a person of unsound mind, the term relates to the capacity of the person to transact business. The unsoundness of mind which will justify such an appointment must be more than mere debility or impairment of memory; it must be such as to deprive the person affected of ability to manage his estate. Emerick v Emerick, 83 Iowa 411, 49 NW 1017.
See **sound mind.**

untenant (un-ten'ant). To evict or remove a tenant from the premises of the landlord.

untenantable condition. A condition of premises rendering them unfit for the purpose for which they were leased, particularly where the lease expressly designates the use to be made of the premises. Tyson v Weil, 169 Ala 558, 53 So 912. A condition of premises rendering them unfit for occupation for any worthwhile purpose. 32 Am J1st L & T § 506.

untenanted. Not occupied by a tenant; not occupied by any person.

unthrift (un-thrift'). A prodigal; a spendthrift.

until. To a certain date or event, either inclusive or exclusive of the date or event, according to the manifest intention revealed by the entire context. 52 Am J1st Time § 25 A technical term apt for the creation of a determinable fee. Consolidated School Dist. v Walter, 243 Minn 153, 66 NW2d 881, 53 ALR2d 218.
No general rule can be laid down to determine whether the word "until," as a limit of time, is a word of inclusion or exclusion. Anno: 16 ALR 1094; 52 Am J1st Time § 25.
The word may have an inclusive or exclusive meaning, according to the use to which it is applied, the nature of the transaction which it specifies, and the connection in which it is used; and it may be held to include the day to which it is prefixed. State ex rel. Birdgell v Jorgenson, 25 ND 539, 142 NW 450.
A contractual provision for payment of a specified rate of interest "until maturity" of the obligation is an express limitation of that interest rate to the period prior to maturity so as to render applicable after maturity a statutory provision for interest at a stipulated rate "if there is no agreement ... for a different rate." Thompson v Getz (CA1 Mass) 178 F2d 325, 16 ALR2d 898.

untimely. Occurring out of time, as in the case of the death of a person who has not reached maturity.

Not in compliance with limitation of time, as in the case of a suit commenced after the running of the period fixed by an applicable statute of limitations.

As to when an application to a lower court for a rehearing may be said to be "untimely," see Anno: 10 ALR2d 1076.

untrue. Lacking truth. Lacking fidelity.

unum austurium (u'num âs-tū'ri-um). A rent reserved in ancient deeds payable to the lord in goshawks.

Unumquodque dissolvi potest eodem ligamine quo ligatum est (ū-num-quod'kwe dis-sol'vī po'test e-ō'dem li-gā'mi-ne quō li-gā'tum est). Everything can be undone by the same means by which it was done.

Unumquodque dissolvitur eodem ligamine quo ligatur (ū-num-quod'kwe dis-sol'vi-ter e-ō'dem li-gā'mi-ne quō li-gā'ter). Every obligation is dissolved in the same manner in which it is made binding. See Broom's Legal Maxims 884.

Unumquodque dissolvitur eo ligamine quo ligatur (ū-num-quod'kwe dis-sol'vi-ter e'ō li-gā'mi-ne quō li-gā'ter). Every obligation is dissolved in the same manner in which it is made binding.

"Like other old maxims, this has received qualifications, and, indeed, was never true to the letter." Munroe v Perkins, 26 Mass (9 Pick) 298.

Unumquodque eodem modo quo colligatum est dissolvitur (ū-num-quod'kwe e-ō'dem mo'dō quo kol-li-gā'tum est dis-sol'vi-ter). Every obligation is dissolved in the same manner in which it is made binding. See Broom's Legal Maxims 891.

Unumquodque est id quod est principalius in ipso (ū-num-quod'que est id quod est prin-si-pā'li-us in ip'sō). Anything which is the principal part is the thing itself.

Unumquodque ligamen dissolvitur eodem ligamine quod ligatur (ū-num-quod'kwe li-gā'men dis-sol'vi-ter e-ō'dem li-gā'me-ne quod li-gā'ter). Every obligation is dissolved in the same manner in which it is made binding. Esmond v Van Benschoten (NY) 12 Barb 366, 375.

Unumquodque principiorum est sibimet ipsi fides; et perspicua vera non sunt probanda (ū-num-quod'kwe prin-si-pi-ō'rum est si-bi-met ip'sī fī'dēz; et per-spi'ku-a vē'ra non sunt prō-ban'da). Every principle is its own proof, and plain truths need not be proved.

unused portion. That portion of an estate not consumed by the tenant entitled to make use thereof. Hardy v Mayhew, 158 Cal 95, 110 P 113.

unusual case. A case which is noteworthy because of either fact or principle involved. A case without precedent.

As the expression is used in a workmen's compensation act requiring the insurer to pay medical bills after the first two weeks in "unusual cases," the statute has been held to refer to injuries which develop unexpected or unusual complications, requiring the services of experts or unusual treatment. Moore's Case, 255 Mass 533, 535, 152 NE 66, 67.

unusual noise. See **excessive** or **unusual noise.**

unusual punishment. See **cruel and unusual punishment.**

unvalued policy. Same as **open policy.**

unwarrantable. Not warrantable; unjustifiable; indefensible.

unwarranted. Not warranted.

unwritten constitution. A system of fundamental laws or principles for the government of a nation which is binding notwithstanding it is not incorporated in a formal writing or document.

Although a constitution may be either written or unwritten, in the United States, the word "Constitution," as applied to the organization of the federal and state governments, always implies a writing. 16 Am J2d Const L § 1.

unwritten contract. An oral contract.

A contract is unwritten if the contract itself cannot be proved wholly by writings. Illinois Cent. R. Co. v Moore (CA5 Miss) 112 F2d 959.

unwritten law. The law as established by cases rather than as enacted by a legislative body. Equity as introduced into the United States. State ex rel. Rhodes v Saunders, 66 NH 39, 25 A 588. The theory that a man should not be punished for a homicide where his victim was the seducer of his wife or daughter.

unwritten law of nations. That part of international law which does not rest upon treaties but which springs from (1) abstract reasoning, (2) custom and usage, (3) the conclusions of publicists based on ancient and admitted practice, and (4) judicial precedents. 30 Am J1st Internat L § 2.

U. P. Abbreviation of **United Press.**

up a stream. Toward the source.

up-draft. An upward movement of air, of concern in the operation of aircraft. 8 Am J2d Avi § 96.

Descriptions running the boundary line up or upon, a river, stream, or creek have generally been construed to refer to the water in its entirety as the monument, and have been regarded as extending to embrace the land to the thread of the stream. Anno: 74 ALR 597.

upkeep. The maintenance of premises or of machinery. The cost of maintenance.

uplands. Elevated lands. Lands above the flood plain of a river. Lands upon a plateau or in a mountainous region.

upon. Literally, "up and on," but, in common usage, and equivalent of "on." An apt word in limiting the time for future enjoyment of an estate. Anno: 49 ALR 193, s. 127 ALR 614.

upon a motor vehicle. Being in physical contact with the vehicle. Anno: 39 ALR2d 956. In physical contact with a motor vehicle, although not seated in the place provided for the seating of passengers. 29A Am J Rev ed Ins § 1241. In physical contact with the vehicle, preparing to enter the vehicle, or in close proximity thereto after alighting therefrom. 29A Am J Rev ed Ins § 1241.

upon condition. See **condition.**

upon information and belief. Qualifying a statement as made, not as a fact, but as believed to be true from information. 5 Am J2d Arr § 14.

See **allegation on information and belief.**

upon personal knowledge. Upon knowledge derived from the exercise of one's own senses. Anno: 96 ALR 694.

upon sight. Same as **at sight.**

upon the failure of heirs. Upon an absence of heirs capable of taking by descent or devise. 27 Am J2d Esch § 11.

upon the faith of a document. In the belief held in good faith that the possessor was the true owner of the document. Warner v Martin (US) 11 How 209, 13 L Ed 667.

upper bench. See **court of upper bench.**

upper house. Inept terminology for the Senate of the United States Congress, the senate of a state legislature, and the House of Lords in Great Britain.

upper owner. A riparian owner whose land is upstream in reference to the land of another such owner. An owner of land from which surface water drains onto adjoining premises.

upper story. Any story of a building above the ground floor. Rose v King, 49 Ohio St 213, 30 NE 267.

upset. An overturning, but not necessarily a complete overturning; a loss of equilibrium. 7 Am J2d Auto Ins § 62.

As to whether damage to vehicle resulting from wind or other phenomenon of nature is as within coverage of automobile policy insuring against collision or upset. Anno: 14 ALR2d 807.

upset bid. A bid for property sold at judicial sale, in an amount greater than the bid of the purchaser, offered upon application to set aside the sale. 30A Am J Rev ed Jud S §§ 105-113.

upset insurance. Automobile insurance protecting the insured against damage to the vehicle caused by an upset.

upset price. See **minimum price.**

up to. A phrase excluding the time or place to which it pertains. 52 Am J1st Time § 25; 12 Am J2d Bound § 52.

uranium (ū-rā′ni-um). A radioactive element; special nuclear material. 6 Am J2d Atomic E § 8.
See **fissionable uranium.**

urban (ėr′ban). Pertaining to the city, not to the country.

urban easements (ėr′ban ēz′ments). The easements belonging to property abutting on streets, including the rights that one's windows should not be darkened; that the free enjoyment of pure air should not be substantially interfered with, and that the free and usual access to the premises should not be impaired. Storms v Manhattan Railway Co. 178 NY 493, 71 NE 3.

urban homestead. A homestead situated within the limits of a village or city. 26 Am J1st Home § 33.

urban redevelopment. A plan for the redevelopment, for all types of uses, of areas in a municipality suffering from blight or decay, through a program of co-operation between government and private enterprise. Anno: 44 ALR2d 1417.
See **slum clearance.**

urban servitude. Same as **urban easement.**

urban surface streetcar passenger service. The transportation of passengers over the streets in suitable cars so operated as to permit passengers to enter and leave at reasonable intervals, irrespective of the fact that a car may be engaged in interurban traffic over a portion of its route. Milwaukee v Milwaukee Elec. R. & Light Co. 173 Wis 400, 180 NW 339, 181 NW 821, 13 ALR 802.

urban transportation. The transportation of passengers over the streets of a city or of a city and its environs in busses or street cars so operated as to permit passengers to enter and leave at reasonable intervals.

urban way. A street in a municipality.

urbs (erbs). A city; a fortified city.

ure (ur). Use; operation; custom; practice.

urea (ū′rē-ạ). A substance found in urine.

uremia (ū-rē′mi-ạ). A disease of the kidneys in which urea is taken into the blood. Gridley v Boggs, 62 Cal 190, 198.

uremic poisoning (ū-rē′mic poi′zn-ing). A poisoning resulting from a diseased condition of the kidneys. People v Harris, 136 NY 423, 433.

urgency. A special condition calling for immediate action or relief. Anno: 111 ALR 703.

urinal (ū′ri-nạl). A toilet. 39 Am J1st Nuis § 83. A container for urine, of particular use in the care of a bedridden person.

urn. A receptacle for the ashes from a cremation.

U. S. Abbreviation of United States. The brand placed by the federal government upon certain kinds of chattels belonging to it, particularly horses and mules. 46 Am J1st Sales § 311.

U.S.A. Abbreviation of **United States of America.**

usable value. The value of the use of a chattel for a definite period of time. 22 Am J2d Damg § 153.

usage. A uniform course of conduct in some particular business or calling, even though it is that of only one person. 21 Am J2d Cust & U § 1.

Usage is habitual or customary practice. Orlich v Rubio Sav. Bank, 240 Iowa 1074, 38 NW2d 622, 10 ALR2d 340.

See **custom; general usage; trade usage.**

usage of trade. See **trade usage.**

usance (ū′zans). The customary time allowed for the payment of bills of exchange.

U. S. brand. The branded mark of the letters "U.S." upon government property.

U. S. Pharm. Abbreviation of **United States Pharmacopoeia.**

U.S.S.Ct. Abbreviation of United States Supreme Court.

use. (ūs). Noun: A beneficial ownership recognized in equity. A trust. The right granted by a patent for an invention. 40 Am J1st Pat § 140. The employment or enjoyment of property. Utility; advantage. The long-continued possession and employment of a thing for the purpose for which it is adapted, as distinguished from a possession or employment that is merely temporary or occasional. Anno: 139 ALR 376, 377 (construing statute imposing tax upon sale for use). 47 Am J1st Sales T § 25. The act of employing; the act of using; applying to one's service; the state of being used, employed, applied, etc. Turner v Smith, 269 Ky 840, 108 SW2d 1019, 113 ALR 468.

A devise by the husband of all his property to his wife, to administer for her own use and the welfare of the children, creates a trust for the children, of their statutory share, and the words are mandatory, not merely directory. Re Yost (Alberta) [1927] 1 West Week 925 [1927] 2 DLR 1001.

A use is where the legal estate of lands was in a certain person, and a trust was also reposed in him that some other person, called the cestui que use, should take and enjoy the rents and profits. Before the Statute of Uses, a use was a mere confidence in a friend, that the feoffee to whom the lands were given should permit the feoffor and his heirs, and such other person as he might designate, to receive the profits of the land. The whole system of uses, however, was changed by the statute 27 Henry VIII Ch 10, known as the Statute of Uses, by which the use was transferred into possession by converting the estate or interest of the cestui que use into a legal estate, and by destroying the intermediate estate of the feoffee. The injustice and inconvenience which followed, caused the lawyers to invent and establish a system of trusts which were recognized as valid by the court of chancery. The Statute of Uses was thereby circumvented. Ware v Richardson, 3 Md 505.

In several cases involving life estates, the word "use" (a word of partial dominion over the property) has been held not to be interpreted as granting the power of consumption to the life tenant. Anno: 108 ALR 571.

In a conveyance to a trustee "for the use and benefit" of a church, it was held that there was no implication of a condition, restriction, or negative covenant against alienation, but that the words were merely declaratory of the purposes of the grant. National Surety Co. v Jarrett, 95 W Va 420, 121 SE 291, 36 ALR 1171, 1176.

As to meaning of the term "use," as it appears in omnibus clause of automobile liability policy, see Anno: 5 ALR2d 607.

See **shifting use; springing use; Statute of Uses; zoning.**

use (ūz). Verb: To employ. To apply to one's service. To occupy. Murphy v Traynor, 110 Colo 466, 135 P2d 230.

The words "used in manufacture," as they appear in a statute providing for local taxation of machinery, import a degree of permanence, are of broad significance, and do not lend themselves to a narrow or technical construction. Hamilton Mfg. Co. v Lowell, 274 Mass 477, 175 NE 73, 74 ALR 1213.

As to meaning of the term "used or occupied," as it appears in the provision of a lease relative to a forfeiture where the premises are used for an unlawful purpose, see Anno: 145 ALR 1063.

use and benefit. See **use.**

use and occupancy insurance. See **business interruption insurance; rent insurance.**

use and occupation. Characterizing the possession of a tenant who has no lease.

use by the public. See **public use.**

used car. A secondhand automobile. 47 Am J1st Sech D § 11.

used goods. See **secondhand goods.**

used necessarily. See **necessarily used.**

used on the highway. Driven, parked, or left standing on the highway. 7 Am J2d Auto § 155.

used or kept for one's trade or business. Kept as reasonably necessary, convenient, or suitable for one's trade or business. Julius v Druckrey, 214 Wis 643, 254 NW 358, 94 ALR 293 (phrase appearing in exemption statute).

used or occupied. See **use.**

used or situated on the leased premises. Property of the tenant relating to the maintenance and operation of the leased premises as a farm or which may acquire a situs or location at the leased premises by reason of, or in connection with, the use of the premises by the lessee. Dorman v Crooks State Bank, 55 SD 209, 225 NW 661, 64 ALR 614, (phrase appearing in provision of farm lease giving the lessor a lien upon lessee's property).

useful. Serviceable. Beneficial.

The word "usefulness" implies capabilities for use, and appertains to the future as well as the present. Chesapeake, Ohio & Southwestern Railroad Co. v Dyer County, 87 Tenn 812, 11 SW 943.

An invention is useful, as the word is used in the patent laws, if it is capable of being beneficially used for the purpose for which it was designated. Or, as sometimes stated, if it will operate to perform the functions and secure the results intended, and its use is not contrary to law, moral principles, or public policy. A device which may be used for innocent amusement may possess utility. See Callison v Dean (CA10 Okla) 70 F2d 55.

useful art. See **new and useful art.**

usefulness. See **useful.**

use of automobile. See **operating motor vehicle; use of highway.**

use of highway. Driving a vehicle on the highway. Walking along the highway; standing still on the highway. 7 Am J2d Auto § 245.

Stalled or disabled vehicles, or vehicles stopped for repairs, are using the highway within the meaning of statutory provisions relating to lights. 7 Am J2d Auto § 155.

As used in a statute providing that the operation by a nonresident of a motor vehicle on a public highway shall be deemed equivalent to an appointment by the nonresident of the secretary of state as his attorney upon whom summons may be served, the word applies not only where the nonresident's automobile is in motion, but also where it is standing or parked at the time when an accident occurs. Hand v Frazer, 139 Misc 446, 248 NYS 557.

use of intoxicating liquor. Personal use as a beverage. An habitual or customary use, rather than an occasional or exceptional use. Anno: 26 ALR 1284 (expression appearing in application for life insurance).

Within the meaning of the liquor law, the term includes the keeping or possessing. Commonwealth v One Dodge Motor Truck, 326 Pa 120, 191 A 590, 110 ALR 919.

use of property. See **use.**

use of sewer. A use in fact, an actual use, as distinguished from the privilege of making use of a sewer or of having one available for use. Southern R. Co. v Richmond, 175 Va 308, 8 SE2d 271, 127 ALR 1368.

use of ticket. Obtaining the admission, transportation, etc. to which one is entitled as the holder of a ticket.

Where a passenger's ticket stipulates that it is to be "used" within a specified time, the general rule is that the condition is complied with if he commences the trip within the time limited, although such time may expire before the actual completion of the trip. 14 Am J2d Car § 826.

use of the mails. The employment of the mails for the delivery of a letter, writing, paper, publication, or articles within the classification of parcels post.

The use of the mails may consist of knowingly causing to be delivered by mail a letter or writing according to the direction thereon and the fact that a clerk who actually mailed the letter was innocent is no defense for one accused of using the mails to defraud who caused the clerk to mail the letter. Creech v Hudspeth (CA10 Kan) 112 F2d 603.

use plaintiff. The owner of the beneficial interest for whose benefit suit is brought by the holder of the legal title as nominal plaintiff. Edgewood Lumber Co. v Hull, 32 Tenn App 577, 223 SW2d 210, 17 ALR2d 228.

user (ū'zėr). Use; actual possession and enjoyment. The right to use. An essential quality of the right of property. Eaton v Boston, C. & M. R. R. Co. 51 NH 504. Exercising the right to use property.

user de action. The institution or bringing of an action.

use restriction. See **restrictive covenant.**

uses. See **use; Statute of Uses.**

use tax. A tax levied upon the use, storage, or consumption of tangible personal property purchased outside the taxing state or taxing district, being a supplement or complement of a sales tax, imposed to prevent residents of a jurisdiction having a sales tax from making purchases outside the jurisdiction in order to avoid such tax. 47 Am J1st Sales T § 42.

The Iowa use tax statute does not impose a tax on the use in Iowa of all personal property, but only such property as was purchased for use in Iowa. Morrison-Knudsen Co. v State Tax Com. 242 Iowa 33, 44 NW2d 449, 41 ALR2d 523.

use upon use. A limitation of one beneficial interest upon another, so that only the first is executed by the Statute of Uses as to carry the legal title, the second use remaining a mere equitable interest. 28 Am J2d Est § 344.

usher. One who escorts the patrons of a theater or other place of amusement, or persons in attendance at a church, to their seats or pews.

using mails to defraud. The use of the mails in perpetrating a fraud. A crime in violation of the federal statutes, the essence of which consists in the making of false promises which the parties never intended to perform, or false representations which they never intended to make good, by means of which they obtain money or other property. Barnard v United States (CA9 Cal) 16 F2d 451.

U.S.M. Abbreviation of **United States Mail; United States Marines; United States Mint.**

U.S.M.A. Abbreviation of United States Military Academy.

usque (us'kwē). Until; as far as.

usque ad coelum (us'kwe ad sē'lum). As far as the sky.

usque ad filum aquae (us'kwe ad fī'lum a'kwē). As far as the thread of the water or stream. 56 Am J1st Water § 51.

usque ad Orcum (us'kwe ad ôr'kum). As far below as the infernal regions.

usquebaugh (us'kwẹ-bâ). (Gaelic). Whisky.

U.S.S. An abbreviation of United States ship.

U.S.S.S. Abbreviation of United States Steamship.

usual. Accustomed; ordinary. Common; habitual. Such as occurs in the ordinary course of events. Not extraordinary. Webb v New Mexico Pub. Co. 47 NM 279, 141 P2d 333, 148 ALR 1002.

usual abode. See **usual place of abode.**

usual and ordinary flow of the stream. The waters of a river annually flowing therein before, during, and after the regularly occurring accretions in the volume thereof both from rainfall and melting snows. Herminghaus v Southern California Edison Co. 200 Cal 81, 252 P 607.

usual business hours. That period or portion of the day during which the business of the community is ordinarily transacted. Derosia v Winona & St. Peter Railroad Co. 18 Minn 133.

usual course of business. Business according to the usages and customs of commercial transactions. 11 Am J2d B & N § 411.

As applied to the indorsement of commercial paper, the term may be said generally to include the concurrent indorsement and delivery for value under such circumstances that a business man of ordinary intelligence and capacity would give his money, goods, or credit for it when offered for the purpose for which this was transferred; and it would not be in due course if such a person would at once suspect the integrity of the paper itself, or the credit and standing of the party offering it. Matlock v Scheuerman, 51 Or 49, 93 P 823.

usual course of trade. The **usual course of business.** 11 Am J2d B & N § 411.

usual covenants. The covenant to warrant and defend, the covenant of seisin, or of good right to convey, the covenant against encumbrances, and the covenant for quiet enjoyment. 20 Am J2d Cov § 43.

The covenant for further assurance is an additional covenant. Adams v Seymour, 191 Va 372, 61 SE2d 23.

usual place of abode. The place at which a person usually lives. 25 Am J2d Dom § 8. The place where a person is usually to be found, at least during some part of the day. Berryhill v Sepp, 106 Minn 458, 119 NW 404. A person's customary or settled place of residence as distinguished from a place where he may be sojourning temporarily. Anno: 127 ALR 1272.

As to the meaning of the expression "usual place of abode," within the rule which authorizes service of summons upon an individual by leaving copies at his usual place of abode, see Anno: 46 ALR2d 1239.

usual place of business. A place actually occupied, either continually or at regular periods, by a person or his employees, in the pursuit of a business, trade, or occupation which occupies his time, attention, and labor. Stephenson v Primrose (Ala) 8 Porter 155. Inclusive in some instances of the usual place of labor or employment in the service of another. 56 Am J1st Ven § 28.

Although the phrase "usual place of business", apart from special circumstances throwing light upon its meaning, may be given a comprehensive meaning and includes the usual place of labor or employment in the service of another, a statute limiting suits to be brought in the county in which the plaintiff has his usual place of business has been held, in the light of its history, not to include the place where one pursues a trade or calling or his place of employment. Hanley v Eastern S.S. Corp. 221 Mass 125, 109 NE 167.

usual place of residence. One's domicil. Ruby v Pierce, 74 Neb 754, 104 NW 1142.
See **domicil.**

usuarius (ū-sū-ā'ri-us). Same as **usuary.**

usuary (us'ū-a-ri). (Civil law.) A bailee who had the bare use of the chattel.

usucapio (ū-sū-kā'pi-ō). A term of the Roman law for the acquisition of title to property by continued possession. Townsend v Jemison (US) 9 How 407, 13 L Ed 194.

Usucapio constituta est ut aliquis litium finis esset (ū-sū-kā'pi-ō kon-sti-tū'ta est ut a'li-quis lī'she-um fī'nis es'set). (Civil law.) Prescription was instituted in order that there might be some end to litigation. See Broom's Legal Maxims 894, footnote.

usufruct (ū'zū-frukt). The right to the use, enjoyment, profits, and avails of property belonging to another. Winsberg v Winsberg, 233 La 67, 96 So 2d 44.

usufructuary right (ū-zū-fruk'tū-ạ-ri rīt). Same as **usufruct**.

usura (ū-sū'ra). (Civil law.) Interest paid on borrowed money; usury.

usurae asses (ū-sū'rē as'sēz). Same as **usurae centesimae**.

usurae centesimae (ū-sū'rē sen-te'si-mē). The term of the Roman law for the highest rate of legal interest.

In calculating, the Romans divided the principal sum into one hundred parts, one of which they allowed to be taken monthly. This was the highest rate permitted and it amounted to twelve per cent a year. They called this usurae centesimae. The as, or Roman pound, was used to express any integral sum, and was divisible into twelve parts or unciae. Hence, these twelve monthly payments or unciae were held to amount to one pound a year, or as usurarius; and so the usurae asses were synonymous with the usurae centesimae, and all lower rates of interest were designated according to their relation to this centesimal usury, or usurae asses. See 2 Bl Comm 462, footnote.

usura manifesta (ū-sū'ra ma-ni-fes'ta). (Civil law.) Unconcealed usury; open usury.

usura maritima (ū-sū'ra ma-ri-tī'ma). An agreement for the repayment of a marine loan with extraordinary interest. See 2 Bl Comm 458.

usurare (ū-sū-rā're). To pay interest.

usura velata (ū-sū'ra ve-lā'ta). (Civil law.) Veiled or concealed usury, as by adding interest to the principal.

usu rem capere (ū'sū rem kā'pe-re). To gain a thing by use of it, to acquire a prescriptive right to it. See 2 Bl Comm 264.

usurious (ū-zū'ri-us). Amounting to or constituting usury.
See **usury**.

usurious contract. See **usury**.

usurious rate. See **usury**.

usurpation. The seizure of position or authority without right. Intruding upon and exercising the powers of a public office, having neither title nor color of title to the office. Hamlin v Kassafer, 15 Or 456, 15 P 778. An unlawful assumption of the use of real property which belongs to another. An absolute ouster or dispossession of a patron by a stranger who with no right to do so presented a clerk to a benefice who was thereupon admitted to the living and instituted therein. See 3 Bl Comm 242. An invasion of the kingdom by foreign enemies to give laws and usurp the government, or an internal armed force in rebellion, assuming the power of government, by making laws, and punishing for not obeying those laws; an invasion from abroad, or an internal rebellion, when armies are employed to support it; when the laws are dormant and silent, and the firing of towns is unavoidable. City Fire Ins. Co. v Corlies (NY) 21 Wend 367.

usurpation of franchise. Exercising the privileges and powers of a corporation in the name of the corporation but without power or authority to act for or represent the corporation. Grant v Elder, 64 Colo 104, 170 P 198.

usurper. See **usurpation**.

usury. An unlawful contract upon the loan of money, to receive the same again with exorbitant increase. Lassman v Jacobson, 125 Minn 218, 146 NW 350. The exaction, or an agreement for the exaction, of a greater sum for the loan, use, or forbearance of money, goods, or things in action than interest at the highest rate allowed by law. 55 Am J1st Usury § 2.

It is the agreement, not necessarily its performance, which renders a debt usurious, the intent actually to get excessive interest being the controlling element, considering the elements of the agreement as and when made. Seebold v Eustermann, 216 Minn 566, 13 NW2d 739, 152 ALR 586.

Any premium, profit, bonus, or charge exacted or required by the lendor in excess of money actually loaned, with interest at the legal rate, is usurious. Hall v Mortgage Secur. Corp. 119 W Va 140, 192 SE 145, 111 ALR 118.

To be a usurious contract, there must be a loan or forbearance of money, or its equivalent, and an unlawful intent and understanding that the loan be paid with an exaction, for the use of the loan, of something in excess of what is permitted by law. State v Miller, 177 Kan 324, 279 P2d 223, 52 ALR2d 691.

The three essential elements of usury are (1) a loan or forbearance of money, (2) an agreement for a return of the money in all events; and (3) an agreement to pay more than the legal rate of interest for its use. Seebold v Eustermann, 216 Minn 566, 13 NW2d 739, 152 ALR 586.

The taking of exorbitant, that is, interest exceeding forty per cent, was a misdemeanor at common law in England before the enactment of prohibitory statutes; and as late as 1814, it was thought that an indictment for usury might lie at common law, but it is now generally considered that usury is not an offense unless made so by statute. 55 Am J1st Usury § 172.

See **lawful interest**; **legal interest**; **legal rate of interest**.

usus (ū'sus). Use; a use.

usus bellici (u'sus bel'li-sī). Use in warfare; warlike use.

Usus est dominium fiduciarium (ū'sus est do-mi'nī-um fī-dū-she-ā'ri-um). A use is a fiduciary ownership.

usus fori (ū'sus fo'rī). The practice of the court.

usus fructus (ū'sus fruk'tus). Same as **usufruct**.

usus loquendi (ū'sus lo-quen'dī). The usage of speaking; the customary language. Hurtado v California, 110 US 516, 534, 28 L Ed 232, 238, 4 S Ct 111, 292.

ut (ut). That; in order that; as; so as.

ut antiquum (ut an-ti'qu-um). As in ancient times.

utas (ū'tās). Same as **octave**.

ut audivi (ut â-dī'vī). As I have heard.

ut credo (ut krē'dō). As I believe.

ut currere solebat (ut ker're-re so-lē'bat). As it is accustomed to flow.

ut de feodo (ut dē fē'dō). As of fee.

utensils (ū-ten'sils). Tools, pots, pans, or implements, especially those used in the kitchen. Anno: 2 ALR 818.
    The word more especially means an implement or vessel for domestic or farming use. "Utensils" is a translation of "utensiles," used in article 2102 of the Code Napoleon. In France it has been held to include a "machine à battre," or threshing machine and in French law is used as synonymous with "agricultural instruments" of all kinds. In some states of the Union mowers and combined harvesters have been held to be "farming utensils or implements," as used in exemption statutes. Cook v Massey, 38 Idaho 264, 220 P 1088, 35 ALR 200, 205.

uterine brother (ū'tẹ-rin bruth'ẻr). A half-brother by the mother's side. See 2 Bl Comm 232.

utero gestation (ū'tẹ-rō jes-tā'shọn). Pregnancy.

utero matris. See **in utero matris.**

utfangthefe. Same as **outfangthef.**

uti (ū'ti). Same as **ut.**

Utile non debet per inutile vitiari (u'ti-le non de'bet per in-u'ti-le vi-she-ā'rī). That which is useful or valid ought not to be vitiated by that which is superfluous or invalid.
    "Courts lean in favor of the preservation of all such valid parts of a will as can be separated from those that are invalid, without defeating the general intention of the testator." Edgerly v Barker, 66 NH 434, 31 A 900.

Utile per inutile non vitiatur (ū'ti-le per in-ū'ti-le non vi-she-ā'ter). That which is useful is not vitiated by that which is superfluous. State of West Virginia v Richards, 32 W Va 348, 9 SE 245.

utilis (ū'ti-lis). Useful; profitable; advantageous.

utilitarian. Looking toward or stressing the point of utility.

utility. Usefulness, especially to a number of persons. An essential of patentability; capable of beneficial use in society. 40 Am J1st Pat §§ 22-24.

utilization facility (ūti-li-zā'shọn fạ-sil'i-ti). (1) Any equipment or device, except an atomic weapon, determined by rule of the Atomic Energy Commission to be capable of making use of special nuclear material in such quantity as to be of significance to the common defense and security, or in such manner as to affect the health and safety of the public, peculiarly adapted for making use of atomic energy in such quantity as to be of significance to the common defense and security, or in such manner as to affect the health and safety of the public; or (2) any important component part especially designed for such equipment or device as determined by the Commission. USC § 2014(aa).

uti possidetis (ū'tī pos-si-dē'tis). As you possess, an expression which when used in a treaty signifies that the respective nation parties may retain the property which they have captured.

Utitur jure auctoris (ū'ti-ter jū're âk-tō'ris). He enjoys the right of his assignor.

utlagatas (ut-la-gā'tās). An outlaw.

utlagatum. See **capias utlagatum.**

utlage. An outlaw.

utlagh. An outlaw.

utmost care. The highest degree of care to be exercised in a particular situation, consistent with the nature of the undertaking and the circumstances of the case. Dodge v Boston & Bangor S.S. Co. 148 Mass 207, 19 NE 373.
    As applied to the care required of passenger carriers, the term implies the highest degree of practicable care and diligence consistent with the mode of transportation adopted, and with the practical prosecution of the carrier's business. 14 Am J2d Car § 916.

utmost care and skill. The highest degree of care and skill known which may be used under the same or similar circumstances. Phelan v Louisville Electrical Co. 122 Ky 476, 91 SW 703.

utmost degree of care. See **utmost care.**

ut poena ad paucos, metus ad omnes perveniat (ut pē'na ad pâ'kos, me'tus ad om'nēz per-ve'ni-at). That few may suffer, but all may dread punishment. See 4 Bl Comm 11.

utraque parte. See **ex utraque parte.**

ut res magis valeat quam pereat (ut rēz' mā'jis va'le-at quam pe're-at). That it may rather become operative than null.
    The most common application of the maxim is in connection with the duty of courts, in passing upon the constitutionality of statutes, to uphold them whenever it can rationally be done. 16 Am J2d Const L § 175.

utrisque parentibus conjuncti. See **ex utrisque parentibus conjuncti.**

utroque jure. See **in utroque jure.**

utrum. See **assize of utrum.**

ut statuta illa, et omnes articulos in eisdem contentos, in singulis locis ubi expedire viderit, publice proclamari, et firmiter teneri et observari faciat (ut sta-tū'ta il'la, et om'nēz ar-ti'ku-los in e-is'dem konten'tos, in sin'gu-lis lō'sis u'bi ex-pe-dī're vi'de-rit, pub'li-se pro-kla-mā'rī, et fir'mi-ter te-nē'rī et obser-vā'rī fā'shē-at). That he cause those statutes and all of the articles contained in them to be publicly proclaimed and to be strictly kept and observed. See 1 Bl Comm 185.

ut supra (ut sūp'rā). As above; as above stated.

utter bar. Same as **outer bar.**

utter barrister. Same as **outer barrister.**

uttering and publishing counterfeit. Declaring or asserting, directly or indirectly, by words or acts, that money or a note offered to another is good. 20 Am J2d Counterf § 4.

uttering forged instrument. An offering to another of a forged instrument with knowledge of the falsity of the writing and with intent to defraud. 36 Am J2d Forg § 20.

uttering worthless check. Obtaining goods or money by drawing and delivering a check on a bank in which the drawer has no funds or credit. 32 Am J2d False Pret § 19.

utterly. To the utmost; to the full extent; fully, totally; as, utterly without fault.

u-turn. A turn made by the driver of a vehicle upon the highway whereby the course of the vehicle is reversed. 8 Am J2d Auto § 805.

ux. See **et ux.**

uxor (u′xor). A wife.

uxore rapta et abducta. See **de uxore rapta et abducta.**

Uxor et filius sunt nomina naturae (u′xor et fi′li-us sunt nō′mi-na na-tū′rē). Wife and son are names of nature.

uxoricide (uk-sō′ri-sīd). The killing of a woman by her husband.

Uxor non est sui juris, sed sub potestate viri (u′xor non est su′ī jū′ris, sed sub po-tes-tā′te vi′rī). A wife has no power of her own, but is under the control of her husband.

Uxor non est sui juris, sed sub potestate viri, cui in vita contradicere non potest (u′xor non est su′ī ju′ris, sed sub po-tes-tā′te vi′rī, kī in vī′ta kon-trā di′se-re non po′test). A wife has no power of her own, but is under the control of her husband, whom she cannot in his lifetime gainsay.

Uxor sequitur domicilium viri (u′xor se′qui-ter do-mi-si′lī-um vi′rī). The wife follows the domicil of her husband.

V

v. An abbreviation of **versus** and also of **vide**.

vacancy in office. A matter of a public office being without an incumbent who has a right to exercise its functions and take its fees or emoluments. 42 Am J1st Pub Of § 131. The condition of a public office which is unoccupied and without an incumbent who has a lawful right to continue therein until the happening of some future event. 42 Am J1st Pub Of § 131. A matter of a corporate office or directorship being without an incumbent. 19 Am J2d Corp § 1086.

The word "vacant" involves no technical or peculiar meanings; as applied to a public office it means empty, unoccupied, without an incumbent. State ex rel. McKittrick v Wilson, 350 Mo 486, 166 SW2d 499, 143 ALR 1465.

A vacancy in public office results from the death of the incumbent, or from his resignation or removal from office. It may exist where there is a newly created office, where the person elected or appointed to the office fails to qualify or dies before qualifying or before the commencement of his term. 42 Am J1st Pub Of § 135.

A provision authorizing corporate directors to fill vacancies is ordinarily held not applicable to newly created directorships. Automatic Steel Products Co. v Johnston (Sup) 31 Del Ch 469, 64 A2d 416, 6 ALR2d 170.

vacant and unoccupied building. A building in which no one is living or residing and which is empty for all practical purposes. 29A Am J Rev ed Ins § 907.

vacant building. A building without inanimate objects. 29A Am J Rev ed Ins § 907.

vacantia bona (va-kan'she-a bō'na). (Civil law.) Goods which no one claimed and which by the law of nature belonged to the first occupant or finder. See 1 Bl Comm 298.

vacant land. Lands of the government, national or state, which are absolutely free, unclaimed, and unoccupied, exclusive of lands belonging to the state by purchase. 42 Am J1st Pub L § 13.

vacant succession (suk sesh'ǫn). An inheritance which no one claims and the heirs who are entitled to which are unknown.

vacare (va-kā're). To be empty or vacant.

vacate. To annul or set aside. To cease the occupancy of premises, leaving them empty.

To vacate, in its English form, has acquired an active sense through a long period of transition, by popular usage and in consequence of its early adoption as a technical and legal term, although it was originally used only as a passive verb. To leave empty; to cease from occupying; to annul; to make void, express the different meanings which it has acquired. Originally it meant to be empty, void or vacant; to be void of, free from, or without; to lack or want a thing. Walsh v Commonwealth, 89 Pa 419.

vacatio (vā-kā'she-ō). (Civil law.) A freedom from something; an immunity; an exemption.

vacation. A setting aside. An annulment of a prior act or determination. A respite from work or study. A period without school.

vacation club deposit. A type of deposit in a bank or trust company, made in accordance with a plan which provides for the making of regular deposits during the year and the withdrawal of the money for use in taking a vacation. 10 Am J2d Banks § 357.

vacation of attachment or garnishment. See **dissolution of attachment or garnishment**.

vacation of adjudication. The setting aside of an adjudication of bankruptcy. 9 Am J2d Bankr § 274.
See **vacation of judgment**.

vacation of award. The setting aside of an award made in an arbitration. 5 Am J2d Arb & A § 167.

vacation of court. The time between the end of one term of court and the beginning of another. Ex parte Earman, 85 Fla 297, 95 So 755, 31 ALR 1226; Conkling v Ridgely & Co. 112 Ill 36, 1 NE 261. Broadly, any considerable period of time when the court does not function, whether such is a period when the court is in recess or a period between terms. 20 Am J2d Cts § 50.

vacation of execution. A special proceeding in the original action by which relief from an execution is granted. 30 Am J2d Exec §§ 711 et seq.

vacation of highway. The termination of the existence of a highway by direct action of the public authorities. 25 Am J1st High § 117.

vacation of injunction. See **dissolution of injunction**.

vacation of judgment. The destruction or elimination of a judgment in its entirety. 30A Am J Rev ed Judgm § 630.

vacation of judicial sale. The setting aside of a judicial sale by a direct attack upon the order of sale or the sale for want of jurisdiction, fraud, collusion, accident, mutual mistake, breach of trust, or misconduct of the purchaser or other person connected with the sale. 30A Am J Rev ed Jud S §§ 247 et seq.

vacation of return. A setting aside on motion of a sheriff's return of an execution. 30 Am J2d Exec § 572.

vacatur (vȧ-kā'ter). Let it be vacated. An order of court vacating a proceeding.

vaccination. The inoculation of a person with a prepared substance, known as vaccine, intended to produce immunity to a specific disease. 25 Am J1st Hlth § 35.

vacuo. See **in vacuo**.

vadari (va-dā'rī). (Civil law.) To hold to bail; to give bail.

vades (vā'dēz). (Civil law.) Pledges; sureties.

vadiare (vā-di-ā're). To wage; to gage; to give security.

vadiare duellum (vā-di-ā're du-el'lum). To wage battel; to engage in trial by combat.

vadiare legem (vā-di-ā're lē'jem). To wage law.
See **wager of law**.

vadiatio legis (vā-di-ā'she-ō lē'jis). Wager of law.
See **wager of law**.

vadio (vā'diō). Pledge.
See **estate in pledge**.

vadium (vā'di-um). A pledge.
See **estate in pledge**.

vadium mortuum. Same as **mortuum vadium.**

vadium ponere (vā'di-um pō'ne-re). To take pledges; to take bail.

vadium vivum. Same as **vivum vadium.**

vadlet. The eldest son of the king.

vagabond (vag'ạ-bond). A tramp; a wanderer. An idle person. A rascal. One using any subtle craft, means, or device to deceive or impose on another. Anno: 14 ALR 1489.

Vagabundum nuncupamus eum qui nullibi domicilium contraxit habitationis (va-ga-bun'dum nun-ku-pā'mus e'um quī nul'li-bi do-mi-si'li-um kon-trā'xit ha-bi-tā"she-ō'nis). We call him a vagabond who has nowhere acquired a domicil of residence.

vagrancy. At common law, the wandering or going about from place to place by an idle person without lawful visible means of support, subsisting on charity, and refraining from working for a living, although able to work. 55 Am J1st Vag § 1.

In most of the states, there has been a departure in some particulars, even to a considerable extent, from the common-law definition.

vagrant. One in a state of vagrancy; one guilty of vagrancy.

At common law, a vagrant was originally understood to be an idle person without visible means of support, who, though able to work for his maintenance, refused to do so. The idea connected with the word "vagrant" or "vagrancy" also had connected with it, and as a part of it, not only an idle person, but one whose business, pursuit, or occupation, or want of it, was vicious to society, and one who loitered or stayed about immoral places. The English vagrant acts, as in effect defined by old English statutes and referred to in 4 Bl Comm 169, also tended to show that this was the idea of a vagrant. Under modern legislation in many states of the Union, vagrants are defined to be and are punished for pursuing a business or occupation or profession of a vicious, illegal, or demoralizing tendency, and the idea conveyed and intended to be conveyed thereby was and is as to the status, course of conduct, business, pursuit, or occupation of such persons who are denounced as vagrants, and proven by showing many specific acts which make up their general course of conduct, status, business, pursuit, or occupation, in contradistinction to their committing a specific act. The idea further is that such persons are denominated "vagrants" because their course of conduct, status, business, pursuit, or occupation is habitual in its nature. Anno: 14 ALR 1483.

See **vagrancy.**

vagrant waters. Flood waters, sometimes known as enemy waters. Herminghaus v Southern California Edison Co. 200 Cal 81, 252 P 607.

vagueness (vāg'nes). Uncertainty; indefiniteness; obscurity.

vail'q'vail'pur.' Same as **Valeat quantum valere potest.**

vain act. A futile act. A useless act. Cantwell v Cantwell, 237 Ind 168, 143 NE2d 275, cert dismd and app den 356 US 225, 2 L Ed 2d 712, 78 S Ct 700, reh den 356 US 954, 2 L Ed 2d 847, 78 S Ct 913. An act ineffectual in accomplishing the object in view. 34 Am J1st Mand § 37.

vain thing. See **vain act.**

vale (vāl). A beautiful word for a poet, meaning valley. (Spanish.) A promissory note.

Valeat quantum valere potest (va'le-at quan'tum va-lē're pō'test). Let it have effect to such extent as it can have effect.

The maxim is applicable to almost every legal transaction. In wills, the method of the courts has been not to set aside the intent because it cannot take effect so fully as the testator desired, but to let it work as far as it can. Edgerly v Barker, 66 NH 434, 31 A 900.

valentia (vạ-len'she-ạ). Value; price.

valid. Effective; operative; not void; sufficient in law. See **lawful; legality.**

validating act. Same as **curative act.**

validation. Rendering legal that which was previously illegal. Giving legality to a bond or other security issued by a public body which otherwise will remain illegal and unenforceable. Confirmation.

validation of statute. Amending a statute which is unconstitutional by removing its objectionable provisions, or supplying provisions, to conform it to the requirements of the Constitution. 16 Am J2d Const L § 179.

validation of ticket. The confirmation of a return ticket of a passenger, made by an agent of the carrier, usually at the place constituting the outer terminus of the trip.

valid defense. A defense required as a condition of the vacation of a judgment, being a defense having such merit that the law will recognize it and give effect thereto when sufficient proof thereof is forthcoming.

It is not essential that the defense extend to the whole cause of action. State ex rel. Comrs. of Land Office v Jones, 198 Okla 187, 176 P2d 992, 174 ALR 1.

valid excuse. A good, sufficient, and satisfactory excuse. Dennis v Massachusetts Ben. Asso. 120 NY 496, 24 NE 843 (excuse for failure to pay assessment by mutual benefit association).

validity. The state of being valid and effective. See **valid.**

validity of statute. The effectiveness of a statute in reference to constitutionality, the power of the Congress or a legislature to enact the statute, the manner of enactment, and the form of the statute. 50 Am J1st Stat § 471.

The validity of a statute is drawn in question whenever the power to enact it as it is by its terms, or as it is made to read by construction, is fairly open to denial and is denied. Baltimore & P. R. Co. v Hopkins, 130 US 210, 32 L Ed 908, 9 S Ct 503.

valid marriage. A marriage effective to create the relationship of husband and wife. Marriage which is not void.

valley. An area of lowlands or depressions of considerable size, with bottoms of gentle slope as compared to the sides; that is to say, it is the space inclosed between two ranges of mountains or hills. Whaley v Northern Pacific Railway Co. (CC Mont) 167 F 664, 669.

valor beneficiorum (va'lor be-ne-fi"she-ō'rum). The value of benefices. See 1 Bl Comm 285.

valor maritagii (va'lor ma-ri-tā'ji-ī). The value of the right of marriage.

This value was the amount or sum of money which a suitable person who desired to marry an infant ward would be willing to pay to the ward's guardian for the marriage. See 2 Bl Comm 70.

valuable consideration. A consideration in money or in something having monetary value. 17 Am J2d Contr § 95. A consideration in money, money's worth, the release of a right, or the compromise of a demand. 37 Am J2d Frd Conv § 18. Something received of monetary value or bearing a value measurable in money. 23 Am J2d Deeds § 63.

Valuable consideration for a deed is not necessarily coincident with valuable consideration such as will make a promise binding. It may consist of marriage, an agreement to marry; a promise of support, antecedent services, etc. 23 Am J2d Deeds § 63.

valuable effects. Items of personal property having at least some value. 32 Am J2d False Pret § 41.

valuable for mining. A term characterizing a reservation by the United States of certain lands.

Lands are valuable for minerals when they contain minerals in such quantities as to justify expenditures in extraction and are, on the whole, more valuable for mining than for agriculture. 36 Am J1st Min & M § 12.

valuable papers. Papers considered worthy of being preserved as records of the facts purported to be stated and perpetuated therein. Brogan v Barnard, 115 Tenn 260, 90 SW 858.

valuable security. A pledge of a valuable chattel. A document, such as a stock certificate, bond, or mortgage.

Checks, notes, etc., obtained from the person executing or signing the same have been held to constitute valuable security within the meaning of statutes declaring it to be a criminal offense to "obtain any valuable security" by false pretenses. Reg v Greenhalgh (Eng) 6 Cox CC 257.

valuable thing. See **thing of value.**

valuation. A determination of the value of particular property, as for the purpose of taxation. The price set upon anything; the estimated or rated worth of anything; the estimated value or worth of a thing. See State v Central Pacific Railroad Co. 7 Nev 99, 104.

See **assessment; fair valuation.**

Valuation Reserve. See **Mandatory Securities Valuation Reserve.**

value. The worth of a thing in money, goods, or other property. The effect in exchange of the relative social desire for compared objects expressed in terms of a common denominator. International Harvester Co. v Kentucky, 234 US 216, 222, 58 L Ed 1284, 1287, 34 S Ct 853. Somewhat of a guess, a prediction, or a prophecy; an educated guess which may or may not correspond with ultimate realities. McMurtry v Commissioner (CA1) 203 F2d 659. The amount which a thing will bring in money in the market. State v Doepke, 68 Mo 208. The market value. World F. & M. Ins. Co. v Palmer (CA5 Miss) 182 F2d 707, 17 ALR2d 1217.

For rate-making purposes, value must be measured by the sound judgment and common sense of impartial tribunals. Petersburg Gas Co. v Petersburg, 132 Va 82, 110 SE 533, 20 ALR 542.

A proceeding for the appointment of a guardian of the estate of an alleged incompetent cannot strictly be said to have a "value in controversy" exceeding $20, so as to come within the protection of the Seventh Amendment of the United States Constitution as to the right of trial by jury, even though the result of the determination as to competency may affect extensive property holdings. Ward v Booth (CA9 Hawaii) 197 F2d 963, 33 ALR2d 1134.

See **market value.**

valued policy. A policy of insurance in which the value of the subject matter insured is fixed by agreement and stated in the policy. 29A Am J Rev ed Ins § 1586.

If there is anything in the policy which clearly indicates an intention on the part of the insurer to value the risk and loss, in whatever words expressed, the policy is valued. American Ins. Co. v Gentile Bros. Co. (CA5 Fla) 109 F2d 732.

value in controversy. See **value.**

value of life insurance policy. For inheritance tax purposes, its face value, less a proper rebate for the period during which payment may be deferred. Anno: 73 ALR2d 232.

See **cash surrender value.**

value of the marriage. The value of the right of marriage; the sum of money which a suitable person who desires to marry an infant ward will pay her guardian in order to accomplish the marriage. See 2 Bl Comm 70.

value received. A formalized recital of consideration without elaboration. 49 Am J1st Stat of F § 373.

As the expression is used in a promissory note, it does not necessarily import a consideration in money, and a promise to pay may legally be the consideration, without any money passing. The consideration may be as varied as the transactions of men. Not only does the phrase not necessarily import a consideration of money, but it does not conclusively import a consideration of any kind; for it is competent, notwithstanding these words, to show that no consideration has been, in fact, received. Osgood v Bringolf, 32 Iowa 265, 270.

The words as used in a written instrument, other than a negotiable or sealed instrument, have generally been held to create a presumption, or make a prima facie case, of a sufficient consideration to support the instrument. Thus, the recital "value received" in an assignment of a life insurance policy, being in the nature of an admission by the assignor of the receipt of a consideration, creates a prima facie case that there was a sufficient consideration to make the assignment effective. Finegan v Prudential Ins. Co. 300 Mass 147, 14 NE2d 172, 116 ALR 535.

See **for value received; valuable consideration.**

value rule. A rule of damages applied in an action for breach of contract by a contractor-builder, that the owner is entitled to recover the difference in value between the building as constructed and as it should have been constructed. Shell v Schmidt, 164 Cal App 2d 350, 330 P2d 817, 76 ALR2d 792, cert den 359 US 959, 3 L Ed 2d 766, 79 S Ct 799.

valvasor (val'vạ-sôr). A title of dignity, next beneath peer. See 1 Bl Comm 403.

Vana est illa potentia quae nunquam venit in actum (vā'na est il'la po-ten'she-a kwē nun'quam vē'nit in ak'tum). A power or authority is a vain one which is never exercised.

vandalism (van'dạl-izm). Wilful or malicious injury to, or the destruction of, property. General Acci-

Fire & Life Assur. Corp. v Azar, 103 Ga App 215, 119 SE2d 82. Wilful, wanton, and ruthless acts intended to damage or destroy property. 7 Am J2d Auto Ins § 75. Any unusual destruction of property wrought in the doing of a wrongful act. Great American Ins. Co. v Dedmon, 260 Ala 330, 72 So 2d 421, 43 ALR2d 599 (construction of term in automobile comprehensive policy).

As to what constitutes "vandalism" within the meaning of an automobile comprehensive policy, see Anno: 43 ALR2d 604.

Vani timores sunt aestimandi, qui non cadunt in constantem virem (vă'nī ti-mō'rēz sunt ē-sti-man'dī, quī non ka'dunt in kon-stan'tem vi'rem). Those fears are to be regarded as groundless which do not affect a man of ordinary firmness.

Vani timoris justa excusatio non est (vă'nī ti-mō'ris jus'ta ex-ku-zā'she-ō non est). An idle fear is not a lawful excuse. Williams v Kansas City Southern Railway Co. 257 Mo 87, 165 SW 788.

vara (vä'rạ). A land measure used in Spanish-American grants.

The true vara is slightly less than 33-1/3 inches, but by usage it is estimated at 33-1/3 inches in Texas and at 33 inches in California. United States v Perot, 98 US 428, 25 L Ed 251.

varech (var'ek). (French.) Seaweed.

variable annuity. An annuity under a contract which guarantees the annuitant that upon reaching a specified age he will receive periodic payments, the amount of which is not fixed and has no assured minimum, but will vary according to the success of the investment policy of the company which issues the contract. Securities & Exchange Com. v Variable Annuity Life Ins. Co. 359 US 65, 3 L Ed 2d 640, 79 S Ct 618.

variance. An exception from the application of a zoning regulation granted by proper authority to relieve against practical difficulties and unnecessary hardship. 58 Am J1st Zon §§ 194 et seq. A disagreement or difference between two parts of the same proceeding which ought to agree, especially the pleading and proof. 41 Am J1st Pl § 370. A difference between a party's allegations and his proofs. A substantial departure from the issue in the evidence adduced concerning a matter which in point of law is essential to the charge or claim. 41 Am J1st Pl §§ 370 et seq. A discrepancy between the allegations in the indictment or information and the proof as to some matter which is legally essential to the charge. State v Crean, 43 Mont 47, 114 P 603.

In a criminal case, a variance is an essential difference between the accusation and the proof, and the variance is not material unless it is such as might mislead the defense, or expose the defendant to the injury of being put twice in jeopardy for the same offense. Brashears v State, 38 Okla Crim 175, 259 P 665.

vary. To alter; to modify. To change to something else.

Power given to trustees to invest and reinvest the trust funds and to "vary" the securities has been held to authorize the trustees to change the investment from one form of securities to another. Merchants' Loan & Trust Co. v Northern Trust Co. 250 Ill 86, 95 NE 59.

See **variance.**

vas (vas). (Civil law.) A surety or pledge.

vas deferens (vās dē'fe-renz). A duct which carries seminal fluid from the testicles.

vas deferens mulieris (vās dē'fe-renz mu-li-e'ris). The Fallopian tube in the body of a woman.

vasectomy (vas-ek'tọ-mi). The removal of the vas deferens or of a part thereof; a surgical operation whereby a male is sterilized so as to be incapable of procreation, but not of performing the sexual act. 21 Am J2d Crim L § 612.

vassal (vas'ạl). A grantee of land, a tenant, a feudatory, a landholder, under the feudal system.

Originally no stigma was attached to the word but the abuses which crept into feudal tenure altered its meaning so that it came to signify a slave or bondman. See 2 Bl Comm 53.

vassalus (vas-sal'us). A vassal.

Vassalus, qui abnegavit feudum ejusve conditionem, exspoliabitur (vas-sal'lus, quī ab-ne-gā'vit fū'dum e-jus've kon-di-she-ō'nem, ex"spo-li-ā'bi-ter). The vassal who has denied either his fee or the terms of it shall be deprived of it. See 3 Bl Comm 234.

vastitas (vās'ti-tās). An empty space; a waste.
See **de vasto.**

vasto (vas'to). To plunder; to commit waste.

vastum (vās'tum). Waste. A common lying open to the cattle of all tenants of one landlord.

vauderie. Witchcraft.

vaudeville (vâd-vil). A type of entertainment.

A term used in the theatrical trade as describing a species of entertainment composed of a number of isolated acts and attractions so put together as to form a balanced show. The acts run in sequence. The theaters where they are played are referred to as vaudeville houses. Hart v B. F. Keith Vaudeville Exchange (CA2 NY) 12 F2d 341, 47 ALR 775.

vaudeville house. See **vaudeville.**

vault. A repository for the remains of a dead person. Dries v Charles Evans Cemetery Co. 109 Pa Super 498, 167 A 237. A crypt or burial chamber. 14 Am J2d Cem § 1. A chamber or room, particularly in a bank, for the safekeeping of money and valuables.

vavasor (vav'ạ-sọr). Same as **valvasor.**

vectigal (vek'ti-gal). (Civil law.) A tax; an impost; a duty.

vectura (vek-tū'ra). Freight.

veer. To change course suddenly.

vegetable. An edible plant.

vegetarianism (vej-ē-tā'ri-ạn-izm). The belief and practice in confining diet to vegetables, excluding all meat. Anno: 12 ALR2d 874-876, § 5.

vehicle. An instrumentality for the carrying of goods or people. 29A Am J Rev ed Ins § 1237. A broader term than **motor vehicle.** Golding-Keene Co. v Fidelity-Phoenix Fire Ins. Co. 96 NH 64, 69 A2d 56, 12 ALR2d 591. Any carriage or contrivance used or capable of being used as a means of transportation on land. National Fire Ins. Co. v Elliott (CA8 Mo) 7 F2d 522, 42 ALR 1121, 1126. A graphic expression for a means of communication.

The word is commonly understood as something which moves or runs on the land, not something which flies in the air, although etymologically the term might be considered as broad enough to cover a conveyance propelled in the air. McBoyle v United States, 283 US 25, 75 L Ed 816, 51 S Ct 340.

As to what constitutes a "vehicle" within the

meaning of insurance coverage or exception. Anno: 12 ALR2d 598.

vein. A fissure in rock filled with quartz or other substance bearing mineral. A stratum or rock in which mineral appears. 36 Am J1st Min & M § 110. A vessel which carries blood from some part of the body to the heart.
See **apex of vein; blanket vein; lode.**

vel (vel). Whether; or.

velata. See **donatio velata.**

velle. (Civil law.) To be willing; to consent.

Velle non creditur qui obsequitur imperio patris vel domini (vel′le non krē′di-ter quī ob-se′qui-ter im-pe′riō pā′tris vel dō′mi-nī). (Civil law.) He is not deemed to consent who obeys the command of his father or master.

vel non (vel non). Or not.

venaria (vē-nā′ri-a). Wild animals which are hunted.

venatio (vē-nā′she-ō). Hunting.

venationes, et sylvaticas vagationes cum canibus et accipitribus (ve-nā-she-ō′nēz, et sil-va′ti-kās va-gā-she-ō′nēz kum kā′ni-bus et ak-si-pi′tri-bus). Hunting and prowling about the woods with dogs and hawks. See 2 Bl Comm 412.

vendee (ven-dē′). The purchaser under a sale or contract of sale of real property. In less frequent use, the purchaser under a sale or contract of sale of personal property.

vendee's lien. The lien of a purchaser of real estate under an executory contract of purchase upon the land covered by the contract for the amount paid by him upon the purchase price. 55 Am J1st V & P § 548.

Vendens eandem rem duobus falsarius est (ven′denz e-an′dem rem du-ō′bus fal-sā′ri-us est). A person who sells the same thing to two persons is fraudulent.

vender (ven′dėr). To sell. Also, same as **vendor.**

vendetta (ven-det′ä). A private blood feud, often hereditary, in which a family seeks to avenge an injury to or a murder of one of its members upon the offender or his family. Stephens v Howell Sales Co. (DC NY) 16 F2d 805, 808.

vending. Selling goods. Giving expression to one's opinions. A right secured by the Federal copyright law which does not differ from the "right to vend" secured by the Federal patent law, it being in both instances the intention of Congress to provide an exclusive right to sell. Bauer v O'Donnell, 229 US 1, 17, 57 L Ed 1041, 1046, 33 S Ct 616.

vending machine. A machine which vends small items of merchandise without a clerk or other employee in attendance, the machine delivering the parcel upon being activated by a coin dropped in a slot.

vendition (ven-dish′ǫn). A selling; a sale.

venditioni exponas (ven-di″she-ō′ni ex-pō-nas). A writ authorizing and requiring an execution officer to sell the property seized by him under an execution. 30 Am J2d Exec § 307.

venditio per mutuam manuum complexionem (ven-di′she-o per mu′tu-am ma′nu-um kom-plek-she-ō′nem). A sale by the mutual clasping of hands; a handsale. See 2 Bl Comm 448.

venditor. A vendor; a seller.

venditor regis (ven′di-tor rē′jis). The salesman of the king,—a person who seized and sold the goods of a debtor of the king, to satisfy the debt.

vendor. The seller in a sale or contract of sale of real property. In less frequent use, the seller in a sale or contract of sale of personal property.

vendor and purchaser. A title much used in digests, encyclopedias, and textbooks for a discussion of sales and contracts to sell real property, the title "sales" being used for the comparable discussion involving personal property.

vendor's express lien. See **vendor's lien.**

vendor's implied lien. See **vendor's lien.**

vendor's lien. The implied lien of a vendor of real estate, who has conveyed the legal title, as security for the unpaid purchase money. 55 Am J1st V & P § 462. The express lien of a vendor of real estate under a provision of the contract that he is to retain title until the purchase money is paid, the vendee being put in possession of the premises. 55 Am J1st V & P § 447. The lien which the vendor of goods has at common law for the whole or the unpaid portion of the purchase price of the goods, where he has parted with title but not with possession, being in the nature of a pledge for the security of the vendor in reference to the unpaid purchase money in the event of the insolvency of the buyer. 46 Am J1st Sales § 518.

vendor's option. See **seller's option.**

vendue (ven-dū′). A sale; an auction sale.

venia aetatis (ve′ni-a ē-tā′tis). (Civil law.) The privilege of age, the privilege of a person who by reason of his age is entitled to act in his own right.

Venia facilitas incentivum est delinquendi (ve′ni-a fa-si′li-tās in-sen-tī′vum est de-lin-quen′dī). Facility of pardon is an incentive or encouragement to crime.

venire (vę-nī′rē). A writ directing the summoning of jurors by the sheriff or other officer with authority to act in this respect. The list of jurors annexed to the writ of venire. 31 Am J Rev ed Jury § 74. A term sometimes used for array or panel.

venire de novo. Same as **venire facias de novo.**

venire facias (vę-nī′rē fā′shi-as). A writ for summoning jurors. A writ summoning a person to service as a grand juror. Powers v United States, 223 US 303, 56 L Ed 448, 32 S Ct 281.

venire facias ad respondendum (vē-nī′re fā′she-as ad res-pon-den′dum). A writ by which a defendant was ordered to appear and answer a charge of misdemeanor.

venire facias de novo (vē-nī′re fā′she-as dē nō′vō). An award, the effect of which is a new trial, granted by the appellate court for error occurring during the course of the trial. A proceeding of ancient origin, resulting in a new trial, granted for some cause apparent on the record. 39 Am J1st New Tr § 3. In modern terminology, the same as **new trial.**

venire facias judicationis (vē-nī′re fā′she-as jū-di-kā″she-ō′nis). The common-law writ by which the sheriff causes to come from the body of his county, a certain number of qualified citizens who are to act as jurors in the court. Durrah v State, 44 Miss 789, 796.

venire facias tot matronas (vē-nī′re fā′she-as tot ma-trō′nas). A venire to summon a jury of matrons.
See **jury of matrons.**

veniremen (vẹ-nī'rē-mẹn). Persons whose names are drawn from the jury wheel for a venire or special venire and who are summoned by a writ of venire and are thereby upon the jury panel for a term of court, a part of a term, or for choosing jurors for a particular case. 31 Am J Rev ed Jury § 3.

venire proceedings (vẹ-nī'rē prọ-sē'dings). Proceedings in the impaneling or selection of the jury.

Venit et defendit vim et injuriam (vē'nit et dē-fen'dit vim et in-jū'ri-am). He comes and denies the force and injury.

Venit et dicit (vē'nit et di'sit). He comes and says.

vente a rémére (vônt ah rā"me-rā'). (French.) An agreement or contract of sale with conditions, and a right or power of redemption annexed; an agreement or paction by which the vendor reserves to himself the power of taking back the thing sold, by returning the price paid for it. Livingston's Executrix v Story (US) 11 Pet 351, 387, 9 L Ed 746, 760.

venting system. A system of pipes and other installations on gas-burning appliances which carry off fumes. 26 Am J2d Electr § 239.

ventre inspiciendo. See de ventre inspiciendo.

ventre sa mere. See en ventre sa mere.

venture (ven'tụr). Verb: To take chances. See Allan v Hargadine-McKittrick Dry Goods Co. 315 Mo 254, 264, 286 SW 16. Noun: A taking of chances. Embarking upon a business enterprise.

venue (ven'ū). The county or district wherein a cause is to be tried. 56 Am J1st Ven § 2. The county or district in which an indictment is returned. 27 Am J1st Indict § 12. In the original meaning, the county district, or neighborhood from which the jury was to come. Eck v State Tax Com. 204 Md 245, 103 A2d 850, 48 ALR2d 415.

Not to be confused with "jurisdiction," since jurisdiction may not be conferred by consent or waiver, whereas the venue of an action as fixed by statute may be changed by the consent of the parties and an objection that the plaintiff brought his suit in the wrong county may be waived by failure to make a timely objection, thereby permitting the court to proceed and render a valid judgment. Hardenburgh v Hardenburgh, 115 Mont 469, 146 P2d 151.

venue of affidavit. The place where an affidavit is taken; the designation in an affidavit of the place where taken. 3 Am J2d Affi § 14.

veracity (vē-ras'i-ti). Truthfulness. Honesty. Wachstetter v State, 99 Ind 290.

vera copula (vē'ra ko'pu-la). Perfect coition; complete sexual intercourse. Anno: 65 ALR2d 781, § 4.

vera lex, recta ratio, naturae congruens (vē'ra lex, rek'ta rā'she-ō, na-tu'rē kon'gru-enz). True law, right reason, agreeable to nature.

veray. True.

verba (ver'ba). Words.
See haec verba.

Verba accipienda sunt cum effectu ut sortiantur effectum (ver'ba ak-si-pi-en'da sunt kum ef-fek'tū ut sor-she-an'ter ef-fek'tum). Words are to be taken with effect, so that they may be productive of effect.

Verba accipienda sunt secundum subjectam materiam (ver'ba ak-si-pi-en'da sunt se-kun'dum subjek'tam ma-te'ri-am). Words are to be taken according to their subject matter.

Verba accipienda ut sortiantur effectum (ver'ba ak-si-pi-en'da ut sor-she-an'ter ef-fek'tum). Words should be so taken that they may be productive of effect.

Verba aequivoca ac in dubio sensu posita, intelliguntur digniori et potentiori sensu (ver'ba ē-qui'vo-ka ak in dū'bi-ō sen'sū po'zi-ta, in-tel-li-gun'ter dig-ni-ō'rī et po-ten-she-ō'rī sen'sū). Equivocal words and those which are used in a doubtful sense are to be understood according to their more worthy and effective signification.

Verba aliquid operari debent; debent intelligi ut aliquid operentur (ver'ba a'li-quid ō-pe-rā'rī de'bent; de'bent in-tel'li-jī ut a'li-quid ō-pe-ren'ter). Words ought to be effective in some way; they ought to be understood as being in some way operative or effective.

Verba aliquid operari debent; verba cum effectu sunt accipienda (ver'ba al'li-quid ō-pe-rā'rī de'bent; ver'ba kum ef-fek'tū sunt ak-si-pi-en'da). Words ought to be operative in some way; words ought to be taken so that they may have effect.

Verba artis ex arte (ver'ba ar'tis ex ar'te). Words of art should be interpreted by the art.

Verba chartarum fortius accipiuntur contra proferentem (ver'ba kar-tā'rum for'ti-us ak-si-pi-un'ter kon'trā prō-fe-ren'tem). The language of the contract shall be construed most strictly against the person who offers it. Owens v Graetzel, 146 Md 361, 126 A 224, 39 ALR 943, 949.

Verba cum effectu accipienda sunt (ver'ba kum ef-fek'tū ak-si-pi-en'da sunt). Words should be so taken as to have effect.

Verba currentis monetae tempus solutionis designant (ver'ba ker-ren'tis mo-nē'tē tem'pus so-lū-she-ō'nis de-sig'nant). The words "current money" refer to the time of payment.

Verba debent intelligi cum effectu (ver'ba de'bent in-tel'li-jī kum ef-fek'tū). Words ought to be understood so as to have effect.

Verba debent intelligi cum effectu, ut res magis valeat quam pereat (ver'ba de'bent in-tel'li-jī kum ef-fek'tū, ut rēz mā'jis va'le-at quam per'e-at). Language ought to be understood with such effect that the subject matter will rather have effect than be lost. See 2 Bl Comm 380.

Verba debent intelligi ut aliquid operentur (ver'ba de'bent in-tel'li-jī ut a'li-quid ō-pe-ren'ter). Words ought to be so understood that they may have some effect.

Verba dicta de persona, intelligi debent de conditione personae (ver'ba dik'ta dē per-sō'na, in-tel'li-jī de'-bent dē kon-di"she-ō'ne per-sō'nē). Words which are spoken concerning a person ought to be understood as referring to the condition of the person.

Verba fortius accipiuntur contra proferentem (ver'ba for'she-us ak-si-pi-un'ter kon'trā prō-fe-ren'tem). Language should be taken more strictly against him who makes use of it. See 2 Bl Comm 380.

Verba generalia generaliter sunt intelligenda (ver'ba je-ne-rā'li-a je-ne-rā'li-ter sunt in-tel-li-jen'da). General words ought to be understood generally.

Verba generalia restringuntur ad habilitatem rei vel aptitudinem personae (ver'ba je-ne-rā'li-a re-strin-gun'ter ad ha-bi'li-tā'tem rē'ī vel ap-ti-tū'di-nem per-sō'nē). (Civil law.) General words should be confined to the character of the thing or the aptitude of the person.

Verba generalia restringuntur ad habilitatem rei vel personae (ver'ba je-ne-rā'li-a re-strin-gun'ter ad ha-bi''li-tā'tem rē'ī vel per-sō'nē). General words should be confined or restricted to the character of the thing or the person. See Broom's Legal Maxims 646.

Verba illata (relata) inesse videntur (ver'ba il-lā'ta (re-lā'ta) in-es'se vi-den'ter). Words which are referred to are deemed to be included.

Verba in differenti materia per prius, non per posterius, intelligenda sunt (ver'ba in dif-fer-en'tī ma-te'ri-a per prī'us, non per pos-te'ri-us, in-tel''li-jen'da sunt). (Civil law.) Words concerning a different matter are to be understood by the matter preceding, and not by that following.

Verba intelligenda sunt in casu possibili (ver'ba in-tel-li-jen'da sunt in kā'sū pos-si'bi-lī). (Civil law.) Words are to be understood as referring to a possible case.

Verba intentioni debent inservire(ver'ba in-ten''she-ō'nī dē'bent in-ser-vī're). Language ought to serve to express the intent.
From this maxim of the law, it follows that the construction of language must be reasonable and agreeable to common understanding. Edgerly v Barker, 66 NH 434, 31 A 900.

Verba intentioni, et non e contra, debent inservire (ver'ba in-ten-she-ō'nī, et non ē kon'tra dē'bent in-ser-vī're). Words ought to serve intention, and not the contrary.

Verba ita sunt intelligenda, ut res magis valeat quam pereat (ver'ba i'ta sunt in-tel-li-jen'da, ut rēz mā'jis va'le-at quam pe're-at). Words should be so understood that the thing should have effect rather than be null.

verbal. By word of mouth; spoken; oral; parol. See **parol**.

verbal abuse. Abusive language.

verbal acts. Statements which characterize or illustrate an act or transaction. People v Carlton, 57 Cal 83; Cox v State, 64 Ga 374. A statement which, because of its materiality in showing the motive, character, and object of an act, is admissible in evidence as against an objection that it is hearsay or self-serving. 29 Am J2d Ev § 710.

verbal will. Same as **oral will.**

Verba mere aequivoca, si per communem usum loquendi in intellectu certo sumuntur, talis intellectus praeferendus est (ver'ba mē'rē ē-qui'vo-ka, sī per kom-mu-nem ū'sum lo-quen'dī in in-tel-lek'tū ser'tō su-mun'ter, tā'lis in-tel-lek'tus prē-fe-ren'dus est). (Civil law.) The words being merely equivocal, if by common usage of speech they take a certain meaning, such meaning is to be preferred.

Verba nihil operari melius est quam absurde (ver'ba ni'hil ō''pe-rā'rī me'li-us est quam ab-ser'de). (Civil law.) It is better that words have no effect than to have an absurd one.

Verba non tam intuenda, quam causa et natura rei, ut mens contrahentium ex eis potius quam ex verbis appareat (ver'ba non tam in-tu-en'da, quam kā'zạ et na-tū'ra re'ī, ut menz kon-tra-hen'she-um ex ē'is po'she-us quam ex ver'bis ap-pā're-at). (Civil law.) Words are not to be regarded as much as the cause and nature of the thing, so that the intent of the contracting parties may appear from these rather than from the words.

Verba offendi possunt, imo ab eis recedere licet, ut verba ad sanum intellectum reducantur (ver'ba of-fen'dī pos'sunt, i'mō ab ē'is re-sē'de-re lī'set, ut ver'ba ad sa'num in-tel-lek'tum re-du-kan'ter). (Civil law.) Words can be stricken out, nay rather it is proper to depart from them, so that they may be reduced to a sensible meaning.

Verba ordinationis quando verificari possunt in sua vera significatione, trahi ad extraneum intellectum non debent (ver'ba or-di-nā-she-ō'nis quan'dō ve-ri-fi-kā'rī pos'sunt in sū'a vē'ra sig-ni-fi-kā''she-ō'ne, trā'hī ad ex-trā'ne-um in-tel-lek'tum non dē'bent). (Civil law.) When the words of an ordinance can be verified in their true signification, they ought not to be twisted into a foreign meaning.

Verba posteriora propter certitudinem addita, ad priora quae certitudine indigent, sunt referenda (ver'ba pos-te''ri-ō'ra prop'ter ser-ti-tū'di-nem ad'-di-ta, ad prī-ō'ra kwē ser-ti-tū'di-ne in'di-jent, sunt re-fe-ren'da). Subsequent words which are added for the sake of certainty ought to be referred to prior ones lacking in certainty. See Broom's Legal Maxims 586.

verba precaria (ver'ba pre-kā'ri-a). Precatory words. See **precatory words.**

Verba pro re et subjecta materia accipi debent (ver'ba prō rē et sub-jek'ta ma-te'ri-a ak'si-pī dē'bent). (Civil law.) Words ought to be taken favorably to the thing and the subject matter.

Verba quae aliquid operari possunt non debent esse superflua (ver'ba kwē a'li-quid ō''pe-rā'rī pos'sunt non dē'bent es'se su-per'flu-a). (Civil law.) Words which can have any effect ought not to be regarded as superfluous.

Verba quantumvis generalia ad aptitudinem restringuntur, etiamsi nullam aliam paterentur restrictionem (ver'ba quan-tum'vis je-ne-rā'li-a ad ap-ti-tū'di-nem re-strin-gun'ter, e-she-am'sī nul'lam a'li-am pa-te-ren'ter re-strik''she-ō'nem). (Civil law.) Words, however general, are confined to fitness, although they disclose no other restriction.

Verba relata hoc maxime operantur per referentiam ut in eis inesse videntur (ver'ba re-lā'ta hōk ma'ksi-me ō-pe-ran'ter per re-fe-ren'she-am ut in ē'is in-es'se vi-den'ter). Words incorporated by reference have as great effect through reference, as they are deemed to be included in them. See Broom's Legal Maxims 673.

Verba relata inesse videntur (ver'ba re-lā'ta in-es'se vi-den'ter). Words which are incorporated by reference are deemed to be included. Commonwealth v Hart, 65 Mass (11 Cush) 130, 137.

Verba restringuntur ad habilitatem rei vel personae (ver'ba re-strin-gun'ter ad ha-bi-li-tā'tem rē'ī vel per-sō'nē). Words are restricted or confined according to the character of the person or the thing.

Verba secundum materiam subjectam intelligi nemo est qui nescit (ver'ba se-kun'dum ma-te'ri-am sub-jek'tam in-tel'li-jī nē'mō est quī ne'sit). There is no one who does not know that words are to be understood according to their subject matter.

Verba semper accipienda sunt in mitiori sensu (ver'ba sem'per ak-si''pī-en'da sunt in mi-she-ō'rī sen'sū). Words should always be taken in their milder sense.

Verba strictae significationis ad latam extendi possunt, si subsit ratio (ver'ba strik'tē sig-ni-fi-kā''she-ō'nis ad lā'tem ex-ten'dī pos'sunt, sī sub'sit rā'she-ō). (Civil law.) Words of strict significance can be extended to a broad meaning, if reason requires it.

Verba sunt indices animi (ver'ba sunt in'di-sēz a'nimī). Words are the indexes of the mind.

verbatim (vėr-bā'tim). In the very same words. Word for word.

verbatim transcript. A transcript of the testimony of a witness in the exact words of the witness, being neither condensed nor narrative in form. 4 Am J2d A & E § 435.

verbis aut cantilenis (vėr'bis ât kant-i-len'is). By words or in song.
"The publication may be verbis aut cantilenis, as when the libel is maliciously repeated or sung in the presence of others." Adams v Lawson, 58 Va (17 Gratt) 250.

Verbis plane expressis omnino standum est (ver'bis pla'nē ex-pres'sis om-nī'nō stan'dum est). Words which plainly express their meaning must in all respects be sustained. The Pedro, 175 US 354, 364, 44 L Ed 195, 199, 175 S Ct 138.

Verbis standum ubi nulla ambiguitas (ver'bis stan'dum u'bi nul'la am-bi-gū'i-tās). Where there is no ambiguity, the words are to be adhered to.

verbo in verbum. Word for word.

verbosity. The use of unnecessary words, particularly in a pleading. 27 Am J2d Equity § 187.

Verbum imperfecti temporis rem adhuc imperfectam significat (ver'bum im-per-fek'tī tem'po-ris rem ad'hŭk im-per-fek'tam sig-ni'fi-kat). A verb in the imperfect tense signifies an uncompleted matter.

verderors of the forest (vėr'dėr-ǫrs). See **sweinmote court.**
See **advisory verdict; chance verdict; compromise verdict; general verdict; privy verdict; public verdict; quotient verdict; sealed verdict; special verdict.**

verdict. The final determination of the jury. Fidelity & Co. v Huse & Carleton, 272 Mass 448, 172 NE 590, 72 ALR 1143. The final decision of a jury concerning matters of fact submitted to it by the court for determination. 53 Am J1st Trial § 1005. Not an indebtedness; not personal property, within the meaning of a garnishment statute. Bassett v McCarty, 3 Wash 2d 488, 101 P2d 575.

verdict against evidence. A verdict which is contrary to the evidence, or to the weight of the evidence, or which is not sustained by sufficient evidence. 39 Am J1st New Tr § 129.

verdict against law. See **verdict contrary to law.**

verdict contrary to law. The verdict of a jury who in arriving at it have failed or neglected to follow the directions of the judge upon matters of law. 39 Am J1st New Tr § 126.
According to the weight of authority, even if the instructions are erroneous, they constitute the law of the case and it is the duty of the jury to follow them. 39 Am J1st New Tr § 127.

verdict of guilty. A determination of the jury in a criminal case, leading to a final judgment of guilt. A proper form of verdict in a civil case where the issue is raised by a plea of not guilty. Peters v Johnson, Jackson & Co. 50 W Va 644, 41 SE 190.

verdict of non licet (ver'dikt ov non lī'set). A jury's verdict expressing doubt and asking further time for deliberation.

verdict of not guilty. An acquittal of the accused in a criminal case. A proper form of verdict in a civil case where the issue is raised by a plea of not guilty.

Peters v Johnson, Jackson & Co. 50 W Va 644, 41 SE 190.

veredicto non obstante (vē-re-dik'tō non ob-stan'te). Notwithstanding the verdict.
See **judgment notwithstanding the verdict.**

Veredictum, quasi dictum veritatis; ut judicium, quasi juris dictum (vē-re-dik'tum, quā'sī dik'tum ve-ri-tā'tis; ut ju-di'she-um, quā'sī jū'ris dik'tum). A verdict is, as it were, the expression of the truth; as a judgment is, as it were, the expression of the law.

verge (vėrj). The space included within a radius of twelve miles from the residence of the king of England.

vergens ad inopiam (ver'genz ad in-ō'pi-am). Verging or declining toward poverty.

verge of the court. Same as **verge.**

verifiable certainty (ver'i-fī-ạ-bl sėr'tạn-ti). A test of judicial notice, referring to facts which can be verified to a certainty by reference to competent authoritative sources. 29 Am J2d Ev § 25.

verification. A sworn statement of the truth of the facts stated in an instrument. 3 Am J2d Affi § 20. A statement under oath by a party who pleads that his pleading is true of his own knowledge or to the best of his knowledge and belief. 41 Am J1st Pl § 284. Testing the accuracy of a statement or an account.

verified account. A statement of account verified under oath as to the accuracy thereof. 1 Am J2d Acctg § 12.

verified pleading. See **verification.**

verify. To test the accuracy of a statement or an account. To substantiate the truth of a statement or of an account by formal oath, in other words, to make a verification. Watts v Gerking, 111 Or 641, 228 P 135, 34 ALR 1489, 1495.
See **verification.**

veritas (ver'i-tas). Truth; accuracy; correctness.

Veritas demonstrationis tollit errorem nominis (ve'ri-tās dē-mōn-strā"she-ō'nis tol'lit er-rō'rem nō'minis). Correctness of description cures error of name.

Veritas habenda est in juratore; justitia et judicium in judice (ve'ri-tās hā-ben'da est in ju-rā'tor; jū-sti'she-a et jū-di'she-um in jū'di-se). Truth should be possessed by a juror; justice and judgment by a judge.

Veritas nihil veretur nisi abscondi (ve'ri-tās ni'hil ve-rē'ter nī'sī ab-skon'dī). Truth fears nothing except concealment.

Veritas nimium altercando amittitur (ve'ri-tas ni'mi-um al-ter-kan'dō a-mit'ti-ter). Truth is lost by too much altercation.

Veritas nominis tollit errorem demonstrationis (ve'ri-tas nō'mi-nis tol'lit er-rō'rem dē-mōn-strā"she-ō'nis). Correctness of name cures error in description. Joiner v Joiner, 55 NC (2 Jones Eq) 68, 72.

veritatem dicere (vē-ri-tā'tem dī'se-re). To speak the truth; the preliminary examination of a juryman touching his qualifications. See 3 Bl Comm 364.

Veritatem qui non libere pronunciat, proditor est veritatis (ve'ri-tā'tem quī non li'be-re prō-nun'she-at, prō'di-tor est ve"ri-tā'tis). He who does not express the truth freely is a traitor to the truth.

verity of judgment. Conclusiveness of judgment.

vermin (vėr'min). Rats, mice, lice, or other representatives of small animal life of destructive or filthy and troublesome tendencies. 32 Am J1st L & T § 247.

vernacular (vėr-nak'ṳ-lặr). Characterizing the language of the people as distinguished from the language of the dictionary or of literary persons. 17 Am J2d Contr § 247.

veronal. A drug; a barbiturate. Mansbacher v Prudential Ins. Co. 273 NY 140, 7 NE2d 18, 111 ALR 618, reh den 274 NY 487, 8 NE2d 616.

vers. An abbreviation of **versus.**

versari (ver-sā'rī). (Civil law.) To be engaged, occupied or employed in; to be versed in or conversant with.

versus (vėr'sus). Against. The meaning of "versus" and its abbreviation "vs." is well understood and it is quite as appropriate, even in a pleading, as the word "against" could be. They have, in fact, become engrafted upon the English language, at least so far as they are used in this country in legal proceedings. Smith v Butler, 25 NH 521, 523.

vert (vėrt). Verdant; green; green growth; pertaining to the forest.

vertical price-fixing agreement. An agreement between the manufacturer or dealer in an article with purchasers who buy numbers of such article for resale in the course of business, having the purpose of controlling the resale or retail price. 52 Am J1st Tradem § 173.

vertical union. Same as **industrial union.**

vertigo (vėr'ti-gō). Dizziness.

verus (vē'rus). True; genuine.

very high degree of care. Due care in the face of imminent danger. 38 Am J1st Negl § 31.

very matrimony (vėr'i mat'ri-mọ-ni). A term used in the ancient canon law, signifying a valid marriage.
Under that law the contract per verba de praesenti did not require consummation in order to become "very matrimony;" but it ipso facto et ipso jure constituted the relation of man and wife. See 17 ERC 10.

vessel. A marine structure intended for transportation of goods or passengers. 48 Am J1st Ship § 35. Anything floating in and on the water, built and used for navigation, regardless of form, rig, or motive power. Cope v Vallette Drydock Co. 119 US 625, 30 L Ed 501, 7 S Ct 336. Watercraft of every description, other than a seaplane on the water, used or capable of being used as a means of transportation on water. 46 USC § 527(2) (Federal Boating Act).
See **burdened vessel; favored vessel; overtaking vessel; public vessel.**

vessel belonging to or employed in the government of the United States. A vessel under the control of the United States. Ackerlind v United States, 240 US 531, 60 L Ed 783, 36 S Ct 438 (phrase appearing in tariff act). A ship registered by the United States for the foreign trade or licensed or enrolled by the United States for the coasting trade. 48 Am J1st Ship § 40.

vessel of the United States. Any vessel registered, enrolled, or licensed under the laws of the United States, whether permanently or temporarily. 46 USC § 911(2)(4) (Ship Mortgage Act).

vessels. A generic term within the meaning of tariff regulations and laws. 21 Am J2d Cust D § 49.
See **vessel.**

vest. To pass to a person, as where the title to property comes to the heir upon the death of the owner intestate. To descend; to take effect. D. M. Ferry & Co. v Forquer, 61 Mont 336, 202 P 193, 29 ALR 642. To give an immediate fixed right of present or future enjoyment. Stewart v Harriman, 56 NH 25.
The use of the term "vest in," in reference to surviving remaindermen, does not operate, in the absence of other controlling language, to prevent the ascertainment of surviving remaindermen at the death of the testator. Anno: 114 ALR 26.

vested. Fixed in interest. Indefeasible. 57 Am J1st Wills § 1230.

vested estate. An absolute, unconditional, and indefeasible interest. 57 Am J1st Wills § 1230. An estate which is not contingent or expectant; an estate carrying a fixed right of present or future enjoyment. 28 Am J2d Est § 6. An estate which gives a certain and fixed right of present or future enjoyment; that is, an interest clothed with a present legal and existing right of alienation. Allison v Allison, 101 Va 537, 44 SE 904.
An estate is vested in possession when there exists a right of present enjoyment, and vested in interest when there is a present right of future enjoyment. Re Kohrs, 122 Mont 145, 199 P2d 856, 5 ALR2d 1046; Carroll v Newark, 108 NJL 323, 158 A 458, 79 ALR 509.
An estate is said to be vested in interest, when there is a present fixed right in someone of future enjoyment of it; it is not vested, but is contingent, when either the person who is to enjoy it, or the event upon which the estate is to arise is uncertain. See Johnston's Estate, 185 Pa 179, 39 A 879.

vested future estate. An estate which exists when there is a person in being who would have an immediate right to the possession of the lands upon the ceasing of the intermediate or precedent estate. Palmer v Dunham, 52 Hun 468, 471, 6 NYS 46.
See **vested remainder.**

vested gift. A gift which vests immediately in interest, albeit the enjoyment is postponed. 24 Am J1st Gifts § 31.

vested in interest. See **vested estate.**

vested in possession. See **vested estate.**

vested interest. A fixed right to the enjoyment of property in an ascertained person which is subject to no condition other than the termination of a precedent estate. Stevens v Carroll, 64 Or 417, 129 P 1044.
An interest when vested, whether it entitles the owner to the possession now or at a future period, is fixed and present; so that the right of ownership, to the extent of the estate, may be aliened. Allison v Allison, 101 Va 537, 44 SE 904.
See **vested estate; vested right.**

vested legacy. A legacy provided absolutely and unconditionally, although sometimes payable at a future time. Magoffin v Patton (Pa) 4 Rawle 113, 116.

vested remainder. A remainder limited to an ascertained person or persons with no further condition imposed upon the taking effect in possession than the determination of the precedent estate. 28 Am J2d Est § 217. An estate invariably fixed, to remain to a determinate person, after the precedent estate is spent. 2 Bl Comm § 168. An estate passing absolutely by will or conveyance, where possession or enjoyment is postponed until the termination of the particular estate upon which it is limited. Re Phearman, 211 Iowa 1137, 232 NW 826, 82 ALR 674.

A remainder is vested if, at every moment during its continuance, it is a present estate, whenever and however the preceding freehold estate determines. Sands v Fly, 200 Tenn 414, 292 SW2d 706, 57 ALR2d 188.

Wherever the preceding estate is limited, so as to determine on an event which certainly must happen, and the remainder is so limited to a person in esse, and ascertained, that the preceding estate may by any means determine before the expiration of the estate limited in remainder, such remainder is vested. Fearne, Contingent Remainders p 216, quoted in 28 Am J2d Est § 217.

Unless the intent of the testator is made to appear to the contrary, a devise or bequest will be construed in favor of a vested remainder instead of a contingent remainder. Re Phearman, 211 Iowa 1137, 232 NW 826, 82 ALR 674.

vested right. An immediate fixed right of present or future enjoyment; an immediate right of present enjoyment, or a present fixed right of future enjoyment. 16 Am J2d Const L § 421; 28 Am J2d Est § 6. A right in the form of a title, legal or equitable, to the present or future enjoyment of property, or to the present or future enforcement of a demand, or a legal exemption from a demand made by another. Hagerty v Administrator, Unemployment Compensation Act, 137 Conn 129, 75 A2d 406, 20 ALR2d 960.

The term includes title, legal or equitable, to the present or future enforcement of a demand or a legal exemption from a demand made by another, though it must be something more than such a mere expectation as may be based on an anticipated continuance of general laws. Massa v Mastri, 125 Conn 144, 3 A2d 839, 120 ALR 939.

To be vested, a right must have become a title, legal or equitable, to the present or future enjoyment of property, or to the present or future enforcement of a demand, or a legal exemption from a demand made by another. Hagerty v Administrator, Unemployment Compensation Act, 137 Conn 129, 75 A2d 406, 20 ALR2d 960.

See **vested estate; vested interest.**

vested subject to divesting. A phrase characterizing an estate intermediate a vested interest and a contingent interest. 57 Am J1st Wills § 1217. A remainder which will be defeated upon the occurrence of the contingency stated in the limitation. 28 Am J2d Est § 320.

vested water rights. See **accrued water rights.**

vestibule (ves'ti-būl). An inclosed space at the end of a railroad car or streetcar through which passengers enter or leave the main part of the car. An inclosed space immediately inside the door of a public building or a building frequented by the public.

vestigial words or phrases (ves-tij'i-al werds or frā'zes). Words or phrases which have been permitted to remain in a statute after it has been amended, but which are rendered useless and meaningless by the amendment. Saltonstall v Birtwell, 164 US 54, 70, 41 L Ed 348, 353, 17 S Ct 19.

vestigium (ves-tij'i-um) A vestige; a trace; a scintilla.

vestimentum (ves-ti-men'tum). Investiture; seisin.

vesting order (ves'ting ôr'dėr). An order or decree of a court of equity transferring title to land.

vestire (ves-tī're). To vest; to invest, as with title.

vestry. See **vestrymen.**

vestrymen (ves'tri-man). Church members composing the vestry or body which manages the temporal affairs of the church. 44 Am J1st Quo W § 83.

vestura terrae (ves-tū'ra ter'rē). The clothing of the land. Vesture.

vesture (ves'tŭr). Clothing. In more frequent use, grass, grain, or other plants which cover the earth. Simpson v Coe, 4 NH 301, 303.

veteran. One who has served as an enlisted man or a commissioned officer in any of the Armed Services. 56 Am J1st Vet & V A § 2.

Veterans' Acts. Statutes making special provision for the benefit or welfare of veterans of the Armed Services and their dependents, or extending to veterans privileges or preferences not accorded to other classes of citizens, particularly in reference to appointment in the public service. 15 Am J2d Civ S § 15.

Veterans' Administration. The federal agency, established in 1930, responsible for the administration of federal statutes providing direct benefits for veterans and their dependents, their duties, powers, and functions being in part those formerly vested in various hospitals, bureaus, agencies, and offices of the federal government. 56 Am J1st Vet & V A § 3.

veterans' benefits. Benefits provided by law for veterans of the Armed Forces. 56 Am J1st Vet & V A § 2.

veterans' cemetery. A national cemetery. 24 USC § 281.

veterans' homes. National homes for veterans, now under the jurisdiction of the Veterans' Administration. Also homes maintained by states for veterans. 56 Am J1st Vet & V A § 7.

veterans' hospital. A hospital primarily for the care of veterans of the Armed Services. 56 Am J1st Vet & V A § 6.

veterans' insurance. Insurance issued to persons in the Armed Forces and maintained in force by them or converted to life insurance in another form after discharge or separation from the service. 29A Am J Rev ed Ins § 1970.

Veterans of Foreign Wars. An organization of veterans of the Armed Forces, distinctive particularly in the limitation of membership to veterans with service on foreign fields.

veterans' organizations. Organizations of veterans of the Armed Services, having the primary purposes of strengthening and preserving comradeship, promoting and advancing mutual helpfulness among members, the protection of their widows and orphans, and the stimulation of patriotism. 56 Am J1st Vet & V A § 17.

veterans' preference. See **Veterans' Acts.**

veterans' settlement. A settlement on public lands under a project primarily for the benefit of veterans. 56 Am J1st Vet & V A § 14.

vetera statuta (vē'te-ra sta-tū'ta). Ancient statutes; a name given to those statutes which were enacted from the time of Magna Charta in 1215 through the reign of Edward the Second in 1327.

Veteres enim haeredes pro dominis appellabant (ve′te-rēz e′nim hē-rē′dēz prō dō′mi-nis ap-pel-lā′bant). For the ancients called heirs, "owners" or "masters." Emeric v Alvarado, 64 Cal 529, 558, 2 P 418.

veterinarian (vet″ẹ-ri-nā′ri-ạn). One who practices medicine or surgery in the limited field of the treatment of animals. Staples v Steed, 167 Ala 214, 52 So 646.

veterinary hospital. A place for the care of sick or disabled animals. Wergin v Voss, 179 Wis 603, 192 NW 51, 26 ALR 933.

vetitio principii (ve-ti′she-ō prin-si′pi-ī). A supposition of what is not granted; a begging the question. Case upon the Statute for Distribution, Wythe (Va) 302, 309.

vetitum namium (vē′ti-tum nā′mi-um). A forbidden taking—a remedy by means of a second or reciprocal distress for a wrongful distress. See 3 Bl Comm 148.

veto. A qualified right of a governor of a state to prevent an enactment of the legislature from becoming law. 49 Am J1st States § 47. The refusal of the executive to approve a bill passed by the legislative body, having the effect of nullifying such legislative action unless the bill is passed by the requisite number of votes upon reconsideration by the legislative body after such disapproval by the executive. 50 Am J1st Stat § 111.

The disapproval by the President of the United States of a bill after it has passed both houses of Congress, or by the governor of a state of the Union after the bill has passed both houses of the state legislature. The veto is essentially a legislative act. The fact that the President or the governor is limited to negation or concurrence, and cannot affirmatively initiate or amend legislation, does not take away the legislative character of his act, any more than want of power in the Senate of the United States to originate revenue bills changes its character as a co-ordinate branch of Congress. Commonwealth ex rel. Elkin v Barnett, 199 Pa 161, 48 A 976.

See **pocket veto.**

veto power. The power of the executive to veto a legislative act. 16 Am J2d Const L §§ 213, 214.
See **veto.**

vetus depositio pecuniae (ve′tus de-po-zi′she-ō pe-kū′ni-ē). The former concealment of the money.

vetustas (ve-tus′tās). (Civil law.) Antiquity; time out of mind.

vexatae quaestiones (vek-sa′tē kwest-she-ō′nēz). Vexata questions; moot questions.

vexata quaestio (vek-sā′ta kwest′she-ō). Singular of **vexatae quaestiones.**

vexatious appeal. A frivolous or unjustified appeal taken for the purpose of hindering or delaying justice. 5 Am J2d A & E § 1024.

vexatious litigation. Same as **vexatious suit.**

vexatious motion. A motion presented or filed for the purpose of vexation or delay, rather than to subserve the ends of justice. 37 Am J1st Motions § 4.

vexatious proceeding. Same as **vexatious suit.**

vexatious refusal to pay claim. A ground for subjecting an insurance company to a penalty. A refusal to pay founded, not upon what appear to be the facts, but only upon a possibility that later investigation may develop facts justifying refusal to pay. 29A Am J Rev ed Ins § 1697.

A refusal is held not to be vexatious if founded on what at the time appeared to be facts justifying the refusal, even though at the trial it may be shown that the true facts were exactly opposite of what they appeared to be at first. Buffalo Ins. Co. v Bommarito (CA8 Mo) 42 F2d 53, 70 ALR 1211.

vexatious suit. Litigation for the purpose of harassing, annoying, and vexing an opponent, rather than for the adjudication of rights, being invoked, not for the attainment of justice, but to further or satisfy a malicious motive. 28 Am J Rev ed Inj § 210.

vi (vī). With violence; with force; forcibly; violently.

via (vī′ạ). Preposition: By way of. Noun: A way.

Lord Coke, adopting the civil law, divided private ways into three kinds: a footway, called "iter;" a footway and horseway, called "actus;" and a cartway which embraced both of the other two, called "via." To these was added a "driftway," a road over which cattle could be driven. Jones v Venable, 120 Ga 1, 47 NE 549.

via alta (al′tạ). A highway.

viable (vī′ạ-bl). Capable of living, physically fit to live; of a fetus, having reached such a stage of development as to permit continued existence under normal conditions, outside of the womb. Williams v Marion Rapid Transit, 152 Ohio St 114, 87 NE2d 334, 10 ALR2d 1051.

viability (vī-ạ-bil′i̇-ti). Ability to live; the capability of a newborn infant to survive.

via amicabili (vī′a a-mi-kā′bi-lī). In a friendly way.

Via antiqua via est tuta (vī′a an-ti′qua vī′a est tū′ta). The old way is the safe way.

"I consider myself bound by those principles, which were known and established as law in courts of equity in England, at the time of the institution of this court." Manning v Manning (NY) 1 Johns Ch 527, 530.

viaduct (vī′ạ-dukt). A long bridge, especially one which spans a valley or gorge. A structure carrying traffic over other lines of traffic. Re Yesler Way, 94 Wash 427, 162 P 536.

viaggio (vee-ag′he-o). A voyage.

viagium (vī-ā′ji-um). A voyage.

viam (vī′am). A way.
See **extra viam.**

via other ports (vī′ạ uth′ėr pōrts). A phrase in a bill of lading relating to the route of the vessel.

These words in a recital in a bill of lading that the goods are received for transportation on a vessel bound for the port of destination "via other ports," do not have the effect of broadening a provision of the charter party giving the vessel "liberty to call at any port or ports in any order, for any purpose." Anno: 33 ALR2d 166.

via publica (vī′a pub′li-ka). A public way.

via regia (vī′a rē′ji-a). The king's highway; any public road or highway in England.

viator (vi-ā′tor). A traveler; a wayfarer.
See **caveat viator.**

Via trita est tutissima (vī′a trī′ta est tū-tis′si-ma). The beaten path is the safest. See Broom's Legal Maxims 134.

Via trita, via tuta (vī'a trī'ta, vī'a tū'ta). The beaten path is the safe path. See Ex parte Crane (US) 5 Pet 190, 223, 8 L Ed 92, 104.

vi aut clam (vī ât klam). By force or fraud.

vi aut metu. Same as **vis aut meta.**

vibration. A process of agitating or shaking. A kind of oscillation. Re Junghans, 28 Cust & Pat App (Pat) 1237, 120 F2d 638.

vibrator. An instrument used in massage. Cornbrooks v Terminal Barber Shops, 282 NY 217, 26 NE2d 25.

vicar (vik'ạr). One of the clergy. In the Anglican and Episcopal churches, a deputy of another minister. In the Roman Catholic Church, a deputy of a bishop; the Pope himself as a representative of Christ.

vicarious (vī-kā'ri-us). Through the agency or by means of a representative, agent or servant.

vicarious liability. A liability imposed upon one person because of the act or omission of another, such as his employee.

vicarius (vī-kā'ri-us). (Eccles.) A vicar, an officiating minister deputed by an appropriating corporation or religious house to perform divine services in a parish of the corporation. See 1 Bl Comm 387.
See **vicar.**

Vicarius non habet vicarium (vī-kā'ri-us non hā'bet vī-kā'ri-um). A vicar has no deputy. See 1 Bl Comm 390.

The maxim has been construed more freely as meaning that a person who acts in a representative capacity cannot employ a representative, on the principle that delegated authority cannot be redelegated. See Broom's Legal Maxims 840.

vice (vīs). Preposition: As a substitute for; in the place of; instead of, as a vice president, a vice consul. Noun: Evil, sinful, and immoral conduct in a collective sense, as in "vice district" or "vice conditions in a city." An imperfection in an animal.

vice admiral. A naval officer ranking immediately below admiral and immediately above rear admiral, his rank being comparable to that of lieutenant general of the army. 36 Am J1st Mil § 55.

vice-admiralty courts (vīs-ad'mi-rạl-ti kōrts). Inferior courts of admiralty in the American Colonies and other settlements, from which appeals lay to the courts of admiralty in England, though they could also be brought before the king in council. See 3 Bl Comm 69.

vice-comes (vī''sẹ-kō'mēz). Same as **viscount.**

Vicecomes non misit breve (vī-sē-kō'mēz non mi'sit brē've). The sheriff has not sent the writ.

vice-commercial agent. A person substituted temporarily for a commercial agent of the consular service. United States v Eaton, 169 US 331, 42 L Ed 767, 18 S Ct 374.

vice consul. A person in the consular service, subordinate to or serving temporarily in place of a consul. United States v Eaton, 169 US 331, 336, 42 L Ed 767, 769, 18 S Ct 374.

vice district. A district in a city, given over to licensed prostitution. A district in a city, wherein houses of prostitution abound.

vice-domini. Same as **vidames.**

vicem seu personam ecclesiae gerere (vī'sem sū per-sō'nam e-kle'si-e je're-re). To represent the church. See 1 Bl Comm 384.

vice mayor. A municipal officer empowered to act as mayor during the absence of the mayor from the municipality during a disability of the mayor rendering him unfit to perform the duties of the office, or temporarily during a vacancy in the office of mayor resulting from the death of the mayor or his removal from office.

vice president. An officer next in rank below a president. Pond v National Mortg. & Debenture Co. 6 Kan App 718, 50 P 973. A corporate officer empowered to act as the chief executive of the corporation in the absence of, or during vacancy in the office of, the president, and sometimes given executive duties by the board of directors or bylaws of the corporation. 19 Am J2d Corp § 1171.

Vice President of the United States. An office provided by the Constitution of the United States, the incumbent of which is elected with the President and serves the same term of office as the President, the salient feature of which is the succession of the incumbent to the powers and duties of the office of the President upon the removal of the latter from office or his death, resignation, or inability to discharge the duties of the office. Any employee who represents the employer in the discharge of those personal or absolute duties which every employer owes to his employees.

vice-principal. One entrusted with the conduct of an employer's business, especially in the direction or superintendence of other employees. 35 Am J1st M & S § 129.

Among those employees who have been held to be vice principals are those charged with the duty of providing machinery and appliances, the place to work, the inspection and repair of premises and appliances, the selection and retention of servants, establishment of proper rules and regulations, and the instruction of servants. Moore v Dublin Cotton Mills, 127 Ga 609, 56 SE 839.

vice versa (vī'sē vėr'sạ). The other way about; under a reversed position of the parties.

vicinage (vis'i-nāj). The area surrounding a particular place, especially the place where the cause of action is alleged to have arisen or where a crime is alleged to have been committed. 56 Am J1st Ven § 2. The neighborhood or vicinity. 31 Am J Rev ed Jury § 6. The county, district, or other subdivision of venue.

At common law, the right of trial by jury includes the right of a prisoner to have the jury obtained from the vicinage or county where the crime is supposed to have been committed. The reason for this is that the accused may have the benefit, on his trial, of his own good reputation and standing with the neighbors, if these he has preserved, and also of such knowledge as the jury may possess of the witnesses who may give evidence against him. 31 Am J Rev ed Jury § 5.

vicineto (vi-sī'ne-tō). Neighborhood; vicinage.

vicinetum (vī-si-nē'tum). Neighborhood; vicinity.

vicinity. A place near to a place designated, but not adjoining or abutting on it. 23 Am J2d Deeds § 243.

The word is not an absolute but a relative one, and what is in the vicinity of a place under one set of circumstances may not be so under other circumstances. In a sparsely settled region a person residing fifteen miles from a road might be regarded as being in the vicinity of it. Sterling v Carter, 105 Kan

423, 185 P 11; Burton v Douglas, 141 Wis 110, 123 NW 631.
See **immediate vicinity; vicinage.**

Vicini viciniora praesumuntur scire (vī-sī'nī vī-sī-ni-ō'ra prē-zu-mun'ter sī're). Neighbors are presumed to know neighborhood matters.

vicious (vish'us). Partaking of vice; wicked; harmful.

vicious animal. An animal dangerous by nature. 4 Am J2d Ani §§ 80 et seq. A domestic animal with a propensity for injuring persons. 4 Am J2d Ani §§ 85 et seq. Any individual of a vicious species, or a vicious individual of a harmless species. Mellicker v Sedlacek, 189 Iowa 946, 179 NW 197, 11 ALR 259, 267.

vicious for false Latin (for fâls lat'in). Defective because of an error in Latin in which all proceedings were formerly written.
In the earlier English cases, it was considered that any stranger, as amicus curiae, might move the court of matters apparent in the writ, and the court ex officio was bound to abate the writ, if it was vicious for false Latin or default of form. Haley v Eureka County Bank, 21 Nev 127, 26 P 64.

vicious propensity. Such a propensity as exists in an animal which might attack or injure the safety of persons without being provoked to do so. Mellicker v Sedlacek, 189 Iowa 946, 179 NW 197, 11 ALR 259, 267.

vi clam aut precario (vī klam ât prē-kā'ri-ō). Forcibly, secretly or by sufferance.
An easement cannot be acquired by prescription if its enjoyment is characterized by either of these attributes. Lehigh Valley Railroad Co. v McFarlan, 43 NJL 605, 622.

vicontiel (vī-kon'ti-el). Pertaining to a sheriff.

victim. One who has suffered the commission of a crime, tort, or wrong.

Victoria (vik-tō'ri-ạ). The queen of England from June 20th, 1837, until January 22nd, 1901.

victualer (vit'l-ėr). One who serves food or drink for consumption on the premises. Friend v Childs Dining Hall Co. 231 Mass 65, 120 NE 407, 5 ALR 1100.

victualing house (vit'l-ing hous). A house where provision is made for strangers to eat; an eating house. Anno: 9 ALR 429.

victuals (vit'ls). Those things which are food for man in themselves or when mixed with something else. Anno: 9 ALR 429. Food ready to eat. Friend v Childs Dining Hall Co. 231 Mass 65, 120 NE 407, 5 ALR 1100, 1105.

victus (vik'tus). (Civil law.) The means of living or support. The vanquished; the unsuccessful party to an action.

Victus victori in expensis condemnandus est (vik'tus vik-tō'ri in ex-pen'sis kon-dem-nan'dus est). The losing party is adjudged to pay the costs to the successful party. See 3 Bl Comm 399.

vicus (vī'kus). A village.

vidame (vē-däm'). A title of dignity, next beneath peer. See 1 Bl Comm 403.

vide (vī'dē). See; refer to.

videlicet (vi-del'i-set). That is to say; namely. To wit. Words particularizing a general statement and explaining obscurities therein, without being repugnant to the statement. 57 Am J1st Wills § 1156. A formal statement in a pleading intended to dispense with strict proof. Lindekugel v Spokane, P. & S. R. Co. 149 Or 634, 42 P2d 907, 99 ALR 721.
When any fact alleged in a pleading is preceded by the words "to wit," or "that is to say," such fact is said to be laid under a videlicet. The object of a videlicet is to dispense with strict proof. The office of a videlicet is to note that the party does not undertake to prove the precise circumstances alleged. Lindekugel v Spokane, P. & S. R. Co. 149 Or 634, 42 P2d 907, 99 ALR 721.
The following note of the famous Sergeant Williams is appended to Dakin's Case, 2 Wms. Saund. 290, 291: "So a videlicet may sometimes restrain the generality of the former words, where they are not express and special, but stand indifferent, so as to be capable of being restrained without apparent injury to them; as if lands be granted to a man and his heirs, that is to say, the heirs of his body, it is an estate tail." See Hall v Hall, 84 Vt 259, 78 A 971.

Videtur qui surdus et mutus ne poet faire alienation (vi-dē'ter quī ser'dus et mu'tus nē po'et fār a-li-en-ā'shọn). He who is deaf and dumb is deemed not to be able to make an alienation. See Brower v Fisher (NY) 4 Johns Ch 441, 443.

vidimus (vid'i-mus). We have seen.

vidua (vid'ū-ạ). A widow.

vidua regis (vid'u-a rē'jis). The widow of the king; the widow of a tenant in capite.

viduitate (vi-du-i-tā'te). Widowhood.

viduity (vi-dū'i̯-ti). Widowhood.

vie (vē). (French.) Life.
See **auter vie; cestui que vie; de sa vie; en vie.**

vi et armis (vī et ar'mis). With force and arms; that is, with actual violence. Taylor v State, 25 Tenn (6 Humph) 284, 286.
See **trespass vi et armis.**

view. An opinion. The range of vision at a particular place. A prospect. An easement. 26 Am J2d Em D § 175. A negative easement. 25 Am J2d Ease § 8.
See **easements of light, air, and view.**

view and delivery. A right of common to be exercised only in the places indicated by the owner of the premises.

view by court. A view of the scene of matters involved in an action taken by the judge in a trial to the court without a jury. 53 Am J1st Trial § 1128.
See **view of premises.**

view by jury. An arranged visit by the jury to the scene of matters involved in the action or of premises involved in the issues of the case, made pursuant to a order of court. 53 Am J1st Trial § 441. In criminal procedure, the taking of the jury, during the trial, to see and examine the place where the crime is alleged to have been committed. 21 Am J2d Crim L § 295. A method of procedure which does not involve the judicial powers of the court at the time it is employed. Carpenter v Carpenter, 78 NH 440, 101 A 628.

viewer. A member of a commission locating a highway. 25 Am J1st High § 26. A member of a body appointed by the court to determine the amount of special assessments against properties benefited by the improvement. 48 Am J1st Spec A §§ 140 et seq.
See **fence viewer.**

viewers' report. A report by viewers of their findings and determinations. 22 Am J1st Ferr § 6.

view of frank-pledge (vū of frangk'plej). An inspection by the sheriff of the frank-pledges in the district.

view of premises. The acts of the court in departing from the courtroom and examining premises pertinent to the issues of the case. 20 Am J2d Cts § 40. A requisite on the part of an execution officer in making a levy under the writ. 30 Am J2d Exec § 237.
See **view by jury.**

view of the body. An essential of an inquest conducted by coroner or medical examiner. 18 Am J2d Corn § 11.
The expression means more than looking, seeing, beholding. It means inspection; investigation; an inquiry into the cause of the death. Lancaster County v Holyoke, 37 Neb 328, 55 NW 950.

vigilant. Alert.
The vigilant are aided by equity. 27 Am J2d Equity § 130.

Vigilantibus et non dormientibus aequitas subvenient (vi-jil-an'ti-bus et non dor-mi-en'ti-bus ē'qui-tās sub-ve'ni-ent). Equity comes to the aid of the vigilant, but not to those who slumber.

Vigilantibus, et non dormientibus, jura subveniunt (vi-jil-an'ti-bus, et non dor-mi-en'ti-bus, jū'ra sub-ve'ni-unt). The laws assist the vigilant and not those who slumber.
To one supinely inattentive to his own concerns, and improvidently and credulously confiding in the naked and interested assertions of another, the maxim emphatically applies. See Bostwick v Mutual Life Ins. Co. 116 Wis 392, 89 NW 538.

Vigilantibus, et non dormientibus servat lex (vi-jil-an'ti-bus, et non dor-mi-en'ti-bus ser'vat lex). The law aids the vigilant, but not those who slumber.
The maxim does not apply where the defendant by his assurances put the plaintiff to sleep. Bostwick v Mutual Life Ins. Co. 116 Wis 392, 89 NW 538.

Vigilantibus, et non dormientibus succurunt jura (vi-jil-an'ti-bus et non dor-mi-en'ti-bus su-ker'unt jū'ra). The laws assist the vigilant, and not those who slumber.
The maxim is grounded on that wise policy of the law which at every turn of life casts upon all persons the duty of exercising some care for their own protection. Bostwick v Mutual Life Ins. Co. 116 Wis 392, 89 NW 538.

Vigilantibus non dormientibus aequitas subvenit (vi-jil-an'ti-bus non dor-mi-en'ti-bus ē'qui-tās sub-ve'-nit). Equity comes to the aid of the vigilant, but not to those who slumber. Doster v Manistee Nat. Bank, 67 Ark 325, 329, 55 SW 137.

Vigilantibus non dormientibus jura subveniunt (vi-jil-an'ti-bus non dor-mi-en'ti-bus jū'ra sub-ve'ni-unt). The law, and equity as well, aids the vigilant, and not those who slumber upon their rights. Jacob C. Slemmer's Appeal, 58 Pa 168.

vigilia (vi-ji'li-a). A vigil; a guard; a watch.

vigore cujus (vi-gō're kū'jus). By the force of which.

viis et modis (vī'is et mō'dis). By ways and means; by substituted service.

vi laica amovenda (vī la'i-ka ā-mō-ven'da). Removing the force of the laity. The purpose of a writ to prevent a layman from entering into a contest or strife between churchmen.

vilis. (Latin.) Cheap. Inferior.

vill (vil). A hamlet or village.

villa (vil'ạ). A dwelling house in the country. (Spanish.) A village.

village. A municipal corporation of limited population. A small municipality characterized by business and residential structures reasonably contiguous. State ex rel. Lorenzino v McKinley County, 20 NM 67, 145 P 1083. An assemblage of houses in an area which may be incorporated or unincorporated. 37 Am J1st Mun Corp § 5.

village proper. The actual and physical village for the purpose of taxation. Atherton v Essex Junction, 83 Vt 218, 74 A 1118.

Villana faciunt servitia, sed certa et determinata (vil-la'na fā'she-unt ser-vi'she-a, sed ser'ta et de-ter-mi-nā'ta). They perform villein services, but certain and fixed. See 2 Bl Comm 99.

villanum socagium (vil-lā'num so-kā'ji-um). Villein socage.

villanus (vil-lā'nus). Same as **villein.**

ville. See **bas-ville.**

villein (vil'ẹn). A tenant of the lowest order in the feudal period. See 2 Bl Comm 22. Possessed by the lord of the manor, the same as one of a flock. Jackson v Phillips, 96 Mass (14 Allen) 539, 562.

villeinage (vil'en-ạj). A kind of estate in land, which was superior to downright slavery, but inferior to every other condition. See 2 Bl Comm 92.

villein in gross (in grōs). A villein at large; that is, a villein who was annexed to the person of the lord as a sort of body servant.
He was transferable by deed from one owner to another, but had no connection with the soil. See 2 Bl Comm 93.

villeinous judgment (vil'en-ous juj'mẹnt). An ancient form of judgment in a prosecution for the crime of conspiring to indict an innocent person for a felony. See 4 Bl Comm 136.

villein regardant (vil'en rẹ-gär'dạnt). A villein annexed to the manor or lands of the lord, not attached to the person of the lord. See 2 Bl Comm 93.

villein services (vil'en sėr'vises). The services required of a villein by the lord of the manor.

villein socage (sok'ạj). Sometimes called privileged villeinage. A kind of villeinage such as has been held of the kings of England since the Norman Conquest.
The services were villein services, but they were fixed and certain; the tenant could not alien but was compelled to surrender to the lord. See 2 Bl Comm 99.

villenous judgment. A judgment which commits the accused to prison and deprives him of certain civil rights. 21 Am J2d Crim L § 616.

Vim vi repellere licet (vim vī re-pel'le-re lī'set). It is lawful to repel force with force.
When an officer transcends his powers, obedience to him may become even an offense. If he is without jurisdiction, then issues the terse command of the maxim. See State v Durham, 141 NC 741, 53 SE 720.

Vim vi repellere licet, modo fiat moderamine inculpatae tutelae, non ad sumendam vindictam, sed ad propulsandam injuriam (vim vī re-pel'le-re lī'set, mō′dō fī′at mō-de-rā′mi-ne in-kul-pā′tē tū-tē′lē, non ad su-men′dam vin-di-kā′tam, sed ad prō-pul-san′dam in-jū′ri-am). It is lawful to repel force with force, but let it be done in the moderate manner of self-defense, not to take revenge, but to repel or ward off injury.

vinculo matrimonii (vin′ku-lō mā-tri-mō′ni-ī). The bonds of marriage.

vinculum (ving′kū-lum). A chain; a bond.

vinculum personarum ab eodem stipite descendentium (vin′ku-lum per-so-nā′rum ab e-ō′dem sti′pi-to de-sen-den′she-um). The relation of persons descended from the same stock or common ancestor; Blackstone's definition of "consanguinity." See 2 Bl Comm 202.

vindicatory (vin′di-kā-tō̱-ri). The part of a statute which imposes punishment or penalty for violation. 50 Am J1st Stat § 151.

vindices injuriarum (vin′di-sēz in-ju-ri-ā′rum). The avengers of wrongs,—the king and his courts. See 4 Bl Comm 185.

vindictive damages. Same as **exemplary damages.** 22 Am J2d Damg § 236.

vine. A plant characterized by tendrils which attach to a wall, trellis, frame, or other support; a cultivated plant of such character, such as grapes. 21 Am J2d Crops § 4.

vineyard. A tract of land whereon grape vines are grown and cultivated.

vinous (vī′nus). Having the character of wine.

vinous liquor (vī′nus lik′er). Liquor made from the juice of the grape or of other fruits or berries by the process of fermentation. 30 Am J Rev ed Intox L § 13.

Alcohol may be obtained from all vinous liquors by distillation. See Eureka Vinegar Co. v Gazette Printing Co. (CC Ark) 35 F 570, 572.

vintner (vint′nėr). A wine seller.

vinum (vī′num). Wine.

violate. To break; to infringe; to disobey: as, to violate a statute. To force; to ravish. State v Montgomery, 79 Iowa 737, 739, 45 NW 292.

violation of blockade. A cause under prize law for the forfeiture of ship, and in some cases its cargo, to capture and condemnation. 56 Am J1st War § 174.

To constitute a violation of blockade, three things must be proved: first, the existence of an actual blockade; second, the knowledge of the party supposed to have offended; and third, some act of violation, either by going in or coming out with a cargo laden after the commencement of the blockade. 56 Am J1st War § 175.

violation of law. To fail to observe the law whether by act of commission or omission. State v Case, 53 Mo 246, 250. In its ordinary sense, the expression includes the violation of a positive law, whether the law is a civil or a criminal law. See Bloom v Franklin Life Ins. Co. 97 Ind 478.

As to what constitutes a "violation of law as to age," within the meaning of the phrase as it appears in an exclusion clause of an automobile insurance policy, see Anno: 72 ALR 1079.

violation of privacy. The actionable wrong of interfering with another person's seclusion by subjecting him to unwarranted and undesired publicity.

The usual form of violation has been the publication of another's name or picture for selfish purposes or for purposes of trade. 41 Am J1st Priv §§ 20 et seq.

violation of sepulter. A crime, as well as a civil wrong, in disturbing the repose of the dead by an unauthorized exhumation and removal of remains or the desecration of a grave by an act affecting the grave or the body therein interred. 22 Am J2d Dead B § 18.

violation of statute. See **violation of law.**

violence. Physical force applied so as to injure or damage. Alexander v State, 40 Tex Crim 395, 411, 49 SW 229, 50 SW 716.

The snatching or jerking the property of another from his person, where such property is so attached to his person or clothing as to afford resistance, or an antecedent or contemporaneous struggle over the taking of the property will constitute that violence essential for robbery, but a mere filching of loose property from the pocket with no more force than is necessary to lift and remove the property from the pocket is not a taking by force or violence, and is a mere larceny. See State v Parker, 262 Mo 169, 170 SW 1121.

See **physical force; physical violence.**

violent. Acting with physical force. See **violence.**

violent death. Death caused by an external agency; not occurring in the ordinary course of nature from disease or a wasting of the body.

violent means. An act not occurring in the ordinary course of events, involving the application of force, however slight. Schonberg v New York Life Ins. Co. 235 La 461, 104 So 2d 171.
See **accidental means.**

violent presumption. A presumption which is very strong and forcible, although not necessarily a conclusive or irrebuttable one.

It is an inference which the law unhesitatingly requires to be drawn from given facts; it is a conclusion quite self-evident from the premises. Shealy & Finn v Edwards, 75 Ala 411, 419.

Viperina est expositio quae corrodit viscera textus (vī-pe-rī′na est ex-pō-zi′she-ō kwē kor-rō′dit vi′se-ra tex′tus). It is a snake-like explanation which gnaws away the vitals of the text.

vir (vir). A man; a husband.

Vires acquirit eundo (vī′rēz ak-quī′rit e-un′dō). It gains strength by continuing.

When a word has been stretched beyond its ordinary legal meaning, it is difficult to know where to stop. Mann v Executors of Mann (NY) 1 Johnson Ch 231, 237.

Vir et uxor consentur in lege una persona (vir et u′xor kon-sen′ter in lē′je ū′na per-sō′na). Husband and wife are considered in law as one person.

virgata regia (vir-gā′ta rē′ji-a). The verge of the king.
See **verge.**

Virgin Islands of the United States. A number of islands in the chain of islands separating the Caribbean Sea and the Atlantic Ocean, east of Puerto Rico, the three largest of which are St. Thomas, St. John, and St. Croix, acquired by the United States from Denmark in 1917.

virginitate (vir-ji-ni-tā′te). Virginity.

viride observantia. See **in viride observantia.**

virilia (vī-ril′i-ạ). The testicles.

viri magnae dignitatis (vi′rī mag′nē dig-ni-tā′tis). Men of high rank.

viripotens (vi-rī-pō′tenz). Capable of performing the sexual act; the reverse of impotent.

virtual possession (vėr′tū-ạl pọ-zesh′ọn). That kind of actual possession consisting of an occupancy in fact of a part of a tract claimed in the name of the whole, where there is sufficient evidence of the bounds of the whole that is claimed as one entirety, and the circumstances are such that the law extends the possession of the part that is occupied to these bounds.
It is so called to distinguish it from the actual possession consisting in an occupancy in fact of the whole of the tract claimed, which is called "substantial possession". Wheeler v Clark, 114 Tenn 117, 85 SW 258.

virtual representation. The principle whereunder members of a class are deemed represented in a suit by one of the class named as a party specifically, although they themselves are not named. 39 Am J1st Parties § 44. A doctrine frequently applied in the case of actions by or against voluntary unincorporated associations or clubs. 6 Am J2d Asso & C § 55.

virtue. Moral excellence. Chastity. Effect. Efficacy.

virtuous (vėr′tū-us). Pure; chaste; undefiled.

virtuous female. A female who has not had sexual intercourse unlawfully, out of wedlock, knowingly and voluntarily. State v Dacke, 59 Wash 238, 109 P 1050.

virtute cujus (vir-tū′te kū′jus). By virtue of which.

virtute officii (vir-tū′te of-fi′she-ī). Characterizing acts of an officer which are within the authority of the officer when properly performed, but which are improperly performed. Haffner v United States F. & G. Co. 35 Idaho 517, 207 P 716.

virtute officii sui (vir-tū′te of-fi′she-ī sū′ī). By virtue of his office.

vis (vis). Force.

visa (vē′zạ). Noun: A stamp of approval, required by some countries, to be affixed to a passport by an authorized officer, usually a consular officer, of the country to be visited. A recognition of the validity of the passport and having otherwise such significance as the country which requires it may attach thereto. United States v Phelps (DC Vt) 14 F2d 679. Verb: To affix a visa to a passport.

vis armata (vis ar-mā′ta). An armed force.

viscera (vis′ẹ-rạ). The internal organs of the body.

visceribus (vis-se′ri-bus). The bowels and other internal organs.

viscount (vī′kount). A nobleman ranking next above a baron and next below a count.
The title appears to have been created by Henry the Sixth when in 1439 he made John Beaumont a peer, by the name of Viscount Beaumont. See 1 Bl Comm 398.

vis divina (vis di-vī′na). Divine force, that is, an act of God; vis major.

visé (vē′zā). A term derived from the French for an indorsement upon a passport showing that it has been examined by an officer of the country wherein it is presented in obtaining admittance to the country.

vis et metus (vis et me′tus). Force and fear.

vis fluminis (vis flu′mi-nis). The force of the current.

visible. Noticeable; apparent; open; conspicuous. Discoverable; in sight; obvious; manifest; clear; distinct; plain; patent; unmistakable. Perceptible by the eye, apparent or obvious. Anno: 14 ALR 1497.

visible contusion (viz′i-bl). Any injury to or morbid change in either the subcutaneous tissue or the skin, whether such results directly from external violence operating upon the exterior of the body or from internal injuries resulting from violence. 29A Am J Rev ed Ins § 1173.

visible dirt. Mud, dust, trash, or filth which is open to view, as where it appears in milk. Anno: 122 ALR 1084.

visible easement. See open and visible easement.

visible mark or injury. A perceptible, discernible clear, distinct, and evident mark upon or injury to the body, whether manifest by its abnormal nature or upon observation or examination. 29A Am J Rev ed Ins § 1170.

visible marks of force or violence. Marks clearly evidencing the use of force or violence employed in gaining an entrance to premises. 29A Am J Rev ed Ins § 1336.

visible means of support. Something or someone in sight from which or from whom the obtaining of support is naturally to be presumed, as a farm upon which a person is living or a husband with whom a woman is living.

visible possession. See open and notorious possession.

vis impressa (vis im-pres′sa). The original force employed in the commission of a tort or injury done with force.
If the proximate cause of the injury is but a continuation of the original force, or vis impressa, the effect is immediate, and the appropriate remedy is trespass vi et armis. But if the original force, or vis impressa, had ceased to act before the injury commenced, the effect is mediate, and the appropriate remedy is trespass on the case. See Ricker v Freeman, 50 NH 420.

vis inermis (vis in-er′mis). An unarmed force.

vision. Eyesight. Awareness of things to come, particularly of things to be desired in the interest of mankind.
See sight.

visit and search. The right of a belligerent growing out of the greater right of capture, being the right to visit and search a neutral vessel on the high seas for goods of the enemy and contraband of war which such vessel may be carrying. 56 Am J1st War § 152. The right of an officer of the customs to hail, stop, and board a vessel and to search it and the cargo aboard in the course of enforcing the payment of customs duties. 21 Am J2d Cust & D § 113.

visitation. A form of personal inquiry whereby an administrative agency exercises investigatory or inquisitorial powers, particularly in reference to public institutions such as state hospitals, prisons, and reformatories. 1 Am J2d Admin L § 85. The act of examining into the affairs of a corporation. 19 Am J2d Corp § 1441. The right, referred to in earlier cases, of the founder of a charity or his heirs to a judicial investigation into alleged mismanagement of the trust property. 15 Am J2d Char § 113. The exercise of control by the founder or founders of a college or university over the management of the affairs of the institution. 15 Am J2d Colleges § 10. The right of a parent to visit his child who is in the custody of the guardian. Anno: 6 ALR 1150, 1151. The right of divorced parent denied the custody of a minor child to visit such child at such times and places as the court may fix in its decree. 24 Am J2d Div & S § 801. The right provided by a decree annulling a marriage and granting the custody of a child to one of the parties, whereby the other is permitted to visit such child. 4 Am J2d Annul § 103. The right of friends or relatives of an insane person to visit him in the institution in which he is confined. 29 Am J Rev ed Ins Per § 37. The privilege accorded relatives of a person confined in a penal institution of visiting him there.

visitation and search. Same as **visit and search.**

visitation books. Books kept by attendants upon the military court, called heralds, in which they registered "such marriages and descents as were verified to them on oath" in their regular circuits of the kingdom.
These books were competent evidence in matters of pedigree. See 3 Bl Comm 105.

visitatione Dei (vi-si-tā-she-ō'ne Dē'ī). Divine visitation; divine dispensation.

visitor. One who comes upon premises to see the owner or occupant, whether for social, business, or professional reasons. Narrowly defined, a person who comes only for health or pleasure, and who engages in no business while visiting, and remains only for a reasonable time. Ex parte Archy, 9 Cal 147, 168. One exercising functions applicable to a right of visitation.
See **business visitor; guest; visitation.**

visitorial power. A power existing by virtue of a right of visitation.
See **visitation.**

vis laica (vis lā'i-ka). A lay force, a force composed of laymen.

Vis legibus est inimica (vis lē'ji-bus est in-i-mī'ka). Force or violence is the enemy of law.

vis major (vis mā'jor). A higher force; an irresistible force. An event which cannot be definitely foreseen or controlled. Krause v Board of School Trustees, 162 Ind 278, 284, 70 NE 264.
The Latin expression "vis major," or "force majeure," is not exactly the equivalent of an act of God. The test of "vis major" is whether under the particular circumstances there was such an insuperable interference without the party's intervention as could not have been prevented by the exercise of prudence, diligence, and care; and, unlike an act of God, it may consist, for instance, of governmental intervention resulting from the necessities of war. 1 Am J2d Act of God § 4.

visne. Same as **vicinage.**

visnetum (vis-nē'tum). Same as **vicinage.**

visores (vi-sō'rēz). The equivalent of viewers.

vis proxima (vis pro'xi-ma). Same as **vis impressa.**

visual flight rules. Air traffic rules and regulations applicable to flights at a time when visibility is not impaired by weather conditions or other circumstances. 14 CFR §§ 60.1 et seq.

visus (vī'sus). A view.

visu scriptionis (vī'su skrip-she-ō'nis). The observing of the act of writing.

visus franci plegii (vī'sus fran'sī plē'ji-ī). View of frank-pledge.
See **view of frank-pledge.**

vita (vī'ta). Life.
See **in vita.**

Vita et membra sunt in potestate legis (vī'ta et mem'-bra sunt in po-tes-tā'te lē'jus). Life and limbs are in the power of the law.

vitalized (vī'tal-īzd). Endowed with life.
Any human embryo which is not dead is vitalized. It is no less endowed with life before reaching the stage of development known as quickening than after. See State v Patterson, 105 Kan 9, 181 P 609.

vital statistics (vī'tal stā-tis'tiks). Those statistics which have been compiled under public authority relative primarily to the subject of health, but commonly including therein the registrations of births, deaths, marriages, and the like. 25 Am J1st Hlth § 47.

Vital Statistics Act. One of the Uniform Laws. 30 Am J2d Ev §§ 1007, 1009.

vitamin (vī'ta-min). An organic substance found in most foods, but in varying amounts, essential to a proper functioning of the human body. A drug where administered or used as a medicine; otherwise a food product. Anno: 98 ALR2d 1088, § 5[b].

vi termini. See **ex vi termini.**

vitiate (vish'i-āt). To weaken, particularly in reference to moral stamina. To invalidate.

viticulture (vit'i-kul-tūr). Cultivation of the vine, particularly the grape vine.

vitious intromission. A term of the Scottish law for meddling with the assets left by a decedent. 31 Am J2d Ex & Ad § 661.

vitium (vi'she-um). Vice; error; mistake.

vitium clerici (vi'she-um kle'ri-sī). The error or mistake of a clerk; a clerical error.

Vitium clerici nocere non debet (vi'she-um kle'ri-sī no-sē're non de'bet). A clerical error ought not to prejudice.

Vitium est quod fugi debet, ne, si rationem non invenias, mox legem sine ratione esse clames (vi'she-um est quod fū'jī de'bet, nē, sī rā-she-ō'nem non in-ve'ni-as, mox lē'jem sī'nē rā-she-ō'ne es'se klā'mēz). It is a mistake which ought to be avoided, that if you cannot discover the reason, you presently exclaim that the law is without reason.

vitium scriptoris (vi'she-um skrip-tō'ris). The error or mistake of a copyist or scribe.

vitreous (vit'rē-us). Having the nature of or resembling glass.

viva aqua (vī'va a'qua). Living water; flowing water.

viva pecunia (vī'va pe-kū'ni-a). An ancient expression for living things, such as cattle, which are accepted as the equivalent of money.

vivarium (vī-vā'ri-um). A place for raising wild animals under conditions fairly close to those of their natural environment.

viva voce (vī'va vo'se). The living voice. Word of mouth. Characterizing the testimony of a witness given in person, rather than by deposition or transcript of testimony given in former trial.
See **voting viva voce.**

vivos (vī'vos). The living.
See **inter vivos**.

vivo vadium (vī'vō va'di-um). Same as **vivum vadium**.

vivum vadium (vī'vum va'di-um). Living pledge. An estate which arises where a person borrows a specific sum and grants property to the lender to hold until the rents and profits shall repay the sum so borrowed, whereupon the property reverts to the borrower. Spect v Spect, 88 Cal 437, 26 P 203.

vix (vix). Scarcely; hardly; with difficulty.

Vix ulla lex fieri potest quae omnibus commoda sit, sed si majori parti prospiciat, utilis est (vix ul'la lex fī'e-ri po'test kwē om'ni-bus kom'mo-da sit, sed sī ma-jō'rī par'tī pro-spi'she-at, ū'ti-lis est). Scarcely any law can be made which is convenient to everyone, but if it provides for the majority, it is of advantage.

vixen (vik'sn). A common scold. 15 Am J2d Com S § 2.

viz. An abbreviation of videlicit, meaning namely; that is to say.

vocabula artis (vo-ka'bu-la ar'tis). Words of art; technical terms.

Vocabula artium explicanda sunt secundum definitiones prudentium (vo-ka'bu-la ar'she-um ex-pli-kan'da sunt se-kun'dum de-fi-ni-she-ō'nēz pru-den'-she-um). Technical terms should be explained according to the definitions of experienced persons.

vocans (vo'kanz). A voucher; a person who vouches for someone else.

vocare (vo-kā're). To call; to summon.

vocat (vo'kat). Called; summoned.

vocation. A trade, profession, occupation, or calling, whether lawful or unlawful. Anno: 43 ALR 800; 50 ALR 1176.

vocational rehabilitation. Training to restore physical ability and earning power, as well as the capacity to enjoy life, of persons who have been disabled by injury or sickness. A primary project for the benefit of disabled members and veterans of the Armed Forces. 56 Am J1st Vet & V A § 15.

vocatus (vo-kā'tus). One who has been called or summoned; a person who has been vouched for; a vouchee.

vociferatio (vo-si-fe-rā'she-ō). Hue and cry.
See **hue and cry**.

vociferous (vō-sif'ę-rus). Clamorous; noisy; as, vociferous heralds. With great noise in calling, shouting, etc. Anderson v State (Tex Crim) 20 SW 358, 359.

vociferous demand (vō-sif'ę-rus). A demand asserted in loud and boisterous language, sometimes constituting a breach of the peace, especially where tainted by profanity. 12 Am J2d Breach P § 35.

void. Noun: An empty space. Adjective: Constituting a nullity. Binding on neither party and not subject to ratification. Anno: 31 ALR 1002. Sometimes construed as "voidable." Hall v Baylous, 109 W Va 1, 153 SE 293, 69 ALR 527.

The words "to be void and of no effect" are often used in statutes and legal documents, such as deeds, leases, bonds, mortgages and others, in the sense of voidable, merely, that is, capable of being avoided, and not as meaning that the act or transaction is absolutely a nullity as if it never had existed, incapable of giving rise to any rights or obligations under any circumstances. Thus we speak of conveyances void as to creditors, meaning that creditors may avoid them, but not others. Leases which contain a forfeiture of the lessee's estate for non-payment of rent, or breach of other condition, declare that on the happening of the contingency the demise shall thereupon become null and void, meaning that the forfeiture may be enforced by re-entry, at the option of the lessor. A deed obtained by fraud is sometimes said to be void, meaning that the party defrauded may elect to treat it as void. Ewell v Daggs, 108 US 143, 149, 27 L Ed 682, 684, 2 S Ct 408.

A statutory provision that, in the absence of compliance therewith, a sale in bulk shall be "void" as against creditors of the seller, means that the sale shall be voidable. Evans v Herbranson, 241 Iowa 268, 41 NW2d 113, 15 ALR2d 925.

voidable. Defective but capable of confirmation or ratification. 50 Am J1st Stat § 287. Obligatory as to other persons until disaffirmed by the person entitled to confirm or disaffirm. Anno: 31 ALR 1002.

voidable assignment. An assignment by a debtor which is fraudulent as to creditors hindered or delayed thereby in reference to realization upon their claims. 6 Am J2d Assign for Crs § 63.
See **voidable preference**.

voidable contract. A contract which, although defective so as to be avoided by one of the parties, is valid and binding until it is avoided by a disaffirmance. Williston, Contracts 3d ed § 15; Restatement, Contracts § 113; 17 Am J2d Contr § 7.

The view of some authorities that an executory contract of an infant is invalid until confirmed has been adversely criticized, and in some jurisdictions there are statutes to the effect that both executed and executory agreements of an infant are valid until disaffirmed. 27 Am J1st Inf § 12.

voidable deed. An instrument which, although defective, is operative to convey the property until set aside by the court. 23 Am J2d Deeds § 137.

voidable judgment. A judgment which is apparently valid, but in truth wanting in some material respect; in other words, a judgment which is erroneous. Southern Surety Co. v Texas Oil Clearing House (Tex Com App) 281 SW 1045, 1046. A judgment which, because of defect, is subject to being reversed, vacated, or superseded but which is binding everywhere until a successful attack has been made upon it. 30A Am J Rev ed Judgm § 44.

voidable lien. A lien which is subject to disaffirmance by the lienee. A lien given by a bankrupt which may be avoided at the instance of his trustee in bankruptcy.
See **fraudulent transfer; voidable preference**.

voidable marriage. A marriage which, although prohibited by law, or subject to annulment, under the circumstances, may be made legal and binding upon both parties through subsequent ratification by the parties. 35 Am J1st Mar §§ 46, 85 et seq.

voidable preference. A preferential transfer made by an insolvent within such period of time prior to insolvency proceedings as to render the transfer voidable under insolvency laws. 29 Am J Rev ed Insolv § 82. A transfer of property by one since adjudicated a bankrupt which is subject to avoidance so as to permit the trustee in bankruptcy to recover for the estate the assets thus transferred. 9 Am J2d Bankr §§ 1056 et seq.

For statement of elements of a voidable prefer-

VOIDABLE [1349] VOLSTEAD

ence under the Bankruptcy Act, see 9 Am J2d Bankr § 1057.

voidable process. Process which is defective but amendable so as to be rendered fully effective by correction of the defects therein. 42 Am J1st Proc § 20.

voidable release. A release which is binding until set aside for cause such as infancy, mental incompetency, or fraudulent representation. 45 Am J1st Rel § 17.

void agreement. See **void contract.**

voidance (voi′dans). A vacancy. Ejection from a benefice.

void as to creditors. Voidable as to creditors. 37 Am J2d Frd Conv § 106.

void contract. An absolute nullity from the contractual aspect. The equivalent of no contract at all. Williston, Contracts 3d ed § 15; 17 Am J2d Contr § 7. A contract which cannot be validated by ratification or other act or omission. 17 Am J2d Contr § 7.

void deed. A deed which is invalid in law for any purpose whatsoever. 23 Am J2d Deeds § 137.

void divorce. A divorce absolutely ineffective in severing the marital relation.
See **void judgment.**

void grant. A patent or other grant of public lands which is absolutely inoperative for want of title in the government or want of authority to convey. 42 Am J1st Pub L § 38.

voiding. Declaring void that which is voidable. Emptying.

void judgment. A judgment which in legal effect is no judgment; a judgment under which no rights are acquired or divested; a judgment which neither binds nor bars anyone. Stafford v Gallope, 123 NC 19, 21, 31 SE 265. A judgment which because of want of jurisdiction is entitled to no respect whatever but may be entirely disregarded or declared inoperative by any court in which effect is sought to be given to it. 30A Am J Rev ed Judgm § 45. A judgment which is an absolute nullity, so that its invalidity may be asserted upon either direct or collateral attack by any person whose rights are affected, at any time and at any place. Southern Surety Co. v Texas Oil Clearing House (Tex Com App) 281 SW 1045, 1046.

void marriage. A marriage absolutely prohibited by law and not subject to ratification. A marriage which is expressly declared a nullity ab initio by statute. 35 Am J1st Mar § 46.

void process. Process which is defective to the extent of being a nullity and not amendable, either because in violation of statute which prohibits it or because it is not in substantial compliance with statutory requirements. 42 Am J1st Proc § 20. Such process as the court has no power to award, or has not acquired jurisdiction to issue in the particular case, or which does not in some material respect comply in form with the legal requisites of such process, or which loses its vitality in consequence of noncompliance with a condition subsequent, obedience to which is rendered essential. Fischer v Langbein, 103 NY 84, 90, 8 NE 251.

void release. A release which is forged, prohibited by express statute, contrary to public policy, or given by one without power to grant a release. 45 Am J1st Rel § 17.

void tax. A tax imposed without basis in law, as where the statute under which it is levied is unconstitutional or so indefinite, uncertain, or inconsistent as to be entirely inoperative. 51 Am J1st Tax § 303. A tax which never had any effect, which never created any lien or raised any obligation to pay.

A void tax is no tax. It is as if there never had been any attempt at assessment. The owner of property is under no duty, either at law or in equity, to pay it. There is no equitable reason for requiring the owner to pay such a tax before a cloud upon his title made by a tax sale shall be removed. Morrill v Lovett, 95 Me 165, 49 A 666.

voir dire (vwor dēr). To speak the truth. An oath administered to one called as a witness or juror preliminary to an examination of him in reference to his qualifications or disqualifications as witness or juror. 31 Am J Rev ed Jury § 136.

voir dire examination (vwor dēr eg-zam-i-nā′shon). The examination of a prospective juror by a litigant, usually through the latter's counsel, for the purpose of determining whether such prospective juror is qualified to act as a juror and for the further purpose of aiding the litigant in the exercise of his peremptory challenges. 31 Am J Rev ed Jury § 136. The preliminary examination of one called as a witness to determine competency. 58 Am J1st Witn § 211.

voiture (vwo-tür). (French.) Carriage; coach; vehicle.

voiturier (vwo-tür-yā). (French.) Carrier. One engaged in transportation.

volatile estates (vol′a-til). Movables of a solid character, such as tables and other heavy furniture. See 2 Bl Comm 428.

volens. (Latin.) Willing, but not necessarily wishing.
It is said in the Kambour Case, 77 N H at page 47, that "volens means wishing, not willing; and it by no means follows from the fact that a person is willing to chance being injured, that he wishes, or even is willing to be injured." Whether volens means wishing rather than willing may be questioned, but if one may be willing to chance being injured, he at least is willing to be injured rather than not take the chance of it, for otherwise his action would not be taken. Smith v Twin State Gas & Electric Co. 83 NH 439, 61 ALR 1015, 144 A 57.

volenti non fit injuria (vo-len′tī non fit in-jū′ri-a). One is not legally injured if he has consented to the act complained of or was willing that it should occur. Anno: 17 ALR2d 348, § 3. The maxim upon which the principal of assumption of risk is based. 35 Am J1st M & S § 293.

The maxim is frequently applied to a plaintiff who is complaining of a nuisance to which he voluntarily exposed himself. 39 Am J1st Nuis § 196. If a vendee blindly trusts where he should not and closes his eyes where ordinary prudence requires him to see, he is willing to be deceived, and the maxim applies. 55 Am J1st V & P § 67.

volition. Choice or determination by one's own will.
See **rational volition.**

volitional insanity. Irresistible impulse. 26 Am J1st Homi §§ 78, 80.

volo (vo′lō). I will; I wish.

Volstead Act (vol′sted akt). The federal statute which established national prohibition of the liquor traffic under the Eighteenth Amendment to the

United States Constitution. 41 Stat at Large 305 Ch 83; Anno: 10 ALR 1553.

volt. The unit of force of an electric current; the force which causes a current of 1 ampere to flow through a conductor whose resistance is 1 ohm. Peoria Water Works Co. v Peoria R. Co. (CC Ill) 181 F 990.

voltage. The force of electricity expressed in a given number of volts. Harrison v Kansas City Electric Light Co. 198 Mo 606, 93 SW 951.
See **volt.**

Voluit sed non dixit (vo'lu-it sed non dik'sit). He willed but he did not say.

volume. A book, especially one of a set of books, as Volume 14 of American Jurisprudence, 2d. Quantity in bulk or mass. Amount of space in cubic contents.

volumus (vo'lu-mus). We will; we wish.

voluntarily. Freely. Of one's own accord.
When used in its ordinary sense, the word means "willingly," or "without compulsion," but it sometimes means more than this; and whenever in order to make a statute effective it is necessary to construe the word "voluntarily" as implying knowledge, it is the duty of the court to so construe it. Sweeney v Sweeney, 96 Vt 196, 118 A 882, 26 ALR 1066, 1067.

voluntarius daemon (vo-lun-tā'ri-us dē'mon). A person who is voluntarily demented, a person who has become voluntarily intoxicated.

voluntary. Intended. Not by compulsion or by accident. Anno: 2 ALR 62.

voluntary abandonment. See **voluntary separation.**

voluntary admission. See **voluntary statement.**

voluntary affidavit (af-i-dā'vit). An affidavit made on an occasion where the law does not require a sworn statement. See 4 Bl Comm 137.

voluntary appearance. An appearance in an action by a defendant in person or through his attorney, the effect of which is a waiver of the service of summons or other formal notice. Harrison v Morton, 87 Md 671, 674, 40 A 897.

voluntary assignment. A transfer, without compulsion of law, by a debtor, of his property to an assignee, in trust, to apply the same, or the proceeds thereof, to the payment of his debts, and to return the surplus, if any, to the debtor. Farwell v Nilsson, 133 Ill 45, 49, 24 NE 74.

voluntary assignment for creditors. See **voluntary assignment.**

voluntary association. An unincorporated society or body of individuals, formed for social, political, moral, religious, benevolent, protective, or mutual purposes, or to promote some public, scientific or educational object, or to facilitate business, and not for purposes of trade or direct pecuniary profit. 40 Am J1st Partn § 7. An association in which one may seek, or be accepted into, membership as a matter of choice.
If membership is required by law, such as in the case of some public officers or employees, or if membership in a professional society is necessary, in a substantial sense, for the practice of one's profession, such an organization is not voluntary. 6 Am J2d Asso & C § 1.

voluntary assumption of risk. See **assumption of risk.**

voluntary bankruptcy. Bankruptcy instituted by an adjudication upon the petition of a debtor seeking such an adjudication. 9 Am J2d Bankr § 175.

voluntary bond. A bond executed by a public officer where no constitutional or statutory provision requires a bond of him. 43 Am J1st Pub Of § 411.

voluntary cohabitation. As a defense to an action for annulment of a marriage, cohabitation with knowledge of all essential facts relied upon as the ground for annulment. Sampson v Sampson, 332 Mich 214, 50 NW2d 764.

voluntary confession. See **confession.**

voluntary conveyance. See **voluntary deed.**

voluntary deed. A deed executed and given without consideration. As to creditors, a conveyance made without any consideration or for an unsubstantial consideration. 37 Am J2d Frd Conv § 23.
A voluntary grant, within the meaning of a statute declaring that realty received by a railroad by voluntary grant shall be held and used for the purpose of such grant only, means a conveyance without valuable consideration. Brown v Weare, 348 Mo 135, 152 SW2d 649, 136 ALR 286.

voluntary deposit (dē-poz'it). (Civil law.) A deposit effected by the mere consent of the parties.

voluntary discontinuance. The dismissal of an action or the taking of a nonsuit by the plaintiff. 24 Am J2d Dism § 2.

voluntary dissolution. The dissolution of a corporation upon a vote of the stockholders, subject to statutory conditions respecting the percentage of the stock voted in favor of dissolution, or at the instance of the directors with the consent of a certain proportion of the stockholders. 19 Am J2d Corp §§ 1596 et seq.
See **voluntary liquidation.**

voluntary domicil. A domicil which a person acquires voluntarily, as distinguished from a domicil by operation of law, as in the case of a married woman or infant.

voluntary escape. An escape of a prisoner occurring where an officer having the prisoner lawfully in his custody voluntarily permits him to escape or go at large. 27 Am J2d Escape § 22.

voluntary expatriation. See **expatriation.**

voluntary exposure to danger. Intentionally doing some act which reasonable and ordinary prudence would pronounce dangerous.
The approach to an unknown and unexpected danger does not make the act a voluntary exposure thereto. The result of the act does not necessarily determine the motive which prompted the action. The act may be voluntary, yet the exposure may be involuntary. The danger being unknown, the injury is accidental. Equitable Acci. Ins. Co. v Osborn, 90 Ala 201, 9 So 869.

voluntary grant. See **voluntary deed.**

voluntary ignorance. The failure to make a reasonable use of a means readily available for obtaining information. 37 Am J2d Fraud § 248.

voluntary license. Same as **simple license.**

voluntary liquidation. The closing of a solvent bank and the liquidation of the business pursuant to the vote of the stockholders holding a certain percentage (usually 2/3) of the shares of the bank. 10 Am J2d Banks § 828.
See **voluntary dissolution.**

voluntary manslaughter. A homicide, in which the act of killing, although intentional, is committed under the influence of passion or in heat of blood, produced by an adequate or reasonable provocation and before a reasonable time has elapsed for the blood to cool and reason to resume its habitual control, such act not being the result of wickedness of heart, cruelty, or recklessness of disposition. 26 Am J1st Homi § 19.

voluntary nonsuit. A judgment given against the plaintiff when he fails to appear as required of him, or where he refuses or neglects to proceed to the trial of a case after it has been put in issue. 24 Am J2d Dism § 3. A nonsuit which is entered against a plaintiff when he throws up his case and consents to a judgment in favor of the defendant for costs.

The plaintiff has the right to do this at any time before the jury retires, or if there is no jury, at any time before the decision is announced. See Sandoval v Rosser, 86 Tex 682, 686, 26 SW 933.

voluntary oath (ōth). See **voluntary affidavit.**

voluntary overexertion. Conscious and intentional overexertion or a reckless disregard of consequences likely to ensue from great physical effort. Rustin v Standard Life & Acci. Ins. Co. 58 Neb 792, 79 NW 712.

voluntary partition. A partition of real estate made by the owners of undivided interests by mutual consent, effected by mutual conveyances or releases to each person of the share which he is to hold, executed by the other owner or owners. 40 Am J1st Partit § 16.

voluntary payment. A payment of an illegal demand, with a full knowledge of all the facts which render the demand illegal, without an immediate and urgent necessity therefor, unless it is to release his person or property from detention or to prevent an immediate seizure of his person or property.

A payment is not to be regarded as compulsory unless made to emancipate the person or property from an actual and existing duress, imposed by the parties to whom the money is paid, and if a payment is otherwise voluntary, the fact that a person making a payment files a written protest at the time does not change its character. 40 Am J1st Paym § 159.

In determining whether a payment of taxes was voluntary or involuntary the real question is whether there was such an immediate and urgent necessity for the payment as to imply that it was made under compulsion. Without such an immediate and urgent necessity, such a payment will be deemed voluntary. United States v New York & C. Mail S. S. Co. 200 US 488, 50 L Ed 569, 26 S Ct 327.

A payment of taxes may be voluntary, although made unwillingly. Anno: 64 ALR 11, s. 84 ALR 294.

It is well established in the absence of statute that the right of a party who has paid a tax, local assessment, or license fee, to recover the same back, depends upon whether or not the payment was voluntary. If the payment was voluntary it cannot be recovered back; if it may be deemed involuntary a recovery may be had. A payment is voluntary in the sense that no action lies to recover back the amount, not only where it is made willingly and without objection, but in all cases where there is no compulsion or duress, or any necessity of making the payment as a means of saving the property from legal restraint or the grasp of legal process. Anno: 84 ALR 294.

Where a taxpayer pays taxes before their payment can be enforced by distraint or the imposition of other penalties, such premature payment has been held to be a voluntary payment and therefore not recoverable, even though the taxes were invalid. Cunard S.S. Co. v Elting (CA2 NY) 97 F2d 373.

See **volunteer.**

voluntary payment of taxes. See **voluntary payment.**

voluntary peonage (vol'un-tạ-ri pē'ọn-ạj). An antithetical expression.

Peonage is sometimes classed as voluntary or involuntary, but this implies simply a difference in the mode of origin, none in the character of the servitude. The one exists where the debtor voluntarily contracts to enter the service of his creditor. The other is forced upon the debtor by some provision of law. But peonage, however created, is compulsory service,—involuntary servitude. The peon can release himself therefrom, it is true, by the payment of the debt, but otherwise the service is enforced. A clear distinction exists between peonage and the voluntary performance of labor or rendering of services in payment of a debt. In the latter case the debtor, though contracting to pay his indebtedness by labor or service, and subject like any other contractor to an action for damages for a breach of that contract, can elect at any time to break it, and no law or force compels performance or a continuance of the service. Ex parte Hollman, 79 SC 9, 60 SE 19.

voluntary petition. A petition in bankruptcy wherein petitioner asks that he be adjudicated a bankrupt. 9 Am J2d Bankr § 207.

voluntary reorganization. The reorganization of a corporation by the voluntary action of the stockholders and creditors, or, where statute permits, by the creditors and a prescribed percentage of the stockholders. 19 Am J2d Corp §§ 1518 et seq.

voluntary sacrifice. An element of liability to contribution in general average.

To satisfy the requirement of a voluntary sacrifice, that there may be a general average contribution toward a marine loss, it is not enough that there be a deliberate intent to do an act that may or may not lead to a loss; there must be a purpose to sacrifice the thing at all events, or at least to put it in a situation in which the danger of eventual destruction is increased. 48 Am J1st Ship § 627.

voluntary self-destruction. The taking of one's own life purposely and intentionally. Courtemanche v Independent Order of Foresters, 136 Mich 30, 98 NW 749.

voluntary separation. A common ground of divorce provided by statute, the condition being a separation that is voluntary, on the part of at least one of the parties, not forced as would be the case if the husband was inducted into the Armed Forces or confined in prison. 24 Am J2d Div & S § 151.

voluntary settlement. A dissolution and winding up of the affairs of a partnership, effected by the partners without court action.

See **compromise; settlement; voluntary payment.**

voluntary statement. A statement by the accused in a criminal prosecution, proceeding from the spontaneous suggestion of his own mind, free from the influence of any extraneous disturbing cause.

A reason why admissions by defendants are only

admissible when voluntary is that they should be received with great caution, because they may not be true, for the mind of an accused, when oppressed by the calamity of his situation, is often influenced, by hope or fear, to make an untrue statement, when, as a matter of fact, the truth would be better. Tuttle v People, 33 Colo 243, 79 P 1035.

See **confession**.

voluntary stranding. The stranding of his ship by the master to save the ship and her cargo from the greater expense which her sinking then imminent would cause. Fowler v Rathbone (US) 12 Wall 102, 20 L Ed 281, 285.

voluntary transfer. See **voluntary assignment; voluntary deed**.

voluntary trust. An obligation arising out of a personal confidence reposed in, and voluntarily accepted by, one for the benefit of another. Bath Sav. Institution v Hathorn, 88 Me 122, 33 A 836.

voluntary validity (vă-lid'ĭ-ti). The effect of a tacit or implied consent of the parties to continue in force a compact which one of them has breached.

voluntary waste. Waste committed by acts of commission such as destroying, altering, or removing buildings, or cutting down trees, as distinguished from the mere failure to exercise care to preserve and protect the estate. 56 Am J1st Waste § 4.

voluntary withdrawal. A termination of employment at the instance of the employee. Quitting the service of the employer. 35 Am J1st M & S § 26.

voluntas (vo-lun'tās). Will; intent; intention; a will; a testament.

Voluntas donatoris in charta doni sui manifeste expressa observetur (vo-lun'tās do-nā-tor'is in kar'ta dō'nī sū'ī ma-ni'fes-te ex-pres'sa ob-zer-vē'ter). The will or intention of the donor which is clearly expressed in his deed of gift should be observed.

Voluntas et propositum distinguunt maleficia (vo-lun'tās et pro-po'zi-tum dis-tin'gu-unt ma-le-fi'she-a). The intent and the purpose distinguish offenses.

Voluntas facit quod in testamento scriptum valeat (vo-lun'tās fā'sit quod in tes-ta-men'to skrip'tum va'le-at). (Civil law.) The intention is that which makes valid the writing in a will.

Voluntas in delictis non exitus spectatur (vo-lun'tās in de-lik'tis non ek'si-tūs spek-tā'ter). In crimes, the intent, and not the result, is regarded.

Voluntas pro facto (vo-lun'tās prō fak'tō). The will for the deed.

Voluntas pro facto reputatur (vo-lun'tās prō fak'tō re-pu-tā'ter). The will is regarded as the deed. Commonwealth v Barlow, 4 Mass 439.

Voluntas regis in curia, non in camera (vo-lun'tās rē'jis in kū'ri-a, non in ka-mē'ra). The will of the king in court, not in his chamber.

Voluntas reputabitur pro facto (vo-lun'tās rep-ū-tab'-i-ter prō fak'to). The intent is to be regarded as the act.

"In some Year Books of the fourteenth century we find our lawyers appealing to . . . a dangerous maxim." See 2 Pollocks & Maitland's History of English Law p 475, note.

Voluntas reputatur pro facto (vo-lun'tās re-pu-tā'ter prō fak'to). The will is regarded as the deed. See Broom's Legal Maxims 311.

Voluntas testatoris ambulatoria est usque ad mortem (vo-lun'tās tes-ta-tō'ris am-bu"la-tō'ri-a est us'kwe ad mor'tem). The will of the testator is changeable up to the moment of his death.

Voluntas testatoris habet interpretationem latam et benignam (vo-lun'tās tes-ta-tō'ris hā'bet in-ter-pre-tā"she-ō'nem lā'tam et be-nig'nam). The intention of the testator should have a broad and liberal interpretation.

Voluntas testatoris pro lege habetur (vo-lun-tās tes-ta-tō'ris prō lē'jē hab'e-tēr). The will of the testator is regarded as the law. The intention of the testator is the law of the case. Panaud v Jones, 1 Cal 488, 511.

Voluntas ultima testatoris est perimplenda secundum veram intentionem suam (vo-lun'tās ul'ti-ma tes-ta-tō'ris est per-im-plen'da se-kun'dum vē'ram in-ten-she'o-nem sū'am). The last will of a testator should be carried out according to his true intention.

voluntate. See **ex voluntate**.

volunteer. One who enlists in one of the Armed Forces of his own volition, not under the compulsion of a military draft. One who works for another without engagement of services. One, who, without duty, moral or otherwise, pays the debt or discharges the obligation of another. 50 Am J1st Subro § 21. One who pays a debt, although not a party to, or interested in, the contract or transaction in which the debt arose. 40 Am J1st Paym § 22.

One who pays the debt of another to protect an interest of his own is not a volunteer and is therefore entitled to subrogation. McMillan v O'Brien, 219 Cal 775, 29 P2d 183, 91 ALR 383.

See **voluntary payment**.

vote. Verb: To express one's choice for a candidate or for or against a proposition submitted at an election. Anno: 14 ALR 1262. The choice expressed by a voter at an election, whether in reference to candidates or a proposition submitted to the voters. The exercise of the right of suffrage. Anno: 14 ALR 1262. The entire number of votes cast at an election.

See **preferential voting; proportional representation; suffrage**.

vote of the people. A plurality or majority vote, as the case may be, of the qualified electors.

In statutes providing for the issuance of bonds when authorized by "a vote of the people," the words "authorized by the vote" can but mean by a majority, as there are but two answers to be made to the question submitted,—an affirmative and a negative one; and, to be authorized, the matter of the proposition must receive the greater number or majority of the votes. It could not be a plurality, as might be when there are more than two candidates for office, and the one receiving the highest number of votes is elected, but may not have received a majority of the votes. The word "people," as used here, must mean "electors" or "voters. " Bryan v Stephenson, 50 Neb 620, 70 NW 252.

voter. One who expresses his choice of candidates or measures offered or proposed at an election by marking a ballot or indicating his choice by appropriate act upon a voting machine. One possessing the legal qualifications of an elector, so as to be entitled to vote. Re Denny, 150 Ind 104, 59 NE 359.

See **elector**.

votes cast at election. The number of voters voting. Gottstein v Lister, 88 Wash 462, 153 P 595.

In the absence of a certification of the number of electors voting, the court must presume that the highest number of votes cast for candidates for any one office represents the number of electors voting. State ex rel. Howie v Brantley, 113 Miss 786, 74 So 662.

In ascertaining whether a school bond issue has been approved by the requisite two-thirds of the qualified voters voting thereon, void ballots are not to be considered as voting thereon, even though in tabulating the result of the election the canvassing board has included them in its total of ballots cast. Anno: 4 ALR2d 612.

As to whether the majority vote required for the adoption of a proposition or measure submitted at a general election is to be determined on the basis of the entire vote cast upon such proposition or measure or the total number of votes cast at the election, see 26 Am J2d Elect § 311.

voting. See **vote.**

voting agreement. An agreement between the stockholders of a corporation, sometimes called a pooling agreement, intended to combine votes with a view to concerted action for a common object, and which control the votes of one or more of the parties by limiting their voting rights or conferring them upon others. 19 Am J2d Corp § 680.

See **voting trust.**

voting booth. The place provided in an election precinct or district for holding the election. A booth which can be transported on the street as need arises for its use in a particular ward, district, or precinct. The space provided at the polls for the purpose of enabling the voter to cast his vote in secrecy.

voting by ballot. The method of implementing constitutional and statutory requirements for secrecy in voting.

In common speech, the word "ballot" is used to mean the ticket used in voting; the act of voting; the result of voting. But from earliest times "voting by ballot" has been a term used to contradistinguish open, viva voce, or public voting, and secret voting. "The material guaranty of the provision of the (state) constitution, that all elections by the people shall be by ballot, is inviolable secrecy as to the person for whom an elector shall vote." People ex rel. Detroit v Board of Inspectors of Election, 139 Mich 548, 102 NW 1029.

Voting by New Residents in Presidential Election Act. One of the uniform laws. 25 Am J2d Elect § 69.

voting contest. A contest conducted by a mercantile establishment for the purpose of increasing sales, ballots being given with purchases, the same to be used in voting for someone, usually a girl, as the most popular person. National Sales Co. v Manciet, 83 Or 34, 162 P 1055.

voting district. See **election district.**

voting hours. The period of time on election day during which qualified voters may vote, such being determined by statute.

voting illegally. See **illegal voting.**

voting machine. A machine used by voters in expressing their choice of candidates or their preference for or against propositions or measures submitted at an election, the same keeping the totals of the votes cast for the various candidates and measures, so that, at the closing of the polls, the results may be obtained by the election inspectors upon opening the machine. 26 Am J2d Elect § 232.

voting precinct (prē'sinkt). Same as **election district.**

Voting Rights Act. A federal statute enacted in 1965, prohibiting any state or political subdivision from imposing or applying any voting qualification or prerequisite to voting, or any standard, practice, or procedure, denying the right of any citizen of the United States to vote on account of race or color, such prohibition applying to all types of elections, federal, state, and local. 42 USC § 1973.

voting thereon. See **votes cast at election.**

voting trust. Simply stated, a device whereby persons owning stock with voting powers divorce the voting rights thereof from the ownership, retaining the latter to all intents and purposes and transferring the former to trustees in whom the voting rights of all depositors in the trust are pooled. Smith v Biggs Boiler Works Co. 33 Del Ch 183, 91 A2d 193, 34 ALR2d 1125.

A trust created by an agreement between a group of the stockholders of a corporation and the trustee or by a group of identical agreements between individual stockholders and a common trustee, whereby it is provided that for a term of years, or for a period contingent upon a certain event, or until the agreement is terminated, control over the stock owned by such stockholders, either for certain purposes or for all purposes, is to be lodged in the trustee, either with or without a reservation to the owners, or persons designated by them, of the power to direct how such control shall be used. Annotation: 98 ALR2d 379, § 1[d]; 19 Am J2d Corp § 685.

The term generally contemplates the transfer of corporate stock to trustees, the issuance of new stock certificates to trustees, and the issuance by them of trust certificates to the beneficial owners of the stock, with the right to vote in the trustees and the right to receive dividends in the trust certificate holders. Anno: 105 ALR 124.

voting viva voce (vō'ting vī'va vo'se). Voting publicly; voting without secrecy in respect of the exercise of choice. 26 Am J2d Elect § 234.

vouch (vouch). To give assurance as to the honesty and ability of another. To affirm the truth of a statement. To give one's testimony.

The word "witness" in its strict legal sense, means one that gives evidence in a cause before a court; and the phrase "vouched by witnesses," seems to import the same as "testified by witnesses" called into court, and in this sense, a note subscribed by two persons as and for witnesses, cannot be said to be vouched by two witnesses, until those persons are vouched, or called and do testify before the court respecting it. See Barker v Coit (Conn) 1 Root 224, 225.

See **vouching in.**

vouched by witnesses. See **vouch.**

vouchee (vou-chē'). A person who is called or summoned; a person who is called upon to defend the title to land under a warranty of title. One for whom another vouches.

voucher. A receipt or other evidence of payment. An account book in which charges and acquittances are entered. Whitwell v Willard, 42 Mass 216, 218. A cancelled check. 40 Am J1st Paym § 288. A written instrument which attests, warrants, maintains, and bears witness. State v Hickman, 8 NJL 299, 301. Most literally, one who vouches.

When used in connection with the disbursement of moneys, the word implies some written or

printed instrument in the nature of a receipt, note, account, bill of particulars, or something of that character which shows on what account or by what authority a particular payment has been made, and which may be kept or filed away by the party receiving it, for his own convenience or protection, or that of the public. People v Swigert, 107 Ill 494, 504.
See **vouch.**

vouching in. The practice whereby persons liable over to a defendant are brought into the action as parties of record having opportunity to defend. 30A Am J Rev ed Judgm § 417. Requesting one bound by a covenant of warranty to defend the title.

vox Dei (vox De'ī). The voice of God.

Vox emissa volat; litera scripta manet (vox ē-mis'sa vo'lat; li'te-ra skrip'ta mā'net). Speech flies away; written letters endure. See Broom's Legal Maxims 666.

vox et preterea nihil (voks et pre-tēr'i-ạ nī'hil). Voice and nothing more; that is, nothing but wind. See Mitchell v Hazen, 4 Conn 495.

Vox populi vox Dei (vox po'pu-li vox De'ī). The voice of the people is the voice of God.

voyage. A long journey, particularly by ship or aircraft. The sailing of a vessel from one port or place to another port or place.
The purpose for which the voyage is to be conducted, whether for trading, freighting, or fishing, is often mentioned in marine policies, but this mention or designation cannot vary or extend the voyage as described in the policy, unless some usage connected with the particular business is shown. Burgess v Equitable Marine Ins. Co. 126 Mass 70.

voyage policy. A policy of marine insurance which establishes the duration of the risk by specifying the voyage, setting out the termini or places of beginning and termination, as from one port to another. 29A Am J Rev ed Ins § 324.

voyeur (vwo-yür). (French.) A pervert, the perversion being in obtaining sexual gratification in looking at an exposed body or sexual scene.

vs. An abbreviation of **versus.**

vulcanization (vul'kạn-i-zā'shọn). The process whereby crude rubber is converted to a form fit for use in the manufacture of tires and other products of industry, one type of such process being known to the trade as "cold vulcanization." Vultex Corp. v Heveatex Corp. (CA1 Mass) 100 F2d 838.

vulgar (vul'gär). Unrefined. Wanting in culture. Lack of taste in language, particularly in using coarse and indecent terms.

vulgaris opinio (vul-gā'ris o-pi'ni-ō). Common opinion or repute.

vulgaris purgatio (vul-gā'ris per-gā'she-ō). Common purgation,—the judicium Dei, that is, the trial by water-ordeal or fire-ordeal was often called vulgaris purgatio to distinguish it from the canonical purgation, which was by the oath of the accused. See 4 Bl Comm 342.
See **judicium Dei.**

vulgarity. The state of being vulgar.
See **vulgar.**

vulgar purgation (vul'gär pėr-gā'shọn). Same as **vulgaris purgatio.**

Vulgate Edition. An edition of the Year Books, otherwise known as the Folio Edition or Edition of 1679.
See **Year Books.**

vulgo concepi (vul'gō kon-sep'tī). Bastards.

vulgo quaesiti (Latin.) A term of the civil law for offspring of promiscuous cohabitation; children who are said to be children of the people, for the reason that identification of the father or fathers is impossible.

vulva (vul'vạ). The external female genitals. State v Wisdom, 122 Or 148, 257 P 826.

W

W. Abbreviation of west.

W.² Abbreviation of West One-half, used frequently in describing land according to the government survey.

WAAC. Abbreviation of Women's Auxiliary Army Corps, which was replaced by the **Women's Army Corps.**

WAC. Abbreviation of **Women's Army Corps.**

wadia (wa′di-a). Same as **guadia.**

WAF. Abbreviation of **Women in the Air Force.**

wage. Verb: To conduct or carry on. Noun: A return for services.
See **wages.**

Wage and Hour Law. The federal statute regulating the hours and wages of employees engaged in interstate commerce or in the production of goods for interstate commerce. 29 USC §§ 201 et seq.

wage continuation plan. See **sick pay.**

wage-earner. Literally, one who earns wages. For the purpose of the exception from involuntary adjudication in bankruptcy, an individual who works for wages, salary, or hire at a rate of compensation not exceeding $1,500 per year. Bankruptcy Act § 1(32); 11 USC § 1(32). For the purposes of eligibility to relief under the Bankruptcy Act by a wage-earner's plan, an individual whose principal income is derived from wages, salary, or commissions, without reference to the amount. Bankruptcy Act § 606(8); 11 USC § 1006(8); 9 Am J2d Bankr § 1387.

wage-earner's plan. A proceeding provided by Chapter XIII of the Bankruptcy Act, the function of which is to assist the financial rehabilitation of a debtor who qualifies as a wage-earner, without adjudicating him a bankrupt. 9 Am J2d Bankr §§ 1382 et seq.

wage his law. See **trial by wager of law.**

wager. An agreement or stipulation to the effect that the parties shall gain or lose upon the happening of an uncertain event, in which event they have no interest except that arising from the possibility of such gain or loss. 24 Am J1st Gaming § 2. In common terms, a bet or gamble.

As the synonymous words "wager" and "bet" are used in criminal statutes, they do not import the kind of agreement contemplated by the law of contracts under which there must be an actual meeting of the minds of the contracting parties in order to form an agreement. So to hold would allow the defendants to escape punishment in all cases in which feigned accomplices were employed to detect them and in which there is no evidence against the defendants except the testimony of feigned accomplices. People v Ghio, 82 Cal App 28, 255 P 205.

wagering contract. An insurance policy not supported by an insurable interest on the part of the insured. 29 Am J Rev ed Ins §§ 432 et seq. An ordinary gambling contract.
See **gambling contract.**

wagering gain. A gain in winning a wager. Jennings v Commissioner (CA5 Tex) 110 F2d 945.

wager insurance policy. Same as **wager policy.**

wager of battel. See **trial by wager of battel.**

wager of law. See **trial by wager of law.**

wager of law of nonsummons (ov lâ ov nonsum′ǫns). A form of a plea in a real action.

wager policy. A contract purporting to be one of insurance but which does not qualify as such for want of a sufficient insurable interest. 29 Am J Rev ed Ins § 434. A gambling policy; for example, a policy of life insurance wherein the person for whose use the policy was issued has no pecuniary interest in the life of the insured. Gambs v Covenant Mut. Life Ins. Co. 50 Mo 44, 47.

Under the doctrine of wager life insurance policies, it is widely held to be against public policy to permit speculation in human life by allowing one having no insurable interest in the life of another to secure for himself as beneficiary a policy of insurance on such life. Butterworth v Mississippi Valley Trust Co. 362 Mo 133, 240 SW2d 676, 30 ALR2d 1298.

wages. Compensation for manual labor, skilled or unskilled, paid at stated times, and measured by the day, week, month, or season. Sums paid as hire or reward to domestic or menial servants, artisans, mechanics, laborers, and other employees of like class, as distinguished from the compensation of clerks, officers of corporations, and public officers. 35 Am J1st M & S § 63. Compensation paid one for personal services of some kind. 22 Am J1st Exemp § 65. Anything constituting a reward for a workman's labor, whether the pay is by the hour, the day, the week, the month, or by the job or piece. 9 Am J2d Bankr § 537. (Pertaining to priority of wage claim.) Inclusive of board, lodging, or "other facilities" customarily furnished by an employer to his employees. 29 USC § 203(m). (Definition of Fair Labor Standards Act.) All remuneration payable for personal services, including commissions, bonuses, and gratuities customarily incident to the course of employment, whether received in cash or other medium. Fuller Brush Co. v Industrial Com. 99 Utah 97, 104 P2d 201, 129 ALR 511. All remuneration for employment, including the cash value of all remuneration paid in any medium other than cash. Social Secur. Board v Nierotko, 327 US 358, 90 L Ed 718, 66 S Ct 637, 162 ALR 1445.

Labor is remunerated by wages and by "salaries;" wages being the remuneration of subordinates, and "salaries" of officials. Springfield Coal Mining Co. v State Industrial Com. 291 Ill 408, 126 NE 133, 22 ALR 859, 862.

Sums set apart by an employer under a pension scheme declared to be for the purpose of giving the employees a share of the earnings of the business over and above their wages are not wages within the meaning of a statute giving a preference to wages in the distribution of assets by a receiver. Dolge v Dolge, 70 App Div 517, 75 NYS 386.

"Wages," defined in an Unemployment Compensation Act as "all remuneration for employment," do not include a pension paid by the employer to a retired employee. Kneeland v Administrator, Unemployment Compensation Act, 138 Conn 630, 88 A2d 376, 32 ALR2d 896.

As to what constitutes "wages" within pension law basing benefits thereon, see Anno: 14 ALR2d 634.

As to what constitutes wages for purpose of social security benefits and unemployment compensation, see 48 Am J1st Soc Sec § 14.

As to what constitutes "wages" within priority provision of Bankruptcy Act, see 9 Am J2d Bankr § 537.

As to "wages" within priority provision in statutes relative to distribution of the assets of an insolvent, see 29 Am J Rev ed Insolv § 49.

See **prevailing rate of wages; salary.**

wage-worker. One who works for wages. A **wage-earner.**

Wagner Act. The first National Labor Relations Act, which became law in 1935, enacted to give greater protection to the right of employees to organize and bargain collectively, and designating certain actions by employers as unfair labor practices. 31 Am J Rev ed Lab § 180.

wagon. A four-wheeled vehicle, drawn by horses or oxen, almost unknown in the age of motor vehicles, for the transportation of goods, wares, merchandise, and personal property of all descriptions, as well as of persons. Quigley v Gorham, 5 Cal 418.

wagon train. A line of vehicles moving together, common in the period of settlement of the West when travelers moving in wagons joined for protection and the comfort of companions.

waifs (wāfs). Abandoned children. Homeless persons, especially persons unable to care for themselves. Goods stolen, and waived or abandoned by a thief in his flight, in fear of apprehension.

Such goods became the property of the king, by way of punishing the owner for his failure to pursue the thief and retake his goods. See 1 Bl Comm 296.

wainable (wā'nạ-bl). Capable of cultivation; tillable.

wainage (wā'nạj). Carts, wagons and tools of husbandry.

wain-bote (wān'bōt). Timber to be used for the repair of wagons and carts.

wainscoting. Panels of wood on the wall of a room, especially on the lower part of the wall.

waiting period. Same as **waiting time.**

waiting room. A room provided by a carrier for the comfort and convenience of prospective passengers and those who accompany them or who are waiting for them. 44 Am J1st RR § 260.

waiting time. A period of time immediately after an injury, for which, as provided by the statute, workmen's compensation is not payable. 58 Am J1st Workm Comp § 319. A certain period of time following the effective date of health, hospital, or medical insurance during which the coverage is not applicable or during which coverage for certain specified diseases or disabilities is not applicable.

See **cooling time.**

waive. Noun: An obsolete term for a woman who by her conduct has deprived herself of the protection of the law to which she would ordinarily be entitled. Verb: To throw away; to relinquish voluntarily that right which one might have enforced by choice. See Anglo-Nevada Assur. Corp. v Nadeau, 90 Cal 393, 27 P 302. To make or effect a waiver.

See **waiver.**

waiver. The intentional relinquishment of a known right, claim, or privilege. Phillips v Lagaly (CA10 Okla) 214 F2d 527, 50 ALR2d 626; Smith v Smith, 235 Minn 412, 51 NW2d 276, 32 ALR2d 1135. A voluntary and intentional relinquishment of a known and existing right, or such conduct as warrants an inference of the relinquishment of such right. An election to dispense with something of value or to forego some advantage which one might, at his option, have demanded. 29A Am J Rev ed Ins § 1009. The intentional surrender of a known right or privilege, such surrender modifying other existing rights or privileges, or varying the terms of a contract. Lenoir Memorial Hospital, Inc. v Stancil, 263 NC 630, 139 SE2d 901.

The term implies the intentional relinquishment of a known right after knowledge of the facts. It implies the intentional forbearance to enforce a right, and necessarily, therefore, assumes the existence of an opportunity for choice between the relinquishment and the enforcement of the right. Anno: 53 ALR 528.

Waiver presupposes a full knowledge of a right existing, and an intentional surrender of relinquishment of that right. It contemplates something done designedly or knowingly, which modifies or changes existing rights, or varies or changes the terms and provisions of a contract. It is the voluntary surrender of a right. Sovereign Camp, W.W. v Newsom, 142 Ark 132, 219 SW 759, 14 ALR 903.

To establish a waiver, there must be shown an act or omission on the part of the one charged with the waiver fairly evidencing an intention permanently to surrender the right alleged to have been waived. Dunbar v Farnum, 109 Vt 313, 196 A 237, 114 ALR 996.

A waiver as to insurance presupposes a right to declare a forfeiture and such subsequent conduct by the insurer as to justify a conclusion that the insurer did not intend to assert its rights in that respect. Seavey v Erickson, 244 Minn 232, 69 NW2d 889, 52 ALR2d 1144.

waiver by election. A defense which arises when a plaintiff who has sought two remedies which are inconsistent with each other, waives one of them by a decisive act of affirmance or disaffirmance, with knowledge of the facts. Robb v Vos, 155 US 13, 43, 39 L Ed 52, 63, 15 S Ct 4.

waiver of appeal. See **waiver of right to appeal.**

waiver of contract. A voluntary and intentional relinquishment or renunciation of a contract right by some positive act or omission inconsistent with the existence of such right. Long v Clark, 90 Kan 535, 135 P 673.

waiver of exemption. The voluntary relinquishment by a debtor of his right to assert the exemption of his property, or a part of his property, from the claims of creditors to which he is otherwise entitled by statute. Wyman v Gay, 90 Me 36, 38, 37 A 325.

waiver of homestead. See **declaration of abandonment of homestead.**

waiver of immunity. A means authorized by statute by which a witness in advance of giving testimony or producing evidence, may renounce the fundamental right and privilege guaranteed to him by the Constitution, that no person shall be compelled in any criminal case to be a witness against himself. Re Grae, 282 NY 428, 26 NE2d 963, 127 ALR 1276.

waiver of notice of dishonor. An oral or written, express or implied relinquishment by an indorser of a negotiable instrument, either before or after the time for giving notice has arrived, of his right to be notified of the dishonor of the instrument. 11 Am J2d B & N §§ 831 et seq.

waiver of presentment. An oral or written, express or implied relinquishment by a party to a negotiable instrument of the right to have the instrument presented for payment. 11 Am J2d B & N §§ 831 et seq.

waiver of proof of loss. A voluntary relinquishment by an insurer having knowledge of all the facts of its right to a written proof of loss to which it is otherwise entitled by the contract of insurance or statute. 29A Am J Rev ed Ins § 1424.

waiver of protest. An oral or written, express or implied relinquishment by a party to a negotiable instrument of his right to have the instrument protested upon dishonor. 11 Am J2d B & N §§ 831 et seq.

waiver of right to appeal. The relinquishment of the right to appeal from a judgment by express agreement or by the party's voluntary act or conduct. 4 Am J2d A & E § 235. Any act evidencing an intent to enjoy a benefit from, or base some interest upon, the judgment. Oatman v Hampton, 43 Idaho 675, 256 P 529.

waiver of tort. The relinquishment by a plaintiff of his right to sue in tort by electing to sue in contract in a case where the plaintiff is entitled to such an election.

wake. A gathering of persons maintaining a vigil over the remains of a departed friend or relative, sometimes having a festive nature in keeping with a custom of the land.

walk. Noun: A sidewalk. Verb: To move on one's feet from one place to another.
  Walking in the open air for exercise, is held not to be within a Sunday law prohibiting unnecessary walking on that day. Sullivan v Maine Central R. Co. 82 Me 196, 19 A 169.

walker. See **nightwalker; pedestrian; walk**.

walking. See **walk**.

walkout. A concerted withdrawal by employees from the place of employment as a result of a labor dispute.
  See **division wall; party wall**.

wall. An upright structure of wood, stone, brick, or other hard and durable material, serving as the side of a building or as a partition inside a building, sometimes as a support holding land in place, sometimes as a fortification protecting against attack by a military or other hostile force.

wallia (wal'li-a). A wall; a sea-wall.

wall in common. Same as **party wall**.

wampum (wom'pum). The bead money of the North American Indians. In common, if not approved usage, money of any kind.

wantage (won'tăj). Same as **ullage**.

want of consideration. Absence of consideration; failure of consideration; insufficiency of consideration.
  See **failure of consideration; sufficient consideration**.

want of issue. The failure of issue; the condition or state of being childless.
  See **definite failure of issue; indefinite failure of issue**.

want of jurisdiction. The want of authority to take cognizance of and decide the case; the want of power to hear and determine a cause. 20 Am J2d Cts § 88.

want of ordinary care. The failure to exercise ordinary care.
  See **ordinary care**.

want of probable cause. The absence of probable cause.
  See **probable cause**.

want of precedent. Characterizing the novelty of an action. Rozell v Rozell, 281 NY 106, 22 NE2d 254, 123 ALR 1015.

want of prosecution. A ground of involuntary dismissal or nonsuit, consisting in the plaintiff's failure to appear and prosecute his case or his failure to prosecute his case diligently. 24 Am J2d Dism § 59.

want of repair of way. A defective condition relating to inert objects or structural imperfections; not inclusive of the negligent or unlawful use of a way by a moving object, or the negligent operation of a stationary instrumentality. 25 Am J1st High § 360.

wanton. Undisciplined. Lewd and immoral. Unchaste. In reckless indifference or disregard of the rights of others and the likelihood of injury to another. Conchin v El Paso & Southwestern Railroad Co. 13 Ariz 259, 108 P 260.

wanton act. An act performed with knowledge that injury to another is likely to result from the act and with reckless indifference to such consequence. Wunderlich v Franklin (CA5 Ala) 100 F2d 164; Southern Railway Co. v Bennefield, 172 Ala 588, 55 So 252.

wanton conduct. See **wanton act; wanton omission**.

wanton injury. See **wanton act; wanton omission**.

wantonly. Wilfully, in reckless disregard of the rights of others and of the likelihood of injury to another. Commonwealth v Byard, 200 Mass 175, 86 NE 285. Heartlessly; evincing a wicked or mischievous intent. Jennings v Cooper (Mo App) 230 SW 325.

wanton misconduct. See **wanton act; wanton omission**.

wanton negligence. A paradoxical expression, since the term "wanton" infers premeditation, knowledge, or consciousness, while "negligence" implies inadvertence; apparently signifying an act done or omitted to be done in such reckless disregard of the security and safety of another as to imply bad faith. 38 Am J1st Negl § 48; 52 Am J1st Torts § 23. An act or omission in complete absence of care for the safety of others, exhibiting indifference to consequences, but not necessarily ill will. Higbee Co. v Jackson, 101 Ohio St 75, 128 NE 61, 14 ALR 131, 20 NCCA 144. In the criminal law, culpable negligence; negligence amounting to a disregard of consequences or indifference to the rights or safety of others. 21 Am J2d Crim L § 84.
  Wanton negligence involves the creation of an unreasonable risk of bodily harm to another, together with a high degree of probability that substantial harm will result. Bryan v Southern Pacific R. Co. 79 Ariz 253, 286 P2d 761, 50 ALR2d 1.
  Inherent in wanton negligence is the idea of moral fault arising from the doing or failing to do an act with consciousness that the act or omission would probably cause serious injury, and with reckless indifference to consequences. Alabama Great Southern R. Co. v Louisville & N. R. Co. (CA5 Ala) 224 F2d 1, 50 ALR2d 1302.

wantonness. See **wanton act; wanton omission**.

wanton omission. The omission to perform an act, with knowledge that such omission is likely to result in injury to another. 52 Am J1st Torts § 23.

wants. See **needs; needs of business.**

wapentakes (wŏp′n-tāks). The hundreds in certain of the more northern counties of England. See 1 Bl Comm 115
See **hundred.**

war. A state of activity in which a nation prosecutes its rights or its claims by force of arms. 56 Am J1st War § 12. An armed struggle or contest by force carried on for any purpose between two or more nations or states exercising at least de facto authority over persons within a given territory and commanding an army prepared to observe the laws of war. 56 Am J1st War § 2. The exercise of force by bodies politic against each other and under the authority of their respective governments with a purpose of coercion. Carce v State, 83 Tex Crim 292, 202 SW 951. An armed conflict between sovereign powers, characterized by declared and open hostilities. West v Palmetto State Life Ins. Co. 202 SC 422, 25 SE2d 475, 145 ALR 1461. A conflict between nations, commencing with a formal declaration of war. West v Palmetto State Life Ins. Co. 202 SC 422, 25 SE2d 475, 145 ALR 1461.

Although Congress has, in certain enactments, recognized the operation of United States military forces in Korea and has appropriated funds for their support, the conflict is not a "war" in the constitutional or legal sense in the absence of a declaration of war by Congress. Beley v Pennsylvania Mut. Life Ins. Co. 373 Pa 231, 95 A2d 202, 36 ALR2d 996.

As to what constitutes a "war" within the meaning of the term as it appears in the provisions of a life or accident insurance policy, see Anno: 36 ALR2d 1037.

As to what constitutes a "war" within the meaning of the term in reference to an excuse for nonperformance of a contract, see Anno: 137 ALR 1249.

See **duration of war; law of war; perfect war.**

warantia. Another spelling of **warrantia.**

warantus. Another spelling of **warrantus.**

war bond. A bond issued by the United States government in time of war for the purpose of obtaining funds for the conduct of the war. 43 Am J1st Pub Sec § 15.

ward. A subdivision of a municipal corporation. 36 Am J1st Mun Corp § 45. One under guardianship because incapable of managing his own affairs. Harrison v Harrison, 21 NM 372, 155 P 356. An infant under guardianship. One under special protection, as ward of the state or ward of the court.

warda (war′da). A ward; a guard.

ward and watch. See **watch and ward.**

warden. A caretaker; a keeper; a guard; a guardian; the superintendent of a prison.
See **church wardens; game warden.**

War Department. Formerly one of the primary departments of the Federal Government, headed by the Secretary of War.
See **Defense Department.**

ward heeler. A term of contempt for one who solicits votes and works for the leader of his party in a ward, particularly one whose activities are questionable from the standpoint of legality or good taste.

ward-holding (wârd-hōl′ding). Tenure by military service.

ward-mote (wârd′mōt). A London ward court.

ward of chancery. An infant under the special protection of a court of equity. 27 Am J1st Inf § 101.

ward of court. An infant under the special protection of the court to which he is entitled. 27 Am J1st Inf §§ 101 et seq.

After submitting themselves to the jurisdiction of the court, the parents cannot by their agreement deprive it of power to control the custody and maintenance of the child. Such a child is in a very real sense the ward of the court. It has power to change the custody of the child; to enforce the parental obligation to provide maintenance, and, if necessary, to remove the child from the custody of both parents. Emrich v McNeil, 75 App DC 309, 126 F2d 841, 146 ALR 1146.

wards and liveries. See **court of wards and liveries.**

ward school. See **district school.**

wardship (wârd′ship). The right of the lord, as "guardian in chivalry," under feudal tenure, to receive and retain, as guardian of the person and estate, the profits of the lands of an infant male heir, his tenant, until the heir, if a male, was twenty-one, and if a female, until she was sixteen. See 2 Bl Comm 67.

In socage tenure, the guardian was the heir's nearest relative to whom the inheritance could not descend. He was accountable for profits and ceased to be guardian when the ward was fourteen. See 2 Bl Comm 87.

In copyhold tenure, wardship was an incident of tenure, and the lord was the legal guardian of his infant tenant. See 2 Bl Comm 97.

wardship in chivalry. See **wardship.**

wardship in copyhold. See **wardship.**

wardship in socage. See **wardship.**

ward-wit (wârd′wit). An exemption or immunity from the service of watch and ward. See **watch and ward.**

warectare (wa-rek-tā′re). To plow up land with the intention of allowing it to lie fallow.

warehouse. A structure, usually one of considerable size, used for the storage of goods of the owner or tenant or the goods of others. 29A Am J Rev ed Ins § 898.
See **bonded warehouse; field warehousing.**

warehouseman. A person engaged in a business of storing goods for hire. UCC § 7—102(1) (h). One who receives and stores goods of others as a business. National Union Bank v Shearer, 225 Pa 470, 74 A 351. A person lawfully engaged in the business of storing goods for profit. 56 Am J1st Wareh § 2.

warehouseman's lien. The right of a warehouseman to retain possession of the goods of another, stored with him, until the satisfaction of his charge or charges for the storage, interest, and advances made by him for insurance, labor, and other expenses in reference to the stored goods. 56 Am J1st Wareh §§ 105 et seq.

warehouseman's risk. A policy of insurance covering the contents of a warehouse, sometimes limited to the interest which the warehouseman has in the stored property, at other times covering only margins uninsured by other policies on the stored property. Home Ins Co. v Baltimore Warehouse Co. 93 US 527, 23 L Ed 868.

warehouse purposes. Characterizing the use of premises for no use other than the storing and safeguarding of goods and effects. 29A Am J Rev ed Ins § 898.

warehouse receipt. In the most simple sense, an instrument importing that the goods of a named person are in the hands of a named warehouseman. Union Trust Co. v Wilson, 198 US 530, 49 L Ed 1154, 25 S Ct 766. A receipt issued by a person engaged in the business of storing goods for hire. UCC § 1—201(45). A written contract between the owner of goods and a warehouseman under which the latter agrees to store the goods and the former to pay for the storage. Sinsheimer v Whitely, 111 Cal 378, 43 P 1109. In a more formal and elaborate character, a symbolic representation of the stored property itself; a document of title to goods. Uniform Sales Act § 76; 56 Am J1st Wareh § 29.

Warehouse Receipts Act. One of the uniform laws, specifically repealed by the Commercial Code. 15 Am J2d Com C § 6.

warenna (wa-ren'na). A warren.
See **warren.**

warentare (wa-ren'tā're). To warrant; to guarantee.

wares. Goods or things kept for sale in a mercantile establishment. 37 Am J2d Frd Conv § 252. Merchandise. The Conqueror, 166 US 110, 41 L Ed 937, 17 S Ct 510. Articles of merchandise, goods, or commodities. Ellis v Commonwealth, 186 Ky 494, 217 SW 368, 11 ALR 1030, 1031.

warlike operations. Warfare; operations in waging war. Anno: 95 L Ed 91.

war-making power. See **war power.**

war memorial. A structure, usually a building available for public meetings and public games or amusements, erected to the memory of deceased veterans of the armed services, a part of the structure being a chapel wherein proper respect may be paid to the departed heroes. Anno: 12 ALR2d 891, § 7.

warning. An advising of danger. Recommending caution. A notice of town meetings. 52 Am J1st Towns § 13.

A railroad crossing is, itself, a place of danger, and is an effectual warning of danger, a warning which must always be heeded. Koch v Southern California Railway Co. 148 Cal 677, 84 P 176.

war power. The power of the government of the United States to wage war to the point of success, that is the overcoming of the enemy. Hirabayashi v United States, 320 US 81, 87 L Ed 1774, 63 S Ct 1375.

The national defense is an absolute necessity of our existence. The people of the United States have prepared themselves for such a situation by confiding to Congress the power to declare war and to support and maintain armies for the national defense. This is necessarily a master power, to be exercised without the hampering interference of anyone. The call of men to the colors is within, and necessarily within, the exercise of this power. To whom the call goes out, and who is to make an answering response are matters germane to, and indeed necessarily involved in, the exercise of the war-making power. Questions which necessarily arise, or may be expected to arise, must be determined in some way and by some tribunal. The war-making power may therefore provide the required system and constitute the needed tribunals. Local Draft Board No. 1 v Connors (CA9 Mont) 124 F2d 388.

war prisoner. See **prisoner of war.**

warrandice (wor'an-dis). A warranty.
See **absolute warrandice.**

warrant. Noun: A form of process, such as a warrant for the arrest of a person. 42 Am J1st Proc § 2. An order authorizing a payment of money by another person to a third person. An order or draft on the treasury of a public body, payable on presentation when funds are available, or at a fixed date with interest, if authorized by statute. Marshall v State, 88 Fla 329, 102 So 650. A notice of a town meeting. 52 Am J1st Towns § 13. Justification or sanction for some act or course of conduct. Verb: To enter into an obligation of warranty; to become a warrantor. To give authorization or sanction for some act or course of conduct.
See **scrip.**

warrantee (wor-an-tē'). A person to whom a warranty is made.

warrant for search. See **search warrant.**

warrantia (wa-ran'she-a). A warranty; a guaranty.

warrantia chartae (war-ran'she-a kar'tē). A writ for the enforcement of a warranty contained in a deed.

warrantia custodiae (war-ran'she-a kus-to'di-ē). An old writ under which the plaintiff contested the right of the lord of the manor to guardianship in chivalry of the lands of the heir where the land had been warranted to be free thereof.

warrantia diei. See **de warrantia diei.**

warrant in bankruptcy (wor'ant in bangk'rup-si). An order issued by the court in a bankruptcy proceeding directing the marshal to take possession of the property of the bankrupt.

warrant in deed. A warrant under seal. State v Shaw, 73 Vt 149, 168, 50 A 863.
See **warranty deed.**

warrant in law. A rational and reasonable basis in the law. 2 Am J2d Admin L § 619. Force of law; authority of law. State v Shaw, 73 Vt 149, 168, 50 A 863.

warrantizo. A technical word used in ancient deeds, meaning "I warrant," which was employed to bind the grantor to warrant and defend the title and possession of the grantee, when deeds first came to be used for the purpose of authenticating the transfer of title to lands.

warrant of arrest. A legal process issued by competent authority, directing the arrest of a person or persons upon grounds stated therein, usually directed to a regular officer of the law, but occasionally issued to a private person named in it. 5 Am J2d Arr § 7.

warrant of attachment. Same as **writ of attachment.**

warrant of attorney. Same as **power of attorney.**

warrant of attorney to confess judgment. Same as **power of attorney to confess judgment.**

warrant of commitment. See **commitment.**

warrant of distress. See **distress warrant.**

warrant of extradition. See **extradition warrant.**

warrant officer. An officer of the armed forces whose office is held under a warrant rather than a commission. 36 Am J1st Mil § 51. Ranking above a non-

WARRANT [1360] WASH

commissioned officer and below a commissioned officer.

warrant of possession. A warrant evicting the defendant and placing a purchaser at execution sale in possession. Hill v Kitchens, 39 Ga App 789, 148 SE 754.

warrantor (wor'ạn-tọr). The maker or obligor in a warranty.

warrant to sue and defend (tö sū and dẹ-fend'). A warrant from the English crown specially authorizing a person to appoint an attorney to sue and defend actions in his behalf.

warrantus (wa-ran'tus). A warrantor.

warranty. An agreement to be responsible for all damages that arise from the falsity of a statement or assurance of a fact. Holcomb & H. Mfg. Co. v Auto Inter-Urban Co. 140 Wash 581, 250 P 34, 51 ALR 39. An express or implied statement of something undertaken as part of a contract of sale of personal property, but collateral to its object. 46 Am J1st Sales § 299. A promise of indemnity against defects in an article sold. State ex rel. Duffy v Western Auto Supply Co. 134 Ohio St 163, 16 NE2d 256, 119 ALR 1236. A covenant against failure of an article for a certain specified purpose, or for a certain specific reason. Barton v Dowis, 315 Mo 226, 285 SW 988, 51 ALR 494. An absolute undertaking by a seller, in praesenti as well as in futuro, for the quality, condition, or quantity of the thing sold. 46 Am J1st Sales § 299. One of the title covenants in a deed. 20 Am J2d Cov C § 50. The obligation undertaken in contracting to defend another person in an action which may be instituted against him. Flanders v Seelye, 105 US 718, 726, 26 L Ed 1217, 1220. In the law of insurance:—a statement, description, or undertaking on the part of the insured, appearing in the policy of insurance or in another instrument properly incorporated in the policy, relating contractually to the risk insured, and which, in the absence of statute, must be literally true or fulfilled. 29 Am J Rev ed Ins §§ 708, 710.

A warranty promises indemnity against defects in an article sold, while insurance indemnifies against loss or damage resulting from perils outside of and unrelated to defects in the article itself. State ex rel. Duffy v Western Auto Supply Co. 134 Ohio St 163, 16 NE2d 256, 119 ALR 1236.

The term "warranty" in an insurance contract ordinarily imports an assurance on the part of the policyholder that a certain situation exists or will continue, which diminishes the likelihood that the event insured against will occur; and hence "warranty" and "condition precedent" are often used interchangeably. Fidelity-Phenix Fire Ins. Co. v Pilot Freight Carriers, Inc. (CA4 NC) 193 F2d 812, 31 ALR2d 839.

See **covenant of warranty.**

warranty deed. A deed conveying land and containing the usual covenants of title. Bowen v Thrall, 28 Vt 382, 385.

See **title covenants.**

warranty in sale by sample. A warranty that the article delivered or the bulk of the commodity will correspond with the sample in kind and quality. 46 Am J1st Sales §§ 362, 364.

warranty of fitness. An implied warranty by the seller of a chattel sold for a particular use that the chattel is fit for such purpose, provided the buyer is relying upon the skill, judgment, or experience of the seller. 46 Am J1st Sales § 346.

warranty of soundness. A warranty by the seller of an animal, particularly a horse, that it is free of defect or infirmity rendering it unfit for convenient use. 46 Am J1st Sales § 396.

warranty of soundness from sound price (ov sound'nes frum sound prīs). The rule of the civil law, in opposition to that of the common law, that a warranty of soundness against hidden or latent defects will be implied where a full or sound price is paid.

This warranty will include all faults known or unknown to the seller, though it is not considered as including defects patent and known to the buyer. 46 Am J1st Sales § 340.

warranty of title. An implied warranty on the part of the seller in a sale or contract to sell personal property that he has, or will have at the time when property is to pass, the right to sell the goods; that the buyer shall enjoy quiet possession as against any lawful claims existing at the time of the sale; and that the goods at the time of the sale shall be free from charge or encumbrance in favor of any third person, not declared or known to the buyer before or at the time when the contract or sale is made. 46 Am J1st Sales § 403.

For warranty of title to real estate, see **covenant of warranty.**

warren (wor'en). A game preserve; private grounds for the keeping of game and wild fowl. See **beasts of the warren; fowls of warren; free warren.**

war risk insurance. Term insurance, covering death and total permanent disability, issued to servicemen of World War I, ultimately converted by many of them to United States Government Life Insurance. 29A Am J Rev ed Ins § 1974.

Warsaw Convention. A multilateral treaty concluded at Warsaw, Poland, in 1929, to which the United States is a party, providing for the unification of certain rules relating to international transportation by air. 8 Am J2d Avi § 16.

warship (wâr-ship). A naval vessel, whether of the United States or a foreign country.

war veteran. See **veteran.**

wash. Erosion by water. A gravel deposit made by an overflowing stream. Another term for **wort.**

wash bank. An unstable bank of a river. Kerr v Bougher, 16 Ohio App 434.

washed land. Submerged land. 56 Am J1st Wat § 448.

washing rack. A rack upon which motor vehicles are placed for cleaning with steam. 24 Am J1st Gas Sta § 23.

washout. A hole in a highway caused by the washing away by stream or surface water of a part of the embankment. 25 Am J1st High § 615. A loss of part of the embankment of a railroad by flood or surface water. A slang term for one who has failed in a particular endeavor or for an enterprise or undertaking which has ended in failure.

washout signal. A signal for a quick stop.

wash sale. A sale of securities or commodities involving no actual change in the beneficial ownership, the seller not expecting to make or the buyer to receive delivery, being a method of manipulating prices. 50 Am J1st Stock Ex § 26. A stock-exchange term for a so-called sale which is merely a bet upon the market. United States v New York Coffee & Sugar Exchange, 263 US 611, 616, 68 L Ed 475, 476, 44 S Ct 225.

Wasserman test (wos′ėr-mạn test). A test for syphilis which has been known to the medical world since about the year 1906, being a standard and well-recognized test, operating with efficiency when made by a physician familiar with its use. Peterson v Widule, 157 Wis 641, 147 NW 966.

waste. In the popular sense, the failure to conserve. Loss of assets in the estate of a decedent through mismanagement by the executor or administrator. 31 Am J2d Ex & Ad § 265. In the technical sense, the destruction, misuse, alteration, or neglect of premises by one lawfully in possession thereof, to the prejudice of the estate or interest therein of another. 56 Am J1st Waste § 2. The destruction or material alteration of any part of a tenement by a tenant for life or years, to the injury of the person entitled to the inheritance. An unlawful act or omission of duty on the part of a tenant which results in permanent injury to the inheritance. Anno: 3 ALR 674; 56 Am J1st Waste § 2. An unreasonable or improper use, abuse, mismanagement, or omission of duty touching real estate by one rightfully in possession which results in substantial injury to the freehold. Gade v National Creamery Co. 324 Mass 515, 87 NE2d 180, 10 ALR2d 1006. Refuse discarded in the process of converting raw material into a manufactured article. Patton v United States, 159 US 500, 40 L Ed 233, 16 S Ct 89.

The primary distinction between waste and trespass is that in the former case the wrong is done by one rightfully in possession. Camden Trust Co. v Handle, 132 NJ Eq 97, 26 A2d 865, 154 ALR 602.

See **impeachable for waste**; **meliorating waste**; **permissive waste**; **unimpeachable for waste**.

waste-book (wāst′buk). A book of original entry of accounts in which all transactions are entered; a blotter.

waste gate (wāst gāt). Same as **spill**.

waste land. Land unfit for cultivation. Malone v McLaurin, 40 Miss 161.

waste water. See **surplus water**.

wasting assets corporation. A corporation engaged in mining or cutting timber or some such business, so that dividends are in fact paid out of capital, the assets being consumed in the regular course of operations. Hayes v St. Louis Union Trust Co. 317 Mo 1028, 298 SW 91, 56 ALR 1276.

wasting his estate. Squandering one's funds or property or impairing one's own health, and ability to labor and have earnings, by drunkenness and riotous living. 24 Am J2d Div & S § 94.

wasting property. Property, such as an oil well, quarry, or mine, the substance of which is consumed in exploitation. See **wasting assets corporation**.

wastors (wās′tọrs). Thieves.

watch. A timepiece carried on the person. A force of guards or watchmen on duty at one time. That part of the officers and crew of a vessel on duty at one time.

R. H. Dana, in his Dictionary of Sea Terms defines the word as "a certain portion of a ship's company, appointed to stand a given length of time. In the merchant service all hands are divided into two watches, larboard and starboard, with a mate to command each." The men are divided as equally as possible with reference to their qualities as able seamen. The customary watch is of four hours' duration, alternating between the starboard and the larboard or port watches. O'Hara v Luckenbach S.S. Co. 269 US 364, 371, 70 L Ed 313, 316, 46 S Ct 157.

See **anchor watch**; **constant watch**; **lookout**; **sea watch**.

watch and chain. A timepiece with chain attached for convenience in carrying upon the person. An article of gold and silver manufacture. 29 Am J Rev ed Innk § 91.

watch and ward. The duty of constables.

Ward, guard, or custodia, as it was variously called, was a duty performed mainly in the daytime and looked chiefly to the apprehension of rioters and highway robbers. Watch was a duty which the constables performed only at night, beginning where ward left off and ending when ward began. It was kept in every borough and town, especially in summer, to apprehend all rogues, vagabonds and nightwalkers and make them give an account of themselves. See 1 Bl Comm 356.

watcher. A person appointed by a political party to be present at the polling place on election day and observe the conduct of the election and the counting of the votes. 26 Am J2d Elect § 233. One who observes the commission of a crime. 26 Am J1st Homi § 65.

watchmaker's materials. A stock of articles required in the trade of watchmaking or watch repair. Maril v Connecticut F. Ins. Co. 95 Ga 604, 23 SE 463.

watchman. One employed to keep a lookout for fire, flood, burglars, thieves, or vandals by way of protection of person or property. As employed by a municipality, a policeman, within the meaning of the common-law rule as to power to arrest without a warrant. Porter v State, 124 Ga 297, 52 SE 283. As employed on a vessel at sea, a seaman and member of the crew. The Herdis (DC Md) 22 F2d 304, 305.

The word is in its very nature loose and indefinite in meaning, and the law cannot supply this defect by giving a definition, because it is not a technical term of the law, and because the nature of a watchman's functions vary in different places and according to the dangers to which the property is exposed, and even according to the nature and value of the property. Anno: 87 ALR 1114.

water. The liquid substance formed by the combination of hydrogen and oxygen represented by the symbol H_2O.

While water is to be defined as a mineral, the rules of law as to its use must logically vary from those applicable to coal, ore, and the like. It is a fluid, and mobile, "a fugitive," while coal and ores have a permanent place. The analogy to natural gas and oil is more apt. Their natural use, however, is as merchandise. Water, although in a large measure a commodity of commerce, is essential to the natural use of land for agriculture and other purposes, and to the support of human life itself. See Erickson v Crookston Waterworks Power & Light Co. 100 Minn 481, 111 NW 391.

See H_2O.

water-bailiff (wâ′tėr-bā″lif). An English port officer whose duty it was to search ships.

water boundary. A watercourse or body of water constituting a boundary of a tract of land described by reference thereto. 12 Am J2d Bound §§ 12 et seq.
See **thalweg.**

water carrier. A carrier operating vessels.

Water Carrier Act. A federal statute regulating water carriers engaged in interstate or foreign commerce. 49 USC §§ 901 et seq.

water charge. A charge, rental, or toll for water furnished by a waterworks company or a municipal water plant. Zubieta v Tarner, 76 Nev 243, 351 P2d 982. A charge imposed for the use of water for irrigation. 30 Am J Rev ed Irrig §§ 54, 67.

water closet. A toilet kept sanitary by flushing it with water. Commonwealth v Roberts, 155 Mass 281, 29 NE 522, 16 LRA 400.

water company. A company which maintains and operates a waterworks. A public service corporation whose main purpose is to supply water to the inhabitants of a municipality, with the right to use the streets and highways for its mains and pipes. 56 Am J1st Watwk § 2.

watercourse. A stream of water flowing in a definite direction or course in a bed with banks. A natural channel, having a well-defined existence, with running water supplied from a definite source. Snyder v Platte Valley Pub. Power & Irrig. Dist. 144 Neb 308, 13 NW2d 160, 160 ALR 1154; Re Johnson Creek, 159 Wash 629, 294 P 566. A physical condition created by a stream having a well-defined and substantial existence. Chicago Rock Island & Pacific R. Co. v Groves, 20 Okla 101, 93 P 755. For some purposes, any well-defined channel or arroyo in which surface waters flow in times of heavy rains. Croeger v Twin Buttes R. Co. 13 Ariz 348, 114 P 553 (application of statute prohibiting obstruction of watercourses).
See **artificial watercourse.**

watercraft. In the broad sense, a ship or boat. Any sort of boat or vessel capable of being used as a means of transportation on water. Bartlett v Steam Dredge, 107 Mich 74. A small vessel, usually engaged in coastwise or domestic navigation. The Saxon (DC SC) 269 F 639.

water damage insurance. Insurance on property against loss or damage by rain, flood, or other accumulation of water from natural causes. 29A Am J Rev ed Ins § 1332.

water district. A quasi corporation having and exercising certain limited powers for the carrying out of the public purpose of providing a water supply. 37 Am J1st Mun Corp § 6.
See **irrigation district.**

watered stock. Shares issued by a corporation without an increment of capital corresponding to the number issued. Shares of stock issued by a corporation as fully paid, but which have in fact been issued without any consideration or at a discount, as in exchange for over valued property or services. 18 Am J2d Corp § 266.

water fixtures. See **plumbing.**

water front. The land at the edge of a river or other body of water. The area of a city with a port, which is immediately adjacent to the harbor. Not inclusive of the harbor itself. Long Beach v Lisenby, 175 Cal 575, 166 P 333.

water-front commission. An administrative body in charge of port or harbor facilities. Application of Waterfront Com. of New York Harbor, 26 Misc 2d 767, 206 NYS2d 123, affd 13 App Div 2d 725, 217 NYS2d 487.

water gas. See **wet gas.**

water license. A license to use the waters of a stream, as for power. 56 Am J1st Water § 258.
See **water privilege.**

water-logged. Render unmanageable or sluggish because of excessive amount of water in the hold.

water lots. Land lots bounded by a river or other body of water. Land lots near enough to a river or other body of water as to have an increased value. Morris v United States, 174 US 196, 262, 43 L Ed 946, 970, 19 S Ct 649.

watermark. A mark in paper produced by pressure in the process of manufacturing, observable when held against the light. 52 Am J1st Tradem § 6.
See **high-water mark; low-water mark.**

water meter. See **meter.**

water nuisance. A wrongful interference with waters or water rights. The wrongful ponding or casting of water upon the premises of another, or an unsanitary, disagreeable, harmful, or dangerous condition caused by an accumulation of water, or by the pollution thereof. 56 Am J1st Water § 432.

water on the brain (on the brān). A disease in which there is an effusion of water into, and pressing upon, the brain.
"An affliction than which no other is more eminently calculated to produce mental imbecility or incapacity for the serious and deliberate concerns of this life." Griffin v Griffin, R. M. Charlton's Rep (Ga) 217, 222.

water ordeal. See **trial by water.**

water-packed. Characterizing a bale of cotton sprinkled with water to such extent as to increase the weight materially. Wallace v Crosthwait, 196 Ala 356, 71 So 666.

water pollution. The infection and contamination of a public water supply by dirt, bacteria, and coli, or any other infectious and contaminating material which renders the water unfit for domestic use and unsafe and dangerous to individuals. 56 Am J1st Watwk § 75. The deterioration in the quality of water in a natural watercourse or other body of water caused by industrial operations, the production of oil or gas, mining operations, or the disposal of waste, refuse, or sewage. 56 Am J1st Water § 415. Any defilement or corruption of the water of a watercourse which prevents its use for any of its reasonable or proper purposes. 56 Am J1st Water § 405. The defilement, contamination, or corruption of the waters of a well or percolating waters. 56 Am J1st Water §§ 136, 143. The pollution of a well or water on neighboring property by the escape of gas or noxious substance from a gasworks. 26 Am J2d Electr § 265.

waterpower. The power existing in water by virtue of the fall of a stream, either in the natural state of the stream or as induced by a dam which impounds the water, applied to the use of man in turning the wheels of machines or in the generation of electricity. Rhodes v Whitehead, 27 Tex 304.

water privilege. An incorporeal hereditament of an independent nature, not constituting a servitude upon some other thing. Union Falls Power Co. v

Marinette County, 238 Wis 134, 298 NW 598, 134 ALR 958.
See **water license; water right.**

waterproof. Resistant to water under ordinary circumstances.
The term is a relative one, but as applied to the walls and floor of a basement, it imports that they are so constructed as to keep out moisture and dampness under such circumstances and weather conditions as may reasonably be foreseen and anticipated. Ozark Grocer Co. v Crandall, 131 Ark 481, 199 SW 551.

water rate. Same as **water charge.**

water rental. Same as **water charge.**

water right. In the general sense, the legal right to use water. An easement, either in gross or appurtenant to other property, in the use of water. 56 Am J1st Water §§ 242, 243. A usufructuary right or interest in a stream or other body of water, or the right to the use of another's premises for the conveyance of water. 56 Am J1st Water § 242.
See **water license; water privilege.**

water runs and ought to run as it is by nature accustomed to run. A maxim of the common law taken from the civil law. Wholey v Caldwell, 108 Cal 95, 41 P 31; San Gabriel Valley Country Club v Los Angeles County, 182 Cal 392, 188 P 554, 9 ALR 1200.

waterscape (wâ'tẽr-skāp). An aqueduct.

watershed. The area drained by a river or other natural stream of water. The area drained by a river system.

water skiing (wâ'tẽr skē-ing). A comparatively modern sport in which the participant, being on skis, is pulled across the water by a motorboat.

waters of the United States. See **inland waters.**

water supply district. See **irrigation district; water district.**

water table. The underground level to which percolating water rises. Bauman v New York, 227 NY 25, 124 NE 141, 8 ALR 595.

water tax. A charge for water furnished by a municipal water plant; not a "tax" in the true sense of the term. 51 Am J1st Tax § 16.
See **water charge.**

waterway. A water course. A natural way for the drainage of surface water. 56 Am J1st Water § 76. In a broader sense, inclusive of a canal or other artificial channel, even a ditch.

water well. See **well.**

waterworks. The system employed by a water company or municipality in furnishing water for residences, places of business, factories, or industrial plants. 56 Am J1st Watwk § 2.
The word has been construed to mean and include a water supply system in its entirety, or any integral part thereof, including mains, hydrants, standpipes, impounding reservoirs, purification plants and other enumerated items. Simpson v Highwood, 372 Ill 212, 23 NE2d 62, 124 ALR 1459.
See **water company; water charge.**

waterworks license. A municipal license issued to a water company, authorizing it to engage in the business of supplying water to the public. 56 Am J1st Watwk § 3.

watt (wot). An electrical unit representing power, equal to the product of the volts times the amperes. Peoria Water Works Co. v Peoria R. Co. (CC Ill) 181 F 990.

wave. See **displacement waves.**

waveson (wāv'sǫn). Goods from a wreck which float upon the sea.

waviata. See **bona waviata.**

way. A means of passage for a vessel in leaving the wharf and proceeding to sea. 48 Am J1st Ship § 263. The course which workmen will under ordinary circumstances take in order to go from one part of the employer's premises to another as their duties require. Anno: 23 ALR 718; 35 Am J1st M & S § 425. A road, sidewalk, or path. Kister v Reeser, 98 Pa 1. In a more technical sense, a right of way, that is, the right of one person, or several persons, or of the community at large to pass over the land of another. 25 Am J1st High § 3.
The words "way" and "road" are frequently used interchangeably, but properly, "way" is more generic, and includes many things, besides roads. Kister v Reeser, 98 Pa 1.
See **areaway; airway; highway; private way; right of way.**

way appurtenant. See **appurtenant way.**

waybill. A paper containing a list of the goods in a shipment by carrier and instructions respecting the shipment, in possession of the carrier's employees on the means of transportation which carries the shipment.

way by dedication. See **dedication.**

way by necessity. Same as **way of necessity.**

way by prescription. A highway established by prescription, that is, by the use of the land by the public as a highway for the prescriptive period. 25 Am J1st High § 11.
See **prescription.**

way ex vi termini (wā ex vī ter'mi-nī). A definite way in public use, standing without substantial change or variation. 25 Am J2d Ease § 63.

wayfarer. A traveler; a transient. 29 Am J Rev ed Innk § 12.

way-going crop. Same as the doctrine of emblements or away-going crops. 21 Am J2d Crops § 25.
See **away-going crops.**

way in gross. An easement of way in gross. 25 Am J2d Ease § 12.
See **easement in gross.**

wayleave. A private way, particularly the way reserved over the surface for the purpose of mining and removing minerals. 36 Am J1st Min & M § 33.

wayleave rent. Rental charged for the use of a right of way which serves a mine or quarry. See Speck v Cottonwood Coal Co. (CA9 Mont) 116 F2d 489.

waynagium (wā-nā'ji-um). Same as **wainage.**

way of necessity. A way acquired by an owner of land so situated that it is physically inaccessible to a public highway. Tomten v Thomas, 125 Mont 159, 232 P2d 723, 26 ALR2d 1285. An easement founded on an implied grant or implied reservation, arising where there is a conveyance of a part of a tract of land of such nature and extent that either the part conveyed or the part retained is shut off from access to a road to the outer world by the land from which it is severed or by this land and the land of strangers, there being in such a situation an implied grant of a way across the grantor's remaining land to the part conveyed, or conversely, an implied reservation of a way to the grantor's remaining land across the portion of the land conveyed. 25 Am J2d Ease § 34.

What are "ways of necessity" within the meaning of constitutional or statutory provisions for condemnation of land to provide a way of necessity is a question that can be answered satisfactorily only by reference to the authorities in the particular jurisdiction. Some courts adhere to the view of absolute necessity; others are more liberal in construction of the term. 26 Am J2d Em D § 47.

way reserved. See **reserved way.**

ways and means committee. A legislative committee the primary duty of which is the consideration of ways and means for raising revenue for the support of the government and the expenses incurred in the performance of its duties.

waywardens (wā'wâr"dns). The supervisors of a public road or highway.

WCTU. Abbreviation of **Women's Christian Temperance Union.**

we. The personal pronoun in the plural of the nominative case. Sufficiently connected with the persons executing the instrument where it appears in the body of the deed, that they are bound, although their names do not appear in the instrument above their signatures. 23 Am J2d Deeds § 49.

weakness of mind. See **feeble minded.**

weal (wēl). Welfare.

weald (wēld). A wood.

wealreaf. Larceny from a buried corpse.

wealth. In the popular sense, riches. In economics, anything having a monetary value; anything capable of being bought or sold.

weapon. Anything used or designed to be used in destroying, defeating, or injuring an enemy; an instrument of offensive or defensive combat. 56 Am J1st Weap § 2. Something with which to fight. Harris v Cameron, 81 Wis 239, 51 NW 437.

See **dangerous weapon; deadly weapon.**

wear. Clothing. Impairment or deterioration from use. Another term for **weir.**

wear and tear. The gradual deterioration of premises resulting from use, lapse of time, and the elements. 32 Am J1st L & T § 811.

wearing apparel. Dress or clothing of all kinds. Stewart v McClung, 12 Or 431, 8 P 447.

Wearing apparel, purchased and worn by the husband alone, constitutes a family expense within the meaning of a statute making the expenses of the family chargeable upon the property of the wife. Gilman v Matthews, 20 Colo App 170, 76 P 366.

See **necessary wearing apparel.**

wearing away of premiums. The gradual diminution of the premiums at which government and other bonds and securities are sold in the market, toward their par value, as the time of the maturity of the securities approaches.

weather. Noun: The manifestation of nature in warmth or coldness of the atmosphere, rain, snow, sunshine, or cloudiness. Verb: To wear away or disintegrate through exposure to the atmosphere.

See **bad weather.**

weather working days. A term of art used in provisions of charter parties relative to the number of days permitted for loading the ship, signifying days upon which the weather is such as to permit loading operations. Pederson v Eugster & Co. (DC La) 14 F 422.

Webb-Keynon Act. A federal statute, enacted prior to National Prohibition, the purpose of which was to subject interstate traffic in intoxicating liquor to the law of the place to which it is consigned. 30 Am J Rev ed Intox L § 47.

wedlock. The state of being married; matrimony.

weed. A useless plant, often crowding out cultivated plants.

The word has a common, everyday meaning to the mind of every man. It may also have a technical meaning to the botanist or the chemist. It is a nuisance to the farmer, the gardener, or the owner of a well-kept lawn, although it may possess valuable medicinal properties. But courts will notice judicially that a high, rank growth of weeds in a populous community has a strong tendency to produce sickness and impair health. St. Louis v Galt, 179 Mo 8, 13.

week. A period of seven days. 30A Am J Rev ed Jud S § 55. A period of seven days, usually reckoned from one Sunday to the next, that is, inclusive of Sunday at the beginning and Saturday at the end. Re Tyson, 13 Colo 482, 22 P 810. A period of seven calendar days' duration, without reference to the particular day on which the period commences to run, unless such a day is fixed by the agreement of the parties or the subject matter of the transaction. Hollister v Vanderlin, 165 Pa 248, 30 A 1002.

weekday. Any day of the week other than Sunday. In common usage of the present, any day of the week other than Saturday or Sunday.

weekend custody. Part-time custody of a minor child of divorced parents awarded to one of the parents, particularly custody over the weekend. 24 Am J2d Div & S § 800.

weekly newspaper. A newspaper which, according to its usual custom, is published once a week. 39 Am J1st Newsp § 4.

A Sunday edition of a daily paper has been held not to be a weekly newspaper. 39 Am J1st Newsp § 4.

week to week tenancy. See **tenancy from week to week.**

weevil. A beetle, the larvae of which are often destructive of stored property, particularly grain in an elevator. 56 Am J1st Wareh § 137. A pest destructive to alfalfa. Oregon-Washington R. & Nav. Co. v Washington, 270 US 87, 70 L Ed 482, 46 S Ct 279.

See **boll weevil.**

wehading. Another term for **trial by wager of battel.**

weighage (wā'āj). A duty or toll imposed by the English law to be paid for weighing merchandise, as of or weighing wool at the king's beam, or for weighing other avoirdupois goods. Hoffman v Jersey City, 34 NJL 172, 176.

weigher. See **weighmaster.**

weighmaster. A public officer appointed for the weighing of grain at a public elevator. 56 Am J1st Wareh § 18.

weighmaster's certificate. A certificate given by a weighmaster showing the weight of a quantity of grain or other goods as determined by the weighmaster. Vega S. S. Co. v Consolidated Elevator Co. 75 Minn 308, 77 NW 973.

weight. The heaviness of a person or a thing expressed in standard units, such as pounds and ounces.

See **false weights; gross weight; net weight.**

weighted average. A seldom-used method of assessing a stock of merchandise for taxation. Anno: 66 ALR2d 836.

weighted voting. A plan of representation in a legislative body whereunder the members, in voting upon measures, cast, not merely one vote per member, but a number of votes, such number varying between members according to the number of constituents represented by them.

weight of evidence. The effect of evidence as proof; the probative force of evidence. 30 Am J2d Ev § 1080.

weights of auncel. See **auncel weight.**

weigh with gold scales. To weigh, measure, determine, or decide with the utmost precision. State v Pugh, 101 NC 737.

weir (wēr). A dam or obstruction in a watercourse which backs up or diverts the stream. Merrifield v Canal Comrs. 212 Ill 456, 72 NE 405, 587. A structure built in a stream for penning fish. A contrivance placed in a flume for the purpose of regulating the amount of water passing from the feeder through the flume, and sometimes used to prevent a consumer from receiving more water than the amount to which he is entitled. Merrifield v Canal Comrs. 212 Ill 456, 72 NE 405.

welfare. In the broadest sense, the good of the people. The well-being of an individual. In a more limited sense familiar in modern usage, public relief for the poor, as provided under relief or welfare acts. 41 Am J1st Poor L §§ 13 et seq.

The whole is no greater than the sum of all the parts. The state still retains an interest in the individual's welfare, however reckless he may be, for when the individual health, safety, and welfare are sacrificed or neglected, the state must suffer. Allgeyer v Louisiana, 165 US 578, 41 L Ed 832, 17 S Ct 427.

See **general welfare; public welfare.**

welfare board. An administrative board of county, town, or township administering poor relief.

welfare laws. Statutes providing for the support, care, and housing of persons unable to support or care for themselves. Laws for the public relief of the poor. 41 Am J1st Poor L §§ 13 et seq.

welfare statutes. Same as **welfare laws.**

well. The shaft of an elevator. An excavation or hole dug, bored, or drilled into the earth for the purpose of obtaining water from subterranean sources. Anno: 55 ALR 1536, s. 109 ALR 419.

The term ordinarily includes, as appurtenant thereto, so much of the land upon which it is located as is necessary for its use and operation, and the fixtures and appliances used in connection therewith. The term may also include the water in the excavation. Davis v Spaulding, 157 Mass 431, 32 NE 650.

See **gas well; salt well.**

well and truly. Words of obligation.

In a bond conditioned that the principal shall well and truly perform the duties of the office, the words are not merely a stipulation for the officer's honesty, but import as well that he shall perform them with reasonable skill and diligence. Minor v Mechanics' Bank of Alexandria (US) 1 Pet 46, 69, 7 L Ed 47, 57.

well-defined channel. A channel clearly in existence, with bed of stream bordered by banks. An essential feature of a watercourse. 56 Am J1st Water § 6.

As to what constitutes a well-defined channel for natural drainage of surface water, see Anno: 81 ALR 262.

well knowing. A term of possible use as precatory.

An absolute devise by a lawyer to his wife, followed by the precatory words "well knowing that she will bequeath the property to the children," creates a trust, considering the knowledge of the testator as a lawyer and the intent manifested by the words. Doe's Will, 192 Wis 333, 212 NW 781.

well informed in the law. See **learned in the law.**

welsher (welsh'er). A person who fails to pay when he loses a bet. A person who makes bets or receives money to bet and absconds without paying his losses or returning the money entrusted to him. People v Monroe, 349 Ill 270, 182 NE 439, 85 ALR 605.

Welsh mortgage. A conveyance of land by way of giving security, similar to the vivum vadium. 36 Am J1st Mtg § 12.

See **vivum vadium.**

wera (wē'ra). Same as **weregild.**

were (wēr). Same as **weregild.**

weregild (wēr'gild). A fine or price paid, under the ancient law of the Saxons, for killing a man.

A part of the sum so paid went to the king and the rest to the near relatives of the deceased. See 4 Bl Comm 188, 313, 413.

It is generally accepted that the infliction of death did not create a civil liability at common law or under the Roman civil law. 22 Am J2d Dth § 1.

wergild (wėr'gild). Same as **weregild.**

west. A word indicating a compass point, being due west unless qualified or controlled by other words. 23 Am J2d Deeds § 248.

westerly. Toward the west, as in "traveling westerly." From the west, as in "westerly wind."

west half. See **west one-half.**

Westminster (west-mins'tėr). A municipality in itself, constituting a part of greater London.

See **Statute of Westminster.**

west one-half. Ordinarily a fraction of a section of land according to the government survey. The half of any tract of land, lying to the west, parol evidence being admissible for identification. 23 Am J2d Deeds § 254.

See **fraction of section.**

West-Saxon Lage. The laws of the West Saxons.

These laws were in force at the beginning of the eleventh century in the counties to the south and west of what is now England, from Kent to Devonshire. See 1 Bl Comm 65.

wet. Adjective: Moist or saturated with water. Noun: One opposed to prohibition or strict limitation of the sale of alcoholic beverages. State v Shumaker, 200 Ind 623, 157 NE 769, 162 NE 441, 163 NE 272, 58 ALR 954.

wetback. An alien who has gained an illegal entry

into the United States by wading or swimming a stream on the border.

wet gas. Gasoline rendered impure by the addition of water. Manufactured gas in the process of being "washed" or "scrubbed" for the removal of some elements. Water gas produced by the application of steam to incandescent carbon. Gas produced by an oil well in the form in which it issues from the well. Standard Oil Co. v United States (CA9 Cal) 107 F2d 402.

wether (weth'ėr). A male sheep which has been castrated.

whale. A mammal of the sea; a subject of property upon capture or taking. 35 Am J2d Fish § 4.

whaler (whā'ler). A whaling ship.

whaling. The taking of whale. The enterprise or expedition in sailing the oceans and taking whale.
See **mating.**

wharf. A structure in aid of navigation, constituting access for a vessel in loading or unloading. Prior v Swartz, 62 Conn 132, 25 A 398. A bank or structure erected on the shore of a harbor, river, or canal for convenience in loading and unloading vessels; a space artificially prepared for the reception of merchandise from a ship or vessel, so as to render convenient the loading and unloading of such vessel. 56 Am J1st Whar § 2.
See **dock; harbor.**

wharfage. Same as **dockage.**

wharfage lien. A maritime lien for wharfage or dockage, arising where the contract was made by a person having authority to pledge the vessel for performance of the contract and the course of dealing or circumstances of the transaction are not inconsistent with the creation of a lien. 56 Am J1st Whar § 38.

wharfinger. One who keeps a wharf for the purpose of receiving goods thereon for hire. 56 Am J1st Whar § 2.

wharfinger's receipt. An instrument having legal effect the same as that of a warehouse receipt. Hale v Milwaukee Dock Co. 29 Wis 482.
See **warehouse receipt.**

wharf lines. See **harbor lines.**

wharf master. Same as **harbor master.**

whatever is placed upon the land belongs to the land. A maxim subject to exceptions, as in the case of something affixed by a tenant. King v Morris, 74 NJL 810, 68 A 162.

what remains. Residue. That which is unexpended or unconsumed.
A life tenant under a will providing for a remainder over of what remains, so much as may remain unexpended, or some synonymous term, is entitled to the possession, control, and use of the entire devised property to be disposed of as he see fit, though he may make no testamentary disposition of the property or fraudulently dispose of the same for the purpose of defeating the estate in remainder. There is quite a divergence of opinion upon the question of the right to make gifts inter vivos. Anno: 69 ALR 831.

wheat. A grain produced by cultivation and used for making flour and other foods for man.

wheel. An instrumentality upon which loads may be rolled or power transmitted to machinery, without which approach to civilization is difficult, if not impossible. An ancient instrument of punishment for crime upon which the culprit was put to death by tearing his limbs apart.

wheelchair. A chair for a sick or disabled person.

wheelwright. A person who makes or repairs wheels.
A person who conducts a garage in which he repairs automobiles has been held to be a wheelwright within the meaning of a statute providing for a mechanic's lien for blacksmiths and "wheelwrights" who perform work or labor on wagons, carriages, farm implements, and other articles repaired by them. Weber Implement & Auto Co. v Pearson, 131 Ark 101, 200 SW 273.

wheelwright's lien. A lien for services of a wheelwright, the lien attaching to the wheel and the vehicle. Anno: 62 ALR 1495.

when. At what time. Sometimes indicating a condition. Jones v Palace Realty Co. 226 NC 303, 37 SE2d 906. Prima facie a word of contingency in a legacy or device. 57 Am J1st Wills § 1222. In a limitation of a remainder, ordinarily relating to the time of enjoyment rather than the time of vesting. Anno: 103 ALR 599.

when able. A qualification of a promise to pay, referring to the financial means of the obligor. 11 Am J2d B & N § 174.

when able to pay. When one has the financial means to pay. 34 Am J1st Lim Ac § 140.

when and as. A phrase importing contingency, not readily yielding to inferences of a contrary intention in the context of the will. 57 Am J1st Wills § 1222.

when, as, and if issued. An elaboration of the familiar term **when issued.**

when cause of action accrues. See **accrual of cause of action.**

when convenient. A qualification of a promise to pay, meaning when the promisor is able to pay or has the means of doing so. 34 Am J1st Lim Ac § 140.

when cut. An expression found in contracts for the sale of standing timber, having significance in reference to the size of the trees covered by the contract, making it clear that trees which reach the size specified in the contract at the time of the actual cutting thereof are included. 34 Am J1st Logs § 22.

whenever. At whatever time. A colloquialism for when.

when issued. A familiar term in transactions in stock and bonds on stock exchanges, involving securities contemplated for issuance but unissued at the time. 50 Am J1st Stock Ex § 25.

when issued stock. See **when issued.**

where. In or at a certain place. In the event of.

whereas. A term favored in the drafting of resolutions, meaning when if fact.

whereby. By means of which.
Where a complaint alleged that the defendant made his note "whereby he promised and agreed to pay," it was held that the effect of the pleading was the same as if it had alleged that the defendant had made his note and, by it, promised and agreed to pay. Acme Food Co. v Older, 64 W Va 255, 61 SE 235.

Where one of two innocent parties must suffer, he through whose agency the loss has occurred must bear it. A maxim and equitable principle. 27 Am J2d Equity § 146.

Where there is a right there is a remedy. A maxim of equity. 27 Am J2d Equity § 120.

whether sane or insane. A clause in a life insurance policy which extends the scope of an exception of suicide. 29A Am J Rev ed Ins § 1146.

whether valid or not. A familiar term in insurance policies, relative to other insurance on the same risk. 29A Am J Rev ed Ins § 966.

Whig (hwig). A political party of strength prior to the near approach of the War between the States, giving way to the Republican party.

while. During a relevant period of time. 29 Am J Rev ed Ins § 592.

The word "while" in an insurance policy is one of time or circumstance and not of causation. Washington Nat. Ins. Co. v Burke (Ky) 258 SW2d 709, 38 ALR2d 861.

while intoxicated. See **driving while intoxicated.**

while operating, driving, riding in or on. A clause defining the risk covered by an accident insurance policy in terms of causation. Provident Life & Acci. Ins. Co. v Nitsch (CA5 Tex) 123 F2d 600, 138 ALR 399. For construction of the clause generally, see Anno: 138 ALR 405.

whiplash. The characterization of a personal injury involving the neck, common in automobile accidents, the typical case occurring when the car in which the victim is riding is struck in the rear by another car or truck, the impact serving to throw his head back with violence. Yellow Cab Co. v McCullers, 98 Ga App 601, 106 SE2d 535. A telltale employed to warn a trainman on top of a car of a train of a structure over the tracks. 35 Am J1st M & S § 224.
See **telltale.**

whipping. A form of corporal punishment. State v Chambers, 22 W Va 779.

whipping-post (whip'ing-pōst). A post to which offenders were first tied and then were whipped.

whipping strap. Same as **telltale.**

whipping wife. A right, privilege, or indoor sport of a husband under the early common law, long since denied him by statute or judicial decision. 26 Am J1st H & W § 12.

whip to force payment. A graphic expression for the use of criminal process to enforce collection of a debt. 1 Am J2d Abuse P § 15.

whirlwind. See **cyclone.**

whiskey. Another spelling of **whisky.**

whisky. A distilled, spirituous, and intoxicating liquor, ordinarily distilled from grain, but sometimes produced from other commodities, even by diluting alcohol with water and mixing it with other ingredients. 30 Am J Rev ed Intox L § 12. Regarded as a drug under some circumstances. 25 Am J2d Drugs § 1.

Whisky Rebellion. An uprising by settlers in western Pennsylvania, in 1794, against the imposition of a tax on whisky.

Whisky Ring. A conspiracy formed in 1872 between certain distillers and revenue officers of the United States to defraud the government of internal revenue.

The government lost more than a million and a half dollars revenue and two hundred and thirty-eight persons were indicted.

Whiteacre (hwīt'ā-kėr). The name of a supposititious parcel of land often used in moot cases or in argument.

white bonnet. A sham bidder or puffer at an auction sale. McMillan v Harris, 110 Ga 72, 35 SE 334.

white damp. A noxious gas encountered in coal mines, commonly known as carbon monoxide, and having the effect of destroying the hemoglobin of the red corpuscles, or the oxygen-carrying property of the blood, thus producing a weakening of the physical and mental powers and often resulting in death. Jellico Coal Mining Co. v Walls, 160 Ky 730, 732, 170 SW 19.

white-heart test. The test of good faith according to honest performance, without reference to negligence. Appel v Morford, 62 Cal App 2d 36, 144 P2d 95; New Jersey Mortg. & Invest. Corp. v Calvetti, 68 NJ Super 181, 71 A2d 321.

white list. A list of names of employees and domestic servants of the various embassies and legations from foreign countries, prepared by the Protocol Division of the State Department. Trost v Tompkins (Mun Ct App Dist Col) 44 A2d 226.

white meats (hwīt mēts). Milk, butter, cheese, and eggs.

white mule. Another term for **moonshine.**

white person. One of the Caucasian or white race, as distinguished from a person of the yellow, brown, black, or red race. Ozawa v United States, 260 US 178, 67 L Ed 199, 43 S Ct 65. By a very literal construction, one who is white of skin, so that even a dark-skinned Causasian is not within the classification. United States v Bhagat Singh Phind, 261 US 204, 67 L Ed 616, 43 S Ct 338; Wadia v United States (CA2 NY) 101 F2d 7.

white race. One of the races of men, often called the Caucasian race.
See **white person.**

white rent. Rent which was payable in silver money, as distinguished from grain rent payable in baser money.

white slave act. A name freely applied to statutes creating and defining offenses relative to inducing or enticing women or girls into prostitution.

white slavery. Holding women or girls in prostitution.

White Slave Traffic Act. A federal statute, often called the Mann Act, which prohibits and penalizes as a felony the act of any person who transports, causes to be transported, or aids or assists in transporting any woman or girl in interstate or foreign commerce for the purpose of prostitution or debauchery or any other immoral purpose, or who knowingly procures or obtains, causes to be procured or obtained, or aids or assists in procuring or obtaining any ticket or tickets or any form of transportation to be used by any woman or girl in interstate or foreign commerce for the purpose of prostitution or debauchery or for any other immoral purpose. 18 USC § 398; 42 Am J1st Prost § 11.

Who is to watch the guards? Sometimes a fair question. Briscoe v Bank of Kentucky (US) 11 Pet 257, 9 L Ed 709, 745.

whole. Hale; hearty; sound; not diseased or injured. Undivided; constituting the entire extent or amount.

whole blood. The blood or relationship of children who have both of their parents in common.

whole chest. A term of the tea trade for an amount of tea, variable in amount from 100 to 150 pounds, or even more, but, in any event, the whole of the container.

wholesale. Characterizing a sale by a manufacturer or wholesaler to a retail merchant, jobber, dealer, or other wholesaler, for resale; not inclusive of a sale by a wholesaler to a user or consumer. Herbertson v Cruse, 115 Colo 274, 170 P2d 1312, 172 ALR 1312. Characterizing a sale in large quantities to dealers rather than to consuming customers. 30 Am J Rev ed Intox L § 216. Implying the selling of goods in unbroken pieces or parcels, as by the barrel, pipe, cask, etc., or in a number of such pieces or parcels. Gorsuth v Butterfield, 2 Wis 237, 243.

wholesale dealer. Same as **wholesaler.**

wholesaler. A middle man; one who buys from the manufacturer and sells to the retailer.

As a rule, wholesaler dealers are those who sell only to merchants who buy to sell to the consumer, whereas retail dealers sell direct to the consumer, and not to other retail merchants. Re Metz Bros. Brewing Co. 88 Neb 164, 129 NW 443.

wholesale price. The price paid by the retailer, often known as the cost price. Sylvester v Ammons, 126 Iowa 140, 101 NW 782.

The term has a fixed, certain, and well-defined meaning in the mercantile world, and signifies the price fixed on merchandise by one who buys it in large quantities of the producer or manufacturer, and sells the same to jobbers, or to retail dealers therein. Fawkner v Smith Wall Paper Co. 88 Iowa 169, 172.

As to the use of parol evidence in explanation of the term "wholesale factory price," see Anno: 89 ALR 1248.

wholesome. Sound in body and mind. Healthful; invigorating. Improving, rather than depraving.

wholly dependent. Characterizing a person in complete dependence upon another, having no other source or means of maintenance of any consequence. Anno: 39 ALR 314.

wholly dependent on. Dependent for support and maintenance upon no one else than the person designated. London Guarantee & Acci. Co. v Industrial Com. of Colorado, 78 Colo 478, 242 P 680.

wholly destroyed. See **total loss.**

wholly disabled. See **total disability.**

wholly retired. See **retired.**

whom it may concern. See **for whom it may concern; on account of whom it may concern.**

whore (hōr). A woman who practices unlawful commerce with men, particularly one who does so for hire; a harlot; a concubine; a prostitute.

A woman may acquire the character of a whore without being generally accessible to men. She may be the mistress of one and chaste toward all others. But in common parlance a vast difference is recognized between such a person and her who yields only to the solicitations of her affianced. Such a person may not justly be called a whore. Sheehey v Cokley, 43 Iowa 183.

whorehouse (hōr′hous). A bawdyhouse; a house of ill fame; a house kept for common prostitution. Wright v Page (NY) 36 Barb 438, 440.

See **house of ill fame; house of prostitution.**

whoremaster. A pimp; a procurer.

wick (wik). A town; a village; a castle.

widen. To make wider, as in the alteration of a highway. 25 Am J1st High § 107.

widow. A woman of single status because of the death of her husband. A woman who survives the man to whom she was married at the time of his death. Meeker v Draffen, 201 NY 205, 94 NE 626. A woman whose husband has died and who has not married again. Re McArthur, 210 Cal 439, 292 P 469, 72 ALR 1318.

The word means a woman who has lost her husband by death, and has no application to a divorced woman. O'Malley v O'Malley, 46 Mont 549, 129 P 501.

There is authority which holds that the term, as used in some statutes, may be applied to a woman in respect of her deceased husband, although she has remarried since his death. Re McArthur, 210 Cal 439, 292 P 469, 72 ALR 1318.

The right of action for wrongful death given by statute for the benefit of a widow for the death of her husband is not divested by her subsequent marriage. 22 Am J2d Dth § 67.

The right of the widow of an insured to the balance due under a national service life insurance policy after the death of the named insured, under a statutory provision giving the "widow" a preference over brothers and sisters of the insured, is not barred by her remarriage. Riley v United States (CA4 W Va) 212 F2d 692, 44 ALR2d 1182.

As to meaning of term under the Federal Longshoremen's and Harbor Workers' Compensation Act, see Anno: 98 L Ed 740.

widow-bench. The share to which a widow is entitled in the estate of her deceased husband, exclusive of any jointure.

widower. A man of single status because of the death of his wife.

As it is used in the statutes of descent, the word has been held to mean one who has been reduced to single status by the ordinary and usual vicissitudes of life, and not one who, by felonious act, has himself created that condition. Perry v Strawbridge, 209 Mo 621, 108 SW 641.

widow's allowance. An allowance made the widow of a decedent, under the laws of some states, for her maintenance and support.

It is neither an interest in the estate nor something which goes to her by descent, but is a preferred claim against the estate and is a part of the expense of administration. Grover v Clover, 69 Colo 72, 169 P 578.

widow's chamber. A widow's apparel and the furniture of her bedchamber, which were given to her by the custom of London. See 4 Bl Comm 518.

widow's quarantine. See **quarantine.**

widow's terce (tėrs). The widow's third, a widow's right of dower.

See **dower.**

widow's third (thėrd). A widow's right of dower. See **dower.**

width of highway. The extent of a highway laterally as fixed by statute, by prescription, or by the proceeding in which it, the highway, was established. 25 Am J1st High § 35.

wifa. A notice which indicates that the land upon which it is posted is in the exclusive possession of the occupant.

wife. A married woman. The spouse of a man. A woman who has a husband living. Names v State, 20 Ind App 168, 50 NE 401.

As the word is used in designating a beneficiary in a will, it is descriptive of the person of a particular individual, and unless there is something in the will indicating the contrary, a gift to the wife of a designated married man is a gift to the person who was his wife at the time when the will was made and not to a wife whom he has subsequently married. See 57 Am J1st Wills § 1385.

As a designation of the beneficiary of life insurance:—descriptio personae, so that the fact that one who otherwise answers the description does not, or did not at the inception of the insurance, have the legal status of wife of the insured does not prevent her from taking as beneficiary, if it is otherwise clear that she is the person intended, assuming that she is eligible to designation as beneficiary and that the misdescription of her as "wife" does not amount to a breach of warranty or misrepresentation avoiding the insurance. 29A Am J Rev ed Ins § 1660.

wife and children. Sometimes a designation of beneficiaries of a life insurance policy.

While some courts hold that a policy payable to the wife of the insured and "their children" includes children by another wife, the prevailing view is that the beneficiaries are limited to children common to both. 29A Am J Rev ed Ins § 1658.

wife-beating. See **whipping wife.**

wife's equity to a settlement. See **equity for a settlement.**

wife's right of survivorship. The title of a surviving wife at common law, arising upon the death of her husband, to choses in action which belonged to her at the time of the marriage or came to her during coverture, and were not reduced to possession by the husband. 26 Am J1st H & W § 59.

wife's separate equitable estate. See **separate estate of wife.**

wife's separate estate. See **separate estate of wife.**

wife's society. See **society of wife.**

Wigglesworth Mortality Table. A life expectancy table once recognized as standard. 29 Am J2d Ev § 895.

wild animal. An animal ferae naturae; an animal wild by nature. 4 Am J2d Ani § 2. An animal such as a deer in the forest, a quail in the air, or a fish in public waters. Fleet v Hegeman (NY) 14 Wend 42, 45.

wild beast test. The test of insanity, as a defense in a criminal case, according to whether or not the defendant was wholly deprived of understanding and memory. Anno: 44 ALR 584.

wildcat engine. A railroad locomotive running "wild"; that is, without an engineer or other attendant. Mars v Delaware & Hudson Canal Co. (Sup) 8 NYS 104, 105.

wildcat leases. Oil and gas leases secured on lands situated in undeveloped territory in the hope that oil or gas will be found there. Germer v Donaldson (CA3 Pa) 18 F2d 697.

wildcat strike. A strike of laborers not authorized by the union which represents them.

wild fowl. Birds wild by nature, especially game birds such as ducks, geese, or pheasants. 4 Am J2d Ani § 2.

wild grass. A grass plant growing without cultivation, valuable in use for forage.

wild land. Land in a state of nature, never having been cultivated. Conner v Shepherd, 15 Mass 164.

Wild's Case. See **first resolution in Wild's Case; second resolution in Wild's Case.**

wild train. A railroad train which is run as an extra train or without any reference to the regular schedule time. Larson v St. Paul, Minneapolis & Manitoba Railway Co. 43 Minn 423, 424, 45 NW 722.

See **wildcat engine.**

wild well. An oil or gas well that is producing oil or gas but which has not been brought under control so that the product can be captured for use.

wilful. A word of several meanings, the meaning in the particular case often being influenced by the context. Spies v United States, 317 US 492, 87 L Ed 418, 63 S Ct 364. Voluntary, as distinguished from accidental. 21 Am J2d Crim L § 87. Intentional or deliberate, yet not necessarily with an evil purpose in mind. Fulton v Wilmington Star Mining Co. (CA7 Ill) 133 F 193; Kite v Hamblen, 192 Tenn 643, 241 SW2d 601. Stubborn, obstinate, perverse. United States v Murdock, 290 US 389, 78 L Ed 381, 54 S Ct 223. Inflexible. Refractory. Wick v Gunn, 66 Okla 316, 169 P 1087, 4 ALR 107. Intentional and with a bad purpose. State v Clifton, 152 NC 800, 67 SE 751. Having a bad purpose, evil intent, or legal malice. Caldwell v State, 55 Tex Crim 164, 115 SW 597.

The word wilful as used in a statute which denies compensation to an employee for an injury sustained when due to a wilful failure or refusal to perform a duty required by statute imports, not only the mere exercise of the will in failing to comply with the statute, but also an intention to do an act that he knows, or ought to know, is wrongful or forbidden by law, and involves the idea of premeditation and determination to do such act. 58 Am J1st Workm Comp § 203.

It has been said that "wilfulness", as used in the Federal internal revenue statutes imposing criminal penalties, includes some element of evil motive and want of justification in view of the financial circumstances of the taxpayer, and as used in statutes imposing civil penalties it may, while often connoting a bad purpose, be used to characterize an act which is intentional, or knowing, or voluntary, as distinguished from accidental. Paddock v Siemonet, 147 Tex 571, 218 SW2d 428, 7 ALR2d 1062.

wilful act. An act done intentionally, or on purpose, and not accidentally. Leicester v Hoadley, 66 Kan 172, 71 P 318.

See **wilful.**

wilful and malicious act. See **malicious act; wilful act.**

wilful and malicious injury. An injury to property inflicted intentionally and in disregard of duty. Re Dixon (DC NY) 21 F2d 565. Within the meaning of the exception of certain liabilities from discharge in bankruptcy: injury to person or property inflicted intentionally and deliberately without cause or excuse and with no regard for the legal rights of the injured one. An injury inflicted by an act against good morals and wrongful in itself, committed with indifference to the safety of the injured person, and without just cause or excuse. Anno: 13 ALR2d 170; 9 Am J2d Bankr § 786.

A misappropriation of partnership funds by a

former partner to his own use after dissolution of the partnership is a "wilful and malicious injury" to the property of another within the provision of the Bankruptcy Act excepting such a debt from a discharge in bankruptcy. Fooshe v Sunshine, 96 Cal App 2d 336, 215 P2d 66, 16 ALR2d 1142.

wilful and wanton act. An act premeditated or performed with knowledge that injury is likely to result therefrom. 38 Am J1st Negl § 48.

wilful and wanton misconduct. A deliberate and intentional wrong. Antonen v Swanson, 74 SD 1, 48 NW2d 161, 28 ALR2d 1 (phrase in statute respecting liability of motorist for injury to guest).

Under a statute which imposes liability on the driver of a car for injury to a guest-passenger only where occasioned by the driver's "wilful or wanton misconduct", such a disposition or mental state is shown by a person when, notwithstanding his conscious and timely knowledge of an approach to an unusual danger and of common probability of injury to others, he proceeds into the presence of danger with indifference to consequences and with absence of all care. Rodney v Staman, 371 Pa 1, 89 A2d 313, 32 ALR2d 976.

See **wanton act.**

wilful and wanton negligence. A paradoxical expression, since the adjectives imply premeditation or consciousness of danger to another, while negligence implied inadvertence, but described as a reckless disregard of the safety of the person or property of another by failing, after discovering the peril, to exercise ordinary care to prevent the impending injury. Hinkle v Minneapolis, A. & C. R. Co. 162 Minn 112, 202 NW 340, 41 ALR 1377.

wilful burning. An element of the offense of arson. A conscious and intentional act of setting a fire. 5 Am J2d Arson § 11.

wilful default. A conscious abstention by an obligor from doing that which reasonably and under the terms of the obligation he should have done. Anno: 75 ALR 352. An intentional, although not necessarily malicious, wanton, or evil, failure to comply with a statute which prescribes the performance of an act intended for preservation of the safety of others. 35 Am J1st M & S § 213.

wilful desertion of spouse. A desertion of one's spouse with evil intent and malice; a desertion in disregard of the duty to one's spouse. 27 Am J1st H & W § 437. As a ground for divorce:—abandonment of one's spouse with an intent to terminate the marriage relation or an intent not to return. 24 Am J2d Div & S § 98.

For definition of term as it pertains to the refusal of sexual intercourse as grounds for divorce. Anno: 175 ALR 711.

wilful disobedience. Intentional disobedience by a free agent who knows what he is doing, although not necessarily acting with malice or evil intent. May v New York Motion Picture Co. 45 Cal App 396, 187 P 785.

wilful failure. See **wilful default.**

wilful injury. An injury produced by an act intended to have such effect. Parker v Pennsylvania Co. 134 Ind 673, 34 NE 504. An injury inflicted designedly and intentionally. Wunderlich v Franklin (CA5 Ala) 100 F2d 164. An injury accompanied by a design, purpose and intent to do wrong and to inflict the injury, or an injury inflicted by means of an act or omission with knowledge on the part of the wrongdoer that the injury would be the natural and probable result of such act or omission. Louisville & Nashville Railroad Co. v Anchors, 114 Ala 492, 499, 22 So 279.

See **wilful and malicious injury.**

wilfully. With a purpose or willingness to commit an act or to omit the performance of an act, irrespective of intent to violate the law or to injure another. Howe v Martin, 23 Okla 561, 102 P 128. Deliberately and with a specific purpose. Hartzel v United States, 322 US 680, 88 L Ed 1534, 64 S Ct 1233. Knowingly, obstinately, and persistently, but not necessarily maliciously. 34 Am J1st Mal § 2. A technical word in an indictment or information. 27 Am J1st Indict § 67. Implying a certain state of mind for the performance of an act proscribed by statute. Screws v United States, 325 US 91, 89 L Ed 1495, 65 S Ct 1031, 162 ALR 1330. Intentionally, deliberately, with a bad or evil purpose, contrary to known duty. State ex rel. Fletcher v Naumann, 213 Iowa 418, 239 NW 93, 81 ALR 483.

This word when used in a criminal statute generally means an act done with a bad purpose, or without justifiable excuse, or stubbornly, obstinately, perversely, and is also employed to characterize a thing done without ground for believing it is lawful, or conduct marked by careless disregard whether or not one has the right so to act. United States v Murdock, 290 US 389, 78 L Ed 381, 54 S Ct 223.

wilfully and knowingly. A term characterizing the offense of obstruction of highway.

Some courts hold that a person may be guilty of "wilfully and knowingly" obstructing a public road where he actively participates in the doing of the act which results in the obstruction, even though he does not know that the place obstructed is legally a public road, while others take the view that one cannot be deemed guilty of "wilfully" obstructing such a road where he acts under the bona fide belief that no public road exists at the place where the obstruction is placed. 25 Am J1st High § 326.

wilfully and maliciously. A technical word in an indictment or information. 27 Am J1st Indict § 67. See **maliciously; wilfully.**

wilfully and unlawfully. A technical word in an indictment or information. 27 Am J1st Indict § 67. See **unlawfully; wilfully.**

wilfully false. Fraudulent. Made with actual intent to mislead. 29 Am J Rev ed Ins § 721.

See **wilful misstatement.**

wilfully misapply. Not the equivalent of embezzle.

As the expression is used in an embezzlement statute making it an offense wilfully to misapply funds, the words have no settled technical meaning, such as the word "embezzle" has in the statutes or the words "steal, take, and carry away" have at common law, and they do not of themselves describe any offense. Batchelor v United States, 156 US 426, 429, 39 L Ed 478, 479, 15 S Ct 446.

wilful misconduct. Deliberate disobedience of the law, inclusive of acts of omission as well as acts of commission. The intentional doing, or omitting to do something, either with the knowledge that such act or omission is likely to result in harm or with a wanton and reckless disregard of the consequences. Gulf, M. & O. R. Co. v Freund (CA8 Mo) 183 F2d 1005, 21 ALR2d 729. Such conduct as manifests a disposition to perversity, and under such surrounding circumstances and existing conditions that the party doing the act or failing to act must be conscious from his knowledge of such circumstances and conditions that his conduct will in all common probability result in injury. Universal Concrete Pipe Co. v Bassett, 130 Ohio St 567, 200 NE 843, 119 ALR 646.

The expression means something different from and more than negligence, however gross. There must be actual knowledge, or that which in the law is esteemed to be the equivalent of actual knowledge, of the peril to be apprehended from the failure to act, coupled with the conscious failure to act to the end of averting injury. Helme v Great Western Milling Co. 13 Cal App 416, 185 P 510.

Wilful misconduct depends upon facts of the particular case and necessarily involves deliberate, intentional, or wanton conduct in doing or omitting to perform acts, with knowledge or appreciation of the fact on the part of the culpable person that danger is likely to result therefrom. Cowgill v Boock, 189 Or 282, 218 P2d 445, 19 ALR2d 405.

As to what constitutes wilful misconduct in reference to the application of statute respecting liability of motorist for injury to guest, see Anno: 136 ALR 1271.

See **serious and wilful misconduct.**

wilful misstatement. A material false statement voluntarily made, with knowledge of its falsity, although not necessarily with intent to deceive. Anno: 4 ALR 559.

See **wilfully false.**

wilful neglect of child. An act or omission by a parent in reference to the care and support of a child which is deliberate and intentional, not by accident or inadvertence. 39 Am J1st P & C § 107.

See **neglect of child.**

wilful negligence. A paradoxical expression, since "negligence" conveys the idea of inadvertence, but apparently signifying an act done or omitted in such reckless disregard of the security and safety of another as to imply bad faith. 52 Am J1st Torts § 23.

wilfulness. See **wilful.**

wilful refusal. A refusal that is both intentional and unreasonable. Vermilye v Postal Telegraph-Cable Co. 205 Mass 598, 91 NE 904.

A wife's continued and persistent refusal to have sexual intercourse with her husband unless he wore a contraceptive sheath does not entitle the husband to a decree of nullity on the ground of "wilful refusal to consummate the marriage," authorized by statute. Baxter v Baxter [1948] AC 274 [1947] 2 All Eng 886, 4 ALR2d 216.

wilful trespasser. One who trespasses with knowledge that he is a trespasser.

One who knowingly and wilfully encroaches or enters upon the land of another and takes his minerals without color or claim of right, or who dishonestly or in bad faith mines minerals of another and converts them to his own use, is a wilful trespasser; one who does so under color of right or in good faith by mistake is an innocent trespasser. Hughett v Caldwell County, 313 Ky 85, 230 SW2d 92, 21 ALR2d 373.

wilful violation. A deliberate and purposeful failure to comply with a statute. Anno: 97 L Ed 270.

See **wilful default.**

wilful voting. An expression which savors of illegality.

To vote wilfully when the voter knows that he is not qualified to vote, means to vote designedly or purposely, and a person votes thus only when he has no right to vote and knows that he has no right. State v Savre, 129 Iowa 122, 105 NW 387.

will. Volition; purpose; desire. An instrument by which a person makes a disposition of his property, to take effect after his decease. Barney v Hayes, 11 Mont 571, 29 P 282. An instrument executed by a competent person, in the manner prescribed by statute, whereby he makes a disposition of his property to take effect on and after his death, such disposition remaining ambulatory and revocable during his lifetime. A legal declaration of a man's intention, which he wills to be performed after his death; the just sentence of the testator's wishes concerning what he would have done after his death. 57 Am J1st Wills § 2.

The term includes every kind of testamentary act taking effect from the mind of the testator and manifested by an instrument in writing executed and attested in conformity to the statute. In fact, in some jurisdictions, there is a recognized privilege of nuncupation under which, subject to certain conditions and restrictions, a will may be made without the execution of a written instrument by the testator. 57 Am J1st Wills § 2.

See **bequest; devise; holographic will; joint will; legacy; mutual will; nuncupative will; oral will; reciprocal wills; seaman's will; soldier's will.**

will and wish. A precatory term creative of a trust in a proper case. Temple v Russel, 251 Mass 231, 146 NE 679, 49 ALR 1.

will contest. See **contest.**

willful. Another spelling of **wilful.**

William I. William the First, king of England from October 14th, 1066, until September 9th, 1087.

William II. William the Second, king of England from September 26th, 1087, until August 2nd, 1100.

William III. William the Third, king of England from February 13th, 1689, until March 8th, 1702.

William of Normandy. Same as **William I.**

Williams Case. A divorce case which established the rule that a decree of divorce entitled to full faith and credit, so far as it is a termination of the marriage, may be obtained upon constructive or substituted service of process upon a defendant who is not a resident of the state. Williams v North Carolina, 317 US 287, 87 L Ed 279, 63 S Ct 207, 14 ALR 1273.

William the Conqueror. The king of England from 1066 to 1087.

Same as **William I.**

willing customer. See **ready, able and willing buyer.**

willingly. Of one's own volition.

See **voluntarily.**

Wills Act. See **Statute of Wills.**

will see you paid. Usually a collateral rather than an original promise. Anno: 99 ALR 85.

Wilson Act. A federal statute relating to the liquor traffic, better known as the **Original Packages Act.** 30 Am J Rev ed Intox L § 45. An act of Congress providing that intoxicating liquors coming into a state should be as completely under the control of the state as if the liquor had been manufactured therein. Delamater v South Dakota, 205 US 93, 51 L Ed 724, 27 S Ct 447. A federal statute of August

27, 1894, supplementing the Sherman Anti-Trust Act, being directed against monopolies. 36 Am J1st Monop etc § 141.

Winchester bushel. A measure of volume established in England in 1701, containing 2,150.42 cubic inches, the same as the present standard bushel in the United States.

winding up (wīn'ding up). The dissolution of a corporation or partnership.
See **dissolution; liquidation.**

windmill. A device whereby force of the wind is captured and placed to use.

window envelope. A common form of envelope used in the transmission of letters by mail, a rectangular bit of the front being of transparent material, so that the address typed on the letter enclosed shows through, serving thereby as an address for the envelope.

window peeking. See **Peeking Tom.**

windows. See **ancient windows; light, air, and view.**

window tax. An English tax levied on the windows of buildings in 1696.

windshakes. Fallen apples. Separations appearing between the rings shown in log or timber, probably caused by the stress of violent winds during growth of the tree.

windshield. Any means of protection against the wind. A transparent screen, usually of glass, in the front of an automobile or other motor vehicle, protecting the driver and occupants of the vehicle against the force of the wind, also against dust, dirt, rain, snow, etc. blown by the wind.

windstorm. A violent storm characterized by the vehemence of the wind and its sudden changes.

In order to amount to a windstorm, a movement of air need not have either the cyclonic or the whirling features which usually accompany tornadoes or cyclones, but it must assume the aspect of a storm —that is, an outburst of tumultuous force. Anno: 126 ALR 708, s. 166 ALR 381; 29A Am J Rev ed Ins § 1329.

windstorm insurance. Insurance covering property against loss or damage by hurricane, tornado, cyclone, or wind of tumultuous force or unusual violence. 29A Am J Rev ed Ins § 1329. Protection under extended coverage provisions of an automobile insurance policy. 7 Am J2d Auto Ins § 77.

windy shots. A technical term for blasts of explosive which send rocks and debris flying through the air. 31 Am J2d Explos § 36.

wine. A vinous alcoholic beverage. 30 Am J Rev ed Intox L § 13. A drinkable vinous beverage containing more than one per cent, by volume, of alcohol. People v Mueller, 168 Cal 526, 528, 143 P 750.

wine gallon. At least one proof gallon. 21 Am J2d Cust D § 86.
See **proof gallon.**

wing fence. A railroad fence so placed in reference to the cattle guard at a railroad crossing as to prevent cattle or other livestock from straying onto the right of way. McKee v Chicago R.I. & P. R. Co. 83 Iowa 616, 50 NW 209.

winterize. To prepare an automobile or other motor vehicle for use during the cold season, paying special attention to the type of oil or grease most suitable for operation in severely cold weather.

winze (winz). A shaft in a mine, leading from one level to another.

wire. Noun: Metal drawn and shaped in a manufacturing process into a long string having a thickness variable with the use to be made of the product. A telegram. Verb: To install wires, particularly electric wires. To send a telegram.
See **electric line; live wire.**

wireless. Communication by radio. Fisher's Blend Station v State Tax Com. 297 US 650, 80 L Ed 956, 56 S Ct 608; Marconi Wireless Tel. Co. v Com. 218 Mass 558, 106 NE 310, revd in part on other grounds 246 US 147, 62 L Ed 632, 38 S Ct 295.

wiretapping. Intercepting a telephone conversation or a telegraph message by tapping the line of communication, that is, connecting a receiving instrument to the line. 29 Am J2d Ev §§ 428 et seq.; 41 Am J1st Priv § 29; 52 Am J1st Teleg & T § 65.

wish. To desire. In some instances, to order or command. Warner v Burlington Fed. Sav. & L. Asso. 168 ALR 1265, 1272, 114 Vt 463, 49 A2d 93.

For discussion of the effect of the word in creating a precatory trust, see Anno: 49 ALR 84.

wish and desire. A precatory term creative of a trust in a proper case. Anno: 49 ALR 91.

wista. The one-half of a hide of land.
See **hide.**

wit. Noun: In a broad sense, mental faculty. In the usual sense, the ability to make clever remarks in speech or written discourse. An abbreviation of the word "witness," sometimes used in the attestation of a deed. Richbourg v Rose, 53 Fla 173, 44 So 69. Verb: To know; to learn by taking notice of something.
See **to wit.**

witan (wit'an). The king's council.

witchcraft. A supernatural phenomenon. Henderson v Jackson, 138 Iowa 326, 111 NW 821. Sorcery. An offense which at one time carried the penalty of being burnt at the stake.

In such a prosecution in 1665, Sir Matthew Hale charged the jury that he made no doubt at all there were such creatures as witches, first, because "the Scriptures had affirmed as much; secondly, the wisdom of all nations had provided laws against such persons." 6 How St Tr 700.

The most notable prosecutions for witchcraft in America were those at Salem, in what was then the Colony of Massachusetts, in 1692.

wite (wīt). (Anglo-Saxon.) A penalty or punishment for a criminal offense.

witenagemote (wit'e-na-ge-mōt"). Sometimes written "wittena-gemote," and also known as "michelsynoth," and "michelgemote,"—the meeting of wise men, the great council, the great meeting.

It was the ancient assembly of the Saxon witans, great and wise men, to aid and advise the king. It was the forerunner of the English parliament. See 1 Bl Comm 147, et seq.

with. Close or near to. In the company of. In addition to.

with all faults. A clause in a contract of sale indicating that the article is taken by the purchaser as it stands. 37 Am J2d Fraud § 388.

with all ways. An expression in a deed from which an easement or easements of way may be implied. Anno: 34 ALR 240.

with child. Pregnant. Anno: 46 ALR2d 1401, § 7[a].

with consent. Having the consent of, as in respect of the "power" by and with the consent of the Senate to make treaties .... US Const Art 2 § 2 cl 2.

with customary dispatch. Within the period normally required for accomplishment of a specific undertaking. Pedersen v Eugster & Co. (DC La) 14 F 422.

withdrawal fee. A fee imposed against a borrowing member of a building and loan association upon his termination of membership. Georgia State Bldg. & Loan Asso. v Grant, 82 Miss 424, 34 So 84.

withdrawal of appearance. The voluntary vacation of an appearance, usually to be had only by leave of court, sometimes only for good cause shown. 5 Am J2d Appear § 36.

withdrawal of bid. The recalling of a bid made in the course of the letting of a public contract. 43 Am J1st Pub Wks § 62.

withdrawal of case from jury. See **taking case from jury.**

withdrawal of charges. See **nolle prosequi.**

withdrawal of deposit. Closing a bank account by taking the fund on deposit.

withdrawal of juror. A means of obtaining a continuance or postponement of a trial after the jury are impaneled and sworn, where some necessity therefor in the furtherance of justice exists. The remedy for a mistrial. 53 Am J1st Trial § 966.

withdrawal of membership. The termination of a membership in a building and loan association before the stock of the member has matured, accompanied by the apportionment to the member of his share of the assets of the association as of the time of withdrawal. 13 Am J2d B & L Assoc § 30. See **withdrawal fee.**

withdrawal of pleading. The recalling by a party of statements made by him in his pleading or of the entire pleading as the exigencies of the case require, usually done by way of correcting mistakes. 41 Am J1st Pl § 318.

withdrawal of public land. The act of Congress or the President, as authorized by Congress, in declaring certain public land not open to settlement, location, sale, or entry. 42 Am J1st Pub L § 12.

withdrawal of stipulation. The recall of a stipulation filed in an action by the party who filed it, with the consent of the adverse party or by leave of court upon cause shown. 50 Am J1st Stip § 11.

withdrawal of subscription. The revocation of a subscription to corporate stock, made by notice to the person in charge of the organization of the corporation, prior to incorporation. Anno: 101 ALR 232.

withdrawal value. The amount to which a member of a building and loan association is entitled upon his withdrawal from the association before his shares have reached maturity value. 13 Am J2d B & L Assoc § 30.

withernam. See **in withernam.**

with exchange. See **stipulation for exchange.**

with force and arms. Technical words used in indictments for offenses amounting to an actual disturbance of the peace. 27 Am J1st Indict § 67.

withhold. To keep something from another. To retain in one's possession that which belongs to or is claimed by another. Ballew v United States, 160 US 187, 194, 40 L Ed 388, 392, 16 S Ct 263.

Withhold implies rather a temporary suspension, than a total and final denial or rejection; as to withhold compensation. United States v Dumas, 149 US 278, 284, 37 L Ed 734, 736, 13 S Ct 872.

withholding pension money. A criminal offense by an agent or attorney for a pensioner who has received pension money to which the latter is immediately entitled. 40 Am J1st Pens § 48.

withholding tax. A method of implementing the pay-as-you-go system of paying income tax on wages and salaries, employers being required to withhold a portion of each salary or wage payment due an employee and turn it over to the government, the employee taking credit for the various amounts withheld in his tax return. The retention by the person making distribution of a decedent's estate of the death duties payable on the specific shares. People v Union Trust Co. 255 Ill 168, 99 NE 377, error dismd 234 US 748, 58 L Ed 1575, 34 S Ct 673; Re Walker, 184 Minn 164, 238 NW 58, 76 ALR 1450.

within. Inclusive of territory. Not going beyond or exceeding the limits prescribed. Anno: 30 ALR 1135. Inclusive of a period of time.

See **from and after; within a year.**

within a motor vehicle. Inside the vehicle in a place ordinarily occupied by one driving or riding. Anno: 39 ALR2d 961.

within a year. A period of 365 days, not a calendar year from January to January. Paetz v State, 129 Wis 174, 107 NW 1090 (phrase in statute providing for increased punishment where defendant has two convictions).

See **infra annum clause.**

within house. See **house confinement clause.**

with interest. Bearing interest.

Where any written instrument provides for the payment of money "with interest," without specifying the rate, the term implies that the amount to be paid will draw interest at the statutory rate. See O'Brien v Young, 95 NY 428.

with interest annually. The equivalent of a promise to pay the interest annually. Anno: 10 ALR 1004.

within the premises. On the premises. At any point on the premises.

For the meaning of the phrase as it pertains to representations, warranties, or conditions in reference to a watchman on premises covered by an insurance policy, see Anno: 87 ALR 1117.

within the radius. Including all territory falling within the measured circle. Sacks v Legg, 219 Ill App 144.

with liberty. See **liberty of port.**

with malice aforethought. A technical word in an indictment, indicating premeditated design. 27 Am J1st Indict § 67. Essentially, as an element of murder, the same as malice, a wicked and corrupt disregard of the life and safety of another. 26 Am J1st Homi § 40.

In the term "malice aforethought," the word aforethought describes, not the intent to take life, but the malice. State v Fiske, 63 Conn 388, 391, 28 A 572.

without. On the outside. Beyond. Lacking.

without compensation. See **taking for public use.**

without day. Without designation of day, as in an **adjournment sine die.**

without deduction. A provision against impairment of gift by deduction which might otherwise be made.

As to definition of phrase in reference to relief of bequest of the burden of tax, see Anno: 51 ALR 466.

without defalcation. An expression, sometimes written "without offset," in an instrument for the payment of money, intended to preclude a setoff against the amount payable under the terms of the instrument. Anno: 79 ALR 126; 98 ALR 606; 20 Am J2d Countcl § 29. A phrase formerly used in promissory notes to confer or emphasize negotiability and to cut off defenses between the original parties as against holders in due course. 11 Am J2d B & N § 198.

without due process of law. See **due process of law.**

without grace. See **days of grace.**

without her consent. See **rape.**

without impeachment of waste. A phrase employed in an instrument creating a tenancy for the purpose of relieving the tenant from acts or conduct otherwise constituting waste, provided such acts or conduct are not unjust, unconscientious, malicious or wanton. 56 Am J1st Waste §§ 7, 8.

without issue. See **die without issue.**

without justification. See **without legal cause.**

without legal cause. The equivalent of without justification.

The use of the phrase in a pleading has been held not objectionable as constituting a mere conclusion of law. It was also held that the pleader was not required to elaborate the phrase. Freeman v Macon Gas Light & Water Co. 126 Ga 843, 56 SE 61.

without liability for waste. See **without impeachment of waste.**

without living heirs of the body. A phrase in a will employed to import a definite failure of issue. Glover v Condell, 163 Ill 566, 45 NE 173.

See **heirs of the body.**

without notice. See **bona fide holder for value without notice; bona fide purchaser.**

without offset. Same as **without defalcation.**

without prejudice. A judicial act without effect as a final determination or res judicata. United States ex rel. Almeida v Baldi (CA3 Pa) 195 F2d 815, 33 ALR2d 1407; Ogens v Northern Industrial Chemical Co. 304 Mass 401, 24 NE2d 1, 126 ALR 280.

The term imports that no right or remedy of the parties is affected. The use of the phrase simply shows that there has been no decision of the case upon the merits, and prevents the defendant from setting up the defense of res adjudicata. Olson v Coalfield School Dist. 54 ND 657, 661, 210 NW 180, 181.

See **dismissal without prejudice.**

without protest. See **waiver of protest.**

without receiving value. A phrase having reference to accommodation paper, meaning "without receiving value for the instrument," not "without receiving consideration for lending one's name." 11 Am J2d B & N § 121.

without recourse. A form of qualified indorsement, exonerating the indorser from liability as such. Bank of St. Albans v Gilliland (NY) 23 Wend 311. Words used or directly implied by an assignor to negative any guaranty of the assigned obligation. 6 Am J2d Assign § 107.

without recourse to me. Same as **without recourse.**

without reserve. A term characterizing an auction sale conducted without right on the part of the owner of the property to withdraw goods from the sale or to bid them in by himself or through another. Anno: 37 ALR2d 1054; 7 Am J2d Auct § 18.

without stint (stint). Without limit or restriction on number or amount.

without the state. Indicating absence from the state or residence outside the state, dependent upon the context of the entire statute or instrument.

A debtor is not "without the state," within the meaning of a statute of limitations, where, being a citizen of, domiciled, and resident within the state, with his family, he temporarily for business purposes, goes to another state and remains there for several months at a time on different occasions. Sage v Hawley, 16 Conn 106.

without this, that. Words employed in an answer by way of a special traverse.

See **absque hoc; special traverse.**

without waiver or prejudice. A phrase negativing admission of liability.

The expression has among both lawyers and business men a well-understood value, and imports into any writing in which it appears that the parties have agreed that, as between themselves the receipt of the money by one, and its payment by the other, shall not, because of the facts of the receipt and payment, have any legal effect upon the rights of the parties in the premises; that such rights will be as open to settlement by negotiation or legal controversy as if the money had not been turned over by the one to the other. Genet v President etc. of Delaware & Hudson Canal Co. 170 NY 278, 63 NE 350

with prejudice. The effect of a final adjudication as res judicata.

See **dismissal with prejudice.**

with quick child. See **quick with child.**

with strong hand. With force or violence. Characterizing a violent entry upon real property, an entry with weapons or with menace of life or limb. 35 Am J2d Forc E & D § 4.

with the appurtenances. Including the appurtenances; a phrase often used in deeds where unnecessary. See Morgan v Mason, 20 Ohio 401.

with the mainour. With the goods in hand.

A thief was said to be taken with the mainour when taken with the stolen goods upon him, in manu, in his hand. When so taken, the thief could be arraigned and tried without being first indicted. This practice was discontinued under Edward the Third, in England, but in Scotland it was followed in Blackstone's time. See 4 Bl Comm 307.

with the will annexed. See **administrator with the will annexed.**

witness. Verb: To see or observe. To act as an observer for the purpose of attesting. Noun: One who has observed so as to be able to give an account of something. An individual who has knowledge of a fact or occurrence sufficient to testify in respect to it. Re Losee, 13 Misc 299, 34 NYS 1120. In the usual application of the word in law, one who tes-

WITNESS [1375] WORDS

tifies in a cause or gives evidence before a judicial tribunal. A person summoned by subpoena or otherwise to testify in a case. Also, a person called to be present at some transaction so as to be able to attest to its having taken place 58 Am J1st Witn § 2.

A person who files an income tax return under oath, disclosing the commission of a crime, is a witness within the meaning of the Fifth Amendment to the Federal Constitution providing that no one shall in any criminal case be compelled to be a witness against himself. See Sullivan v United States (CA4 SC) 15 F2d 809, 812.

witness against himself. See **self-incrimination.**

witness fees. Fees paid witnesses for their attendance at court. Commonly included as taxable costs. 20 Am J2d Costs § 53.

witnessing part. See **attestation clause.**

witness my hand. A formal clause, indicating a signature. Salazar v Taylor, 18 Colo 538.

witness my hand and seal. A formal clause indicating a signature and the seal of the person thus signing. Salazar v Taylor, 18 Colo 538.

witness to instrument. See **attesting witness.**

witness whereof. See **in witness whereof.**

witten-gemote. Same as **witenagemote.**

wittingly. By design or forethought, not by accident.

W.O. Abbreviation of warrant officer.

wolf. A wild animal; a carnivorous mammal, most closely resembling the dog. A slang term for a man who seeks to prey upon women.

wolf's head (wŭlfs hed). An outlaw.

woman. An adult female human being. God's gift.

woman chaser. A slang term for a man who is overly interested in women, especially for sexual relations.

Women in the Air Force. An integral part of the Air Force military personnel.

Women's Army Corps. A component of the Army, organized and maintained for the purpose of making available to the service women volunteers, trained in noncombat occupational skills.

Women's Christian Temperance Union. An organization active in the cause of temperance and the strict control, if not outright prohibition, of traffic in intoxicating liquors.

women's suffrage. The right of women to vote. The political and civil right granted by law to women, permitting them to participate in the government, to take part in the choice of officers, or in the decision of public questions, and to vote at elections held for those purposes. Gougar v Timberlake, 148 Ind 38, 40, 46 NE 339.

women's suffrage amendment. The Nineteenth Amendment to the Constitution of the United States, declaring that the right of citizens of the United States to vote shall not be denied or abridged by the United States or by any state on account of sex.

wood alcohol. Same as **methyl alcohol.**

wood-corn (wŭd'kôrn). Grain which was paid for the liberty of picking up wood.

wood-geld (wŭd'geld). A payment which was made for the privilege of taking wood from a forest.

wood is to be intended of that which is cut down. An ancient maxim. Dexter v Taber (NY) 12 Johns 239.

wood leave. A license to go upon premises, cut down standing trees, and remove them from the premises.

wood measure. The measurement of standing timber, that is ascertaining the circumference, without including the bark. Craddock Mfg. Co. v Faison, 138 Va 665, 123 SE 535, 39 ALR 1309.

See **cord; log measure; lumber measure.**

wood pulp. The product of grinding and wetting wood of certain trees, used in the manufacture of certain kinds of paper, also in the production of methyl alcohol.

woods. A forest.

woodsrider. One whose vocation or avocation includes riding through the woods or forest.

Wood-street Compter. The name which was given to an ancient London prison.

woodwork. Articles made of wood. The trim in a house around doors and windows, and wainscotting.

wool-sack (wŭl'sak). A name given to the seat of the lord chancellor in the house of lords.

wool-sorter's disease. A disease named for its one-time prevalence among people handling wool and hides. Anno: 20 ALR 7.

The disease is usually caused by contact with diseased or putrid animal matter. A blister-like swelling develops into a pustule. Great swelling and pustular infection of glands follow. Prostration ensues and the patient usually dies within from five to eight days. Stedman v United States Mut. Acci. Asso. 123 NY 304, 25 NE 399.

word. Letters in combination, having meaning as written or in sound, and conveying thought as a unit of language. "A word is not a crystal, transparent and unchanged, it is the skin of a living thought and may vary greatly in color and content according to the circumstances and the time in which it is used." Holmes, J., in Towne v Eisner, 245 US 418, 425, 62 L Ed 372, 38 S Ct 158.

words actionable per quod. See **libelous per quod; slanderous per quod.**

words actionable per se. See **libelous per se; slanderous per se.**

words of art. Technical words; terms inexpressive to others which have a meaning to members of a particular profession, line of work, or study.

words of censure. See **censure.**

words of condition. See **condition; words of limitation.**

words of covenant. See **covenant.**

words of demise (dẹ-mīz'). Words in a lease or agreement whereby the lessor undertakes to transfer and vest the possession in the lessee forthwith.

The fact that the actual term of the lease is to begin at a later date does not prevent the words from being words of demise, for there may be a present demise to commence in futuro. See Shaw v Farnsworth, 108 Mass 357, 360.

words of inheritance. Words of limitation indicating the character of an estate granted or devised. Words in the habendum of a deed which set forth the estate to be held and enjoyed by the grantee. 23 Am J2d Deeds § 38. Words necessary in the grant of an easement in order to make it a perpetual interest.

Chappell v New York, New Haven & Hartford R. Co. 62 Conn 195, 24 A 997.
See **estate of inheritance**.

words of limitation. Words appearing in a grant or devise which indicate the character of the estate created. Words which describe the extent or quality of the estate conveyed to the first taker. 28 Am J2d Est § 102. Words used in an instrument or devise creating an estate in real property which circumscribe the continuance of the estate. Summit v Yount, 109 Ind 506, 9 NE 582.

words of negotiability. Words in an instrument for the payment of money, such as "to order," "to bearer," or the equivalent in meaning, which render the instrument negotiable or have the effect, at least, of signs of negotiability. 11 Am J2d B & N § 105.

words of obloquy. See **obloquy**.

words of procreation (ov prō-krē-ā'shon). Words essential to the creation of an estate-tail; as, an estate to A "and the heirs of his body."

words of purchase. Such words, used in a will or conveyance of real property, as give an estate originally, to the heirs, and not through the medium of, or by descent from, the ancestor. Ball v Payne, 27 Va (6 Rand) 73, 75. Words which describe any means of acquiring an estate other than by descent, so that persons who are to take an estate by that means are themselves to become the root of a new inheritance or the stock of a new descent. 28 Am J2d Est § 102.

words of purchase or of limitation. The distinction between marking out the bounds of an estate conveyed and describing the means of acquiring an estate. 28 Am J2d Est § 102.

words of qualification. See **qualification**.

words of reproach. See **reproach**.

work. Noun: Employment. Any form of physical or mental exertion, or both combined, for the attainment of some object other than recreation or amusement. 31 Am J Rev ed Lab § 1. Physical or mental exertion, whether burdensome or not, controlled or required by an employer and pursued necessarily and primarily for his benefit and the benefit of his business. 31 Am J Rev ed Lab § 626. Effort directed to an end. Commonwealth v Griffith, 204 Mass 18, 90 NE 394 (holding the services of an actor to be work). Verb: To labor. To perform services. To persuade, particularly in the sense of persuasion for the purpose of perpetrating a fraud. Palmerlee v Nottage, 119 Minn 351, 138 NW 312.
See **availability for work**; **commencement of work**; **inability to work**; **labor**; **stoppage of work**.

work and labor. See **implied contract**.

work animal. An animal, such as a horse, mule, or ox, kept for pulling the plow or pulling loads, carriages or loaded vehicles on the highway, especially an animal by which one earns a living or which is used in a business. 31 Am J2d Exemp § 61.
See **work horse**.

workaway (wėrk'awā). One carried on a train or ship in return for his services, that is, a person working his way.

work beast. Same as **work animal**.

workday. A day for work, as distinguished from a Sunday or holiday. A day's work.
See **day's work**; **hours of labor**; **working days**.

worker. One who works whether at physical labor or labor which requires mental as well as physical effort. 31 Am J Rev ed Lab § 1.

work float. A raft used in the performance of work on water, such as raising sunken logs or boats.

work horse. A horse employed to perform work, as distinguished from one kept solely for pleasure. Tishomingo Sav. Institute v Young, 87 Miss 473, 40 So 9. A horse used in farming, in pulling a carriage, or in hauling heavy loads. A horse which performs the common work required of it on the owner's premises or in the owner's business or trade. Not inclusive of a horse kept for racing or one bought as a speculation. 31 Am J2d Exemp § 70. Slang for a person who works long hours or at heavy labor.

workhouse. A municipal prison. Farmer v St. Paul, 65 Minn 176, 67 NW 990. A place of imprisonment under sentence for crime. People v Stavrakas, 335 Ill 570, 167 NE 852. A place or prison where persons convicted of minor offenses and misdemeanors may be confined and kept at labor. 41 Am J1st Pris & P § 2.

working capital. A fund kept on hand by a corporation for the purpose of paying current obligations and keeping its credit good, without awaiting the collecting of its revenues. 43 Am J1st Pub Util § 125. In a broader and less technical sense, capital actually employed in a business.

working claim. Performing acts for the purpose of making a mining claim productive, such as developing or extracting an ore body after it has been discovered. Cole v Ralph, 252 US 286, 307, 64 L Ed 567, 582, 40 S Ct 321.

working conditions. The condition of the premises and facilities for the labor force at a place of employment.

working days. The days as they succeed each other, exclusive of Sundays and holidays. For the purposes of loading a ship, all days except Sundays and holidays. Pedersen v. Eugster & Co. (DC La) 14 F 422, 423.
See **day's work**; **hours of labor**.

working face. That place in a mine at which the coal or ore is extracted from the stratum in which it is found.

working hours. See **day's work**; **hours of labor**; **Hours of Service Act**.

working interest. The production of an oil well upon which royalty payable under a lease is computed. 24 Am J1st Gas & O § 87.

working lay days. An expression found in a provision of charter parties relative to the period of time during which the charterer may detain the vessel for loading or unloading, making it clear that Sundays and holidays are to be excluded in the computation. Brooks v Minturn, 1 Cal 481, 483.

working place. The place wherein the operations of an employer are carried on. 35 Am J1st M & S § 424.
See **working conditions**.

working place of miners. A room or other place in a coal mine in which the work of excavation is being carried on and which is immediately affected by such operation. 35 Am J1st M & S § 215.

working time. The potential of earnings in employment. Time spent at physical or mental exertion on behalf of the employer; for some purposes, dependent upon the nature of the employment, even wait-

ing time, sleeping time, travel time, lunch time, etc. 31 Am J Rev ed Lab §§ 626 et seq.
See **day's work; hours of labor; working days.**

workman. A working man. A man employed for wages in labor, whether in tilling the soil or manufacturing, whether an artificer or common laborer. Anno: 129 ALR 990. Any person who occupies the status of servant under the law of master and servant. One engaged under a contract of employment between him and an alleged employer. 58 Am J1st Workm Comp § 132. A term not intended to embrace every person of whatever rank in the service of an employer, but used in a restrictive sense, intended to establish a classification of those in service on the basis of the character of work ordinarily connoted by the term. 58 Am J1st Workm Comp § 91.

This term as used in constitutional and charter provisions has generally been construed as not including a public officer. Anno: 5 ALR2d 416.

In general parlance, the word workman perhaps connotes a grade inferior to that of an "employee," but no such distinction appears in the workmen's compensation statutes. A superintendent has been held to be included in the comprehensive sense of such a statute, and likewise a professional football player. 58 Am J1st Workm Comp § 133.

workmanlike manner. The customary way of doing the work in the vicinity of the place where the work is to be done. Shores Lumber Co. v Stitt, 102 Wis 450, 456, 78 NW 562. A manner of work adequate for the performance undertaken. 17 Am J2d Contr § 371.

workmanlike performance. The performance of a contract with the use of the degree of diligence, attention, and skill adequate for the performance of the particular undertaking. 17 Am J2d Contr § 371.

workmanship. The character of work as demonstrated by the completed article or job. Anno: 34 ALR 544.

workmen's compensation. A general and comprehensive term applied to and embracing those laws providing for compensation for loss resulting from the injury, disablement, or death of workmen through industrial accident, casualty, or disease, such laws possessing the common feature or characteristic of providing such compensation otherwise than on the basis of tort liability and in accordance with a definite schedule based generally upon the loss or impairment of the workmen's wage-earning power. Lewis & Clark County v Industrial Acci. Board, 52 Mont 6, 155 P 268. The payment made under such a law to a disabled workman or the spouse, children, or representatives of a deceased workman.

workmen's compensation acts. Statutes which provide for the payment of compensation to an employee injured in his employment or, in case of his death, to his dependents, eliminating common-law defenses such as assumption of risk, contributory negligence, and negligence of fellow servant, and provide a system for the determination of the amount of compensation to be paid. 58 Am J1st Workm Comp § 2.

workmen's compensation commission. A special agency established by statute for the administration of the provisions of a workmen's compensation act. 58 Am J1st Workm Comp § 370.

work of art. See **art.**

work of necessity. Work coming within an exception to a Sunday observance law as required under an emergency which will not reasonably admit of delay or in satisfaction of a need so pressing in its nature as to rescue the act performed from the imputation of a wilful desecration of a day made sacred for certain purposes in morals as well as in law. Work needful and desirable, even though not physically and absolutely necessary. 50 Am J1st Sun & H § 16.

work-product doctrine. The principle that material collected and prepared for a case by counsel is not subject to disclosure by way of discovery at the instance of the party adverse to counsel's client. 23 Am J2d Dep § 195.

work relief. Relieving the needs of the poor by providing jobs for them or for the heads of families. 41 Am J1st Poor L § 4.

works. An establishment for manufacturing, or for performing industrial labor of any sort. Elliott v Payne, 293 Mo 581, 239 SW 851, 23 ALR 706, 712. An industrial plant. A factory. The parts of a machine.
See **working place.**

worksheet. A sheet whereon there appears the calculations and rough notes from which an account is prepared or an income tax return made out for filing. 1 Am J2d Accts § 12. A plan for the performance of a particular job or undertaking.

workshop. A small factory. A repair shop. Anno: 83 ALR 1045. Any place where goods or products are manufactured or repaired, cleaned or sorted, in whole or in part, for sale or for wages. Ritchie v People, 155 Ill 98, 40 NE 454 (statutory definition).

workshop of fraud. A graphic expression for the background of a fraudulent enterprise. The Friendship (US) 3 Wheat 12, 4 L Ed 322.

workshop of justice. The judicial system. A court.
See **officina justitiae.**

workshop of nations. Any project typified by international co-operation.

works of charity. Acts of a charitable nature. Bucher v Cheshire R. Co. 125 US 555, 31 L Ed 795, 8 S Ct 974. Covering everything morally fit and proper to be done on Sunday, under the particular circumstances of the case. 50 Am J1st Sun & H § 19.

works of internal improvement. Those enterprises which ordinarily might in human experience be expected to be undertaken for profit or benefit to the property interests of private promoters, as distinguished from those things which primarily and preponderantly merely facilitate the essential functions of government. State v Froehlich, 115 Wis 32, 91 NW 115.

The term, as used in a constitutional provision forbidding the state to engage in such works, is not to be construed as limited only to channels of trade and commerce, such as canals, turnpikes, railroads, and the like, although, in order to come within this provision, the improvement must be of a more or less fixed and permanent character. State ex rel. Wilkinson v Murphy, 237 Ala 332, 186 So 487, 121 ALR 283.
See **internal improvement.**

works of necessity. See **work of necessity.**

Works Progress Administration. A federal agency of the period of the Great Depression, the primary purpose of which was to give employment to needy persons upon work designated by the agency. 41 Am J1st Poor L § 33.

work stoppage. See **stoppage of work.**

work time. See **working time.**

work week. See **hours of labor.**

World Bank. A bank, otherwise known as the International Bank for Reconstruction and Development, having an official existence since Dec. 27, 1945, the primary purpose of which is to assist the economic development of member countries by facilitating investment of capital for productive purposes, and thereby promote growth of international trade and improvement of standards of living.

worldly. Concerned with the enjoyments of this present existence; secular, not religious, spiritual, or holy. Commonwealth ex rel. Woodruff v American Baseball Club, 290 Pa 136, 138 A 497, 53 ALR 1027. Of or pertaining to the world or the present state of existence; temporal; earthly. Devoted to, interested in, or connected with this present life, and its cares, advantages, or pleasures, to the exclusion of those of a future life. Anderson v Gibson, 116 Ohio St 684, 157 NE 377, 54 ALR 92.

worldly goods. Goods to be enjoyed by one in his present state of existence. That property which one must leave behind when he departs this life. Subject to construction as including both real and personal property of a testator. 57 Am J1st Wills § 1343.

World Peace Foundation. An organization having the purpose of promoting and maintaining world peace. Parkhurst v Treasurer, 228 Mass 196, 117 NE 39.

World War Veteran. See **veteran.**

worm fence. Another term for **rail fence.**

worry. See **mental anguish.**

worrying animals. The act of a dog in chasing, running after, and barking at animals. Bunn v Shaw, 3 NJ 195, 69 A2d 576, 15 ALR2d 574.

worship. Intense admiration. An expression of reverence or devotion for a deity. The act of paying honors to the Supreme Being; religious reverence and homage; adoration paid to God, or a Being viewed as God. Hamsher v Hamsher, 132 Ill 273, 23 NE 1123.
"We know of no technical definition of the word by any court. It includes prayer, praise, thanksgiving. In the ordinary church meeting the congregation is regarded as engaged in religious worship while listening to the sermon, reading the Holy Scriptures or hearing them read, or engaged in the singing. Devotional religious exercises constitute worship. Prayer is a chief part of the worship. Prayer is always worship. Reading the Bible and singing may be worship." People ex rel. Ring v Board of Education, 245 Ill 334, 92 NE 251.

See **public worship; religious worship.**

worsted (wus'ted). A specific kind of wool. Long-staple wool. Seeberger v Cahn, 137 US 95, 34 L Ed 599, 11 S Ct 28. Cloth made from long-staple wool.

wort (wert). The mixture of malt, hops, and water from which beer is produced.

worth. Monetary value. Importance. Merit.
"Few philologists get on juries. We believe that only a philologist would appreciate the difference between the word compensation and the word price or worth as used in instructions to be considered by juries in assessing damages." Herb v Hallowell, 304 Pa 128, 154 A 582, 85 ALR 1004.

worthier title rule. The early rule of the common law that an heir may not take by devise where he may take the same title by descent, title by descent being regarded as the worthier and better title. 23 Am J2d Desc & D § 3. A rule sometimes advanced as the rationale of the common-law rule against remainders to the heirs of the grantor. 28 Am J2d Est § 175.
The inter vivos branch of the doctrine of worthier title, adopted in nearly all American jurisdictions which have had occasion to consider it, favors a reversion in the grantor rather than a remainder to his heirs. McKenna v Seattle First Nat. Bank, 35 Wash 2d 662, 214 P2d 664, 16 ALR2d 679.

worthiest of blood. The theory of the rule of primogeniture.
See **primogeniture.**

worthless. Deprived of worth; of no value or use. Spring City Foundry Co. v Commissioner, 292 US 182, 78 L Ed 1200, 54 S Ct 644.

worthless check. A check payment of which has been refused for want of funds on deposit to the credit of the drawer.

worthless draft. A dishonored draft.

worthless stock. Stock in a corporation, the assets of which, properly valued, are less than its liabilities. Foster v Commissioner (CA1) 112 F2d 109.

worthy. Having worth or merit. Deserving of honor or respect.
See **law worthy; oathworthy.**

worthy cause or institution. A cause or institution of a charitable character. Re Funk, 353 Pa 321, 45 A2d 67, 163 ALR 780.

wound. A severance or breakage of the skin. Anno: 16 ALR 958, s. 58 ALR 1320. Any abrasion, breach or rupture of the skin or mucous membrane of the body, whereby animal venom or virus, or some impure, poisonous, or irritating matter, may gain entrance to the underlying tissues and contaminate the blood. Fidelity and Casualty Co. v Thompson (CA8 Colo) 154 F 484, 487. An injury to the body of a person or animal, especially one caused by violence, by which the continuity of the covering, as skin, mucous membrane, or conjunctivea, is broken. Anno: 117 ALR 767. A lesion of the body. A hurt, loss, or injury, or any morbid change in the structure of organs or parts of the body. 29A Am J Rev ed Ins § 1173. As the term appears in an application for life insurance:—an injury to the body causing an impairment of health or strength, or rendering the person more liable to contract disease, or less able to resist its effects. Bancroft v Home Beneficial Asso. 120 NY 14, 23 NE 997.
The Supreme Court of Illinois defines the word as meaning a lesion of the body and defines lesion as a hurt, loss, or injury. Hence, that court's definition excludes the necessity of a breaking or cutting of the skin and is broad enough to include an injury to the subcutaneous tissue and to the skin, which has resulted from carbon monoxide poisoning and is revealed by scarlet blotches. Warbende v Prudential Ins. Co. (CA7 Ill) 97 F2d 749.
Ordinarily, whether or not a particular injury constitutes a wound, within the meaning of statutes relating to wounding with intent to maim, seems to depend upon whether there is a complete sever-

ance or breakage of the skin. From an early date, the word wound in such a statute has been construed to mean that there must be a breaking of the skin. This breaking must consist in the separation of the whole skin; a separation of the cuticle or upper skin only, or the fact that one's skin is bruised where struck by a stick, is not sufficient. Similarly, a scratch does not constitute a wound within the provisions of a maiming statute. A disruption or breaking of the internal skin or membrane, however, as that within the mouth or the membrane lining the urethra, will suffice. 36 Am J1st May § 5.

wounded feelings. Distress from insults, indignity, or humiliation. 22 Am J2d Damg § 237.

wounding. Inflicting a wound.
See **wound.**

W.P.A. Abbreviation of Works Progress Administration.

wreck. Verb: To tear down. To drive a vehicle or handle an object in such manner as to destroy or damage it greatly. To disorganize or cause serious injury to anything. Mochel v Iowa State Traveling Men's Asso. 203 Iowa 623, 213 NW 259, 51 ALR 1327. Noun: A ship which, in consequence of injuries received, is rendered unnavigable, or unable to pursue her voyage, without repairs exceeding the half of her value. 48 Am J1st Ship § 647. Such goods as after a shipwreck are cast upon land by the sea, and left there. 48 Am J1st Ship § 647. A person in very poor physical condition. A dowdy woman.

Under the Federal income tax law, allowing deduction for loss caused by shipwreck, in computing net income, the word does not mean complete loss; damage to the ship suffices. Nor need such damage be caused by storm or natural causes. A wreck through collision is within the act, whether due to the negligence of the other vessel or of employees of the wrecked ship. See Shearer v Anderson (CA2 NY) 16 F2d 995, 51 ALR 534.

For definition of term "wrecking," as it appears in a provision of an accident insurance policy relative to accidents in connection with automobiles or other motor vehicles, see Anno: 138 ALR 414.
See **train wreck.**

wreckage. See **wreck; wreck of the sea.**

wrecker. A motor vehicle employed in dragging wrecked vehicles off the highway. A work train on a railroad used primarily in clearing the track of wrecks. One engaged in the work of tearing down buildings. 27 Am J1st Ind Contr § 44.

wrecking. See **wreck.**

wrecking or disablement. See **wreck.**

wreck of the sea. Such goods as after a shipwreck are cast upon land by the sea and left there. 1 Am J2d Aband § 24; 48 Am J1st Ship § 647.

wrench (rench). Verb: To twist with violence. Noun: A common tool used to turn nuts on bolts. A sprain caused by the twisting of a joint, such as in the ankle.

wrestling. A sport, by amateur and professional, in which two participants engage, the purpose of each being to pin the shoulders of the other to the mat on which they struggle.

wrist drop. A paralysis evidenced by inability of the subject to extend his hand directly outward from the wrist.

writ. A process. 42 Am J1st Proc § 2. A process authorizing or commanding the arrest of a person or the seizure of property, sometimes the seizure of property specifically described in the writ, at other times the seizure of any property of the defendant, not exempt from seizure, sufficient to satisfy the amount of a judgment against the defendant. Caples v State, 3 Okla Crim 72, 104 P 493.

See **alias writ; prerogative writ; supervisory writ; teste.**

writ ad faciendum et recipiendum. See **ad faciendum et recipiendum.**

writ de annua pensione. See **annua pensione.**

writ de apostata capiendo. See **de apostata capiendo.**

writ de excommunicato capiendo. See **de excommunicato capiendo; de ex communicato recapiendo.**

writ de lunatico inquirendo (rit lū-nat′i-kō in-kwi-ren′dō). See **de lunatico inquirendo.**

writ de ventre inspiciendo. See **de ventre inspiciendo.**

write-in. A name written or inserted on a ballot at a place provided on the ballot, indicating the choice of a voter for a particular office, such person's name not being on the official ballot. 26 Am J2d Elect § 268.

Under an election law providing that the voter might "insert" the name of a person whose name did not appear on the ballot, the use of a sticker, instead of writing the name has been upheld. Fletcher v Wall, 172 Ill 426, 50 NE 230.

write-in candidate. A candidate for election whose name is not on the ballot as such is prepared for the voters but who campaigns to have people vote for him by writing or inserting his name on the ballot.
See **write-in.**

writer to the signet. A Scottish term for solicitor at law.

writing. An instrument. Anything which is written. Legible characters in pen or pencil. Handwriting, typewriting, or printing. 11 Am J2d B & N § 57. The expression of ideas by visible letters.

It may be on paper, wood, stone, or other material. The ten commandments were written with the finger of God on tables of stone: Exodus xxxi, 18. The general rule undoubtedly is that whenever a statute or usage requires a writing, it must be made on paper or parchment; but it is not necessary that it be in ink. It may be in pencil. Numerous authorities sustain this view, as applied to contracts and promissory notes. A prudent man will not write his will in pencil, but it is valid if he does so. Myers v Vanderbilt, 84 Pa 510.

A Missouri statute defines the term "written instrument" as including every instrument, partly printed and partly written, or wholly printed with a written signature thereto. State v Carragin, 210 Mo 351, 109 SW 553.

writing obligatory (ob′li-gạ-tọ-ri). A bond; a promise under seal.

writings of an author. The literary and scientific productions of an author. United States v Chase, 135 US 255, 258, 34 L Ed 117, 119, 10 S Ct 756. Copyrightable material. Drop Dead Co. v S. C. Johnson & Sons, Inc. (CA9 Cal) 326 F2d 87.

As used in section 8, of the first article of the Federal Constitution conferring upon Congress the power to secure to authors the exclusive right to their respective "writings," the word means the literary productions of those authors, and Congress has declared these to include all forms of writing, printing, engraving, etching, etc., by which the ideas in the mind of the author are given visible expression. 18 Am J2d Copyr § 35.

writ of amoveas manus. See **amoveas manus.**

writ of annuity. A common-law process available to the grantee of a rent charge for the enforcement of his right. 4 Am J2d Annui § 2.

writ of arrest. An intermediate remedy or process to secure the presence of the party until final judgment. Matoon v Eder, 6 Cal 57, 61.
See **warrant of arrest.**

writ of assistance. Process, sometimes called a writ of possession, issued by a court of equity to secure the possession of land after the title or right of possession has been finally determined. 6 Am J2d Assist § 1. A process for enforcing the right of a purchaser at a judicial sale to possession. 30A Am J Rev ed Jud S § 197. A writ under which the purchaser at an execution sale may obtain possession of the property. 6 Am J2d Assist § 6. A writ issued by an American colonial court authorizing officers of the king to call for aid and to search any premises.

The writ of assistance is a summary proceeding resorted to under the rules of chancery practice to give effect to the decree, and presupposes that the rights of the parties are only such as follow upon the decree and any sale had pursuant thereto. San Jose v Fulton, 45 Cal 316, 318.

writ of assize (ov a-sīz'). A remedy which the law has provided for a freehold rent, when it is unjustly taken away.

The writ also lay to try the mere possessory title to an estate. Farley v Craig, 11 NJL 262, 272.

writ of association. A writ issued under the authority of statutes of Edward I and II whereby certain persons (usually the clerk of assize and his subordinate officers) were directed to associate themselves with the justices and serjeants so that a sufficient supply of commissioners for the assizes might always be had. See 3 Bl Comm 59.

writ of attachment. A writ, otherwise known as a warrant or order of attachment, issued at or near the beginning of a suit, the object of which is to seize and hold property of the defendant subject to the claim upon which suit is brought for the ultimate purpose of satisfying the claim out of the seized property after an adjudication in the action in favor of the plaintiff upon such claim. 6 Am J2d Attach § 276.
See **alias writ; pluries writs.**

writ of attaint (rit of a-tānt'). See **attaint.**

writ of audita querela. See **audita querela.**

writ of certiorari. See **certiorari.**

writ of conspiracy. A writ which only lay at common law where the conspiracy was to indict the plaintiff either of treason or felony, by which his life was in danger, and he had been acquitted of the indictment by verdict.

All the other cases of conspiracy in the books were but actions on the case. Hutchins v Hutchins (NY) 7 Hill 104, 107.

writ of consultation. A writ by which a cause which had been removed from the ecclesiastical court to the king's court was sent back again to the ecclesiastical court.

writ of coram nobis. See **coram nobis.**

writ of coram vobis. See **coram vobis.**

writ of covenant (kuv'ĕ-nant). A writ to recover damages for the breach of a covenant.

writ of debt. The common-law writ in an action of debt. Lacaze v State (Pa) 1 Addison 58, 86.
See **debet et detinet.**

writ of deceit. A writ which lay against a person who had acted in the name of another and had deceived and injured him.

writ of delivery. A writ to enforce the delivery of chattels under a judgment.

writ of detinue (det'i-nū). The writ in an action of detinue.
See **detinue.**

writ of distress. See **distress.**

writ of dower. The common-law process in obtaining an assignment of dower under the judgment of the court. 25 Am J2d Dow § 180.

writ of ejectment (ĕ-jekt'ment). The writ in an action of ejectment.

writ of elegit. See **elegit.**

writ of entry. The common-law writ in an action which is merely possessory, serving only to regain that possession whereof the demandant or plaintiff or his ancestors have been unjustly deprived by the tenant or possessor of the freehold, or those under whom he claims. See 3 Bl Comm 180.

writ of entry ad terminum qui praeteriit (rit ov en'tri ad ter'mi-num quī prē-ter'i-it). A writ of entry for the term which has passed.

A common-law writ which lay for an owner who deemed it more expedient to admit that his tenant at sufferance had gained a tortious freehold, than to oust him by actual entry, as he had a lawful right to do. See 3 Bl Comm 175.

writ of error. A commission by which the judges of one court are authorized to examine a record on which a judgment was given in another court, and to affirm or reverse that judgment according to law. Cohen v Virginia (US) 6 Wheat 264, 5 L Ed 257. The authorization of a proceeding whereby the record of a case is transferred from one court to a higher court whose function it is to review the record for ascertainment and correction of errors at law. People v Barber, 348 Ill 40, 180 NE 633, 92 ALR 1131.

writ of error coram nobis. See **coram nobis.**

writ of error coram vobis. See **coram vobis.**

writ of estrepement. A writ invoking an ancient remedy for the prevention of waste. 56 Am J1st Waste § 30. A writ of ancient origin, the purpose of which was originally to prevent waste, after judgment obtained in any action real and before possession delivered.

Its scope was enlarged by the Statute of Gloucester (6 Edward I, ch. 13) to include cases of waste pending suit and to extend the writ to cases in which no recovery of land was sought. It was not only a preventive remedy, but was remedial and corrective, because the holder of land might not only be prevented from doing waste, but if he should do any, notwithstanding the prohibition, the plaintiff might recover damages for such waste, even up to the time when possession should be delivered to him. See 56 Am J1st Waste § 30.

writ of execution. A direct command of the court to the sheriff to carry out the mandate of the writ which normally is the enforcement of a judgment. 30 Am J2d Exec § 28.
See **alias writ of execution; pluries writs.**

writ of exigent. See **exigent.**

writ of extendi facias. See **extendi facias.**

writ of extent. See **extendi facias; extent; extent in chief.**

writ of false judgment. See **false judgment.**

writ of formedon. See **formedon.**

writ of garnishment. See **garnishment.**

writ of habeas corpus. See **habeas corpus.**

writ of habeas corpus cum causa (hā'bē-as kor'pus kum kâ'za). Same as **ad faciendum et recipiendum.**

writ of habere facias possessionem (rit of hạ-bē're fā'she-ạs po-ze-she-ō'nem). See **habere facias possessionem.**

writ of injunction. The writ of process issued in a suit for an injunction pursuant to an order or decree therein for the relief demanded. 28 Am J Rev ed Inj § 2.

writ of inquest. See **writ of inquiry.**

writ of inquiry. A writ for the assessment of damages by the sheriff and a jury.
Our courts possess the same power to assess damages as a jury in England upon a writ of inquiry, issued to the sheriff for that purpose. There, in these cases, the court must issue a writ to the sheriff, commanding him by twelve men to inquire into the damages and make return to the court; which process is called a writ of inquiry. The sheriff sits as judge, and there is a regular tiral by twelve jurors to assess the damages. Lennon v Rawitzer, 57 Conn 583, 584, 19 A 334.

writ of mainprise (ov mān'prīz). A writ directed to the sheriff, commanding him to take sureties for a prisoner's appearance, and to set him at large. See 3 Bl Comm 128.

writ of mandamus. The process or writ which issues in a proceeding in mandamus where the plaintiff or petitioner is granted relief by way of mandamus. 35 Am J1st Mand § 380.
See **alternative writ of mandamus; peremptory writ of mandamus.**

writ of mandate. Same as **writ of mandamus.**

writ of mesne (mēn). A writ which lay for a tenant paravail against a mesne lord for permitting a distress to be levied by the lord paramount by reason of the default of the mesne lord, to the damage of the plaintiff, the tenant paravail.

writ of monstraverunt (mōn-strā-vē'runt). A writ which lay for a tenant who was distrained for his default in the performance of duties or the rendition of services which were not incumbent upon him.

writ of ne exeat. See **ne exeat.**

writ of partition. A common-law writ for the partition of land between cotenants which has given way both in this country and in England to the remedy in equity or under statute. 40 Am J1st Partit §§ 58, 59.

writ of pone (ov pōn). A writ issued after the return of the original writ and the nonappearance of the defendant, ordering the sheriff to attach or take sureties for his appearance. See 3 Bl Comm 280.

writ of possession. A process for the enforcement of a judgment determining the title to real estate. 3 Am J2d Adv P § 91. The process whereby a judgment in favor of a plaintiff in ejectment or an action substituted by statute for ejectment is executed. 25 Am J2d Eject § 133. A term sometimes used for **writ of assistance.**
See **habere facias possessionem; writ of restitution.**

writ of praecipe. See **praecipe.**

writ of prevention. A writ to prohibit the bringing of an action or suit.

writ of privilege (rit of priv'i-lej). A writ for the release of a member of parliament who had been arrested on civil process.

writ of procedendo. See **procedendo; procedendo ad judicium; procedendo de loquela.**

writ of proclamation. A writ directed to the sheriff of the county of the defendant's residence, commanding the sheriff to make three proclamations of the pendency of outlawry proceedings against the defendant. This was a statutory requirement, the purpose of which was to prevent secret outlawries. See 3 Bl Comm 283.

writ of prohibitio de vasto (rit of pro-hi-bi-she-ō dē vas'tō). See **prohibitio de vasto, directa parti.**

writ of prohibition. A writ which commands the person or tribunal to whom it is directed not to do something which, by the suggestion of the relator, the court is informed he is about to do. Better defined as a writ to prevent a tribunal possessing judicial or quasi-judicial powers from exercising jurisdiction over matters not within its cognizance, or exceeding its jurisdiction in matters of which it has cognizance. 42 Am J1st Prohib § 2.

writ of prohibition of waste. A common-law writ, which anciently lay for the owner of the inheritance against the commission of waste by a tenant in dower, or by the curtesy, or a guardian in chivalry, which issued out of chancery, was directed to the sheriff and commanded him to prevent waste from being committed, and in the execution of which the sheriff might, if necessary, call to his aid the posse comitatus.
Subsequently the scope of the writ was so enlarged as to make it available for the purpose of preventing waste by a tenant for life or for years. See 56 Am J1st Waste § 30.

writ of pro retorno habendo (rit of prō re-tor'nō haben'dō). A writ issued in an action of replevin upon the entry of a judgment for the defendant, commanding the return to the defendant of property taken from him under the writ of replevin.

writ of protection. A writ protecting a witness threatened with civil arrest. 5 Am J2d Arr § 100. A writ for the release of a person in the king's service who had been arrested on civil process.

writ of quare impedit. See **quare impedit.**

writ of quod permittat prosternere. See **quod permittat prosternere.**

writ of quo warranto (rit of kwō wo-ran'tō). See **quo warranto.**

writ of recaption (rit of rẹ-kap'shọn). See **recaption.**

writ of replevin. Process issued in an action of replevin authorizing an officer to seize the property involved in the action. 46 Am J1st Replev § 79.
See **replevin.**

writ of restitution. The process for the enforcement of a judgment for the plaintiff in forcible entry and detainer. 35 Am J2d Forc E & D § 53. The final process in action or proceeding by a landlord to obtain possession from the tenant. 32 Am J1st L & T § 1028. A common-law writ for the restoration to a successful appellant of the amount which he had been compelled to pay under the judgment or decree reversed, a remedy which has given way in modern practice to more summary relief. 5 Am J2d A & E § 1001.

writ of review (rit of rẹ-vū'). A writ which is substantially the common-law writ of certiorari and is denominated in the codes a "special proceeding."
The return to the writ brings up the record of the inferior court, officer, or tribunal, not for the purpose of ascertaining an issue of fact, but to determine whether or not the functions of the court, officer, or tribunal have been exercised erroneously, or that the jurisdiction employed has been exceeded. The only inquiry to be considered upon the return to the writ is a question of law, in the examination of which the parties are not entitled to a jury trial, thus taking the proceedings out of the reason usually assigned for excluding equitable jurisdiction. Hall v Dunn, 52 Or 475, 97 P 811.

writ of right. An ancient writ for the recovery of real property wrongfully withheld from the owner.
The term was also applied to that class of writs which the sovereign was bound by Magna Charta to issue, and which are distinguishable from prerogative writs.

writ of right close (klōz). A writ which lay for the king's tenants in ancient demesne, and others of a similar nature, to try the right of their lands and tenements in the court of the lord exclusively. See 3 Bl Comm 195.

writ of scire facias. See **scire facias.**

writ of second deliverance. See **second deliverance.**

writ of second surcharge. See **second surcharge.**

writ of sequestration (rit of sẹ-kwes-trā'shọn). See **sequestration.**

writ of subpoena (rit of sub or su-pē'nạ). See **subpoena.**

writ of summons (rit of sum'ọnz). See **summons.**

writ of supersedeas. See **supersedeas.**

writ of supervisory control. See **supervisory writ.**

writ of supplicavit (rit of sup-pli-kā'vit). A mandatory writ which issued out of the court of king's bench or chancery to compel a justice, in case of his refusal, to take a recognizance to keep the peace. See 4 Bl Comm 253. A writ for the enforcement of the right of consortium. 26 Am J1st H & W § 17. A process of the chancery court which protected the wife against the husband's violence, and in cases where it was found unsafe for her to abide with him, as incident to such proceedings, compelled the husband to provide maintenance for her while she was separate and apart from him, by reason of his violent conduct toward her. Edgerton v Edgerton, 12 Mont 122, 29 P 966.

writ of tolt. See **tolt.**

writ of venire facias. See **venire facias.**

writ of waste. A writ invoking an ancient remedy to recover damages for waste committed and the estate itself in the same action. 56 Am J1st Waste § 30.

written. See **writing.**

written constitution. The typical constitution as known in the United States. 16 Am J2d Const L § 1.
The usual form of constitution in the United States.
See **constitution.**

written contract. A contract in writing, as distinguished from an oral contract.
See **specialty.**

written evidence. See **documentary evidence; X-ray photograph.**

written instrument. See **writing.**

written law. The law which is written in statutes, ordinances, bylaws, treaties and written constitutions as distinguished from the unwritten or common law. See 1 Bl Comm 62.

written notice. See **notice in writing.**

written signature. See **signature.**

written slander. A poorly conceived term for libel. 33 Am J1st L & S § 3.

wrong. The infringement of a legal right belonging to a definite specific person. Kamm v Flink, 113 NJL 582, 175 A 62, 99 ALR 1. In common usage, an act in violation of a moral principle.
The word, as the word "injury," in law imports the invasion of a legal right, and to say that a person has committed a wrong, is to say that he has subjected himself to a cause of action. See Eller v Carolina & N. W. R. Co. 140 NC 140, 52 SE 305.
Sometimes that may be right in law which is otherwise from a moral standpoint, since there is no wrong in legal contemplation as to that upon which the law's instrumentalities have set the seal of right. Laun v Kipp, 155 Wis 347, 145 NW 183, 5 ALR 655.
As the word was used by the fathers of the common law in their saying that for every "wrong" there should be a remedy, they meant a violation of the municipal law, the law of civil conduct, not a transgression of the divine law, as such, nor a breach of etiquette. Western Union Tel. Co. v Ferguson, 157 Ind 64, 60 NE 674.
Under a statutory test to the effect that a person is not excused from liability as an idiot, imbecile, lunatic, or insane person, except upon proof that at the time of committing the alleged criminal act, he was laboring under such a defect of reason as not to know the nature and quality of the act he was doing, or not to know that the act was wrong, the word "wrong" does not always and necessarily mean legal wrong, although it sometimes includes such a wrong. People v Schmidt, 216 NY 324, 110 NE 945.

wrongdoer. One who commits a wrong against another. A tortfeasor.

wrongful. Unlawful, inequitable, contrary to natural justice, or in violation of the principles of good morals. Board of Comrs. v Armstrong, 91 Ind 528, 536.

wrongful abstraction. An unauthorized and illegal taking or withholding of funds or securities from the possession and control of one's employer and the appropriation of such funds or securities to the benefit of the taker or to the benefit of another. 50 Am J1st Suret § 336.

wrongful act. Any act which in the ordinary course will infringe upon the rights of another to his damage, unless it is done in the exercise of an equal or superior right. Brennan v United Hatters of North America, 73 NJL 729, 65 A 165; Louis Kamm, Inc. v Flink, 113 NJL 582, 175 A 62, 99 ALR 1.

The words are comprehensive enough to include negligent acts, but they are intended primarily to cover cases where the act was wanton or was intentionally committed, or where one may have counseled or procured another to do it, when, in contemplation of law, the act of counseling or advising makes the wrongful act his own. See Foreman v Taylor Coal Co. 112 Ky 845, 66 SW 1044.

wrongful attachment. Wrongfully obtaining or tortiously employing an order for, or writ, of attachment, as where no ground for attachment exists, where property of the defendant not liable to attachment is seized, or where property of a third person is seized as that of the defendant. A wrong for which a remedy exists in a suit on the attachment bond, an action for malicious attachment, an action for abuse of process, or a suit for malicious prosecution. 6 Am J2d Attach § 596.
See **wrongful levy.**

wrongful commitment. Commitment of a person to an institution for the insane upon proceedings in contravention of the constitutional rights of the persons affected. 29 Am J Rev ed Ins Per § 38.
See **false imprisonment.**

wrongful conduct. See **wrongful act.**

wrongful death. An action provided by constitution or statute to recover from one whose wrongful act, neglect or default has resulted in the death of another person. 22 Am J2d Dth § 2.

wrongful delivery. An unauthorized delivery by the depositary of an escrow. 28 Am J2d Escr § 23.

wrongful distress. A distress which is unlawful and actionable, as where there was no rent in arrears, or where acts rendering the landlord a trespasser ab initio are committed in making the levy, or where a second distress is barred by a prior distress, or where the distress is excessive and a sale is made under it. See 32 Am J1st L & T § 645.

wrongful execution. An actionable wrong predicated upon irregular procedure, irregularity in the judgment upon which the writ was obtained, the doing of an act outside the authority conferred by the writ, an improper seizure of property, a wrongful sale, or the enforcement of an execution in violation of an injunction. 30 Am J2d Exec §§ 755 et seq.
See **wrongful levy.**

wrongful garnishment. Improperly obtaining or tortiously employing the remedy of garnishment. A wrong akin to wrongful attachment. 6 Am J2d Attach § 596.

See **wrongful attachment.**

wrongful injunction. An injunction sued out maliciously without just cause. 28 Am J Rev ed Inj § 334.

wrongful levy. A levy made by the sheriff or other officer upon exempt property; a levy which is excessive in reference to the amount of property seized; a levy upon the property of a person other than one named in the writ; or any levy constituting an improper and illegal exercise of authority as a cover for illegal conduct on the part of the officer. 47 Am J1st Sher § 48.
See **wrongful attachment; wrongful execution.**

wrongfully. Unlawfully, unjustly, or in a manner contrary to sound moral principles. Board of Comrs. v Armstrong, 91 Ind 528, 536.

wrongful removal. Exceeding jurisdiction in removing a public officer without following the method provided by statute. 43 Am J1st Pub Of § 240.

wrongful search. See **unreasonable search.**

wrongful search and seizure. See **unreasonable search and seizure.**

wrongful seizure. See **unreasonable seizure.**

wrong name. See **misnomer.**

wrongous imprisonment (rong'us im-priz'n-ment). The term used in the Scots law for "false imprisonment." Evans v M'Loughlan (Eng) 15 ERC 173.

Wunderlich Act. A federal statute the principle effect of which is broadening of the criteria for judicial review of administrative decisions pursuant to the "disputes clauses" of Government contracts so as to render administrative conclusions of law not binding on a reviewing court and an administrative finding of facts not binding on a reviewing court if fraudulent, capricious, so grossly erroneous as necessarily to imply bad faith, or not supported by substantial evidence. Anno: 10 L Ed 2d 1217.

wye (wī). See **y.**

wyte. An immunity or exemption from amercement. See **amercement.**

X

X. Roman numeral ten.

x. A sign of multiplication, meaning times or by, as 3x6. A familiar legend indicating position upon a map or drawing, as: "x marks the spot where ...." The unknown quantity.

X-ray. Noun: An electromagnetic ray used in the diagnosis and treatment of certain bodily conditions of disease and injury because of its penetrating character. The instrumentality by which the electromagnetic ray is employed. Verb: To employ the electromagnetic ray in treatment or examination of the body. To take an X-ray photograph.

The rays were discovered by Roentgen and have been known and recognized by scientists, both in and out of the medical profession since 1895. Henslin v Wheaton, 91 Minn 219, 97 NW 882.

X-ray photograph. A distinctive kind of photograph or picture produced by the employment of electromagnetic rays in an instrumentality directed to the human body, constituting, under interpretation by an expert, a reliable representation of bones, foreign substances lodged in the body, or the condition of tissues of the body. 29 Am J2d Ev § 799.

X-ray photographs, properly identified, authenticated and explained in detail by doctors testifying in behalf of the respective parties, and exhibited to and examined in detail by the jury during the trial, are, irrespective of the jury's ability to understand such photographs, within the operation of a statute which permits a jury to take with it to the jury room "any written evidence." Texas Employers' Ins. Asso. v Crow, 148 Tex 113, 221 SW2d 235, 10 ALR2d 913.

X-ray specialist. A radiologist; a doctor of medicine qualified as an expert in the employment of the X-ray and its use in the diagnosis and treatment of disease.

X-ray technician. A person trained in the use of an X-ray machine, although not as a radiologist.

Y

Y. A popular designation for the Young Men's Christian Association, also for a building wherein activities of such association are conducted.

y. Forked tracks at the end of a streetcar line upon which a streetcar is reversed for the return trip.

yacht (yot). A watercraft of elaborate construction used for pleasure, usually powered by sails but having a motor by way of auxiliary power. 12 Am J2d Boats § 1. A vessel entitled to enrolment and license as an American vessel employed for the purpose of pleasure, not for the transportation of passengers or merchandise for pay. 48 Am J1st Ship § 51.

yacht basin. A place for the mooring of yachts and other pleasure craft.

yard. A unit of lineal measure, the equivalent of three feet. An area surrounding, or adjacent to one or more sides of, a dwelling house, for the use, comfort, and recreation of the residents.
See **railroad yard**; **stockyard**.

yard engine. Same as **switch engine**.

yard master. A railroad employee in charge of a railroad yard.

yardmen. Gardeners employed in the care and maintenance of lawn or garden. Employees of a railroad who work in a railroad yard.

yard restriction. A restriction in a zoning law stipulating the minimum side or rear yard area, or the percentage of the area of a building lot that may be occupied by the building. 58 Am J1st Zon § 52.

Yazoo Frauds Act. A Georgia statute enacted in 1795, and subsequently declared unconstitutional by the courts, which purported to authorize the sale to individuals of certain public lands, including lands which now comprise all of the state of Mississippi and half of the state of Alabama.

yea and nay. Yes and no.

year. A determinate period, consisting for all practical purposes of 365 days, except as 366 days appear in a leap year. 52 Am J1st Time § 10. A calendar year in the absence of qualification. Dycema v Story & C. Piano Co. 220 Mich 600, 190 NW 638, 27 ALR 660. A season, particularly a farming season in which crops are planted, cultivated, and harvested, or a season as known to proprietors of vacation resorts.
See **current year**; **leap year**; **solar year**; **term of years**; **within a year**.

year and a day. A limitation of time for some purposes. Lyon v Cleveland, 170 Pa 611, 33 A 143 (former limitation upon sale of land under a judgment). The familiar rule in prosecutions for homicide that if death does not ensue within a year and a day after the infliction of a wound, it will be presumed that death, when it finally does occur, proceeded from some other cause. 26 Am J1st Homi § 269.

The statute of Gloucester provided that an appeal of death must be sued out within a year and a day from the day of the victim's death, and this was said to be declaratory of the common law. The rule of a year and a day was also applied at common law to inquisitions of deodands, brought to forfeit to the king any personal chattel that was the immediate cause of a person's death. The reason for the rule was that the law does not look upon such a wound as the cause of a man's death if he lived longer than a year and a day. Louisville, Evansville & St. Louis Railroad Co. v Clarke, 152 US 230, 240, 38 L Ed 422, 424, 14 S Ct 579.

Year Books. The earliest reports of cases heard in the courts of King's Bench, Common Pleas, and before the Justices Itinerant, in England, covering the period from about 1270 to 1530.

The reports for this period are presently extant in manuscripts in a more or less regular series from the 18th year of the reign of Edward I down through the 27th year of the reign of Henry VIIIth, and are attempted verbatim accounts of what was said in open court by the Justices and counsel, written in abbreviated Anglo-French, and, perhaps, the earliest of which were taken down privately by counsel and students of the law, and, it would seem, toward the end of the period by professional private scribes as a business venture. In short, they are contemporary reports of English law not only of the utmost value but the like of which is to be found in no other legal system.

The reports for individual years (consisting of the four terms of court: Hilary, Easter, Trinity, and Michaelmas) were collected and bound together and hence came to be known as the Year Books. It has been conclusively established that these reports were not made by the prothonotaries, or chief scribes of the court at the expense of the crown, as Blackstone erroneously reports, but rather that they were the result of the private enterprise of the English Bar.

The Year Books had a wide private circulation in manuscript form down to the time when printing came into common use. Except for reports from the reigns of Edward I, Edward II, and Richard II (for which there is still abundant manuscript authority extant today) reports for various individual years and groups of years, without any attention to chronological order, were printed in many editions during the 16th-century. A "Quarto" edition of previously printed reports was printed in ten volumes at the end of the 16th and the beginning of the 17th century. In 1678-1680 there was printed what is known as the "Folio" or "Vulgate" edition of the Year Books which, in addition to reprinting the hithertofore black-letter printed texts of the Year Books from the reign of Edward III down through the 27th year of the reign of Henry VIII (omitting the reports from the reign of Richard II, some of which were first printed in modern times), printed for the first time, from one manuscript, the reports of 1-19 Edward II. This "edition of 1679", as it is sometimes called, was made up of eleven volumes.

In modern times the English Records Commission has published in modern form in the Rolls Series the reports of 20-35 Edward I, and 11-20 Edward III; the Selden Society has published Year Books 1-12 Edward II and 1 Henry VI; the Ames Foundation of Harvard has published the Year Books 11-13 Richard II; and, Sweet & Maxwell, the Year Books 9-10 Henry V.

Note: The foregoing dissertation on the Year Books is the work of Mr. Ralph V. Rogers of the Editorial Staff of the Lawyers Cooperative Publishing Company. Such contribution is acknowledged with appreciation. W.S.A.

year, day, and waste. An ancient right of the king.
"In petit treason and felony the offender also forfeits all his chattel interests absolutely, and the profits of all estates of freehold during life, and, after his death, all his lands and tenements in fee simple (but not those in tail) to the crown, for a very short period of time; for the king shall have them for a year and a day, and may commit therein what waste he pleases; which is called the king's year, day and waste." See 4 Bl Comm 385.

year-end bonus. A bonus paid to employees near the end of the calendar year, often during the week before Christmas.

yearling (yēr′ling). A domestic animal past one year old and in its second year.

year of mourning. The year following the death of a married man during which his widow was not permitted to remarry, for the reason, it has been said, that is if a widow remarried soon after her husband's death, the determination of the parentage of a child born to her a matter of months after her second marriage would present difficulty. See 1 Bl Comm 457.

year of our Lord. The beginning of the Christian era.
In England, in court proceedings, the date sometimes refers to the year of the king's reign and sometimes to the beginning of the Christian era, but since in this country our only national era, that of our independence, is not used in courts of justice, and we use but the one, the Christian era, it is not a fatal defect in either criminal or civil proceedings to omit the words "of our Lord," after the word "year." Commonwealth v Doran, 80 Mass (14 Gray) 37, 38.

year to year estate. See **estate from year to year; tenancy from year to year.**

year-to-year renewal. The option of the maker of a note for indefinite renewal. 11 Am J2d B & N § 306.

year to year tenancy. See **tenancy from year to year.**

yellow-dog contract. A contract of employment containing a condition binding the employee not to join or remain a member of a labor union. 31 Am J Rev ed Lab § 9.

yellow light. A traffic signal indicating the necessity of caution.

yellow line. A barrier painted on the middle thread of paving as a control of traffic on the highway.

yeoman (yō′man). A freeholder. A solid citizen. An enlisted man in the Navy engaged in office or clerical work.

Yiddish (yid′ish). A dialect of the German language which includes words from other languages, particularly Hebrew, spoken at one time by many Jews in Europe and elsewhere throughout the world, but of diminishing use at the present time.

yield. Noun: The amount of a crop by bushel or pound grown on a specified area of land. The return upon an investment. Verb: To produce; to earn, as a principal sum yields interest, or a farm yields a crop. To perform, as, to yield services incident to land tenure. To give way. To concede.

yield right of way. Permitting another vehicle to proceed without interference.

Y. M. C. A. Abbreviation of **Young Men's Christian Association.**

yoke. A measure of land, being the area of land ploughable by an ox-team in one day. A pair of oxen. A symbol of bondage, deriving from the name of the wooden frame used in harnessing a pair of oxen for work.

Yom Kippur (Yom Kip′ūr). A sacred holiday of the Jews, otherwise known as the Day of Atonement.

York. See **custom of York.**

York-Antwerp rules. Rules formulated by a conference of representatives of commercial interests in the interest of uniformity in bills of lading and contracts of affreightment involved in international commerce, the principles of which appear in modern uniform laws. 13 Am J2d Car §§ 264 et seq.

you-drive-it. See **drive-it-yourself system.**

Young Men's Christian Association. An organization of national and international scope for the improvement and betterment of men and boys, particularly in their formative years.

Young Turks. A name applied to the members of a political party, especially members in Congress or a state legislature, who break away from control of the party by the existing leadership.

Young Women's Christian Association. An organization of national and international scope for the improvement and betterment of women and girls, particularly in their formative years.

youth. Young people considered as a class, inclusive of both male and female.

youth rally. A meeting of young people called for discussion of a particular subject of interest. A meeting of young persons constituting a church activity. 24 Am J2d Disturb M § 2.

Y. W. C. A. Abbreviation of **Young Women's Christian Association.**

Z

zealot (zel'ǫt). A person who is zealous to an excessive degree, especially in the cause of a religion.

zealous witness. A witness eager to be of service to a party, usually the party who called him.

zingara (zing'ga-rä). Any female in a band of gypsies.

zingaro (zing'ga-rō). A gypsy.

zig zagging. A driver veering back and forth across the highway. 8 Am J2d Auto § 952.

Zollverein (tsol'fer-īn"). A customs union of German states, existing prior to the establishment of the German Empire.

zone. A district established by a zoning law. 58 Am J1st Zon § 3. A specific area noted in the establishment of a parcel post rate. 41 Am J1st P O § 61. One of the sections of the country under a division made in the fixing of rates charged by railroads.

See **time zone; zoning.**

zone of employment. See **working place.**

zoning. The division of a municipality into districts for the application of municipal regulations. Miller v Board of Public Works, 195 Cal 477, 234 P 381, 38 ALR 1479, error dismd 273 US 781, 71 L Ed 889, 47 S Ct 460. The creation and application of structural and use restrictions imposed upon the owners of real estate within prescribed districts or zones. 58 Am J1st Zon § 1. Literally, separating commercial or industrial districts of a city or town from the residential districts, and prohibiting the establishment of places of business or industry in any district designated as residential. State ex rel. Civello v New Orleans, 154 La 271, 97 So 440, 33 ALR 260, 268.

Zoning regulations are divided into two classes: (1) Those which regulate the height or bulk of buildings within certain designated districts—in other words, those regulations which have to do with structural and architectural designs of the buildings; and (2) those which prescribe the use to which buildings within certain designated districts may be put. Both modes of regulation have received the sanction of the Supreme Court of the United States. Miller v Board of Public Works, 195 Cal 477, 234 P 381, 38 ALR 1479, 1483.

See **partial zoning; spot zoning.**

zoning commission. An administrative agency of a municipality to which the administration of zoning laws and regulations is entrusted. 58 Am J1st Zon § 178.

zoning map. A map showing the districts established by a zoning law, sometimes annexed to the ordinance, made a part of it, and given a controlling effect. Anno: 159 ALR 857.

zoning regulations. See **zoning.**

zoo. A place provided by a municipal corporation for the housing, care, and exhibition of animals.

zoological garden. A zoo maintained in elaborate surroundings.

See **zoo.**

zymurgy (zī'mėr-ji). The branch of chemistry concerned with the process of fermentation, particularly in the making of wine or the brewing of beer. Fletcher v Paige, 124 Mont 114, 220 P2d 84, 19 ALR2d 1108.

ABBREVIATIONS OF LEGAL REPORTS, TREATISES, AND PHRASES

A

A	Atlantic
A2d	Atlantic 2d Series
ABAJ	See Am Bar Asso J
ABA Rep	See Am Bar Asso Rep
Abb (F)	Abbott, US Circuit & Dist Cts
Abb Adm (F)	Abbott's Admiralty 1 vol
Abb App Dec (NY)	Abbott's NY Ct of Appeals Decisions
Abb NC (NY)	Abbott's New Cases
Abb NY Dig 2d	Abbott's New York Digest 2d
Abbott, Civ Jury Trials	Abbott on Civil Jury Trials
Abbott, Crim Tr Pr	Abbott on Criminal Trial Practice
Abb Pr (NY)	Abbott's Practice
Abb Pr NS (NY)	Abbott's Practice New Series
AC	Advance California Reports
AC (Can)	Appeal Cases (Canada)
AC (Eng)	Appeal Cases
ACA	Advance California Appellate
acct	account
Acton (Eng)	Acton [12 Eng Reprint]
Adam	Justiciary Reports (Scot)
Adams Leg J (Pa)	Adams Legal Journal
Ad & El (Eng)	Adolphus & Ellis (King's Bench) [110–113 Eng Reprint]
Ad & El NS (Eng)	See QB
Addams Eccl (Eng)	Addams, Ecclesiastical [162 Eng Reprint]
Addison (Pa)	Addison—1 vol
Adm & Eccl (Eng)	See LR—Adm & Eccl
AFTR	American Federal Tax Reports
Aik (Vt)	Aiken
Air L Rev	Air Law Review
AK Marsh (Ky)	A. K. Marshall
Ala	Alabama
Ala App	Alabama Appeals
Ala LJ	Alabama Law Journal
Alaska	Alaska
Alaska Fed Rep	Alaska Federal Reports
Albany L Rev	Albany Law Review
Alberta L (Can)	Alberta Law Reports
Alcock & N (Ir)	Alcock & Napier 1 vol
Aleyn (Eng)	Aleyn, Select Cases [82 Eng Reprint]
Allen (Mass)	Allen

[1389]

All Eng	All England Law Reports
ALR	American Law Reports Annotated
ALR2d	American Law Reports Annotated 2d Series
Am & Eng Enc Law	American & English Encyclopedia of Law
Am & Eng Enc Law & Pr	American & English Encyclopedia of Law & Practice
Am & Eng Pat Cas	American & English Patent Cases
Am Bankr	American Bankruptcy
Am Bankr NS	American Bankruptcy New Series
Am Bar Asso J	American Bar Association Journal
Am Bar Asso Rep	American Bar Association Reports
Ambl (Eng)	Ambler [27 Eng Reprint]
AMC	American Maritime Cases
Am Cent Dig	American Digest (Century Edition)
Am Civ LJ	American Civil Law Journal (NY)
Am Dec	American Decisions
Am J1st	American Jurisprudence (First Edition)
Am J2d	American Jurisprudence (Second Edition)
Am J Int L	American Journal of International Law, New York
Am J Leg Forms Anno	American Jurisprudence Legal Forms Annotated
Am J Pl & Pr Forms Anno	American Jurisprudence Pleading & Practice Forms Annotated
Am J Proof of Facts	American Jurisprudence Proof of Facts
Am J Trials	American Jurisprudence Trials
Am Jud Soc	American Judicature Society
Am Jurist	American Jurist
Am Labor Legis Rev	American Labor Legislation Review
Am Lead Cas (H & W)	American Leading Cases (Hare & Wallace)
Am L Inst	American Law Institute, Restatement of the Law
Am LJ	American Law Journal (Phila)
Am LJ NS	American Law Journal, New Series (Phila)
Am L Rec	American Law Record
Am L Reg	American Law Register
Am L Reg NS	American Law Register, New Series
Am L Rev	American Law Review
Am LT Bankr Rep	American Law Times Bankruptcy Reports
Am LT Rep	American Law Times Reports
Am Neg Cas	American Negligence Cases
Am Neg Rep	American Negligence Reports
Am Pol Science Rev	American Political Science Review
Am Property	American Law of Property
Am Pr Rep NS	American Practice Reports, New Series
Am Rep	American Reports
Am St Rep	American State Reports
Am Trade Mark Cas	American Trade Mark Cases (Cox)
Am Vets	American Law of Veterans
Ander (Eng)	Anderson [123 Eng Reprint]
Anderson UCC	Anderson's Uniform Commercial Code
Andrews (Eng)	Andrews [95 Eng Reprint]
Ann Cas	American & English Annotated Cases

Ann Cas 1912D .... American Annotated Cases (annuals)
anon. .... anonymous
Anstr (Eng) .... Anstruther (Exchequer) [145 Eng Reprint]
Anthon NP (NY) .... Anthon's Nisi Prius (Common Law)
App Cas (Eng) .... See LR—App Cas
App DC .... Appeal Cases, District of Columbia
App Div (NY) .... Appellate Division
App Div 2d (NY) .... Appellate Division, Second Series
arg. .... arguendo
Ariz .... Arizona
Ark .... Arkansas
Ark LJ .... Arkansas Law Journal
Armstrong M & O (Ir) .... Armstrong, Macartney & Ogle
Arnold (Eng) .... Arnold
Arnold & H (Eng) .... Arnold & Hodges
Ashm (Pa) .... Ashmead
Asp Mar L Cas (Eng) ..... Aspinall's Maritime Law Cases
Atk (Eng) .... Atkyns (Chancery) [26 Eng Reprint]
Austr CLR .... Australia Commonwealth Law Reports
Austr Jur .... Australian Jurist
Austr LJ .... Australian Law Journal
Austr LT .... Australian Law Times
Averbach Acci Cas .... Averbach on Handling Accident Cases
Aviation Q .... United States Aviation Quarterly

B

Bagl (Cal) .... Bagley
Bagl & Har (Cal) .... Bagley & Harman
Bail Eq (SC) .... Bailey Equity
Bail L (SC) .... Bailey Law
Baldw (F) .... Baldwin, US Circuit Ct
Ball & B (Ir) .... Ball & Beatty
Ballentine's Law Dict ..... Ballentine's Self-Pronouncing Law Dictionary
Bann & Ard (F) .... Banning & Arden (Patent Cases)
Barb (NY) .... Barbour (Supreme)
Barb Ch (NY) .... Barbour, Chancery Reports
Barber (Ark) .... Barber
Barn & Ad (Eng) .... Barnewall & Adolphus (King's Bench) [109, 110 Eng Reprint]
Barn & Ald (Eng) .... Barnewall & Alderson (King's Bench) [106 Eng Reprint]
Barn & C (Eng) .... Barnewall & Cresswell (King's Bench) [107–109 Eng Reprint]
Barnard Ch (Eng) .... Barnardiston's Chancery [27 Eng Reprint]
Barnard KB (Eng) .... Barnardiston's King's Bench [94 Eng Reprint]
Barnes Notes (Eng) ...... Barnes' Notes of Cases [94 Eng Reprint]
Barr (Pa) .... Barr
Barron & H Fed Pr & Proc Barron & Holtzoff's Federal Practice & Procedure
Barrows (RI) .... Barrows
Batty (Ir) .... Batty

Baxt (Tenn)	Baxter
Bay (SC)	Bay
Beasl (NJ)	Beasley
Beatty Ir Ch	Beatty, Irish Chancery
Beav (Eng)	Beavan [48–55 Eng Reprint]
Beaver Co LJ (Pa)	Beaver County Law Journal
Beck (Colo)	Beck
Bee Adm (F)	Bee, US Dist Ct (Admiralty)
Bell CC (Eng)	Bell, Crown Cases Reserved [169 Eng Reprint]
Bellewe (Eng)	Bellewe [72 Eng Reprint]
Belli's Mod Trials	Belli's Modern Trials
Bell Sc App Cas (Scot)	Bell, Scotch Appeal Cases
Belt's Supp (Eng)	Belt, Supplement to Vessey Senior's English Chancery [28 Eng Reprint]
Ben (F)	Benedict, US Dist Ct
Benedict, Admiralty	Benedict on Admiralty
Benl (Eng)	Benloe, or Bendloe [73 Eng Reprint]
Benl & D (Eng)	Benlow & Dalison [123 Eng Reprint]
Berks Co LJ (Pa)	Berk's County Law Journal
Best & S (Eng)	Best & Smith (Queen's Bench) [121, 122 Eng Reprint]
b.f.p.	bona fide purchaser
Bibb (Ky)	Bibb
Bi-Mo L Rev	Bi-Monthly Law Review
Bing (Eng)	Bingham (Common Pleas) [130, 131 Eng Reprint]
Bing NC (Eng)	Bingham, New Cases (Common Pleas) [131–133 Eng Reprint]
Binn (Pa)	Binney
Biss (F)	Bissell, US Circuit Ct
b/l	bill of lading
Bl (Eng)	See H Bl or W Bl
Black (US)	Black, US Supreme Ct
Blackf (Ind)	Blackford
Blackstone's Commen	Blackstone's Commentaries
Blair Co LR (Pa)	Blair County Law Reports
Bland Ch (Md)	Bland's Chancery
Blatchf (F)	Blatchford, US Circuit Ct
Blatchf & H (F)	Blatchford & Howland, US Dist Ct
Blatchf Pr Cas (F)	Blatchford, Prize Cases
Bligh (Eng)	Bligh [4 Eng Reprint]
Bligh NS (Eng)	Bligh, New Series [4–6 Eng Reprint]
B Mon (Ky)	Ben Monroe
Bogert, Trusts	Bogert on Trusts & Trustees
Bond (F)	Bond, US Circuit Ct
Bos & P (Eng)	Bosanquet & Puller [126, 127 Eng Reprint]
Bos & P NR (Eng)	Bosanquet & Puller's New Reports (Common Pleas) [127 Eng Reprint]
Boston U L Rev	Boston University Law Review
Bosw (NY)	Bosworth (Superior)
Boyce (Del)	Boyce

Bradb (NY)	Bradbury's Pleading & Practice
Bradf (Ia)	Bradford
Bradf (NY)	Bradford (Surrogate)
Bradw (Ill)	Bradwell
Branch (Fla)	Branch
Br & Col Pr Cas (Eng)	British & Colonial Prize Cases
Brayton (Vt)	Brayton
BRC (British Empire)	British Ruling Cases
Breese (Ill)	Breese
Brev (SC)	Brevard
Brewst (Pa)	Brewster
Bridg (Eng)	See J Bridg or O Bridg
Brightly Election Cas (Pa)	Brightly, Leading Election Cases
Brightly NP (Pa)	Brightly, Nisi Prius
Brit Col (Can)	British Columbia
Bro Ch (Eng)	Brown, Chancery [28, 29 Eng Reprint]
Brock (F)	Brockenbrough, US Circuit Ct
Brod & B (Eng)	Broderip & Bingham (Common Pleas) [129 Eng Reprint]
Brod & F (Eng)	Broderick & Freemantle
Bro NP (mich)	Brown Nisi Prius
Brooke Abr (Eng)	Brooke's Abridgment [73 Eng Reprint]
Brooke, NC (Eng)	See Brooke Abr
Brooklyn L Rev	Brooklyn Law Review
Bro PC (Eng)	Brown, Parliamentary Cases [1–3 Eng Reprint]
Brown Adm (F)	Brown's Admiralty
Brown & H (Miss)	Brown & Hemingway
Brown & L (Eng)	Browning & Lushington [167 Eng Reprint]
Browne (Pa)	Browne
Brown, Ga Pl & Pr Anno	Brown, Georgia Pleading & Practice & Legal Forms Annotated
Brownl & G (Eng)	Brownlow & Goldesborough (Common Pleas) [123 Eng Reprint]
Brunner Col Cas (F)	Brunner's Collected Cases
BTA (F)	US Board of Tax Appeals
Buch Eq (NJ)	Buchanan's New Jersey Equity Reports
Buck Bankr (Eng)	Buck, Bankruptcy Cases
Bucks Co LR (Pa)	Bucks County Law Reporter
Bull (Ohio)	See WL Bull
Bull NP (Eng)	Buller's Law of Nisi Prius
Bulstr (Eng)	Bulstrode [80, 81 Eng Reprint]
Bunbury (Eng)	Bunbury [145 Eng Reprint]
Burdick, Crime	Burdick's Law of Crime
Burdick, Roman Law	Burdick's Principles of Roman Law
Burnett (Wis)	Burnett
Burn's JP (Eng)	Burn's Justice of Peace
Burr (Eng)	Burrow (King's Bench) [97, 98 Eng Reprint]
Burrell (Eng)	Burrell, Admiralty Edition [167 Eng Reprint]
Burrnett (Ore)	Burrnett
Burr Sett Cas (Eng)	Burrow's Settlement Cases

Busbee Eq (NC) .... Busbee Equity
Busbee L (NC) .... Busbee Law
Bush (Ky) .... Bush
Business L J .... Business Law Journal
Buxton (NC) .... Buxton
BWCC (Eng) .... Butterworth's Workmen's Compensation Cases

C

Cab & El (Eng) .... Cababe & Ellis
Cadwalader .... Cadwalader's Cases, US District Court, Eastern District of Pennsylvania
Caines (NY) .... Caines (Common Law)
Caines Cas (NY) .... Caines' Cases (Common Law)
Caines Term Rep (NY) .... See Caines Cas
Cal .... California
Cal 2d .... California, 2d Series
Cal 2d (Adv—) .... California, 2d Series (Advance Parts)
Cal App .... California Appellate
Cal App 2d .... California Appellate Reports, 2d Series
Cal App 2d (Adv—) ...... California Appellate Reports, 2d Series (Advance Parts)
Cal App Supp .... California Appellate Supplement (Appellate Dept. of Superior Court)
Cal App 2d Supp .... California Appellate Supplement (Appellate Dept. of Superior Court) 2d Series
Cald (Eng) .... Caldecott's Settlement Cases
Cal Dec .... California Decisions
Cal Jur .... California Jurisprudence
Call (Va) .... Call
Callman, Unfair Comp .... Callman on Unfair Competition & Trade Marks
Cal L Rev .... California Law Review
Cal Rptr .... California Reporter
Cal Sup (Cal) .... See Cal App Supp
Calth (Eng) .... Calthrop [80 Eng Reprint]
Cal Unrep .... California Unreported Cases
Cambria Co (Pa) .... Cambria County Reports
Cambria Co LJ .... Cambria County Law Journal
Cameron (Can) .... Cameron
Cameron Cas (Can) .... Cameron's Supreme Court Cases
Cameron Pr (Can) .... Cameron's Practice
Campb (Eng) .... Campbell (Nisi Prius) [170, 171 Eng Reprint]
Campb (Pa) .... Campbell's Legal Gazette Reports
Canal Zone .... Canal Zone
Can Bankr .... Canadian Bankruptcy Reports
Can Crim Cas .... Canadian Criminal Cases, Annotated
Can Exch .... Exchequer Court of Canada Reports
Can LJ .... Canada Law Journal
Can LJ NS .... Canada Law Journal New Series
Can LT .... Canadian Law Times
Can LT Occ N .... Canadian Law Times, Occasional Notes

Can R AC	Canadian Reports, Appeal Cases
Can R App Cas	See Can R AC
Can Ry Cas	Canada Railway Cases
Can SC	Canada Supreme Court Reports
Cantor, Med & Surg	Cantor's Traumatic Medicine & Surgery for the Attorney
Cape P Div (South Africa)	Cape Provincial Division Reports
Car & K (Eng)	Carrington & Kirwan (Nisi Prius) [174, 175 Eng Reprint]
Car & M (Eng)	Carrington & Marshman (Nisi Prius) [174 Eng Reprint]
Car & P (Eng)	Carrington & Payne (Nisi Prius) [171–173 Eng Reprint]
Cardozo, Growth of the Law	Cardozo's Growth of the Law
Cardozo, Judicial Process	Cardozo's Nature of the Judicial Process
Car Law Repos (NC)	Carolina Law Repository
Car LJ (SC)	Carolina Law Journal
Carmody-Wait, NY Prac	Carmody-Wait Cyclopedia of New York Practice
Cart Cas (Can)	Cartwright's Cases
Carter (Eng)	Carter [124 Eng Reprint]
Carth (Eng)	Carthew (King's Bench) [90 Eng Reprint]
Cary (Eng)	Cary [21 Eng Reprint]
ca. sa.	Capias ad satisfaciendum (writ of execution for arrest and imprisonment until a claim could be satisfied)
Case & Com	Case & Comment
Casey (Pa)	Casey
Cas t Finch (Eng)	Cases temp. Finch [23 Eng Reprint]
Cas t Hardw (Eng)	Cases temp. Hardwicke [95 Eng Reprint]
Cas t King (Eng)	Select Cases temp. King [25 Eng Reprint]
Cas t Talb (Eng)	Cases temp. Talbot [25 Eng Reprint]
Cates (Tenn)	Cates
CB (Eng)	Common Bench [135–139 Eng Reprint]
CBNS (Eng)	Common Bench, New Series [140–144 Eng Reprint]
CCA (US)	Circuit Court of Appeals
Cent Dig	American Digest (Century Edition)
Cent LJ (Mo)	Central Law Journal
Cent R (Pa)	Central Reporter
cf.	conferre (compare)
Ch (Eng)	See LR—Ch—
Chaffe & Admin Law	Chaffe & Nathanson's Administrative Law, Cases & Materials
Chand (NH)	Chandler
Chand (Wis)	Chandler
Chaney (Mich)	Chaney
Charlet (Ga)	See RM Charlt or TUP Charlt
Chase Dec (F)	Chase, US Circuit CT Decisions
Ch Cas (Eng)	Select Cases in Chancery [22 Eng Reprint] 3 parts
Ch Chamb (Can)	Chancery Chambers
Ch Div (Eng)	See LR—Ch Div—
Chester Co (Pa)	Chester County Reports
Cheves Eq (SC)	Cheves Equity

Cheves L (SC) .... Cheves Law
Chicago Leg News (Ill) .... Chicago Legal News
Chicago LJ .... Chicago Law Journal
Chicago L Record (Ill) .... Chicago Law Record
Chi-Kent Rev .... Chicago-Kent Review
Chip (Vt) .... Chipman; See D Chip or N Chip
Chitty .... See Chitty BC
Chitty BC (Eng) .... Chitty Bail Court Reports
Chitty, Contracts .... Chitty on Contracts
Choyce Cas (Eng) .... Choyce Cases in Chancery [21 Eng Reprint]
Ch Rep .... See Rep in Ch
Ch Sent (NY) .... Chancery Sentinel
c.i.f. .... costs, insurance, and freight
Cin Law Bull (Ohio) ...... See WL Bull
Cin L Rev .... University of Cincinnati Law Review
Cin Super (Ohio) .... Cincinnati Superior Court Reporter
Cir Ct Dec (Ohio) .... Circuit Court Decisions
City Ct (NY) .... See NY City Ct
City Ct Supp (NY) .... See NY City Ct Supp
City Hall Rec (NY) .... See NY City Hall Rec
City Hall Rep (NY) .... Lomas' City Hall Reporter
City Rec (NY) .... City Record
Civ Proc (NY) .... See NY Civ Proc
Civ Proc NS (NY) .... See NY Civ Proc NS
CJ .... Corpus Juris
CJS .... Corpus Juris Secundum
Clark (Ala) .... Clark
Clark (Pa) .... Clark's Pennsylvania Law Journal
Clark & F (Eng) .... Clark & Finnelly (House of Lords) [6–8 Eng Reprint]
Clark & F NS (Eng) ...... Clark & Finnelly, New Series
Clarke (Ia) .... Clarke (Edition)
Clarke (Mich) .... Clarke
Clarke (Pa) .... Clarke
Clarke Ch (NY) .... Clarke's Chancery Reports
Clark, Receivers .... Clark on Receivers
Clark's Summary .... Clark's Summary of American Law
Clayton (Eng) .... Clayton (York Assizes)
Cleve LR (Ohio) .... Cleveland Law Reporter
Cleve L Rec (Ohio) .... Cleveland Law Record
Cleve L Reg (Ohio) .... Cleveland Law Register
Cliff (F) .... Clifford, US Circuit Ct
CLR (Austr) .... Commonwealth Law Reports
CMR .... Court Martial Reports
CMR, Cit & Ind .... Court Martial Reports, Citators & Indexes
CMR JAG AF .... Court Martial Reports of the Judge Advocate General
                                of the Air Force

CMR JAG & US Ct of Mil
   App .... Court Martial Reports of the Judge Advocate General

of the Armed Forces and the US Court of Military Appeals
c/o .... care of
Co Ct Rep (Pa) .... County Court Reports
c.o.d. .... cash on delivery (collect)
Code R (NY) .... See NY Code R
Code R NS (NY) .... See NY Code R NS
Cof Prob Dec (Cal) .... Coffey's Probate Decisions
Co Inst (Eng) .... Coke's Institutes
Coke (Eng) .... Coke (King's Bench) [76, 77 Eng Reprint]
Col & Caines Cas (NY).... Coleman & Caines' Cases (Common Law)
Col Cas (NY) .... Coleman Cases (Common Law)
Coldw (Tenn) .... Coldwell
Co Litt (Eng) .... Coke on Littleton (1st Institute)
Colles (Eng) .... Colles (Parliamentary Cases) [1 Eng Reprint]
Collier & E Am Bankr .... Collier & Eaton's American Bankruptcy
Collier, Bankr .... Collier's Bankruptcy
Col L Rev .... Columbia Law Review
Colly Ch Cas (Eng) .... Collyer, Chancery Cases [63 Eng Reprint]
Colo .... Colorado
Colo App .... Colorado Appeals
Colo LR .... Colorado Law Reporter
Comb (Eng) .... Comberbach (King's Bench) [90 Eng Reprint]
Comp Armed Forces ...... Compendium of Laws—Armed Forces
Comp Gen (US) .... Decisions of Comptroller General of the United States
Com Pl R (Pa)........... Common Pleas Reporter
Comst (NY) .... Comstock Court of Appeals
Comyns (Eng) .... Comyns (King's Bench) [92 Eng Reprint]
Comyns' Dig (Eng) .... Comyns Digest of Laws of England
Conference (NC) .... Conference Reports
Conn .... Connecticut
Connoly (NY)............ Connoly (Surrogate)
Connor & L (Ir) .... Connor & Lawson
Conn Supp .... Connecticut Supplement
Const Rep (SC) .... Constitutional Reports
Cooke (Eng) .... Cooke, Cases of Practice [125 Eng Reprint]
Cooke (Tenn) .... Cooke
Cooke & Al (Ir) .... Cooke & Alcock Reports, Irish King's Bench
Cooley, Const Limit ...... Cooley on Constitutional Limitations
Coop Ch (Eng) .... Cooper's Chancery [35 Eng Reprint]
Cooper G (Eng) .... See G Cooper
Cooper Pr Cas (Eng) ...... Cooper's Practice Cases [47 Eng Reprint]
Coop t Brougham (Eng) ... Cooper, Cases temp. Brougham [47 Eng Reprint]
Coop t Cott (Eng) .... Cooper, Cases temp. Cottenham [47 Eng Reprint]
Coop t Eld (Eng) .... Cooper, Cases temp. Eldon
Corbin, Contracts .... Corbin on Contracts
Cornell LQ............... Cornell Law Quarterly
Couch, Insurance .... Couch on Insurance
Couch, Insurance 2d ...... Couch on Insurance, 2d edition

Court & Macl (Scot) ...... Courteney & Maclean
Coutlee Unrep (Can) ...... Coutlee's Unreported Cases
Cow (NY) .... Cowen (Common Law)
Cow Crim (NY) .... Cowen's Criminal Reports
Cowp (Eng) .... Cowper (King's Bench) [98 Eng Reprint]
Cox CC (Eng) .... Cox's Criminal Cases
Cox Ch Cas (Eng) .... Cox, Chancery Cases [29, 30 Eng Reprint]
Coxe (N.J) .... Coxe
CP (Eng) .... See LR—CP—
CP Div (Eng) .... See LR—CP Div—
CP Moore (Eng) .... See JB Moore
Crabbe (F) .... Crabbe, US Dist Ct
Craig & Ph (Eng) .... Craig & Phillips (Chancery) [41 Eng Reprint]
Cranch (US) .... Cranch, US Supreme Ct
Cranch CC (F) .... Cranch, US Circuit Ct, Dist of Col App Cases
Cranch Pat Dec (US) ..... Cranch's Patent Decisions
Craw (Ark) .... Crawford
Craw & D (Ir) .... Crawford & Dix (Abridged Cases)
Craw & DCC (Ir) .... Crawford & Dix Circuit Cases
Craw Co Leg J (Pa) ...... Crawford County Legal Journal
Crim App (Eng) .... Criminal Appeal
Crim R (Can) .... Criminal Reports
Critch (Ohio St) .... Critchfield
C Rob (Eng) .... Christopher Robinson [165 Eng Reprint]
Cro Car (Eng) .... Croke, temp. Charles I [79 Eng Reprint]
Cro Eliz (Eng) .... Croke, temp. Elizabeth [78 Eng Reprint]
Cro Jac (Eng) .... Croke, temp. James I [79 Eng Reprint]
Cromp & J (Eng) .... Crompton & Jarvis (Exchequer) [148, 149 Eng Reprint]
Cromp & M (Eng) .... Crompton & Meeson [149 Eng Reprint]
Cromp M & R (Eng) ...... Crompton, Meeson & Roscoe (Exchequer) [149, 150 Eng Reprint]
c.t.a. .... cum testamento annexo (with the will annexed)
Ct Cl (F) .... US Court of Claims
Ct Cl (Ill) .... Court of Claims
Cumberland LJ (Pa) ...... Cumberland Law Journal
Cummins (Idaho) .... Cummins
Cunningham (Eng) .... Cunningham (King's Bench) [94 Eng Reprint]
Curt CC (F) .... Curtis, US Circuit Ct Decisions
Curt Eccl (Eng) .... Curteis, Ecclesiastical Reports [163 Eng Reprint]
Cush (Mass) .... Cushing
Cust & Pat App (Cust) (F) . Customs and Patent Appeals Reports (Customs)
Cust & Pat App (Pat) (F) .. Customs and Patent Appeals Reports (Patents)

D

Daily Leg (Pa) .... Daily Legal Record
Daily Leg News (Pa) ...... Daily Legal News
Dak .... Dakota
Dak L Rev .... Dakota Law Review
Dalison (Eng) .... Dalison, (Common Pleas) [123 Eng Reprint]

Dall (F)	Dallas, US Reports
Dall (Pa)	Dallas, Pennsylvania Reports
Dall (US)	Dallas, US Supreme Ct Reports
Dallam Dig (Tex)	Dallam's Digest
Daly (NY)	Daly (Common Pleas)
Dana (Ky)	Dana
Dan Exch (Eng)	Daniell's Exchequer & Equity [159 Eng Reprint]
Dass Ed (Kan)	Dassler's Edition
Dauph Co (Pa)	Dauphin County
Dav & M (Eng)	Davison & Merivale
Davies (Eng)	See Davis
Davis (Eng)	Davis [80 Eng Reprint]
Davis, Admin Law	Davis' Administrative Law Treatise
Davis Land Ct Dec (Mass)	Davis Land Court Decisions
Davis, Mass Convey Hdbk	Davis' Massachusetts Conveyancer's Handbook
Davys (Eng)	See Davis
Day (Conn)	Day
Dayton (Ohio)	Dayton Misc Decisions
d.b.a.	de bonis asportatis (trespass to personalty)
d.b.e.	de bene esse (sufficient for the time being)
d.b.n.	de bonis non
DC	See Dist Col
D Chip (Vt)	D. Chipman
Deacon & C Bankr Cas (Eng)	Deacon & Chitty, Bankruptcy
Deacon Bankr (Eng)	Deacon, Bankruptcy
Deady (F)	Deady (US Circuit & Dist Cts)
Deane & S Eccl (Eng)	Deane & Swabey, Ecclesiastical [164 Eng Reprint]
Dears & BCC (Eng)	Dearsley & Bell, Crown Cases [169 Eng Reprint]
Dears CC (Eng)	Dearsley, Crown Cases [169 Eng Reprint]
Dec Dig	American Digest (Decennial Edition)
De G & J (Eng)	De Gex & Jones (Chancery) [44, 45 Eng Reprint]
De G & S (Eng)	De Gex & Smale [63, 64 Eng Reprint]
De G Bankr (Eng)	De Gex, Bankruptcy Reports
De GF & J (Eng)	De Gex, Fisher & Jones (Chancery) [45 Eng Reprint]
De GJ & S (Eng)	De Gex, Jones & Smith (Chancery) [46 Eng Reprint]
De GM & G (Eng)	De Gex, Macnaghten & Gordon (Chancery) [42–44 Eng Reprint]
Del	Delaware
Del Ch	Delaware Chancery
Del Co (Pa)	Delaware County Reports
Del Co LJ (Pa)	Delaware County Law Journal
dem.	demise
Dem (NY)	Demarest (Surrogate)
Den CC (Eng)	Denison, Crown Cases [169 Eng Reprint]
Denio (NY)	Denio (Common Law)
Denver LJ	Denver Law Journal
Desauss Eq (SC)	Desaussure, SC Equity
Detroit L Rev	Detroit Law Review

Dev & B Eq (NC)	Devereux & Battle Equity
Dev & BL (NC)	Devereux & Battle Law
Dev Ct Cl (F)	Devereux, US Court of Claims
Dev Eq (NC)	Devereux Equity
Dev L (NC)	Devereux Law
Dicey, Confl Laws	Dicey on Conflict of Laws
Dicey, Domicil	Dicey's Law of Domicil
Dick (NJ)	Dickinson's New Jersey Equity
Dick Ch (Eng)	Dickens [21 Eng Reprint]
Dick L Rev	Dickinson Law Review
Dill (F)	Dillon, US Circuit Ct
Dillon, Mun Corp	Dillon on Municipal Corporation
Disn (Ohio)	Disney
Dist Col	District of Columbia
Dist Col App	See App DC
Dix Dec (NY)	Dix's School Decisions, New York
DLN	See Daily Leg News
DLR (Can)	Dominion Law Reports
DLR2d (Can)	Dominion Law Reports, Second Series
DL Rec	See Daily Leg
do.	ditto
Dodson Adm (Eng)	Dodson, Admiralty [165 Eng Reprint]
Donnelly (Eng)	Donnelly (Chancery) [47 Eng Reprint]
Dorion (Can)	Dorion
Dougl (Mich)	Douglass
Dougl KB (Eng)	Douglas, King's Bench [99 Eng Reprint]
Dow & C (Eng)	Dow & Clark (House of Lords) [6 Eng Reprint]
Dowl (Eng)	See Dowl PC
Dowl & L (Eng)	Dowling & Lowndes (Bail Court)
Dowl & R (Eng)	Dowling & Ryland (King's Bench)
Dowl & R Mag Cas (Eng)	Dowling & Ryland's Magistrates' Cases
Dowl & R NP (Eng)	Dowling & Ryland's Nisi Prius Cases [171 Eng Reprint]
Dowl NS (Eng)	Dowling, New Series
Dowl PC (Eng)	Dowling, Practice Cases
Dow PC (Eng)	Dow, House of Lords (Parliamentary) Cases [3 Eng Reprint]
Drake, Attachment	Drake on Attachment
Draper (Can)	Draper
Drew (Eng)	Drewry (Vice-Chancellor) [61, 62 Eng Reprint]
Drew & S (Eng)	Drewry & Smale (Vice-Chancellor) [62 Eng Reprint]
Drinkw (Eng)	Drinkwater
Drury (Ir)	Drury
Drury & Wal (Ir)	Drury & Walsh
Drury & War (Ir)	Drury & Warren
Dud Eq (SC)	Dudley, SC Equity
Dud L (SC)	Dudley, SC Law
Dudley (Ga)	Dudley
Duer (NY)	Duer (Superior)
Dunl B & M (Scot)	Dunlop, Bell & Murray

Dunlop (Scot)	Dunlop
Dunn (Eng)	Dunning
Duponceau, US Cts	Duponceau on Jurisdiction of United States Courts
Durn & E (Eng)	See TR
Dutch (NJ)	Dutcher
Duv (Ky)	Duvall
d.v.n.	devisavit vel non (issue of fact as to whether a will in question was made by the testator)
Dyer (Eng)	Dyer (King's Bench) [73 Eng Reprint]

E

East (Eng)	East [102–104 Eng Reprint]
East LR (Can)	Eastern Law Reporter
East PC (Eng)	East's Pleas of the Crown
Ebersole (Ia)	Ebersole's Reports
ECL (Eng)	English Common Law
Edelman, Maritime Injury	Edelman's Maritime Injury & Death
Eden (Eng)	Eden [28 Eng Reprint]
Edinb LJ	Edinburgh Law Journal
Edm Sel Cas (NY)	Edmond's Select Cases (Common Law)
ED Smith (NY)	E. D. Smith (Common Pleas)
Edw (Mo)	Edwards' Reports
Edw Adm (Eng)	Edwards, Admiralty [165 Eng Reprint]
Edw Ch (NY)	Edward's Chancery Reports
e.g.	exempli gratia (for example)
El & Bl (Eng)	Ellis & Blackburn [118–120 Eng Reprint]
El & El (Eng)	Ellis & Ellis [120, 121 Eng Reprint]
El B & S (Eng)	Ellis, Best & Smith, English Queen's Bench Reports
El Bl & El (Eng)	Ellis, Blackburn & Ellis (Queen's Bench) [120 Eng Reprint]
El Cas (NY)	New York Election Cases (Armstrong's)
Emerson & Haber, Pol & Civ Rts	Emerson & Haber's Political & Civil Rights in the United States
Enc Pl & Pr	Encyclopedia of Pleading & Practice
Eng (Ark)	English
Eng & Ir App	See LR—HL—
Eng L & Eq	English Law & Equity
Eng Rep Anno	English Reports Annotated
Eng Reprint	English Reprint
Eq (Eng)	See LR—Eq—
Eq Cas Abr (Eng)	Equity Cases Abridgment [21, 22 Eng Reprint]
Eq R (Eng)	Equity Reports
ERC (Eng)	English Ruling Cases
Erie Co Leg J	Erie County Legal Journal
Erie Co LJ (Pa)	Erie County Law Journal
Esp (Eng)	Espinasse [170 Eng Reprint]
Estee (Hawaii)	Estee's District Court of Hawaii
et al.	et alii (and others)

et seq.	et sequitur (and as follows)
et ux.	et uxor (and wife)
Exch (Eng)	Exchequer [154–156 Eng Reprint]. See also LR—Exch—
Exch Ct (Can)	See Can Exch
Exch Div (Eng)	See LR—Exch Div—
Exec Order	Executive Orders of the President of the United States
exr.	executor
ex rel.	ex relatione (on the relation of)

F

F	Federal Reporter
F2d	Federal Reporter, 2d series
Fairf (Me)	Fairfield
Falc Marine Dict	Falconer's Marine Dictionary
Fayette Leg J (Pa)	Fayette Legal Journal
FC (Scott)	Faculty Collection of Decisions
FCA	Federal Code Annotated
FCC	Federal Communications Commission
F Carrier Cas	Federal Carrier Cases
F Cas No —	Federal Cases Number
Fearne, Contingent Remainders	Fearne on Contingent Remainders
Fed Com BJ	Federal Communications Bar Journal
Fed LQ	Federal Law Quarterly (Indianapolis)
Fiduciary R (Pa)	Fiduciary Reporter
fi. fa.	fieri facias (writ of execution of property)
Finch (Eng)	See Cas t Finch
Finkel, Medical Cyc	Finkel, et al., Lawyers' Medical Cyclopedia
Fisher Pat Cas (F)	Fisher, US Patent Cases
Fisher Pr Cas (F)	Fisher, US Prize Cases
Fisher Pr Cas (Pa)	Fisher Pennsylvania Prize Cases
Fitzg (Eng)	Fitzgibbon [94 Eng Reprint]
Fla	Florida
Fla Dig	See Thompson's Fla Dig
Fla Jur	Florida Jurisprudence
Fla LJ	Florida Law Journal
Fla L Rev	University of Florida Law Review
Flan & K (Ir)	Flanagan & Kelly
Fla Stat Anno	Annotations to Official Florida Statutes
Fletcher, Corporations	Fletcher's Cyclopedia Corporations
Flipp (F)	Flippin, US Circuit Ct
F Moore (Eng)	Francis Moore (King's Bench) [72 Eng Reprint]
f.o.b.	free on board
Fonbl Eq (Eng)	Fonblanque, Equity
Fordham L Rev	Fordham Law Review
Forman (Ill)	Forman
Forrest (Eng)	Forrest [145 Eng Reprint]
Fortescue (Eng)	Fortescue [92 Eng Reprint]

Fort LJ	Fortnightly Law Journal
Fost (NH)	Foster
Fost & F (Eng)	Foster & Finlason (Nisi Prius) [175, 176 Eng Reprint]
Fost CL (Eng)	Foster, Crown Law [168 Eng Reprint]
Foster (Pa)	Foster Legal Chronicle Reports
Fox & S (Ir)	Fox & Smith
FPC	Federal Power Commission
France (Colo)	France
Fraser (Scot)	Fraser
FRD	Federal Rules Decisions
Freem Ch (Eng)	Freeman, Chancery [22 Eng Reprint]
Freem Ch (Miss)	Freeman's Chancery
Freem KB (Eng)	Freeman's King's Bench Reports [89 Eng Reprint]
French (NH)	French
F Supp	Federal Supplement
FTC	Federal Trade Commission Reports
Fuller (Mich)	Fuller

G

Ga	Georgia
Ga App	Georgia Appeals
Ga BJ	Georgia Bar Journal
Ga Dec	Georgia Decisions
Galb (Fla)	Galbraith
Galb & M (Fla)	Galbraith & Meek
Gale & D (Eng)	Gale & Davison (Queen's Bench)
Ga LJ	Georgia Law Journal
Gall (F)	Gallison, US Circuit Ct
Gamboa, Philippine Law	Gamboa's Introduction to Philippine Law
G & G (Mo)	Goldsmith & Guthrie
Ga Prac	See Stand Ga Prac
Ga Supp to vol 33	Georgia Supplement
Gault (Ga)	Gault
G Cooper (Eng)	George Cooper (Chancery) [35 Eng Reprint]
Georgetown LJ	Georgetown Law Journal (Wash D. C.)
Geo Wash L Rev	George Washington Law Review
G Greene (Iowa)	George Greene
Gibbons (NY)	Gibbons (Surrogate)
Giff (Eng)	Giffard (Vice-Chancellor) [65, 66 Eng Reprint]
Gil (Minn)	Gilfillan
Gilb Cas L & Eq (Eng)	Gilbert's Cases, Law & Equity [93 Eng Reprint]
Gilb Eq (Eng)	Gilbert, Equity [25 Eng Reprint]
Gildersleeve (N Mex)	Gildersleeve
Gill (Md)	Gill
Gill & J (Md)	Gill & Johnson
Gilm (Ill)	Gilman
Gilmer (Va)	Gilmer
Gilpin (F)	Gilpin, US Dist Ct
Glyn & J (Eng)	Glyn & Jameson (Bankruptcy)

Godb (Eng) .... Godbolt (King's Bench) [78 Eng Reprint]
Goebel (Ohio) .... Goebel's Probate Ct
Goodrich-Amram .... Goodrich-Amram Procedural Rules Service
Gouldsb (Eng) .... Gouldsborough (King's Bench) [75 Eng Reprint]
Gow NP (Eng) .... Gow's Nisi Prius Cases [171 Eng Reprint]
Grant Cas (Pa) .... Grant's Cases
Grant Ch (Can) .... Grant, Chancery
Gratt (Va) .... Grattan
Gray (Mass) .... Gray
Gray, Perpetuities .... Gray's Rule Against Perpetuities
Green (NJ) .... Green's New Jersey Law or Equity
Greene G (Iowa) .... See G Greene
Gunby (La) .... Gunby's Appeal Decisions

H

Hagg Adm (Eng) .... Haggard, Admiralty Reports [166 Eng Reprint]
Hagg Consist (Eng) .... Haggard's Consistory Reports [161 Eng Reprint]
Hagg Eccl (Eng) .... Haggard's Ecclesiastical Reports [162 Eng Reprint]
Hale PC (Eng) .... Hale's Pleas of the Crown
Hall (NY) .... Hall (Superior)
Hall & Tw (Eng) .... Hall & Twell (Chancery) [47 Eng Reprint]
Hall, J., Criminal Law .... Hall, Jerome on General Principles of Criminal Law
Halsted (NJ) .... Halsted
Handy (Ohio) .... Handy (Miscellaneous)
Hardin (Ky) .... Hardin
Hardr (Eng) .... Hardres (Exchequer) [145 Eng Reprint]
Hardw (Eng) .... See Cas t Hardw
Hare (Eng) .... Hare (Vice-Chancellor) [66–68 Eng Reprint]
Harp Eq (SC) .... Harper, SC Equity
Harper & James, Torts .... Harper & James on Torts
Harp L (SC) .... Harper, SC Law
Harr (Del) .... Harrington
Harr (NJ) .... Harrison
Harr & G (Md) .... Harris & Gill
Harr & J (Md) .... Harris & Johnson
Harr & McH (Md) .... Harris & McHenry
Harr & W (Eng) .... Harrison & Wollaston
Harr Ch (Mich) .... Harrington's Chancery
Harv L Rev .... Harvard Law Review
Haskell (F) .... Haskell, US Circuit & Dist Cts
Hatcher's Kan Dig .... Hatcher's Kansas Digest
Hawaii .... Hawaiian
Hawaii Dist .... US District Ct of Hawaii
Hawks (NC) .... Hawks
Hay & M (Eng) .... Hay & Marriott (Admiralty) [165 Eng Reprint]
Hayes & J (Ir) .... Hayes & Jones (Exchequer)
Hayes Exch (Ir) .... Hayes (Exchequer)
Hayw (NC) .... Haywood, NC Reports
Hayw (Tenn) .... Haywood, Tenn Reports

Hayw & H (F)	Hayward & Hazelton
Haz Pa Reg (Pa)	Hazard's Pennsylvania Register
H Bl (Eng)	Henry Blackstone [126 Eng Reprint]
Head (Tenn)	Head
Heisk (Tenn)	Heiskell
Hem & M (Eng)	Hemming & Miller (Vice-Chancellor) [71 Eng Reprint]
Hempst (F)	Hempstead, US Circuit Ct
Hen & M (Va)	Hening & Munford
Henderson, Income Tax	Henderson's Introduction to Federal Income Taxation
Het (Eng)	Hetley [124 Eng Reprint]
Hicks, Ethics	Hicks' Organization and Ethics of Bench and Bar
Hicks, Leg Research	Hicks on Materials and Methods of Legal Research
Hicks, Men & Books	Hicks on Men and Books Famous in the Law
Hill (NY)	Hill (Common Law)
Hill & D Supp (NY)	Lalor's Supplement to Hill & Denio (Common Law)
Hill Eq (SC)	Hill, SC Equity
Hill L (SC)	Hill, SC Law
Hilt (NY)	Hilton (Common Pleas)
Hitch, Pr & Proc	Hitch's Practice & Procedure in the Probate Court of Massachusetts
HL (Eng)	See LR—HL—
HL Cas (Eng)	House of Lords Cases [9–11 Eng Reprint]
HL Sc App Cas	See LR—HL Sc App Cas—
Hobart (Eng)	Hobart (King's Bench) [80 Eng Reprint]
Hodges (Eng)	Hodges
Hodg Ont Elect	Hodgins' Election Cases, Ontario
Hoffm Ch (NY)	Hoffman's Chancery Reports
Hoffm Dec (F)	Hoffman's Decisions, US Dist Ct
Hoffm Land Cas (F)	Hoffman's Land Cases, US Dist Ct
Hoffm Ops (F)	Hoffman's Opinions, US Dist Ct
Hogan (Ir)	Hogan
Holmes (F)	Holmes, US Circuit Ct
Holmes, Collected Legal Papers	Holmes' Collected Legal Papers
Holmes, Common Law	Holmes' Common Law
Holt Adm (Eng)	Holt's Admiralty
Holt Eq (Eng)	Holt's Equity [71 Eng Reprint]
Holt KB (Eng)	Holt's King's Bench [90 Eng Reprint]
Holt NP (Eng)	Holt's Nisi Prius [171 Eng Reprint]
Hopk Adm (Pa)	Hopkinson's Admiralty
Hopk Ch (NY)	Hopkins' Chancery
Hopk Works (Pa)	Hopkinson's Works
Hopw & C (Eng)	Hopwood & Coltman
Hopw & P (Eng)	Hopwood & Philbrick
Horn & H (Eng)	Horn & Hurlstone (Exchequer)
Hornstein, Corporation Law	Hornstein's Corporation Law & Practice
Hosea (Ohio)	Hosea (Superior)
Houst (Del)	Houston

Houst Crim (Del)	Houston, Criminal Cases
How (Miss)	Howard
How (US)	Howard, US Supreme Ct
How App Cas (NY)	Howard, NY Ct of Appeals Cases
How NP (Mich)	Howell, Nisi Prius
How Pr (NY)	Howard, Practice Reports
How Pr NS (NY)	Howard, Practice Reports, New Series
How St Tr (Eng)	Howell, State Trials
Hud & B (Ir)	Hudson & Brooke
Hughes (F)	Hughes, US Circuit Ct
Hughes (Ky)	Hughes
Humph (Tenn)	Humphrey
Hun (NY)	Hun (Supreme)
Hurlst & C (Eng)	Hurlstone & Coltman (Exchequer) [158, 159 Eng Reprint]
Hurlst & N (Eng)	Hurlstone & Norman (Exchequer) [156–158 Eng Reprint]
Hurlst & W (Eng)	Hurlstone & Walmsley
Hursh, Products Liability	Hursh's American Law of Products Liability
Hutton (Eng)	Hutton (Common Pleas) [123 Eng Reprint]

I

ibid.	ibidem (in the same place)
id.	idem (the same)
Idaho	Idaho
Idaho LJ	Idaho Law Journal
Idd TR (Ohio)	Iddings' Term Reports
i.e.	id est (that is)
Ill	Illinois
Ill 2d	Illinois 2d Series
Ill App	Illinois Appellate Court
Ill App 2d	Illinois Appellate, Second Series
Ill Cir Ct	Illinois Circuit Court
Ill L Rev	Illinois Law Review
Ind	Indiana
Ind & Lab Rel Rev	Industrial & Labor Relations Review
Ind App	Indiana Appellate Court
Indian App (Eng)	See LR—Ind App—
Indian LR 21 Calc	Indian Law Reports, Calcutta Series
Indian LR 1 Mad	Indian Law Reports, Madras Series
Ind Leg Per	Index to Legal Periodicals
Ind LJ	Indiana Law Journal
Ind Super (Ind)	See Wils Super
Ind Terr	Indian Territory
Ins LJ	Insurance Law Journal
Inters Com	Interstate Commerce
Inters Com Com	Interstate Commerce Commission
Int Rev Bull	Internal Revenue Bulletin
Iowa	Iowa

Iowa L Rev	Iowa Law Review
Ir Ch	Irish Chancery (1850–1866)
Ir CL	Irish Common Law (1849–1866)
Ir—CL	Irish Common Law (1867–1878)
Ired Eq (NC)	Iredell's Equity Reports
Ired L (NC)	Iredell's Law Reports
Ir Eq	Irish Equity (1839–1852)
Ir—Eq	Irish Equity (1867–1878)
Ir Jur	Irish Jurist
Ir L	Irish Law Reports (1839–1852)
Ir LR	Irish Law Reports
Ir LT	Irish Law Times
Ir R	See Ir LR
Ir Term	Irish Term Reports
Irvine Just Cas	Irvine's Justiciary Cases

J

Jac & W (Eng)	Jacob & Walker [37 Eng Reprint]
Jacob (Eng)	Jacob [37 Eng Reprint]
Jaeger, Labor Law	Jaeger's Cases and Statutes on Labor Law
JAG (Def Dept)	Judge Advocate General (Defense Department) Court-Martial Reports; Holdings & Decisions of Judge Advocate General Boards of Review & United States Court of Military Appeals
JAG CMR (AF)	Judge Advocate General Court-Martial Reports
JAG Comp CMO (Navy)	Judge Advocate General Compilation of Court-Martial Orders
JAG Dig Op	Judge Advocate General Digest of Opinions
J Air Law	Journal of Air Law
J Am Jud Soc	Journal of the American Judicature Society, Chicago
Jarman, Wills	Jarman on Wills
JB Moore (Eng)	John Bayly Moore
J Bridg (Eng)	Sir John Bridgman [123 Eng Reprint]
J Crim Law	Journal of American Institute Criminal Law & Criminology, Chicago
Jebb & B (Ir)	Jebb & Bourke
Jebb & S (Ir)	Jebb & Symes
Jebb CC (Ir)	Jebb's Crown Cases
Jeff (Va)	Jefferson
Jenkins (Eng)	Jenkins (Exchequer) [145 Eng Reprint]
JJ Marsh (Ky)	J. J. Marshall
J Jur	Journal of Jurisprudence
J Kelyng (Eng)	Sir John Kelyng Crown Cases (King's Bench) [84 Eng Reprint]
Johns (NM)	Johnson
Johns (NY)	Johnson (Common Law)
Johns & H (Eng)	Johnson & Hemming (Chancery) [70 Eng Reprint]
Johns Cas (NY)	Johnson's Cases (Common Law)
Johns Ch (NY)	Johnson's Chancery

Johns VC (Eng) .... Johnson's Vice-Chancellor [70 Eng Reprint]
Jones (Eng) .... See T Jones or W Jones
Jones (Ir) .... Jones
Jones & L (Ir) .... Jones & La Touche
Jones & S (NY) .... Jones & Spencer (Superior)
Jones Eq (NC) .... Jones, Equity Reports
Jones L (NC) .... Jones, Law Reports
Joyce, Insurance .... Joyce on Insurance
JP (Eng) .... Justice of the Peace
JP Smith (Eng) .... See Smith (Eng)
J Psychological Medicine .. Journal of Psychological Medicine & Medical Jurisprudence
J Radio Law .... Journal of Radio Law
Jur (Eng) .... The Jurist
Jurid Rev .... Juridical Review, Edinburgh
Jur NS (Eng) .... The Jurist, New Series
Justice of the Peace (Pa) .. Justice of the Peace
Justice's LR (Pa) .... Justice's Law Reporter

K

Kan .... Kansas
Kan App .... Kansas Appeals
Kan Dig .... See Hatcher's Kan Dig
Kay (Eng) .... Kay [69 Eng Reprint]
Kay & J (Eng) .... Kay & Johnson (Vice-Chancellor) [69, 70 Eng Reprint]
KB (Eng) .... Law Reports, King's Bench
Keble (Eng) .... Keble (King's Bench) [83, 84 Eng Reprint]
Keen (Eng) .... Keen (Rolls Court) [48 Eng Reprint]
Keigwin, Common
   Law Pleading .... Keigwin's Cases in Common Law Pleading
Keilw (Eng) .... Keilway (King's Bench) [72 Eng Reprint]
Kelyng J (Eng) .... See J Kelyng
Kelynge W (Eng) .... See W Kelynge
Kent's Commen .... Kent's Commentaries
Kenyon Ld (Eng) .... See Ld Kenyon
Keyes (NY) .... Keyes
King (Eng) .... See Cas t King
Kirby (Conn) .... Kirby
Knapp PCC (Eng) .... Knapp's Privy Council Cases [12 Eng Reprint]
Kulp (Pa) .... See Luzerne Leg Reg R
Ky .... Kentucky
Ky LJ .... Kentucky Law Journal
Ky LR .... Kentucky Law Reporter
Ky Ops .... Kentucky Opinions

L

La .... Louisiana
La Ann .... Louisiana Annual Reports
La App .... Louisiana Appeals

La App (Orleans)	See Orleans App
Lab Rel Rep	Labor Relations Reporter
Lack Bar (Pa)	Lackawanna Bar
Lack Bar R (Pa)	Lackawanna Bar Reports
Lack Co (Pa)	Lackawanna County Reports
Lack Jur (Pa)	Lackawanna Jurist
Lack Leg News (Pa)	Lackawanna Legal News
Lack Leg Rec (Pa)	Lackawanna Legal Record
Lalor (NY)	Lalor's Supplement to Hill & Denio (NY)
La L Rev	Louisiana Law Review
Lanc Bar (Pa)	Lancaster Bar
Lanc L Rev (Pa)	Lancaster Law Review
Land Dec (US)	Lands Decisions (US)
Lane (Eng)	Lane [145 Eng Reprint]
Lans (NY)	Lansing (Supreme)
Lans Ch (NY)	Lansing's Chancery Decisions
LAR	Labor Arbitration Reports (BNA)
Latch (Eng)	Latch [82 Eng Reprint]
Law & Contempt Problems	Law & Contemporary Problems (Duke University)
Law Journal (Eng)	See LJ
Law Notes (Eng)	Law Notes
Lawrence LJ (Pa)	Lawrence Law Journal
Law Reports (Eng)	See LR
Ld Kenyon (Eng)	Lord Kenyon (King's Bench) [96 Eng Reprint]
Ld Raym (Eng)	Lord Raymond (King's Bench) [91, 92 Eng Reprint]
Lea (Tenn)	Lea
Leach CL (Eng)	Leach's Cases in Crown Law [168 Eng Reprint]
Lead Cas in Eq (Eng)	See White & T Lead Cas in Eq
Lebanon Co LJ (Pa)	Lebanon County Legal Journal
L ed (US)	Lawyers' Edition, Supreme Ct Reports
L ed 2d	Lawyers' Edition, Second Series
Lee Eccl (Eng)	Lee, Ecclesiastical Judgments [161 Eng Reprint]
Legal Chron (Pa)	See Foster
Legal Gaz (Pa)	Legal Gazette, Philadelphia
Legal Gaz R (Pa)	See Campb
Leg & Ins Rep (Pa)	Legal & Insurance Reporter
Leg Int (Pa)	See Phila Leg Int
Leg Ops (Pa)	Legal Opinions
Leg R (Tenn)	Legal Reporter parallel to Shannon Cas
Leg Rec (Pa)	Legal Record
Leh Co LJ (Pa)	Lehigh County Law Journal
Leh VLR (Pa)	Lehigh Valley Law Reporter
Leigh (Va)	Leigh Reports
Leigh & CCC (Eng)	Leigh & Cave English Crown Cases [169 Eng Reprint]
Leon (Eng)	Leonard (King's Bench) [74 Eng Reprint]
Lev (Eng)	Levinz (King's Bench) [83 Eng Reprint]
Lewin CC (Eng)	Lewin, Crown Cases [168 Eng Reprint]
Ley (Eng)	Ley [80 Eng Reprint]
LGR (Eng)	Local Government Reports

Lilly Assize (Eng)	Lilly's Reports & Pleadings of Cases in Assize [170 Eng Reprint]
Litt (Ky)	Littell
Littleton (Eng)	Littleton [124 Eng Reprint]
Litt Sel Cas (Ky)	Littell's Select Cases
Livingstone Jud Ops (NY)	Livingstone's Judicial Opinions (Mayor) Court, NY
LJ Adm NS (Eng)	See LJ Prob NS
LJ Bankr NS (Eng)	Law Journal Reports, New Series, Bankruptcy
LJ Ch (Eng)	Law Journal Chancery
LJ Ch NS (Eng)	Law Journal Reports, New Series, Chancery
LJCP (Eng)	Law Journal Reports, Common Pleas
LJCP NS (Eng)	Law Journal Reports, Common Pleas, New Series
LJ Exch (Eng)	Law Journal Reports, Exchequer
LJ Exch in Eq (Eng)	English Law Journal, Exchequer in Equity
LJ Exch NS (Eng)	Law Journal Reports, Exchequer, New Series
LJKB (Eng)	Law Journal Reports, King's Bench
LJKB NS (Eng)	Law Journal Reports, King's Bench, New Series
LJ Mag Cas (Eng)	Law Journal Reports, Magistrates' Cases
LJ Mag Cas NS (Eng)	Law Journal Reports, Magistrates' Cases, New Series
LJ Mat (Eng)	See LJ Prob
LJNC (Eng)	Law Journal, Notes of Cases
LJ News (Eng)	Law Journal Newspaper
LJPC (Eng)	Law Journal, Privy Council
LJPC NS (Eng)	Law Journal, Privy Council, New Series
LJPD & A (Eng)	See LJ Prob NS
LJ Prob (Eng)	Law Journal, Probate & Matrimonial
LJ Prob NS (Eng)	Law Journal, Probate & Matrimonial, New Series
LJQB (Eng)	Law Journal Reports, Queen's Bench
LJQB NS (Eng)	Law Journal Reports, Queen's Bench, New Series
LJR (Eng)	Law Journal Reports 1947–1949
Lloyd & Goold (t Plunkett) (Ir)	Lloyd & Goold (temp. Plunkett)
Lloyd & Goold (t Sugden) (Ir)	Lloyd & Goold (temp. Sugden)
Lloyd List (Eng)	Lloyd's List
Lock Rev Cas (NY)	Lockwood's Reversed Cases (Common Law)
Lofft (Eng)	Lofft (King's Bench) [98 Eng Reprint]
Loss, Sec Reg	Loss' Security Regulations
Low Dec (F)	Lowell's Decisions
Lower Can	Lower Canada Reports
Lower Can Jur	Lower Canada Jurist
Lower Can SQ	Lower Canada Reports—Seigniorial Questions
Lowndes & M (Eng)	Lowndes & Maxwell
LRA	Lawyers' Reports, Annotated
LRA NS	Lawyers' Reports, Annotated, New Series
LRA1915A	Lawyers' Reports, Annotated annuals begin with 1915
LR—Adm & Eccl (Eng)	Law Reports, Admiralty and Ecclesiastical
LR—App Cas (Eng)	Law Reports, Appeal Cases
LR—CC (Eng)	Law Reports, Crown Cases

LR—Ch (Eng)	Law Reports, Chancery Appeal Cases
LR—Ch Div (Eng)	Law Reports, Chancery Division
LR—CP (Eng)	Law Reports, Common Pleas
LR—CP Div (Eng)	Law Reports, Common Pleas Division
LR—Eq (Eng)	Law Reports, Equity
LR—Exch (Eng)	Law Reports, Exchequer
LR—Exch Div (Eng)	Law Reports, Exchequer Division
LR—HL (Eng)	Law Reports, House of Lords
LR—HL Sc App Cas (Eng)	Law Reports, Scotch and Divorce Appeal Cases, House of Lords
LR—Indian App (Eng)	Law Reports, Indian Appeals
LR—PC (Eng)	Law Reports, Privy Council
LR—Prob & D (Eng)	Law Reports, Probate & Divorce
LR—Prob & M (Eng)	See LR—Prob & D
LR—Prob Div (Eng)	Law Reports, Probate, Divorce and Admiralty Division
LR—QB (Eng)	Law Reports, Queen's Bench
LR—QB Div (Eng)	Law Reports, Queen's Bench Division
L.S.	locus sigilli (place of the seal)
LT (Eng)	Law Times Journal
Ltd.	Limited
LT Jo (Eng)	Law Times, Newspaper
LT NS (Eng)	Law Times, New Series
Luders Elec Cas (Eng)	Luders' Election Cases
Lush (Eng)	Lushington (Admiralty) [167 Eng Reprint]
Lutw (Eng)	Lutwyche [125 Eng Reprint]
Lutw Reg Cas (Eng)	Lutwyche's Registration Appeal Cases
Luzerne Leg Obs (Pa)	Luzerne Legal Observer
Luzerne Leg Reg (Pa)	Luzerne Legal Register
Luzerne Leg Reg R (Pa)	Luzerne Legal Register Reports
Luzerne LJ (Pa)	Luzerne Law Journal
Lycoming R (Pa)	Lycoming Reporter

M

McAll (F)	McAllister, US Circuit Ct
MacArth (Dist Col)	MacArthur
MacArth & M (Dist Col)	MacArthur & Mackay
MacArth Pat Cas (F)	MacArthur's Patent Cases
McCahon (Kan)	McCahon, Kansas Reports
McCart (NJ)	McCarter
M'Clel (Eng)	M'Cleland (Exchequer) [148 Eng Reprint]
M'Clel & Y (Eng)	M'Cleland & Young (Exchequer) [148 Eng Reprint]
M'Cord Eq (SC)	M'Cord, SC Equity Reports
M'Cord L (SC)	M'Cord, SC Law Reports
McCormick, Damages	McCormick on Damages
McCrary (F)	McCrary, US Circuit Ct
McGloin (La)	McGloin
Mackey (Dist Col)	Mackey
McLean (F)	McLean, US Circuit Ct

Maclean & R (Scot)	Maclean & Robinson, Scotch Appeal Cases [9 Eng Reprint]
McMull Eq (SC)	McMullan, SC Equity Reports
McMull L (SC)	McMullan, SC Law Reports
Macn & G (Eng)	Macnaghten & Gordon [41, 42 Eng Reprint]
Macpherson (Scot)	Macpherson
Macq Sc App Cas	Macqueen Scotch Appeal Cases
McQuillin, Municipal Corporations	McQuillin on Municipal Corporations
Madd Ch (Eng)	Maddock, Chancery Reports [56 Eng Reprint]
Magis & Const (Pa)	Magistrate & Constable
Maine L Rev	Maine Law Review
Malcolm, Ethics	Malcolm, Legal and Judicial Ethics
Manitoba L (Can)	Manitoba Law Reports
Mann & G (Eng)	Manning & Granger (Common Pleas) [133–135 Eng Reprint]
Mann & R (Eng)	Manning & Ryland (King's Bench)
Mann G & S (Eng)	See CB
Manson (Eng)	Manson
Man Unrep Cas (La)	Manning's Unreported Cases
March NC (Eng)	March, New Cases (King's Bench & Common Pleas) [82 Eng Reprint]
Marq L Rev (Wis)	Marquette Law Review
Marsh (Eng)	Marshall (Common Pleas)
Marsh (Ky)	See AK Marsh or JJ Marsh
Mart (Ga)	Martin
Mart (Ind)	Martin
Mart (La)	Martin
Mart & Y (Tenn)	Martin & Yeager
Martin (NC)	Martin
Mart NS (La)	Martin's New Series
Marv (Del)	Marvell
Mason (F)	Mason, US Circuit Ct
Mass	Massachusetts Reports
Mass LQ	Massachusetts Law Quarterly, Boston
Mass LR	Massachusetts Law Reporter, Boston
Matson (Conn)	Matson
Maule & S (Eng)	Maule & Selwyn (King's Bench) [105 Eng Reprint]
MC (F)	Maritime Cases
MCC	Motor Carrier Cases
Md	Maryland
Md Ch	Maryland Chancery
Md L Rev	Maryland Law Review
Me	Maine
Mechem, Agency	Mechem on Agency
Med Leg J	Medical Legal Journal
Mees & W (Eng)	Meeson & Welsby (Exchequer) [150–153 Eng Reprint]
Megone (Eng)	Megone
Meigs (Tenn)	Meigs

Mercer L Rev	Mercer Law Review
Meriv (Eng)	Merivale (Chancery) [35, 36 Eng Reprint]
Met (Ky)	Metcalfe
Met (Mass)	Metcalf
Miami L Rev	Miami Law Review (Fla)
Mich	Michigan
Mich Adv	Michigan Reports Advanced Sheets
Michie, Banks	Michie's Banks & Banking
Mich L Rev	Michigan Law Review
Mich NP	Michigan Nisi Prius Cases
Miles (Pa)	Miles
Mil Jur, Cas & Mat	Military Jurisprudence, Cases & Materials
Mill Const (SC)	Mill SC Constitutional Law
Mills (NY)	Mills (Surrogate)
Minn	Minnesota
Minn L Rev	Minnesota Law Review
Minor (Ala)	Minor
Misc (NY)	Miscellaneous Reports
Miss	Mississippi Reports
Miss LJ	Mississippi Law Journal
Mo	Missouri
Moak (Eng)	Moak
Mo App	Missouri Appeals
Mod (Eng)	Modern (King's Bench) [86–88 Eng Reprint]
Model Bus Corp Act Anno	Atkins, et al., Model Business Corporation Act, annotated
Molloy (Ir)	Molloy
Mo L Rev	Missouri Law Review
Mon	See B Mon or TB Mon
Monaghan (Pa)	Monaghan
Mon Leg R (Pa)	Monroe Legal Reporter
Mont	Montana
Mont & Ayr Bankr (Eng)	Montagu & Ayrton, Bankruptcy
Mont & B Bankr (Eng)	Montagu & Bligh, Bankruptcy
Mont & C Bankr (Eng)	Montagu & Chitty, Bankruptcy
Mont & M Bankr (Eng)	Montagu & MacArthur, Bankruptcy
Mont Bankr (Eng)	Montagu Reports, Bankruptcy
Mont D & De G (Eng)	Montagu, Deacon & De Gex
Montg Co LR (Pa)	Montgomery County Law Reporter
Month L Bull (NY)	Monthly Law Bulletin
Month Leg Exam (NY)	Monthly Legal Examiner, NY
Month LJ	Monthly Journal of Law, Washington
Month L Rev	Monthly Law Review
Mont L Rev	Montana Law Review
Montreal L—QB (Can)	Montreal Law Reports, Queen's Bench
Montreal L—SC (Can)	Montreal Law Reports, Superior Court
Moody & M (Eng)	Moody & Malkin (Nisi Prius) [173 Eng Reprint]
Moody & R (Eng)	Moody & Robinson (Nisi Prius) [174 Eng Reprint]
Moody CC (Eng)	Moody, Crown Cases [168, 169 Eng Reprint]

Moore (Eng)	See F Moore or JB Moore
Moore & P (Eng)	Moore & Payne (Common Pleas)
Moore & S (Eng)	Moore & Scott (Common Pleas)
Moore, Fed Practice	Moore's Federal Practice
Moore Ind App (Eng)	Moore's Indian Appeals Reports [18–20 Eng Reprint]
Moore KB (Eng)	See F Moore
Moore PCC (Eng)	Moore, Privy Council Cases [12–15 Eng Reprint]
Moore PCC NS (Eng)	Moore, Privy Council Cases, New Series [15–17 Eng Reprint]
Morrell (Eng)	Morrell Bankruptcy Cases
Morris (Iowa)	Morris
Morris Crim (Miss)	Morris' State Cases (Criminal)
Mosely (Eng)	Mosely (Chancery) [25 Eng Reprint]
Mottla, NY Evidence	Mottla, New York Evidence—Proof of Cases
MPR (Can)	Maritime Provinces Reports
ms.	manuscript
Munf (Va)	Munford
Munic LR (Pa)	Municipal Law Reporter
Murph (NC)	Murphey
Murph & H (Eng)	Murphy & Hurlstone (Exchequer)
Murray (Scot)	Murray
Myl & C (Eng)	Mylne & Craig (Chancery) [40, 41 Eng Reprint]
Myl & K (Eng)	Mylne & Keen (Chancery) [39, 40 Eng Reprint]
Myrick Prob (Cal)	Myrick's Probate Reports

N

Nat L Rep (US)	National Law Reporter
N.B.	nota bene (note well)
NC	North Carolina State
NCCA	Negligence & Compensation Cases, Annotated
NCCA NS	Negligence & Compensation Cases, Annotated, New Series
NCCA3d	Negligence & Compensation Cases, Annotated, 3d Series
N Chip (Vt)	N. Chipman
NC Conf Rep (NC)	North Carolina Conference Reports
NC L Rev	North Carolina Law Review
NC Term Rep	North Carolina Term Reports
ND	North Dakota
NE	Northeastern Reporter
NE2d	Northeastern Reporter, 2d Series
Neb	Nebraska
Neb (Unof)	Nebraska Unofficial Reports
Nelson (Eng)	Nelson (Chancery) [21 Eng Reprint]
Nev	Nevada
Nev & M (Eng)	Nevile & Manning (King's Bench)
Nev & Macn (Eng)	Nevile & Macnamara (King's Bench)
Nev & P (Eng)	Nevile & Perry (King's Bench)
Newberry Adm (F)	Newberry, US Admiralty (Dist Ct)
New Br (Can)	New Brunswick

New Br Eq (Can)	New Brunswick Equity Reports
New Br Eq Cas (Can)	New Brunswick Equity Cases
Newfoundl LR	Newfoundland Law Reports
Newfoundl R	Newfoundland Reports
Newfoundl Sel Cas	Newfoundland Select Cases
New Reports (Eng)	New Reports
New Sess Cas (Eng)	New Sessions Cases
New So WL	New South Wales Law Reports
New So W St	New South Wales State Reports
New So WWN	New South Wales Weekly Notes
New Zeal L	New Zealand Law Reports
NH	New Hampshire
Newhall, Estates	Newhall's Settlement of Estates and Fiduciary Law in Massachusetts
Nichols-Cahill	Nichols-Cahill Annotated New York Civil Practice Acts
Nichols, Eminent Domain	Nichols' Law of Eminent Domain
Nichols, Fed Procedure	Nichols, et al., Cyclopedia of Federal Procedure
N Ir	Northern Ireland Law
NJ	New Jersey
NJ Eq	New Jersey Equity
NJL	New Jersey Law
NJLJ	New Jersey Law Journal
NJ Misc	New Jersey Miscellaneous
NJ Super	New Jersey Superior Court
NLRB (F)	National Labor Relations Board Decisions
NM	New Mexico
Nolan (Eng)	Nolan's Magistrate's Cases
nol-pros	nolle prosequi
Norris & L, Perpetuities	Norris & Leach on Rule Against Perpetuities
Norris, Seamen	Norris' Law of Seamen
North Co R (Pa)	Northampton County Reporter
North U L Rev	Northwestern University Law Review (formerly Illinois Law Review)
Northum Leg J (Pa)	Northumberland Legal Journal
Northum Leg N (Pa)	Northumberland County Legal News
Notes of Cases (Eng)	Notes of Cases, Ecclesiastical & Maritime
Notre Dame Law	Notre Dame Law
Nott & M'C (SC)	Nott & M'Cord, SC Law Reports
Nov Sc	Nova Scotia Supreme Court Reports
Noy (Eng)	Noy's King's Bench Reports [74 Eng Reprint]
NW	Northwestern Reporter
NW2d	Northwestern Reporter, 2d Series
NW Terr (Can)	See Terr L
NY	New York (Court of Appeals)
NY Anno Cas	New York Annotated Cases (Practice & Code)
NY City Ct	New York City Court Reports
NY City Ct Supp	New York City Court Reports, Supplement
NY City Hall Rec	New York City Hall Recorder
NY Civ Proc	New York Civil Procedure Reports

NY Civ Proc NS	New York Civil Procedure Reports, New Series
NY Code R	New York Code Reporter
NY Code R NS	New York Code Reports, New Series
NY Crim	New York Criminal Reports
NY Jur	New York Jurisprudence
NY Leg Obs	New York Legal Observer
NY L Gaz	New York Law Gazette
NY LJ	New York Law Journal
NY L Rec	New York Law Record
NY L Rev	New York Law Review
NYS	New York Supplement
NYS2d	New York Supplement Reports, 2d Series
NYSR	New York State Reporter
NY St Dept	New York State Department Reports
NY Super	New York Superior Ct Reports
NY Trans App	New York Transcript Appeal
NYU LQ Rev	New York University Law Quarterly Review
NYU L Rev	New York University Law Review
NY Week Dig	New York Weekly Digest

O

O Bridg (Eng)	Orlando Bridgman [124 Eng Reprint]
Off Gaz	Official Gazette, US Patent Office, Wash., D.C.
Ohio	Ohio
Ohio App	Ohio Appeals
Ohio CA	Ohio Court of Appeals
Ohio CC	Ohio Circuit Court Reports
Ohio CC NS	Ohio Circuit Court Reports, New Series
Ohio CD	Ohio Circuit Decisions
Ohio Dec	See Ohio Dec NP
Ohio Dec NP	Ohio Decisions Nisi Prius
Ohio Dec Reprint	Ohio Decisions Reprint (Circuit Ct)
Ohio F Dec	Ohio Federal Decisions
Ohio Jur	Ohio Jurisprudence
Ohio Jur 2d	Ohio Jurisprudence, Second Series
Ohio L Abs	Ohio Law Abstract
Ohio Leg News	Ohio Legal News
Ohio LJ	See WL Bull
Ohio Low Dec	Ohio Lower Court Decisions
Ohio LR	Ohio Law Reporter
Ohio NP	Ohio Nisi Prius Reports
Ohio NP NS	Ohio Nisi Prius Reports, New Series
Ohio Ops	Ohio Opinions
Ohio Prob	Ohio Probate Court Reports
Ohio S & CP Dec	See Ohio Dec NP
Ohio St	Ohio State
Ohio St LJ	Ohio State Law Journal
Ohio Supp	Ohio Supplement
Ohio Unrep	Ohio Supreme Ct Unreported Cases 1 vol (Misc)

Ohlinger, Fed Practice .... Ohlinger's Federal Practice
Okla .... Oklahoma
Okla Crim .... Oklahoma Criminal Reports
Olcott Adm (F) .... Olcott, US Dist Ct (Admiralty)
Oleck, Corporations ..... Oleck's Modern Corporation Law
Olwine's LJ (Pa) .... Olwine's Law Journal
Ont App .... Ontario Appeals
Ont Elect .... Ontario Election Cases
Ont L .... Ontario Law Reports
Ont Pr .... Ontario Practice Reports
Ont R .... Ontario Reports
Ont Week N .... Ontario Weekly Notes
Ont Week R .... Ontario Weekly Reporter
Ops Atty Gen .... Opinions of the US Attorneys-General
Or .... Oregon
Orleans App (La) .... Louisiana Court of Appeals, Parish of Orleans
Out (Pa) .... Outerbridge
Overt (Tenn) .... Overton
Owen (Eng) .... Owen (King's Bench) [74 Eng Reprint]

P

P .... Pacific
P2d .... Pacific 2d Series
Pa .... Pennsylvania
Pa Bar Asso Q .... Pennsylvania Bar Association Quarterly
Pa Co .... Pennsylvania County Court
Pa Corp R .... Pennsylvania Corporation Reporter
Pa D & C .... Pennsylvania District & County Reports
Pa Dist .... Pennsylvania District Reporter
Page, Wills .... Page on Wills
Paige (NY) .... Paige (Chancery)
Paine (F) .... Paine, US Circuit Ct
Pa LJ .... Clark's Pennsylvania Law Journal
Palmer (Eng) .... Palmer [81 Eng Reprint]
Pa L Rec .... Pennsylvania Law Record
Pa L Rev .... University of Pennsylvania Law Review
Pa Prac .... See Stand Pa Prac
Pa Rec .... Pennsylvania Record
Park Crim (NY) .... Parker's Criminal Cases
Parker (Eng) .... Parker [145 Eng Reprint]
Pars Sel Eq Cas (Pa) .... Parsons Select Equity Cases
Pa St .... Pennsylvania State Reports
Pa Summary .... Summary of Pennsylvania Jurisprudence
Pa Super .... Pennsylvania Superior Court Reports
Paterson Sc App Cas .... Paterson, Scotch Appeal Cases
Paton Sc App Cas ...... Paton, Scotch Appeal Cases
Patton & H (Va) .... Patton & Heath
PC (Eng) .... See LR—PC—
Peake NP Add Cas (Eng) .. Peake, Additional Cases Nisi Prius [170 Eng Reprint]

Peake NP Cas (Eng)	Peake, Nisi Prius Cases [170 Eng Reprint]
Pears (Pa)	Pearson
Peck (Tenn)	Peck
Peere-Wms (Eng)	See P Wms
Pen (NJ)	Pennington
Penn (Del)	Pennewill
Pennyp (Pa)	Pennypacker Unreported Pennsylvania Cases
Pennyp Col Cas	Pennypacker's Colonial Cases
Penr & W (Pa)	Penrose & Watts
Perry & D (Eng)	Perry & Davison
Pet (US)	Peter
Pet Adm (F)	Peters' Admiralty, US Dist Ct
Pet CC (F)	Peters, US Circuit Ct
Phila (Pa)	Philadelphia
Phila Leg Int (Pa)	Philadelphia Legal Intelligencer
Philippine	Philippine Reports
Phill Ch (Eng)	Phillips' Chancery Reports [41 Eng Reprint]
Phill Eq (NC)	Phillips' Equity.
Phillim Eccl (Eng)	J. Phillimore Ecclesiastical Reports [161 Eng Reprint]
Phill L (NC)	Phillips' Law
Pick (Mass)	Pickering
Pike & Fischer, Admin Law	Pike & Fischer's Administrative Law
Pinney (Wis)	Pinney
Pittsb (Pa)	Pittsburgh
Pittsb Leg J (Pa)	Pittsburgh Legal Journal
Pittsb Leg J NS (Pa)	Pittsburgh Legal Journal, New Series
Pittsb L Rev	University of Pittsburgh Law Review
Plowd (Eng)	Plowden's King's Bench Reports [75 Eng Reprint]
Pollexfen (Eng)	Pollexfen [86 Eng Reprint]
Pollock, Torts	Pollock on Torts
Popham (Eng)	Popham (King's Bench) [79 Eng Reprint]
Port (Ala)	Porter
Porto Rico	See Puerto Rico
Posey Unrep Cas (Tex)	Posey Unreported Cases
Powell, Real Property	Powell on Real Property
Powers (NY)	Powers (Surrogate)
p.p.a.	per power of attorney
Prec in Ch (Eng)	Precedents in Chancery [24 Eng Reprint]
Pr Edw Isl (Eng)	Prince Edward Island
Price (Eng)	Price [145–147 Eng Reprint]
Prob (Eng)	Probate Division
Prob & D (Eng)	See LR—Prob & D—
Prob & M (Eng)	See LR—Prob & D—
Prob Div (Eng)	See LR—Prob Div—
Prosser, Torts	Prosser on Torts
Puerto Rico	Puerto Rico
Puerto Rico F	Puerto Rico Federal Reports
Pulsifer (Me)	Pulsifer
PUR	Public Utilities Reports

PUR NS .... Public Utilities Reports, New Series
PUR1915A .... Public Utilities Reports: Annuals begin with 1915
P Wms (Eng) .... Peere Williams [24 Eng Reprint]

Q

QB (Eng) .... Queen's Bench [113–118 Eng Reprint]
QB (Eng) .... See LR—QB—
QB (Eng) .... Law Reports, Queen's Bench Division
QB Div (Eng) .... See LR—QB Div—
q.c.f. .... quare clausum fregit (because he broke the close)
q.t. .... qui tam (who as well)
Quart LJ (Va) .... Quarterly Law Journal
Quart L Rev (Va) .... Quarterly Law Review
Quebec KB (Can) .... See Rap Jud Quebec—KB—
Quebec L (Can) .... Quebec Law Reports
Quebec Pr (Can) .... Quebec Practice
Quebec QB (Can) .... See Rap Jud Quebec—QB—
Quebec SC (Can) .... See Rap Jud Quebec—CS—
Queensl JP (Austr) .... Queensland Justice of the Peace
Queensl LJ (Austr) .... Queensland Law Journal
Queensl SC (Austr) .... Queensland Supreme Court Reports
Queensl St (Austr) .... Queensland State Reports
Queensl WN (Austr) ...... Queensland Weekly Notes
Quincy (Mass) .... Quincy
q.v. .... quod vide (which see)

R

Rag Super Ct Dec (Calif) .. Ragland Superior Court Decisions, California
Railway & Corp Law J .... Railway & Corporation Law Journal
Ramsay App Cas (Can) .... Ramsay's Appeal Cases
Rand (Va) .... Randolph
Rap Jud Quebec—CS—
 (Can) .... Rapports Judiciaries de Quebec
Rap Jud Quebec—KB—
 (Can) .... Rapports Judiciaries de Quebec
Rap Jud Quebec—QB—
 (Can) .... Rapports Judiciaries de Quebec
Rawle (Pa) .... Rawle
Raym Ld .... See Ld Raym
Raym T .... See T Raym
RCL .... Ruling Case Law
Redf (NY) .... Redfield (Surrogate)
Remington, Bankruptcy ... Remington on Bankruptcy
Rep in Ch (Eng) .... Reports in Chancery [21 Eng Reprint]
Rep Pat Cas (Eng) .... Reports of Patents, Designs & Trade-Marks Cases
Reprint (Eng) .... See Eng Reprint
Rep t Finch (Eng) .... See Cas t Finch
Rep t Hardw .... Reports temp. Hardwicke [27 Eng Reprint]
Rep t Talb (Eng) .... See Cas t Talb

Rettie (Scot)	Rettie
Rev de Jur (Can)	Revue de Jurisprudence
Rev de Leg (Can)	Revue de Legislation et du Jurisprudence
Revised R (Eng)	Revised Reports
Rev Leg (Can)	La Revue Legale
RI	Rhode Island
Rice Eq (SC)	Rice, SC Equity Reports
Rice L (SC)	Rice, SC Law Reports
Richardson, Law Practice	Richardson's Establishing a Law Practice
Rich Cas (SC)	Richardson, SC Equity Cases
Rich Eq (SC)	Richardson, SC Equity Reports
Rich L (SC)	Richardson, SC Law Reports
RI Ct Rec	Rhode Island Court Records
RI Dec	Rhode Island Decisions
Ridgew (Ir)	Ridgeway Reports
Ridgew Ir PC	Ridgeway Irish Appeal or Parliamentary Cases
Ridgew L & S (Ir)	Ridgeway, Lapp & Schoales
Ridgew t Hardw (Eng)	Ridgeway temp. Hardwicke [27 Eng Reprint]
Riley Eq (SC)	Riley, SC Equity Reports
Riley L (SC)	Riley, SC Law Reports
RLB Dec	Railroad Labor Board Decisions
RM Charlt (Ga)	R. M. Charlton
Rob (Eng)	See C Rob or W Rob
Rob (La)	Robinson
Rob (Va)	Robinson
Robb (NJ)	Robbins' New Jersey Equity Reports
Rob Cons Cas (Tex)	Robards' Conscript Cases
Robinson, Crim Law & Proc	Robinson's Cases on Criminal Law and Procedure
Robinson Sc App Cas	Robinson, Scotch Appeals Cases
Robt (NY)	Robertson (Superior)
Robt Eccl (Eng)	Robertson's Ecclesiastical [163 Eng Reprint]
Robt Sc App Cas	Robertson's Scotch Appeal Cases
Rolle (Eng)	Rolle's King's Bench Reports [81 Eng Reprint]
Rolle Abr (Eng)	Rolle's Abridgment of Common Law
Rolls Ct Rep (Eng)	Rolls Court Reports
Romilly NC (Eng)	Romilly's Notes of Cases
Root (Conn)	Root
Rose Bankr (Eng)	Rose, Bankruptcy
Runnell (Ia)	Runnell's Reports
Russ & Ches (Nov Sc)	Russell & Chesley, Nova Scotia
Russ & M (Eng)	Russell & Mylne's Chancery Reports [39 Eng Reprint]
Russ & RCC (Eng)	Russell & Ryan's Crown Cases [168 Eng Reprint]
Russ Ch (Eng)	Russell's Chancery Reports [38 Eng Reprint]
Russ Con El (Mass)	Russell's Contested Elections, Mass
Russ Eq (Nova Sc)	Russell's Equity Cases
Ryan & M (Eng)	Ryan & Moody's Nisi Prius Reports [171 Eng Reprint]
Ry & C Cas (Eng)	Railway & Canal Cases
Ry & C Traffic Cas (Eng)	Railway & Canal Traffic Cases

S

Sadler (Pa)	Sadler's Cases
Sal (Ia)	Salinger
Salk (Eng)	Salkeld [91 Eng Reprint]
Sandf (NY)	Sandford (Superior)
Sandf Ch (NY)	Sandford's Chancery Reports
San Fran Law Bull	San Francisco Law Bulletin
San Fran LJ	San Francisco Law Journal
Sask L (Can)	Saskatchewan Law
Saund (Eng)	See Wms' Saund
Saund & C (Eng)	Saunders & Cole
Savile (Eng)	Savile [123 Eng Reprint]
Sawy (F)	Sawyer, US Circuit Ct
Sax (NJ)	Saxton
Sayer (Eng)	Sayer [96 Eng Reprint]
Sayre, Adm Cas	Sayre's Cases on Admiralty
SC	South Carolina State Reports
SC (Scot)	Scottish Court of Session Cases, New Series
Scam (Ill)	Scammon
Sch & Lef (Ir)	Schoales & Lefroy
Schuy Leg Rec (Pa)	Schuylkill Legal Record
Schuy Reg (Pa)	Schuylkill Register
sci. fa.	scire facias (revival of judgment)
SC LJ	South Carolina Law Journal
Scot Jur (Scot)	Scottish Jurist
Scot LR (Scot)	Scottish Law Reporter
Scots LT (Scot)	Scots Law Times
Scott (Eng)	Scott's Reports
Scott NR (Eng)	Scott's New Reports
Scott, Trusts	Scott on Trusts
S Ct (US)	Supreme Court Reporter
SD	South Dakota
SEC (F)	Securities & Exchange Commission Decisions
Seld (NY)	Selden
Seld Notes (NY)	Selden's Notes (Court of Appeals)
Sen Doc	Senate Document
Sen J	Senate Journal
Sen Rep	Senate Reports
Serg & R (Pa)	Sergeant & Rawle
Sess Cas (Eng)	Session Cases [93 Eng Reprint]
Shannon Cas (Tenn)	Shannon's Unreported Tennessee Cases
Shaw & D (Scot)	Shaw & Dunlop
Shaw & M Sc App Cas (Scot)	Shaw & Maclean's Scotch Appeal Cases
Shaw Sc App Cas (Scot)	Shaw's Scotch Appeal Cases, House of Lords
Sheldon (NY)	Sheldon (Superior)
Shep (Ala)	Shepherd, Reports
Shep Sel Cas (Ala)	Shepherds' Select Cases, Ala
Shower KB (Eng)	Shower's King's Bench Reports [89 Eng Reprint]

Shower PC (Eng)	Shower's Parliamentary Cases [1 Eng Reprint]
Sid (Eng)	Siderfin's King's Bench Reports [82 Eng Reprint]
Silv Ct App (NY)	Silvernail's Court of Appeals Reports
Silv Sup (NY)	Silvernail's Supreme Court Reports
Sim (Eng)	Simons' Vice-Chancery Reports [57–60 Eng Reprint]
Sim & Stu (Eng)	Simons & Stuart's Vice-Chancery Reports [57 Eng Reprint]
Simes & S, Future Interests	Simes & Smith on the Law of Future Interests
Sim NS (Eng)	Simons' Vice-Chancery, New Series [61 Eng Reprint]
Singer Prob Cas (Pa)	Singer's Probate Cases
Skill Pol Rep (NY)	Skillman's NY Police Reports
Skinner (Eng)	Skinner's King's Bench Reports [90 Eng Reprint]
Smale & G (Eng)	Smale & Giffard [65 Eng Reprint]
Smedes & M (Miss)	Smedes & Marshall
Smedes & M Ch (Miss)	Smedes & Marshall, Chancery Reports
Smith (Cal)	Smith
Smith (Dak)	Smith
Smith (Eng)	Smith
Smith (Ind)	Smith
Smith (Me)	Smith
Smith (Mo App)	Smith
Smith (NH)	Smith
Smith (NY)	See ED Smith
Smith (Pa)	P. F. Smith
Smith (Wis)	Smith
Smith CCM (Me)	Smith Circuit Courts-Martial
Smith Lead Cas (H & W) (Eng)	Smith's Leading Cases (Hare & W)
Smith Reg Cas (Eng)	Smith's Registration Cases (Eng)
Sneed (Ky)	Sneed
Sneed (Tenn)	Sneed
So	Southern
So 2d	Southern 2d Series
So African L	South African Law Reports
So African LJ	South African Law J
So Austr L	South Australian Law Reports
So Austr St	South Australian State Reports
So Cal L Rev	Southern California Law Review
So LJ	Southern Law Journal and Reporter, Nashville, Tennessee
Sol Jo (Eng)	Solicitors' Journal
So LQ	Southern Law Quarterly
So L Rev	Southern Law Review, St. Louis
So L Rev NS	Southern Law Review, New Series, St. Louis, Missouri
Som Leg J (Pa)	Somerset Legal Journal
South (NJ)	Southard
Spears	See Speers
Speers Eq (SC)	Speers, SC Equity Reports

Speers L (SC)	Speers, SC Law Reports
Spen (NJ)	Spencer
Spinks Eccl & Adm (Eng)	Spinks, Ecclesiastical & Admiralty [164 Eng Reprint]
Spinks Prize Cas (Eng)	Spinks' Prize Cases [164 Eng Reprint]
Spooner (Wis)	Spooner
Sprague (F)	Sprague, US Dist Ct Decisions (Admiralty)
ss.	scilicet (to wit)
Stand Ga Prac	Standard Georgia Practice
Stand Pa Prac	Standard Pennsylvania Practice
Stanford L Rev	Stanford Law Review (Calif)
Starkie (Eng)	Starkie [171 Eng Reprint]
Stat at L	US Statutes at Large
State Tr (Eng)	See How St Tr
State Tr NS (Eng)	See How St Tr NS
Stecher, Agency & Partnership	Stecher's Cases on Agency and Partnership
Stevens & G (Ga)	Stevens & Graham's Reports
Stew (Ala)	Stewart
Stew (NJ)	Stewart, NJ Equity
Stew (SD)	Stewart
Stew & P (Ala)	Stewart & Porter
Stewart Vice-Adm (Nov Sc)	Stewart, Vice-Admiralty
Stiles (Ia)	Stiles
Stiness (RI)	Stiness
St John's L Rev	St. John's Law Review (Brooklyn, N. Y.)
Stock (NJ)	Stockton
Stockett (Md)	Stockett
Stockton Adm (New Br)	Stockton, Admiralty
Story (F)	Story, US Circuit Ct
Strange (Eng)	Strange [93 Eng Reprint]
Street, Legal Liability	Street on Foundations of Legal Liability
St Rep Queensl (Austr)	Queensland State Reports
Strobh Eq (SC)	Strobhart, SC Equity
Strobh L (SC)	Strobhart, SC Law
Stuart KB (Quebec)	Stuart, Lower Canada King's Bench
Stuart Vice-Adm (Quebec)	Stuart, Vice-Admiralty
Style (Eng)	Style [82 Eng Reprint]
Summers, Oil & Gas	Summers on Oil & Gas
Sumn (F)	Sumner, US Circuit Ct
Super Ct (RI)	Rhode Island Superior Court
Susquehanna Leg Chron (Pa)	Susquehanna Legal Chronicle
SW	Southwestern
SW2d	Southwestern 2d Series
Swabey Adm (Eng)	Swabey's Admiralty [166 Eng Reprint]
Swabey & T (Eng)	Swabey & Tristram [164 Eng Reprint]
Swan (Tenn)	Swan
Swanst (Eng)	Swanston [36 Eng Reprint]
Sweeney (NY)	Sweeney (Superior)

Syracuse L Rev .... Syracuse Law Review

T

Talb (Eng) .... See Cas t Talb
Tamlyn (Eng) .... Tamlyn [48 Eng Reprint]
Taney (F) .... Taney, US Circuit Ct
Tappan (Ohio) .... Tappan (Common Pleas)
Taunt (Eng) .... Taunton [127–129 Eng Reprint]
Tax LR .... Tax Law Reporter
Tax L Rev .... Tax Law Review
Taylor (NC) .... Taylor
Taylor KB (Can) .... Taylor, Upper Canada King's Bench Reports
TB Mon (Ky) .... T. B. Monroe
T Ct (F) .... Tax Court of US
T Ct Mem (F) .... Tax Court of US Memorandum
Temple & M (Eng) .... Temple & Mew (Crown Cases)
Temple LQ (Pa) .... Temple Law Quarterly
Tenn .... Tennessee
Tenn App .... Tennessee Civil Appeals
Tenn Cas .... See Shannon Cas
Tenn CCA .... Tennessee Court of Civil Appeals
Tenn Ch .... Tennessee Chancery
Tenn Ch App .... Tennessee Chancery Appeal
Tenn L Rev .... Tennessee Law Review
Term Rep (NC) .... Term Reports
Terr L (Can) .... North-West Territories Law Reports
Terry (Del) .... Terry
Tex .... Texas Reports
Tex App .... Texas Appeal Reports (Criminal Cases)
Tex App Civ Cas (White &
  W) .... Texas Civil Appeal Cases (White & Willson)
Tex App Civ Cas (Willson) . Texas Civil Appeal Cases (Willson)
Tex Civ App .... Texas Civil Appeals
Tex Com App .... Texas Commission of Appeals
Tex Crim .... Texas Criminal Reports
Tex Dec .... Texas Decisions
Tex Jur .... Texas Jurisprudence
Tex Jur 2d .... Texas Jurisprudence, 2d Edition
Tex LJ .... Texas Law Journal
Tex L Rev .... Texas Law Review
Tex Supp .... Texas Supplement
Tex Unrep Cas .... Texas Unreported Cases, Supreme Court
Thacher Crim Cas (Mass) .. Thacher Criminal Cases
Thomp & C (NY) .... Thompson & Cook (Supreme)
Thompson's Fla Dig ...... Thompson's Digest of Laws, Florida
Thompson Unrep (Pa) ..... Thompson's Unreported Cases
Thomp Tenn Cas .... Thompson Unreported Tennessee Cases
Tiffany, Landlord & Ten .. Tiffany on Landlord & Tenant
Tiffany, Real Property ... Tiffany on Real Property

Times L (Eng)	Times Law Reports
T Jones (Eng)	T. Jones [84 Eng Reprint]
Tothill (Eng)	Tothill [21 Eng Reprint]
Toulmin, Anti-Trust Laws	Toulmin's Anti-Trust Laws
TR (Eng)	Term Reports [99–101 Eng Reprint]
Tracey, Evidence	Tracey's Cases on Evidence
Trade Mark R	Trade Mark Reporter
Trans App (NY)	Transcript Appeals
T Raym (Eng)	Sir Thomas Raymond [83 Eng Reprint]
Treadway Const (SC)	Treadway, SC Constitutional Law
Treas Regs	United States Treasury Regulations
Tucker (NY)	Tucker (Surrogate)
Tucker & C (Dist Col)	Tucker and Clephane
Tulane L Rev	Tulane Law Review
TUP Charlt (Ga)	T. U. P. Charlton
Turn & R (Eng)	Turner & Russell (Chancery) [37 Eng Reprint]
Tyler (Vt)	Tyler
Tyrw (Eng)	Tyrwhitt (Exchequer)
Tyrw & G (Eng)	Tyrwhitt & Granger (Exchequer)

U

UC App (Can)	Upper Canada Appeal Reports
UC Ch (Can)	Upper Canada Chancery Reports
UC Cham (Can)	Upper Canada Chambers Reports
UCCP (Can)	Upper Canada Common Pleas
UC Err & App (Can)	Upper Canada, Error and Appeal
U Chicago L Rev	University of Chicago Law Review
U Cin L Rev	University of Cincinnati Law Review
UC Jur (Can)	Upper Canada Jurist
UC KB (Can)	Upper Canada King's Bench Reports, Old Series
UCLJ (Can)	Upper Canada Law Journal
UC LJ NS (Can)	Upper Canada Law Journal, NS
UCMJ	Uniform Code of Military Justice
UC Pr (Can)	Upper Canada Practice Reports
UCQB (Can)	Upper Canada Queen's Bench Reports
UCQB OS (Can)	Upper Canada Queen's (King's) Bench Reports, Old Series
U Det L Rev	University of Detroit Law Review
U Fla L Rev	University of Florida Law Review
U Ill L Forum	University of Illinois Law Forum
U Iowa L Rev	University of Iowa Law Review
ULA	Uniform Laws Annotated
U Mo L Bull	University of Missouri Law Bulletin
U Pa L Rev	University of Pennsylvania Law Review
U Pitts L Rev	University of Pittsburgh Law Review
US	United States Reports
US App DC	See App DC
US Av	United States Aviation Reports
USC	United States Code

USCA	United States Code Annotated
US CCA	See CCA
USCMA	Official Reports, United States Court of Military Appeals
USCMA, Adv Op	United States Court of Military Appeals, Advance Opinions
US Ct Cl	See Ct Cl
US Dig (L ed) Anno	United States Supreme Court Digest Annotated
US Pat Quart	United States Patent Quarterly
USTC	United States Tax Cases
US Treas Regs	See Treas Regs
Utah	Utah
Utah 2d	Utah, Second Series
Utah L Rev	Utah Law Review

V

Va	Virginia
Va Cas (Va)	Virginia Cases
Va Dec	Virginia Decisions
Va L Dig	Virginia Law Digest
Va LJ	Virginia Law Journal
Va L Rev	Virginia Law Review
Vand L Rev (Tenn)	Vanderbilt Law Review
Vaughan (Eng)	Vaughan (Common Pleas) [124 Eng Reprint]
Vaux (Pa)	Vaux
Vent (Eng)	Ventris (Common Pleas) [86 Eng Reprint]
Vern (Eng)	Vernon's Chancery Reports [23 Eng Reprint]
Vern & S (Ir)	Vernon & Scriven
Ves & B (Eng)	Vesey & Beames (Chancery) [35 Eng Reprint]
Ves Jr (Eng)	Vesey, Junior (Chancery) [30–34 Eng Reprint]
Ves Jr Supp (Eng)	Supplement to Vesey, Junior [34 Eng Reprint]
Ves Sr (Eng)	Vesey, Senior (Chancery) [27, 28 Eng Reprint]
Ves Sr Supp (Eng)	Supplement to Vesey, Senior [28 Eng Reprint]
Vict L (Austr)	Victorian Law Reports
Vict Rep (Austr)	Victorian Reports
Vin Abr (Eng)	Viner's Abridgment of Law & Equity
Vin Supp	Supplement to Viner's Abridgment of Law and Equity
Virgin Islands	Virgin Islands
viz.	videlicet (namely)
Vroom (NJ)	Vroom
Vt	Vermont

W

Walk (Miss)	Walker
Walk (Pa)	Walker
Walk Ch (Mich)	Walker's Chancery Reports
Wall (US)	Wallace
Wallis (Ir)	Wallis (Chancery)
Wall Jr (F)	Wallace (J. W.) Junior, US Circuit Ct
Wall Sr (F)	Wallace (J. B.) Senior, US Circuit Ct

Walsh, Real Property	Walsh's Commentaries on Law of Real Property
Ware (F)	Ware, US Dist Ct
Wash	Washington
Wash 2d	Washington 2d Series
34A Wash 2d	Washington Court Rules
Wash (Va)	Washington, Virginia Reports
Wash CC (F)	Washington, US Circuit Ct
Wash Co (Pa)	Washington County Reports
Wash Dec	Washington Decisions
Wash Jur	Washington Jurist
Wash LR (Dist Col)	Washington Law Reporter
Wash Terr	Washington Territory
Wash UL Rev	Washington University Law Review
Watts (Pa)	Watts
Watts & S (Pa)	Watts & Sergeant
W Bl (Eng)	Sir William Blackstone [96 Eng Reprint]
WC & Ins (Eng)	Workmen's Compensation & Insurance Reports
WCC (Eng)	Workmen's Compensation Cases
Webster Pat Cas (Eng)	Webster Patent Cases
Week Dig (NY)	See NY Week Dig
Week LR (Eng)	Weekly Law Reports
Week R (Eng)	Weekly Reporter
Welsby H & G (Eng)	See Exch
Wend (NY)	Wendell (Common Law)
West (Eng)	West [9 Eng Reprint]
West Austr L	West Australian Law Reports
West Ch (Eng)	West Chancery [25 Eng Reprint]
West LJ (Ohio)	Western Law Journal
West L Month (Ohio)	Western Law Monthly
West LR (Can)	Western Law Reporter
Westmore Co LJ (Pa)	Westmoreland County Law Journal
West t H	See West Ch
West Week (Can)	Western Weekly
West Week N (Can)	Western Weekly Notes
West Week NS (Can)	Western Weekly New Series
Whart (Pa)	Wharton
Wharton, Crim Evidence	Wharton's Criminal Evidence
Wharton, Crim Proc	Wharton's Criminal Law & Procedure
Wheat (US)	Wheaton, US Supreme Ct
Wheel (Tex)	Wheelock's Reports
Wheeler CC (NY)	Wheeler's Criminal Cases
White & T Lead Cas in Eq (Eng)	White & Tudor, Leading Cases in Equity
White & W (Tex)	White & Willson
Whitman Pat Cas (US)	Whitman, Patent Cases
Wightw (Eng)	Wightwick (Exchequer) [145 Eng Reprint]
Wigmore, Evidence	Wigmore on Evidence
Wilcox (Pa)	Wilcox
Willes (Eng)	Willes (Common Pleas) [125 Eng Reprint]

Williston, Contracts	Williston on Contracts
Willson (Tex)	Willson
Wilmot's Notes (Eng)	Wilmot's Notes of Opinions (King's Bench) [97 Eng Reprint]
Wils (Eng)	Wilson [95 Eng Reprint]
Wils & S (Scot)	Wilson & Shaw, Scotch Appeal Cases
Wils Ch (Eng)	Wilson's Chancery [37 Eng Reprint]
Wils Exch (Eng)	Wilson's Exchequer [159 Eng Reprint]
Wils Super (Ind)	Wilson, Indiana Superior Ct
Winch (Eng)	Winch [124 Eng Reprint]
Winst Eq (NC)	Winston Equity Reports
Winst L (NC)	Winston Law Reports
Wis	Wisconsin
Wis 2d	Wisconsin, Second Series
Wis L Rev	Wisconsin Law Review
Witkin, Cal Summary	Witkin's Summary of California Law
W Jones (Eng)	Sir William Jones [82 Eng Reprint]
W Kelynge (Eng)	William Kelynge [25 Eng Reprint]
WL Bull (Ohio)	Weekly Law Bulletin
WL Gaz (Ohio)	Western Law Gazette
Wms (Eng)	See P Wms
Wms' Saund (Eng)	Saunders (Sir Edmund) Reports, edited by Williams [85 Eng Reprint]
WN (Eng)	Weekly Notes
WNC (Pa)	Weekly Notes of Cases
Woodb & M (F)	Woodbury & Minot, US Circuit Ct
Woods (F)	Woods, US Circuit Ct
Woodw Dec (Pa)	Woodward's Decisions
Woolw (F)	Woolworth, US Circuit Ct
Wright (Ohio)	Wright (Supreme Court)
W Rob (Eng)	William Robinson [166 Eng Reprint]
W Rob Adm (Eng)	W. Robinson's English Admiralty Reports
W Va	West Virginia
WW & D (Eng)	Willmore, Wollaston & Davison
WW & H (Eng)	Willmore, Wollaston & Hodges
WW Harr (Del)	See Harr (Del)
Wyo	Wyoming
Wythe (Va)	See Wythe
Wythe Ch (Va)	See Wythe

Y

Yale LJ	Yale Law Journal
Yates Sel Cas (NY)	Yates Select Cases (Common Law)
YB (Eng)	Year Books
Yeates (Pa)	Yeates
Yelv (Eng)	Yelverton [80 Eng Reprint]
Yerg (Tenn)	Yerger
York Leg Rec (Pa)	York Legal Record
Young Adm Dec (Nov Sc)	Young's Admiralty Decisions

Younge & C Ch Cas (Eng) . Younge & Collyer Chancery Cases [62, 63 Eng Reprint]
Younge & C Exch (Eng) ... Younge & Collyer, Exchequer Equity [160 Eng Reprint]
Younge & J (Eng) .... Younge & Jervis [148 Eng Reprint]
Younge Exch (Eng) .... Younge, Exchequer [159 Eng Reprint]
Yukon Terr .... Yukon Territory

Z

Zab (NJ) .... Zabriskie's Reports
Zane (Utah) .... Zane